The International Atlas

Revised Third Edition

World Longitudes & Latitudes
Time Changes and Time Zones

Compiled and Programmed by
Thomas G. Shanks

ACS Publications, Inc.
San Diego, California

First Edition published 1985. Second Edition 1988. Third Edition 1991.

International Standard Book Number 0-935127-16-X

Printed in the United States of America

Published by ACS Publications, Inc.
PO Box 34487
San Diego, CA 92163-4487

First printing, 1985
Second printing, 1988
Third printing, 1991

HOW TO USE THIS INTERNATIONAL ATLAS

The entries in the index of this book point to the first page for each country. The countries are listed alphabetically by their most commonly used English names. Each country's listing includes: Time Tables, cities, towns, islands and (in some cases) political or geographical divisions (e.g., provinces). Items within a country are arranged alphabetically with spaces within a name and diacritical marks ignored in alphabetizing.

For each item (city, town, island, etc.), the division number (if any), Time Table number (if any), latitude, longitude, and longitude time equivalent (hours, minutes and seconds from Greenwich) are given, in that order. If only one Time Table for the entire country is given, no table number is listed. If no divisions are given for the country, no division number follows the city name.

SAMPLE LISTING for Germany:

(City, Town, etc.)	(Province/ Division #)	(Time Table #)	(Latitude)	(Longitude)	(Time Equivalent to Greenwich)
Bonn	2	7	50N44	7E05	– 0:28:20

[Province/Division and Time Table # are omitted in countries having only one Time Table and no major political or geographic divisions.]

To find the hours from Greenwich in effect during the period in which you are interested, determine the correct Time Table number listed after the city name (preceding the latitude). Follow instructions in "Time Tables" section (below).

LATITUDE AND LONGITUDE

If there is more than one city with the same name, check the division number (if given), or compare the coordinates of nearby cities to determine which city is to be used. For each city, the latitude, longitude and time equivalent of the longitude are printed on the same line. The time equivalent of the longitude is given in hours, minutes and seconds from Greenwich, with positive values for western longitudes and negative values for eastern longitudes.

TIME TABLES

Note that the entries are given in the sequence: day/month/year hour:minute.

The first listing in each Time Table shows when the country began observing a **Standard Time.** Local Mean Time (LMT) is assumed prior to that date. (Local Mean Time closely approximates Sundial Time.)

The initial line of each Time Table gives the **date** on which observation of a Standard Time began (and Local Mean Time ended). The second line gives the **longitude meridian** on which the Standard Time was based. The third line repeats the date on which Standard Time began, followed by the **exact time** the switch was made to Standard Time and then by the **time equivalent** to Greenwich (in hours and minutes). Western longitudes have positive values for the time equivalent; eastern longitudes have negative values.

A time zone need not be an integral number of hours (or degrees of longitude) from Greenwich. In many instances, the first time zone was determined by the longitude of the capital city. For example, France's first Standard Time was based on longitude 2E20 equivalent to 9 minutes east of Greenwich. Whenever a country's Standard Time was changed, the resulting time zone is indicated by an entry "Begin Standard. . .," followed by the date and time of the change, as well as the effective hours from Greenwich Time.

Many entries may follow a "Begin Standard. . ." entry. The Time Tables have an **entry for each change of time zone or time type** (such as "Standard Time," "Daylight Time," "War Time," "Summer Time"). **That entry is in effect until the next time change**, whether the period is one day or thirty-five years. These entries give the time adjustments for Daylight, War and Summer Time. **These adjustments are not always even-hour increments from Greenwich**. In most instances Daylight or War Time has the effect of shifting the time one hour further east (adding one hour to the local time). However, Summer Time changes have also been 20 minutes, 30 minutes, 40 minutes and 2 hours.

To find the hours from Greenwich in effect for a period with which you are concerned, scan down the column of dates to the last date and time entry **before** the date and time you want. The time equivalent from Greenwich listed there is correct for the date you seek. Positive values are west of Greenwich; negative values are east.

Some Time Tables give a reference to another table in the same country instead of a time change. If the date being used is in the period before the next entry in the first table, refer to the second table.

The following example uses the Time Table for Bangladesh which is reproduced here:

```
      Time Table
  Before  1/01/1890 LMT
  Begin Standard   88E20
  1/01/1890   0:00 -5:53
  Begin Standard   97E30
10/01/1941   0:00 -6:30
 1/10/1941   0:00 -7:30
15/05/1942   0:00 -6:30
 1/09/1942   0:00 -7:30
 1/09/1947   0:00 -6:30
  Begin Standard   90E00
30/09/1951   0:00 -6:00
```

This region began to standardize time in 1890, using as Standard Time the Local Mean Time of Calcutta, longitude 88E20, 5 hours and 53 minutes east of Greenwich Mean Time (GMT). This lasted until 10 January 1941, when the Standard Time was changed to 6 hours and 30 minutes east of Greenwich.

Two Daylight Time periods followed, the first beginning on 1 October 1941 and lasting until 15 May 1942; the second beginning on 1 September 1942 and lasting until 1 September 1947. (Remember: **dates are given as day/month/year**! Thus, 01/10/1941 is October 1, 1984.) Finally, the time standard was changed to zone 6 east (6 hours east of Greenwich) on 30 September 1951 and has continued since that date without further change.

ANOTHER EXAMPLE:

Gretchen was born in Bonn, Germany, on 28 April 1946 at 4:29 AM.

1) Locate **Germany** (alphabetically) in *The International Atlas*.
2) Locate **Bonn** (alphabetically) within Germany.
3) Copy the **latitude, longitude and longitude equivalent from Greenwich** as given.
4) Following the city name is a **division number** (2) referring to where Bonn is located in Germany. This could be used to verify the correct Bonn (if more than one exists).
5) Preceding the latitude is a **number referring to the Time Table** (7). This refers you to Time Table #7 for time type and zone changes in Bonn, Germany.
6) In Time Table #7, the following entries appear:

```
     Time Table # 7
  Begin Standard   15E00
 9/04/1927 23:00 -1:00
 1/04/1940  2:00 -2:00
 2/11/1942  3:00 -1:00
29/03/1943  2:00 -2:00
 4/10/1943  3:00 -1:00
 3/04/1944  2:00 -2:00
 2/10/1944  3:00 -1:00
 2/04/1945  2:00 -2:00
16/09/1945  2:00 -1:00
14/04/1946  2:00 -2:00
 7/10/1946  2:00 -1:00
 6/04/1947  3:00 -2:00
```

This tells you that Bonn, Germany used times that were two hours east of Greenwich (– 2:00) beginning the 14th of April in 1946 at 2:00 AM. Bonn then changed, on the 7th of October, 1946, to times one hour east of Greenwich (– 1:00). The change took place at 2:00 AM on the 7th of October.

7) Since Gretchen was born **between** the two dates given above, her time would be based on a **two-hour** difference from Greenwich.
8) Thus, Gretchen's 4:29 AM birthtime is equivalent to 2:29 AM in Greenwich. Her UT (Universal Time) would be 2:29.

STILL ANOTHER EXAMPLE:

Jens was born in Flateyri, Iceland on 14th July 1953 at 15:13 (3:13 PM).

1) Locate **Iceland** (alphabetically) in *The International Atlas.*
2) Locate **Flateyri** (alphabetically) within Iceland.
3) Copy the **latitude, longitude and longitude equivalent from Greenwich** as given.

SAMPLE LISTING for Iceland:

(City, Town, etc.)	(Province/ Division #)	(Time Table #)	(Latitude)	(Longitude)	(Time Equivalent to Greenwich)
Flateyri			65N59	23W42	1:34:48

4) Note that there is **not** a division number following the city name. Iceland has no division numbers.
5) There is also **no number preceding the latitude** to refer you to a Time Table. That is because Iceland has **only one** Time Table, which appears directly above the listing of cities.
6) In that Time Table, the following entries appear:

3/04/1949	2:00	0:00
30/10/1949	2:00	1:00
2/04/1950	2:00	0:00
22/10/1950	2:00	1:00
1/04/1951	2:00	0:00
28/10/1951	2:00	1:00
6/04/1952	2:00	0:00
26/10/1952	2:00	1:00
5/04/1953	2:00	0:00
26/10/1953	2:00	1:00
4/04/1954	2:00	0:00
24/10/1954	2:00	1:00
3/04/1955	2:00	0:00
23/10/1955	2:00	1:00
1/04/1956	2:00	0:00

This tells you that Flatyri, Iceland used times that were equivalent to Greenwich (0:00 hours from Greenwich), beginning the 5th of April 1953 at 2:00 AM. Flateyri then changed, on the 26th of October, 1953, to times one hour west of Greenwich (1:00). The change took place at 2:00 AM on the 26th of October.

7) Since Jens was born **between** the two dates given above, his time would be based on a **zero-hour** difference from Greenwich.
8) Thus, Jens's 15:13 (3:13 PM) birthtime is equivalent to 15:13 (3:13 PM) in Greenwich. His UT (Universal Time) would be 15:13 (3:13 PM).

COMO USAR EL ATLAS INTERNACIONAL

Las anotaciones que estan en el índice de este libro indican a la primer página de cada país. Los paises estan por orden alfabetico y por el nombre en Inglés usado mas comunmente. Cada país incluye: Tablas de Tiempo, ciudades, pueblos, islas (y en algunos casos) divisiones políticas y geográficas (por ejemplo: provincias) Los articulos dentro de cada país están por orden alfabetico ignorando en su alfabetización los espacios y acentos especiales.

Para cada articulo las (ciudades, pueblos, islas, etc.) el número de división (si tiene), número de Tabla (si tiene) latitud, longitud y el equivalente de tiempo de longitud (horas, minutos y segundos de Greenwich) son indicados en ese orden. Si nada mas una Tabla es dada para todo el país ningun número de tiempo es mostrado, si no se han dado divisiones para el país, ningún número sigue al nombre de la ciudad.

EJEMPLO para Alemania:

(Ciudad, Pueblo, etc.)	(#Provincia/ División)	(#de la Tabla de Tiempo)	(Latitud)	(Longitud)	(Tiempo Equivalente a Greenwich)
Bonn	2	7	50N44	7E05	−0:28:20

[La Provincia/Division y Tabla de Tiempo son omitidas en paises que solo tienen una Tabla y no tienen divisiones politicas ó geográficas importantes]

Para encontrar las horas vigentes durante el periodo en el que esta interesado, determine el número correcto de la Tabla que esta después del nombre de la ciudad (precediendo la latitud). Proceda con las instrucciones que siguen en la sección de "Tablas de Tiempo" (abajo).

LATITUD Y LONGITUD:
Si hay mas de una ciudad con el mismo nombre verifique el número de su división (si tiene), ó compare los coordinantes de las ciudades cercanas para así determinar cual se ha de usar. Para cada ciudad la latitud, longitud y tiempo equivalente de su longitud estan impresos en el mismo renglón. El tiempo equivalente de su longitud es indicado en horas, minutos y segundos de Greenwich, con valores positivos para las longitudes occidentales y valores negativos para las longitudes orientales.

TABLAS DE TIEMPO:
Observe: Las anotaciones estan indicadas en este orden: dia/mes/año hora:minuto.

La primera anotación en cada Tabla muestra cuando el país empezó a observar el Tiempo Standard. Anterior a esa fecha se asumió el Tiempo Local Medio (LMT, siglas en Inglés). El Tiempo Local Medio se aproxima muy cercanamente al Tiempo del Cuadrante Solar (Sundial Time).

El primer renglón de cada Tabla indica la fecha en la cual la observación del Tiempo Standard empezó y cuando (el Tiempo Local Medio se terminó). El segundo renglón da el meridiano de longitud en el cual el Tiempo Standard fue basado. El tercer renglón repite la fecha en la cual el tiempo Standard empezó, seguido por el tiempo exacto cuando el cambio fue hecho al Tiempo Standard y después seguido por el tiempo equivalente a Greenwich (en horas, con minutos y segundos donde se puedan aplicar). Las longitudes occidentales tienen valores positivos para su tiempo equivalente; las longitudes orientales tienen valores negativos.

Una zona de tiempo no necesita tener un número de horas íntegro (o grados de longitud) de Greenwich. En varios casos, la primer zona de tiempo es determinada por la longitud de su capital. Por ejemplo, el primer Tiempo Standard de Francia fué basado en la longitud 2E20 equivalente a 9 minutos al este de Greenwich. Cada vez que el Tiempo Standard de un país fué cambiado, el resultado del cambio de la zona de tiempo es indicado con una anotación que dice "Begin Standard. . ." (Comienzo de Standard. . .) seguido por la fecha y el tiempo del cambio, asi como las horas vigentes del Tiempo de Greenwich.

Muchas anotaciones pueden seguir a otra que diga "Begin Standard . . ." Las Tablas tienen una anotación para cada cambio de zona de tiempo ó tipo de tiempo (Tiempo de Luz Natural, Tiempo de Guerra ó Tiempo de Verano). Esta anotaciónes efectiva hasta que el próximo cambio de tiempo suceda. Aunque sea un periodo de un día ó de treinta y cinco años. Estas anotaciones dan la converción para los Tiempos de Luz Natural, de Guerra y de Verano. Estos ajustes no son siempre en incrementos de horas-pares de Greenwich. En la mayoría de los casos los Tiempos de Luz Natural o de Guerra tienen el efecto de cambiar la hora mas al este (añadiendo una hora al tiempo local). Aún sin embargo, los cambios del Tiempo de Verano han sido también 20 minutos, 30 minutos, 40 minutos y dos horas.

Para encontrar las horas de Greenwich que estan en efecto en el periodo en el cual esta ud. interesado, busque siguiendo la columa de fechas hasta la penúltima fecha y tiempo anotados antes de llegar al tiempo que busca. El tiempo equivalente de Greenwich anotado ahí es el correcto para la fecha que ud. busca. Los valores positivos estan al oeste de Greenwich; y los negativos al este.

Algunas Tablas dan referencia a otra Tabla en el mismo país en lugar de dar el cambio de tiempo. Si la fecha que ud. necesita esta en el periodo anterior a la próxima anotación en la primer Tabla, refierase a la segunda Tabla.

Los siguientes ejemplos usan la Tabla de Bangladesh, la cual es reproducida aquí:

```
     Time Table
 Before  1/01/1890 LMT
 Begin Standard   88E20
  1/01/1890   0:00 -5:53
 Begin Standard   97E30
10/01/1941   0:00 -6:30
 1/10/1941   0:00 -7:30
15/05/1942   0:00 -6:30
 1/09/1942   0:00 -7:30
 1/09/1947   0:00 -6:30
 Begin Standard   90E00
30/09/1951   0:00 -6:00
```

Esta región empezó a usar el Tiempo Standard en 1890, usando como Tiempo Standard el Tiempo Local Medio de Calcutta, con una longitud de 88E20, 5 horas y 53 minutos al este del Tiempo Medio de Greenwich (GMT; siglas en Inglés) este duró hasta el 10 de enero de 1941, cuando el Tiempo Standard fue cambiado a 6 horas y 30 minutos al este de Greenwich.

Dos periodos de Tiempo de Luz Natural (Daylight Time) siguieron, el primero empezó el 1 de octubre de 1941 y duró hasta el 15 de mayo de 1942; el segundo empezó el 1 de septiembre de 1942 y duró hasta el 1 de septiembre de 1947. (¡Recuerde: las fechas son dia/mes/año! Así, 01/10/1941 es octubre 1, 1941). Finalmente, el Tiempo Standard fué cambiado a la zona 6 este (6 horas al este de Greenwich) El 30 de septiembre de 1951 y ha continuado desde esa fecha sin ningún cambio.

OTRO EJEMPLO:
Gretchen nació en Bonn, Alemania, el 28 de abril de 1946 a las 4:29 AM.

1) Localize Alemania (en orden alfabetico) en *el Atlas Internacional*.
2) Localize Bonn (en orden alfabetico) en Alemania.
3) Copie la latitud, longitud y la longitud equivalente de Greenwich como se muestra.
4) Enseguida del nombre de la ciudad esta un número de división (2) que se refiere a donde Bonn esta localizada en Alemania. Este se puede usar para verificar si es el Bonn correcto, (si mas de uno existe).
5) Precediendo a la latitud esta un número (7) refiriendose a la Tabla de Tiempo. Este número da referencia ala Tabla #7 para el tipo de tiempo y cambios de zona en Bonn, Alemania.
6) En la tabla #7 las siguientes anotaciones aparecen:

```
    Time Table # 7
 Begin Standard   15E00
 9/04/1927 23:00 -1:00
 1/04/1940  2:00 -2:00
 2/11/1942  3:00 -1:00
29/03/1943  2:00 -2:00
 4/10/1943  3:00 -1:00
 3/04/1944  2:00 -2:00
 2/10/1944  3:00 -1:00
 2/04/1945  2:00 -2:00
16/09/1945  2:00 -1:00
14/04/1946  2:00 -2:00
 7/10/1946  2:00 -1:00
 6/04/1947  3:00 -2:00
```

Esto indica que Bonn, Alemania usó tiempos que estaban 2 horas al este de Greenwich. (– 2:00) empezando el 14 de abril de 1946 a las 2:00 AM. Bonn entonces cambió al 7 de octubre de 1946 a 1 hora al este de Greenwich (– 1:00). El cambio tomó lugar a las 2:00 AM el 7 de octubre.

7) Como Gretchen nació entre las dos fechas indicadas arriba, su tiempo seria basado con una diferencia de 2 horas de Greenwich.
8) Así, el tiempo de nacimiento de Gretchen, 4:29 AM es equivalente a las 2:29 de Greenwich. Su Tiempo Universal (UT; siglas en Inglés) sería 2:29.

TODAVIA OTRO EJEMPLO:

Jens nació en Flateyri, Islanda, el 14 de julio de 1953 a las 15:13 (3:13 PM)

1) Localize Islanda (en orden alfabetico) en *el Atlas Internacional*.
2) Localize Flateyri (en orden alfabetico) dentro de Islanda.
3) Copie la latitud, longitud y la longitud equivalente de Greenwich como se ha indicado.

EJEMPLO para Islanda:

(Ciudad, Pueblo, etc.)	(#Provincia/ División)	(#de la Tabla de Tiempo)	(Latitud)	(Longitud)	(Tiempo Equivalente a Greenwich)
Flateyri			65N59	23W42	1:38:48

4) Anote que no hay número de división enseguida del nombre de la ciudad. Islanda no tiene números de división.
5) Tampoco hay número precediendo la latitud para referir a una Tabla de Tiempo. Esto es porque Islanda tiene únicamente 1 Tabla, la cual aparece directamente arriba de la lista de ciudades.
6) En esta Tabla las siguientes anotaciones aparecen:

3/04/1949	2:00	0:00
30/10/1949	2:00	1:00
2/04/1950	2:00	0:00
22/10/1950	2:00	1:00
1/04/1951	2:00	0:00
28/10/1951	2:00	1:00
6/04/1952	2:00	0:00
26/10/1952	2:00	1:00
5/04/1953	2:00	0:00
26/10/1953	2:00	1:00
4/04/1954	2:00	0:00
24/10/1954	2:00	1:00
3/04/1955	2:00	0:00
23/10/1955	2:00	1:00
1/04/1956	2:00	0:00

Esto le indica que Flateyri, Islanda, uso tiempos que fueron equivalentes a Greenwich (0:00 horas de Greenwich) empezando el 5 de abril de 1953 a las 2:00 AM. Flateyri entonces cambió, el 26 de octubre de 1953, a los tiempos de una hora al oeste de Greenwich (1:00). El cambio surgió a las 2:00 AM el 26 de octubre.

7) Como Jens nació entre las dos fechas indicadas arriba, su tiempo sería basado en una diferencia de cero-horas de Greenwich.
8) Así, el tiempo de nacimiento de Jens 15:13 (3:13 PM) es equivalente a 15:13 (3:13 PM) en Greenwich. Su Tiempo Universal sería 15:13 (3:13 PM)

COMMENT UTILISER CET ATLAS INTERNATIONAL

L'index indique la première page de la rubrique consacrée à chaque pays. Les pays sont rangés par lettre alphabétique en utilisant leur nom le plus commun en langue anglaise. Pour chaque pays il est donné: Tableaux horaires, villes principales et secondaires, îles et (dans certains cas) divisions politiques ou géographiques (les provinces). Pour un pays donné chaque élément se trouve rangé par ordre alphabétique (l'espacement à l'intérieur d'un mot et les signes diacritiques ne sont pas donnés dans le classement alphabétique).

Le numéro indiquant la division politique ou géographique (lorsqu'il y en a une) le numéro du tableau horaire, la latitude, la longitude et l'heure à la longitude (la différence par rapport à Greenwich exprimée en heures, minutes or secondes) sont donnés dans cet ordre. S'il n'y a qu'un seul tableau horaire pour tout le pays, aucun numéro n'est mentionné et s'il n'y a pas de division, on ne trouvera également aucun numéro à la suite du nom de la ville.

VOICI UN EXEMPLE pris en Allemagne:

(Ville)	(Provinces/ Division no)	(Tableau Horaire no)	(Latitude)	(Longitude)	(heure par rapport à Greenwich)
Bonn	2	7	50N44	7E05	−0:28:20

[Ces chiffres sont omis lorsque le pays n'a qu'un seul tableau horaire et aucune division administrative ou géographique]

Pour trouver l'heure par rapport à Greenwich pour la période qui vous interesse, notez le numéro du tableau horaire qui se trouve aprés le nom de la ville (avant la latitude). Suivez les instructions concernant les tableaux horaires (voir ci-dessous).

LATITUDE ET LONGITUDE

S'il y a plus d'une ville du même nom, vérifiez le numéro de division (s'il est donné) ou comparez avec les coordonnées de villes voisines afin de savoir quelle ville vous devez choisir. Pour chaque ville, la latitude, la longitude et l'heure à la longitude sont sur une même ligne. L'heure par rapport à Greenwich de la longitude est donnée en heures, minutes et secondes avec le signe + pour les longitudes ouest et le signe — pour les longitudes est.

TABLEAUX HORAIRES

Pour chaque rubrique on trouve dans l'ordre suivant le jour/le mois/l'année l'heure: les minutes.

Le tableau horaire nous apprend tout d'abord quand le pays a commencé à utiliser l'heure légale. Avant cette date on suppose que c'était l'heure locale qui était en vigueur. (L'heure locale est trés proche de l'heure solaire).

La première ligne de chaque tableau donne la date où l'heure légale remplaça l'heure locale. La deuxième ligne donne la longitude qui sert à determiner l'heure légale. La troisiéme ligne donne à nouveau la date d'entrée en vigueur de l'heure légale, suivie par l'heure où le changement eut lieu, et par l'heure de Greenwich (GMT) (en heures; et minutes). L'heure à la longitude est positive dans le cas des longitudes ouest, elle est négative dans le cas des longitudes est.

Le chiffre représentant la zone horaire n'est pas obligatoirement un nombre entier d'heures (ou degrés de longitude) par rapport à Greenwich. Dans de nombreux cas, la première zone horaire fut déterminée par la longitude de la capitale du pays. Par exemple, la première heure légale adoptée par la France fut basée sur la longitude 2E20, soit 9 minutes à l'est de Greenwich. Toutes les fois que l'heure légale a été modifiée la nouvelle zone horaire qui en résulte, est indiquée par un article commenant par les mots: "Begin Standard . . ." suivie de la date et de l'heure du changement, ainsi que de l'heure par rapport a Greenwich qui a pris effet.

D'autres articles peuvent suivre l'article commençant par "Begin Standard..." Les tableaux horaires ont un article différent pour chaque changement de zone horaire ou type d'heure (comme par exemple "Heure légale," "heure d'été," "heure en temps de guerre," "heure d'été"). Les renseignements donnés dans cet article sont valables jusqu'au prochain changement d'heure, cette période pouvant aller d'un jour à 35 ans. Ces articles donnent les ajustements horaires pour les heures d'été, pour celles de temps de guerre. Ces ajustements ne sont pas toujours des accroissements de l'ordre de l'heure par rapport à Greenwich. Dans la plupart des cas, l'heure d'été ou l'heure de temps de guerre cause un déplacement d'une heure à l'est de Greenwich (ajoutant une heure à l'heure locale). Cependant l'heure d'été a quelquefois changé de 20, 30, 40 minutes ou même de 2 heures.

Pour trouver l'heure par rapport à Greenwich en usage pendant la période considérée, parcourez la liste des dates jusqu'à la date qui précède immédiatement la date et l'heure que vous cherchez. L'heure par rapport à Greenwich que vous trouverez en face de cette date est celle que vous cherchez. Les chiffres positifs sont à l'ouest de Greenwich, les chiffres négatifs sont à l'est de Greenwich.

Quelques tableaux horaires donnent une référence à un autre tableau du même pays au lieu de donner un changement d'heure. Si la date dont vous vous servez se situe dans une période qui suit le dernier article du premier tableau, reportez vous au deuxième tableau.

L'exemple suivant utilise le tableau horaire du Bangladesh. Voici ce que l'on peut lire:

```
        Time Table
  Before   1/01/1890 LMT
   Begin Standard   88E20
   1/01/1890   0:00 -5:53
   Begin Standard   97E30
10/01/1941   0:00 -6:30
  1/10/1941   0:00 -7:30
15/05/1942   0:00 -6:30
  1/09/1942   0:00 -7:30
  1/09/1947   0:00 -6:30
   Begin Standard   90E00
30/09/1951   0:00 -6:00
```

Cette région adopte l'heure légale en 1890, prennant comme heure légale, l'heure locale de Calcutta, longitude 33E20, 5 heures et 53 minutes à l'est de l'heure de Greenwich (GMT). Ceci dura jusqu'au 10 janvier 1941, où l'heure légale devint 6 heures et 30 minutes à l'est de Greenwich.

Il y eut ensuite deux périodes pendant lesquelles une heure d'été fut utilisée. La première du I octobre 1941 jusqu'au 15 mai 1942 et la deuxième du 1 septembre 1942 au 1 septembre 1947. (Souvenez vous que les dates sont données dans l'ordre suivant jour/mois/année! Ainsi, 01/10/1941 c'est le Ier octobre 1941.) Finalement, l'heure légale est devenue celle du fuseau 6 à l'est de Greenwich (6 heures à l'est de Greenwich) le 30 septembre 1951 et n'a pas été modifiée depuis cette date.

VOICI UN AUTRE EXEMPLE:
Gretchen est née à Bonn (Allemagne) le 28 avril 1946 à 4:29 du matin.

1) Trouvez l'Allemagne dans la liste alphabétique *de l'Atlas International.*
2) Trouvez Bonn à la lettre B dans l'article sur l'Allemagne.
3) Relevez la latitude, la longitude et l'heure de la longitude par rapport à Greenwich.
4) A la suite du nom de la ville il y a un numéro de division (2) qui représente l'endroit ou se trouve Bonn en Allemagne. Ce chiffre peut être utile pour vérifier qu'il s'agit bien du Bonn que vous cherchez (dans le cas où il existe plusieurs villes du même nom).
5) Avant la latitude il y a un chiffre qui est celui du tableau horaire (7). Il s'agit du tableau horaire numéro 7 qui donne le type d'heure et les changements de zone pour Bonn (Allemagne).
6) Dans le tableau No. 7, les renseignements suivants apparaissent:

```
    Time Table # 7
  Begin Standard   15E00
  9/04/1927 23:00 -1:00
  1/04/1940  2:00 -2:00
  2/11/1942  3:00 -1:00
 29/03/1943  2:00 -2:00
  4/10/1943  3:00 -1:00
  3/04/1944  2:00 -2:00
  2/10/1944  3:00 -1:00
  2/04/1945  2:00 -2:00
 16/09/1945  2:00 -1:00
 14/04/1946  2:00 -2:00
  7/10/1946  2:00 -1:00
  6/04/1947  3:00 -2:00
```

Ceci nous apprend que Bonn (Allemagne) a utilisé une heure qui était de 2 heures à l'est de Greenwich (– 2:00) à partir du 14 avril 1946 à 2:00 de une du matin. Puis Bonn à changé son heure le 7 octobre 1946. La nouvelle était de 1 heure à l'est de Greenwich (– 1:00). Le changement eût lieu à 2:00 du matin le 7 octobre.

7) Puisque Gretchen est née entre les deux dates ci-dessus, l'heure de naissance montre donc une différence de 2 heures par rapport à Greenwich.
8) Par conséquent, l'heure de sa naissance: 4:29 du matin équivaut à 2:29 du matin (heure de Greenwich). Son heure universelle (Universal Time) serait 2:29.

UN AUTRE EXEMPLE:
Jens est né à Flateyri, en Islande, le 14 juillet 1953 à 15:13 (3:13 PM).
1) Cherchez l'Islande à la lettre I *dans l'Atlas International*.
2) Cherchez Flateyri à la lettre F dans l'article Islande.
3) Relevez la latitude, la longitude, et la longitude par rapport à Greenwich comme suit:

VOICI UN EXEMPLE pris en Islande (Iceland):

(Ville Pays etc.)	(Provinces/ Division no)	(Tableau Horaire no)	(Latitude)	(Longitude)	(heure par rapport à Greenwich)
Flateyri			65N59	23W42	– 1:34:48

4) Remarquez aussi que le nom de la ville n'est pas suivi d'un chiffre. L'Islande n'a pas été divisée en sections.
5) Devant la latitude, il n'y a aucun chiffre qui vous renvoie à un tableau horaire. C'est parceque l'islande n'a qu'un seul tableau horaire. Celui-ci se trouve avant la liste des villes.
6) Dans ce tableau horaire, se trouvent les renseignements suivants:

3/04/1949	2:00	0:00
30/10/1949	2:00	1:00
2/04/1950	2:00	0:00
22/10/1950	2:00	1:00
1/04/1951	2:00	0:00
28/10/1951	2:00	1:00
6/04/1952	2:00	0:00
26/10/1952	2:00	1:00
5/04/1953	2:00	0:00
26/10/1953	2:00	1:00
4/04/1954	2:00	0:00
24/10/1954	2:00	1:00
3/04/1955	2:00	0:00
23/10/1955	2:00	1:00
1/04/1956	2:00	0:00

No apprend que Flateyri (Islande) a utilisé l'heure de Greenwich à partir du 5 avril 1953 à 2:00 du matin. L'heure utilisée a ensuite été d'une heure à l'ouest de Greenwich. Le changement eût lieu à 2:00 du matin, le 26 octobre.

7) Etant donné que Jens est né entre les 2 dates ci-dessus, son heure sera calculée avec une différence nulle par rapport à Greenwich.
8) Ainsi, l'heure où Jens est né: 15:13 (soit 3:13 de l'après-midi) sera 15:13 à Greenwich. Son heure universelle (Universal Time) sera 15:13.

ZUR BENUTZUNG DIESES INTERNATIONALEN ATLAS

Die Eintragungen in dem Register dieses Buches zeigen auf die erste Seite für jedes Land. Die Länder sind alphabetisch nach ihren meist benutzten englischen Namen geordnet. Die Eintragung jedes Landes schliesst das folgende ein: Zeitpläne, Städte, Dörfer, Inseln und (in einigen Fällen) politische oder geographische Teilungen (z.B. Provinzen). Einzelheiten innerhalb eines Landes werden alphabetisch geordnet. Abstände innerhalb eines Names und Unterscheidungszeichen werden bei der Alphabetizierung ignoriert.

Für jede Einzelheit (Stadt, Dorf, Insel, usw) werden die Teilungsnummer (wenn überhaupt), die Breite, die Länge, und das Zeitäquivalent der Länge (Stunden, Minuten und Sekunden von Greenwich) in dieser Ordnung gegeben. Wenn nur einen Zeitplan für das ganze Land vorhanden ist, wird keine Plannummer eingetragen. Wenn keine Teilungen für das Land gegeben werden, folgt auch keine Teilungsnummer nach dem Stadtname.

EINE MUSTEREINTRAGUNG Für Die Bundesrepublik Deutschland:

(Stadt, Dorf, usw)	(Provinz/ Teilung #)	(Zeitplan #)	(Breite)	(Länge)	(Zeitäquivalent zu Greenwich)
Bonn	2	7	50N44	7E05	– 0:28:20

[Provinz/Teilung und Zeitplannummer werden in den Ländern, die nur einen Zeitplan und keine grösseren politischen oder geographischen Teilungen haben, ausgelassen.]

Um die Stunden von Greenwich zu finden, die während der Periode, in der Sie interessiert sind, in Kraft sind, müssen Sie die richtige Zeitplannummer, die nach dem Stadtname eingetragen ist (vor der Breite) feststellen. Folgen Sie die Anweisung in dem „Zietplan" Abschnitt (unten).

DIE BREITE UND DIE LÄNGE

Wenn mehr als eine Stadt mit dem gleichen Name da ist, prüfen Sie die Teilungsnummer nach (wenn eine gegeben ist), oder vergleichen Sie die Koordinate der naheliegenden Städten, um festzustellen welche Stadt benutzt werden soll. Für jede Stadt, sind die Breite, die Länge und das Zeitäquivalent der Länge auf der gleichen Linie gedruckt. Das Zeitäquivalent der Länge wird in Stunden, Minuten und Sekunden von Greenwich, mit positiven Werten für westliche Längen und negativen Werten für östliche Längen, gegeben.

ZEITPLÄNE

Merken Sie, dass die Eintragungen in der folgenden Sequenz gegeben werden: Tag/Monat/ Jahr Stunde:Minute.

Die erste Eintragung in jedem Zeitplan zeigt wann das Land eine Normalzeit einzuhalten begann. Örtliche mittlere Zeit (LMT) wird vor dem Datum angenommen. (Örtliche mittlere Zeit nährt sich die Sonnenuhrzeit.).

In der ersten Linie jedes Zeitplans steht das Datum an dem die Einhaltung der Normalzeit begann (und wann die örtliche mittlere Zeit endete). In der zweiten Linie steht der Längenmeridian an dem die Normalzeit basiert ist. Die dritte Linie wiederholt das Datum, an dem die Normalzeit begann. Darauf folgt die genaue Zeit, in der der Wechsel zur Normalzeit gemacht worden ist, und danach folgt das Zeitäquivalent zu Greenwich (in Stunden und Minuten). Westliche Längen haben positive Werte für das Zeitäquivalent; östliche Längen haben negative Werte.

Eine Zeitzone braucht nichteine vollständige Nummer von Stunden (oder Grade der Länge) von Greenwich zu sein. In vielen Fällen wurde die erste Zeitzone durch die Länge der

Hauptstadt festgestellt. Zum Beispiel, die erste französische Normalzeit wurde auf die Länge 2E20 basiert, die gleich war zu neun Minuten östlich von Greenwich. Wann auch immer die Normalzeit eines Landes geändert wurde, wurde die herrührende Zeitzone durch eine Eintragung „Begin Standard...," angezeigt. Darauf folgten das Datum und die Zeit des Wechsels, so wie die effektiven Stunden von Greenwich Zeit.

Viele Eintragungen folgen eine „Begin Standard..." Eintragung. Die Zeitpläne haben eine Eintragung für jeden Wechsel der Zeitzone oder der Zeitart (wie „Standard Time," „Daylight Time," „War Time," „Summer Time"). Jene Eintragung ist in Kraft bis zu dem nächsten Zeitwechsel, obgleich die Periode ein Tag oder fünfunddreissig Jahre ist. In diesen Eintragungen werden die Anpassungen für Tagestlicht-, Kriegs-und Sommerzeit gegeben. Nicht immer sind diese Anpassungen Steigerungen mit gerade Stunden von Greenwich. In den meisten Fällen, Tageslichtzeit oder Kriegszeit hat die Wirkung, dass die Zeit eine Stunde weiter ostwärts geschoben wird (dies addiert eine Stunde zu örtlicher Zeit). Aber die Wechsel der Sommerzeit sind auch 20 Minuten, 30 Minuten, 40 Minuten und zwei Stunden gewesen.

Um die Stunden von Greenwich zu finden, die während der Periode, in der Sie interessiert sind, in Kraft sind, suchen Sie in der Säule des Datums die letzte Datum-und Zeiteintragung vor dem Datum und der Zeit, die sie wollen. Das Zeitäquivalent von Greenwich, das dort eingetragen ist, ist das richtige für das gesuchte Datum. Positive Werte sind westlich von Greenwich, negative Werte sind östlich von Greenwich.

Manche Zeitpläne geben eine Verweisung auf einen anderen Zeitplan statt eines Zeitwechsels. Wenn das Datum, das benutzt wird, in der Periode vor der nächsten Eintragung in dem ersten Zeitplan ist, beziehen Sie sich auf den zweiten Zeitplan.

Das folgende Beispiel benutzt den Zeitplan für Bangladesh, der hier reproduziert ist:

```
     Time Table
 Before   1/01/1890 LMT
 Begin Standard   88E20
 1/01/1890   0:00 -5:53
 Begin Standard   97E30
10/01/1941   0:00 -6:30
 1/10/1941   0:00 -7:30
15/05/1942   0:00 -6:30
 1/09/1942   0:00 -7:30
 1/09/1947   0:00 -6:30
 Begin Standard   90E00
30/09/1951   0:00 -6:00
```

Diese Gegend begann in 1890 die Zeit zu normalisieren. Sie benutzte die örtliche mittlere Zeit von Calcutta, die Länge 88E20, 5 Stunden und 53 Minuten östlich von Greenwich mittlere Zeit (GMT), als die Normalzeit. Dieses System wurde benutzt bis zum 10. Januar 1941, als die Normalzeit zu 6 Stunden und 30 Minuten östlich von Greenwich geändert wurde.

Zwei Tageslichtzeitperioden folgten. Die erste Periode begann am 1. Oktober 1941 und dauerte bis zum 15. Mai 1942; die zweite Periode begann am 1. September 1942 und dauerte bis zum 1. September 1947. (Erinnern Sie sich daran, dass die Datumen in der Ordnung Tag/Monat/Jahr geschrieben wurden! Infolgedessen, 01/10/1941 ist 1. Oktober 1941.) Schliesslich, die Zeitnorm wurde am 30. September 1951 zur zone 6 ost (6 Stunden östlich von Greenwich) geändert und seitdem wird es ohne Änderungen fortgesetzt.

EIN WEITERES BEISPIEL:
Gretchen ist in Bonn, Bundesrepublik Deutschland am 28. April 1946 um 4.29 geboren.

1) Finden Sie die Bundesrepublik Deutschland (alphabetisch) in *Dem Internationalen Atlas*.
2) Finden Sie Bonn (alphabetisch) innerhalb der Bundesrepublik Deutschland.
3) Schreiben Sie die Breite, die Länge und das Längeäquivalent von Greenwich auf, wie sie dort gegeben werden.
4) Nach dem Stadtname ist die Teilungsnummer (2), die sich auf die Ortsangabe von Bonn in Deutschland bezieht. Diese Nummer könnte benutzt werden um die richtige Bonn (wenn mehr als eine existiert) zu prüfen.
5) Vor der Breite steht eine Nummer, die sich auf den Zeitplan (7) bezieht. Diese Nummer verweist auf den Zeitplan #7 für die Zeitart und den Zonenwechsel in Bonn, Bundesrepublik Deutschland.

6) Im Zeitplan #7 stehen die folgende Eintragungen:

```
     Time Table # 7
  Begin Standard   15E00
  9/04/1927 23:00 -1:00
  1/04/1940  2:00 -2:00
  2/11/1942  3:00 -1:00
 29/03/1943  2:00 -2:00
  4/10/1943  3:00 -1:00
  3/04/1944  2:00 -2:00
  2/10/1944  3:00 -1:00
  2/04/1945  2:00 -2:00
 16/09/1945  2:00 -1:00
 14/04/1946  2:00 -2:00
  7/10/1946  2:00 -1:00
  6/04/1947  3:00 -2:00
```

Diese Information Zeigt, dass am 14. April 1946 um 2.00 Bonn, Bundesrepublik Deutschland angefangen hat, Zeiten zu benutzen, die zwei Stunden östlich von Greenwich waren (– 2:00). Am 7. Oktober 1946 wechselte Bonn zu Zeiten, die eine Stunde östlich von Greenwich waren (– 1:00). Die Anderung fand um 2.00 am 7. Oktober statt.

7) Weil Gretchen zwischen den zwei oben gegebene Datumen geboren ist, wäre ihre Zeit auf einem zwei stundigen Unterschied von Greenwich basiert.

8) Infolgedessen, die 4.29 Geburtszeit von Gretchen ist gleich 2.29 in Greenwich. Ihre UT (Universale Zeit) wäre 2.29.

NOCH EIN WEITERES BEISPIEL:

Jens ist in Flateyre, Island am 14. Juli 1953 um 15.13 (3.13 nachmittags) geboren.

1) Finden Sie Island (alphabetisch) in *Dem Internationalen Atlas.*

2) Finden Sie Flateyri (alphabetisch) innerhalb Island.

3) Schreiben Sie die Breite, die Länge und das Längeäquivalent von Greenwich auf, wie sie dort gegeben werden.

EINE MUSTEREINTRAGUNG für Island (Iceland)

(Stadt, Dorf, usw)	(Provinz/ Teilung #)	(Zeitplan #)	(Breite)	(Länge)	(Zeitäquivalentzu Greenwich)
Flateyri			65N59	23W42	1:34:48

4) Merken Sie, dass Keine Teilungsnummer die Stadtname folgt. Island hat keine Teilungsnummern.

5) Da ist auch keine Nummer vor der Breite, um auf einen Zeitplan zu verweisen. Dies ist der Fall, weil Island nur einen Zeitplan hat, der direkt über die Liste der Städte steht.

6) In jenem Zeitplan stehen die folgenden Eintragungen:

```
  3/04/1949  2:00  0:00
 30/10/1949  2:00  1:00
  2/04/1950  2:00  0:00
 22/10/1950  2:00  1:00
  1/04/1951  2:00  0:00
 28/10/1951  2:00  1:00
  6/04/1952  2:00  0:00
 26/10/1952  2:00  1:00
  5/04/1953  2:00  0:00
 26/10/1953  2:00  1:00
  4/04/1954  2:00  0:00
 24/10/1954  2:00  1:00
  3/04/1955  2:00  0:00
 23/10/1955  2:00  1:00
  1/04/1956  2:00  0:00
```

Diese Information zeigt, dass am 5. April 1953 um 2.00 Flateyri, Island angefangen hat Zeiten zu benutzen, die Greenwich gleich waren (0:00 Stunden von Greenwich). Am 26. Oktober 1953 hat Flateyri zu Zeiten eine Stunde östlich von Greenwich (1:00) gewechselt. Der Wechsel fand um 2.00 am 26. Oktober Statt.

7) Weil Jens zwischen den zwei oben gegebene Datumen geboren ist, wäre seine Zeit auf einem null Stundigen Unterschied Von Greenwich basiert.

8) Infolgedessen, die 15.13 (3.13 nachmittags) Geburtszeit von Jens ist 15.13 (3.13 nachmittags) in Greenwich gleich. Seine UT (Universale Ziet) wäre 15.13 (3.13 nachmittags).

HOW TO CALCULATE SIDEREAL TIME FOR AN EVENT

	Example 1	Example 2	Example 3
	11 May, 1931 1:30 PM Toronto, ON	11 November, 1931 6:15 PM Papeete, French Polynesia	11 May, 1931 00:15 AM Beijing, China
1) Convert the time of the event to the 24-hour clock.	13:30:00	18:15:00	00:15:00
2) Find the hours from Greenwich for the time being observed on that day from the time table given for that location. Add or subtract to the result of 1) according to the sign of the time observed, to convert to Universal Time (UT). Generally, you will add for Western longitudes and subtract for eastern longitudes. There are exceptions to this general rule but the correct operation is always given by the sign in the Time Table.	4:00:00 (daylight) 17:30:00	10:00:00 28:15:00	– 8:00:00 – 07:45:00
3) If the result of 2) is greater than 24 hours, subtract 24 hours and add 1 day to obtain the Greenwich date of the event. If the result of 2) is negative, add 24 hours and subtract 1 day to obtain the Greenwich date.		– 24:00:00 04:15:00 *(12 Nov. 1931)*	24:00:00 16:15:00 *(10 May, 1931)*
4) Use the UT from 2) or 3) and Table I to determine the solar/sidereal time correction (acceleration). Add this value to the UT.	02:52 17:32:52	00:42 04:15:42	02:40 16:17:40
5) Find the 0 hour sidereal time for the Greenwich date from *The American Ephemeris* or other reference and add to the result of 4).	15:11:16 32:43:68	03:20:39 07:36:21	15:07:19 31:24:59
6) Subtract from the result of 5) the longitude time equivalent obtained for the location of the event from *The International Atlas*. For eastern longitudes one would add the longitude time equivalent since subtraction of a negative value is equivalent to addition. If the result is between 0 and 24 hours you have calculated the sidereal time. Otherwise, go to step 7).	– 05:17:32 27:26:36	– 09:58:16 – 02:21:55	07:45:40 39:10:39
7) To the result of 6) add or subtract 24 hours, as appropriate, to put the sidereal time in the range between 0 to 24 hours. This adjustment does not require adjusting the date.	– 24:00:00 03:26:36	24:00:00 21:38:05	– 24:00:00 15:10:39

COMO CALCULAR EL TIEMPO SIDEREAL PARA UN EVENTO

	Ejemplo 1	**Ejemplo 2**	**Ejemplo 3**
	11 Mayo, 1931 1:30 PM Toronto, ON	11 Noviembre, 1931 6:15 PM Papeete, Polinesia Francesa	11 Mayo, 1931 00:15 AM Beijing, China
1) Convierta el tiempo del evento al reloj de 24 horas.	13:30:00	18:15:00	00:15:00
2) Encuentre las horas de Greenwich para el tiempo que esta siendo observado en ese dia de la Tabla de Tiempo dada para ese lugar, súmele o restele al resultado de 1) de acuerdo al signo del tiempo siendo observado, para convertirse al Tiempo Universal (UL) generalmente, tendrá que sumar para las longitudes occidentes y restar para las longitudes orientales. Esta regla general tiene sus excepciones pero la operación correcta es siempre dada por el signo en la Tabla.	4:00:00 (luz Natural) 17:30:00	10:00:00 28:15:00	– 8:00:00 – 07:45:00
3) Si el resultado del número 2) es mas alto de 24 horas, reste 24 horas y súme 1 dia para obtener la fecha del evento de Greenwich. Si el resultado del numero 2) es negativo, sumele 24 horas y restele 1 dia para obtener la fecha de Greenwich.		– 24:00:00 04:15:00 *(12 Nov. 1931)*	24:00:00 16:15:00 *(10 May, 1931)*
4) Use el Tiempo Universal (UT) del 2) ó 3) y la Tabla I para determinar la corrección del Solar/Sidereal (aceleración). Súmele este valor al Tiempo Universal (UT).	02:52 17:32:52	00:42 04:15:42	02:40 16:17:40
5) Encuentre la hora 0 del Tiempo Sidereal para la fecha de Greenwich del *The American Ephemeris* ó algún otro libro de referencia y súme el resultado de 4).	15:11:16 32:43:68	03:20:39 07:36:21	15:07:19 31:24:59
6) Reste del resultado del número 5) el tiempo equivalente de la longitud obtenida para la localidad del evento *del Atlas Internacional*. Para las longitudes orientales uno sumaría el tiempo de longitud equivalente porque la substracción de un valor negativo equivale a la suma. Si el resultado es entre 0 y 24 horas ud. ha calculado el Tiempo Sidereal, de otra manera continue con el paso 7).	– 05:17:32 27:26:36	– 09:58:16 – 02:21:55	07:45:40 39:10:39
7) Al resultado del 6) súmele o restele 24 horas, tal como sea apropiado, para poner el tiempo sidereal en el rango entre 0 a 24 horas. Este ajuste no requiere ajustar la fecha.	– 24:00:00 03:26:36	24:00:00 21:38:05	– 24:00:00 15:10:39

COMMENT CALCULER L'HEURE SIDERALE D'UN EVENEMENT

	Exemple 1	**Exemple 2**	**Exemple 3**
	11 Mai, 1931 1:30 PM Toronto, ON	11 Novembre, 1931 6:15 PM Papeete, Polynésie Française	11 Mai, 1931 00:15 AM Beijing, Chine
1) Donnez l'heure en chiffres allant de 1-24.	13:30:00	18:15:00	00:15:00
2) Trouvez la différence par rapport à l'heure de Greenwich pour l'époque où l'évènement a eu lieu grâce au tableau horaire du lieu en question. Ajoutez ou retranchez du résultat de 1), suivant le signe dont est affecté cette différence, afin d'obtenir l'heure universelle (Universal Time — UT) En général vous devrez ajouter dans le cas de longitudes ouest et soustraire dans celui des longitudes est. Il existe des exceptions à cette régle mais l'opération exacte est indiquée par le tableau horaire.	4:00:00 (luniére du jour) 17:30:00	10:00:00 28:15:00	– 8:00:00 – 07:45:00
3) Si le résultat obtenu en 2), est supérieur à 24 heures, retranchez 24 heures et ajoutez 1 jour pour avoir la date de Greenwich de l'évènement. Si le résultat de 2) est négatif, ajoutez 24 heures et enlevez 1 jour pour avoir la date de Greenwich.		– 24:00:00 04:15:00 *(12 Nov. 1931)*	24:00:00 16:15:00 *(10 May, 1931)*
4) Utilisez l'heure universelle obtenue en 2) ou 3) et le tableau I pour déterminer la correction (l'accélération) solaire/sidérale et ajoutez ce chiffre à l'heure universelle.	02:52 17:32:52	00:42 04:15:42	02:40 16:17:40
5) Trouvez le temp sidéral pour l'heure zéro à la date de Greenwich *dans l'Américan Ephemeris* ou dans tout autre ouvrage de référence. Ajoutez ce chiffre à 4).	15:11:16 32:43:68	03:20:39 07:36:21	15:07:19 31:24:59
6) Cherchez l'heure à la longitude du lieu où s'est déroulé l'évènement et soustrayez ce chiffre du resultat obtenu en 5) *de l'atlas International*. Pour les longitudes est on devra ajouter l'heure à la longitude puisque la soustraction d'une quantité négative équivaut à une addition. Si le résultat se situe entre 0 et 24 heures vous avez calculé l'heure sidérale. Sinon passez au numéro 7).	– 05:17:32 27:26:36	– 09:58:16 – 02:21:55	07:45:40 39:10:39
7) Ajoutez ou soustrayez 24, suivant le cas, au résultat de 6) afin d'obtenir un chiffre entre 0 et 24 pour l'heure sidérale. Cette correction n'entraine pas un ajustement de la date.	– 24:00:00 03:26:36	24:00:00 21:38:05	– 24:00:00 15:10:39

WIE MAN DIE STERNZEIT FÜR EIN EREIGNIS RECHNET

	Beispiel 1	Beispiel 2	Beispiel 3
	11 Mai, 1931 1:30 PM Toronto, ON	11 November, 1931 6:15 PM Papeete, Französisch Polynesien	11 Mai, 1931 00:15 AM Beijing, China
1) Rechnen Sie die Zeit des Ereignis auf die Vierundzwanzigstundenuhr.	13:30:00	18:15:00	00:15:00
2) Finden Sie die Stunden von Greenwich für die Zeit, die beobachtet wird an jenem Tag, von dem vorhandenem Zeitplan für jene Ortsangabe. Addieren Sie oder ziehen Sie das Ergebnis von 1) ab, nach dem Zeichen der beobachteten Zeit, um auf die universale Zeit (UT) umzurechnen. Normalerweise, werden Sie für westliche Längen addieren und für östliche Längen abziehen. Da sind Ausnahmen von dieser allgemeinen Regel, aber der richtige Vorgang wird von dem Zeichen im Zeitplan gegeben.	4:00:00 (tageslichtzeit) 17:30:00	10:00:00 28:15:00	– 8:00:00 – 07:45:00
3) Wenn das Ergebnis von 2) grösser als 24 Stunden ist, ziehen Sie 24 Stunden ab und addieren Sie einen Tag, um das Greenwich Datum des Ereignis zu bekommen. Wenn das Ergebnis von 2) negativ ist, addieren Sie 24 Stunden und ziehen Sie einen Tag ab, um das Greenwich Datum zu bekommen.		– 24:00:00 04:15:00 *(12 Nov. 1931)*	24:00:00 16:15:00 *(10 May, 1931)*
4) Benutzen Sie die UT von 2) oder 3) und den Plan I, um die Sonnen/Sternzeit verbesserung (Beschleunigung) festzustellen. Addieren Sie diesen Wert zur UT.	02:52 17:32:52	00:42 04:15:42	02:40 16:17:40
5) Finden Sie die 0 stundige Sternzeit für das Greenwich Datum von *The American Ephemeris* oder von anderen Referenz und addieren Sie das Ergebnis von 4).	15:11:16 32:43:68	03:20:39 07:36:21	15:07:19 31:24:59
6) Ziehen Sie von dem Ergebnis von 5) das längliche Zeitäquivalent ab, das für die Ortsangabe des Ereignis von *Dem Internationalen Atlas* erhalten wird. Für östliche Längen addierte man das längliche Zeitäquivalent, weil das Abziehen von negativen Werten zur Addition gleich ist. Wenn das Ergebnis zwischen 0 und 24 Stunden ist, müssen Sie die Sternzeit rechnen. Sonst, gehen Sie zur Stufe 7) weiter.	– 05:17:32 27:26:36	– 09:58:16 – 02:21:55	07:45:40 39:10:39
7) Zur Ergebnis von 6) addieren Sie oder ziehen Sie 24 Stunden ab, wo passend, um die Sternzeit in den Bereich zwischen 0 und 24 Stunden zu stellen. Diese Anpassung fordert nicht die Anpassung des Datums.	– 24:00:00 03:26:36	24:00:00 21:38:05	– 24:00:00 15:10:39

Table I
Solar-Sidereal Time Correction (Acceleration)

MIN	0h	1h	2h	3h	4h	5h	6h	7h	8h	9h	10h	11h	12h	13h	14h	15h	16h	17h	18h	19h	20h	21h	22h	23h	MIN
	m s	m s	m s	m s	m s	m s	m s	m s	m s	m s	m s	m s	m s	m s	m s	m s	m s	m s	m s	m s	m s	m s	m s	m s	
0	0 0	0 10	0 20	0 30	0 39	0 49	0 59	1 9	1 19	1 29	1 39	1 48	1 58	2 8	2 18	2 28	2 38	2 48	2 57	3 7	3 17	3 27	3 37	3 47	0
1	0 0	0 10	0 20	0 30	0 40	0 49	0 59	1 9	1 19	1 29	1 39	1 49	1 58	2 8	2 18	2 28	2 38	2 48	2 58	3 7	3 17	3 27	3 37	3 47	1
2	0 0	0 10	0 20	0 30	0 40	0 50	0 59	1 9	1 19	1 29	1 39	1 49	1 59	2 8	2 18	2 28	2 38	2 48	2 58	3 8	3 17	3 27	3 37	3 47	2
3	0 0	0 10	0 20	0 30	0 40	0 50	0 60	1 9	1 19	1 29	1 39	1 49	1 59	2 9	2 18	2 28	2 38	2 48	2 58	3 8	3 18	3 27	3 37	3 47	3
4	0 1	0 11	0 20	0 30	0 40	0 50	0 60	1 10	1 20	1 29	1 39	1 49	1 59	2 9	2 19	2 29	2 38	2 48	2 58	3 8	3 18	3 28	3 37	3 47	4
5	0 1	0 11	0 21	0 30	0 40	0 50	0 60	1 10	1 20	1 30	1 39	1 49	1 59	2 9	2 19	2 29	2 39	2 48	2 58	3 8	3 18	3 28	3 38	3 48	5
6	0 1	0 11	0 21	0 31	0 40	0 50	1 0	1 10	1 20	1 30	1 40	1 49	1 59	2 9	2 19	2 29	2 39	2 49	2 58	3 8	3 18	3 28	3 38	3 48	6
7	0 1	0 11	0 21	0 31	0 41	0 50	1 0	1 10	1 20	1 30	1 40	1 50	1 59	2 9	2 19	2 29	2 39	2 49	2 59	3 8	3 18	3 28	3 38	3 48	7
8	0 1	0 11	0 21	0 31	0 41	0 51	1 0	1 10	1 20	1 30	1 40	1 50	1 60	2 9	2 19	2 29	2 39	2 49	2 59	3 9	3 18	3 28	3 38	3 48	8
9	0 1	0 11	0 21	0 31	0 41	0 51	1 1	1 10	1 20	1 30	1 40	1 50	1 60	2 10	2 19	2 29	2 39	2 49	2 59	3 9	3 19	3 28	3 38	3 48	9
10	0 2	0 11	0 21	0 31	0 41	0 51	1 1	1 11	1 20	1 30	1 40	1 50	1 60	2 10	2 20	2 29	2 39	2 49	2 59	3 9	3 19	3 29	3 38	3 48	10
11	0 2	0 12	0 22	0 31	0 41	0 51	1 1	1 11	1 21	1 31	1 40	1 50	2 0	2 10	2 20	2 30	2 40	2 49	2 59	3 9	3 19	3 29	3 39	3 49	11
12	0 2	0 12	0 22	0 32	0 41	0 51	1 1	1 11	1 21	1 31	1 41	1 50	2 0	2 10	2 20	2 30	2 40	2 50	2 59	3 9	3 19	3 29	3 39	3 49	12
13	0 2	0 12	0 22	0 32	0 42	0 51	1 1	1 11	1 21	1 31	1 41	1 51	2 0	2 10	2 20	2 30	2 40	2 50	2 60	3 9	3 19	3 29	3 39	3 49	13
14	0 2	0 12	0 22	0 32	0 42	0 52	1 1	1 11	1 21	1 31	1 41	1 51	2 1	2 10	2 20	2 30	2 40	2 50	2 60	3 10	3 19	3 29	3 39	3 49	14
15	0 2	0 12	0 22	0 32	0 42	0 52	1 2	1 11	1 21	1 31	1 41	1 51	2 1	2 11	2 20	2 30	2 40	2 50	2 60	3 10	3 20	3 29	3 39	3 49	15
16	0 3	0 12	0 22	0 32	0 42	0 52	1 2	1 12	1 21	1 31	1 41	1 51	2 1	2 11	2 21	2 30	2 40	2 50	3 0	3 10	3 20	3 30	3 39	3 49	16
17	0 3	0 13	0 23	0 32	0 42	0 52	1 2	1 12	1 22	1 32	1 41	1 51	2 1	2 11	2 21	2 31	2 40	2 50	3 0	3 10	3 20	3 30	3 40	3 49	17
18	0 3	0 13	0 23	0 33	0 42	0 52	1 2	1 12	1 22	1 32	1 42	1 51	2 1	2 11	2 21	2 31	2 41	2 51	3 0	3 10	3 20	3 30	3 40	3 50	18
19	0 3	0 13	0 23	0 33	0 43	0 52	1 2	1 12	1 22	1 32	1 42	1 52	2 1	2 11	2 21	2 31	2 41	2 51	3 1	3 10	3 20	3 30	3 40	3 50	19
20	0 3	0 13	0 23	0 33	0 43	0 53	1 2	1 12	1 22	1 32	1 42	1 52	2 2	2 11	2 21	2 31	2 41	2 51	3 1	3 11	3 20	3 30	3 40	3 50	20
21	0 3	0 13	0 23	0 33	0 43	0 53	1 3	1 12	1 22	1 32	1 42	1 52	2 2	2 12	2 21	2 31	2 41	2 51	3 1	3 11	3 21	3 30	3 40	3 50	21
22	0 4	0 13	0 23	0 33	0 43	0 53	1 3	1 13	1 22	1 32	1 42	1 52	2 2	2 12	2 22	2 31	2 41	2 51	3 1	3 11	3 21	3 31	3 40	3 50	22
23	0 4	0 14	0 23	0 33	0 43	0 53	1 3	1 13	1 23	1 32	1 42	1 52	2 2	2 12	2 22	2 32	2 41	2 51	3 1	3 11	3 21	3 31	3 41	3 50	23
24	0 4	0 14	0 24	0 34	0 43	0 53	1 3	1 13	1 23	1 33	1 43	1 52	2 2	2 12	2 22	2 32	2 42	2 52	3 1	3 11	3 21	3 31	3 41	3 51	24
25	0 4	0 14	0 24	0 34	0 44	0 53	1 3	1 13	1 23	1 33	1 43	1 53	2 2	2 12	2 22	2 32	2 42	2 52	3 2	3 11	3 21	3 31	3 41	3 51	25
26	0 4	0 14	0 24	0 34	0 44	0 54	1 3	1 13	1 23	1 33	1 43	1 53	2 3	2 12	2 22	2 32	2 42	2 52	3 2	3 12	3 21	3 31	3 41	3 51	26
27	0 4	0 14	0 24	0 34	0 44	0 54	1 4	1 13	1 23	1 33	1 43	1 53	2 3	2 13	2 22	2 32	2 42	2 52	3 2	3 12	3 22	3 31	3 41	3 51	27
28	0 5	0 14	0 24	0 34	0 44	0 54	1 4	1 14	1 23	1 33	1 43	1 53	2 3	2 13	2 23	2 32	2 42	2 52	3 2	3 12	3 22	3 32	3 41	3 51	28
29	0 5	0 15	0 24	0 34	0 44	0 54	1 4	1 14	1 24	1 33	1 43	1 53	2 3	2 13	2 23	2 33	2 42	2 52	3 2	3 12	3 22	3 32	3 42	3 51	29
30	0 5	0 15	0 25	0 34	0 44	0 54	1 4	1 14	1 24	1 34	1 43	1 53	2 3	2 13	2 23	2 33	2 43	2 52	3 2	3 12	3 22	3 32	3 42	3 52	30
31	0 5	0 15	0 25	0 35	0 45	0 54	1 4	1 14	1 24	1 34	1 44	1 54	2 3	2 13	2 23	2 33	2 43	2 53	3 3	3 12	3 22	3 32	3 42	3 52	31
32	0 5	0 15	0 25	0 35	0 45	0 55	1 4	1 14	1 24	1 34	1 44	1 54	2 4	2 13	2 23	2 33	2 43	2 53	3 3	3 13	3 22	3 32	3 42	3 52	32
33	0 5	0 15	0 25	0 35	0 45	0 55	1 5	1 14	1 24	1 34	1 44	1 54	2 4	2 14	2 23	2 33	2 43	2 53	3 3	3 13	3 23	3 32	3 42	3 52	33
34	0 6	0 15	0 25	0 35	0 45	0 55	1 5	1 15	1 24	1 34	1 44	1 54	2 4	2 14	2 24	2 33	2 43	2 53	3 3	3 13	3 23	3 33	3 42	3 52	34
35	0 6	0 16	0 25	0 35	0 45	0 55	1 5	1 15	1 25	1 34	1 44	1 54	2 4	2 14	2 24	2 34	2 43	2 53	3 3	3 13	3 23	3 33	3 43	3 52	35
36	0 6	0 16	0 26	0 35	0 45	0 55	1 5	1 15	1 25	1 35	1 44	1 54	2 4	2 14	2 24	2 34	2 44	2 53	3 3	3 13	3 23	3 33	3 43	3 53	36
37	0 6	0 16	0 26	0 36	0 46	0 55	1 5	1 15	1 25	1 35	1 45	1 54	2 4	2 14	2 24	2 34	2 44	2 54	3 3	3 13	3 23	3 33	3 43	3 53	37
38	0 6	0 16	0 26	0 36	0 46	0 56	1 5	1 15	1 25	1 35	1 45	1 55	2 5	2 14	2 24	2 34	2 44	2 54	3 4	3 14	3 23	3 33	3 43	3 53	38
39	0 6	0 16	0 26	0 36	0 46	0 56	1 6	1 15	1 25	1 35	1 45	1 55	2 5	2 15	2 24	2 34	2 44	2 54	3 4	3 14	3 24	3 33	3 43	3 53	39
40	0 7	0 16	0 26	0 36	0 46	0 56	1 6	1 16	1 25	1 35	1 45	1 55	2 5	2 15	2 25	2 34	2 44	2 54	3 4	3 14	3 24	3 34	3 43	3 53	40
41	0 7	0 17	0 26	0 36	0 46	0 56	1 6	1 16	1 26	1 35	1 45	1 55	2 5	2 15	2 25	2 35	2 44	2 54	3 4	3 14	3 24	3 34	3 44	3 53	41
42	0 7	0 17	0 27	0 36	0 46	0 56	1 6	1 16	1 26	1 36	1 45	1 55	2 5	2 15	2 25	2 35	2 45	2 54	3 4	3 14	3 24	3 34	3 44	3 54	42
43	0 7	0 17	0 27	0 37	0 46	0 56	1 6	1 16	1 26	1 36	1 46	1 55	2 5	2 15	2 25	2 35	2 45	2 55	3 4	3 14	3 24	3 34	3 44	3 54	43
44	0 7	0 17	0 27	0 37	0 47	0 57	1 6	1 16	1 26	1 36	1 46	1 56	2 6	2 15	2 25	2 35	2 45	2 55	3 5	3 15	3 24	3 34	3 44	3 54	44
45	0 7	0 17	0 27	0 37	0 47	0 57	1 7	1 16	1 26	1 36	1 46	1 56	2 6	2 16	2 25	2 35	2 45	2 55	3 5	3 15	3 25	3 34	3 44	3 54	45
46	0 8	0 17	0 27	0 37	0 47	0 57	1 7	1 17	1 26	1 36	1 46	1 56	2 6	2 16	2 26	2 35	2 45	2 55	3 5	3 15	3 25	3 35	3 44	3 54	46
47	0 8	0 18	0 27	0 37	0 47	0 57	1 7	1 17	1 27	1 36	1 46	1 56	2 6	2 16	2 26	2 36	2 45	2 55	3 5	3 15	3 25	3 35	3 45	3 54	47
48	0 8	0 18	0 28	0 37	0 47	0 57	1 7	1 17	1 27	1 37	1 46	1 56	2 6	2 16	2 26	2 36	2 46	2 55	3 5	3 15	3 25	3 35	3 45	3 55	48
49	0 8	0 18	0 28	0 38	0 47	0 57	1 7	1 17	1 27	1 37	1 47	1 56	2 6	2 16	2 26	2 36	2 46	2 56	3 5	3 15	3 25	3 35	3 45	3 55	49
50	0 8	0 18	0 28	0 38	0 48	0 57	1 7	1 17	1 27	1 37	1 47	1 57	2 6	2 16	2 26	2 36	2 46	2 56	3 6	3 15	3 25	3 35	3 45	3 55	50
51	0 8	0 18	0 28	0 38	0 48	0 58	1 8	1 17	1 27	1 37	1 47	1 57	2 7	2 17	2 26	2 36	2 46	2 56	3 6	3 16	3 26	3 35	3 45	3 55	51
52	0 9	0 18	0 28	0 38	0 48	0 58	1 8	1 18	1 27	1 37	1 47	1 57	2 7	2 17	2 27	2 36	2 46	2 56	3 6	3 16	3 26	3 36	3 45	3 55	52
53	0 9	0 19	0 28	0 38	0 48	0 58	1 8	1 18	1 28	1 37	1 47	1 57	2 7	2 17	2 27	2 37	2 46	2 56	3 6	3 16	3 26	3 36	3 46	3 55	53
54	0 9	0 19	0 29	0 38	0 48	0 58	1 8	1 18	1 28	1 38	1 47	1 57	2 7	2 17	2 27	2 37	2 47	2 56	3 6	3 16	3 26	3 36	3 46	3 56	54
55	0 9	0 19	0 29	0 39	0 48	0 58	1 8	1 18	1 28	1 38	1 48	1 57	2 7	2 17	2 27	2 37	2 47	2 57	3 6	3 16	3 26	3 36	3 46	3 56	55
56	0 9	0 19	0 29	0 39	0 49	0 58	1 8	1 18	1 28	1 38	1 48	1 58	2 7	2 17	2 27	2 37	2 47	2 57	3 7	3 16	3 26	3 36	3 46	3 56	56
57	0 9	0 19	0 29	0 39	0 49	0 59	1 9	1 18	1 28	1 38	1 48	1 58	2 8	2 17	2 27	2 37	2 47	2 57	3 7	3 17	3 26	3 36	3 46	3 56	57
58	0 10	0 19	0 29	0 39	0 49	0 59	1 9	1 19	1 28	1 38	1 48	1 58	2 8	2 18	2 28	2 37	2 47	2 57	3 7	3 17	3 27	3 37	3 46	3 56	58
59	0 10	0 20	0 29	0 39	0 49	0 59	1 9	1 19	1 29	1 38	1 48	1 58	2 8	2 18	2 28	2 38	2 47	2 57	3 7	3 17	3 27	3 37	3 47	3 56	59
60	0 10	0 20	0 30	0 39	0 49	0 59	1 9	1 19	1 29	1 39	1 48	1 58	2 8	2 18	2 28	2 38	2 48	2 57	3 7	3 17	3 27	3 37	3 47	3 57	60

Table II
Calendar Table

This table gives the date when the listed countries changed to the Gregorian calendar (N.S.) from the Julian calendar (O.S.), except for China and Japan, which never used the Julian calendar.

Western countries not listed here changed to the Gregorian calendar before the 19th century.

Country	Province	Year	Gregorian Date	Julian Date
BULGARIA	Part	1915	14 November	1 November
	Part	1920	17 September	4 September
CHINA		1912	12 February	Chinese Calendar
GREECE	Adopted Julian	1846		
	Part	1916	28 July	15 July
	Rest	1920	18 March	5 March
JAPAN		1893	1 January	Japanese Calendar
POLAND	Austrian & German	1582	15 October	5 October
	Russian	1918	14 January	1 January
ROMANIA	Catholic	1919	18 March	5 March
	Gr. Orothodox	1920	18 March	5 March
SOVIET UNION	Western	1918	14 January	1 January
	Estonia	1918	15 February	2 February
	Latvia	1918	15 February	2 February
	Lithuania	1918	15 February	2 February
	Eastern	1920	18 March	5 March
	All	1929	instituted a 5 day week and altered calendar accordingly.	
		1932	instituted a 6 day week and again changed calendar.	
		1940	27 June returned to N.S.	
TURKEY	European	1908		
	Asian	1914		
YUGOSLAVIA		1919	18 March	5 March

AFGHĀNESTĀN — AFGANISTÁN — AFGHANISTAN

Time Table
Before 1/Jan/1890 LMT
Begin Standard 60E00
1/Jan/1890 0:00 -4:00
Begin Standard 67E30
1/Jan/1945 0:00 -4:30

Place	Lat	Long	Offset
Āchīn	34N08	70E42	-4:42:48
Adraskan	33N39	62E16	-4:09:04
'Alam Lek	37N02	65E57	-4:23:48
'Alī Khēl	33N57	69E43	-4:38:52
Amurd	38N12	71E21	-4:45:24
Anār Darreh	32N46	61E39	-4:06:36
Andkhvoy	36N56	65E08	-4:20:32
Andowj	37N02	71E27	-4:45:48
Āqcheh	36N56	66E11	-4:24:44
Āq Koprūk	36N05	66E51	-4:27:24
Asadābād	34N52	71E09	-4:44:36
Āsmār	35N02	71E22	-4:45:28
Āybak	36N16	68E01	-4:32:04
Bābā Valī Şāḩeb	31N40	65E40	-4:22:40
Badrao	34N46	69E40	-4:38:40
Baghlān	36N13	68E46	-4:35:04
Baghlīn	36N14	65E55	-4:23:40
Baghrān Khowleh	33N01	64E58	-4:19:52
Bahrām Chāh	29N26	64E03	-4:16:12
Bailugh	32N41	66E46	-4:27:04
Bālā Bāgh	34N24	70E14	-4:40:56
Bālā Morghāb	35N35	63E20	-4:13:20
Balkh	36N46	66E54	-4:27:36
Bāmīān	34N50	67E50	-4:31:20
Band	33N17	68E39	-4:34:36
Banow	35N38	69E15	-4:37:00
Barakī Barak	33N56	68E55	-4:35:40
Barg-E Maţāl	35N40	71E21	-4:45:24
Barghanak	33N56	62E26	-4:09:44
Barī Gāv	33N52	67E49	-4:31:16
Barīkowţ	35N18	71E32	-4:46:08
Bātsawul	34N15	70E52	-4:43:28
Bāzār-E Panjvā'ī	31N32	65E28	-4:21:52
Belcherāgh	35N50	65E14	-4:20:56
Bībānak	32N11	64E11	-4:16:44
Boyni Qara	36N19	66E53	-4:27:32
'Chaghcharān	34N32	65E15	-4:21:00
Chahār Bāgh	37N00	65E14	-4:20:56
Chahār Bāgh	35N58	69E38	-4:38:32
Chahār Borjak	30N17	62E03	-4:08:12
Chahār Deh-Ye Ghowrband	34N59	68E44	-4:34:56
Chakhānsūr	31N10	62E04	-4:08:16
Chamkanī	33N48	69E49	-4:39:16
Chārīkār	35N01	69E11	-4:36:44
Chehel Dokhtarān	35N06	62E19	-4:09:16
Chelīk-E Yās Khān	37N05	66E14	-4:24:56
Chesht-E Sharīf	34N21	63E44	-4:14:56
Dahaneh-Ye Ghowrī	35N54	68E30	-4:34:00
Dahaneh-Ye Kāshār	35N09	66E14	-4:24:56
Dahan-E Qowmghī	34N28	66E31	-4:26:04
Ḏang	31N37	65E41	-4:22:44
Darakht-E Yahyá	31N50	68E08	-4:32:32
Darvāzahgêy	31N48	67E44	-4:30:56
Darz Āb	35N58	65E22	-4:21:28
Daulatābād (Shirin Tagāo)	36N26	64E55	-4:19:40
Deh Bālā	34N04	70E29	-4:41:56
Delārām	32N11	63E25	-4:13:40
Deshu	30N26	63E19	-4:13:16
Dīwāl Qol	34N19	67E54	-4:31:36
Do Āb-E Mīkh-E Zarrīn	35N16	68E00	-4:32:00
Dowlatābād	36N59	66E50	-4:27:20
Dowlatābād	36N26	64E55	-4:19:40
Dowlat Yār	34N33	65E47	-4:23:08
Dowshī	35N37	68E41	-4:34:44
Eshkāshem	36N42	71E34	-4:46:16
Eslām Qal'Eh	34N40	61E04	-4:04:16
Farāh	32N22	62E07	-4:08:28
Fārsī	33N47	63E15	-4:13:00
Feyẕābād	37N06	70E34	-4:42:16
Gardēz	33N37	69E07	-4:36:28
Garm Āb	32N14	65E01	-4:20:04
Gereshk	31N48	64E34	-4:18:16
Ghaznī	33N33	68E26	-4:33:44
Ghūrīān	34N21	61E30	-4:06:00
Gīzāb	33N23	66E16	-4:25:04
Golrān	35N06	61E41	-4:06:44
Gowmal Kalay	32N29	68E55	-4:35:40
Hazāreh Toghāy	37N11	67E13	-4:28:52
Herāt	34N20	62E12	-4:08:48
Jabal Os Sarāj	35N07	69E14	-4:36:56
Jaldak	31N58	66E43	-4:26:52
Jalālābād	34N26	70E28	-4:41:52
Jorm	36N52	70E51	-4:43:24
Kaboul → Kābul	34N31	69E12	-4:36:48
Kābul	34N31	69E12	-4:36:48
Kāl Qal'Eh	32N38	62E32	-4:10:08
Kamdēsh	35N24	71E20	-4:45:20
Kārīz-E Elyās	35N25	61E20	-4:05:20
Karokh	34N28	62E35	-4:10:20
Khānābād	36N41	69E07	-4:36:28
Khāsh	31N31	62E52	-4:11:28
Khenjān	35N36	70E59	-4:43:56
Khevāj	38N13	71E02	-4:44:08
Kheyr Khāneh	34N57	63E37	-4:14:28
Khivach	38N13	71E02	-4:44:08
Kholm	36N42	67E41	-4:30:44
Khowst	33N22	69E57	-4:39:48
Khūgīānī Sānī	31N31	66E12	-4:24:48
Khvājeh Ra'ūf	33N19	64E43	-4:18:52
Kohsān	34N39	61E12	-4:04:48
Konar-E Khāş	34N39	70E54	-4:43:36
Koshk-E Kohneh	34N52	62E31	-4:10:04
Kowt-E 'Ashrow	34N27	68E48	-4:35:12
Kūchnay Darvīshān	30N59	64E11	-4:16:44
Kugas	38N21	70E48	-4:43:12
Landay	30N31	63E47	-4:15:08
Langar	37N02	73E47	-4:55:08
Lar Gerd	35N29	66E40	-4:26:40
Lāsh-E Joveyn	31N43	61E37	-4:06:28
Lashkar Gāh	31N30	64E21	-4:17:24
Mahmūd-E 'Erāqī	35N01	69E20	-4:37:20
Malek Dīn	32N25	68E04	-4:32:16
Mandel	33N17	61E52	-4:07:28
Marghī	34N58	66E31	-4:26:04
Ma'Rūt	31N34	67E03	-4:28:12
Mashūray	32N12	68E21	-4:33:24
Mazār-E Sharīf	36N42	67E06	-4:28:24
Mehtar Lām	34N39	70E10	-4:40:40
Mengeh Jek	37N02	66E07	-4:24:28
Meydān Kalay	32N25	66E44	-4:26:56
Meydān Khvolah	33N36	69E51	-4:39:24
Meymaneh	35N55	64E47	-4:19:08
Mīrābād	30N25	61E50	-4:07:20
Mīr Bachcheh Kūt	34N45	69E08	-4:36:32
Mogor	32N52	67E47	-4:31:08
Mūsá Qal'Eh	32N22	64E46	-4:19:04
Nārīn Ghar	36N01	69E06	-4:36:24
Nāwah	32N19	67E53	-4:31:32
Nayak	34N44	66E57	-4:27:48
Now Zād	32N24	64E28	-4:17:52
Orgūn	32N51	69E07	-4:36:28
Orūzgān (Qala-I-Hazār Qadam)	32N56	66E38	-4:26:32
Owbeh	34N22	63E10	-4:12:40
Paghmān	34N36	68E57	-4:35:48
Panjāb	34N22	67E01	-4:28:04
Peshīn Jān	33N25	61E28	-4:05:52
Pol-E Khomrī	35N56	68E43	-4:34:52
Por Chaman	33N08	63E51	-4:15:24
Qalāt	32N07	66E54	-4:27:36
Qal'Eh Kāh	32N18	61E31	-4:06:04
Qal'Eh Shahr	35N33	65E34	-4:22:16
Qal'Eh-Ye Now	34N59	63E08	-4:12:32
Qal'Eh-Ye Now	35N27	67E08	-4:28:32
Qal'Eh-Ye Panjeh	37N00	72E36	-4:50:24
Qal'Eh-Ye Sāber	34N02	69E01	-4:36:04
Qal'Eh-Ye Sarkārī	35N54	67E17	-4:29:08
Qandahār	31N32	65E30	-4:22:00
Qarah Bāgh	34N56	61E46	-4:07:04
Qarāvol	37N14	68E46	-4:35:04
Qarqīn	37N25	66E03	-4:24:12
Qeyşār	35N41	64E17	-4:17:08
Qondūz	37N45	68E51	-4:35:24
Rashīd Qal'Eh	31N31	67E31	-4:30:04
Rechāh Lām	34N58	70E51	-4:43:24
Rokheh	35N16	69E28	-4:37:52
Rostāq	37N07	69E49	-4:39:16
Rūdbār	30N09	62E36	-4:10:24
Sākhar	32N57	65E32	-4:22:08
Salām Khān	31N47	66E45	-4:27:00
Sangar Sarāy	34N24	70E38	-4:42:32
Sang-E Māsheh	33N08	67E27	-4:29:48
Sayghān	35N11	67E42	-4:30:48
Shāhī Kowt	34N16	70E34	-4:42:16
Shāh-I-Mashhad	35N03	63E58	-4:15:52
Shāh Jūy	32N31	67E25	-4:29:40
Shahrak	34N06	64E18	-4:17:12
Shahr-E Monjān	36N02	70E46	-4:43:04
Shahr-E Şafā	31N50	66E22	-4:25:28
Shahrestān	34N22	66E47	-4:27:08
Sheberghān	36N41	65E45	-4:23:00
Shēkhābād	34N05	68E45	-4:35:00
Shesh Gāv	33N45	68E33	-4:34:12
Shīndand	33N18	62E08	-4:08:32
Shīnkay	31N57	67E26	-4:29:44
Shīn Naray	31N19	66E43	-4:26:52
Sorūbī	34N36	69E43	-4:38:52
Spīn Būldak	31N01	66E24	-4:25:36
Tagow Bāy	35N42	66E03	-4:24:12
Tahāneh-Ye Ney Basteh	32N59	60E53	-4:03:32
Tāloqān	36N44	69E33	-4:38:12
Tarīn Kowt	32N52	65E38	-4:22:32
Tāshkurghān → Kholm	36N42	67E41	-4:30:44
Teylān	35N32	64E47	-4:19:08
Teyvareh	33N21	64E25	-4:17:40
Tīr Pol	34N36	61E15	-4:05:00
Tojg	32N04	61E48	-4:07:12
Tokzār	35N52	66E26	-4:25:44
Towr Kham	34N08	71E05	-4:44:20
Towrzī	32N38	65E53	-4:23:32
Towrzī	30N11	65E59	-4:23:56
Tsowkêy	34N41	70E56	-4:43:44
Tūlak	33N58	63E44	-4:14:56
Ujum	38N22	70E51	-4:43:24
Üst	36N56	72E53	-4:51:32
Wānow	32N38	65E54	-4:23:36
Wazay	33N22	69E26	-4:37:44
Yakchāl	31N47	64E41	-4:18:44
Yakhchāl	31N47	64E41	-4:18:44
Zaranj	31N06	61E53	-4:07:32
Zarghūn Shahr	32N51	68E25	-4:33:40
Zaydābād	34N17	69E07	-4:36:28
Zendeh Jān	34N21	61E45	-4:07:00
Zīārat-E Shāh Maqşūd	31N59	65E30	-4:22:00
Zībāk	36N32	71E21	-4:45:24

SHQIPËRI — ALBANIEN — ALBANIE — ALBANIA

Time Table
Before 1/Jan/1914 LMT
Begin Standard 15E00

Date	Time	Offset
1/Jan/1914	0:00	-1:00
16/Jun/1940	0:00	-2:00
2/Nov/1942	3:00	-1:00
29/Mar/1943	2:00	-2:00
10/Apr/1943	3:00	-1:00
4/May/1974	0:00	-2:00
2/Oct/1974	0:00	-1:00
1/May/1975	0:00	-2:00
2/Oct/1975	0:00	-1:00
2/May/1976	0:00	-2:00
3/Oct/1976	0:00	-1:00
8/May/1977	0:00	-2:00
2/Oct/1977	0:00	-1:00
6/May/1978	0:00	-2:00
1/Oct/1978	0:00	-1:00
5/May/1979	0:00	-2:00
30/Sep/1979	0:00	-1:00
3/May/1980	0:00	-2:00
4/Oct/1980	0:00	-1:00
26/Apr/1981	0:00	-2:00
27/Sep/1981	0:00	-1:00
2/May/1982	0:00	-2:00
3/Oct/1982	0:00	-1:00
18/Apr/1983	0:00	-2:00
1/Oct/1983	0:00	-1:00
1/Apr/1984	0:00	-2:00
1/Oct/1984	0:00	-1:00
31/Mar/1985	1:00	-2:00
29/Sep/1985	2:00	-1:00
30/Mar/1986	1:00	-2:00
28/Sep/1986	2:00	-1:00
29/Mar/1987	1:00	-2:00
27/Sep/1987	2:00	-1:00
27/Mar/1988	1:00	-2:00
25/Sep/1988	2:00	-1:00
26/Mar/1989	1:00	-2:00
24/Sep/1989	2:00	-1:00
25/Mar/1990	1:00	-2:00
30/Sep/1990	2:00	-1:00
31/Mar/1991	1:00	-2:00
29/Sep/1991	2:00	-1:00
29/Mar/1992	1:00	-2:00
27/Sep/1992	2:00	-1:00
28/Mar/1993	1:00	-2:00
26/Sep/1993	2:00	-1:00
27/Mar/1994	1:00	-2:00
25/Sep/1994	2:00	-1:00
26/Mar/1995	1:00	-2:00
24/Sep/1995	2:00	-1:00
31/Mar/1996	1:00	-2:00
29/Sep/1996	2:00	-1:00
30/Mar/1997	1:00	-2:00
28/Sep/1997	2:00	-1:00
29/Mar/1998	1:00	-2:00
27/Sep/1998	2:00	-1:00
28/Mar/1999	1:00	-2:00
26/Sep/1999	2:00	-1:00
26/Mar/2000	1:00	-2:00
24/Sep/2000	2:00	-1:00

Place	Lat	Long	Offset
Berat	40N42	19E57	-1:19:48
Burrel	41N37	20E00	-1:20:00
Cërrik	41N02	19E57	-1:19:48
Çorovodë	40N30	20E13	-1:20:52
Delvinë	39N57	20E06	-1:20:24
Durazzo → Durrës	41N19	19E26	-1:17:44
Durrës	41N19	19E26	-1:17:44
Elbasan	41N06	20E05	-1:20:20
Ersekë	40N20	20E41	-1:22:44
Fier	40N43	19E34	-1:18:16
Gjirokastër	40N05	20E10	-1:20:40
Gramsh	40N52	20E11	-1:20:44
Himarë	40N07	19E44	-1:18:56
Kavajë	41N11	19E33	-1:18:12
Konispol	39N39	20E10	-1:20:40

ALBANIA — ALBANIE — ALBANIEN — SHQIPËRI

Place	Lat	Long	Offset
Koplik	42N13	19E26	-1:17:44
Korçë	40N37	20E46	-1:23:04
Koritsa → Korçë	40N37	20E46	-1:23:04
Krujë	41N30	19E48	-1:19:12
Kuçovë → Stalin	40N48	19E54	-1:19:36
Kukës	42N05	20E24	-1:21:36
Laç	41N38	19E43	-1:18:52
Lezhë	41N47	19E39	-1:18:36
Librazhd	41N11	20E19	-1:21:16
Lushnje	40N56	19E42	-1:18:48
Peqin	41N03	19E45	-1:19:00
Përmet	40N14	20E21	-1:21:24
Peshkopi	41N41	20E26	-1:21:44
Pogradec	40N54	20E39	-1:22:36
Prenjas	41N04	20E32	-1:22:08
Pukë	42N03	19E54	-1:19:36
Rrëshen	41N47	19E54	-1:19:36
Rrogozhinë	41N05	19E40	-1:18:40
Sarandë	39N52	20E00	-1:20:00
Scutari → Shkodër	42N05	19E30	-1:18:00
Selenicë	40N32	19E38	-1:18:32
Shkodër	42N05	19E30	-1:18:00
Stalin (Kuçovë)	40N48	19E54	-1:19:36
Tepelenë	40N18	20E01	-1:20:04
Tirana → Tiranë	41N20	19E50	-1:19:20
Tiranë	41N20	19E50	-1:19:20
Tropojë	42N24	20E10	-1:20:40
Ulzë	41N41	19E54	-1:19:36
Valona → Vlorë	40N27	19E30	-1:18:00
Vlonë → Vlorë	40N27	19E30	-1:18:00
Vlorë	40N27	19E30	-1:18:00
Zerqan	41N30	20E21	-1:21:24

ALGERIA — ARGELIA — ALGERIEN — ALGÉRIE

Time Table

Date	Time	Offset
Before 15/Mar/1891		LMT
Begin Standard		2E20
15/Mar/1891	0:01	-0:09
Begin Standard		0W00
11/Mar/1911	0:00	0:00
14/Jun/1916	23:00	-1:00
1/Oct/1916	24:00	0:00
24/Mar/1917	23:00	-1:00
7/Oct/1917	24:00	0:00
9/Mar/1918	23:00	-1:00
6/Oct/1918	24:00	0:00
1/Mar/1919	23:00	-1:00
5/Oct/1919	24:00	0:00
14/Feb/1920	23:00	-1:00
23/Oct/1920	24:00	0:00
14/Mar/1921	23:00	-1:00
21/Jun/1921	24:00	0:00
11/Sep/1939	23:00	-1:00
19/Nov/1939	1:00	0:00
Begin Standard		1E00
25/Feb/1940	2:00	-1:00
2/Apr/1944	2:00	-2:00
8/Oct/1944	2:00	-1:00
2/Apr/1945	2:00	-2:00
16/Sep/1945	1:00	-1:00
Begin Standard		0W00
7/Oct/1946	0:00	0:00
Begin Standard		1E00
29/Jan/1956	0:00	-1:00
Begin Standard		0W00
14/Apr/1963	0:00	0:00
25/Apr/1971	23:00	-1:00
26/Sep/1971	24:00	0:00
6/May/1977	0:00	-1:00
Begin Standard		1E00
21/Oct/1977	0:00	-1:00
24/Mar/1978	1:00	-2:00
22/Sep/1978	3:00	-1:00
Begin Standard		0W00
26/Oct/1979	0:00	0:00
25/Apr/1980	0:00	-1:00
31/Oct/1980	2:00	0:00
Begin Standard		1E00
1/May/1981	0:00	-1:00

Place	Lat	Long	Offset
Abadla	31N01	2W44	0:10:56
Abalessa	22N54	4E50	-0:19:20
Acheb	28N23	9E05	-0:36:20
Adrar	27N54	0W17	0:01:08
Afar	25N30	8E22	-0:33:28
Aflou	34N07	2E06	-0:08:24
Aïn Arnat	36N11	5E19	-0:21:16
Aïn Azel	35N49	5E31	-0:22:04
Aïn Beïda	35N48	7E24	-0:29:36
Aïn Benian	36N48	2E55	-0:11:40
Aïn Berda	36N39	7E35	-0:30:20
Aïn Bessem	36N18	3E40	-0:14:40
Aïn Defla	36N16	1E58	-0:07:52
Aïn Deheb	34N51	1E33	-0:06:12
Aïn el Beïda	35N48	7E24	-0:29:36
Aïn el Hadjel	35N40	3E53	-0:15:32
Aïn el Kebira	36N22	5E30	-0:22:00
Aïn Milia	36N02	6E34	-0:26:16
Aïn Oulmène	35N55	5E18	-0:21:12
Aïn Oussera	35N27	2E54	-0:11:36
Aïn Sefra	32N45	0W35	0:02:20
Aïn Taghrout	36N08	5E05	-0:20:20
Aïn Tedelès	36N00	0E18	-0:01:12
Aïn Témouchent	35N18	1W08	0:04:32
Aïn Touta	35N23	5E54	-0:23:36
Aïn Wessara	35N27	2E54	-0:11:36
Aïn Yagout	35N47	6E25	-0:25:40
Akabli	26N42	1E22	-0:05:28
Akbou	36N28	4E32	-0:18:08
Alger (Algiers)	36N47	3E03	-0:12:12
Algier → Alger	36N47	3E03	-0:12:12
Algiers → Alger	36N47	3E03	-0:12:12
Amguid	26N26	5E22	-0:21:28
Amsel	22N37	5E26	-0:21:44
Annaba (Bône)	36N54	7E46	-0:31:04
Aomar	36N30	3E47	-0:15:08
Aoulef	26N58	1E05	-0:04:20
Arak	25N18	3E45	-0:15:00
Argel → Alger	36N47	3E03	-0:12:12
Arziw	35N51	0W19	0:01:16
Assekaifaf	27N08	8E50	-0:35:20
Awled Djellal	34N28	5E02	-0:20:08
Awlef	26N58	1E05	-0:04:20
Azazga	36N44	4E22	-0:17:28
Azeffoun	36N53	4E25	-0:17:40
Baniou	35N25	4E21	-0:17:24
Barika	35N23	5E22	-0:21:28
Batna	35N34	6E11	-0:24:44
Béchar	31N37	2W13	0:08:52
Bejaïa (Bougie)	36N45	5E05	-0:20:20
Bekkaria	35N22	8E15	-0:33:00
Ben Badis	34N57	0W55	0:03:40
Béni Abbas	30N08	2W10	0:08:40
Beni Saf	35N19	1W23	0:05:32
Ben Mehidi	36N46	7E54	-0:31:36
Ben Smih	36N23	7E31	-0:30:04
Berriyyane	32N50	3E46	-0:15:04
Berrouaghia	36N08	2E55	-0:11:40
Besbes	36N42	7E51	-0:31:24
Beskra	34N51	5E44	-0:22:56
Bidon Cinq → Post Maurice Cortier	22N18	1E05	-0:04:20
Bir Chouhada	35N53	6E18	-0:25:12
Bir el Ater	34N44	8E03	-0:32:12
Bir Ghbalou	36N16	3E35	-0:14:20
Biskra	34N51	5E44	-0:22:56
Blida	36N28	2E50	-0:11:20
Bloumet	23N27	6E06	-0:24:24
Bône → Annaba	36N54	7E46	-0:31:04
Bordj Amguid	26N26	5E22	-0:21:28
Bordj Bou Arreridj	36N04	4E46	-0:19:04
Bordj Bounaama	35N51	1E36	-0:06:24
Bordj el Oussif	32N20	8E02	-0:32:08
Bordj Fly Sainte Marie	27N20	3W50	0:15:20
Bordj Menaïel	36N44	3E43	-0:14:52
Bordj Omar Idriss	28N09	6E43	-0:26:52
Bou Bernous	27N18	2W59	0:11:56
Bouchegouf	36N28	7E44	-0:30:56
Boudjellil	36N20	4E21	-0:17:24
Boudouaou	36N43	3E25	-0:13:40
Boufarik	36N34	2E55	-0:11:40
Bougaa	36N20	5E05	-0:20:20
Bougie → Bejaïa	36N45	5E05	-0:20:20
Bougtob	34N02	0E05	-0:00:20
Bougzoul	35N42	2E51	-0:11:24
Bou Hadjar	36N30	8E06	-0:32:24
Bouïra	36N23	3E54	-0:15:36
Bou Ismail	36N38	2E41	-0:10:44
Bou Kadir	36N04	1E07	-0:04:28
Bou Khadra	35N45	8E02	-0:32:08
Bou Medfaa	36N22	2E28	-0:09:52
Bouqteb	34N02	0E05	-0:00:20
Bou Saâda	35N12	4E11	-0:16:44
Bou Smail	36N38	2E41	-0:10:44
Bouteldja	36N47	8E12	-0:32:48
Bou Zadjar	35N35	1W09	0:04:36
Brézina	33N04	1E14	-0:04:56
Briziana	33N04	1E14	-0:04:56
Charouine	29N01	0W16	0:01:04
Chelghoum el Aïd	36N10	6E10	-0:24:40
Chenachane	26N00	4W15	0:17:00
Cherchell	36N36	2E12	-0:08:48
Chetaibi	37N04	7E23	-0:29:32
Collo	37N00	6E34	-0:26:16
Colomb-Béchar → Béchar	31N37	2W13	0:08:52
Constantine	36N22	6E37	-0:26:28
Damous	36N33	1E42	-0:06:48
Delles	36N55	3E55	-0:15:40
Dellys	36N55	3E55	-0:15:40
Djamaa	33N32	6E00	-0:24:00
Djanet	24N34	9E29	-0:37:56
Djelfa	34N40	3E15	-0:13:00
Djidjelli	36N48	5E46	-0:23:04
Dome à Collenias	27N15	9E42	-0:38:48
Draa el Mizan	36N32	3E50	-0:15:20
Drean	36N41	7E46	-0:31:04
Dzioua	33N14	5E14	-0:20:56
Ech Cheliff (Orléansville)	36N10	1E20	-0:05:20
Edarene	25N27	8E22	-0:33:28
Edjeleh	27N38	9E50	-0:39:20
Eféri	24N22	9E30	-0:38:00
El Abiadh Sidi Cheikh	32N56	0E42	-0:02:48
El Adeb Larache	27N22	8E52	-0:35:28
El Affroun	36N30	2E38	-0:10:32
El Agreb	30N48	5E30	-0:22:00
El Aouinet	35N52	7E54	-0:31:36
El Arba	36N37	3E13	-0:12:52
El Aricha	34N09	1W10	0:04:40
El Asnam (Orléansville)	36N10	1E20	-0:05:20
El Bayadh	33N40	1E01	-0:04:04
El Beyyadh	33N40	1E01	-0:04:04
El Boulaïda	36N28	2E50	-0:11:20
El Djazaïr (Algiers)	36N47	3E03	-0:12:12
El Djelfa	34N40	3E15	-0:13:00
El Eulma	36N08	5E40	-0:22:40
El Ghazawet	35N06	1W51	0:07:24
El Goléa	30N30	2E50	-0:11:20
El Grara	32N46	4E34	-0:18:16
El Hadjar	36N48	7E45	-0:31:00
El Idrissia	34N30	2E37	-0:10:28
El Kala	36N50	8E30	-0:34:00
El Kerma	35N36	0W35	0:02:20
El Kouif	35N29	8E19	-0:33:16
El Kseur	36N46	4E49	-0:19:16
El Malah	35N24	1W05	0:04:20
El Marsa el Kebir	35N45	0W43	0:02:52
El Meghaïer	33N55	5E58	-0:23:52
El Menia	30N30	2E50	-0:11:20
El Mghayyar	33N55	5E58	-0:23:52
El Milia	36N48	6E14	-0:24:56
El Miliyya	36N48	6E14	-0:24:56
El Mohammadia	35N33	0E03	-0:00:12
El Oued	33N20	6E58	-0:27:52
El Qala	36N50	8E30	-0:34:00
El Qoll	37N00	6E34	-0:26:16
El Tarf	36N45	8E20	-0:33:20
El Wad	33N20	6E58	-0:27:52
El Wanza	35N57	8E04	-0:32:16
Erg el Agreb	30N48	5E30	-0:22:00
Foggaret el Arab	27N03	2E59	-0:11:56
Foggaret ez Zoua	27N20	3E00	-0:12:00
Fort Flatters → Zaouia el Kahla	28N09	6E43	-0:26:52
Fort Gardel	24N52	8E21	-0:33:24
Fort Lallemand	31N13	6E17	-0:25:08
Fort Mac Mahon	29N51	1E45	-0:07:00
Fort Miribel	29N31	2E55	-0:11:40
Frenda	35N02	1E01	-0:04:04
Gdyel	35N48	0W26	0:01:44
Ghardaïa	32N31	3E37	-0:14:28
Ghazaouet	35N06	1W51	0:07:24
Ghilizane	35N44	0E30	-0:02:00
Gouraya	36N34	1E55	-0:07:40
Guelma	36N28	7E26	-0:29:44
Guerara	32N46	4E34	-0:18:16
Guerzim	29N45	1W47	0:07:08
Hadjout	36N31	2E25	-0:09:40
Hammamet	35N27	7E58	-0:31:52
Hassi Bel Guebbour	28N46	6E27	-0:25:48
Hassi el Ghella	35N28	1W03	0:04:12
Hassi Mameche	35N52	0E04	-0:00:16
Hassi Messaoud	31N43	5E59	-0:23:56
Hassi R'Mel	32N35	3E24	-0:13:36
Hassi Zehana	35N01	0W53	0:03:32
Hennaya	34N58	1W22	0:05:28
Hirhafok	23N49	5E45	-0:23:00
Idelès	23N58	5E53	-0:23:32
Ifata	25N29	7E58	-0:31:52
Ighil Izane	35N44	0E30	-0:02:00
Igli	30N25	2W12	0:08:48
Illizi	26N29	8E28	-0:33:52
In Aménas	28N05	9E30	-0:38:00
In Amguel	23N40	5E10	-0:20:40
In Amnas	28N05	9E30	-0:38:00
In Belbel	27N54	1E10	-0:04:40
In Ecker	24N09	5E03	-0:20:12
In Ezzane	23N28	11E12	-0:44:48
In Guezzam	19N32	5E42	-0:22:48
In Rhar	27N10	1E59	-0:07:56
In Salah	27N12	2E28	-0:09:52
Jdioula	35N57	0E50	-0:03:20
Jijel	36N48	5E46	-0:23:04
Kenadsa	31N48	2W26	0:09:44
Kerzaz	29N30	1W37	0:06:28
Khadra	36N15	0E35	-0:02:20
Khemis	36N16	2E13	-0:08:52
Khemis el Khechna	36N39	3E20	-0:13:20
Khemis Miliana	36N16	2E13	-0:08:52
Khenchela	35N28	7E11	-0:28:44
Khenchla	35N28	7E11	-0:28:44
Kherrata	36N31	5E26	-0:21:44
Kolea	36N38	2E46	-0:11:04
Ksar Chellala	35N13	2E18	-0:09:12
Ksar el Boukhari	35N51	2E52	-0:11:28
Laghouat	33N50	2E59	-0:11:56
Lakhdaria	36N34	3E35	-0:14:20
L'Arbaa Naït Irathen	36N38	4E12	-0:16:48
La Reculée	28N00	9E30	-0:38:00
Le Guelta	36N22	0E50	-0:03:20
Le Kreïder	34N06	0E02	-0:00:08
Lemdiyya	36N12	2E50	-0:11:20
Maghnia	34N50	1W50	0:07:20
Maghniyya	34N50	1W50	0:07:20
Mansourah	36N04	4E28	-0:17:52
Mascara	35N45	0E01	-0:00:04

ALGÉRIE ALGERIEN ARGELIA ALGERIA

Place	Lat	Long	Offset
Mazoula	28N20	7E50	-0:31:20
M'Chedallah	36N21	4E16	-0:17:04
M'Daourouch	36N05	7E49	-0:31:16
Méchéria	33N35	0W18	0:01:12
Mechriyya	33N35	0W18	0:01:12
Mechroha	36N21	7E51	-0:31:24
Médéa	36N12	2E50	-0:11:20
Medjana	36N08	4E41	-0:18:44
Mehdia	35N26	1E40	-0:06:40
Melyana	36N15	2E15	-0:09:00
Merouana	35N38	5E55	-0:23:40
Mers el Kébir	35N45	0W43	0:02:52
Meskiana	35N39	7E41	-0:30:44
Mestghanem	35N51	0E07	-0:00:28
Metlili Chaamba	32N18	3E40	-0:14:40
Metlili ech Chaâmba	32N18	3E40	-0:14:40
Mila	36N27	6E16	-0:25:04
Miliana	36N15	2E15	-0:09:00
Misserghin	35N37	0W45	0:03:00
Mohammadia	35N33	0E03	-0:00:12
Morsott	35N40	8E01	-0:32:04
Mostaganem	35N51	0E07	-0:00:28
Mouaskar	35N45	0E01	-0:00:04
M'Sila	35N46	4E31	-0:18:04
Nacereddine	36N08	3E26	-0:13:44
Nechmeya	36N36	7E31	-0:30:04
Nédroma	35N01	1W45	0:07:00
Negrine	34N30	7E30	-0:30:00
Ohanet	28N45	8E55	-0:35:40
Oran (Ouahran)	35N43	0W43	0:02:52
Orléansville → El Asnam	36N10	1E20	-0:05:20
Ouahran → Oran	35N43	0W43	0:02:52
Ouallene	24N37	1E14	-0:04:56
Ouan Taredert	27N33	9E32	-0:38:08
Ouargla	31N59	5E25	-0:21:40
Oued Athmenia	36N15	6E17	-0:25:08
Oued Cheham	36N23	7E46	-0:31:04
Oued Fodda	36N11	1E32	-0:06:08
Oued Rhiou	35N58	0E55	-0:03:40
Oued Tlelat	35N34	0W27	0:01:48
Ouenza	35N57	8E04	-0:32:16
Ouled Agla	35N58	4E45	-0:19:00
Ouled Djellal	34N28	5E02	-0:20:08
Philippeville → Skikda	36N50	6E58	-0:27:52
Poste Weygand	24N28	0E39	-0:02:36
Post Maurice Cortier (Bidon Cinq)	22N18	1E05	-0:04:20
Qacentina (Constantine)	36N22	6E37	-0:26:28
Qasr el-Boukhari	35N51	2E52	-0:11:28
Qnadsa	31N48	2W26	0:09:44
Rahouia	35N32	1E01	-0:04:04
Râs el Aïoun	35N30	8E18	-0:33:12
Ras el Ma	34N31	0W46	0:03:04
Ras el Oued	35N57	5E03	-0:20:12
Reggane	26N42	0E10	-0:00:40
Remchi	35N04	1W26	0:05:44
Rhourde-El-Baguel	31N24	6E57	-0:27:48
Rouiba	36N44	3E17	-0:13:08
Saïda	34N50	0E09	-0:00:36
Sali	26N58	0W01	0:00:04
Sba	28N13	0W08	0:00:32
Sedrata	36N08	7E32	-0:30:08
Seraidi	36N55	7E41	-0:30:44
Sétif	36N09	5E26	-0:21:44
Sfizef	35N14	0W15	0:01:00
Sidi Aïch	36N37	4E42	-0:18:48
Sidi Aïssa	35N53	3E48	-0:15:12
Sidi Akacha	36N28	1E18	-0:05:12
Sidi Ali	36N06	0E25	-0:01:40
Sidi bel Abbès	35N13	0W10	0:00:40
Sidi Mohammed Ben Ali	36N09	0E51	-0:03:24
Sidi Okba	34N48	5E54	-0:23:36
Sig	35N32	0W11	0:00:44
Silet	22N44	4E37	-0:18:28
Skikda (Philippeville)	36N50	6E58	-0:27:52
Souguer	35N12	1E30	-0:06:00
Sougueur	35N12	1E30	-0:06:00
Souk Ahras	36N23	8E00	-0:32:00
Souq Ahras	36N23	8E00	-0:32:00
Sour el Ghozlane	36N10	3E45	-0:15:00
Stif	36N09	5E26	-0:21:44
Stile	34N20	5E51	-0:23:24
Still	34N20	5E51	-0:23:24
Tabelbala	29N23	3W15	0:13:00
Tablat	36N24	3E19	-0:13:16
Tadjemout	25N37	3E48	-0:15:12
Tadjenanet	36N08	5E59	-0:23:56
Tagdempt → Tiaret	35N28	1E21	-0:05:24
Taghit	30N55	2W02	0:08:08
Tahart	22N51	5E12	-0:20:48
Tahifet	22N58	5E55	-0:23:40
Tamadjert	25N36	7E20	-0:29:20
Tamanrasset	22N56	5E30	-0:22:00
Tamenghest	22N56	5E30	-0:22:00
Tan Emellel	27N30	9E45	-0:39:00
Tan Kena	26N33	9E35	-0:38:20
Taougrite	36N15	0E55	-0:03:40
Taoura	36N09	8E03	-0:32:12
Tarat	26N13	9E18	-0:37:12
Tarhaouaout	22N20	5E58	-0:23:52
Tarhit	30N55	2W02	0:08:08
Tazoult-Lambese	35N29	6E15	-0:25:00
Tazrouk	23N25	6E16	-0:25:04
Tbessa	35N28	8E09	-0:32:36
Tébessa	35N28	8E09	-0:32:36
Télagh	34N47	0W34	0:02:16
Telergma	36N07	6E21	-0:25:24
Ténès	36N31	1E14	-0:04:56
Teniet el Had	35N47	2E01	-0:08:04
Tétouan	35N34	5W23	0:21:32
Tetuán → Tétouan	35N34	5W23	0:21:32
Thenia	36N43	3E34	-0:14:16
Theniet el Hadd	35N47	2E01	-0:08:04
Tiaret	35N28	1E21	-0:05:24
Tidjenaouine	22N33	5E15	-0:21:00
Tif	27N00	1E37	-0:06:28
Tighennif	35N20	0E21	-0:01:24
Tiguentourine	27N50	9E18	-0:37:12
Tigzirt	36N54	4E08	-0:16:32
Tihert	35N28	1E21	-0:05:24
Tilimsen	34N52	1W15	0:05:00
Tilrhemt	33N10	3E21	-0:13:24
Timellouline	29N15	8E54	-0:35:36
Timimoun	29N14	0E16	-0:01:04
Timmoudi	29N19	1W09	0:04:36
Timoudi	29N19	1W09	0:04:36
Tindouf	27N50	8W04	0:32:16
Tin-Zaouaten	19N55	2E52	-0:11:28
Ti-N-Zaouatene	19N55	2E52	-0:11:28
Tipasa	36N35	2E27	-0:09:48
Tissemsilt	35N35	1E50	-0:07:20
Tit	27N00	1E37	-0:06:28
Tit	23N00	5E10	-0:20:40
Titaf	27N26	0W13	0:00:52
Tizi-Ouzou	36N48	4E02	-0:16:08
Tizzeine	25N21	8E50	-0:35:20
Tlemcen	34N52	1W15	0:05:00
Tletat ed Douair	35N59	2E55	-0:11:40
Tolga	34N46	5E22	-0:21:28
Touggourt	33N10	6E00	-0:24:00
Toustain	36N40	8E15	-0:33:00
Wahran (Oran)	35N43	0W43	0:02:52
Wargla	31N59	5E25	-0:21:40
Zahana	35N32	0W25	0:01:40
Zaouia el Kahla (Fort Flatters)	28N09	6E43	-0:26:52
Zarzaïtine	28N18	9E48	-0:39:12
Zemmora	35N44	0E45	-0:03:00
Zeralda	36N41	2E53	-0:11:32
Ziama Mansouria	36N40	5E29	-0:21:56
Département 96	36N47	3E00	-0:12:00
Département 97	36N35	2E45	-0:11:00
Département 98	37N00	7E45	-0:31:00
Département 99	37N00	7E45	-0:31:00
Département 100	36N30	6E15	-0:25:00
Département 101	36N47	3E00	-0:12:00
Département 102	35N50	0W00	0:00:00
Département 103	35N50	0W00	0:00:00
Département 104	35N40	0W30	0:02:00
Département 105	36N47	3E00	-0:12:00
Département 106	36N10	3E45	-0:15:00
Département 107	35N20	0W45	0:03:00
Département 108	35N40	0W30	0:02:00
Département 109	36N40	4E00	-0:16:00

ANDORRE ANDORRA

Time Table
Before 1/Jan/1901 LMT
Begin Standard 0W00

Date	Time	Offset
1/Jan/1901	0:00	0:00

Begin Standard 15E00

Date	Time	Offset
29/Sep/1946	24:00	-1:00
31/Mar/1985	2:00	-2:00
29/Sep/1985	3:00	-1:00
30/Mar/1986	2:00	-2:00
28/Sep/1986	3:00	-1:00
29/Mar/1987	2:00	-2:00
27/Sep/1987	3:00	-1:00
27/Mar/1988	2:00	-2:00
25/Sep/1988	3:00	-1:00
26/Mar/1989	2:00	-2:00
24/Sep/1989	3:00	-1:00
25/Mar/1990	2:00	-2:00
30/Sep/1990	3:00	-1:00
31/Mar/1991	2:00	-2:00
29/Sep/1991	3:00	-1:00
29/Mar/1992	2:00	-2:00
27/Sep/1992	3:00	-1:00
28/Mar/1993	2:00	-2:00
26/Sep/1993	3:00	-1:00
27/Mar/1994	2:00	-2:00
25/Sep/1994	3:00	-1:00
26/Mar/1995	2:00	-2:00
24/Sep/1995	3:00	-1:00
31/Mar/1996	2:00	-2:00
29/Sep/1996	3:00	-1:00
30/Mar/1997	2:00	-2:00
28/Sep/1997	3:00	-1:00
29/Mar/1998	2:00	-2:00
27/Sep/1998	3:00	-1:00
28/Mar/1999	2:00	-2:00
26/Sep/1999	3:00	-1:00
26/Mar/2000	2:00	-2:00
24/Sep/2000	3:00	-1:00

Place	Lat	Long	Offset
Andorra	42N30	1E31	-0:06:04
Ordino	42N34	1E31	-0:06:04

ANGOLA PORTUGUESE WEST AFRICA ANGOLA

Time Table
Before 1/Jan/1892 LMT
Begin Standard 13E01

Date	Time	Offset
1/Jan/1892	0:00	-0:52

Begin Standard 15E00

Date	Time	Offset
26/May/1911	0:00	-1:00

Place	Lat	Long	Offset
Aguema	12S03	21E49	-1:27:16
Alto Cauale	7S34	16E16	-1:05:04
Alto Chicapa	10S53	19E14	-1:16:56
Alto Cuito	13S27	18E49	-1:15:16
Alto-Uama	12S14	15E33	-1:02:12
Amboíva	11S32	14E44	-0:58:56
Ambriz	7S50	13E06	-0:52:24
Ambrizete	7S14	12E52	-0:51:28
Andulo	11S30	16E45	-1:07:00
Artur de Paiva	14S28	16E20	-1:05:20
Baía dos Tigres	16S36	11E43	-0:46:52
Baía Farta	12S40	13E11	-0:52:44
Bailundo	12S12	15E52	-1:03:28
Baixo Longa	15S42	18E30	-1:15:20
Balombo	12S21	14E46	-0:59:04
Bando	15S00	20E30	-1:22:00
Barra do Cuanza	9S09	13E00	-0:52:00
Barra do Dande	8S28	13E22	-0:53:28
Bela Vista	7S50	13E40	-0:54:40
Bela Vista	12S35	16E13	-1:04:52
Bembe	7S02	14E18	-0:57:12
Benguela	12S35	13E25	-0:53:40
Benza	6S16	12E57	-0:51:48
Bessa Monteiro	7S07	13E44	-0:54:56
Béu	6S14	15E28	-1:01:52
Bibala	14S46	13E21	-0:53:24
Bimbe	11S49	15E49	-1:03:16

Bom Jesus	9s09	13E34	-0:54:16
Bongo	8s48	17E49	-1:11:16
Botera	11s37	14E17	-0:57:08
Branco	12s30	20E32	-1:22:08
Brito Godins	8s57	16E32	-1:06:08
Buco Zau	4s46	12E33	-0:50:12
Buela	5s55	14E33	-0:58:12
Bula Atumba	8s40	14E48	-0:59:12
Bungo	7s26	15E23	-1:01:32
Buto	15s46	15E09	-1:00:36
Caála	12s51	15E33	-1:02:12
Cabinda	5s33	12E12	-0:48:48
Cabiri	8s52	13E39	-0:54:36
Cabo Ledo	9s39	13E17	-0:53:08
Cabulo	10s15	16E40	-1:06:40
Cabuta	9s50	14E48	-0:59:12
Cachimo	8s21	21E20	-1:25:20
Cachingues	13s05	16E43	-1:06:52
Cacólo	10s07	19E17	-1:17:08
Caconda	13s43	15E06	-1:00:24
Cacuaco	8s47	13E22	-0:53:28
Cacula	14s29	14E10	-0:56:40
Cacuri	8s14	18E20	-1:13:20
Cacuso	9s26	15E43	-1:02:52
Cafima	16s39	16E27	-1:05:48
Cafu	16s27	15E14	-1:00:56
Cahama	16s17	14E19	-0:57:16
Caianda	11s02	23E31	-1:34:04
Caimbambo	12s58	14E01	-0:56:04
Cainde	15s42	13E12	-0:52:48
Cairofa	14s05	12E54	-0:51:36
Caitou	14s28	13E06	-0:52:24
Caiundo	15s46	17E28	-1:09:52
Cakeni	17s48	19E27	-1:17:48
Calala	12s59	23E30	-1:34:00
Calego	12s10	23E36	-1:34:24
Calemba	16s04	15E44	-1:02:56
Calola	16s30	17E51	-1:11:24
Calólo	10s00	14E53	-0:59:32
Caluango	8s21	19E40	-1:18:40
Calucinga	11s18	16E12	-1:04:48
Calulo	10s00	14E53	-0:59:32
Calumbolaca	9s09	13E48	-0:55:12
Calunda	12s06	23E23	-1:33:32
Caluquembe	13s47	14E44	-0:58:56
Camabatela	8s11	15E22	-1:01:28
Camacupa	12s03	17E30	-1:10:00
Camatambo	6s30	15E18	-1:01:12
Camaxilo	8s21	18E56	-1:15:44
Camba Cassai	9s40	19E18	-1:17:12
Cambulo	7s48	21E14	-1:24:56
Camucuio	14s12	13E20	-0:53:20
Cando	16s30	18E19	-1:13:16
Cangamba	13s40	19E54	-1:19:36
Cangandala	9s45	16E33	-1:06:12
Cangola	7s58	15E52	-1:03:28
Cangombe	14s24	19E59	-1:19:56
Cangongo	9s24	17E30	-1:10:00
Cangumbe	12s00	19E17	-1:17:08
Canhoca	9s15	14E41	-0:58:44
Canjinge	10s12	21E17	-1:25:08
Canzar	7s38	21E32	-1:26:08
Caombo	8s43	16E51	-1:07:24
Capage	13s21	21E05	-1:24:20
Capala	13s37	14E45	-0:59:00
Capangombe	15s05	13E08	-0:52:32
Capelengue	9s12	19E43	-1:18:52
Capelongo	14s28	16E20	-1:05:20
Capenda Camulemba	9s24	18E27	-1:13:48
Capuça I	17s22	21E18	-1:25:12
Capuna	15s38	19E43	-1:18:52
Capunda	14s57	14E03	-0:56:12
Cariango	10s37	15E20	-1:01:20
Cassai	10s33	21E59	-1:27:56
Cassamba	13s06	20E18	-1:21:12
Cassinga	15s08	16E05	-1:04:20
Cassoalala	9s30	14E22	-0:57:28
Cassoango	13s42	20E56	-1:23:44
Cassongue	11s51	15E03	-1:00:12
Cassunda	10s57	21E03	-1:24:12
Cateco Cangola	8s27	15E48	-1:03:12
Catende	11s14	21E30	-1:26:00
Catete	9s06	13E43	-0:54:52
Catota	13s52	17E15	-1:09:00
Catuala	16s29	19E03	-1:16:12
Catumbela	12s25	13E34	-0:54:16
Caúngula	8s25	18E40	-1:14:40
Cavelo	17s33	19E21	-1:17:24
Caxito	8s33	13E36	-0:54:24
Caxopa	11s52	20E52	-1:23:28
Cazage	11s02	20E45	-1:23:00
Cazombo	11s54	22E52	-1:31:28
Cela	11s25	15E07	-1:00:28
Ceptia	12s56	17E35	-1:10:20
Chamangonge	11s16	20E24	-1:21:36
Chanhanga	16s04	14E07	-0:56:28
Chá Pungana	13s44	18E39	-1:14:36
Chenele	12s54	23E54	-1:35:36
Chepaúa	12s58	22E43	-1:30:52
Chiange	15s45	13E48	-0:55:12
Chianje	15s45	13E48	-0:55:12
Chibango	13s38	21E56	-1:27:44
Chibemba	15s45	14E05	-0:56:20
Chibia	15s11	13E41	-0:54:44
Chicomba	14s09	14E57	-0:59:48
Chicuma	13s23	14E51	-0:59:24
Chiengo	13s20	21E55	-1:27:40
Chila	12s04	14E29	-0:57:56
Chilongo	13s55	16E35	-1:06:20
Chiluage	9s30	21E47	-1:27:08
Chimaco	15s12	21E56	-1:27:44
Chimakela	15s24	16E58	-1:07:52
Chimbua	16s32	15E08	-1:00:32
Chingamba	12s49	18E20	-1:13:20
Chingoroi	13s37	14E01	-0:56:04
Chinguar	12s36	16E20	-1:05:20
Chiquelequele	16s40	19E06	-1:16:24
Chiquita	8s38	17E05	-1:08:20
Chissengue	9s14	20E42	-1:22:48
Chissilo	13s34	16E30	-1:06:00
Chitado	17s20	13E54	-0:55:36
Chitata	13s47	15E43	-1:02:52
Chitembo	13s34	16E40	-1:06:40
Chiumbe	12s29	16E08	-1:04:32
Chiúme	15s03	21E14	-1:24:56
Cinco de Outubro	9s34	17E50	-1:11:20
Ciuma	13s14	15E40	-1:02:40
Coemba	12s08	18E05	-1:12:20
Conda	11s06	14E20	-0:57:20
Condé	10s50	14E37	-0:58:28
Copolo	10s22	14E07	-0:56:28
Covelo	12s06	13E55	-0:55:40
Cuále	8s06	16E03	-1:04:12
Cuamato	17s05	15E09	-1:00:36
Cuando	16s32	22E07	-1:28:28
Cuangar	17s36	18E39	-1:14:36
Cuango	14s30	18E59	-1:15:56
Cuango	9s10	17E58	-1:11:52
Cuango	6s17	16E41	-1:06:44
Cubal	13s02	14E19	-0:57:16
Cuchi	14s36	16E58	-1:07:52
Cucumbi	10s17	19E05	-1:16:20
Cuilo Futa	6s25	15E44	-1:02:56
Cuimba	6s08	14E38	-0:58:32
Cuio	12s58	12E58	-0:51:52
Cuito-Cuanavale	15s10	19E10	-1:16:40
Cuma	12s52	15E05	-1:00:20
Curoca Norte	16s18	12E58	-0:51:52
Curunga	12s51	21E12	-1:24:48
Dala	8s05	15E50	-1:03:20
Dala	11s03	20E17	-1:21:08
Dala Cachibo	10s28	14E39	-0:58:36
Dalatando	9s18	14E54	-0:59:36
Damba	6s41	15E08	-1:00:32
Dange	8s09	14E46	-0:59:04
Dange-Iá-Menha	9s32	14E39	-0:58:36
Demba Chio	9s41	13E41	-0:54:44
Didimbo	17s30	21E45	-1:27:00
Dima	15s27	20E10	-1:20:40
Dinde	14s12	13E44	-0:54:56
Dinge	4s58	12E22	-0:49:28
Dirico	17s58	20E47	-1:23:08
Djamba	16s46	13E59	-0:55:56
Dombe Grande	12s58	13E11	-0:52:44
Dondo	9s38	14E25	-0:57:40
Dongo	14s36	15E48	-1:03:12
Donque	15s28	14E06	-0:56:24
Dumbo	14s06	17E24	-1:09:36
Duque de Bragança	9s06	15E57	-1:03:48
Ebanga	12s44	14E44	-0:58:56
Ebo	11s02	14E41	-0:58:44
Emílio de Carvalho	5s55	12E57	-0:51:48
Evale	16s33	15E44	-1:02:56
Fazenda Libongo	8s24	13E24	-0:53:36
Ferreira	12s53	22E48	-1:31:12
Folgares	14s54	15E08	-1:00:32
Forte República	7s45	16E23	-1:05:32
Foz do Cunene	17s16	11E50	-0:47:20
Gabela	10s48	14E20	-0:57:20
Gago Coutinho	14s08	21E25	-1:25:40
Galangue	13s48	16E09	-1:04:36
Gambos	14s51	14E30	-0:58:00
Ganda	13s02	14E40	-0:58:40
Gando	12s30	17E25	-1:09:40
General Machado	12s03	17E30	-1:10:00
Golungo Alto	9s08	14E46	-0:59:04
Guilherme Capelo	5s13	12E08	-0:48:32
Gumba	11s40	16E34	-1:06:16
Gungo	11s48	14E08	-0:56:32
Haco	10s12	15E44	-1:02:56
Honga	15s09	15E12	-1:00:48
Hoque	14s39	13E54	-0:55:36
Huambo (Nova Lisboa)	12s44	15E47	-1:03:08
Huíla	15s04	13E32	-0:54:08
Humbe	16s40	14E55	-0:59:40
Humpata	15s02	13E24	-0:53:36
Iango	9s11	17E39	-1:10:36
Icoca	6s11	16E19	-1:05:16
Impulo	13s53	13E39	-0:54:36
Indungo	14s48	16E17	-1:05:08
Iôna	16s50	12E20	-0:49:20
Jamba	13s50	15E30	-1:02:00
Jáu	15s12	13E31	-0:54:04
Kassinga	15s08	16E05	-1:04:20
Kuito	12s22	16E56	-1:07:44
Lagos	16s04	17E03	-1:08:12
Lândana	5s13	12E08	-0:48:32
Lela	5s03	12E29	-0:49:56
Lépi	12s52	15E26	-1:01:44
Léua	11s34	20E32	-1:22:08
Libibi	14s42	17E44	-1:10:56
Limbueta	12s30	18E42	-1:14:48
Litunga	13s17	16E43	-1:06:52
Loanda → Luanda	8s48	13E14	-0:52:56
Lobito	12s20	13E34	-0:54:16
Lóla	14s22	13E42	-0:54:48
Lombe	9s27	16E13	-1:04:52
Longa	14s42	18E32	-1:14:08
Lóvua	7s20	20E16	-1:21:04
Lóvua	11s36	23E53	-1:35:32
Luachimo	7s20	20E47	-1:23:08
Luanda	8s48	13E14	-0:52:56
Luangue	7s19	19E38	-1:18:32
Luao	12s12	15E52	-1:03:28
Luati	14s35	21E13	-1:24:52
Luatira	12s52	17E14	-1:08:56
Lubalo	9s12	19E16	-1:17:04
Lubango	14s55	13E30	-0:54:00
Lucala	9s16	15E15	-1:01:00
Lucano	11s16	21E38	-1:26:32
Lucapa	8s36	20E54	-1:23:36
Luceque	14s41	15E04	-1:00:16
Lucira	13s51	12E31	-0:50:04
Lucusse	12s32	20E48	-1:23:12
Luena	11s47	19E52	-1:19:28
Lufico	6s24	13E23	-0:53:32
Luia	8s26	21E45	-1:27:00
Luiana	17s23	23E03	-1:32:12
Luimbale	12s15	15E19	-1:01:16
Luita	8s04	19E25	-1:17:40
Lumai	13s31	21E21	-1:25:24
Lumbala	12s39	22E34	-1:30:16
Lumbala	14s08	21E25	-1:25:40
Lunge	12s12	16E05	-1:04:20
Lupire	14s36	19E29	-1:17:56
Luremo	8s31	17E50	-1:11:20
Luso	11s47	19E52	-1:19:28
Lutembo	13s26	21E16	-1:25:04
Luvo	5s51	14E05	-0:56:20
Mabaia	7s13	14E03	-0:56:12
Macocolo	6s47	16E08	-1:04:32
Macolo	7s05	16E48	-1:07:12
Macondo	12s35	23E44	-1:34:56
Macusse	17s51	20E21	-1:21:24
Madimba	6s31	14E21	-0:57:24
Mafembage	14s32	21E42	-1:26:48
Maianga	14s12	21E45	-1:27:00
Malange	9s32	16E20	-1:05:20
Malanje	9s32	16E20	-1:05:20
Mamué	13s35	13E13	-0:52:52
Maquela do Zombo	6s03	15E07	-1:00:28
Mariano Machado	13s02	14E40	-0:58:40
Marimba	8s28	17E08	-1:08:32
Marunga	17s27	20E02	-1:20:08
Masibi	11s08	22E42	-1:30:48
Massangano	9s37	14E15	-0:57:00
Matala	14s46	15E04	-1:00:16
Mavinga	15s50	20E21	-1:21:24
Mbanza Congo	6s16	14E15	-0:57:00
Melunga	17s16	16E24	-1:05:36
Menongue	14s36	17E48	-1:11:12
Miconge	4s26	12E51	-0:51:24
Mienga	17s17	19E48	-1:19:12
Milando	8s45	17E36	-1:10:24
Missão Santa Cruz	16s14	21E57	-1:27:48
Moçâmedes	15s10	12E09	-0:48:36
Mona Quimbundo	9s55	19E58	-1:19:52
Mõngua	16s43	15E23	-1:01:32
Monte Verde	8s43	16E51	-1:07:24
Mossamedes → Moçâmedes	15s10	12E09	-0:48:36
Muacandala	10s02	19E40	-1:18:40
Muangai	12s32	19E51	-1:19:24
Muá Ximica	9s50	18E41	-1:14:44
Mucári	9s30	16E54	-1:07:36
Mucoma	15s18	13E39	-0:54:36
Mucope	16s24	14E53	-0:59:32
Mucope	8s42	21E43	-1:26:52
Muculo	16s47	14E51	-0:59:24
Mucusso	17s51	20E21	-1:21:24
Mufuma	9s04	17E06	-1:08:24
Muginga	8s20	17E37	-1:10:28
Muié	14s25	20E36	-1:22:24
Mulanda	14s41	21E48	-1:27:12
Mulondo	15s39	15E14	-1:00:56
Munenga	10s02	14E41	-0:58:44
Mungau	13s56	21E55	-1:27:40
Munhango	12s12	18E42	-1:14:48
Mupa	16s10	15E44	-1:02:56
Muquequete	14s50	14E16	-0:57:04
Muriége	9s58	21E11	-1:24:44
Murila	10s44	20E20	-1:21:20
Mussende	10s32	16E05	-1:04:20
Mussolo	9s59	17E19	-1:09:16
Mussuco	17s08	19E05	-1:16:20
Mussuma	14s14	21E59	-1:27:56
Mutumbo	13s14	17E17	-1:09:08
Muxaluando	8s07	14E17	-0:57:08
Muxima	9s31	13E56	-0:55:44
Muzeze	15s03	17E43	-1:10:52
Namachire	11s26	22E43	-1:30:52
Namacunde	17s18	15E50	-1:03:20
Nambuangongo	8s01	14E12	-0:56:48
Nana Candundo	11s31	23E03	-1:32:12
Naulila	17s12	14E42	-0:58:48
Ndalatando	9s18	14E54	-0:59:36
Negage	7s45	15E16	-1:01:04
Negola	14s10	14E30	-0:58:00
Neriquinha	15s45	21E42	-1:26:48
Ngiva	17s03	15E47	-1:03:08
Ngunza	11s13	13E50	-0:55:20
Nhareia	11s25	17E03	-1:08:12
Nhundo	14s25	21E23	-1:25:32
Ninda	14s47	21E24	-1:25:36
Nóqui	5s51	13E25	-0:53:40
Norton de Matos	12s21	14E46	-0:59:04
Nova Caipemba	7s26	14E38	-0:58:32
Nova Chaves	10s34	21E17	-1:25:08
Nova Gaia	10s09	17E31	-1:10:04
Nova Lisboa → Huambo	12s44	15E47	-1:03:08
Nova Sintra	12s09	17E16	-1:09:04
Novo Redondo	11s13	13E50	-0:55:20
N'Riquinha	15s45	21E42	-1:26:48
N'Vinda	13s04	18E57	-1:15:48
Nzeto	7s14	12E52	-0:51:28
Oncócua	16s34	13E28	-0:53:52
Otchinjau	16s30	13E57	-0:55:48
Paiva Couceiro	14s51	14E30	-0:58:00
Pango Aluquém	8s43	14E27	-0:57:48
Pereira de Eça	17s03	15E47	-1:03:08
Pipas	14s56	12E12	-0:48:48
Porto Alexandre	15s49	11E53	-0:47:32

ANGOLA — PORTUGUESE WEST AFRICA — ANGOLA

Place	Lat	Long	Offset
Porto Amboim	10s44	13E44	-0:54:56
Porto Rico	6s08	12E30	-0:50:00
Portugália	7s20	20E47	-1:23:08
Púlpito do Sul	15s46	12E00	-0:48:00
Pungo Andongo	9s40	15E35	-1:02:20
Quela	9s16	17E02	-1:08:08
Quelo	6s27	12E48	-0:51:12
Quibala	10s46	14E59	-0:59:56
Quibaxi	8s29	14E36	-0:58:24
Quiculungo	8s31	15E19	-1:01:16
Quilenda	10s33	14E22	-0:57:28
Quilengues	14s05	14E04	-0:56:16
Quimbango	11s01	17E26	-1:09:44
Quimbele	6s28	16E13	-1:04:52
Quimbo	13s59	16E05	-1:04:20
Quimbonge	8s36	18E30	-1:14:00
Quimbumbe	7s50	14E03	-0:56:12
Quinjenje	12s49	14E55	-0:59:40
Quinzáu	6s51	12E46	-0:51:04
Quipeio	12s26	15E30	-1:02:00
Quipemba	7s12	15E06	-1:00:24
Quirima	10s48	18E09	-1:12:36
Quirimbo	10s36	14E12	-0:56:48
Quissongo	10s01	15E07	-1:00:28
Quitapa	10s23	18E14	-1:12:56
Quitexe	7s56	15E02	-1:00:08
Quixico	7s59	14E25	-0:57:40
Quixinge	9s52	14E23	-0:57:32
Quizenga	9s21	15E28	-1:01:52
Ricupe	14s37	21E25	-1:25:40
Robert Williams	12s51	15E33	-1:02:12
Roçadas	16s43	15E01	-1:00:04
Ruacaná	17s25	14E12	-0:56:48
Sacandica	5s58	15E56	-1:03:44
Sacaola	12s57	22E25	-1:29:40
Sachicapa	10s21	19E59	-1:19:56
Sachimbo	9s14	20E16	-1:21:04
Sa da Bandeira	14s41	13E29	-0:53:56
Sagaba	11s17	23E07	-1:32:28
Samacimbo	13s33	16E59	-1:07:56
Samba Caju	8s46	15E24	-1:01:36
Sambo	12s57	16E05	-1:04:20
Sambungo	8s39	20E43	-1:22:52
Sandongo	15s30	21E28	-1:25:52
Sandumba	13s45	17E29	-1:09:56
Sanga	11s07	15E22	-1:01:28
Santo António do Zaire	6s07	12E18	-0:49:12
Sanza Pombo	7s19	15E59	-1:03:56
São José de Encoge	7s38	14E41	-0:58:44
São Nicolau	14s15	12E21	-0:49:24
São Salvador do Congo	6s16	14E15	-0:57:00
Sapu	12s29	19E26	-1:17:44
Saricumbe	12s12	19E46	-1:19:04
Saupite	13s54	17E43	-1:10:52
Saurimo	9s39	20E24	-1:21:36
Saútar	11s06	18E27	-1:13:48
Sessa	13s56	20E38	-1:22:32
Sombo	8s42	20E57	-1:23:48
Songo	7s22	14E51	-0:59:24
Soyo	6s07	12E18	-0:49:12
Tabi	8s10	13E18	-0:53:12
Tampa	15s30	13E27	-0:53:48
Tando Zinze	5s22	12E26	-0:49:44
Tembo Aluma	7s42	17E17	-1:09:08
Tomboco	6s48	13E18	-0:53:12
Toto	7s08	14E16	-0:57:04
Tuta	14s37	20E45	-1:23:00
Uamba	7s12	16E25	-1:05:40
Uiche	12s03	21E02	-1:24:08
Uíge	7s37	15E03	-1:00:12
Umpulo	12s38	17E42	-1:10:48
Urimba	10s56	16E32	-1:06:08
Veríssimo Sarmento	8s10	20E39	-1:22:36
Vila Arriaga	14s46	13E21	-0:53:24
Vila Luso	11s47	19E52	-1:19:28
Vila Nova	12s38	16E03	-1:04:12
Vila Nova do Seles	11s24	14E15	-0:57:00
Vouga	12s11	16E47	-1:07:08
Xá-Cassau	9s02	20E14	-1:20:56
Xamindele	7s08	14E16	-0:57:04
Xangongo	16s43	15E01	-1:00:04
Zenza do Itombe	9s16	14E13	-0:56:52
Zundi	10s28	16E48	-1:07:12

ANGUILLA — ANGUILLA

Time Table

Before 2/Mar/1912		LMT
Begin Standard		60w00
2/Mar/1912	0:00	4:00

Place	Lat	Long	Offset
Anguilla	18N12	63w04	4:12:16
Crocus Hill → The Valley	18N13	63w04	4:12:16
Sombrero	18N36	63w26	4:13:44
The Valley	18N13	63w04	4:12:16

ANTIGUA AND BARBUDA — ANTIGUA AND BARBUDA

Time Table

Before 2/Mar/1912		LMT
Begin Standard		75w00
2/Mar/1912	0:00	5:00
Begin Standard		60w00
1/Jan/1951	0:00	4:00

Place	Lat	Long	Offset
All Saints	17N03	61w48	4:07:12
Antigua	17N03	61w48	4:07:12
Barbuda	17N38	61w48	4:07:12
Bolands	17N02	61w53	4:07:32
Cadrington	17N38	61w50	4:07:20
Falmouth	17N00	61w47	4:07:08
Fort Byham	17N08	61w48	4:07:12
Freetown	17N03	61w42	4:06:48
Liberta	17N02	61w47	4:07:08
Old Road	17N01	61w50	4:07:20
Parham	17N05	61w46	4:07:04
Redonda	16N55	62w19	4:09:16
Saint Johns	17N06	61w51	4:07:24
Urlins	17N02	61w52	4:07:28
Willikies	17N05	61w42	4:06:48

ARGENTINE — ARGENTINIEN — ARGENTINA

Time Table

Before 1/Nov/1894		LMT
Begin Standard		64w11
1/Nov/1894	0:00	4:17
Begin Standard		60w00
1/May/1920	0:00	4:00
1/Dec/1930	0:00	3:00
31/Mar/1931	24:00	4:00
15/Oct/1931	0:00	3:00
29/Feb/1932	24:00	4:00
1/Nov/1932	0:00	3:00
28/Feb/1933	24:00	4:00
1/Nov/1933	0:00	3:00
28/Feb/1934	24:00	4:00
1/Nov/1934	0:00	3:00
28/Feb/1935	24:00	4:00
1/Nov/1935	0:00	3:00
29/Feb/1936	24:00	4:00
1/Nov/1936	0:00	3:00
28/Feb/1937	24:00	4:00
1/Nov/1937	0:00	3:00
28/Feb/1938	24:00	4:00
1/Nov/1938	0:00	3:00
28/Feb/1939	24:00	4:00
1/Nov/1939	0:00	3:00
29/Feb/1940	24:00	4:00
1/Jul/1940	0:00	3:00
14/Jun/1941	24:00	4:00
15/Oct/1941	0:00	3:00
31/Jul/1943	24:00	4:00
15/Oct/1943	0:00	3:00
28/Feb/1946	24:00	4:00
1/Oct/1946	0:00	3:00
30/Sep/1963	24:00	4:00
15/Dec/1963	0:00	3:00
29/Feb/1964	24:00	4:00
15/Oct/1964	0:00	3:00
28/Feb/1965	24:00	4:00
15/Oct/1965	0:00	3:00
28/Feb/1966	24:00	4:00
15/Oct/1966	0:00	3:00
31/Mar/1967	24:00	4:00
1/Oct/1967	0:00	3:00
6/Apr/1968	24:00	4:00
6/Oct/1968	0:00	3:00
5/Apr/1969	24:00	4:00
Begin Standard		45w00
5/Oct/1969	0:00	3:00
23/Jan/1974	0:00	2:00
1/May/1974	0:00	3:00
6/Oct/1974	0:00	2:00
6/Apr/1975	0:00	3:00
5/Oct/1975	0:00	2:00
4/Apr/1976	0:00	3:00
3/Oct/1976	0:00	2:00
3/Apr/1977	0:00	3:00
2/Nov/1985	0:00	2:00
14/Mar/1986	0:00	3:00
25/Oct/1986	0:00	2:00
13/Feb/1987	0:00	3:00
25/Oct/1987	0:00	2:00
7/Feb/1988	0:00	3:00
1/Dec/1988	0:00	2:00
16/Mar/1989	0:00	3:00
15/Oct/1989	0:00	2:00
4/Mar/1990	0:00	3:00

Abra Pampa	22s43	65w42	4:22:48
Acebal	33s14	60w50	4:03:20
Acevedo	33s45	60w27	4:01:48
Achiras	33s10	65w00	4:20:00
Acuña	29s55	57w58	3:51:52
Adrogué → Almirante Brown	34s48	58w23	3:53:32
Aguada Cecilio	40s51	65w51	4:23:24
Aguada de Guerra	41s04	68w25	4:33:40
Aguaray	22s16	63w44	4:14:56
Aguayo	31s40	65w54	4:23:36
Aguilares	27s26	65w37	4:22:28
Aimogasta	28s33	66w49	4:27:16
Albardón	31s26	68w32	4:34:08
Alberti	35s02	60w16	4:01:04
Alcira (Gigena)	32s45	64w20	4:17:20
Alcorta	33s32	61w07	4:04:28
Aldea Apeleg	44s41	70w51	4:43:24
Aldo Bonzi	34s42	58w31	3:54:04
Alejandro Roca	33s21	63w43	4:14:52
Alejo Ledesma	33s37	62w37	4:10:28
Alemania	25s36	65w38	4:22:32
Algarrobo	38s53	63w08	4:12:32
Algarrobo del Águila	36s26	67w09	4:28:36
Algarrobo Verde	31s44	68w18	4:33:12
Allen	38s58	67w50	4:31:20
Almafuerte	32s12	64w15	4:17:00
Almirante Brown	34s48	58w23	3:53:32
Alpachiri	37s22	63w46	4:15:04
Alsina	33s54	59w23	3:57:32
Alta Gracia	31s40	64w26	4:17:44
Alto Río Senguerr	45s02	70w50	4:43:20
Aluminé	39s13	70w57	4:43:48
Alvear	29s06	56w33	3:46:12
Amaichá del Valle	26s36	65w55	4:23:40
Ameghino	34s50	62w27	4:09:48
Aminga	28s50	66w54	4:27:36
Anasagasti	35s01	59w24	3:57:36
Añatuya	28s28	62w50	4:11:20
Ancasti	28s49	65w30	4:22:00
Anchorena	35s41	65w27	4:21:48
Andacollo	37s11	70w41	4:42:44
Andalgalá	27s36	66w19	4:25:16
Añelo	38s21	68w47	4:35:08
Angastaco	25s38	66w11	4:24:44
Angel Etcheverry	35s02	58w04	3:52:16
Angualasto	30s03	69w09	4:36:36
Antilla	26s07	64w36	4:18:24
Antofagasta de la Sierra	26s04	67w25	4:29:40
Antonio de Biedma	47s29	66w30	4:26:00
Apeadero Funke	35s28	58w59	3:55:56
Apolinario Saravia	24s25	64w02	4:16:08
Apóstoles	27s55	55w46	3:43:04
Arana	35s00	57w54	3:51:36
Arboledas	36s53	61w29	4:05:56
Arequito	33s09	61w28	4:05:52
Arias	33s38	62w25	4:09:40
Arizona	35s43	65w18	4:21:12
Armstrong	32s47	61w36	4:06:24
Arraga	28s04	64w14	4:16:56
Arrecifes	34s03	60w07	4:00:28
Arroyito	31s25	63w03	4:12:12
Astica	30s56	67w23	4:29:32
Astra	45s44	67w30	4:30:00
Atalaya	35s02	57w32	3:50:08
Atucha	33s58	59w18	3:57:12
Auca Mahuida	37s53	68w31	4:34:04
Avellaneda	29s07	59w40	3:58:40
Avellaneda	34s39	58w23	3:53:32
Ayacucho	37s09	58w29	3:53:56
Azcuénaga	34s23	59w21	3:57:24
Azucena	37s29	59w18	3:57:12
Azul	36s47	59w51	3:59:24
Bahía Blanca	38s43	62w17	4:09:08
Bahía Bustamante	45s08	66w32	4:26:08
Bahía Laura	48s24	66w29	4:25:56
Bajada del Agrio	38s23	70w02	4:40:08
Balcarce	37s50	58w15	3:53:00
Balcosna	27s53	65w43	4:22:52
Balde	33s20	66w38	4:26:32
Ballesteros	32s33	62w59	4:11:56
Balnearia	31s00	62w40	4:10:40
Banda del Río Salí	26s50	65w10	4:20:40
Bandera	28s54	62w16	4:09:04
Bandera Bajada	27s14	63w31	4:14:04
Baradero	33s48	59w30	3:58:00
Barda del Medio	38s43	68w10	4:32:40
Bariloche → San Carlos de Bariloche	41s09	71w18	4:45:12
Barranqueras	27s29	58w56	3:55:44
Barreal	31s38	69w28	4:37:52
Barrow	38s18	60w14	4:00:56
Bartolomé Bavio → General Mansilla	35s05	57w45	3:51:00
Bartolomé de las Casas	25s24	59w34	3:58:16
Basail	27s52	59w18	3:57:12
Basavilbaso	32s22	58w53	3:55:32
Batavia	34s47	65w41	4:22:44
Beazley	33s45	66w39	4:26:36
Belén	27s39	67w02	4:28:08
Belén de Escobar	34s21	58w47	3:55:08
Bella Vista	28s30	59w03	3:56:12
Bella Vista	27s02	65w18	4:21:12
Bella Vista	34s33	58w41	3:54:44
Bell Ville	32s37	62w42	4:10:48
Beltrán	27s50	64w04	4:16:16
Benavidez	34s25	58w42	3:54:48
Benjamín Zorrilla	39s06	65w29	4:21:56
Berazategui	34s46	58w13	3:52:52
Berisso	34s52	57w53	3:51:32
Bermejo	31s37	67w39	4:30:36
Bernasconi	37s54	63w43	4:14:52
Berón de Astrada	27s33	57w32	3:50:08
Bolívar	36s15	61w06	4:04:24
Bosques	34s49	58w14	3:52:56
Bovril	31s21	59w26	3:57:44
Bowen	35s00	67w31	4:30:04
Bragado	35s08	60w30	4:02:00
Brea Pozo	28s15	63w57	4:15:48
Buchanan	34s58	58w13	3:52:52
Buchardo	34s43	63w31	4:14:04
Buena Esperanza	34s45	65w15	4:21:00
Buenos Aires	34s36	58w27	3:53:48
Buen Pasto	45s05	69w28	4:37:52
Burruyacú	26s30	64w45	4:19:00
Burzaco	34s49	58w24	3:53:36
Buta Ranquil	37s03	69w50	4:39:20
Cabildo	38s29	61w54	4:07:36
Cabo Blanco	47s12	65w45	4:23:00
Cabo Raso	44s21	65w14	4:20:56
Cacharí	36s24	59w32	3:58:08
Cachí	25s06	66w11	4:24:44
Cafayate	26s05	65w58	4:23:52
Calafate	50s20	72w18	4:49:12
Calchaquí	29s54	60w18	4:01:12
Caleta Olivia	46s26	67w32	4:30:08
Caleufú	35s35	64w33	4:18:12
Calilegua	23s47	64w47	4:19:08
Calingasta	31s19	69w25	4:37:40
Camarones	44s48	65w42	4:22:48
Campana	34s10	58w57	3:55:48
Campo Gallo	26s35	62w51	4:11:24
Campo Grande	27s13	54w58	3:39:52
Campo Largo	26s48	60w50	4:03:20
Campo Quijano	24s55	65w39	4:22:36
Campo Santo	24s40	65w06	4:20:24
Cañada de Gómez	32s49	61w24	4:05:36
Cañada Honda	31s59	68w33	4:34:12
Cañada Verde → Villa Huidobro	34s50	64w35	4:18:20
Cañadón Seco	46s33	67w35	4:30:20
Canals	33s33	62w53	4:11:32
Candelaria	27s28	55w44	3:42:56
Candelaria	32s04	65w49	4:23:16
Canning	34s53	58w30	3:54:00
Cañuelas	35s03	58w44	3:54:56
Capilla del Monte	30s51	64w31	4:18:04
Capilla del Señor	34s18	59w06	3:56:24
Capitán Bermúdez	32s49	60w43	4:02:52
Capitán Sarmiento	34s10	59w48	3:59:12
Carcarañá	32s51	61w09	4:04:36
Carhué	37s11	62w44	4:10:56
Carlos Beguerie	35s29	59w06	3:56:24
Carlos Casares	35s38	61w21	4:05:24
Carlos Keen	34s29	59w14	3:56:56
Carlos Pellegrini	32s03	61w48	4:07:12
Carlos Tejedor	35s23	62w25	4:09:40
Carmen de Areco	34s22	59w49	3:59:16
Carmen de Patagones	40s48	62w59	4:11:56
Casbas	36s45	62w30	4:10:00
Caseros	34s36	58w33	3:54:12
Casilda	33s03	61w10	4:04:40
Castelar	34s40	58w40	3:54:40
Castelli	36s06	57w47	3:51:08
Castro Barros	30s35	65w44	4:22:56
Catamarca	28s28	65w47	4:23:08
Catriló	36s26	63w24	4:13:36
Cebollar	29s06	66w33	4:26:12
Centenario	38s48	68w08	4:32:32
Centro Río Mayo	45s35	71w06	4:44:24
Cereales	36s49	63w51	4:15:24
Ceres	29s53	61w57	4:07:48
Cerrillos	24s54	65w29	4:21:56
Cerro Azul	27s38	55w29	3:41:56
Chabás	33s15	61w22	4:05:28
Chacabuco	34s38	60w29	4:01:56
Chajarí	30s46	57w59	3:51:56
Chamaicó	35s03	64w58	4:19:52
Chamical (Gobernador Gordillo)	30s21	66w19	4:25:16
Chañar	30s32	65w58	4:23:52
Chaquiago	27s32	66w21	4:25:24
Charadai	27s38	59w54	3:59:36
Charata	27s13	61w12	4:04:48
Chascomús	35s34	58w01	3:52:04
Chasicó	40s18	68w58	4:35:52
Chavarría	28s57	58w35	3:54:20
Chelforó	39s04	66w32	4:26:08
Chenaut	34s15	59w13	3:56:52
Chepes	31s21	66w36	4:26:24
Chilecito	29s10	67w30	4:30:00
Chilecito	33s53	69w03	4:36:12
Chillar	37s18	59w59	3:59:56
Chimbas	31s29	68w32	4:34:08
Chimpay	39s10	66w09	4:24:36
Chivilcoy	34s53	60w01	4:00:04
Choele-Choel	39s16	65w41	4:22:44
Cholila	42s31	71w27	4:45:48
Chos Malal	37s23	70w16	4:41:04
Choya	28s30	64w52	4:19:28
Chuchimba	28s45	66w09	4:24:36
Chumbicha	28s52	66w14	4:24:56
Cinco Saltos	38s49	68w04	4:32:16
Cipolletti	38s56	67w59	4:31:56
Ciudad General Belgrano	34s43	58w32	3:54:08
Clara	31s50	58w49	3:55:16
Claraz	37s54	59w17	3:57:08
Claypole	34s48	58w20	3:53:20
Clodomira	27s35	64w08	4:16:32
Clorinda	25s17	57w43	3:50:52
Cochagual	31s54	68w23	4:33:32
Colalao del Valle	26s22	65w57	4:23:48
Colán Conhué	43s16	69w51	4:39:24
Colón	33s53	61w07	4:04:28
Colón	32s13	58w08	3:52:32
Colonia Alvear	35s00	67w40	4:30:40
Colonia Caroya	31s02	64w05	4:16:20
Colonia Dora	28s36	62w57	4:11:48
Colonia Elisa	26s56	59w32	3:58:08
Colonia Hogar Ricardo Gutiérrez	34s51	58w51	3:55:24
Colonia José Mármol	26s59	60w44	4:02:56
Colonia Las Heras	46s33	68w57	4:35:48
Colonias Unidas	26s42	59w38	3:58:32
Colonia Villafañe	26s12	59w05	3:56:20
Comallo	40s40	63w30	4:14:00
Comandante Fontana	25s20	59w41	3:58:44
Comandante Leal	30s53	65w47	4:23:08
Comandante Luis Piedrabuena	49s59	68w54	4:35:36
Comandante Nicanor Otamendi	38s07	57w51	3:51:24
Comodoro Py	35s19	60w31	4:02:04
Comodoro Rivadavia	45s52	67w30	4:30:00
Cona Niyeo	41s53	67w00	4:28:00
Concarán	32s34	65w15	4:21:00
Concepción	28s23	57w53	3:51:32
Concepción	27s20	65w35	4:22:20
Concepción de la Sierra	27s59	55w31	3:42:04
Concepción del Uruguay	32s29	58w14	3:52:56
Concordia	31s24	58w02	3:52:08
Contraalmirante Cordero	38s44	68w10	4:32:40
Copacabana	28s12	67w29	4:29:56
Copetonas	38s43	60w27	4:01:48
Córdoba	31s24	64w11	4:16:44
Coronda	31s58	60w55	4:03:40
Coronel Brandsen	35s10	58w14	3:52:56
Coronel Dorrego	38s42	61w17	4:05:08
Coronel Du Graty	27s40	60w56	4:03:44
Coronel Eugenio del Busto	38s57	64w15	4:17:00
Coronel Moldes	25s16	65w29	4:21:56
Coronel Moldes	33s38	64w36	4:18:24
Coronel Pringles	37s58	61w22	4:05:28
Coronel Suárez	37s28	61w55	4:07:40
Coronel Vidal	37s27	57w43	3:50:52
Corpus	27s07	55w31	3:42:04
Corral de Bustos	33s17	62w12	4:08:48
Corrientes	27s28	58w50	3:55:20
Cortaderas	32s30	65w00	4:20:00
Cortines	34s34	59w13	3:56:52
Corzuela	26s57	60w58	4:03:52
Cosquín	31s15	64w29	4:17:56
Crespo	32s02	60w19	4:01:16
Cruz Alta	33s01	61w49	4:07:16
Cruz del Eje	30s44	64w48	4:19:12
Cuadro Nacional	34s37	68w17	4:33:08
Cubanea	41s02	70w16	4:41:04
Cuchillo-Có	38s20	64w37	4:18:28
Curuzú Cuatiá	29s47	58w03	3:52:12
Cutral-Có	38s56	69w14	4:36:56
Daireaux	36s36	61w45	4:07:00
Dalmacio Vélez Sarsfield	32s36	63w35	4:14:20
Darregueira	37s42	63w10	4:12:40
Darwin	39s12	65w46	4:23:04
Deán Funes	30s26	64w21	4:17:24
Del Campillo	34s22	64w29	4:17:56
Del Carril	35s31	59w30	3:58:00
Del Viso	34s27	58w48	3:55:12
Desiderio Tello	31s13	66w19	4:25:16
Devoto	31s24	62w19	4:09:16
Diadema Argentina	45s46	67w40	4:30:40
Diamante	32s04	60w39	4:02:36
Diego Gaynor	34s17	59w14	3:56:56
Dique Florentino Ameghino	43s40	66w25	4:25:40
Dolavon	43s18	65w42	4:22:48
Dolores	36s20	57w40	3:50:40
Domselaar	35s04	58w18	3:53:12
Donadeu	26s43	62w44	4:10:56
Don Torcuato	34s30	58w38	3:54:32
Eduardo Castex	35s54	64w18	4:17:12
Egaña	36s59	59w06	3:56:24
El Aguilar	23s12	65w42	4:22:48
El Bolsón	41s58	71w31	4:46:04
El Caburé	26s01	62w22	4:09:28
El Carmen	24s23	65w16	4:21:04
El Carril	25s05	65w28	4:21:52
El Cholar	37s25	70w39	4:42:36
El Chorrillo	33s18	66w16	4:25:04
El Colorado	26s18	59w22	3:57:28
El Corcovado	43s32	71w36	4:46:24
El Cuy	39s56	68w20	4:33:20
Eldorado	26s24	54w38	3:38:32
El Galpón	25s23	64w38	4:18:32
El Huecú	37s37	70w36	4:42:24
Elías Romero	34s46	58w52	3:55:28
El Mayoco	42s39	70w59	4:43:56
El Milagro	31s01	65w59	4:23:56
El Naranjo	25s44	64w59	4:19:56
Elortondo	33s42	61w37	4:06:28
El Palomar	34s36	58w36	3:54:24
El Pintado	24s38	61w27	4:05:48
El Piquete	24s13	64w39	4:18:36
El Puesto	27s57	67w38	4:30:32
El Quebrachal	25s17	64w04	4:16:16
El Tala	26s07	65w17	4:21:08
El Talar	34s27	58w39	3:54:36
El Trébol	32s12	61w42	4:06:48
El Tunal	24s48	65w45	4:23:00
El Turbio	51s41	72w05	4:48:20

Elvira	35s14	59w29	3:57:56
El Volcán	33s15	66w12	4:24:48
Embarcación	23s13	64w06	4:16:24
Empalme San Vicente	34s58	58w22	3:53:28
Empedrado	27s57	58w48	3:55:12
Enrique Fynn	34s50	59w08	3:56:32
Enrique Urien	27s34	60w32	4:02:08
Ensenada	34s51	57w55	3:51:40
Entrerios	32s00	59w20	3:57:20
Epuyén	42s14	71w21	4:45:24
Ernestina	35s16	59w34	3:58:16
Escalada	34s10	59w07	3:56:28
Esperanza	31s27	60w56	4:03:44
Espinillo	24s58	58w34	3:54:16
Esquel	42s54	71w19	4:45:16
Esquina	30s01	59w32	3:58:08
Esquina Negra	35s02	58w03	3:52:12
Esquiú	29s23	65w17	4:21:08
Estanislao del Campo	25s03	60w06	4:00:24
Esteban Echeverría	34s50	58w28	3:53:52
Esteros	26s37	63w39	4:14:36
Eugenio Bustos	33s46	69w04	4:36:16
Eva Perón → La Plata	34s55	57w57	3:51:48
Ezeiza	34s51	58w32	3:54:08
Ezpeleta	34s46	58w15	3:53:00
Facundo	45s18	69w58	4:39:52
Famaillá	27s03	65w24	4:21:36
Famatina	28s55	67w31	4:30:04
Fatima	34s26	59w00	3:56:00
Federación	31s00	57w54	3:51:36
Federal	30s57	58w48	3:55:12
Fernández	27s55	63w54	4:15:36
Ferreyra	31s28	64w08	4:16:32
Fiambalá	27s41	67w38	4:30:32
Firmat	33s27	61w29	4:05:56
Fitz Roy	47s02	67w15	4:29:00
Florencio Varela	34s49	58w17	3:53:08
Fontana	27s25	59w02	3:56:08
Formosa	26s11	58w11	3:52:44
Forres	27s53	63w58	4:15:52
Fortín Uno	38s51	65w17	4:21:08
Fortuna	35s07	65w23	4:21:32
Fraga	33s30	65w48	4:23:12
Francisco A. Berra	35s23	58w51	3:55:24
Francisco Alvarez	34s38	58w52	3:55:28
Fray Luis Beltrán	39s19	65w46	4:23:04
Freyre	31s10	62w06	4:08:24
Frías	28s39	65w09	4:20:36
Gaimán	43s17	65w29	4:21:56
Gálvez	32s02	61w13	4:04:52
Gandara	35s26	58w06	3:52:24
Gan Gan	42s30	68w16	4:33:04
Gaona	25s12	64w05	4:16:20
Gardey	37s17	59w21	3:57:24
Garín	34s26	58w44	3:54:56
Garza	28s09	63w32	4:14:08
Gastre	42s17	69w14	4:36:56
General Acha	37s23	64w36	4:18:24
General Alvear	36s03	60w01	4:00:04
General Alvear	34s58	67w42	4:30:48
General Arenales	34s18	61w18	4:05:12
General Belgrano	35s46	58w30	3:54:00
General Cabrera	32s48	63w52	4:15:28
General Campos	31s32	58w24	3:53:36
General Conesa	36s30	57w20	3:49:20
General Conesa	40s06	64w26	4:17:44
General Daniel Cerri	38s42	62w24	4:09:36
General Enrique Mosconi	22s36	63w49	4:15:16
General Galarza	32s43	59w24	3:57:36
General Guido	36s40	57w46	3:51:04
General Gutiérrez	32s57	68w48	4:35:12
General Hornos	34s53	58w56	3:55:44
General José de San Martín	26s33	59w21	3:57:24
General Juan Madariaga	37s00	57w09	3:48:36
General La Madrid	37s16	61w17	4:05:08
General Las Heras	34s56	58w57	3:55:48
General Lavalle	36s24	56w58	3:47:52
General Levalle	34s01	63w56	4:15:44
General Lorenzo Vintter	40s44	64w29	4:17:56
General Mansilla (Bartolomé Bavio)	35s05	57w45	3:51:00
General Martín Miguel de Güemes	24s40	65w03	4:20:12
General O'Brien	34s54	60w45	4:03:00
General Pacheco	34s28	58w38	3:54:32
General Paz	27s45	57w37	3:50:28
General Paz	35s31	58w19	3:53:16
General Pico	35s40	63w44	4:14:56
General Pinedo	27s19	61w17	4:05:08
General Pinto	34s46	61w53	4:07:32
General Pizarro	24s13	64w01	4:16:04
General Roca	39s02	67w35	4:30:20
General Rodríguez	34s36	58w57	3:55:48
General Rojo	33s28	60w17	4:01:08
General San Martín	37s59	63w34	4:14:16
General San Martín	34s34	58w32	3:54:08
General Sarmiento	34s33	58w43	3:54:52
General Viamonte (Los Toldos)	35s01	61w01	4:04:04
General Villegas	35s02	63w01	4:12:04
Gigena → Alcira	32s45	64w20	4:17:20
Glew	34s53	58w23	3:53:32
Gobernador Andonaegui	34s10	59w19	3:57:16
Gobernador Costa	44s04	70w35	4:42:20
Gobernador Gregores	48s46	70w15	4:41:00
Gobernador Ingeniero Valentín Virasoro	28s03	56w02	3:44:08
Gobernador Juan E. Martínez	28s55	58w56	3:55:44
Gobernador Monteverde	34s48	58w16	3:53:04
Gobernador Racedo	31s34	60w04	4:00:16
Gobernador Udaondo	35s18	58w36	3:54:24
Godoy Cruz	32s55	68w50	4:35:20
Goldney	34s37	59w18	3:57:12
González Catán	34s46	58w39	3:54:36
González Chaves	38s02	60w06	4:00:24
González Moreno	35s33	63w22	4:13:28
González Risos	34s52	59w13	3:56:52
Goudge	34s40	68w08	4:32:32
Goya	29s08	59w16	3:57:04
Goyeneche	35s20	58w43	3:54:52
Gramilla	27s18	64w37	4:18:28
Gran Guardia	25s52	58w53	3:55:32
Gualeguay	33s09	59w20	3:57:20
Gualeguaychú	33s01	58w31	3:54:04
Gualjaina	42s42	70w30	4:42:00
Guaminí	37s02	62w25	4:09:40
Guandacol	29s31	68w32	4:34:08
Guardia Escolta	28s59	62w08	4:08:32
Guardia Mitre	40s26	63w41	4:14:44
Guatimozín	33s27	62w27	4:09:48
Guatraché	37s40	63w32	4:14:08
Guernica	34s56	58w25	3:53:40
Guillermo E. Hudson	34s47	58w10	3:52:40
Hasenkamp	31s31	59w51	3:59:24
Helvecia	31s06	60w05	4:00:20
Henderson	36s18	61w43	4:06:52
Hernando	32s25	63w44	4:14:56
Herradura	26s29	58w18	3:53:12
Herrera	28s29	63w04	4:12:16
Hipólito Yrigoyen	32s55	66w20	4:25:20
Holdich	45s57	68w13	4:32:52
Huaco	30s09	68w31	4:34:04
Hualfín	27s14	66w50	4:27:20
Huanguelén	37s02	61w57	4:07:48
Huillapima	28s44	65w59	4:23:56
Huinca Renancó	34s50	64w23	4:17:32
Humahuaca	23s12	65w21	4:21:24
Humberto Primo	30s52	61w22	4:05:28
Hurlingham	34s36	58w38	3:54:32
Ibarreta	25s13	59w51	3:59:24
Ibicuy	33s44	59w10	3:56:40
Icaño	28s54	65w19	4:21:16
Icaño	28s41	62w54	4:11:36
Iglesia	30s24	69w13	4:36:52
Ingeniero Jacobacci	41s18	69w35	4:38:20
Ingeniero Juan Allan	34s53	58w11	3:52:44
Ingeniero Luiggi	35s25	64w29	4:17:56
Ingeniero Maschwitz	34s23	58w44	3:54:56
Ingeniero Romulo Otamendi	34s13	58w54	3:55:36
Ingeniero White	38s47	62w16	4:09:04
Ingeniero Williams	34s54	59w22	3:57:28
Ingenio La Esperanza	24s13	64w51	4:19:24
Ingenio Santa Ana	27s28	65w41	4:22:44
Intendente Alvear	35s14	63w35	4:14:20
Intiyaco	28s39	60w05	4:00:20
Isidro Casanova	34s42	58w35	3:54:20
Isla Verde	33s14	62w24	4:09:36
Itá-Ibaté	27s26	57w20	3:49:20
Itatí	27s16	58w15	3:53:00
Ituzaingó	27s36	56w41	3:46:44
Ituzaingó	34s40	58w40	3:54:40
Jacinto Aráuz	38s04	63w26	4:13:44
Jagüé	28s38	68w24	4:33:36
James Craik	32s09	63w28	4:13:52
Jaramillo	47s11	67w09	4:28:36
Jardín América	27s03	55w14	3:40:56
Jáuregui	34s36	59w10	3:56:40
Jeppener	35s17	58w12	3:52:48
Jesús María	30s59	64w06	4:16:24
Joaquín V. González	25s05	64w11	4:16:44
Jocolí	32s35	68w41	4:34:44
José C. Paz	34s30	58w45	3:55:00
José de San Martín	44s02	70w29	4:41:56
José María Blanco (Tres Lomas)	36s27	62w51	4:11:24
José Santos Arévalo	35s10	59w14	3:56:56
Juan Atucha	35s32	59w21	3:57:24
Juan B. Arruabarrena	30s20	58w19	3:53:16
Juan de Garay	38s52	64w34	4:18:16
Juan E. Barra	37s48	60w29	4:01:56
Juan Jorba	33s37	65w16	4:21:04
Juan José Castelli	25s57	60w37	4:02:28
Juan N. Fernández	38s00	59w16	3:57:04
Juan Tronconi	35s30	59w15	3:57:00
Juárez	37s40	59w48	3:59:12
Jujuy → San Salvador de Jujuy	24s11	65w18	4:21:12
Junín	34s35	60w57	4:03:48
Junín de los Andes	39s56	71w05	4:44:20
Justiniano Posse	32s53	62w40	4:10:40
Justo Daract	33s52	65w11	4:20:44
Koluel Kayke	46s43	68w14	4:32:56
La Banda	27s44	64w15	4:17:00
Laborde	33s09	62w51	4:11:24
Laboulaye	34s07	63w24	4:13:36
La Candelaria	26s06	65w06	4:20:24
La Carlota	33s26	63w18	4:13:12
La Choza	34s47	59w07	3:56:28
La Ciénaga	27s30	66w57	4:27:48
La Clotilde	27s08	60w40	4:02:40
La Cocha	27s47	65w34	4:22:16
La Consulta	33s44	69w07	4:36:28
La Cruz	29s10	56w38	3:46:32
La Cumbre	30s58	64w30	4:18:00
La Dormida	33s21	67w55	4:31:40
La Falda	31s05	64w30	4:18:00
Laferrere	34s45	58w35	3:54:20
La Fragua	26s05	64w20	4:17:20
La Francia	31s24	62w38	4:10:32
La Gallareta	29s34	60w23	4:01:32
Lago Argentino → Calafate	50s20	72w18	4:49:12
Lago Blanco	45s55	71w15	4:45:00
Lago Futalaufquen	42s53	71w37	4:46:28
Lago Posadas	47s32	71w45	4:47:00
Lago Viedma	49s48	72w07	4:48:28
La Guardia	29s33	65w27	4:21:48
Laguna Larga	31s46	63w48	4:15:12
Laguna Limpia	26s29	59w41	3:58:44
La Leonesa	27s03	58w43	3:54:52
La Madrid	27s38	65w15	4:21:00
Lamarque	39s24	65w42	4:22:48
La Matanza → San Justo	34s40	58w33	3:54:12
La Mendieta	24s19	64w58	4:19:52
La Merced	28s10	65w41	4:22:44
La Merced	24s58	65w29	4:21:56
La Noria	35s10	58w48	3:55:12
Lanús	34s43	58w24	3:53:36
La Paz	30s45	59w39	3:58:36
La Paz	33s28	67w33	4:30:12
La Plata	34s55	57w57	3:51:48
Laprida	37s33	60w49	4:03:16
Laprida	28s23	64w33	4:18:12
La Puerta	28s10	65w48	4:23:12
La Quiaca	22s06	65w37	4:22:28
La Rioja	29s26	66w51	4:27:24
La Rubia	30s06	61w48	4:07:12
La Sabana	27s52	59w57	3:59:48
Las Arrias	30s21	63w35	4:14:20
Las Breñas	27s05	61w05	4:04:20
Las Casuarinas	31s48	68w19	4:33:16
Las Catitas	33s18	68w02	4:32:08
Las Cejas	26s53	64w44	4:18:56
Las Chacras	35s05	59w10	3:56:40
Las Coloradas	39s33	70w35	4:42:20
Las Flores	36s03	59w07	3:56:28
Las Flores	30s19	69w12	4:36:48
Las Garcitas	26s35	59w48	3:59:12
Las Heras	32s51	68w49	4:35:16
Las Lajas	38s31	70w22	4:41:28
Las Lajitas	24s41	64w15	4:17:00
Las Lomitas	24s42	60w36	4:02:24
Las Malvinas	34s50	68w15	4:33:00
Las Marianas	35s04	59w31	3:58:04
Las Ovejas	37s01	70w45	4:43:00
Las Palmas	27s04	58w42	3:54:48
Las Palmas	34s05	59w10	3:56:40
Las Plumas	43s43	67w15	4:29:00
Las Rosas	32s28	61w34	4:06:16
Las Termas	27s29	64w52	4:19:28
Las Tinajas	27s27	62w55	4:11:40
Las Toscas	28s21	59w17	3:57:08
Las Varillas	31s52	62w43	4:10:52
La Toma	33s03	65w37	4:22:28
La Trinidad	27s24	65w31	4:22:04
Lavaisse	33s49	65w25	4:21:40
Lavalle	29s01	59w11	3:56:44
Lavalle	28s12	65w08	4:20:32
La Verde	27s08	59w23	3:57:32
La Verde	34s44	59w16	3:57:04
La Viña	25s27	65w35	4:22:20
Leandro N. Alem	27s36	55w19	3:41:16
Leleque	42s23	71w03	4:44:12
Leones	32s39	62w18	4:09:12
León Rougés	27s13	65w32	4:22:08
Libertad	34s42	58w41	3:54:44
Libertador General San Martín	26s48	55w02	3:40:08
Libertador General San Martín (Ledesma	23s48	64w48	4:19:12
Lilo Viejo	26s56	62w58	4:11:52
Lima	34s03	59w12	3:56:48
Limay Mahuida	37s12	66w42	4:26:48
Lincoln	34s52	61w32	4:06:08
Lobería	38s09	58w47	3:55:08
Lobos	35s11	59w06	3:56:24
Lomas de Zamora	34s46	58w24	3:53:36
Loma Verde	35s16	58w24	3:53:36
Loncopué	38s04	70w37	4:42:28
Londres	27s43	67w07	4:28:28
Longchamps	34s52	58w23	3:53:32
Loreto	27s46	57w17	3:49:08
Los Antiguos	46s33	71w37	4:46:28
Los Berros	31s57	68w39	4:34:36
Los Blancos	23s36	62w36	4:10:24
Los Cardales	34s20	58w59	3:55:56
Los Cerrillos	31s57	65w28	4:21:52
Los Conquistadores	30s36	58w28	3:53:52
Los Frentones	26s25	61w25	4:05:40
Los Juríes	28s28	62w06	4:08:24
Los Menucos	40s50	68w08	4:32:32
Los Palacios	29s22	68w11	4:32:44

ARGENTINA

Los Polvorines	34s30	58w41	3:54:44
Los Quirquinchos	33s22	61w43	4:06:52
Los Telares	28s59	63w26	4:13:44
Louge	36s57	61w40	4:06:40
Lozano	34s51	59w03	3:56:12
Luán Toro	36s12	65w06	4:20:24
Lucas González	32s24	59w33	3:58:12
Luis Guillón	34s48	58w27	3:53:48
Luján	33s03	68w52	4:35:28
Luján	32s22	65w57	4:23:48
Luján	34s34	59w07	3:56:28
Lules	26s56	65w21	4:21:24
Macachín	37s09	63w39	4:14:36
Machagai	26s56	60w03	4:00:12
Maciá	32s10	59w23	3:57:32
Magdalena	35s04	57w32	3:50:08
Maipú	36s52	57w52	3:51:28
Maipú	32s58	68w47	4:35:08
Makallé	27s13	59w17	3:57:08
Malanzán	30s48	66w37	4:26:28
Malargüe	35s28	69w35	4:38:20
Malaspina	44s56	66w54	4:27:36
Malbrán	29s21	62w27	4:09:48
Malligasta	29s11	67w26	4:29:44
Malvinas	29s37	58w59	3:55:56
Manantiales Behr	45s41	67w31	4:30:04
Mancha Blanca	40s47	65w27	4:21:48
Manuel Derqui	27s50	58w48	3:55:12
Manzone	34s29	58w52	3:55:28
Maquinchao	41s15	68w44	4:34:56
Marayes	31s29	67w20	4:29:20
Marcos Juárez	32s42	62w06	4:08:24
Marcos Paz	34s46	58w50	3:55:20
Mar del Plata	38s00	57w33	3:50:12
Margarita Belén	27s16	58w58	3:55:52
María Ignacia (Vela)	37s24	59w30	3:58:00
Mariano Acosta	34s43	58w48	3:55:12
Mariano I. Loza	29s22	58w12	3:52:48
Mariano J. Haedo	34s38	58w36	3:54:24
Mariano Moreno → Moreno			
	38s44	70w01	4:40:04
María Teresa	34s01	61w54	4:07:36
Mascasín	31s22	66w59	4:27:56
Mata Amarilla	49s36	71w13	4:44:52
Matanza → San Justo			
	34s40	58w33	3:54:12
Matheu	34s22	58w50	3:55:20
Maximo Paz	34s56	58w37	3:54:28
Mayor Buratovich	39s15	62w37	4:10:28
Maza	36s50	63w19	4:13:16
Mazarredo	47s05	66w42	4:26:48
Mburucuyá	28s03	58w14	3:52:56
Mechita	35s04	60w24	4:01:36
Médanos	38s50	62w41	4:10:44
Media Agua	31s59	68w25	4:33:40
Melincué	33s39	61w27	4:05:48
Mencué	40s25	69w38	4:38:32
Mendoza	32s53	68w49	4:35:16
Mercedes	29s12	58w05	3:52:20
Mercedes	33s40	65w28	4:21:52
Mercedes	34s39	59w27	3:57:48
Merlo	32s21	65w02	4:20:08
Merlo	34s40	58w45	3:55:00
Metán	25s29	64w57	4:19:48
Miguel Riglos	36s51	63w42	4:14:48
Mina Pirquitas	22s41	66w31	4:26:04
Ministro Ramos Mexía	40s30	67w17	4:29:08
Ministro Rivadavia	34s51	58w22	3:53:28
Miraflores	28s36	65w55	4:23:40
Miramar	38s16	57w51	3:51:24
Miramar	30s54	62w40	4:10:40
Misión San Francisco de Laishí	26s14	58w38	3:54:32
Mocoretá	30s38	57w58	3:51:52
Moisés Ville	30s43	61w29	4:05:56
Molinos	25s25	66w19	4:25:16
Monte Buey	32s55	62w27	4:09:48
Montecarlo	26s34	54w47	3:39:08
Monte Caseros	30s15	57w39	3:50:36
Monte Comán	34s36	67w54	4:31:36
Monte Maíz	33s12	62w36	4:10:24
Monte Quemado	25s48	62w52	4:11:28
Monteros	27s10	65w30	4:22:00
Moreno	34s39	58w48	3:55:12
Morón	34s39	58w37	3:54:28
Morrison	32s36	62w50	4:11:20
Morteros	30s42	62w00	4:08:00
Muñiz	34s33	58w42	3:54:48
Mutquín	28s19	66w10	4:24:40
Nahuel Huapí	41s03	71w09	4:44:36
Nahuel Niyeu	40s30	66w33	4:26:12
Napenay	26s44	60w37	4:02:28
Naschel	32s55	65w23	4:21:32
Navarro	35s01	59w16	3:57:04
Navia	34s47	66w35	4:26:20
Necochea	38s33	58w45	3:55:00
Neuquén	38s57	68w04	4:32:16
Nihuil	35s02	68w40	4:34:40
Niquivil	30s25	68w42	4:34:48
Noetinger	32s22	62w19	4:09:16
Nogoyá	32s24	59w48	3:59:12
Nonogasta	29s18	67w30	4:30:00
Norberto de la Riestra	35s16	59w46	3:59:04
Ñorquincó	41s51	70w54	4:43:36
Nuestra Señora de Talavera	25s26	63w48	4:15:12
Nueva California	32s45	68w20	4:33:20
Nueva Francia	28s11	64w12	4:16:48
Nueva Galia	35s07	65w15	4:21:00
Nueva Lubecka	44s32	70w24	4:41:36
Nueve de Julio	35s27	60w52	4:03:28
Oberá	27s29	55w08	3:40:32
Olascoaga	35s12	60w36	4:02:24
Olavarría	36s54	60w17	4:01:08
Oliden	35s11	57w57	3:51:48
Oliva	32s03	63w34	4:14:16
Olivera	34s38	59w15	3:57:00
Olta	30s37	66w16	4:25:04
Oncativo	31s55	63w40	4:14:40
Open Door	34s30	59w05	3:56:20
Ordoqui	35s54	61w10	4:04:40
Orense	38s40	59w47	3:59:08
Oriente	38s44	60w37	4:02:28
Otumpa	27s19	62w13	4:08:52
Pagancillo	29s34	68w03	4:32:12
Palmira	33s03	68w34	4:34:16
Palo Santo	25s34	59w21	3:57:24
Palpalá	24s15	65w12	4:20:48
Pampa Almirón	26s42	59w08	3:56:32
Pampa del Castillo	45s48	68w05	4:32:20
Pampa del Chañar	30s11	68w43	4:34:52
Pampa del Indio	26s02	59w55	3:59:40
Pampa del Infierno	26s31	61w10	4:04:40
Pampa de los Guanacos	26s14	61w51	4:07:24
Paraná	31s44	60w32	4:02:08
Parera	35s08	64w32	4:18:08
Paso de Indios	43s52	69w06	4:36:24
Paso de los Libres	29s43	57w05	3:48:20
Paso del Rey	34s39	58w46	3:55:04
Paso Limay	40s33	70w26	4:41:44
Patquía	30s03	66w53	4:27:32
Pavón	34s23	59w03	3:56:12
Pedernales	35s15	59w39	3:58:36
Pedro Luro	39s29	62w41	4:10:44
Pedro R. Fernández	28s45	58w39	3:54:36
Pehuajó	35s48	61w53	4:07:32
Pellegrini	36s16	63w09	4:12:36
Pérez	33s00	60w46	4:03:04
Pergamino	33s53	60w35	4:02:20
Perico	24s23	65w06	4:20:24
Perito Moreno	46s36	70w56	4:43:44
Perugorría	29s20	58w37	3:54:28
Pichanal	23s19	64w13	4:16:52
Pichi-Mahuída	38s50	64w57	4:19:48
Pico Truncado	46s48	67w58	4:31:52
Picún Leufú	39s31	69w15	4:37:00
Piedra del Águila	40s03	70w05	4:40:20
Piedras Blancas	31s11	59w56	3:59:44
Pigüé	37s37	62w25	4:09:40
Pila	36s01	58w08	3:52:32
Pilar	31s41	63w54	4:15:36
Pilar	31s27	61w15	4:05:00
Pilar	34s27	58w54	3:55:36
Pinas	31s09	65w29	4:21:56
Piñero	34s32	58w45	3:55:00
Pinto	29s09	62w39	4:10:36
Pipinas	35s32	57w20	3:49:20
Pirané	25s43	59w06	3:56:24
Pirovano	36s30	61w34	4:06:16
Pituil	28s34	67w27	4:29:48
Plátanos	34s47	58w11	3:52:44
Plaza Huincul	38s55	69w09	4:36:36
Plomer	34s48	59w02	3:56:08
Plottier	38s58	68w14	4:32:56
Poblet	35s04	57w57	3:51:48
Polvaredas	35s35	59w30	3:58:00
Pomán	28s24	66w13	4:24:52
Pontevedra	34s45	58w42	3:54:48
Porteña	31s01	62w04	4:08:16
Posadas	27s23	55w53	3:43:32
Pozo del Molle	32s02	62w55	4:11:40
Pozo del Tigre	24s54	60w19	4:01:16
Pozo Hondo	27s10	64w30	4:18:00
Presidencia de la Plaza	27s01	59w51	3:59:24
Presidencia Roca	26s08	59w36	3:58:24
Presidencia Roque Sáenz Peña	26s47	60w27	4:01:48
Presidente Derqui	34s29	58w51	3:55:24
Pringles	38s00	61w23	4:05:32
Puán	37s33	62w43	4:10:52
Pucheta	29s54	57w34	3:50:16
Pueblo Ledesma	23s50	64w46	4:19:04
Pueblo Libertador	30s13	59w23	3:57:32
Puelches	38s09	65w55	4:23:40
Puerto Belgrano	38s54	62w06	4:08:24
Puerto Bermejo	26s56	58w30	3:54:00
Puerto Constanza	33s50	59w03	3:56:12
Puerto Delicia	26s12	54w35	3:38:20
Puerto Deseado	47s45	65w54	4:23:36
Puerto Esperanza	26s01	54w39	3:38:36
Puerto Iguazú	25s34	54w34	3:38:16
Puerto Libertad	25s55	54w36	3:38:24
Puerto Lobos	42s00	65w06	4:20:24
Puerto Madryn	42s46	65w03	4:20:12
Puerto Pirámides	42s34	64w17	4:17:08
Puerto Piray	26s28	54w42	3:38:48
Puerto Victoria	26s20	54w39	3:38:36
Puerto Visser	45s24	67w08	4:28:32
Punta Alta	38s53	62w05	4:08:20
Punta Delgada	42s46	63w38	4:14:32
Punta de los Llanos	30s09	66w33	4:26:12
Punta Porá	25s13	58w31	3:54:04
Quemú Quemú	36s03	63w33	4:14:12
Quequén	38s32	58w42	3:54:48
Quilino	30s12	64w29	4:17:56
Quilmes	34s44	58w16	3:53:04
Quimilí	27s38	62w25	4:09:40
Quines	32s13	65w48	4:23:12
Quirós	28s47	65w07	4:20:28
Quitilipi	26s52	60w13	4:00:52
Rafaela	31s16	61w29	4:05:56
Rafael Calzada	34s48	58w22	3:53:28
Rafael Castillo	34s43	58w37	3:54:28
Ramos Mejía	34s38	58w34	3:54:16
Ranchillos	26s57	65w03	4:20:12
Rancul	35s03	64w42	4:18:48
Ranelagh	34s48	58w12	3:52:48
Rapelli	26s24	64w29	4:17:56
Rauch	36s46	59w06	3:56:24
Rawson	34s36	60w04	4:00:16
Rawson	43s18	65w06	4:20:24
Real del Padre	34s50	67w46	4:31:04
Realicó	35s02	64w15	4:17:00
Recalde	36s39	61w05	4:04:20
Reconquista	29s09	59w39	3:58:36
Recreo	29s16	65w04	4:20:16
Remecó	37s38	63w39	4:14:36
Resistencia	27s27	58w59	3:55:56
Reynaldo Cullen	31s19	60w39	4:02:36
Rinconada	22s26	66w10	4:24:40
Río Ceballos	31s10	64w20	4:17:20
Río Chico	41s43	70w30	4:42:00
Río Colorado	39s01	64w05	4:16:20
Río Cuarto	33s08	64w21	4:17:24
Río Gallegos	51s38	69w13	4:36:52
Río Grande	53s47	67w42	4:30:48
Río Luján	34s17	58w54	3:55:36
Río Mayo	45s41	70w16	4:41:04
Río Pico	44s13	71w21	4:45:24
Río Piedras	25s18	64w54	4:19:36
Río Segundo	31s40	63w55	4:15:40
Río Tercero	32s11	64w06	4:16:24
Rivadavia	35s28	62w57	4:11:48
Rivadavia	33s11	68w28	4:33:52
Rivadavia	24s11	62w53	4:11:32
Rivadavia	31s33	68w37	4:34:28
Rivera	37s12	63w14	4:12:56
Roberto Payró	35s10	57w39	3:50:36
Rodeo	30s12	69w06	4:36:24
Rodolfo Iselín	34s39	68w01	4:32:04
Rojas	34s12	60w44	4:02:56
Roldán	32s54	60w54	4:03:36
Roque Pérez	35s25	59w20	3:57:20
Rosario	32s57	60w40	4:02:40
Rosario de la Frontera	25s48	64w58	4:19:52
Rosario de Lerma	24s59	65w35	4:22:20
Rosario del Tala	32s18	59w09	3:56:36
Roversi	27s35	61w57	4:07:48
Rufino	34s16	62w42	4:10:48
Ruiz de Montoya	26s59	55w03	3:40:12
Saavedra	37s45	62w22	4:09:28
Sachayoj	26s41	61w50	4:07:20
Saladas	28s15	58w38	3:54:32
Saladillo	35s38	59w46	3:59:04
Salado	28s18	67w15	4:29:00
Salavina	28s48	63w25	4:13:40
Saldungaray	38s12	61w47	4:07:08
Salliqueló	36s45	62w56	4:11:44
Salsacate	31s19	65w05	4:20:20
Salta	24s47	65w25	4:21:40
Salto	34s17	60w15	4:01:00
Salto de las Rosas	34s43	68w14	4:32:56
Salvador María	35s18	59w10	3:56:40
Salvador Mazza	22s04	63w43	4:14:52
Sampacho	33s23	64w43	4:18:52
Samuhú	27s31	60w24	4:01:36
San Agustín	38s01	58w21	3:53:24
San Agustín	31s59	64w23	4:17:32
San Agustín de Valle Fértil	30s38	67w27	4:29:48
San Andrés de Giles	34s27	59w27	3:57:48
San Antonio	24s22	65w20	4:21:20
San Antonio	28s56	65w06	4:20:24
San Antonio de Areco	34s15	59w28	3:57:52
San Antonio de los Cobres	24s11	66w21	4:25:24
San Antonio de Padua	34s40	58w42	3:54:48
San Antonio Oeste	40s44	64w56	4:19:44
San Bernardo	27s17	60w42	4:02:48
San Blas de los Sauces	28s24	67w05	4:28:20
San Carlos	27s45	55w54	3:43:36
San Carlos	33s46	69w02	4:36:08
San Carlos	25s56	65w56	4:23:44
San Carlos Centro	31s44	61w06	4:04:24
San Carlos de Bariloche	41s09	71w18	4:45:12
San Cayetano	38s20	59w37	3:58:28
San Cosme	27s22	58w31	3:54:04
San Cristóbal	30s19	61w14	4:04:56
San Eladio	34s46	59w11	3:56:44
San Enrique	35s47	60w22	4:01:28
San Fernando	34s26	58w34	3:54:16
San Francisco	31s26	62w05	4:08:20
San Francisco del Chañar	29s47	63w56	4:15:44
San Francisco del Monte de Oro	32s36	66w08	4:24:32
San Gregorio	34s19	62w02	4:08:08
San Ignacio	27s16	55w32	3:42:08
San Isidro	28s27	65w44	4:22:56
San Isidro	34s27	58w30	3:54:00
San Javier	27s53	55w08	3:40:32
San Javier	30s35	59w57	3:59:48
San Jerónimo Norte	31s33	61w05	4:04:20
San Jorge	31s54	61w52	4:07:28
San José	28s23	65w42	4:22:48
San José	27s46	55w47	3:43:08

San José de Feliciano 30s23 58w45 3:55:00
San José de Jáchal 30s14 68w45 4:35:00
San José de la Esquina 33s06 61w42 4:06:48
San Juan 31s32 68w31 4:34:04
San Julián 49s18 67w43 4:30:52
San Justo 30s47 60w35 4:02:20
San Justo 34s40 58w33 3:54:12
San Lorenzo 28s08 58w46 3:55:04
San Lorenzo 32s45 60w44 4:02:56
San Luis 33s18 66w21 4:25:24
San Luis del Palmar 27s31 58w34 3:54:16
San Manuel 37s47 58w50 3:55:20
San Martín 29s14 65w46 4:23:04
San Martín 33s04 68w28 4:33:52
San Martín → General San Martín 34s34 58w32 3:54:08
San Martín de los Andes 40s10 71w21 4:45:24
San Miguel 28s00 57w36 3:50:24
San Miguel → General Sarmiento 34s33 58w43 3:54:52
San Miguel del Monte 35s27 58w48 3:55:12
San Miguel de Tucumán 26s49 65w13 4:20:52
San Nicolás 33s20 60w13 4:00:52
San Nicolás de los Arroyos 33s20 60w13 4:00:52
Sañogasta 29s18 67w36 4:30:24
San Pedro 33s40 59w40 3:58:40
San Pedro 24s14 64w52 4:19:28
San Pedro 27s57 65w10 4:20:40
San Rafael 34s36 68w20 4:33:20
San Ramón 27s42 64w17 4:17:08
San Ramón de la Nueva Orán 23s08 64w20 4:17:20
San Roque 28s34 58w43 3:54:52
San Roque 30s17 68w41 4:34:44
San Salvador 29s16 57w31 3:50:04
San Salvador 31s37 58w30 3:54:00
San Salvador de Jujuy 24s11 65w18 4:21:12
San Solano 31s29 65w55 4:23:40
Santa Ana 27s22 55w34 3:42:16
Santa Catalina 21s57 66w04 4:24:16
Santa Clara 29s33 68w31 4:34:04
Santa Cruz 50s01 68w31 4:34:04
Santa Elena 30s57 59w48 3:59:12
Santa Fe 31s38 60w42 4:02:48
Santa Isabel 36s15 66w56 4:27:44
Santa Isabel 33s54 61w42 4:06:48
Santa Lucía 28s59 59w06 3:56:24
Santa Lucía 31s32 68w29 4:33:56
Santa Magdalena 34s30 63w56 4:15:44
Santa María 26s41 66w02 4:24:08
Santa Rita de Catuna 30s57 66w13 4:24:52
Santa Rosa 28s02 67w37 4:30:28
Santa Rosa 36s37 64w17 4:17:08
Santa Rosa 23s22 64w30 4:18:00
Santa Rosa 32s20 65w12 4:20:48
Santa Rosa de Leales 27s09 65w15 4:21:00
Santa Rosa de Río Primero 31s09 63w23 4:13:32
Santa Rosa de Toay 36s37 64w17 4:17:08
Santa Sylvina 27s49 61w09 4:04:36
Santa Teresa 33s26 60w47 4:03:08
Santiago del Estero 27s47 64w16 4:17:04
Santiago Larre 35s34 59w10 3:56:40
Santo Domingo 29s16 63w56 4:15:44
Santo Tomé 28s33 56w03 3:44:12
Santo Tomé 31s40 60w46 4:03:04
San Vicente 28s30 64w09 4:16:36
San Vicente 34s58 58w22 3:53:28
Sarmiento 45s36 69w05 4:36:20
Sastre 31s45 61w50 4:07:20
Saturnino M. Laspiur 31s42 62w29 4:09:56
Sauce 30s05 58w46 3:55:04
Saujil 28s11 66w14 4:24:56
Seclantas 25s18 66w15 4:25:00
Seguí 31s57 60w08 4:00:32
Seis de Septiembre → Morón 34s39 58w37 3:54:28
Selva 29s46 62w03 4:08:12
Serodino 32s37 60w57 4:03:48
Serrezuela 30s38 65w23 4:21:32
Sierra Chica 36s50 60w13 4:00:52
Sierra Colorada 40s35 67w48 4:31:12
Sierras Bayas 36s57 60w09 4:00:36
Simoca 27s16 65w21 4:21:24
Solca 30s46 66w28 4:25:52
Sol de Julio 29s33 63w27 4:13:48
Solís 34s18 59w20 3:57:20
Strobel 32s03 60w37 4:02:28
Stroeder 40s11 62w37 4:10:28
Sucre 34s30 59w07 3:56:28
Suipacha 34s45 59w41 3:58:44
Sumampa 29s22 63w28 4:13:52
Sunchales 30s56 61w34 4:06:16
Suncho Corral 27s56 63w27 4:13:48
Susques 23s25 66w29 4:25:56
Tabacal 23s16 64w15 4:17:00
Tablada 34s42 58w32 3:54:08
Tacañitas 28s38 62w36 4:10:24
Taco Pozo 25s37 63w17 4:13:08
Tafí Viejo 26s44 65w16 4:21:04
Tama 30s31 66w32 4:26:08
Tamberías 31s28 69w25 4:37:40
Tamel Aike 48s19 70w58 4:43:52
Tandil 37s19 59w09 3:56:36
Tapalquén 36s21 60w01 4:00:04
Tapiales 34s42 58w31 3:54:04
Tartagal 22s32 63w49 4:15:16
Tartagal 28s40 59w52 3:59:28
Tecka 43s29 70w48 4:43:12
Tehuelches 46s56 67w27 4:29:48
Telén 36s16 65w30 4:22:00
Tellier 47s39 66w03 4:24:12
Telsen 42s24 66w57 4:27:48
Teodelina 34s11 61w32 4:06:08
Tigre 34s25 58w34 3:54:16
Tilcara 23s34 65w22 4:21:28
Tilisarao 32s44 65w18 4:21:12
Tinogasta 28s04 67w34 4:30:16
Tintina 27s02 62w43 4:10:52
Toay 36s40 64w21 4:17:24
Tobas 28s08 62w42 4:10:48
Tolloche 25s30 63w32 4:14:08
Tomás Jofré 34s43 59w19 3:57:16
Tornquist 38s06 62w14 4:08:56
Torrent 28s50 56w28 3:45:52
Torres 34s26 59w08 3:56:32
Tortuguitas 34s28 58w46 3:55:04
Tostado 29s14 61w46 4:07:04
Totoras 32s35 61w11 4:04:44
Trancas 26s13 65w17 4:21:08
Trelew 43s15 65w18 4:21:12
Trenel 35s42 64w08 4:16:32
Trenque Lauquen 35s58 62w42 4:10:48
Tres Algarrobos 35s12 62w46 4:11:04
Tres Arroyos 38s23 60w17 4:01:08
Tres Cerros 48s13 67w33 4:30:12
Tres de Febrero → Caseros 34s36 58w33 3:54:12
Tres Isletas 26s21 60w26 4:01:44
Tres Lagos 49s37 71w30 4:46:00
Trevelín 43s04 71w28 4:45:52
Tricao Malal 37s03 70w19 4:41:16
Tristán Suárez 34s53 58w34 3:54:16
Tucumán → San Miguel de Tucumán 26s49 65w13 4:20:52
Tucunuco 30s36 68w38 4:34:32
Tudcum 30s14 69w15 4:37:00
Tulumaya (Lavalle) 32s43 68w35 4:34:20
Tumbaya 23s51 65w28 4:21:52
Tunuyán 33s34 69w01 4:36:04
Tupungato 33s22 69w08 4:36:32
Ucacha 33s02 63w31 4:14:04
Udaquiola 36s34 58w31 3:54:04
Ullún 31s28 68w42 4:34:48
Unión 35s09 65w57 4:23:48
Unquillo 31s14 64w19 4:17:16
Urdinarrain 32s41 58w53 3:55:32
Uribelarrea 35s09 58w54 3:55:36
Urundel 23s33 64w25 4:17:40
Urutaú 25s42 63w04 4:12:16
Ushuaia 54s48 68w18 4:33:12
Uspallata 32s35 69w20 4:37:20
Vagues 34s19 59w26 3:57:44
Valcheta 40s42 66w09 4:24:36
Valle Hermoso 31s07 64w29 4:17:56
Varela 34s07 66w27 4:25:48
Vedia 34s30 61w32 4:06:08
Veinticinco de Mayo 35s26 60w10 4:00:40
Veinticinco de Mayo 34s35 68w33 4:34:12
Venado Tuerto 33s45 61w58 4:07:52
Vera (Jobson) 29s28 60w13 4:00:52
Verónica 35s22 57w20 3:49:20
Viale 31s53 60w01 4:00:04
Viamonte 33s44 63w06 4:12:24
Vicente Casares 34s57 58w38 3:54:32
Vicente López 34s32 58w28 3:53:52
Vichigasta 29s29 67w31 4:30:04
Victoria 32s37 60w10 4:00:40
Victorica 36s13 65w27 4:21:48
Victorino de la Plaza 36s36 62w40 4:10:40
Vicuña Mackenna 33s54 64w23 4:17:32
Viedma 40s48 63w00 4:12:00
Vieytes 35s16 57w35 3:50:20
Vilelas 27s57 62w38 4:10:32
Villa Aberastain 31s39 68w35 4:34:20
Villa Alberdi 27s35 65w37 4:22:28
Villa Allende 31s18 64w18 4:17:12
Villa Ana 28s29 59w37 3:58:28
Villa Ángela 27s35 60w43 4:02:52
Villa Atamisqui 28s29 63w48 4:15:12
Villa Atuel 34s50 67w54 4:31:36
Villa Berthet 27s17 60w25 4:01:40
Villa Bustos 29s17 67w02 4:28:08
Villa Cañás 34s00 61w36 4:06:24
Villa Carlos Paz 31s24 64w31 4:18:04
Villa Castelli 29s00 68w11 4:32:44
Villa Colón (Caucete) 31s39 68w17 4:33:08
Villa Concepción del Tío 31s19 62w50 4:11:20
Villa Constitución 33s14 60w20 4:01:20
Villa del Carmen 32s57 65w03 4:20:12
Villa del Rosario 31s35 63w32 4:14:08
Villa del Rosario 30s47 57w55 3:51:40
Villa de María 29s54 63w43 4:14:52
Villa de Mayo 34s30 58w41 3:54:44
Villa de Soto 30s51 64w59 4:19:56
Villa Diego 33s01 60w37 4:02:28
Villa Dolores 31s56 65w12 4:20:48
Villa El Alto 28s18 65w22 4:21:28
Villa Elisa 32s10 58w24 3:53:36
Villa General Roca 32s39 66w28 4:25:52
Villaguay 31s51 59w01 3:56:04
Villa Guillermina 28s14 59w28 3:57:52
Villa Hernandarias 31s13 59w59 3:59:56
Villa Huidobro (Cañada Verde) 34s50 64w35 4:18:20
Villa Iris 38s10 63w15 4:13:00
Villa Krause 31s34 68w32 4:34:08
Villa La Angostura 40s47 71w40 4:46:40
Villa La Paz 33s27 67w38 4:30:32
Villa Larca 32s37 64w59 4:19:56
Villa Larroque 33s02 59w01 3:56:04
Villa Lía 34s07 59w26 3:57:44
Villalonga 39s53 62w35 4:10:20
Villa Madero 34s42 58w30 3:54:00
Villa María 32s25 63w15 4:13:00
Villa María Grande 31s39 59w54 3:59:36
Villa Matoque 25s49 63w49 4:15:16
Villa Mazán 28s40 66w34 4:26:16
Villa Mercedes 30s07 68w42 4:34:48
Villa Nueva 32s54 68w47 4:35:08
Villa Nueva 32s26 63w15 4:13:00
Villa Numancia 34s55 58w24 3:53:36
Villa Ocampo 28s28 59w22 3:57:28
Villa Ojo de Agua 29s31 63w42 4:14:48
Villa Quinteros 27s14 65w33 4:22:12
Villa Ramírez 32s11 60w12 4:00:48
Villa Regina 39s06 67w04 4:28:16
Villa Reynolds 33s43 65w23 4:21:32
Villa Rosa 34s25 58w52 3:55:28
Villars 34s50 58w56 3:55:44
Villa Ruiz 34s25 59w15 3:57:00
Villa San José 32s12 58w13 3:52:52
Villa San Martín 28s18 64w12 4:16:48
Villa Unión 29s18 68w12 4:32:48
Villa Unión 29s24 62w47 4:11:08
Villa Valeria 34s20 64w55 4:19:40
Villa Zorraquín 31s19 58w02 3:52:08
Vinchina 28s46 68w10 4:32:40
Vipos 26s29 65w22 4:21:28
Vista Alegre 38s45 68w11 4:32:44
Vista Flores 33s38 69w09 4:36:36
Vivoratá 37s40 57w39 3:50:36
Volcán 23s54 65w27 4:21:48
Warnes 34s55 60w31 4:02:04
Weisburd 27s18 62w36 4:10:24
Wheelwright 33s47 61w13 4:04:52
Winifreda 36s15 64w14 4:16:56
Yapeyú 29s28 56w49 3:47:16
Zanjón 27s55 64w15 4:17:00
Zapala 38s54 70w04 4:40:16
Zapiola 35s03 59w03 3:56:12
Zárate 34s06 59w02 3:56:08
Zelaya 34s21 58w52 3:55:28
Zenon Videla Dorna 35s33 58w53 3:55:32

AUSTRALIA AUSTRALIEN AUSTRALIE

Time Table # 1
Before 1/02/1895 LMT
Begin Standard 150E00
1/02/1895 0:00 -10:00
1/01/1917 0:01 -11:00
25/03/1917 2:00 -10:00
1/01/1942 2:00 -11:00
29/03/1942 2:00 -10:00
27/09/1942 2:00 -11:00
28/03/1943 2:00 -10:00
3/10/1943 2:00 -11:00
26/03/1944 2:00 -10:00
31/10/1971 2:00 -11:00
27/02/1972 2:00 -10:00
29/10/1972 2:00 -11:00
4/03/1973 2:00 -10:00
28/10/1973 2:00 -11:00
3/03/1974 2:00 -10:00
27/10/1974 2:00 -11:00
2/03/1975 2:00 -10:00
26/10/1975 2:00 -11:00
7/03/1976 2:00 -10:00
31/10/1976 2:00 -11:00
6/03/1977 2:00 -10:00
30/10/1977 2:00 -11:00
5/03/1978 2:00 -10:00
29/10/1978 2:00 -11:00
4/03/1979 2:00 -10:00
28/10/1979 2:00 -11:00
2/03/1980 2:00 -10:00
26/10/1980 2:00 -11:00
1/03/1981 2:00 -10:00
25/10/1981 2:00 -11:00
4/04/1982 2:00 -10:00
31/10/1982 2:00 -11:00
6/03/1983 2:00 -10:00
30/10/1983 2:00 -11:00
4/03/1984 2:00 -10:00
28/10/1984 2:00 -11:00
3/03/1985 2:00 -10:00
27/10/1985 2:00 -11:00
16/03/1986 2:00 -10:00
19/10/1986 2:00 -11:00
15/03/1987 2:00 -10:00
25/10/1987 2:00 -11:00
20/03/1988 2:00 -10:00
30/10/1988 2:00 -11:00
19/03/1989 2:00 -10:00
29/10/1989 2:00 -11:00
18/03/1990 2:00 -10:00
28/10/1990 2:00 -11:00
17/03/1991 2:00 -10:00
27/10/1991 2:00 -11:00
15/03/1992 2:00 -10:00
25/10/1992 2:00 -11:00
21/03/1993 2:00 -10:00
31/10/1993 2:00 -11:00
20/03/1994 2:00 -10:00
30/10/1994 2:00 -11:00
19/03/1995 2:00 -10:00
29/10/1995 2:00 -11:00
17/03/1996 2:00 -10:00
27/10/1996 2:00 -11:00
16/03/1997 2:00 -10:00
26/10/1997 2:00 -11:00
15/03/1998 2:00 -10:00
25/10/1998 2:00 -11:00
21/03/1999 2:00 -10:00
31/10/1999 2:00 -11:00
19/03/2000 2:00 -10:00
....

Time Table # 2
Before 1/02/1895 LMT
Begin Standard 150E00
1/02/1895 0:00 -10:00
1/01/1917 0:01 -11:00
25/03/1917 2:00 -10:00
1/01/1942 2:00 -11:00
29/03/1942 2:00 -10:00
27/09/1942 2:00 -11:00
28/03/1943 2:00 -10:00
3/10/1943 2:00 -11:00
26/03/1944 2:00 -10:00
31/10/1971 2:00 -11:00
27/02/1972 2:00 -10:00
29/10/1972 2:00 -11:00
4/03/1973 2:00 -10:00
28/10/1973 2:00 -11:00
3/03/1974 2:00 -10:00
27/10/1974 2:00 -11:00
2/03/1975 2:00 -10:00
26/10/1975 2:00 -11:00
7/03/1976 2:00 -10:00
31/10/1976 2:00 -11:00
6/03/1977 2:00 -10:00
30/10/1977 2:00 -11:00
5/03/1978 2:00 -10:00
29/10/1978 2:00 -11:00
4/03/1979 2:00 -10:00
28/10/1979 2:00 -11:00
2/03/1980 2:00 -10:00
26/10/1980 2:00 -11:00
1/03/1981 2:00 -10:00
25/10/1981 2:00 -11:00
7/03/1982 2:00 -10:00
31/10/1982 2:00 -11:00
6/03/1983 2:00 -10:00
30/10/1983 2:00 -11:00
4/03/1984 2:00 -10:00
28/10/1984 2:00 -11:00
3/03/1985 2:00 -10:00
27/10/1985 2:00 -11:00
16/03/1986 2:00 -10:00
19/10/1986 2:00 -11:00
15/03/1987 2:00 -10:00
25/10/1987 2:00 -11:00
20/03/1988 2:00 -10:00
30/10/1988 2:00 -11:00
19/03/1989 2:00 -10:00
29/10/1989 2:00 -11:00
18/03/1990 2:00 -10:00
28/10/1990 2:00 -11:00
17/03/1991 2:00 -10:00
27/10/1991 2:00 -11:00
15/03/1992 2:00 -10:00
25/10/1992 2:00 -11:00
21/03/1993 2:00 -10:00
31/10/1993 2:00 -11:00
20/03/1994 2:00 -10:00
30/10/1994 2:00 -11:00
19/03/1995 2:00 -10:00
29/10/1995 2:00 -11:00
17/03/1996 2:00 -10:00
27/10/1996 2:00 -11:00
16/03/1997 2:00 -10:00
26/10/1997 2:00 -11:00
15/03/1998 2:00 -10:00
25/10/1998 2:00 -11:00
21/03/1999 2:00 -10:00
31/10/1999 2:00 -11:00
19/03/2000 2:00 -10:00
....

Time Table # 3
Before 1/09/1895 LMT
Begin Standard 150E00
1/09/1895 0:00 -10:00
1/10/1916 2:00 -11:00
25/03/1917 2:00 -10:00
28/10/1917 2:00 -11:00
3/03/1918 2:00 -10:00
27/10/1918 2:00 -11:00
2/03/1919 2:00 -10:00
1/01/1942 2:00 -11:00
29/03/1942 2:00 -10:00
27/09/1942 2:00 -11:00
28/03/1943 2:00 -10:00
3/10/1943 2:00 -11:00
26/03/1944 2:00 -10:00
1/10/1967 2:00 -11:00
31/03/1968 2:00 -10:00
27/10/1968 2:00 -11:00
9/03/1969 2:00 -10:00
26/10/1969 2:00 -11:00
8/03/1970 2:00 -10:00
25/10/1970 2:00 -11:00
14/03/1971 2:00 -10:00
31/10/1971 2:00 -11:00
27/02/1972 2:00 -10:00
29/10/1972 2:00 -11:00
4/03/1973 2:00 -10:00
28/10/1973 2:00 -11:00
3/03/1974 2:00 -10:00
27/10/1974 2:00 -11:00
2/03/1975 2:00 -10:00
26/10/1975 2:00 -11:00
7/03/1976 2:00 -10:00
31/10/1976 2:00 -11:00
6/03/1977 2:00 -10:00
30/10/1977 2:00 -11:00
5/03/1978 2:00 -10:00
29/10/1978 2:00 -11:00
4/03/1979 2:00 -10:00
28/10/1979 2:00 -11:00
2/03/1980 2:00 -10:00
26/10/1980 2:00 -11:00
1/03/1981 2:00 -10:00
25/10/1981 2:00 -11:00
28/03/1982 2:00 -10:00
31/10/1982 2:00 -11:00
27/03/1983 2:00 -10:00
30/10/1983 2:00 -11:00
4/03/1984 2:00 -10:00
28/10/1984 2:00 -11:00
3/03/1985 2:00 -10:00
27/10/1985 2:00 -11:00
2/03/1986 2:00 -10:00
19/10/1986 2:00 -11:00
15/03/1987 2:00 -10:00
25/10/1987 2:00 -11:00
20/03/1988 2:00 -10:00
30/10/1988 2:00 -11:00
19/03/1989 2:00 -10:00
29/10/1989 2:00 -11:00
18/03/1990 2:00 -10:00
28/10/1990 2:00 -11:00
17/03/1991 2:00 -10:00
27/10/1991 2:00 -11:00
15/03/1992 2:00 -10:00
25/10/1992 2:00 -11:00
21/03/1993 2:00 -10:00
31/10/1993 2:00 -11:00
20/03/1994 2:00 -10:00
30/10/1994 2:00 -11:00
19/03/1995 2:00 -10:00
29/10/1995 2:00 -11:00
17/03/1996 2:00 -10:00
27/10/1996 2:00 -11:00
16/03/1997 2:00 -10:00
26/10/1997 2:00 -11:00
15/03/1998 2:00 -10:00
25/10/1998 2:00 -11:00
21/03/1999 2:00 -10:00
31/10/1999 2:00 -11:00
19/03/2000 2:00 -10:00
....

Time Table # 4
Before 1/01/1895 LMT
Begin Standard 150E00
1/01/1895 0:00 -10:00
1/01/1917 0:01 -11:00
25/03/1917 2:00 -10:00
1/01/1942 2:00 -11:00
29/03/1942 2:00 -10:00
27/09/1942 2:00 -11:00
28/03/1943 2:00 -10:00
3/10/1943 2:00 -11:00
26/03/1944 2:00 -10:00
31/10/1971 2:00 -11:00
27/02/1972 2:00 -10:00
....

Time Table # 5
Before 1/12/1895 LMT
Begin Standard 120E00
1/12/1895 0:00 -8:00
1/01/1917 0:01 -9:00
25/03/1917 2:00 -8:00
1/01/1942 2:00 -9:00
29/03/1942 2:00 -8:00
27/09/1942 2:00 -9:00
28/03/1943 2:00 -8:00
27/10/1974 2:00 -9:00
2/03/1975 2:00 -8:00
30/10/1983 2:00 -9:00
4/03/1984 2:00 -8:00
....

Time Table # 6
Before 1/02/1895 LMT
Begin Standard 105E00
1/02/1895 0:00 -7:00
....

Time Table # 7
Before 1/02/1895 LMT
Begin Standard 150E00
1/02/1895 0:00 -10:00
Begin Standard 135E00
23/08/1896 0:00 -9:00
Begin Standard 142E30
1/05/1899 0:00 -9:30
1/01/1917 0:01 -10:30
25/03/1917 2:00 -9:30
1/01/1942 2:00 -10:30
29/03/1942 2:00 -9:30
27/09/1942 2:00 -10:30
28/03/1943 2:00 -9:30
3/10/1943 2:00 -10:30
26/03/1944 2:00 -9:30
31/10/1971 2:00 -10:30
27/02/1972 2:00 -9:30
29/10/1972 2:00 -10:30
4/03/1973 2:00 -9:30
28/10/1973 2:00 -10:30
3/03/1974 2:00 -9:30
27/10/1974 2:00 -10:30
2/03/1975 2:00 -9:30
26/10/1975 2:00 -10:30
7/03/1976 2:00 -9:30
31/10/1976 2:00 -10:30
6/03/1977 2:00 -9:30
30/10/1977 2:00 -10:30
5/03/1978 2:00 -9:30
29/10/1978 2:00 -10:30
4/03/1979 2:00 -9:30
28/10/1979 2:00 -10:30
2/03/1980 2:00 -9:30
26/10/1980 2:00 -10:30
1/03/1981 2:00 -9:30
25/10/1981 2:00 -10:30
4/04/1982 2:00 -9:30
31/10/1982 2:00 -10:30
6/03/1983 2:00 -9:30
30/10/1983 2:00 -10:30
4/03/1984 2:00 -9:30
28/10/1984 2:00 -10:30
3/03/1985 2:00 -9:30
27/10/1985 2:00 -10:30
16/03/1986 2:00 -9:30
19/10/1986 2:00 -10:30
15/03/1987 2:00 -9:30
25/10/1987 2:00 -10:30
20/03/1988 2:00 -9:30
30/10/1988 2:00 -10:30
19/03/1989 2:00 -9:30
29/10/1989 2:00 -10:30
18/03/1990 2:00 -9:30
28/10/1990 2:00 -10:30
17/03/1991 2:00 -9:30
27/10/1991 2:00 -10:30
15/03/1992 2:00 -9:30
25/10/1992 2:00 -10:30
21/03/1993 2:00 -9:30
31/10/1993 2:00 -10:30
20/03/1994 2:00 -9:30
30/10/1994 2:00 -10:30
19/03/1995 2:00 -9:30
29/10/1995 2:00 -10:30
17/03/1996 2:00 -9:30
27/10/1996 2:00 -10:30
16/03/1997 2:00 -9:30
26/10/1997 2:00 -10:30
15/03/1998 2:00 -9:30
25/10/1998 2:00 -10:30
21/03/1999 2:00 -9:30
31/10/1999 2:00 -10:30
19/03/2000 2:00 -9:30
....

Time Table # 8
Before 1/02/1895 LMT
Begin Standard 135E00
1/02/1895 0:00 -9:00
Begin Standard 142E30
1/05/1899 0:00 -9:30
1/01/1917 0:01 -10:30
25/03/1917 2:00 -9:30
1/01/1942 2:00 -10:30
29/03/1942 2:00 -9:30
27/09/1942 2:00 -10:30
28/03/1943 2:00 -9:30
3/10/1943 2:00 -10:30
26/03/1944 2:00 -9:30
....

Time Table # 9
Before 1/02/1895 LMT
Begin Standard 135E00
1/02/1895 0:00 -9:00
Begin Standard 142E30
1/05/1899 0:00 -9:30
1/01/1917 0:01 -10:30
25/03/1917 2:00 -9:30
1/01/1942 2:00 -10:30
29/03/1942 2:00 -9:30
27/09/1942 2:00 -10:30
28/03/1943 2:00 -9:30
3/10/1943 2:00 -10:30
26/03/1944 2:00 -9:30
31/10/1971 2:00 -10:30
27/02/1972 2:00 -9:30
29/10/1972 2:00 -10:30
4/03/1973 2:00 -9:30
28/10/1973 2:00 -10:30
3/03/1974 2:00 -9:30
27/10/1974 2:00 -10:30
2/03/1975 2:00 -9:30
26/10/1975 2:00 -10:30
7/03/1976 2:00 -9:30
31/10/1976 2:00 -10:30
6/03/1977 2:00 -9:30
30/10/1977 2:00 -10:30
5/03/1978 2:00 -9:30
29/10/1978 2:00 -10:30
4/03/1979 2:00 -9:30
28/10/1979 2:00 -10:30
2/03/1980 2:00 -9:30
26/10/1980 2:00 -10:30
1/03/1981 2:00 -9:30
25/10/1981 2:00 -10:30
7/03/1982 2:00 -9:30
31/10/1982 2:00 -10:30
6/03/1983 2:00 -9:30
30/10/1983 2:00 -10:30
4/03/1984 2:00 -9:30
28/10/1984 2:00 -10:30
3/03/1985 2:00 -9:30
27/10/1985 2:00 -10:30
16/03/1986 2:00 -9:30
19/10/1986 2:00 -10:30
15/03/1987 2:00 -9:30
25/10/1987 2:00 -10:30
20/03/1988 2:00 -9:30
30/10/1988 2:00 -10:30
19/03/1989 2:00 -9:30
29/10/1989 2:00 -10:30
18/03/1990 2:00 -9:30
28/10/1990 2:00 -10:30
17/03/1991 2:00 -9:30
27/10/1991 2:00 -10:30
15/03/1992 2:00 -9:30
25/10/1992 2:00 -10:30
21/03/1993 2:00 -9:30
31/10/1993 2:00 -10:30
20/03/1994 2:00 -9:30
30/10/1994 2:00 -10:30
19/03/1995 2:00 -9:30
29/10/1995 2:00 -10:30
17/03/1996 2:00 -9:30
27/10/1996 2:00 -10:30
16/03/1997 2:00 -9:30
26/10/1997 2:00 -10:30
15/03/1998 2:00 -9:30
25/10/1998 2:00 -10:30
21/03/1999 2:00 -9:30
31/10/1999 2:00 -10:30
19/03/2000 2:00 -9:30
....

Time Table # 10
Before 1/02/1895 LMT
Begin Standard 150E00
1/02/1895 0:00 -10:00
Begin Standard 157E30
1/03/1981 0:00 -10:30
25/10/1981 2:00 -11:30
7/03/1982 2:00 -10:30
31/10/1982 2:00 -11:30
6/03/1983 2:00 -10:30
30/10/1983 2:00 -11:30
4/03/1984 2:00 -10:30
28/10/1984 2:00 -11:30
3/03/1985 2:00 -10:30
27/10/1985 2:00 -11:00
16/03/1986 2:00 -10:30
19/10/1986 2:00 -11:00
15/03/1987 2:00 -10:30
25/10/1987 2:00 -11:00
20/03/1988 2:00 -10:30
30/10/1988 2:00 -11:00
19/03/1989 2:00 -10:30
29/10/1989 2:00 -11:00
18/03/1990 2:00 -10:30
28/10/1990 2:00 -11:00
17/03/1991 2:00 -10:30
27/10/1991 2:00 -11:00
15/03/1992 2:00 -10:30
25/10/1992 2:00 -11:00
21/03/1993 2:00 -10:30
31/10/1993 2:00 -11:00
20/03/1994 2:00 -10:30
30/10/1994 2:00 -11:00
19/03/1995 2:00 -10:30
29/10/1995 2:00 -11:00
17/03/1996 2:00 -10:30
27/10/1996 2:00 -11:00
16/03/1997 2:00 -10:30
26/10/1997 2:00 -11:00
15/03/1998 2:00 -10:30
25/10/1998 2:00 -11:00
21/03/1999 2:00 -10:30
31/10/1999 2:00 -11:00
19/03/2000 2:00 -10:30

DIVISIONS

1. Australian Capital Territory
2. New South Wales
3. Northern Territory
4. Queensland
5. South Australia
6. Tasmania
7. Victoria
8. Western Australia
9. Christmas Island
10. Lord Howe Island

Abbotsford 2 1 33s51 151E08-10:04:32
Abermain 2 1 32s49 151E25-10:05:40
Abminga 5 9 26s07 134E52 -8:59:28
Abydos 8 5 21s25 118E54 -7:55:36
Adaminaby 2 1 36s03 148E43 -9:54:52
Adamstown 2 1 32s56 151E44-10:06:56
Adavale 4 4 25s55 144E36 -9:38:24
Adelaida → Adelaide 5
9 34s55 138E35 -9:14:20
Adelaide 5 9 34s55 138E35 -9:14:20
Adelaide River 3
8 13s15 131E06 -8:44:24
Agery 5 9 34s10 137E44 -9:10:56
Agnew 8 5 28s01 120E30 -8:02:00
Aileron 3 8 22s39 133E20 -8:53:20
Airport West 7 2 37s44 144E53 -9:39:32
Ajana 8 5 27s57 114E38 -7:38:32
Albany 8 5 35s02 117E53 -7:51:32
Alberga 5 9 27s12 135E28 -9:01:52
Albion 7 2 37s47 144E49 -9:39:16
Albion Park 2 1 34s34 150E47-10:03:08
Albury 7 2 36s05 146E55 -9:47:40
Alderley 4 4 22s39 139E44 -9:18:56
Alexandra 7 2 37s12 145E43 -9:42:52
Alexandria 3 8 19s05 136E40 -9:06:40
Alford 5 9 33s49 137E49 -9:11:16
Alice Downs 8 5 17s45 127E56 -8:31:44
Alice Springs 3
8 23s42 133E53 -8:55:32
Allanson 8 5 33s20 116E06 -7:44:24

Allora 4 4 28s02 151E59-10:07:56
Almaden 4 4 17s20 144E41 -9:38:44
Alpha 4 4 23s39 146E38 -9:46:32
Alroy Downs 3 8 19s18 136E04 -9:04:16
Altona 8 5 27s34 120E00 -8:00:00
Altona 7 2 37s52 144E50 -9:39:20
Altona North 7 2 37s50 144E51 -9:39:24
American River 5 9 35s47 137E47 -9:11:08
Amery 8 5 31s09 117E05 -7:48:20
Amiens 4 4 28s35 151E49-10:07:16
Ammaroo 3 8 21s45 135E15 -9:01:00
Andamooka 5 9 30s27 137E12 -9:08:48
Angas Downs 3 8 24s49 132E14 -8:48:56
Angaston 5 9 34s30 139E02 -9:16:08
Anglesea 7 2 38s25 144E11 -9:36:44
Angus Place 2 1 33s20 150E06-10:00:24
Anna Creek 5 9 28s51 136E08 -9:04:32
Annandale 4 4 21s57 148E22 -9:53:28
Anna Plains 8 5 19s17 121E37 -8:06:28
Anthony Lagoon 3 8 17s59 135E32 -9:02:08
Apollo Bay 7 2 38s45 143E40 -9:34:40
Appin 2 1 34s12 150E47-10:03:08
Aramac 4 4 22s59 145E14 -9:40:56
Ararat 7 2 37s17 142E56 -9:31:44
Aratula 4 4 27s59 152E32-10:10:08
Arckaringa 5 9 27s56 134E45 -8:59:00
Ardlethan 2 1 34s21 146E54 -9:47:36
Ardoch 4 4 27s26 144E08 -9:36:32
Ardrossan 5 9 34s25 137E55 -9:11:40
Argadargada 3 8 21s40 136E40 -9:06:40
Arltunga 3 8 23s26 134E41 -8:58:44
Armadale 8 5 32s09 116E00 -7:44:00
Armidale 2 1 30s31 151E39-10:06:36
Arncliffe 2 1 33s56 151E09-10:04:36
Arno Bay 5 9 33s54 136E34 -9:06:16
Artarmon 2 1 33s49 151E11-10:04:44
Arthurton 5 9 34s16 137E45 -9:11:00
Ascot 4 4 27s26 153E04-10:12:16
Ashburton 7 2 37s52 145E05 -9:40:20
Ashburton Downs 8 5 23s24 117E04 -7:48:16
Ashfield 2 1 33s53 151E08-10:04:32
Ashford 2 1 29s20 151E06-10:04:24
Ashley 2 1 29s19 149E49 -9:59:16
Aspendale 7 2 38s02 145E07 -9:40:28
Asquith 2 1 33s41 151E06-10:04:24
Atherton 4 4 17s16 145E29 -9:41:56
Attadale 8 5 32s01 115E48 -7:43:12
Auburn 5 9 34s01 138E41 -9:14:44
Auburn 2 1 33s51 151E02-10:04:08
Augathella 4 4 25s48 146E35 -9:46:20
Augusta 8 5 34s19 115E10 -7:40:40
Augustus Downs 4 4 18s33 139E52 -9:19:28
Aurukun Mission 4 4 13s19 141E45 -9:27:00
Austinmer 2 1 34s18 150E56-10:03:44
Australia Plains 5 9 34s06 139E09 -9:16:36
Australind 8 5 33s16 115E44 -7:42:56
Auvergne 3 8 15s41 130E01 -8:40:04
Avoca 7 2 37s05 143E28 -9:33:52
Avoca Beach 2 1 33s29 151E29-10:05:56
Avon 5 9 34s17 138E20 -9:13:20
Avondale Heights 7 2 37s46 144E51 -9:39:24
Avon Downs 3 8 20s05 137E30 -9:10:00
Awaba 2 1 33s01 151E33-10:06:12
Axedale 7 2 36s47 144E30 -9:38:00
Ayr 4 4 19s35 147E24 -9:49:36
Ayton 4 4 15s56 145E22 -9:41:28
Babakin 8 5 32s07 118E01 -7:52:04
Babinda 4 4 17s20 145E55 -9:43:40
Bacchus Marsh 7 2 37s41 144E27 -9:37:48
Badgery's Creek 2 1 33s53 150E44-10:02:56
Bairnsdale 7 2 37s50 147E38 -9:50:32
Bajool 4 4 23s39 150E39-10:02:36
Bakers Hill 8 5 31s45 116E27 -7:45:48
Balaklava 5 9 34s09 138E25 -9:13:40
Balcanoona 5 9 30s31 139E18 -9:17:12
Bald Hills 4 4 27s19 153E01-10:12:04
Balfes Creek 4 4 20s13 145E55 -9:43:40
Balfour Downs 8 5 22s50 120E50 -8:03:20
Balgo Hill Mission 8 5 20s09 127E48 -8:31:12
Balgowlah 2 1 33s48 151E16-10:05:04
Balhannah 5 9 35s00 138E50 -9:15:20
Balingup 8 5 33s48 115E58 -7:43:52
Balladonia 8 5 32s27 123E51 -8:15:24
Ballan 7 2 37s36 144E14 -9:36:56
Ballarat 7 2 37s34 143E52 -9:35:28
Ballidu 8 5 30s36 116E46 -7:47:04
Ballina 2 1 28s52 153E33-10:14:12
Balmain 2 1 33s51 151E11-10:04:44
Balmoral 7 2 37s15 141E51 -9:27:24
Balranald 2 2 34s38 143E33 -9:34:12
Balwyn 7 2 37s49 145E05 -9:40:20
Bamaga 4 4 10s52 142E24 -9:29:36
Bambaroo 4 4 18s52 146E12 -9:44:48
Bamboo Creek 8 5 20s56 120E13 -8:00:52
Bamboo Springs 8 5 22s04 119E38 -7:58:32
Banana 4 4 24s28 150E07-10:00:28
Bangholme 7 2 38s02 145E11 -9:40:44
Banka Banka 3 8 18s48 134E01 -8:56:04
Banksmeadow 2 1 33s58 151E13-10:04:52
Bankstown 2 1 33s55 151E02-10:04:08
Bannister 8 5 32s40 116E33 -7:46:12
Bannockburn 7 2 38s03 144E10 -9:36:40
Baradine 2 1 30s56 149E04 -9:56:16
Barakula 4 4 26s26 150E31-10:02:04
Baralaba 4 4 24s11 149E49 -9:59:16
Baratta 5 9 31s59 139E06 -9:16:24
Barcaldine 4 4 23s33 145E17 -9:41:08
Bardoc 8 5 30s20 121E17 -8:05:08
Bargara 4 4 24s49 152E27-10:09:48
Bargo 2 1 34s18 150E35-10:02:20
Barmedman 2 1 34s09 147E23 -9:49:32
Barmera 5 9 34s15 140E28 -9:21:52
Barraba 2 1 30s22 150E36-10:02:24
Barringun 2 1 29s01 145E43 -9:42:52
Barrow Creek 3 8 21s33 133E53 -8:55:32
Barton 5 9 30s31 132E39 -8:50:36
Barwidgee 8 5 27s02 120E52 -8:03:36
Bass Hill 2 1 33s54 151E00-10:04:00
Batchelor 3 8 13s04 131E01 -8:44:04
Batemans Bay 2 1 35s43 150E11-10:00:44
Bathurst 2 1 33s25 149E35 -9:58:20
Bathurst Island Mission 3 8 11s45 130E38 -8:42:32
Batlow 2 1 35s31 148E09 -9:52:36
Baulkham Hills 2 1 33s46 151E00-10:04:00
Bayswater 7 2 37s51 145E16 -9:41:04
Bayswater North 7 2 37s49 145E17 -9:41:08
Bayview 2 1 33s40 151E18-10:05:12
Beachport 5 9 37s30 140E01 -9:20:04
Beacon 8 5 30s26 117E51 -7:51:24
Beacon Hill 2 1 33s45 151E15-10:05:00
Beaconsfield 6 3 41s12 146E48 -9:47:12
Beaconsfield 7 2 38s03 145E22 -9:41:28
Beagle Bay Mission 8 5 16s58 122E40 -8:10:40
Bealiba 7 2 36s48 143E33 -9:34:12
Beaudesert 4 4 27s59 153E00-10:12:00
Beaufort 7 2 37s26 143E23 -9:33:32
Beaumaris 7 2 37s59 145E02 -9:40:08
Bedfordale 8 5 32s10 116E03 -7:44:12
Bedourie 4 4 24s21 139E28 -9:17:52
Beeac 7 2 38s12 143E38 -9:34:32
Beech Forest 7 2 38s38 143E34 -9:34:16
Beechmont 4 4 28s07 153E11-10:12:44
Beechworth 7 2 36s22 146E41 -9:46:44
Beecroft 2 1 33s45 151E04-10:04:16
Beenleigh 4 4 27s43 153E12-10:12:48
Beerburrum 4 4 26s58 152E58-10:11:52
Beerwah 4 4 26s51 152E58-10:11:52
Bega 2 1 36s40 149E50 -9:59:20
Belfield 2 1 33s54 151E05-10:04:20
Belgrave 7 2 37s55 145E21 -9:41:24
Bellambi 2 1 34s21 150E55-10:03:40
Bellarine 7 2 38s08 144E37 -9:38:28
Bellata 2 1 29s55 149E47 -9:59:08
Bellbird 2 1 32s51 151E21-10:05:24
Bellbrook 2 1 30s49 152E31-10:10:04
Bellingen 2 1 30s27 152E54-10:11:36
Belmont 7 2 38s10 144E21 -9:37:24
Belmont 2 1 33s02 151E40-10:06:40
Belmore 2 1 33s55 151E05-10:04:20
Belrose 2 1 33s44 151E13-10:04:52
Beltana 5 9 30s48 138E25 -9:13:40
Benagerie 5 9 31s25 140E24 -9:21:36
Benalla 7 2 36s33 145E59 -9:43:56
Bencubbin 8 5 30s48 117E52 -7:51:28
Bendemeer 2 1 30s53 151E10-10:04:40
Bendigo 7 2 36s46 144E17 -9:37:08
Benger 8 5 33s11 115E52 -7:43:28
Benlidi 4 4 24s34 144E52 -9:39:28
Bennettswood 7 2 37s51 145E07 -9:40:28
Bentleigh 7 2 37s55 145E02 -9:40:08
Beresford 5 9 29s14 136E40 -9:06:40
Bermagui 2 1 36s25 150E04-10:00:16
Berowra 2 1 33s37 151E09-10:04:36
Berri 5 9 34s17 140E36 -9:22:24
Berridale 2 1 36s22 148E50 -9:55:20
Berrigan 2 1 35s40 145E49 -9:43:16
Berrima 2 1 34s30 150E20-10:01:20
Berry 2 1 34s47 150E42-10:02:48
Berwick 7 2 38s02 145E21 -9:41:24
Betoota 4 4 25s42 140E44 -9:22:56
Beulah 7 2 35s56 142E26 -9:29:44
Beverley 8 5 32s06 116E56 -7:47:44
Beverly Hills 2 1 33s57 151E05-10:04:20
Bexley 2 1 33s57 151E08-10:04:32
Big Bell 8 5 27s21 117E40 -7:50:40
Billiluna 8 5 19s37 127E41 -8:30:44
Biloela 4 4 24s24 150E30-10:02:00
Bilpin 2 1 33s30 150E31-10:02:04
Bimbowrie 5 9 32s03 140E09 -9:20:36
Bindebango 4 4 27s45 147E24 -9:49:36
Bingara 2 1 29s52 150E34-10:02:16
Binna Burra 4 4 28s13 153E14-10:12:56
Binnaway 2 1 31s33 149E23 -9:57:32
Birdsville 4 4 25s54 139E22 -9:17:28
Birdum 3 8 15s39 133E13 -8:52:52
Birdwood 5 9 34s49 138E57 -9:15:48
Birregurra 7 2 38s20 143E48 -9:35:12
Birrindudu 3 8 18s22 129E27 -8:37:48
Blackall 4 4 24s25 145E28 -9:41:52
Blackburn 7 2 37s49 145E09 -9:40:36
Blackbutt 4 4 26s53 152E06-10:08:24
Blackheath 2 1 33s38 150E17-10:01:08
Black Rock 7 2 37s59 145E01 -9:40:04
Black Springs 2 1 33s52 149E42 -9:58:48
Blacktown 2 1 33s46 150E55-10:03:40
Blackwater 4 4 23s35 148E53 -9:55:32
Blackwood 7 2 37s29 144E19 -9:37:16
Blackwood 5 9 35s02 138E37 -9:14:28
Blair Athol 4 4 22s42 147E33 -9:50:12
Blakehurst 2 1 33s59 151E07-10:04:28
Blaxland 2 1 33s45 150E36-10:02:24
Blayney 2 1 33s32 149E15 -9:57:00
Blenheim 4 4 27s39 152E20-10:09:20
Blinman 5 9 31s06 138E41 -9:14:44
Bloods Creek 5 9 26s28 135E17 -9:01:08
Bloomsbury 4 4 20s43 148E35 -9:54:20
Blyth 5 9 33s51 138E29 -9:13:56
Boatman 4 4 27s16 146E55 -9:47:40
Bobbin Head 2 1 33s39 151E08-10:04:32
Bodalla 2 1 36s05 150E03-10:00:12
Bodallin 8 5 31s22 118E52 -7:55:28
Boddington 8 5 32s48 116E28 -7:45:52
Bogan Gate 2 1 33s07 147E48 -9:51:12
Bogantungan 4 4 23s39 147E18 -9:49:12
Boggabilla 4 4 28s37 150E21-10:01:24
Boggabri 2 1 30s42 150E02-10:00:08
Bohemia Downs 8 5 18s53 126E14 -8:24:56
Bokal 8 5 33s29 116E54 -7:47:36
Bolangum 7 2 36s46 142E53 -9:31:32
Bolgart 8 5 31s16 116E30 -7:46:00
Bolivar 5 9 34s46 138E36 -9:14:24
Bollon 4 4 28s05 147E15 -9:49:00
Bolwarra 4 4 17s24 144E11 -9:36:44
Bomaderry 2 1 34s51 150E37-10:02:28
Bombala 2 1 36s54 149E14 -9:56:56
Bonbeach 7 2 38s04 145E08 -9:40:32
Bon Bon 5 9 30s26 135E28 -9:01:52
Bondi 2 1 33s53 151E17-10:05:08
Bongaree 4 4 27s05 153E10-10:12:40
Bonnie Rock 8 5 30s32 118E21 -7:53:24
Bonnyrigg 2 1 33s54 150E54-10:03:36
Boogardie 8 5 28s02 117E47 -7:51:08
Bookabie 5 9 31s50 132E41 -8:50:44
Bookaloo 5 9 31s55 137E22 -9:09:28
Boolaloo 8 5 22s35 115E51 -7:43:24
Booleroo Centre 5 9 32s53 138E21 -9:13:24
Booligal 2 1 33s52 144E53 -9:39:32
Boologooro 8 5 24s21 114E02 -7:36:08
Boomarra 4 4 19s33 140E20 -9:21:20
Boomi 2 1 28s44 149E35 -9:58:20
Boonah 4 4 28s00 152E41-10:10:44
Boorindal 2 1 30s21 146E08 -9:44:32
Booroorban 2 1 34s56 144E46 -9:39:04
Boorowa 2 1 34s26 148E43 -9:54:52
Boorthanna 5 9 28s38 135E54 -9:03:36
Bopeechee 5 9 29s36 137E23 -9:09:32
Borambola 2 1 35s12 147E41 -9:50:44
Borden 8 5 34s05 118E16 -7:53:04
Bordertown 5 9 36s19 140E47 -9:23:08
Boronia 7 2 37s52 145E17 -9:41:08
Borroloola 3 8 16s04 136E17 -9:05:08
Bossley Park 2 1 33s52 150E54-10:03:36
Botany 2 1 33s57 151E12-10:04:48
Bothwell 6 3 42s23 147E00 -9:48:00
Boulder 8 5 30s47 121E29 -8:05:56
Boulia 4 4 22s54 139E54 -9:19:36
Bourke 2 1 30s05 145E56 -9:43:44
Bowelling 8 5 33s25 116E29 -7:45:56
Bowen 4 4 20s01 148E15 -9:53:00
Bowenfels 2 1 33s31 150E07-10:00:28
Bowmans 5 9 34s09 138E16 -9:13:04
Bowral 2 1 34s28 150E25-10:01:40
Bowraville 2 1 30s39 152E51-10:11:24
Box Hill 7 2 37s49 145E08 -9:40:32
Boyanup 8 5 33s29 115E44 -7:42:56
Boyup Brook 8 5 33s50 116E24 -7:45:36
Braeside 8 5 21s12 121E01 -8:04:04
Braeside 7 2 37s59 145E07 -9:40:28
Braidwood 2 1 35s27 149E48 -9:59:12
Bransby 4 4 28s14 142E04 -9:28:16
Branxholme 7 2 37s51 141E47 -9:27:08
Branxton 2 1 32s39 151E22-10:05:28
Braybrook 7 2 37s47 144E51 -9:39:24
Breadalbane 4 4 23s49 139E35 -9:18:20
Bredbo 2 1 35s57 149E10 -9:56:40
Breeza Plains 4 4 14s50 144E07 -9:36:28
Brewarrina 2 1 29s57 146E52 -9:47:28
Brewongle 2 1 33s29 149E43 -9:58:52
Bridgetown 8 5 33s57 116E08 -7:44:32
Bright 7 2 36s44 146E58 -9:47:52
Brighton 7 2 37s55 145E00 -9:40:00
Brighton 5 9 35s01 138E31 -9:14:04
Brighton Downs 4 4 23s22 141E34 -9:26:16
Brighton-Le-Sands 2 1 33s58 151E09-10:04:36
Brindabella 2 1 35s23 148E45 -9:55:00
Bringelly 2 1 33s56 150E44-10:02:56
Brinkley 5 9 35s14 139E13 -9:16:52
Brinkworth 5 9 33s42 138E24 -9:13:36
Brisbane 4 4 27s28 153E02-10:12:08
Brixton 4 4 23s32 144E57 -9:39:48
Broad Arrow 8 5 30s20 121E27 -8:05:48
Broadford 7 2 37s13 145E03 -9:40:12
Broadmeadows 7 2 37s40 144E54 -9:39:36
Brocks Creek 3 8 13s28 131E25 -8:45:40
Broke 2 1 32s45 151E06-10:04:24
Broken Hill 2 7 31s57 141E27 -9:25:48
Bronte Park 6 3 42s08 146E30 -9:46:00
Brookton 8 5 32s22 117E01 -7:48:04
Brookvale 2 1 33s46 151E17-10:05:08
Brooloo 4 4 26s29 152E42-10:10:48
Broome 8 5 17s58 122E14 -8:08:56
Bruce Rock 8 5 31s53 118E09 -7:52:36
Brunette Downs 3 8 18s38 135E57 -9:03:48
Brungle 2 1 35s10 148E14 -9:52:56
Brunswick 7 2 37s46 144E58 -9:39:52
Brunswick Junction 8 5 33s15 115E51 -7:43:24
Bruthen 7 2 37s43 147E48 -9:51:12
Buckingham 8 5 33s24 116E19 -7:45:16
Buckleboo 5 9 32s55 136E12 -9:04:48
Bulga 2 1 32s39 151E01-10:04:04

Place	Zone	Lat	Long	Time
Bulgroo 4	4	25s48	143E59	-9:35:56
Bulimba 4	4	27s25	153E04	-10:12:16
Bullabulling 8	5	31s01	120E32	-8:02:08
Bullara 8	5	22s40	114E03	-7:36:12
Bullfinch 8	5	30s59	119E06	-7:56:24
Bulli 2	1	34s20	150E55	-10:03:40
Bullioh 7	2	36s12	147E20	-9:49:20
Bullock Creek 4	4	17s43	144E31	-9:38:04
Bulloo Downs 4	4	28s31	142E57	-9:31:48
Bullsbrook 8	5	31s40	116E01	-7:44:04
Bulyee 8	5	32s22	117E31	-7:50:04
Bunbury 8	5	33s19	115E38	-7:42:32
Bundaberg 4	4	24s52	152E21	-10:09:24
Bundanoon 2	1	34s39	150E18	-10:01:12
Bundarra 2	1	30s10	151E05	-10:04:20
Bundeena 2	1	34s05	151E09	-10:04:36
Bundooma 3	8	24s54	134E16	-8:57:04
Bundoora 7	2	37s42	145E04	-9:40:16
Bungendore 2	1	35s15	149E27	-9:57:48
Bungonia 2	1	34s51	149E57	-9:59:48
Buninyong 7	2	37s39	143E53	-9:35:32
Buntine 8	5	29s59	116E34	-7:46:16
Bunyip 7	2	38s06	145E43	-9:42:52
Burakin 8	5	30s31	117E10	-7:48:40
Burcher 2	1	33s32	147E18	-9:49:12
Burekup 8	5	33s19	115E49	-7:43:16
Burketown 4	4	17s43	139E34	-9:18:16
Burleigh Heads 4	4	28s06	153E27	-10:13:48
Burnie 6	3	41s04	145E54	-9:43:36
Burnside 5	9	34s57	138E40	-9:14:40
Burpengary 4	4	27s10	152E57	-10:11:48
Burra 5	9	33s40	138E56	-9:15:44
Burracoppin 8	5	31s23	118E29	-7:53:56
Burramurra 3	8	20s30	137E20	-9:09:20
Burrawang 2	1	34s36	150E31	-10:02:04
Burren Junction 2	1	30s06	148E58	-9:55:52
Burrundie 3	8	13s32	131E42	-8:46:48
Burtundy 2	1	33s44	142E16	-9:29:04
Burtville 8	5	28s47	122E39	-8:10:36
Burwood 7	2	37s51	145E06	-9:40:24
Burwood 2	1	33s53	151E06	-10:04:24
Busby 2	1	33s54	150E53	-10:03:32
Bushy Park 4	4	21s16	139E43	-9:18:52
Busselton 8	5	33s39	115E20	-7:41:20
Bute 5	9	33s52	138E01	-9:12:04
Butru 4	4	21s30	139E43	-9:18:52
Byford 8	5	32s13	116E00	-7:44:00
Byro 8	5	26s05	116E09	-7:44:36
Byrock 2	1	30s40	146E24	-9:45:36
Byron Bay 2	1	28s39	153E37	-10:14:28
Cables 8	5	27s59	123E23	-8:13:32
Caboolture 4	4	27s05	152E57	-10:11:48
Cabramatta 2	1	33s54	150E56	-10:03:44
Cabramurra 2	1	35s58	148E23	-9:53:32
Cadoux 8	5	30s47	117E08	-7:48:32
Cairns 4	4	16s55	145E46	-9:43:04
Calen 4	4	20s54	148E46	-9:55:04
Calingiri 8	5	31s06	116E27	-7:45:48
Callanna 5	9	29s38	137E55	-9:11:40
Callington 5	9	35s07	139E02	-9:16:08
Calliope 4	4	24s00	151E12	-10:04:48
Caloote 5	9	34s58	139E16	-9:17:04
Caloundra 4	4	26s48	153E09	-10:12:36
Calvert Hills 3	8	17s15	137E20	-9:09:20
Camberwell 7	2	37s50	145E04	-9:40:16
Camboon 4	4	25s03	150E26	-10:01:44
Cambooya 4	4	27s42	151E52	-10:07:28
Cambrai 5	9	34s39	139E17	-9:17:08
Cambridge Park 2	1	33s45	150E43	-10:02:52
Camden 2	1	34s03	150E42	-10:02:48
Camfield 3	8	17s09	131E21	-8:45:24
Camooweal 4	4	19s55	138E07	-9:12:28
Campbellfield 7	2	37s41	144E57	-9:39:48
Campbells River 2	1	33s54	149E37	-9:58:28
Campbell Town 6	3	41s56	147E29	-9:49:56
Campbelltown 2	1	34s04	150E49	-10:03:16
Campbelltown 5	9	34s53	138E40	-9:14:40
Camperdown 7	2	38s14	143E09	-9:32:36
Campsie 2	1	33s55	151E06	-10:04:24
Canbelego 2	1	31s33	146E19	-9:45:16
Canberra 1	1	35s17	149E08	-9:56:32
Candelo 2	1	36s46	149E42	-9:58:48
Canley Vale 2	1	33s53	150E57	-10:03:48
Cann River 7	2	37s34	149E10	-9:56:40
Canowindra 2	1	33s34	148E38	-9:54:32
Canterbury 7	2	37s49	145E05	-9:40:20
Canterbury 2	1	33s55	151E07	-10:04:28
Canungra 4	4	28s01	153E10	-10:12:40
Cape Jervis 5	9	35s36	138E06	-9:12:24
Capella 4	4	23s05	148E02	-9:52:08
Capertee 2	1	33s09	149E59	-9:59:56
Captains Flat 2	1	35s35	149E27	-9:57:48
Carabost 2	1	35s36	147E44	-9:50:56
Cardabia 8	5	23s06	113E48	-7:35:12
Cardiff 2	1	32s57	151E41	-10:06:44
Cardwell 4	4	18s16	146E02	-9:44:08
Carey Downs 8	5	25s38	115E27	-7:41:48
Carinda 2	1	30s28	147E41	-9:50:44
Caringbah 2	1	34s03	151E08	-10:04:32
Carlingford 2	1	33s47	151E03	-10:04:12
Carlton 2	1	33s58	151E08	-10:04:32
Carmila 4	4	21s55	149E25	-9:57:40
Carnamah 8	5	29s42	115E53	-7:43:32
Carnarvon 8	5	24s53	113E40	-7:34:40
Carnegie 8	5	25s43	122E59	-8:11:56
Carpolac 7	2	36s44	141E19	-9:25:16
Carramar 2	1	33s53	150E58	-10:03:52
Carrathool 2	1	34s24	145E26	-9:41:44
Carrieton 5	9	32s26	138E32	-9:14:08
Carrum 7	2	38s05	145E08	-9:40:32
Carrum Downs 7	2	38s06	145E11	-9:40:44
Carrum North 7	2	38s03	145E09	-9:40:36
Cashmere Downs 8	5	28s58	119E35	-7:58:20
Casino 2	1	28s52	153E03	-10:12:12
Casterton 7	2	37s35	141E24	-9:25:36
Castlecrag 2	1	33s48	151E13	-10:04:52
Castle Hill 2	1	33s44	151E00	-10:04:00
Castlemaine 7	2	37s04	144E13	-9:36:52
Caulfield 7	2	37s53	145E03	-9:40:12
Cavendish 7	2	37s31	142E02	-9:28:08
Cecil Park 2	1	33s52	150E51	-10:03:24
Cecil Plains 4	4	27s32	151E12	-10:04:48
Ceduna 5	9	32s07	133E40	-8:54:40
Cessnock 2	1	32s50	151E21	-10:05:24
Chadstone 7	2	37s53	145E05	-9:40:20
Charbon 2	1	32s54	149E58	-9:59:52
Charleston 5	9	34s55	138E54	-9:15:36
Charlestown 2	1	32s58	151E42	-10:06:48
Charleville 4	4	26s24	146E15	-9:45:00
Charlton 7	2	36s16	143E21	-9:33:24
Charters Towers 4	4	20s05	146E16	-9:45:04
Chatswood 2	1	33s48	151E12	-10:04:48
Chatsworth 4	4	21s58	140E19	-9:21:16
Cheepie 4	4	26s39	145E01	-9:40:04
Chelsea 7	2	38s03	145E07	-9:40:28
Cheltenham 7	2	37s58	145E03	-9:40:12
Cheltenham 2	1	33s46	151E05	-10:04:20
Chermside 4	4	27s23	153E02	-10:12:08
Cherrabun 8	5	18s29	125E19	-8:21:16
Chester Hill 2	1	33s53	151E00	-10:04:00
Chewton 7	2	37s05	144E16	-9:37:04
Chidlow 8	5	31s52	116E14	-7:44:56
Childers 4	4	25s14	152E17	-10:09:08
Chillagoe 4	4	17s09	144E32	-9:38:08
Chilwell 7	2	38s10	144E21	-9:37:24
Chinchilla 4	4	26s45	150E38	-10:02:32
Chittering 8	5	31s29	116E06	-7:44:24
Christmas Creek 8	5	18s53	125E55	-8:23:40
Christmas Island 9	6	10s25	105E43	-7:02:52
Chullora 2	1	33s54	151E04	-10:04:16
City Beach 8	5	31s56	115E45	-7:43:00
Clackline 8	5	31s43	116E31	-7:46:04
Clampton 8	5	29s56	119E06	-7:56:24
Clandulla 2	1	32s55	149E57	-9:59:48
Claraville 4	4	18s40	141E43	-9:26:52
Clare 2	1	33s25	143E55	-9:35:40
Clare 5	9	33s50	138E36	-9:14:24
Clarence Town 2	1	32s35	151E47	-10:07:08
Clarendon 5	9	35s07	138E38	-9:14:32
Clarke River 4	4	19s13	145E27	-9:41:48
Clayton 7	2	37s56	145E07	-9:40:28
Clermont 4	4	22s49	147E39	-9:50:36
Cleve 5	9	33s42	136E30	-9:06:00
Cleveland 4	4	27s32	153E17	-10:13:08
Clifton 4	4	27s56	151E54	-10:07:36
Clifton Hills 5	9	26s52	138E50	-9:15:20
Clive 4	4	22s46	149E18	-9:57:12
Cloncurry 4	4	20s42	140E30	-9:22:00
Clontarf 2	1	33s48	151E16	-10:05:04
Clovelly 2	1	33s55	151E16	-10:05:04
Clunes 7	2	37s18	143E47	-9:35:08
Cluny 4	4	24s31	139E35	-9:18:20
Cobar 2	1	31s30	145E49	-9:43:16
Cobargo 2	1	36s23	149E53	-9:59:32
Cobbitty 2	1	34s01	150E41	-10:02:44
Cobden 7	2	38s20	143E05	-9:32:20
Cobram 7	2	35s55	145E39	-9:42:36
Coburg 7	2	37s45	144E58	-9:39:52
Cockburn 5	9	32s05	141E00	-9:24:00
Coen 4	4	13s56	143E12	-9:32:48
Coffs Harbour 2	1	30s18	153E08	-10:12:32
Cohuna 7	2	35s49	144E13	-9:36:52
Colac 7	2	38s20	143E35	-9:34:20
Colbinabbin 7	2	36s35	144E49	-9:39:16
Coldstream 7	2	37s44	145E23	-9:41:32
Coledale 2	1	34s17	150E57	-10:03:48
Coleraine 7	2	37s36	141E42	-9:26:48
Colinton 2	1	35s51	149E09	-9:56:36
Collarenebri 2	1	29s33	148E35	-9:54:20
Collaroy 2	1	33s44	151E18	-10:05:12
Collerina 2	1	29s41	146E38	-9:46:32
Collie 8	5	33s21	116E09	-7:44:36
Collingwood 7	2	37s48	145E00	-9:40:00
Collinsville 4	4	20s34	147E51	-9:51:24
Colona 5	9	31s38	132E05	-8:48:20
Colo Vale 2	1	34s24	150E29	-10:01:56
Colton 5	9	33s29	134E56	-8:59:44
Colyton 2	1	33s47	150E48	-10:03:12
Comboyne 2	1	31s36	152E29	-10:09:56
Comet 4	4	23s37	148E33	-9:54:12
Como 2	1	34s00	151E04	-10:04:16
Conara Junction 6	3	41s50	147E26	-9:49:44
Concord 2	1	33s52	151E06	-10:04:24
Concord West 2	1	33s51	151E05	-10:04:20
Condamine 4	4	26s56	150E08	-10:00:32
Condobolin 2	1	33s05	147E09	-9:48:36
Congelin 8	5	32s50	116E54	-7:47:36
Conjola 2	1	35s13	150E27	-10:01:48
Connemara 4	4	24s13	142E17	-9:29:08
Coober Pedy 5	9	29s01	134E43	-8:58:52
Coogee 8	5	32s07	115E46	-7:43:04
Coogee 2	1	33s55	151E16	-10:05:04
Cook 5	9	30s37	130E25	-8:41:40
Cookardinia 2	1	35s34	147E14	-9:48:56
Cookernup 8	5	33s00	115E54	-7:43:36
Cooktown 4	4	15s28	145E15	-9:41:00
Coolabah 2	1	31s02	146E43	-9:46:52
Cooladdi 4	4	26s39	145E28	-9:41:52
Coolah 2	1	31s50	149E42	-9:58:48
Coolamon 2	1	34s49	147E12	-9:48:48
Coolangatta 4	4	28s10	153E32	-10:14:08
Coolawanyah 8	5	21s47	117E48	-7:51:12
Coolgardie 8	5	30s57	121E10	-8:04:40
Coolup 8	5	32s44	115E53	-7:43:32
Cooma 2	1	36s14	149E08	-9:56:32
Coomberdale 8	5	30s28	116E02	-7:44:08
Coomera 4	4	27s52	153E19	-10:13:16
Coominya 4	4	27s23	152E30	-10:10:00
Coonabarabran 2	1	31s16	149E17	-9:57:08
Coonalpyn 5	9	35s42	139E51	-9:19:24
Coonamble 2	1	30s57	148E23	-9:53:32
Coonana 8	5	31s01	123E07	-8:12:28
Coondambo 5	9	31s04	135E52	-9:03:28
Coongoola 4	4	27s39	145E54	-9:43:36
Coopers Plains 4	4	27s34	153E02	-10:12:08
Coorabie 5	9	31s54	132E18	-8:49:12
Cooranbong 2	1	33s04	151E27	-10:05:48
Coorow 8	5	29s53	116E01	-7:44:04
Cooroy 4	4	26s25	152E55	-10:11:40
Cootamundra 2	1	34s39	148E02	-9:52:08
Cooyar 4	4	26s59	151E50	-10:07:20
Copley 5	9	30s32	138E25	-9:13:40
Cordillo Downs 5	9	26s43	140E38	-9:22:32
Coreinbob 2	1	35s13	147E38	-9:50:32
Corfield 4	4	21s43	143E22	-9:33:28
Corinda 4	4	17s53	138E35	-9:14:20
Corio 7	2	38s04	144E23	-9:37:32
Corny Point 5	9	34s55	137E03	-9:08:12
Corowa 7	2	36s02	146E23	-9:45:32
Corrigin 8	5	32s21	117E52	-7:51:28
Corrimal 2	1	34s22	150E54	-10:03:36
Corryong 7	2	36s12	147E54	-9:51:36
Corunna Downs 8	5	21s28	119E51	-7:59:24
Cotherstone 4	4	22s37	148E14	-9:52:56
Cottesloe 8	5	31s59	115E45	-7:43:00
Coulta 5	9	34s23	135E29	-9:01:56
Countegany 2	1	36s11	149E27	-9:57:48
Cowaramup 8	5	33s52	115E05	-7:40:20
Coward Springs 5	9	29s24	136E49	-9:07:16
Cowarie 5	9	27s43	138E20	-9:13:20
Cowell 5	9	33s41	136E55	-9:07:40
Cowes 7	2	38s27	145E14	-9:40:56
Cowley 4	4	26s54	144E49	-9:39:16
Cowra 2	1	33s50	148E41	-9:54:44
Cradock 5	9	32s04	138E30	-9:14:00
Crafers-Bridgewater 5	9	35s01	138E47	-9:15:08
Cranbourne 7	2	38s06	145E17	-9:41:08
Cranbrook 8	5	34s18	117E32	-7:50:08
Cranebrook 2	1	33s43	150E42	-10:02:48
Cravensville 7	2	36s24	147E34	-9:50:16
Cressy 7	2	38s02	143E38	-9:34:32
Creswell Downs 3	8	17s57	135E55	-9:03:40
Creswick 7	2	37s26	143E54	-9:35:36
Crib Point 7	2	38s22	145E12	-9:40:48
Cringila 2	1	34s28	150E53	-10:03:32
Cromer 2	1	33s44	151E17	-10:05:08
Cronulla 2	1	34s03	151E09	-10:04:36
Crookwell 2	1	34s28	149E28	-9:57:52
Crossman 8	5	32s47	116E36	-7:46:24
Crow's Nest 4	4	27s16	152E03	-10:08:12
Crows Nest 2	1	33s50	151E12	-10:04:48
Croydon 4	4	18s12	142E14	-9:28:56
Croydon 7	2	37s48	145E17	-9:41:08
Croydon 2	1	33s53	151E07	-10:04:28
Croydon Park 2	1	33s54	151E07	-10:04:28
Crystal Brook 5	9	33s21	138E13	-9:12:52
Cudgegong 2	1	32s48	149E49	-9:59:16
Cudgewa 7	2	36s12	147E46	-9:51:04
Cue 8	5	27s25	117E54	-7:51:36
Culbin 8	5	33s10	116E50	-7:47:20
Culcairn 2	1	35s40	147E03	-9:48:12
Cullen Bullen 2	1	33s18	150E01	-10:00:04
Cumborah 2	1	29s44	147E46	-9:51:04
Cummins 5	9	34s16	135E44	-9:02:56
Cunderdin 8	5	31s39	117E15	-7:49:00
Cunliffe 5	9	34s05	137E45	-9:11:00
Cunnamulla 4	4	28s04	145E41	-9:42:44
Cunningham 4	4	28s09	151E51	-10:07:24
Curl Curl 2	1	33s46	151E18	-10:05:12
Curlewis 2	1	31s07	150E16	-10:01:04
Curnamona 5	9	31s39	139E32	-9:18:08
Curramulka 5	9	34s42	137E42	-9:10:48
Currarong 2	1	35s01	150E49	-10:03:16
Currency Creek 5	9	35s28	138E46	-9:15:04
Currie 6	3	39s56	143E52	-9:35:28
Curtin Springs 3	8	25s20	131E45	-8:47:00
Cygnet River 5	9	35s42	137E31	-9:10:04
Daintree 4	4	16s15	145E19	-9:41:16
Dajarra 4	4	21s41	139E31	-9:18:04
Dalby 4	4	27s11	151E16	-10:05:04
Dale Bridge 8	5	32s05	116E49	-7:47:16
Dalgaranga 8	5	27s46	117E02	-7:48:08
Dalgety 2	1	36s30	148E50	-9:55:20
Dalgety Downs 8	5	25s17	116E15	-7:45:00
Dalwallinu 8	5	30s17	116E40	-7:46:40
Daly River 3	8	13s45	130E50	-8:43:20

Daly Waters 3 8 16s15 133E22 -8:53:28
Dampier 8 5 20s39 116E45 -7:47:00
Dandaragan 8 5 30s40 115E42 -7:42:48
Dandenong 7 2 37s59 145E12 -9:40:48
Dapto 2 1 34s30 150E47-10:03:08
Dardadine 8 5 33s14 116E50 -7:47:20
Dardanup 8 5 33s24 115E45 -7:43:00
Darkan 8 5 33s20 116E44 -7:46:56
Darke Peak 5 9 33s28 136E12 -9:04:48
Darlington 7 2 38s00 143E03 -9:32:12
Darlington 8 5 31s55 116E05 -7:44:20
Darnick 2 1 32s51 143E37 -9:34:28
Darra 4 4 27s34 152E58-10:11:52
Dartmoor 7 2 37s55 141E17 -9:25:08
Darwin 3 8 12s28 130E50 -8:43:20
Darwin River 3 8 12s49 130E58 -8:43:52
Davenport 6 3 41s11 146E19 -9:45:16
Davenport Downs 4 4 24s08 141E07 -9:24:28
Dayboro 4 4 27s11 152E50-10:11:20
Daylesford 7 2 37s21 144E09 -9:36:36
Deakin 8 5 30s46 128E58 -8:35:52
Deepwater 2 1 29s27 151E51-10:07:24
Deep Well 3 8 24s25 134E05 -8:56:20
Deer Park 7 2 37s47 144E47 -9:39:08
Dee Why 2 1 33s45 151E17-10:05:08
De Grey 8 5 20s10 119E12 -7:56:48
Delamere 5 9 35s35 138E11 -9:12:44
Delegate 2 1 37s03 148E58 -9:55:52
Deloraine 6 3 41s31 146E39 -9:46:36
Delta Downs 4 4 17s00 141E18 -9:25:12
Delungra 2 1 29s39 150E50-10:03:20
Denham 8 5 25s55 113E32 -7:34:08
Denial Bay 5 9 32s06 133E32 -8:54:08
Deniliquin 2 1 35s32 144E58 -9:39:52
Denmark 8 5 34s57 117E21 -7:49:24
Derby 8 5 17s18 123E38 -8:14:32
Derby 6 3 41s09 147E47 -9:51:08
Derrinallum 7 2 37s57 143E13 -9:32:52
Derwent Bridge 6 3 42s08 146E13 -9:44:52
Devonport 6 3 41s11 146E21 -9:45:24
Diamantina Lakes 4 4 23s46 141E09 -9:24:36
Diamond Creek 7 2 37s41 145E09 -9:40:36
Dimboola 7 2 36s27 142E02 -9:28:08
Dimbulah 4 4 17s09 145E07 -9:40:28
Dingley 7 2 37s58 145E07 -9:40:28
Dingo 4 4 23s39 149E20 -9:57:20
Dirranbandi 4 4 28s35 148E14 -9:52:56
Dobbyn 4 4 19s48 140E00 -9:20:00
Donald 7 2 36s22 143E00 -9:32:00
Doncaster 7 2 37s47 145E08 -9:40:32
Doncaster East 7 2 37s47 145E10 -9:40:40
Dongara 8 5 29s15 114E56 -7:39:44
Donnybrook 8 5 33s35 115E49 -7:43:16
Donors Hills 4 4 18s42 140E33 -9:22:12
Doomadgee Mission 4 4 17s56 138E49 -9:15:16
Doondi 4 4 28s15 148E28 -9:53:52
Doonside 2 1 33s46 150E52-10:03:28
Dooralong 2 1 33s12 151E22-10:05:28
Dorrigo 2 1 30s21 152E43-10:10:52
Doughboy 2 1 35s15 149E39 -9:58:36
Douglas Park 2 1 34s11 150E43-10:02:52
Dover 6 3 43s19 147E01 -9:48:04
Dover Heights 2 1 33s53 151E17-10:05:08
Doveton 7 2 38s00 145E14 -9:40:56
Dowerin 8 5 31s12 117E02 -7:48:08
Dromana 7 2 38s21 144E58 -9:39:52
Drouin 7 2 38s08 145E51 -9:43:24
Drummoyne 2 1 33s51 151E09-10:04:36
Drysdale 7 2 38s11 144E34 -9:38:16
Duaringa 4 4 23s43 149E40 -9:58:40
Dubbo 2 1 32s15 148E36 -9:54:24
Dublin 5 9 34s27 138E21 -9:13:24
Duchess 4 4 21s22 139E52 -9:19:28
Duffield 3 8 25s50 134E40 -8:58:40
Dulkaninna 5 9 29s01 138E27 -9:13:48
Dumbleyung 8 5 33s19 117E44 -7:50:56
Dundas 2 1 33s48 151E02-10:04:08
Dundoo 4 4 27s39 144E39 -9:38:36
Dunedoo 2 1 32s01 149E24 -9:57:36
Dungog 2 1 32s24 151E46-10:07:04
Dunheved 2 1 33s45 150E47-10:03:08
Dunmarra 3 8 16s42 133E25 -8:53:40
Dunolly 7 2 36s52 143E44 -9:34:56
Dunwich 4 4 27s31 153E23-10:13:32
Dural 2 1 33s41 151E02-10:04:08
Duranillin 8 5 33s31 116E48 -7:47:12
Durham Downs 4 4 27s05 141E54 -9:27:36
Durrie 4 4 25s38 140E16 -9:21:04
Dwellingup 8 5 32s43 116E02 -7:44:08
Eaglehawk 7 2 36s43 144E15 -9:37:00
Earaheedy 8 5 25s34 121E39 -8:06:36
Earlwood 2 1 33s56 151E08-10:04:32
East Burwood 7 2 37s51 145E09 -9:40:36
East Freemantle 8 5 32s02 115E46 -7:43:04
East Hills 2 1 33s58 150E59-10:03:56
East Lindfield 2 1 33s46 151E11-10:04:44
Eastwood 2 1 33s48 151E05-10:04:20
Eaton 8 5 33s19 115E43 -7:42:52
Echuca 7 2 36s08 144E46 -9:39:04
Echunga 5 9 35s07 138E48 -9:15:12
Edah 8 5 28s17 117E10 -7:48:40
Eden 2 1 37s04 149E54 -9:59:36
Eden Valley 5 9 34s39 139E06 -9:16:24
Edeowie 5 9 31s27 138E27 -9:13:48
Edgeroi 2 1 30s07 149E48 -9:59:12
Edith 2 1 33s48 149E55 -9:59:40
Edithburgh 5 9 35s06 137E44 -9:10:56
Edith River 3 8 14s11 132E02 -8:48:08
Edithvale 7 2 38s02 145E07 -9:40:28
Edjudina 8 5 29s48 122E23 -8:09:32
Edmonton 4 4 17s01 145E45 -9:43:00
Edmund 8 5 23s46 116E02 -7:44:08
Edwards Creek 5 9 28s21 135E51 -9:03:24
Egg Lagoon 6 3 39s39 143E58 -9:35:52
Eidsvold 4 4 25s22 151E07-10:04:28
Eildon 7 2 37s14 145E56 -9:43:44
Einasleigh 4 4 18s31 144E05 -9:36:20
Elanora Heights 2 1 33s42 151E17-10:05:08
Elgin 8 5 33s31 115E37 -7:42:28
Elizabeth 5 9 34s43 138E40 -9:14:40
Ellavalla 8 5 25s05 114E22 -7:37:28
Elleker 8 5 35s00 117E43 -7:50:52
Ellendale 8 5 17s56 124E48 -8:19:12
Elliott 3 8 17s33 133E32 -8:54:08
Elliston 5 9 33s39 134E55 -8:59:40
Elmhurst 7 2 37s11 143E15 -9:33:00
Elmore 7 2 36s30 144E37 -9:38:28
Eltham 7 2 37s44 145E09 -9:40:36
Elwood 7 2 37s53 144E59 -9:39:56
Emerald 4 4 23s32 148E10 -9:52:40
Emerald 7 2 37s56 145E26 -9:41:44
Emita 6 3 40s00 147E54 -9:51:36
Emmaville 2 1 29s26 151E36-10:06:24
Emmet 4 4 24s40 144E28 -9:37:52
Emu Downs 5 9 33s54 138E59 -9:15:56
Emu Park 4 4 23s15 150E50-10:03:20
Emu Plains 2 1 33s45 150E41-10:02:44
Enfield 5 9 34s53 138E35 -9:14:20
Enfield 2 1 33s53 151E06-10:04:24
Engadine 2 1 34s04 151E01-10:04:04
Enngonia 2 1 29s19 145E51 -9:43:24
Ensay 7 2 37s23 147E50 -9:51:20
Epping 7 2 37s39 145E02 -9:40:08
Epping 2 1 33s46 151E05-10:04:20
Eradu 8 5 28s41 115E02 -7:40:08
Erica 7 2 37s59 146E22 -9:45:28
Erldunda 3 8 25s14 133E12 -8:52:48
Erlistoun 8 5 28s20 122E08 -8:08:32
Ermington 2 1 33s48 151E04-10:04:16
Ernaballa Mission 5 9 26s17 132E07 -8:48:28
Eromanga 4 4 26s40 143E16 -9:33:04
Errabiddy 8 5 25s28 117E07 -7:48:28
Erskine Park 2 1 33s49 150E47-10:03:08
Erudina 5 9 31s28 139E23 -9:17:32
Esk 4 4 27s15 152E25-10:09:40
Esmeralda 4 4 18s50 142E34 -9:30:16
Esperance 8 5 33s51 121E53 -8:07:32
Essendon 7 2 37s46 144E55 -9:39:40
Etadunna 5 9 28s43 138E38 -9:14:32
Ethel Creek 8 5 22s54 120E09 -8:00:36
Eton 4 4 21s16 148E58 -9:55:52
Ettalong 2 1 33s31 151E21-10:05:24
Eucla 8 5 31s43 128E52 -8:35:28
Eucumbene 2 1 36s07 148E38 -9:54:32
Eudunda 5 9 34s11 139E04 -9:16:16
Eugowra 2 1 33s26 148E23 -9:53:32
Eulo 4 4 28s10 145E03 -9:40:12
Eumungerie 2 1 31s57 148E37 -9:54:28
Euroa 7 2 36s45 145E35 -9:42:20
Euston 2 1 34s35 142E44 -9:30:56
Eva Downs 3 8 18s01 134E52 -8:59:28
Evandale 6 3 41s34 147E14 -9:48:56
Ewaninga 3 8 23s58 133E58 -8:55:52
Exeter 2 1 34s38 150E19-10:01:16
Exmouth Gulf 8 5 22s23 114E07 -7:36:28
Eyre 8 5 32s15 126E18 -8:25:12
Fairfield 2 1 33s52 150E57-10:03:48
Fairview 4 4 15s33 144E19 -9:37:16
Fairy Meadow 2 1 34s23 150E54-10:03:36
Falls Creek 2 1 34s59 150E36-10:02:24
Farrell Flat 5 9 33s50 138E47 -9:15:08
Fawkner 7 2 37s43 144E58 -9:39:52
Ferguson 8 5 33s26 115E51 -7:43:24
Fernvale 4 4 27s27 152E39-10:10:36
Ferny Creek 7 2 37s53 145E21 -9:41:24
Fingal 6 3 41s39 147E58 -9:51:52
Finke 3 8 25s34 134E35 -8:58:20
Finley 2 1 35s39 145E35 -9:42:20
Finniss 5 9 35s24 138E49 -9:15:16
First King 8 5 31s49 124E21 -8:17:24
Fisher 5 9 30s33 130E58 -8:43:52
Fish River 3 8 17s55 137E45 -9:11:00
Fitzroy 7 2 37s48 144E59 -9:39:56
Fitzroy Crossing 8 5 18s11 125E35 -8:22:20
Five Dock 2 1 33s52 151E08-10:04:32
Flinton 4 4 27s54 149E34 -9:58:16
Flying Fish Cove 9 6 10s25 105E43 -7:02:52
Footscray 7 2 37s48 144E54 -9:39:36
Forbes 2 1 33s23 148E01 -9:52:04
Fords Bridge 2 1 29s45 145E26 -9:41:44
Forest Hill 4 4 27s35 152E22-10:09:28
Forest Hill 2 1 35s09 147E27 -9:49:48
Forest Hill 7 2 37s50 145E11 -9:40:44
Forestville 2 1 33s46 151E13-10:04:52
Forrest 8 5 30s51 128E06 -8:32:24
Forsayth 4 4 18s35 143E36 -9:34:24
Forster 2 1 32s11 152E31-10:10:04
Fort Constantine 4 4 20s28 140E37 -9:22:28
Fort Dundas 3 8 11s24 130E29 -8:41:56
Fort Hurd 3 8 11s39 130E18 -8:41:12
Fossil Downs 8 5 18s08 125E38 -8:22:32
Foster 7 2 38s39 146E12 -9:44:48
Fowlers Bay 5 9 31s59 132E27 -8:49:48
Fox Valley 2 1 33s45 151E06-10:04:24
Frankston 7 2 38s08 145E07 -9:40:28
Fraser Range 8 5 32s03 122E48 -8:11:12
Freestone 4 4 28s08 152E08-10:08:32
Fremantle 8 5 32s03 115E45 -7:43:00
Frenchs Forest 2 1 33s45 151E14-10:04:56
Frewena 3 8 19s25 135E25 -9:01:40
Frome Downs 5 9 31s13 139E46 -9:19:04
Galena 8 5 27s50 114E41 -7:38:44
Gallipoli 3 8 19s10 137E55 -9:11:40
Galvin 7 2 37s51 144E49 -9:39:16
Garah 2 1 29s04 149E38 -9:58:32
Gascoyne Junction 8 5 25s03 115E12 -7:40:48
Gatton 4 4 27s33 152E17-10:09:08
Gawler 5 9 34s37 138E44 -9:14:56
Gayndah 4 4 25s37 151E36-10:06:24
Geebung 4 4 27s22 153E03-10:12:12
Geehi 2 1 36s24 148E11 -9:52:44
Geelong 7 2 38s08 144E21 -9:37:24
Geelong West 7 2 38s08 144E20 -9:37:20
Geeveston 6 3 43s10 146E55 -9:47:40
Gellibrand 7 2 38s32 143E32 -9:34:08
Gembrook 7 2 37s57 145E33 -9:42:12
Genoa 7 2 37s29 149E35 -9:58:20
Georges Hall 2 1 33s55 150E59-10:03:56
Georgetown 4 4 18s18 143E33 -9:34:12
George Town 6 3 41s06 146E50 -9:47:20
Geraldton 8 5 28s46 114E36 -7:38:24
Gerringong 2 1 34s45 150E50-10:03:20
Gibb River 8 5 15s39 126E38 -8:26:32
Gibson 8 5 33s39 121E48 -8:07:12
Gidgee 8 5 27s16 119E22 -7:57:28
Gifford Creek 8 5 24s05 116E11 -7:44:44
Gilbert River 4 4 18s09 142E52 -9:31:28
Gilgai 8 5 31s15 119E56 -7:59:44
Gilgandra 2 1 31s42 148E39 -9:54:36
Gilmore 2 1 35s20 148E11 -9:52:44
Gingin 8 5 31s21 115E42 -7:42:48
Gin Gin 4 4 25s00 151E58-10:07:52
Giralia 8 5 22s41 114E21 -7:37:24
Girgarre 7 2 36s24 144E59 -9:39:56
Girilambone 2 1 31s15 146E54 -9:47:36
Giru 4 4 19s31 147E06 -9:48:24
Gisborne 7 2 37s29 144E35 -9:38:20
Gladesville 2 1 33s50 151E08-10:04:32
Gladstone 4 4 23s51 151E16-10:05:04
Gladstone 5 9 33s17 138E22 -9:13:28
Glass House Mountains 4 4 26s53 152E58-10:11:52
Glen Alice 2 1 33s02 150E13-10:00:52
Glenbrook 2 1 33s46 150E37-10:02:28
Glencoe 5 9 37s42 140E37 -9:22:28
Glen Davis 2 1 33s08 150E17-10:01:08
Glen Eagle 8 5 32s17 116E11 -7:44:44
Gleneagle 4 4 27s57 152E59-10:11:56
Glenelg 5 9 34s59 138E31 -9:14:04
Glenfield 2 1 33s58 150E54-10:03:36
Glen Florrie 8 5 22s55 115E59 -7:43:56
Glen Forest 8 5 31s54 116E06 -7:44:24
Glengyle 4 4 24s48 139E37 -9:18:28
Glenhaven 2 1 33s42 151E00-10:04:00
Glenhuntly 7 2 37s54 145E03 -9:40:12
Glen Innes 2 1 29s44 151E44-10:06:56
Glenmorgan 4 4 27s15 149E41 -9:58:44
Glenore Grove 4 4 27s32 152E24-10:09:36
Glenorie 2 1 33s33 151E00-10:04:00
Glenormiston 4 4 22s55 138E48 -9:15:12
Glenreagh 2 1 30s03 152E59-10:11:56
Glenroy 8 5 21s46 114E49 -7:39:16
Glenroy 8 5 17s22 126E06 -8:24:24
Glenroy 7 2 37s42 144E55 -9:39:40
Glen Waverley 7 2 37s53 145E10 -9:40:40
Gloucester 2 1 31s59 151E58-10:07:52
Gnalta 2 1 31s03 142E20 -9:29:20
Gnaraloo 8 5 23s51 113E31 -7:34:04
Gnowangerup 8 5 33s56 117E59 -7:51:56
Gold Coast → Southport 4 4 27s58 153E25-10:13:40
Golspie 2 1 34s17 149E40 -9:58:40
Goodna 4 4 27s37 152E54-10:11:36
Goodooga 2 1 29s07 147E27 -9:49:48
Goolgowi 2 1 33s59 145E42 -9:42:48
Goolwa 5 9 35s31 138E47 -9:15:08
Goomalling 8 5 31s19 116E49 -7:47:16
Goombalie 2 1 29s59 145E23 -9:41:32
Goombungee 4 4 27s18 151E51-10:07:24
Goomburra 4 4 28s03 152E07-10:08:28
Goondiwindi 4 4 28s32 150E19-10:01:16
Goongarrie 8 5 30s03 121E09 -8:04:36
Gordon Downs 8 5 18s44 128E35 -8:34:20
Gordonvale 4 4 17s05 145E47 -9:43:08
Gore 4 4 28s17 151E29-10:05:56
Gore Hill 2 1 33s49 151E11-10:04:44
Gorokan 2 1 33s16 151E30-10:06:00
Gosford 2 1 33s26 151E21-10:05:24
Gosnells 8 5 32s04 116E00 -7:44:00
Goulburn 2 1 34s45 149E43 -9:58:52
Grafton 2 1 29s41 152E56-10:11:44
Grange 5 9 34s54 138E30 -9:14:00
Granite Downs 5 9 26s57 133E30 -8:54:00
Granite Peak 8 5 25s38 121E21 -8:05:24
Grantham 4 4 27s34 152E12-10:08:48
Grants Patch 8 5 30s27 121E07 -8:04:28
Granville 2 1 33s50 151E01-10:04:04
Grass Patch 8 5 33s14 121E43 -8:06:52
Grass Valley 8 5 31s38 116E48 -7:47:12
Grassy 6 3 40s03 144E04 -9:36:16
Gravesend 2 1 29s35 150E19-10:01:16
Grays Point 2 1 34s04 151E05-10:04:20

AUSTRALIA

Greater Wollongong → Wollongong 2
1 34s25 150E54 -10:03:36
Greenbushes 8 5 33s51 116E03 -7:44:12
Greendale 2 1 33s55 150E39 -10:02:36
Greenmount 8 5 31s54 116E03 -7:44:12
Greenmount 4 4 27s47 151E54 -10:07:36
Greenock 5 9 34s27 138E55 -9:15:40
Greenough 8 5 28s57 114E44 -7:38:56
Greenwell Point 2
1 34s55 150E44 -10:02:56
Greenwich 2 1 33s50 151E11 -10:04:44
Gregadoo 2 1 35s14 147E27 -9:49:48
Greg Greg 2 1 36s03 148E02 -9:52:08
Grenfell 2 1 33s54 148E10 -9:52:40
Greta 2 1 32s41 151E24 -10:05:36
Greystanes 2 1 33s49 150E55 -10:03:40
Griffith 2 1 34s17 146E03 -9:44:12
Guildford 2 1 33s51 150E59 -10:03:56
Gulargambone 2 1 31s20 148E28 -9:53:52
Gulgong 2 1 32s22 149E32 -9:58:08
Gumeracha 5 9 34s49 138E53 -9:15:32
Gunbar 2 1 34s01 145E25 -9:41:40
Gundagai 2 1 35s04 148E07 -9:52:28
Gunnedah 2 1 30s59 150E15 -10:01:00
Gunyidi 8 5 30s08 116E04 -7:44:16
Guyra 2 1 30s14 151E40 -10:06:40
Gwabegar 2 1 30s36 148E58 -9:55:52
Gwalia 8 5 28s55 121E20 -8:05:20
Gwambygine 8 5 31s59 116E48 -7:47:12
Gymea Bay 2 1 34s02 151E05 -10:04:20
Gympie 4 4 26s11 152E40 -10:10:40
Haast Bluff 3 8 23s30 131E50 -8:47:20
Haberfield 2 1 33s53 151E08 -10:04:32
Haddon Downs 5 9 26s21 140E50 -9:23:20
Haden 4 4 27s14 151E53 -10:07:32
Hadfield 7 2 37s42 144E56 -9:39:44
Haig 8 5 31s01 126E05 -8:24:20
Halbury 5 9 34s05 138E31 -9:14:04
Halifax 4 4 18s35 146E18 -9:45:12
Hall 1 1 35s10 149E04 -9:56:16
Hallam 7 2 38s01 145E06 -9:40:24
Halls Creek 8 5 18s16 127E46 -8:31:04
Hamel 8 5 32s52 115E55 -7:43:40
Hamelin Pool 8 5 26s26 114E11 -7:36:44
Hamilton 7 2 37s45 142E02 -9:28:08
Hamilton Hill 8
5 32s05 115E46 -7:43:04
Hamilton Hotel 4
4 22s50 140E35 -9:22:20
Hamley Bridge 5
9 34s21 138E41 -9:14:44
Hammondville 2 1 33s57 150E57 -10:03:48
Hampden 5 9 34s09 139E03 -9:16:12
Hampton 7 2 37s56 145E00 -9:40:00
Hampton Park 7 2 38s02 145E15 -9:41:00
Hanwood 2 1 34s20 146E03 -9:44:12
Harbord 2 1 33s45 151E26 -10:05:44
Harcourt 7 2 37s00 144E15 -9:37:00
Harkaway 7 2 38s00 145E21 -9:41:24
Harlin 4 4 26s59 152E22 -10:09:28
Harrisfield 7 2 37s57 145E11 -9:40:44
Harrismith 8 5 32s56 117E52 -7:51:28
Harris Park 2 1 33s49 151E01 -10:04:04
Harrisville 4 4 27s49 152E40 -10:10:40
Hartley 2 1 33s33 150E11 -10:00:44
Harts Range 3 8 23s00 134E55 -8:59:40
Harvey 8 5 33s05 115E54 -7:43:36
Hastings 7 2 38s18 145E11 -9:40:44
Hatches Creek 3
8 20s56 135E12 -9:00:48
Hatfield 2 1 33s52 143E45 -9:35:00
Hawker 5 9 31s53 138E25 -9:13:40
Hawkwood 4 4 25s47 150E50 -10:03:20
Hawthorn 7 2 37s49 145E02 -9:40:08
Hay 2 1 34s30 144E51 -9:39:24
Hazelbrook 2 1 33s44 150E27 -10:01:48
Hazelgrove 2 1 33s40 149E52 -9:59:28
Healesville 7 2 37s40 145E31 -9:42:04
Heathcote 7 2 36s55 144E42 -9:38:48
Heathcote 2 1 34s05 151E01 -10:04:04
Heatherton 7 2 37s58 145E06 -9:40:24
Heathmont 7 2 37s49 145E15 -9:41:00
Hebel 4 4 28s59 147E48 -9:51:12
Heidelberg 7 2 37s45 145E04 -9:40:16
Helensburgh 2 1 34s11 150E59 -10:03:56
Helen Springs 3
8 18s26 133E52 -8:55:28
Helidon 4 4 27s33 152E08 -10:08:32
Henbury 3 8 24s35 133E15 -8:53:00
Henley Beach 5 9 34s55 138E30 -9:14:00
Henty 2 1 35s31 147E02 -9:48:08
Hepburn Springs 7
2 37s19 144E09 -9:36:36
Herberton 4 4 17s23 145E23 -9:41:32
Hermannsburg 3 8 23s57 132E45 -8:51:00
Hermidale 2 1 31s33 146E43 -9:46:52
Herne Hill 8 5 31s50 116E01 -7:44:04
Herrick 6 3 41s06 147E52 -9:51:28
Hesso 5 9 32s08 137E27 -9:09:48
Heywood 7 2 38s08 141E38 -9:26:32
Higginsville 8 5 31s45 121E43 -8:06:52
Highbury 4 4 16s25 143E09 -9:32:36
Highett 7 2 37s57 145E03 -9:40:12
Hillside 8 5 21s44 119E23 -7:57:32
Hillston 2 1 33s29 145E32 -9:42:08
Hindmarsh Valley 5
9 35s30 138E38 -9:14:32
Hobart 6 3 42s53 147E19 -9:49:16
Holbrook 2 1 35s44 147E19 -9:49:16
Holland Park 4 4 27s31 153E03 -10:12:12
Holleton 8 5 31s57 119E02 -7:56:08
Holmesglen 7 2 37s53 145E06 -9:40:24
Holroyd 2 1 33s50 150E58 -10:03:52
Home Hill 4 4 19s40 147E25 -9:49:40
Homestead 4 4 20s22 145E39 -9:42:36

Hooker Creek 3 8 18s20 130E40 -8:42:40
Hookina 5 9 31s45 138E20 -9:13:20
Hopetoun 8 5 33s57 120E07 -8:00:28
Hopetoun 7 2 35s44 142E22 -9:29:28
Hope Valley 5 9 34s50 138E44 -9:14:56
Hornsby 2 1 33s42 150E06 -10:00:24
Horsham 7 2 36s43 142E13 -9:28:52
Horsley 2 1 33s51 150E51 -10:03:24
Howard 4 4 25s19 152E34 -10:10:16
Howes Valley 2 1 32s50 150E51 -10:03:24
Hoxton Park 2 1 33s55 150E51 -10:03:24
Hoyleton 5 9 34s01 138E33 -9:14:12
Hughenden 4 4 20s51 144E12 -9:36:48
Hughes 5 9 30s42 129E31 -8:38:04
Humeburn 4 4 27s24 145E14 -9:40:56
Humula 2 1 35s29 147E45 -9:51:00
Hungerford 4 4 29s00 144E25 -9:37:40
Hunters Hill 2 1 33s50 151E09 -10:04:36
Huonville 6 3 43s01 147E02 -9:48:08
Hurstbridge 7 2 37s38 145E12 -9:40:48
Hurstville 2 1 33s58 151E06 -10:04:24
Huskisson 2 1 35s02 150E40 -10:02:40
Hyden 8 5 32s27 118E53 -7:55:32
Hythe 6 3 43s25 146E59 -9:47:56
Ilbunga 5 9 26s25 135E03 -9:00:12
Ilford 2 1 32s58 149E51 -9:59:24
Ilfracombe 4 4 23s30 144E30 -9:38:00
Immarna 5 9 30s30 132E09 -8:48:36
Inala 4 4 27s35 152E58 -10:11:52
Indooroopilly 4
4 27s30 152E58 -10:11:52
Ingham 4 4 18s39 146E10 -9:44:40
Ingleburn 2 1 34s00 150E52 -10:03:28
Ingleside 2 1 33s41 151E13 -10:04:52
Inglewood 4 4 28s25 151E05 -10:04:20
Inglewood 7 2 36s34 143E52 -9:35:28
Injune 4 4 25s51 148E34 -9:54:16
Inman Valley 5 9 35s30 138E28 -9:13:52
Innamincka 5 9 27s45 140E44 -9:22:56
Innisfail 4 4 17s32 146E02 -9:44:08
Innisplain 4 4 28s10 152E55 -10:11:40
Inveralochy 2 1 34s57 149E39 -9:58:36
Inverell 2 1 29s47 151E07 -10:04:28
Inverleigh 7 2 38s06 144E03 -9:36:12
Inverloch 7 2 38s38 145E43 -9:42:52
Inverway 3 8 17s50 129E38 -8:38:32
Ipswich 4 4 27s36 152E46 -10:11:04
Irishtown 6 3 40s55 145E08 -9:40:32
Iron Baron 5 9 32s59 137E09 -9:08:36
Iron Knob 5 9 32s44 137E08 -9:08:32
Iron Range 4 4 12s42 143E18 -9:33:12
Irwin 8 5 29s12 115E04 -7:40:16
Isis 4 4 25s12 152E13 -10:08:52
Isisford 4 4 24s16 144E26 -9:37:44
Island Bend 2 1 36s19 148E29 -9:53:56
Ivanhoe 2 1 32s54 144E18 -9:37:12
Ivanhoe 7 2 37s46 145E03 -9:40:12
Jacana 7 2 37s42 144E55 -9:39:40
Jamberoo 2 1 34s39 150E47 -10:03:08
Jambin 4 4 24s12 150E22 -10:01:28
Jamestown 5 9 33s12 138E36 -9:14:24
Jamison Town 2 1 33s46 150E41 -10:02:44
Jandowae 4 4 26s47 151E06 -10:04:24
Jannali 2 1 34s01 151E04 -10:04:16
Jarrahdale 8 5 32s20 116E04 -7:44:16
Jeparit 7 2 36s09 141E59 -9:27:56
Jerangle 2 1 35s52 149E22 -9:57:28
Jericho 4 4 23s36 146E08 -9:44:32
Jerilderie 2 1 35s22 145E44 -9:42:56
Jervis Bay 2 1 35s08 150E42 -10:02:48
Jiggalong Mission 8
5 23s25 120E47 -8:03:08
Jimboomba 4 4 27s50 153E02 -10:12:08
Jindabyne 2 1 36s25 148E38 -9:54:32
Jingellic 2 1 35s56 147E42 -9:50:48
Jitarning 8 5 32s48 117E59 -7:51:56
Jubilee Downs 8
5 18s22 125E17 -8:21:08
Julia Creek 4 4 20s39 141E45 -9:27:00
Junee 2 1 34s52 147E35 -9:50:20
Kadina 5 9 33s58 137E43 -9:10:52
Kajabbi 4 4 20s02 140E02 -9:20:08
Kalamunda 8 5 31s57 116E03 -7:44:12
Kalannie 8 5 30s21 117E04 -7:48:16
Kalbar 4 4 27s56 152E37 -10:10:28
Kalgan 8 5 34s53 118E01 -7:52:04
Kalgoorlie 8 5 30s45 121E28 -8:05:52
Kallista 7 2 37s53 145E22 -9:41:28
Kalorama 7 2 37s49 145E22 -9:41:28
Kalumburu 8 5 14s18 126E39 -8:26:36
Kamballie 8 5 30s48 121E30 -8:06:00
Kandos 2 1 32s52 149E58 -9:59:52
Kangarilla 5 9 35s09 138E40 -9:14:40
Kangaroo Flat 5
9 34s33 138E40 -9:14:40
Kangaroo Ground 7
2 37s41 145E13 -9:40:52
Kangaroo Valley 2
1 34s44 150E32 -10:02:08
Kaniva 7 2 36s23 141E15 -9:25:00
Kanowna 8 5 30s36 121E36 -8:06:24
Kapunda 5 9 34s21 138E54 -9:15:36
Karonie 8 5 30s58 122E32 -8:10:08
Karoonda 5 9 35s06 139E54 -9:19:36
Karridale 8 5 34s13 115E05 -7:40:20
Karumba 4 4 17s29 140E50 -9:23:20
Karunjie 8 5 16s18 127E12 -8:28:48
Katanning 8 5 33s42 117E33 -7:50:12
Katherine 3 8 14s28 132E16 -8:49:04
Kathleen Valley 8
5 27s23 120E38 -8:02:32
Katoomba 2 1 33s42 150E18 -10:01:12
Keilor 7 2 37s43 144E50 -9:39:20
Keith 5 9 36s06 140E21 -9:21:24
Kellerberrin 8 5 31s38 117E43 -7:50:52

Kellyville 2 1 33s43 150E57 -10:03:48
Kelmscott 8 5 32s07 116E01 -7:44:04
Kempsey 2 1 31s05 152E50 -10:11:20
Kendall 2 1 31s38 152E43 -10:10:52
Kendenup 8 5 34s29 117E39 -7:50:36
Kensington 2 1 33s55 151E14 -10:04:56
Kenthurst 2 1 33s40 151E00 -10:04:00
Kenwick 8 5 32s02 115E58 -7:43:52
Keon Park 7 2 37s42 145E01 -9:40:04
Kerang 7 2 35s44 143E55 -9:35:40
Kersbrook 5 9 34s47 138E51 -9:15:24
Kew 7 2 37s49 145E02 -9:40:08
Keyneton 5 9 34s34 139E08 -9:16:32
Keysborough 7 2 38s00 145E10 -9:40:40
Keysbrook 8 5 32s26 115E59 -7:43:56
Khancoban 2 1 36s12 148E05 -9:52:20
Kiama 2 1 34s41 150E51 -10:03:24
Kiandra 2 1 35s53 148E30 -9:54:00
Kilcoy 4 4 26s57 152E33 -10:10:12
Kildurk 3 8 16s26 129E37 -8:38:28
Killara 2 1 33s46 151E09 -10:04:36
Killarney 4 4 28s20 152E18 -10:09:12
Killarney Heights 2
1 33s46 151E13 -10:04:52
Kilmore 7 2 37s18 144E57 -9:39:48
Kilsyth 7 2 37s48 145E19 -9:41:16
Kimba 5 9 33s09 136E25 -9:05:40
Kimberley Downs 8
5 17s24 124E22 -8:17:28
Kingaroy 4 4 26s33 151E50 -10:07:20
Kingoonya 5 9 30s54 135E18 -9:01:12
Kingscote 5 9 35s40 137E38 -9:10:32
Kingsford 2 1 33s56 151E14 -10:04:56
Kingsgrove 2 1 33s57 151E06 -10:04:24
Kingsthorpe 4 4 27s29 151E49 -10:07:16
Kingston 4 4 27s40 153E07 -10:12:28
Kingston Southeast 5
9 36s50 139E51 -9:19:24
Kingsville 7 2 37s49 144E52 -9:39:28
Kingswood 2 1 33s46 150E43 -10:02:52
Kitchener 8 5 31s02 124E11 -8:16:44
Knox 7 2 37s53 145E18 -9:41:12
Kogan 4 4 27s03 150E46 -10:03:04
Kogarah 2 1 33s58 151E08 -10:04:32
Kojonup 8 5 33s50 117E09 -7:48:36
Kondinin 8 5 32s30 118E16 -7:53:04
Kookynie 8 5 29s20 121E29 -8:05:56
Koolamarra 4 4 20s12 140E14 -9:20:56
Koolatah 4 4 15s53 142E27 -9:29:48
Kooloonong 7 2 34s53 143E09 -9:32:36
Koolyanobbing 8
5 30s50 119E35 -7:58:20
Koolywurtie 5 9 34s38 137E37 -9:10:28
Koondrook 7 2 35s39 144E08 -9:36:32
Koonibba 5 9 31s58 133E27 -8:53:48
Koorawatha 2 1 34s02 148E33 -9:54:12
Koorda 8 5 30s50 117E29 -7:49:56
Koo-Wee-Rup 7 2 38s12 145E30 -9:42:00
Kooyong 7 2 37s50 145E02 -9:40:08
Koriella 7 2 37s10 145E39 -9:42:36
Koroit 7 2 38s17 142E22 -9:29:28
Korumburra 7 2 38s26 145E49 -9:43:16
Koumala 4 4 21s37 149E15 -9:57:00
Kukerin 8 5 33s11 118E05 -7:52:20
Kulgera 3 8 25s50 133E18 -8:53:12
Kulin 8 5 32s40 118E10 -7:52:40
Kulnura 2 1 33s14 151E13 -10:04:52
Kulpara 5 9 34s04 138E02 -9:12:08
Kulwin 7 2 35s02 142E33 -9:30:12
Kumarl 8 5 32s47 121E33 -8:06:12
Kumbarilla 4 4 27s19 150E53 -10:03:32
Kundip 8 5 33s42 120E10 -8:00:40
Kungurri 4 4 21s05 148E44 -9:54:56
Kununurra 8 5 15s47 128E44 -8:34:56
Kuridala 4 4 21s17 140E30 -9:22:00
Ku-Ring-Gai 2 1 33s45 151E08 -10:04:32
Kurnell 2 1 34s01 151E13 -10:04:52
Kurrajong 2 1 33s33 150E40 -10:02:40
Kurri Kurri 2 1 32s49 151E29 -10:05:56
Kwinana 8 5 32s15 115E48 -7:43:12
Kwobrup 8 5 33s37 117E46 -7:51:04
Kyabra 4 4 26s18 143E10 -9:32:40
Kyabram 7 2 36s19 145E03 -9:40:12
Kyancutta 5 9 33s08 135E34 -9:02:16
Kybean 2 1 36s22 149E25 -9:57:40
Kydra 2 1 36s27 149E23 -9:57:32
Kyeamba 2 1 35s26 147E37 -9:50:28
Kyneton 7 2 37s15 144E27 -9:37:48
Kynuna 4 4 21s35 141E55 -9:27:40
Kyogle 2 1 28s37 153E00 -10:12:00
Kywong 2 1 34s59 146E44 -9:46:56
Lacmalac 2 1 35s19 148E19 -9:53:16
Lady Barron 6 3 40s12 148E14 -9:52:56
Ladysmith 2 1 35s12 147E31 -9:50:04
La Grange 8 5 18s41 121E45 -8:07:00
Laidley 4 4 27s38 152E24 -10:09:36
Lake Albert 2 1 35s10 147E23 -9:49:32
Lake Bathurst 2
1 35s01 149E36 -9:58:24
Lake Biddy 8 5 33s00 118E57 -7:55:48
Lake Camm 8 5 32s59 119E35 -7:58:20
Lake Cargelligo 2
1 33s18 146E23 -9:45:32
Lake Grace 8 5 33s06 118E28 -7:53:52
Lake Illawarra 2
1 34s33 150E52 -10:03:28
Lake King 8 5 33s05 119E40 -7:58:40
Lakemba 2 1 33s55 151E05 -10:04:20
Lake Nash 3 8 21s00 137E55 -9:11:40
Lakes Entrance 7
2 37s53 147E59 -9:51:56
Lake Varley 8 5 32s46 119E27 -7:57:48
Lalor Park 2 1 33s45 150E56 -10:03:44
Lameroo 5 9 35s20 140E31 -9:22:04
Lancefield 7 2 37s17 144E44 -9:38:56

Landor 8 5 25s09 116E54 -7:47:36
Landsborough 4 4 26s49 152E58-10:11:52
Lane Cove 2 1 33s49 151E10-10:04:40
Langhorne Creek 5 9 35s18 139E02 -9:16:08
Lankeys Creek 2 1 35s49 147E39 -9:50:36
Lansdowne 8 5 17s53 126E39 -8:26:36
Lansdowne 2 1 33s54 150E59-10:03:56
La Perouse 2 1 33s59 151E14-10:04:56
Lara 7 2 38s01 144E24 -9:37:36
Laravale 4 4 28s05 152E56-10:11:44
Larrimah 3 8 15s35 133E12 -8:52:48
Latham 8 5 29s45 116E26 -7:45:44
Latrobe 6 3 41s14 146E24 -9:45:36
Launceston 6 3 41s26 147E08 -9:48:32
Laura 4 4 15s34 144E28 -9:37:52
Laurel Hill 2 1 35s37 148E05 -9:52:20
Lavers Hill 7 2 38s40 143E24 -9:33:36
Laverton 8 5 28s38 122E25 -8:09:40
Laverton 7 2 37s52 144E45 -9:39:00
Lawgi 4 4 24s34 150E39-10:02:36
Lawn Hill 4 4 18s35 138E35 -9:14:20
Lawson 2 1 33s43 150E26-10:01:44
Leeton 2 1 34s33 146E24 -9:45:36
Legume 4 4 28s25 152E19-10:09:16
Leichhardt 2 1 33s53 151E07-10:04:28
Leigh Creek 5 9 30s28 138E25 -9:13:40
Lennonville 8 5 27s58 117E50 -7:51:20
Lenswood 5 9 34s55 138E49 -9:15:16
Leongatha 7 2 38s29 145E57 -9:43:48
Leonora 8 5 28s53 121E20 -8:05:20
Leopold 7 2 38s11 144E28 -9:37:52
Leopold Downs 8 5 17s52 125E25 -8:21:40
Leppington 2 1 33s58 150E49-10:03:16
Lethbridge 2 1 33s44 150E48-10:03:12
Leumeah 2 1 34s03 150E50-10:03:20
Leura 2 1 33s43 150E20-10:01:20
Lexton 7 2 37s17 143E31 -9:34:04
Lidcombe 2 1 33s52 151E03-10:04:12
Lilli Pilli 2 1 34s04 151E07-10:04:28
Lilydale 6 3 41s15 147E13 -9:48:52
Lilydale 7 2 37s45 145E21 -9:41:24
Lilyfield 2 1 33s52 151E10-10:04:40
Limbunya 3 8 17s14 129E50 -8:39:20
Limestone 8 5 21s11 119E50 -7:59:20
Lincoln Gap 5 9 32s37 137E35 -9:10:20
Lindfield 2 1 33s47 151E10-10:04:40
Linton 7 2 37s41 143E34 -9:34:16
Linville 4 4 26s51 152E16-10:09:04
Linwood 5 9 34s21 138E46 -9:15:04
Lismore 2 1 28s48 153E17-10:13:08
Lismore 7 2 37s58 143E20 -9:33:20
Lithgow 2 1 33s29 150E09-10:00:36
Little Billabong 2 1 35s35 147E32 -9:50:08
Little River 7 2 37s58 144E30 -9:38:00
Liveringa 8 5 18s03 124E10 -8:16:40
Liverpool 2 1 33s54 150E56-10:03:44
Llandilo 2 1 33s43 150E45-10:03:00
Llanelly 7 2 36s44 143E51 -9:35:24
Lobethal 5 9 34s54 138E52 -9:15:28
Loch 7 2 38s22 145E43 -9:42:52
Lochiel 5 9 33s56 138E10 -9:12:40
Lock 5 9 33s34 135E46 -9:03:04
Lockhart 2 1 35s14 146E43 -9:46:52
Loftus 2 1 34s03 151E03-10:04:12
Longford 7 2 38s10 147E05 -9:48:20
Long Jetty 2 1 33s22 151E29-10:05:56
Long Plains 5 9 34s21 138E22 -9:13:28
Long Point 2 1 34s01 150E54-10:03:36
Longreach 4 4 23s26 144E15 -9:37:00
Longueville 2 1 33s50 151E10-10:04:40
Longwarry 7 2 38s07 145E46 -9:43:04
Loongana 8 5 30s57 127E02 -8:28:08
Lord Howe Island 8 10 31s33 159E05-10:36:20
Lorna Glen 8 5 26s14 121E33 -8:06:12
Lorne 7 2 38s33 143E59 -9:35:56
Louth 2 1 30s32 145E07 -9:40:28
Lower Chittering 8 5 31s34 116E06 -7:44:24
Lower Plenty 7 2 37s44 145E06 -9:40:24
Lower Portland 2 1 33s27 150E53-10:03:32
Lowood 4 4 27s28 152E35-10:10:20
Loxton 5 9 34s27 140E35 -9:22:20
Lucindale 5 9 36s59 140E22 -9:21:28
Lucy Creek 3 8 22s25 136E20 -9:05:20
Luddenham 2 1 33s53 150E41-10:02:44
Lue 2 1 32s39 149E51 -9:59:24
Lugarno 2 1 33s59 151E03-10:04:12
Lurnea 2 1 33s56 150E54-10:03:36
Lyndhurst 4 4 19s12 144E23 -9:37:32
Lyndhurst 5 9 30s17 138E21 -9:13:24
Lyndhurst 7 2 38s03 145E15 -9:41:00
Lyndoch 5 9 34s37 138E53 -9:15:32
Lyndon 8 5 23s37 115E15 -7:41:00
Lysterfield 7 2 37s56 145E18 -9:41:12
Mabel Creek 5 9 29s01 134E17 -8:57:08
McArthur River 3 8 16s27 136E07 -9:04:28
Macclesfield 5 9 35s10 138E50 -9:15:20
MacDonald Downs 3 8 22s27 135E13 -9:00:52
McDouall Peak 5 9 29s51 134E55 -8:59:40
Mackay 4 4 21s09 149E11 -9:56:44
McKinlay 4 4 21s16 141E17 -9:25:08
Macksville 2 1 30s43 152E55-10:11:40
Maclean 2 1 29s28 153E13-10:12:52
Macleod 7 2 37s43 145E04 -9:40:16
Macquarie Fields 2 1 33s59 150E53-10:03:32

Maddington 8 5 32s03 115E59 -7:43:56
Madura 8 5 31s55 127E00 -8:28:00
Maffra 7 2 37s58 146E59 -9:47:56
Maggieville 4 4 17s27 141E10 -9:24:40
Maidstone 7 2 37s47 144E52 -9:39:28
Mainoru 3 8 14s02 134E05 -8:56:20
Maitland 2 1 32s44 151E33-10:06:12
Maitland 5 9 34s22 137E40 -9:10:40
Malabar 2 1 33s58 151E15-10:05:00
Malbon 4 4 21s04 140E18 -9:21:12
Malbooma 5 9 30s41 134E11 -8:56:44
Malcolm 8 5 28s56 121E30 -8:06:00
Maldon 7 2 37s00 144E04 -9:36:16
Mallala 5 9 34s26 138E30 -9:14:00
Mallapunyah 3 8 16s59 135E49 -9:03:16
Mallina 8 5 20s53 118E02 -7:52:08
Malmsbury 7 2 37s12 144E23 -9:37:32
Malpas 5 9 34s43 140E37 -9:22:28
Malvern 7 2 37s52 145E02 -9:40:08
Malvern Hills 4 4 24s29 145E10 -9:40:40
Mandora 8 5 19s44 120E51 -8:03:24
Mandurah 8 5 32s32 115E43 -7:42:52
Mangoplah 2 1 35s23 147E15 -9:49:00
Mangrove Mountain 2 1 33s19 151E14-10:04:56
Manilla 2 1 30s45 150E43-10:02:52
Maningrida 3 8 12s03 134E13 -8:56:52
Manjimup 8 5 34s14 116E09 -7:44:36
Manly 2 1 33s48 151E17-10:05:08
Mannahill 5 9 32s26 139E59 -9:19:56
Mannus 2 1 35s48 147E57 -9:51:48
Manoora 5 9 34s00 138E49 -9:15:16
Mansfield 7 2 37s03 146E05 -9:44:20
Many Peaks 4 4 24s33 151E23-10:05:32
Maranalgo 8 5 29s23 117E48 -7:51:12
Maranboy 3 8 14s30 132E45 -8:51:00
Marathon 4 4 20s49 143E34 -9:34:16
Marayong 2 1 33s45 150E54-10:03:36
Marble Bar 8 5 21s11 119E44 -7:58:56
Marburg 4 4 27s34 152E35-10:10:20
Marda 8 5 30s13 119E17 -7:57:08
Mardie 8 5 21s11 115E57 -7:43:48
Mareeba 4 4 17s00 145E26 -9:41:44
Margaret River 8 5 33s57 115E04 -7:40:16
Margaret River 8 5 18s38 126E52 -8:27:28
Maribyrnong 7 2 37s46 144E54 -9:39:36
Marion 5 9 35s01 138E34 -9:14:16
Marion Downs 4 4 23s22 139E39 -9:18:36
Marlborough 4 4 22s49 149E53 -9:59:32
Maroon 4 4 28s10 152E44-10:10:56
Maroubra 2 1 33s57 151E16-10:05:04
Marrabel 5 9 34s08 138E53 -9:15:32
Marradong 8 5 32s52 116E27 -7:45:48
Marrawah 6 3 40s56 144E41 -9:38:44
Marree 5 9 29s39 138E04 -9:12:16
Marrickville 2 1 33s55 151E09-10:04:36
Marsden 2 1 33s45 147E32 -9:50:08
Marsden Park 2 1 33s42 150E50-10:03:20
Marsfield 2 1 33s47 151E07-10:04:28
Martinsville 2 1 33s03 151E25-10:05:40
Marulan 2 1 34s43 150E00-10:00:00
Marulan South 2 1 34s46 150E02-10:00:08
Marvel Loch 8 5 31s28 119E28 -7:57:52
Maryborough 4 4 25s32 152E42-10:10:48
Maryborough 7 2 37s03 143E45 -9:35:00
Mary Kathleen 4 4 20s49 139E58 -9:19:52
Marysville 7 2 37s31 145E45 -9:43:00
Maryvale 4 4 28s05 152E15-10:09:00
Mascot 2 1 33s56 151E12-10:04:48
Matakana 2 1 33s00 145E54 -9:43:36
Mataranka 3 8 14s56 133E07 -8:52:28
Matraville 2 1 33s58 151E18-10:05:12
Maude 2 1 34s28 144E18 -9:37:12
Maydena 6 3 42s55 146E30 -9:46:00
Meadow Flat 2 1 33s26 149E56 -9:59:44
Meadows 5 9 35s11 138E46 -9:15:04
Meandarra 4 4 27s20 149E53 -9:59:32
Meckering 8 5 31s38 117E01 -7:48:04
Meeberrie 8 5 26s58 115E58 -7:43:52
Meekatharra 8 5 26s36 118E29 -7:53:56
Meenaar 8 5 31s38 116E53 -7:47:32
Meentheena 8 5 21s17 120E28 -8:01:52
Meka 8 5 27s26 116E48 -7:47:12
Melbourne 7 2 37s49 144E58 -9:39:52
Melrose 8 5 27s56 121E19 -8:05:16
Melrose 2 1 32s42 146E58 -9:47:52
Melton 7 2 37s41 144E35 -9:38:20
Melton 5 9 34s05 137E59 -9:11:56
Melville 8 5 32s03 115E49 -7:43:16
Menai 2 1 34s01 151E01-10:04:04
Menangina 8 5 29s50 121E54 -8:07:36
Menindee 2 1 32s24 142E26 -9:29:44
Meningie 5 9 35s42 139E20 -9:17:20
Menzies 8 5 29s41 121E02 -8:04:08
Merbein 7 2 34s11 142E04 -9:28:16
Meredith 7 2 37s51 144E04 -9:36:16
Merewether 2 1 32s57 151E46-10:07:04
Meribah 5 9 34s42 140E51 -9:23:24
Merimbula 2 1 36s53 149E54 -9:59:36
Merinda 4 4 20s01 148E10 -9:52:40
Merlynston 7 2 37s43 144E58 -9:39:52
Mermaid Beach 4 4 28s03 153E27-10:13:48
Merredin 8 5 31s29 118E16 -7:53:04
Merriwa 2 1 32s08 150E21-10:01:24
Merrygoen 2 1 31s50 149E14 -9:56:56
Merrylands 2 1 33s50 150E59-10:03:56
Merton 7 2 36s59 145E42 -9:42:48
Michelago 2 1 35s43 149E10 -9:56:40
Middalya 8 5 23s55 114E45 -7:39:00

Middle Swan 8 5 31s52 116E00 -7:44:00
Middleton 4 4 22s22 141E32 -9:26:08
Midland 8 5 31s53 116E00 -7:44:00
Milang 5 9 35s25 138E58 -9:15:52
Mildura 7 2 34s12 142E09 -9:28:36
Miles 4 4 26s40 150E11-10:00:44
Mileura 8 5 26s23 117E20 -7:49:20
Miling 8 5 30s30 116E21 -7:45:24
Millendon 8 5 31s48 116E02 -7:44:08
Millicent 5 9 37s36 140E22 -9:21:28
Millmerran 4 4 27s52 151E16-10:05:04
Millstream 8 5 21s35 117E04 -7:48:16
Milparinka 2 1 29s44 141E53 -9:27:32
Milton 2 1 35s19 150E26-10:01:44
Minderoo 8 5 22s00 115E02 -7:40:08
Mingary 5 9 32s08 140E44 -9:22:56
Mingela 4 4 19s53 146E38 -9:46:32
Mingenew 8 5 29s11 115E26 -7:41:44
Minilya 8 5 23s51 113E58 -7:35:52
Minlaton 5 9 34s46 137E36 -9:10:24
Minnie Creek 8 5 24s02 115E42 -7:42:48
Minnipa 5 9 32s51 135E09 -9:00:36
Mintaro 5 9 33s55 138E43 -9:14:52
Minto 2 1 34s01 150E51-10:03:24
Miranda 2 1 34s02 151E06-10:04:24
Mirboo North 7 2 38s24 146E10 -9:44:40
Miriam Vale 4 4 24s20 151E34-10:06:16
Mistake Creek 3 8 17s06 129E04 -8:36:16
Mitcham 5 9 34s59 138E36 -9:14:24
Mitcham 7 2 37s49 145E12 -9:40:48
Mitchell 4 4 26s29 147E58 -9:51:52
Mitchell River Mission 4 4 15s28 141E44 -9:26:56
Mittagong 2 1 34s27 150E27-10:01:48
Moama 2 1 36s07 144E47 -9:39:08
Moana 5 9 35s13 138E29 -9:13:56
Moe 7 2 38s10 146E15 -9:45:00
Mole Creek 6 3 41s33 146E24 -9:45:36
Molong 2 1 33s06 148E52 -9:55:28
Monarto South 5 9 35s08 139E08 -9:16:32
Mona Vale 2 1 33s41 151E18-10:05:12
Monbulk 7 2 37s52 145E25 -9:41:40
Monkira 4 4 24s49 140E34 -9:22:16
Montejinni 3 8 16s40 131E45 -8:47:00
Montmorency 7 2 37s43 145E07 -9:40:28
Monto 4 4 24s52 151E07-10:04:28
Mont Park 7 2 37s43 145E04 -9:40:16
Montrose 7 2 37s49 145E21 -9:41:24
Moolawatana 5 9 29s55 139E43 -9:18:52
Mooloogool 8 5 26s06 119E05 -7:56:20
Moonta 5 9 34s04 137E35 -9:10:20
Moonyoonooka 8 5 28s47 114E43 -7:38:52
Moora 8 5 30s39 116E00 -7:44:00
Moorabbin 7 2 37s56 145E02 -9:40:08
Mooraberree 4 4 25s14 140E59 -9:23:56
Moorarie 8 5 25s56 117E35 -7:50:20
Moore 4 4 26s53 152E18-10:09:12
Moorebank 2 1 33s56 150E56-10:03:44
Moorooka 4 4 27s32 153E02-10:12:08
Mooroolbark 7 2 37s47 145E19 -9:41:16
Morawa 8 5 29s13 116E00 -7:44:00
Morayfield 4 4 27s07 152E57-10:11:48
Mordialloc 7 2 38s00 145E05 -9:40:20
Moree 2 1 29s28 149E51 -9:59:24
Morella 4 4 22s59 143E52 -9:35:28
Moreton 4 4 12s28 142E38 -9:30:32
Morgan 5 9 34s02 139E40 -9:18:40
Morisset 2 1 33s06 151E29-10:05:56
Morney 4 4 25s22 141E28 -9:25:52
Mornington 7 2 38s13 145E03 -9:40:12
Morphett Vale 5 9 35s07 138E31 -9:14:04
Mortana 5 9 33s02 134E07 -8:56:28
Mortlake 7 2 38s05 142E48 -9:31:12
Mortlake 2 1 33s51 151E07-10:04:28
Moruya 2 1 35s55 150E05-10:00:20
Morven 4 4 26s25 147E07 -9:48:28
Morwell 7 2 38s14 146E24 -9:45:36
Mosman 2 1 33s49 151E14-10:04:56
Mosman Park 8 5 32s01 115E46 -7:43:04
Mossgiel 2 1 33s15 144E34 -9:38:16
Mossman 4 4 16s28 145E22 -9:41:28
Moss Vale 2 1 34s33 150E22-10:01:28
Moulamein 2 1 35s05 144E02 -9:36:08
Mount Alford 4 4 28s04 152E36-10:10:24
Mount Augustus 8 5 24s19 116E54 -7:47:36
Mount Barker 8 5 34s38 117E40 -7:50:40
Mount Barker 5 9 35s04 138E52 -9:15:28
Mount Buller 7 2 37s10 146E27 -9:45:48
Mount Cavenagh 3 8 25s58 133E15 -8:53:00
Mount Colah 2 1 33s41 151E07-10:04:28
Mount Compass 5 9 35s22 138E37 -9:14:28
Mount Crawford 5 9 34s40 138E57 -9:15:48
Mount Crosby 4 4 27s32 152E48-10:11:12
Mount Dandenong 7 2 37s50 145E22 -9:41:28
Mount Doreen 3 8 22s03 131E18 -8:45:12
Mount Druitt 2 1 33s46 150E49-10:03:16
Mount Dutton 5 9 27s50 135E43 -9:02:52
Mount Eba 5 9 30s12 135E40 -9:02:40
Mount Edwards 4 4 28s01 152E31-10:10:04
Mount Evelyn 7 2 37s47 145E23 -9:41:32
Mount Gambier 5 9 37s50 140E46 -9:23:04
Mount Garnet 4 4 17s41 145E07 -9:40:28
Mount Gravatt 4 4 27s33 153E06-10:12:24

Mount Hawthorn 8 5 31s55 115E50 -7:43:20
Mount Helena 8 5 31s53 116E13 -7:44:52
Mount Hope 5 9 34s07 135E23 -9:01:32
Mount Howitt 4 4 26s31 142E16 -9:29:04
Mount Isa 4 4 20s44 139E30 -9:18:00
Mount Kokeby 8 5 32s13 116E58 -7:47:52
Mount Lawley 8 5 31s56 115E52 -7:43:28
Mount Magnet 8 5 28s04 117E49 -7:51:16
Mount Manara 2 1 32s29 143E56 -9:35:44
Mount Margaret 4 4 26s54 143E21 -9:33:24
Mount Martha 7 2 38s17 145E01 -9:40:04
Mount Mee 4 4 27s04 152E46-10:11:04
Mount Molloy 4 4 16s41 145E20 -9:41:20
Mount Monger 8 5 30s59 121E53 -8:07:32
Mount Morgan 4 4 23s39 150E23-10:01:32
Mount Mulligan 4 4 16s51 144E52 -9:39:28
Mount Perry 4 4 25s11 151E39-10:06:36
Mount Pleasant 5 9 34s47 139E02 -9:16:08
Mount Pritchard 2 1 33s54 150E54-10:03:36
Mount Rebecca 5 9 26s48 135E10 -9:00:40
Mount Riddock 3 8 23s03 134E40 -8:58:40
Mount Sandiman 8 5 24s24 115E23 -7:41:32
Mount Sarah 5 9 26s57 135E22 -9:01:28
Mount Surprise 4 4 18s09 144E19 -9:37:16
Mount Sylvia 4 4 27s44 152E14-10:08:56
Mount Torrens 5 9 34s52 138E57 -9:15:48
Mount Vernon 8 5 24s13 118E14 -7:52:56
Mount Victoria 2 1 33s35 150E15-10:01:00
Mount Waverley 7 2 37s53 145E08 -9:40:32
Mount Wedge 3 8 22s45 132E09 -8:48:36
Mount Wedge 5 9 33s29 135E10 -9:00:40
Mount Willoughby 5 9 27s58 134E08 -8:56:32
Moyagee 8 5 27s45 117E54 -7:51:36
Muccan 8 5 20s38 120E04 -8:00:16
Muchea 8 5 31s35 115E59 -7:43:56
Muckadilla 4 4 26s35 148E23 -9:53:32
Mudgee 2 1 32s36 149E35 -9:58:20
Mudgeeraba 4 4 28s04 153E22-10:13:28
Mukinbudin 8 5 30s54 118E13 -7:52:52
Mulga Downs 8 5 22s08 118E26 -7:53:44
Mulgathing 5 9 30s15 134E00 -8:56:00
Mulgoa 2 1 33s50 150E40-10:02:40
Mulgowie 4 4 27s43 152E22-10:09:28
Mulgrave 7 2 37s56 145E12 -9:40:48
Mulgul 8 5 24s49 118E26 -7:53:44
Mullengudgery 2 1 31s41 147E26 -9:49:44
Mullewa 8 5 28s33 115E31 -7:42:04
Mullumbimby 2 1 28s33 153E30-10:14:00
Mundaring 8 5 31s54 116E10 -7:44:40
Mundijong 8 5 32s18 115E59 -7:43:56
Mundiwindi 8 5 23s52 120E09 -8:00:36
Mundrabilla 8 5 31s52 127E51 -8:31:24
Mundubbera 4 4 25s36 151E18-10:05:12
Mungallala 4 4 26s27 147E33 -9:50:12
Mungana 4 4 17s07 144E24 -9:37:36
Mungar Junction 4 4 25s36 152E36-10:10:24
Mungeranie 5 9 28s00 138E36 -9:14:24
Mungindi 2 1 28s58 148E59 -9:55:56
Muntadgin 8 5 31s45 118E34 -7:54:16
Murchison 7 2 36s37 145E14 -9:40:56
Murgon 4 4 26s15 151E57-10:07:48
Murra Murra 4 4 28s16 146E48 -9:47:12
Murray Bridge 5 9 35s07 139E17 -9:17:08
Murray Downs 3 8 21s04 134E40 -8:58:40
Murrin Murrin 8 5 28s55 121E49 -8:07:16
Murrumburrah 2 1 34s33 148E21 -9:53:24
Murrurundi 2 1 31s46 150E50-10:03:20
Murtee 2 2 31s35 143E30 -9:34:00
Murtoa 7 2 36s37 142E28 -9:29:52
Murwillumbah 2 1 28s19 153E24-10:13:36
Musgrave 4 4 14s47 143E30 -9:34:00
Muswellbrook 2 1 32s16 150E53-10:03:32
Muttaburra 4 4 22s36 144E33 -9:38:12
Mylor 5 9 35s03 138E45 -9:15:00
Myponga 5 9 35s24 138E28 -9:13:52
Myroodah 8 5 18s08 124E16 -8:17:04
Myrtleville 2 1 34s29 149E49 -9:59:16
Nagambie 7 2 36s47 145E10 -9:40:40
Nairne 5 9 35s02 138E54 -9:15:36
Nambi 8 5 28s54 121E41 -8:06:44
Nambour 4 4 26s38 152E58-10:11:52
Nambucca Heads 2 1 30s39 153E00-10:12:00
Nanango 4 4 26s40 152E00-10:08:00
Nannine 8 5 26s53 118E20 -7:53:20
Nannup 8 5 33s59 115E45 -7:43:00
Nanson 8 5 28s34 114E46 -7:39:04
Nantawarra 5 9 34s00 138E14 -9:12:56
Nappamerry 4 4 27s36 141E07 -9:24:28
Naracoorte 5 9 36s58 140E44 -9:22:56
Naradhan 2 1 33s37 146E19 -9:45:16
Narangba 4 4 27s12 152E58-10:11:52
Narellan 2 1 34s02 150E44-10:02:56
Narembeen 8 5 32s04 118E24 -7:53:36
Naretha 8 5 31s00 124E50 -8:19:20
Nariel 7 2 36s26 147E50 -9:51:20
Nar-Nar-Goon 7 2 38s05 145E34 -9:42:16
Narooma 2 1 36s14 150E03-10:00:12

Narrabeen 2 1 33s43 151E18-10:05:12
Narrabri 2 1 30s19 149E47 -9:59:08
Narrandera 2 1 34s45 146E33 -9:46:12
Narraweena 2 1 33s45 151E16-10:05:04
Narre Warren 7 2 38s02 145E19 -9:41:16
Narre Warren North 7 2 37s59 145E19 -9:41:16
Narrogin 8 5 32s56 117E10 -7:48:40
Narromine 2 1 32s14 148E15 -9:53:00
Narwietooma 3 8 23s15 132E35 -8:50:20
Natimuk 7 2 36s45 141E57 -9:27:48
Nattai River 2 1 34s04 150E27-10:01:48
Navarre 7 2 36s54 143E07 -9:32:28
Neales Flat 5 9 34s15 139E10 -9:16:40
Nedlands 8 5 31s59 115E49 -7:43:16
Neerim South 7 2 38s01 145E58 -9:43:52
Nerang 4 4 28s00 153E20-10:13:20
Nerriga 2 1 35s07 150E05-10:00:20
Nerrima 8 5 18s24 124E29 -8:17:56
Netherdale 4 4 21s08 148E32 -9:54:08
Nevertire 2 1 31s52 147E39 -9:50:36
New Angledool 2 1 29s07 147E57 -9:51:48
Newborough 7 2 38s11 146E17 -9:45:08
Newcastle 2 1 32s56 151E46-10:07:04
Newcastle Waters 3 8 17s24 133E24 -8:53:36
Newdegate 8 5 33s06 119E01 -7:56:04
Newlyn 7 2 37s25 143E59 -9:35:56
Newmarket 4 4 27s25 153E01-10:12:04
New Norcia 8 5 30s58 116E13 -7:44:52
New Norfolk 6 3 42s47 147E03 -9:48:12
Newport 7 2 37s51 144E53 -9:39:32
Newport 2 1 33s40 151E19-10:05:16
Newstead 7 2 37s07 144E04 -9:36:16
Newtown 7 2 38s09 144E20 -9:37:20
Nhill 7 2 36s20 141E39 -9:26:36
Nhulunbuy 3 8 12s11 136E47 -9:07:08
Nicholson 8 5 18s02 128E54 -8:35:36
Nimmitabel 2 1 36s31 149E16 -9:57:04
Nindigully 4 4 28s21 148E49 -9:55:16
Nipan 4 4 24s47 150E01-10:00:04
Nive Downs 4 4 25s30 146E32 -9:46:08
Noarlunga 5 9 35s11 138E30 -9:14:00
Nobby 4 4 27s51 151E54-10:07:36
Noble Park 7 2 37s58 145E10 -9:40:40
Noccundra 4 4 27s50 142E36 -9:30:24
Nockatunga 4 4 27s43 142E43 -9:30:52
Nonning 5 9 32s30 136E30 -9:06:00
Noojee 7 2 37s55 146E00 -9:44:00
Nookawarra 8 5 26s19 116E52 -7:47:28
Noonamah 3 8 12s38 131E04 -8:44:16
Noonkanbah 8 5 18s30 124E50 -8:19:20
Noorat 7 2 38s12 142E56 -9:31:44
Noosaville 4 4 26s24 153E04-10:12:16
Norlane 7 2 38s06 144E21 -9:37:24
Normanby 4 4 27s28 153E01-10:12:04
Normanhurst 2 1 33s43 151E06-10:04:24
Normanton 4 4 17s40 141E05 -9:24:20
Normanville 5 9 35s27 138E19 -9:13:16
Nornalup 8 5 35s00 116E49 -7:47:16
Norseman 8 5 32s12 121E46 -8:07:04
Northam 8 5 31s39 116E40 -7:46:40
Northampton 8 5 28s21 114E37 -7:38:28
North Auburn 2 1 33s50 151E02-10:04:08
North Balwyn 7 2 37s48 145E05 -9:40:20
North Bannister 8 5 32s35 116E26 -7:45:44
North Beach 8 5 31s52 115E45 -7:43:00
North Bourke 2 1 30s03 145E57 -9:43:48
North Box Hill 7 2 37s48 145E07 -9:40:28
Northbridge 2 1 33s49 151E13-10:04:52
Northcliffe 8 5 34s36 116E07 -7:44:28
Northcote 7 2 37s46 145E00 -9:40:00
North Dandalup 8 5 32s31 115E58 -7:43:52
North Essendon 7 2 37s45 144E54 -9:39:36
North Fitzroy 7 2 37s47 144E59 -9:39:56
North Manly 2 1 33s46 151E16-10:05:04
North Maroota 2 1 33s29 150E56-10:03:44
Northmead 2 1 33s47 151E00-10:04:00
North Narrabeen 2 1 33s42 151E18-10:05:12
North Parramatta 2 1 33s48 151E00-10:04:00
North Rocks 2 1 33s46 151E02-10:04:08
North Ryde 2 1 33s48 151E07-10:04:28
North Sydney 2 1 33s50 151E13-10:04:52
North Tamborine 4 4 27s56 153E11-10:12:44
North Turramurra 2 1 33s43 150E09-10:00:36
North Yelta 5 9 34s03 137E37 -9:10:28
Notting Hill 7 2 37s54 145E08 -9:40:32
Nowendoc 2 1 31s32 151E43-10:06:52
Nowingi 7 2 34s36 142E14 -9:28:56
Nowra 2 1 34s53 150E36-10:02:24
Nullagine 8 5 21s53 120E06 -8:00:24
Nullarbor 5 9 31s26 130E55 -8:43:40
Numeralla 2 1 36s11 149E20 -9:57:20
Numurkah 7 2 36s06 145E26 -9:41:44
Nunawading 7 2 37s49 145E10 -9:40:40
Nundah 4 4 27s24 153E04-10:12:16
Nungarin 8 5 31s11 118E06 -7:52:24
Nunjikompita 5 9 32s16 134E19 -8:57:16
Nuriootpa 5 9 34s29 139E00 -9:16:00
Nutwood Downs 3 8 15s49 134E10 -8:56:40
Nyabing 8 5 33s32 118E09 -7:52:36
Nyah West 7 2 35s11 143E22 -9:33:28
Nymagee 2 1 32s04 146E20 -9:45:20

Nyngan 2 1 31s34 147E11 -9:48:44
Oakbank 5 9 34s59 138E51 -9:15:24
Oakdale 8 5 34s26 119E00 -7:56:00
Oakey 4 4 27s26 151E43-10:06:52
Oaklands 5 9 35s00 137E41 -9:10:44
Oakleigh 7 2 37s54 145E06 -9:40:24
Oakleigh South 7 2 37s56 145E05 -9:40:20
Oak Park 7 2 37s43 144E55 -9:39:40
Oatlands 6 3 42s18 147E21 -9:49:24
Oatley 2 1 33s59 151E05-10:04:20
Oban 4 4 21s14 139E03 -9:16:12
Oberne 2 1 35s24 147E50 -9:51:20
Oberon 2 1 33s43 149E52 -9:59:28
O'Connell 2 1 33s32 149E44 -9:58:56
Oenpelli Mission 3 8 12s20 133E04 -8:52:16
Officer 7 2 38s04 145E25 -9:41:40
Ogilvie 8 5 28s09 114E38 -7:38:32
Ogmore 4 4 22s37 149E40 -9:58:40
Olary 5 9 32s17 140E19 -9:21:16
Old Cork 4 4 22s56 141E52 -9:27:28
Old Noranside 4 4 22s13 140E04 -9:20:16
Olinda 2 1 32s50 150E08-10:00:32
Olinda 7 2 37s51 145E22 -9:41:28
Olio 4 4 21s54 143E13 -9:32:52
Omeo 7 2 37s06 147E36 -9:50:24
One Tree Hill 5 9 34s43 138E46 -9:15:04
Ongerup 8 5 33s58 118E29 -7:53:56
Onslow 8 5 21s39 115E06 -7:40:24
Oodnadatta 5 9 27s33 135E28 -9:01:52
Ooldea 5 9 30s27 131E50 -8:47:20
Ooratippra 3 8 22s00 136E00 -9:04:00
Ora Banda 8 5 30s22 121E04 -8:04:16
Orange 2 1 33s17 149E06 -9:56:24
Oraparinna 5 9 31s22 138E43 -9:14:52
Orbost 7 2 37s42 148E27 -9:53:48
Orchard Hills 2 1 33s47 150E43-10:02:52
Ord River 8 5 17s23 128E51 -8:35:24
Orientos 4 4 28s05 141E14 -9:24:56
Ormond 7 2 37s54 145E03 -9:40:12
Orroroo 5 9 32s44 138E37 -9:14:28
Otford 2 1 34s12 151E01-10:04:04
Ourimbah 2 1 33s22 151E23-10:05:32
Ournie 2 1 35s56 147E51 -9:51:24
Ouse 6 3 42s29 146E42 -9:46:48
Outer Harbour 5 9 34s47 138E30 -9:14:00
Ouyen 7 2 35s04 142E20 -9:29:20
Owen 5 9 34s16 138E33 -9:14:12
Oxford Falls 2 1 33s44 151E15-10:05:00
Oxley 2 1 34s12 144E06 -9:36:24
Padstow 2 1 33s57 151E02-10:04:08
Paisley 7 2 37s51 144E51 -9:39:24
Pakenham 7 2 38s04 145E29 -9:41:56
Pallamana 5 9 35s02 139E12 -9:16:48
Palm Beach 2 1 33s36 151E19-10:05:16
Palm Beach 4 4 28s08 153E28-10:13:52
Palmer 5 9 34s51 139E10 -9:16:40
Palmerville 4 4 15s59 144E05 -9:36:20
Papunya 3 8 23s16 131E54 -8:47:36
Parachilna 5 9 31s08 138E23 -9:13:32
Parafield 5 9 34s47 138E38 -9:14:32
Paratoo 5 9 32s42 139E22 -9:17:28
Parker Range 8 5 31s38 119E35 -7:58:20
Parkerville 8 5 31s53 116E09 -7:44:36
Parkes 2 1 33s08 148E11 -9:52:44
Parklea 2 1 33s44 150E57-10:03:48
Park Orchards 7 2 37s46 145E13 -9:40:52
Paroo 8 5 26s16 119E46 -7:59:04
Parramatta 2 1 33s49 151E00-10:04:00
Pascoe Vale 7 2 37s44 144E56 -9:39:44
Paskeville 5 9 34s02 137E54 -9:11:36
Patchewollock 7 2 35s23 142E11 -9:28:44
Paterson 2 1 32s36 151E37-10:06:28
Paxton 2 1 32s54 151E16-10:05:04
Payneham 5 9 34s53 138E38 -9:14:32
Paynes Find 8 5 29s15 117E41 -7:50:44
Peak Crossing 4 4 27s47 152E44-10:10:56
Peak Hill 8 5 25s38 118E43 -7:54:52
Peak Hill 2 1 32s44 148E12 -9:52:48
Peakhurst 2 1 33s58 151E04-10:04:16
Peakview 2 1 36s04 149E24 -9:57:36
Pedirka 5 9 26s40 135E14 -9:00:56
Peebinga 5 9 34s56 140E55 -9:23:40
Peedamullah 8 5 21s50 115E38 -7:42:32
Peel 2 1 33s19 149E38 -9:58:32
Pemberton 8 5 34s28 116E01 -7:44:04
Pendle Hill 2 1 33s48 150E57-10:03:48
Penguin 6 3 41s07 146E04 -9:44:16
Pennant Hills 2 1 33s44 151E04-10:04:16
Penneshaw 5 9 35s44 137E56 -9:11:44
Penola 5 9 37s23 140E50 -9:23:20
Penong 5 9 31s55 133E01 -8:52:04
Penrith 2 1 33s45 150E42-10:02:48
Pentland 4 4 20s32 145E24 -9:41:36
Perenjori 8 5 29s26 116E17 -7:45:08
Perth 8 5 31s57 115E51 -7:43:24
Peterborough 5 9 32s58 138E50 -9:15:20
Petersham 2 1 33s54 151E09-10:04:36
Petrie 4 4 27s16 152E59-10:11:56
Pialba 4 4 25s17 152E51-10:11:24
Piawaning 8 5 30s51 116E22 -7:45:28
Pickering Brook 8 5 32s03 116E08 -7:44:32
Picton 2 1 34s11 150E36-10:02:24
Picton Junction 8 5 33s21 115E41 -7:42:44

Pilga 8 5 21s29 119E25 -7:57:40
Pilliga 2 1 30s21 148E54 -9:55:36
Pimba 5 9 31s15 136E47 -9:07:08
Pindar 8 5 28s29 115E48 -7:43:12
Pine Creek 3 8 13s49 131E49 -8:47:16
Pine Hill 4 4 23s39 146E58 -9:47:52
Pine Point 5 9 34s34 137E52 -9:11:28
Pingaring 8 5 32s45 118E37 -7:54:28
Pingelly 8 5 32s32 117E05 -7:48:20
Pingrup 8 5 33s32 118E31 -7:54:04
Pinjarra 8 5 32s37 115E53 -7:43:32
Pinnaroo 5 9 35s16 140E55 -9:23:40
Pioneer 8 5 31s48 121E43 -8:06:52
Pithara 8 5 30s24 116E40 -7:46:40
Pittsworth 4 4 27s43 151E38-10:06:32
Plumpton 2 1 33s45 150E50-10:03:20
Point Cloates 8 5 22s35 113E41 -7:34:44
Point Cook 7 2 37s56 144E45 -9:39:00
Point McLeay 5 9 35s32 139E06 -9:16:24
Point Pass 5 9 34s05 139E03 -9:16:12
Point Samson 8 5 20s36 117E12 -7:48:48
Pokataroo 2 1 29s35 148E42 -9:54:48
Poochera 5 9 32s43 134E51 -8:59:24
Pooncarie 2 1 33s23 142E34 -9:30:16
Pooraka 5 9 34s50 138E37 -9:14:28
Poowong 7 2 38s21 145E46 -9:43:04
Port Adelaide 5 9 34s51 138E30 -9:14:00
Port Alma 4 4 23s35 150E51-10:03:24
Portarlington 7 2 38s07 144E39 -9:38:36
Port Arthur 6 3 43s09 147E51 -9:51:24
Port Augusta 5 9 32s30 137E46 -9:11:04
Port Broughton 5 9 33s36 137E56 -9:11:44
Port Campbell 7 2 38s37 143E00 -9:32:00
Port Clinton 5 9 34s14 138E01 -9:12:04
Port Darwin 3 8 12s28 130E50 -8:43:20
Port Elliot 5 9 35s32 138E41 -9:14:44
Porters Retreat 2 1 34s00 149E48 -9:59:12
Port Fairy 7 2 38s23 142E14 -9:28:56
Port Germein 5 9 33s01 138E00 -9:12:00
Port Hacking 2 1 34s04 151E08-10:04:32
Port Hedland 8 5 20s19 118E34 -7:54:16
Port Hughes 5 9 34s04 137E32 -9:10:08
Port Keats Mission 3 8 14s13 129E32 -8:38:08
Port Kembla 2 1 34s29 150E54-10:03:36
Port Kenny 5 9 33s10 134E42 -8:58:48
Portland 7 2 38s21 141E36 -9:26:24
Portland 2 1 33s22 150E00-10:00:00
Port Lincoln 5 9 34s44 135E52 -9:03:28
Port MacDonnell 5 9 38s03 140E42 -9:22:48
Port Macquarie 2 1 31s26 152E55-10:11:40
Port Melbourne 7 2 37s51 144E56 -9:39:44
Port Neill 5 9 34s07 136E20 -9:05:20
Port Noarlunga 5 9 35s09 138E28 -9:13:52
Port Pirie 5 9 33s11 138E01 -9:12:04
Portsea 7 2 38s19 144E43 -9:38:52
Port Vincent 5 9 34s47 137E51 -9:11:24
Port Wakefield 5 9 34s11 138E09 -9:12:36
Prahran 7 2 37s51 144E59 -9:39:56
Prairie 4 4 20s52 144E36 -9:38:24
Preston 7 2 37s45 145E01 -9:40:04
Price 5 9 34s17 138E00 -9:12:00
Proserpine 4 4 20s24 148E34 -9:54:16
Prospect 5 9 34s54 138E35 -9:14:20
Prospect 2 1 33s48 150E56-10:03:44
Prospect Hill 5 9 35s13 138E44 -9:14:56
Proston 4 4 26s10 151E36-10:06:24
Punchbowl 2 1 33s56 151E03-10:04:12
Purga 4 4 27s43 152E44-10:10:56
Putty 2 1 32s57 150E40-10:02:40
Pyalong 7 2 37s07 144E54 -9:39:36
Pymble 2 1 33s45 151E09-10:04:36
Quairading 8 5 32s01 117E25 -7:49:40
Quakers Hill 2 1 33s43 150E53-10:03:32
Quambatook 7 2 35s51 143E31 -9:34:04
Queanbeyan 2 1 35s21 149E14 -9:56:56
Queenscliff 7 2 38s16 144E40 -9:38:40
Queenstown 6 3 42s05 145E33 -9:42:12
Quilpie 4 4 26s37 144E15 -9:37:00
Quindanning 8 5 33s03 116E34 -7:46:16
Quirindi 2 1 31s31 150E41-10:02:44
Quorn 5 9 32s21 138E03 -9:12:12
Raglan 2 1 33s26 149E36 -9:58:24
Railton 6 3 41s21 146E25 -9:45:40
Ramsgate 2 1 33s59 151E08-10:04:32
Rand 2 1 35s36 146E35 -9:46:20
Randwick 2 1 33s55 151E15-10:05:00
Ranford 8 5 32s48 116E31 -7:46:04
Ranken Store 3 8 19s35 136E55 -9:07:40
Rankins Springs 2 1 33s50 146E16 -9:45:04
Rapid Bay 5 9 35s32 138E12 -9:12:48
Rathdowney 4 4 28s12 152E52-10:11:28
Ravensbourne 4 4 27s22 152E10-10:08:40
Ravenshoe 4 4 17s37 145E29 -9:41:56
Ravensthorpe 8 5 33s35 120E02 -8:00:08
Rawlinna 8 5 31s01 125E20 -8:21:20
Raymond Terrace 2 1 32s46 151E44-10:06:56
Redcliffe 4 4 27s14 153E07-10:12:28
Red Cliffs 7 2 34s19 142E11 -9:28:44
Red Hill 8 5 21s59 116E03 -7:44:12
Redland Bay 4 4 27s37 153E18-10:13:12
Regent 7 2 37s44 145E00 -9:40:00
Regents Park 2 1 33s53 151E02-10:04:08
Regentville 2 1 33s47 150E40-10:02:40
Reid 8 5 30s49 128E26 -8:33:44
Renmark 5 9 34s11 140E45 -9:23:00
Renner Springs 3 8 18s20 133E48 -8:55:12
Research 7 2 37s42 145E11 -9:40:44
Reservoir 7 2 37s43 145E00 -9:40:00
Revesby 2 1 33s57 151E01-10:04:04
Reynella 5 9 35s06 138E32 -9:14:08
Rhodes 2 1 33s50 151E05-10:04:20
Richmond 4 4 20s44 143E08 -9:32:32
Richmond 2 1 33s36 150E46-10:03:04
Richmond 7 2 37s49 145E00 -9:40:00
Ringwood 7 2 37s49 145E14 -9:40:56
Ringwood North 7 2 37s48 145E14 -9:40:56
Riversleigh 4 4 19s02 138E44 -9:14:56
Riverstone 2 1 33s40 150E52-10:03:28
Riverton 5 9 34s09 138E45 -9:15:00
Riverwood 2 1 33s57 151E03-10:04:12
Robe 5 9 37s11 139E45 -9:19:00
Robertson 2 1 34s35 150E35-10:02:20
Robertstown 5 9 34s00 139E05 -9:16:20
Robinvale 7 2 34s36 142E46 -9:31:04
Rochester 7 2 36s22 144E42 -9:38:48
Rockbank 7 2 37s43 144E39 -9:38:36
Rockdale 2 1 33s57 151E08-10:04:32
Rock Flat 2 1 36s21 149E12 -9:56:48
Rockhampton 4 4 23s23 150E31-10:02:04
Rockhampton Downs 3 8 18s57 135E01 -9:00:04
Rockingham 8 5 32s17 115E44 -7:42:56
Rocky Gully 8 5 34s30 116E48 -7:47:12
Rodinga 3 8 24s34 134E05 -8:56:20
Roebourne 8 5 20s47 117E09 -7:48:36
Roelands 8 5 33s18 115E50 -7:43:20
Rogans Hill 2 1 33s44 151E01-10:04:04
Rokewood 7 2 37s54 143E43 -9:34:52
Rokewood Junction 7 2 37s51 143E41 -9:34:44
Roleystone 8 5 32s08 116E04 -7:44:16
Rolleston 4 4 24s28 148E37 -9:54:28
Rollingstone 4 4 19s03 146E24 -9:45:36
Roma 4 4 26s35 148E47 -9:55:08
Romsey 7 2 37s21 144E45 -9:39:00
Rooty Hill 2 1 33s46 150E50-10:03:20
Roper River Mission 3 8 14s44 134E44 -8:58:56
Roper Valley 3 8 14s56 134E00 -8:56:00
Rosanna 7 2 37s45 145E04 -9:40:16
Roseberth 4 4 25s47 139E37 -9:18:28
Rosebery 6 3 41s46 145E32 -9:42:08
Rosebud 7 2 38s21 144E54 -9:39:36
Rosedale 4 4 24s38 151E55-10:07:40
Rosevale 4 4 27s51 152E29-10:09:56
Roseville 2 1 33s47 151E11-10:04:44
Rosewood 4 4 27s39 152E35-10:10:20
Rosewood 2 1 35s41 147E52 -9:51:28
Roseworthy 5 9 34s32 138E44 -9:14:56
Ross 6 3 42s02 147E29 -9:49:56
Rossmore 2 1 33s57 150E46-10:03:04
Rothsay 8 5 29s17 116E53 -7:47:32
Roto 2 1 33s03 145E28 -9:41:52
Rouse Hill 2 1 33s41 150E56-10:03:44
Rowena 2 1 29s49 148E54 -9:55:36
Rowland Flat 5 9 34s35 138E56 -9:15:44
Rowville 7 2 37s56 145E14 -9:40:56
Roxborough Downs 4 4 22s30 138E50 -9:15:20
Royalla 2 1 35s31 149E09 -9:56:36
Roy Hill 8 5 22s38 119E57 -7:59:48
Rozelle 2 1 33s52 151E10-10:04:40
Rudall 5 9 33s41 136E16 -9:05:04
Rumbalara 3 8 25s20 134E29 -8:57:56
Rum Jungle 3 8 13s01 131E00 -8:44:00
Rumula 4 4 16s35 145E20 -9:41:20
Rupari 5 9 35s37 139E09 -9:16:36
Rydal 2 1 33s29 150E02-10:00:08
Rydalmere 2 1 33s49 151E02-10:04:08
Ryde 2 1 33s49 151E06-10:04:24
Rye 7 2 38s23 144E49 -9:39:16
Rylstone 2 1 32s48 149E58 -9:59:52
Saddleworth 5 9 34s05 138E47 -9:15:08
Safety Bay 8 5 32s18 115E43 -7:42:52
Saint Albans 7 2 37s44 144E48 -9:39:12
Saint Albans 2 1 33s17 150E59-10:03:56
Saint Arnaud 7 2 36s37 143E15 -9:33:00
Saint George 4 4 28s02 148E35 -9:54:20
Saint Helens 6 3 41s20 148E15 -9:53:00
Saint Ives 2 1 33s44 151E10-10:04:40
Saint Kilda 7 2 37s52 144E59 -9:39:56
Saint Kilda 5 9 34s44 138E32 -9:14:08
Saint Lawrence 4 4 22s21 149E31 -9:58:04
Saint Marys 6 3 41s35 148E10 -9:52:40
Saint Marys 2 1 33s47 150E47-10:03:08
Sale 7 2 38s06 147E04 -9:48:16
Salisbury 5 9 34s46 138E38 -9:14:32
Salmon Gums 8 5 32s59 121E38 -8:06:32
Salt Ash 2 1 32s47 151E55-10:07:40
Samford 4 4 27s23 152E53-10:11:32
Sanderston 5 9 34s46 139E13 -9:16:52
Sandgate 4 4 27s20 153E05-10:12:20
Sandilands 5 9 34s31 137E46 -9:11:04
Sandringham 4 4 24s05 139E04 -9:16:16
Sandringham 7 2 37s57 145E00 -9:40:00
Sandstone 8 5 27s59 119E17 -7:57:08
San Remo 7 2 38s31 145E22 -9:41:28
Sans Souci 2 1 33s59 151E08-10:04:32
Saratoga 2 1 33s28 151E21-10:05:24
Sarina 4 4 21s26 149E13 -9:56:52
Sassafras 7 2 37s52 145E21 -9:41:24
Sawyers Valley 8 5 31s54 116E13 -7:44:52
Scaddan 8 5 33s27 121E43 -8:06:52
Scarborough 8 5 31s54 115E45 -7:43:00
Scarsdale 7 2 37s40 143E40 -9:34:40
Sceale Bay 5 9 33s01 134E12 -8:56:48
Schofields 2 1 33s42 150E52-10:03:28
Scone 2 1 32s03 150E52-10:03:28
Scoresby 7 2 37s54 145E14 -9:40:56
Scottsdale 6 3 41s10 147E31 -9:50:04
Seaforth 2 1 33s48 151E15-10:05:00
Seaholme 7 2 37s52 144E50 -9:39:20
Sea Lake 7 2 35s30 142E51 -9:31:24
Sebastopol 7 2 37s36 143E51 -9:35:24
Second Valley 5 9 35s33 138E14 -9:12:56
Sedan 5 9 34s35 139E18 -9:17:12
Seemore Downs 8 5 30s42 125E15 -8:21:00
Selby 7 2 37s55 145E22 -9:41:28
Selwyn 4 4 21s32 140E30 -9:22:00
Serpentine 8 5 32s22 115E59 -7:43:56
Sevenhill 5 9 33s53 138E38 -9:14:32
Seven Hills 2 1 33s46 150E57-10:03:48
Seymour 7 2 37s02 145E08 -9:40:32
Shannons Flat 2 1 35s54 148E58 -9:55:52
Shaw River 8 5 20s43 119E20 -7:57:20
Shelbourne 7 2 36s52 144E01 -9:36:04
Shellharbour 2 1 34s35 150E52-10:03:28
Shepparton 7 2 36s23 145E25 -9:41:40
Sheringa 5 9 33s51 135E15 -9:01:00
Shooters Hill 2 1 33s54 149E52 -9:59:28
Silverton 2 7 31s53 141E13 -9:24:52
Singleton 2 1 32s34 151E10-10:04:40
Skipton 7 2 37s41 143E22 -9:33:28
Smithfield 5 9 34s41 138E41 -9:14:44
Smithfield 2 1 33s51 150E57-10:03:48
Smithton 6 3 40s51 145E07 -9:40:28
Smoky Bay 5 9 32s22 133E56 -8:55:44
Smythesdale 7 2 37s38 143E41 -9:34:44
Snowtown 5 9 33s47 138E13 -9:12:52
Sodwalls 2 1 33s31 149E59 -9:59:56
Sofala 2 1 33s05 149E42 -9:58:48
Somersby 2 1 33s25 151E17-10:05:08
Somerville 7 2 38s13 145E10 -9:40:40
Sommariva 4 4 26s24 146E36 -9:46:24
Sorell 6 3 42s47 147E33 -9:50:12
Sorrento 7 2 38s20 144E45 -9:39:00
Soudan 3 8 20s05 137E00 -9:08:00
South Barwon 7 2 38s17 144E30 -9:38:00
Southbrook 4 4 27s41 151E43-10:06:52
Southern Cross 8 5 31s13 119E19 -7:57:16
South Melbourne 7 2 37s50 144E57 -9:39:48
South Perth 8 5 31s59 115E51 -7:43:24
Southport 4 4 27s58 153E25-10:13:40
Spalding 5 9 33s30 138E37 -9:14:28
Spearwood 8 5 32s07 115E47 -7:43:08
Spotswood 7 2 37s50 144E53 -9:39:32
Springsure 4 4 24s07 148E05 -9:52:20
Springton 5 9 34s43 139E05 -9:16:20
Springvale 8 5 17s48 127E41 -8:30:44
Springvale 4 4 23s33 140E42 -9:22:48
Springvale 7 2 37s57 145E09 -9:40:36
Springvale South 7 2 37s58 145E09 -9:40:36
Springwood 2 1 33s42 150E33-10:02:12
Stamford 4 4 21s16 143E49 -9:35:16
Stanley 6 3 40s46 145E18 -9:41:12
Stansbury 5 9 34s55 137E47 -9:11:08
Stanthorpe 4 4 28s39 151E57-10:07:48
Station Peak 8 5 21s10 118E11 -7:52:44
Staughton Vale 7 2 37s51 144E17 -9:37:08
Stawell 7 2 37s04 142E46 -9:31:04
Stephens Creek 2 7 31s50 141E30 -9:26:00
Stirling 3 8 21s44 133E45 -8:55:00
Stirling 5 9 35s00 138E43 -9:14:52
Stockton 2 1 32s55 151E47-10:07:08
Stonehenge 4 4 24s22 143E17 -9:33:08
Stony Crossing 2 1 35s05 143E35 -9:34:20
Strahan 6 3 42s09 145E19 -9:41:16
Strathalbyn 5 9 35s16 138E54 -9:15:36
Strathfield 2 1 33s52 151E06-10:04:24
Strathpine 4 4 27s19 152E59-10:11:56
Streaky Bay 5 9 32s48 134E13 -8:56:52
Streatham 7 2 37s41 143E04 -9:32:16
Stretton 8 5 32s32 117E41 -7:50:44
Stroud Road 2 1 32s20 151E56-10:07:44
Sturdee 5 9 31s52 132E23 -8:49:32
Sturt Creek 8 5 19s10 128E10 -8:32:40
Subiaco 8 5 31s57 115E49 -7:43:16
Sunbury 7 2 37s35 144E44 -9:38:56
Sundown 5 9 26s14 133E12 -8:52:48
Sunny Corner 2 1 33s23 149E53 -9:59:32
Sunshine 7 2 37s47 144E50 -9:39:20
Surat 4 4 27s09 149E04 -9:56:16
Surfers Paradise 4 4 28s00 153E26-10:13:44
Sussex Inlet 2 1 35s11 150E36-10:02:24
Sutherland 2 1 34s02 151E04-10:04:16
Sutherlands 5 9 34s10 139E13 -9:16:52
Sutton 2 1 35s10 149E15 -9:57:00
Sutton Forest 2 1 34s35 150E19-10:01:16
Swan Hill 7 2 35s21 143E34 -9:34:16
Swansea 6 3 42s08 148E04 -9:52:16
Swansea 2 1 33s05 151E38-10:06:32
Sydenham 7 2 37s42 144E46 -9:39:04

AUSTRALIA AUSTRALIEN AUSTRALIE

Sydenham West 7 2 37s41 144E39 -9:38:36
Sydney 2 1 33s52 151E13-10:04:52
Sylvania 2 1 34s01 151E07-10:04:28
Sylvania Heights 2 1 34s02 151E06-10:04:24
Syndal 7 2 37s53 145E09 -9:40:36
Tahmoor 2 1 34s13 150E36-10:02:24
Tailem Bend 5 9 35s16 139E27 -9:17:48
Talawanta 4 4 18s38 140E16 -9:21:04
Talbingo 2 1 35s34 148E18 -9:53:12
Talbot 7 2 37s11 143E43 -9:34:52
Talbot Brook 8 5 32s01 116E40 -7:46:40
Talia 5 9 33s19 134E54 -8:59:36
Tallanalla 8 5 33s06 116E07 -7:44:28
Tallangatta 7 2 36s13 147E15 -9:49:00
Tallong 2 1 34s44 150E05-10:00:20
Tally Ho 7 2 37s52 145E09 -9:40:36
Talmalmo 2 1 35s56 147E30 -9:50:00
Talwood 4 4 28s30 149E30 -9:58:00
Tamala 8 5 26s42 113E45 -7:35:00
Tambellup 8 5 34s02 117E39 -7:50:36
Tambo 4 4 24s53 146E15 -9:45:00
Tamborine 4 4 27s53 153E08-10:12:32
Tamworth 2 1 31s05 150E55-10:03:40
Tanami 3 8 19s59 129E43 -8:38:52
Tanbar 4 4 25s50 141E55 -9:27:40
Tanunda 5 9 34s32 138E57 -9:15:48
Tara 4 4 27s17 150E28-10:01:52
Tarago 2 1 35s04 149E39 -9:58:36
Taralga 2 1 34s24 149E49 -9:59:16
Tarana 2 1 33s32 149E54 -9:59:36
Tarcoola 5 9 30s41 134E33 -8:58:12
Tarcoon 2 1 30s16 146E43 -9:46:52
Tarcutta 2 1 35s17 147E44 -9:50:56
Tardun 8 5 28s48 115E45 -7:43:00
Taree 2 1 31s54 152E28-10:09:52
Tarlee 5 9 34s16 138E46 -9:15:04
Tarneit 7 2 37s52 144E41 -9:38:44
Tarong 4 4 26s46 151E51-10:07:24
Taroom 4 4 25s39 149E49 -9:59:16
Tarraleah 6 3 42s18 146E27 -9:45:48
Tathra 2 1 36s44 149E59 -9:59:56
Tea Tree 3 8 22s11 133E17 -8:53:08
Teatree Gully 5 9 34s49 138E44 -9:14:56
Temora 2 1 34s26 147E32 -9:50:08
Templers 5 9 34s28 138E45 -9:15:00
Templestowe 7 2 37s45 145E07 -9:40:28
Templeton 4 4 18s26 142E28 -9:29:52
Tennant Creek 3 8 19s40 134E10 -8:56:40
Tenterfield 2 1 29s03 152E01-10:08:04
Tent Hill 4 4 27s36 152E14-10:08:56
Tepko 5 9 34s58 139E11 -9:16:44
Teralba 2 1 32s58 151E37-10:06:28
Terang 7 2 38s14 142E55 -9:31:40
Terrey Hills 2 1 33s41 151E14-10:04:56
Terrigal 2 1 33s27 151E27-10:05:48
Texas 4 4 28s51 151E11-10:04:44
Thallon 4 4 28s38 148E52 -9:55:28
Thangoo 8 5 18s10 122E22 -8:09:28
Thangool 4 4 24s29 150E35-10:02:20
Thargomindah 4 4 28s00 143E49 -9:35:16
Tharwa 1 1 35s31 149E04 -9:56:16
The Basin 7 2 37s51 145E19 -9:41:16
Theebine 4 4 25s57 152E33-10:10:12
The Entrance 2 1 33s21 151E30-10:06:00
The Granites 3 8 20s35 130E21 -8:41:24
The Lynd 4 4 18s56 144E30 -9:38:00
The Oaks 2 1 34s04 150E34-10:02:16
Theodore 4 4 24s57 150E05-10:00:20
Theresa Park 2 1 34s01 150E39-10:02:36
The Rock 2 1 35s16 147E07 -9:48:28
Thevenard 5 9 32s09 133E38 -8:54:32
Thirlmere 2 1 34s12 150E34-10:02:16
Thirroul 2 1 34s19 150E56-10:03:44
Thomastown 7 2 37s41 145E01 -9:40:04
Thornbury 7 2 37s45 145E00 -9:40:00
Thornleigh 2 1 33s44 151E05-10:04:20
Thornton 4 4 27s49 152E23-10:09:32
Thredbo Village 2 1 36s29 148E19 -9:53:16
Three Rivers 8 5 25s07 119E09 -7:56:36
Three Springs 8 5 29s32 115E45 -7:43:00
Thursday Island 4 4 10s35 142E13 -9:28:52
Thylungra 4 4 26s04 143E28 -9:33:52
Tiaro 4 4 25s44 152E35-10:10:20
Tilcha 5 9 29s36 140E54 -9:23:36
Tilpa 2 1 30s57 144E24 -9:37:36
Timboon 7 2 38s29 142E59 -9:31:56
Tinapagee 2 1 29s28 144E23 -9:37:32
Tingha 2 1 29s57 151E13-10:04:52
Tintaldra 7 2 36s03 147E56 -9:51:44
Tintinara 5 9 35s54 140E03 -9:20:12
Tipperary 3 8 13s44 131E02 -8:44:08
Tobermorey 3 8 22s15 138E00 -9:12:00
Tobermory 4 4 27s17 143E41 -9:34:44
Tocumwal 2 1 35s49 145E34 -9:42:16
Todmorden 5 9 27s08 134E48 -8:59:12
Tomerong 2 1 35s04 150E35-10:02:20
Tom Price 8 5 22s41 117E43 -7:50:52
Tongo 2 1 30s30 143E45 -9:35:00
Toobeah 4 4 28s25 149E52 -9:59:28
Toodyay 8 5 31s33 116E28 -7:45:52
Toogoolawah 4 4 27s06 152E23-10:09:32
Tooma 2 1 35s58 148E03 -9:52:12
Toompine 4 4 27s13 144E22 -9:37:28
Toongabbie 2 1 33s47 150E57-10:03:48
Toora 7 2 38s40 146E20 -9:45:20
Toowoomba 4 4 27s33 151E57-10:07:48
Top Springs 3 8 16s38 131E50 -8:47:20
Toronto 2 1 33s01 151E36-10:06:24
Torquay 7 2 38s21 144E19 -9:37:16
Torrens Creek 4 4 20s46 145E02 -9:40:08
Tottenham 2 1 32s14 147E21 -9:49:24
Toukley 2 1 33s16 151E33-10:06:12
Tower Hill 4 4 22s03 144E36 -9:38:24
Townsville 4 4 19s16 146E48 -9:47:12
Towrang 2 1 34s42 149E51 -9:59:24
Trafalgar 7 2 38s12 146E09 -9:44:36
Trangie 2 1 32s02 147E59 -9:51:56
Traralgon 7 2 38s12 146E32 -9:46:08
Trawalla 7 2 37s26 143E29 -9:33:56
Trayning 8 5 31s07 117E48 -7:51:12
Trentham 7 2 37s23 144E19 -9:37:16
Triabunna 6 3 42s30 147E55 -9:51:40
Trida 2 1 33s01 145E01 -9:40:04
Truganina 7 2 37s49 144E43 -9:38:52
Trundle 2 1 32s55 147E43 -9:50:52
Truro 5 9 34s25 139E07 -9:16:28
Tuckanarra 8 5 27s07 118E05 -7:52:20
Tugun 4 4 28s09 153E30-10:14:00
Tullamarine 7 2 37s41 144E52 -9:39:28
Tullamore 2 1 32s38 147E34 -9:50:16
Tullibigeal 2 1 33s25 146E44 -9:46:56
Tully 4 4 17s56 145E56 -9:43:44
Tumbarumba 2 1 35s47 148E01 -9:52:04
Tumblong 2 1 35s09 148E00 -9:52:00
Tumby Bay 5 9 34s22 136E06 -9:04:24
Tumut 2 1 35s18 148E13 -9:52:52
Tungkillo 5 9 34s49 139E04 -9:16:16
Turee Creek 8 5 23s37 118E39 -7:54:36
Turkey Creek 8 5 17s02 128E12 -8:32:48
Turner 8 5 17s50 128E17 -8:33:08
Turramurra 2 1 33s44 151E08-10:04:32
Tweed Heads 4 4 28s10 153E31-10:14:04
Two Wells 5 9 34s36 138E30 -9:14:00
Tyabb 7 2 38s16 145E11 -9:40:44
Ulladulla 2 1 35s21 150E29-10:01:56
Ulmarra 2 1 29s37 153E02-10:12:08
Ulverstone 6 3 41s09 146E10 -9:44:40
Unanderra 2 1 34s27 150E52-10:03:28
Ungarie 2 1 33s38 146E58 -9:47:52
Unley 5 9 34s57 138E35 -9:14:20
Upper Beaconsfield 7 2 38s01 145E25 -9:41:40
Upper Castlereagh 2 1 33s43 150E40-10:02:40
Upper Ferntree Gully 7 2 37s54 145E19 -9:41:16
Upwey 7 2 37s54 145E20 -9:41:20
Uralla 2 1 30s39 151E30-10:06:00
Urana 2 1 35s20 146E16 -9:45:04
Urandangi 4 4 21s36 138E18 -9:13:12
Urangan 4 4 25s18 152E54-10:11:36
Urania 5 9 34s31 137E36 -9:10:24
Uranquinty 2 1 35s12 147E15 -9:49:00
Urarey 8 5 27s26 122E18 -8:09:12
Utopia 3 8 22s14 134E33 -8:58:12
Vanrook 4 4 16s57 141E57 -9:27:48
Vaucluse 2 1 33s51 151E17-10:05:08
Vermont 7 2 37s50 145E12 -9:40:48
Verran 5 9 33s51 136E18 -9:05:12
Victor Harbor 5 9 35s34 138E37 -9:14:28
Victoria Park 8 5 31s58 115E55 -7:43:40
Victoria Point 4 4 27s35 153E18-10:13:12
Victoria River Downs 3 8 16s24 131E00 -8:44:00
Virginia 5 9 34s40 138E34 -9:14:16
Wadderin Hill 8 5 32s00 118E27 -7:53:48
Wagerup 8 5 32s55 115E54 -7:43:36
Wagga Wagga 2 1 35s07 147E22 -9:49:28
Wagin 8 5 33s18 117E21 -7:49:24
Wahroonga 2 1 33s43 151E07-10:04:28
Waikerie 5 9 34s11 139E59 -9:19:56
Waitara 2 1 33s43 151E07-10:04:28
Waitpinga 5 9 35s37 138E29 -9:13:56
Walcha 2 1 30s59 151E36-10:06:24
Walgett 2 1 30s01 148E07 -9:52:28
Walkaway 8 5 28s57 114E48 -7:39:12
Wallacia 2 1 33s52 150E39-10:02:36
Wallal Downs 8 5 19s47 120E40 -8:02:40
Wallangarra 4 4 28s56 151E56-10:07:44
Wallaroo 5 9 33s56 137E38 -9:10:32
Wallaroo Mines 5 9 33s57 137E41 -9:10:44
Wallerawang 2 1 33s25 150E04-10:00:16
Wallgrove 2 1 33s47 150E51-10:03:24
Wallsend 2 1 32s55 151E40-10:06:40
Walpeup 7 2 35s08 142E02 -9:28:08
Walpole 8 5 34s57 116E44 -7:46:56
Walsh 4 4 16s39 143E54 -9:35:36
Walwa 2 1 35s58 147E45 -9:51:00
Wamuran 4 4 27s02 152E52-10:11:28
Wanaaring 2 1 29s42 144E09 -9:36:36
Wanbi 5 9 34s46 140E19 -9:21:16
Wandana 5 9 32s04 133E49 -8:55:16
Wandering 8 5 32s40 116E40 -7:46:40
Wandoan 4 4 26s08 149E57 -9:59:48
Wangaratta 7 2 36s22 146E20 -9:45:20
Wangary 5 9 34s33 135E29 -9:01:56
Wangi Wangi 2 1 33s04 151E35-10:06:20
Wanneroo 8 5 31s45 115E48 -7:43:12
Wantirna 7 2 37s51 145E14 -9:40:56
Wantirna South 7 2 37s52 145E14 -9:40:56
Waratah 6 3 41s27 145E32 -9:42:08
Waratah 2 1 32s54 151E44-10:06:56
Warbreccan 4 4 24s18 142E51 -9:31:24
Warburton 7 2 37s46 145E41 -9:42:44
Warenda 4 4 22s37 140E32 -9:22:08
Warialda 2 1 29s32 150E34-10:02:16
Waroona 8 5 32s50 115E55 -7:43:40
Warra 4 4 26s56 150E55-10:03:40
Warracknabeal 7 2 36s15 142E24 -9:29:36
Warragul 7 2 38s10 145E56 -9:43:44
Warrandyte 7 2 37s45 145E13 -9:40:52
Warrandyte South 7 2 37s46 145E14 -9:40:56
Warrawagine 8 5 20s51 120E42 -8:02:48
Warrawee 2 1 33s44 151E07-10:04:28
Warrawong 2 1 34s29 150E53-10:03:32
Warren 2 1 31s42 147E50 -9:51:20
Warriewood 2 1 33s42 151E18-10:05:12
Warrina 5 9 28s12 135E50 -9:03:20
Warrnambool 7 2 38s23 142E29 -9:29:56
Warwick 4 4 28s13 152E02-10:08:08
Waterloo 3 8 16s38 129E18 -8:37:12
Waterloo 8 5 33s20 115E47 -7:43:08
Waterloo 5 9 33s59 138E53 -9:15:32
Watervale 5 9 33s57 138E38 -9:14:32
Watheroo 8 5 30s17 116E04 -7:44:16
Watson 5 9 30s29 131E31 -8:46:04
Watsonia 7 2 37s43 145E05 -9:40:20
Watsons Bay 2 1 33s51 151E17-10:05:08
Watsons Creek 7 2 37s40 145E13 -9:40:52
Wattle Flat 2 1 33s08 149E41 -9:58:44
Wattle Glen 7 2 37s40 145E11 -9:40:44
Waubra 7 2 37s21 143E39 -9:34:36
Wauchope 3 8 20s36 134E15 -8:57:00
Wauchope 2 1 31s27 152E44-10:10:56
Waukaringa 5 9 32s18 139E26 -9:17:44
Wave Hill 3 8 17s29 130E57 -8:43:48
Waverley 2 1 33s54 151E16-10:05:04
Wedderburn 7 2 36s25 143E37 -9:34:28
Weebo 8 5 28s01 121E03 -8:04:12
Wee Jasper 2 1 35s09 148E41 -9:54:44
Weethalle 2 1 33s53 146E38 -9:46:32
Wee Waa 2 1 30s14 149E26 -9:57:44
Weilmoringle 2 1 29s15 146E51 -9:47:24
Weipa 4 4 12s41 141E52 -9:27:28
Welbourn Hill 5 9 27s21 134E06 -8:56:24
Wellard 8 5 32s19 115E50 -7:43:20
Wellington 2 1 32s33 148E57 -9:55:48
Wellington Point 4 4 27s29 153E15-10:13:00
Welshpool 7 2 38s39 146E26 -9:45:44
Wenlock 4 4 13s06 142E58 -9:31:52
Wentworth 7 2 34s07 141E55 -9:27:40
Wentworth Falls 2 1 33s43 150E22-10:01:28
Wentworthville 2 1 33s48 150E58-10:03:52
Wernadinga 4 4 18s07 139E58 -9:19:52
Werribee 7 2 37s54 144E40 -9:38:40
Werribee South 7 2 37s56 144E42 -9:38:48
Werrimull 7 2 34s24 141E26 -9:25:44
Werrington 2 1 33s45 150E46-10:03:04
Werris Creek 2 1 31s21 150E39-10:02:36
Westbrook 4 4 27s36 151E52-10:07:28
Westby 2 1 35s30 147E25 -9:49:40
Westgate 4 4 26s35 146E12 -9:44:48
West Heidelberg 7 2 37s45 145E02 -9:40:08
West Hoxton 2 1 33s55 150E49-10:03:16
Weston 2 1 32s49 151E28-10:05:52
West Pymble 2 1 33s46 151E08-10:04:32
West Ryde 2 1 33s48 151E05-10:04:20
West Toodyay 8 5 31s33 116E27 -7:45:48
West Torrens 5 9 34s56 138E32 -9:14:08
West Wallsend 2 1 32s54 151E35-10:06:20
West Wyalong 2 1 33s55 147E13 -9:48:52
Wetherill Park 2 1 33s51 150E54-10:03:36
Whalan 2 1 33s45 150E49-10:03:16
Wheelers Hill 7 2 37s55 145E11 -9:40:44
Whim Creek 8 5 20s50 117E50 -7:51:20
White Cliffs 8 5 28s26 122E57 -8:11:48
White Cliffs 2 1 30s51 143E05 -9:32:20
Whitemark 6 3 40s07 148E01 -9:52:04
Whitewood 4 4 21s28 143E36 -9:34:24
Whittlesea 7 2 37s31 145E07 -9:40:28
Whyalla 5 9 33s02 137E35 -9:10:20
Wickepin 8 5 32s46 117E30 -7:50:00
Widgiemooltha 8 5 31s30 121E34 -8:06:16
Wilberforce 2 1 33s33 150E50-10:03:20
Wilcannia 2 2 31s34 143E23 -9:33:32
Wilgena 5 9 30s46 134E44 -8:58:56
Willaston 5 9 34s36 138E45 -9:15:00
Willeroo 3 8 15s17 131E35 -8:46:20
William Creek 5 9 28s55 136E21 -9:05:24
Williams 8 5 33s01 116E52 -7:47:28
Williamsdale 2 1 35s35 149E09 -9:56:36
Williamstown 7 2 37s52 144E54 -9:39:36
Williamstown 5 9 34s40 138E53 -9:15:32
Williamtown 2 1 32s49 151E50-10:07:20
Willoughby 2 1 33s48 151E12-10:04:48
Willowra 3 8 21s15 132E35 -8:50:20
Willunga 5 9 35s17 138E33 -9:14:12
Wilmington 5 9 32s39 138E07 -9:12:28
Wilson 5 9 32s00 138E22 -9:13:28
Wiluna 8 5 26s36 120E13 -8:00:52
Winchelsea 7 2 38s15 143E59 -9:35:56
Windang 2 1 34s32 150E53-10:03:32
Windera 4 4 26s03 151E50-10:07:20
Windorah 4 4 25s26 142E39 -9:30:36
Windsor 2 1 33s37 150E49-10:03:16
Windsor 5 9 34s25 138E20 -9:13:20
Wingello 2 1 34s42 150E09-10:00:36

AUSTRALIE — AUSTRALIEN — AUSTRALIA

Place		Lat	Long	LMT
Wingham 2	1	31s52	152e22	-10:09:28
Winning 8	5	23s09	114e32	-7:38:08
Wintinna 5	9	27s44	134e07	-8:56:28
Winton 4	4	22s23	143e02	-9:32:08
Wirraminna 5	9	31s12	136e15	-9:05:00
Wirrulla 5	9	32s24	134e31	-8:58:04
Wisemans Ferry 2	1	33s24	150e59	-10:03:56
Wittenoom 8	5	22s17	118e19	-7:53:16
Woden 1	1	35s22	149e08	-9:56:32
Wodgina 8	5	21s11	118e40	-7:54:40
Wodonga 7	2	36s07	146e54	-9:47:36
Wokalup 8	5	33s06	115e53	-7:43:32
Wollogorang 3	8	17s13	137e57	-9:11:48
Wollombi 2	1	32s56	151e09	-10:04:36
Wollongong 2	1	34s25	150e54	-10:03:36
Wombarra 2	1	34s16	150e58	-10:03:52
Wonarah 3	8	19s55	136e20	-9:05:20
Wondai 4	4	26s19	151e52	-10:07:28
Wondinong 8	5	27s52	118e25	-7:53:40
Wongan Hills 8	5	30s53	116e42	-7:46:48
Wonga Park 7	2	37s44	145e16	-9:41:04
Wonthaggi 7	2	38s36	145e35	-9:42:20
Woocalla 5	9	31s42	137e13	-9:08:52
Woodchester 5	9	35s13	138e57	-9:15:48
Woodenbong 2	1	28s23	152e37	-10:10:28
Woodend 7	2	37s22	144e32	-9:38:08
Woodford 4	4	26s57	152e47	-10:11:08
Woodridge 4	4	27s38	153e06	-10:12:24
Woods 5	9	34s15	138e31	-9:14:04
Woodside 7	2	38s31	146e52	-9:47:28
Woodside 5	9	34s57	138e52	-9:15:28
Woods Point 7	2	37s35	146e15	-9:45:00
Woodstock 4	4	22s15	141e57	-9:27:48
Woodville 5	9	34s53	138e32	-9:14:08
Wool Bay 5	9	35s00	137e45	-9:11:00
Woolgangie 8	5	31s10	120e32	-8:02:08
Woolgoolga 2	1	30s07	153e12	-10:12:48
Woollahra 2	1	33s53	151e15	-10:05:00
Woomargama 2	1	35s50	147e15	-9:49:00
Woomera 5	9	31s31	137e10	-9:08:40
Woonona 2	1	34s21	150e55	-10:03:40
Woorabinda 4	4	24s08	149e28	-9:57:52
Wooramel 8	5	25s44	114e17	-7:37:08
Woorim 4	4	27s08	153e12	-10:12:48
Wooroloo 8	5	31s48	116e19	-7:45:16
Woronora 2	1	34s01	151e03	-10:04:12
Wowan 4	4	23s55	150e12	-10:00:48
Woy Woy 2	1	33s30	151e20	-10:05:20
Wubin 8	5	30s06	116e38	-7:46:32
Wudinna 5	9	33s03	135e28	-9:01:52
Wundowie 8	5	31s46	116e22	-7:45:28
Wuraming 8	5	32s48	116e16	-7:45:04
Wurarga 8	5	28s25	116e17	-7:45:08
Wyalkatchem 8	5	31s10	117e22	-7:49:28
Wyandra 4	4	27s15	145e59	-9:43:56
Wycheproof 7	2	36s05	143e14	-9:32:56
Wydgee 8	5	28s51	117e49	-7:51:16
Wyee 2	1	33s11	151e29	-10:05:56
Wymah 7	2	36s02	147e17	-9:49:08
Wynbring 5	9	30s33	133e32	-8:54:08
Wyndham 8	5	15s28	128e06	-8:32:24
Wynnum 4	4	27s27	153e10	-10:12:40
Wynyard 6	3	40s59	145e41	-9:42:44
Wyong 2	1	33s17	151e25	-10:05:40
Wyreema 4	4	27s39	151e52	-10:07:28
Yaapeet 7	2	35s46	142e03	-9:28:12
Yagoona 2	1	33s55	151e02	-10:04:08
Yalata 5	9	31s29	131e52	-8:47:28
Yalgoo 8	5	28s20	116e41	-7:46:44
Yalleroi 4	4	24s04	145e45	-9:43:00
Yallourn 7	2	38s11	146e21	-9:45:24
Yallourn North 7	2	38s09	146e22	-9:45:28
Yamba 2	1	29s26	153e22	-10:13:28
Yampi Sound 8	5	15s15	123e30	-8:14:00
Yanac 7	2	36s08	141e26	-9:25:44
Yanchep 8	5	31s33	115e41	-7:42:44
Yanco 2	1	34s36	146e25	-9:45:40
Yandal 8	5	27s33	121e07	-8:04:28
Yangan 4	4	28s12	152e13	-10:08:52
Yankalilla 5	9	35s28	138e21	-9:13:24
Yanna 4	4	26s56	146e03	-9:44:12
Yanrey 8	5	22s31	114e48	-7:39:12
Yantabulla 2	1	29s21	145e00	-9:40:00
Yaraka 4	4	24s53	144e04	-9:36:16
Yardea 5	9	32s23	135e32	-9:02:08
Yarlarweelor 8	5	25s35	117e59	-7:51:56
Yarloop 8	5	32s57	115e54	-7:43:36
Yarra Glen 7	2	37s40	145e23	-9:41:32
Yarragon 7	2	38s12	146e04	-9:44:16
Yarraloola 8	5	21s34	115e52	-7:43:28
Yarram 7	2	38s33	146e41	-9:46:44
Yarraman 4	4	26s50	151e59	-10:07:56
Yarrangobilly 2	1	35s39	148e28	-9:53:52
Yarraville 7	2	37s49	144e53	-9:39:32
Yarrawonga 7	2	36s01	146e00	-9:44:00
Yass 2	1	34s50	148e55	-9:55:40
Yea 7	2	37s13	145e26	-9:41:44
Yeeda 8	5	17s36	123e39	-8:14:36
Yeelanna 5	9	34s09	135e45	-9:03:00
Yeelirrie 8	5	27s17	120e06	-8:00:24
Yelarbon 4	4	28s34	150e45	-10:03:00
Yellowdine 8	5	31s18	119e39	-7:58:36
Yelma 8	5	26s30	121e40	-8:06:40
Yelvertoft 4	4	20s13	138e53	-9:15:32
Yenda 2	1	34s15	146e11	-9:44:44
Yennora 2	1	33s52	150e58	-10:03:52
Yeoval 2	1	32s45	148e40	-9:54:40
Yeppoon 4	4	23s08	150e45	-10:03:00
Yerilla 8	5	29s28	121e49	-8:07:16
Yering 7	2	37s41	145e23	-9:41:32
Yetholme 2	1	33s27	149e49	-9:59:16
Yetman 2	1	28s54	150e46	-10:03:04
Yilliminning 8	5	32s54	117e22	-7:49:28
Yinkanie 5	9	34s20	140e19	-9:21:16
Yinnietharra 8	5	24s39	116e11	-7:44:44
Yirrkala Mission 3	8	12s14	136e56	-9:07:44
York 8	5	31s53	116e46	-7:47:04
Yorketown 5	9	35s02	137e36	-9:10:24
Youanmi 8	5	28s37	118e49	-7:55:16
Young 2	1	34s19	148e18	-9:53:12
Yoweragabbie 8	5	28s13	117e39	-7:50:36
Yuendumu 3	8	22s16	131e49	-8:47:16
Yuin 8	5	27s58	116e02	-7:44:08
Yuna 8	5	28s20	115e00	-7:40:00
Yundamindra 8	5	29s07	122e02	-8:08:08
Yunderup 8	5	32s35	115e46	-7:43:04
Yunta 5	9	32s35	139e33	-9:18:12
Zanthus 8	5	31s02	123e34	-8:14:16
Zeehan 6	3	41s53	145e20	-9:41:20

ÖSTERREICH — AUTRICHE — AUSTRIA

Time Table
Before 1/04/1893 LMT
Begin Standard 15e00

Date	Time	Offset
1/04/1893	0:00	-1:00
30/04/1916	23:00	-2:00
1/10/1916	1:00	-1:00
16/04/1917	2:00	-2:00
17/09/1917	3:00	-1:00
15/04/1918	2:00	-2:00
16/06/1918	3:00	-1:00
5/04/1920	2:00	-2:00
13/09/1920	3:00	-1:00
1/04/1940	2:00	-2:00
2/11/1942	3:00	-1:00
29/03/1943	2:00	-2:00
4/10/1943	3:00	-1:00
3/04/1944	2:00	-2:00
2/10/1944	3:00	-1:00
2/04/1945	2:00	-2:00
18/11/1945	3:00	-1:00
14/04/1946	2:00	-2:00
7/10/1946	3:00	-1:00
6/04/1947	2:00	-2:00
5/10/1947	3:00	-1:00
18/04/1948	2:00	-2:00
3/10/1948	3:00	-1:00
6/04/1980	2:00	-2:00
27/09/1980	24:00	-1:00
29/03/1981	2:00	-2:00
27/09/1981	3:00	-1:00
28/03/1982	2:00	-2:00
26/09/1982	3:00	-1:00
27/03/1983	2:00	-2:00
25/09/1983	3:00	-1:00
25/03/1984	2:00	-2:00
30/09/1984	3:00	-1:00
31/03/1985	2:00	-2:00
29/09/1985	3:00	-1:00
30/03/1986	2:00	-2:00
28/09/1986	3:00	-1:00
29/03/1987	2:00	-2:00
27/09/1987	3:00	-1:00
27/03/1988	2:00	-2:00
25/09/1988	3:00	-1:00
26/03/1989	2:00	-2:00
24/09/1989	3:00	-1:00
25/03/1990	2:00	-2:00
30/09/1990	3:00	-1:00
31/03/1991	2:00	-2:00
29/09/1991	3:00	-1:00
29/03/1992	2:00	-2:00
27/09/1992	3:00	-1:00
28/03/1993	2:00	-2:00
26/09/1993	3:00	-1:00
27/03/1994	2:00	-2:00
25/09/1994	3:00	-1:00
26/03/1995	2:00	-2:00
24/09/1995	3:00	-1:00
31/03/1996	2:00	-2:00
29/09/1996	3:00	-1:00
30/03/1997	2:00	-2:00
28/09/1997	3:00	-1:00
29/03/1998	2:00	-2:00
27/09/1998	3:00	-1:00
28/03/1999	2:00	-2:00
26/09/1999	3:00	-1:00
26/03/2000	2:00	-2:00
24/09/2000	3:00	-1:00

Place	Lat	Long	LMT
Absam	47n18	11e30	-0:46:00
Absdorf	48n24	15e59	-1:03:56
Abtenau	47n33	13e21	-0:53:24
Ach	48n09	12e50	-0:51:20
Achau	48n05	16e23	-1:05:32
Achenkirch	47n31	11e42	-0:46:48
Aderklaa	48n17	16e32	-1:06:08
Admont	47n34	14e27	-0:57:48
Aflenz Kurort	47n32	15e14	-1:00:56
Afritz	46n43	13e48	-0:55:12
Aich	47n25	13e49	-0:55:16
Aigen im Mühlkreis	48n39	13e58	-0:55:52
Alberschwende	47n27	9e49	-0:39:16
Alland	48n03	16e05	-1:04:20
Allentsteig	48n42	15e20	-1:01:20
Alm	47n24	12e54	-0:51:36
Altenburg	48n38	15e35	-1:02:20
Altenfelden	48n29	13e58	-0:55:52
Altheim	48n15	13e13	-0:52:52
Althofen	46n54	14e27	-0:57:48
Altmünster	47n54	13e45	-0:55:00
Altstätten	47n28	9e30	-0:38:00
Ampflwang	48n05	13e34	-0:54:16
Amstetten	48n07	14e53	-0:59:32
Andorf	48n23	13e35	-0:54:20
Angern	48n22	16e50	-1:07:20
Anif	47n45	13e04	-0:52:16
Annaberg	47n31	13e26	-0:53:44
Annaberg	47n52	15e22	-1:01:28
Ansfelden	47n53	13e55	-0:55:40
Apetlon	47n45	16e50	-1:07:20
Arbesbach	48n29	14e57	-0:59:48
Arnoldstein	46n33	13e43	-0:54:52
Aschach an der Donau	48n22	14e02	-0:56:08
Aspach	48n11	13e18	-0:53:12
Aspang Markt	47n33	16e06	-1:04:24
Attersee	47n55	13e33	-0:54:12
Attnang	48n01	13e43	-0:54:52
Au	47n19	9e59	-0:39:56
Aurolzmünster	48n15	13e27	-0:53:48
Ausserfragant	46n56	13e06	-0:52:24
Axams	47n14	11e18	-0:45:12
Baad	47n19	10e07	-0:40:28
Bach	47n16	10e24	-0:41:36
Bad Aussee	47n36	13e47	-0:55:08
Baden	48n00	16e14	-1:04:56
Bad Fusch	47n12	12e51	-0:51:24
Badgastein	47n07	13e08	-0:52:32
Bad Gleichenberg	46n52	15e54	-1:03:36
Bad Goisern	47n38	13e37	-0:54:28
Bad Hall	48n02	14e13	-0:56:52
Bad Hofgastein	47n10	13e06	-0:52:24
Bad Ischl	47n43	13e37	-0:54:28
Bad Kleinkirchheim	46n49	13e49	-0:55:16
Bad Leonfelden	48n33	14e19	-0:57:16
Bad Sankt Leonhard im Lavanttal	46n58	14e48	-0:59:12
Bad Schallerbach	48n14	13e55	-0:55:40
Bad Tatzmannsdorf	47n20	16e13	-1:04:52
Bad Vöslau	47n57	16e16	-1:05:04
Bad Wimsbach-Neydharting	48n04	13e54	-0:55:36
Berg	46n45	13e09	-0:52:36
Bergheim	47n50	13e02	-0:52:08
Berndorf	47n57	16e08	-1:04:32
Berwang	47n24	10e45	-0:43:00
Bezau	47n23	9e54	-0:39:36
Bichlbach	47n25	10e47	-0:43:08
Biedermannsdorf	48n05	16e21	-1:05:24
Birkfeld	47n21	15e42	-1:02:48
Birnbaum	46n41	12e54	-0:51:36
Bisamberg	48n20	16e22	-1:05:28
Bischofshofen	47n25	13e13	-0:52:52
Bleiberg ob Villach	46n37	13e41	-0:54:44
Bleiburg	46n35	14e48	-0:59:12
Bludenz	47n09	9e49	-0:39:16
Böckstein	47n05	13e07	-0:52:28
Bramberg am Wildkogel	47n16	12e21	-0:49:24
Brand	47n06	9e44	-0:38:56
Brandenberg	47n29	11e53	-0:47:32
Braunau am Inn	48n15	13e02	-0:52:08
Bregenz	47n30	9e46	-0:39:04
Breitsetten	48n12	16e42	-1:06:48
Brenner	47n00	11e30	-0:46:00
Brixen im Thale	47n27	12e15	-0:49:00
Brixlegg	47n25	11e53	-0:47:32
Bruck	47n17	12e49	-0:51:16
Bruck an der Leitha	47n57	16e44	-1:06:56
Bruck an der Mur	47n25	15e16	-1:01:04
Brunn am Gebirge	48n07	16e17	-1:05:08
Burgkirchen	48n12	13e06	-0:52:24
Bürs	47n09	9e48	-0:39:12
Dalaas	47n07	10e00	-0:40:00
Damüls	47n17	9e53	-0:39:32
Dellach	46n40	13e05	-0:52:20
Deutschfeistritz	47n11	15e20	-1:01:20
Deutschlandsberg	46n49	15e13	-1:00:52
Deutsch Wagram	48n18	16e34	-1:06:16
Diersbach	48n25	13e34	-0:54:16
Döbriach	46n47	13e39	-0:54:36
Döllach	46n58	12e54	-0:51:36
Dölsach	46n49	12e51	-0:51:24
Dorf Dienten	47n22	13e00	-0:52:00
Dorfgastein	47n15	13e06	-0:52:24
Dornbirn	47n25	9e44	-0:38:56
Drösing	48n32	16e54	-1:07:36
Dürnkrut	48n28	16e51	-1:07:24
Ebbs	47n38	12e13	-0:48:52
Ebenau	47n47	13e11	-0:52:44
Ebene Reichenau	46n51	13e54	-0:55:36
Ebensee	47n48	13e46	-0:55:04

AUSTRIA AUTRICHE ÖSTERREICH

Ebergassing 48N03 16E31 -1:06:04
Eberndorf 46N35 14E38 -0:58:32
Eberschwang 48N09 13E34 -0:54:16
Eberstein 46N48 14E34 -0:58:16
Eferding 48N18 14E02 -0:56:08
Egg 47N26 9E54 -0:39:36
Eggelsberg 48N05 13E00 -0:52:00
Eggenburg 48N39 15E50 -1:03:20
Ehrenhausen 46N43 15E35 -1:02:20
Ehrwald 47N24 10E55 -0:43:40
Eisenkappel 46N29 14E35 -0:58:20
Eisentadt 47N51 16E32 -1:06:08
Eisgarn 48N54 15E06 -1:00:24
Ellmau 47N31 12E18 -0:49:12
Elmen 47N20 10E32 -0:42:08
Elsbethen 47N45 13E05 -0:52:20
Engelhartszell 48N31 13E44 -0:54:56
Enns 48N13 14E29 -0:57:56
Enzenkirchen 48N23 13E39 -0:54:36
Enzesfeld 47N55 16E10 -1:04:40
Erl 47N41 12E11 -0:48:44
Erlach 47N43 16E13 -1:04:52
Erlsbach 46N55 12E15 -0:49:00
Erpfendorf 47N35 12E28 -0:49:52
Eugendorf 47N52 13E07 -0:52:28
Feichten 47N02 10E44 -0:42:56
Feistritz an der Gail
46N34 13E36 -0:54:24
Feld am See 46N47 13E45 -0:55:00
Feldbach 46N57 15E54 -1:03:36
Feldkirch 47N14 9E36 -0:38:24
Feldkirchen in Kärnten
46N43 14E05 -0:56:20
Ferlach 46N31 14E18 -0:57:12
Ferleiten 47N10 12E49 -0:51:16
Fieberbrunn 47N29 12E33 -0:50:12
Fladnitz 46N59 15E47 -1:03:08
Flandorf 48N21 16E23 -1:05:32
Flirsch 47N09 10E24 -0:41:36
Fohnsdorf 47N13 14E41 -0:58:44
Frankenburg 48N05 13E30 -0:54:00
Frankenmarkt 47N59 13E25 -0:53:40
Freiland 47N58 15E34 -1:02:16
Freinberg 48N34 13E31 -0:54:04
Freistadt 48N31 14E31 -0:58:04
Friedberg 47N27 16E03 -1:04:12
Friedburg 48N01 13E15 -0:53:00
Friesach 46N57 14E24 -0:57:36
Frohnleiten 47N16 15E20 -1:01:20
Fügen 47N21 11E51 -0:47:24
Fulpmes 47N10 11E21 -0:45:24
Fürstenfeld 47N03 16E05 -1:04:20
Fusch 47N13 12E49 -0:51:16
Fuschl am See 47N48 13E18 -0:53:12
Gaaden 48N03 16E12 -1:04:48
Gablitz 48N14 16E09 -1:04:36
Galtür 46N58 10E11 -0:40:44
Gaming 47N56 15E06 -1:00:24
Gänserndorf 48N20 16E43 -1:06:52
Gargellen 46N58 9E56 -0:39:44
Gaspoltshofen 48N08 13E46 -0:55:04
Gastein → Badgastein
47N07 13E08 -0:52:32
Gattendorf 48N01 16E59 -1:07:56
Gaweinstal 48N28 16E35 -1:06:20
Gerasdorf 48N18 16E28 -1:05:52
Gerlos 47N14 12E02 -0:48:08
Glanegg 46N44 14E11 -0:56:44
Gleisdorf 47N06 15E44 -1:02:56
Gloggnitz 47N40 15E57 -1:03:48
Gmünd 46N54 13E32 -0:54:08
Gmünd 48N47 15E00 -1:00:00
Gmunden 47N55 13E48 -0:55:12
Golling an der Salzach
47N36 13E10 -0:52:40
Göpfritz 48N43 15E24 -1:01:36
Gosau 47N34 13E31 -0:54:04
Gössl 47N38 13E54 -0:55:36
Göstling 47N48 14E55 -0:59:40
Götzendorf 48N01 16E35 -1:06:20
Götzis 47N20 9E38 -0:38:32
Gramatneusiedl 48N02 16E29 -1:05:56
Gratkorn 47N08 15E21 -1:01:24
Graz 47N05 15E27 -1:01:48
Greifenburg 46N45 13E11 -0:52:44
Greifenstein 48N21 16E25 -1:05:40
Grein 48N14 14E51 -0:59:24
Gresten 48N00 15E02 -1:00:08
Gries am Brenner 47N03 11E29 -0:45:56
Gries im Sellrain 47N12 11E09 -0:44:36
Grieskirchen 48N14 13E50 -0:55:20
Griffen 46N42 14E44 -0:58:56
Grimmenstein 47N38 16E06 -1:04:24
Gröbming 47N26 13E54 -0:55:36
Grödig 47N44 13E02 -0:52:08
Grossarl 47N14 13E12 -0:52:48
Gross-Enzersdorf 48N12 16E33 -1:06:12
Gross-Gerungs 48N34 14E57 -0:59:48
Grossgmain 47N43 12E55 -0:51:40
Grosskrut 48N38 16E43 -1:06:52
Grossraming 47N53 14E33 -0:58:12
Grosssölk 47N25 13E58 -0:55:52
Grünau im Almtal 47N51 13E57 -0:55:48
Gschnitz 47N03 11E22 -0:45:28
Gugging 48N19 16E15 -1:05:00
Gumpoldskirchen 48N03 16E17 -1:05:08
Gundertshausen 48N05 12E59 -0:51:56
Gunskirchen 48N08 13E57 -0:55:48
Guntersdorf 48N39 16E03 -1:04:12
Guntramsdorf 48N03 16E19 -1:05:16
Gurk 46N52 14E18 -0:57:12
Güssing 47N04 16E20 -1:05:20
Gusswerk 47N45 15E18 -1:01:12
Haag 48N07 14E34 -0:58:16
Haag am Hausruck 48N11 13E38 -0:54:32

Hadersfeld 48N20 16E15 -1:05:00
Hagenbrunn 48N20 16E25 -1:05:40
Haiding 48N13 13E58 -0:55:52
Haiming 47N15 10E53 -0:43:32
Hainburg an der Donau
48N09 16E57 -1:07:48
Hainfeld 48N02 15E46 -1:03:04
Hainzenberg 47N13 11E54 -0:47:36
Hallein 47N41 13E06 -0:52:24
Hallstatt 47N33 13E39 -0:54:36
Hard 47N29 9E41 -0:38:44
Hartberg 47N17 15E59 -1:03:56
Häselgehr 47N19 10E30 -0:42:00
Haugsdorf 48N42 16E05 -1:04:20
Haus 47N25 13E49 -0:55:16
Heidenreichenstein
48N52 15E07 -1:00:28
Heiligenblut 47N02 12E50 -0:51:20
Helfenberg 48N32 14E08 -0:56:32
Hellmonsödt 48N26 14E18 -0:57:12
Hennersdorf 48N07 16E22 -1:05:28
Hermagor 46N37 13E22 -0:53:28
Herzogenburg 48N17 15E42 -1:02:48
Hieflau 47N36 14E44 -0:58:56
Himberg 48N05 16E26 -1:05:44
Hinterbichl 47N01 12E20 -0:49:20
Hinterbrühl 48N05 16E15 -1:05:00
Hinterriss 47N28 11E28 -0:45:52
Hintersdorf 48N18 16E13 -1:04:52
Hintersee 47N42 13E17 -0:53:08
Hinterstoder 47N41 14E09 -0:56:36
Hintertux 47N07 11E41 -0:46:44
Hittisau 47N27 9E57 -0:39:48
Hochburg 48N07 12E52 -0:51:28
Hochfilzen 47N28 12E37 -0:50:28
Hochfinstermünz 46N56 10E29 -0:41:56
Höchst 47N28 9E38 -0:38:32
Hofkirchen an der Trattnac
48N13 13E44 -0:54:56
Höflein an der Donau
48N21 16E17 -1:05:08
Hohenau an der March
48N36 16E55 -1:07:40
Hohenems 47N22 9E41 -0:38:44
Hohentauern 47N26 14E29 -0:57:56
Hohenthurn 46N33 13E40 -0:54:40
Hollabrunn 48N34 16E05 -1:04:20
Hollenstein an der Ybbs
47N48 14E46 -0:59:04
Holzgau 47N16 10E21 -0:41:24
Hopfgarten 47N27 12E10 -0:48:40
Hopfgarten in Defereggen
46N55 12E31 -0:50:04
Horn 48N40 15E40 -1:02:40
Huben 47N03 10E58 -0:43:52
Huben 46N56 12E34 -0:50:16
Hüttau 47N25 13E18 -0:53:12
Hüttschlag 47N10 13E14 -0:52:56
Igls 47N14 11E25 -0:45:40
Imst 47N14 10E44 -0:42:56
Innerbraz 47N09 9E55 -0:39:40
Innerfragant 46N58 13E04 -0:52:16
Innervillgraten 46N48 12E23 -0:49:32
Innsbruck 47N16 11E24 -0:45:36
Irdning 47N33 14E01 -0:56:04
Ischgl 47N01 10E17 -0:41:08
Jenbach 47N24 11E47 -0:47:08
Jennersdorf 46N57 16E08 -1:04:32
Jerzens 47N10 10E45 -0:43:00
Jochberg 47N23 12E24 -0:49:36
Judenau 48N17 16E00 -1:04:00
Judenburg 47N10 14E40 -0:58:40
Julbach 48N40 13E52 -0:55:28
Kaibing 47N12 15E50 -1:03:20
Kaiserhaus 47N32 11E55 -0:47:40
Kaltenleutgeben 48N07 16E12 -1:04:48
Kalwang 47N26 14E46 -0:59:04
Kapellen 47N38 15E37 -1:02:28
Kapellerfeld 48N19 16E30 -1:06:00
Kapelln 48N15 15E45 -1:03:00
Kapfenberg 47N26 15E18 -1:01:12
Kaprun 47N16 12E46 -0:51:04
Karlstift 48N35 14E45 -0:59:00
Karres 47N13 10E47 -0:43:08
Kathal 47N06 14E42 -0:58:48
Kefermarkt 48N26 14E32 -0:58:08
Kellerberg 46N40 13E42 -0:54:48
Kernhof 47N49 15E32 -1:02:08
Kierling 48N19 16E17 -1:05:08
Kilb 48N06 15E24 -1:01:36
Kindberg 47N31 15E27 -1:01:48
Kirchbach in Steiermark
46N54 15E44 -1:02:56
Kirchberg am Wagram
48N26 15E53 -1:03:32
Kirchberg in Tirol
47N27 12E19 -0:49:16
Kirchbichl 47N31 12E05 -0:48:20
Kirchdorf an der Krems
47N56 14E07 -0:56:28
Kirchheim 48N12 13E23 -0:53:32
Kirchschlag in der Buckligen Welt
47N31 16E18 -1:05:12
Kitzbühel 47N27 12E23 -0:49:32
Klagenfurt 46N37 14E18 -0:57:12
Klein Glödnitz 46N51 14E08 -0:56:32
Klopein 46N36 14E35 -0:58:20
Klösterle 47N08 10E05 -0:40:20
Klosterneuburg 48N18 16E20 -1:05:20
Knappenberg 46N56 14E35 -0:58:20
Knittelfeld 47N14 14E50 -0:59:20
Köflach 47N04 15E05 -1:00:20
Kolbnitz 46N52 13E19 -0:53:16
Königsbrunn 48N21 16E25 -1:05:40
Königstetten 48N18 16E09 -1:04:36

Korneuburg 48N21 16E20 -1:05:20
Kössen 47N40 12E24 -0:49:36
Kötschach 46N40 13E00 -0:52:00
Krampen 47N40 15E32 -1:02:08
Kramsach 47N27 11E52 -0:47:28
Krems an der Donau
48N25 15E36 -1:02:24
Kremsbrücke 46N57 13E37 -0:54:28
Kremsmünster 48N03 14E08 -0:56:32
Kreuzen 46N40 13E35 -0:54:20
Krimml 47N13 12E11 -0:48:44
Kritzendorf 48N20 16E18 -1:05:12
Kuchl 47N37 13E09 -0:52:36
Kufstein 47N35 12E10 -0:48:40
Kühnsdorf 46N37 14E37 -0:58:28
Kundl 47N28 11E59 -0:47:56
Laa an der Thaya 48N43 16E23 -1:05:32
Laaben 48N06 15E52 -1:03:28
Laab im Walde 48N09 16E11 -1:04:44
Laakirchen 47N58 13E49 -0:55:16
Lainbach 47N38 14E46 -0:59:04
Lambach 48N05 13E53 -0:55:32
Lambrechten 48N19 13E31 -0:54:04
Lamprechtshausen 47N59 12E57 -0:51:48
Landeck 47N08 10E34 -0:42:16
Landl 47N35 12E02 -0:48:08
Lanersbach 47N09 11E44 -0:46:56
Langau 48N49 15E42 -1:02:48
Längenfeld 47N04 10E58 -0:43:52
Langenlois 48N28 15E40 -1:02:40
Langenzersdorf 48N18 16E22 -1:05:28
Lanzendorf 48N06 16E26 -1:05:44
Lassee 48N13 16E49 -1:07:16
Laterns 47N16 9E43 -0:38:52
Lauffen 47N40 13E37 -0:54:28
Launsdorf 46N46 14E27 -0:57:48
Lauterach 47N29 9E44 -0:38:56
Laxenburg 48N04 16E21 -1:05:24
Lech 47N12 10E09 -0:40:36
Lechleiten 47N16 10E12 -0:40:48
Leibnitz 46N47 15E32 -1:02:08
Leisach 46N48 12E45 -0:51:00
Lembach im Mühlkreis
48N29 13E53 -0:55:32
Lend 47N18 13E04 -0:52:16
Lendorf 46N50 13E26 -0:53:44
Leoben 47N23 15E06 -1:00:24
Leogang 47N26 12E45 -0:51:00
Leonding 48N16 14E15 -0:57:00
Leopoldsdorf 48N06 16E24 -1:05:36
Lermoos 47N24 10E53 -0:43:32
Lessach 47N11 13E49 -0:55:16
Lienz 46N50 12E47 -0:51:08
Liezen 47N35 14E15 -0:57:00
Lilienfeld 48N03 15E36 -1:02:24
Linz 48N18 14E18 -0:57:12
Lofer 47N35 12E41 -0:50:44
Lunz am See 47N51 15E03 -1:00:12
Lustenau 47N26 9E39 -0:38:36
Mallnitz 46N59 13E10 -0:52:40
Malta 46N57 13E30 -0:54:00
Mandling 47N24 13E34 -0:54:16
Mank 48N06 15E20 -1:01:20
Mannersdorf am Leithagebirge
47N58 16E36 -1:06:24
Mannersdorf an der Rabnitz
47N25 16E31 -1:06:04
Marchegg 48N17 16E55 -1:07:40
Marchtrenk 48N11 14E07 -0:56:28
Maria Enzersdorf 48N06 16E17 -1:05:08
Maria Gail 46N36 13E52 -0:55:28
Maria Lanzendorf 48N06 16E25 -1:05:40
Maria Luggau 46N42 12E45 -0:51:00
Mariazell 47N47 15E19 -1:01:16
Martinsberg 48N22 15E09 -1:00:36
Matrei am Brenner 47N08 11E27 -0:45:48
Matrei in Osttirol
47N00 12E32 -0:50:08
Mattersburg 47N44 16E25 -1:05:40
Mattighofen 48N06 13E09 -0:52:36
Mattsee 47N58 13E06 -0:52:24
Mauerbach 48N15 16E10 -1:04:40
Mauerkirchen 48N11 13E08 -0:52:32
Mautern 47N24 14E50 -0:59:20
Mauterndorf 47N08 13E40 -0:54:40
Mauthausen 48N14 14E32 -0:58:08
Mauthen 46N40 13E00 -0:52:00
Mayerling 48N03 16E06 -1:04:24
Mayrhofen 47N10 11E52 -0:47:28
Melk 48N14 15E20 -1:01:20
Mellau 47N21 9E53 -0:39:32
Metnitz 46N59 14E13 -0:56:52
Mettmach 48N10 13E21 -0:53:24
Micheldorf 47N52 14E08 -0:56:32
Milders 47N06 11E16 -0:45:04
Millstatt 46N48 13E35 -0:54:20
Mistelbach an de Zaya
48N34 16E35 -1:06:20
Mittelberg 47N20 10E10 -0:40:40
Mitterding 48N22 13E24 -0:53:36
Mitterndorf 47N33 13E55 -0:55:40
Mittersill 47N16 12E29 -0:49:56
Mittewald an der Drau
46N46 12E36 -0:50:24
Möderbrugg 47N17 14E29 -0:57:56
Mödling 48N05 16E17 -1:05:08
Möllbrücke 46N50 13E22 -0:53:28
Möllersdorf 48N02 16E18 -1:05:12
Molln 47N53 14E15 -0:57:00
Mönchdorf 48N21 14E48 -0:59:12
Mönchhof 47N52 16E56 -1:07:44
Mondsee 47N52 13E21 -0:53:24
Mönichkirchen 47N31 16E02 -1:04:08
Moosbrunn 48N01 16E28 -1:05:52
Mörbisch 47N45 16E40 -1:06:40

Place	Lat.	Long.	Time
Mörtschach	46N55	12E55	-0:51:40
Muckendorf an der Donau	48N20	16E09	-1:04:36
Mühlbach am Hochkönig	47N22	13E08	-0:52:32
Mühldorf	48N22	15E21	-1:01:24
Mühlleiten	48N10	16E34	-1:06:16
Münchendorf	48N02	16E23	-1:05:32
Munderfing	48N05	13E11	-0:52:44
Münzkirchen	48N29	13E34	-0:54:16
Murau	47N07	14E01	-0:56:04
Mureck	46N42	15E46	-1:03:04
Mürzsteg	47N40	15E29	-1:01:56
Mürzzuschlag	47N36	15E41	-1:02:44
Musau	47N32	10E40	-0:42:40
Mutters	47N14	11E23	-0:45:32
Namlos	47N21	10E40	-0:42:40
Nassereith	47N19	10E50	-0:43:20
Natters	47N14	11E22	-0:45:28
Nauders	46N53	10E30	-0:42:00
Navis	47N07	11E32	-0:46:08
Nenzing	47N11	9E42	-0:38:48
Nesselwängle	47N29	10E37	-0:42:28
Neufelden	48N29	14E00	-0:56:00
Neuhaus	47N47	15E11	-1:00:44
Neukirchen	47N52	13E42	-0:54:48
Neukirchen	47N15	12E17	-0:49:08
Neukirchen am Walde	48N24	13E46	-0:55:04
Neumarkt am Wallersee	47N57	13E14	-0:52:56
Neumarkt im Hansruckkreis	48N16	13E45	-0:55:00
Neumarkt in Steiermark	47N04	14E25	-0:57:40
Neunkirchen	47N43	16E05	-1:04:20
Neureisenberg	48N01	16E30	-1:06:00
Neusiedl am See	47N57	16E51	-1:07:24
Neustift im Stubaital	47N07	11E19	-0:45:16
Niedersulz	48N29	16E40	-1:06:40
Nikolsdorf	46N47	12E55	-0:51:40
Nofels	47N15	9E34	-0:38:16
Nussdorf am Attersee	47N53	13E31	-0:54:04
Oberaurach	47N24	12E26	-0:49:44
Oberdrauburg	46N45	12E58	-0:51:52
Obergurgl	46N52	11E01	-0:44:04
Ober-Kirchbach	48N17	16E12	-1:04:48
Obermieming	47N18	10E59	-0:43:56
Obermühl	48N27	13E55	-0:55:40
Obernberg am Inn	48N19	13E20	-0:53:20
Oberndorf bei Salzburg	47N57	12E56	-0:51:44
Oberndorf in Tirol	47N30	12E23	-0:49:32
Oberpettnau	47N18	11E08	-0:44:32
Oberpullendorf	47N31	16E31	-1:06:04
Obertilliach	46N42	12E37	-0:50:28
Obertraun	47N33	13E41	-0:54:44
Obertrum	47N56	13E05	-0:52:20
Obervellach	46N56	13E12	-0:52:48
Oberwart	47N17	16E13	-1:04:52
Oberwölz Stadt	47N13	14E17	-0:57:08
Oberzeiring	47N15	14E29	-0:57:56
öblarn	47N27	13E59	-0:55:56
Obsteig	47N18	10E56	-0:43:44
Oepping	48N36	13E56	-0:55:44
Oetz	47N12	10E54	-0:43:36
Ohlsdorf	47N57	13E47	-0:55:08
Oppenberg	47N29	14E16	-0:57:04
Ottenschlag	48N25	15E13	-1:00:52
Ottnang	48N06	13E40	-0:54:40
Pack	46N58	14E59	-0:59:56
Palfau	47N42	14E48	-0:59:12
Parndorf	47N59	16E51	-1:07:24
Partenen	46N58	10E03	-0:40:12
Patergassen	46N49	13E52	-0:55:28
Paternion	46N43	13E38	-0:54:32
Peilstein im Mühlviertel	48N37	13E53	-0:55:32
Pellendorf	48N06	16E27	-1:05:48
Perchau	47N06	14E27	-0:57:48
Perchtoldsdorf	48N07	16E17	-1:05:08
Perg	48N15	14E37	-0:58:28
Pernitz	47N54	15E58	-1:03:52
Pertisau	47N26	11E42	-0:46:48
Pettenbach	47N57	14E01	-0:56:04
Pettneu am Arlberg	47N09	10E20	-0:41:20
Peuerbach	48N21	13E56	-0:55:44
Pfaffstätten	48N01	16E16	-1:05:04
Pfunds	46N58	10E33	-0:42:12
Pians	47N08	10E30	-0:42:00
Piberegg	47N05	15E05	-1:00:20
Pichl bei Wels	48N11	13E54	-0:55:36
Piesendorf	47N17	12E43	-0:50:52
Pinkafeld	47N22	16E07	-1:04:28
Plangeross	46N59	10E52	-0:43:28
Pöchlarn	48N12	15E13	-1:00:52
Podersdorf am See	47N51	16E50	-1:07:20
Pöllau	47N18	15E51	-1:03:24
Pörtschach	46N37	14E08	-0:56:32
Poysdorf	48N40	16E38	-1:06:32
Prägraten	47N01	12E23	-0:49:32
Pram	48N14	13E37	-0:54:28
Prambachkirchen	48N19	13E55	-0:55:40
Predlitz	47N04	13E55	-0:55:40
Pregarten	48N12	14E32	-0:58:08
Pressbaum	48N11	16E05	-1:04:20
Pruggern	47N25	13E52	-0:55:28
Prutz	47N05	10E40	-0:42:40
Puchberg am Schneeberg	47N47	15E54	-1:03:36
Pulkau	48N42	15E51	-1:03:24
Purgg	47N32	14E04	-0:56:16
Purgstall	48N03	15E08	-1:00:32
Purkersdorf	48N12	16E11	-1:04:44
Raab	48N21	13E39	-0:54:36
Raabs an der Thaya	48N51	15E30	-1:02:00
Raasdorf	48N15	16E34	-1:06:16
Radenthein	46N48	13E43	-0:54:52
Radkersburg	46N41	15E59	-1:03:56
Radstadt	47N23	13E27	-0:53:48
Ragnitz	46N50	15E35	-1:02:20
Raiding	47N34	16E32	-1:06:08
Rainbach im Innkreis	48N27	13E32	-0:54:08
Ramingstein	47N04	13E50	-0:55:20
Ranalt	47N02	11E13	-0:44:52
Rangersdorf	46N51	12E58	-0:51:52
Rankweil	47N17	9E39	-0:38:36
Rannersdorf	48N08	16E28	-1:05:52
Ranten	47N09	14E05	-0:56:20
Rattenberg	47N26	11E54	-0:47:36
Rauchenwarth	48N05	16E32	-1:06:08
Rauris	47N13	13E00	-0:52:00
Regau	47N59	13E41	-0:54:44
Reichenau	47N42	15E50	-1:03:20
Reichraming	47N53	14E27	-0:57:48
Reisach	46N39	13E09	-0:52:36
Reith bei Seefeld	47N18	11E12	-0:44:48
Rennweg	47N01	13E37	-0:54:28
Retz	48N45	15E57	-1:03:48
Reutte	47N29	10E43	-0:42:52
Riedau	48N18	13E38	-0:54:32
Ried im Innkreis	48N13	13E30	-0:54:00
Ried im Oberinntal	47N03	10E39	-0:42:36
Riegersdorf	46N33	13E47	-0:55:08
Riezlern	47N21	10E11	-0:40:44
Rohrbach in Oberösterreich	48N34	13E59	-0:55:56
Rottenmann	47N31	14E22	-0:57:28
Rust	47N48	16E41	-1:06:44
Saalbach	47N23	12E38	-0:50:32
Saalfelden	47N25	12E51	-0:51:24
Sachsenburg	46N50	13E21	-0:53:24
Salzburg	47N48	13E02	-0:52:08
Sandl	48N33	14E38	-0:58:32
Sankt Aegyd am Neuwalde	47N52	15E35	-1:02:20
Sankt Andrä	46N46	14E49	-0:59:16
Sankt Andrä vor dem Hagenthale	48N19	16E13	-1:04:52
Sankt Anton am Arlberg	47N08	10E16	-0:41:04
Sankt Gallen	47N41	14E37	-0:58:28
Sankt Gallenkirch	47N01	9E59	-0:39:56
Sankt Georgen	46N43	14E55	-0:59:40
Sankt Georgen im Attergau	47N56	13E29	-0:53:56
Sankt Gilgen	47N46	13E22	-0:53:28
Sankt Jakob im Lesachtal	46N41	12E56	-0:51:44
Sankt Jakob in Defereggen	46N55	12E20	-0:49:20
Sankt Johann am Tauern	47N22	14E29	-0:57:56
Sankt Johann im Pongau	47N21	13E12	-0:52:48
Sankt Johann im Walde	46N54	12E37	-0:50:28
Sankt Johann in Tirol	47N31	12E26	-0:49:44
Sankt Leonhard im Pitztal	47N04	10E51	-0:43:24
Sankt Lorenzen im Lesachtal	46N42	12E47	-0:51:08
Sankt Martin	47N28	13E23	-0:53:32
Sankt Michael im Lungau	47N06	13E38	-0:54:32
Sankt Paul im Lavanttal	46N42	14E52	-0:59:28
Sankt Pölten	48N12	15E37	-1:02:28
Sankt Stefan an der Gail	46N37	13E31	-0:54:04
Sankt Valentin	48N10	14E32	-0:58:08
Sankt Veit an der Glan	46N46	14E21	-0:57:24
Sankt Veit im Pongau	47N20	13E09	-0:52:36
Sankt Wolfgang im Salzkammergut	47N44	13E27	-0:53:48
Sattledt	48N04	14E03	-0:56:12
Schalchen	48N07	13E10	-0:52:40
Schardenberg	48N32	13E30	-0:54:00
Schärding	48N27	13E26	-0:53:44
Scharfling	47N48	13E25	-0:53:40
Scharnitz	47N23	11E17	-0:45:08
Scheffau an der Lammer	47N35	13E12	-0:52:48
Scheibbs	48N00	15E10	-1:00:40
Scheiblingstein	48N16	16E13	-1:04:52
Scheifling	47N09	14E24	-0:57:36
Schladming	47N23	13E41	-0:54:44
Schneegattern	48N01	13E18	-0:53:12
Schönberg	48N43	13E52	-0:55:28
Schönberg im Stubaital	47N11	11E25	-0:45:40
Schönwies	47N11	10E39	-0:42:36
Schörfling	47N56	13E36	-0:54:24
Schrems	48N47	15E04	-1:00:16
Schrick	48N30	16E37	-1:06:28
Schröcken	47N15	10E05	-0:40:20
Schruns	47N04	9E55	-0:39:40
Schwadorf	48N04	16E35	-1:06:20
Schwanenstadt	48N03	13E46	-0:55:04
Schwarzach	47N27	9E45	-0:39:00
Schwarzach im Pongau	47N19	13E09	-0:52:36
Schwaz	47N20	11E42	-0:46:48
Schwechat	48N08	16E29	-1:05:56
Schwerting	48N01	12E57	-0:51:48
Seckau	47N16	14E47	-0:59:08
See	47N05	10E28	-0:41:52
See	47N48	13E27	-0:53:48
Seeboden	46N49	13E30	-0:54:00
Seefeld in Tirol	47N20	11E11	-0:44:44
Seehaus	47N45	13E57	-0:55:48
Seekirchen Markt	47N54	13E08	-0:52:32
Seetal	47N09	13E57	-0:55:48
Seewalchen am Attersee	47N57	13E35	-0:54:20
Seewiesen	47N37	15E16	-1:01:04
Seitenstetten	48N02	14E39	-0:58:36
Seiz	47N23	14E55	-0:59:40
Semmering	47N38	15E49	-1:03:16
Serfaus	47N02	10E36	-0:42:24
Seyring	48N20	16E29	-1:05:56
Siegenfeld	48N02	16E10	-1:04:40
Siezenheim	47N48	12E59	-0:51:56
Silbertal	47N05	9E59	-0:39:56
Sillian	46N45	12E25	-0:49:40
Sittendorf	48N05	16E10	-1:04:40
Solbad Hall in Tirol	47N17	11E31	-0:46:04
Sölden	46N58	11E00	-0:44:00
Söll	47N30	12E11	-0:48:44
Sollenau	47N53	16E15	-1:05:00
Sonntagberg	47N59	14E45	-0:59:00
Spannberg	48N27	16E44	-1:06:56
Sparbach	48N04	16E11	-1:04:44
Spital am Pyhrn	47N39	14E20	-0:57:20
Spittal an der Drau	46N48	13E30	-0:54:00
Spitz	48N22	15E25	-1:01:40
Staatz	48N40	16E29	-1:05:56
Stadl an der Mur	47N05	13E58	-0:55:52
Stadl-Paura	48N05	13E53	-0:55:32
Stadt Haag	48N07	14E34	-0:58:16
Stainz	46N54	15E16	-1:01:04
Stams	47N16	10E59	-0:43:56
Stanz	47N28	15E30	-1:02:00
Stanzach	47N23	10E34	-0:42:16
Steeg	47N14	10E17	-0:41:08
Stegersbach	47N10	16E10	-1:04:40
Steinach	47N05	11E28	-0:45:52
Steinfeld	46N45	13E15	-0:53:00
Steyr	48N03	14E25	-0:57:40
Stockerau	48N23	16E13	-1:04:52
Strass bei Jenbach	47N23	11E49	-0:47:16
Strasswalchen	47N59	13E15	-0:53:00
Strengen	47N08	10E27	-0:41:48
Strobl	47N43	13E29	-0:53:56
Stumm	47N17	11E53	-0:47:32
Suben	48N25	13E26	-0:53:44
Tamsweg	47N08	13E48	-0:55:12
Tannheim	47N30	10E31	-0:42:04
Tauplitz	47N33	14E00	-0:56:00
Taxenbach	47N17	12E58	-0:51:52
Techendorf	46N43	13E17	-0:53:08
Telfes	47N10	11E22	-0:45:28
Telfes	47N18	11E04	-0:44:16
Ternberg	47N58	14E22	-0:57:28
Ternitz	47N44	16E03	-1:04:12
Teufenbach	47N08	14E21	-0:57:24
Thal-Assling	46N47	12E38	-0:50:32
Thalgau	47N50	13E15	-0:53:00
Thörl	47N31	15E13	-1:00:52
Thüringen	47N12	9E45	-0:39:00
Timelkam	48N00	13E36	-0:54:24
Tösens	47N01	10E36	-0:42:24
Traiskirchen	48N01	16E18	-1:05:12
Traismauer	48N21	15E44	-1:02:56
Traun	48N13	14E14	-0:56:56
Traunkirchen	47N50	13E47	-0:55:08
Treffen	46N40	13E52	-0:55:28
Tribuswinkel	48N00	16E16	-1:05:04
Trieben	47N29	14E30	-0:58:00
Trins	47N05	11E25	-0:45:40
Trofaich	47N25	15E00	-1:00:00
Tschagguns	47N05	9E54	-0:39:36
Tulbing	48N16	16E09	-1:04:36
Tulln	48N20	16E03	-1:04:12
Turnau	47N33	15E20	-1:01:20
Türnitz	47N57	15E30	-1:02:00
Turrach	46N57	13E52	-0:55:28
Tweng	47N11	13E36	-0:54:24
Twinberg	46N55	14E50	-0:59:20
Überackern	48N11	12E52	-0:51:28
Ulrichberg	48N41	13E54	-0:55:36
Umhausen	47N08	10E56	-0:43:44
Unken	47N39	12E43	-0:50:52
Unterkirchen	47N25	11E12	-0:44:48
Untermauerbach	48N14	16E12	-1:04:48
Untertauern	47N18	13E30	-0:54:00
Unterzeiring	47N15	14E31	-0:58:04
Uttendorf	47N17	12E34	-0:50:16
Uttendorf	48N09	13E07	-0:52:28
Veitsch	47N35	15E30	-1:02:00
Velden	46N37	14E03	-0:56:12
Velm	48N03	16E27	-1:05:48
Vent	46N52	10E56	-0:43:44
Viechtwang	47N55	13E57	-0:55:48
Vienna → Wien	48N13	16E20	-1:05:20
Vienne → Wien	48N13	16E20	-1:05:20
Viktring	46N35	14E16	-0:57:04
Villach	46N36	13E50	-0:55:20
Vils	47N33	10E38	-0:42:32
Virgen	47N00	12E27	-0:49:48
Vitis	48N45	15E10	-1:00:40
Vöcklabruck	48N01	13E39	-0:54:36

AUSTRIA — AUTRICHE — ÖSTERREICH

Place	Lat.	Long.	Time
Vöcklamarkt	48N00	13E29	-0:53:56
Voitsberg	47N03	15E10	-1:00:40
Volders	47N17	11E34	-0:46:16
Völkermarkt	46N39	14E38	-0:58:32
Vomp	47N20	11E41	-0:46:44
Vorau	47N25	15E54	-1:03:36
Vorchdorf	48N00	13E55	-0:55:40
Vordernberg	47N28	15E00	-1:00:00
Vösendorf	48N07	16E20	-1:05:20
Wagrain	47N20	13E18	-0:53:12
Wagram → Deutsch Wagram	48N18	16E34	-1:06:16
Waidhofen an der Thaya	48N49	15E18	-1:01:12
Waidhofen an der Ybbs	47N58	14E47	-0:59:08
Waidring	47N35	12E34	-0:50:16
Waizenkirchen	48N20	13E52	-0:55:28
Walchsee	47N39	12E19	-0:49:16
Wald	47N27	14E40	-0:58:40
Wald im Pinzgau	47N15	12E14	-0:48:56
Waldkirchen am Wesen	48N26	13E49	-0:55:16
Wallern	47N43	16E56	-1:07:44
Warth	47N15	10E11	-0:40:44
Wattens	47N17	11E36	-0:46:24
Weichselboden	47N40	15E10	-1:00:40
Weiden am See	47N55	16E52	-1:07:28
Weidling	48N17	16E19	-1:05:16
Weidlingbach	48N16	16E15	-1:05:00
Weissbach bei Lofer	47N31	12E45	-0:51:00
Weissbriach	46N41	13E15	-0:53:00
Weissenbach	48N05	16E13	-1:04:52
Weissenbach am Attersee	47N48	13E32	-0:54:08
Weissenbach am Lech	47N26	10E39	-0:42:36
Weissenstein	46N41	13E44	-0:54:56
Weitensfeld	46N51	14E11	-0:56:44
Weitra	48N42	14E54	-0:59:36
Weiz	47N13	15E37	-1:02:28
Wels	48N10	14E02	-0:56:08
Wenns	47N10	10E44	-0:42:56
Weppersdorf	47N35	16E26	-1:05:44
Werfen	47N28	13E11	-0:52:44
Wernberg	46N37	13E56	-0:55:44
Wernstein	48N30	13E28	-0:53:52
Wesenufer	48N27	13E49	-0:55:16
Westendorf	47N26	12E13	-0:48:52
Wien (Vienna)	48N13	16E20	-1:05:20
Wienerherberg	48N03	16E33	-1:06:12
Wiener Neudorf	48N05	16E19	-1:05:16
Wiener Neustadt	47N49	16E15	-1:05:00
Wies	46N43	15E16	-1:01:04
Wieselburg	48N08	15E09	-1:00:36
Wieting	46N52	14E32	-0:58:08
Wildalpen	47N39	14E59	-0:59:56
Wildon	46N53	15E31	-1:02:04
Wilfersdorf	48N35	16E38	-1:06:32
Wilhelmsburg	48N06	15E36	-1:02:24
Wimsbach	48N04	13E54	-0:55:36
Windischgarsten	47N44	14E20	-0:57:20
Windorf	48N27	14E02	-0:56:08
Winklern	46N52	12E52	-0:51:28
Wolfpassing	48N19	16E11	-1:04:44
Wolfsberg	46N51	14E51	-0:59:24
Wolfsegg am Hausruck	48N06	13E40	-0:54:40
Wolfurt	47N28	9E45	-0:39:00
Wolkersdorf	48N23	16E31	-1:06:04
Wördern	48N20	16E13	-1:04:52
Wörgl	47N29	12E04	-0:48:16
Würnsdorf	48N18	15E10	-1:00:40
Ybbs an der Donau	48N11	15E05	-1:00:20
Ybbsitz	47N56	14E53	-0:59:32
Zams	47N09	10E35	-0:42:20
Zederhaus	47N09	13E30	-0:54:00
Zeiselmauer	48N20	16E11	-1:04:44
Zell am Moos	47N54	13E19	-0:53:16
Zell am See	47N19	12E47	-0:51:08
Zell am Ziller	47N14	11E53	-0:47:32
Zeltweg	47N11	14E45	-0:59:00
Ziersdorf	48N31	15E55	-1:03:40
Zin	47N17	11E14	-0:44:56
Zinkenbach	47N44	13E25	-0:53:40
Zirl	47N17	11E14	-0:44:56
Zürs	47N10	10E10	-0:40:40
Zwettl	48N37	15E10	-1:00:40
Zwieselstein	46N56	11E02	-0:44:08
Zwölfaxing	48N06	16E28	-1:05:52

BAHAMAS — BAHAMA-INSELN — BAHAMA

Time Table
Before 2/03/1912 LMT
Begin Standard 75W00

Date	Time	Offset
2/03/1912	0:00	5:00
26/04/1964	2:00	4:00
25/10/1964	2:00	5:00
25/04/1965	2:00	4:00
31/10/1965	2:00	5:00
24/04/1966	2:00	4:00
30/10/1966	2:00	5:00
30/04/1967	2:00	4:00
29/10/1967	2:00	5:00
28/04/1968	2:00	4:00
27/10/1968	2:00	5:00
27/04/1969	2:00	4:00
26/10/1969	2:00	5:00
26/04/1970	2:00	4:00
25/10/1970	2:00	5:00
25/04/1971	2:00	4:00
31/10/1971	2:00	5:00
30/04/1972	2:00	4:00
29/10/1972	2:00	5:00
29/04/1973	2:00	4:00
28/10/1973	2:00	5:00
28/04/1974	2:00	4:00
27/10/1974	2:00	5:00
27/04/1975	2:00	4:00
26/10/1975	2:00	5:00
25/04/1976	2:00	4:00
31/10/1976	2:00	5:00
24/04/1977	2:00	4:00
30/10/1977	2:00	5:00
30/04/1978	2:00	4:00
29/10/1978	2:00	5:00
29/04/1979	2:00	4:00
28/10/1979	2:00	5:00
27/04/1980	2:00	4:00
26/10/1980	2:00	5:00
26/04/1981	2:00	4:00
25/10/1981	2:00	5:00
25/04/1982	2:00	4:00
31/10/1982	2:00	5:00
24/04/1983	2:00	4:00
30/10/1983	2:00	5:00
29/04/1984	2:00	4:00
28/10/1984	2:00	5:00
28/04/1985	2:00	4:00
27/10/1985	2:00	5:00
27/04/1986	2:00	4:00
26/10/1986	2:00	5:00
5/04/1987	2:00	4:00
25/10/1987	2:00	5:00
3/04/1988	2:00	4:00
30/10/1988	2:00	5:00
2/04/1989	2:00	4:00
29/10/1989	2:00	5:00
1/04/1990	2:00	4:00
28/10/1990	2:00	5:00
7/04/1991	2:00	4:00
27/10/1991	2:00	5:00
5/04/1992	2:00	4:00
25/10/1992	2:00	5:00
4/04/1993	2:00	4:00
31/10/1993	2:00	5:00
3/04/1994	2:00	4:00
30/10/1994	2:00	5:00
2/04/1995	2:00	4:00
29/10/1995	2:00	5:00
7/04/1996	2:00	4:00
27/10/1996	2:00	5:00
6/04/1997	2:00	4:00
26/10/1997	2:00	5:00
5/04/1998	2:00	4:00
25/10/1998	2:00	5:00
4/04/1999	2:00	4:00
31/10/1999	2:00	5:00
2/04/2000	2:00	4:00
29/10/2000	2:00	5:00

Place	Lat.	Long.	Time
Acklins Island	22N26	73W58	4:55:52
Adelaide	25N00	77W31	5:10:04
Albert Town	22N36	74W21	4:57:24
Alice Town	25N44	79W17	5:17:08
Andros Island	24N26	77W57	5:11:48
Andros Town	24N43	77W47	5:11:08
Arthurs Town	24N38	75W42	5:02:48
Bannerman Town	24N38	76W10	5:04:40
Bennets Harbour	24N35	75W38	5:02:32
Berry Islands	25E34	77W45	5:11:00
Bimini Islands	25N44	79W15	5:17:00
Blanket Sound	24N51	77W54	5:11:36
Bullock Harbour	25N47	77W51	5:11:24
Cat Island	24N27	75W30	5:02:00
Cherokee Sound	26N17	77W04	5:08:16
Clarence Town	23N06	74W59	4:59:56
Crooked Island	22N45	74W13	4:56:52
Deadmans Cay	23N14	75W14	5:00:56
Dunmore Town	25N30	76W39	5:06:36
Eleuthera Island	25N10	76W14	5:04:56
Free Town	26N34	78W27	5:13:48
Freeport	26N30	78W45	5:15:00
George Town	23N30	75W46	5:03:04
Governors Harbour	25N10	76W14	5:04:56
Grand Bahama Island	26N38	78W25	5:13:40
Great Abaco Island	26N28	77W05	5:08:20
Great Exuma Island	23N32	75W50	5:03:20
Great Guana Cay	24N00	76W20	5:05:20
Great Inagua Island	21N05	73W18	4:53:12
High Rock	26N36	76W18	5:05:12
Hope Town	26N33	76W57	5:07:48
Kemps Bay	24N02	77W33	5:10:12
Little Inagua Island	21N30	73W00	4:52:00
Long Island	23N15	75W07	5:00:28
Mangrove Cay	24N15	77W39	5:10:36
Marsh Harbour	26N33	77W03	5:08:12
Mastic Point	25N03	77W57	5:11:48
Matthew Town	20N57	73W40	4:54:40
Mayaguana Island	22N23	72W57	4:51:48
Mores Island	26N18	77W33	5:10:12
Nassau	25N05	77W21	5:09:24
Nicolls Town	25N08	78W00	5:12:00
Old Bight	24N15	75W21	5:01:24
Pirate Well	22N26	73W04	4:52:16
Point Nelson	23N38	74W50	4:59:20
Ragged Island	22N12	75W44	5:02:56
Rock Sound	24N54	76W12	5:04:48
Rolleville	23N41	76W00	5:04:00
Samana Cay	23N06	73W42	4:54:48
Sandilands Village	25N02	77W18	5:09:12
Savannah Sound	25N06	76W09	5:04:36
The Bight	24N19	75W24	5:01:36
West End	26N41	78W58	5:15:52

BAHRAIN — BAHREIN — BAHREÏN — TYROS — AL-BAḤRAYN

Time Table
Before 1/01/1920 LMT
Begin Standard 60E00
1/01/1920 0:00 -4:00
Begin Standard 45E00
1/06/1972 0:00 -3:00

Place	Lat.	Long.	Time
Al-Manāmah	26N13	50E35	-3:22:20
Al-Muḥarraq	26N16	50E37	-3:22:28
'Awālī	26N05	50E33	-3:22:12
Manama → Al-Manāmah	26N13	50E35	-3:22:20
Sitrah	26N09	50E38	-3:22:32

Time Table
Before 1/Jan/1890 LMT
Begin Standard 88E20
1/Jan/1890 0:00 -5:53
Begin Standard 97E30
1/Oct/1941 0:00 -6:30
Begin Standard 82E30
15/May/1942 0:00 -5:30
Begin Standard 97E30
1/Sep/1942 0:00 -6:30
Begin Standard 90E00
30/Sep/1951 0:00 -6:00

Abbaynagar	23N01	89E28	-5:57:52
Alamdānga	23N46	88E57	-5:55:48
Alampur	23N49	89E06	-5:56:24
Ālfādānga	23N18	89E42	-5:58:48
Āmādi	22N28	89E19	-5:57:16
Āmjhupi	23N45	88E42	-5:54:48
Āmla	23N54	88E56	-5:55:44
Amtāli	22N08	90E14	-6:00:56
Āngāria	22N29	90E22	-6:01:28
Arāihāzār	23N47	90E40	-6:02:40
Ārāni	24N17	88E52	-5:55:28
Ārpāra	23N23	89E23	-5:57:32
Āsāsuni	22N32	89E10	-5:56:40
Ātgharia	24N06	89E14	-5:56:56
Bādura	22N16	90E21	-6:01:24
Baga	22N26	90E28	-6:01:52
Bāgātipāra	24N18	88E57	-5:55:48
Bāgherhāt	22N40	89E48	-5:59:12
Bāgherpāra	23N14	89E21	-5:57:24
Bāghia	23N27	90E29	-6:01:56
Bāhādurābād Ghāt	25N09	89E42	-5:58:48
Baharpur	23N41	89E34	-5:58:16
Baidya Bāzār	23N39	90E37	-6:02:28
Bāisrasi	23N27	90E02	-6:00:08
Baje Phukura	23N09	89E45	-5:59:00
Bākarganj	22N33	90E21	-6:01:24
Bākhrābād	23N43	90E53	-6:03:32
Baksir Chāndpur	23N30	89E44	-5:58:56
Bāliākāndi	23N38	89E33	-5:58:12
Bāliāti	23N59	90E03	-6:00:12
Bāmna	22N19	90E06	-6:00:24
Banagrām	22N35	89E55	-5:59:40
Bānaripāra	22N47	90E10	-6:00:40
Bānchhārāmpur	23N46	90E48	-6:03:12
Bangeswardi	23N29	89E44	-5:58:56
Bānibaha	23N42	89E37	-5:58:28
Bāniyāchung	24N31	91E22	-6:05:28
Bankhari	23N44	90E03	-6:00:12
Bara Doāni	22N06	89E59	-5:59:56
Barahānuddin	22N30	90E43	-6:02:52
Barāigrām	24N19	89E10	-5:56:40
Bārākpur	22N55	89E32	-5:58:08
Bārguna	22N09	90E07	-6:00:28
Barisāl	22N42	90E22	-6:01:28
Barkal	22N44	92E23	-6:09:32
Barkhanpur	23N50	89E33	-5:58:12
Bārthi	23N02	90E12	-6:00:48
Bāsāil	24N14	90E04	-6:00:16
Bāuphal	22N25	90E33	-6:02:12
Belonia	23N15	91E27	-6:05:48
Bera	24N05	89E37	-5:58:28
Bera	23N59	89E40	-5:58:40
Betāgi	22N25	90E11	-6:00:44
Betil	24N14	89E43	-5:58:52
Bhairab Bāzār	24N04	90E58	-6:03:52
Bhandāria	22N29	90E04	-6:00:16
Bhānga	23N22	89E59	-5:59:56
Bhātai	23N36	89E11	-5:56:44
Bhātiāpāra Ghāt	23N13	89E42	-5:58:48
Bhātsāla	22N33	90E30	-6:02:00
Bhattapratāp	22N45	89E48	-5:59:12
Bheramara	24N02	88E58	-5:55:52
Bhola	22N41	90E39	-6:02:36
Bhūshana	23N24	89E40	-5:58:40
Bībi Chīni	22N28	90E12	-6:00:48
Binodepur	23N26	89E30	-5:58:00
Bīraba	23N51	90E34	-6:02:16
Bishahari	23N10	89E01	-5:56:04
Bishaykhāli	23N28	89E09	-5:56:36
Boalia	23N35	88E57	-5:55:48
Bogra	24N51	89E22	-5:57:28
Brāhmanbāria	23N59	91E07	-6:04:28
Budhhāta	22N36	89E10	-5:56:40
Bunagāti	23N19	89E25	-5:57:40
Buruz Bāgān	23N03	89E00	-5:56:00
Chakaria	21N45	92E05	-6:08:20
Chandanpratap	23N33	89E24	-5:57:36
Chandapāra	22N46	90E16	-6:01:04
Chandar	23N54	89E58	-5:59:52
Chandīpur	23N59	89E01	-5:56:04
Chāndpur	22N08	91E55	-6:07:40
Chāndpur	23N13	90E39	-6:02:36
Chandra Dighalia	23N04	89E46	-5:59:04
Changācha	23N16	89E01	-5:56:04
Char Bansi	22N59	90E43	-6:02:52
Chārghāt	24N17	88E45	-5:55:00
Char Hāim	23N04	90E38	-6:02:32
Char Lākhpur	24N04	90E40	-6:02:40
Char Lālmohan	22N13	90E42	-6:02:48
Chātmohar	24N13	89E15	-5:57:00
Chaugācha	23N16	89E01	-5:56:04
Chaumuhāni	22N56	91E07	-6:04:28
Chhanka	23N59	89E55	-5:59:40
Chhātak	25N02	91E40	-6:06:40
Chhota Bāisdia	22N00	90E27	-6:01:48
Chilmāri	25N33	89E43	-5:58:52
Chittagong	22N20	91E50	-6:07:20
Chuādānga	23N38	88E51	-5:55:24
Churāmankāti	23N14	89E09	-5:56:36
Comilla	23N27	91E12	-6:04:48
Cox's Bāzār	21N26	91E59	-6:07:56
Dacca	23N43	90E25	-6:01:40
Daibagnyahāti	22N33	89E52	-5:59:28
Dāmurhuda	23N36	88E47	-5:55:08
Dānga	23N54	90E36	-6:02:24
Dāriāpur	23N36	89E27	-5:57:48
Dārsana	23N32	88E52	-5:55:28
Dasmina	22N17	90E35	-6:02:20
Dāsuria	24N07	89E08	-5:56:32
Dattapāra	23N01	90E53	-6:03:32
Daudkāndi	23N32	90E43	-6:02:52
Daulatkhan	22N38	90E49	-6:03:16
Daulatpur	24N00	88E52	-5:55:28
Daulatpur	22N53	89E31	-5:58:04
Daulatpur (Ramchandrapur)	23N58	89E50	-5:59:20
Debhāta	22N33	88E58	-5:55:52
Debīr Char	22N24	90E41	-6:02:44
Deopāra	22N55	90E15	-6:01:00
Dhāmrai	23N55	90E13	-6:00:52
Dhāmura	22N53	90E12	-6:00:48
Dhaneswargāti	23N25	89E20	-5:57:20
Dhirāsrām	23N57	90E25	-6:01:40
Dhopākholai	23N08	89E10	-5:56:40
Dhulāsār	21N52	90E14	-6:00:56
Dīghalia	23N07	89E39	-5:58:36
Dinājpur	25N38	88E38	-5:54:32
Dohār	23N35	90E09	-6:00:36
Duāigaon	24N14	90E51	-6:03:24
Dulāi	23N57	89E31	-5:58:04
Dumria	22N47	89E26	-5:57:44
Durbādānga	22N57	89E15	-5:57:00
Elliotganj	23N31	90E52	-6:03:28
Farīdganj	23N08	90E45	-6:03:00
Farīdpur	24N10	89E26	-5:57:44
Farīdpur	23N36	89E50	-5:59:20
Farīdpur Station	24N10	89E10	-5:56:40
Fatulla	23N38	90E29	-6:01:56
Feni	23N00	91E24	-6:05:36
Gaibānda	25N19	89E33	-5:58:12
Gāla	24N18	89E54	-5:59:36
Galāchipa	22N10	90E25	-6:01:40
Gārādāha	24N14	89E34	-5:58:16
Gaurambha	22N39	89E34	-5:58:16
Gauribaradia	23N45	89E52	-5:59:28
Gaurnadi	22N58	90E14	-6:00:56
Gāzīpura	22N46	90E43	-6:02:52
Ghātākhān	23N02	90E26	-6:01:44
Ghior	23N54	89E53	-5:59:32
Ghorāsāl	23N56	90E38	-6:02:32
Ghoshpur	23N27	89E39	-5:58:36
Gilātala	22N36	89E41	-5:58:44
Goalundo Ghāt	23N43	89E46	-5:59:04
Gobra	23N45	89E12	-5:56:48
Godāgāri	24N28	88E20	-5:53:20
Gohāla	23N15	89E59	-5:59:56
Gopālganj	23N01	89E50	-5:59:20
Gopālpur	24N12	89E01	-5:56:04
Gosairhāt	23N05	90E26	-6:01:44
Gouripur	24N46	90E34	-6:02:16
Habiganj	24N23	91E25	-6:05:40
Hājīganj	23N15	90E50	-6:03:20
Haldībunia	22N26	89E38	-5:58:32
Hānār Char	23N08	90E38	-6:02:32
Hāntālbunia	22N44	89E31	-5:58:04
Harinākunda	23N39	89E03	-5:56:12
Harirāmpur	23N42	89E57	-5:59:48
Hilli	25N17	89E01	-5:56:04
Hogalbāria	23N53	88E51	-5:55:24
Husainpur	24N25	90E40	-6:02:40
Iluhār	22N48	90E06	-6:00:24
Ishurdi	24N08	89E05	-5:56:20
Iswarīpur	22N19	89E07	-5:56:28
Jāfarpur	22N29	89E06	-5:56:24
Jagannāthganj Ghāt	24N45	89E49	-5:59:16
Jagati	23N54	89E06	-5:56:24
Jaintiāpur	25N08	92E07	-6:08:28
Jalirpār	23N13	89E58	-5:59:52
Jamālpur	24N55	89E56	-5:59:44
Jāmurki	24N09	90E02	-6:00:08
Jangal Bādhāl	23N07	89E21	-5:57:24
Jāria Jhānjail	25N02	90E39	-6:02:36
Jātrāpur	22N44	89E45	-5:59:00
Jaydebpur	24N00	90E26	-6:01:44
Jaynagar	22N36	90E42	-6:02:48
Jessore	23N10	89E13	-5:56:52
Jhālakāti	22N39	90E12	-6:00:48
Jhenida	23N33	89E10	-5:56:40
Jhingergācha	23N07	89E07	-5:56:28
Jibannagar	23N25	88E50	-5:55:20
Jiudhara	22N24	89E44	-5:58:56
Kabadak	22N13	89E19	-5:57:16
Kachua	22N39	89E53	-5:59:32
Kachua	23N21	90E54	-6:03:36
Kājālia	23N01	89E57	-5:59:48
Kālaia	22N23	90E36	-6:02:24
Kalapāra	21N59	90E14	-6:00:56
Kalāroa	22N52	89E02	-5:56:08
Kālia	23N03	89E38	-5:58:32
Kāliākair	24N05	90E14	-6:00:56
Kālīganj	23N25	89E08	-5:56:32
Kālīganj	22N28	89E02	-5:56:08
Kālikāpur	22N43	89E26	-5:57:44
Kālikāpur	23N46	89E55	-5:59:40
Kalipara	22N09	89E16	-5:57:04
Kālkini	23N06	90E16	-6:01:04
Kālupāra	22N58	90E10	-6:00:40
Kāmarkhāli Ghāt	23N32	89E33	-5:58:12
Kāmrānga	23N14	90E47	-6:03:08
Kānāipur	23N33	89E47	-5:59:08
Kanakeswar	23N09	90E25	-6:01:40
Kāpāsia	24N07	90E32	-6:02:08
Kapilmuni	22N42	89E20	-5:57:20
Kaptai	22N21	92E17	-6:09:08
Karatia	24N14	89E58	-5:59:52
Kāsiāni	23N14	89E45	-5:59:00
Kāsimpur	23N59	90E19	-6:01:16
Kāsināthpur	23N58	89E37	-5:58:28
Kāthuli	23N52	88E40	-5:54:40
Kātiādi	24N15	90E48	-6:03:12
Kaukhāli	22N38	90E04	-6:00:16
Kāzīr Char	22N46	90E33	-6:02:12
Kedārpur	23N18	90E27	-6:01:48
Kesabpur	22N55	89E13	-5:56:52
Khoksa	23N48	89E17	-5:57:08
Khulna	22N48	89E33	-5:58:12
Kishorganj	24N26	90E46	-6:03:04
Kotchāndpur	23N24	89E01	-5:56:04
Kotwālīpāra	22N59	89E59	-5:59:56
Krishnapur	23N30	89E56	-5:59:44
Kumārkhāli	23N51	89E15	-5:57:00
Kurīgrām	25N49	89E39	-5:58:36
Kurmani	22N47	89E53	-5:59:32
Kushtia	23N55	89E07	-5:56:28
Lakshmīpur	22N57	90E50	-6:03:20
Lālmai	23N19	91E07	-6:04:28
Lālmanir Hāt	25N54	89E27	-5:57:48
Lālpur	24N11	88E58	-5:55:52
Lohāgara	23N11	89E39	-5:58:36
Londa	22N06	90E25	-6:01:40
Machhuakhali	22N05	90E21	-6:01:24
Mādārīpur	23N10	90E12	-6:00:48
Madhukhāli	23N33	89E38	-5:58:32
Māgura	23N29	89E25	-5:57:40
Mahādebpur	23N51	89E53	-5:59:32
Mahespur	23N21	88E55	-5:55:40
Mahendraganj	25N20	89E45	-5:59:00
Mahilāra	22N56	90E16	-6:01:04
Maijdi	22N52	91E06	-6:04:24
Majlispur	24N13	90E53	-6:03:32
Makrampur	22N44	90E14	-6:00:56
Mangalpaita	23N19	89E11	-5:56:44
Mānikganj	23N52	90E00	-6:00:00
Manirāmpur	23N01	89E14	-5:56:56
Manohardi	24N08	90E43	-6:02:52
Masua	24N16	90E46	-6:03:04
Masura	23N16	90E24	-6:01:36
Matbāri	22N18	89E57	-5:59:48
Mathurāpur	24N02	88E47	-5:55:08
Mathurāpur	23N17	89E15	-5:57:00
Mātibhānga	22N49	89E56	-5:59:44
Matlab Bāzār	23N20	90E43	-6:02:52
Maulvi Bāzār	24N29	91E47	-6:07:08
Mautala	22N25	89E05	-5:56:20
Maynāmati	23N29	91E07	-6:04:28
Medākul	23N03	90E11	-6:00:44
Medua	22N38	90E44	-6:02:56
Mehendiganj	22N49	90E32	-6:02:08
Meherpur	23N46	88E38	-5:54:32
Miksimil	22N52	89E23	-5:57:32
Mīrpur	23N47	90E21	-6:01:24
Mīrpur	23N56	88E59	-5:55:56
Mirzāganj	22N21	90E14	-6:00:56
Mīrzakālu	22N29	90E48	-6:03:12
Mirzāpur	24N06	90E06	-6:00:24
Mobārakpur	22N58	89E10	-5:56:40
Mohanpur	23N24	90E36	-6:02:24
Mollāhāt	22N56	89E48	-5:59:12
Morghar	23N40	89E37	-5:58:28
Morrelganj	22N28	89E51	-5:59:24
Muhammadpur	23N24	89E36	-5:58:24
Muksūdpur	23N18	89E51	-5:59:24
Muktāgācha	24N46	90E14	-6:00:56
Mulādi	22N54	90E25	-6:01:40
Mulghar	22N46	89E45	-5:59:00
Mungla	22N19	89E36	-5:58:24
Munshiganj	23N33	90E32	-6:02:08
Nāgarpur	24N03	89E53	-5:59:32
Nāgirāt	23N38	89E18	-5:57:12
Nahāta	23N20	89E31	-5:58:04
Naihāti	22N49	89E37	-5:58:28
Nākālia	24N02	89E40	-5:58:40
Nālchiti	22N38	90E17	-6:01:08
Naldānga	23N26	89E11	-5:56:44
Nalgora	22N52	90E39	-6:02:36
Naliagrām	23N36	89E37	-5:58:28
Naoāpāra	22N45	89E39	-5:58:36
Naogaon	24N47	88E56	-5:55:44
Nāopāra	24N09	88E54	-5:55:36

BANGLADESH BANGLADESCH EAST PAKISTAN BANGLA DESH

Place	Lat	Long	Offset
Narāl	23N10	89E30	-5:58:00
Narasinhapur	23N10	90E36	-6:02:24
Nārāyanganj	23N37	90E30	-6:02:00
Naria	23N18	90E25	-6:01:40
Nārikelbāria	23N17	89E21	-5:57:24
Narsingdi	23N55	90E43	-6:02:52
Nasirābād	24N45	90E24	-6:01:36
Nator	24N25	88E59	-5:55:56
Nātudaha	23N39	88E41	-5:54:44
Nawābganj	24N36	88E17	-5:53:08
Nawābganj	23N40	90E10	-6:00:40
Nawāpāra	23N02	89E23	-5:57:32
Nayāgaon	23N32	90E46	-6:03:04
Nāzir Hāt	22N38	91E47	-6:07:08
Nāzirpur	22N43	89E58	-5:59:52
Netrakona	24N53	90E43	-6:02:52
Nilphāmāri	25N56	88E51	-5:55:24
Noākhāli	22N49	91E06	-6:04:24
Nurnagar	22N20	89E03	-5:56:12
Pābna	24N00	89E15	-5:57:00
Pachāgarh	26N20	88E34	-5:54:16
Pāchh Elāsin	24N08	89E54	-5:59:36
Pāikgācha	22N35	89E20	-5:57:20
Pākrāganj	24N00	90E41	-6:02:44
Pāksey	24N05	89E03	-5:56:12
Pākundia	24N20	90E42	-6:02:48
Pālang	23N13	90E21	-6:01:24
Palāspol	22N43	89E05	-5:56:20
Pangsa	23N47	89E25	-5:57:40
Pānkhāli	22N37	89E31	-5:58:04
Pārbatipur	25N39	88E55	-5:55:40
Pātghāti	22N53	89E55	-5:59:40
Pātharghāta	22N02	89E58	-5:59:52
Pāthrāil	24N12	89E56	-5:59:44
Pātua	22N06	90E23	-6:01:32
Patuākhāli	22N21	90E21	-6:01:24
Pātuli	24N13	89E54	-5:59:36
Phulbāria	23N22	89E50	-5:59:20
Phuljhuri	22N12	90E04	-6:00:16
Phultala	22N59	89E28	-5:57:52
Pirojpur	22N34	89E59	-5:59:56
Porādaha	23N51	89E01	-5:56:04
Pratāpnagar	22N23	89E13	-5:56:52
Pubāil	23N56	90E29	-6:01:56
Rāenda	22N18	89E51	-5:59:24
Raghunāthpur	23N12	89E31	-5:58:04
Rāipur	23N03	90E46	-6:03:04
Rāipura	23N59	90E53	-6:03:32
Raita	24N07	88E57	-5:55:48
Rājābari	23N23	90E28	-6:01:52
Rājāpur	22N34	90E09	-6:00:36
Rājbāri	23N46	89E39	-5:58:36
Rājendrapur	24N06	90E27	-6:01:48
Rājshāhi	24N22	88E36	-5:54:24
Rāmdia	23N42	89E32	-5:58:08
Rāmganj	23N06	90E51	-6:03:24
Rāmgarh	22N59	91E44	-6:06:56
Rāmpāl	22N34	89E39	-5:58:36
Rampur Boalia → Rājshāhi	24N22	88E36	-5:54:24
Rāmu	21N25	92E07	-6:08:28
Rāngāmāti	22N38	92E12	-6:08:48
Rangpur	25N45	89E15	-5:57:00
Rohitpur	23N42	90E19	-6:01:16
Ruhea	26N10	88E25	-5:53:40
Rupdia	23N08	89E18	-5:57:12
Rupganj	23N48	90E31	-6:02:04
Sābhār	23N51	90E15	-6:01:00
Sadarpur	23N28	90E02	-6:00:08
Sādhuhāti	23N34	89E01	-5:56:04
Safipur	23N01	90E22	-6:01:28
Sahasrail	23N19	89E43	-5:58:52
Saidābād	24N18	89E43	-5:58:52
Saidpur	25N47	88E54	-5:55:36
Sailkupa	23N41	89E15	-5:57:00
Sālikha	23N18	89E22	-5:57:28
Sandwīp	22N29	91E26	-6:05:44
Sānkdaha	22N46	89E10	-5:56:40
Sāntāhār	24N48	88E59	-5:55:56
Sānthia	24N03	89E33	-5:58:12
Sāra	24N07	89E02	-5:56:08
Sārankhola	22N18	89E47	-5:59:08
Sardah	24N18	88E44	-5:54:56
Sātbāria	23N52	89E26	-5:57:44
Satkānia	22N04	92E03	-6:08:12
Sātkhira	22N43	89E06	-5:56:24
Senhāti	22N53	89E33	-5:58:12
Shāhzādpur	24N10	89E36	-5:58:24
Sherpur	24N41	89E25	-5:57:40
Sherpur	25N01	90E01	-6:00:04
Siālghuni	22N33	90E27	-6:01:48
Sibālay	23N50	89E47	-5:59:08
Sibchar	23N21	90E09	-6:00:36
Sibpur	24N02	90E44	-6:02:56
Singa (North)	23N16	89E30	-5:58:00
Singair	23N49	90E08	-6:00:32
Singāti	22N44	89E43	-5:58:52
Sirājganj	24N27	89E43	-5:58:52
Sonādugi	22N47	90E40	-6:02:40
Sonāpur	23N42	89E30	-5:58:00
Srīdharpur	23N04	89E25	-5:57:40
Srīnagar	23N32	90E18	-6:01:12
Srīpur	24N12	90E29	-6:01:56
Srīpur	23N36	89E24	-5:57:36
Sthal	24N12	89E44	-5:58:56
Sujānagar	23N57	89E25	-5:57:40
Sunāmganj	25N04	91E24	-6:05:36
Swarupkāti	22N45	90E06	-6:00:24
Syāmnagar	22N21	89E07	-5:56:28
Sylhet	24N54	91E52	-6:07:28
Tala	22N46	89E16	-5:57:04
Tālma	23N29	89E54	-5:59:36
Tangail	24N15	89E55	-5:59:40
Tāzumuddin	22N29	90E53	-6:03:32
Terakhāda	22N56	89E40	-5:58:40
Tetulbāria	21N58	90E03	-6:00:12
Thākurgaon	26N02	88E28	-5:53:52
Tilli	23N57	89E57	-5:59:48
Tungi	23N53	90E24	-6:01:36
Ulānia	22N12	90E29	-6:01:56
Ulāpāra	24N19	89E34	-5:58:16
Ulpur	23N04	89E50	-5:59:20
Ulusara	24N16	90E36	-6:02:24
Umedpur	22N31	89E59	-5:59:56
Zopui	23N39	92E14	-6:08:56

BARBADOS BARBADE

Time Table

Before 1/Jan/1924 LMT

Date	Time	Offset
Begin Standard		59w37
1/Jan/1924	0:00	3:58
Begin Standard		60w00
1/Jan/1932	0:00	4:00
12/Jun/1977	2:00	3:00
2/Oct/1977	2:00	4:00
16/Apr/1978	2:00	3:00
1/Oct/1978	2:00	4:00
15/Apr/1979	2:00	3:00
30/Sep/1979	2:00	4:00
20/Apr/1980	2:00	3:00
25/Sep/1980	2:00	4:00

Place	Lat	Long	Offset
Bathsheba	13N13	59w31	3:58:04
Bridgetown	13N06	59w37	3:58:28
Bulkeley	13N07	59w32	3:58:08
Crab Hill	13N19	59w38	3:58:32
Hastings	13N04	59w35	3:58:20
Holetown	13N11	59w39	3:58:36
Oistins	13N04	59w32	3:58:08
Saint Andrew	13N15	59w33	3:58:12
Speightstown	13N15	59w39	3:58:36

BELGIUM BELGIË BÉLGICA BELGIEN BELGIQUE

Time Table

Before 1/Jan/1880 LMT

Date	Time	Offset
Begin Standard		4E21
1/Jan/1880	0:00	-0:17
Begin Standard		0w00
1/May/1892	12:00	0:00
Begin Standard		15E00
4/Aug/1914	0:00	-1:00
30/Apr/1916	23:00	-2:00
1/Oct/1916	1:00	-1:00
16/Apr/1917	2:00	-2:00
17/Sep/1917	3:00	-1:00
15/Apr/1918	2:00	-2:00
16/Sep/1918	3:00	-1:00
Begin Standard		0w00
1/Mar/1919	23:00	-1:00
4/Oct/1919	24:00	0:00
14/Feb/1920	23:00	-1:00
23/Oct/1920	24:00	0:00
14/Mar/1921	23:00	-1:00
25/Oct/1921	24:00	0:00
25/Mar/1922	23:00	-1:00
7/Oct/1922	24:00	0:00
21/Apr/1923	23:00	-1:00
6/Oct/1923	24:00	0:00
29/Mar/1924	23:00	-1:00
4/Oct/1924	24:00	0:00
4/Apr/1925	23:00	-1:00
3/Oct/1925	24:00	0:00
17/Apr/1926	23:00	-1:00
2/Oct/1926	24:00	0:00
9/Apr/1927	23:00	-1:00
1/Oct/1927	24:00	0:00
14/Apr/1928	23:00	-1:00
7/Oct/1928	24:00	0:00
21/Apr/1929	2:00	-1:00
6/Oct/1929	3:00	0:00
13/Apr/1930	2:00	-1:00
5/Oct/1930	3:00	0:00
19/Apr/1931	2:00	-1:00
4/Oct/1931	3:00	0:00
17/Apr/1932	2:00	-1:00
2/Oct/1932	3:00	0:00
26/Mar/1933	2:00	-1:00
8/Oct/1933	3:00	0:00
8/Apr/1934	2:00	-1:00
7/Oct/1934	3:00	0:00
31/Mar/1935	2:00	-1:00
6/Oct/1935	3:00	0:00
19/Apr/1936	2:00	-1:00
4/Oct/1936	3:00	0:00
4/Apr/1937	2:00	-1:00
3/Oct/1937	3:00	0:00
27/Mar/1938	2:00	-1:00
2/Oct/1938	3:00	0:00
16/Apr/1939	2:00	-1:00
19/Nov/1939	3:00	0:00
Begin Standard		15E00
24/Feb/1940	23:00	-1:00
19/May/1940	2:00	-2:00
2/Nov/1942	3:00	-1:00
29/Mar/1943	2:00	-2:00
4/Oct/1943	3:00	-1:00
3/Apr/1944	2:00	-2:00
17/Sep/1944	3:00	-1:00
2/Apr/1945	2:00	-2:00
16/Sep/1945	3:00	-1:00
19/May/1946	2:00	-2:00
7/Oct/1946	3:00	-1:00
3/Apr/1977	2:00	-2:00
1/Oct/1977	2:00	-1:00
2/Apr/1978	2:00	-2:00
25/Sep/1978	2:00	-1:00
1/Apr/1979	2:00	-2:00
30/Sep/1979	3:00	-1:00
6/Apr/1980	2:00	-2:00
28/Sep/1980	3:00	-1:00
29/Mar/1981	2:00	-2:00
27/Sep/1981	3:00	-1:00
28/Mar/1982	2:00	-2:00
26/Sep/1982	3:00	-1:00
27/Mar/1983	2:00	-2:00
25/Sep/1983	3:00	-1:00
25/Mar/1984	2:00	-2:00
30/Sep/1984	3:00	-1:00
31/Mar/1985	2:00	-2:00
29/Sep/1985	3:00	-1:00
30/Mar/1986	2:00	-2:00
28/Sep/1986	3:00	-1:00
29/Mar/1987	2:00	-2:00
27/Sep/1987	3:00	-1:00
27/Mar/1988	2:00	-2:00
25/Sep/1988	3:00	-1:00
26/Mar/1989	2:00	-2:00
24/Sep/1989	3:00	-1:00
25/Mar/1990	2:00	-2:00
30/Sep/1990	3:00	-1:00
31/Mar/1991	2:00	-2:00
29/Sep/1991	3:00	-1:00
29/Mar/1992	2:00	-2:00
27/Sep/1992	3:00	-1:00
28/Mar/1993	2:00	-2:00
26/Sep/1993	3:00	-1:00
27/Mar/1994	2:00	-2:00
25/Sep/1994	3:00	-1:00
26/Mar/1995	2:00	-2:00
24/Sep/1995	3:00	-1:00
31/Mar/1996	2:00	-2:00
29/Sep/1996	3:00	-1:00
30/Mar/1997	2:00	-2:00
28/Sep/1997	3:00	-1:00
29/Mar/1998	2:00	-2:00
27/Sep/1998	3:00	-1:00
28/Mar/1999	2:00	-2:00
26/Sep/1999	3:00	-1:00
26/Mar/2000	2:00	-2:00
24/Sep/2000	3:00	-1:00

BELGIQUE BELGIEN BÉLGICA BELGIË BELGIUM

Place	Lat	Long	Time
Aalst (Alost)	50N56	4E02	-0:16:08
Aalter	51N05	3E27	-0:13:48
Aarschot	50N59	4E50	-0:19:20
Achêne	50N16	5E03	-0:20:12
Adegem	51N12	3E29	-0:13:56
Agimont	50N10	4E48	-0:19:12
Alle	49N51	4E58	-0:19:52
Alost → Aalst	50N56	4E02	-0:16:08
Amay	50N33	5E19	-0:21:16
Amberes → Antwerpen	51N13	4E25	-0:17:40
Andenne	50N29	5E06	-0:20:24
Anderlecht	50N50	4E18	-0:17:12
Anderlues	50N24	4E16	-0:17:04
Andinkerke	51N04	2E36	-0:10:24
Annevoie Rouillon	50N21	4E50	-0:19:20
Ans	50N39	5E32	-0:22:08
Anseremme	50N15	4E54	-0:19:36
Antoing	50N34	3E27	-0:13:48
Antwerp → Antwerpen	51N13	4E25	-0:17:40
Antwerpen (Anvers)	51N13	4E25	-0:17:40
Anvers → Antwerpen	51N13	4E25	-0:17:40
Ardooie	50N59	3E12	-0:12:48
Arendonk	51N19	5E05	-0:20:20
Arlon	49N41	5E49	-0:23:16
As	51N01	5E35	-0:22:20
Asse	50N55	4E12	-0:16:48
Assebroek	51N12	3E16	-0:13:04
Assenede	51N14	3E45	-0:15:00
Ath	50N38	3E47	-0:15:08
Athus	49N34	5E50	-0:23:20
Aubange	49N35	5E48	-0:23:12
Auby sur Semois	49N49	5E10	-0:20:40
Auderghem	50N49	4E26	-0:17:44
Avelgem	50N46	3E26	-0:13:44
Averbode	51N02	4E59	-0:19:56
Aywaille	50N28	5E40	-0:22:40
Baarle Hertog	51N27	4E56	-0:19:44
Baasrode	51N02	4E10	-0:16:40
Balen	51N10	5E09	-0:20:36
Bastogne	50N00	5E43	-0:22:52
Battice	50N39	5E49	-0:23:16
Baudour	50N29	3E49	-0:15:16
Beaubru	49N46	5E05	-0:20:20
Beaufays	50N34	5E38	-0:22:32
Beaumont	50N14	4E14	-0:16:56
Beauraing	50N07	4E58	-0:19:52
Beernem	51N09	3E20	-0:13:20
Beerse	51N19	4E52	-0:19:28
Beho	50N13	6E00	-0:24:00
Bekkevoort	50N57	4E58	-0:19:52
Bellegem	50N47	3E16	-0:13:04
Bellevaux Ligneuville	50N24	6E00	-0:24:00
Beloeil	50N33	3E43	-0:14:52
Belsele	51N09	4E05	-0:16:20
Berchem	51N12	4E26	-0:17:44
Berchem	50N47	3E30	-0:14:00
Berchem Sainte Agathe	50N52	4E17	-0:17:08
Bergen → Mons	50N27	3E56	-0:15:44
Beringen	51N03	5E13	-0:20:52
Berlaar	51N07	4E39	-0:18:36
Bertogne	50N05	5E40	-0:22:40
Bertrix	49N51	5E15	-0:21:00
Beveren	51N13	4E15	-0:17:00
Beverlo	51N05	5E12	-0:20:48
Bierwart	50N34	5E01	-0:20:04
Bièvre	49N56	5E01	-0:20:04
Bilzen	50N52	5E31	-0:22:04
Binche	50N24	4E10	-0:16:40
Bissegem	50N49	3E13	-0:12:52
Blankenberge	51N19	3E08	-0:12:32
Bocholt	51N10	5E35	-0:22:20
Bohan	49N52	4E53	-0:19:32
Bomal	50N23	5E32	-0:22:08
Bonheiden	51N02	4E32	-0:18:08
Bon Secours	50N30	3E36	-0:14:24
Booischot	51N03	4E46	-0:19:04
Boom	51N05	4E22	-0:17:28
Borgerhout	51N13	4E26	-0:17:44
Borgloon	50N48	5E20	-0:21:20
Bouillon	49N48	5E04	-0:20:16
Boussu	50N26	3E48	-0:15:12
Braine l'Alleud	50N41	4E22	-0:17:28
Braine le Château	50N41	4E16	-0:17:04
Braine le Comte	50N36	4E08	-0:16:32
Brasschaat	51N17	4E27	-0:17:48
Bray	50N26	4E06	-0:16:24
Brecht	51N21	4E38	-0:18:32
Bredene	51N14	2E58	-0:11:52
Bree	51N08	5E36	-0:22:24
Bruges → Brugge	51N13	3E14	-0:12:56
Brugge (Bruges)	51N13	3E14	-0:12:56
Brûly	49N58	4E31	-0:18:04
Bruselas → Bruxelles	50N50	4E20	-0:17:20
Brussel → Bruxelles	50N50	4E20	-0:17:20
Brussels → Bruxelles	50N50	4E20	-0:17:20
Bruxelles (Brussels) (Brussel)	50N50	4E20	-0:17:20
Buggenhout	51N01	4E12	-0:16:48
Büllingen	50N25	6E16	-0:25:04
Bütgenbach	50N26	6E12	-0:24:48
Celles	50N14	5E01	-0:20:04
Champlon	50N07	5E28	-0:21:52
Charleroi	50N25	4E26	-0:17:44
Châtelet	50N24	4E31	-0:18:04
Châtelineau	50N25	4E31	-0:18:04
Chaudfontaine	50N35	5E38	-0:22:32
Cherain	50N11	5E52	-0:23:28
Chièvres	50N35	3E48	-0:15:12
Chimay	50N03	4E19	-0:17:16
Chiny	49N44	5E20	-0:21:20
Chislenghien (Gellingen)	50N39	3E52	-0:15:28
Ciney	50N18	5E06	-0:20:24
Comblain Au Pont	50N28	5E35	-0:22:20
Coo	50N24	5E52	-0:23:28
Corbion	49N48	5E00	-0:20:00
Couillet	50N23	4E27	-0:17:48
Courcelles	50N28	4E22	-0:17:28
Courtrai → Kortrijk	50N50	3E16	-0:13:04
Court Saint Étienne	50N39	4E34	-0:18:16
Couvin	50N03	4E29	-0:17:56
Crupet	50N21	4E48	-0:19:12
Cuesmes	50N26	3E55	-0:15:40
Damme	51N15	3E17	-0:13:08
Deerlijk	50N51	3E21	-0:13:24
De Haan	51N16	3E02	-0:12:08
Deinze	50N59	3E32	-0:14:08
Denderleeuw	50N53	4E04	-0:16:16
Dendermonde	51N02	4E07	-0:16:28
De Panne	51N06	2E35	-0:10:20
De Pinte	51N00	3E39	-0:14:36
Dessel	51N14	5E07	-0:20:28
Destelbergen	51N03	3E48	-0:15:12
Deurne	51N13	4E28	-0:17:52
Diest	50N59	5E03	-0:20:12
Diksmuide (Dixmude)	51N02	2E52	-0:11:28
Dilbeek	50N51	4E16	-0:17:04
Dinant	50N16	4E55	-0:19:40
Dixmude → Diksmuide	51N02	2E52	-0:11:28
Doornik → Tournai	50N36	3E23	-0:13:32
Dour	50N24	3E47	-0:15:08
Drongen	51N03	3E40	-0:14:40
Dudzele	51N17	3E14	-0:12:56
Duffel	51N06	4E31	-0:18:04
Durbuy	50N21	5E28	-0:21:52
Écaussinnes D'Enghen	50N34	4E10	-0:16:40
Edegem	51N09	4E27	-0:17:48
Edingen → Enghien	50N42	4E02	-0:16:08
Eeklo	51N11	3E34	-0:14:16
Éghezée	50N36	4E54	-0:19:36
Eine	50N52	3E37	-0:14:28
Ekeren	51N17	4E25	-0:17:40
Eksel	51N09	5E23	-0:21:32
Ellezelles	50N44	3E41	-0:14:44
Emptinne	50N19	5E07	-0:20:28
Enghien (Edingen)	50N42	4E02	-0:16:08
Engis	50N35	5E25	-0:21:40
Érezée	50N18	5E33	-0:22:12
Erquelinnes	50N18	4E07	-0:16:28
Ertvelde	51N11	3E45	-0:15:00
Esneux	50N32	5E34	-0:22:16
Essen	51N28	4E28	-0:17:52
Étalle	49N41	5E36	-0:22:24
Etterbeek	50N50	4E23	-0:17:32
Eupen	50N38	6E02	-0:24:08
Evere	50N52	4E24	-0:17:36
Evergem	51N07	3E42	-0:14:48
Fallais	50N37	5E10	-0:20:40
Familleureux	50N31	4E12	-0:16:48
Fauvillers	49N51	5E40	-0:22:40
Fleurus	50N29	4E33	-0:18:12
Flobecq (Vloesberg)	50N44	3E44	-0:14:56
Floreffe	50N26	4E45	-0:19:00
Florennes	50N15	4E37	-0:18:28
Florenville	49N42	5E18	-0:21:12
Forest	50N48	4E19	-0:17:16
Fosses la Ville	50N24	4E42	-0:18:48
Fraire	50N16	4E30	-0:18:00
Frameries	50N24	3E54	-0:15:36
Frasnes Lez Buissenal	50N40	3E36	-0:14:24
Furnes → Veurne	51N04	2E40	-0:10:40
Gand → Gent	51N03	3E43	-0:14:52
Ganshoren	50N52	4E18	-0:17:12
Gante → Gent	51N03	3E43	-0:14:52
Gaurain Ramecroix	50N35	3E29	-0:13:56
Gedinne	49N59	4E56	-0:19:44
Geel	51N10	5E00	-0:20:00
Gelinden	50N46	5E15	-0:21:00
Gellingen → Ghislenghien	50N39	3E52	-0:15:28
Geluwe	50N48	3E04	-0:12:16
Gembloux	50N34	4E41	-0:18:44
Genappe	50N36	4E27	-0:17:48
Genk	50N58	5E30	-0:22:00
Gent (Gand)	51N03	3E43	-0:14:52
Gentbrugge	51N03	3E45	-0:15:00
Genval	50N43	4E29	-0:17:56
Geraardsbergen	50N46	3E52	-0:15:28
Gerpinnes	50N20	4E31	-0:18:04
Ghent → Gent	51N03	3E43	-0:14:52
Ghislenghien	50N39	3E52	-0:15:28
Ghlin	50N28	3E53	-0:15:32
Gierle	51N16	4E51	-0:19:24
Gilly	50N26	4E30	-0:18:00
Gistel	51N10	2E57	-0:11:48
Godinne	50N21	4E52	-0:19:28
Gosselies	50N28	4E25	-0:17:40
Grammont → Geraardsbergen	50N46	3E52	-0:15:28
Grand Halleux	50N19	5E54	-0:23:36
Grandrieu	50N12	4E10	-0:16:40
Grez Doiceau	50N44	4E42	-0:18:48
Grimbergen	50N56	4E23	-0:17:32
Grobbendonk	51N12	4E43	-0:18:52
Gruitrode	51N05	5E35	-0:22:20
Haaltert	50N54	4E00	-0:16:00
Habay la Neuve	49N44	5E39	-0:22:36
Hakendover	50N48	4E59	-0:19:56
Halle	50N44	4E13	-0:16:52
Halma	50N05	5E08	-0:20:32
Hamme	51N06	4E08	-0:16:32
Hamme Mille	50N47	4E43	-0:18:52
Hamoir	50N26	5E32	-0:22:08
Hamont	51N15	5E33	-0:22:12
Handzame	51N02	3E00	-0:12:00
Hannut	50N40	5E05	-0:20:20
Han sur Lesse	50N08	5E11	-0:20:44
Harchies	50N29	3E41	-0:14:44
Harelbeke	50N51	3E18	-0:13:12
Hasselt	50N56	5E20	-0:21:20
Hastière Lavaux	50N13	4E50	-0:19:20
Havelange	50N23	5E14	-0:20:56
Havré	50N28	4E02	-0:16:08
Hechtel	51N08	5E21	-0:21:24
Heer	50N10	4E50	-0:19:20
Heist Aan Zee	51N21	3E15	-0:13:00
Heist Op Den Berg	51N05	4E43	-0:18:52
Hekelgem	50N54	4E06	-0:16:24
Helchteren	51N03	5E22	-0:21:28
Hemiksem	51N09	4E21	-0:17:24
Henri Chapelle	50N40	5E56	-0:23:44
Herbeumont	49N47	5E14	-0:20:56
Herentals	51N11	4E50	-0:19:20
Herk De Stad	50N56	5E10	-0:20:40
Herselt	51N03	4E53	-0:19:32
Herstal	50N40	5E38	-0:22:32
Herve	50N38	5E48	-0:23:12
Het Zoute	51N21	3E18	-0:13:12
Heule	50N50	3E14	-0:12:56
Heusden	51N02	5E16	-0:21:04
Heverlee	50N52	4E42	-0:18:48
Hoboken	51N10	4E21	-0:17:24
Hofstade	50N58	4E02	-0:16:08
Hooglede	50N59	3E05	-0:12:20
Hoogstraten	51N24	4E46	-0:19:04
Hornu	50N26	3E49	-0:15:16
Hotton	50N16	5E27	-0:21:48
Houdeng Aimeries	50N29	4E08	-0:16:32
Houffalize	50N08	5E47	-0:23:08
Houthalen	51N02	5E22	-0:21:28
Houthulst	50N59	2E57	-0:11:48
Humbeek	50N58	4E23	-0:17:32
Huy	50N31	5E14	-0:20:56
Ichtegem	51N06	3E00	-0:12:00
Ieper (Ypres)	50N51	2E53	-0:11:32
Ingelmunster	50N55	3E15	-0:13:00
Ixelles	50N50	4E22	-0:17:28
Izegem	50N55	3E12	-0:12:48
Jabbeke	51N11	3E05	-0:12:20
Jalhay	50N34	5E58	-0:23:52
Jambes	50N28	4E52	-0:19:28
Jamoigne	49N42	5E25	-0:21:40
Jemappes	50N27	3E53	-0:15:32
Jemeppe	50N37	5E30	-0:22:00
Jette	50N52	4E20	-0:17:20
Jodoigne	50N43	4E52	-0:19:28
Jumet	50N26	4E25	-0:17:40
Jupille	50N39	5E38	-0:22:32
Kain	50N38	3E22	-0:13:28
Kalmthout	51N23	4E28	-0:17:52
Kapellen	51N19	4E26	-0:17:44
Kapelle Op Den Bos	51N01	4E22	-0:17:28
Kaprijke	51N13	3E36	-0:14:24
Kasterlee	51N15	4E57	-0:19:48
Kaulille	51N11	5E31	-0:22:04
Keerbergen	51N00	4E37	-0:18:28
Kemmel	50N47	2E49	-0:11:16
Kerkhove	50N48	3E30	-0:14:00
Kessel	51N08	4E37	-0:18:28
Knesselare	51N08	3E25	-0:13:40
Knokke	51N21	3E17	-0:13:08
Koekelare	51N05	2E58	-0:11:52
Koersel	51N04	5E16	-0:21:04
Koksijde	51N07	2E38	-0:10:32
Kontich	51N08	4E27	-0:17:48
Koolskamp	51N00	3E12	-0:12:48
Kortemark	51N02	3E02	-0:12:08
Kortrijk (Courtrai)	50N50	3E16	-0:13:04
Kruishoutem	50N54	3E31	-0:14:04
Kuurne	50N51	3E17	-0:13:08
La Bouverie	50N24	3E52	-0:15:28
Laeken	50N53	4E21	-0:17:24
La Gleize	50N25	5E51	-0:23:24
La Louvière	50N28	4E11	-0:16:44
Lanaken	50N53	5E39	-0:22:36
Landen	50N45	5E05	-0:20:20
Langemark	50N55	2E55	-0:11:40
Lanklaar	51N01	5E44	-0:22:56
La Roche En Ardenne	50N11	5E35	-0:22:20
Lauwe	50N48	3E11	-0:12:44
Lebbeke	51N00	4E08	-0:16:32
Lede	50N58	3E58	-0:15:52
Lembeek	50N43	4E13	-0:16:52
Lendelede	50N53	3E14	-0:12:56
Leopoldsburg	51N07	5E15	-0:21:00
Lessen → Lessines	50N43	3E50	-0:15:20
Lessines (Lessen)	50N43	3E50	-0:15:20
Leuven (Louvain)	50N53	4E42	-0:18:48
Leuze	50N34	4E54	-0:19:36
Leuze	50N36	3E36	-0:14:24
Libramont	49N55	5E23	-0:21:32
Lichtaart	51N14	4E54	-0:19:36
Lichtervelde	51N02	3E09	-0:12:36
Liedekerke	50N52	4E05	-0:16:20
Liège (Luik)	50N38	5E34	-0:22:16
Lieja → Liège	50N38	5E34	-0:22:16
Lier (Lierre)	51N08	4E34	-0:18:16
Lierneux	50N18	5E48	-0:23:12
Limbourg	50N37	5E56	-0:23:44

BELGIUM BELGIË BÉLGICA BELGIEN BELGIQUE

Place	Lat	Long	Time
Lissewege	51N18	3E11	-0:12:44
Lobbes	50N21	4E15	-0:17:00
Lochristi	51N06	3E50	-0:15:20
Lokeren	51N06	4E00	-0:16:00
Lommel	51N14	5E18	-0:21:12
Londerzeel	51N00	4E18	-0:17:12
Longchamps	50N03	5E42	-0:22:48
Longvilly	50N01	5E50	-0:23:20
Louvain → Leuven	50N53	4E42	-0:18:48
Louveigné	50N32	5E42	-0:22:48
Löwen → Leuven	50N53	4E42	-0:18:48
Luik → Liège	50N38	5E34	-0:22:16
Lummen	50N59	5E12	-0:20:48
Lustin	50N23	4E53	-0:19:32
Lüttich → Liège	50N38	5E34	-0:22:16
Maaseik	51N06	5E48	-0:23:12
Machelen	50N55	4E26	-0:17:44
Macon	50N03	4E13	-0:16:52
Maissin	49N58	5E11	-0:20:44
Maldegem	51N13	3E27	-0:13:48
Malines → Mechelen	51N02	4E28	-0:17:52
Malmédy	50N25	6E02	-0:24:08
Manderfeld	50N20	6E20	-0:25:20
Marbais	50N33	4E31	-0:18:04
Marche En Famenne	50N12	5E20	-0:21:20
Marche Les Dames	50N29	4E58	-0:19:52
Marchienne Au Pont	50N24	4E23	-0:17:32
Mariembourg	50N06	4E31	-0:18:04
Martelange	49N50	5E44	-0:22:56
Méan	50N22	5E20	-0:21:20
Mechelen (Malines)	51N02	4E28	-0:17:52
Mechlin → Mechelen	51N02	4E28	-0:17:52
Meer	51N27	4E44	-0:18:56
Meerbeke	50N50	4E02	-0:16:08
Meerhout	51N08	5E05	-0:20:20
Meerle	51N28	4E48	-0:19:12
Membre	49N52	4E54	-0:19:36
Menen	50N48	3E07	-0:12:28
Merchtem	50N58	4E14	-0:16:56
Merelbeke	51N00	3E45	-0:15:00
Merkem	50N57	2E51	-0:11:24
Merksem	51N15	4E27	-0:17:48
Merksplas	51N22	4E52	-0:19:28
Mettet	50N19	4E40	-0:18:40
Meulebeke	50N57	3E17	-0:13:08
Middelkerke	51N11	2E49	-0:11:16
Moen	50N46	3E24	-0:13:36
Moerbeke	50N45	3E55	-0:15:40
Moerbeke	51N10	3E56	-0:15:44
Mol	51N11	5E06	-0:20:24
Molenbeek Saint Jean	50N51	4E19	-0:17:16
Momignies	50N02	4E10	-0:16:40
Monceau sur Sambre	50N25	4E22	-0:17:28
Mons (Bergen)	50N27	3E56	-0:15:44
Moorsel	50N57	4E06	-0:16:24
Moorslede	50N53	3E04	-0:12:16
Moresnet	50N43	5E59	-0:23:56
Morlanwelz	50N27	4E14	-0:16:56
Mortsel	51N10	4E28	-0:17:52
Mouscron	50N44	3E13	-0:12:52
Moxhe	50N38	5E05	-0:20:20
Muizen	51N01	4E31	-0:18:04
Naast	50N33	4E05	-0:16:20
Nadrin	50N10	5E41	-0:22:44
Nalinnes	50N19	4E26	-0:17:44
Namen → Namur	50N28	4E52	-0:19:28
Namur	50N28	4E52	-0:19:28
Nazareth	50N58	3E36	-0:14:24
Nederbrakel	50N48	3E46	-0:15:04
Nederzwalm Hermelgem	50N53	3E41	-0:14:44
Neeroeteren	51N05	5E42	-0:22:48
Neerpelt	51N13	5E25	-0:21:40
Neufchâteau	49N50	5E26	-0:21:44
Neufvilles	50N34	4E00	-0:16:00
Neuville En Condroz	50N32	5E27	-0:21:48
Niel	51N07	4E20	-0:17:20
Nieuwpoort	51N08	2E45	-0:11:00
Nieuwpoort Bad	51N09	2E42	-0:10:48
Nijlen	51N10	4E39	-0:18:36
Nijvel → Nivelles	50N36	4E20	-0:17:20
Nimy	50N28	3E57	-0:15:48
Ninove	50N50	4E01	-0:16:04
Nismes	50N05	4E33	-0:18:12
Nivelles (Nijvel)	50N36	4E20	-0:17:20
Nonceveux	50N28	5E44	-0:22:56
Noville	50N40	5E23	-0:21:32
Oedelem	51N10	3E20	-0:13:20
Ohey	50N26	5E08	-0:20:32
Olen	51N09	4E51	-0:19:24
Oombergen	50N54	3E50	-0:15:20
Oostakker	51N06	3E46	-0:15:04
Oostduinkerke	51N07	2E41	-0:10:44
Oostende (Ostende)	51N13	2E55	-0:11:40
Oosterzele	50N57	3E48	-0:15:12
Oostkamp	51N09	3E14	-0:12:56
Oostmalle	51N18	4E44	-0:18:56
Oostrozebeke	50N55	3E20	-0:13:20
Oostvleteren	50N56	2E44	-0:10:56
Ophain Bois Seigneur Isaac	50N40	4E21	-0:17:24
Ophasselt	50N49	3E53	-0:15:32
Opwijk	50N58	4E11	-0:16:44
Oreye	50N44	5E22	-0:21:28
Ostende → Oostende	51N13	2E55	-0:11:40
Ottignies	50N40	4E34	-0:18:16
Oudenaarde	50N51	3E36	-0:14:24
Oudenburg	50N46	3E53	-0:15:32
Ouffet	50N26	5E28	-0:21:52
Overijse	50N46	4E32	-0:18:08
Overpelt	51N13	5E25	-0:21:40
Paal	51N02	5E11	-0:20:44
Paliseul	49N54	5E08	-0:20:32
Pamel	50N50	4E04	-0:16:16
Pecq	50N41	3E20	-0:13:20
Peer	51N08	5E28	-0:21:52
Pepinster	50N34	5E49	-0:23:16
Péronnes	50N26	4E08	-0:16:32
Péruwelz	50N31	3E35	-0:14:20
Pervijze	51N05	2E47	-0:11:08
Petegem	50N58	3E32	-0:14:08
Philippeville	50N12	4E32	-0:18:08
Pittem	51N00	3E16	-0:13:04
Ploegsteert	50N43	2E53	-0:11:32
Poelkapelle	50N55	2E57	-0:11:48
Pont À Celles	50N30	4E21	-0:17:24
Pont De Bonne	50N27	5E17	-0:21:08
Poperinge	50N51	2E43	-0:10:52
Poppel	51N27	5E02	-0:20:08
Presles	50N23	4E35	-0:18:20
Putte	51N04	4E38	-0:18:32
Puurs	51N05	4E17	-0:17:08
Quaregnon	50N26	3E51	-0:15:24
Quiévrain	50N24	3E41	-0:14:44
Raeren	50N41	6E07	-0:24:28
Rebecq Rognon	50N40	4E08	-0:16:32
Recogne	49N55	5E22	-0:21:28
Renaix → Ronse	50N45	3E36	-0:14:24
Retie	51N16	5E04	-0:20:16
Riemst	50N48	5E36	-0:22:24
Rijkevorsel	51N21	4E46	-0:19:04
Robertville	50N27	6E07	-0:24:28
Rochefort	50N10	5E13	-0:20:52
Rochehaut	49N51	5E00	-0:20:00
Roclenge sur Geer	50N45	5E36	-0:22:24
Roesbrugge Haringe	50N55	2E37	-0:10:28
Roeselare (Roulers)	50N57	3E08	-0:12:32
Rœulx	50N30	4E06	-0:16:24
Ronse (Renaix Gleiche)	50N45	3E36	-0:14:24
Rotem	51N03	5E44	-0:22:56
Roulers → Roeselare	50N57	3E08	-0:12:32
Ruddervoorde	51N06	3E12	-0:12:48
Ruiselede	51N03	3E24	-0:13:36
Rumbeke	50N56	3E10	-0:12:40
Rumst	51N05	4E25	-0:17:40
Saint Gérard	50N21	4E45	-0:19:00
Saint Gilles	50N49	4E20	-0:17:20
Saint Hubert	50N01	5E23	-0:21:32
Saint Nicolas → Sint Niklaas	51N10	4E08	-0:16:32
Saintes	50N42	4E10	-0:16:40
Saint Séverin	50N32	5E25	-0:21:40
Saint Troud	50N48	5E12	-0:20:48
Saint Vith	50N17	6E08	-0:24:32
Salmchâteau	50N16	5E54	-0:23:36
Sart	50N31	5E56	-0:23:44
Schaerbeek	50N51	4E23	-0:17:32
Scherpenheuve	50N59	4E59	-0:19:56
Schilde	51N14	4E34	-0:18:16
Schoten	51N15	4E30	-0:18:00
Seneffe	50N31	4E15	-0:17:00
Seraing	50N36	5E29	-0:21:56
Silenrieux	50N14	4E24	-0:17:36
Sinsin	50N17	5E15	-0:21:00
Sint Amandsberg	51N04	3E45	-0:15:00
Sint Andries	51N12	3E10	-0:12:40
Sint Denijs Westrem	51N01	3E40	-0:14:40
Sint Gillis Waas	51N13	4E08	-0:16:32
Sint Joris Weert	50N48	4E39	-0:18:36
Sint Joris Winge	50N55	4E52	-0:19:28
Sint Katelijne Waver	51N04	4E32	-0:18:08
Sint Kruis	51N13	3E15	-0:13:00
Sint Lenaarts	51N21	4E41	-0:18:44
Sint Michiels	51N11	3E12	-0:12:48
Sint Niklaas (Saint Nicolas)	51N10	4E08	-0:16:32
Sint Pieters Leeuw	50N47	4E14	-0:16:56
Sint Truiden	50N48	5E12	-0:20:48
Sirault	50N30	3E47	-0:15:08
Sleidinge	51N08	3E41	-0:14:44
Soheit Tinlot	50N29	5E22	-0:21:28
Soignies (Zinnik)	50N35	4E04	-0:16:16
Solre sur Sambre	50N18	4E08	-0:16:32
Sougne Remouchamps	50N29	5E40	-0:22:40
Soy	50N17	5E31	-0:22:04
Spa	50N30	5E52	-0:23:28
Stabroek	51N20	4E22	-0:17:28
Staden	50N59	3E01	-0:12:04
Stavelot	50N23	5E56	-0:23:44
Stekene	51N12	4E02	-0:16:08
Stoumont	50N25	5E48	-0:23:12
Tamines	50N26	4E36	-0:18:24
Templeuve	50N38	3E16	-0:13:04
Temse	51N08	4E13	-0:16:52
Tenneville	50N06	5E32	-0:22:08
Termonde → Dendermonde	51N02	4E07	-0:16:28
Tervuren	50N49	4E31	-0:18:04
Terwagne	50N27	5E20	-0:21:20
Tessenderlo	51N04	5E05	-0:20:20
Theux	50N32	5E49	-0:23:16
Thorembais Les Béguines	50N40	4E49	-0:19:16
Thourout	51N04	3E06	-0:12:24
Thuin	50N20	4E17	-0:17:08
Tielt	51N00	3E19	-0:13:16
Tienen	50N48	4E57	-0:19:48
Tilff	50N34	5E35	-0:22:20
Tintigny	49N41	5E31	-0:22:04
Tirlemont	50N48	4E56	-0:19:44
Tongeren	50N47	5E28	-0:21:52
Tongerlo	51N07	4E54	-0:19:36
Torhout	51N04	3E06	-0:12:24
Tournai	50N36	3E23	-0:13:32
Tournhout	51N19	4E57	-0:19:48
Trazegnies	50N28	4E19	-0:17:16
Trois Ponts	50N22	5E52	-0:23:28
Tubize	50N41	4E12	-0:16:48
Turnhout	51N19	4E57	-0:19:48
Uccle	50N48	4E19	-0:17:16
Vencimont	50N02	4E55	-0:19:40
Verviers	50N35	5E52	-0:23:28
Veurne (Furnes)	51N04	2E40	-0:10:40
Vielsalm	50N17	5E55	-0:23:40
Villers Devant Orval	49N37	5E19	-0:21:16
Villers la Ville	50N35	4E32	-0:18:08
Vilvoorde	50N56	4E26	-0:17:44
Virelles	50N04	4E20	-0:17:20
Virginal Samme	50N38	4E12	-0:16:48
Virton	49N34	5E32	-0:22:08
Visé	50N44	5E42	-0:22:48
Vloesberg → Flobecq	50N44	3E44	-0:14:56
Vorst	51N04	5E01	-0:20:04
Vosselaar	51N19	4E53	-0:19:32
Vresse	49N52	4E56	-0:19:44
Waarschoot	51N09	3E36	-0:14:24
Waasmunster	51N06	4E05	-0:16:20
Waimes	50N25	6E07	-0:24:28
Walcourt	50N15	4E25	-0:17:40
Waregem	50N53	3E25	-0:13:40
Waremme	50N41	5E15	-0:21:00
Warneton	50N45	2E57	-0:11:48
Wasmes	50N33	3E32	-0:14:08
Waterloo	50N43	4E23	-0:17:32
Watou	50N51	2E37	-0:10:28
Waulsort	50N13	4E52	-0:19:28
Wavre	50N43	4E37	-0:18:28
Weelde	51N25	5E00	-0:20:00
Welkenraedt	50N40	5E59	-0:23:56
Wellin	50N05	5E07	-0:20:28
Wenduine	51N18	3E05	-0:12:20
Wépion	50N25	4E52	-0:19:28
Werbomont	50N23	5E41	-0:22:44
Wervik	50N47	3E02	-0:12:08
Westende	51N10	2E46	-0:11:04
Westerlo	51N05	4E55	-0:19:40
Westkapelle	51N19	3E18	-0:13:12
Westmalle	51N18	4E41	-0:18:44
Westrem	50N58	3E52	-0:15:28
Wetteren	51N00	3E53	-0:15:32
Wevelgem	50N48	3E10	-0:12:40
Wezemaal	50N57	4E46	-0:19:04
Willebroek	51N04	4E22	-0:17:28
Wilrijk	51N10	4E24	-0:17:36
Wingene	51N04	3E16	-0:13:04
Woluwe Saint Pierre	50N50	4E25	-0:17:40
Wolvertem	50N57	4E18	-0:17:12
Wondelgem	51N05	3E43	-0:14:52
Wuustwezel	51N23	4E36	-0:18:24
Ypres → Ieper	50N51	2E53	-0:11:32
Yvoir	50N20	4E53	-0:19:32
Zaventem	50N53	4E28	-0:17:52
Zedelgem	51N09	3E08	-0:12:32
Zeebrugge	51N20	3E12	-0:12:48
Zele	51N04	4E02	-0:16:08
Zelzate	51N12	3E49	-0:15:16
Zemst	50N59	4E28	-0:17:52
Zinnik → Soignies	50N35	4E04	-0:16:16
Zolder	51N01	5E18	-0:21:12
Zomergem	51N07	3E33	-0:14:12
Zonhoven	50N59	5E21	-0:21:24
Zonnebeke	50N52	2E59	-0:11:56
Zottegem	50N52	3E48	-0:15:12
Zwevegem	50N48	3E20	-0:13:20
Zwevezele	51N02	3E12	-0:12:48

BELIZE — BRITISH HONDURAS — BELICE — BELIZE

Time Table
Before 1/Apr/1912 LMT
Begin Standard 90W00

Date	Time	Offset
1/Apr/1912	0:00	6:00
6/Oct/1918	0:00	5:30
12/Feb/1919	0:00	6:00
5/Oct/1919	0:00	5:30
13/Feb/1920	0:00	6:00
3/Oct/1920	0:00	5:30
13/Feb/1921	0:00	6:00
2/Oct/1921	0:00	5:30
12/Feb/1922	0:00	6:00
8/Oct/1922	0:00	5:30
11/Feb/1923	0:00	6:00
7/Oct/1923	0:00	5:30
10/Feb/1924	0:00	6:00
5/Oct/1924	0:00	5:30
15/Feb/1925	0:00	6:00
4/Oct/1925	0:00	5:30
14/Feb/1926	0:00	6:00
3/Oct/1926	0:00	5:30
13/Feb/1927	0:00	6:00
2/Oct/1927	0:00	5:30
12/Feb/1928	0:00	6:00
7/Oct/1928	0:00	5:30
10/Feb/1929	0:00	6:00
6/Oct/1929	0:00	5:30
9/Feb/1930	0:00	6:00
5/Oct/1930	0:00	5:30
15/Feb/1931	0:00	6:00
4/Oct/1931	0:00	5:30
14/Feb/1932	0:00	6:00
2/Oct/1932	0:00	5:30
12/Feb/1933	0:00	6:00
8/Oct/1933	0:00	5:30
11/Feb/1934	0:00	6:00
7/Oct/1934	0:00	5:30
10/Feb/1935	0:00	6:00
6/Oct/1935	0:00	5:30
12/Feb/1936	0:00	6:00
4/Oct/1936	0:00	5:30
14/Feb/1937	0:00	6:00
3/Oct/1937	0:00	5:30
13/Feb/1938	0:00	6:00
9/Oct/1938	0:00	5:30
12/Feb/1939	0:00	6:00
8/Oct/1939	0:00	5:30
11/Feb/1940	0:00	6:00
6/Oct/1940	0:00	5:30
9/Feb/1941	0:00	6:00
5/Oct/1941	0:00	5:30
15/Feb/1942	0:00	6:00
4/Oct/1942	0:00	5:30
14/Feb/1943	0:00	6:00
5/Dec/1973	0:00	5:00
9/Feb/1974	0:00	6:00
18/Dec/1982	0:00	5:00
12/Feb/1983	0:00	6:00

Place	Lat	Long	Offset
Belice → Belize City	17N30	88W12	5:52:48
Belize City	17N30	88W12	5:52:48
Belmopan	17N15	88W46	5:55:04
Benque Viejo	17N05	89W08	5:56:32
Caledonia	18N14	88W29	5:53:56
Casemero Palma	16N20	88W47	5:55:08
Corozal	18N24	88W24	5:53:36
Hill Bank	17N35	88W42	5:54:48
Indian Church	17N45	88W40	5:54:40
Middlesex	17N02	88W31	5:54:04
Monkey River	16N22	88W29	5:53:56
Orange Walk	18N06	88W33	5:54:12
Palmar Camp	16N26	88W53	5:55:32
Punta Gorda	16N07	88W48	5:55:12
San Antonio	16N15	89W02	5:56:08
Sierra de Agua	17N32	88W54	5:55:36
Stann Creek	16N58	88W13	5:52:52

BENIN — ABOMEY — DAHOMEY — BENIN

Time Table
Before 1/Jan/1912 LMT
Begin Standard 0W00

Date	Time	Offset
1/Jan/1912	0:00	0:00

Begin Standard 15E00

Date	Time	Offset
26/Feb/1934	0:00	-1:00

Place	Lat	Long	Offset
Abomey	7N11	1E59	-0:07:56
Adjohon	6N42	2E28	-0:09:52
Agouna	7N34	1E42	-0:06:48
Allada	6N39	2E09	-0:08:36
Angara-Débou	11N19	3E03	-0:12:12
Athiémé	6N35	1E40	-0:06:40
Banikoara	11N18	2E26	-0:09:44
Bassila	9N01	1E40	-0:06:40
Batia	10N54	1E29	-0:05:56
Béroubouay	10N32	2E44	-0:10:56
Bétérou	9N12	2E16	-0:09:04
Bimbéréké	10N13	2E40	-0:10:40
Birni	10N00	1E31	-0:06:04
Bohicon	7N12	2E04	-0:08:16
Borodarou	10N59	2E53	-0:11:32
Boukombé	10N11	1E06	-0:04:24
Cotonou	6N21	2E26	-0:09:44
Djougou	9N42	1E40	-0:06:40
Gogonou	10N50	2E50	-0:11:20
Grand-Popo	6N17	1E50	-0:07:20
Guené	11N44	3E13	-0:12:52
Guessou-Sud	10N03	2E38	-0:10:32
Kandi	11N08	2E56	-0:11:44
Kérou	10N50	2E06	-0:08:24
Kétou	7N22	2E36	-0:10:24
Kilibo	8N34	2E36	-0:10:24
Kouandé	10N20	1E42	-0:06:48
Lokossa	6N38	1E43	-0:06:52
Malanville	11N52	3E23	-0:13:32
Natitingou	10N19	1E22	-0:05:28
Ndali	9N51	2E43	-0:10:52
Nikki	9N56	3E12	-0:12:48
Ouidah	6N22	2E05	-0:08:20
Parakou	9N21	2E37	-0:10:28
Pira	8N30	1E44	-0:06:56
Pobé	6N58	2E41	-0:10:44
Porto-Novo	6N29	2E37	-0:10:28
Sakété	6N43	2E40	-0:10:40
Savalou	7N56	1E58	-0:07:52
Savé	8N02	2E29	-0:09:56
Segbana	10N56	3E42	-0:14:48
Sinindé	10N21	2E23	-0:09:32
Tanguiéta	10N37	1E16	-0:05:04
Tchaourou	8N53	2E36	-0:10:24
Tchetti	7N50	1E40	-0:06:40
Tobré	10N12	2E08	-0:08:32
Zagnanado	7N16	2E21	-0:09:24

BERMUDAS — BERMUDES — BERMUDA

Time Table
Before 1/Jan/1930 LMT
Begin Standard 60W00

Date	Time	Offset
1/Jan/1930	2:00	4:00
28/Apr/1974	2:00	3:00
27/Oct/1974	2:00	4:00
27/Apr/1975	2:00	3:00
26/Oct/1975	2:00	4:00
25/Apr/1976	2:00	3:00
31/Oct/1976	2:00	4:00
24/Apr/1977	2:00	3:00
30/Oct/1977	2:00	4:00
30/Apr/1978	2:00	3:00
29/Oct/1978	2:00	4:00
29/Apr/1979	2:00	3:00
28/Oct/1979	2:00	4:00
27/Apr/1980	2:00	3:00
26/Oct/1980	2:00	4:00
26/Apr/1981	2:00	3:00
25/Oct/1981	2:00	4:00
25/Apr/1982	2:00	3:00
31/Oct/1982	2:00	4:00
24/Apr/1983	2:00	3:00
30/Oct/1983	2:00	4:00
29/Apr/1984	2:00	3:00
28/Oct/1984	2:00	4:00
28/Apr/1985	2:00	3:00
27/Oct/1985	2:00	4:00
27/Apr/1986	2:00	3:00
26/Oct/1986	2:00	4:00
5/Apr/1987	2:00	3:00
25/Oct/1987	2:00	4:00
3/Apr/1988	2:00	3:00
30/Oct/1988	2:00	4:00
2/Apr/1989	2:00	3:00
29/Oct/1989	2:00	4:00
1/Apr/1990	2:00	3:00
28/Oct/1990	2:00	4:00
7/Apr/1991	2:00	3:00
27/Oct/1991	2:00	4:00
5/Apr/1992	2:00	3:00
25/Oct/1992	2:00	4:00
4/Apr/1993	2:00	3:00
31/Oct/1993	2:00	4:00
3/Apr/1994	2:00	3:00
30/Oct/1994	2:00	4:00
2/Apr/1995	2:00	3:00
29/Oct/1995	2:00	4:00
7/Apr/1996	2:00	3:00
27/Oct/1996	2:00	4:00
6/Apr/1997	2:00	3:00
26/Oct/1997	2:00	4:00
5/Apr/1998	2:00	3:00
25/Oct/1998	2:00	4:00
4/Apr/1999	2:00	3:00
31/Oct/1999	2:00	4:00
2/Apr/2000	2:00	3:00
29/Oct/2000	2:00	4:00

Place	Lat	Long	Offset
Evans Bay	32N15	64W52	4:19:28
Flatts	32N19	64W44	4:18:56
Hamilton	32N17	64W46	4:19:04
Ireland Point	32N20	64W50	4:19:20
Kindley Field	32N22	64W40	4:18:40
Paget	32N18	64W46	4:19:04
Riddles Bay	32N15	64W49	4:19:16
Saint George	32N22	64W40	4:18:40
Somerset	32N18	64W52	4:19:28
Spanish Point	32N18	64W48	4:19:12
The Flats Village	32N19	64W44	4:18:56
Tuckers Town	32N20	64W42	4:18:48

BHUTAN

BHUTÁN

BHOUTAN

DRUK-YUL

Time Table
Before 15/Aug/1947 LMT
Begin Standard 82E30
15/Aug/1947 0:00 -5:30
Begin Standard 90E00
1/Oct/1987 0:00 -6:00

Place	Lat	Long	Time
Chhukha Dzong	27N09	89E36	-5:58:24
Lhuntsi Dzong	27N39	91E09	-6:04:36
Paro	27N26	89E25	-5:57:40
Phuntsholing	26N53	89E23	-5:57:32
Punakha	27N37	89E52	-5:59:28
Taga Dzong	27N04	89E53	-5:59:32
Tashi Gang Dzong	27N19	91E34	-6:06:16
Thimbu	27N28	89E39	-5:58:36
Tongsa Dzong	27N31	90E30	-6:02:00
Wangdu Phodrang	27N29	89E54	-5:59:36

BOLIVIA

BOLIVIEN

BOLIVIE

Time Table
Before 1/Jan/1890 LMT
Begin Standard 68w09
1/Jan/1890 0:00 4:33
15/Oct/1931 0:00 3:33
Begin Standard 60w00
21/Mar/1932 0:00 4:00

Place	Lat	Long	Time
Achacachi	16s03	68w43	4:34:52
Aiquile	18s10	65w10	4:20:40
Amarete (Charazani)	15s14	68w58	4:35:52
Ancoraimes	15s54	68w58	4:35:52
Andamarca	18s49	67w31	4:30:04
Añez	17s19	63w43	4:14:52
Antequera	18s29	66w53	4:27:32
Anzaldo	17s50	65w55	4:23:40
Apolo	14s43	68w31	4:34:04
Arampampa	17s55	66w04	4:24:16
Arani	17s34	65w46	4:23:04
Arque	17s48	66w23	4:25:32
Atocha	20s56	66w14	4:24:56
Ayacucho	17s51	63w20	4:13:20
Ayo Ayo	17s05	68w00	4:32:00
Azurduy	19s59	64w29	4:17:56
Baures	13s35	63w35	4:14:20
Bella Flor	11s09	67w49	4:31:16
Betanzos	19s34	65w27	4:21:48
Boyuibe	20s25	63w17	4:13:08
Buena Vista	17s27	63w40	4:14:40
Cabezas	18s46	63w24	4:13:36
Cachuela Esperanza	10s32	65w38	4:22:32
Caiza	20s02	65w40	4:22:40
Calamarca	16s55	68w09	4:32:36
Calcha	21s06	67w31	4:30:04
Camargo	20s39	65w13	4:20:52
Camiri	20s03	63w31	4:14:04
Capinota	17s43	66w14	4:24:56
Caquiaviri	17s03	68w38	4:34:32
Caracollo	17s39	67w10	4:28:40
Caranavi	15s46	67w36	4:30:24
Carandaiti	20s45	63w04	4:12:16
Caraparí	21s49	63w46	4:15:04
Cataricahua	18s14	66w49	4:27:16
Cerdas	20s48	66w29	4:25:56
Chaguaya	21s49	64w50	4:19:20
Challapata	18s54	66w47	4:27:08
Chaqui	19s36	65w32	4:22:08
Charagua	19s48	63w13	4:12:52
Charaña	17s36	69w28	4:37:52
Charazani → Amarete	15s14	68w58	4:35:52
Chayanta	18s27	66w30	4:26:00
Chulumani	16s24	67w31	4:30:04
Chuma	15s24	68w56	4:35:44
Cliza	17s36	65w56	4:23:44
Cobija	11s02	68w44	4:34:56
Cochabamba	17s24	66w09	4:24:36
Cohoni	16s44	67w51	4:31:24
Colcapirhua	17s25	66w15	4:25:00
Colquechaca	18s40	66w01	4:24:04
Colquencha	17s00	68w17	4:33:08
Colquiri	17s25	67w08	4:28:32
Comarapa	17s54	64w29	4:17:56
Concepción	11s29	66w31	4:26:04
Concepción	16s15	62w04	4:08:16
Copacabana	16s10	69w05	4:36:20
Coripata	16s18	67w36	4:30:24
Corocoro	17s12	68w29	4:33:56
Coroico	16s10	67w44	4:30:56
Corque	18s21	67w42	4:30:48
Cosapa	18s11	68w40	4:34:40
Cotagaita	20s50	65w41	4:22:44
Cotoca	17s49	63w03	4:12:12
Cuevo	20s27	63w32	4:14:08
Culpina	20s50	64w58	4:19:52
Curahuara	17s40	68w02	4:32:08
El Carmen	18s49	58w33	3:54:12
El Cerro	17s31	61w34	4:06:16
El Palmar	21s54	63w39	4:14:36
Entre Ríos	21s32	64w12	4:16:48
Eucaliptus	17s35	67w31	4:30:04
Exaltación	13s16	65w15	4:21:00
General Saavedra	17s15	63w10	4:12:40
Guadalupe	18s33	64w05	4:16:20
Guanay	15s28	67w52	4:31:28
Guaqui	16s35	68w51	4:35:24
Guayaramerín	10s48	65w23	4:21:32
Gutiérrez	19s25	63w34	4:14:16
Huacaraje	13s33	63w45	4:15:00
Huachacalla	18s45	68w17	4:33:08
Huanchaca	20s20	66w39	4:26:36
Huanuni	18s16	66w51	4:27:24
Huari	19s00	66w48	4:27:12
Huarina	16s12	68w38	4:34:32
Ichoca	17s12	67w17	4:29:08
Independencia	17s07	66w53	4:27:32
Ipitá	19s20	63w32	4:14:08
Irupana	16s28	67w28	4:29:52
Itapaya	17s34	66w21	4:25:24
Ivo	20s27	63w26	4:13:44
Ixiamas	13s45	68w09	4:32:36
La Estrella	16s30	63w45	4:15:00
La Guardia	17s54	63w20	4:13:20
Lagunillas	19s38	63w43	4:14:52
La Paz	16s30	68w09	4:32:36
Las Piedras	11s06	66w10	4:24:40
Las Taperas	17s54	60w23	4:01:32
Llallagua	18s25	66w38	4:26:32
Llanquera	18s06	67w47	4:31:08
Llica	19s52	68w16	4:33:04
Loreto	15s13	64w40	4:18:40
Los Chacos	14s33	62w11	4:08:44
Luribay	17s06	67w39	4:30:36
Macha	18s49	66w05	4:24:20
Machacamarca	18s10	67w02	4:28:08
Magdalena	13s20	64w08	4:16:32
Manoa	9s40	65w27	4:21:48
Mapiri	15s15	68w10	4:32:40
Mizque	17s56	65w19	4:21:16
Mocomoco	15s22	68w59	4:35:56
Monteagudo	19s49	63w59	4:15:56
Monte Cristo	14s43	61w14	4:04:56
Montero	17s20	63w15	4:13:00
Moraya	21s45	65w32	4:22:08
Morococala	18s10	66w44	4:26:56
Ocurí	18s50	65w50	4:23:20
Oruro	17s59	67w09	4:28:36
Padcaya	21s52	64w48	4:19:12
Padilla	19s19	64w20	4:17:20
Palca	16s34	67w59	4:31:56
Pampa Grande	18s05	64w06	4:16:24
Panacachi	18s23	66w21	4:25:24
Pasorapa	18s16	64w37	4:18:28
Patacamaya	17s14	67w55	4:31:40
Pazña	18s36	66w55	4:27:40
Pelechuco	14s48	69w04	4:36:16
Perotó	14s50	64w31	4:18:04
Perseverancia	14s44	62w48	4:11:12
Pocoata	18s41	66w11	4:24:44
Pocona	17s39	65w24	4:21:36
Pojo	17s45	64w49	4:19:16
Poopó	18s23	66w59	4:27:56
Porco	19s50	65w59	4:23:56
Poroma	18s29	65w30	4:22:00
Portachuelo	17s21	63w24	4:13:36
Postrevalle	18s29	63w51	4:15:24
Potosí	19s35	65w45	4:23:00
Presto	18s55	64w56	4:19:44
Pucará	18s43	64w11	4:16:44
Pucarani	16s23	68w30	4:34:00
Puerto Acosta	15s32	69w15	4:37:00
Puerto Alegre	13s53	61w36	4:06:24
Puerto Heath	12s30	68w40	4:34:40
Puerto Rico	11s05	67w38	4:30:32
Puerto Siles	12s48	65w05	4:20:20
Puerto Suárez	18s57	57w51	3:51:24
Pulacayo	20s25	66w41	4:26:44
Puna	19s46	65w28	4:21:52
Punata	17s32	65w50	4:23:20
Quetena	22s10	67w25	4:29:40
Quiabaya	15s37	68w46	4:35:04
Quillacas	19s14	66w58	4:27:52
Quillacollo	17s26	66w17	4:25:08
Quime	17s02	67w15	4:29:00
Ravelo	18s48	65w32	4:22:08
Reyes	14s19	67w23	4:29:32
Riberalta	10s59	66w06	4:24:24
Río Mulatos	19s42	66w47	4:27:08
Roboré	18s20	59w45	3:59:00
Rurrenabaque	14s28	67w34	4:30:16
Sabaya	19s01	68w23	4:33:32
Sacaba	17s23	66w02	4:24:08
Sacaca	18s05	66w26	4:25:44
Sajama	18s07	69w00	4:36:00
Salinas de Garci Mendoza	19s38	67w43	4:30:52
Samaipata	18s09	63w52	4:15:28
Sanandita	21s40	63w35	4:14:20
San Benito	17s31	65w55	4:23:40
San Borja	14s49	66w51	4:27:24
San Buena Ventura	14s28	67w35	4:30:20
San Ignacio	14s53	65w36	4:22:24
San Ignacio	16s23	60w59	4:03:56
San Javier	14s34	64w42	4:18:48
San Javier	16s20	62w38	4:10:32
San Joaquín	13s04	64w49	4:19:16
San José	14s13	68w05	4:32:20
San José de Chiquitos	17s51	60w47	4:03:08
San Juan del Piray	20s27	64w09	4:16:36
San Lorenzo	21s26	64w47	4:19:08
San Lucas	20s06	65w07	4:20:28
San Matías	16s22	58w24	3:53:36
San Miguel	16s42	61w01	4:04:04
San Pablo de Tiquina	16s13	68w52	4:35:28
San Pedro	14s20	64w50	4:19:20
San Pedro de Buena Vista	18s13	65w59	4:23:56
San Ramón	13s17	64w43	4:18:52
Santa Ana	13s45	65w35	4:22:20
Santa Ana	15s31	67w30	4:30:00
Santa Ana	18s43	58w44	3:54:56
Santa Cruz	17s48	63w10	4:12:40
Santa Rosa	14s10	66w53	4:27:32
Santa Rosa	10s36	67w25	4:29:40
Santa Rosa	17s07	63w35	4:14:20
Santa Rosa de la Roca	16s04	61w32	4:06:08
Santa Rosa del Palmar	16s54	62w24	4:09:36
Santiago	18s19	59w34	3:58:16
Santiago de Huata	16s06	68w53	4:35:32
Santiago de Machaca	17s05	69w16	4:37:04
Santo Corazón	17s59	58w51	3:55:24
Sena	11s32	67w11	4:28:44
Sicasica	17s22	67w45	4:31:00
Sopachuy	19s29	64w31	4:18:04
Sorata	15s47	68w40	4:34:40
Sotomayor	19s18	65w03	4:20:12
Sucre	19s02	65w17	4:21:08
Tapacarí	17s31	66w36	4:26:24
Tarabuco	19s10	64w57	4:19:48
Tarata	17s37	66w01	4:24:04
Tarija	21s31	64w45	4:19:00
Tiahuanacu	16s33	68w42	4:34:48
Tinguipaya	19s11	65w51	4:23:24
Tiraque	17s37	65w04	4:20:16
Todos Santos	16s48	65w08	4:20:32
Toledo	18s10	67w25	4:29:40
Tomás Barrón (Eucaliptus)	17s35	67w31	4:30:04
Tomave	20s06	66w35	4:26:20
Torotoro	18s07	65w46	4:23:04
Totora	17s42	65w09	4:20:36
Totora	17s49	68w07	4:32:28
Totora Palca	19s55	65w26	4:21:44
Trigal	18s17	64w08	4:16:32

BOLIVIE — BOLIVIEN — BOLIVIA

Place	Lat	Long	Offset
Trinidad	14s47	64w47	4:19:08
Tumupasa	14s09	67w55	4:31:40
Tupiza	21s27	65w43	4:22:52
Uncia	18s27	66w37	4:26:28
Uyuni	20s28	66w50	4:27:20
Vallegrande	18s29	64w06	4:16:24
Viacha	16s39	68w18	4:33:12
Villa Abecia	21s00	65w23	4:21:32
Villa Bella	10s23	65w24	4:21:36
Villa Eufronio Viscarra	17s59	65w36	4:22:24
Villa Martín	20s46	67w47	4:31:08
Villa Montes	21s15	63w30	4:14:00
Villa Rivero	17s37	65w48	4:23:12
Villa Serrano	19s06	64w22	4:17:28
Villa Tunari	16s55	65w25	4:21:40
Villa Vaca Guzmán	19s54	63w48	4:15:12
Villazón	22s06	65w36	4:22:24
Vitichi	20s13	65w29	4:21:56
Warnes	17s30	63w10	4:12:40
Yaco	17s09	67w24	4:29:36
Yacuiba	22s02	63w45	4:15:00
Yamparáez	19s10	65w10	4:20:40
Yanacachi	16s23	67w43	4:30:52
Yata	13s20	66w35	4:26:20
Yotala	19s10	65w17	4:21:08
Yotaú	16s03	63w03	4:12:12
Zudañez	19s06	64w44	4:18:56

BOPHUTHATSWANA — BOPHUTHATSWANA

Time Table

Before 8/Feb/1892 LMT		
Begin Standard		22E30
8/Feb/1892	0:00	-1:30
Begin Standard		30E00
1/Mar/1903	0:00	-2:00
20/Sep/1942	2:00	-3:00
21/Mar/1943	2:00	-2:00
19/Sep/1943	2:00	-3:00
19/Mar/1944	2:00	-2:00

Place	Lat	Long	Offset
Battlemount	26s57	23E46	-1:35:04
Buxton	27s38	24E42	-1:38:48
Cardington	27s11	23E30	-1:34:00
Deelpan	26s19	25E36	-1:42:24
Ewbank	26s14	23E35	-1:34:20
Ganyesa	26s35	24E10	-1:36:40
Pudimoe	27s26	24E44	-1:38:56
Setlagodi	26s16	25E06	-1:40:24
Taung	27s33	24E47	-1:39:08
Thaba Nchu	29s17	26E52	-1:47:28
Tlhakgameng	26s27	24E21	-1:37:24
Tshidilamolomo	25s50	24E41	-1:38:44
Tsineng	27s06	23E04	-1:32:16

BOTSWANA — BECHUANALAND — BOTSWANA

Time Table

Before 1/Jan/1885 LMT		
Begin Standard		30E00
1/Jan/1885	0:00	-2:00
19/Sep/1943	2:00	-3:00
19/Mar/1944	2:00	-2:00

Place	Lat	Long	Offset
Artesia → Mosomane	24s04	26E15	-1:45:00
Bobonong	21s58	28E17	-1:53:08
Dibete	23s45	26E26	-1:45:44
Dinokwe	23s24	26E40	-1:46:40
Dodo	18s45	25E20	-1:41:20
Duma	18s45	22E46	-1:31:04
Dutlhe	23s55	23E47	-1:35:08
Dutlwe	23s55	23E47	-1:35:08
Francistown	21s11	27E32	-1:50:08
Gaberones → Gaborone	24s45	25E55	-1:43:40
Gaborone	24s45	25E55	-1:43:40
Gcoverega	19s08	24E15	-1:37:00
Gerufa	19s17	26E02	-1:44:08
Ghanzi	21s38	21E45	-1:27:00
Gumare	19s21	22E12	-1:28:48
Gweta	20s10	25E18	-1:41:12
Hukuntsi	24s02	21E48	-1:27:12
Kakoaka	18s40	24E22	-1:37:28
Kalakamate	20s39	27E21	-1:49:24
Kalkfontein	22s08	20E53	-1:23:32
Kang	23s41	22E50	-1:31:20
Kanye	24s59	25E19	-1:41:16
Kanyu	20s05	24E39	-1:38:36
Kasane	17s50	25E05	-1:40:20
Kasinka	18s13	24E22	-1:37:28
Kavimba	18s02	24E38	-1:38:32
Khakhea	24s51	23E20	-1:33:20
Khasebake	20s41	24E29	-1:37:56
Khomodimo	22s46	23E52	-1:35:28
Khoutsiri	21s22	20E08	-1:20:32
Khuis	26s37	21E45	-1:27:00
Khutshwe	23s19	24E29	-1:37:56
Kokong	24s27	23E03	-1:32:12
Krombi Pits	19s30	25E02	-1:40:08
Kule	23s05	20E05	-1:20:20
Kumba Pits	18s45	24E45	-1:39:00
Kumha Pits	18s45	24E45	-1:39:00
Kwakhanai	21s41	21E19	-1:25:16
Lehututu	23s58	21E51	-1:27:24
Lephepe	23s20	25E50	-1:43:20
Letlhakane	21s27	25E30	-1:42:00
Letlhakeng	24s08	25E02	-1:40:08
Lobatse	25s11	25E40	-1:42:40
Mabeleapodi	20s58	22E36	-1:30:24
Machaneng	23s10	27E26	-1:49:44
Mahalatswe	23s05	26E51	-1:47:24
Maitengwe	20s06	27E13	-1:48:52
Makalamabedi	20s19	23E51	-1:35:24
Mamuno	22s16	20E01	-1:20:04
Manyana	23s23	21E44	-1:26:56
Maralaleng	25s47	22E45	-1:31:00
Matapa	23s11	24E39	-1:38:36
Matlamanyane	19s33	25E57	-1:43:48
Maun	20s00	23E25	-1:33:40
Maunatlala	22s32	27E28	-1:49:52
Metsematluku	24s01	24E40	-1:38:40
Mmadinare	21s57	27E52	-1:51:28
Mochudi	24s28	26E05	-1:44:20
Mogapinyana	22s19	27E27	-1:49:48
Molepolole	24s25	25E30	-1:42:00
Mookane	24s59	24E33	-1:38:12
Mopipi	21s07	24E55	-1:39:40
Mosetse	20s37	26E32	-1:46:08
Moshupa	24s50	25E31	-1:42:04
Mosomane	24s04	26E15	-1:45:00
Mosopa	24s50	25E31	-1:42:04
Motloutse	21s28	27E24	-1:49:36
Mumungwe	21s59	26E24	-1:45:36
Nata	20s12	26E12	-1:44:48
Nokaneng	19s40	22E16	-1:29:04
Nxainxai	19s50	21E13	-1:24:52
Nxaunxau	18s19	21E04	-1:24:16
Odanakumadona	20s53	24E45	-1:39:00
Odiakwe	20s01	25E17	-1:41:08
Old Tate	21s22	27E46	-1:51:04
Ootse	25s02	25E45	-1:43:00
Ootsi	25s02	25E45	-1:43:00
Palapye	22s37	27E06	-1:48:24
Pandamatenga	18s35	25E42	-1:42:48
Phala	23s45	26E57	-1:47:48
Pitsani	25s30	25E35	-1:42:20
Rakops	21s00	24E32	-1:38:08
Ramathlabama	25s40	25E35	-1:42:20
Ramotswa	24s56	25E50	-1:43:20
Ranwanalenaus	19s35	22E47	-1:31:08
Ranwanlenau	19s35	22E47	-1:31:08
Sefare	23s02	27E28	-1:49:52
Sefhare	23s02	27E28	-1:49:52
Sehithwa	20s23	22E45	-1:31:00
Sekoma	24s41	23E50	-1:35:20
Sepopa	18s13	22E13	-1:28:52
Serowe	22s25	26E44	-1:46:56
Serule	21s58	27E20	-1:49:20
Shakawe	18s23	21E50	-1:27:20
Shaleshanto	19s09	23E58	-1:35:52
Shoshong	22s59	26E30	-1:46:00
Takachu	22s37	21E58	-1:27:52
Tlalamabele	21s16	26E20	-1:45:20
Tlapeng	23s15	21E49	-1:27:16
Tonota	21s29	27E29	-1:49:56
Toteng	20s22	22E58	-1:31:52
Tsau	20s12	22E22	-1:29:28
Tsekanyani	19s52	26E39	-1:46:36
Tshabong	26s03	22E29	-1:29:56
Tshane	24s05	21E54	-1:27:36
Tshesebe	21s51	27E35	-1:50:20
Tshukudu	22s30	23E22	-1:33:28
Tshwaane	22s29	22E03	-1:28:12
Tsigara	20s10	25E18	-1:41:12
Two Rivers	26s27	20E37	-1:22:28
Urwi	23s22	20E30	-1:22:00
Werda	25s15	23E16	-1:33:04
Xhumo	21s07	24E42	-1:38:48

Time Table # 1
Before 1/Jan/1914 LMT
Begin Standard 30w00
1/Jan/1914 0:00 2:00
9/Dec/1963 0:00 1:00
1/Mar/1964 0:00 2:00
31/Jan/1965 0:00 1:00
1/Apr/1965 0:00 2:00
1/Dec/1965 0:00 1:00
1/Mar/1966 0:00 2:00
1/Nov/1966 0:00 1:00
1/Mar/1967 0:00 2:00
1/Nov/1967 0:00 1:00
1/Mar/1968 0:00 2:00
2/Nov/1985 0:00 1:00
15/Mar/1986 0:00 2:00
25/Oct/1986 0:00 1:00
14/Feb/1987 0:00 2:00
24/Oct/1987 0:00 1:00
7/Feb/1988 0:00 2:00
16/Oct/1988 0:00 1:00
22/Jan/1989 0:00 2:00
15/Oct/1989 0:00 1:00
11/Feb/1990 0:00 2:00
....

Time Table # 2
Before 1/Jan/1914 LMT
Begin Standard 45w00
1/Jan/1914 0:00 3:00
3/Oct/1931 11:00 2:00
1/Apr/1932 0:00 3:00
3/Oct/1932 0:00 2:00
1/Apr/1933 0:00 3:00
1/Dec/1949 0:00 2:00
16/Apr/1950 0:00 3:00
1/Dec/1950 0:00 2:00
1/Apr/1951 0:00 3:00
1/Dec/1951 0:00 2:00
1/Apr/1952 0:00 3:00
1/Dec/1952 0:00 2:00
1/Apr/1953 0:00 3:00
23/Oct/1963 0:00 2:00
1/Mar/1964 0:00 3:00
31/Jan/1965 0:00 2:00
1/Apr/1965 0:00 3:00
1/Dec/1965 0:00 2:00
1/Mar/1966 0:00 3:00
1/Nov/1966 0:00 2:00
1/Mar/1967 0:00 3:00
1/Nov/1967 0:00 2:00
1/Mar/1968 0:00 3:00
2/Nov/1985 0:00 2:00
15/Mar/1986 0:00 3:00
25/Oct/1986 0:00 2:00
14/Feb/1987 0:00 3:00
24/Oct/1987 0:00 2:00
7/Feb/1988 0:00 3:00
16/Oct/1988 0:00 2:00
22/Jan/1989 0:00 3:00
15/Oct/1989 0:00 2:00
11/Feb/1990 0:00 3:00
....

Time Table # 3
Before 1/Jan/1914 LMT
Begin Standard 45w00
1/Jan/1914 0:00 3:00
9/Dec/1963 0:00 2:00
1/Mar/1964 0:00 3:00
31/Jan/1965 0:00 2:00
1/Apr/1965 0:00 3:00
1/Dec/1965 0:00 2:00
1/Mar/1966 0:00 3:00
1/Nov/1966 0:00 2:00
1/Mar/1967 0:00 3:00
1/Nov/1967 0:00 2:00
1/Mar/1968 0:00 3:00
2/Nov/1985 0:00 2:00
15/Mar/1986 0:00 3:00
25/Oct/1986 0:00 2:00
14/Feb/1987 0:00 3:00
24/Oct/1987 0:00 2:00
7/Feb/1988 0:00 3:00
16/Oct/1988 0:00 2:00
22/Jan/1989 0:00 3:00
15/Oct/1989 0:00 2:00
11/Feb/1990 0:00 3:00
....

Time Table # 4
Before 1/Jan/1914 LMT
Begin Standard 60w00
1/Jan/1914 0:00 4:00
9/Dec/1963 0:00 3:00
1/Mar/1964 0:00 4:00
31/Jan/1965 0:00 3:00
1/Apr/1965 0:00 4:00
1/Dec/1965 0:00 3:00
1/Mar/1966 0:00 4:00
1/Nov/1966 0:00 3:00
1/Mar/1967 0:00 4:00
1/Nov/1967 0:00 3:00
1/Mar/1968 0:00 4:00
2/Nov/1985 0:00 3:00
15/Mar/1986 0:00 4:00
25/Oct/1986 0:00 3:00
14/Feb/1987 0:00 4:00
24/Oct/1987 0:00 3:00
7/Feb/1988 0:00 4:00
16/Oct/1988 0:00 3:00
22/Jan/1989 0:00 4:00
15/Oct/1989 0:00 3:00
11/Feb/1990 0:00 4:00
....

Time Table # 5
Before 1/Jan/1914 LMT
Begin Standard 75w00
1/Jan/1914 0:00 5:00
9/Dec/1963 0:00 4:00
1/Mar/1964 0:00 5:00
31/Jan/1965 0:00 4:00
1/Apr/1965 0:00 5:00
1/Dec/1965 0:00 4:00
1/Mar/1966 0:00 5:00
1/Nov/1966 0:00 4:00
1/Mar/1967 0:00 5:00
1/Nov/1967 0:00 4:00
1/Mar/1968 0:00 5:00
2/Nov/1985 0:00 4:00
15/Mar/1986 0:00 5:00
25/Oct/1986 0:00 4:00
14/Feb/1987 0:00 5:00
24/Oct/1987 0:00 4:00
7/Feb/1988 0:00 5:00

Place	TT	Lat	Long	Offset
Abadia dos Dourados	2	18s28	47w24	3:09:36
Abadiânia	3	16s06	48w48	3:15:12
Abaeté	2	19s09	45w27	3:01:48
Abaetetuba	3	1s42	48w54	3:15:36
Abarracamento	2	22s12	43w30	2:54:00
Abatiá	3	23s19	50w18	3:21:12
Abel	2	22s54	46w08	3:04:32
Abraão	2	23s08	44w10	2:56:40
Abre Campo	2	20s18	42w29	2:49:56
Abreu e Lima	3	7s54	34w53	2:19:32
Abufari	4	5s25	62w59	4:11:56
Abunã	4	9s42	65w23	4:21:32
Acajutiba	3	11s40	38w01	2:32:04
Acará	3	1s57	48w11	3:12:44
Acaraú	3	2s53	40w07	2:40:28
Acari	3	6s31	36w38	2:26:32
Acopiara	3	6s06	39w27	2:37:48
Acorizal	4	15s12	56w22	3:45:28
Açu	3	5s34	36w54	2:27:36
Açucena	2	19s04	42w32	2:50:08
Adamantina	2	21s42	51w04	3:24:16
Adrianópolis	2	22s39	43w30	2:54:00
Afogados da Ingâzeira	3	7s45	37w39	2:30:36
Afonso Bezerra	3	5s30	36w30	2:26:00
Afonso Cláudio	2	20s05	41w08	2:44:32
Afuá	3	0s10	50w23	3:21:32
Agostinho Pôrto	2	22s47	43w23	2:53:32
Agrestina	3	8s27	35w57	2:23:48
Água Boa	2	17s59	42w24	2:49:36
Água Branca	3	9s17	37w55	2:31:40
Água Branca	3	7s31	37w40	2:30:40
Água Branca	3	5s53	42w38	2:50:32
Água Clara	4	20s27	52w52	3:31:28
Água Comprida	2	20s04	48w08	3:12:32
Água Comprida	2	21s54	45w40	3:02:40
Água Doce	3	27s00	51w33	3:26:12
Aguaí	2	22s04	46w58	3:07:52
Água Limpa	3	18s06	48w46	3:15:04
Águas Belas	3	9s07	37w07	2:28:28
Águas da Prata	2	21s56	46w43	3:06:52
Águas de Contendas	2	21s54	45w01	3:00:04
Águas de Lindóia	2	22s29	46w39	3:06:36
Águas Formosas	2	17s05	40w57	2:43:48
Água Viva	2	21s41	42w33	2:50:12
Agudo	3	29s38	53w15	3:33:00
Agudos	2	22s28	49w00	3:16:00
Agulhas Negras	2	22s28	44w27	2:57:48
Aiapuá	4	4s29	62w04	4:08:16
Aimorés	2	19s30	41w04	2:44:16
Aiquara	3	14s07	39w52	2:39:28
Airão	4	1s56	61w22	4:05:28
Aiuaba	3	6s38	40w07	2:40:28
Aiuruoca	2	21s58	44w36	2:58:24
Aiva	2	22s42	43w28	2:53:52
Alagoa	2	22s10	44w38	2:58:32
Alagoa Grande	3	7s03	35w38	2:22:32
Alagoa Nova	3	7s04	35w46	2:23:04
Alagoinhas	3	12s07	38w26	2:33:44
Albertina	2	22s12	46w37	3:06:28
Alcântara	3	2s24	44w24	2:57:36
Alcantilado	4	16s23	53w31	3:34:04
Alcobaça	3	17s30	39w13	2:36:52
Aldeia	2	23s30	46w51	3:07:24
Aldeia de Carapicuíba	2	23s35	46w48	3:07:12
Aldeia Velha	2	22s47	42w55	2:51:40
Aldeinha	2	23s45	46w53	3:07:32
Alegre	2	20s46	41w32	2:46:08
Alegrete	4	29s46	55w46	3:43:04
Além Paraíba	2	21s52	42w41	2:50:44
Alenquer	4	1s56	54w46	3:39:04
Alexandria	3	6s25	38w01	2:32:04
Alfenas	2	21s25	45w57	3:03:48
Alfredo Chaves	2	20s38	40w45	2:43:00
Alhandra	3	7s26	34w54	2:19:36
Aliança	3	7s35	35w13	2:20:52
Aljezur	2	22s40	43w36	2:54:24
Almas	3	11s33	47w09	3:08:36
Almeirim	4	1s32	52w34	3:30:16
Almenara	2	16s11	40w42	2:42:48
Almino Afonso	3	6s09	37w46	2:31:04
Aloândia	3	17s43	49w29	3:17:56
Alpinópolis	2	20s52	46w23	3:05:32
Altamira	3	3s12	52w12	3:28:48
Alterosa	2	21s15	46w08	3:04:32
Altinho	3	8s29	36w04	2:24:16
Altinópolis	2	21s02	47w23	3:09:32
Alto Araguaia	4	17s19	53w12	3:32:48
Alto Coité	4	15s47	54w20	3:37:20
Alto da Serra	2	22s53	44w14	2:56:56
Alto Garças	4	16s56	53w32	3:34:08
Alto Longá	3	5s15	42w12	2:48:48
Alto Paraguai	4	14s30	56w31	3:46:04
Alto Paraíso de Goiás	3	14s07	47w31	3:10:04
Alto Parnaíba	3	9s06	45w57	3:03:48
Alto Rio Doce	2	21s02	43w25	2:53:40
Altos	3	5s03	42w28	2:49:52
Alto Santo	3	5s31	38w15	2:33:00
Alto Sucuriú	4	19s19	52w47	3:31:08
Alvarães	4	3s12	64w50	4:19:20
Alvinópolis	2	20s06	43w03	2:52:12
Amambaí	4	23s05	55w13	3:40:52
Amapá	3	2n03	50w48	3:23:12
Amaraji	3	8s24	35w27	2:21:48
Amaral	2	22s42	43w29	2:53:56
Amarante	3	6s14	42w50	2:51:20
Amarante do Maranhão	3	5s36	46w45	3:07:00
Amargosa	3	13s02	39w36	2:38:24
Amaro Leite	3	13s58	49w09	3:16:36
Amataurá	4	3s29	68w06	4:32:24
Ambaí	2	22s43	43w28	2:53:52
Americana	2	22s45	47w20	3:09:20
Americano	3	1s19	48w04	3:12:16
Amolar	4	18s01	57w30	3:50:00
Amorinópolis	3	16s36	51w08	3:24:32
Amparo	2	22s42	46w45	3:07:00
Anadia	3	9s42	36w18	2:25:12
Anajás	3	0s59	49w57	3:19:48
Anajatuba	3	3s16	44w37	2:58:28
Anamã	4	3s35	61w22	4:05:28
Ananindeua	3	1s22	48w23	3:13:32
Anápolis	3	16s20	48w58	3:15:52
Anapurus	3	3s40	43w06	2:52:24
Anastácio	4	21s31	54w08	3:36:32
Anaurilândia	4	22s03	52w45	3:31:00
Andaraí	3	12s48	41w20	2:45:20
Andradas	2	22s04	46w34	3:06:16
Andrade Araújo	2	22s45	43w26	2:53:44
Andrade Pinto	2	22s14	43w22	2:53:28
Andradina	2	20s54	51w23	3:25:32
Andrelândia	2	21s44	44w18	2:57:12
Angatuba	2	23s29	48w25	3:13:40
Angelim	3	8s53	36w17	2:25:08
Angical	3	12s00	44w42	2:58:48
Angical do Piauí	3	6s05	42w44	2:50:56
Angicos	3	5s40	36w36	2:26:24
Angra dos Reis	2	23s00	44w18	2:57:12
Angustura	2	21s45	42w41	2:50:44
Anhanguera	3	18s19	48w14	3:12:56
Anicuns	3	16s28	49w58	3:19:52
Anil	3	2s32	44w14	2:56:56
Anori	4	3s47	61w38	4:06:32
Anta	2	22s03	42w59	2:51:56
Antas	3	10s23	38w20	2:33:20
Antenor Navarro	3	6s44	38w27	2:33:48
Antonina	3	25s27	48w43	3:14:52
Antonina do Norte	3	6s43	39w58	2:39:52
Antônio Carlos	2	21s19	43w45	2:55:00
Antônio Diogo	3	4s18	38w45	2:35:00
Antônio João	4	23s15	55w31	3:42:04
Antônio Lemos	3	1s22	50w50	3:23:20
Antônio Prado	3	28s51	51w17	3:25:08
Aparecida	2	22s50	45w14	3:00:56
Apeú	3	1s18	47w59	3:11:56
Apiacá	2	21s08	41w34	2:46:16
Apiaí	2	24s31	48w50	3:15:20
Apinajé	3	11s31	48w18	3:13:12
Apodi	3	5s39	37w48	2:31:12
Aporá	3	11s39	38w05	2:32:20
Aporé	3	18s58	52w01	3:28:04
Aporema	3	1n14	50w49	3:23:16
Apucarana	3	23s33	51w29	3:25:56
Apuiarés	3	3s56	39w24	2:37:36
Aquidabã	3	10s17	37w02	2:28:08
Aquidauana	4	20s28	55w48	3:43:12
Aracaju	3	10s55	37w04	2:28:16
Araçariguama	2	23s26	47w04	3:08:16
Aracati	3	4s34	37w46	2:31:04
Araçatuba	2	21s12	50w25	3:21:40
Araci	3	11s20	38w57	2:35:48
Aracitaba	2	21s20	43w23	2:53:32
Aracoiaba	3	4s23	38w49	2:35:16
Aracruz	2	19s49	40w16	2:41:04
Araçuaí	2	16s52	42w04	2:48:16
Aragarças	3	15s55	52w15	3:29:00
Aragoiânia	3	16s57	49w30	3:18:00
Araguacema	3	8s50	49w34	3:18:16
Araguaçu	3	12s49	49w51	3:19:24
Araguaína	3	7s12	48w12	3:12:48
Araguainha	4	16s49	53w05	3:32:20
Araguari	2	18s38	48w11	3:12:44
Araguatins	3	5s38	48w07	3:12:28
Araioses	3	2s53	41w55	2:47:40
Aramari	3	12s04	38w30	2:34:00
Arantina	2	21s56	44w15	2:57:00
Arapeí	2	22s41	44w27	2:57:48
Arapiraca	3	9s45	36w39	2:26:36
Arapongas	3	23s23	51w27	3:25:48
Arapoti	3	24s08	49w50	3:19:20
Araquari	3	26s23	48w43	3:14:52
Araranguá	3	28s56	49w29	3:17:56
Araraquara	2	21s47	48w10	3:12:40
Araras	2	22s22	47w23	3:09:32
Araras	2	22s49	46w36	3:06:24
Arari	3	3s28	44w47	2:59:08
Araripe	3	7s12	40w08	2:40:32
Araripina	3	7s33	40w34	2:42:16
Araruna	3	6s32	35w44	2:22:56
Arassuahí	2	16s52	42w04	2:48:16
Aratiba	3	27s24	52w19	3:29:16
Aratuípe	3	13s05	39w00	2:36:00
Arauá	3	11s16	37w37	2:30:28
Araucária	3	25s35	49w25	3:17:40
Araújos	2	19s56	45w04	3:00:16
Araxá	2	19s35	46w55	3:07:40
Arcadas	2	22s42	46w52	3:07:28
Arcângelo	2	21s18	44w19	2:57:16
Arceburgo	2	21s22	46w56	3:07:44
Arcos	2	20s17	45w32	3:02:08
Arcoverde	3	8s25	37w04	2:28:16
Areado	2	21s21	46w09	3:04:36
Areal	2	22s14	43w07	2:52:28
Areia	3	6s58	35w42	2:22:48
Areia Branca	3	4s56	37w07	2:28:28
Areia Branca	2	22s48	46w51	3:07:24
Areia Branca	2	22s44	43w25	2:53:40
Areias	2	22s35	44w42	2:58:48
Arenápolis	4	14s26	56w49	3:47:16
Arês	3	6s11	35w09	2:20:36
Argirita	2	21s37	42w50	2:51:20
Ariaú	4	3s11	57w14	3:48:56
Aripuanã	4	9s10	60w38	4:02:32
Ariquemes	4	9s56	63w04	4:12:16
Armazém	3	28s16	49w01	3:16:04
Arneiroz	3	6s20	40w08	2:40:32
Aroeiras	3	7s31	35w41	2:22:44
Arraial do Cabo	2	22s58	42w01	2:48:04
Arraias	3	12s56	46w57	3:07:48
Arroio Grande	3	32s14	53w05	3:32:20
Arrozal	2	22s37	44w03	2:56:12
Artur Nogueira	2	22s35	47w09	3:08:36
Aruanã	3	14s54	51w05	3:24:20
Arujá	2	23s24	46w20	3:05:20
Arumanduba	4	1s29	52w29	3:29:56
Árvorezinha	3	28s53	52w10	3:28:40
Assaí	3	23s22	50w49	3:23:16
Assaré	3	6s52	39w52	2:39:28
Assis	2	22s40	50w25	3:21:40
Astolfo Dutra	2	21s19	42w52	2:51:28
Astorga	3	23s13	51w40	3:26:40
Atalaia	3	9s31	36w02	2:24:08
Atibaia	2	23s07	46w33	3:06:12
Augusto Severo	3	5s52	37w19	2:29:16
Auriflama	2	20s41	50w34	3:22:16
Aurilândia	3	16s44	50w28	3:21:52
Aurizona	3	1s17	45w46	3:03:04
Aurora	3	6s57	38w58	2:35:52

Aurora 2 22s46 43w24 2:53:36
Aurora do Norte 3 12s43 46w24 3:05:36
Austin 2 22s43 43w32 2:54:08
Autazes 4 3s35 59w08 3:56:32
Avaí 2 22s08 49w22 3:17:28
Avaré 2 23s05 48w55 3:15:40
Aveiro 4 3s15 55w10 3:40:40
Avelar 2 22s20 43w25 2:53:40
Axinim 4 4s02 59w22 3:57:28
Axixá 3 2s51 44w04 2:56:16
Babaçulândia 3 7s13 47w46 3:11:04
Babilônia 2 22s33 44w28 2:57:52
Baby 2 22s42 43w23 2:53:32
Bacabal 3 4s14 44w47 2:59:08
Bacatuba 3 5s40 43w42 2:54:48
Bacurituba 3 2s43 44w43 2:58:52
Badu 2 22s54 43w04 2:52:16
Baependi 2 21s57 44w53 2:59:32
Bagé 4 31s20 54w06 3:36:24
Bagre 3 1s54 50w12 3:20:48
Bahía → Salvador
3 12s59 38w31 2:34:04
Baía Formosa 3 6s22 35w00 2:20:00
Baião 3 2s41 49w41 3:18:44
Bailique 3 0N58 50w04 3:20:16
Bairrinho 2 22s36 47w06 3:08:24
Bairro Alto 2 23s29 45w21 3:01:24
Baixa Grande 3 11s57 40w11 2:40:44
Baixio 3 6s44 38w43 2:34:52
Baldeador 2 22s53 43w02 2:52:08
Baldim 2 19s17 43w57 2:55:48
Baliza 3 16s15 52w25 3:29:40
Bálsamo 4 20s27 53w57 3:35:48
Balsas 3 7s31 46w02 3:04:08
Bambu 2 22s31 46w26 3:05:44
Bambuí 2 20s01 45w58 3:03:52
Bananal 2 22s41 44w19 2:57:16
Bananeiras 3 6s45 35w37 2:22:28
Bandeira do Sul 2 21s47 46w23 3:05:32
Bandeirantes 3 13s41 50w48 3:23:12
Bandeirantes 4 19s53 54w23 3:37:32
Bandeirantes 3 23s06 50w21 3:21:24
Barão Ataliba Nogueira
2 22s24 46w45 3:07:00
Barão de Aquino 2 22s07 42w39 2:50:36
Barão de Cocais 2 19s56 43w28 2:53:52
Barão de Geraldo
2 22s49 47w06 3:08:24
Barão de Grajaú 3 6s45 43w01 2:52:04
Barão de Juparanã
2 22s21 43w41 2:54:44
Barão de Melgaço
4 16s13 55w58 3:43:52
Barão de Tromaí 3 1s29 45w36 3:02:24
Barbacena 2 21s14 43w46 2:55:04
Barbalha 3 7s19 39w17 2:37:08
Barcelos 4 0s58 62w57 4:11:48
Bariri 2 22s04 48w44 3:14:56
Barra 3 11s05 43w10 2:52:40
Barracão 3 26s15 53w38 3:34:32
Barracão do Barreto
4 8s48 58w24 3:53:36
Barra da Estiva 3 13s38 41w19 2:45:16
Barra de Santa Rosa
3 6s43 36w04 2:24:16
Barra de Santo Antônio
3 9s24 35w30 2:22:00
Barra de São Francisco
2 21s58 42w42 2:50:48
Barra do Bugres 4 15s05 57w11 3:48:44
Barra do Corda 3 5s30 45w15 3:01:00
Barra do Garças 4 15s53 52w15 3:29:00
Barra do Mendes 3 11s43 42w04 2:48:16
Barra do Piraí 2 22s28 43w49 2:55:16
Barra do Ribeiro
3 30s18 51w18 3:25:12
Barra dos Coqueiros
3 10s54 37w03 2:28:12
Barra Mansa 2 22s32 44w11 2:56:44
Barrânia 2 21s33 46w32 3:06:08
Barras 3 4s15 42w18 2:49:12
Barreiras 3 12s08 45w00 3:00:00
Barreirinha 4 2s47 57w03 3:48:12
Barreirinhas 3 2s45 42w50 2:51:20
Barreiros 3 8s49 35w12 2:20:48
Barretos 2 20s33 48w33 3:14:12
Barrinho 2 23s07 45w22 3:01:28
Barro 3 7s11 38w47 2:35:08
Barro Alto 3 15s04 48w58 3:15:52
Barro Duro 3 2s52 42w17 2:49:08
Barueri 2 23s31 46w53 3:07:32
Basílio 3 31s53 53w01 3:32:04
Bataguaçu 4 21s42 52w22 3:29:28
Bataiporã 4 22s20 53w17 3:33:08
Batalha 3 9s41 37w08 2:28:32
Batalha 3 4s01 42w05 2:48:20
Batatais 2 20s53 47w37 3:10:28
Batatuba 2 23s04 46w25 3:05:40
Bateia 2 22s20 45w49 3:03:16
Batovi 4 15s53 53w24 3:33:36
Baturité 3 4s20 38w53 2:35:32
Bauru 2 22s19 49w04 3:16:16
Baús 4 18s19 53w10 3:32:40
Bayeux 3 7s08 34w56 2:19:44
Bebedouro 2 20s56 48w28 3:13:52
Beberibe 3 4s11 38w08 2:32:32
Beja 3 1s36 48w47 3:15:08
Bela Cruz 3 3s03 40w11 2:40:44
Bela Vista 4 22s06 56w31 3:46:04
Bela Vista de Goiás
3 16s58 48w57 3:15:48
Bela Vista do Paraíso
3 23s00 51w12 3:24:48
Belém 3 1s27 48w29 3:13:56

Belém de São Francisco
3 8s46 38w58 2:35:52
Belford Roxo 2 22s46 43w24 2:53:36
Bello Horizonte → Belo Horizonte
2 19s55 43w56 2:55:44
Belmonte 3 15s51 38w54 2:35:36
Belo Horizonte 2 19s55 43w56 2:55:44
Belo Jardim 3 8s20 36w26 2:25:44
Belo Vale 2 20s25 44w01 2:56:04
Belterra 4 2s38 54w57 3:39:48
Bemposta 2 22s09 43w07 2:52:28
Beneditinos 3 5s27 42w22 2:49:28
Benedito Leite 3 7s13 44w34 2:58:16
Benjamin Constant
5 4s22 70w02 4:40:08
Bento Gonçalves 3 29s10 51w31 3:26:04
Bequimão 3 2s26 44w47 2:59:08
Bertioga 2 23s51 46w09 3:04:36
Bertolínia 3 7s38 43w57 2:55:48
Beruri 4 3s54 61w22 4:05:28
Betém 2 22s52 44w17 2:57:08
Bezerros 3 8s14 35w45 2:23:00
Bias Fortes 2 21s36 43w46 2:55:04
Bicas 2 21s43 43w04 2:52:16
Bicas do Meio 2 22s31 45w21 3:01:24
Biguaçu 3 27s30 48w40 3:14:40
Bilac 2 21s24 50w28 3:21:52
Biriguí 2 21s18 50w19 3:21:16
Biritiba-Mirim 2 23s35 46w02 3:04:08
Bitupitá 3 2s54 41w16 2:45:04
Bituruna 3 26s10 51w34 3:26:16
Blumenau 3 26s56 49w03 3:16:12
Boa Barrinha 2 23s18 47w10 3:08:40
Boa Esperança 2 21s05 45w34 3:02:16
Boa Esperança 2 22s48 42w34 2:50:16
Boa Nova 3 14s22 40w10 2:40:40
Boa Vereda 2 22s27 46w14 3:04:56
Boa Viagem 3 5s07 39w44 2:38:56
Boa Vida 2 22s18 42w47 2:51:08
Boa Vista 3 26s17 48w50 3:15:20
Boa Vista 4 2N49 60w40 4:02:40
Bôca da Mata 3 9s41 36w11 2:24:44
Bôca do Acre 5 8s45 67w23 4:29:32
Bôca do Jari 3 1s07 51w58 3:27:52
Bocaina de Minas
2 22s10 44w24 2:57:36
Bocaiúva 2 17s07 43w49 2:55:16
Bodocó 3 7s47 39w55 2:39:40
Boiaçu 4 0s27 61w46 4:07:04
Bojuru 3 31s38 51w26 3:25:44
Bom Conselho 3 9s10 36w41 2:26:44
Bom Despacho 2 19s43 45w15 3:01:00
Bomfim 3 10s21 40w06 2:40:24
Bom Jardim de Goiás
3 16s17 52w07 3:28:28
Bom Jardim de Minas
2 21s57 44w11 2:56:44
Bom Jesus 3 9s04 44w22 2:57:28
Bom Jesus da Lapa
3 13s15 43w25 2:53:40
Bom Jesus da Terra Preta
2 23s15 46w36 3:06:24
Bom Jesus dos Perdões
2 23s08 46w28 3:05:52
Bom Repouso 2 22s28 46w09 3:04:36
Bom Retiro 3 27s48 49w31 3:18:04
Bom Retiro 2 22s10 45w40 3:02:40
Bom Retiro do Sul
3 29s37 51w56 3:27:44
Bom Sucesso 3 23s42 51w45 3:27:00
Bom Sucesso 4 15s43 56w07 3:44:28
Bom Sucesso 2 22s52 45w33 3:02:12
Bom Sucesso 2 23s25 46w24 3:05:36
Bonfim 2 22s58 45w15 3:01:00
Bonfinópolis 3 16s38 48w58 3:15:52
Bonito 4 21s08 56w28 3:45:52
Bonito 3 8s29 35w44 2:22:56
Bonito de Santa Fé
3 7s19 38w31 2:34:04
Borba 4 4s24 59w35 3:58:20
Borborema 2 21s37 49w04 3:16:16
Borda da Mata 2 22s16 46w10 3:04:40
Borda da Mata 2 22s37 47w01 3:08:04
Borrazópolis 3 23s56 51w36 3:26:24
Botelhos 2 21s39 46w24 3:05:36
Botucatu 2 22s52 48w26 3:13:44
Braço do Norte 3 28s17 49w11 3:16:44
Bragança 3 1s03 46w46 3:07:04
Bragança Paulista
2 22s57 46w34 3:06:16
Brás Cubas 2 23s32 46w13 3:04:52
Brasiléia 5 11s00 68w44 4:34:56
Brasília 3 15s47 47w55 3:11:40
Brasília de Minas
2 16s12 44w26 2:57:44
Braúnas 2 19s04 42w43 2:50:52
Brazópolis 2 22s28 45w37 3:02:28
Brejinho de Nazaré
3 11s01 48w34 3:14:16
Brejo 3 3s41 42w47 2:51:08
Brejo de São Felix
3 5s24 43w24 2:53:36
Brejões 3 13s06 39w48 2:39:12
Brejo Grande 3 10s26 36w28 2:25:52
Brejo Santo 3 7s29 39w00 2:36:00
Breves 3 1s40 50w29 3:21:56
Britânia 3 15s14 51w09 3:24:36
Brotas de Macaúbas
3 12s00 42w38 2:50:32
Brumadinho 2 20s08 44w13 2:56:52
Brumado 3 14s13 41w40 2:46:40
Brusque 3 27s06 48w56 3:15:44
Bueno Brandão 2 22s27 46w21 3:05:24
Buenolândia 3 15s48 50w17 3:21:08
Buenópolis 2 17s54 44w11 2:56:44

Buerarema 3 14s57 39w19 2:37:16
Buíque 3 8s37 37w09 2:28:36
Buquim 3 11s09 37w37 2:30:28
Buri 2 23s48 48w35 3:14:20
Buritama 2 21s03 50w08 3:20:32
Buriti 4 16s27 53w27 3:33:48
Buriti 3 3s55 42w57 2:51:48
Buriti Alegre 3 18s09 49w03 3:16:12
Buriti Bravo 3 5s50 43w50 2:55:20
Buriti Cortado 3 5s11 43w06 2:52:24
Buriti dos Lopes
3 3s10 41w52 2:47:28
Buritizeiro 2 17s21 44w58 2:59:52
Butiá 3 30s07 51w58 3:27:52
Caapiranga 4 3s18 61w13 4:04:52
Cabaceiras 3 7s30 36w17 2:25:08
Cabeceiras 3 15s48 46w59 3:07:56
Cabedelo 3 6s58 34w50 2:19:20
Cabo 3 8s17 35w02 2:20:08
Cabo Frio 2 22s53 42w01 2:48:04
Cabo Verde 2 21s28 46w24 3:05:36
Cabreúva 2 23s18 47w08 3:08:32
Cabrobó 3 8s31 39w19 2:37:16
Cabuçu 2 22s50 42w55 2:51:40
Cabuçu 2 22s47 43w32 2:54:08
Cabuçu 2 23s25 46w32 3:06:08
Caçador 3 26s47 51w00 3:24:00
Caçapava 2 23s06 45w42 3:02:48
Caçapava do Sul 3 30s30 53w30 3:34:00
Caçapava Velha 2 23s07 45w39 3:02:36
Cacequi 4 29s53 54w49 3:39:16
Cáceres 4 16s04 57w41 3:50:44
Cachoeira 3 12s36 38w58 2:35:52
Cachoeira Alta 3 18s48 50w58 3:23:52
Cachoeira de Goiás
3 16s44 50w38 3:22:32
Cachoeira de Minas
2 22s21 45w47 3:03:08
Cachoeira do Arari
3 1s01 48w58 3:15:52
Cachoeira do Sul
3 30s02 52w54 3:31:36
Cachoeira Paulista
2 22s40 45w01 3:00:04
Cachoeiras 2 22s39 43w28 2:53:52
Cachoeiras de Macacu
2 22s28 42w39 2:50:36
Cachoeirinha 3 8s29 36w14 2:24:56
Cachoeiro de Itapemirim
2 20s51 41w06 2:44:24
Cacimbinhas 3 9s24 36w59 2:27:56
Caconde 2 21s33 46w38 3:06:32
Caçu 3 18s37 51w04 3:24:16
Caculé 3 14s30 42w13 2:48:52
Caetanópolis 2 19s18 44w24 2:57:36
Caeté 2 19s54 43w40 2:54:40
Caetité 3 14s04 42w29 2:49:56
Cafelândia do Leste Matogrossense
4 16s40 53w25 3:33:40
Cafundó 2 22s31 46w25 3:05:40
Caiapônia 3 16s57 51w49 3:27:16
Caiçara 3 15s34 50w12 3:20:48
Caiçara 3 6s36 35w29 2:21:56
Caiçara 3 5s04 36w03 2:24:12
Caicó 3 6s27 37w06 2:28:24
Caieiras 2 23s22 46w44 3:06:56
Cairari 3 2s33 49w07 3:16:28
Cairu 3 13s30 39w03 2:36:12
Cajamar 2 23s21 46w53 3:07:32
Cajapió 3 2s58 44w48 2:59:12
Cajari 3 3s20 45w01 3:00:04
Cajàzeiras 3 6s54 38w34 2:34:16
Cajueiro 3 9s25 36w08 2:24:32
Cajuru 2 21s17 47w18 3:09:12
Calama 4 8s03 62w53 4:11:32
Calçoene 3 2N30 50w57 3:23:48
Caldas 2 21s56 46w23 3:05:32
Caldas Novas 3 17s45 48w38 3:14:32
Camaçari 3 12s41 38w18 2:33:12
Camacho 2 22s20 47w13 3:08:52
Camamu 3 13s57 39w07 2:36:28
Camanducaia 2 22s46 46w09 3:04:36
Camapuã 4 19s30 54w05 3:36:20
Camaquã 3 30s51 51w49 3:27:16
Camará 4 3s55 62w44 4:10:56
Camaragibe 3 8s01 34w58 2:19:52
Cambaquara 2 23s54 45w27 3:01:48
Cambará 3 23s03 50w05 3:20:20
Camboriú 3 27s01 48w38 3:14:32
Cambuci 2 21s34 41w55 2:47:40
Cambuí 2 22s37 46w04 3:04:16
Cambuquira 2 21s51 45w18 3:01:12
Cametá 3 2s15 49w32 3:18:00
Camiranga 3 1s48 46w17 3:05:08
Camocim 3 2s54 40w50 2:43:20
Campanha 2 21s50 45w24 3:01:36
Campestre 2 21s16 42w56 2:51:44
Campestre 2 21s43 46w15 3:05:00
Campina Grande 3 7s13 35w53 2:23:32
Campinas 2 22s54 47w05 3:08:20
Campina Verde 2 19s31 49w28 3:17:52
Campo Alegre de Goiás
3 17s39 47w45 3:11:00
Campo Belo 2 20s53 45w16 3:01:04
Campo da Bocaina
2 22s17 46w06 3:04:24
Campo do Coelho 2 22s15 42w39 2:50:36
Campo Erê 3 26s23 53w03 3:32:12
Campo Florido 2 19s47 48w35 3:14:20
Campo Formoso 3 10s31 40w20 2:41:20
Campo Grande 4 20s27 54w37 3:38:28
Campo Largo 3 25s26 49w32 3:18:08
Campolide 2 21s36 43w53 2:55:32
Campo Limpo 2 23s12 46w48 3:07:12
Campo Maior 3 4s49 42w10 2:48:40

Place	Zone	Lat	Long	Time
Campo Mourão	3	24s03	52w22	3:29:28
Campo Nôvo	3	27s42	53w48	3:35:12
Campos	2	21s45	41w18	2:45:12
Campos Altos	2	19s41	46w10	3:04:40
Campos Belos	3	13s03	46w53	3:07:32
Campos de Cunha	2	22s55	44w49	2:59:16
Campos do Jordão	2	22s44	45w35	3:02:20
Campos Elyseos	2	22s42	43w17	2:53:08
Campos Gerais	2	21s14	45w46	3:03:04
Campos Novos	3	27s24	51w12	3:24:48
Campos Sales	3	7s04	40w23	2:41:32
Cananéia	2	25s01	47w57	3:11:48
Canápolis	2	18s44	49w13	3:16:52
Canavieiras	3	15s39	38w57	2:35:48
Candeias	3	12s40	38w33	2:34:12
Candeias	2	20s47	45w16	3:01:04
Candelária	3	29s40	52w48	3:31:12
Cândido de Abreu	3	24s35	51w20	3:25:20
Cândido Mendes	3	1s27	45w43	3:02:52
Canela	3	29s22	50w50	3:23:20
Cangas	4	16s05	56w33	3:46:12
Canguaretama	3	6s24	35w08	2:20:32
Canguçu	3	31s24	52w41	3:30:44
Canhotinho	3	8s53	36w12	2:24:48
Canindé	3	4s22	39w19	2:37:16
Canindé de São Francisco	3	9s39	37w48	2:31:12
Canoas	3	29s56	51w11	3:24:44
Canoinhas	3	26s10	50w24	3:21:36
Cansanção	3	10s41	39w31	2:38:04
Cantagalo	2	21s58	42w22	2:49:28
Cantanhede	3	3s39	44w24	2:57:36
Canto do Buriti	3	8s07	42w58	2:51:52
Canto do Pontes	2	22s58	43w04	2:52:16
Canumã	4	4s02	59w04	3:56:16
Canutama	4	6s32	64w20	4:17:20
Capanema	3	25s40	53w48	3:35:12
Capanema	3	1s12	47w11	3:08:44
Capão Bonito	2	24s01	48w20	3:13:20
Capela	3	9s25	36w04	2:24:16
Capela	3	10s30	37w04	2:28:16
Capelinha	2	17s42	42w31	2:50:04
Capinópolis	2	18s41	49w35	3:18:20
Capinzal	3	27s20	51w36	3:26:24
Capistrano	3	4s28	38w55	2:35:40
Capitão de Campos	3	4s28	41w57	2:47:48
Capitari	4	0N51	61w24	4:05:36
Capivari	2	23s00	47w31	3:10:04
Capuáva	2	23s39	46w29	3:05:56
Caquende	2	21s20	44w33	2:58:12
Caracaraí	4	1N50	61w08	4:04:32
Caracol	4	22s01	57w02	3:48:08
Caracol	3	9s17	43w20	2:53:20
Caraguatatuba	2	23s37	45w25	3:01:40
Caraí	2	17s12	41w42	2:46:48
Carandaí	2	20s57	43w48	2:55:12
Carangola	2	20s44	42w02	2:48:08
Carapajó	3	2s16	49w22	3:17:28
Carapeva	2	23s12	45w24	3:01:36
Carapicuíba	2	23s31	46w50	3:07:20
Carapó	4	22s38	54w48	3:39:12
Caratinga	2	19s47	42w08	2:48:32
Carauari	4	4s52	66w54	4:27:36
Caraúbas	3	7s43	36w31	2:26:04
Caraúbas	3	5s47	37w34	2:30:16
Caravelas	3	17s45	39w15	2:37:00
Caràzinho	3	28s18	52w48	3:31:12
Cardoso	2	20s04	49w54	3:19:36
Careaçu	2	22s02	45w42	3:02:48
Careiro	4	3s12	59w45	3:59:00
Cariacica	2	20s16	40w25	2:41:40
Caridade	3	4s13	39w12	2:36:48
Carinhanha	3	14s18	43w47	2:55:08
Carira	3	10s21	37w42	2:30:48
Cariré	3	3s57	40w27	2:41:48
Caririaçu	3	7s02	39w17	2:37:08
Cariús	3	6s32	39w30	2:38:00
Carlópolis	2	23s25	49w41	3:18:44
Carlos Alves	2	21s37	43w07	2:52:28
Carlos Barbosa	3	29s18	51w30	3:26:00
Carlos Chagas	2	17s43	40w45	2:43:00
Carlos Sampaio	2	22s42	43w31	2:54:04
Carmo	2	21s56	42w37	2:50:28
Carmo da Cachoeira	2	21s28	45w13	3:00:52
Carmo de Minas	2	22s07	45w08	3:00:32
Carmo do Paranaíba	2	18s59	46w21	3:05:24
Carmo do Rio Verde	3	15s21	49w42	3:18:48
Carmópolis de Minas	2	20s33	44w38	2:58:32
Carnaíba	3	7s48	37w49	2:31:16
Carolina	3	7s20	47w28	3:09:52
Carpina	3	7s51	35w15	2:21:00
Carrancas	2	21s30	44w39	2:58:36
Carrazedo	3	1s36	51w54	3:27:36
Caruaru	3	8s17	35w58	2:23:52
Carutapera	3	1s13	46w01	3:04:04
Carvalhos	2	22s00	44w28	2:57:52
Carvoeiro	4	1s24	61w59	4:07:56
Casa Branca	2	21s46	47w04	3:08:16
Casa Nova	3	9s25	41w08	2:44:32
Casca	3	28s34	51w59	3:27:56
Cascalho Rico	2	18s34	47w52	3:11:28
Cascatinha	2	22s29	43w09	2:52:36
Cascavel	3	24s57	53w28	3:33:52
Cascavel	3	4s07	38w14	2:32:56
Casimiro de Abreu	2	22s29	42w12	2:48:48
Cássia	2	20s36	46w56	3:07:44
Cássia dos Coqueiros	2	21s17	47w10	3:08:40
Cassilândia	4	19s09	51w45	3:27:00
Cassino	3	32s11	52w10	3:28:40
Cassununga	4	16s03	53w38	3:34:32
Castanhal	3	1s18	47w55	3:11:40
Castelo	2	20s36	41w12	2:44:48
Castelo do Piauí	3	5s20	41w33	2:46:12
Castilho	2	20s52	51w29	3:25:56
Castro	3	24s47	50w00	3:20:00
Cataguarino	2	21s18	42w43	2:50:52
Cataguases	2	21s24	42w41	2:50:44
Catalão	3	18s10	47w57	3:11:48
Catanduva	2	21s08	48w58	3:15:52
Catarina	3	6s12	39w54	2:39:36
Catingueira	3	7s08	37w37	2:30:28
Catingueiro	2	22s10	46w52	3:07:28
Catolé do Rocha	3	6s21	37w45	2:31:00
Catrimani	4	0N27	61w41	4:06:44
Catu	3	12s21	38w23	2:33:32
Catuçaba	2	23s15	45w12	3:00:48
Caucaia	3	3s42	38w39	2:34:36
Caucaia do Alto	2	23s41	47w02	3:08:08
Cava	2	22s41	43w26	2:53:44
Cavalcante	3	13s48	47w30	3:10:00
Cavalheiro	3	17s15	48w02	3:12:08
Caxambu	2	21s59	44w56	2:59:44
Caxias	3	4s50	43w21	2:53:24
Caxias do Sul	3	29s10	51w11	3:24:44
Ceará → Fortaleza	3	3s43	38w30	2:34:00
Ceará-Mirim	3	5s38	35w26	2:21:44
Cedro	3	6s36	39w03	2:36:12
Centenário do Sul	2	22s48	51w37	3:26:28
Central	3	11s08	42w08	2:48:32
Centralina	2	18s34	49w13	3:16:52
Ceres	3	15s17	49w35	3:18:20
Cêrro Azul	3	24s50	49w15	3:17:00
Cêrro Corá	3	6s03	36w21	2:25:24
Cêrro Largo	4	28s09	54w45	3:39:00
Chácara	2	21s41	43w13	2:52:52
Chapada dos Guimarães	4	15s26	55w45	3:43:00
Chapadinha	3	3s44	43w21	2:53:24
Chapecó	3	27s06	52w36	3:30:24
Chaval	3	3s02	41w15	2:45:00
Chaves	3	0s10	49w55	3:19:40
Chiador	2	22s01	43w03	2:52:12
Chopinzinho	3	25s51	52w30	3:30:00
Chorrochó	3	8s59	39w06	2:36:24
Chuí	3	33s41	53w27	3:33:48
Cianorte	3	23s37	52w37	3:30:28
Cícero Dantas	3	10s36	38w23	2:33:32
Cipó	3	11s06	38w31	2:34:04
Cipolândia	4	20s08	55w24	3:41:36
Clevelândia	3	26s24	52w21	3:29:24
Clevelândia do Norte	3	3N49	51w52	3:27:28
Coaraci	3	14s38	39w32	2:38:08
Coari	4	4s05	63w08	4:12:32
Cocal	3	3s28	41w34	2:46:16
Cococi	3	6s25	40w30	2:42:00
Côcos	3	14s10	44w33	2:58:12
Codajás	4	3s50	62w05	4:08:20
Codó	3	4s29	43w53	2:55:32
Codòzinho	3	4s46	44w10	2:56:40
Coelho da Rocha	2	22s47	43w23	2:53:32
Coelho Neto	3	4s15	43w00	2:52:00
Coimbra	2	20s52	42w48	2:51:12
Coimbra	4	19s55	57w47	3:51:08
Colares	3	0s56	48w17	3:13:08
Colatina	2	19s32	40w37	2:42:28
Colinas	3	14s12	48w03	3:12:12
Colinas	3	6s02	44w14	2:56:56
Colombo	3	25s17	49w14	3:16:56
Colônia Leopoldina	3	8s57	35w39	2:22:36
Coluna	2	18s14	42w50	2:51:20
Comendador Gomes	2	19s41	49w05	3:16:20
Comercinho	2	16s19	41w47	2:47:08
Conceição	4	7s24	58w05	3:52:20
Conceição	3	7s33	38w31	2:34:04
Conceição da Aparecida	2	21s06	46w12	3:04:48
Conceição da Barra	2	18s35	39w45	2:39:00
Conceição da Ibitipoca	2	21s43	43w55	2:55:40
Conceição da Pedra	2	22s09	45w27	3:01:48
Conceição das Alagoas	2	19s55	48w23	3:13:32
Conceição de Ipanema	2	19s55	41w41	2:46:44
Conceição de Jacareí	2	23s02	44w09	2:56:36
Conceição do Almeida	3	12s48	39w12	2:36:48
Conceição do Araguaia	3	8s15	49w17	3:17:08
Conceição do Canindé	3	7s54	41w34	2:46:16
Conceição do Coité	3	11s33	39w16	2:37:04
Conceição do Formoso	2	21s25	43w21	2:53:24
Conceição do Mato Dentro	2	19s01	43w25	2:53:40
Conceição do Maú	4	3N35	59w53	3:59:32
Conceição do Norte	3	12s13	47w18	3:09:12
Conceição do Rio Verde	2	21s53	45w05	3:00:20
Conceição dos Ouros	2	22s25	45w47	3:03:08
Conchal	2	22s20	47w10	3:08:40
Concórdia	3	27s14	52w01	3:28:04
Concórdia	4	4s35	66w35	4:26:20
Conde	3	11s49	37w37	2:30:28
Condeixa	3	0s54	48w36	3:14:24
Condeúba	3	14s53	41w59	2:47:56
Congo	3	7s48	36w40	2:26:40
Congonhal	2	22s09	46w02	3:04:08
Congonhinhas	3	23s33	50w33	3:22:12
Conquista	2	19s56	47w33	3:10:12
Conrado	2	22s32	43w33	2:54:12
Conselheiro Lafaiete	2	20s40	43w48	2:55:12
Conselheiro Paulino	2	22s13	42w31	2:50:04
Conselheiro Pena	2	19s10	41w30	2:46:00
Conservatória	2	22s18	43w57	2:55:48
Consolação	2	22s33	45w55	3:03:40
Contendas do Sincorá	3	13s45	41w02	2:44:08
Copatana	4	2s48	67w04	4:28:16
Coração de Jesus	2	16s42	44w22	2:57:28
Coração de Maria	3	12s14	38w45	2:35:00
Cordeiro	2	22s02	42w22	2:49:28
Cordisburgo	2	19s07	44w21	2:57:24
Coreaú	3	3s33	40w39	2:42:36
Coremas	3	7s01	37w58	2:31:52
Coribe	3	13s50	44w28	2:57:52
Corinto	2	18s21	44w27	2:57:48
Cornélio Procópio	3	23s08	50w39	3:22:36
Coroaci	2	18s35	42w17	2:49:08
Coroa Grande	2	22s54	43w52	2:55:28
Coroatá	3	4s08	44w08	2:56:32
Coromandel	2	18s28	47w13	3:08:52
Coronel Fabriciano	2	19s31	42w38	2:50:32
Coronel Murta	2	16s37	42w11	2:48:44
Coronel Pacheco	2	21s35	43w16	2:53:04
Coronel Ponce	4	15s34	55w01	3:40:04
Coronel Vivida	3	25s58	52w34	3:30:16
Corredor	2	23s27	46w19	3:05:16
Córrego do Bom Jesus	2	22s38	46w02	3:04:08
Córrego do Ouro	3	16s18	50w32	3:22:08
Córrego do Ouro	2	21s22	45w47	3:03:08
Córrego Rico	3	15s14	47w48	3:11:12
Correia de Almeida	2	21s17	43w38	2:54:32
Corrente	3	10s27	45w10	3:00:40
Correntes	3	9s08	36w19	2:25:16
Correntezas	2	22s30	42w31	2:50:04
Correntina	3	13s20	44w39	2:58:36
Corumbá	4	19s01	57w39	3:50:36
Corumbá de Goiás	3	15s55	48w48	3:15:12
Corumbaíba	3	18s09	48w34	3:14:16
Coruripe	3	10s08	36w10	2:24:40
Cosmópolis	2	22s38	47w12	3:08:48
Cosmorama	2	20s28	49w47	3:19:08
Costas	2	22s39	45w56	3:03:44
Cotegipe	3	12s02	44w15	2:57:00
Cotia	2	23s37	46w56	3:07:44
Cotubandê	2	22s51	43w01	2:52:04
Couto Magalhães	3	8s17	49w16	3:17:04
Coxim	4	18s30	54w45	3:39:00
Coxipó da Ponte	4	15s38	56w04	3:44:16
Craolândia	3	7s57	47w15	3:09:00
Crateús	3	5s10	40w40	2:42:40
Crato	3	7s14	39w23	2:37:32
Criciúma	3	28s40	49w23	3:17:32
Crisólia	2	22s15	46w25	3:05:40
Crissiumal	4	27s30	54w07	3:36:28
Cristalândia	3	10s36	49w11	3:16:44
Cristalina	3	16s45	47w36	3:10:24
Cristianópolis	3	17s13	48w45	3:15:00
Cristina	2	22s13	45w16	3:01:04
Cristinápolis	3	11s29	37w46	2:31:04
Cristino Castro	3	8s49	44w13	2:56:52
Crixalândia	3	15s18	47w15	3:09:00
Crixás	3	14s27	49w58	3:19:52
Cromínia	3	17s17	49w21	3:17:24
Crucilândia	2	20s23	44w21	2:57:24
Cruz Alta	3	28s39	53w36	3:34:24
Cruz das Almas	2	22s44	46w51	3:07:24
Cruz Descoberta	2	22s45	46w48	3:07:12
Cruzeiro	2	22s34	44w58	2:59:52
Cruzeiro do Oeste	3	23s46	53w04	3:32:16
Cruzeiro do Sul	5	7s38	72w36	4:50:24
Cruzeta	3	6s25	36w47	2:27:08
Cruzília	2	21s50	44w48	2:59:12
Cruz Machado	3	26s01	51w21	3:25:24
Cubatão	2	23s53	46w25	3:05:40
Cubati	3	6s51	36w21	2:25:24
Cucuí	4	1N12	66w50	4:27:20
Cuiabá	4	15s35	56w05	3:44:20
Cuiari	4	1N30	68w11	4:32:44
Cuité	3	6s29	36w09	2:24:36
Cumari	3	18s16	48w11	3:12:44
Cumbe	3	10s21	37w14	2:28:56
Cunani	3	2N52	51w06	3:24:24
Cunha	2	23s05	44w58	2:59:52
Cunhambebe	2	23s00	44w20	2:57:20
Cunha Porã	3	26s54	53w09	3:32:36
Cupins	4	19s51	51w03	3:24:12
Curaçá	3	8s59	39w54	2:39:36
Curimatá	3	10s02	44w17	2:57:08

Curitiba	3	25s25	49w15	3:17:00
Curitibanos	3	27s18	50w36	3:22:24
Curiúva	3	24s02	50w27	3:21:48
Currais Novos	3	6s15	36w31	2:26:04
Curralinho	3	1s48	49w47	3:19:08
Curuçá	3	0s43	47w50	3:11:20
Curuçambaba	3	2s08	49w18	3:17:12
Curumu	3	1s01	51w03	3:24:12
Curupá	3	9s54	45w54	3:03:36
Cururupu	3	1s50	44w52	2:59:28
Curva Grande	3	2s37	45w27	3:01:48
Curvelo	2	18s45	44w25	2:57:40
Custódia	3	8s07	37w39	2:30:36
Cuyabá → Cuiabá	4	15s35	56w05	3:44:20
Damianópolis	3	14s33	46w10	3:04:40
Davinópolis	3	15s58	50w08	3:20:32
Delfim Moreira	2	22s30	45w17	3:01:08
Delfinópolis	2	20s20	46w51	3:07:24
Delmiro Gouveia	3	9s23	37w59	2:31:56
Depósito	4	3N12	60w35	4:02:20
Descanso	3	26s50	53w35	3:34:20
Descoberto	2	21s27	42w58	2:51:52
Destêrro	3	7s17	37w06	2:28:24
Diadema	2	23s42	46w37	3:06:28
Diamante de Ubá	2	21s12	42w55	2:51:40
Diamantina	2	18s15	43w36	2:54:24
Diamantino	4	14s25	56w27	3:45:48
Dianópolis	3	11s38	46w50	3:07:20
Dias	2	22s28	45w34	3:02:16
Dionísio	2	19s49	42w45	2:51:00
Dionísio Cerqueira	3	26s15	53w38	3:34:32
Diorama	3	16s21	51w14	3:24:56
Divino	2	20s37	42w09	2:48:36
Divinolândia	2	21s40	46w45	3:07:00
Divinópolis	2	20s09	44w54	2:59:36
Divisa Nova	2	21s31	46w12	3:04:48
Dois Irmãos	3	9s16	49w05	3:16:20
Dois Riachos	3	9s23	37w05	2:28:20
Dom Aquino	4	15s48	54w53	3:39:32
Dom Cavati	2	19s23	42w06	2:48:24
Domiciano Ribeiro	3	16s56	47w46	3:11:04
Domingos Martins	2	20s22	40w40	2:42:40
Dom Joaquim	2	18s57	43w16	2:53:04
Dom Pedrito	4	30s59	54w40	3:38:40
Dom Pedro	3	4s29	44w27	2:57:48
Dom Silvério	2	20s09	42w58	2:51:52
Dom Viçoso	2	22s13	45w09	3:00:36
Dona Eusébia	2	21s18	42w48	2:51:12
Dorândia	2	22s27	43w57	2:55:48
Dores da Boa Esperança	2	21s06	45w21	3:01:24
Dores do Indaiá	2	19s27	45w36	3:02:24
Dores do Paraibuna	2	21s31	43w39	2:54:36
Douradinho	2	21s45	45w46	3:03:04
Dourados	4	22s13	54w48	3:39:12
Dracena	2	21s32	51w29	3:25:56
Duartina	2	22s24	49w25	3:17:40
Duas Barras	2	22s02	42w32	2:50:08
Dueré	3	11s20	49w17	3:17:08
Duque Bacelar	3	4s09	42w57	2:51:48
Duque de Caxias	2	22s47	43w18	2:53:12
Echaporã	2	22s26	50w12	3:20:48
Edéia	3	17s18	49w55	3:19:40
Éden	2	22s48	43w24	2:53:36
Eirunepé	5	6s40	69w52	4:39:28
Eldorado	2	24s32	48w06	3:12:24
Elesbão Veloso	3	6s13	42w08	2:48:32
Eleutério	2	22s19	46w43	3:06:52
Eliseu Martins	3	8s13	43w42	2:54:48
Elói Mendes	2	21s37	45w34	3:02:16
Emboabas	2	21s18	44w08	2:56:32
Embu	2	23s39	46w51	3:07:24
Embu-Guaçu	2	23s49	46w48	3:07:12
Encantado	3	29s15	51w53	3:27:32
Encruzilhada	3	15s31	40w54	2:43:36
Encruzilhada do Sul	3	30s32	52w31	3:30:04
Engenheiro Passos	2	22s30	44w41	2:58:44
Engenheiro Paulo de Frontin	2	22s33	43w41	2:54:44
Engenho	4	15s10	56w25	3:45:40
Engenho do Mato	2	22s52	43w01	2:52:04
Engenho Nôvo	2	21s49	43w00	2:52:00
Enseada	2	23s29	45w05	3:00:20
Entre Rios	3	11s56	38w05	2:32:20
Entre Rios de Minas	2	20s41	44w04	2:56:16
Entupido	2	22s30	44w51	2:59:24
Envira	5	7s18	70w13	4:40:52
Erechim	3	27s38	52w17	3:29:08
Eremita	2	21s35	45w04	3:00:16
Erval	3	32s02	53w24	3:33:36
Escada	3	8s22	35w14	2:20:56
Espera Feliz	2	20s39	41w55	2:47:40
Esperança	5	4s24	69w52	4:39:28
Esperança	3	7s01	35w51	2:23:24
Esperantina	3	3s54	42w14	2:48:56
Esperantinópolis	3	4s53	44w53	2:59:32
Espinosa	2	14s56	42w50	2:51:20
Espírito Santo → Vila Velha	3	3N13	51w13	3:24:52
Espírito Santo do Dourado	2	22s03	45w58	3:03:52
Esplanada	3	11s47	37w57	2:31:48
Espumoso	3	28s44	52w51	3:31:24
Estância	3	11s16	37w26	2:29:44
Estandarte	3	1s26	45w32	3:02:08
Esteio	3	29s51	51w10	3:24:40
Estiva	2	22s28	46w02	3:04:08
Estrêla	3	29s29	51w58	3:27:52
Estrêla do Indaiá	2	19s31	45w47	3:03:08
Estrêla do Leste	4	16s17	53w34	3:34:16
Estrêla do Norte	3	13s49	49w04	3:16:16
Estrêla do Sul	2	18s46	47w42	3:10:48
Eubanque	2	21s33	43w30	2:54:00
Euclides da Cunha	3	10s31	39w01	2:36:04
Eugênio de Melo	2	23s09	45w47	3:03:08
Eugenópolis	2	21s06	42w11	2:48:44
Extrema	2	22s51	46w19	3:05:16
Exu	3	7s31	39w43	2:38:52
Falcão	2	22s17	44w16	2:57:04
Faro	4	2s11	56w44	3:46:56
Fátima	4	16s11	54w58	3:39:52
Faxinal	3	23s59	51w22	3:25:28
Faxinal do Soturno	3	29s37	53w26	3:33:44
Fazenda de Cima	4	15s56	56w37	3:46:28
Fazenda Nova	3	16s11	50w48	3:23:12
Feijó	5	8s09	70w21	4:41:24
Feira de Santana	3	12s15	38w57	2:35:48
Felixlândia	2	18s47	44w55	2:59:40
Fernandes Belo	3	1s07	46w19	3:05:16
Fernando de Noronha	1	3s51	32w25	2:09:40
Fernandópolis	2	20s16	50w14	3:20:56
Ferraz de Vasconcelos	2	23s32	46w22	3:05:28
Ferreira Gomes	3	0N48	51w08	3:24:32
Ferreiros	2	22s25	43w34	2:54:16
Ferros	2	19s14	43w02	2:52:08
Figueira → Governador Valadares	2	18s51	41w56	2:47:44
Figueira	2	22s42	43w27	2:53:48
Filadélfia	3	7s21	47w30	3:10:00
Firminópolis	3	16s40	50w19	3:21:16
Florânia	3	6s08	36w49	2:27:16
Flores	3	7s51	37w59	2:31:56
Flores da Cunha	3	29s02	51w11	3:24:44
Flôres de Goiás	3	14s34	47w04	3:08:16
Floresta	3	8s36	38w34	2:34:16
Floresta Azul	3	14s51	39w41	2:38:44
Florestina	2	18s29	48w01	3:12:04
Floriano	3	6s47	43w01	2:52:04
Floriano	2	22s27	44w18	2:57:12
Floriano Peixoto	5	9s03	67w24	4:29:36
Floriano Peixoto	3	9s32	35w36	2:22:24
Florianópolis	3	27s35	48w34	3:14:16
Fonte	2	23s25	46w21	3:05:24
Fonte Boa	4	2s32	66w01	4:24:04
Formiga	2	20s27	45w25	3:01:40
Formosa	3	15s32	47w20	3:09:20
Fortaleza	3	3s43	38w30	2:34:00
Fortaleza do Ituxi	4	7s29	66w20	4:25:20
Fortaleza dos Nogueiras	3	6s54	46w09	3:04:36
Foz do Iguaçu	4	25s33	54w35	3:38:20
Foz do Jordão	5	9s23	71w56	4:47:44
Franca	2	20s32	47w24	3:09:36
França	3	11s34	40w36	2:42:24
Francês dos Carvalhos	2	22s05	44w29	2:57:56
Francisco Beltrão	3	26s05	53w04	3:32:16
Francisco Morato	2	23s16	46w45	3:07:00
Francisco Sá	2	16s28	43w30	2:54:00
Franco da Rocha	2	23s20	46w43	3:06:52
Frecheiras	3	2s51	42w05	2:48:20
Frecheirinha	3	3s46	40w48	2:43:12
Frederico Westphalen	3	27s22	53w24	3:33:36
Fronteiras	3	7s05	40w37	2:42:28
Frutal	2	20s02	48w55	3:15:40
Fumaça	2	22s17	44w19	2:57:16
Fundão	2	19s55	40w24	2:41:36
Gabiarra	3	16s15	39w41	2:38:44
Gabriel	3	11s14	41w53	2:47:32
Galheiros	3	13s18	46w25	3:05:40
Galiléia	2	19s00	41w33	2:46:12
Gandu	3	13s45	39w30	2:38:00
Garanhuns	3	8s54	36w29	2:25:56
Garça	2	22s14	49w37	3:18:28
Garcias	4	20s34	52w13	3:28:52
Garibaldi	3	29s15	51w32	3:26:08
Gaspar	3	26s56	48w58	3:15:52
Gaurama	3	27s34	52w03	3:28:12
Gaviões	2	22s34	42w33	2:50:12
General Câmara	3	29s54	51w46	3:27:04
General Carneiro	4	15s42	52w45	3:31:00
General Sampaio	3	4s02	39w29	2:37:56
General Vargas	4	29s42	54w40	3:38:40
Gentio do Ouro	3	11s25	42w30	2:50:00
Getulândia	2	22s40	44w06	2:56:24
Getulina	2	21s49	49w55	3:19:40
Getúlio Vargas	3	27s50	52w16	3:29:04
Gilbués	3	9s50	45w21	3:01:24
Giruá	4	28s02	54w21	3:37:24
Glória	3	9s11	38w18	2:33:12
Glória de Dourados	4	22s21	54w13	3:36:52
Goiana	3	7s33	34w59	2:19:56
Goianá	2	21s32	43w12	2:52:48
Goianápolis	3	16s30	49w01	3:16:04
Goiandira	3	18s08	48w06	3:12:24
Goianésia	3	15s18	49w07	3:16:28
Goiânia	3	16s40	49w16	3:17:04
Goianinha	3	6s16	35w12	2:20:48
Goianira	3	16s30	49w26	3:17:44
Goianorte	3	8s35	48w56	3:15:44
Goiás	3	15s56	50w08	3:20:32
Goiatuba	3	18s01	49w22	3:17:28
Goio-Erê	3	24s12	53w01	3:32:04
Góis	2	22s33	46w18	3:05:12
Gonçalves	2	22s40	45w51	3:03:24
Gonçalves Dias	3	4s57	44w14	2:56:56
Gongogi	3	14s19	39w29	2:37:56
Gouvêa	2	18s27	43w44	2:54:56
Governador Portela	2	22s29	43w30	2:54:00
Governador Valadares	2	18s51	41w56	2:47:44
Goyania → Goiânia	3	16s40	49w16	3:17:04
Gradaús	3	7s43	51w11	3:24:44
Grajaú	3	5s49	46w08	3:04:32
Gramacho	2	22s44	43w18	2:53:12
Gramado	3	29s24	50w54	3:23:36
Gramínea	2	22s10	46w38	3:06:32
Granito	3	7s43	39w36	2:38:24
Granja	3	3s06	40w50	2:43:20
Grão Mogol	2	16s34	42w54	2:51:36
Gravatá	3	8s12	35w34	2:22:16
Groaíras	3	3s53	40w23	2:41:32
Grossos	3	4s59	37w09	2:28:36
Guaçuí	2	20s46	41w41	2:46:44
Guaíba	3	30s06	51w19	3:25:16
Guaipava	2	21s40	45w43	3:02:52
Guaiquica	2	22s25	47w14	3:08:56
Guaíra	2	20s19	48w18	3:13:12
Guaíra	4	24s04	54w15	3:37:00
Guaiúba	3	4s02	38w38	2:34:32
Guajará-Açu	3	1s38	48w07	3:12:28
Guajará-Miri	3	1s29	48w17	3:13:08
Guajará-Mirim	4	10s48	65w22	4:21:28
Guanambi	3	14s13	42w47	2:51:08
Guapiara	2	24s10	48w32	3:14:08
Guapimirim	2	22s32	42w59	2:51:56
Guapó	3	16s49	49w32	3:18:08
Guaporé	3	28s51	51w54	3:27:36
Guarabira	3	6s51	35w29	2:21:56
Guaraçaí	2	21s02	51w11	3:24:44
Guaraci	3	22s57	51w40	3:26:40
Guaraci	2	20s29	48w57	3:15:48
Guaraciaba do Norte	3	4s10	40w46	2:43:04
Guaraciama	2	17s03	43w41	2:54:44
Guaramirim	3	26s27	49w00	3:16:00
Guaranésia	2	21s18	46w48	3:07:12
Guarani	2	21s22	43w03	2:52:12
Guaraniaçu	3	25s06	52w52	3:31:28
Guarani das Missões	4	28s08	54w34	3:38:16
Guarani de Goiás	3	13s59	46w31	3:06:04
Guarapari	2	20s40	40w30	2:42:00
Guarapuava	3	25s23	51w27	3:25:48
Guaraqueçaba	3	25s17	48w21	3:13:24
Guarará	2	21s43	43w02	2:52:08
Guararema	2	23s25	46w02	3:04:08
Guaratinguetá	2	22s49	45w13	3:00:52
Guaratuba	3	25s54	48w34	3:14:16
Guarujá	2	24s00	46w16	3:05:04
Guarulhos	2	23s28	46w32	3:06:08
Guaxupé	2	21s18	46w42	3:06:48
Guia	4	15s22	56w14	3:44:56
Guia de Pacobaíba	2	22s43	43w10	2:52:40
Guia Lopes da Laguna	4	21s26	56w07	3:44:28
Guimarães	3	2s08	44w36	2:58:24
Guiratinga	4	16s21	53w45	3:35:00
Guiricema	2	21s00	42w43	2:50:52
Gurupá	3	1s25	51w39	3:26:36
Gurupi	3	11s43	49w04	3:16:16
Heliodora	2	22s04	45w32	3:02:08
Heliópolis	2	22s45	43w25	2:53:40
Hervel d'Oeste	3	27s13	51w34	3:26:16
Hidrolândia	3	16s58	49w14	3:16:56
Hidrolina	3	14s37	49w25	3:17:40
Horizontina	4	27s37	54w19	3:37:16
Humaitá	4	7s31	63w02	4:12:08
Humberto de Campos	3	2s37	43w27	2:53:48
Iacanga	2	21s54	49w01	3:16:04
Iaciara	3	14s09	46w40	3:06:40
Iaçu	3	12s45	40w13	2:40:52
Iapu	2	19s26	42w13	2:48:52
Iauaretê	4	0N36	69w12	4:36:48
Ibaiti	3	23s50	50w10	3:20:40
Ibertioga	2	21s25	43w58	2:55:52
Ibiá	2	19s29	46w32	3:06:08
Ibiapina	3	3s55	40w54	2:43:36
Ibiara	3	7s30	38w25	2:33:40
Ibicaraí	3	14s51	39w36	2:38:24
Ibicuí	3	14s51	39w59	2:39:56
Ibipetuba	3	11s00	44w32	2:58:08
Ibipira	3	6s31	44w38	2:58:32
Ibiquera	3	12s38	40w57	2:43:48
Ibiraci	2	20s28	47w08	3:08:32
Ibiraçu	2	19s50	40w22	2:41:28
Ibirama	3	27s04	49w31	3:18:04
Ibirapuã	3	17s39	40w07	2:40:28
Ibirataia	3	14s04	39w38	2:38:32
Ibirubá	3	28s38	53w06	3:32:24
Ibitiara	3	12s39	42w13	2:48:52
Ibitiguaia	2	21s57	43w25	2:53:40
Ibitinga	2	21s45	48w49	3:15:16
Ibitiúra De Minas	2	22s04	46w26	3:05:44
Ibituporanga	2	22s45	43w47	2:55:08

Ibiúna	2	23s39	47w13	3:08:52
Ibotirama	3	12s11	43w13	2:52:52
Içana	4	0N21	67w19	4:29:16
Icatu	3	2s46	44w04	2:56:16
Icatuaçu	2	23s44	46w24	3:05:36
Icém	2	20s21	49w12	3:16:48
Icó	3	6s24	38w51	2:35:24
Iconha	2	20s48	40w48	2:43:12
Icoraci	3	1s18	48w28	3:13:52
Iepê	2	22s40	51w05	3:24:20
Igaci	3	9s33	36w38	2:26:32
Igaporã	3	13s46	42w43	2:50:52
Igara	3	10s24	40w07	2:40:28
Igaraí	2	21s25	46w49	3:07:16
Igarapé-Açu	3	1s07	47w37	3:10:28
Igarapé Grande	3	4s41	44w58	2:59:52
Igarapé-Mirí	3	1s59	48w58	3:15:52
Igaratá	2	23s12	46w07	3:04:28
Igreja Nova	3	10s07	36w39	2:26:36
Iguaí	3	14s45	40w04	2:40:16
Iguape	2	24s43	47w33	3:10:12
Iguaraçu	3	23s11	51w50	3:27:20
Iguatemi	4	23s40	54w34	3:38:16
Iguatu	3	6s22	39w18	2:37:12
Ijuí	3	28s23	53w55	3:35:40
Ilhabela	2	23s47	45w21	3:01:24
Ilha das Flôres	3	10s27	36w33	2:26:12
Ilha Fernando de Noronha	1	3s51	32w25	2:09:40
Ilha Grande	4	0s27	65w02	4:20:08
Ilha Trindade	1	20s31	29w19	1:57:16
Ilhas Martin Vaz	1	20s30	28w51	1:55:24
Ilhéos → Ilhéus	3	14s49	39w02	2:36:08
Ilhéus	3	14s49	39w02	2:36:08
Ilicínea	2	20s56	45w50	3:03:20
Imaruí	3	28s21	48w49	3:15:16
Imbariê	2	22s39	43w13	2:52:52
Imbituba	3	28s14	48w40	3:14:40
Imbituva	3	25s12	50w35	3:22:20
Imperatriz	3	5s32	47w29	3:09:56
Inajá	3	8s54	37w49	2:31:16
Inconfidência	2	22s16	43w13	2:52:52
Inconfidentes	2	22s20	46w20	3:05:20
Indaiatuba	2	23s05	47w14	3:08:56
Independência	3	5s23	40w19	2:41:16
Indianópolis	2	19s02	47w55	3:11:40
Indiaporã	2	19s57	50w17	3:21:08
Indiaroba	3	11s32	37w31	2:30:04
Ingá	3	7s17	35w36	2:22:24
Ingaí	2	21s24	44w55	2:59:40
Inhambupe	3	11s47	38w21	2:33:24
Inhapim	2	19s33	42w07	2:48:28
Inhaúma	2	19s29	44w22	2:57:28
Inhomirim	2	22s35	43w10	2:52:40
Inhuma	3	6s40	41w42	2:46:48
Inhumas	3	16s22	49w30	3:18:00
Inimutaba	2	18s45	44w22	2:57:28
Inoã	2	22s55	42w57	2:51:48
Inocência	4	19s47	51w48	3:27:12
Interlândia	3	16s12	49w02	3:16:08
Ipameri	3	17s43	48w09	3:12:36
Ipanguaçu	3	5s30	36w52	2:27:28
Ipatinga	2	19s30	42w32	2:50:08
Ipaumirim	3	6s47	38w43	2:34:52
Ipiabas	2	22s23	43w53	2:55:32
Ipiaú	3	14s08	39w44	2:38:56
Ipiíba	2	22s52	42w57	2:51:48
Ipirá	3	12s10	39w44	2:38:56
Ipiranga	3	25s01	50w35	3:22:20
Ipiranga	4	3s12	66w01	4:24:04
Ipiranga	2	22s43	43w12	2:52:48
Ipixuna	3	4s22	44w34	2:58:16
Ipojuca	3	8s24	35w04	2:20:16
Iporá	3	16s28	51w07	3:24:28
Iporã	3	23s59	53w37	3:34:28
Ipu	3	4s20	40w42	2:42:48
Ipubi	3	7s39	40w07	2:40:28
Ipueiras	3	4s33	40w43	2:42:52
Ipuiúna	2	22s06	46w11	3:04:44
Ipupiara	3	11s49	42w37	2:50:28
Iracema	3	5s48	38w18	2:33:12
Iraí	3	27s11	53w15	3:33:00
Irará	3	12s02	38w46	2:35:04
Irati	3	25s27	50w39	3:22:36
Irauçuba	3	3s45	39w47	2:39:08
Irecê	3	11s18	41w52	2:47:28
Irituia	3	1s46	47w26	3:09:44
Itabaiana	3	7s20	35w20	2:21:20
Itabaiana	3	10s41	37w26	2:29:44
Itabaiana	3	11s16	37w47	2:31:08
Itabapoana	2	21s18	40w58	2:43:52
Itaberá	2	23s51	49w09	3:16:36
Itaberaba	3	12s32	40w18	2:41:12
Itaberaí	3	16s02	49w48	3:19:12
Itabi	3	10s08	37w06	2:28:24
Itabira	2	19s37	43w13	2:52:52
Itaboca	2	22s03	44w05	2:56:20
Itaboraí	2	22s45	42w52	2:51:28
Itabuna	3	14s48	39w16	2:37:04
Itacajá	3	8s19	47w46	3:11:04
Itacaré	3	14s18	39w00	2:36:00
Itacoatiara	4	3s08	58w25	3:53:40
Itacurussá	2	22s55	43w55	2:55:40
Itaetê	3	12s59	40w58	2:43:52
Itagi	3	14s10	40w01	2:40:04
Itaguaçu	2	19s48	40w51	2:43:24
Itaguaí	2	22s52	43w47	2:55:08
Itagujé	3	22s37	51w59	3:27:56
Itaguara	2	20s23	44w29	2:57:56
Itaguaru	3	15s44	49w37	3:18:28
Itaguatins	3	5s47	47w29	3:09:56
Itaí	2	23s24	49w06	3:16:24
Itaiçaba	3	4s40	37w51	2:31:24
Itaim	2	22s24	45w53	3:03:32
Itainópolis	3	7s24	41w31	2:46:04
Itaiópolis	3	26s20	49w56	3:19:44
Itaipava	2	22s23	43w08	2:52:32
Itaipu	2	22s58	43w02	2:52:08
Itaipu	2	22s44	43w26	2:53:44
Itaituba	4	4s17	55w59	3:43:56
Itajá	3	19s07	51w37	3:26:28
Itajaí	3	26s53	48w39	3:14:36
Itajubá	2	22s26	45w27	3:01:48
Itaju do Colônia	3	15s09	39w44	2:38:56
Itajuípe	3	14s41	39w22	2:37:28
Itamaraju	3	17s05	39w31	2:38:04
Itamarandiba	2	17s51	42w51	2:51:24
Itamarati	2	21s25	42w49	2:51:16
Itamari	3	13s47	39w37	2:38:28
Itamataré	3	2s16	46w24	3:05:36
Itambacuri	2	18s01	41w42	2:46:48
Itambé	3	15s15	40w37	2:42:28
Itambi	2	22s44	42w58	2:51:52
Itamonte	2	22s17	44w53	2:59:32
Itanhaém	2	24s11	46w47	3:07:08
Itanhandu	2	22s18	44w57	2:59:48
Itanhém	3	17s09	40w20	2:41:20
Itanhomi	2	19s10	41w52	2:47:28
Itaobim	2	16s34	41w30	2:46:00
Itaocaia	2	22s58	43w01	2:52:04
Itapaci	3	14s57	49w34	3:18:16
Itapagé	3	3s41	39w34	2:38:16
Itapagipe	2	19s54	49w22	3:17:28
Itapé	3	14s54	39w26	2:37:44
Itapebi	3	15s56	39w32	2:38:08
Itapecerica	2	20s28	45w07	3:00:28
Itapecerica da Serra	2	23s43	46w50	3:07:20
Itapechinga	2	22s58	46w35	3:06:20
Itapecuru-Mirim	3	3s24	44w20	2:57:20
Itapemirim	2	21s01	40w50	2:43:20
Itapera	3	2s32	43w47	2:55:08
Itaperuna	2	21s12	41w54	2:47:36
Itapeteiú	2	22s54	42w47	2:51:08
Itapetim	3	7s22	37w11	2:28:44
Itapetinga	3	15s15	40w15	2:41:00
Itapetininga	2	23s36	48w03	3:12:12
Itapeva	2	23s58	48w52	3:15:28
Itapeva	2	22s46	46w13	3:04:52
Itapevi	2	23s33	46w56	3:07:44
Itapicuru	3	11s19	38w15	2:33:00
Itapipoca	3	3s30	39w35	2:38:20
Itapira	2	22s26	46w50	3:07:20
Itapiranga	3	27s08	53w43	3:34:52
Itapiranga	4	2s45	58w01	3:52:04
Itapirapuã	3	15s52	50w36	3:22:24
Itapitanga	3	14s26	39w34	2:38:16
Itapiúna	3	4s33	38w57	2:35:48
Itápolis	2	21s35	48w46	3:15:04
Itaporã	4	22s01	54w54	3:39:36
Itaporã de Goiás	3	8s02	48w39	3:14:36
Itaporanga	2	23s42	49w29	3:17:56
Itaporanga	3	7s18	38w10	2:32:40
Itaporanga d'Ajuda	3	10s59	37w18	2:29:12
Itapuranga	3	15s35	49w59	3:19:56
Itaquaciara	2	23s47	46w51	3:07:24
Itaquaquecetuba	2	23s29	46w21	3:05:24
Itaquara	3	13s27	39w57	2:39:48
Itaquari	2	20s20	40w22	2:41:28
Itaqui	4	29s08	56w33	3:46:12
Itarantim	3	15s39	40w03	2:40:12
Itararé	2	24s07	49w20	3:17:20
Itarumã	3	18s42	51w25	3:25:40
Itatiaia	2	22s30	44w34	2:58:16
Itatiba	2	23s00	46w51	3:07:24
Itatinga	2	23s07	48w36	3:14:24
Itatira	3	4s30	39w37	2:38:28
Itatupã	3	0s37	51w12	3:24:48
Itaú	3	5s50	37w59	2:31:56
Itauçu	3	16s13	49w37	3:18:28
Itaueira	3	7s36	43w02	2:52:08
Itaúna	2	20s04	44w34	2:58:16
Itinga	2	16s36	41w47	2:47:08
Itiquira	4	17s12	54w07	3:36:28
Itirapina	2	22s15	47w49	3:11:16
Itiruçu	3	13s31	40w09	2:40:36
Itiúba	3	10s43	39w51	2:39:24
Itobi	2	21s44	46w58	3:07:52
Itororó	3	15s07	40w06	2:40:24
Itu	2	23s16	47w19	3:09:16
Ituaçu	3	13s49	41w18	2:45:12
Ituberá	3	13s44	39w09	2:36:36
Itueta	2	19s23	41w11	2:44:44
Ituí	2	21s32	42w55	2:51:40
Ituiutaba	2	18s58	49w28	3:17:52
Itumbiara	3	18s25	49w13	3:16:52
Itumirim	2	21s19	44w53	2:59:32
Itupeva	2	23s09	47w04	3:08:16
Itupiranga	3	5s09	49w20	3:17:20
Ituporanga	3	27s25	49w36	3:18:24
Iturama	2	19s44	50w11	3:20:44
Itutinga	2	21s18	44w40	2:58:40
Ituverava	2	20s20	47w47	3:11:08
Iúna	2	20s21	41w32	2:46:08
Iupeba	2	23s41	46w22	3:05:28
Ivaiporã	3	24s15	51w45	3:27:00
Ivatuva	3	23s37	52w13	3:28:52
Jaboatão	3	8s07	35w01	2:20:04
Jaborandi	2	20s40	48w25	3:13:40
Jaboticabal	2	21s16	48w19	3:13:16
Jacaraci	3	14s51	42w26	2:49:44
Jacaré	2	21s20	42w51	2:51:24
Jacareí	2	23s19	45w58	3:03:52
Jacarèzinho	3	23s09	49w59	3:19:56
Jaceruba	2	22s35	43w34	2:54:16
Jaciara	4	15s59	54w57	3:39:48
Jacinto	2	16s10	40w17	2:41:08
Jacinto Machado	3	29s00	49w46	3:19:04
Jaci Paraná	4	9s15	64w23	4:17:32
Jacobina	3	11s11	40w31	2:42:04
Jacuecanga	2	23s01	44w13	2:56:52
Jacuípe	3	12s29	38w38	2:34:32
Jacundá	3	4s33	49w28	3:17:52
Jacupiranga	2	24s42	48w00	3:12:00
Jacutinga	2	22s17	46w37	3:06:28
Jaguaquara	3	13s32	39w58	2:39:52
Jaguarão	3	32s34	53w23	3:33:32
Jaguarari	3	10s16	40w12	2:40:48
Jaguaretama	3	5s37	38w46	2:35:04
Jaguari	4	29s30	54w41	3:38:44
Jaguariaíva	3	24s15	49w42	3:18:48
Jaguaribara	3	5s40	38w37	2:34:28
Jaguaribe	3	5s53	38w37	2:34:28
Jaguaripe	3	13s06	38w53	2:35:32
Jaguariúna	2	22s41	46w59	3:07:56
Jaguaruana	3	4s50	37w47	2:31:08
Jaguaruna	3	28s36	49w02	3:16:08
Jahú → Jaú	2	22s18	48w33	3:14:12
Jaicós	3	7s21	41w08	2:44:32
Jamapará	2	21s55	42w43	2:50:52
Jambeiro	2	23s16	45w41	3:02:44
Janaúba	2	15s48	43w19	2:53:16
Jandaia	3	17s06	50w07	3:20:28
Jandaia do Sul	3	23s36	51w39	3:26:36
Jandaíra	3	11s34	37w47	2:31:08
Jandira	2	23s31	46w54	3:07:36
Januária	2	15s29	44w22	2:57:28
Januário Cicco	3	6s09	35w35	2:22:20
Japaratinga	3	9s05	35w15	2:21:00
Japaratuba	3	10s35	36w57	2:27:48
Japeri	2	22s39	43w40	2:54:40
Japi	3	6s27	35w56	2:23:44
Japiim	5	7s37	72w54	4:51:36
Japoatã	3	10s20	36w48	2:27:12
Japuíba	2	22s35	42w42	2:50:48
Japurá	4	1s48	66w30	4:26:00
Jaraguá	3	15s45	49w20	3:17:20
Jaraguá do Sul	3	26s29	49w04	3:16:16
Jardim	4	21s28	56w09	3:44:36
Jardim	3	7s35	39w16	2:37:04
Jardim de Angicos	3	5s39	35w59	2:23:56
Jardim de Piranhas	3	6s22	37w20	2:29:20
Jardim do Seridó	3	6s35	36w46	2:27:04
Jardinópolis	2	21s02	47w46	3:11:04
Jarinu	2	23s06	46w44	3:06:56
Jaru	4	10s26	62w27	4:09:48
Jataí	3	17s53	51w43	3:26:52
Jati	3	7s41	39w01	2:36:04
Jaú	2	22s18	48w33	3:14:12
Jaupaci	3	16s18	50w54	3:23:36
Jequeri	2	20s27	42w40	2:50:40
Jequié	3	13s51	40w05	2:40:20
Jequitaí	2	17s15	44w28	2:57:52
Jequitinhonha	2	16s26	41w00	2:44:00
Jeremoabo	3	10s04	38w21	2:33:24
Jericó	3	6s33	37w48	2:31:12
Jeroaquara	3	15s23	50w25	3:21:40
Jerônimo Monteiro	2	20s47	41w24	2:45:36
Jerumenha	3	7s05	43w30	2:54:00
Jesuânia	2	22s00	45w18	3:01:12
Jiquiriçá	3	13s14	39w36	2:38:24
Jitaúna	3	14s01	39w57	2:39:48
Joaçaba	3	27s10	51w30	3:26:00
Joaíma	2	16s39	41w02	2:44:08
Joana Coeli	3	1s58	49w23	3:17:32
Joana Peres	3	3s18	49w42	3:18:48
Joanes	3	0s51	48w31	3:14:04
Joanésia	2	19s12	42w40	2:50:40
Joanópolis	2	22s56	46w17	3:05:08
João Alfredo	3	7s52	35w35	2:22:20
João Câmara	3	5s32	35w48	2:23:12
João Neiva	2	19s45	40w24	2:41:36
João Pessoa	3	7s07	34w52	2:19:28
João Pinheiro	2	17s45	46w10	3:04:40
Joaquim Távora	3	23s30	49w58	3:19:52
Joinvile	3	26s18	48w50	3:15:20
Jordânia	2	15s54	40w11	2:40:44
José Bonifácio	2	21s03	49w41	3:18:44
José de Freitas	3	4s45	42w35	2:50:20
Joselândia	4	16s32	56w12	3:44:48
Joviânia	3	17s49	49w30	3:18:00
Juaba	3	2s23	49w33	3:18:12
Juàzeirinho	3	7s04	36w35	2:26:20
Juàzeiro	3	9s25	40w30	2:42:00
Juàzeiro do Norte	3	7s12	39w20	2:37:20
Juçara	3	15s53	50w51	3:23:24
Jucás	3	6s32	39w32	2:38:08
Jucurutu	3	6s02	37w01	2:28:04
Juiz de Fora	2	21s45	43w20	2:53:20
Júlio de Castilhos	3	29s14	53w41	3:34:44
Jundiaí	2	23s11	46w52	3:07:28
Jundiaí do Sul	3	23s27	50w17	3:21:08
Jundiapeba	2	23s33	46w15	3:05:00
Junqueiro	3	9s56	36w29	2:25:56
Junqueirópolis	2	21s32	51w26	3:25:44
Juqueri-Mirim	2	23s21	46w37	3:06:28
Juquiá	2	24s19	47w38	3:10:32
Juquitiba	2	23s57	47w03	3:08:12
Juramento	2	16s50	43w35	2:54:20
Juréia	2	21s17	46w22	3:05:28
Juruá	4	3s27	66w03	4:24:12
Juruaia	2	21s15	46w35	3:06:20
Juruti	4	2s09	56w04	3:44:16
Juscelândia	3	15s20	51w19	3:25:16
Jutaí	5	5s11	68w54	4:35:36

Juti	4	22s52	54w37	3:38:28
Lábrea	4	7s16	64w47	4:19:08
Ladainha	2	17s39	41w44	2:46:56
Ladário	4	19s01	57w35	3:50:20
Lagarto	3	10s54	37w41	2:30:44
Lageado	3	29s27	51w58	3:27:52
Lagoa	2	23s18	45w36	3:02:24
Lagoa Branca	2	21s54	47w02	3:08:08
Lagoa da Prata	2	20s01	45w33	3:02:12
Lagoa Dourada	2	20s55	44w05	2:56:20
Lagoa Formosa	2	18s47	46w24	3:05:36
Lagoa Santa	2	19s38	43w53	2:55:32
Lagoa Vermelha	3	28s13	51w32	3:26:08
Lago da Pedra	3	4s20	45w10	3:00:40
Lagoinha	2	23s06	45w11	3:00:44
Lagolândia	3	15s37	49w02	3:16:08
Laguna	3	28s29	48w47	3:15:08
Laguna Carapã	4	22s27	55w01	3:40:04
Laje	3	13s10	39w25	2:37:40
Lajeado	3	29s27	51w58	3:27:52
Lajedo	3	8s40	36w19	2:25:16
Lajes	3	27s48	50w19	3:21:16
Lajes	3	5s41	36w14	2:24:56
Lajinha	2	20s09	41w37	2:46:28
Lambari	2	21s58	45w21	3:01:24
Landri Sales	3	7s16	43w55	2:55:40
Lapa	3	25s45	49w42	3:18:48
Lapão	3	11s24	41w50	2:47:20
Lapela	3	3s44	44w45	2:59:00
Laranjal	2	21s22	42w28	2:49:52
Laranjeiras	3	10s48	37w10	2:28:40
Laranjeiras do Sul	3	25s25	52w25	3:29:40
Lassance	2	17s54	44w34	2:58:16
Lauro Müller	3	28s24	49w23	3:17:32
Lavras	2	21s14	45w00	3:00:00
Lavras da Mangabeira	3	6s45	38w57	2:35:48
Lavras do Sul	3	30s49	53w55	3:35:40
Lavrinhas	2	22s35	44w54	2:59:36
Leandro	3	5s59	44w55	2:59:40
Lebon Régis	3	26s56	50w42	3:22:48
Leme	2	22s12	47w24	3:09:36
Lençóis	3	12s34	41w23	2:45:32
Leopoldina	2	21s32	42w38	2:50:32
Leopoldo de Bulhões	3	16s37	48w46	3:15:04
Liberdade	2	22s01	44w19	2:57:16
Lídice	2	22s51	44w12	2:56:48
Lima Duarte	2	21s51	43w48	2:55:12
Limeira	2	22s34	47w24	3:09:36
Limoeiro	3	7s52	35w27	2:21:48
Limoeiro do Norte	3	5s08	38w05	2:32:20
Lindóia	2	22s31	46w39	3:06:36
Linfa	2	23s44	46w56	3:07:44
Linhares	2	19s25	40w04	2:40:16
Lins	2	21s40	49w45	3:19:00
Livramento → Santana do Livramento	4	30s53	55w31	3:42:04
Livramento do Brumado	3	13s39	41w50	2:47:20
Lizarda	3	9s36	46w41	3:06:44
Loanda	3	22s54	53w10	3:32:40
Londrina	3	23s18	51w09	3:24:36
Lorena	2	22s44	45w08	3:00:32
Loreto	3	7s05	45w09	3:00:36
Lourenço	3	2N30	51w40	3:26:40
Lourenço Velho	2	22s22	45w19	3:01:16
Louveira	2	23s04	46w58	3:07:52
Luís Alves	3	26s44	48w57	3:15:48
Luís Correia	3	2s53	41w40	2:46:40
Luís Gomes	3	6s25	38w23	2:33:32
Luisiânia	2	21s41	50w17	3:21:08
Luminárias	2	21s30	44w54	2:59:36
Luminosa	2	22s35	45w38	3:02:32
Luz	2	19s48	45w40	3:02:40
Luz	2	22s48	43w05	2:52:20
Luziânia	3	16s15	47w56	3:11:44
Luzilândia	3	3s28	42w22	2:49:28
Macaé	2	22s23	41w47	2:47:08
Macaíba	3	5s51	35w21	2:21:24
Macajuba	3	12s09	40w22	2:41:28
Macambira	3	10s40	37w32	2:30:08
Macapá	3	0N02	51w03	3:24:12
Macarani	3	15s33	40w24	2:41:36
Macau	3	5s07	36w38	2:26:32
Macaúbas	3	13s02	42w42	2:50:48
Maceió	3	9s40	35w43	2:22:52
Machado	2	21s41	45w56	3:03:44
Machados	2	22s30	46w25	3:05:40
Madre de Deus de Minas	2	21s29	44w20	2:57:20
Mãe dos Homens	2	22s52	46w37	3:06:28
Mafra	3	26s07	49w49	3:19:16
Magalhães de Almeida	3	3s24	42w12	2:48:48
Magé	2	22s39	43w02	2:52:08
Magé-Mirim	2	22s40	43w01	2:52:04
Maiauatá	3	1s51	49w02	3:16:08
Mairi	3	11s43	40w08	2:40:32
Mairinque	2	23s33	47w10	3:08:40
Mairiporã	2	23s19	46w35	3:06:20
Mairipotaba	3	17s18	49w28	3:17:52
Major Isidoro	3	9s32	37w00	2:28:00
Malacacheta	2	17s50	42w05	2:48:20
Mallet	3	25s55	50w50	3:23:20
Malta	3	6s54	37w31	2:30:04
Mamanguape	3	6s50	35w07	2:20:28
Mambaí	3	14s28	46w07	3:04:28
Mambucaba	2	23s01	44w31	2:58:04
Manacapuru	4	3s18	60w37	4:02:28
Manáos → Manaus	4	3s08	60w01	4:00:04
Manaus	4	3s08	60w01	4:00:04
Mandaguaçu	3	23s20	52w05	3:28:20
Mandaguari	3	23s32	51w42	3:26:48
Manduri	2	23s01	49w19	3:17:16
Manga	2	14s46	43w56	2:55:44
Mangaratiba	2	22s57	44w02	2:56:08
Mangueirinha	3	25s57	52w09	3:28:36
Manhuaçu	2	20s15	42w02	2:48:08
Manhumirim	2	20s22	41w57	2:47:48
Manicoré	4	5s49	61w17	4:05:08
Manuel Duarte	2	22s06	43w34	2:54:16
Manuel Ribas	3	24s31	51w39	3:26:36
Manuel Urbano	5	8s53	69w18	4:37:12
Maraã	4	1s50	65w22	4:21:28
Marabá	3	5s21	49w07	3:16:28
Maracaí	2	22s36	50w39	3:22:36
Maracaju	4	21s38	55w09	3:40:36
Maracanã	3	0s46	47w27	3:09:48
Maracanaú	3	3s52	38w38	2:34:32
Maracás	3	13s26	40w27	2:41:48
Maragogi	3	9s01	35w13	2:20:52
Maragogipe	3	12s46	38w55	2:35:40
Maraial	3	8s47	35w50	2:23:20
Maranguape	3	3s53	38w40	2:34:40
Marapanim	3	0s42	47w42	3:10:48
Marapicu	2	22s48	43w35	2:54:20
Maraú	3	14s06	39w00	2:36:00
Marau	3	28s27	52w12	3:28:48
Maravilha	3	26s47	53w09	3:32:36
Maravilha	3	9s14	37w21	2:29:24
Marcelino Ramos	3	27s28	51w54	3:27:36
Marco	3	3s08	40w09	2:40:36
Mar de Espanha	2	21s52	43w00	2:52:00
Marechal Cândido Rondon	4	24s34	54w04	3:36:16
Marechal Deodoro	3	9s43	35w54	2:23:36
Maresias	2	23s48	45w33	3:02:12
Maria da Fé	2	22s18	45w23	3:01:32
Mariana	2	20s23	43w25	2:53:40
Marianópolis	3	4s47	44w38	2:58:32
Maria Paula	2	22s54	43w02	2:52:08
Maricá	2	22s55	42w49	2:51:16
Marília	2	22s13	49w56	3:19:44
Maringá	3	23s25	51w55	3:27:40
Marins	2	22s27	45w08	3:00:32
Mariópolis	3	26s20	52w33	3:30:12
Maripá de Minas	2	21s48	42w58	2:51:52
Marmelos	4	6s08	61w50	4:07:20
Martim Francisco	2	22s31	46w57	3:07:48
Martinho Campos	2	19s20	45w13	3:00:52
Martinópole	3	3s15	40w41	2:42:44
Martins	3	6s05	37w55	2:31:40
Martin Vaz	1	20s30	28w51	1:55:24
Martin Vaz, Ilhas	1	20s30	28w51	1:55:24
Martin Vaz Island	1	20s30	28w51	1:55:24
Maruim	3	10s45	37w05	2:28:20
Marzagão	3	17s59	48w39	3:14:36
Massapê	3	3s31	40w19	2:41:16
Mata de São João	3	12s31	38w17	2:33:08
Mata Grande	3	9s07	37w44	2:30:56
Matias Barbosa	2	21s53	43w20	2:53:20
Matinha	3	3s06	45w02	3:00:08
Matipó	2	20s17	42w21	2:49:24
Mato do Gado	2	23s42	47w07	3:08:28
Mato Grosso	4	15s00	59w57	3:59:48
Mato Verde	2	15s23	42w52	2:51:28
Matozinhos	2	19s35	44w07	2:56:28
Matutina	2	19s13	45w58	3:03:52
Mauá	2	23s40	46w27	3:05:48
Maués	4	3s24	57w42	3:50:48
Mauriti	3	7s23	38w46	2:35:04
Maxaranguape	3	5s31	35w16	2:21:04
Mazagão	3	0s07	51w17	3:25:08
Mazagão Velho	3	0s13	51w25	3:25:40
Medeiros Neto	3	17s20	40w14	2:40:56
Medina	2	16s15	41w29	2:45:56
Melgaço	3	1s47	50w44	3:22:56
Mendes	2	22s32	43w44	2:54:56
Mercês	2	21s12	43w21	2:53:24
Meruoca	3	3s28	40w28	2:41:52
Mesquita	2	19s13	42w35	2:50:20
Mesquita	2	22s48	43w26	2:53:44
Miguel Alves	3	4s10	42w54	2:51:36
Miguel Calmon	3	11s26	40w36	2:42:24
Miguel Couto	2	22s43	43w27	2:53:48
Miguelópolis	2	20s12	48w03	3:12:12
Miguel Pereira	2	22s27	43w22	2:53:28
Milagre	2	21s18	47w00	3:08:00
Milagres	3	7s17	38w57	2:35:48
Mimoso	3	15s10	48w05	3:12:20
Mimoso	4	16s17	55w48	3:43:12
Mimoso do Sul	2	21s04	41w22	2:45:28
Minas Novas	2	17s15	42w36	2:50:24
Minduri	2	21s41	44w37	2:58:28
Mineiros	3	17s34	52w34	3:30:16
Miracema do Norte	3	9s33	48w24	3:13:36
Mirador	3	6s22	44w22	2:57:28
Miradouro	2	20s53	42w21	2:49:24
Miraí	2	21s12	42w37	2:50:28
Miranda	4	20s14	56w22	3:45:28
Mirantão	2	22s15	44w30	2:58:00
Mirante do Paranapanema	2	22s17	51w54	3:27:36
Mirinzal	3	2s01	44w43	2:58:52
Miriti	4	6s15	59w00	3:56:00
Missão Velha	3	7s15	39w08	2:36:32
Mocajuba	3	2s35	49w30	3:18:00
Mococa	2	21s28	47w01	3:08:04
Moeda	2	20s20	44w03	2:56:12
Moema	2	19s50	45w24	3:01:36
Mogi das Cruzes	2	23s31	46w11	3:04:44
Mogi-Guaçu	2	22s22	46w57	3:07:48
Mogi-Mirim	2	22s26	46w57	3:07:48
Moinhos	2	22s43	46w20	3:05:20
Moiporá	3	16s34	50w42	3:22:48
Moiraba	3	2s27	49w25	3:17:40
Moju	3	1s53	48w46	3:15:04
Mombaça	3	5s45	39w38	2:38:32
Monção	3	3s30	45w15	3:01:00
Mondaí	3	27s05	53w25	3:33:40
Mongaguá	2	24s06	46w37	3:06:28
Monjolo	2	22s49	42w57	2:51:48
Monsenhor Hipólito	3	6s59	41w07	2:44:28
Monsenhor Paulo	2	21s46	45w33	3:02:12
Monsenhor Tabosa	3	4s47	40w04	2:40:16
Monte Alegre	4	2s01	54w04	3:36:16
Monte Alegre	3	6s04	35w20	2:21:20
Monte Alegre de Goiás	3	13s14	47w10	3:08:40
Monte Alegre de Minas	2	18s52	48w52	3:15:28
Monte Alegre de Sergipe	3	10s02	37w33	2:30:12
Monte Alegre do Piauí	3	9s46	45w18	3:01:12
Monte Alegre do Sul	2	22s40	46w41	3:06:44
Monte Azul	3	15s09	42w53	2:51:32
Monte Azul Paulista	2	20s55	48w38	3:14:32
Monte Belo	2	21s20	46w23	3:05:32
Monte do Carmo	3	10s45	48w07	3:12:28
Monteiro	3	7s53	37w07	2:28:28
Monteiro Lobato	2	22s58	45w50	3:03:20
Montenegro	3	29s42	51w28	3:25:52
Montes Altos	3	5s50	47w04	3:08:16
Monte Santo	3	10s26	39w20	2:37:20
Monte Santo	3	9s54	49w03	3:16:12
Monte Santo de Minas	2	21s12	46w59	3:07:56
Montes Claros	2	16s43	43w52	2:55:28
Monte Sião	2	22s26	46w34	3:06:16
Montividiu	3	17s24	51w14	3:24:56
Monumento	2	22s44	43w51	2:55:24
Morada Nova	3	5s07	38w23	2:33:32
Morada Nova de Minas	2	18s37	45w22	3:01:28
Morretes	3	25s28	48w49	3:15:16
Morrinhos	3	17s44	49w07	3:16:28
Morrinhos	3	3s14	40w07	2:40:28
Morro Agudo	2	22s45	43w29	2:53:56
Morro do Chapéu	3	11s33	41w09	2:44:36
Morro do Pilar	2	19s12	43w23	2:53:32
Morros	3	2s52	44w03	2:56:12
Morungaba	2	22s52	46w48	3:07:12
Mosqueiro	3	1s10	48w28	3:13:52
Mossâmedes	3	16s07	50w11	3:20:44
Mossoró	3	5s11	37w20	2:29:20
Mostardas	3	31s06	50w57	3:23:48
Moura	4	1s27	61w38	4:06:32
Mozarlândia	3	14s47	50w35	3:22:20
Muaná	3	1s32	49w13	3:16:52
Mucambo	3	3s54	40w44	2:42:56
Mucugê	3	13s00	41w23	2:45:32
Muçum	3	29s10	51w53	3:27:32
Mucuri	3	18s05	39w34	2:38:16
Mulungu	3	7s02	35w28	2:21:52
Mundo Novo	3	11s52	40w28	2:41:52
Munhoz	2	22s37	46w22	3:05:28
Muniz Freire	2	20s28	41w25	2:45:40
Muqui	2	20s57	41w20	2:45:20
Murajá	3	0s47	47w57	3:11:48
Muribeca	3	10s26	36w59	2:27:56
Muribeca dos Guararapes	3	8s10	35w01	2:20:04
Murici	3	9s19	35w56	2:23:44
Murinéli	2	22s07	42w39	2:50:36
Muritiba	3	12s39	38w59	2:35:56
Murutinga	4	3s26	59w12	3:56:48
Mutuípe	3	13s15	39w31	2:38:04
Mutum	2	19s49	41w26	2:45:44
Mutunópolis	3	13s40	49w15	3:17:00
Muzambinho	2	21s22	46w32	3:06:08
Nanuque	2	17s50	40w21	2:41:24
Não-Me-Toque	3	28s28	52w49	3:31:16
Natal	3	5s47	35w13	2:20:52
Natércia	2	22s07	45w30	3:02:00
Natividade	3	11s43	47w47	3:11:08
Natividade da Serra	2	23s24	45w26	3:01:44
Naviraí	4	23s08	54w13	3:36:52
Nazaré	3	13s02	39w00	2:36:00
Nazaré	3	6s23	47w40	3:10:40
Nazaré da Mata	3	7s45	35w14	2:20:56
Nazaré do Piauí	3	6s59	42w40	2:50:40
Nazareno	2	21s13	44w37	2:58:28
Nazaré Paulista	2	23s11	46w24	3:05:36
Nazário	3	16s36	49w54	3:19:36
Neópolis	3	10s18	36w35	2:26:20
Nepomuceno	2	21s14	45w15	3:01:00
Nerópolis	3	16s25	49w14	3:16:56
Neves	2	22s51	43w06	2:52:24
Nhamundá	4	2s14	56w43	3:46:52
Nhandeara	2	20s40	50w02	3:20:08
Nhecolândia	4	19s16	57w04	3:48:16
Nhunguaçu	2	22s21	42w53	2:51:32
Nictheroy → Niterói	2	22s53	43w07	2:52:28
Nilópolis	2	22s49	43w25	2:53:40
Nioaque	4	21s08	55w48	3:43:12
Niquelândia	3	14s27	48w27	3:13:48
Niterói	2	22s53	43w07	2:52:28
Nobres	4	14s44	56w20	3:45:20
Nonoai	3	27s21	52w47	3:31:08

Place	Zone	Lat	Long	Time
Nortelândia	4	14s25	56w48	3:47:12
Nossa Senhora da Aparecida	2	22s02	42w48	2:51:12
Nossa Senhora das Dores	3	10s29	37w13	2:28:52
Nossa Senhora do Amparo	2	22s22	44w05	2:56:20
Nossa Senhora do Livramento	4	15s48	56w22	3:45:28
Nova América	3	15s01	49w56	3:19:44
Nova Andradina	4	22s10	53w15	3:33:00
Nova Aurora	3	18s04	48w16	3:13:04
Nova Cintra	2	22s13	46w46	3:07:04
Nova Cruz	3	6s28	35w23	2:21:32
Nova Era	2	19s45	43w03	2:52:12
Nova Esperança	3	23s08	52w13	3:28:52
Nova Fátima	3	23s29	50w33	3:22:12
Nova Friburgo	2	22s16	42w32	2:50:08
Nova Granada	2	20s29	49w19	3:17:16
Nova Iguaçu	2	22s45	43w27	2:53:48
Nova Lima	2	19s59	43w51	2:55:24
Nova Olinda	3	7s06	39w40	2:38:40
Nova Olinda do Norte	4	3s45	59w03	3:56:12
Nova Ponte	2	19s08	47w41	3:10:44
Nova Prata	3	28s47	51w36	3:26:24
Nova Resende	2	21s08	46w25	3:05:40
Nova Roma	3	13s51	46w57	3:07:48
Nova Russas	3	4s42	40w34	2:42:16
Nova Soure	3	11s14	38w29	2:33:56
Nova Timboteua	3	1s12	47w24	3:09:36
Nova Venécia	2	18s43	40w24	2:41:36
Nova Veneza	3	28s39	49w30	3:18:00
Nova Vida	4	10s11	62w47	4:11:08
Nôvo Acôrdo	3	13s10	46w48	3:07:12
Novo Aripuanã	4	5s08	60w22	4:01:28
Novo Brasil	3	16s11	50w38	3:22:32
Nôvo Cruzeiro	2	17s29	41w53	2:47:32
Nôvo Hamburgo	3	29s41	51w08	3:24:32
Novo Horizonte	2	21s28	49w13	3:16:52
Novo Oriente	3	5s32	40w42	2:42:48
Núcleo Colonial São Bento	2	22s44	43w18	2:53:12
Óbidos	4	1s55	55w31	3:42:04
Oeiras	3	7s01	42w08	2:48:32
Oeiras do Pará	3	1s58	49w51	3:19:24
Oiapoque	3	3N50	51w50	3:27:20
Oiticica	3	5s03	41w05	2:44:20
Olaria	2	21s52	43w56	2:55:44
Olaria	2	22s41	43w08	2:52:32
Olegário Maciel	2	22s19	45w35	3:02:20
Ôlho d'Água das Cunhãs	3	4s43	44w34	2:58:16
Ôlho-D'Água das Flores	3	9s33	37w17	2:29:08
Olímpia	2	20s44	48w54	3:15:36
Olímpio Noronha	2	22s04	45w16	3:01:04
Olinda	3	8s01	34w51	2:19:24
Olinda	2	22s49	43w25	2:53:40
Olindina	3	11s22	38w21	2:33:24
Oliveira	2	20s41	44w49	2:59:16
Oliveira dos Brejinhos	3	12s19	42w54	2:51:36
Oliveira Fortes	2	21s20	43w27	2:53:48
Oriximiná	4	1s45	55w52	3:43:28
Orizona	3	17s03	48w18	3:13:12
Orlândia	2	20s43	47w53	3:11:32
Orleães	3	28s21	49w18	3:17:12
Orós	3	6s15	38w55	2:35:40
Ortigueira	3	24s12	50w55	3:23:40
Osasco	2	23s32	46w46	3:07:04
Os Césares	2	22s47	46w49	3:07:16
Osório Fonseca	4	3s40	58w13	3:52:52
Os Ribeiros	2	22s06	46w49	3:07:16
Osvaldo Cruz	2	21s47	50w50	3:23:20
Ourém	3	1s33	47w06	3:08:24
Ouricuri	3	7s53	40w05	2:40:20
Ourinhos	2	22s59	49w52	3:19:28
Ouro Branco	3	6s42	36w57	2:27:48
Ouro Fino	2	22s17	46w22	3:05:28
Ouro Prêto	2	20s23	43w30	2:54:00
Ouvidor	3	18s14	47w50	3:11:20
Pacaembu	2	21s34	51w17	3:25:08
Pacajus	3	4s10	38w28	2:33:52
Pacatuba	3	3s58	38w37	2:34:28
Pachecos	2	22s48	42w50	2:51:20
Paço do Lumiar	3	2s31	44w07	2:56:28
Pacoti	3	4s13	38w56	2:35:44
Padre Bernardo	3	15s21	48w30	3:14:00
Padre Brito	2	21s18	43w59	2:55:56
Padre Paraíso	2	17s06	41w31	2:46:04
Pains	2	20s22	45w40	3:02:40
Paiol da Vargem	2	22s41	46w26	3:05:44
Paiolinho	2	21s52	45w54	3:03:36
Paiva	2	21s18	43w25	2:53:40
Palestina	2	20s23	49w25	3:17:40
Palhano	3	4s44	37w57	2:31:48
Palma	2	21s22	42w19	2:49:16
Palmácia	3	4s08	38w50	2:35:20
Palmares	3	8s41	35w36	2:22:24
Palmares do Sul	3	30s16	50w31	3:22:04
Palmas	3	26s30	52w00	3:28:00
Palmas de Monte Alto	3	14s16	43w10	2:52:40
Palmeira	3	25s25	50w00	3:20:00
Palmeira das Missões	3	27s55	53w17	3:33:08
Palmeira d'Oeste	2	20s23	50w47	3:23:08
Palmeira dos Indios	3	9s25	36w37	2:26:28
Palmeirais	3	5s58	43w04	2:52:16
Palmeiral	2	21s38	46w31	3:06:04
Palmeirante	3	7s49	48w09	3:12:36
Palmeiras	3	12s31	41w34	2:46:16
Palmeirina	3	8s56	36w17	2:25:08
Palmelo	3	17s20	48w27	3:13:48
Palminópolis	3	16s47	50w08	3:20:32
Palmitos	3	27s05	53w08	3:32:32
Panamá	3	18s11	49w21	3:17:24
Panambi	3	28s18	53w30	3:34:00
Panelas	3	8s40	36w01	2:24:04
Panorama	2	21s21	51w51	3:27:24
Pântano	2	22s23	46w01	3:04:04
Pão de Açúcar	3	9s45	37w26	2:29:44
Papagaio	3	6s01	45w21	3:01:24
Paquequer Pequeno	2	22s20	43w02	2:52:08
Pará → Belém	3	1s27	48w29	3:13:56
Paracambi	2	22s37	43w43	2:54:52
Paracatu	2	17s13	46w52	3:07:28
Paracuru	3	3s24	39w04	2:36:16
Paraguaçu	2	21s33	45w44	3:02:56
Paraguaçu Paulista	2	22s25	50w34	3:22:16
Parahyba → João Pessoa	3	7s07	34w52	2:19:28
Paraíba do Sul	2	22s09	43w17	2:53:08
Paraibano	3	6s30	44w01	2:56:04
Paraibuna	2	23s23	45w39	3:02:36
Paraíso	4	19s03	52w59	3:31:56
Paraíso	2	22s19	45w42	3:02:48
Paraíso do Norte	3	23s13	52w38	3:30:32
Paraíso Garcia	2	21s32	43w53	2:55:32
Paraisópolis	2	22s33	45w47	3:03:08
Parambu	3	6s13	40w43	2:42:52
Paramirim	3	13s26	42w15	2:49:00
Paramoti	3	4s06	39w15	2:37:00
Paranã	3	12s33	47w52	3:11:28
Paranabi	2	23s54	45w14	3:00:56
Paranaguá	3	25s31	48w30	3:14:00
Paranaíba	4	19s40	51w11	3:24:44
Paranaidji	3	6s33	47w27	3:09:48
Paranapiacaba	2	23s47	46w19	3:05:16
Paranavaí	3	23s04	52w28	3:29:52
Paranhos	4	23s55	55w25	3:41:40
Paraopeba	2	19s18	44w25	2:57:40
Paratei	2	23s14	46w00	3:04:00
Parati	2	23s13	44w43	2:58:52
Parati-Mirim	2	23s14	44w38	2:58:32
Paratinga	3	12s42	43w10	2:52:40
Paraúna	3	17s02	50w26	3:21:44
Parecis	4	14s09	56w56	3:47:44
Paredes do Sapucaí	2	21s48	45w43	3:02:52
Parelhas	3	6s41	36w39	2:26:36
Parintins	4	2s36	56w44	3:46:56
Paripiranga	3	10s41	37w52	2:31:28
Pariquera-Açu	2	24s43	47w53	3:11:32
Parnaguá	3	10s13	44w38	2:58:32
Parnahyba → Parnaíba	3	2s54	41w47	2:47:08
Parnaíba	3	2s54	41w47	2:47:08
Parnamirim	3	8s05	39w34	2:38:16
Parnamirim	3	5s55	35w15	2:21:00
Parnarama	3	5s41	43w06	2:52:24
Passagem Franca	3	6s10	43w47	2:55:08
Passa Quatro	2	22s23	44w58	2:59:52
Passa Três	2	22s42	44w00	2:56:00
Passa Vinte	2	22s13	44w15	2:57:00
Passo de Camaragibe	3	9s14	35w29	2:21:56
Passo Fundo	3	28s15	52w24	3:29:36
Passos	2	20s43	46w37	3:06:28
Pastos Bons	3	6s36	44w05	2:56:20
Pati do Alferes	2	22s25	43w25	2:53:40
Pato Branco	3	26s13	52w40	3:30:40
Patos	3	7s01	37w16	2:29:04
Patos de Minas	2	18s35	46w32	3:06:08
Patrocínio	2	18s57	46w59	3:07:56
Patrocínio Paulista	2	20s38	47w17	3:09:08
Patu	3	6s06	37w38	2:30:32
Pau Brasil	3	15s27	39w39	2:38:36
Pau d'Arco	3	7s30	49w22	3:17:28
Pau dos Ferros	3	6s07	38w10	2:32:40
Pauini	4	7s40	66w58	4:27:52
Paula Lima	2	21s35	43w29	2:53:56
Paulicéia	2	21s17	51w51	3:27:24
Paulínia	2	22s45	47w10	3:08:40
Paulino Neves	3	2s43	42w33	2:50:12
Paulista	3	7s57	34w53	2:19:32
Paulistana	3	8s09	41w09	2:44:36
Paulistas	2	18s25	42w52	2:51:28
Paulo Afonso	3	9s21	38w14	2:32:56
Paulo de Faria	2	20s02	49w24	3:17:36
Peçanha	2	18s33	42w34	2:50:16
Pé do Morro	2	22s20	44w57	2:59:48
Pedra	3	8s30	36w57	2:27:48
Pedra Azul	2	16s01	41w16	2:45:04
Pedra Bela	2	22s47	46w27	3:05:48
Pedra Branca	3	5s27	39w43	2:38:52
Pedralva	2	22s14	45w28	3:01:52
Pedras	4	2s48	57w16	3:49:04
Pedras de Fogo	3	7s23	35w07	2:20:28
Pedra Selada	2	22s21	44w26	2:57:44
Pedras Negras	4	12s51	62w54	4:11:36
Pedregulho	2	20s16	47w29	3:09:56
Pedreira	2	22s43	46w55	3:07:40
Pedreiras	3	4s34	44w39	2:58:36
Pedrinhas	3	11s12	37w41	2:30:44
Pedro Afonso	3	8s59	48w11	3:12:44
Pedro Avelino	3	5s31	36w23	2:25:32
Pedro do Rio	2	22s20	43w09	2:52:36
Pedro Gomes	4	18s04	54w32	3:38:08
Pedro II	3	4s25	41w28	2:45:52
Pedro Leopoldo	2	19s38	44w03	2:56:12
Pedro Osório	3	31s51	52w45	3:31:00
Pedro Teixeira	2	21s43	43w44	2:54:56
Pedro Velho	3	6s26	35w14	2:20:56
Peixe	3	12s03	48w32	3:14:08
Peixe-Boi	3	1s12	47w18	3:09:12
Pelotas	3	31s46	52w20	3:29:20
Penalva	3	3s18	45w10	3:00:40
Penápolis	2	21s24	50w04	3:20:16
Pendências	3	5s15	36w43	2:26:52
Penedo	3	10s17	36w36	2:26:24
Penha	3	26s46	48w39	3:14:36
Penha Longa	2	22s04	43w05	2:52:20
Pentagna	2	22s09	43w45	2:55:00
Pentecoste	3	3s48	39w17	2:37:08
Pequeri	2	21s50	43w06	2:52:24
Pequizeiro	3	8s32	48w58	3:15:52
Perdizes	2	19s21	47w17	3:09:08
Pereira Barreto	2	20s38	51w07	3:24:28
Pereiras	2	22s42	46w24	3:05:36
Pereiro	3	6s03	38w28	2:33:52
Peri-Mirim	3	2s38	44w54	2:59:36
Peritoró	3	4s20	44w18	2:57:12
Pernambuco → Recife	3	8s03	34w54	2:19:36
Peruíbe	2	24s19	47w00	3:08:00
Pesqueira	3	8s22	36w42	2:26:48
Petrolândia	3	9s05	38w18	2:33:12
Petrolina	3	9s24	40w30	2:42:00
Petrolina de Goiás	3	16s06	49w20	3:17:20
Petrópolis	2	22s31	43w10	2:52:40
Piabas	3	1s12	46w54	3:07:36
Piabetá	2	22s37	43w10	2:52:40
Piacá	3	7s42	47w18	3:09:12
Piaçabuçu	3	10s24	36w25	2:25:40
Piacatu	2	21s38	50w30	3:22:00
Piacatuba	2	21s29	42w47	2:51:08
Piancó	3	7s12	37w57	2:31:48
Piatã	3	13s09	41w48	2:47:12
Piau	2	21s31	43w19	2:53:16
Picinguaba	2	23s22	44w50	2:59:20
Picos	3	7s05	41w28	2:45:52
Picuí	3	6s31	36w21	2:25:24
Piedade	2	22s41	43w05	2:52:20
Piedade do Baruel	2	23s37	46w18	3:05:12
Piedade do Rio Grande	2	21s28	44w12	2:56:48
Pilão Arcado	3	10s09	42w26	2:49:44
Pilar	3	9s36	35w56	2:23:44
Pilar	2	22s42	43w19	2:53:16
Pilar de Goiás	3	14s41	49w27	3:17:48
Pilar do Sul	2	23s49	47w42	3:10:48
Pimenteiras	3	6s14	41w25	2:45:40
Pimentel	3	3s43	45w30	3:02:00
Pindamonhangaba	2	22s55	45w28	3:01:52
Pindobaçu	3	10s44	40w21	2:41:24
Pindorama de Goiás	3	10s55	47w40	3:10:40
Pinhal	2	22s12	46w45	3:07:00
Pinhalzinho	2	22s46	46w36	3:06:24
Pinhão	3	10s34	37w44	2:30:56
Pinheiral	2	22s31	43w59	2:55:56
Pinheirinhos	2	22s26	44w59	2:59:56
Pinheiro	3	2s31	45w05	3:00:20
Pinheiro Machado	3	31s34	53w23	3:33:32
Pinheiros	2	22s32	44w54	2:59:36
Pintos Negreiros	2	22s18	45w13	3:00:52
Pio IX	3	6s50	40w37	2:42:28
Pio XII	3	3s53	45w17	3:01:08
Piquet Carneiro	3	5s48	39w25	2:37:40
Piquete	2	22s36	45w11	3:00:44
Piracaia	2	23s03	46w21	3:05:24
Piracanjuba	3	17s18	49w01	3:16:04
Piracicaba	2	22s43	47w38	3:10:32
Piracuruca	3	3s56	41w42	2:46:48
Piraí	2	22s38	43w54	2:55:36
Piraí do Sul	3	24s31	49w56	3:19:44
Piraju	2	23s12	49w23	3:17:32
Pirajuba	2	19s54	48w42	3:14:48
Pirajuí	2	21s59	49w29	3:17:56
Piranga	2	20s41	43w18	2:53:12
Pirangaí	2	22s34	44w37	2:58:28
Piranguinho	2	22s24	45w32	3:02:08
Piranhas	3	16s31	51w51	3:27:24
Piranhas	3	9s27	37w46	2:31:04
Pirapemas	3	3s43	44w14	2:56:56
Pirapetinga	2	21s54	43w40	2:54:40
Pirapora	2	17s21	44w56	2:59:44
Piraputanga	4	20s26	55w32	3:42:08
Piraquara	3	25s26	49w04	3:16:16
Pirassununga	2	21s59	47w25	3:09:40
Piratini	3	31s27	53w06	3:32:24
Piratininga	2	22s57	43w04	2:52:16
Piratuba	3	27s27	51w48	3:27:12
Piraúba	2	21s17	43w02	2:52:08
Pirenópolis	3	15s51	48w57	3:15:48
Pires do Rio	3	17s18	48w17	3:13:08
Piriá	3	1s40	50w02	3:20:08
Piripiri	3	4s16	41w47	2:47:08
Piritiba	3	11s44	40w34	2:42:16
Pirpirituba	3	6s46	35w30	2:22:00
Pitanga	3	24s46	51w44	3:26:56
Pitangueiras	2	21s02	48w13	3:12:52
Pitangui	2	19s40	44w54	2:59:36
Pium	3	10s27	49w11	3:16:44
Plácido de Castro	5	10s20	67w11	4:28:44
Planalto	3	14s39	40w29	2:41:56
Planalto	3	27s20	53w03	3:32:12
Poá	2	23s32	46w20	3:05:20
Poção	3	8s11	36w42	2:26:48
Pocinhos	3	7s04	36w03	2:24:12
Pocinhos do Rio Verde	2	21s56	46w25	3:05:40

Poções	3	14s31	40w21	2:41:24
Poço Fundo	2	21s48	45w58	3:03:52
Poconé	4	16s15	56w37	3:46:28
Poço Redondo	3	9s49	37w41	2:30:44
Poços de Caldas	2	21s48	46w34	3:06:16
Poço Verde	3	10s42	38w11	2:32:44
Pocrane	2	19s37	41w37	2:46:28
Pojuca	3	12s21	38w20	2:33:20
Pombal	3	6s46	37w47	2:31:08
Pomerode	3	26s45	49w11	3:16:44
Pompéia	2	22s08	50w10	3:20:40
Pompéu	2	19s12	44w59	2:59:56
Ponta de Pedras	3	1s23	48w52	3:15:28
Ponta Grossa	3	25s05	50w09	3:20:36
Pontalete	2	21s27	45w40	3:02:40
Pontalina	3	17s31	49w27	3:17:48
Ponta Porã	4	22s32	55w43	3:42:52
Pontas de Pedra	3	7s38	34w48	2:19:12
Ponte Alta	2	22s26	47w06	3:08:24
Ponte Alta do Bom Jesus	3	12s06	46w29	3:05:56
Ponte Alta do Norte	3	10s45	47w34	3:10:16
Ponte Branca	4	16s27	52w40	3:30:40
Ponte Nova	2	20s24	42w54	2:51:36
Pontes	2	22s26	46w28	3:05:52
Ponte Serrada	3	26s52	51w58	3:27:52
Poranga	3	4s44	40w55	2:43:40
Porangatu	3	13s26	49w10	3:16:40
Porciúncula	2	20s58	42w02	2:48:08
Porecatu	3	22s43	51w24	3:25:36
Portalegre	3	6s02	38w00	2:32:00
Porteiras	3	7s31	39w07	2:36:28
Porteirinha	2	15s44	43w02	2:52:08
Portel	3	1s57	50w49	3:23:16
Porto	3	3s54	42w42	2:50:48
Porto Acre	5	9s34	67w31	4:30:04
Porto Alegre	3	30s04	51w11	3:24:44
Porto Amazonas	3	25s33	49w53	3:19:32
Porto Belo	3	27s10	48w33	3:14:12
Porto Calvo	3	9s04	35w24	2:21:36
Porto das Caixas	2	22s42	42w53	2:51:32
Porto das Flôres	2	22s05	43w34	2:54:16
Porto das Gabarras	3	3s07	44w34	2:58:16
Porto de Moz	3	1s45	52w14	3:28:56
Porto de Pedras	3	9s10	35w17	2:21:08
Porto Esperança	4	19s37	57w27	3:49:48
Porto Esperidião	4	15s51	58w28	3:53:52
Porto Feliz	2	23s13	47w32	3:10:08
Porto Ferreira	2	21s51	47w28	3:09:52
Porto Franco	3	6s20	47w24	3:09:36
Porto Grande	3	0n42	51w24	3:25:36
Porto Lucena	4	27s51	55w01	3:40:04
Porto Mendes	4	24s30	54w20	3:37:20
Porto Murtinho	4	21s42	57w52	3:51:28
Porto Nacional	3	10s42	48w25	3:13:40
Porto Real	2	22s25	44w20	2:57:20
Porto Real do Colégio	3	10s11	36w49	2:27:16
Porto São José	3	22s43	53w10	3:32:40
Porto Seguro	3	16s26	39w05	2:36:20
Porto União	3	26s15	51w05	3:24:20
Porto Válter	5	8s15	72w45	4:51:00
Porto Velho	4	8s46	63w54	4:15:36
Porto Velho do Cunha	2	21s50	42w32	2:50:08
Posse	3	14s05	46w22	3:05:28
Posse dos Coutinhos	2	22s49	42w45	2:51:00
Posses	2	21s43	46w08	3:04:32
Pôsto do Registro	2	22s23	42w35	2:50:20
Poté	2	17s49	41w49	2:47:16
Potengi	3	7s06	40w00	2:40:00
Potiraguá	3	15s36	39w53	2:39:32
Potirendaba	2	21s08	49w08	3:16:32
Pouso Alegre	2	22s13	45w56	3:03:44
Pouso Alto	2	22s11	44w58	2:59:52
Pouso Redondo	3	27s15	49w57	3:19:48
Pouso Sêco	2	22s41	44w10	2:56:40
Poxoréo	4	15s50	54w23	3:37:32
Prado	3	17s21	39w13	2:36:52
Prados	2	21s03	44w05	2:56:20
Praia de Araçatiba	2	23s06	44w15	2:57:00
Praia Grande	3	29s12	49w57	3:19:48
Praia Grande	2	24s01	46w25	3:05:40
Prainha	4	7s16	60w23	4:01:32
Prainha	4	1s48	53w29	3:33:56
Prata	2	19s18	48w55	3:15:40
Prata	3	7s41	37w06	2:28:24
Prata	2	22s45	43w25	2:53:40
Pratápolis	2	20s45	46w52	3:07:28
Pratinha	2	19s46	46w24	3:05:36
Pregos	2	21s46	42w54	2:51:36
Presidente Dutra	3	5s15	44w30	2:58:00
Presidente Epitácio	2	21s46	52w06	3:28:24
Presidente Getúlio	3	27s03	49w37	3:18:28
Presidente Olegário	2	18s25	46w25	3:05:40
Presidente Prudente	2	22s07	51w22	3:25:28
Presidente Venceslau	2	21s52	51w50	3:27:20
Primavera	3	0s56	47w06	3:08:24
Primeira Cruz	3	2s30	43w26	2:53:44
Primeiro de Maio	3	22s48	51w01	3:24:04
Princesa Isabel	3	7s44	38w00	2:32:00
Príncipe da Beira	4	12s25	64w25	4:17:40
Promissão	2	21s32	49w52	3:19:28
Propriá	3	10s13	36w51	2:27:24
Protestantes	2	22s44	46w18	3:05:12
Providência	2	21s40	42w35	2:50:20
Prudentópolis	3	25s12	50w57	3:23:48
Quaraí	4	30s23	56w27	3:45:48
Quatá	2	22s16	50w42	3:22:48
Quatis	2	22s25	44w16	2:57:04
Quebrangulo	3	9s20	36w29	2:25:56
Queimada Nova	3	8s35	41w25	2:45:40
Queimadas	3	10s58	39w38	2:38:32
Queimados	2	22s42	43w34	2:54:16
Queluz → Conselheiro Lafaiete	2	20s40	43w48	2:55:12
Queluz	2	22s32	44w46	2:59:04
Querência do Norte	3	23s00	53w28	3:33:52
Quipapá	3	8s50	36w02	2:24:08
Quirinópolis	3	18s32	50w30	3:22:00
Quiririm	2	23s02	45w38	3:02:32
Quitaúna	2	23s31	46w47	3:07:08
Quixadá	3	4s58	39w01	2:36:04
Quixeramobim	3	5s12	39w17	2:37:08
Quixeré	3	5s05	37w59	2:31:56
Rancharia	2	22s15	50w55	3:23:40
Raul Soares	2	20s05	42w22	2:49:28
Rebouças	3	25s36	50w42	3:22:48
Recife	3	8s03	34w54	2:19:36
Recreio	2	21s32	42w28	2:49:52
Recreio	4	8s11	58w14	3:52:56
Redenção	3	4s13	38w43	2:34:52
Redenção da Serra	2	23s16	45w33	3:02:12
Regeneração	3	6s15	42w41	2:50:44
Registro	2	24s30	47w50	3:11:20
Registro do Araguaia	3	15s44	51w50	3:27:20
Remansão	3	4s25	49w34	3:18:16
Remanso	3	9s41	42w04	2:48:16
Remedios, Fernandes de Noronha	3	3s20	32w25	2:09:40
Renascença	4	3s50	66w21	4:25:24
Reriutaba	3	4s10	40w35	2:42:20
Resende	2	22s28	44w27	2:57:48
Reserva	3	24s38	50w52	3:23:28
Resplandes	3	6s17	45w13	3:00:52
Resplendor	2	19s20	41w15	2:45:00
Restinga Sêca	3	29s49	53w23	3:33:32
Riachão	3	7s22	46w37	3:06:28
Riachão do Dantas	3	11s04	37w44	2:30:56
Riachão do Jacuípe	3	11s48	39w21	2:37:24
Riacho de Santana	3	13s37	42w57	2:51:48
Riacho Grande	2	23s48	46w35	3:06:20
Riachuelo	3	10s44	37w11	2:28:44
Rialma	3	15s18	49w34	3:18:16
Rialto	2	22s35	44w16	2:57:04
Rianápolis	3	15s29	49w28	3:17:52
Ribamar	3	2s33	44w03	2:56:12
Ribas do Rio Pardo	4	20s27	53w46	3:35:04
Ribeira	2	24s40	49w01	3:16:04
Ribeira do Amparo	3	11s03	38w26	2:33:44
Ribeira do Pombal	3	10s50	38w32	2:34:08
Ribeirão	3	8s31	35w23	2:21:32
Ribeirão	2	23s17	45w36	3:02:24
Ribeirão	2	23s35	46w55	3:07:40
Ribeirão de São Joaquim	2	22s17	44w11	2:56:44
Ribeirão do Pinhal	3	23s24	50w18	3:21:12
Ribeirão do Pote	2	23s36	45w50	3:03:20
Ribeirão Fundo	2	22s40	46w15	3:05:00
Ribeirão Grande	2	22s48	45w27	3:01:48
Ribeirão Pires	2	23s43	46w26	3:05:40
Ribeirão Prêto	2	21s10	47w48	3:11:12
Ribeirão Vermelho	2	21s11	45w03	3:00:12
Ribeirãozinho	4	16s27	52w35	3:30:20
Ribeiro Gonçalves	3	7s32	45w14	3:00:56
Ribeiro Junqueira	2	21s28	42w31	2:50:04
Rio Azul	3	25s43	50w47	3:23:08
Rio Bonito	2	22s43	42w37	2:50:28
Rio Branco	5	9s58	67w48	4:31:12
Rio Brilhante	4	21s48	54w33	3:38:12
Rio Casca	2	20s13	42w39	2:50:36
Rio Claro	2	22s24	47w33	3:10:12
Rio Claro	2	22s43	44w09	2:56:36
Rio da Conceição	3	11s24	46w54	3:07:36
Rio das Antas	3	26s55	51w04	3:24:16
Rio das Flores	2	22s10	43w35	2:54:20
Rio de Contas	3	13s36	41w48	2:47:12
Rio de Janeiro	2	22s54	43w14	2:52:56
Rio d'Oeste	3	27s12	49w48	3:19:12
Rio do Ouro	2	22s51	42w59	2:51:56
Rio do Prado	2	16s35	40w34	2:42:16
Rio do Sul	3	27s13	49w39	3:18:36
Rio d'Ouro	2	22s39	43w32	2:54:08
Rio Espera	2	20s51	43w29	2:53:56
Rio Fortuna	3	28s06	49w07	3:16:28
Rio Grande	3	32s02	52w05	3:28:20
Rio Grande do Sul → Rio Grande	3	32s02	52w05	3:28:20
Riograndina	2	22s11	42w30	2:50:00
Riolândia	2	19s59	49w40	3:18:40
Rio Largo	3	9s29	35w51	2:23:24
Rio Negrinho	3	26s15	49w31	3:18:04
Rio Negro	4	19s27	54w58	3:39:52
Rio Negro	3	26s06	49w48	3:19:12
Rio Novo	2	21s29	43w08	2:52:32
Rio Novo do Sul	2	20s52	40w56	2:43:44
Rio Pardo	3	29s59	52w22	3:29:28
Rio Pardo de Minas	2	15s37	42w33	2:50:12
Rio Piracicaba	2	19s55	43w11	2:52:44
Rio Pomba	2	21s17	43w11	2:52:44
Rio Prêto	2	22s06	43w50	2:55:20
Rio Prêto	2	22s48	45w46	3:03:04
Rio Prêto → São José do Rio Prê	2	22s10	42w57	2:51:48
Rio Real	3	11s28	37w56	2:31:44
Rio Sêco	2	22s46	42w40	2:50:40
Rio Tinto	3	6s48	35w05	2:20:20
Rio Verde	3	17s43	50w56	3:23:44
Rio Verde de Mato Grosso	4	18s56	54w52	3:39:28
Rio Vermelho	2	18s18	43w00	2:52:00
Roçado	3	6s40	44w19	2:57:16
Roça Grande	2	21s36	42w58	2:51:52
Rocha	2	21s28	45w49	3:03:16
Rocha Sobrinho	2	22s47	43w25	2:53:40
Rochedinho	4	20s14	54w33	3:38:12
Rochedo	4	19s57	54w52	3:39:28
Rochedo de Minas	2	21s38	43w01	2:52:04
Rodeio	3	26s57	49w23	3:17:32
Rodeiro	2	21s12	42w52	2:51:28
Rolândia	3	23s18	51w22	3:25:28
Rondon	3	23s23	52w48	3:31:12
Rondônia	4	10s52	61w57	4:07:48
Rondonópolis	4	16s28	54w38	3:38:32
Roque	3	3s01	45w23	3:01:32
Rosário	3	2s57	44w14	2:56:56
Rosário de Minas	2	21s43	43w38	2:54:32
Rosário do Sul	4	30s15	54w55	3:39:40
Rosário Oeste	4	14s50	56w25	3:45:40
Roseira	2	22s54	45w18	3:01:12
Roseiras	2	22s49	46w17	3:05:08
Rubiataba	3	15s08	49w48	3:19:12
Rubim	2	16s23	40w32	2:42:08
Rudge Ramos	2	23s41	46w34	3:06:16
Russas	3	4s56	37w58	2:31:52
Ruy Barbosa	3	12s18	40w27	2:41:48
Sabará	2	19s54	43w48	2:55:12
Sabaúna	2	23s29	46w05	3:04:20
Sabinópolis	2	18s40	43w06	2:52:24
Saboeiro	3	6s32	39w54	2:39:36
Sacra Família do Tinguá	2	22s29	43w36	2:54:24
Sacramento	2	19s53	47w27	3:09:48
Salesópolis	2	23s32	45w51	3:03:24
Salgado	3	11s02	37w28	2:29:52
Salgueiro	3	8s04	39w06	2:36:24
Salinas	2	16s10	42w17	2:49:08
Salinópolis	3	0s37	47w20	3:09:20
Salto	2	23s12	47w17	3:09:08
Salto da Divisa	2	16s00	39w57	2:39:48
Salto Grande	2	22s54	49w59	3:19:56
Salutáris	2	22s10	43w17	2:53:08
Salvador	3	12s59	38w31	2:34:04
Salvaterra	3	0s46	48w31	3:14:04
Sambaetiba	2	22s41	42w48	2:51:12
Sambaíba	3	7s08	45w21	3:01:24
Sampaio Correia	2	22s52	42w36	2:50:24
Sanaduva	3	27s57	51w48	3:27:12
San Antônio de Pádua	2	21s32	42w11	2:48:44
Sandovalina	2	22s27	51w44	3:26:56
Sanga Puitã	4	22s40	55w36	3:42:24
Sanharó	3	8s21	36w34	2:26:16
Santa Adélia	2	21s16	48w48	3:15:12
Santa Albertina	2	20s02	50w44	3:22:56
Santa Bábara	3	11s57	38w58	2:35:52
Santa Bárbara do Monte Verde	2	21s58	43w42	2:54:48
Santa Bárbara do Sul	3	28s22	53w15	3:33:00
Santa Branca	2	23s24	45w53	3:03:32
Santa Cecília	3	26s56	50w27	3:21:48
Santa Cruz	2	19s56	40w09	2:40:36
Santa Cruz	3	6s13	36w01	2:24:04
Santa Cruz Cabrália	3	16s17	39w02	2:36:08
Santa Cruz da Vitória	3	14s57	39w48	2:39:12
Santa Cruz de Goiás	3	17s19	48w30	3:14:00
Santa Cruz do Capibaribe	3	7s57	36w12	2:24:48
Santa Cruz do Piauí	3	7s09	41w48	2:47:12
Santa Cruz do Prata	2	21s12	46w45	3:07:00
Santa Cruz do Rio Abaixo	2	23s18	45w24	3:01:36
Santa Cruz do Rio Pardo	2	22s55	49w37	3:18:28
Santa Cruz do Sul	3	29s43	52w26	3:29:44
Santa Fé	3	15s40	51w16	3:25:04
Santa Fé	3	23s01	51w48	3:27:12
Santa Fé do Sul	2	20s13	50w56	3:23:44
Santa Filomena	3	9s07	45w56	3:03:44
Santa Helena	3	2s14	45w18	3:01:12
Santa Helena de Goiás	3	17s43	50w35	3:22:20
Santa Inês	3	13s17	39w48	2:39:12
Santa Isabel	2	23s19	46w14	3:04:56

Santa Isabel do Araguaia	3	6s07	48w19	3:13:16
Santa Isabel do Rio Prêto	2	22s14	44w05	2:56:20
Santa Juliana	2	19s19	47w32	3:10:08
Santa Leopoldina	2	20s06	40w32	2:42:08
Santa Luísa de Baixo	2	22s46	45w49	3:03:16
Santaluz	3	11s15	39w22	2:37:28
Santa Luzia	3	6s53	36w56	2:27:44
Santa Maria	3	29s41	53w48	3:35:12
Santa Maria da Boa Vista	3	8s49	39w49	2:39:16
Santa Maria da Vitória	3	13s24	44w12	2:56:48
Santa Maria de Itabira	2	19s27	43w08	2:52:32
Santa Maria do Suaçuí	2	18s12	42w25	2:49:40
Santa Maria Madalena	2	21s57	42w01	2:48:04
Santana	3	12s59	44w03	2:56:12
Santana da Boa Vista	3	30s52	53w07	3:32:28
Santana da Vargem	2	21s15	45w30	3:02:00
Santana de Caldas	2	21s50	46w24	3:05:36
Santana de Cataguases	2	21s17	42w33	2:50:12
Santana de Parnaíba	2	23s27	46w55	3:07:40
Santana do Acaraú	3	3s27	40w12	2:40:48
Santana do Capivari	2	22s14	44w56	2:59:44
Santana do Cariri	3	7s11	39w44	2:38:56
Santana do Deserto	2	21s57	43w11	2:52:44
Santana do Garambéu	2	21s36	44w06	2:56:24
Santana do Ipanema	3	9s22	37w14	2:28:56
Santana do Livramento	4	30s53	55w31	3:42:04
Santana do Matos	3	5s57	36w39	2:26:36
Santanésia	2	22s30	43w49	2:55:16
Santa Quitéria	3	4s20	40w10	2:40:40
Santa Quitéria do Maranhão	3	3s31	42w32	2:50:08
Santarém	4	2s26	54w42	3:38:48
Santarém Novo	3	0s56	47w23	3:09:32
Santa Rita	3	7s08	34w58	2:19:52
Santa Rita	2	22s41	43w28	2:53:52
Santa Rita de Caldas	2	22s02	46w20	3:05:20
Santa Rita de Jacutinga	2	22s09	44w06	2:56:24
Santa Rita do Araguaia	4	17s20	53w12	3:32:48
Santa Rita do Ibitipoca	2	21s33	43w55	2:55:40
Santa Rita do Sapucaí	2	22s15	45w42	3:02:48
Santa Rita do Weil	4	3s29	69w19	4:37:16
Santa Rosa	3	15s01	47w13	3:08:52
Santa Rosa	4	27s52	54w29	3:37:56
Santa Teresa	2	19s55	40w36	2:42:24
Santa Teresa de Goiás	3	13s38	49w01	3:16:04
Santa Teresinha	3	12s45	39w32	2:38:08
Santa Vitória	2	18s50	50w08	3:20:32
Santa Vitória do Palmar	3	33s31	53w21	3:33:24
Santiago	4	29s11	54w53	3:39:32
Santo Aleixo	2	22s34	43w04	2:52:16
Santo Amaro	2	12s32	38w43	2:34:52
Santo Amaro	3	2s33	43w14	2:52:56
Santo Amaro das Brotas	3	10s47	37w04	2:28:16
Santo Anastácio	2	21s58	51w39	3:26:36
Santo André	2	23s40	46w31	3:06:04
Santo Ângelo	4	28s18	54w16	3:37:04
Santo Antônio	3	29s50	50w32	3:22:08
Santo Antônio	3	6s18	35w27	2:21:48
Santo Antônio da Boa Vista	2	15s52	44w09	2:56:36
Santo Antônio de Jesus	3	12s58	39w16	2:37:04
Santo Antonio de Posse	2	22s36	46w55	3:07:40
Santo Antônio do Amparo	2	20s57	44w55	2:59:40
Santo Antônio do Aventureiro	2	21s45	42w49	2:51:16
Santo Antônio do Içá	4	3s05	67w57	4:31:48
Santo Antônio do Jardim	2	22s07	46w41	3:06:44
Santo Antônio do Leverger	4	15s52	56w05	3:44:20
Santo Antônio do Pinhal	2	22s47	45w41	3:02:44
Santo Antônio do Rio Verde	3	17s57	47w27	3:09:48
Santo Antônio do Sudoeste	3	26s02	53w44	3:34:56
Santo Augusto	3	27s51	53w47	3:35:08
Santo Cristo	4	27s50	54w40	3:38:40
Santo Estevão	3	12s26	39w13	2:36:52
Santos	2	23s57	46w20	3:05:20
Santos Dumont	2	21s28	43w34	2:54:16
São Benedito	3	4s03	40w53	2:43:32
São Benedito das Areias	2	21s19	47w02	3:08:08
São Benedito do Rio Prêto	3	3s20	43w35	2:54:20
São Bento	4	3N02	60w30	4:02:00
São Bento	3	2s42	44w50	2:59:20
São Bento de Caldas	2	22s08	46w18	3:05:12
São Bento do Norte	3	5s04	36w02	2:24:08
São Bento do Sapucaí	2	22s42	45w43	3:02:52
São Bento do Sul	3	26s15	49w23	3:17:32
São Bento do Una	3	8s32	36w22	2:25:28
São Bernardo	3	3s22	42w24	2:49:36
São Bernardo do Campo	2	23s42	46w33	3:06:12
São Borja	4	28s39	56w00	3:44:00
São Brás	3	10s05	36w55	2:27:40
São Caetano de Odivelas	3	0s45	48w02	3:12:08
São Caetano do Sul	2	23s36	46w34	3:06:16
São Caitano	3	8s21	36w06	2:24:24
São Carlos	2	22s01	47w54	3:11:36
São Carlos	3	27s04	52w59	3:31:56
São Cristóvão	3	11s01	37w12	2:28:48
São Domingos	3	13s24	46w19	3:05:16
São Domingos	3	26s34	52w32	3:30:08
São Domingos	2	21s41	42w47	2:51:08
São Domingos da Bocaina	2	21s50	44w01	2:56:04
São Domingos do Capim	3	1s41	47w47	3:11:08
São Domingos do Maranhão	3	5s42	44w22	2:57:28
São Félix	3	11s36	50w39	3:22:36
São Félix de Balsas	3	7s08	44w52	2:59:28
São Félix do Piauí	3	5s56	42w07	2:48:28
São Filipe	3	14s49	41w23	2:45:32
São Francisco	2	15s57	44w52	2:59:28
São Francisco	2	22s36	45w18	3:01:12
São Francisco de Assis	4	29s33	55w08	3:40:32
São Francisco de Goiás	3	15s55	49w16	3:17:04
São Francisco de Paula	3	29s27	50w35	3:22:20
São Francisco do Croará	2	22s42	43w08	2:52:32
São Francisco do Maranhão	3	6s15	42w52	2:51:28
São Francisco do Piauí	3	7s15	42w32	2:50:08
São Francisco do Sul	3	26s14	48w39	3:14:36
São Francisco Xavier	2	22s54	45w58	3:03:52
São Gabriel	4	30s20	54w19	3:37:16
São Gabriel da Palha	2	19s01	40w32	2:42:08
São Gabriel de Goiás	3	15s12	47w34	3:10:16
São Gonçalo	2	21s36	46w19	3:05:16
São Gonçalo	2	22s51	43w04	2:52:16
São Gonçalo do Abaeté	2	18s20	45w49	3:03:16
São Gonçalo do Amarante	3	3s36	38w58	2:35:52
São Gonçalo do Pará	2	19s59	44w51	2:59:24
São Gonçalo do Sapucaí	2	21s54	45w36	3:02:24
São Gonçalo dos Campos	3	12s25	38w58	2:35:52
São Jerônimo	3	29s58	51w43	3:26:52
São Jerônimo da Serra	3	23s43	50w44	3:22:56
São João da Aliança	3	14s42	47w32	3:10:08
São João da Barra	2	21s38	41w03	2:44:12
São João da Boa Vista	2	21s58	46w47	3:07:08
São João da Mata	2	21s56	45w56	3:03:44
São João da Ponte	2	15s56	44w01	2:56:04
São João da Serra	2	21s28	43w27	2:53:48
São João de Côrtes	3	2s12	44w32	2:58:08
São João del Rei	2	21s09	44w16	2:57:04
São João de Meriti	2	22s48	43w22	2:53:28
São João de Pirabas	3	0s46	47w10	3:08:40
São João do Araguaia	3	5s23	48w46	3:15:04
São João do Caiuá	3	22s48	52w22	3:29:28
São João do Cariri	3	7s23	36w31	2:26:04
São João do Jaguaribe	3	5s16	38w16	2:33:04
São João do Paraíso	2	15s19	42w01	2:48:04
São João do Piauí	3	8s21	42w15	2:49:00
São João do Sabugi	3	6s43	37w12	2:28:48
São João dos Patos	3	6s30	43w42	2:54:48
São João do Triunfo	3	25s40	50w20	3:21:20
São João Evangelista	2	18s32	42w45	2:51:00
São João Nepomuceno	2	21s33	43w01	2:52:04
São João Nôvo	2	23s33	47w01	3:08:04
São Joaquim	3	28s18	49w56	3:19:44
São Joaquim da Barra	2	20s35	47w53	3:11:32
São Joaquim dos Melos	3	5s48	44w44	2:58:56
São Jorge	3	23s24	52w17	3:29:08
São José	3	27s38	48w39	3:14:36
São José da Lagoa Tapada	3	6s57	38w10	2:32:40
São José da Laje	3	9s01	36w03	2:24:12
São José das Palmeiras	2	22s33	47w12	3:08:48
São José de Anauá	4	1N00	61w23	4:05:32
São José de Mipibu	3	6s05	35w15	2:21:00
São José de Piranhas	3	7s07	38w30	2:34:00
São José do Alegre	2	22s19	45w32	3:02:08
São José do Barreiro	2	22s38	44w35	2:58:20
São José do Belmonte	3	7s52	38w46	2:35:04
São José do Calçado	2	21s02	41w40	2:46:40
São José do Campestre	3	6s18	35w42	2:22:48
São José do Cedro	3	26s30	53w30	3:34:00
São José do Egito	3	7s28	37w16	2:29:04
São José do Goiabal	2	19s56	42w42	2:50:48
São José do Gurupi	3	1s36	46w13	3:04:52
São José do Norte	3	32s01	52w03	3:28:12
São José do Peixe	3	7s24	42w34	2:50:16
São José do Piriá	3	1s17	46w18	3:05:12
São José do Rio Pardo	2	21s36	46w54	3:07:36
São José do Rio Prêto	2	20s48	49w23	3:17:32
São José do Rio Prêto	2	22s10	42w57	2:51:48
São José dos Campos	2	22s10	45w06	3:00:24
São José dos Campos	2	23s11	45w53	3:03:32
São José dos Lopes	2	21s48	43w53	2:55:32
São José dos Pinhais	3	25s31	49w13	3:16:52
São José do Turvo	2	22s21	43w59	2:55:56
São Leopoldo	3	29s46	51w09	3:24:36
São Lourenço	2	22s07	45w03	3:00:12
São Lourenço da Serra	2	23s52	46w57	3:07:48
São Lourenço d'Oeste	3	26s24	52w46	3:31:04
São Lourenço do Ipixuna	3	4s28	44w54	2:59:36
São Lourenço do Sul	3	31s22	51w58	3:27:52
São Luís	3	2s31	44w16	2:57:04
São Luís de Montes Belos	3	16s32	50w20	3:21:20
São Luís do Curu	3	3s40	39w14	2:36:56
São Luís Do Paraitinga	2	23s14	45w20	3:01:20
São Luís do Quitunde	3	9s20	35w33	2:22:12
São Luís do Tocantins	3	14s17	47w59	3:11:56
São Luís Gonzaga	4	28s24	54w58	3:39:52
São Mamede	3	6s56	37w06	2:28:24
São Manuel	2	22s44	48w34	3:14:16
São Mateus	2	18s44	39w51	2:39:24
São Mateus	2	22s49	43w23	2:53:32
São Mateus do Sul	3	25s52	50w23	3:21:32
São Miguel	3	6s13	38w30	2:34:00
São Miguel do Anta	2	20s42	42w43	2:50:52
São Miguel do Araguaia	3	13s19	50w13	3:20:52
São Miguel d'Oeste	3	26s45	53w34	3:34:16
São Miguel do Guamá	3	1s37	47w27	3:09:48
São Miguel dos Campos	3	9s47	36w05	2:24:20
São Miguel dos Macacos	3	1s11	50w28	3:21:52

São Miguel do Tapuio	3	5s30	41w20	2:45:20
São Paulo	2	23s32	46w37	3:06:28
São Paulo de Olivença	4	3s27	68w48	4:35:12
São Paulo do Potengi	3	5s55	35w45	2:23:00
São Pedro	4	19s53	51w55	3:27:40
São Pedro	2	22s12	46w46	3:07:04
São Pedro de Viseu	3	2s33	49w33	3:18:12
São Pedro do Ivaí	3	23s51	51w51	3:27:24
São Pedro do Piauí	3	5s56	42w43	2:50:52
São Pedro do Sul	4	29s37	54w10	3:36:40
São Rafael	3	5s47	36w55	2:27:40
São Raimundo das Mangabeiras	3	7s01	45w29	3:01:56
São Raimundo de Codó	3	4s21	43w37	2:54:28
São Raimundo Nonato	3	9s01	42w42	2:50:48
São Romão	2	16s22	45w04	3:00:16
São Roque	2	23s32	47w08	3:08:32
São Roque da Fartura	2	21s51	46w45	3:07:00
São Roque do Paraguaçu	3	12s51	38w51	2:35:24
São Salvador → Salvador	3	12s59	38w31	2:34:04
São Sebastião	2	23s48	45w25	3:01:40
São Sebastião da Bela Vista	2	22s10	45w45	3:03:00
São Sebastião da Boa Vista	3	1s42	49w31	3:18:04
São Sebastião da Grama	2	21s43	46w49	3:07:16
São Sebastião da Vitória	2	21s14	44w25	2:57:40
São Sebastião do Barreado	2	22s04	43w38	2:54:32
São Sebastião do Maranhão	2	18s05	42w35	2:50:20
São Sebastião do Paraíso	2	20s55	47w00	3:08:00
São Sebastião do Rio Claro	3	15s45	51w30	3:26:00
São Sebastião do Rio Verde	2	22s13	44w58	2:59:52
São Sebastião dos Peitudos	2	22s19	46w29	3:05:56
São Sebastião dos Robertos	2	22s13	46w32	3:06:08
São Sebastião do Umbuzeiro	3	8s09	37w01	2:28:04
São Sepé	3	30s10	53w34	3:34:16
São Simão	2	18s56	50w30	3:22:00
São Simão	2	21s30	47w33	3:10:12
São Tiago	2	20s55	44w30	2:58:00
São Timóteo	3	13s51	42w11	2:48:44
São Tomé	3	5s58	36w04	2:24:16
São Tomé das Letras	2	21s43	44w59	2:59:56
São Vicente	3	6s13	36w41	2:26:44
São Vicente	2	23s58	46w23	3:05:32
São Vicente de Minas	2	21s42	44w27	2:57:48
São Vicente Ferrer	3	2s53	44w52	2:59:28
São Vicente Ferrer	3	7s35	35w30	2:22:00
Sapé	3	7s06	35w13	2:20:52
Sapé	2	22s16	46w34	3:06:16
Sapeaçu	3	12s44	39w13	2:36:52
Sapucaí	2	22s19	46w42	3:06:48
Sapucaia	2	22s00	42w54	2:51:36
Sapucaí-Mirim	2	22s44	45w45	3:03:00
Saquarema	2	22s56	42w30	2:50:00
Sarandi	3	27s56	52w55	3:31:40
Sarandira	2	21s50	43w11	2:52:44
Sará-Sará	2	23s40	47w05	3:08:20
Sátiro Dias	3	11s36	38w36	2:34:24
Saudade	2	21s56	43w03	2:52:12
Saúde	3	10s56	40w24	2:41:36
Seara	3	27s07	52w17	3:29:08
Sebastião de Lacerda	2	22s17	43w35	2:54:20
Seberi	3	27s29	53w24	3:33:36
Senador Amaral	2	22s35	46w11	3:04:44
Senador Canedo	3	16s43	49w05	3:16:20
Senador Côrtes	2	21s48	42w56	2:51:44
Senador Firmino	2	20s55	43w06	2:52:24
Senador José Bento	2	22s10	46w10	3:04:40
Senador José Porfírio	3	2s39	51w55	3:27:40
Senador Pompeu	3	5s35	39w22	2:37:28
Sena Madureira	5	9s04	68w40	4:34:40
Sengés	3	24s06	49w29	3:17:56
Senhora do Pôrto	2	18s53	43w06	2:52:24
Senhor do Bonfim	3	10s27	40w11	2:40:44
Sento Sé	3	9s40	41w18	2:45:12
Sereno	2	21s19	42w39	2:50:36
Seritinga	2	21s54	44w30	2:58:00
Sernambitiba	2	22s41	42w59	2:51:56
Seropédica	2	22s44	43w43	2:54:52
Serra	2	20s07	40w18	2:41:12
Serra Branca	3	7s29	36w40	2:26:40
Serra do Navio	3	0N59	52w03	3:28:12
Serra do Salitre	2	19s06	46w41	3:06:44

Serra Grande	3	7s15	38w19	2:33:16
Serrana	2	21s14	47w36	3:10:24
Serra Negra	2	22s36	46w42	3:06:48
Serra Negra do Norte	3	6s40	37w24	2:29:36
Serrania	2	21s33	46w03	3:04:12
Serranópolis	3	18s16	52w00	3:28:00
Serranos	2	21s51	44w30	2:58:00
Serra Preta	3	12s09	39w20	2:37:20
Serraria	3	6s49	35w38	2:22:32
Serraria	2	22s01	43w12	2:52:48
Serra Talhada	3	7s59	38w18	2:33:12
Serrinha	3	11s39	39w00	2:36:00
Serrita	3	7s56	39w19	2:37:16
Sêrro	2	18s37	43w23	2:53:32
Sertaneja	3	23s03	50w50	3:23:20
Sertânia	3	8s05	37w16	2:29:04
Sertãozinho	2	22s19	46w03	3:04:12
Sete Barras	2	24s23	47w55	3:11:40
Sete Lagoas	2	19s27	44w14	2:56:56
Sete Pontes	2	22s51	43w05	2:52:20
Siderópolis	3	28s35	49w26	3:17:44
Sidrolândia	4	20s55	54w58	3:39:52
Silva Jardim	2	22s39	42w23	2:49:32
Silvânia	3	16s42	48w38	3:14:32
Silveiras	2	22s33	46w55	3:07:40
Silveiras	2	22s40	44w52	2:59:28
Silvianópolis	2	22s02	45w50	3:03:20
Simão Dias	3	10s44	37w49	2:31:16
Simão Pereira	2	21s58	43w19	2:53:16
Simões	3	7s36	40w49	2:43:16
Siqueira Campos	3	23s42	49w50	3:19:20
Sítio da Abadia	3	14s48	46w16	3:05:04
Sítio Nôvo do Grajaú	3	5s51	46w43	3:06:52
Sobradinho	3	29s24	53w03	3:32:12
Sobral	3	3s42	40w21	2:41:24
So[illegible]amirim	2	23s37	47w12	3:08:48
Socorro	2	22s36	46w32	3:06:08
Solânea	3	6s45	35w39	2:22:36
Soledade	3	28s50	52w30	3:30:00
Soledade de Minas	2	22s04	45w03	3:00:12
Solonópole	3	5s44	39w01	2:36:04
Sombrio	3	29s07	49w40	3:18:40
Sorocaba	2	23s29	47w27	3:09:48
Soure	3	0s44	48w31	3:14:04
Sousa	3	6s45	38w14	2:32:56
Sousânia	3	16s11	49w05	3:16:20
Sousas	2	22s52	46w59	3:07:56
Subaio	2	22s35	42w52	2:51:28
Sucuriju	3	1N39	49w57	3:19:48
Sumaúma	4	7s50	60w02	4:00:08
Sumé	3	7s39	36w55	2:27:40
Sumidouro	2	22s03	42w41	2:50:44
Suruí	2	22s40	43w07	2:52:28
Suzano	2	23s32	46w20	3:05:20
Tabira	3	7s35	37w33	2:30:12
Taboão da Serra	2	23s38	46w46	3:07:04
Tabuão	2	21s59	44w02	2:56:08
Tábuas	2	22s12	43w37	2:54:28
Tabuleiro	2	21s22	43w15	2:53:00
Tabuleiro do Norte	3	5s15	38w07	2:32:28
Tacaratu	3	9s06	38w10	2:32:40
Tacima	3	6s30	35w39	2:22:36
Taguatinga	3	12s25	46w26	3:05:44
Taiaçupeba	2	23s40	46w11	3:04:44
Taiobeiras	2	15s49	42w14	2:48:56
Taipas	3	12s15	47w09	3:08:36
Taipu	3	5s37	35w36	2:22:24
Tairetã	2	22s36	43w42	2:54:48
Tamandaré	3	8s45	35w06	2:20:24
Tamaniquá	4	2s38	65w44	4:22:56
També	3	7s25	35w06	2:20:24
Tamboara	3	23s09	52w33	3:30:12
Tamboril	3	4s50	40w20	2:41:20
Tanabi	2	20s37	49w37	3:18:28
Tangará	3	27s08	51w13	3:24:52
Tanguá	2	22s44	42w43	2:50:52
Tanquinho	3	11s58	39w06	2:36:24
Tanquinho	2	22s48	47w00	3:08:00
Tapauá	4	5s45	63w04	4:12:16
Tapejara	3	28s04	52w00	3:28:00
Tapera	3	28s38	52w52	3:31:28
Taperoá	3	13s31	39w06	2:36:24
Taperoá	3	7s12	36w49	2:27:16
Tapes	3	30s40	51w23	3:25:32
Tapiraí	2	19s52	46w01	3:04:04
Tapiratiba	2	21s28	46w45	3:07:00
Tapurucuara	4	0s24	65w02	4:20:08
Taquara	3	29s39	50w47	3:23:08
Taquaral	3	16s01	49w38	3:18:32
Taquari	4	17s50	53w17	3:33:08
Taquari	3	29s48	51w51	3:27:24
Taquaritinga	2	21s24	48w30	3:14:00
Taraquá	4	0N06	68w28	4:33:52
Tarauacá	5	8s10	70w46	4:43:04
Tarituba	2	23s02	44w36	2:58:24
Taruaçu	2	21s37	42w56	2:51:44
Tarumirim	2	19s16	41w59	2:47:56
Tauá	3	6s01	40w26	2:41:44
Tauari	3	1s07	47w04	3:08:16
Taubaté	2	23s02	45w33	3:02:12
Taumaturgo	5	8s57	72w48	4:51:12
Taunay	4	20s18	56w05	3:44:20
Tavares	3	7s38	37w54	2:31:36
Tebas	2	21s35	42w44	2:50:56
Tefé	4	3s22	64w42	4:18:48
Teixeira	3	7s13	37w15	2:29:00
Teixeiras	2	20s39	42w51	2:51:24
Teixeira Soares	3	25s22	50w27	3:21:48
Tenente Portela	3	27s22	53w45	3:35:00
Tenentes	2	22s48	46w20	3:05:20
Tentugal	3	1s19	46w59	3:07:56

Teófilo Cunha	2	22s39	43w34	2:54:16
Teófilo Otoni	2	17s51	41w30	2:46:00
Terenos	4	20s26	54w50	3:39:20
Teresina	3	5s05	42w49	2:51:16
Teresópolis	2	22s26	42w59	2:51:56
Terra Boa	3	23s45	52w27	3:29:48
Terra Rica	3	22s43	52w38	3:30:32
Terra Roxa d'Oeste	3	24s08	53w59	3:35:56
Terra Santa	4	2s06	56w29	3:45:56
Tesouro	4	16s04	53w34	3:34:16
Tianguá	3	3s44	40w59	2:43:56
Tibagi	3	24s30	50w24	3:21:36
Tietê	2	23s07	47w43	3:10:52
Tijucas	3	27s14	48w38	3:14:32
Tijucas do Sul	3	25s55	49w12	3:16:48
Tijuco Prêto	2	22s56	46w40	3:06:40
Timbaúba	3	7s31	35w19	2:21:16
Timbiras	3	4s15	43w57	2:55:48
Timbó	3	26s50	49w18	3:17:12
Timon	3	5s06	42w49	2:51:16
Tinguá	2	22s36	43w26	2:53:44
Tiradentes	2	21s07	44w11	2:56:44
Tiros	2	19s00	45w58	3:03:52
Tobias Barreto	3	11s11	38w01	2:32:04
Tocantínia	3	9s33	48w22	3:13:28
Tocantinópolis	3	6s20	47w25	3:09:40
Tocos do Mogi	2	22s22	46w06	3:04:24
Toledo	3	24s44	53w45	3:35:00
Toledo	2	22s44	46w23	3:05:32
Tomazina	3	23s46	49w58	3:19:52
Tombos	2	20s55	42w02	2:48:08
Tomé-Açu	3	2s25	48w09	3:12:36
Tonantins	4	2s47	67w47	4:31:08
Toriparu	4	16s20	53w55	3:35:40
Torreões	2	21s52	43w33	2:54:12
Tôrres	3	29s21	49w44	3:18:56
Torrinha	2	22s26	48w09	3:12:36
Touros	3	5s12	35w28	2:21:52
Trabiju	2	22s03	48w18	3:13:12
Tracuateua	3	1s05	46w54	3:07:36
Traipu	3	9s58	37w01	2:28:04
Trairi	3	3s17	39w15	2:37:00
Tremedal	3	14s58	41w24	2:45:36
Tremembé	2	22s58	45w33	3:02:12
Três Corações	2	21s42	45w16	3:01:04
Três Coroas	3	29s32	50w48	3:23:12
Três de Maio	4	27s47	54w14	3:36:56
Três Fronteiras	2	20s13	50w55	3:23:40
Três Ilhas	2	22s04	43w29	2:53:56
Três Lagoas	4	20s48	51w43	3:26:52
Três Passos	3	27s27	53w56	3:35:44
Três Pontas	2	21s22	45w31	3:02:04
Três Ranchos	3	18s22	47w47	3:11:08
Três Rios	2	22s07	43w12	2:52:48
Tribobó	2	22s52	43w01	2:52:04
Trimonte	2	21s43	42w35	2:50:20
Trindade	3	16s40	49w30	3:18:00
Trindade	1	20s31	29w19	1:57:16
Trindade Island	1	20s31	29w19	1:57:16
Triunfo	3	7s50	38w07	2:32:28
Trombudo Central	3	27s18	49w47	3:19:08
Tubarão	3	28s30	49w01	3:16:04
Tucano	3	10s58	38w48	2:35:12
Tucunduva	4	27s39	54w27	3:37:48
Tucuruí	3	3s42	49w27	3:17:48
Tugúrio	2	21s15	43w35	2:54:20
Tuiuti	2	22s47	46w42	3:06:48
Tumiritinga	2	18s58	41w38	2:46:32
Tuntum	3	5s14	44w39	2:58:36
Tupã	2	21s56	50w30	3:22:00
Tupaciguara	2	18s35	48w42	3:14:48
Tupanciretã	3	29s05	53w51	3:35:24
Tupi Paulista	2	21s24	51w34	3:26:16
Tupiraçaba	3	14s29	48w34	3:14:16
Tupirama	3	8s58	48w12	3:12:48
Turiaçu	3	1s41	45w21	3:01:24
Turmalina	2	17s17	42w45	2:51:00
Turvânia	3	16s39	50w09	3:20:36
Turvo	3	28s56	49w41	3:18:44
Tutóia	3	2s45	42w16	2:49:04
Uauá	3	9s50	39w28	2:37:52
Ubá	2	21s07	42w56	2:51:44
Ubaíra	3	13s16	39w39	2:38:36
Ubaitaba	3	14s18	39w20	2:37:20
Ubajara	3	3s51	40w56	2:43:44
Ubatã	3	14s12	39w31	2:38:04
Ubatuba	2	23s26	45w04	3:00:16
Uberaba	2	19s45	47w55	3:11:40
Uberlândia	2	18s56	48w18	3:13:12
Uchoa	2	20s56	49w13	3:16:52
Uiraúna	3	6s31	38w25	2:33:40
Umari	3	6s38	38w42	2:34:48
Umarizal	3	5s59	37w49	2:31:16
Umbaúba	3	11s22	37w39	2:30:36
Umbuzeiro	3	7s41	35w40	2:22:40
Umuarama	3	23s45	53w20	3:33:20
Una	3	15s18	39w04	2:36:16
Unaí	2	16s23	46w53	3:07:32
União	3	4s35	42w52	2:51:28
União da Vitória	3	26s13	51w05	3:24:20
União dos Palmares	3	9s10	36w02	2:24:08
Upanema	3	5s38	37w15	2:29:00
Urandi	3	14s46	42w38	2:50:32
Uraricoera	4	3N27	60w59	4:03:56
Urbano Santos	3	3s12	43w23	2:53:32
Uruaçu	3	14s30	49w10	3:16:40
Uruana	3	15s30	49w41	3:18:44
Uruburetama	3	3s38	39w30	2:38:00
Urucará	4	2s32	57w45	3:51:00
Uruçuca	3	14s35	39w16	2:37:04
Uruçuí	3	7s14	44w33	2:58:12

BRAZIL — BRÉSIL — BRASILIEN — BRASIL

Urucurituba	4	2s41	57w40	3:50:40
Uruguaiana	4	29s45	57w05	3:48:20
Uruoca	3	3s20	40w32	2:42:08
Urupês	2	21s13	49w17	3:17:08
Urussanga	3	28s31	49w19	3:17:16
Urutaí	3	17s28	48w12	3:12:48
Utiariti	4	13s02	58w17	3:53:08
Utinga	2	23s38	46w32	3:06:08
Uvá	3	15s53	50w25	3:21:40
Vacaria	3	28s30	50w56	3:23:44
Val-De-Cães	3	1s23	48w29	3:13:56
Valdelândia	3	15s11	50w02	3:20:08
Valença	3	13s22	39w05	2:36:20
Valença	2	22s15	43w43	2:54:52
Valença do Piauí	3	6s24	41w45	2:47:00
Valente	3	11s34	39w27	2:37:48
Valinhos	2	22s57	47w01	3:08:04
Valparaíso	2	21s13	50w51	3:23:24
Vargem	2	22s53	46w25	3:05:40
Vargem Alegre	2	22s30	43w55	2:55:40
Vargem do Laje	2	22s08	44w49	2:59:16
Vargem Grande	3	3s33	43w56	2:55:44
Vargem Grande	2	22s59	45w17	3:01:08
Vargem Grande do Sul	2	21s50	46w53	3:07:32
Varginha	2	21s33	45w26	3:01:44
Varjão	3	17s03	49w37	3:18:28
Várzea	2	22s30	44w46	2:59:04
Várzea Alegre	3	6s47	39w17	2:37:08
Várzea da Palma	2	17s36	44w44	2:58:56
Várzea das Moças	2	22s57	42w58	2:51:52
Várzea Grande	4	15s39	56w08	3:44:32
Varzeão	3	24s34	49w26	3:17:44
Várzea Paulista	2	23s12	46w50	3:07:20
Vassouras	2	22s25	43w40	2:54:40
Vazante	2	18s00	46w54	3:07:36
Veiros	4	2s05	52w10	3:28:40
Venâncio Aires	3	29s36	52w11	3:28:44
Venceslau Brás	3	23s51	49w48	3:19:12
Veranópolis	3	28s57	51w33	3:26:12
Verava	2	23s47	47w05	3:08:20
Veríssimo	2	19s42	48w18	3:13:12
Vertentes	3	7s54	35w59	2:23:56
Vespasiano	2	19s40	43w55	2:55:40
Viadutos	3	27s34	52w01	3:28:04
Viamão	3	30s05	51w02	3:24:08
Viana	3	3s13	45w00	3:00:00
Vicência	3	7s40	35w20	2:21:20
Vicente de Carvalho	2	23s56	46w19	3:05:16
Viçosa	2	20s45	42w53	2:51:32
Viçosa	3	9s24	36w14	2:24:56
Viçosa do Ceará	3	3s34	41w05	2:44:20
Victoria → Vitória	2	20s19	40w21	2:41:24
Vidal Ramos	3	27s23	49w22	3:17:28
Videira	3	27s00	51w08	3:24:32
Vigia	3	0s48	48w08	3:12:32
Vila Augusta	2	23s28	46w32	3:06:08
Vila, Fernandes de Noronha	3	3s50	32w26	2:09:44
Vila Galvão	2	23s27	46w33	3:06:12
Vila Muriqui	2	22s56	43w57	2:55:48
Vila Progresso	2	22s55	43w03	2:52:12
Vila Rica	4	3s40	61w02	4:04:08
Vilarinho do Monte	3	1s37	52w01	3:28:04
Vila Velha	2	20s20	40w17	2:41:08
Vila Velha	3	3n13	51w13	3:24:52
Vilhena	4	12s43	60w07	4:00:28
Vinhedo	2	23s01	46w59	3:07:56
Viradouro	2	20s53	48w18	3:13:12
Virgem da Lapa	2	16s49	42w21	2:49:24
Virgínia	2	22s20	45w06	3:00:24
Virginópolis	2	18s45	42w45	2:51:00
Virgolândia	2	18s27	42w18	2:49:12
Viseu	3	1s12	46w07	3:04:28
Vista Alegre	2	21s27	42w35	2:50:20
Vitória	2	20s19	40w21	2:41:24
Vitória	4	2s54	52w01	3:28:04
Vitória da Conquista	3	14s51	40w51	2:43:24
Vitória de Santo Antão	3	8s07	35w18	2:21:12
Vitória do Mearim	3	3s28	44w53	2:59:32
Vitorino Freire	3	4s04	45w10	3:00:40
Volta Grande	2	21s46	42w32	2:50:08
Volta Redonda	2	22s32	44w07	2:56:28
Votuporanga	2	20s24	49w59	3:19:56
Werneck	2	22s13	43w19	2:53:16
Xambioá	3	6s25	48w40	3:14:40
Xanxerê	3	26s53	52w23	3:29:32
Xapuri	5	10s39	68w31	4:34:04
Xavantina	4	21s15	52w48	3:31:12
Xaxim	3	26s56	52w31	3:30:04
Xerém	2	22s33	43w18	2:53:12
Xique-Xique	3	10s50	42w44	2:50:56

BRUNEI — BRUNÉI — BRUNEI

Time Table

Before 1/Mar/1926		LMT
Begin Standard		112E30
1/Mar/1926	0:00	-7:30
Begin Standard		120E00
1/Jan/1933	0:00	-8:00

Badas	4N36	114E27	-7:37:48
Bandar Seri Begawan	4N56	114E55	-7:39:40
Bangar	4N43	115E04	-7:40:16
Brooketown	5N02	115E03	-7:40:12
Brunei → Bandar Seri Begawan	4N56	114E55	-7:39:40
Kuala Belait	4N35	114E11	-7:36:44
Labi	4N25	114E22	-7:37:28
Muara	5N02	115E02	-7:40:08
Seria	4N39	114E23	-7:37:32
Tutong	4N50	114E40	-7:38:40

BULGARIA — BULGARIE — BULGARIEN — BÂLGARIJA

Time Table # 1

Before 1/Jan/1880		LMT
Begin Standard		29E14
1/Jan/1880	0:00	-1:57
Begin Standard		30E00
30/Nov/1894	0:00	-2:00
Begin Standard		15E00
2/Nov/1942	3:00	-1:00
29/Mar/1943	2:00	-2:00
4/Oct/1943	3:00	-1:00
3/Apr/1944	2:00	-2:00
2/Oct/1944	0:00	-1:00
Begin Standard		30E00
2/Apr/1945	3:00	-2:00
31/Mar/1979	23:00	-3:00
1/Oct/1979	1:00	-2:00
5/Apr/1980	23:00	-3:00
29/Sep/1980	1:00	-2:00
4/Apr/1981	23:00	-3:00
27/Sep/1981	2:00	-2:00
3/Apr/1982	23:00	-3:00
26/Sep/1982	2:00	-2:00
27/Mar/1983	2:00	-3:00
25/Sep/1983	3:00	-2:00
25/Mar/1984	2:00	-3:00
30/Sep/1984	3:00	-2:00
31/Mar/1985	2:00	-3:00
29/Sep/1985	3:00	-2:00
30/Mar/1986	2:00	-3:00
28/Sep/1986	3:00	-2:00
29/Mar/1987	2:00	-3:00
27/Sep/1987	3:00	-2:00
27/Mar/1988	2:00	-3:00
25/Sep/1988	3:00	-2:00
26/Mar/1989	2:00	-3:00
24/Sep/1989	3:00	-2:00
25/Mar/1990	2:00	-3:00
30/Sep/1990	3:00	-2:00
31/Mar/1991	2:00	-3:00
29/Sep/1991	3:00	-2:00
29/Mar/1992	2:00	-3:00
27/Sep/1992	3:00	-2:00
28/Mar/1993	2:00	-3:00
26/Sep/1993	3:00	-2:00
27/Mar/1994	2:00	-3:00
25/Sep/1994	3:00	-2:00
26/Mar/1995	2:00	-3:00
24/Sep/1995	3:00	-2:00
31/Mar/1996	2:00	-3:00
29/Sep/1996	3:00	-2:00
30/Mar/1997	2:00	-3:00
28/Sep/1997	3:00	-2:00
29/Mar/1998	2:00	-3:00
27/Sep/1998	3:00	-2:00
28/Mar/1999	2:00	-3:00
26/Sep/1999	3:00	-2:00
26/Mar/2000	2:00	-3:00
24/Sep/2000	3:00	-2:00

....

Time Table # 2

Before 1/Jan/1880		LMT
Begin Standard		29E14
1/Jan/1880	0:00	-1:57
Begin Standard		30E00
1/Oct/1910	0:00	-2:00
Begin Standard		15E00
2/Nov/1942	3:00	-1:00
29/Mar/1943	2:00	-2:00
4/Oct/1943	3:00	-1:00
3/Apr/1944	2:00	-2:00
2/Oct/1944	0:00	-1:00
Begin Standard		30E00
2/Apr/1945	3:00	-2:00
31/Mar/1979	23:00	TT#1

Ahtopol	1	42N06	27E57	-1:51:48
Ajtos	1	42N42	27E15	-1:49:00
Alfatar	1	43N57	27E17	-1:49:08
Ardino	2	41N35	25E08	-1:40:32
Asenovgrad	1	42N01	24E52	-1:39:28
Balčik	1	43N25	28E10	-1:52:40
Bansko	2	41N50	23E29	-1:33:56
Batak	1	41N57	24E13	-1:36:52
Bazargic → Tolbuhin	1	43N34	27E50	-1:51:20
Belene	1	43N39	25E07	-1:40:28
Belogradčik	1	43N38	22E41	-1:30:44
Bjala	1	43N27	25E44	-1:42:56
Bjala Slatina	1	43N28	23E56	-1:35:44
Blagoevgrad	2	42N01	23E06	-1:32:24
Blatnica	1	43N42	28E31	-1:54:04
Boljarovo	1	42N09	26E49	-1:47:16
Borovan	1	43N26	23E45	-1:35:00
Botevgrad	1	42N54	23E47	-1:35:08
Bracigovo	1	42N01	24E22	-1:37:28
Bregovo	1	44N09	22E39	-1:30:36
Brest	1	43N38	24E35	-1:38:20
Breznik	1	42N44	22E54	-1:31:36
Burgas	1	42N30	27E28	-1:49:52
Butan	1	43N39	23E45	-1:35:00
Cenovo	1	43N32	25E39	-1:42:36
Čepelare	2	41N44	24E41	-1:38:44
Červen Brjag	1	43N16	24E06	-1:36:24
Čirpan	1	42N12	25E20	-1:41:20
Devin	2	41N45	24E24	-1:37:36
Dimitrovgrad	1	42N03	25E36	-1:42:24
Dimitrovo → Pernik	1	42N36	23W02	1:32:08
Dobrich → Tolbuhin	1	43N34	27E50	-1:51:20
Dolni Dăbnik	1	43N24	24E26	-1:37:44
Dolni Lom	1	43N31	22E47	-1:31:08
Drenovec	1	43N42	22E59	-1:31:56
Drjanovo	1	42N58	25E27	-1:41:48
Dulovo	1	43N49	27E09	-1:48:36
Dve Mogili	1	43N36	25E52	-1:43:28
Elena	1	42N56	25E53	-1:43:32
Elhovo	1	42N10	26E34	-1:46:16
Elin Pelin	1	42N40	23E36	-1:34:24
Eski Dzhumaya → Târgovište	1	43N15	26E34	-1:46:16
Ferdinand Vratza	1	43N25	23E12	-1:32:48
Gabare	1	43N19	23E55	-1:35:40
Gabrovo	1	42N52	25E19	-1:41:16
General Toševo	1	43N42	28E02	-1:52:08
Gigen	1	43N42	24E29	-1:37:56
Gjuesevo	1	42N14	22E28	-1:29:52
Goce Delčev	2	41N34	23E44	-1:34:56
Gorna Dzhumaya → Blagoevgrad	2	42N01	23E06	-1:32:24
Gorna Orjahovica	1	43N07	25E41	-1:42:44
Gramada	1	43N50	22E39	-1:30:36
Grudovo	1	42N21	27E10	-1:48:40
Guljanci	1	43N38	24E42	-1:38:48
Harmanli	1	41N56	25E54	-1:43:36
Haskovo	1	41N56	25E33	-1:42:12
Ihtiman	1	42N26	23E49	-1:35:16
Isperih	1	43N43	26E50	-1:47:20
Ivajlovgrad	2	41N32	26E08	-1:44:32

BÂLGARIJA BULGARIEN BULGARIE BULGARIA

Place		Lat	Long	Offset
Jambol	1	42N29	26E30	-1:46:00
Kalofer	1	42N37	24E59	-1:39:56
Kârdžali	2	41N39	25E22	-1:41:28
Karlovo	1	42N38	24E48	-1:39:12
Karnobat	1	42N39	26E59	-1:47:56
Kavarna	1	43N25	28E20	-1:53:20
Kazanlâk	1	42N38	25E21	-1:41:24
Khaskovo → Haskovo	1	41N56	25E33	-1:42:12
Kjustendil	1	42N17	22E41	-1:30:44
Klisura	1	42N42	24E27	-1:37:48
Kneža	1	43N30	24E05	-1:36:20
Kolarovgrad → Šumen	1	43N16	26E55	-1:47:40
Kostenec	1	42N16	23E49	-1:35:16
Kotel	1	42N53	26E27	-1:45:48
Krivodol	1	43N23	23E29	-1:33:56
Krumovgrad	2	41N28	25E39	-1:42:36
Kubrat	1	43N48	26E30	-1:46:00
Kula	1	43N53	22E31	-1:30:04
Lehčevo	1	43N32	23E32	-1:34:08
Levski	1	43N22	25E08	-1:40:32
Ljubimec	1	41N50	26E05	-1:44:20
Lom	1	43N49	23E14	-1:32:56
Loveč	1	43N08	24E43	-1:38:52
Lukovit	1	43N12	24E10	-1:36:40
Madan	2	41N30	24E57	-1:39:48
Malko Târnovo	1	41N59	27E32	-1:50:08
Marica	1	42N02	25E50	-1:43:20
Medkovec	1	43N37	23E10	-1:32:40
Mezdra	1	43N09	23E42	-1:34:48
Mičurin	1	42N10	27E51	-1:51:24
Mihajlovgrad	1	43N25	23E13	-1:32:52
Mikre	1	43N02	24E31	-1:38:04
Momčilgrad	2	41N32	25E25	-1:41:40
Nesebâr	1	42N39	27E44	-1:50:56
Nikopol	1	43N42	24E54	-1:39:36
Nova Zagora	1	42N29	26E01	-1:44:04
Novi Pazar	1	43N21	27E12	-1:48:48
Obnova	1	43N26	24E59	-1:39:56
Omurtag	1	43N06	26E25	-1:45:40
Opaka	1	43N27	26E10	-1:44:40
Orjahovo	1	43N45	23E57	-1:35:48
Panagjurište	1	42N30	24E11	-1:36:44
Pârvomaj	1	42N06	25E13	-1:40:52
Pavlikeni	1	43N14	25E18	-1:41:12
Pazardžik	1	42N12	24E20	-1:37:20
Pernik	1	42N36	23E02	-1:32:08
Peštera	1	42N02	24E18	-1:37:12
Petrič	2	41N24	23E13	-1:32:52
Philippopolis → Plovdiv	1	42N09	24E45	-1:39:00
Pirdop	1	42N42	24E11	-1:36:44
Pleven	1	43N25	24E37	-1:38:28
Plovdiv	1	42N09	24E45	-1:39:00
Polski Trâmbeš	1	43N22	25E38	-1:42:32
Pomorie	1	42N33	27E39	-1:50:36
Popinci	1	42N25	24E17	-1:37:08
Popovo	1	43N21	26E13	-1:44:52
Pordim	1	43N23	24E51	-1:39:24
Primorsko	1	42N16	27E46	-1:51:04
Provadija	1	43N11	27E26	-1:49:44
Radnevo	1	42N18	25E56	-1:43:44
Radomir	1	42N33	22E58	-1:31:52
Rakovski	1	42N18	24E58	-1:39:52
Razgrad	1	43N32	26E31	-1:46:04
Razlog	2	41N53	23E28	-1:33:52
Rezovo	1	41N59	28E02	-1:52:08
Roman	1	43N09	23E55	-1:35:40
Ruschuk → Ruse	1	43N50	25E57	-1:43:48
Ruse	1	43N50	25E57	-1:43:48
Ryazovo	1	41N59	28E02	-1:52:08
Šabla	1	43N32	28E32	-1:54:08
Samokov	1	42N20	23E33	-1:34:12
Sandanski	2	41N34	23E17	-1:33:08
Sevlievo	1	43N01	25E06	-1:40:24
Shipka	1	42N43	25E20	-1:41:20
Shumen → Šumen	1	43N16	26E55	-1:47:40
Silistra	1	44N07	27E16	-1:49:04
Sliven	1	42N40	26E19	-1:45:16
Slivnica	1	42N51	23E02	-1:32:08
Smoljan	2	41N35	24E41	-1:38:44
Sofia → Sofija	1	42N41	23E19	-1:33:16
Sofija (Sofia)	1	42N41	23E19	-1:33:16
Sozopol	1	42N25	27E42	-1:50:48
Stalin → Varna	1	43N13	27E55	-1:51:40
Stanke Dimitrov	1	42N16	23E07	-1:32:28
Stara Zagora	1	42N25	25E38	-1:42:32
Šumen	1	43N16	26E55	-1:47:40
Svilengrad	1	41N46	26E12	-1:44:48
Svištov	1	43N37	25E20	-1:41:20
Svoge	1	42N58	23E21	-1:33:24
Târgovište	1	43N15	26E34	-1:46:16
Telerig	1	43N51	27E40	-1:50:40
Tervel	1	43N45	27E24	-1:49:36
Teteven	1	42N55	24E16	-1:37:04
Tirnovo → Veliko Târnovo	1	43N04	25E39	-1:42:36
Tolbuhin	1	43N34	27E50	-1:51:20
Topolovgrad	1	42N05	26E20	-1:45:20
Trân	1	42N50	22E39	-1:30:36
Trâstenik	1	43N31	24E28	-1:37:52
Trnovo → Veliko Târnovo	1	43N04	25E39	-1:42:36
Trojan	1	42N51	24E43	-1:38:52
Tŭrgovishte → Târgovište	1	43N15	26E34	-1:46:16
Tŭrnovo → Veliko Târnovo	1	43N04	25E39	-1:42:36
Tutrakan	1	44N03	26E37	-1:46:28
Tvârdica	1	43N42	25E52	-1:43:28
Ugârčin	1	43N06	24E25	-1:37:40
Vâlčedrâm	1	43N42	23E27	-1:33:48
Varna	1	43N13	27E55	-1:51:40
Vâršec	1	43N12	23E17	-1:33:08
Veliko Târnovo	1	43N04	25E39	-1:42:36
Velingrad	1	42N04	24E00	-1:36:00
Vetovo	1	43N42	26E16	-1:45:04
Vetren	1	42N16	24E03	-1:36:12
Vidin	1	43N59	22E52	-1:31:28
Vraca	1	43N12	23E33	-1:34:12
Yambol → Jambol	1	42N29	26E30	-1:46:00
Zafirovo	1	44N00	26E50	-1:47:20
Zavet	1	43N46	26E40	-1:46:40
Zlatica	1	42N43	24E08	-1:36:32
Zlatograd	2	41N23	25E06	-1:40:24
Zornica	1	42N23	26E56	-1:47:44
Zvezdec	1	42N07	27E25	-1:49:40

UPPER VOLTA OBERVOLTA ALTO VOLTA HAUTE-VOLTA BURKINA FASO

Time Table		
Before	1/Jan/1912 LMT	
Begin Standard		0w00
1/Jan/1912	0:00	0:00

Place	Lat	Long	Offset
Aribinda	14N14	0w52	0:03:28
Arli	11N35	1E28	-0:05:52
Arly	11N35	1E28	-0:05:52
Balavé	12N23	4w09	0:16:36
Ban	14N05	2w27	0:09:48
Banfora	10N38	4w46	0:19:04
Banh	14N05	2w27	0:09:48
Bani	14N02	0w02	0:00:08
Baraboulé	14N12	1w51	0:07:24
Barani	13N10	3w53	0:15:32
Barsalogho	13N25	1w03	0:04:12
Bartibougou	12N52	0E48	-0:03:12
Batié	9N53	2w55	0:11:40
Bilanga	12N32	0E02	-0:00:08
Bitou	11N16	0w18	0:01:12
Bittou	11N16	0w18	0:01:12
Bobo Dioulasso	11N12	4w18	0:17:12
Bogandé	12N59	0w08	0:00:32
Bohongou	12N30	0E42	-0:02:48
Boromo	11N45	2w56	0:11:44
Botou	12N25	0E09	-0:00:36
Botou	12N40	2E03	-0:08:12
Boulsa	12N39	0w34	0:02:16
Bouroum	13N37	0w39	0:02:36
Bourzanga	13N41	1w33	0:06:12
Boussé	12N39	1w53	0:07:32
Boussouma	12N55	1w05	0:04:20
Cassou	11N35	2w03	0:08:12
Dani	13N43	0w10	0:00:40
Dano	11N09	3w04	0:12:16
Dédougou	12N28	3w28	0:13:52
Diapaga	12N04	1E47	-0:07:08
Diapangou	12N07	0E11	-0:00:44
Diébougou	10N58	3w15	0:13:00
Djibasso	13N07	4w10	0:16:40
Djibo	14N06	1w38	0:06:32
Dori	14N02	0w02	0:00:08
Fada Ngourma	12N04	0E21	-0:01:24
Faramana	12N03	4w40	0:18:40
Gaoua	10N20	3w11	0:12:44
Garango	11N48	0w34	0:02:16
Gassan	12N49	3w12	0:12:48
Gayéri	12N39	0E29	-0:01:56
Gomboro	13N29	2w46	0:11:04
Gorom-Gorom	14N26	0w14	0:00:56
Gourcy	13N13	2w21	0:09:24
Gourey	13N13	2w21	0:09:24
Houndé	11N30	3w31	0:14:04
Kampti	10N08	3w27	0:13:48
Kantchari	12N29	1E31	-0:06:04
Kassou	11N35	2w03	0:08:12
Kassoum	13N05	3w18	0:13:12
Katchirga	14N03	0E06	-0:00:24
Kaya	13N05	1w05	0:04:20
Kéléso	10N57	3w59	0:15:56
Kiembara	13N15	2w44	0:10:56
Klésso	10N57	3w59	0:15:56
Koloko	11N05	5w19	0:21:16
Kombissiri	12N04	1w20	0:05:20
Komin Yanga	11N42	0E08	-0:00:32
Kongoussi	13N19	1w32	0:06:08
Koudougou	12N15	2w22	0:09:28
Kouéré	10N27	3w59	0:15:56
Koumbia	11N14	3w42	0:14:48
Koundougou	11N44	4w31	0:18:04
Koupéla	12N11	0w21	0:01:24
Kourouma	11N37	4w48	0:19:12
Léo	11N06	2w06	0:08:24
Lokosso	10N19	3w40	0:14:40
Louta	13N30	3w10	0:12:40
Madjoari	11N26	1E15	-0:05:00
Madjori	11N26	1E15	-0:05:00
Mané	12N59	1w21	0:05:24
Manga	11N40	1w04	0:04:16
Markoy	14N39	0E02	-0:00:08
Markoye	14N39	0E02	-0:00:08
Matiacoali	12N22	1E02	-0:04:08
Matiakoali	12N22	1E02	-0:04:08
Nabou	11N27	2w43	0:10:52
Nako	10N38	3w04	0:12:16
Namounou	11N52	1E42	-0:06:48
Nebbou	11N18	1w53	0:07:32
Niangoloko	10N17	4w55	0:19:40
Nobéré	11N33	1w12	0:04:48
Nobili	11N33	1w12	0:04:48
Nouna	12N44	3w52	0:15:28
Nyou	12N46	1w56	0:07:44
Orodara	10N59	4w55	0:19:40
Ouagadougou	12N22	1w31	0:06:04
Ouahigouya	13N35	2w25	0:09:40
Ouargaye	11N32	0E01	-0:00:04
Ouarkoye	12N05	3w40	0:14:40
Oudyoumoudi	14N04	0w28	0:01:52
Ouessa	11N03	2w47	0:11:08
Ougarou	12N09	0E56	-0:03:44
Oursi	14N41	0w27	0:01:48
Pâ	11N33	3w15	0:13:00
Pama	11N15	0E42	-0:02:48
Piéla	12N42	0w08	0:00:32
Pissila	13N10	0w49	0:03:16
Pô	11N10	1w09	0:04:36
Pobé	13N53	1w45	0:07:00
Réo	12N19	2w28	0:09:52
Sabou	12N04	2w14	0:08:56
Sanaba	12N25	3w49	0:15:16
Sanga	11N10	0E10	-0:00:40
Saponé	12N03	1w36	0:06:24
Sara	11N43	3w50	0:15:20
Sebba	13N26	0E32	-0:02:08
Séguénéga	13N27	1w58	0:07:52
Sidéradougou	10N40	4w15	0:17:00
Silli	11N36	2w30	0:10:00
Sindou	10N40	5w10	0:20:40
Soin	12N47	3w49	0:15:16
Solenzo	12N11	4w05	0:16:20
Soubakaniédougou	10N28	5w01	0:20:04
Soulougou	13N01	0E23	-0:01:32
Tansilla	12N26	4w23	0:17:32
Tchériba	12N16	3w05	0:12:20
Tenkodogo	11N47	0w22	0:01:28
Thiou	13N48	2w40	0:10:40
Tiankoura	10N46	3w16	0:13:04
Tikaré	13N17	1w43	0:06:52
Tinié	14N20	1w28	0:05:52
Titao	13N46	2w04	0:08:16
Tôecé	11N50	1w16	0:05:04
Toéssé	11N50	1w16	0:05:04
Toma	12N46	2w53	0:11:32
Tougan	13N04	3w04	0:12:16
Tougouri	13N19	0w31	0:02:04
Uagadugu → Ouagadougou	12N22	1w31	0:06:04
Wagadugu → Ouagadougou	12N22	1w31	0:06:04
Yako	12N58	2w16	0:09:04
Yendéré	10N12	4w58	0:19:52
Zabré	11N10	0w38	0:02:32
Ziniaré	12N35	1w18	0:05:12
Zorgo	12N15	0w36	0:02:24
Zorgongo	12N16	0w48	0:03:12
Zourma	11N22	0w49	0:03:16

BURMA — BIRMANIA — BIRMANIE — BIRMA — MYANMAR

Time Table
Before 1/Jan/1880 LMT
Begin Standard 96E09
1/Jan/1880 0:00 -6:25
Begin Standard 97E30
1/Jan/1920 0:00 -6:30
Begin Standard 135E00
1/May/1942 0:00 -9:00
Begin Standard 97E30
3/May/1945 0:00 -6:30

Place	Lat	Long	Offset
Akyab → Sittwe	20N09	92E54	-6:11:36
Allanmyo	19N22	95E13	-6:20:52
Amarapura	21N54	96E03	-6:24:12
Amherst	16N05	97E35	-6:30:20
An	19N47	94E02	-6:16:08
Anin	15N40	97E46	-6:31:04
Athok	17N12	95E05	-6:20:20
Awegyun	12N44	98E44	-6:34:56
Badupi	21N36	93E25	-6:13:40
Banmauk	24N24	95E51	-6:23:24
Bassein	16N47	94E44	-6:18:56
Baw	23N19	95E50	-6:23:20
Bawdwin	23N06	97E18	-6:29:12
Bawlake	19N11	97E21	-6:29:24
Bawmi	17N19	94E35	-6:18:20
Bhamo	24N16	97E14	-6:28:56
Bilin	17N14	97E15	-6:29:00
Bogale	16N17	95E24	-6:21:36
Bokpyin	11N16	98E46	-6:35:04
Budalin	22N22	95E08	-6:20:32
Buthidaung	20N52	92E32	-6:10:08
Chauk	20N54	94E50	-6:19:20
Chaungwabyin	13N41	98E22	-6:33:28
Chaungzon	16N22	97E32	-6:30:08
Chi-Kyaw	20N17	93E54	-6:15:36
Dagwin	18N04	97E41	-6:30:44
Daik-U	17N47	96E40	-6:26:40
Dalet	19N59	93E51	-6:15:24
Danubyu	17N15	95E35	-6:22:20
Dawlan	16N44	98E01	-6:32:04
Dedaye	16N24	95E53	-6:23:32
Einme	16N54	95E11	-6:20:44
Ela	19N37	96E13	-6:24:52
Falam	22N55	93E40	-6:14:40
Fort Hertz → Putao	27N21	97E24	-6:29:36
Gangaw	22N11	94E07	-6:16:28
Gwa	17N36	94E35	-6:18:20
Gyobingauk	18N13	95E39	-6:22:36
Haka	22N39	93E37	-6:14:28
Heho	20N43	96E49	-6:27:16
Heirnkut	25N14	94E45	-6:19:00
Henzada	17N38	95E28	-6:21:52
Hermyingyi	14N15	98E21	-6:33:24
Hlaingbwe	17N08	97E50	-6:31:20
Hlegu	17N06	96E14	-6:24:56
Hmawbi	17N06	96E02	-6:24:08
Homalin	24N52	94E55	-6:19:40
Hpru-So	19N25	97E08	-6:28:32
Hsenwi	23N18	97E58	-6:31:52
Hsi-Hseng	20N09	97E15	-6:29:00
Hsipaw	22N37	97E18	-6:29:12
Hsuphāng	20N18	98E42	-6:34:48
Indaw	23N40	94E46	-6:19:04
Indin	20N16	92E57	-6:11:48
Ingabu	17N49	95E16	-6:21:04
Insein	16N53	96E07	-6:24:28
Inywa	23N56	96E17	-6:25:08
Kadaingti	17N37	97E32	-6:30:08
Kalagwe	22N31	96E31	-6:26:04
Kalaw	20N38	96E34	-6:26:16
Kalemyo	23N12	94E10	-6:16:40
Kaletwa	21N45	92E48	-6:11:12
Kalewa	23N12	94E17	-6:17:08
Kama	19N02	95E06	-6:20:24
Kamamaung	17N21	97E40	-6:30:40
Kampong Ulu	10N03	98E33	-6:34:12
Kanbalu	23N12	95E31	-6:22:04
Kanbauk	14N36	98E02	-6:32:08
Kanbe	16N42	96E01	-6:24:04
Kangyidaung	16N56	94E54	-6:19:36
Kani	22N26	94E50	-6:19:20
Kanpetlet	21N12	94E02	-6:16:08
Kansau	23N50	93E35	-6:14:20
Kantu-Long	19N57	97E36	-6:30:24
Kanyutkwin	18N21	96E30	-6:26:00
Katha	24N11	96E21	-6:25:24
Kaunghein	25N40	95E26	-6:21:44
Kawa	17N05	96E28	-6:25:52
Kawbein	16N33	97E52	-6:31:28
Kawdut	15N31	97E47	-6:31:08
Kawkareik	16N33	98E14	-6:32:56
Kawludo	18N29	97E19	-6:29:16
Kayan	16N54	96E34	-6:26:16
Ke-Hsi Mānsām	21N56	97E50	-6:31:20
Kēng Hkam	21N01	98E29	-6:33:56
Keng Hkam	21N27	97E03	-6:28:12
Kēng Tung	21N17	99E36	-6:38:24
Khawsa	15N03	97E50	-6:31:20
Khugaung	26N07	98E18	-6:33:12
Kinchang	26N32	98E02	-6:32:08
Klangpi	22N59	93E20	-6:13:20
Koma	15N39	98E12	-6:32:48
Kontha	19N30	96E03	-6:24:12
Kronwa	15N25	98E26	-6:33:44
Kunhing	21N18	98E26	-6:33:44
Kunlong	23N25	98E39	-6:34:36
Kutkai	23N27	97E56	-6:31:44
Kyaikkami	16N04	97E34	-6:30:16
Kyaiklat	16N26	95E44	-6:22:56
Kyaikto	17N18	97E01	-6:28:04
Kya-In	16N02	98E08	-6:32:32
Kyat-Aw	12N29	98E19	-6:33:16
Kyaukhnyat	18N15	97E31	-6:30:04
Kyaukkyi	18N19	96E46	-6:27:04
Kyaukme	22N32	97E02	-6:28:08
Kyaukpa	13N05	98E59	-6:35:56
Kyaukpyu	19N05	93E52	-6:15:28
Kyaukpyu	19N26	93E33	-6:14:12
Kyaukse	21N36	96E08	-6:24:32
Kyauktaw	20N51	92E59	-6:11:56
Kyaunggon	17N06	95E11	-6:20:44
Kyeikdon	16N00	98E24	-6:33:36
Kyeintali	18N00	94E29	-6:17:56
Kyidaunggan	19N53	96E12	-6:24:48
Kyindwe	20N58	93E51	-6:15:24
Kyondo	16N35	98E03	-6:32:12
Kyönkadun	16N04	95E38	-6:22:32
Kyonmange	16N30	95E50	-6:23:20
Kyonpyaw	17N18	95E12	-6:20:48
Kyunchaung	15N33	98E15	-6:33:00
Kyundon	20N31	95E44	-6:22:56
Kyunhla	23N21	95E18	-6:21:12
Kywebwe	18N42	96E25	-6:25:40
Labutta	16N09	94E46	-6:19:04
Lāhe	26N20	95E26	-6:21:44
Lai-Hka	21N16	97E40	-6:30:40
Lāmu	19N14	94E10	-6:16:40
Lashio	22N56	97E45	-6:31:00
Launglon	13N58	98E07	-6:32:28
Lawksawk	21N15	96E52	-6:27:28
Leiktho	19N13	96E35	-6:26:20
Lemyethna	17N36	95E09	-6:20:36
Lenya	11N28	99E00	-6:36:00
Letpadan	17N47	95E45	-6:23:00
Lewe	19N38	96E07	-6:24:28
Loi-Kaw	19N41	97E13	-6:28:52
Loi Mwe	21N11	99E46	-6:39:04
Lonton	25N06	96E17	-6:25:08
Madaya	22N13	96E07	-6:24:28
Māge	26N33	98E33	-6:34:12
Magwe	20N09	94E55	-6:19:40
Makaw	26N27	96E42	-6:26:48
Malān	25N37	96E21	-6:25:24
Male	23N02	95E58	-6:23:52
Maliwun	10N14	98E37	-6:34:28
Manaung	18N51	93E44	-6:14:56
Mandalay	22N00	96E05	-6:24:20
Mān Hpāng	22N41	98E36	-6:34:24
Mān Kāt	22N05	98E01	-6:32:04
Mān Na	23N27	97E14	-6:28:56
Manoron	11N38	99E04	-6:36:16
Mansein	25N12	95E58	-6:23:52
Marang	10N27	98E47	-6:35:08
Martaban	16N32	97E37	-6:30:28
Ma-Ubin	16N44	95E39	-6:22:36
Maungdaw	20N50	92E21	-6:09:24
Maungmagan	14N09	98E06	-6:32:24
Mawchi	18N49	97E09	-6:28:36
Mawkhi	16N17	98E53	-6:35:32
Mawlaik	23N38	94E24	-6:17:36
Mawlamyaing → Moulmein	16N30	97E38	-6:30:32
Maymyo	22N02	96E28	-6:25:52
Mè-Hsa-Tè	19N33	97E38	-6:30:32
Meiktila	20N52	95E52	-6:23:28
Melun	20N14	93E24	-6:13:36
Mergui (Myeik)	12N26	98E36	-6:34:24
Mèsè Atet	18N38	97E39	-6:30:36
Metharaw	16N12	98E08	-6:32:32
Migyaunglaung	14N40	98E09	-6:32:36
Minbu	20N11	94E52	-6:19:28
Minbya	20N22	93E15	-6:13:00
Minbyin	19N17	93E32	-6:14:08
Mindon	19N21	94E44	-6:18:56
Mingin	22N52	94E39	-6:18:36
Minhla	19N58	95E03	-6:20:12
Minhla	17N59	95E43	-6:22:52
Mogaung	25N18	96E56	-6:27:44
Mogok	22N55	96E30	-6:26:00
Mohnyin	24N47	96E22	-6:25:28
Mokpalin	17N26	96E53	-6:27:32
Mon	18N31	96E38	-6:26:32
Möng Hai	20N46	99E49	-6:39:16
Möng Hawm	23N51	98E20	-6:33:20
Möng Hpāyak	20N53	99E54	-6:39:36
Möng Hsat	20N32	99E15	-6:37:00
Möng Küng	21N36	97E32	-6:30:08
Möng Ma	21N37	99E54	-6:39:36
Möng Mit	23N07	96E41	-6:26:44
Möng Nai	20N31	97E52	-6:31:28
Möng Nawng	21N39	98E08	-6:32:32
Möng Pai	19N44	97E05	-6:28:20
Möng Pan	20N19	98E22	-6:33:28
Möng Pawn	20N49	97E28	-6:29:52
Möng Ping	22N22	99E02	-6:36:08
Möng Si	23N40	98E23	-6:33:32
Möng Yai	22N25	98E02	-6:32:08
Möng Yawng	21N11	100E22	-6:41:28
Monyo	17N59	95E30	-6:22:00
Monywa	22N05	95E08	-6:20:32
Moulmein	16N30	97E38	-6:30:32
Moulmeingyun	16N23	95E16	-6:21:04
Mudon	16N15	97E44	-6:30:56
Myaing	21N37	94E51	-6:19:24
Myanaung	18N17	95E19	-6:21:16
Myaungmya	16N36	94E56	-6:19:44
Myawadi	16N41	98E31	-6:34:04
Myebon	20N03	93E22	-6:13:28
Myeik → Mergui	12N26	98E36	-6:34:24
Myingyan	21N28	95E23	-6:21:32
Myitkyinā	25N23	97E24	-6:29:36
Myitta	14N10	98E31	-6:34:04
Myittha	21N25	96E08	-6:24:32
Myo-Gyi	21N27	96E22	-6:25:28
Myohaung	20N36	93E10	-6:12:40
Namhkam	23N50	97E41	-6:30:44
Namhsan	22N58	97E10	-6:28:40
Namlan	22N15	97E24	-6:29:36
Nampawng	22N45	97E52	-6:31:28
Namsang	20N53	97E43	-6:30:52
Namtu	23N05	97E24	-6:29:36
Nanantun	24N45	95E41	-6:22:44
Nangin	10N31	98E31	-6:34:04
Nankye	14N20	98E11	-6:32:44
Natkyizin	14N55	97E57	-6:31:48
Nattalin	18N26	95E33	-6:22:12
Naunglon	16N48	97E45	-6:31:00
Naungpale	19N33	97E08	-6:28:32
Ngape	20N04	94E38	-6:18:32
Ngaputaw	16N32	94E42	-6:18:48
Ngathainggyaung	17N24	95E05	-6:20:20
Nyaunglebin	17N57	96E44	-6:26:56
Oktwin	18N49	96E26	-6:25:44
O-Mu	22N58	99E18	-6:37:12
Pa-An	16N53	97E38	-6:30:32
Pagan	21N10	94E51	-6:19:24
Pakokku	21N20	95E05	-6:20:20
Pala	12N51	98E40	-6:34:40
Palauk	13N16	98E38	-6:34:32
Palaw	12N58	98E39	-6:34:36
Paletwa	21N18	92E51	-6:11:24
Panghkam	23N53	97E37	-6:30:28
Pangtara	20N57	96E40	-6:26:40
Pantanaw	16N59	95E28	-6:21:52
Pantha	23N49	94E33	-6:18:12
Papun	18N04	97E27	-6:29:48
Pasawng	18N52	97E18	-6:29:12
Pauk	21N27	94E27	-6:17:48
Paung	16N37	97E28	-6:29:52
Paungbyin	24N16	94E49	-6:19:16
Paungde	18N29	95E30	-6:22:00
Paunggyi	17N19	96E11	-6:24:44
Pawota	17N46	97E17	-6:29:08
Payagyi	17N29	96E32	-6:26:08
Pe	13N28	98E31	-6:34:04
Pegu	17N20	96E29	-6:25:56
Pènwègon	18N13	96E34	-6:26:16
Pindale	21N11	95E51	-6:23:24
Pinlaung	20N08	96E47	-6:27:08
Pinlebu	24N05	95E21	-6:21:24
Prome (Pyè)	18N49	95E13	-6:20:52
Putao	27N21	97E24	-6:29:36
Pwinbyu	20N22	94E40	-6:18:40
Pyalo	19N09	95E11	-6:20:44
Pyapon	16N17	95E41	-6:22:44
Pyawbwe	20N35	96E04	-6:24:16
Pyaye	19N15	95E06	-6:20:24
Pyinbongyi	17N34	96E34	-6:26:16
Pyingaing	23N09	94E51	-6:19:24
Pyinkayaing	15N58	94E24	-6:17:36
Pyinmana	19N44	96E13	-6:24:52
Pyu	18N29	96E26	-6:25:44
Pyuntaza	17N52	96E44	-6:26:56
Rangoon	16N47	96E10	-6:24:40
Rangun → Rangoon	16N47	96E10	-6:24:40
Sabyin	19N06	94E11	-6:16:44
Sagaing	21N52	95E59	-6:23:56
Salin	20N35	94E39	-6:18:36
Salingyi	21N58	95E03	-6:20:12
Samka	20N09	96E57	-6:27:48
Sandoway	18N28	94E22	-6:17:28
Satthwa	17N46	94E30	-6:18:00
Sawan	24N30	96E19	-6:25:16
Seikpyu	20N55	94E47	-6:19:08
Shandatgyi	19N37	94E43	-6:18:52
Shingbwiyang	26N41	96E13	-6:24:52
Shurkhua	22N15	93E38	-6:14:32
Shwebo	22N34	95E42	-6:22:48
Shwegun	17N09	97E39	-6:30:36
Shwegyin	17N55	96E53	-6:27:32
Shwenyaung	20N46	96E57	-6:27:48
Sinbaungwe	19N43	95E10	-6:20:40
Sinbo	24N46	97E03	-6:28:12
Sindingale	18N17	94E25	-6:17:40
Singkaling Hkāmti	26N00	95E42	-6:22:48
Sinkan	24N08	97E01	-6:28:04
Sittwe (Akyab)	20N09	92E54	-6:11:36
Sumprabum	26N33	97E34	-6:30:16
Syriam	16N46	96E15	-6:25:00
Tabayin	22N42	95E19	-6:21:16
Taikkyi	17N19	95E58	-6:23:52
Ta-Kaw	21N36	98E56	-6:35:44
Tamanthi	25N19	95E18	-6:21:12
Tamu	24N13	94E18	-6:17:12

MYANMAR BIRMA BIRMANIE BIRMANIA BURMA

Place	Lat	Long	Offset
Tangyan	22N29	98E24	-6:33:36
Tapun	18N22	95E27	-6:21:48
Taungbon	15N25	97E50	-6:31:20
Taungdwingyi	20N01	95E33	-6:22:12
Taunggon	23N38	96E32	-6:26:08
Taunggyi	20N47	97E02	-6:28:08
Taungup	18N51	94E14	-6:16:56
Tavoy	14N05	98E12	-6:32:48
Tenasserim	12N05	99E01	-6:36:04
Thabaung	17N02	94E48	-6:19:12
Thabawleikkyi	12N01	99E12	-6:36:48
Thabyu	15N36	98E29	-6:33:56
Thagyettaw	13N45	98E09	-6:32:36
Thanbyuzayat	15N58	97E44	-6:30:56
Thandaung	19N04	96E41	-6:26:44
Tharabwin West	12N17	99E03	-6:36:12
Tharrawaddy	17N39	95E48	-6:23:12
Tharrawaw	17N41	95E28	-6:21:52
Thaton	16N55	97E22	-6:29:28
Thaungdut	24N26	94E42	-6:18:48
Thayetchaung	13N52	98E16	-6:33:04
Thayetmyo	19N19	95E11	-6:20:44
Thazi	20N51	96E05	-6:24:20
Thègon	18N39	95E25	-6:21:40
Theinkun	11N53	99E09	-6:36:36
Thongwa	16N46	96E32	-6:26:08
Thonze	17N38	95E47	-6:23:08
Tiddim	23N23	93E39	-6:14:36
Tigyaing	23N46	96E08	-6:24:32
Tilin	21N42	94E04	-6:16:16
Tingkawk Sakan	26N04	96E44	-6:26:56
Tonbo	18N31	95E05	-6:20:20
Tongta	21N20	99E16	-6:37:04
Tonkwa	23N36	96E58	-6:27:52
Toungoo	18N56	96E26	-6:25:44
Twante	16N43	95E56	-6:23:44
U-Yin	22N53	95E13	-6:20:52
Ving Ngün	22N37	99E16	-6:37:04
Wādat Ga	26N00	97E00	-6:28:00
Wakema	16N36	95E11	-6:20:44
Wān Namton	22N03	99E33	-6:38:12
Wettigan	18N57	95E21	-6:21:24
Winkana	15N44	98E01	-6:32:04
Wundwin	21N05	96E02	-6:24:08
Wuntho	23N54	95E41	-6:22:44
Yamethin	20N26	96E09	-6:24:36
Yandoon	17N02	95E39	-6:22:36
Yanangyaung	20N28	94E53	-6:19:32
Yangon → Rangoon	16N47	96E10	-6:24:40
Ye	15N15	97E51	-6:31:24
Yebawgyi	18N40	94E35	-6:18:20
Yebyu	14N15	98E12	-6:32:48
Yedashe	19N09	96E21	-6:25:24
Yenangyaung	20N28	94E52	-6:19:28
Yenanma	19N46	94E48	-6:19:12
Ye-Ngan	21N09	96E27	-6:25:48
Ye-U	22N46	95E26	-6:21:44
Yeywa	21N41	96E24	-6:25:36
Yinbaing	17N25	97E46	-6:31:04
Yinmabin	22N05	94E54	-6:19:36
Yinnyein	16N48	97E23	-6:29:32
Ywamun	20N31	95E25	-6:21:40
Ywathagyi	22N18	95E42	-6:22:48
Ywathit	19N10	97E30	-6:30:00
Zalun	17N29	95E34	-6:22:16
Zeyawadi	18N33	96E26	-6:25:44

BURUNDI URUNDI BURUNDI

Time Table
Before 1/Jan/1890 LMT
Begin Standard 30E00
1/Jan/1890 0:00 -2:00

Place	Lat	Long	Offset
Bubanza	3S06	29E23	-1:57:32
Bujumbura	3S23	29E22	-1:57:28
Bururi	3S57	29E37	-1:58:28
Gitega	3S26	29E56	-1:59:44
Kibumbu	3S32	29E45	-1:59:00
Kibuye	3S40	29E59	-1:59:56
Kitega → Gitega	3S26	29E56	-1:59:44
Makamba	4S08	29E49	-1:59:16
Matana	3S46	29E41	-1:58:44
Muramvya	3S16	29E37	-1:58:28
Muyaga	3S14	30E33	-2:02:12
Muyinga	2S51	30E20	-2:01:20
Ngozi	2S54	29E50	-1:59:20
Nyanza-Lac	4S21	29E36	-1:58:24
Rutana	3S55	30E00	-2:00:00
Ruyigi	3S29	30E15	-2:01:00
Usumbura → Bujumbura	3S23	29E22	-1:57:28

CAMEROON

CAMERÚN

KAMERUN

CAMEROUN

Time Table
Before 1/Jan/1912 LMT
Begin Standard 15E00
1/Jan/1912 0:00 -1:00

Place	Latitude	Longitude	Offset
Abong Mbang	3N59	13E10	-0:52:40
Afade	12N14	14E38	-0:58:32
Akok	2N46	10E18	-0:41:12
Akom	2N37	10E04	-0:40:16
Akonolinga	3N47	12E15	-0:49:00
Akouaya	6N30	9E40	-0:38:40
Akwaya	6N30	9E40	-0:38:40
Ambam	2N23	11E17	-0:45:08
Ayos	3N54	12E31	-0:50:04
Babungo	6N04	10E26	-0:41:44
Bafang	5N09	10E11	-0:40:44
Bafia	4N44	11E16	-0:45:04
Bafoussam	5N29	10E24	-0:41:36
Bagodo	6N25	13E23	-0:53:32
Bali	5N53	10E01	-0:40:04
Balikumbat	5N54	10E23	-0:41:32
Bamenda	5N56	10E10	-0:40:40
Bamendjou	5N24	10E19	-0:41:16
Bangangté	5N09	10E31	-0:42:04
Bangé	3N01	15E07	-1:00:28
Bangué	3N01	15E07	-1:00:28
Bankim	6N05	11E30	-0:46:00
Banyo	6N45	11E49	-0:47:16
Batouri	4N26	14E22	-0:57:28
Béka	9N04	12E53	-0:51:32
Bélabo	5N00	13E20	-0:53:20
Bélel	7N03	14E26	-0:57:44
Bengbis	3N27	12E27	-0:49:48
Bérem	7N33	13E55	-0:55:40
Bertoua	4N35	13E41	-0:54:44
Bétaré Oya	5N36	14E05	-0:56:20
Bibémi	9N19	13E53	-0:55:32
Bipindi	3N05	10E25	-0:41:40
Bogo	10N44	14E36	-0:58:24
Boki	8N48	13E32	-0:54:08
Botmakak	4N00	10E55	-0:43:40
Boula-Ibi	9N34	13E46	-0:55:04
Boula Ibib	9N34	13E46	-0:55:04
Boumnyebe	3N52	10E49	-0:43:16
Buea	4N09	9E14	-0:36:56
Campo	2N22	9E49	-0:39:16
Dabilda	12N46	14E34	-0:58:16
Dana	10N14	15E18	-1:01:12
Dang-Haoussa	5N52	13E29	-0:53:56
Demsa	9N32	13E14	-0:52:56
Deng Deng	5N12	13E31	-0:54:04
Djaouro Mbali	5N52	13E29	-0:53:56
Djaposten	3N25	13E32	-0:54:08
Djohong	6N50	14E42	-0:58:48
Djoum	2N40	12E40	-0:50:40
Dodéo	7N29	12E04	-0:48:16
Doreissou	10N33	15E08	-1:00:32
Douala	4N03	9E42	-0:38:48
Doumba	5N05	14E18	-0:57:12
Doumba Bélo	5N05	14E18	-0:57:12
Doumé	4N14	13E27	-0:53:48
Doumé	5N32	12E19	-0:49:16
Dschang	5N27	10E04	-0:40:16
Duala → Douala	4N03	9E42	-0:38:48
Dzeng	3N45	12E00	-0:48:00
Ebolowa	2N54	11E09	-0:44:36
Edéa	3N48	10E08	-0:40:32
Elogbatindi	3N27	10E08	-0:40:32
Elokbatindi	3N27	10E08	-0:40:32
Eséka	3N39	10E46	-0:43:04
Essé	4N05	11E53	-0:47:32
Fort-Foureau	12N05	15E02	-1:00:08
Foumban	5N43	10E55	-0:43:40
Foumbot	5N30	10E38	-0:42:32
Galim	7N06	12E29	-0:49:56
Garga Sarali	5N11	14E00	-0:56:00
Garoua	9N18	13E24	-0:53:36
Garoua Boulaï	5N53	14E33	-0:58:12
Gouna	8N32	13E34	-0:54:16
Guider	9N56	13E57	-0:55:48
Jaunde → Yaoundé	3N52	11E31	-0:46:04
Kaélé	10N07	14E27	-0:57:48
Kenzou	4N10	15E02	-1:00:08
Kimi	6N05	11E30	-0:46:00
Kombone	4N37	9E19	-0:37:16
Kontcha	7N58	12E14	-0:48:56
Koumban	7N43	15E12	-1:00:48
Kribi	2N57	9E55	-0:39:40
Kumba	4N38	9E25	-0:37:40
Kumbo	6N12	10E40	-0:42:40
Laro	8N17	12E18	-0:49:12
Lesdiboderi	8N28	12E35	-0:50:20
Linté	5N24	11E42	-0:46:48
Logone Birni	11N47	15E06	-1:00:24
Lokomo	2N41	15E19	-1:01:16
Lolodorf	3N14	10E44	-0:42:56
Lomié	3N10	13E37	-0:54:28
Loum	4N43	9E44	-0:38:56
Makak	3N33	11E02	-0:44:08
Makari	12N35	14E28	-0:57:52
Mali	8N28	12E35	-0:50:20
Mamfe	5N46	9E17	-0:37:08
Mankim	5N01	12E00	-0:48:00
Maroua	10N36	14E20	-0:57:20
Martap	6N54	13E03	-0:52:12
Matsari	5N21	12E14	-0:48:56
Mbalam	2N13	13E49	-0:55:16
Mbalmayo	3N31	11E30	-0:46:00
Mbanga	3N52	10E49	-0:43:16
Mbanga	4N30	9E34	-0:38:16
Mbé	7N43	13E30	-0:54:00
Mbonge	4N33	9E05	-0:36:20
Mbor	6N24	11E19	-0:45:16
Mbouda	5N38	10E15	-0:41:00
Meiganga	6N31	14E11	-0:56:44
Melong	5N07	9E57	-0:39:48
Mengong	2N56	11E25	-0:45:40
Mesaména	3N44	12E50	-0:51:20
Mésondo	3N43	10E28	-0:41:52
Messondo	3N43	10E28	-0:41:52
Meuban	2N27	12E41	-0:50:44
Meyo-Centre	2N33	11E02	-0:44:08
Mfou	3N43	11E38	-0:46:32
Mindif	10N24	14E26	-0:57:44
Mindourou	4N06	14E34	-0:58:16
Mindourou	3N25	13E32	-0:54:08
Minta	4N35	12E48	-0:51:12
Mintom	2N42	13E17	-0:53:08
Mintom II	2N42	13E17	-0:53:08
Mislippi	10N00	15E37	-1:02:28
Mokolo	10N45	13E48	-0:55:12
Moloundou	2N03	15E10	-1:00:40
Monatélé	4N16	11E12	-0:44:48
Mora	11N03	14E09	-0:56:36
Mouangko	3N39	9E49	-0:39:16
Mouanko	3N39	9E49	-0:39:16
Muyuka	4N17	9E25	-0:37:40
Mvangan	2N38	11E44	-0:46:56
Mvangane	2N38	11E44	-0:46:56
Mvengué	3N17	11E01	-0:44:04
Nanga-Eboko	4N41	12E22	-0:49:28
Ndélélé	4N02	14E56	-0:59:44
Ndikiniméki	4N46	10E50	-0:43:20
Ngambé	4N14	10E37	-0:42:28
Ngaoundéré	7N19	13E35	-0:54:20
Ngila	4N43	11E41	-0:46:44
Ngoap	4N09	12E51	-0:51:24
Ngomedzap	3N15	11E12	-0:44:48
Ngoulémakong	3N07	11E25	-0:45:40
Nguélémendouka	4N23	12E55	-0:51:40
Nguila	4N43	11E41	-0:46:44
Nkambe	6N38	10E40	-0:42:40
Nkongsamba	4N57	9E56	-0:39:44
Ntui	4N27	11E38	-0:46:32
Nwa	6N30	11E00	-0:44:00
Nyabéssan	2N24	10E24	-0:41:36
Obala	4N10	11E32	-0:46:08
Obout	3N28	11E44	-0:46:56
Okola	4N01	11E23	-0:45:32
Otélé	3N35	11E15	-0:45:00
Ouak	7N43	13E30	-0:54:00
Oveng	2N25	12E16	-0:49:04
Pété	10N58	14E30	-0:58:00
Poli	8N29	13E15	-0:53:00
Pouss	10N51	15E03	-1:00:12
Rey Bouba	8N40	14E11	-0:56:44
Saa	4N22	11E27	-0:45:48
Sambolabbo	7N05	11E59	-0:47:56
Sangbé	6N03	12E28	-0:49:52
Sangmélima	2N56	11E59	-0:47:56
Somalomo	3N23	12E44	-0:50:56
Tcholliré	8N24	14E10	-0:56:40
Tibati	6N27	12E38	-0:50:32
Tignère	7N22	12E39	-0:50:36
Tiko	4N05	9E22	-0:37:28
Tonga	4N58	10E42	-0:42:48
Tongo	5N11	14E00	-0:56:00
Torok	10N03	14E33	-0:58:12
Touboro	7N43	15E12	-1:00:48
Victoria	4N01	9E12	-0:36:48
Waza	11N25	14E34	-0:58:16
Waza Garou	11N25	14E34	-0:58:16
Woutchaba	5N13	13E05	-0:52:20
Wum	6N23	10E04	-0:40:16
Yabassi	4N28	9E58	-0:39:52
Yagoua	10N20	15E14	-1:00:56
Yaoundé	3N52	11E31	-0:46:04
Yaundé → Yaoundé	3N52	11E31	-0:46:04
Yen	2N27	12E41	-0:50:44
Yokadouma	3N31	15E03	-1:00:12
Yoko	5N32	12E19	-0:49:16
Zina	11N16	14E58	-0:59:52
Zoadiba	3N04	14E02	-0:56:08
Zoétélé	3N15	11E53	-0:47:32
Zoulabot	3N17	14E02	-0:56:08
Zwadība	3N04	14E02	-0:56:08

Time Table # 1

Before 1/Jan/1895 LMT

Begin Standard 75w00

1/Jan/1895	0:00	5:00
14/Apr/1918	2:00	4:00
31/Oct/1918	2:00	5:00
29/Sep/1940	0:00	4:00
30/Sep/1945	2:00	5:00
28/Apr/1974	2:00	4:00
27/Oct/1974	2:00	5:00
27/Apr/1975	2:00	4:00
26/Oct/1975	2:00	5:00
25/Apr/1976	2:00	4:00
31/Oct/1976	2:00	5:00
24/Apr/1977	2:00	4:00
30/Oct/1977	2:00	5:00
30/Apr/1978	2:00	4:00
29/Oct/1978	2:00	5:00
29/Apr/1979	2:00	4:00
28/Oct/1979	2:00	5:00
27/Apr/1980	2:00	4:00
26/Oct/1980	2:00	5:00
26/Apr/1981	2:00	4:00
25/Oct/1981	2:00	5:00
25/Apr/1982	2:00	4:00
31/Oct/1982	2:00	5:00
24/Apr/1983	2:00	4:00
30/Oct/1983	2:00	5:00
29/Apr/1984	2:00	4:00
28/Oct/1984	2:00	5:00
28/Apr/1985	2:00	4:00
27/Oct/1985	2:00	5:00
27/Apr/1986	2:00	4:00
26/Oct/1986	2:00	5:00
5/Apr/1987	2:00	4:00
25/Oct/1987	2:00	5:00
3/Apr/1988	2:00	4:00
30/Oct/1988	2:00	5:00
2/Apr/1989	2:00	4:00
29/Oct/1989	2:00	5:00
1/Apr/1990	2:00	4:00
28/Oct/1990	2:00	5:00
7/Apr/1991	2:00	4:00
27/Oct/1991	2:00	5:00
5/Apr/1992	2:00	4:00
25/Oct/1992	2:00	5:00
4/Apr/1993	2:00	4:00
31/Oct/1993	2:00	5:00
3/Apr/1994	2:00	4:00
30/Oct/1994	2:00	5:00
2/Apr/1995	2:00	4:00
29/Oct/1995	2:00	5:00
7/Apr/1996	2:00	4:00
27/Oct/1996	2:00	5:00
6/Apr/1997	2:00	4:00
26/Oct/1997	2:00	5:00
5/Apr/1998	2:00	4:00
25/Oct/1998	2:00	5:00
4/Apr/1999	2:00	4:00
31/Oct/1999	2:00	5:00
2/Apr/2000	2:00	4:00
29/Oct/2000	2:00	5:00

Time Table # 2

Before 1/Jan/1895 LMT

Begin Standard 75w00

1/Jan/1895	0:00	5:00
14/Apr/1918	2:00	4:00
31/Oct/1918	2:00	5:00
26/Apr/1931	2:00	4:00
27/Sep/1931	2:00	5:00
1/May/1932	2:00	4:00
25/Sep/1932	2:00	5:00
30/Apr/1933	2:00	4:00
1/Oct/1933	2:00	5:00
29/Apr/1934	2:00	4:00
30/Sep/1934	2:00	5:00
28/Apr/1935	2:00	4:00
29/Sep/1935	2:00	5:00
26/Apr/1936	2:00	4:00
27/Sep/1936	2:00	5:00
25/Apr/1937	2:00	4:00
26/Sep/1937	2:00	5:00
24/Apr/1938	2:00	4:00
25/Sep/1938	2:00	5:00
30/Apr/1939	2:00	4:00
24/Sep/1939	2:00	5:00
28/Apr/1940	2:00	4:00
30/Sep/1945	2:00	5:00
28/Apr/1946	2:00	4:00
29/Sep/1946	2:00	5:00
27/Apr/1947	0:00	4:00
28/Sep/1947	0:00	5:00
25/Apr/1948	0:00	4:00
26/Sep/1948	0:00	5:00
24/Apr/1949	2:00	4:00
25/Sep/1949	2:00	5:00
30/Apr/1950	2:00	4:00
24/Sep/1950	2:00	5:00
29/Apr/1951	2:00	4:00
30/Sep/1951	2:00	5:00
27/Apr/1952	2:00	4:00
28/Sep/1952	2:00	5:00
26/Apr/1953	2:00	4:00
27/Sep/1953	2:00	5:00
25/Apr/1954	2:00	4:00
26/Sep/1954	2:00	5:00
24/Apr/1955	2:00	4:00
25/Sep/1955	2:00	5:00
29/Apr/1956	2:00	4:00
30/Sep/1956	2:00	5:00
28/Apr/1957	2:00	4:00
27/Oct/1957	2:00	5:00
27/Apr/1958	2:00	4:00
26/Oct/1958	2:00	5:00
26/Apr/1959	2:00	4:00
25/Oct/1959	2:00	5:00
24/Apr/1960	2:00	4:00
30/Oct/1960	2:00	5:00
30/Apr/1961	2:00	4:00
29/Oct/1961	2:00	5:00
29/Apr/1962	2:00	4:00
28/Oct/1962	2:00	5:00
28/Apr/1963	2:00	4:00
27/Oct/1963	2:00	5:00
26/Apr/1964	2:00	4:00
25/Oct/1964	2:00	5:00
25/Apr/1965	2:00	4:00
31/Oct/1965	2:00	5:00
24/Apr/1966	2:00	4:00
30/Oct/1966	2:00	5:00
30/Apr/1967	2:00	4:00
29/Oct/1967	2:00	5:00
28/Apr/1968	2:00	4:00
27/Oct/1968	2:00	5:00
27/Apr/1969	2:00	4:00
26/Oct/1969	2:00	5:00
26/Apr/1970	2:00	4:00
25/Oct/1970	2:00	5:00
25/Apr/1971	2:00	4:00
24/Oct/1971	2:00	5:00
30/Apr/1972	2:00	4:00
29/Oct/1972	2:00	5:00
29/Apr/1973	2:00	4:00
28/Oct/1973	2:00	5:00
28/Apr/1974	2:00	4:00
27/Oct/1974	2:00	5:00
27/Apr/1975	2:00	4:00
26/Oct/1975	2:00	5:00
25/Apr/1976	2:00	4:00
31/Oct/1976	2:00	5:00
24/Apr/1977	2:00	4:00
30/Oct/1977	2:00	5:00
30/Apr/1978	2:00	4:00
29/Oct/1978	2:00	5:00
29/Apr/1979	2:00	4:00
28/Oct/1979	2:00	5:00
27/Apr/1980	2:00	4:00
26/Oct/1980	2:00	5:00
26/Apr/1981	2:00	4:00
25/Oct/1981	2:00	5:00
25/Apr/1982	2:00	4:00
31/Oct/1982	2:00	5:00
24/Apr/1983	2:00	4:00
30/Oct/1983	2:00	5:00
29/Apr/1984	2:00	4:00
28/Oct/1984	2:00	5:00
28/Apr/1985	2:00	4:00
27/Oct/1985	2:00	5:00
27/Apr/1986	2:00	4:00
26/Oct/1986	2:00	5:00
5/Apr/1987	2:00	4:00
25/Oct/1987	2:00	5:00
3/Apr/1988	2:00	4:00
30/Oct/1988	2:00	5:00
2/Apr/1989	2:00	4:00
29/Oct/1989	2:00	5:00
1/Apr/1990	2:00	4:00
28/Oct/1990	2:00	5:00
7/Apr/1991	2:00	4:00
27/Oct/1991	2:00	5:00
5/Apr/1992	2:00	4:00
25/Oct/1992	2:00	5:00
4/Apr/1993	2:00	4:00
31/Oct/1993	2:00	5:00
3/Apr/1994	2:00	4:00
30/Oct/1994	2:00	5:00
2/Apr/1995	2:00	4:00
29/Oct/1995	2:00	5:00
7/Apr/1996	2:00	4:00
27/Oct/1996	2:00	5:00
6/Apr/1997	2:00	4:00
26/Oct/1997	2:00	5:00
5/Apr/1998	2:00	4:00
25/Oct/1998	2:00	5:00
4/Apr/1999	2:00	4:00
31/Oct/1999	2:00	5:00
2/Apr/2000	2:00	4:00
29/Oct/2000	2:00	5:00

Time Table # 3

Before 1/Jan/1895 LMT

Begin Standard 90w00

1/Jan/1895	0:00	6:00
14/Apr/1918	2:00	5:00
31/Oct/1918	2:00	6:00
29/Sep/1940	0:00	5:00
30/Sep/1945	2:00	6:00
28/Apr/1974	2:00	5:00
27/Oct/1974	2:00	6:00
27/Apr/1975	2:00	5:00
26/Oct/1975	2:00	6:00
25/Apr/1976	2:00	5:00
31/Oct/1976	2:00	6:00
24/Apr/1977	2:00	5:00
30/Oct/1977	2:00	6:00
30/Apr/1978	2:00	5:00
29/Oct/1978	2:00	6:00
29/Apr/1979	2:00	5:00
28/Oct/1979	2:00	6:00
27/Apr/1980	2:00	5:00
26/Oct/1980	2:00	6:00
26/Apr/1981	2:00	5:00
25/Oct/1981	2:00	6:00
25/Apr/1982	2:00	5:00
31/Oct/1982	2:00	6:00
24/Apr/1983	2:00	5:00
30/Oct/1983	2:00	6:00
29/Apr/1984	2:00	5:00
28/Oct/1984	2:00	6:00
28/Apr/1985	2:00	5:00
27/Oct/1985	2:00	6:00
27/Apr/1986	2:00	5:00
26/Oct/1986	2:00	6:00
5/Apr/1987	2:00	5:00
25/Oct/1987	2:00	6:00
3/Apr/1988	2:00	5:00
30/Oct/1988	2:00	6:00
2/Apr/1989	2:00	5:00
29/Oct/1989	2:00	6:00
1/Apr/1990	2:00	5:00
28/Oct/1990	2:00	6:00
7/Apr/1991	2:00	5:00
27/Oct/1991	2:00	6:00
5/Apr/1992	2:00	5:00
25/Oct/1992	2:00	6:00
4/Apr/1993	2:00	5:00
31/Oct/1993	2:00	6:00
3/Apr/1994	2:00	5:00
30/Oct/1994	2:00	6:00
2/Apr/1995	2:00	5:00
29/Oct/1995	2:00	6:00
7/Apr/1996	2:00	5:00
27/Oct/1996	2:00	6:00
6/Apr/1997	2:00	5:00
26/Oct/1997	2:00	6:00
5/Apr/1998	2:00	5:00
25/Oct/1998	2:00	6:00
4/Apr/1999	2:00	5:00
31/Oct/1999	2:00	6:00
2/Apr/2000	2:00	5:00
29/Oct/2000	2:00	6:00

Time Table # 4

Before 9/Dec/1883 LMT

Begin Standard 75w00

9/Dec/1883	0:00	5:00
Begin Standard		60w00
15/Jun/1902	0:00	4:00
14/Apr/1918	2:00	3:00
31/Oct/1918	2:00	4:00
11/Jun/1933	1:00	3:00
10/Sep/1933	1:00	4:00
10/Jun/1934	1:00	3:00
9/Sep/1934	1:00	4:00
9/Jun/1935	1:00	3:00
8/Sep/1935	1:00	4:00
7/Jun/1936	1:00	3:00
6/Sep/1936	1:00	4:00
6/Jun/1937	1:00	3:00
4/Sep/1937	1:00	4:00
5/Jun/1938	1:00	3:00
4/Sep/1938	1:00	4:00
27/May/1939	1:00	3:00
23/Sep/1939	1:00	4:00
19/May/1940	1:00	3:00
21/Sep/1940	1:00	4:00
4/May/1941	1:00	3:00
27/Sep/1941	1:00	4:00
9/Feb/1942	2:00	3:00
30/Sep/1945	2:00	4:00
28/Apr/1946	2:00	3:00
29/Sep/1946	2:00	4:00
27/Apr/1947	2:00	3:00
28/Sep/1947	2:00	4:00
25/Apr/1948	2:00	3:00
26/Sep/1948	2:00	4:00
24/Apr/1949	2:00	3:00
25/Sep/1949	2:00	4:00
30/Apr/1950	2:00	3:00
25/Sep/1950	2:00	4:00
29/Apr/1951	2:00	3:00
30/Sep/1951	2:00	4:00
27/Apr/1952	2:00	3:00
29/Sep/1952	2:00	4:00
26/Apr/1953	2:00	3:00
28/Sep/1953	2:00	4:00
25/Apr/1954	2:00	3:00
26/Sep/1954	2:00	4:00
24/Apr/1955	2:00	3:00
25/Sep/1955	2:00	4:00
29/Apr/1956	2:00	3:00
30/Sep/1956	2:00	4:00
28/Apr/1957	2:00	3:00
27/Oct/1957	2:00	4:00
27/Apr/1958	2:00	3:00
26/Oct/1958	2:00	4:00
26/Apr/1959	2:00	3:00
25/Oct/1959	2:00	4:00
24/Apr/1960	2:00	3:00
30/Oct/1960	2:00	4:00
30/Apr/1961	2:00	3:00
29/Oct/1961	2:00	4:00
29/Apr/1962	2:00	3:00
28/Oct/1962	2:00	4:00
28/Apr/1963	2:00	3:00
27/Oct/1963	2:00	4:00
26/Apr/1964	2:00	3:00
25/Oct/1964	2:00	4:00
25/Apr/1965	2:00	3:00
31/Oct/1965	2:00	4:00
24/Apr/1966	2:00	3:00
30/Oct/1966	2:00	4:00
30/Apr/1967	2:00	3:00
29/Oct/1967	2:00	4:00
28/Apr/1968	2:00	3:00
27/Oct/1968	2:00	4:00
27/Apr/1969	2:00	3:00
26/Oct/1969	2:00	4:00
26/Apr/1970	2:00	3:00
25/Oct/1970	2:00	4:00
25/Apr/1971	2:00	3:00
31/Oct/1971	2:00	4:00
30/Apr/1972	2:00	3:00
29/Oct/1972	2:00	4:00
29/Apr/1973	2:00	3:00
28/Oct/1973	2:00	4:00
28/Apr/1974	2:00	3:00
27/Oct/1974	2:00	4:00
27/Apr/1975	2:00	3:00
26/Oct/1975	2:00	4:00
25/Apr/1976	2:00	3:00
31/Oct/1976	2:00	4:00
24/Apr/1977	2:00	3:00
30/Oct/1977	2:00	4:00
30/Apr/1978	2:00	3:00
29/Oct/1978	2:00	4:00
29/Apr/1979	2:00	3:00
28/Oct/1979	2:00	4:00
27/Apr/1980	2:00	3:00
26/Oct/1980	2:00	4:00
26/Apr/1981	2:00	3:00
25/Oct/1981	2:00	4:00
25/Apr/1982	2:00	3:00
31/Oct/1982	2:00	4:00
24/Apr/1983	2:00	3:00
30/Oct/1983	2:00	4:00
29/Apr/1984	2:00	3:00
28/Oct/1984	2:00	4:00
28/Apr/1985	2:00	3:00
27/Oct/1985	2:00	4:00
27/Apr/1986	2:00	3:00
26/Oct/1986	2:00	4:00
5/Apr/1987	2:00	3:00
25/Oct/1987	2:00	4:00
3/Apr/1988	2:00	3:00
30/Oct/1988	2:00	4:00
2/Apr/1989	2:00	3:00
29/Oct/1989	2:00	4:00
1/Apr/1990	2:00	3:00
28/Oct/1990	2:00	4:00
7/Apr/1991	2:00	3:00
27/Oct/1991	2:00	4:00
5/Apr/1992	2:00	3:00
25/Oct/1992	2:00	4:00
4/Apr/1993	2:00	3:00
31/Oct/1993	2:00	4:00
3/Apr/1994	2:00	3:00
30/Oct/1994	2:00	4:00
2/Apr/1995	2:00	3:00
29/Oct/1995	2:00	4:00
7/Apr/1996	2:00	3:00
27/Oct/1996	2:00	4:00
6/Apr/1997	2:00	3:00
26/Oct/1997	2:00	4:00
5/Apr/1998	2:00	3:00
25/Oct/1998	2:00	4:00
4/Apr/1999	2:00	3:00
31/Oct/1999	2:00	4:00
2/Apr/2000	2:00	3:00
29/Oct/2000	2:00	4:00

Time Table # 5

Before 15/Jun/1902 LMT

Begin Standard 60w00

15/Jun/1902	0:00	4:00
14/Apr/1918	2:00	3:00
31/Oct/1918	2:00	4:00
16/May/1933	0:00	3:00
16/Sep/1933	0:00	4:00
1/Jul/1940	0:00	3:00
2/Sep/1940	0:00	4:00
27/Apr/1941	0:00	3:00
28/Sep/1941	0:00	4:00
9/Feb/1942	2:00	3:00
30/Sep/1945	2:00	4:00
28/Apr/1946	2:00	3:00
29/Sep/1946	2:00	4:00
27/Apr/1947	2:00	3:00
28/Sep/1947	2:00	4:00
25/Apr/1948	2:00	3:00
26/Sep/1948	2:00	4:00
24/Apr/1949	2:00	3:00
25/Sep/1949	2:00	4:00
30/Apr/1950	2:00	3:00
24/Sep/1950	2:00	4:00
29/Apr/1951	2:00	3:00
30/Sep/1951	2:00	4:00
27/Apr/1952	2:00	3:00
28/Sep/1952	2:00	4:00
26/Apr/1953	2:00	3:00
27/Sep/1953	2:00	4:00
25/Apr/1954	2:00	3:00
26/Sep/1954	2:00	4:00
24/Apr/1955	2:00	3:00
25/Sep/1955	2:00	4:00
29/Apr/1956	2:00	3:00
30/Sep/1956	2:00	4:00
28/Apr/1957	2:00	3:00
27/Oct/1957	2:00	4:00
27/Apr/1958	2:00	3:00
26/Oct/1958	2:00	4:00
26/Apr/1959	2:00	3:00
25/Oct/1959	2:00	4:00
24/Apr/1960	2:00	3:00
30/Oct/1960	2:00	4:00
30/Apr/1961	2:00	3:00
29/Oct/1961	2:00	4:00
29/Apr/1962	2:00	3:00
28/Oct/1962	2:00	4:00
28/Apr/1963	2:00	3:00
27/Oct/1963	2:00	4:00
26/Apr/1964	2:00	3:00
25/Oct/1964	2:00	4:00
25/Apr/1965	2:00	3:00
31/Oct/1965	2:00	4:00
24/Apr/1966	2:00	3:00
30/Oct/1966	2:00	4:00
30/Apr/1967	2:00	3:00
29/Oct/1967	2:00	4:00
28/Apr/1968	2:00	3:00
27/Oct/1968	2:00	4:00
27/Apr/1969	2:00	3:00
26/Oct/1969	2:00	4:00
26/Apr/1970	2:00	3:00
25/Oct/1970	2:00	4:00
25/Apr/1971	2:00	3:00
31/Oct/1971	2:00	4:00
30/Apr/1972	2:00	3:00
29/Oct/1972	2:00	4:00
29/Apr/1973	2:00	3:00
28/Oct/1973	2:00	4:00
28/Apr/1974	2:00	3:00
27/Oct/1974	2:00	4:00
27/Apr/1975	2:00	3:00
26/Oct/1975	2:00	4:00
25/Apr/1976	2:00	3:00
31/Oct/1976	2:00	4:00
24/Apr/1977	2:00	3:00
30/Oct/1977	2:00	4:00
30/Apr/1978	2:00	3:00
29/Oct/1978	2:00	4:00
29/Apr/1979	2:00	3:00
28/Oct/1979	2:00	4:00
27/Apr/1980	2:00	3:00
26/Oct/1980	2:00	4:00
26/Apr/1981	2:00	3:00
25/Oct/1981	2:00	4:00
25/Apr/1982	2:00	3:00
31/Oct/1982	2:00	4:00
24/Apr/1983	2:00	3:00
30/Oct/1983	2:00	4:00
29/Apr/1984	2:00	3:00
28/Oct/1984	2:00	4:00
28/Apr/1985	2:00	3:00
27/Oct/1985	2:00	4:00
27/Apr/1986	2:00	3:00
26/Oct/1986	2:00	4:00
5/Apr/1987	2:00	3:00
25/Oct/1987	2:00	4:00
3/Apr/1988	2:00	3:00
30/Oct/1988	2:00	4:00
2/Apr/1989	2:00	3:00
29/Oct/1989	2:00	4:00
1/Apr/1990	2:00	3:00
28/Oct/1990	2:00	4:00
7/Apr/1991	2:00	3:00
27/Oct/1991	2:00	4:00
5/Apr/1992	2:00	3:00
25/Oct/1992	2:00	4:00
4/Apr/1993	2:00	3:00
31/Oct/1993	2:00	4:00
3/Apr/1994	2:00	3:00
30/Oct/1994	2:00	4:00
2/Apr/1995	2:00	3:00
29/Oct/1995	2:00	4:00
7/Apr/1996	2:00	3:00
27/Oct/1996	2:00	4:00
6/Apr/1997	2:00	3:00
26/Oct/1997	2:00	4:00
5/Apr/1998	2:00	3:00
25/Oct/1998	2:00	4:00
4/Apr/1999	2:00	3:00
31/Oct/1999	2:00	4:00
2/Apr/2000	2:00	3:00
29/Oct/2000	2:00	4:00

Time Table # 6

Before 15/Jun/1902 LMT

Begin Standard 60w00

15/Jun/1902	0:00	4:00
14/Apr/1918	2:00	3:00
31/Oct/1918	2:00	4:00
9/Feb/1942	2:00	3:00
30/Sep/1945	2:00	4:00
29/Apr/1962	2:00	3:00
28/Oct/1962	2:00	4:00
28/Apr/1963	2:00	3:00
27/Oct/1963	2:00	4:00
26/Apr/1964	2:00	3:00
25/Oct/1964	2:00	4:00
25/Apr/1965	2:00	3:00
31/Oct/1965	2:00	4:00
24/Apr/1966	2:00	3:00
30/Oct/1966	2:00	4:00
30/Apr/1967	2:00	3:00
29/Oct/1967	2:00	4:00
28/Apr/1968	2:00	3:00
27/Oct/1968	2:00	4:00
27/Apr/1969	2:00	3:00
26/Oct/1969	2:00	4:00
26/Apr/1970	2:00	3:00
25/Oct/1970	2:00	4:00
25/Apr/1971	2:00	3:00
31/Oct/1971	2:00	4:00
30/Apr/1972	2:00	3:00
29/Oct/1972	2:00	4:00
29/Apr/1973	2:00	3:00
28/Oct/1973	2:00	4:00
28/Apr/1974	2:00	3:00
27/Oct/1974	2:00	4:00
27/Apr/1975	2:00	3:00
26/Oct/1975	2:00	4:00
25/Apr/1976	2:00	3:00
31/Oct/1976	2:00	4:00
24/Apr/1977	2:00	3:00
30/Oct/1977	2:00	4:00
30/Apr/1978	2:00	3:00
29/Oct/1978	2:00	4:00
29/Apr/1979	2:00	3:00
28/Oct/1979	2:00	4:00
27/Apr/1980	2:00	3:00
26/Oct/1980	2:00	4:00
26/Apr/1981	2:00	3:00
25/Oct/1981	2:00	4:00

25/Apr/1982	2:00	3:00
31/Oct/1982	2:00	4:00
24/Apr/1983	2:00	3:00
30/Oct/1983	2:00	4:00
29/Apr/1984	2:00	3:00
28/Oct/1984	2:00	4:00
28/Apr/1985	2:00	3:00
27/Oct/1985	2:00	4:00
27/Apr/1986	2:00	3:00
26/Oct/1986	2:00	4:00
5/Apr/1987	2:00	3:00
25/Oct/1987	2:00	4:00
3/Apr/1988	2:00	3:00
30/Oct/1988	2:00	4:00
2/Apr/1989	2:00	3:00
29/Oct/1989	2:00	4:00
1/Apr/1990	2:00	3:00
28/Oct/1990	2:00	4:00
7/Apr/1991	2:00	3:00
27/Oct/1991	2:00	4:00
5/Apr/1992	2:00	3:00
25/Oct/1992	2:00	4:00
4/Apr/1993	2:00	3:00
31/Oct/1993	2:00	4:00
3/Apr/1994	2:00	3:00
30/Oct/1994	2:00	4:00
2/Apr/1995	2:00	3:00
29/Oct/1995	2:00	4:00
7/Apr/1996	2:00	3:00
27/Oct/1996	2:00	4:00
6/Apr/1997	2:00	3:00
26/Oct/1997	2:00	4:00
5/Apr/1998	2:00	3:00
25/Oct/1998	2:00	4:00
4/Apr/1999	2:00	3:00
31/Oct/1999	2:00	4:00
2/Apr/2000	2:00	3:00
29/Oct/2000	2:00	4:00

Time Table # 7

Before 1/Jan/1884 LMT

Begin Standard 75w00

1/Jan/1884	0:00	5:00
14/Apr/1918	2:00	4:00
31/Oct/1918	2:00	5:00
9/Feb/1942	2:00	4:00
30/Sep/1945	2:00	5:00
30/Apr/1967	2:00	4:00
29/Oct/1967	2:00	5:00
28/Apr/1968	2:00	4:00
27/Oct/1968	2:00	5:00
27/Apr/1969	2:00	4:00
26/Oct/1969	2:00	5:00
26/Apr/1970	2:00	4:00
25/Oct/1970	2:00	5:00
25/Apr/1971	2:00	4:00
31/Oct/1971	2:00	5:00
30/Apr/1972	2:00	4:00
29/Oct/1972	2:00	5:00
29/Apr/1973	2:00	4:00
28/Oct/1973	2:00	5:00
28/Apr/1974	2:00	4:00
27/Oct/1974	2:00	5:00
27/Apr/1975	2:00	4:00
26/Oct/1975	2:00	5:00
25/Apr/1976	2:00	4:00
31/Oct/1976	2:00	5:00
24/Apr/1977	2:00	4:00
30/Oct/1977	2:00	5:00
30/Apr/1978	2:00	4:00
29/Oct/1978	2:00	5:00
29/Apr/1979	2:00	4:00
28/Oct/1979	2:00	5:00
27/Apr/1980	2:00	4:00
26/Oct/1980	2:00	5:00
26/Apr/1981	2:00	4:00
25/Oct/1981	2:00	5:00
25/Apr/1982	2:00	4:00
31/Oct/1982	2:00	5:00
24/Apr/1983	2:00	4:00
30/Oct/1983	2:00	5:00
29/Apr/1984	2:00	4:00
28/Oct/1984	2:00	5:00
28/Apr/1985	2:00	4:00
27/Oct/1985	2:00	5:00
27/Apr/1986	2:00	4:00
26/Oct/1986	2:00	5:00
5/Apr/1987	2:00	4:00
25/Oct/1987	2:00	5:00
3/Apr/1988	2:00	4:00
30/Oct/1988	2:00	5:00
2/Apr/1989	2:00	4:00
29/Oct/1989	2:00	5:00
1/Apr/1990	2:00	4:00
28/Oct/1990	2:00	5:00
7/Apr/1991	2:00	4:00
27/Oct/1991	2:00	5:00
5/Apr/1992	2:00	4:00
25/Oct/1992	2:00	5:00
4/Apr/1993	2:00	4:00
31/Oct/1993	2:00	5:00
3/Apr/1994	2:00	4:00
30/Oct/1994	2:00	5:00
2/Apr/1995	2:00	4:00
29/Oct/1995	2:00	5:00
7/Apr/1996	2:00	4:00
27/Oct/1996	2:00	5:00
6/Apr/1997	2:00	4:00
26/Oct/1997	2:00	5:00
5/Apr/1998	2:00	4:00
25/Oct/1998	2:00	5:00
4/Apr/1999	2:00	4:00
31/Oct/1999	2:00	5:00
2/Apr/2000	2:00	4:00
29/Oct/2000	2:00	5:00

Time Table # 8

Before 1/Jan/1884 LMT

Begin Standard 75w00

1/Jan/1884	0:00	5:00
14/Apr/1918	2:00	4:00
31/Oct/1918	2:00	5:00
26/Apr/1931	0:00	4:00
27/Sep/1931	0:00	5:00
30/Apr/1933	0:00	4:00
1/Oct/1933	0:00	5:00
29/Apr/1934	0:00	4:00
30/Sep/1934	0:00	5:00
28/Apr/1935	0:00	4:00
29/Sep/1935	0:00	5:00
24/Apr/1938	0:00	4:00
25/Sep/1938	0:00	5:00
30/Apr/1939	0:00	4:00
24/Sep/1939	0:00	5:00
28/Apr/1940	0:00	4:00
30/Sep/1945	2:00	5:00
28/Apr/1946	2:00	4:00
29/Sep/1946	2:00	5:00
27/Apr/1947	2:00	4:00
28/Sep/1947	2:00	5:00
25/Apr/1948	2:00	4:00
26/Sep/1948	2:00	5:00
24/Apr/1949	2:00	4:00
25/Sep/1949	2:00	5:00
30/Apr/1950	2:00	4:00
24/Sep/1950	2:00	5:00
29/Apr/1951	2:00	4:00
30/Sep/1951	2:00	5:00
27/Apr/1952	2:00	4:00
28/Sep/1952	2:00	5:00
26/Apr/1953	2:00	4:00
27/Sep/1953	2:00	5:00
25/Apr/1954	2:00	4:00
26/Sep/1954	2:00	5:00
24/Apr/1955	2:00	4:00
25/Sep/1955	2:00	5:00
29/Apr/1956	2:00	4:00
30/Sep/1956	2:00	5:00
28/Apr/1957	2:00	4:00
27/Oct/1957	2:00	5:00
27/Apr/1958	2:00	4:00
26/Oct/1958	2:00	5:00
26/Apr/1959	2:00	4:00
25/Oct/1959	2:00	5:00
24/Apr/1960	2:00	4:00
30/Oct/1960	2:00	5:00
30/Apr/1961	2:00	4:00
29/Oct/1961	2:00	5:00
29/Apr/1962	2:00	4:00
28/Oct/1962	2:00	5:00
28/Apr/1963	2:00	4:00
27/Oct/1963	2:00	5:00
26/Apr/1964	2:00	4:00
25/Oct/1964	2:00	5:00
25/Apr/1965	2:00	4:00
31/Oct/1965	2:00	5:00
24/Apr/1966	2:00	4:00
30/Oct/1966	2:00	5:00
30/Apr/1967	2:00	4:00
29/Oct/1967	2:00	5:00
28/Apr/1968	2:00	4:00
27/Oct/1968	2:00	5:00
27/Apr/1969	2:00	4:00
26/Oct/1969	2:00	5:00
26/Apr/1970	2:00	4:00
25/Oct/1970	2:00	5:00
25/Apr/1971	2:00	4:00
31/Oct/1971	2:00	5:00
30/Apr/1972	2:00	4:00
29/Oct/1972	2:00	5:00
29/Apr/1973	2:00	4:00
28/Oct/1973	2:00	5:00
28/Apr/1974	2:00	4:00
27/Oct/1974	2:00	5:00
27/Apr/1975	2:00	4:00
26/Oct/1975	2:00	5:00
25/Apr/1976	2:00	4:00
31/Oct/1976	2:00	5:00
24/Apr/1977	2:00	4:00
30/Oct/1977	2:00	5:00
30/Apr/1978	2:00	4:00
29/Oct/1978	2:00	5:00
29/Apr/1979	2:00	4:00
28/Oct/1979	2:00	5:00
27/Apr/1980	2:00	4:00
26/Oct/1980	2:00	5:00
26/Apr/1981	2:00	4:00
25/Oct/1981	2:00	5:00
25/Apr/1982	2:00	4:00
31/Oct/1982	2:00	5:00
24/Apr/1983	2:00	4:00
30/Oct/1983	2:00	5:00
29/Apr/1984	2:00	4:00
28/Oct/1984	2:00	5:00
28/Apr/1985	2:00	4:00
27/Oct/1985	2:00	5:00
27/Apr/1986	2:00	4:00
26/Oct/1986	2:00	5:00
5/Apr/1987	2:00	4:00
25/Oct/1987	2:00	5:00
3/Apr/1988	2:00	4:00
30/Oct/1988	2:00	5:00
2/Apr/1989	2:00	4:00
29/Oct/1989	2:00	5:00
1/Apr/1990	2:00	4:00
28/Oct/1990	2:00	5:00
7/Apr/1991	2:00	4:00
27/Oct/1991	2:00	5:00
5/Apr/1992	2:00	4:00
25/Oct/1992	2:00	5:00
4/Apr/1993	2:00	4:00
31/Oct/1993	2:00	5:00
3/Apr/1994	2:00	4:00
30/Oct/1994	2:00	5:00
2/Apr/1995	2:00	4:00
29/Oct/1995	2:00	5:00
7/Apr/1996	2:00	4:00
27/Oct/1996	2:00	5:00
6/Apr/1997	2:00	4:00
26/Oct/1997	2:00	5:00
5/Apr/1998	2:00	4:00
25/Oct/1998	2:00	5:00
4/Apr/1999	2:00	4:00
31/Oct/1999	2:00	5:00
2/Apr/2000	2:00	4:00
29/Oct/2000	2:00	5:00

Time Table # 9

Before 1/Jan/1884 LMT

Begin Standard 60w00

1/Jan/1884	0:00	4:00
14/Apr/1918	2:00	3:00
31/Oct/1918	2:00	4:00
11/May/1936	0:00	3:00
5/Oct/1936	0:00	4:00
10/May/1937	0:00	3:00
4/Oct/1937	0:00	4:00
9/May/1938	0:00	3:00
3/Oct/1938	0:00	4:00
15/May/1939	0:00	3:00
2/Oct/1939	0:00	4:00
13/May/1940	0:00	3:00
17/Oct/1940	0:00	4:00
12/May/1941	0:00	3:00
6/Oct/1941	0:00	4:00
11/May/1942	0:00	3:00
30/Sep/1945	2:00	4:00
12/May/1946	2:00	3:00
6/Oct/1946	2:00	4:00
11/May/1947	2:00	3:00
5/Oct/1947	2:00	4:00
9/May/1948	2:00	3:00
3/Oct/1948	2:00	4:00
8/May/1949	2:00	3:00
2/Oct/1949	2:00	4:00
14/May/1950	2:00	3:00
8/Oct/1950	2:00	4:00
29/Apr/1951	2:00	3:00
30/Sep/1951	2:00	4:00
27/Apr/1952	2:00	3:00
29/Sep/1952	2:00	4:00
26/Apr/1953	2:00	3:00
28/Sep/1953	2:00	4:00
25/Apr/1954	2:00	3:00
26/Sep/1954	2:00	4:00
24/Apr/1955	2:00	3:00
25/Sep/1955	2:00	4:00
29/Apr/1956	2:00	3:00
30/Sep/1956	2:00	4:00
28/Apr/1957	2:00	3:00
29/Sep/1957	2:00	4:00
27/Apr/1958	2:00	3:00
28/Sep/1958	2:00	4:00
26/Apr/1959	2:00	3:00
27/Sep/1959	2:00	4:00
24/Apr/1960	2:00	3:00
29/Oct/1960	2:00	4:00
30/Apr/1961	2:00	3:00
28/Oct/1961	2:00	4:00
29/Apr/1962	2:00	3:00
28/Oct/1962	2:00	4:00
28/Apr/1963	2:00	3:00
27/Oct/1963	2:00	4:00
26/Apr/1964	2:00	3:00
25/Oct/1964	2:00	4:00
25/Apr/1965	2:00	3:00
31/Oct/1965	2:00	4:00
24/Apr/1966	2:00	3:00
30/Oct/1966	2:00	4:00
30/Apr/1967	2:00	3:00
29/Oct/1967	2:00	4:00
28/Apr/1968	2:00	3:00
27/Oct/1968	2:00	4:00
27/Apr/1969	2:00	3:00
26/Oct/1969	2:00	4:00
26/Apr/1970	2:00	3:00
25/Oct/1970	2:00	4:00
25/Apr/1971	2:00	3:00
31/Oct/1971	2:00	4:00
30/Apr/1972	2:00	3:00
29/Oct/1972	2:00	4:00
29/Apr/1973	2:00	3:00
28/Oct/1973	2:00	4:00
28/Apr/1974	2:00	3:00
27/Oct/1974	2:00	4:00
27/Apr/1975	2:00	3:00
26/Oct/1975	2:00	4:00
25/Apr/1976	2:00	3:00
31/Oct/1976	2:00	4:00
24/Apr/1977	2:00	3:00
30/Oct/1977	2:00	4:00
30/Apr/1978	2:00	3:00
29/Oct/1978	2:00	4:00
29/Apr/1979	2:00	3:00
28/Oct/1979	2:00	4:00
27/Apr/1980	2:00	3:00
26/Oct/1980	2:00	4:00
26/Apr/1981	2:00	3:00
25/Oct/1981	2:00	4:00
25/Apr/1982	2:00	3:00
31/Oct/1982	2:00	4:00
24/Apr/1983	2:00	3:00
30/Oct/1983	2:00	4:00
29/Apr/1984	2:00	3:00
28/Oct/1984	2:00	4:00
28/Apr/1985	2:00	3:00
27/Oct/1985	2:00	4:00
27/Apr/1986	2:00	3:00
26/Oct/1986	2:00	4:00
5/Apr/1987	2:00	3:00
25/Oct/1987	2:00	4:00
3/Apr/1988	2:00	2:00
30/Oct/1988	2:00	4:00
2/Apr/1989	2:00	3:00
29/Oct/1989	2:00	4:00
1/Apr/1990	2:00	3:00
28/Oct/1990	2:00	4:00
7/Apr/1991	2:00	3:00
27/Oct/1991	2:00	4:00
5/Apr/1992	2:00	3:00
25/Oct/1992	2:00	4:00
4/Apr/1993	2:00	3:00
31/Oct/1993	2:00	4:00
3/Apr/1994	2:00	3:00
30/Oct/1994	2:00	4:00
2/Apr/1995	2:00	3:00
29/Oct/1995	2:00	4:00
7/Apr/1996	2:00	3:00
27/Oct/1996	2:00	4:00
6/Apr/1997	2:00	3:00
26/Oct/1997	2:00	4:00
5/Apr/1998	2:00	3:00
25/Oct/1998	2:00	4:00
4/Apr/1999	2:00	3:00
31/Oct/1999	2:00	4:00
2/Apr/2000	2:00	3:00
29/Oct/2000	2:00	4:00

Time Table # 10

Before 1/Jan/1884 LMT

Begin Standard 60w00

1/Jan/1884	0:00	4:00
14/Apr/1918	2:00	3:00
27/Oct/1918	2:00	4:00
25/May/1919	2:00	3:00
1/Nov/1919	0:00	4:00
9/Feb/1942	2:00	3:00
30/Sep/1945	2:00	4:00
25/Apr/1965	0:00	2:00
31/Oct/1965	2:00	4:00
27/Apr/1980	2:00	3:00
26/Oct/1980	2:00	4:00
26/Apr/1981	2:00	3:00
25/Oct/1981	2:00	4:00
25/Apr/1982	2:00	3:00
31/Oct/1982	2:00	4:00
24/Apr/1983	2:00	3:00
30/Oct/1983	2:00	4:00
29/Apr/1984	2:00	3:00
28/Oct/1984	2:00	4:00
28/Apr/1985	2:00	3:00
27/Oct/1985	2:00	4:00
27/Apr/1986	2:00	3:00
26/Oct/1986	2:00	4:00
5/Apr/1987	2:00	3:00
25/Oct/1987	2:00	4:00
3/Apr/1988	2:00	3:00
30/Oct/1988	2:00	4:00
2/Apr/1989	2:00	3:00
29/Oct/1989	2:00	4:00
1/Apr/1990	2:00	3:00
28/Oct/1990	2:00	4:00
7/Apr/1991	2:00	3:00
27/Oct/1991	2:00	4:00
5/Apr/1992	2:00	3:00
25/Oct/1992	2:00	4:00
4/Apr/1993	2:00	3:00
31/Oct/1993	2:00	4:00
3/Apr/1994	2:00	3:00
30/Oct/1994	2:00	4:00
2/Apr/1995	2:00	3:00
29/Oct/1995	2:00	4:00
7/Apr/1996	2:00	3:00
27/Oct/1996	2:00	4:00
6/Apr/1997	2:00	3:00
26/Oct/1997	2:00	4:00
5/Apr/1998	2:00	3:00
25/Oct/1998	2:00	4:00
4/Apr/1999	2:00	3:00
31/Oct/1999	2:00	4:00
2/Apr/2000	2:00	3:00
29/Oct/2000	2:00	4:00

Time Table # 11

Before 15/Jun/1902 LMT

Begin Standard 60w00

15/Jun/1902	0:00	4:00
14/Apr/1918	2:00	3:00
31/Oct/1918	2:00	4:00
9/Feb/1942	2:00	3:00
30/Sep/1945	2:00	4:00
30/Apr/1972	2:00	TT#5

Time Table # 12

Before 15/Jun/1902 LMT

Begin Standard 60w00

15/Jun/1902	0:00	4:00
1/Apr/1916	0:00	3:00
1/Oct/1916	0:00	4:00
14/Apr/1918	2:00	3:00
31/Oct/1918	2:00	4:00
9/May/1920	0:00	3:00
28/Aug/1920	24:00	4:00
6/May/1921	0:00	3:00
4/Sep/1921	24:00	4:00
30/Apr/1922	0:00	3:00
4/Sep/1922	24:00	4:00
6/May/1923	0:00	3:00
3/Sep/1923	24:00	4:00
4/May/1924	0:00	3:00
14/Sep/1924	24:00	4:00
3/May/1925	0:00	3:00
27/Sep/1925	24:00	4:00
16/May/1926	0:00	3:00
12/Sep/1926	24:00	4:00
1/May/1927	0:00	3:00
25/Sep/1927	24:00	4:00
13/May/1928	0:00	3:00
8/Sep/1928	24:00	4:00
12/May/1929	0:00	3:00
2/Sep/1929	24:00	4:00
11/May/1930	0:00	3:00
14/Sep/1930	24:00	4:00
10/May/1931	0:00	3:00
27/Sep/1931	24:00	4:00
1/May/1932	0:00	3:00
25/Sep/1932	24:00	4:00
30/Apr/1933	0:00	3:00
1/Oct/1933	24:00	4:00
20/May/1934	0:00	3:00
15/Sep/1934	24:00	4:00
2/Jun/1935	0:00	3:00
29/Sep/1935	24:00	4:00
1/Jun/1936	0:00	3:00
13/Sep/1936	24:00	4:00
2/May/1937	0:00	3:00
26/Sep/1937	24:00	4:00
1/May/1938	0:00	3:00
25/Sep/1938	24:00	4:00
28/May/1939	0:00	3:00
24/Sep/1939	24:00	4:00
5/May/1940	0:00	3:00
29/Sep/1940	24:00	4:00
4/May/1941	0:00	3:00
28/Sep/1941	24:00	4:00
9/Feb/1942	2:00	3:00
30/Sep/1945	2:00	4:00
28/Apr/1946	2:00	3:00
29/Sep/1946	2:00	4:00
27/Apr/1947	2:00	3:00
28/Sep/1947	2:00	4:00
25/Apr/1948	2:00	3:00
26/Sep/1948	2:00	4:00
24/Apr/1949	2:00	3:00
25/Sep/1949	2:00	4:00
29/Apr/1951	2:00	3:00
30/Sep/1951	2:00	4:00
27/Apr/1952	2:00	3:00
28/Sep/1952	2:00	4:00
26/Apr/1953	2:00	3:00
27/Sep/1953	2:00	4:00
25/Apr/1954	2:00	3:00
26/Sep/1954	2:00	4:00
29/Apr/1956	2:00	3:00
30/Sep/1956	2:00	4:00
28/Apr/1957	2:00	3:00
29/Sep/1957	2:00	4:00
27/Apr/1958	2:00	3:00
26/Oct/1958	2:00	4:00
26/Apr/1959	2:00	3:00
27/Sep/1959	2:00	4:00
29/Apr/1962	2:00	TT#5

Time Table # 13

Before 15/Jun/1902 LMT

Begin Standard 60w00

15/Jun/1902	0:00	4:00
14/Apr/1918	2:00	3:00
31/Oct/1918	2:00	4:00
9/Feb/1942	2:00	3:00
30/Sep/1945	2:00	4:00
28/Apr/1946	2:00	3:00
29/Sep/1946	2:00	4:00
27/Apr/1947	2:00	3:00
28/Sep/1947	2:00	4:00
25/Apr/1948	2:00	3:00
26/Sep/1948	2:00	4:00
24/Apr/1949	2:00	3:00
25/Sep/1949	2:00	4:00
30/Apr/1950	2:00	3:00
24/Sep/1950	2:00	4:00
29/Apr/1951	2:00	3:00
30/Sep/1951	2:00	4:00
27/Apr/1952	2:00	3:00
28/Sep/1952	2:00	4:00
26/Apr/1953	2:00	3:00
27/Sep/1953	2:00	4:00
25/Apr/1954	2:00	3:00
26/Sep/1954	2:00	4:00
24/Apr/1955	2:00	3:00
25/Sep/1955	2:00	4:00
29/Apr/1956	2:00	3:00
30/Sep/1956	2:00	4:00
28/Apr/1957	2:00	3:00
27/Oct/1957	2:00	4:00
27/Apr/1958	2:00	3:00
26/Oct/1958	2:00	4:00
26/Apr/1959	2:00	3:00
25/Oct/1959	2:00	4:00
24/Apr/1960	2:00	3:00
30/Oct/1960	2:00	4:00
24/Apr/1961	2:00	3:00
29/Oct/1961	2:00	4:00
29/Apr/1962	2:00	TT#5

Time Table # 14

Before 15/Jun/1902 LMT

Begin Standard 60w00

15/Jun/1902	0:00	4:00
14/Apr/1918	2:00	3:00
31/Oct/1918	2:00	4:00
9/Feb/1942	2:00	3:00
30/Sep/1945	2:00	4:00
26/Apr/1953	2:00	3:00
27/Sep/1953	2:00	4:00

30/Apr/1972 2:00 TT#5
....
Time Table # 15
Before 15/Jun/1902 LMT
Begin Standard 60w00
15/Jun/1902 0:00 4:00
14/Apr/1918 2:00 3:00
31/Oct/1918 2:00 4:00
9/Feb/1942 2:00 3:00
30/Sep/1945 2:00 4:00
28/Apr/1946 2:00 3:00
29/Sep/1946 2:00 4:00
29/Apr/1951 2:00 3:00
30/Sep/1951 2:00 4:00
26/Apr/1953 2:00 3:00
27/Sep/1953 2:00 4:00
30/Apr/1972 2:00 TT#5
....
Time Table # 16
Before 15/Jun/1902 LMT
Begin Standard 60w00
15/Jun/1902 0:00 4:00
14/Apr/1918 2:00 3:00
31/Oct/1918 2:00 4:00
2/May/1937 0:00 3:00
26/Sep/1937 0:00 4:00
24/Apr/1938 0:00 3:00
25/Sep/1938 0:00 4:00
26/May/1939 0:00 3:00
24/Sep/1939 0:00 4:00
5/May/1940 0:00 3:00
29/Sep/1940 0:00 4:00
4/May/1941 0:00 3:00
28/Sep/1941 0:00 4:00
9/Feb/1942 2:00 3:00
30/Sep/1945 2:00 4:00
28/Apr/1946 2:00 3:00
29/Sep/1946 2:00 4:00
27/Apr/1947 2:00 3:00
28/Sep/1947 2:00 4:00
25/Apr/1948 2:00 3:00
26/Sep/1948 2:00 4:00
24/Apr/1949 2:00 3:00
25/Sep/1949 2:00 4:00
30/Apr/1950 2:00 3:00
29/Oct/1950 2:00 4:00
29/Apr/1951 2:00 3:00
30/Sep/1951 2:00 4:00
27/Apr/1952 2:00 3:00
28/Sep/1952 2:00 4:00
26/Apr/1953 2:00 3:00
27/Sep/1953 2:00 4:00
25/Apr/1954 2:00 3:00
26/Sep/1954 2:00 4:00
24/Apr/1955 2:00 3:00
25/Sep/1955 2:00 4:00
29/Apr/1956 2:00 3:00
30/Sep/1956 2:00 4:00
26/Apr/1959 2:00 3:00
25/Oct/1959 2:00 4:00
24/Apr/1960 2:00 3:00
30/Oct/1960 2:00 4:00
30/Apr/1961 2:00 3:00
29/Oct/1961 2:00 4:00
29/Apr/1962 2:00 3:00
28/Oct/1962 2:00 4:00
28/Apr/1963 2:00 3:00
27/Oct/1963 2:00 4:00
26/Apr/1964 2:00 3:00
25/Oct/1964 2:00 4:00
30/Apr/1967 2:00 3:00
29/Oct/1967 2:00 4:00
28/Apr/1968 2:00 3:00
27/Oct/1968 2:00 4:00
27/Apr/1969 2:00 3:00
26/Oct/1969 2:00 4:00
26/Apr/1970 2:00 3:00
25/Oct/1970 2:00 4:00
25/Apr/1971 2:00 3:00
31/Oct/1971 2:00 4:00
30/Apr/1972 2:00 3:00
29/Oct/1972 2:00 4:00
29/Apr/1973 2:00 3:00
28/Oct/1973 2:00 4:00
28/Apr/1974 2:00 3:00
27/Oct/1974 2:00 4:00
27/Apr/1975 2:00 3:00
26/Oct/1975 2:00 4:00
25/Apr/1976 2:00 3:00
31/Oct/1976 2:00 4:00
24/Apr/1977 2:00 3:00
30/Oct/1977 2:00 4:00
30/Apr/1978 2:00 3:00
29/Oct/1978 2:00 4:00
29/Apr/1979 2:00 3:00
28/Oct/1979 2:00 4:00
27/Apr/1980 2:00 3:00
26/Oct/1980 2:00 4:00
26/Apr/1981 2:00 3:00
25/Oct/1981 2:00 4:00
25/Apr/1982 2:00 3:00
31/Oct/1982 2:00 4:00
24/Apr/1983 2:00 3:00
30/Oct/1983 2:00 4:00
29/Apr/1984 2:00 3:00
28/Oct/1984 2:00 4:00
28/Apr/1985 2:00 3:00
27/Oct/1985 2:00 4:00
27/Apr/1986 2:00 3:00
26/Oct/1986 2:00 4:00
5/Apr/1987 2:00 3:00
25/Oct/1987 2:00 4:00
3/Apr/1988 2:00 3:00
30/Oct/1988 2:00 4:00
2/Apr/1989 2:00 3:00
29/Oct/1989 2:00 4:00
1/Apr/1990 2:00 3:00
28/Oct/1990 2:00 4:00
7/Apr/1991 2:00 3:00
27/Oct/1991 2:00 4:00
5/Apr/1992 2:00 3:00
25/Oct/1992 2:00 4:00
4/Apr/1993 2:00 3:00
31/Oct/1993 2:00 4:00
3/Apr/1994 2:00 3:00
30/Oct/1994 2:00 4:00
2/Apr/1995 2:00 3:00
29/Oct/1995 2:00 4:00
7/Apr/1996 2:00 3:00
27/Oct/1996 2:00 4:00
6/Apr/1997 2:00 3:00
26/Oct/1997 2:00 4:00
5/Apr/1998 2:00 3:00
25/Oct/1998 2:00 4:00
4/Apr/1999 2:00 3:00
31/Oct/1999 2:00 4:00
2/Apr/2000 2:00 3:00
29/Oct/2000 2:00 4:00
....
Time Table # 17
Before 15/Jun/1902 LMT
Begin Standard 60w00
15/Jun/1902 0:00 4:00
14/Apr/1918 2:00 3:00
31/Oct/1918 2:00 4:00
9/Feb/1942 2:00 3:00
30/Sep/1945 2:00 4:00
28/Apr/1946 2:00 3:00
29/Sep/1946 2:00 4:00
24/Apr/1949 2:00 3:00
25/Sep/1949 2:00 4:00
24/May/1951 2:00 3:00
4/Sep/1951 2:00 4:00
26/Apr/1953 2:00 3:00
27/Sep/1953 2:00 4:00
25/Apr/1954 2:00 3:00
26/Sep/1954 2:00 4:00
24/Apr/1955 2:00 3:00
25/Sep/1955 2:00 4:00
28/Apr/1957 2:00 3:00
27/Oct/1957 2:00 4:00
27/Apr/1958 2:00 3:00
26/Oct/1958 2:00 4:00
24/Apr/1960 2:00 TT#5
....
Time Table # 18
Before 15/Jun/1902 LMT
Begin Standard 60w00
15/Jun/1902 0:00 4:00
14/Apr/1918 2:00 3:00
31/Oct/1918 2:00 4:00
9/Feb/1942 2:00 3:00
30/Sep/1945 2:00 4:00
28/Apr/1946 2:00 3:00
29/Sep/1946 2:00 4:00
25/Apr/1948 2:00 3:00
26/Sep/1948 2:00 4:00
6/Jun/1949 2:00 3:00
6/Sep/1949 2:00 4:00
23/May/1950 2:00 3:00
4/Sep/1950 2:00 4:00
24/May/1951 2:00 3:00
4/Sep/1951 2:00 4:00
24/May/1952 2:00 3:00
2/Sep/1952 2:00 4:00
26/Apr/1953 2:00 3:00
27/Sep/1953 2:00 4:00
25/Apr/1954 2:00 3:00
26/Sep/1954 2:00 4:00
24/Apr/1955 2:00 3:00
25/Sep/1955 2:00 4:00
29/Apr/1956 2:00 3:00
30/Sep/1956 2:00 4:00
28/Apr/1957 2:00 3:00
27/Oct/1957 2:00 4:00
27/Apr/1958 2:00 3:00
26/Oct/1958 2:00 4:00
26/Apr/1959 2:00 3:00
25/Oct/1959 2:00 4:00
24/Apr/1960 2:00 3:00
30/Oct/1960 2:00 4:00
30/Apr/1961 2:00 3:00
29/Oct/1961 2:00 4:00
29/Apr/1962 2:00 3:00
28/Oct/1962 2:00 4:00
28/Apr/1963 2:00 3:00
27/Oct/1963 2:00 4:00
26/Apr/1964 2:00 3:00
25/Oct/1964 2:00 4:00
25/Apr/1965 2:00 3:00
31/Oct/1965 2:00 4:00
24/Apr/1966 2:00 3:00
30/Oct/1966 2:00 4:00
28/Apr/1968 2:00 TT#5
....
Time Table # 19
Before 15/Jun/1902 LMT
Begin Standard 60w00
15/Jun/1902 0:00 4:00
14/Apr/1918 2:00 3:00
31/Oct/1918 2:00 4:00
9/Feb/1942 2:00 3:00
30/Sep/1945 2:00 4:00
28/Apr/1946 2:00 3:00
29/Sep/1946 2:00 4:00
27/Apr/1947 2:00 3:00
28/Sep/1947 2:00 4:00
25/Apr/1948 2:00 3:00
26/Sep/1948 2:00 4:00
24/Apr/1949 2:00 3:00
25/Sep/1949 2:00 4:00
30/Apr/1950 2:00 3:00
24/Sep/1950 2:00 4:00
29/Apr/1951 2:00 3:00
30/Sep/1951 2:00 4:00
27/Apr/1952 2:00 3:00
28/Sep/1952 2:00 4:00
26/Apr/1953 2:00 3:00
27/Sep/1953 2:00 4:00
25/Apr/1954 2:00 3:00
26/Sep/1954 2:00 4:00
24/Apr/1955 2:00 3:00
25/Sep/1955 2:00 4:00
29/Apr/1956 2:00 3:00
30/Sep/1956 2:00 4:00
28/Apr/1957 2:00 3:00
27/Oct/1957 2:00 4:00
27/Apr/1958 2:00 3:00
26/Oct/1958 2:00 4:00
26/Apr/1959 2:00 3:00
25/Oct/1959 2:00 4:00
24/Apr/1960 2:00 3:00
30/Oct/1960 2:00 4:00
30/Apr/1961 2:00 3:00
29/Oct/1961 2:00 4:00
29/Apr/1962 2:00 3:00
28/Oct/1962 2:00 4:00
28/Apr/1963 2:00 3:00
27/Oct/1963 2:00 4:00
26/Apr/1964 2:00 3:00
25/Oct/1964 2:00 4:00
25/Apr/1965 2:00 3:00
31/Oct/1965 2:00 4:00
24/Apr/1966 2:00 3:00
30/Oct/1966 2:00 4:00
25/Apr/1971 2:00 TT#5
....
Time Table # 20
Before 15/Jun/1902 LMT
Begin Standard 60w00
15/Jun/1902 0:00 4:00
14/Apr/1918 2:00 3:00
31/Oct/1918 2:00 4:00
9/Feb/1942 2:00 3:00
30/Sep/1945 2:00 4:00
27/Apr/1947 2:00 3:00
28/Sep/1947 2:00 4:00
24/Apr/1949 2:00 3:00
25/Sep/1949 2:00 4:00
29/Apr/1951 2:00 3:00
30/Sep/1951 2:00 4:00
26/Apr/1953 2:00 3:00
27/Sep/1953 2:00 4:00
30/Apr/1972 2:00 TT#5
....
Time Table # 21
Before 15/Jun/1902 LMT
Begin Standard 60w00
15/Jun/1902 0:00 4:00
14/Apr/1918 2:00 3:00
31/Oct/1918 2:00 4:00
27/Apr/1931 0:00 3:00
6/Sep/1931 0:00 4:00
9/Feb/1942 2:00 3:00
30/Sep/1945 2:00 4:00
28/Apr/1946 2:00 3:00
29/Sep/1946 2:00 4:00
27/Apr/1947 2:00 3:00
28/Sep/1947 2:00 4:00
29/Apr/1951 2:00 3:00
30/Sep/1951 2:00 4:00
26/Apr/1953 2:00 3:00
27/Sep/1953 2:00 4:00
30/Apr/1972 2:00 TT#5
....
Time Table # 22
Before 15/Jun/1902 LMT
Begin Standard 60w00
15/Jun/1902 0:00 4:00
14/Apr/1918 2:00 3:00
31/Oct/1918 2:00 4:00
9/Feb/1942 2:00 3:00
30/Sep/1945 2:00 4:00
28/Apr/1946 2:00 3:00
29/Sep/1946 2:00 4:00
27/Apr/1947 2:00 3:00
28/Sep/1947 2:00 4:00
25/Apr/1948 2:00 3:00
26/Sep/1948 2:00 4:00
24/Apr/1949 2:00 3:00
25/Sep/1949 2:00 4:00
29/Apr/1951 2:00 3:00
30/Sep/1951 2:00 4:00
27/Apr/1952 2:00 3:00
28/Sep/1952 2:00 4:00
26/Apr/1953 2:00 3:00
27/Sep/1953 2:00 4:00
25/Apr/1954 2:00 3:00
26/Sep/1954 2:00 4:00
24/Apr/1955 2:00 3:00
25/Sep/1955 2:00 4:00
28/Apr/1957 2:00 3:00
27/Oct/1957 2:00 4:00
26/Apr/1959 2:00 3:00
25/Oct/1959 2:00 4:00
30/Apr/1961 2:00 3:00
29/Oct/1961 2:00 4:00
28/Apr/1963 2:00 3:00
27/Oct/1963 2:00 4:00
24/Apr/1966 2:00 3:00
30/Oct/1966 2:00 4:00
30/Apr/1967 2:00 TT#5
....
Time Table # 23
Before 16/May/1902 LMT
Begin Standard 60w00
16/May/1902 0:00 4:00
14/Apr/1918 2:00 3:00
31/Oct/1918 2:00 4:00
9/Feb/1942 2:00 3:00
30/Sep/1945 2:00 4:00
28/Apr/1946 2:00 3:00
29/Sep/1946 2:00 4:00
25/Apr/1948 2:00 3:00
26/Sep/1948 2:00 4:00
24/Apr/1949 2:00 3:00
25/Sep/1949 2:00 4:00
30/Apr/1950 2:00 3:00
24/Sep/1950 2:00 4:00
29/Apr/1951 2:00 3:00
30/Sep/1951 2:00 4:00
27/Apr/1952 2:00 3:00
28/Sep/1952 2:00 4:00
25/Apr/1953 2:00 3:00
26/Sep/1953 2:00 4:00
25/Apr/1954 2:00 3:00
26/Sep/1954 2:00 4:00
24/Apr/1955 2:00 3:00
25/Sep/1955 2:00 4:00
29/Apr/1956 2:00 3:00
30/Sep/1956 2:00 4:00
26/Apr/1959 2:00 3:00
25/Oct/1959 2:00 4:00
24/Apr/1960 2:00 3:00
30/Oct/1960 2:00 4:00
29/Apr/1962 2:00 3:00
28/Oct/1962 2:00 4:00
28/Apr/1963 2:00 3:00
27/Oct/1963 2:00 4:00
26/Apr/1964 2:00 3:00
25/Oct/1964 2:00 4:00
25/Apr/1965 2:00 3:00
31/Oct/1965 2:00 4:00
30/Apr/1972 2:00 TT#5
....
Time Table # 24
Before 15/Jun/1902 LMT
Begin Standard 60w00
15/Jun/1902 0:00 4:00
14/Apr/1918 2:00 3:00
31/Oct/1918 2:00 4:00
9/Feb/1942 2:00 3:00
30/Sep/1945 2:00 4:00
28/Apr/1946 2:00 3:00
29/Sep/1946 2:00 4:00
1/May/1947 2:00 3:00
30/Sep/1947 2:00 4:00
26/Apr/1953 2:00 3:00
27/Sep/1953 2:00 4:00
30/Apr/1972 2:00 TT#5
....
Time Table # 25
Before 15/Jun/1902 LMT
Begin Standard 60w00
15/Jun/1902 0:00 4:00
14/Apr/1918 2:00 3:00
31/Oct/1918 2:00 4:00
9/Feb/1942 2:00 3:00
30/Sep/1945 2:00 4:00
28/Apr/1946 2:00 3:00
29/Sep/1946 2:00 4:00
27/Apr/1947 2:00 3:00
28/Sep/1947 2:00 4:00
25/Apr/1948 2:00 3:00
26/Sep/1948 2:00 4:00
24/Apr/1949 2:00 3:00
25/Sep/1949 2:00 4:00
30/Apr/1950 2:00 3:00
24/Sep/1950 2:00 4:00
29/Apr/1951 2:00 3:00
30/Sep/1951 2:00 4:00
27/Apr/1952 2:00 3:00
28/Sep/1952 2:00 4:00
26/Apr/1953 2:00 3:00
27/Sep/1953 2:00 4:00
25/Apr/1954 2:00 3:00
26/Sep/1954 2:00 4:00
24/Apr/1955 2:00 3:00
25/Sep/1955 2:00 4:00
29/Apr/1956 2:00 3:00
30/Sep/1956 2:00 4:00
28/Apr/1957 2:00 3:00
29/Sep/1957 2:00 4:00
27/Apr/1958 2:00 TT#5
....
Time Table # 26
Before 15/Jun/1902 LMT
Begin Standard 60w00
15/Jun/1902 0:00 4:00
14/Apr/1918 2:00 3:00
31/Oct/1918 2:00 4:00
9/Feb/1942 2:00 3:00
30/Sep/1945 2:00 4:00
28/Apr/1946 2:00 3:00
29/Sep/1946 2:00 4:00
27/Apr/1947 2:00 3:00
28/Sep/1947 2:00 4:00
25/Apr/1948 2:00 3:00
26/Sep/1948 2:00 4:00
24/Apr/1949 2:00 3:00
25/Sep/1949 2:00 4:00
29/Apr/1951 2:00 3:00
30/Sep/1951 2:00 4:00
27/Apr/1952 2:00 3:00
28/Sep/1952 2:00 4:00
26/Apr/1953 2:00 3:00
27/Sep/1953 2:00 4:00
25/Apr/1954 2:00 3:00
26/Sep/1954 2:00 4:00
24/Apr/1955 2:00 3:00
25/Sep/1955 2:00 4:00
29/Apr/1956 2:00 3:00
30/Sep/1956 2:00 4:00
29/Apr/1962 2:00 3:00
28/Oct/1962 2:00 4:00
28/Apr/1963 2:00 3:00
27/Oct/1963 2:00 4:00
26/Apr/1964 2:00 3:00
25/Oct/1964 2:00 4:00
25/Apr/1965 2:00 3:00
31/Oct/1965 2:00 4:00
24/Apr/1966 2:00 3:00
30/Oct/1966 2:00 4:00
28/Apr/1968 2:00 TT#5
....
Time Table # 27
Before 15/Jun/1902 LMT
Begin Standard 60w00
15/Jun/1902 0:00 4:00
14/Apr/1918 2:00 3:00
31/Oct/1918 2:00 4:00
9/Feb/1942 2:00 3:00
30/Sep/1945 2:00 4:00
28/Apr/1946 2:00 3:00
29/Sep/1946 2:00 4:00
27/Apr/1947 2:00 3:00
28/Sep/1947 2:00 4:00
25/Apr/1948 2:00 3:00
26/Sep/1948 2:00 4:00
24/Apr/1949 2:00 3:00
25/Sep/1949 2:00 4:00
30/Apr/1950 2:00 3:00
24/Sep/1950 2:00 4:00
29/Apr/1951 2:00 3:00
30/Sep/1951 2:00 4:00
27/Apr/1952 2:00 3:00
28/Sep/1952 2:00 4:00
26/Apr/1953 2:00 3:00
27/Sep/1953 2:00 4:00
25/Apr/1954 2:00 3:00
26/Sep/1954 2:00 4:00
24/Apr/1955 2:00 3:00
25/Sep/1955 2:00 4:00
29/Apr/1956 2:00 3:00
30/Sep/1956 2:00 4:00
28/Apr/1957 2:00 3:00
29/Sep/1957 2:00 4:00
27/Apr/1958 2:00 TT#5
....
Time Table # 28
Before 15/Jun/1902 LMT
Begin Standard 60w00
15/Jun/1902 0:00 4:00
14/Apr/1918 2:00 3:00
31/Oct/1918 2:00 4:00
29/Apr/1934 2:00 3:00
30/Sep/1934 2:00 4:00
28/Apr/1940 2:00 3:00
2/Sep/1940 2:00 4:00
27/Apr/1941 2:00 3:00
28/Sep/1941 2:00 4:00
9/Feb/1942 2:00 3:00
30/Sep/1945 2:00 4:00
28/Apr/1946 2:00 3:00
29/Sep/1946 2:00 4:00
27/Apr/1947 2:00 3:00
28/Sep/1947 2:00 TT#6
....
Time Table # 29
Before 15/Jun/1902 LMT
Begin Standard 60w00
15/Jun/1902 0:00 4:00
14/Apr/1918 2:00 3:00
31/Oct/1918 2:00 4:00
28/Apr/1940 2:00 3:00
29/Sep/1940 2:00 4:00
9/Feb/1942 2:00 3:00
30/Sep/1945 2:00 4:00
27/Apr/1947 2:00 3:00
28/Sep/1947 2:00 TT#6
....
Time Table # 30
Before 1/Jan/1884 LMT
Begin Standard 60w00
1/Jan/1884 0:00 4:00
14/Apr/1918 2:00 3:00
31/Oct/1918 2:00 4:00
9/Feb/1942 2:00 3:00
30/Sep/1945 2:00 4:00
30/Apr/1967 2:00 3:00
29/Oct/1967 2:00 4:00
28/Apr/1968 2:00 3:00
27/Oct/1968 2:00 4:00
27/Apr/1969 2:00 3:00
26/Oct/1969 2:00 4:00
26/Apr/1970 2:00 3:00
25/Oct/1970 2:00 4:00
25/Apr/1971 2:00 3:00
31/Oct/1971 2:00 4:00
30/Apr/1972 2:00 3:00
29/Oct/1972 2:00 4:00
29/Apr/1973 2:00 3:00
28/Oct/1973 2:00 4:00
28/Apr/1974 2:00 3:00
27/Oct/1974 2:00 4:00
27/Apr/1975 2:00 3:00
26/Oct/1975 2:00 4:00
25/Apr/1976 2:00 3:00
31/Oct/1976 2:00 4:00
24/Apr/1977 2:00 3:00
30/Oct/1977 2:00 4:00
30/Apr/1978 2:00 3:00
29/Oct/1978 2:00 4:00
29/Apr/1979 2:00 3:00
28/Oct/1979 2:00 4:00

27/Apr/1980 2:00 3:00
26/Oct/1980 2:00 4:00
26/Apr/1981 2:00 3:00
25/Oct/1981 2:00 4:00
25/Apr/1982 2:00 3:00
31/Oct/1982 2:00 4:00
24/Apr/1983 2:00 3:00
30/Oct/1983 2:00 4:00
29/Apr/1984 2:00 3:00
28/Oct/1984 2:00 4:00
28/Apr/1985 2:00 3:00
27/Oct/1985 2:00 4:00
27/Apr/1986 2:00 3:00
26/Oct/1986 2:00 4:00
5/Apr/1987 2:00 3:00
25/Oct/1987 2:00 4:00
3/Apr/1988 2:00 3:00
30/Oct/1988 2:00 4:00
2/Apr/1989 2:00 3:00
29/Oct/1989 2:00 4:00
1/Apr/1990 2:00 3:00
28/Oct/1990 2:00 4:00
7/Apr/1991 2:00 3:00
27/Oct/1991 2:00 4:00
5/Apr/1992 2:00 3:00
25/Oct/1992 2:00 4:00
4/Apr/1993 2:00 3:00
31/Oct/1993 2:00 4:00
3/Apr/1994 2:00 3:00
30/Oct/1994 2:00 4:00
2/Apr/1995 2:00 3:00
29/Oct/1995 2:00 4:00
7/Apr/1996 2:00 3:00
27/Oct/1996 2:00 4:00
6/Apr/1997 2:00 3:00
26/Oct/1997 2:00 4:00
5/Apr/1998 2:00 3:00
25/Oct/1998 2:00 4:00
4/Apr/1999 2:00 3:00
31/Oct/1999 2:00 4:00
2/Apr/2000 2:00 3:00
29/Oct/2000 2:00 4:00

....

Time Table # 31
Before 15/Jun/1902 LMT
Begin Standard 60w00
15/Jun/1902 0:00 4:00
14/Apr/1918 2:00 3:00
31/Oct/1918 2:00 4:00
9/Feb/1942 2:00 3:00
30/Sep/1945 2:00 4:00
28/Apr/1946 2:00 3:00
29/Sep/1946 2:00 4:00
24/Apr/1949 2:00 3:00
25/Sep/1949 2:00 4:00
29/Apr/1951 2:00 3:00
30/Sep/1951 2:00 4:00
26/Apr/1953 2:00 3:00
27/Sep/1953 2:00 4:00
30/Apr/1972 2:00 TT#5

....

Time Table # 32
Before 15/Jun/1902 LMT
Begin Standard 60w00
15/Jun/1902 0:00 4:00
14/Apr/1918 2:00 3:00
31/Oct/1918 2:00 4:00
9/Feb/1942 2:00 3:00
30/Sep/1945 2:00 4:00
24/Apr/1949 2:00 3:00
25/Sep/1949 2:00 4:00
30/Apr/1972 2:00 TT#5

....

Time Table # 33
Before 1/Jan/1884 LMT
Begin Standard 75w00
1/Jan/1884 0:00 5:00
14/Apr/1918 2:00 4:00
27/Oct/1918 2:00 5:00
25/May/1919 2:00 4:00
1/Nov/1919 0:00 5:00
9/Feb/1942 2:00 4:00
30/Sep/1945 2:00 5:00
25/Apr/1965 0:00 3:00
31/Oct/1965 2:00 5:00
27/Apr/1980 2:00 4:00
26/Oct/1980 2:00 5:00
26/Apr/1981 2:00 4:00
25/Oct/1981 2:00 5:00
25/Apr/1982 2:00 4:00
31/Oct/1982 2:00 5:00
24/Apr/1983 2:00 4:00
30/Oct/1983 2:00 5:00
29/Apr/1984 2:00 4:00
28/Oct/1984 2:00 5:00
28/Apr/1985 2:00 4:00
27/Oct/1985 2:00 5:00
27/Apr/1986 2:00 4:00
26/Oct/1986 2:00 5:00
5/Apr/1987 2:00 4:00
25/Oct/1987 2:00 5:00
3/Apr/1988 2:00 4:00
30/Oct/1988 2:00 5:00
2/Apr/1989 2:00 4:00
29/Oct/1989 2:00 5:00
1/Apr/1990 2:00 4:00
28/Oct/1990 2:00 5:00
7/Apr/1991 2:00 4:00
27/Oct/1991 2:00 5:00
5/Apr/1992 2:00 4:00
25/Oct/1992 2:00 5:00
4/Apr/1993 2:00 4:00
31/Oct/1993 2:00 5:00
3/Apr/1994 2:00 4:00
30/Oct/1994 2:00 5:00
2/Apr/1995 2:00 4:00
29/Oct/1995 2:00 5:00
7/Apr/1996 2:00 4:00
27/Oct/1996 2:00 5:00
6/Apr/1997 2:00 4:00
26/Oct/1997 2:00 5:00
5/Apr/1998 2:00 4:00
25/Oct/1998 2:00 5:00
4/Apr/1999 2:00 4:00
31/Oct/1999 2:00 5:00
2/Apr/2000 2:00 4:00
29/Oct/2000 2:00 5:00

....

Time Table # 34
Before 1/Jan/1895 LMT
Begin Standard 75w00
1/Jan/1895 0:00 5:00
14/Apr/1918 2:00 4:00
31/Oct/1918 2:00 5:00
29/Sep/1940 0:00 4:00
30/Sep/1945 2:00 5:00
28/Apr/1946 2:00 4:00
29/Sep/1946 2:00 5:00
27/Apr/1947 0:00 4:00
28/Sep/1947 0:00 5:00
26/Apr/1953 2:00 4:00
27/Sep/1953 2:00 TT#1

....

Time Table # 35
Before 1/Jan/1895 LMT
Begin Standard 75w00
1/Jan/1895 0:00 5:00
14/Apr/1918 2:00 4:00
31/Oct/1918 2:00 5:00
29/Sep/1940 0:00 4:00
30/Sep/1945 2:00 5:00
26/Apr/1953 2:00 4:00
27/Sep/1953 2:00 TT#1

....

Time Table # 36
Before 1/Jan/1895 LMT
Begin Standard 75w00
1/Jan/1895 0:00 5:00
14/Apr/1918 2:00 4:00
31/Oct/1918 2:00 5:00
29/Sep/1940 0:00 4:00
30/Sep/1945 2:00 5:00
27/Apr/1947 0:00 4:00
28/Sep/1947 0:00 5:00
26/Apr/1953 2:00 4:00
27/Sep/1953 2:00 TT#1

....

Time Table # 37
Before 1/Jan/1895 LMT
Begin Standard 75w00
1/Jan/1895 0:00 5:00
14/Apr/1918 2:00 4:00
31/Oct/1918 2:00 5:00
29/Sep/1940 0:00 4:00
30/Sep/1945 2:00 5:00
27/Apr/1947 0:00 4:00
28/Sep/1947 0:00 TT#1

....

Time Table # 38
Before 1/Jan/1895 LMT
Begin Standard 75w00
1/Jan/1895 0:00 5:00
14/Apr/1918 2:00 4:00
31/Oct/1918 2:00 5:00
29/Sep/1940 0:00 4:00
30/Sep/1945 2:00 5:00
25/Apr/1948 0:00 4:00
26/Sep/1948 0:00 5:00
29/Apr/1951 2:00 4:00
30/Sep/1951 2:00 TT#1

....

Time Table # 39
Before 1/Jan/1895 LMT
Begin Standard 75w00
1/Jan/1895 0:00 5:00
14/Apr/1918 2:00 4:00
31/Oct/1918 2:00 5:00
26/Apr/1931 2:00 4:00
27/Sep/1931 2:00 5:00
29/Sep/1940 0:00 4:00
30/Sep/1945 2:00 5:00
28/Apr/1946 2:00 4:00
9/Nov/1946 2:00 5:00
27/Apr/1947 0:00 4:00
28/Sep/1947 0:00 5:00
25/Apr/1948 0:00 4:00
26/Sep/1948 0:00 5:00
24/Apr/1949 2:00 4:00
25/Sep/1949 2:00 5:00
30/Apr/1950 2:00 4:00
24/Sep/1950 2:00 5:00
29/Apr/1951 2:00 4:00
30/Sep/1951 2:00 5:00
27/Apr/1952 2:00 4:00
28/Sep/1952 2:00 5:00
26/Apr/1953 2:00 4:00
27/Sep/1953 2:00 5:00
25/Apr/1954 2:00 4:00
26/Sep/1954 2:00 5:00
24/Apr/1955 2:00 4:00
25/Sep/1955 2:00 5:00
29/Apr/1956 2:00 4:00
30/Sep/1956 2:00 5:00
28/Apr/1957 2:00 4:00
27/Oct/1957 2:00 5:00
27/Apr/1958 2:00 4:00
26/Oct/1958 2:00 5:00
26/Apr/1959 2:00 4:00
25/Oct/1959 2:00 5:00
24/Apr/1960 2:00 4:00
30/Oct/1960 2:00 5:00
30/Apr/1961 2:00 4:00
29/Oct/1961 2:00 5:00
29/Apr/1962 2:00 4:00
28/Oct/1962 2:00 5:00
28/Apr/1963 2:00 4:00
27/Oct/1963 2:00 5:00
26/Apr/1964 2:00 4:00
25/Oct/1964 2:00 5:00
25/Apr/1965 2:00 4:00
31/Oct/1965 2:00 5:00
24/Apr/1966 2:00 4:00
30/Oct/1966 2:00 5:00
30/Apr/1967 2:00 4:00
29/Oct/1967 2:00 5:00
28/Apr/1968 2:00 4:00
27/Oct/1968 2:00 5:00
27/Apr/1969 2:00 4:00
26/Oct/1969 2:00 5:00
26/Apr/1970 2:00 4:00
25/Oct/1970 2:00 5:00
25/Apr/1971 2:00 4:00
24/Oct/1971 2:00 5:00
30/Apr/1972 2:00 4:00
29/Oct/1972 2:00 TT#1

....

Time Table # 40
Before 1/Jan/1895 LMT
Begin Standard 75w00
1/Jan/1895 0:00 5:00
14/Apr/1918 2:00 4:00
31/Oct/1918 2:00 5:00
29/Sep/1940 0:00 4:00
30/Sep/1945 2:00 5:00
28/Apr/1946 2:00 TT#2

....

Time Table # 41
Before 1/Jan/1895 LMT
Begin Standard 75w00
1/Jan/1895 0:00 5:00
14/Apr/1918 2:00 4:00
31/Oct/1918 2:00 5:00
30/Apr/1939 2:00 4:00
24/Sep/1939 2:00 5:00
28/Apr/1940 2:00 4:00
30/Sep/1945 2:00 5:00
27/Apr/1947 0:00 4:00
28/Sep/1947 0:00 5:00
26/Apr/1953 2:00 4:00
27/Sep/1953 2:00 5:00
28/Apr/1957 2:00 4:00
27/Oct/1957 2:00 TT#1

....

Time Table # 42
Before 1/Jan/1895 LMT
Begin Standard 75w00
1/Jan/1895 0:00 5:00
14/Apr/1918 2:00 4:00
31/Oct/1918 2:00 5:00
29/Sep/1940 0:00 4:00
30/Sep/1945 2:00 5:00
27/Apr/1947 2:00 4:00
30/Sep/1947 2:00 5:00
26/Apr/1953 2:00 4:00
27/Sep/1953 2:00 TT#1

....

Time Table # 43
Before 1/Jan/1895 LMT
Begin Standard 75w00
1/Jan/1895 0:00 5:00
14/Apr/1918 2:00 4:00
31/Oct/1918 2:00 5:00
29/Sep/1940 0:00 4:00
30/Sep/1945 2:00 5:00
28/Apr/1946 2:00 4:00
1/Sep/1946 2:00 5:00
27/Apr/1947 0:00 4:00
28/Sep/1947 0:00 5:00
26/Apr/1953 2:00 4:00
27/Sep/1953 2:00 TT#1

....

Time Table # 44
Before 1/Jan/1895 LMT
Begin Standard 75w00
1/Jan/1895 0:00 5:00
14/Apr/1918 2:00 4:00
31/Oct/1918 2:00 5:00
29/Sep/1940 0:00 4:00
30/Sep/1945 2:00 5:00
28/Apr/1946 2:00 4:00
29/Sep/1946 2:00 5:00
27/Apr/1947 0:00 4:00
28/Sep/1947 0:00 5:00
25/Apr/1948 0:00 4:00
26/Sep/1948 0:00 5:00
24/Apr/1949 2:00 4:00
25/Sep/1949 2:00 5:00
26/Apr/1953 2:00 4:00
27/Sep/1953 2:00 TT#1

....

Time Table # 45
Before 1/Jan/1895 LMT
Begin Standard 75w00
1/Jan/1895 0:00 5:00
14/Apr/1918 2:00 4:00
31/Oct/1918 2:00 5:00
29/Apr/1934 2:00 TT#2

....

Time Table # 46
Before 1/Jan/1895 LMT
Begin Standard 75w00
1/Jan/1895 0:00 5:00
14/Apr/1918 2:00 4:00
31/Oct/1918 2:00 5:00
29/Sep/1940 0:00 4:00
30/Sep/1945 2:00 5:00
26/Apr/1953 2:00 4:00
27/Sep/1953 2:00 5:00
25/Apr/1954 2:00 4:00
26/Sep/1954 2:00 TT#1

....

Time Table # 47
Before 1/Jan/1895 LMT
Begin Standard 75w00
1/Jan/1895 0:00 5:00
14/Apr/1918 2:00 4:00
31/Oct/1918 2:00 5:00
29/Sep/1940 0:00 4:00
30/Sep/1945 2:00 5:00
27/Apr/1952 2:00 4:00
28/Sep/1952 2:00 5:00
26/Apr/1953 2:00 4:00
27/Sep/1953 2:00 TT#1

....

Time Table # 48
Before 1/Jan/1895 LMT
Begin Standard 75w00
1/Jan/1895 0:00 5:00
14/Apr/1918 2:00 4:00
31/Oct/1918 2:00 5:00
1/May/1932 2:00 4:00
25/Sep/1932 2:00 5:00
1/May/1933 2:00 4:00
1/Oct/1933 2:00 5:00
29/Apr/1934 2:00 4:00
30/Sep/1934 2:00 5:00
28/Apr/1935 2:00 4:00
29/Sep/1935 2:00 5:00
26/Apr/1936 2:00 4:00
27/Sep/1936 2:00 5:00
25/Apr/1937 2:00 4:00
26/Sep/1937 2:00 5:00
24/Apr/1938 2:00 4:00
25/Sep/1938 2:00 5:00
29/Sep/1940 0:00 4:00
30/Sep/1945 2:00 5:00
28/Apr/1946 2:00 4:00
29/Sep/1946 2:00 5:00
27/Apr/1947 0:00 4:00
28/Sep/1947 0:00 5:00
25/Apr/1948 0:00 4:00
26/Sep/1948 0:00 5:00
24/Apr/1949 2:00 4:00
25/Sep/1949 2:00 5:00
30/Apr/1950 2:00 4:00
24/Sep/1950 2:00 5:00
29/Apr/1951 2:00 4:00
30/Sep/1951 2:00 5:00
27/Apr/1952 2:00 4:00
28/Sep/1952 2:00 5:00
26/Apr/1953 2:00 4:00
27/Sep/1953 2:00 5:00
25/Apr/1954 2:00 4:00
26/Sep/1954 2:00 5:00
24/Apr/1955 2:00 4:00
25/Sep/1955 2:00 5:00
29/Apr/1956 2:00 4:00
30/Sep/1956 2:00 5:00
28/Apr/1957 2:00 4:00
27/Oct/1957 2:00 5:00
27/Apr/1958 2:00 4:00
26/Oct/1958 2:00 5:00
24/Apr/1960 2:00 4:00
30/Oct/1960 2:00 5:00
30/Apr/1961 2:00 4:00
29/Oct/1961 2:00 5:00
29/Apr/1962 2:00 4:00
28/Oct/1962 2:00 5:00
28/Apr/1963 2:00 4:00
27/Oct/1963 2:00 5:00
26/Apr/1964 2:00 4:00
25/Oct/1964 2:00 5:00
30/Apr/1967 2:00 TT#2

....

Time Table # 49
Before 1/Jan/1895 LMT
Begin Standard 75w00
1/Jan/1895 0:00 5:00
14/Apr/1918 2:00 4:00
31/Oct/1918 2:00 5:00
29/Sep/1940 0:00 4:00
30/Sep/1945 2:00 5:00
30/Apr/1946 2:00 4:00
30/Sep/1946 2:00 5:00
26/Apr/1953 2:00 4:00
27/Sep/1953 2:00 TT#1

....

Time Table # 50
Before 1/Jan/1895 LMT
Begin Standard 75w00
1/Jan/1895 0:00 5:00
14/Apr/1918 2:00 4:00
31/Oct/1918 2:00 5:00
3/May/1930 0:00 4:00
7/Sep/1930 0:00 5:00
2/May/1931 0:00 4:00
13/Sep/1931 0:00 5:00
1/May/1932 0:00 4:00
2/Oct/1932 0:00 5:00
30/Apr/1933 0:00 4:00
1/Oct/1933 0:00 5:00
29/Apr/1934 0:00 4:00
30/Sep/1934 0:00 5:00
28/Apr/1935 0:00 4:00
29/Sep/1935 0:00 5:00
29/Apr/1936 0:00 4:00
27/Sep/1936 0:00 5:00
25/Apr/1937 0:00 4:00
26/Sep/1937 0:00 5:00
24/Apr/1938 0:00 4:00
25/Sep/1938 0:00 5:00
30/Apr/1939 0:00 4:00
24/Sep/1939 0:00 5:00
28/Apr/1940 0:00 4:00
30/Sep/1945 2:00 5:00
28/Apr/1946 2:00 4:00
29/Sep/1946 2:00 5:00
27/Apr/1947 0:00 4:00
28/Sep/1947 0:00 5:00
25/Apr/1948 0:00 4:00
26/Sep/1948 0:00 5:00
24/Apr/1949 2:00 4:00
27/Nov/1949 2:00 5:00
30/Apr/1950 2:00 TT#2

....

Time Table # 51
Before 1/Jan/1895 LMT
Begin Standard 75w00
1/Jan/1895 0:00 5:00
14/Apr/1918 2:00 4:00
31/Oct/1918 2:00 5:00
21/Jun/1930 2:00 4:00
13/Sep/1930 2:00 5:00
21/Jun/1931 2:00 4:00
13/Sep/1931 2:00 5:00
19/Jun/1932 2:00 4:00
11/Sep/1932 2:00 5:00
18/Jun/1933 2:00 4:00
10/Sep/1933 2:00 5:00
14/Jul/1935 2:00 4:00
15/Sep/1935 2:00 5:00
29/Sep/1940 0:00 4:00
30/Sep/1945 2:00 5:00
28/Apr/1946 2:00 4:00
29/Sep/1946 2:00 5:00
27/Apr/1947 0:00 4:00
28/Sep/1947 0:00 5:00
25/Apr/1948 0:00 4:00
26/Sep/1948 0:00 5:00
24/Apr/1949 2:00 4:00
25/Sep/1949 2:00 5:00
30/Apr/1950 2:00 4:00
24/Sep/1950 2:00 5:00
29/Apr/1951 2:00 4:00
30/Sep/1951 2:00 5:00
27/Apr/1952 2:00 4:00
28/Sep/1952 2:00 5:00
26/Apr/1953 2:00 4:00
27/Sep/1953 2:00 5:00
25/Apr/1954 2:00 4:00
26/Sep/1954 2:00 5:00
24/Apr/1955 2:00 4:00
25/Sep/1955 2:00 5:00
29/Apr/1956 2:00 4:00
30/Sep/1956 2:00 5:00
28/Apr/1957 2:00 4:00
27/Oct/1957 2:00 5:00
27/Apr/1958 2:00 4:00
26/Oct/1958 2:00 5:00
26/Apr/1959 2:00 4:00
25/Oct/1959 2:00 5:00
24/Apr/1960 2:00 4:00
30/Oct/1960 2:00 5:00
30/Apr/1961 2:00 4:00
29/Oct/1961 2:00 5:00
29/Apr/1962 2:00 4:00
28/Oct/1962 2:00 5:00
28/Apr/1963 2:00 4:00
27/Oct/1963 2:00 5:00
26/Apr/1964 2:00 4:00
25/Oct/1964 2:00 5:00
25/Apr/1965 2:00 4:00
31/Oct/1965 2:00 5:00
24/Apr/1966 2:00 4:00
30/Oct/1966 2:00 5:00
28/Apr/1968 2:00 TT#2

....

Time Table # 52
Before 1/Jan/1895 LMT
Begin Standard 75w00
1/Jan/1895 0:00 5:00
14/Apr/1918 2:00 4:00
31/Oct/1918 2:00 5:00
26/Apr/1931 2:00 4:00
27/Sep/1931 2:00 5:00
2/Jul/1937 0:00 4:00
5/Sep/1937 0:00 5:00
2/Jul/1938 0:00 4:00
4/Sep/1938 0:00 5:00
2/Jul/1939 0:00 4:00
3/Sep/1939 0:00 5:00
2/Jul/1940 0:00 4:00
8/Sep/1940 0:00 5:00
29/Sep/1940 0:00 4:00
30/Sep/1945 2:00 5:00
28/Apr/1946 2:00 TT#2

....

Time Table # 53
Before 1/Jan/1895 LMT
Begin Standard 75w00
1/Jan/1895 0:00 5:00
14/Apr/1918 2:00 4:00
31/Oct/1918 2:00 5:00
29/Sep/1940 0:00 4:00
30/Sep/1945 2:00 5:00
28/Apr/1957 2:00 4:00
27/Oct/1957 2:00 TT#1

....

Time Table # 54
Before 1/Jan/1895 LMT
Begin Standard 75w00
1/Jan/1895 0:00 5:00
14/Apr/1918 2:00 4:00
31/Oct/1918 2:00 5:00
28/Apr/1940 2:00 4:00

```
30/Sep/1945  2:00  5:00
27/Apr/1947  0:00  4:00
28/Sep/1947  0:00  5:00
25/Apr/1948  0:00  4:00
26/Sep/1948  0:00  5:00
24/Apr/1949  2:00  4:00
25/Sep/1949  2:00  5:00
30/Apr/1950  2:00  4:00
24/Sep/1950  2:00  5:00
29/Apr/1951  2:00  4:00
30/Sep/1951  2:00  5:00
27/Apr/1952  2:00  4:00
28/Sep/1952  2:00  5:00
26/Apr/1953  2:00  4:00
27/Sep/1953  2:00  5:00
25/Apr/1954  2:00  4:00
26/Sep/1954  2:00  5:00
24/Apr/1955  2:00  4:00
25/Sep/1955  2:00  5:00
29/Apr/1956  2:00  4:00
30/Sep/1956  2:00  5:00
28/Apr/1957  2:00  4:00
27/Oct/1957  2:00  5:00
27/Apr/1958  2:00  4:00
26/Oct/1958  2:00  5:00
26/Apr/1959  2:00  4:00
25/Oct/1959  2:00  5:00
24/Apr/1960  2:00  4:00
30/Oct/1960  2:00  5:00
30/Apr/1961  2:00  4:00
29/Oct/1961  2:00  5:00
29/Apr/1962  2:00  4:00
28/Oct/1962  2:00  5:00
28/Apr/1963  2:00  4:00
27/Oct/1963  2:00  5:00
26/Apr/1964  2:00  4:00
25/Oct/1964  2:00  5:00
25/Apr/1965  2:00  4:00
31/Oct/1965  2:00  TT#1
......................
   Time Table # 55
 Before  1/Jan/1895 LMT
 Begin Standard   75w00
 1/Jan/1895  0:00  5:00
14/Apr/1918  2:00  4:00
31/Oct/1918  2:00  5:00
29/Sep/1940  0:00  4:00
30/Sep/1945  2:00  5:00
 4/May/1947  2:00  4:00
28/Sep/1947  2:00  5:00
26/Apr/1953  2:00  4:00
27/Sep/1953  2:00  TT#1
......................
   Time Table # 56
 Before  1/Jan/1895 LMT
 Begin Standard   75w00
 1/Jan/1895  0:00  5:00
14/Apr/1918  2:00  4:00
31/Oct/1918  2:00  5:00
29/Sep/1940  0:00  4:00
30/Sep/1945  2:00  5:00
28/Apr/1946  2:00  4:00
29/Sep/1946  2:00  5:00
27/Apr/1947  0:00  4:00
28/Sep/1947  0:00  5:00
25/Apr/1948  0:00  4:00
26/Sep/1948  0:00  5:00
24/Apr/1949  2:00  4:00
25/Sep/1949  2:00  5:00
30/Apr/1950  2:00  4:00
24/Sep/1950  2:00  5:00
29/Apr/1951  2:00  4:00
30/Sep/1951  2:00  5:00
27/Apr/1952  2:00  4:00
28/Sep/1952  2:00  5:00
26/Apr/1953  2:00  4:00
27/Sep/1953  2:00  5:00
25/Apr/1954  2:00  4:00
 5/Sep/1954  2:00  5:00
24/Apr/1955  2:00  4:00
 4/Sep/1955  2:00  5:00
29/Apr/1956  2:00  4:00
30/Sep/1956  2:00  5:00
28/Apr/1957  2:00  4:00
 1/Sep/1957  2:00  5:00
27/Apr/1958  2:00  4:00
31/Aug/1958  2:00  5:00
26/Apr/1959  2:00  4:00
 6/Sep/1959  2:00  5:00
24/Apr/1960  2:00  4:00
 4/Sep/1960  2:00  5:00
29/Apr/1962  2:00  4:00
 2/Sep/1962  2:00  5:00
28/Apr/1963  2:00  4:00
 1/Sep/1963  2:00  5:00
26/Apr/1964  2:00  TT#2
......................
   Time Table # 57
 Before  1/Jan/1895 LMT
 Begin Standard   75w00
 1/Jan/1895  0:00  5:00
14/Apr/1918  2:00  4:00
31/Oct/1918  2:00  5:00
28/Apr/1940  2:00  4:00
30/Sep/1945  2:00  5:00
28/Apr/1946  2:00  4:00
29/Sep/1946  2:00  5:00
27/Apr/1947  0:00  4:00
28/Sep/1947  0:00  5:00
25/Apr/1948  0:00  4:00
26/Sep/1948  0:00  5:00
30/Apr/1950  2:00  4:00
24/Sep/1950  2:00  5:00
26/Apr/1953  2:00  4:00
27/Sep/1953  2:00  5:00
25/Apr/1954  2:00  4:00
26/Sep/1954  2:00  5:00
24/Apr/1955  2:00  4:00
25/Sep/1955  2:00  5:00
29/Apr/1956  2:00  4:00
30/Sep/1956  2:00  5:00
28/Apr/1957  2:00  4:00
27/Oct/1957  2:00  5:00
26/Apr/1959  2:00  4:00
25/Oct/1959  2:00  5:00
24/Apr/1960  2:00  4:00
30/Oct/1960  2:00  5:00
29/Apr/1962  2:00  TT#2
......................
   Time Table # 58
 Before  1/Jan/1895 LMT
 Begin Standard   75w00
 1/Jan/1895  0:00  5:00
14/Apr/1918  2:00  4:00
31/Oct/1918  2:00  5:00
29/Sep/1940  0:00  4:00
30/Sep/1945  2:00  5:00
27/Apr/1947  0:00  4:00
28/Sep/1947  0:00  5:00
26/Apr/1953  2:00  4:00
27/Sep/1953  2:00  5:00
25/Apr/1954  2:00  4:00
26/Sep/1954  2:00  TT#1
......................
   Time Table # 59
 Before  1/Jan/1895 LMT
 Begin Standard   75w00
 1/Jan/1895  0:00  5:00
14/Apr/1918  2:00  4:00
31/Oct/1918  2:00  5:00
29/Sep/1940  0:00  4:00
30/Sep/1945  2:00  5:00
24/Apr/1949  2:00  4:00
25/Sep/1949  2:00  5:00
29/Apr/1951  2:00  4:00
30/Sep/1951  2:00  5:00
26/Apr/1953  2:00  4:00
27/Sep/1953  2:00  TT#1
......................
   Time Table # 60
 Before  1/Jan/1895 LMT
 Begin Standard   75w00
 1/Jan/1895  0:00  5:00
14/Apr/1918  2:00  4:00
31/Oct/1918  2:00  5:00
29/Sep/1940  0:00  4:00
30/Sep/1945  2:00  5:00
27/Apr/1947  0:00  TT#2
......................
   Time Table # 61
 Before  1/Jan/1895 LMT
 Begin Standard   75w00
 1/Jan/1895  0:00  5:00
14/Apr/1918  2:00  4:00
31/Oct/1918  2:00  5:00
29/Sep/1940  0:00  4:00
30/Sep/1945  2:00  5:00
 1/May/1947  2:00  4:00
28/Sep/1947  2:00  5:00
26/Apr/1953  2:00  4:00
27/Sep/1953  2:00  TT#1
......................
   Time Table # 62
 Before  1/Jan/1895 LMT
 Begin Standard   75w00
 1/Jan/1895  0:00  5:00
14/Apr/1918  2:00  4:00
31/Oct/1918  2:00  5:00
29/Sep/1940  0:00  4:00
30/Sep/1945  2:00  5:00
27/Apr/1947  0:00  4:00
28/Sep/1947  0:00  5:00
24/Apr/1949  2:00  4:00
25/Sep/1949  2:00  5:00
29/Apr/1951  2:00  4:00
30/Sep/1951  2:00  5:00
26/Apr/1953  2:00  4:00
27/Sep/1953  2:00  TT#1
......................
   Time Table # 63
 Before  1/Jan/1895 LMT
 Begin Standard   75w00
 1/Jan/1895  0:00  5:00
14/Apr/1918  2:00  4:00
31/Oct/1918  2:00  5:00
29/Apr/1934  2:00  4:00
30/Sep/1934  2:00  5:00
28/Apr/1935  2:00  4:00
29/Sep/1935  2:00  5:00
26/Apr/1936  2:00  4:00
27/Sep/1936  2:00  5:00
16/May/1937  2:00  4:00
26/Sep/1937  2:00  5:00
24/Apr/1938  2:00  4:00
25/Sep/1938  2:00  5:00
30/Apr/1939  2:00  4:00
10/Sep/1939  2:00  5:00
28/Apr/1940  2:00  4:00
30/Sep/1945  2:00  5:00
28/Apr/1946  2:00  4:00
29/Sep/1946  2:00  5:00
26/Apr/1953  2:00  4:00
27/Sep/1953  2:00  TT#1
......................
   Time Table # 64
 Before  1/Jan/1895 LMT
 Begin Standard   75w00
 1/Jan/1895  0:00  5:00
14/Apr/1918  2:00  4:00
31/Oct/1918  2:00  5:00
29/Sep/1940  0:00  4:00
30/Sep/1945  2:00  5:00
28/Apr/1957  2:00  4:00
27/Oct/1957  2:00  5:00
27/Apr/1958  2:00  4:00
27/Sep/1958  2:00  TT#1
......................
   Time Table # 65
 Before  1/Jan/1895 LMT
 Begin Standard   75w00
 1/Jan/1895  0:00  5:00
14/Apr/1918  2:00  4:00
31/Oct/1918  2:00  5:00
29/Sep/1940  0:00  4:00
30/Sep/1945  2:00  5:00
28/Apr/1957  2:00  4:00
27/Oct/1957  2:00  5:00
27/Apr/1958  2:00  4:00
26/Oct/1958  2:00  5:00
30/Apr/1961  2:00  4:00
29/Oct/1961  2:00  5:00
29/Apr/1962  2:00  4:00
28/Oct/1962  2:00  5:00
28/Apr/1963  2:00  4:00
27/Oct/1963  2:00  5:00
26/Apr/1964  2:00  4:00
25/Oct/1964  2:00  5:00
25/Apr/1965  2:00  4:00
31/Oct/1965  2:00  5:00
24/Apr/1966  2:00  4:00
30/Oct/1966  2:00  TT#1
......................
   Time Table # 66
 Before  1/Jan/1895 LMT
 Begin Standard   75w00
 1/Jan/1895  0:00  5:00
14/Apr/1918  2:00  4:00
31/Oct/1918  2:00  5:00
 2/Jul/1931  0:00  4:00
 1/Sep/1931  0:00  5:00
 1/Jul/1932  0:00  4:00
 1/Sep/1932  0:00  5:00
29/Sep/1940  0:00  4:00
30/Sep/1945  2:00  5:00
28/Apr/1946  2:00  TT#2
......................
   Time Table # 67
 Before  1/Jan/1895 LMT
 Begin Standard   75w00
 1/Jan/1895  0:00  5:00
14/Apr/1918  2:00  4:00
31/Oct/1918  2:00  5:00
 5/May/1930  0:00  4:00
 2/Sep/1930  0:00  5:00
 4/May/1931  0:00  4:00
 8/Sep/1931  0:00  5:00
 2/May/1932  0:00  4:00
 6/Sep/1932  0:00  5:00
 8/May/1933  0:00  4:00
 5/Sep/1933  0:00  5:00
 7/May/1934  0:00  4:00
 4/Sep/1934  0:00  5:00
 6/May/1935  0:00  4:00
 3/Sep/1935  0:00  5:00
 4/May/1936  0:00  4:00
 8/Sep/1936  0:00  5:00
 3/May/1937  0:00  4:00
 7/Sep/1937  0:00  5:00
 2/May/1938  0:00  4:00
 6/Sep/1938  0:00  5:00
 8/May/1939  0:00  4:00
 5/Sep/1939  0:00  5:00
 6/May/1940  0:00  4:00
 3/Sep/1940  0:00  5:00
29/Sep/1940  0:00  4:00
30/Sep/1945  2:00  5:00
28/Apr/1946  2:00  4:00
29/Sep/1946  2:00  5:00
27/Apr/1947  0:00  4:00
28/Sep/1947  0:00  5:00
25/Apr/1948  0:00  4:00
26/Sep/1948  0:00  5:00
24/Apr/1949  2:00  4:00
25/Sep/1949  2:00  5:00
30/Apr/1950  2:00  4:00
24/Sep/1950  2:00  5:00
29/Apr/1951  2:00  4:00
30/Sep/1951  2:00  5:00
27/Apr/1952  2:00  4:00
28/Sep/1952  2:00  5:00
26/Apr/1953  2:00  4:00
27/Sep/1953  2:00  5:00
25/Apr/1954  2:00  4:00
26/Sep/1954  2:00  5:00
24/Apr/1955  2:00  4:00
25/Sep/1955  2:00  5:00
29/Apr/1956  2:00  4:00
30/Sep/1956  2:00  5:00
26/Apr/1959  2:00  TT#2
......................
   Time Table # 68
 Before  1/Jan/1895 LMT
 Begin Standard   75w00
 1/Jan/1895  0:00  5:00
14/Apr/1918  2:00  4:00
31/Oct/1918  2:00  5:00
28/Apr/1940  2:00  4:00
30/Sep/1945  2:00  5:00
27/Apr/1947  0:00  4:00
28/Sep/1947  0:00  5:00
26/Apr/1953  2:00  4:00
27/Sep/1953  2:00  TT#1
......................
   Time Table # 69
 Before  1/Jan/1895 LMT
 Begin Standard   75w00
 1/Jan/1895  0:00  5:00
14/Apr/1918  2:00  4:00
31/Oct/1918  2:00  5:00
29/Sep/1940  0:00  4:00
30/Sep/1945  2:00  5:00
27/Apr/1947  0:00  4:00
28/Sep/1947  0:00  5:00
25/Apr/1948  0:00  4:00
26/Sep/1948  0:00  5:00
24/Apr/1949  2:00  4:00
25/Sep/1949  2:00  5:00
30/Apr/1950  2:00  4:00
 1/Oct/1950  2:00  5:00
29/Apr/1951  2:00  4:00
30/Sep/1951  2:00  5:00
27/Apr/1952  2:00  4:00
28/Sep/1952  2:00  5:00
26/Apr/1953  2:00  4:00
27/Sep/1953  2:00  5:00
25/Apr/1954  2:00  4:00
26/Sep/1954  2:00  5:00
24/Apr/1955  2:00  4:00
25/Sep/1955  2:00  5:00
29/Apr/1956  2:00  4:00
30/Sep/1956  2:00  5:00
28/Apr/1957  2:00  4:00
27/Oct/1957  2:00  5:00
27/Apr/1958  2:00  4:00
26/Oct/1958  2:00  5:00
26/Apr/1959  2:00  4:00
27/Sep/1959  2:00  5:00
24/Apr/1960  2:00  TT#2
......................
   Time Table # 70
 Before  1/Jan/1895 LMT
 Begin Standard   75w00
 1/Jan/1895  0:00  5:00
14/Apr/1918  2:00  4:00
31/Oct/1918  2:00  5:00
 5/May/1935  2:00  4:00
14/Sep/1935  2:00  5:00
 3/May/1936  2:00  4:00
12/Sep/1936  2:00  5:00
16/May/1937  2:00  4:00
11/Sep/1937  2:00  5:00
24/Apr/1938  2:00  4:00
11/Sep/1938  2:00  5:00
30/Apr/1939  2:00  4:00
10/Sep/1939  2:00  5:00
27/Apr/1940  2:00  4:00
30/Sep/1945  2:00  5:00
31/Mar/1946  2:00  4:00
29/Sep/1946  2:00  5:00
27/Apr/1947  0:00  TT#2
......................
   Time Table # 71
 Before  1/Jan/1895 LMT
 Begin Standard   75w00
 1/Jan/1895  0:00  5:00
14/Apr/1918  2:00  4:00
31/Oct/1918  2:00  5:00
27/Apr/1930  0:00  4:00
28/Sep/1930  0:00  5:00
17/May/1931  0:00  4:00
13/Sep/1931  0:00  5:00
 1/May/1932  0:00  4:00
25/Sep/1932  0:00  5:00
14/May/1933  0:00  4:00
10/Sep/1933  0:00  5:00
 6/May/1934  0:00  4:00
 4/Sep/1934  0:00  5:00
11/May/1935  0:00  4:00
 3/Sep/1935  0:00  5:00
10/May/1936  0:00  4:00
 8/Sep/1936  0:00  5:00
 9/May/1937  0:00  4:00
 7/Sep/1937  0:00  5:00
 1/May/1938  0:00  4:00
 6/Sep/1938  0:00  5:00
30/Apr/1939  0:00  4:00
 5/Sep/1939  0:00  5:00
27/Apr/1940  0:00  4:00
30/Sep/1945  2:00  5:00
28/Apr/1946  2:00  4:00
14/Sep/1946  2:00  5:00
27/Apr/1947  0:00  4:00
28/Sep/1947  0:00  5:00
25/Apr/1948  0:00  4:00
26/Sep/1948  0:00  5:00
24/Apr/1949  2:00  4:00
25/Sep/1949  2:00  5:00
30/Apr/1950  2:00  4:00
24/Sep/1950  2:00  5:00
29/Apr/1951  2:00  4:00
30/Sep/1951  2:00  5:00
27/Apr/1952  2:00  4:00
28/Sep/1952  2:00  5:00
26/Apr/1953  2:00  4:00
27/Sep/1953  2:00  5:00
25/Apr/1954  2:00  4:00
26/Sep/1954  2:00  5:00
24/Apr/1955  2:00  4:00
25/Sep/1955  2:00  5:00
29/Apr/1956  2:00  4:00
30/Sep/1956  2:00  5:00
28/Apr/1957  2:00  4:00
29/Sep/1957  2:00  5:00
27/Apr/1958  2:00  4:00
26/Oct/1958  2:00  5:00
26/Apr/1959  2:00  4:00
27/Sep/1959  2:00  5:00
24/Apr/1960  2:00  TT#2
......................
   Time Table # 72
 Before  1/Jan/1895 LMT
 Begin Standard   75w00
 1/Jan/1895  0:00  5:00
14/Apr/1918  2:00  4:00
31/Oct/1918  2:00  5:00
28/Apr/1940  2:00  4:00
30/Sep/1945  2:00  5:00
28/Apr/1946  2:00  4:00
29/Sep/1946  2:00  5:00
27/Apr/1947  0:00  4:00
28/Sep/1947  0:00  5:00
25/Apr/1948  0:00  4:00
26/Sep/1948  0:00  5:00
24/Apr/1949  2:00  4:00
25/Sep/1949  2:00  5:00
30/Apr/1950  2:00  4:00
24/Sep/1950  2:00  5:00
26/Apr/1953  2:00  4:00
27/Sep/1953  2:00  5:00
25/Apr/1954  2:00  4:00
26/Sep/1954  2:00  5:00
29/Apr/1956  2:00  4:00
30/Sep/1956  2:00  5:00
27/Apr/1958  2:00  4:00
26/Oct/1958  2:00  5:00
26/Apr/1959  2:00  4:00
25/Oct/1959  2:00  5:00
30/Apr/1961  2:00  4:00
29/Oct/1961  2:00  5:00
26/Apr/1970  2:00  TT#2
......................
   Time Table # 73
 Before  1/Jan/1895 LMT
 Begin Standard   75w00
 1/Jan/1895  0:00  5:00
14/Apr/1918  2:00  4:00
31/Oct/1918  2:00  5:00
29/Sep/1940  0:00  4:00
30/Sep/1945  2:00  5:00
27/Apr/1947  0:00  4:00
28/Sep/1947  0:00  5:00
27/Apr/1952  2:00  4:00
28/Sep/1952  2:00  5:00
26/Apr/1953  2:00  4:00
27/Sep/1953  2:00  TT#1
......................
   Time Table # 74
 Before  1/Jan/1895 LMT
 Begin Standard   75w00
 1/Jan/1895  0:00  5:00
 4/Jun/1916  2:00  4:00
13/Aug/1916  2:00  5:00
14/Apr/1918  2:00  4:00
31/Oct/1918  2:00  5:00
17/Jun/1929  2:00  4:00
 3/Sep/1929  2:00  5:00
 9/Jun/1930  0:00  4:00
 2/Sep/1930  0:00  5:00
15/Jun/1931  0:00  4:00
 8/Sep/1931  0:00  5:00
30/May/1932  0:00  4:00
18/Sep/1932  0:00  5:00
 4/Jun/1933  0:00  4:00
17/Sep/1933  0:00  5:00
 6/May/1934  0:00  4:00
16/Sep/1934  0:00  5:00
 5/May/1935  0:00  4:00
15/Sep/1935  0:00  5:00
 3/May/1936  0:00  4:00
13/Sep/1936  0:00  5:00
 2/May/1937  0:00  4:00
12/Sep/1937  0:00  5:00
25/Apr/1938  0:00  4:00
12/Sep/1938  0:00  5:00
 1/May/1939  0:00  4:00
10/Sep/1939  0:00  5:00
29/Apr/1940  0:00  4:00
30/Sep/1945  2:00  5:00
28/Apr/1946  2:00  4:00
29/Sep/1946  2:00  5:00
27/Apr/1947  0:00  4:00
28/Sep/1947  0:00  5:00
25/Apr/1948  0:00  4:00
26/Sep/1948  0:00  5:00
24/Apr/1949  0:00  4:00
27/Nov/1949  0:00  5:00
30/Apr/1950  2:00  4:00
26/Nov/1950  2:00  TT#2
......................
   Time Table # 75
 Before  1/Jan/1895 LMT
 Begin Standard   75w00
 1/Jan/1895  0:00  5:00
14/Apr/1918  2:00  4:00
31/Oct/1918  2:00  5:00
31/May/1931  2:00  4:00
 4/Oct/1931  2:00  5:00
29/May/1932  2:00  4:00
 2/Oct/1932  2:00  5:00
 4/Jun/1933  2:00  4:00
10/Sep/1933  2:00  5:00
 4/Jul/1937  0:00  4:00
12/Sep/1937  0:00  5:00
 3/Jul/1938  0:00  4:00
 4/Sep/1938  0:00  5:00
 2/Jul/1939  0:00  4:00
 3/Sep/1939  0:00  5:00
 4/Jul/1940  0:00  4:00
30/Sep/1945  2:00  5:00
28/Apr/1946  2:00  4:00
29/Sep/1946  2:00  5:00
27/Apr/1947  0:00  4:00
28/Sep/1947  0:00  5:00
25/Apr/1948  0:00  4:00
26/Sep/1948  0:00  5:00
```

26/Apr/1953 2:00 4:00
27/Sep/1953 2:00 5:00
25/Apr/1954 2:00 4:00
26/Sep/1954 2:00 TT#1
....

Time Table # 76
Before 1/Jan/1895 LMT
Begin Standard 75w00
1/Jan/1895 0:00 5:00
14/Apr/1918 2:00 4:00
31/Oct/1918 2:00 5:00
26/Apr/1931 0:00 4:00
27/Sep/1931 0:00 5:00
2/May/1932 0:00 4:00
26/Sep/1932 0:00 5:00
8/May/1933 0:00 4:00
25/Sep/1933 0:00 5:00
7/May/1934 0:00 4:00
1/Oct/1934 0:00 5:00
6/May/1935 0:00 4:00
30/Sep/1935 0:00 5:00
26/Apr/1936 0:00 4:00
28/Sep/1936 0:00 5:00
24/Apr/1937 0:00 4:00
27/Sep/1937 0:00 5:00
2/May/1938 0:00 4:00
26/Sep/1938 0:00 5:00
8/May/1939 0:00 4:00
25/Sep/1939 0:00 5:00
6/May/1940 0:00 4:00
30/Sep/1945 2:00 5:00
5/May/1946 2:00 4:00
30/Sep/1946 2:00 5:00
20/Apr/1947 2:00 4:00
4/Oct/1947 2:00 5:00
25/Apr/1948 0:00 4:00
26/Sep/1948 0:00 5:00
24/Apr/1949 2:00 4:00
25/Sep/1949 2:00 5:00
30/Apr/1950 2:00 4:00
24/Sep/1950 2:00 5:00
29/Apr/1951 2:00 4:00
30/Sep/1951 2:00 5:00
27/Apr/1952 2:00 4:00
28/Sep/1952 2:00 5:00
26/Apr/1953 2:00 4:00
27/Sep/1953 2:00 5:00
25/Apr/1954 2:00 4:00
26/Sep/1954 2:00 5:00
30/Apr/1955 2:00 4:00
24/Sep/1955 2:00 5:00
29/Apr/1956 2:00 TT#2
....

Time Table # 77
Before 1/Jan/1895 LMT
Begin Standard 75w00
1/Jan/1895 0:00 5:00
14/Apr/1918 2:00 4:00
31/Oct/1918 2:00 5:00
29/Sep/1940 0:00 4:00
30/Sep/1945 2:00 5:00
27/Apr/1947 0:00 4:00
28/Sep/1947 0:00 5:00
25/Apr/1948 0:00 4:00
26/Sep/1948 0:00 5:00
24/Apr/1949 2:00 4:00
25/Sep/1949 2:00 5:00
29/Apr/1951 2:00 TT#2
....

Time Table # 78
Before 1/Jan/1895 LMT
Begin Standard 75w00
1/Jan/1895 0:00 5:00
14/Apr/1918 2:00 4:00
31/Oct/1918 2:00 5:00
1/Jul/1930 2:00 4:00
1/Sep/1930 2:00 5:00
29/Sep/1940 0:00 4:00
30/Sep/1945 2:00 5:00
28/Apr/1946 2:00 TT#2
....

Time Table # 79
Before 1/Jan/1895 LMT
Begin Standard 75w00
1/Jan/1895 0:00 5:00
14/Apr/1918 2:00 4:00
31/Oct/1918 2:00 5:00
29/Sep/1940 0:00 4:00
30/Sep/1945 2:00 5:00
28/Apr/1946 2:00 4:00
29/Sep/1946 2:00 5:00
27/Apr/1947 0:00 4:00
28/Sep/1947 0:00 5:00
25/Apr/1948 0:00 4:00
26/Sep/1948 0:00 5:00
24/Apr/1949 2:00 4:00
25/Sep/1949 2:00 5:00
30/Apr/1950 2:00 4:00
24/Sep/1950 2:00 5:00
29/Apr/1951 2:00 4:00
30/Sep/1951 2:00 5:00
27/Apr/1952 2:00 4:00
28/Sep/1952 2:00 5:00
26/Apr/1953 2:00 4:00
27/Sep/1953 2:00 5:00
25/Apr/1954 2:00 4:00
26/Sep/1954 2:00 5:00
24/Apr/1955 2:00 4:00
25/Sep/1955 2:00 5:00
29/Apr/1956 2:00 4:00
30/Sep/1956 2:00 5:00
28/Apr/1957 2:00 4:00
27/Oct/1957 2:00 5:00
27/Apr/1958 2:00 4:00
26/Oct/1958 2:00 5:00
26/Apr/1959 2:00 4:00
25/Oct/1959 2:00 5:00
24/Apr/1960 2:00 4:00
30/Oct/1960 2:00 5:00
30/Apr/1961 2:00 4:00
29/Oct/1961 2:00 5:00
29/Apr/1962 2:00 4:00
28/Oct/1962 2:00 5:00
28/Apr/1963 2:00 4:00
27/Oct/1963 2:00 5:00
26/Apr/1964 2:00 4:00
25/Oct/1964 2:00 5:00
25/Apr/1965 2:00 4:00
31/Oct/1965 2:00 TT#1
....

Time Table # 80
Before 1/Jan/1895 LMT
Begin Standard 75w00
1/Jan/1895 0:00 5:00
14/Apr/1918 2:00 4:00
31/Oct/1918 2:00 5:00
4/Jul/1937 2:00 4:00
29/Aug/1937 2:00 5:00
15/Apr/1946 2:00 4:00
15/Sep/1946 2:00 5:00
27/Apr/1947 0:00 4:00
28/Sep/1947 0:00 5:00
25/Apr/1948 0:00 4:00
26/Sep/1948 0:00 5:00
24/Apr/1949 2:00 4:00
30/Sep/1949 2:00 TT#2
....

Time Table # 81
Before 1/Jan/1895 LMT
Begin Standard 75w00
1/Jan/1895 0:00 5:00
14/Apr/1918 2:00 4:00
31/Oct/1918 2:00 5:00
29/Sep/1940 0:00 4:00
30/Sep/1945 2:00 5:00
27/Apr/1947 0:00 4:00
28/Sep/1947 0:00 5:00
25/Apr/1948 0:00 4:00
26/Sep/1948 0:00 5:00
24/Apr/1949 2:00 4:00
25/Sep/1949 2:00 5:00
30/Apr/1950 2:00 4:00
24/Sep/1950 2:00 5:00
29/Apr/1951 2:00 4:00
30/Sep/1951 2:00 5:00
27/Apr/1952 2:00 4:00
28/Sep/1952 2:00 5:00
26/Apr/1953 2:00 4:00
27/Sep/1953 2:00 5:00
25/Apr/1954 2:00 4:00
26/Sep/1954 2:00 5:00
24/Apr/1955 2:00 4:00
25/Sep/1955 2:00 5:00
29/Apr/1956 2:00 4:00
30/Sep/1956 2:00 5:00
28/Apr/1957 2:00 4:00
27/Oct/1957 2:00 5:00
27/Apr/1958 2:00 4:00
27/Sep/1958 2:00 5:00
26/Apr/1959 2:00 4:00
27/Sep/1959 2:00 5:00
24/Apr/1960 2:00 TT#2
....

Time Table # 82
Before 1/Jan/1895 LMT
Begin Standard 75w00
1/Jan/1895 0:00 5:00
14/Apr/1918 2:00 4:00
31/Oct/1918 2:00 5:00
29/Sep/1940 0:00 4:00
30/Sep/1945 2:00 5:00
27/Apr/1947 2:00 4:00
26/Oct/1947 2:00 5:00
26/Apr/1953 2:00 4:00
27/Sep/1953 2:00 TT#1
....

Time Table # 83
Before 1/Jan/1895 LMT
Begin Standard 75w00
1/Jan/1895 0:00 5:00
14/Apr/1918 2:00 4:00
31/Oct/1918 2:00 5:00
29/Sep/1940 0:00 4:00
30/Sep/1945 2:00 5:00
27/Apr/1947 2:00 4:00
1/Oct/1947 2:00 5:00
26/Apr/1953 2:00 4:00
27/Sep/1953 2:00 TT#1
....

Time Table # 84
Before 1/Jan/1895 LMT
Begin Standard 75w00
1/Jan/1895 0:00 5:00
14/Apr/1918 2:00 4:00
31/Oct/1918 2:00 5:00
29/Sep/1940 0:00 4:00
30/Sep/1945 2:00 5:00
28/Apr/1946 2:00 4:00
29/Sep/1946 2:00 5:00
27/Apr/1947 0:00 4:00
28/Sep/1947 0:00 5:00
25/Apr/1948 0:00 4:00
26/Sep/1948 0:00 5:00
24/Apr/1949 2:00 4:00
25/Sep/1949 2:00 5:00
30/Apr/1950 2:00 4:00
24/Sep/1950 2:00 5:00
29/Apr/1951 2:00 4:00
30/Sep/1951 2:00 5:00
27/Apr/1952 2:00 4:00
28/Sep/1952 2:00 5:00
26/Apr/1953 2:00 4:00
27/Sep/1953 2:00 5:00
25/Apr/1954 2:00 4:00
26/Sep/1954 2:00 TT#1
....

Time Table # 85
Before 1/Jan/1895 LMT
Begin Standard 75w00
1/Jan/1895 0:00 5:00
14/Apr/1918 2:00 4:00
31/Oct/1918 2:00 5:00
29/Sep/1940 0:00 4:00
30/Sep/1945 2:00 5:00
1/May/1946 2:00 4:00
30/Sep/1946 2:00 5:00
27/Apr/1947 0:00 4:00
28/Sep/1947 0:00 5:00
26/Apr/1953 2:00 4:00
27/Sep/1953 2:00 TT#1
....

Time Table # 86
Before 1/Jan/1895 LMT
Begin Standard 75w00
1/Jan/1895 0:00 5:00
14/Apr/1918 2:00 4:00
31/Oct/1918 2:00 5:00
29/Sep/1940 0:00 4:00
30/Sep/1945 2:00 5:00
26/Apr/1970 2:00 TT#2
....

Time Table # 87
Before 1/Jan/1895 LMT
Begin Standard 75w00
1/Jan/1895 0:00 5:00
14/Apr/1918 2:00 4:00
31/Oct/1918 2:00 5:00
16/May/1932 0:00 4:00
6/Sep/1932 0:00 5:00
16/May/1933 0:00 4:00
5/Sep/1933 0:00 5:00
16/May/1934 0:00 4:00
4/Sep/1934 0:00 5:00
16/May/1935 0:00 4:00
3/Sep/1935 0:00 5:00
2/Jul/1936 0:00 4:00
2/Sep/1936 0:00 5:00
2/Jul/1937 0:00 4:00
2/Sep/1937 0:00 5:00
2/Jul/1938 0:00 4:00
2/Sep/1938 0:00 5:00
2/Jul/1939 0:00 4:00
2/Sep/1939 0:00 5:00
2/Jul/1940 0:00 4:00
30/Sep/1945 2:00 TT#2
....

Time Table # 88
Before 1/Jan/1895 LMT
Begin Standard 75w00
1/Jan/1895 0:00 5:00
14/Apr/1918 2:00 4:00
31/Oct/1918 2:00 5:00
25/Apr/1937 0:00 4:00
5/Sep/1937 0:00 5:00
24/Apr/1938 0:00 4:00
4/Sep/1938 0:00 5:00
30/Apr/1939 0:00 4:00
3/Sep/1939 0:00 5:00
5/May/1940 0:00 4:00
30/Sep/1945 2:00 5:00
25/Apr/1948 0:00 4:00
26/Sep/1948 0:00 5:00
24/Apr/1949 2:00 4:00
30/Sep/1949 2:00 5:00
29/Apr/1951 2:00 4:00
30/Sep/1951 2:00 5:00
26/Apr/1953 2:00 4:00
27/Sep/1953 2:00 5:00
24/Apr/1955 2:00 4:00
25/Sep/1955 2:00 TT#1
....

Time Table # 89
Before 1/Jan/1895 LMT
Begin Standard 75w00
1/Jan/1895 0:00 5:00
14/Apr/1918 2:00 4:00
31/Oct/1918 2:00 5:00
28/Apr/1940 2:00 4:00
30/Sep/1945 2:00 5:00
28/Apr/1946 2:00 4:00
29/Sep/1946 2:00 5:00
20/Apr/1947 2:00 4:00
27/Sep/1947 2:00 5:00
25/Apr/1948 0:00 4:00
26/Sep/1948 0:00 5:00
24/Apr/1949 2:00 4:00
25/Sep/1949 2:00 5:00
30/Apr/1950 2:00 4:00
24/Sep/1950 2:00 5:00
29/Apr/1951 2:00 4:00
30/Sep/1951 2:00 5:00
27/Apr/1952 2:00 4:00
28/Sep/1952 2:00 5:00
26/Apr/1953 2:00 4:00
27/Sep/1953 2:00 5:00
25/Apr/1954 2:00 4:00
26/Sep/1954 2:00 5:00
24/Apr/1955 2:00 4:00
25/Sep/1955 2:00 5:00
29/Apr/1956 2:00 4:00
30/Sep/1956 2:00 5:00
28/Apr/1957 2:00 4:00
27/Oct/1957 2:00 5:00
27/Apr/1958 2:00 4:00
27/Sep/1958 2:00 5:00
26/Apr/1959 2:00 4:00
25/Oct/1959 2:00 5:00
24/Apr/1960 2:00 4:00
30/Oct/1960 2:00 5:00
30/Apr/1961 2:00 4:00
29/Oct/1961 2:00 5:00
26/Apr/1964 2:00 4:00
25/Oct/1964 2:00 5:00
24/Apr/1966 2:00 TT#2
....

Time Table # 90
Before 1/Jan/1895 LMT
Begin Standard 75w00
1/Jan/1895 0:00 5:00
14/Apr/1918 2:00 4:00
31/Oct/1918 2:00 5:00
13/Jun/1921 0:00 4:00
5/Sep/1921 0:00 5:00
12/Jun/1922 0:00 4:00
4/Sep/1922 0:00 5:00
9/Jun/1924 0:00 4:00
8/Sep/1924 0:00 5:00
8/Jun/1925 0:00 4:00
7/Sep/1925 0:00 5:00
11/Jun/1928 0:00 4:00
3/Sep/1928 0:00 5:00
10/Jun/1929 0:00 4:00
12/Sep/1929 0:00 5:00
15/Jun/1930 0:00 4:00
7/Sep/1930 0:00 5:00
15/Jun/1931 0:00 4:00
7/Sep/1931 0:00 5:00
9/May/1932 0:00 4:00
26/Sep/1932 0:00 5:00
22/May/1933 0:00 4:00
25/Sep/1933 0:00 5:00
29/Apr/1934 0:00 4:00
30/Sep/1934 0:00 5:00
28/Apr/1935 0:00 4:00
29/Sep/1935 0:00 5:00
26/Apr/1936 0:00 4:00
27/Sep/1936 0:00 5:00
25/Apr/1937 0:00 4:00
26/Sep/1937 0:00 5:00
24/Apr/1938 0:00 4:00
25/Sep/1938 0:00 5:00
30/Apr/1939 0:00 4:00
24/Sep/1939 0:00 5:00
28/Apr/1940 0:00 4:00
30/Sep/1945 2:00 TT#2
....

Time Table # 91
Before 1/Jan/1895 LMT
Begin Standard 75w00
1/Jan/1895 0:00 5:00
14/Apr/1918 2:00 4:00
31/Oct/1918 2:00 5:00
25/Apr/1937 2:00 TT#2
....

Time Table # 92
Before 1/Jan/1895 LMT
Begin Standard 75w00
1/Jan/1895 0:00 5:00
14/Apr/1918 2:00 4:00
31/Oct/1918 2:00 5:00
2/Jul/1933 0:00 4:00
1/Sep/1933 0:00 5:00
29/Sep/1940 0:00 4:00
30/Sep/1945 2:00 5:00
28/Apr/1946 2:00 TT#2
....

Time Table # 93
Before 1/Jan/1895 LMT
Begin Standard 75w00
1/Jan/1895 0:00 5:00
14/Apr/1918 2:00 4:00
31/Oct/1918 2:00 5:00
29/Sep/1940 0:00 4:00
30/Sep/1945 2:00 5:00
30/Apr/1950 2:00 4:00
24/Sep/1950 2:00 5:00
29/Apr/1951 2:00 4:00
30/Sep/1951 2:00 5:00
27/Apr/1952 2:00 4:00
28/Sep/1952 2:00 5:00
26/Apr/1953 2:00 4:00
27/Sep/1953 2:00 5:00
25/Apr/1954 2:00 4:00
26/Sep/1954 2:00 5:00
24/Apr/1955 2:00 4:00
25/Sep/1955 2:00 5:00
29/Apr/1956 2:00 4:00
30/Sep/1956 2:00 5:00
24/Apr/1960 2:00 TT#2
....

Time Table # 94
Before 1/Jan/1895 LMT
Begin Standard 75w00
1/Jan/1895 0:00 5:00
14/Apr/1918 2:00 4:00
31/Oct/1918 2:00 5:00
28/Apr/1929 2:00 4:00
29/Sep/1929 0:00 5:00
27/Apr/1930 2:00 4:00
28/Sep/1930 2:00 5:00
26/Apr/1931 2:00 4:00
27/Sep/1931 2:00 5:00
1/May/1932 2:00 4:00
25/Sep/1932 2:00 5:00
30/Apr/1933 2:00 4:00
24/Sep/1933 2:00 5:00
29/Apr/1934 0:00 4:00
30/Sep/1934 0:00 5:00
28/Apr/1935 0:00 4:00
29/Sep/1935 0:00 5:00
26/Apr/1936 0:00 4:00
27/Sep/1936 0:00 5:00
25/Apr/1937 0:00 4:00
26/Sep/1937 0:00 5:00
24/Apr/1938 0:00 4:00
25/Sep/1938 0:00 5:00
30/Apr/1939 0:00 4:00
24/Sep/1939 0:00 5:00
28/Apr/1940 0:00 4:00
30/Sep/1945 2:00 TT#2
....

Time Table # 95
Before 1/Jan/1888 LMT
Begin Standard 75w00
1/Jan/1888 0:00 5:00
14/Apr/1918 2:00 4:00
31/Oct/1918 2:00 5:00
2/May/1920 0:00 4:00
23/Oct/1920 0:00 5:00
1/May/1921 0:00 4:00
2/Oct/1921 0:00 5:00
30/Apr/1922 0:00 4:00
1/Oct/1922 0:00 5:00
13/May/1923 0:00 4:00
30/Sep/1923 0:00 5:00
18/May/1924 0:00 4:00
28/Sep/1924 0:00 5:00
3/May/1925 2:00 4:00
27/Sep/1925 2:00 5:00
2/May/1926 0:00 4:00
26/Sep/1926 0:00 5:00
1/May/1927 2:00 4:00
25/Sep/1927 2:00 5:00
29/Apr/1928 2:00 4:00
30/Sep/1928 2:00 5:00
28/Apr/1929 0:00 4:00
29/Sep/1929 0:00 5:00
27/Apr/1930 2:00 4:00
28/Sep/1930 2:00 5:00
26/Apr/1931 2:00 4:00
27/Sep/1931 2:00 5:00
1/May/1932 0:00 4:00
25/Sep/1932 0:00 5:00
30/Apr/1933 0:00 4:00
1/Oct/1933 0:00 5:00
29/Apr/1934 0:00 4:00
30/Sep/1934 0:00 5:00
28/Apr/1935 0:00 4:00
29/Sep/1935 0:00 5:00
26/Apr/1936 0:00 4:00
27/Sep/1936 0:00 5:00
25/Apr/1937 0:00 4:00
26/Sep/1937 0:00 5:00
24/Apr/1938 0:00 4:00
25/Sep/1938 0:00 5:00
30/Apr/1939 0:00 4:00
1/Oct/1939 0:00 5:00
28/Apr/1940 0:00 4:00
30/Sep/1945 2:00 5:00
28/Apr/1946 2:00 4:00
29/Sep/1946 2:00 5:00
27/Apr/1947 0:00 4:00
28/Sep/1947 0:00 5:00
25/Apr/1948 0:00 4:00
26/Sep/1948 0:00 5:00
24/Apr/1949 2:00 4:00
27/Nov/1949 2:00 TT#2
....

Time Table # 96
Before 1/Jan/1895 LMT
Begin Standard 75w00
1/Jan/1895 0:00 5:00
14/Apr/1918 2:00 4:00
31/Oct/1918 2:00 5:00
29/Sep/1940 0:00 4:00
30/Sep/1945 2:00 5:00
27/Apr/1947 0:00 4:00
28/Sep/1947 0:00 5:00
25/Apr/1948 0:00 4:00
26/Sep/1948 0:00 5:00
24/Apr/1949 2:00 4:00
25/Sep/1949 2:00 5:00
30/Apr/1950 2:00 4:00
24/Sep/1950 2:00 5:00
29/Apr/1951 2:00 4:00
30/Sep/1951 2:00 5:00
27/Apr/1952 2:00 4:00
28/Sep/1952 2:00 5:00
26/Apr/1953 2:00 4:00
27/Sep/1953 2:00 5:00
25/Apr/1954 2:00 4:00
26/Sep/1954 2:00 5:00
24/Apr/1955 2:00 4:00
25/Sep/1955 2:00 5:00
29/Apr/1956 2:00 4:00
30/Sep/1956 2:00 5:00
28/Apr/1957 2:00 4:00
27/Oct/1957 2:00 5:00
27/Apr/1958 2:00 4:00
26/Oct/1958 2:00 5:00
28/Apr/1963 2:00 TT#2
....

Time Table # 97
Before 1/Jan/1895 LMT
Begin Standard 75w00
1/Jan/1895 0:00 5:00
14/Apr/1918 2:00 4:00
31/Oct/1918 2:00 5:00
29/Sep/1940 0:00 4:00
30/Sep/1945 2:00 5:00
28/Apr/1946 2:00 4:00
29/Sep/1946 2:00 5:00
27/Apr/1947 0:00 4:00
28/Sep/1947 0:00 5:00
25/Apr/1948 0:00 4:00

26/Sep/1948 0:00 5:00
24/Apr/1949 2:00 4:00
25/Sep/1949 2:00 5:00
29/Apr/1951 2:00 4:00
30/Sep/1951 2:00 5:00
26/Apr/1953 2:00 4:00
27/Sep/1953 2:00 TT#1
....
Time Table # 98
Before 1/Jan/1895 LMT
Begin Standard 75w00
1/Jan/1895 0:00 5:00
14/Apr/1918 2:00 4:00
31/Oct/1918 2:00 5:00
9/May/1936 2:00 4:00
12/Sep/1936 2:00 5:00
29/Sep/1940 0:00 4:00
30/Sep/1945 2:00 5:00
28/Apr/1946 2:00 4:00
29/Sep/1946 2:00 5:00
25/Apr/1948 0:00 TT#2
....
Time Table # 99
Before 1/Jan/1895 LMT
Begin Standard 75w00
1/Jan/1895 0:00 5:00
14/Apr/1918 2:00 4:00
31/Oct/1918 2:00 5:00
29/Sep/1940 0:00 4:00
30/Sep/1945 2:00 5:00
2/Jun/1946 2:00 4:00
1/Sep/1946 2:00 5:00
27/Apr/1947 0:00 TT#2
....
Time Table # 100
Before 1/Jan/1895 LMT
Begin Standard 75w00
1/Jan/1895 0:00 5:00
14/Apr/1918 2:00 4:00
31/Oct/1918 2:00 5:00
29/Sep/1940 0:00 4:00
30/Sep/1945 2:00 5:00
28/Apr/1946 2:00 4:00
29/Sep/1946 2:00 5:00
25/Apr/1948 0:00 4:00
26/Sep/1948 0:00 5:00
24/Apr/1949 2:00 4:00
25/Sep/1949 2:00 5:00
29/Apr/1951 2:00 4:00
30/Sep/1951 2:00 5:00
26/Apr/1953 2:00 4:00
27/Sep/1953 2:00 TT#1
....
Time Table # 101
Before 1/Jan/1895 LMT
Begin Standard 75w00
1/Jan/1895 0:00 5:00
14/Apr/1918 2:00 4:00
31/Oct/1918 2:00 5:00
12/Jun/1929 0:00 4:00
2/Sep/1929 0:00 5:00
15/Jun/1930 0:00 4:00
1/Sep/1930 0:00 5:00
14/Jun/1931 0:00 4:00
7/Sep/1931 0:00 5:00
12/Jun/1932 0:00 4:00
5/Sep/1932 0:00 5:00
11/Jun/1933 0:00 4:00
4/Sep/1933 0:00 5:00
16/May/1936 0:00 4:00
7/Sep/1936 0:00 5:00
29/May/1937 0:00 4:00
6/Sep/1937 0:00 5:00
15/Jun/1938 0:00 4:00
6/Sep/1938 0:00 5:00
7/May/1939 0:00 4:00
24/Sep/1939 0:00 5:00
5/May/1940 0:00 4:00
30/Sep/1945 0:00 TT#2
....
Time Table # 102
Before 1/Jan/1895 LMT
Begin Standard 75w00
1/Jan/1895 0:00 5:00
14/Apr/1918 2:00 4:00
31/Oct/1918 2:00 5:00
24/Apr/1938 0:00 4:00
4/Sep/1938 0:00 5:00
30/Apr/1939 0:00 4:00
1/Oct/1939 0:00 5:00
5/May/1940 0:00 4:00
30/Sep/1945 2:00 5:00
28/Apr/1946 2:00 4:00
29/Sep/1946 2:00 5:00
27/Apr/1947 0:00 4:00
28/Sep/1947 0:00 5:00
25/Apr/1948 0:00 4:00
26/Sep/1948 0:00 5:00
24/Apr/1949 2:00 4:00
25/Sep/1949 2:00 5:00
30/Apr/1950 2:00 4:00
24/Sep/1950 2:00 5:00
29/Apr/1951 2:00 4:00
30/Sep/1951 2:00 5:00
26/Apr/1953 2:00 4:00
27/Sep/1953 2:00 5:00
25/Apr/1954 2:00 4:00
26/Sep/1954 2:00 5:00
24/Apr/1955 2:00 4:00
25/Sep/1955 2:00 5:00
27/Apr/1958 2:00 4:00
26/Oct/1958 2:00 5:00
26/Apr/1959 2:00 4:00
25/Oct/1959 2:00 5:00
24/Apr/1960 2:00 4:00
30/Oct/1960 2:00 5:00
29/Apr/1962 2:00 4:00
28/Oct/1962 2:00 5:00
28/Apr/1963 2:00 4:00
27/Oct/1963 2:00 TT#1
....
Time Table # 103
Before 1/Jan/1895 LMT
Begin Standard 75w00
1/Jan/1895 0:00 5:00
14/Apr/1918 2:00 4:00
31/Oct/1918 2:00 5:00
1/May/1932 0:00 4:00
25/Sep/1932 0:00 5:00
1/May/1933 0:00 4:00
1/Oct/1933 0:00 5:00
29/Apr/1934 0:00 4:00
30/Sep/1934 0:00 5:00
28/Apr/1935 0:00 4:00
29/Sep/1935 0:00 5:00
26/Apr/1936 0:00 4:00
27/Sep/1936 0:00 5:00
25/Apr/1937 0:00 4:00
26/Sep/1937 0:00 5:00
24/Apr/1938 0:00 4:00
25/Sep/1938 0:00 5:00
30/Apr/1939 0:00 4:00
24/Sep/1939 0:00 5:00
28/Apr/1940 0:00 4:00
30/Sep/1945 2:00 TT#2
....
Time Table # 104
Before 1/Jan/1895 LMT
Begin Standard 75w00
1/Jan/1895 0:00 5:00
14/Apr/1918 2:00 4:00
31/Oct/1918 2:00 5:00
31/May/1931 2:00 4:00
31/Aug/1931 2:00 5:00
1/May/1933 2:00 4:00
1/Oct/1933 2:00 5:00
1/Jun/1934 2:00 4:00
16/Sep/1934 2:00 5:00
2/Jun/1935 2:00 4:00
3/Sep/1935 2:00 5:00
1/Jun/1936 2:00 4:00
7/Sep/1936 2:00 5:00
25/Apr/1937 2:00 TT#2
....
Time Table # 105
Before 1/Jan/1895 LMT
Begin Standard 75w00
1/Jan/1895 0:00 5:00
14/Apr/1918 2:00 4:00
31/Oct/1918 2:00 5:00
1/Jun/1940 2:00 4:00
30/Sep/1945 2:00 5:00
28/Apr/1946 2:00 4:00
29/Sep/1946 2:00 5:00
27/Apr/1947 0:00 4:00
28/Sep/1947 0:00 5:00
25/Apr/1948 0:00 4:00
26/Sep/1948 0:00 5:00
24/Apr/1949 2:00 4:00
25/Sep/1949 2:00 5:00
30/Apr/1950 2:00 4:00
24/Sep/1950 2:00 5:00
29/Apr/1951 2:00 4:00
30/Sep/1951 2:00 5:00
27/Apr/1952 2:00 4:00
28/Sep/1952 2:00 5:00
26/Apr/1953 2:00 4:00
27/Sep/1953 2:00 5:00
25/Apr/1954 2:00 4:00
26/Sep/1954 2:00 5:00
24/Apr/1955 2:00 4:00
25/Sep/1955 2:00 5:00
29/Apr/1956 2:00 4:00
30/Sep/1956 2:00 5:00
28/Apr/1957 2:00 4:00
27/Oct/1957 2:00 5:00
24/Apr/1960 2:00 TT#2
....
Time Table # 106
Before 1/Jan/1895 LMT
Begin Standard 75w00
1/Jan/1895 0:00 5:00
14/Apr/1918 2:00 4:00
31/Oct/1918 2:00 5:00
29/Sep/1940 0:00 4:00
30/Sep/1945 2:00 5:00
4/May/1947 2:00 4:00
28/Sep/1947 2:00 5:00
25/Apr/1948 0:00 TT#2
....
Time Table # 107
Before 1/Jan/1895 LMT
Begin Standard 75w00
1/Jan/1895 0:00 5:00
14/Apr/1918 2:00 4:00
31/Oct/1918 2:00 5:00
28/Apr/1940 2:00 4:00
30/Sep/1945 2:00 5:00
27/Apr/1947 0:00 TT#2
....
Time Table # 108
Before 1/Jan/1895 LMT
Begin Standard 75w00
1/Jan/1895 0:00 5:00
14/Apr/1918 2:00 4:00
31/Oct/1918 2:00 5:00
29/Sep/1940 0:00 4:00
30/Sep/1945 2:00 5:00
28/Apr/1957 2:00 4:00
1/Sep/1957 2:00 5:00
27/Apr/1958 2:00 4:00
2/Sep/1958 2:00 5:00
29/Apr/1962 2:00 4:00
2/Sep/1962 2:00 TT#1
....
Time Table # 109
Before 1/Jan/1895 LMT
Begin Standard 75w00
1/Jan/1895 0:00 5:00
14/Apr/1918 2:00 4:00
31/Oct/1918 2:00 5:00
29/Sep/1940 0:00 4:00
30/Sep/1945 2:00 5:00
28/Apr/1957 2:00 4:00
27/Oct/1957 2:00 5:00
27/Apr/1958 2:00 4:00
26/Oct/1958 2:00 TT#1
....
Time Table # 110
Before 1/Jan/1895 LMT
Begin Standard 75w00
1/Jan/1895 0:00 5:00
14/Apr/1918 2:00 4:00
31/Oct/1918 2:00 5:00
2/May/1920 0:00 4:00
1/Oct/1920 0:00 5:00
1/May/1921 0:00 4:00
16/Sep/1921 0:00 5:00
15/May/1922 0:00 4:00
18/Sep/1922 0:00 5:00
13/May/1923 0:00 4:00
16/Sep/1923 0:00 5:00
11/May/1924 0:00 4:00
14/Sep/1924 0:00 5:00
10/May/1925 0:00 4:00
15/Sep/1925 0:00 5:00
12/May/1926 0:00 4:00
14/Sep/1926 0:00 5:00
1/May/1927 0:00 4:00
11/Sep/1927 0:00 5:00
29/Apr/1928 0:00 4:00
30/Sep/1928 0:00 5:00
19/May/1929 0:00 4:00
15/Sep/1929 0:00 5:00
18/May/1930 0:00 4:00
14/Sep/1930 0:00 5:00
17/May/1931 0:00 4:00
13/Sep/1931 0:00 5:00
15/May/1932 0:00 4:00
25/Sep/1932 0:00 5:00
30/Apr/1933 0:00 4:00
1/Oct/1933 0:00 5:00
29/Apr/1934 0:00 4:00
30/Sep/1934 0:00 5:00
28/Apr/1935 0:00 4:00
29/Sep/1935 0:00 5:00
25/Apr/1936 0:00 4:00
12/Sep/1936 0:00 5:00
25/Apr/1937 0:00 4:00
26/Sep/1937 0:00 5:00
1/May/1938 0:00 4:00
25/Sep/1938 0:00 5:00
30/Apr/1939 0:00 4:00
1/Oct/1939 0:00 5:00
28/Apr/1940 0:00 4:00
30/Sep/1945 2:00 TT#2
....
Time Table # 111
Before 1/Jan/1895 LMT
Begin Standard 75w00
1/Jan/1895 0:00 5:00
14/Apr/1918 2:00 4:00
31/Oct/1918 2:00 5:00
29/Sep/1940 0:00 4:00
30/Sep/1945 2:00 5:00
28/Apr/1946 2:00 4:00
29/Sep/1946 2:00 5:00
27/Apr/1947 0:00 4:00
28/Sep/1947 0:00 5:00
25/Apr/1948 0:00 4:00
26/Sep/1948 0:00 5:00
24/Apr/1949 2:00 4:00
25/Sep/1949 2:00 5:00
30/Apr/1950 2:00 4:00
24/Sep/1950 2:00 5:00
29/Apr/1951 2:00 4:00
30/Sep/1951 2:00 5:00
27/Apr/1952 2:00 4:00
28/Sep/1952 2:00 5:00
26/Apr/1953 2:00 4:00
27/Sep/1953 2:00 5:00
25/Apr/1954 2:00 4:00
26/Sep/1954 2:00 5:00
24/Apr/1955 2:00 4:00
25/Sep/1955 2:00 5:00
29/Apr/1956 2:00 4:00
30/Sep/1956 2:00 5:00
28/Apr/1957 2:00 4:00
27/Oct/1957 2:00 5:00
27/Apr/1958 2:00 4:00
27/Sep/1958 2:00 5:00
26/Apr/1959 2:00 4:00
27/Sep/1959 2:00 5:00
25/Apr/1960 2:00 4:00
25/Sep/1960 2:00 5:00
30/Apr/1961 2:00 TT#2
....
Time Table # 112
Before 1/Jan/1895 LMT
Begin Standard 75w00
1/Jan/1895 0:00 5:00
14/Apr/1918 2:00 4:00
31/Oct/1918 2:00 5:00
29/Sep/1940 0:00 4:00
30/Sep/1945 2:00 5:00
25/Apr/1948 0:00 4:00
26/Sep/1948 0:00 5:00
24/Apr/1949 2:00 4:00
25/Sep/1949 2:00 5:00
29/Apr/1951 2:00 4:00
30/Sep/1951 2:00 5:00
27/Apr/1952 2:00 4:00
28/Sep/1952 2:00 5:00
26/Apr/1953 2:00 4:00
27/Sep/1953 2:00 5:00
25/Apr/1954 2:00 4:00
26/Sep/1954 2:00 5:00
24/Apr/1955 2:00 4:00
25/Sep/1955 2:00 TT#1
....
Time Table # 113
Before 1/Jan/1895 LMT
Begin Standard 75w00
1/Jan/1895 0:00 5:00
14/Apr/1918 2:00 4:00
31/Oct/1918 2:00 5:00
29/Apr/1934 2:00 4:00
30/Sep/1934 2:00 5:00
29/Sep/1940 0:00 4:00
30/Sep/1945 2:00 5:00
27/Apr/1947 0:00 4:00
28/Sep/1947 0:00 5:00
25/Apr/1948 0:00 4:00
26/Sep/1948 0:00 5:00
24/Apr/1949 2:00 4:00
25/Sep/1949 2:00 5:00
30/Apr/1950 2:00 4:00
24/Sep/1950 2:00 5:00
29/Apr/1951 2:00 4:00
30/Sep/1951 2:00 5:00
27/Apr/1952 2:00 4:00
28/Sep/1952 2:00 5:00
26/Apr/1953 2:00 4:00
27/Sep/1953 2:00 5:00
25/Apr/1954 2:00 4:00
26/Sep/1954 2:00 5:00
24/Apr/1955 2:00 4:00
25/Sep/1955 2:00 5:00
29/Apr/1956 2:00 4:00
30/Sep/1956 2:00 5:00
28/Apr/1957 2:00 4:00
29/Sep/1957 2:00 5:00
27/Apr/1958 2:00 TT#2
....
Time Table # 114
Before 1/Jan/1895 LMT
Begin Standard 75w00
1/Jan/1895 0:00 5:00
14/Apr/1918 2:00 4:00
31/Oct/1918 2:00 5:00
29/Sep/1940 0:00 4:00
30/Sep/1945 2:00 5:00
27/Apr/1946 2:00 4:00
27/Sep/1946 2:00 5:00
27/Apr/1947 0:00 4:00
28/Sep/1947 0:00 5:00
25/Apr/1948 0:00 4:00
26/Sep/1948 0:00 5:00
30/Apr/1949 2:00 4:00
24/Sep/1949 2:00 5:00
30/Apr/1950 2:00 TT#2
....
Time Table # 115
Before 1/Jan/1895 LMT
Begin Standard 75w00
1/Jan/1895 0:00 5:00
14/Apr/1918 2:00 4:00
31/Oct/1918 2:00 5:00
29/Sep/1940 0:00 4:00
30/Sep/1945 2:00 5:00
27/Apr/1947 0:00 4:00
28/Sep/1947 0:00 5:00
24/Apr/1949 2:00 4:00
25/Sep/1949 2:00 5:00
29/Apr/1951 2:00 TT#2
....
Time Table # 116
Before 1/Jan/1895 LMT
Begin Standard 75w00
1/Jan/1895 0:00 5:00
14/Apr/1918 2:00 4:00
31/Oct/1918 2:00 5:00
29/Sep/1940 0:00 4:00
30/Sep/1945 2:00 5:00
1/May/1946 2:00 4:00
30/Sep/1946 2:00 5:00
27/Apr/1947 0:00 4:00
28/Sep/1947 0:00 5:00
26/Apr/1953 2:00 4:00
27/Sep/1953 2:00 TT#1
....
Time Table # 117
Before 1/Jan/1895 LMT
Begin Standard 75w00
1/Jan/1895 0:00 5:00
14/Apr/1918 2:00 4:00
31/Oct/1918 2:00 5:00
29/Sep/1940 0:00 4:00
30/Sep/1945 2:00 5:00
27/Apr/1947 0:00 4:00
28/Sep/1947 0:00 5:00
25/Apr/1948 0:00 4:00
26/Sep/1948 0:00 5:00
24/Apr/1949 2:00 4:00
25/Sep/1949 2:00 5:00
30/Apr/1950 2:00 4:00
24/Sep/1950 2:00 5:00
29/Apr/1951 2:00 4:00
30/Sep/1951 2:00 5:00
27/Apr/1952 2:00 4:00
28/Sep/1952 2:00 5:00
26/Apr/1953 2:00 4:00
27/Sep/1953 2:00 5:00
25/Apr/1954 2:00 4:00
26/Sep/1954 2:00 5:00
24/Apr/1955 2:00 4:00
25/Sep/1955 2:00 5:00
29/Apr/1956 2:00 4:00
30/Sep/1956 2:00 5:00
28/Apr/1957 2:00 4:00
27/Oct/1957 2:00 5:00
27/Apr/1958 2:00 4:00
26/Oct/1958 2:00 5:00
24/Apr/1960 2:00 4:00
30/Oct/1960 2:00 5:00
30/Apr/1961 2:00 4:00
29/Oct/1961 2:00 5:00
29/Apr/1962 2:00 4:00
28/Oct/1962 2:00 5:00
28/Apr/1963 2:00 4:00
27/Oct/1963 2:00 5:00
26/Apr/1964 2:00 4:00
25/Oct/1964 2:00 5:00
25/Apr/1965 2:00 4:00
31/Oct/1965 2:00 5:00
24/Apr/1966 2:00 4:00
30/Oct/1966 2:00 5:00
28/Apr/1968 2:00 TT#2
....
Time Table # 118
Before 1/Jan/1895 LMT
Begin Standard 75w00
1/Jan/1895 0:00 5:00
14/Apr/1918 2:00 4:00
31/Oct/1918 2:00 5:00
28/Apr/1940 2:00 4:00
30/Sep/1945 2:00 5:00
25/Apr/1948 0:00 4:00
26/Sep/1948 0:00 5:00
24/Apr/1949 2:00 4:00
25/Sep/1949 2:00 5:00
30/Apr/1950 2:00 4:00
24/Sep/1950 2:00 5:00
29/Apr/1951 2:00 4:00
30/Sep/1951 2:00 5:00
26/Apr/1953 2:00 4:00
27/Sep/1953 2:00 5:00
25/Apr/1954 2:00 4:00
26/Sep/1954 2:00 5:00
24/Apr/1955 2:00 4:00
25/Sep/1955 2:00 5:00
29/Apr/1956 2:00 4:00
30/Sep/1956 2:00 5:00
24/Apr/1960 2:00 4:00
30/Oct/1960 2:00 5:00
30/Apr/1961 2:00 4:00
29/Oct/1961 2:00 5:00
26/Apr/1964 2:00 TT#2
....
Time Table # 119
Before 1/Jan/1895 LMT
Begin Standard 75w00
1/Jan/1895 0:00 5:00
14/Apr/1918 2:00 4:00
31/Oct/1918 2:00 5:00
15/May/1932 2:00 4:00
11/Sep/1932 2:00 5:00
3/Jun/1933 2:00 4:00
3/Sep/1933 2:00 5:00
3/Jun/1934 2:00 4:00
2/Sep/1934 2:00 5:00
2/Jun/1935 2:00 4:00
1/Sep/1935 2:00 5:00
8/Jun/1936 2:00 4:00
6/Sep/1936 2:00 5:00
6/Jun/1937 2:00 4:00
5/Sep/1937 2:00 5:00
4/Jun/1938 2:00 4:00
3/Sep/1938 2:00 5:00
4/Jun/1939 2:00 4:00
2/Sep/1939 2:00 5:00
2/Jun/1940 2:00 4:00
30/Sep/1945 2:00 5:00
30/Apr/1946 2:00 4:00
30/Sep/1946 2:00 5:00
27/Apr/1947 0:00 TT#2
....
Time Table # 120
Before 1/Jan/1895 LMT
Begin Standard 75w00
1/Jan/1895 0:00 5:00
14/Apr/1918 2:00 4:00
31/Oct/1918 2:00 5:00
29/Sep/1940 0:00 4:00
30/Sep/1945 2:00 5:00
15/Apr/1946 2:00 4:00
15/Sep/1946 2:00 5:00
26/Apr/1953 2:00 4:00
27/Sep/1953 2:00 TT#1
....
Time Table # 121
Before 1/Jan/1895 LMT
Begin Standard 75w00
1/Jan/1895 0:00 5:00
14/Apr/1918 2:00 4:00
31/Oct/1918 2:00 5:00
29/Sep/1940 0:00 4:00
30/Sep/1945 2:00 5:00
26/Apr/1970 2:00 4:00
25/Oct/1970 2:00 5:00
25/Apr/1971 2:00 4:00
31/Oct/1971 2:00 5:00
30/Apr/1972 2:00 4:00
29/Oct/1972 2:00 TT#1
....

Time Table # 122

Before	1/Jan/1895	LMT
Begin Standard		75w00
1/Jan/1895	0:00	5:00
14/Apr/1918	2:00	4:00
31/Oct/1918	2:00	5:00
29/Sep/1940	0:00	4:00
30/Sep/1945	2:00	5:00
27/Apr/1947	0:00	4:00
28/Sep/1947	0:00	5:00
25/Apr/1948	0:00	4:00
26/Sep/1948	0:00	5:00
24/Apr/1949	2:00	4:00
25/Sep/1949	2:00	5:00
30/Apr/1950	2:00	4:00
24/Sep/1950	2:00	5:00
29/Apr/1951	2:00	4:00
30/Sep/1951	2:00	5:00
27/Apr/1952	2:00	4:00
28/Sep/1952	2:00	5:00
26/Apr/1953	2:00	4:00
27/Sep/1953	2:00	5:00
25/Apr/1954	2:00	4:00
26/Sep/1954	2:00	5:00
24/Apr/1955	2:00	4:00
25/Sep/1955	2:00	5:00
29/Apr/1956	2:00	4:00
30/Sep/1956	2:00	5:00
28/Apr/1957	2:00	4:00
27/Oct/1957	2:00	5:00
27/Apr/1958	2:00	4:00
26/Oct/1958	2:00	5:00
26/Apr/1959	2:00	4:00
27/Sep/1959	2:00	5:00
30/Apr/1961	2:00	4:00
29/Oct/1961	2:00	5:00
28/Apr/1963	2:00	4:00
27/Oct/1963	2:00	5:00
26/Apr/1964	2:00	4:00
25/Oct/1964	2:00	5:00
25/Apr/1965	2:00	4:00
31/Oct/1965	2:00	TT#1

Time Table # 123

Before	1/Jan/1895	LMT
Begin Standard		75w00
1/Jan/1895	0:00	5:00
14/Apr/1918	2:00	4:00
31/Oct/1918	2:00	5:00
29/Sep/1940	0:00	4:00
30/Sep/1945	2:00	5:00
30/Apr/1950	2:00	4:00
24/Sep/1950	2:00	5:00
29/Apr/1951	2:00	4:00
30/Sep/1951	2:00	5:00
27/Apr/1952	2:00	4:00
28/Sep/1952	2:00	5:00
25/Apr/1954	2:00	4:00
26/Sep/1954	2:00	5:00
24/Apr/1955	2:00	4:00
25/Sep/1955	2:00	5:00
29/Apr/1956	2:00	4:00
30/Sep/1956	2:00	5:00
28/Apr/1957	2:00	4:00
27/Oct/1957	2:00	5:00
26/Apr/1959	2:00	4:00
25/Oct/1959	2:00	5:00
24/Apr/1960	2:00	4:00
30/Oct/1960	2:00	5:00
30/Apr/1961	2:00	4:00
29/Oct/1961	2:00	5:00
29/Apr/1962	2:00	4:00
28/Oct/1962	2:00	5:00
28/Apr/1963	2:00	4:00
27/Oct/1963	2:00	5:00
26/Apr/1964	2:00	4:00
25/Oct/1964	2:00	5:00
24/Apr/1966	2:00	TT#2

Time Table # 124

Before	1/Jan/1895	LMT
Begin Standard		75w00
1/Jan/1895	0:00	5:00
14/Apr/1918	2:00	4:00
31/Oct/1918	2:00	5:00
30/Mar/1919	23:00	4:00
26/Oct/1919	0:00	5:00
2/May/1920	2:00	4:00
26/Sep/1920	0:00	5:00
15/May/1921	2:00	4:00
15/Sep/1921	2:00	5:00
14/May/1922	2:00	4:00
17/Sep/1922	2:00	5:00
13/May/1923	2:00	4:00
19/Sep/1923	2:00	5:00
4/May/1924	2:00	4:00
21/Sep/1924	2:00	5:00
3/May/1925	2:00	4:00
20/Sep/1925	2:00	5:00
2/May/1926	2:00	4:00
19/Sep/1926	2:00	5:00
1/May/1927	2:00	4:00
25/Sep/1927	2:00	5:00
29/Apr/1928	2:00	4:00
30/Sep/1928	2:00	5:00
28/Apr/1929	0:00	4:00
29/Sep/1929	0:00	5:00
27/Apr/1930	2:00	4:00
28/Sep/1930	2:00	5:00
26/Apr/1931	2:00	4:00
27/Sep/1931	2:00	5:00
1/May/1932	2:00	4:00
25/Sep/1932	2:00	5:00
30/Apr/1933	2:00	4:00
1/Oct/1933	2:00	5:00
29/Apr/1934	2:00	4:00
30/Sep/1934	2:00	5:00
28/Apr/1935	2:00	4:00
29/Sep/1935	2:00	5:00
26/Apr/1936	2:00	4:00
27/Sep/1936	2:00	5:00
25/Apr/1937	2:00	4:00
26/Sep/1937	2:00	5:00
24/Apr/1938	2:00	4:00
25/Sep/1938	2:00	5:00
30/Apr/1939	2:00	4:00
24/Sep/1939	2:00	5:00
28/Apr/1940	2:00	4:00
30/Sep/1945	2:00	5:00
28/Apr/1946	2:00	4:00
29/Sep/1946	2:00	5:00
27/Apr/1947	0:00	4:00
28/Sep/1947	0:00	5:00
25/Apr/1948	0:00	4:00
26/Sep/1948	0:00	5:00
24/Apr/1949	0:00	4:00
27/Nov/1949	0:00	5:00
30/Apr/1950	2:00	4:00
26/Nov/1950	2:00	TT#2

Time Table # 125

Before	1/Jan/1895	LMT
Begin Standard		75w00
1/Jan/1895	0:00	5:00
14/Apr/1918	2:00	4:00
31/Oct/1918	2:00	5:00
29/Sep/1940	0:00	4:00
30/Sep/1945	2:00	5:00
25/Apr/1971	2:00	4:00
24/Oct/1971	2:00	5:00
30/Apr/1972	2:00	4:00
29/Oct/1972	2:00	TT#1

Time Table # 126

Before	1/Jan/1895	LMT
Begin Standard		75w00
1/Jan/1895	0:00	5:00
14/Apr/1918	2:00	4:00
31/Oct/1918	2:00	5:00
29/Sep/1940	0:00	4:00
30/Sep/1945	2:00	5:00
27/Apr/1947	2:00	4:00
31/Aug/1947	2:00	5:00
26/Apr/1953	2:00	4:00
27/Sep/1953	2:00	TT#1

Time Table # 127

Before	1/Jan/1895	LMT
Begin Standard		75w00
1/Jan/1895	0:00	5:00
14/Apr/1918	2:00	4:00
31/Oct/1918	2:00	5:00
29/Sep/1940	0:00	4:00
30/Sep/1945	2:00	5:00
29/Apr/1951	2:00	4:00
30/Sep/1951	2:00	5:00
25/Apr/1954	2:00	4:00
26/Sep/1954	2:00	5:00
24/Apr/1955	2:00	4:00
25/Sep/1955	2:00	5:00
29/Apr/1956	2:00	4:00
30/Sep/1956	2:00	5:00
28/Apr/1957	2:00	4:00
27/Oct/1957	2:00	5:00
27/Apr/1958	2:00	4:00
26/Oct/1958	2:00	TT#1

Time Table # 128

Before	1/Jan/1895	LMT
Begin Standard		75w00
1/Jan/1895	0:00	5:00
14/Apr/1918	2:00	4:00
31/Oct/1918	2:00	5:00
29/Apr/1930	0:00	4:00
2/Sep/1930	0:00	5:00
27/Apr/1931	0:00	4:00
8/Sep/1931	0:00	5:00
25/Apr/1932	0:00	4:00
6/Sep/1932	0:00	5:00
1/May/1933	0:00	4:00
5/Sep/1933	0:00	5:00
30/Apr/1934	0:00	4:00
4/Sep/1934	0:00	5:00
29/Apr/1935	0:00	4:00
3/Sep/1935	0:00	5:00
26/Apr/1936	2:00	TT#2

Time Table # 129

Before	1/Jan/1895	LMT
Begin Standard		75w00
1/Jan/1895	0:00	5:00
14/Apr/1918	2:00	4:00
31/Oct/1918	2:00	5:00
4/May/1924	2:00	4:00
21/Sep/1924	2:00	5:00
3/May/1925	2:00	4:00
20/Sep/1925	2:00	5:00
2/May/1926	2:00	4:00
19/Sep/1926	2:00	5:00
1/May/1927	2:00	4:00
25/Sep/1927	2:00	5:00
29/Apr/1928	2:00	4:00
30/Sep/1928	2:00	5:00
28/Apr/1929	0:00	4:00
29/Sep/1929	0:00	5:00
27/Apr/1930	2:00	4:00
28/Sep/1930	2:00	5:00
26/Apr/1931	2:00	4:00
27/Sep/1931	2:00	5:00
1/May/1932	2:00	4:00
25/Sep/1932	2:00	5:00
30/Apr/1933	2:00	4:00
1/Oct/1933	2:00	5:00
29/Apr/1934	2:00	4:00
30/Sep/1934	2:00	5:00
28/Apr/1935	2:00	4:00
29/Sep/1935	2:00	5:00
26/Apr/1936	2:00	4:00
27/Sep/1936	2:00	5:00
25/Apr/1937	2:00	4:00
26/Sep/1937	2:00	5:00
24/Apr/1938	2:00	4:00
25/Sep/1938	2:00	5:00
30/Apr/1939	2:00	4:00
24/Sep/1939	2:00	5:00
28/Apr/1940	2:00	4:00
30/Sep/1945	2:00	5:00
27/Apr/1947	0:00	4:00
28/Sep/1947	0:00	5:00
25/Apr/1948	0:00	4:00
26/Sep/1948	0:00	5:00
24/Apr/1949	2:00	4:00
27/Nov/1949	2:00	TT#2

Time Table # 130

Before	1/Jan/1895	LMT
Begin Standard		75w00
1/Jan/1895	0:00	5:00
14/Apr/1918	2:00	4:00
31/Oct/1918	2:00	5:00
30/Apr/1933	2:00	TT#2

Time Table # 131

Before	1/Jan/1895	LMT
Begin Standard		75w00
1/Jan/1895	0:00	5:00
14/Apr/1918	2:00	4:00
31/Oct/1918	2:00	5:00
29/Sep/1940	0:00	4:00
30/Sep/1945	2:00	5:00
26/Apr/1953	2:00	4:00
27/Sep/1953	2:00	5:00
24/Apr/1955	2:00	4:00
25/Sep/1955	2:00	5:00
29/Apr/1956	2:00	4:00
30/Sep/1956	2:00	5:00
28/Apr/1957	2:00	4:00
27/Oct/1957	2:00	TT#1

Time Table # 132

Before	1/Jan/1895	LMT
Begin Standard		75w00
1/Jan/1895	0:00	5:00
14/Apr/1918	2:00	4:00
31/Oct/1918	2:00	5:00
29/Sep/1940	0:00	4:00
30/Sep/1945	2:00	5:00
27/Apr/1947	2:00	4:00
28/Sep/1947	0:00	5:00
25/Apr/1948	0:00	4:00
26/Sep/1948	0:00	5:00
24/Apr/1949	2:00	4:00
25/Sep/1949	2:00	5:00
30/Apr/1950	2:00	4:00
24/Sep/1950	2:00	5:00
25/Apr/1954	2:00	4:00
26/Sep/1954	2:00	5:00
28/Apr/1968	2:00	TT#2

Time Table # 133

Before	1/Jan/1895	LMT
Begin Standard		75w00
1/Jan/1895	0:00	5:00
14/Apr/1918	2:00	4:00
31/Oct/1918	2:00	5:00
29/Sep/1940	0:00	4:00
30/Sep/1945	2:00	5:00
30/Apr/1946	2:00	4:00
30/Sep/1946	2:00	5:00
3/May/1947	2:00	4:00
27/Sep/1947	2:00	5:00
25/Apr/1948	0:00	4:00
26/Sep/1948	0:00	5:00
24/Apr/1949	2:00	4:00
25/Sep/1949	2:00	5:00
30/Apr/1950	2:00	4:00
24/Sep/1950	2:00	5:00
29/Apr/1951	2:00	4:00
30/Sep/1951	2:00	5:00
27/Apr/1952	2:00	4:00
28/Sep/1952	2:00	5:00
26/Apr/1953	2:00	4:00
27/Sep/1953	2:00	5:00
25/Apr/1954	2:00	4:00
26/Sep/1954	2:00	5:00
24/Apr/1955	2:00	4:00
25/Sep/1955	2:00	5:00
29/Apr/1956	2:00	4:00
30/Sep/1956	2:00	5:00
28/Apr/1957	2:00	4:00
27/Oct/1957	2:00	5:00
27/Apr/1958	2:00	4:00
26/Oct/1958	2:00	5:00
26/Apr/1959	2:00	4:00
27/Sep/1959	2:00	5:00
24/Apr/1960	2:00	TT#2

Time Table # 134

Before	1/Jan/1895	LMT
Begin Standard		75w00
1/Jan/1895	0:00	5:00
14/Apr/1918	2:00	4:00
31/Oct/1918	2:00	5:00
29/Sep/1940	0:00	4:00
30/Sep/1945	2:00	5:00
27/Apr/1947	2:00	4:00
28/Sep/1947	0:00	5:00
25/Apr/1948	0:00	4:00
26/Sep/1948	0:00	TT#1

Time Table # 135

Before	1/Jan/1884	LMT
Begin Standard		75w00
1/Jan/1884	0:00	5:00
14/Apr/1918	2:00	4:00
31/Oct/1918	2:00	5:00
9/Feb/1942	2:00	4:00
30/Sep/1945	2:00	5:00
26/Apr/1953	2:00	4:00
27/Sep/1953	2:00	TT#7

Time Table # 136

Before	1/Jan/1884	LMT
Begin Standard		75w00
1/Jan/1884	0:00	5:00
14/Apr/1918	2:00	4:00
31/Oct/1918	2:00	5:00
9/Feb/1942	2:00	4:00
30/Sep/1945	2:00	5:00
25/Apr/1948	2:00	4:00
26/Sep/1948	2:00	5:00
24/Apr/1949	2:00	4:00
25/Sep/1949	2:00	5:00
29/Apr/1951	2:00	4:00
30/Sep/1951	2:00	5:00
26/Apr/1953	2:00	4:00
27/Sep/1953	2:00	TT#7

Time Table # 137

Before	1/Jan/1884	LMT
Begin Standard		75w00
1/Jan/1884	0:00	5:00
14/Apr/1918	2:00	4:00
31/Oct/1918	2:00	5:00
28/Apr/1940	2:00	4:00
30/Sep/1945	2:00	5:00
25/Apr/1948	2:00	4:00
26/Sep/1948	2:00	5:00
24/Apr/1949	2:00	4:00
25/Sep/1949	2:00	5:00
30/Apr/1950	2:00	4:00
24/Sep/1950	2:00	5:00
29/Apr/1951	2:00	4:00
30/Sep/1951	2:00	5:00
27/Apr/1952	2:00	4:00
28/Sep/1952	2:00	5:00
26/Apr/1953	2:00	4:00
27/Sep/1953	2:00	5:00
25/Apr/1954	2:00	4:00
26/Sep/1954	2:00	5:00
24/Apr/1955	2:00	4:00
25/Sep/1955	2:00	5:00
29/Apr/1956	2:00	4:00
30/Sep/1956	2:00	5:00
28/Apr/1957	2:00	4:00
27/Oct/1957	2:00	5:00
27/Apr/1958	2:00	4:00
26/Oct/1958	2:00	5:00
26/Apr/1959	2:00	4:00
25/Oct/1959	2:00	5:00
24/Apr/1960	2:00	4:00
30/Oct/1960	2:00	5:00
30/Apr/1961	2:00	4:00
29/Oct/1961	2:00	5:00
29/Apr/1962	2:00	4:00
28/Oct/1962	2:00	5:00
28/Apr/1963	2:00	4:00
27/Oct/1963	2:00	5:00
26/Apr/1964	2:00	4:00
25/Oct/1964	2:00	5:00
25/Apr/1965	2:00	4:00
31/Oct/1965	2:00	5:00
24/Apr/1966	2:00	4:00
30/Oct/1966	2:00	TT#7

Time Table # 138

Before	1/Jan/1884	LMT
Begin Standard		75w00
1/Jan/1884	0:00	5:00
14/Apr/1918	2:00	4:00
31/Oct/1918	2:00	5:00
1/May/1932	0:00	4:00
25/Sep/1932	0:00	5:00
30/Apr/1933	0:00	4:00
30/Sep/1933	0:00	5:00
29/Apr/1934	0:00	4:00
1/Oct/1934	0:00	5:00
26/Apr/1936	0:00	4:00
27/Sep/1936	0:00	5:00
25/Apr/1937	0:00	4:00
26/Sep/1937	0:00	5:00
24/Apr/1938	0:00	4:00
25/Sep/1938	0:00	5:00
30/Apr/1939	0:00	4:00
24/Sep/1939	0:00	5:00
28/Apr/1940	0:00	4:00
29/Sep/1940	0:00	5:00
9/Feb/1942	2:00	4:00
30/Sep/1945	2:00	5:00
25/Apr/1948	2:00	4:00
26/Sep/1948	2:00	5:00
24/Apr/1949	2:00	4:00
25/Sep/1949	2:00	5:00
30/Apr/1950	2:00	4:00
24/Sep/1950	2:00	5:00
29/Apr/1951	2:00	4:00
30/Sep/1951	2:00	5:00
27/Apr/1952	2:00	4:00
28/Sep/1952	2:00	5:00
26/Apr/1953	2:00	4:00
27/Sep/1953	2:00	5:00
25/Apr/1954	2:00	4:00
26/Sep/1954	2:00	5:00
24/Apr/1955	2:00	4:00
25/Sep/1955	2:00	5:00
29/Apr/1956	2:00	4:00
30/Sep/1956	2:00	TT#7

Time Table # 139

Before	1/Jan/1884	LMT
Begin Standard		75w00
1/Jan/1884	0:00	5:00
14/Apr/1918	2:00	4:00
31/Oct/1918	2:00	5:00
28/Apr/1940	0:00	4:00
30/Sep/1945	2:00	TT#7

Time Table # 140

Before	1/Jan/1884	LMT
Begin Standard		75w00
1/Jan/1884	0:00	5:00
14/Apr/1918	2:00	4:00
31/Oct/1918	2:00	5:00
1/May/1921	0:00	4:00
2/Oct/1921	0:00	5:00
30/Apr/1922	0:00	4:00
1/Oct/1922	0:00	5:00
13/May/1923	0:00	4:00
30/Sep/1923	0:00	5:00
27/Apr/1924	0:00	4:00
28/Sep/1924	0:00	5:00
26/Apr/1925	0:00	4:00
27/Sep/1925	0:00	5:00
25/Apr/1926	0:00	4:00
26/Sep/1926	0:00	5:00
27/Apr/1927	0:00	4:00
25/Sep/1927	0:00	5:00
29/Apr/1928	0:00	4:00
30/Sep/1928	0:00	5:00
28/Apr/1929	0:00	4:00
29/Sep/1929	0:00	5:00
27/Apr/1930	0:00	4:00
28/Sep/1930	0:00	5:00
26/Apr/1931	0:00	4:00
27/Sep/1931	0:00	5:00
24/Apr/1932	0:00	4:00
25/Sep/1932	0:00	5:00
30/Apr/1933	0:00	4:00
24/Sep/1933	0:00	5:00
29/Apr/1934	0:00	4:00
30/Sep/1934	0:00	5:00
28/Apr/1935	0:00	4:00
29/Sep/1935	0:00	5:00
26/Apr/1936	0:00	4:00
27/Oct/1936	0:00	5:00
25/Apr/1937	0:00	4:00
26/Sep/1937	0:00	5:00
24/Apr/1938	0:00	4:00
25/Sep/1938	0:00	5:00
30/Apr/1939	0:00	4:00
24/Sep/1939	0:00	5:00
28/Apr/1940	0:00	4:00
30/Sep/1945	2:00	5:00
30/Apr/1967	2:00	TT#8

Time Table # 141

Before	1/Jan/1884	LMT
Begin Standard		75w00
1/Jan/1884	0:00	5:00
14/Apr/1918	2:00	4:00
31/Oct/1918	2:00	5:00
9/Feb/1942	2:00	4:00
30/Sep/1945	2:00	5:00
24/Apr/1949	2:00	4:00
25/Sep/1949	2:00	5:00
29/Apr/1951	2:00	4:00
30/Sep/1951	2:00	5:00
26/Apr/1953	2:00	4:00
27/Sep/1953	2:00	TT#7

Time Table # 142

Before	1/Jan/1884	LMT
Begin Standard		75w00
1/Jan/1884	0:00	5:00
14/Apr/1918	2:00	4:00
31/Oct/1918	2:00	5:00
30/Apr/1933	0:00	4:00
1/Oct/1933	0:00	5:00
29/Apr/1934	0:00	4:00
30/Sep/1934	0:00	5:00
4/May/1935	0:00	4:00
29/Sep/1935	0:00	5:00
3/May/1936	0:00	4:00
27/Sep/1936	0:00	5:00
2/May/1937	0:00	4:00
26/Sep/1937	0:00	5:00
7/May/1938	0:00	4:00
25/Sep/1938	0:00	5:00
6/May/1939	0:00	4:00
1/Oct/1939	0:00	5:00
5/May/1940	0:00	4:00
30/Sep/1945	2:00	5:00
28/Apr/1946	2:00	4:00
29/Sep/1946	2:00	5:00
27/Apr/1947	2:00	4:00
28/Sep/1947	2:00	5:00
25/Apr/1948	2:00	4:00
26/Sep/1948	2:00	5:00
24/Apr/1949	2:00	4:00
25/Sep/1949	2:00	5:00
30/Apr/1950	2:00	4:00
29/Oct/1950	2:00	5:00
27/Apr/1952	2:00	4:00
28/Sep/1952	2:00	5:00
26/Apr/1953	2:00	4:00

27/Sep/1953 2:00 5:00
25/Apr/1954 2:00 4:00
26/Sep/1954 2:00 5:00
24/Apr/1955 2:00 4:00
25/Sep/1955 2:00 5:00
29/Apr/1956 2:00 4:00
30/Sep/1956 2:00 5:00
27/Apr/1958 2:00 4:00
26/Oct/1958 2:00 TT#7
....
Time Table # 143
Before 1/Jan/1884 LMT
Begin Standard 75w00
1/Jan/1884 0:00 5:00
14/Apr/1918 2:00 4:00
31/Oct/1918 2:00 5:00
30/Apr/1933 0:00 4:00
1/Oct/1933 0:00 5:00
29/Apr/1934 0:00 4:00
30/Sep/1934 0:00 5:00
28/Apr/1935 0:00 4:00
29/Sep/1935 0:00 5:00
26/Apr/1936 0:00 4:00
27/Oct/1936 0:00 5:00
25/Apr/1937 0:00 4:00
26/Sep/1937 0:00 5:00
24/Apr/1938 0:00 4:00
25/Sep/1938 0:00 5:00
30/Apr/1939 0:00 4:00
24/Sep/1939 0:00 5:00
28/Apr/1940 0:00 4:00
30/Sep/1945 2:00 5:00
28/Apr/1946 2:00 4:00
29/Sep/1946 2:00 5:00
27/Apr/1947 2:00 4:00
28/Sep/1947 2:00 5:00
25/Apr/1948 2:00 4:00
26/Sep/1948 2:00 5:00
24/Apr/1949 2:00 4:00
25/Sep/1949 2:00 5:00
30/Apr/1950 2:00 4:00
30/Sep/1950 2:00 TT#8
....
Time Table # 144
Before 1/Jan/1884 LMT
Begin Standard 75w00
1/Jan/1884 0:00 5:00
14/Apr/1918 2:00 4:00
31/Oct/1918 2:00 5:00
26/Apr/1925 0:00 4:00
27/Sep/1925 0:00 5:00
25/Apr/1926 0:00 4:00
26/Sep/1926 0:00 5:00
27/Apr/1927 0:00 4:00
25/Sep/1927 0:00 5:00
29/Apr/1928 0:00 4:00
30/Sep/1928 0:00 5:00
28/Apr/1929 0:00 4:00
29/Sep/1929 0:00 5:00
27/Apr/1930 0:00 4:00
28/Sep/1930 0:00 5:00
26/Apr/1931 0:00 4:00
27/Sep/1931 0:00 5:00
1/May/1932 0:00 4:00
25/Sep/1932 0:00 5:00
30/Apr/1933 0:00 4:00
1/Oct/1933 0:00 5:00
29/Apr/1934 0:00 4:00
30/Sep/1934 0:00 5:00
28/Apr/1935 0:00 4:00
29/Sep/1935 0:00 5:00
26/Apr/1936 0:00 4:00
27/Oct/1936 0:00 5:00
25/Apr/1937 0:00 4:00
26/Sep/1937 0:00 5:00
24/Apr/1938 0:00 4:00
25/Sep/1938 0:00 5:00
30/Apr/1939 0:00 4:00
24/Sep/1939 0:00 5:00
28/Apr/1940 0:00 4:00
30/Sep/1945 2:00 5:00
28/Apr/1946 2:00 TT#8
....
Time Table # 145
Before 1/Jan/1884 LMT
Begin Standard 75w00
1/Jan/1884 0:00 5:00
14/Apr/1918 2:00 4:00
31/Oct/1918 2:00 5:00
12/Jun/1938 0:00 4:00
11/Sep/1938 0:00 5:00
4/Jun/1939 0:00 4:00
24/Sep/1939 0:00 5:00
26/May/1940 0:00 4:00
30/Sep/1945 2:00 5:00
27/Apr/1947 2:00 4:00
28/Sep/1947 2:00 5:00
25/Apr/1948 2:00 4:00
26/Sep/1948 2:00 5:00
24/Apr/1949 2:00 4:00
25/Sep/1949 2:00 5:00
29/Apr/1950 2:00 4:00
29/Oct/1950 2:00 5:00
29/Apr/1951 2:00 TT#8
....
Time Table # 146
Before 1/Jan/1884 LMT
Begin Standard 75w00
1/Jan/1884 0:00 5:00
14/Apr/1918 2:00 4:00
31/Oct/1918 2:00 5:00
29/Apr/1934 0:00 4:00
30/Sep/1934 0:00 5:00
11/Jun/1935 0:00 4:00
30/Sep/1935 0:00 5:00
26/Apr/1936 0:00 4:00
27/Oct/1936 0:00 5:00
25/Apr/1937 0:00 4:00
26/Sep/1937 0:00 5:00
24/Apr/1938 0:00 4:00
25/Sep/1938 0:00 5:00
30/Apr/1939 0:00 4:00
24/Sep/1939 0:00 5:00
28/Apr/1940 0:00 4:00
30/Sep/1945 2:00 5:00
27/Apr/1947 2:00 4:00
28/Sep/1947 2:00 5:00
25/Apr/1948 2:00 4:00
26/Sep/1948 2:00 5:00
24/Apr/1949 2:00 4:00
25/Sep/1949 2:00 5:00
30/Apr/1950 2:00 4:00
29/Oct/1950 2:00 5:00
29/Apr/1951 2:00 4:00
30/Sep/1951 2:00 5:00
27/Apr/1952 2:00 4:00
28/Sep/1952 2:00 5:00
26/Apr/1953 2:00 4:00
27/Sep/1953 2:00 5:00
25/Apr/1954 2:00 4:00
26/Sep/1954 2:00 5:00
24/Apr/1955 2:00 4:00
25/Sep/1955 2:00 5:00
29/Apr/1956 2:00 4:00
30/Sep/1956 2:00 5:00
28/Apr/1957 2:00 4:00
27/Oct/1957 2:00 5:00
30/Apr/1961 2:00 TT#8
....
Time Table # 147
Before 1/Jan/1884 LMT
Begin Standard 75w00
1/Jan/1884 0:00 5:00
14/Apr/1918 2:00 4:00
31/Oct/1918 2:00 5:00
29/Apr/1934 2:00 4:00
30/Sep/1934 2:00 5:00
28/Apr/1935 2:00 4:00
29/Sep/1935 2:00 5:00
24/Apr/1938 2:00 4:00
25/Sep/1938 2:00 5:00
23/Apr/1939 2:00 4:00
24/Sep/1939 2:00 5:00
21/Apr/1940 0:00 4:00
30/Sep/1945 2:00 5:00
28/Apr/1946 2:00 4:00
29/Sep/1946 2:00 5:00
27/Apr/1947 2:00 4:00
28/Sep/1947 2:00 5:00
25/Apr/1948 2:00 4:00
26/Sep/1948 2:00 5:00
24/Apr/1949 2:00 4:00
25/Sep/1949 2:00 5:00
30/Apr/1950 2:00 4:00
24/Sep/1950 2:00 5:00
29/Apr/1951 2:00 4:00
30/Sep/1951 2:00 5:00
27/Apr/1952 2:00 4:00
28/Sep/1952 2:00 5:00
26/Apr/1953 2:00 4:00
27/Sep/1953 2:00 5:00
25/Apr/1954 2:00 4:00
26/Sep/1954 2:00 5:00
24/Apr/1955 2:00 4:00
25/Sep/1955 2:00 5:00
29/Apr/1956 2:00 4:00
30/Sep/1956 2:00 5:00
28/Apr/1957 2:00 4:00
27/Oct/1957 2:00 5:00
27/Apr/1958 2:00 4:00
26/Oct/1958 2:00 5:00
26/Apr/1959 2:00 4:00
25/Oct/1959 2:00 5:00
24/Apr/1960 2:00 4:00
23/Oct/1960 2:00 5:00
30/Apr/1961 2:00 TT#8
....
Time Table # 148
Before 1/Jan/1884 LMT
Begin Standard 75w00
1/Jan/1884 0:00 5:00
14/Apr/1918 2:00 4:00
31/Oct/1918 2:00 5:00
29/Apr/1934 0:00 4:00
30/Sep/1934 0:00 5:00
28/Apr/1935 0:00 4:00
29/Sep/1935 0:00 5:00
24/Apr/1938 0:00 4:00
25/Sep/1938 0:00 5:00
30/Apr/1939 0:00 4:00
24/Sep/1939 0:00 5:00
28/Apr/1940 0:00 4:00
30/Sep/1945 2:00 5:00
27/Apr/1947 2:00 TT#8
....
Time Table # 149
Before 1/Jan/1884 LMT
Begin Standard 75w00
1/Jan/1884 0:00 5:00
14/Apr/1918 2:00 4:00
31/Oct/1918 2:00 5:00
25/Apr/1937 0:00 4:00
26/Sep/1937 0:00 5:00
24/Apr/1938 0:00 4:00
25/Sep/1938 0:00 5:00
30/Apr/1939 0:00 4:00
1/Oct/1939 0:00 5:00
28/Apr/1940 0:00 4:00
30/Sep/1945 2:00 5:00
27/Apr/1947 2:00 4:00
28/Sep/1947 2:00 5:00
25/Apr/1948 2:00 4:00
26/Sep/1948 2:00 5:00
24/Apr/1949 2:00 4:00
27/Sep/1949 2:00 5:00
30/Apr/1950 2:00 TT#8
....
Time Table # 150
Before 1/Jan/1884 LMT
Begin Standard 75w00
1/Jan/1884 0:00 5:00
14/Apr/1918 2:00 4:00
31/Oct/1918 2:00 5:00
30/Apr/1933 0:00 4:00
1/Oct/1933 0:00 5:00
29/Apr/1934 0:00 4:00
30/Sep/1934 0:00 5:00
24/Apr/1938 0:00 4:00
25/Sep/1938 0:00 5:00
30/Apr/1939 0:00 4:00
24/Sep/1939 0:00 5:00
28/Apr/1940 0:00 4:00
30/Sep/1945 2:00 5:00
27/Apr/1947 2:00 TT#8
....
Time Table # 151
Before 1/Jan/1884 LMT
Begin Standard 75w00
1/Jan/1884 0:00 5:00
25/Mar/1917 2:00 4:00
24/Apr/1917 0:00 5:00
14/Apr/1918 2:00 4:00
31/Oct/1918 2:00 5:00
31/Mar/1919 2:30 4:00
25/Oct/1919 2:30 5:00
2/May/1920 2:30 4:00
3/Oct/1920 2:30 5:00
1/May/1921 2:00 4:00
2/Oct/1921 2:30 5:00
30/Apr/1922 2:00 4:00
1/Oct/1922 2:30 5:00
17/May/1924 2:00 4:00
28/Sep/1924 2:30 5:00
3/May/1925 2:00 4:00
27/Sep/1925 2:30 5:00
2/May/1926 2:00 4:00
26/Sep/1926 2:30 5:00
1/May/1927 0:00 4:00
25/Sep/1927 0:00 5:00
29/Apr/1928 0:00 4:00
30/Sep/1928 0:00 5:00
28/Apr/1929 0:00 4:00
29/Sep/1929 0:00 5:00
27/Apr/1930 0:00 4:00
28/Sep/1930 0:00 5:00
26/Apr/1931 0:00 4:00
27/Sep/1931 0:00 5:00
1/May/1932 0:00 4:00
25/Sep/1932 0:00 5:00
30/Apr/1933 0:00 4:00
1/Oct/1933 0:00 5:00
29/Apr/1934 0:00 4:00
30/Sep/1934 0:00 5:00
28/Apr/1935 0:00 4:00
29/Sep/1935 0:00 5:00
26/Apr/1936 0:00 4:00
27/Oct/1936 0:00 5:00
25/Apr/1937 0:00 4:00
26/Sep/1937 0:00 5:00
24/Apr/1938 0:00 4:00
25/Sep/1938 0:00 5:00
30/Apr/1939 0:00 4:00
24/Sep/1939 0:00 5:00
28/Apr/1940 0:00 4:00
30/Sep/1945 2:00 5:00
28/Apr/1946 2:00 4:00
29/Sep/1946 2:00 5:00
27/Apr/1947 2:00 4:00
28/Sep/1947 2:00 5:00
25/Apr/1948 2:00 4:00
26/Sep/1948 2:00 5:00
24/Apr/1949 2:00 4:00
30/Oct/1949 2:00 5:00
30/Apr/1950 2:00 4:00
29/Oct/1950 2:00 5:00
29/Apr/1951 2:00 TT#8
....
Time Table # 152
Before 1/Jan/1884 LMT
Begin Standard 75w00
1/Jan/1884 0:00 5:00
14/Apr/1918 2:00 4:00
31/Oct/1918 2:00 5:00
26/Apr/1931 0:00 4:00
27/Sep/1931 0:00 5:00
1/May/1932 0:00 4:00
25/Sep/1932 0:00 5:00
30/Apr/1933 0:00 4:00
1/Oct/1933 0:00 5:00
29/Apr/1934 0:00 4:00
30/Sep/1934 0:00 5:00
28/Apr/1935 0:00 4:00
29/Sep/1935 0:00 5:00
26/Apr/1936 0:00 4:00
27/Oct/1936 0:00 5:00
25/Apr/1937 0:00 4:00
26/Sep/1937 0:00 5:00
24/Apr/1938 0:00 4:00
25/Sep/1938 0:00 5:00
30/Apr/1939 0:00 4:00
24/Sep/1939 0:00 5:00
28/Apr/1940 0:00 4:00
30/Sep/1945 2:00 5:00
28/Apr/1946 2:00 4:00
29/Sep/1946 2:00 5:00
27/Apr/1947 2:00 4:00
28/Sep/1947 2:00 5:00
25/Apr/1948 2:00 4:00
26/Sep/1948 2:00 5:00
24/Apr/1949 2:00 4:00
30/Oct/1949 2:00 5:00
27/Apr/1952 2:00 4:00
28/Sep/1952 2:00 5:00
26/Apr/1953 2:00 4:00
27/Sep/1953 2:00 5:00
25/Apr/1954 2:00 4:00
26/Sep/1954 2:00 5:00
24/Apr/1955 2:00 4:00
25/Sep/1955 2:00 5:00
29/Apr/1956 2:00 4:00
30/Sep/1956 2:00 5:00
28/Apr/1957 2:00 4:00
27/Oct/1957 2:00 5:00
27/Apr/1958 2:00 4:00
26/Oct/1958 2:00 5:00
26/Apr/1959 2:00 4:00
25/Oct/1959 2:00 5:00
24/Apr/1960 2:00 4:00
30/Oct/1960 2:00 5:00
30/Apr/1961 2:00 4:00
29/Oct/1961 2:00 5:00
28/Apr/1963 2:00 4:00
27/Oct/1963 2:00 TT#7
....
Time Table # 153
Before 1/Jan/1884 LMT
Begin Standard 75w00
1/Jan/1884 0:00 5:00
14/Apr/1918 2:00 4:00
31/Oct/1918 2:00 5:00
2/May/1920 0:00 4:00
3/Oct/1920 0:00 5:00
1/May/1921 0:00 4:00
2/Oct/1921 0:00 5:00
30/Apr/1922 0:00 4:00
1/Oct/1922 0:00 5:00
13/May/1923 0:00 4:00
30/Sep/1923 0:00 5:00
27/Apr/1924 0:00 4:00
28/Sep/1924 0:00 5:00
26/Apr/1925 0:00 4:00
27/Sep/1925 0:00 5:00
25/Apr/1926 0:00 4:00
26/Sep/1926 0:00 5:00
27/Apr/1927 0:00 4:00
25/Sep/1927 0:00 5:00
29/Apr/1928 0:00 4:00
30/Sep/1928 0:00 5:00
28/Apr/1929 0:00 4:00
29/Sep/1929 0:00 5:00
27/Apr/1930 0:00 4:00
28/Sep/1930 0:00 5:00
26/Apr/1931 0:00 4:00
27/Sep/1931 0:00 5:00
1/May/1932 0:00 4:00
25/Sep/1932 0:00 5:00
30/Apr/1933 0:00 4:00
1/Oct/1933 0:00 5:00
29/Apr/1934 0:00 4:00
30/Sep/1934 0:00 5:00
28/Apr/1935 0:00 4:00
29/Sep/1935 0:00 5:00
26/Apr/1936 0:00 4:00
27/Oct/1936 0:00 5:00
25/Apr/1937 0:00 4:00
26/Sep/1937 0:00 5:00
24/Apr/1938 0:00 4:00
25/Sep/1938 0:00 5:00
30/Apr/1939 0:00 4:00
24/Sep/1939 0:00 5:00
28/Apr/1940 0:00 4:00
30/Sep/1945 2:00 5:00
28/Apr/1946 2:00 4:00
29/Sep/1946 2:00 5:00
27/Apr/1947 2:00 4:00
28/Sep/1947 2:00 5:00
25/Apr/1948 2:00 4:00
26/Sep/1948 2:00 5:00
24/Apr/1949 2:00 4:00
27/Nov/1949 2:00 TT#8
....
Time Table # 154
Before 1/Jan/1884 LMT
Begin Standard 75w00
1/Jan/1884 0:00 5:00
14/Apr/1918 2:00 4:00
31/Oct/1918 2:00 5:00
9/Feb/1942 2:00 4:00
30/Sep/1945 2:00 5:00
25/Apr/1948 2:00 4:00
26/Sep/1948 2:00 5:00
24/Apr/1949 2:00 4:00
25/Sep/1949 2:00 5:00
29/Apr/1951 2:00 4:00
30/Sep/1951 2:00 5:00
27/Apr/1952 2:00 4:00
28/Sep/1952 2:00 5:00
26/Apr/1953 2:00 4:00
27/Sep/1953 2:00 5:00
25/Apr/1954 2:00 4:00
26/Sep/1954 2:00 5:00
24/Apr/1955 2:00 4:00
25/Sep/1955 2:00 5:00
29/Apr/1956 2:00 4:00
30/Sep/1956 2:00 TT#7
....
Time Table # 155
Before 1/Jan/1884 LMT
Begin Standard 75w00
1/Jan/1884 0:00 5:00
14/Apr/1918 2:00 4:00
31/Oct/1918 2:00 5:00
19/Jun/1938 0:00 4:00
25/Sep/1938 0:00 5:00
4/Jun/1939 0:00 4:00
24/Sep/1939 0:00 5:00
26/May/1940 0:00 4:00
30/Sep/1945 2:00 5:00
27/Apr/1947 2:00 4:00
28/Sep/1947 2:00 5:00
25/Apr/1948 2:00 4:00
26/Sep/1948 2:00 5:00
24/Apr/1949 2:00 4:00
25/Sep/1949 2:00 5:00
30/Apr/1950 2:00 4:00
29/Oct/1950 2:00 5:00
29/Apr/1951 2:00 TT#8
....
Time Table # 156
Before 1/Jan/1884 LMT
Begin Standard 75w00
1/Jan/1884 0:00 5:00
14/Apr/1918 2:00 4:00
31/Oct/1918 2:00 5:00
24/Apr/1938 0:00 4:00
25/Sep/1938 0:00 5:00
30/Apr/1939 0:00 4:00
24/Sep/1939 0:00 5:00
28/Apr/1940 0:00 4:00
30/Sep/1945 2:00 5:00
25/Apr/1948 2:00 TT#8
....
Time Table # 157
Before 1/Jan/1884 LMT
Begin Standard 75w00
1/Jan/1884 0:00 5:00
14/Apr/1918 2:00 4:00
31/Oct/1918 2:00 5:00
26/Apr/1931 0:00 4:00
27/Sep/1931 0:00 5:00
30/Apr/1933 0:00 4:00
24/Sep/1933 0:00 5:00
29/Apr/1934 0:00 4:00
30/Sep/1934 0:00 5:00
25/Apr/1937 0:00 4:00
26/Sep/1937 0:00 5:00
24/Apr/1938 0:00 4:00
25/Sep/1938 0:00 5:00
30/Apr/1939 0:00 4:00
24/Sep/1939 0:00 5:00
28/Apr/1940 0:00 4:00
30/Sep/1945 2:00 5:00
28/Apr/1946 2:00 4:00
29/Sep/1946 2:00 5:00
27/Apr/1947 2:00 4:00
28/Sep/1947 2:00 5:00
25/Apr/1948 2:00 4:00
26/Sep/1948 2:00 5:00
24/Apr/1949 2:00 4:00
25/Sep/1949 2:00 5:00
29/Apr/1956 2:00 4:00
30/Sep/1956 2:00 5:00
26/Apr/1959 2:00 4:00
25/Oct/1959 2:00 5:00
30/Apr/1961 2:00 TT#8
....
Time Table # 158
Before 1/Jan/1884 LMT
Begin Standard 75w00
1/Jan/1884 0:00 5:00
14/Apr/1918 2:00 4:00
31/Oct/1918 2:00 5:00
9/Feb/1942 2:00 4:00
30/Sep/1945 2:00 5:00
25/Apr/1948 2:00 4:00
26/Sep/1948 2:00 TT#7
....
Time Table # 159
Before 1/Jan/1884 LMT
Begin Standard 75w00
1/Jan/1884 0:00 5:00
14/Apr/1918 2:00 4:00
31/Oct/1918 2:00 5:00
26/Apr/1936 0:00 4:00
27/Oct/1936 0:00 5:00
25/Apr/1937 0:00 4:00
26/Sep/1937 0:00 5:00
24/Apr/1938 0:00 4:00
25/Sep/1938 0:00 5:00
30/Apr/1939 0:00 4:00
24/Sep/1939 0:00 5:00
28/Apr/1940 0:00 4:00
30/Sep/1945 2:00 5:00
27/Apr/1947 2:00 4:00
28/Sep/1947 2:00 5:00
25/Apr/1948 2:00 4:00
26/Sep/1948 2:00 5:00
24/Apr/1949 2:00 4:00
25/Sep/1949 2:00 5:00
30/Apr/1950 2:00 4:00
24/Sep/1950 2:00 5:00
29/Apr/1951 2:00 4:00
30/Sep/1951 2:00 5:00
27/Apr/1952 2:00 4:00
26/Oct/1952 2:00 TT#8
....
Time Table # 160
Before 1/Jan/1884 LMT
Begin Standard 75w00
1/Jan/1884 0:00 5:00
14/Apr/1918 2:00 4:00
31/Oct/1918 2:00 5:00
26/Apr/1936 0:00 4:00
27/Oct/1936 0:00 5:00
25/Apr/1937 0:00 4:00

26/Sep/1937 0:00 5:00
24/Apr/1938 0:00 4:00
25/Sep/1938 0:00 5:00
30/Apr/1939 0:00 4:00
1/Oct/1939 0:00 5:00
28/Apr/1940 0:00 4:00
30/Sep/1945 2:00 TT#8
....

Time Table # 161
Before 1/Jan/1884 LMT
Begin Standard 75w00
1/Jan/1884 0:00 5:00
14/Apr/1918 2:00 4:00
31/Oct/1918 2:00 5:00
9/Feb/1942 2:00 4:00
30/Sep/1945 2:00 5:00
25/Apr/1948 2:00 4:00
26/Sep/1948 2:00 5:00
26/Apr/1953 2:00 4:00
27/Sep/1953 2:00 TT#7
....

Time Table # 162
Before 1/Jan/1884 LMT
Begin Standard 75w00
1/Jan/1884 0:00 5:00
14/Apr/1918 2:00 4:00
31/Oct/1918 2:00 5:00
9/Feb/1942 2:00 4:00
30/Sep/1945 2:00 5:00
24/Apr/1949 2:00 4:00
25/Sep/1949 2:00 5:00
29/Apr/1951 2:00 4:00
30/Sep/1951 2:00 5:00
27/Apr/1952 2:00 4:00
28/Sep/1952 2:00 5:00
26/Apr/1953 2:00 4:00
27/Sep/1953 2:00 5:00
25/Apr/1954 2:00 4:00
26/Sep/1954 2:00 TT#7
....

Time Table # 163
Before 1/Jan/1884 LMT
Begin Standard 75w00
1/Jan/1884 0:00 5:00
14/Apr/1918 2:00 4:00
31/Oct/1918 2:00 5:00
9/Feb/1942 2:00 4:00
30/Sep/1945 2:00 5:00
27/Apr/1947 2:00 4:00
28/Sep/1947 2:00 TT#7
....

Time Table # 164
Before 1/Jan/1884 LMT
Begin Standard 75w00
1/Jan/1884 0:00 5:00
14/Apr/1918 2:00 4:00
31/Oct/1918 2:00 5:00
29/Apr/1928 0:00 4:00
30/Sep/1928 0:00 5:00
28/Apr/1929 0:00 4:00
29/Sep/1929 0:00 5:00
27/Apr/1930 0:00 4:00
28/Sep/1930 0:00 5:00
26/Apr/1931 0:00 4:00
27/Sep/1931 0:00 5:00
1/May/1932 0:00 4:00
25/Sep/1932 0:00 5:00
30/Apr/1933 0:00 4:00
1/Oct/1933 0:00 5:00
29/Apr/1934 0:00 4:00
30/Sep/1934 0:00 5:00
28/Apr/1935 0:00 4:00
29/Sep/1935 0:00 5:00
26/Apr/1936 0:00 4:00
27/Oct/1936 0:00 5:00
25/Apr/1937 0:00 4:00
26/Sep/1937 0:00 5:00
24/Apr/1938 0:00 4:00
25/Sep/1938 0:00 5:00
30/Apr/1939 0:00 4:00
24/Sep/1939 0:00 5:00
28/Apr/1940 0:00 4:00
30/Sep/1945 2:00 5:00
28/Apr/1946 2:00 4:00
29/Sep/1946 2:00 5:00
27/Apr/1947 2:00 4:00
28/Sep/1947 2:00 5:00
25/Apr/1948 2:00 4:00
26/Sep/1948 2:00 5:00
24/Apr/1949 2:00 4:00
30/Oct/1949 2:00 5:00
30/Apr/1950 2:00 4:00
29/Oct/1950 2:00 5:00
29/Apr/1951 2:00 TT#8
....

Time Table # 165
Before 1/Jan/1884 LMT
Begin Standard 75w00
1/Jan/1884 0:00 5:00
14/Apr/1918 2:00 4:00
31/Oct/1918 2:00 5:00
30/Apr/1939 0:00 4:00
24/Sep/1939 0:00 5:00
28/Apr/1940 0:00 4:00
30/Sep/1945 2:00 5:00
28/Apr/1946 2:00 4:00
29/Sep/1946 2:00 5:00
27/Apr/1947 2:00 4:00
28/Sep/1947 2:00 5:00
25/Apr/1948 2:00 4:00
26/Sep/1948 2:00 5:00
24/Apr/1949 2:00 4:00
25/Sep/1949 2:00 5:00
30/Apr/1950 2:00 4:00
29/Oct/1950 2:00 5:00
29/Apr/1951 2:00 4:00
30/Sep/1951 2:00 5:00
27/Apr/1952 2:00 4:00
28/Sep/1952 2:00 5:00
26/Apr/1953 2:00 4:00
27/Sep/1953 2:00 5:00
25/Apr/1954 2:00 4:00
26/Sep/1954 2:00 5:00
24/Apr/1955 2:00 4:00
25/Sep/1955 2:00 5:00
29/Apr/1956 2:00 4:00
30/Sep/1956 2:00 5:00
28/Apr/1957 2:00 4:00
27/Oct/1957 2:00 5:00
27/Apr/1958 2:00 4:00
26/Oct/1958 2:00 5:00
26/Apr/1959 2:00 4:00
25/Oct/1959 2:00 5:00
24/Apr/1960 2:00 4:00
30/Oct/1960 2:00 5:00
30/Apr/1961 2:00 4:00
29/Oct/1961 2:00 5:00
29/Apr/1962 2:00 4:00
28/Oct/1962 2:00 5:00
28/Apr/1963 2:00 4:00
27/Oct/1963 2:00 5:00
26/Apr/1964 2:00 4:00
25/Oct/1964 2:00 TT#7
....

Time Table # 166
Before 1/Jan/1884 LMT
Begin Standard 75w00
1/Jan/1884 0:00 5:00
14/Apr/1918 2:00 4:00
31/Oct/1918 2:00 5:00
9/Feb/1942 2:00 4:00
30/Sep/1945 2:00 5:00
25/Apr/1948 2:00 4:00
26/Sep/1948 2:00 5:00
29/Apr/1951 2:00 4:00
30/Sep/1951 2:00 TT#7
....

Time Table # 167
Before 1/Jan/1884 LMT
Begin Standard 75w00
1/Jan/1884 0:00 5:00
14/Apr/1918 2:00 4:00
31/Oct/1918 2:00 5:00
26/Apr/1931 0:00 4:00
27/Sep/1931 0:00 5:00
1/May/1932 0:00 4:00
25/Sep/1932 0:00 5:00
30/Apr/1933 0:00 4:00
1/Oct/1933 0:00 5:00
29/Apr/1934 0:00 4:00
30/Sep/1934 0:00 5:00
28/Apr/1935 0:00 4:00
29/Sep/1935 0:00 5:00
26/Apr/1936 0:00 4:00
27/Oct/1936 0:00 5:00
25/Apr/1937 0:00 4:00
26/Sep/1937 0:00 5:00
24/Apr/1938 0:00 4:00
25/Sep/1938 0:00 5:00
30/Apr/1939 0:00 4:00
24/Sep/1939 0:00 5:00
28/Apr/1940 0:00 4:00
30/Sep/1945 2:00 5:00
28/Apr/1946 2:00 4:00
29/Sep/1946 2:00 5:00
27/Apr/1947 2:00 4:00
28/Sep/1947 2:00 5:00
25/Apr/1948 2:00 4:00
26/Sep/1948 2:00 5:00
24/Apr/1949 2:00 4:00
25/Sep/1949 2:00 5:00
30/Apr/1950 2:00 4:00
29/Oct/1950 2:00 5:00
27/Apr/1952 2:00 4:00
28/Sep/1952 2:00 5:00
26/Apr/1953 2:00 4:00
27/Sep/1953 2:00 5:00
25/Apr/1954 2:00 4:00
26/Sep/1954 2:00 5:00
24/Apr/1955 2:00 4:00
25/Sep/1955 2:00 5:00
29/Apr/1956 2:00 4:00
23/Sep/1956 2:00 5:00
28/Apr/1957 2:00 TT#8
....

Time Table # 168
Before 1/Jan/1884 LMT
Begin Standard 75w00
1/Jan/1884 0:00 5:00
14/Apr/1918 2:00 4:00
31/Oct/1918 2:00 5:00
1/May/1932 0:00 4:00
25/Sep/1932 0:00 5:00
30/Apr/1933 0:00 4:00
1/Oct/1933 0:00 5:00
29/Apr/1934 0:00 4:00
30/Sep/1934 0:00 5:00
28/Apr/1935 0:00 4:00
29/Sep/1935 0:00 5:00
26/Apr/1936 0:00 4:00
27/Oct/1936 0:00 5:00
25/Apr/1937 0:00 4:00
26/Sep/1937 0:00 5:00
24/Apr/1938 0:00 4:00
25/Sep/1938 0:00 5:00
30/Apr/1939 0:00 4:00
24/Sep/1939 0:00 5:00
28/Apr/1940 0:00 4:00
30/Sep/1945 2:00 5:00
28/Apr/1946 2:00 TT#8
....

Time Table # 169
Before 1/Jan/1884 LMT
Begin Standard 75w00
1/Jan/1884 0:00 5:00
14/Apr/1918 2:00 4:00
31/Oct/1918 2:00 5:00
26/Apr/1936 0:00 4:00
27/Oct/1936 0:00 5:00
25/Apr/1937 0:00 4:00
26/Sep/1937 0:00 5:00
24/Apr/1938 0:00 4:00
25/Sep/1938 0:00 5:00
30/Apr/1939 0:00 4:00
24/Sep/1939 0:00 5:00
28/Apr/1940 0:00 4:00
30/Sep/1945 2:00 5:00
26/Apr/1953 2:00 4:00
27/Sep/1953 2:00 TT#7
....

Time Table # 170
Before 1/Jan/1884 LMT
Begin Standard 75w00
1/Jan/1884 0:00 5:00
14/Apr/1918 2:00 4:00
31/Oct/1918 2:00 5:00
26/Apr/1936 0:00 4:00
27/Oct/1936 0:00 5:00
25/Apr/1937 0:00 4:00
26/Sep/1937 0:00 5:00
24/Apr/1938 0:00 4:00
25/Sep/1938 0:00 5:00
30/Apr/1939 0:00 4:00
24/Sep/1939 0:00 5:00
28/Apr/1940 0:00 4:00
30/Sep/1945 2:00 5:00
25/Apr/1948 2:00 4:00
26/Sep/1948 2:00 5:00
24/Apr/1949 2:00 4:00
25/Sep/1949 2:00 5:00
30/Apr/1950 2:00 4:00
29/Oct/1950 2:00 5:00
29/Apr/1951 2:00 TT#8
....

Time Table # 171
Before 1/Jan/1884 LMT
Begin Standard 75w00
1/Jan/1884 0:00 5:00
14/Apr/1918 2:00 4:00
31/Oct/1918 2:00 5:00
27/Apr/1930 2:00 4:00
28/Sep/1930 2:00 5:00
26/Apr/1931 2:00 4:00
27/Sep/1931 2:00 5:00
1/May/1932 2:00 4:00
25/Sep/1932 2:00 5:00
30/Apr/1933 2:00 4:00
1/Oct/1933 2:00 5:00
8/May/1937 2:00 4:00
26/Sep/1937 2:00 5:00
24/Apr/1938 2:00 4:00
25/Sep/1938 2:00 5:00
30/Apr/1939 2:00 4:00
28/Sep/1939 2:00 5:00
28/Apr/1940 2:00 4:00
30/Sep/1945 2:00 5:00
27/Apr/1947 2:00 4:00
28/Sep/1947 2:00 5:00
25/Apr/1948 2:00 4:00
26/Sep/1948 2:00 5:00
24/Apr/1949 2:00 4:00
25/Sep/1949 2:00 5:00
30/Apr/1950 2:00 4:00
24/Sep/1950 2:00 5:00
29/Apr/1951 2:00 4:00
30/Sep/1951 2:00 5:00
27/Apr/1952 2:00 4:00
28/Sep/1952 2:00 5:00
26/Apr/1953 2:00 4:00
27/Sep/1953 2:00 5:00
25/Apr/1954 2:00 4:00
26/Sep/1954 2:00 5:00
24/Apr/1955 2:00 4:00
25/Sep/1955 2:00 5:00
29/Apr/1956 2:00 4:00
30/Sep/1956 2:00 5:00
28/Apr/1957 2:00 4:00
27/Oct/1957 2:00 5:00
27/Apr/1958 2:00 4:00
26/Oct/1958 2:00 5:00
26/Apr/1959 2:00 4:00
25/Oct/1959 2:00 5:00
24/Apr/1960 2:00 4:00
30/Oct/1960 2:00 5:00
30/Apr/1961 2:00 4:00
29/Oct/1961 2:00 5:00
29/Apr/1962 2:00 4:00
28/Oct/1962 2:00 5:00
28/Apr/1963 2:00 4:00
27/Oct/1963 2:00 5:00
26/Apr/1964 2:00 4:00
25/Oct/1964 2:00 TT#7
....

Time Table # 172
Before 1/Jan/1884 LMT
Begin Standard 75w00
1/Jan/1884 0:00 5:00
14/Apr/1918 2:00 4:00
31/Oct/1918 2:00 5:00
29/Mar/1919 23:00 4:00
25/Oct/1919 2:00 5:00
1/May/1920 0:00 4:00
2/Oct/1920 0:00 5:00
1/May/1921 0:00 4:00
2/Oct/1921 0:00 5:00
31/May/1923 0:00 4:00
30/Sep/1923 0:00 5:00
4/May/1924 0:00 4:00
28/Sep/1924 0:00 5:00
3/May/1925 0:00 4:00
27/Sep/1925 0:00 5:00
3/May/1926 0:00 4:00
26/Sep/1926 0:00 5:00
1/May/1927 0:00 4:00
25/Sep/1927 0:00 5:00
29/Apr/1928 0:00 4:00
30/Sep/1928 0:00 5:00
28/Apr/1929 0:00 4:00
29/Sep/1929 0:00 5:00
27/Apr/1930 0:00 4:00
28/Sep/1930 0:00 5:00
26/Apr/1931 0:00 4:00
27/Sep/1931 0:00 5:00
1/May/1932 0:00 4:00
25/Sep/1932 0:00 5:00
30/Apr/1933 0:00 4:00
1/Oct/1933 0:00 5:00
29/Apr/1934 0:00 4:00
30/Sep/1934 0:00 5:00
28/Apr/1935 0:00 4:00
29/Sep/1935 0:00 5:00
26/Apr/1936 0:00 4:00
27/Oct/1936 0:00 5:00
25/Apr/1937 0:00 4:00
26/Sep/1937 0:00 5:00
24/Apr/1938 0:00 4:00
25/Sep/1938 0:00 5:00
30/Apr/1939 0:00 4:00
1/Oct/1939 0:00 5:00
28/Apr/1940 0:00 4:00
30/Sep/1945 2:00 5:00
28/Apr/1946 2:00 4:00
29/Sep/1946 2:00 5:00
27/Apr/1947 2:00 4:00
28/Sep/1947 2:00 5:00
25/Apr/1948 2:00 4:00
26/Sep/1948 2:00 5:00
24/Apr/1949 2:00 4:00
30/Oct/1949 2:00 5:00
30/Apr/1950 2:00 TT#8
....

Time Table # 173
Before 1/Jan/1884 LMT
Begin Standard 75w00
1/Jan/1884 0:00 5:00
14/Apr/1918 2:00 4:00
31/Oct/1918 2:00 5:00
27/Apr/1930 0:00 4:00
28/Sep/1930 0:00 5:00
26/Apr/1931 0:00 4:00
27/Sep/1931 0:00 5:00
24/Apr/1932 0:00 4:00
25/Sep/1932 0:00 5:00
30/Apr/1933 0:00 4:00
1/Oct/1933 0:00 5:00
29/Apr/1934 0:00 4:00
30/Sep/1934 0:00 5:00
28/Apr/1935 0:00 4:00
29/Sep/1935 0:00 5:00
26/Apr/1936 0:00 4:00
27/Oct/1936 0:00 5:00
25/Apr/1937 0:00 4:00
26/Sep/1937 0:00 5:00
24/Apr/1938 0:00 4:00
25/Sep/1938 0:00 5:00
30/Apr/1939 0:00 4:00
24/Sep/1939 0:00 5:00
28/Apr/1940 0:00 4:00
30/Sep/1945 2:00 5:00
29/Apr/1946 2:00 4:00
29/Sep/1946 2:00 5:00
27/Apr/1947 2:00 4:00
28/Sep/1947 2:00 5:00
25/Apr/1948 2:00 4:00
26/Sep/1948 2:00 5:00
24/Apr/1949 2:00 4:00
25/Sep/1949 2:00 5:00
30/Apr/1950 2:00 4:00
29/Oct/1950 2:00 5:00
29/Apr/1951 2:00 4:00
30/Sep/1951 2:00 5:00
27/Apr/1952 2:00 4:00
28/Sep/1952 2:00 5:00
26/Apr/1953 2:00 4:00
27/Sep/1953 2:00 5:00
25/Apr/1954 2:00 4:00
26/Sep/1954 2:00 5:00
24/Apr/1955 2:00 4:00
25/Sep/1955 2:00 5:00
29/Apr/1956 2:00 4:00
30/Sep/1956 2:00 5:00
28/Apr/1957 2:00 4:00
27/Oct/1957 2:00 5:00
27/Apr/1958 2:00 4:00
26/Oct/1958 2:00 5:00
26/Apr/1959 2:00 4:00
25/Oct/1959 2:00 5:00
24/Apr/1960 2:00 4:00
30/Oct/1960 2:00 5:00
30/Apr/1961 2:00 4:00
29/Oct/1961 2:00 5:00
29/Apr/1962 2:00 4:00
28/Oct/1962 2:00 5:00
28/Apr/1963 2:00 4:00
27/Oct/1963 2:00 TT#7
....

Time Table # 174
Before 1/Jan/1884 LMT
Begin Standard 75w00
1/Jan/1884 0:00 5:00
14/Apr/1918 2:00 4:00
31/Oct/1918 2:00 5:00
25/Apr/1937 0:00 4:00
26/Sep/1937 0:00 5:00
24/Apr/1938 0:00 4:00
25/Sep/1938 0:00 5:00
30/Apr/1939 0:00 4:00
24/Sep/1939 0:00 5:00
28/Apr/1940 0:00 4:00
30/Sep/1945 2:00 5:00
25/Apr/1948 2:00 TT#8
....

Time Table # 175
Before 1/Jan/1884 LMT
Begin Standard 75w00
1/Jan/1884 0:00 5:00
14/Apr/1918 2:00 4:00
31/Oct/1918 2:00 5:00
2/Apr/1919 2:00 4:00
5/Oct/1919 2:00 5:00
2/May/1920 2:00 4:00
3/Oct/1920 2:00 5:00
1/May/1921 2:00 4:00
2/Oct/1921 2:00 5:00
22/May/1924 1:00 4:00
28/Sep/1924 2:00 5:00
15/Jun/1925 1:00 4:00
1/Sep/1925 2:00 5:00
2/May/1926 0:00 4:00
26/Sep/1926 0:00 5:00
2/May/1927 0:00 4:00
25/Sep/1927 0:00 5:00
29/Apr/1928 0:00 4:00
30/Sep/1928 0:00 5:00
28/Apr/1929 0:00 4:00
29/Sep/1929 0:00 5:00
27/Apr/1930 0:00 4:00
28/Sep/1930 0:00 5:00
26/Apr/1931 0:00 4:00
27/Sep/1931 0:00 5:00
1/May/1932 0:00 4:00
2/Oct/1932 0:00 5:00
7/May/1933 0:00 4:00
1/Oct/1933 0:00 5:00
6/May/1934 0:00 4:00
7/Oct/1934 0:00 5:00
5/May/1935 0:00 4:00
6/Oct/1935 0:00 5:00
3/May/1936 0:00 4:00
4/Oct/1936 0:00 5:00
2/May/1937 0:00 4:00
3/Oct/1937 0:00 5:00
24/Apr/1938 0:00 4:00
4/Sep/1938 0:00 5:00
30/Apr/1939 0:00 4:00
3/Sep/1939 0:00 5:00
28/Apr/1940 0:00 4:00
8/Sep/1940 0:00 5:00
9/Feb/1942 2:00 4:00
30/Sep/1945 2:00 5:00
27/Apr/1947 2:00 TT#8
....

Time Table # 176
Before 1/Jan/1884 LMT
Begin Standard 75w00
1/Jan/1884 0:00 5:00
14/Apr/1918 2:00 4:00
31/Oct/1918 2:00 5:00
9/Feb/1942 2:00 4:00
30/Sep/1945 2:00 5:00
25/Apr/1948 2:00 4:00
26/Sep/1948 2:00 5:00
24/Apr/1949 2:00 4:00
25/Sep/1949 2:00 5:00
29/Apr/1951 2:00 4:00
30/Sep/1951 2:00 5:00
27/Apr/1952 2:00 4:00
28/Sep/1952 2:00 5:00
26/Apr/1953 2:00 4:00
27/Sep/1953 2:00 5:00
25/Apr/1954 2:00 4:00
26/Sep/1954 2:00 TT#7
....

Time Table # 177
Before 1/Jan/1884 LMT
Begin Standard 75w00
1/Jan/1884 0:00 5:00
14/Apr/1918 2:00 4:00
31/Oct/1918 2:00 5:00
29/Apr/1934 0:00 4:00
30/Sep/1934 0:00 5:00
28/Apr/1935 0:00 4:00
29/Sep/1935 0:00 5:00
26/Apr/1936 0:00 4:00
27/Oct/1936 0:00 5:00
25/Apr/1937 0:00 4:00
26/Sep/1937 0:00 5:00
24/Apr/1938 0:00 4:00
25/Sep/1938 0:00 5:00
30/Apr/1939 0:00 4:00
24/Sep/1939 0:00 5:00
28/Apr/1940 0:00 4:00
30/Sep/1945 2:00 5:00
5/May/1946 2:00 4:00
28/Sep/1946 2:00 5:00
4/May/1947 2:00 4:00
27/Sep/1947 2:00 5:00
25/Apr/1948 2:00 4:00
26/Sep/1948 2:00 5:00
24/Apr/1949 2:00 4:00
25/Sep/1949 2:00 5:00
30/Apr/1950 2:00 4:00
29/Oct/1950 2:00 5:00
29/Apr/1951 2:00 TT#8
....

Time Table # 178
Before 1/Jan/1884 LMT
Begin Standard 75w00
1/Jan/1884 0:00 5:00
14/Apr/1918 2:00 4:00
31/Oct/1918 2:00 5:00
26/Apr/1931 0:00 4:00
27/Sep/1931 0:00 5:00
30/Apr/1933 0:00 4:00
1/Oct/1933 0:00 5:00
29/Apr/1934 0:00 4:00
30/Sep/1934 0:00 5:00
28/Apr/1935 0:00 4:00
29/Sep/1935 0:00 5:00
25/Apr/1937 0:00 4:00
26/Sep/1937 0:00 5:00
24/Apr/1938 0:00 4:00
25/Sep/1938 0:00 5:00
30/Apr/1939 0:00 4:00
24/Sep/1939 0:00 5:00
28/Apr/1940 0:00 4:00
30/Sep/1945 2:00 5:00
27/Apr/1947 2:00 4:00
28/Sep/1947 2:00 5:00
25/Apr/1948 2:00 4:00
26/Sep/1948 2:00 5:00
24/Apr/1949 2:00 4:00
25/Sep/1949 2:00 5:00
30/Apr/1950 2:00 4:00
29/Oct/1950 2:00 5:00
29/Apr/1951 2:00 TT#8
....
Time Table # 179
Before 1/Jan/1884 LMT
Begin Standard 75w00
1/Jan/1884 0:00 5:00
14/Apr/1918 2:00 4:00
31/Oct/1918 2:00 5:00
26/Apr/1931 0:00 4:00
27/Sep/1931 0:00 5:00
30/Apr/1933 0:00 4:00
1/Oct/1933 0:00 5:00
29/Apr/1934 0:00 4:00
30/Sep/1934 0:00 5:00
28/Apr/1935 0:00 4:00
29/Sep/1935 0:00 5:00
26/Apr/1936 0:00 4:00
27/Oct/1936 0:00 5:00
25/Apr/1937 0:00 4:00
26/Sep/1937 0:00 5:00
24/Apr/1938 0:00 4:00
25/Sep/1938 0:00 5:00
30/Apr/1939 0:00 4:00
24/Sep/1939 0:00 5:00
28/Apr/1940 0:00 4:00
30/Sep/1945 2:00 5:00
27/Apr/1947 2:00 4:00
28/Sep/1947 2:00 5:00
25/Apr/1948 2:00 4:00
26/Sep/1948 2:00 5:00
24/Apr/1949 2:00 4:00
25/Sep/1949 2:00 5:00
30/Apr/1950 2:00 4:00
24/Sep/1950 2:00 5:00
26/Apr/1953 2:00 4:00
27/Sep/1953 2:00 5:00
25/Apr/1954 2:00 4:00
26/Sep/1954 2:00 5:00
24/Apr/1955 2:00 4:00
25/Sep/1955 2:00 5:00
29/Apr/1956 2:00 4:00
30/Sep/1956 2:00 5:00
28/Apr/1957 2:00 4:00
27/Oct/1957 2:00 5:00
27/Apr/1958 2:00 4:00
26/Oct/1958 2:00 5:00
29/Apr/1962 2:00 4:00
28/Oct/1962 2:00 5:00
28/Apr/1963 2:00 4:00
27/Oct/1963 2:00 TT#7
....
Time Table # 180
Before 1/Jan/1895 LMT
Begin Standard 75w00
1/Jan/1895 0:00 5:00
14/Apr/1918 2:00 4:00
31/Oct/1918 2:00 5:00
29/Apr/1934 2:00 4:00
30/Sep/1934 2:00 5:00
28/Apr/1935 2:00 4:00
29/Sep/1935 2:00 5:00
16/Apr/1936 2:00 4:00
16/Sep/1936 2:00 5:00
25/Apr/1937 2:00 TT#2
....
Time Table # 181
Before 1/Jan/1895 LMT
Begin Standard 75w00
1/Jan/1895 0:00 5:00
14/Apr/1918 2:00 4:00
31/Oct/1918 2:00 5:00
2/Jun/1935 2:00 4:00
25/Aug/1935 2:00 5:00
24/Apr/1938 2:00 4:00
5/Sep/1938 2:00 5:00
30/Apr/1939 2:00 4:00
4/Sep/1939 2:00 5:00
28/Apr/1940 2:00 4:00
30/Sep/1945 2:00 5:00
28/Apr/1946 2:00 4:00
29/Sep/1946 2:00 5:00
27/Apr/1947 0:00 4:00
28/Sep/1947 0:00 5:00
25/Apr/1948 0:00 4:00
26/Sep/1948 0:00 5:00
24/Apr/1949 2:00 4:00
25/Sep/1949 2:00 5:00
30/Apr/1950 2:00 4:00
24/Sep/1950 2:00 5:00
29/Apr/1951 2:00 4:00
30/Sep/1951 2:00 5:00
27/Apr/1952 2:00 4:00
28/Sep/1952 2:00 5:00
26/Apr/1953 2:00 4:00
27/Sep/1953 2:00 5:00
25/Apr/1954 2:00 4:00
26/Sep/1954 2:00 5:00
24/Apr/1955 2:00 4:00
25/Sep/1955 2:00 5:00
29/Apr/1956 2:00 4:00
30/Sep/1956 2:00 5:00
28/Apr/1957 2:00 4:00
27/Oct/1957 2:00 5:00
27/Apr/1958 2:00 4:00
26/Oct/1958 2:00 5:00
26/Apr/1959 2:00 4:00
25/Oct/1959 2:00 5:00
24/Apr/1960 2:00 4:00
30/Oct/1960 2:00 5:00
30/Apr/1961 2:00 4:00
29/Oct/1961 2:00 5:00
29/Apr/1962 2:00 4:00
28/Oct/1962 2:00 5:00
28/Apr/1963 2:00 4:00
27/Oct/1963 2:00 5:00
26/Apr/1964 2:00 4:00
25/Oct/1964 2:00 5:00
25/Apr/1965 2:00 4:00
31/Oct/1965 2:00 5:00
28/Apr/1968 2:00 TT#2
....
Time Table # 182
Before 1/Jan/1895 LMT
Begin Standard 75w00
1/Jan/1895 0:00 5:00
14/Apr/1918 2:00 4:00
31/Oct/1918 2:00 5:00
5/May/1934 2:00 4:00
15/Sep/1934 2:00 5:00
5/May/1935 2:00 4:00
14/Sep/1935 2:00 5:00
3/May/1936 2:00 4:00
12/Sep/1936 2:00 5:00
2/May/1937 2:00 4:00
11/Sep/1937 2:00 5:00
24/Apr/1938 2:00 4:00
10/Sep/1938 2:00 5:00
30/Apr/1939 2:00 4:00
10/Sep/1939 2:00 5:00
28/Apr/1940 2:00 TT#2
....
Time Table # 183
Before 1/Jan/1895 LMT
Begin Standard 75w00
1/Jan/1895 0:00 5:00
14/Apr/1918 2:00 4:00
31/Oct/1918 2:00 5:00
29/May/1933 2:00 4:00
4/Sep/1933 2:00 5:00
21/May/1934 2:00 4:00
3/Sep/1934 2:00 5:00
19/May/1935 2:00 4:00
16/Sep/1935 2:00 5:00
18/May/1936 2:00 4:00
19/Sep/1936 2:00 5:00
16/May/1937 2:00 4:00
18/Sep/1937 2:00 5:00
24/Apr/1938 2:00 4:00
17/Sep/1938 2:00 5:00
30/Apr/1939 2:00 TT#2
....
Time Table # 184
Before 1/Jan/1895 LMT
Begin Standard 75w00
1/Jan/1895 0:00 5:00
14/Apr/1918 2:00 4:00
31/Oct/1918 2:00 5:00
12/May/1935 2:00 4:00
2/Sep/1935 2:00 5:00
3/May/1936 2:00 4:00
30/Aug/1936 2:00 5:00
16/May/1937 2:00 4:00
6/Sep/1937 2:00 5:00
3/Jul/1938 2:00 4:00
5/Sep/1938 2:00 5:00
30/Apr/1939 2:00 4:00
4/Sep/1939 2:00 5:00
28/Apr/1940 2:00 TT#2
....
Time Table # 185
Before 1/Jan/1895 LMT
Begin Standard 75w00
1/Jan/1895 0:00 5:00
14/Apr/1918 2:00 4:00
31/Oct/1918 2:00 5:00
26/Apr/1931 2:00 4:00
27/Sep/1931 2:00 5:00
1/May/1932 2:00 4:00
25/Sep/1932 2:00 5:00
30/Apr/1933 2:00 4:00
1/Oct/1933 2:00 5:00
29/Apr/1934 2:00 4:00
30/Sep/1934 2:00 5:00
28/Apr/1935 2:00 4:00
29/Sep/1935 2:00 5:00
26/Apr/1936 2:00 4:00
27/Sep/1936 2:00 5:00
25/Apr/1937 2:00 4:00
26/Sep/1937 2:00 5:00
24/Apr/1938 2:00 4:00
25/Sep/1938 2:00 5:00
30/Apr/1939 2:00 4:00
1/Oct/1939 2:00 TT#2
....
Time Table # 186
Before 1/Jan/1895 LMT
Begin Standard 75w00
1/Jan/1895 0:00 5:00
14/Apr/1918 2:00 4:00
31/Oct/1918 2:00 5:00
26/Apr/1936 2:00 4:00
27/Sep/1936 2:00 5:00
29/Sep/1940 0:00 4:00
30/Sep/1945 2:00 5:00
28/Apr/1946 2:00 4:00
29/Sep/1946 2:00 5:00
27/Apr/1947 0:00 4:00
28/Sep/1947 0:00 5:00
26/Apr/1953 2:00 4:00
27/Sep/1953 2:00 TT#1
....
Time Table # 187
Before 1/Jan/1895 LMT
Begin Standard 75w00
1/Jan/1895 0:00 5:00
14/Apr/1918 2:00 4:00
31/Oct/1918 2:00 5:00
30/Jun/1931 2:00 4:00
31/Aug/1931 2:00 5:00
30/Apr/1933 2:00 TT#2
....
Time Table # 188
Before 1/Jan/1895 LMT
Begin Standard 75w00
1/Jan/1895 0:00 5:00
14/Apr/1918 2:00 4:00
31/Oct/1918 2:00 5:00
15/Jun/1935 2:00 4:00
15/Sep/1935 2:00 5:00
28/Apr/1940 2:00 TT#2
....
Time Table # 189
Before 1/Jan/1884 LMT
Begin Standard 75w00
1/Jan/1884 0:00 5:00
14/Apr/1918 2:00 4:00
31/Oct/1918 2:00 5:00
26/Apr/1931 0:00 4:00
27/Sep/1931 0:00 5:00
26/Apr/1936 0:00 4:00
27/Oct/1936 0:00 5:00
25/Apr/1937 0:00 4:00
26/Sep/1937 0:00 5:00
24/Apr/1938 0:00 4:00
25/Sep/1938 0:00 5:00
30/Apr/1939 0:00 4:00
1/Oct/1939 0:00 5:00
28/Apr/1940 0:00 4:00
30/Sep/1945 2:00 5:00
28/Apr/1946 2:00 4:00
29/Sep/1946 2:00 5:00
27/Apr/1947 2:00 4:00
28/Sep/1947 2:00 5:00
25/Apr/1948 2:00 4:00
26/Sep/1948 2:00 5:00
30/Apr/1949 2:00 4:00
4/Sep/1949 2:00 5:00
30/Apr/1950 2:00 TT#8
....
Time Table # 190
Before 1/Jan/1884 LMT
Begin Standard 75w00
1/Jan/1884 0:00 5:00
14/Apr/1918 2:00 4:00
31/Oct/1918 2:00 5:00
29/Apr/1934 2:00 4:00
30/Sep/1934 2:00 5:00
26/Apr/1936 2:00 4:00
27/Oct/1936 2:00 5:00
24/Apr/1938 2:00 4:00
25/Sep/1938 2:00 5:00
30/Apr/1939 2:00 4:00
24/Sep/1939 2:00 5:00
28/Apr/1940 2:00 4:00
29/Sep/1940 2:00 5:00
27/Apr/1941 2:00 4:00
28/Sep/1941 2:00 5:00
9/Feb/1942 2:00 4:00
30/Sep/1945 2:00 5:00
27/Apr/1947 2:00 TT#8
....
Time Table # 191
Before 1/Jan/1884 LMT
Begin Standard 75w00
1/Jan/1884 0:00 5:00
14/Apr/1918 2:00 4:00
31/Oct/1918 2:00 5:00
24/Apr/1938 2:00 4:00
25/Sep/1938 2:00 5:00
30/Apr/1939 2:00 4:00
1/Oct/1939 2:00 5:00
28/Apr/1940 2:00 4:00
30/Sep/1945 2:00 5:00
27/Apr/1947 2:00 TT#8
....
Time Table # 192
Before 1/Jan/1884 LMT
Begin Standard 75w00
1/Jan/1884 0:00 5:00
14/Apr/1918 2:00 4:00
31/Oct/1918 2:00 5:00
3/May/1937 0:00 4:00
26/Sep/1937 0:00 5:00
24/Apr/1938 0:00 4:00
25/Sep/1938 0:00 5:00
30/Apr/1939 0:00 4:00
24/Sep/1939 0:00 5:00
28/Apr/1940 0:00 4:00
30/Sep/1945 2:00 5:00
27/Apr/1947 2:00 TT#8
....
Time Table # 193
Before 1/Jan/1884 LMT
Begin Standard 75w00
1/Jan/1884 0:00 5:00
14/Apr/1918 2:00 4:00
31/Oct/1918 2:00 5:00
30/Apr/1939 0:00 4:00
24/Sep/1939 0:00 TT#7
....
Time Table # 194
Before 1/Jan/1884 LMT
Begin Standard 75w00
1/Jan/1884 0:00 5:00
14/Apr/1918 2:00 4:00
31/Oct/1918 2:00 5:00
24/Apr/1938 0:00 4:00
25/Sep/1938 0:00 5:00
30/Apr/1939 0:00 4:00
1/Oct/1939 0:00 5:00
28/Apr/1940 0:00 4:00
30/Sep/1945 2:00 5:00
27/Apr/1947 2:00 TT#8
....
Time Table # 195
Before 1/Jan/1884 LMT
Begin Standard 75w00
1/Jan/1884 0:00 5:00
14/Apr/1918 2:00 4:00
31/Oct/1918 2:00 5:00
25/Apr/1937 0:00 4:00
26/Sep/1937 0:00 5:00
24/Apr/1938 0:00 4:00
25/Sep/1938 0:00 5:00
30/Apr/1939 0:00 4:00
1/Oct/1939 0:00 5:00
28/Apr/1940 0:00 4:00
30/Sep/1945 2:00 5:00
27/Apr/1947 2:00 TT#8
....
Time Table # 196
Before 1/Jan/1884 LMT
Begin Standard 75w00
1/Jan/1884 0:00 5:00
14/Apr/1918 2:00 4:00
31/Oct/1918 2:00 5:00
1/May/1937 0:00 4:00
26/Sep/1937 0:00 5:00
24/Apr/1938 0:00 4:00
25/Sep/1938 0:00 5:00
30/Apr/1939 0:00 4:00
24/Sep/1939 0:00 5:00
28/Apr/1940 0:00 4:00
30/Sep/1945 2:00 5:00
25/Apr/1948 2:00 TT#8
....
Time Table # 197
Before 1/Jan/1884 LMT
Begin Standard 75w00
1/Jan/1884 0:00 5:00
14/Apr/1918 2:00 4:00
31/Oct/1918 2:00 5:00
30/Apr/1939 0:00 4:00
1/Oct/1939 0:00 5:00
28/Apr/1940 0:00 4:00
30/Sep/1945 2:00 TT#7
....
Time Table # 198
Before 1/Jan/1884 LMT
Begin Standard 75w00
1/Jan/1884 0:00 5:00
14/Apr/1918 2:00 4:00
31/Oct/1918 2:00 5:00
24/Apr/1938 0:00 4:00
25/Sep/1938 0:00 5:00
30/Apr/1939 0:00 4:00
1/Oct/1939 0:00 5:00
28/Apr/1940 0:00 4:00
30/Sep/1945 2:00 5:00
30/Apr/1967 2:00 TT#8
....
Time Table # 199
Before 1/Jan/1884 LMT
Begin Standard 75w00
1/Jan/1884 0:00 5:00
14/Apr/1918 2:00 4:00
31/Oct/1918 2:00 5:00
9/Feb/1942 2:00 4:00
30/Sep/1945 2:00 5:00
24/Apr/1949 2:00 4:00
25/Sep/1949 2:00 5:00
26/Apr/1953 2:00 4:00
27/Sep/1953 2:00 TT#7
....
Time Table # 200
Before 1/Jan/1884 LMT
Begin Standard 75w00
1/Jan/1884 0:00 5:00
14/Apr/1918 2:00 4:00
31/Oct/1918 2:00 5:00
9/Feb/1942 2:00 4:00
30/Sep/1945 2:00 5:00
24/Apr/1949 2:00 4:00
25/Sep/1949 2:00 TT#7
....
Time Table # 201
Before 1/Jan/1884 LMT
Begin Standard 75w00
1/Jan/1884 0:00 5:00
14/Apr/1918 2:00 4:00
31/Oct/1918 2:00 5:00
19/May/1936 0:00 4:00
27/Sep/1936 0:00 5:00
25/Apr/1937 0:00 4:00
26/Sep/1937 0:00 5:00
24/Apr/1938 0:00 4:00
25/Sep/1938 0:00 5:00
30/Apr/1939 0:00 4:00
24/Sep/1939 0:00 5:00
28/Apr/1940 0:00 4:00
30/Sep/1945 2:00 5:00
27/Apr/1947 2:00 4:00
28/Sep/1947 2:00 5:00
25/Apr/1948 2:00 4:00
26/Sep/1948 2:00 5:00
24/Apr/1949 2:00 4:00
25/Sep/1949 2:00 5:00
30/Apr/1950 2:00 4:00
30/Sep/1950 2:00 TT#8
....
Time Table # 202
Before 1/Jan/1884 LMT
Begin Standard 75w00
1/Jan/1884 0:00 5:00
14/Apr/1918 2:00 4:00
31/Oct/1918 2:00 5:00
30/Apr/1933 0:00 4:00
1/Oct/1933 0:00 5:00
29/Apr/1934 0:00 4:00
30/Sep/1934 0:00 5:00
28/Apr/1935 0:00 4:00
29/Sep/1935 0:00 5:00
26/Apr/1936 0:00 4:00
27/Oct/1936 0:00 5:00
25/Apr/1937 0:00 4:00
26/Sep/1937 0:00 5:00
24/Apr/1938 0:00 4:00
25/Sep/1938 0:00 5:00
30/Apr/1939 0:00 4:00
24/Sep/1939 0:00 5:00
28/Apr/1940 0:00 4:00
30/Sep/1945 2:00 5:00
28/Apr/1946 2:00 4:00
29/Sep/1946 2:00 5:00
27/Apr/1947 2:00 4:00
28/Sep/1947 2:00 5:00
25/Apr/1948 2:00 4:00
26/Sep/1948 2:00 5:00
24/Apr/1949 2:00 4:00
30/Oct/1949 2:00 5:00
30/Apr/1950 2:00 4:00
29/Oct/1950 2:00 5:00
29/Apr/1951 2:00 TT#8
....
Time Table # 203
Before 1/Jan/1891 LMT
Begin Standard 90w00
1/Jan/1891 0:00 6:00
14/Apr/1918 2:00 5:00
31/Oct/1918 2:00 6:00
9/Feb/1942 2:00 5:00
30/Sep/1945 2:00 6:00
12/May/1963 2:00 5:00
7/Sep/1963 2:00 6:00
26/Apr/1964 2:00 5:00
13/Sep/1964 2:00 6:00
25/Apr/1965 2:00 5:00
12/Sep/1965 2:00 6:00
30/Apr/1967 2:00 5:00
29/Oct/1967 2:00 6:00
28/Apr/1968 2:00 5:00
27/Oct/1968 2:00 6:00
27/Apr/1969 2:00 5:00
26/Oct/1969 2:00 6:00
26/Apr/1970 2:00 5:00
25/Oct/1970 2:00 6:00
25/Apr/1971 2:00 5:00
31/Oct/1971 2:00 6:00
30/Apr/1972 2:00 5:00
29/Oct/1972 2:00 6:00
29/Apr/1973 2:00 5:00
28/Oct/1973 2:00 6:00
28/Apr/1974 2:00 5:00
27/Oct/1974 2:00 6:00
27/Apr/1975 2:00 5:00
26/Oct/1975 2:00 6:00
25/Apr/1976 2:00 5:00
31/Oct/1976 2:00 6:00
24/Apr/1977 2:00 5:00
30/Oct/1977 2:00 6:00
30/Apr/1978 2:00 5:00
29/Oct/1978 2:00 6:00
29/Apr/1979 2:00 5:00
28/Oct/1979 2:00 6:00
27/Apr/1980 2:00 5:00
26/Oct/1980 2:00 6:00
26/Apr/1981 2:00 5:00
25/Oct/1981 2:00 6:00
25/Apr/1982 2:00 5:00
31/Oct/1982 2:00 6:00
24/Apr/1983 2:00 5:00
30/Oct/1983 2:00 6:00
29/Apr/1984 2:00 5:00
28/Oct/1984 2:00 6:00
28/Apr/1985 2:00 5:00
27/Oct/1985 2:00 6:00
27/Apr/1986 2:00 5:00
26/Oct/1986 2:00 6:00
5/Apr/1987 2:00 5:00
25/Oct/1987 2:00 6:00
3/Apr/1988 2:00 5:00
30/Oct/1988 2:00 6:00
2/Apr/1989 2:00 5:00
29/Oct/1989 2:00 6:00
1/Apr/1990 2:00 5:00

28/Oct/1990 2:00 6:00
7/Apr/1991 2:00 5:00
27/Oct/1991 2:00 6:00
5/Apr/1992 2:00 5:00
25/Oct/1992 2:00 6:00
4/Apr/1993 2:00 5:00
31/Oct/1993 2:00 6:00
3/Apr/1994 2:00 5:00
30/Oct/1994 2:00 6:00
2/Apr/1995 2:00 5:00
29/Oct/1995 2:00 6:00
7/Apr/1996 2:00 5:00
27/Oct/1996 2:00 6:00
6/Apr/1997 2:00 5:00
26/Oct/1997 2:00 6:00
5/Apr/1998 2:00 5:00
25/Oct/1998 2:00 6:00
4/Apr/1999 2:00 5:00
31/Oct/1999 2:00 6:00
2/Apr/2000 2:00 5:00
29/Oct/2000 2:00 6:00
....

Time Table # 204
Before 1/Jan/1891 LMT
Begin Standard 90w00
1/Jan/1891 0:00 6:00
14/Apr/1918 2:00 5:00
31/Oct/1918 2:00 6:00
16/May/1937 2:00 5:00
26/Sep/1937 2:00 6:00
9/Feb/1942 2:00 5:00
30/Sep/1945 2:00 6:00
24/Apr/1949 2:00 5:00
25/Sep/1949 2:00 6:00
30/Apr/1950 2:00 5:00
24/Sep/1950 2:00 6:00
29/Apr/1951 2:00 5:00
30/Sep/1951 2:00 6:00
12/May/1963 2:00 5:00
7/Sep/1963 2:00 6:00
26/Apr/1964 2:00 5:00
13/Sep/1964 2:00 6:00
25/Apr/1965 2:00 5:00
12/Sep/1965 2:00 6:00
30/Apr/1967 2:00 5:00
29/Oct/1967 2:00 6:00
28/Apr/1968 2:00 5:00
27/Oct/1968 2:00 6:00
27/Apr/1969 2:00 5:00
26/Oct/1969 2:00 6:00
26/Apr/1970 2:00 5:00
25/Oct/1970 2:00 6:00
25/Apr/1971 2:00 5:00
31/Oct/1971 2:00 6:00
30/Apr/1972 2:00 5:00
29/Oct/1972 2:00 6:00
29/Apr/1973 2:00 5:00
28/Oct/1973 2:00 6:00
28/Apr/1974 2:00 5:00
27/Oct/1974 2:00 6:00
27/Apr/1975 2:00 5:00
26/Oct/1975 2:00 6:00
25/Apr/1976 2:00 5:00
31/Oct/1976 2:00 6:00
24/Apr/1977 2:00 5:00
30/Oct/1977 2:00 6:00
30/Apr/1978 2:00 5:00
29/Oct/1978 2:00 6:00
29/Apr/1979 2:00 5:00
28/Oct/1979 2:00 6:00
27/Apr/1980 2:00 5:00
26/Oct/1980 2:00 6:00
26/Apr/1981 2:00 5:00
25/Oct/1981 2:00 6:00
25/Apr/1982 2:00 5:00
31/Oct/1982 2:00 6:00
24/Apr/1983 2:00 5:00
30/Oct/1983 2:00 6:00
29/Apr/1984 2:00 5:00
28/Oct/1984 2:00 6:00
28/Apr/1985 2:00 5:00
27/Oct/1985 2:00 6:00
27/Apr/1986 2:00 5:00
26/Oct/1986 2:00 6:00
5/Apr/1987 2:00 5:00
25/Oct/1987 2:00 6:00
3/Apr/1988 2:00 5:00
30/Oct/1988 2:00 6:00
2/Apr/1989 2:00 5:00
29/Oct/1989 2:00 6:00
1/Apr/1990 2:00 5:00
28/Oct/1990 2:00 6:00
7/Apr/1991 2:00 5:00
27/Oct/1991 2:00 6:00
5/Apr/1992 2:00 5:00
25/Oct/1992 2:00 6:00
4/Apr/1993 2:00 5:00
31/Oct/1993 2:00 6:00
3/Apr/1994 2:00 5:00
30/Oct/1994 2:00 6:00
2/Apr/1995 2:00 5:00
29/Oct/1995 2:00 6:00
7/Apr/1996 2:00 5:00
27/Oct/1996 2:00 6:00
6/Apr/1997 2:00 5:00
26/Oct/1997 2:00 6:00
5/Apr/1998 2:00 5:00
25/Oct/1998 2:00 6:00
4/Apr/1999 2:00 5:00
31/Oct/1999 2:00 6:00
2/Apr/2000 2:00 5:00
29/Oct/2000 2:00 6:00
....

Time Table # 205
Before 1/Jan/1891 LMT
Begin Standard 90w00
1/Jan/1891 0:00 6:00
14/Apr/1918 2:00 5:00
31/Oct/1918 2:00 6:00
9/Feb/1942 2:00 5:00
30/Sep/1945 2:00 6:00
25/Apr/1948 2:00 5:00
26/Sep/1948 2:00 6:00
12/May/1963 2:00 5:00
7/Sep/1963 2:00 6:00
26/Apr/1964 2:00 5:00
13/Sep/1964 2:00 6:00
25/Apr/1965 2:00 5:00
12/Sep/1965 2:00 6:00
30/Apr/1967 2:00 5:00
29/Oct/1967 2:00 6:00
28/Apr/1968 2:00 5:00
27/Oct/1968 2:00 6:00
27/Apr/1969 2:00 5:00
26/Oct/1969 2:00 6:00
26/Apr/1970 2:00 5:00
25/Oct/1970 2:00 6:00
25/Apr/1971 2:00 5:00
31/Oct/1971 2:00 6:00
30/Apr/1972 2:00 5:00
29/Oct/1972 2:00 6:00
29/Apr/1973 2:00 5:00
28/Oct/1973 2:00 6:00
28/Apr/1974 2:00 5:00
27/Oct/1974 2:00 6:00
27/Apr/1975 2:00 5:00
26/Oct/1975 2:00 6:00
25/Apr/1976 2:00 5:00
31/Oct/1976 2:00 6:00
24/Apr/1977 2:00 5:00
30/Oct/1977 2:00 6:00
30/Apr/1978 2:00 5:00
29/Oct/1978 2:00 6:00
29/Apr/1979 2:00 5:00
28/Oct/1979 2:00 6:00
27/Apr/1980 2:00 5:00
26/Oct/1980 2:00 6:00
26/Apr/1981 2:00 5:00
25/Oct/1981 2:00 6:00
25/Apr/1982 2:00 5:00
31/Oct/1982 2:00 6:00
24/Apr/1983 2:00 5:00
30/Oct/1983 2:00 6:00
29/Apr/1984 2:00 5:00
28/Oct/1984 2:00 6:00
28/Apr/1985 2:00 5:00
27/Oct/1985 2:00 6:00
27/Apr/1986 2:00 5:00
26/Oct/1986 2:00 6:00
5/Apr/1987 2:00 5:00
25/Oct/1987 2:00 6:00
3/Apr/1988 2:00 5:00
30/Oct/1988 2:00 6:00
2/Apr/1989 2:00 5:00
29/Oct/1989 2:00 6:00
1/Apr/1990 2:00 5:00
28/Oct/1990 2:00 6:00
7/Apr/1991 2:00 5:00
27/Oct/1991 2:00 6:00
5/Apr/1992 2:00 5:00
25/Oct/1992 2:00 6:00
4/Apr/1993 2:00 5:00
31/Oct/1993 2:00 6:00
3/Apr/1994 2:00 5:00
30/Oct/1994 2:00 6:00
2/Apr/1995 2:00 5:00
29/Oct/1995 2:00 6:00
7/Apr/1996 2:00 5:00
27/Oct/1996 2:00 6:00
6/Apr/1997 2:00 5:00
26/Oct/1997 2:00 6:00
5/Apr/1998 2:00 5:00
25/Oct/1998 2:00 6:00
4/Apr/1999 2:00 5:00
31/Oct/1999 2:00 6:00
2/Apr/2000 2:00 5:00
29/Oct/2000 2:00 6:00
....

Time Table # 206
Before 1/Jan/1891 LMT
Begin Standard 90w00
1/Jan/1891 0:00 6:00
17/Apr/1916 0:00 5:00
19/Jun/1916 0:00 6:00
14/Apr/1918 2:00 5:00
31/Oct/1918 2:00 6:00
9/Feb/1942 2:00 5:00
30/Sep/1945 2:00 6:00
28/Apr/1946 2:00 5:00
29/Sep/1946 2:00 6:00
1/Jun/1963 2:00 5:00
1/Sep/1963 2:00 6:00
26/Apr/1964 2:00 5:00
13/Sep/1964 2:00 6:00
25/Apr/1965 2:00 5:00
12/Sep/1965 2:00 6:00
30/Apr/1966 2:00 5:00
29/Oct/1966 2:00 6:00
30/Apr/1967 2:00 5:00
29/Oct/1967 2:00 6:00
28/Apr/1968 2:00 5:00
27/Oct/1968 2:00 6:00
27/Apr/1969 2:00 5:00
26/Oct/1969 2:00 6:00
26/Apr/1970 2:00 5:00
25/Oct/1970 2:00 6:00
25/Apr/1971 2:00 5:00
31/Oct/1971 2:00 6:00
30/Apr/1972 2:00 5:00
29/Oct/1972 2:00 6:00
29/Apr/1973 2:00 5:00
28/Oct/1973 2:00 6:00
28/Apr/1974 2:00 5:00
27/Oct/1974 2:00 6:00
27/Apr/1975 2:00 5:00
26/Oct/1975 2:00 6:00
25/Apr/1976 2:00 5:00
31/Oct/1976 2:00 6:00
24/Apr/1977 2:00 5:00
30/Oct/1977 2:00 6:00
30/Apr/1978 2:00 5:00
29/Oct/1978 2:00 6:00
29/Apr/1979 2:00 5:00
28/Oct/1979 2:00 6:00
27/Apr/1980 2:00 5:00
26/Oct/1980 2:00 6:00
26/Apr/1981 2:00 5:00
25/Oct/1981 2:00 6:00
25/Apr/1982 2:00 5:00
31/Oct/1982 2:00 6:00
24/Apr/1983 2:00 5:00
30/Oct/1983 2:00 6:00
29/Apr/1984 2:00 5:00
28/Oct/1984 2:00 6:00
28/Apr/1985 2:00 5:00
27/Oct/1985 2:00 6:00
27/Apr/1986 2:00 5:00
26/Oct/1986 2:00 6:00
5/Apr/1987 2:00 5:00
25/Oct/1987 2:00 6:00
3/Apr/1988 2:00 5:00
30/Oct/1988 2:00 6:00
2/Apr/1989 2:00 5:00
29/Oct/1989 2:00 6:00
1/Apr/1990 2:00 5:00
28/Oct/1990 2:00 6:00
7/Apr/1991 2:00 5:00
27/Oct/1991 2:00 6:00
5/Apr/1992 2:00 5:00
25/Oct/1992 2:00 6:00
4/Apr/1993 2:00 5:00
31/Oct/1993 2:00 6:00
3/Apr/1994 2:00 5:00
30/Oct/1994 2:00 6:00
2/Apr/1995 2:00 5:00
29/Oct/1995 2:00 6:00
7/Apr/1996 2:00 5:00
27/Oct/1996 2:00 6:00
6/Apr/1997 2:00 5:00
26/Oct/1997 2:00 6:00
5/Apr/1998 2:00 5:00
25/Oct/1998 2:00 6:00
4/Apr/1999 2:00 5:00
31/Oct/1999 2:00 6:00
2/Apr/2000 2:00 5:00
29/Oct/2000 2:00 6:00
....

Time Table # 207
Before 1/Jan/1891 LMT
Begin Standard 90w00
1/Jan/1891 0:00 6:00
14/Apr/1918 2:00 5:00
31/Oct/1918 2:00 6:00
9/Feb/1942 2:00 5:00
30/Sep/1945 2:00 6:00
27/Apr/1947 2:00 5:00
31/Aug/1947 2:00 6:00
12/May/1963 2:00 5:00
7/Sep/1963 2:00 6:00
26/Apr/1964 2:00 5:00
13/Sep/1964 2:00 6:00
25/Apr/1965 2:00 5:00
12/Sep/1965 2:00 6:00
24/Apr/1966 2:00 5:00
11/Sep/1966 2:00 6:00
30/Apr/1967 2:00 5:00
29/Oct/1967 2:00 6:00
28/Apr/1968 2:00 5:00
27/Oct/1968 2:00 6:00
27/Apr/1969 2:00 5:00
26/Oct/1969 2:00 6:00
26/Apr/1970 2:00 5:00
25/Oct/1970 2:00 6:00
25/Apr/1971 2:00 5:00
31/Oct/1971 2:00 6:00
30/Apr/1972 2:00 5:00
29/Oct/1972 2:00 6:00
29/Apr/1973 2:00 5:00
28/Oct/1973 2:00 6:00
28/Apr/1974 2:00 5:00
27/Oct/1974 2:00 6:00
27/Apr/1975 2:00 5:00
26/Oct/1975 2:00 6:00
25/Apr/1976 2:00 5:00
31/Oct/1976 2:00 6:00
24/Apr/1977 2:00 5:00
30/Oct/1977 2:00 6:00
30/Apr/1978 2:00 5:00
29/Oct/1978 2:00 6:00
29/Apr/1979 2:00 5:00
28/Oct/1979 2:00 6:00
27/Apr/1980 2:00 5:00
26/Oct/1980 2:00 6:00
26/Apr/1981 2:00 5:00
25/Oct/1981 2:00 6:00
25/Apr/1982 2:00 5:00
31/Oct/1982 2:00 6:00
24/Apr/1983 2:00 5:00
30/Oct/1983 2:00 6:00
29/Apr/1984 2:00 5:00
28/Oct/1984 2:00 6:00
28/Apr/1985 2:00 5:00
27/Oct/1985 2:00 6:00
27/Apr/1986 2:00 5:00
26/Oct/1986 2:00 6:00
5/Apr/1987 2:00 5:00
25/Oct/1987 2:00 6:00
3/Apr/1988 2:00 5:00
30/Oct/1988 2:00 6:00
2/Apr/1989 2:00 5:00
29/Oct/1989 2:00 6:00
1/Apr/1990 2:00 5:00
28/Oct/1990 2:00 6:00
7/Apr/1991 2:00 5:00
27/Oct/1991 2:00 6:00
5/Apr/1992 2:00 5:00
25/Oct/1992 2:00 6:00
4/Apr/1993 2:00 5:00
31/Oct/1993 2:00 6:00
3/Apr/1994 2:00 5:00
30/Oct/1994 2:00 6:00
2/Apr/1995 2:00 5:00
29/Oct/1995 2:00 6:00
7/Apr/1996 2:00 5:00
27/Oct/1996 2:00 6:00
6/Apr/1997 2:00 5:00
26/Oct/1997 2:00 6:00
5/Apr/1998 2:00 5:00
25/Oct/1998 2:00 6:00
4/Apr/1999 2:00 5:00
31/Oct/1999 2:00 6:00
2/Apr/2000 2:00 5:00
29/Oct/2000 2:00 6:00
....

Time Table # 208
Before 1/Jan/1891 LMT
Begin Standard 90w00
1/Jan/1891 0:00 6:00
14/Apr/1918 2:00 5:00
31/Oct/1918 2:00 6:00
9/Feb/1942 2:00 5:00
30/Sep/1945 2:00 6:00
27/Apr/1947 2:00 5:00
28/Sep/1947 2:00 6:00
25/Apr/1948 2:00 5:00
26/Sep/1948 2:00 6:00
3/Jul/1949 2:00 5:00
25/Sep/1949 2:00 6:00
2/Jul/1950 2:00 5:00
30/Sep/1950 2:00 6:00
12/May/1963 2:00 5:00
7/Sep/1963 2:00 6:00
26/Apr/1964 2:00 5:00
13/Sep/1964 2:00 6:00
25/Apr/1965 2:00 5:00
12/Sep/1965 2:00 6:00
24/Apr/1966 2:00 5:00
11/Sep/1966 2:00 6:00
30/Apr/1967 2:00 5:00
29/Oct/1967 2:00 6:00
28/Apr/1968 2:00 5:00
27/Oct/1968 2:00 6:00
27/Apr/1969 2:00 5:00
26/Oct/1969 2:00 6:00
26/Apr/1970 2:00 5:00
25/Oct/1970 2:00 6:00
25/Apr/1971 2:00 5:00
31/Oct/1971 2:00 6:00
30/Apr/1972 2:00 5:00
29/Oct/1972 2:00 6:00
29/Apr/1973 2:00 5:00
28/Oct/1973 2:00 6:00
28/Apr/1974 2:00 5:00
27/Oct/1974 2:00 6:00
27/Apr/1975 2:00 5:00
26/Oct/1975 2:00 6:00
25/Apr/1976 2:00 5:00
31/Oct/1976 2:00 6:00
24/Apr/1977 2:00 5:00
30/Oct/1977 2:00 6:00
30/Apr/1978 2:00 5:00
29/Oct/1978 2:00 6:00
29/Apr/1979 2:00 5:00
28/Oct/1979 2:00 6:00
27/Apr/1980 2:00 5:00
26/Oct/1980 2:00 6:00
26/Apr/1981 2:00 5:00
25/Oct/1981 2:00 6:00
25/Apr/1982 2:00 5:00
31/Oct/1982 2:00 6:00
24/Apr/1983 2:00 5:00
30/Oct/1983 2:00 6:00
29/Apr/1984 2:00 5:00
28/Oct/1984 2:00 6:00
28/Apr/1985 2:00 5:00
27/Oct/1985 2:00 6:00
27/Apr/1986 2:00 5:00
26/Oct/1986 2:00 6:00
5/Apr/1987 2:00 5:00
25/Oct/1987 2:00 6:00
3/Apr/1988 2:00 5:00
30/Oct/1988 2:00 6:00
2/Apr/1989 2:00 5:00
29/Oct/1989 2:00 6:00
1/Apr/1990 2:00 5:00
28/Oct/1990 2:00 6:00
7/Apr/1991 2:00 5:00
27/Oct/1991 2:00 6:00
5/Apr/1992 2:00 5:00
25/Oct/1992 2:00 6:00
4/Apr/1993 2:00 5:00
31/Oct/1993 2:00 6:00
3/Apr/1994 2:00 5:00
30/Oct/1994 2:00 6:00
2/Apr/1995 2:00 5:00
29/Oct/1995 2:00 6:00
7/Apr/1996 2:00 5:00
27/Oct/1996 2:00 6:00
6/Apr/1997 2:00 5:00
26/Oct/1997 2:00 6:00
5/Apr/1998 2:00 5:00
25/Oct/1998 2:00 6:00
4/Apr/1999 2:00 5:00
31/Oct/1999 2:00 6:00
2/Apr/2000 2:00 5:00
29/Oct/2000 2:00 6:00
....

Time Table # 209
Before 1/Jan/1891 LMT
Begin Standard 90w00
1/Jan/1891 0:00 6:00
14/Apr/1918 2:00 5:00
31/Oct/1918 2:00 6:00
9/Feb/1942 2:00 5:00
30/Sep/1945 2:00 6:00
24/Apr/1949 2:00 5:00
25/Sep/1949 2:00 6:00
24/Apr/1955 2:00 5:00
25/Sep/1955 2:00 6:00
12/May/1963 2:00 5:00
7/Sep/1963 2:00 6:00
26/Apr/1964 2:00 5:00
13/Sep/1964 2:00 6:00
25/Apr/1965 2:00 5:00
12/Sep/1965 2:00 6:00
30/Apr/1967 2:00 5:00
29/Oct/1967 2:00 6:00
28/Apr/1968 2:00 5:00
27/Oct/1968 2:00 6:00
27/Apr/1969 2:00 5:00
26/Oct/1969 2:00 6:00
26/Apr/1970 2:00 5:00
25/Oct/1970 2:00 6:00
25/Apr/1971 2:00 5:00
31/Oct/1971 2:00 6:00
30/Apr/1972 2:00 5:00
29/Oct/1972 2:00 6:00
29/Apr/1973 2:00 5:00
28/Oct/1973 2:00 6:00
28/Apr/1974 2:00 5:00
27/Oct/1974 2:00 6:00
27/Apr/1975 2:00 5:00
26/Oct/1975 2:00 6:00
25/Apr/1976 2:00 5:00
31/Oct/1976 2:00 6:00
24/Apr/1977 2:00 5:00
30/Oct/1977 2:00 6:00
30/Apr/1978 2:00 5:00
29/Oct/1978 2:00 6:00
29/Apr/1979 2:00 5:00
28/Oct/1979 2:00 6:00
27/Apr/1980 2:00 5:00
26/Oct/1980 2:00 6:00
26/Apr/1981 2:00 5:00
25/Oct/1981 2:00 6:00
25/Apr/1982 2:00 5:00
31/Oct/1982 2:00 6:00
24/Apr/1983 2:00 5:00
30/Oct/1983 2:00 6:00
29/Apr/1984 2:00 5:00
28/Oct/1984 2:00 6:00
28/Apr/1985 2:00 5:00
27/Oct/1985 2:00 6:00
27/Apr/1986 2:00 5:00
26/Oct/1986 2:00 6:00
5/Apr/1987 2:00 5:00
25/Oct/1987 2:00 6:00
3/Apr/1988 2:00 5:00
30/Oct/1988 2:00 6:00
2/Apr/1989 2:00 5:00
29/Oct/1989 2:00 6:00
1/Apr/1990 2:00 5:00
28/Oct/1990 2:00 6:00
7/Apr/1991 2:00 5:00
27/Oct/1991 2:00 6:00
5/Apr/1992 2:00 5:00
25/Oct/1992 2:00 6:00
4/Apr/1993 2:00 5:00
31/Oct/1993 2:00 6:00
3/Apr/1994 2:00 5:00
30/Oct/1994 2:00 6:00
2/Apr/1995 2:00 5:00
29/Oct/1995 2:00 6:00
7/Apr/1996 2:00 5:00
27/Oct/1996 2:00 6:00
6/Apr/1997 2:00 5:00
26/Oct/1997 2:00 6:00
5/Apr/1998 2:00 5:00
25/Oct/1998 2:00 6:00
4/Apr/1999 2:00 5:00
31/Oct/1999 2:00 6:00
2/Apr/2000 2:00 5:00
29/Oct/2000 2:00 6:00
....

Time Table # 210
Before 1/Jan/1891 LMT
Begin Standard 90w00
1/Jan/1891 0:00 6:00
14/Apr/1918 2:00 5:00
31/Oct/1918 2:00 6:00
9/Feb/1942 2:00 5:00
30/Sep/1945 2:00 6:00
27/Apr/1952 2:00 5:00
28/Sep/1952 2:00 6:00
26/Apr/1953 2:00 5:00
27/Sep/1953 2:00 6:00
25/Apr/1954 2:00 5:00
26/Sep/1954 2:00 6:00
24/Apr/1955 2:00 5:00
25/Sep/1955 2:00 6:00
12/May/1963 2:00 5:00
7/Sep/1963 2:00 6:00
26/Apr/1964 2:00 5:00
13/Sep/1964 2:00 6:00
25/Apr/1965 2:00 5:00

Date	Time	Offset
12/Sep/1965	2:00	6:00
30/Apr/1967	2:00	5:00
29/Oct/1967	2:00	6:00
28/Apr/1968	2:00	5:00
27/Oct/1968	2:00	6:00
27/Apr/1969	2:00	5:00
26/Oct/1969	2:00	6:00
26/Apr/1970	2:00	5:00
25/Oct/1970	2:00	6:00
25/Apr/1971	2:00	5:00
31/Oct/1971	2:00	6:00
30/Apr/1972	2:00	5:00
29/Oct/1972	2:00	6:00
29/Apr/1973	2:00	5:00
28/Oct/1973	2:00	6:00
28/Apr/1974	2:00	5:00
27/Oct/1974	2:00	6:00
27/Apr/1975	2:00	5:00
26/Oct/1975	2:00	6:00
25/Apr/1976	2:00	5:00
31/Oct/1976	2:00	6:00
24/Apr/1977	2:00	5:00
30/Oct/1977	2:00	6:00
30/Apr/1978	2:00	5:00
29/Oct/1978	2:00	6:00
29/Apr/1979	2:00	5:00
28/Oct/1979	2:00	6:00
27/Apr/1980	2:00	5:00
26/Oct/1980	2:00	6:00
26/Apr/1981	2:00	5:00
25/Oct/1981	2:00	6:00
25/Apr/1982	2:00	5:00
31/Oct/1982	2:00	6:00
24/Apr/1983	2:00	5:00
30/Oct/1983	2:00	6:00
29/Apr/1984	2:00	5:00
28/Oct/1984	2:00	6:00
28/Apr/1985	2:00	5:00
27/Oct/1985	2:00	6:00
27/Apr/1986	2:00	5:00
26/Oct/1986	2:00	6:00
5/Apr/1987	2:00	5:00
25/Oct/1987	2:00	6:00
3/Apr/1988	2:00	5:00
30/Oct/1988	2:00	6:00
2/Apr/1989	2:00	5:00
29/Oct/1989	2:00	6:00
1/Apr/1990	2:00	5:00
28/Oct/1990	2:00	6:00
7/Apr/1991	2:00	5:00
27/Oct/1991	2:00	6:00
5/Apr/1992	2:00	5:00
25/Oct/1992	2:00	6:00
4/Apr/1993	2:00	5:00
31/Oct/1993	2:00	6:00
3/Apr/1994	2:00	5:00
30/Oct/1994	2:00	6:00
2/Apr/1995	2:00	5:00
29/Oct/1995	2:00	6:00
7/Apr/1996	2:00	5:00
27/Oct/1996	2:00	6:00
6/Apr/1997	2:00	5:00
26/Oct/1997	2:00	6:00
5/Apr/1998	2:00	5:00
25/Oct/1998	2:00	6:00
4/Apr/1999	2:00	5:00
31/Oct/1999	2:00	6:00
2/Apr/2000	2:00	5:00
29/Oct/2000	2:00	6:00

Time Table # 211

Before 26/Apr/1853 LMT

Begin Standard 90w00

Date	Time	Offset
26/Apr/1853	2:00	6:00
14/Apr/1918	2:00	5:00
31/Oct/1918	2:00	6:00
16/May/1937	2:00	5:00
26/Sep/1937	2:00	6:00
9/Feb/1942	2:00	5:00
30/Sep/1945	2:00	6:00
12/May/1946	2:00	5:00
13/Oct/1946	2:00	6:00
27/Apr/1947	2:00	5:00
28/Sep/1947	2:00	6:00
25/Apr/1948	2:00	5:00
26/Sep/1948	2:00	6:00
24/Apr/1949	2:00	5:00
25/Sep/1949	2:00	6:00
1/May/1950	2:00	5:00
30/Sep/1950	2:00	6:00
29/Apr/1951	2:00	5:00
30/Sep/1951	2:00	6:00
26/Apr/1953	2:00	5:00
27/Sep/1953	2:00	6:00
25/Apr/1954	2:00	5:00
26/Sep/1954	2:00	6:00
24/Apr/1955	2:00	5:00
25/Sep/1955	2:00	6:00
12/May/1963	2:00	5:00
7/Sep/1963	2:00	6:00
26/Apr/1964	2:00	5:00
13/Sep/1964	2:00	6:00
25/Apr/1965	2:00	5:00
12/Sep/1965	2:00	6:00
30/Apr/1967	2:00	5:00
29/Oct/1967	2:00	6:00
28/Apr/1968	2:00	5:00
27/Oct/1968	2:00	6:00
27/Apr/1969	2:00	5:00
26/Oct/1969	2:00	6:00
26/Apr/1970	2:00	5:00
25/Oct/1970	2:00	6:00
25/Apr/1971	2:00	5:00
31/Oct/1971	2:00	6:00
30/Apr/1972	2:00	5:00
29/Oct/1972	2:00	6:00
29/Apr/1973	2:00	5:00
28/Oct/1973	2:00	6:00
28/Apr/1974	2:00	5:00
27/Oct/1974	2:00	6:00
27/Apr/1975	2:00	5:00
26/Oct/1975	2:00	6:00
25/Apr/1976	2:00	5:00
31/Oct/1976	2:00	6:00
24/Apr/1977	2:00	5:00
30/Oct/1977	2:00	6:00
30/Apr/1978	2:00	5:00
29/Oct/1978	2:00	6:00
29/Apr/1979	2:00	5:00
28/Oct/1979	2:00	6:00
27/Apr/1980	2:00	5:00
26/Oct/1980	2:00	6:00
26/Apr/1981	2:00	5:00
25/Oct/1981	2:00	6:00
25/Apr/1982	2:00	5:00
31/Oct/1982	2:00	6:00
24/Apr/1983	2:00	5:00
30/Oct/1983	2:00	6:00
29/Apr/1984	2:00	5:00
28/Oct/1984	2:00	6:00
28/Apr/1985	2:00	5:00
27/Oct/1985	2:00	6:00
27/Apr/1986	2:00	5:00
26/Oct/1986	2:00	6:00
5/Apr/1987	2:00	5:00
25/Oct/1987	2:00	6:00
3/Apr/1988	2:00	5:00
30/Oct/1988	2:00	6:00
2/Apr/1989	2:00	5:00
29/Oct/1989	2:00	6:00
1/Apr/1990	2:00	5:00
28/Oct/1990	2:00	6:00
7/Apr/1991	2:00	5:00
27/Oct/1991	2:00	6:00
5/Apr/1992	2:00	5:00
25/Oct/1992	2:00	6:00
4/Apr/1993	2:00	5:00
31/Oct/1993	2:00	6:00
3/Apr/1994	2:00	5:00
30/Oct/1994	2:00	6:00
2/Apr/1995	2:00	5:00
29/Oct/1995	2:00	6:00
7/Apr/1996	2:00	5:00
27/Oct/1996	2:00	6:00
6/Apr/1997	2:00	5:00
26/Oct/1997	2:00	6:00
5/Apr/1998	2:00	5:00
25/Oct/1998	2:00	6:00
4/Apr/1999	2:00	5:00
31/Oct/1999	2:00	6:00
2/Apr/2000	2:00	5:00
29/Oct/2000	2:00	6:00

Time Table # 212

Before 1/Jan/1891 LMT

Begin Standard 90w00

Date	Time	Offset
1/Jan/1891	0:00	6:00
14/Apr/1918	2:00	5:00
31/Oct/1918	2:00	6:00
9/Feb/1942	2:00	5:00
30/Sep/1945	2:00	6:00
28/Apr/1946	2:00	5:00
15/Aug/1946	2:00	6:00
27/Apr/1947	2:00	5:00
17/Aug/1947	2:00	6:00
29/Apr/1956	2:00	5:00
30/Sep/1956	2:00	6:00
30/Apr/1961	2:00	5:00
24/Sep/1961	2:00	6:00
29/Apr/1962	2:00	5:00
28/Oct/1962	2:00	6:00
28/Apr/1963	2:00	5:00
22/Sep/1963	2:00	6:00
24/Apr/1966	2:00	5:00
11/Sep/1966	2:00	6:00
30/Apr/1967	2:00	5:00
29/Oct/1967	2:00	6:00
28/Apr/1968	2:00	5:00
27/Oct/1968	2:00	6:00
27/Apr/1969	2:00	5:00
26/Oct/1969	2:00	6:00
26/Apr/1970	2:00	5:00
25/Oct/1970	2:00	6:00
25/Apr/1971	2:00	5:00
31/Oct/1971	2:00	6:00
30/Apr/1972	2:00	5:00
29/Oct/1972	2:00	6:00
29/Apr/1973	2:00	5:00
28/Oct/1973	2:00	6:00
28/Apr/1974	2:00	5:00
27/Oct/1974	2:00	6:00
27/Apr/1975	2:00	5:00
26/Oct/1975	2:00	6:00
25/Apr/1976	2:00	5:00
31/Oct/1976	2:00	6:00
24/Apr/1977	2:00	5:00
30/Oct/1977	2:00	6:00
30/Apr/1978	2:00	5:00
29/Oct/1978	2:00	6:00
29/Apr/1979	2:00	5:00
28/Oct/1979	2:00	6:00
27/Apr/1980	2:00	5:00
26/Oct/1980	2:00	6:00
26/Apr/1981	2:00	5:00
25/Oct/1981	2:00	6:00
25/Apr/1982	2:00	5:00
31/Oct/1982	2:00	6:00
24/Apr/1983	2:00	5:00
30/Oct/1983	2:00	6:00
29/Apr/1984	2:00	5:00
28/Oct/1984	2:00	6:00
28/Apr/1985	2:00	5:00
27/Oct/1985	2:00	6:00
27/Apr/1986	2:00	5:00
26/Oct/1986	2:00	6:00
5/Apr/1987	2:00	5:00
25/Oct/1987	2:00	6:00
3/Apr/1988	2:00	5:00
30/Oct/1988	2:00	6:00
2/Apr/1989	2:00	5:00
29/Oct/1989	2:00	6:00
1/Apr/1990	2:00	5:00
28/Oct/1990	2:00	6:00
7/Apr/1991	2:00	5:00
27/Oct/1991	2:00	6:00
5/Apr/1992	2:00	5:00
25/Oct/1992	2:00	6:00
4/Apr/1993	2:00	5:00
31/Oct/1993	2:00	6:00
3/Apr/1994	2:00	5:00
30/Oct/1994	2:00	6:00
2/Apr/1995	2:00	5:00
29/Oct/1995	2:00	6:00
7/Apr/1996	2:00	5:00
27/Oct/1996	2:00	6:00
6/Apr/1997	2:00	5:00
26/Oct/1997	2:00	6:00
5/Apr/1998	2:00	5:00
25/Oct/1998	2:00	6:00
4/Apr/1999	2:00	5:00
31/Oct/1999	2:00	6:00
2/Apr/2000	2:00	5:00
29/Oct/2000	2:00	6:00

Time Table # 213

Before 1/Jan/1891 LMT

Begin Standard 90w00

Date	Time	Offset
1/Jan/1891	0:00	6:00
14/Apr/1918	2:00	5:00
31/Oct/1918	2:00	6:00
9/Feb/1942	2:00	5:00
30/Sep/1945	2:00	6:00
24/Apr/1949	2:00	5:00
25/Sep/1949	2:00	6:00
12/May/1963	2:00	5:00
7/Sep/1963	2:00	6:00
26/Apr/1964	2:00	5:00
13/Sep/1964	2:00	6:00
25/Apr/1965	2:00	5:00
12/Sep/1965	2:00	6:00
30/Apr/1967	2:00	5:00
29/Oct/1967	2:00	6:00
28/Apr/1968	2:00	5:00
27/Oct/1968	2:00	6:00
27/Apr/1969	2:00	5:00
26/Oct/1969	2:00	6:00
26/Apr/1970	2:00	5:00
25/Oct/1970	2:00	6:00
25/Apr/1971	2:00	5:00
31/Oct/1971	2:00	6:00
30/Apr/1972	2:00	5:00
29/Oct/1972	2:00	6:00
29/Apr/1973	2:00	5:00
28/Oct/1973	2:00	6:00
28/Apr/1974	2:00	5:00
27/Oct/1974	2:00	6:00
27/Apr/1975	2:00	5:00
26/Oct/1975	2:00	6:00
25/Apr/1976	2:00	5:00
31/Oct/1976	2:00	6:00
24/Apr/1977	2:00	5:00
30/Oct/1977	2:00	6:00
30/Apr/1978	2:00	5:00
29/Oct/1978	2:00	6:00
29/Apr/1979	2:00	5:00
28/Oct/1979	2:00	6:00
27/Apr/1980	2:00	5:00
26/Oct/1980	2:00	6:00
26/Apr/1981	2:00	5:00
25/Oct/1981	2:00	6:00
25/Apr/1982	2:00	5:00
31/Oct/1982	2:00	6:00
24/Apr/1983	2:00	5:00
30/Oct/1983	2:00	6:00
29/Apr/1984	2:00	5:00
28/Oct/1984	2:00	6:00
28/Apr/1985	2:00	5:00
27/Oct/1985	2:00	6:00
27/Apr/1986	2:00	5:00
26/Oct/1986	2:00	6:00
5/Apr/1987	2:00	5:00
25/Oct/1987	2:00	6:00
3/Apr/1988	2:00	5:00
30/Oct/1988	2:00	6:00
2/Apr/1989	2:00	5:00
29/Oct/1989	2:00	6:00
1/Apr/1990	2:00	5:00
28/Oct/1990	2:00	6:00
7/Apr/1991	2:00	5:00
27/Oct/1991	2:00	6:00
5/Apr/1992	2:00	5:00
25/Oct/1992	2:00	6:00
4/Apr/1993	2:00	5:00
31/Oct/1993	2:00	6:00
3/Apr/1994	2:00	5:00
30/Oct/1994	2:00	6:00
2/Apr/1995	2:00	5:00
29/Oct/1995	2:00	6:00
7/Apr/1996	2:00	5:00
27/Oct/1996	2:00	6:00
6/Apr/1997	2:00	5:00
26/Oct/1997	2:00	6:00
5/Apr/1998	2:00	5:00
25/Oct/1998	2:00	6:00
4/Apr/1999	2:00	5:00
31/Oct/1999	2:00	6:00
2/Apr/2000	2:00	5:00
29/Oct/2000	2:00	6:00

Time Table # 214

Before 1/Jan/1891 LMT

Begin Standard 90w00

Date	Time	Offset
1/Jan/1891	0:00	6:00
14/Apr/1918	2:00	5:00
31/Oct/1918	2:00	6:00
9/Feb/1942	2:00	5:00
30/Sep/1945	2:00	6:00
28/Apr/1946	2:00	5:00
13/Oct/1946	2:00	6:00
27/Apr/1947	2:00	5:00
28/Sep/1947	2:00	6:00
25/Apr/1948	2:00	5:00
26/Sep/1948	2:00	6:00
1/May/1950	2:00	5:00
30/Sep/1950	2:00	6:00
29/Apr/1951	2:00	5:00
30/Sep/1951	2:00	6:00
27/Apr/1952	2:00	5:00
28/Sep/1952	2:00	6:00
26/Apr/1953	2:00	5:00
27/Sep/1953	2:00	6:00
25/Apr/1954	2:00	5:00
26/Sep/1954	2:00	6:00
24/Apr/1955	2:00	5:00
25/Sep/1955	2:00	6:00
29/Apr/1956	2:00	5:00
30/Sep/1956	2:00	6:00
28/Apr/1957	2:00	5:00
29/Sep/1957	2:00	6:00
27/Apr/1958	2:00	5:00
28/Sep/1958	2:00	6:00
28/Apr/1963	2:00	5:00
22/Sep/1963	2:00	6:00
24/Apr/1966	2:00	5:00
30/Oct/1966	2:00	6:00
30/Apr/1967	2:00	5:00
29/Oct/1967	2:00	6:00
28/Apr/1968	2:00	5:00
27/Oct/1968	2:00	6:00
27/Apr/1969	2:00	5:00
26/Oct/1969	2:00	6:00
26/Apr/1970	2:00	5:00
25/Oct/1970	2:00	6:00
25/Apr/1971	2:00	5:00
31/Oct/1971	2:00	6:00
30/Apr/1972	2:00	5:00
29/Oct/1972	2:00	6:00
29/Apr/1973	2:00	5:00
28/Oct/1973	2:00	6:00
28/Apr/1974	2:00	5:00
27/Oct/1974	2:00	6:00
27/Apr/1975	2:00	5:00
26/Oct/1975	2:00	6:00
25/Apr/1976	2:00	5:00
31/Oct/1976	2:00	6:00
24/Apr/1977	2:00	5:00
30/Oct/1977	2:00	6:00
30/Apr/1978	2:00	5:00
29/Oct/1978	2:00	6:00
29/Apr/1979	2:00	5:00
28/Oct/1979	2:00	6:00
27/Apr/1980	2:00	5:00
26/Oct/1980	2:00	6:00
26/Apr/1981	2:00	5:00
25/Oct/1981	2:00	6:00
25/Apr/1982	2:00	5:00
31/Oct/1982	2:00	6:00
24/Apr/1983	2:00	5:00
30/Oct/1983	2:00	6:00
29/Apr/1984	2:00	5:00
28/Oct/1984	2:00	6:00
28/Apr/1985	2:00	5:00
27/Oct/1985	2:00	6:00
27/Apr/1986	2:00	5:00
26/Oct/1986	2:00	6:00
5/Apr/1987	2:00	5:00
25/Oct/1987	2:00	6:00
3/Apr/1988	2:00	5:00
30/Oct/1988	2:00	6:00
2/Apr/1989	2:00	5:00
29/Oct/1989	2:00	6:00
1/Apr/1990	2:00	5:00
28/Oct/1990	2:00	6:00
7/Apr/1991	2:00	5:00
27/Oct/1991	2:00	6:00
5/Apr/1992	2:00	5:00
25/Oct/1992	2:00	6:00
4/Apr/1993	2:00	5:00
31/Oct/1993	2:00	6:00
3/Apr/1994	2:00	5:00
30/Oct/1994	2:00	6:00
2/Apr/1995	2:00	5:00
29/Oct/1995	2:00	6:00
7/Apr/1996	2:00	5:00
27/Oct/1996	2:00	6:00
6/Apr/1997	2:00	5:00
26/Oct/1997	2:00	6:00
5/Apr/1998	2:00	5:00
25/Oct/1998	2:00	6:00
4/Apr/1999	2:00	5:00
31/Oct/1999	2:00	6:00
2/Apr/2000	2:00	5:00
29/Oct/2000	2:00	6:00

Time Table # 215

Before 1/Jan/1891 LMT

Begin Standard 90w00

Date	Time	Offset
1/Jan/1891	0:00	6:00
14/Apr/1918	2:00	5:00
31/Oct/1918	2:00	6:00
16/May/1937	2:00	5:00
26/Sep/1937	2:00	6:00
9/Feb/1942	2:00	5:00
30/Sep/1945	2:00	6:00
28/Apr/1946	2:00	5:00
29/Sep/1946	2:00	6:00
25/Apr/1948	2:00	5:00
26/Sep/1948	2:00	6:00
24/Apr/1949	2:00	5:00
25/Sep/1949	2:00	6:00
1/May/1950	2:00	5:00
30/Sep/1950	2:00	6:00
29/Apr/1951	2:00	5:00
30/Sep/1951	2:00	6:00
27/Apr/1952	2:00	5:00
28/Sep/1952	2:00	6:00
26/Apr/1953	2:00	5:00
27/Sep/1953	2:00	6:00
25/Apr/1954	2:00	5:00
26/Sep/1954	2:00	6:00
24/Apr/1955	2:00	5:00
25/Sep/1955	2:00	6:00
12/May/1963	2:00	5:00
7/Sep/1963	2:00	6:00
26/Apr/1964	2:00	5:00
13/Sep/1964	2:00	6:00
25/Apr/1965	2:00	5:00
12/Sep/1965	2:00	6:00
30/Apr/1967	2:00	5:00
29/Oct/1967	2:00	6:00
28/Apr/1968	2:00	5:00
27/Oct/1968	2:00	6:00
27/Apr/1969	2:00	5:00
26/Oct/1969	2:00	6:00
26/Apr/1970	2:00	5:00
25/Oct/1970	2:00	6:00
25/Apr/1971	2:00	5:00
31/Oct/1971	2:00	6:00
30/Apr/1972	2:00	5:00
29/Oct/1972	2:00	6:00
29/Apr/1973	2:00	5:00
28/Oct/1973	2:00	6:00
28/Apr/1974	2:00	5:00
27/Oct/1974	2:00	6:00
27/Apr/1975	2:00	5:00
26/Oct/1975	2:00	6:00
25/Apr/1976	2:00	5:00
31/Oct/1976	2:00	6:00
24/Apr/1977	2:00	5:00
30/Oct/1977	2:00	6:00
30/Apr/1978	2:00	5:00
29/Oct/1978	2:00	6:00
29/Apr/1979	2:00	5:00
28/Oct/1979	2:00	6:00
27/Apr/1980	2:00	5:00
26/Oct/1980	2:00	6:00
26/Apr/1981	2:00	5:00
25/Oct/1981	2:00	6:00
25/Apr/1982	2:00	5:00
31/Oct/1982	2:00	6:00
24/Apr/1983	2:00	5:00
30/Oct/1983	2:00	6:00
29/Apr/1984	2:00	5:00
28/Oct/1984	2:00	6:00
28/Apr/1985	2:00	5:00
27/Oct/1985	2:00	6:00
27/Apr/1986	2:00	5:00
26/Oct/1986	2:00	6:00
5/Apr/1987	2:00	5:00
25/Oct/1987	2:00	6:00
3/Apr/1988	2:00	5:00
30/Oct/1988	2:00	6:00
2/Apr/1989	2:00	5:00
29/Oct/1989	2:00	6:00
1/Apr/1990	2:00	5:00
28/Oct/1990	2:00	6:00
7/Apr/1991	2:00	5:00
27/Oct/1991	2:00	6:00
5/Apr/1992	2:00	5:00
25/Oct/1992	2:00	6:00
4/Apr/1993	2:00	5:00
31/Oct/1993	2:00	6:00
3/Apr/1994	2:00	5:00
30/Oct/1994	2:00	6:00
2/Apr/1995	2:00	5:00
29/Oct/1995	2:00	6:00
7/Apr/1996	2:00	5:00
27/Oct/1996	2:00	6:00
6/Apr/1997	2:00	5:00
26/Oct/1997	2:00	6:00
5/Apr/1998	2:00	5:00
25/Oct/1998	2:00	6:00
4/Apr/1999	2:00	5:00
31/Oct/1999	2:00	6:00
2/Apr/2000	2:00	5:00
29/Oct/2000	2:00	6:00

Time Table # 216

Before 1/Jan/1891 LMT

Begin Standard 90w00

Date	Time	Offset
1/Jan/1891	0:00	6:00
14/Apr/1918	2:00	5:00
31/Oct/1918	2:00	6:00
9/Feb/1942	2:00	5:00
30/Sep/1945	2:00	6:00
24/Apr/1949	2:00	5:00
25/Sep/1949	2:00	6:00
29/Apr/1951	2:00	5:00
30/Sep/1951	2:00	6:00
26/Apr/1953	2:00	5:00
27/Sep/1953	2:00	6:00
25/Apr/1954	2:00	5:00
26/Sep/1954	2:00	6:00
24/Apr/1955	2:00	5:00
25/Sep/1955	2:00	6:00

12/May/1963 2:00 5:00
7/Sep/1963 2:00 6:00
26/Apr/1964 2:00 5:00
13/Sep/1964 2:00 6:00
25/Apr/1965 2:00 5:00
12/Sep/1965 2:00 6:00
30/Apr/1967 2:00 5:00
29/Oct/1967 2:00 6:00
28/Apr/1968 2:00 5:00
27/Oct/1968 2:00 6:00
27/Apr/1969 2:00 5:00
26/Oct/1969 2:00 6:00
26/Apr/1970 2:00 5:00
25/Oct/1970 2:00 6:00
25/Apr/1971 2:00 5:00
31/Oct/1971 2:00 6:00
30/Apr/1972 2:00 5:00
29/Oct/1972 2:00 6:00
29/Apr/1973 2:00 5:00
28/Oct/1973 2:00 6:00
28/Apr/1974 2:00 5:00
27/Oct/1974 2:00 6:00
27/Apr/1975 2:00 5:00
26/Oct/1975 2:00 6:00
25/Apr/1976 2:00 5:00
31/Oct/1976 2:00 6:00
24/Apr/1977 2:00 5:00
30/Oct/1977 2:00 6:00
30/Apr/1978 2:00 5:00
29/Oct/1978 2:00 6:00
29/Apr/1979 2:00 5:00
28/Oct/1979 2:00 6:00
27/Apr/1980 2:00 5:00
26/Oct/1980 2:00 6:00
26/Apr/1981 2:00 5:00
25/Oct/1981 2:00 6:00
25/Apr/1982 2:00 5:00
31/Oct/1982 2:00 6:00
24/Apr/1983 2:00 5:00
30/Oct/1983 2:00 6:00
29/Apr/1984 2:00 5:00
28/Oct/1984 2:00 6:00
28/Apr/1985 2:00 5:00
27/Oct/1985 2:00 6:00
27/Apr/1986 2:00 5:00
26/Oct/1986 2:00 6:00
5/Apr/1987 2:00 5:00
25/Oct/1987 2:00 6:00
3/Apr/1988 2:00 5:00
30/Oct/1988 2:00 6:00
2/Apr/1989 2:00 5:00
29/Oct/1989 2:00 6:00
1/Apr/1990 2:00 5:00
28/Oct/1990 2:00 6:00
7/Apr/1991 2:00 5:00
27/Oct/1991 2:00 6:00
5/Apr/1992 2:00 5:00
25/Oct/1992 2:00 6:00
4/Apr/1993 2:00 5:00
31/Oct/1993 2:00 6:00
3/Apr/1994 2:00 5:00
30/Oct/1994 2:00 6:00
2/Apr/1995 2:00 5:00
29/Oct/1995 2:00 6:00
7/Apr/1996 2:00 5:00
27/Oct/1996 2:00 6:00
6/Apr/1997 2:00 5:00
26/Oct/1997 2:00 6:00
5/Apr/1998 2:00 5:00
25/Oct/1998 2:00 6:00
4/Apr/1999 2:00 5:00
31/Oct/1999 2:00 6:00
2/Apr/2000 2:00 5:00
29/Oct/2000 2:00 6:00
....

Time Table # 217
Before 16/Jul/1877 LMT
Begin Standard 90w00
16/Jul/1877 0:00 6:00
23/Apr/1916 0:00 5:00
17/Sep/1916 0:00 6:00
14/Apr/1918 2:00 5:00
31/Oct/1918 2:00 6:00
16/May/1937 2:00 5:00
26/Sep/1937 2:00 6:00
9/Feb/1942 2:00 5:00
30/Sep/1945 2:00 6:00
12/May/1946 2:00 5:00
13/Oct/1946 2:00 6:00
27/Apr/1947 2:00 5:00
28/Sep/1947 2:00 6:00
25/Apr/1948 2:00 5:00
26/Sep/1948 2:00 6:00
24/Apr/1949 2:00 5:00
25/Sep/1949 2:00 6:00
1/May/1950 2:00 5:00
30/Sep/1950 2:00 6:00
29/Apr/1951 2:00 5:00
30/Sep/1951 2:00 6:00
27/Apr/1952 2:00 5:00
28/Sep/1952 2:00 6:00
26/Apr/1953 2:00 5:00
27/Sep/1953 2:00 6:00
25/Apr/1954 2:00 5:00
26/Sep/1954 2:00 6:00
24/Apr/1955 2:00 5:00
25/Sep/1955 2:00 6:00
29/Apr/1956 2:00 5:00
30/Sep/1956 2:00 6:00
28/Apr/1957 2:00 5:00
29/Sep/1957 2:00 6:00
27/Apr/1958 2:00 5:00
28/Sep/1958 2:00 6:00
26/Apr/1959 2:00 5:00
25/Oct/1959 2:00 6:00
24/Apr/1960 2:00 5:00
25/Sep/1960 2:00 6:00
28/Apr/1963 2:00 5:00
22/Sep/1963 2:00 6:00
24/Apr/1966 2:00 5:00
30/Oct/1966 2:00 6:00
30/Apr/1967 2:00 5:00
29/Oct/1967 2:00 6:00
28/Apr/1968 2:00 5:00
27/Oct/1968 2:00 6:00
27/Apr/1969 2:00 5:00
26/Oct/1969 2:00 6:00
26/Apr/1970 2:00 5:00
25/Oct/1970 2:00 6:00
25/Apr/1971 2:00 5:00
31/Oct/1971 2:00 6:00
30/Apr/1972 2:00 5:00
29/Oct/1972 2:00 6:00
29/Apr/1973 2:00 5:00
28/Oct/1973 2:00 6:00
28/Apr/1974 2:00 5:00
27/Oct/1974 2:00 6:00
27/Apr/1975 2:00 5:00
26/Oct/1975 2:00 6:00
25/Apr/1976 2:00 5:00
31/Oct/1976 2:00 6:00
24/Apr/1977 2:00 5:00
30/Oct/1977 2:00 6:00
30/Apr/1978 2:00 5:00
29/Oct/1978 2:00 6:00
29/Apr/1979 2:00 5:00
28/Oct/1979 2:00 6:00
27/Apr/1980 2:00 5:00
26/Oct/1980 2:00 6:00
26/Apr/1981 2:00 5:00
25/Oct/1981 2:00 6:00
25/Apr/1982 2:00 5:00
31/Oct/1982 2:00 6:00
24/Apr/1983 2:00 5:00
30/Oct/1983 2:00 6:00
29/Apr/1984 2:00 5:00
28/Oct/1984 2:00 6:00
28/Apr/1985 2:00 5:00
27/Oct/1985 2:00 6:00
27/Apr/1986 2:00 5:00
26/Oct/1986 2:00 6:00
5/Apr/1987 2:00 5:00
25/Oct/1987 2:00 6:00
3/Apr/1988 2:00 5:00
30/Oct/1988 2:00 6:00
2/Apr/1989 2:00 5:00
29/Oct/1989 2:00 6:00
1/Apr/1990 2:00 5:00
28/Oct/1990 2:00 6:00
7/Apr/1991 2:00 5:00
27/Oct/1991 2:00 6:00
5/Apr/1992 2:00 5:00
25/Oct/1992 2:00 6:00
4/Apr/1993 2:00 5:00
31/Oct/1993 2:00 6:00
3/Apr/1994 2:00 5:00
30/Oct/1994 2:00 6:00
2/Apr/1995 2:00 5:00
29/Oct/1995 2:00 6:00
7/Apr/1996 2:00 5:00
27/Oct/1996 2:00 6:00
6/Apr/1997 2:00 5:00
26/Oct/1997 2:00 6:00
5/Apr/1998 2:00 5:00
25/Oct/1998 2:00 6:00
4/Apr/1999 2:00 5:00
31/Oct/1999 2:00 6:00
2/Apr/2000 2:00 5:00
29/Oct/2000 2:00 6:00
....

Time Table # 218
Before 1/Jan/1891 LMT
Begin Standard 90w00
1/Jan/1891 0:00 6:00
14/Apr/1918 2:00 5:00
31/Oct/1918 2:00 6:00
9/Feb/1942 2:00 5:00
30/Sep/1945 2:00 6:00
24/Apr/1949 2:00 5:00
25/Sep/1949 2:00 6:00
1/May/1950 2:00 5:00
30/Sep/1950 2:00 6:00
29/Apr/1951 2:00 5:00
30/Sep/1951 2:00 6:00
27/Apr/1952 2:00 5:00
28/Sep/1952 2:00 6:00
26/Apr/1953 2:00 5:00
27/Sep/1953 2:00 6:00
25/Apr/1954 2:00 5:00
26/Sep/1954 2:00 6:00
24/Apr/1955 2:00 5:00
25/Sep/1955 2:00 6:00
12/May/1963 2:00 5:00
7/Sep/1963 2:00 6:00
26/Apr/1964 2:00 5:00
13/Sep/1964 2:00 6:00
25/Apr/1965 2:00 5:00
12/Sep/1965 2:00 6:00
30/Apr/1967 2:00 5:00
29/Oct/1967 2:00 6:00
28/Apr/1968 2:00 5:00
27/Oct/1968 2:00 6:00
27/Apr/1969 2:00 5:00
26/Oct/1969 2:00 6:00
26/Apr/1970 2:00 5:00
25/Oct/1970 2:00 6:00
25/Apr/1971 2:00 5:00
31/Oct/1971 2:00 6:00
30/Apr/1972 2:00 5:00
29/Oct/1972 2:00 6:00
29/Apr/1973 2:00 5:00
28/Oct/1973 2:00 6:00
28/Apr/1974 2:00 5:00
27/Oct/1974 2:00 6:00
27/Apr/1975 2:00 5:00
26/Oct/1975 2:00 6:00
25/Apr/1976 2:00 5:00
31/Oct/1976 2:00 6:00
24/Apr/1977 2:00 5:00
30/Oct/1977 2:00 6:00
30/Apr/1978 2:00 5:00
29/Oct/1978 2:00 6:00
29/Apr/1979 2:00 5:00
28/Oct/1979 2:00 6:00
27/Apr/1980 2:00 5:00
26/Oct/1980 2:00 6:00
26/Apr/1981 2:00 5:00
25/Oct/1981 2:00 6:00
25/Apr/1982 2:00 5:00
31/Oct/1982 2:00 6:00
24/Apr/1983 2:00 5:00
30/Oct/1983 2:00 6:00
29/Apr/1984 2:00 5:00
28/Oct/1984 2:00 6:00
28/Apr/1985 2:00 5:00
27/Oct/1985 2:00 6:00
27/Apr/1986 2:00 5:00
26/Oct/1986 2:00 6:00
5/Apr/1987 2:00 5:00
25/Oct/1987 2:00 6:00
3/Apr/1988 2:00 5:00
30/Oct/1988 2:00 6:00
2/Apr/1989 2:00 5:00
29/Oct/1989 2:00 6:00
1/Apr/1990 2:00 5:00
28/Oct/1990 2:00 6:00
7/Apr/1991 2:00 5:00
27/Oct/1991 2:00 6:00
5/Apr/1992 2:00 5:00
25/Oct/1992 2:00 6:00
4/Apr/1993 2:00 5:00
31/Oct/1993 2:00 6:00
3/Apr/1994 2:00 5:00
30/Oct/1994 2:00 6:00
2/Apr/1995 2:00 5:00
29/Oct/1995 2:00 6:00
7/Apr/1996 2:00 5:00
27/Oct/1996 2:00 6:00
6/Apr/1997 2:00 5:00
26/Oct/1997 2:00 6:00
5/Apr/1998 2:00 5:00
25/Oct/1998 2:00 6:00
4/Apr/1999 2:00 5:00
31/Oct/1999 2:00 6:00
2/Apr/2000 2:00 5:00
29/Oct/2000 2:00 6:00
....

Time Table # 219
Before 1/Jan/1884 LMT
Begin Standard 90w00
1/Jan/1884 0:00 6:00
14/Apr/1918 2:00 5:00
27/Oct/1918 2:00 6:00
25/May/1919 2:00 5:00
1/Nov/1919 0:00 6:00
9/Feb/1942 2:00 5:00
30/Sep/1945 2:00 6:00
25/Apr/1965 0:00 4:00
31/Oct/1965 2:00 6:00
27/Apr/1980 2:00 5:00
26/Oct/1980 2:00 6:00
26/Apr/1981 2:00 5:00
25/Oct/1981 2:00 6:00
25/Apr/1982 2:00 5:00
31/Oct/1982 2:00 6:00
24/Apr/1983 2:00 5:00
30/Oct/1983 2:00 6:00
29/Apr/1984 2:00 5:00
28/Oct/1984 2:00 6:00
28/Apr/1985 2:00 5:00
27/Oct/1985 2:00 6:00
27/Apr/1986 2:00 5:00
26/Oct/1986 2:00 6:00
5/Apr/1987 2:00 5:00
25/Oct/1987 2:00 6:00
3/Apr/1988 2:00 5:00
30/Oct/1988 2:00 6:00
2/Apr/1989 2:00 5:00
29/Oct/1989 2:00 6:00
1/Apr/1990 2:00 5:00
28/Oct/1990 2:00 6:00
7/Apr/1991 2:00 5:00
27/Oct/1991 2:00 6:00
5/Apr/1992 2:00 5:00
25/Oct/1992 2:00 6:00
4/Apr/1993 2:00 5:00
31/Oct/1993 2:00 6:00
3/Apr/1994 2:00 5:00
30/Oct/1994 2:00 6:00
2/Apr/1995 2:00 5:00
29/Oct/1995 2:00 6:00
7/Apr/1996 2:00 5:00
27/Oct/1996 2:00 6:00
6/Apr/1997 2:00 5:00
26/Oct/1997 2:00 6:00
5/Apr/1998 2:00 5:00
25/Oct/1998 2:00 6:00
4/Apr/1999 2:00 5:00
31/Oct/1999 2:00 6:00
2/Apr/2000 2:00 5:00
29/Oct/2000 2:00 6:00
....

Time Table # 220
Before 1/Jan/1895 LMT
Begin Standard 90w00
1/Jan/1895 0:00 6:00
14/Apr/1918 2:00 5:00
31/Oct/1918 2:00 6:00
29/Sep/1940 0:00 5:00
30/Sep/1945 2:00 6:00
25/Apr/1948 0:00 5:00
26/Sep/1948 0:00 6:00
24/Apr/1949 2:00 5:00
25/Sep/1949 2:00 6:00
30/Apr/1950 2:00 5:00
24/Sep/1950 2:00 6:00
29/Apr/1951 2:00 5:00
30/Sep/1951 2:00 6:00
27/Apr/1952 2:00 5:00
28/Sep/1952 2:00 6:00
26/Apr/1953 2:00 5:00
27/Sep/1953 2:00 6:00
25/Apr/1954 2:00 5:00
26/Sep/1954 2:00 6:00
24/Apr/1955 2:00 5:00
25/Sep/1955 2:00 TT#3
....

Time Table # 221
Before 1/Jan/1895 LMT
Begin Standard 90w00
1/Jan/1895 0:00 6:00
14/Apr/1918 2:00 5:00
31/Oct/1918 2:00 6:00
29/Sep/1940 0:00 5:00
30/Sep/1945 2:00 6:00
27/Apr/1947 0:00 5:00
28/Sep/1947 0:00 6:00
24/Apr/1949 2:00 5:00
25/Sep/1949 2:00 6:00
30/Apr/1950 2:00 5:00
24/Sep/1950 2:00 6:00
29/Apr/1951 2:00 5:00
30/Sep/1951 2:00 6:00
27/Apr/1952 2:00 5:00
28/Sep/1952 2:00 6:00
26/Apr/1953 2:00 5:00
27/Sep/1953 2:00 6:00
25/Apr/1954 2:00 5:00
26/Sep/1954 2:00 TT#3
....

Time Table # 222
Before 1/Jan/1895 LMT
Begin Standard 90w00
1/Jan/1895 0:00 6:00
14/Apr/1918 2:00 5:00
31/Oct/1918 2:00 6:00
16/May/1937 2:00 5:00
26/Sep/1937 2:00 6:00
29/Apr/1951 2:00 5:00
23/Sep/1951 2:00 6:00
27/Apr/1952 2:00 5:00
28/Sep/1952 2:00 6:00
26/Apr/1953 2:00 5:00
27/Sep/1953 2:00 6:00
25/Apr/1954 2:00 5:00
26/Sep/1954 2:00 6:00
24/Apr/1955 2:00 5:00
25/Sep/1955 2:00 6:00
29/Apr/1956 2:00 5:00
30/Sep/1956 2:00 6:00
28/Apr/1957 2:00 5:00
27/Oct/1957 2:00 6:00
27/Apr/1958 2:00 5:00
26/Oct/1958 2:00 6:00
26/Apr/1959 2:00 5:00
25/Oct/1959 2:00 6:00
24/Apr/1960 2:00 5:00
30/Oct/1960 2:00 6:00
30/Apr/1961 2:00 5:00
29/Oct/1961 2:00 6:00
29/Apr/1962 2:00 5:00
28/Oct/1962 2:00 6:00
28/Apr/1963 2:00 5:00
27/Oct/1963 2:00 6:00
26/Apr/1964 2:00 5:00
25/Oct/1964 2:00 6:00
25/Apr/1965 2:00 5:00
31/Oct/1965 2:00 6:00
24/Apr/1966 2:00 5:00
30/Oct/1966 2:00 6:00
30/Apr/1967 2:00 5:00
29/Oct/1967 2:00 6:00
28/Apr/1968 2:00 5:00
27/Oct/1968 2:00 6:00
27/Apr/1969 2:00 5:00
26/Oct/1969 2:00 6:00
26/Apr/1970 2:00 5:00
25/Oct/1970 2:00 6:00
25/Apr/1971 2:00 5:00
31/Oct/1971 2:00 6:00
30/Apr/1972 2:00 5:00
29/Oct/1972 2:00 6:00
29/Apr/1973 2:00 5:00
28/Oct/1973 2:00 6:00
28/Apr/1974 2:00 5:00
27/Oct/1974 2:00 6:00
27/Apr/1975 2:00 5:00
26/Oct/1975 2:00 6:00
25/Apr/1976 2:00 TT#3
....

Time Table # 223
Before 1/Sep/1906 LMT
Begin Standard 105w00
1/Sep/1906 0:00 7:00
14/Apr/1918 2:00 6:00
31/Oct/1918 2:00 7:00
13/Apr/1919 2:00 6:00
27/May/1919 2:00 7:00
9/Feb/1942 2:00 6:00
30/Sep/1945 2:00 7:00
30/Apr/1972 2:00 6:00
29/Oct/1972 2:00 7:00
29/Apr/1973 2:00 6:00
28/Oct/1973 2:00 7:00
28/Apr/1974 2:00 6:00
27/Oct/1974 2:00 7:00
27/Apr/1975 2:00 6:00
26/Oct/1975 2:00 7:00
25/Apr/1976 2:00 6:00
31/Oct/1976 2:00 7:00
24/Apr/1977 2:00 6:00
30/Oct/1977 2:00 7:00
30/Apr/1978 2:00 6:00
29/Oct/1978 2:00 7:00
29/Apr/1979 2:00 6:00
28/Oct/1979 2:00 7:00
27/Apr/1980 2:00 6:00
26/Oct/1980 2:00 7:00
26/Apr/1981 2:00 6:00
25/Oct/1981 2:00 7:00
25/Apr/1982 2:00 6:00
31/Oct/1982 2:00 7:00
24/Apr/1983 2:00 6:00
30/Oct/1983 2:00 7:00
29/Apr/1984 2:00 6:00
28/Oct/1984 2:00 7:00
28/Apr/1985 2:00 6:00
27/Oct/1985 2:00 7:00
27/Apr/1986 2:00 6:00
26/Oct/1986 2:00 7:00
5/Apr/1987 2:00 6:00
25/Oct/1987 2:00 7:00
3/Apr/1988 2:00 6:00
30/Oct/1988 2:00 7:00
2/Apr/1989 2:00 6:00
29/Oct/1989 2:00 7:00
1/Apr/1990 2:00 6:00
28/Oct/1990 2:00 7:00
7/Apr/1991 2:00 6:00
27/Oct/1991 2:00 7:00
5/Apr/1992 2:00 6:00
25/Oct/1992 2:00 7:00
4/Apr/1993 2:00 6:00
31/Oct/1993 2:00 7:00
3/Apr/1994 2:00 6:00
30/Oct/1994 2:00 7:00
2/Apr/1995 2:00 6:00
29/Oct/1995 2:00 7:00
7/Apr/1996 2:00 6:00
27/Oct/1996 2:00 7:00
6/Apr/1997 2:00 6:00
26/Oct/1997 2:00 7:00
5/Apr/1998 2:00 6:00
25/Oct/1998 2:00 7:00
4/Apr/1999 2:00 6:00
31/Oct/1999 2:00 7:00
2/Apr/2000 2:00 6:00
29/Oct/2000 2:00 7:00
....

Time Table # 224
Before 1/Sep/1906 LMT
Begin Standard 105w00
1/Sep/1906 0:00 7:00
14/Apr/1918 2:00 6:00
31/Oct/1918 2:00 7:00
13/Apr/1919 2:00 6:00
27/May/1919 2:00 7:00
9/Feb/1942 2:00 6:00
30/Sep/1945 2:00 7:00
15/May/1946 2:00 6:00
5/Oct/1946 2:00 7:00
27/Apr/1947 2:00 6:00
27/Sep/1947 2:00 7:00
30/Apr/1972 2:00 6:00
29/Oct/1972 2:00 7:00
29/Apr/1973 2:00 6:00
28/Oct/1973 2:00 7:00
28/Apr/1974 2:00 6:00
27/Oct/1974 2:00 7:00
27/Apr/1975 2:00 6:00
26/Oct/1975 2:00 7:00
25/Apr/1976 2:00 6:00
31/Oct/1976 2:00 7:00
24/Apr/1977 2:00 6:00
30/Oct/1977 2:00 7:00
30/Apr/1978 2:00 6:00
29/Oct/1978 2:00 7:00
29/Apr/1979 2:00 6:00
28/Oct/1979 2:00 7:00
27/Apr/1980 2:00 6:00
26/Oct/1980 2:00 7:00
26/Apr/1981 2:00 6:00
25/Oct/1981 2:00 7:00
25/Apr/1982 2:00 6:00
31/Oct/1982 2:00 7:00
24/Apr/1983 2:00 6:00
30/Oct/1983 2:00 7:00
29/Apr/1984 2:00 6:00
28/Oct/1984 2:00 7:00
28/Apr/1985 2:00 6:00
27/Oct/1985 2:00 7:00
27/Apr/1986 2:00 6:00
26/Oct/1986 2:00 7:00
5/Apr/1987 2:00 6:00
25/Oct/1987 2:00 7:00
3/Apr/1988 2:00 6:00
30/Oct/1988 2:00 7:00
2/Apr/1989 2:00 6:00
29/Oct/1989 2:00 7:00
1/Apr/1990 2:00 6:00
28/Oct/1990 2:00 7:00
7/Apr/1991 2:00 6:00
27/Oct/1991 2:00 7:00
5/Apr/1992 2:00 6:00
25/Oct/1992 2:00 7:00

4/Apr/1993 2:00 6:00
31/Oct/1993 2:00 7:00
3/Apr/1994 2:00 6:00
30/Oct/1994 2:00 7:00
2/Apr/1995 2:00 6:00
29/Oct/1995 2:00 7:00
7/Apr/1996 2:00 6:00
27/Oct/1996 2:00 7:00
6/Apr/1997 2:00 6:00
26/Oct/1997 2:00 7:00
5/Apr/1998 2:00 6:00
25/Oct/1998 2:00 7:00
4/Apr/1999 2:00 6:00
31/Oct/1999 2:00 7:00
2/Apr/2000 2:00 6:00
29/Oct/2000 2:00 7:00
....
Time Table # 225
Before 1/Sep/1906 LMT
Begin Standard 105w00
1/Sep/1906 0:00 7:00
14/Apr/1918 2:00 6:00
31/Oct/1918 2:00 7:00
13/Apr/1919 2:00 6:00
27/May/1919 2:00 7:00
25/Apr/1920 2:00 6:00
31/Oct/1920 2:00 7:00
24/Apr/1921 2:00 6:00
25/Sep/1921 2:00 7:00
30/Apr/1922 2:00 6:00
24/Sep/1922 2:00 7:00
29/Apr/1923 2:00 6:00
30/Sep/1923 2:00 7:00
9/Feb/1942 2:00 6:00
30/Sep/1945 2:00 7:00
27/Apr/1947 2:00 6:00
27/Sep/1947 2:00 7:00
23/Apr/1967 2:00 6:00
29/Oct/1967 2:00 7:00
27/Apr/1969 2:00 6:00
26/Oct/1969 2:00 7:00
30/Apr/1972 2:00 6:00
29/Oct/1972 2:00 7:00
29/Apr/1973 2:00 6:00
28/Oct/1973 2:00 7:00
28/Apr/1974 2:00 6:00
27/Oct/1974 2:00 7:00
27/Apr/1975 2:00 6:00
26/Oct/1975 2:00 7:00
25/Apr/1976 2:00 6:00
31/Oct/1976 2:00 7:00
24/Apr/1977 2:00 6:00
30/Oct/1977 2:00 7:00
30/Apr/1978 2:00 6:00
29/Oct/1978 2:00 7:00
29/Apr/1979 2:00 6:00
28/Oct/1979 2:00 7:00
27/Apr/1980 2:00 6:00
26/Oct/1980 2:00 7:00
26/Apr/1981 2:00 6:00
25/Oct/1981 2:00 7:00
25/Apr/1982 2:00 6:00
31/Oct/1982 2:00 7:00
24/Apr/1983 2:00 6:00
30/Oct/1983 2:00 7:00
29/Apr/1984 2:00 6:00
28/Oct/1984 2:00 7:00
28/Apr/1985 2:00 6:00
27/Oct/1985 2:00 7:00
27/Apr/1986 2:00 6:00
26/Oct/1986 2:00 7:00
5/Apr/1987 2:00 6:00
25/Oct/1987 2:00 7:00
3/Apr/1988 2:00 6:00
30/Oct/1988 2:00 7:00
2/Apr/1989 2:00 6:00
29/Oct/1989 2:00 7:00
1/Apr/1990 2:00 6:00
28/Oct/1990 2:00 7:00
7/Apr/1991 2:00 6:00
27/Oct/1991 2:00 7:00
5/Apr/1992 2:00 6:00
25/Oct/1992 2:00 7:00
4/Apr/1993 2:00 6:00
31/Oct/1993 2:00 7:00
3/Apr/1994 2:00 6:00
30/Oct/1994 2:00 7:00
2/Apr/1995 2:00 6:00
29/Oct/1995 2:00 7:00
7/Apr/1996 2:00 6:00
27/Oct/1996 2:00 7:00
6/Apr/1997 2:00 6:00
26/Oct/1997 2:00 7:00
5/Apr/1998 2:00 6:00
25/Oct/1998 2:00 7:00
4/Apr/1999 2:00 6:00
31/Oct/1999 2:00 7:00
2/Apr/2000 2:00 6:00
29/Oct/2000 2:00 7:00
....
Time Table # 226
Before 1/Sep/1906 LMT
Begin Standard 105w00
1/Sep/1906 0:00 7:00
14/Apr/1918 2:00 6:00
31/Oct/1918 2:00 7:00
13/Apr/1919 2:00 6:00
27/May/1919 2:00 7:00
9/Feb/1942 2:00 6:00
30/Sep/1945 2:00 7:00
27/Apr/1947 2:00 6:00
27/Sep/1947 2:00 7:00
30/Apr/1972 2:00 6:00
29/Oct/1972 2:00 7:00
29/Apr/1973 2:00 6:00
28/Oct/1973 2:00 7:00
28/Apr/1974 2:00 6:00
27/Oct/1974 2:00 7:00
27/Apr/1975 2:00 6:00
26/Oct/1975 2:00 7:00
25/Apr/1976 2:00 6:00
31/Oct/1976 2:00 7:00
24/Apr/1977 2:00 6:00
30/Oct/1977 2:00 7:00
30/Apr/1978 2:00 6:00
29/Oct/1978 2:00 7:00
29/Apr/1979 2:00 6:00
28/Oct/1979 2:00 7:00
27/Apr/1980 2:00 6:00
26/Oct/1980 2:00 7:00
26/Apr/1981 2:00 6:00
25/Oct/1981 2:00 7:00
25/Apr/1982 2:00 6:00
31/Oct/1982 2:00 7:00
24/Apr/1983 2:00 6:00
30/Oct/1983 2:00 7:00
29/Apr/1984 2:00 6:00
28/Oct/1984 2:00 7:00
28/Apr/1985 2:00 6:00
27/Oct/1985 2:00 7:00
27/Apr/1986 2:00 6:00
26/Oct/1986 2:00 7:00
5/Apr/1987 2:00 6:00
25/Oct/1987 2:00 7:00
3/Apr/1988 2:00 6:00
30/Oct/1988 2:00 7:00
2/Apr/1989 2:00 6:00
29/Oct/1989 2:00 7:00
1/Apr/1990 2:00 6:00
28/Oct/1990 2:00 7:00
7/Apr/1991 2:00 6:00
27/Oct/1991 2:00 7:00
5/Apr/1992 2:00 6:00
25/Oct/1992 2:00 7:00
4/Apr/1993 2:00 6:00
31/Oct/1993 2:00 7:00
3/Apr/1994 2:00 6:00
30/Oct/1994 2:00 7:00
2/Apr/1995 2:00 6:00
29/Oct/1995 2:00 7:00
7/Apr/1996 2:00 6:00
27/Oct/1996 2:00 7:00
6/Apr/1997 2:00 6:00
26/Oct/1997 2:00 7:00
5/Apr/1998 2:00 6:00
25/Oct/1998 2:00 7:00
4/Apr/1999 2:00 6:00
31/Oct/1999 2:00 7:00
2/Apr/2000 2:00 6:00
29/Oct/2000 2:00 7:00
....
Time Table # 227
Before 1/Jan/1884 LMT
Begin Standard 105w00
1/Jan/1884 0:00 7:00
14/Apr/1918 2:00 6:00
27/Oct/1918 2:00 7:00
25/May/1919 2:00 6:00
1/Nov/1919 0:00 7:00
9/Feb/1942 2:00 6:00
30/Sep/1945 2:00 7:00
25/Apr/1965 0:00 5:00
31/Oct/1965 2:00 7:00
27/Apr/1980 2:00 6:00
26/Oct/1980 2:00 7:00
26/Apr/1981 2:00 6:00
25/Oct/1981 2:00 7:00
25/Apr/1982 2:00 6:00
31/Oct/1982 2:00 7:00
24/Apr/1983 2:00 6:00
30/Oct/1983 2:00 7:00
29/Apr/1984 2:00 6:00
28/Oct/1984 2:00 7:00
28/Apr/1985 2:00 6:00
27/Oct/1985 2:00 7:00
27/Apr/1986 2:00 6:00
26/Oct/1986 2:00 7:00
5/Apr/1987 2:00 6:00
25/Oct/1987 2:00 7:00
3/Apr/1988 2:00 6:00
30/Oct/1988 2:00 7:00
2/Apr/1989 2:00 6:00
29/Oct/1989 2:00 7:00
1/Apr/1990 2:00 6:00
28/Oct/1990 2:00 7:00
7/Apr/1991 2:00 6:00
27/Oct/1991 2:00 7:00
5/Apr/1992 2:00 6:00
25/Oct/1992 2:00 7:00
4/Apr/1993 2:00 6:00
31/Oct/1993 2:00 7:00
3/Apr/1994 2:00 6:00
30/Oct/1994 2:00 7:00
2/Apr/1995 2:00 6:00
29/Oct/1995 2:00 7:00
7/Apr/1996 2:00 6:00
27/Oct/1996 2:00 7:00
6/Apr/1997 2:00 6:00
26/Oct/1997 2:00 7:00
5/Apr/1998 2:00 6:00
25/Oct/1998 2:00 7:00
4/Apr/1999 2:00 6:00
31/Oct/1999 2:00 7:00
2/Apr/2000 2:00 6:00
29/Oct/2000 2:00 7:00
....
Time Table # 228
Before 1/Sep/1905 LMT
Begin Standard 105w00
1/Sep/1905 0:00 7:00
14/Apr/1918 2:00 6:00
31/Oct/1918 2:00 7:00
9/Feb/1942 2:00 6:00
30/Sep/1945 2:00 7:00
27/Apr/1947 2:00 6:00
28/Sep/1947 2:00 7:00
26/Apr/1959 2:00 6:00
25/Oct/1959 2:00 7:00
30/Apr/1972 2:00 6:00
....
Time Table # 229
Before 1/Sep/1905 LMT
Begin Standard 105w00
1/Sep/1905 0:00 7:00
14/Apr/1918 2:00 6:00
31/Oct/1918 2:00 7:00
9/Feb/1942 2:00 6:00
30/Sep/1945 2:00 7:00
27/Apr/1947 2:00 6:00
28/Sep/1947 2:00 7:00
26/Apr/1959 2:00 6:00
25/Oct/1959 2:00 7:00
28/Apr/1968 2:00 6:00
....
Time Table # 230
Before 1/Sep/1905 LMT
Begin Standard 105w00
1/Sep/1905 0:00 7:00
14/Apr/1918 2:00 6:00
31/Oct/1918 2:00 7:00
9/Feb/1942 2:00 6:00
30/Sep/1945 2:00 7:00
27/Apr/1947 2:00 6:00
28/Sep/1947 2:00 7:00
26/Apr/1959 2:00 6:00
25/Oct/1959 2:00 7:00
30/Apr/1961 2:00 6:00
....
Time Table # 231
Before 1/Sep/1905 LMT
Begin Standard 105w00
1/Sep/1905 0:00 7:00
14/Apr/1918 2:00 6:00
31/Oct/1918 2:00 7:00
9/Feb/1942 2:00 6:00
30/Sep/1945 2:00 7:00
27/Apr/1947 2:00 6:00
28/Sep/1947 2:00 7:00
26/Apr/1959 2:00 6:00
25/Oct/1959 2:00 7:00
24/Apr/1960 2:00 6:00
....
Time Table # 232
Before 1/Sep/1905 LMT
Begin Standard 105w00
1/Sep/1905 0:00 7:00
14/Apr/1918 2:00 6:00
31/Oct/1918 2:00 7:00
9/Feb/1942 2:00 6:00
30/Sep/1945 2:00 7:00
27/Apr/1947 2:00 6:00
28/Sep/1947 2:00 7:00
25/Apr/1954 2:00 6:00
....
Time Table # 233
Before 1/Sep/1905 LMT
Begin Standard 105w00
1/Sep/1905 0:00 7:00
14/Apr/1918 2:00 6:00
31/Oct/1918 2:00 7:00
9/Feb/1942 2:00 6:00
30/Sep/1945 2:00 7:00
27/Apr/1947 2:00 6:00
28/Sep/1947 2:00 7:00
27/Apr/1952 2:00 6:00
28/Sep/1952 2:00 7:00
26/Apr/1953 2:00 6:00
27/Sep/1953 2:00 7:00
25/Apr/1954 2:00 6:00
26/Sep/1954 2:00 7:00
26/Apr/1959 2:00 6:00
25/Oct/1959 2:00 7:00
24/Apr/1960 2:00 6:00
....
Time Table # 234
Before 1/Sep/1905 LMT
Begin Standard 105w00
1/Sep/1905 0:00 7:00
14/Apr/1918 2:00 6:00
31/Oct/1918 2:00 7:00
9/Feb/1942 2:00 6:00
30/Sep/1945 2:00 7:00
27/Apr/1947 2:00 6:00
28/Sep/1947 2:00 7:00
25/Apr/1948 2:00 6:00
26/Sep/1948 2:00 7:00
29/Apr/1951 2:00 6:00
23/Sep/1951 2:00 7:00
27/Apr/1952 2:00 6:00
28/Sep/1952 2:00 7:00
26/Apr/1953 2:00 6:00
27/Sep/1953 2:00 7:00
25/Apr/1954 2:00 6:00
26/Sep/1954 2:00 7:00
3/Apr/1955 2:00 6:00
25/Sep/1955 2:00 7:00
26/Apr/1959 2:00 6:00
25/Oct/1959 2:00 7:00
24/Apr/1960 2:00 6:00
....
Time Table # 235
Before 1/Sep/1905 LMT
Begin Standard 105w00
1/Sep/1905 0:00 7:00
14/Apr/1918 2:00 6:00
31/Oct/1918 2:00 7:00
9/Feb/1942 2:00 6:00
30/Sep/1945 2:00 7:00
27/Apr/1947 2:00 6:00
28/Sep/1947 2:00 7:00
25/Apr/1948 2:00 6:00
26/Sep/1948 2:00 7:00
24/Apr/1949 2:00 6:00
25/Sep/1949 2:00 7:00
30/Apr/1950 2:00 6:00
24/Sep/1950 2:00 7:00
29/Apr/1951 2:00 6:00
23/Sep/1951 2:00 7:00
27/Apr/1952 2:00 6:00
28/Sep/1952 2:00 7:00
26/Apr/1953 2:00 6:00
27/Sep/1953 2:00 7:00
26/Apr/1959 2:00 6:00
25/Oct/1959 2:00 7:00
24/Apr/1960 2:00 6:00
....
Time Table # 236
Before 1/Sep/1905 LMT
Begin Standard 105w00
1/Sep/1905 0:00 7:00
14/Apr/1918 2:00 6:00
31/Oct/1918 2:00 7:00
9/Feb/1942 2:00 6:00
30/Sep/1945 2:00 7:00
27/Apr/1947 2:00 6:00
28/Sep/1947 2:00 7:00
24/Apr/1955 2:00 6:00
25/Sep/1955 2:00 7:00
26/Apr/1959 2:00 6:00
25/Oct/1959 2:00 7:00
24/Apr/1960 2:00 6:00
....
Time Table # 237
Before 1/Sep/1905 LMT
Begin Standard 105w00
1/Sep/1905 0:00 7:00
14/Apr/1918 2:00 6:00
31/Oct/1918 2:00 7:00
9/Feb/1942 2:00 6:00
30/Sep/1945 2:00 7:00
27/Apr/1947 2:00 6:00
28/Sep/1947 2:00 7:00
25/Apr/1948 2:00 6:00
26/Sep/1948 2:00 7:00
24/Apr/1949 2:00 6:00
25/Sep/1949 2:00 7:00
26/Apr/1959 2:00 6:00
25/Oct/1959 2:00 7:00
28/Apr/1968 2:00 6:00
....
Time Table # 238
Before 1/Sep/1905 LMT
Begin Standard 105w00
1/Sep/1905 0:00 7:00
14/Apr/1918 2:00 6:00
31/Oct/1918 2:00 7:00
9/Feb/1942 2:00 6:00
30/Sep/1945 2:00 7:00
27/Apr/1947 2:00 6:00
28/Sep/1947 2:00 7:00
27/Apr/1952 2:00 6:00
28/Sep/1952 2:00 7:00
26/Apr/1953 2:00 6:00
27/Sep/1953 2:00 7:00
25/Apr/1954 2:00 6:00
26/Sep/1954 2:00 7:00
24/Apr/1955 2:00 6:00
25/Sep/1955 2:00 7:00
26/Apr/1959 2:00 6:00
25/Oct/1959 2:00 7:00
24/Apr/1960 2:00 6:00
....
Time Table # 239
Before 1/Sep/1905 LMT
Begin Standard 105w00
1/Sep/1905 0:00 7:00
14/Apr/1918 2:00 6:00
31/Oct/1918 2:00 7:00
9/Feb/1942 2:00 6:00
30/Sep/1945 2:00 7:00
27/Apr/1947 2:00 6:00
28/Sep/1947 2:00 7:00
26/Apr/1953 2:00 6:00
27/Sep/1953 2:00 7:00
25/Apr/1954 2:00 6:00
26/Sep/1954 2:00 7:00
24/Apr/1955 2:00 6:00
25/Sep/1955 2:00 7:00
26/Apr/1959 2:00 6:00
25/Oct/1959 2:00 7:00
24/Apr/1960 2:00 6:00
....
Time Table # 240
Before 1/Sep/1905 LMT
Begin Standard 105w00
1/Sep/1905 0:00 7:00
14/Apr/1918 2:00 6:00
31/Oct/1918 2:00 7:00
9/Feb/1942 2:00 6:00
30/Sep/1945 2:00 7:00
27/Apr/1947 2:00 6:00
28/Sep/1947 2:00 7:00
25/Apr/1954 2:00 6:00
26/Sep/1954 2:00 7:00
24/Apr/1955 2:00 6:00
25/Sep/1955 2:00 7:00
26/Apr/1959 2:00 6:00
25/Oct/1959 2:00 7:00
24/Apr/1960 2:00 6:00
....
Time Table # 241
Before 1/Sep/1905 LMT
Begin Standard 105w00
1/Sep/1905 0:00 7:00
14/Apr/1918 2:00 6:00
31/Oct/1918 2:00 7:00
9/Feb/1942 2:00 6:00
30/Sep/1945 2:00 7:00
27/Apr/1947 2:00 6:00
28/Sep/1947 2:00 7:00
25/Apr/1948 2:00 6:00
26/Sep/1948 2:00 7:00
24/Apr/1949 2:00 6:00
25/Sep/1949 2:00 7:00
26/Apr/1959 2:00 6:00
25/Oct/1959 2:00 7:00
24/Apr/1960 2:00 6:00
....
Time Table # 242
Before 1/Sep/1905 LMT
Begin Standard 105w00
1/Sep/1905 0:00 7:00
14/Apr/1918 2:00 6:00
31/Oct/1918 2:00 7:00
9/Feb/1942 2:00 6:00
30/Sep/1945 2:00 7:00
27/Apr/1947 2:00 6:00
28/Sep/1947 2:00 7:00
27/Apr/1952 2:00 6:00
28/Sep/1952 2:00 7:00
25/Apr/1954 2:00 6:00
....
Time Table # 243
Before 1/Sep/1905 LMT
Begin Standard 105w00
1/Sep/1905 0:00 7:00
14/Apr/1918 2:00 6:00
31/Oct/1918 2:00 7:00
9/Feb/1942 2:00 6:00
30/Sep/1945 2:00 7:00
27/Apr/1947 2:00 6:00
28/Sep/1947 2:00 7:00
26/Apr/1953 2:00 6:00
27/Sep/1953 2:00 7:00
25/Apr/1954 2:00 6:00
26/Sep/1954 2:00 7:00
26/Apr/1959 2:00 6:00
25/Oct/1959 2:00 7:00
24/Apr/1960 2:00 6:00
....
Time Table # 244
Before 1/Sep/1905 LMT
Begin Standard 105w00
1/Sep/1905 0:00 7:00
14/Apr/1918 2:00 6:00
31/Oct/1918 2:00 7:00
9/Feb/1942 2:00 6:00
30/Sep/1945 2:00 7:00
27/Apr/1947 2:00 6:00
28/Sep/1947 2:00 7:00
25/Apr/1948 2:00 6:00
26/Sep/1948 2:00 7:00
24/Apr/1949 2:00 6:00
25/Sep/1949 2:00 7:00
30/Apr/1950 2:00 6:00
24/Sep/1950 2:00 7:00
29/Apr/1951 2:00 6:00
23/Sep/1951 2:00 7:00
27/Apr/1952 2:00 6:00
28/Sep/1952 2:00 7:00
26/Apr/1953 2:00 6:00
27/Sep/1953 2:00 7:00
25/Apr/1954 2:00 6:00
26/Sep/1954 2:00 7:00
24/Apr/1955 2:00 6:00
25/Sep/1955 2:00 7:00
26/Apr/1959 2:00 6:00
25/Oct/1959 2:00 7:00
24/Apr/1960 2:00 6:00
....
Time Table # 245
Before 1/Sep/1905 LMT
Begin Standard 105w00
1/Sep/1905 0:00 7:00
14/Apr/1918 2:00 6:00
31/Oct/1918 2:00 7:00
9/Feb/1942 2:00 6:00
30/Sep/1945 2:00 7:00
27/Apr/1947 2:00 6:00
28/Sep/1947 2:00 7:00
27/Apr/1952 2:00 6:00
28/Sep/1952 2:00 7:00
26/Apr/1953 2:00 6:00
27/Sep/1953 2:00 7:00
25/Apr/1954 2:00 6:00
3/Oct/1954 2:00 7:00
24/Apr/1955 2:00 6:00
25/Sep/1955 2:00 7:00
26/Apr/1959 2:00 6:00
25/Oct/1959 2:00 7:00
24/Apr/1960 2:00 6:00
....
Time Table # 246
Before 1/Sep/1905 LMT
Begin Standard 105w00
1/Sep/1905 0:00 7:00
14/Apr/1918 2:00 6:00
31/Oct/1918 2:00 7:00
9/Feb/1942 2:00 6:00
30/Sep/1945 2:00 7:00
27/Apr/1947 2:00 6:00
28/Sep/1947 2:00 7:00
27/Apr/1952 2:00 6:00
28/Sep/1952 2:00 7:00
26/Apr/1953 2:00 6:00

27/Sep/1953 2:00 7:00
25/Apr/1954 2:00 6:00
26/Sep/1954 2:00 7:00
24/Apr/1955 2:00 6:00
25/Sep/1955 2:00 7:00
26/Apr/1959 2:00 6:00
25/Oct/1959 2:00 7:00
28/Apr/1968 2:00 6:00
....
Time Table # 247
Before 1/Sep/1905 LMT
Begin Standard 105w00
1/Sep/1905 0:00 7:00
14/Apr/1918 2:00 6:00
31/Oct/1918 2:00 7:00
9/Feb/1942 2:00 6:00
30/Sep/1945 2:00 7:00
27/Apr/1947 2:00 6:00
28/Sep/1947 2:00 7:00
25/Apr/1948 2:00 6:00
26/Sep/1948 2:00 7:00
24/Apr/1949 2:00 6:00
25/Sep/1949 2:00 7:00
30/Apr/1950 2:00 6:00
24/Sep/1950 2:00 7:00
29/Apr/1951 2:00 6:00
23/Sep/1951 2:00 7:00
27/Apr/1952 2:00 6:00
28/Sep/1952 2:00 7:00
26/Apr/1953 2:00 6:00
27/Sep/1953 2:00 7:00
25/Apr/1954 2:00 6:00
1/Jan/1955 2:00 7:00
26/Apr/1959 2:00 6:00
25/Oct/1959 2:00 7:00
24/Apr/1960 2:00 6:00
....
Time Table # 248
Before 1/Sep/1906 LMT
Begin Standard 105w00
1/Sep/1906 0:00 7:00
14/Apr/1918 2:00 6:00
31/Oct/1918 2:00 7:00
13/Apr/1919 2:00 6:00
27/May/1919 2:00 7:00
9/Feb/1942 2:00 6:00
30/Sep/1945 2:00 7:00
25/Apr/1948 2:00 6:00
26/Sep/1948 2:00 7:00
28/Apr/1957 2:00 6:00
27/Oct/1957 2:00 7:00
30/Apr/1972 2:00 6:00
29/Oct/1972 2:00 7:00
29/Apr/1973 2:00 6:00
28/Oct/1973 2:00 7:00
28/Apr/1974 2:00 6:00
27/Oct/1974 2:00 7:00
27/Apr/1975 2:00 6:00
26/Oct/1975 2:00 7:00
25/Apr/1976 2:00 6:00
31/Oct/1976 2:00 7:00
24/Apr/1977 2:00 6:00
30/Oct/1977 2:00 7:00
30/Apr/1978 2:00 6:00
29/Oct/1978 2:00 7:00
29/Apr/1979 2:00 6:00
28/Oct/1979 2:00 7:00
27/Apr/1980 2:00 6:00
26/Oct/1980 2:00 7:00
26/Apr/1981 2:00 6:00
25/Oct/1981 2:00 7:00
25/Apr/1982 2:00 6:00
31/Oct/1982 2:00 7:00
24/Apr/1983 2:00 6:00
30/Oct/1983 2:00 7:00
29/Apr/1984 2:00 6:00
28/Oct/1984 2:00 7:00
28/Apr/1985 2:00 6:00
27/Oct/1985 2:00 7:00
27/Apr/1986 2:00 6:00
26/Oct/1986 2:00 7:00
5/Apr/1987 2:00 6:00
25/Oct/1987 2:00 7:00
3/Apr/1988 2:00 6:00
30/Oct/1988 2:00 7:00
2/Apr/1989 2:00 6:00
29/Oct/1989 2:00 7:00
1/Apr/1990 2:00 6:00
28/Oct/1990 2:00 7:00
7/Apr/1991 2:00 6:00
27/Oct/1991 2:00 7:00
5/Apr/1992 2:00 6:00
25/Oct/1992 2:00 7:00
4/Apr/1993 2:00 6:00
31/Oct/1993 2:00 7:00
3/Apr/1994 2:00 6:00
30/Oct/1994 2:00 7:00
2/Apr/1995 2:00 6:00
29/Oct/1995 2:00 7:00
7/Apr/1996 2:00 6:00
27/Oct/1996 2:00 7:00
6/Apr/1997 2:00 6:00
26/Oct/1997 2:00 7:00
5/Apr/1998 2:00 6:00
25/Oct/1998 2:00 7:00
4/Apr/1999 2:00 6:00
31/Oct/1999 2:00 7:00
2/Apr/2000 2:00 6:00
29/Oct/2000 2:00 7:00
....
Time Table # 249
Before 1/Sep/1905 LMT
Begin Standard 105w00
1/Sep/1905 0:00 7:00
14/Apr/1918 2:00 6:00
31/Oct/1918 2:00 7:00
9/Feb/1942 2:00 6:00
30/Sep/1945 2:00 7:00
27/Apr/1947 2:00 6:00
28/Sep/1947 2:00 7:00
25/Apr/1948 2:00 6:00
26/Sep/1948 2:00 7:00
24/Apr/1949 2:00 6:00
25/Sep/1949 2:00 7:00
30/Apr/1950 2:00 6:00
24/Sep/1950 2:00 7:00
29/Apr/1951 2:00 6:00
23/Sep/1951 2:00 7:00
27/Apr/1952 2:00 6:00
28/Sep/1952 2:00 7:00
26/Apr/1953 2:00 6:00
27/Sep/1953 2:00 7:00
25/Apr/1954 2:00 6:00
26/Sep/1954 2:00 7:00
24/Apr/1955 2:00 6:00
25/Sep/1955 2:00 7:00
26/Apr/1959 2:00 6:00
25/Oct/1959 2:00 7:00
30/Apr/1961 2:00 6:00
....
Time Table # 250
Before 1/Sep/1905 LMT
Begin Standard 105w00
1/Sep/1905 0:00 7:00
14/Apr/1918 2:00 6:00
31/Oct/1918 2:00 7:00
9/Feb/1942 2:00 6:00
30/Sep/1945 2:00 7:00
27/Apr/1947 2:00 6:00
28/Sep/1947 2:00 7:00
27/Apr/1952 2:00 6:00
28/Sep/1952 2:00 7:00
26/Apr/1953 2:00 6:00
27/Sep/1953 2:00 7:00
2/May/1954 2:00 6:00
3/Oct/1954 2:00 7:00
26/Apr/1959 2:00 6:00
25/Oct/1959 2:00 7:00
24/Apr/1960 2:00 6:00
....
Time Table # 251
Before 1/Sep/1905 LMT
Begin Standard 105w00
1/Sep/1905 0:00 7:00
14/Apr/1918 2:00 6:00
31/Oct/1918 2:00 7:00
9/Feb/1942 2:00 6:00
30/Sep/1945 2:00 7:00
28/Apr/1946 2:00 6:00
13/Oct/1946 2:00 7:00
27/Apr/1947 2:00 6:00
28/Sep/1947 2:00 7:00
29/Apr/1951 2:00 6:00
30/Sep/1951 2:00 7:00
26/Apr/1953 2:00 6:00
27/Sep/1953 2:00 7:00
25/Apr/1954 2:00 6:00
26/Sep/1954 2:00 7:00
24/Apr/1955 2:00 6:00
25/Sep/1955 2:00 7:00
26/Apr/1959 2:00 6:00
25/Oct/1959 2:00 7:00
24/Apr/1960 2:00 6:00
....
Time Table # 252
Before 1/Sep/1905 LMT
Begin Standard 105w00
1/Sep/1905 0:00 7:00
14/Apr/1918 2:00 6:00
31/Oct/1918 2:00 7:00
9/Feb/1942 2:00 6:00
30/Sep/1945 2:00 7:00
27/Apr/1947 2:00 6:00
28/Sep/1947 2:00 7:00
25/Apr/1948 2:00 6:00
26/Sep/1948 2:00 7:00
24/Apr/1949 2:00 6:00
25/Sep/1949 2:00 7:00
30/Apr/1950 2:00 6:00
3/Sep/1950 2:00 7:00
29/Apr/1951 2:00 6:00
23/Sep/1951 2:00 7:00
27/Apr/1952 2:00 6:00
28/Sep/1952 2:00 7:00
26/Apr/1953 2:00 6:00
27/Sep/1953 2:00 7:00
25/Apr/1954 2:00 6:00
26/Sep/1954 2:00 7:00
24/Apr/1955 2:00 6:00
25/Sep/1955 2:00 7:00
29/Apr/1956 2:00 6:00
30/Sep/1956 2:00 7:00
28/Apr/1957 2:00 6:00
29/Sep/1957 2:00 7:00
26/Apr/1959 2:00 6:00
25/Oct/1959 2:00 7:00
24/Apr/1960 2:00 6:00
....
Time Table # 253
Before 1/Sep/1905 LMT
Begin Standard 105w00
1/Sep/1905 0:00 7:00
14/Apr/1918 2:00 6:00
31/Oct/1918 2:00 7:00
9/Feb/1942 2:00 6:00
30/Sep/1945 2:00 7:00
27/Apr/1947 2:00 6:00
28/Sep/1947 2:00 7:00
25/Apr/1948 2:00 6:00
26/Sep/1948 2:00 7:00
24/Apr/1949 2:00 6:00
25/Sep/1949 2:00 7:00
30/Apr/1950 2:00 6:00
24/Sep/1950 2:00 7:00
29/Apr/1951 2:00 6:00
23/Sep/1951 2:00 7:00
27/Apr/1952 2:00 6:00
28/Sep/1952 2:00 7:00
26/Apr/1953 2:00 6:00
27/Sep/1953 2:00 7:00
25/Apr/1954 2:00 6:00
26/Sep/1954 2:00 7:00
24/Apr/1955 2:00 6:00
25/Sep/1955 2:00 7:00
29/Apr/1956 2:00 6:00
30/Sep/1956 2:00 7:00
28/Apr/1957 2:00 6:00
27/Oct/1957 2:00 7:00
26/Apr/1959 2:00 6:00
25/Oct/1959 2:00 7:00
24/Apr/1960 2:00 6:00
25/Sep/1960 2:00 7:00
30/Apr/1961 2:00 6:00
24/Sep/1961 2:00 7:00
30/Apr/1972 2:00 6:00
....
Time Table # 254
Before 1/Sep/1905 LMT
Begin Standard 105w00
1/Sep/1905 0:00 7:00
14/Apr/1918 2:00 6:00
31/Oct/1918 2:00 7:00
1/May/1941 2:00 6:00
1/Oct/1941 2:00 7:00
9/Feb/1942 2:00 6:00
30/Sep/1945 2:00 7:00
1/May/1946 2:00 6:00
1/Oct/1946 2:00 7:00
27/Apr/1947 2:00 6:00
28/Sep/1947 2:00 7:00
25/Apr/1948 2:00 6:00
26/Sep/1948 2:00 7:00
24/Apr/1949 2:00 6:00
25/Sep/1949 2:00 7:00
30/Apr/1950 2:00 6:00
24/Sep/1950 2:00 7:00
29/Apr/1951 2:00 6:00
23/Sep/1951 2:00 7:00
27/Apr/1952 2:00 6:00
28/Sep/1952 2:00 7:00
26/Apr/1953 2:00 6:00
27/Sep/1953 2:00 7:00
25/Apr/1954 2:00 6:00
26/Sep/1954 2:00 7:00
24/Apr/1955 2:00 6:00
2/Oct/1955 2:00 7:00
29/Apr/1956 2:00 6:00
30/Sep/1956 2:00 7:00
28/Apr/1957 2:00 6:00
29/Sep/1957 2:00 7:00
24/Apr/1960 2:00 6:00
25/Sep/1960 2:00 7:00
30/Apr/1961 2:00 6:00
....
Time Table # 255
Before 1/Sep/1905 LMT
Begin Standard 105w00
1/Sep/1905 0:00 7:00
14/Apr/1918 2:00 6:00
31/Oct/1918 2:00 7:00
4/May/1930 0:00 6:00
5/Oct/1930 0:00 7:00
3/May/1931 0:00 6:00
4/Oct/1931 0:00 7:00
1/May/1932 0:00 6:00
2/Oct/1932 0:00 7:00
7/May/1933 0:00 6:00
1/Oct/1933 0:00 7:00
6/May/1934 0:00 6:00
7/Oct/1934 0:00 7:00
11/Apr/1937 0:00 6:00
10/Oct/1937 0:00 7:00
10/Apr/1938 0:00 6:00
2/Oct/1938 0:00 7:00
9/Apr/1939 0:00 6:00
8/Oct/1939 0:00 7:00
14/Apr/1940 0:00 6:00
13/Oct/1940 0:00 7:00
13/Apr/1941 0:00 6:00
12/Oct/1941 0:00 7:00
9/Feb/1942 2:00 6:00
30/Sep/1945 2:00 7:00
14/Apr/1946 2:00 6:00
13/Oct/1946 2:00 7:00
27/Apr/1947 2:00 6:00
28/Sep/1947 2:00 7:00
25/Apr/1948 2:00 6:00
26/Sep/1948 2:00 7:00
24/Apr/1949 2:00 6:00
25/Sep/1949 2:00 7:00
30/Apr/1950 2:00 6:00
24/Sep/1950 2:00 7:00
29/Apr/1951 2:00 6:00
23/Sep/1951 2:00 7:00
27/Apr/1952 2:00 6:00
28/Sep/1952 2:00 7:00
26/Apr/1953 2:00 6:00
27/Sep/1953 2:00 7:00
25/Apr/1954 2:00 6:00
26/Sep/1954 2:00 7:00
24/Apr/1955 2:00 6:00
25/Sep/1955 2:00 7:00
29/Apr/1956 2:00 6:00
30/Sep/1956 2:00 7:00
28/Apr/1957 2:00 6:00
29/Sep/1957 2:00 7:00
26/Apr/1959 2:00 6:00
25/Oct/1959 2:00 7:00
24/Apr/1960 2:00 6:00
....
Time Table # 256
Before 1/Sep/1905 LMT
Begin Standard 105w00
1/Sep/1905 0:00 7:00
14/Apr/1918 2:00 6:00
31/Oct/1918 2:00 7:00
9/Feb/1942 2:00 6:00
30/Sep/1945 2:00 7:00
28/Apr/1946 2:00 6:00
13/Oct/1946 2:00 7:00
27/Apr/1947 2:00 6:00
28/Sep/1947 2:00 7:00
25/Apr/1948 2:00 6:00
26/Sep/1948 2:00 7:00
26/Apr/1959 2:00 6:00
25/Oct/1959 2:00 7:00
30/Apr/1972 2:00 6:00
....
Time Table # 257
Before 1/Sep/1905 LMT
Begin Standard 105w00
1/Sep/1905 0:00 7:00
14/Apr/1918 2:00 6:00
31/Oct/1918 2:00 7:00
9/Feb/1942 2:00 6:00
30/Sep/1945 2:00 7:00
27/Apr/1947 2:00 6:00
28/Sep/1947 2:00 7:00
25/Apr/1948 2:00 6:00
26/Sep/1948 2:00 7:00
24/Apr/1949 2:00 6:00
25/Sep/1949 2:00 7:00
26/Apr/1959 2:00 6:00
25/Oct/1959 2:00 7:00
30/Apr/1972 2:00 6:00
....
Time Table # 258
Before 1/Sep/1905 LMT
Begin Standard 105w00
1/Sep/1905 0:00 7:00
14/Apr/1918 2:00 6:00
31/Oct/1918 2:00 7:00
9/Feb/1942 2:00 6:00
30/Sep/1945 2:00 7:00
27/Apr/1947 2:00 6:00
28/Sep/1947 2:00 7:00
27/Apr/1952 2:00 6:00
28/Sep/1952 2:00 7:00
25/Apr/1954 2:00 6:00
26/Sep/1954 2:00 7:00
24/Apr/1955 2:00 6:00
25/Sep/1955 2:00 7:00
26/Apr/1959 2:00 6:00
25/Oct/1959 2:00 7:00
24/Apr/1960 2:00 6:00
....
Time Table # 259
Before 1/Sep/1905 LMT
Begin Standard 105w00
1/Sep/1905 0:00 7:00
14/Apr/1918 2:00 6:00
31/Oct/1918 2:00 7:00
9/Feb/1942 2:00 6:00
30/Sep/1945 2:00 7:00
28/Apr/1946 2:00 6:00
13/Oct/1946 2:00 7:00
27/Apr/1947 2:00 6:00
28/Sep/1947 2:00 7:00
25/Apr/1948 2:00 6:00
26/Sep/1948 2:00 7:00
24/Apr/1949 2:00 6:00
25/Sep/1949 2:00 7:00
28/Apr/1957 2:00 6:00
27/Oct/1957 2:00 7:00
26/Apr/1959 2:00 6:00
25/Oct/1959 2:00 7:00
24/Apr/1960 2:00 6:00
25/Sep/1960 2:00 7:00
30/Apr/1961 2:00 6:00
24/Sep/1961 2:00 7:00
30/Apr/1972 2:00 6:00
....
Time Table # 260
Before 1/Sep/1905 LMT
Begin Standard 105w00
1/Sep/1905 0:00 7:00
14/Apr/1918 2:00 6:00
31/Oct/1918 2:00 7:00
9/Feb/1942 2:00 6:00
30/Sep/1945 2:00 7:00
27/Apr/1947 2:00 6:00
28/Sep/1947 2:00 7:00
26/Apr/1953 2:00 6:00
27/Sep/1953 2:00 7:00
24/Apr/1955 2:00 6:00
25/Sep/1955 2:00 7:00
26/Apr/1959 2:00 6:00
25/Oct/1959 2:00 7:00
24/Apr/1960 2:00 6:00
....
Time Table # 261
Before 1/Sep/1905 LMT
Begin Standard 105w00
1/Sep/1905 0:00 7:00
14/Apr/1918 2:00 6:00
31/Oct/1918 2:00 7:00
3/Jun/1934 2:00 6:00
2/Sep/1934 2:00 7:00
1/May/1935 2:00 6:00
31/Aug/1935 2:00 7:00
1/May/1936 2:00 6:00
31/Aug/1936 2:00 7:00
1/May/1937 2:00 6:00
31/Aug/1937 2:00 7:00
1/May/1938 2:00 6:00
31/Aug/1938 2:00 7:00
1/May/1939 2:00 6:00
31/Aug/1939 2:00 7:00
1/May/1940 2:00 6:00
30/Sep/1940 2:00 7:00
1/May/1941 2:00 6:00
30/Sep/1941 2:00 7:00
9/Feb/1942 2:00 6:00
30/Sep/1945 2:00 7:00
28/Apr/1946 2:00 6:00
29/Sep/1946 2:00 7:00
27/Apr/1947 2:00 6:00
28/Sep/1947 2:00 7:00
1/May/1948 2:00 6:00
1/Nov/1948 2:00 7:00
24/Apr/1949 2:00 6:00
25/Sep/1949 2:00 7:00
30/Apr/1950 2:00 6:00
24/Sep/1950 2:00 7:00
29/Apr/1951 2:00 6:00
23/Sep/1951 2:00 7:00
27/Apr/1952 2:00 6:00
28/Sep/1952 2:00 7:00
26/Apr/1953 2:00 6:00
27/Sep/1953 2:00 7:00
25/Apr/1954 2:00 6:00
3/Oct/1954 2:00 7:00
24/Apr/1955 2:00 6:00
25/Sep/1955 2:00 7:00
29/Apr/1956 2:00 6:00
30/Sep/1956 2:00 7:00
28/Apr/1957 2:00 6:00
29/Sep/1957 2:00 7:00
26/Apr/1959 2:00 6:00
25/Oct/1959 2:00 7:00
24/Apr/1960 2:00 6:00
....
Time Table # 262
Before 1/Sep/1905 LMT
Begin Standard 105w00
1/Sep/1905 0:00 7:00
14/Apr/1918 2:00 6:00
31/Oct/1918 2:00 7:00
9/Feb/1942 2:00 6:00
30/Sep/1945 2:00 7:00
27/Apr/1947 2:00 6:00
28/Sep/1947 2:00 7:00
29/Apr/1951 2:00 6:00
23/Sep/1951 2:00 7:00
27/Apr/1952 2:00 6:00
28/Sep/1952 2:00 7:00
26/Apr/1953 2:00 6:00
27/Sep/1953 2:00 7:00
25/Apr/1954 2:00 6:00
26/Sep/1954 2:00 7:00
24/Apr/1955 2:00 6:00
25/Sep/1955 2:00 7:00
26/Apr/1959 2:00 6:00
25/Oct/1959 2:00 7:00
24/Apr/1960 2:00 6:00
....
Time Table # 263
Before 1/Sep/1905 LMT
Begin Standard 105w00
1/Sep/1905 0:00 7:00
14/Apr/1918 2:00 6:00
31/Oct/1918 2:00 7:00
4/May/1931 0:00 6:00
9/Feb/1942 2:00 6:00
30/Sep/1945 2:00 7:00
27/Apr/1947 2:00 6:00
28/Sep/1947 2:00 7:00
25/Apr/1948 2:00 6:00
26/Sep/1948 2:00 7:00
24/Apr/1949 2:00 6:00
25/Sep/1949 2:00 7:00
25/Apr/1954 2:00 6:00
....
Time Table # 264
Before 1/Sep/1905 LMT
Begin Standard 105w00
1/Sep/1905 0:00 7:00
14/Apr/1918 2:00 6:00
31/Oct/1918 2:00 7:00
3/Jun/1921 2:00 6:00
30/Sep/1921 2:00 7:00
1/May/1932 1:00 6:00
2/Oct/1932 1:00 7:00
7/May/1933 1:00 6:00
1/Oct/1933 1:00 7:00
24/Apr/1938 0:00 6:00
2/Oct/1938 0:00 7:00
30/Apr/1939 0:00 6:00
1/Oct/1939 0:00 7:00
28/Apr/1940 0:00 6:00
30/Sep/1940 0:00 7:00
13/Apr/1941 0:00 6:00
12/Oct/1941 0:00 7:00
9/Feb/1942 2:00 6:00
30/Sep/1945 2:00 7:00
28/Apr/1946 2:00 6:00
13/Oct/1946 2:00 7:00
27/Apr/1947 2:00 6:00
28/Sep/1947 2:00 7:00
25/Apr/1948 2:00 6:00
26/Sep/1948 2:00 7:00
24/Apr/1949 2:00 6:00
25/Sep/1949 2:00 7:00
30/Apr/1950 2:00 6:00
24/Sep/1950 2:00 7:00

29/Apr/1951 2:00 6:00
23/Sep/1951 2:00 7:00
27/Apr/1952 2:00 6:00
28/Sep/1952 2:00 7:00
26/Apr/1953 2:00 6:00
27/Sep/1953 2:00 7:00
25/Apr/1954 2:00 6:00
26/Sep/1954 2:00 7:00
24/Apr/1955 2:00 6:00
25/Sep/1955 2:00 7:00
29/Apr/1956 2:00 6:00
30/Sep/1956 2:00 7:00
28/Apr/1957 2:00 6:00
27/Oct/1957 2:00 7:00
26/Apr/1959 2:00 6:00
25/Oct/1959 2:00 7:00
24/Apr/1960 2:00 6:00
25/Sep/1960 2:00 7:00
30/Apr/1961 2:00 6:00
24/Sep/1961 2:00 7:00
28/Apr/1968 2:00 6:00
....
Time Table # 265
Before 1/Jan/1884 LMT
Begin Standard 120w00
1/Jan/1884 0:00 8:00
14/Apr/1918 2:00 7:00
31/Oct/1918 2:00 8:00
1/May/1921 2:00 7:00
1/Oct/1921 2:00 8:00
30/Apr/1922 2:00 7:00
5/Sep/1922 2:00 8:00
6/May/1923 2:00 7:00
9/Sep/1923 2:00 8:00
9/Feb/1942 2:00 7:00
30/Sep/1945 2:00 8:00
28/Apr/1946 2:00 7:00
29/Sep/1946 2:00 8:00
27/Apr/1947 2:00 7:00
28/Sep/1947 2:00 8:00
25/Apr/1948 2:00 7:00
26/Sep/1948 2:00 8:00
24/Apr/1949 2:00 7:00
25/Sep/1949 2:00 8:00
30/Apr/1950 2:00 7:00
24/Sep/1950 2:00 8:00
29/Apr/1951 2:00 7:00
30/Sep/1951 2:00 8:00
27/Apr/1952 2:00 7:00
28/Sep/1952 2:00 8:00
26/Apr/1953 2:00 7:00
27/Sep/1953 2:00 8:00
25/Apr/1954 2:00 7:00
26/Sep/1954 2:00 8:00
24/Apr/1955 2:00 7:00
25/Sep/1955 2:00 8:00
29/Apr/1956 2:00 7:00
30/Sep/1956 2:00 8:00
28/Apr/1957 2:00 7:00
29/Sep/1957 2:00 8:00
27/Apr/1958 2:00 7:00
28/Sep/1958 2:00 8:00
26/Apr/1959 2:00 7:00
27/Sep/1959 2:00 8:00
24/Apr/1960 2:00 7:00
25/Sep/1960 2:00 8:00
30/Apr/1961 2:00 7:00
24/Sep/1961 2:00 8:00
29/Apr/1962 2:00 7:00
28/Oct/1962 2:00 8:00
28/Apr/1963 2:00 7:00
27/Oct/1963 2:00 8:00
26/Apr/1964 2:00 7:00
25/Oct/1964 2:00 8:00
25/Apr/1965 2:00 7:00
31/Oct/1965 2:00 8:00
24/Apr/1966 2:00 7:00
30/Oct/1966 2:00 8:00
30/Apr/1967 2:00 7:00
29/Oct/1967 2:00 8:00
28/Apr/1968 2:00 7:00
27/Oct/1968 2:00 8:00
27/Apr/1969 2:00 7:00
26/Oct/1969 2:00 8:00
26/Apr/1970 2:00 7:00
25/Oct/1970 2:00 8:00
25/Apr/1971 2:00 7:00
31/Oct/1971 2:00 8:00
30/Apr/1972 2:00 7:00
29/Oct/1972 2:00 8:00
29/Apr/1973 2:00 7:00
28/Oct/1973 2:00 8:00
28/Apr/1974 2:00 7:00
27/Oct/1974 2:00 8:00
27/Apr/1975 2:00 7:00
26/Oct/1975 2:00 8:00
25/Apr/1976 2:00 7:00
31/Oct/1976 2:00 8:00
24/Apr/1977 2:00 7:00
30/Oct/1977 2:00 8:00
30/Apr/1978 2:00 7:00
29/Oct/1978 2:00 8:00
29/Apr/1979 2:00 7:00
28/Oct/1979 2:00 8:00
27/Apr/1980 2:00 7:00
26/Oct/1980 2:00 8:00
26/Apr/1981 2:00 7:00
25/Oct/1981 2:00 8:00
25/Apr/1982 2:00 7:00
31/Oct/1982 2:00 8:00
24/Apr/1983 2:00 7:00
30/Oct/1983 2:00 8:00
29/Apr/1984 2:00 7:00
28/Oct/1984 2:00 8:00
28/Apr/1985 2:00 7:00
27/Oct/1985 2:00 8:00
27/Apr/1986 2:00 7:00
26/Oct/1986 2:00 8:00
5/Apr/1987 2:00 7:00
25/Oct/1987 2:00 8:00
3/Apr/1988 2:00 7:00
30/Oct/1988 2:00 8:00
2/Apr/1989 2:00 7:00
29/Oct/1989 2:00 8:00
1/Apr/1990 2:00 7:00
28/Oct/1990 2:00 8:00
7/Apr/1991 2:00 7:00
27/Oct/1991 2:00 8:00
5/Apr/1992 2:00 7:00
25/Oct/1992 2:00 8:00
4/Apr/1993 2:00 7:00
31/Oct/1993 2:00 8:00
3/Apr/1994 2:00 7:00
30/Oct/1994 2:00 8:00
2/Apr/1995 2:00 7:00
29/Oct/1995 2:00 8:00
7/Apr/1996 2:00 7:00
27/Oct/1996 2:00 8:00
6/Apr/1997 2:00 7:00
26/Oct/1997 2:00 8:00
5/Apr/1998 2:00 7:00
25/Oct/1998 2:00 8:00
4/Apr/1999 2:00 7:00
31/Oct/1999 2:00 8:00
2/Apr/2000 2:00 7:00
29/Oct/2000 2:00 8:00
....
Time Table # 266
Before 1/Jan/1884 LMT
Begin Standard 120w00
1/Jan/1884 0:00 8:00
14/Apr/1918 2:00 7:00
31/Oct/1918 2:00 8:00
9/Feb/1942 2:00 7:00
30/Sep/1945 2:00 8:00
27/Apr/1947 2:00 7:00
28/Sep/1947 2:00 8:00
25/Apr/1948 2:00 7:00
26/Sep/1948 2:00 8:00
24/Apr/1949 2:00 7:00
25/Sep/1949 2:00 8:00
30/Apr/1950 2:00 7:00
24/Sep/1950 2:00 8:00
29/Apr/1951 2:00 7:00
30/Sep/1951 2:00 8:00
27/Apr/1952 2:00 7:00
28/Sep/1952 2:00 8:00
26/Apr/1953 2:00 7:00
27/Sep/1953 2:00 8:00
25/Apr/1954 2:00 7:00
26/Sep/1954 2:00 8:00
24/Apr/1955 2:00 7:00
25/Sep/1955 2:00 8:00
29/Apr/1956 2:00 7:00
30/Sep/1956 2:00 8:00
28/Apr/1957 2:00 7:00
29/Sep/1957 2:00 8:00
27/Apr/1958 2:00 7:00
28/Sep/1958 2:00 8:00
26/Apr/1959 2:00 7:00
27/Sep/1959 2:00 8:00
24/Apr/1960 2:00 7:00
25/Sep/1960 2:00 8:00
30/Apr/1961 2:00 7:00
24/Sep/1961 2:00 8:00
29/Apr/1962 2:00 7:00
28/Oct/1962 2:00 8:00
28/Apr/1963 2:00 7:00
27/Oct/1963 2:00 8:00
26/Apr/1964 2:00 7:00
25/Oct/1964 2:00 8:00
25/Apr/1965 2:00 7:00
31/Oct/1965 2:00 8:00
24/Apr/1966 2:00 7:00
30/Oct/1966 2:00 8:00
30/Apr/1967 2:00 7:00
29/Oct/1967 2:00 8:00
28/Apr/1968 2:00 7:00
27/Oct/1968 2:00 8:00
27/Apr/1969 2:00 7:00
26/Oct/1969 2:00 8:00
26/Apr/1970 2:00 7:00
25/Oct/1970 2:00 8:00
25/Apr/1971 2:00 7:00
31/Oct/1971 2:00 8:00
30/Apr/1972 2:00 7:00
29/Oct/1972 2:00 8:00
29/Apr/1973 2:00 7:00
28/Oct/1973 2:00 8:00
28/Apr/1974 2:00 7:00
27/Oct/1974 2:00 8:00
27/Apr/1975 2:00 7:00
26/Oct/1975 2:00 8:00
25/Apr/1976 2:00 7:00
31/Oct/1976 2:00 8:00
24/Apr/1977 2:00 7:00
30/Oct/1977 2:00 8:00
30/Apr/1978 2:00 7:00
29/Oct/1978 2:00 8:00
29/Apr/1979 2:00 7:00
28/Oct/1979 2:00 8:00
27/Apr/1980 2:00 7:00
26/Oct/1980 2:00 8:00
26/Apr/1981 2:00 7:00
25/Oct/1981 2:00 8:00
25/Apr/1982 2:00 7:00
31/Oct/1982 2:00 8:00
24/Apr/1983 2:00 7:00
30/Oct/1983 2:00 8:00
29/Apr/1984 2:00 7:00
28/Oct/1984 2:00 8:00
28/Apr/1985 2:00 7:00
27/Oct/1985 2:00 8:00
27/Apr/1986 2:00 7:00
26/Oct/1986 2:00 8:00
5/Apr/1987 2:00 7:00
25/Oct/1987 2:00 8:00
3/Apr/1988 2:00 7:00
30/Oct/1988 2:00 8:00
2/Apr/1989 2:00 7:00
29/Oct/1989 2:00 8:00
1/Apr/1990 2:00 7:00
28/Oct/1990 2:00 8:00
7/Apr/1991 2:00 7:00
27/Oct/1991 2:00 8:00
5/Apr/1992 2:00 7:00
25/Oct/1992 2:00 8:00
4/Apr/1993 2:00 7:00
31/Oct/1993 2:00 8:00
3/Apr/1994 2:00 7:00
30/Oct/1994 2:00 8:00
2/Apr/1995 2:00 7:00
29/Oct/1995 2:00 8:00
7/Apr/1996 2:00 7:00
27/Oct/1996 2:00 8:00
6/Apr/1997 2:00 7:00
26/Oct/1997 2:00 8:00
5/Apr/1998 2:00 7:00
25/Oct/1998 2:00 8:00
4/Apr/1999 2:00 7:00
31/Oct/1999 2:00 8:00
2/Apr/2000 2:00 7:00
29/Oct/2000 2:00 8:00
....
Time Table # 267
Before 1/Jan/1884 LMT
Begin Standard 120w00
1/Jan/1884 0:00 8:00
14/Apr/1918 2:00 7:00
31/Oct/1918 2:00 8:00
9/Feb/1942 2:00 7:00
30/Sep/1945 2:00 8:00
28/Apr/1946 2:00 7:00
13/Oct/1946 2:00 8:00
27/Apr/1947 2:00 7:00
28/Sep/1947 2:00 8:00
25/Apr/1948 2:00 7:00
26/Sep/1948 2:00 8:00
24/Apr/1949 2:00 7:00
25/Sep/1949 2:00 8:00
30/Apr/1950 2:00 7:00
24/Sep/1950 2:00 8:00
29/Apr/1951 2:00 7:00
30/Sep/1951 2:00 8:00
27/Apr/1952 2:00 7:00
28/Sep/1952 2:00 8:00
26/Apr/1953 2:00 7:00
27/Sep/1953 2:00 8:00
25/Apr/1954 2:00 7:00
26/Sep/1954 2:00 8:00
24/Apr/1955 2:00 7:00
25/Sep/1955 2:00 8:00
29/Apr/1956 2:00 7:00
30/Sep/1956 2:00 8:00
28/Apr/1957 2:00 7:00
29/Sep/1957 2:00 8:00
27/Apr/1958 2:00 7:00
28/Sep/1958 2:00 8:00
26/Apr/1959 2:00 7:00
27/Sep/1959 2:00 8:00
24/Apr/1960 2:00 7:00
25/Sep/1960 2:00 8:00
30/Apr/1961 2:00 7:00
24/Sep/1961 2:00 8:00
29/Apr/1962 2:00 7:00
28/Oct/1962 2:00 8:00
28/Apr/1963 2:00 7:00
27/Oct/1963 2:00 8:00
26/Apr/1964 2:00 7:00
25/Oct/1964 2:00 8:00
25/Apr/1965 2:00 7:00
31/Oct/1965 2:00 8:00
24/Apr/1966 2:00 7:00
30/Oct/1966 2:00 8:00
30/Apr/1967 2:00 7:00
29/Oct/1967 2:00 8:00
28/Apr/1968 2:00 7:00
27/Oct/1968 2:00 8:00
27/Apr/1969 2:00 7:00
26/Oct/1969 2:00 8:00
26/Apr/1970 2:00 7:00
25/Oct/1970 2:00 8:00
25/Apr/1971 2:00 7:00
31/Oct/1971 2:00 8:00
30/Apr/1972 2:00 7:00
29/Oct/1972 2:00 8:00
29/Apr/1973 2:00 7:00
28/Oct/1973 2:00 8:00
28/Apr/1974 2:00 7:00
27/Oct/1974 2:00 8:00
27/Apr/1975 2:00 7:00
26/Oct/1975 2:00 8:00
25/Apr/1976 2:00 7:00
31/Oct/1976 2:00 8:00
24/Apr/1977 2:00 7:00
30/Oct/1977 2:00 8:00
30/Apr/1978 2:00 7:00
29/Oct/1978 2:00 8:00
29/Apr/1979 2:00 7:00
28/Oct/1979 2:00 8:00
27/Apr/1980 2:00 7:00
26/Oct/1980 2:00 8:00
26/Apr/1981 2:00 7:00
25/Oct/1981 2:00 8:00
25/Apr/1982 2:00 7:00
31/Oct/1982 2:00 8:00
24/Apr/1983 2:00 7:00
30/Oct/1983 2:00 8:00
29/Apr/1984 2:00 7:00
28/Oct/1984 2:00 8:00
28/Apr/1985 2:00 7:00
27/Oct/1985 2:00 8:00
27/Apr/1986 2:00 7:00
26/Oct/1986 2:00 8:00
5/Apr/1987 2:00 7:00
25/Oct/1987 2:00 8:00
3/Apr/1988 2:00 7:00
30/Oct/1988 2:00 8:00
2/Apr/1989 2:00 7:00
29/Oct/1989 2:00 8:00
1/Apr/1990 2:00 7:00
28/Oct/1990 2:00 8:00
7/Apr/1991 2:00 7:00
27/Oct/1991 2:00 8:00
5/Apr/1992 2:00 7:00
25/Oct/1992 2:00 8:00
4/Apr/1993 2:00 7:00
31/Oct/1993 2:00 8:00
3/Apr/1994 2:00 7:00
30/Oct/1994 2:00 8:00
2/Apr/1995 2:00 7:00
29/Oct/1995 2:00 8:00
7/Apr/1996 2:00 7:00
27/Oct/1996 2:00 8:00
6/Apr/1997 2:00 7:00
26/Oct/1997 2:00 8:00
5/Apr/1998 2:00 7:00
25/Oct/1998 2:00 8:00
4/Apr/1999 2:00 7:00
31/Oct/1999 2:00 8:00
2/Apr/2000 2:00 7:00
29/Oct/2000 2:00 8:00
....
26/Apr/1936 2:00 8:0o
7/May/1939 2:00 8:0o
30/Apr/1961 2:00 8:0o
Time Table # 268
Before 20/Aug/1900 LMT
Begin Standard 0w02
20/Aug/1900 0:00 0:00
14/Apr/1918 2:00 -0:60
Begin Standard 0w00
27/Oct/1918 2:00 0:00
Begin Standard 0w02
30/Mar/1919 2:00 0:00
25/May/1919 2:00 -0:60
Begin Standard 0w00
26/Oct/1919 2:00 -1:00
1/Nov/1919 0:00 0:00
9/Feb/1942 2:00 -1:00
30/Sep/1945 2:00 0:00
Begin Standard 0w01
26/Apr/1964 2:00 0:00
Begin Standard 0w00
25/Oct/1964 2:00 0:00
25/Apr/1965 0:00 -2:00
31/Oct/1965 2:00 0:00
Begin Standard 0w01
24/Apr/1966 2:00 0:00
Begin Standard 0w00
30/Oct/1966 2:00 0:00
Begin Standard 0w01
30/Apr/1967 2:00 0:00
Begin Standard 0w00
29/Oct/1967 2:00 0:00
Begin Standard 0w01
28/Apr/1968 2:00 0:00
Begin Standard 0w00
27/Oct/1968 2:00 0:00
Begin Standard 0w01
27/Apr/1969 2:00 0:00
Begin Standard 0w00
26/Oct/1969 2:00 0:00
Begin Standard 0w01
26/Apr/1970 2:00 0:00
Begin Standard 0w00
25/Oct/1970 2:00 0:00
Begin Standard 0w01
25/Apr/1971 2:00 0:00
Begin Standard 0w00
31/Oct/1971 2:00 0:00
Begin Standard 0w01
30/Apr/1972 2:00 0:00
Begin Standard 0w00
29/Oct/1972 2:00 0:00
Begin Standard 0w01
29/Apr/1973 2:00 0:00
Begin Standard 0w00
28/Oct/1973 2:00 0:00
Begin Standard 0w01
6/Jan/1974 2:00 0:00
Begin Standard 0w00
27/Oct/1974 2:00 0:00
Begin Standard 0w01
23/Feb/1975 2:00 0:00
Begin Standard 0w00
26/Oct/1975 2:00 0:00
27/Apr/1980 2:00 -1:00
26/Oct/1980 2:00 0:00
26/Apr/1981 2:00 -1:00
25/Oct/1981 2:00 0:00
25/Apr/1982 2:00 -1:00
31/Oct/1982 2:00 0:00
24/Apr/1983 2:00 -1:00
30/Oct/1983 2:00 0:00
29/Apr/1984 2:00 -1:00
28/Oct/1984 2:00 0:00
28/Apr/1985 2:00 -1:00
27/Oct/1985 2:00 0:00
27/Apr/1986 2:00 -1:00
26/Oct/1986 2:00 0:00
5/Apr/1987 2:00 -1:00
25/Oct/1987 2:00 0:00
3/Apr/1988 2:00 -1:00
30/Oct/1988 2:00 0:00
2/Apr/1989 2:00 -1:00
29/Oct/1989 2:00 0:00
1/Apr/1990 2:00 -1:00
28/Oct/1990 2:00 0:00
7/Apr/1991 2:00 -1:00
27/Oct/1991 2:00 0:00
5/Apr/1992 2:00 -1:00
25/Oct/1992 2:00 0:00
4/Apr/1993 2:00 -1:00
31/Oct/1993 2:00 0:00
3/Apr/1994 2:00 -1:00
30/Oct/1994 2:00 0:00
2/Apr/1995 2:00 -1:00
29/Oct/1995 2:00 0:00
7/Apr/1996 2:00 -1:00
27/Oct/1996 2:00 0:00
6/Apr/1997 2:00 -1:00
26/Oct/1997 2:00 0:00
5/Apr/1998 2:00 -1:00
25/Oct/1998 2:00 0:00
4/Apr/1999 2:00 -1:00
31/Oct/1999 2:00 0:00
2/Apr/2000 2:00 -1:00
29/Oct/2000 2:00 0:00
....
Time Table # 269
Before 1/Jan/1884 LMT
Begin Standard 52w43
1/Jan/1884 0:00 3:31
14/Apr/1918 2:00 2:31
31/Oct/1918 2:00 3:31
Begin Standard 52w30
30/Mar/1935 0:00 3:30
11/May/1936 0:00 2:30
5/Oct/1936 0:00 3:30
10/May/1937 0:00 2:30
4/Oct/1937 0:00 3:30
9/May/1938 0:00 2:30
3/Oct/1938 0:00 3:30
15/May/1939 0:00 2:30
2/Oct/1939 0:00 3:30
13/May/1940 0:00 2:30
17/Oct/1940 0:00 3:30
12/May/1941 0:00 2:30
6/Oct/1941 0:00 3:30
11/May/1942 0:00 2:30
30/Sep/1945 2:00 3:30
12/May/1946 2:00 2:30
6/Oct/1946 2:00 3:30
11/May/1947 2:00 2:30
5/Oct/1947 2:00 3:30
9/May/1948 2:00 2:30
3/Oct/1948 2:00 3:30
8/May/1949 2:00 2:30
2/Oct/1949 2:00 3:30
14/May/1950 2:00 2:30
8/Oct/1950 2:00 3:30
29/Apr/1951 2:00 2:30
30/Sep/1951 2:00 3:30
27/Apr/1952 2:00 2:30
29/Sep/1952 2:00 3:30
26/Apr/1953 2:00 2:30
28/Sep/1953 2:00 3:30
25/Apr/1954 2:00 2:30
26/Sep/1954 2:00 3:30
24/Apr/1955 2:00 2:30
25/Sep/1955 2:00 3:30
29/Apr/1956 2:00 2:30
30/Sep/1956 2:00 3:30
28/Apr/1957 2:00 2:30
29/Sep/1957 2:00 3:30
27/Apr/1958 2:00 2:30
28/Sep/1958 2:00 3:30
26/Apr/1959 2:00 2:30
27/Sep/1959 2:00 3:30
24/Apr/1960 2:00 2:30
29/Oct/1960 2:00 3:30
30/Apr/1961 2:00 2:30
28/Oct/1961 2:00 3:30
29/Apr/1962 2:00 2:30
28/Oct/1962 2:00 3:30
28/Apr/1963 2:00 2:30
27/Oct/1963 2:00 3:30
26/Apr/1964 2:00 2:30
25/Oct/1964 2:00 3:30
25/Apr/1965 2:00 2:30
31/Oct/1965 2:00 3:30
Begin Standard 60w00
15/Mar/1966 2:00 4:00
24/Apr/1966 2:00 3:00
30/Oct/1966 2:00 4:00
30/Apr/1967 2:00 3:00
29/Oct/1967 2:00 4:00
28/Apr/1968 2:00 3:00
27/Oct/1968 2:00 4:00
27/Apr/1969 2:00 3:00
26/Oct/1969 2:00 4:00
26/Apr/1970 2:00 3:00
25/Oct/1970 2:00 4:00
25/Apr/1971 2:00 3:00
31/Oct/1971 2:00 4:00
30/Apr/1972 2:00 3:00
29/Oct/1972 2:00 4:00
29/Apr/1973 2:00 3:00
28/Oct/1973 2:00 4:00
28/Apr/1974 2:00 3:00
27/Oct/1974 2:00 4:00
27/Apr/1975 2:00 3:00
26/Oct/1975 2:00 4:00
25/Apr/1976 2:00 3:00

31/Oct/1976 2:00 4:00
24/Apr/1977 2:00 3:00
30/Oct/1977 2:00 4:00
30/Apr/1978 2:00 3:00
29/Oct/1978 2:00 4:00
29/Apr/1979 2:00 3:00
28/Oct/1979 2:00 4:00
27/Apr/1980 2:00 3:00
26/Oct/1980 2:00 4:00
26/Apr/1981 2:00 3:00
25/Oct/1981 2:00 4:00
25/Apr/1982 2:00 3:00
31/Oct/1982 2:00 4:00
24/Apr/1983 2:00 3:00
30/Oct/1983 2:00 4:00
29/Apr/1984 2:00 3:00
28/Oct/1984 2:00 4:00
28/Apr/1985 2:00 3:00
27/Oct/1985 2:00 4:00
27/Apr/1986 2:00 3:00
26/Oct/1986 2:00 4:00
5/Apr/1987 2:00 3:00
25/Oct/1987 2:00 4:00
3/Apr/1988 2:00 2:00
30/Oct/1988 2:00 4:00
2/Apr/1989 2:00 3:00
29/Oct/1989 2:00 4:00
1/Apr/1990 2:00 3:00
28/Oct/1990 2:00 4:00
7/Apr/1991 2:00 3:00
27/Oct/1991 2:00 4:00
5/Apr/1992 2:00 3:00
25/Oct/1992 2:00 4:00
4/Apr/1993 2:00 3:00
31/Oct/1993 2:00 4:00
3/Apr/1994 2:00 3:00
30/Oct/1994 2:00 4:00
2/Apr/1995 2:00 3:00
29/Oct/1995 2:00 4:00
7/Apr/1996 2:00 3:00
27/Oct/1996 2:00 4:00
6/Apr/1997 2:00 3:00
26/Oct/1997 2:00 4:00
5/Apr/1998 2:00 3:00
25/Oct/1998 2:00 4:00
4/Apr/1999 2:00 3:00
31/Oct/1999 2:00 4:00
2/Apr/2000 2:00 3:00
29/Oct/2000 2:00 4:00
....
Time Table # 270
Before 20/Aug/1900 LMT
Begin Standard 135w00
20/Aug/1900 0:00 9:00
14/Apr/1918 2:00 8:00
27/Oct/1918 2:00 9:00
25/May/1919 2:00 8:00
1/Nov/1919 0:00 9:00
9/Feb/1942 2:00 8:00
30/Sep/1945 2:00 9:00
25/Apr/1965 0:00 7:00
31/Oct/1965 2:00 9:00
Begin Standard 120w00
1/Jul/1966 2:00 8:00
27/Apr/1980 2:00 7:00
26/Oct/1980 2:00 8:00
26/Apr/1981 2:00 7:00
25/Oct/1981 2:00 8:00
25/Apr/1982 2:00 7:00
31/Oct/1982 2:00 8:00
24/Apr/1983 2:00 7:00
30/Oct/1983 2:00 8:00
29/Apr/1984 2:00 7:00
28/Oct/1984 2:00 8:00
28/Apr/1985 2:00 7:00
27/Oct/1985 2:00 8:00
27/Apr/1986 2:00 7:00
26/Oct/1986 2:00 8:00
5/Apr/1987 2:00 7:00
25/Oct/1987 2:00 8:00
3/Apr/1988 2:00 7:00
30/Oct/1988 2:00 8:00
2/Apr/1989 2:00 7:00
29/Oct/1989 2:00 8:00
1/Apr/1990 2:00 7:00
28/Oct/1990 2:00 8:00
7/Apr/1991 2:00 7:00
27/Oct/1991 2:00 8:00
5/Apr/1992 2:00 7:00
25/Oct/1992 2:00 8:00
4/Apr/1993 2:00 7:00
31/Oct/1993 2:00 8:00
3/Apr/1994 2:00 7:00
30/Oct/1994 2:00 8:00
2/Apr/1995 2:00 7:00
29/Oct/1995 2:00 8:00
7/Apr/1996 2:00 7:00
27/Oct/1996 2:00 8:00
6/Apr/1997 2:00 7:00
26/Oct/1997 2:00 8:00
5/Apr/1998 2:00 7:00
25/Oct/1998 2:00 8:00
4/Apr/1999 2:00 7:00
31/Oct/1999 2:00 8:00
2/Apr/2000 2:00 7:00
29/Oct/2000 2:00 8:00
....
Time Table # 271
Before 9/Dec/1883 LMT
Begin Standard 75w00
9/Dec/1883 0:00 5:00
Begin Standard 60w00
15/Jun/1902 0:00 4:00
14/Apr/1918 2:00 3:00
31/Oct/1918 2:00 4:00
9/Feb/1942 2:00 3:00
30/Sep/1945 2:00 4:00
24/Apr/1966 2:00 TT#4
....
Time Table # 272
Before 9/Dec/1883 LMT
Begin Standard 75w00
9/Dec/1883 0:00 5:00
Begin Standard 60w00
15/Jun/1902 0:00 4:00
14/Apr/1918 2:00 3:00
31/Oct/1918 2:00 4:00
29/Apr/1934 2:00 3:00
30/Sep/1934 2:00 4:00
9/Feb/1942 2:00 3:00
30/Sep/1945 2:00 4:00
1/Apr/1946 2:00 3:00
28/Sep/1946 2:00 4:00
25/Apr/1948 2:00 3:00
26/Sep/1948 2:00 4:00
15/May/1950 2:00 3:00
2/Oct/1950 2:00 4:00
29/Apr/1951 2:00 3:00
30/Sep/1951 2:00 4:00
26/Apr/1953 2:00 3:00
28/Sep/1953 2:00 4:00
26/Apr/1954 2:00 3:00
27/Sep/1954 2:00 4:00
30/Apr/1956 2:00 3:00
1/Oct/1956 2:00 4:00
28/Apr/1957 2:00 3:00
30/Sep/1957 2:00 4:00
1/May/1961 2:00 3:00
2/Oct/1961 2:00 4:00
27/Apr/1964 2:00 3:00
26/Oct/1964 2:00 4:00
24/Apr/1966 2:00 TT#4
....
Time Table # 273
Before 9/Dec/1883 LMT
Begin Standard 75w00
9/Dec/1883 0:00 5:00
Begin Standard 60w00
15/Jun/1902 0:00 4:00
14/Apr/1918 2:00 3:00
31/Oct/1918 2:00 4:00
9/Feb/1942 2:00 3:00
30/Sep/1945 2:00 4:00
24/Apr/1949 2:00 3:00
25/Sep/1949 2:00 4:00
30/Apr/1950 2:00 3:00
25/Sep/1950 2:00 4:00
29/Apr/1951 2:00 3:00
30/Sep/1951 2:00 4:00
27/Apr/1952 2:00 3:00
29/Sep/1952 2:00 4:00
26/Apr/1953 2:00 3:00
28/Sep/1953 2:00 4:00
25/Apr/1954 2:00 3:00
26/Sep/1954 2:00 4:00
24/Apr/1955 2:00 3:00
25/Sep/1955 2:00 4:00
29/Apr/1956 2:00 3:00
30/Sep/1956 2:00 4:00
28/Apr/1957 2:00 3:00
1/Sep/1957 2:00 4:00
27/Apr/1958 2:00 3:00
31/Aug/1958 2:00 4:00
26/Apr/1959 2:00 3:00
27/Sep/1959 2:00 4:00
18/Jun/1961 2:00 3:00
5/Sep/1961 2:00 4:00
17/May/1964 2:00 3:00
11/Oct/1964 2:00 4:00
24/Apr/1966 2:00 TT#4
....
Time Table # 274
Before 9/Dec/1883 LMT
Begin Standard 75w00
9/Dec/1883 0:00 5:00
Begin Standard 60w00
15/Jun/1902 0:00 4:00
14/Apr/1918 2:00 3:00
31/Oct/1918 2:00 4:00
9/Feb/1942 2:00 3:00
30/Sep/1945 2:00 4:00
29/Apr/1951 2:00 3:00
30/Sep/1951 2:00 4:00
27/Apr/1952 2:00 3:00
29/Sep/1952 2:00 4:00
26/Apr/1953 2:00 3:00
28/Sep/1953 2:00 4:00
29/Apr/1956 2:00 3:00
30/Sep/1956 2:00 4:00
27/Apr/1957 2:00 3:00
30/Sep/1957 2:00 4:00
24/Apr/1966 2:00 TT#4
....
Time Table # 275
Before 9/Dec/1883 LMT
Begin Standard 75w00
9/Dec/1883 0:00 5:00
Begin Standard 60w00
15/Jun/1902 0:00 4:00
14/Apr/1918 2:00 3:00
31/Oct/1918 2:00 4:00
9/Feb/1942 2:00 3:00
30/Sep/1945 2:00 4:00
26/Apr/1953 2:00 3:00
28/Sep/1953 2:00 4:00
27/Apr/1957 2:00 3:00
29/Sep/1957 2:00 4:00
24/Apr/1966 2:00 TT#4
....
Time Table # 276
Before 9/Dec/1883 LMT
Begin Standard 75w00
9/Dec/1883 0:00 5:00
Begin Standard 60w00
15/Jun/1902 0:00 4:00
14/Apr/1918 2:00 3:00
31/Oct/1918 2:00 4:00
9/Feb/1942 2:00 3:00
30/Sep/1945 2:00 4:00
28/Apr/1946 2:00 3:00
29/Sep/1946 2:00 4:00
25/Apr/1948 2:00 3:00
26/Sep/1948 2:00 4:00
24/Apr/1949 2:00 3:00
25/Sep/1949 2:00 4:00
30/Apr/1950 2:00 3:00
25/Sep/1950 2:00 4:00
29/Apr/1951 2:00 3:00
30/Sep/1951 2:00 4:00
27/Apr/1952 2:00 3:00
29/Sep/1952 2:00 4:00
26/Apr/1953 2:00 3:00
28/Sep/1953 2:00 4:00
25/Apr/1954 2:00 3:00
26/Sep/1954 2:00 4:00
24/Apr/1955 2:00 3:00
25/Sep/1955 2:00 4:00
29/Apr/1956 2:00 3:00
30/Sep/1956 2:00 4:00
28/Apr/1957 2:00 3:00
29/Sep/1957 2:00 4:00
27/Apr/1958 2:00 3:00
27/Sep/1958 2:00 4:00
26/Apr/1959 2:00 TT#4
....
Time Table # 277
Before 9/Dec/1883 LMT
Begin Standard 75w00
9/Dec/1883 2:00 5:00
Begin Standard 60w00
15/Jun/1902 0:00 4:00
14/Apr/1918 2:00 3:00
31/Oct/1918 2:00 4:00
9/Feb/1942 2:00 3:00
30/Sep/1945 2:00 4:00
26/Apr/1953 2:00 3:00
28/Sep/1953 2:00 4:00
24/Apr/1966 2:00 TT#4
....
Time Table # 278
Before 9/Dec/1883 LMT
Begin Standard 75w00
9/Dec/1883 0:00 5:00
Begin Standard 60w00
15/Jun/1902 0:00 4:00
14/Apr/1918 2:00 3:00
31/Oct/1918 2:00 4:00
9/Feb/1942 2:00 3:00
30/Sep/1945 2:00 4:00
25/Apr/1954 2:00 3:00
26/Sep/1954 2:00 4:00
24/Apr/1955 2:00 3:00
25/Sep/1955 2:00 4:00
26/Apr/1959 2:00 3:00
25/Oct/1959 2:00 4:00
24/Apr/1960 2:00 3:00
26/Sep/1960 2:00 4:00
29/Apr/1962 2:00 3:00
28/Oct/1962 2:00 4:00
28/Apr/1963 2:00 3:00
27/Oct/1963 2:00 4:00
24/Apr/1966 2:00 TT#4
....
Time Table # 279
Before 9/Dec/1883 LMT
Begin Standard 75w00
9/Dec/1883 0:00 5:00
Begin Standard 60w00
15/Jun/1902 0:00 4:00
14/Apr/1918 2:00 3:00
31/Oct/1918 2:00 4:00
9/Feb/1942 2:00 3:00
30/Sep/1945 2:00 4:00
25/Apr/1948 2:00 TT#4
....
Time Table # 280
Before 9/Dec/1883 LMT
Begin Standard 75w00
9/Dec/1883 0:00 5:00
Begin Standard 60w00
15/Jun/1902 0:00 4:00
14/Apr/1918 2:00 3:00
31/Oct/1918 2:00 4:00
19/May/1924 0:00 3:00
8/Sep/1924 0:00 4:00
4/May/1925 0:00 3:00
28/Sep/1925 0:00 4:00
3/May/1926 0:00 3:00
8/Sep/1926 0:00 4:00
2/May/1927 0:00 3:00
26/Sep/1927 0:00 4:00
21/May/1928 0:00 3:00
5/Sep/1928 0:00 4:00
13/May/1929 0:00 3:00
4/Sep/1929 0:00 4:00
2/Jun/1930 0:00 3:00
3/Sep/1930 0:00 4:00
18/May/1931 0:00 3:00
14/Sep/1931 0:00 4:00
29/May/1932 0:00 3:00
25/Sep/1932 0:00 4:00
28/May/1933 0:00 3:00
1/Oct/1933 0:00 4:00
27/May/1934 0:00 3:00
30/Sep/1934 0:00 4:00
26/May/1935 0:00 3:00
29/Sep/1935 0:00 4:00
24/May/1936 0:00 3:00
27/Sep/1936 0:00 4:00
23/May/1937 0:00 3:00
26/Sep/1937 0:00 4:00
22/May/1938 0:00 3:00
25/Sep/1938 0:00 4:00
21/May/1939 0:00 3:00
24/Sep/1939 0:00 4:00
26/May/1940 0:00 3:00
29/Sep/1940 0:00 4:00
25/May/1941 0:00 3:00
28/Sep/1941 0:00 4:00
9/Feb/1942 2:00 TT#4
....
Time Table # 281
Before 9/Dec/1883 LMT
Begin Standard 75w00
9/Dec/1883 0:00 5:00
Begin Standard 60w00
15/Jun/1902 0:00 4:00
14/Apr/1918 2:00 3:00
31/Oct/1918 2:00 4:00
9/Feb/1942 2:00 3:00
30/Sep/1945 2:00 4:00
27/Apr/1958 2:00 3:00
26/Oct/1958 2:00 4:00
26/Apr/1959 2:00 3:00
25/Oct/1959 2:00 4:00
24/Apr/1966 2:00 TT#4
....
Time Table # 282
Before 9/Dec/1883 LMT
Begin Standard 75w00
9/Dec/1883 0:00 5:00
Begin Standard 60w00
15/Jun/1902 0:00 4:00
14/Apr/1918 2:00 3:00
31/Oct/1918 2:00 4:00
28/Apr/1940 2:00 3:00
1/Sep/1940 2:00 4:00
9/Feb/1942 2:00 3:00
30/Sep/1945 2:00 4:00
28/Apr/1946 2:00 3:00
29/Sep/1946 2:00 4:00
27/Apr/1947 2:00 3:00
28/Sep/1947 2:00 4:00
25/Apr/1948 2:00 3:00
26/Sep/1948 2:00 4:00
24/Apr/1949 2:00 3:00
25/Sep/1949 2:00 4:00
30/Apr/1950 2:00 3:00
25/Sep/1950 2:00 4:00
29/Apr/1951 2:00 3:00
30/Sep/1951 2:00 4:00
26/Apr/1953 2:00 3:00
28/Sep/1953 2:00 4:00
25/Apr/1954 2:00 3:00
26/Sep/1954 2:00 4:00
27/Apr/1958 2:00 3:00
26/Oct/1958 2:00 4:00
26/Apr/1959 2:00 3:00
25/Oct/1959 2:00 4:00
24/Apr/1960 2:00 3:00
30/Oct/1960 2:00 4:00
30/Apr/1961 2:00 3:00
29/Oct/1961 2:00 4:00
29/Apr/1962 2:00 3:00
28/Oct/1962 2:00 4:00
24/Apr/1966 2:00 TT#4
....
Time Table # 283
Before 9/Dec/1883 LMT
Begin Standard 75w00
9/Dec/1883 0:00 5:00
Begin Standard 60w00
15/Jun/1902 0:00 4:00
14/Apr/1918 2:00 3:00
31/Oct/1918 2:00 4:00
9/Feb/1942 2:00 3:00
30/Sep/1945 2:00 4:00
28/Apr/1946 2:00 3:00
29/Sep/1946 2:00 4:00
25/Apr/1948 2:00 3:00
26/Sep/1948 2:00 4:00
24/Apr/1949 2:00 3:00
25/Sep/1949 2:00 4:00
29/Apr/1951 2:00 3:00
30/Sep/1951 2:00 4:00
27/Apr/1952 2:00 3:00
29/Sep/1952 2:00 4:00
26/Apr/1953 2:00 3:00
28/Sep/1953 2:00 4:00
25/Apr/1954 2:00 3:00
26/Sep/1954 2:00 4:00
24/Apr/1955 2:00 3:00
25/Sep/1955 2:00 4:00
29/Apr/1956 2:00 3:00
30/Sep/1956 2:00 4:00
28/Apr/1957 2:00 3:00
27/Oct/1957 2:00 4:00
27/Apr/1958 2:00 3:00
26/Oct/1958 2:00 4:00
29/Apr/1962 2:00 3:00
28/Oct/1962 2:00 4:00
28/Apr/1963 2:00 3:00
27/Oct/1963 2:00 4:00
26/Apr/1964 2:00 3:00
25/Oct/1964 2:00 4:00
24/Apr/1966 2:00 TT#4
....
Time Table # 284
Before 9/Dec/1883 LMT
Begin Standard 75w00
9/Dec/1883 0:00 5:00
Begin Standard 60w00
15/Jun/1902 0:00 4:00
14/Apr/1918 2:00 3:00
31/Oct/1918 2:00 4:00
9/Feb/1942 2:00 3:00
30/Sep/1945 2:00 4:00
30/Apr/1950 2:00 3:00
25/Sep/1950 2:00 4:00
29/Apr/1951 2:00 3:00
30/Sep/1951 2:00 4:00
26/Apr/1953 2:00 3:00
8/Sep/1953 2:00 4:00
25/Apr/1954 2:00 3:00
7/Sep/1954 2:00 4:00
29/May/1955 2:00 3:00
5/Sep/1955 2:00 4:00
1/Jun/1956 2:00 3:00
3/Sep/1956 2:00 4:00
28/Apr/1957 2:00 3:00
29/Sep/1957 2:00 4:00
27/Apr/1958 2:00 3:00
27/Sep/1958 2:00 4:00
26/Apr/1959 2:00 3:00
27/Sep/1959 2:00 4:00
24/Apr/1966 2:00 TT#4
....
Time Table # 285
Before 1/Jan/1884 LMT
Begin Standard 52w43
1/Jan/1884 0:00 3:31
8/Apr/1917 2:00 2:31
17/Sep/1917 2:00 3:31
14/Apr/1918 2:00 2:31
31/Oct/1918 2:00 3:31
5/May/1919 23:00 2:31
12/Aug/1919 23:00 3:31
2/May/1920 23:00 2:31
31/Oct/1920 23:00 3:31
1/May/1921 23:00 2:31
30/Oct/1921 23:00 3:31
7/May/1922 23:00 2:31
29/Oct/1922 23:00 3:31
6/May/1923 23:00 2:31
28/Oct/1923 23:00 3:31
4/May/1924 23:00 2:31
26/Oct/1924 23:00 3:31
3/May/1925 23:00 2:31
25/Oct/1925 23:00 3:31
2/May/1926 23:00 2:31
31/Oct/1926 23:00 3:31
1/May/1927 23:00 2:31
30/Oct/1927 23:00 3:31
6/May/1928 23:00 2:31
28/Oct/1928 23:00 3:31
5/May/1929 23:00 2:31
27/Oct/1929 23:00 3:31
4/May/1930 23:00 2:31
26/Oct/1930 23:00 3:31
3/May/1931 23:00 2:31
25/Oct/1931 23:00 3:31
1/May/1932 23:00 2:31
30/Oct/1932 23:00 3:31
7/May/1933 23:00 2:31
29/Sep/1933 23:00 3:31
6/May/1934 23:00 2:31
28/Oct/1934 23:00 3:31
Begin Standard 52w30
30/Mar/1935 0:00 3:30
5/May/1935 23:00 2:30
27/Oct/1935 23:00 3:30
11/May/1936 0:00 2:30
5/Oct/1936 0:00 3:30
10/May/1937 0:00 2:30
4/Oct/1937 0:00 3:30
9/May/1938 0:00 2:30
3/Oct/1938 0:00 3:30
15/May/1939 0:00 2:30
2/Oct/1939 0:00 3:30
13/May/1940 0:00 2:30
17/Oct/1940 0:00 3:30
12/May/1941 0:00 2:30
6/Oct/1941 0:00 3:30
11/May/1942 0:00 2:30
30/Sep/1945 2:00 3:30
12/May/1946 2:00 2:30
6/Oct/1946 2:00 3:30
11/May/1947 2:00 2:30
5/Oct/1947 2:00 3:30
9/May/1948 2:00 2:30
3/Oct/1948 2:00 3:30
8/May/1949 2:00 2:30
2/Oct/1949 2:00 3:30
14/May/1950 2:00 2:30
8/Oct/1950 2:00 3:30
29/Apr/1951 2:00 2:30
30/Sep/1951 2:00 3:30
27/Apr/1952 2:00 2:30
29/Sep/1952 2:00 3:30
26/Apr/1953 2:00 2:30
28/Sep/1953 2:00 3:30
25/Apr/1954 2:00 2:30
26/Sep/1954 2:00 3:30
24/Apr/1955 2:00 2:30
25/Sep/1955 2:00 3:30
29/Apr/1956 2:00 2:30
30/Sep/1956 2:00 3:30
28/Apr/1957 2:00 2:30
29/Sep/1957 2:00 3:30
27/Apr/1958 2:00 2:30
28/Sep/1958 2:00 3:30
26/Apr/1959 2:00 2:30
27/Sep/1959 2:00 3:30
24/Apr/1960 2:00 2:30
29/Oct/1960 2:00 3:30

30/Apr/1961 2:00 2:30
28/Oct/1961 2:00 3:30
29/Apr/1962 2:00 2:30
28/Oct/1962 2:00 3:30
28/Apr/1963 2:00 2:30
27/Oct/1963 2:00 3:30
26/Apr/1964 2:00 2:30
25/Oct/1964 2:00 3:30
25/Apr/1965 2:00 2:30
31/Oct/1965 2:00 3:30
24/Apr/1966 2:00 2:30
30/Oct/1966 2:00 3:30
30/Apr/1967 2:00 2:30
29/Oct/1967 2:00 3:30
28/Apr/1968 2:00 2:30
27/Oct/1968 2:00 3:30
27/Apr/1969 2:00 2:30
26/Oct/1969 2:00 3:30
26/Apr/1970 2:00 2:30
25/Oct/1970 2:00 3:30
25/Apr/1971 2:00 2:30
31/Oct/1971 2:00 3:30
30/Apr/1972 2:00 2:30
29/Oct/1972 2:00 3:30
29/Apr/1973 2:00 2:30
28/Oct/1973 2:00 3:30
28/Apr/1974 2:00 2:30
27/Oct/1974 2:00 3:30
27/Apr/1975 2:00 2:30
26/Oct/1975 2:00 3:30
25/Apr/1976 2:00 2:30
31/Oct/1976 2:00 3:30
24/Apr/1977 2:00 2:30
30/Oct/1977 2:00 3:30
30/Apr/1978 2:00 2:30
29/Oct/1978 2:00 3:30
29/Apr/1979 2:00 2:30
28/Oct/1979 2:00 3:30
27/Apr/1980 2:00 2:30
26/Oct/1980 2:00 3:30
26/Apr/1981 2:00 2:30
25/Oct/1981 2:00 3:30
25/Apr/1982 2:00 2:30
31/Oct/1982 2:00 3:30
24/Apr/1983 2:00 2:30
30/Oct/1983 2:00 3:30
29/Apr/1984 2:00 2:30
28/Oct/1984 2:00 3:30
28/Apr/1985 2:00 2:30
27/Oct/1985 2:00 3:30
27/Apr/1986 2:00 2:30
26/Oct/1986 2:00 3:30
5/Apr/1987 2:00 2:30
25/Oct/1987 2:00 3:30
3/Apr/1988 2:00 1:30
30/Oct/1988 2:00 3:30
2/Apr/1989 2:00 2:30
29/Oct/1989 2:00 3:30
1/Apr/1990 2:00 2:30
28/Oct/1990 2:00 3:30
7/Apr/1991 2:00 2:30
27/Oct/1991 2:00 3:30
5/Apr/1992 2:00 2:30
25/Oct/1992 2:00 3:30
4/Apr/1993 2:00 2:30
31/Oct/1993 2:00 3:30
3/Apr/1994 2:00 2:30
30/Oct/1994 2:00 3:30
2/Apr/1995 2:00 2:30
29/Oct/1995 2:00 3:30
7/Apr/1996 2:00 2:30
27/Oct/1996 2:00 3:30
6/Apr/1997 2:00 2:30
26/Oct/1997 2:00 3:30
5/Apr/1998 2:00 2:30
25/Oct/1998 2:00 3:30
4/Apr/1999 2:00 2:30
31/Oct/1999 2:00 3:30
2/Apr/2000 2:00 2:30
29/Oct/2000 2:00 3:30
....

Time Table # 286
Before 1/Jan/1884 LMT
Begin Standard 52w43
1/Jan/1884 0:00 3:31
14/Apr/1918 2:00 2:31
31/Oct/1918 2:00 3:31
Begin Standard 52w30
30/Mar/1935 0:00 3:30
11/May/1942 0:00 2:30
30/Sep/1945 2:00 3:30
12/May/1946 2:00 2:30
6/Oct/1946 2:00 3:30
11/May/1947 2:00 2:30
5/Oct/1947 2:00 3:30
9/May/1948 2:00 2:30
3/Oct/1948 2:00 3:30
8/May/1949 2:00 2:30
2/Oct/1949 2:00 3:30
14/May/1950 2:00 2:30
8/Oct/1950 2:00 3:30
29/Apr/1951 2:00 2:30
30/Sep/1951 2:00 3:30
27/Apr/1952 2:00 2:30
29/Sep/1952 2:00 3:30
26/Apr/1953 2:00 2:30
28/Sep/1953 2:00 3:30
25/Apr/1954 2:00 2:30
26/Sep/1954 2:00 3:30
24/Apr/1955 2:00 2:30
25/Sep/1955 2:00 3:30
29/Apr/1956 2:00 2:30
30/Sep/1956 2:00 3:30
28/Apr/1957 2:00 2:30
29/Sep/1957 2:00 3:30
27/Apr/1958 2:00 2:30
28/Sep/1958 2:00 3:30
26/Apr/1959 2:00 2:30
27/Sep/1959 2:00 3:30
24/Apr/1960 2:00 2:30
29/Oct/1960 2:00 3:30
30/Apr/1961 2:00 2:30
28/Oct/1961 2:00 3:30
29/Apr/1962 2:00 2:30
28/Oct/1962 2:00 3:30
28/Apr/1963 2:00 2:30
27/Oct/1963 2:00 3:30
26/Apr/1964 2:00 2:30
25/Oct/1964 2:00 3:30
25/Apr/1965 2:00 2:30
31/Oct/1965 2:00 3:30
24/Apr/1966 2:00 2:30
30/Oct/1966 2:00 3:30
30/Apr/1967 2:00 2:30
29/Oct/1967 2:00 3:30
28/Apr/1968 2:00 2:30
27/Oct/1968 2:00 3:30
27/Apr/1969 2:00 2:30
26/Oct/1969 2:00 3:30
26/Apr/1970 2:00 2:30
25/Oct/1970 2:00 3:30
25/Apr/1971 2:00 2:30
31/Oct/1971 2:00 3:30
30/Apr/1972 2:00 2:30
29/Oct/1972 2:00 3:30
29/Apr/1973 2:00 2:30
28/Oct/1973 2:00 3:30
28/Apr/1974 2:00 2:30
27/Oct/1974 2:00 3:30
27/Apr/1975 2:00 2:30
26/Oct/1975 2:00 3:30
25/Apr/1976 2:00 2:30
31/Oct/1976 2:00 3:30
24/Apr/1977 2:00 2:30
30/Oct/1977 2:00 3:30
30/Apr/1978 2:00 2:30
29/Oct/1978 2:00 3:30
29/Apr/1979 2:00 2:30
28/Oct/1979 2:00 3:30
27/Apr/1980 2:00 2:30
26/Oct/1980 2:00 3:30
26/Apr/1981 2:00 2:30
25/Oct/1981 2:00 3:30
25/Apr/1982 2:00 2:30
31/Oct/1982 2:00 3:30
24/Apr/1983 2:00 2:30
30/Oct/1983 2:00 3:30
29/Apr/1984 2:00 2:30
28/Oct/1984 2:00 3:30
28/Apr/1985 2:00 2:30
27/Oct/1985 2:00 3:30
27/Apr/1986 2:00 2:30
26/Oct/1986 2:00 3:30
5/Apr/1987 2:00 2:30
25/Oct/1987 2:00 3:30
3/Apr/1988 2:00 1:30
30/Oct/1988 2:00 3:30
2/Apr/1989 2:00 2:30
29/Oct/1989 2:00 3:30
1/Apr/1990 2:00 2:30
28/Oct/1990 2:00 3:30
7/Apr/1991 2:00 2:30
27/Oct/1991 2:00 3:30
5/Apr/1992 2:00 2:30
25/Oct/1992 2:00 3:30
4/Apr/1993 2:00 2:30
31/Oct/1993 2:00 3:30
3/Apr/1994 2:00 2:30
30/Oct/1994 2:00 3:30
2/Apr/1995 2:00 2:30
29/Oct/1995 2:00 3:30
7/Apr/1996 2:00 2:30
27/Oct/1996 2:00 3:30
6/Apr/1997 2:00 2:30
26/Oct/1997 2:00 3:30
5/Apr/1998 2:00 2:30
25/Oct/1998 2:00 3:30
4/Apr/1999 2:00 2:30
31/Oct/1999 2:00 3:30
2/Apr/2000 2:00 2:30
29/Oct/2000 2:00 3:30
....

Time Table # 287
Before 1/Jan/1884 LMT
Begin Standard 60w00
1/Jan/1884 0:00 4:00
14/Apr/1918 2:00 3:00
31/Oct/1918 2:00 4:00
9/Feb/1942 2:00 3:00
Begin Standard 75w00
28/Sep/1942 2:00 4:00
30/Sep/1945 2:00 5:00
27/Apr/1952 2:00 4:00
28/Sep/1952 2:00 5:00
Begin Standard 60w00
6/Oct/1952 2:00 4:00
30/Apr/1967 2:00 3:00
29/Oct/1967 2:00 4:00
28/Apr/1968 2:00 3:00
27/Oct/1968 2:00 4:00
27/Apr/1969 2:00 3:00
Begin Standard 75w00
23/Oct/1969 2:00 4:00
26/Oct/1969 2:00 TT#7
....

Time Table # 288
Before 1/Jan/1884 LMT
Begin Standard 60w00
1/Jan/1884 0:00 4:00
14/Apr/1918 2:00 3:00
31/Oct/1918 2:00 4:00
9/Feb/1942 2:00 3:00
Begin Standard 75w00
28/Sep/1942 2:00 4:00
30/Sep/1945 2:00 5:00
Begin Standard 60w00
6/Oct/1952 2:00 4:00
30/Apr/1967 2:00 3:00
29/Oct/1967 2:00 4:00
28/Apr/1968 2:00 3:00
27/Oct/1968 2:00 4:00
27/Apr/1969 2:00 3:00
Begin Standard 75w00
23/Oct/1969 2:00 4:00
26/Oct/1969 2:00 TT#7
....

Time Table # 289
Before 1/Jan/1884 LMT
Begin Standard 60w00
1/Jan/1884 0:00 4:00
14/Apr/1918 2:00 3:00
31/Oct/1918 2:00 4:00
9/Feb/1942 2:00 3:00
Begin Standard 75w00
28/Sep/1942 2:00 4:00
30/Sep/1945 2:00 5:00
Begin Standard 60w00
6/Oct/1952 2:00 4:00
26/Apr/1953 2:00 3:00
27/Sep/1953 2:00 4:00
30/Apr/1967 2:00 3:00
29/Oct/1967 2:00 4:00
28/Apr/1968 2:00 3:00
27/Oct/1968 2:00 4:00
27/Apr/1969 2:00 3:00
Begin Standard 75w00
23/Oct/1969 2:00 4:00
26/Oct/1969 2:00 TT#7
....

Time Table # 290
Before 1/Jan/1884 LMT
Begin Standard 60w00
1/Jan/1884 0:00 4:00
14/Apr/1918 2:00 3:00
31/Oct/1918 2:00 4:00
26/Apr/1936 0:00 3:00
27/Oct/1936 0:00 4:00
25/Apr/1937 0:00 3:00
26/Sep/1937 0:00 4:00
24/Apr/1938 0:00 3:00
25/Sep/1938 0:00 4:00
30/Apr/1939 0:00 3:00
24/Sep/1939 0:00 4:00
28/Apr/1940 0:00 3:00
Begin Standard 75w00
28/Sep/1942 2:00 4:00
30/Sep/1945 2:00 5:00
Begin Standard 60w00
6/Oct/1952 2:00 4:00
30/Apr/1967 2:00 3:00
29/Oct/1967 2:00 4:00
28/Apr/1968 2:00 3:00
27/Oct/1968 2:00 4:00
27/Apr/1969 2:00 3:00
Begin Standard 75w00
23/Oct/1969 2:00 4:00
26/Oct/1969 2:00 TT#7
....

Time Table # 291
Before 1/Jan/1884 LMT
Begin Standard 60w00
1/Jan/1884 0:00 4:00
14/Apr/1918 2:00 3:00
31/Oct/1918 2:00 4:00
9/Feb/1942 2:00 3:00
Begin Standard 75w00
28/Sep/1942 2:00 4:00
30/Sep/1945 2:00 5:00
24/Apr/1949 2:00 4:00
25/Sep/1949 2:00 5:00
Begin Standard 60w00
6/Oct/1952 2:00 4:00
30/Apr/1967 2:00 3:00
29/Oct/1967 2:00 4:00
28/Apr/1968 2:00 3:00
27/Oct/1968 2:00 4:00
27/Apr/1969 2:00 3:00
Begin Standard 75w00
23/Oct/1969 2:00 4:00
26/Oct/1969 2:00 TT#7
....

Time Table # 292
Before 1/Jan/1884 LMT
Begin Standard 75w00
1/Jan/1884 0:00 5:00
14/Apr/1918 2:00 4:00
31/Oct/1918 2:00 5:00
25/Apr/1937 0:00 4:00
26/Sep/1937 0:00 5:00
24/Apr/1938 0:00 4:00
25/Sep/1938 0:00 5:00
28/Apr/1940 0:00 4:00
30/Sep/1945 2:00 5:00
27/Apr/1947 2:00 4:00
28/Sep/1947 2:00 5:00
26/Apr/1953 2:00 4:00
27/Sep/1953 2:00 5:00
Begin Standard 60w00
1/Nov/1953 2:00 4:00
Begin Standard 75w00
29/Oct/1961 2:00 5:00
29/Apr/1962 2:00 4:00
28/Oct/1962 2:00 5:00
26/Apr/1964 2:00 TT#8
....

Time Table # 293
Before 1/Jan/1884 LMT
Begin Standard 75w00
1/Jan/1884 0:00 5:00
14/Apr/1918 2:00 4:00
31/Oct/1918 2:00 5:00
2/May/1937 0:00 4:00
26/Sep/1937 0:00 5:00
24/Apr/1938 0:00 4:00
25/Sep/1938 0:00 5:00
30/Apr/1939 0:00 4:00
1/Oct/1939 0:00 5:00
28/Apr/1940 0:00 4:00
30/Sep/1945 2:00 5:00
28/Apr/1946 2:00 4:00
29/Sep/1946 2:00 5:00
23/Mar/1947 0:00 4:00
28/Sep/1947 0:00 5:00
25/Apr/1948 2:00 4:00
26/Sep/1948 2:00 5:00
24/Apr/1949 2:00 4:00
25/Sep/1949 2:00 5:00
1/Jan/1950 0:00 4:00
31/Dec/1951 24:00 5:00
26/Apr/1953 2:00 4:00
27/Sep/1953 2:00 5:00
Begin Standard 60w00
1/Nov/1953 2:00 4:00
Begin Standard 75w00
29/Oct/1961 2:00 5:00
29/Apr/1962 2:00 TT#8
....

Time Table # 294
Before 1/Jan/1884 LMT
Begin Standard 75w00
1/Jan/1884 0:00 5:00
14/Apr/1918 2:00 4:00
31/Oct/1918 2:00 5:00
25/Apr/1937 0:00 4:00
26/Sep/1937 0:00 5:00
24/Apr/1938 0:00 4:00
25/Sep/1938 0:00 5:00
30/Apr/1939 0:00 4:00
24/Sep/1939 0:00 5:00
28/Apr/1940 0:00 4:00
30/Sep/1945 2:00 5:00
28/Apr/1946 2:00 4:00
29/Sep/1946 2:00 5:00
27/Apr/1947 2:00 4:00
28/Sep/1947 2:00 5:00
25/Apr/1948 2:00 4:00
26/Sep/1948 2:00 5:00
24/Apr/1949 2:00 4:00
25/Sep/1949 2:00 5:00
2/Apr/1950 2:00 4:00
29/Oct/1950 2:00 5:00
29/Apr/1951 2:00 4:00
30/Sep/1951 2:00 5:00
27/Apr/1952 2:00 4:00
28/Sep/1952 2:00 5:00
26/Apr/1953 2:00 4:00
27/Sep/1953 2:00 5:00
Begin Standard 60w00
1/Nov/1953 2:00 4:00
Begin Standard 75w00
29/Oct/1961 2:00 5:00
29/Apr/1962 2:00 TT#8
....

Time Table # 295
Before 1/Jan/1884 LMT
Begin Standard 75w00
1/Jan/1884 0:00 5:00
14/Apr/1918 2:00 4:00
31/Oct/1918 2:00 5:00
9/Feb/1942 2:00 4:00
30/Sep/1945 2:00 5:00
Begin Standard 60w00
1/Nov/1953 2:00 4:00
Begin Standard 75w00
29/Oct/1961 2:00 5:00
30/Apr/1967 2:00 TT#7
....

Time Table # 296
Before 1/Jan/1884 LMT
Begin Standard 75w00
1/Jan/1884 0:00 5:00
14/Apr/1918 2:00 4:00
31/Oct/1918 2:00 5:00
9/Feb/1942 2:00 4:00
30/Sep/1945 2:00 5:00
Begin Standard 60w00
1/Nov/1953 2:00 4:00
Begin Standard 75w00
29/Oct/1961 2:00 5:00
Begin Standard 60w00
1/Nov/1962 2:00 4:00
30/Apr/1967 2:00 3:00
29/Oct/1967 2:00 4:00
28/Apr/1968 2:00 3:00
27/Oct/1968 2:00 4:00
27/Apr/1969 2:00 3:00
Begin Standard 75w00
23/Oct/1969 2:00 4:00
26/Oct/1969 2:00 TT#7
....

Time Table # 297
Before 1/Jan/1884 LMT
Begin Standard 60w00
1/Jan/1884 0:00 4:00
14/Apr/1918 2:00 3:00
31/Oct/1918 2:00 4:00
9/Feb/1942 2:00 3:00
30/Sep/1945 2:00 4:00
30/Apr/1967 2:00 3:00
29/Oct/1967 2:00 4:00
28/Apr/1968 2:00 3:00
27/Oct/1968 2:00 4:00
27/Apr/1969 2:00 3:00
Begin Standard 75w00
23/Oct/1969 2:00 4:00
26/Oct/1969 2:00 TT#7
....

Time Table # 298
Before 1/Jan/1884 LMT
Begin Standard 120w00
1/Jan/1884 0:00 8:00
14/Apr/1918 2:00 7:00
27/Oct/1918 2:00 8:00
25/May/1919 2:00 7:00
1/Nov/1919 0:00 8:00
9/Feb/1942 2:00 7:00
30/Sep/1945 2:00 8:00
25/Apr/1965 0:00 6:00
31/Oct/1965 2:00 8:00
Begin Standard 105w00
29/Apr/1979 2:00 7:00
27/Apr/1980 2:00 6:00
26/Oct/1980 2:00 7:00
26/Apr/1981 2:00 6:00
25/Oct/1981 2:00 7:00
25/Apr/1982 2:00 6:00
31/Oct/1982 2:00 7:00
24/Apr/1983 2:00 6:00
30/Oct/1983 2:00 7:00
29/Apr/1984 2:00 6:00
28/Oct/1984 2:00 7:00
28/Apr/1985 2:00 6:00
27/Oct/1985 2:00 7:00
27/Apr/1986 2:00 6:00
26/Oct/1986 2:00 7:00
5/Apr/1987 2:00 6:00
25/Oct/1987 2:00 7:00
3/Apr/1988 2:00 6:00
30/Oct/1988 2:00 7:00
2/Apr/1989 2:00 6:00
29/Oct/1989 2:00 7:00
1/Apr/1990 2:00 6:00
28/Oct/1990 2:00 7:00
7/Apr/1991 2:00 6:00
27/Oct/1991 2:00 7:00
5/Apr/1992 2:00 6:00
25/Oct/1992 2:00 7:00
4/Apr/1993 2:00 6:00
31/Oct/1993 2:00 7:00
3/Apr/1994 2:00 6:00
30/Oct/1994 2:00 7:00
2/Apr/1995 2:00 6:00
29/Oct/1995 2:00 7:00
7/Apr/1996 2:00 6:00
27/Oct/1996 2:00 7:00
6/Apr/1997 2:00 6:00
26/Oct/1997 2:00 7:00
5/Apr/1998 2:00 6:00
25/Oct/1998 2:00 7:00
4/Apr/1999 2:00 6:00
31/Oct/1999 2:00 7:00
2/Apr/2000 2:00 6:00
29/Oct/2000 2:00 7:00
....

Time Table # 299
Before 1/Jan/1884 LMT
Begin Standard 120w00
1/Jan/1884 0:00 8:00
14/Apr/1918 2:00 7:00
31/Oct/1918 2:00 8:00
9/Feb/1942 2:00 7:00
30/Sep/1945 2:00 8:00
27/Apr/1947 2:00 7:00
28/Sep/1947 2:00 8:00
25/Apr/1948 2:00 7:00
26/Sep/1948 2:00 8:00
24/Apr/1949 2:00 7:00
25/Sep/1949 2:00 8:00
30/Apr/1950 2:00 7:00
24/Sep/1950 2:00 8:00
29/Apr/1951 2:00 7:00
30/Sep/1951 2:00 8:00
27/Apr/1952 2:00 7:00
28/Sep/1952 2:00 8:00
26/Apr/1953 2:00 7:00
27/Sep/1953 2:00 8:00
25/Apr/1954 2:00 7:00
26/Sep/1954 2:00 8:00
24/Apr/1955 2:00 7:00
25/Sep/1955 2:00 8:00
29/Apr/1956 2:00 7:00
30/Sep/1956 2:00 8:00
28/Apr/1957 2:00 7:00
29/Sep/1957 2:00 8:00
27/Apr/1958 2:00 7:00
28/Sep/1958 2:00 8:00
26/Apr/1959 2:00 7:00
27/Sep/1959 2:00 8:00
24/Apr/1960 2:00 7:00
25/Sep/1960 2:00 8:00
30/Apr/1961 2:00 7:00
24/Sep/1961 2:00 8:00
29/Apr/1962 2:00 7:00
28/Oct/1962 2:00 8:00
28/Apr/1963 2:00 7:00
27/Oct/1963 2:00 8:00
26/Apr/1964 2:00 7:00
25/Oct/1964 2:00 8:00
25/Apr/1965 2:00 7:00
31/Oct/1965 2:00 8:00
24/Apr/1966 2:00 7:00
30/Oct/1966 2:00 8:00
30/Apr/1967 2:00 7:00
29/Oct/1967 2:00 8:00
28/Apr/1968 2:00 7:00

27/Oct/1968 2:00 8:00
27/Apr/1969 2:00 7:00
26/Oct/1969 2:00 8:00
26/Apr/1970 2:00 7:00
25/Oct/1970 2:00 8:00
25/Apr/1971 2:00 7:00
31/Oct/1971 2:00 8:00
30/Apr/1972 2:00 7:00
Begin Standard 105w00
30/Aug/1972 2:00 7:00
....

Time Table # 300
Before 20/Aug/1900 LMT
Begin Standard 135w00
20/Aug/1900 0:00 9:00
14/Apr/1918 2:00 8:00
27/Oct/1918 2:00 9:00
25/May/1919 2:00 8:00
1/Nov/1919 0:00 9:00
9/Feb/1942 2:00 8:00
30/Sep/1945 2:00 9:00
25/Apr/1965 0:00 7:00
31/Oct/1965 2:00 9:00
Begin Standard 120w00
1/Jul/1967 2:00 8:00
27/Apr/1980 2:00 7:00
26/Oct/1980 2:00 8:00
26/Apr/1981 2:00 7:00
25/Oct/1981 2:00 8:00
25/Apr/1982 2:00 7:00
31/Oct/1982 2:00 8:00
24/Apr/1983 2:00 7:00
30/Oct/1983 2:00 8:00
29/Apr/1984 2:00 7:00
28/Oct/1984 2:00 8:00
28/Apr/1985 2:00 7:00
27/Oct/1985 2:00 8:00
27/Apr/1986 2:00 7:00
26/Oct/1986 2:00 8:00
5/Apr/1987 2:00 7:00
25/Oct/1987 2:00 8:00
3/Apr/1988 2:00 7:00
30/Oct/1988 2:00 8:00
2/Apr/1989 2:00 7:00
29/Oct/1989 2:00 8:00
1/Apr/1990 2:00 7:00
28/Oct/1990 2:00 8:00
7/Apr/1991 2:00 7:00
27/Oct/1991 2:00 8:00
5/Apr/1992 2:00 7:00
25/Oct/1992 2:00 8:00
4/Apr/1993 2:00 7:00
31/Oct/1993 2:00 8:00
3/Apr/1994 2:00 7:00
30/Oct/1994 2:00 8:00
2/Apr/1995 2:00 7:00
29/Oct/1995 2:00 8:00
7/Apr/1996 2:00 7:00
27/Oct/1996 2:00 8:00
6/Apr/1997 2:00 7:00
26/Oct/1997 2:00 8:00
5/Apr/1998 2:00 7:00
25/Oct/1998 2:00 8:00
4/Apr/1999 2:00 7:00
31/Oct/1999 2:00 8:00
2/Apr/2000 2:00 7:00
29/Oct/2000 2:00 8:00
....

Time Table # 301
Before 20/Aug/1900 LMT
Begin Standard 135w00
20/Aug/1900 0:00 9:00
14/Apr/1918 2:00 8:00
27/Oct/1918 2:00 9:00
25/May/1919 2:00 8:00
1/Nov/1919 0:00 9:00
9/Feb/1942 2:00 8:00
30/Sep/1945 2:00 9:00
25/Apr/1965 0:00 7:00
31/Oct/1965 2:00 9:00
Begin Standard 120w00
28/Oct/1973 2:00 8:00
27/Apr/1980 2:00 7:00
26/Oct/1980 2:00 8:00
26/Apr/1981 2:00 7:00
25/Oct/1981 2:00 8:00
25/Apr/1982 2:00 7:00
31/Oct/1982 2:00 8:00
24/Apr/1983 2:00 7:00
30/Oct/1983 2:00 8:00
29/Apr/1984 2:00 7:00
28/Oct/1984 2:00 8:00
28/Apr/1985 2:00 7:00
27/Oct/1985 2:00 8:00
27/Apr/1986 2:00 7:00
26/Oct/1986 2:00 8:00
5/Apr/1987 2:00 7:00
25/Oct/1987 2:00 8:00
3/Apr/1988 2:00 7:00
30/Oct/1988 2:00 8:00
2/Apr/1989 2:00 7:00
29/Oct/1989 2:00 8:00
1/Apr/1990 2:00 7:00
28/Oct/1990 2:00 8:00
7/Apr/1991 2:00 7:00
27/Oct/1991 2:00 8:00
5/Apr/1992 2:00 7:00
25/Oct/1992 2:00 8:00
4/Apr/1993 2:00 7:00
31/Oct/1993 2:00 8:00
3/Apr/1994 2:00 7:00
30/Oct/1994 2:00 8:00
2/Apr/1995 2:00 7:00
29/Oct/1995 2:00 8:00
7/Apr/1996 2:00 7:00
27/Oct/1996 2:00 8:00
6/Apr/1997 2:00 7:00
26/Oct/1997 2:00 8:00
5/Apr/1998 2:00 7:00
25/Oct/1998 2:00 8:00
4/Apr/1999 2:00 7:00
31/Oct/1999 2:00 8:00
2/Apr/2000 2:00 7:00
29/Oct/2000 2:00 8:00

DIVISIONS

1. Alberta
2. British Columbia
3. Manitoba
4. New Brunswick
5. Newfoundland (Island)
6. Newfoundland, Labrador
7. Northwest Territories
8. Nova Scotia
9. Ontario
10. Prince Edward Island
11. Quebec
12. Saskatchewan
13. Yukon

Abbey 12 228 50N43 108w45 7:15:00
Abbotsford 2 266 49N03 122w17 8:09:08
Abercorn 11 7 45N02 72w40 4:50:40
Aberdeen 12 264 52N19 106w17 7:05:08
Abernethy 12 233 50N45 103w25 6:53:40
Acadia Valley 1 223 51N08 110w13 7:20:52
Acme 1 223 51N30 113w30 7:34:00
Acton 9 34 43N37 80w02 5:20:08
Acton Vale 11 7 45N39 72w34 4:50:16
Adamsville 11 144 45N17 72w47 4:51:08
Admiral 12 228 49N43 108w01 7:12:04
Advocate Harbour 8 11 45N20 64w47 4:19:08
Aetna 1 223 49N08 113w15 7:33:00
Agassiz 2 266 49N14 121w46 8:07:04
Aguanish 11 30 50N13 62w05 4:08:20
Ailsa Craig 9 36 43N08 81w33 5:26:12
Airdrie 1 224 51N18 114w02 7:36:08
Aishihik 13 300 61N35 137w30 9:10:00
Aiyansh 2 266 55N17 129w03 8:36:12
Ajax 9 40 43N51 79w02 5:16:08
Aklavik 7 298 68N12 135w00 9:00:00
Albert Canyon 2 266 51N08 117w52 7:51:28
Albert Harbour 7 33 72N47 77w40 5:10:40
Alberton 10 6 46N49 64w04 4:16:16
Albion 2 267 49N11 122w33 8:10:12
Albreda 2 266 52N38 119w09 7:56:36
Aldergrove 2 266 49N04 122w28 8:09:52
Alert Bay 2 266 50N35 126w55 8:27:40
Alexander 3 203 49N50 100w17 6:41:08
Alexandria 2 266 52N38 122w27 8:09:48
Alexandria 9 38 45N19 74w38 4:58:32
Alexis Creek 2 266 52N05 123w17 8:13:08
Alfred 9 1 45N34 74w53 4:59:32
Algoma Mills 9 1 46N10 82w50 5:31:20
Alice Arm 2 266 55N29 129w29 8:37:56
Alix 1 223 52N24 113w11 7:32:44
Alkali Lake 2 266 51N47 122w14 8:08:56
Allan 12 229 51N53 106w04 7:04:16
Alliance 1 223 52N26 111w47 7:27:08
Allison Harbour 2 266 51N03 127w30 8:30:00
Alliston 9 36 44N09 79w52 5:19:28
Alma 10 6 45N52 64w06 4:16:24
Alma 11 169 48N33 71w39 4:46:36
Almonte 9 1 45N14 76w12 5:04:48
Alsask 12 228 51N23 109w59 7:19:56
Altario 1 223 51N55 110w09 7:20:36
Alton 9 1 43N52 80w04 5:20:16
Altona 3 203 49N06 97w33 6:30:12
Alvinston 9 1 42N49 81w52 5:27:28
Amaranth 3 203 50N36 98w43 6:34:52
Amery 3 203 56N34 94w03 6:16:12
Amherst 8 13 45N49 64w14 4:16:56
Amherstburg 9 1 42N06 83w06 5:32:24
Amherstview 9 76 44N13 76w38 5:06:32
Amisk 1 223 52N33 111w04 7:24:16
Amos 11 136 48N35 78w07 5:12:28
Amqui 11 288 48N28 67w26 4:29:44
Anahim Lake 2 266 52N28 125w18 8:21:12
Anama Bay 3 203 51N56 98w05 6:32:20
Ancaster 9 74 43N12 80w00 5:20:00
Ancienne Lorette 11 164 46N48 71w21 4:45:24
Andrew 1 223 53N53 112w21 7:29:24
Aneroid 12 228 49N43 107w20 7:09:20
Angus 9 34 44N19 79w53 5:19:32
Angusville 3 203 50N44 101w01 6:44:04
Anjou 11 151 45N36 73w33 4:54:12
Annapolis Royal 8 11 44N45 65w31 4:22:04
Antigonish 8 14 45N35 61w55 4:07:40
Anzac 1 223 56N27 111w02 7:24:08
Apenes 2 266 49N16 124w41 8:18:44
Apple Hill 9 1 45N13 74w46 4:59:04
Apsley 9 1 44N45 78w06 5:12:24
Arborfield 12 249 53N06 103w39 6:54:36
Arborg 3 203 50N55 97w15 6:29:00
Arcola 12 203 49N37 102w30 6:50:00
Arctic Bay 7 33 73N02 85w11 5:40:44
Arctic Red River 7 298 67N27 133w46 8:55:04
Arden 3 203 50N17 99w14 6:36:56
Ardill 12 231 49N53 105w49 7:03:16
Argentia 5 286 47N18 53w59 3:35:56
Arichat 8 11 45N31 61w01 4:04:04
Armadale 9 1 43N50 79w15 5:17:00
Armstrong 2 266 50N27 119w12 7:56:48
Armstrong Station 9 1 50N18 89w02 5:56:08
Arnold 2 266 49N08 122w03 8:08:12
Arnprior 9 39 45N26 76w21 5:05:24
Arrowwood 1 223 50N44 113w09 7:32:36
Arthabaska 11 178 46N02 71w55 4:47:40
Arthur 9 1 43N50 80w32 5:22:08
Arundel 11 7 45N58 74w37 4:58:28
Arvida 11 189 48N25 71w11 4:44:44
Asbestos 11 137 45N46 71w57 4:47:48
Ashcroft 2 266 50N43 121w17 8:05:08
Ashern 3 203 51N11 98w21 6:33:24
Asquith 12 228 52N08 107w13 7:08:52
Assiniboia 12 234 49N38 105w59 7:03:56
Athabasca 1 223 54N43 113w17 7:33:08
Athalmer 2 223 50N32 116w02 7:44:08
Athens 9 37 44N38 75w57 5:03:48
Atherley 9 187 44N36 79w22 5:17:28
Atikokan 9 3 48N45 91w37 6:06:28
Atlin 2 266 59N35 133w42 8:54:48
Attawapiskat 9 1 52N55 82w26 5:29:44
Atwater 12 232 50N47 102w10 6:48:40
Atwood 9 36 43N40 81w01 5:24:04
Aurora 9 180 44N00 79w28 5:17:52
Austin 3 203 49N57 98w56 6:35:44
Avola 2 266 51N47 119w19 7:57:16
Avonlea 12 238 50N00 105w04 7:00:16
Avonmore 9 1 45N10 74w58 4:59:52
Ayers Cliff 11 192 45N10 72w03 4:48:12
Aylmer East 11 153 45N24 75w51 5:03:24
Aylmer West 9 41 42N46 80w59 5:23:56
Aylsham 12 249 53N11 103w49 6:55:16
Ayr 9 40 43N17 80w27 5:21:48
Ayton 9 42 44N03 80w56 5:23:44
Babine 2 266 55N19 126w37 8:26:28
Baddeck 8 11 46N07 60w45 4:03:00
Baden 9 36 43N24 80w39 5:22:36
Badger 5 286 48N59 56w02 3:44:08
Bagotville 11 7 48N21 70w53 4:43:32
Baie Comeau 11 295 49N13 68w10 4:32:40
Baie des Ha! Ha! 11 30 50N56 58w56 3:55:44
Baie de Shawinigan 11 171 46N34 72w45 4:51:00
Baie du Renard 11 30 49N17 61w50 4:07:20
Baie d'Urfé 11 138 45N25 73w55 4:55:40
Baie Johan Beetz 11 30 50N17 62w48 4:11:12
Baie Saint Claire 11 297 49N54 64w30 4:18:00
Baie Saint Paul 11 7 47N27 70w30 4:42:00
Baie Trinité 11 297 49N25 67w18 4:29:12
Baie Verte 5 286 49N56 56w11 3:44:44
Baieville 11 7 46N08 72w43 4:50:52
Baker Lake 7 219 64N15 96w00 6:24:00
Bala 9 1 45N01 79w37 5:18:28
Balcarres 12 235 50N48 103w33 6:54:12
Baldur 3 203 49N23 99w15 6:37:00
Balmertown 9 3 51N04 93w44 6:14:56
Balzac 1 224 51N10 114w01 7:36:04
Bamberton 2 265 48N35 123w31 8:14:04
Bamfield 2 266 48N50 125w08 8:20:32
Bancroft 9 43 45N03 77w51 5:11:24
Banff 1 223 51N10 115w34 7:42:16
Barkerville 2 266 53N04 121w31 8:06:04
Barnwell 1 223 49N46 112w15 7:29:00
Barons 1 223 50N00 113w05 7:32:20
Barrhead 1 223 54N08 114w24 7:37:36
Barrie 9 44 44N24 79w40 5:18:40
Barriefield 9 76 44N14 76w28 5:05:52
Barrington 8 11 43N34 65w34 4:22:16
Barrows 3 203 52N49 101w27 6:45:48
Barrys Bay 9 36 45N29 77w41 5:10:44
Bartletts Harbour 5 286 50N57 57w00 3:48:00
Bashaw 1 223 52N35 112w58 7:31:52
Bassano 1 223 50N47 112w28 7:29:52
Bass River 8 11 45N25 63w47 4:15:08
Batawa 9 1 44N10 77w36 5:10:24
Bath 9 40 44N11 76w47 5:07:08
Bathurst 4 272 47N36 65w39 4:22:36
Bathurst Inlet 7 227 66N50 108w01 7:12:04
Battle Harbour 6 269 52N16 55w35 3:42:20
Bay Bulls 5 286 47N19 52w49 3:31:16
Bay de Verde 5 286 48N05 52w54 3:31:36
Bay L'Argent 5 286 47N33 54w54 3:39:36
Bay Roberts 5 286 47N36 53w16 3:33:04
Bayside 9 40 44N07 77w30 5:10:00
Beachville 9 36 43N05 80w49 5:23:16
Beaconsfield 11 138 45N26 73w50 4:55:20
Beardmore 9 1 49N36 87w57 5:51:48
Bear Lake 2 266 56N11 126w51 8:27:24
Bear River 8 11 44N34 65w39 4:22:36
Beaton 2 266 50N44 117w44 7:50:56
Beauceville Est 11 193 46N12 70w46 4:43:04
Beauharnois 11 138 45N19 73w52 4:55:28
Beaumont 5 286 49N34 55w36 3:42:24
Beauport 11 164 46N52 71w11 4:44:44
Beaupré 11 7 47N03 70w54 4:43:36
Beaurivage 11 7 46N25 71w14 4:44:56
Beauséjour 3 204 50N04 96w33 6:26:12
Beaver Creek 13 301 62N22 140w52 9:23:28
Beaverdell 2 266 49N26 119w05 7:56:20
Beaverlodge 1 223 55N13 119w26 7:57:44
Beaverton 9 36 44N26 79w09 5:16:36
Bécancour 11 7 46N20 72w26 4:49:44
Bedford 11 7 45N07 72w59 4:51:56
Beebe 11 195 45N01 72w09 4:48:36
Beechy 12 228 50N51 107w25 7:09:40
Beeton 9 36 44N05 79w47 5:19:08
Beiseker 1 223 51N23 113w32 7:34:08
Bella Bella 2 266 52N09 128w07 8:32:28
Bella Coola 2 266 52N22 126w46 8:27:04
Belle Island 5 286 51N55 55w20 3:41:20

Belle Isle 5 286 51N55 55w20 3:41:20
Belle Plaine 12 238 50N24 105w09 7:00:36
Belle River 9 1 42N18 82w43 5:30:52
Belleville 9 181 44N10 77w23 5:09:32
Bellevue 1 223 49N35 114w22 7:37:28
Bell Ewart 9 1 44N16 79w33 5:18:12
Bellin 11 7 60N01 70w01 4:40:04
Bells Corners 9 95 45N19 75w50 5:03:20
Belmont 3 203 49N24 99w27 6:37:48
Belmont 9 1 42N53 81w05 5:24:20
Beloeil 11 7 45N34 73w12 4:52:48
Bengough 12 231 49N24 105w08 7:00:32
Benito 3 203 51N55 101w31 6:46:04
Bentley 1 223 52N28 114w04 7:36:16
Berens River 3 203 52N22 97w02 6:28:08
Beresford 4 271 47N42 65w42 4:22:48
Bernierville 11 7 46N06 71w34 4:46:16
Berthierville 11 7 46N05 73w10 4:52:40
Berwick 8 11 45N03 64w44 4:18:56
Bethune 12 231 50N43 105w08 7:00:32
Betsiamites 11 295 48N56 68w38 4:34:32
Bewdley 9 1 44N05 78w19 5:13:16
Bic 11 295 48N22 68w42 4:34:48
Bienfait 12 203 49N08 102w47 6:51:08
Big Bar Creek 2 266 51N12 122w06 8:08:24
Big Beaver 12 231 49N08 105w10 7:00:40
Big Creek 2 266 51N44 123w03 8:12:12
Biggar 12 228 52N04 108w00 7:12:00
Big River 12 228 53N50 107w01 7:08:04
Big Valley 1 223 52N02 112w46 7:31:04
Bindloss 1 223 50N52 110w16 7:21:04
Binscarth 3 203 50N37 101w16 6:45:04
Birch Hills 12 230 52N59 105w25 7:01:40
Birch Island 2 266 51N36 119w55 7:59:40
Birch River 3 203 52N23 101w06 6:44:24
Birchy Bay 5 286 49N21 54w44 3:38:56
Birken 2 266 50N29 122w36 8:10:24
Birtle 3 203 50N25 101w03 6:44:12
Bishop's Falls 5 286 49N01 55w30 3:42:00
Bishopton 11 194 45N35 71w35 4:46:20
Bissett 3 203 51N02 95w40 6:22:40
Black Creek 2 266 49N50 125w08 8:20:32
Black Creek 9 2 43N00 79w01 5:16:04
Black Diamond 1 224 50N42 114w14 7:36:56
Blackfalds 1 223 52N23 113w47 7:35:08
Black Hawk 9 3 48N48 93w59 6:15:56
Black Hills 13 301 63N29 138w52 9:15:28
Black Lake 11 196 46N03 71w21 4:45:24
Blacks Harbour 4 271 45N03 66w47 4:27:08
Bladworth 12 229 51N18 106w09 7:04:36
Blaine Lake 12 229 52N50 106w54 7:07:36
Blaineys 2 266 48N53 123w47 8:15:08
Blair 9 60 43N23 80w23 5:21:32
Blairmore 1 223 49N36 114w26 7:37:44
Blanc Sablon 11 30 51N25 57w07 3:48:28
Blenheim 9 1 42N20 82w00 5:28:00
Blind River 9 35 46N10 82w58 5:31:52
Bloedel 2 266 50N07 125w23 8:21:32
Bloomfield 9 36 43N59 77w14 5:08:56
Blue Ridge 1 223 54N08 115w22 7:41:28
Blue River 2 266 52N05 119w17 7:57:08
Bluesky 1 223 56N04 118w14 7:52:56
Blumenhof 12 228 50N01 107w41 7:10:44
Blyth 9 1 43N44 81w26 5:25:44
Blytheswood 9 1 42N07 82w36 5:30:24
Boat Basin 2 266 49N29 126w25 8:25:40
Bobcaygeon 9 1 44N33 78w33 5:14:12
Boiestown 4 271 46N27 66w25 4:25:40
Boischâtel 11 164 46N54 71w08 4:44:32
Bois des Filion 11 151 45N40 73w45 4:55:00
Boissevain 3 205 49N14 100w03 6:40:12
Bolton 9 1 43N53 79w44 5:18:56
Bonanza 13 301 63N55 139w19 9:17:16
Bonaventure 11 288 48N03 65w29 4:21:56
Bonavista 5 286 48N39 53w07 3:32:28
Bonne Bay (Woody Point) 5 286 49N30 57w56 3:51:44
Bonnyville 1 223 54N16 110w44 7:22:56
Bonshaw 10 6 46N12 63w21 4:13:24
Borden 12 228 52N25 107w13 7:08:52
Boston Bar 2 266 49N52 121w26 8:05:44
Bothwell 9 47 42N38 81w52 5:27:28
Botwood 5 286 49N09 55w21 3:41:24
Boucherville 11 151 45N36 73w27 4:53:48
Bourget 9 1 45N26 75w09 5:00:36
Bowden 1 223 51N55 114w02 7:36:08
Bow Island 1 223 49N52 111w22 7:25:28
Bowmanville 9 48 43N55 78w41 5:14:44
Bowsman 3 203 52N14 101w14 6:44:56
Boxey 5 286 47N25 55w34 3:42:16
Box Grove 9 1 43N51 79w14 5:16:56

Boyd's Cove 5 286 49N27 54w39 3:38:36
Boyle 1 223 54N35 112w49 7:31:16
Boyne 9 1 43N29 79w50 5:19:20
Bracebridge 9 49 45N02 79w19 5:17:16
Brackendale 2 266 49N46 123w09 8:12:36
Bradford 9 36 44N07 79w34 5:18:16
Bradner 2 266 49N06 122w25 8:09:40
Bradore Bay 11 30 51N28 57w14 3:48:56
Braeside 9 1 45N28 76w24 5:05:36
Bralorne 2 266 50N47 122w49 8:11:16
Bramalea 9 50 43N44 79w43 5:18:52
Brampton 9 50 43N41 79w46 5:19:04
Branch 5 286 46N53 53w57 3:35:48
Brandon 3 206 49N50 99w57 6:39:48
Brantford 9 51 43N08 80w16 5:21:04
Brantville 4 271 47N22 64w58 4:19:52
Bredenbury 12 232 50N57 102w03 6:48:12
Brem River 2 266 50N26 124w39 8:18:36
Brentwood Bay 2 265 48N35 123w28 8:13:52
Breslau 9 60 43N28 80w25 5:21:40
Breton 1 223 53N07 114w28 7:37:52
Bridge Lake 2 266 51N29 120w43 8:02:52
Bridgenorth 9 40 44N23 78w23 5:13:32
Bridgeport 9 60 43N29 80w29 5:21:56
Bridgetown 8 11 44N51 65w18 4:21:12
Bridgewater 8 15 44N23 64w31 4:18:04
Brig Bay 5 286 51N04 56w55 3:47:40
Brigden 9 1 42N49 82w17 5:29:08
Brighton 9 40 44N02 77w44 5:10:56
Brigus 5 286 47N32 53w13 3:32:52
Brilliant 2 266 49N19 117w38 7:50:32
Britannia 9 50 43N37 79w41 5:18:44
Britannia Beach 2 267 49N38 123w12 8:12:48
Broadview 12 232 50N20 102w30 6:50:00
Brochet 3 203 57N53 101w40 6:46:40
Brock 12 228 51N27 108w42 7:14:48
Brocks Beach 9 1 44N27 80w06 5:20:24
Brockville 9 52 44N35 75w41 5:02:44
Brome 11 179 45N12 72w34 4:50:16
Bromptonville 11 160 45N28 71w57 4:47:48
Brookfield 8 11 45N15 63w17 4:13:08
Brooklin 9 1 43N57 78w57 5:15:48
Brooklyn 8 11 44N03 64w42 4:18:48
Brookmere 2 266 49N49 120w53 8:03:32
Brooks 1 223 50N35 111w53 7:27:32
Brossard 11 151 45N26 73w29 4:53:56
Brougham 9 1 43N55 79w06 5:16:24
Brownsburg 11 157 45N41 74w25 4:57:40
Brownsville 9 1 42N52 80w50 5:23:20
Brownvale 1 223 56N08 117w53 7:51:32
Bruce Mines 9 1 46N18 83w48 5:35:12
Bruderheim 1 223 53N47 112w56 7:31:44
Bruno 12 229 52N15 105w30 7:02:00
Brussels 9 35 43N44 81w15 5:25:00
Bryson 11 7 45N41 76w37 5:06:28
Buchanan 12 232 51N43 102w45 6:51:00
Buchans 5 286 48N49 56w52 3:47:28
Buckingham 11 140 45N35 75w25 5:01:40
Buctouche 4 271 46N28 64w43 4:18:52
Buffalo Narrows 12 228 55N51 108w30 7:14:00
Bull Harbour 2 266 50N54 127w55 8:31:40
Burdett 1 223 49N50 111w32 7:26:08
Burford 9 40 43N06 80w26 5:21:44
Burgeo 5 286 47N37 57w37 3:50:28
Burgessville 9 1 43N01 80w39 5:22:36
Burin 5 286 47N02 55w10 3:40:40
Burleigh Falls 9 1 44N34 78w13 5:12:52
Burlington 5 286 49N45 56w02 3:44:08
Burlington 9 182 43N19 79w47 5:19:08
Burnaby 2 267 49N15 122w57 8:11:48
Burnhamthorpe 9 1 43N37 79w36 5:18:24
Burns Lake 2 266 54N14 125w46 8:23:04
Burnt Island 5 286 47N36 58w53 3:55:32
Burstall 12 228 50N40 109w54 7:19:36
Burton 2 266 49N59 117w54 7:51:36
Burwash 9 35 46N19 80w48 5:23:12
Burwash Landing 13 301 61N21 139w00 9:16:00
Bury 11 7 45N28 71w30 4:46:00
Buttonville 9 1 43N52 79w22 5:17:28
Byng Inlet 9 1 45N46 80w33 5:22:12
Cabano 11 296 47N41 68w53 4:35:32
Cabri 12 228 50N37 108w28 7:13:52
Cache Creek 2 266 50N48 121w19 8:05:16
Cadillac 12 228 49N44 107w43 7:10:52
Cadomin 1 223 53N02 117w20 7:49:20
Calabogie 9 1 45N18 76w43 5:06:52
Calder 12 203 51N10 101w45 6:47:00
Caledon 9 1 43N52 80w00 5:20:00
Caledon East 9 37 43N52 79w52 5:19:28
Caledonia 8 11 44N22 65w02 4:20:08
Caledonia 9 34 43N04 79w56 5:19:44
Calgary 1 224 51N03 114w05 7:36:20
Callander 9 36 46N13 79w23 5:17:32
Calling Lake 1 223 55N15 113w12 7:32:48
Calmar 1 223 53N16 113w49 7:35:16

Cambridge (Galt) 9 66 43N22 80w19 5:21:16
Cambridge Bay 7 227 69N03 105w05 7:00:20
Campbellford 9 54 44N18 77w48 5:11:12
Campbell Island 2 266 52N10 128w09 8:32:36
Campbell River 2 266 50N01 125w15 8:21:00
Campbells Bay 11 7 45N44 76w36 5:06:24
Campbellton 4 273 48N00 66w40 4:26:40
Campbellton 5 286 49N17 54w56 3:39:44
Campbellton 10 6 46N47 64w18 4:17:12
Campbellville 9 1 43N29 79w59 5:19:56
Camperville 3 203 51N59 100w09 6:40:36
Camrose 1 223 53N01 112w50 7:31:20
Canal Flats 2 223 50N09 115w48 7:43:12
Candiac 11 151 45N23 73w31 4:54:04
Cando 12 228 52N23 108w14 7:12:56
Canim Lake 2 266 51N46 120w54 8:03:36
Canmore 1 223 51N05 115w21 7:41:24
Cannifton 9 181 44N12 77w23 5:09:32
Canning 8 11 45N09 64w25 4:17:40
Cannington 9 36 44N21 79w02 5:16:08
Canoe 2 266 50N45 119w13 7:56:52
Canol 7 298 65N14 126w56 8:27:44
Canora 12 232 51N37 102w26 6:49:44
Canso 8 11 45N20 61w00 4:04:00
Canterbury 4 271 45N53 67w29 4:29:56
Canyon 13 300 60N52 137w02 9:08:08
Canyon Creek 1 223 54N22 115w05 7:40:20
Cap Chat 11 288 49N06 66w42 4:26:48
Cap de la Madeleine 11 7 46N22 72w31 4:50:04
Cape Broyle 5 286 47N06 52w57 3:31:48
Cape Chidley 6 269 60W23 64w26 4:17:44
Cape Dorset 7 33 64N14 76w32 5:06:08
Cape Harrison 6 269 54N55 57w55 3:51:40
Cape la Hune 5 286 47N33 56w52 3:47:28
Cape Tormentine 4 271 46N08 63w47 4:15:08
Capilano 2 267 49N23 123w09 8:12:36
Caplan 11 288 48N06 65w41 4:22:44
Cap Pelé 4 271 46N13 64w18 4:17:12
Capreol 9 1 46N43 80w56 5:23:44
Cap Santé 11 191 46N40 71w47 4:47:08
Caraquet 4 271 47N48 64w57 4:19:48
Carberry 3 203 49N52 99w20 6:37:20
Carbon 1 223 51N29 113w09 7:32:36
Carbonear 5 286 47N45 53w13 3:32:52
Carcross 13 270 60N10 134w42 8:58:48
Cardigan 10 6 46N14 62w37 4:10:28
Cardinal 9 1 44N47 75w23 5:01:32
Cardinal Heights 9 95 45N27 75w37 5:02:28
Cardston 1 223 49N12 113w18 7:33:12
Carleton Place 9 1 45N08 76w09 5:04:36
Carlisle 9 1 43N23 79w59 5:19:56
Carlyle 12 203 49N38 102w16 6:49:04
Carmacks 13 300 62N05 136w18 9:05:12
Carman 3 203 49N32 98w00 6:32:00
Carmangay 1 223 50N08 113w07 7:32:28
Carmanville 5 286 49N24 54w17 3:37:08
Carnduff 12 203 49N10 101w50 6:47:20
Caron 12 252 50N28 105w52 7:03:28
Carp 9 55 45N21 76w02 5:04:08
Carrot River 12 249 53N17 103w35 6:54:20
Carseland 1 223 50N51 113w28 7:33:52
Carstairs 1 223 51N34 114w06 7:36:24
Cartwright 3 203 49N06 99w20 6:37:20
Cartwright 6 269 53N42 57w01 3:48:04
Cascade 2 266 49N01 118w13 7:52:52
Casselman 9 1 45N19 75w05 5:00:20
Cassiar 2 266 59N16 129w40 8:38:40
Cassidy 2 266 49N04 123w53 8:15:32
Castlegar 2 266 49N19 117w40 7:50:40
Castlemore 9 50 43N47 79w41 5:18:44
Castor 1 223 52N13 111w53 7:27:32
Casummit Lake 9 3 51N28 92w24 6:09:36
Catalina 5 286 48N31 53w05 3:32:20
Cataraqui 9 76 44N16 76w32 5:06:08
Caughnawaga 11 151 45N25 73w41 4:54:44
Causapscal 11 289 48N22 67w14 4:28:56
Cawston 2 266 49N11 119w45 7:59:00
Caycuse 2 266 48N53 124w22 8:17:28
Cayuga 9 53 42N56 79w51 5:19:24
Cedar Grove 9 1 43N52 79w12 5:16:48
Cedar Springs 9 1 42N17 82w02 5:28:08
Cedarvale 2 266 55N01 128w20 8:33:20
Ceepeecee 2 266 49N52 126w43 8:26:52
Central Butte 12 229 50N47 106w30 7:06:00
Cereal 1 223 51N25 110w48 7:23:12
Ceylon 12 243 49N28 104w36 6:58:24
Chalk River 9 1 46N01 77w27 5:09:48

Chamberlain 12
231 50N50 105w34 7:02:16
Chambly 11 168 45N27 73w17 4:53:08
Champagne 13 300 60N47 136w29 9:05:56
Champion 1 223 50N14 113w09 7:32:36
Chandler 11 288 48N21 64w41 4:18:44
Change Islands 5
286 49N40 54w25 3:37:40
Channel Port Aux Basques 5
286 47N34 59w09 3:56:36
Chapleau 9 1 47N50 83w24 5:33:36
Chaplin 12 229 50N28 106w40 7:06:40
Charing Cross 9
1 42N20 82w06 5:28:24
Charlemagne 11
151 45N43 73w29 4:53:56
Charlesbourg 11
164 46N51 71w16 4:45:04
Charlie Lake 2
299 56N16 120w57 8:03:48
Charlottetown 10
28 46N14 63w08 4:12:32
Charny 11 164 46N43 71w16 4:45:04
Chase 2 266 50N49 119w41 7:58:44
Chase River 2
266 49N08 123w55 8:15:40
Châteauguay 11
151 45N23 73w45 4:55:00
Châteauguay Centre 11
151 45N21 73w45 4:55:00
Châteauguay Heights 11
151 45N23 73w44 4:54:56
Château Richer 11
7 46N58 71w01 4:44:04
Chatham 4 274 47N02 65w28 4:21:52
Chatham 9 56 42N24 82w11 5:28:44
Chatham Head 4
271 47N00 65w33 4:22:12
Chatsworth 9 1 44N27 80w54 5:23:36
Chauvin 1 223 52N42 110w07 7:20:28
Cheam View 2 266 49N15 121w41 8:06:44
Chelmsford 9 1 46N35 81w12 5:24:48
Chemainus 2 266 48N55 123w43 8:14:52
Chénéville 11 7 45N53 75w03 5:00:12
Cherry Creek 2
266 49N17 124w47 8:19:08
Cherrywood 9 1 43N52 79w08 5:16:32
Chesley 9 36 44N17 81w05 5:24:20
Chester Basin 8
11 44N34 64w19 4:17:16
Chesterfield Inlet 7
219 63N21 90w42 6:02:48
Chesterville 9 1 45N06 75w14 5:00:56
Chéticamp 8 11 46N38 61w01 4:04:04
Chetwynd 2 299 55N42 121w40 8:06:40
Chibougamau 11 7 49N55 74w22 4:57:28
Chicoutimi 11
142 48N26 71w04 4:44:16
Chilanko Forks 2
266 52N06 124w10 8:16:40
Chilliwack 2 266 49N10 121w57 8:07:48
Chinook 1 223 51N27 110w56 7:23:44
Chinook Cove 2
266 51N14 120w10 8:00:40
Chipewyan 1 223 58N42 111w08 7:24:32
Chipman 4 271 46N11 65w53 4:23:32
Chisholm Mills 1
223 54N55 114w08 7:36:32
Choiceland 12
249 53N27 104w25 6:57:40
Chu Chua 2 266 51N21 120w10 8:00:40
Churchill 3 203 58N46 94w10 6:16:40
Churchill Falls 6
9 53N35 64w27 4:17:48
Churchville 9 50 43N38 79w45 5:19:00
Chute À Blondeau 9
1 45N35 74w29 4:57:56
Chute Panet 11
170 46N51 71w51 4:47:24
Cinema 2 266 53N11 122w30 8:10:00
Claireville 9 50 43N45 79w38 5:18:32
Clairmont 1 223 55N16 118w47 7:55:08
Clandonald 1 223 53N34 110w44 7:22:56
Claremont 9 1 43N58 79w07 5:16:28
Clarence Creek 9
1 45N30 75w13 5:00:52
Clarenceville 11
7 45N04 73w15 4:53:00
Clarenville 5
286 48N10 53w58 3:35:52
Claresholm 1 223 50N02 113w35 7:34:20
Clarke City 11
297 50N12 66w38 4:26:32
Clarksburg 9 1 44N43 80w27 5:21:48
Clark's Harbour 8
11 43N26 65w38 4:22:32
Clarkson 9 45 43N31 79w37 5:18:28
Clavet 12 264 52N00 106w23 7:05:32
Clayhurst 2 299 56N15 120w01 8:00:04
Clearbrook 2 266 49N08 122w26 8:09:44
Clearwater 2 266 51N38 120w02 8:00:08
Clearwater 3 203 49N08 99w01 6:36:04
Clementsport 8
11 44N40 65w37 4:22:28
Clermont 11 141 47N41 70w14 4:40:56
Clifford 9 36 43N58 80w58 5:23:52
Climax 12 228 49N13 108w23 7:13:32
Clinton 2 266 51N05 121w35 8:06:20
Clinton 9 36 43N37 81w32 5:26:08
Clo Oose 2 266 48N40 124w49 8:19:16
Cloverdale 2 266 49N06 122w44 8:10:56
Clyde 1 223 54N09 113w39 7:34:36
Clyde 7 33 70N25 68w30 4:34:00
Coaldale 1 223 49N43 112w37 7:30:28
Coal Harbour 2
266 50N36 127w35 8:30:20
Coalhurst 1 223 49N45 112w56 7:31:44
Coalmont 2 266 49N31 120w41 8:02:44
Coal River 2 266 59N45 126w55 8:27:40
Coalspur 1 223 53N11 117w01 7:48:04
Coaticook 11 143 45N08 71w48 4:47:12
Cobalt 9 57 47N24 79w41 5:18:44
Cobble Hill 2
266 48N41 123w36 8:14:24
Cobden 9 1 45N38 76w53 5:07:32
Coboconk 9 36 44N39 78w48 5:15:12
Cobourg 9 183 43N58 78w10 5:12:40
Cochrane 1 224 51N11 114w28 7:37:52
Cochrane 9 58 49N04 81w01 5:24:04
Coderre 12 231 50N10 106w23 7:05:32
Codesa 1 223 55N45 118w04 7:52:16
Cod Island 6 269 57N45 61w50 4:07:20
Codroy 5 286 47N53 59w24 3:57:36
Codroy Pond 5
286 48N04 58w52 3:55:28
Codys 4 271 45N52 65w50 4:23:20
Colborne 9 40 44N00 77w53 5:11:32
Colborne 9 36 42N51 80w19 5:21:16
Colchester 9 1 41N59 82w56 5:31:44
Cold Lake 1 223 54N27 110w10 7:20:40
Coldsprings 9 40 44N17 78w18 5:13:12
Coldwater 9 34 44N42 79w40 5:18:40
Coleman 1 223 49N38 114w30 7:38:00
Coleville 12 228 51N43 109w16 7:17:04
Colinet 5 286 47N13 53w33 3:34:12
Colinton 1 223 54N37 113w15 7:33:00
Colleymount 2
266 54N01 126w09 8:24:36
Collingwood 9 59 44N29 80w13 5:20:52
Collins Bay 9 76 44N15 76w36 5:06:24
Colonsay 12 237 51N59 105w53 7:03:32
Colwood 2 265 48N26 123w29 8:13:56
Comber 9 1 42N14 82w33 5:30:12
Come by Chance 5
286 47N51 53w58 3:35:52
Comox 2 266 49N40 124w55 8:19:40
Conche 5 286 50N53 55w54 3:43:36
Concord 9 34 43N48 79w29 5:17:56
Conestogo 9 60 43N32 80w30 5:22:00
Congress 12 238 49N46 106w00 7:04:00
Coniston 9 119 46N29 80w51 5:23:24
Conklin 1 223 55N38 111w05 7:24:20
Conquest 12 228 51N32 107w17 7:09:08
Conrad 13 270 60N04 134w33 8:58:12
Consecon 9 35 44N00 77w31 5:10:04
Consort 1 223 52N01 110w46 7:23:04
Consul 12 223 49N21 109w30 7:18:00
Contrecoeur 11
135 45N51 73w14 4:52:56
Conway 10 6 46N40 63w59 4:15:56
Cook's Harbour 5
286 51N36 55w52 3:43:28
Cookshire 11 149 45N25 71w38 4:46:32
Cooks Mills 9
128 43N00 79w11 5:16:44
Cookstown 9 35 44N11 79w42 5:18:48
Copper Cliff 9
119 46N28 81w04 5:24:16
Coppermine 7 227 67N50 115w05 7:40:20
Copper Mountain 2
266 49N20 120w33 8:02:12
Coquitlam 2 267 49N17 122w47 8:11:08
Coral Harbour 7
33 64N08 83w10 5:32:40
Cormorant 3 203 54N14 100w35 6:42:20
Corner Brook 5
286 48N57 57w57 3:51:48
Cornwall 9 45 45N02 74w44 4:58:56
Coronation 1 223 52N05 111w27 7:25:48
Corunna 9 112 42N53 82w26 5:29:44
Coteau Landing 11
177 45N15 74w13 4:56:52
Coteau Station 11
177 45N17 74w14 4:56:56
Côte Saint Luc 11
151 45N28 73w40 4:54:40
Côte Saint Michel 11
151 45N34 73w36 4:54:24
Cottam 9 1 42N08 82w45 5:31:00
Courtenay 2 266 49N41 125w00 8:20:00
Courtice 9 40 43N55 78w46 5:15:04
Courtland 9 36 42N51 80w38 5:22:32
Courtright 9 1 42N49 82w28 5:29:52
Coutts 1 223 49N00 111w57 7:27:48
Cowansville 11
144 45N12 72w45 4:51:00
Cow Head 5 286 49N55 57w48 3:51:12
Cowichan Bay 2
266 48N44 123w40 8:14:40
Cowley 1 223 49N34 114w05 7:36:20
Cox's Cove 5 286 49N07 58w05 3:52:20
Crabtree Mills 11
145 45N58 73w28 4:53:52
Craig 2 266 49N18 124w15 8:17:00
Craigellachie 2
266 50N59 118w43 7:54:52
Craigmyle 1 223 51N40 112w15 7:29:00
Craik 12 231 51N03 105w49 7:03:16
Cranberry Portage 3
203 54N35 101w23 6:45:32
Cranbrook 2 223 49N31 115w46 7:43:04
Craven 12 238 50N39 104w50 6:59:20
Crawford Bay 2
266 49N42 116w48 7:47:12
Creemore 9 35 44N19 80w06 5:20:24
Creighton 12 208 54N45 101w54 6:47:36
Creighton Mine 9
119 46N28 81w11 5:24:44
Cremona 1 223 51N33 114w29 7:37:56
Crescent Beach 2
267 49N04 122w53 8:11:32
Crescent Spur 2
266 53N35 120w41 8:02:44
Creston 2 266 49N06 116w31 7:46:04
Creston 5 286 47N09 55w11 3:40:44
Criss Creek 2
266 51N03 120w44 8:02:56
Crofton 2 266 48N52 123w38 8:14:32
Crooked River 12
249 52N51 103w44 6:54:56
Crossfield 1 224 51N26 114w02 7:36:08
Crow Lake 9 3 49N12 93w57 6:15:48
Crown Hill 9 1 44N26 79w39 5:18:36
Crowsnest 2 223 49N38 114w41 7:38:44
Croydon Station 2
266 53N05 119w44 7:58:56
Crumlin 9 1 43N01 81w09 5:24:36
Crystal Beach 9
2 42N52 79w04 5:16:16
Crystal City 3
203 49N09 98w56 6:35:44
Cudworth 12 230 52N30 105w45 7:03:00
Cultus Lake 2
266 49N04 121w58 8:07:52
Cumberland 2 266 49N37 125w01 8:20:04
Cumberland House 12
232 53N58 102w16 6:49:04
Cupar 12 238 50N57 104w12 6:56:48
Cut Knife 12 228 52N44 109w01 7:16:04
Cypress River 3
203 49N34 99w05 6:36:20
Dafoe 12 231 51N46 104w32 6:58:08
Dalesville 11
157 45N42 74w24 4:57:36
Dalhousie 4 275 48N04 66w23 4:25:32
Dalmeny 12 264 52N20 106w46 7:07:04
Dalroy 1 223 51N07 113w39 7:34:36
Daniel's Harbour 5
286 50N14 57w35 3:50:20
Danville 11 146 45N47 72w01 4:48:04
D'Arcy 2 266 50N33 122w29 8:09:56
Darlingford 3
203 49N12 98w22 6:33:28
Dartmouth 8 16 44N40 63w34 4:14:16
Dauphin 3 207 51N09 100w03 6:40:12
Daveluyville 11
135 46N12 72w08 4:48:32
Davidson 12 229 51N18 105w59 7:03:56
Davis Cove 5 286 47N40 54w18 3:37:12
Dawson 13 301 64N04 139w25 9:17:40
Dawson Creek 2
299 55N46 120w14 8:00:56
Daysland 1 223 52N52 112w15 7:29:00
Decker Lake 2
266 54N17 125w50 8:23:20
Deep Cove 2 267 49N22 122w56 8:11:44
Deep River 9 1 46N06 77w30 5:10:00
Deer Lake 5 286 49N10 57w26 3:49:44
Delaware 9 1 42N55 81w25 5:25:40
Delburne 1 223 52N12 113w14 7:32:56
Delhi 9 36 42N51 80w30 5:22:00
Delia 1 223 51N38 112w23 7:29:32
Delisle 12 228 51N55 107w08 7:08:32
Delmas 12 228 52N55 108w36 7:14:24
Deloraine 3 203 49N12 100w29 6:41:56
Deloro 9 37 44N31 77w37 5:10:28
Delson 11 151 45N22 73w33 4:54:12
Delta 9 1 44N37 76w08 5:04:32
Delta Beach 3
203 50N11 98w19 6:33:16
Demmitt 1 223 55N26 119w54 7:59:36
Denare Beach 12
232 54N40 102w05 6:48:20
Denbigh 9 1 45N08 77w16 5:09:04
Departure Bay 2
266 49N12 123w58 8:15:52
Deroche 2 266 49N11 122w04 8:08:16
Derry West 9 50 43N39 79w42 5:18:48
Derwent 1 223 53N39 110w58 7:23:52
Deschaillons 11
7 46N32 72w07 4:48:28
Deschambault 11
191 46N39 71w56 4:47:44
Deschambault Lake 12
230 54N55 103w22 6:53:28
Deschênes 11 153 45N23 75w48 5:03:12
Deseronto 9 40 44N12 77w03 5:08:12
Desmarais 1 223 55N56 113w49 7:35:16
Destruction Bay 13
301 61N15 138w48 9:15:12
Deux Montagnes 11
7 45N32 73w53 4:55:32
Devine 2 266 50N32 122w30 8:10:00
Devon 1 225 53N22 113w44 7:34:56
Dewdney 2 266 49N10 122w12 8:08:48
Didsbury 1 223 51N40 114w08 7:36:32
Dieppe 4 4 46N06 64w45 4:19:00
Digby 8 17 44N37 65w47 4:23:08
Dingwall 8 11 46N54 60w28 4:01:52
Dinorwic 9 3 49N41 92w30 6:10:00
Dinsmore 12 228 51N20 107w26 7:09:44
Disraëli 11 197 45N54 71w21 4:45:24
Dixie 9 1 43N36 79w36 5:18:24
Dixville 11 143 45N04 71w46 4:47:04
Doaktown 4 271 46N33 66w08 4:24:32
Dodsland 12 228 51N48 108w49 7:15:16
Doe River 2 299 56N00 120w05 8:00:20
Dog Creek 2 266 51N35 122w15 8:09:00
Dolbeau 11 147 48N53 72w14 4:48:56
Dollard des Ormeaux 11
7 45N29 73w49 4:55:16
Dollarton 2 267 49N18 122w56 8:11:44
Dome Creek 2 266 53N44 121w01 8:04:04
Dominion 8 11 46N13 60w01 4:00:04

Domremy 12	230	52N47	105w44	7:02:56
Donalda 1	223	52N35	112w34	7:30:16
Donnacona 11	191	46N40	71w47	4:47:08
Donnelly 1	223	55N44	117w06	7:48:24
Doon 9	60	43N23	80w26	5:21:44
Dorchester 4	271	45N54	64w31	4:18:04
Dorchester 9	36	42N59	81w04	5:24:16
Dorchester Crossing 4	271	46N10	64w34	4:18:16
Doré Lake 12	228	54N31	107w06	7:08:24
Dorion Vaudreuil 11	202	45N23	74w01	4:56:04
Dorval 11	151	45N27	73w44	4:54:56
Doting Cove 5	286	49N27	53w57	3:35:48
Douglas 9	61	45N31	76w56	5:07:44
Douglas Lake 2	266	50N10	120w12	8:00:48
Douglas Station 3	203	49N53	99w46	6:39:04
Downsview 9	124	43N44	79w30	5:18:00
Doyles 5	286	47N50	59w12	3:56:48
Drayton 9	36	43N46	80w40	5:22:40
Drayton Valley 1	223	53N13	114w59	7:39:56
Dresden 9	1	42N35	82w11	5:28:44
Drumbo 9	60	43N14	80w33	5:22:12
Drumheller 1	223	51N28	112w42	7:30:48
Drummondville 11	148	45N53	72w29	4:49:56
Dryden 9	220	49N47	92w50	6:11:20
Dublin 9	35	43N31	81w17	5:25:08
Duck Bay 3	203	52N10	100w09	6:40:36
Duck Lake 12	229	52N47	106w13	7:04:52
Dunbarton 9	1	43N49	79w06	5:16:24
Dunblane 12	229	51N11	106w52	7:07:28
Duncan 2	266	48N47	123w42	8:14:48
Dundalk 9	1	44N10	80w24	5:21:36
Dundarave 2	267	49N23	123w14	8:12:56
Dundas 9	74	43N16	79w58	5:19:52
Dundurn 12	264	51N49	106w30	7:06:00
Dunham 11	144	45N08	72w48	4:51:12
Dunnville 9	63	42N54	79w36	5:18:24
Dunrea 3	203	49N25	99w44	6:38:56
Dunster 2	266	53N08	119w50	7:59:20
Dunville 5	286	47N16	53w54	3:35:36
Durham 9	36	44N10	80w49	5:23:16
Durrell 5	286	49N40	54w44	3:38:56
Dutton 9	64	42N39	81w30	5:26:00
Dyment 9	3	49N37	92w19	6:09:16
Dysart 12	238	50N56	104w02	6:56:08
Eagle Bay 2	266	50N56	119w12	7:56:48
Eaglesham 1	223	55N47	117w53	7:51:32
Ear Falls 9	3	50N38	93w13	6:12:52
Earl Grey 12	240	50N56	104w45	6:59:00
East Angus 11	149	45N29	71w40	4:46:40
East Braintree 3	203	49N37	95w38	6:22:32
Eastchester 8	21	44N23	64w19	4:17:16
East Coulee 1	223	51N20	112w19	7:29:16
Eastend 12	228	49N31	108w48	7:15:12
East Kelowna 2	266	49N51	119w25	7:57:40
Eastmain 11	7	52N15	78w30	5:14:00
Eastman 11	7	45N18	72w19	4:49:16
East Pine 2	299	55N43	121w13	8:04:52
Eastport 5	286	48N39	53w45	3:35:00
East Sooke 2	266	48N22	123w43	8:14:52
East York 9	124	43N41	79w20	5:17:20
Eatonia 12	228	51N13	109w23	7:17:32
Ebenezer 9	50	43N46	79w40	5:18:40
Eckville 1	223	52N21	114w22	7:37:28
Ecum Secum 8	11	44N58	62w08	4:08:32
Edam 12	228	53N12	108w46	7:15:04
Eden Mills 9	60	43N35	80w09	5:20:36
Edgeley 9	1	43N48	79w31	5:18:04
Edgerton 1	223	52N45	110w27	7:21:48
Edgewood 2	266	49N47	118w08	7:52:32
Edmonton 1	225	53N33	113w28	7:33:52
Edmundston 4	271	47N22	68w20	4:33:20
Edson 1	223	53N35	116w26	7:45:44
Eganville 9	59	45N32	77w06	5:08:24
Egremont 1	223	54N02	113w08	7:32:32
Elbow 12	229	51N07	106w35	7:06:20
Elder Mills 9	1	43N49	79w38	5:18:32
Elfros 12	242	51N43	103w52	6:55:28
Elgin 9	1	44N36	76w13	5:04:52
Elizabeth Harbour 7	219	70N35	92w50	6:11:20
Elkhorn 3	203	49N58	101w14	6:44:56
Elko 2	223	49N18	115w07	7:40:28
Elk Point 1	223	53N34	110w54	7:23:36
Elliot Lake 9	1	46N23	82w39	5:30:36
Elliston 5	286	48N38	53w03	3:32:12
Elm Creek 3	203	49N41	98w00	6:32:00
Elmira 9	60	43N36	80w33	5:22:12
Elmira 10	6	46N27	62w04	4:08:16
Elmsdale 8	11	44N58	63w30	4:14:00
Elmvale 9	35	44N35	79w52	5:19:28
Elmwood 9	35	44N14	81w03	5:24:12
Elnora 1	223	51N59	113w12	7:32:48
Elora 9	36	43N41	80w26	5:21:44
Elphinstone 3	203	50N33	100w19	6:41:16
Elrose 12	228	51N13	108w01	7:12:04
Elsa 13	270	63N55	135w28	9:01:52
Embro 9	1	43N09	80w54	5:23:36
Embrun 9	1	45N16	75w17	5:01:08
Emerson 3	203	49N00	97w12	6:28:48
Emeryville 9	1	42N18	82w45	5:31:00
Emo 9	3	48N38	93w50	6:15:20
Empress 1	223	50N57	110w00	7:20:00
Endako 2	266	54N05	125w02	8:20:08
Endeavour 12	232	52N08	102w40	6:50:40
Enderby 2	266	50N33	119w08	7:56:32
Englee 5	286	50N44	56w06	3:44:24
Englehart 9	46	47N49	79w52	5:19:28
Englewood 2	266	50N33	126w53	8:27:32
English Harbour West 5	286	47N28	55w29	3:41:56
Enilda 1	223	55N25	116w18	7:45:12
Entwistle 1	223	53N36	115w00	7:40:00
Erickson 2	266	49N05	116w28	7:45:52
Erickson 3	203	50N30	99w55	6:39:40
Erieau 9	1	42N16	81w56	5:27:44
Erie Beach 9	2	42N53	78w57	5:15:48
Erie Beach 9	1	42N16	82w00	5:28:00
Eriksdale 3	203	50N52	98w06	6:32:24
Erin 9	1	43N45	80w07	5:20:28
Erindale 9	45	43N32	79w39	5:18:36
Errington 2	266	49N17	124w22	8:17:28
Erwood 12	232	52N50	102w10	6:48:40
Eskimo Point 7	219	61N07	94w03	6:16:12
Espanola 9	35	46N15	81w46	5:27:04
Esquimalt 2	265	48N26	123w24	8:13:36
Essex 9	1	42N10	82w49	5:31:16
Esterhazy 12	232	50N40	102w08	6:48:32
Estevan 12	203	49N07	103w05	6:52:20
Estevan Point 2	266	49N23	126w33	8:26:12
Eston 12	228	51N10	108w46	7:15:04
Estuary 12	228	50N56	109w46	7:19:04
Ethelbert 3	203	51N31	100w22	6:41:28
Etobicoke 9	65	43N39	79w34	5:18:16
Evansburg 1	223	53N36	115w01	7:40:04
Everett 9	1	44N11	79w57	5:19:48
Evesham 12	228	52N24	109w50	7:19:20
Exeter 9	36	43N21	81w29	5:25:56
Exshaw 1	223	51N03	115w09	7:40:36
Extension 2	266	49N06	123w57	8:15:48
Eyebrow 12	241	50N47	106w09	7:04:36
Fairmont Hot Springs 2	223	50N19	115w53	7:43:32
Fairport 9	1	43N49	79w05	5:16:20
Fairport Beach 9	1	43N48	79w06	5:16:24
Fairview 1	223	56N04	118w23	7:53:32
Falconbridge 9	1	46N35	80w48	5:23:12
Falher 1	223	55N44	117w12	7:48:48
Falkland 2	266	50N30	119w33	7:58:12
Fanny Bay 2	266	49N30	124w50	8:19:20
Farnham 11	150	45N17	72w59	4:51:56
Fauquier 2	266	49N53	118w05	7:52:20
Faust 1	223	55N19	115w38	7:42:32
Fawcett 1	223	54N32	114w05	7:36:20
Fenelon Falls 9	36	44N32	78w45	5:15:00
Fergus 9	184	43N42	80w22	5:21:28
Ferguson 2	266	50N41	117w28	7:49:52
Fernie 2	223	49N30	115w03	7:40:12
Ferryland 5	286	47N02	52w53	3:31:32
Field 2	266	51N24	116w29	7:45:56
Fife Lake 12	231	49N12	105w43	7:02:52
Fillmore 12	233	49N50	103w25	6:53:40
Finch 9	1	45N11	75w07	5:00:28
Fingal 9	1	42N43	81w19	5:25:16
Finmoore 2	266	53N59	123w37	8:14:28
Finnegan 1	223	51N07	112w05	7:28:20
Fisher Branch 3	203	51N05	97w37	6:30:28
Fisherville 9	124	43N47	79w28	5:17:52
Five Islands 8	11	45N25	64w02	4:16:08
Flanders 9	3	48N44	92w05	6:08:20
Flat Bay 5	286	48N24	58w36	3:54:24
Flat River 10	6	46N01	62w52	4:11:28
Flaxcombe 12	228	51N29	109w36	7:18:24
Flesherton 9	1	44N16	80w33	5:22:12
Fletcher 9	1	42N18	82w18	5:29:12
Fleur de Lys 5	286	50N07	56w08	3:44:32
Flin Flon 3	208	54N46	101w53	6:47:32
Flower's Cove 5	286	51N18	56w44	3:46:56
Foam Lake 12	232	51N39	103w33	6:54:12
Fogo 5	286	49N43	54w17	3:37:08
Foleyet 9	1	48N16	82w30	5:30:00
Fond du Lac 12	228	59N19	107w10	7:08:40
Fontenelle 11	288	48N52	64w52	4:19:28
Foothills 1	223	53N04	116w48	7:47:12
Foremost 1	223	49N29	111w25	7:25:40
Forest 9	35	43N06	82w00	5:28:00
Forestburg 1	223	52N35	112w04	7:28:16
Forest Grove 2	266	51N46	121w06	8:04:24
Forestville 11	295	48N45	69w06	4:36:24
Fort Albany 9	1	52N15	81w37	5:26:28
Fort Assiniboine 1	223	54N20	114w46	7:39:04
Fort Chimo 11	7	58N06	68w25	4:33:40
Fort Chipewyan 1	223	58N42	111w08	7:24:32
Fort Coulonge 11	7	45N51	76w44	5:06:56
Forteau 6	269	51N28	56w58	3:47:52
Fort Erie 9	2	42N54	78w56	5:15:44
Fort Fitzgerald 1	223	59N53	111w37	7:26:28
Fort Frances 9	3	48N36	93w24	6:13:36
Fort Franklin 7	298	65N11	123w46	8:15:04
Fort Fraser 2	266	54N04	124w33	8:18:12
Fort George 11	7	53N50	79w00	5:16:00
Fort Good Hope 7	298	66N15	128w38	8:34:32
Fortierville 11	135	46N29	72w02	4:48:08
Fort Langley 2	267	49N10	122w35	8:10:20
Fort Liard 7	298	60N15	123w28	8:13:52
Fort Macleod 1	223	49N43	113w25	7:33:40
Fort McMurray 1	223	56N44	111w23	7:25:32
Fort McPherson 7	298	67N27	134w53	8:59:32
Fort Nelson 2	266	58N49	122w39	8:10:36
Fort Norman 7	298	64N54	125w34	8:22:16
Fort Providence 7	227	61N21	117w39	7:50:36
Fort Qu'Appelle 12	231	50N56	103w09	6:52:36
Fort Reliance 7	227	62N42	109w08	7:16:32
Fort Resolution 7	227	61N10	113w40	7:34:40
Fort Saint James 2	266	54N26	124w15	8:17:00
Fort Saint John 2	299	56N15	120w51	8:03:24
Fort Saskatchewan 1	225	53N43	113w13	7:32:52
Fort Severn 9	1	56N00	87w38	5:50:32
Fort Simpson 7	298	61N52	121w23	8:05:32
Fort Smith 7	227	60N00	111w53	7:27:32
Fort Steele 2	223	49N37	115w38	7:42:32
Fortune 5	286	47N04	55w50	3:43:20
Fortune Harbour 5	286	49N31	55w15	3:41:00
Fort Vermilion 1	223	58N24	116w00	7:44:00
Fort William → Thunder Bay 9	121	48N23	89w15	5:57:00
Fortymile 13	301	64N26	140w33	9:22:12
Fourchu 8	11	45N43	60w15	4:01:00
Foxboro 9	181	44N15	77w26	5:09:44
Fox Harbour 6	269	52N22	55w41	3:42:44
Fox Valley 12	228	50N29	109w28	7:17:52
Francis 12	243	50N05	103w55	6:55:40
François 5	286	47N35	56w45	3:47:00
François Lake 2	266	54N04	125w44	8:22:56
Frankford 9	34	44N12	77w36	5:10:24
Franklin River 2	266	49N06	124w49	8:19:16
Fraser Lake 2	266	54N04	124w51	8:19:24
Fraser Mills 2	267	49N14	122w52	8:11:28
Fredericton 4	276	45N58	66w39	4:26:36
Fredericton Junction 4	271	45N40	66w37	4:26:28
Freeport 8	11	44N17	66w19	4:25:16
Freeport 9	60	43N25	80w25	5:21:40
Frenchman Butte 12	228	53N35	109w38	7:18:32
Frobisher 12	203	49N12	102w26	6:49:44
Frobisher Bay 7	33	63N44	68w28	4:33:52
Frontier 12	228	49N12	108w34	7:14:16
Fruitvale 2	266	49N07	117w33	7:50:12
Fulford Harbour 2	266	48N46	123w27	8:13:48
Fusilier 12	228	51N51	109w46	7:19:04
Gabarus 8	11	45N50	60w09	4:00:36
Gabriola 2	266	49N12	123w50	8:15:20
Gagetown 4	271	45N47	66w09	4:24:36
Gagnon 11	295	51N53	68w10	4:32:40
Gainsborough 12	203	49N10	101w26	6:45:44
Galahad 1	223	52N31	111w56	7:27:44
Galiano 2	266	48N52	123w21	8:13:24
Galt → Cambridge 9	66	43N22	80w19	5:21:16
Gambo 5	286	48N46	54w14	3:36:56
Gananoque 9	67	44N20	76w10	5:04:40
Gander 5	286	48N57	54w37	3:38:28
Gander Bay 5	286	49N18	54w29	3:37:56
Ganges 2	266	48N51	123w30	8:14:00
Gang Ranch 2	266	51N33	122w20	8:09:20
Gardenton 3	203	49N05	96w40	6:26:40
Garibaldi 2	266	49N58	123w09	8:12:36
Garnish 5	286	47N14	55w22	3:41:28
Garson 9	119	46N34	80w52	5:23:28
Garthby Station (Beaulac) 11	197	45N50	71w23	4:45:32
Gasline 9	103	42N53	79w11	5:16:44
Gaspé 11	287	48N50	64w29	4:17:56
Geary 4	271	45N46	66w29	4:25:56
Georgetown 9	68	43N39	79w55	5:19:40
Georgetown 10	6	46N11	62w32	4:10:08
Geraldton 9	1	49N44	86w57	5:47:48
Germansen Landing 2	266	55N47	124w43	8:18:52
Gethsémani 11	30	50N13	60w40	4:02:40
Gibbons 1	225	53N50	113w20	7:33:20
Gibsons 2	267	49N24	123w30	8:14:00
Gilbert Plains 3	203	51N09	100w29	6:41:56
Gillam 3	203	56N21	94w43	6:18:52

Gimli 3 209 50N38 96w59 6:27:56
Girouxville 1 223 55N45 117w20 7:49:20
Giscome 2 266 54N04 122w22 8:09:28
Gjoa Haven 7 219 68N38 95w57 6:23:48
Glace Bay 8 14 46N12 59w57 3:59:48
Glacier 2 266 51N16 117w31 7:50:04
Gladstone 3 203 50N13 98w57 6:35:48
Glaslyn 12 228 53N21 108w22 7:13:28
Gleichen 1 223 50N52 113w03 7:32:12
Glenarchy 9 45 43N29 79w46 5:19:04
Glenavon 12 231 50N10 103w10 6:52:40
Glenboro 3 203 49N32 99w15 6:37:00
Glencoe 9 35 42N45 81w43 5:26:52
Glendon 1 223 54N15 111w10 7:24:40
Glen Lake 2 265 48N26 123w31 8:14:04
Glen Miller 9 40 44N08 77w35 5:10:20
Glen Robertson 9 1 45N21 74w30 4:58:00
Glen Ross 9 1 44N16 77w36 5:10:24
Glen Williams 9 1 43N40 79w55 5:19:40
Glenwood 5 286 48N59 54w52 3:39:28
Glenwoodville 1 223 49N22 113w21 7:33:24
Glovertown 5 286 48N41 54w02 3:36:08
Godbout 11 297 49N19 67w37 4:30:28
Goderich 9 69 43N45 81w43 5:26:52
Gods Lake 3 203 54N40 94w09 6:16:36
Gogama 9 1 47N40 81w43 5:26:52
Goldboro 8 11 45N11 61w39 4:06:36
Gold Bridge 2 266 50N51 122w50 8:11:20
Golden 2 266 51N18 116w58 7:47:52
Golden Prairie 12 223 50N14 109w38 7:18:32
Gold River 2 266 49N41 126w08 8:24:32
Gold Rock 9 3 49N27 92w43 6:10:52
Gooderham 9 1 44N54 78w23 5:13:32
Goodeve 12 232 51N04 103w10 6:52:40
Goodlands 3 203 49N05 100w35 6:42:20
Goodwood 9 37 44N02 79w12 5:16:48
Goose Bay 6 269 53N20 60w25 4:01:40
Gordon River 2 266 48N47 124w21 8:17:24
Gore 8 11 45N07 63w43 4:14:52
Gore Bay 9 1 45N55 82w28 5:29:52
Goshen 8 11 45N23 61w59 4:07:56
Govan 12 244 51N18 105w00 7:00:00
Govenlock 12 223 49N15 109w48 7:19:12
Gracefield 11 7 46N06 76w03 5:04:12
Grafton 9 40 44N00 78w01 5:12:04
Granby 11 8 45N24 72w44 4:50:56
Grand Bank 5 286 47N06 55w46 3:43:04
Grand Bay 4 280 45N18 66w12 4:24:48
Grand Beach 3 210 50N35 96w40 6:26:40
Grand Bend 9 1 43N15 81w45 5:27:00
Grand Bruit 5 286 47N41 58w13 3:52:52
Grand Centre 1 223 54N25 110w13 7:20:52
Grande Anse 4 271 47N48 65w11 4:20:44
Grand Entrée 11 30 47N33 61w34 4:06:16
Grande Prairie 1 223 55N10 118w48 7:55:12
Grande Rivière 11 288 48N24 64w30 4:18:00
Grandes Piles 11 152 46N41 72w44 4:50:56
Grand Étang 8 11 46N33 61w02 4:04:08
Grand Falls 5 286 48N56 55w40 3:42:40
Grand Falls 4 271 47N03 67w44 4:30:56
Grand Forks 2 266 49N02 118w27 7:53:48
Grand'Mère 11 152 46N37 72w41 4:50:44
Grand Rapids 3 203 53N08 99w20 6:37:20
Grand Valley 9 1 43N54 80w19 5:21:16
Grandview 3 203 51N10 100w45 6:43:00
Granum 1 223 49N52 113w30 7:34:00
Grassy Lake 1 223 49N49 111w43 7:26:52
Grassy Plains 2 266 53N57 125w54 8:23:36
Gravelbourg 12 231 49N53 106w34 7:06:16
Gravenhurst 9 34 44N55 79w22 5:17:28
Grayson 12 232 50N44 102w40 6:50:40
Great Falls 3 211 50N27 96w02 6:24:08
Greenfield Park 11 151 45N29 73w29 4:53:56
Green Lake 12 228 54N17 107w47 7:11:08
Greenlal (Saint Grégoire de Greenlay) 7 45N34 72w01 4:48:04
Greenspond 5 286 49N04 53w34 3:34:16
Green Valley 9 1 45N16 74w36 4:58:24
Greenwood 2 266 49N05 118w41 7:54:44
Grenfell 12 232 50N25 102w56 6:51:44
Grenville 11 7 45N37 74w36 4:58:24
Grenville Bay 11 7 45N38 74w36 4:58:24
Gretna 3 203 49N02 97w35 6:30:20
Griffin 12 245 49N40 103w26 6:53:44
Grimsby 9 70 43N12 79w34 5:18:16
Grimshaw 1 223 56N11 117w36 7:50:24
Grindstone Island (Cap Aux Meules) 11 30 47N23 61w52 4:07:28
Griswold 3 203 49N45 100w25 6:41:40
Grondines (Saint Charles des Grondines) 7 46N36 72w03 4:48:12
Gronlid 12 249 53N06 104w28 6:57:52
Grouard Mission 1 223 55N31 116w09 7:44:36
Groundbirch 2 299 55N47 120w55 8:03:40
Grunthal 3 203 49N25 96w52 6:27:28
Guelph 9 71 43N33 80w15 5:21:00
Gull Lake 12 228 50N08 108w27 7:13:48
Gunnar 12 228 59N23 108w53 7:15:32
Guysborough 8 11 45N23 61w30 4:06:00
Gypsumville 3 203 51N45 98w35 6:34:20
Hafford 12 228 52N48 107w20 7:09:20
Hagensborg 2 266 52N23 126w33 8:26:12
Hagerman Corners 9 1 43N50 79w18 5:17:12
Hagersville 9 60 42N58 80w03 5:20:12
Hague 12 229 52N30 106w25 7:05:40
Haileybury 9 72 47N27 79w38 5:18:32
Haines Junction 13 300 60N45 137w30 9:10:00
Halbrite 12 250 49N20 103w32 6:54:08
Halfmoon Bay 2 266 49N31 123w54 8:15:36
Haliburton 9 73 45N03 78w03 5:12:12
Halifax 8 12 44N39 63w36 4:14:24
Hamilton 9 74 43N15 79w51 5:19:24
Hamiota 3 203 50N11 100w36 6:42:24
Ham Nord 11 7 45N54 71w39 4:46:36
Hampden 5 286 49N33 56w51 3:47:24
Hampstead 11 151 45N29 73w38 4:54:32
Hampton 4 277 45N32 65w51 4:23:24
Hampton 9 40 43N58 78w45 5:15:00
Ham Sud 11 7 45N46 71w36 4:46:24
Hanceville 2 266 51N55 123w03 8:12:12
Handsworth 12 231 49N48 103w00 6:52:00
Haney 2 267 49N13 122w36 8:10:24
Hanley 12 229 51N37 106w27 7:05:48
Hanmer 9 119 46N30 80w56 5:23:44
Hanna 1 223 51N38 111w54 7:27:36
Hanover 9 36 44N09 81w02 5:24:08
Hansard 2 266 54N05 121w52 8:07:28
Hant's Harbour 5 286 48N01 53w16 3:33:04
Hantsport 8 11 45N04 64w11 4:16:44
Harbour Breton 5 286 47N29 55w48 3:43:12
Harbour Buffett 5 286 47N31 54w05 3:36:20
Harbour Deep 5 286 50N22 56w31 3:46:04
Harbour Grace 5 286 47N42 53w13 3:32:52
Harbourville 8 11 45N09 64w49 4:19:16
Hardisty 1 223 52N40 111w18 7:25:12
Hare Bay 5 286 48N51 54w01 3:36:04
Harris 12 228 51N44 107w35 7:10:20
Harrison, Cape 6 269 54N55 57w55 3:51:40
Harrison Hot Springs 2 266 49N18 121w47 8:07:08
Harrison Mills 2 266 49N14 121w57 8:07:48
Harriston 9 36 43N54 80w53 5:23:32
Harrow 9 1 42N02 82w55 5:31:40
Harrowsmith 9 35 44N24 76w40 5:06:40
Hartland 4 271 46N18 67w32 4:30:08
Hartley Bay 2 266 53N25 129w15 8:37:00
Hartney 3 203 49N28 100w30 6:42:00
Harvey 4 271 45N43 64w43 4:18:52
Hastings 9 36 44N18 77w57 5:11:48
Hatchet Lake 8 12 44N35 63w40 4:14:40
Hatzic 2 266 49N09 122w15 8:09:00
Hauterive 11 295 49N12 68w16 4:33:04
Havelock 9 1 44N26 77w53 5:11:32
Havre Aubert 11 30 47N14 61w51 4:07:24
Havre Saint Pierre 11 297 50N14 63w36 4:14:24
Hawarden 12 229 51N23 106w36 7:06:24
Hawkesbury 9 185 45N36 74w37 4:58:28
Hawk Junction 9 1 48N05 84w34 5:38:16
Hawk Lake 9 3 49N48 93w59 6:15:56
Hay Lakes 1 223 53N13 113w03 7:32:12
Hay River 7 227 60N51 115w40 7:42:40
Hays 1 223 50N06 111w48 7:27:12
Hazelton 2 266 55N15 127w40 8:30:40
Hazlet 12 228 50N25 108w36 7:14:24
Head Bay d'Espoir 5 286 47N56 55w45 3:43:00
Hearst 9 59 49N41 83w40 5:34:40
Heart's Content 5 286 47N53 53w22 3:33:28
Hebron 6 269 58N20 62w45 4:11:00
Hectanooga 8 11 44N06 66w02 4:24:08
Hedley 2 266 49N21 120w04 8:00:16
Heidelberg 9 60 43N31 80w37 5:22:28
Heisler 1 223 52N41 112w13 7:28:52
Hemford 8 11 44N30 64w47 4:19:08
Henryville 11 7 45N08 73w11 4:52:44
Hensall 9 35 43N26 81w30 5:26:00
Hepburn 12 264 52N31 106w43 7:06:52
Hepworth 9 1 44N37 81w09 5:24:36
Herbert 12 228 50N26 107w12 7:08:48
Herb Lake 3 203 54N47 99w47 6:39:08
Hermitage 5 286 47N33 55w56 3:43:44
Herring Cove 8 12 44N34 63w34 4:14:16
Herschel 12 228 51N38 108w21 7:13:24
Hespeler 9 66 43N26 80w18 5:21:12
Hickman's Harbour 5 286 48N06 53w44 3:34:56
Highgate 9 1 42N30 81w49 5:27:16
High Prairie 1 223 55N26 116w29 7:45:56
High River 1 223 50N35 113w52 7:35:28
Highwater 11 7 45N01 72w26 4:49:44
Hilda 1 223 50N28 110w03 7:20:12
Hillcrest Mines 1 223 49N34 114w23 7:37:32
Hillsborough 4 271 45N56 64w39 4:18:36
Hillsburgh 9 1 43N47 80w09 5:20:36
Hines Creek 1 223 56N15 118w36 7:54:24
Hinton 1 223 53N25 117w34 7:50:16
Hixon 2 266 53N27 122w36 8:10:24
Hodgeville 12 229 50N08 106w58 7:07:52
Hodgson 3 203 51N13 97w34 6:30:16
Holberg 2 266 50N31 128w01 8:32:04
Holden 1 223 53N14 112w14 7:28:56
Holdfast 12 231 50N58 105w25 7:01:40
Holland 3 203 49N32 98w55 6:35:40
Holland Landing 9 1 44N06 79w29 5:17:56
Holman Island 7 227 70N43 117w43 7:50:52
Holton 6 269 54N40 57w25 3:49:40
Hondo 1 223 55N04 114w02 7:36:08
Honeymoon Bay 2 266 48N49 124w10 8:16:40
Hooping Harbour 5 286 50N37 56w17 3:45:08
Hope 2 266 49N23 121w26 8:05:44
Hopedale 6 269 55N28 60w13 4:00:52
Hornby 9 1 43N34 79w50 5:19:20
Hornepayne 9 1 49N13 84w47 5:39:08
Horsefly 2 266 52N20 121w24 8:05:36
Hosmer 2 223 49N35 114w57 7:39:48
Houston 2 266 54N24 126w38 8:26:32
Howick 11 138 45N11 73w51 4:55:24
Howley 5 286 49N10 57w07 3:48:28
Howser 2 266 50N18 116w57 7:47:48
Hubbards 8 11 44N38 64w04 4:16:16
Huberdeau 11 135 45N58 74w38 4:58:32
Hudson 11 7 45N27 74w09 4:56:36
Hudson Bay 12 232 52N52 102w25 6:49:40
Hudson Hope 2 299 56N02 121w55 8:07:40
Hull 11 153 45N26 75w43 5:02:52
Humboldt 12 246 52N12 105w07 7:00:28
Hunter River 10 6 46N21 63w21 4:13:24
Huntingdon 2 266 49N00 122w16 8:09:04
Huntingdon 11 154 45N05 74w10 4:56:40
Huntingville 11 160 45N20 71w51 4:47:24
Huntsville 9 40 45N20 79w13 5:16:52
Hussar 1 223 51N03 112w41 7:30:44
Huttonsville 9 50 43N38 79w48 5:19:12
Huxley 1 223 51N56 113w14 7:32:56
Hydraulic 2 266 52N36 121w42 8:06:48
Hythe 1 223 55N20 119w33 7:58:12
Iberville 11 168 45N18 73w14 4:52:56
Igloolik 7 33 69N24 81w49 5:27:16
Île À la Crosse 12 228 55N27 107w53 7:11:32
Île Cadieux 11 202 45N25 74w01 4:56:04
Île Perrot 11 202 45N23 73w57 4:55:48
Ilford 3 203 56N04 95w35 6:22:20
Imperial 12 231 51N22 105w27 7:01:48
Imperial Mills 1 223 55N00 111w44 7:26:56
Indian Brook 8 11 46N23 60w32 4:02:08
Indian Head 12 247 50N32 103w40 6:54:40
Ingersoll 9 60 43N02 80w53 5:23:32
Ingleside 9 1 45N00 75w00 5:00:00
Inglewood 9 36 43N47 79w56 5:19:44
Inglis 3 203 50N57 101w15 6:45:00
Ingonish 8 11 46N42 60w22 4:01:28
Innerkip 9 1 43N13 80w42 5:22:48
Innisfail 1 223 52N02 113w57 7:35:48
Innisfree 1 223 53N22 111w32 7:26:08
Instow 12 228 49N44 108w16 7:13:04
Inuvik 7 298 68N25 133w30 8:54:00
Invermay 12 232 51N48 103w09 6:52:36
Invermere 2 223 50N30 116w02 7:44:08
Inverness 8 11 46N14 61w18 4:05:12
Inverness 11 7 46N15 71w31 4:46:04
Inwood 3 203 50N34 97w32 6:30:08
Inwood 9 1 42N49 81w59 5:27:56
Ioco 2 267 49N18 122w52 8:11:28
Iona 8 11 45N58 60w48 4:03:12
Iosegun Lake 1 223 54N29 116w50 7:47:20
Irma 1 223 52N55 111w14 7:24:56
Iron Bridge 9 1 46N17 83w14 5:32:56
Iroquois 9 1 44N51 75w19 5:01:16
Iroquois Falls 9 75 48N46 80w41 5:22:44
Irricana 1 223 51N19 113w37 7:34:28
Irvine 1 226 49N57 110w16 7:21:04

Irvines Landing 2 266 49N38 124w03 8:16:12
Island Falls 12 232 55N32 102w21 6:49:24
Island Lake 3 203 53N58 94w47 6:19:08
Isle aux Morts 5 286 47N35 58w59 3:55:56
Islets Caribou 11 297 49N30 67w14 4:28:56
Ituna 12 231 51N10 103w30 6:54:00
Ivujivik 11 7 62N24 77w55 5:11:40
Jackhead Harbour 3 203 51N52 97w16 6:29:04
Jackson Park 9 132 42N17 83w01 5:32:04
Jackson's Arm 5 286 49N52 56w47 3:47:08
Jacquet River 4 271 47N55 66w00 4:24:00
James Island 2 265 48N37 123w22 8:13:28
Jansen 12 231 51N47 104w43 6:58:52
Jarvie 1 223 54N27 113w59 7:35:56
Jarvis 9 35 42N53 80w06 5:20:24
Jasper 1 223 52N53 118w05 7:52:20
Jeune Landing 2 266 50N27 127w30 8:30:00
Joe Batt's Arm 5 286 49N44 54w10 3:36:40
Joggins 8 11 45N42 64w27 4:17:48
Johnsons Crossing 13 270 60N29 133w16 8:53:04
Joliette 11 155 46N01 73w27 4:53:48
Jonquière 11 156 48N24 71w15 4:45:00
Judique 8 11 45N52 61w30 4:06:00
Juniper 4 271 46N33 67w13 4:28:52
Juskatla 2 266 53N37 132w18 8:49:12
Kaladar 9 1 44N39 77w07 5:08:28
Kaleden 2 266 49N23 119w35 7:58:20
Kamloops 2 266 50N40 120w20 8:01:20
Kamsack 12 232 51N34 101w54 6:47:36
Kandahar 12 231 51N46 104w21 6:57:24
Kapuskasing 9 35 49N25 82w26 5:29:44
Kaslo 2 266 49N55 116w55 7:47:40
Katepwa Beach 12 229 50N42 103w38 6:54:32
Kawartha Park 9 1 44N32 78w12 5:12:48
Kedgwick 4 271 47N39 67w21 4:29:24
Keefers 2 266 50N02 121w33 8:06:12
Keels 5 286 48N36 53w24 3:33:36
Keene 9 40 44N15 78w10 5:12:40
Keewatin 9 221 49N46 94w34 6:18:16
Kegaska 11 30 50N12 61w17 4:05:08
Keg River 1 223 57N48 117w52 7:51:28
Keithley Creek 2 266 52N45 121w24 8:05:36
Kelliher 12 231 51N15 103w44 6:54:56
Kelowna 2 266 49N53 119w29 7:57:56
Kelsey Bay 2 266 50N24 125w57 8:23:48
Kelvington 12 231 52N10 103w30 6:54:00
Kemano 2 266 53N34 127w56 8:31:44
Kemptville 9 1 45N01 75w38 5:02:32
Kenaston 12 229 51N30 106w18 7:05:12
Kendal 12 231 50N15 103w37 6:54:28
Kennetcook 8 11 45N11 63w44 4:14:56
Kénogami 11 156 48N26 71w14 4:44:56
Keno Hill 13 270 63N55 135w18 9:01:12
Kenora 9 222 49N47 94w29 6:17:56
Kensington 10 6 46N26 63w38 4:14:32
Kent Bridge 9 1 42N31 82w04 5:28:16
Kentville 8 18 45N05 64w30 4:18:00
Keremeos 2 266 49N12 119w50 7:59:20
Kerrobert 12 228 51N55 109w08 7:16:32
Kersley 2 266 52N49 122w25 8:09:40
Keswick 9 1 44N15 79w28 5:17:52
Kildare (Saint Ambroise de Kildare) 11 155 46N05 73w32 4:54:08
Kildonan 2 266 49N00 125w00 8:20:00
Kilgard 2 266 49N03 122w12 8:08:48
Killaloe Station 9 35 45N33 77w25 5:09:40
Killam 1 223 52N47 111w51 7:27:24
Killarney 3 203 49N12 99w42 6:38:48
Killarney 9 1 45N58 81w31 5:26:04
Kimberley 2 223 49N41 115w59 7:43:56
Kimsquit 2 266 52N49 126w58 8:27:52
Kincaid 12 231 49N39 107w00 7:08:00
Kincardine 9 60 44N11 81w38 5:26:32
Kincolith 2 266 55N00 129w57 8:39:48
Kindersley 12 228 51N27 109w10 7:16:40
King City 9 1 43N56 79w32 5:18:08
Kingsgate 2 266 49N00 116w11 7:44:44
King's Point 5 286 49N35 56w11 3:44:44
Kingston 8 11 44N59 64w57 4:19:48
Kingston 9 76 44N14 76w30 5:06:00
Kingston Mills 9 76 44N17 76w27 5:05:48
Kingsville 9 1 42N02 82w45 5:31:00
Kinistino 12 230 52N57 105w00 7:00:00
Kinmount 9 35 44N47 78w39 5:14:36
Kinnaird 2 266 49N17 117w39 7:50:36
Kinuso 1 223 55N20 115w25 7:41:40
Kipling 12 232 50N10 102w38 6:50:32
Kirkland 11 138 45N27 73w52 4:55:28
Kirkland Lake 9 77 48N09 80w02 5:20:08
Kisbey 12 203 49N38 102w41 6:50:44
Kispiox 2 266 55N21 127w41 8:30:44
Kississing 3 203 55N07 101w07 6:44:28
Kitchener 9 78 43N27 80w29 5:21:56
Kitimat 2 266 54N03 128w33 8:34:12
Kitscoty 1 223 53N20 110w20 7:21:20
Kitwanga 2 266 55N06 128w03 8:32:12
Kleena Kleene 2 266 51N58 124w59 8:19:56
Kleinburg 9 1 43N50 79w38 5:18:32
Klemtu 2 266 52N36 128w31 8:34:04
Koidern 13 301 61N58 140w25 9:21:40
Koksilah 2 266 48N40 123w38 8:14:32
Komoka 9 35 42N57 81w26 5:25:44
Krydor 12 228 52N47 107w03 7:08:12
Kyle 12 228 50N50 108w02 7:12:08
Kyuquot 2 266 50N02 127w23 8:29:32
La Baie 11 7 48N19 70w53 4:43:32
Labelle 11 7 46N16 74w44 4:58:56
Labrador City 6 9 52N57 66w55 4:27:40
La Broquerie 3 203 49N28 96w27 6:25:48
L'Acadie 11 168 45N19 73w21 4:53:24
Lac À la Tortue 11 152 46N37 72w38 4:50:32
Lac Allard 11 297 50N38 63w28 4:13:52
Lac Bellemare 11 7 46N34 72w55 4:51:40
Lac Brome 11 179 45N13 72w31 4:50:04
Lac Etchemin 11 7 46N24 70w30 4:42:00
Lac Frontière 11 7 46N42 70w00 4:40:00
Lachine 11 151 45N26 73w40 4:54:40
Lachute 11 157 45N38 74w20 4:57:20
Lac la Biche 1 223 54N46 111w58 7:27:52
Lac la Hache 2 266 51N49 121w28 8:05:52
Lac Masson 11 7 46N02 74w04 4:56:16
Lac Mégantic 11 198 45N36 70w53 4:43:32
Lacolle 11 7 45N05 73w22 4:53:28
Lacombe 1 223 52N28 113w44 7:34:56
Lac Saguay 11 7 46N30 75w09 5:00:36
Lac Seul 9 3 50N20 92w16 6:09:04
Ladner 2 267 49N05 123w05 8:12:20
Ladysmith 2 266 48N58 123w49 8:15:16
Laflèche 11 151 45N30 73w28 4:53:52
Laflèche 12 231 49N43 106w35 7:06:20
Lafontaine 11 167 45N48 74w01 4:56:04
La Guadeloupe (Saint Evariste) 11 7 45N57 70w56 4:43:44
Lajord 12 238 50N14 104w09 6:56:36
Lake Cowichan 2 266 48N50 124w03 8:16:12
Lake Errock 2 266 49N13 122w02 8:08:08
Lakefield 9 40 44N26 78w16 5:13:04
Lake Harbour 7 33 62N51 69w53 4:39:32
Lake Louise 1 223 51N26 116w11 7:44:44
Lake Megantic 11 198 45N36 70w53 4:43:32
Lakeside 8 12 44N38 63w41 4:14:44
La Loche 12 228 56N29 109w27 7:17:48
La Malbaie 11 141 47N39 70w10 4:40:40
Lamaline 5 286 46N52 55w49 3:43:16
Lambeth 9 1 42N54 81w18 5:25:12
Lamèque 4 271 47N47 64w38 4:18:32
La Minerve 11 7 46N15 74w56 4:59:44
Lamming Mills 2 266 53N22 120w18 8:01:12
Lamont 1 223 53N46 112w48 7:31:12
Lampman 12 203 49N23 102w45 6:51:00
Lanark 9 1 45N01 76w22 5:05:28
Lancaster 9 1 45N08 74w30 4:58:00
Landis 12 228 52N12 108w28 7:13:52
Lang 12 238 49N56 104w23 6:57:32
Langbank 12 203 50N05 102w20 6:49:20
Lang Bay 2 266 49N47 124w21 8:17:24
Langenburg 12 203 50N50 101w43 6:46:52
Langford 2 265 48N27 123w30 8:14:00
Langham 12 264 52N22 106w57 7:07:48
Langley 2 267 49N06 122w39 8:10:36
Langruth 3 203 50N24 98w38 6:34:32
Langton 9 1 42N45 80w35 5:22:20
Lanigan 12 231 51N52 105w02 7:00:08
L'Annonciation 11 7 46N25 74w52 4:59:28
Lanoraie 11 7 45N58 73w13 4:52:52
Lansdowne 9 35 44N24 76w01 5:04:04
Lantzville 2 266 49N15 124w05 8:16:20
La Patrie 11 7 45N24 71w15 4:45:00
La Pocatière 11 7 47N22 68w41 4:34:44
La Prairie 11 151 45N25 73w30 4:54:00
Lardeau 2 266 50N09 116w57 7:47:48
L'Ardoise 8 11 45N37 60w45 4:03:00
Lark Harbour 5 286 49N06 58w23 3:53:32
La Ronge 12 230 55N06 105w17 7:01:08
Larrys River 8 11 45N13 61w23 4:05:32
La Salle 9 132 42N14 83w06 5:32:24
La Salle 11 151 45N26 73w38 4:54:32
La Sarre 11 158 48N48 79w12 5:16:48
L'Ascension 11 7 46N33 74w50 4:59:20
La Scie 5 286 49N57 55w36 3:42:24
Lashburn 12 248 53N08 109w36 7:18:24
L'Assomption 11 7 45N50 73w25 4:53:40
La Tabatière 11 30 50N50 58w58 3:55:52
Laterrière 11 7 48N18 71w06 4:44:24
La Tuque 11 159 47N26 72w47 4:51:08
Laurentides 11 7 45N51 73w46 4:55:04
Laurier 3 203 50N54 99w33 6:38:12
Laurier 11 135 46N32 71w38 4:46:32
Laurierville 11 7 46N18 71w39 4:46:36
Lauzon 11 164 46N50 71w10 4:44:40
Laval 11 151 45N35 73w45 4:55:00
Lavaltrie 11 7 45N53 73w17 4:53:08
Lavillette 4 271 47N16 65w18 4:21:12
Lawn 5 286 46N57 55w32 3:42:08
Leader 12 228 50N53 109w31 7:18:04
Leamington 9 1 42N03 82w36 5:30:24
Leaside 9 79 43N42 79w22 5:17:28
Leask 12 229 53N00 106w45 7:07:00
Leduc 1 225 53N16 113w33 7:34:12
Leechtown 2 266 48N30 123w42 8:14:48
Lefroy 9 1 44N16 79w34 5:18:16
Legal 1 225 53N57 113w35 7:34:20
Leinan 12 228 50N30 107w46 7:11:04
Lemberg 12 231 50N44 103w13 6:52:52
LeMoyne 11 151 45N31 73w29 4:53:56
Lennoxville 11 160 45N22 71w51 4:47:24
Leoville 12 228 53N37 107w35 7:10:20
L'Épiphanie 11 7 45N51 73w30 4:54:00
Léry 11 138 45N21 73w48 4:55:12
Les Écureuils 11 191 46N39 71w43 4:46:52
Lester Pearson Intl Airport 9 124 43N40 79w37 5:18:28
Lestock 12 231 51N18 104w00 6:56:00
Lethbridge 1 223 49N42 112w50 7:31:20
Lethbridge 5 286 48N21 53w52 3:35:28
Levack 9 1 46N38 81w23 5:25:32
Lévis 11 164 46N48 71w11 4:44:44
Lewisporte 5 286 49N15 55w03 3:40:12
Lewisville 4 4 46N06 64w46 4:19:04
Lewvan 12 231 50N00 104w06 6:56:24
Likely 2 266 52N37 121w34 8:06:16
Lillooet 2 266 50N42 121w56 8:07:44
Limerick 12 231 49N40 106w15 7:05:00
Limoges 9 1 45N20 75w15 5:01:00
Lincoln 9 70 43N10 79w29 5:17:56
Lindsay 9 80 44N21 78w44 5:14:56
Lion's Head 9 1 44N59 81w15 5:25:00
Lipton 12 238 50N54 103w50 6:55:20
Lisieux 12 231 49N17 105w59 7:03:56
Lismore 8 11 45N42 62w16 4:09:04
Listowel 9 36 43N44 80w57 5:23:48
Little Bay Islands 5 286 49N39 55w47 3:43:08
Little Bullhead 3 203 51N40 96w51 6:27:24
Little Catalina 5 286 48N33 53w02 3:32:08
Little Current 9 1 45N58 81w56 5:27:44
Little Fort 2 266 51N25 120w12 8:00:48
Little Harbour Deep 5 286 50N15 56w33 3:46:12
Lively 9 119 46N26 81w09 5:24:36
Liverpool 8 19 44N02 64w43 4:18:52
Lloydminster 1 248 53N17 110w00 7:20:00
Lloydminster 12 248 53N17 110w00 7:20:00
Lockeport 8 20 43N42 65w07 4:20:28
Lockport 3 217 50N05 96w56 6:27:44
Lodgepole 1 223 53N06 115w19 7:41:16
Lomond 1 223 50N21 112w39 7:30:36
London 9 81 42N59 81w14 5:24:56
Londonderry 8 11 45N29 63w36 4:14:24
Long Harbour 5 286 47N26 53w48 3:35:12
Longueuil 11 151 45N32 73w30 4:54:00
Longview 1 223 50N32 114w14 7:36:56
Longworth 2 266 53N55 121w28 8:05:52
Lorette 3 217 49N44 96w52 6:27:28
Loretteville 11 164 46N51 71w21 4:45:24
L'Orignal 9 1 45N37 74w42 4:58:48
Lorne 4 271 47N53 66w08 4:24:32
Louisbourg 8 11 45N55 59w58 3:59:52
Louisdale 8 11 45N36 61w04 4:04:16
Louiseville 11 7 46N15 72w57 4:51:48
Louisville 9 1 42N28 82w07 5:28:28
Lourdes 5 286 48N39 59w00 3:56:00
Love 12 249 53N29 104w09 6:56:36
Low 11 7 45N48 75w57 5:03:48
Lower Post 2 266 59N55 128w30 8:34:00
Lower West Pubnico 8 11 43N38 65w48 4:23:12
Lower Wood's Harbour 8 11 43N31 65w44 4:22:56
Lucan 9 82 43N11 81w24 5:25:36
Lucknow 9 36 43N57 81w31 5:26:04
Lucky Lake 12 228 51N00 107w10 7:08:40
Lumby 2 266 50N15 118w58 7:55:52
Lumsden 5 286 49N19 53w37 3:34:28
Lumsden 12 238 50N34 104w53 6:59:32
Lund 2 266 49N58 124w44 8:18:56
Lundar 3 203 50N42 98w02 6:32:08
Lunenburg 8 21 44N23 64w19 4:17:16
Luscar 1 223 53N04 117w24 7:49:36
Luseland 12 228 52N05 109w30 7:18:00
Lyn 9 1 44N35 75w47 5:03:08
Lynden 9 40 43N14 80w09 5:20:36
Lynn Lake 3 203 56N51 101w03 6:44:12

Lynn Valley 2	267	49N23	123w01	8:12:04
Lyster Station 11	7	46N22	71w37	4:46:28
Lytton 2	266	50N14	121w34	8:06:16
Mabou 8	11	46N05	61w22	4:05:28
Macalister 2	266	52N27	122w24	8:09:36
Macamic 11	135	48N46	79w00	5:16:00
MacGregor 3	203	49N57	98w49	6:35:16
Macklin 12	228	52N20	109w56	7:19:44
MacTier 9	1	45N08	79w47	5:19:08
Madawaska 9	1	45N30	77w59	5:11:56
Madeleine Centre 11	288	49N15	65w21	4:21:24
Madoc 9	83	44N30	77w28	5:09:52
Madsen 9	3	50N58	93w55	6:15:40
Mafeking 3	203	52N41	101w06	6:44:24
Magnet 3	203	51N19	99w30	6:38:00
Magog 11	190	45N16	72w09	4:48:36
Magpie 11	297	50N19	64w30	4:18:00
Magrath 1	223	49N25	112w52	7:31:28
Mahone Bay 8	11	44N27	64w23	4:17:32
Mahood Falls 2	266	51N50	120w39	8:02:36
Maidstone 9	132	42N13	82w53	5:31:32
Maidstone 12	228	53N06	109w18	7:17:12
Maitland 8	11	45N19	63w30	4:14:00
Maitland 9	1	44N38	75w37	5:02:28
Malagash 8	11	45N46	63w23	4:13:32
Malahat 2	265	48N32	123w34	8:14:16
Malartic 11	135	48N08	78w08	5:12:32
Mallaig 1	223	54N13	111w22	7:25:28
Mallorytown 9	1	44N29	75w53	5:03:32
Ma-Me-O Beach 1	223	52N58	113w59	7:35:56
Mandeville 11	7	46N22	73w22	4:53:28
Manigotagan 3	203	51N06	96w18	6:25:12
Manitou 3	203	49N15	98w31	6:34:04
Manitou Beach 12	229	51N43	105w26	7:01:44
Manitowaning 9	1	45N45	81w49	5:27:16
Maniwaki 11	7	46N23	75w58	5:03:52
Mankota 12	231	49N25	107w04	7:08:16
Mannville 1	223	53N20	111w10	7:24:40
Manor 12	203	49N36	102w05	6:48:20
Manotick 9	95	45N13	75w41	5:02:44
Manseau 11	7	46N22	72w00	4:48:00
Mansonville 11	7	45N03	72w23	4:49:32
Manyberries 1	223	49N24	110w42	7:22:48
Maple Bay 2	266	48N49	123w36	8:14:24
Maple Creek 12	223	49N55	109w27	7:17:48
Maple Grove 9	40	43N55	78w44	5:14:56
Maple Grove 11	138	45N19	73w50	4:55:20
Maple Ridge 2	267	49N13	122w36	8:10:24
Marathon 9	1	48N40	86w25	5:45:40
Marbleton 11	194	45N37	71w35	4:46:20
Marcelin 12	229	52N55	106w47	7:07:08
Margaree 8	11	46N24	61w05	4:04:20
Margaree Harbour 8	11	46N26	61w07	4:04:28
Margaret Bay 2	266	51N20	127w29	8:29:56
Maricourt (Wakeham Bay) 11	7	61N36	71w58	4:47:52
Marieville 11	168	45N26	73w10	4:52:40
Markdale 9	1	44N19	80w39	5:22:36
Markham 9	40	43N52	79w16	5:17:04
Marlboro 1	223	53N33	116w45	7:47:00
Marmora 9	36	44N29	77w41	5:10:44
Martintown 9	1	45N09	74w42	4:58:48
Marwayne 1	223	53N32	110w20	7:21:20
Maryfield 12	203	49N48	101w32	6:46:08
Marystown 5	286	47N10	55w09	3:40:36
Marysville 2	223	49N38	115w57	7:43:48
Marysville 4	276	45N59	66w35	4:26:20
Mascouche 11	151	45N45	73w36	4:54:24
Masefield 12	231	49N09	107w48	7:11:12
Mason Creek 2	266	55N40	124w29	8:17:56
Masset 2	266	54N02	132w09	8:48:36
Massey 9	1	46N12	82w05	5:28:20
Matachewan 9	1	47N56	80w39	5:22:36
Matane 11	290	48N51	67w32	4:30:08
Matapédia 11	291	47N58	66w57	4:27:48
Mather 3	203	49N06	99w07	6:36:28
Matheson 9	46	48N32	80w28	5:21:52
Matheson Island 3	203	51N44	96w56	6:27:44
Matsqui 2	266	49N12	122w25	8:09:40
Mattagami Heights 9	1	48N29	81w22	5:25:28
Mattawa 9	1	46N19	78w42	5:14:48
Maxville 9	35	45N17	74w51	4:59:24
Mayerthorpe 1	223	53N57	115w08	7:40:32
Maymont 12	228	52N33	107w40	7:10:40
Mayne 2	266	48N51	123w18	8:13:12
Mayo 13	270	63N35	135w54	9:03:36
Mayo Landing 13	270	63N36	135w51	9:03:24
Mazenod 12	238	49N53	106w14	7:04:56
McAdam 4	278	45N36	67w20	4:29:20
McAuley 3	203	50N16	101w23	6:45:32
McBride 2	266	53N18	120w10	8:00:40
McCallum 5	286	47N38	56w15	3:45:00
McCreary 3	203	50N46	99w30	6:38:00
McGregor 9	132	42N09	82w58	5:31:52
McKenzie Island 9	3	51N05	93w48	6:15:12
McLean 12	236	50N30	104w04	6:56:16
McLennan 1	223	55N42	116w54	7:47:36
McLeod Lake 2	266	54N59	123w02	8:12:08
McLure 2	266	51N03	120w14	8:00:56
McMahon 12	228	50N05	107w32	7:10:08
McMasterville 11	7	45N33	73w15	4:53:00
Meacham 12	229	52N08	105w45	7:03:00
Meadow Lake 12	228	54N08	108w26	7:13:44
Meaford 9	36	44N36	80w35	5:22:20
Meaghers Grant 8	11	44N55	63w15	4:13:00
Meander River 1	223	59N02	117w42	7:50:48
Medicine Hat 1	226	50N03	110w40	7:22:40
Medstead 12	228	53N19	108w02	7:12:08
Meductic 4	271	46N00	67w29	4:29:56
Mégantic 11	198	45N36	70w53	4:43:32
Melbourne 9	1	42N49	81w33	5:26:12
Meldrum Bay 9	1	45N56	83w07	5:32:28
Meldrum Creek 2	266	52N07	122w20	8:09:20
Melfort 12	249	52N52	104w36	6:58:24
Melita 3	203	49N16	101w00	6:44:00
Melocheville 11	138	45N19	73w56	4:55:44
Melville 12	232	50N55	102w48	6:51:12
Meota 12	228	53N02	108w27	7:13:48
Merasheen 5	286	47N25	54w21	3:37:24
Mercier (Saint Philomène) 11	138	45N19	73w45	4:55:00
Mercoal 1	223	53N10	117w05	7:48:20
Merivale Gardens 9	95	45N19	75w44	5:02:56
Merlin 9	1	42N14	82w14	5:28:56
Merrickville 9	1	44N55	75w50	5:03:20
Merritt 2	266	50N07	120w47	8:03:08
Merritton 9	110	43N08	79w13	5:16:52
Mervin 12	228	53N20	108w53	7:15:32
Mesachie Lake 2	266	48N49	124w07	8:16:28
Metcalfe 9	1	45N14	75w28	5:01:52
Metchosin 2	265	48N22	123w33	8:14:12
Meteghan 8	11	44N11	66w10	4:24:40
Metiskow 1	223	52N24	110w38	7:22:32
Metlakatla 2	266	54N20	130w27	8:41:48
Meyronne 12	231	49N39	106w50	7:07:20
Miami 3	203	49N21	98w11	6:32:44
Miami Beach 9	1	44N13	79w29	5:17:56
Michel 2	223	49N43	114w49	7:39:16
Midale 12	250	49N22	103w27	6:53:48
Middle Bay 11	30	51N28	57w30	3:50:00
Middlebro 3	203	49N01	95w21	6:21:24
Middle Brook 5	286	48N45	54w13	3:36:52
Middle Musquodoboit 8	11	45N03	63w09	4:12:36
Middle Stewiacke 8	11	45N13	63w08	4:12:32
Middleton 8	11	44N57	65w04	4:20:16
Midgic 4	271	45N59	64w18	4:17:12
Midhurst 9	1	44N27	79w44	5:18:56
Midland 9	60	44N45	79w53	5:19:32
Midnapore 1	224	50N55	114w05	7:36:20
Milden 12	228	51N30	107w31	7:10:04
Mildmay 9	36	44N03	81w07	5:24:28
Mile Seven Hundred Thirty Three 13	270	60N03	131w07	8:44:28
Milestone 12	251	50N00	104w30	6:58:00
Milford Station 8	11	45N03	63w26	4:13:44
Milk River 1	223	49N09	112w05	7:28:20
Mill Bay 2	265	48N39	123w34	8:14:16
Millbrook 9	37	44N09	78w27	5:13:48
Millertown 5	286	48N49	56w33	3:46:12
Millertown Junction 5	286	49N01	56w21	3:45:24
Millet 1	223	53N06	113w28	7:33:52
Milliken 9	1	43N49	79w18	5:17:12
Millstream 2	265	48N30	123w31	8:14:04
Milner 2	266	49N20	122w42	8:10:48
Milo 1	223	50N34	112w53	7:31:32
Milton 9	84	43N31	79w53	5:19:32
Milverton 9	85	43N34	80w55	5:23:40
Mindemoya 9	1	45N44	82w10	5:28:40
Minden 9	1	44N55	78w43	5:14:52
Mine Centre 9	3	48N45	92w37	6:10:28
Mingan 11	297	50N18	64w02	4:16:08
Miniota 3	203	50N08	101w00	6:44:00
Minitonas 3	203	52N07	101w00	6:44:00
Minnedosa 3	203	50N14	99w51	6:39:24
Minto 3	203	49N25	100w01	6:40:04
Minto 4	271	46N05	66w05	4:24:20
Minto 13	300	62N34	136w51	9:07:24
Minton 12	231	49N05	105w35	7:02:20
Mirror 1	223	52N28	113w07	7:32:28
Miscou Centre 4	271	47N57	64w34	4:18:16
Mission City 2	266	49N08	122w18	8:09:12
Mississauga 9	86	43N35	79w37	5:18:28
Mistatim 12	249	52N52	103w22	6:53:28
Mitchell 9	36	43N28	81w12	5:24:48
Mitchell Corners 9	40	43N57	78w48	5:15:12
Moberly Lake 2	299	55N48	121w45	8:07:00
Moisie 11	297	50N11	66w05	4:24:20
Molanosa 12	230	54N30	105w33	7:02:12
Moncton 4	4	46N06	64w47	4:19:08
Monkton 9	1	43N35	81w05	5:24:20
Mono Road Station 9	1	43N51	79w51	5:19:24
Montague 10	6	46N10	62w39	4:10:36
Montauban Les Mines 11	7	46N50	72w20	4:49:20
Montebello 11	7	45N39	74w56	4:59:44
Monte Creek 2	266	50N39	119w57	7:59:48
Mont Joli 11	292	48N35	68w11	4:32:44
Mont Laurier 11	7	46N33	75w30	5:02:00
Montmagny 11	199	46N59	70w33	4:42:12
Montréal 11	151	45N31	73w34	4:54:16
Montréal Est 11	151	45N38	73w31	4:54:04
Montreal Lake 12	230	54N03	105w46	7:03:04
Montréal Nord 11	151	45N36	73w38	4:54:32
Mont Royal 11	151	45N31	73w39	4:54:36
Mont Saint Hilaire 11	7	45N34	73w12	4:52:48
Moose Creek 9	35	45N15	74w58	4:59:52
Moose Heights 2	266	53N05	122w30	8:10:00
Moose Jaw 12	252	50N23	105w32	7:02:08
Moose Lake 3	203	53N43	100w20	6:41:20
Moosomin 12	203	50N07	101w40	6:46:40
Moosonee 9	46	51N17	80w39	5:22:36
Morden 3	203	49N11	98w05	6:32:20
Morell 10	6	46N25	62w42	4:10:48
Morinville 1	225	53N48	113w39	7:34:36
Morpeth 9	1	42N23	81w51	5:27:24
Morrin 1	223	51N40	112w47	7:31:08
Morris 3	203	49N21	97w22	6:29:28
Morrisburg 9	35	44N54	75w11	5:00:44
Morse 12	228	50N25	107w03	7:08:12
Morson 9	3	49N03	94w18	6:17:12
Mortlach 12	231	50N28	106w03	7:04:12
Mosers River 8	11	44N59	62w15	4:09:00
Mossbank 12	231	49N55	105w59	7:03:56
Mossleigh 1	223	50N43	113w20	7:33:20
Mountain Park 1	223	52N55	117w14	7:48:56
Mount Albert 9	36	44N08	79w19	5:17:16
Mount Brydges 9	35	42N54	81w29	5:25:56
Mount Carmel 5	286	47N09	53w29	3:33:56
Mount Charles 9	50	43N41	79w40	5:18:40
Mount Forest 9	36	43N59	80w44	5:22:56
Mount Hope 9	1	43N09	79w55	5:19:40
Mount Pleasant 9	40	43N05	80w19	5:21:16
Mount Stewart 10	6	46N22	62w52	4:11:28
Mount Uniacke 8	11	44N54	63w50	4:15:20
Moyie 2	223	49N17	115w50	7:43:20
Mulgrave 8	11	45N37	61w23	4:05:32
Mundare 1	223	53N36	112w20	7:29:20
Munson 1	223	51N34	112w45	7:31:00
Murray Bay → La Malbaie 11	141	47N39	70w10	4:40:40
Murray Harbour 10	6	46N00	62w31	4:10:04
Murrayville 2	266	49N10	122w36	8:10:24
Musgrave 2	266	48N45	123w32	8:14:08
Musgravetown 5	286	48N24	53w53	3:35:32
Musquodoboit Harbour 8	11	44N47	63w09	4:12:36
Mutton Bay 11	30	50N47	59w02	3:56:08
Myrnam 1	223	53N40	111w14	7:24:56
Nachvak 6	269	59N03	63w53	4:15:32
Naicam 12	231	52N25	104w30	6:58:00
Nain 6	269	56N32	61w41	4:06:44
Nakina 9	1	50N10	86w42	5:46:48
Nakusp 2	266	50N15	117w48	7:51:12
Nampa 1	223	56N02	117w08	7:48:32
Namu 2	266	51N49	127w52	8:31:28
Namur 11	7	45N54	74w56	4:59:44
Nanaimo 2	266	49N10	123w56	8:15:44
Nanoose Bay 2	266	49N16	124w12	8:16:48
Nanton 1	223	50N21	113w46	7:35:04
Napanee 9	87	44N15	76w57	5:07:48
Napierville 11	7	45N11	73w25	4:53:40
Napinka 3	203	49N17	100w50	6:43:20
Naramata 2	266	49N36	119w35	7:58:20
Nashville 9	1	43N50	79w40	5:18:40
Nashwaaksis 4	276	45N59	66w39	4:26:36
Natal 2	223	49N44	114w50	7:39:20
Natashquan 11	30	50N12	61w49	4:07:16
Naughton 9	119	46N24	81w12	5:24:48
Neepawa 3	203	50N13	99w29	6:37:56
Neguac 4	271	47N15	65w05	4:20:20
Neidpath 12	228	50N08	107w15	7:09:00
Neilburg 12	228	52N50	109w38	7:18:32
Nelson 2	266	49N29	117w17	7:49:08
Nelson House 3	203	55N47	98w51	6:35:24
Neudorf 12	232	50N44	102w59	6:51:56
Neustadt 9	36	44N05	81w00	5:24:00
Newboro 9	1	44N39	76w19	5:05:16
Newbrook 1	223	54N19	112w57	7:31:48
Newburgh 9	40	44N19	76w52	5:07:28
Newbury 9	35	42N41	81w48	5:27:12

New Carlisle 11 288 48N01 65w20 4:21:20
Newcastle 4 279 47N00 65w34 4:22:16
Newcastle 9 88 43N55 78w35 5:14:20
Newcastle Mine 1 223 51N28 112w46 7:31:04
New Dayton 1 223 49N25 112w23 7:29:32
New Denver 2 266 49N59 117w22 7:49:28
New Dundee 9 60 43N21 80w31 5:22:04
Newgate 2 223 49N00 115w10 7:40:40
New Germany 8 11 44N33 64w43 4:18:52
New Glasgow 8 31 45N35 62w39 4:10:36
New Hamburg 9 36 43N23 80w42 5:22:48
New Hazelton 2 266 55N15 127w35 8:30:20
New Liskeard 9 89 47N30 79w40 5:18:40
Newmarket 9 186 44N03 79w28 5:17:52
New Norway 1 223 52N53 112w58 7:31:52
Newport 11 288 48N16 64w45 4:19:00
New Richmond 11 288 48N10 65w52 4:23:28
New Road 8 11 44N45 63w28 4:13:52
New Ross 8 11 44N44 64w27 4:17:48
Newtonville 9 40 43N56 78w30 5:14:00
Newtown 5 286 49N12 53w31 3:34:04
New Waterford 8 11 46N15 60w05 4:00:20
New Westminster 2 267 49N12 122w54 8:11:36
Niagara Falls 9 90 43N06 79w04 5:16:16
Niagara on the Lake 9 91 43N15 79w04 5:16:16
Nicola 2 266 50N10 120w40 8:02:40
Nicolet 11 161 46N13 72w37 4:50:28
Ninette 3 203 49N22 99w43 6:38:52
Ninga 3 203 49N13 99w51 6:39:24
Nipawin 12 249 53N22 104w00 6:56:00
Nipigon 9 1 49N01 88w16 5:53:04
Nippers Harbour 5 286 49N48 55w52 3:43:28
Nithi River 2 266 54N01 125w01 8:20:04
Nitinat 2 266 48N55 124w29 8:17:56
Niverville 3 217 49N37 97w01 6:28:04
Nobel 9 1 45N25 80w06 5:20:24
Nobleton 9 1 43N54 79w40 5:18:40
Nokomis 12 241 51N30 105w00 7:00:00
Nominingue 11 7 46N24 75w02 5:00:08
Noralee 2 266 53N59 126w26 8:25:44
Noranda 11 162 48N15 79w02 5:16:08
Nordegg 1 223 52N28 116w04 7:44:16
Norland 9 1 44N43 78w49 5:15:16
Norman Wells 7 298 65N17 126w51 8:27:24
Norquay 12 232 51N53 102w05 6:48:20
Norris Arm 5 286 49N05 55w15 3:41:00
Norris Point 5 286 49N31 57w53 3:51:32
North Aulatsivik Island 6 269 59N50 64w00 4:16:00
North Battleford 12 253 52N47 108w17 7:13:08
North Bay 9 92 46N19 79w28 5:17:52
North Bend 2 266 49N53 121w27 8:05:48
Northbrook 9 1 44N44 77w10 5:08:40
Northern Arm 5 286 49N10 55w23 3:41:32
Northfield 2 266 49N11 123w59 8:15:56
North Glanford 9 1 43N11 79w54 5:19:36
North Gower 9 1 45N08 75w43 5:02:52
North Portal 12 203 49N00 102w33 6:50:12
North Rustico 10 6 46N27 63w19 4:13:16
North Sydney 8 22 46N13 60w15 4:01:00
North Vancouver 2 267 49N19 123w04 8:12:16
North West River 6 269 53N32 60w08 4:00:32
North Woodslee 9 1 42N13 82w43 5:30:52
North York 9 124 43N46 79w25 5:17:40
Norton 4 271 45N38 65w42 4:22:48
Nortonville 9 50 43N43 79w44 5:18:56
Norval 9 50 43N39 79w51 5:19:24
Norway House 3 203 53N59 97w50 6:31:20
Norwich 9 36 42N59 80w36 5:22:24
Norwood 9 1 44N23 77w59 5:11:56
Notre Dame 4 271 46N19 64w43 4:18:52
Notre Dame de Lourdes 3 203 49N32 98w33 6:34:12
Notre Dame de Pierreville 11 7 46N06 72w53 4:51:32
Notre Dame du Laus 11 7 46N05 75w37 5:02:28
Notre Dame du Nord 11 7 47N36 79w30 5:18:00
Nouvelle 11 288 48N08 66w19 4:25:16
Novar 9 36 45N27 79w15 5:17:00
Nutak 6 269 57N30 62w05 4:08:20
Oak Bay 2 265 48N27 123w18 8:13:12
Oakburn 3 203 50N35 100w32 6:42:08
Oak Lake 3 203 49N47 100w38 6:42:32
Oakland 9 1 42N09 82w36 5:30:24
Oak Point 3 203 50N30 98w00 6:32:00
Oakview Beach 9 1 44N29 80w03 5:20:12
Oakville 3 203 49N56 97w58 6:31:52
Oakville 9 45 43N27 79w41 5:18:44
Oakwood 9 1 44N20 78w53 5:15:32
Obed 1 223 53N33 117w12 7:48:48
Ocean Falls 2 266 52N21 127w40 8:30:40
Ocean Park 2 267 49N02 122w53 8:11:32
Ochre River 3 203 51N03 99w47 6:39:08
Odessa 9 40 44N17 76w43 5:06:52
Ogema 12 243 49N35 104w55 6:59:40
Oil Springs 9 1 42N47 82w07 5:28:28
Okanagan Centre 2 266 50N03 119w27 7:57:48
Okanagan Falls 2 266 49N21 119w34 7:58:16
Okanagan Landing 2 266 50N14 119w22 7:57:28
Okkak 6 269 57N31 61w56 4:07:44
Okotoks 1 224 50N44 113w59 7:35:56
Old Crow 13 301 67N35 139w50 9:19:20
Old Fort Bay 11 30 51N26 57w49 3:51:16
Old Perlican 5 286 48N05 53w01 3:32:04
Olds 1 223 51N47 114w06 7:36:24
O'Leary 10 6 46N42 64w13 4:16:52
Oliver 2 266 49N11 119w33 7:58:12
Omagh 9 1 43N30 79w49 5:19:16
Omemee 9 36 44N18 78w33 5:14:12
Omerville 11 190 45N17 72w07 4:48:28
One Hundred Fifty Mile House 2 266 52N07 121w56 8:07:44
One Hundred Mile House 2 266 51N39 121w18 8:05:12
Onoway 1 223 53N42 114w12 7:36:48
Oona River 2 266 53N57 130w18 8:41:12
Ootsa Lake 2 266 53N47 126w03 8:24:12
Opasquia 9 3 53N16 93w35 6:14:20
Optic Lake 3 203 54N46 101w13 6:44:52
Orangeville 9 93 43N55 80w06 5:20:24
Orillia 9 187 44N37 79w25 5:17:40
Orkney 12 228 49N08 107w55 7:11:40
Orléans 9 95 45N28 75w31 5:02:04
Ormiston 12 231 49N45 105w22 7:01:28
Ormstown 11 135 45N08 74w00 4:56:00
Oromocto 4 276 45N51 66w29 4:25:56
Orono 9 40 43N59 78w37 5:14:28
Orwell 9 1 42N46 81w02 5:24:08
Osgoode 9 1 45N08 75w36 5:02:24
Oshawa 9 94 43N54 78w51 5:15:24
Osoyoos 2 266 49N02 119w28 7:57:52
Ottawa 9 95 45N25 75w42 5:02:48
Otterburne 3 203 49N30 97w03 6:28:12
Otterburn Park 11 7 45N33 73w13 4:52:52
Otter Lake 11 7 45N51 76w26 5:05:44
Otterville 9 1 42N55 80w36 5:22:24
Outlook 12 228 51N30 107w03 7:08:12
Outremont 11 151 45N31 73w38 4:54:32
Owen Sound 9 96 44N34 80w56 5:23:44
Oxbow 12 203 49N14 102w11 6:48:44
Oxford 8 32 45N44 63w52 4:15:28
Oxford House 3 203 54N56 95w16 6:21:04
Oyama 2 266 50N07 119w22 7:57:28
Oyen 1 223 51N22 110w28 7:21:52
Pacific 2 266 54N46 128w17 8:33:08
Pacquet 5 286 49N59 55w53 3:43:32
Paddle Prairie 1 223 57N57 117w29 7:49:56
Paincourt 9 1 42N23 82w17 5:29:08
Paisley 9 83 44N18 81w16 5:25:04
Pakenham 9 1 45N20 76w17 5:05:08
Paldi 2 266 48N48 123w51 8:15:24
Palling 2 266 54N21 125w55 8:23:40
Palmerston 9 35 43N50 80w51 5:23:24
Pangman 12 243 49N39 104w39 6:58:32
Pangnirtung 7 10 66N08 65w44 4:22:56
Papineauville 11 7 45N37 75w01 5:00:04
Paradise Hill 12 228 53N32 109w28 7:17:52
Parent 11 7 47N55 74w37 4:58:28
Paris 9 40 43N12 80w23 5:21:32
Parkdale 10 28 46N15 63w07 4:12:28
Parkhill 9 36 43N09 81w41 5:26:44
Parksville 2 266 49N19 124w19 8:17:16
Parrsboro 8 11 45N24 64w20 4:17:20
Parry Sound 9 97 45N21 80w02 5:20:08
Parson's Pond 5 286 50N02 57w43 3:50:52
Pasadena 5 286 49N01 57w36 3:50:24
Pass Island 5 286 47N29 56w11 3:44:44
Pavilion 2 266 50N52 121w50 8:07:20
Paynton 12 228 53N01 108w56 7:15:44
Peace River 1 223 56N14 117w17 7:49:08
Peachland 2 266 49N46 119w44 7:58:56
Peers 1 223 53N40 116w00 7:44:00
Peesane 12 249 52N52 103w36 6:54:24
Pefferlaw 9 35 44N19 79w12 5:16:48
Pelham 9 128 43N02 79w17 5:17:08
Pelican Narrows 12 232 55N10 102w56 6:51:44
Pelican Rapids 3 203 52N45 100w42 6:42:48
Pelly 12 232 51N52 101w55 6:47:40
Pelly Crossing 13 300 62N50 136w35 9:06:20
Pemberton 2 266 50N20 122w48 8:11:12
Pembroke 9 98 45N49 77w07 5:08:28
Pemmican Portage 12 232 53N56 102w17 6:49:08
Penetang 9 99 44N47 79w55 5:19:40
Penetanguishene 9 99 44N47 79w55 5:19:40
Penhold 1 223 52N08 113w52 7:35:28
Pennant Station 12 228 50N33 108w12 7:12:48
Penny 2 266 53N50 121w17 8:05:08
Pense 12 238 50N25 105w00 7:00:00
Penticton 2 266 49N30 119w35 7:58:20
Percé 11 288 48N31 64w13 4:16:52
Perdue 12 228 52N04 107w32 7:10:08
Perkinsfield 9 1 44N42 79w57 5:19:48
Perow 2 266 54N31 126w26 8:25:44
Perrault Falls 9 3 50N19 93w11 6:12:44
Perth 9 100 44N54 76w15 5:05:00
Perth-Andover 4 271 46N45 67w42 4:30:48
Petawawa 9 1 45N54 77w17 5:09:08
Peterborough 9 101 44N18 78w19 5:13:16
Petitcodiac 4 271 45N56 65w10 4:20:40
Petrolia 9 35 42N52 82w09 5:28:36
Petty Harbour 5 285 47N28 52w43 3:30:52
Philipsburg 11 163 45N02 73w05 4:52:20
Piapot 12 228 50N00 109w11 7:16:44
Pibroch 1 223 54N16 113w52 7:35:28
Piccadilly 5 286 48N34 58w55 3:55:40
Pickardville 1 223 54N03 113w53 7:35:32
Pickering 9 40 43N52 79w02 5:16:08
Pickering Beach 9 40 43N50 78w59 5:15:56
Pickle Crow 9 3 51N30 90w04 6:00:16
Picton 9 102 44N00 77w08 5:08:32
Pictou 8 23 45N41 62w43 4:10:52
Picture Butte 1 223 49N53 112w47 7:31:08
Pierrefonds 11 138 45N29 73w52 4:55:28
Pierreville 11 135 46N04 72w49 4:51:16
Pikangikum 9 3 51N49 94w00 6:16:00
Pikwitonei 3 203 55N35 97w09 6:28:36
Pilley's Island 5 286 49N31 55w44 3:42:56
Pilot Butte 12 255 50N28 104w25 6:57:40
Pilot Mound 3 203 49N16 98w55 6:35:40
Pincher Creek 1 223 49N29 113w57 7:35:48
Pincourt 11 202 45N23 74w00 4:56:00
Pine Beach 11 7 45N32 73w57 4:55:48
Pine Falls 3 203 50N35 96w15 6:25:00
Pine Glen 9 95 45N19 75w43 5:02:52
Pinehouse Lake 12 229 55N31 106w36 7:06:24
Pine Point 7 227 61N01 114w15 7:37:00
Pine River 3 203 51N47 100w32 6:42:08
Pioneer Mine 2 266 50N46 122w46 8:11:04
Pitt Meadows 2 267 49N13 122w41 8:10:44
Placentia 5 286 47N14 53w58 3:35:52
Plamondon 1 223 54N51 112w19 7:29:16
Plantagenet 9 1 45N32 75w00 5:00:00
Plaster Rock 4 271 46N54 67w24 4:29:36
Plattsville 9 60 43N18 80w37 5:22:28
Pleasant 9 50 43N41 79w49 5:19:16
Pleasant Bay 8 11 46N49 60w48 4:03:12
Pleasantdale 12 230 52N35 104w30 6:58:00
Plenty 12 228 51N47 108w36 7:14:24
Plessisville 11 135 46N14 71w47 4:47:08
Plumas 3 203 50N25 99w02 6:36:08
Pointe À la Frégate 11 288 49N12 64w55 4:19:40
Pointe À la Garde 11 288 48N05 66w32 4:26:08
Pointe À Maurier 11 30 50N20 59w48 3:59:12
Pointe Au Chêne 11 7 45N38 74w45 4:59:00
Pointe Aux Trembles 11 151 45N39 73w30 4:54:00
Pointe Calumet 11 7 45N30 73w58 4:55:52
Pointe Claire 11 135 45N26 73w50 4:55:20
Pointe des Cascades 11 202 45N20 73w58 4:55:52
Pointe du Moulin 11 138 45N22 73w52 4:55:28
Point Edward 9 112 43N00 82w24 5:29:36
Pointe Gatineau 11 153 45N28 75w42 5:02:48
Point Leamington 5 286 49N20 55w24 3:41:36
Point Sapin 4 271 46N58 64w50 4:19:20
Poltimore 11 7 45N47 75w43 5:02:52
Pomquet 8 11 45N38 61w51 4:07:24
Pond Inlet 7 33 72N41 78w00 5:12:00
Ponoka 1 223 52N42 113w35 7:34:20
Pontbriand 11 174 46N09 71w15 4:45:00
Ponteix 12 228 49N49 107w30 7:10:00
Pont Rouge 11 191 46N45 71w42 4:46:48
Popkum 2 266 49N12 121w44 8:06:56

Poplar Hill 9 3 52N05 94w18 6:17:12
Poplar Point 3 203 50N04 97w57 6:31:48
Portage la Prairie 3 212 49N59 98w18 6:33:12
Port Alberni 2 266 49N14 124w48 8:19:12
Port Alice 2 266 50N23 127w27 8:29:48
Port Alma 9 1 42N11 82w15 5:29:00
Port Anson 5 286 49N32 55w50 3:43:20
Port Arthur → Thunder Bay 9 121 48N23 89w15 5:57:00
Port au Port 5 286 48N33 58w44 3:54:56
Port aux Basques → Channel Port Aux Ba 286 47N34 59w09 3:56:36
Port Blandford 5 286 48N21 54w10 3:36:40
Port Borden 10 6 46N15 63w42 4:14:48
Port Burwell 9 1 42N39 80w49 5:23:16
Port Carling 9 1 45N07 79w35 5:18:20
Port Cartier Ouest 11 297 50N01 66w52 4:27:28
Port Clements 2 266 53N42 132w11 8:48:44
Port Colborne 9 103 42N53 79w14 5:16:56
Port Coquitlam 2 267 49N16 122w46 8:11:04
Port Credit 9 45 43N33 79w35 5:18:20
Port Dover 9 36 42N47 80w12 5:20:48
Port Edward 2 266 54N14 130w18 8:41:12
Port Elgin 9 36 44N26 81w24 5:25:36
Port Elgin 4 271 46N03 64w05 4:16:20
Port Essington 2 266 54N09 129w57 8:39:48
Port Greville 8 11 45N24 64w33 4:18:12
Port Hammond 2 267 49N13 122w39 8:10:36
Port Hardy 2 266 50N43 127w29 8:29:56
Port Hawkesbury 8 11 45N37 61w21 4:05:24
Port Hill 10 6 46N35 63w53 4:15:32
Port Hood 8 11 46N01 61w32 4:06:08
Port Hope 9 104 43N57 78w18 5:13:12
Port Kells 2 267 49N09 122w41 8:10:44
Port Lambton 9 1 42N39 82w30 5:30:00
Port Maitland 9 63 42N52 79w34 5:18:16
Port Maitland 8 11 43N59 66w09 4:24:36
Port Mann 2 267 49N13 122w48 8:11:12
Port McNeill 2 266 50N35 127w06 8:28:24
Port McNicoll 9 1 44N45 79w49 5:19:16
Port Mellon 2 266 49N32 123w29 8:13:56
Port Menier 11 297 49N48 64w20 4:17:20
Port Moody 2 267 49N17 122w51 8:11:24
Port Morien 8 11 46N08 59w52 3:59:28
Port Mouton 8 11 43N56 64w51 4:19:24
Port Nelson 3 203 57N03 92w36 6:10:24
Portneuf 11 191 46N42 71w53 4:47:32
Portneuf Station 11 191 46N43 71w54 4:47:36
Portneuf Sur Mer 11 295 48N37 69w06 4:36:24
Port Neville 2 266 50N29 126w05 8:24:20
Port Nouveau Québec 11 297 58N32 65w54 4:23:36
Port Perry 9 1 44N06 78w57 5:15:48
Port Radium 7 227 66N05 118w02 7:52:08
Port Renfrew 2 266 48N33 124w25 8:17:40
Port Rexton 5 286 48N23 53w20 3:33:20
Port Rowan 9 36 42N37 80w28 5:21:52
Port Saint Servan 11 30 51N19 58w02 3:52:08
Port Saunders 5 286 50N39 57w18 3:49:12
Port Simpson 2 266 54N33 130w25 8:41:40
Port Stanley 9 1 42N40 81w13 5:24:52
Portugal Cove South 5 286 46N42 53w15 3:33:00
Port Union 9 35 43N47 79w08 5:16:32
Port Union 5 286 48N30 53w05 3:32:20
Port Washington 2 266 48N49 123w19 8:13:16
Poste de la Baleine 11 7 55N17 77w45 5:11:00
Poste Mistassini 11 7 50N25 73w52 4:55:28
Pouce Coupe 2 299 55N43 120w08 8:00:32
Pouch Cove 5 285 47N46 52w46 3:31:04
Povungnituk 11 7 60N02 77w10 5:08:40
Powassan 9 36 46N05 79w22 5:17:28
Powell River 2 266 49N52 124w33 8:18:12
Prairie River 12 231 52N52 103w00 6:52:00
Preeceville 12 232 51N58 102w40 6:50:40
Prelate 12 228 50N51 109w23 7:17:32
Prémont 11 7 46N22 73w03 4:52:12
Prescott 9 105 44N43 75w31 5:02:04
Prestville 1 223 55N45 118w06 7:52:24
Prince Albert 9 1 44N05 78w58 5:15:52
Prince Albert 12 254 53N12 105w46 7:03:04
Prince George 2 266 53N55 122w45 8:11:00
Prince Rupert 2 266 54N19 130w19 8:41:16
Princeton 2 266 49N27 120w31 8:02:04
Princeton 5 286 48N25 53w36 3:34:24
Princeton 9 60 43N10 80w32 5:22:08
Princeville 11 135 46N10 71w53 4:47:32
Pritzler Harbour 7 33 62N07 67w20 4:29:20
Procter 2 266 49N37 116w57 7:47:48
Proulxville 11 7 46N40 72w30 4:50:00
Provost 1 223 52N21 110w16 7:21:04
Pubnico 8 11 43N42 65w47 4:23:08
Puce 9 1 42N18 82w47 5:31:08
Pugwash 8 11 45N51 63w40 4:14:40
Punchaw 2 266 53N28 123w13 8:12:52
Punnichy 12 231 51N23 104w18 6:57:12
Pushthrough 5 286 47N39 56w10 3:44:40
Qualicum Beach 2 266 49N21 124w27 8:17:48
Qu'Appelle 12 239 50N33 103w52 6:55:28
Québec 11 164 46N49 71w14 4:44:56
Queen Charlotte 2 266 53N16 132w05 8:48:20
Queensport 8 11 45N20 61w16 4:05:04
Queensville 9 1 44N08 79w28 5:17:52
Quesnel 2 266 52N59 122w30 8:10:00
Quill Lake 12 231 52N05 104w15 6:57:00
Quinton 12 231 51N23 104w24 6:57:36
Quyon 11 7 45N31 76w14 5:04:56
Radford 13 301 63N45 139w07 9:16:28
Radisson 12 228 52N27 107w23 7:09:32
Radium Hot Springs 2 223 50N38 116w03 7:44:12
Radville 12 243 49N27 104w17 6:57:08
Radway 1 223 54N04 112w57 7:31:48
Rae 7 227 62N50 116w03 7:44:12
Rainy River 9 3 48N43 94w29 6:17:56
Raleigh 5 286 51N34 55w44 3:42:56
Ramea 5 286 47N31 57w23 3:49:32
Rancheria 13 270 60N05 130w40 8:42:40
Rankin Inlet 7 219 62N45 92w10 6:08:40
Rapid City 3 203 50N08 100w02 6:40:08
Rathwell 3 203 49N40 98w32 6:34:08
Rattling Brook 5 286 49N38 56w10 3:44:40
Ravenscrag 12 228 49N30 109w05 7:16:20
Rawdon 11 7 46N03 73w44 4:54:56
Raymond 1 223 49N27 112w39 7:30:36
Raymore 12 255 50N25 104w31 6:58:04
Red Bay 6 269 51N44 56w25 3:45:40
Redcliff 1 226 50N05 110w47 7:23:08
Red Deer 1 223 52N16 113w48 7:35:12
Red Lake 9 3 51N03 93w49 6:15:16
Red Lake Road 9 3 49N58 93w22 6:13:28
Red Mill 11 7 46N25 72w28 4:49:52
Red Pass 2 266 52N59 118w59 7:55:56
Red Rock 9 1 48N58 88w15 5:53:00
Red Rock 2 266 53N39 122w41 8:10:44
Redstone 2 266 52N08 123w42 8:14:48
Redvers 12 203 49N33 101w39 6:46:36
Redwater 1 223 53N57 113w06 7:32:24
Refuge Cove 2 266 50N07 124w50 8:19:20
Regina 12 255 50N25 104w39 6:58:36
Regina Beach 12 258 50N47 105w00 7:00:00
Reindeer Station 7 298 68N42 134w06 8:56:24
Renata 2 266 49N26 118w06 7:52:24
Rencontre East 5 286 47N38 55w12 3:40:48
Renews 5 286 46N56 52w56 3:31:44
Renfrew 9 106 45N28 76w41 5:06:44
Rennie 3 213 49N51 95w33 6:22:12
Renous 4 271 46N49 65w48 4:23:12
Repentigny 11 151 45N44 73w28 4:53:52
Repulse Bay 7 219 66N32 86w15 5:45:00
Resolute 7 219 74N41 94w54 6:19:36
Reston 3 203 49N35 101w02 6:44:08
Revelstoke 2 266 50N59 118w12 7:52:48
Rexton 4 271 46N39 64w52 4:19:28
Rhein 12 232 51N22 102w10 6:48:40
Richan 9 3 49N59 92w49 6:11:16
Richard's Harbour 5 286 47N37 56w24 3:45:36
Richelieu 11 168 45N27 73w15 4:53:00
Richer 3 203 49N39 96w28 6:25:52
Richibucto 4 271 46N41 64w52 4:19:28
Richmond 2 267 49N10 123w10 8:12:40
Richmond 9 34 45N11 75w50 5:03:20
Richmond 11 165 45N40 72w09 4:48:36
Richmond Hill 9 107 43N52 79w27 5:17:48
Richvale 9 1 43N51 79w26 5:17:44
Ridgedale 12 249 53N04 104w09 6:56:36
Ridgetown 9 108 42N26 81w54 5:27:36
Ridgeville 3 203 49N04 97w01 6:28:04
Ridgeway 9 2 42N53 79w03 5:16:12
Rigaud 11 7 45N29 74w18 4:57:12
Rigolet 6 269 54N20 58w35 3:54:20
Rimbey 1 223 52N38 114w14 7:36:56
Rimouski 11 293 48N26 68w33 4:34:12
Riondel 2 266 49N46 116w52 7:47:28
Ripon 11 7 45N47 75w06 5:00:24
River Drive Park 9 1 44N08 79w31 5:18:04
River Hébert 8 11 45N42 64w23 4:17:32
Riverhurst 12 229 50N53 106w52 7:07:28
River John 8 11 45N45 63w03 4:12:12
River Jordan 2 266 48N25 124w03 8:16:12
River of Ponds 5 286 50N32 57w24 3:49:36
Rivers 3 203 50N02 100w12 6:40:48
Rivers Inlet 2 266 51N41 127w15 8:29:00
Riverton 3 203 50N59 96w59 6:27:56
Rivière À Claude 11 288 49N13 65w54 4:23:36
Rivière Au Tonnerre 11 297 50N16 64w47 4:19:08
Rivière Bleue 11 296 47N26 69w03 4:36:12
Rivière Bois Clair 11 191 46N34 71w50 4:47:20
Rivière de la Chaloupe 11 30 49N08 62w32 4:10:08
Rivière du Loup 11 294 47N50 69w32 4:38:08
Rivière Matane 11 288 48N39 67w20 4:29:20
Rivière Mékinac 11 7 46N47 72w48 4:51:12
Rivière Pentecôte 11 297 49N47 67w10 4:28:40
Rivière Trois Pistoles 11 295 48N07 69w10 4:36:40
Robert's Arm 5 286 49N29 55w49 3:43:16
Robertsonville 11 174 46N09 71w13 4:44:52
Roberval 11 141 48N31 72w13 4:48:52
Robinsons 5 286 48N15 58w48 3:55:12
Roblin 3 203 51N14 101w21 6:45:24
Rocanville 12 203 50N24 101w43 6:46:52
Roche Percée 12 203 49N03 102w45 6:51:00
Rock Bay 2 266 50N20 125w29 8:21:56
Rockcliffe Park 9 95 45N27 75w41 5:02:44
Rock Creek 2 266 49N06 118w58 7:55:52
Rock Forest 11 160 45N20 71w59 4:47:56
Rockglen 12 231 49N10 105w57 7:03:48
Rock Island 11 195 45N01 72w06 4:48:24
Rockwood 9 60 43N37 80w08 5:20:32
Rockyford 1 223 51N13 113w08 7:32:32
Rocky Harbour 5 286 49N36 57w55 3:51:40
Rocky Mountain House 1 223 52N22 114w55 7:39:40
Roddickton 5 286 50N52 56w08 3:44:32
Rodney 9 109 42N34 81w41 5:26:44
Rogersville 4 271 46N44 65w26 4:21:44
Roland 3 203 49N25 97w55 6:31:40
Rolla 2 299 55N54 120w09 8:00:36
Rorketon 3 203 51N26 99w32 6:38:08
Rosebank Station 9 1 43N47 79w07 5:16:28
Rose Blanche 5 286 47N37 58w41 3:54:44
Rosedale 1 223 51N25 112w38 7:30:32
Rosedale 2 266 49N11 121w48 8:07:12
Rose Lake 2 266 54N24 126w02 8:24:08
Rosemary 1 223 50N46 112w05 7:28:20
Rosemère 11 7 45N38 73w48 4:55:12
Rosetown 12 256 51N33 108w00 7:12:00
Rose Valley 12 231 52N18 103w50 6:55:20
Rossburn 3 203 50N40 100w52 6:43:28
Rosseau 9 1 45N16 79w39 5:18:36
Rossland 2 266 49N05 117w48 7:51:12
Ross River 13 270 61N59 132w27 8:49:48
Rosthern 12 229 52N40 106w17 7:05:08
Rothesay 4 280 45N23 66w00 4:24:00
Rothwell 4 271 46N04 66w04 4:24:16
Rouleau 12 238 50N11 104w55 6:59:40
Round Harbour 5 286 47N37 56w00 3:44:00
Routhierville 11 288 48N11 67w09 4:28:36
Rouyn 11 162 48N15 79w01 5:16:04
Roxboro 11 151 45N31 73w48 4:55:12
Roxton Pond (Sainte Pudentienne) 11 8 45N29 72w40 4:50:40
Royal Oak 2 265 48N30 123w23 8:13:32
Rupert House 11 7 51N30 78w45 5:15:00
Ruscom Station 9 1 42N13 82w39 5:30:36
Ruskin 2 266 49N12 122w28 8:09:52
Russell 3 203 50N47 101w15 6:45:00
Russell 9 1 45N17 75w17 5:01:08
Ruthven 9 1 42N03 82w40 5:30:40
Rutland 2 266 49N53 119w24 7:57:36
Rutter 9 1 46N06 80w40 5:22:40
Rycroft 1 223 55N45 118w43 7:54:52
Rykerts 2 266 49N00 116w35 7:46:20

Ryley 1 223 53N17 112w26 7:29:44
Sabrevois 11 168 45N12 73w14 4:52:56
Sachs Harbour 7
298 72N00 125w00 8:20:00
Sackville 4 279 45N54 64w22 4:17:28
Saddle Lake 1
223 54N00 111w40 7:26:40
Saglek Bay 6 269 58N35 63w00 4:12:00
Saglouc 11 7 62N14 75w38 5:02:32
Sahtlam 2 266 48N48 123w54 8:15:36
Saint Adrien 11
7 45N49 71w43 4:46:52
Saint Agapit 11
7 46N34 71w27 4:45:48
Saint Agatha 9
60 43N26 80w36 5:22:24
Saint Aimé (Massueville) 11
7 45N55 72w56 4:51:44
Saint Alban's 5
286 47N52 55w51 3:43:24
Saint Albert 1
225 53N38 113w38 7:34:32
Saint Albert 11
7 46N00 72w05 4:48:20
Saint Alexandre de Kamouraska 11
7 47N41 69w38 4:38:32
Saint Alexis des Monts 11
7 46N28 73w08 4:52:32
Saint André Avellin 11
7 45N43 75w03 5:00:12
Saint André Est 11
157 45N34 74w20 4:57:20
Saint Andrews 4
271 45N08 67w06 4:28:24
Saint Anselme 11
7 46N37 70w58 4:43:52
Saint Anthony 5
286 51N22 55w35 3:42:20
Saint Antoine 11
167 45N46 73w59 4:55:56
Saint Antoine 4
271 46N22 64w45 4:19:00
Saint Apollinaire (Francoeur) 11
135 46N37 71w31 4:46:04
Saint Augustin Deux Montagnes 11
167 45N38 73w59 4:55:56
Saint Augustin Saguenay 11
30 51N14 58w39 3:54:36
Saint Basile 4
271 47N21 68w14 4:32:56
Saint Basile de Portneuf 11
191 46N45 71w49 4:47:16
Saint Basile le Grand 11
7 45N32 73w17 4:53:08
Saint Bernard de Dorchester 11
7 46N30 71w08 4:44:32
Saint Blaise 11
168 45N13 73w17 4:53:08
Saint Bonaventure 11
7 45N58 72w41 4:50:44
Saint Boniface 3
214 49N55 97w06 6:28:24
Saint Boniface de Shawinigan 11
171 46N30 72w49 4:51:16
Saint Brendan's 5
286 48N52 53w40 3:34:40
Saint Bride's 5
286 46N55 54w10 3:36:40
Saint Brieux 12
230 52N38 104w52 6:59:28
Saint Bruno 11
151 45N32 73w21 4:53:24
Saint Calixte de Kilkenny 11
7 45N57 73w51 4:55:24
Saint Casimir 11
135 46N40 72w08 4:48:32
Saint Catharines 9
110 43N10 79w15 5:17:00
Saint Célestin (Annaville) 11
7 46N13 72w26 4:49:44
Saint Césaire 11
7 45N25 73w00 4:52:00
Saint Charles de Drummond 11
148 45N54 72w28 4:49:52
Saint Charles Richelieu 11
7 45N41 73w11 4:52:44
Saint Chrysostome 11
7 45N06 73w46 4:55:04
Saint Clair Beach 9
132 42N19 82w51 5:31:24
Saint Claude 3
203 49N40 98w22 6:33:28
Saint Clements 9
1 43N31 80w39 5:22:36
Saint Constant 11
151 45N22 73w37 4:54:28
Saint Cuthbert 11
135 46N09 73w14 4:52:56
Saint Cyrille de Wendover 11
148 45N56 72w26 4:49:44
Saint Damien de Brandon 11
135 46N20 73w29 4:53:56
Saint David's 5
286 48N12 58w52 3:55:28
Saint Davids 9
91 43N10 79w06 5:16:24
Saint Denis Rivière Richelieu 11
7 45N47 73w09 4:52:36
Saint Donat de Montcalm 11
7 46N19 74w13 4:56:52
Sainte Adèle 11
7 45N57 74w07 4:56:28
Sainte Agathe (de Lotbinière) 11
7 46N23 71w24 4:45:36

Sainte Agathe 3
217 49N34 97w10 6:28:40
Sainte Agathe des Monts 11
7 46N03 74w17 4:57:08
Sainte Amélie 3
203 50N59 99w21 6:37:24
Sainte Anne de Beaupré 11
135 47N02 70w56 4:43:44
Sainte Anne de Bellevue 11
202 45N24 73w57 4:55:48
Sainte Anne de la Pérade 11
7 46N35 72w12 4:48:48
Sainte Anne de Madawaska 4
271 47N15 68w02 4:32:08
Sainte Anne des Chênes 3
203 49N40 96w40 6:26:40
Sainte Anne des Monts 11
288 49N08 66w30 4:26:00
Sainte Anne des Plaines 11
7 46N46 73w48 4:55:12
Sainte Clothilde 11
7 45N59 72w14 4:48:56
Sainte Croix 11
191 46N38 71w44 4:46:56
Saint Édouard de Maskinongé 11
7 46N20 73w09 4:52:36
Sainte Félicité 11
288 48N54 67w20 4:29:20
Sainte Foy 11
164 46N47 71w17 4:45:08
Sainte Geneviève 11
138 45N29 73w52 4:55:28
Sainte Geneviève de Batiscan 11
7 46N32 72w20 4:49:20
Sainte Hélène de Bagot 11
7 45N44 72w44 4:50:56
Sainte Julie 11
7 45N35 73w19 4:53:16
Sainte Julienne 11
7 45N58 73w43 4:54:52
Saint Eleanor's 10
29 46N25 63w49 4:15:16
Saint Éleuthère 11
7 47N29 69w17 4:37:08
Saint Éloi 11
295 48N02 69w14 4:36:56
Sainte Marthe de Gaspé 11
288 49N12 66w10 4:24:40
Sainte Martine 11
138 45N15 73w48 4:55:12
Saint Émile de Montcalm 11
7 46N06 74w00 4:56:00
Saint Émile de Québec 11
164 46N52 71w20 4:45:20
Saint Émile de Suffolk 11
7 45N56 74w55 4:59:40
Sainte Rosalie 11
201 45N38 72w54 4:51:36
Sainte Rose du Lac 3
203 51N03 99w32 6:38:08
Sainte Scholastique 11
167 45N39 74w05 4:56:20
Sainte Sophie de Mégantic 11
7 46N09 71w42 4:46:48
Sainte Thècle 11
135 46N49 72w31 4:50:04
Sainte Thérèse de Blainville 11
7 45N38 73w51 4:55:24
Saint Étienne des Grès 11
7 46N26 72w46 4:51:04
Saint Eugène 9 1 45N30 74w28 4:57:52
Saint Eustache 11
7 45N33 73w54 4:55:36
Saint Evariste → La Guadeloupe 11
7 45N57 70w56 4:43:44
Saint Fabien 11
295 48N18 68w52 4:35:28
Saint Félicien 11
166 48N39 72w26 4:49:44
Saint Félix de Kingsey 11
7 45N48 72w12 4:48:48
Saint Félix de Valois 11
7 46N10 73w26 4:53:44
Saint Ferdinand (Bernierville) 11
7 46N06 71w34 4:46:16
Saint Flavien 11
7 46N31 71w36 4:46:24
Saint Fortunat 11
7 45N58 71w36 4:46:24
Saint François du Lac 11
135 46N04 72w50 4:51:20
Saint Gabriel 11
7 46N17 73w23 4:53:32
Saint Gabriel DeGaspé 11
288 48N31 64w32 4:18:08
Saint Gabriel de Rimouski 11
295 48N25 68w10 4:32:40
Saint George 4
271 45N08 66w49 4:27:16
Saint George 9
40 43N15 80w15 5:21:00
Saint George's 5
286 48N26 58w29 3:53:56
Saint Georges 11
152 46N37 72w40 4:50:40
Saint Georges de Windsor 11
7 45N42 71w50 4:47:20
Saint Gérard 11
139 45N46 71w25 4:45:40
Saint Germain de Grantham 11
148 45N50 72w34 4:50:16
Saint Gilles 11
7 46N31 71w22 4:45:28
Saint Grégoire (Larochelle) 11
135 46N16 72w30 4:50:00

Saint Guillaume d'Upton 11
7 45N53 72w46 4:51:04
Saint Hilaire Est 11
7 45N34 73w11 4:52:44
Saint Hippolyte de Kilkenny 11
167 45N56 74w01 4:56:04
Saint Hubert 11
151 45N30 73w25 4:53:40
Saint Hugues 11
7 45N48 72w52 4:51:28
Saint Hyacinthe 11
201 45N37 72w57 4:51:48
Saint Ignace 4
271 46N42 65w05 4:20:20
Saint Isidore 4
271 47N33 65w03 4:20:12
Saint Isidore d'Auckland 11
7 45N16 71w31 4:46:04
Saint Isidore de Laprairie 11
151 45N18 73w41 4:54:44
Saint Jacobs 9
60 43N32 80w33 5:22:12
Saint Jacques 11
7 45N57 73w34 4:54:16
Saint Jean 11
168 45N19 73w16 4:53:04
Saint Jean Baptiste 3
203 49N16 97w21 6:29:24
Saint Jean Baptiste de Rouville 11
201 45N31 73w07 4:52:28
Saint Jean des Piles 11
152 46N41 72w45 4:51:00
Saint Jean Port Joli 11
7 47N13 70w16 4:41:04
Saint Jean sur Richelieu 11
168 45N19 73w16 4:53:04
Saint Jérôme 11
167 45N47 74w00 4:56:00
Saint Joachim 9
1 42N16 82w38 5:30:32
Saint John 4 280 45N16 66w03 4:24:12
Saint Johns → Saint Jean 11
168 45N19 73w16 4:53:04
Saint John's 5
285 47N34 52w43 3:30:52
Saint Joseph 4
271 45N59 64w34 4:18:16
Saint Joseph d'Alma → Alma 11
169 48N33 71w39 4:46:36
Saint Joseph de Beauce 11
7 46N18 70w53 4:43:32
Saint Joseph de Mékinac 11
7 46N55 72w42 4:50:48
Saint Joseph de Sorel 11
173 46N02 73w07 4:52:28
Saint Joseph du Lac 11
7 45N32 74w00 4:56:00
Saint Jovite 11
7 46N07 74w36 4:58:24
Saint Justin 11
135 46N15 73w05 4:52:20
Saint Lambert 11
151 45N30 73w30 4:54:00
Saint Laurent 3
203 50N24 97w56 6:31:44
Saint Laurent 11
151 45N30 73w40 4:54:40
Saint Laurent d'Orléans 11
164 46N52 71w01 4:44:04
Saint Lawrence 5
286 46N55 55w24 3:41:36
Saint Lazare 3
203 50N26 101w16 6:45:04
Saint Léandre 11
290 48N44 67w36 4:30:24
Saint Léonard 4
271 47N10 67w56 4:31:44
Saint Léonard 11
151 45N35 73w35 4:54:20
Saint Léonard d'Aston 11
7 46N06 72w22 4:49:28
Saint Liboire 11
201 45N39 72w46 4:51:04
Saint Louis 12
230 52N56 105w49 7:03:16
Saint Louis de Champlain 11
7 46N25 72w36 4:50:24
Saint Louis de Kent 4
271 46N44 64w58 4:19:52
Saint Luc 11 168 45N22 73w18 4:53:12
Saint Malo 11 7 45N12 71w30 4:46:00
Saint Marc 11
135 45N41 73w12 4:52:48
Saint Marc des Carrières 11
7 46N41 72w03 4:48:12
Saint Marcelline de Kildare 11
7 46N07 73w36 4:54:24
Saint Martins 4
271 45N21 65w32 4:22:08
Saint Mary's 5
286 46N55 53w34 3:34:16
Saint Mary's 9
36 43N16 81w08 5:24:32
Saint Mathieu de Laprairie 11
151 45N19 73w31 4:54:04
Saint Michel de Napierville 11
7 45N14 73w34 4:54:16
Saint Michel des Saints 11
7 46N41 73w55 4:55:40
Saint Michel de Vaudreuil 11
202 45N24 74w01 4:56:04
Saint Narcisse 11
7 46N34 72w28 4:49:52
Saint Nicéphore 11
148 45N50 72w25 4:49:40

Saint Nicolas 11 7 46N42 71w24 4:45:36
Saint Norbert d'Arthabaska 11 7 46N07 71w50 4:47:20
Saint Pacôme 11 7 47N24 69w57 4:39:48
Saint Pamphile 11 7 46N58 69w47 4:39:08
Saint Pascal 11 135 47N32 69w49 4:39:16
Saint Paul 1 223 53N59 111w17 7:25:08
Saint Paul de Chester (Chesterville) 11 135 45N57 71w49 4:47:16
Saint Paulin 11 7 46N25 73w01 4:52:04
Saint Paul L'Ermite 11 7 45N45 73w28 4:53:52
Saint Peters 8 11 45N40 60w52 4:03:28
Saint Peters Bay 10 6 46N25 62w35 4:10:20
Saint Philippe d'Argenteuil 11 157 45N37 74w25 4:57:40
Saint Philippe de Laprairie 11 151 45N21 73w28 4:53:52
Saint Philomène 11 138 45N19 73w45 4:55:00
Saint Pie 11 201 45N30 72w54 4:51:36
Saint Pierre 11 151 45N26 73w39 4:54:36
Saint Pierre de Broughton 11 135 46N15 71w12 4:44:48
Saint Pierre Jolys 3 203 49N26 96w59 6:27:56
Saint Polycarpe 11 135 45N18 74w18 4:57:12
Saint Prosper de Dorchester 11 135 46N13 70w29 4:41:56
Saint Quentin 4 271 47N30 67w23 4:29:32
Saint Raymond 11 170 46N54 71w50 4:47:20
Saint Rédempter de Lévis 11 164 46N42 71w17 4:45:08
Saint Rémi 11 135 45N16 73w37 4:54:28
Saint Rémi d'Amherst 11 7 46N01 74w46 4:59:04
Saint Roch de L'Achigan 11 7 45N51 73w36 4:54:24
Saint Romuald d'Etchemin 11 164 46N45 71w14 4:44:56
Saint Rose du Dégelis → Dégelis 11 296 47N33 68w39 4:34:36
Saint Sauveur des Monts 11 167 45N52 74w10 4:56:40
Saint Sébastien 11 7 45N07 73w09 4:52:36
Saint Shotts 5 286 46N38 53w35 3:34:20
Saint Stanislas de Kosta 11 177 45N11 74w08 4:56:32
Saint Stephen 4 281 45N12 67w17 4:29:08
Saint Sylvestre 11 7 46N22 71w14 4:44:56
Saint Théodore d'Acton 11 7 45N41 72w35 4:50:20
Saint Thomas 9 111 42N47 81w12 5:24:48
Saint Timothée 11 177 45N18 74w02 4:56:08
Saint Tite 11 135 46N44 72w34 4:50:16
Saint Tite des Caps 11 7 47N08 70w47 4:43:08
Saint Ubald 11 7 46N45 72w16 4:49:04
Saint Urbain de Charlevoix 11 7 47N33 70w32 4:42:08
Saint Valerien 11 201 45N30 72w52 4:51:28
Saint Vincent's 5 286 46N48 53w38 3:34:32
Saint Walburg 12 228 53N39 109w12 7:16:48
Saint Williams 9 35 42N40 80w25 5:21:40
Saint Yvon 11 288 49N10 64w48 4:19:12
Saint Zénon 11 7 46N33 73w49 4:55:16
Salaberry de Valleyfield 11 177 45N15 74w08 4:56:32
Salem 9 1 43N42 80w27 5:21:48
Salmo 2 266 49N12 117w17 7:49:08
Salmon Arm 2 266 50N42 119w16 7:57:04
Salmon Bay 11 30 51N26 57w36 3:50:24
Salmon Valley 2 266 54N05 122w41 8:10:44
Saltair 2 266 48N57 123w46 8:15:04
Saltcoats 12 232 51N03 102w12 6:48:48
Salt Spring Island 2 266 48N47 123w30 8:14:00
Salvage 5 286 48N41 53w38 3:34:32
Sandhill 9 1 43N50 79w49 5:19:16
Sandspit 2 266 53N14 131w50 8:47:20
Sandwick 2 266 49N42 124w59 8:19:56
Sangudo 1 223 53N53 114w54 7:39:36
Sardis 2 266 49N08 121w57 8:07:48
Sarnia 9 112 42N58 82w23 5:29:32
Sarsfield 9 1 45N27 75w21 5:01:24
Saseenos 2 265 48N24 123w40 8:14:40
Saskatoon 12 264 52N07 106w38 7:06:32
Saturna 2 266 48N43 123w11 8:12:44
Sault Au Mouton 11 295 48N33 69w15 4:37:00
Sault Sainte Marie 9 113 46N31 84w20 5:37:20
Savona 2 266 50N45 120w50 8:03:20
Sawyerville 11 7 45N20 71w34 4:46:16
Sayward 2 266 50N22 125w55 8:23:40
Scapa 1 223 51N52 111w59 7:27:56
Scarborough 9 124 43N44 79w16 5:17:04
Sceptre 12 228 50N51 109w15 7:17:00
Schefferville 11 297 54N48 66w50 4:27:20
Schomberg 9 1 44N00 79w41 5:18:44
Schreiber 9 1 48N48 87w15 5:49:00
Schumacher 9 1 48N28 81w18 5:25:12
Scotland 9 40 43N01 80w22 5:21:28
Scotsburn 8 11 45N39 62w51 4:11:24
Scotstown 11 7 45N32 71w17 4:45:08
Scott 12 228 52N23 108w50 7:15:20
Scout Lake 12 231 49N22 106w00 7:04:00
Seaforth 9 36 43N33 81w24 5:25:36
Seal Cove 4 271 44N39 66w51 4:27:24
Seal Cove 5 286 47N28 53w05 3:32:20
Sebringville 9 36 43N24 81w04 5:24:16
Sechelt 2 266 49N28 123w45 8:15:00
Sedalia 1 223 51N41 110w40 7:22:40
Sedgewick 1 223 52N46 111w41 7:26:44
Seeleys Bay 9 1 44N29 76w14 5:04:56
Selkirk 3 215 50N09 96w52 6:27:28
Selkirk 9 1 42N49 79w56 5:19:44
Semans 12 231 51N25 104w44 6:58:56
Senate 12 223 49N18 109w41 7:18:44
Senlac 12 228 52N29 109w41 7:18:44
Senneterre 11 200 48N23 77w15 5:09:00
Senneville 11 202 45N27 73w57 4:55:48
Sept Îles (Seven Islands) 11 297 50N12 66w23 4:25:32
Seton Portage 2 266 50N43 122w18 8:09:12
Seven Islands → Sept Îles 11 297 50N12 66w23 4:25:32
Seven Persons 1 226 49N52 110w54 7:23:36
Seventy Mile House 2 266 51N18 121w24 8:05:36
Sexsmith 1 223 55N21 118w47 7:55:08
Shakespeare 9 134 43N22 80w49 5:23:16
Shalalth 2 266 50N44 122w13 8:08:52
Shallow Lake 9 1 44N36 81w05 5:24:20
Shamattawa 3 203 55N52 92w05 6:08:20
Shannonville 9 40 44N12 77w13 5:08:52
Shanty Bay 9 1 44N25 79w36 5:18:24
Sharbot Lake 9 1 44N46 76w41 5:06:44
Sharon 9 1 44N06 79w26 5:17:44
Sharon 9 1 42N53 81w22 5:25:28
Shaunavon 12 257 49N40 108w25 7:13:40
Shawbridge 11 167 45N52 74w05 4:56:20
Shawinigan 11 171 46N33 72w45 4:51:00
Shawinigan Falls → Shawinigan 11 171 46N33 72w45 4:51:00
Shawinigan Sud 11 171 46N31 72w45 4:51:00
Shawnigan Lake 2 265 48N38 123w35 8:14:20
Shawville 11 7 45N36 76w30 5:06:00
Shedden 9 53 42N44 81w21 5:25:24
Shediac 4 282 46N13 64w32 4:18:08
Sheet Harbour 8 11 44N55 62w32 4:10:08
Sheho 12 232 51N38 103w12 6:52:48
Shekatika Bay 11 30 51N17 58w20 3:53:20
Shelburne 8 31 43N46 65w19 4:21:16
Shelburne 9 1 44N04 80w12 5:20:48
Shellbrook 12 229 53N13 106w24 7:05:36
Shelley 2 266 54N00 122w37 8:10:28
Shell Lake 12 228 53N18 107w07 7:08:28
Shemogue 4 271 46N09 64w11 4:16:44
Shepard 1 224 50N57 113w55 7:35:40
Sherbrooke 8 11 45N08 61w59 4:07:56
Sherbrooke 11 172 45N24 71w54 4:47:36
Sherkston 9 103 42N53 79w08 5:16:32
Sherridon 3 203 55N07 101w05 6:44:20
Sherwood 9 1 43N50 79w31 5:18:04
Sherwood 10 28 46N17 63w08 4:12:32
Sherwood Park 1 225 53N31 113w19 7:33:16
Ship Cove 5 286 47N06 54w05 3:36:20
Shippegan 4 271 47N45 64w42 4:18:48
Shirley 2 266 48N23 123w54 8:15:36
Shoal Harbour 5 286 48N11 53w59 3:35:56
Shoal Lake 3 203 50N26 100w34 6:42:16
Shoe Cove 5 285 47N45 52w44 3:30:56
Shoreacres 2 266 49N26 117w32 7:50:08
Shuswap 2 266 50N45 119w00 7:56:00
Sibbald 1 223 51N23 110w09 7:20:36
Sicamous 2 266 50N50 119w00 7:56:00
Sidney 2 265 48N39 123w24 8:13:36
Sifton 3 203 51N21 100w07 6:40:28
Sillery 11 164 46N46 71w15 4:45:00
Silton 12 258 50N48 104w55 6:59:40
Silverdale 2 266 49N09 122w24 8:09:36
Silverton 2 266 49N57 117w21 7:49:24
Simcoe 9 36 42N50 80w18 5:21:12
Simmie 12 228 49N57 108w06 7:12:24
Simoom Sound 2 266 50N45 126w45 8:27:00
Sinclair Mills 2 266 54N02 121w41 8:06:44
Sioux Lookout 9 3 50N06 91w55 6:07:40
Sioux Narrows 9 3 49N25 94w06 6:16:24
Sipiwesk 3 203 55N27 97w24 6:29:36
Sirdar 2 266 49N15 116w37 7:46:28
Skeena Crossing 2 266 55N06 127w49 8:31:16
Skidegate 2 266 53N15 132w00 8:48:00
Skownan 3 203 51N57 99w36 6:38:24
Slave Lake 1 223 55N17 114w46 7:39:04
Slocan 2 266 49N46 117w28 7:49:52
Smeaton 12 230 53N30 104w49 6:59:16
Smiley 12 228 51N37 109w29 7:17:56
Smith 1 223 55N10 114w02 7:36:08
Smithers 2 266 54N47 127w10 8:28:40
Smithfield 9 40 44N04 77w41 5:10:44
Smiths Falls 9 114 44N54 76w01 5:04:04
Smithville 9 70 43N06 79w33 5:18:12
Smoky Lake 1 223 54N07 112w28 7:29:52
Snag 13 301 62N24 140w22 9:21:28
Snelgrove 9 50 43N44 79w49 5:19:16
Snowden 12 230 53N30 104w41 6:58:44
Snowdrift 7 227 62N23 110w47 7:23:08
Snow Lake 3 203 54N53 100w02 6:40:08
Soda Creek 2 266 52N21 122w18 8:09:12
Sointula 2 266 50N38 127w01 8:28:04
Sombra 9 1 42N43 82w29 5:29:56
Somenos 2 266 48N49 123w44 8:14:56
Somerset 3 203 49N24 98w39 6:34:36
Sonningdale 12 228 52N24 107w40 7:10:40
Sooke 2 266 48N23 123w43 8:14:52
Sorel 11 173 46N02 73w07 4:52:28
Souris 3 203 49N38 100w15 6:41:00
Souris 10 6 46N21 62w15 4:09:00
Southampton 8 11 45N35 64w15 4:17:00
Southampton 9 115 44N29 81w23 5:25:32
South Aulatsivik Island 6 269 56N45 61w30 4:06:00
Southbank 2 266 54N02 125w46 8:23:04
South Baymouth 9 1 45N33 82w01 5:28:04
South Branch 5 286 47N55 59w02 3:56:08
South Brookfield 8 11 44N23 64w58 4:19:52
Southey 12 258 50N56 104w30 6:58:00
South Fort George 2 266 53N54 122w45 8:11:00
South Indian Lake 3 203 56N46 98w57 6:35:48
South Pender 2 266 48N45 123w14 8:12:56
South Porcupine 9 46 48N28 81w13 5:24:52
South Revelstoke 2 266 50N48 118w11 7:52:44
South River 9 116 45N45 79w25 5:17:40
South Slocan 2 266 49N28 117w32 7:50:08
South Wellington 2 266 49N06 123w53 8:15:32
South Westminster 2 267 49N12 122w52 8:11:28
South Woodslee 9 1 42N14 82w43 5:30:52
Spalding 12 231 52N20 104w30 6:58:00
Spaniard's Bay 5 286 47N37 53w17 3:33:08
Spanish 9 1 46N12 82w21 5:29:24
Sparta 9 1 42N42 81w05 5:24:20
Spence Bay 7 219 69N32 93w31 6:14:04
Spencerville 9 1 44N51 75w33 5:02:12
Spences Bridge 2 266 50N25 121w21 8:05:24
Sperling 2 266 49N08 122w33 8:10:12
Spirit River 1 223 55N47 118w50 7:55:20
Spiritwood 12 228 53N22 107w31 7:10:04
Sprague 3 203 49N02 95w38 6:22:32
Springbrook 9 50 43N39 79w47 5:19:08
Springdale 5 286 49N30 56w04 3:44:16
Springfield 4 271 46N01 67w03 4:28:12
Springfield 9 64 42N50 80w56 5:23:44
Springhill 8 11 45N39 64w03 4:16:12
Springhouse 2 266 51N55 122w07 8:08:28
Spruce Brook 5 286 48N45 58w11 3:52:44
Spruce Grove 1 223 53N32 113w55 7:35:40
Spruce Lake 12 228 53N32 109w14 7:16:56
Spurfield 1 223 55N13 114w16 7:37:04
Spuzzum 2 266 49N41 121w25 8:05:40
Spy Hill 12 203 50N36 101w41 6:46:44
Squamish 2 266 49N42 123w09 8:12:36
Squatteck 11 296 47N53 68w43 4:34:52
Squaw Rapids 12 249 53N41 103w20 6:53:20
Squilax 2 266 50N52 119w35 7:58:20
Standard 1 223 51N07 112w59 7:31:56
Stanley 4 271 46N17 66w44 4:26:56

Stanley Mills 9 50 43N46 79w44 5:18:56
Stanstead 11 195 45N01 72w05 4:48:20
Starbuck 3 203 49N46 97w36 6:30:24
Star City 12 249 52N53 104w21 6:57:24
Stavely 1 223 50N10 113w38 7:34:32
Stayner 9 36 44N25 80w05 5:20:20
Steeles Corners 9 124 43N48 79w25 5:17:40
Steelhead 2 266 49N13 122w19 8:09:16
Steep Rock 3 203 51N26 98w48 6:35:12
Steinbach 3 203 49N32 96w41 6:26:44
Stellarton 8 31 45N34 62w40 4:10:40
Stephenville 5 286 48N33 58w35 3:54:20
Stephenville Crossing 5 286 48N30 58w26 3:53:44
Stettler 1 223 52N19 112w43 7:30:52
Stevensville 9 2 42N57 79w04 5:16:16
Stewart 2 266 55N56 129w59 8:39:56
Stewart Valley 12 228 50N36 107w50 7:11:20
Stewiacke 8 11 45N08 63w21 4:13:24
Stillwater 2 266 49N46 124w18 8:17:12
Stirling 1 223 49N30 112w31 7:30:04
Stirling 9 35 44N18 77w33 5:10:12
Stittsville 9 1 45N15 75w55 5:03:40
Stoner 2 266 53N36 122w40 8:10:40
Stonewall 3 216 50N09 97w21 6:29:24
Stoney Creek 9 74 43N13 79w46 5:19:04
Stony Plain 1 223 53N02 114w00 7:36:00
Stony Rapids 12 230 59N16 105w50 7:03:20
Storthoaks 12 203 49N22 101w38 6:46:32
Stouffville 9 35 43N58 79w15 5:17:00
Stoughton 12 231 49N41 103w03 6:52:12
Straffordville 9 1 42N45 80w47 5:23:08
Strasbourg 12 238 51N04 104w57 6:59:48
Stratford 9 117 43N22 80w57 5:23:48
Stratford Centre 11 7 45N47 71w16 4:45:04
Strathclair 3 203 50N24 100w24 6:41:36
Strathlorne 8 11 46N11 61w17 4:05:08
Strathmore 1 223 51N03 113w23 7:33:32
Strathroy 9 36 42N57 81w38 5:26:32
Streatham 2 266 53N52 126w12 8:24:48
Streetsville 9 118 43N35 79w42 5:18:48
Strome 1 223 52N48 112w04 7:28:16
Stuie 2 266 52N22 126w02 8:24:08
Sturgeon Falls 9 1 46N22 79w55 5:19:40
Sturgeon Landing 12 232 54N16 101w49 6:47:16
Sturgis 12 232 51N58 102w32 6:50:08
Sudbury 9 119 46N30 81w00 5:24:00
Suffield 1 223 50N12 111w10 7:24:40
Sulphur 13 301 63N47 138w53 9:15:32
Summerford 5 286 49N29 54w47 3:39:08
Summerland 2 266 49N39 119w33 7:58:12
Summerside 10 29 46N24 63w47 4:15:08
Summerville 9 1 43N37 79w34 5:18:16
Summit Lake 2 266 54N17 122w38 8:10:32
Sunderland 9 120 44N16 79w04 5:16:16
Sundre 1 223 51N48 114w38 7:38:32
Sundridge 9 35 45N46 79w24 5:17:36
Sunnybrae 8 11 45N24 62w30 4:10:00
Sunnynook 1 223 51N17 111w40 7:26:40
Sunnyside 5 286 47N51 53w55 3:35:40
Sunnyslope 1 223 51N40 113w32 7:34:08
Sunset Prairie 2 299 55N50 120w48 8:03:12
Surrey 2 267 49N10 122w47 8:11:08
Sussex 4 283 45N43 65w31 4:22:04
Sutton 11 7 45N06 72w37 4:50:28
Sutton West 9 1 44N18 79w22 5:17:28
Swan Hills 1 223 54N52 115w45 7:43:00
Swan Lake 3 203 49N24 98w46 6:35:04
Swan River 3 203 52N06 101w16 6:45:04
Swift Current 12 259 50N17 107w50 7:11:20
Sydenham 9 36 44N25 76w36 5:06:24
Sydney 8 5 46N09 60w11 4:00:44
Sydney Mines 8 24 46N14 60w14 4:00:56
Sylvan Lake 1 223 52N19 114w05 7:36:20
Taber 1 223 49N47 112w08 7:28:32
Tadoussac 11 295 48N09 69w43 4:38:52
Tahsis 2 266 49N55 126w39 8:26:36
Takla Landing 2 266 55N29 125w58 8:23:52
Takysie Lake 2 266 53N54 125w53 8:23:32
Talbotville Royal 9 111 42N48 81w15 5:25:00
Tamworth 9 1 44N29 77w00 5:08:00
Tara 9 36 44N28 81w09 5:24:36
Tatla Lake 2 266 51N55 124w36 8:18:24
Tatlayoko Lake 2 266 51N39 124w24 8:17:36
Tavistock 9 36 43N19 80w50 5:23:20
Taylor 2 299 56N10 120w41 8:02:44
Taymouth 4 271 46N11 66w37 4:26:28
Tecumseh 9 132 42N19 82w54 5:31:36
Teeswater 9 1 44N00 81w17 5:25:08
Telegraph Cove 2 266 50N33 126w50 8:27:20
Telegraph Creek 2 266 57N55 131w10 8:44:40
Telkwa 2 266 54N42 127w03 8:28:12
Témiscaming 11 7 46N43 79w06 5:16:24
Templeton 11 153 45N29 75w36 5:02:24
Terence Bay 8 11 44N28 63w43 4:14:52
Terrace 2 266 54N31 128w35 8:34:20
Terrace Bay 9 1 48N47 87w09 5:48:36
Terra Nova 5 286 48N30 54w13 3:36:52
Terrasse Vaudreuil 11 202 45N24 73w59 4:55:56
Terrebonne 11 151 45N42 73w38 4:54:32
Terrenceville 5 286 47N40 54w44 3:38:56
Teslin 13 270 60N09 132w45 8:51:00
Teston 9 1 43N52 79w32 5:18:08
Tête À la Baleine 11 30 50N41 59w20 3:57:20
Tête Jaune Cache 2 266 52N57 119w26 7:57:44
Teulon 3 203 50N23 97w16 6:29:04
Thamesford 9 1 43N04 81w00 5:24:00
Thamesville 9 35 42N33 81w59 5:27:56
Theodore 12 232 51N25 102w54 6:51:36
The Pas 3 203 53N50 101w15 6:45:00
Thessalon 9 1 46N15 83w34 5:34:16
Thetford Mines 11 174 46N05 71w18 4:45:12
Thetis Island 2 266 49N59 123w40 8:14:40
Thibaudeau 3 203 57N05 94w08 6:16:32
Thicket Portage 3 203 55N19 97w42 6:30:48
Thistle Creek 13 301 63N04 139w29 9:17:56
Thompson 3 203 55N45 97w45 6:31:00
Thorburn 8 11 45N34 62w33 4:10:12
Thorhild 1 223 54N10 113w07 7:32:28
Thornbury 9 35 44N34 80w26 5:21:44
Thorndale 9 35 43N06 81w08 5:24:32
Thorold 9 110 43N07 79w12 5:16:48
Thorold South 9 110 43N06 79w12 5:16:48
Thorsby 1 223 53N14 114w03 7:36:12
Three Hills 1 223 51N42 113w16 7:33:04
Three Mile Plains 8 11 44N58 64w07 4:16:28
Three Rivers → Trois Rivières 11 175 46N21 72w33 4:50:12
Thrums 2 266 49N19 117w30 7:50:00
Thunder Bay 9 121 48N23 89w15 5:57:00
Thurso 11 7 45N36 75w15 5:01:00
Tignish 10 6 46N57 64w02 4:16:08
Tilbury 9 1 42N16 82w26 5:29:44
Tilley 1 223 50N27 111w39 7:26:36
Tillsonburg 9 122 42N51 80w44 5:22:56
Timmins 9 123 48N28 81w20 5:25:20
Tingwick 11 146 45N50 71w58 4:47:52
Tintagel 2 266 54N12 125w35 8:22:20
Tisdale 12 249 52N51 104w04 6:56:16
Tofield 1 223 53N22 112w40 7:30:40
Tofino 2 266 49N09 125w54 8:23:36
Tompkins 5 286 47N48 59w13 3:56:52
Tompkins 12 228 50N04 108w47 7:15:08
Topley 2 266 54N49 126w18 8:25:12
Torbay 5 285 47N40 52w44 3:30:56
Torbrook 8 11 44N55 64w59 4:19:56
Toronto 9 124 43N39 79w23 5:17:32
Torquay 12 231 49N08 103w31 6:54:04
Tors Cove 5 286 47N13 52w51 3:31:24
Tottenham 9 36 44N01 79w49 5:19:16
Touraine 11 153 45N34 75w47 5:03:08
Tracadie 5 286 47N31 64w54 4:19:36
Tracy 11 173 46N01 73w09 4:52:36
Trafalgar 9 45 43N29 79w43 5:18:52
Trail 2 266 49N06 117w42 7:50:48
Transcona 3 203 53N47 97w00 6:28:00
Treherne 3 203 49N38 98w41 6:34:44
Trenton 8 31 45N37 62w38 4:10:32
Trenton 9 188 44N06 77w35 5:10:20
Trepassey 5 286 46N44 53w22 3:33:28
Tribune 12 231 49N15 103w50 6:55:20
Trinity 5 286 48N59 53w55 3:35:40
Trochu 1 223 51N50 113w13 7:32:52
Trois Rivières 11 175 46N21 72w33 4:50:12
Trout River 5 286 49N29 58w08 3:52:32
Truax 12 238 49N55 104w58 6:59:52
Truro 8 25 45N22 63w16 4:13:04
Tsawwassen 2 267 49N01 123w06 8:12:24
Tugaske 12 241 50N53 106w16 7:05:04
Tuktoyaktuk 7 298 69N27 133w02 8:52:08
Tullamore 9 50 43N47 79w46 5:19:04
Tulsequah 2 266 58N35 133w35 8:54:20
Tungsten 7 298 62N00 127w40 8:30:40
Tunungayualok Island 6 269 56N05 61w05 4:04:20
Tupper 2 299 55N31 120w02 8:00:08
Tupperville 9 1 42N36 82w16 5:29:04
Turin 1 223 49N58 112w31 7:30:04
Turner Valley 1 223 50N40 114w17 7:37:08
Turtle Creek 4 271 45N58 64w53 4:19:32
Turtleford 12 228 53N23 108w56 7:15:44
Tuxford 12 260 50N35 105w35 7:02:20
Tweed 9 1 44N29 77w19 5:09:16
Twillingate 5 286 49N39 54w46 3:39:04
Two Hills 1 223 53N43 111w45 7:27:00
Uchi Lake 9 3 51N05 92w35 6:10:20
Ucluelet 2 266 48N57 125w33 8:22:12
Union 9 1 42N42 81w12 5:24:48
Union Bay 2 266 49N35 124w53 8:19:32
Unionville 9 36 43N52 79w18 5:17:12
Unity 12 228 52N27 109w10 7:16:40
Upper Blackville 4 271 46N39 65w52 4:23:28
Upper Fraser 2 266 54N07 121w56 8:07:44
Upper Hat Creek 2 266 50N38 121w35 8:06:20
Upper Island Cove 5 286 47N39 53w12 3:32:48
Upper Liard 13 270 60N02 128w55 8:35:40
Upper Musquodoboit 8 11 45N08 62w57 4:11:48
Upper Sheila 4 271 47N28 64w56 4:19:44
Upper Sumas 2 266 49N01 122w12 8:08:48
Upton 11 7 45N39 72w41 4:50:44
Uranium City 12 228 59N34 108w36 7:14:24
Usk 2 266 54N38 128w25 8:33:40
Uxbridge 9 34 44N06 79w07 5:16:28
Val Alain 11 7 46N24 71w45 4:47:00
Valcourt 11 7 45N29 72w18 4:49:12
Val David 11 7 46N01 74w12 4:56:48
Val des Bois 11 7 45N54 75w35 5:02:20
Val d'Or 11 176 48N07 77w47 5:11:08
Valemount 2 266 52N50 119w15 7:57:00
Valleyfield 5 286 49N08 53w37 3:34:28
Valleyfield 11 177 45N15 74w08 4:56:32
Valleyview 1 223 55N04 117w17 7:49:08
Val Marie 12 231 49N14 107w44 7:10:56
Val Saint Michel 11 7 46N52 71w27 4:45:48
Vananda 2 266 49N45 124w33 8:18:12
Vancouver 2 267 49N16 123w07 8:12:28
Vanderhoof 2 266 54N01 124w01 8:16:04
Vanguard 12 228 49N55 107w20 7:09:20
Vanier 9 95 45N26 75w40 5:02:40
Vankleek Hill 9 1 45N31 74w39 4:58:36
Varennes 11 151 45N41 73w26 4:53:44
Vars 9 1 45N21 75w21 5:01:24
Vaudreuil (Saint Michel de Vaudreuil) 202 45N24 74w01 4:56:04
Vaughan 9 125 43N47 79w36 5:18:24
Vauxhall 1 223 50N04 112w07 7:28:28
Vedder Crossing 2 266 49N06 121w57 8:07:48
Vegreville 1 223 53N30 112w03 7:28:12
Vellore 9 1 43N50 79w34 5:18:16
Verchères 11 135 45N47 73w21 4:53:24
Verdun 11 151 45N27 73w34 4:54:16
Verigin 12 232 51N35 102w08 6:48:32
Vermilion 1 223 53N22 110w51 7:23:24
Vermilion Bay 9 3 49N51 93w24 6:13:36
Verner 9 1 46N25 80w07 5:20:28
Vernon 2 266 50N16 119w16 7:57:04
Vernon 9 1 45N10 75w28 5:01:52
Vernon River 10 6 46N12 62w50 4:11:20
Verona 9 1 44N29 76w42 5:06:48
Vesuvius Bay 2 266 48N53 123w35 8:14:20
Vibank 12 231 50N20 103w55 6:55:40
Viceroy 12 231 49N27 105w22 7:01:28
Victoria 2 265 48N25 123w22 8:13:28
Victoria 10 6 46N13 63w29 4:13:56
Victoria Beach 3 210 50N43 96w33 6:26:12
Victoria Harbour 9 1 44N45 79w46 5:19:04
Victoriaville 11 178 46N03 71w57 4:47:48
Vienna 9 1 42N41 80w48 5:23:12
Viking 1 223 53N06 111w46 7:27:04
Ville de Laval → Laval 11 151 45N35 73w45 4:55:00
Ville La Salle 11 151 45N26 73w38 4:54:32
Ville Marie 11 7 47N19 79w26 5:17:44
Ville Saint Georges 11 7 46N07 70w40 4:42:40
Vilna 1 223 54N07 111w55 7:27:40
Virden 3 203 49N51 100w55 6:43:40
Virgil 9 91 43N13 79w08 5:16:32
Virginiatown 9 1 48N08 79w35 5:18:20
Viscount 12 229 51N57 105w39 7:02:36
Vita 3 203 49N08 96w34 6:26:16
Vittoria 9 1 42N46 80w19 5:21:16
Vonda 12 229 52N19 106w06 7:04:24
Vulcan 1 223 50N24 113w15 7:33:00
Wabamun 1 223 53N33 114w28 7:37:52
Wabana 5 286 47N38 52w57 3:31:48
Wabasca 1 223 56N00 113w53 7:35:32
Wabowden 3 203 54N55 98w38 6:34:32
Wabush 6 9 52N50 66w55 4:27:40
Wadena 12 231 51N57 103w47 6:55:08
Wadhams 2 266 51N30 127w31 8:30:04
Wainwright 1 223 52N49 110w52 7:23:28
Wakaw 12 230 52N39 105w44 7:02:56
Wakeham Bay → Maricourt 11 7 61N36 71w58 4:47:52

CANADA

Walcott 2	266	54N31	126w51	8:27:24
Waldheim 12	229	52N37	106w38	7:06:32
Waldo 2	223	49N13	115w13	7:40:52
Waldron 12	232	50N51	102w30	6:50:00
Walhachin 2	266	50N45	120w59	8:03:56
Walkerton 9	36	44N07	81w09	5:24:36
Wallaceburg 9	126	42N36	82w23	5:29:32
Wallacetown 9	1	42N38	81w28	5:25:52
Walnut Grove 2	266	49N11	122w39	8:10:36
Walsh 1	223	49N57	110w03	7:20:12
Walsingham 9	1	42N41	80w32	5:22:08
Walton 8	11	45N14	64w00	4:16:00
Wanham 1	223	55N44	118w24	7:53:36
Wapella 12	203	50N15	102w00	6:48:00
Wardlow 1	223	50N54	111w33	7:26:12
Wardner 2	223	49N25	115w26	7:41:44
Wardsville 9	1	42N39	81w45	5:27:00
Warkworth 9	1	44N12	77w53	5:11:32
Warman 12	264	52N20	106w34	7:06:16
Warner 1	223	49N17	112w12	7:28:48
Warspite 1	223	54N06	112w37	7:30:28
Warwick 11	135	45N56	71w59	4:47:56
Wasaga Beach 9	1	44N31	80w01	5:20:04
Washago 9	62	44N45	79w20	5:17:20
Washicoutai 11	30	50N17	60w42	4:02:48
Waskada 3	203	49N06	100w46	6:43:04
Waskatenau 1	223	54N07	112w47	7:31:08
Waterdown 9	40	43N20	79w53	5:19:32
Waterford 9	127	42N56	80w17	5:21:08
Waterloo 9	60	43N28	80w31	5:22:04
Waterloo 11	179	45N21	72w31	4:50:04
Waterton Park 1	223	49N03	113w55	7:35:40
Waterville 8	11	45N03	64w41	4:18:44
Waterville 11	160	45N16	71w54	4:47:36
Watford 9	35	42N57	81w53	5:27:32
Watino 1	223	55N43	117w37	7:50:28
Watrous 12	229	51N40	105w28	7:01:52
Watson 12	236	52N07	104w31	6:58:04
Watson Lake 13	268	60N07	128w48	8:35:12
Waubaushene 9	36	44N45	79w42	5:18:48
Waugh 3	203	49N40	95w13	6:20:52
Wawa 9	1	47N59	84w47	5:39:08
Wawanesa 3	203	49N36	99w41	6:38:44
Wawota 12	203	49N55	102w00	6:48:00
Wayne 1	223	51N23	112w39	7:30:36
Webb 12	228	50N11	108w12	7:12:48
Webbwood 9	1	41N16	81w53	5:27:32
Webster 1	223	55N26	118w42	7:54:48
Websters Corners 2	266	49N13	122w30	8:10:00
Wedgeport 8	11	43N44	65w59	4:23:56
Weedon 11	139	45N42	71w28	4:45:52
Weir River 3	203	56N49	94w04	6:16:16
Welcome 9	40	43N58	78w21	5:13:24
Weldon 12	230	53N00	105w08	7:00:32
Welland 9	128	42N59	79w15	5:17:00
Welland Junction 9	128	42N57	79w14	5:16:56
Wellesley 9	1	43N28	80w45	5:23:00
Wellington 2	266	49N13	124w01	8:16:04
Wellington 9	36	43N57	77w21	5:09:24
Wellington Station 10	6	46N27	64w00	4:16:00
Wells 2	266	53N06	121w34	8:06:16
Welsford 4	271	45N27	66w20	4:25:20
Wembley 1	223	55N09	119w08	7:56:32
Wesleyville 5	286	49N09	53w34	3:34:16
Westbank 2	266	49N50	119w38	7:58:32
West Bay 8	11	45N43	61w10	4:04:40
Westbourne 3	203	50N09	98w35	6:34:20
Westbridge 2	266	49N10	118w59	7:55:56
Westbrook 9	76	44N16	76w38	5:06:32
Western Shore 8	11	44N32	64w19	4:17:16
Westholme 2	266	49N52	123w42	8:14:48
West Kildonan 3	217	49N56	97w07	6:28:28
Westlock 1	223	54N09	113w52	7:35:28
West Lorne 9	64	42N36	81w36	5:26:24
Westmount 11	151	45N29	73w36	4:54:24
Weston 9	129	43N42	79w31	5:18:04
Westport 5	286	49N47	56w38	3:46:32
Westport 8	11	44N16	66w21	4:25:24
Westport 9	37	44N41	76w26	5:05:44
West Saint Modeste 6	269	51N36	56w42	3:46:48
West Vancouver 2	267	49N22	123w12	8:12:48
Westville 8	15	45N34	62w43	4:10:52
Westwold 2	266	50N28	119w45	7:59:00
Wetaskiwin 1	223	52N58	113w22	7:33:28
Weyburn 12	261	49N41	103w52	6:55:28
Weymouth 8	11	44N25	66w00	4:24:00
Wheatley 9	1	42N06	82w27	5:29:48
Whitbourne 5	286	47N25	53w32	3:34:08
Whitby 9	130	43N52	78w56	5:15:44
Whitchurch-Stouffville 9	35	43N58	79w15	5:17:00
Whitecourt 1	223	54N09	115w41	7:42:44
White Fox 12	249	53N27	104w05	6:56:20
Whitehorse 13	270	60N43	135w03	9:00:12
Whitelaw 1	223	56N07	118w04	7:52:16
Whitemouth 3	203	49N57	95w59	6:23:56
White River 9	1	48N35	85w15	5:41:00
White Rock 2	267	49N02	122w49	8:11:16
Whitevale 9	1	43N53	79w09	5:16:36
Whitewood 12	203	50N20	102w15	6:49:00
Whitney 9	131	45N30	78w14	5:12:56
Whonock 2	266	49N11	122w28	8:09:52
Whycocomagh 8	11	45N59	61w07	4:04:28
Wiarton 9	36	44N45	81w09	5:24:36
Wickham 11	148	45N45	72w30	4:50:00
Wilcox 12	238	50N07	104w44	6:58:56
Wildfield 9	1	43N49	79w44	5:18:56
Wildwood 1	223	53N37	115w14	7:40:56
Wilkie 12	228	52N25	108w43	7:14:52
Williamsburg 9	1	44N58	75w15	5:01:00
Williams Lake 2	266	52N08	122w09	8:08:36
Williamsport 5	286	50N32	56w19	3:45:16
Williamstown 9	1	45N08	74w35	4:58:20
Willingdon 1	223	53N50	112w08	7:28:32
Willowbrook 12	232	51N13	102w47	6:51:08
Willow Bunch 12	231	49N24	105w37	7:02:28
Willowdale 9	124	43N47	79w26	5:17:44
Willow River 2	266	54N04	122w28	8:09:52
Wilsons Beach 4	271	44N56	66w56	4:27:44
Winchester 9	1	45N06	75w21	5:01:24
Windermere 2	223	50N30	115w58	7:43:52
Windfall 1	223	54N11	116w15	7:45:00
Windsor 4	271	48N57	55w40	3:42:40
Windsor 8	26	44N59	64w08	4:16:32
Windsor 9	132	42N18	83w01	5:32:04
Windsor 11	7	45N34	72w00	4:48:00
Winfield 1	223	52N58	114w26	7:37:44
Wingham 9	42	43N53	81w19	5:25:16
Winisk 9	1	55N15	85w12	5:40:48
Winkler 3	203	49N11	97w56	6:31:44
Winlaw 2	266	49N37	117w34	7:50:16
Winnipeg 3	217	49N53	97w09	6:28:36
Winnipeg Beach 3	218	50N31	96w58	6:27:52
Winnipegosis 3	203	51N39	99w56	6:39:44
Winter Harbour 2	266	50N31	128w02	8:32:08
Winterton 5	286	47N58	53w20	3:33:20
Wishart 12	231	51N34	104w00	6:56:00
Witless Bay 5	286	47N16	52w50	3:31:20
Woking 1	223	55N35	118w46	7:55:04
Wolf Bay 11	30	50N16	60w08	4:00:32
Wolfe Island 9	1	44N12	76w26	5:05:44
Wolfville 8	11	45N05	64w22	4:17:28
Wolseley 12	231	50N25	103w19	6:53:16
Woodbine Racetrack 9	124	43N44	79w38	5:18:32
Woodbridge 9	124	43N47	79w36	5:18:24
Woodfibre 2	266	49N40	123w15	8:13:00
Woodhill 9	50	43N45	79w41	5:18:44
Wood Islands 10	6	45N58	62w45	4:11:00
Woodridge 3	203	49N17	96w09	6:24:36
Woodstock 4	284	46N09	67w34	4:30:16
Woodstock 9	133	43N08	80w45	5:23:00
Woodville 9	36	44N24	78w59	5:15:56
Wotton 11	7	45N44	71w48	4:47:12
Woundedmoose 13	301	63N33	138w39	9:14:36
Wrentham 1	223	49N32	112w10	7:28:40
Wrigley 7	298	63N16	123w37	8:14:28
Wroxton 12	232	51N14	101w53	6:47:32
Wymark 12	228	50N07	107w44	7:10:56
Wynyard 12	231	51N47	104w10	6:56:40
Wyoming 9	35	42N57	82w07	5:28:28
Yahk 2	266	49N05	116w05	7:44:20
Yale 2	266	49N34	121w26	8:05:44
Yamachiche 11	7	46N16	72w50	4:51:20
Yamaska (Saint Michel) 11	7	46N00	72w55	4:51:40
Yarker 9	1	44N23	76w46	5:07:04
Yarmouth 8	27	43N50	66w07	4:24:28
Yarrow 2	266	49N05	122w02	8:08:08
Yellow Grass 12	262	49N49	104w08	6:56:32
Yellowknife 7	227	62N27	114w21	7:37:24
Yennadon 2	266	49N14	122w34	8:10:16
Ymir 2	266	49N17	117w13	7:48:52
York 9	124	43N41	79w29	5:17:56
York Factory 3	203	57N00	92w18	6:09:12
Yorkton 12	263	51N13	102w28	6:49:52
York University 9	124	43N46	79w31	5:18:04
Youbou 2	266	48N53	124w13	8:16:52
Young 12	229	51N47	105w46	7:03:04
Youngstown 1	223	51N32	111w13	7:24:52
Yukon Crossing 13	300	62N21	136w30	9:06:00
Zealandia 12	228	51N37	107w45	7:11:00
Zeballos 2	266	49N49	126w50	8:27:20
Zeneta 12	232	50N44	102w02	6:48:08
Zenon Park 12	249	53N04	103w45	6:55:00
Zurich 9	1	43N26	81w37	5:26:28

CAPE VERDE

CAP-VERT

KAP VERDE

CABO VERDE

Time Table

Before 1/Jan/1907 LMT		
Begin Standard		30w00
1/Jan/1907	0:00	2:00
1/Sep/1942	0:00	1:00
15/Oct/1945	0:00	2:00
Begin Standard		15w00
25/Nov/1975	2:00	1:00

Assomada	15N06	23w41	1:34:44
Mindelo	16N53	25w00	1:40:00
Palmeira	16N46	22w59	1:31:56
Pedra Lume	16N46	22w54	1:31:36
Porto Inglês	15N08	23w13	1:32:52
Praia	14N55	23w31	1:34:04
Ribeira Brava	16N37	24w19	1:37:16
Ribeira Grande	17N11	25w04	1:40:16
Sal Rei	16N11	22w55	1:31:40
Santa Maria	16N36	22w54	1:31:36
São Filipe	14N54	24w31	1:38:04
Tarrafal	16N58	25w19	1:41:16
Tarrafal	15N17	23w46	1:35:04
Vila da Ribeira Brava	16N37	24w18	1:37:12
Villa de Nova Sintra	14N52	24w43	1:38:52

ISLAS CAIMÁN KAIMAN-INSELN ÎLES CAÏMANES CAYMAN ISLANDS

Time Table
Before 1/Jan/1890 LMT
Begin Standard 76w48
1/Jan/1890 0:00 5:07
Begin Standard 75w00
1/Feb/1912 0:00 5:00

Place	Lat	Long	Offset
Cayman Brac	19N43	79w49	5:19:16
Georgetown	19N18	81w23	5:25:32
Grand Cayman	19N20	81w15	5:25:00
Little Cayman	19N41	80w03	5:20:12
West Bay	19N22	81w25	5:25:40

UBANGI-SHARI RÉP. CENTRAFRICAINE CENTRAL AFRICAN REPUBLIC

Time Table
Before 1/Jan/1912 LMT
Begin Standard 15E00
1/Jan/1912 0:00 -1:00

Place	Lat	Long	Offset
Abba	5N20	15E11	-1:00:44
Adelaye	7N07	22E49	-1:31:16
Alindao	5N02	21E13	-1:24:52
Ancien Goubéré	5N51	26E46	-1:47:04
Andjeguéré	6N41	21E03	-1:24:12
Baboua	5N48	14E49	-0:59:16
Bade	6N41	17E07	-1:08:28
Baïna Bondio	5N10	16E33	-1:06:12
Bakala	3N46	17E33	-1:10:12
Bakala	6N11	20E22	-1:21:28
Bakouma	5N42	22E47	-1:31:08
Balakété	6N56	19E54	-1:19:36
Bambari	5N45	20E40	-1:22:40
Bambio	3N54	16E59	-1:07:56
Bambouti	5N24	27E12	-1:48:48
Bamingui	7N34	20E11	-1:20:44
Bangassou	4N50	23E07	-1:32:28
Bangbari	5N12	22E21	-1:29:24
Bangi → Bangui	4N22	18E35	-1:14:20
Bangui	4N22	18E35	-1:14:20
Bani	7N07	22E49	-1:31:16
Bania	4N00	16E07	-1:04:28
Banima	5N26	23E54	-1:35:36
Baoro	5N40	15E58	-1:03:52
Batangafo	7N18	18E18	-1:13:12
Batibia	5N56	21E09	-1:24:36
Bayanga	2N53	16E19	-1:05:16
Béle-Kété	6N01	17E26	-1:09:44
Bélézé	3N51	16E19	-1:05:16
Benima	5N26	23E54	-1:35:36
Berbérati	4N16	15E47	-1:03:08
Bianga	4N51	20E25	-1:21:40
Bigéné	3N25	15E38	-1:02:32
Bimbo	4N18	18E33	-1:14:12
Birao	10N17	22E47	-1:31:08
Boali	4N48	18E07	-1:12:28
Bocaranga	6N59	15E39	-1:02:36
Boda	4N19	17E28	-1:09:52
Bodanga Dawili	5N33	16E45	-1:07:00
Bodoukpa	5N43	17E36	-1:10:24
Bodoupa	5N43	17E36	-1:10:24
Bogangolo	5N34	18E15	-1:13:00
Bohorg	6N23	15E37	-1:02:28
Bolaï I	4N20	17E21	-1:09:24
Bolay I	4N20	17E21	-1:09:24
Bossangoa	6N29	17E27	-1:09:48
Bossembélé	5N16	17E39	-1:10:36
Bossemtele II	5N41	16E38	-1:06:32
Bossentele	5N41	16E38	-1:06:32
Bouala	6N23	15E37	-1:02:28
Bouar	5N57	15E36	-1:02:24
Bouca	6N30	18E17	-1:13:08
Boulouba	6N49	22E15	-1:29:00
Bouméntana	6N59	16E56	-1:07:44
Bouraéré	4N44	17E25	-1:09:40
Boykétté	5N28	20E50	-1:23:20
Boyo	5N43	21E33	-1:26:12
Bozoum	6N19	16E23	-1:05:32
Bria	6N32	21E59	-1:27:56
Carnot	4N56	15E52	-1:03:28
Damara	4N58	18E42	-1:14:48
Dekoa	6N19	19E04	-1:16:16
Délembé	9N53	22E37	-1:30:28
Délimbé	9N53	22E37	-1:30:28
Dembia	5N07	24E25	-1:37:40
Denguiro	5N38	23E02	-1:32:08
Digui	5N28	20E50	-1:23:20
Djema	6N03	25E19	-1:41:16
Djoubissi	6N12	20E45	-1:23:00
Djouho Battinga	6N38	20E34	-1:22:16
Dobane	6N24	24E42	-1:38:48
Doumdégué	7N29	18E58	-1:15:52
Fodé	5N29	23E18	-1:33:12
Fort-Crampel	6N59	19E11	-1:16:44
Fort de Possel	5N01	19E15	-1:17:00
Fort-Sibut	5N44	19E05	-1:16:20
Gadzi	4N47	16E42	-1:06:48
Gambo	4N39	22E16	-1:29:04
Gamboula	4N08	15E09	-1:00:36
Garba	9N12	20E30	-1:22:00
Gbaoui Bodanga	5N33	16E45	-1:07:00
Golongoso	9N00	19E09	-1:16:36
Gordil	9N44	21E35	-1:26:20
Gréfodé	5N43	21E33	-1:26:12
Grima	3N59	17E06	-1:08:24
Grimari	5N44	20E03	-1:20:12
Grivai Pamia	7N03	19E26	-1:17:44
Guita Koulouba	5N56	23E19	-1:33:16
Hyrra Banda	5N57	22E04	-1:28:16
Ippy	6N15	21E12	-1:24:48
Ira Banda	5N57	22E04	-1:28:16
Kabo	7N39	18E37	-1:14:28
Kaboro	6N59	17E33	-1:10:12
Kabou	5N20	21E43	-1:26:52
Kaga Bandoro	6N59	19E11	-1:16:44
Kaka	6N01	26E30	-1:46:00
Kambakota	7N10	17E54	-1:11:36
Kazanga	5N10	23E06	-1:32:24
Kazima	5N16	26E11	-1:44:44
Kembé	4N36	21E54	-1:27:36
Kéré	5N16	26E11	-1:44:44
Kitéssa	5N20	25E20	-1:41:20
Kongbo	4N44	21E23	-1:25:32
Koropele	4N44	17E11	-1:08:44
Kossindi	3N51	16E19	-1:05:16
Kouango	4N58	19E59	-1:19:56
Kouki	7N10	17E18	-1:09:12
Koumbal	9N26	22E39	-1:30:36
Koundé	6N07	14E38	-0:58:32
Lavougba	5N46	23E21	-1:33:24
Les Moroubas	6N11	20E13	-1:20:52
Limassa	4N14	22E02	-1:28:08
Mambéllé	3N51	16E42	-1:06:48
Mangoupa	5N53	24E40	-1:38:40
Marali	6N01	18E24	-1:13:36
Marcounda	7N37	16E59	-1:07:56
Markounda	7N37	16E59	-1:07:56
Mayaka	5N17	16E52	-1:07:28
Mbage	5N30	25E13	-1:40:52
Mbaïki	3N53	18E00	-1:12:00
Mbala	7N48	20E51	-1:23:24
Mboula	4N27	16E29	-1:05:56
Mbrés	6N40	19E48	-1:19:12
Mélé	9N46	21E33	-1:26:12
Miaméré	8N52	19E50	-1:19:20
Mingala	5N06	21E49	-1:27:16
Mobaye	4N19	21E11	-1:24:44
Mongoumba	3N38	18E36	-1:14:24
Mopoï	5N08	26E55	-1:47:40
Morouba	6N11	20E13	-1:20:52
Mouka	7N16	21E52	-1:27:28
Moyenne-Sido	8N13	18E43	-1:14:52
Nao	4N35	15E09	-1:00:36
Ndanda	5N12	22E21	-1:29:24
Ndarassa	6N49	22E15	-1:29:00
Ndélé	8N24	20E39	-1:22:36
Ngadza	5N10	20E12	-1:20:48
Ngolo	9N56	22E16	-1:29:04
Ngoto	4N00	17E21	-1:09:24
Ngotto	4N00	17E21	-1:09:24
Ngouroundou	6N27	22E37	-1:30:28
Nguiroungou	6N27	22E37	-1:30:28
Niem	6N12	15E14	-1:00:56
Nola	3N32	16E04	-1:04:16
Obo	5N24	26E30	-1:46:00
Ouadda	8N04	22E24	-1:29:36
Ouamiri	6N12	20E45	-1:23:00
Ouanda Djallé	8N54	22E48	-1:31:12
Ouandago	7N10	18E42	-1:14:48
Ouango	4N19	22E33	-1:30:12
Paoua	7N15	16E26	-1:05:44
Possel	5N01	19E15	-1:17:00
Rafaï	4N58	23E56	-1:35:44
Saba	7N50	17E49	-1:11:16
Sabo	7N50	17E49	-1:11:16
Salo	3N12	16E07	-1:04:28
Samba	6N49	21E12	-1:24:48
Satema	4N18	21E42	-1:26:48
Sibut	5N44	19E05	-1:16:20
Sido	8N13	18E43	-1:14:52
Soboko	6N49	24E50	-1:39:20
Tagbara	5N56	21E09	-1:24:36
Taley	6N40	16E23	-1:05:32
Tiroungoulou	9N34	22E09	-1:28:36
Togho	6N01	17E26	-1:09:44
Vougba	5N10	23E06	-1:32:24
Voulou	8N33	22E36	-1:30:24
Yakotoko	5N20	25E20	-1:41:20
Yalinga	6N31	23E15	-1:33:00
Yaloká	5N19	17E05	-1:08:20
Yaloke	5N19	17E05	-1:08:20
Yao	5N19	19E36	-1:18:24
Yao Malikidza	5N19	19E36	-1:18:24
Zaorosongou	5N02	16E13	-1:04:52
Zemio	5N02	25E08	-1:40:32
Zinga	3N43	18E35	-1:14:20
Zouginindja	5N24	21E40	-1:26:40

CHAD TSCHAD TCHAD

Time Table		
Before	1/Jan/1912	LMT
Begin Standard		15E00
1/Jan/1912	0:00	-1:00
14/Oct/1979	0:00	-2:00
8/Mar/1980	0:00	-1:00

Place	Lat	Long	Offset
Abéché	13N49	20E49	-1:23:16
Abou Deïa	11N27	19E17	-1:17:08
Adré	13N28	22E12	-1:28:48
Al Bidia	10N33	20E13	-1:20:52
Alo	11N47	20E53	-1:23:32
Am Dam	12N46	20E29	-1:21:56
Am Géréda	12N52	21E10	-1:24:40
Am Loubia	13N39	20E08	-1:20:32
Am-Raya	14N00	16E35	-1:06:20
Am Saterna	12N26	21E25	-1:25:40
Am Sigan	11N41	19E51	-1:19:24
Am Timan	11N02	20E17	-1:21:08
Aozi	21N04	18E41	-1:14:44
Aozou	21N49	17E25	-1:09:40
Arada	15N01	20E40	-1:22:40
Ardélik	12N26	21E25	-1:25:40
Ati	13N13	18E20	-1:13:20
Badanga	11N36	17E26	-1:09:44
Baïbokoum	7N46	15E43	-1:02:52
Ba-Illi	10N30	16E34	-1:06:16
Bardaï	21N22	16E59	-1:07:56
Béboto	8N16	16E56	-1:07:44
Bédaya	8N55	17E52	-1:11:28
Bédi	11N06	18E33	-1:14:12
Bédiondo	8N39	17E12	-1:08:48
Béguigui	9N00	18E56	-1:15:44
Beinamar	8N40	15E23	-1:01:32
Benoy	8N59	16E19	-1:05:16
Béré	9N20	16E09	-1:04:36
Biltine	14N32	20E55	-1:23:40
Binder	9N58	14E28	-0:57:52
Binder Foulbé	9N58	14E28	-0:57:52
Bir Gara	13N11	15E58	-1:03:52
Birket Fatimé	12N54	19E05	-1:16:20
Bitkin	11N59	18E13	-1:12:52
Bitkine	11N59	18E13	-1:12:52
Bokoro	12N23	17E03	-1:08:12
Bol	13N28	14E43	-0:58:52
Boli	10N50	18E43	-1:14:52
Bomboyo	12N01	15E28	-1:01:52
Bongor	10N17	15E22	-1:01:28
Boumou	9N02	16E26	-1:05:44
Bousso	10N29	16E43	-1:06:52
Chakarnaba	14N13	20E51	-1:23:24
Dik	9N58	17E31	-1:10:04
Djangatiti Dafana	11N46	21E19	-1:25:16
Djébren	11N14	19E01	-1:16:04
Djébrène	11N14	19E01	-1:16:04
Djédaa	13N31	18E34	-1:14:16
Djéké Djéké	8N25	18E12	-1:12:48
Djember	10N25	17E50	-1:11:20
Djouna	10N27	20E04	-1:20:16
Doba	8N39	16E51	-1:07:24
Dourbali	11N49	15E52	-1:03:28
Dourkoulé	14N27	22E13	-1:28:52
Fada	17N14	21E33	-1:26:12
Faya	17N55	19E07	-1:16:28
Fianga	9N55	15E09	-1:00:36
Fort-Archambault → Sarh	9N09	18E23	-1:13:32
Fort-Lamy → Ndjamena	12N07	15E03	-1:00:12
Gabil	11N09	18E12	-1:12:48
Gagal	9N01	15E08	-1:00:32
Gélengdeng	10N56	15E32	-1:02:08
Gézenti	21N41	18E18	-1:13:12
Gidari	9N17	16E40	-1:06:40
Gondey	9N09	19E19	-1:17:16
Gongo	9N00	18E56	-1:15:44
Goré	7N53	16E40	-1:06:40
Goro	8N37	18E08	-1:12:32
Goubone	20N43	17E08	-1:08:32
Goundi	9N22	17E22	-1:09:28
Gounou Gaya	9N38	15E31	-1:02:04
Gouro	19N33	19E33	-1:18:12
Goz Beïda	12N13	21E25	-1:25:40
Guélendeng	10N56	15E32	-1:02:08
Guéré	9N12	18E10	-1:12:40
Guéréda	14N31	22E05	-1:28:20
Guidari	9N17	16E40	-1:06:40
Ham	10N00	15E41	-1:02:44
Haraz	13N57	19E26	-1:17:44
Haraz-Djombo	13N57	19E26	-1:17:44
Haraze	9N55	20E48	-1:23:12
Haraze-Mangueigne	9N55	20E48	-1:23:12
Ianga	9N07	18E11	-1:12:44
Iriba	15N07	22E15	-1:29:00
Kagopal	8N17	16E27	-1:05:48
Karé	10N07	19E48	-1:19:12
Kélo	9N19	15E48	-1:03:12
Korbol	10N01	17E43	-1:10:52
Koro Toro	16N05	18E30	-1:14:00
Kouga	9N56	21E03	-1:24:12
Koumra	8N55	17E33	-1:10:12
Krim Krim	8N58	15E48	-1:03:12
Kyabé	9N27	18E57	-1:15:48
Laï	9N24	16E18	-1:05:12
Laïri	10N49	17E06	-1:08:24
Lamé	9N15	14E32	-0:58:08
Largeau	17N55	19E07	-1:16:28
Léré	9N39	14E13	-0:56:52
Logone Gana	11N33	15E09	-1:00:36
Madadi	18N28	20E45	-1:23:00
Mai Aché	12N00	15E44	-1:02:56
Malam	11N27	20E59	-1:23:56
Manda	9N12	18E10	-1:12:40
Mandélia	11N43	15E15	-1:01:00
Mandjafa	11N11	15E25	-1:01:40
Mangalmé	12N21	19E37	-1:18:28
Mangeigne	10N31	21E19	-1:25:16
Mao	14N07	15E19	-1:01:16
Masalasef	11N43	17E08	-1:08:32
Massaguet	12N28	15E26	-1:01:44
Massakory	13N00	15E44	-1:02:56
Massalassef	11N43	17E08	-1:08:32
Massenya	11N24	16E10	-1:04:40
May Aché	12N00	15E44	-1:02:56
Mayo	9N07	18E11	-1:12:44
Mbasay	7N39	15E40	-1:02:40
Mbassay	7N39	15E40	-1:02:40
Mbéré	10N49	15E44	-1:02:56
Melfi	11N04	17E56	-1:11:44
Meskine	11N25	15E21	-1:01:24
Miltou	10N14	17E26	-1:09:44
Mito	10N49	15E44	-1:02:56
Modra	20N43	17E42	-1:10:48
Mogroum	11N06	15E25	-1:01:40
Moïssala	8N21	17E46	-1:11:04
Molou	13N42	21E44	-1:26:56
Mondo	13N47	15E32	-1:02:08
Mongo	12N11	18E42	-1:14:48
Mongororo	12N01	22E28	-1:29:52
Mougdi	11N30	17E34	-1:10:16
Moundou	8N34	16E05	-1:04:20
Mounyaz	10N41	21E18	-1:25:12
Moura	13N47	21E13	-1:24:52
Mouraya	11N27	20E59	-1:23:56
Mousgougou	10N47	16E09	-1:04:36
Moussoro	13N39	16E29	-1:05:56
Mouzarak	13N11	15E58	-1:03:52
Ndjamena	12N07	15E03	-1:00:12
Ngouri	13N38	15E22	-1:01:28
Niellim	9N42	17E49	-1:11:16
Niéré	14N30	21E09	-1:24:36
Nokou	14N35	14E47	-0:59:08
Oum Chalouba	15N48	20E46	-1:23:04
Oum Hadjer	13N18	19E41	-1:18:44
Ounianga Kébir	19N04	20E29	-1:21:56
Ouri	21N34	19E13	-1:16:52
Pala	9N22	14E54	-0:59:36
Rig-Rig	14N16	14E21	-0:57:24
Salal	14N51	17E13	-1:08:52
Sarh	9N09	18E23	-1:13:32
Séssé	11N30	17E34	-1:10:16
Singako	9N50	19E29	-1:17:56
Takalaou	10N07	19E48	-1:19:12
Tapol	8N31	15E35	-1:02:20
Tchagin Golo	10N03	16E19	-1:05:16
Tchaguine Golo	10N03	16E19	-1:05:16
Tédji	11N46	21E19	-1:25:16
Wour	21N21	15E57	-1:03:48
Yao	12N51	17E34	-1:10:16
Yebbi Bou	20N58	18E04	-1:12:16
Yebbi Souma	21N08	17E56	-1:11:44
Zakouma	10N54	19E49	-1:19:16
Zigey	14N43	15E47	-1:03:08
Ziguéy	14N43	15E47	-1:03:08
Zouar	20N27	16E32	-1:06:08

```
Time Table # 1
Before 1/Jan/1890 LMT
Begin Standard 70w40
1/Jan/1890 0:00 4:43
Begin Standard 75w00
1/Jan/1910 0:00 5:00
Begin Standard 60w00
1/Sep/1932 0:00 4:00
12/Oct/1969 0:00 3:00
15/Mar/1970 0:00 4:00
11/Oct/1970 0:00 3:00
14/Mar/1971 0:00 4:00
10/Oct/1971 0:00 3:00
12/Mar/1972 0:00 4:00
15/Oct/1972 0:00 3:00
11/Mar/1973 0:00 4:00
14/Oct/1973 0:00 3:00
10/Mar/1974 0:00 4:00
13/Oct/1974 0:00 3:00
9/Mar/1975 0:00 4:00
12/Oct/1975 0:00 3:00
14/Mar/1976 0:00 4:00
10/Oct/1976 0:00 3:00
13/Mar/1977 0:00 4:00
9/Oct/1977 0:00 3:00
12/Mar/1978 0:00 4:00
15/Oct/1978 0:00 3:00
11/Mar/1979 0:00 4:00
14/Oct/1979 0:00 3:00
9/Mar/1980 0:00 4:00
12/Oct/1980 0:00 3:00
15/Mar/1981 0:00 4:00
11/Oct/1981 0:00 3:00
14/Mar/1982 0:00 4:00
10/Oct/1982 0:00 3:00
13/Mar/1983 0:00 4:00
9/Oct/1983 0:00 3:00
11/Mar/1984 0:00 4:00
14/Oct/1984 0:00 3:00
10/Mar/1985 0:00 4:00
13/Oct/1985 0:00 3:00
9/Mar/1986 0:00 4:00
12/Oct/1986 0:00 3:00
15/Mar/1987 0:00 4:00
11/Oct/1987 0:00 3:00
13/Mar/1988 0:00 4:00
9/Oct/1988 0:00 3:00
12/Mar/1989 0:00 4:00
15/Oct/1989 0:00 3:00
11/Mar/1990 0:00 4:00
14/Oct/1990 0:00 3:00
10/Mar/1991 0:00 4:00
13/Oct/1991 0:00 3:00
15/Mar/1992 0:00 4:00
11/Oct/1992 0:00 3:00
14/Mar/1993 0:00 4:00
10/Oct/1993 0:00 3:00
13/Mar/1994 0:00 4:00
9/Oct/1994 0:00 3:00
12/Mar/1995 0:00 4:00
15/Oct/1995 0:00 3:00
10/Mar/1996 0:00 4:00
13/Oct/1996 0:00 3:00
9/Mar/1997 0:00 4:00
12/Oct/1997 0:00 3:00
15/Mar/1998 0:00 4:00
11/Oct/1998 0:00 3:00
14/Mar/1999 0:00 4:00
10/Oct/1999 0:00 3:00
12/Mar/2000 0:00 4:00
.......................
Time Table # 2
Before 1/Jan/1890 LMT
Begin Standard 70w40
1/Jan/1890 0:00 4:43
Begin Standard 75w00
1/Jan/1910 0:00 5:00
1/Sep/1918 0:00 4:00
2/Jul/1919 0:00 5:00
1/Sep/1927 0:00 4:00
1/Apr/1928 0:00 5:00
1/Sep/1928 0:00 4:00
1/Apr/1929 0:00 5:00
1/Sep/1929 0:00 4:00
1/Apr/1930 0:00 5:00
1/Sep/1930 0:00 4:00
1/Apr/1931 0:00 5:00
1/Sep/1931 0:00 4:00
1/Apr/1932 0:00 5:00
Begin Standard 60w00
1/Sep/1932 0:00 4:00
12/Oct/1969 0:00 3:00
15/Mar/1970 0:00 4:00
11/Oct/1970 0:00 3:00
14/Mar/1971 0:00 4:00
10/Oct/1971 0:00 3:00
12/Mar/1972 0:00 4:00
15/Oct/1972 0:00 3:00
11/Mar/1973 0:00 4:00
14/Oct/1973 0:00 3:00
10/Mar/1974 0:00 4:00
13/Oct/1974 0:00 3:00
9/Mar/1975 0:00 4:00
12/Oct/1975 0:00 3:00
14/Mar/1976 0:00 4:00
10/Oct/1976 0:00 3:00
13/Mar/1977 0:00 4:00
9/Oct/1977 0:00 3:00
12/Mar/1978 0:00 4:00
15/Oct/1978 0:00 3:00
11/Mar/1979 0:00 4:00
14/Oct/1979 0:00 3:00
9/Mar/1980 0:00 4:00
12/Oct/1980 0:00 3:00
15/Mar/1981 0:00 4:00
11/Oct/1981 0:00 3:00
14/Mar/1982 0:00 4:00
10/Oct/1982 0:00 3:00
13/Mar/1983 0:00 4:00
9/Oct/1983 0:00 3:00
11/Mar/1984 0:00 4:00
14/Oct/1984 0:00 3:00
10/Mar/1985 0:00 4:00
13/Oct/1985 0:00 3:00
9/Mar/1986 0:00 4:00
12/Oct/1986 0:00 3:00
15/Mar/1987 0:00 4:00
11/Oct/1987 0:00 3:00
13/Mar/1988 0:00 4:00
9/Oct/1988 0:00 3:00
12/Mar/1989 0:00 4:00
15/Oct/1989 0:00 3:00
11/Mar/1990 0:00 4:00
14/Oct/1990 0:00 3:00
10/Mar/1991 0:00 4:00
13/Oct/1991 0:00 3:00
15/Mar/1992 0:00 4:00
11/Oct/1992 0:00 3:00
14/Mar/1993 0:00 4:00
10/Oct/1993 0:00 3:00
13/Mar/1994 0:00 4:00
9/Oct/1994 0:00 3:00
12/Mar/1995 0:00 4:00
15/Oct/1995 0:00 3:00
10/Mar/1996 0:00 4:00
13/Oct/1996 0:00 3:00
9/Mar/1997 0:00 4:00
12/Oct/1997 0:00 3:00
15/Mar/1998 0:00 4:00
11/Oct/1998 0:00 3:00
14/Mar/1999 0:00 4:00
10/Oct/1999 0:00 3:00
12/Mar/2000 0:00 4:00
.......................
Time Table # 3
Before 1/Jan/1890 LMT
Begin Standard 70w40
1/Jan/1890 0:00 4:43
Begin Standard 75w00
1/Jan/1910 0:00 5:00
1/Sep/1931 0:00 4:00
1/Apr/1932 0:00 5:00
Begin Standard 60w00
1/Sep/1932 0:00 4:00
12/Oct/1969 0:00 3:00
15/Mar/1970 0:00 4:00
11/Oct/1970 0:00 3:00
14/Mar/1971 0:00 4:00
10/Oct/1971 0:00 3:00
12/Mar/1972 0:00 4:00
15/Oct/1972 0:00 3:00
11/Mar/1973 0:00 4:00
14/Oct/1973 0:00 3:00
10/Mar/1974 0:00 4:00
13/Oct/1974 0:00 3:00
9/Mar/1975 0:00 4:00
12/Oct/1975 0:00 3:00
14/Mar/1976 0:00 4:00
10/Oct/1976 0:00 3:00
13/Mar/1977 0:00 4:00
9/Oct/1977 0:00 3:00
12/Mar/1978 0:00 4:00
15/Oct/1978 0:00 3:00
11/Mar/1979 0:00 4:00
14/Oct/1979 0:00 3:00
9/Mar/1980 0:00 4:00
12/Oct/1980 0:00 3:00
15/Mar/1981 0:00 4:00
11/Oct/1981 0:00 3:00
14/Mar/1982 0:00 4:00
10/Oct/1982 0:00 3:00
13/Mar/1983 0:00 4:00
9/Oct/1983 0:00 3:00
11/Mar/1984 0:00 4:00
14/Oct/1984 0:00 3:00
10/Mar/1985 0:00 4:00
13/Oct/1985 0:00 3:00
9/Mar/1986 0:00 4:00
12/Oct/1986 0:00 3:00
15/Mar/1987 0:00 4:00
11/Oct/1987 0:00 3:00
13/Mar/1988 0:00 4:00
9/Oct/1988 0:00 3:00
12/Mar/1989 0:00 4:00
15/Oct/1989 0:00 3:00
11/Mar/1990 0:00 4:00
14/Oct/1990 0:00 3:00
10/Mar/1991 0:00 4:00
13/Oct/1991 0:00 3:00
15/Mar/1992 0:00 4:00
11/Oct/1992 0:00 3:00
14/Mar/1993 0:00 4:00
10/Oct/1993 0:00 3:00
13/Mar/1994 0:00 4:00
9/Oct/1994 0:00 3:00
12/Mar/1995 0:00 4:00
15/Oct/1995 0:00 3:00
10/Mar/1996 0:00 4:00
13/Oct/1996 0:00 3:00
9/Mar/1997 0:00 4:00
12/Oct/1997 0:00 3:00
15/Mar/1998 0:00 4:00
11/Oct/1998 0:00 3:00
14/Mar/1999 0:00 4:00
10/Oct/1999 0:00 3:00
12/Mar/2000 0:00 4:00
.......................
Time Table # 4
Before 1/Jan/1890 LMT
Begin Standard 109w22
1/Jan/1890 0:00 7:17
Begin Standard 105w00
1/Sep/1932 0:00 7:00
12/Oct/1969 0:00 6:00
15/Mar/1970 0:00 7:00
11/Oct/1970 0:00 6:00
14/Mar/1971 0:00 7:00
10/Oct/1971 0:00 6:00
12/Mar/1972 0:00 7:00
15/Oct/1972 0:00 6:00
11/Mar/1973 0:00 7:00
14/Oct/1973 0:00 6:00
10/Mar/1974 0:00 7:00
13/Oct/1974 0:00 6:00
9/Mar/1975 0:00 7:00
12/Oct/1975 0:00 6:00
14/Mar/1976 0:00 7:00
10/Oct/1976 0:00 6:00
13/Mar/1977 0:00 7:00
9/Oct/1977 0:00 6:00
12/Mar/1978 0:00 7:00
15/Oct/1978 0:00 6:00
11/Mar/1979 0:00 7:00
14/Oct/1979 0:00 6:00
9/Mar/1980 0:00 7:00
12/Oct/1980 0:00 6:00
15/Mar/1981 0:00 7:00
11/Oct/1981 0:00 6:00
Begin Standard 90w00
14/Mar/1982 0:00 6:00
10/Oct/1982 0:00 5:00
13/Mar/1983 0:00 6:00
9/Oct/1983 0:00 5:00
11/Mar/1984 0:00 6:00
14/Oct/1984 0:00 5:00
10/Mar/1985 0:00 6:00
13/Oct/1985 0:00 5:00
9/Mar/1986 0:00 6:00
12/Oct/1986 0:00 5:00
15/Mar/1987 0:00 6:00
11/Oct/1987 0:00 5:00
13/Mar/1988 0:00 6:00
9/Oct/1988 0:00 5:00
12/Mar/1989 0:00 6:00
15/Oct/1989 0:00 5:00
11/Mar/1990 0:00 6:00
14/Oct/1990 0:00 5:00
10/Mar/1991 0:00 6:00
13/Oct/1991 0:00 5:00
15/Mar/1992 0:00 6:00
11/Oct/1992 0:00 5:00
14/Mar/1993 0:00 6:00
10/Oct/1993 0:00 5:00
13/Mar/1994 0:00 6:00
9/Oct/1994 0:00 5:00
12/Mar/1995 0:00 6:00
15/Oct/1995 0:00 5:00
10/Mar/1996 0:00 6:00
13/Oct/1996 0:00 5:00
9/Mar/1997 0:00 6:00
12/Oct/1997 0:00 5:00
15/Mar/1998 0:00 6:00
11/Oct/1998 0:00 5:00
14/Mar/1999 0:00 6:00
10/Oct/1999 0:00 5:00
12/Mar/2000 0:00 6:00
```

Place	Table	Lat	Long	Offset
Achao	1	42s28	73w30	4:54:00
Alemania	1	25s10	69w55	4:39:40
Algarrobal	1	28s08	70w39	4:42:36
Algarrobo	1	33s22	71w40	4:46:40
Almirante Latorre	1	29s38	70w58	4:43:52
Altamira	1	25s47	69w51	4:39:24
Alto del Carmen	1	28s46	70w30	4:42:00
Ancud	1	41s52	73w50	4:55:20
Andacollo	1	30s14	71w06	4:44:24
Angol	1	37s48	72w43	4:50:52
Antofagasta	1	23s39	70w24	4:41:36
Apoquindo	2	33s24	70w32	4:42:08
Arauco	1	37s15	73w19	4:53:16
Arica	1	18s29	70w20	4:41:20
Ascotán	1	21s44	68w18	4:33:12
Balmaceda	1	45s55	71w41	4:46:44
Baquedano	1	23s20	69w51	4:39:24
Barrancas	2	33s27	70w46	4:43:04
Belén	1	18s29	69w31	4:38:04
Bellavista	2	33s31	70w37	4:42:28
Buin	2	33s44	70w45	4:43:00
Bulnes	1	36s44	72w18	4:49:12
Cabildo	1	32s26	71w05	4:44:20
Calama	1	22s28	68w56	4:35:44
Calbuco	1	41s46	73w08	4:52:32
Caldera	1	27s04	70w50	4:43:20
Camiña	1	19s18	69w26	4:37:44
Cañete	1	37s48	73w24	4:53:36
Carén	1	30s51	70w47	4:43:08
Carmen Alto	1	23s11	69w40	4:38:40
Carmen de Huechuraba	2	33s21	70w40	4:42:40
Carrascal	2	33s25	70w43	4:42:52
Carrizal Bajo	1	28s05	71w10	4:44:40
Cartagena	1	33s33	71w37	4:46:28
Castro	1	42s29	73w46	4:55:04
Catalina	1	25s13	69w43	4:38:52
Cauquenes	1	35s58	72w21	4:49:24
Cerro Moreno	1	23s28	70w25	4:41:40
Chañaral	1	26s21	70w37	4:42:28
Chanco	1	35s44	72w32	4:50:08
Cherquenco	1	38s41	72w00	4:48:00
Chiapa	1	19s32	69w13	4:36:52
Chile Chico	1	46s33	71w44	4:46:56
Chillán	1	36s36	72w07	4:48:28
Chimbarongo	1	34s42	71w03	4:44:12
Chincolco	1	32s13	70w50	4:43:20
Chiuchiu	1	22s21	68w39	4:34:36
Chonchi	1	42s38	73w47	4:55:08
Chuquicamata	1	22s19	68w56	4:35:44
Cobija	1	22s33	70w16	4:41:04
Cobquecura	1	36s08	72w47	4:51:08
Codpa	1	18s50	69w44	4:38:56
Coelemu	1	36s29	72w42	4:50:48
Coihaique	1	45s34	72w04	4:48:16
Colbún	1	35s42	71w25	4:45:40
Colina	2	33s12	70w41	4:42:44
Collipulli	1	37s57	72w26	4:49:44
Coltauco	1	34s18	71w06	4:44:24
Combarbalá	1	31s11	71w02	4:44:08
Concepción	1	36s50	73w03	4:52:12
Conchalí	2	33s24	70w39	4:42:36
Conchi	1	22s02	68w38	4:34:32
Concón	3	32s55	71w31	4:46:04
Constitución	1	35s20	72w25	4:49:40
Copiapó	1	27s22	70w20	4:41:20
Coquimbo	1	29s58	71w21	4:45:24
Coronel	1	37s01	73w08	4:52:32
Corral	1	39s52	73w26	4:53:44
Corte Alto	1	40s57	73w10	4:52:40
Coya Sur	1	22s25	69w38	4:38:32
Cruz Grande	1	29s25	71w18	4:45:12
Cunco	1	38s55	72w02	4:48:08
Cuncumén	1	31s53	70w38	4:42:32
Curacautín	1	38s26	71w53	4:47:32
Curacaví	1	33s24	71w09	4:44:36
Curanilahue	1	37s28	73w21	4:53:24
Curanipe	1	35s50	72w38	4:50:32
Curepto	1	35s05	72w01	4:48:04
Curicó	1	34s59	71w14	4:44:56
Dalcahue	1	42s23	73w40	4:54:40
Domeyko	1	28s57	70w54	4:43:36
Easter Island → Isla de Pascua	4	27s07	109w22	7:17:28
El Alto	2	33s30	70w43	4:42:52
El Arrayán	2	33s21	70w28	4:41:52
El Carmen	2	33s21	70w43	4:42:52
El Cortijo	2	33s22	70w42	4:42:48
El Monte	1	33s41	71w01	4:44:04
El Palqui	1	30s45	70w59	4:43:56
El Peral	2	33s35	70w34	4:42:16
El Salado	1	26s25	70w19	4:41:16
El Salto	2	33s23	70w38	4:42:32
El Tofo	1	29s27	71w15	4:45:00
El Tránsito	1	28s52	70w17	4:41:08
El Volcán	1	33s49	70w11	4:40:44
Empedrado	1	35s36	72w17	4:49:08
Freirina	1	28s30	71w06	4:44:24
Fresia	1	41s09	73w27	4:53:48
Frutillar	1	41s07	73w03	4:52:12
Galvarino	1	38s24	72w47	4:51:08
Graneros	1	34s04	70w44	4:42:56
Guayacán	1	29s58	71w22	4:45:28
Hanga Roa	4	27s09	109w26	7:17:44
Hualañé	1	34s59	71w49	4:47:16
Huara	1	19s59	69w47	4:39:08
Huasco	1	28s28	71w14	4:44:56
Huentelauquén	1	31s35	71w32	4:46:08
Illapel	1	31s38	71w10	4:44:40
Imilac	1	24s14	68w53	4:35:32
Inca de Oro	1	26s45	69w54	4:39:36
Incaguasi	1	29s13	71w03	4:44:12
Iquique	1	20s13	70w10	4:40:40
Isla de Maipo	1	33s45	70w54	4:43:36
Isla de Pascua	4	27s07	109w22	7:17:28
Islón	1	29s54	71w12	4:44:48
José Francisco Vergara	1	22s28	69w38	4:38:32
La Aurora	2	33s36	70w38	4:42:32
La Bandera	2	33s34	70w39	4:42:36
La Blanca	2	33s31	70w41	4:42:44
La Calera	1	32s47	71w12	4:44:48
La Cisterna	2	33s33	70w41	4:42:44
La Dehesa	2	33s22	70w33	4:42:12
La Florida	2	33s33	70w34	4:42:16
La Granja	2	33s32	70w39	4:42:36
La Higuera	1	29s30	71w17	4:45:08
La Ligua	1	32s27	71w14	4:44:56
Lanco	1	39s24	72w46	4:51:04
La Negra	1	23s45	70w19	4:41:16
La Obra	2	33s36	70w30	4:42:00
La Purísima	2	33s34	70w39	4:42:36
La Reina	2	33s27	70w33	4:42:12
Las Cabras	1	34s18	71w19	4:45:16
Las Condes	2	33s22	70w31	4:42:04
La Serena	1	29s54	71w16	4:45:04
Las Rejas	2	33s28	70w44	4:42:56
Las Rosas	2	33s35	70w37	4:42:28
Las Vizcachas	2	33s36	70w32	4:42:08
La Unión	1	40s17	73w05	4:52:20
Lautaro	1	38s31	72w27	4:49:48
Lebu	1	37s37	73w39	4:54:36
Lepihué	1	41s37	73w36	4:54:24
Licantén	1	34s59	72w00	4:48:00
Limache	1	33s01	71w16	4:45:04
Linares	1	35s51	71w36	4:46:24
Liucura	1	38s39	71w05	4:44:20
Llanquihue	1	41s15	73w01	4:52:04
Llanta	1	26s20	69w49	4:39:16
Llico	1	34s46	72w05	4:48:20
Lo Aranguiz	2	33s23	70w40	4:42:40
Lo Barnechea	2	33s21	70w31	4:42:04
Lo Benitez	2	33s34	70w42	4:42:48
Lo Bernales	2	33s34	70w34	4:42:16

CHILE

Lo Boza	2	33s23	70w46	4:43:04
Lo Espejo	2	33s32	70w43	4:42:52
Lo Hermida	2	33s29	70w33	4:42:12
Loma Blanca	2	33s30	70w47	4:43:08
Lo Miranda	1	34s11	70w54	4:43:36
Loncoche	1	39s22	72w38	4:50:32
Longaví	1	35s58	71w41	4:46:44
Lo Ortuzar	2	33s28	70w45	4:43:00
Lo Prado Arriba	2	33s26	70w45	4:43:00
Los Andes	1	32s50	70w37	4:42:28
Los Ángeles	1	37s28	72w21	4:49:24
Los Cuatro Álamos	2	33s32	70w44	4:42:56
Los Lagos	1	39s51	72w50	4:51:20
Los Muermos	1	41s24	73w29	4:53:56
Los Quillayes	2	33s34	70w37	4:42:28
Los Sauces	1	37s58	72w50	4:51:20
Los Vilos	1	31s55	71w31	4:46:04
Lota	1	37s05	73w10	4:52:40
Machalí	1	34s11	70w40	4:42:40
Macul	2	33s30	70w34	4:42:16
Magallanes → Punta Arenas	1	53s09	70w55	4:43:40
Maipú	2	33s31	70w46	4:43:04
Mamiña	1	20s05	69w14	4:36:56
Mantos Blancos	1	23s25	70w05	4:40:20
María Elena	1	22s21	69w40	4:38:40
Mataveri	4	27s10	109w27	7:17:48
Maullín	1	41s38	73w37	4:54:28
Mejillones	1	23s06	70w27	4:41:48
Melipilla	1	33s42	71w13	4:44:52
Molina	1	35s07	71w17	4:45:08
Monte Grande	1	30s06	70w31	4:42:04
Monte Patria	1	30s42	70w58	4:43:52
Mulchén	1	37s43	72w14	4:48:56
Nacimiento	1	37s30	72w40	4:50:40
Navidad	1	33s57	71w50	4:47:20
Neurara	1	24s10	68w29	4:33:56
Ninhue	1	36s24	72w24	4:49:36
Nogales	1	32s44	71w15	4:45:00
Nueva Imperial	1	38s44	72w57	4:51:48
Ñuñoa	2	33s28	70w36	4:42:24
Oficina Alianza	1	20s46	69w42	4:38:48
Oficina Chile	1	25s09	69w54	4:39:36
Oficina Pedro de Valdivia	1	22s36	69w40	4:38:40
Oficina Victoria	1	20s44	69w42	4:38:48
Ollagüe	1	21s14	68w16	4:33:04
Osorno	1	40s34	73w09	4:52:36
Ovalle	1	30s36	71w12	4:44:48
Paiguano	1	30s01	70w32	4:42:08
Paposo	1	25s01	70w28	4:41:52
Papudo	1	32s31	71w27	4:45:48
Parral	1	36s09	71w50	4:47:20
Pascua, Isla de	4	27s07	109w22	7:17:28
Pemuco	1	36s58	72w06	4:48:24
Peñalolén	2	33s29	70w32	4:42:08
Pencahue	1	35s24	71w49	4:47:16
Peralillo	1	34s29	71w29	4:45:56
Petorca	1	32s15	70w56	4:43:44
Petrohué	1	41s08	72w25	4:49:40
Pica	1	20s30	69w21	4:37:24
Pichilemu	1	34s23	72w00	4:48:00
Pintados	1	20s37	69w38	4:38:32
Pisagua	1	19s36	70w13	4:40:52
Pitrufquén	1	38s59	72w39	4:50:36
Polcura	1	37s17	71w43	4:46:52
Porvenir	1	53s18	70w22	4:41:28
Potrerillos	1	26s26	69w29	4:37:56
Pozo Almonte	1	20s16	69w48	4:39:12
Providencia	2	33s26	70w37	4:42:28
Pueblo Hundido	1	26s23	70w03	4:40:12
Puente Alto	2	33s37	70w35	4:42:20
Puerto Aisén	1	45s24	72w42	4:50:48
Puerto Ingeniero Ibáñez	1	46s18	71w56	4:47:44
Puerto Montt	1	41s28	72w57	4:51:48
Puerto Natales	1	51s44	72w31	4:50:04
Puerto Octay	1	40s58	72w54	4:51:36
Puerto Saavedra	1	38s47	73w24	4:53:36
Puerto Varas	1	41s19	72w59	4:51:56
Punitaqui	1	30s50	71w16	4:45:04
Punta Arenas	1	53s09	70w55	4:43:40
Punta de Díaz	1	28s03	70w37	4:42:28
Punta del Cobre	1	27s30	70w16	4:41:04
Purranque	1	40s55	73w10	4:52:40
Putaendo	1	32s38	70w44	4:42:56
Putre	1	18s12	69w35	4:38:20
Putú	1	35s13	72w17	4:49:08
Puyehue	1	40s40	72w37	4:50:28
Quemchi	1	42s09	73w29	4:53:56
Quilicura	2	33s22	70w45	4:43:00
Quilimarí	1	32s07	71w30	4:46:00
Quillagua	1	21s39	69w33	4:38:12
Quillota	1	32s53	71w16	4:45:04
Quilpué	1	33s03	71w27	4:45:48
Quinta Normal	2	33s27	70w42	4:42:48
Quintero	1	32s47	71w32	4:46:08
Quirihue	1	36s17	72w32	4:50:08
Rancagua	1	34s10	70w45	4:43:00
Recinto	1	36s48	71w44	4:46:56
Renca	2	33s24	70w44	4:42:56
Rengo	1	34s25	70w52	4:43:28
Riachuelo	1	40s49	73w21	4:53:24
Riñihue	1	39s49	72w27	4:49:48
Río Blanco	1	32s55	70w19	4:41:16
Río Bueno	1	40s19	72w58	4:51:52
Río Negro	1	40s47	73w14	4:52:56
Rivadavia	1	29s58	70w34	4:42:16
Rupanco	1	40s46	72w42	4:50:48
Salala	1	30s41	71w32	4:46:08
Salamanca	1	31s47	70w58	4:43:52
Samo Alto	1	30s25	70w58	4:43:52
San Antonio	1	27s53	70w03	4:40:12
San Antonio	1	33s35	71w38	4:46:32
San Bernardo	2	33s36	70w43	4:42:52
San Carlos	1	36s25	71w58	4:47:52
San Carlos	2	33s36	70w35	4:42:20
San Carlos de Chena	2	33s35	70w44	4:42:56
San Felipe	1	32s45	70w44	4:42:56
San Fernando	1	34s35	71w00	4:44:00
San Francisco de Mostazal	1	33s59	70w43	4:42:52
San Javier de Loncomilla	1	35s35	71w45	4:47:00
San Juan de Pirque	2	33s38	70w30	4:42:00
San Marco	2	33s37	70w38	4:42:32
San Marcos	1	30s56	71w03	4:44:12
San Miguel	2	33s30	70w40	4:42:40
San Pablo	1	40s24	73w01	4:52:04
San Pedro	1	21s57	68w34	4:34:16
San Pedro	1	33s54	71w28	4:45:52
San Pedro de Atacama	1	22s55	68w13	4:32:52
San Rafael	1	35s19	71w32	4:46:08
San Rosendo	1	37s16	72w43	4:50:52
Santa Ana de Chena	2	33s34	70w47	4:43:08
Santa Bárbara	1	37s40	72w01	4:48:04
Santa Cruz	1	34s38	71w22	4:45:28
Santa Eduviges	2	33s33	70w39	4:42:36
Santa Elena del Gomero	2	33s29	70w46	4:43:04
Santa Emilia	2	33s23	70w39	4:42:36
Santa Julia	2	33s30	70w38	4:42:32
Santa Rosa de Huechuraba	2	33s21	70w41	4:42:44
Santa Rosa de Locobe	2	33s26	70w33	4:42:12
Santa Teresa de lo Ovalle	2	33s23	70w47	4:43:08
Santiago	2	33s27	70w40	4:42:40
San Vicente de Tagua-Tagua	2	34s26	71w05	4:44:20
Sewell	1	34s05	70w23	4:41:32
Sierra Gorda	1	22s54	69w19	4:37:16
Socaire	1	23s36	67w51	4:31:24
Talagante	1	33s40	70w56	4:43:44
Talca	1	35s26	71w40	4:46:40
Talcahuano	1	36s43	73w07	4:52:28
Taltal	1	25s24	70w29	4:41:56
Tana	1	19s27	69w57	4:39:48
Tegualda	1	41s02	73w26	4:53:44
Temuco	1	38s44	72w36	4:50:24
Teno	1	34s52	71w11	4:44:44
Tierra Amarilla	1	27s29	70w17	4:41:08
Toco	1	22s05	69w35	4:38:20
Toconao	1	23s11	68w01	4:32:04
Tocopilla	1	22s05	70w12	4:40:48
Toltén	1	39s13	73w14	4:52:56
Tomé	1	36s37	72w57	4:51:48
Tongoy	1	30s15	71w30	4:46:00
Traiguén	1	38s15	72w41	4:50:44
Valdivia	1	39s48	73w14	4:52:56
Vallenar	1	28s35	70w46	4:43:04
Valparaíso	3	33s02	71w38	4:46:32
Vichuquén	1	34s53	72w00	4:48:00
Victoria	1	38s13	72w20	4:49:20
Vicuña	1	30s02	70w44	4:42:56
Villa Alemana	1	33s03	71w23	4:45:32
Villarrica	1	39s16	72w13	4:48:52
Viña del Mar	3	33s02	71w34	4:46:16
Vista Alegre	2	33s30	70w43	4:42:52
Vitacura	2	33s24	70w36	4:42:24
Yumbel	1	37s08	72w32	4:50:08
Yungay	1	37s07	72w01	4:48:04

Time Table # 1
Before 1 Jan 1928 LMT
Begin Standard 120E00
1 Jan 1928 0:00 -8:00
4 May 1986 0:00 -9:00
14 Sep 1986 0:00 -8:00
12 Apr 1987 0:00 -9:00
13 Sep 1987 0:00 -8:00
10 Apr 1988 0:00 -9:00
11 Sep 1988 0:00 -8:00
16 Apr 1989 0:00 -9:00
17 Sep 1989 0:00 -8:00
15 Apr 1990 0:00 -9:00
16 Sep 1990 0:00 -8:00
14 Apr 1991 0:00 -9:00
15 Sep 1991 0:00 -8:00

Time Table # 2
Before 1 Jan 1928 LMT
Begin Standard 120E00
1 Jan 1928 0:00 -8:00
3 Jun 1940 0:00 -9:00
1 Oct 1940 0:00 -8:00
16 Mar 1941 0:00 -9:00
1 Oct 1941 0:00 -8:00
4 May 1986 0:00 -9:00
14 Sep 1986 0:00 -8:00
12 Apr 1987 0:00 -9:00
13 Sep 1987 0:00 -8:00
10 Apr 1988 0:00 -9:00
11 Sep 1988 0:00 -8:00
16 Apr 1989 0:00 -9:00
17 Sep 1989 0:00 -8:00
15 Apr 1990 0:00 -9:00
16 Sep 1990 0:00 -8:00
14 Apr 1991 0:00 -9:00
15 Sep 1991 0:00 -8:00

Time Table # 3
Before 1 Jan 1928 LMT
Begin Standard 120E00
1 Jan 1928 0:00 -8:00
16 Mar 1941 0:00 -9:00
1 Oct 1941 0:00 -8:00
4 May 1986 0:00 -9:00
14 Sep 1986 0:00 -8:00
12 Apr 1987 0:00 -9:00
13 Sep 1987 0:00 -8:00
10 Apr 1988 0:00 -9:00
11 Sep 1988 0:00 -8:00
16 Apr 1989 0:00 -9:00
17 Sep 1989 0:00 -8:00
15 Apr 1990 0:00 -9:00
16 Sep 1990 0:00 -8:00
14 Apr 1991 0:00 -9:00
15 Sep 1991 0:00 -8:00

Time Table # 4
Before 30 Oct 1904 LMT
Begin Standard 120E00
30 Oct 1904 0:00 -8:00
20 Apr 1946 3:30 -9:00
1 Dec 1946 3:30 -8:00
13 Apr 1947 3:30 -9:00
30 Dec 1947 3:30 -8:00
2 May 1948 3:30 -9:00
31 Oct 1948 3:30 -8:00
3 Apr 1949 3:30 -9:00
30 Oct 1949 3:30 -8:00
2 Apr 1950 3:30 -9:00
29 Oct 1950 3:30 -8:00
1 Apr 1951 3:30 -9:00
28 Oct 1951 3:30 -8:00
6 Apr 1952 3:30 -9:00
25 Oct 1952 3:30 -8:00
5 Apr 1953 3:30 -9:00
1 Nov 1953 3:30 -8:00
21 Mar 1954 3:30 -9:00
31 Oct 1954 3:30 -8:00
20 Mar 1955 3:30 -9:00
6 Nov 1955 3:30 -8:00
18 Mar 1956 3:30 -9:00
4 Nov 1956 3:30 -8:00
24 Mar 1957 3:30 -9:00
3 Nov 1957 3:30 -8:00
23 Mar 1958 3:30 -9:00
2 Nov 1958 3:30 -8:00
22 Mar 1959 3:30 -9:00
1 Nov 1959 3:30 -8:00
20 Mar 1960 3:30 -9:00
6 Nov 1960 3:30 -8:00
19 Mar 1961 3:30 -9:00
5 Nov 1961 3:30 -8:00
18 Mar 1962 3:30 -9:00
4 Nov 1962 3:30 -8:00
24 Mar 1963 3:30 -9:00
3 Nov 1963 3:30 -8:00
22 Mar 1964 3:30 -9:00
1 Nov 1964 3:30 -8:00
18 Apr 1965 3:30 -9:00
17 Oct 1965 3:30 -8:00
17 Apr 1966 3:30 -9:00
16 Oct 1966 3:30 -8:00
16 Apr 1967 3:30 -9:00
22 Oct 1967 3:30 -8:00
21 Apr 1968 3:30 -9:00
20 Oct 1968 3:30 -8:00
20 Apr 1969 3:30 -9:00
19 Oct 1969 3:30 -8:00
19 Apr 1970 3:30 -9:00
18 Oct 1970 3:30 -8:00
18 Apr 1971 3:30 -9:00
17 Oct 1971 3:30 -8:00
16 Apr 1972 3:30 -9:00
22 Oct 1972 3:30 -8:00
22 Apr 1973 3:30 -9:00
21 Oct 1973 2:20 -8:00
30 Dec 1973 3:30 -9:00
20 Oct 1974 3:30 -8:00
20 Apr 1975 3:30 -9:00
19 Oct 1975 3:30 -8:00
18 Apr 1976 3:30 -9:00
17 Oct 1976 3:30 -8:00
17 Apr 1977 3:30 -9:00
16 Oct 1977 3:30 -8:00
13 May 1979 3:30 -9:00
21 Oct 1979 3:30 -8:00
11 May 1980 3:30 -9:00
19 Oct 1980 3:30 -8:00

Time Table # 5
Before 1 Jan 1912 LMT
Begin Standard 120E00
1 Jan 1912 0:00 -8:00
19 Mar 1961 3:30 -9:00
5 Nov 1961 3:30 -8:00
18 Mar 1962 3:30 -9:00
4 Nov 1962 3:30 -8:00
17 Mar 1963 0:00 -9:00
3 Nov 1963 3:30 -8:00
22 Mar 1964 3:30 -9:00
1 Nov 1964 3:30 -8:00
21 Mar 1965 0:00 -9:00
31 Oct 1965 0:00 -8:00
17 Apr 1966 3:30 -9:00
16 Oct 1966 3:30 -8:00
16 Apr 1967 3:30 -9:00
22 Oct 1967 3:30 -8:00
21 Apr 1968 3:30 -9:00
20 Oct 1968 3:30 -8:00
20 Apr 1969 3:30 -9:00
19 Oct 1969 3:30 -8:00
19 Apr 1970 3:30 -9:00
18 Oct 1970 3:30 -8:00
18 Apr 1971 3:30 -9:00
17 Oct 1971 3:30 -8:00
16 Apr 1972 0:00 -9:00
15 Oct 1972 0:00 -8:00
15 Apr 1973 0:00 -9:00
21 Oct 1973 0:00 -8:00
21 Apr 1974 0:00 -9:00
20 Oct 1974 3:30 -8:00
20 Apr 1975 3:30 -9:00
19 Oct 1975 3:30 -8:00
18 Apr 1976 3:30 -9:00
17 Oct 1976 3:30 -8:00
17 Apr 1977 3:30 -9:00
16 Oct 1977 3:30 -8:00
16 Apr 1978 0:00 -9:00
15 Oct 1978 0:00 -8:00
15 Apr 1979 0:00 -9:00
21 Oct 1979 0:00 -8:00
20 Apr 1980 0:00 -9:00
19 Oct 1980 0:00 -8:00

Time Table # 6
Before 1 Jan 1896 LMT
Begin Standard 120E00
1 Jan 1896 0:00 -8:00
1 May 1945 0:00 -9:00
1 Oct 1945 0:00 -8:00
1 May 1946 0:00 -9:00
1 Oct 1946 0:00 -8:00
1 May 1947 0:00 -9:00
1 Oct 1947 0:00 -8:00
1 May 1948 0:00 -9:00
1 Oct 1948 0:00 -8:00
1 May 1949 0:00 -9:00
1 Oct 1949 0:00 -8:00
1 May 1950 0:00 -9:00
1 Oct 1950 0:00 -8:00
1 May 1951 0:00 -9:00
1 Oct 1951 0:00 -8:00
1 Mar 1952 0:00 -9:00
1 Nov 1952 0:00 -8:00
1 Apr 1953 0:00 -9:00
1 Nov 1953 0:00 -8:00
1 Apr 1954 0:00 -9:00
1 Nov 1954 0:00 -8:00
1 Apr 1955 0:00 -9:00
1 Oct 1955 0:00 -8:00
1 Apr 1956 0:00 -9:00
1 Oct 1956 0:00 -8:00
1 Apr 1957 0:00 -9:00
1 Oct 1957 0:00 -8:00
1 Apr 1958 0:00 -9:00
1 Oct 1958 0:00 -8:00
1 Apr 1959 0:00 -9:00
1 Oct 1959 0:00 -8:00
1 Jun 1960 0:00 -9:00
1 Oct 1960 0:00 -8:00
1 Jun 1961 0:00 -9:00
1 Oct 1961 0:00 -8:00
1 Apr 1974 0:00 -9:00
1 Oct 1974 0:00 -8:00
1 Apr 1975 0:00 -9:00
1 Oct 1975 0:00 -8:00
30 Jun 1980 0:00 -9:00
30 Sep 1980 0:00 -8:00

Time Table # 7
Before 1 Jan 1928 LMT
Begin Standard 82E30
1 Jan 1928 0:00 -5:30
Begin Standard 75E00
1 Jan 1940 0:00 -5:00
Begin Standard 120E00
1 May 1980 0:00 -8:00
4 May 1986 0:00 -9:00
14 Sep 1986 0:00 -8:00
12 Apr 1987 0:00 -9:00
13 Sep 1987 0:00 -8:00
10 Apr 1988 0:00 -9:00
11 Sep 1988 0:00 -8:00
16 Apr 1989 0:00 -9:00
17 Sep 1989 0:00 -8:00
15 Apr 1990 0:00 -9:00
16 Sep 1990 0:00 -8:00
14 Apr 1991 0:00 -9:00
15 Sep 1991 0:00 -8:00

Time Table # 8
Before 1 Jan 1928 LMT
Begin Standard 90E00
1 Jan 1928 0:00 -6:00
Begin Standard 120E00
1 May 1980 0:00 -8:00
4 May 1986 0:00 -9:00
14 Sep 1986 0:00 -8:00
12 Apr 1987 0:00 -9:00
13 Sep 1987 0:00 -8:00
10 Apr 1988 0:00 -9:00
11 Sep 1988 0:00 -8:00
16 Apr 1989 0:00 -9:00
17 Sep 1989 0:00 -8:00
15 Apr 1990 0:00 -9:00
16 Sep 1990 0:00 -8:00
14 Apr 1991 0:00 -9:00
15 Sep 1991 0:00 -8:00

Time Table # 9
Before 1 Jan 1928 LMT
Begin Standard 105E00
1 Jan 1928 0:00 -7:00
Begin Standard 120E00
1 May 1980 0:00 -8:00
4 May 1986 0:00 -9:00
14 Sep 1986 0:00 -8:00
12 Apr 1987 0:00 -9:00
13 Sep 1987 0:00 -8:00
10 Apr 1988 0:00 -9:00
11 Sep 1988 0:00 -8:00
16 Apr 1989 0:00 -9:00
17 Sep 1989 0:00 -8:00
15 Apr 1990 0:00 -9:00
16 Sep 1990 0:00 -8:00
14 Apr 1991 0:00 -9:00
15 Sep 1991 0:00 -8:00

Time Table # 10
Before 1 Jan 1928 LMT
Begin Standard 120E00
1 Jan 1928 0:00 -8:00
Begin Standard 105E00
1 Jan 1952 0:00 -7:00
Begin Standard 120E00
1 May 1980 0:00 -8:00
4 May 1986 0:00 -9:00
14 Sep 1986 0:00 -8:00
12 Apr 1987 0:00 -9:00
13 Sep 1987 0:00 -8:00
10 Apr 1988 0:00 -9:00
11 Sep 1988 0:00 -8:00
16 Apr 1989 0:00 -9:00
17 Sep 1989 0:00 -8:00
15 Apr 1990 0:00 -9:00
16 Sep 1990 0:00 -8:00
14 Apr 1991 0:00 -9:00
15 Sep 1991 0:00 -8:00

Time Table # 11
Before 1 Jan 1928 LMT
Begin Standard 127E30
1 Jan 1928 0:00 -8:30
Begin Standard 120E00
1 Mar 1932 10:00 -8:00
Begin Standard 135E00
1 Jan 1940 0:00 -9:00
Begin Standard 120E00
1 May 1966 0:00 -8:00
4 May 1986 0:00 -9:00
14 Sep 1986 0:00 -8:00
12 Apr 1987 0:00 -9:00
13 Sep 1987 0:00 -8:00
10 Apr 1988 0:00 -9:00
11 Sep 1988 0:00 -8:00
16 Apr 1989 0:00 -9:00
17 Sep 1989 0:00 -8:00
15 Apr 1990 0:00 -9:00
16 Sep 1990 0:00 -8:00
14 Apr 1991 0:00 -9:00
15 Sep 1991 0:00 -8:00

Time Table # 12
Before 1 Jan 1928 LMT
Begin Standard 127E30
1 Jan 1928 0:00 -8:30
Begin Standard 120E00
1 Mar 1932 10:00 -8:00
Begin Standard 135E00
1 Jan 1940 0:00 -9:00
Begin Standard 127E30
1 May 1966 0:00 -8:30
Begin Standard 120E00
1 May 1980 0:00 -8:00
4 May 1986 0:00 -9:00
14 Sep 1986 0:00 -8:00
12 Apr 1987 0:00 -9:00
13 Sep 1987 0:00 -8:00
10 Apr 1988 0:00 -9:00
11 Sep 1988 0:00 -8:00
16 Apr 1989 0:00 -9:00
17 Sep 1989 0:00 -8:00
15 Apr 1990 0:00 -9:00
16 Sep 1990 0:00 -8:00
14 Apr 1991 0:00 -9:00
15 Sep 1991 0:00 -8:00

DIVISIONS

1. Anhui (Anhwei)
2. Beijing Shi (Peking)
3. Fujian (Fukien)
4. Gansu (Kansu)
5. Guangdong (Kwangtung)
6. Guangxi Zhuangzu Zizhiqu (Kwangsi Chuan
7. Guizhou (Kweichow)
8. Hebei (Hopeh)
9. Heilongjiang (Heilungkiang)
10. Henan (Honan)
11. Hubei (Hupei)
12. Hunan
13. Jiangsu (Kiangsu)
14. Jiangxi (Kiangsi)
15. Jilin (Kirin)
16. Liaoning
17. Nei Mongol Zizhiqu (Inner Mongolia)
18. Ningxia Huizu Zizhiqu (Ningsia Hui)
19. Qinghai (Tsinghai)
20. Shaanxi (Shensi)
21. Shandong (Shantung)
22. Shanghai Shi (Shanghai)
23. Shanxi (Shansi)
24. Sichuan (Szechwan)
25. T'aiwan (Taiwan)
26. Tianjin Shi (Tientsin)
27. Xinjiang Uygur Zizhiqu (Sinkiang)
28. Xizang Zizhiqu (Tibet)
29. Yunnan
30. Zhejiang (Chekiang)
31. Hong Kong
32. Macau

Place	Time Table	Latitude	Longitude	Offset
Aba 24	9	33N06	101E59	-6:47:56
Abagnar Qi 17	1	43N58	116E04	-7:44:16
Abag Qi 17	1	43N53	114E33	-7:38:12
Abate 27	7	39N03	77E36	-5:10:24
Aberdeen (Xianggangzi) 31	4	22N15	114E09	-7:36:36
Acheng 9	12	45N32	126E59	-8:27:56
Aerhuola 17	11	51N01	120E10	-8:00:40
Aershatu 17	1	44N11	113E36	-7:34:24
Aguit 17	9	41N52	112E56	-7:31:44
Aheqi 27	7	40N52	77E58	-5:11:52
Ahu 13	1	34N27	118E39	-7:54:36
Aidong 6	9	24N46	107E21	-7:09:24
Aigenmiao 17	11	43N36	120E50	-8:03:20
Aihui (Heihe) 9	12	50N16	127E28	-8:29:52
Ailinzhuang 26	1	39N27	117E36	-7:50:24
Airgin Sum 17	1	42N58	111E08	-7:24:32
Aisike 27	7	39N43	76E08	-5:04:32
Aisinaike 27	7	39N47	75E47	-5:03:08
Aizhaipuzi 16	11	40N57	124E01	-8:16:04
Ajipuzicun 16	11	42N16	123E33	-8:14:12
Aketao 27	7	39N08	75E57	-5:03:48
Aketilepa 27	7	39N57	74E03	-4:56:12
Akqi 27	7	40N52	77E58	-5:11:52
Aksay 4	8	39N28	94E15	-6:17:00
Aksu 27	7	41N10	80E20	-5:21:20
Akto 27	7	39N08	75E57	-5:03:48
Alashanyouqi 17	9	40N02	103E33	-6:54:12
Alasitan 27	7	37N01	76E59	-5:07:56
Alatan'aola → Xinbaerhuyouqi 17	11	48N41	116E53	-7:47:32
Aletai 27	8	47N52	88E07	-5:52:28
Alitanguo 28	8	35N10	83E30	-5:34:00
Altay 27	8	47N52	88E07	-5:52:28
Alxa Zuoqi 17	9	38N50	105E32	-7:02:08
Ameng 29	9	23N50	104E32	-6:58:08
Amili 28	8	28N25	95E52	-6:23:28
Amoy → Xiamen 3	1	24N28	118E07	-7:52:28
Amugulang → Xinbaerhuzuoqi 17	11	48N14	118E18	-7:53:12
Amuyimusu 17	1	42N25	113E21	-7:33:24
Amuzhong 28	8	30N33	84E28	-5:37:52
Anbanjing 29	9	23N57	100E55	-6:43:40
Anbei 27	8	40N45	96E06	-6:24:24
Anbei 17	9	40N49	108E56	-7:15:44
Anbianbu 20	9	37N39	108E11	-7:12:44
Anbo 16	11	39N51	122E19	-8:09:16
Anbu 5	1	23N28	116E44	-7:46:56
Anchang 30	1	30N09	120E30	-8:02:00
Anch'ing → Anqing 1	1	30N31	117E02	-7:48:08
Anci (Langfang) 8	1	39N31	116E41	-7:46:44
Anda 9	12	46N24	125E19	-8:21:16
Andilangan 27	8	37N36	83E50	-5:35:20
Andingpu 18	9	37N58	107E02	-7:08:08
Anding Zhan 2	1	39N38	116E29	-7:45:56
Andong 30	1	30N16	121E13	-8:04:52
Anduo 28	8	32N18	91E04	-6:04:16
Anfeng 13	1	32N44	120E24	-8:01:36
Anfeng 13	1	33N06	120E08	-8:00:32
Anfengqiao 3	1	26N41	118E08	-7:52:32
Anfu 14	1	27N23	114E37	-7:38:28
Anfuzhen 24	9	29N21	105E28	-7:01:52
Anfuzhen 24	9	28N47	104E41	-6:58:44
Ang'angxi 9	12	47N09	123E48	-8:15:12
An'ganka 9	12	52N18	126E17	-8:25:08
Angao 10	1	33N08	112E22	-7:29:28
Angduo 24	8	32N20	98E55	-6:35:40
Angren 28	8	29N25	86E40	-5:46:40
Anguang 15	12	45N31	123E45	-8:15:00
Anguchang 24	9	29N30	103E39	-6:54:36
Anguo 8	1	38N25	115E19	-7:41:16
Anguozhuang 8	1	39N44	117E59	-7:51:56
Anhai 3	1	24N45	118E27	-7:53:48
Anhua 12	1	28N18	111E14	-7:24:56
Anhuai 1	1	33N04	117E50	-7:51:20
Anji 30	1	30N43	119E41	-7:58:44

Anjiang 8 1 40N45 117E38 -7:50:32
Anju 11 1 31N45 113E11 -7:32:44
Anju 24 9 30N21 105E27 -7:01:48
Anjuzhen 24 9 29N59 106E02 -7:04:08
Ankang 20 9 32N42 109E05 -7:16:20
Anking → Anqing 1
1 30N31 117E02 -7:48:08
Ankou 5 1 25N03 113E24 -7:33:36
Anlinnuoer 8 1 41N11 114E31 -7:38:04
Anliu 5 1 23N42 115E42 -7:42:48
Anlong 7 9 25N02 105E31 -7:02:04
Anlu 11 1 31N17 113E40 -7:34:40
Annlangnlang 9
12 51N33 125E49 -8:23:16
Anning 29 9 24N59 102E18 -6:49:12
Anningdu 4 9 36N56 104E31 -6:58:04
Anping 12 1 26N33 113E22 -7:33:28
Anping 8 1 38N16 115E30 -7:42:00
Anping 10 1 34N01 115E07 -7:40:28
Anping 8 1 39N43 116E53 -7:47:32
Anping 16 11 41N11 123E26 -8:13:44
Anpu 5 8 21N27 110E00 -7:20:00
Anqing 1 1 30N31 117E02 -7:48:08
Anqiu 21 1 36N25 119E10 -7:56:40
Anren 30 1 28N04 119E20 -7:57:20
Anren 12 1 26N42 113E16 -7:33:04
Anrenzhen 24 9 30N31 103E38 -6:54:32
Ansai 20 9 36N54 109E10 -7:16:40
Anschan → Anshan 16
11 41N08 122E59 -8:11:56
Anshan 16 11 41N08 122E59 -8:11:56
Anshun 7 9 26N15 105E56 -7:03:44
Anting 22 2 31N18 121E09 -8:04:36
Antou 3 1 26N07 118E11 -7:52:44
Antu (Songjiang) 15
12 42N32 128E18 -8:33:12
Antung → Dandong 16
11 40N08 124E20 -8:17:20
Anxi 4 8 40N32 95E51 -6:23:24
Anxi 3 1 25N06 118E12 -7:52:48
Anxi 14 1 25N15 115E06 -7:40:24
Anxi 30 1 30N25 120E01 -8:00:04
Anxian 24 9 31N40 104E32 -6:58:08
Anxiang 12 1 29N23 112E09 -7:28:36
Anxin (Xin'anzhen) 8
1 38N55 115E55 -7:43:40
Anxing 13 1 31N24 119E06 -7:56:24
Anyang 10 1 36N06 114E21 -7:37:24
Anyi 14 1 28N50 115E31 -7:42:04
Anyuan 3 1 26N36 116E38 -7:46:32
Anyuan 14 1 27N37 113E54 -7:35:36
Anyuan 14 1 25N08 115E28 -7:41:52
Anyuanyi → Tianzhu 4
9 37N14 102E59 -6:51:56
Anyue 24 9 30N06 105E21 -7:01:24
Anze 23 1 36N11 112E16 -7:29:04
Anzhen 13 1 31N36 120E28 -8:01:52
Anzhou 8 1 38N52 115E49 -7:43:16
Anzhuang 22 2 31N04 121E01 -8:04:04
Anzicun 2 1 39N46 115E50 -7:43:20
Aohaibolihu 16
11 42N01 121E32 -8:06:08
Aohandaba 16 11 42N05 121E59 -8:07:56
Aohan Qi (Xinhui) 17
11 42N19 119E59 -7:59:56
Aojiang 30 1 27N37 120E33 -8:02:12
Aojiao 3 1 23N37 117E26 -7:49:44
Aoliyingzi 16 11 42N14 121E58 -8:07:52
Aomen → Macau 32
5 22N14 113E35 -7:34:20
Aoshang 12 1 25N42 113E00 -7:32:00
Aotou 5 1 22N44 114E33 -7:38:12
Arun Qi 17 11 48N07 123E28 -8:13:52
Arxan 17 11 47N11 119E57 -7:59:48
Asar 17 11 47N56 117E38 -7:50:32
Atushi 27 7 39N42 75E48 -5:03:12
Ayulhai 17 1 44N36 115E36 -7:42:24
Babailiqiao 13 1 32N26 118E57 -7:55:48
Bachagou 16 11 40N36 122E54 -8:11:36
Bache 13 1 31N05 120E40 -8:02:40
Bacheng 13 1 31N27 120E52 -8:03:28
Bachi 5 1 24N48 115E49 -7:43:16
Bachu 27 7 39N50 78E20 -5:13:20
Badajia 13 1 33N57 120E17 -8:01:08
Badaohao 16 11 41N47 121E57 -8:07:48
Badaohe 8 1 40N24 118E42 -7:54:48
Badaohe 16 11 40N02 122E17 -8:09:08
Badaying 8 1 41N22 117E28 -7:49:52
Badazhou 6 9 24N36 105E04 -7:00:16
Badong 11 1 31N02 110E20 -7:21:20
Badou 21 1 36N27 117E55 -7:51:40
Badouling 1 1 32N10 117E36 -7:50:24
Badu 6 9 24N15 105E41 -7:02:44
Badu 3 1 26N51 119E35 -7:58:20
Badu 14 1 28N32 117E57 -7:51:48
Bagehadu 28 8 35N25 84E50 -5:39:20
Bag Narin 19 8 38N57 94E08 -6:16:32
Bag Tal 17 11 43N20 122E16 -8:09:04
Bahechuan 16 11 40N59 124E49 -8:19:16
Baibao 8 1 39N04 115E31 -7:42:04
Baibei 14 1 27N47 115E53 -7:43:32
Baibuting 30 1 30N33 120E46 -8:03:04
Baicao 8 1 41N13 116E07 -7:44:28
Baicaochang 24 9 32N08 103E59 -6:55:56
Baicha 14 1 29N11 115E37 -7:42:28
Baicheng 15 12 45N38 122E46 -8:11:04
Baidian 1 1 30N47 119E14 -7:56:56
Baidiao 24 9 28N07 101E28 -6:45:52
Baidunzi 27 8 43N11 95E19 -6:21:16
Baigezhuang 8 1 39N54 118E09 -7:52:36
Baigong 5 1 24N18 116E14 -7:44:56
Baigou 8 1 39N07 116E01 -7:44:04
Baiguoshu 1 1 30N45 119E07 -7:56:28
Baigusi 24 9 33N10 103E52 -6:55:28
Baihe 20 9 32N17 110E02 -7:20:08
Baihe 30 1 29N12 120E55 -8:03:40
Baihebu 2 1 40N39 116E10 -7:44:40
Baihegang 22 2 31N16 121E08 -8:04:32
Baihekou 11 1 31N46 110E13 -7:20:52
Baihou 5 1 24N18 116E48 -7:47:12
Baihua 24 9 29N07 104E37 -6:58:28
Baijian 8 1 39N36 115E16 -7:41:04
Baijiang 30 1 29N51 119E20 -7:57:20
Baijiawu 8 1 39N30 116E28 -7:45:52
Baijie 24 9 29N17 106E31 -7:06:04
Baijietan 24 9 28N44 105E30 -7:02:00
Baiju 13 1 33N04 120E20 -8:01:20
Baikeshu 1 1 30N26 118E55 -7:55:40
Baikuerte 27 7 39N58 75E33 -5:02:12
Bailaiqiao 1 1 32N40 118E23 -7:53:32
Bailang 28 8 29N11 89E12 -5:56:48
Bailang 17 11 46N57 120E05 -8:00:20
Baile 8 1 39N55 114E51 -7:39:24
Bailian 5 1 24N09 112E22 -7:29:28
Bailicun 6 9 25N45 110E33 -7:22:12
Bailin 3 1 27N12 120E10 -8:00:40
Bailin 12 1 26N20 113E18 -7:33:12
Bailin 24 9 29N11 105E57 -7:03:48
Bailin 24 9 28N45 106E26 -7:05:44
Bailingmiao → Darhan Muminggan Lianheqi
9 41N50 110E27 -7:21:48
Bailonggang 22 2 31N15 121E44 -8:06:56
Bailuchang 24 9 28N56 105E57 -7:03:48
Bailuoji 11 1 29N37 113E15 -7:33:00
Baima 13 1 31N35 119E10 -7:56:40
Baima 24 9 30N03 103E44 -6:54:56
Baima 24 9 29N09 104E16 -6:57:04
Baimachang 24 9 29N18 107E30 -7:10:00
Baimachang 24 9 29N40 103E54 -6:55:36
Baimachang 16 11 41N59 122E30 -8:10:00
Baimaguan 2 1 40N41 116E52 -7:47:28
Baimakou 29 9 25N55 102E06 -6:48:24
Baimamiao 4 9 36N58 108E08 -7:12:32
Baimamiao 24 9 29N33 104E59 -6:59:56
Baimao 13 1 31N39 120E52 -8:03:28
Baimao 13 1 31N35 120E54 -8:03:36
Baimashi 30 1 29N15 118E42 -7:54:48
Baimazhai 14 1 28N06 115E50 -7:43:20
Baimiaozi 9 12 46N18 123E35 -8:14:20
Baimiaozi 16 11 40N34 120E36 -8:02:24
Baimiaozi 24 9 29N47 106E29 -7:05:56
Baimiaozi 16 11 41N55 122E12 -8:08:48
Baimuqiao 13 1 32N01 120E19 -8:01:16
Bainiqiao 11 1 29N35 114E09 -7:36:36
Baipeng 6 9 24N09 109E25 -7:17:40
Baipu 13 1 32N15 120E46 -8:03:04
Baiqibao 16 11 41N48 122E30 -8:10:00
Baiqiu 10 1 32N44 112E38 -7:30:32
Baiquan 9 12 47N36 126E07 -8:24:28
Baiquan 30 1 30N06 122E08 -8:08:32
Baiqueyuan 10 1 31N48 115E05 -7:40:20
Bairin Zuoqi 17
11 44N00 119E00 -7:56:00
Bairuopu 12 1 28N12 112E46 -7:31:04
Baisha 5 9 19N17 109E27 -7:17:48
Baisha 30 1 29N26 119E16 -7:57:04
Baisha 3 1 25N40 118E59 -7:55:56
Baisha 3 1 25N24 117E16 -7:49:04
Baisha 10 1 34N22 112E32 -7:30:08
Baisha 14 1 26N58 115E22 -7:41:28
Baisha 5 1 24N39 113E31 -7:34:04
Baisha 10 1 34N20 113E14 -7:32:56
Baisha 24 9 28N55 105E45 -7:03:00
Baisha 24 9 29N04 106E07 -7:04:28
Baishaba 24 9 30N03 106E21 -7:05:24
Baishanji 1 1 33N48 116E40 -7:46:40
Baishantu 16 11 42N21 122E35 -8:10:20
Baishapu 11 1 29N58 115E04 -7:40:16
Baishatan 21 1 36N52 121E38 -8:06:32
Baishe 14 1 27N02 116E20 -7:45:20
Baishecun 2 1 40N10 116E18 -7:45:12
Baishi 3 1 27N18 119E45 -7:59:00
Baishi 3 1 26N48 119E46 -7:59:04
Baishidu 12 1 25N26 113E01 -7:32:04
Baishiyi 24 9 29N29 106E22 -7:05:28
Baishizhai 16 11 40N57 122E58 -8:11:52
Baishui 12 1 28N42 113E04 -7:32:16
Baishui 30 1 30N34 119E39 -7:58:36
Baishui 24 9 30N06 105E38 -7:02:32
Baishuifan 11 1 30N17 115E43 -7:42:52
Baishuijiang 20
9 33N29 106E01 -7:04:04
Baishun 5 1 25N12 114E01 -7:36:04
Baishuxia 12 1 27N22 113E41 -7:34:44
Baita 13 1 31N48 119E35 -7:58:20
Baitazi 17 11 42N19 120E19 -8:01:16
Baitazibeigou 16
11 42N17 120E48 -8:03:12
Baitou 24 9 30N37 103E36 -6:54:24
Baitoutan 24 9 32N30 106E56 -7:07:44
Baitu 13 1 31N59 119E21 -7:57:24
Baitugang 10 1 33N28 112E22 -7:29:28
Baiwang 6 9 24N14 108E32 -7:14:08
Baiwen 23 1 38N15 111E06 -7:24:24
Baixi 24 9 29N39 106E28 -7:05:52
Baixiang 8 1 37N32 114E34 -7:38:16
Baixingt 17 11 43N08 121E03 -8:04:12
Baiyan 30 1 28N04 120E02 -8:00:08
Baiyan 30 1 31N08 119E38 -7:58:32
Baiyang 10 1 34N25 112E12 -7:28:48
Baiyanghe 27 8 43N13 88E28 -5:53:52
Baiyin 4 9 36N47 104E07 -6:56:28
Baiyinheshuo 17
11 44N31 119E51 -7:59:24
Baiyintaohai 17
11 43N12 120E23 -8:01:32
Baiyü 24 8 31N18 98E49 -6:35:16
Baiyu 2 1 40N01 115E37 -7:42:28
Baiyundu 3 1 26N10 118E47 -7:55:08
Baiyunguan 2 1 39N54 116E19 -7:45:16
Baizhongpu 10 1 33N22 114E50 -7:39:20
Baizi 24 9 30N06 105E43 -7:02:52
Bajiaotai 16 11 41N14 121E14 -8:04:56
Bajiazi 16 11 42N17 122E37 -8:10:28
Bajiazi 16 11 42N21 121E27 -8:05:48
Bajiazi 16 11 41N36 123E53 -8:15:32
Bakeshu 16 11 42N26 124E37 -8:18:28
Bakun 28 7 32N32 80E26 -5:21:44
Balidianzi 16 11 41N13 124E49 -8:19:16
Balihan 17 11 41N29 118E41 -7:54:44
Balin 17 11 48N19 122E19 -8:09:16
Balipu 8 1 39N53 117E48 -7:51:12
Baliyingzi 16 11 41N59 121E14 -8:04:56
Balizhuang 8 1 39N16 116E28 -7:45:52
Balizhuang 2 1 39N52 116E28 -7:45:52
Balong 19 8 36N17 97E20 -6:29:20
Bama 6 9 24N21 107E08 -7:08:32
Bamao 30 1 29N26 120E59 -8:03:56
Bamencheng 26 1 39N35 117E37 -7:50:28
Bamiancheng 16
11 43N13 124E02 -8:16:08
Bamumo 28 8 32N30 93E15 -6:13:00
Banbidian 2 1 39N54 116E32 -7:46:08
Banbuji 1 1 33N34 116E44 -7:46:56
Bancun 1 1 30N53 118E48 -7:55:12
Bandan'gou 8 1 39N08 115E11 -7:40:44
Bandiantaolehai 17
9 41N41 104E06 -6:56:24
Bangbu 1 1 32N58 117E24 -7:49:36
Bangda 29 9 27N59 98E40 -6:34:40
Bangeluo 28 8 32N27 90E35 -6:02:20
Bangjun 26 1 39N59 117E16 -7:49:04
Bangkou 22 2 31N40 121E26 -8:05:44
Bangshi 16 11 40N23 122E46 -8:11:04
Bangwei 6 9 23N46 107E34 -7:10:16
Bangzhen 22 2 31N39 121E29 -8:05:56
Banjin 13 1 32N19 120E24 -8:01:36
Banjita 16 11 41N11 120E52 -8:03:28
Banjuangou 8 1 40N44 115E11 -7:40:44
Banlamen 16 11 41N51 122E27 -8:09:48
Banlashanzi 16
11 41N26 123E28 -8:13:52
Banliyuan 1 1 30N50 118E58 -7:55:52
Banmian 3 1 26N02 118E06 -7:52:24
Banpu 13 1 34N28 119E18 -7:57:12
Banqiao 30 1 30N06 120E27 -8:01:48
Banqiao 11 1 31N46 112E31 -7:30:04
Banqiao 13 1 31N55 118E39 -7:54:36
Banqiao 24 9 29N31 105E59 -7:03:56
Banqiao 2 1 39N56 115E51 -7:43:24
Banqiaochang 24
9 29N54 104E21 -6:57:24
Banqiaoji 1 1 32N19 116E37 -7:46:28
Banqiaoxi 24 9 29N41 103E47 -6:55:08
Banquan 21 1 35N07 118E42 -7:54:48
Banshanpu 12 1 27N42 113E24 -7:33:36
Banshi 14 1 25N20 115E23 -7:41:32
Banshigou 16 11 41N09 120E58 -8:03:52
Bantaji 1 1 32N41 118E35 -7:54:20
Banxiancun 30 1 30N33 119E42 -7:58:48
Banzhuyuan 24 9 28N44 106E18 -7:05:12
Banzi 3 1 24N18 117E19 -7:49:16
Bao'an 11 1 30N11 114E43 -7:38:52
Bao'an 5 1 22N34 114E07 -7:36:28
Baoan 22 2 31N46 121E21 -8:05:24
Baoancun 9 12 48N13 125E52 -8:23:28
Baoan → Zhuolu 8
1 40N22 115E12 -7:40:48
Baochang 13 1 32N04 121E25 -8:05:40
Baochang → Taibus Qi 17
1 41N56 115E22 -7:41:28
Baocheng 20 9 33N08 107E09 -7:08:36
Baode 23 1 39N06 111E11 -7:24:44
Baodi 26 1 39N44 117E17 -7:49:08
Baoding 8 1 38N52 115E29 -7:41:56
Baofeng 10 1 33N55 113E02 -7:32:08
Baofu 30 1 30N31 119E29 -7:57:56
Baoguosi 24 9 29N35 103E25 -6:53:40
Baohekou 8 1 40N32 118E15 -7:53:00
Baoji 20 9 34N23 107E09 -7:08:36
Baoji 13 1 33N08 118E19 -7:53:16
Baojiagou 8 1 40N05 115E22 -7:41:28
Baojiapu 16 11 40N51 122E14 -8:08:56
Baojiatou 30 1 30N11 119E48 -7:59:12
Baojiawazi 16 11 41N38 123E24 -8:13:36
Baojing 12 1 28N43 109E25 -7:17:40
Baokang → Keerqinzuozhongqi 17
11 44N07 123E18 -8:13:12
Baolin 24 9 30N24 105E02 -7:00:08
Baolizhen 16 11 42N56 123E46 -8:15:04
Baolunyuan 24 9 32N22 105E40 -7:02:40
Baomachang 24 9 29N58 104E12 -6:56:48
Baonian 13 1 31N55 119E21 -7:57:24
Baoning 6 9 23N31 106E24 -7:05:36
Baoqing 9 12 46N21 132E14 -8:48:56
Baoquan 21 1 36N16 119E04 -7:56:16
Baoshan 29 9 26N19 104E27 -6:57:48
Baoshan 29 9 25N09 99E09 -6:36:36
Baoshan 10 1 32N39 113E54 -7:35:36
Baoshan 22 2 31N25 121E29 -8:05:56
Baoting 5 9 18N42 109E45 -7:19:00
Baotou (Paotow) 17
9 40N40 109E59 -7:19:56
Baotun 16 11 42N29 122E52 -8:11:28
Baowei 6 9 22N39 106E50 -7:07:20
Baoxikou 5 1 23N16 115E14 -7:40:56
Baoxingchang 24
9 29N38 105E41 -7:02:44
Baoxinji 10 1 32N35 115E00 -7:40:00
Baoyi 1 1 32N13 116E42 -7:46:48
Baoying 13 1 33N16 119E20 -7:57:20
Baozhuchang 24 9 29N48 104E15 -6:57:00
Baozidian 8 1 40N11 117E48 -7:51:12
Bapanling 16 11 40N58 123E08 -8:12:32
Baqing 28 8 32N15 93E30 -6:14:00

Place		Lat	Long	Time
Barkam 24	9	31N50	102E40	-6:50:40
Barkol 27	8	43N50	93E30	-6:14:00
Barun Su 17	1	42N27	111E01	-7:24:04
Bashikejike 27	8	37N30	85E50	-5:43:20
Bashiqiao 13	1	31N40	120E22	-8:01:28
Basiyingzi 16	11	42N05	121E37	-8:06:28
Basuo → Dongfang 5	9	19N05	108E39	-7:14:36
Batan 13	1	34N10	120E04	-8:00:16
Batang 24	9	30N02	99E02	-6:36:08
Baweigang 13	1	31N57	120E14	-8:00:56
Baxian 8	1	39N06	116E23	-7:45:32
Baxian (Yudongxi) 24	9	29N23	106E32	-7:06:08
Bayan 9	12	46N05	127E24	-8:29:36
Bayanchagan 9	12	47N19	124E03	-8:16:12
Bayange 17	9	39N19	107E31	-7:10:04
Bayanheshuomiao 17	11	48N51	119E46	-7:59:04
Bayanjie 17	11	49N36	124E37	-8:18:28
Bayanluke 17	11	50N52	119E33	-7:58:12
Bayannaobao 17	9	39N44	107E40	-7:10:40
Bayan Obo 17	9	41N58	110E02	-7:20:08
Bayan Tal 17	11	43N44	123E16	-8:13:04
Bayantala 17	11	43N44	123E16	-8:13:04
Bayiji 13	1	34N18	117E41	-7:50:44
Bayingzi 16	11	41N28	120E46	-8:03:04
Bay Kurt 27	7	39N58	75E33	-5:02:12
Bazai 5	1	24N32	114E10	-7:36:40
Bazhong 24	9	31N51	106E39	-7:06:36
Bazi 5	1	24N46	113E10	-7:32:40
Baziqiao 13	1	32N07	119E52	-7:59:28
Bei'an 9	12	48N16	126E36	-8:26:24
Beianhe 2	1	40N04	116E06	-7:44:24
Beibaihua 8	1	38N57	114E51	-7:39:24
Beibaozhen 22	2	31N33	121E38	-8:06:32
Beibei 24	9	29N49	106E26	-7:05:44
Beicai 22	2	31N12	121E34	-8:06:16
Beicang 26	1	39N13	117E07	-7:48:28
Beidaihe 8	1	39N54	119E29	-7:57:56
Beidaoqiao 27	8	44N12	89E38	-5:58:32
Beidouzhen 24	9	30N02	104E26	-6:57:44
Beidun 3	1	26N42	118E57	-7:55:48
Beifangcun 2	1	40N20	116E42	-7:46:48
Beifangzi 16	11	41N22	121E03	-8:04:12
Beigang 11	1	29N20	113E41	-7:34:44
Beiguo 13	1	31N47	120E33	-8:02:12
Beihai (Pakhoi) 6	9	21N29	109E05	-7:16:20
Beihedian 8	1	39N13	115E45	-7:43:00
Beiheishang'gou 8	1	39N53	118E15	-7:53:00
Beihuaidian 26	1	39N16	117E33	-7:50:12
Beijialing 16	11	41N08	124E02	-8:16:08
Beijiao 3	1	26N22	119E58	-7:59:52
Beijiean 13	1	32N15	121E12	-8:04:48
Beijijiazhuang 8	1	40N01	114E51	-7:39:24
Beijing (Peking) 2	1	39N55	116E25	-7:45:40
Beikan 13	1	32N23	121E21	-8:05:24
Beilifang 16	11	41N59	121E57	-8:07:48
Beiling 5	1	24N36	115E20	-7:41:20
Beiliu 6	9	22N42	110E22	-7:21:28
Beiliuwangshui 8	1	38N57	115E03	-7:40:12
Beilizhen 5	9	19N10	108E43	-7:14:52
Beilizigu 26	1	39N30	117E28	-7:49:52
Beimaizhu 26	1	39N31	117E44	-7:50:56
Beiminjiatun 16	11	42N38	122E43	-8:10:52
Beimuzhen 24	9	29N31	105E05	-7:00:20
Beipanxiaozhen 22	2	31N44	121E26	-8:05:44
Beipiao 16	11	41N49	120E46	-8:03:04
Beiqi 16	11	40N27	122E20	-8:09:20
Beiqiao 22	2	31N03	121E24	-8:05:36
Beisanjia 16	11	42N04	124E42	-8:18:48
Beishakou 8	1	39N08	116E07	-7:44:28
Beishan 6	9	24N28	108E35	-7:14:20
Beishangcun 26	1	39N28	116E58	-7:47:52
Beishipian 2	1	40N43	116E55	-7:47:40
Beishuangdong 8	1	40N32	117E24	-7:49:36
Beishuiquan 8	1	40N05	114E40	-7:38:40
Beisi 19	8	34N59	95E07	-6:20:28
Beisu 8	1	38N13	114E46	-7:39:04
Beitaitou 21	1	37N06	118E31	-7:54:04
Beitang 26	1	39N07	117E42	-7:50:48
Beitanshiqiao 22	2	31N05	121E38	-8:06:32
Beiwei 13	1	32N05	121E12	-8:04:48
Beiwenquan 24	9	29N51	106E24	-7:05:36
Beiwu 2	1	40N04	116E48	-7:47:12
Beiwudu 10	1	33N39	113E39	-7:34:36
Beixiadai 13	1	32N12	120E08	-8:00:32
Beixiejiadang 8	1	40N30	114E50	-7:39:20
Beixili 9	12	51N47	125E45	-8:23:00
Beixin'an 2	1	39N55	116E08	-7:44:32
Beixindian 2	1	39N44	116E44	-7:46:56
Beixing 9	12	48N29	125E40	-8:22:40
Beixinjing 22	2	31N13	121E22	-8:05:28
Beixinliu 8	1	39N16	116E31	-7:46:04
Beixinzhen 13	1	31N49	121E31	-8:06:04
Beiyan 21	1	36N33	118E42	-7:54:48
Beiyin 13	1	31N07	120E47	-8:03:08
Beiyindai 16	11	42N35	122E22	-8:09:28
Beiyuan 2	1	40N01	116E24	-7:45:36
Beizangzong 28	8	30N14	90E44	-6:02:56
Beizhaijiawopeng 16	11	41N14	122E41	-8:10:44
Beizhen (Gaoshanzi) 16	11	41N36	121E47	-8:07:08
Beizhen 21	1	37N22	118E01	-7:52:04
Beizhouzhuang 13	1	31N52	120E24	-8:01:36
Beizifu 17	11	42N09	120E29	-8:01:56
Benniu 13	1	31N52	119E48	-7:59:12
Benxi (Penhsi) 16	11	41N18	123E45	-8:15:00
Benxi (Xiaoshi) 16	11	41N17	124E07	-8:16:28
Bianba 28	8	30N49	94E59	-6:19:56
Bian'er 24	9	31N14	101E28	-6:45:52
Bian'gezhuang 8	1	39N28	115E53	-7:43:32
Bianlinzhen 21	1	37N26	116E32	-7:46:08
Bianminchang 24	9	29N41	105E04	-7:00:16
Biannilupucun 16	11	41N30	123E42	-8:14:48
Bianquanwopu 16	11	41N21	120E48	-8:03:12
Bibo 24	9	29N02	99E20	-6:37:20
Bidian 10	1	32N38	113E03	-7:32:12
Bieguzhuang 8	1	39N19	116E39	-7:46:36
Bieshan 26	1	39N58	117E29	-7:49:56
Bieteluobaoluosika 17	11	48N35	119E56	-7:59:44
Bihu 30	1	28N21	119E48	-7:59:12
Bijiang 29	9	26N30	98E55	-6:35:40
Bijie 7	9	27N18	105E20	-7:01:20
Bikeqi 17	9	40N49	111E13	-7:24:52
Bilian 30	1	28N21	120E33	-8:02:12
Bin'an 9	12	45N50	127E45	-8:31:00
Bingcha 13	1	32N30	120E52	-8:03:28
Bingfang 13	1	32N15	121E20	-8:05:20
Binhai (Dongkan) 13	1	34N03	119E51	-7:59:24
Binxian 9	12	45N44	127E29	-8:29:56
Binxian 20	9	35N00	108E08	-7:12:32
Binxian 21	1	37N28	117E56	-7:51:44
Binyang 6	9	23N18	108E46	-7:15:04
Biqiao 1	1	31N02	119E02	-7:56:08
Bishan 24	9	29N37	106E13	-7:04:52
Biyang 10	1	32N44	113E20	-7:33:20
Bo'ai 10	1	35N10	113E04	-7:32:16
Bobai 6	9	22N12	109E52	-7:19:28
Bohetai 16	11	42N01	123E13	-8:12:52
Bojizhang 8	1	41N49	117E46	-7:51:04
Bokalike 19	8	36N47	91E41	-6:06:44
Bole 27	7	44N53	82E05	-5:28:20
Boli 9	12	45N46	130E31	-8:42:04
Boligeqiu 16	11	42N14	121E40	-8:06:40
Bolishan 15	12	43N50	123E31	-8:14:04
Boluo 5	1	23N11	114E17	-7:37:08
Boluo 5	1	24N27	113E03	-7:32:12
Boluochi 16	11	41N24	119E56	-7:59:44
Boluokeng 5	1	24N05	113E22	-7:33:28
Bomei 5	1	22N57	115E46	-7:43:04
Boping 21	1	36N36	116E07	-7:44:28
Bose 6	9	23N54	106E37	-7:06:28
Boshan 21	1	36N29	117E50	-7:51:20
Bowang 13	1	31N34	118E50	-7:55:20
Boxian 1	1	33N53	115E45	-7:43:00
Boxing 21	1	37N08	118E07	-7:52:28
Boxodoi 17	1	42N34	115E18	-7:41:12
Boyang 14	1	28N59	116E40	-7:46:40
Bozhen 8	1	38N07	116E32	-7:46:08
Bubuduo 28	8	30N06	84E38	-5:38:32
Bucun 21	1	36N37	117E27	-7:49:48
Budayuan 16	11	40N56	125E19	-8:21:16
Buerjin 27	8	47N43	86E53	-5:47:32
Buertuokai 27	7	39N35	74E58	-4:59:52
Bugt 17	11	48N46	121E57	-8:07:48
Bugt 17	11	42N20	120E43	-8:02:52
Buhanhua 16	11	42N39	122E46	-8:11:04
Buhuai 28	7	33N22	80E36	-5:22:24
Buji 19	8	33N58	95E22	-6:21:28
Buluni-Tokhoi 27	8	47N02	87E19	-5:49:16
Buluntai 28	8	36N34	92E38	-6:10:32
Buluntouhai 27	8	47N02	87E19	-5:49:16
Burqin 27	8	47N43	86E53	-5:47:32
Butha Qi (Zalantun) 17	11	48N02	122E43	-8:10:52
Buyiqiao 13	1	31N47	119E48	-7:59:12
Buziji 13	1	33N49	118E14	-7:52:56
Caigou 10	1	33N16	114E32	-7:38:08
Caihuaping 12	1	26N54	113E23	-7:33:32
Caijiachang 24	9	29N44	106E29	-7:05:56
Caijiagang 24	9	28N55	106E21	-7:05:24
Caijialou 16	11	41N24	121E06	-8:04:24
Caijiapo 20	9	34N17	107E39	-7:10:36
Caijiazhuang 8	1	40N48	114E44	-7:38:56
Caitingqiao 8	1	39N54	117E39	-7:50:36
Caiwan 6	9	25N50	110E50	-7:23:20
Caixi 3	1	25N15	116E28	-7:45:52
Caiyu 2	1	39N39	116E37	-7:46:28
Caizhuang 10	1	34N17	114E08	-7:36:32
Caka 19	9	36N48	99E19	-6:37:16
Cangbu 11	1	30N49	114E35	-7:38:20
Cangniutun 8	1	39N23	115E54	-7:43:36
Cangqian 30	1	30N17	120E25	-8:01:40
Cangqian 30	1	30N18	120E00	-8:00:00
Cangshangtun 26	1	40N03	117E32	-7:50:08
Cangwu 6	9	23N22	111E13	-7:24:52
Cangxi 24	9	31N48	105E57	-7:03:48
Cangyuan 29	9	23N12	99E16	-6:37:04
Cangzhou 8	1	38N19	116E51	-7:47:24
Canton → Guangzhou 5	1	23N06	113E16	-7:33:04
Caochi 24	9	30N19	104E24	-6:57:36
Caocun 13	1	31N42	118E56	-7:55:44
Caodian 11	1	32N32	111E11	-7:24:44
Caodian 30	1	28N39	120E23	-8:01:32
Caodian 10	1	33N21	112E39	-7:30:36
Cao'e 30	1	30N01	120E52	-8:03:28
Caofang 3	1	26N04	116E35	-7:46:20
Caogezhai 8	1	40N09	117E50	-7:51:20
Caohe 8	1	38N57	115E32	-7:42:08
Caohe 22	2	31N09	121E25	-8:05:40
Caohecheng 16	11	40N46	124E02	-8:16:08
Caohekou 16	11	40N54	123E53	-8:15:32
Caohezhang 16	11	41N04	124E03	-8:16:12
Caojian 29	9	25N38	99E07	-6:36:28
Caojiawopeng 16	11	42N00	122E20	-8:09:20
Caojiawopu 16	11	42N37	122E19	-8:09:16
Caojiawu 8	1	39N24	116E31	-7:46:04
Caojiazhen 13	1	31N55	121E38	-8:06:32
Caojiezi 24	9	29N53	106E24	-7:05:36
Caojing 22	2	30N47	121E24	-8:05:36
Caojun 14	1	29N41	116E17	-7:45:08
Caolaoji 1	1	33N06	117E22	-7:49:28
Caomaji 21	1	34N52	116E17	-7:45:08
Caonian 13	1	32N56	120E20	-8:01:20
Caopeng 22	2	31N44	121E17	-8:05:08
Caoping 30	1	28N48	118E22	-7:53:28
Caopu 13	1	34N34	118E52	-7:55:28
Caoqiao 13	1	31N32	119E59	-7:59:56
Caoshi 1	1	33N32	116E29	-7:45:56
Caoshi 16	11	42N17	125E16	-8:21:04
Caota 30	1	29N42	120E08	-8:00:32
Caotang 13	1	31N16	118E59	-7:55:56
Caoxi 14	1	28N42	117E18	-7:49:12
Caoxian 21	1	34N53	115E33	-7:42:12
Caoyangxi 3	1	26N34	118E47	-7:55:08
Cecheng 8	1	39N06	116E48	-7:47:12
Ceheng 7	9	25N10	105E48	-7:03:12
Cele 27	7	37N00	80E47	-5:23:08
Cenxi 6	9	22N59	111E00	-7:24:00
Cetian 3	1	25N44	116E22	-7:45:28
Chaanling 11	1	29N39	113E49	-7:35:16
Chabogongba 28	7	31N47	81E14	-5:24:56
Chabuchaer 27	7	43N42	81E04	-5:24:16
Chachu 28	7	33N16	81E41	-5:26:44
Chadian 7	9	26N48	105E48	-7:03:12
Chadian 26	1	39N14	117E45	-7:51:00
Chadian 24	9	30N14	105E56	-7:03:44
Chadianzi 24	9	30N31	104E22	-6:57:28
Chaersen 17	11	46N19	121E54	-8:07:36
Chagandianlisu 17	9	41N47	103E29	-6:53:56
Chahancheluo 8	1	41N39	114E22	-7:37:28
Chahanwusu → Dulan 19	8	36N16	98E28	-6:33:52
Chahayang 9	12	48N24	124E15	-8:17:00
Chahe 19	8	33N48	97E22	-6:29:28
Chahe 13	1	33N16	119E02	-7:56:08
Chahe 8	1	39N50	115E21	-7:41:24
Chahuamiao 1	1	33N00	115E56	-7:43:44
Chaigou 21	1	36N15	119E36	-7:58:24
Chaihe 9	12	44N47	129E42	-8:38:48
Chaijiawan 12	1	29N10	113E06	-7:32:24
Chaiqiao 30	1	29N51	121E56	-8:07:44
Chaishudian 2	1	40N46	116E30	-7:46:00
Chaiwobao 27	8	43N33	87E59	-5:51:56
Chaiwopu 27	8	43N33	87E59	-5:51:56
Chajia 24	9	29N37	104E27	-6:57:48
Chajian 1	1	32N40	118E46	-7:55:04
Chajianling 8	1	39N14	114E36	-7:38:24
Chajiaqiao 13	1	34N00	120E07	-8:00:28
Chakaer 27	7	36N32	80E43	-5:22:52
Chakou 23	1	38N03	113E36	-7:34:24
Chakou 8	1	38N53	116E41	-7:46:44
Chalaxung 19	8	34N10	97E44	-6:30:56
Chalengkou 19	8	37N57	93E40	-6:14:40
Chaling 12	1	26N47	113E33	-7:34:12
Chalisi 24	9	32N55	102E04	-6:48:16
Chaluhe 15	12	43N43	126E00	-8:24:00
Chamdo → Qamdo 28	8	31N11	97E15	-6:29:00
Chamojie 17	11	49N25	124E45	-8:19:00
Chanchiang → Zhanjiang 5	8	21N12	110E23	-7:21:32
Chanfang 2	1	39N56	115E55	-7:43:40
Chang'an 6	9	26N00	109E34	-7:18:16
Changan → Xi'an 20	9	34N15	108E52	-7:15:28
Chang'anzhen 30	1	30N28	120E27	-8:01:48
Changbai 15	12	41N26	128E11	-8:32:44
Changbu 5	1	23N48	115E26	-7:41:44
Changcaocun 2	1	39N49	115E47	-7:43:08
Changchaoling 30	1	31N00	119E40	-7:58:40
Changcheng 5	9	19N24	108E42	-7:14:48
Changcheng 1	1	31N49	116E54	-7:47:36
Changchiak'ou → Zhangjiakou 8	1	40N50	114E53	-7:39:32
Ch'angchih → Changzhi 23	1	36N11	113E08	-7:32:32
Changchou → Zhangzhou 3	1	24N33	117E39	-7:50:36
Changchow → Changzhou 13	1	31N47	119E57	-7:59:48
Changchun 15	12	43N53	125E19	-8:21:16
Changchunling 15	12	45N22	125E28	-8:21:52
Changdao (Sihou) 21	1	37N56	120E42	-8:02:48
Changde 12	1	29N02	111E41	-7:26:44
Changdian 2	1	40N01	116E32	-7:46:08
Changfeng 1	1	32N27	117E09	-7:48:36
Changgang 5	1	24N38	113E05	-7:32:20
Changgangzi 16	11	41N26	122E41	-8:10:44
Changge 10	1	34N15	113E50	-7:35:20
Changgou 2	1	39N34	115E53	-7:43:32
Changguoyu 2	1	39N44	115E52	-7:43:28
Changguandian 1	1	32N58	115E16	-7:41:04

Changguowei 30 1 29N15 121E56 -8:07:44
Changhai 16 11 39N18 122E35 -8:10:20
Chang-Hai → Shanghai 22 2 31N14 121E28 -8:05:52
Changhe 30 3 30N11 120E11 -8:00:44
Changhua 30 1 30N11 119E13 -7:56:52
Changhua 25 6 24N05 120E32 -8:02:08
Changji 27 8 44N01 87E19 -5:49:16
Changjiang 5 1 25N19 113E56 -7:35:44
Changjiang 5 9 19N17 109E02 -7:16:08
Changjiangbu 11 1 30N52 113E43 -7:34:52
Changjiapuzi 16 11 40N51 123E43 -8:14:52
Changjiazhuang 8 1 40N35 115E24 -7:41:36
Changjie 30 1 29N16 121E40 -8:06:40
Changjing 13 1 31N45 120E29 -8:01:56
Changkai 14 1 28N04 116E18 -7:45:12
Changkalajier 27 7 40N09 76E59 -5:07:56
Changkeng 30 1 30N19 121E57 -8:07:48
Changkiakow → Zhangjiakou 8 1 40N50 114E53 -7:39:32
Changle 3 1 26N00 119E31 -7:58:04
Changle 21 1 36N42 118E49 -7:55:16
Changle 30 1 29N25 120E37 -8:02:28
Changlejie 12 1 28N52 113E19 -7:33:16
Changleqiao 30 1 30N21 119E51 -7:59:24
Changlezhen 13 1 31N56 121E15 -8:05:00
Changli 21 1 36N57 119E45 -7:59:00
Changli 8 1 39N43 119E11 -7:56:44
Changling 15 12 44N15 123E58 -8:15:52
Changlingfeng 8 1 40N11 118E24 -7:53:36
Changlingji 10 1 32N30 114E54 -7:39:36
Changlingzi 16 11 39N33 121E19 -8:05:16
Changlingzi 16 11 39N47 122E43 -8:10:52
Changlinhe 1 1 31N40 117E29 -7:49:56
Changning 29 9 24N55 99E35 -6:38:20
Changning (Anningqiao) 24 9 28N21 104E53 -6:59:32
Changning 8 1 39N59 114E55 -7:39:40
Changning 12 1 26N19 112E21 -7:29:24
Ch'angpin 25 6 23N19 121E27 -8:05:48
Changping 2 1 40N14 116E14 -7:44:56
Changputong 29 9 28N05 98E29 -6:33:56
Changqiao 3 1 24N15 117E39 -7:50:36
Changqiao 3 1 26N49 118E50 -7:55:20
Changqing 21 1 36N34 116E43 -7:46:52
Changsa 5 9 19N51 110E53 -7:23:32
Changsha 12 1 28N12 112E58 -7:31:52
Changsha 5 1 24N13 116E07 -7:44:28
Changshageng 24 9 30N00 104E35 -6:58:20
Changshan 24 9 29N30 104E13 -6:56:52
Changshan 30 1 28N55 118E30 -7:54:00
Changshan 21 1 36N54 117E50 -7:51:20
Changsheng 14 1 26N16 116E01 -7:44:04
Changshengqiao 24 9 29N31 106E39 -7:06:36
Changshitai 17 11 42N33 120E43 -8:02:52
Changshitou 19 9 35N03 99E11 -6:36:44
Changshou 24 9 29N51 107E06 -7:08:24
Changshoudian 11 1 31N26 112E35 -7:30:20
Changshoujie 12 1 28N44 113E57 -7:35:48
Changshu 13 1 31N39 120E45 -8:03:00
Changshui 10 1 34N21 111E29 -7:25:56
Changtai 16 11 41N34 122E00 -8:08:00
Changtai 30 1 28N34 118E37 -7:54:28
Changtai 3 1 24N40 117E46 -7:51:04
Changtancun 16 11 41N33 123E02 -8:12:08
Ch'angte → Changde 12 1 29N02 111E41 -7:26:44
Changteh → Anyang 10 1 36N06 114E21 -7:37:24
Changting 9 12 44N32 128E47 -8:35:08
Changting 3 1 25N52 116E20 -7:45:20
Changtumiao 17 1 43N30 114E34 -7:38:16
Changwu 9 12 46N00 125E36 -8:22:24
Changwu 20 9 35N09 107E42 -7:10:48
Changxindianzhen 2 1 39N49 116E12 -7:44:48
Changxing 30 1 31N01 119E54 -7:59:36
Changxingdian 16 11 41N27 121E44 -8:06:56
Changxingdian 16 11 41N33 123E23 -8:13:32
Changxingzhen 16 11 41N40 122E14 -8:08:56
Changxuanling 11 1 31N08 114E20 -7:37:20
Changyi 21 1 36N51 119E23 -7:57:32
Changyuan 10 1 35N13 114E39 -7:38:36
Changyukou 8 1 40N46 115E08 -7:40:32
Changzhi 23 1 36N11 113E08 -7:32:32
Changzhou (Changchow) 13 1 31N47 119E57 -7:59:48
Chankiang → Zhanjiang 5 8 21N12 110E23 -7:21:32
Chankou 4 9 35N52 104E27 -6:57:48
Chantang 1 1 33N41 117E37 -7:50:28
Chao'an 5 1 23N41 116E38 -7:46:32
Chaocheng 21 1 36N05 115E35 -7:42:20
Ch'aochou 25 6 22N33 120E32 -8:02:08
Ch'aochou → Chao'an 5 1 23N41 116E38 -7:46:32
Chaomidian 26 1 39N04 117E01 -7:48:04
Chaoshui 21 1 37N42 120E55 -8:03:40

Chaoshui 9 12 49N44 127E21 -8:29:24
Chaoxian 1 1 31N36 117E52 -7:51:28
Chaoyang 15 12 44N34 126E20 -8:25:20
Chaoyang 5 1 23N17 116E37 -7:46:28
Chaoyang 16 11 41N35 120E28 -8:01:52
Chaoyangchuan 15 12 42N54 129E21 -8:37:24
Chaoyangcun 17 11 50N02 124E16 -8:17:04
Chaoyanggou 16 11 42N07 121E04 -8:04:16
Chaoyangpo 15 12 43N37 124E42 -8:18:48
Chaoyangshan 15 12 43N02 125E40 -8:22:40
Chaozhuang 10 1 34N18 114E56 -7:39:44
Chasidaba 16 11 42N19 121E19 -8:05:16
Chatian 30 1 27N54 118E58 -7:55:52
Chating 13 1 31N21 119E25 -7:57:40
Chawa'nanake 28 8 31N36 89E41 -5:58:44
Chayuan 12 1 27N40 112E57 -7:31:48
Chayuan 30 1 29N20 121E34 -8:06:16
Chayue 1 1 30N49 119E21 -7:57:24
Chebeigou 15 12 43N28 127E04 -8:28:16
Ch'ech'eng 25 6 22N05 120E42 -8:02:48
Chedaoyu 8 1 40N22 117E57 -7:51:48
Chedun 3 1 24N09 117E19 -7:49:16
Chefang 13 3 31N15 120E45 -8:03:00
Chefang 16 11 41N35 121E26 -8:05:44
Chefoo → Yantai 21 1 37N33 121E20 -8:05:20
Chehe 6 9 25N00 107E38 -7:10:32
Cheheqiao 8 1 40N21 118E16 -7:53:04
Chejiatun 16 11 41N57 123E01 -8:12:04
Chejiawopeng 16 11 42N29 123E07 -8:12:28
Chek Kang 31 4 22N26 114E21 -7:37:24
Chemaogang 22 2 31N33 121E52 -8:07:28
Chen Barag Qi 17 11 49N21 119E31 -7:58:04
Chenbofang 8 1 37N27 115E18 -7:41:12
Chencai 30 1 29N37 120E22 -8:01:28
Chenchiang → Zhenjiang 13 1 32N13 119E26 -7:57:44
Chencun 5 1 22N58 113E13 -7:32:52
Chendai 3 1 23N48 117E24 -7:49:36
Chenfang 14 1 28N01 117E32 -7:50:08
Cheng'an 8 1 36N27 114E41 -7:38:44
Chengbu 12 1 26N18 110E13 -7:20:52
Chengchow → Zhengzhou 10 1 34N48 113E39 -7:34:36
Chengde (Xiabancheng) 8 1 40N47 118E08 -7:52:32
Chengde 8 1 40N58 117E53 -7:51:32
Chengdu (Chengtu) 24 9 30N39 104E04 -6:56:16
Chenggang 14 1 26N32 115E26 -7:41:44
Chenghai 5 1 23N30 116E46 -7:47:04
Chenghuang 6 9 22N32 109E39 -7:18:36
Chengjia 5 1 24N50 112E50 -7:31:20
Chengjiahe 11 1 32N18 112E27 -7:29:48
Chengjiang 29 9 24N45 102E54 -6:51:36
Chengjiangzhen 24 9 29N52 106E23 -7:05:32
Chengjiazhen 24 9 29N24 104E36 -6:58:24
Chengkou 24 9 31N54 108E41 -7:14:44
Chenglingji 12 1 29N26 113E09 -7:32:36
Chenglong 14 1 24N51 114E41 -7:38:44
Chengmai 5 9 19N48 110E02 -7:20:08
Chengmao 13 1 31N10 120E53 -8:03:32
Chengpu 3 1 25N46 118E48 -7:55:12
Chengqian 21 1 35N21 117E21 -7:49:24
Chengqianwei 14 1 28N09 116E13 -7:44:52
Chengteh → Chengde 8 1 40N58 117E53 -7:51:32
Chengtu → Chengdu 24 9 30N39 104E04 -6:56:16
Ch'engtzuliao 25 6 25N06 121E27 -8:05:48
Chengwu 21 1 34N58 115E52 -7:43:28
Chengxian 4 9 33N43 105E41 -7:02:44
Chengyang 21 1 36N18 120E22 -8:01:28
Chengyang 30 1 29N59 119E44 -7:58:56
Chengzi 2 1 39N58 116E02 -7:44:08
Chengzi 8 1 41N57 117E16 -7:49:04
Chengzitan 16 11 39N30 122E30 -8:10:00
Ch'enhsien → Chenxian 12 1 25N48 112E59 -7:31:56
Chenji 13 1 33N50 119E11 -7:56:44
Chenjiachang 24 9 30N04 105E15 -7:01:00
Chenjiachang 24 9 29N35 104E52 -6:59:28
Chenjiagang 13 1 34N25 119E49 -7:59:16
Chenjiahe 12 1 29N28 109E59 -7:19:56
Chenjiaji 11 3 30N42 114E21 -7:37:24
Chenjiapang 13 1 31N14 119E42 -7:58:48
Chenjiapu 8 1 40N31 115E37 -7:42:28
Chenjiaqiao 22 2 31N27 121E16 -8:05:04
Chenjiatun 16 11 40N57 121E01 -8:04:04
Chenjiatun 16 11 42N20 124E06 -8:16:24
Chenjiawan 13 1 31N02 120E35 -8:02:20
Chenjiaxiang 11 1 31N29 113E45 -7:35:00
Chenjiazhen 22 2 31N30 121E48 -8:07:12
Chenjiazui 26 1 39N17 116E59 -7:47:56
Chenkeng 3 1 25N06 116E15 -7:45:00
Chenlingjiao 1 1 30N23 118E47 -7:55:08
Chenliu 10 1 34N43 114E31 -7:38:04
Chenlong 22 2 31N17 121E25 -8:05:40
Chenqiao 10 1 34N58 114E32 -7:38:08
Chenquingqiao 9 12 49N08 127E16 -8:29:04

Chenshanzhuang 26 1 39N43 117E30 -7:50:00
Chenshichang 24 9 29N17 106E00 -7:04:00
Chentang 6 9 23N54 110E39 -7:22:36
Chenxi 12 1 27N51 109E59 -7:19:56
Chenxian 12 1 25N48 112E59 -7:31:56
Chenxiangtun 16 11 41N36 123E30 -8:14:00
Chenyang 13 1 33N47 120E10 -8:00:40
Chenyang → Shenyang 16 11 41N48 123E27 -8:13:48
Chepaizi 27 8 44N55 84E30 -5:38:00
Chesu 28 8 30N31 82E37 -5:30:28
Cheung Shue Tan 31 4 22N26 114E12 -7:36:48
Chezhen 21 1 37N54 117E37 -7:50:28
Chiahsien 25 6 23N05 120E35 -8:02:20
Chiahsing → Jiaxing 30 1 30N46 120E45 -8:03:00
Chiai 25 6 23N29 120E27 -8:01:48
Chiali 25 6 23N10 120E10 -8:00:40
Chiamussu → Jiamusi 9 12 46N50 130E21 -8:41:24
Chiangmen → Jiangmen 5 1 22N35 113E05 -7:32:20
Chiangtu → Yangzhou 13 1 32N24 119E26 -7:57:44
Chiangyin → Jiangyin 13 1 31N55 120E16 -8:01:04
Chian → Ji'an 14 1 27N07 114E58 -7:39:52
Chiaohsi 25 6 24N49 121E46 -8:07:04
Chiaohsien → Jiaoxian 21 1 36N18 119E58 -7:59:52
Chiaopan 25 6 24N50 121E21 -8:05:24
Chiaotso → Jiaozuo 10 1 35N15 113E13 -7:32:52
Chiapaot'ai 25 6 24N11 121E00 -8:04:00
Chibakou 11 1 29N36 113E01 -7:32:04
Chicheng 8 1 40N54 115E46 -7:43:04
Chichi 25 6 23N50 120E47 -8:03:08
Ch'ich'ihaerh → Qiqihaer 9 12 47N19 123E55 -8:15:40
Chidu 28 8 31N50 94E30 -6:18:00
Chiehyang → Jieyang 5 1 23N35 116E21 -7:45:24
Chifeng (Ulanhad) 17 11 42N18 119E00 -7:56:00
Chigu 14 1 27N34 114E40 -7:38:40
Chihe 1 1 32N32 117E58 -7:51:52
Ch'ihfeng → Chifeng 17 11 42N18 119E00 -7:56:00
Chihpen 25 6 22N42 121E02 -8:04:08
Ch'ihshang 25 6 23N07 121E12 -8:04:48
Chihsi → Jixi 9 12 45N17 130E59 -8:43:56
Chihtungtsun 25 6 22N44 120E14 -8:00:56
Chihu 3 1 24N07 117E51 -7:51:24
Chikou 1 1 30N44 117E32 -7:50:08
Ch'iku 25 6 23N08 120E07 -8:00:28
Chilingchang 24 9 28N58 105E31 -7:02:04
Chilin → Jilin 15 12 43N51 126E33 -8:26:12
Chilung (Keelung) 25 6 25N08 121E44 -8:06:56
Chinan → Jinan 21 1 36N40 116E57 -7:47:48
Chinchiang → Quanzhou 3 1 24N54 118E35 -7:54:20
Chinchou → Jinzhou 16 11 41N07 121E08 -8:04:32
Ch'ingchiang → Qingjiang 13 1 33N35 119E02 -7:56:08
Chingshih → Jinshi 12 1 29N39 111E52 -7:27:28
Ch'ingtao → Qingdao 21 1 36N06 120E19 -8:01:16
Chingtechen → Jingdezhen 14 1 29N16 117E11 -7:48:44
Ch'ingt'ung 25 6 25N02 121E43 -8:06:52
Chinguan 8 1 38N32 115E29 -7:41:56
Chinhsien 16 11 41N07 121E08 -8:04:32
Chinhsien → Jinxian 16 11 39N04 121E40 -8:06:40
Chinhua → Jinhua 30 1 29N07 119E39 -7:58:36
Ch'inhuangtao → Qinhuangdao 8 1 39N56 119E36 -7:58:24
Chining → Jining 21 1 35N25 116E36 -7:46:24
Chining → Jining 17 9 40N57 113E02 -7:32:08
Chinkiang → Zhenjiang 13 1 32N13 119E26 -7:57:44
Chinkuashih 25 6 25N07 121E51 -8:07:24
Chinmen 3 1 24N27 118E21 -7:53:24
Chinshan 25 6 25N13 121E38 -8:06:32
Chinshui 25 6 24N36 120E53 -8:03:32
Chinwangtao → Qinhuangdao 8 1 39N56 119E36 -7:58:24
Chiping 21 1 36N37 116E16 -7:45:04
Ch'ishan 25 6 22N53 120E28 -8:01:52
Chishanji 21 1 36N56 122E23 -8:09:32
Chishi 3 1 27N42 117E58 -7:51:52
Chishisi 5 1 25N32 113E11 -7:32:44
Chishui 7 9 28N29 105E38 -7:02:32
Chishuihe 24 9 27N50 105E32 -7:02:08
Ch'itu 25 6 25N06 121E43 -8:06:52
Chiuchiang → Jiujiang 14 1 29N44 115E59 -7:43:56
Chixi 14 1 28N22 116E22 -7:45:28
Chizhen 1 1 31N55 118E12 -7:52:48

Place	Zone	Lat	Long	Time
Chizizhen 10	1	32N22	115E11	-7:40:44
Chong'an 3	1	27N45	118E02	-7:52:08
Chongde 30	1	30N32	120E26	-8:01:44
Chonggu 22	2	31N12	121E10	-8:04:40
Chonghe 9	12	44N43	127E45	-8:31:00
Chongkanzhen 24	9	30N09	105E37	-7:02:28
Chongli (Xiwanzi) 8	1	40N54	115E16	-7:41:04
Chongming 22	2	31N37	121E24	-8:05:36
Chongqing 24	9	30N39	103E41	-6:54:44
Chongqing (Chungking) 24	9	29N34	106E35	-7:06:20
Chongren 30	1	29N37	120E43	-8:02:52
Chongren 14	1	27N46	116E01	-7:44:04
Chongru 3	1	27N01	120E10	-8:00:40
Chongshi 14	1	25N24	115E28	-7:41:52
Chongwu 3	1	24N53	118E55	-7:55:40
Chongxi 15	12	42N07	128E59	-8:35:56
Chongxin 4	9	35N13	107E29	-7:09:56
Chongyang 11	1	29N33	114E00	-7:36:00
Chongyi 5	1	25N44	114E18	-7:37:12
Chongzuo 6	9	22N21	107E26	-7:09:44
Chouchiak'ou → Shangshui 10	1	33N33	114E34	-7:38:16
Chouk'ou → Shangshui 10	1	33N33	114E34	-7:38:16
Chuanbu 13	1	31N17	119E49	-7:59:16
Chuanergu 26	1	39N20	117E43	-7:50:52
Chuan'gang 13	1	31N57	121E04	-8:04:16
Chuangjiapuzi 16	11	40N50	124E06	-8:16:24
Chuanliao 30	1	28N17	120E13	-8:00:52
Chuansha 22	2	31N12	121E42	-8:06:48
Chuanshan 30	1	29N53	121E57	-8:07:48
Chuanxindian 16	11	41N25	120E30	-8:02:00
Ch'üchiang → Shaoguan 5	1	24N50	113E37	-7:34:28
Chuchou → Zhuzhou 12	1	27N50	113E09	-7:32:36
Chucun 1	1	33N04	116E32	-7:46:08
Chuen Lung 31	4	22N24	114E06	-7:36:24
Chuhe 10	1	34N03	113E35	-7:34:20
Chukou 12	1	25N44	113E22	-7:33:28
Chun'an 30	1	29N35	118E58	-7:55:52
Chunan 25	6	24N41	120E52	-8:03:28
Chunchi 3	1	27N22	119E20	-7:57:20
Chung Hau 31	4	22N16	114E00	-7:36:00
Chungho 25	6	25N00	121E30	-8:06:00
Chungking → Chongqing 24	9	29N34	106E35	-7:06:20
Chungli 25	6	24N57	121E13	-8:04:52
Chungliao 25	6	22N41	121E28	-8:05:52
Chungp'u 25	6	23N25	120E31	-8:02:04
Chungshan → Zhongshan 5	1	22N31	113E22	-7:33:28
Chunheji 10	1	32N12	115E22	-7:41:28
Chunhua 13	1	31N56	118E56	-7:55:44
Chunhua 20	9	34N50	108E31	-7:14:04
Chunyang 15	12	43N43	129E28	-8:37:52
Chunze 28	8	29N51	88E41	-5:54:44
Chuosijia 24	9	31N53	101E59	-6:47:56
Chushan 25	6	23N45	120E40	-8:02:40
Chutung 25	6	24N44	121E05	-8:04:20
Chuwang 10	1	36N02	114E52	-7:39:28
Chuwei 25	6	25N08	121E27	-8:05:48
Chuxian 1	1	32N19	118E17	-7:53:08
Chuxiong 29	9	25N02	101E30	-6:46:00
Chuzhai 10	1	33N22	113E37	-7:34:28
Ciba 24	9	29N07	105E55	-7:03:40
Cicheng 30	1	30N00	121E22	-8:05:28
Cigou 10	1	33N51	113E35	-7:34:20
Cijiawu 2	1	39N48	115E59	-7:43:56
Cikou 11	1	29N42	114E46	-7:39:04
Cili 12	1	29N17	111E00	-7:24:00
Ciqikou 24	9	29N35	106E26	-7:05:44
Cishan 8	1	36N37	114E07	-7:36:28
Cishangang 1	1	30N55	119E31	-7:58:04
Cixi 30	1	30N11	121E15	-8:05:00
Cixian 8	1	36N22	114E23	-7:37:32
Ciyutuo 16	11	41N31	122E53	-8:11:32
Cizhuping 24	9	29N11	103E36	-6:54:24
Conghua 5	1	23N32	113E32	-7:34:08
Congjiang 7	9	25N41	108E47	-7:15:08
Cuigezhuang 2	1	40N01	116E28	-7:45:52
Cuigezhuang 8	1	40N02	117E54	-7:51:36
Cuihuangkou 26	1	39N32	117E11	-7:48:44
Cuijiatun 16	11	40N57	121E09	-8:04:36
Cuijiazhuang 16	11	40N57	122E44	-8:10:56
Cuiqiao 10	1	34N12	114E36	-7:38:24
Cunqian 14	1	28N30	115E10	-7:40:40
Cuntan 24	9	29N37	106E36	-7:06:24
Cuqiao 24	9	30N36	103E59	-6:55:56
Da'an 15	12	45N28	124E18	-8:17:12
Daan 6	9	23N19	110E34	-7:22:16
Da'an 5	1	23N05	115E37	-7:42:28
Da'an 24	9	29N23	106E01	-7:04:04
Daba 16	11	42N06	122E00	-8:08:00
Dabagou 16	11	42N27	122E00	-8:08:00
Dabaizhuang 26	1	39N27	117E23	-7:49:32
Dabali 16	11	41N51	120E37	-8:02:28
Dabancheng 27	8	43N21	88E19	-5:53:16
Dabangdian 11	1	31N37	113E41	-7:34:44
Dabaojiagangzi 16	11	42N09	123E33	-8:14:12
Dabaozhuang 2	1	40N18	116E58	-7:47:52
Dabaozi 8	1	40N11	115E10	-7:40:40
Dabasi 24	9	28N55	105E09	-7:00:36
Dabayingzi 16	11	42N11	121E35	-8:06:20
Dabeiwa 8	1	40N48	117E31	-7:50:04
Dabeiyingzi 16	11	42N05	122E08	-8:08:32
Dabobeizhuang 26	1	39N18	117E59	-7:51:56
Dabu 5	1	24N19	116E43	-7:46:52
Dabu 5	1	23N52	116E54	-7:47:36
Dabu 5	1	24N20	114E35	-7:38:20
Dacaitun 16	11	41N38	121E18	-8:05:12
Dacangzigou 16	11	40N59	121E01	-8:04:04
Dacaocun 2	1	40N34	117E07	-7:48:28
Dachakou 1	1	29N38	118E18	-7:53:12
Dachang 8	1	39N53	116E59	-7:47:56
Dachang 13	3	32N12	118E45	-7:55:00
Dachang 22	2	31N18	121E25	-8:05:40
Dacheng 14	1	28N34	115E31	-7:42:04
Dachengji 13	1	33N52	119E26	-7:57:44
Dachenjiabao 13	1	32N11	120E22	-8:01:28
Dachixu 3	1	25N10	116E46	-7:47:04
Dachongyu 8	1	40N23	117E41	-7:50:44
Dacun 24	9	27N55	101E08	-6:44:32
Dacun 13	1	31N12	119E40	-7:58:40
Dadaolizhuang 2	1	39N59	116E59	-7:47:56
Dadaotun 16	11	41N46	122E13	-8:08:52
Dadayungou 16	11	41N23	123E25	-8:13:40
Dadian 1	1	33N36	117E16	-7:49:04
Dadianzi 16	11	42N11	124E02	-8:16:08
Dadingjiawopu 16	11	41N13	122E16	-8:09:04
Dadonggejiang 2	1	39N51	116E48	-7:47:12
Dadongzhou 16	11	41N44	124E00	-8:16:00
Dadugang 29	9	22N23	100E55	-6:43:40
Dadukou 24	9	29N28	106E29	-7:05:56
Dadukou 3	1	25N44	119E05	-7:56:20
Dadukou 24	9	28N45	105E13	-7:00:52
Daerhanwangfu 17	11	44N19	122E15	-8:09:00
Da'erhao 8	1	41N45	116E01	-7:44:04
Dafan 11	1	29N41	114E40	-7:38:40
Dafan 16	11	42N38	122E11	-8:08:44
Dafang 7	9	27N04	105E31	-7:02:04
Dafangshen 16	11	42N36	123E04	-8:12:16
Dafangshen 16	11	42N25	123E14	-8:12:56
Dafangshen 16	11	42N34	123E28	-8:13:52
Dafanhe 16	11	42N13	123E43	-8:14:52
Dafanpuzi 16	11	41N37	122E50	-8:11:20
Dafeng 13	1	33N12	120E30	-8:02:00
Dafoutuo 2	1	40N24	115E58	-7:43:52
Dafu 1	1	29N55	118E35	-7:54:20
Dagang 13	1	32N12	119E39	-7:58:36
Dagang 13	1	33N12	120E07	-8:00:28
Dagang 5	1	22N49	113E23	-7:33:32
Dagangtou 30	1	28N18	119E44	-7:58:56
Daganwangzhai 16	11	40N49	122E33	-8:10:12
Dagaokan 16	11	40N46	122E22	-8:09:28
Dagaolifangcun 16	11	41N10	122E28	-8:09:52
Dagaolitun 16	11	42N26	123E53	-8:15:32
Dagaoyang 30	1	30N35	120E26	-8:01:44
Dagcanglhamo 4	9	34N02	102E30	-6:50:00
Dagongtun 17	11	42N48	121E58	-8:07:52
Dagu 26	1	38N59	117E41	-7:50:44
Daguan 29	9	27N44	104E16	-6:57:04
Daguan 1	1	31N14	117E01	-7:48:04
Dagufen'gou 2	1	40N41	116E20	-7:45:20
Dagujia 16	11	42N22	124E52	-8:19:28
Dagujiazi 16	11	42N20	123E20	-8:13:20
Dagushan 16	11	41N03	123E02	-8:12:08
Dagutang 14	1	29N38	116E06	-7:44:24
Dahanchang 26	1	39N29	117E05	-7:48:20
Dahantun 16	11	42N10	122E41	-8:10:44
Dahe 13	1	31N42	120E37	-8:02:28
Dahebei 26	1	39N10	117E39	-7:50:36
Daheiyugou 16	11	41N21	121E55	-8:07:40
Dahekou 13	1	32N16	119E05	-7:56:20
Dahengdu 30	1	29N03	121E30	-8:06:00
Daheqiao 14	1	29N25	115E16	-7:41:04
Dahong 13	1	31N53	121E17	-8:05:08
Dahongmen 2	1	39N50	116E25	-7:45:40
Dahongqi 16	11	41N52	122E36	-8:10:24
Dahongtaizi 16	11	41N41	121E23	-8:05:32
Dahoucun 8	1	38N51	115E37	-7:42:28
Dahu 3	1	26N22	119E06	-7:56:24
Dahu 3	1	26N04	117E19	-7:49:16
Dahua 6	9	23N44	107E59	-7:11:56
Dahuan 5	1	22N33	113E29	-7:33:56
Dahuangdi 16	11	42N08	122E27	-8:09:48
Dahuangji 10	1	35N06	115E15	-7:41:00
Dahuangpu 26	1	39N26	117E16	-7:49:04
Dahuangshanpu 16	11	41N16	121E23	-8:05:32
Dahuashan 2	1	40N17	117E04	-7:48:16
Dahuasi 24	9	30N05	104E08	-6:56:32
Dahujiang 14	1	26N10	114E57	-7:39:48
Dahushan 16	11	41N37	122E09	-8:08:36
Daibu 1	1	32N19	117E12	-7:48:48
Daibu 13	1	31N18	119E30	-7:58:00
Daifang 14	1	27N32	115E41	-7:42:44
Daiguantun 8	1	39N57	117E50	-7:51:20
Daihaiyingzi 16	11	42N30	121E26	-8:05:44
Daiji 10	1	33N48	115E03	-7:40:12
Daijiagou 24	9	30N00	106E33	-7:06:12
Daijiayao 13	1	32N56	120E19	-8:01:16
Dailing 9	12	47N01	129E02	-8:36:08
Dainan 13	1	32N43	120E06	-8:00:24
Dainkog 24	8	32N31	97E59	-6:31:56
Dairen → Lüda 16	11	38N53	121E35	-8:06:20
Daishan 30	1	30N14	122E12	-8:08:48
Daisizhen 24	9	29N14	105E09	-7:00:36
Daixi 30	1	30N40	120E01	-8:00:04
Daixian 23	1	39N08	113E01	-7:32:04
Daixiqiao 13	1	31N36	120E04	-8:00:16
Dajidian 8	1	38N50	115E26	-7:41:44
Dajindian 10	1	34N24	112E58	-7:31:52
Dajing 30	1	28N24	121E07	-8:04:28
Dajing 12	1	28N59	113E19	-7:33:16
Dajishan 14	1	24N38	114E26	-7:37:44
Dajitai 16	11	42N20	121E11	-8:04:44
Dajiuba 27	8	36N50	89E35	-5:58:20
Daju 8	1	39N12	115E31	-7:42:04
Da Juh 19	8	36N40	94E04	-6:16:16
Dakangpu 16	11	41N32	121E06	-8:04:24
Dakanzi 16	11	40N52	122E53	-8:11:32
Dakeng 14	1	26N18	115E32	-7:42:08
Dakengkou 5	1	24N33	113E37	-7:34:28
Dakongcheng 26	1	39N30	117E09	-7:48:36
Dakongwan 16	11	40N51	122E19	-8:09:16
Dakou 10	1	34N27	112E44	-7:30:56
Dakoutun 26	1	39N35	117E14	-7:48:56
Dakumu 17	11	48N51	124E18	-8:17:12
Dakunlun 21	1	36N34	117E52	-7:51:28
Dalad Qi 17	9	40N28	110E02	-7:20:08
Dalahan (Shiqizhan) 9	12	52N06	125E46	-8:23:04
Dalaji 17	11	51N38	120E06	-8:00:24
Dalan 5	1	23N19	114E47	-7:39:08
Dalang 5	1	22N57	113E56	-7:35:44
Dalantuozi 16	11	41N28	122E47	-8:11:08
Dalayaozi 8	1	40N49	117E41	-7:50:44
Dalengtu 17	9	41N11	113E45	-7:35:00
Dali 20	9	34N47	109E57	-7:19:48
Dali 29	9	25N38	100E09	-6:40:36
Daliangdi 17	1	41N54	115E45	-7:43:00
Dalianhe 16	11	40N57	123E15	-8:13:00
Daliankeng 8	1	40N54	117E45	-7:51:00
Dalianwukou 30	1	30N17	119E00	-7:56:00
Dalikou 3	1	26N52	118E00	-7:52:00
Dalin 17	11	43N43	122E45	-8:11:00
Dalin 24	9	30N17	104E07	-6:56:28
Daling 16	11	41N27	121E15	-8:05:00
Dalingbeigou 16	11	40N42	123E08	-8:12:32
Daliushugou 16	11	40N46	122E14	-8:08:56
Daliutai 16	11	41N25	121E55	-8:07:40
Daliutun 16	11	42N14	122E46	-8:11:04
Daliuzhen 8	1	38N51	116E19	-7:45:16
Daliuzhuang 10	1	33N04	114E03	-7:36:12
Dalizi 15	12	41N45	126E49	-8:27:16
Dalong 28	8	28N54	90E33	-6:02:12
Dalongchang 2	1	39N50	116E06	-7:44:24
Dalonghua 8	1	39N18	115E18	-7:41:12
Dalongtian 5	1	24N14	115E44	-7:42:56
Dalu 16	11	41N27	123E19	-8:13:16
Dalubeikou 26	1	38N59	117E12	-7:48:48
Daluojiazhuang 13	1	32N09	120E08	-8:00:32
Daluotaozi 16	11	41N17	122E52	-8:11:28
Daluoxi 3	1	25N14	118E36	-7:54:24
Daluping 14	1	26N11	114E30	-7:38:00
Daluxi 3	1	24N28	117E01	-7:48:04
Dama 1	1	32N03	118E02	-7:52:08
Damanling 8	1	40N36	115E08	-7:40:32
Damaopu 16	11	41N16	121E07	-8:04:28
Damengjialazi 16	11	41N04	120E53	-8:03:32
Damengzhuang 26	1	39N32	116E59	-7:47:56
Damianzhen 24	9	30N36	104E10	-6:56:40
Damiao 18	9	37N18	104E39	-6:58:36
Damiao 17	11	42N26	118E22	-7:53:28
Damiao 13	1	34N20	117E23	-7:49:32
Damiao 16	11	42N33	122E18	-8:09:12
Damiaochang 24	9	29N39	106E05	-7:04:20
Damiaogou 16	11	41N06	123E52	-8:15:28
Damiaojiang 13	1	31N00	120E28	-8:01:52
Damiaoshang 8	1	39N56	115E12	-7:40:48
Damin 30	1	28N56	120E29	-8:01:56
Daming 8	1	36N19	115E06	-7:40:24
Damingzhen 16	11	42N34	123E36	-8:14:24
Damintun 16	11	41N52	122E56	-8:11:44
Damozhuang 2	1	39N53	115E40	-7:42:40
Damutougou 17	11	42N28	118E56	-7:55:44
Danahu 27	8	42N28	93E32	-6:14:08
Danan'gou 8	1	40N32	117E49	-7:51:16
Danba 24	9	31N00	101E50	-6:47:20
Dancheng 10	1	33N39	115E11	-7:40:44
Danchengji 10	1	33N47	116E17	-7:45:08
Dandong 16	11	40N08	124E20	-8:17:20
Danfeng 20	9	33N40	110E17	-7:21:08
Danfengzhen 29	9	24N50	103E56	-6:55:44
Dangba 8	1	40N46	118E32	-7:54:08
Dangchang 4	9	34N03	104E23	-6:57:32
Dangcheng 8	1	38N46	114E34	-7:38:16
Danghui 2	1	40N03	117E04	-7:48:16
Dangkou 13	1	31N32	120E34	-8:02:16
Dangshan 1	1	34N26	116E21	-7:45:24
Dangtu 1	1	31N34	118E30	-7:54:00
Dangxiong 28	8	30N31	91E08	-6:04:32
Dangyang 11	1	30N50	111E38	-7:26:32
Dangyu 8	1	40N00	118E01	-7:52:04
Daning 6	9	24N39	111E51	-7:27:24
Daning 23	1	36N33	110E38	-7:22:32
Daningbashi 27	7	38N45	75E04	-5:00:16
Daniupucun 16	11	41N23	122E37	-8:10:28
Danleng 24	9	30N01	103E30	-6:54:00
Danleng 24	9	29N18	103E10	-6:52:40
Danleng 24	9	29N58	103E31	-6:54:04
Danshan 24	9	30N06	104E54	-6:59:36
Danshui 5	1	22N49	114E27	-7:37:48
Dantuzhen 13	1	32N12	119E31	-7:58:04
Danxian (Nada) 5	9	19N35	109E17	-7:17:08
Danyang 3	1	26N22	119E30	-7:58:00
Danyang 13	1	32N00	119E35	-7:58:20

Daocheng 24 9 29N06 100E38 -6:42:32
Daodemiao 17 11 43N41 120E19 -8:01:16
Daodi 8 1 39N32 118E11 -7:52:44
Daoguanhe 11 1 30N54 114E57 -7:39:48
Daohu 1 1 29N42 117E29 -7:49:56
Daolazui 8 1 40N06 115E06 -7:40:24
Daoliban 16 11 41N52 121E37 -8:06:28
Daolin 12 1 27N59 112E42 -7:30:48
Daolinggang 10 1 34N02 114E34 -7:38:16
Daolipu 24 9 30N12 105E09 -7:00:36
Daomaguan 8 1 39N07 114E38 -7:38:32
Daoshiwu 1 1 30N18 118E57 -7:55:48
Daoshuqiao 13 1 31N51 119E41 -7:58:44
Daotiandi 9 12 48N53 130E03 -8:40:12
Daotou 21 1 37N14 120E20 -8:01:20
Daoxian 12 1 25N35 111E27 -7:25:48
Daozhen 7 9 28N42 107E56 -7:11:44
Daozi 15 12 45N00 123E43 -8:14:52
Dapanzhuang 8 1 37N20 115E28 -7:41:52
Dapaozi 17 11 45N27 122E07 -8:08:28
Dapeng 5 1 22N34 114E29 -7:37:56
Daping 5 1 23N11 115E49 -7:43:16
Daping 5 1 24N24 115E58 -7:43:52
Dapingshan 6 9 25N30 109E39 -7:18:36
Dapishi 12 1 26N30 112E54 -7:31:36
Dapu 13 1 31N19 119E56 -7:59:44
Dapu 5 1 23N16 113E32 -7:34:08
Dapu 16 11 40N34 124E12 -8:16:48
Dapujie 12 1 27N01 112E46 -7:31:04
Da Qaidam 19 8 37N53 95E07 -6:20:28
Daqian 30 1 30N55 120E11 -8:00:44
Daqiangmen 13 1 31N29 120E27 -8:01:48
Daqiangzi 17 11 42N21 120E29 -8:01:56
Daqiao 5 1 24N56 113E09 -7:32:36
Daqiao 22 2 30N59 121E14 -8:04:56
Daqiao 24 9 28N52 105E40 -7:02:40
Daqiao 30 1 29N39 121E26 -8:05:44
Daqiao 3 1 26N38 118E54 -7:55:36
Daqiao 14 1 28N11 114E16 -7:37:04
Daqiao 13 1 32N21 119E41 -7:58:44
Daqiaojie 1 1 30N46 119E14 -7:56:56
Daqiaokou 12 1 27N06 113E38 -7:34:32
Daqiaotou 30 1 30N47 120E52 -8:03:28
Daqiaozhai 7 9 25N21 106E15 -7:05:00
Daqing 8 1 39N13 118E51 -7:55:24
Daqinggou 8 1 41N16 114E10 -7:36:40
Daqinggou 16 11 41N12 125E07 -8:20:28
Daqiu 3 1 25N24 119E39 -7:58:36
Daquan 4 8 41N21 95E17 -6:21:08
Daquanshan 23 1 40N14 113E47 -7:35:08
Daquantou 8 1 39N31 114E46 -7:39:04
Daquanyan 16 11 42N37 123E32 -8:14:08
Darbod (Taikang) 9
12 46N52 124E27 -8:17:48
Darhan Muminggan Lianheqi 17
9 41N50 110E27 -7:21:48
Darlag 19 9 33N48 99E52 -6:39:28
Dasanjiazi 16 11 42N31 122E54 -8:11:36
Dashafa 8 1 39N19 116E19 -7:45:16
Dashalitu 16 11 42N31 122E30 -8:10:00
Dashan 21 1 38N02 117E39 -7:50:36
Dashankou 8 1 40N17 115E49 -7:43:16
Dashanpu 24 9 29N25 104E49 -6:59:16
Dashaping 11 1 29N24 113E51 -7:35:24
Dashengfenchang 13
1 31N53 121E34 -8:06:16
Dashengpu 16 11 41N13 121E02 -8:04:08
Dashentang 26 1 39N13 117E56 -7:51:44
Dashetai 17 9 40N58 109E19 -7:17:16
Dashi 24 9 30N39 105E37 -7:02:28
Dashiqiao 10 1 33N57 113E53 -7:35:32
Dashiqiao 24 9 30N07 106E12 -7:04:48
Dashiqiao 24 9 30N28 106E29 -7:05:56
Dashiqiao 16 11 41N52 123E17 -8:13:08
Dashitou 15 12 43N19 128E28 -8:33:52
Dashitou 27 8 42N49 95E19 -6:21:16
Dashizhai 17 11 46N16 121E25 -8:05:40
Dashu 13 1 31N13 120E56 -8:03:44
Dashun 30 1 28N06 119E52 -7:59:28
Dashutang 29 9 23N00 103E55 -6:55:40
Dashuwan 2 1 40N37 117E19 -7:49:16
Dasi (Huangfansi) 19
9 38N15 100E22 -6:41:28
Dasiji 1 1 33N48 115E55 -7:43:40
Dasizhan 9 12 45N53 130E24 -8:41:36
Datachang 24 9 28N55 104E21 -6:57:24
Datai 2 1 39N58 115E54 -7:43:36
Dataizi 16 11 41N17 121E46 -8:07:04
Datan 8 1 41N35 116E00 -7:44:00
Datan 16 11 39N31 122E11 -8:08:44
Datang 6 9 22N23 108E23 -7:13:32
Datang 6 9 24N11 109E00 -7:16:00
Datang 5 1 24N47 113E43 -7:34:52
Datang 14 1 25N17 114E56 -7:39:44
Datian 3 1 25N42 117E49 -7:51:16
Datian 5 1 24N06 116E19 -7:45:16
Datianwei 14 1 25N54 115E10 -7:40:40
Datong 23 1 40N05 113E18 -7:33:12
Datong 1 1 30N48 117E45 -7:51:00
Datong 1 1 32N50 118E52 -7:55:28
Datong 9 12 46N03 124E50 -8:19:20
Datong 19 9 37N03 101E45 -6:47:00
Datongzhen 13 1 32N12 121E19 -8:05:16
Datoushan 8 1 41N50 117E08 -7:48:32
Datuan 22 2 30N58 121E44 -8:06:56
Datun 16 11 40N59 122E55 -8:11:40
Datun 15 12 43N49 125E12 -8:20:48
Datun 16 11 40N37 119E57 -7:59:48
Datuopu 12 1 28N03 112E58 -7:31:52
Dawa 16 11 41N00 122E03 -8:08:12
Dawa 16 11 41N54 123E32 -8:14:08
Dawan 6 9 23N52 109E29 -7:17:56
Dawang 21 1 36N58 118E31 -7:54:04
Dawangcun 1 1 30N45 118E59 -7:55:56
Dawangdian 8 1 39N04 115E26 -7:41:44
Dawangdong 8 1 38N53 116E21 -7:45:24
Dawangsangou 16
11 41N43 121E36 -8:06:24
Dawangzhai 22 2 31N22 121E25 -8:05:40
Dawangzhuang 8 1 39N23 116E28 -7:45:52
Dawangzhuang 8 1 38N59 115E56 -7:43:44
Dawatun 16 11 41N05 121E01 -8:04:04
Daweizhuang 26 1 39N34 116E53 -7:47:32
Daweizigou 16 11 42N38 123E09 -8:12:36
Dawenkou 21 1 35N59 117E07 -7:48:28
Dawu 24 9 31N07 101E08 -6:44:32
Dawu 11 1 31N34 114E06 -7:36:24
Dawudapu 16 11 41N36 123E03 -8:12:12
Dawujiawopeng 16
11 41N55 122E29 -8:09:56
Dawujiazi 16 11 42N16 121E52 -8:07:28
Dawulah 16 11 41N56 121E05 -8:04:20
Daxian 24 9 31N18 107E30 -7:10:00
Daxin 6 9 22N50 107E26 -7:09:44
Daxin 13 1 33N54 118E30 -7:54:00
Daxing (Huangcun) 2
1 39N44 116E20 -7:45:20
Daxing 13 1 31N50 121E40 -8:06:40
Daxingchang 24 9 30N17 103E26 -6:53:44
Daxingcun 13 1 31N45 121E40 -8:06:40
Daxingzhai 29 9 23N13 102E21 -6:49:24
Daxinji 13 1 34N03 119E28 -7:57:52
Daxinzhuang 2 1 40N23 116E44 -7:46:56
Daxinzhuang 8 1 39N26 118E20 -7:53:20
Daxiyang 30 1 30N21 121E58 -8:07:52
Daxu 6 9 25N09 110E21 -7:21:24
Daxu 30 1 29N32 121E52 -8:07:28
Daxujia 13 1 34N18 117E34 -7:50:16
Dayakou 29 9 22N46 100E18 -6:41:12
Dayanchi 24 9 27N41 101E55 -6:47:40
Dayang 3 1 25N56 118E48 -7:55:12
Dayang 21 1 36N04 116E31 -7:46:04
Dayangcha 15 12 42N04 126E43 -8:26:52
Dayanggou 16 11 41N14 123E51 -8:15:24
Dayangshu 17 11 49N45 124E35 -8:18:20
Dayao 29 9 25N43 101E13 -6:44:52
Dayao 12 1 27N59 113E42 -7:34:48
Dayaoshan 6 9 24N05 110E17 -7:21:08
Daye 11 1 30N06 114E57 -7:39:48
Dayi 24 9 30N37 103E31 -6:54:04
Dayiji 13 1 32N32 119E14 -7:56:56
Daying 8 1 37N19 115E43 -7:42:52
Daying 16 11 39N53 123E07 -8:12:28
Daying 23 1 39N19 113E46 -7:35:04
Daying 8 1 39N05 116E06 -7:44:24
Daying 10 1 33N59 112E51 -7:31:24
Daying 10 1 34N27 113E59 -7:35:56
Dayingzi 16 11 41N08 122E50 -8:11:20
Dayingzi 17 11 41N19 118E19 -7:53:16
Dayingzi 16 11 41N28 120E21 -8:01:24
Dayiqiao 13 1 31N44 120E45 -8:03:00
Dayong 12 1 29N06 110E29 -7:21:56
Dayong 5 1 22N28 113E16 -7:33:04
Dayou 13 1 34N12 119E52 -7:59:28
Dayu 14 1 25N24 114E22 -7:37:28
Dayuba 24 9 29N15 103E34 -6:54:16
Dayushupu 16 11 41N32 121E24 -8:05:36
Dazaoliyingzi 16
11 42N07 121E20 -8:05:20
Dazaomiao 13 1 32N06 121E29 -8:05:56
Dazhangzi 8 1 40N38 118E07 -7:52:28
Dazhaotai 16 11 41N14 123E03 -8:12:12
Dazhengjiatun 16
11 39N37 122E52 -8:11:28
Dazhengzhuangzi 8
1 39N16 116E46 -7:47:04
Dazhi 10 1 34N29 113E17 -7:33:08
Dazhiba 29 9 27N09 99E52 -6:39:28
Dazhifang 16 11 41N21 123E12 -8:12:48
Dazhou 30 1 28N53 118E58 -7:55:52
Dazhu 24 9 30N48 107E12 -7:08:48
Dazhuangke 2 1 40N32 115E42 -7:42:48
Dazhubao 24 9 28N59 103E38 -6:54:32
Dazhuyuan 5 1 23N43 115E57 -7:43:48
Dazifangshen 16
11 42N27 124E12 -8:16:48
Daziling 16 11 41N21 121E26 -8:05:44
Daziying 16 11 41N42 123E36 -8:14:24
Dazu 24 9 29N43 105E42 -7:02:48
Dazui 11 1 30N16 114E02 -7:36:08
De'an 14 1 29N20 115E46 -7:43:04
Debao 6 9 23N21 106E31 -7:06:04
Dechang 24 9 27N24 102E10 -6:48:40
Dedu 9 12 48N31 126E14 -8:24:56
Defengzhuang 17
9 41N02 113E16 -7:33:04
Dêgê 24 8 31N50 98E40 -6:34:40
Dehua 3 1 25N32 118E15 -7:53:00
Dehuang 10 1 35N12 114E25 -7:37:40
Dehui 15 12 44N34 125E43 -8:22:52
Delapu 28 8 31N35 90E35 -6:02:20
Delingha 19 8 37N14 97E11 -6:28:44
Dengcheng 10 1 33N41 114E27 -7:37:48
Dengfeng 10 1 34N29 113E04 -7:32:16
Denggongchang 24
9 30N24 103E49 -6:55:16
Dengguanzhen 24
9 29N10 104E56 -6:59:44
Dengkou 17 9 40N20 106E59 -7:07:56
Denglongshu 8 1 41N20 115E15 -7:41:00
Dengmingsi 8 1 37N53 116E42 -7:46:48
Dêngqên 28 8 31N32 95E27 -6:21:48
Dengshahe 16 11 39N13 122E04 -8:08:16
Dengta 5 1 24N01 114E49 -7:39:16
Dengxian 10 1 32N42 112E01 -7:28:04
Dengyoufang 8 1 41N34 114E32 -7:38:08
Deping 21 1 37N28 116E57 -7:47:48
Dêqên 29 9 28N38 98E52 -6:35:28
Deqing 5 10 23N09 111E46 -7:27:00
Deqing 30 1 30N33 120E05 -8:00:20
Derenwu 2 1 39N40 116E46 -7:47:04
Dêrong 24 9 28N47 99E14 -6:36:56
Desheng 6 9 24N45 108E28 -7:13:52
Deshengchang 24
9 29N06 105E25 -7:01:40
Deshengpo 7 9 26N58 103E59 -6:55:56
Deshengtai 16 11 42N14 123E45 -8:15:00
Deshengyingzi 16
11 41N44 123E14 -8:12:56
Deshun 13 1 31N58 120E29 -8:01:56
Dexing 14 1 28N54 117E36 -7:50:24
Dexingjie 16 11 39N54 122E50 -8:11:20
Deyang 24 9 31N14 104E22 -6:57:28
Dezhou 21 1 37N27 116E18 -7:45:12
Dezong 28 8 32N09 90E20 -6:01:20
Dianbai 5 8 21N30 111E01 -7:24:04
Diancun 2 1 39N55 116E14 -7:44:56
Dianfangba 24 9 32N54 103E35 -6:54:20
Dianhu 13 1 33N58 119E38 -7:58:32
Dianji 21 1 36N32 120E27 -8:01:48
Dianjiang 24 9 30N21 107E23 -7:09:32
Dianqianhe 1 1 30N44 116E02 -7:44:08
Dianshang 1 1 31N10 118E51 -7:55:24
Diantou 3 1 27N18 120E11 -8:00:44
Dianzi 16 11 41N37 122E05 -8:08:20
Diaobingshan 16
11 42N28 123E33 -8:14:12
Diao'ecun 8 1 40N43 115E49 -7:43:16
Diaohetou 8 1 39N17 116E41 -7:46:44
Diaopu 13 1 32N22 119E54 -7:59:36
Diaoshuilouzi 16
11 40N59 122E22 -8:09:28
Diaotai 30 1 29N40 119E39 -7:58:36
Diaowo 8 1 39N30 116E04 -7:44:16
Dicun 1 1 33N46 117E32 -7:50:08
Didao 9 12 45N22 130E51 -8:43:24
Dieleemu 27 8 46N22 88E43 -5:54:52
Diemuchuoke 28 7 32N42 79E29 -5:17:56
Dierbao 8 1 40N20 114E32 -7:38:08
Difang 21 1 35N23 117E52 -7:51:28
Dige 10 1 34N22 114E28 -7:37:52
Digong 16 11 42N11 122E03 -8:08:12
Dihaer 27 8 42N35 89E49 -5:59:16
Dingan 5 9 19N44 110E21 -7:21:24
Dingbian 20 9 37N40 107E41 -7:10:44
Dingbianji 20 9 36N37 108E41 -7:14:44
Dingbu 1 1 31N18 119E10 -7:56:40
Dingeryu 8 1 39N37 114E55 -7:39:40
Dingfeng 22 2 31N20 121E45 -8:07:00
Dinggou 13 1 32N34 119E39 -7:58:36
Dinghai 30 1 30N02 122E06 -8:08:24
Dingjia 24 9 29N24 106E09 -7:04:36
Dingjiagou 16 11 40N40 122E35 -8:10:20
Dingjiandian 13
1 32N06 120E52 -8:03:28
Dingjiasuo 13 1 32N32 120E40 -8:02:40
Dingjiazhuang 13
1 32N11 120E16 -8:01:04
Dingjie 28 8 28N29 88E06 -5:52:24
Dingkouzhen 17 9 39N55 106E40 -7:06:40
Dingnan 14 1 24N48 114E59 -7:39:56
Dingri 28 8 28N35 86E38 -5:46:32
Dingshuzhen 13 1 31N17 119E50 -7:59:20
Dingtao 10 1 35N04 115E34 -7:42:16
Dingxi 4 9 35N33 104E32 -6:58:08
Dingxian 8 1 38N32 114E59 -7:39:56
Dingxiang 23 1 38N30 113E00 -7:32:00
Dingxiao 7 9 25N13 105E07 -7:00:28
Dingxing 8 1 39N17 115E46 -7:43:04
Dingyan 13 1 32N23 120E45 -8:03:00
Dingyuan 1 1 32N32 117E40 -7:50:40
Dingzhouying 8 1 40N20 115E43 -7:42:52
Dingzichang 24 9 28N54 106E08 -7:04:32
Dipai 5 1 23N50 114E06 -7:36:24
Dipu 30 1 30N38 119E41 -7:58:44
Diqiyingzi 16 11 42N11 121E29 -8:05:56
Disihao 17 11 50N28 124E35 -8:18:20
Dizangsi 16 11 41N26 120E57 -8:03:48
Dizhou 6 9 23N00 106E20 -7:05:20
Dong'an 10 1 33N24 114E24 -7:37:36
Dong'an 1 1 30N30 118E48 -7:55:12
Dong'an 13 1 31N35 119E44 -7:58:56
Dong'an 9 12 47N20 134E10 -8:56:40
Dong'an 12 1 26N17 111E07 -7:24:28
Dongan → Mishan 9
12 45N33 131E52 -8:47:28
Dongao 30 1 29N12 121E25 -8:05:40
Dongba 13 1 31N18 119E03 -7:56:12
Dongba 2 1 39N58 116E32 -7:46:08
Dongbahe 2 1 39N58 116E27 -7:45:48
Dongbaimiao 2 1 40N34 116E05 -7:44:20
Dongbei 14 1 27N15 116E06 -7:44:24
Dongbeicha 15 12 41N43 127E23 -8:29:32
Dongbeijipo 21 1 36N06 117E08 -7:48:32
Dongbulizhadamu 19
8 34N27 93E12 -6:12:48
Dongchan 24 9 30N20 105E20 -7:01:20
Dongchang 13 1 31N52 121E38 -8:06:32
Dongchangjie 13
1 32N04 119E18 -7:57:12
Dongcheng 30 1 28N56 121E16 -8:05:04
Dongchong 3 1 26N35 119E52 -7:59:28
Dongchuan 29 9 26N10 103E01 -6:52:04
Dongcun 22 2 30N57 121E46 -8:07:04
Dongdaoan 8 1 38N21 117E12 -7:48:48
Dongduluo 8 1 39N04 115E15 -7:41:00
Dong'e (Tongcheng) 21
1 36N14 116E16 -7:45:04
Dong'ezhen 21 1 36N11 116E16 -7:45:04
Dongfang (Basuo) 5
9 19N05 108E39 -7:14:36
Dongfeng 3 1 27N20 118E53 -7:55:32
Dongfeng 15 12 42N40 125E28 -8:21:52
Dongfengtai 8 1 39N34 117E45 -7:51:00
Donggang 5 1 22N58 115E57 -7:43:48

Donggangzi 9 12 45N53 129E49 -8:39:16
Donggongsuo 13 1 32N07 121E25 -8:05:40
Donggou 1 1 32N17 118E59 -7:55:56
Donggou 16 11 39N54 124E09 -8:16:36
Donggu 14 1 26N46 115E22 -7:41:28
Dongguan 14 1 27N49 116E25 -7:45:40
Dongguan 5 1 23N03 113E46 -7:35:04
Dongguan 30 1 30N22 119E28 -7:57:52
Dongguan 24 9 30N47 106E16 -7:05:04
Dongguang 8 1 37N53 116E30 -7:46:00
Dongguanpu 13 3 31N13 120E43 -8:02:52
Dongguanyingzi 16
11 41N55 120E38 -8:02:32
Donggugang 8 1 39N10 116E49 -7:47:16
Donghai (Niushan) 13
1 34N30 118E47 -7:55:08
Donghezhen 13 1 31N08 120E17 -8:01:08
Donghu 12 1 26N28 113E07 -7:32:28
Donghuanggou 16
11 40N43 123E29 -8:13:56
Dongjia 21 1 37N18 118E24 -7:53:36
Dongjiangkou 20
9 33N37 108E49 -7:15:16
Dongjie 3 1 25N53 116E22 -7:45:28
Dongjielang 11 1 31N03 115E57 -7:43:48
Dongjingcheng 9
12 44N07 129E09 -8:36:36
Dongjingji 8 1 40N02 114E01 -7:36:04
Dongjingling 16
11 41N18 123E15 -8:13:00
Dongjiu 28 8 29N58 94E53 -6:19:32
Dongkaihecheng 16
11 41N04 122E38 -8:10:32
Dongkeng 30 1 27N48 119E42 -7:58:48
Dongkeng 14 1 24N59 114E54 -7:39:36
Dongkou 21 1 35N29 115E20 -7:41:20
Donglan 6 9 24N40 107E18 -7:09:12
Donglaohuyu 16
11 42N28 124E17 -8:17:08
Donglaojunpu 16
11 41N24 121E22 -8:05:28
Dongli 5 8 20N50 110E20 -7:21:20
Dongliang 16 11 42N00 121E25 -8:05:40
Dongliangjia 8 1 40N52 118E17 -7:53:08
Donglidian 21 1 36N02 118E23 -7:53:32
Donglinchang 24
9 29N39 104E07 -6:56:28
Dongling 16 11 41N50 123E35 -8:14:20
Dongliu 1 1 30N14 116E53 -7:47:32
Dongliu 1 1 32N06 118E58 -7:55:52
Dongliujiazi 16
11 42N21 122E44 -8:10:56
Donglizhuang 8 1 39N21 116E47 -7:47:08
Donglong 5 1 23N36 116E50 -7:47:20
Donglucun 9 12 49N28 128E50 -8:35:20
Dongmen 12 1 28N29 114E02 -7:36:08
Dongming 21 1 35N18 115E08 -7:40:32
Dongnangou 16 11 41N25 122E02 -8:08:08
Dongning 9 12 44N04 131E07 -8:44:28
Dongping 21 1 35N55 116E18 -7:45:12
Dongping 5 10 21N43 112E15 -7:29:00
Dongping 3 1 27N24 118E39 -7:54:36
Dongpu 30 1 30N03 120E34 -8:02:16
Dongqian 30 1 30N52 120E23 -8:01:32
Dongqiao 11 1 31N12 112E48 -7:31:12
Dongqing 13 1 31N49 120E03 -8:00:12
Dongqingduizi 16
11 41N02 122E08 -8:08:32
Dongsanjiazi 16
11 41N54 122E48 -8:11:12
Dongsanlintang 22
2 31N09 121E31 -8:06:04
Dongsanpu 1 1 33N38 117E09 -7:48:36
Dongshaer 28 8 28N41 89E09 -5:56:36
Dongshajiao 30 1 30N19 122E09 -8:08:36
Dongshan 13 1 31N04 120E24 -8:01:36
Dongshan 5 9 19N50 110E14 -7:20:56
Dongshan 3 1 23N42 117E24 -7:49:36
Dongshanqiao 13
1 31N52 118E46 -7:55:04
Dongshe 13 1 32N07 121E12 -8:04:48
Dongsheng 17 9 39N49 109E59 -7:19:56
Dongsheshanzi 16
11 42N15 123E09 -8:12:36
Dongshi 3 1 24N42 118E27 -7:53:48
Dongshi 5 1 24N43 115E59 -7:43:56
Dongshuiyan 8 1 39N15 115E23 -7:41:32
Dongtai 13 1 32N51 120E20 -8:01:20
Dongtaipingzhen 17
11 45N18 122E05 -8:08:20
Dongtangou 8 1 39N23 118E22 -7:53:28
Dongting 8 1 38N29 115E08 -7:40:32
Dongtinghu 1 1 30N53 119E30 -7:58:00
Dongtingxi 12 1 28N34 110E36 -7:22:24
Dongtou 30 1 27N50 121E09 -8:04:36
Dongtuhulu 16 11 41N55 121E33 -8:06:12
Dongtuoshanzi 16
11 42N10 123E08 -8:12:32
Dongtuozi 16 11 41N17 121E53 -8:07:32
Dongwangfu 17 11 44N47 120E53 -8:03:32
Dongwangzhuang 13
1 32N16 120E32 -8:02:08
Dongwuquan 8 1 39N20 115E43 -7:42:52
Dongxi 1 28N47 106E39 -7:06:36
Dongxi 30 1 28N35 120E02 -8:00:08
Dongxi 24 9 28N46 106E39 -7:06:36
Dongxi 24 9 30N24 104E33 -6:58:12
Dongxia 1 1 31N11 119E05 -7:56:20
Dongxiagaogao 16
11 42N36 122E30 -8:10:00
Dongxiang 14 1 28N13 116E35 -7:46:20
Dongxing 9 12 46N23 127E52 -8:31:28
Dongxingchang 24
9 29N16 103E55 -6:55:40
Dongxingchang 24
9 29N36 105E04 -7:00:16
Dongxinghe 8 1 39N46 114E49 -7:39:16
Dongxinpu 16 11 41N00 123E18 -8:13:12
Dongxinzhen 13 1 31N57 121E42 -8:06:48
Dongyang 9 12 48N03 124E17 -8:17:08
Dongyang 30 1 29N16 120E14 -8:00:56
Dongyangqiao 13
1 30N52 120E34 -8:02:16
Dongyao 10 1 35N56 113E58 -7:35:52
Dongyian 8 1 39N22 115E46 -7:43:04
Dongyou 3 1 27N10 118E37 -7:54:28
Dongyuemiao 13 1 31N36 119E14 -7:56:56
Dongyuezhen 24 9 30N24 103E32 -6:54:08
Dongzhang 3 1 25N44 119E17 -7:57:08
Dongzhaocun 2 1 40N02 116E46 -7:47:04
Dongzhaozhuang 8
1 39N57 118E24 -7:53:36
Dongzhenbeng 22
2 30N59 121E01 -8:04:04
Dongzhi 1 1 30N07 116E59 -7:47:56
Dongzhizhuang 2
1 40N25 116E50 -7:47:20
Dongzhuangpu 8 1 40N34 115E42 -7:42:48
Dongziya 26 1 38N50 116E44 -7:46:56
Doudian 2 1 39N39 116E03 -7:44:12
Dougouzi 9 12 49N57 127E01 -8:28:04
Dougouzi 16 11 41N16 122E34 -8:10:16
Douhutun 16 11 42N06 124E50 -8:19:20
Doujiapu 16 11 41N05 122E12 -8:08:48
Doujiazhuang 2 1 40N22 116E59 -7:47:56
Doumen 5 1 22N12 113E16 -7:33:04
Doumen 8 1 39N18 115E53 -7:43:32
Doushanhe 10 1 31N38 114E42 -7:38:48
Douyu 8 1 37N53 114E30 -7:38:00
Douzhangzhuang 26
1 39N23 116E55 -7:47:40
Douzishan 24 9 29N04 104E57 -6:59:48
Du'an 6 9 24N06 108E10 -7:12:40
Duancun 8 1 38N52 115E56 -7:43:44
Duanjialing 8 1 39N59 117E09 -7:48:36
Duboweitun 17 11 50N42 120E14 -8:00:56
Duchang 14 1 29N15 116E13 -7:44:52
Ducun 13 1 31N07 120E27 -8:01:48
Duerji 17 11 45N39 121E49 -8:07:16
Dugede 28 8 30N54 90E48 -6:03:12
Dugui Qarag 17 9 39N38 108E40 -7:14:40
Duhu 5 10 22N04 112E56 -7:31:44
Duilongdeqing 28
8 29N56 90E42 -6:02:48
Duji 8 1 37N44 116E50 -7:47:20
Duji 10 1 34N11 115E48 -7:43:12
Dujiahang 22 2 31N03 121E29 -8:05:56
Dukazi 28 8 30N54 92E52 -6:11:28
Dukou 29 9 26N40 101E39 -6:46:36
Dulan (Chahanwusu) 19
8 36N16 98E28 -6:33:52
Dulata 27 7 43N26 80E50 -5:23:20
Dulin 8 1 38N22 116E43 -7:46:52
Duliu 8 1 39N13 116E16 -7:45:04
Duliu 26 1 39N01 116E54 -7:47:36
Dumei 3 1 24N47 117E21 -7:49:24
Dunhou 14 1 27N02 114E58 -7:39:52
Dunhua 15 12 43N21 128E13 -8:32:52
Dunhuang 4 8 40N12 94E41 -6:18:44
Duntou 30 1 29N21 119E46 -7:59:04
Duogu'nao 24 9 31N32 103E14 -6:52:56
Duojundian 26 1 39N22 117E31 -7:50:04
Duolun (Dolonnur) 17
1 42N15 116E18 -7:45:12
Duolundabohuer 19
8 33N25 93E54 -6:15:36
Duomaer 28 7 34N15 79E45 -5:19:00
Duomula 28 8 34N07 82E30 -5:30:00
Duopatela 28 8 28N28 88E14 -5:52:56
Duoyuezhen 24 9 30N11 103E42 -6:54:48
Duozhu 5 1 22N59 114E43 -7:38:52
Duozhuang 21 1 35N35 118E12 -7:52:48
Duping 7 9 27N11 108E20 -7:13:20
Dushan 7 9 25N53 107E30 -7:10:00
Dushan 1 1 31N36 116E14 -7:44:56
Dushantou 30 1 30N46 119E47 -7:59:08
Dushanzi 27 8 44N20 84E51 -5:39:24
Dusheng 8 1 38N23 116E33 -7:46:12
Dushichang 24 9 29N10 106E31 -7:06:04
Dushikou 8 1 41N17 115E38 -7:42:32
Dushu 10 1 33N21 113E09 -7:32:36
Dutianjie 29 9 24N38 101E31 -6:46:04
Dutou 13 1 31N19 120E54 -8:03:36
Dutun 8 1 39N46 117E02 -7:48:08
Duxun 3 1 23N55 117E37 -7:50:28
Duyun 7 9 26N12 107E31 -7:10:04
Duze 30 1 29N07 118E56 -7:55:44
Ebian 24 9 29N10 103E20 -6:53:20
Echeng 11 1 30N24 114E51 -7:39:24
Ejin Horo Qi 17
9 39N27 109E40 -7:18:40
Ejin Qi 17 9 41N50 100E50 -6:43:20
Emei 24 9 29N36 103E31 -6:54:04
Emin 27 8 46N32 83E39 -5:34:36
Emu 15 12 43N45 128E10 -8:32:40
Encha 8 1 37N25 115E42 -7:42:48
Enle 29 9 24N00 101E07 -6:44:28
Enping 5 10 22N11 112E17 -7:29:08
Enshi 11 1 30N17 109E19 -7:17:16
Enyang 24 9 31N48 106E31 -7:06:04
Erdaobaihe 15 12 42N22 128E07 -8:32:28
Erdaofang 16 11 41N54 123E57 -8:15:48
Erdaofang 16 11 41N37 122E34 -8:10:16
Erdaofangshen 16
11 42N09 123E17 -8:13:08
Erdaogangzi 16
11 41N57 122E09 -8:08:36
Erdaogangzi 16
11 42N04 123E06 -8:12:24
Erdaohe 15 12 43N37 127E35 -8:30:20
Erdaohezi 9 12 45N07 127E16 -8:29:04
Erdaohezi 9 12 45N08 129E39 -8:38:36
Erdaojingzi 16
11 41N49 122E20 -8:09:20
Erdaoliangzi 16
11 40N50 119E04 -7:56:16
Erdaoliangzi 8 1 40N31 118E03 -7:52:12
Erdaowan 9 12 47N58 124E33 -8:18:12
Erdiao 13 1 32N12 121E12 -8:04:48
Erenhot 17 1 43N46 112E05 -7:28:20
Ergun Youqi 17
11 50N14 120E10 -8:00:40
Ergun Zuoqi 17
11 50N47 121E31 -8:06:04
Erhlin 25 6 23N54 120E22 -8:01:28
Erhshui 25 6 23N49 120E36 -8:02:24
Erhulai 16 11 41N23 125E08 -8:20:32
Erjiazhen 13 1 32N02 121E13 -8:04:52
Erlanghe 1 1 30N19 116E04 -7:44:16
Erlangmiao 10 1 33N46 112E23 -7:29:32
Erling 13 1 31N53 119E36 -7:58:24
Erlongshan 9 12 47N20 132E28 -8:49:52
Erlongshan 9 12 50N04 126E47 -8:27:08
Erlongshantun 9
12 48N28 126E31 -8:26:04
Ermendegou 16 11 42N02 121E56 -8:07:44
Erpuzi 8 1 40N29 115E33 -7:42:12
Ershijiazi 16 11 41N17 120E32 -8:02:08
Ershilipu 26 1 40N07 117E24 -7:49:36
Ershiqizhan 9 12 53N23 123E16 -8:13:04
Ershiwuzhan 9 12 53N22 123E55 -8:15:40
Ertai 27 8 46N07 90E06 -6:00:24
Ertai 27 7 44N14 80E52 -5:23:28
Ertaizi 16 11 42N35 124E00 -8:16:00
Ertaizi 16 11 40N47 120E54 -8:03:36
Ertaizi 16 11 41N52 121E56 -8:07:44
Ertaizi 16 11 42N05 123E35 -8:14:20
Eryuan 29 9 26N06 99E55 -6:39:40
Erzaohang 22 2 31N05 121E49 -8:07:16
Erzhan 15 12 43N58 128E44 -8:34:56
Erzhuang 26 1 39N24 117E22 -7:49:28
Eshan 29 9 24N11 102E22 -6:49:28
Ewenkiku Zizhiqi 17
11 49N07 119E40 -7:58:40
Fahuaqiao 22 2 30N52 121E25 -8:05:40
Faku 16 11 42N30 123E24 -8:13:36
Falun 24 9 29N58 104E29 -6:57:56
Fanchang 1 1 31N07 118E12 -7:52:48
Fanch'eng → Xiangfan 11
1 32N03 112E01 -7:28:04
Fanchuan 13 1 32N40 119E42 -7:58:48
Fangbian 13 1 31N42 119E06 -7:56:24
Fangcheng 10 1 33N16 112E59 -7:31:56
Fangcheng 8 1 39N16 115E28 -7:41:52
Fangcheng 6 9 21N49 108E22 -7:13:28
Fangcun 30 1 29N04 118E36 -7:54:24
Fangcun 3 1 26N50 118E15 -7:53:00
Fangdao 3 1 27N01 118E06 -7:52:24
Fangguan 8 1 39N20 115E58 -7:43:52
Fangji 10 1 31N54 115E35 -7:42:20
Fangjiachang 24
9 30N05 104E16 -6:57:04
Fangjiazhuang 30
1 30N45 119E53 -7:59:32
Fangliao 25 6 22N22 120E35 -8:02:20
Fangmutun 16 11 42N34 124E34 -8:18:16
Fangniu 29 9 27N40 100E25 -6:41:40
Fangshan 2 1 39N42 115E58 -7:43:52
Fangshan 25 6 22N16 120E39 -8:02:36
Fangshanzhen 16
11 41N54 122E05 -8:08:20
Fangshen 16 11 42N02 124E04 -8:16:16
Fangshengpu 24 9 30N20 104E54 -6:59:36
Fangsi 21 1 36N56 116E29 -7:45:56
Fangtai 22 2 31N19 121E12 -8:04:48
Fangxi 14 1 28N23 114E38 -7:38:32
Fangxian 11 1 32N02 110E45 -7:23:00
Fangxianzhen 13
1 32N00 119E44 -7:58:56
Fangzheng 9 12 45N50 128E50 -8:35:20
Fangzi 21 1 36N36 119E07 -7:56:28
Fanjiadai 13 1 32N04 120E15 -8:01:00
Fanjiadian 16 11 41N41 121E50 -8:07:20
Fanjiatun 15 12 43N43 125E06 -8:20:24
Fanjiazhuang 26
1 39N12 117E20 -7:49:20
Fanqiao 30 1 28N48 121E10 -8:04:40
Fanshan 30 1 27N21 120E24 -8:01:36
Fanshan 8 1 40N13 115E25 -7:41:40
Fanshang 13 1 31N40 120E01 -8:00:04
Fanshui 13 1 33N07 119E25 -7:57:40
Fanxian 21 1 35N57 115E38 -7:42:32
Fanzhen 21 1 36N14 117E21 -7:49:24
Fatshan → Foshan 5
1 23N03 113E09 -7:32:36
Feicheng 21 1 36N15 116E46 -7:47:04
Feidong 1 1 31N52 117E29 -7:49:56
Feiheji 1 1 33N36 115E36 -7:42:24
Feiketu 9 12 45N46 127E09 -8:28:36
Feiliqiao 1 1 31N05 119E05 -7:56:20
Feilong 24 9 30N25 106E20 -7:05:20
Feilong 24 9 30N36 105E54 -7:03:36
Feilongguan 24 9 28N57 105E05 -7:00:20
Feiluan 3 1 26N35 119E35 -7:58:20
Feixi 1 1 31N42 117E10 -7:48:40
Feixian 21 1 35N18 117E57 -7:51:48
Feixiang 8 1 36N34 114E49 -7:39:16
Fendaozi 16 11 41N35 120E51 -8:03:24
Fengcheng 4 9 38N32 101E50 -6:47:20
Fengcheng 14 1 28N10 115E46 -7:43:04
Fengcheng 16 11 40N27 124E02 -8:16:08
Fengcheng 22 2 30N55 121E38 -8:06:32
Fengdengwu 8 1 39N42 117E55 -7:51:40
Fengdian 24 9 30N41 104E51 -6:59:24

Name		Lat	Long	Time
Fengdu 24	9	29N58	107E41	-7:10:44
Fengfeng 8	1	36N28	114E14	-7:36:56
Fenggang 7	9	27N58	107E47	-7:11:08
Fenggang 14	1	28N34	116E34	-7:46:16
Fenggaopu 24	9	29N24	105E41	-7:02:44
Fenghua 30	1	29N40	121E24	-8:05:36
Fenghuang 6	9	24N25	107E17	-7:09:08
Fenghuang 12	1	27N58	109E19	-7:17:16
Fenghuang 5	1	23N58	116E44	-7:46:56
Fenghuang 22	2	31N21	121E44	-8:06:56
Fenghuangchang 24	9	29N44	106E19	-7:05:16
Fenghuanjing 1	1	31N11	117E49	-7:51:16
Fenghui 30	1	29N56	120E58	-8:03:52
Fengjia 21	1	37N03	121E42	-8:06:48
Fengjia 16	11	42N35	122E30	-8:10:00
Fengjiabao 4	9	36N12	104E49	-6:59:16
Fengjiakou 8	1	38N11	116E44	-7:46:56
Fengjianjiao 30	1	30N41	120E51	-8:03:24
Fengjiatun 16	11	41N14	122E00	-8:08:00
Fengjiawopeng 16	11	42N19	123E40	-8:14:40
Fengjiaxiang 22	2	30N56	121E06	-8:04:24
Fengjie 24	9	31N03	109E31	-7:18:04
Fengjing 22	2	30N53	121E01	-8:04:04
Fengkou 11	1	30N05	113E18	-7:33:12
Fengle 9	12	45N47	125E26	-8:21:44
Fengle 3	1	27N13	118E11	-7:52:44
Fenglezhen 10	1	36N14	114E18	-7:37:12
Fengliang 5	1	23N59	116E14	-7:44:56
Fenglin 30	1	28N19	120E46	-8:03:04
Fenglin 25	6	23N45	121E26	-8:05:44
Fenglingtou 14	1	28N26	117E50	-7:51:20
Fengman 15	12	43N46	126E41	-8:26:44
Fengnan (Xugezhuang) 8	1	39N34	118E06	-7:52:24
Fengning (Dagezhen) 8	1	41N12	116E32	-7:46:08
Fengpin 25	6	23N36	121E31	-8:06:04
Fengpingzi 4	9	32N46	105E12	-7:00:48
Fengqiao 30	1	29N46	120E26	-8:01:44
Fengqiao 13	3	31N19	120E33	-8:02:12
Fengqing 29	9	24N46	99E52	-6:39:28
Fengqiu 10	1	35N05	114E25	-7:37:40
Fengrun 8	1	39N50	118E07	-7:52:28
Fengshan 8	1	41N14	117E05	-7:48:20
Fengshan 9	12	46N22	128E30	-8:34:00
Fengshan 6	9	22N01	109E59	-7:19:56
Fengshi 3	1	24N42	116E34	-7:46:16
Fengshun 5	1	23N48	116E11	-7:44:44
Fengtai 1	1	32N44	116E43	-7:46:52
Fengtai 2	1	39N51	116E16	-7:45:04
Fengtian 14	1	25N46	115E30	-7:42:00
Fengtian 14	1	27N24	114E43	-7:38:52
Fengtien → Shenyang 16	11	41N48	123E27	-8:13:48
Fengting 3	1	25N16	118E54	-7:55:36
Fengwan 5	1	24N48	113E50	-7:35:20
Fengxi 11	1	31N48	109E50	-7:19:20
Fengxian 22	2	30N55	121E27	-8:05:48
Fengxian 4	9	33N57	106E44	-7:06:56
Fengxian 13	1	34N42	116E34	-7:46:16
Fengxiang 20	9	34N29	107E29	-7:09:56
Fengxin 14	1	28N43	115E23	-7:41:32
Fengyang 1	1	32N52	117E34	-7:50:16
Fengyang 3	1	24N49	117E53	-7:51:32
Fengyi 24	9	31N44	103E53	-6:55:32
Fengyu 3	1	26N31	119E18	-7:57:12
Fengyüan 25	6	24N15	120E43	-8:02:52
Fengzhen 17	9	40N24	113E09	-7:32:36
Fengzhou 12	1	25N41	113E52	-7:35:28
Fengzhuangtou 1	1	31N00	118E39	-7:54:36
Fenjie 13	1	32N17	120E20	-8:01:20
Fenshui 16	11	40N41	122E32	-8:10:08
Fenshui'ao 14	1	25N20	114E43	-7:38:52
Fenshuidunshen 13	1	31N30	120E01	-8:00:04
Fenshuiling 24	9	30N20	105E15	-7:01:00
Fenshuiling 24	9	28N51	105E35	-7:02:20
Fenshuipu 24	9	30N05	104E05	-6:56:20
Fenshuizhen 24	9	29N44	103E55	-6:55:40
Fenshuizui 11	1	30N35	113E38	-7:34:32
Fentou 8	1	38N53	116E32	-7:46:08
Fenyang 23	1	37N17	111E48	-7:27:12
Fenyi 14	1	27N47	114E42	-7:38:48
Fogang (Shijiao) 5	1	23N52	113E32	-7:34:08
Folamasi 16	11	41N56	121E27	-8:05:48
Foochow → Fuzhou 3	1	26N06	119E17	-7:57:08
Foping 20	9	33N21	107E59	-7:11:56
Fort Bayard → Zhanjiang 5	8	21N12	110E23	-7:21:32
Foshan 5	1	23N03	113E09	-7:32:36
Fotan 3	1	24N12	117E53	-7:51:32
Fou-Chouen → Fushun 16	11	41N52	123E53	-8:15:32
Fouhsin → Fuxin 16	11	42N03	121E46	-8:07:04
Fouling → Fuling 24	9	29N42	107E21	-7:09:24
Fou-Tcheou → Fuzhou 3	1	26N06	119E17	-7:57:08
Fouyang → Fuyang 1	1	32N54	115E49	-7:43:16
Fowliang → Jingdezhen 14	1	29N16	117E11	-7:48:44
Foyedong 16	11	40N41	119E12	-7:56:48
Foziling 1	1	31N20	116E17	-7:45:08
Fu'an 13	1	32N41	120E41	-8:02:44
Fu'an 3	1	27N08	119E40	-7:58:40
Fuanjie 3	1	25N29	117E53	-7:51:32
Fubao 24	9	28N47	106E05	-7:04:20
Fuchang 11	1	30N06	113E08	-7:32:32
Fucheng 8	1	37N52	116E07	-7:44:28
Fuchikou 11	1	29N51	115E27	-7:41:48
Fuchow → Fuzhou 14	1	28N01	116E20	-7:45:20
Fuding 3	1	27N21	120E12	-8:00:48
Fuerli 2	1	39N40	116E41	-7:46:44
Fufeng 20	9	34N20	107E51	-7:11:24
Fugong 29	9	27N09	98E52	-6:35:28
Fugou 10	1	34N04	114E24	-7:37:36
Fuhai 27	8	47N06	87E23	-5:49:32
Fuhe 5	1	23N22	113E37	-7:34:28
Fuhsien → Fuxian 16	11	39N37	122E01	-8:08:04
Fuhu 30	1	29N11	118E04	-7:52:16
Fuji 24	9	29N09	105E23	-7:01:32
Fuji 10	1	34N24	114E48	-7:39:12
Fujiafeng 26	1	39N11	117E32	-7:50:08
Fujiatun 16	11	41N42	123E44	-8:14:56
Fujiawopu 16	11	40N58	122E14	-8:08:56
Fujiazhen 24	9	29N57	104E18	-6:57:12
Fujiazhuangcun 16	11	41N15	122E20	-8:09:20
Fujie 1	1	31N09	119E27	-7:57:48
Fujin 9	12	47N14	132E00	-8:48:00
Fukang 27	8	44N10	87E59	-5:51:56
Fukou 3	1	26N28	117E40	-7:50:40
Fukou 3	1	25N45	118E28	-7:53:52
Fule 29	9	25N27	104E19	-6:57:16
Fuli 25	6	23N11	121E14	-8:04:56
Fuliji 1	1	33N46	116E58	-7:47:52
Fuling 24	9	29N42	107E21	-7:09:24
Fulitun 9	12	46N42	131E10	-8:44:40
Fulong 6	9	22N57	107E41	-7:10:44
Fulongchang 24	9	30N03	103E38	-6:54:32
Fulongquan 15	12	44N22	124E36	-8:18:24
Fuluchang 24	9	29N38	106E08	-7:04:32
Fuluzhen 24	9	29N18	103E40	-6:54:40
Fumin 29	9	25N16	102E26	-6:49:44
Fumin 13	1	31N54	121E10	-8:04:40
Fumintun 15	12	42N29	126E22	-8:25:28
Fuminzhen 22	2	31N37	121E39	-8:06:36
Funan 1	1	32N39	115E32	-7:42:08
Funing 13	1	33N47	119E48	-7:59:12
Funing 8	1	39N54	119E14	-7:56:56
Funing 29	9	23N33	105E35	-7:02:20
Funiuchang 24	9	29N03	106E33	-7:06:12
Fuping 20	9	34N47	109E07	-7:16:28
Fuqiao 13	1	31N36	121E12	-8:04:48
Fuqikou 1	1	29N44	117E48	-7:51:12
Fuqing 3	1	25N44	119E22	-7:57:28
Fuschun → Fushun 16	11	41N52	123E53	-8:15:32
Fushan 21	1	37N29	121E16	-8:05:04
Fushan 13	1	31N49	120E46	-8:03:04
Fushan 23	1	35N58	111E51	-7:27:24
Fushuigang 11	1	31N21	113E40	-7:34:40
Fushun 24	9	29N11	105E00	-7:00:00
Fushun (Funan) 16	11	41N52	123E53	-8:15:32
Fushuncheng 16	11	41N53	123E51	-8:15:24
Fusin → Fuxin 16	11	42N03	121E46	-8:07:04
Fusong 15	12	42N18	127E20	-8:29:20
Fusui 6	9	22N32	107E56	-7:11:44
Futang 5	10	24N26	112E09	-7:28:36
Futang 30	1	30N40	119E35	-7:58:20
Futian 14	1	27N26	114E56	-7:39:44
Futianhe 11	1	31N30	115E05	-7:40:20
Futianpu 12	1	27N22	112E47	-7:31:08
Futschou → Fuzhou 3	1	26N06	119E17	-7:57:08
Futuyu 8	1	39N18	114E50	-7:39:20
Fuwen 27	8	47N13	89E39	-5:58:36
Fuxi 3	1	27N14	119E50	-7:59:20
Fuxi 5	1	25N14	113E52	-7:35:28
Fuxian 20	9	36N02	109E13	-7:16:52
Fuxian (Wafangdian) 16	11	39N37	122E01	-8:08:04
Fuxin 16	11	42N08	121E45	-8:07:00
Fuxin 16	11	42N03	121E46	-8:07:04
Fuxing 24	9	30N24	104E53	-6:59:32
Fuxing 24	9	29N54	105E43	-7:02:52
Fuxing 24	9	30N27	106E04	-7:04:16
Fuxingchang 24	9	29N40	105E13	-7:00:52
Fuxinghao 17	11	42N35	120E32	-8:02:08
Fuyang 30	1	30N03	119E57	-7:59:48
Fuyang 5	1	23N36	116E37	-7:46:28
Fuyang 1	1	32N54	115E49	-7:43:16
Fuyu 9	12	47N49	124E27	-8:17:48
Fuyu 15	12	45N10	124E50	-8:19:20
Fuyuan 9	12	48N21	134E18	-8:57:12
Fuyuan 29	9	25N39	104E12	-6:56:48
Fuzhai 30	1	29N32	120E02	-8:00:08
Fuzhong 6	9	24N28	111E22	-7:25:28
Fuzhou 14	1	28N01	116E20	-7:45:20
Fuzhou (Foochow) 3	1	26N06	119E17	-7:57:08
Fuzhuang 21	1	34N57	118E17	-7:53:08
Fuzhuangyi 8	1	38N02	116E08	-7:44:32
Gaer (Geeryasha) 28	7	31N44	80E21	-5:21:24
Gaijiatun 16	11	40N50	122E37	-8:10:28
Gaixian 16	11	40N24	122E22	-8:09:28
Ganchangba 24	9	28N52	103E41	-6:54:44
Ganfang 14	1	28N40	114E51	-7:39:24
Ganfosi 24	9	29N36	104E03	-6:56:12
Gangcheng 21	1	35N52	116E52	-7:47:28
Ganghu 28	8	32N05	86E45	-5:47:00
Gangkou 12	1	29N12	113E19	-7:33:16
Gangkou 1	1	30N44	118E54	-7:55:36
Gangkou 14	1	29N45	115E44	-7:42:56
Gangkou 14	1	29N21	117E58	-7:51:52
Gangkou 5	1	22N38	113E22	-7:33:28
Gangkou 5	1	22N36	114E54	-7:39:36
Gangkouzhen 13	1	31N45	120E40	-8:02:40
Gangoa 19	9	37N15	100E28	-6:41:52
Gangou 8	1	40N30	119E27	-7:57:48
Gangoumen 8	1	41N40	116E35	-7:46:20
Gangouyi 4	9	36N01	105E03	-7:00:12
Gangqiao 24	9	30N13	105E22	-7:01:28
Gangshangji 14	1	28N06	116E30	-7:46:00
Gangtou 8	1	38N04	113E56	-7:35:44
Gangtouli 13	1	31N42	119E02	-7:56:08
Gangu 4	9	34N45	105E20	-7:01:20
Gangwa 2	1	39N48	116E10	-7:44:40
Gangwei 3	1	24N20	118E01	-7:52:04
Ganhezi 27	8	44N08	88E32	-5:54:08
Ganhu 27	8	44N33	94E09	-6:16:36
Ganjiang 24	9	29N42	103E38	-6:54:32
Ganlu 13	1	31N32	120E35	-8:02:20
Ganluchang 24	9	29N54	104E47	-6:59:08
Ganluo 24	9	29N03	102E59	-6:51:56
Gannan 9	12	47N54	123E30	-8:14:00
Ganpingsi 4	9	35N13	102E30	-6:50:00
Ganpu 30	1	30N24	120E53	-8:03:32
Ganquan 20	9	36N25	109E16	-7:17:04
Gansen 28	8	37N25	92E15	-6:09:00
Gantan 30	1	29N37	119E34	-7:58:16
Gantang 6	9	22N58	109E00	-7:16:00
Gantang 3	1	26N56	119E40	-7:58:40
Gantian 12	1	27N30	113E10	-7:32:40
Ganxi 12	1	29N02	109E32	-7:18:08
Ganxi 14	1	28N08	118E06	-7:52:24
Ganyanchi 18	9	36N39	105E18	-7:01:12
Ganyu (Qing Kou) 13	1	34N52	119E10	-7:56:40
Ganzê 24	9	31N40	100E01	-6:40:04
Ganzhenyi 11	1	30N33	113E21	-7:33:24
Ganzhou 14	1	25N54	114E55	-7:39:40
Ganzhou 14	1	28N49	115E25	-7:41:40
Ganzhou → Zhangye 4	9	38N56	100E27	-6:41:48
Ganzhuermiao 17	11	48N24	118E08	-7:52:32
Gao'an 14	1	28N25	115E22	-7:41:28
Gaobaita 2	1	39N53	116E30	-7:46:00
Gaobei 14	1	26N37	114E38	-7:38:32
Gaobeidian 2	1	39N54	116E33	-7:46:12
Gaobu 14	1	27N48	117E01	-7:48:04
Gaochang 24	9	28N49	104E24	-6:57:36
Gaocheng 8	1	38N04	114E49	-7:39:16
Gaocheng 13	1	31N28	119E48	-7:59:12
Gaocheng 11	1	31N57	113E25	-7:33:40
Gaochengzhai 16	11	41N24	123E43	-8:14:52
Gaochun 13	1	31N20	118E52	-7:55:28
Gaocun 21	1	37N05	122E12	-8:08:48
Gaodianzi 11	1	30N40	110E01	-7:20:04
Gaogongmiao 1	1	33N25	115E53	-7:43:32
Gaogou 13	1	34N03	119E15	-7:57:00
Gaohe 5	1	22N47	112E57	-7:31:48
Gaohebu 1	1	30N44	116E50	-7:47:20
Gaojiabu 20	9	38N30	110E11	-7:20:44
Gaojiadi 8	1	41N33	114E58	-7:39:52
Gaojiadian 16	11	42N40	124E28	-8:17:52
Gaojian 30	1	29N04	121E14	-8:04:56
Gaojiapuzi 16	11	41N22	123E36	-8:14:24
Gaojiaqiao 30	1	30N43	120E38	-8:02:32
Gaojiatun 16	11	41N06	121E19	-8:05:16
Gaojiawopeng 16	11	41N28	122E10	-8:08:40
Gaojiawopu 16	11	41N50	122E47	-8:11:08
Gaojiazhen 24	9	30N05	107E51	-7:11:24
Gaokan 16	11	40N46	122E23	-8:09:32
Gaokeng 14	1	27N40	113E58	-7:35:52
Gaolan 4	9	36N25	103E56	-6:55:44
Gaolao 16	11	41N54	120E59	-8:03:56
Gaoli 8	1	39N17	115E38	-7:42:32
Gaoliang 24	9	29N45	105E15	-7:01:00
Gaoliban 16	11	41N39	121E58	-8:07:52
Gaolifangshen 16	11	42N27	123E21	-8:13:24
Gaolimen 16	11	40N22	124E02	-8:16:08
Gaoling 2	1	40N32	117E01	-7:48:04
Gaolinying 8	1	39N06	115E38	-7:42:32
Gaoliying 2	1	40N10	116E29	-7:45:56
Gaoliyingzi 16	11	41N56	124E17	-8:17:08
Gaolong 12	1	26N56	113E45	-7:35:00
Gaolou 8	1	39N59	116E50	-7:47:20
Gaolouchang 24	9	29N51	104E41	-6:58:44
Gaolouchang 24	9	30N03	105E58	-7:03:52
Gaoluo 23	1	37N27	113E55	-7:35:40
Gaomi 21	1	36N23	119E44	-7:58:56
Gaopi 5	1	24N14	116E39	-7:46:36
Gaoping 23	1	35N48	112E52	-7:31:28
Gaoping 24	9	30N28	105E45	-7:03:00
Gaopingba 24	9	30N47	106E06	-7:04:24
Gaoqiao 7	9	28N06	106E36	-7:06:24
Gaoqiao 30	1	30N08	119E56	-7:59:44
Gaoqiao 3	1	26N36	117E46	-7:51:04
Gaoqiao 13	1	32N14	119E38	-7:58:32
Gaoqiao 22	2	31N21	121E34	-8:06:16
Gaoqiaomen 1	3	32N01	118E51	-7:55:24
Gaoqiaozhen 16	11	40N55	121E00	-8:04:00
Gaoqing (Tianzhen) 21	1	37N11	117E47	-7:51:08
Gaoqipu 16	11	41N32	121E40	-8:06:40
Gaosha 3	1	26N27	117E56	-7:51:44
Gaoshaling 26	1	38N51	117E36	-7:50:24
Gaoshan 3	1	25N29	119E34	-7:58:16
Gaoshan 24	9	29N26	104E28	-6:57:52
Gaoshanbao 2	1	40N40	117E29	-7:49:56
Gaoshangbao 8	1	39N11	118E30	-7:54:00
Gaoshanpu 7	9	27N10	105E14	-7:00:56
Gaoshantai 16	11	42N22	122E28	-8:09:52

Gaoshanzi 16	11	41N34	122E02	-8:08:08
Gaoshengchang 24	9	29N59	105E31	-7:02:04
Gaoshengzhen 16	11	41N20	122E12	-8:08:48
Gaoshi 24	9	29N36	104E44	-6:58:56
Gaoshikan 24	9	29N12	105E04	-7:00:16
Gaosichang 24	9	30N17	104E52	-6:59:28
Gaotai 4	9	39N20	99E58	-6:39:52
Gaotaishan 16	11	42N02	122E52	-8:11:28
Gaotan 1	1	30N23	117E23	-7:49:32
Gaotan 5	1	23N12	115E22	-7:41:28
Gaotan 20	9	32N22	108E36	-7:14:24
Gaotang 21	1	36N54	116E14	-7:44:56
Gaotangji 1	1	32N24	116E01	-7:44:04
Gaotingsi 12	1	26N05	112E53	-7:31:32
Gaotuozi 16	11	41N08	122E40	-8:10:40
Gaoxian 24	9	28N20	104E38	-6:58:32
Gaoxingru 14	1	26N28	115E14	-7:40:56
Gaoxinji 10	1	34N11	115E33	-7:42:12
Gaoya 21	1	36N22	118E49	-7:55:16
Gaoyang 10	1	34N30	114E40	-7:38:40
Gaoyapu 24	9	29N14	106E19	-7:05:16
Gaoyi 8	1	37N36	114E36	-7:38:24
Gaoyou 13	1	32N47	119E27	-7:57:48
Gaoyou 14	1	28N25	115E31	-7:42:04
Gaozhangjia 4	9	36N06	107E18	-7:09:12
Gaozhou 5	8	21N55	110E50	-7:23:20
Gaozi 13	1	32N11	119E18	-7:57:12
Gaoziba 24	9	29N01	106E00	-7:04:00
Gaozuo 13	1	33N57	118E03	-7:52:12
Garyi 24	8	30N54	98E56	-6:35:44
Gechang 1	1	31N05	119E27	-7:57:48
Gecun 13	1	32N10	119E37	-7:58:28
Gedian 11	1	30N32	114E38	-7:38:32
Gedun 3	1	27N39	118E26	-7:53:44
Gegang 1	1	30N04	117E38	-7:50:32
Gegenmiao 17	11	45N58	122E15	-8:09:00
Gegong 1	1	30N05	117E11	-7:48:44
Gegou 21	1	35N24	118E32	-7:54:08
Gegu 26	1	38N59	117E30	-7:50:00
Gehu 30	1	27N46	119E16	-7:57:04
Gejiatun 16	11	40N27	119E55	-7:59:40
Gejiu (Kokiu) 29	9	23N22	103E06	-6:52:24
Gelan 24	9	30N03	107E04	-7:08:16
Gelaochang 24	9	29N36	103E39	-6:54:36
Geluji 21	1	37N08	121E50	-8:07:20
Gengji 10	1	33N47	112E47	-7:31:08
Gengma 29	9	23N34	99E06	-6:36:24
Gengputou 13	1	31N12	119E55	-7:59:40
Gengzhuang 16	11	40N59	122E42	-8:10:48
Geyuan 14	1	28N31	117E44	-7:50:56
Girang Kzong 28	8	28N28	85E16	-5:41:04
Golin Baixing 17	11	44N53	121E58	-8:07:52
Golmud 19	8	36N22	94E55	-6:19:40
Gong'an 11	1	30N02	112E04	-7:28:16
Gonganbao 27	8	44N59	86E18	-5:45:12
Gonganpucun 16	11	41N19	123E27	-8:13:48
Gongbuchang 2	1	40N17	116E15	-7:45:00
Gongchangling 16	11	41N06	123E30	-8:14:00
Gongcheng 6	9	24N49	110E46	-7:23:04
Gongchenqiao 30	3	30N20	120E08	-8:00:32
Gongchuan 6	9	23N40	107E50	-7:11:20
Gongchuan 3	1	26N06	117E24	-7:49:36
Gongcun 8	1	39N28	116E10	-7:44:40
Gongdaoqiao 13	1	32N36	119E22	-7:57:28
Gongdian 14	1	28N06	116E56	-7:47:44
Gongfang 14	1	27N36	115E34	-7:42:16
Gongge 28	8	29N17	90E46	-6:03:04
Gonghe 19	9	36N20	100E48	-6:43:12
Gonghui 8	1	41N12	114E37	-7:38:28
Gongjialu 22	2	31N17	121E40	-8:06:40
Gongjiatun 16	11	40N55	120E37	-8:02:28
Gongjiazhai 16	11	41N57	124E01	-8:16:04
Gongjing 24	9	29N21	104E43	-6:58:52
Gongjingying 8	1	39N12	116E11	-7:44:44
Gongkou 21	1	35N38	119E47	-7:59:08
Gongli 21	1	35N55	117E24	-7:49:36
Gongling 3	1	26N18	119E40	-7:58:40
Gongliu 27	7	43N30	82E15	-5:29:00
Gongpengzi 15	12	45N09	125E39	-8:22:36
Gongping 5	1	23N05	115E24	-7:41:36
Gongpingxu 12	1	26N12	112E51	-7:31:24
Gongshan 29	9	25N50	103E13	-6:52:52
Gongshiya 28	8	31N25	84E37	-5:38:28
Gongsizhen 13	1	31N41	121E48	-8:07:12
Gongtangtou 13	1	31N48	118E42	-7:54:48
Gongxi 14	1	27N38	115E52	-7:43:28
Gongxian 10	1	34N48	113E03	-7:32:12
Gongyefu 17	11	42N16	118E32	-7:54:08
Gongyemiao 17	11	43N40	121E06	-8:04:24
Gongyingzi 16	11	40N54	119E41	-7:58:44
Gongzhutun 16	11	42N10	123E00	-8:12:00
Gongzui 24	9	29N19	103E28	-6:53:52
Gonjo 28	8	30N43	98E19	-6:33:16
Goqên 28	8	29N15	96E59	-6:27:56
Goubangzi 16	11	41N22	121E46	-8:07:04
Gougezhuang 8	1	38N53	116E11	-7:44:44
Goujiaozhen 24	9	30N36	106E33	-7:06:12
Goukou 17	11	48N39	122E06	-8:08:24
Goulicun 13	1	31N40	120E00	-8:00:00
Goutou 26	1	39N49	117E11	-7:48:44
Gouyadong 12	1	25N10	112E55	-7:31:40
Guabu 1	1	32N16	118E53	-7:55:32
Guahe 8	1	39N12	115E00	-7:40:00
Guaihe 10	1	33N28	112E59	-7:31:56
Guaimozi 16	11	41N31	125E26	-8:21:44
Guajiasi 16	11	41N15	120E54	-8:03:36
Gu'an 8	1	39N26	116E18	-7:45:12
Guanbuqiao 11	1	29N56	114E21	-7:37:24
Guanchao 14	1	26N41	114E58	-7:39:52
Guancheng 30	1	30N11	121E25	-8:05:40
Guancheng 24	9	30N01	103E54	-6:55:36
Guancun 13	1	31N30	119E43	-7:58:52
Guandanghu 11	1	30N06	113E37	-7:34:28
Guandi 8	1	41N48	116E52	-7:47:28
Guandi 17	11	42N37	118E27	-7:53:48
Guandian 1	1	32N40	118E04	-7:52:16
Guandu 5	1	24N17	113E53	-7:35:32
Guandu 24	9	30N04	106E25	-7:05:40
Guang'an 24	9	30N28	106E39	-7:06:36
Guangchang 14	1	26N50	116E14	-7:44:56
Guangde 1	1	30N54	119E26	-7:57:44
Guangfeng 14	1	28N25	118E11	-7:52:44
Guangfu 24	9	30N13	104E41	-6:58:44
Guangfu 22	2	31N21	121E19	-8:05:16
Guangfu 13	1	31N18	120E23	-8:01:32
Guangfuyingzi 16	11	42N14	120E58	-8:03:52
Guanghua 11	1	32N25	111E36	-7:26:24
Guangji 11	1	29N52	115E34	-7:42:16
Guangling 23	1	39N47	114E17	-7:37:08
Guangling 13	1	32N06	120E13	-8:00:52
Guangnan 29	9	24N10	105E06	-7:00:24
Guangningsi 8	1	40N27	118E31	-7:54:04
Guangningsi 16	11	39N08	121E45	-8:07:00
Guangping 8	1	36N30	114E57	-7:39:48
Guangrao 21	1	37N02	118E25	-7:53:40
Guangsbunchang 24	9	29N22	105E31	-7:02:04
Guangshan 10	1	32N02	114E52	-7:39:28
Guangshui 11	1	31N40	114E00	-7:36:00
Guangxing 24	9	29N04	106E33	-7:06:12
Guangyuan 24	9	32N26	105E52	-7:03:28
Guangze 3	1	27N32	117E20	-7:49:20
Guangzhen 30	1	30N45	121E07	-8:04:28
Guangzhou (Canton) 5	1	23N06	113E16	-7:33:04
Guangzong 8	1	37N06	115E08	-7:40:32
Guanhu 13	1	34N26	117E59	-7:51:56
Guanjian 24	9	29N59	105E59	-7:03:56
Guankou 11	1	30N35	115E20	-7:41:20
Guankou 24	9	30N39	103E26	-6:53:44
Guanlin 13	1	31N32	119E42	-7:58:48
Guanling 7	9	25N57	105E29	-7:01:56
Guanlipu 16	11	41N37	123E18	-8:13:12
Guanmenshan 17	11	47N23	122E20	-8:09:20
Guannan (Xin'anzhen) 13	1	34N07	119E23	-7:57:32
Guanputou 26	1	38N58	117E04	-7:48:16
Guanqian 1	1	30N42	117E39	-7:50:36
Guanqian 3	1	27N48	118E31	-7:54:04
Guanqian 3	1	25N57	116E33	-7:46:12
Guanqian 3	1	26N12	117E57	-7:51:48
Guanqiao 3	1	25N03	118E06	-7:52:24
Guanqiao 21	1	34N58	117E14	-7:48:56
Guanqiaopu 11	1	31N08	112E54	-7:31:36
Guanshanchang 24	9	28N46	103E42	-6:54:48
Guanshi 12	1	26N43	112E53	-7:31:32
Guanshui 16	11	40N55	124E33	-8:18:12
Guantang 13	1	31N37	119E06	-7:56:24
Guantangqiao 13	1	32N09	119E27	-7:57:48
Guantao (Nanguantao) 8	1	36N35	115E19	-7:41:16
Guanting 10	1	34N19	113E47	-7:35:08
Guanting 8	1	40N13	115E37	-7:42:28
Guantou 30	1	28N03	120E41	-8:02:44
Guantou 3	1	26N08	119E33	-7:58:12
Guantunpu 17	9	40N28	113E24	-7:33:36
Guanxian 24	9	31N00	103E40	-6:54:40
Guanxian 21	1	36N30	115E27	-7:41:48
Guanxun 3	1	24N19	117E45	-7:51:00
Guanyin 24	9	30N16	103E51	-6:55:24
Guanyinchang 24	9	29N15	104E02	-6:56:08
Guanyinchang 24	9	30N28	105E16	-7:01:04
Guanyingzicun 16	11	41N52	121E53	-8:07:32
Guanyinpu 24	9	28N58	104E53	-6:59:32
Guanyinqiao 24	9	29N05	104E46	-6:59:04
Guanyinqiao 24	9	29N46	104E12	-6:56:48
Guanyinshan 13	1	32N01	120E58	-8:03:52
Guanyinsi 13	1	31N48	118E57	-7:55:48
Guanyintan 24	9	29N35	105E14	-7:00:56
Guanyintang 13	1	32N09	121E09	-8:04:36
Guanyintang 2	1	39N52	116E31	-7:46:04
Guanyintang 11	1	31N01	112E35	-7:30:20
Guanyinzhen 24	9	29N06	104E24	-6:57:36
Guanyinzhou 11	1	29N30	113E09	-7:32:36
Guanyun (Dayishan) 13	1	34N20	119E17	-7:57:08
Guanzhuang 14	1	28N58	117E24	-7:49:36
Guanzhuang 8	1	37N12	114E30	-7:38:00
Guanzhuang 10	1	32N49	114E16	-7:37:04
Guazhou 13	1	32N15	119E23	-7:57:32
Gubeikou 2	1	40N42	117E09	-7:48:36
Gubentaoligai 16	11	42N16	122E13	-8:08:52
Gucheng 11	1	32N18	111E35	-7:26:20
Gucheng 1	1	33N59	117E29	-7:49:56
Gucheng 3	1	25N53	116E11	-7:44:44
Gucheng 13	1	32N46	118E32	-7:54:08
Gucheng (Zhengjiakou) 8	1	37N22	115E56	-7:43:44
Gucheng 30	1	30N29	119E46	-7:59:04
Gucheng 2	1	40N32	116E02	-7:44:08
Gucheng 8	1	39N08	115E42	-7:42:48
Guchengcang 10	1	32N34	115E20	-7:41:20
Guchengzi 16	11	42N33	123E45	-8:15:00
Guchengzi 16	11	40N58	122E36	-8:10:24
Guchengzi 16	11	40N40	120E31	-8:02:04
Guchengzi 16	11	41N44	123E35	-8:14:20
Gudianzi 1	1	31N49	116E05	-7:44:20
Gufang 30	1	29N04	119E32	-7:58:08
Gugang 12	1	28N17	113E46	-7:35:04
Guguan 4	9	40N27	99E13	-6:36:52
Guhe 1	1	31N54	117E58	-7:51:52
Guichi 1	1	30N40	117E28	-7:49:52
Guicun 10	1	33N37	114E11	-7:36:44
Guide 19	9	36N03	101E28	-6:45:52
Guidexiang 24	9	29N51	104E47	-6:59:08
Guiding 7	9	26N34	107E14	-7:08:56
Guidong 12	1	26N05	113E57	-7:35:48
Guifujie 3	1	27N20	120E01	-8:00:04
Guihuayuan 24	9	30N37	105E25	-7:01:40
Guiji 1	1	32N51	116E33	-7:46:12
Guijingqiao 13	1	31N21	119E40	-7:58:40
Guiler 17	11	46N11	121E45	-8:07:00
Guilin (Kweilin) 6	9	25N17	110E17	-7:21:08
Guilinchang 24	9	30N13	105E50	-7:03:20
Guilinzhen 24	9	30N15	104E53	-6:59:32
Guimeishan 14	1	24N44	114E52	-7:39:28
Guinan 19	9	35N24	100E57	-6:43:48
Guiping 6	9	23N20	110E09	-7:20:36
Guiren 13	1	33N42	118E12	-7:52:48
Guitou 5	1	24N58	113E25	-7:33:40
Guixi 14	1	28N16	117E10	-7:48:40
Guixian 6	9	23N06	109E39	-7:18:36
Guiyang (Kweiyang) 7	9	26N35	106E43	-7:06:52
Guiyang 12	1	25N46	112E43	-7:30:52
Gujiabeng 30	1	30N45	120E59	-8:03:56
Gujiang 14	1	27N11	114E49	-7:39:16
Gujiatun 16	11	40N39	124E08	-8:16:32
Gujiatuo 24	9	29N14	106E12	-7:04:48
Gujiazhai 22	2	31N22	121E28	-8:05:52
Gujiazi 16	11	42N02	123E01	-8:12:04
Gujiazi 16	11	41N44	124E11	-8:16:44
Gukou 3	1	26N27	118E38	-7:54:32
Gulang 4	9	37N36	102E58	-6:51:52
Guleitou 3	1	23N47	117E36	-7:50:24
Guli 13	1	31N38	120E50	-8:03:20
Gulian 17	11	52N55	122E19	-8:09:16
Gulicun 13	1	31N52	118E41	-7:54:44
Gulong 9	12	45N51	124E14	-8:16:56
Gulu 28	8	28N06	89E17	-5:57:08
Guluogongba 28	8	34N20	84E50	-5:39:20
Gumiao 10	1	32N26	113E16	-7:33:04
Gunzigou 16	11	41N31	123E58	-8:15:52
Guobei 24	9	29N33	105E08	-7:00:32
Guodian 30	1	30N27	120E33	-8:02:12
Guoji 10	1	32N59	113E06	-7:32:24
Guojiadian 16	11	41N51	121E30	-8:06:00
Guojiajiang 13	1	32N17	120E50	-8:03:20
Guojiatun 16	11	42N00	122E51	-8:11:24
Guojiatun 16	11	40N52	122E04	-8:08:16
Guojiatun 8	1	41N31	117E02	-7:48:08
Guojiawopeng 16	11	42N03	122E46	-8:11:04
Guojiayao 8	1	40N37	115E39	-7:42:36
Guojiayuan 13	1	32N10	120E35	-8:02:20
Guojiga 27	7	43N47	80E48	-5:23:12
Guoleizhuang 8	1	40N44	114E36	-7:38:24
Guolutan 10	1	32N04	115E40	-7:42:40
Guosu 8	1	38N24	114E00	-7:36:00
Guoyang 1	1	33N32	116E12	-7:44:48
Guoyangzhen 23	1	38N54	112E50	-7:31:20
Guozhuang 21	1	35N25	117E10	-7:48:40
Guozhuangmiao 13	1	31N49	119E01	-7:56:04
Gupei 13	1	34N09	117E54	-7:51:36
Gurban Anggir 19	8	37N45	97E30	-6:30:00
Gurban Obo 17	1	43N14	112E28	-7:29:52
Gushan 21	1	36N30	116E53	-7:47:32
Gushan 13	1	31N44	120E33	-8:02:12
Gushan 16	11	39N53	123E36	-8:14:24
Gushanbeizifu 17	11	42N10	120E30	-8:02:00
Gushankou 2	1	39N38	115E49	-7:43:16
Gushantun 17	11	48N18	123E47	-8:15:08
Gushanzi 16	11	40N22	120E03	-8:00:12
Gushanzi 16	11	41N03	123E03	-8:12:12
Gushi 30	1	28N34	119E24	-7:57:36
Gushi 10	1	32N12	115E41	-7:42:44
Gushu 8	1	39N55	117E35	-7:50:20
Gushu 16	11	42N36	123E26	-8:13:44
Gushuji 10	1	34N15	115E48	-7:43:12
Gusong 24	9	28N18	105E14	-7:00:56
Gutian 3	1	25N15	116E46	-7:47:04
Gutian 3	1	25N43	116E57	-7:47:48
Gutian 3	1	26N36	118E46	-7:55:04
Guxi 24	9	30N18	105E52	-7:03:28
Guxian 14	1	27N09	115E31	-7:42:04
Guxian 21	1	37N35	121E09	-8:04:36
Guxian 10	1	32N26	113E37	-7:34:28
Guxiandu 14	1	29N06	116E50	-7:47:20
Guxiansi 1	1	32N01	116E20	-7:45:20
Guxiong 13	1	31N55	118E38	-7:54:32
Guyang 17	9	41N03	110E03	-7:20:12
Guyang 10	1	34N58	114E58	-7:39:52
Guye 8	1	39N44	118E25	-7:53:40
Guyi 3	1	25N38	118E47	-7:55:08
Guyi 24	9	30N22	103E33	-6:54:12
Guyin 29	9	23N58	105E47	-7:03:08
Guyuan 18	9	35N58	106E45	-7:07:00
Guyuan (Pingdingbu) 8	1	41N40	115E41	-7:42:44
Guzhang 12	1	28N31	109E57	-7:19:48
Guzhen 5	1	22N37	113E11	-7:32:44
Guzhen 1	1	33N19	117E21	-7:49:24
Guzhu 14	1	26N58	116E16	-7:45:04

Gyangtse → Jiangzi 28
8 28N57 89E35 -5:58:20
Habahe 27 8 47N53 86E12 -5:44:48
Habaqi 16 11 42N36 122E52 -8:11:28
Habaqi 16 11 42N38 122E02 -8:08:08
Habaqila 17 9 42N01 106E02 -7:04:08
Hadat 17 11 49N40 119E40 -7:58:40
Hadayingzi 16 11 42N22 121E40 -8:06:40
Haerhpin 9 12 45N45 126E41 -8:26:44
Haernao 16 11 41N46 120E28 -8:01:52
Hai'an 13 1 32N34 120E28 -8:01:52
Haibei 9 12 47N39 126E51 -8:27:24
Haicheng 3 1 24N25 117E51 -7:51:24
Haicheng 16 11 40N52 122E45 -8:11:00
Haidian 2 1 39N59 116E18 -7:45:12
Haidun 30 1 29N36 121E49 -8:07:16
Haifeng 5 1 22N59 115E21 -7:41:24
Haifengzheng 13
1 31N53 121E46 -8:07:04
Haifuzhen 13 1 31N59 121E42 -8:06:48
Haihezhen 13 1 33N44 120E02 -8:00:08
Haikang 5 8 20N56 110E04 -7:20:16
Haikou 5 9 20N03 110E19 -7:21:16
Haikou 30 1 28N20 120E06 -8:00:24
Haikou 3 1 25N43 119E28 -7:57:52
Haikou 14 1 29N04 117E46 -7:51:04
Hailar → Hailaer 17
11 49N12 119E42 -7:58:48
Hailasen 17 11 46N13 121E00 -8:04:00
Hailin 9 12 44N35 129E22 -8:37:28
Hailong (Meihekou) 15
12 42N32 125E38 -8:22:32
Hailun 9 12 47N28 126E58 -8:27:52
Haimen 5 1 23N14 116E38 -7:46:32
Haimen 13 1 31N55 121E10 -8:04:40
Haimen 30 1 28N41 121E27 -8:05:48
Haimiao 21 1 37N13 119E51 -7:59:24
Haining (Xiashi) 30
1 30N32 120E41 -8:02:44
Haiqiao 22 2 31N47 121E19 -8:05:16
Haiqing 9 12 47N53 134E40 -8:58:40
Haitangxi 24 9 29N33 106E35 -7:06:20
Haitou 5 9 19N34 108E58 -7:15:52
Haitou 13 1 34N56 119E10 -7:56:40
Haitouji 21 1 35N23 115E19 -7:41:16
Haitun 19 8 38N50 96E41 -6:26:44
Haiyan 19 9 36N54 101E12 -6:44:48
Haiyan 30 1 30N31 120E57 -8:03:48
Haiyang (Dongcun) 21
1 36N46 121E10 -8:04:40
Haiyuan 18 9 36N35 105E40 -7:02:40
Haizhou 5 1 22N40 113E10 -7:32:40
Haizhou 13 1 34N34 119E11 -7:56:44
Haizhoumiao 16
11 42N00 121E39 -8:06:36
Haizhouyingzi 16
11 42N07 121E46 -8:07:04
Hajiadian 8 1 41N32 117E10 -7:48:40
Halaaobao 17 9 42N11 107E20 -7:09:20
Halaerjige 16 11 42N24 122E11 -8:08:44
Halagetu 16 11 42N34 122E40 -8:10:40
Halahai 15 12 44N39 125E07 -8:20:28
Halahushao 16 11 42N11 121E44 -8:06:56
Halamutai 27 8 46N10 84E52 -5:39:28
Halataojie 16 11 42N30 122E06 -8:08:24
Halawotelake 27
8 37N17 90E20 -6:01:20
Halimatazi 16 11 42N37 122E35 -8:10:20
Hamakeza 17 11 47N05 120E52 -8:03:28
Hamatang 16 11 40N12 124E20 -8:17:20
Hami (Kumul) 27
8 42N48 93E27 -6:13:48
Hanailike 27 7 39N16 76E26 -5:05:44
Hanchang 24 9 30N26 103E43 -6:54:52
Hancheng 20 9 35N29 110E25 -7:21:40
Hancheng 8 1 39N39 118E02 -7:52:08
Hanchuan 11 1 30N39 113E48 -7:35:12
Hanchung → Hanzhong 20
9 33N08 107E02 -7:08:08
Hancun 8 1 39N24 116E36 -7:46:24
Handan 8 1 36N37 114E29 -7:37:56
Handaokou 10 1 34N16 116E24 -7:45:36
Han'gang 10 1 34N39 114E38 -7:38:32
Hangbu 30 1 28N53 118E49 -7:55:16
Hangchow → Hangzhou 30
3 30N15 120E10 -8:00:40
Hanggai 30 1 30N35 119E23 -7:57:32
Hanggin Houqi 17
9 40N55 107E15 -7:09:00
Hanggin Qi 17 9 39N56 108E54 -7:15:36
Hang Hau Town 31
4 22N19 114E16 -7:37:04
Hangkou 14 1 29N03 114E27 -7:37:48
Hangou 26 1 39N18 117E07 -7:48:28
Hang-Tcheou → Hangzhou 30
3 30N15 120E10 -8:00:40
Hangtou 22 2 31N01 121E35 -8:06:20
Hangtschou → Hangzhou 30
3 30N15 120E10 -8:00:40
Hangu 26 1 39N15 117E47 -7:51:08
Hangu 24 9 28N58 104E30 -6:58:00
Hanguang 5 1 24N16 113E08 -7:32:32
Hanguchang 24 9 29N32 106E21 -7:05:24
Hangugang 26 1 39N15 116E56 -7:47:44
Hangzhou (Hangchow) 30
3 30N15 120E10 -8:00:40
Hanjiagou 16 11 40N42 120E47 -8:03:08
Hanjiang 3 1 25N30 119E06 -7:56:24
Hanjiapuzi 16 11 40N48 123E14 -8:12:56
Hanjiashu 26 1 39N11 117E04 -7:48:16
Hanjiawa 1 1 31N16 119E18 -7:57:12
Hankow → Wuhan 11
3 30N36 114E17 -7:37:08
Hanku → Hangu 26
1 39N15 117E47 -7:51:08
Hanmiao 17 11 44N33 119E59 -7:59:56
Hansanjiazi 16
11 41N44 122E57 -8:11:48
Hansantai 27 8 45N23 84E06 -5:36:24
Hanshan 1 1 31N44 118E08 -7:52:32
Hantan → Handan 8
1 36N37 114E29 -7:37:56
Hanxinzhuang 2 1 40N16 116E44 -7:46:56
Hanyang 24 9 29N44 103E44 -6:54:56
Hanyangping 20 9 32N41 108E34 -7:14:16
Hanyin 20 9 32N42 108E50 -7:15:20
Hanyuan 24 9 29N22 102E38 -6:50:32
Hanyuangai 24 9 29N30 102E31 -6:50:04
Hanzhong 20 9 33N08 107E02 -7:08:08
Hanzhuang 21 1 34N38 117E24 -7:49:36
Haohekou 12 1 28N38 112E49 -7:31:16
Haojiadian 11 1 31N47 113E44 -7:34:56
Haoli → Hegang 9
12 47N24 130E17 -8:41:08
Haoluqi 30 1 30N38 119E34 -7:58:16
Haoxue 11 1 30N00 112E20 -7:29:20
Haozhikou 24 9 29N36 105E02 -7:00:08
Harbin 9 12 45N45 126E41 -8:26:44
Harqin 16 11 41N08 119E38 -7:58:32
Harqin Qi (Jinshan) 17
11 41N56 118E36 -7:54:24
Har Su 17 11 48N09 122E25 -8:09:40
Hasafen 27 8 45N14 90E20 -6:01:20
Hashitai 9 12 49N24 125E18 -8:21:12
Haya'er 19 8 37N00 93E18 -6:13:12
Hebaochang 24 9 29N33 105E32 -7:02:08
Hebei 16 11 40N43 122E12 -8:08:48
Hebei 16 11 41N01 123E51 -8:15:24
Hebeitun 26 1 39N35 117E07 -7:48:28
Hebi 10 1 35N59 114E11 -7:36:44
Hebian 24 9 30N29 105E08 -7:00:32
Hebo 24 8 31N29 98E58 -6:35:52
Hebu 14 1 27N50 115E22 -7:41:28
Hebukesaier 27 8 46N47 85E43 -5:42:52
Hebutu 16 11 42N19 122E20 -8:09:20
Hecao 2 1 40N21 116E47 -7:47:08
Hechi 6 9 24N42 108E02 -7:12:08
Hechuan 24 9 30N00 106E16 -7:05:04
Hedian 10 1 32N45 114E18 -7:37:12
Heerkan 24 9 29N32 103E56 -6:55:44
Hefei 1 1 31N51 117E17 -7:49:08
Hefengchang 24 9 30N26 104E43 -6:58:52
Hegang 9 12 47N24 130E22 -8:41:28
Hehou 14 1 28N40 114E28 -7:37:52
Heichengzhen 18
9 36N16 106E06 -7:04:24
Heichengzi 16 11 42N10 121E01 -8:04:04
Heidayingzi 8 1 40N52 116E12 -7:44:48
Heidouwo 26 1 39N42 117E15 -7:49:00
Heigoutaicun 16
11 41N30 123E01 -8:12:04
Heihe (Naquka) 28
8 31N34 92E00 -6:08:00
Heihe → Aihun 9
12 50N16 127E28 -8:29:52
Heilangkou 26 1 39N37 117E24 -7:49:36
Heilin 13 1 35N01 118E58 -7:55:52
Heilongguan 23 1 36N19 111E11 -7:24:44
Heilongtan 2 1 40N44 116E31 -7:46:04
Heilongtan 2 1 40N02 116E11 -7:44:44
Heiniuyingzi 16
11 41N07 120E19 -8:01:16
Heiquan 4 9 39N32 99E42 -6:38:48
Heishan 16 11 41N41 122E07 -8:08:28
Heishanguan 8 1 38N33 113E41 -7:34:44
Heishantou 17 11 50N13 119E28 -7:57:52
Heishantou 15 12 42N28 125E33 -8:22:12
Heishui 16 11 42N09 119E28 -7:57:52
Heishuisi 20 9 36N08 108E42 -7:14:48
Heitang 7 9 26N29 105E09 -7:00:36
Heiyanghebao 8 1 39N07 118E15 -7:53:00
Heiyantang 24 9 27N28 101E11 -6:44:44
Heiyanzi 8 1 39N13 118E08 -7:52:32
Hejiachang 24 9 29N24 104E56 -6:59:44
Hejian 8 1 38N26 116E05 -7:44:20
Hejian 8 1 39N25 116E25 -7:45:40
Hejiang 24 9 28N49 105E50 -7:03:20
Hejiangzhen 24 9 29N16 104E16 -6:57:04
Hejiaqiao 12 1 27N24 113E21 -7:33:24
Hejiawopeng 16
11 41N32 122E07 -8:08:28
Hejiaying 8 1 39N55 118E19 -7:53:16
Hejiazhen 24 9 29N52 104E26 -6:57:44
Hejin 23 1 35N39 110E40 -7:22:40
Hekou 4 9 36N09 103E22 -6:53:28
Hekou 7 9 28N22 108E14 -7:12:56
Hekou 12 1 29N57 111E04 -7:24:16
Hekou 29 9 22N38 103E56 -6:55:44
Hekou 11 1 31N22 114E26 -7:37:44
Hekouchang 24 9 29N21 104E21 -6:57:24
Hekouji 1 1 32N09 116E04 -7:44:16
Hekoujie 29 9 26N31 100E39 -6:42:36
Helaluo 24 9 33N56 102E10 -6:48:40
Helangou 16 11 41N00 123E25 -8:13:40
Heli 9 12 47N05 130E16 -8:41:04
Heliuji 1 1 33N02 116E57 -7:47:48
Helixi 1 1 30N40 118E59 -7:55:56
Helong 15 12 42N32 128E59 -8:35:56
Hemujing 8 1 37N54 115E22 -7:41:28
Henan 19 9 34N35 101E34 -6:46:16
Hengchow → Hengyang 12
1 26N54 112E36 -7:30:24
Hengdaochuan 16
11 41N15 125E31 -8:22:04
Hengdaohe 16 11 42N02 123E51 -8:15:24
Hengdaohezi 15
12 43N13 126E44 -8:26:56
Hengdaozi 15 12 43N18 127E18 -8:29:12
Hengdong 12 1 27N03 112E57 -7:31:48
Hengfan 30 1 30N20 119E45 -7:59:00
Hengfeng 14 1 28N24 117E34 -7:50:16
Henggang 14 1 29N32 115E27 -7:41:48
Henggouzi 15 12 43N12 124E47 -8:19:08
Henghutou 16 11 42N05 124E00 -8:16:00
Hengjie 13 1 31N13 119E30 -7:58:00
Hengjing 13 3 31N11 120E32 -8:02:08
Hengjinghong 30
1 30N34 120E59 -8:03:56
Hengli 5 1 23N12 114E37 -7:38:28
Henglin 13 1 31N42 120E06 -8:00:24
Henglu 15 12 41N26 126E04 -8:24:16
Henglutou 30 1 30N19 119E19 -7:57:16
Hengmian 22 2 31N09 121E38 -8:06:32
Hengshan 12 1 27N15 112E51 -7:31:24
Hengshan 13 1 31N01 120E32 -8:02:08
Hengshan 20 9 37N56 108E53 -7:15:32
Hengshanchang 24
9 30N33 105E24 -7:01:36
Hengshanqiao 13
1 31N46 120E07 -8:00:28
Hengshanxia 1 1 30N18 118E44 -7:54:56
Hengshi 5 1 23N52 113E15 -7:33:00
Hengshi 11 1 29N32 114E41 -7:38:44
Hengshi 14 1 26N05 114E38 -7:38:32
Hengshui 8 1 37N43 115E40 -7:42:40
Hengtangshi 13 1 31N41 121E02 -8:04:08
Hengtianchi 24 9 29N07 105E01 -7:00:04
Hengtianxi 24 9 29N05 105E03 -7:00:12
Hengxi 30 1 28N46 120E29 -8:01:56
Hengxi 13 1 31N43 118E46 -7:55:04
Hengxi 30 1 29N42 121E35 -8:06:20
Hengxian 6 9 22N42 109E13 -7:16:52
Hengxiang 13 1 32N12 120E15 -8:01:00
Hengxikou 30 1 29N26 121E26 -8:05:44
Hengyang 12 1 26N54 112E36 -7:30:24
Heping 3 1 27N10 117E18 -7:49:12
Heping 5 10 22N01 112E59 -7:31:56
Heping 5 1 23N17 116E29 -7:45:56
Heping 5 1 24N28 114E58 -7:39:52
Heping 30 1 30N50 119E54 -7:59:36
Hepu (Lianzhou) 6
9 21N39 109E11 -7:16:44
Heqiao 13 1 32N55 118E22 -7:53:28
Heqiao 13 1 31N30 119E53 -7:59:32
Heqing 29 9 26N34 100E12 -6:40:48
Hequ 23 1 39N26 111E08 -7:24:32
Heruncun 16 11 40N58 123E27 -8:13:48
Heshachang 24 9 30N37 105E40 -7:02:40
Heshangqiao 10 1 34N15 113E47 -7:35:08
Heshe 5 9 19N41 109E42 -7:18:48
Heshengqiao 11 1 30N00 114E22 -7:37:28
Heshi 3 1 25N04 118E37 -7:54:28
Heshi 24 9 29N10 104E22 -6:57:28
Heshituoluogai 27
8 46N35 86E01 -5:44:04
Heshui 5 10 22N48 112E29 -7:29:56
Heshui 5 1 24N24 114E56 -7:39:44
Heshuijian 1 1 30N33 116E05 -7:44:20
Heshun 23 1 37N21 113E35 -7:34:20
Heshun 3 1 27N30 117E24 -7:49:36
Heshuo 27 8 42N15 86E53 -5:47:32
Hetai 5 10 23N22 112E19 -7:29:16
Hetanbu 14 1 28N21 117E11 -7:48:44
Hetang 13 1 31N43 120E27 -8:01:48
Hetang 24 9 28N58 106E03 -7:04:12
Hetang 3 1 26N40 119E09 -7:56:36
Hetian 3 1 25N41 116E26 -7:45:44
Hetian 5 1 23N19 115E38 -7:42:32
Hetian 27 7 37N08 79E54 -5:19:36
Hetou 5 1 24N18 113E29 -7:33:56
Hetoudian 21 1 37N02 120E35 -8:02:20
Hetupu 1 1 30N50 116E03 -7:44:12
Hewopu 16 11 41N14 122E24 -8:09:36
Hewu 12 1 26N41 113E40 -7:34:40
Hexi 3 1 24N52 117E15 -7:49:00
Hexi 30 1 31N03 119E49 -7:59:16
Hexi 29 9 24N09 102E39 -6:50:36
Hexian 6 9 24N15 111E43 -7:26:52
Hexian 1 1 31N43 118E22 -7:53:28
Hexibao 4 9 38N34 102E11 -6:48:44
Hexingchang 24 9 30N05 104E35 -6:58:20
Hexingjie 13 1 31N55 120E36 -8:02:24
Hexiwu 26 1 39N38 116E58 -7:47:52
Heyan 17 11 42N30 120E29 -8:01:56
Heyang 20 9 35N15 110E06 -7:20:24
Heyang 21 1 35N27 118E33 -7:54:12
Heyuan 5 1 23N44 114E41 -7:38:44
Heze (Caozhou) 21
1 35N17 115E27 -7:41:48
Hezhang 7 9 27N00 104E37 -6:58:28
Hezhao 8 1 37N08 115E17 -7:41:08
Hezhen 30 1 29N56 120E10 -8:00:40
Hezheng 4 9 35N25 103E10 -6:52:40
Hezijian 2 1 40N13 116E03 -7:44:12
Hezixu 14 1 24N54 115E14 -7:40:56
Hezuo 4 9 34N58 102E57 -6:51:48
Hiaohexi 11 1 31N21 114E02 -7:36:08
Hoboksar 27 8 46N47 85E43 -5:42:52
Hoch'uan → Hechuan 24
9 30N00 106E16 -7:05:04
Ho Chung 31 4 22N22 114E14 -7:36:56
Hofei → Hefei 1
1 31N51 117E17 -7:49:08
Hohhot 17 9 40N51 111E40 -7:26:40
Hoihow → Haikou 5
9 20N03 110E19 -7:21:16
Hokang → Hegang 9
12 47N24 130E17 -8:41:08
Hok So Wan 31 4 22N13 114E14 -7:36:56
Honan → Luoyang 10
1 34N41 112E28 -7:29:52
Hong'an 11 1 31N18 114E37 -7:38:28
Hongchang 10 1 34N05 113E20 -7:33:20
Hongchoudai 30 1 29N03 121E11 -8:04:44
Hongcun 14 1 27N10 116E48 -7:47:12

Hongcun 1 1 31N01 119E15 -7:57:00
Honghe 29 9 23N23 102E35 -6:50:20
Honghu 11 1 29N48 113E27 -7:33:48
Honghuaerji 17 11 48N15 120E01 -8:00:04
Honghuaji 10 1 33N52 114E26 -7:37:44
Honghualiangzi 17 11 48N06 123E12 -8:12:48
Honghuamu 9 12 48N33 125E39 -8:22:36
Hongjiang 12 1 27N07 109E56 -7:19:44
Hongjiang 3 1 26N49 120E03 -8:00:12
Hong Kong → Victoria 31 4 22N17 114E09 -7:36:36
Honglai 3 1 25N08 118E32 -7:54:08
Honglanbu 13 1 31N37 118E57 -7:55:48
Honglinqiao 1 1 30N59 118E59 -7:55:56
Hongliutai 27 7 39N48 77E26 -5:09:44
Hongliuyuan 4 8 41N04 95E26 -6:21:44
Honglongdian 1 1 30N30 119E00 -7:56:00
Honglu 3 1 25N44 119E20 -7:57:20
Hongluan 14 1 28N31 117E01 -7:48:04
Hongluoxian 16 11 41N01 120E53 -8:03:32
Hongmeichang 2 1 39N50 115E51 -7:43:24
Hongmendu 29 9 26N10 102E37 -6:50:28
Hongmenkou 29 9 27N22 100E30 -6:42:00
Hongmenpu 24 9 30N37 104E08 -6:56:32
Hongmiaozi 24 9 28N47 104E02 -6:56:08
Hongpailou 24 9 30N38 104E01 -6:56:04
Hongqi 15 12 44N23 126E32 -8:26:08
Hongqiao 30 1 28N14 121E01 -8:04:04
Hongqiao 22 2 31N29 121E49 -8:07:16
Hongqiao 8 1 39N50 117E44 -7:50:56
Hongqiao 22 2 31N12 121E22 -8:05:28
Hongshan 9 12 48N02 129E00 -8:36:00
Hongshan 21 1 36N37 118E00 -7:52:00
Hongshanzi 17 1 42N34 117E14 -7:48:56
Hongshi 15 12 43N00 127E04 -8:28:16
Hongshi 16 11 41N21 119E32 -7:58:08
Hongshidou 16 11 41N52 122E11 -8:08:44
Hongshili 16 11 40N41 125E03 -8:20:12
Hongshui 4 9 37N24 104E00 -6:56:00
Hongshuichuan 8 1 40N06 117E55 -7:51:40
Hongshuyangzi 2 1 40N36 116E36 -7:46:24
Hongtang 3 1 26N06 119E14 -7:56:56
Hongtian 3 1 25N52 117E15 -7:49:00
Hongtong 23 1 36N19 111E39 -7:26:36
Hongtugou 19 8 38N08 91E10 -6:04:40
Hongtuwan 17 9 41N03 113E39 -7:34:36
Hongxin 1 1 32N43 117E47 -7:51:08
Hongxing 2 1 39N48 116E27 -7:45:48
Hongxingqiao 30 1 30N55 119E52 -7:59:28
Hongyang 3 1 26N32 119E27 -7:57:48
Hongyang 5 1 23N28 116E13 -7:44:52
Hongyanzi 16 11 40N38 120E31 -8:02:04
Hongze 13 1 33N19 118E53 -7:55:32
Hopi → Hebi 10 1 35N59 114E11 -7:36:44
Hoppo → Hepu 6 9 21N39 109E11 -7:16:44
Ho Pui 31 4 22N25 114E03 -7:36:12
Horinger 17 9 40N26 111E55 -7:27:40
Horqin Youyi Qianqi (Ulan Hot) 17 11 46N05 122E05 -8:08:20
Horqin Youyi Zhongqi 17 11 45N09 121E24 -8:05:36
Horqin Zuoyi Houqi 17 11 42N58 122E20 -8:09:20
Horqin Zuoyi Zhongqi 17 11 44N07 123E18 -8:13:12
Houbaishu 13 1 31N49 119E10 -7:56:40
Houbao 16 11 41N54 125E14 -8:20:56
Houcheng 13 1 31N55 120E26 -8:01:44
Houdahepao 16 11 41N49 123E01 -8:12:04
Houguangzhengtai 16 11 41N13 122E07 -8:08:28
Hougujiazi 16 11 42N21 123E22 -8:13:28
Houhuangtukan 16 11 41N02 122E29 -8:09:56
Houjiangfushan 2 1 40N03 117E09 -7:48:36
Houjiaping 24 9 30N02 104E38 -6:58:32
Houjiaying 26 1 39N51 117E15 -7:49:00
Houjie 5 1 22N58 113E39 -7:34:36
Houjiumen 16 11 42N38 123E18 -8:13:12
Houkou 8 1 37N34 115E09 -7:40:36
Houliujia 16 11 40N47 122E19 -8:09:16
Houluan 8 1 39N13 116E32 -7:46:08
Houma 23 1 35N36 111E21 -7:25:24
Houmanzhoutun 16 11 42N29 123E14 -8:12:56
Houmen 5 1 22N51 115E09 -7:40:36
Houqianjiayu 16 11 40N50 120E41 -8:02:44
Houqiao 2 1 40N04 116E39 -7:46:36
Houshan 13 1 31N03 120E21 -8:01:24
Houwuliangdian 16 11 41N31 121E55 -8:07:40
Houwutaigou 16 11 41N46 121E42 -8:06:48
Houxijie 30 1 28N46 118E49 -7:55:16
Houxinlitun 16 11 41N05 122E33 -8:10:12
Houxinqiu 16 11 42N34 122E43 -8:10:52
Houyatai 16 11 41N26 121E49 -8:07:16
Houying 8 1 39N42 118E18 -7:53:12
Houyingzi 16 11 40N24 123E50 -8:15:20
Houzhangcun 2 1 40N08 116E11 -7:44:44
Houzhou 13 1 31N35 119E22 -7:57:28
Houzitun 16 11 41N04 121E18 -8:05:12
Hoxtolgay 27 8 46N35 86E01 -5:44:04
Hsiakuan → Xiaguan 29 9 25N34 100E14 -6:40:56
Hsiamen → Xiamen 3 1 24N28 118E07 -7:52:28
Hsiangt'an → Xiangtan 12 1 27N51 112E54 -7:31:36
Hsiangyang → Xiangfan 11 1 32N03 112E01 -7:28:04
Hsian → Xi'an 20 9 34N15 108E52 -7:15:28
Hsichih 25 6 25N04 121E39 -8:06:36
Hsientung 25 6 25N09 121E44 -8:06:56
Hsienyang → Xianyang 20 9 34N22 108E42 -7:14:48
Hsihu 25 6 23N58 120E28 -8:01:52
Hsilo 25 6 23N48 120E27 -8:01:48
Hsinch'eng 25 6 24N08 121E39 -8:06:36
Hsinchu 25 6 24N48 120E58 -8:03:52
Hsinchuang 25 6 25N02 121E27 -8:05:48
Hsinghua → Xinghua 13 1 32N57 119E50 -7:59:20
Hsingt'ai → Xingtai 8 1 37N04 114E29 -7:37:56
Hsinhailien → Lianyungang 13 1 34N39 119E16 -7:57:04
Hsinhsiang → Xinxiang 10 1 35N20 113E51 -7:35:24
Hsinhua 25 6 23N02 120E18 -8:01:12
Hsining → Xining 19 9 36N38 101E55 -6:47:40
Hsinking → Changchun 15 12 43N53 125E19 -8:21:16
Hsinp'u → Lianyungang 13 1 34N39 119E16 -7:57:04
Hsinshih 25 6 23N05 120E17 -8:01:08
Hsintien 25 6 24N57 121E32 -8:06:08
Hsinyang → Xinyang 10 1 32N08 114E04 -7:36:16
Hsiyü 25 6 23N36 119E30 -7:58:00
Hsüanhua → Xuanhua 8 1 40N37 115E03 -7:40:12
Hsüch'ang → Xuchang 10 1 34N03 113E49 -7:35:16
Hsüchou → Xuzhou 13 1 34N16 117E11 -7:48:44
Hsüehchia 25 6 23N14 120E10 -8:00:40
Hua'an 3 1 25N02 117E34 -7:50:16
Huabu 30 1 29N00 118E20 -7:53:20
Huacao 22 2 31N14 121E19 -8:05:16
Huacheng 5 1 24N04 115E38 -7:42:32
Huachi 4 9 36N43 107E52 -7:11:28
Huade 17 9 41N46 114E16 -7:37:04
Huadian 15 12 42N58 126E43 -8:26:52
Huafeng 13 1 32N14 121E16 -8:05:04
Huagutang 1 1 30N55 119E18 -7:57:12
Huai'an 13 1 33N32 119E10 -7:56:40
Huai'an (Chaigoubu) 8 1 40N39 114E27 -7:37:48
Huaibin 10 1 32N28 115E24 -7:41:36
Huaide 15 12 43N32 124E50 -8:19:20
Huaidezhen 15 12 43N54 124E47 -8:19:08
Huaidezhen 24 9 28N59 105E15 -7:01:00
Huaihuazhenshi 30 1 31N05 119E41 -7:58:44
Huaiji 5 1 24N01 112E18 -7:29:12
Huailai (Shacheng) 8 1 40N23 115E33 -7:42:12
Huailin 1 1 31N26 117E36 -7:50:24
Huainan 1 1 32N40 117E00 -7:48:00
Huaining 1 1 30N25 116E38 -7:46:32
Huairou 2 1 40N19 116E37 -7:46:28
Huaite → Huaide 15 12 43N32 124E50 -8:19:20
Huaiyang 10 1 33N44 114E53 -7:39:32
Huaiyuan 1 1 32N57 117E12 -7:48:48
Huaji 1 1 32N46 115E20 -7:41:20
Huajiang 6 9 25N50 110E21 -7:21:24
Huajianzi 16 11 40N48 122E12 -8:08:48
Huajiapuzi 16 11 40N52 123E14 -8:12:56
Huajiayingzi 16 11 42N20 121E00 -8:04:00
Huakou 3 1 25N13 117E35 -7:50:20
Hualien 25 6 23N59 121E36 -8:06:24
Hualingpuzi 16 11 41N31 123E54 -8:15:36
Hualong 19 9 36N05 102E36 -6:50:24
Huameiao 14 1 26N32 115E47 -7:43:08
Huanan 9 12 46N13 130E32 -8:42:08
Huang'aicun 1 1 31N43 118E40 -7:54:40
Huang'an 21 1 35N28 115E42 -7:42:48
Huang'anshi 12 1 29N06 113E34 -7:34:16
Huangbai 15 12 41N17 126E21 -8:25:24
Huangbaozi 4 9 39N54 99E26 -6:37:44
Huangbeipu 16 11 42N21 123E25 -8:13:40
Huangcaoping 12 1 25N42 113E27 -7:33:48
Huangchong 5 10 22N18 113E03 -7:32:12
Huangchuan 10 1 32N09 115E03 -7:40:12
Huangcun 2 1 39N56 116E11 -7:44:44
Huangdaizhen 13 3 31N26 120E33 -8:02:12
Huangdan 24 9 29N10 103E44 -6:54:56
Huangdi 8 1 40N57 118E24 -7:53:36
Huangdi 16 11 40N14 120E15 -8:01:00
Huangdu 22 2 31N16 121E13 -8:04:52
Huangdu 1 1 30N47 118E51 -7:55:24
Huangduqiao 30 1 29N18 120E55 -8:03:40
Huanggang 11 1 30N27 114E52 -7:39:28
Huanggangji 21 1 34N39 116E03 -7:44:12
Huanggangkou 14 1 28N32 114E33 -7:38:12
Huanggangshi 1 1 33N09 115E55 -7:43:40
Huangguayingzi 16 11 41N46 120E46 -8:03:04
Huangguoshu 7 9 26N02 105E32 -7:02:08
Huanghu 30 1 30N27 119E48 -7:59:12
Huanghua 8 1 38N22 117E21 -7:49:24
Huanghuadianzi 16 11 41N44 122E48 -8:11:12
Huanghuashi 12 1 28N14 113E14 -7:32:56
Huangjialing 16 11 42N12 122E55 -8:11:40
Huangjialu 22 2 31N00 121E45 -8:07:00
Huangjiatun 16 11 41N11 122E54 -8:11:36
Huangjiazhai 13 1 32N01 121E36 -8:06:24
Huangjinbu 14 1 28N27 116E47 -7:47:08
Huangjing 13 1 31N39 121E06 -8:04:24
Huangjinggou 24 9 29N37 104E35 -6:58:20
Huangjinjing 24 9 29N44 104E38 -6:58:32
Huangjinzi 9 12 50N02 127E20 -8:29:20
Huangjuezhen 24 9 29N50 106E27 -7:05:48
Huangkan 2 1 40N22 116E28 -7:45:52
Huangkeng 3 1 27N35 117E39 -7:50:36
Huangkou 27 8 42N46 93E58 -6:15:52
Huanglaomen 14 1 29N30 115E49 -7:43:16
Huangli 13 1 31N39 119E42 -7:58:48
Huanglian 24 9 29N17 106E18 -7:05:12
Huangling 20 9 35N41 109E09 -7:16:36
Huanglingji 11 1 30N25 114E03 -7:36:12
Huanglong 11 1 31N58 112E28 -7:29:52
Huanglong 20 9 35N45 109E42 -7:18:48
Huanglongxi 24 9 30N19 103E58 -6:55:52
Huangmao 14 1 28N07 114E04 -7:36:16
Huangmapi 5 1 23N30 114E33 -7:38:12
Huangmei 11 1 30N04 115E56 -7:43:44
Huangnihe 1 1 31N06 117E22 -7:49:28
Huangnihe 15 12 43N32 127E59 -8:31:56
Huangpi 14 1 26N39 115E51 -7:43:24
Huangpi 11 1 30N53 114E22 -7:37:28
Huangqi 3 1 26N21 119E54 -7:59:36
Huangqiao 13 1 32N15 120E13 -8:00:52
Huangshahe 6 9 26N03 110E58 -7:23:52
Huangshajie 12 1 29N03 113E08 -7:32:32
Huangshan 21 1 36N57 122E18 -8:09:12
Huangshanguan 21 1 37N32 120E16 -8:01:04
Huangshapu 12 1 26N50 113E26 -7:33:44
Huangshapu 12 1 25N08 112E44 -7:30:56
Huangshaqiao 14 1 28N56 114E40 -7:38:40
Huangshatuo 16 11 41N12 122E31 -8:10:04
Huangshi 11 1 30N13 115E05 -7:40:20
Huangshi 12 1 29N00 111E02 -7:24:08
Huangshi 3 1 25N23 119E04 -7:56:16
Huangshidu 14 1 27N44 116E44 -7:46:56
Huangshiguan 14 1 26N15 115E54 -7:43:36
Huangshui 24 9 30N32 103E55 -6:55:40
Huangtan 3 1 26N41 117E17 -7:49:08
Huangtan 30 1 27N44 119E58 -7:59:52
Huangtang 13 1 31N47 119E40 -7:58:40
Huangtang 5 1 23N44 114E58 -7:39:52
Huangtang 13 1 31N46 120E21 -8:01:24
Huangtankou 30 1 28N50 118E53 -7:55:32
Huangtantuan 11 1 30N53 113E33 -7:34:12
Huangtian 5 1 23N52 114E58 -7:39:52
Huangtianfan 30 1 29N10 120E08 -8:00:32
Huangtu 13 1 31N52 120E03 -8:00:12
Huangtu 3 1 27N36 118E00 -7:52:00
Huangtuchang 24 9 30N41 104E18 -6:57:12
Huangtugang 11 1 31N25 115E05 -7:40:20
Huangtukan 16 11 41N21 122E45 -8:11:00
Huangtuliangzi 8 1 41N14 118E39 -7:54:36
Huangtuling 12 1 27N18 113E30 -7:34:00
Huangtupo 2 1 39N47 116E16 -7:45:04
Huangwan 30 1 30N22 120E48 -8:03:12
Huangxian 21 1 37N38 120E29 -8:01:56
Huangxu 13 1 32N06 119E37 -7:58:28
Huangyaguan 26 1 40N14 117E26 -7:49:44
Huangyan 30 1 28N39 121E15 -8:05:00
Huangyanzhuang 8 1 40N01 118E21 -7:53:24
Huangyuan 19 9 36N40 101E12 -6:44:48
Huangyuzeng 16 11 42N05 124E11 -8:16:44
Huangze 30 1 29N35 120E55 -8:03:40
Huangzhai 30 1 29N27 120E00 -8:00:00
Huangzhong 19 9 36N31 101E40 -6:46:40
Huangzhu 5 9 19N29 110E24 -7:21:36
Huangzhuang 8 1 39N53 117E05 -7:48:20
Huangzhuang 10 1 34N05 112E15 -7:29:00
Huangzhuang 26 1 39N29 117E31 -7:50:04
Huaning 29 9 24N14 102E56 -6:51:44
Huaniugouzi 16 11 41N34 122E35 -8:10:20
Huaniupuzi 16 11 41N23 123E31 -8:14:04
Huanjiang 6 9 24N54 108E21 -7:13:24
Huanren 16 11 41N14 125E21 -8:21:24
Huantai (Suozhen) 21 1 36N59 118E06 -7:52:24
Huantan 11 1 31N49 113E04 -7:32:16
Huanxi 12 1 26N34 113E36 -7:34:24
Huanxian 4 9 36N39 107E18 -7:09:12
Huanxiling 16 11 41N17 123E54 -8:15:36
Huaqiao 30 1 28N56 121E27 -8:05:48
Huaqiao 14 1 29N32 117E11 -7:48:44
Huaqiao 24 9 30N28 103E52 -6:55:28
Huaqiao 12 1 27N28 110E02 -7:20:08
Huaqiaozhen 24 9 30N47 106E41 -7:06:44
Huarong 12 1 29N30 112E34 -7:30:16
Huashan 13 1 34N39 116E44 -7:46:56
Huashaoying 8 1 40N12 114E36 -7:38:24

Huashi 13 1 31N50 120E28 -8:01:52
Huatangpu 12 1 25N48 112E52 -7:31:28
Huating 4 9 35N09 106E38 -7:06:32
Huatong 16 11 40N03 121E56 -8:07:44
Huatong 6 9 23N01 106E36 -7:06:24
Huaxian (Daokou) 10 1 35N37 114E32 -7:38:08
Huaxian 20 9 34N30 109E40 -7:18:40
Huaxian 5 1 23N22 113E12 -7:32:48
Huayan 24 9 30N01 105E02 -7:00:08
Huayang 24 9 30N32 104E04 -6:56:16
Huayangzhen 20 9 33N25 107E44 -7:10:56
Huayingtai 16 11 40N43 122E19 -8:09:16
Huayuan 15 12 42N17 127E07 -8:28:28
Huayuan 12 1 28N34 109E13 -7:16:52
Huayuan 11 1 31N16 113E58 -7:35:52
Huayuanzui 13 1 33N00 118E16 -7:53:04
Huazhou 5 8 21N40 110E33 -7:22:12
Huazi 16 11 41N25 123E29 -8:13:56
Huazigou 16 11 41N50 121E01 -8:04:04
Huazikou 1 1 32N13 118E57 -7:55:48
Hubuleng 17 9 41N19 111E08 -7:24:32
Hucaogang 13 1 32N00 120E29 -8:01:56
Hucheng 3 1 25N26 118E27 -7:53:48
Huchi 1 1 31N08 117E40 -7:50:40
Huchow → Huzhou 30 1 30N52 120E06 -8:00:24
Hucun 8 1 39N02 115E56 -7:43:44
Hudangtou 22 2 30N48 121E22 -8:05:28
Huder 17 11 50N00 121E37 -8:06:28
Hudong 5 1 22N51 115E56 -7:43:44
Huerlumada 28 8 32N45 90E00 -6:00:00
Hufengzhen 24 9 29N43 106E07 -7:04:28
Hufu 13 1 31N16 119E47 -7:59:08
Hugou 1 1 33N23 117E08 -7:48:32
Huhehot → Hohhot 17 9 40N51 111E40 -7:26:40
Huhsi 25 6 23N35 119E39 -7:58:36
Hui'an 3 1 25N04 118E47 -7:55:08
Huian 22 2 31N47 121E45 -8:07:00
Huibu 14 1 28N18 115E15 -7:41:00
Huichang 14 1 25N34 115E49 -7:43:16
Huichang 8 1 39N04 115E04 -7:40:16
Huichou → Huizhou 5 1 23N05 114E24 -7:37:36
Huichuan 4 9 35N11 104E02 -6:56:08
Huidong 24 9 26N41 102E36 -6:50:24
Huidui 26 1 39N04 117E16 -7:49:04
Huihe 17 11 48N12 119E17 -7:57:08
Huihe 13 1 31N45 121E43 -8:06:52
Huilai 5 1 23N04 116E18 -7:45:12
Huili 24 9 26N43 102E10 -6:48:40
Huiliuji 1 1 32N50 115E58 -7:43:52
Huilong 24 9 30N35 105E49 -7:03:16
Huilong 3 1 27N30 118E24 -7:53:36
Huilong 3 1 25N22 116E24 -7:45:36
Huilong 5 1 24N09 113E58 -7:35:52
Huilong 24 9 30N28 105E26 -7:01:44
Huilongchang 24 9 30N41 106E34 -7:06:16
Huilongchang 24 9 29N17 105E01 -7:00:04
Huilongchang 24 9 29N41 104E17 -6:57:08
Huilongchang 24 9 30N18 103E39 -6:54:36
Huimin 21 1 37N29 117E29 -7:49:56
Huinan (Chaoyang) 15 12 42N40 126E00 -8:24:00
Huining 4 9 35N41 105E08 -7:00:32
Huishan 13 1 31N35 120E16 -8:01:04
Huishui 7 9 26N07 106E24 -7:05:36
Huiting 10 1 34N05 116E04 -7:44:16
Huitong 12 1 26N54 109E31 -7:18:04
Huitongqiao 29 9 24N43 98E56 -6:35:44
Huixian 4 9 33N47 106E16 -7:05:04
Huiyang → Huizhou 5 1 23N05 114E24 -7:37:36
Huiyao 3 1 27N16 118E05 -7:52:20
Huize 29 9 26N27 103E09 -6:52:36
Huizhou 5 1 23N05 114E24 -7:37:36
Hujia 22 2 31N25 121E37 -8:06:28
Hujia 16 11 41N20 121E52 -8:07:28
Hujiadian 24 9 29N41 104E07 -6:56:28
Hujiajie 16 11 41N06 122E10 -8:08:40
Hujiasi 24 9 29N16 105E13 -7:00:52
Hujiawopu 16 11 42N34 122E11 -8:08:44
Hujiayu 8 1 39N28 115E27 -7:41:48
Hujiazhuang 8 1 39N51 117E07 -7:48:28
Hujiazhuang 22 2 31N21 121E25 -8:05:40
Hujie 29 9 24N56 100E32 -6:42:08
Hukeng 14 1 27N29 114E18 -7:37:12
Hukou 14 1 29N45 116E13 -7:44:52
Hulan 9 12 46N00 126E38 -8:26:32
Hulan Ergi 9 12 47N13 123E39 -8:14:36
Hulei 3 1 24N50 116E48 -7:47:12
Hulin 9 12 45N46 132E59 -8:51:56
Huludao 16 11 40N43 121E00 -8:04:00
Hulufa 2 1 39N42 116E12 -7:44:48
Hulun → Hailaer 17 11 49N12 119E42 -7:58:48
Huluyu 2 1 40N14 116E53 -7:47:32
Huma 9 12 51N43 126E38 -8:26:32
Humayingzi 8 1 41N06 116E48 -7:47:12
Hunchun 15 12 42N54 130E22 -8:41:28
Hungchiang → Hongjiang 12 1 27N07 109E56 -7:19:44
Hungmao 25 6 24N55 120E58 -8:03:52
Hunhe 16 11 41N43 123E22 -8:13:28
Hunjiang (Badaojiang) 15 12 41N56 126E29 -8:25:56
Hunyuan 23 1 39N48 113E41 -7:34:44
Huocheng 27 7 44N12 80E26 -5:21:44
Huoergeluo 17 11 45N35 120E56 -8:03:44
Huokou 3 1 26N28 119E16 -7:57:04
Huolong 13 1 32N04 121E17 -8:05:08
Huolongmen 9 12 49N48 125E47 -8:23:08
Huolu 8 1 38N05 114E18 -7:37:12
Huoqiu 1 1 32N20 116E16 -7:45:04
Huorili 17 11 49N00 124E41 -8:18:44
Huoshan 1 1 31N25 116E20 -7:45:20
Huoshaoliao 25 6 25N00 121E45 -8:07:00
Huotong 3 1 26N53 119E25 -7:57:40
Huotuolaihuduke 17 9 40N19 104E18 -6:57:12
Huoxian 23 1 36N37 111E40 -7:26:40
Huoxian 2 1 39N46 116E46 -7:47:04
Huoyan 10 1 33N42 113E40 -7:34:40
Huqiao 13 1 31N25 119E24 -7:57:36
Hure Qi 17 11 42N44 121E40 -8:06:40
Hushan 5 1 22N09 113E10 -7:32:40
Hushan 9 12 45N35 130E35 -8:42:20
Hushan 30 1 28N36 118E59 -7:55:56
Hushi 24 9 28N57 105E22 -7:01:28
Hushitai 16 11 41N57 123E30 -8:14:00
Hushu 13 1 31N52 118E59 -7:55:56
Hushu 30 3 30N18 120E08 -8:00:32
Hutangqiao 13 1 31N46 119E57 -7:59:48
Hutou 3 1 25N15 118E03 -7:52:12
Hutou 3 1 26N04 118E46 -7:55:04
Hutou 13 1 31N37 119E37 -7:58:28
Hutou 13 1 32N14 120E17 -8:01:08
Hutouya 21 1 37N13 119E46 -7:59:04
Hutubi 27 8 44N07 86E57 -5:47:48
Huwan 10 1 31N41 114E53 -7:39:32
Huwei 25 6 23N43 120E26 -8:01:44
Huxi 14 1 26N12 114E44 -7:38:56
Huxian 20 9 34N09 108E32 -7:14:08
Huyangzhen 10 1 32N25 112E45 -7:31:00
Huyuesi 1 1 30N23 118E45 -7:55:00
Huyutou 3 1 26N44 119E49 -7:59:16
Huzhen 30 1 28N50 120E15 -8:01:00
Huzhou 30 1 30N52 120E06 -8:00:24
Huzhu 19 9 37N00 102E00 -6:48:00
Huzhuangtun 16 11 40N43 122E33 -8:10:12
Huzi 11 1 30N56 113E42 -7:34:48
Hwaian 13 1 33N32 119E10 -7:56:40
Hwainan → Huainan 1 1 32N40 117E00 -7:48:00
Hwaining → Anqing 1 1 30N31 117E02 -7:48:08
Hwangshih → Huangshi 11 1 30N13 115E05 -7:40:20
Ichang → Yichang 11 1 30N42 111E17 -7:25:08
Ich'un → Yichun 9 12 47N42 128E55 -8:35:40
Ih Tal 17 11 43N13 122E15 -8:09:00
Ilan 25 6 24N46 121E45 -8:07:00
Ining → Yining 27 7 43N54 81E21 -5:25:24
Ipin → Yibin 24 9 28N47 104E38 -6:58:32
Iyang → Yiyang 12 1 28N36 112E20 -7:29:20
Jainca 19 9 35N59 102E02 -6:48:08
Jalaid Qi 17 11 46N40 122E55 -8:11:40
Jargalang 17 11 43N06 122E54 -8:11:36
Jarud Qi 17 11 44N37 120E58 -8:03:52
Jehol → Chengde 8 1 40N58 117E53 -7:51:32
Jeminary 27 8 47N32 85E38 -5:42:32
Jenli 25 6 23N15 120E08 -8:00:32
Jiaban 7 9 25N38 107E07 -7:08:28
Jiaban 6 9 25N10 107E03 -7:08:12
Jiacha 28 8 29N11 92E44 -6:10:56
Jiading 22 2 31N23 121E15 -8:05:00
Jiagedan 17 11 51N35 120E55 -8:03:40
Jiahashitai 17 11 46N25 122E17 -8:09:08
Jiahe 12 1 25N43 112E05 -7:28:20
Jiajiachang 24 9 30N26 104E21 -6:57:24
Jiajiachang 24 9 29N44 105E06 -7:00:24
Jiajiagou 16 11 42N20 121E46 -8:07:04
Jiajiagou 16 11 41N44 120E58 -8:03:52
Jiajiang 24 9 29N45 103E34 -6:54:16
Jiajiayuan 13 1 32N18 120E55 -8:03:40
Jiakou 30 1 30N10 119E03 -7:56:12
Jiali 28 8 30N47 93E24 -6:13:36
Jialou 10 1 32N54 113E26 -7:33:44
Jialu 1 1 30N26 118E50 -7:55:20
Jiamingzhen 24 9 29N16 105E20 -7:01:20
Jiamusi (Kiamusze) 9 12 46N50 130E21 -8:41:24
Jiamuyingzi 16 11 41N56 121E43 -8:06:52
Ji'an 15 12 41N06 126E08 -8:24:32
Ji'an 14 1 27N07 114E58 -7:39:52
Jian'an 15 12 43N04 125E03 -8:20:12
Jianba 13 1 31N59 120E35 -8:02:20
Jianbi 13 1 32N11 119E35 -7:58:20
Ji'anchang 24 9 30N31 106E02 -7:04:08
Jianchang 16 11 40N51 119E46 -7:59:04
Jianchang 16 11 39N58 122E35 -8:10:20
Jianchang 16 11 41N16 124E29 -8:17:56
Jianchangying 8 1 40N06 118E49 -7:55:16
Jianchapu 8 1 39N06 116E31 -7:46:04
Jianchaxi 24 9 30N22 104E03 -6:56:12
Jianchaxi 7 9 28N08 108E04 -7:12:16
Jianchuan 29 9 26N34 99E53 -6:39:32
Jiande 30 1 29N29 119E16 -7:57:04
Jiang'an 24 9 28N44 105E05 -7:00:20
Jiangba 13 1 33N08 118E45 -7:55:00
Jiangbei (Lianglukou) 24 9 29N44 106E38 -7:06:32
Jiangbeixu 14 1 26N20 115E26 -7:41:44
Jiangbian 29 9 24N03 103E37 -6:54:28
Jiangbianzhai 29 9 23N49 100E11 -6:40:44
Jiangcheng 8 1 38N52 115E22 -7:41:28
Jiangcheng 29 9 22N40 101E48 -6:47:12
Jiangcun 14 1 28N17 117E49 -7:51:16
Jiangdihe 29 9 25N55 101E31 -6:46:04
Jiangdu 13 1 32N26 119E34 -7:58:16
Jiangduo 13 1 32N22 120E15 -8:01:00
Jiange 24 9 32N06 105E29 -7:01:56
Jianggeer 27 7 36N41 76E07 -5:04:28
Jianghua (Shuikou) 12 1 24N58 111E38 -7:26:32
Jianghuaqiao 13 1 32N05 120E00 -8:00:00
Jiangji 10 1 32N19 115E44 -7:42:56
Jiangjia 13 1 31N58 121E28 -8:05:52
Jiangjia 13 1 31N40 121E09 -8:04:36
Jiangjiadian 16 11 41N41 121E03 -8:04:12
Jiangjiagou 16 11 41N44 121E44 -8:06:56
Jiangjiaji 10 1 31N59 115E16 -7:41:04
Jiangjiatun 16 11 41N42 122E25 -8:09:40
Jiangjiatun 16 11 41N42 122E02 -8:08:08
Jiangjin 24 9 29N17 106E16 -7:05:04
Jiangjing 3 1 25N34 119E25 -7:57:40
Jiangjunmiao 27 8 44N43 90E05 -6:00:20
Jiangjunqiao 24 9 31N18 100E55 -6:43:40
Jiangkou 14 1 27N44 114E49 -7:39:16
Jiangkou 20 9 33N39 107E12 -7:08:48
Jiangkou 11 1 29N38 110E20 -7:21:20
Jiangkou 30 1 29N43 121E25 -8:05:40
Jiangkou 3 1 27N27 118E03 -7:52:12
Jiangkou 3 1 25N29 119E12 -7:56:48
Jiangkou 14 1 27N21 115E31 -7:42:04
Jiangkou 6 9 23N31 110E17 -7:21:08
Jiangkou 7 9 27N37 108E48 -7:15:12
Jiangkou 11 1 30N26 111E42 -7:26:48
Jiangkou 24 9 30N14 103E55 -6:55:40
Jiangkouji 1 1 32N50 116E16 -7:45:04
Jiangkoutang 12 1 27N30 112E44 -7:30:56
Jiangle 3 1 26N42 117E25 -7:49:40
Jiangliadian 8 1 42N33 117E27 -7:49:48
Jiangling 11 1 30N20 112E06 -7:28:24
Jianglingxi 24 9 31N28 107E13 -7:08:52
Jiangmen 5 1 22N35 113E05 -7:32:20
Jiangmifeng 15 12 43N58 126E45 -8:27:00
Jiangning 1 3 31N58 118E50 -7:55:20
Jiangpu 13 1 32N04 118E37 -7:54:28
Jiangqiao 9 12 46N48 123E45 -8:15:00
Jiangqiaotou 30 1 30N37 120E38 -8:02:32
Jiangshan 30 1 28N45 118E37 -7:54:28
Jiangshe 13 1 31N34 120E08 -8:00:32
Jiangshui 8 1 37N13 113E59 -7:35:56
Jiangtian 3 1 25N52 119E34 -7:58:16
Jiangtun 16 11 41N37 122E22 -8:09:28
Jiangtun 5 1 23N41 112E37 -7:30:28
Jiangwakou 26 1 39N31 117E42 -7:50:48
Jiangwan 22 2 31N18 121E29 -8:05:56
Jiangwan 14 1 29N25 118E02 -7:52:08
Jiangxi 29 9 22N51 101E50 -6:47:20
Jiangxiacun 13 1 31N44 121E50 -8:07:20
Jiangxiang 1 1 32N16 117E37 -7:50:28
Jiangxikou 3 1 27N36 118E23 -7:53:32
Jiangya 12 1 29N17 110E39 -7:22:36
Jiangyi 14 1 29N12 115E46 -7:43:04
Jiangyin 13 1 31N55 120E16 -8:01:04
Jiangyou 24 9 31N47 104E45 -6:59:00
Jiangyu 21 1 36N16 118E40 -7:54:40
Jiangyu 12 1 27N50 112E46 -7:31:04
Jiangyuanzhen 24 9 30N35 103E48 -6:55:12
Jiangzaogang 13 1 32N01 121E03 -8:04:12
Jiangzhasiji 28 8 30N28 88E55 -5:55:40
Jiangzhong 28 8 29N10 93E32 -6:14:08
Jiangzi 28 8 28N57 89E35 -5:58:20
Jianhe 26 1 39N14 118E03 -7:52:12
Jianhe 7 9 26N27 108E33 -7:14:12
Jianhu 13 1 33N28 119E50 -7:59:20
Jianli 11 1 29N49 112E53 -7:31:32
Jianling 10 1 32N45 113E12 -7:32:48
Jianning 3 1 26N50 116E49 -7:47:16
Jian'ou 3 1 27N03 118E19 -7:53:16
Jianping (Yebaishou) 16 11 41N24 119E37 -7:58:28
Jianqiao 30 3 30N20 120E12 -8:00:48
Jianqigou 16 11 40N54 123E17 -8:13:08
Jianshan 30 1 29N58 120E16 -8:01:04
Jianshan 30 1 29N14 120E44 -8:02:56
Jianshi 11 1 30N36 109E38 -7:18:32
Jianshui 29 9 23N38 102E49 -6:51:16
Jiantiao 30 1 29N04 121E36 -8:06:24
Jiantou 8 1 39N26 115E41 -7:42:44
Jiantouji 21 1 34N35 117E34 -7:50:16
Jianyang 24 9 30N24 104E32 -6:58:08
Jianyang 13 1 33N27 119E40 -7:58:40
Jianyang 3 1 27N22 118E04 -7:52:16
Jiaocheng 23 1 37N33 112E02 -7:28:08
Jiaodao 2 1 39N39 116E06 -7:44:24
Jiaodianzi 16 11 41N32 121E49 -8:07:16
Jiaodonggou 16 11 40N50 123E58 -8:15:52
Jiaohe 8 1 38N01 116E17 -7:45:08
Jiaohe 15 12 43N42 127E19 -8:29:16
Jiaojiapuzi 16 11 40N47 123E48 -8:15:12

Jiaoling 5 1 24N41 116E10 -7:44:40
Jiaomei 3 1 24N32 117E54 -7:51:36
Jiaonan (Wanggezhuang) 21
1 35N51 119E59 -7:59:56
Jiaoshanhe 11 1 29N38 112E33 -7:30:12
Jiaoxi 13 1 31N49 120E10 -8:00:40
Jiaoxian 21 1 36N18 119E58 -7:59:52
Jiaoyang 30 1 27N56 119E16 -7:57:04
Jiaozhuang 10 1 33N14 114E02 -7:36:08
Jiaozuo 10 1 35N15 113E13 -7:32:52
Jiapu 30 1 31N06 119E56 -7:59:44
Jiashan 30 1 30N51 120E54 -8:03:36
Jiashan 1 1 32N47 118E00 -7:52:00
Jiashi 27 7 39N28 76E45 -5:07:00
Jiasi 24 9 29N06 106E24 -7:05:36
Jiatan 24 9 30N12 106E29 -7:05:56
Jiatanchang 24 9 29N09 106E16 -7:05:04
Jiawang 13 1 34N27 117E27 -7:49:48
Jiaxian 10 1 33N58 113E13 -7:32:52
Jiaxian 20 9 38N01 110E31 -7:22:04
Jiaxiang 21 1 35N25 116E21 -7:45:24
Jiaxing 30 1 30N46 120E45 -8:03:00
Jiayin 9 12 48N53 130E24 -8:41:36
Jiayu 11 1 29N58 113E55 -7:35:40
Jiaze 13 1 31N42 119E47 -7:59:08
Jiazhai 10 1 34N33 115E48 -7:43:12
Jiazhuang 26 1 39N19 117E22 -7:49:28
Jiazi 5 1 22N55 116E04 -7:44:16
Jiazier 27 7 38N40 76E33 -5:06:12
Jicheng 8 1 39N23 116E17 -7:45:08
Jidingxilin 28 8 32N52 92E21 -6:09:24
Jiebu 14 1 28N15 115E02 -7:40:08
Jiedong 12 1 26N02 113E00 -7:32:00
Jiegou 1 1 33N21 117E55 -7:51:40
Jiehe 21 1 35N16 117E04 -7:48:16
Jieji 13 1 33N33 118E24 -7:53:36
Jiejiang 13 1 31N58 120E43 -8:02:52
Jiejinkou 9 12 47N57 132E50 -8:51:20
Jielingkou 8 1 40N09 119E15 -7:57:00
Jielongchang 24
9 29N13 106E32 -7:06:08
Jiemian 3 1 25N56 118E02 -7:52:08
Jiepai 24 9 29N28 104E43 -6:58:52
Jiepai 12 1 26N41 112E46 -7:31:04
Jiepai 14 1 29N34 115E06 -7:40:24
Jiepai 1 1 30N55 119E32 -7:58:08
Jiepaiji 1 1 32N15 117E50 -7:51:20
Jiesheng 5 1 22N45 115E25 -7:41:40
Jieshi 24 9 29N27 105E17 -7:01:08
Jieshi 5 1 22N51 115E49 -7:43:16
Jieshou 13 1 33N00 119E27 -7:57:48
Jieshou 1 1 33N18 115E20 -7:41:20
Jieshou 3 1 27N22 117E40 -7:50:40
Jiexi 5 1 23N28 115E56 -7:43:44
Jiexiu 23 1 37N05 111E51 -7:27:24
Jieyang 5 1 23N35 116E21 -7:45:24
Jiezhongdian 10
1 32N41 112E29 -7:29:56
Jigongying 7 9 26N18 104E48 -6:59:12
Jigongzhen 10 1 34N02 115E32 -7:42:08
Jiguanshan 16 11 41N18 123E36 -8:14:24
Jiguanshan 16 11 40N32 123E55 -8:15:40
Jiguanshan 16 11 42N08 124E15 -8:17:00
Jigzhi 19 9 33N28 101E29 -6:45:56
Jihe 11 1 32N15 112E48 -7:31:12
Jiheier 27 7 38N11 75E46 -5:03:04
Jijiadianzi 21 1 35N31 118E59 -7:55:56
Jijiamiao 24 9 29N18 104E06 -6:56:24
Jijiapuzi 16 11 41N16 124E12 -8:16:48
Jijiashi 13 1 32N08 120E18 -8:01:12
Jijiaying 8 1 40N20 115E24 -7:41:36
Jike 24 9 31N00 99E41 -6:38:44
Jilalin 17 11 51N19 119E55 -7:59:40
Jilantai 17 9 39N47 105E45 -7:03:00
Jilemutu 17 11 52N14 120E47 -8:03:08
Jilibulake 19 8 33N05 93E10 -6:12:40
Jilin (Kirin) 15
12 43N51 126E33 -8:26:12
Jilong 28 8 28N29 85E20 -5:41:20
Jimei 3 1 24N37 118E07 -7:52:28
Jimingcun 8 1 39N19 116E09 -7:44:36
Jiminghe 11 1 30N36 115E32 -7:42:08
Jimo 21 1 36N23 120E27 -8:01:48
Jimsar 27 8 44N00 89E04 -5:56:16
Jimuganayaji 27
7 38N36 75E39 -5:02:36
Jimusaer 27 8 44N00 89E04 -5:56:16
Jinan (Tsinan) 21
1 36N40 116E57 -7:47:48
Jin'an 30 1 28N38 119E18 -7:57:12
Jinbang 3 1 25N01 118E01 -7:52:04
Jincang 15 12 43N20 130E30 -8:42:00
Jinchanggouliang 17
11 41N56 120E19 -8:01:16
Jincheng 16 11 41N12 121E25 -8:05:40
Jincheng 23 1 35N30 112E50 -7:31:20
Jinchengshai 12
1 26N43 111E00 -7:24:00
Jinchuan 24 9 31N25 102E08 -6:48:32
Jinchuanqiao 24
9 27N18 101E48 -6:47:12
Jincun 30 1 31N08 119E49 -7:59:16
Jindaichang 24 9 29N43 104E49 -6:59:16
Jinfeng 3 1 26N01 119E36 -7:58:24
Jinfosi 4 9 39N29 99E00 -6:36:00
Jing'an 14 1 28N52 115E20 -7:41:20
Jin'gangpo 24 9 29N38 106E25 -7:05:40
Jingangtou 12 1 27N54 113E40 -7:34:40
Jingangtuo 24 9 29N10 106E07 -7:04:28
Jing'anji 13 1 34N30 116E55 -7:47:40
Jingbian 20 9 37N25 108E21 -7:13:24
Jingcheng 3 1 24N36 117E30 -7:50:00
Jingde 1 1 30N19 118E31 -7:54:04
Jingdezhen (Kingtechen) 14
1 29N16 117E11 -7:48:44

Jingdong 29 9 24N28 100E52 -6:43:28
Jingeryu 2 1 39N43 115E36 -7:42:24
Jinggang 12 1 28N28 112E46 -7:31:04
Jinggangshan 14
1 26N36 114E05 -7:36:20
Jinggongqiao 14
1 29N45 117E11 -7:48:44
Jinggu 29 9 23N32 100E41 -6:42:44
Jingguanzhen 24
9 29N55 106E33 -7:06:12
Jinghai 26 1 38N56 116E55 -7:47:40
Jinghai 5 1 23N03 116E31 -7:46:04
Jinghaiwei 21 1 36N52 122E13 -8:08:52
Jinghe 27 8 44N39 82E50 -5:31:20
Jinghong 29 9 22N01 100E49 -6:43:16
Jinghuiling 8 1 40N22 117E27 -7:49:48
Jingjiang 13 1 32N01 120E15 -8:01:00
Jingjiang 29 9 26N19 100E33 -6:42:12
Jingjiayu 16 11 41N40 123E51 -8:15:24
Jinglou 10 1 32N39 112E56 -7:31:44
Jingmen 11 1 31N00 112E09 -7:28:36
Jingning 30 1 27N59 119E38 -7:58:32
Jingning 18 9 35N25 105E56 -7:03:44
Jingou 16 11 41N38 120E35 -8:02:20
Jingoutun 8 1 41N03 117E27 -7:49:48
Jingshan 11 1 31N02 113E05 -7:32:20
Jingtai 4 9 37N17 104E09 -6:56:36
Jingu 3 1 25N13 118E07 -7:52:28
Jingxi 6 9 23N08 106E29 -7:05:56
Jingxian 8 1 37N42 116E16 -7:45:04
Jingxian 12 1 26N40 109E25 -7:17:40
Jingxian 1 1 30N42 118E24 -7:53:36
Jingxin 5 1 24N14 115E56 -7:43:44
Jingxing 8 1 38N02 114E08 -7:36:32
Jingxing 9 12 47N04 123E01 -8:12:04
Jingyan 24 9 29N40 104E04 -6:56:16
Jingyu 15 12 42N22 126E50 -8:27:20
Jingyuan 18 9 35N30 106E48 -7:07:12
Jingyuan 4 9 36N38 104E37 -6:58:28
Jingzhi 21 1 36N19 119E23 -7:57:32
Jingzichang 24 9 29N00 104E41 -6:58:44
Jinhu 13 1 33N00 119E02 -7:56:08
Jinhua 30 1 29N07 119E39 -7:58:36
Jinhui 22 2 30N59 121E29 -8:05:56
Jining 21 1 35N25 116E36 -7:46:24
Jining 17 9 40N57 113E02 -7:32:08
Jinjiadian 17 11 41N39 118E18 -7:53:12
Jinjiang 3 1 24N50 118E35 -7:54:20
Jinjiangjie 29 9 26N19 100E33 -6:42:12
Jinjiawopeng 16
11 41N38 122E16 -8:09:04
Jinjiawopu 16 11 42N32 122E10 -8:08:40
Jinjiazhen 16 11 42N49 123E40 -8:14:40
Jinjing 3 1 24N37 118E36 -7:54:24
Jinjing 12 1 28N31 113E25 -7:33:40
Jinkeng 3 1 27N15 117E14 -7:48:56
Jinkou 21 1 36N35 120E46 -8:03:04
Jinkou 11 1 30N22 114E10 -7:36:40
Jinkou 14 1 29N18 115E15 -7:41:00
Jinkuang 24 9 28N20 101E54 -6:47:36
Jinlijing 24 9 29N48 104E45 -6:59:00
Jinlingsi 16 11 41N42 120E49 -8:03:16
Jinlingyu 26 1 40N06 117E32 -7:50:08
Jinlingzhen 21 1 36N49 118E11 -7:52:44
Jinlonggou 9 12 51N45 125E51 -8:23:24
Jinning 29 9 24N41 102E35 -6:50:20
Jinniu 11 1 29N59 114E38 -7:38:32
Jinniu 1 1 31N24 117E12 -7:48:48
Jinping 29 9 22N50 103E10 -6:52:40
Jinping 7 9 26N38 109E03 -7:16:12
Jinpingchang 24
9 28N54 104E43 -6:58:52
Jinpo 8 1 39N18 115E15 -7:41:00
Jinqiao 1 1 31N46 116E50 -7:47:20
Jinrui 14 1 27N57 114E12 -7:36:48
Jinsha 13 1 32N06 121E05 -8:04:20
Jinsha 7 9 27N18 106E10 -7:04:40
Jinsha 3 1 26N12 118E39 -7:54:36
Jinshan 22 2 30N54 121E09 -8:04:36
Jinshan 9 12 51N51 126E30 -8:26:00
Jinshanwei 22 2 30N44 121E19 -8:05:16
Jinshanxiang 24
9 30N35 104E52 -6:59:28
Jinshanzui 22 2 30N44 121E22 -8:05:28
Jinshi 12 1 29N39 111E52 -7:27:28
Jinshijing 24 9 29N23 104E08 -6:56:32
Jinshuzhen 13 1 31N23 120E24 -8:01:36
Jinsiniangqiao 30
1 30N43 121E15 -8:05:00
Jinta 4 9 40N03 98E53 -6:35:32
Jintan 13 1 31N45 119E34 -7:58:16
Jintang 24 9 30N19 102E19 -6:49:16
Jintang 24 9 30N54 104E19 -6:57:16
Jintian 14 1 27N10 114E27 -7:37:48
Jinxi 16 11 40N45 120E50 -8:03:20
Jinxi 14 1 27N54 116E43 -7:46:52
Jinxian (Dalinghe) 16
11 41N11 121E22 -8:05:28
Jinxian 14 1 28N22 116E14 -7:44:56
Jinxian 8 1 38N02 115E02 -7:40:08
Jinxian 16 11 39N04 121E40 -8:06:40
Jinxiang 21 1 35N05 116E18 -7:45:12
Jinxiang 30 1 27N26 120E35 -8:02:20
Jinyun 30 1 28N40 120E03 -8:00:12
Jinze 13 1 31N02 120E56 -8:03:44
Jinzhai 1 1 31N44 115E54 -7:43:36
Jinzhaizhen 1 1 31N32 115E46 -7:43:04
Jinzhen 13 1 33N39 118E17 -7:53:08
Jinzhou (Chinchou) 16
11 41N07 121E08 -8:04:32
Jinzisi 24 9 29N09 106E22 -7:05:28
Jishou 12 1 28N17 109E29 -7:17:56
Jishui 10 1 33N46 115E24 -7:41:36
Jishui 14 1 27N14 115E06 -7:40:24
Jitai 27 8 44N01 89E28 -5:57:52

Jitan 14 1 24N56 115E43 -7:42:52
Jitianzhen 24 9 30N19 104E01 -6:56:04
Jituo 28 7 34N15 82E05 -5:28:20
Jiubao 14 1 25N57 115E48 -7:43:12
Jiubingtai 16 11 41N39 124E07 -8:16:28
Jiucheng 8 1 39N23 116E44 -7:46:56
Jiucheng 8 1 38N12 117E18 -7:49:12
Jiuchuchang 24 9 29N55 104E38 -6:58:32
Jiudaoliang 11 1 31N35 110E12 -7:20:48
Jiudian 13 1 32N10 120E57 -8:03:48
Jiudongle 4 9 38N49 101E05 -6:44:20
Jiudu 30 1 30N31 119E53 -7:59:32
Jiufanxian 10 1 35N51 115E41 -7:42:44
Jiufeng 3 1 25N33 119E08 -7:56:32
Jiufeng 3 1 24N20 117E02 -7:48:08
Jiugang 8 1 39N03 116E12 -7:44:48
Jiugongan 11 1 29N52 112E00 -7:28:00
Jiugongkou 8 1 39N50 114E43 -7:38:52
Jiuguan 30 1 30N51 120E16 -8:01:04
Jiuguan 21 1 37N26 121E53 -8:07:32
Jiuguantao 8 1 36N40 115E25 -7:41:40
Jiuhe 5 1 23N32 115E04 -7:40:16
Jiuhongshui 4 9 37N14 103E57 -6:55:48
Jiuhu 21 1 37N03 117E36 -7:50:24
Jiuhuai'an 8 1 40N24 114E31 -7:38:04
Jiuhuajie 1 1 30N25 117E51 -7:51:24
Jiuhuaxian 5 1 23N30 113E16 -7:33:04
Jiuhuinan 15 12 42N37 126E14 -8:24:56
Jiujiang 5 1 22N51 113E02 -7:32:08
Jiujiang 14 1 29N36 115E52 -7:43:28
Jiujiang 14 1 29N44 115E59 -7:43:56
Jiujiawopeng 16
11 40N59 121E22 -8:05:28
Jiujiji 10 1 35N09 114E48 -7:39:12
Jiujing 24 9 29N05 103E54 -6:55:36
Jiukou 11 1 30N52 112E38 -7:30:32
Jiuli 24 9 29N32 103E32 -6:54:08
Jiuliguan 10 1 31N50 114E14 -7:36:56
Jiulong 5 1 24N08 112E55 -7:31:40
Jiulong 24 9 29N00 101E50 -6:47:20
Jiulongchang 24
9 29N32 106E05 -7:04:20
Jiulonggang 1 1 32N38 117E03 -7:48:12
Jiulong → Kowloon 31
4 22N18 114E10 -7:36:40
Jiulongpo 24 9 29N29 106E32 -7:06:08
Jiulongzhen 13 1 31N54 121E34 -8:06:16
Jiumangya 19 8 37N40 91E50 -6:07:20
Jiumen 16 11 40N42 120E27 -8:01:48
Jiumianyang 11 1 30N16 113E13 -7:32:52
Jiumiao 16 11 42N24 121E36 -8:06:24
Jiumu 3 1 28N11 118E27 -7:53:48
Jiuninghe 26 1 39N28 117E46 -7:51:04
Jiuningyang 3 1 25N38 117E21 -7:49:24
Jiupu 8 1 40N21 115E18 -7:41:12
Jiupu 13 1 32N50 118E45 -7:55:00
Jiuquan (Suzhou) 4
9 39N45 98E34 -6:34:16
Jiurongcheng 21
1 37N21 122E32 -8:10:08
Jiushangshui 10
1 33N32 114E32 -7:38:08
Jiushenqiu 10 1 33N11 115E08 -7:40:32
Jiusiyang 13 1 33N41 118E39 -7:54:36
Jiusongyu 2 1 40N27 116E58 -7:47:52
Jiutai 15 12 44N08 125E50 -8:23:20
Jiuwuqing 26 1 39N31 116E52 -7:47:28
Jiuxian 10 1 33N32 113E17 -7:33:08
Jiuxian 12 1 25N54 113E22 -7:33:28
Jiuxian 8 1 37N53 117E06 -7:48:24
Jiuxian 24 9 30N27 103E51 -6:55:24
Jiuxian 24 9 29N51 106E13 -7:04:52
Jiuxian 1 1 31N11 118E04 -7:52:16
Jiuxian 1 1 33N15 115E35 -7:42:20
Jiuxian 3 1 25N14 116E31 -7:46:04
Jiuxiangcheng 10
1 33N13 114E49 -7:39:16
Jiuyingkou 8 1 39N42 114E44 -7:38:56
Jiuyingzi 16 11 42N03 121E38 -8:06:32
Jiuyuanqu 23 1 35N09 111E51 -7:27:24
Jiuyuhang 30 1 30N17 119E56 -7:59:44
Jiuyunjie 27 8 44N12 88E05 -5:52:20
Jiuzhan 15 12 43N57 126E29 -8:25:56
Jiuzhen 3 1 24N05 117E42 -7:50:48
Jiuzhou 8 1 39N30 116E33 -7:46:12
Jiuzhuangwo 8 1 40N11 115E36 -7:42:24
Jiwangmiao 22 2 31N14 121E17 -8:05:08
Jiwangtun 16 11 41N02 122E58 -8:11:52
Jiwen 17 11 50N32 123E15 -8:13:00
Jixi 1 1 30N06 118E35 -7:54:20
Jixi 9 12 45N17 130E59 -8:43:56
Jixian 26 1 40N03 117E24 -7:49:36
Jixian 10 1 35N26 114E05 -7:36:20
Jixian 8 1 37N36 115E31 -7:42:04
Jixiangsi 24 9 30N39 105E32 -7:02:08
Jixiashi 30 1 28N22 118E44 -7:54:56
Jixingji 1 1 32N55 116E46 -7:47:04
Jiyang 2 1 39N38 115E59 -7:43:56
Jiyang 3 1 27N10 118E07 -7:52:28
Jiyang 21 1 36N59 117E11 -7:48:44
Jiyi 20 9 35N50 110E23 -7:21:32
Jiyuan 10 1 35N08 112E35 -7:30:20
Jize 8 1 36N54 114E52 -7:39:28
Jomba 28 8 31N27 98E15 -6:33:00
Jongkha 28 8 28N57 85E15 -5:41:00
Juancheng 21 1 35N35 115E29 -7:41:56
Judian 29 9 27N20 99E36 -6:38:24
Juehedian 26 1 39N26 117E06 -7:48:24
Juexi 30 1 29N27 121E57 -8:07:48
Juexizhen 24 9 28N55 104E16 -6:57:04
Juidongshan 3 1 23N46 117E31 -7:50:04
Juisui 25 6 23N30 121E21 -8:05:24
Jukao 13 1 32N24 120E33 -8:02:12
Julebu 23 1 40N09 113E36 -7:34:24
Juliuhe 16 11 42N03 122E55 -8:11:40

Julu 8 1 37N13 115E01 -7:40:04
Junan (Shizilu) 21
1 35N11 118E51 -7:55:24
Juncheng 8 1 38N57 114E41 -7:38:44
Jungar Qi 17 9 39N49 111E10 -7:24:40
Junkou 3 1 26N42 116E49 -7:47:16
Junlian 24 9 28N08 104E35 -6:58:20
Junliangcheng 26
1 39N04 117E27 -7:49:48
Junling 14 1 28N17 116E28 -7:45:52
Junxian 11 1 32N31 111E30 -7:26:00
Jurong 13 1 31N57 119E10 -7:56:40
Jushiguan 29 9 24N47 97E38 -6:30:32
Juxi 30 1 27N30 119E08 -7:56:32
Juxian 21 1 35N37 118E54 -7:55:36
Juxing 13 1 31N56 121E33 -8:06:12
Juye 21 1 35N23 116E06 -7:44:24
Juyongguan 2 1 40N18 116E04 -7:44:16
Kagelike 27 8 37N20 87E02 -5:48:08
Kaichengqiao 1 1 31N18 117E44 -7:50:56
Kaifeng 10 1 34N51 114E21 -7:37:24
Kaihe 21 1 35N42 116E20 -7:45:20
Kaihua 30 1 29N09 118E23 -7:53:32
Kaijian 5 10 23N42 111E48 -7:27:12
Kaijiang 24 9 31N05 107E55 -7:11:40
Kaikukang 9 12 53N07 124E46 -8:19:04
Kaili 7 9 26N35 107E55 -7:11:40
Kailu 17 11 43N36 121E14 -8:04:56
Kaimenshan 16 11 41N03 123E08 -8:12:32
Kaiping 5 10 22N23 112E35 -7:30:20
Kaiping 8 1 39N41 118E16 -7:53:04
Kaishantun 15 12 42N43 129E43 -8:38:52
Kaixian 24 9 31N13 108E25 -7:13:40
Kaiyang 7 9 26N58 106E40 -7:06:40
Kaiyuan 29 9 23N44 103E11 -6:52:44
Kaiyuan 16 11 42N32 124E01 -8:16:04
Kaiyuancheng 16
11 42N37 124E04 -8:16:16
Kaizhou 16 11 41N22 121E19 -8:05:16
Kala 27 8 36N47 83E48 -5:35:12
Kala 28 8 28N16 89E23 -5:57:32
Kalabula 27 8 43N24 83E06 -5:32:24
Kalagan 17 11 50N30 119E55 -7:59:40
Kalashankou 19 8 35N06 91E51 -6:07:24
Kalasi 27 8 48N43 86E59 -5:47:56
Kalgan → Zhangjiakou 8
1 40N50 114E53 -7:39:32
Kalima 16 11 41N32 122E40 -8:10:40
Kamba 28 8 28N17 88E32 -5:54:08
Kam Tin 31 4 22N27 114E03 -7:36:12
Kanchow → Ganzhou 14
1 25N54 114E55 -7:39:40
Kangbao 8 1 41N53 114E40 -7:38:40
Kangding 24 9 30N03 102E02 -6:48:08
Kangdu 14 1 27N00 116E36 -7:46:24
Kanggezhuang 2 1 40N26 116E44 -7:46:56
Kangjinjing 9 12 46N12 126E48 -8:27:12
Kangma 28 8 28N34 89E51 -5:59:24
Kangmaer 28 8 30N45 85E34 -5:42:16
Kangnichumike 28
7 33N10 80E59 -5:23:56
Kangping 16 11 42N44 123E21 -8:13:24
Kangpu 29 9 27N43 99E00 -6:36:00
Kangshan 25 6 22N48 120E17 -8:01:08
Kangsu 27 7 39N45 75E02 -5:00:08
Kangtuyingzi 16
11 41N47 121E31 -8:06:04
Kangxianzhuang 8
1 39N06 116E27 -7:45:48
Kangzhuang 2 1 40N23 115E53 -7:43:32
Kanhsien → Ganzhou 14
1 25N54 114E55 -7:39:40
Kanmen 30 1 28N06 121E16 -8:05:04
Kanshan 30 1 30N12 120E25 -8:01:40
Kanshi 3 1 24N56 116E54 -7:47:36
Kansu 27 7 39N45 75E02 -5:00:08
Kanton → Guangzhou 5
1 23N06 113E16 -7:33:04
Kantuanji 1 1 32N59 116E19 -7:45:16
Kanzi 16 11 39N34 122E39 -8:10:36
Kaohiung → Kaohsiung 25
6 22N38 120E17 -8:01:08
Kaohsiung 25 6 22N38 120E17 -8:01:08
Kaohsiunghsien 25
6 22N38 120E21 -8:01:24
Kaolun → Kowloon 31
4 22N18 114E10 -7:36:40
Kaoping → Changzhi 23
1 36N11 113E08 -7:32:32
Kaoshanji 2 1 40N11 117E17 -7:49:08
Kaoshanpu 11 1 30N54 114E32 -7:38:08
Kaoyu 13 1 32N47 119E27 -7:57:48
Karamai → Kelamayi 27
8 45N30 84E55 -5:39:40
Karamay → Kelamayi 27
8 45N30 84E55 -5:39:40
Kareke 27 7 38N23 76E58 -5:07:52
Kashgar → Kashi 27
7 39N29 75E59 -5:03:56
Kashi (Shufu) (Kashgar) 27
7 39N29 75E59 -5:03:56
Kashing → Jiaxing 30
1 30N46 120E45 -8:03:00
Kebeiti 27 7 36N47 79E29 -5:17:56
Kedian 11 1 31N23 112E51 -7:31:24
Kedong 9 12 48N02 126E15 -8:25:00
Kedu 7 9 26N33 104E21 -6:57:24
Keelung → Chilung 25
6 25N08 121E44 -8:06:56
Keerzong 28 7 32N11 79E59 -5:19:56
Kegonzhake 28 8 33N00 87E53 -5:51:32
Kekexili 19 8 35N11 93E35 -6:14:20
Kekeyaer 27 7 38N02 75E05 -5:00:20
Kelamayi 27 8 45N30 84E55 -5:39:40
Kelan 23 1 38N43 111E32 -7:26:08

Kelegou 8 1 41N57 118E11 -7:52:44
Keluotun 9 12 49N16 125E44 -8:22:56
Kengkou 30 1 28N27 120E26 -8:01:44
Kengkou 1 1 29N48 117E22 -7:49:28
Kengtian 3 1 25N54 119E26 -7:57:44
Kenli (Xishuanghe) 21
1 37N40 118E35 -7:54:20
Kequan 10 1 36N04 114E00 -7:36:00
Keshan 9 12 48N02 125E51 -8:23:24
Keshitage 27 7 37N23 78E05 -5:12:20
Ketang 5 1 22N58 115E28 -7:41:52
Keyihe 17 11 50N40 122E27 -8:09:48
Kharbine → Haerbin 9
12 45N45 126E41 -8:26:44
Kiamusze → Jiamusi 9
12 46N50 130E21 -8:41:24
Kiangpeih 24 9 29N36 106E35 -7:06:20
Kiangtu → Yangzhou 13
1 32N24 119E26 -7:57:44
Kiangyin → Jiangyin 13
1 31N55 120E16 -8:01:04
Kian → Ji'an 14
1 27N07 114E58 -7:39:52
Kiaohsien → Jiaoxian 21
1 36N18 119E58 -7:59:52
Kienli → Jianli 11
1 29N49 112E53 -7:31:32
Kiirun → Chilung 25
6 25N08 121E44 -8:06:56
Kingtechen → Jingdezhen 14
1 29N16 117E11 -7:48:44
Kinhwa → Jinhua 30
1 29N07 119E39 -7:58:36
Kirin → Jilin 15
12 43N51 126E33 -8:26:12
Kityang → Jieyang 5
1 23N35 116E21 -7:45:24
Kiukiang → Jiujiang 14
1 29N44 115E59 -7:43:56
Kokiu → Gejiu 29
9 23N22 103E06 -6:52:24
Kongcheng 1 1 31N02 117E05 -7:48:20
Kongfang 14 1 27N58 116E53 -7:47:32
Kongjiamatou 8 1 39N07 116E10 -7:44:40
Kongjiatun 16 11 40N42 124E04 -8:16:16
Kongjiawopeng 17
11 43N58 122E41 -8:10:44
Kongjiazhuang 8
1 40N47 114E48 -7:39:12
Konglong 11 1 29N56 115E54 -7:43:36
Konglongshan 8 1 40N33 117E17 -7:49:08
Kongmoon → Jiangmen 5
1 22N35 113E05 -7:32:20
Kongtan 24 9 29N10 104E42 -6:58:48
Kongyangcun 13 1 31N23 118E54 -7:55:36
Kongzhen 13 1 31N29 119E00 -7:56:00
Korla 27 8 41N44 86E09 -5:44:36
Kou'an 13 1 32N19 119E52 -7:59:28
K'ouhu 25 6 23N35 120E11 -8:00:44
Koutou 8 1 38N35 114E24 -7:37:36
Kowloon (Jiulong) 31
4 22N18 114E10 -7:36:40
Kowloon City 31
4 22N19 114E11 -7:36:44
Kuanbang 16 11 40N29 120E04 -8:00:16
Kuancheng 8 1 40N38 118E27 -7:53:48
Kuancheng 8 1 40N37 118E31 -7:54:04
Kuandian 16 11 40N43 124E44 -8:18:56
Kuanhsi 25 6 24N48 121E10 -8:04:40
Kuanmiao 25 6 22N58 120E19 -8:01:16
Kuanshan 25 6 23N03 121E09 -8:04:36
Kuanyin 25 6 25N02 121E04 -8:04:16
KuanyÜn → Guanyun 13
1 34N20 119E17 -7:57:08
Kudanggou 16 11 41N06 124E00 -8:16:00
Kueisui → Hohhot 17
9 40N51 111E40 -7:26:40
Kueiyang → Guiyang 7
9 26N35 106E43 -7:06:52
Kuerbin 9 12 49N25 128E59 -8:35:56
K'uerhlo → Korla 27
8 41N44 86E09 -5:44:36
Kuga 27 8 41N43 82E54 -5:31:36
Kuidesu 16 11 41N46 119E29 -7:57:56
Kuidou 3 1 25N10 118E11 -7:52:44
Kuitan 5 1 23N05 115E58 -7:43:52
Kuitun 27 8 44N24 85E10 -5:40:40
KÜkong → Shaoguan 5
1 24N50 113E37 -7:34:28
Kuldja → Yining 27
7 43N54 81E21 -5:25:24
Kuliushucun 2 1 40N07 116E34 -7:46:16
Kulongshan 8 1 41N43 116E54 -7:47:36
Kulongshanpuzi 16
11 41N16 123E59 -8:15:56
Kuluqi 17 11 50N23 124E13 -8:16:52
Kumukuli 27 8 37N33 88E50 -5:55:20
Kumushi 27 8 42N14 88E11 -5:52:44
KÜmÜx 27 8 42N14 88E11 -5:52:44
Kungchuling → Huaide 15
12 43N32 124E50 -8:19:20
Kunghsi 25 6 24N37 121E16 -8:05:04
Kung-Pei-Tien 25
6 25N06 121E38 -8:06:32
Kunming 29 9 25N05 102E40 -6:50:40
Kunshan 13 1 31N23 120E57 -8:03:48
Kunting 30 1 29N48 121E56 -8:07:44
Kuntuolun 17 1 45N13 115E21 -7:41:24
Kuohsing 25 6 24N02 120E51 -8:03:24
Kuokegan 27 8 37N30 89E55 -5:59:40
Kuruqi 17 11 48N58 123E50 -8:15:20
Kushui 27 8 42N11 94E25 -6:17:40
Kwangchow → Guangzhou 5
1 23N06 113E16 -7:33:04

Kweihwa → Hohhot 17
9 40N51 111E40 -7:26:40
Kweijang → Guiyang 7
9 26N35 106E43 -7:06:52
Kweilin → Guilin 6
9 25N17 110E17 -7:21:08
Kweisui → Hohhot 17
9 40N51 111E40 -7:26:40
Kweisui, Sui 17
9 40N17 111E37 -7:26:28
Kweiyang → Guiyang 7
9 26N35 106E43 -7:06:52
Kweiyer 7 9 26N35 106E13 -7:04:52
Kwun Tong 31 4 22N19 114E12 -7:36:48
La'a 24 9 29N44 101E26 -6:45:44
Laduozong 28 8 31N27 97E19 -6:29:16
Lafa 15 12 43N50 127E19 -8:29:16
Lagangzong 28 8 28N05 91E04 -6:04:16
Lagantu 17 9 42N20 108E22 -7:13:28
Lage 28 8 29N26 85E51 -5:43:24
Lagedu 29 9 26N24 101E11 -6:44:44
Lagu 29 9 26N26 101E30 -6:46:00
Lagubu 28 8 29N08 87E14 -5:48:56
Laguyu 16 11 41N43 123E49 -8:15:16
Laha 9 12 48N10 124E39 -8:18:36
Lai'an 1 1 32N27 118E25 -7:53:40
Laibin 6 9 23N42 109E22 -7:17:28
Laifang 3 1 25N56 116E54 -7:47:36
Laifeng 11 1 29N31 109E15 -7:17:00
Laifeng 24 9 30N14 105E17 -7:01:08
Laifengzhen 24 9 29N26 106E13 -7:04:52
Laigou 1 1 33N56 117E06 -7:48:24
Laishan 21 1 37N24 121E23 -8:05:32
Laishui 8 1 39N23 115E42 -7:42:48
Laisu 24 9 29N16 105E47 -7:03:08
Laitan 24 9 29N06 106E10 -7:04:40
Laiwu 21 1 36N12 117E42 -7:50:48
Laixi (Shuiji) 21
1 36N51 120E29 -8:01:56
Laiyang 21 1 36N58 120E44 -8:02:56
Laiyang 12 1 26N26 112E30 -7:30:00
Laiyuan 8 1 39N18 114E44 -7:38:56
Laiyuan 3 1 25N36 117E01 -7:48:04
Lalatuncun 16 11 41N44 122E00 -8:08:00
Lamadong 16 11 40N39 119E39 -7:58:36
Lamagoumen 2 1 40N52 116E39 -7:46:36
Lamahuang 16 11 42N27 121E33 -8:06:12
Lamaya 24 9 29N50 99E53 -6:39:32
Lamayingzi 16 11 42N09 121E50 -8:07:20
Lam Uk Wei 31 4 22N26 114E22 -7:37:28
Lancang 29 9 23N00 100E02 -6:40:08
Lanchow → Lanzhou 4
9 36N03 103E41 -6:54:44
Lancun 21 1 36N24 120E10 -8:00:40
Landi 21 1 36N35 119E59 -7:59:56
Langao 20 9 32N13 109E02 -7:16:08
Langda 28 8 31N12 96E59 -6:27:56
Langdai 7 9 26N06 105E20 -7:01:20
Langfang → Anci 8
1 39N31 116E41 -7:46:44
Langju 14 1 27N52 116E36 -7:46:24
Langkazi 28 8 28N59 90E25 -6:01:40
Langmazong 28 8 30N52 89E58 -5:59:52
Langping 11 1 30N38 110E21 -7:21:24
Langqiao 1 1 30N30 118E24 -7:53:36
Langruzong 28 8 31N50 91E25 -6:05:40
Langshan 17 9 41N12 107E22 -7:09:28
Langshan 8 1 40N22 115E41 -7:42:44
Langtian 5 1 25N11 113E28 -7:33:52
Langtoutun 17 11 46N51 121E54 -8:07:36
Langtuozi 16 11 41N01 121E43 -8:06:52
Langu 3 1 27N56 118E11 -7:52:44
Langwo 16 11 41N13 121E44 -8:06:56
Langwozhuang 8 1 39N05 115E37 -7:42:28
Langxi 1 1 31N08 119E10 -7:56:40
Langzhong 24 9 31N35 105E59 -7:03:56
Langzishan 16 11 41N02 123E23 -8:13:32
Lanjiang 24 9 30N24 105E11 -7:00:44
Lankao (Lanfeng) 10
1 34N50 114E49 -7:39:16
Lankou 5 1 23N59 115E05 -7:40:20
Lanling 9 12 45N15 126E12 -8:24:48
Lanping 29 9 26N29 99E23 -6:37:32
Lanqibao 16 11 40N56 122E25 -8:09:40
Lanqikoucun 16
11 40N52 122E26 -8:09:44
Lanqipuzi 16 11 42N12 123E15 -8:13:00
Lanshan 12 1 25N18 111E52 -7:27:28
Lanshantou 21 1 35N07 119E21 -7:57:24
Lantang 5 1 23N25 114E56 -7:39:44
Lantian 20 9 34N03 109E12 -7:16:48
Lantianba 24 9 28N52 105E26 -7:01:44
Lantianchang 2 1 39N58 116E17 -7:45:08
Lantschou → Lanzhou 4
9 36N03 103E41 -6:54:44
Lanxi 9 12 46N15 126E14 -8:24:56
Lanxi 30 1 29N12 119E28 -7:57:52
Lanxian 23 1 38N22 111E46 -7:27:04
Lanzhou (Lanchow) 4
9 36N03 103E41 -6:54:44
Laobian 16 11 41N58 123E10 -8:12:40
Laobian 16 11 40N42 122E21 -8:09:24
Laochang 29 9 24N34 104E11 -6:56:44
Laochang 24 9 29N30 106E36 -7:06:24
Laocheng 16 11 42N37 124E04 -8:16:16
Laodafang 16 11 41N40 122E40 -8:10:40
Laodaodian 9 12 51N16 126E40 -8:26:40
Laofengkou 27 8 46N11 83E38 -5:34:32
Laofu 17 11 42N13 118E17 -7:53:08
Laogang 22 2 31N01 121E49 -8:07:16
Laoge 13 1 32N49 119E52 -7:59:28
Laoguan 12 1 27N38 113E36 -7:34:24
Laoguanpu 16 11 40N53 120E51 -8:03:24
Laohaotuo 16 11 41N25 122E46 -8:11:04
Laoheba 24 9 28N51 103E49 -6:55:16

Laoheishan 9 12 43N45 130E52 -8:43:28
Laoheshangtai 16 11 40N43 120E49 -8:03:16
Laohokow → Guanghua 11 1 32N25 111E36 -7:26:24
Laohuk'ou 25 6 24N53 121E03 -8:04:12
Laohumiao 2 1 39N58 116E20 -7:45:20
Laohutuozi 16 11 42N25 122E34 -8:10:16
Laojunguan 8 1 40N22 114E47 -7:39:08
Laojunmiao → Yumen 4 9 39N56 97E51 -6:31:24
Laoka 9 12 52N47 125E52 -8:23:28
Laolongtan 24 9 30N01 104E48 -6:59:12
Laomocun 1 1 30N51 119E11 -7:56:44
Laoshan (Licun) 21 1 36N10 120E25 -8:01:40
Laowushi 13 1 31N43 121E00 -8:04:00
Laoxinkou 11 1 30N12 112E50 -7:31:20
Laoyemiao 16 11 41N03 119E53 -7:59:32
Laoyezhuang 13 1 32N16 120E04 -8:00:16
Laoyingpan 14 1 26N34 115E10 -7:40:40
Laozha 13 1 31N35 121E07 -8:04:28
Laozhen 1 1 31N34 118E19 -7:53:16
Laozhong 10 1 33N56 114E51 -7:39:24
Laozhuangzi 8 1 39N44 118E05 -7:52:20
Laozishan 13 1 33N11 118E36 -7:54:24
Lasa (Lhasa) 28 8 29N40 91E09 -6:04:36
Lazha 24 9 26N26 101E50 -6:47:20
Lazhulong 28 7 35N08 81E33 -5:26:12
Lazi 28 8 29N10 87E42 -5:50:48
Le'an 14 1 27N24 115E48 -7:43:12
Lechang 5 1 25N09 113E21 -7:33:24
Lecheng 5 9 19N14 110E34 -7:22:16
Ledong 5 9 18N45 109E12 -7:16:48
Ledu 19 9 36N32 102E25 -6:49:40
Leibo 24 9 28N19 103E21 -6:53:24
Leishendian 24 9 28N58 106E40 -7:06:40
Leixi 12 1 27N10 112E52 -7:31:28
Leiyang 12 1 26N24 112E51 -7:31:24
Leizhuang 8 1 39N47 118E34 -7:54:16
Leling 21 1 37N45 117E12 -7:48:48
Lemin 5 8 21N11 109E42 -7:18:48
Lengduqiao 1 1 30N27 119E15 -7:57:00
Lenghu 19 8 38N30 93E15 -6:13:00
Lengjiagou 16 11 41N40 121E37 -8:06:28
Lengshuichang 24 9 29N27 106E26 -7:05:44
Lengshuikeng 14 1 27N55 117E08 -7:48:32
Lengshuitan 12 1 26N27 111E35 -7:26:20
Lengzipu 16 11 41N42 122E47 -8:11:08
Leping 14 1 28N57 117E05 -7:48:20
Leshan 24 9 29N34 103E45 -6:55:00
Leting 8 1 39N27 118E53 -7:55:32
Leye 6 9 24N48 106E34 -7:06:16
Leyu 13 1 31N55 120E43 -8:02:52
Lezhi 24 9 30N17 105E02 -7:00:08
Lhasa → Lasa 28 8 29N40 91E09 -6:04:36
Lhorong 28 8 30N45 96E09 -6:24:36
Liancheng 3 1 25N44 116E46 -7:47:04
Liang'anchang 24 9 30N30 104E56 -6:59:44
Liangbao 23 1 34N37 110E45 -7:23:00
Liangbingbao 9 12 45N48 128E19 -8:33:16
Liangbingtai 15 12 43N12 128E47 -8:35:08
Liangchahe 24 9 29N03 106E18 -7:05:12
Liangcheng 21 1 35N35 119E35 -7:58:20
Liangcun 14 1 26N36 115E34 -7:42:16
Liangdang 4 9 33N56 106E12 -7:04:48
Liangdawa 8 1 40N39 117E37 -7:50:28
Liangfengwu 24 9 30N11 105E22 -7:01:28
Lianggezhuang 8 1 39N21 115E22 -7:41:28
Lianghe 29 9 24N51 98E25 -6:33:40
Lianghe 9 12 45N09 128E45 -8:35:00
Liangheguan 20 9 32N52 109E19 -7:17:16
Lianghekou 24 9 28N55 106E03 -7:04:12
Lianghekou 4 9 33N42 104E25 -6:57:40
Lianghekou 24 9 29N14 108E40 -7:14:40
Lianghekou 24 9 31N27 102E13 -6:48:52
Liangiu 21 1 35N12 117E47 -7:51:08
Liangjia 24 9 29N29 105E33 -7:02:12
Liangjiadian 16 11 39N10 121E54 -8:07:36
Liangjiafang 8 1 41N04 117E18 -7:49:12
Liangjianfang 8 1 40N45 117E20 -7:49:20
Liangjiang 6 9 23N23 108E22 -7:13:28
Liangjiangkou 15 12 42N38 128E05 -8:32:20
Liangjiawazi 16 11 40N40 120E42 -8:02:48
Liangjiazi 16 11 42N13 122E31 -8:10:04
Liangkou 5 1 23N43 113E43 -7:34:52
Lianglukou 24 9 29N18 106E15 -7:05:00
Liangmen 10 1 35N34 114E54 -7:39:36
Liangmentou 30 1 28N58 121E12 -8:04:48
Liangmushi 30 1 30N46 119E35 -7:58:20
Liangpa 6 9 24N10 106E13 -7:04:52
Liangpeng 30 1 30N47 119E38 -7:58:32
Liangping 24 9 30N41 107E49 -7:11:16
Liangtinghe 1 1 30N20 116E12 -7:44:48
Liangtoumen 30 1 29N31 120E45 -8:03:00
Liangtun 16 11 40N14 122E34 -8:10:16
Liangwangzhuang 26 1 39N01 116E58 -7:47:52
Liangxiangzhen 2 1 39N44 116E08 -7:44:32
Liangying 5 1 23N14 116E21 -7:45:24
Liangyuan 1 1 32N00 117E34 -7:50:16
Liangzhu 30 1 30N23 120E03 -8:00:12
Lianhe 15 12 42N36 125E37 -8:22:28
Lianhua 14 1 27N07 113E57 -7:35:48
Lianhuachi 2 1 40N28 116E33 -7:46:12
Lianhuapao 9 12 45N32 129E50 -8:39:20
Lianjiang 3 1 26N12 119E31 -7:58:04
Lianjiang 5 8 21N38 110E15 -7:21:00
Lianjiechang 24 9 29N41 104E30 -6:58:00
Liannan (Sanjiang) 5 10 24N38 112E10 -7:28:40
Lianping 5 1 24N22 114E31 -7:38:04
Lianpu 3 1 26N02 118E38 -7:54:32
Lianshanguan 16 11 40N58 123E46 -8:15:04
Lianshi 30 1 30N42 120E26 -8:01:44
Lianshui 13 1 33N47 119E16 -7:57:04
Liansiji 10 1 33N58 114E24 -7:37:36
Liantang 13 1 31N37 120E38 -8:02:32
Lianxian 5 1 24N48 112E25 -7:29:40
Lianyin 9 12 53N28 123E51 -8:15:24
Lianyuan (Lantian) 12 1 27N42 111E19 -7:25:16
Lianyungang (Xinpu) 13 1 34N39 119E16 -7:57:04
Lianyungang 13 1 34N44 119E30 -7:58:00
Lianzhou → Hepu 6 9 21N39 109E11 -7:16:44
Liaobinta 16 11 42N08 123E04 -8:12:16
Liaocheng 21 1 36N30 115E59 -7:43:56
Liaojiangshi 12 1 26N05 113E17 -7:33:08
Liaoyang 16 11 41N17 123E11 -8:12:44
Liaoyangwopu 16 11 43N00 123E28 -8:13:52
Liaoyuan 15 12 42N54 125E07 -8:20:28
Liaozhong 16 11 41N31 122E44 -8:10:56
Libishan 1 1 30N45 119E20 -7:57:20
Libo 7 9 25N28 107E53 -7:11:32
Libu 6 9 23N41 111E30 -7:26:00
Lichang 24 9 28N53 104E26 -6:57:44
Licheng 21 1 36N41 117E00 -7:48:00
Licheng 23 1 36N30 113E21 -7:33:24
Lichuan 14 1 27N18 116E53 -7:47:32
Lichuan 11 1 30N18 108E51 -7:15:24
Licun 8 1 38N32 117E08 -7:48:32
Lidao 21 1 37N15 122E32 -8:10:08
Lidarentuncun 16 11 41N32 123E12 -8:12:48
Lidesi 1 1 33N33 115E53 -7:43:32
Lidian 24 9 28N57 103E44 -6:54:56
Lidu 24 9 30N35 106E04 -7:04:16
Liemienzhen 24 9 30N29 106E05 -7:04:20
Lienchou → Hepu 6 9 21N39 109E11 -7:16:44
Liershizhai 16 11 41N49 123E43 -8:14:52
Ligang 30 1 30N04 121E52 -8:07:28
Ligezhuang 8 1 39N42 118E12 -7:52:48
Ligezhuang 2 1 39N49 115E56 -7:43:44
Lihu 5 1 23N23 116E03 -7:44:12
Liji 13 1 33N48 117E48 -7:51:12
Liji 10 1 31N59 115E51 -7:43:24
Lijia 16 11 41N43 122E20 -8:09:20
Lijia 21 1 37N49 118E01 -7:52:04
Lijiaba 24 9 29N37 105E33 -7:02:12
Lijiadian 16 11 42N07 121E14 -8:04:56
Lijiajie 24 9 29N49 105E30 -7:02:00
Lijiakou 8 1 39N12 116E29 -7:45:56
Lijiang 29 9 26N57 100E15 -6:41:00
Lijiapuzi 16 11 40N59 123E38 -8:14:32
Lijiaqiao 13 1 31N38 120E00 -8:00:00
Lijiaqiao 2 1 40N03 116E40 -7:46:40
Lijiaqiao 8 1 39N47 117E47 -7:51:08
Lijiatun 16 11 41N19 121E23 -8:05:32
Lijiatuo 24 9 29N28 106E33 -7:06:12
Lijiawobao 16 11 41N00 122E26 -8:09:44
Lijiaxiang 30 1 30N57 119E59 -7:59:56
Lijiazao 8 1 39N17 118E19 -7:53:16
Lijin 16 11 41N40 121E20 -8:05:20
Lijin 21 1 37N29 118E16 -7:53:04
Likang 25 6 22N47 120E29 -8:01:56
Likou 10 1 33N51 113E20 -7:33:20
Likou 13 3 31N24 120E37 -8:02:28
Likou 1 1 29N53 117E28 -7:49:52
Lilianchengzhen 8 1 39N12 116E43 -7:46:52
Lilasi 28 8 29N22 84E30 -5:38:00
Lili 13 1 31N00 120E42 -8:02:48
Liling 12 1 27N40 113E30 -7:34:00
Limen 3 1 27N07 119E19 -7:57:16
Liminzhen 10 1 34N31 115E56 -7:43:44
Limu 6 9 25N02 110E51 -7:23:24
Lin'an 30 1 30N14 119E43 -7:58:52
Lincai 10 1 33N50 114E56 -7:39:44
Lincang 29 9 23N45 102E20 -6:49:20
Lincheng 8 1 37N27 114E29 -7:37:56
Lincheng 30 1 30N55 119E47 -7:59:08
Linch'ing → Linqing 21 1 36N53 115E41 -7:42:44
Lindian 9 12 47N11 124E52 -8:19:28
Lindong 3 1 26N03 118E49 -7:55:16
Lindong 8 1 39N51 117E41 -7:50:44
Linfen 23 1 36N05 111E32 -7:26:08
Ling'an 30 1 30N36 120E30 -8:02:00
Lingao 5 9 19N54 109E40 -7:18:40
Lingbi 1 1 33N33 117E33 -7:50:12
Lingchuan 6 9 25N26 110E15 -7:21:00
Lingchuan 23 1 35N46 113E26 -7:33:44
Lingda 1 1 31N12 119E18 -7:57:12
Lingdianzhen 13 1 31N51 121E25 -8:05:40
Lingdou 3 1 26N22 118E56 -7:55:44
Lingekeke 28 8 29N59 87E33 -5:50:12
Lingfengwei 14 1 24N44 115E35 -7:42:20
Linghe 21 1 36N23 119E03 -7:56:12
Linghu 30 1 30N44 120E10 -8:00:40
Lingjiachang 24 9 29N28 104E54 -6:59:36
Lingjiaqiao 30 3 30N09 120E04 -8:00:16
Lingkar Dzong 28 8 28N45 90E36 -6:02:24
Lingkou 30 1 29N16 120E38 -8:02:32
Lingkou 13 1 31N57 119E38 -7:58:32
Lingling 12 1 26N13 111E37 -7:26:28
Linglongta 16 11 40N54 119E59 -7:59:56
Lingma 6 9 23N22 107E53 -7:11:32
Lingqiu 23 1 39N24 114E13 -7:36:52
Lingshan 6 9 22N28 109E17 -7:17:08
Lingshan 21 1 36N33 120E27 -8:01:48
Lingshanwei 21 1 35N58 120E13 -8:00:52
Lingshi 23 1 36N54 111E43 -7:26:52
Lingshou 8 1 38N18 114E24 -7:37:36
Lingshui 5 9 18N31 110E01 -7:20:04
Lingtangqiao 13 1 32N43 119E14 -7:56:56
Lingu 28 8 29N26 87E36 -5:50:24
Lingwu 18 9 38N06 106E21 -7:05:24
Lingxian 12 1 26N30 113E46 -7:35:04
Lingxian 21 1 37N21 116E34 -7:46:16
Lingxiazhu 30 1 29N03 119E46 -7:59:04
Lingyuan 16 11 41N15 119E16 -7:57:04
Lingzhuangzi 26 1 39N04 117E09 -7:48:36
Lingzinan 8 1 39N29 115E15 -7:41:00
Linhai 30 1 28N51 121E07 -8:04:28
Linhe 17 9 40N51 107E30 -7:10:00
Linhezhuang 26 1 40N04 117E39 -7:50:36
Linhsia → Linxia 4 9 35N35 103E13 -6:52:52
Linhuaiguan 1 1 32N55 117E40 -7:50:40
Linhuanji 1 1 33N42 116E33 -7:46:12
Lini → Linyi 21 1 35N04 118E22 -7:53:28
Linjiang 4 9 33N01 105E01 -7:00:04
Linjiang 3 1 27N50 118E26 -7:53:44
Linjiang 14 1 28N04 115E21 -7:41:24
Linjiang 15 12 41N44 126E55 -8:27:40
Linjiangchang 24 9 29N14 105E58 -7:03:52
Linjianghu 14 1 28N41 117E54 -7:51:36
Linjiangsi 24 9 30N15 104E37 -6:58:28
Linjiatai 16 11 40N43 123E57 -8:15:48
Linkou 9 12 45N15 130E16 -8:41:04
Linli 12 1 29N18 111E30 -7:26:00
Linnancang 8 1 39N50 117E37 -7:50:28
Linping → Yuhang 30 1 30N25 120E18 -8:01:12
Linpu 30 1 30N03 120E15 -8:01:00
Linqi 30 1 29N51 119E06 -7:56:24
Linqi 10 1 35N48 113E53 -7:35:32
Linqing 21 1 36N53 115E41 -7:42:44
Linqu 21 1 36N32 118E31 -7:54:04
Linquan 1 1 33N06 115E13 -7:40:52
Linru 10 1 34N11 112E49 -7:31:16
Linruzhen 10 1 34N17 112E35 -7:30:20
Linshan 30 1 30N09 120E59 -8:03:56
Linshanhe 11 1 30N44 114E52 -7:39:28
Linshengpu 16 11 41N34 123E20 -8:13:20
Linshui 24 9 30N21 106E59 -7:07:56
Lintan 4 9 34N37 103E40 -6:54:40
Lintao 4 9 35N27 103E46 -6:55:04
Lintingkou 26 1 39N39 117E30 -7:50:00
Lintong 20 9 34N21 109E11 -7:16:44
Linwu 12 1 25N16 112E20 -7:29:20
Linwu 21 1 36N14 119E17 -7:57:08
Linxi 17 11 43N30 118E00 -7:52:00
Linxi 8 1 36N52 115E32 -7:42:08
Linxia 4 9 35N35 103E13 -6:52:52
Linxian 23 1 37N58 110E59 -7:23:56
Linxian 11 1 36N04 113E50 -7:35:20
Linxiang 12 1 29N28 113E30 -7:34:00
Linyi 21 1 35N04 118E22 -7:53:28
Linyi 21 1 37N13 116E51 -7:47:24
Linyi 23 1 35N15 110E59 -7:23:56
Linying 10 1 33N50 113E57 -7:35:48
Linyüan 25 6 22N30 120E23 -8:01:32
Linyü → Shanhaiguan 8 1 40N01 119E44 -7:58:56
Linze 13 1 33N03 119E38 -7:58:32
Linze 4 9 39N19 100E17 -6:41:08
Linzhai 5 1 24N18 115E03 -7:40:12
Linzhang 8 1 36N21 114E36 -7:38:24
Linzhi 28 8 29N25 94E22 -6:17:28
Linzikou 12 1 28N42 112E46 -7:31:04
Lipayan 16 11 42N13 123E23 -8:13:32
Liping 7 9 26N17 109E00 -7:16:00
Lipiyu 16 11 41N09 123E36 -8:14:24
Lipu 6 9 24N25 110E29 -7:21:56
Liqiao 24 9 29N03 104E48 -6:59:12
Lirangdian 8 1 39N14 116E14 -7:44:56
Liren 13 1 33N55 118E47 -7:55:08
Lirentuncun 16 11 41N24 122E59 -8:11:56
Lishan 16 11 41N10 123E00 -8:12:00
Lishan 11 1 31N50 113E16 -7:33:04
Lishangzhuang 8 1 39N35 118E11 -7:52:44
Lishanke 16 11 40N41 119E53 -7:59:32
Lishe 30 1 29N48 121E28 -8:05:52
Lishi 24 9 29N10 105E42 -7:02:48
Lishi 23 1 37N32 111E09 -7:24:36
Lishi 13 3 31N14 120E37 -8:02:28
Lishizhen 24 9 29N04 106E15 -7:05:00
Lishizhen 24 9 29N20 105E24 -7:01:36
Lishu 15 12 43N21 124E37 -8:18:28
Lishui 13 1 31N39 119E01 -7:56:04
Lishui 30 1 28N27 119E54 -7:59:36
Lishuzhen 9 12 45N05 130E41 -8:42:44
Lisizhuang 8 1 38N55 115E07 -7:40:28
Lisui 2 1 40N05 116E44 -7:46:56

Lita 14 1 27N22 116E34 -7:46:16
Litang 24 9 30N00 100E16 -6:41:04
Litang 6 9 23N11 109E05 -7:16:20
Litian 14 1 26N58 114E10 -7:36:40
Litouqiao 1 1 31N15 118E54 -7:55:36
Liuanzhuang 26 1 39N14 117E11 -7:48:44
Liuba 20 9 33N32 107E07 -7:08:28
Liubotong 1 1 31N26 116E00 -7:44:00
Liucao 22 2 31N07 121E41 -8:06:44
Liuchen 6 9 23N09 110E29 -7:21:56
Liucheng 30 1 28N36 119E34 -7:58:16
Liucheng 6 9 24N32 109E21 -7:17:24
Liucheng 5 1 24N03 115E08 -7:40:32
Liuchengba 24 9 27N27 102E53 -6:51:32
Liuchow → Liuzhou 6 9 24N19 109E24 -7:17:36
Liucun 1 1 30N44 119E23 -7:57:32
Liudaogou 15 12 41N34 127E12 -8:28:48
Liudaohe 2 1 40N39 116E12 -7:44:48
Liudongqiao 1 1 31N03 119E32 -7:58:08
Liudu 3 1 26N44 119E33 -7:58:12
Liuduo 13 1 34N01 120E17 -8:01:08
Liuduzhuang 26 1 39N27 117E50 -7:51:20
Liuerbao 16 11 41N13 122E55 -8:11:40
Liufang 14 1 27N56 116E22 -7:45:28
Liufangling 11 1 30N27 114E27 -7:37:48
Liufentzu 25 6 24N57 121E35 -8:06:20
Liugezhuang 8 1 38N33 116E30 -7:46:00
Liugezhuang 8 1 40N03 118E16 -7:53:04
Liugou 8 1 40N57 118E18 -7:53:12
Liuguan 11 1 29N56 113E08 -7:32:32
Liuguantun 16 11 41N20 121E21 -8:05:24
Liuhang 22 2 31N21 121E22 -8:05:28
Liuhe 11 1 30N20 115E36 -7:42:24
Liuhe 10 1 33N20 112E48 -7:31:12
Liuhe 11 1 30N46 113E12 -7:32:48
Liuhe 15 12 42N15 125E43 -8:22:52
Liuhe 13 1 31N30 121E15 -8:05:00
Liuhe 8 1 39N31 118E17 -7:53:08
Liuhegou 16 11 41N56 122E44 -8:10:56
Liuheita 16 11 42N09 123E56 -8:15:44
Liuhejie 29 9 24N26 101E35 -6:46:20
Liuhekou 8 1 40N39 118E09 -7:52:36
Liuhuang 5 1 23N58 116E28 -7:45:52
Liuhudang 16 11 42N31 122E22 -8:09:28
Liujia 6 9 24N54 107E49 -7:11:16
Liujiachang 24 9 29N46 103E49 -6:55:16
Liujiachuan 8 1 40N07 114E47 -7:39:08
Liujiadai 13 1 31N57 120E23 -8:01:32
Liujiadian 17 11 50N07 124E17 -8:17:08
Liujiadu 13 1 32N15 120E33 -8:02:12
Liujiafen 2 1 39N58 115E47 -7:43:08
Liujiagangzi 16 11 41N28 122E33 -8:10:12
Liujiagou 21 1 37N47 120E53 -8:03:32
Liujiahe 11 1 32N06 113E21 -7:33:24
Liujiahe 16 11 40N40 123E58 -8:15:52
Liujiang 8 1 40N04 119E34 -7:58:16
Liujiashan 8 1 40N14 114E49 -7:39:16
Liujiatun 16 11 41N52 122E44 -8:10:56
Liujiatun 16 11 41N51 122E05 -8:08:20
Liujiatun 16 11 42N08 122E44 -8:10:56
Liujiawopeng 16 11 42N16 123E01 -8:12:04
Liujiazhen 13 1 32N04 121E30 -8:06:00
Liujiazi 16 11 41N00 120E13 -8:00:52
Liujiazi 16 11 42N36 122E15 -8:09:00
Liujiazi 16 11 41N48 123E47 -8:15:08
Liujingcun 8 1 39N27 115E26 -7:41:44
Liujisu 26 1 40N01 117E13 -7:48:52
Liukeshu 27 8 44N59 90E12 -6:00:48
Liuku 29 9 25N48 98E52 -6:35:28
Liulidian 13 1 31N31 119E17 -7:57:08
Liuligou 16 11 41N24 121E29 -8:05:56
Liulihezhen 2 1 39N36 116E01 -7:44:04
Liulin 11 1 31N34 113E14 -7:32:56
Liuliwei 5 1 24N20 114E03 -7:36:12
Liulongtai 16 11 41N32 120E56 -8:03:44
Liumachang 24 9 29N51 104E54 -6:59:36
Liumaogou 9 12 48N12 127E13 -8:28:52
Liupangtun 16 11 41N36 123E28 -8:13:52
Liuqianhutun 16 11 42N01 123E41 -8:14:44
Liuqiao 13 1 32N11 120E51 -8:03:24
Liuquan 13 1 34N27 117E20 -7:49:20
Liuquan 8 1 39N22 116E18 -7:45:12
Liurenba 11 1 29N57 114E49 -7:39:16
Liushi 30 1 28N03 120E51 -8:03:24
Liushi 8 1 38N33 115E44 -7:42:56
Liushilipu 1 1 32N45 115E58 -7:43:52
Liushudian 21 1 35N54 119E30 -7:58:00
Liushudixia 16 11 42N26 121E14 -8:04:56
Liushui 15 12 44N17 124E15 -8:17:00
Liushuigou 11 1 31N34 112E27 -7:29:48
Liushuquan 8 1 39N21 118E06 -7:52:24
Liusiqiao 14 1 29N47 116E21 -7:45:24
Liusong 8 1 39N40 117E08 -7:48:32
Liuta 10 1 35N52 115E18 -7:41:12
Liutai 17 9 41N20 113E43 -7:34:52
Liutaizi 16 11 41N46 122E39 -8:10:36
Liutang 6 9 24N58 110E21 -7:21:24
Liutiaozhaicun 16 11 41N29 123E12 -8:12:48
Liutuan 21 1 36N56 119E22 -7:57:28
Liutuhutun 16 11 40N44 120E32 -8:02:08
Liuwanglou 13 1 34N48 116E28 -7:45:52
Liuwei 13 1 32N16 119E28 -7:57:52
Liuwudian 3 1 24N36 118E13 -7:52:52
Liuxia 30 3 30N15 120E03 -8:00:12
Liuyang 12 1 28N09 113E38 -7:34:32
Liuyuan 10 1 36N10 114E34 -7:38:16
Liuyuankou 10 1 34N54 114E20 -7:37:20
Liuzhai 6 9 25N15 107E20 -7:09:20
Liuzhou 6 9 24N19 109E24 -7:17:36
Liuzhuang 13 1 33N10 120E19 -8:01:16
Lixi 14 1 27N39 116E19 -7:45:16
Lixi 14 1 29N15 114E46 -7:39:04
Lixian 12 1 29N30 111E37 -7:26:28
Lixian 8 1 38N29 115E34 -7:42:16
Lixian 2 1 39N33 116E26 -7:45:44
Lixin 3 1 26N52 116E42 -7:46:48
Lixin 1 1 33N06 116E08 -7:44:32
Lixing 1 1 33N28 115E28 -7:41:52
Lixingzhuang 8 1 39N25 117E56 -7:51:44
Liyang 23 1 37N28 113E37 -7:34:28
Liyang 13 1 31N26 119E29 -7:57:56
Liyuanbao 12 1 25N16 112E55 -7:31:40
Liyujiang 12 1 25N57 113E15 -7:33:00
Lize 24 9 30N08 106E11 -7:04:44
Lizhai 22 2 31N34 121E45 -8:07:00
Lizhou 24 9 28N08 102E10 -6:48:40
Lizhu 30 1 29N56 120E30 -8:02:00
Lizhuang 1 1 34N24 116E30 -7:46:00
Lizhuang 24 9 28N47 104E46 -6:59:04
Lizhuangqiao 13 1 31N48 119E37 -7:58:28
Liziwei 24 9 30N19 106E39 -7:06:36
Loho → Luohe 10 1 33N35 114E01 -7:36:04
Lojang → Luoyang 10 1 34N41 112E28 -7:29:52
Long'an 6 9 25N03 109E00 -7:16:00
Long'anqiao 9 12 47N31 124E27 -8:17:48
Longbu 14 1 25N32 115E24 -7:41:36
Longchang 24 9 29N21 105E17 -7:01:08
Longchang 16 11 40N53 123E08 -8:12:32
Longchuan 29 9 24N14 97E45 -6:31:00
Longchuan 5 1 24N07 115E17 -7:41:08
Longcun 5 1 23N34 115E33 -7:42:12
Longde 18 9 35N28 106E22 -7:05:28
Longdongtuo 24 9 29N59 106E21 -7:05:24
Longdou 3 1 27N25 117E24 -7:49:36
Longdu 13 1 31N51 118E56 -7:55:44
Longfengchang 24 9 30N26 105E38 -7:02:32
Longfengkan 16 11 41N51 124E01 -8:16:04
Longfengyutun 16 11 40N39 122E57 -8:11:48
Longgang 29 9 24N41 101E09 -6:44:36
Longgang 14 1 29N38 114E57 -7:39:48
Longgang 13 1 33N22 120E04 -8:00:16
Longgangzi 16 11 42N09 123E26 -8:13:44
Longguan 8 1 40N47 115E34 -7:42:16
Longgudu 14 1 27N45 116E14 -7:44:56
Longhua 8 1 41N17 117E37 -7:50:28
Longhua 22 2 31N09 121E26 -8:05:44
Longhua 5 1 22N42 113E59 -7:35:56
Longhua 5 1 23N37 114E14 -7:36:56
Longhui (Taohuaping) 12 1 27N00 110E59 -7:23:56
Longhui 14 1 25N32 114E47 -7:39:08
Longhui 24 9 29N32 104E48 -6:59:12
Longhutang 13 1 31N52 119E59 -7:59:56
Longji 24 9 29N23 106E04 -7:04:16
Longjiadian 16 11 42N10 120E47 -8:03:08
Longjiang 5 1 22N59 116E13 -7:44:52
Longjiang 24 9 29N48 105E03 -7:00:12
Longjiang 9 12 47N19 123E12 -8:12:48
Longjiang 5 1 22N53 113E04 -7:32:16
Longjie 24 9 29N53 104E32 -6:58:08
Longjin 14 1 28N37 116E37 -7:46:28
Longjing 5 1 23N53 112E52 -7:31:28
Longka 28 8 31N10 84E00 -5:36:00
Longka 28 7 33N12 79E47 -5:19:08
Longkangji 1 1 33N09 116E54 -7:47:36
Long Ke 31 4 22N23 114E22 -7:37:28
Longkou 14 1 26N11 115E15 -7:41:00
Longkou 21 1 37N38 120E18 -8:01:12
Longkou 10 1 32N56 114E57 -7:39:48
Longkou 11 1 29N57 113E47 -7:35:08
Longkouqiao 27 7 39N40 77E09 -5:08:36
Longli 7 9 26N26 106E58 -7:07:52
Longlin 6 9 24N49 105E31 -7:02:04
Longling 29 9 24N39 98E40 -6:34:40
Longmen 30 1 29N53 119E57 -7:59:48
Longmen 3 1 24N56 118E04 -7:52:16
Longmen 3 1 25N06 116E58 -7:47:52
Longmen 5 1 23N44 114E15 -7:37:00
Longmen 24 9 29N27 104E59 -6:59:56
Longmen 24 9 29N12 106E13 -7:04:52
Longmen 9 12 48N55 126E54 -8:27:36
Longmenchang 24 9 30N53 106E10 -7:04:40
Longmensuo 8 1 40N56 115E54 -7:43:36
Longmenzhang 24 9 28N59 106E13 -7:04:52
Longming 6 9 22N59 107E11 -7:08:44
Longmu 5 1 24N16 115E28 -7:41:52
Longnan 14 1 24N54 114E48 -7:39:12
Longnüsi 24 9 30N23 106E11 -7:04:44
Longping 11 1 29N53 115E41 -7:42:44
Longqiantai 16 11 41N23 120E52 -8:03:28
Longqu 10 1 34N16 114E49 -7:39:16
Longqu 13 1 34N54 116E47 -7:47:08
Longquan 30 1 28N04 119E07 -7:56:28
Longquanguan 23 1 38N55 113E51 -7:35:24
Longquanyi 24 9 30N34 104E16 -6:57:04
Longquanzhen 24 9 30N21 104E39 -6:58:36
Longshan 12 1 29N28 109E20 -7:17:20
Longshan 1 1 33N36 116E18 -7:45:12
Longshansuo 30 1 30N05 121E33 -8:06:12
Longsheng 6 9 25N48 110E00 -7:20:00
Longsheng 24 9 30N36 105E21 -7:01:24
Longshizhen 24 9 30N12 106E26 -7:05:44
Longshizhen 24 9 29N23 105E10 -7:00:40
Longshu 24 9 29N33 105E45 -7:03:00
Longtaichang 24 9 30N04 105E34 -7:02:16
Longtan 13 1 32N11 119E04 -7:56:16
Longtan 13 1 31N20 118E45 -7:55:00
Longtan 24 9 28N20 108E52 -7:15:28
Longtan 5 1 23N40 113E24 -7:33:36
Longtansi 24 9 30N42 104E10 -6:56:40
Longtanzhen 24 9 29N19 104E35 -6:58:20
Longtian 3 1 25N38 119E28 -7:57:52
Longtian'an 13 1 31N10 120E49 -8:03:16
Longtou 16 11 38N51 121E18 -8:05:12
Longtoupu 12 1 27N54 113E12 -7:32:48
Longtouwei 14 1 25N14 115E24 -7:41:36
Longwan 8 1 38N57 116E10 -7:44:40
Longwangmiao 16 11 41N38 121E04 -8:04:16
Longwangmiao 16 11 42N35 123E42 -8:14:48
Longwangmiao 4 8 40N36 95E52 -6:23:28
Longwangmiao 8 1 36N12 115E13 -7:40:52
Longwen 5 1 24N36 116E21 -7:45:24
Longwo 5 1 23N28 115E17 -7:41:08
Longwokou 13 1 32N18 119E52 -7:59:28
Longxi 4 9 34N56 104E47 -6:59:08
Longxi 24 9 29N59 106E09 -7:04:36
Longxian 20 9 34N51 106E59 -7:07:56
Longxian 24 9 29N09 105E50 -7:03:20
Longxi → Zhangzhou 3 1 24N33 117E39 -7:50:36
Longyan 3 1 25N08 117E02 -7:48:08
Longyao 8 1 37N23 114E41 -7:38:44
Longyou 30 1 29N02 119E10 -7:56:40
Longyuanba 14 1 24N56 114E27 -7:37:48
Longzhaogou 16 11 40N49 124E36 -8:18:24
Longzhen 9 12 48N41 126E42 -8:26:48
Longzhou 6 9 22N22 106E52 -7:07:28
Longzi 28 8 28N25 92E31 -6:10:04
Lonzhen 24 9 30N00 103E59 -6:55:56
Loshan → Leshan 24 9 29N34 103E45 -6:55:00
Lotung 25 6 24N41 121E46 -8:07:04
Loude 21 1 35N54 117E18 -7:49:12
Loujiaying 17 1 42N04 116E04 -7:44:16
Loutang 22 2 31N26 121E12 -8:04:48
Loyang → Luoyang 10 1 34N41 112E28 -7:29:52
Lu'an 1 1 31N44 116E31 -7:46:04
Luancheng 8 1 37N53 114E39 -7:38:36
Luancheng 6 9 22N45 108E51 -7:15:24
Luanchuan 10 1 33N51 111E36 -7:26:24
Luanhe 8 1 40N57 117E44 -7:50:56
Luannan (Bencheng) 8 1 39N32 118E39 -7:54:36
Luanping (Anjiangying) 8 1 40N57 117E20 -7:49:20
Luanshishan 16 11 42N10 123E41 -8:14:44
Luanxian 8 1 39N45 118E44 -7:54:56
Lubao 5 1 23N22 112E55 -7:31:40
Lubu 5 10 23N09 112E13 -7:28:52
Lucaogou 27 8 42N26 96E55 -6:27:40
Luchang 24 9 26N23 102E18 -6:49:12
Lücheng 13 1 31N55 119E44 -7:58:56
Lucheng 13 1 31N47 120E02 -8:00:08
Lucheng 6 9 24N21 106E00 -7:04:00
Luchou 25 6 25N05 121E28 -8:05:52
Luchow 1 1 31N54 117E18 -7:49:12
Luchow → Luzhou 24 9 28N54 105E27 -7:01:48
Luchuan 6 9 22N19 110E11 -7:20:44
Luci 30 1 29N52 119E47 -7:59:08
Lucikou 14 1 28N56 116E04 -7:44:16
Lucun 21 1 36N12 118E01 -7:52:04
Lucun 1 1 30N49 119E26 -7:57:44
Lüda (Dairen) 16 11 38N53 121E35 -8:06:20
Ludao 9 12 43N51 129E19 -8:37:16
Ludian 29 9 27N11 103E33 -6:54:12
Luding 24 9 29N55 102E15 -6:49:00
Ludonghe 29 9 25N53 103E33 -6:54:12
Lueyang 20 9 33N20 106E10 -7:04:40
Lüfangsicun 16 11 41N25 123E22 -8:13:28
Lufeng 29 9 25N07 102E07 -6:48:28
Lufeng 5 1 22N57 115E38 -7:42:32
Lugang 1 1 31N17 118E22 -7:53:28
Lugang 14 1 27N23 115E36 -7:42:24
Lugongshi 13 1 31N38 121E12 -8:04:48
Lugouqiao 2 1 39N51 116E13 -7:44:52
Lugu 24 9 28N21 102E09 -6:48:36
Lühedian 10 1 32N33 114E28 -7:37:52
Luhsien → Luzhou 24 9 28N54 105E27 -7:01:48
Luhuo 24 9 31N26 100E48 -6:43:12
Lujia 22 2 31N22 121E18 -8:05:12
Lujia 22 2 31N15 121E37 -8:06:28
Lujia 13 1 31N19 121E03 -8:04:12
Lujiabang 13 1 31N20 121E01 -8:04:04
Lujiachang 24 9 30N14 105E34 -7:02:16
Lujiagangzi 16 11 42N05 122E59 -8:11:56
Lujiang 1 1 31N14 117E17 -7:49:08
Lujiao 12 1 29N10 112E52 -7:31:28
Lujiaoxi 24 9 28N55 105E48 -7:03:12
Lujiaqiao 13 1 31N47 120E27 -8:01:48
Lujiaqiao 24 9 28N50 106E21 -7:05:24
Lujiatun 16 11 40N44 122E11 -8:08:44
Lujiatun 16 11 41N58 122E38 -8:10:32
Lujiatun 16 11 42N18 124E15 -8:17:00
Lujiatun 16 11 41N10 121E56 -8:07:44
Lujiazhou 14 1 28N16 114E35 -7:38:20
Lukang 25 6 24N03 120E25 -8:01:40

Lukeqin 27 8 42N44 89E42 -5:58:48
Lukong 24 9 29N31 105E39 -7:02:36
Lukou 13 1 31N48 118E52 -7:55:28
Lukou 14 1 27N14 114E04 -7:36:16
Lukoupu 12 1 29N30 113E26 -7:33:44
Lukouyu 12 1 28N24 113E18 -7:33:12
Lükqün 27 8 42N44 89E42 -5:58:48
Luliang 29 9 25N05 103E36 -6:54:24
Luliao 25 6 25N07 121E39 -8:06:36
Lulong 8 1 39N54 118E50 -7:55:20
Luluo 8 1 37N06 113E58 -7:35:52
Lumaling 28 8 29N53 92E37 -6:10:28
Lumu 13 3 31N22 120E37 -8:02:28
Lunan 29 9 24N49 103E16 -6:53:04
Lungch'i → Zhangzhou 3
1 24N33 117E39 -7:50:36
Lunge'nake 28 8 31N45 85E55 -5:43:40
Lungt'an 25 6 24N52 121E12 -8:04:48
Lunjiao 5 1 22N53 113E13 -7:32:52
Lunongzha 13 1 31N59 120E55 -8:03:40
Lunzhen 21 1 36N47 116E34 -7:46:16
Luoba 24 9 29N08 106E11 -7:04:44
Luoba 5 1 24N51 114E13 -7:36:52
Luobei (Fengxiang) 9
12 47N34 130E50 -8:43:20
Luobo 24 9 28N22 101E38 -6:46:32
Luobu 6 9 24N30 109E40 -7:18:40
Luobumiao 17 9 40N19 107E30 -7:10:00
Luobuqiongzi 28
8 29N02 89E15 -5:57:00
Luochanghe 1 1 31N01 117E18 -7:49:12
Luocheng 24 9 29N23 104E01 -6:56:04
Luocheng 6 9 24N51 108E59 -7:15:56
Luochuan 20 9 35N55 109E26 -7:17:44
Luoci 29 9 25N19 102E18 -6:49:12
Luodian 22 2 31N25 121E20 -8:05:20
Luoding 5 10 22N47 111E31 -7:26:04
Luoduoke 28 7 33N28 79E40 -5:18:40
Luoduzhen 24 9 30N22 106E35 -7:06:20
Luofa 26 1 39N25 116E50 -7:47:20
Luofang 14 1 27N52 115E06 -7:40:24
Luofang 14 1 28N40 115E04 -7:40:16
Luofu 5 1 24N32 115E35 -7:42:20
Luogang 5 1 24N25 115E38 -7:42:32
Luogang 5 1 23N11 113E30 -7:34:00
Luoguhe 17 11 53N18 121E30 -8:06:00
Luohe 10 1 33N35 114E01 -7:36:04
Luoheya 21 1 35N46 118E54 -7:55:36
Luohua 3 1 26N35 118E43 -7:54:52
Luoji 1 1 32N06 117E16 -7:49:04
Luojiachang 24 9 30N49 106E32 -7:06:08
Luojiang 24 9 31N21 104E28 -6:57:52
Luojiatang 30 3 30N18 120E13 -8:00:52
Luojiatun 16 11 40N55 122E04 -8:08:16
Luojiatun 8 1 40N11 118E34 -7:54:16
Luojiatun 16 11 42N06 122E44 -8:10:56
Luojiawei 14 1 26N55 115E02 -7:40:08
Luoke 5 1 24N07 114E28 -7:37:52
Luokeng 5 1 24N32 113E23 -7:33:32
Luokou 14 1 25N46 115E39 -7:42:36
Luokou 14 1 28N54 117E24 -7:49:36
Luolong 24 9 28N49 104E46 -6:59:04
Luonan 20 9 34N05 110E04 -7:20:16
Luoning 10 1 34N25 111E42 -7:26:48
Luoping 29 9 24N59 104E21 -6:57:24
Luopu 27 7 37N02 80E15 -5:21:00
Luoqi 24 9 29N48 106E56 -7:07:44
Luoqiao 3 1 26N28 119E01 -7:56:04
Luoquanzhen 24 9 29N50 104E31 -6:58:04
Luoshan 8 1 39N55 117E33 -7:50:12
Luoshan 10 1 32N13 114E32 -7:38:08
Luoshan 11 1 29N41 113E18 -7:33:12
Luoshe 30 1 30N41 120E04 -8:00:16
Luoshe 13 1 31N39 120E11 -8:00:44
Luoshuihe 23 1 39N27 114E19 -7:37:16
Luotian 11 1 30N48 115E22 -7:41:28
Luotuodian 10 1 32N13 113E49 -7:35:16
Luotuoqiao 30 1 29N56 121E32 -8:06:08
Luowenba 24 9 31N48 107E48 -7:11:12
Luowenyu 8 1 40N16 117E57 -7:51:48
Luoxi 14 1 29N05 114E58 -7:39:52
Luoyang 13 1 31N39 120E05 -8:00:20
Luoyang (Loyang) 10
1 34N41 112E28 -7:29:52
Luoyuan 3 1 26N31 119E32 -7:58:08
Luozha 28 8 28N24 90E49 -6:03:16
Luozhexi 24 9 29N02 103E54 -6:55:36
Luqiao 30 1 28N35 121E22 -8:05:28
Luqiao 1 1 32N34 117E14 -7:48:56
Luqu 4 9 34N41 102E22 -6:49:28
Lushan 10 1 33N45 112E53 -7:31:32
Lushan 24 9 30N15 102E58 -6:51:52
Lushanguanliju 14
1 29N33 115E58 -7:43:52
Lushi 10 1 34N05 111E01 -7:24:04
Lüshikou 30 1 29N16 120E17 -8:01:08
Lushui 29 9 26N00 98E51 -6:35:24
Lüshun (Port Arthur) 16
11 38N48 121E16 -8:05:04
Lüsi 13 1 32N03 121E36 -8:06:24
Lutai 10 1 33N32 115E03 -7:40:12
Lü-Ta → Lüda 16
11 38N53 121E35 -8:06:20
Lütan 10 1 34N07 114E27 -7:37:48
Lütan 30 1 28N57 119E46 -7:59:04
Lutang 12 1 25N39 112E46 -7:31:04
Lütian 5 1 23N48 113E56 -7:35:44
Lutian 14 1 26N33 114E38 -7:38:32
Lutou 11 1 32N16 112E53 -7:31:32
Luxi (Mangshi) 29
9 24N20 98E25 -6:33:40
Luxi 29 9 24N32 103E41 -6:54:44
Lüxia 3 1 26N41 120E06 -8:00:24
Luxian 24 9 28N55 105E29 -7:01:56
Lüxiang 22 2 30N50 121E10 -8:04:40

Luxiang 13 1 31N32 120E45 -8:03:00
Luxikou 11 1 29N54 113E42 -7:34:48
Luxu 13 1 31N01 120E50 -8:03:20
Lüxuqiao 13 1 31N50 119E31 -7:58:04
Luyan 30 1 30N25 120E53 -8:03:32
Lüyang 16 11 41N23 121E40 -8:06:40
Luyeh 25 6 22N55 121E08 -8:04:32
Luyi 10 1 33N53 115E28 -7:41:52
Luyu 22 2 31N34 121E41 -8:06:44
Luyuan 13 1 31N51 120E38 -8:02:32
Luyuan 2 1 39N54 116E27 -7:45:48
Luzhai 6 9 24N31 109E50 -7:19:20
Luzhi 13 1 31N16 120E52 -8:03:28
Luzhou 24 9 28N54 105E27 -7:01:48
Lwanhsien → Luanxian 8
1 39N45 118E44 -7:54:56
Ma'anshan 1 1 31N42 118E30 -7:54:00
Maanshan 24 9 29N52 104E59 -6:59:56
Maba 13 1 32N59 118E48 -7:55:12
Mabaoquan 2 1 40N09 115E53 -7:43:32
Mabi 23 1 35N59 112E15 -7:29:00
Mabi 3 1 26N21 119E36 -7:58:24
Mabian 24 9 28N48 103E41 -6:54:44
Mabuguai 11 1 29N49 112E42 -7:30:48
Macau (Aomen) 32
5 22N14 113E35 -7:34:20
Machang 13 1 34N06 119E02 -7:56:08
Machang 16 11 42N05 119E42 -7:58:48
Machangcun 8 1 38N54 115E26 -7:41:44
Machangfu 29 9 25N14 103E45 -6:55:00
Macheng 11 1 31N13 115E00 -7:40:00
Macunqiao 10 1 33N50 116E13 -7:44:52
Madang 14 1 29N58 116E40 -7:46:40
Madian 13 1 32N15 119E58 -7:59:52
Madida 15 12 42N57 130E48 -8:43:12
Madingzi 16 11 42N08 120E52 -8:03:28
Madiyi 12 1 28N14 110E30 -7:22:00
Madoi 19 8 34N53 98E24 -6:33:36
Maerkansu 27 7 39N19 73E53 -4:55:32
Ma'erna 24 9 31N13 102E02 -6:48:08
Mafang 2 1 40N02 117E01 -7:48:04
Mafangchang 24 9 29N24 106E06 -7:04:24
Mafangcun 2 1 40N09 116E24 -7:45:36
Mafengtun 16 11 40N49 122E54 -8:11:36
Magezhuang 8 1 40N08 117E59 -7:51:56
Maguan 29 9 22N59 104E19 -6:57:16
Maguanying 2 1 39N52 116E17 -7:45:08
Maguzhan 28 8 31N15 88E00 -5:52:00
Mahai 19 8 38N17 94E13 -6:16:52
Mahao 15 12 43N10 127E59 -8:31:56
Mahuiling 14 1 29N24 115E48 -7:43:12
Maichen 5 8 20N29 109E59 -7:19:56
Maigaiti 27 7 38N55 77E38 -5:10:32
Maiqihamiao 17
11 43N22 120E46 -8:03:04
Maishi 11 1 29N11 113E58 -7:35:52
Maixie 14 1 27N38 115E29 -7:41:56
Majia 13 1 32N32 118E50 -7:55:20
Majiacun 30 1 30N08 119E58 -7:59:52
Majiahe 4 9 35N20 104E46 -6:59:04
Majian 30 1 29N19 119E36 -7:58:24
Majian 30 1 29N43 120E00 -8:00:00
Majiang 6 9 23N48 111E09 -7:24:36
Majiang 7 9 26N28 107E28 -7:09:52
Majiangzong 28 8 30N27 90E03 -6:00:12
Majiaoba 24 9 32N14 104E35 -6:58:20
Majiaping 4 9 36N31 103E20 -6:53:20
Majiasi 26 1 39N03 117E05 -7:48:20
Majiawopu 16 11 41N46 121E06 -8:04:24
Majiayan 12 1 27N26 112E56 -7:31:44
Majiazhai 16 11 42N22 124E04 -8:16:16
Majiazhou 14 1 26N46 114E47 -7:39:08
Majie 29 9 23N50 105E07 -7:00:28
Majie 29 9 25N03 103E45 -6:55:00
Majin 30 1 29N18 118E24 -7:53:36
Majinzhuangzi 16
11 41N55 123E53 -8:15:32
Majuqiao 2 1 39N46 116E32 -7:46:08
Majuzigou 16 11 41N49 121E38 -8:06:32
Maku 8 1 39N33 114E46 -7:39:04
Makung (P'enghu) 25
6 23N34 119E34 -7:58:16
Malanyu 8 1 40N11 117E42 -7:50:48
Maliangping 11 1 31N29 111E20 -7:25:20
Malianjingzi 4 8 41N32 95E23 -6:21:32
Malienkang 25 6 25N10 121E39 -8:06:36
Maliuchang 24 9 29N05 104E07 -6:56:28
Maliuping 24 9 29N55 106E23 -7:05:32
Ma Liu Shui 31 4 22N25 114E12 -7:36:48
Malizhen 29 9 23N10 104E35 -6:58:20
Malugou 15 12 43N39 128E27 -8:33:48
Maluzhen 22 2 31N20 121E16 -8:05:04
Mamahuolang 16
11 42N24 124E12 -8:16:48
Mamajiecun 16 11 41N26 122E51 -8:11:24
Mamiao 21 1 35N04 116E10 -7:44:40
Mamuchi 21 1 35N41 118E17 -7:53:08
Manas 27 8 44N18 86E13 -5:44:52
Ma'nasi 27 8 44N18 86E13 -5:44:52
Manban 29 9 23N04 103E11 -6:52:44
Manbian 29 9 24N19 100E32 -6:42:08
Mancheng 8 1 38N56 115E20 -7:41:20
Manchouli → Manzhouli 17
11 49N35 117E22 -7:49:28
Mandehu 16 11 42N07 121E33 -8:06:12
Manduhu 16 11 41N36 122E38 -8:10:32
Mandun 29 9 22N17 100E05 -6:40:20
Mangchang 6 9 25N08 107E31 -7:10:04
Mange 28 8 32N25 83E35 -5:34:20
Mangnuiyingzi 16
11 41N37 120E43 -8:02:52
Mangui 17 11 52N03 122E13 -8:08:52
Mangya 19 8 37N40 90E50 -6:03:20
Maniganggo 24 9 32N01 99E11 -6:36:44
Manjiang 15 12 41N57 127E36 -8:30:24

Manjing 24 9 29N55 104E07 -6:56:28
Manni 28 8 34N48 87E15 -5:49:00
Manpitou 5 10 22N17 112E52 -7:31:28
Mantou 16 11 42N27 122E26 -8:09:44
Manzhouli 17 11 49N35 117E22 -7:49:28
Maoba 11 1 30N02 108E59 -7:15:56
Maocifan 11 1 31N40 112E53 -7:31:32
Maocun 13 1 34N25 117E16 -7:49:04
Maodianzi 24 9 29N45 104E55 -6:59:40
Maodianzi 24 9 30N42 104E25 -6:57:40
Mao'ertuo 24 9 29N19 106E24 -7:05:36
Maojiagou 16 11 40N58 120E51 -8:03:24
Maojiaji 11 1 31N32 114E16 -7:37:04
Maojiakou 11 1 29N53 112E58 -7:31:52
Maojiaping 8 1 40N34 114E43 -7:38:52
Maojiapuzi 16 11 41N10 123E32 -8:14:08
Maojiatun 16 11 41N05 121E58 -8:07:52
Maojiazao 23 1 39N53 113E26 -7:33:44
Maolin 15 12 43N58 123E24 -8:13:36
Maolin 1 1 30N32 118E14 -7:52:56
Maoming 5 8 21N39 110E54 -7:23:36
Maomu 4 9 40N18 99E28 -6:37:52
Ma On Shan Tsuen 31
4 22N24 114E14 -7:36:56
Maoping 11 1 30N23 110E33 -7:22:12
Maoshan 8 1 40N17 117E26 -7:49:44
Maoshi 12 1 26N57 113E05 -7:32:20
Maowen 24 9 31N30 103E39 -6:54:36
Maoxing 9 12 45N32 124E33 -8:18:12
Maozhou 8 1 38N51 116E06 -7:44:24
Maping 3 1 24N16 117E54 -7:51:36
Maping 11 1 31N36 113E32 -7:34:08
Mapujiang 8 1 40N24 114E56 -7:39:44
Maqiangou 8 1 39N30 115E02 -7:40:08
Maqiao 11 1 29N48 114E22 -7:37:28
Maqiao 30 1 30N28 120E42 -8:02:48
Mara 28 8 28N11 94E08 -6:16:32
Markam 28 8 29N40 98E30 -6:34:00
Markit 27 8 38N55 77E38 -5:10:32
Marong 24 9 31N07 99E20 -6:37:20
Mase 29 9 27N16 104E08 -6:56:32
Masha 3 1 27N26 117E50 -7:51:20
Mashan 14 1 27N33 113E46 -7:35:04
Mashan 9 12 45N13 130E35 -8:42:20
Mashan 6 9 23N50 108E16 -7:13:04
Mashenqiao 26 1 40N04 117E36 -7:50:24
Mashi 14 1 29N05 114E22 -7:37:28
Mashi 5 1 25N01 114E09 -7:36:36
Matajing 24 9 29N32 104E00 -6:56:00
Matang 12 1 29N17 113E05 -7:32:20
Matang 13 1 32N20 121E04 -8:04:16
Matou 1 1 30N48 118E29 -7:53:56
Matou 8 1 36N29 114E26 -7:37:44
Matou 2 1 39N46 116E49 -7:47:16
Matou 8 1 39N18 116E45 -7:47:00
Matou 2 1 39N33 116E07 -7:44:28
Matou 3 1 25N14 118E22 -7:53:28
Matou 14 1 29N49 115E35 -7:42:20
Matou 25 6 23N11 120E14 -8:00:56
Matouji 21 1 35N02 115E07 -7:40:28
Matouxi 24 9 30N15 106E31 -7:06:04
Matouying 8 1 39N18 118E47 -7:55:08
Matouzhen 21 1 34N39 118E18 -7:53:12
Matouzhen 13 1 33N32 118E56 -7:55:44
Mawangtang 30 1 30N42 120E42 -8:02:48
Mawuba 24 9 29N50 108E11 -7:12:44
Maxiang 3 1 24N41 118E15 -7:53:00
Mayang 12 1 27N41 109E35 -7:18:20
Mayao 30 1 30N50 120E23 -8:01:32
Mayu 30 1 27N48 120E26 -8:01:44
Mazha 5 1 23N27 114E00 -7:36:00
Mazhan 21 1 36N04 118E45 -7:55:00
Mazhangfang 16
11 40N44 120E53 -8:03:32
Mazhangfang 16
11 42N23 122E26 -8:09:44
Mazhuang 10 1 32N54 114E03 -7:36:12
Mazhuang 8 1 37N47 115E17 -7:41:08
Mazhuang 8 1 39N11 116E15 -7:45:00
Mazigou 8 1 40N28 114E48 -7:39:12
Meichang 26 1 39N22 117E10 -7:48:40
Meichuan 11 1 30N10 115E36 -7:42:24
Meicun 13 1 31N33 120E24 -8:01:36
Meicun 3 1 25N30 116E56 -7:47:44
Meicun 1 1 30N22 119E01 -7:56:04
Meicun 1 1 30N40 119E04 -7:56:16
Meierkaisong 28
8 30N54 84E31 -5:38:04
Meihsien → Meixian 5
1 24N21 116E08 -7:44:32
Meihua 3 1 26N02 119E40 -7:58:40
Meihuajie 5 1 25N14 113E05 -7:32:20
Meikeng 5 1 23N59 114E05 -7:36:20
Meili 13 1 31N42 120E53 -8:03:32
Meilie 3 1 26N18 117E38 -7:50:32
Meilin 1 1 30N35 119E04 -7:56:16
Meilin 5 1 23N18 115E58 -7:43:52
Meilong 5 1 22N56 115E17 -7:41:08
Meiluyingzi 16
11 42N18 122E10 -8:08:40
Meinung 25 6 22N54 120E32 -8:02:08
Meishan 30 1 31N06 119E43 -7:58:52
Meishan 24 9 30N02 103E49 -6:55:16
Meitan 7 9 27N46 107E35 -7:10:20
Meitian 12 1 25N21 112E47 -7:31:08
Meixi 30 1 30N48 119E45 -7:59:00
Meixian 12 1 28N52 113E38 -7:34:32
Meixian 5 1 24N21 116E08 -7:44:32
Meiyao 17 11 49N37 124E30 -8:18:00
Meizhai 7 9 25N30 108E50 -7:15:20
Meizhou 3 1 23N50 117E20 -7:49:20
Meizhu 1 1 31N16 119E13 -7:56:52
Menchang 26 1 38N54 117E01 -7:48:04
Menda 17 11 43N40 123E08 -8:12:32
Mendatai 19 8 38N51 94E39 -6:18:36

Mengban 29	9	23N08	100E19	-6:41:16
Mengbang 29	9	21N28	101E19	-6:45:16
Mengcheng 1	1	33N17	116E33	-7:46:12
Mengcun 8	1	38N06	117E05	-7:48:20
Mengdapu 16	11	41N35	123E12	-8:12:48
Menggu 29	9	26N34	102E57	-6:51:48
Menggubao 16	11	42N27	122E23	-8:09:32
Menggudai 17	9	38N10	108E15	-7:13:00
Menghai 29	9	22N00	100E26	-6:41:44
Menghe 13	1	32N03	119E47	-7:59:08
Menghun 29	9	21N44	100E23	-6:41:32
Mengjiacun 1	1	31N33	118E46	-7:55:04
Mengjiagang 9	12	46N22	130E40	-8:42:40
Mengjiatai 16	11	42N06	123E21	-8:13:24
Mengjiawan 20	9	38N35	109E25	-7:17:40
Mengjiawopeng 16	11	41N22	121E51	-8:07:24
Mengjiayuanjia 8	1	40N52	118E08	-7:52:32
Mengjiazhai 22	2	31N18	121E19	-8:05:16
Mengka 29	9	25N10	98E01	-6:32:04
Menglian 29	9	22N20	99E38	-6:38:32
Mengluchang 24	9	29N19	103E35	-6:54:20
Mengmucun 13	1	31N59	119E01	-7:56:04
Mengqigou 16	11	42N00	121E08	-8:04:32
Mengshan 6	9	24N07	110E33	-7:22:12
Mengtong 24	9	30N44	105E53	-7:03:32
Mengwang 29	9	22N26	100E34	-6:42:16
Mengyin 21	1	35N45	117E57	-7:51:48
Mengzhe 29	9	22N02	100E16	-6:41:04
Mengzhi 29	9	24N10	99E46	-6:39:04
Mengzi 29	9	23N22	103E20	-6:53:20
Menjiaqiangzi 16	11	42N29	121E19	-8:05:16
Menkoutang 1	1	31N01	119E27	-7:57:48
Mentougou 2	1	39N56	116E03	-7:44:12
Menyuan 19	9	37N27	101E48	-6:47:12
Mianchi 10	1	34N48	111E49	-7:27:16
Mianduhe 17	11	49N05	121E06	-8:04:24
Mianhu 5	1	23N28	116E09	-7:44:36
Mianhuadi 16	11	41N15	120E49	-8:03:16
Mianning 24	9	28N39	102E09	-6:48:36
Mianxian 20	9	33N09	106E48	-7:07:12
Mianyang 24	9	31N30	104E49	-6:59:16
Mianyang 11	1	30N23	113E25	-7:33:40
Mianzhu 24	9	31N20	104E09	-6:56:36
Miaoergou 27	8	45N32	83E52	-5:35:28
Miaofengshan 2	1	40N04	116E13	-7:44:52
Miaogou 16	11	41N12	120E40	-8:02:40
Miaojiagou 16	11	42N16	123E22	-8:13:28
Miaojiatun 16	11	40N54	120E55	-8:03:40
Miaokou 10	1	35N48	114E09	-7:36:36
Miaoli 25	6	24N34	120E49	-8:03:16
Miaopu 1	1	31N00	118E44	-7:54:56
Miaoqian 1	1	30N33	117E44	-7:50:56
Miaotou 13	1	30N58	120E33	-8:02:12
Miaowan 10	1	33N07	114E41	-7:38:44
Miaoyang 16	11	40N49	124E24	-8:17:36
Miaozhen 22	2	31N43	121E21	-8:05:24
Miaozigou 24	9	30N17	104E35	-6:58:20
Midu 29	9	25N22	100E31	-6:42:04
Miehuapu 26	1	39N11	117E44	-7:50:56
Miesaituo 19	8	35N52	93E40	-6:14:40
Mihuangzhuang 8	1	39N07	116E12	-7:44:48
Mijiang 15	12	43N01	130E08	-8:40:32
Mile 29	9	24N26	103E26	-6:53:44
Miluo 12	1	28N50	113E04	-7:32:16
Minfeng 27	8	37N05	82E40	-5:30:40
Mingcheng 15	12	43N11	125E59	-8:23:56
Minggang 10	1	32N29	114E03	-7:36:12
Minggao 10	1	34N20	112E15	-7:29:00
Minghuang 13	1	31N41	119E56	-7:59:44
Mingjuesi 13	1	31N34	118E53	-7:55:32
Mingshantou 12	1	29N18	112E33	-7:30:12
Mingshui 27	8	42N06	96E04	-6:24:16
Mingshui 9	12	47N10	125E55	-8:23:40
Mingwan 13	1	31N04	120E17	-8:01:08
Mingxi 3	1	26N24	117E13	-7:48:52
Mingyuegou 15	12	43N07	128E54	-8:35:36
Mingyuelu 27	7	39N34	75E26	-5:01:44
Minhang 22	2	31N01	121E24	-8:05:36
Minhou 3	1	26N12	119E06	-7:56:24
Minjiadianzi 16	11	41N35	121E41	-8:06:44
Minjiaji 11	1	31N08	115E01	-7:40:04
Minle 5	1	22N59	112E58	-7:31:52
Minle 4	9	38N27	100E56	-6:43:44
Minqiao 13	1	32N53	119E13	-7:56:52
Minqin 4	9	38N42	103E11	-6:52:44
Minqing 3	1	26N12	118E51	-7:55:24
Minquan 10	1	34N41	115E11	-7:40:44
Minxian 4	9	34N26	104E02	-6:56:08
Miquan 27	8	44N06	87E35	-5:50:20
Mishan 9	12	45N33	131E52	-8:47:28
Misikan 28	8	35N45	89E25	-5:57:40
Mituo 24	9	28N53	105E37	-7:02:28
Mixian 10	1	34N31	113E22	-7:33:28
Mixin 24	9	30N23	105E46	-7:03:04
Miyi 24	9	27N00	102E08	-6:48:32
Miyun 2	1	40N22	116E50	-7:47:20
Mizhi 20	9	37N49	110E02	-7:20:08
Mocheng 13	1	31N35	120E43	-8:02:52
Mohe 17	11	53N29	122E19	-8:09:16
Moji 27	7	38N59	74E24	-4:57:36
Mojiang 29	9	23N28	101E39	-6:46:36
Moke 24	9	30N14	100E01	-6:40:04
Molimiao 17	11	43N34	121E54	-8:07:36
Molingguan 13	1	31N50	118E50	-7:55:20
Monggon Qulu 17	11	48N35	119E49	-7:59:16
Mong Tung Hang 31	4	22N20	114E02	-7:36:08
Mopo 10	1	33N07	113E02	-7:32:08
Morin Dawa 17	11	48N28	124E27	-8:17:48
Moshanpu 12	1	29N34	112E41	-7:30:44
Moshiyu 16	11	41N15	124E05	-8:16:20
Motou 13	1	32N18	120E34	-8:02:16
Motuo 28	8	29N20	95E15	-6:21:00
Mouding 29	9	25N24	101E35	-6:46:20
Moukden → Shenyang 16	11	41N48	123E27	-8:13:48
Mowang 11	1	30N31	113E34	-7:34:16
Mowu 3	1	26N50	117E42	-7:50:48
Moxi 24	9	30N18	105E41	-7:02:44
Moyu 27	7	37N17	79E44	-5:18:56
Mozhugongka 28	8	29N50	91E45	-6:07:00
Mozichang 24	9	29N20	103E53	-6:55:32
Mucha 25	6	24N59	121E34	-8:06:16
Muchangpu 1	1	31N55	116E35	-7:46:20
Muchengzhen 24	9	29N47	103E29	-6:53:56
Muchuan 24	9	28N55	103E58	-6:55:52
Mucun 14	1	26N44	114E00	-7:36:00
Mudanjiang 9	12	44N35	129E36	-8:38:24
Mudongzhen 24	9	29N35	106E51	-7:07:24
Mudu 13	3	31N15	120E30	-8:02:00
Mu'er 24	9	29N48	106E37	-7:06:28
Mugang 11	1	29N44	115E14	-7:40:56
Mui Wo 31	4	22N16	113E59	-7:35:56
Mujiapucun 16	11	41N06	122E48	-8:11:12
Mujiayu 2	1	40N24	116E55	-7:47:40
Mukden → Shenyang 16	11	41N48	123E27	-8:13:48
Mula 24	9	29N40	100E39	-6:42:36
Mulan 9	12	45N57	128E03	-8:32:12
Mulei 27	8	43N49	90E11	-6:00:44
Muli 24	9	27N50	101E15	-6:45:00
Muling 9	12	44N56	130E31	-8:42:04
Muling 9	12	44N31	130E13	-8:40:52
Mumen 24	9	32N09	106E28	-7:05:52
Muping 21	1	37N24	121E35	-8:06:20
Muqi 16	11	41N46	124E39	-8:18:36
Mutanchiang → Mudanjiang 9	12	44N35	129E36	-8:38:24
Mutankiang → Mudanjiang 9	12	44N35	129E36	-8:38:24
Mutouchengzi 16	11	41N20	119E59	-7:59:56
Mutouhao 24	9	28N49	105E04	-7:00:16
Muwopu 16	11	41N03	121E12	-8:04:48
Muxihe 11	1	31N03	115E21	-7:41:24
Muyang 3	1	27N06	119E34	-7:58:16
Muzhen 1	1	30N43	117E56	-7:51:44
Nabula 28	7	31N55	80E10	-5:20:40
Nahe 9	12	48N28	124E52	-8:19:28
Naidong 28	8	29N14	91E46	-6:07:04
Nailin 17	11	41N53	119E15	-7:57:00
Naiman Qi 17	11	42N55	120E43	-8:02:52
Naizifang 8	1	39N36	116E47	-7:47:08
N'aizishen 15	12	43N41	127E29	-8:29:56
Najinkouzi 9	12	50N23	126E57	-8:27:48
Nakechake 28	8	30N11	83E09	-5:32:36
Nakou 3	1	27N09	117E38	-7:50:32
Nalao 6	9	24N22	105E23	-7:01:32
Naliang 6	9	21N43	107E51	-7:11:24
Nalige 27	8	43N28	83E44	-5:34:56
Nalisan 16	11	42N06	122E12	-8:08:48
Nalong 29	9	23N35	106E05	-7:04:20
Namling Dzong → Nanmulin 28	8	29N41	89E04	-5:56:16
Nan'an 3	1	24N58	118E23	-7:53:32
Nan'anba 24	9	28N46	104E38	-6:58:32
Nan'ao 5	1	23N27	117E02	-7:48:08
Nanao 25	6	24N28	121E48	-8:07:12
Nanba 24	9	32N20	104E58	-6:59:52
Nanbaita 8	1	38N58	115E39	-7:42:36
Nanbaixia 21	1	35N45	117E23	-7:49:32
Nanbaozhen 22	2	31N32	121E37	-8:06:28
Nanbu 24	9	31N23	106E02	-7:04:08
Nancaicun 26	1	39N28	117E01	-7:48:04
Nancha 9	12	47N08	129E19	-8:37:16
Nanchang (Liantang) 14	1	28N34	115E56	-7:43:44
Nanchang 14	1	28N41	115E53	-7:43:32
Nancheng 14	1	27N35	116E40	-7:46:40
Nancheng 3	1	25N39	118E26	-7:53:44
Nancheng → Hanzhong 20	9	33N08	107E02	-7:08:08
Nanching → Nanjing 13	3	32N03	118E47	-7:55:08
Nanchong 24	9	30N48	106E04	-7:04:16
Nanchuan 24	9	29N08	107E07	-7:08:28
Nanchuang 25	6	24N36	120E59	-8:03:56
Nanch'ung → Nanchong 24	9	30N48	106E04	-7:04:16
Nancun 21	1	36N32	120E06	-8:00:24
Nancun 23	1	39N46	114E07	-7:36:28
Nandashan 12	1	29N01	112E43	-7:30:52
Nandu 13	1	31N27	119E19	-7:57:16
Nanduluohe 2	1	40N11	117E13	-7:48:52
Nanfangquan 13	1	31N26	120E16	-8:01:04
Nanfen 16	11	41N06	123E44	-8:14:56
Nanfeng 14	1	27N15	116E32	-7:46:08
Nanfeng 14	1	29N16	116E32	-7:46:08
Nangang 1	1	31N22	116E59	-7:47:56
Nan'gangwa 2	1	39N46	116E09	-7:44:36
Nangaocun 8	1	39N25	115E58	-7:43:52
Nangezhuang 2	1	39N31	116E23	-7:45:32
Nangong 8	1	37N24	115E22	-7:41:28
Nangou 15	12	43N17	128E37	-8:34:28
Nangqên 19	8	32N22	96E21	-6:25:24
Nanguan 23	1	37N00	112E31	-7:30:04
Nanhai → Foshan 5	1	23N03	113E09	-7:32:36
Nanhe 8	1	37N01	114E41	-7:38:44
Nanhedian 10	1	33N23	112E25	-7:29:40
Nanhekan 24	9	30N24	103E27	-6:53:48
Nanhezhao 8	1	39N05	115E56	-7:43:44
Nanhsi 25	6	23N11	120E29	-8:01:56
Nanhu 4	8	39N57	94E13	-6:16:52
Nanhua 29	9	25N14	101E13	-6:44:52
Nanhualou 16	11	42N30	123E53	-8:15:32
Nanhuang 21	1	36N58	121E47	-8:07:08
Nanhui 22	2	31N03	121E45	-8:07:00
Nanhutou 9	12	43N44	128E55	-8:35:40
Nanjiang 13	1	32N44	120E52	-8:03:28
Nanjiang 24	9	32N33	107E30	-7:10:00
Nanjiangqiao 12	1	28N58	113E44	-7:34:56
Nanjie 24	9	29N11	105E00	-7:00:00
Nanjing 14	1	24N41	114E25	-7:37:40
Nanjing (Nanking) 13	3	32N03	118E47	-7:55:08
Nanjing 24	9	28N49	105E12	-7:00:48
Nanjing 3	1	24N32	117E22	-7:49:28
Nanjingyi 24	9	30N02	104E42	-6:58:48
Nankang 14	1	29N24	116E04	-7:44:16
Nankang 14	1	25N42	114E44	-7:38:56
Nanking → Nanjing 13	3	32N03	118E47	-7:55:08
Nankou 3	1	26N38	117E24	-7:49:36
Nankouzhen 2	1	40N14	116E07	-7:44:28
Nanku 13	1	31N06	120E37	-8:02:28
Nanle 10	1	36N04	115E10	-7:40:40
Nanling 1	1	30N56	118E20	-7:53:20
Nanling 5	1	23N21	115E25	-7:41:40
Nanling 16	11	41N37	120E56	-8:03:44
Nanlinqiao 11	1	29N35	114E19	-7:37:16
Nanliucun 2	1	40N10	116E04	-7:44:16
Nanlongba 7	9	28N02	107E31	-7:10:04
Nanma 29	9	24N17	101E03	-6:44:12
Nanmatang 13	1	32N18	120E38	-8:02:32
Nanmeng 8	1	39N11	116E22	-7:45:28
Nanmulin 28	8	29N41	89E04	-5:56:16
Nanning 6	9	22N48	108E20	-7:13:20
Nanniwan 20	9	36N29	109E40	-7:18:40
Nanpengchang 24	9	29N21	106E38	-7:06:32
Nanpi 8	1	38N02	116E42	-7:46:48
Nanpiao 16	11	41N12	120E39	-8:02:36
Nanping 3	1	26N38	118E10	-7:52:40
Nanping 15	12	42N16	129E09	-8:36:36
Nanping 15	12	43N24	129E05	-8:36:20
Nanping 6	9	21N50	107E28	-7:09:52
Nanping 24	9	33N07	104E20	-6:57:20
Nanpingji 1	1	33N30	116E51	-7:47:24
Nanpu 8	1	39N16	118E12	-7:52:48
Nanqingtuo 8	1	39N37	117E53	-7:51:32
Nanqu 16	11	40N44	122E08	-8:08:32
Nanquan 21	1	36N24	120E17	-8:01:08
Nanshahe 21	1	35N03	117E12	-7:48:48
Nanshan 8	1	39N21	115E34	-7:42:16
Nanshan 3	1	26N38	118E20	-7:53:20
Nanshanba 3	1	25N34	116E32	-7:46:08
Nanshanchengzi 16	11	42N09	125E19	-8:21:16
Nanshankou 27	8	43N09	93E41	-6:14:44
Nanshanlingcun 26	1	39N09	117E26	-7:49:44
Nanshui 5	1	22N02	113E16	-7:33:04
Nansifa 2	1	39N27	116E27	-7:45:48
Nantai 16	11	40N55	122E47	-8:11:08
Nantang 14	1	26N08	115E12	-7:40:48
Nantangdun 13	1	31N15	120E56	-8:03:44
Nantangmei 8	1	38N51	114E56	-7:39:44
Nantian 30	1	29N08	121E56	-8:07:44
Nantian 30	1	27N57	119E56	-7:59:44
Nantianmen 16	11	40N56	123E04	-8:12:16
Nantong 13	1	32N02	120E53	-8:03:32
Nantou 5	1	22N33	113E55	-7:35:40
Nant'ou 25	6	23N55	120E41	-8:02:44
Nantschang → Nanchang 14	1	28N41	115E53	-7:43:32
Nantuantingzhuang 8	1	40N17	118E17	-7:53:08
Nantung → Nantong 13	1	32N02	120E53	-8:03:32
Nanwan 10	1	32N09	113E57	-7:35:48
Nanwengkouzi 17	11	51N10	125E25	-8:21:40
Nanwenquan 24	9	29N26	106E35	-7:06:20
Nanxi 3	1	26N24	118E24	-7:53:36
Nanxi 24	9	28N51	104E58	-6:59:52
Nanxi 1	1	31N31	115E38	-7:42:32
Nanxian 12	1	29N20	112E19	-7:29:16
Nanxiang 22	2	31N17	121E18	-8:05:12
Nanxikou 24	9	30N43	106E07	-7:04:28
Nanxin 21	1	35N33	117E12	-7:48:48
Nanxin 8	1	39N11	115E38	-7:42:32
Nanxinzhuang 8	1	36N39	115E15	-7:41:00
Nanxiong 5	1	25N10	114E20	-7:37:20
Nanxun 30	1	30N53	120E26	-8:01:44
Nanya 3	1	26N52	118E19	-7:53:16
Nanyang 10	1	33N00	112E32	-7:30:08
Nanyang 13	1	33N25	120E13	-8:00:52
Nanyang 3	1	27N24	119E39	-7:58:36
Nanyangcun 13	1	31N53	121E43	-8:06:52
Nanyanggangzi 9	12	48N43	125E27	-8:21:48
Nanyu 3	1	25N59	119E14	-7:56:56
Nanyuan 2	1	39N48	116E23	-7:45:32
Nanyue 12	1	27N13	112E43	-7:30:52
Nanyulin 8	1	40N09	115E23	-7:41:32
Nanzamu 16	11	41N56	124E23	-8:17:32
Nanzha 13	1	31N51	120E15	-8:01:00
Nanzhai 13	1	31N34	120E02	-8:00:08
Nanzhang 11	1	31N50	111E41	-7:26:44
Nanzhang 8	1	39N03	115E46	-7:43:04
Nanzhao 10	1	33N30	112E27	-7:29:48
Nanzhaoji 1	1	32N38	115E58	-7:43:52
Nanzhen 3	1	26N59	119E57	-7:59:48
Nanzhenjie 13	1	31N48	119E17	-7:57:08
Nanzhuang 2	1	40N22	116E21	-7:45:24
Nanzhuang 8	1	40N43	114E58	-7:39:52
Napo 6	9	23N16	105E54	-7:03:36

Narat 27 8 43N28 83E44 -5:34:56
Narenbulake 17 11 49N52 120E23 -8:01:32
Nashuixi 11 1 30N09 108E40 -7:14:40
Natong 6 9 23N01 107E50 -7:11:20
Naxi 24 9 28N47 105E22 -7:01:28
Naxuebiruzong 28 8 31N30 93E51 -6:15:24
Nayong 7 9 26N50 105E13 -7:00:52
Neichiang → Neijiang 24 9 29N35 105E03 -7:00:12
Neihu 25 6 25N05 121E34 -8:06:16
Neihuang 10 1 35N59 114E55 -7:39:40
Neijiang 24 9 29N35 105E03 -7:00:12
Neikiang → Neijiang 24 9 29N35 105E03 -7:00:12
Neiqiu 8 1 37N17 114E31 -7:38:04
Neishuishan 25 6 25N09 121E43 -8:06:52
Neiwufuquan 8 1 40N11 117E39 -7:50:36
Neixiang 10 1 33N12 111E57 -7:27:48
Nengjia 16 11 41N38 120E46 -8:03:04
New Kowloon (Xinjiulong) 31 4 22N20 114E10 -7:36:40
Ngamring 28 8 30N25 87E36 -5:50:24
Ngau Tau Kok → Kwun Tong 31 4 22N19 114E12 -7:36:48
Nianbadu 30 1 28N17 118E28 -7:53:52
Niangmake 24 9 30N14 99E40 -6:38:40
Niangnianggong 16 11 41N00 121E13 -8:04:52
Niangniangmiao 17 11 42N34 118E05 -7:52:20
Niangniangwa 8 1 40N33 117E30 -7:50:00
Niangzizhuang 8 1 40N02 118E05 -7:52:20
Nianpan 16 11 41N48 124E02 -8:16:08
Nianyugou 16 11 42N00 123E59 -8:15:56
Nianyushan 14 1 29N11 117E04 -7:48:16
Nianzhuang 13 1 34N19 117E47 -7:51:08
Nianzigang 11 1 31N03 114E18 -7:37:12
Nianzishan 9 12 47N32 122E52 -8:11:28
Nicheng 22 2 30N55 121E49 -8:07:16
Nide 19 8 31N51 96E19 -6:25:16
Niedu 14 1 25N28 114E08 -7:36:32
Nierong 28 8 32N09 92E11 -6:08:44
Nihe 16 11 41N27 121E13 -8:04:52
Nijiaqiao 22 2 31N14 121E21 -8:05:24
Nileke 27 7 43N47 82E20 -5:29:20
Nilka 27 7 43N47 82E20 -5:29:20
Ning'an 9 12 44N22 129E25 -8:37:40
Ningbo 30 1 29N52 121E31 -8:06:04
Ningcheng (Tianyi) 17 11 41N33 119E20 -7:57:20
Ningde 3 1 26N43 119E33 -7:58:12
Ningdu 14 1 26N31 115E58 -7:43:52
Ninggang 14 1 26N50 114E02 -7:36:08
Ningguo 1 1 30N38 118E58 -7:55:52
Ninghai 30 1 29N17 121E25 -8:05:40
Ninghe (Lutai) 26 1 39N20 117E48 -7:51:12
Ninghepu 8 1 40N43 116E07 -7:44:28
Ninghsian 30 1 29N54 121E32 -8:06:08
Ninghua 3 1 26N15 116E38 -7:46:32
Ningjin 8 1 37N37 114E55 -7:39:40
Ningjin 8 1 37N39 116E48 -7:47:12
Ningling 10 1 34N27 115E21 -7:41:24
Ningming 6 9 22N07 107E05 -7:08:20
Ningnan 24 9 27N11 102E36 -6:50:24
Ningpo → Ningbo 30 1 29N52 121E31 -8:06:04
Ningqiang 20 9 32N44 106E19 -7:05:16
Ningshan 20 9 33N04 108E39 -7:14:36
Ningsia → Yinchuan 18 9 38N30 106E18 -7:05:12
Ningwu 23 1 39N01 112E21 -7:29:24
Ningxi 30 1 28N35 121E00 -8:04:00
Ningxian 4 9 35N31 108E01 -7:12:04
Ningxiang 12 1 28N15 112E33 -7:30:12
Ningyang 21 1 35N47 116E47 -7:47:08
Ningyuan 12 1 25N37 111E46 -7:27:04
Ningyuanbao 4 9 38N38 102E30 -6:50:00
Ningyuanpu 8 1 40N44 114E54 -7:39:36
Niqiu 1 1 33N25 115E38 -7:42:32
Nishan 28 8 33N35 85E30 -5:42:00
Niubaotun 2 1 39N46 116E41 -7:46:44
Niubu 1 1 31N02 117E39 -7:50:36
Niuchutuncun 16 11 41N28 122E58 -8:11:52
Niudouguang 14 1 24N51 115E44 -7:42:56
Niu'erhe 17 11 51N30 121E49 -8:07:16
Niufentai 17 11 47N05 120E02 -8:00:08
Niufozhen 24 9 29N23 105E02 -7:00:08
Niuhang 14 1 28N44 115E51 -7:43:24
Niuhuaxi 24 9 29N29 103E48 -6:55:12
Niujingjie 29 9 25N46 100E33 -6:42:12
Niuke 28 7 30N41 82E01 -5:28:04
Niulanshan 2 1 40N13 116E39 -7:46:36
Niumaowu 16 11 40N58 124E59 -8:19:56
Niupeng 22 2 31N32 121E50 -8:07:20
Niupichang 24 9 30N35 103E40 -6:54:40
Niushitun 10 1 35N18 114E24 -7:37:36
Niutan 24 9 29N05 105E21 -7:01:24
Niuti 10 1 32N58 113E35 -7:34:20
Niutian 14 1 27N17 115E44 -7:42:56
Niutoushan 15 12 45N09 126E45 -8:27:00
Niutoushan 1 1 31N04 119E37 -7:58:28
Niutuo 8 1 39N15 116E20 -7:45:20
Niuxichang 24 9 28N47 104E31 -6:58:04
Niuxintai 16 11 41N21 123E53 -8:15:32
Niuxintun 16 11 41N56 121E21 -8:05:24
Niuyuanzi 8 1 40N20 117E47 -7:51:08
Niuzhuang 21 1 37N21 118E29 -7:53:56
Niuzhuang 16 11 40N58 122E32 -8:10:08
Nixi 29 9 27N58 99E27 -6:37:48
Nixis 24 9 30N08 106E19 -7:05:16
Nixizhen 24 9 29N02 104E16 -6:57:04
Nong'an 15 12 44N25 125E10 -8:20:40
North Point 31 4 22N17 114E12 -7:36:48
Nuanchitang 16 11 41N02 120E41 -8:02:44
Nuanli 29 9 23N26 100E51 -6:43:24
Nuannuan 25 6 25N06 121E44 -8:06:56
Nunshui 14 1 28N53 117E51 -7:51:24
Nuanzhouying 3 1 25N22 117E22 -7:49:28
Nü'erhe 16 11 41N04 121E00 -8:04:00
Nujiang 28 8 29N58 97E25 -6:29:40
Nunjiang 9 12 49N10 125E11 -8:20:44
Nunshan 9 12 48N59 125E14 -8:20:56
Nürenbei 24 9 30N11 106E04 -7:04:16
Nyenyam 28 8 28N11 85E58 -5:43:52
Orogen Zizhiqi 17 11 50N34 123E40 -8:14:40
Otog Qi 17 9 39N08 108E00 -7:12:00
Oumiao 11 1 31N55 112E09 -7:28:36
Padingge 28 8 32N52 88E39 -5:54:36
Pahsien 24 9 30N38 103E40 -6:54:40
Paifangchang 24 9 30N31 106E38 -7:06:32
Paiho 25 6 23N21 120E25 -8:01:40
Pailoutou 22 2 30N56 121E16 -8:05:04
Pailoutun 16 11 40N44 122E49 -8:11:16
Paisha 25 6 23N40 119E35 -7:58:20
Paitan 5 1 23N31 113E46 -7:35:04
Paizhou 11 1 30N13 113E56 -7:35:44
Pajiangkou 5 1 23N46 113E14 -7:32:56
Pakhoi → Beihai 6 9 21N29 109E05 -7:16:20
Pak Kong 31 4 22N23 114E15 -7:37:00
Pan'an 30 1 29N06 120E27 -8:01:48
Pan'ao 24 9 30N09 103E37 -6:54:28
Panch'iao 25 6 25N01 121E27 -8:05:48
Pandian 21 1 36N38 116E27 -7:45:48
Panfang 14 1 27N54 115E57 -7:43:48
Pangfou → Bangbu 1 1 32N58 117E24 -7:49:36
Panggezhuang 2 1 39N38 116E19 -7:45:16
Panggezhuang 8 1 39N16 115E49 -7:43:16
Pangjiabu 8 1 40N36 115E27 -7:41:48
Pangp'u → Bangbu 1 1 32N58 117E24 -7:49:36
Pangzidian 24 9 30N38 105E04 -7:00:16
Panjiapie 13 1 32N54 120E42 -8:02:48
Panjiatun 16 11 41N04 121E38 -8:06:32
Panlong 13 1 31N58 121E35 -8:06:20
Panlong 22 2 31N11 121E16 -8:05:04
Panlong 14 1 25N52 114E52 -7:39:28
Panlongzhen 24 9 29N31 105E17 -7:01:08
Panshan 16 11 41N12 122E04 -8:08:16
Panxi 30 1 30N35 119E20 -7:57:20
Panxian 7 9 25N50 104E36 -6:58:24
Panxidu 21 1 35N39 115E52 -7:43:28
Panyu 5 1 22N57 113E20 -7:33:20
Panzhuang 26 1 39N20 117E28 -7:49:52
Paochi → Baoji 20 9 34N23 107E09 -7:08:36
Paoki → Baoji 20 9 34N23 107E09 -7:08:36
Paoshenmiao 8 1 41N12 118E17 -7:53:08
Paotai Yingzi 17 1 41N48 115E12 -7:40:48
Paoting → Baoding 8 1 38N52 115E29 -7:41:56
Paotow → Baotou 17 9 40N40 109E59 -7:19:56
Paoying → Baoying 13 1 33N16 119E20 -7:57:20
Paozi 16 11 42N13 122E19 -8:09:16
Pari 28 8 27N44 89E09 -5:56:36
Pautou → Baotou 17 9 40N40 109E59 -7:19:56
Peian → Beian 9 12 48N15 126E30 -8:26:00
Peiching → Beijing 2 1 39N55 116E25 -7:45:40
Peihai → Beihai 6 9 21N29 109E05 -7:16:20
Peijiatun 16 11 39N19 121E41 -8:06:44
Peikang 25 6 23N34 120E18 -8:01:12
Peinan 25 6 22N47 121E07 -8:04:28
Peip'ing → Beijing 2 1 39N55 116E25 -7:45:40
Peixian (Yunhe) 13 1 34N21 117E59 -7:51:56
Peixian 13 1 34N44 116E59 -7:47:56
Peiziyan 21 1 35N07 115E01 -7:40:04
Pékin → Beijing 2 1 39N55 116E25 -7:45:40
Peking → Beijing 2 1 39N55 116E25 -7:45:40
Penggong 30 1 30N27 119E57 -7:59:48
Penggongmiao 12 1 26N07 113E34 -7:34:16
Penghu 3 1 25N24 118E11 -7:52:44
Pengjiachang 24 9 30N36 103E53 -6:55:32
Pengjialouzi 16 11 41N56 123E40 -8:14:40
Pengjiawan 10 1 32N16 114E04 -7:36:16
Pengjiawu 8 1 39N41 117E10 -7:48:40
Pengkou 3 1 25N32 116E42 -7:46:48
Penglai (Dengzhou) 21 1 37N48 120E42 -8:02:48
Penglaizhen 24 9 30N36 105E14 -7:00:56
Penglang 13 1 31N23 121E05 -8:04:20
Pengnan 24 9 30N25 105E53 -7:03:32
Pengpu → Bangbu 1 1 32N58 117E24 -7:49:36
Pengshan 24 9 30N13 103E52 -6:55:28
Pengshi 11 1 30N28 113E10 -7:32:40
Pengshui 24 9 29N18 108E09 -7:12:36
Pengxi 24 9 30N49 105E40 -7:02:40
Pengxian 24 9 31N00 103E50 -6:55:20
Pengze 14 1 29N53 116E33 -7:46:12
Pengzhai 5 1 24N23 115E06 -7:40:24
Pengzhuangzi 8 1 40N06 114E51 -7:39:24
Penhsi → Benxi 16 11 41N18 123E45 -8:15:00
Penki → Benxi 16 11 41N18 123E45 -8:15:00
Pianguan 23 1 39N24 111E30 -7:26:00
Pianjiaojie 29 9 26N01 100E32 -6:42:08
Pianling 16 11 41N24 123E58 -8:15:52
Picheng 13 1 32N07 119E42 -7:58:48
Pigezhuang 2 1 39N39 116E15 -7:45:00
Pikou 16 11 39N24 122E20 -8:09:20
Piluchang 24 9 29N13 105E37 -7:02:28
Pilusi 13 1 32N05 120E05 -8:00:20
Ping'an 15 12 45N20 123E42 -8:14:48
Ping'an 24 9 30N36 104E42 -6:58:48
Ping'an 16 11 41N11 123E26 -8:13:44
Ping'anbu 8 1 41N45 116E13 -7:44:52
Ping'ancheng 8 1 40N03 117E48 -7:51:12
Ping'andi 16 11 42N34 121E52 -8:07:28
Pingba 7 9 26N22 106E09 -7:04:36
Pingba 11 1 31N19 113E18 -7:33:12
Pingchang 24 9 31N35 107E03 -7:08:12
Pingchao 13 1 32N07 120E45 -8:03:00
Pingding 23 1 37N48 113E37 -7:34:28
Pingdingpu 16 11 42N22 123E55 -8:15:40
Pingdingshan 10 1 33N45 113E17 -7:33:08
Pingdingshan 16 11 41N26 124E45 -8:19:00
Pingdu 21 1 36N47 119E54 -7:59:36
Pingfang 11 1 30N07 113E48 -7:35:12
Pingfang 16 11 41N17 120E40 -8:02:40
Pingfang 16 11 41N28 120E48 -8:03:12
Pingfang 17 11 42N14 120E38 -8:02:32
Pingfang 17 11 42N27 120E38 -8:02:32
Pingfang 2 1 39N56 116E33 -7:46:12
Pingfangdu 16 11 41N45 121E12 -8:04:48
Pingfangzi 16 11 41N31 121E21 -8:05:24
Pinggu 2 1 40N09 117E07 -7:48:28
Pingguo 6 9 23N19 107E39 -7:10:36
Pinghai 3 1 25N14 119E15 -7:57:00
Pinghai 5 1 22N39 114E53 -7:39:32
Pinghe 29 9 22N51 102E30 -6:50:00
Pinghe 3 1 24N25 117E22 -7:49:28
P'inghsiang → Pingxiang 6 9 22N09 106E43 -7:06:52
Pinghu 5 1 22N42 114E08 -7:36:32
Pinghu 30 1 30N42 121E01 -8:04:04
Pinghu 3 1 26N46 118E48 -7:55:12
Pinghu 11 1 30N56 115E22 -7:41:28
Pingjiang 12 1 28N44 113E34 -7:34:16
Pingjing 8 1 39N20 116E06 -7:44:24
Pinglan 5 1 22N22 113E27 -7:33:48
Pingle 6 9 24N37 110E40 -7:22:40
Pingle 6 9 24N31 106E59 -7:07:56
Pingli 20 9 32N19 109E21 -7:17:24
Pingliang 4 9 35N27 107E10 -7:08:40
Pinglidian 21 1 37N17 119E59 -7:59:56
Pingling 5 1 23N39 114E23 -7:37:32
Pinglucheng 23 1 39N50 112E19 -7:29:16
Pingluo 18 9 38N57 106E35 -7:06:20
Pingluopu 16 11 41N56 123E20 -8:13:20
Pingnan 6 9 23N30 110E30 -7:22:00
Pingnan 3 1 26N56 119E02 -7:56:08
Pingqiao 13 1 33N24 119E13 -7:56:52
Pingquan 8 1 40N59 118E34 -7:54:16
Pingshan 5 1 23N26 113E15 -7:33:00
Pingshan 5 1 22N43 114E22 -7:37:28
Ping Shan 31 4 22N27 114E00 -7:36:00
Pingshan 8 1 38N15 114E10 -7:36:40
Pingshan 3 1 25N36 117E52 -7:51:28
Pingshang 21 1 35N11 119E07 -7:56:28
Pingshi 10 1 32N32 113E03 -7:32:12
Pingshi 5 1 25N20 113E02 -7:32:08
Pingshui 30 1 29N53 120E38 -8:02:32
Pingtaizi 2 1 40N44 116E25 -7:45:40
Pingtan 24 9 29N38 105E16 -7:01:04
Pingtan 24 9 29N50 105E56 -7:03:44
Pingtan 3 1 25N31 119E47 -7:59:08
Pingtan 5 1 23N04 114E38 -7:38:32
Pingtang 7 9 25N50 107E19 -7:09:16
Pingtian 5 1 25N19 113E31 -7:34:04
P'ingtung 25 6 22N40 120E29 -8:01:56
Pingwang 13 1 30N59 120E38 -8:02:32
Pingwu 24 9 32N29 104E37 -6:58:28
Pingxiang 14 1 27N38 113E50 -7:35:20
Pingxiang 6 9 22N09 106E43 -7:06:52
Pingyang 30 1 27N41 120E33 -8:02:12
Pingyang 9 12 48N13 124E23 -8:17:32
Pingyao 30 1 30N24 119E58 -7:59:52
Pingyao 23 1 37N16 112E09 -7:28:36
Pingyi 21 1 35N34 117E37 -7:50:28
Pingyin 21 1 36N19 116E22 -7:45:28
Pingyu 10 1 32N57 114E41 -7:38:44
Pingyuan 21 1 37N11 116E25 -7:45:40
Pingyuan 5 1 24N36 115E54 -7:43:36
Pingzhai 29 9 24N07 104E22 -6:57:28
Pingzhuang 17 11 42N03 119E22 -7:57:28
Pinkiang → Haerbin 9 12 45N45 126E41 -8:26:44
Pipa 24 9 29N07 105E05 -7:00:20
Piqiang 27 7 40N20 77E38 -5:10:32
Piqiao 13 1 31N34 119E27 -7:57:48
Pishan 27 7 37N37 78E18 -5:13:12
Pitou 5 1 23N34 116E05 -7:44:20
Pitou 5 1 24N26 114E22 -7:37:28
Pitou 14 1 25N01 114E35 -7:38:20
Pixian 24 9 30N49 103E49 -6:55:16
Pogan 14 1 27N40 116E46 -7:47:04
Pogan 14 1 28N18 116E46 -7:47:04

Place	Zone	Lat	Long	Time
Pohsien → Boxian 1	1	33N53	115E45	-7:43:00
Poli 21	1	35N57	118E17	-7:53:08
Poli 21	1	35N43	119E47	-7:59:08
Port Arthur → Lüshun 16	11	38N48	121E16	-8:05:04
Port Edward → Weihai 21	1	37N28	122E07	-8:08:28
Poshan → Boshan 21	1	36N29	117E50	-7:51:20
Poshiwu 30	1	30N22	119E36	-7:58:24
Potaizi 16	11	41N34	121E08	-8:04:32
P'otzu 25	6	23N28	120E14	-8:00:56
Pucheng 20	9	34N59	109E29	-7:17:56
Pucheng 3	1	27N55	118E31	-7:54:04
Pudi 29	9	27N58	99E05	-6:36:20
Puding 7	9	26N21	105E40	-7:02:40
Puduhe 29	9	25N39	102E39	-6:50:36
Pu'er 29	9	23N07	101E00	-6:44:00
Pu'erdu 29	9	28N08	104E24	-6:57:36
Puge 24	9	27N28	102E31	-6:50:04
Puhe 16	11	41N57	123E36	-8:14:24
Puji 12	1	27N59	113E25	-7:33:40
Puji 11	1	29N58	112E32	-7:30:08
Pujiang 30	1	29N28	119E53	-7:59:32
Pujiang 24	9	30N12	103E30	-6:54:00
Pukou 3	1	26N16	119E35	-7:58:20
Pukou 13	3	32N07	118E43	-7:54:52
Pulan 28	7	30N16	81E14	-5:24:56
Puli 25	6	23N58	120E57	-8:03:48
Pulü 24	9	29N50	106E11	-7:04:44
Puluo 27	7	36N11	81E30	-5:26:00
Pumei 29	9	23N28	105E15	-7:01:00
Punan 3	1	24N39	117E41	-7:50:44
Puning 5	1	23N18	116E12	-7:44:48
Puqi 11	1	29N43	113E53	-7:35:32
Puqi 30	1	28N11	121E01	-8:04:04
Puqian 5	1	23N34	114E38	-7:38:32
Puqian 5	9	20N03	110E36	-7:22:24
Pushang 21	1	36N08	119E42	-7:58:48
Putai 25	6	23N23	120E09	-8:00:36
Putangqiao 13	1	31N34	118E59	-7:55:56
Putian 3	1	25N28	119E02	-7:56:08
Putian 14	1	29N16	114E58	-7:39:52
Putuo 30	1	29N58	122E17	-8:09:08
Puxi 3	1	25N10	119E08	-7:56:32
Puxian 23	1	36N30	111E02	-7:24:08
Puxingchang 24	9	30N41	105E06	-7:00:24
Puyang 10	1	35N42	114E59	-7:39:56
Puyuan 30	1	30N41	120E38	-8:02:32
Puzhen 13	3	32N09	118E41	-7:54:44
Qagan 17	11	49N14	118E08	-7:52:32
Qahar Youyi Zhongqi 17	9	41N09	112E38	-7:30:32
Qamdo 28	8	31N11	97E15	-6:29:00
Qarak 27	7	38N23	76E58	-5:07:52
Qeh 17	9	42N18	100E59	-6:43:56
Qiakemake 27	7	40N05	75E24	-5:01:36
Qian'an 15	12	45N00	124E01	-8:16:04
Qian'an 8	1	39N59	118E40	-7:54:40
Qiancaijiatun 16	11	41N14	121E38	-8:06:32
Qiandiwu 8	1	39N16	116E38	-7:46:32
Qiandong 5	1	23N41	116E55	-7:47:40
Qiandun 13	1	31N16	121E00	-8:04:00
Qianertaizi 16	11	42N04	122E42	-8:10:48
Qianfang 14	1	28N32	116E13	-7:44:52
Qian Gorlos 15	12	45N08	124E47	-8:19:08
Qiangzilu 2	1	40N26	117E13	-7:48:52
Qianhonghepu 16	11	41N23	123E07	-8:12:28
Qianhuang 13	1	31N36	119E58	-7:59:52
Qianji 13	1	33N55	118E56	-7:55:44
Qianjiadian 17	11	43N42	122E35	-8:10:20
Qianjiang 6	9	23N37	109E00	-7:16:00
Qianjiang 11	1	30N25	112E51	-7:31:24
Qianjian'gangzi 16	11	41N34	122E26	-8:09:44
Qianjiangtai 16	11	41N46	122E03	-8:08:12
Qianjiaqiao 22	2	30N53	121E31	-8:06:04
Qianjiaying 8	1	39N35	118E21	-7:53:24
Qianjiazhuang 13	1	32N16	120E17	-8:01:08
Qianjing 13	1	31N33	121E15	-8:05:00
Qianjinmiao 3	1	25N09	118E20	-7:53:20
Qiankeng 30	1	30N43	119E47	-7:59:08
Qiankoutou 8	1	39N42	117E01	-7:48:04
Qianlijiazhuang 8	1	39N25	118E17	-7:53:08
Qianluanshanzi 16	11	42N17	122E27	-8:09:48
Qianmajiagushanzi 16	11	42N23	123E33	-8:14:12
Qianmintun 16	11	41N49	123E15	-8:13:00
Qianning 24	9	30N30	101E31	-6:46:04
Qianpai 5	8	22N22	111E11	-7:24:44
Qianqi 30	1	27N20	120E20	-8:01:20
Qianqianjianglugou 16	11	41N59	120E58	-8:03:52
Qiansandaoliangzi 16	11	42N06	120E44	-8:02:56
Qianshahezi 16	11	41N46	123E01	-8:12:04
Qianshan 5	1	22N16	113E33	-7:34:12
Qianshan 13	1	31N06	120E24	-8:01:36
Qianshan 1	1	30N38	116E33	-7:46:12
Qianshuangshanzi 16	11	41N22	121E13	-8:04:52
Qiansuo 30	1	28N44	121E27	-8:05:48
Qiantangzhen 24	9	30N12	106E18	-7:05:12
Qianwei 16	11	40N12	120E06	-8:00:24
Qianwei 24	9	29N12	103E57	-6:55:48
Qianxi 7	9	26N57	106E00	-7:04:00
Qianxi 8	1	40N09	118E19	-7:53:16
Qianxiatazi 16	11	42N23	123E53	-8:15:32
Qianyamen 16	11	42N04	121E26	-8:05:44
Qianyang 12	1	27N11	110E04	-7:20:16
Qianyaopu 16	11	42N02	123E37	-8:14:28
Qi'anzhen 13	1	32N11	121E03	-8:04:12
Qianzhou 13	1	31N42	120E13	-8:00:52
Qiaodun 30	1	27N29	120E18	-8:01:12
Qiaogou 10	1	32N26	115E45	-7:43:00
Qiaohengjin 24	9	29N30	99E50	-6:39:20
Qiaojia 29	9	26N57	102E52	-6:51:28
Qiaojiang 22	2	31N15	121E19	-8:05:16
Qiaokou 12	1	25N55	113E10	-7:32:40
Qiaolima 28	7	34N35	81E00	-5:24:00
Qiaolin 13	1	31N57	118E32	-7:54:08
Qiaomu 23	1	39N34	114E27	-7:37:48
Qiaopurikebazha 27	7	38N48	76E19	-5:05:16
Qiaoqi 13	1	31N49	120E18	-8:01:12
Qiaoshe 14	1	28N48	115E58	-7:43:52
Qiaosi 30	3	30N21	120E18	-8:01:12
Qiaotou 10	1	33N05	112E46	-7:31:04
Qiaotou 13	1	32N11	119E14	-7:56:56
Qiaotou 24	9	29N18	104E39	-6:58:36
Qiaotou 16	11	41N13	123E44	-8:14:56
Qiaotou 29	9	28N17	99E22	-6:37:28
Qiaotoucun 1	1	30N36	119E08	-7:56:32
Qiaotouji 1	1	31N45	117E34	-7:50:16
Qiaotoupu 1	1	30N33	118E50	-7:55:20
Qiaotouyi 12	1	28N24	112E58	-7:31:52
Qiaotouzhen 1	1	30N49	119E13	-7:56:52
Qiaowan 27	8	40N36	96E55	-6:27:40
Qiaowei 6	9	22N51	109E50	-7:19:20
Qiaoxia 13	1	31N09	119E35	-7:58:20
Qiaoxiajie 30	1	28N10	120E34	-8:02:16
Qiaozhen 22	2	31N39	121E24	-8:05:36
Qibao 22	2	31N09	121E20	-8:05:20
Qichun 11	1	30N17	115E26	-7:41:44
Qidong 12	1	26N44	112E04	-7:28:16
Qidong 13	1	31N49	121E40	-8:06:40
Qidu 1	1	30N16	117E46	-7:51:04
Qiemo 27	8	38N08	85E32	-5:42:08
Qiesanglinzi 16	11	41N42	123E30	-8:14:00
Qieshikou 2	1	39N59	116E24	-7:45:36
Qiezixi 24	9	29N25	106E30	-7:06:00
Qifosi 24	9	29N27	105E58	-7:03:52
Qigong 24	9	28N38	100E38	-6:42:32
Qigongtai 16	11	41N50	123E08	-8:12:32
Qihe (Yancheng) 21	1	36N48	116E44	-7:46:56
Qiji 8	1	37N16	115E21	-7:41:24
Qijiadian 9	12	46N48	125E36	-8:22:24
Qijian 24	9	30N14	106E09	-7:04:36
Qijiang 24	9	29N02	106E39	-7:06:36
Qijiapuzi 16	11	40N54	122E31	-8:10:04
Qijiawan 11	1	30N53	114E13	-7:36:52
Qijiawopeng 16	11	41N02	121E26	-8:05:44
Qijiazi 16	11	41N54	122E58	-8:11:52
Qika 17	11	50N35	119E16	-7:57:04
Qikou 8	1	38N35	117E31	-7:50:04
Qilian 19	9	38N05	100E12	-6:40:48
Qilihe 16	11	41N21	121E16	-8:05:04
Qilihe 16	11	41N30	121E15	-8:05:00
Qilihezi 16	11	40N56	121E02	-8:04:08
Qiling 5	1	24N05	115E27	-7:41:48
Qilingzicun 16	11	41N05	123E06	-8:12:24
Qilinmen 1	3	32N04	118E55	-7:55:40
Qilinzhen 13	1	31N56	121E21	-8:05:24
Qiliping 11	1	31N27	114E39	-7:38:36
Qiliqiao 13	1	31N35	120E48	-8:03:12
Qilizhen 20	9	35N43	108E59	-7:15:56
Qilizhen 13	1	32N19	121E05	-8:04:20
Qimafang 8	1	40N08	114E31	-7:38:04
Qimen 1	1	29N52	117E42	-7:50:48
Qimen 5	1	25N18	113E15	-7:33:00
Qimoudi 8	1	39N35	115E32	-7:42:08
Qincaigou 16	11	40N38	120E37	-8:02:28
Qing'an 9	12	46N52	127E30	-8:30:00
Qingbaikou 2	1	40N01	115E50	-7:43:20
Qingcaoge 1	1	30N50	116E46	-7:47:04
Qingcheng 21	1	37N12	117E40	-7:50:40
Qingchengzi 16	11	40N44	123E36	-8:14:24
Qingchuan 24	9	32N36	105E09	-7:00:36
Qingcungang 22	2	30N56	121E34	-8:06:16
Qingdao (Tsingtao) 21	1	36N06	120E19	-8:01:16
Qingdian 26	1	39N51	117E22	-7:49:28
Qingduizi 16	11	39N50	123E18	-8:13:12
Qingduizi 16	11	41N28	121E53	-8:07:32
Qingfeng 10	1	35N54	115E07	-7:40:28
Qingfengtuo 8	1	40N59	116E04	-7:44:16
Qingfu 24	9	28N29	104E35	-6:58:20
Qinggang 9	12	46N43	126E07	-8:24:28
Qingguang 26	1	39N11	117E02	-7:48:08
Qingguji 21	1	34N45	115E47	-7:43:08
Qinghe 2	1	40N01	116E20	-7:45:20
Qinghe 16	11	42N32	124E09	-8:16:36
Qinghe 27	8	46N36	90E39	-6:02:36
Qinghe 16	11	40N02	122E35	-8:10:20
Qinghecheng 16	11	41N28	124E15	-8:17:00
Qinghechengzi 16	11	41N44	121E25	-8:05:40
Qinghemen 16	11	41N45	121E25	-8:05:40
Qinghezhen 21	1	37N16	117E39	-7:50:36
Qinghu 30	1	28N40	118E34	-7:54:16
Qinghua 14	1	29N24	117E46	-7:51:04
Qinghuayuan 2	1	40N00	116E19	-7:45:16
Qinghuazhen 10	1	32N55	112E19	-7:29:16
Qingjian 20	9	37N10	110E00	-7:20:00
Qingjiang 30	1	28N16	121E06	-8:04:24
Qingjiang 24	9	29N17	105E34	-7:02:16
Qingjiang 13	1	33N35	119E02	-7:56:08
Qingjiang 14	1	28N05	115E29	-7:41:56
Qingjujie 24	9	30N42	106E07	-7:04:28
Qinglian 5	1	24N27	112E45	-7:31:00
Qingliu 3	1	26N12	116E52	-7:47:28
Qingliuzhen 24	9	29N56	105E19	-7:01:16
Qinglong 14	1	25N28	114E28	-7:37:52
Qinglong 8	1	40N24	118E54	-7:55:36
Qinglong 7	9	25N50	105E10	-7:00:40
Qinglongchang 24	9	29N51	105E40	-7:02:40
Qinglongchang 24	9	30N20	103E51	-6:55:24
Qinglongchang 24	9	28N50	106E31	-7:06:04
Qinglonggang 13	1	31N51	121E15	-8:05:00
Qinglongguan 24	9	30N25	104E48	-6:59:12
Qinglongji 1	1	34N05	116E37	-7:46:28
Qingmuguan 24	9	29N41	106E18	-7:05:12
Qingningsi 22	2	31N16	121E33	-8:06:12
Qingping 24	9	29N00	106E21	-7:05:24
Qingping 24	9	30N14	106E12	-7:04:48
Qingping 21	1	36N47	116E06	-7:44:24
Qingpu 22	2	31N09	121E06	-8:04:24
Qingshan 11	3	30N38	114E23	-7:37:32
Qingshan 30	1	30N43	120E03	-8:00:12
Qingshan 30	1	30N15	119E52	-7:59:28
Qingshan 30	1	30N36	119E41	-7:58:44
Qingshan 1	1	31N33	116E22	-7:45:28
Qingshanpu 11	1	29N27	114E01	-7:36:04
Qingshen 24	9	29N50	103E50	-6:55:20
Qingshui 4	9	39N23	99E09	-6:36:36
Qingshui 24	9	30N10	104E03	-6:56:12
Qingshui 4	9	34N42	106E21	-7:05:24
Qingshuijian 2	1	39N59	115E58	-7:43:52
Qingtan 11	1	31N48	112E48	-7:31:12
Qingtang 14	1	26N28	115E48	-7:43:12
Qingtang 5	1	24N14	113E51	-7:35:24
Qingtian 30	1	28N10	120E17	-8:01:08
Qingtong 24	9	29N28	103E27	-6:53:48
Qingtongxia 18	9	37N58	106E02	-7:04:08
Qingtuosi 21	1	35N29	118E20	-7:53:20
Qingtuozi 26	1	39N08	117E45	-7:51:00
Qingtuozi 16	11	41N05	121E28	-8:05:52
Qingxi 1	1	31N40	118E00	-7:52:00
Qingxi 24	9	30N40	106E14	-7:04:56
Qingxi 9	12	49N19	127E10	-8:28:40
Qingxian 8	1	38N34	116E46	-7:47:04
Qingxizhen 24	9	29N09	103E55	-6:55:40
Qingyang 4	9	36N06	107E47	-7:11:08
Qingyang 1	1	30N38	117E48	-7:51:12
Qingyang 9	12	45N20	128E47	-8:35:08
Qingyangzhen 13	1	31N46	120E15	-8:01:00
Qingyuan 5	1	23N42	113E02	-7:32:08
Qingyuan 16	11	42N13	124E56	-8:19:44
Qingyuan 30	1	27N38	119E04	-7:56:16
Qingyuan → Baoding 8	1	38N52	115E29	-7:41:56
Qingyun (Xiejiaji) 21	1	37N52	117E21	-7:49:24
Qingyunbao 16	11	42N34	123E50	-8:15:20
Qingzhen 7	9	26N29	106E22	-7:05:28
Qingzhen 30	1	30N45	120E30	-8:02:00
Qingzhou 5	1	23N39	116E57	-7:47:48
Qinhuangdao (Chinwangtao) 8	1	39N56	119E36	-7:58:24
Qinjia 9	12	46N47	127E00	-8:28:00
Qinlan 1	1	32N37	119E08	-7:56:32
Qinnan 13	1	33N16	119E55	-7:59:40
Qinshui 23	1	35N41	112E11	-7:28:44
Qintong 13	1	32N39	120E08	-8:00:32
Qinxian 23	1	36N48	112E41	-7:30:44
Qinyang 10	1	35N06	112E57	-7:31:48
Qinyuan 23	1	36N30	112E15	-7:29:00
Qinzhou 6	9	21N59	108E36	-7:14:24
Qionghai (Jiaji) 5	9	19N20	110E30	-7:22:00
Qionglai 24	9	30N25	103E27	-6:53:48
Qiongzhong 5	9	19N02	109E49	-7:19:16
Qipandi 8	1	39N46	115E12	-7:40:48
Qipanshan 8	1	42N05	117E30	-7:50:00
Qiqian 17	11	52N12	120E30	-8:03:16
Qiqihar (Tsitsihar) 9	12	47N19	123E55	-8:15:40
Qishudang 24	9	29N13	104E39	-6:58:36
Qishuyan 13	1	31N44	120E04	-8:00:16
Qitai 27	8	44N01	89E28	-5:57:52
Qitaihe 9	12	45N48	130E53	-8:43:32
Qitaizi 16	11	41N33	122E11	-8:08:44
Qitamu 15	12	44N22	126E20	-8:25:20
Qitangzhen 24	9	29N47	106E16	-7:05:04
Qiting 11	1	31N02	114E44	-7:38:56
Qitingqiao 13	1	31N26	119E52	-7:59:28
Qitou 3	1	24N54	117E29	-7:49:56
Qiubei 29	9	24N07	104E12	-6:56:48
Qiuchang 24	9	28N59	104E42	-6:58:48
Qiuji 13	1	33N51	118E01	-7:52:04
Qiujia 13	1	31N49	121E51	-8:07:24
Qiujiatun 16	11	41N20	121E00	-8:04:00
Qiujin 14	1	29N10	115E42	-7:42:48
Qiuxizhen 24	9	29N56	104E41	-6:58:44
Qiweigang 13	1	32N01	119E59	-7:59:56
Qixia 21	1	37N17	120E48	-8:03:12
Qixian 10	1	34N33	114E47	-7:39:08
Qixian (Zhaoge) 10	1	35N38	114E11	-7:36:44
Qixianji 1	1	33N28	117E01	-7:48:04

Qixiashan 1 1 32N10 118E57 -7:55:48
Qixingqiao 30 1 30N49 120E51 -8:03:24
Qiyahe 17 11 53N02 120E33 -8:02:12
Qiyang 12 1 26N29 111E43 -7:26:52
Qiyi 10 1 32N30 112E54 -7:31:36
Qiying 4 9 36N38 106E25 -7:05:40
Qizhou 11 1 30N04 115E20 -7:41:20
Quangang 14 1 28N10 115E34 -7:42:16
Quanjiang 14 1 27N43 113E59 -7:35:56
Quanjiao 1 1 32N06 118E16 -7:53:04
Quanmian 16 11 42N02 122E13 -8:08:52
Quannan 14 1 24N44 114E31 -7:38:04
Quanshang 3 1 26N25 116E55 -7:47:40
Quanshengpu 16 11 41N59 123E22 -8:13:28
Quanshui 16 11 41N18 124E11 -8:16:44
Quanshuitou 2 1 40N24 116E39 -7:46:36
Quantou 16 11 42N52 124E07 -8:16:28
Quanxishi 12 1 26N51 112E45 -7:31:00
Quanyanhezi 16 11 40N52 123E26 -8:13:44
Quanzhou (Chuanchou) 3 1 24N54 118E35 -7:54:20
Qubei 28 8 28N18 86E53 -5:47:32
Quchijie 12 1 28N03 111E53 -7:27:32
Qudi 21 1 37N06 117E15 -7:49:00
Queerhe 16 11 40N57 121E35 -8:06:20
Quelizhen 22 2 30N54 121E26 -8:05:44
Queshan 10 1 32N48 114E01 -7:36:04
Qufu 21 1 35N36 117E02 -7:48:08
Qugou 19 9 36N10 100E56 -6:43:44
Qugou 8 1 39N17 116E15 -7:45:00
Qujiadian 16 11 43N13 123E53 -8:15:32
Qujiang 14 1 28N15 115E45 -7:43:00
Qujiang 5 1 24N48 113E17 -7:33:08
Qujiang 5 1 24N41 113E35 -7:34:20
Qujing 29 9 25N32 103E41 -6:54:44
Qujiu 6 9 22N28 107E40 -7:10:40
Quke 28 8 28N16 87E24 -5:49:36
Qukou 8 1 39N46 117E07 -7:48:28
Qumalai 19 8 34N35 95E27 -6:21:48
Qunshen'guan 8 1 39N49 117E59 -7:51:56
Qushui 28 8 29N22 90E43 -6:02:52
Qushui 24 9 30N41 106E02 -7:04:08
Qutang 13 1 32N30 120E21 -8:01:24
Quxi 30 1 28N00 120E31 -8:02:04
Quxi 5 1 23N36 116E26 -7:45:44
Quxia 13 1 32N06 120E09 -8:00:36
Quxian 24 9 30N51 106E59 -7:07:56
Quxian 30 1 28N58 118E52 -7:55:28
Quxingji 10 1 34N52 114E39 -7:38:36
Quxiong 28 8 31N09 96E00 -6:24:00
Quyang 8 1 38N34 114E42 -7:38:48
Quzhou 8 1 36N46 114E57 -7:39:48
Quzong 28 8 30N08 96E00 -6:24:00
Ranghe 10 1 33N43 112E51 -7:31:24
Rao'er 14 1 28N48 117E40 -7:50:40
Raohe 9 12 46N47 134E00 -8:56:00
Raoping 5 1 23N43 117E01 -7:48:04
Raoyang 8 1 38N16 115E44 -7:42:56
Raoyanghe 16 11 41N46 122E26 -8:09:44
Rawu 28 8 29N30 96E45 -6:27:00
Rela 28 8 29N27 89E45 -5:59:00
Renbu 28 8 29N10 89E59 -5:59:56
Rencun 10 1 36N19 113E50 -7:35:20
Ren'gang 13 1 32N01 120E50 -8:03:20
Rengezhuang 8 1 39N45 118E10 -7:52:40
Renhe 10 1 33N32 114E02 -7:36:08
Renhe 14 1 27N41 115E15 -7:41:00
Renhechang 24 9 30N30 105E56 -7:03:44
Renheji 10 1 31N56 115E07 -7:40:28
Renhua 5 1 25N06 113E44 -7:34:56
Renhuai 7 9 27N48 106E18 -7:05:12
Renjiawopeng 16 11 41N27 122E18 -8:09:12
Renjiaxu 30 1 30N49 121E00 -8:04:00
Renju 5 1 24N51 115E54 -7:43:36
Renliuchang 24 9 29N13 106E39 -7:06:36
Renlong 24 9 30N32 105E47 -7:03:08
Renmei 3 1 25N50 117E56 -7:51:44
Renmin 9 12 46N37 125E32 -8:22:08
Rennie's Mill 31 4 22N18 114E15 -7:37:00
Renqiao 1 1 33N27 117E16 -7:49:04
Renqiu 8 1 38N43 116E05 -7:44:20
Renshan 5 1 22N50 114E48 -7:39:12
Renshou 3 1 27N08 117E51 -7:51:24
Renshou 24 9 30N00 104E08 -6:56:32
Rentuo 24 9 29N14 106E23 -7:05:32
Renyichang 24 9 29N29 105E28 -7:01:52
Reshui 17 11 42N09 119E18 -7:57:12
Reshuitang 29 9 24N10 103E09 -6:52:36
Rikaze (Shigatse) 28 8 29N17 88E53 -5:55:32
Rizhao 21 1 35N27 119E29 -7:57:56
Rong'an 6 9 25N10 109E20 -7:17:20
Rongbaca 24 9 31N48 99E40 -6:38:40
Rongchang 24 9 29N24 105E36 -7:02:24
Rongcheng 21 1 37N08 122E23 -8:09:32
Rongcheng 8 1 39N03 115E52 -7:43:28
Rongding 24 9 28N57 103E40 -6:54:40
Rongjiang 7 9 25N52 108E37 -7:14:28
Rongwanshi 12 1 28N10 112E57 -7:31:48
Rongxian 6 9 22N50 110E38 -7:22:32
Rongxian 24 9 29N28 104E25 -6:57:40
Rucheng 12 1 25N34 113E41 -7:34:44
Rudong 5 8 21N39 111E23 -7:25:32
Rudong 13 1 32N19 121E12 -8:04:48
Rugao 13 1 32N25 120E36 -8:02:24
Rui'an 30 1 27N49 120E38 -8:02:32
Ruichang 14 1 29N41 115E40 -7:42:40
Ruicheng 23 1 34N45 110E45 -7:23:00
Ruijin 14 1 25N50 116E00 -7:44:00
Runan 10 1 33N01 114E22 -7:37:28
Runheji 1 1 32N30 116E05 -7:44:20
Ruo'ergai 24 9 33N16 102E55 -6:51:40
Ruoheng 30 1 28N24 121E31 -8:06:04
Ruoqiang 27 8 38N30 88E05 -5:52:20
Ruoxi 14 1 29N18 115E20 -7:41:20
Rushan (Xiacun) 21 1 36N54 121E29 -8:05:56
Ruyang 10 1 34N10 112E26 -7:29:44
Ryojun → Lüshun 16 11 38N48 121E16 -8:05:04
Saga 28 8 29N30 85E22 -5:41:28
Saihan Toroi 17 9 41N41 100E26 -6:41:44
Sai Keng 31 4 22N26 114E16 -7:37:04
Sai Kung 31 4 22N23 114E15 -7:37:00
Saileati 27 7 38N57 74E45 -4:59:00
Saima 16 11 41N00 124E14 -8:16:56
Saiqi 3 1 27N00 119E43 -7:58:52
Saitula 27 7 36N21 78E02 -5:12:08
Sajia 28 8 28N55 88E05 -5:52:20
San'anzhuling 28 8 28N33 93E00 -6:12:00
Sanbao 27 8 43N00 93E19 -6:13:16
Sanbao 2 1 40N20 116E02 -7:44:08
Sanbaoyingzi 16 11 41N34 120E56 -8:03:44
Sancang 13 1 32N45 120E43 -8:02:52
Sancha 13 1 31N52 119E06 -7:56:24
Sancha 2 1 40N27 116E26 -7:45:44
Sanchaba 24 9 30N19 104E14 -6:56:56
Sanchahe 15 12 44N59 126E04 -8:24:16
Sanchakou 26 1 39N47 117E19 -7:49:16
Sanchang 13 1 31N54 121E15 -8:05:00
Sanchazi 16 11 41N07 124E15 -8:17:00
Sanchazicun 16 11 42N03 123E59 -8:15:56
Sanchenglong 17 11 44N02 120E58 -8:03:52
Sanchih 25 6 25N16 121E30 -8:06:00
Sanchung 25 6 25N04 121E30 -8:06:00
Sanch'ungch'iao 25 6 25N12 121E35 -8:06:20
Sandaogang 9 12 46N08 130E05 -8:40:20
Sandaogou 16 11 41N39 121E45 -8:07:00
Sandaogou 8 1 39N33 115E27 -7:41:48
Sandaohe 27 8 44N21 85E37 -5:42:28
Sandaoliangzi 16 11 41N20 122E07 -8:08:28
Sandaolingzi 16 11 40N58 124E08 -8:16:32
Sandaozhen 9 12 47N25 126E25 -8:25:40
Sandian 11 1 30N56 114E48 -7:39:12
Sandouping 11 1 30N48 110E49 -7:23:16
Sandu 30 1 29N46 120E12 -8:00:48
Sandu 12 1 26N02 113E16 -7:33:04
Sandu 14 1 29N12 114E40 -7:38:40
Sandu 7 9 25N59 107E52 -7:11:28
Sanduan 16 11 41N10 121E27 -8:05:48
Sandun 30 3 30N19 120E05 -8:00:20
Sandun 13 1 31N52 121E50 -8:07:20
Sanduo 13 1 32N49 119E42 -7:58:48
Sangchungshih 25 6 25N04 121E29 -8:05:56
Sanggin Dalai 17 9 38N11 105E17 -7:01:08
Sanglin 14 1 27N54 114E46 -7:39:04
Sangluoshu 21 1 37N31 117E43 -7:50:52
Sangou 8 1 41N02 118E11 -7:52:44
Sangshuyuan 27 8 42N23 88E30 -5:54:00
Sanguandian 1 1 31N19 118E05 -7:52:20
Sanguang 22 2 31N47 121E16 -8:05:04
Sanguanmiao 10 1 32N25 114E04 -7:36:16
Sanguanyingzi 16 11 41N39 120E44 -8:02:56
Sanguliu 16 11 40N45 124E14 -8:16:56
Sangya 28 8 30N52 91E40 -6:06:40
Sangyuanbao 8 1 40N15 115E32 -7:42:08
Sangyuanbu 13 1 31N37 118E53 -7:55:32
Sangyuanzhen 24 9 30N30 103E26 -6:53:44
Sangzhi 12 1 29N18 110E02 -7:20:08
Sangzidian 21 1 36N46 116E55 -7:47:40
Sanhe 5 1 24N24 116E34 -7:46:16
Sanhe 8 1 39N59 117E04 -7:48:16
Sanhechang 24 9 31N22 106E48 -7:07:12
Sanhechang 24 9 30N04 105E01 -7:00:04
Sanhecun 15 12 42N28 129E39 -8:38:36
Sanheji 1 1 32N42 117E55 -7:51:40
Sanhekou 13 1 31N50 120E08 -8:00:32
Sanhetun 16 11 42N38 123E38 -8:14:32
Sanhezhan 9 12 52N34 126E02 -8:24:08
Sanhezhen 1 1 31N30 117E14 -7:48:56
Sanhezhuang 2 1 40N04 116E18 -7:45:12
Sanhsing 25 6 24N40 121E39 -8:06:36
Sanhu 14 1 27N55 115E24 -7:41:36
Sanhui 24 9 29N57 105E53 -7:03:32
Sanhui 24 9 30N06 106E36 -7:06:24
Sani 25 6 24N25 120E46 -8:03:04
Sanjiadian 2 1 39N58 116E06 -7:44:24
Sanjiadian 8 1 39N22 115E58 -7:43:52
Sanjiadian 2 1 40N09 116E36 -7:46:24
Sanjiang 6 9 25N42 109E23 -7:17:32
Sanjiang 24 9 29N33 104E03 -6:56:12
Sanjiangzhen 24 9 30N31 103E48 -6:55:12
Sanjiaocheng 4 9 36N47 104E40 -6:58:40
Sanjiaopao 16 11 41N22 122E17 -8:09:08
Sanjiaoshancun 16 11 40N42 122E49 -8:11:16
Sanjiazhen 24 9 30N17 105E32 -7:02:08
Sanjiazi 16 11 40N54 121E59 -8:07:56
Sanjiazi 17 11 42N33 121E38 -8:06:32
Sanjiazi 16 11 42N02 122E20 -8:09:20
Sanjiazi 16 11 41N53 121E42 -8:06:48
Sanjiazi 16 11 40N42 123E16 -8:13:04
Sanjiaziyingzi 16 11 41N52 120E49 -8:03:16
Sanjie 29 9 25N01 101E02 -6:44:08
Sanjie 1 1 32N35 118E08 -7:52:32
Sankeng 5 1 23N36 112E48 -7:31:12
Sankeshu 16 11 42N38 122E25 -8:09:40
Sanlicheng 11 1 31N48 114E12 -7:36:48
Sanlidian 1 1 30N48 118E15 -7:53:00
Sanlifan 11 1 30N51 115E15 -7:41:00
Sanlintang 22 2 31N08 121E29 -8:05:56
Sanlipu 13 1 31N46 119E03 -7:56:12
Sanliuji 1 1 32N08 116E19 -7:45:16
Sanmen 30 1 29N06 121E24 -8:05:36
Sanmenxia (Shanxian) 10 1 34N45 111E05 -7:24:20
Sanming 3 1 26N14 117E36 -7:50:24
Sanpu 13 1 34N09 117E10 -7:48:40
Sanqiao 30 1 30N35 119E58 -7:59:52
Sanqutan 14 1 27N17 115E04 -7:40:16
Sanquzhen 24 9 29N39 105E37 -7:02:28
Sanrao 5 1 23N59 116E50 -7:47:20
Sansha 3 1 26N58 120E12 -8:00:48
Sanshengchang 17 11 44N51 120E21 -8:01:24
Sanshierzhan 17 11 53N16 121E49 -8:07:16
Sanshijia 17 11 41N44 119E15 -7:57:00
Sanshijia 16 11 41N05 119E03 -7:56:12
Sanshilibao 16 11 39N15 121E48 -8:07:12
Sanshiling 1 1 30N51 119E29 -7:57:56
Sanshisanzhan 17 11 53N10 121E27 -8:05:48
Sanshui 5 1 23N11 112E53 -7:31:32
Santai 16 11 41N48 121E53 -8:07:32
Santai 16 11 41N56 123E11 -8:12:44
Santai 27 7 44N35 81E18 -5:25:12
Santai 24 9 31N10 105E02 -7:00:08
Santai 27 7 39N14 77E42 -5:10:48
Santai 8 1 38N58 115E49 -7:43:16
Santaizi 16 11 41N21 121E36 -8:06:24
Santang 14 1 28N44 116E32 -7:46:08
Santanghu 27 8 44N13 93E22 -6:13:28
Santiaoqiao 22 2 31N36 121E22 -8:05:28
Santuanjiang 22 2 30N54 121E43 -8:06:52
Santunying 8 1 40N14 118E12 -7:52:48
Sanxi 1 1 30N22 118E25 -7:53:40
Sanxi 30 1 27N42 120E04 -8:00:16
Sanxing 13 1 31N47 121E35 -8:06:20
Sanxing 13 1 31N58 121E07 -8:04:28
Sanxingchang 24 9 30N19 104E09 -6:56:36
Sanxingchang 24 9 30N32 104E38 -6:58:32
Sanxingjie 13 1 32N06 121E01 -8:04:04
Sanyang 11 1 31N20 113E10 -7:32:40
Sanyang 14 1 27N57 114E22 -7:37:28
Sanyang 14 1 28N37 116E15 -7:45:00
Sanyangzhen 13 1 31N55 121E29 -8:05:56
Sanyanjing 16 11 41N28 122E27 -8:09:48
Sanyanqiao 12 1 28N39 113E43 -7:34:52
Sanyuan 20 9 34N35 108E54 -7:15:36
Sanyuanpu 15 12 42N02 125E44 -8:22:56
Sanyuhao 8 1 42N30 117E34 -7:50:16
Sanyuzhen 13 1 32N08 121E19 -8:05:16
Sanzha 8 1 41N44 114E39 -7:38:36
Sanzhan 9 12 49N42 125E20 -8:21:20
Sanzhan 9 12 49N36 126E38 -8:26:32
Sanzuodian 17 11 41N36 118E49 -7:55:16
Saodatun 16 11 42N02 123E31 -8:14:04
Saxike 28 8 30N44 86E22 -5:45:28
Schanghai → Shanghai 22 2 31N14 121E28 -8:05:52
Schihkiatschwang → Shijiazhuang 8 1 38N03 114E28 -7:37:52
Seda 24 9 32N20 100E41 -6:42:44
Seergu 24 9 32N00 103E33 -6:54:12
Segang 10 1 31N58 114E18 -7:37:12
Sêndo 28 8 31N40 95E12 -6:20:48
Senjitu 8 1 41N56 116E25 -7:45:40
Sêrxü 24 8 33N04 97E45 -6:31:00
Seshu 8 1 39N33 115E37 -7:42:28
Shacheng 8 1 40N25 115E31 -7:42:04
Shadi 14 1 26N08 114E49 -7:39:16
Shadian 10 1 35N30 114E26 -7:37:44
Shading 28 8 31N20 94E40 -6:18:40
Shadui 24 9 31N30 100E10 -6:40:40
Shafu 5 10 22N25 113E01 -7:32:04
Shaguotun 16 11 41N10 120E38 -8:02:32
Shahe 6 9 22N06 109E43 -7:18:52
Shahe 8 1 36N56 114E30 -7:38:00
Shahe 13 1 34N44 118E58 -7:55:52
Shahe 21 1 37N01 119E43 -7:58:52
Shahedian 10 1 33N01 113E44 -7:34:56
Shaheji 1 1 32N26 118E14 -7:52:56
Shahepu 16 11 41N08 121E01 -8:04:04
Shaheyi 8 1 39N53 118E31 -7:54:04
Shaheying 16 11 40N50 120E46 -8:03:04
Shahezhen 21 1 35N49 116E23 -7:45:32
Shahezhen 2 1 40N08 116E15 -7:45:00
Shahezi 9 12 46N05 129E20 -8:37:20
Shahu 11 1 30N11 113E39 -7:34:36
Shaikou 3 1 27N19 117E35 -7:50:20
Shajian 3 1 24N46 117E38 -7:50:32
Shajianzi 16 11 41N01 125E26 -8:21:44
Shajiazhuang 13 1 32N13 120E53 -8:03:32
Shajing 5 1 23N36 114E06 -7:36:24
Shajingzi 4 9 37N42 105E09 -7:00:36
Shakeng 17 1 42N13 116E35 -7:46:20
Shakou 5 1 24N25 113E32 -7:34:08
Shaling 16 11 41N20 123E01 -8:12:04
Shaling 16 11 41N09 122E22 -8:09:28
Shalingpu 16 11 41N47 123E11 -8:12:44

Shalingzi 8	1	40N42	114E55	-7:39:40
Shaliuhe 19	8	36N28	98E57	-6:35:48
Shaliuhe 8	1	39N53	117E56	-7:51:44
Shaluhe 9	12	51N08	126E00	-8:24:00
Shaman 27	7	38N50	75E36	-5:02:24
Shamei 3	1	24N32	118E25	-7:53:40
Shanbiao 10	1	35N28	113E57	-7:35:48
Shancheng 4	9	37N01	107E00	-7:08:00
Shanchengzhen 15	12	42N23	125E26	-8:21:44
Shandan 4	9	38N45	101E15	-6:45:00
Shandianhe 17	1	42N22	116E15	-7:45:00
Shandong 24	9	29N31	106E25	-7:05:40
Shang'ao 1	1	30N41	119E25	-7:57:40
Shangba 13	3	32N11	118E46	-7:55:04
Shangbahe 11	1	30N40	115E05	-7:40:20
Shangbai 30	1	30N29	119E58	-7:59:52
Shangbancheng 8	1	40N50	118E03	-7:52:12
Shangbatang 19	8	32N46	96E20	-6:25:20
Shangcai 10	1	33N16	114E15	-7:37:00
Shangcang 26	1	39N54	117E23	-7:49:32
Shangchen 30	1	30N07	119E53	-7:59:32
Shangcheng 10	1	31N48	115E24	-7:41:36
Shangchewan 11	1	29N48	113E01	-7:32:04
Shangch'iu → Shangqiu 10	1	34N27	115E42	-7:42:48
Shangdang 13	1	32N06	119E24	-7:57:36
Shangdayangqi 17	11	51N09	124E02	-8:16:08
Shangdian 10	1	34N07	112E23	-7:29:32
Shangdianmiao 30	1	30N56	120E51	-8:03:24
Shangdouying 8	1	40N36	115E33	-7:42:12
Shangdu 17	9	41N29	113E34	-7:34:16
Shangduichunshi 16	11	41N00	123E02	-8:12:08
Shangdundu 14	1	27N56	116E15	-7:45:00
Shangfu 14	1	28N40	114E59	-7:39:56
Shanggaixin 29	9	23N25	100E02	-6:40:08
Shanggan 3	1	25N56	119E22	-7:57:28
Shanggang 13	1	33N30	120E04	-8:00:16
Shanggangzi 16	11	42N26	123E03	-8:12:12
Shanggao 14	1	28N18	114E54	-7:39:36
Shanggecun 13	1	31N49	119E07	-7:56:28
Shanggu 8	1	40N47	118E28	-7:53:52
Shangguanying 8	1	41N18	117E07	-7:48:28
Shanghai 22	2	31N14	121E28	-8:05:52
Shanghailingao 16	11	41N57	120E55	-8:03:40
Shanghang 3	1	25N06	116E25	-7:45:40
Shanghe 21	1	37N19	117E07	-7:48:28
Shanghekou 16	11	40N26	124E47	-8:19:08
Shanghetou 26	1	39N12	116E59	-7:47:56
Shanghewantun 16	11	41N42	123E23	-8:13:32
Shanghuang 13	1	31N33	119E34	-7:58:16
Shanghuangqi 8	1	41N29	116E31	-7:46:04
Shanghucun 8	1	40N45	115E45	-7:43:00
Shangjao → Shangrao 14	1	28N26	117E58	-7:51:52
Shangjiafen 16	11	41N18	121E10	-8:04:40
Shangjiahe 16	11	41N51	124E28	-8:17:52
Shangjiaodao 30	1	29N00	119E54	-7:59:36
Shangjiatai 16	11	40N53	123E35	-8:14:20
Shangjie 14	1	27N06	116E06	-7:44:24
Shangjiuwu 10	1	33N59	113E01	-7:32:04
Shangkasa 28	7	33N45	80E12	-5:20:48
Shangkou 21	1	36N59	118E53	-7:55:32
Shanglanjiagou 16	11	40N52	120E37	-8:02:28
Shanglin 8	1	38N19	116E05	-7:44:20
Shanglin 16	11	41N31	122E14	-8:08:56
Shanglin 6	9	23N28	108E33	-7:14:12
Shanglishi 14	1	27N52	113E46	-7:35:04
Shangliuhezicun 16	11	41N28	123E32	-8:14:08
Shangliulinzi 16	11	41N02	123E13	-8:12:52
Shangmagushan 16	11	41N41	124E10	-8:16:40
Shangmatai 26	1	39N22	117E15	-7:49:00
Shangmatun 16	11	40N57	123E22	-8:13:28
Shangmingdian 13	1	31N12	120E57	-8:03:48
Shangmingju 8	1	39N41	115E12	-7:40:48
Shangnan 20	9	33N31	110E45	-7:23:00
Shangpandaoling 16	11	41N42	121E14	-8:04:56
Shangpeibu 13	1	31N28	119E13	-7:56:52
Shangping 5	1	24N43	115E27	-7:41:48
Shangping 5	1	24N29	114E38	-7:38:32
Shangping 3	1	25N57	117E33	-7:50:12
Shangpuzi 16	11	41N37	121E35	-8:06:20
Shangqianbu 30	1	30N27	120E04	-8:00:16
Shangqiao 1	1	31N02	117E42	-7:50:48
Shangqing 3	1	25N53	118E36	-7:54:24
Shangqing 14	1	28N02	117E00	-7:48:00
Shangqingshuicun 2	1	39N56	115E38	-7:42:32
Shangqiu (Zhuji) 10	1	34N27	115E42	-7:42:48
Shangqiu 10	1	34N23	115E37	-7:42:28
Shangrao 14	1	28N26	117E58	-7:51:52
Shangshe 23	1	38N15	113E20	-7:33:20
Shangshibatai 16	11	42N02	120E51	-8:03:24
Shangshui 10	1	33N33	114E34	-7:38:16
Shangsi 6	9	22N09	107E57	-7:11:48
Shangtan 1	1	30N27	118E42	-7:54:48
Shangtang 13	1	33N23	118E02	-7:52:08
Shangweiniuchang 16	11	40N54	120E44	-8:02:56
Shangxian 20	9	33N51	109E54	-7:19:36
Shangxingzhen 13	1	31N32	119E15	-7:57:00
Shangxinhe 13	3	32N02	118E43	-7:54:52
Shangxinqiu 16	11	42N27	121E37	-8:06:28
Shangyangbao 16	11	42N30	124E14	-8:16:56
Shangyangcun 1	1	30N48	118E40	-7:54:40
Shangye 21	1	35N26	117E59	-7:51:56
Shangyi (Nanhaoqian) 8	1	41N04	114E03	-7:36:12
Shangying 15	12	44N10	127E17	-8:29:08
Shangyinkou 24	9	32N52	103E04	-6:52:16
Shangyou 14	1	25N51	114E30	-7:38:00
Shangyu 30	1	30N02	120E54	-8:03:36
Shangyuan 16	11	41N39	120E55	-8:03:40
Shangyun 29	9	23N01	99E50	-6:39:20
Shangzhai 23	1	39N13	114E17	-7:37:08
Shangzhaoshugou 16	11	42N12	121E58	-8:07:52
Shangzhazi 8	1	40N52	117E42	-7:50:48
Shangzhenzhuang 2	1	40N20	117E06	-7:48:24
Shangzhi 9	12	45N13	127E59	-8:31:56
Shangzhuangtai 8	1	39N41	115E25	-7:41:40
Shanhaiguan 8	1	40N01	119E44	-7:58:56
Shanhaikwan → Shanhaiguan 8	1	40N01	119E44	-7:58:56
Shanhe 28	7	33N38	79E50	-5:19:20
Shanhecun 9	12	45N38	128E27	-8:33:48
Shanhetun 9	12	44N44	127E12	-8:28:48
Shanjiazhuang 8	1	38N52	115E45	-7:43:00
Shankou 6	9	21N38	109E43	-7:18:52
Shankou 3	1	26N40	117E46	-7:51:04
Shankou 14	1	28N58	115E12	-7:40:48
Shankou 14	1	28N48	114E29	-7:37:56
Shanlenggang 24	9	28N33	103E23	-6:53:32
Shanli 1	1	29N52	117E21	-7:49:24
Shanlian 30	1	30N42	120E19	-8:01:16
Shanmenjie 1	1	30N40	118E52	-7:55:28
Shanmulong 29	9	24N39	98E05	-6:32:20
Shannanguan 1	1	31N36	116E52	-7:47:28
Shanpo 11	1	30N06	114E20	-7:37:20
Shanrendong 17	11	46N50	123E08	-8:12:32
Shanrenqiao 13	1	31N16	120E27	-8:01:48
Shanshan 27	8	42N52	90E10	-6:00:40
Shanshenmiao 8	1	40N45	117E11	-7:48:44
Shanting 21	1	35N09	117E29	-7:49:56
Shantou (Swatow) 5	1	23N23	116E41	-7:46:44
Shanwei 5	1	22N47	115E21	-7:41:24
Shanxian 21	1	34N48	116E03	-7:44:12
Shanxian → Sanmenxia 10	1	34N45	111E05	-7:24:20
Shanxiawu 12	1	28N52	113E52	-7:35:28
Shanxu 6	9	22N21	107E58	-7:11:52
Shanyang 3	1	26N43	119E13	-7:56:52
Shanyang 13	1	31N19	120E16	-8:01:04
Shanyang 20	9	33N35	109E49	-7:19:16
Shanyao 3	1	25N13	118E55	-7:55:40
Shanyaqiao 13	1	31N15	119E25	-7:57:40
Shanyin 23	1	39N33	112E50	-7:31:20
Shanzhangjiafen 2	1	40N37	116E44	-7:46:56
Shanzui 8	1	40N48	118E13	-7:52:52
Shanzuizi 16	11	41N55	120E30	-8:02:00
Shaobo 13	1	32N30	119E32	-7:58:08
Shaodenggao 16	11	42N13	121E47	-8:07:08
Shaodian 10	1	33N10	114E18	-7:37:12
Shaodian 13	1	34N08	118E25	-7:53:40
Shaoguan 5	1	24N50	113E37	-7:34:28
Shaogudian 21	1	36N57	115E32	-7:42:08
Shaoguyingzi 16	11	41N33	120E27	-8:01:48
Shaohing → Shaoxing 30	1	30N00	120E35	-8:02:20
Shaohsing → Shaoxing 30	1	30N00	120E35	-8:02:20
Shaojiaolou 22	2	31N05	121E32	-8:06:08
Shaokuan → Shaoguan 5	1	24N50	113E37	-7:34:28
Shaowu 3	1	27N20	117E28	-7:49:52
Shaoxing 30	1	30N00	120E35	-8:02:20
Shaoyang 12	1	27N15	111E28	-7:25:52
Shaoyang 12	1	27N00	111E18	-7:25:12
Shaoyun 24	9	29N30	105E57	-7:03:48
Shaozihe 16	11	40N13	123E33	-8:14:12
Shaquan 27	8	44N33	83E25	-5:33:40
Shaquzhen 24	9	30N33	103E45	-6:55:00
Shashi 11	1	30N19	112E14	-7:28:56
Shashibu 14	1	25N48	114E54	-7:39:36
Shasi → Shashi 11	1	30N19	112E14	-7:28:56
Shatangjiang 13	1	31N25	120E01	-8:00:04
Shatian 12	1	25N53	113E44	-7:34:56
Shatian 5	1	23N59	113E56	-7:35:44
Sha Tin 31	4	22N23	114E11	-7:36:44
Shatuji 21	1	35N18	115E45	-7:43:00
Shatuosi 24	9	31N20	108E51	-7:15:24
Shawan 30	1	27N52	119E28	-7:57:52
Shawan 24	9	29N25	103E33	-6:54:12
Shawan 27	8	44N34	85E48	-5:43:12
Shawo 14	1	28N52	114E47	-7:39:08
Shawo 10	1	34N28	114E37	-7:38:28
Shawo 10	1	31N44	115E08	-7:40:32
Shaxi 14	1	28N34	118E06	-7:52:24
Shaxi 14	1	26N53	115E34	-7:42:16
Shaxi 5	1	24N38	113E42	-7:34:48
Shaxi 13	1	31N34	121E04	-8:04:16
Shaxian 3	1	26N24	117E47	-7:51:08
Shaxikou 3	1	26N33	118E02	-7:52:08
Shaximiao 24	9	29N57	106E19	-7:05:16
Shayang 11	1	30N42	112E33	-7:30:12
Shayuan 30	1	27N45	120E38	-8:02:32
Shazhen 21	1	36N23	115E47	-7:43:08
Shazhou 13	1	31N52	120E32	-8:02:08
Shazihe 24	9	32N12	106E42	-7:06:48
Shebu 12	1	27N40	112E48	-7:31:12
Shecheng 23	1	37N14	113E05	-7:32:20
Shefu 14	1	26N11	115E22	-7:41:28
Shegangshi 12	1	28N32	113E36	-7:34:24
Shehong 24	9	30N56	105E22	-7:01:28
Shehongmiao 24	9	30N44	106E03	-7:04:12
Shekki → Zhongshan 5	1	22N31	113E22	-7:33:28
Shek Kong 31	4	22N26	114E06	-7:36:24
Shekou 11	3	30N44	114E20	-7:37:20
Shenchi 23	1	39N09	112E19	-7:29:16
Shencun 1	1	31N04	118E51	-7:55:24
Shendang 30	1	30N34	120E49	-8:03:16
Shenduncun 30	1	30N48	120E25	-8:01:40
Shengang 14	1	27N20	116E18	-7:45:12
Shengang 13	1	31N54	120E08	-8:00:32
Shengfang 8	1	39N04	116E42	-7:46:48
Shenggongjing 30	1	31N07	119E48	-7:59:12
Shenghongqing 11	1	30N12	114E56	-7:39:44
Shengjiachi 24	9	30N28	105E03	-7:00:12
Shengjiaqiao 22	2	31N27	121E24	-8:05:36
Shengjiatun 16	11	41N14	121E22	-8:05:28
Shengjin'gao 16	11	42N04	120E43	-8:02:52
Shengou 10	1	34N08	113E13	-7:32:52
Shengqing 16	11	41N34	121E36	-8:06:24
Shengshan 30	1	30N50	120E15	-8:01:00
Shengshui 21	1	35N45	119E39	-7:58:36
Shengshuihezi 15	12	42N27	125E59	-8:23:56
Shengtian 12	1	27N14	113E06	-7:32:24
Shengxian 30	1	29N36	120E48	-8:03:12
Shengze 13	1	30N55	120E39	-8:02:36
Shengzigou 16	11	41N35	124E04	-8:16:16
Shenhu 3	1	24N38	118E39	-7:54:36
Shenji 10	1	34N47	115E09	-7:40:36
Shenjia 9	12	46N06	126E46	-8:27:04
Shenjiadian 9	12	46N35	130E38	-8:42:32
Shenjiatai 16	11	41N22	120E50	-8:03:20
Shenjiawan 22	2	31N43	121E19	-8:05:16
Shenjiazhuang 13	1	32N18	120E26	-8:01:44
Shenjing 5	10	21N59	112E28	-7:29:52
Shenjing 8	1	40N24	114E49	-7:39:16
Shenjingzi 16	11	41N47	123E41	-8:14:44
Shenk'eng 25	6	25N00	121E36	-8:06:24
Shenkou 14	1	28N42	116E02	-7:44:08
Shenmu 20	9	38N56	110E19	-7:21:16
Shennan 8	1	38N59	114E56	-7:39:44
Shenqiu 10	1	33N24	115E02	-7:40:08
Shenquan 5	1	22N59	116E20	-7:45:20
Shentuan 21	1	35N30	119E17	-7:57:08
Shenxian 21	1	36N15	115E41	-7:42:44
Shenxian 8	1	38N01	115E33	-7:42:12
Shenxing 8	1	39N02	115E19	-7:41:16
Shenyang (Mukden) 16	11	41N48	123E27	-8:13:48
Shenze 8	1	38N11	115E11	-7:40:44
Shenzha 28	8	30N57	88E38	-5:54:32
Sheqi 10	1	33N03	112E57	-7:31:48
Shetou 13	1	31N39	119E27	-7:57:48
Shexian 13	1	36N33	113E40	-7:34:40
Shexian 1	1	29N53	118E26	-7:53:44
Sheyang 13	1	33N46	120E18	-8:01:12
Sheyang 13	1	33N20	119E38	-7:58:32
Shezhu 13	1	31N19	119E16	-7:57:04
Shiba 1	1	32N45	118E07	-7:52:28
Shibadu 12	1	28N01	110E51	-7:23:24
Shiban 24	9	30N18	104E28	-6:57:52
Shibanxi 24	9	29N17	103E51	-6:55:24
Shibaocheng 27	8	39N48	96E10	-6:24:40
Shibi 3	1	26N43	120E02	-8:00:08
Shibing 7	9	26N50	108E04	-7:12:16
Shibishan 14	1	29N21	116E45	-7:47:00
Shibu 21	1	36N45	119E27	-7:57:48
Shibuzi 21	1	36N09	119E06	-7:56:24
Shicha 14	1	28N24	115E50	-7:43:20
Shichangyu 16	11	41N12	123E14	-8:12:56
Shicheng 16	11	40N39	124E17	-8:17:08
Shicheng 3	1	25N18	119E21	-7:57:24
Shicheng 14	1	26N22	116E22	-7:45:28
Shidai 1	1	30N20	117E56	-7:51:44
Shidao 21	1	36N53	122E23	-8:09:32
Shideng 29	9	26N44	99E11	-6:36:44
Shidong 24	9	30N25	105E20	-7:01:20
Shidong 24	9	28N59	105E27	-7:01:48
Shidongzigou 8	1	40N41	118E23	-7:53:32
Shiercun 30	1	30N31	119E34	-7:58:16
Shi'erwei 13	1	32N15	119E14	-7:56:56
Shifang 3	1	25N01	116E14	-7:44:56
Shifo 24	9	29N58	103E50	-6:55:20
Shifobao 16	11	41N28	121E27	-8:05:48
Shifochang 24	9	30N19	105E07	-7:00:28
Shifodian 10	1	32N06	115E46	-7:43:04
Shifosi 16	11	42N08	123E20	-8:13:20
Shifoya 16	11	40N12	123E10	-8:12:40
Shigaise → Rikaze 28	8	29N17	88E53	-5:55:32
Shigang 13	1	32N14	121E00	-8:04:00

Shigang 13 1 32N13 120E58 -8:03:52
Shigangmen 22 2 31N21 121E17 -8:05:08
Shigaopu 24 9 30N16 104E01 -6:56:04
Shigezhuang 26 1 39N18 116E53 -7:47:32
Shigezhuang 8 1 38N57 116E19 -7:45:16
Shigezhuang 8 1 38N59 115E36 -7:42:24
Shigouyi 18 9 37N44 106E26 -7:05:44
Shigu 14 1 29N27 117E14 -7:48:56
Shigu 29 9 26N50 99E55 -6:39:40
Shiguaigou 17 9 40N42 110E20 -7:21:20
Shiguantun 16 11 41N38 123E39 -8:14:36
Shigulingyu 2 1 40N38 116E54 -7:47:36
Shihchiachuang → Shijiazhuang 8 1 38N03 114E28 -7:37:52
Shihch'i → Zhongshan 5 1 22N31 113E22 -7:33:28
Shihe 16 11 39N19 121E52 -8:07:28
Shihengyuanyu 13 1 31N50 121E45 -8:07:00
Shihezi 27 8 44N18 86E02 -5:44:08
Shihkiachwang → Shijiazhuang 8 1 38N03 114E28 -7:37:52
Shihti 25 6 25N02 121E44 -8:06:56
Shihting 25 6 24N59 121E39 -8:06:36
Shihu 26 1 40N04 117E17 -7:49:08
Shihu 15 12 41N29 126E18 -8:25:12
Shihuajie 11 1 32N20 111E25 -7:25:40
Shihudang 22 2 30N58 121E07 -8:04:28
Shihuixi 24 9 29N02 105E04 -7:00:16
Shihuiyaozi 16 11 42N08 123E47 -8:15:08
Shihuxia 8 1 40N48 117E22 -7:49:28
Shijiaba 24 9 30N18 104E46 -6:59:04
Shijiagangzi 16 11 42N19 123E34 -8:14:16
Shijiagou 16 11 42N27 123E28 -8:13:52
Shijiao 5 1 23N36 112E59 -7:31:56
Shijiaqiao 30 1 30N46 120E06 -8:00:24
Shijiaqiao 13 1 32N18 119E26 -7:57:44
Shijiawu 8 1 39N21 116E15 -7:45:00
Shijiaxiang 24 9 29N38 104E59 -6:59:56
Shijiayaozhuang 13 1 32N13 120E29 -8:01:56
Shijiazhai 8 1 38N56 114E18 -7:37:12
Shijiazhen 13 1 31N51 121E10 -8:04:40
Shijiazhuang 8 1 38N03 114E28 -7:37:52
Shijiazi 16 11 42N39 122E06 -8:08:24
Shijiazi 16 11 42N07 122E18 -8:09:12
Shijiedu 1 1 30N57 119E13 -7:56:52
Shijing 21 1 35N30 118E57 -7:55:48
Shijing 8 1 39N54 114E58 -7:39:52
Shijing 3 1 24N40 118E24 -7:53:36
Shijingshan 2 1 39N56 116E07 -7:44:28
Shijiusuo 21 1 35N24 119E29 -7:57:56
Shikewusumiao 17 9 40N13 108E52 -7:15:28
Shikuang 13 1 31N54 121E24 -8:05:36
Shiliangji 10 1 33N54 115E14 -7:40:56
Shilibao 2 1 39N55 116E29 -7:45:56
Shilihe 16 11 41N31 123E22 -8:13:28
Shiling 30 1 30N26 119E35 -7:58:20
Shilipeng 13 1 31N14 119E35 -7:58:20
Shilipu 8 1 39N11 115E59 -7:43:56
Shilipu 8 1 40N15 117E58 -7:51:52
Shilipu 2 1 39N29 116E18 -7:45:12
Shiliuban 3 1 24N08 117E33 -7:50:12
Shilong 5 1 23N07 113E48 -7:35:12
Shilong 24 9 30N15 106E34 -7:06:16
Shilong 6 9 23N54 109E40 -7:18:40
Shilou 5 1 22N58 113E29 -7:33:56
Shima 24 9 29N38 105E50 -7:03:20
Shima 3 1 24N27 117E49 -7:51:16
Shimachang 24 9 29N03 105E36 -7:02:24
Shimachang 24 9 28N59 105E55 -7:03:40
Shimamiao 13 1 32N08 119E20 -7:57:20
Shimantan 10 1 33N17 113E28 -7:33:52
Shimei 13 1 32N14 120E10 -8:00:40
Shimen 8 1 39N44 118E52 -7:55:28
Shimen 30 1 30N37 120E26 -8:01:44
Shimen 8 1 40N06 117E42 -7:50:48
Shimen 24 9 29N36 106E27 -7:05:48
Shimen 24 9 29N09 106E02 -7:04:08
Shimen 12 1 29N28 111E17 -7:25:08
Shimencun 30 1 30N23 119E41 -7:58:44
Shimencun 13 1 31N21 119E34 -7:58:16
Shimendong 30 1 28N16 120E07 -8:00:28
Shimengou 16 11 40N40 123E43 -8:14:52
Shimenjie 14 1 29N34 116E44 -7:46:56
Shimenlou 14 1 28N58 114E51 -7:39:24
Shimenying 2 1 39N54 116E05 -7:44:20
Shimenzi 17 11 48N30 121E31 -8:06:04
Shimian 24 9 29N18 102E22 -6:49:28
Shimiaozi 16 11 40N39 123E31 -8:14:04
Shinan 6 9 22N43 109E54 -7:19:36
Shipai 13 1 31N30 120E55 -8:03:40
Shipai 5 1 23N08 113E21 -7:33:24
Shipanpu 24 9 30N28 104E23 -6:57:32
Shipantuo 24 9 30N25 106E13 -7:04:52
Shiping 29 9 23N47 102E30 -6:50:00
Shiping 7 9 28N20 107E42 -7:10:48
Shipu 13 1 31N15 121E03 -8:04:12
Shipu 30 1 29N13 121E55 -8:07:40
Shiqian 7 9 27N31 108E20 -7:13:20
Shiqiao 24 9 30N25 104E31 -6:58:04
Shiqiao 10 1 33N12 112E36 -7:30:24
Shiqiao 14 1 26N58 114E23 -7:37:32
Shiqiao 1 1 30N30 119E11 -7:56:44
Shiqiaopu 24 9 30N05 105E23 -7:01:32
Shiqiaozi 16 11 41N27 123E43 -8:14:52
Shiqi → Zhongshan 5 1 22N31 113E22 -7:33:28
Shiquan 30 1 30N30 120E48 -8:03:12
Shiquan 20 9 33N03 108E17 -7:13:08
Shisanling 2 1 40N19 116E16 -7:45:04
Shisanzhan 9 12 51N21 125E43 -8:22:52

Shishan 16 11 41N16 121E30 -8:06:00
Shishi 3 1 24N48 118E38 -7:54:32
Shishou 11 1 29N43 112E19 -7:29:16
Shisiazhan 9 12 51N36 125E42 -8:22:48
Shisixian 16 11 40N53 122E59 -8:11:56
Shitai 1 1 30N13 117E27 -7:49:48
Shitan 5 1 23N10 113E47 -7:35:08
Shitan 12 1 27N44 112E42 -7:30:48
Shitang 30 1 28N16 121E36 -8:06:24
Shitang 6 9 25N38 110E50 -7:23:20
Shitangwan 13 1 31N40 120E13 -8:00:52
Shiting 8 1 39N31 115E41 -7:42:44
Shiting 12 1 27N36 113E16 -7:33:04
Shitoufangzi 9 12 48N38 126E08 -8:24:32
Shitougouzi 9 12 49N19 125E55 -8:23:40
Shitoumiao 17 9 41N41 106E50 -7:07:20
Shitoumiaozi 16 11 41N38 121E26 -8:05:44
Shitoushan 2 1 40N27 116E13 -7:44:52
Shitoushuangmiao 17 11 41N28 118E55 -7:55:40
Shituan 24 9 30N09 105E01 -7:00:04
Shitunwei 16 11 41N07 121E31 -8:06:04
Shiwan 5 1 23N01 113E04 -7:32:16
Shiwan 20 9 37N35 109E01 -7:16:04
Shiwan 12 1 27N17 112E57 -7:31:48
Shiwan 12 1 28N12 113E49 -7:35:16
Shiwenchang 16 11 41N43 123E54 -8:15:36
Shiwu 15 12 43N48 124E13 -8:16:52
Shixi 14 1 28N16 115E36 -7:42:24
Shixi 14 1 28N16 117E45 -7:51:00
Shixia 8 1 40N20 114E59 -7:39:56
Shixian 15 12 43N05 129E47 -8:39:08
Shixiancun 13 3 31N12 120E29 -8:01:56
Shixiechang 24 9 29N51 106E41 -7:06:44
Shixing 5 1 24N58 114E03 -7:36:12
Shixun 3 1 24N44 118E11 -7:52:44
Shiyachang 24 9 30N27 106E31 -7:06:04
Shiyan 24 9 30N22 104E27 -6:57:48
Shiyan 11 1 32N38 110E44 -7:22:56
Shiyangchang 24 9 30N42 105E57 -7:03:48
Shiyangchang 24 9 29N56 105E37 -7:02:28
Shiyanqiao 24 9 29N19 105E22 -7:01:28
Shiyiwei 13 1 31N59 120E43 -8:02:52
Shiyizhan 9 12 51N13 125E52 -8:23:28
Shiyu 24 9 29N46 106E06 -7:04:24
Shizhangzi 16 11 40N24 119E48 -7:59:12
Shizheng 5 1 24N32 115E50 -7:43:20
Shizhenjie 14 1 28N51 116E56 -7:47:44
Shizhong 30 1 30N44 120E16 -8:01:04
Shizhong 3 1 24N57 117E06 -7:48:24
Shizhongtan 24 9 30N26 104E35 -6:58:20
Shizhu 30 1 28N48 120E06 -8:00:24
Shizhu 24 9 29N56 108E09 -7:12:36
Shizhuang 13 1 32N08 120E31 -8:02:04
Shizhuangzi 16 11 42N24 122E53 -8:11:32
Shizhuangzi 2 1 40N38 116E59 -7:47:56
Shizhuzi 16 11 41N18 121E35 -8:06:20
Shizichang 24 9 29N32 106E14 -7:04:56
Shizigu 8 1 39N23 118E08 -7:52:32
Shizikou 5 1 24N12 113E38 -7:34:32
Shizilin 22 2 31N26 121E25 -8:05:40
Shizipo 8 1 40N21 115E07 -7:40:28
Shizipu 1 1 30N59 119E07 -7:56:28
Shizui 23 1 38N52 113E42 -7:34:48
Shizui 15 12 43N08 126E06 -8:24:24
Shou'anzhen 24 9 30N16 103E37 -6:54:28
Shouchang 30 1 29N22 119E13 -7:56:52
Shoufeng 25 6 23N52 121E30 -8:06:00
Shouguang 21 1 36N53 118E42 -7:54:48
Shouning 3 1 27N27 119E30 -7:58:00
Shoushan 16 11 41N12 123E03 -8:12:12
Shouwangfen 8 1 40N35 117E48 -7:51:12
Shouxian 1 1 32N35 116E47 -7:47:08
Shouyang 23 1 37N59 113E09 -7:32:36
Shuajingsi 24 9 32N00 103E05 -6:52:20
Shuangbai 29 9 24N54 101E32 -6:46:08
Shuangcheng 9 12 45N21 126E17 -8:25:08
Shuangchengzi 8 1 40N11 118E03 -7:52:12
Shuangdian 13 1 32N23 120E51 -8:03:24
Shuangdun 13 1 32N13 121E08 -8:04:32
Shuangfeng 13 1 31N31 121E02 -8:04:08
Shuangfeng 12 1 27N24 112E05 -7:28:20
Shuangfeng 13 1 31N31 121E01 -8:04:04
Shuangfengyi 24 9 29N27 105E09 -7:00:36
Shuangfu 8 1 39N48 117E44 -7:50:56
Shuangfuchang 24 9 29N41 103E31 -6:54:04
Shuangfuchang 24 9 30N08 103E32 -6:54:08
Shuanggang 15 12 45N07 122E59 -8:11:56
Shuanggang 14 1 28N11 117E30 -7:50:00
Shuanggetun 9 12 48N58 129E57 -8:39:48
Shuanggou 13 1 34N03 117E37 -7:50:28
Shuanggou 11 1 32N12 112E21 -7:29:24
Shuanggou 13 1 33N16 118E10 -7:52:40
Shuanggufen 24 9 29N38 104E11 -6:56:44
Shuanghe 11 1 31N41 112E46 -7:31:04
Shuanghe 24 9 29N40 104E48 -6:59:12
Shuanghe 24 9 30N07 105E10 -7:00:40
Shuanghe 24 9 30N15 104E44 -6:58:56
Shuanghe 1 1 31N33 116E46 -7:47:04
Shuanghechang 24 9 28N51 104E51 -6:59:24
Shuanghechang 24 9 29N25 106E17 -7:05:08
Shuanghechang 24 9 29N12 105E43 -7:02:52

Shuanghechang 24 9 29N18 105E36 -7:02:24
Shuang-Hsi 25 6 25N01 121E39 -8:06:36
Shuangjiang 29 9 23N37 99E41 -6:38:44
Shuangjiang 14 1 26N48 116E28 -7:45:52
Shuangjiang 24 9 30N13 105E45 -7:03:00
Shuangjiangqiao 29 9 25N19 98E51 -6:35:24
Shuangjianji 1 1 33N12 116E40 -7:46:40
Shuangjingzi 16 11 42N28 123E42 -8:14:48
Shuangkou 26 1 39N15 117E02 -7:48:08
Shuangliao 15 12 43N31 123E30 -8:14:00
Shuanglin 30 1 30N47 120E19 -8:01:16
Shuanglingzi 16 11 40N50 123E06 -8:12:24
Shuanglingzi 16 11 40N54 124E10 -8:16:40
Shuangliu 24 9 30N34 103E55 -6:55:40
Shuangliushu 10 1 31N56 115E12 -7:40:48
Shuanglongtai 16 11 40N56 122E39 -8:10:36
Shuangmiao 1 1 32N09 116E52 -7:47:28
Shuangmiao 30 1 28N24 120E45 -8:03:00
Shuangmiaozi 16 11 42N02 121E52 -8:07:28
Shuangmiaozi 16 11 42N25 122E17 -8:09:08
Shuangpai 12 1 25N57 111E32 -7:26:08
Shuangpaishi 13 1 31N24 118E59 -7:55:56
Shuangqiao 1 1 32N29 116E41 -7:46:44
Shuangqiao 1 1 30N59 118E47 -7:55:08
Shuangqiao 2 1 39N54 116E37 -7:46:28
Shuangshanzi 8 1 40N21 119E08 -7:56:32
Shuangshipu 24 9 29N14 104E42 -6:58:48
Shuangshiqiao 24 9 29N23 104E29 -6:57:56
Shuangshiqiao 24 9 29N22 105E51 -7:03:24
Shuangshu 26 1 39N34 117E01 -7:48:04
Shuangshutai 17 11 43N50 121E15 -8:05:00
Shuangtaizi 16 11 42N25 123E11 -8:12:44
Shuangtaizi 16 11 41N00 122E34 -8:10:16
Shuangtaizi 16 11 41N11 121E14 -8:04:56
Shuangtaizi 16 11 41N34 121E12 -8:04:48
Shuangtaizi 16 11 42N21 124E10 -8:16:40
Shuangtang 14 1 28N01 116E44 -7:46:56
Shuangtang 8 1 39N03 116E17 -7:45:08
Shuangtang 26 1 38N53 116E54 -7:47:36
Shuangtangdian 1 1 30N59 118E51 -7:55:24
Shuangtuo 26 1 39N14 117E20 -7:49:20
Shuangtuozhen 8 1 39N29 118E23 -7:53:32
Shuangxi 30 1 30N24 119E50 -7:59:20
Shuangxi 3 1 27N01 119E03 -7:56:12
Shuangyang 15 12 43N32 125E42 -8:22:48
Shuangyangdian 16 11 41N07 121E16 -8:05:04
Shuangyaocun 26 1 38N55 117E03 -7:48:12
Shuangyashan 9 12 46N37 131E22 -8:45:28
Shucheng 1 1 31N27 116E57 -7:47:48
Shufu → Kashi 27 7 39N29 75E59 -5:03:56
Shugudali 9 12 52N47 124E02 -8:16:08
Shuheyingzi 16 11 42N18 122E16 -8:09:04
Shuhezhen 22 2 31N35 121E35 -8:06:20
Shuhong 30 1 28N39 120E09 -8:00:36
Shuibatang 7 9 28N39 107E03 -7:08:12
Shuibei 13 1 31N40 119E39 -7:58:36
Shuibei 14 1 28N04 115E01 -7:40:04
Shuichaoyang 3 1 26N22 117E57 -7:51:48
Shuicheng 7 9 26N41 104E50 -6:59:20
Shuidiangou 17 11 47N43 122E40 -8:10:40
Shuidong 1 1 30N47 118E57 -7:55:48
Shuidong 13 1 31N23 119E37 -7:58:28
Shuidongjie 1 1 31N07 119E33 -7:58:12
Shuiduixia 1 1 30N17 118E50 -7:55:20
Shuihai 13 1 33N02 120E26 -8:01:44
Shuihouling 1 1 30N43 116E26 -7:45:44
Shuiji 3 1 27N26 118E20 -7:53:20
Shuijiahuangdi 16 11 42N14 123E28 -8:13:52
Shuijian 2 1 40N09 115E58 -7:43:52
Shuijing 29 9 26N10 99E09 -6:36:36
Shuijingtang 7 9 28N50 108E11 -7:12:44
Shuikou 5 1 24N00 115E55 -7:43:40
Shuikou 12 1 26N18 113E46 -7:35:04
Shuikou 24 9 29N29 103E42 -6:54:48
Shuikou 7 9 25N54 109E06 -7:16:24
Shuikou 3 1 26N59 117E41 -7:50:44
Shuikou 3 1 26N22 118E44 -7:54:56
Shuikouchang 24 9 29N33 103E40 -6:54:40
Shuikouguan 6 9 22N30 106E34 -7:06:16
Shuikoushan 12 1 26N30 112E30 -7:30:00
Shuikouxu 5 1 25N09 114E28 -7:37:52
Shuiliandong 16 11 42N12 125E09 -8:20:36
Shuimenzi 16 11 39N36 122E19 -8:09:16
Shuimingqiao 1 1 31N03 119E09 -7:56:36
Shuimoqipan 27 7 39N51 76E42 -5:06:48

Shuiquan'gou 16 11 41N58 121E50 -8:07:20
Shuiquanzi 16 11 40N53 121E05 -8:04:20
Shuiquanzi 16 11 42N15 121E32 -8:06:08
Shuitangzi 24 9 29N18 101E10 -6:44:40
Shuiting 30 1 29N10 119E14 -7:56:56
Shuitou 3 1 24N43 118E25 -7:53:40
Shuitou 5 1 23N53 113E37 -7:34:28
Shuitou 30 1 27N38 120E16 -8:01:04
Shuitouwei 14 1 26N06 115E28 -7:41:52
Shuituzhen 24 9 29N47 106E31 -7:06:04
Shuiyang 1 1 31N14 118E47 -7:55:08
Shuiye 10 1 36N08 114E07 -7:36:28
Shuizhai 21 1 36N54 117E24 -7:49:36
Shuizhuyang 3 1 26N59 119E13 -7:56:52
Shujiawazi 16 11 42N20 121E57 -8:07:48
Shulan 15 12 44N27 126E57 -8:27:48
Shule 27 7 39N23 76E06 -5:04:24
Shulu (Xinji) 8 1 37N54 115E13 -7:40:52
Shun'an 1 1 30N57 117E57 -7:51:48
Shunchang 3 1 26N50 117E48 -7:51:12
Shunde 5 1 22N50 113E14 -7:32:56
Shundian 10 1 34N15 113E20 -7:33:20
Shundianqiao 13 3 31N24 120E41 -8:02:44
Shunge 19 8 37N25 95E27 -6:21:48
Shunhechang 24 9 29N57 104E42 -6:58:48
Shunlongchang 24 9 30N04 103E27 -6:53:48
Shunshanpu 16 11 42N08 122E21 -8:09:24
Shuntianhu 5 1 24N08 114E48 -7:39:12
Shunyi 2 1 40N08 116E38 -7:46:32
Shuoduzong 28 8 30N48 95E47 -6:23:08
Shuojiaji 13 1 33N42 119E44 -7:58:56
Shuping 24 9 29N19 104E43 -6:58:52
Shuyang 13 1 34N08 118E47 -7:55:08
Shwangliao → Liaoyuan 15 12 42N54 125E07 -8:20:28
Siackan 11 1 30N56 113E55 -7:35:40
Si'an 30 1 30N54 119E39 -7:58:36
Siangtan → Xiangtan 12 1 27N51 112E54 -7:31:36
Sian → Xi'an 20 9 34N15 108E52 -7:15:28
Sianzhuang 13 1 33N05 119E13 -7:56:52
Sibao 3 1 25N55 116E42 -7:46:48
Sibati 27 8 47N12 88E15 -5:53:00
Sibochi 24 9 28N50 104E32 -6:58:08
Sibotu 27 8 47N12 88E15 -5:53:00
Sichakou 8 1 41N39 116E26 -7:45:44
Sichuanzhai 29 9 23N02 101E44 -6:46:56
Sicun 13 1 31N55 119E18 -7:57:12
Sidao 2 1 39N51 116E26 -7:45:44
Sidaohe 8 1 40N24 117E17 -7:49:08
Sidu 5 1 24N12 115E15 -7:41:00
Sidu 3 1 23N48 117E18 -7:49:12
Siduan 22 2 30N59 121E48 -8:07:12
Sienyang → Xianyang 20 9 34N22 108E42 -7:14:48
Si'erpu 16 11 40N47 120E41 -8:02:44
Sifangtai 16 11 41N33 121E19 -8:05:16
Sifangtai 16 11 41N02 122E46 -8:11:04
Sifangtai 16 11 41N35 122E57 -8:11:48
Sifangtai 9 12 46N55 127E00 -8:28:00
Sifen 12 1 27N32 113E30 -7:34:00
Sifentoudun 13 1 32N18 121E21 -8:05:24
Sihai 2 1 40N33 116E24 -7:45:36
Sihecun 8 1 39N56 117E07 -7:48:28
Sihong 13 1 33N28 118E11 -7:52:44
Sihu 13 1 34N38 117E59 -7:51:56
Sihui 5 1 23N19 112E40 -7:30:40
Sijiaba 13 1 32N02 121E18 -8:05:12
Sijianfang 16 11 42N29 122E17 -8:09:08
Sijiazi 16 11 41N47 120E06 -8:00:24
Sijing 22 2 31N07 121E16 -8:05:04
Sijupu 24 9 30N02 106E18 -7:05:12
Sikeshu 27 8 44N25 84E14 -5:36:56
Siking → Xi'an 20 9 34N15 108E52 -7:15:28
Silangcheng 17 1 42N19 115E43 -7:42:52
Silijiang 26 1 39N43 117E28 -7:49:52
Simao 29 9 22N50 101E00 -6:44:00
Simen 16 11 40N44 123E49 -8:15:16
Simeng 24 9 29N56 103E44 -6:54:56
Simianshan 24 9 28N49 105E09 -7:00:36
Simingchang 24 9 29N02 105E45 -7:03:00
Sinan 7 9 27N54 108E18 -7:13:12
Sinhai → Lianyungang 13 1 34N39 119E16 -7:57:04
Sining → Xining 19 9 36N38 101E55 -6:47:40
Sinmin 16 11 41N59 122E48 -8:11:12
Sinsiang → Xinxiang 10 1 35N20 113E51 -7:35:24
Sipaozi 16 11 41N26 122E13 -8:08:52
Siping 15 12 43N12 124E20 -8:17:20
Sipingjie 15 12 42N31 125E08 -8:20:32
Sipu 17 9 40N48 113E43 -7:34:52
Siqian 5 1 24N40 114E06 -7:36:24
Siqian 5 10 22N31 112E52 -7:31:28
Sishangcun 2 1 40N16 116E33 -7:46:12
Sishili 13 1 32N09 120E45 -8:03:00
Sishilijie 14 1 29N08 116E44 -7:46:56
Sishilipu 8 1 40N12 118E08 -7:52:32
Sishui 21 1 35N39 117E15 -7:49:00
Sitai 8 1 41N16 114E23 -7:37:32
Sitai 27 7 39N23 77E56 -5:11:44
Sitaizi 16 11 41N17 122E16 -8:09:04
Sitaizi 16 11 42N29 123E20 -8:13:20
Sitaizui 8 1 40N49 115E20 -7:41:20
Situ 8 1 39N20 115E39 -7:42:36
Siu Lek Yuen 31 4 22N23 114E12 -7:36:48
Sixian 1 1 33N30 117E56 -7:51:44
Sixitou 30 1 27N31 119E57 -7:59:48
Siyang 13 1 33N43 118E41 -7:54:44
Sizhijian 17 1 42N25 114E36 -7:38:24
Siziwang Qi 17 9 41N33 111E31 -7:26:04
Soch'e → Suoche 27 7 38N25 77E16 -5:09:04
Solon 17 11 46N36 121E13 -8:04:52
Song'ao 30 1 29N36 121E41 -8:06:44
Songbahutun 16 11 41N28 121E11 -8:04:44
Songbu 11 1 31N05 114E48 -7:39:12
Songcun 30 1 30N26 119E43 -7:58:52
Songgaizhen 24 9 29N03 105E54 -7:03:36
Songgang 5 1 22N49 113E51 -7:35:24
Songhe 11 1 31N10 113E20 -7:33:20
Songhuajiang 15 12 44N46 125E54 -8:23:36
Songjiachang 24 9 28N47 104E55 -6:59:40
Songjiang 22 2 31N01 121E14 -8:04:56
Songjiangzhen 15 12 42N12 126E56 -8:27:44
Songjiapu 24 9 29N38 104E44 -6:58:56
Songjiaying 8 1 40N38 115E14 -7:40:56
Songkan 7 9 28N27 106E50 -7:07:20
Songkou 5 1 24N32 116E24 -7:45:36
Songkou 3 1 25N48 118E36 -7:54:24
Songlinba 5 1 24N00 115E59 -7:43:56
Songlindian 8 1 39N25 115E54 -7:43:36
Songling 17 11 48N02 121E12 -8:04:48
Songlukelujia 28 8 29N15 84E49 -5:39:16
Songmen 30 1 28N19 121E34 -8:06:16
Songming 29 9 25N24 102E59 -6:51:56
Songpan 24 9 32N40 103E24 -6:53:36
Songshancun 16 11 41N02 121E09 -8:04:36
Songshu 16 11 39N50 122E06 -8:08:24
Songshugou 8 1 41N02 117E49 -7:51:16
Songtangmiao 1 1 31N08 119E16 -7:57:04
Songtao 7 9 28N06 109E05 -7:16:20
Songtun 16 11 39N54 123E56 -8:15:44
Songxi 3 1 27N33 118E46 -7:55:04
Songxi 3 1 26N16 116E59 -7:47:56
Songxia 3 1 25N44 119E36 -7:58:24
Songxia 30 1 30N07 120E51 -8:03:24
Songxian 10 1 34N10 112E05 -7:28:20
Songyan 23 1 37N13 113E43 -7:34:52
Songyin 22 2 30N54 121E13 -8:04:52
Songzhangzi 16 11 41N13 119E08 -7:56:32
Songzhuang 13 1 32N06 121E17 -8:05:08
Sonid Youqi 17 1 42N32 112E58 -7:31:52
Sonid Zuoqi 17 1 43N58 113E59 -7:35:56
Soochow → Suzhou 13 3 31N18 120E37 -8:02:28
Ssuchunghsi 25 6 22N06 120E44 -8:02:56
Ssup'ing → Siping 15 12 43N12 124E20 -8:17:20
Stanley 31 4 22N13 114E12 -7:36:48
Su'ao 3 1 25N38 119E42 -7:58:48
Suao 25 6 24N36 121E51 -8:07:24
Subashi 27 7 38N22 74E57 -4:59:48
Subei 4 8 39N27 95E03 -6:20:12
Suchang 24 9 30N34 103E34 -6:54:16
Suchou → Suzhou 13 3 31N18 120E37 -8:02:28
Süchow → Xuzhou 13 1 34N16 117E11 -7:48:44
Sufu → Kashi 27 7 39N29 75E59 -5:03:56
Suhaitu 27 8 44N50 93E39 -6:14:36
Suianzhan 9 12 53N07 125E20 -8:21:20
Suichang 30 1 28N34 119E14 -7:56:56
Suichuan 14 1 26N26 114E32 -7:38:08
Suide 20 9 37N32 110E12 -7:20:48
Suiding 27 7 44N03 80E49 -5:23:16
Suifenhe 9 12 44N24 131E10 -8:44:40
Suifu → Yibin 24 9 28N47 104E38 -6:58:32
Suihua 9 12 46N37 127E00 -8:28:00
Suijiang 29 9 28N31 104E07 -6:56:28
Suileng 9 12 47N18 127E10 -8:28:40
Suining 24 9 30N31 105E34 -7:02:16
Suining 12 1 26N21 110E00 -7:20:00
Suining 13 1 33N54 117E56 -7:51:44
Suiping 10 1 33N10 113E57 -7:35:48
Suixi 1 1 33N56 116E46 -7:47:04
Suixi 5 8 21N25 110E15 -7:21:00
Suixian 10 1 34N26 115E05 -7:40:20
Suixian 11 1 31N42 113E20 -7:33:20
Suiyang 7 9 27N56 107E18 -7:09:12
Suiyang 9 12 44N26 130E53 -8:43:32
Suiyangdian 11 1 32N04 112E55 -7:31:40
Suizhong 16 11 40N20 120E19 -8:01:16
Suji 24 9 29N35 103E37 -6:54:28
Sujiabu 1 1 31N38 116E22 -7:45:28
Sujiaqiao 8 1 39N24 116E10 -7:44:40
Sujiatun 16 11 41N40 123E22 -8:13:28
Sujiawan 24 9 29N48 104E57 -6:59:48
Sujiawu 8 1 39N17 115E55 -7:43:40
Sujiazui 13 1 33N40 119E29 -7:57:56
Sumatou 24 9 30N28 104E03 -6:56:12
Sumzom 28 8 29N45 96E10 -6:24:40
Sungchiang → Songjiang 22 2 31N01 121E14 -8:04:56
Sungezhuang 2 1 40N15 116E39 -7:46:36
Sunhezhen 2 1 40N03 116E31 -7:46:04
Suning 8 1 38N25 115E50 -7:43:20
Sunjiabu 1 1 30N55 118E54 -7:55:36
Sunjiadizi 16 11 42N09 124E09 -8:16:36
Sunjiagou 16 11 40N45 120E39 -8:02:36
Sunjiajiang 8 1 40N10 115E32 -7:42:08
Sunjiakanzi 16 11 40N42 123E02 -8:12:08
Sunjiawan 16 11 41N59 121E42 -8:06:48
Sunjiazhai 22 2 30N55 121E52 -8:07:28
Sunlongwan 16 11 41N19 122E57 -8:11:48
Sunwu 9 12 49N27 127E20 -8:29:20
Sunwui → Jiangmen 5 1 22N35 113E05 -7:32:20
Sunying 10 1 34N30 114E21 -7:37:24
Suoche (Yarkand) 27 7 38N25 77E16 -5:09:04
Suoshu 13 1 31N57 119E00 -7:56:00
Suoxian 28 8 31N50 93E45 -6:15:00
Supoqiao 24 9 30N40 103E59 -6:55:56
Suqian 13 1 33N59 118E18 -7:53:12
Suqiao 8 1 39N03 116E29 -7:45:56
Suqiao 10 1 34N08 113E47 -7:35:08
Susong 1 1 30N09 116E06 -7:44:24
Sutschou → Suzhou 13 3 31N18 120E37 -8:02:28
Sütschou → Xuzhou 13 1 34N16 117E11 -7:48:44
Suxi 30 1 29N25 120E07 -8:00:28
Suxian 1 1 33N38 116E58 -7:47:52
Suzhi 17 1 42N17 113E42 -7:34:48
Suzhou (Soochow) 13 3 31N18 120E37 -8:02:28
Suzhuang 2 1 40N04 116E44 -7:46:56
Suzigou 16 11 40N25 123E25 -8:13:40
Swatow → Shantou 5 1 23N23 116E41 -7:46:44
Szeping → Siping 15 12 43N12 124E20 -8:17:20
Tabei 16 11 39N44 122E29 -8:09:56
Tacheng 27 8 46N45 82E57 -5:31:48
Tachia 25 6 24N21 120E37 -8:02:28
Tachoshui 25 6 24N20 121E44 -8:06:56
Taer 19 8 34N09 98E50 -6:35:20
Ta'erwan 11 1 31N49 113E25 -7:33:40
Tafanlieh 25 6 21N58 120E46 -8:03:04
Taguke 28 8 32N07 84E35 -5:38:20
Taha 9 12 47N33 124E14 -8:16:56
Tahsi 25 6 24N57 121E53 -8:07:32
Tahu 25 6 24N26 120E52 -8:03:28
Tai'an 24 9 30N05 105E47 -7:03:08
Tai'an 16 11 41N23 122E27 -8:09:48
Tai'an 21 1 36N12 117E07 -7:48:28
Tai'angang 13 1 31N43 121E40 -8:06:40
Taibai 20 9 34N00 107E18 -7:09:12
Taibus Qi (Baochang) 17 1 41N56 115E22 -7:41:28
Taicang 13 1 31N26 121E07 -8:04:28
T'aichou → Taizhou 13 1 32N30 119E58 -7:59:52
T'aichung 25 6 24N09 120E41 -8:02:44
Taichu → T'aichung 25 6 24N09 120E41 -8:02:44
Taicunzhen 13 1 31N27 119E03 -7:56:12
Taigu 23 1 37N28 112E30 -7:30:00
Tai Hang 31 4 22N17 114E11 -7:36:44
Taihe 1 1 33N11 115E36 -7:42:24
Taihe 14 1 26N49 114E55 -7:39:40
Taihe 24 9 30N10 105E56 -7:03:44
Taihezhen 15 12 44N47 123E29 -8:13:56
Taihezhen 24 9 30N06 106E03 -7:04:12
Taihezhen 24 9 30N07 103E50 -6:55:20
Taihoku → T'aipei 25 6 25N03 121E30 -8:06:00
T'aihsi 25 6 23N42 120E11 -8:00:44
T'aihsien → Taizhou 13 1 32N30 119E58 -7:59:52
Taihu 1 1 30N26 116E16 -7:45:04
Taijiang 7 9 26N32 108E22 -7:13:28
Taijimiao 17 9 40N55 113E46 -7:35:04
Taijüan → Taiyuan 23 1 37N55 112E30 -7:30:00
Taikang 10 1 34N04 114E50 -7:39:20
Taikou 11 1 31N53 111E07 -7:24:28
Tailai 9 12 46N23 123E27 -8:13:48
Tai Lam Chung 31 4 22N22 114E01 -7:36:04
Tai Long 31 4 22N25 114E22 -7:37:28
Tai Long 31 4 22N13 113E59 -7:35:56
T'aima 25 6 22N37 120E59 -8:03:56
Taimei 5 1 23N19 114E29 -7:37:56
Tai Mong Tsai 31 4 22N24 114E18 -7:37:12
T'ainan 25 6 23N00 120E12 -8:00:48
T'ainanhsien 25 6 23N18 120E19 -8:01:16
Taining 3 1 26N54 117E09 -7:48:36
Tai O 31 4 22N15 113E51 -7:35:24
T'aipei 25 6 25N03 121E30 -8:06:00
T'aipeihsien 25 6 25N01 121E27 -8:05:48
Taiping 1 1 30N18 118E12 -7:52:48
Taiping 5 1 22N49 113E41 -7:34:44
Taiping 24 9 30N24 103E37 -6:54:28
Taiping 6 9 22N40 107E05 -7:08:20
Taipingchang 29 9 27N25 103E04 -6:52:16
Taipingchang 24 9 29N33 103E33 -6:54:12
Taipingchang 24 9 29N53 106E04 -7:04:16
Taipingchang 24 9 29N55 103E49 -6:55:16
Taipingchang 24 9 30N10 106E21 -7:05:24
Taipingchang 24 9 30N39 105E54 -7:03:36
Taipingchang 24 9 30N25 103E46 -6:55:04
Taipingchuan 15 12 42N36 127E20 -8:29:20
Taipingchuan 15 12 44N23 123E11 -8:12:44

Taipingdian 11 1 32N08 111E45 -7:27:00
Taipingkou 11 1 29N50 113E35 -7:34:20
Taipingling 15 12 43N26 128E09 -8:32:36
Taipingshan 16 11 41N36 123E41 -8:14:44
Taipingshan 16 11 40N34 122E25 -8:09:40
Taipingshao 16 11 40N54 125E08 -8:20:32
Taipingsi 24 9 29N24 103E34 -6:54:16
Taipingxigou 17 11 42N36 121E13 -8:04:52
Taipingzhai 16 11 42N14 124E07 -8:16:28
Taipingzhen 4 9 35N42 107E37 -7:10:28
Taipingzhen 24 9 29N24 105E47 -7:03:08
Taipingzhen 24 9 30N26 104E12 -6:56:48
Taipingzhen 9 12 46N44 130E44 -8:42:56
Taipingzhuang 26 1 40N08 117E36 -7:50:24
Taipingzhuang 16 11 42N38 123E45 -8:15:00
Taipingzhuang 2 1 40N03 116E24 -7:45:36
Tai Po Tsai 31 4 22N21 114E15 -7:37:00
Tairiqiao 22 2 30N59 121E33 -8:06:12
Taishan 23 1 39N01 113E36 -7:34:24
Taishan 5 10 22N16 112E44 -7:30:56
Taishanchang 24 9 30N32 106E42 -7:06:48
Tai Shui Hang 31 4 22N25 14E13 -0:56:52
Taishun 30 1 27N33 119E43 -7:58:52
Tai Tong 31 4 22N25 114E01 -7:36:04
Taitouying 8 1 40N02 119E12 -7:56:48
T'aitung 25 6 22N45 121E09 -8:04:36
Tai Wan 31 4 22N10 114E15 -7:37:00
Tai Wan Tau 31 4 22N18 114E17 -7:37:08
Taixi 3 1 24N42 116E56 -7:47:44
Taixian 13 1 32N31 120E09 -8:00:36
Taixing 13 1 32N11 120E01 -8:00:04
Taixizhen 30 1 31N03 119E49 -7:59:16
Taiyang 30 1 30N12 119E19 -7:57:16
Taiyanggong 2 1 39N58 116E25 -7:45:40
Taiyuan 23 1 37N55 112E30 -7:30:00
Taizhao 28 8 30N01 93E08 -6:12:32
Taizhou 13 1 32N30 119E58 -7:59:52
Takao → Kaohsiung 25 6 22N38 120E17 -8:01:08
Takela 27 7 37N54 76E44 -5:06:56
Takenake 28 7 34N11 81E20 -5:25:20
Takow → Kaohsiung 25 6 22N38 120E17 -8:01:08
Talagou 16 11 41N37 120E32 -8:02:08
Talien → Lüda 16 11 38N53 121E35 -8:06:20
Talimuashili 27 7 39N08 77E03 -5:08:12
Tamusuke 27 7 38N03 76E53 -5:07:32
Tanbu 14 1 28N08 114E12 -7:36:48
Tanbu 21 1 35N51 118E17 -7:53:08
Tancheng 21 1 34N37 118E23 -7:53:32
Tandian 16 11 40N39 124E46 -8:19:04
Tangba 24 9 30N00 105E46 -7:03:04
Tangchi 9 12 47N00 123E46 -8:15:04
Tangchigou 16 11 41N04 124E11 -8:16:44
Tangcun 30 1 29N50 118E54 -7:55:36
Tangcun 5 1 25N26 113E10 -7:32:40
Tangdaohe 8 1 40N38 118E58 -7:55:52
Tang'erli 8 1 39N09 116E43 -7:46:52
Tangfang 8 1 39N29 118E01 -7:52:04
Tangfang 16 11 41N20 120E34 -8:02:16
Tangfang 29 9 27N00 101E08 -6:44:32
Tangfangqiao 13 1 31N45 120E50 -8:03:20
Tangfeng 8 1 38N07 115E30 -7:42:00
Tanggangzi 16 11 41N01 122E54 -8:11:36
Tanggengtou 1 1 30N55 119E03 -7:56:12
Tanggou 13 1 33N59 118E57 -7:55:48
Tanggu 26 1 39N01 117E40 -7:50:40
Tangguantun 26 1 38N43 116E55 -7:47:40
Tanggulashan (Tuotuoheyan) 28 8 34N05 92E45 -6:11:00
Tanggushiluke 27 7 38N45 80E55 -5:23:40
Tanghe 10 1 32N43 112E48 -7:31:12
Tanghekou 2 1 40N44 116E38 -7:46:32
Tanghu 8 1 39N11 115E24 -7:41:36
Tanghuang 13 1 31N41 119E25 -7:57:40
Tangijatuo 24 9 29N36 106E39 -7:06:36
Tangjia 5 1 22N23 113E36 -7:34:24
Tangjiagou 1 1 30N48 117E28 -7:49:52
Tangjiang 14 1 25N51 114E44 -7:38:56
Tangjiapao 16 11 41N59 122E14 -8:08:56
Tangjiaqiao 13 1 31N24 119E12 -7:56:48
Tangjiqiaozhen 22 2 31N13 121E31 -8:06:04
Tangkou 1 1 30N06 118E11 -7:52:44
Tangling 3 1 26N14 119E24 -7:57:36
Tanglitun 16 11 41N45 123E57 -8:15:48
Tangmai 28 8 30N08 95E11 -6:20:44
Tangmazhai 16 11 41N10 122E44 -8:10:56
Tangpu 30 1 29N51 120E47 -8:03:08
Tangpu 14 1 28N28 114E58 -7:39:52
Tangqi 30 1 30N29 120E11 -8:00:44
Tangqiao 1 1 31N13 119E15 -7:57:00
Tangsanying 8 1 41N38 117E40 -7:50:40
Tangschan → Tangshan 8 1 39N38 118E11 -7:52:44
Tangshan 2 1 40N10 116E22 -7:45:28
Tangshan 8 1 39N38 118E11 -7:52:44
Tangshan 13 1 32N05 119E03 -7:56:12
Tangshi 13 1 31N33 120E51 -8:03:24
Tangtou 21 1 35N16 118E35 -7:54:20
Tangtou 13 1 31N38 120E19 -8:01:16
Tangtou 7 9 27N42 108E17 -7:13:08
Tangtouxia 5 1 22N50 114E06 -7:36:24
Tangxi 30 1 29N04 119E23 -7:57:32
Tangxian 8 1 38N45 114E58 -7:39:52
Tangxianzhen 11 1 31N59 113E07 -7:32:28
Tangyi 21 1 36N32 115E47 -7:43:08
Tangyin 14 1 27N32 116E16 -7:45:04
Tangyin 10 1 35N55 114E21 -7:37:24
Tangyuan 9 12 46N42 129E55 -8:39:40
Tangzha 13 1 32N05 120E49 -8:03:16
Tanjiafang 21 1 36N41 118E36 -7:54:24
Tanjiahe 10 1 31N58 113E56 -7:35:44
Tanjiang 5 1 24N07 116E32 -7:46:08
Tanjiaqiao 1 1 30N11 118E15 -7:53:00
Tankou 14 1 25N48 114E50 -7:39:20
Tanshui 25 6 25N10 121E26 -8:05:44
Tantou 14 1 26N53 115E26 -7:41:44
Tantou 30 1 29N07 121E09 -8:04:36
Tantou 3 1 26N03 119E35 -7:58:20
Tantung → Datong 19 9 37N03 101E45 -6:47:00
Tanxi 14 1 28N58 115E38 -7:42:32
Tanxia 5 1 23N58 115E34 -7:42:16
Tanyi 21 1 35N14 118E09 -7:52:36
Tao'an 15 12 45N22 122E47 -8:11:08
Taochong 1 1 31N04 118E06 -7:52:24
Taocun 21 1 37N10 121E05 -8:04:20
Taodigou 8 1 40N52 116E14 -7:44:56
Taoerdeng 16 11 40N44 119E02 -7:56:08
Taohe 8 1 39N12 116E50 -7:47:20
Taohua 13 1 31N23 120E04 -8:00:16
Taohuachiyingzi 16 11 42N18 121E06 -8:04:24
Taohuanbuligai 16 11 42N13 122E14 -8:08:56
Taohuatu 16 11 41N40 120E40 -8:02:40
Taohuayuan 1 1 30N34 118E42 -7:54:48
Taohuazhen 8 1 40N04 114E59 -7:39:56
Taojiagou 24 9 29N48 104E48 -6:59:12
Taojiahe 11 1 30N55 115E56 -7:43:44
Taojialiang 17 11 42N36 121E25 -8:05:40
Taolahusu 17 1 42N34 116E48 -7:47:12
Taolaizhao 15 12 44N51 125E57 -8:23:48
Taolakepa 28 8 32N05 85E22 -5:41:28
Taole 18 9 38N46 106E40 -7:06:40
Taolin 13 1 34N30 118E30 -7:54:00
Taoling 1 1 30N21 118E16 -7:53:04
Taoluo 21 1 35N17 119E24 -7:57:36
T'aonan → Taoan 15 12 45N22 122E47 -8:11:08
Taowu 13 1 31N47 118E46 -7:55:04
Taoxi 3 1 25N18 116E05 -7:44:20
Taoxi 30 1 28N44 119E36 -7:58:24
Taoxi 1 1 31N33 117E00 -7:48:00
Taoxiantun 16 11 41N39 123E27 -8:13:48
Taoyuan 3 1 25N48 117E32 -7:50:08
Taoyuan 12 1 28N46 111E20 -7:25:20
Taozhu 30 1 28N50 121E31 -8:06:04
Taozhuang 30 1 30N58 120E48 -8:03:12
Taqian 14 1 29N03 117E03 -7:48:12
Taqiao 14 1 28N24 117E02 -7:48:08
Taqiao 1 1 31N28 118E25 -7:53:40
Taqin 28 7 30N57 81E20 -5:25:20
Tarhu 17 9 41N09 107E58 -7:11:52
Tashan 16 11 40N51 120E56 -8:03:44
Tashan 16 11 40N48 122E39 -8:10:36
Tashikuergan 27 7 37N49 75E14 -5:00:56
Tashimalike 27 7 39N06 75E41 -5:02:44
Tashiyi 11 1 29N43 112E48 -7:31:12
Tashuik'u 25 6 25N13 121E30 -8:06:00
Tasitan 27 7 39N17 76E07 -5:04:28
Tatelang 27 8 38N28 85E35 -5:42:20
Tatsienlu 24 9 30N03 102E02 -6:48:08
Tat'ung → Datong 23 1 40N05 113E18 -7:33:12
Tawu 25 6 22N22 120E54 -8:03:36
Taxi 9 12 49N26 126E08 -8:24:32
Taxusi 24 8 32N58 98E10 -6:32:40
Tayayi 8 1 39N25 115E03 -7:40:12
Tayuan 9 12 51N27 124E16 -8:17:04
Tayüan 25 6 25N04 121E11 -8:04:44
Tazhuang 26 1 39N55 117E13 -7:48:52
Tazicheng 9 12 46N35 123E06 -8:12:24
Tazishan 24 9 29N28 104E14 -6:56:56
Tch'ang-Cha → Changsha 12 1 28N12 112E58 -7:31:52
Tcheng-Tcheou → Zhengzhou 10 1 34N48 113E39 -7:34:36
Tchong-K'ing → Chongqing 24 9 29N34 106E35 -7:06:20
Techou → Dezhou 21 1 37N27 116E18 -7:45:12
Tekes 27 7 43N10 81E43 -5:26:52
Tekesi 27 7 43N10 81E43 -5:26:52
Teladuomu 28 8 29N38 84E13 -5:36:52
Teng'aopu 16 11 41N05 122E49 -8:11:16
Tengchong 29 9 25N04 98E29 -6:33:56
Tengjiabao 11 1 31N10 115E29 -7:41:56
Tengqiao 5 9 18N22 109E46 -7:19:04
Tengtian 14 1 27N04 115E40 -7:42:40
Tengxian 6 9 23N21 110E53 -7:23:32
Tengxian 21 1 35N08 117E10 -7:48:40
Têwo 24 9 34N02 103E05 -6:52:20
Tianbao 3 1 24N36 117E35 -7:50:20
Tianchang 1 1 32N41 119E01 -7:56:04
Tiancunpu 8 1 39N06 115E41 -7:42:44
Tiandeng 6 9 23N09 107E10 -7:08:40
Tiandong 6 9 23N36 107E08 -7:08:32
Tian'e 6 9 25N01 107E20 -7:09:20
Tianfanjie 14 1 29N20 116E50 -7:47:20
Tiangang 15 12 43N24 125E54 -8:23:36
Tiangang 15 12 43N55 127E00 -8:28:00
Tiangongsi 8 1 39N14 115E53 -7:43:32
Tianhe 14 1 27N01 114E30 -7:38:00
Tianhekou 11 1 32N08 113E25 -7:33:40
Tianhelong 17 11 43N56 120E39 -8:02:36
Tianhuang 21 1 35N29 117E18 -7:49:12
Tianjia 24 9 29N40 105E08 -7:00:32
Tianjia 16 11 41N07 122E03 -8:08:12
Tianjiaba 11 1 32N08 110E03 -7:20:12
Tianjiatun 16 11 41N39 123E44 -8:14:56
Tianjiawopu 16 11 42N28 122E38 -8:10:32
Tianjiazhen 11 1 29N56 115E26 -7:41:44
Tianjin (Tientsin) 26 1 39N08 117E12 -7:48:48
Tianjing 13 1 31N27 120E46 -8:03:04
Tianjun 19 8 37N25 98E58 -6:35:52
Tiankai 2 1 39N38 115E51 -7:43:24
Tianlin 6 9 24N14 106E03 -7:04:12
Tianlin 24 9 29N49 105E19 -7:01:16
Tianmashan 22 2 31N04 121E08 -8:04:32
Tianmen 11 1 30N40 113E08 -7:32:32
Tianpu 13 1 31N56 121E07 -8:04:28
Tianqiaochang 16 11 40N52 121E02 -8:04:08
Tianqiaoling 15 12 43N26 129E38 -8:38:32
Tianquan 24 9 30N10 102E48 -6:51:12
Tianshenggang 13 1 32N03 120E45 -8:03:00
Tianshifu 16 11 41N17 124E21 -8:17:24
Tianshui 4 9 34N30 105E58 -7:03:52
Tianshuijing 4 8 40N17 95E21 -6:21:24
Tianshuijing 16 11 41N19 121E48 -8:07:12
Tianshuituo 8 1 39N20 118E12 -7:52:48
Tianshuizhan 16 11 41N00 123E34 -8:14:16
Tiantai 30 1 29N09 121E02 -8:04:08
Tiantang 5 10 22N32 111E55 -7:27:40
Tiantou 30 1 28N48 120E39 -8:02:36
Tiantou 14 1 26N19 115E57 -7:43:48
Tianwangsi 13 1 31N45 119E12 -7:56:48
Tianxin 14 1 28N11 114E35 -7:38:20
Tianxin 12 1 27N21 111E00 -7:24:00
Tianxin 12 1 27N53 113E06 -7:32:24
Tianxingqiao 13 1 32N05 119E57 -7:59:48
Tianxiyang 3 1 26N31 118E33 -7:54:12
Tianyang 6 9 23N51 106E34 -7:06:16
Tianyangping 24 9 29N11 105E16 -7:01:04
Tianzhen 23 1 40N28 114E06 -7:36:24
Tianzhongying 1 1 33N13 115E22 -7:41:28
Tianzhu 4 9 37N14 102E59 -6:51:56
Tianzhu 7 9 26N50 109E00 -7:16:00
Tianzhuang 12 1 25N43 113E40 -7:34:40
Tianzhuang 8 1 39N25 117E54 -7:51:36
Tianzhuangtai 16 11 40N50 122E08 -8:08:32
Tiaodengchang 24 9 30N47 106E22 -7:05:28
Tiechang 7 9 26N34 103E58 -6:55:52
Tiechang 5 1 24N10 115E30 -7:42:00
Tiechang 15 12 41N44 126E11 -8:24:44
Tiechang 8 1 40N04 118E12 -7:52:48
Tiechangpu 24 9 29N29 104E20 -6:57:20
Tiefo 24 9 29N45 104E33 -6:58:12
T'iehling → Tieling 16 11 42N18 123E49 -8:15:16
Tiekou 21 1 37N16 121E13 -8:04:52
Tieli 9 12 46N59 128E02 -8:32:08
Tieling 16 11 42N18 123E49 -8:15:16
Tielutou 14 1 27N49 115E48 -7:43:12
T'ienching → Tianjin 26 1 39N08 117E12 -7:48:48
T'ienchung 25 6 23N52 120E35 -8:02:20
T'ienshui → Tianshui 4 9 34N30 105E58 -7:03:52
Tientsin → Tianjin 26 1 39N08 117E12 -7:48:48
Tieshan 11 1 30N14 114E52 -7:39:28
Tieshanguan 5 1 23N30 113E54 -7:35:36
Tihua → Wulumuqi 27 8 43N48 87E35 -5:50:20
Tinghsien → Dingxian 8 1 38N32 114E59 -7:39:56
Ting Kau 31 4 22N22 114E05 -7:36:20
Tingkou 21 1 36N34 119E46 -7:59:04
Tinglin 22 2 30N53 121E17 -8:05:08
Tingliuhe 8 1 39N34 118E49 -7:55:16
Tingqian 11 1 30N10 115E54 -7:43:36
Tingsiqiao 11 1 29N50 114E12 -7:36:48
Tingzitou 30 1 30N12 119E46 -7:59:04
Tin Sam 31 4 22N22 114E11 -7:36:44
Titou 11 1 29N52 112E42 -7:30:48
Toba 28 8 31N18 97E40 -6:30:40
Togtoh 17 9 40N22 111E11 -7:24:44
Toli 27 8 45N57 83E37 -5:34:28
Tong'an 3 1 24N46 118E08 -7:52:32
Tong'anqiao 13 1 31N22 120E27 -8:01:48
Tongbai 8 1 39N35 116E44 -7:46:56
Tongbai 10 1 32N22 113E24 -7:33:36
Tongbei 9 12 47N45 126E46 -8:27:04
Tongcheng 1 1 31N03 116E58 -7:47:52
Tongcheng 1 1 32N53 118E58 -7:55:52
Tongcheng 11 1 29N11 113E49 -7:35:16
Tongchengzha 1 1 31N30 118E07 -7:52:28
Tongchengzhuang 26 1 39N22 117E36 -7:50:24
Tongchuan 20 9 35N01 109E01 -7:16:04
Tongdao 12 1 26N23 109E23 -7:17:32
Tongde 19 9 35N17 100E42 -6:42:48
Tongerbao 16 11 41N26 123E02 -8:12:08

Name		Lat	Long	Time
Tonggou 15	12	41N53	125E46	-8:23:04
Tonggu 5	10	21N53	112E55	-7:31:40
Tonggu 14	1	28N33	114E21	-7:37:24
Tongguan 20	9	34N38	110E20	-7:21:20
Tongguan 29	9	23N18	101E23	-6:45:32
Tongguan 12	1	28N29	112E48	-7:31:12
Tongguanyi 24	9	29N20	106E23	-7:05:32
Tongguye 27	7	37N22	78E48	-5:15:12
Tonghai 29	9	24N07	102E49	-6:51:16
Tonghaikou 11	1	30N14	113E08	-7:32:32
Tonghe 10	1	32N56	112E45	-7:31:00
Tonghe 9	12	45N59	128E45	-8:35:00
Tonghua (Kuaidamao) 15	12	41N41	125E55	-8:23:40
Tongjiang 24	9	31N58	107E14	-7:08:56
Tongjiang 9	12	47N40	132E30	-8:50:00
Tongjiangchang 24	9	29N37	103E43	-6:54:52
Tongjiangkou 16	11	42N37	123E41	-8:14:44
Tongjing 13	1	31N47	118E33	-7:54:12
Tongjuzhen 8	1	38N36	117E11	-7:48:44
Tongli 13	3	31N10	120E43	-8:02:52
Tongliang 24	9	29N51	106E03	-7:04:12
Tongliao 17	11	43N39	122E14	-8:08:56
Tongling 1	1	30N53	117E46	-7:51:04
Tongling 6	9	23N28	109E40	-7:18:40
Tonglu 30	1	29N48	119E40	-7:58:40
Tongmu 14	1	27N57	113E55	-7:35:40
Tongmu 6	9	24N09	110E04	-7:20:16
Tongnan 24	9	30N11	105E48	-7:03:12
Tongqin 30	1	28N52	119E56	-7:59:44
Tongquansi 24	9	30N23	104E50	-6:59:20
Tongren 19	9	35N32	101E54	-6:47:36
Tongren 7	9	27N38	109E03	-7:16:12
Tongrengchang 24	9	30N02	106E42	-7:06:48
Tongshan 11	1	29N38	114E29	-7:37:56
Tongshi 21	1	35N26	117E43	-7:50:52
Tongshuping 14	1	27N17	114E54	-7:39:36
Tongtai 13	1	32N38	120E47	-8:03:08
Tongtan 24	9	28N56	105E17	-7:01:08
Tongtianheyan 28	8	33N50	92E28	-6:09:52
Tongwei 4	9	35N07	105E27	-7:01:48
Tongxi 24	9	29N59	106E08	-7:04:32
Tongxian 2	1	39N55	116E39	-7:46:36
Tongxianchang 24	9	30N14	105E24	-7:01:36
Tongxiang 30	1	30N38	120E32	-8:02:08
Tongxin 18	9	37N02	106E09	-7:04:36
Tongxinchang 24	9	29N42	106E26	-7:05:44
Tongxing 24	9	30N35	106E12	-7:04:48
Tongxu 10	1	34N29	114E28	-7:37:52
Tongyu 15	12	44N48	123E05	-8:12:20
Tongyuan 30	1	30N28	120E52	-8:03:28
Tongyuan 14	1	28N04	116E08	-7:44:32
Tongyuanpu 16	11	40N49	123E54	-8:15:36
Tongzhaipu 10	1	32N48	112E44	-7:30:56
Tongzi 7	9	28N08	106E49	-7:07:16
Tongzidixia 16	11	41N08	120E34	-8:02:16
Toubei 14	1	26N44	116E05	-7:44:20
T'ouch'eng 25	6	24N52	121E49	-8:07:16
Toudaogou 8	1	40N58	117E59	-7:51:56
Toudaogou 16	11	41N37	121E40	-8:06:40
Toudaogou 15	12	42N46	129E12	-8:36:48
Toukansi 30	1	29N22	119E06	-7:56:24
Touliu 25	6	23N43	120E32	-8:02:08
Tounan 25	6	23N41	120E28	-8:01:52
Toupeng 30	1	30N19	120E31	-8:02:04
Toutai 9	12	45N40	124E50	-8:19:20
Toutai 16	11	41N41	121E11	-8:04:44
Toutaizi 16	11	42N19	122E49	-8:11:16
Toutuohe 1	1	31N06	116E25	-7:45:40
Touzhan 17	11	49N27	119E41	-7:58:44
Tsamkong → Zhanjiang 5	8	21N12	110E23	-7:21:32
Ts'anghsien → Cangzhou 8	1	38N19	116E51	-7:47:24
T'sangwu → Wuzhou 6	9	23N30	111E27	-7:25:48
Ts'aot'un 25	6	23N59	120E41	-8:02:44
Tschangscha → Changsha 12	1	28N12	112E58	-7:31:52
Tschangtschun → Changchun 15	12	43N53	125E19	-8:21:16
Tschengtu → Chengdu 24	9	30N39	104E04	-6:56:16
Tschingtau → Qingdao 21	1	36N06	120E19	-8:01:16
Tschungking → Chongqing 24	9	29N34	106E35	-7:06:20
Tsethang → Zedang 28	8	29N16	91E46	-6:07:04
Tsinan → Jinan 21	1	36N40	116E57	-7:47:48
Tsingkiang → Qingjiang 13	1	33N35	119E02	-7:56:08
Tsingtao → Qingdao 21	1	36N06	120E19	-8:01:16
Tsingyuan → Baoding 8	1	38N52	115E29	-7:41:56
Tsining → Jining 21	1	35N25	116E36	-7:46:24
Tsitsihar → Qiqihaer 9	12	47N19	123E55	-8:15:40
Tsoying 25	6	22N41	120E17	-8:01:08
Tsuen Wan (Quanwan) 31	4	22N22	114E07	-7:36:28
Tsuni → Zunyi 7	9	27N39	106E57	-7:07:48
Tuanfeng 11	1	30N38	114E51	-7:39:24
Tuannian 24	9	29N55	106E03	-7:04:12
Tuanpi 11	1	30N44	115E13	-7:40:52
Tuanshan 16	11	40N02	123E34	-8:14:16
Tuanwang 21	1	36N45	120E38	-8:02:32
Tuanxi 7	9	27N28	107E08	-7:08:32
T'uch'ang 25	6	24N35	121E29	-8:05:56
Tucheng 16	11	38N53	121E15	-8:05:00
Tucheng 7	9	28N12	105E58	-7:03:52
T'uch'eng 25	6	24N59	121E26	-8:05:44
Tuchengzi 16	11	40N29	124E24	-8:17:36
Tuchengzi 16	11	42N27	122E44	-8:10:56
Tuchengzi 8	1	41N20	116E29	-7:45:56
Tuchengzicun 16	11	41N52	120E41	-8:02:44
Tuchengziwuhao 17	9	40N56	113E58	-7:35:52
Tudian 30	1	30N35	120E37	-8:02:28
Tudichang 24	9	30N06	103E56	-6:55:44
Tuditang 11	1	30N12	114E18	-7:37:12
Tuen Mun 31	4	22N24	113E58	-7:35:52
Tuergate 27	7	40N28	75E21	-5:01:24
Tuhepu 16	11	40N54	122E49	-8:11:16
Tuhuangba 24	9	31N40	108E21	-7:13:24
Tuibo 15	12	44N01	127E47	-8:31:08
Tulaodian 16	11	41N13	121E27	-8:05:48
Tuling 3	1	25N11	118E50	-7:55:20
Tulufan 27	8	42N56	89E10	-5:56:40
Tumen 15	12	42N58	129E49	-8:39:16
Tumenpu 24	9	29N49	103E39	-6:54:36
Tumenzi 4	9	37N43	103E09	-6:52:36
Tumoteqi 17	9	40N52	111E28	-7:25:52
Tumu 8	1	40N23	115E36	-7:42:24
Tunchang 5	9	19N28	110E08	-7:20:32
T'unch'i → Tunxi 1	1	29N44	118E18	-7:53:12
T'ungchou → Tongxian 2	1	39N55	116E39	-7:46:36
T'ungch'uan → Tongchuan 20	9	35N01	109E01	-7:16:04
Tungho 25	6	22N58	121E18	-8:05:12
T'unghsien → Tongxian 2	1	39N55	116E39	-7:46:36
T'unghua → Tonghua 15	12	41N41	125E55	-8:23:40
Tunghwa → Tonghua 15	12	41N41	125E55	-8:23:40
Tungkang 25	6	22N28	120E26	-8:01:44
T'ungliao → Tongliao 17	11	43N39	122E14	-8:08:56
Tung O 31	4	22N12	114E08	-7:36:32
T'ungshan 13	1	34N18	117E16	-7:49:04
Tungshih 25	6	24N15	120E49	-8:03:16
Tunliu 23	1	36N19	112E54	-7:31:36
Tunxi 1	1	29N44	118E18	-7:53:12
Tuobalage 28	8	31N37	88E10	-5:52:40
Tuocheng 5	1	24N05	115E13	-7:40:52
Tuoheji 1	1	33N26	117E26	-7:49:44
Tuokedingling 28	8	32N45	84E55	-5:39:40
Tuokexun 27	8	42N47	88E38	-5:54:32
Tuoli 2	1	39N46	116E01	-7:44:04
Tuoli 27	8	45N57	83E37	-5:34:28
Tuolunduo 17	11	50N35	120E05	-8:00:20
Tuowu 24	9	28N58	102E13	-6:48:52
Tuqiao 13	1	31N39	120E24	-8:01:36
Tuqiao 24	9	30N24	105E28	-7:01:52
Tuqiao 13	1	31N56	119E03	-7:56:12
Tuqiaozhen 24	9	30N32	104E50	-6:59:20
Tuquan 17	11	45N26	121E50	-8:07:20
Tuquiaochang 24	9	29N47	106E01	-7:04:04
Turfan → Tulufan 27	8	42N56	89E10	-5:56:40
Turpan → Tulufan 27	8	42N56	89E10	-5:56:40
Tushan 13	1	34N14	117E51	-7:51:24
Tutaizi 16	11	41N01	122E38	-8:10:32
Tutang 14	1	29N21	116E24	-7:45:36
Tuwang 24	9	29N06	105E48	-7:03:12
Tuxiaqiao 30	1	28N47	121E29	-8:05:56
Tuxsun 27	8	42N47	88E38	-5:54:32
Tuyün → Duyun 7	9	26N12	107E31	-7:10:04
Tzekung → Zigong 24	9	29N24	104E47	-6:59:08
Tzeliutsing → Zigong 24	9	29N24	104E47	-6:59:08
Tzukung → Zigong 24	9	29N24	104E47	-6:59:08
Tzupo → Boshan 21	1	36N29	117E50	-7:51:20
Tzupo → Zibo 21	1	36N47	118E01	-7:52:04
Ulan 19	8	36N59	98E26	-6:33:44
Ulanhot → Wulanhaote 17	11	46N05	122E05	-8:08:20
Ulugqat 27	7	39N48	74E21	-4:57:24
Uma 17	11	52N36	120E37	-8:02:28
Urad Zhonghou Lianheqi 17	9	41N42	108E49	-7:15:16
Urho 27	8	46N48	89E45	-5:59:00
Urumchi → Wulumuqi 27	8	43N48	87E35	-5:50:20
Usu 27	8	44N27	84E37	-5:38:28
Uzunbulak 27	8	45N23	84E06	-5:36:24
Victoria (Xianggang) 31	4	22N17	114E09	-7:36:36
Waao 29	9	24N20	104E40	-6:58:40
Wabu 1	1	32N17	116E55	-7:47:40
Wadagou 17	11	42N27	120E58	-8:03:52
Wadian 10	1	32N48	112E30	-7:30:00
Wafang 17	11	41N44	118E54	-7:55:36
Wagang 24	9	28N04	103E10	-6:52:40
Waichagoumen 15	12	40N54	125E45	-8:23:00
Waigang 22	2	31N22	121E11	-8:04:44
Waigoumen 8	1	41N24	116E13	-7:44:52
Waihuantan 1	1	30N25	118E40	-7:54:40
Waikuatang 13	3	31N20	120E41	-8:02:44
Waisanzao 22	2	30N57	121E52	-8:07:28
Walang 24	9	28N33	100E54	-6:43:36
Wali 8	1	39N42	118E20	-7:53:20
Wamiao 11	1	30N49	113E02	-7:32:08
Wan'an 14	1	26N30	114E49	-7:39:16
Wan'an 3	1	26N56	117E22	-7:49:28
Wan'anchang 24	9	30N39	104E25	-6:57:40
Wanbaoshan 15	12	44N12	125E11	-8:20:44
Wanchangchang 24	9	29N43	104E19	-6:57:16
Wande 21	1	36N21	116E56	-7:47:44
Wandingzhen 29	9	24N10	98E04	-6:32:16
Wanfang 16	11	41N57	122E52	-8:11:28
Wanfoxia 4	8	40N04	95E55	-6:23:40
Wang'anzhen 8	1	39N19	114E54	-7:39:36
Wangbaotaicun 16	11	41N10	123E18	-8:13:12
Wangbenying 2	1	40N28	116E06	-7:44:24
Wangbintun 16	11	41N58	123E43	-8:14:52
Wangchang 24	9	29N05	104E40	-6:58:40
Wangchang 24	9	28N52	105E55	-7:03:40
Wangchangtuizigou 16	11	41N14	120E32	-8:02:08
Wangcheng 12	1	28N23	112E48	-7:31:12
Wangcun 21	1	36N41	117E41	-7:50:44
Wangcunkou 30	1	28N22	118E59	-7:55:56
Wangdalong 24	9	29N25	99E03	-6:36:12
Wangdian 30	1	30N37	120E44	-8:02:56
Wangdu 8	1	38N43	115E09	-7:40:36
Wangfu 16	11	42N05	121E29	-8:05:56
Wanggangpu 16	11	41N38	123E09	-8:12:36
Wanggao 6	9	24N38	111E30	-7:26:00
Wanggezhuang 8	1	40N00	117E52	-7:51:28
Wanggoutun 16	11	41N40	121E53	-8:07:32
Wanghai 16	11	40N26	120E30	-8:02:00
Wanghechenggou 16	11	41N52	121E13	-8:04:52
Wanghu 23	1	39N47	113E54	-7:35:36
Wanghuzhuang 26	1	38N50	117E05	-7:48:20
Wangingsha 5	1	22N44	113E33	-7:34:12
Wangji 13	1	34N00	117E46	-7:51:04
Wangji 13	1	33N52	118E44	-7:54:56
Wangjia 13	1	32N07	120E59	-8:03:56
Wangjia 13	1	31N59	121E13	-8:04:52
Wangjiadian 26	1	40N03	117E29	-7:49:56
Wangjiadian 11	1	31N26	113E58	-7:35:52
Wangjiagou 16	11	42N33	123E16	-8:13:04
Wangjiajing 16	11	39N56	122E11	-8:08:44
Wangjiang 1	1	30N09	116E41	-7:46:44
Wangjiangjing 13	1	30N53	120E43	-8:02:52
Wangjiaputun 16	11	40N39	122E50	-8:11:20
Wangjiapuzi 16	11	41N05	123E34	-8:14:16
Wangjiapuzi 16	11	40N41	122E24	-8:09:36
Wangjiaqiao 1	1	30N50	119E18	-7:57:12
Wangjiashan 8	1	40N19	114E45	-7:39:00
Wangjiashao 29	9	23N57	102E18	-6:49:12
Wangjiatai 26	1	39N17	117E29	-7:49:56
Wangjiaying 8	1	39N06	115E59	-7:43:56
Wangjiaying 2	1	40N36	116E34	-7:46:16
Wangjiazhai 22	2	31N21	121E37	-8:06:28
Wangjiazui 13	1	31N16	120E18	-8:01:12
Wangkantou 30	1	29N12	120E09	-8:00:36
Wangkou 26	1	38N56	116E44	-7:46:56
Wangkui 9	12	46N50	126E30	-8:26:00
Wanglanzhuang 8	1	39N26	118E01	-7:52:04
Wangling 12	1	27N13	113E26	-7:33:44
Wangliu 10	1	32N25	115E40	-7:42:40
Wangmiao 12	1	26N50	112E52	-7:31:28
Wangmulazi 16	11	41N42	124E02	-8:16:08
Wangong 17	11	49N10	118E53	-7:55:32
Wangpingchang 24	9	29N17	105E45	-7:03:00
Wangqing 15	12	43N20	129E48	-8:39:12
Wangqingmen 16	11	41N42	125E23	-8:21:32
Wangqingtuo 26	1	39N11	116E53	-7:47:32
Wangqinzhuang 26	1	39N15	117E05	-7:48:20
Wangqucun 13	1	31N22	120E19	-8:01:16
Wangshanhutun 16	11	42N03	122E37	-8:10:28
Wangshi 1	1	33N11	116E04	-7:44:16
Wangsi 8	1	38N00	116E55	-7:47:40
Wangsiying 24	9	30N34	103E29	-6:53:56
Wangtai 21	1	36N05	119E59	-7:59:56
Wangtai 3	1	26N39	117E57	-7:51:48
Wangtan 30	1	29N45	120E40	-8:02:40
Wangtian 14	1	25N59	116E04	-7:44:16
Wangting 13	1	31N26	120E26	-8:01:44
Wangtongshitai 16	11	42N05	123E11	-8:12:44
Wangtuan 21	1	37N17	122E04	-8:08:16
Wangtuan 8	1	37N32	116E08	-7:44:32
Wangtuanji 1	1	33N12	116E21	-7:45:24
Wangu 24	9	30N19	106E05	-7:04:20
Wanguzhen 24	9	29N41	105E57	-7:03:48
Wangwenzhuang 26	1	38N53	117E15	-7:49:00
Wangxiangshang 13	1	31N29	120E15	-8:01:00
Wangxiangtai 8	1	40N02	115E09	-7:40:36
Wangxiuqiao 13	1	31N38	121E03	-8:04:12
Wangyangzhen 24	9	29N44	104E14	-6:56:56
Wangyedian 17	11	41N36	118E17	-7:53:08

Wangyefu 17 11 41N50 118E23 -7:53:32
Wangyehmiao → Wulanhaote 17
11 46N05 122E05 -8:08:20
Wangyiguantun 16
11 42N36 123E19 -8:13:16
Wangzhai 1 1 34N09 116E47 -7:47:08
Wangzhimawo 8 1 39N39 117E40 -7:50:40
Wangzhong 21 1 35N08 116E58 -7:47:52
Wangzhuang 1 1 33N07 117E29 -7:49:56
Wangzhuangbu 23
1 39N27 113E56 -7:35:44
Wangzhuangji 13
1 34N09 118E23 -7:53:32
Wangzhuangzi 8 1 39N17 118E14 -7:52:56
Wanhedian 11 1 32N16 113E16 -7:33:04
Wanhsien → Wanxian 24
9 30N52 108E22 -7:13:28
Wanhuyu 20 9 38N24 110E40 -7:22:40
Wanjiabu 14 1 28N51 115E39 -7:42:36
Wanjiaqiao 1 1 30N25 119E07 -7:56:28
Wanjiatun 16 11 40N03 119E51 -7:59:24
Wanjindian 10 1 32N50 114E46 -7:39:04
Wanli 13 1 31N06 120E16 -8:01:04
Wanli 25 6 25N11 121E41 -8:06:44
Wannian 14 1 28N42 117E03 -7:48:12
Wanning 5 9 18N53 110E26 -7:21:44
Wanquan 8 1 40N52 114E45 -7:39:00
Wanshan 24 9 30N23 106E06 -7:04:24
Wanshouchang 24
9 29N26 105E55 -7:03:40
Wantan 11 1 30N03 110E18 -7:21:12
Wanxian 24 9 30N52 108E22 -7:13:28
Wanxian 8 1 38N50 115E09 -7:40:36
Wanyuan 24 9 32N04 108E02 -7:12:08
Wanzai 14 1 28N06 114E27 -7:37:48
Wanzhuang 8 1 39N34 116E36 -7:46:24
Waxuecun 22 2 31N07 121E38 -8:06:32
Wayaopu 1 1 30N33 118E53 -7:55:32
Weichang (Zhuizishan) 8
1 42N00 117E32 -7:50:08
Weichuan 10 1 34N17 113E58 -7:35:52
Weicun 13 1 31N59 119E55 -7:59:40
Weifang 21 1 36N42 119E04 -7:56:16
Weihai 21 1 37N28 122E07 -8:08:28
Weihaiwei → Weihai 21
1 37N28 122E07 -8:08:28
Weijiagou 8 1 40N28 115E08 -7:40:32
Weijiatang 13 1 31N25 118E55 -7:55:40
Weijiazhuang 2 1 39N37 116E22 -7:45:28
Weijiazui 1 1 30N29 117E20 -7:49:20
Weijingtang 13 3 31N27 120E39 -8:02:36
Weinan 20 9 34N29 109E29 -7:17:56
Weining 7 9 26N43 104E18 -6:57:12
Weining 16 11 41N21 123E49 -8:15:16
Weishan (Xiazhen) 21
1 34N52 117E09 -7:48:36
Weishan 29 9 25N15 100E20 -6:41:20
Weishan 30 1 29N20 120E25 -8:01:40
Weishancheng 10
1 32N34 113E24 -7:33:36
Weishanhe 16 11 40N47 123E31 -8:14:04
Weishanzhuang 2
1 39N40 116E25 -7:45:40
Weishi 10 1 34N25 114E11 -7:36:44
Weitang 8 1 40N24 117E24 -7:49:36
Weitian 3 1 27N43 118E46 -7:55:04
Weiting 13 1 31N22 120E47 -8:03:08
Weitou 3 1 24N34 118E34 -7:54:16
Weituo 24 9 30N03 106E08 -7:04:32
Weiwan 21 1 36N43 115E54 -7:43:36
Weixi 29 9 27N14 99E12 -6:36:48
Weixi 24 9 30N12 106E39 -7:06:36
Weixian (Hanting) 21
1 36N52 119E07 -7:56:28
Weixian 8 1 36N57 115E15 -7:41:00
Weixian 8 1 36N22 114E56 -7:39:44
Weixin 29 9 27N48 105E06 -7:00:24
Weiyuan 24 9 29N33 104E39 -6:58:36
Weiyuankou 11 1 30N09 115E15 -7:41:00
Weiyuanpu 16 11 42N39 124E16 -8:17:04
Weizhuang 8 1 39N02 115E20 -7:41:20
Weizi 16 11 40N04 123E10 -8:12:40
Weizigou 17 11 42N05 120E34 -8:02:16
Weizigou 16 11 42N25 122E47 -8:11:08
Weizigou 16 11 41N05 120E38 -8:02:32
Weizigoumen 8 1 41N58 116E49 -7:47:16
Weiziyu 16 11 41N29 124E31 -8:18:04
Wen'an 8 1 38N52 116E28 -7:45:52
Wenchang 5 9 19N41 110E48 -7:23:12
Wencheng 30 1 27N50 120E05 -8:00:20
Wenchow → Wenzhou 30
1 28N01 120E39 -8:02:36
Wendaohezi 16 11 41N46 124E09 -8:16:36
Wendeng 21 1 37N12 122E04 -8:08:16
Wendilou 16 11 41N13 121E08 -8:04:32
Wenfang 14 1 28N02 117E19 -7:49:16
Weng'an 7 9 26N53 107E22 -7:09:28
Wengbo 28 8 31N23 86E40 -5:46:40
Wengcheng 5 1 24N23 113E51 -7:35:24
Wengdang 28 8 28N50 90E03 -6:00:12
Wengjiabu 30 1 30N23 120E21 -8:01:24
Wengong 24 9 30N11 104E09 -6:56:36
Wenguantun 16 11 41N53 123E30 -8:14:00
Wengyang 30 1 28N03 120E58 -8:03:52
Wengyuan 5 1 24N21 114E08 -7:36:32
Wenheng 3 1 25N42 116E45 -7:47:00
Wenjiachang 24 9 30N41 103E55 -6:55:40
Wenjiang 24 9 30N42 103E49 -6:55:16
Wenjiangban 3 1 26N01 117E51 -7:51:24
Wenjiazhen 14 1 28N20 116E05 -7:44:20
Wenling 30 1 28N22 121E20 -8:05:20
Wenlong 14 1 24N48 114E54 -7:39:36
Wenmingsi 12 1 25N33 113E20 -7:33:20
Wenniu 29 9 24N18 104E31 -6:58:04
Wenquan 27 7 44N59 81E04 -5:24:16
Wenquan 5 1 23N37 113E43 -7:34:52
Wenquansi 16 11 41N20 124E04 -8:16:16
Wenshan 29 9 23N30 104E20 -6:57:20
Wenshang 21 1 35N44 116E29 -7:45:56
Wenshui 7 9 28N28 106E30 -7:06:00
Wenshui 23 1 37N28 112E01 -7:28:04
Wenxi 23 1 35N26 111E11 -7:24:44
Wenxian 4 9 32N58 104E46 -6:59:04
Wenxingchang 24
9 29N52 106E29 -7:05:56
Wenzhou 30 1 28N01 120E39 -8:02:36
Wenzhu 14 1 27N01 113E58 -7:35:52
Wenzhuangzicun 16
11 42N16 123E51 -8:15:24
Wobaer 27 7 39N19 75E32 -5:02:08
Woerdeke 27 7 39N41 77E53 -5:11:32
Wofosi 8 1 40N09 115E18 -7:41:12
Woluogu 8 1 39N40 117E46 -7:51:04
Wong Ka Wai 31 4 22N24 113E58 -7:35:52
Wonlushi 16 11 42N31 123E03 -8:12:12
Wu'an 8 1 36N40 114E12 -7:36:48
Wubaozhen 24 9 29N14 104E29 -6:57:56
Wubu 20 9 37N33 110E39 -7:22:36
Wuchang → Wuhan 11
3 30N36 114E17 -7:37:08
Wucheng 14 1 29N10 115E59 -7:43:56
Wucheng 8 1 37N09 115E53 -7:43:32
Wucheng (Jiucheng) 21
1 37N13 116E02 -7:44:08
Wucheng 1 1 29N36 118E10 -7:52:40
Wucheng 10 1 33N28 113E44 -7:34:56
Wuch'i 25 6 24N16 120E31 -8:02:04
Wuchin → Changzhou 13
1 31N47 119E57 -7:59:48
Wuchow → Wuzhou 6
9 23N30 111E27 -7:25:48
Wuchuan 5 8 21N25 110E40 -7:22:40
Wuchuan 7 9 28N25 107E56 -7:11:44
Wuchuan 17 9 41N05 111E23 -7:25:32
Wuchung → Wuzhong 18
9 37N57 106E10 -7:04:40
Wucun 8 1 38N57 115E19 -7:41:16
Wuda 18 9 39N30 106E40 -7:06:40
Wudaogou 15 12 42N08 125E51 -8:23:24
Wudaogou 15 12 41N43 127E05 -8:28:20
Wudaolianggou 16
11 40N59 120E35 -8:02:20
Wudi 21 1 37N44 117E35 -7:50:20
Wudian 1 1 32N42 117E18 -7:49:12
Wudian 11 1 31N57 112E46 -7:31:04
Wuding 29 9 25N32 102E23 -6:49:32
Wudu 4 9 33N24 104E50 -6:59:20
Wudu 14 1 28N23 118E14 -7:52:56
Wudu 30 1 27N37 119E00 -7:56:00
Wuduhe 11 1 31N03 111E03 -7:24:12
Wuerqihan 17 11 49N37 121E45 -8:07:00
Wufeng 11 1 30N11 110E33 -7:22:12
Wufengxi 24 9 30N37 104E29 -6:57:56
Wufu 30 1 30N06 120E58 -8:03:52
Wugang 12 1 26N44 110E38 -7:22:32
Wugong 20 9 34N20 108E04 -7:12:16
Wugouying 10 1 33N28 114E08 -7:36:32
Wugunuoer 17 11 49N10 119E19 -7:57:16
Wuhai 17 9 39N39 106E41 -7:06:44
Wuhan 11 3 30N36 114E17 -7:37:08
Wuhe 5 1 24N26 115E25 -7:41:40
Wuhe 1 1 33N10 117E54 -7:51:36
Wuhsien → Huzhou 30
1 30N52 120E06 -8:00:24
Wuhsing → Huzhou 30
1 30N52 120E06 -8:00:24
Wuhsi → Wuxi 13
1 31N35 120E18 -8:01:12
Wuhu 1 1 31N11 118E35 -7:54:20
Wuhu 1 1 31N21 118E22 -7:53:28
Wuhua 5 1 23N57 115E48 -7:43:12
Wuhuanchi 16 11 42N20 121E51 -8:07:24
Wuhuang 24 9 29N58 104E46 -6:59:04
Wuhudongmiao 17
9 38N19 107E20 -7:09:20
Wuji 13 1 34N12 119E02 -7:56:08
Wuji 8 1 38N13 114E57 -7:39:48
Wujiabeigou 16
11 40N57 123E50 -8:15:20
Wujiang 1 1 31N52 118E28 -7:53:52
Wujiang 14 1 27N14 115E15 -7:41:00
Wujiang 13 3 31N10 120E38 -8:02:32
Wujiangdu 7 9 27N16 106E48 -7:07:12
Wujianpu 24 9 29N10 105E50 -7:03:20
Wujiapai 26 1 39N32 117E18 -7:49:12
Wujiapu 26 1 38N52 117E07 -7:48:28
Wujiazhen 24 9 29N38 105E24 -7:01:36
Wujiazhuang 8 1 40N35 115E20 -7:41:20
Wujiazhuang 13 1 32N18 120E10 -8:00:40
Wujiazi 9 12 46N27 123E34 -8:14:16
Wujiazi 16 11 42N13 122E08 -8:08:32
Wujiazi 17 11 42N30 121E10 -8:04:40
Wujing 5 1 25N16 114E36 -7:38:24
Wukang 30 1 30N33 119E58 -7:59:52
Wukeshu 15 12 44N48 126E08 -8:24:32
Wukeshu 15 12 46N02 123E45 -8:15:00
Wulai 25 6 24N52 121E33 -8:06:12
Wulajia 9 12 48N23 129E58 -8:39:52
Wulanheduojia 17
1 42N40 113E20 -7:33:20
Wulanhutong 8 1 41N44 114E49 -7:39:16
Wulanmutou 16 11 42N23 121E21 -8:05:24
Wulanwusu 27 8 44N20 85E50 -5:43:20
Wulanwusu 17 9 41N39 107E48 -7:11:12
Wulasitai 17 11 43N15 121E27 -8:05:48
Wulateqianqi 17
9 40N39 109E05 -7:16:20
Wulaxi 24 9 28N38 101E40 -6:46:40
Wulian (Hongning) 21
1 35N47 119E15 -7:57:00
Wuliangdian 16
11 41N52 122E16 -8:09:04
Wulichuan 10 1 33N49 111E08 -7:24:32
Wuling 10 1 35N53 114E36 -7:38:24
Wulitaizi 16 11 41N28 123E21 -8:13:24
Wulizhuang 13 1 33N49 118E57 -7:55:48
Wulong 24 9 29N20 107E43 -7:10:52
Wulong 16 11 41N39 124E13 -8:16:52
Wulongbei 16 11 40N21 124E16 -8:17:04
Wuluhayingzi 16
11 42N20 121E34 -8:06:16
Wulumuch'i → Wulumuqi 27
8 43N48 87E35 -5:50:20
Wulumuqi (Urumchi) 27
8 43N48 87E35 -5:50:20
Wuluo 7 9 26N09 108E15 -7:13:00
Wumiaoxiang 24 9 30N23 104E17 -6:57:08
Wuming 6 9 23N10 108E18 -7:13:12
Wunamu 27 8 46N06 85E44 -5:42:56
Wuning 14 1 29N17 115E06 -7:40:24
Wunuer 17 11 48N53 121E15 -8:05:00
Wupaowan 24 9 29N50 103E59 -6:55:56
Wuping 3 1 25N08 116E06 -7:44:24
Wuqi 20 9 37N08 108E10 -7:12:40
Wuqi 3 1 27N10 120E23 -8:01:32
Wuqia 27 7 39N42 75E13 -5:00:52
Wuqiagou 27 8 46N48 89E45 -5:59:00
Wuqiang (Xiaofan) 8
1 38N03 115E58 -7:43:52
Wuqing (Yangcun) 26
1 39N23 117E04 -7:48:16
Wusha 1 1 30N39 117E18 -7:49:12
Wushan 1 1 32N04 117E03 -7:48:12
Wushan 13 1 31N44 118E58 -7:55:52
Wushan 4 9 34N38 105E04 -7:00:16
Wushan 24 9 31N05 109E48 -7:19:12
Wusheng 30 1 29N56 119E25 -7:57:40
Wusheng 24 9 30N21 106E17 -7:05:08
Wushengchang 24
9 29N00 103E43 -6:54:52
Wushengi 17 9 38N58 109E01 -7:16:04
Wushi 6 9 22N11 110E11 -7:20:44
Wushi 13 1 31N44 120E59 -8:03:56
Wushu 14 1 26N20 114E56 -7:39:44
Wusih → Wuxi 13
1 31N35 120E18 -8:01:12
Wusong 22 2 31N23 121E29 -8:05:56
Wusu 27 8 44N27 84E37 -5:38:28
Wusuo 3 1 25N02 116E02 -7:44:08
Wuta 13 1 31N31 120E39 -8:02:36
Wutai 27 7 39N28 78E09 -5:12:36
Wutai 17 9 41N18 113E59 -7:35:56
Wutai 27 7 44N36 82E06 -5:28:24
Wutai 23 1 38N44 113E17 -7:33:08
Wutaizi 16 11 42N27 123E17 -8:13:08
Wutan 12 1 28N29 111E40 -7:26:40
Wutanchang 24 9 29N15 106E04 -7:04:16
Wutang 13 1 31N31 119E10 -7:56:40
Wutangdun 30 1 30N38 120E08 -8:00:32
Wutangjie 30 1 29N59 122E22 -8:09:28
Wutianzhen 1 1 30N23 117E12 -7:48:48
Wutong 6 9 25N18 110E01 -7:20:04
Wutonghaolai 17
11 42N55 120E15 -8:01:00
Wutongqiao 24 9 29N26 103E51 -6:55:24
Wutongwozi 27 8 42N27 95E17 -6:21:08
Wutsin → Changzhou 13
1 31N47 119E57 -7:59:48
Wutun 3 1 27N51 118E04 -7:52:16
Wutungkiao → Wutongqiao 24
9 29N26 103E51 -6:55:24
Wutuohuo 17 9 40N51 101E48 -6:47:12
Wuwei (Liangzhou) 4
9 37N58 102E49 -6:51:16
Wuwei 1 1 31N18 117E54 -7:51:36
Wuxi 1 1 31N20 118E39 -7:54:36
Wuxi (Wuhsi) 13
1 31N35 120E18 -8:01:12
Wuxi 24 9 31N25 109E34 -7:18:16
Wuxiang 23 1 36N51 113E00 -7:32:00
Wuxingchang 13 1 31N13 119E23 -7:57:32
Wuxuan 6 9 23N36 109E42 -7:18:48
Wuyang 10 1 33N26 113E34 -7:34:16
Wuyang 14 1 25N41 115E55 -7:43:40
Wuyang 12 1 26N41 110E20 -7:21:20
Wuyi 30 1 28N54 119E48 -7:59:12
Wuyi 8 1 37N49 115E54 -7:43:36
Wuyi 1 1 32N13 118E26 -7:53:44
Wuying 9 12 48N05 129E15 -8:37:00
Wuyuan 17 9 41N06 108E29 -7:13:56
Wuyuan 14 1 29N15 117E49 -7:51:16
Wuyun 9 12 49N16 129E37 -8:38:28
Wuyunqiao 14 1 26N02 114E52 -7:39:28
Wuzaizi 16 11 42N28 123E57 -8:15:48
Wuzhai 23 1 38N58 111E55 -7:27:40
Wuzhan 9 12 45N51 126E17 -8:25:08
Wuzhen 30 1 30N46 120E29 -8:01:56
Wuzhong 18 9 37N57 106E10 -7:04:40
Wuzhou (Wuchow) 6
9 23N30 111E27 -7:25:48
Wuzong 13 1 32N14 121E03 -8:04:12
Xiaang 30 1 30N45 120E07 -8:00:28
Xiaba 5 1 24N54 116E06 -7:44:24
Xiabai 13 1 31N12 119E50 -7:59:20
Xiabai 30 1 30N29 120E00 -8:00:00
Xiabanghu 11 1 30N31 112E38 -7:30:32
Xiabian 16 11 40N51 120E30 -8:02:00
Xiabuji 14 1 28N19 116E20 -7:45:20
Xiacang 26 1 39N47 117E24 -7:49:36
Xiache 5 1 24N40 115E08 -7:40:32
Xiachengzi 9 12 44N41 130E27 -8:41:48
Xiacun 2 1 40N21 116E14 -7:44:56
Xiadao 3 1 26N34 118E16 -7:53:04
Xiadian 21 1 37N06 120E19 -8:01:16
Xiadian 8 1 39N57 116E55 -7:47:40

Xiadian 11 1 31N26 114E17 -7:37:08
Xiadianjie 3 1 25N13 118E27 -7:53:48
Xiafeidi 16 11 42N18 124E21 -8:17:24
Xiafu 5 1 25N01 113E41 -7:34:44
Xiafu 5 1 23N52 115E45 -7:43:00
Xiagaixin 29 9 22N36 99E59 -6:39:56
Xiagang 13 1 31N55 120E13 -8:00:52
Xiagezhuang 21 1 36N41 120E25 -8:01:40
Xiaguan 23 1 39N07 114E09 -7:36:36
Xiaguan 13 3 32N06 118E44 -7:54:56
Xiaguan 29 9 25N34 100E14 -6:40:56
Xiaguanjunchang 16 11 41N28 121E40 -8:06:40
Xiaguanpi 3 1 24N04 117E06 -7:48:24
Xiagucheng 4 9 36N47 102E53 -6:51:32
Xiagucun 1 1 30N56 119E09 -7:56:36
Xiahada 16 11 41N58 124E08 -8:16:32
Xiahailangzhai 16 11 41N35 123E46 -8:15:04
Xiahe 4 9 35N18 102E30 -6:50:00
Xiahuangjintun 16 11 41N57 123E48 -8:15:12
Xiahuayuan 8 1 40N29 115E17 -7:41:08
Xiajiabaozi 16 11 42N16 124E37 -8:18:28
Xiajialou 16 11 42N25 123E39 -8:14:36
Xiajiang 14 1 27N32 115E08 -7:40:32
Xiajiangdun 13 1 31N14 120E24 -8:01:36
Xiajiangwu 1 1 30N29 119E00 -7:56:00
Xiajiayuan 13 1 32N13 120E38 -8:02:32
Xiajiezi 24 9 27N28 101E35 -6:46:20
Xiajin 21 1 36N55 115E57 -7:43:48
Xiakou 30 1 28N28 118E31 -7:54:04
Xialianggang 8 1 39N14 115E07 -7:40:28
Xialufang 24 9 31N11 103E38 -6:54:32
Xiamaguan 18 9 37N14 106E28 -7:05:52
Xiamen (Amoy) 3 1 24N28 118E07 -7:52:28
Xiamianzhen 24 9 30N08 106E32 -7:06:08
Xiamin'ansutai 16 11 41N54 120E53 -8:03:32
Xiamocun 1 1 31N09 119E22 -7:57:28
Xi'an (Sian) 20 9 34N15 108E52 -7:15:28
Xianchenggu 8 1 36N53 115E17 -7:41:08
Xiandu 3 1 25N04 117E44 -7:50:56
Xianfeng 11 1 29N41 109E02 -7:16:08
Xianfeng 3 1 25N42 117E53 -7:51:32
Xiang'an 1 1 31N12 117E46 -7:51:04
Xiangcheng 10 1 33N53 113E29 -7:33:56
Xiangcheng 13 1 31N29 120E44 -8:02:56
Xiangcheng 24 9 28N59 99E45 -6:39:00
Xiangcheng 10 1 33N28 114E53 -7:39:32
Xiangfan 11 1 32N03 112E01 -7:28:04
Xiangfuguan 14 1 28N30 115E26 -7:41:44
Xiangfusi 24 9 30N06 104E24 -6:57:36
Xianggang → Victoria 31 4 22N17 114E09 -7:36:36
Xianggongshi 12 1 28N25 113E32 -7:34:08
Xianggongzhuang 8 1 39N48 118E19 -7:53:16
Xianghe 8 1 39N46 116E59 -7:47:56
Xiangheguan 10 1 33N08 113E26 -7:33:44
Xianghuazhen 22 2 31N31 121E43 -8:06:52
Xiangjia 13 3 31N20 120E31 -8:02:04
Xiangjia 13 1 31N19 120E23 -8:01:32
Xiangjiachang 24 9 30N08 104E18 -6:57:12
Xiangning 23 1 36N01 110E45 -7:23:00
Xiangride 19 8 36N02 98E08 -6:32:32
Xiangshan 30 1 29N28 121E51 -8:07:24
Xiangshan 2 1 39N59 116E12 -7:44:48
Xiangshizhen 24 9 29N17 105E09 -7:00:36
Xiangshui 5 1 23N15 114E10 -7:36:40
Xiangshui 13 1 34N12 119E34 -7:58:16
Xiangtan 12 1 27N51 112E54 -7:31:36
Xiangtang 14 1 28N26 115E58 -7:43:52
Xiangxiang 12 1 27N43 112E27 -7:29:48
Xiangyang 8 1 39N13 115E25 -7:41:40
Xiangyangkou 2 1 40N06 115E47 -7:43:08
Xiangyin 12 1 28N40 112E53 -7:31:32
Xiangyuan 23 1 36N32 113E00 -7:32:00
Xiangyun 29 9 25N30 100E30 -6:42:00
Xiangzhenpu 1 1 30N52 117E21 -7:49:24
Xiangzhou 6 9 23N55 109E49 -7:19:16
Xiangzhou 21 1 36N12 119E24 -7:57:36
Xiangzhu 30 1 29N02 120E04 -8:00:16
Xianinggang 12 1 28N20 112E56 -7:31:44
Xianjiang 30 1 27N48 120E30 -8:02:00
Xianju 30 1 28N51 120E44 -8:02:56
Xianning 11 1 29N53 114E17 -7:37:08
Xiannübu 14 1 25N36 114E40 -7:38:40
Xianru 15 12 43N11 128E02 -8:32:08
Xianshichang 24 9 28N43 105E44 -7:02:56
Xianshuigu 26 1 38N59 117E23 -7:49:32
Xiantan 24 9 29N21 104E53 -6:59:32
Xiantan 24 9 28N50 106E12 -7:04:48
Xiantang 5 1 23N48 114E46 -7:39:04
Xianxian 8 1 38N13 116E06 -7:44:24
Xianyang 20 9 34N22 108E42 -7:14:48
Xianyang 3 1 28N02 118E30 -7:54:00
Xianyou 3 1 25N23 118E40 -7:54:40
Xianzhong 12 1 28N36 113E48 -7:35:12
Xiao'ao 3 1 26N14 119E39 -7:58:36
Xiaoazhang 29 9 23N42 104E58 -6:59:52
Xiaobangniulu 16 11 41N34 122E46 -8:11:04
Xiaobeigou 16 11 41N55 120E46 -8:03:04
Xiaobeihe 16 11 42N39 123E58 -8:15:52
Xiaobeihe 16 11 41N22 122E50 -8:11:20
Xiaocaohu 27 8 43N06 88E30 -5:54:00
Xiaocheng 3 1 26N20 119E47 -7:59:08
Xiaochengdu 30 1 30N59 120E04 -8:00:16
Xiaochengzi 17 11 46N33 122E54 -8:11:36
Xiaochengzi 17 11 42N56 123E12 -8:12:48
Xiaochi 1 1 30N33 116E23 -7:45:32
Xiaochikou 11 1 29N46 115E59 -7:43:56
Xiaodanyang 1 1 31N38 118E43 -7:54:52
Xiaodong 6 9 22N14 108E39 -7:14:36
Xiao'ergou 17 11 49N12 123E42 -8:14:48
Xiaofangshen 16 11 42N13 123E54 -8:15:36
Xiaofanshan 8 1 40N16 115E19 -7:41:16
Xiaofen 13 1 31N45 119E39 -7:58:36
Xiaofeng 30 1 30N36 119E32 -7:58:08
Xiaogan 11 1 30N55 113E54 -7:35:36
Xiaogangkou 14 1 28N14 115E50 -7:43:20
Xiaogaojiatun 16 11 41N02 121E59 -8:07:56
Xiaogencaigangzi 16 11 41N48 122E42 -8:10:48
Xiaogu 24 9 29N08 104E01 -6:56:04
Xiaoguai 27 8 45N13 85E02 -5:40:08
Xiaogushan 16 11 39N49 123E12 -8:12:48
Xiaohaizhen 13 1 31N58 120E59 -8:03:56
Xiaohaladaokou 17 11 42N37 119E32 -7:58:08
Xiaohan 10 1 35N48 114E52 -7:39:28
Xiaohe 13 1 32N01 119E52 -7:59:28
Xiaohekou 20 9 33N19 107E25 -7:09:40
Xiaoheyan 17 11 42N26 119E38 -7:58:32
Xiaoheying 24 9 32N37 104E23 -6:57:32
Xiaohongmen 2 1 39N49 116E26 -7:45:44
Xiaohu 3 1 27N20 118E14 -7:52:56
Xiaohuying 8 1 41N09 117E13 -7:48:52
Xiaoji 13 1 32N38 119E48 -7:59:12
Xiaoji 21 1 36N45 121E01 -8:04:04
Xiaoji 12 1 27N08 113E15 -7:33:00
Xiaojiachang 24 9 30N18 106E28 -7:05:52
Xiaojiagang 11 1 31N06 113E55 -7:35:40
Xiaojialing 14 1 29N35 116E32 -7:46:08
Xiaojiang 14 1 25N08 114E59 -7:39:56
Xiaojianji 1 1 33N23 116E29 -7:45:56
Xiaojiawu 8 1 39N36 116E36 -7:46:24
Xiaojiayingzi 8 1 40N17 118E47 -7:55:08
Xiaojieling 11 1 31N36 115E09 -7:40:36
Xiaojin 24 9 31N00 102E21 -6:49:24
Xiaojingfang 8 1 39N22 116E34 -7:46:16
Xiaojiu 9 12 45N15 127E47 -8:31:08
Xiaokaoshantun 16 11 42N10 123E53 -8:15:32
Xiaokuli 17 11 50N18 120E20 -8:01:20
Xiaokunshan 22 2 31N02 121E07 -8:04:28
Xiaolan 5 1 22N41 113E14 -7:32:56
Xiaoliangshan 16 11 42N05 122E32 -8:10:08
Xiaoling 9 12 45N20 127E18 -8:29:12
Xiaoling 16 11 42N18 123E23 -8:13:32
Xiaolingzi 16 11 41N07 123E19 -8:13:16
Xiaolinzhuang 16 11 41N36 124E01 -8:16:04
Xiaolipu 21 1 36N24 116E35 -7:46:20
Xiaolongtan 29 9 23N51 103E10 -6:52:40
Xiaolüzhuang 13 1 31N57 119E25 -7:57:40
Xiaomei 30 1 27N50 118E58 -7:55:52
Xiaomiaozi 8 1 41N24 114E25 -7:37:40
Xiaonanhai 24 9 29N23 106E27 -7:05:48
Xiaopikou 21 1 35N47 115E53 -7:43:32
Xiaopingyang 6 9 23N22 109E13 -7:16:52
Xiaoqiao 3 1 26N57 118E30 -7:54:00
Xiaoqiaotou 1 1 30N43 119E27 -7:57:48
Xiaoqingchuizi 16 11 42N30 123E39 -8:14:36
Xiaoquandong 4 8 41N14 95E26 -6:21:44
Xiaosanjiazi 16 11 42N34 123E23 -8:13:32
Xiaoshakou 11 1 29N58 113E16 -7:33:04
Xiaoshan 30 3 30N10 120E15 -8:01:00
Xiaoshangqiao 10 1 33N43 113E58 -7:35:52
Xiaoshi 14 1 27N27 116E49 -7:47:16
Xiaoshixiang 1 1 30N36 116E38 -7:46:32
Xiaoshu 30 1 30N48 119E46 -7:59:04
Xiaoshun 30 1 29N11 119E51 -7:59:24
Xiaosigou 8 1 40N53 118E33 -7:54:12
Xiaosijia 17 11 42N24 120E46 -8:03:04
Xiaotang 16 11 41N38 119E33 -7:58:12
Xiaotanghe 15 12 42N04 127E10 -8:28:40
Xiaotao 3 1 25N46 117E08 -7:48:32
Xiaotazi 16 11 42N17 123E08 -8:12:32
Xiaotian 1 1 31N12 116E33 -7:46:12
Xiaotianji 1 1 32N45 115E36 -7:42:24
Xiaotun 16 11 42N24 123E44 -8:14:56
Xiaotunzicun 16 11 41N14 123E20 -8:13:20
Xiaowa 16 11 41N03 122E04 -8:08:16
Xiaowan 3 1 26N53 116E36 -7:46:24
Xiaowangmiao 30 1 29N41 121E21 -8:05:24
Xiaoxi 14 1 25N48 115E21 -7:41:24
Xiaoxian 1 1 34N11 116E56 -7:47:44
Xiaoxincheng 8 1 39N24 115E11 -7:40:44
Xiaoxintian 2 1 39N58 116E22 -7:45:28
Xiaoxizhen 30 1 30N51 119E50 -7:59:20
Xiaoyangjiadian 16 11 42N23 122E24 -8:09:36
Xiaoyangqi 17 11 50N48 124E12 -8:16:48
Xiaoyantai 16 11 41N26 123E10 -8:12:40
Xiaoyaozhen 10 1 33N46 114E16 -7:37:04
Xiaoyi 23 1 37N10 111E46 -7:27:04
Xiaoying 21 1 37N18 118E04 -7:52:16
Xiaoying 2 1 40N12 116E33 -7:46:12
Xiaoyingcun 8 1 39N28 116E41 -7:46:44
Xiaoyuan 24 9 30N00 104E56 -6:59:44
Xiaozhan 26 1 38N55 117E25 -7:49:40
Xiaozhongdian 29 9 27N40 99E46 -6:39:04
Xiaozhuang 16 11 41N30 121E27 -8:05:48
Xiaozhujiawan 13 1 31N24 121E01 -8:04:04
Xiapu 3 1 26N52 120E01 -8:00:04
Xiapu 14 1 27N49 114E26 -7:37:44
Xiaqialafangzi 16 11 41N48 121E44 -8:06:56
Xiaqiubao 21 1 37N01 119E54 -7:59:36
Xiasantumen 8 1 38N50 114E48 -7:39:12
Xiashe 30 1 30N33 120E11 -8:00:44
Xiashesi 12 1 27N46 112E57 -7:31:48
Xiashi → Haining 30 1 30N32 120E41 -8:02:44
Xiashu 13 1 32N11 119E10 -7:56:40
Xiashuerfowei 17 11 50N23 120E47 -8:03:08
Xiashuiquan 16 11 41N52 123E38 -8:14:32
Xiataizi 8 1 40N37 117E45 -7:51:00
Xiatang 10 1 33N45 112E39 -7:30:36
Xiatang 13 1 31N29 118E41 -7:54:44
Xiatangtian 30 1 30N55 120E12 -8:00:48
Xiataohuatu 16 11 41N42 120E36 -8:02:24
Xiawa 17 11 42N39 120E35 -8:02:20
Xiawajiang 22 2 30N59 121E51 -8:07:24
Xiawaziyu 16 11 41N15 123E38 -8:14:32
Xiaxi 13 1 31N43 119E45 -7:59:00
Xiaxian 23 1 35N11 111E15 -7:25:00
Xiaxiangcheng 24 9 28N42 99E59 -6:39:56
Xiaxikou 3 1 26N15 118E59 -7:55:56
Xiaxinhe 13 1 31N40 119E31 -7:58:04
Xiayang 3 1 26N46 117E59 -7:51:56
Xiayang 3 1 24N39 116E52 -7:47:28
Xiayang 30 1 28N48 119E41 -7:58:44
Xiayi 10 1 34N14 116E06 -7:44:24
Xiaying 21 1 37N03 119E25 -7:57:40
Xiaying 26 1 40N10 117E25 -7:49:40
Xiayunling 2 1 39N43 115E44 -7:42:56
Xiazhang 21 1 36N08 116E57 -7:47:48
Xiazhen 14 1 28N39 118E21 -7:53:24
Xiazhuang 8 1 39N54 117E01 -7:48:04
Xiazhuang 8 1 39N38 115E26 -7:41:44
Xiazhuang 3 1 27N22 119E01 -7:56:04
Xiazhuang 21 1 35N28 118E43 -7:54:52
Xiazikou 8 1 39N01 115E25 -7:41:40
Xiban 24 9 30N32 106E12 -7:04:48
Xibaqianmou 16 11 40N59 121E35 -8:06:20
Xibeiyingzi 16 11 41N55 121E38 -8:06:32
Xibu 1 1 31N46 118E17 -7:53:08
Xicang 13 1 31N34 120E29 -8:01:56
Xichang 24 9 27N58 102E13 -6:48:52
Xichang 16 11 42N15 124E12 -8:16:48
Xicheng 9 12 48N10 125E29 -8:21:56
Xichong 24 9 31N00 105E52 -7:03:28
Xicicun 8 1 39N29 116E08 -7:44:32
Xicun 14 1 27N46 114E14 -7:36:56
Xidachuan 15 12 41N46 127E34 -8:30:16
Xidapo 15 12 43N12 130E02 -8:40:08
Xidaying 2 1 39N41 116E14 -7:44:56
Xidian 30 1 29N32 121E26 -8:05:44
Xiditou 26 1 39N16 117E23 -7:49:32
Xiecun 8 1 39N00 115E31 -7:42:04
Xiedian 10 1 33N27 113E28 -7:33:52
Xiefang 3 1 26N12 116E41 -7:46:44
Xiegeer 28 8 28N38 87E04 -5:48:16
Xieji 10 1 34N32 115E29 -7:41:56
Xiejia 15 12 42N24 125E42 -8:22:48
Xiejiagangzi 16 11 41N55 122E20 -8:09:20
Xiejiapu 1 1 31N15 119E09 -7:56:36
Xiejunmiao 24 9 30N15 103E40 -6:54:40
Xielipuke 28 8 31N30 82E45 -5:31:00
Xiemachang 24 9 29N46 106E22 -7:05:28
Xiepu 30 1 30N02 121E37 -8:06:28
Xieqiao 13 1 32N03 120E22 -8:01:28
Xieqiao 30 1 30N29 120E34 -8:02:16
Xietang 13 3 31N18 120E44 -8:02:56
Xiexi 13 1 31N54 118E54 -7:55:36
Xiexinggou 16 11 41N51 121E05 -8:04:20
Xifeng 7 9 27N02 106E30 -7:06:00
Xifeng 16 11 42N43 124E40 -8:18:40
Xifengkou 8 1 40N24 118E19 -7:53:16
Xifocun 16 11 41N26 122E33 -8:10:12
Xigangzi 9 12 49N58 127E20 -8:29:20
Xigaolizhuangzi 16 11 41N40 122E55 -8:11:40
Xigaotan 8 1 38N18 116E13 -7:44:52
Xigaotun 16 11 40N27 122E36 -8:10:24
Xiguanjiatun 16 11 42N35 123E10 -8:12:40
Xiguanyingzi 16 11 41N50 120E37 -8:02:28
Xihaikou 16 11 40N50 121E05 -8:04:20
Xihe 1 1 31N01 118E28 -7:53:52
Xihe 11 1 31N41 113E27 -7:33:48
Xihe 4 9 34N01 105E17 -7:01:08
Xiheying 8 1 39N53 114E42 -7:38:48
Xihezhuang 26 1 39N20 118E02 -7:52:08
Xihua 10 1 33N47 114E31 -7:38:04
Xihuangcang 13 1 31N43 121E40 -8:06:40
Xihuanzidong 16 11 41N31 122E28 -8:09:52
Xihuashan 14 1 25N28 114E20 -7:37:20
Xihuashan 2 1 40N07 116E54 -7:47:36
Xihuishan 16 11 41N41 122E38 -8:10:32

Xiji 18 9 35N58 105E44 -7:02:56
Xiji 2 1 39N49 116E52 -7:47:28
Xijialong 29 9 23N31 103E51 -6:55:24
Xijiang 14 1 25N50 115E49 -7:43:16
Xijianshanzi 16
11 40N47 120E48 -8:03:12
Xijiapuzitun 16
11 41N26 123E50 -8:15:20
Xikou 17 11 46N40 120E40 -8:02:40
Xikou 1 1 29N44 118E02 -7:52:08
Xikou 30 1 28N52 119E11 -7:56:44
Xikou 3 1 25N26 118E45 -7:55:00
Xikou 1 29N14 114E24 -7:37:36
Xikou 1 1 30N40 118E41 -7:54:44
Xikou 1 29N11 114E23 -7:37:32
Xikouxu 3 1 25N24 117E03 -7:48:12
Xikouzi 17 11 53N06 120E40 -8:02:40
Xilai 24 9 30N20 103E29 -6:53:56
Xilaiqiao 13 1 32N03 119E54 -7:59:36
Xilaizhen 13 1 32N07 120E25 -8:01:40
Xilin 28 8 28N33 87E48 -5:51:12
Xilintuo 28 8 30N08 88E04 -5:52:16
Xiliuhe 8 1 38N58 116E32 -7:46:08
Xiliushuyingzi 16
11 42N25 121E54 -8:07:36
Xiluncun 9 12 47N08 126E26 -8:25:44
Ximagou 8 1 40N16 117E50 -7:51:20
Ximakou 11 1 30N33 113E47 -7:35:08
Ximalatu 17 11 47N00 122E01 -8:08:04
Ximalin 8 1 40N48 114E29 -7:37:56
Ximiao 17 9 41N09 100E17 -6:41:08
Ximucheng 16 11 40N42 122E54 -8:11:36
Xin'an 15 12 43N46 125E40 -8:22:40
Xin'an 5 1 23N02 114E56 -7:39:44
Xinan 3 1 25N26 117E35 -7:50:20
Xin'an 14 1 26N44 116E13 -7:44:52
Xin'an 13 1 31N47 120E09 -8:00:36
Xin'an 13 1 31N30 120E22 -8:01:28
Xin'an 8 1 39N09 116E38 -7:46:32
Xin'andian 10 1 32N37 114E03 -7:36:12
Xin'andu 1 1 30N52 116E53 -7:47:32
Xin'anji 10 1 33N22 115E13 -7:40:52
Xin'anpu 16 11 42N39 123E27 -8:13:48
Xin'anqiao 13 1 32N16 121E07 -8:04:28
Xin'ansuo 29 9 23N16 103E27 -6:53:48
Xin'anzhen 15 12 44N06 123E46 -8:15:04
Xin'anzhen 26 1 39N45 117E32 -7:50:08
Xi'nanzhuang 8 1 40N48 118E23 -7:53:32
Xinba 13 1 32N08 120E39 -8:02:36
Xinba 13 1 32N16 119E45 -7:59:00
Xinba 1 1 30N24 116E52 -7:47:28
Xinbao'an 8 1 40N27 115E24 -7:41:36
Xin Barag Youqi (Altan Emel) 17
11 48N41 116E53 -7:47:32
Xin Barag Zuoqi (Amgalang) 17
11 48N14 118E18 -7:53:12
Xinbin 16 11 41N42 125E02 -8:20:08
Xinbin 22 2 30N56 121E04 -8:04:16
Xinbo 8 1 42N19 117E44 -7:50:56
Xincai 10 1 32N44 114E59 -7:39:56
Xincang 30 1 30N25 120E42 -8:02:48
Xincang 30 1 30N44 121E11 -8:04:44
Xinchang 29 9 25N10 104E18 -6:57:12
Xinchang 30 1 29N30 120E53 -8:03:32
Xinchang 13 1 31N42 121E46 -8:07:04
Xinchang 22 2 31N02 121E38 -8:06:32
Xinchang 24 9 29N20 104E15 -6:57:00
Xinchang 24 9 29N38 104E33 -6:58:12
Xinchang 24 9 30N29 106E21 -7:05:24
Xinchang 24 9 30N16 104E29 -6:57:56
Xinchang 29 9 28N03 103E46 -6:55:04
Xinchangzi 24 9 29N40 103E46 -6:55:04
Xincheng (Gaobeidian) 8
1 39N20 115E51 -7:43:24
Xincheng 6 9 24N09 108E46 -7:15:04
Xincheng 14 1 25N34 114E36 -7:38:24
Xincheng 30 1 30N48 120E36 -8:02:24
Xincheng 26 1 38N59 117E33 -7:50:12
Xinchengzi 16 11 42N03 123E30 -8:14:00
Xinchepaizi 27 8 44N55 84E30 -5:38:00
Xincunji 1 1 32N53 115E31 -7:42:04
Xindai 30 1 30N49 121E05 -8:04:20
Xindi 17 11 42N21 120E31 -8:02:04
Xindian 9 12 45N55 127E50 -8:31:20
Xindian 10 1 33N07 112E38 -7:30:32
Xindian 10 1 31N33 115E16 -7:41:04
Xindian 10 1 33N38 113E51 -7:35:24
Xindian 11 1 29N40 113E40 -7:34:40
Xindian 8 1 37N07 114E49 -7:39:16
Xindian 21 1 37N29 118E28 -7:53:52
Xindian 2 1 40N11 116E11 -7:44:44
Xindian 2 1 40N47 116E49 -7:47:16
Xindian 8 1 39N10 116E27 -7:45:48
Xindian 24 9 29N19 105E40 -7:02:40
Xindianbu 1 1 32N24 116E22 -7:45:28
Xindianzi 24 9 29N46 105E11 -7:00:44
Xindianzi 24 9 29N43 104E01 -6:56:04
Xindianzi 8 1 40N04 118E01 -7:52:04
Xindianzi 24 9 28N49 103E35 -6:54:20
Xindianzi 24 9 29N03 103E46 -6:55:04
Xindianzi 24 9 29N52 106E06 -7:04:24
Xindu 6 9 23N59 111E46 -7:27:04
Xinfatuncun 16
11 41N13 122E28 -8:09:52
Xinfeng 13 1 33N19 120E30 -8:02:00
Xinfeng 5 1 24N04 114E12 -7:36:48
Xinfeng 5 1 24N05 116E53 -7:47:32
Xinfeng 1 1 31N09 118E40 -7:54:40
Xinfeng 13 1 32N05 119E34 -7:58:16
Xinfeng 30 1 30N43 120E55 -8:03:40
Xinfeng 14 1 25N24 114E56 -7:39:44
Xinfeng 14 1 27N26 116E40 -7:46:40
Xing'an 17 11 48N49 121E45 -8:07:00
Xing'an 6 9 25N37 110E31 -7:22:04
Xin'gang 13 1 31N56 120E57 -8:03:48
Xingang 13 1 32N03 120E25 -8:01:40
Xing'antun 17 11 51N31 120E08 -8:00:32
Xingcheng 16 11 40N37 120E43 -8:02:52
Xingguo 14 1 26N21 115E19 -7:41:16
Xinghai 19 9 35N31 99E36 -6:38:24
Xinghe 17 9 40N48 113E58 -7:35:52
Xinghua 13 1 32N57 119E50 -7:59:20
Xingliu 1 1 33N04 115E41 -7:42:44
Xinglong 24 9 30N20 106E07 -7:04:28
Xinglong 18 9 35N38 106E08 -7:04:32
Xinglong 11 1 32N05 112E51 -7:31:24
Xinglong 8 1 40N26 117E34 -7:50:16
Xinglong 24 9 30N36 106E20 -7:05:20
Xinglongchang 24
9 29N54 105E26 -7:01:44
Xinglongchang 24
9 30N25 104E06 -6:56:24
Xinglongchang 24
9 29N34 106E09 -7:04:36
Xinglongcun 17
11 49N50 125E12 -8:20:48
Xinglongdian 16
11 42N16 124E00 -8:16:00
Xinglongdian 16
11 41N59 123E03 -8:12:12
Xinglonggou 16
11 41N46 120E38 -8:02:32
Xinglonggou 16
11 40N45 123E08 -8:12:32
Xinglongpao 9 12 46N27 125E47 -8:23:08
Xinglongtai 16
11 42N30 123E48 -8:15:12
Xingning 5 1 24N09 115E45 -7:43:00
Xingou 11 1 30N41 113E57 -7:35:48
Xingou 11 1 30N08 112E56 -7:31:44
Xingren 7 9 25N27 105E13 -7:00:52
Xingrenbu 18 9 37N06 105E12 -7:00:48
Xingshanbao 9 12 45N30 125E45 -8:23:00
Xingtai 8 1 37N04 114E29 -7:37:56
Xingtan 5 1 22N46 113E07 -7:32:28
Xingtang 8 1 38N26 114E33 -7:38:12
Xingtian 3 1 27N30 118E02 -7:52:08
Xinguan 1 1 33N38 118E05 -7:52:20
Xingwenping 24 9 29N24 103E23 -6:53:32
Xingxian 23 1 38N36 111E15 -7:25:00
Xingxing 30 1 30N39 121E09 -8:04:36
Xingyi 7 9 25N06 104E58 -6:59:52
Xingyi 8 1 38N18 115E01 -7:40:04
Xingzhuangzi 8 1 40N34 115E00 -7:40:00
Xingzi 14 1 29N28 116E01 -7:44:04
Xinhe 13 1 31N59 121E21 -8:05:24
Xinhe 26 1 39N03 117E37 -7:50:28
Xinhe 30 1 28N30 121E27 -8:05:48
Xinhe 8 1 37N32 115E14 -7:40:56
Xinhekou 9 12 48N22 130E45 -8:43:00
Xinheng 5 1 23N38 116E18 -7:45:12
Xinhezhen 22 2 31N35 121E31 -8:06:04
Xinhezhuang 1 1 31N10 118E46 -7:55:04
Xinhua 12 1 27N37 111E02 -7:24:08
Xinhuang 30 1 30N37 120E55 -8:03:40
Xinhui 5 1 22N32 113E02 -7:32:08
Xining (Sining) 19
9 36N38 101E55 -6:47:40
Xiniu 5 1 24N10 113E07 -7:32:28
Xiniu 13 1 31N25 120E07 -8:00:28
Xiniuguchengzi 16
11 41N01 122E24 -8:09:36
Xinji 21 1 35N19 115E36 -7:42:24
Xinji 26 1 39N52 117E10 -7:48:40
Xinji 10 1 33N24 114E44 -7:38:56
Xinjiaji 21 1 36N56 116E59 -7:47:56
Xinjian 14 1 28N34 115E47 -7:43:08
Xinjian 13 1 31N33 119E39 -7:58:36
Xinjian 30 1 28N46 120E02 -8:00:08
Xinjiang 5 1 24N29 113E52 -7:35:28
Xinjiang 13 1 32N05 120E40 -8:02:40
Xinjiang 23 1 35N40 111E11 -7:24:44
Xinjianglang 30
1 30N58 120E54 -8:03:36
Xinjiapu 2 1 40N32 115E57 -7:43:48
Xinjiazhuang 8 1 40N31 114E58 -7:39:52
Xinjie 29 9 26N48 101E15 -6:45:00
Xinjieji 9 12 52N08 126E24 -8:25:36
Xinjin (Pulandian) 16
11 39N24 121E58 -8:07:52
Xinjin 24 9 30N25 103E49 -6:55:16
Xinjingzi 27 8 42N13 87E36 -5:50:24
Xinjuntun 8 1 39N39 117E57 -7:51:48
Xinkaigang 13 1 31N55 120E56 -8:03:44
Xinkengdong 12 1 26N09 113E46 -7:35:04
Xinle (Dongchangshou) 8
1 38N24 114E47 -7:39:08
Xinli 15 12 44N41 126E45 -8:27:00
Xinlitun 16 11 42N00 122E09 -8:08:36
Xinlizhuang 8 1 39N17 116E10 -7:44:40
Xinmin 16 11 42N00 122E48 -8:11:12
Xinmintun 16 11 41N39 123E02 -8:12:08
Xinning 12 1 26N19 110E45 -7:23:00
Xinping 29 9 24N06 101E58 -6:47:52
Xinpu 5 1 24N31 116E08 -7:44:32
Xinqianhu 21 1 37N59 118E15 -7:53:00
Xinqiao 24 9 30N33 105E33 -7:02:12
Xinqiao 13 1 31N32 119E04 -7:56:16
Xinqiao 22 2 31N04 121E18 -8:05:12
Xinqiao 24 9 29N32 106E28 -7:05:52
Xinqiao 24 9 30N10 103E50 -6:55:20
Xinqiaotou 1 1 31N00 119E24 -7:57:36
Xinqiaozhen 24 9 29N36 103E39 -6:54:36
Xinqiu 16 11 41N53 119E41 -7:58:44
Xinqizhou 14 1 28N56 115E50 -7:43:20
Xinqu 27 8 44N57 85E15 -5:41:00
Xinquan 3 1 25N23 116E38 -7:46:32
Xinsanyu 13 1 31N58 120E07 -8:00:28
Xinshao 12 1 27N11 111E20 -7:25:20
Xinshengzhen 24
9 29N29 104E39 -6:58:36
Xinshi 30 1 30N37 120E19 -8:01:16
Xinshi 13 1 32N04 120E02 -8:00:08
Xinshizhen 24 9 30N20 104E35 -6:58:20
Xintai 21 1 35N54 117E44 -7:50:56
Xintaimen 16 11 40N50 120E23 -8:01:32
Xintaizi 16 11 42N07 123E36 -8:14:24
Xintang 5 1 23N08 113E36 -7:34:24
Xintang 30 1 31N02 119E59 -7:59:56
Xintang 11 1 30N13 109E30 -7:18:00
Xintangcun 13 1 31N53 119E31 -7:58:04
Xintanpu 11 1 29N43 114E54 -7:39:36
Xintian 12 1 25N53 112E05 -7:28:20
Xintun 16 11 42N11 123E45 -8:15:00
Xinvi 8 1 40N04 118E21 -7:53:24
Xinwei 14 1 25N21 115E48 -7:43:12
Xinwen (Suncun) 21
1 35N53 117E40 -7:50:40
Xinxian 23 1 38N25 112E48 -7:31:12
Xinxian 10 1 31N38 114E51 -7:39:24
Xinxiang 10 1 35N20 113E51 -7:35:24
Xinxing 5 9 19N57 109E32 -7:18:08
Xinxing 5 10 22N40 112E52 -7:31:28
Xinxing 15 12 43N16 129E48 -8:39:12
Xinxu 3 1 24N57 117E34 -7:50:16
Xinxu 5 1 22N52 114E20 -7:37:20
Xinyang 10 1 32N08 114E04 -7:36:16
Xinyao 3 1 27N39 118E52 -7:55:28
Xinye 10 1 32N33 112E21 -7:29:24
Xinyi (Dongzhen) 5
8 22N13 110E50 -7:23:20
Xinyi (Xin'anzhen) 13
1 34N22 118E21 -7:53:24
Xinying 18 9 36N03 105E35 -7:02:20
Xinyu 14 1 27N49 114E57 -7:39:48
Xinyuan 27 8 43N08 82E31 -5:30:04
Xinzao 5 1 23N02 113E26 -7:33:44
Xinzha 29 9 23N41 101E09 -6:44:36
Xinzhai 8 1 39N24 118E46 -7:55:04
Xinzhai 21 1 36N24 118E37 -7:54:28
Xinzhai 29 9 24N33 99E08 -6:36:32
Xinzhan 10 1 33N33 114E50 -7:39:20
Xinzhang 8 1 39N05 116E46 -7:47:04
Xinzhangzi 8 1 40N45 117E50 -7:51:20
Xinzhao 17 9 39N32 107E52 -7:11:28
Xinzhazhen 13 1 31N50 119E52 -7:59:28
Xinzhen 22 2 31N24 121E24 -8:05:36
Xinzhen 8 1 39N01 116E22 -7:45:28
Xinzhen 10 1 35N37 114E03 -7:36:12
Xinzheng 10 1 34N25 113E43 -7:34:52
Xinzhou 5 9 19N48 109E18 -7:17:12
Xinzhou 11 1 30N50 114E47 -7:39:08
Xinzhuang 21 1 35N05 117E56 -7:51:44
Xinzhuang 2 1 39N56 116E31 -7:46:04
Xinzhuangtou 8 1 39N25 115E45 -7:43:00
Xinzhuangzi 16
11 41N05 121E23 -8:05:32
Xinzhuangzi 2 1 40N14 116E59 -7:47:56
Xinzhuangzi 8 1 40N32 115E10 -7:40:40
Xinzhuangzi 26 1 38N52 117E21 -7:49:24
Xinzhuangzi 8 1 39N20 118E25 -7:53:40
Xiongjiachang 7
9 26N31 105E39 -7:02:36
Xiongxian 8 1 38N59 116E05 -7:44:20
Xiongyuecheng 16
11 40N10 122E08 -8:08:32
Xiping 30 1 28N27 119E29 -7:57:56
Xiping 10 1 33N23 114E02 -7:36:08
Xiping'anhe 16
11 40N47 122E01 -8:08:04
Xiqia 1 1 31N03 119E37 -7:58:28
Xiqilichiquan 17
11 49N59 119E27 -7:57:48
Xiqin 3 1 26N33 118E06 -7:52:24
Xisanshilipu 1 1 32N40 117E31 -7:50:04
Xisantai 16 11 39N38 121E37 -8:06:28
Xishan 14 1 28N34 115E37 -7:42:28
Xishan 8 1 39N38 118E10 -7:52:40
Xishanqiao 13 3 31N57 118E43 -7:54:52
Xishanxicun 8 1 40N01 116E50 -7:47:20
Xishijiazi 16 11 41N46 120E55 -8:03:40
Xishiqiao 13 1 31N53 120E06 -8:00:24
Xishu 8 1 36N41 113E49 -7:35:16
Xishui 11 1 30N27 115E13 -7:40:52
Xishuiyu 2 1 40N25 116E16 -7:45:04
Xisuhupu 16 11 41N41 123E14 -8:12:56
Xitai 16 11 40N37 120E12 -8:00:48
Xitan 3 1 23N47 117E08 -7:48:32
Xitang 30 1 30N57 120E53 -8:03:32
Xitangqiao 13 1 31N49 120E38 -8:02:32
Xitangqiao 30 1 30N37 121E01 -8:04:04
Xitaoyuan 16 11 40N57 122E11 -8:08:44
Xiti 28 8 33N27 82E48 -5:31:12
Xiting 13 1 32N07 121E00 -8:04:00
Xituan 8 1 39N29 115E47 -7:43:08
Xiujiangpu 16 11 41N17 123E02 -8:12:08
Xiuning 1 1 29N47 118E10 -7:52:40
Xiushan 24 9 28N29 108E52 -7:15:28
Xiushui 14 1 29N04 114E33 -7:38:12
Xiushuihe 16 11 42N22 123E01 -8:12:04
Xiuyan 16 11 40N17 123E18 -8:13:12
Xiwei 3 1 25N22 117E46 -7:51:04
Xiweizigou 16 11 42N01 121E59 -8:07:56
Xiwenquan 24 9 29N42 106E07 -7:04:28
Xiwu 30 1 29N40 121E30 -8:06:00
Xiwukou 1 1 30N24 118E54 -7:55:36
Xixi 3 1 26N45 118E42 -7:54:48
Xixia 10 1 33N22 111E28 -7:25:52
Xixian 23 1 36N43 110E52 -7:23:28
Xixian 10 1 32N21 114E44 -7:38:56
Xixiang 20 9 32N48 107E55 -7:11:40
Xixiangyang 8 1 39N33 116E02 -7:44:08
Xixiaojie 16 11 40N42 122E12 -8:08:48
Xixiashu 13 1 31N57 119E49 -7:59:16

Xixing 30	3	30N11	120E13	-8:00:52
Xiyang 13	1	31N49	120E43	-8:02:52
Xiyang 13	1	31N52	119E23	-7:57:32
Xiyang 3	1	25N50	117E25	-7:49:40
Xiyang 23	1	37N37	113E42	-7:34:48
Xiyangji 1	1	33N25	116E22	-7:45:28
Xiyangjiao 13	1	31N43	120E23	-8:01:32
Xiyangshugou 16	11	40N41	122E44	-8:10:56
Xiyangzhuang 13	1	31N50	119E22	-7:57:28
Xiyingzi 16	11	41N55	122E34	-8:10:16
Xiyou 21	1	37N24	119E56	-7:59:44
Xiyushi 30	1	30N36	119E26	-7:57:44
Xizhou 30	1	29N29	121E39	-8:06:36
Xizi 17	11	41N48	119E16	-7:57:04
Xuancheng 1	1	30N58	118E45	-7:55:00
Xuan'en 11	1	30N00	109E20	-7:17:20
Xuanfeng 14	1	27N42	114E08	-7:36:32
Xuanhan 24	9	31N24	107E43	-7:10:52
Xuanhua 8	1	40N37	115E03	-7:40:12
Xuanhuadian 11	1	31N42	114E29	-7:37:56
Xuanjiabao 13	1	32N17	120E01	-8:00:04
Xuanjiangying 8	1	41N25	116E45	-7:47:00
Xuantan 24	9	29N12	105E34	-7:02:16
Xuanwei 29	9	26N07	104E05	-6:56:20
Xuanzhuang 8	1	39N29	118E07	-7:52:28
Xubu 23	1	40N02	113E43	-7:34:52
Xuchang 10	1	34N03	113E49	-7:35:16
Xuchang 24	9	29N06	104E31	-6:58:04
Xucheng 21	1	35N56	116E27	-7:45:48
Xucun 30	1	30N27	120E22	-8:01:28
Xudazhuang 1	1	33N44	117E53	-7:51:32
Xueao 30	1	29N27	121E30	-8:06:00
Xueba 28	8	29N58	93E48	-6:15:12
Xuebu 13	1	31N43	119E22	-7:57:28
Xuecheng 21	1	34N50	117E16	-7:49:04
Xuedian 10	1	34N30	113E44	-7:34:56
Xuefanggou 16	11	41N57	121E01	-8:04:04
Xuefeng 13	1	33N21	118E22	-7:53:28
Xuehu 10	1	34N08	116E27	-7:45:48
Xueshuiwen 9	12	49N10	129E45	-8:39:00
Xuetangpuzi 16	11	40N38	123E53	-8:15:32
Xueyanqiao 13	1	31N30	120E06	-8:00:24
Xuezhen 1	1	31N35	118E38	-7:54:32
Xuguanzhen 13	3	31N23	120E30	-8:02:00
Xuguichenxiaodian 13	1	32N07	121E20	-8:05:20
Xuguit Qi (Yakeshi) 17	11	49N17	120E41	-8:02:44
Xuji 1	1	31N50	116E22	-7:45:28
Xujiabu 14	1	29N27	116E18	-7:45:12
Xujiadong 12	1	25N54	113E02	-7:32:08
Xujiadu 14	1	28N18	114E44	-7:38:56
Xujiagou 16	11	42N17	124E04	-8:16:16
Xujiapuzi 16	11	40N44	123E18	-8:13:12
Xujiatou 13	1	31N19	119E25	-7:57:40
Xujiazhai 22	2	31N11	121E46	-8:07:04
Xujiazhai 22	2	31N23	121E17	-8:05:08
Xuliying 8	1	39N28	116E02	-7:44:08
Xunhe 9	12	49N18	128E04	-8:32:16
Xunhua 19	9	35N49	102E26	-6:49:44
Xunjiansi 8	1	40N50	116E04	-7:44:16
Xunke 9	12	49N35	128E25	-8:33:40
Xunle 6	9	25N17	108E12	-7:12:48
Xunmukou 10	1	34N03	114E42	-7:38:48
Xunshansuo 21	1	37N10	122E29	-8:09:56
Xunwu 14	1	24N58	115E38	-7:42:32
Xunxian 10	1	35N43	114E31	-7:38:04
Xupu 12	1	27N44	110E24	-7:21:36
Xupu 13	1	31N45	120E54	-8:03:36
Xushe 13	1	31N24	119E39	-7:58:36
Xushi 13	1	31N40	120E57	-8:03:48
Xushui 8	1	39N02	115E39	-7:42:36
Xutian 10	1	34N10	114E03	-7:36:12
Xuwan 14	1	27N55	116E31	-7:46:04
Xuwen 5	8	20N21	110E11	-7:20:44
Xuxiandai 30	1	30N40	120E47	-8:03:08
Xuxiang 13	1	31N33	120E13	-8:00:52
Xuyi 13	1	33N01	118E29	-7:53:56
Xuyong 24	9	28N10	105E24	-7:01:36
Xuzhou (Süchow) 13	1	34N16	117E11	-7:48:44
Xuzhuang 13	1	31N09	120E32	-8:02:08
Yaan 24	9	30N03	103E02	-6:52:08
Yabuli 9	12	44N55	128E35	-8:34:20
Yachengzhen 5	9	18N25	109E11	-7:16:44
Yadong 28	8	27N29	88E55	-5:55:40
Yafuquan 27	7	39N12	76E09	-5:04:36
Yahagong 29	9	28N24	99E11	-6:36:44
Yahe 9	12	45N21	130E24	-8:41:36
Yahe 13	1	31N44	119E52	-7:59:28
Yahongqiao 8	1	39N45	117E51	-7:51:24
Yajiang 24	9	30N02	101E05	-6:44:20
Yakou 3	1	24N46	118E46	-7:55:04
Yaliji 8	1	36N06	114E56	-7:39:44
Yalu 17	11	48N34	122E09	-8:08:36
Yamatengwumulu 19	8	38N38	97E05	-6:28:20
Yamenkou 2	1	39N53	116E12	-7:44:48
Yamenying 17	11	43N25	122E19	-8:09:16
Yamu 27	8	43N48	94E48	-6:19:12
Yan'an 20	9	36N36	109E28	-7:17:52
Yanbian 24	9	26N55	101E30	-6:46:00
Yanbu 5	1	23N05	113E10	-7:32:40
Yanbutou 11	1	29N52	115E04	-7:40:16
Yanchang 20	9	36N33	110E01	-7:20:04
Yancheng 10	1	33N36	113E57	-7:35:48
Yancheng 13	1	33N24	120E09	-8:00:36
Yanchi 18	9	37N52	107E22	-7:09:28
Yanchi 2	1	40N02	115E53	-7:43:32
Yanchuan 20	9	36N56	110E05	-7:20:20
Yandun 27	8	42N20	94E09	-6:16:36
Yanfeng 29	9	25N53	101E01	-6:44:04
Yang'an 21	1	37N38	117E09	-7:48:36
Yan'gang 3	1	26N02	116E22	-7:45:28
Yangbajing 28	8	30N06	90E33	-6:02:12
Yangce 10	1	32N58	113E14	-7:32:56
Yangcha 15	12	41N11	126E15	-8:25:00
Yangchang 24	9	30N22	103E42	-6:54:48
Yangcheng 23	1	35N29	112E25	-7:29:40
Yangcheng 13	1	31N24	120E47	-8:03:08
Yangchiang → Yangjiang 5	10	21N51	111E56	-7:27:44
Yangchow → Yangzhou 13	1	32N24	119E26	-7:57:44
Yangchu 21	1	37N11	120E47	-8:03:08
Yangch'üan → Yangquan 23	1	37N52	113E36	-7:34:24
Yangchun 5	10	22N10	111E46	-7:27:04
Yangcun 5	1	23N26	114E30	-7:38:00
Yangcun 8	1	39N09	115E50	-7:43:20
Yangcun 14	1	28N07	117E40	-7:50:40
Yangcunqiao 30	1	29N36	119E28	-7:57:52
Yangdachengzi 15	12	43N59	124E25	-8:17:40
Yangdalinzi 15	12	42N38	125E07	-8:20:28
Yangdang 11	1	32N23	112E39	-7:30:36
Yangdian 30	1	31N08	119E45	-7:59:00
Yang'erzhuang 8	1	38N18	117E30	-7:50:00
Yangfang 2	1	40N07	116E07	-7:44:28
Yangfangpu 8	1	40N48	115E01	-7:40:04
Yangfengang 26	1	39N07	116E52	-7:47:28
Yangfenzhen 30	1	30N28	120E03	-8:00:12
Yangganzhen 1	1	31N00	119E15	-7:57:00
Yanggao 23	1	40N25	113E44	-7:34:56
Yanggezhuang 2	1	40N09	116E48	-7:47:12
Yanggu 10	1	34N44	114E48	-7:39:12
Yanggu 21	1	36N08	115E48	-7:43:12
Yangguanpu 10	1	32N13	115E31	-7:42:04
Yanghang 22	2	31N22	121E26	-8:05:44
Yanghe 13	1	33N47	118E23	-7:53:32
Yanghexi 24	9	29N39	108E40	-7:14:40
Yanghu 1	1	32N34	116E30	-7:46:00
Yanghua 24	9	30N11	104E45	-6:59:00
Yangji 10	1	34N25	116E06	-7:44:24
Yangji 8	1	36N44	113E56	-7:35:44
Yangji 13	1	34N19	119E28	-7:57:52
Yangjia 13	1	34N19	119E28	-7:57:52
Yangjia 30	1	30N41	120E15	-8:01:00
Yangjiachang 24	9	29N23	104E21	-6:57:24
Yangjiachang 24	9	29N45	105E21	-7:01:24
Yangjiafeng 11	1	30N49	112E47	-7:31:08
Yangjiagou 26	1	39N18	117E54	-7:51:36
Yangjiajie 24	9	30N18	104E39	-6:58:36
Yangjian 13	1	31N39	120E33	-8:02:12
Yangjiang 5	10	21N51	111E56	-7:27:44
Yangjiaogou 21	1	37N16	118E50	-7:55:20
Yangjiaqiao 13	1	31N53	121E42	-8:06:48
Yangjiaqiao 13	1	32N02	121E26	-8:05:44
Yangjiaqiao 12	1	27N44	112E46	-7:31:04
Yangjiatao 8	1	39N49	117E51	-7:51:24
Yangjiawopu 16	11	42N21	122E57	-8:11:48
Yangjiazeng 2	1	40N12	117E04	-7:48:16
Yangjiazhangzi 16	11	40N48	120E33	-8:02:12
Yangjie 29	9	24N49	100E22	-6:41:28
Yangjishi 12	1	26N39	113E14	-7:32:56
Yangkou 3	1	26N47	117E51	-7:51:24
Yangkoushi 30	1	28N39	118E53	-7:55:32
Yanglinjie 12	1	29N07	113E27	-7:33:48
Yangliupu 1	1	30N52	118E37	-7:54:28
Yangliupu 24	9	30N09	104E03	-6:56:12
Yangliuqing 26	1	39N08	117E01	-7:48:04
Yangloudong 11	1	29N31	113E44	-7:34:56
Yanglousi 12	1	29N30	113E38	-7:34:32
Yangluo 11	1	30N41	114E34	-7:38:16
Yangluomayu 16	11	40N47	122E54	-8:11:36
Yangmachang 24	9	30N39	103E45	-6:55:00
Yangmahe 24	9	30N29	104E31	-6:58:04
Yangmeisi 14	1	25N42	114E30	-7:38:00
Yangmiao 10	1	34N11	114E53	-7:39:32
Yangmiao 30	1	30N51	120E49	-8:03:16
Yangmugou 16	11	40N36	124E28	-8:17:52
Yangmugou 16	11	41N11	123E50	-8:15:20
Yangmulin 8	1	40N06	115E12	-7:40:48
Yangpingguan 20	9	32N51	106E09	-7:04:36
Yangpu 3	1	27N14	119E08	-7:56:32
Yangqi 13	1	31N23	119E57	-7:59:48
Yangquan 23	1	37N52	113E36	-7:34:24
Yangriwan 11	1	31N37	110E49	-7:23:16
Yangshan 16	11	41N13	120E24	-8:01:36
Yangshan 21	1	35N13	116E13	-7:44:52
Yangshan 5	1	24N28	112E38	-7:30:32
Yangshigangzi 16	11	41N42	122E59	-8:11:56
Yangshitun 16	11	42N06	123E44	-8:14:56
Yangshugemen 8	1	40N55	118E18	-7:53:12
Yangshugoudonggou 16	11	41N43	120E41	-8:02:44
Yangshuling 8	1	41N02	118E47	-7:55:08
Yangshuo 6	9	24N45	110E24	-7:21:36
Yangtan 1	1	30N42	119E11	-7:56:44
Yangting 21	1	37N24	122E07	-8:08:28
Yangtou 5	1	23N26	115E24	-7:41:36
Yanguan 30	1	30N26	120E32	-8:02:08
Yangwan 14	1	28N22	116E46	-7:47:04
Yangwan 13	1	31N03	120E22	-8:01:28
Yangxi 1	1	30N11	118E39	-7:54:36
Yangxi 14	1	27N18	114E10	-7:36:40
Yangxian 20	9	33N03	107E47	-7:11:08
Yangxiang 13	1	31N29	119E35	-7:58:20
Yangxiang 13	1	31N12	121E01	-8:04:04
Yangxiangtun 16	11	40N58	122E48	-8:11:12
Yangxiaodian 1	1	31N46	116E45	-7:47:00
Yangxin 11	1	29N51	115E12	-7:40:48
Yangxin 21	1	37N39	117E34	-7:50:16
Yangxiudian 2	1	39N44	116E32	-7:46:08
Yangyuan (Xicheng) 8	1	40N01	114E10	-7:36:40
Yangze 3	1	26N57	118E23	-7:53:32
Yangzhong 13	1	32N16	119E49	-7:59:16
Yangzhou 13	1	32N24	119E26	-7:57:44
Yangzhuang 13	1	33N36	118E58	-7:55:52
Yangzhujuanzi 16	11	41N38	122E46	-8:11:04
Yangzi 11	1	31N19	112E36	-7:30:24
Yangzishao 15	12	42N28	126E09	-8:24:36
Yanhaiyingzi 16	11	41N52	123E05	-8:12:20
Yanhe 7	9	28N37	108E35	-7:14:20
Yanhe 11	1	31N16	115E07	-7:40:28
Yanhecheng 2	1	40N04	115E43	-7:42:52
Yanheying 8	1	40N02	119E03	-7:56:12
Yanhui 23	1	37N54	113E51	-7:35:24
Yanji 15	12	42N57	129E32	-8:38:08
Yanji (Longjing) 15	12	42N47	129E26	-8:37:44
Yanji 10	1	34N17	115E39	-7:42:36
Yanji 10	1	34N41	115E27	-7:41:48
Yanjia 16	11	40N57	121E41	-8:06:44
Yanjiabao 13	1	32N19	120E07	-8:00:28
Yanjiadian 16	11	39N48	121E49	-8:07:16
Yanjiahe 10	1	31N48	114E50	-7:39:20
Yanjiajie 16	11	41N02	121E32	-8:06:08
Yanjiao 8	1	39N56	116E48	-7:47:12
Yanjiapu 8	1	39N52	118E00	-7:52:00
Yanjiatuozi 16	11	42N27	123E47	-8:15:08
Yanjiawopeng 16	11	40N59	121E17	-8:05:08
Yanjin 10	1	35N11	114E11	-7:36:44
Yanjing 28	8	29N00	98E34	-6:34:16
Yanjing 24	9	29N56	106E21	-7:05:24
Yanling 10	1	34N07	114E11	-7:36:44
Yanling 13	1	31N54	119E30	-7:58:00
Yanliumiao 1	1	32N01	116E52	-7:47:28
Yanmeimeizi 8	1	39N42	115E03	-7:40:12
Yanqi 27	8	42N00	86E15	-5:45:00
Yanqian 3	1	24N54	116E14	-7:44:56
Yanqian 3	1	26N15	117E28	-7:49:52
Yanqianhu 16	11	42N16	123E12	-8:12:48
Yanqiao 13	1	31N41	120E17	-8:01:08
Yanqidoumen 1	1	31N17	118E42	-7:54:48
Yanqing 2	1	40N28	115E58	-7:43:52
Yanshan 14	1	28N18	117E41	-7:50:44
Yanshan 8	1	38N05	117E13	-7:48:52
Yanshan 29	9	23N41	104E21	-6:57:24
Yanshankou 8	1	39N59	117E42	-7:50:48
Yanshi 3	1	25N17	117E10	-7:48:40
Yanshou 9	12	45N28	128E20	-8:33:20
Yansi 1	1	29N48	118E20	-7:53:20
Yantai (Chefoo) 21	1	37N33	121E20	-8:05:20
Yantai 2	1	39N47	116E38	-7:46:32
Yantan 30	1	28N55	120E11	-8:00:44
Yantan 24	9	29N17	104E52	-6:59:28
Yantan 30	1	28N28	120E44	-8:02:56
Yantian 3	1	26N53	119E53	-7:59:32
Yantian 14	1	27N21	114E22	-7:37:28
Yanting 24	9	31N19	105E23	-7:01:32
Yantongshan 15	12	43N17	126E00	-8:24:00
Yantongshan 8	1	40N42	115E06	-7:40:24
Yanwangshan 16	11	41N36	123E57	-8:15:48
Yanweigang 13	1	34N30	119E48	-7:59:12
Yanxi 3	1	24N46	117E47	-7:51:08
Yanxia 11	1	29N34	114E50	-7:39:20
Yanxidu 14	1	26N51	114E58	-7:39:52
Yanxing 29	9	25N23	101E42	-6:46:48
Yanyegongsi 13	1	32N02	121E41	-8:06:44
Yanyuan 24	9	27N29	101E32	-6:46:08
Yanzhou 21	1	35N33	116E50	-7:47:20
Yanziji 13	3	32N09	118E49	-7:55:16
Yanzijiao 29	9	23N38	100E12	-6:40:48
Yanzikou 7	9	27N31	105E21	-7:01:24
Yao'an 29	9	25N32	101E12	-6:44:48
Yaoba 24	9	28N45	105E39	-7:02:36
Yaocun 21	1	35N41	116E57	-7:47:48
Yaocun 8	1	39N09	115E32	-7:42:08
Yaocun 10	1	36N12	113E50	-7:35:20
Yaodafangshen 16	11	42N27	122E59	-8:11:56
Yaoerwan 8	1	40N49	115E27	-7:41:48
Yaogongbu 30	1	29N51	120E18	-8:01:12
Yaohongcaopao 16	11	40N55	122E26	-8:09:44
Yaohuamen 1	3	32N08	118E52	-7:55:28
Yaohuangdi 16	11	41N32	122E48	-8:11:12
Yaojiaji 11	1	31N14	114E22	-7:37:28
Yaojiaqiao 13	1	32N10	119E46	-7:59:04
Yaojiatun 16	11	41N18	121E57	-8:07:48
Yaojiawopeng 16	11	41N47	122E25	-8:09:40
Yaojie 4	9	36N26	102E59	-6:51:56
Yaoling 5	1	24N49	113E58	-7:35:52
Yaolugou 16	11	40N34	119E24	-7:57:36
Yaoluzi 16	11	41N26	121E34	-8:06:16
Yaopi 12	1	26N52	113E38	-7:34:32
Yaopu 1	1	32N14	118E20	-7:53:20
Yaoqianhutun 16	11	41N32	123E36	-8:14:24
Yaoshizhen 24	9	30N11	105E30	-7:02:00
Yaotou 14	1	26N38	114E48	-7:39:12

Yaotun 9 12 49N28 127E30 -8:30:00
Yaotun 16 11 40N59 122E18 -8:09:12
Yaotutun 16 11 42N06 123E29 -8:13:56
Yaowan 13 1 34N12 118E03 -7:52:12
Yaowangmiao 16 11 40N47 120E10 -8:00:40
Yaoxian 20 9 34N56 108E53 -7:15:32
Yaozhan 9 12 52N53 125E13 -8:20:52
Yaqian 14 1 26N38 114E30 -7:38:00
Yarkand → Suoche 27 7 38N25 77E16 -5:09:04
Yashanjie 1 1 30N51 119E03 -7:56:12
Yating 6 9 25N03 106E05 -7:04:20
Yau Tong 31 4 22N18 114E13 -7:36:52
Yaxi 7 9 27N32 106E45 -7:07:00
Yaxian 5 9 18N20 109E30 -7:18:00
Yaxigang 13 1 31N23 119E10 -7:56:40
Yayuan 15 12 41N47 126E11 -8:24:44
Yazi 21 1 37N04 121E17 -8:05:08
Yazichangcun 16 11 41N16 122E26 -8:09:44
Yazikou 27 7 39N48 74E21 -4:57:24
Yecheng 27 7 37N54 77E25 -5:09:40
Yehliu 25 6 25N12 121E41 -8:06:44
Yeji 1 1 31N52 115E55 -7:43:40
Yemadu 27 7 43N36 81E50 -5:27:20
Yemagong 28 8 29N28 89E06 -5:56:24
Yemaotai 16 11 42N20 122E53 -8:11:32
Yematan 19 8 34N40 98E16 -6:33:04
Yench'eng → Yancheng 13 1 33N24 120E09 -8:00:36
Yenchi → Yanji 15 12 42N57 129E32 -8:38:08
Yengisar 27 7 38N57 76E03 -5:04:12
Yenshuichen 25 6 23N20 120E16 -8:01:04
Yeshenpu 16 11 40N51 122E32 -8:10:08
Yexian 10 1 33N37 113E20 -7:33:20
Yexian 21 1 37N13 119E54 -7:59:36
Yexie 22 2 30N56 121E19 -8:05:16
Yeyuan 21 1 36N22 118E27 -7:53:48
Yezhuang 8 1 39N10 116E18 -7:45:12
Yezhuhe 8 1 40N53 118E13 -7:52:52
Yi 17 11 42N08 118E48 -7:55:12
Yi'an 9 12 47N55 125E20 -8:21:20
Yibao 30 1 30N25 119E53 -7:59:32
Yibin (Ipin) 24 9 28N47 104E38 -6:58:32
Yibutan 24 9 28N54 104E40 -6:58:40
Yicanghe 13 1 32N47 120E43 -8:02:52
Yichang (Ichang) 11 1 30N42 111E17 -7:25:08
Yicheng 11 1 31N43 112E07 -7:28:28
Yicheng 8 1 36N48 114E17 -7:37:08
Yicheng 21 1 34N46 117E37 -7:50:28
Yichexun 29 9 26N50 103E28 -6:53:52
Yichuan 20 9 36N04 110E06 -7:20:24
Yichuan 10 1 34N26 112E24 -7:29:36
Yichun 9 12 47N42 128E55 -8:35:40
Yichun 14 1 27N50 114E23 -7:37:32
Yicun 8 1 38N57 115E37 -7:42:28
Yidan 15 12 43N24 125E25 -8:21:40
Yidie 23 1 37N08 110E30 -7:22:00
Yidu 11 1 30N22 111E22 -7:25:28
Yidu 21 1 36N41 118E28 -7:53:52
Yidun 24 9 29N56 99E22 -6:37:28
Yifeng 10 1 33N19 113E47 -7:35:08
Yifeng 14 1 28N26 114E46 -7:39:04
Yigaolou 30 1 30N56 120E20 -8:01:20
Yigou 10 1 35N51 114E20 -7:37:20
Yihe 5 1 23N50 114E53 -7:39:32
Yihechang 24 9 30N23 106E24 -7:05:36
Yihezhuang 21 1 37N53 118E23 -7:53:32
Yihezhuang 16 11 41N15 122E57 -8:11:48
Yihuang 14 1 27N34 116E10 -7:44:40
Yijiangzhen 1 1 30N55 118E28 -7:53:52
Yijiawan 12 1 27N58 113E01 -7:32:04
Yijiazi 16 11 42N29 122E41 -8:10:44
Yijingpu 8 1 40N08 117E47 -7:51:08
Yijinqiao 1 1 30N54 117E12 -7:48:48
Yijun 20 9 35N24 109E00 -7:16:00
Yikengaolu 17 9 42N17 98E19 -6:33:16
Yikou 3 1 26N45 117E00 -7:48:00
Yilaha 9 12 48N50 125E10 -8:20:40
Yilan 9 12 46N19 129E34 -8:38:16
Yilaxi 15 12 43N47 126E08 -8:24:32
Yili 24 9 30N45 105E58 -7:03:52
Yiliang 29 9 24N54 103E09 -6:52:36
Yiliang 29 9 27N35 104E01 -6:56:04
Yiliekede 17 11 48N51 121E37 -8:06:28
Yilin 13 1 33N36 119E37 -7:58:28
Yiling 13 1 32N30 119E46 -7:59:04
Yiliping 19 8 37N55 93E30 -6:14:00
Yilong 9 12 47N28 125E23 -8:21:32
Yilong 24 9 31N34 106E19 -7:05:16
Yilong 29 9 25N20 103E14 -6:52:56
Yimachi 16 11 42N11 122E15 -8:09:00
Yimatu 16 11 41N55 121E25 -8:05:40
Yimen 29 9 24N43 102E10 -6:48:40
Yimen 1 1 33N39 116E02 -7:44:08
Yimuhe 17 11 52N45 120E07 -8:00:28
Yinan (Jiehu) 21 1 35N37 118E30 -7:54:00
Yinchuan 18 9 38N30 106E18 -7:05:12
Yinfang 8 1 39N07 114E52 -7:39:28
Yingcheng 11 1 30N57 113E32 -7:34:08
Yingchengzi 15 12 44N08 125E56 -8:23:44
Yingchengzi 16 11 38N58 121E23 -8:05:32
Yingchengzi 16 11 41N50 124E04 -8:16:16
Yingchengzi 16 11 42N22 124E14 -8:16:56
Yingen 17 9 41N09 104E45 -6:59:00
Yingfang 2 1 40N14 116E17 -7:45:08
Yinggehai 5 9 18N31 108E44 -7:14:56
Yinggen 5 9 19N04 109E48 -7:19:12
Yinghe 1 1 32N16 116E31 -7:46:04
Yingjisha 27 7 38N57 76E03 -5:04:12
Yingkou 16 11 40N40 122E14 -8:08:56
Yingkou (Dashiqiao) 16 11 40N38 122E30 -8:10:00
Yingpan 7 9 25N48 106E18 -7:05:12
Yingpan 29 9 24N44 99E38 -6:38:32
Yingpanjie 29 9 25N27 98E24 -6:33:36
Yingqiao 10 1 33N58 113E39 -7:34:36
Yingshan 24 9 31N08 106E31 -7:06:04
Yingshan 11 1 30N45 115E39 -7:42:36
Yingshan 11 1 31N38 113E50 -7:35:20
Yingshang 1 1 32N38 116E15 -7:45:00
Yingshouyingzi 8 1 40N33 117E38 -7:50:32
Yingshouyingzi 8 1 40N49 117E55 -7:51:40
Yingtan 14 1 28N14 117E00 -7:48:00
Yingtaogou 16 11 42N08 121E57 -8:07:48
Yingtaoyuan 16 11 41N10 123E05 -8:12:20
Yingtian 12 1 28N50 112E56 -7:31:44
Yingxiangjie 24 9 29N24 105E11 -7:00:44
Yingxianpu 16 11 41N20 121E31 -8:06:04
Yining (Kuldja) 27 7 43N55 81E14 -5:24:56
Yinjiadai 13 1 32N03 120E07 -8:00:28
Yinjiang 7 9 28N02 108E28 -7:13:52
Yinjiawopeng 17 11 42N34 121E01 -8:04:04
Yinkeng 14 1 26N14 115E34 -7:42:16
Yinliu 26 1 39N59 117E23 -7:49:32
Yinmahe 15 12 44N07 125E44 -8:22:56
Yinong 24 9 30N19 101E01 -6:44:04
Yinping 13 1 34N15 118E39 -7:54:36
Yinqiaotou 13 1 31N52 119E13 -7:56:52
Yinshanzhen 24 9 29N41 104E58 -6:59:52
Yinwogou 8 1 41N55 117E55 -7:51:40
Yinxian 30 1 29N50 121E38 -8:06:32
Yinxiang 13 3 31N55 118E49 -7:55:16
Yinxianji 1 1 32N07 116E32 -7:46:08
Yinyangjie 16 11 42N16 121E23 -8:05:32
Yinyuan 29 9 23N26 101E54 -6:47:36
Yinzhan'ao 5 1 23N33 113E07 -7:32:28
Yi'ong 28 8 30N17 94E51 -6:19:24
Yi Pak 31 4 22N19 114E00 -7:36:00
Yipinchang 24 9 29N17 106E34 -7:06:16
Yipinglang 29 9 25N11 101E51 -6:47:24
Yiqian 14 1 26N34 116E11 -7:44:44
Yirshi 17 11 47N20 119E45 -7:59:00
Yisaduo 28 8 28N50 96E44 -6:26:56
Yishan 6 9 24N40 108E35 -7:14:20
Yishan 30 1 27N32 120E32 -8:02:08
Yishui 21 1 35N50 118E41 -7:54:44
Yisikan 17 11 49N09 124E47 -8:19:08
Yisuhe 12 1 27N46 112E54 -7:31:36
Yitajing 27 8 42N32 94E12 -6:16:48
Yitang 11 1 31N06 113E42 -7:34:48
Yitang 21 1 35N10 118E16 -7:53:04
Yiting 30 1 29N15 119E57 -7:59:48
Yitong 15 12 43N20 125E17 -8:21:08
Yitulihe 17 11 50N38 121E34 -8:06:16
Yiwu 27 8 43N15 94E15 -6:19:00
Yiwu 29 9 22N00 101E28 -6:45:52
Yiwu 30 1 29N18 120E04 -8:00:16
Yixi 5 1 23N45 116E38 -7:46:32
Yixian 1 1 29N55 117E56 -7:51:44
Yixian 8 1 39N21 115E29 -7:41:56
Yixian 16 11 41N32 121E15 -8:05:00
Yixiken 9 12 52N57 125E40 -8:22:40
Yixing 13 1 31N22 119E50 -7:59:20
Yixingbu 26 1 39N12 117E12 -7:48:48
Yixingchang 24 9 30N37 106E38 -7:06:32
Yixu 3 1 26N02 119E16 -7:57:04
Yiyang 12 1 28N36 112E20 -7:29:20
Yiyang 10 1 34N30 112E10 -7:28:40
Yiyang 14 1 28N23 117E25 -7:49:40
Yiyuan (Nanma) 21 1 36N11 118E08 -7:52:32
Yiyuankou 8 1 40N10 119E35 -7:58:20
Yizhang 12 1 25N26 112E56 -7:31:44
Yizheng 13 1 32N16 119E12 -7:56:48
Yizikong 7 9 25N38 104E28 -6:57:52
Yong'an 3 1 25N58 117E22 -7:49:28
Yongan 24 9 30N44 106E16 -7:05:04
Yong'an 24 9 29N13 104E46 -6:59:04
Yonganbao 16 11 40N15 119E52 -7:59:28
Yong'anchang 24 9 30N24 103E58 -6:55:52
Yong'anshi 12 1 28N13 113E19 -7:33:16
Yongchang 4 9 38N17 101E59 -6:47:56
Yongchang 30 1 29N13 119E20 -7:57:20
Yongchangzhen 13 1 31N42 121E44 -8:06:56
Yongcheng 10 1 33N58 116E21 -7:45:24
Yongchuan 24 9 29N21 105E54 -7:03:36
Yongchun 3 1 25N21 118E21 -7:53:24
Yongdeng 4 9 36N48 103E14 -6:52:56
Yongdian 16 11 40N34 124E48 -8:19:12
Yongding 3 1 24N46 116E43 -7:46:52
Yongfeng 1 1 29N44 116E49 -7:47:16
Yongfeng 14 1 27N19 115E24 -7:41:36
Yongfengchang 24 9 30N33 105E05 -7:00:20
Yongfu 3 1 25N05 117E20 -7:49:20
Yongguzhai 1 1 34N05 116E50 -7:47:20
Yongheshi 12 1 28N18 113E51 -7:35:24
Yongi 15 12 43N40 126E30 -8:26:00
Yongji 23 1 34N51 110E29 -7:21:56
Yongjia 30 1 28N11 120E42 -8:02:48
Yongjia 24 9 29N34 106E01 -7:04:04
Yongkang 1 1 32N32 117E24 -7:49:36
Yongkang 30 1 28N53 120E02 -8:00:08
Yongkou 3 1 26N16 118E19 -7:53:16
Yongle 9 12 45N45 125E12 -8:20:48
Yongle 8 1 39N32 115E59 -7:43:56
Yongledian 2 1 39N43 116E46 -7:47:04
Yonglong 22 2 31N34 121E48 -8:07:12
Yonglonghe 11 1 30N46 112E48 -7:31:12
Yongnian (Linmingguan) 8 1 36N47 114E30 -7:38:00
Yongnianchang 24 9 29N08 104E51 -6:59:24
Yongning 18 9 38N20 106E17 -7:05:08
Yongning 6 9 22N42 108E50 -7:15:20
Yongning 29 9 27N47 100E38 -6:42:32
Yongning 3 1 24N43 118E42 -7:54:48
Yongningcheng 2 1 40N34 116E11 -7:44:44
Yongping 29 9 25N28 99E33 -6:38:12
Yongping 14 1 28N12 117E45 -7:51:00
Yongqing 8 1 39N19 116E29 -7:45:56
Yongqing 24 9 30N00 105E27 -7:01:48
Yongquan 30 1 28N46 121E19 -8:05:16
Yongren 29 9 26N08 101E40 -6:46:40
Yongshan 29 9 28N15 103E24 -6:53:36
Yongshanqiao 14 1 29N06 117E17 -7:49:08
Yongsheng 29 9 26N42 100E43 -6:42:52
Yongshou 20 9 34N43 108E05 -7:12:20
Yongshun 12 1 28N57 109E41 -7:18:44
Yongshunchang 24 9 30N06 105E26 -7:01:44
Yongtai 3 1 25N54 118E58 -7:55:52
Yongxin 14 1 26N56 114E18 -7:37:12
Yongxin 24 9 28N59 106E32 -7:06:08
Yongxing 20 9 39N08 110E31 -7:22:04
Yongxing 12 1 26N08 113E06 -7:32:24
Yongxing 16 11 40N11 123E52 -8:15:28
Yongxing 13 1 31N56 120E55 -8:03:40
Yongxing 24 9 30N13 105E06 -7:00:24
Yongxing 24 9 30N34 105E35 -7:02:20
Yongxingchang 24 9 29N02 104E34 -6:58:16
Yongxingchang 24 9 29N37 106E23 -7:05:32
Yongxingchang 24 9 30N20 103E44 -6:54:56
Yongxiu 14 1 29N04 115E49 -7:43:16
Yongyang 14 1 26N57 114E46 -7:39:04
Yongzhai 14 1 27N59 115E26 -7:41:44
Yopurga 27 7 39N15 76E45 -5:07:00
Youcheng 14 1 29N14 116E48 -7:47:12
Youfang 13 1 32N09 119E50 -7:59:20
Youhe 10 1 32N19 113E50 -7:35:20
Youjidong 16 11 42N12 121E07 -8:04:28
Youlan 14 1 28N34 116E10 -7:44:40
Youtingpu 24 9 29N26 105E45 -7:03:00
Youxi 30 1 28N45 121E06 -8:04:24
Youxi 3 1 26N11 118E09 -7:52:36
Youxi 24 9 29N12 106E09 -7:04:36
Youxian 12 1 27N00 113E21 -7:33:24
Youxizhen 24 9 30N35 106E18 -7:05:12
Youyang 24 9 28N58 108E41 -7:14:44
Youyi 9 12 46N44 131E44 -8:46:56
Youyu 23 1 40N09 112E32 -7:30:08
Youzhagou 1 1 31N04 118E46 -7:55:04
Youzhou 8 1 40N09 115E42 -7:42:48
Yuan'an 11 1 31N04 111E26 -7:25:44
Yuanao 3 1 26N29 119E48 -7:59:12
Yuanbachang 24 9 29N44 105E27 -7:01:48
Yuanhua 30 1 30N25 120E46 -8:03:04
Yuanjiang 29 9 23N34 102E03 -6:48:12
Yuankeng 3 1 26N48 117E44 -7:50:56
Yüanli 25 6 24N27 120E39 -8:02:36
Yüanlin 25 6 23N58 120E34 -8:02:16
Yuanling 12 1 28N20 110E16 -7:21:04
Yuanmou 29 9 25N38 101E54 -6:47:36
Yuanshancun 13 1 31N08 120E20 -8:01:20
Yuanshi 8 1 37N45 114E32 -7:38:08
Yuantan 10 1 32N47 112E53 -7:31:32
Yuantan 5 1 23N39 113E12 -7:32:48
Yuantongsi 24 9 30N13 104E15 -6:57:00
Yuantouzhu 13 1 31N32 120E14 -8:00:56
Yuanxiang 10 1 34N14 115E19 -7:41:16
Yuanxiangzhen 13 1 31N39 119E15 -7:57:00
Yuanxing 24 9 30N36 104E59 -6:59:56
Yuanyang 29 9 23N12 102E52 -6:51:28
Yuanyang (Yangwu) 10 1 35N04 113E57 -7:35:48
Yuanyangpu 24 9 30N10 105E15 -7:01:00
Yuanyangqiao 24 9 29N41 106E33 -7:06:12
Yuba 28 8 29N27 97E42 -6:30:48
Yuchaozhuang 8 1 39N35 117E50 -7:51:20
Yucheng 21 1 36N56 116E39 -7:46:36
Yucheng 30 1 30N32 120E51 -8:03:24
Yuci 23 1 37N45 112E41 -7:30:44
Yudaokou 8 1 42N14 116E48 -7:47:12
Yudong 13 1 32N02 121E22 -8:05:28
Yudu 14 1 25N59 115E24 -7:41:36
Yuebo 24 9 29N03 104E12 -6:56:48
Yuecheng 10 1 32N39 114E49 -7:39:16
Yuechi 24 9 30N33 106E26 -7:05:44
Yuejiatun 16 11 41N10 120E43 -8:02:52
Yuejiawopeng 16 11 41N35 122E20 -8:09:20
Yuekou 11 1 30N32 113E03 -7:32:12
Yuelai 13 1 31N56 121E27 -8:05:48
Yuelaichang 24 9 29N44 106E32 -7:06:08
Yuelaichang 24 9 28N53 106E22 -7:05:28
Yuemenpu 24 9 30N28 106E34 -7:06:16
Yuen Long 31 4 22N26 114E02 -7:36:08
Yuepu 22 2 31N25 121E26 -8:05:44
Yuepuhu 27 7 39N15 76E45 -5:07:00
Yueqing 30 1 28N08 120E58 -8:03:52

Place			Lat.	Long.	Time
Yuewang	13	1	31N33	121E09	-8:04:36
Yuexi	24	9	28N42	102E28	-6:49:52
Yuexi	1	1	30N50	116E24	-7:45:36
Yueyang	12	1	29N23	113E06	-7:32:24
Yuezi	14	1	24N54	115E02	-7:40:08
Yufa	2	1	39N31	116E19	-7:45:16
Yufeng	24	9	30N37	105E11	-7:00:44
Yugan	14	1	28N41	116E41	-7:46:44
Yugou	13	1	33N42	118E55	-7:55:40
Yuguan	8	1	39N56	119E22	-7:57:28
Yuguo	16	11	41N52	123E15	-8:13:00
Yuhang (Linping)	30	1	30N25	120E18	-8:01:12
Yuhebu	20	9	38N01	109E37	-7:18:28
Yuhu	30	1	27N53	120E08	-8:00:32
Yuhuaizhuang	26	1	39N24	117E40	-7:50:40
Yuhuan	30	1	28N10	121E12	-8:04:48
Yujiachang	24	9	29N57	104E04	-6:56:16
Yujiacun	13	1	31N45	121E48	-8:07:12
Yujiang	14	1	28N11	116E47	-7:47:08
Yujiaqiao	13	1	31N30	119E25	-7:57:40
Yujiawan	27	8	44N32	86E45	-5:47:00
Yuke	8	1	37N58	115E39	-7:42:36
Yukou	2	1	40N12	117E00	-7:48:00
Yulao	5	10	23N31	111E46	-7:27:04
Yuli	21	1	37N00	121E25	-8:05:40
Yüli	25	6	23N20	121E18	-8:05:12
Yuliang	1	1	29N52	118E30	-7:54:00
Yuliangpu	17	11	43N26	121E55	-8:07:40
Yulin	6	9	22N36	110E07	-7:20:28
Yulin	20	9	38N20	109E29	-7:17:56
Yulin	5	9	18N16	109E32	-7:18:08
Yulincun	2	1	40N12	116E42	-7:46:48
Yulong	24	9	29N58	104E22	-6:57:28
Yumen (Laojunmiao)	4	9	39N56	97E51	-6:31:24
Yumenzhen	4	8	40N17	97E07	-6:28:28
Yumin	27	8	46N02	82E37	-5:30:28
Yunan (Ducheng)	5	10	23N11	111E29	-7:25:56
Yuncao	1	1	31N26	118E04	-7:52:16
Yuncheng	21	1	35N35	115E54	-7:43:36
Yuncheng	23	1	35N00	110E59	-7:23:56
Yundanyingzi	16	11	42N00	121E34	-8:06:16
Yungchia → Wenzhou	30	1	28N01	120E39	-8:02:36
Yungchi → Jilin	15	12	43N51	126E33	-8:26:12
Yungho	25	6	25N01	121E31	-8:06:04
Yungning → Nanning	6	9	22N48	108E20	-7:13:20
Yung Shue Wan	31	4	22N14	114E06	-7:36:24
Yunhe	30	1	28N06	119E34	-7:58:16
Yunhe → Peixian	13	1	34N21	117E59	-7:51:56
Yunjin	24	9	29N06	105E40	-7:02:40
Yunlong	29	9	25N50	99E17	-6:37:08
Yunlong	24	9	30N31	104E46	-6:59:04
Yunluchang	24	9	29N45	105E57	-7:03:48
Yunmeng	11	1	31N02	113E41	-7:34:44
Yunmenling	14	1	25N15	115E49	-7:43:16
Yunmenzhen	24	9	30N06	106E20	-7:05:20
Yunnanfu → Kunming	29	9	25N05	102E40	-6:50:40
Yunting	13	1	31N53	120E19	-8:01:16
Yunxi	11	1	32N49	110E13	-7:20:52
Yunxi	12	1	29N28	113E16	-7:33:04
Yunxian	29	9	24N30	100E03	-6:40:12
Yunxian (Yunyang)	11	1	32N49	110E49	-7:23:16
Yunxiao	3	1	24N04	117E20	-7:49:20
Yunyang	24	9	30N58	109E05	-7:16:20
Yunyang	10	1	33N28	112E42	-7:30:48
Yunzhong	14	1	29N13	117E40	-7:50:40
Yunzhou	8	1	41N01	115E44	-7:42:56
Yuping	7	9	27N07	108E47	-7:15:08
Yuqi	13	1	31N43	120E11	-8:00:44
Yuqia	19	8	38N07	94E35	-6:18:20
Yuqian'gou	16	11	41N41	121E28	-8:05:52
Yuqing	7	9	27N05	107E44	-7:10:56
Yushan	14	1	28N41	118E15	-7:53:00
Yushan	10	1	33N19	113E41	-7:34:44
Yushan	3	1	26N54	118E36	-7:54:24
Yushanzhen	24	9	29N38	108E19	-7:13:16
Yushu	15	12	44N46	126E34	-8:26:16
Yushu (Jiegu)	19	8	33N01	97E00	-6:28:00
Yushugou	27	8	44N07	87E05	-5:48:20
Yushulinzi	17	11	41N30	119E07	-7:56:28
Yushulinzi	15	12	40N59	125E57	-8:23:48
Yushupu	16	11	41N10	122E08	-8:08:32
Yushutai	15	12	43N30	124E17	-8:17:08
Yushutai	16	11	41N42	123E26	-8:13:44
Yushuwan	2	1	40N04	115E35	-7:42:20
Yusichang	24	9	29N14	105E25	-7:01:40
Yutai (Guting)	21	1	35N02	116E40	-7:46:40
Yutian	14	1	26N27	114E36	-7:38:24
Yutian	8	1	39N53	117E45	-7:51:00
Yutian	27	7	36N51	81E40	-5:26:40
Yuting	1	1	29N50	117E57	-7:51:48
Yutou	30	1	28N36	118E30	-7:54:00
Yützu → Yuci	23	1	37N45	112E41	-7:30:44
Yuwangcheng	11	1	31N31	114E29	-7:37:56
Yuxi	29	9	24N21	102E34	-6:50:16
Yuxi	3	1	25N36	119E18	-7:57:12
Yuxi	13	1	32N03	121E11	-8:04:44
Yuxi	24	9	30N19	105E47	-7:03:08
Yuxian	10	1	34N10	113E28	-7:33:52
Yuxian	8	1	39N48	114E33	-7:38:12
Yuxian	23	1	38N09	113E25	-7:33:40
Yuxiangpu	10	1	34N27	114E57	-7:39:48
Yuxiangtou	13	1	31N14	120E53	-8:03:32
Yuxikou	1	1	31N26	118E17	-7:53:08
Yuyao	30	1	30N04	121E10	-8:04:40
Zaijiafangzi	16	11	41N17	122E39	-8:10:36
Zaizhuangzi	8	1	40N02	117E43	-7:50:52
Zanggezhuang	21	1	37N28	120E57	-8:03:48
Zangji	10	1	33N01	113E52	-7:35:28
Zangwan	14	1	29N27	117E23	-7:49:32
Zanhuang	8	1	37N38	114E26	-7:37:44
Zanri	24	9	28N58	100E50	-6:43:20
Zanyang	10	1	34N00	116E13	-7:44:52
Zaohe	13	1	34N03	118E07	-7:52:28
Zaoheshi	14	1	26N53	114E41	-7:38:44
Zaojiang	8	1	37N30	115E43	-7:42:52
Zaojiaochang	24	9	29N58	106E11	-7:04:44
Zaojiatuo	8	1	39N23	118E11	-7:52:44
Zaolin	14	1	26N24	114E24	-7:37:36
Zaoshi	12	1	26N22	112E50	-7:31:20
Zaoshi	11	1	30N51	113E20	-7:33:20
Zaoxi	30	1	30N13	119E30	-7:58:00
Zaoyang	11	1	32N10	112E43	-7:30:52
Zaozhuang	21	1	34N53	117E34	-7:50:16
Zayü	28	8	28N48	97E27	-6:29:48
Zedang	28	8	29N16	91E46	-6:07:04
Zeguo	30	1	28N32	121E20	-8:05:20
Zengcheng	5	1	23N19	113E49	-7:35:16
Zengjiawan	8	1	39N22	118E24	-7:53:36
Zepu	27	7	38N13	77E16	-5:09:04
Zhada	28	7	31N30	79E30	-5:18:00
Zhage	29	9	26N20	103E51	-6:55:24
Zhagenasongduo	19	8	33N12	94E33	-6:18:12
Zhag'yab	28	8	30N32	98E00	-6:32:00
Zhahasutai	27	8	42N58	85E20	-5:41:20
Zhaihe	10	1	32N08	114E54	-7:39:36
Zhaili	3	1	27N42	117E22	-7:49:28
Zhailing	8	1	41N00	116E53	-7:47:32
Zhaiqiao	13	1	31N35	119E55	-7:59:40
Zhaitang	2	1	39N57	115E42	-7:42:48
Zhaitun	16	11	41N46	122E06	-8:08:24
Zhakou	30	1	30N23	120E47	-8:03:08
Zhakou	30	3	30N13	120E08	-8:00:32
Zhakou	11	1	29N59	112E10	-7:28:40
Zhalantun → Butehaqi	17	11	48N02	122E43	-8:10:52
Zhalanyingzi	16	11	41N29	120E37	-8:02:28
Zhalun	28	7	32N25	81E35	-5:26:20
Zhaluomude	17	11	49N13	120E22	-8:01:28
Zhancheng	21	1	37N41	117E46	-7:51:04
Zhangbei	8	1	41N04	114E48	-7:39:12
Zhangcang	21	1	35N54	119E57	-7:59:48
Zhangcun	1	1	33N20	115E59	-7:43:56
Zhangcun	14	1	28N50	117E57	-7:51:48
Zhangcun	30	1	30N28	119E22	-7:57:28
Zhangcun	30	1	30N40	119E57	-7:59:48
Zhangdang	16	11	41N54	124E05	-8:16:20
Zhangde	10	1	34N07	113E27	-7:33:48
Zhangdiyingzi	9	12	50N30	127E16	-8:29:04
Zhangdu	1	1	30N38	118E13	-7:52:52
Zhangfang	2	1	39N35	115E41	-7:42:44
Zhangfengji	21	1	35N14	116E01	-7:44:04
Zhanggang	11	1	30N34	112E51	-7:31:24
Zhanggezhuang	21	1	36N47	119E47	-7:59:08
Zhanggezhuang	2	1	40N08	116E56	-7:47:44
Zhanggou	16	11	42N07	124E06	-8:16:24
Zhangguizhuang	26	1	39N07	117E18	-7:49:12
Zhanggutai	16	11	42N40	122E28	-8:09:52
Zhanghezhuang	8	1	38N56	114E56	-7:39:44
Zhanghuang	6	9	22N01	109E27	-7:17:48
Zhanghuanggang	13	1	32N07	120E30	-8:02:00
Zhanghuban	3	1	26N23	118E29	-7:53:56
Zhangji	13	1	34N08	117E24	-7:49:36
Zhangjiachang	24	9	29N33	104E54	-6:59:36
Zhangjiachang	24	9	29N57	103E48	-6:55:12
Zhangjiachang	24	9	29N26	104E34	-6:58:16
Zhangjiadian	8	1	39N44	114E54	-7:39:36
Zhangjiagou	11	1	30N18	113E22	-7:33:28
Zhangjiaji	11	1	32N09	112E23	-7:29:32
Zhangjiajie	16	11	41N28	124E08	-8:16:32
Zhangjiakou (Kalgan)	8	1	40N50	114E53	-7:39:32
Zhangjiapang	11	1	30N25	115E47	-7:43:08
Zhangjiapu	16	11	41N18	122E02	-8:08:08
Zhangjiaqiao	13	1	31N36	120E36	-8:02:24
Zhangjiaqiao	24	9	30N02	104E15	-6:57:00
Zhangjiatou	13	1	31N38	119E05	-7:56:20
Zhangjiatun	8	1	40N37	114E57	-7:39:48
Zhangjiatun	16	11	41N05	121E44	-8:06:56
Zhangjiawa	8	1	40N10	117E52	-7:51:28
Zhangjiawan	2	1	39N51	116E41	-7:46:44
Zhangjiawopu	16	11	41N10	122E17	-8:09:08
Zhangjiayingzi	16	11	42N04	120E57	-8:03:48
Zhangjingqiao	13	1	31N39	120E27	-8:01:48
Zhangjinhe	11	1	30N14	112E35	-7:30:20
Zhangliangdian	10	1	33N42	113E02	-7:32:08
Zhangliantang	22	2	31N01	121E02	-8:04:08
Zhangling	21	1	36N32	119E29	-7:57:56
Zhanglu	21	1	36N16	115E33	-7:42:12
Zhangmang	10	1	32N03	114E32	-7:38:08
Zhangming	24	9	31N49	104E51	-6:59:24
Zhangmuqiao	1	1	31N26	116E44	-7:46:56
Zhangmushi	12	1	27N01	112E38	-7:30:32
Zhangmutou	5	1	22N55	114E05	-7:36:20
Zhangping	3	1	25N19	117E25	-7:49:40
Zhangpu	3	1	24N09	117E36	-7:50:24
Zhangpu	13	1	31N17	120E57	-8:03:48
Zhangqiangzhen	16	11	42N39	122E59	-8:11:56
Zhangqiao	1	1	32N21	117E38	-7:50:32
Zhangqiu (Mingshui)	21	1	36N43	117E30	-7:50:00
Zhangsanta	17	9	39N37	110E14	-7:20:56
Zhangsanying	8	1	41N34	117E39	-7:50:36
Zhangshitai	16	11	41N50	122E51	-8:11:24
Zhangshuping	11	1	31N20	111E02	-7:24:08
Zhangshuxia	12	1	25N54	112E45	-7:31:00
Zhangtaitai	16	11	40N59	121E05	-8:04:20
Zhangtaizi	16	11	41N22	123E16	-8:13:04
Zhangting	30	1	30N02	121E19	-8:05:16
Zhangwan	3	1	26N43	119E36	-7:58:24
Zhangwenpu	2	1	40N26	116E04	-7:44:16
Zhangwu	30	1	30N47	119E33	-7:58:12
Zhangwu	16	11	42N22	122E31	-8:10:04
Zhangwutaimen	16	11	42N16	122E42	-8:10:48
Zhangxinliuji	1	1	33N43	115E48	-7:43:12
Zhangyan	13	1	31N48	119E44	-7:58:56
Zhangyan	22	2	30N48	121E16	-8:05:04
Zhangyangongtun	16	11	40N58	120E46	-8:03:04
Zhangye	4	9	38N56	100E27	-6:41:48
Zhangze	22	2	30N55	121E15	-8:05:00
Zhangzhishan	13	1	31N56	121E01	-8:04:04
Zhangzhou (Longxi)	3	1	24N33	117E39	-7:50:36
Zhangzhu	13	1	31N16	119E37	-7:58:28
Zhangzhuang	21	1	37N03	116E32	-7:46:08
Zhangzhuang	13	1	31N57	119E52	-7:59:28
Zhangzhuang	21	1	36N02	118E01	-7:52:04
Zhanhua (Fuguo)	21	1	37N42	118E08	-7:52:32
Zhanji	10	1	34N14	115E52	-7:43:28
Zhanjiajing	24	9	29N15	104E55	-6:59:40
Zhanjiang	5	8	21N12	110E23	-7:21:32
Zhanjiaqiao	12	1	29N19	113E34	-7:34:16
Zhanjiaqiao	30	1	30N25	120E08	-8:00:32
Zhanyang	3	1	25N30	119E28	-7:57:52
Zhanyi	29	9	25N38	103E43	-6:54:52
Zhanyu	15	12	44N31	122E37	-8:10:28
Zhao'an	3	1	23N47	117E12	-7:48:48
Zhaobeikou	8	1	38N55	116E06	-7:44:24
Zhaochuan	8	1	40N41	115E18	-7:41:12
Zhaocun	2	1	39N35	116E14	-7:44:56
Zhaodong	9	12	46N05	125E59	-8:23:56
Zhaogezhuang	21	1	37N27	120E37	-8:02:28
Zhaogezhuang	8	1	39N45	118E24	-7:53:36
Zhaoguang	9	12	48N07	126E43	-8:26:52
Zhaohe	10	1	33N12	112E49	-7:31:16
Zhaohuazhen	24	9	29N02	105E08	-7:00:32
Zhaojiagou	16	11	40N47	123E27	-8:13:48
Zhaojiapuzi	16	11	40N51	123E49	-8:15:16
Zhaojiaqiao	30	1	30N44	121E12	-8:04:48
Zhaojiatangfang	16	11	42N07	122E57	-8:11:48
Zhaojiatun	16	11	41N24	121E53	-8:07:32
Zhaojiawopeng	16	11	42N30	123E06	-8:12:24
Zhaojiaying	8	1	38N58	116E42	-7:46:48
Zhaojue	24	9	28N15	102E50	-6:51:20
Zhaomaozhuang	8	1	39N28	117E59	-7:51:56
Zhaomutun	16	11	41N10	121E38	-8:06:32
Zhaoping	6	9	24N03	110E52	-7:23:28
Zhaoqiao	14	1	28N42	114E45	-7:39:00
Zhaoqing (Gaoyao)	5	10	23N03	112E27	-7:29:48
Zhaosu	27	7	43N06	81E08	-5:24:32
Zhaotan	1	1	29N42	116E48	-7:47:12
Zhaotong	29	9	27N19	103E48	-6:55:12
Zhaotun	16	11	41N54	121E59	-8:07:56
Zhaoxian	8	1	37N45	114E46	-7:39:04
Zhaoxian	21	1	35N44	118E55	-7:55:40
Zhaoxing	9	12	47N43	131E19	-8:45:16
Zhaoya	24	9	29N00	105E35	-7:02:20
Zhaoyi	2	1	39N55	116E43	-7:46:52
Zhaoyuan	9	12	45N31	125E09	-8:20:36
Zhaoyuan	21	1	37N22	120E24	-8:01:36
Zhaozhou	9	12	45N41	125E21	-8:21:24
Zhaozhuang	1	1	34N14	116E38	-7:46:32
Zhaozhuang	13	1	34N45	116E27	-7:45:48
Zhaozhuangzi	26	1	39N10	117E20	-7:49:20
Zhapu	30	1	30N36	121E05	-8:04:20
Zhashui	20	9	33N40	109E01	-7:16:04
Zhaxigang	28	7	32N32	79E41	-5:18:44
Zhayi	24	9	28N34	99E09	-6:36:36
Zhaze	13	1	32N09	119E29	-7:57:56
Zhecheng	10	1	34N06	115E19	-7:41:16
Zhegao	1	1	31N46	117E45	-7:51:00

Zhegu 28 8 28N43 91E43 -6:06:52
Zhêhor 24 9 31N41 100E24 -6:41:36
Zhelang 5 1 22N43 115E32 -7:42:08
Zhelin 14 1 29N14 115E30 -7:42:00
Zhelin 22 2 30N50 121E29 -8:05:56
Zhelin 5 1 23N36 117E06 -7:48:24
Zhen'an 20 9 33N27 109E01 -7:16:04
Zhenbeikou 18 9 39N15 106E17 -7:05:08
Zhenbiancheng 2
1 40N10 115E49 -7:43:16
Zhenchang 13 1 32N04 121E02 -8:04:08
Zhenchang 8 1 39N47 115E24 -7:41:36
Zhenfeng 7 9 25N23 105E41 -7:02:44
Zheng'an 7 9 28N31 107E29 -7:09:56
Zheng'anpu 16 11 41N43 121E56 -8:07:44
Zhengcun 8 1 39N13 115E40 -7:42:40
Zhengding 8 1 38N10 114E34 -7:38:16
Zhengdongyu 13 1 31N59 120E10 -8:00:40
Zhengfang 14 1 28N42 117E53 -7:51:32
Zhengguanchang 24
9 29N54 106E35 -7:06:20
Zhengguo 5 1 23N25 113E53 -7:35:32
Zhenghe 3 1 27N22 118E50 -7:55:20
Zhengji 13 1 34N26 117E01 -7:48:04
Zhengjiadiancun 16
11 41N05 122E20 -8:09:20
Zhengjiawu 30 1 29N29 120E05 -8:00:20
Zhenglan Qi (Dund Hot) 17
1 42N16 115E49 -7:43:16
Zhengning 4 9 35N22 108E24 -7:13:36
Zhengping 14 1 25N22 114E46 -7:39:04
Zhen'guosi 2 1 39N51 116E21 -7:45:24
Zhengxiangbai Qi (Qagan Nur) 17
1 42N16 114E52 -7:39:28
Zhengyang 10 1 32N37 114E23 -7:37:32
Zhengyangguan 1
1 32N28 116E32 -7:46:08
Zhengyi 13 1 31N23 120E52 -8:03:28
Zhengzhou (Chengchow) 10
1 34N48 113E39 -7:34:36
Zhengzhuang 30 1 28N11 119E01 -7:56:04
Zhengzi 24 9 29N22 104E16 -6:57:04
Zhengzichang 24
9 29N08 106E38 -7:06:32
Zhenhai 30 1 29N57 121E42 -8:06:48
Zhenhai 3 1 24N16 118E06 -7:52:24
Zhenhai 5 10 21N53 112E25 -7:29:40
Zhenjiang 16 11 40N44 125E28 -8:21:52
Zhenjiang 13 1 32N13 119E26 -7:57:44
Zhenjiangguan 24
9 32N25 103E35 -6:54:20
Zhenjiaqiao 13 1 32N08 120E49 -8:03:16
Zhenjinqiao 24 9 30N12 104E22 -6:57:28
Zhenkang 29 9 24N06 99E16 -6:37:04
Zhenlai 15 12 45N52 123E14 -8:12:56
Zhenning 7 9 26N05 105E46 -7:03:04
Zhenping 10 1 33N08 112E19 -7:29:16
Zhenru 22 2 31N15 121E24 -8:05:36
Zhentou 14 1 27N04 114E56 -7:39:44
Zhentoudian 14 1 29N10 117E29 -7:49:56
Zhentoushi 12 1 28N01 113E20 -7:33:20
Zhenxi 24 9 29N29 104E33 -6:58:12
Zhenxiaguan 30 1 27N12 120E28 -8:01:52
Zhenxing 16 11 42N38 124E53 -8:19:32
Zhenxiong 29 9 27N27 104E50 -6:59:20
Zhenyu 3 1 27N08 120E18 -8:01:12
Zhenyuan 4 9 35N46 107E18 -7:09:12
Zhenyuan 7 9 26N53 108E19 -7:13:16
Zhenze 13 1 30N55 120E30 -8:02:00
Zhenzhumen 15 12 41N53 126E45 -8:27:00
Zhenzichang 24 9 29N52 104E12 -6:56:48
Zhenzichang 24 9 30N38 104E20 -6:57:20
Zhenzichang 24 9 29N59 105E11 -7:00:44
Zhenzijie 24 9 28N48 106E40 -7:06:40
Zhenziling 16 11 42N10 124E12 -8:16:48
Zhenzizhen 8 1 39N50 118E20 -7:53:20
Zheqiao 12 1 26N27 112E48 -7:31:12
Zherong 3 1 27N16 119E54 -7:59:36
Zheshan 30 1 30N15 120E24 -8:01:36
Zhetang 13 1 31N45 118E55 -7:55:40
Zhidan 20 9 37N00 108E40 -7:14:40
Zhidoi 19 8 33N08 94E50 -6:19:20
Zhierling 23 1 40N26 114E16 -7:37:04
Zhigou 21 1 35N55 119E13 -7:56:52
Zhijiang 12 1 27N27 109E41 -7:18:44
Zhijin 7 9 26N41 105E37 -7:02:28
Zhili 30 1 30N52 120E16 -8:01:04
Zhitan 14 1 29N35 117E16 -7:49:04
Zhitang 13 1 31N33 121E01 -8:04:04
Zhitang 13 1 31N36 120E58 -8:03:52
Zhitouji 13 1 33N28 118E18 -7:53:12
Zhiwucun 30 1 30N38 119E47 -7:59:08
Zhixi 5 1 23N57 114E33 -7:38:12
Zhixia 30 1 29N42 119E36 -7:58:24
Zhixiqiao 13 1 31N49 119E29 -7:57:56
Zhiyang 10 1 33N47 113E07 -7:32:28
Zhizushan 16 11 41N50 121E24 -8:05:36
Zhonganpu 16 11 41N37 121E58 -8:07:52
Zhong'aozhen 24
9 29N46 105E41 -7:02:44
Zhongba 28 8 29N54 83E40 -5:34:40
Zhongba 5 1 23N43 115E22 -7:41:28
Zhongbu 1 1 31N40 117E45 -7:51:00
Zhongbu 14 1 28N50 117E16 -7:49:04
Zhongbu 1 1 31N25 117E45 -7:51:00
Zhongchuan 3 1 26N58 119E27 -7:57:48
Zhongcun 20 9 33N27 110E05 -7:20:20
Zhongdai 30 1 30N46 120E59 -8:03:56
Zhongdian 29 9 27N50 99E40 -6:38:40
Zhongdu 13 1 33N04 118E46 -7:55:04
Zhongdu 24 9 28N46 103E58 -6:55:52
Zhongduan 3 1 25N17 116E41 -7:46:44
Zhongerchong 16
11 41N58 123E58 -8:15:52
Zhonggang 1 1 32N38 115E45 -7:43:00

Zhonggong 21 1 36N30 117E01 -7:48:04
Zhonggoumen 8 1 41N00 116E26 -7:45:44
Zhonggu 16 11 42N27 124E00 -8:16:00
Zhongguan 30 1 30N39 120E11 -8:00:44
Zhonghe 7 9 27N11 103E52 -6:55:28
Zhonghechang 24
9 30N12 104E49 -6:59:16
Zhongheying 29 9 23N48 103E36 -6:54:24
Zhonghezhen 24 9 30N34 104E06 -6:56:24
Zhonghuamen 13 3 32N01 118E46 -7:55:04
Zhonghuopu 11 1 29N44 113E59 -7:35:56
Zhongjianchang 24
9 28N46 106E13 -7:04:52
Zhongjiang 24 9 31N00 104E18 -6:57:12
Zhongjiatai 16
11 40N48 122E46 -8:11:04
Zhonglou 21 1 35N24 119E02 -7:56:08
Zhongluotan 5 1 23N23 113E23 -7:33:32
Zhongluyantai 16
11 41N32 123E17 -8:13:08
Zhongmeihe 1 1 31N19 116E45 -7:47:00
Zhongmou 10 1 34N46 114E01 -7:36:04
Zhongning 18 9 37N27 105E38 -7:02:32
Zhongpingchang 11
1 31N15 110E10 -7:20:40
Zhongqiao 1 1 31N11 119E11 -7:56:44
Zhongsha 3 1 26N24 116E36 -7:46:24
Zhongshan 3 1 26N12 117E26 -7:49:44
Zhongshan (Shiqizhen) 5
1 22N31 113E22 -7:33:28
Zhongtou 10 1 34N00 113E21 -7:33:24
Zhongwei 18 9 37N33 105E10 -7:00:40
Zhongwopu 4 9 38N30 102E59 -6:51:56
Zhongxian 24 9 30N29 108E05 -7:12:20
Zhongxian 14 1 27N17 116E47 -7:47:08
Zhongxiang 11 1 31N11 112E33 -7:30:12
Zhongxiangzhen 24
9 29N50 104E08 -6:56:32
Zhongxin 5 1 24N14 114E44 -7:38:56
Zhongxin 16 11 40N47 124E08 -8:16:32
Zhongxin 5 1 23N16 113E38 -7:34:32
Zhongxing 13 1 32N17 119E34 -7:58:16
Zhongxing 24 9 30N12 103E32 -6:54:08
Zhongxingchang 24
9 29N07 105E18 -7:01:12
Zhongxinzhen 24
9 30N30 104E03 -6:56:12
Zhongxinzhen 24
9 30N16 106E15 -7:05:00
Zhongyangqu 16
11 40N47 122E05 -8:08:20
Zhongyaozhan 9
12 50N46 125E54 -8:23:36
Zhongyi 11 1 31N08 114E52 -7:39:28
Zhongying 8 1 39N38 117E06 -7:48:24
Zhongzangcun 8 1 38N52 115E38 -7:42:32
Zhongzhan 5 1 25N16 114E24 -7:37:36
Zhongzhuang 8 1 39N25 114E47 -7:39:08
Zhouba 24 9 29N06 103E43 -6:54:52
Zhoubachang 24 9 28N59 103E52 -6:55:28
Zhoucun 21 1 36N47 117E48 -7:51:12
Zhoudangfan 10 1 31N54 114E31 -7:38:04
Zhoujiachang 24
9 30N33 104E25 -6:57:40
Zhoujiadai 13 1 32N12 120E26 -8:01:44
Zhoujiadu 22 2 31N11 121E29 -8:05:56
Zhoujiagou 24 9 30N08 104E30 -6:58:00
Zhoujiatun 16 11 41N29 121E50 -8:07:20
Zhoujiatun 16 11 41N04 120E47 -8:03:08
Zhoujiatun 16 11 41N16 120E58 -8:03:52
Zhoujiatun 16 11 41N34 121E05 -8:04:20
Zhoujiawopu 16
11 42N31 122E45 -8:11:00
Zhoujiayao 16 11 41N19 122E48 -8:11:12
Zhoujingxiang 13
1 31N32 120E23 -8:01:32
Zhoukoudianzhen 2
1 39N41 115E56 -7:43:44
Zhoulichang 24 9 29N55 105E09 -7:00:36
Zhouning 3 1 27N16 119E12 -7:56:48
Zhoupo 24 9 29N48 104E01 -6:56:04
Zhoupu 22 2 31N07 121E34 -8:06:16
Zhouqu 4 9 33N43 104E10 -6:56:40
Zhouquan 30 1 30N35 120E21 -8:01:24
Zhoushu 13 1 31N28 120E59 -8:03:56
Zhoushuizi 16 11 38N57 121E34 -8:06:16
Zhoutieqiao 13 1 31N26 120E00 -8:00:00
Zhouwangmiao 30
1 30N28 120E29 -8:01:56
Zhouxi 14 1 29N13 116E20 -7:45:20
Zhouxiang 30 1 30N10 121E08 -8:04:32
Zhouxinzhen 13 1 31N30 120E18 -8:01:12
Zhouzhai 13 1 32N02 121E31 -8:06:04
Zhouzhi 20 9 34N12 108E10 -7:12:40
Zhouzhuang 13 1 32N15 120E08 -8:00:32
Zhouzhuang 8 1 39N09 115E18 -7:41:12
Zhouzhuang 13 1 31N06 120E51 -8:03:24
Zhuanghang 22 2 30N54 121E23 -8:05:32
Zhuanghe 16 11 39N43 123E01 -8:12:04
Zhuangji 10 1 34N20 115E15 -7:41:00
Zhuangtou 8 1 40N55 117E57 -7:51:48
Zhuangtouyingzi 16
11 41N43 120E32 -8:02:08
Zhuangtouyingzi 16
11 41N50 120E43 -8:02:52
Zhuangxi 24 9 30N33 104E31 -6:58:04
Zhuangyuanqiao 30
1 27N54 120E48 -8:03:12
Zhuanqiao 22 2 31N04 121E23 -8:05:32
Zhuantouwan 11 1 31N29 112E24 -7:29:36
Zhuanwantai 16
11 41N20 122E22 -8:09:28
Zhuao 30 1 29N05 121E16 -8:05:04
Zhucang 7 9 27N18 107E26 -7:09:44
Zhucheng 21 1 36N00 119E24 -7:57:36

Zhudi 22 2 31N12 121E18 -8:05:12
Zhudian 11 1 30N33 115E12 -7:40:48
Zhuergan 17 11 52N04 120E48 -8:03:12
Zhufengzhen 1 1 30N35 118E56 -7:55:44
Zhufuo 24 9 29N02 105E51 -7:03:24
Zhuganpu 10 1 32N13 114E39 -7:38:36
Zhugao 24 9 30N37 104E40 -6:58:40
Zhuge 30 1 29N15 119E18 -7:57:12
Zhuge 21 1 36N00 118E32 -7:54:08
Zhugentan 24 9 29N25 103E50 -6:55:20
Zhugou 21 1 36N52 120E15 -8:01:00
Zhugouzhen 10 1 32N47 113E42 -7:34:48
Zhugusi 19 9 37N01 102E27 -6:49:48
Zhuhe 11 1 29N44 113E06 -7:32:24
Zhuhongyu 16 11 40N48 123E00 -8:12:00
Zhuji 30 1 29N43 120E14 -8:00:56
Zhujiabeng 13 3 31N21 120E41 -8:02:44
Zhujiabian 13 1 31N38 119E11 -7:56:44
Zhujiachang 24 9 29N48 104E20 -6:57:20
Zhujiachang 24 9 30N03 104E13 -6:56:52
Zhujiafang 16 11 41N20 122E40 -8:10:40
Zhujiahang 22 2 30N51 121E19 -8:05:16
Zhujiahe 13 1 31N08 120E53 -8:03:32
Zhujiajiao 22 2 31N06 121E02 -8:04:08
Zhujiajiaotou 22
2 31N24 121E11 -8:04:44
Zhujiangqing 14
1 27N18 114E44 -7:38:56
Zhujiaqiao 1 1 30N26 119E03 -7:56:12
Zhujiawan 11 1 30N56 114E10 -7:36:40
Zhujiawan 8 1 40N08 114E56 -7:39:44
Zhujiawan 1 1 32N28 117E29 -7:49:56
Zhujiawopeng 16
11 42N27 122E13 -8:08:52
Zhujiesi 19 8 33N34 97E21 -6:29:24
Zhukeng 5 1 23N49 112E55 -7:31:40
Zhukou 3 1 26N58 117E16 -7:49:04
Zhukou 10 1 34N07 115E04 -7:40:16
Zhukou 30 1 27N41 118E53 -7:55:32
Zhulanbu 14 1 25N36 115E46 -7:43:04
Zhulin 11 1 32N20 113E38 -7:34:32
Zhulin 13 1 31N45 119E27 -7:57:48
Zhulongqiao 1 1 32N21 118E09 -7:52:36
Zhuluke 16 11 41N36 119E54 -7:59:36
Zhumadian 10 1 32N58 114E03 -7:36:12
Zhuolu 8 1 40N22 115E12 -7:40:48
Zhuoni 4 9 34N32 103E24 -6:53:36
Zhuotian 3 1 25N38 116E13 -7:44:52
Zhuoxian 8 1 39N30 115E58 -7:43:52
Zhuozi 17 9 40N52 112E33 -7:30:12
Zhuqianzongpuzi 16
11 42N17 123E18 -8:13:12
Zhuqiao 30 1 30N26 120E36 -8:02:24
Zhuqiao 22 2 31N07 121E44 -8:06:56
Zhuqiao 21 1 37N22 120E05 -8:00:20
Zhurushan 11 1 30N26 113E48 -7:35:12
Zhushan 11 1 32N10 110E19 -7:21:16
Zhusigang 1 1 31N14 118E23 -7:53:32
Zhutan 14 1 28N04 114E10 -7:36:40
Zhutang 1 1 31N06 118E39 -7:54:36
Zhutang 13 1 31N47 120E24 -8:01:36
Zhutian 14 1 28N43 117E01 -7:48:04
Zhuting 12 1 27N24 113E04 -7:32:16
Zhuting 14 1 27N48 114E02 -7:36:08
Zhuwo 2 1 40N02 115E48 -7:43:12
Zhuwotuo 24 9 30N31 104E34 -6:58:16
Zhuwumiao 1 1 30N54 116E19 -7:45:16
Zhuxi 30 1 28N10 118E53 -7:55:32
Zhuxi 24 9 29N32 105E40 -7:02:40
Zhuxi 11 1 32N09 109E42 -7:18:48
Zhuxianzhen 10 1 34N37 114E16 -7:37:04
Zhuxichang 14 1 28N58 114E06 -7:36:24
Zhuya 21 1 36N38 118E12 -7:52:48
Zhuyang 21 1 36N16 117E22 -7:49:28
Zhuyangxi 24 9 29N03 105E57 -7:03:48
Zhuyangzhen 23 1 34N20 110E44 -7:22:56
Zhuyuan 24 9 29N34 104E08 -6:56:32
Zhuzeqiao 13 1 31N34 119E20 -7:57:20
Zhuzhenji 13 1 32N31 118E42 -7:54:48
Zhuzhou (Chuchow) 12
1 27N50 113E09 -7:32:36
Zhuzikou 12 1 29N17 112E41 -7:30:44
Zibo (Zhangdian) 21
1 36N47 118E01 -7:52:04
Zichang 20 9 37N19 109E33 -7:18:12
Zichuan 21 1 36N38 117E55 -7:51:40
Zigong (Tzukung) 24
9 29N24 104E47 -6:59:08
Zigui 11 1 31N00 110E31 -7:22:04
Zigutaicun 16 11 42N01 121E16 -8:05:04
Zihedian 21 1 36N48 118E22 -7:53:28
Zihukou 12 1 28N44 112E33 -7:30:12
Zihukou 14 1 28N55 118E08 -7:52:32
Ziiyang 20 9 32N31 108E48 -7:15:12
Zijiao 21 1 37N21 117E25 -7:49:40
Zijin 5 1 23N40 115E11 -7:40:44
Zijingguan 8 1 39N23 115E12 -7:40:48
Zikatse → Rikaze 28
8 29N17 88E53 -5:55:32
Zikoufang 3 1 26N22 117E24 -7:49:36
Zili 29 9 26N50 100E27 -6:41:48
Zishan 14 1 25N57 115E35 -7:42:20
Zisuntang 1 1 30N38 118E42 -7:54:48
Zitong 24 9 31N43 105E10 -7:00:40
Ziwuji 1 1 32N55 115E58 -7:43:52
Zixi 14 1 27N42 117E02 -7:48:08
Zixi 14 1 28N01 117E46 -7:51:04
Zixing 12 1 26N00 113E23 -7:33:32
Ziyang 24 9 30N07 104E39 -6:58:36
Ziyuan 6 9 26N01 110E31 -7:22:04
Ziyun 7 9 25N43 106E05 -7:04:20
Zizhong 24 9 29N48 104E50 -6:59:20
Zizhou 20 9 37N37 109E41 -7:18:44
Zogang 28 8 29N55 97E44 -6:30:56
Zongchang 24 9 28N52 104E36 -6:58:24

CHINA — CHINE — PEOPLE'S REPUBLIC — ZHONGGUO

Place		Lat	Long	Time
Zongyang 1	1	30N42	117E12	-7:48:48
Zoumagang 24	9	29N28	106E18	-7:05:12
Zoumayi 8	1	39N07	114E34	-7:38:16
Zouping 21	1	36N53	117E42	-7:50:48
Zouxian 21	1	35N24	117E00	-7:48:00
Zunhua 8	1	40N12	117E58	-7:51:52
Zunsuzhi 17	1	44N40	112E50	-7:31:20
Zunyi 7	9	27N39	106E57	-7:07:48
Zuo'an 14	1	26N10	114E16	-7:37:04
Zuodeng 6	9	23N27	106E57	-7:07:48
Zuogezhuang 8	1	39N01	116E37	-7:46:28
Zuomaozigou 16	11	42N12	120E41	-8:02:44
Zuoquan 23	1	37N03	113E30	-7:34:00
Zuosuo 24	9	27N45	100E54	-6:43:36
Zuotema 27	7	35N50	80E45	-5:23:00
Zuowei 8	1	40N41	114E43	-7:38:52
Zuoxiunulemiao 17	11	48N08	115E38	-7:42:32
Zuoyun 23	1	40N02	112E54	-7:31:36

CISKEI — CISKEI

Time Table

Before 8 Feb 1892	LMT	
Begin Standard		22E30
8 Feb 1892	0:00	-1:30
Begin Standard		30E00
1 Mar 1903	0:00	-2:00
20 Sep 1942	2:00	-3:00
21 Mar 1943	2:00	-2:00
19 Sep 1943	2:00	-3:00
19 Mar 1944	2:00	-2:00

Place	Lat	Long	Time
Alice	32s47	26E50	-1:47:20
Bell	33s15	27E23	-1:49:32
Berlin	32s54	27E35	-1:50:20
Bisho	32s50	27E20	-1:49:20
Braunschweig	32s48	27E22	-1:49:28
Fort Beaufort	32s46	26E40	-1:46:40
Frankfort	32s44	27E26	-1:49:44
Hamburg	33s17	27E28	-1:49:52
Keiskammahoek	32s41	27E09	-1:48:36
Peddie	33s14	27E07	-1:48:28
Potsdam	32s56	27E42	-1:50:48
Seymour	32s33	26E46	-1:47:04
Whittlesea	32s10	26E50	-1:47:20
Wooldridge	33s13	27E15	-1:49:00

COLOMBIA — KOLUMBIEN — COLOMBIE

Time Table

Before 13 Mar 1884	LMT	
Begin Standard		74w05
13 Mar 1884	0:00	4:56
Begin Standard		75w00
23 Nov 1914	0:00	5:00

Place	Lat	Long	Time
Abejorral	5N47	75w26	5:01:44
Ábrego	8N05	73w13	4:52:52
Acacías	3N59	73w46	4:55:04
Acandí	8N32	77w14	5:08:56
Achí	8N34	74w33	4:58:12
Agrado	2N15	75w46	5:03:04
Aguachica	8N19	73w38	4:54:32
Aguadas	5N37	75w27	5:01:48
Agua de Dios	4N23	74w40	4:58:40
Agustín Codazzi	10N02	73w14	4:52:56
Aipe	3N13	75w15	5:01:00
Algeciras	2N35	75w18	5:01:12
Amalfi	6N55	75w04	5:00:16
Ambalema	4N47	74w46	4:59:04
Andes	5N40	75w53	5:03:32
Anorí	7N05	75w08	5:00:32
Anserma	5N13	75w48	5:03:12
Antioquia	6N33	75w50	5:03:20
Apía	5N05	75w58	5:03:52
Aracataca	10N36	74w12	4:56:48
Arambaza	2s04	73w06	4:52:24
Arauca	7N05	70w45	4:43:00
Arauquita	7N02	71w25	4:45:40
Arboletes	8N51	76w26	5:05:44
Arica	2s08	71w47	4:47:08
Arjona	10N15	75w21	5:01:24
Armenia	4N31	75w41	5:02:44
Armero	4N58	74w54	4:59:36
Ataco	3N35	75w23	5:01:32
Ayapel	8N19	75w09	5:00:36
Baranoa	10N48	74w55	4:59:40
Baraya	3N10	75w04	5:00:16
Barbacoas	1N41	78w09	5:12:36
Bárbara	0s53	72w30	4:50:00
Barbosa	6N26	75w20	5:01:20
Barbosa	5N57	73w37	4:54:28
Barichara	6N38	73w14	4:52:56
Barrancabermeja	7N03	73w52	4:55:28
Barrancas	10N57	72w50	4:51:20
Barranquilla	10N59	74w48	4:59:12
Belén	6N00	72w55	4:51:40
Belén	1N26	75w56	5:03:44
Bello	6N20	75w33	5:02:12
Boavita	6N20	72w35	4:50:20
Bogotá	4N36	74w05	4:56:20
Bolívar	5N50	76w01	5:04:04
Bolívar	1N50	76w58	5:07:52
Bolívar	4N21	76w10	5:04:40
Bucaramanga	7N08	73w09	4:52:36
Buenaventura	3N53	77w04	5:08:16
Buenos Aires	3N02	76w38	5:06:32
Buesaco	1N23	77w09	5:08:36
Buga	3N54	76w17	5:05:08
Bugalagrande	4N11	76w09	5:04:36
Cabuyaro	4N18	72w49	4:51:16
Cáceres	7N35	75w20	5:01:20
Caicedonia	4N20	75w50	5:03:20
Calamar	10N15	74w55	4:59:40
Calamar	1N58	72w41	4:50:44
Calarcá	4N31	75w38	5:02:32
Caldas	6N05	75w38	5:02:32
Cali	3N27	76w31	5:06:04
Campoalegre	2N41	75w20	5:01:20
Campo de la Cruz	10N23	74w53	4:59:32
Cananguchal	0N51	75w47	5:03:08
Cañasgordas	6N45	76w01	5:04:04
Candelaria	3N25	76w20	5:05:20
Caqueza	4N25	73w55	4:55:40
Carmen de Apicalá	4N09	74w44	4:58:56
Carolina	6N43	75w17	5:01:08
Cartagena	10N25	75w32	5:02:08
Cartago	4N45	75w55	5:03:40
Caucasia	8N00	75w12	5:00:48
Cereté	8N53	75w48	5:03:12
Chafurray	3N10	73w14	4:52:56
Chaparral	3N43	75w28	5:01:52
Charalá	6N17	73w10	4:52:40
Cháviva	4N22	72w20	4:49:20
Chía	4N52	74w04	4:56:16
Chigorodó	7N41	76w42	5:06:48
Chimichagua	9N15	73w49	4:55:16
Chinácota	7N37	72w36	4:50:24
Chinchiná	4N58	75w36	5:02:24
Chinú	9N06	75w24	5:01:36
Chiquinquirá	5N37	73w50	4:55:20
Chiriguaná	9N22	73w36	4:54:24
Chiscas	6N33	72w29	4:49:56
Chita	6N11	72w28	4:49:52
Chitagá	7N09	72w40	4:50:40
Chocontá	5N09	73w41	4:54:44
Ciénaga	11N01	74w15	4:57:00
Ciénaga de Oro	8N53	75w37	5:02:28
Cisneros	6N33	75w04	5:00:16
Colombia	3N24	74w49	4:59:16
Concepción	6N46	72w42	4:50:48
Condoto	5N06	76w37	5:06:28
Contratación	6N18	73w29	4:53:56
Convención	8N28	73w21	4:53:24
Corozal	9N19	75w18	5:01:12
Cravo Norte	6N18	70w12	4:40:48
Cúcuta	7N54	72w31	4:50:04
Cumbal	0N54	77w47	5:11:08
Dabeiba	7N01	76w16	5:05:04
Dagua	3N40	76w41	5:06:44
Darién	3N56	76w31	5:06:04
Dolores	3N33	74w54	4:59:36
Don Matías	6N30	75w22	5:01:28
Duitama	5N50	73w02	4:52:08
El Banco	9N00	73w58	4:55:52
El Bordo	2N06	76w58	5:07:52
El Calvario	4N22	73w40	4:54:40
El Carmen	8N30	73w27	4:53:48
El Carmen de Bolívar	9N43	75w08	5:00:32
El Cerrito	3N42	76w19	5:05:16
El Cocuy	6N25	72w27	4:49:48
El Diviso	1N22	78w14	5:12:56
El Encanto	1s37	73w14	4:52:56
El Guamo	10N02	74w59	4:59:56
El Pato	2N50	74w48	4:59:12
El Piñón	10N24	74w50	4:59:20
El Tambo	1N26	77w23	5:09:32
El Tigre	2N28	68w15	4:33:00
El Trapiche	3N03	77w33	5:10:12
El Yopal	5N21	72w23	4:49:32
Envigado	6N10	75w35	5:02:20
Espinal	4N09	74w53	4:59:32
Facatativá	4N49	74w22	4:57:28
Firavitoba	5N40	73w00	4:52:00
Flandes	4N18	74w49	4:59:16
Florencia	1N36	75w36	5:02:24
Florida	3N21	76w15	5:05:00
Floridablanca	7N04	73w06	4:52:24
Fonseca	10N54	72w51	4:51:24
Fontibón	4N40	74w09	4:56:36
Fredonia	5N55	75w41	5:02:44
Fresno	5N09	75w01	5:00:04
Frontino	6N46	76w08	5:04:32
Fuente de Oro	3N28	73w37	4:54:28
Fundación	10N31	74w11	4:56:44
Fusagasugá	4N21	74w22	4:57:28
Gachetá	4N49	73w36	4:54:24
Gamarra	8N20	73w45	4:55:00
Garagoa	5N05	73w21	4:53:24
Garzón	2N12	75w38	5:U2:32
Gigante	2N23	75w33	5:02:12
Girardot	4N18	74w48	4:59:12
Gómez Plata	6N41	75w12	5:00:48
Gramalote	7N53	72w48	4:51:12
Granada	3N34	73w45	4:55:00
Guacarí	3N46	76w20	5:05:20
Guadalupe	2N01	75w45	5:03:00
Guamal	9N09	74w14	4:56:56
Guamal	3N52	73w44	4:54:56
Guamo	4N02	74w58	4:59:52
Guapí	2N36	77w54	5:11:36
Guateque	5N00	73w28	4:53:52
Güicán	6N28	72w25	4:49:40
Hobo	2N35	75w27	5:01:48

COLOMBIE KOLUMBIEN COLOMBIA

Place	Lat	Long	Time
Honda	5N12	74w45	4:59:00
Ibagué	4N27	75w14	5:00:56
Ipiales	0N50	77w37	5:10:28
Istmina	5N10	76w39	5:06:36
Itagüí	6N10	75w36	5:02:24
Ituango	7N04	75w45	5:03:00
Jamundí	3N15	76w32	5:06:08
Jericó	5N47	75w47	5:03:08
La Chorrera	0s44	73w01	4:52:04
La Cruz	1N35	76w58	5:07:52
La Dorada	5N27	74w40	4:58:40
La Gloria	8N37	73w48	4:55:12
La Horqueta	3N06	72w50	4:51:20
La Palma	5N22	74w24	4:57:36
La Paz	10N23	73w10	4:52:40
La Pedrera	1s18	69w43	4:38:52
La Plata	2N23	75w53	5:03:32
La Tagua	0s03	74w40	4:58:40
La Unión	1N36	77w09	5:08:36
La Virginia	4N54	75w53	5:03:32
Leiva	5N38	73w34	4:54:16
Lérida	0N10	70w42	4:42:48
Leticia	4s09	69w57	4:39:48
Líbano	4N55	75w04	5:00:16
Linares	1N23	77w31	5:10:04
Loreto	3s48	70w15	4:41:00
Lorica	9N14	75w49	5:03:16
Maceo	6N33	74w47	4:59:08
Macujer	0N23	72w55	4:51:40
Madrid	4N44	74w16	4:57:04
Magangué	9N14	74w45	4:59:00
Mahates	10N14	75w12	5:00:48
Maicao	11N23	72w13	4:48:52
Majagual	8N33	74w38	4:58:32
Málaga	6N42	72w44	4:50:56
Manatí	10N27	74w58	4:59:52
Manizales	5N05	75w32	5:02:08
María la Baja	9N59	75w17	5:01:08
Mariquita	5N12	74w54	4:59:36
Matarca	0s30	72w38	4:50:32
Medellín	6N15	75w35	5:02:20
Melgar	4N12	74w39	4:58:36
Melúa	3N55	72w50	4:51:20
Mercaderes	1N47	77w10	5:08:40
Miraflores	5N12	73w12	4:52:48
Miraflores	1N25	72w13	4:48:52
Miranda	3N15	76w14	5:04:56
Mitú	1N08	70w03	4:40:12
Mocoa	1N09	76w37	5:06:28
Mogotes	6N30	72w58	4:51:52
Mompós	9N14	74w26	4:57:44
Moniquirá	5N52	73w36	4:54:24
Montelíbano	8N05	75w29	5:01:56
Montería	8N46	75w53	5:03:32
Mosquera	2N30	78w29	5:13:56
Natagaima	3N37	75w06	5:00:24
Nechí	8N07	74w46	4:59:04
Neira	5N10	75w32	5:02:08
Neiva	2N56	75w18	5:01:12
Nobsa	5N46	72w57	4:51:48
Nueva Antioquia	6N05	69w26	4:37:44
Nuquí	5N42	77w17	5:09:08
Ocaña	8N15	73w20	4:53:20
Orocué	4N48	71w20	4:45:20
Ortega	3N56	75w13	5:00:52
Ovejas	9N32	75w14	5:00:56
Pacho	5N08	74w10	4:56:40
Pácora	5N31	75w27	5:01:48
Pailitas	8N58	73w38	4:54:32
Palermo	2N54	75w26	5:01:44
Palmar de Varela	10N45	74w45	4:59:00
Palmira	3N32	76w16	5:05:04
Pamplona	7N23	72w39	4:50:36
Pasto	1N13	77w17	5:09:08
Patía	2N04	77w04	5:08:16
Pavón	3N37	72w15	4:49:00
Payan	1N49	78w08	5:12:32
Paz de Ariporo	5N53	71w54	4:47:36
Paz de Río	5N59	72w47	4:51:08
Pedraza	10N11	74w55	4:59:40
Pensilvania	5N31	75w05	5:00:20
Pereira	4N49	75w43	5:02:52
Pesca	5N33	73w03	4:52:12
Petrólea	8N30	72w35	4:50:20
Pichimá	4N24	77w21	5:09:24
Piedecuesta	6N59	73w03	4:52:12
Piendamó	2N38	76w30	5:06:00
Pinillos	8N55	74w28	4:57:52
Pital	2N16	75w49	5:03:16
Pitalito	1N51	76w02	5:04:08
Pivijay	10N28	74w37	4:58:28
Pizarro	4N58	77w22	5:09:28
Planeta Rica	8N25	75w36	5:02:24
Plato	9N47	74w47	4:59:08
Popayán	2N27	76w36	5:06:24
Pradera	3N25	76w15	5:05:00
Pueblonuevo	8N31	75w15	5:01:00
Puerto Alfonso	2s11	71w01	4:44:04
Puerto Asís	0N30	76w31	5:06:04
Puerto Berrío	6N29	74w24	4:57:36
Puerto Boyacá	5N45	74w39	4:58:36
Puerto Carreño	6N12	67w22	4:29:28
Puerto Colombia	10N59	74w58	4:59:52
Puerto Leguízamo	0s12	74w46	4:59:04
Puerto Limón	3N23	73w30	4:54:00
Puerto López	4N05	72w58	4:51:52
Puerto Nariño	4N56	67w48	4:31:12
Puerto Reyes	0s59	73w17	4:53:08
Puerto Rico	1N54	75w10	5:00:40
Puerto Rondón	6N17	71w06	4:44:24
Puerto Salgar	5N28	74w39	4:58:36
Puerto Tejada	3N14	76w24	5:05:36
Puerto Toledo	0s59	74w09	4:56:36
Puerto Umbría	0N52	76w33	5:06:12
Puerto Villamizar	8N19	72w26	4:49:44
Puerto Wilches	7N21	73w54	4:55:36
Purificación	3N51	74w55	4:59:40
Quibdó	5N42	76w40	5:06:40
Quimbaya	4N38	75w47	5:03:08
Ramiriquí	5N24	73w20	4:53:20
Remedios	7N02	74w41	4:58:44
Restrepo	4N15	73w33	4:54:12
Restrepo	3N48	76w31	5:06:04
Ricaurte	1N13	77w59	5:11:56
Río de Oro	8N17	73w23	4:53:32
Ríohacha	11N33	72w55	4:51:40
Ríonegro	6N09	75w22	5:01:28
Ríonegro	7N16	73w09	4:52:36
Río Sucio	5N25	75w42	5:02:48
Ríosucio	7N27	77w07	5:08:28
Rivera	2N47	75w15	5:01:00
Roldanillo	4N24	76w09	5:04:36
Rovira	4N14	75w14	5:00:56
Sabanalarga	10N38	74w55	4:59:40
Sahagún	8N57	75w27	5:01:48
Salamina	5N25	75w29	5:01:56
Salaquí	7N18	77w33	5:10:12
Salgar	5N58	75w59	5:03:56
Samacá	5N29	73w29	4:53:56
Samaniego	1N20	77w35	5:10:20
Sampués	9N11	75w23	5:01:32
San Agustín	1N53	76w16	5:05:04
San Andrés	6N49	72w52	4:51:28
San Andrés	12N35	81w42	5:26:48
San Antero	9N23	75w46	5:03:04
San Antonio	3N55	75w28	5:01:52
San Bernardo del Viento	9N21	75w57	5:03:48
San Carlos de Guaroa	3N44	73w14	4:52:56
Sandoná	1N17	77w28	5:09:52
San Estanislao	10N24	75w09	5:00:36
San Felipe	1N55	67w06	4:28:24
San Francisco	1N11	76w53	5:07:32
San Gil	6N33	73w08	4:52:32
San Jacinto	9N50	75w08	5:00:32
San José del Guaviare	2N35	72w38	4:50:32
San José de Ocuné	4N15	70w20	4:41:20
San Juan del César	10N46	73w01	4:52:04
San Juan Nepomuceno	9N57	75w05	5:00:20
San Lope	6N12	71w56	4:47:44
San Marcos	8N39	75w08	5:00:32
San Martín	3N42	73w42	4:54:48
San Onofre	9N44	75w32	5:02:08
San Pablo	1N40	77w00	5:08:00
San Pedro	9N24	75w04	5:00:16
San Pelayo	8N58	75w51	5:03:24
Santa Ana	9N19	74w35	4:58:20
Santa Bárbara	5N53	75w35	5:02:20
Santa Clara	2s43	69w43	4:38:52
Santa Marta	11N15	74w13	4:56:52
Santander	3N01	76w28	5:05:52
Santa Rita	1N04	73w58	4:55:52
Santa Rosa	2N31	68w13	4:32:52
Santa Rosa de Cabal	4N52	75w38	5:02:32
Santa Rosa de Osos	6N39	75w28	5:01:52
Santa Rosa de Viterbo	5N53	72w59	4:51:56
Santo Tomás	10N46	74w45	4:59:00
San Vicente de Chucurí	6N54	73w25	4:53:40
San Vicente del Caguán	2N07	74w46	4:59:04
Sardina	2N02	67w07	4:28:28
Sardinata	8N05	72w48	4:51:12
Segovia	7N07	74w42	4:58:48
Sevilla	4N16	75w57	5:03:48
Silvia	2N37	76w21	5:05:24
Simití	7N58	73w57	4:55:48
Sincé	9N15	75w09	5:00:36
Sincelejo	9N18	75w24	5:01:36
Sitionuevo	10N47	74w43	4:58:52
Soacha	4N35	74w13	4:56:52
Soatá	6N20	72w41	4:50:44
Socorro	6N29	73w16	4:53:04
Sogamoso	5N43	72w56	4:51:44
Soledad	10N55	74w46	4:59:04
Sonsón	5N42	75w18	5:01:12
Sopetrán	6N30	75w46	5:03:04
Suaita	6N07	73w27	4:53:48
Sucre	8N49	74w44	4:58:56
Sucuaro	4N34	68w50	4:35:20
Tamalameque	8N52	73w49	4:55:16
Támara	5N50	72w10	4:48:40
Tame	6N28	71w44	4:46:56
Tarapacá	2s52	69w44	4:38:56
Tello	3N04	75w08	5:00:32
Teruel	2N44	75w33	5:02:12
Tesalia	2N29	75w44	5:02:56
Tierralta	8N11	76w04	5:04:16
Timaná	1N58	75w56	5:03:44
Timbío	2N20	76w40	5:06:40
Tocaima	4N28	74w38	4:58:32
Toledo	7N19	72w28	4:49:52
Tolú	9N31	75w35	5:02:20
Tres Esquinas	0N43	75w16	5:01:04
Trinidad	5N25	71w40	4:46:40
Trujillo	4N10	76w19	5:05:16
Tuluá	4N06	76w11	5:04:44
Tumaco	1N49	78w46	5:15:04
Tunja	5N31	73w22	4:53:28
Túquerres	1N05	77w37	5:10:28
Turbaco	10N20	75w25	5:01:40
Turbo	8N06	76w43	5:06:52
Ubaté	5N19	73w49	4:55:16
Uré	7N46	75w31	5:02:04
Uribe	3N13	74w24	4:57:36
Uribia	11N43	72w16	4:49:04
Urrao	6N20	76w11	5:04:44
Valdivia	7N11	75w27	5:01:48
Valle	6N29	73w07	4:52:28
Valledupar	10N29	73w15	4:53:00
Vélez	6N01	73w41	4:54:44
Venadillo	4N43	74w55	4:59:40
Villanueva	10N37	72w59	4:51:56
Villapinzón	5N13	73w36	4:54:24
Villarrica	3N58	74w37	4:58:28
Villavicencio	4N09	73w37	4:54:28
Villeta	5N01	74w28	4:57:52
Yaguará	2N40	75w31	5:02:04
Yarumal	6N58	75w24	5:01:36
Yolombó	6N36	75w01	5:00:04
Yumbo	3N35	76w28	5:05:52
Zambrano	9N45	74w49	4:59:16
Zapatoca	6N49	73w17	4:53:08
Zaragoza	7N30	74w52	4:59:28
Zarzal	4N24	76w04	5:04:16
Zipaquirá	5N02	74w00	4:56:00

COMORES KOMOREN COMORAS COMOROS

Time Table
Before 1 Jul 1911 LMT
Begin Standard 45E00
1 Jul 1911 0:00 -3:00

Place	Lat	Long	Time
Anjouan Island	12s15	44E25	-2:57:40
Antsahe	12s21	44E32	-2:58:08
Bandeli	12s55	45E13	-3:00:52
Boeni	12s55	45E06	-3:00:24
Chingoni	12s48	45E08	-3:00:32
Dembéni	11s50	43E24	-2:53:36
Domoni	12s15	44E32	-2:58:08
Dzaoudzi	12s47	45E17	-3:01:08
Fomboni	12s16	43E45	-2:55:00
Foumbouni	11s50	43E30	-2:54:00
Grande Comore Island	11s35	43E20	-2:53:20
Hahaia	11s33	43E17	-2:53:08
Koimbani	11s37	43E23	-2:53:32
Kombani	11s37	43E23	-2:53:32
Mamoutzou	12s47	45E14	-3:00:56
Mohéli Island	12s15	43E45	-2:55:00
Mitsamiouli	11s23	43E18	-2:53:12
Moroni	11s41	43E16	-2:53:04
Moya	12s18	44E27	-2:57:48
M'Ramani	12s21	44E32	-2:58:08
Mutsamudu	12s09	44E25	-2:57:40
N'Tsaoueni	11s27	43E18	-2:53:12
Panda Gongoue	11s50	43E24	-2:53:36
Salimani	11s47	43E17	-2:53:08
Sima	12s11	44E17	-2:57:08

CONGO — KONGO — CONGO

Time Table
Before 1/Jan/1912 LMT
Begin Standard 15E00
1/Jan/1912 0:00 -1:00

Place	Lat	Long	Offset
Abala	1S21	15E30	-1:02:00
Bandéko	1N56	17E28	-1:09:52
Bérandjoko	3N06	17E17	-1:09:08
Bétou	3N03	18E31	-1:14:04
Bikié	3S06	13E52	-0:55:28
Bimé	4S09	15E11	-1:00:44
Bitatolo	4S09	15E14	-1:00:56
Boémbé	2S54	15E39	-1:02:36
Boko	4S47	14E38	-0:58:32
Boko Songo	4S26	13E37	-0:54:28
Bomandjokou	0N34	14E23	-0:57:32
Boukiéro	4S12	15E18	-1:01:12
Brazzaville	4S16	15E17	-1:01:08
Conkouati	4S00	11E13	-0:44:52
Dembo	3S56	12E35	-0:50:20
Divenié	2S41	12E05	-0:48:20
Djambala	2S33	14E45	-0:59:00
Djiri	4S08	15E19	-1:01:16
Djokoumatombi	0N47	15E22	-1:01:28
Dolisie	4S12	12E41	-0:50:44
Dongou	2N02	18E04	-1:12:16
Doumanga	2S41	12E40	-0:50:40
Dounguila	2S53	11E58	-0:47:52
Ekoungounou	0S33	15E38	-1:02:32
Ekovamou	0N07	16E31	-1:06:04
Enyellé	2N49	18E06	-1:12:24
Epéna	1N22	17E29	-1:09:56
Etoumbi	0S01	14E57	-0:59:48
Ewo	0S53	14E49	-0:59:16
Gagnia	1S28	16E02	-1:04:08
Gamboma	1S53	15E51	-1:03:24
Gampoko	4S16	15E10	-1:00:40
Gampoui	4S08	15E22	-1:01:28
Gampoul	4S08	15E22	-1:01:28
Gandou	2N24	17E27	-1:09:48
Gangalingolo	4S20	15E09	-1:00:36
Gare Simon	4S15	15E11	-1:00:44
Goma Tsétsé	4S14	15E08	-1:00:32
Gonaka	2S56	13E14	-0:52:56
Ikalou	4S03	11E48	-0:47:12
Ikélemba	1N14	16E31	-1:06:04
Iko	0S35	16E01	-1:04:04
Impe	2S44	15E17	-1:01:08
Impfondo	1N37	18E04	-1:12:16
Inoni	3S04	15E39	-1:02:36
Itatolo	4S09	15E15	-1:01:00
Kaonga	4S09	15E12	-1:00:48
Kayes	4S25	11E41	-0:46:44
Kébara	2S27	14E25	-0:57:40
Kélékélé	4S20	15E08	-1:00:32
Kellé	0S06	14E33	-0:58:12
Kéma	4S11	15E13	-1:00:52
Kémah	4S11	15E13	-1:00:52
Ketta	1N28	15E56	-1:03:44
Kibangou	3S27	12E21	-0:49:24
Kibouendé	4S19	15E11	-1:00:44
Kibouendé	4S17	15E09	-1:00:36
Kibouendé I	4S11	15E09	-1:00:36
Kibouendé II	4S12	15E09	-1:00:36
Kimongo	4S29	12E58	-0:51:52
Kimpombo	4S17	15E10	-1:00:40
Kindanba	3S44	14E31	-0:58:04
Kingoma	4S09	15E15	-1:01:00
Kingoué	3S43	14E09	-0:56:36
Kinkala	4S22	14E46	-0:59:04
Kinsoundi	4S10	15E15	-1:01:00
Kintélé	4S09	15E21	-1:01:24
Kintsana	4S19	15E10	-1:00:40
Komono	3S15	13E14	-0:52:56
Koubansaki	4S22	15E09	-1:00:36
Koungoulou	3S32	13E20	-0:53:20
Lebango	0N22	14E49	-0:59:16
Lékana	2S19	14E36	-0:58:24
Lengoué	1N13	15E43	-1:02:52
Lifoula	4S06	15E25	-1:01:40
Linzolo	4S25	15E07	-1:00:28
Liouesso	1N02	15E43	-1:02:52
Liranga	0S40	17E36	-1:10:24
Loboko	0S45	16E38	-1:06:32
Londela-Kaye	4S51	13E24	-0:53:36
Loubetsi	3S12	12E10	-0:48:40
Loudima Poste	4S07	13E04	-0:52:16
Loukanga	4S20	15E09	-1:00:36
Loumou	4S08	15E09	-1:00:36
Madingo	4S07	11E22	-0:45:28
Madingou	4S09	13E34	-0:54:16
Madjingo	1N23	14E06	-0:56:24
Makabana	2S48	12E29	-0:49:56
Makoua	0N01	15E39	-1:02:36
Malinga	2S25	12E14	-0:48:56
Manianga	4S10	15E19	-1:01:16
Manpaka	4S18	15E12	-1:00:48
Masa	3S45	15E29	-1:01:56
Massina	4S08	15E19	-1:01:16
Mayala	4S21	15E09	-1:00:36
Mayama	3S51	14E54	-0:59:36
Mayoko	2S18	12E49	-0:51:16
Mbalouro	4S09	15E21	-1:01:24
Mbalourou	4S09	15E21	-1:01:24
Mbé	3N18	15E54	-1:03:36
Mbinda	2S00	12E55	-0:51:40
Mboté	3S56	12E43	-0:50:52
Mikatou	4S16	15E08	-1:00:32
Mindouli	4S17	14E21	-0:57:24
Mingo	1S55	14E59	-0:59:56
Mobenzélé	0N54	17E51	-1:11:24
Mokou	4S13	15E13	-1:00:52
Mossaka	1S13	16E48	-1:07:12
Mossendjo	2S57	12E44	-0:50:56
Moutomoukadi	4S41	13E15	-0:53:00
Mouyondzi	3S58	13E57	-0:55:48
Mpé	2S54	14E43	-0:58:52
Mpila	4S14	15E18	-1:01:12
Mpouya	2S37	16E13	-1:04:52
Mvouti	4S15	12E29	-0:49:56
Ndemba	0N11	14E19	-0:57:16
Ndjo	1S15	14E30	-0:58:00
Ndongo	2S19	13E38	-0:54:32
Ndouba	0S11	14E09	-0:56:36
Ngabé	3S12	16E11	-1:04:44
Ngamaba	4S14	15E16	-1:01:04
Ngamba	4S15	15E18	-1:01:12
Ngamouéri	4S14	15E14	-1:00:56
Ngo	2S29	15E45	-1:03:00
Nsah	2S22	15E19	-1:01:16
Nsouélé	4S12	15E11	-1:00:44
Ntsama	0S32	14E38	-0:58:32
Nzaba	4S06	15E16	-1:01:04
Obaba	2S00	16E10	-1:04:40
Obouya	0S56	15E43	-1:02:52
Odziba	3S35	15E31	-1:02:04
Okalataka	0S20	14E59	-0:59:56
Okoyo	1S28	15E04	-1:00:16
Olloua	0S56	14E34	-0:58:16
Olombo	1S18	15E53	-1:03:32
Ouesso	1N37	16E04	-1:04:16
Owando	0S29	15E55	-1:03:40
Oyo	0N01	15E54	-1:03:36
Pangala	3S19	14E34	-0:58:16
Pikounda	0N33	16E42	-1:06:48
Pointe-Noire	4S48	11E51	-0:47:24
Saint-François de Boundji	1S03	15E22	-1:01:28
Sembé	1N39	14E36	-0:58:24
Sexcello	3S58	11E38	-0:46:32
Sibiti	3S41	13E21	-0:53:24
Simon	4S15	15E11	-1:00:44
Souanké	2N05	14E03	-0:56:12
Soufflay	2N01	14E54	-0:59:36
Tchaba	4S06	15E16	-1:01:04
Tchékapika	1S17	16E11	-1:04:44
Tchitondi	4S33	12E08	-0:48:32
Yengo	0N22	15E29	-1:01:56
Zanaga	2S51	13E50	-0:55:20

COOK ISLANDS — ÎLES COOK — COOK-INSELN — ISLAS COOK

Time Table
Before 1/Jan/1901 LMT
Begin Standard 157W30
1/Jan/1901 0:00 10:30
Begin Standard 150W00

Date	Time	Offset
12/Nov/1978	0:00	9:30
4/Mar/1979	0:00	10:00
28/Oct/1979	0:00	9:30
2/Mar/1980	0:00	10:00
26/Oct/1980	0:00	9:30
1/Mar/1981	0:00	10:00
25/Oct/1981	0:00	9:30
7/Mar/1982	0:00	10:00
31/Oct/1982	0:00	9:30
6/Mar/1983	0:00	10:00
30/Oct/1983	0:00	9:30
4/Mar/1984	0:00	10:00
28/Oct/1984	0:00	9:30
3/Mar/1985	0:00	10:00
27/Oct/1985	0:00	9:30
2/Mar/1986	0:00	10:00
26/Oct/1986	0:00	9:30
1/Mar/1987	0:00	10:00
25/Oct/1987	0:00	9:30
6/Mar/1988	0:00	10:00
30/Oct/1988	0:00	9:30
5/Mar/1989	0:00	10:00
29/Oct/1989	0:00	9:30
4/Mar/1990	0:00	10:00
28/Oct/1990	0:00	9:30
3/Mar/1991	0:00	10:00
27/Oct/1991	0:00	9:30
1/Mar/1992	0:00	10:00
25/Oct/1992	0:00	9:30
7/Mar/1993	0:00	10:00
31/Oct/1993	0:00	9:30
6/Mar/1994	0:00	10:00
30/Oct/1994	0:00	9:30
5/Mar/1995	0:00	10:00
29/Oct/1995	0:00	9:30
3/Mar/1996	0:00	10:00
27/Oct/1996	0:00	9:30
2/Mar/1997	0:00	10:00
26/Oct/1997	0:00	9:30
1/Mar/1998	0:00	10:00
25/Oct/1998	0:00	9:30
7/Mar/1999	0:00	10:00
31/Oct/1999	0:00	9:30
5/Mar/2000	0:00	10:00

DIVISIONS

1. Aitutaki
2. Atiu
3. Mangaia
4. Manuae
5. Mauke
6. Mitiaro
7. Palmerston
8. Rarotonga
9. Suwarrow
10. Tatutea

Place	Lat	Long	Offset
Aitutaki Island 1	18S52	159W45	10:39:00
Arorangi 8	21S13	159W49	10:39:16
Arutunga 1	18S53	159W46	10:39:04
Atiu Island	20S01	158W09	10:32:36
Avarua 8	21S12	159W46	10:39:04
Avatiu 8	21S12	159W47	10:39:08
Mangaia Island 3	21S55	157W55	10:31:40
Manuae Island 4	19S21	158W56	10:35:44
Matavera 8	21S13	159W44	10:38:56
Mauke Island 5	20S09	157W23	10:29:32
Mitiaro Island 6	19S49	157W43	10:30:52
Muri 8	21S14	159W43	10:38:52
Ngatangiia 8	21S14	159W43	10:38:52
Nukuoa 5	20S08	157W23	10:29:32
Oneroa 3	21S54	157W58	10:31:52
Palmerston Island 7	18S04	163W10	10:52:40
Pokoinu 8	21S12	159W49	10:39:16
Rarotonga Island 8	21S14	159W46	10:39:04
Suwarrow Island 9	13S15	163W05	10:52:20
Taunganui	20S01	158W09	10:32:36
Tatutea Island 10	13S15	163W05	10:52:20
Titikaveka 8	21S15	159W45	10:39:00

COSTA RICA

COSTA RICA

Time Table		
Before 1/Jan/1890 LMT		
Begin Standard		84w05
1/Jan/1890	0:00	5:36
Begin Standard		90w00
15/Jan/1921	0:00	6:00
25/Feb/1979	0:00	5:00
3/Jun/1979	0:00	6:00
24/Feb/1980	0:00	5:00
1/Jun/1980	0:00	6:00
19/Jan/1991	0:00	5:00
1/Jul/1991	0:00	6:00

Place	Lat	Long	Time
Alajuela	10N01	84w13	5:36:52
Altamira	10N30	84w23	5:37:32
Amubri	9N31	82w56	5:31:44
Arenal	10N29	84w53	5:39:32
Atenas	9N58	84w23	5:37:32
Bagaces	10N31	85w15	5:41:00
Boruca	9N00	83w20	5:33:20
Buenos Aires	9N10	83w20	5:33:20
Cabuya	9N36	85w06	5:40:24
Cabuyal	10N40	85w40	5:42:40
Cañas	10N25	85w07	5:40:28
Caño Negro	10N54	84w44	5:38:56
Carrillo	9N52	85w30	5:42:00
Cartago	9N52	83w55	5:35:40
Colorado	10N46	83w35	5:34:20
Convento	9N21	83w30	5:34:00
Curubandé	10N43	85w26	5:41:44
Dominical	9N13	83w51	5:35:24
Esparta	9N59	84w40	5:38:40
Filadelfia	10N26	85w34	5:42:16
Golfito	8N38	83w11	5:32:44
Grecia	10N05	84w18	5:37:12
Guadalupe	9N57	84w03	5:36:12
Guápiles	10N13	83w46	5:35:04
Hacienda Miravalles	10N41	85w14	5:40:56
Heredia	10N00	84w07	5:36:28
Juan Viñas	9N54	83w45	5:35:00
La Cruz	11N04	85w39	5:42:36
La Cuesta	8N30	82w50	5:31:20
La Fortuna	10N30	84w35	5:38:20
Lagarto	10N07	84w56	5:39:44
La Mansión	10N06	85w22	5:41:28
La Piedra	9N29	83w40	5:34:40
Las Juntas	10N16	85w00	5:40:00
La Unión de Coto	8N36	83w03	5:32:12
Lepanto	9N57	85w02	5:40:08
Liberia	10N38	85w27	5:41:48
Limón	10N00	83w02	5:32:08
Los Chiles	11N02	84w43	5:38:52
Miramar	10N06	84w44	5:38:56
Moravia	9N51	83w26	5:33:44
Murciélago	10N55	85w44	5:42:56
Naranjo	10N06	84w22	5:37:28
Nicoya	10N09	85w27	5:41:48
Orotina	9N54	84w31	5:38:04
Palmares	10N03	84w26	5:37:44
Palmares	9N21	83w40	5:34:40
Palmar Sur	8N58	83w29	5:33:56
Paquera	9N50	84w56	5:39:44
Paraíso	9N50	83w51	5:35:24
Parismina	10N12	83w38	5:34:32
Parrita	9N30	84w19	5:37:16
Playa Bonita	9N39	84w27	5:37:48
Portegolpe	10N20	85w46	5:43:04
Potrero Grande	9N00	83w11	5:32:44
Puerto Cortés	8N58	83w32	5:34:08
Puerto Jiménez	8N33	83w19	5:33:16
Puerto Limón → Limón	10N00	83w02	5:32:08
Puerto Potrero	10N28	85w47	5:43:08
Puerto Viejo	10N26	83w59	5:35:56
Puerto Viejo	9N39	82w45	5:31:00
Puntarenas	9N58	84w50	5:39:20
Quepos	9N27	84w09	5:36:36
Quesada	10N19	84w26	5:37:44
Rincón	8N42	83w29	5:33:56
San Antonio	10N12	85w26	5:41:44
San Francisco	9N49	85w15	5:41:00
San Ignacio	9N48	84w09	5:36:36
San Isidro del General	9N22	83w42	5:34:48
San José	9N56	84w05	5:36:20
San Juanillo	10N02	85w44	5:42:56
San Marcos	9N40	84w01	5:36:04
San Pablo	9N54	84w26	5:37:44
San Pedro	9N56	84w03	5:36:12
San Ramón	10N06	84w28	5:37:52
Santa Cruz	10N16	85w36	5:42:24
Santa María	9N39	83w57	5:35:48
Santa Rosa	10N51	85w38	5:42:32
Santiago	9N51	84w18	5:37:12
Santo Domingo	9N59	84w05	5:36:20
San Vito	8N50	82w58	5:31:52
Sardinal	10N31	85w39	5:42:36
Siquirres	10N06	83w30	5:34:00
Suretka	9N34	82w56	5:31:44
Tambor	9N43	85w01	5:40:04
Tilarán	10N28	84w59	5:39:56
Tres Ríos	9N54	83w58	5:35:52
Turrialba	9N54	83w41	5:34:44
Upala	10N47	85w02	5:40:08
Veintisiete de Abril	10N15	85w45	5:43:00
Venecia	10N22	84w17	5:37:08
Vesta	9N43	83w03	5:32:12
Zarcero	10N11	84w23	5:37:32

KUBA

CUBA

Time Table		
Before 1/Jan/1890 LMT		
Begin Standard		82w24
1/Jan/1890	0:00	5:30
Begin Standard		75w00
19/Jul/1925	12:00	5:00
10/Jun/1928	0:00	4:00
10/Oct/1928	0:00	5:00
2/Jun/1940	0:00	4:00
1/Sep/1940	0:00	5:00
1/Jun/1941	0:00	4:00
7/Sep/1941	0:00	5:00
7/Jun/1942	0:00	4:00
6/Sep/1942	0:00	5:00
3/Jun/1945	0:00	4:00
2/Sep/1945	0:00	5:00
2/Jun/1946	0:00	4:00
1/Sep/1946	0:00	5:00
1/Jun/1965	0:00	4:00
30/Sep/1965	0:00	5:00
29/May/1966	0:00	4:00
2/Oct/1966	0:00	5:00
8/Apr/1967	0:00	4:00
10/Sep/1967	0:00	5:00
14/Apr/1968	0:00	4:00
8/Sep/1968	0:00	5:00
27/Apr/1969	0:00	4:00
26/Oct/1969	0:00	5:00
26/Apr/1970	0:00	4:00
25/Oct/1970	0:00	5:00
25/Apr/1971	0:00	4:00
30/Oct/1971	0:00	5:00
30/Apr/1972	0:00	4:00
8/Oct/1972	0:00	5:00
29/Apr/1973	0:00	4:00
8/Oct/1973	0:00	5:00
28/Apr/1974	0:00	4:00
8/Oct/1974	0:00	5:00
27/Apr/1975	0:00	4:00
26/Oct/1975	0:00	5:00
25/Apr/1976	0:00	4:00
31/Oct/1976	0:00	5:00
24/Apr/1977	0:00	4:00
30/Oct/1977	0:00	5:00
7/May/1978	0:00	4:00
8/Oct/1978	0:00	5:00
18/Mar/1979	0:00	4:00
14/Oct/1979	0:00	5:00
16/Mar/1980	0:00	4:00
12/Oct/1980	0:00	5:00
10/May/1981	0:00	4:00
11/Oct/1981	0:00	5:00
9/May/1982	0:00	4:00
10/Oct/1982	0:00	5:00
8/May/1983	0:00	4:00
9/Oct/1983	0:00	5:00
6/May/1984	0:00	4:00
14/Oct/1984	0:00	5:00
5/May/1985	0:00	4:00
13/Oct/1985	0:00	5:00
16/Mar/1986	0:00	4:00
12/Oct/1986	0:00	5:00
22/Mar/1987	0:00	4:00
11/Oct/1987	0:00	5:00
20/Mar/1988	0:00	4:00
9/Oct/1988	0:00	5:00
19/Mar/1989	0:00	4:00
8/Oct/1989	0:00	5:00
1/Apr/1990	0:00	4:00
14/Oct/1990	0:00	5:00
17/Mar/1991	0:00	4:00
13/Oct/1991	0:00	5:00
15/Mar/1992	0:00	4:00
11/Oct/1992	0:00	5:00
14/Mar/1993	0:00	4:00
10/Oct/1993	0:00	5:00
20/Mar/1994	0:00	4:00
9/Oct/1994	0:00	5:00
19/Mar/1995	0:00	4:00
8/Oct/1995	0:00	5:00
17/Mar/1996	0:00	4:00
13/Oct/1996	0:00	5:00
16/Mar/1997	0:00	4:00
12/Oct/1997	0:00	5:00
15/Mar/1998	0:00	4:00
11/Oct/1998	0:00	5:00
14/Mar/1999	0:00	4:00
10/Oct/1999	0:00	5:00
19/Mar/2000	0:00	4:00
8/Oct/2000	0:00	5:00

Place	Lat	Long	Time
Agramonte	22N41	81w07	5:24:28
Aguacate	22N59	81w49	5:27:16
Aguada de Pasajeros	22N23	80w51	5:23:24
Alacranes	22N46	81w34	5:26:16
Alquízar	22N48	82w35	5:30:20
Alto Cedro	20N31	75w58	5:03:52
Antilla	20N50	75w45	5:03:00
Artemisa	22N49	82w46	5:31:04
Báez	22N13	79w45	5:19:00
Bahía Honda	22N54	83w10	5:32:40
Baire	20N19	76w20	5:05:20
Banes	20N58	75w43	5:02:52
Baracoa	20N21	74w30	4:58:00
Baraguá	21N41	78w38	5:14:32
Batabanó	22N43	82w17	5:29:08
Bauta	22N59	82w33	5:30:12
Bayamo	20N23	76w39	5:06:36
Bejucal	22N56	82w23	5:29:32
Bello	23N07	82w24	5:29:36
Bolondrón	22N46	81w27	5:25:48
Cabaiguán	22N05	79w30	5:18:00
Cabañas	22N58	82w55	5:31:40
Cacocum	20N44	76w23	5:05:32
Caibarién	22N31	79w28	5:17:52
Caimanera	19N59	75w09	5:00:36
Camagüey	21N23	77w55	5:11:40
Camajuaní	22N28	79w44	5:18:56
Campechuela	20N14	77w17	5:09:08
Candelaria	22N44	82w58	5:31:52
Cárdenas	23N02	81w12	5:24:48
Casilda	21N46	79w59	5:19:56
Céspedes	21N35	78w17	5:13:08
Chambas	22N12	78w55	5:15:40
Chaparra	21N10	76w29	5:05:56
Cidra	22N56	81w32	5:26:08
Ciego de Avila	21N51	78w46	5:15:04
Cienfuegos	22N09	80w27	5:21:48
Cifuentes	22N39	80w03	5:20:12
Colón	22N43	80w54	5:23:36
Consolación del Norte	22N45	83w33	5:34:12
Consolación del Sur	22N30	83w31	5:34:04
Contramaestre	20N18	76w15	5:05:00
Corralillo	22N59	80w35	5:22:20
Cruces	22N21	80w16	5:21:04
Cuatro Caminos	22N54	82w23	5:29:32
Cueto	20N39	75w56	5:03:44
Cumanayagua	22N09	80w12	5:20:48
Delicias	21N11	76w34	5:06:16
El Cobre	20N03	75w57	5:03:48
El Cristo	20N07	75w45	5:03:00
El Santo	22N42	79w41	5:18:44
Encrucijada	22N37	79w52	5:19:28
Esmeralda	21N51	78w07	5:12:28
Florida	21N32	78w14	5:12:56
Fomento	22N06	79w43	5:18:52
Gibara	21N07	76w08	5:04:32
Guáimaro	21N03	77w21	5:09:24
Guamo Embarcadero	20N37	76w58	5:07:52
Guanabacoa	23N08	82w18	5:29:12
Guanajay	22N55	82w42	5:30:48
Guane	22N12	84w05	5:36:20
Guantánamo	20N08	75w12	5:00:48
Guantánamo Bay	19N55	79w09	5:16:36
Guayabal	20N42	77w36	5:10:24
Güines	22N50	82w02	5:28:08
Güira de Melena	22N48	82w30	5:30:00
Havana → La Habana	23N08	82w22	5:29:28
Havane, La → La Habana	23N08	82w22	5:29:28
Holguín	20N53	76w15	5:05:00
Imías	20N04	74w38	4:58:32
Jagüey Grande	22N32	81w08	5:24:32
Jamaica	20N12	75w09	5:00:36
Jatibonico	21N56	79w10	5:16:40
Jiguaní	20N22	76w26	5:05:44
Jobabo	20N54	77w17	5:09:08
Jovellanos	22N48	81w12	5:24:48
Juan Gualberto Gómez	22N52	81w33	5:26:12
Júcaro	21N37	78w51	5:15:24
La Coloma	22N15	83w34	5:34:16
La Esperanza	22N27	80w06	5:20:24
La Esperanza	22N46	83w44	5:34:56
Laguna Blanca	20N27	76w07	5:04:28
La Habana (Havana)	23N08	82w22	5:29:28
La Havane → La Habana	23N08	82w22	5:29:28
La Isabela	22N57	80w01	5:20:04
La Maya	20N10	75w39	5:02:36
La Rioja	20N46	76w36	5:06:24
Las Villas	22N15	80w00	5:20:00

CUBA KUBA

Place	Lat	Long	Offset
Limonar	22N57	81w24	5:25:36
Los Arabos	22N44	80w43	5:22:52
Los Palacios	22N35	83w15	5:33:00
Lugareño	21N33	77w28	5:09:52
Mabay	20N16	76w40	5:06:40
Madruga	22N55	81w51	5:27:24
Majagua	21N55	79w00	5:16:00
Manacas	22N36	80w19	5:21:16
Manatí	21N19	76w56	5:07:44
Manguito	22N35	80w55	5:23:40
Manicaragua	22N09	79w58	5:19:52
Mantua	22N17	84w17	5:37:08
Manzanillo	20N21	77w07	5:08:28
Marianao	23N05	82w26	5:29:44
Mariel	22N59	82w45	5:31:00
Martí	21N09	77w27	5:09:48
Martí	22N57	80w55	5:23:40
Matanzas	23N03	81w35	5:26:20
Maximo Gomez	22N55	81w02	5:24:08
Mayajigua	22N14	79w04	5:16:16
Mayarí	20N40	75w41	5:02:44
Mayarí Arriba	20N25	75w32	5:02:08
Melena del Sur	22N47	82w09	5:28:36
Minas	21N29	77w37	5:10:28
Minas de Matahambre	22N35	83w57	5:35:48
Morón	22N06	78w38	5:14:32
Nicaro	20N42	75w33	5:02:12
Niquero	20N03	77w35	5:10:20
Nueva Gerona	21N53	82w48	5:31:12
Nueva Paz	22N46	81w45	5:27:00
Nuevitas	21N33	77w16	5:09:04
Oriente	20N35	76w00	5:04:00
Palma Soriano	20N13	76w00	5:04:00
Palmira	22N14	80w23	5:21:32
Palos	22N48	81w44	5:26:56
Pedro Betancourt	22N44	81w17	5:25:08
Perico	22N46	81w01	5:24:04
Pina	22N01	78w43	5:14:52
Pinar del Río	22N25	83w42	5:34:48
Placetas	22N19	79w40	5:18:40
Playa Baracoa	23N03	82w34	5:30:16
Portillo	19N55	77w11	5:08:44
Preston	20N46	75w39	5:02:36
Puerto Manatí	21N22	76w50	5:07:20
Puerto Padre	21N12	76w36	5:06:24
Punta Alegre	22N23	78w49	5:15:16
Quemado de Güines	22N48	80w15	5:21:00
Rancho Veloz	22N53	80w23	5:21:32
Ranchuelo	22N23	80w09	5:20:36
Remedios	22N30	79w33	5:18:12
Río Cauto	20N33	76w55	5:07:40
Rodas	22N20	80w33	5:22:12
Sagua de Tánamo	20N35	75w14	5:00:56
Sagua la Grande	22N49	80w05	5:20:20
San Antonio de los Baños	22N53	82w30	5:30:00
San Cristóbal	22N43	83w03	5:32:12
Sancti-Spíritus	21N56	79w27	5:17:48
San Germán	20N36	76w08	5:04:32
San José de las Lajas	22N58	82w09	5:28:36
San Juan y Martínez	22N16	83w50	5:35:20
San Luis	20N12	75w51	5:03:24
San Luis	22N17	83w46	5:35:04
San Nicolás de Bari	22N47	81w55	5:27:40
Santa Clara	22N24	79w58	5:19:52
Santa Cruz del Norte	23N09	81w55	5:27:40
Santa Cruz del Sur	20N43	78w00	5:12:00
Santa Fé	21N45	82w45	5:31:00
Santa Isabel de las Lajas	22N25	80w18	5:21:12
Santa Lucía	21N02	76w00	5:04:00
Santa Lucía	22N40	83w58	5:35:52
Santa Lucía	20N59	77w25	5:09:40
Santiago	20N01	75w49	5:03:16
Santiago de Cuba	20N01	75w49	5:03:16
Santo Domingo	22N35	80w15	5:21:00
Sibanicú	21N14	77w31	5:10:04
Sierra Morena	22N57	80w32	5:22:08
Surgidero	22N41	82w18	5:29:12
Tiguabos	20N14	75w21	5:01:24
Trinidad	21N48	79w59	5:19:56
Tunas de Zaza	21N38	79w33	5:18:12
Unión de Reyes	22N48	81w32	5:26:08
Varadero	23N09	81w16	5:25:04
Vertientes	21N16	78w09	5:12:36
Victoria de las Tunas	20N58	76w57	5:07:48
Viñales	22N37	83w43	5:34:52
Yaguajay	22N19	79w14	5:16:56
Yara	20N16	76w57	5:07:48
Zaza del Medio	22N00	79w23	5:17:32
Zulueta	22N22	79w34	5:18:16

CYPRUS KIBRIS CHIPRE ZYPERN KÍPROS

Time Table
Before 14/Nov/1921 LMT
Begin Standard 30E00

14/Nov/1921	0:00	-2:00
13/Apr/1975	0:00	-3:00
12/Oct/1975	0:00	-2:00
15/May/1976	0:00	-3:00
11/Oct/1976	0:00	-2:00
3/Apr/1977	0:00	-3:00
25/Sep/1977	0:00	-2:00
2/Apr/1978	0:00	-3:00
2/Oct/1978	0:00	-2:00
1/Apr/1979	0:00	-3:00
30/Sep/1979	0:00	-2:00
6/Apr/1980	0:00	-3:00
28/Sep/1980	3:00	-2:00
29/Mar/1981	0:00	-3:00
27/Sep/1981	1:00	-2:00
28/Mar/1982	0:00	-3:00
26/Sep/1982	1:00	-2:00
27/Mar/1983	0:00	-3:00
25/Sep/1983	1:00	-2:00
25/Mar/1984	0:00	-3:00
30/Sep/1984	1:00	-2:00
31/Mar/1985	0:00	-3:00
29/Sep/1985	1:00	-2:00
30/Mar/1986	0:00	-3:00
28/Sep/1986	1:00	-2:00
29/Mar/1987	0:00	-3:00
27/Sep/1987	1:00	-2:00
27/Mar/1988	0:00	-3:00
25/Sep/1988	1:00	-2:00
26/Mar/1989	0:00	-3:00
24/Sep/1989	1:00	-2:00
25/Mar/1990	0:00	-3:00
30/Sep/1990	1:00	-2:00
31/Mar/1991	0:00	-3:00
29/Sep/1991	1:00	-2:00
29/Mar/1992	0:00	-3:00
27/Sep/1992	1:00	-2:00
28/Mar/1993	0:00	-3:00
26/Sep/1993	1:00	-2:00
27/Mar/1994	0:00	-3:00
25/Sep/1994	1:00	-2:00
26/Mar/1995	0:00	-3:00
24/Sep/1995	1:00	-2:00
31/Mar/1996	0:00	-3:00
29/Sep/1996	1:00	-2:00
30/Mar/1997	0:00	-3:00
28/Sep/1997	1:00	-2:00
29/Mar/1998	0:00	-3:00
27/Sep/1998	1:00	-2:00
28/Mar/1999	0:00	-3:00
26/Sep/1999	1:00	-2:00
26/Mar/2000	0:00	-3:00
24/Sep/2000	1:00	-2:00

Place	Lat	Long	Offset
Aiyialoúsa	35N32	34E11	-2:16:44
Akáki	35N08	33E08	-2:12:32
Akrotíri	34N36	32E57	-2:11:48
Ammókhostos (Famagusta)	35N07	33E57	-2:15:48
Aradhíppou	34N57	33E35	-2:14:20
Ársos	34N50	32E46	-2:11:04
Ássia	35N09	33E36	-2:14:24
Athiaínou	35N04	33E32	-2:14:08
Dháli	35N01	33E25	-2:13:40
Dherínia	35N03	33E57	-2:15:48
Episkopí	34N40	32E54	-2:11:36
Famagusta → Ammókhostos	35N07	33E57	-2:15:48
Kirínia (Kyrenia)	35N20	33E19	-2:13:16
Kithraía	35N15	33E29	-2:13:56
Koúklia	34N42	32E34	-2:10:16
Kyrenia → Kirínia	35N20	33E19	-2:13:16
Lápithos	35N20	33E10	-2:12:40
Larnaca → Lárnax	34N55	33E38	-2:14:32
Lárnax (Larnaca)	34N55	33E38	-2:14:32
Lemesós (Limassol)	34N40	33E02	-2:12:08
Leonárison	35N28	34E08	-2:16:32
Lévka	35N07	32E51	-2:11:24
Levkónoikon	35N15	33E45	-2:15:00
Levkosía (Nicosia)	35N10	33E22	-2:13:28
Limassol → Lemesós	34N40	33E02	-2:12:08
Lísi	35N06	33E41	-2:14:44
Marathóvounon	35N13	33E37	-2:14:28
Mórfou	35N12	32E59	-2:11:56
Néa Páfos (Paphos)	34N45	32E25	-2:09:40
Nicosia → Levkosía	35N10	33E22	-2:13:28
Pákhna	34N46	32E48	-2:11:12
Palaikhóri	34N55	33E05	-2:12:20
Páno Panayiá	34N55	32E38	-2:10:32
Páno Plátres	34N53	32E52	-2:11:28
Paphos → Néa Páfos	34N45	32E25	-2:09:40
Paralímni	35N02	33E59	-2:15:56
Péyia	34N53	32E23	-2:09:32
Pólis	35N02	32E25	-2:09:40
Rizokárpason	35N36	34E23	-2:17:32
Tríkomon	35N17	33E52	-2:15:28
Troödos	34N55	32E53	-2:11:32
Yermasóyia	34N43	33E05	-2:12:20
Yialoúsa → Aiyialoúsa	35N32	34E11	-2:16:44
Zódhia	35N10	33E00	-2:12:00

CZECHOSLOVAKIA CHECOSLOVAQUIA TCHÉCOSLOVAQUIE ČESKOSLOVENSKO

Time Table
Before 1/Jan/1850 LMT
Begin Standard 14E26
1/Jan/1850 0:00 -0:58
Begin Standard 15E00

1/Oct/1891	0:00	-1:00
30/Apr/1916	23:00	-2:00
1/Oct/1916	1:00	-1:00
16/Apr/1917	2:00	-2:00
17/Sep/1917	3:00	-1:00
15/Apr/1918	2:00	-2:00
16/Sep/1918	3:00	-1:00
1/Apr/1940	2:00	-2:00
2/Nov/1942	3:00	-1:00
29/Mar/1943	2:00	-2:00
4/Oct/1943	3:00	-1:00
3/Apr/1944	2:00	-2:00
17/Sep/1944	3:00	-1:00
8/Apr/1945	2:00	-2:00
18/Nov/1945	3:00	-1:00
6/May/1946	0:00	-2:00
7/Oct/1946	3:00	-1:00
20/Apr/1947	2:00	-2:00
5/Oct/1947	3:00	-1:00
18/Apr/1948	2:00	-2:00
3/Oct/1948	3:00	-1:00
9/Apr/1949	2:00	-2:00
2/Oct/1949	3:00	-1:00
1/Apr/1979	2:00	-2:00
30/Sep/1979	3:00	-1:00
6/Apr/1980	2:00	-2:00
28/Sep/1980	3:00	-1:00
29/Mar/1981	1:00	-2:00
27/Sep/1981	2:00	-1:00
28/Mar/1982	1:00	-2:00
26/Sep/1982	2:00	-1:00
27/Mar/1983	1:00	-2:00
25/Sep/1983	2:00	-1:00
25/Mar/1984	1:00	-2:00
30/Sep/1984	2:00	-1:00
31/Mar/1985	1:00	-2:00
29/Sep/1985	2:00	-1:00
30/Mar/1986	1:00	-2:00
28/Sep/1986	2:00	-1:00
29/Mar/1987	1:00	-2:00
27/Sep/1987	2:00	-1:00
27/Mar/1988	1:00	-2:00
25/Sep/1988	2:00	-1:00
26/Mar/1989	1:00	-2:00
24/Sep/1989	2:00	-1:00
25/Mar/1990	1:00	-2:00
30/Sep/1990	2:00	-1:00
31/Mar/1991	1:00	-2:00
29/Sep/1991	2:00	-1:00
29/Mar/1992	1:00	-2:00
27/Sep/1992	2:00	-1:00
28/Mar/1993	1:00	-2:00
26/Sep/1993	2:00	-1:00
27/Mar/1994	1:00	-2:00
25/Sep/1994	2:00	-1:00
26/Mar/1995	1:00	-2:00
24/Sep/1995	2:00	-1:00
31/Mar/1996	1:00	-2:00
29/Sep/1996	2:00	-1:00
30/Mar/1997	1:00	-2:00
28/Sep/1997	2:00	-1:00
29/Mar/1998	1:00	-2:00
27/Sep/1998	2:00	-1:00
28/Mar/1999	1:00	-2:00
26/Sep/1999	2:00	-1:00
26/Mar/2000	1:00	-2:00
24/Sep/2000	2:00	-1:00

Place	Lat	Long	Offset
Aš	50N10	12E10	-0:48:40
Aussig → Ústí nad Labem	50N40	14E02	-0:56:08
Austerlitz → Slavkov u Brna	49N09	16E52	-1:07:28
Bánovce nad Bebravou	48N43	18E14	-1:12:56
Banská Bystrica	48N44	19E07	-1:16:28

ČESKOSLOVENSKO TCHÉCOSLOVAQUIE CHECOSLOVAQUIA CZECHOSLOVAKIA

Banská Štiavnica	48N28	18E56	-1:15:44
Bardejov	49N18	21E16	-1:25:04
Bechyně	49N18	14E29	-0:57:56
Bečov nad Teplou	50N02	12E19	-0:49:16
Bělá nad Radbuzou	49N36	12E44	-0:50:56
Bělá pod Bezdězem	50N30	14E50	-0:59:20
Bělčice	49N30	13E53	-0:55:32
Benátky nad Jizerou	50N17	14E51	-0:59:24
Benešov nad Ploučnicí	50N45	14E22	-0:57:28
Beroun	49N58	14E04	-0:56:16
Bezdružice	49N55	12E59	-0:51:56
Bílina	50N35	13E45	-0:55:00
Blansko	49N22	16E39	-1:06:36
Blatná	49N26	13E53	-0:55:32
Blovice	49N35	13E33	-0:54:12
Blšany	50N10	13E29	-0:53:56
Bochov	50N06	13E02	-0:52:08
Bohušovice nad Ohří	50N29	14E07	-0:56:28
Bohutín	49N40	13E55	-0:55:40
Boletice nad Labem	50N45	14E13	-0:56:52
Bolíkov	49N02	15E22	-1:01:28
Bonětice	49N41	12E49	-0:51:16
Bor	49N43	12E47	-0:51:08
Borová Lada	48N59	13E40	-0:54:40
Borovany	48N54	14E39	-0:58:36
Borovy	49N33	13E18	-0:53:12
Boskovice	49N29	16E40	-1:06:40
Boží Dar	50N24	12E55	-0:51:40
Brandýsek	50N10	14E10	-0:56:40
Brandýs nad Labem	50N10	14E41	-0:58:44
Branka	49N50	12E33	-0:50:12
Břasy	49N50	13E35	-0:54:20
Bratislava	48N09	17E07	-1:08:28
Břeclav	48N46	16E53	-1:07:32
Březnice	49N33	13E57	-0:55:48
Brezno	48N50	19E39	-1:18:36
Březno	50N24	13E26	-0:53:44
Březová	50N06	12E39	-0:50:36
Březové Hory	49N41	13E58	-0:55:52
Brno	49N12	16E37	-1:06:28
Brod	49N51	12E45	-0:51:00
Brodeslavy	49N56	13E34	-0:54:16
Broumov	50N35	16E20	-1:05:20
Broumov	49N54	12E37	-0:50:28
Brünn → Brno	49N12	16E37	-1:06:28
Bruntál	49N59	17E28	-1:09:52
Brüx → Most	50N32	13E39	-0:54:36
Bučina	48N58	13E36	-0:54:24
Budišov nad Budišovkou	49N47	17E38	-1:10:32
Budweis → české Budějovice	48N59	14E28	-0:57:52
Budyně nad Ohří	50N22	14E09	-0:56:36
Buštěhrad	50N09	14E10	-0:56:40
Bylnice	49N04	18E01	-1:12:04
Byšice-Liblice	50N19	14E38	-0:58:32
Bystřany	50N38	13E51	-0:55:24
Bystřice	49N45	14E41	-0:58:44
Bystřice pod Hostýnem	49N24	17E40	-1:10:40
Bytča	49N14	18E36	-1:14:24
Čachrov	49N16	13E18	-0:53:12
Čadca	49N26	18E48	-1:15:12
Čaňa	48N37	21E18	-1:25:12
Carlsbad → Karlovy Vary	50N11	12E52	-0:51:28
Čáslav	49N54	15E23	-1:01:32
Čechtice	49N37	15E03	-1:00:12
Čelákovice	50N10	14E46	-0:59:04
Čepřovice	49N10	13E59	-0:55:56
Čerčany	49N51	14E43	-0:58:52
Černá v Pošumaví	48N44	14E07	-0:56:28
Černá v Pošumaví Údolní ná	48N44	14E07	-0:56:28
Černošín	49N49	12E53	-0:51:32
Čerňovice	49N49	13E06	-0:52:24
Červený Kostelec	50N29	16E06	-1:04:24
Česká Kamenice	50N47	14E26	-0:57:44
Česká Kublice	49N22	12E52	-0:51:28
Česká Lípa	50N42	14E32	-0:58:08
Česká Třebová	49N54	16E27	-1:05:48
České Budějovice	48N59	14E28	-0:57:52
Český Brod	50N02	14E58	-0:59:52
Český Krumlov	48N49	14E19	-0:57:16
Český Těšín	49N45	18E37	-1:14:28
Chabařovice	50N40	13E56	-0:55:44
Cheb	50N01	12E25	-0:49:40
Chlum	48N52	13E55	-0:55:40
Choceň	50N00	16E13	-1:04:52
Chocenice	49N33	13E31	-0:54:04
Chodov	50N11	12E43	-0:50:52
Chomutov	50N28	13E26	-0:53:44
Chotěboř	49N43	15E40	-1:02:40
Chotěšov	49N39	13E12	-0:52:48
Chrást	49N48	13E29	-0:53:56
Chříbská	50N50	14E29	-0:57:56
Chříč	49N57	13E39	-0:54:36
Chrudim	49N57	15E48	-1:03:12
Chudeč	49N58	13E05	-0:52:20
Chudenín	49N18	13E06	-0:52:24
Chyše	50N05	13E15	-0:53:00
Čierna (nad Tisou)	48N25	22E05	-1:28:20
Čierny Balog	48N45	19E40	-1:18:40
Cínovec	50N43	13E45	-0:55:00
Čistá	50N03	12E42	-0:50:48
Čkyně	49N07	13E49	-0:55:16
Cvikov	50N48	14E40	-0:58:40
Dačice	49N05	15E26	-1:01:44
Dalovice	50N11	12E55	-0:51:40
Děčín	50N48	14E13	-0:56:52
Defurovy Lažany	49N27	13E40	-0:54:40
Detva	48N31	19E28	-1:17:52
Dívčice	49N06	14E19	-0:57:16
Dlouhá Ves	49N12	13E31	-0:54:04
Dobřany	49N40	13E18	-0:53:12
Dobříš	49N47	14E11	-0:56:44
Dobroměřice	50N23	13E46	-0:55:04
Dobruška	50N17	16E10	-1:04:40
Dobšiná	48N49	20E23	-1:21:32
Doksy	50N35	14E38	-0:58:32
Dolany	49N27	13E15	-0:53:00
Dolní Jiřetín	50N35	13E33	-0:54:12
Dolní Žandov	50N02	12E34	-0:50:16
Dolný Kubín	49N12	19E17	-1:17:08
Domažlice	49N27	12E56	-0:51:44
Doupov	50N10	13E08	-0:52:32
Dražeň	49N54	13E18	-0:53:12
Draženov	49N28	12E52	-0:51:28
Drienov	48N53	21E17	-1:25:08
Drnholec	48N52	16E29	-1:05:56
Dubá	50N34	14E33	-0:58:12
Dubí	50N42	13E45	-0:55:00
Dubňany	48N55	17E06	-1:08:24
Dubnica nad Váhom	48N58	18E09	-1:12:36
Duchcov	50N37	13E45	-0:55:00
Dunajská Streda	48N01	17E35	-1:10:20
Dvůr Králové (nad Labem)	50N26	15E48	-1:03:12
Dýšina	49N46	13E29	-0:53:56
Eger → Cheb	50N01	12E25	-0:49:40
Fil'akovo	48N17	19E51	-1:19:24
Františkovy Lázně	50N04	12E21	-0:49:24
Frenštát pod Radhoštěm	49N33	18E14	-1:12:56
Frýdek-Místek	49N41	18E22	-1:13:28
Frýdlant	50N56	15E05	-1:00:20
Gablonz → Jablonec nad Nisou	50N44	15E10	-1:00:40
Galanta	48N12	17E43	-1:10:52
Gerlova Hut'	49N10	13E17	-0:53:08
Giraltovce	49N07	21E31	-1:26:04
Gottwaldov	49N13	17E41	-1:10:44
Habartov	50N08	12E33	-0:50:12
Halenkov	49N19	18E08	-1:12:32
Hamr	50N35	13E35	-0:54:20
Handlová	48N44	18E46	-1:15:04
Hanušovce nad Topl'ou	49N02	21E30	-1:26:00
Hanušovice	50N05	16E55	-1:07:40
Hartmanice	49N10	13E27	-0:53:48
Havířov	49N47	18E27	-1:13:48
Havlíčkův Brod	49N36	15E35	-1:02:20
Heřmanova Hut'	49N44	13E04	-0:52:16
Hlinsko	49N45	15E55	-1:03:40
Hlohovec	48N25	17E47	-1:11:08
Hlohovice	49N53	13E38	-0:54:32
Hluboká nad Vltavou	49N03	14E27	-0:57:48
Hlučín	49N54	18E12	-1:12:48
Hodonín	48N51	17E08	-1:08:32
Holešov	49N20	17E35	-1:10:20
Holíč	48N49	17E10	-1:08:40
Holice	50N04	15E59	-1:03:56
Holýšov	49N36	13E05	-0:52:20
Horažd'ovice	49N20	13E43	-0:54:52
Hořice	50N22	15E38	-1:02:32
Horní Jiřetín	50N35	13E32	-0:54:08
Horní Počernice	50N06	14E38	-0:58:32
Horní Slavkov	50N07	12E46	-0:51:04
Horní Vltavice	48N57	13E46	-0:55:04
Hořovice	49N50	13E54	-0:55:36
Horšovský Týn	49N32	12E56	-0:51:44
Hory Matky Boží	49N16	13E27	-0:53:48
Hostěradice	48N57	16E15	-1:05:00
Hostivice	50N04	14E15	-0:57:00
Hošt'ka	50N30	14E20	-0:57:20
Hostomice	50N35	13E46	-0:55:04
Hostouň	49N34	12E46	-0:51:04
Hradec Králové	50N12	15E50	-1:03:20
Hrádek nad Nisou	50N48	14E51	-0:59:24
Hranice	49N33	17E44	-1:10:56
Hranice	50N15	12E10	-0:48:40
Hrdlovka	50N36	13E40	-0:54:40
Hřensko	50N50	14E14	-0:56:56
Hriňová	48N36	19E31	-1:18:04
Hrob	50N39	13E44	-0:54:56
Hronov	50N29	16E12	-1:04:48
Hrotovice	49N06	16E07	-1:04:28
Hrušovany	48N50	16E23	-1:05:32
Hulín	49N19	17E28	-1:09:52
Humenné	48N56	21E55	-1:27:40
Humpolec	49N32	15E22	-1:01:28
Husinec	49N03	13E58	-0:55:52
Hustopeče	48N57	16E44	-1:06:56
Iglau → Jihlava	49N24	15E36	-1:02:24
Ivančice	49N06	16E23	-1:05:32
Jablonec nad Nisou	50N44	15E10	-1:00:40
Jablonica	48N37	17E25	-1:09:40
Jablonné v Podještědí	50N48	14E47	-0:59:08
Jablunkov	49N35	18E47	-1:15:08
Jáchymov	50N20	12E55	-0:51:40
Jägerndorf → Krnov	50N05	17E41	-1:10:44
Janovice nad Úhlava	49N21	13E14	-0:52:56
Jaroměř	50N21	15E55	-1:03:40
Jaroměřice	49N05	15E53	-1:03:32
Javorná	49N13	13E18	-0:53:12
Javorník	50N23	17E00	-1:08:00
Jelšava	48N39	20E14	-1:20:56
Jemnice	49N01	15E35	-1:02:20
Jesenice	50N04	13E29	-0:53:56
Jeseník	50N14	17E13	-1:08:52
Jestřebí	50N38	14E36	-0:58:24
Jetřichovice	50N49	14E25	-0:57:40
Jevíčko	49N38	16E43	-1:06:52
Jičín	50N26	15E21	-1:01:24
Jihlava	49N24	15E36	-1:02:24
Jílové	50N46	14E07	-0:56:28
Jince	49N47	13E59	-0:55:56
Jindřichovice	50N15	12E37	-0:50:28
Jindřichův Hradec	49N09	15E00	-1:00:00
Jinín	49N13	13E58	-0:55:52
Jiřetín	50N50	14E35	-0:58:20
Jiříkov	50N59	13E35	-0:54:20
Jirkov	50N30	13E27	-0:53:48
Joachimsthal → Jáchymov	50N20	12E55	-0:51:40
Jur	48N15	17E13	-1:08:52
Kadaň	50N20	13E15	-0:53:00
Kadov	49N24	13E47	-0:55:08
Kamenický Šenov	50N45	14E29	-0:57:56
Kaplice	48N45	14E30	-0:58:00
Karlovy Vary (Carlsbad)	50N11	12E52	-0:51:28
Karlsbad → Karlovy Vary	50N11	12E52	-0:51:28
Karviná	49N50	18E30	-1:14:00
Kaschau → Košice	48N43	21E15	-1:25:00
Käsmark → Kežmarok	49N08	20E25	-1:21:40
Kašperske Hory	49N09	13E33	-0:54:12
Kassa → Košice	48N43	21E15	-1:25:00
Katovice	49N16	13E49	-0:55:16
Katusice	50N26	14E50	-0:59:20
Kbelnice	49N18	13E59	-0:55:56
Kdyně	49N23	13E02	-0:52:08
Kežmarok	49N08	20E25	-1:21:40
Kladno	50N08	14E05	-0:56:20
Kladruby	49N43	12E59	-0:51:56
Klášterec	50N24	13E10	-0:52:40
Klatovy	49N24	13E18	-0:53:12
Kočov	49N49	12E44	-0:50:56
Kojetín	49N21	17E18	-1:09:12
Kokašice	49N53	12E57	-0:51:48
Kokava nad Rimavicou	48N34	19E50	-1:19:20
Kolárovo	47N52	18E02	-1:12:08
Kolín	50N01	15E13	-1:00:52
Komárno	47N45	18E09	-1:12:36
Komorn → Komárno	47N45	18E09	-1:12:36
Komotau → Chomutov	50N28	13E26	-0:53:44
Konice	49N35	16E53	-1:07:32
Königgrätz → Hradec Králové	50N12	15E50	-1:03:20
Kopisty	50N34	13E35	-0:54:20
Koryta	49N24	13E13	-0:52:52
Košice	48N43	21E15	-1:25:00
Kosmonosy	50N26	15E00	-1:00:00
Košt'ahy	50N39	13E45	-0:55:00
Kostelec nad Labem	50N11	14E35	-0:58:20
Koštice	50N24	13E55	-0:55:40
Kralovice	49N59	13E29	-0:53:56
Kralupy nad Vltavou	50N11	14E18	-0:57:12
Kralupy u Chomutova	50N25	13E20	-0:53:20
Kraslice	50N18	12E31	-0:50:04
Krásná Lípa	50N54	14E31	-0:58:04
Krásný Dvůr	50N10	13E24	-0:53:36
Kravaře	50N38	14E23	-0:57:32
Kremnica	48N43	18E54	-1:15:36
Křimice	49N46	13E15	-0:53:00
Křivoklát	50N02	13E54	-0:55:36
Krnov	50N05	17E41	-1:10:44
Kroměříž	49N18	17E24	-1:09:36
Krompachy	48N56	20E52	-1:23:28
Krsy	49N54	13E03	-0:52:12
Krupá	50N08	13E41	-0:54:44
Krupka	50N43	13E46	-0:55:04
Kunovice	49N03	17E29	-1:09:56
Kunžak	49N07	15E11	-1:00:44
Kuřim	49N18	16E32	-1:06:08
Kutná Hora	49N57	15E16	-1:01:04
Kúty	48N40	17E03	-1:08:12
Kvilda	49N01	13E35	-0:54:20
Kyjov	49N01	17E08	-1:08:32
Kynšperk nad Ohří	50N04	12E32	-0:50:08
Lanškroun	49N55	16E37	-1:06:28
Lány	50N06	13E58	-0:55:52
Lázně Kynžvart	50N01	12E38	-0:50:32
Ledce	49N49	13E20	-0:53:20
Lenora	48N55	13E54	-0:55:36
Lestkov	49N54	12E52	-0:51:28
Levice	48N13	18E37	-1:14:28
Levoča	49N02	20E36	-1:22:24
Libčeves	50N26	13E50	-0:55:20
Libčice nad Vltavou	50N10	14E20	-0:57:20
Liběchov	50N20	14E28	-0:57:52
Liberec	50N46	15E03	-1:00:12
Líbeznice	50N10	14E30	-0:58:00
Liblín	49N55	13E32	-0:54:08
Libochovice	50N22	14E03	-0:56:12
Libušín	50N09	14E04	-0:56:16
Lipany	49N10	20E58	-1:23:52
Lipník nad Bečvou	49N31	17E35	-1:10:20
Liptovská Teplička	48N59	20E06	-1:20:24
Liptovský Mikuláš	49N06	19E37	-1:18:28
Líšina	49N37	13E10	-0:52:40
Lískova	49N25	12E43	-0:50:52
Lišov	49N01	14E37	-0:58:28
Litoměřice	50N35	14E09	-0:56:36
Litomyšl	49N52	16E19	-1:05:16
Litovel	49N42	17E05	-1:08:20

CZECHOSLOVAKIA CHECOSLOVAQUIA TCHÉCOSLOVAQUIE ČESKOSLOVENSKO

Litvínov	50N37	13E36	-0:54:24
Lnáře	49N28	13E47	-0:55:08
Lochovice	49N51	13E59	-0:55:56
Loket	50N09	12E43	-0:50:52
Lom	50N37	13E40	-0:54:40
Lomnice nad Popelkou	50N32	15E22	-1:01:28
Loučim	49N22	13E07	-0:52:28
Louny	50N19	13E46	-0:55:04
Lovosice	50N31	14E03	-0:56:12
Loza	49N53	13E18	-0:53:12
Lubenec	50N06	13E20	-0:53:20
Lubná	50N04	13E42	-0:54:48
Luby	50N12	12E25	-0:49:40
Lučenec	48N20	19E40	-1:18:40
Lužná	50N06	13E45	-0:55:00
Lysá pod Makytou	49N12	18E13	-1:12:52
Makov	49N23	18E30	-1:14:00
Malacky	48N27	17E00	-1:08:00
Manětín	49N59	13E14	-0:52:56
Margecany	48N54	21E01	-1:24:04
Mariánské Lázně	49N59	12E43	-0:50:52
Marienbad → Mariánské Lázně	49N59	12E43	-0:50:52
Martin	49N05	18E55	-1:15:40
Měčín	49N29	13E25	-0:53:40
Meclov	49N31	12E52	-0:51:28
Měděnec	50N25	13E05	-0:52:20
Medzilaborce	49N16	21E55	-1:27:40
Mělník	50N20	14E29	-0:57:56
Merklín	49N34	13E07	-0:52:28
Městečko	50N03	13E52	-0:55:28
Město Touškov	49N46	13E15	-0:53:00
Michalovce	48N45	21E55	-1:27:40
Michalovy Hory	49N55	12E47	-0:51:08
Mikulášovice	50N58	14E20	-0:57:20
Mikulov	48N49	16E39	-1:06:36
Milevsko	49N27	14E22	-0:57:28
Mimoň	50N40	14E44	-0:58:56
Miroslav	48N57	16E18	-1:05:12
Mirošov	49N41	13E40	-0:54:40
Mladá Boleslav	50N23	14E59	-0:59:56
Mladotice	49N58	13E18	-0:53:12
Mnichov	50N03	12E49	-0:51:16
Mníšek pod Brdy	49N52	14E16	-0:57:04
Mochov	50N08	14E50	-0:59:20
Mochtín	49N22	13E21	-0:53:24
Modra	48N21	17E17	-1:09:08
Modřice	49N07	16E37	-1:06:28
Mohelnice	49N46	16E55	-1:07:40
Moravská Ostrava → Ostrava	49N50	18E17	-1:13:08
Moravská Třebová	49N45	16E40	-1:06:40
Moravské Budějovice	49N03	15E49	-1:03:16
Moravsky Krumlov	49N03	16E19	-1:05:16
Most	50N32	13E39	-0:54:36
Moutnice	49N02	16E46	-1:07:04
Mšec	50N10	13E54	-0:55:36
Mšeno	50N27	14E38	-0:58:32
Muráň	48N46	20E02	-1:20:08
Mutějovice	50N09	13E41	-0:54:44
Myjava	48N45	17E34	-1:10:16
Mýto	49N47	13E44	-0:54:56
Náchod	50N25	16E10	-1:04:40
Nalžovské Hory	49N20	13E33	-0:54:12
Námestovo	49N25	19E30	-1:18:00
Napajedla	49N10	17E31	-1:10:04
Nejdek	50N17	12E42	-0:50:48
Němčice	49N26	13E05	-0:52:20
Neopmuk	49N29	13E35	-0:54:20
Nepomuk	49N29	13E36	-0:54:24
Neratovice	50N14	14E31	-0:58:04
Neštěmice	50N40	14E07	-0:56:28
Netolice	49N03	14E12	-0:56:48
Neusohl → Banská Bystrica	48N44	19E07	-1:16:28
Nezvěstice	49N39	13E32	-0:54:08
Nitra	48N20	18E05	-1:12:20
Nová Baňa	48N26	18E39	-1:14:36
Nová Bystřice	49N01	15E06	-1:00:24
Nováky	48N43	18E34	-1:14:16
Nová Paka	50N29	15E31	-1:02:04
Nová Role	50N15	12E47	-0:51:08
Nové Hardy	48N47	14E37	-0:58:28
Nové Město	50N21	16E09	-1:04:36
Nové Město nad Váhom	48N46	17E49	-1:11:16
Nové Město na Moravě	49N34	16E04	-1:04:16
Nové Sedlo	50N10	12E42	-0:50:48
Nové Strašecí	50N07	13E53	-0:55:32
Nové Údolí	48N48	13E48	-0:55:12
Nové Zámky	47N59	18E11	-1:12:44
Nový Bohumín	49N56	18E20	-1:13:20
Nový Bor	50N45	14E33	-0:58:12
Nový Jičín	49N36	18E00	-1:12:00
Nymburk	50N11	15E03	-1:00:12
Nýřany	49N43	13E12	-0:52:48
Nýrsko	49N18	13E09	-0:52:36
Odry	49N39	17E50	-1:11:20
Olešná	49N46	13E48	-0:55:12
Olmütz → Olomouc	49N36	17E16	-1:09:04
Olomouc	49N36	17E16	-1:09:04
Oloví	50N11	12E33	-0:50:12
Olšany	49N24	13E38	-0:54:32
Opava	49N56	17E54	-1:11:36
Orlová	49N50	18E24	-1:13:36
Osek	50N37	13E40	-0:54:40
Oselce	49N26	13E40	-0:54:40
Ostrau → Ostrava	49N50	18E17	-1:13:08
Ostrava	49N50	18E17	-1:13:08
Ostromeč	49N37	12E58	-0:51:52
Ostrov	50N17	12E57	-0:51:48
Otěšice	49N33	13E07	-0:52:28
Otrokovice	49N13	17E31	-1:10:04
Pacov	49N28	15E00	-1:00:00
Padrt'	49N40	13E46	-0:55:04
Pardubice	50N02	15E47	-1:03:08
Partizánske	48N39	18E23	-1:13:32
Pavlice	48N59	15E53	-1:03:32
Pchery	50N10	14E08	-0:56:32
Pelhřimov	49N26	15E13	-1:00:52
Pernink	50N20	12E45	-0:51:00
Perštejn	50N23	13E08	-0:52:32
Peruc	50N19	13E59	-0:55:56
Pezinok	48N18	17E17	-1:09:08
Piešt'any	48N36	17E50	-1:11:20
Pilsen → Plzeň	49N45	13E23	-0:53:32
Písek	49N19	14E10	-0:56:40
Planá	49N52	12E44	-0:50:56
Plánice	49N24	13E29	-0:53:56
Plasy	49N56	13E24	-0:53:36
Plzeň	49N45	13E23	-0:53:32
Poběžovice	49N31	12E48	-0:51:12
Podbořany	50N11	13E25	-0:53:40
Poděbrady	50N08	15E07	-1:00:28
Podhůří	49N28	13E40	-0:54:40
Podmokly	50N46	14E13	-0:56:52
Podvousy	49N32	13E08	-0:52:32
Pohořelice	48N59	16E32	-1:06:08
Polička	49N43	16E16	-1:05:04
Polná	49N29	15E43	-1:02:52
Poprad	49N03	20E18	-1:21:12
Postoloprty	50N20	13E40	-0:54:40
Považská Bystrica	49N08	18E27	-1:13:48
Povrly	50N40	14E10	-0:56:40
Pozsony → Bratislava	48N09	17E07	-1:08:28
Prachatice	49N01	14E00	-0:56:00
Prag → Praha	50N05	14E26	-0:57:44
Praga → Praha	50N05	14E26	-0:57:44
Prague → Praha	50N05	14E26	-0:57:44
Praha (Prague)	50N05	14E26	-0:57:44
Prameny	50N03	12E46	-0:51:04
Přelouč	50N02	15E34	-1:02:16
Přerov	49N27	17E27	-1:09:48
Prešov	49N00	21E15	-1:25:00
Pressburg → Bratislava	48N09	17E07	-1:08:28
Přeštice	49N34	13E20	-0:53:20
Příbor	49N39	18E10	-1:12:40
Příbram	49N42	14E01	-0:56:04
Prievidza	48N47	18E37	-1:14:28
Přimda	49N41	12E41	-0:50:44
Přísečnice	50N27	13E06	-0:52:24
Proboštov	50N39	13E50	-0:55:20
Prostějov	49N29	17E07	-1:08:28
Prostiboř	49N40	12E54	-0:51:36
Prunéřov	50N25	13E16	-0:53:04
Pšov	50N10	13E29	-0:53:56
Púchov	49N08	18E20	-1:13:20
Radnice	49N51	13E37	-0:54:28
Radošice	49N33	13E39	-0:54:36
Radotin	50N00	14E22	-0:57:28
Rajhrad	49N05	16E37	-1:06:28
Rakovník	50N05	13E43	-0:54:52
Reichenberg → Liberec	50N46	15E03	-1:00:12
Rejštejn	49N09	13E31	-0:54:04
Řetenice	50N38	13E46	-0:55:04
Řevničov	50N08	13E45	-0:55:00
Rimavská Sobota	48N23	20E02	-1:20:08
Rokycany	49N45	13E36	-0:54:24
Rosice	49N11	16E23	-1:05:32
Roudnice (nad Labem)	50N22	14E16	-0:57:04
Roželov	49N33	13E48	-0:55:12
Rožmitál pod Třemšínem	49N36	13E52	-0:55:28
Rožňava	48N40	20E32	-1:22:08
Rožnov pod Radhoštěm	49N28	18E10	-1:12:40
Roztoky	50N09	14E22	-0:57:28
Rumburk	50N57	14E32	-0:58:08
Rusovce	48N04	17E10	-1:08:40
Ružomberok	49N06	19E18	-1:17:12
Rychnov nad Kněžnou	50N10	16E17	-1:05:08
Rýmařov	49N56	17E16	-1:09:04
Sabinov	49N06	21E06	-1:24:24
Šafárikovo	48N27	20E20	-1:21:20
Šahy	48N05	18E57	-1:15:48
Šal'a	48N09	17E52	-1:11:28
Seč	49N36	13E30	-0:54:00
Sečovce	48N43	21E40	-1:26:40
Sečovská Polianka	48N47	21E42	-1:26:48
Sedlčany	49N40	14E26	-0:57:44
Sedlice	49N23	13E56	-0:55:44
Semily	50N36	15E20	-1:01:20
Seňa	48N34	21E15	-1:25:00
Senec	48N14	17E24	-1:09:36
Senica	48N41	17E22	-1:09:28
Sered'	48N17	17E44	-1:10:56
Sezimovo Ústí	49N23	14E42	-0:58:48
Silnice	48N54	13E44	-0:54:56
Skalica	48N51	17E14	-1:08:56
Skalná	50N07	12E23	-0:49:32
Skášov	49N31	13E26	-0:53:44
Slabce	50N00	13E44	-0:54:56
Slaný	50N11	14E04	-0:56:16
Šlapanice	49N10	16E44	-1:06:56
Slavkov u Brna	49N09	16E52	-1:07:28
Slavonice	49N00	15E21	-1:01:24
Šluknov	51N00	14E27	-0:57:48
Smečno	50N10	14E03	-0:56:12
Smědeč	48N56	14E09	-0:56:36
Snina	48N59	22E07	-1:28:28
Soběšice	49N12	13E41	-0:54:44
Soběslav	49N15	14E44	-0:58:56
Sobrance	48N45	22E11	-1:28:44
Sokolov	50N09	12E40	-0:50:40
Sol'	48N56	21E36	-1:26:24
Souš	50N32	13E34	-0:54:16
Spálené Poříčí	49N37	13E36	-0:54:24
Spišská Nová Ves	48N57	20E34	-1:22:16
Spořice	50N26	13E25	-0:53:40
Srní	49N06	13E27	-0:53:48
Stachy	49N06	13E40	-0:54:40
Staňkov	49N34	13E04	-0:52:16
Stará Boleslav	50N12	14E42	-0:58:48
Stará Role	50N14	12E47	-0:51:08
Stará Voda	50N00	12E36	-0:50:24
Staré Sedliště	49N45	12E42	-0:50:48
Starý Plzenec	49N42	13E28	-0:53:52
Šternberk	49N44	17E18	-1:09:12
Štětí	50N25	14E23	-0:57:32
Stod	49N39	13E10	-0:52:40
Stožec	48N51	13E50	-0:55:20
Strakonice	49N16	13E55	-0:55:40
Strašice	49N44	13E46	-0:55:04
Strašín	49N08	13E38	-0:54:32
Stráž	49N04	14E54	-0:59:36
Strážnice	48N54	17E18	-1:09:12
Strážný	48N54	13E42	-0:54:48
Strážov	49N18	13E15	-0:53:00
Strážske	48N53	21E50	-1:27:20
Streda nad Bodrogem	48N23	21E46	-1:27:04
Střelské Hoštice	49N18	13E46	-0:55:04
Stříbro	49N46	13E00	-0:52:00
Stropkov	49N12	21E40	-1:26:40
Studená	49N11	15E17	-1:01:08
Studénka	49N42	18E05	-1:12:20
Stupava	48N17	17E02	-1:08:08
Štúrovo	47N48	18E49	-1:15:16
Stvolny	50N03	13E15	-0:53:00
Šumná	48N56	15E52	-1:03:28
Šumperk	49N58	16E58	-1:07:52
Šurany	48N06	18E14	-1:12:56
Sušice	49N14	13E32	-0:54:08
Svatava	50N11	12E35	-0:50:20
Švermov	50N09	14E05	-0:56:20
Světlá nad Sázavou	49N40	15E25	-1:01:40
Svidník	49N18	21E35	-1:26:20
Švihov	49N29	13E17	-0:53:08
Svit	49N03	20E12	-1:20:48
Svitávka	49N30	16E37	-1:06:28
Svitavy	49N45	16E27	-1:05:48
Svor	50N47	14E36	-0:58:24
Svržno	49N35	12E46	-0:51:04
Tábor	49N25	14E41	-0:58:44
Tachov	49N48	12E38	-0:50:32
Tanvald	50N45	15E19	-1:01:16
Tchořovice	49N27	13E48	-0:55:12
Telč	49N11	15E27	-1:01:48
Teplá	49N59	12E52	-0:51:28
Teplice	50N39	13E48	-0:55:12
Teplitz → Teplice	50N39	13E48	-0:55:12
Terezín	50N31	14E08	-0:56:32
Teschen → Český Těšín	49N45	18E37	-1:14:28
Tetschen → Děčín	50N48	14E13	-0:56:52
Theresienstadt → Terezín	50N31	14E08	-0:56:32
Tišnov	49N21	16E25	-1:05:40
Tisovec	48N43	19E57	-1:19:48
Tlučiná	49N44	13E14	-0:52:56
Točník	49N27	13E19	-0:53:16
Topol'čany	48N34	18E10	-1:12:40
Toužim	50N04	13E00	-0:52:00
Třebechovice pod Orebem	50N12	16E00	-1:04:00
Třebenice	50N29	14E00	-0:56:00
Třebíč	49N13	15E53	-1:03:32
Třeboň	49N00	14E47	-0:59:08
Třemošna	49N49	13E20	-0:53:20
Trenčín	48N54	18E04	-1:12:16
Třešt'	49N18	15E30	-1:02:00
Trhomné	49N55	13E05	-0:52:20
Trhové Sviny	48N51	14E39	-0:58:36
Třinec	49N41	18E40	-1:14:40
Trnava	48N23	17E35	-1:10:20
Troppau → Opava	49N56	17E54	-1:11:36
Trstená	49N22	19E37	-1:18:28
Trutnov	50N34	15E55	-1:03:40
Tuchlovice	50N06	14E00	-0:56:00
Turčiansky Svätý Martin → Martin	49N05	18E55	-1:15:40
Turna nad Bodvou	48N37	20E53	-1:23:32
Turnov	50N35	15E10	-1:00:40
Turzovka	49N25	18E39	-1:14:36
Týn nad Vltavou	49N14	14E26	-0:57:44
Ubl'a	48N55	22E23	-1:29:32
Úborsko	49N20	13E09	-0:52:36
Uherské Hradiště	49N05	17E28	-1:09:52
Uherský Brod	49N02	17E39	-1:10:36
Újezd	50N03	14E44	-0:58:56
Ujęzd	49N26	13E27	-0:53:48
Úlice	49N45	13E09	-0:52:36
Úněšov	49N53	13E09	-0:52:36
Unhošt'	50N04	14E08	-0:56:32
Úšava	49N46	12E40	-0:50:40
Úštěk	50N36	14E20	-0:57:20
Ústí nad Labem	50N40	14E02	-0:56:08
Ústí nad Orlicí	49N58	16E24	-1:05:36
Útery	49N57	13E01	-0:52:04
Úvaly	50N03	14E47	-0:59:08
Vacov	49N09	13E45	-0:55:00
Valašské Klobouky	49N08	18E01	-1:12:04
Valašské Meziříčí	49N28	17E58	-1:11:52
Valtice	48N44	16E45	-1:07:00
Varnsdorf	50N52	14E40	-0:58:40
Vejprty	50N30	13E02	-0:52:08

ČESKOSLOVENSKO TCHÉCOSLOVAQUIE CHECOSLOVAQUIA CZECHOSLOVAKIA

Place	Lat.	Long.	LMT
Velemín	50N33	13E59	-0:55:56
Velešín	48N50	14E28	-0:57:52
Velhartice	49N16	13E23	-0:53:32
Velká Bíteš	49N17	16E13	-1:04:52
Vel'ké Kapušany	48N33	22E04	-1:28:16
Velké Meziříčí	49N21	16E00	-1:04:00
Velké Němčie	48N59	16E40	-1:06:40
Velké Pavlovice	48N54	16E19	-1:05:16
Velký Bor	49N22	13E42	-0:54:48
Velký Šenov	51N00	14E25	-0:57:40
Velký Sevljus	49N09	23E02	-1:32:08
Veltrusy	50N14	14E18	-0:57:12
Velvary	50N15	14E15	-0:57:00
Veselí nad Lužnicí	49N11	14E43	-0:58:52
Veselí nad Moravou	48N58	17E22	-1:09:28
Vidim	50N28	14E31	-0:58:04
Vimperk	49N03	13E47	-0:55:08
Višňové	48N59	16E09	-1:04:36
Vítkov	49N46	17E45	-1:11:00
Vlachovo Březí	49N05	13E57	-0:55:48
Vlašim	49N42	14E54	-0:59:36
Vodňany	49N09	14E11	-0:56:44
Vojkovice	50N15	13E02	-0:52:08
Vojtanov	50N06	12E19	-0:49:16
Volary	48N55	13E54	-0:55:36
Volyně	49N10	13E53	-0:55:32
Votice	49N38	14E39	-0:58:36
Vráble	48N15	18E19	-1:13:16
Vranov (nad Topl'ou)	48N54	21E41	-1:26:44
Vrchlabí	50N38	15E37	-1:02:28
Vroutek	50N08	13E24	-0:53:36
Vrútky	49N07	18E55	-1:15:40
Všepadly	49N28	13E06	-0:52:24
Všeruby	49N51	13E14	-0:52:56
Vsetín	49N21	17E59	-1:11:56
Vyškov	49N16	17E00	-1:08:00
Vyšná Radvaň	49N07	21E56	-1:27:44
Vysoké Mýto	49N57	16E10	-1:04:40
Vyšší Brod	48N37	14E19	-0:57:16
Zábřeh	49N53	16E52	-1:07:28
Zadní Chodov	49N54	12E44	-0:50:56
Zákolany	50N10	14E14	-0:56:56
Zákupy	50N42	14E40	-0:58:40
Žalany	50N35	13E55	-0:55:40
Žamberk	50N05	16E28	-1:05:52
Žandov	50N44	14E24	-0:57:36
Žarnovica	48N29	18E44	-1:14:56
Žatec	50N18	13E32	-0:54:08
Zavlekov	49N20	13E30	-0:54:00
Zbiroh	49N52	13E47	-0:55:08
Zborovy	49N23	13E31	-0:54:04
Zbraslav	49N59	14E24	-0:57:36
Zbůch	49N41	13E14	-0:52:56
Žd'ár	50N03	13E28	-0:53:52
Žd'ár	49N52	12E35	-0:50:20
Žd'ár nad Sazavou	49N34	15E57	-1:03:48
Ždiar	49N17	20E16	-1:21:04
Zdice	49N55	13E59	-0:55:56
Zdíkovec	49N05	13E42	-0:54:48
Žebrák	49N52	13E56	-0:55:44
Zelená Lhota	49N14	13E10	-0:52:40
Železná Ruda	49N09	13E14	-0:52:56
Žiar nad Hronom	48N36	18E52	-1:15:28
Žichovice	49N16	13E37	-0:54:28
Židlochovice	49N02	16E37	-1:06:28
Žihle	50N03	13E22	-0:53:28
Žilina	49N14	18E46	-1:15:04
Žirovnice	49N15	15E11	-1:00:44
Žitenice	50N35	14E08	-0:56:32
Zlaté Moravce	48N25	18E24	-1:13:36
Zlín → Gottwaldov	49N13	17E41	-1:10:44
Zlonice	50N15	14E07	-0:56:28
Žlutice	50N03	13E10	-0:52:40
Znaim → Znojmo	48N52	16E02	-1:04:08
Znojmo	48N52	16E02	-1:04:08
Zruč nad Sázavou	49N45	15E07	-1:00:28
Zvíkovec	49N56	13E42	-0:54:48
Zvolen	48N35	19E08	-1:16:32

DANMARK DÄNEMARK DANEMARK DINAMARCA DENMARK

Time Table		
Before 1/Jan/1890	LMT	
Begin Standard	12E35	
1/Jan/1890	0:00	-0:50
Begin Standard	15E00	
1/Jan/1894	0:00	-1:00
14/May/1916	23:00	-2:00
30/Sep/1916	23:00	-1:00
15/May/1940	0:00	-2:00
2/Nov/1942	3:00	-1:00
29/Mar/1943	2:00	-2:00
4/Oct/1943	3:00	-1:00
3/Apr/1944	2:00	-2:00
2/Oct/1944	3:00	-1:00
2/Apr/1945	2:00	-2:00
15/Aug/1945	3:00	-1:00
1/May/1946	2:00	-2:00
1/Sep/1946	3:00	-1:00
4/May/1947	2:00	-2:00
10/Aug/1947	3:00	-1:00
9/May/1948	2:00	-2:00
8/Aug/1948	3:00	-1:00
6/Apr/1980	2:00	-2:00
28/Sep/1980	3:00	-1:00
29/Mar/1981	2:00	-2:00
27/Sep/1981	3:00	-1:00
28/Mar/1982	2:00	-2:00
26/Sep/1982	3:00	-1:00
27/Mar/1983	2:00	-2:00
25/Sep/1983	3:00	-1:00
25/Mar/1984	2:00	-2:00
30/Sep/1984	3:00	-1:00
31/Mar/1985	2:00	-2:00
29/Sep/1985	3:00	-1:00
30/Mar/1986	2:00	-2:00
28/Sep/1986	3:00	-1:00
29/Mar/1987	2:00	-2:00
27/Sep/1987	3:00	-1:00
27/Mar/1988	2:00	-2:00
25/Sep/1988	3:00	-1:00
26/Mar/1989	2:00	-2:00
24/Sep/1989	3:00	-1:00
25/Mar/1990	2:00	-2:00
30/Sep/1990	3:00	-1:00
31/Mar/1991	2:00	-2:00
29/Sep/1991	3:00	-1:00
29/Mar/1992	2:00	-2:00
27/Sep/1992	3:00	-1:00
28/Mar/1993	2:00	-2:00
26/Sep/1993	3:00	-1:00
27/Mar/1994	2:00	-2:00
25/Sep/1994	3:00	-1:00
26/Mar/1995	2:00	-2:00
24/Sep/1995	3:00	-1:00
31/Mar/1996	2:00	-2:00
29/Sep/1996	3:00	-1:00
30/Mar/1997	2:00	-2:00
28/Sep/1997	3:00	-1:00
29/Mar/1998	2:00	-2:00
27/Sep/1998	3:00	-1:00
28/Mar/1999	2:00	-2:00
26/Sep/1999	3:00	-1:00
26/Mar/2000	2:00	-2:00
24/Sep/2000	3:00	-1:00

Place	Lat.	Long.	LMT
Aalborg → Ålborg	57N03	9E56	-0:39:44
Aarhus → Århus	57N09	10E13	-0:40:52
Åbenrå	55N02	9E26	-0:37:44
Åbybro	57N09	9E45	-0:39:00
Ærøskøbing	54N53	10E25	-0:41:40
Ågård	55N35	9E26	-0:37:44
Agerbæk	55N36	8E48	-0:35:12
Agerskov	55N07	9E08	-0:36:32
Åkirkeby	55N04	14E56	-0:59:44
Ålbæk	57N36	10E25	-0:41:40
Ålborg	57N03	9E56	-0:39:44
Allerslev	55N05	12E03	-0:48:12
Allinge	55N16	14E49	-0:59:16
Alnor	54N55	9E36	-0:38:24
Ans	56N19	9E36	-0:38:24
Ansager	55N42	8E45	-0:35:00
Århus	56N09	10E13	-0:40:52
Arnborg	56N01	8E59	-0:35:56
Arnum	55N15	8E59	-0:35:56
Årøsund	55N16	9E45	-0:39:00
Arrild	55N09	8E58	-0:35:52
Års	56N48	9E32	-0:38:08
Årslev	55N18	10E29	-0:41:56
Årup	55N23	10E04	-0:40:16
Askov	55N28	9E06	-0:36:24
Asnæs	55N49	11E31	-0:46:04
Asperup	55N29	9E55	-0:39:40
Assens	55N16	9E55	-0:39:40
Asserbo	56N01	12E01	-0:48:04
Augustenborg	54N57	9E53	-0:39:32
Auning	56N26	10E23	-0:41:32
Avlum	56N16	8E48	-0:35:12
Avnbøl	54N58	9E39	-0:38:36
Bække	55N34	9E09	-0:36:36
Bagenkop	54N45	10E41	-0:42:44
Ballen	55N49	10E39	-0:42:36
Ballerup	55N44	12E22	-0:49:28
Bandholm	54N50	11E29	-0:45:56
Bårse	55N07	11E58	-0:47:52
Beder	56N04	10E13	-0:40:52
Bellinge	55N20	10E20	-0:41:20
Besser	55N52	10E39	-0:42:36
Billund	55N44	9E07	-0:36:28
Birkerød	55N50	12E26	-0:49:44
Bjæverskov	55N27	12E02	-0:48:08
Bjernede	55N27	11E38	-0:46:32
Bjerringbro	56N23	9E40	-0:38:40
Blåhøj	55N51	9E01	-0:36:04
Blokhus	57N15	9E35	-0:38:20
Blovstrød	55N52	12E24	-0:49:36
Boeslunde	55N18	11E17	-0:45:08
Bogense	55N34	10E06	-0:40:24
Bolderslev	54N59	9E18	-0:37:12
Bording	56N12	9E17	-0:37:08
Bording Kirkeby	56N10	9E15	-0:37:00
Børkop	55N39	9E39	-0:38:36
Borre	55N00	12E28	-0:49:52
Borreby	55N14	11E19	-0:45:16
Bov	54N50	9E23	-0:37:32
Bovrup	54N59	9E36	-0:38:24
Brabrand	56N09	10E07	-0:40:28
Brædstrup	55N58	9E37	-0:38:28
Bramdrupdam	55N31	9E28	-0:37:52
Bramming	55N28	8E42	-0:34:48
Brande	55N57	9E07	-0:36:28
Bred	55N22	10E07	-0:40:28
Bredebro	55N03	8E49	-0:35:16
Bredsten	55N42	9E24	-0:37:36
Bregninge	55N41	11E19	-0:45:16
Bregninge	55N01	10E37	-0:42:28
Brenderup	55N29	9E59	-0:39:56
Broager	54N53	9E41	-0:38:44
Brobyværk	55N14	10E15	-0:41:00
Brønderslev	57N16	9E58	-0:39:52
Brøns	55N11	8E44	-0:34:56
Brørup	55N29	9E01	-0:36:04
Brovst	57N06	9E32	-0:38:08
Brudager	55N07	10E41	-0:42:44
Brundby	55N49	10E37	-0:42:28
Bryrup	56N01	9E31	-0:38:04
Bylderup	54N57	9E07	-0:36:28
Christiansfeld	55N21	9E29	-0:37:56
Copenhagen → København	55N40	12E35	-0:50:20
Copenhague → København	55N40	12E35	-0:50:20
Dageløkke	55N04	10E53	-0:43:32
Dalmose	55N18	11E26	-0:45:44
Dalum	55N22	10E22	-0:41:28
Dannemare	54N45	11E12	-0:44:48
Daugård	55N44	9E43	-0:38:52
Dianalund	55N32	11E30	-0:46:00
Dragør	55N36	12E41	-0:50:44
Dronninglund	57N09	10E18	-0:41:12
Dybbøl	54N55	9E45	-0:39:00
Dyreborg	55N04	10E13	-0:40:52
Ebberup	55N15	9E59	-0:39:56
Ebeltoft	56N12	10E41	-0:42:44
Egernsund	54N54	9E37	-0:38:28
Egtved	55N37	9E18	-0:37:12
Ejby	55N30	12E07	-0:48:28
Ejby	55N26	9E57	-0:39:48
Ejstrup	55N59	9E17	-0:37:08
Elsinore → Helsingør	56N02	12E37	-0:50:28
Engestofte	54N46	11E34	-0:46:16
Engesvang	56N10	9E21	-0:37:24
Engum	55N44	9E40	-0:38:40
Esbjaerg → Esbjerg	55N28	8E27	-0:33:48
Esbjerg	55N28	8E27	-0:33:48
Eskilstrup	54N51	11E54	-0:47:36
Espe	55N12	10E25	-0:41:40
Espergærde	56N00	12E34	-0:50:16
Fåborg	55N06	10E15	-0:41:00
Fakse	55N15	12E08	-0:48:32
Fakse Ladeplads	55N13	12E11	-0:48:44
Faldsled	55N09	10E09	-0:40:36
Fårevejle	55N48	11E27	-0:45:48
Farsø	56N47	9E21	-0:37:24
Farum	55N48	12E22	-0:49:28
Fårvang	56N16	9E44	-0:38:56
Fasterholt	56N01	9E07	-0:36:28
Femmøller	56N14	10E35	-0:42:20
Fensmark	55N17	11E49	-0:47:16
Ferritslev	55N18	10E36	-0:42:24
Filskov	55N48	9E02	-0:36:08
Fjællebroen	55N03	10E24	-0:41:36
Fjenneslev	55N26	11E40	-0:46:40
Fjerritslev	57N05	9E16	-0:37:04
Foldingbro	55N26	9E01	-0:36:04
Fredensborg	55N58	12E24	-0:49:36
Fredericia	55N35	9E46	-0:39:04
Frederiksberg	55N25	11E34	-0:46:16
Frederiksberg	55N41	12E32	-0:50:08
Frederikshavn	57N26	10E32	-0:42:08
Frederikssund	55N50	12E04	-0:48:16
Frederiksværk	55N58	12E02	-0:48:08
Fuglebjerg	55N18	11E34	-0:46:16
Gadbjerg	55N46	9E20	-0:37:20
Gadevang	55N58	12E18	-0:49:12
Galten	56N09	9E55	-0:39:40
Gårslev	55N38	9E43	-0:38:52
Gavnø	55N11	11E44	-0:46:56
Gedser	54N35	11E57	-0:47:48
Gelsted	55N24	9E59	-0:39:56
Genner	55N07	9E26	-0:37:44
Gentofte	55N45	12E33	-0:50:12
Gershøj	55N43	11E59	-0:47:56
Gesten	55N31	9E12	-0:36:48
Gilleleje	56N07	12E19	-0:49:16
Gislev	55N13	10E37	-0:42:28
Gislinge	55N44	11E33	-0:46:12
Gisselfeld	55N18	11E59	-0:47:56
Give	55N51	9E15	-0:37:00
Gjedved	55N56	9E51	-0:39:24
Gjern	56N14	9E45	-0:39:00
Gladsakse	55N44	12E29	-0:49:56
Glamsbjerg	55N16	10E07	-0:40:28
Glejbjerg	55N33	8E50	-0:35:20
Glostrup	55N40	12E24	-0:49:36
Glud	55N49	10E00	-0:40:00
Glumsø	55N21	11E42	-0:46:48
Glyngøre	56N46	8E52	-0:35:28
Gørding	55N29	8E48	-0:35:12
Gørlev	55N32	11E14	-0:44:56
Græsted	56N04	12E17	-0:49:08
Gram	55N17	9E04	-0:36:16
Gråsten	54N55	9E36	-0:38:24
Gredstedbro	55N24	8E45	-0:35:00
Grejsdal	55N45	9E32	-0:38:08
Grenå	56N25	10E53	-0:43:32
Greve	55N36	12E15	-0:49:00
Greve Strand	55N35	12E14	-0:48:56

Place	Lat.	Long.	Time
Grevinge	55N48	11E34	-0:46:16
Grindsted	55N45	8E56	-0:35:44
Guderup	54N59	9E53	-0:39:32
Gudhjem	55N13	14E59	-0:59:56
Gudme	55N09	10E43	-0:42:52
Guldborg	54N52	11E45	-0:47:00
Gylling	55N53	10E11	-0:40:44
Haderslev	55N15	9E30	-0:38:00
Hadsten	56N20	10E03	-0:40:12
Hadsund	56N43	10E07	-0:40:28
Hals	57N00	10E19	-0:41:16
Hammel	56N15	9E52	-0:39:28
Hammerum	56N08	9E04	-0:36:16
Hanstholm	57N07	8E38	-0:34:32
Haraldsted	55N30	11E47	-0:47:08
Harboør	56N37	8E12	-0:32:48
Hårby	55N13	10E07	-0:40:28
Hareskov	55N46	12E25	-0:49:40
Hårlev	55N21	12E15	-0:49:00
Harndrup	55N28	10E02	-0:40:08
Hasle	55N11	14E43	-0:58:52
Haslev	55N20	11E58	-0:47:52
Hasmark	55N33	10E28	-0:41:52
Hastrup	55N26	12E11	-0:48:44
Hatting	55N51	9E46	-0:39:04
Havdrup	55N32	12E08	-0:48:32
Havnbjerg	55N02	9E48	-0:39:12
Havnsø	55N45	11E20	-0:45:20
Hedehusene	55N39	12E12	-0:48:48
Hedensted	55N46	9E42	-0:38:48
Hejlsminde	55N22	9E37	-0:38:28
Hejnsvig	55N41	8E59	-0:35:56
Hellebæk	56N04	12E34	-0:50:16
Hellevad	55N05	9E13	-0:36:52
Helsinge	56N01	12E12	-0:48:48
Helsingør (Elsinore)	56N02	12E37	-0:50:28
Herfølge	55N25	12E10	-0:48:40
Herlev	55N43	12E27	-0:49:48
Herlufmagle	55N19	11E46	-0:47:04
Herlufsholm	55N15	11E46	-0:47:04
Herning	56N08	8E59	-0:35:56
Herritslev	54N42	11E41	-0:46:44
Hesselager	55N10	10E45	-0:43:00
Hillerød	55N56	12E19	-0:49:16
Hinnerup	56N16	10E04	-0:40:16
Hirtshals	57N35	9E58	-0:39:52
Hjembæk	55N42	11E25	-0:45:40
Hjøllund	56N05	9E25	-0:37:40
Hjordkær	55N01	9E19	-0:37:16
Hjørring	57N28	9E59	-0:39:56
Hobro	56N38	9E48	-0:39:12
Hoed	56N19	10E49	-0:43:16
Højby	55N55	11E37	-0:46:28
Højby	55N20	10E27	-0:41:48
Højer	54N58	8E43	-0:34:52
Højerup	55N17	12E27	-0:49:48
Holbæk	55N43	11E43	-0:46:52
Holckenhavn	55N17	10E47	-0:43:08
Holeby	54N43	11E28	-0:45:52
Holme	56N07	10E11	-0:40:44
Holstebro	56N21	8E38	-0:34:32
Holsted	55N30	8E55	-0:35:40
Holte	55N49	12E28	-0:49:52
Holtug	55N21	12E25	-0:49:40
Høng	55N31	11E18	-0:45:12
Hoptrup	55N11	9E28	-0:37:52
Horbelev	54N49	12E04	-0:48:16
Hornbæk	56N05	12E28	-0:49:52
Horne	55N06	10E11	-0:40:44
Hørning	56N05	10E03	-0:40:12
Hornslet	56N19	10E20	-0:41:20
Hornsyld	55N45	9E51	-0:39:24
Horsens	55N52	9E52	-0:39:28
Hørsholm	55N53	12E30	-0:50:00
Horslunde	54N54	11E14	-0:44:56
Hørup	54N56	9E55	-0:39:40
Hørve	55N45	11E28	-0:45:52
Hov	55N55	10E16	-0:41:04
Hovborg	55N36	8E57	-0:35:48
Høve	55N50	11E30	-0:46:00
Hovedgård	55N57	9E58	-0:39:52
Hoven	55N51	8E46	-0:35:04
Humble	54N50	10E42	-0:42:48
Humlebæk	55N58	12E33	-0:50:12
Hundested	55N58	11E52	-0:47:28
Hundslund	55N55	10E04	-0:40:16
Hunseby	54N48	11E32	-0:46:08
Hurup	56N45	8E25	-0:33:40
Hvalsø	55N36	11E50	-0:47:20
Hvide Sande	55N59	8E08	-0:32:32
Hvidovre	55N39	12E29	-0:49:56
Hyllinge	55N16	11E37	-0:46:28
Ikast	56N08	9E10	-0:36:40
Ilskov	56N14	9E06	-0:36:24
Jægerspris	55N51	11E59	-0:47:56
Jelling	55N45	9E26	-0:37:44
Jels	55N21	9E12	-0:36:48
Juelsminde	55N43	10E01	-0:40:04
Jyderup	55N40	11E26	-0:45:44
Jyllinge	55N45	12E07	-0:48:28
Kalundborg	55N41	11E06	-0:44:24
Kalvehave	55N00	12E10	-0:48:40
Karise	55N18	12E13	-0:48:52
Karlslunde	55N34	12E14	-0:48:56
Karrebæksminde	55N11	11E40	-0:46:40
Karup	56N18	9E10	-0:36:40
Kattrup	55N57	9E56	-0:39:44
Kerteminde	55N27	10E40	-0:42:40
Kettinge	54N42	11E45	-0:47:00
Kibæk	56N02	8E51	-0:35:24
Kirkeby	56N09	9E27	-0:37:48
Kirke Stillinge	55N26	11E15	-0:45:00
Kjellerup	56N17	9E26	-0:37:44

Place	Lat.	Long.	Time
Kjøbenhavn → København	55N40	12E35	-0:50:20
Kliplev	54N56	9E25	-0:37:40
Klitmøller	57N02	8E31	-0:34:04
Knebel	56N13	10E30	-0:42:00
Knuthenborg	54N50	11E30	-0:46:00
København (Copenhagen)	55N40	12E35	-0:50:20
Køge	55N27	12E11	-0:48:44
Kolby Kås	55N48	10E33	-0:42:12
Kolding	55N31	9E29	-0:37:56
Kølkær	56N04	9E06	-0:36:24
Kollund	54N51	9E27	-0:37:48
Kølvrå	56N18	9E08	-0:36:32
Køng	55N07	11E50	-0:47:20
Kongens Lyngby	55N46	12E31	-0:50:04
Kopenhagen → København	55N40	12E35	-0:50:20
Korinth	55N08	10E21	-0:41:24
Korsør	55N20	11E09	-0:44:36
Kragenæs	54N55	11E22	-0:45:28
Kraghave	54N48	11E53	-0:47:32
Kregme	55N57	12E04	-0:48:16
Krogager	55N42	8E51	-0:35:24
Kruså	54N50	9E25	-0:37:40
Kværndrup	55N10	10E32	-0:42:08
Kvanløse	55N39	11E41	-0:46:44
Kvistgård	55N59	12E30	-0:50:00
Kyndby	55N48	11E56	-0:47:44
Ladby	55N26	10E38	-0:42:32
Langeskov	55N22	10E36	-0:42:24
Låsby	56N09	9E49	-0:39:16
Laven	56N07	9E43	-0:38:52
Lemvig	56N32	8E18	-0:33:12
Lillerød	55N52	12E22	-0:49:28
Lille Værløse	55N47	12E23	-0:49:32
Lindelse	54N52	10E44	-0:42:56
Lindved	55N47	9E35	-0:38:20
Liseleje	56N01	11E59	-0:47:56
Løgstør	56N58	9E15	-0:37:00
Løgten	56N17	10E19	-0:41:16
Løgumgårde	55N05	8E57	-0:35:48
Løgumkloster	55N03	8E57	-0:35:48
Lohals	55N08	10E55	-0:43:40
Løjt Kirkeby	55N05	9E28	-0:37:52
Løkken	57N22	9E43	-0:38:52
Løsning	55N48	9E42	-0:38:48
Lumsås	55N57	11E31	-0:46:04
Lundby	55N07	11E53	-0:47:32
Lunde	55N29	10E21	-0:41:24
Lundeborg	55N08	10E47	-0:43:08
Lunderskov	55N29	9E18	-0:37:12
Lynæs	55N57	11E52	-0:47:28
Lynge	55N51	12E17	-0:49:08
Malling	56N02	10E10	-0:40:40
Måløv	55N45	12E20	-0:49:20
Mariager	56N39	10E00	-0:40:00
Maribo	54N46	11E31	-0:46:04
Marstal	54N51	10E31	-0:42:04
Martofte	55N33	10E40	-0:42:40
Mårup	55N57	10E35	-0:42:20
Menstrup	55N13	11E36	-0:46:24
Mern	55N03	12E04	-0:48:16
Middelfart	55N30	9E45	-0:39:00
Møgeltønder	54N56	8E49	-0:35:16
Mogenstrup	55N11	11E53	-0:47:32
Mommark	54N55	10E03	-0:40:12
Mørkøv	55N40	11E32	-0:46:08
Mullerup	55N30	11E13	-0:44:52
Munkebo	55N27	10E34	-0:42:16
Næsby	55N25	10E22	-0:41:28
Næstved	55N14	11E46	-0:47:04
Nakskov	54N50	11E09	-0:44:36
Neksø	55N04	15E09	-1:00:36
Nibe	56N59	9E38	-0:38:32
Nivå	55N56	12E31	-0:50:04
Nordborg	55N03	9E45	-0:39:00
Nordby	55N58	10E34	-0:42:16
Nørre Åby	55N27	9E54	-0:39:36
Nørre Alslev	54N54	11E54	-0:47:36
Nørre Broby	55N15	10E14	-0:40:56
Nørre Nærå	55N34	10E17	-0:41:08
Nørre Snede	55N58	9E25	-0:37:40
Nørresundby	57N04	9E55	-0:39:40
Nørre Vejrup	55N31	8E47	-0:35:08
Norsminde	56N01	10E16	-0:41:04
Nørup	55N43	9E19	-0:37:16
Nyborg	55N19	10E48	-0:43:12
Nykøbing	56N48	8E52	-0:35:28
Nykøbing	55N55	11E41	-0:46:44
Nykøbing	54N46	11E53	-0:47:32
Nysø	55N08	12E02	-0:48:08
Nysted	54N40	11E45	-0:47:00
Odden	55N58	11E22	-0:45:28
Odder	55N58	10E10	-0:40:40
Odense	55N24	10E23	-0:41:32
Ødsted	55N39	9E25	-0:37:40
Oksbøl	55N38	8E17	-0:33:08
Ølby Lyng	55N29	12E09	-0:48:36
Ølgod	55N49	8E37	-0:34:28
Ollerup	55N04	10E30	-0:42:00
Ølsemagle	55N30	12E10	-0:48:40
Ølstykke	55N47	12E11	-0:48:44
Onsbjerg	55N51	10E35	-0:42:20
Orehoved	54N57	11E52	-0:47:28
Ørslev	55N02	11E59	-0:47:56
Ørsted	55N20	10E04	-0:40:16
Østbirk	55N58	9E46	-0:39:04
Osted	55N34	11E58	-0:47:52
Øster Højst	55N00	9E03	-0:36:12
Otterup	55N31	10E24	-0:41:36
Over Jerstal	55N12	9E18	-0:37:12
Padborg	54N49	9E22	-0:37:28
Pårup	55N24	10E20	-0:41:20
Pårup	56N08	9E21	-0:37:24

Place	Lat.	Long.	Time
Pedersborg	55N27	11E34	-0:46:16
Pederstrup	54N54	11E16	-0:45:04
Præstø	55N07	12E03	-0:48:12
Rågeleje	56N06	12E10	-0:48:40
Randbøl	55N42	9E16	-0:37:04
Randers	56N28	10E03	-0:40:12
Rask Mølle	55N52	9E37	-0:38:28
Ravsted	55N01	9E08	-0:36:32
Regstrup	55N40	11E37	-0:46:28
Rens	54N54	9E06	-0:36:24
Ribe	55N21	8E46	-0:35:04
Ringe	55N14	10E29	-0:41:56
Ringkøbing	56N05	8E15	-0:33:00
Ringsted	55N27	11E49	-0:47:16
Rinkenæs	54N54	9E34	-0:38:16
Risø	55N42	12E06	-0:48:24
Ristinge	54N50	10E38	-0:42:32
Rødby	54N42	11E24	-0:45:36
Rødbyhavn	54N39	11E21	-0:45:24
Rødding	55N23	9E06	-0:36:24
Rødekro	55N04	9E21	-0:37:24
Rødovre	55N41	12E29	-0:49:56
Rødvig	55N15	12E23	-0:49:32
Rønde	56N18	10E29	-0:41:56
Rønne	55N06	14E42	-0:58:48
Rørvig	55N57	11E46	-0:47:04
Roskilde	55N39	12E05	-0:48:20
Roslev	56N42	8E59	-0:35:56
Rudbøl	54N54	8E45	-0:35:00
Rudkøbing	54N56	10E43	-0:42:52
Ruds Vedby	55N33	11E23	-0:45:32
Rungsted	55N53	12E33	-0:50:12
Ry	56N05	9E46	-0:39:04
Ryslinge	55N15	10E33	-0:42:12
Sæby	57N20	10E32	-0:42:08
Sæby	55N33	11E19	-0:45:16
Særslev	55N31	10E11	-0:40:44
Særslev	55N43	11E23	-0:45:32
Sakskøbing	54N48	11E39	-0:46:36
Salten	56N05	9E35	-0:38:20
Sandvig	55N17	14E47	-0:59:08
Seest	55N29	9E27	-0:37:48
Sejs	56N09	9E36	-0:38:24
Silkeborg	56N10	9E34	-0:38:16
Sindal	57N28	10E13	-0:40:52
Skåde	56N06	10E13	-0:40:52
Skælskør	55N15	11E19	-0:45:16
Skærbæk	55N31	9E38	-0:38:32
Skærbæk	55N09	8E46	-0:35:04
Skævinge	55N55	12E10	-0:48:40
Skagen	57N44	10E36	-0:42:24
Skanderborg	56N02	9E56	-0:39:44
Skårup	55N05	10E42	-0:42:48
Skelde	54N51	9E44	-0:38:56
Skibby	55N45	11E58	-0:47:52
Skive	56N34	9E02	-0:36:08
Skjern	55N57	8E30	-0:34:00
Skodborg	55N25	9E09	-0:36:36
Skodsborg	55N49	12E34	-0:50:16
Skørping	56N50	9E53	-0:39:32
Skovby	54N53	10E00	-0:40:00
Skovlund	55N44	8E43	-0:34:52
Skrydstrup	55N14	9E15	-0:37:00
Slagelse	55N24	11E22	-0:45:28
Slangerup	55N51	12E11	-0:48:44
Snaptun	55N49	10E04	-0:40:16
Snedsted	56N54	8E32	-0:34:08
Snekkersten	56N00	12E36	-0:50:24
Snøde	55N05	10E55	-0:43:40
Snoghøj	55N31	9E43	-0:38:52
Søby	54N56	10E16	-0:41:04
Søllerød	55N49	12E31	-0:50:04
Søllested	54N49	11E17	-0:45:08
Sommersted	55N19	9E19	-0:37:16
Sønderborg	54N55	9E47	-0:39:08
Sønderby	55N47	10E01	-0:40:04
Sønder Felding	55N57	8E47	-0:35:08
Sønderhav	54N51	9E30	-0:38:00
Sønder Nærå	55N18	10E30	-0:42:00
Sønder Omme	55N50	8E54	-0:35:36
Søndersø	55N29	10E16	-0:41:04
Sorø	55N26	11E34	-0:46:16
Søvind	55N54	10E01	-0:40:04
Spang	54N56	9E50	-0:39:20
Spodsbjerg	54N56	10E50	-0:43:20
Spørring	56N18	10E09	-0:40:36
Stakroge	55N53	8E51	-0:35:24
Stege	54N59	12E18	-0:49:12
Stenlille	55N32	11E36	-0:46:24
Stenløse	55N46	12E12	-0:48:48
Stenstrup	55N07	10E31	-0:42:04
Stige	55N26	10E25	-0:41:40
Stilling	56N04	10E00	-0:40:00
Stokkemarke	54N50	11E23	-0:45:32
Store Andst	55N29	9E14	-0:36:56
Store Heddinge	55N19	12E25	-0:49:40
Store Magleby	55N36	12E38	-0:50:32
Store Merløse	55N33	11E40	-0:46:40
Strib	55N32	9E47	-0:39:08
Strøby	55N23	12E18	-0:49:12
Struer	56N29	8E37	-0:34:28
Stubbekøbing	54N53	12E03	-0:48:12
Sundby	54N42	11E48	-0:47:12
Sunds	56N12	9E01	-0:36:04
Sværdborg	55N05	11E54	-0:47:36
Svaneke	55N08	15E09	-1:00:36
Svanninge	55N07	10E15	-0:41:00
Svebølle	55N38	11E20	-0:45:20
Svendborg	55N03	10E37	-0:42:28
Svenstrup	56N59	9E52	-0:39:28
Svinninge	55N43	11E28	-0:45:52
Tandslet	54N55	9E59	-0:39:56
Tappernøje	55N10	11E59	-0:47:56
Tårbæk	55N47	12E36	-0:50:24
Tarm	55N55	8E32	-0:34:08

DANMARK DÄNEMARK DANEMARK DINAMARCA DENMARK

Place	Lat	Long	Offset
Tårnby	55N38	12E36	-0:50:24
Tåstrup	55N39	12E19	-0:49:16
Taulov	55N33	9E37	-0:38:28
Tebstrup	55N59	9E53	-0:39:32
Terslev	55N22	11E59	-0:47:56
Tersløse	55N31	11E30	-0:46:00
Them	56N06	9E33	-0:38:12
Thisted	56N57	8E42	-0:34:48
Thorsø	56N18	9E48	-0:39:12
Thurø	55N03	10E40	-0:42:40
Thyborøn	56N42	8E13	-0:32:52
Thyregod	55N54	9E16	-0:37:04
Tibirke	56N03	12E07	-0:48:28
Tinglev	54N56	9E15	-0:37:00
Tingsted	54N49	11E56	-0:47:44
Tirsted	54N44	11E21	-0:45:24
Tirstrup	56N18	10E42	-0:42:48
Tisvildeleje	56N03	12E05	-0:48:20
Tofterup	55N39	8E50	-0:35:20
Toftlund	55N11	9E04	-0:36:16
Tølløse	55N37	11E45	-0:47:00
Tommerup Stationsby	55N19	10E13	-0:40:52
Tønder	54N56	8E54	-0:35:36
Torning	56N17	9E20	-0:37:20
Torrild	55N59	10E04	-0:40:16
Tørring	55N51	9E29	-0:37:56
Tranderup	54N52	10E22	-0:41:28
Tranebjerg	55N50	10E36	-0:42:24
Tranekær	55N00	10E51	-0:43:24
Troense	55N02	10E39	-0:42:36
Troldhede	55N59	8E45	-0:35:00
Tulstrup	56N07	9E46	-0:39:04
Tune	55N36	12E11	-0:48:44
Tuse	55N43	11E37	-0:46:28
Ubby	55N37	11E13	-0:44:52
Udby	55N05	11E57	-0:47:48
Ugerløse	55N35	11E40	-0:46:40
Uldum	55N51	9E36	-0:38:24
Ulfborg	56N16	8E20	-0:33:20
Ullerslev	55N22	10E40	-0:42:40
Undløse	55N36	11E35	-0:46:20
Væggerløse	54N42	11E56	-0:47:44
Vallensbæk	55N38	12E22	-0:49:28
Vallø	55N24	12E15	-0:49:00
Vamdrup	55N25	9E17	-0:37:08
Vandel	55N42	9E13	-0:36:52
Varde	55N38	8E29	-0:33:56
Vedbæk	55N51	12E34	-0:50:16
Vejen	55N29	9E09	-0:36:36
Vejlby	56N12	10E13	-0:40:52
Vejle	55N42	9E32	-0:38:08
Vemmenæs	54N59	10E40	-0:42:40
Veng	56N07	9E53	-0:39:32
Verninge	55N18	10E13	-0:40:52
Vester Egede	55N16	11E59	-0:47:56
Vesterø Havn	57N18	10E56	-0:43:44
Vester Skerninge	55N03	10E28	-0:41:52
Vester Sottrup	54N57	9E43	-0:38:52
Viborg	56N26	9E24	-0:37:36
Viby	55N33	12E02	-0:48:08
Videbæk	56N05	8E38	-0:34:32
Vig	55N51	11E36	-0:46:24
Vigersted	55N29	11E54	-0:47:36
Vildbjerg	56N12	8E46	-0:35:04
Vindeby	55N03	10E38	-0:42:32
Vinderslev	56N15	9E26	-0:37:44
Vinderup	56N29	8E47	-0:35:08
Vinding	55N41	9E35	-0:38:20
Vindinge	55N19	10E45	-0:43:00
Virklund	56N07	9E34	-0:38:16
Viskinge	55N40	11E16	-0:45:04
Vissenbjerg	55N23	10E08	-0:40:32
Vojens	55N15	9E19	-0:37:16
Vonsild	55N27	9E29	-0:37:56
Vorbasse	55N38	9E05	-0:36:20
Vordingborg	55N01	11E55	-0:47:40
Vrå	57N21	9E57	-0:39:48

JIBUTI FRENCH SOMALILAND AFARS ET ISSAS DJIBOUTI

Time Table

Before	1/Jul/1911	LMT
Begin Standard		45E00
1/Jul/1911	0:00	-3:00

Place	Lat	Long	Offset
Ali-Sabieh	11N09	42E42	-2:50:48
Dikhil	11N06	42E22	-2:49:28
Djibouti	11N36	43E09	-2:52:36
Hol-Hol	11N19	42E57	-2:51:48
Jibuti → Djibouti	11N36	43E09	-2:52:36
Moulhoulé	12N36	43E12	-2:52:48
Obock	11N59	43E16	-2:53:04
Tadjoura	11N47	42E54	-2:51:36

DOMINIQUE DOMINICA

Time Table

Before	1/Jul/1911	LMT
Begin Standard		60w00
1/Jul/1911	0:01	4:00

Place	Lat	Long	Offset
Berekua	15N14	61w19	4:05:16
Castle Bruce	15N26	61w16	4:05:04
Coulihaut	15N30	61w29	4:05:56
Delices	15N17	61w16	4:05:04
La Plaine	15N20	61w15	4:05:00
Mahaut	15N21	61w25	4:05:40
Marigot	15N32	61w18	4:05:12
Portsmouth	15N35	61w28	4:05:52
Roseau	15N18	61w24	4:05:36
Saint Joseph	15N26	61w26	4:05:44
Salisbury	15N26	61w27	4:05:48
Vieille Case	15N36	61w24	4:05:36
Wesley	15N34	61w19	4:05:16

REPÚBLICA DOMINICANA SANTO DOMINGO DOMINICAN REPUBLIC

Time Table

Before	1/Jan/1890	LMT
Begin Standard		70w00
1/Jan/1890	0:00	4:40
Begin Standard		75w00
1/Apr/1933	12:00	5:00
30/Oct/1966	0:00	4:00
28/Feb/1967	0:00	5:00
26/Oct/1969	0:00	4:30
21/Feb/1970	0:00	5:00
25/Oct/1970	0:00	4:30
20/Jan/1971	0:00	5:00
31/Oct/1971	0:00	4:30
21/Jan/1972	0:00	5:00
29/Oct/1972	0:00	4:30
21/Jan/1973	0:00	5:00
27/Oct/1973	0:00	4:00
21/Jan/1974	0:00	5:00
Begin Standard		60w00
27/Oct/1974	0:00	4:00

Place	Lat	Long	Offset
Azua	18N27	70w44	4:42:56
Bajos de Haina	18N25	70w02	4:40:08
Baní	18N17	70w20	4:41:20
Banica	19N06	71w41	4:46:44
Barahona	18N12	71w06	4:44:24
Benemérita de San Cristóbal	18N25	70w06	4:40:24
Bonao	18N56	70w25	4:41:40
Cabral	18N15	71w13	4:44:52
Ciudad Trujillo → Santo Domingo	18N28	69w54	4:39:36
Concepción de la Vega	19N13	70w31	4:42:04
Cotuí	19N03	70w09	4:40:36
Dajabón	19N33	71w42	4:46:48
Duarte	18N29	69w52	4:39:28
Elías Piña	18N53	71w42	4:46:48
El Seibo	18N46	69w02	4:36:08
Enriquillo	17N54	71w14	4:44:56
Hato Mayor (del Rey)	18N46	69w15	4:37:00
La Romana	18N25	68w58	4:35:52
La Vega	19N14	70w31	4:42:04
Mao	19N34	71w05	4:44:20
Miches	18N59	69w03	4:36:12
Moca	19N24	70w31	4:42:04
Monte Cristi	19N51	71w39	4:46:36
Nagua	19N23	69w50	4:39:20
Neiba	18N28	71w25	4:45:40
Pedernales	18N02	71w45	4:47:00
Puerto Plata	19N48	70w41	4:42:44
Sabana de la Mar	19N04	69w23	4:37:32
Sabaneta	19N30	71w21	4:45:24
Salcedo	19N23	70w25	4:41:40
Salvaleón de Higüey	18N37	68w42	4:34:48
Samana	19N13	69w19	4:37:16
Sánchez	19N14	69w36	4:38:24
San Cristobal	18N24	70w07	4:40:28
San Felipe de Puerto Plata	19N48	70w41	4:42:44
San Francisco de Macorís	19N18	70w15	4:41:00
San José de Ocoa	18N33	70w30	4:42:00
San Juan (de la Maguana)	18N48	71w14	4:44:56
San Pedro de Macorís	18N27	69w18	4:37:12
Santa Bárbara de Samaná	19N13	69w19	4:37:16
Santa Cruz de el Seibo	18N46	69w02	4:36:08
Santiago (de los Caballeros)	19N27	70w42	4:42:48

DOMINICAN REPUBLIC — SANTO DOMINGO — REPÚBLICA DOMINICANA

Place	Lat	Long	Time
Santo Domingo	18N28	69w54	4:39:36
Seibo	18N46	69w02	4:36:08
Vicente Noble	18N23	71w11	4:44:44
Villa Vázquez	19N45	71w27	4:45:48

ECUADOR — ÉQUATEUR

Time Table # 1
Before 1/Jan/1890 LMT
Begin Standard 78w30
1/Jan/1890 0:00 5:14
Begin Standard 75w00
1/Jan/1931 0:00 5:00
....

Time Table # 2
Before 1/Jan/1931 LMT
Begin Standard 75w00
1/Jan/1931 0:00 5:00
Begin Standard 90w00
1/Jan/1986 0:00 6:00

Place	TT	Lat	Long	Time
Alamor	1	4s02	80w02	5:20:08
Alausí	1	2s12	78w50	5:15:20
Alfaro	1	2s12	79w50	5:19:20
Ambato	1	1s15	78w37	5:14:28
Archipiélago de Colón	2	0s30	90w30	6:02:00
Arenillas	1	3s33	80w04	5:20:16
Atuntaqui	1	0N20	78w13	5:12:52
Azogues	1	2s44	78w50	5:15:20
Baba	1	1s47	79w40	5:18:40
Babahoyo	1	1s49	79w31	5:18:04
Baeza	1	0s27	77w53	5:11:32
Bahía de Caráquez	1	0s36	80w25	5:21:40
Balzar	1	1s22	79w54	5:19:36
Baños	1	1s24	78w25	5:13:40
Biblián	1	2s42	78w52	5:15:28
Cajabamba	1	1s42	78w45	5:15:00
Calceta	1	0s51	80w10	5:20:40
Cañar	1	2s33	78w56	5:15:44
Cariamanga	1	4s20	79w35	5:18:20
Catacocha	1	4s04	79w38	5:18:32
Catamayo	1	3s59	79w21	5:17:24
Catarama	1	1s35	79w28	5:17:52
Cayambe	1	0N03	78w08	5:12:32
Celica	1	4s07	79w59	5:19:56
Chone	1	0s41	80w06	5:20:24
Chunchi	1	2s17	78w55	5:15:40
Corazón	1	1s12	79w06	5:16:24
Cuenca	1	2s53	78w59	5:15:56
Daule	1	0N24	80w00	5:20:00
Daule	1	1s50	79w56	5:19:44
El Angel	1	0N37	77w56	5:11:44
El Corazón	1	1s12	79w06	5:16:24
El Progreso	2	0s54	89w33	5:58:12
Esmeraldas	1	0N59	79w42	5:18:48
Francisco de Orellana	1	0s28	76w58	5:07:52
Galápagos	2	0s30	90w30	6:02:00
Galapagos Islands	2	0s30	90w30	6:02:00
General Plaza (Limón)	1	2s58	78w25	5:13:40
Girón	1	3s10	79w08	5:16:32
Gonzanamá	1	4s15	79w27	5:17:48
Gualaceo	1	2s54	78w47	5:15:08
Gualaquiza	1	3s24	78w33	5:14:12
Guamote	1	1s56	78w43	5:14:52
Guano	1	1s35	78w38	5:14:32
Guaranda	1	1s36	79w00	5:16:00
Guayaquil	1	2s10	79w50	5:19:20
Ibarra	1	0N21	78w07	5:12:28
Isabela, Isla	2	0s30	91w06	6:04:24
Isabela Island	2	0s30	91w06	6:04:24
Isla San Cristóbal	2	0s50	89w26	5:57:44
Isla Santa Cruz	2	0s38	90w23	6:01:32
Jipijapa	1	1s20	80w35	5:22:20
Junín	1	0s56	80w13	5:20:52
Las Ramas	1	1s50	79w48	5:19:12
Latacunga	1	0s56	78w37	5:14:28
Limón → General Plaza	1	2s58	78w25	5:13:40
Loja	1	4s00	79w13	5:16:52
Macará	1	4s23	79w57	5:19:48
Macas	1	2s19	78w07	5:12:28
Machachi	1	0s30	78w34	5:14:16
Machala	1	3s16	79w58	5:19:52
Manta	1	0s57	80w44	5:22:56
Méndez	1	2s43	78w19	5:13:16
Milagro	1	2s07	79w36	5:18:24
Montecristi	1	1s03	80w40	5:22:40
Morro	1	2s39	80w19	5:21:16
Muisne	1	0N36	80w02	5:20:08
Naranjal	1	2s42	79w37	5:18:28
Nuevo Rocafuerte	1	0s56	75w24	5:01:36
Otavalo	1	0N14	78w16	5:13:04
Paján	1	1s34	80w25	5:21:40
Palmira	1	2s05	78w43	5:14:52
Pasaje	1	3s20	79w49	5:19:16
Paute	1	2s47	78w50	5:15:20
Pelileo	1	1s19	78w32	5:14:08
Píllaro	1	1s10	78w32	5:14:08
Piñas	1	3s42	79w42	5:18:48
Portoviejo	1	1s03	80w27	5:21:48
Puebloviejo	1	1s34	79w30	5:18:00
Puerto Baquerizo Moreno	2	0s54	89w36	5:58:24
Puerto Bolívar	1	3s16	79w59	5:19:56
Pujilí	1	0s57	78w41	5:14:44
Puyo	1	1s28	77w59	5:11:56
Quevedo	1	1s02	79w29	5:17:56
Quito	1	0s13	78w30	5:14:00
Riobamba	1	1s40	78w38	5:14:32
Rocafuerte	1	0s55	80w28	5:21:52
Salinas	1	2s13	80w58	5:23:52
Samborondón	1	1s57	79w44	5:18:56
San Cristóbal, Isla	2	0s50	89w26	5:57:44
San Cristóbal Island	2	0s50	89w26	5:57:44
San Gabriel	1	0N36	77w49	5:11:16
Sangolquí	1	0s19	78w27	5:13:48
San José	1	1s42	79w01	5:16:04
San Lorenzo	1	1N17	78w50	5:15:20
San Lucas	1	3s45	79w15	5:17:00
San Miguel	1	1s44	79w01	5:16:04
San Miguel de Salcedo	1	1s02	78w34	5:14:16
Santa Ana	1	1s13	80w23	5:21:32
Santa Cruz, Isla	2	0s38	90w23	6:01:32
Santa Cruz Island	2	0s38	90w23	6:01:32
Santa Elena	1	2s14	80w51	5:23:24
Santa Isabel	1	3s21	79w19	5:17:16
Santa Rosa	1	3s27	79w58	5:19:52
Santa Rosa de Sucumbíos	1	0N22	77w10	5:08:40
Santo Domingo de los Colorados	1	0s15	79w09	5:16:36
Saquisilí	1	0s51	78w40	5:14:40
Saraguro	1	3s36	79w13	5:16:52
Sigsig	1	3s01	78w45	5:15:00
Sucre	1	1s16	80w26	5:21:44
Sucúa	1	2s28	78w10	5:12:40
Tabacundo	1	0N03	78w12	5:12:48
Tena	1	0s59	77w49	5:11:16
Tulcán	1	0N48	77w43	5:10:52
Valdez	1	1N15	79w00	5:16:00
Valladolid	1	4s33	79w08	5:16:32
Veintiocho de Mayo	1	3s50	78w52	5:15:28
Ventanas	1	1s23	79w25	5:17:40
Villamil	2	0s56	91w01	6:04:04
Vinces	1	1s32	79w45	5:19:00
Yaguachi	1	2s07	79w41	5:18:44
Yaupi	1	2s59	77w50	5:11:20
Zamora	1	4s04	78w58	5:15:52
Zapotillo	1	4s25	80w31	5:22:04
Zaruma	1	3s41	79w37	5:18:28
Zumba	1	4s52	79w09	5:16:36

EGYPT — EGIPTO — ÉGYPTE — ÄGYPTEN — MIṢR

Time Table
Before 1/Oct/1900 LMT
Begin Standard 30E00

Date	Time	Offset
1/Oct/1900	0:00	-2:00
15/Jul/1940	0:00	-3:00
1/Oct/1940	0:00	-2:00
15/Apr/1941	0:00	-3:00
16/Sep/1941	0:00	-2:00
1/Apr/1942	0:00	-3:00
27/Oct/1942	0:00	-2:00
1/Apr/1943	0:00	-3:00
1/Nov/1943	0:00	-2:00
1/Apr/1944	0:00	-3:00
1/Nov/1944	0:00	-2:00
16/Apr/1945	0:00	-3:00
1/Nov/1945	0:00	-2:00
10/May/1957	0:00	-3:00
1/Oct/1957	0:00	-2:00
1/May/1958	0:00	-3:00
1/Oct/1958	0:00	-2:00
1/May/1959	1:00	-3:00
30/Sep/1959	3:00	-2:00
1/May/1960	1:00	-3:00
30/Sep/1960	3:00	-2:00
1/May/1961	1:00	-3:00
30/Sep/1961	3:00	-2:00
1/May/1962	1:00	-3:00
30/Sep/1962	3:00	-2:00
1/May/1963	1:00	-3:00
30/Sep/1963	3:00	-2:00
1/May/1964	1:00	-3:00
30/Sep/1964	3:00	-2:00
1/May/1965	1:00	-3:00
30/Sep/1965	3:00	-2:00
1/May/1966	1:00	-3:00
1/Oct/1966	3:00	-2:00
1/May/1967	1:00	-3:00
1/Oct/1967	3:00	-2:00
1/May/1968	1:00	-3:00
1/Oct/1968	3:00	-2:00
1/May/1969	1:00	-3:00
1/Oct/1969	3:00	-2:00
1/May/1970	1:00	-3:00
1/Oct/1970	3:00	-2:00
1/May/1971	1:00	-3:00
1/Oct/1971	3:00	-2:00
1/May/1972	1:00	-3:00
1/Oct/1972	3:00	-2:00
1/May/1973	1:00	-3:00
1/Oct/1973	3:00	-2:00
1/May/1974	1:00	-3:00
1/Oct/1974	3:00	-2:00
1/May/1975	1:00	-3:00
1/Oct/1975	3:00	-2:00
1/May/1976	1:00	-3:00
1/Oct/1976	3:00	-2:00
1/May/1977	1:00	-3:00
1/Oct/1977	3:00	-2:00
1/May/1978	1:00	-3:00
1/Oct/1978	3:00	-2:00
1/May/1979	1:00	-3:00
1/Oct/1979	3:00	-2:00
1/May/1980	1:00	-3:00
1/Oct/1980	3:00	-2:00
1/May/1981	1:00	-3:00
1/Oct/1981	3:00	-2:00
25/Jul/1982	1:00	-3:00
1/Oct/1982	3:00	-2:00
12/Jul/1983	1:00	-3:00
1/Oct/1983	3:00	-2:00
1/May/1984	1:00	-3:00
1/Oct/1984	3:00	-2:00
1/May/1985	1:00	-3:00
1/Oct/1985	3:00	-2:00
6/May/1989	1:00	-3:00
1/Oct/1989	3:00	-2:00
1/May/1990	1:00	-3:00
1/Oct/1990	3:00	-2:00
1/May/1991	1:00	-3:00
1/Oct/1991	3:00	-2:00

Place	Lat	Long	Time
Abā al-Waqf	28N35	30E46	-2:03:04
'Abd al-Shāhīd	29N55	31E13	-2:04:52
Abnūb	27N16	31E09	-2:04:36
Abū al-Ghayṭ	30N09	31E11	-2:04:44
Abū al-Maṭāmīr	30N55	30E11	-2:00:44
Abū an-Numrus	29N57	31E12	-2:04:48
Abū Dā'ūd as-Sibākh	30N55	31E34	-2:06:16
Abū Ghālib	30N16	30E56	-2:03:44
Abū Ḥammād al-Maḥaṭṭah	30N32	31E40	-2:06:40
Abū Ḥummuṣ	31N06	30E19	-2:01:16
Abū Jandīr	29N14	30E41	-2:02:44
Abū Jirj	28N32	30E47	-2:03:08
Abū Kabīr	30N44	31E40	-2:06:40
Abūksāh	29N23	30E42	-2:02:48
Abū Qīr	31N19	30E04	-2:00:16
Abū Qurqāṣ	27N56	30E50	-2:03:20
Abū Ṣīr	29N53	31E13	-2:04:52
Abu Ṣīr al-Malaq	29N15	31E05	-2:04:20
Abū Ṣīr-Banā	30N55	31E15	-2:05:00
Abū Ṣulṭan	30N25	32E19	-2:09:16
Abū Ṣuwayr al-Maḥaṭṭah	30N34	32E07	-2:08:28

Abū Tīj 27N02 31E19 -2:05:16
Abū Za'Bal 30N15 31E21 -2:05:24
Abū Zanīmah 29N03 33E06 -2:12:24
Abyār 30N50 30E52 -2:03:28
Aḍ-Ḍab'Ah 31N02 28E26 -1:53:44
Aḍ-Ḍaljamūn 30N48 30E50 -2:03:20
Ad-Dayr 25N20 32E35 -2:10:20
Ad-Dayr 30N20 31E16 -2:05:04
Ad-Dilinjāt 30N50 30E30 -2:02:00
Aḍ-Ḍuhayr 31N10 32E00 -2:08:00
Ad-Duqqī 30N04 31E15 -2:05:00
Ajā 30N57 31E17 -2:05:08
Ajhūr al-Kubrā 30N18 31E09 -2:04:36
Akhmīm 26N34 31E44 -2:06:56
Al-Ab'ādīyah 31N22 31E07 -2:04:28
Al-'Abbāsah ash-Sharqīyah 30N32 31E43 -2:06:52
Al-'Ajamīyīn 29N20 30E43 -2:02:52
Al-'Akrīshah 31N08 30E09 -2:00:36
Al-'Alamayn 30N49 28E57 -1:55:48
Al-'Alāqimah 30N37 31E38 -2:06:32
Al-'Amār al-Kubrā 30N21 31E08 -2:04:32
Alamein → Al-'Alamayn 30N49 28E57 -1:55:48
Al-'Āmirīyah 31N01 29E48 -1:59:12
Al-'Arīsh 31N08 33E48 -2:15:12
Al-Ashmūnayn 27N47 30E49 -2:03:16
Al-'Atāminah 27N20 30E50 -2:03:20
Al-Aṭāwilah 27N14 31E13 -2:04:52
Al-'Āṭf 29N39 31E16 -2:05:04
Al-'Awjā' 30N58 30E32 -2:02:08
Al-'Ayyāsh ash-Sharqī 31N33 31E13 -2:04:52
Al-'Ayyāṭ 29N37 31E15 -2:05:00
Al'Azīzah 31N11 31E57 -2:07:48
Al-'Azīzīyah 30N29 31E18 -2:05:12
Al-'Azīzīyah 29N52 31E15 -2:05:00
Al-Badārī 26N59 31E25 -2:05:40
Al-Badrashayn 29N51 31E16 -2:05:04
Al-Bahnasā 28N32 30E39 -2:02:36
Al-Bajalāt 31N10 31E37 -2:06:28
Al-Bājūr 30N26 31E02 -2:04:08
Al-Bakātūsh 31N03 30E48 -2:03:12
Al-Balāmūn 30N49 31E26 -2:05:44
Al-Balāshūn 30N26 31E26 -2:05:44
Al-Ballaḥ 30N46 32E19 -2:09:16
Al-Ballāṣ 26N01 32E46 -2:11:04
Al-Balyanā 26N14 32E00 -2:08:00
Al-Barājīl 30N04 31E09 -2:04:36
Al-Barāmūn 31N07 31E26 -2:05:44
Al-Barnūjī 30N56 30E23 -2:01:32
Al-Barshā 27N43 30E54 -2:03:36
Al-Baslaqūn 31N06 30E08 -2:00:32
Al-Basqalūn 28N42 30E44 -2:02:56
Al-Baṭānūn 30N37 30E59 -2:03:56
Al-Bawīṭī 28N21 28E52 -1:55:28
Al-Bayahū 28N16 30E44 -2:02:56
Al-Bayḍā' 31N10 30E05 -2:00:20
Al-Birīgāt 30N30 30E49 -2:03:16
Al-Burj 31N35 30E59 -2:03:56
Al-Burjāyah 28N09 30E44 -2:02:56
Al-Burumbul 29N19 31E14 -2:04:56
Al-Buṣaylī 31N20 30E24 -2:01:36
Alejandría → Al-Iskandarīyah 31N12 29E54 -1:59:36
Alexandria → Al-Iskandarīyah 31N12 29E54 -1:59:36
Alexandrie → Al-Iskandarīyah 31N12 29E54 -1:59:36
Al-Fahmīyīn 29N36 31E17 -2:05:08
Al-Fant 28N46 30E53 -2:03:32
Al-Fashn 28N49 30E54 -2:03:36
Al-Fayyūm 29N19 30E50 -2:03:20
Al-Firdān 30N41 32E20 -2:09:20
Al-Gharaq as-Sulṭānī 29N08 30E42 -2:02:48
Al-Ghayatah 30N57 30E06 -2:00:24
Al-Ghazālī 30N49 31E49 -2:07:16
Al-Ghurdaqah 27N14 33E50 -2:15:20
Al-Ḥaddādī 31N20 30E47 -2:03:08
Al-Ḥaddayn 30N44 30E38 -2:02:32
Al-Ḥājir 30N41 31E49 -2:07:16
Al-Ḥammām 30N50 29E23 -1:57:32
Al-Ḥamrah 31N10 30E52 -2:03:28
Al-Ḥāmūl 31N19 31E10 -2:04:40
Al-Ḥawāmidīyah 29N54 31E15 -2:05:00
Al-Ḥawātikah 27N16 31E01 -2:04:04
Al-Ḥawwārīyah 30N58 29E41 -1:58:44
Al-Ḥayy 29N39 31E18 -2:05:12
Al-Ḥayz 28N02 28E39 -1:54:36
Al-Ḥībah 28N45 30E55 -2:03:40
Al-Ḥusaynīyah 30N52 31E55 -2:07:40
Al-Ibrāhīmīyah 30N57 31E35 -2:06:20
Al-'Idwah 29N21 30E55 -2:03:40
Al-Ikhṣāṣ al-Qiblīyah 29N42 31E17 -2:05:08
Al-'Imārīyah 27N37 30E53 -2:03:32
Al-Iskandarīyah (Alexandria) 31N12 29E54 -1:59:36
Al-Ismā'īlīyah (Ismailia) 30N35 32E16 -2:09:04
Al-'Izzīyah 27N13 30E59 -2:03:56
Al-Jadīdah 25N34 28E51 -1:55:24
Al-Jafādūn 28N50 30E48 -2:03:12
Al-Jamālīyah 31N11 31E51 -2:07:24
Al-Jarnūs 28N36 30E43 -2:02:52
Al-Jīzah (Giza) 30N01 31E13 -2:04:52
Al-Junaynah 31N06 31E41 -2:06:44
Al-Jundīyah 28N34 30E50 -2:03:20
Al-Kāb 30N57 32E18 -2:09:12
Al-Kafr ash-Sharqī 37N17 31E10 -2:04:40
Al-Karnak 25N43 32E39 -2:10:36
Al-Kawm al-Akhḍar 30N58 30E17 -2:01:08
Al-Kawm aṭ-Ṭawīl 31N12 31E05 -2:04:20
Al-Khānkah 30N13 31E21 -2:05:24
Al-Kharaqānīyah 30N10 31E10 -2:04:40
Al-Khārijah 25N26 30E33 -2:02:12
Al-Khuṣūṣ 30N09 31E19 -2:05:16
Al-Kūbrī 30N02 32E33 -2:10:12
Al-Kunayyisah 29N59 31E11 -2:04:44
Al-Kuntillah 30N00 34E41 -2:18:44
Al-Kurdī 31N05 30E49 -2:03:16
Al-Lāhūn 29N13 30E59 -2:03:56
Al-Lisht 29N34 31E14 -2:04:56
Al-Ma'ābidah 27N20 31E01 -2:04:04
Al-Madīnah al-Fikrīyah 27N56 30E49 -2:03:16
Al-Maḥallah al-Kubrā 30N58 31E10 -2:04:40
Al-Maḥārīq 25N37 30E39 -2:02:36
Al-Maḥmūdīyah 31N11 30E32 -2:02:08
Al-Maḥraṣ 27N49 30E48 -2:03:12
Al-Maḥsamah 30N34 32E01 -2:08:04
Al-Maks 31N09 29E51 -1:59:24
Al-Ma'mūrah 31N18 30E03 -2:00:12
Al-Manāwāt 29N55 31E14 -2:04:56
Al-Manshāh 26N28 31E48 -2:07:12
Al-Manṣūrah 31N03 31E23 -2:05:32
Al-Manṣūrīyah 30N08 31E05 -2:04:20
Al-Manzilah 31N09 31E56 -2:07:44
Al-Marāghah 26N42 31E36 -2:06:24
Al-Marāzīq 29N49 31E16 -2:05:04
Al-Ma'ṣarah 27N42 30E52 -2:03:28
Al-Ma'ṣarah 31N13 31E19 -2:05:16
Al-Ma'ṣarah 29N54 31E17 -2:05:08
Al-Maṭarīyah 31N11 32E02 -2:08:08
Al-Maymūn 29N14 31E12 -2:04:48
Al-Minshāt al-Kubrā 31N03 30E54 -2:03:36
Al-Minyā 28N06 30E45 -2:03:00
Al-Minyā 29N45 31E18 -2:05:12
Al-Minyā 29N14 30E45 -2:03:00
Al-Munājāt al-Kubrā 30N50 32E01 -2:08:04
Al-Muntazah 31N17 30E01 -2:00:04
Al-Musharrak Qiblī 29N23 30E34 -2:02:16
Al-Mu'Tamadīyah 31N02 31E05 -2:04:20
Al-Muṭī'Ah 27N08 31E18 -2:05:12
Al-Narrānīyah 29N58 31E10 -2:04:40
Al-Nasser 24N32 32E55 -2:11:40
Al-Qāhirah (Cairo) 30N03 31E15 -2:05:00
Al-Qāiyāt 28N40 30E41 -2:02:44
Al-Qalaj 30N11 31E21 -2:05:24
Al-Qanāṭir al-Khayrīyah 30N12 31E08 -2:04:32
Al-Qanāyāt 30N37 31E28 -2:05:52
Al-Qanṭarah 30N52 32E19 -2:09:16
Al-Qaṣābī 31N16 30E41 -2:02:44
Al-Qaṣr 25N42 28E53 -1:55:32
Al-Qaṣṣāṣīn 30N34 31E56 -2:07:44
Al-Qaṭṭā 30N13 30E58 -2:03:52
Al-Qaṭṭāwīyah 30N33 31E40 -2:06:40
Al-Qays 28N29 30E47 -2:03:08
Al-Qurayn 30N37 31E44 -2:06:56
Al-Quṣaymah 30N40 34E22 -2:17:28
Al-Quṣayr 26N06 34E17 -2:17:08
Al-Quṣayr 27N27 30E52 -2:03:28
Al-Qūṣīyah 27N26 30E49 -2:03:16
Al-'Udaysāt 25N35 32E29 -2:09:56
Al-Uqṣur (Luxor) 25N41 32E39 -2:10:36
Al-Wafā'īyah 30N46 30E36 -2:02:24
Al-Walīdīyah 27N12 31E10 -2:04:40
Al-Wāṣifīyah 30N35 32E10 -2:08:40
Al-Wāsiṭah 29N20 31E12 -2:04:48
Al-Wazīrīyah 31N11 30E57 -2:03:48
Al-Widy 29N31 31E16 -2:05:04
Al-Zarqa 31N13 31E38 -2:06:32
An-Nakhl 29N55 33E45 -2:15:00
An-Narrānīyah 29N58 31E10 -2:04:40
An-Nazlat 29N19 30E39 -2:02:36
An-Nubayrah 30N54 30E35 -2:02:20
An-Nuwayrah 29N06 30E59 -2:03:56
'Arab Muṭayr 27N16 31E14 -2:04:56
Armant 25N37 32E32 -2:10:08
Ar-Radīsīyah Baḥrī 24N57 32E53 -2:11:32
Ar-Raḥāminah 31N18 31E45 -2:07:00
Ar-Raḥmānīyah 31N06 30E38 -2:02:32
Ar-Rāshidah 25N35 28E56 -1:55:44
Ar-Rawḍah 27N48 30E52 -2:03:28
Ar-Rawḍah 29N27 31E00 -2:04:00
Ar-Rayramūn 27N45 30E52 -2:03:28
Ar-Rubayqī 30N10 31E46 -2:07:04
Ar-Ru'ūs 29N21 31E04 -2:04:16
Aryamūn 31N11 30E54 -2:03:36
Aṣfūn al-Maṭā'inah 25N23 32E32 -2:10:08
Ashmūn 30N18 30E58 -2:03:52
Ash-Shallūfah 30N07 32E34 -2:10:16
Ash-Shanāwīyah 29N08 31E08 -2:04:32
Ash-Shawāshinah 29N22 30E36 -2:02:24
Ash-Shaykh Faḍl 28N29 30E50 -2:03:20
Ash-Shaykh 'Ibādah 27N48 30E52 -2:03:28
Ash-Shaykh Timay 27N53 30E51 -2:03:24
Ash-Shīn 31N01 30E53 -2:03:32
Ash-Shuhadā' 30N36 30E54 -2:03:36
Aṣ-Ṣaff 29N34 31E17 -2:05:08
Aṣ-Ṣāliḥīyah 30N47 31E59 -2:07:56
As-Sallūm 31N34 25E09 -1:40:36
Aṣ-Ṣanāfīn al-Qiblīyah 30N27 31E18 -2:05:12
As-Sanṭah 30N45 31E08 -2:04:32
As-Sarīrīyah 28N20 30E45 -2:03:00
As-Sinbillāwayn 30N53 31E27 -2:05:48
Aṣ-Ṣūfīyah 30N55 31E46 -2:07:04
As-Su'ūdīyah 29N33 31E14 -2:04:56
As-Suways (Suez) 29N58 32E33 -2:10:12
Aswān 24N05 32E53 -2:11:32
Asyūṭ 27N11 31E11 -2:04:44
Aṭfīḥ 29N24 31E15 -2:05:00
Ath-Thamad 29N41 34E18 -2:17:12
At-Tabbīn 29N47 31E18 -2:05:12
Aṭ-Ṭalibīyah 30N00 31E11 -2:04:44
At-Tall al-Kabīr 30N34 31E47 -2:07:08
At-Taṭālīyah 27N20 30E50 -2:03:20
Aṭ-Ṭawd 30N47 30E37 -2:02:28
Aṭ-Ṭayrīyah 30N39 30E46 -2:03:04
Aṭ-Ṭayyibah 28N16 30E39 -2:02:36
Aṭ-Ṭīnah 31N03 32E18 -2:09:12
Aṭ-Ṭūr 28N14 33E37 -2:14:28
Awīsh al-Ḥajar 31N01 31E19 -2:05:16
Awlād Mūsā 30N48 31E44 -2:06:56
Awsīm 30N07 31E08 -2:04:32
Az-Zankalūn 30N33 31E27 -2:05:48
Az-Zaqāzīq 30N35 31E31 -2:06:04
Az-Zawāmil 30N21 31E26 -2:05:44
Bābil 30N41 31E00 -2:04:00
Badahl 28N56 30E54 -2:03:36
Badr 30N33 30E43 -2:02:52
Bahīj 30N56 29E35 -1:58:20
Bahnāy 30N23 31E04 -2:04:16
Bahnayā 30N41 31E23 -2:05:32
Bahtīm 30N08 31E17 -2:05:08
Baḥṭīṭ 30N29 31E38 -2:06:32
Bahūt 31N10 31E19 -2:05:16
Balanṣūrah 27N55 30E41 -2:02:44
Balaqs 30N10 31E17 -2:05:08
Balaqṭar 31N05 30E13 -2:00:52
Balāṭ 25N33 29E16 -1:57:04
Balṭīm 31N33 31E05 -2:04:20
Bamhā 29N35 31E14 -2:04:56
Banhā 30N28 31E11 -2:04:44
Banī 'Adī al-Baḥrīyah 27N15 30E55 -2:03:40
Banī 'Adī al-Qiblīyah 27N15 30E56 -2:03:44
Banī Aḥmad 28N03 30E46 -2:03:04
Banī 'Alī 28N29 30E43 -2:02:52
Banī Ḥasan ash-Shurūq 27N54 30E51 -2:03:24
Banī Khālid 27N50 30E44 -2:02:56
Banī Majdūl 30N02 31E07 -2:04:28
Banī Mazār 28N30 30E48 -2:03:12
Banī Muḥammadīyāt 27N17 31E05 -2:04:20
Banī Mūsā 29N08 31E03 -2:04:12
Banī Rāfi' 27N22 30E53 -2:03:32
Banī Salāmah 30N19 30E51 -2:03:24
Banī Sha'Rān 27N19 30E51 -2:03:24
Banī Shuqayr 27N23 30E59 -2:03:56
Banī Suwayf 29N05 31E05 -2:04:20
Banī 'Ubayd 31N01 31E39 -2:06:36
Banī 'Ubayd 27N57 30E46 -2:03:04
Banī Zayd 27N13 31E09 -2:04:36
Bārīs 24N40 30E36 -2:02:24
Barnasht 29N41 31E15 -2:05:00
Barq al-'Izz 31N01 31E26 -2:05:44
Barrīyat al-Uṣayfir 31N18 30E40 -2:02:40
Basandīlah 31N12 31E26 -2:05:44
Bashtīl 30N05 31E11 -2:04:44
Bāsūs 30N08 31E13 -2:04:52
Basyūn 30N57 30E49 -2:03:16
Baṭrah 31N10 31E27 -2:05:48
Bayāḍ an-Naṣārā 29N04 31E08 -2:04:32
Benha → Banhā 30N28 31E11 -2:04:44
Beni Suef → Banī Suwayf 29N05 31E05 -2:04:20
Bibā 28N55 30E59 -2:03:56
Bībān 30N47 30E40 -2:02:40
Bilbays 30N25 31E34 -2:06:16
Bilifyā 29N07 31E03 -2:04:12
Bilqās Qism Awwal 31N13 31E21 -2:05:24
Biltāj 31N00 30E59 -2:03:56
Biltān 30N23 31E10 -2:04:40
Bimbān 24N26 32E53 -2:11:32
Birimbāl 31N21 30E30 -2:02:00
Birimbāl al-Qadīmah 31N10 31E44 -2:06:56
Birkat as-Sab' 30N38 31E05 -2:04:20
Birkat Ghiṭās 31N07 30E16 -2:01:04
Birmā 30N51 30E54 -2:03:36
Birqāsh 30N10 31E02 -2:04:08
Bīshat Qā'Id 30N38 31E32 -2:06:08
Biyalā 31N10 31E13 -2:04:52
Būlāq 25N12 30E32 -2:02:08
Būlāq ad-Dakrūr 30N02 31E11 -2:04:44
Būr Ibrāhīm 29N57 32E34 -2:10:16
Burj al-'Arab 30N55 29E32 -1:58:08
Burj Mughayzil 31N27 30E23 -2:01:32
Būr Safājah 26N44 33E56 -2:15:44
Būr Sa'īd (Port Said) 31N16 32E18 -2:09:12
Būr Tawfīq 29N57 32E34 -2:10:16
Burṭus 30N09 31E08 -2:04:32
Būsh 29N09 31E08 -2:04:32
Caire, Le → Al-Qāhirah 30N03 31E15 -2:05:00
Cairo → Al-Qāhirah 30N03 31E15 -2:05:00
Coptos → Qifṭ 26N00 32E49 -2:11:16
Dahmarū 28N41 30E49 -2:03:16
Dahshūr 29N45 31E14 -2:04:56
Daljā' 27N39 30E42 -2:02:48
Damanhūr Shubra 30N07 31E14 -2:04:56
Damanhūr 31N02 30E28 -2:01:52
Damāṣ 30N48 31E20 -2:05:20
Damāṭ 30N57 30E57 -2:03:48
Damietta → Dumyāṭ 31N25 31E48 -2:07:12
Dandīl 29N10 31E02 -2:04:08
Dāqūf 28N24 30E38 -2:02:32
Darājīl 30N39 30E52 -2:03:28

Name	Lat	Long	Time
Dār as-Salām	29N59	31E13	-2:04:52
Darāw	24N25	32E56	-2:11:44
Darawah	30N13	31E06	-2:04:24
Darb al-Ḥājj	30N10	31E33	-2:06:12
Dashlūṭ	27N34	30E42	-2:02:48
Dayr Jabal aṭ-Ṭayr	28N17	30E45	-2:03:00
Dayr Mawās	27N38	30E51	-2:03:24
Dayrūṭ	27N33	30E49	-2:03:16
Dayrūṭ	31N13	30E30	-2:02:00
Dayrūṭ ash-Sharīf	27N35	30E49	-2:03:16
Dhahab	28N29	34E32	-2:18:08
Dikirnis	31N05	31E35	-2:06:20
Dishāshah	28N59	30E51	-2:03:24
Dishnā	26N07	32E28	-2:09:52
Disūq	31N08	30E39	-2:02:36
Diyā al-Kawm	30N38	31E05	-2:04:20
Diyarb Najm	30N45	31E26	-2:05:44
Diyu al-Wasta	30N54	31E30	-2:06:00
Dukhmays	31N07	31E04	-2:04:16
Dumayrah	31N08	31E22	-2:05:28
Dumyāṭ (Damietta)	31N25	31E48	-2:07:12
Dundīṭ	30N41	31E18	-2:05:12
Durunkah	27N08	31E10	-2:04:40
Edfu → Idfū	24N58	32E52	-2:11:28
El Alamein → Al-ʿAlamayn	30N49	28E57	-1:55:48
Fā'id	30N19	32E19	-2:09:16
Faiyum → Al-Fayyūm	29N19	30E50	-2:03:20
Fanārah	30N17	32E21	-2:09:24
Fāqūs	30N44	31E48	-2:07:12
Fāriskūr	31N20	31E43	-2:06:52
Farnawā	30N59	30E39	-2:02:36
Farsīs	30N40	31E14	-2:04:56
Fayyum → Al-Fayyūm	29N19	30E50	-2:03:20
Fidīmīn	29N23	30E46	-2:03:04
Fuwah	31N12	30E33	-2:02:12
Gerza	29N26	31E11	-2:04:44
Ghammāzah al-Kubrā	29N43	31E18	-2:05:12
Ghamrīn	30N30	30E55	-2:03:40
Ghazālat al-Khīs	30N34	31E34	-2:06:16
Girga	26N20	31E54	-2:07:36
Giza → Al-Jīzah	30N01	31E13	-2:04:52
Ḥalā'ib	22N13	36E38	-2:26:32
Ḥawr	27N52	30E44	-2:02:56
Ḥawsh ʿĪsā	30N55	30E17	-2:01:08
Ḥawwārat ʿAdlān	29N12	30E58	-2:03:52
Ḥawwārat al-Maqṭaʿ	29N15	30E54	-2:03:36
Heliopolis	30N06	31E19	-2:05:16
Hihyā	30N40	31E36	-2:06:24
Ḥulwān	29N51	31E20	-2:05:20
Hūrayn	30N39	31E08	-2:04:32
Ibnahs	30N34	31E07	-2:04:28
Ibshān	31N10	31E10	-2:04:40
Ibshawāy	29N22	30E41	-2:02:44
Idfīnā	31N18	30E31	-2:02:04
Idfū	24N58	32E52	-2:11:28
Idkū	31N18	30E18	-2:01:12
Idmū	28N09	30E41	-2:02:44
Ihnāsiyat al-Madīnah	29N05	30E56	-2:03:44
Ihwah	29N03	31E00	-2:04:00
Īkinjī Maryūt	31N00	29E45	-1:59:00
Ikrāsh	30N45	31E30	-2:06:00
Ikwah	30N41	31E28	-2:05:52
Imbābah	30N04	31E13	-2:04:52
Inshāṣ ar-Raml	30N23	31E27	-2:05:48
Iqfahṣ	28N47	30E49	-2:03:16
Ishmant	29N12	31E11	-2:04:44
Ismailia → Al-Ismāʿīlīyah	30N35	32E16	-2:09:04
Isnā	25N18	32E33	-2:10:12
Isṭanhā	30N28	31E07	-2:04:28
Ithnayn	30N41	32E21	-2:09:24
Itlīdim	27N52	30E48	-2:03:12
Itmīdah	30N46	31E20	-2:05:20
Iṭsā	29N15	30E48	-2:03:12
Ityāy al-Bārūd	30N53	30E40	-2:02:40
ʿIzab al-Baṣāriṭah	31N23	31E47	-2:07:08
ʿIzbat Abū Ṣuql	31N09	33E49	-2:15:16
Jabal an-Nūr	28N57	31E02	-2:04:08
Jabal aṭ-Ṭayr	28N14	30E45	-2:03:00
Jabal ʿUwaybid	30N09	32E12	-2:08:48
Jamsah	27N38	33E35	-2:14:20
Janāj	31N00	30E46	-2:03:04
Janzūr	30N41	31E02	-2:04:08
Jaradū	29N18	30E42	-2:02:48
Jarrīs	27N55	30E46	-2:03:04
Jazīrat Muḥammad	30N07	31E12	-2:04:48
Jināḥ	25N20	30E31	-2:02:04
Jirjā	26N20	31E53	-2:07:32
Jīzayy	30N28	30E51	-2:03:24
Jummayzat Banī ʿAmr	30N48	31E32	-2:06:08
Junayfah	30N12	32E25	-2:09:40
Jurays wa ʿIzbatuhā	30N19	30E55	-2:03:40
Kafr ad-Dawwār	31N08	30E07	-2:00:28
Kafr ad-Difrāwī	31N03	30E40	-2:02:40
Kafr al-ʿĀ'id	30N27	31E35	-2:06:20
Kafr al-Baṭṭīkh	31N24	31E44	-2:06:56
Kafr al Jarā'idah	31N13	31E16	-2:05:04
Kafr ash-Shaykh	31N07	30E56	-2:03:44
Kafrat Ṭā'il Mūsā	30N53	29E44	-1:58:56
Kafr at-Tamīmī	30N37	31E21	-2:05:24
Kafr az-Zayyāt	30N49	30E49	-2:03:16
Kafr Diyamā	30N48	30E52	-2:03:28
Kafr el-Zaiyat → Kafr az-Zayyāt	30N49	30E49	-2:03:16
Kafr Ḥakīm	30N05	31E07	-2:04:28
Kafr Kilā al-Bāb	30N41	31E09	-2:04:36
Kafr Rabīʿ	30N42	30E50	-2:03:20
Kafr Saʿd	31N19	31E39	-2:06:36
Kafr Salīm	31N09	30E06	-2:00:24
Kafr Ṣaqr	30N48	31E37	-2:06:28
Kafr Shanawān	30N30	31E01	-2:04:04
Kafr Shibīn	30N18	31E18	-2:05:12
Kafr Shukr	30N33	31E16	-2:05:04
Kafr Ṭarkhān al-Gharbī	29N29	31E13	-2:04:52
Kafr Yaʿqūb	30N46	30E46	-2:03:04
Kahk	29N25	30E38	-2:02:32
Kairo → Al-Qāhirah	30N03	31E15	-2:05:00
Karnak → Al-Karnak	25N43	32E39	-2:10:36
Kawm ar-Rāhib	28N20	30E37	-2:02:28
Kawm Birah	30N05	31E08	-2:04:32
Kawm Ḥamādah	30N46	30E42	-2:02:48
Kawm Ishfīn	30N11	31E15	-2:05:00
Kawm Ishū	31N07	30E00	-2:00:00
Kawm Umbū	24N28	32E57	-2:11:48
Khamsah	30N25	32E23	-2:09:32
Khirbitā	30N45	30E40	-2:02:40
Kirdāsah	30N02	31E07	-2:04:28
Kudyat al-Islām	27N32	30E45	-2:03:00
Kufūr Bilshāy	30N51	30E48	-2:03:12
Kufūr Najm	30N44	31E35	-2:06:20
Kutāmat al-Ghābah	30N55	30E54	-2:03:36
Le Caire → Al-Qāhirah	30N03	31E15	-2:05:00
Luxor → Al-Uqṣur	25N41	32E39	-2:10:36
Maghāghah	28N39	30E50	-2:03:20
Mahalla el-Kubra → Al-Maḥallah al-Kub	30N58	31E10	-2:04:40
Maḥallat Kayl	31N01	30E17	-2:01:08
Maḥallat Marḥūm	30N48	30E57	-2:03:48
Maḥallat Minūf	30N53	30E58	-2:03:52
Maḥallat Zayyād	31N02	31E14	-2:04:56
Malāṭīyah	28N42	30E51	-2:03:24
Mallawī	27N44	30E50	-2:03:20
Manfalūṭ	27N19	30E58	-2:03:52
Maʿnīyā	30N50	30E39	-2:02:36
Manqabād	27N12	31E07	-2:04:28
Manqaṭīn	28N20	30E40	-2:02:40
Mansafīs	28N00	30E49	-2:03:16
Mansura → Al-Manṣūrah	31N03	31E23	-2:05:32
Manyal Shīḥah	29N57	31E14	-2:04:56
Marṣafā wa Kafr Aḥmad Hashīsh	30N25	31E15	-2:05:00
Marsa Maṭrūḥ	31N21	27E14	-1:48:56
Masarah	27N29	30E50	-2:03:20
Maʿṣarat Samālūṭ	28N19	30E43	-2:02:52
Mashalah	30N44	31E08	-2:04:32
Mashtūl as-Sūq	30N22	31E22	-2:05:28
Masīr	31N03	31E00	-2:04:00
Maṣraʿ	27N14	31E02	-2:04:08
Maṭāy	28N25	30E46	-2:03:04
Matbūl	31N05	31E02	-2:04:08
Maṭir Ṭāris	29N22	30E54	-2:03:36
Matruh → Marsa Maṭrūḥ	31N21	27E14	-1:48:56
Maydūm	29N22	31E10	-2:04:40
Medinat al-Faiyum → Al-Fayyūm	29N19	30E50	-2:03:20
Mersa Matruh → Marsa Maṭrūḥ	31N21	27E14	-1:48:56
Milīj	30N36	31E03	-2:04:12
Minbāl	28N24	30E41	-2:02:44
Minshāt Adh Dhahab	28N00	30E42	-2:02:48
Minshat al-Amir Muhammad ʿAli	29N10	30E38	-2:02:32
Minshāt al-Bakkārī	30N01	31E08	-2:04:32
Minshāt al-Ikhwah	30N56	31E21	-2:05:24
Minshāt al-Mughālaqah	27N44	30E47	-2:03:08
Minshāt Būlīn	31N11	30E10	-2:00:40
Minshāt Sulṭān	30N32	30E55	-2:03:40
Minūf	30N28	30E56	-2:03:44
Minya → Al-Minyā	28N06	30E45	-2:03:00
Minyā al-Qamḥ	30N31	31E21	-2:05:24
Minyat an-Naṣr	31N07	31E39	-2:06:36
Minyat Sandūb	31N00	31E23	-2:05:32
Mīr	27N27	30E44	-2:02:56
Mīt Abū Ghālib	31N17	31E40	-2:06:40
Mīt al-ʿĀmil	30N54	31E21	-2:05:24
Mīt Badr Ḥalāwah	30N51	31E14	-2:04:56
Mīt Bashshār	30N31	31E24	-2:05:36
Mīt Fāris	31N02	31E36	-2:06:24
Mīt Ghamr	30N43	31E16	-2:05:04
Mīt Ḥalfah	30N10	31E14	-2:04:56
Mīt Ḥamal	30N26	31E32	-2:06:08
Mīt Kinānah	30N23	31E16	-2:05:04
Mīt Ruhaynah	29N51	31E15	-2:05:00
Mīt Yazīd	30N30	31E20	-2:05:20
Munā al-Amīr	29N54	31E15	-2:05:00
Mūshā	27N08	31E18	-2:05:12
Mustāy	30N37	31E09	-2:04:36
Musṭurud	30N08	31E17	-2:05:08
Mūt	25N29	28E59	-1:55:56
Muṭūbis	31N18	30E31	-2:02:04
Muzūrah	28N53	30E48	-2:03:12
Nabarūh	31N06	31E18	-2:05:12
Nabq	28N04	34E25	-2:17:40
Nādir	30N33	30E51	-2:03:24
Nafīshah	30N34	32E15	-2:09:00
Nāhyā	30N03	31E07	-2:04:28
Naj' Ḥammādī	26N03	32E15	-2:09:00
Naqādah	25N54	32E43	-2:10:52
Nashwah	30N30	31E29	-2:05:56
Naṣr	30N36	30E23	-2:01:32
Nawasā al-Ghayṭ	30N58	31E19	-2:05:16
Nawāy	27N47	30E46	-2:03:04
Nazālī Ṭāhā'	28N11	30E42	-2:02:48
Nazlat al-ʿAmūdayn	28N14	30E42	-2:02:48
Nazlat al-Badramān	27N40	30E44	-2:02:56
Nazlat as-Sammān	29N59	31E08	-2:04:32
Nazlat Khalīfah	30N01	31E10	-2:04:40
Nazlat Quftan Bāshā	28N57	30E49	-2:03:16
Nazlat Thābit	28N25	30E47	-2:03:08
Niklā al-ʿInab	30N55	30E46	-2:03:04
Niṣf Thānī Bashbīsh	31N07	31E11	-2:04:44
Nūbah	30N29	31E33	-2:06:12
Nudaybah	30N59	30E22	-2:01:28
Nuwaybiʿ al-Muzayyinah	28N58	34E39	-2:18:36
Port Said → Būr Saʿīd	31N16	32E18	-2:09:12
Port Taufiq → Būr Tawfīq	29N57	32E34	-2:10:16
Qāfilah	31N04	30E16	-2:01:04
Qahā	30N17	31E12	-2:04:48
Qahbūna	30N48	31E54	-2:07:36
Qalabshū	31N26	31E19	-2:05:16
Qalamshāh	29N10	30E50	-2:03:20
Qalandūl	27N49	30E50	-2:03:20
Qallīn	31N03	30E51	-2:03:24
Qalyūb	30N11	31E12	-2:04:48
Qaṣr al-Farāfirah	27N03	27E58	-1:51:52
Qaṣr al-Jibālī	29N20	30E38	-2:02:32
Qaṣr Baghdād	30N44	30E53	-2:03:32
Qaṣr Qārūn	29N25	30E25	-2:01:40
Qāy	29N09	30E57	-2:03:48
Qena → Qinā	26N10	32E43	-2:10:52
Qifṭ (Coptos)	26N00	32E49	-2:11:16
Qiman al-ʿArūs	29N18	31E10	-2:04:40
Qinā	26N10	32E43	-2:10:52
Qulubbā	27N45	30E50	-2:03:20
Qulūṣanā	28N21	30E44	-2:02:56
Qunbush al-Ḥamrā'	29N00	30E59	-2:03:56
Qūṣ	25N55	32E45	-2:11:00
Quṭūr	30N59	30E57	-2:03:48
Quwaysinā	30N34	31E09	-2:04:36
Ra's al-Barr	31N31	31E50	-2:07:20
Ra's al-Khalīj	31N15	31E39	-2:06:36
Ra's an-Naqb	29N36	34E51	-2:19:24
Rashīd (Rosetta)	31N24	30E25	-2:01:40
Rosetta → Rashīd	31N24	30E25	-2:01:40
Rummānah	31N01	32E40	-2:10:40
Ṣā al-Ḥajar	30N58	30E46	-2:03:04
Ṣafanīyah	28N49	30E48	-2:03:12
Ṣafṭ al-ʿInab	30N49	30E41	-2:02:44
Ṣaft al-Khammār	28N02	30E42	-2:02:48
Ṣaft al-Laban	30N02	31E10	-2:04:40
Ṣafṭ al-Mulūk	30N49	30E41	-2:02:44
Ṣafṭ Rāshīn	28N58	30E55	-2:03:40
Ṣafṭ Turāb	30N54	31E07	-2:04:28
Ṣahrajat al-Kubrā wa Kafr Jirjis Yu.	30N38	31E17	-2:05:08
Sakhā	31N05	30E57	-2:03:48
Sakkara → Ṣaqqārah	29N51	31E13	-2:04:52
Salāmūn	31N04	31E28	-2:05:52
Salāqūs	28N44	30E50	-2:03:20
Salum → As-Sallūm	31N34	25E09	-1:40:36
Salwā Baḥrī	24N44	32E56	-2:11:44
Samādūn	30N20	30E57	-2:03:48
Samālūt	28N18	30E42	-2:02:48
Samannūd	30N58	31E15	-2:05:00
Ṣanabū	27N30	30E47	-2:03:08
Sanafā	30N47	31E21	-2:05:24
Ṣān al-Ḥajar al-Qiblīyah	30N58	31E52	-2:07:28
Sandafā al-Fa'r	28N32	30E40	-2:02:40
Sandūb	31N01	31E23	-2:05:32
Sanhūr	29N25	30E46	-2:03:04
Sanhūr al-Madīnah	31N07	30E44	-2:02:56
Sanjahā	30N50	31E38	-2:06:32
Sāqiyat Makkī	30N00	31E13	-2:04:52
Ṣaqqārah	29N51	31E13	-2:04:52
Sarābiyūm	30N23	32E17	-2:09:08
Sawhāj	26N33	31E42	-2:06:48
Ṣawl	29N21	31E14	-2:04:56
Saylah	29N21	30E58	-2:03:52
Shābah	31N11	30E46	-2:03:04
Shabās al-Milḥ	31N12	30E39	-2:02:36
Shabās ash-Shuhadā'	31N05	30E45	-2:03:00
Shabās ʿUmayr	31N06	30E48	-2:03:12
Shabrāmant	29N56	31E12	-2:04:48
Shabshīr al-Ḥiṣṣah	30N52	31E04	-2:04:16
Shakshūk	29N28	30E42	-2:02:48
Shālimah	31N14	30E52	-2:03:28
Shandīd	30N55	30E40	-2:02:40
Shanshūr	30N21	31E00	-2:04:00
Sharnūb	31N01	30E35	-2:02:20
Shārūnah	28N36	30E51	-2:03:24
Shaṭānūf	30N14	31E04	-2:04:16
Shawnī	30N45	30E55	-2:03:40
Shibīn al-Kawm	30N33	31E01	-2:04:04
Shibīn al-Qanāṭir	30N19	31E19	-2:05:16
Shiblanjah	30N28	31E16	-2:05:04
Shinarā	28N47	30E46	-2:03:04
Shinbārī	30N07	31E09	-2:04:36
Shirbīn	31N11	31E32	-2:06:08
Shirshābah	30N47	31E10	-2:04:40
Shisht al-Anʿām	30N52	30E44	-2:02:56
Shubrā al-Khaymah	30N06	31E15	-2:05:00
Shubrā Bābil	30N54	31E11	-2:04:44
Shubrā Khalfūn	30N29	31E05	-2:04:20
Shubrā Khīt	31N02	30E43	-2:02:52
Shuṭab	27N08	31E14	-2:04:56

MIṢR ÄGYPTEN ÉGYPTE EGIPTO EGYPT

Place	Lat	Long	Offset
Sibirbāy	30N49	31E01	-2:04:04
Sīdī 'Abd ar-Raḥmān	30N58	29E44	-1:58:56
Sīdī Barrānī	31N36	25E55	-1:43:40
Sīdī Ghāzī	31N12	31E03	-2:04:12
Sīdī Ḥunaysh	31N10	27E37	-1:50:28
Sīdī Ṡālim	31N17	30E48	-2:03:12
Sīnarū	29N22	30E45	-2:03:00
Sindiyūn	30N15	31E12	-2:04:48
Sinnahwā	30N25	31E21	-2:05:24
Sinnūris	29N25	30E52	-2:03:28
Sirs al-Layyānah	30N26	30E58	-2:03:52
Sirsinā	30N36	30E54	-2:03:36
Sirsinā	29N24	30E58	-2:03:52
Siryāqūs	30N12	31E19	-2:05:16
Sīwah	29N12	25E31	-1:42:04
Sohāg → Sawhāj	26N33	31E42	-2:06:48
Subk al-Ahad	30N18	31E02	-2:04:08
Sudūd	30N25	30E54	-2:03:36
Suez → As-Suways	29N58	32E33	-2:10:12
Sumusṭā al-Waqf	28N55	30E51	-2:03:24
Sunbāṭ	30N48	31E12	-2:04:48
Ṣurad	30N59	30E54	-2:03:36
Ṫafahnā al-'Azab	30N36	31E15	-2:05:00
Ṭahmā wa Minshāt 'Abd as-Sayyid	29N38	31E14	-2:04:56
Ṭahṭā	26N46	31E30	-2:06:00
Ṭahwāy	30N22	30E52	-2:03:28
Tāj al-'Izz	30N57	31E35	-2:06:20
Talā	30N41	30E56	-2:03:44
Ṭalkhā	31N03	31E22	-2:05:28
Ṫallah	28N05	30E44	-2:02:56
Tall Banī 'Umrān	27N40	30E54	-2:03:36
Tall Rāk	30N54	31E43	-2:06:52
Ṭalyā	30N16	31E00	-2:04:00
Ṭamalāy	30N30	30E51	-2:03:24
Ṭāmiyah	29N29	30E58	-2:03:52
Ṭammūh	29N56	31E16	-2:05:04
Ṭanān	30N15	31E14	-2:04:56
Ṭanbidī	28N38	30E47	-2:03:08
Ṫandah	27N41	30E46	-2:03:04
Ṭanṭā	30N47	31E00	-2:04:00
Ṭārūṭ	30N32	31E28	-2:05:52
Ṭawwah Banī Ibrāhīm	28N05	30E41	-2:02:44
Tīdah	31N15	30E50	-2:03:20
Tilbānah	30N59	31E27	-2:05:48
Ṭimā	26N54	31E26	-2:05:44
Ṫimay al-Amdīd	30N57	31E32	-2:06:08
Tīrah	31N05	31E14	-2:04:56
Tirsā	29N25	30E49	-2:03:16
Tirsā	29N58	31E12	-2:04:48
Tizmant ash-Sharqīyah	29N03	31E03	-2:04:12
Ṭubhār	29N19	30E42	-2:02:48
Ṭūkh	30N21	31E12	-2:04:48
Ṭūkh	27N41	30E49	-2:03:16
Ṭūkh al-Aqlām	30N52	31E26	-2:05:44
Ṭūkh al-Khayl	28N06	30E40	-2:02:40
Ṭūkh Dalakah	30N39	30E55	-2:03:40
Ṫūnat al-Jabal	27N46	30E44	-2:02:56
Tunaydah	25N31	29E21	-1:57:24
Ṭurā	29N56	31E16	-2:05:04
Ṫur'At Ghunaym	31N16	31E29	-2:05:56
Tuṭūn	29N09	30E46	-2:03:04
Umm al-Quṣūr	27N23	30E54	-2:03:36
Umm Dīnār	30N12	31E04	-2:04:16
Umm Khunān	29N55	31E15	-2:05:00
Orein	30N58	30E42	-2:02:48
Wāqid	30N42	30E44	-2:02:56
Warrāq al-'Arab	30N06	31E12	-2:04:48
Warrāq al-Ḥaḍar	30N06	31E13	-2:04:52
Warrāq al-Ḣadar wa Ambūtbah wa Mīt	30N06	31E13	-2:04:52
Ẓafar al-Qadīmah	30N58	31E37	-2:06:28
Żagazig → Az-Zaqāzīq	30N35	31E31	-2:06:04
Zarqūn	31N07	30E28	-2:01:52
Zāwiyat Abū Musallam	29N56	31E10	-2:04:40
Zāwiyat Abū Musallum	29N56	31E10	-2:04:40
Zāwiyat al-Amwāt	28N04	30E50	-2:03:20
Zawiyat al-Judhāmī	28N42	30E54	-2:03:36
Zāwiyat Nābit	30N07	31E09	-2:04:36
Zāwiyat Razīn	30N25	30E51	-2:03:24
Zāwiyat Saqr	30N56	30E12	-2:00:48
Zawiyat Shammās	31N31	26E24	-1:45:36
Zāwiyat 'Abd al-Qādir	31N02	29E49	-1:59:16
Zāwiyat Sīdī Ghāzī	31N03	30E05	-2:00:20
Zāwiyet an-Najjār	30N11	31E17	-2:05:08
Ziftā	30N43	31E15	-2:05:00
Zufaytat Mashtūl	30N20	31E21	-2:05:24

EL SALVADOR EL SALVADOR

Time Table

Before 1/Jan/1921 LMT		
Begin Standard		90w00
1/Jan/1921	0:00	6:00
3/May/1987	0:00	5:00
27/Sep/1987	0:00	6:00
1/May/1988	0:00	5:00
25/Sep/1988	0:00	6:00

Place	Lat	Long	Offset
Acajutla	13N36	89w50	5:59:20
Aguilares	13N58	89w12	5:56:48
Ahuachapán	13N55	89w51	5:59:24
Apopa	13N48	89w11	5:56:44
Arcatao	14N05	88w45	5:55:00
Atiquizaya	13N58	89w46	5:59:04
Carolina	13N51	88w19	5:53:16
Chalatenango	14N03	88w56	5:55:44
Chalchuapa	13N59	89w41	5:58:44
Chinameca	13N30	88w21	5:53:24
Chirilagua	13N13	88w08	5:52:32
Ciudad Barrios	13N46	88w16	5:53:04
Cojutepeque	13N43	88w56	5:55:44
Concepción de Ataco	13N52	89w51	5:59:24
Concepción Quezaltepeque	14N06	88w58	5:55:52
Conchagua	13N19	87w52	5:51:28
Corinto	13N49	87w58	5:51:52
El Congo	13N54	89w30	5:58:00
El Cuco	13N10	88w07	5:52:28
El Tamarindo	13N11	87w54	5:51:36
El Tránsito	13N22	88w21	5:53:24
Estanzuelas	13N38	88w30	5:54:00
Garita Palmera	13N44	90w05	6:00:20
Guatajiagua	13N40	88w13	5:52:52
Ilobasco	13N51	88w51	5:55:24
Intipucá	13N12	88w04	5:52:16
Izalco	13N45	89w40	5:58:40
Jiquilisco	13N19	88w35	5:54:20
Jocoro	13N37	88w01	5:52:04
Jucuapa	13N31	88w24	5:53:36
La Libertad	13N29	89w19	5:57:16
La Palma	14N19	89w11	5:56:44
La Tasajera	13N16	88w52	5:55:28
La Unión	13N20	87w51	5:51:24
Lolotique	13N33	88w21	5:53:24
Metapán	14N20	89w27	5:57:48
Nahuizalco	13N46	89w45	5:59:00
Nueva Concepción	14N08	89w18	5:57:12
Nueva San Salvador	13N41	89w17	5:57:08
Puerto El Triunfo	13N17	88w33	5:54:12
Quezaltepeque	13N50	89w17	5:57:08
San Alejo	13N26	87w58	5:51:52
San Francisco Gotera	13N42	88w06	5:52:24
San Jorge	13N25	88w21	5:53:24
San Marcelino	13N22	89w03	5:56:12
San Marcos	13N39	89w11	5:56:44
San Miguel	13N29	88w11	5:52:44
San Rafael Oriente	13N23	88w21	5:53:24
San Salvador	13N42	89w12	5:56:48
San Sebastián	13N44	88w50	5:55:20
Santa Ana	13N59	89w34	5:58:16
Santa Elena	13N22	88w25	5:53:40
Santa Rosa de Lima	13N37	87w53	5:51:32
Santa Tecla → Nueva San Salvador	13N41	89w17	5:57:08
San Vicente	13N38	88w48	5:55:12
Sensuntepeque	13N52	88w38	5:54:32
Sonsonate	13N43	89w44	5:58:56
Soyapango	13N42	89w09	5:56:36
Suchitoto	13N56	89w02	5:56:08
Usulután	13N21	88w27	5:53:48
Villa Delgado	13N43	89w10	5:56:40
Zacatecoluca	13N30	88w52	5:55:28

ENGLAND ANGLETERRE ANGLIA INGLATERRA

Time Table # 1

Date	Time	Offset
Before 1/Jan/1848	LMT	
Begin Standard		0w00
1/Jan/1848	0:00	0:00
21/May/1916	2:00	-1:00
1/Oct/1916	3:00	0:00
8/Apr/1917	2:00	-1:00
17/Sep/1917	3:00	0:00
24/Mar/1918	2:00	-1:00
30/Sep/1918	3:00	0:00
30/Mar/1919	2:00	-1:00
29/Sep/1919	3:00	0:00
28/Mar/1920	2:00	-1:00
25/Oct/1920	3:00	0:00
3/Apr/1921	2:00	-1:00
3/Oct/1921	3:00	0:00
26/Mar/1922	2:00	-1:00
8/Oct/1922	3:00	0:00
22/Apr/1923	2:00	-1:00
16/Sep/1923	3:00	0:00
13/Apr/1924	2:00	-1:00
21/Sep/1924	3:00	0:00
19/Apr/1925	2:00	-1:00
4/Oct/1925	3:00	0:00
18/Apr/1926	2:00	-1:00
3/Oct/1926	3:00	0:00
10/Apr/1927	2:00	-1:00
2/Oct/1927	3:00	0:00
22/Apr/1928	2:00	-1:00
7/Oct/1928	3:00	0:00
21/Apr/1929	2:00	-1:00
6/Oct/1929	3:00	0:00
13/Apr/1930	2:00	-1:00
5/Oct/1930	3:00	0:00
19/Apr/1931	2:00	-1:00
4/Oct/1931	3:00	0:00
17/Apr/1932	2:00	-1:00
2/Oct/1932	3:00	0:00
9/Apr/1933	2:00	-1:00
8/Oct/1933	3:00	0:00
22/Apr/1934	2:00	-1:00
7/Oct/1934	3:00	0:00
14/Apr/1935	2:00	-1:00
6/Oct/1935	3:00	0:00
19/Apr/1936	2:00	-1:00
4/Oct/1936	3:00	0:00
18/Apr/1937	2:00	-1:00
3/Oct/1937	3:00	0:00
10/Apr/1938	2:00	-1:00
2/Oct/1938	3:00	0:00
16/Apr/1939	2:00	-1:00
19/Nov/1939	3:00	0:00
25/Feb/1940	2:00	-1:00
4/May/1941	2:00	-2:00
10/Aug/1941	3:00	-1:00
5/Apr/1942	2:00	-2:00
9/Aug/1942	3:00	-1:00
4/Apr/1943	2:00	-2:00
15/Aug/1943	3:00	-1:00
2/Apr/1944	2:00	-2:00
17/Sep/1944	3:00	-1:00
2/Apr/1945	2:00	-2:00
15/Jul/1945	3:00	-1:00
7/Oct/1945	3:00	0:00
14/Apr/1946	2:00	-1:00
6/Oct/1946	3:00	0:00
16/Mar/1947	2:00	-1:00
13/Apr/1947	2:00	-2:00
10/Aug/1947	3:00	-1:00
2/Nov/1947	3:00	0:00
14/Mar/1948	2:00	-1:00
31/Oct/1948	3:00	0:00
3/Apr/1949	2:00	-1:00
30/Oct/1949	3:00	0:00
16/Apr/1950	2:00	-1:00
22/Oct/1950	3:00	0:00
15/Apr/1951	2:00	-1:00
21/Oct/1951	3:00	0:00
20/Apr/1952	2:00	-1:00
26/Oct/1952	3:00	0:00
19/Apr/1953	2:00	-1:00
4/Oct/1953	3:00	0:00
11/Apr/1954	2:00	-1:00
3/Oct/1954	3:00	0:00
17/Apr/1955	2:00	-1:00
2/Oct/1955	3:00	0:00
22/Apr/1956	2:00	-1:00
7/Oct/1956	3:00	0:00
14/Apr/1957	2:00	-1:00
6/Oct/1957	3:00	0:00
20/Apr/1958	2:00	-1:00
5/Oct/1958	3:00	0:00
19/Apr/1959	2:00	-1:00
4/Oct/1959	3:00	0:00
10/Apr/1960	2:00	-1:00
2/Oct/1960	3:00	0:00
26/Mar/1961	2:00	-1:00
29/Oct/1961	3:00	0:00
25/Mar/1962	2:00	-1:00
28/Oct/1962	3:00	0:00
31/Mar/1963	2:00	-1:00
27/Oct/1963	3:00	0:00
22/Mar/1964	2:00	-1:00
25/Oct/1964	3:00	0:00
21/Mar/1965	2:00	-1:00
24/Oct/1965	3:00	0:00
20/Mar/1966	2:00	-1:00
23/Oct/1966	3:00	0:00
19/Mar/1967	2:00	-1:00
29/Oct/1967	3:00	0:00
Begin Standard		15E00
18/Feb/1968	2:00	-1:00
Begin Standard		0w00
31/Oct/1971	3:00	0:00
19/Mar/1972	2:00	-1:00
29/Oct/1972	3:00	0:00
18/Mar/1973	2:00	-1:00
28/Oct/1973	3:00	0:00
17/Mar/1974	2:00	-1:00
27/Oct/1974	3:00	0:00
16/Mar/1975	2:00	-1:00
26/Oct/1975	3:00	0:00
21/Mar/1976	2:00	-1:00
24/Oct/1976	3:00	0:00
20/Mar/1977	2:00	-1:00
23/Oct/1977	3:00	0:00
19/Mar/1978	2:00	-1:00
29/Oct/1978	3:00	0:00
18/Mar/1979	2:00	-1:00
28/Oct/1979	3:00	0:00
16/Mar/1980	2:00	-1:00
26/Oct/1980	3:00	0:00
29/Mar/1981	1:00	-1:00
25/Oct/1981	2:00	0:00
28/Mar/1982	1:00	-1:00
24/Oct/1982	2:00	0:00
27/Mar/1983	1:00	-1:00
23/Oct/1983	2:00	0:00
25/Mar/1984	1:00	-1:00
28/Oct/1984	2:00	0:00
31/Mar/1985	1:00	-1:00
27/Oct/1985	2:00	0:00
30/Mar/1986	1:00	-1:00
26/Oct/1986	2:00	0:00
29/Mar/1987	1:00	-1:00
25/Oct/1987	2:00	0:00
27/Mar/1988	1:00	-1:00
23/Oct/1988	2:00	0:00
26/Mar/1989	1:00	-1:00
29/Oct/1989	2:00	0:00
25/Mar/1990	1:00	-1:00
28/Oct/1990	2:00	0:00
31/Mar/1991	1:00	-1:00
27/Oct/1991	2:00	0:00
29/Mar/1992	1:00	-1:00
25/Oct/1992	2:00	0:00
28/Mar/1993	1:00	-1:00
24/Oct/1993	2:00	0:00
27/Mar/1994	1:00	-1:00
23/Oct/1994	2:00	0:00
26/Mar/1995	1:00	-1:00
29/Oct/1995	2:00	0:00
31/Mar/1996	1:00	-1:00
27/Oct/1996	2:00	0:00
30/Mar/1997	1:00	-1:00
26/Oct/1997	2:00	0:00
29/Mar/1998	1:00	-1:00
25/Oct/1998	2:00	0:00
28/Mar/1999	1:00	-1:00
24/Oct/1999	2:00	0:00
26/Mar/2000	1:00	-1:00
29/Oct/2000	2:00	0:00

Time Table # 2

Date	Time	Offset
Before 1/Jan/1855	LMT	
Begin Standard		0w00
1/Jan/1855	0:00	0:00
21/May/1916	2:00	TT#1

Time Table # 3

Date	Time	Offset
Before 14/Sep/1852	LMT	
Begin Standard		0w00
14/Sep/1852	0:00	0:00
21/May/1916	2:00	TT#1

Time Table # 4

Date	Time	Offset
Before 2/Nov/1852	LMT	
Begin Standard		0w00
2/Nov/1852	0:00	0:00
21/May/1916	2:00	TT#1

Time Table # 5

Date	Time	Offset
Before 2/Aug/1880	LMT	
Begin Standard		0w00
2/Aug/1880	0:00	0:00
21/May/1916	2:00	TT#1

Place	TT	Lat	Long	Offset
Abbess Roding	1	51N47	0E17	-0:01:08
Abbey Town	1	54N50	3w17	0:13:08
Abbotsbury	1	50N40	2w36	0:10:24
Abbots Langley	1	51N43	0w25	0:01:40
Abingdon	2	51N41	1w17	0:05:08
Abinger	1	51N12	0w24	0:01:36
Abram	1	53N31	2w35	0:10:20
Abridge	1	51N39	0E07	-0:00:28
Accrington	1	53N46	2w21	0:09:24
Acle	1	52N38	1E33	-0:06:12
Acton	1	51N30	0w16	0:01:04
Acton Bridge	1	53N16	2w36	0:10:24
Acton Turville	1	51N32	2w17	0:09:08
Adderbury	1	52N00	1w17	0:05:08
Addingham	1	53N57	1w53	0:07:32
Addington	1	51N18	0E23	-0:01:32
Addlestone	1	51N22	0w30	0:02:00
Adlington	1	53N37	2w36	0:10:24
Adwick le Street	1	53N34	1w11	0:04:44
Ainsdale	1	53N36	3w02	0:12:08
Ainsworth	1	53N35	2w22	0:09:28
Aintree	1	53N29	2w56	0:11:44
Albrighton	1	52N38	2w16	0:09:04
Albury	1	51N13	0w30	0:02:00
Alcester	1	52N13	1w52	0:07:28
Aldbourne	1	51N31	1w37	0:06:28
Aldbrough	1	53N50	0w07	0:00:28
Aldbury	1	51N48	0w36	0:02:24
Aldeburgh	1	52N09	1E35	-0:06:20
Aldenham	1	51N40	0w21	0:01:24
Alderley Edge	1	53N18	2w15	0:09:00
Aldermaston	1	51N23	1w09	0:04:36
Aldershot	1	51N15	0w47	0:03:08
Aldridge	1	52N36	1w55	0:07:40
Alford	1	53N16	0E10	-0:00:40
Alfreton	1	53N06	1w23	0:05:32
Alfriston	1	50N48	0E10	-0:00:40
Allendale Town	1	54N54	2w15	0:09:00
Allestree	1	52N57	1w29	0:05:56
Allhallows	1	51N28	0E39	-0:02:36
Allonby	1	54N46	3w25	0:13:40
Almondsbury	3	51N34	2w34	0:10:16
Alnmouth	1	55N23	1w36	0:06:24
Alnwick	1	55N25	1w42	0:06:48
Alperton	1	51N33	0w18	0:01:12
Alphington	4	50N42	3w31	0:14:04
Alston	1	54N49	2w26	0:09:44
Altarnun	2	50N37	4w30	0:18:00
Altham	1	53N47	2w21	0:09:24
Alton	1	51N09	0w59	0:03:56
Altrincham	1	53N24	2w21	0:09:24
Alvanley	1	53N16	2w45	0:11:00
Alvechurch	1	52N21	1w57	0:07:48
Alveston	1	51N36	2w32	0:10:08
Amble	1	55N20	1w34	0:06:16
Amblecote	1	52N28	2w09	0:08:36
Ambleside	1	54N26	2w58	0:11:52
Amersham	1	51N40	0w38	0:02:32
Amesbury	1	51N10	1w45	0:07:00
Ampleforth	1	54N12	1w06	0:04:24
Ampthill	1	52N02	0w30	0:02:00
Ancaster	1	52N59	0w32	0:02:08
Anderton	1	53N17	2w32	0:10:08
Andover	1	51N13	1w28	0:05:52
Angmering	1	50N48	0w28	0:01:52
Anlaby	1	53N45	0w27	0:01:48
Annfield Plain	1	54N51	1w45	0:07:00
Anstey	1	52N40	1w11	0:04:44
Appleby	1	54N36	2w29	0:09:56
Appledore	2	51N03	4w10	0:16:40
Appleton	1	53N21	2w33	0:10:12
Appley Bridge	1	53N35	2w43	0:10:52
Ardsley	1	53N32	1w28	0:05:52
Arley	1	53N19	2w30	0:10:00
Armthorpe	1	53N32	1w03	0:04:12
Arnold	1	53N00	1w08	0:04:32
Arundel	1	50N51	0w34	0:02:16
Ascot	1	51N25	0w41	0:02:44
Ash	1	51N17	1E16	-0:05:04
Ash	1	51N15	0w44	0:02:56
Ashbourne	1	53N02	1w44	0:06:56
Ashburton	2	50N31	3w45	0:15:00
Ashby-de-la-Zouch	1	52N46	1w28	0:05:52
Ashford	1	51N08	0E53	-0:03:32
Ashford	1	51N26	0w27	0:01:48
Ashingdon	1	51N36	0E42	-0:02:48
Ashington	1	55N12	1w35	0:06:20
Ashley	1	53N21	2w20	0:09:20
Ashley Green	1	51N44	0w35	0:02:20
Ashtead	1	51N19	0w18	0:01:12
Ashton	1	53N13	2w45	0:11:00
Ashton-in-Makerfield	1	53N29	2w39	0:10:36
Ashton-under-Lyne	1	53N29	2w06	0:08:24
Ashton upon Mersey	1	53N26	2w19	0:09:16
Ashwater	2	50N44	4w16	0:17:04
Askern	1	53N37	1w09	0:04:36
Askrigg	1	54N19	2w04	0:08:16
Aspatria	1	54N46	3w20	0:13:20
Aspull	1	53N34	2w35	0:10:20
Astley Bridge	1	53N36	2w26	0:09:44
Astley Green	1	53N29	2w27	0:09:48
Aston	1	53N18	2w40	0:10:40
Aston Clinton	1	51N48	0w44	0:02:56
Atherstone	1	52N35	1w31	0:06:04
Atherton	1	53N31	2w31	0:10:04
Attleborough	1	52N31	1E01	-0:04:04
Audenshaw	1	53N28	2w08	0:08:32
Aughton	1	53N32	2w56	0:11:44
Aughton Park	1	53N33	2w53	0:11:32
Austonley	1	53N34	1w50	0:07:20
Avanley	1	53N16	2w45	0:11:00
Avebury	1	51N27	1w51	0:07:24
Aveley	1	51N30	0E16	-0:01:04
Avonmouth	1	51N31	2w42	0:10:48
Awbridge	1	50N59	1w30	0:06:00
Axbridge	1	51N18	2w49	0:11:16
Axminster	2	50N47	3w00	0:12:00
Axmouth	2	50N42	3w02	0:12:08
Aylesbury	1	51N50	0w50	0:03:20
Aylesford	1	51N18	0E29	-0:01:56
Aylesham	1	51N13	1E13	-0:04:52
Aylsham	1	52N49	1E15	-0:05:00
Aysgarth	1	54N17	2w00	0:08:00
Backford	1	53N15	2w54	0:11:36
Bacton	1	52N52	1E28	-0:05:52
Bacup	1	53N43	2w12	0:08:48
Badger's Mount	1	51N20	0E09	-0:00:36
Bagshot	1	51N22	0w42	0:02:48
Baildon	1	53N52	1w46	0:07:04
Baker Street	1	51N30	0E21	-0:01:24
Bakewell	1	53N13	1w40	0:06:40
Balcombe	1	51N04	0w08	0:00:32
Balderstone	1	53N47	2w34	0:10:16
Balderton	1	53N03	0w47	0:03:08
Baldock	1	51N59	0w12	0:00:48
Balsham	1	52N08	0E20	-0:01:20
Bamburgh	1	55N36	1w42	0:06:48
Bampton	1	51N00	3w29	0:13:56
Bampton	1	51N44	1w33	0:06:12
Banbury	1	52N04	1w20	0:05:20
Banks	1	53N41	2w56	0:11:44
Banstead	1	51N19	0w12	0:00:48
Banwell	1	51N20	2w52	0:11:28
Barber Booth	1	53N22	1w50	0:07:20
Bardney	1	53N12	0w21	0:01:24
Barking	1	51N33	0E06	-0:00:24
Barkingside	1	51N36	0E05	-0:00:20
Barkisland	1	53N41	1w55	0:07:40
Barlby	1	53N48	1w03	0:04:12
Barnard Castle	1	54N33	1w55	0:07:40
Barnes	1	51N29	0w15	0:01:00
Barnet	1	51N40	0w13	0:00:52
Barnetby le Wold	1	53N35	0w25	0:01:40
Barnoldswick	1	53N55	2w11	0:08:44
Barnsley	1	53N34	1w28	0:05:52
Barnstaple	2	51N05	4w04	0:16:16
Barnston	1	53N21	3w05	0:12:20
Barnt Green	1	52N22	1w59	0:07:56
Barnton	1	53N16	2w33	0:10:12
Barrowford	1	53N52	2w13	0:08:52
Barrow-in-Furness	1	54N07	3w14	0:12:56
Barton Mills	1	52N20	0E31	-0:02:04
Barton-under-Needwood	1	52N45	1w43	0:06:52
Barton-upon-Humber	1	53N41	0w27	0:01:48
Barwell	1	52N32	1w21	0:05:24
Basildon	1	51N35	0E25	-0:01:40
Basing	2	51N20	1w10	0:04:40
Basingstoke	2	51N15	1w05	0:04:20
Baslow	1	53N15	1w38	0:06:32
Bassenthwaite	1	54N41	3w12	0:12:48
Bate Heath	1	53N19	2w28	0:09:52
Bath	2	51N23	2w22	0:09:28
Batley	1	53N44	1w37	0:06:28
Battersea	1	51N28	0w10	0:00:40
Battle	1	50N55	0E29	-0:01:56
Battlesbridge	1	51N37	0E34	-0:02:16
Bawdeswell	1	52N45	1E01	-0:04:04
Bawtry	1	53N26	1w01	0:04:04
Baxenden	1	53N44	2w20	0:09:20
Bayford	1	51N46	0w06	0:00:24
Beaconsfield	1	51N37	0w39	0:02:36
Beaminster	2	50N49	2w45	0:11:00
Bean	1	51N25	0E17	-0:01:08
Bearstead	1	51N16	0E35	-0:02:20
Beauchamp Roding	1	51N46	0E18	-0:01:12
Beaulieu	1	50N49	1w27	0:05:48
Beccles	1	52N28	1E34	-0:06:16
Becconsall	1	53N42	2w50	0:11:20
Beckenham	1	51N24	0w02	0:00:08
Beckington	2	51N16	2w18	0:09:12
Bedale	1	54N17	1w35	0:06:20
Bedford	1	52N08	0w29	0:01:56
Bedfordshire	1	52N05	0w30	0:02:00
Bedmond	1	51N43	0w25	0:01:40
Bedworth	1	52N28	1w29	0:05:56
Beeston	1	52N56	1w12	0:04:48
Belford	1	55N36	1w49	0:07:16
Bellingdon	1	51N44	0w38	0:02:32
Bellingham	1	55N09	2w16	0:09:04
Belmont	1	53N38	2w30	0:10:00
Belper	1	53N01	1w29	0:05:56
Belthorn	1	53N43	2w26	0:09:44
Bembridge	2	50N41	1w05	0:04:20
Benover	1	51N13	0E26	-0:01:44
Benson	1	51N38	1w05	0:04:20
Bentley	1	53N33	1w09	0:04:36
Bere Alston	2	50N29	4w11	0:16:44
Bere Regis	1	50N46	2w14	0:08:56
Berkeley	1	51N42	2w27	0:09:48

Berkhamsted	1	51N46	0w35	0:02:20
Berkshire	1	51N30	1w20	0:05:20
Bermondsey	1	51N30	0w05	0:00:20
Berwick	1	50N49	0E15	-0:01:00
Berwick-upon-Tweed	1	55N46	2w00	0:08:00
Betchworth	1	51N14	0w16	0:01:04
Bethersden	1	51N08	0E48	-0:03:12
Bethnal Green	1	51N32	0w03	0:00:12
Betsham	1	51N25	0E19	-0:01:16
Beverley	1	53N52	0w26	0:01:44
Bewdley	1	52N22	2w19	0:09:16
Bexhill on Sea	1	50N50	0E29	-0:01:56
Bexley	1	51N26	0E10	-0:00:40
Bicester	1	51N54	1w09	0:04:36
Bickerstaffe	1	53N32	2w50	0:11:20
Bicknacre	2	51N42	0E35	-0:02:20
Bicknor	1	51N18	0E40	-0:02:40
Biddenden	1	51N07	0E39	-0:02:36
Biddulph	1	53N08	2w10	0:08:40
Bideford	2	51N01	4w13	0:16:52
Bidford-on-Avon	1	52N10	1w51	0:07:24
Bidston	1	53N24	3w05	0:12:20
Biggleswade	1	52N05	0w17	0:01:08
Billericay	2	51N38	0E25	-0:01:40
Billesdon	1	52N37	0w55	0:03:40
Billinge	1	53N30	2w42	0:10:48
Billingham	1	54N36	1w17	0:05:08
Billingshurst	1	51N01	0w28	0:01:52
Bilston	2	52N34	2w04	0:08:16
Bingham	1	52N57	0w57	0:03:48
Bingley	1	53N51	1w50	0:07:20
Birch	1	53N34	2w13	0:08:52
Birchington	2	51N23	1E19	-0:05:16
Birch Vale	1	53N23	1w57	0:07:48
Birkdale	1	53N37	3w02	0:12:08
Birkenhead	1	53N24	3w02	0:12:08
Birling	1	51N19	0E25	-0:01:40
Birmingham	1	52N30	1w50	0:07:20
Birstall	1	52N41	1w07	0:04:28
Birtley	1	54N54	1w34	0:06:16
Bishop Auckland	1	54N40	1w40	0:06:40
Bishop's Castle	1	52N29	3w00	0:12:00
Bishop's Cleeve	1	51N57	2w04	0:08:16
Bishops Frome	1	52N08	2w29	0:09:56
Bishops Lydeard	1	51N04	3w12	0:12:48
Bishop's Stortford	1	51N53	0E09	-0:00:36
Bishopsteignton	2	50N34	3w31	0:14:04
Bishopstoke	1	50N59	1w19	0:05:16
Bishop's Waltham	1	50N58	1w12	0:04:48
Bisley	1	51N20	0w38	0:02:32
Bisley	1	51N45	2w08	0:08:32
Blackburn	1	53N45	2w29	0:09:56
Blackden Heath	1	53N14	2w20	0:09:20
Blackhall Colliery	1	54N44	1w14	0:04:56
Blackheath	1	51N12	0w31	0:02:04
Blackmore	1	51N41	0E19	-0:01:16
Blackpool	1	53N50	3w03	0:12:12
Blackrod	1	53N35	2w35	0:10:20
Blagdon	1	51N20	2w43	0:10:52
Blakeney	1	51N46	2w29	0:09:56
Blakeney	1	52N58	1E00	-0:04:00
Blandford Forum	1	50N52	2w11	0:08:44
Blaydon	1	54N58	1w42	0:06:48
Blean	1	51N19	1E02	-0:04:08
Bletchingley	1	51N14	0w06	0:00:24
Bletchley	1	52N00	0w46	0:03:04
Blindley Heath	1	51N12	0w04	0:00:16
Blockley	1	52N01	1w45	0:07:00
Bloxham	1	52N02	1w22	0:05:28
Bluebell Hill	1	51N20	0E30	-0:02:00
Blyth	1	55N07	1w30	0:06:00
Bobbing	1	51N21	0E43	-0:02:52
Bobbingworth	1	51N44	0E13	-0:00:52
Bodiam	1	51N00	0E33	-0:02:12
Bodmin	2	50N29	4w43	0:18:52
Bognor Regis	1	50N47	0w41	0:02:44
Bold Heath	1	53N24	2w42	0:10:48
Boldon	1	54N57	1w27	0:05:48
Bollington	1	53N18	2w06	0:08:24
Bollington	1	53N22	2w25	0:09:40
Bolsover	1	53N14	1w18	0:05:12
Bolton	1	53N35	2w26	0:09:44
Bolton Abbey	1	53N59	1w53	0:07:32
Bolton Bridge	1	53N58	1w57	0:07:48
Bolton-le-Sands	1	54N06	2w47	0:11:08
Bolton upon Dearne	1	53N31	1w19	0:05:16
Boot	1	54N24	3w17	0:13:08
Boothstown	1	53N30	2w25	0:09:40
Bootle	1	53N28	3w00	0:12:00
Borden	1	51N20	0E42	-0:02:48
Boreham	2	51N46	0E33	-0:02:12
Borehamwood	1	51N40	0w16	0:01:04
Boroughbridge	1	54N06	1w23	0:05:32
Borough Green	1	51N17	0E19	-0:01:16
Borrowdale	1	54N31	3w10	0:12:40
Boscastle	2	50N41	4w42	0:18:48
Bostock Green	1	53N13	2w30	0:10:00
Boston	1	52N59	0w01	0:00:04
Botley	1	50N56	1w18	0:05:12
Bottesford	1	52N56	0w48	0:03:12
Boughton Green	1	51N14	0E32	-0:02:08
Boughton Malherbe	1	51N13	0E42	-0:02:48
Boughton Street	1	51N18	0E59	-0:03:56
Bourne	1	52N46	0w23	0:01:32
Bournebridge	1	51N38	0E11	-0:00:44
Bourne End	1	51N45	0w32	0:02:08
Bournemouth	1	50N43	1w54	0:07:36
Bourton-on-TheWater	1	51N53	1w45	0:07:00
Bovey Tracey	2	50N36	3w40	0:14:40

Bovingdon	1	51N44	0w32	0:02:08
Bowdon	1	53N23	2w22	0:09:28
Bowers Gifford	1	51N34	0E32	-0:02:08
Bowgreave	1	53N52	2w45	0:11:00
Bowness-on-Windermere	1	54N22	2w55	0:11:40
Box	2	51N26	2w15	0:09:00
Boxley	1	51N18	0E33	-0:02:12
Boxmoor	1	51N45	0w29	0:01:56
Bracebridge Heath	1	53N13	0w33	0:02:12
Brackley	1	52N02	1w09	0:04:36
Bracknell	1	51N26	0w45	0:03:00
Bradford	1	53N48	1w45	0:07:00
Bradford-on-Avon	2	51N20	2w15	0:09:00
Brading	1	50N41	1w09	0:04:36
Bradshaw	1	53N36	2w24	0:09:36
Bradwell-on-Sea	1	51N44	0E54	-0:03:36
Bradworthy	2	50N54	4w22	0:17:28
Braintree	1	51N53	0E32	-0:02:08
Bramford	2	52N04	1E06	-0:04:24
Bramhall	1	53N22	2w10	0:08:40
Bramham	1	54N00	1w15	0:05:00
Bramley	1	51N12	0w34	0:02:16
Brampton	1	52N19	0w14	0:00:56
Brampton	1	54N57	2w43	0:10:52
Brancaster	1	52N58	0E39	-0:02:36
Brandon	1	52N27	0E37	-0:02:28
Brandon	1	54N46	1w39	0:06:36
Brasted	1	51N16	0E17	-0:01:08
Brasted Chart	1	51N16	0E06	-0:00:24
Braunton	2	51N07	4w10	0:16:40
Bream's Eaves	1	51N45	2w34	0:10:16
Bredbury	1	53N25	2w06	0:08:24
Bredgar	1	51N18	0E42	-0:02:48
Bredhurst	1	51N20	0E35	-0:02:20
Brentford	1	51N29	0w18	0:01:12
Brentwood	1	51N38	0E18	-0:01:12
Bretherton	1	53N41	2w48	0:11:12
Brewood	2	52N41	2w10	0:08:40
Bridge Trafford	1	53N14	2w49	0:11:16
Bridgnorth	1	52N33	2w25	0:09:40
Bridgwater	1	51N08	3w00	0:12:00
Bridlington	1	54N05	0w12	0:00:48
Bridport	2	50N44	2w46	0:11:04
Brierfield	1	53N50	2w14	0:08:56
Brierley Hill	2	52N29	2w07	0:08:28
Brigg	1	53N34	0w30	0:02:00
Brighouse	1	53N42	1w47	0:07:08
Brighstone	1	50N38	1w24	0:05:36
Brightlingsea	1	51N49	1E02	-0:04:08
Brighton	1	50N50	0w08	0:00:32
Brill	1	51N49	1w03	0:04:12
Brimfield	1	52N18	2w42	0:10:48
Brimington	1	53N16	1w23	0:05:32
Brindle	1	53N43	2w36	0:10:24
Brindley Heath	1	51N12	0w03	0:00:12
Brinscall	1	53N41	2w34	0:10:16
Bristol	3	51N27	2w35	0:10:20
Brixham	1	50N24	3w30	0:14:00
Brixworth	1	52N20	0w54	0:03:36
Broadbottom	1	53N26	2w01	0:08:04
Broad Chalke	1	51N02	1w57	0:07:48
Broad Clyst	4	50N46	3w26	0:13:44
Broadheath	1	53N24	2w21	0:09:24
Broadley Common	1	51N45	0E04	-0:00:16
Broadstairs	1	51N22	1E27	-0:05:48
Broad Street	1	51N17	0E38	-0:02:32
Broadway	1	52N02	1w51	0:07:24
Broadwindsor	2	50N49	2w48	0:11:12
Brockenhurst	1	50N49	1w34	0:06:16
Brockham	1	51N14	0w17	0:01:08
Brockworth	1	51N51	2w09	0:08:36
Broken Cross	1	53N15	2w10	0:08:40
Broken Cross	1	53N15	2w29	0:09:56
Bromborough	1	53N19	2w59	0:11:56
Bromley	1	51N24	0E02	-0:00:08
Brompton	1	51N23	0E33	-0:02:12
Brompton	1	54N22	1w25	0:05:40
Bromsgrove	1	52N20	2w03	0:08:12
Bromyard	1	52N11	2w30	0:10:00
Brookland	1	50N59	0E50	-0:03:20
Brookmans Park	1	51N43	0w12	0:00:48
Brook Street	1	51N37	0E17	-0:01:08
Brookwood	1	51N18	0w38	0:02:32
Broomfield	1	51N14	0E38	-0:02:32
Broomfield	2	51N46	0E28	-0:01:52
Broseley	1	52N37	2w29	0:09:56
Brotton	1	54N34	0w56	0:03:44
Brough	1	53N44	0w35	0:02:20
Brough	1	54N32	2w19	0:09:16
Broughton	1	53N49	2w43	0:10:52
Broughton	1	52N23	0w46	0:03:04
Broughton in Furness	1	54N17	3w12	0:12:48
Brownhills	1	52N39	1w55	0:07:40
Broxbourne	1	51N45	0w01	0:00:04
Bruton	1	51N07	2w27	0:09:48
Bryn	1	53N30	2w39	0:10:36
Bryn Gates	1	53N30	2w37	0:10:28
Buckden	1	52N17	0w16	0:01:04
Buckden	1	54N12	2w05	0:08:20
Buckfastleigh	2	50N29	3w46	0:15:04
Buckingham	1	52N00	1w00	0:04:00
Buckingham Palace	1	51N30	0w08	0:00:32
Buckinghamshire	1	51N45	0w48	0:03:12
Buckland	1	51N15	0w15	0:01:00
Buckland Brewer	2	50N57	4w14	0:16:56
Buckland Common	1	51N45	0w39	0:02:36
Bude	2	50N50	4w33	0:18:12
Budleigh Salterton	1	50N38	3w20	0:13:20
Bugle	2	50N24	4w47	0:19:08
Bulkington	1	52N29	1w25	0:05:40

Bulpham	1	51N33	0E22	-0:01:28
Bumbles Green	1	51N44	0E02	-0:00:08
Bungay	1	52N28	1E26	-0:05:44
Buntingford	1	51N57	0w01	0:00:04
Burbage	1	52N31	1w20	0:05:20
Burbage	1	53N15	1w56	0:07:44
Burford	1	51N49	1w38	0:06:32
Burgess Hill	1	50N57	0w07	0:00:28
Burgh Heath	1	51N18	0w13	0:00:52
Burham	1	51N20	0E29	-0:01:56
Burnage	1	53N26	2w12	0:08:48
Burnham	1	51N33	0w39	0:02:36
Burnham Market	1	52N57	0E44	-0:02:56
Burnham-on-Crouch	1	51N38	0E49	-0:03:16
Burnham-on-Sea	1	51N15	3w00	0:12:00
Burnley	1	53N48	2w14	0:08:56
Burpham	1	51N15	0w33	0:02:12
Burrowhill	1	51N21	0w36	0:02:24
Burscough	1	53N35	2w51	0:11:24
Burscough Bridge	1	53N36	2w51	0:11:24
Burslem	1	53N02	2w12	0:08:48
Burton	1	53N16	3w01	0:12:04
Burton Fleming	1	54N08	0w20	0:01:20
Burton Latimer	1	52N23	0w41	0:02:44
Burton-upon-Trent	1	52N49	1w36	0:06:24
Burtonwood	1	53N26	2w39	0:10:36
Burwell	1	52N16	0E19	-0:01:16
Bury	1	50N54	0w34	0:02:16
Bury	1	53N36	2w17	0:09:08
Bury Saint Edmunds	1	52N15	0E43	-0:02:52
Bushey	1	51N39	0w22	0:01:28
Bushey Heath	1	51N38	0w20	0:01:20
Buttermere	1	54N33	3w17	0:13:08
Butterwick	1	52N59	0E05	-0:00:20
Buxton	1	53N15	1w55	0:07:40
Byfield	1	52N11	1w14	0:04:56
Byfleet	1	51N20	0w29	0:01:56
Byley	1	53N13	2w25	0:09:40
Cadishead	1	53N25	2w26	0:09:44
Cadnam	1	50N55	1w35	0:06:20
Caister-on-Sea	2	52N39	1E44	-0:06:56
Caistor	1	53N30	0w20	0:01:20
Calder Bridge	1	54N27	3w29	0:13:56
Calderbrook	1	53N39	2w05	0:08:20
Caldy	1	53N21	3w10	0:12:40
Callington	2	50N30	4w18	0:17:12
Calne	2	51N27	2w00	0:08:00
Calshot	1	50N49	1w19	0:05:16
Calstock	2	50N30	4w12	0:16:48
Camberley	1	51N21	0w45	0:03:00
Camberwell	1	51N27	0w05	0:00:20
Cambo	1	55N10	1w57	0:07:48
Cambois	1	55N10	1w31	0:06:04
Camborne	2	50N12	5w19	0:21:16
Cambridge	2	52N13	0E08	-0:00:32
Cambridgeshire	2	52N20	0E05	-0:00:20
Camelford	2	50N37	4w41	0:18:44
Cannington	1	51N09	3w04	0:12:16
Cannock	2	52N42	2w09	0:08:36
Canterbury	1	51N17	1E05	-0:04:20
Cantorbéry → Canterbury	1	51N17	1E05	-0:04:20
Canvey	1	51N32	0E36	-0:02:24
Capenhurst	1	53N15	2w57	0:11:48
Capstone	1	51N21	0E34	-0:02:16
Carisbrooke	1	50N41	1w19	0:05:16
Carlisle	1	54N54	2w55	0:11:40
Carlton	1	52N58	1w05	0:04:20
Carnforth	1	54N08	2w46	0:11:04
Carrington	1	53N26	2w24	0:09:36
Carshalton	1	51N22	0w10	0:00:40
Castle Acre	1	52N42	0E41	-0:02:44
Castle Cary	1	51N06	2w31	0:10:04
Castle Donington	1	52N51	1w19	0:05:16
Castleford	1	53N44	1w21	0:05:24
Castleside	1	54N50	1w52	0:07:28
Castleton	1	53N35	2w11	0:08:44
Castleton	1	53N21	1w46	0:07:04
Castleton	1	54N28	0w56	0:03:44
Caterham	1	51N17	0w04	0:00:16
Catterick	1	54N22	1w38	0:06:32
Catterick Camp	1	54N22	1w43	0:06:52
Catton	1	54N55	2w15	0:09:00
Cawood	1	53N50	1w07	0:04:28
Cawston	1	52N46	1E10	-0:04:40
Cerne Abbas	5	50N49	2w29	0:09:56
Chacewater	2	50N15	5w10	0:20:40
Chadderton	1	53N33	2w08	0:08:32
Chadwell Saint Mary	1	51N29	0E22	-0:01:28
Chainhurst	1	51N12	0E29	-0:01:56
Chaldon	1	51N17	0w07	0:00:28
Chalfont Common	1	51N38	0w33	0:02:12
Chalfont Saint Giles	1	51N38	0w34	0:02:16
Chalfont Saint Peter	1	51N37	0w33	0:02:12
Chalford	1	51N45	2w09	0:08:36
Chalk	1	51N26	0E25	-0:01:40
Chandler's Cross	1	51N40	0w27	0:01:48
Chandler's Ford	1	50N59	1w23	0:05:32
Chapel-en-le-Frith	1	53N20	1w54	0:07:36
Chapeltown	1	53N38	2w24	0:09:36
Chard	2	50N53	2w58	0:11:52
Charing	1	51N13	0E48	-0:03:12
Charlbury	1	51N53	1w29	0:05:56
Charlesworth	1	53N26	1w59	0:07:56
Charlton Kings	1	51N53	2w03	0:08:12
Charminster	5	50N43	2w28	0:09:52
Charmouth	2	50N45	2w55	0:11:40
Charnock Richard	1	53N38	2w41	0:10:44

Chartridge	1	51N44	0W39	0:02:36
Chart Sutton	1	51N13	0E35	-0:02:20
Chasetown	1	52N41	1W56	0:07:44
Chatham	1	51N23	0E32	-0:02:08
Chattenden	1	51N25	0E32	-0:02:08
Chatteris	1	52N27	0E03	-0:00:12
Chatton	1	55N33	1W55	0:07:40
Cheadle	1	52N59	1W59	0:07:56
Cheadle	1	53N24	2W13	0:08:52
Cheadle Hulme	1	53N22	2W12	0:08:48
Cheddar	1	51N17	2W46	0:11:04
Chelford	1	53N16	2W16	0:09:04
Chellaston	1	52N53	1W27	0:05:48
Chelmorton	1	53N13	1W50	0:07:20
Chelmsford	2	51N44	0E28	-0:01:52
Chelsea	1	51N29	0W10	0:00:40
Cheltenham	1	51N54	2W04	0:08:16
Chenies	1	51N41	0W32	0:02:08
Chertsey	1	51N24	0W30	0:02:00
Chesham	1	51N43	0W38	0:02:32
Chesham Bois	1	51N41	0W37	0:02:28
Cheshire	1	53N15	2W30	0:10:00
Cheshunt	1	51N43	0W02	0:00:08
Chessington	1	51N21	0W18	0:01:12
Chester	1	53N12	2W54	0:11:36
Chesterfield	1	53N15	1W25	0:05:40
Chester-le-Street	1	54N52	1W34	0:06:16
Chevening	1	51N18	0E08	-0:00:32
Chevington Drift	1	55N17	1W36	0:06:24
Chew Magna	3	51N22	2W35	0:10:20
Chichester	1	50N50	0W48	0:03:12
Chickerell	5	50N37	2W30	0:10:00
Chiddingstone Causeway	1	51N12	0E10	-0:00:40
Chieveley	1	51N27	1W19	0:05:16
Chignall Saint James	2	51N46	0E25	-0:01:40
Chignall Smealy	2	51N47	0E25	-0:01:40
Chigwell	1	51N38	0E05	-0:00:20
Chigwell Row	1	51N37	0E07	-0:00:28
Childer Thornton	1	53N17	2W57	0:11:48
Chilham	1	51N15	0E57	-0:03:48
Chinley	1	53N20	1W56	0:07:44
Chinnor	1	51N43	0W56	0:03:44
Chippenham	1	51N28	2W07	0:08:28
Chipperfield	1	51N42	0W29	0:01:56
Chipping Campden	1	52N03	1W46	0:07:04
Chipping Norton	1	51N56	1W32	0:06:08
Chipping Ongar	1	51N43	0E15	-0:01:00
Chipping Sodbury	1	51N33	2W24	0:09:36
Chipstead	1	51N17	0E09	-0:00:36
Chiseldon	1	51N31	1W44	0:06:56
Chislehurst	1	51N25	0E04	-0:00:16
Chiswellgreen	1	51N44	0W22	0:01:28
Chobham	1	51N21	0W36	0:02:24
Cholsey	1	51N34	1W10	0:04:40
Chorley	1	53N39	2W39	0:10:36
Chorleywood	1	51N39	0W31	0:02:04
Christchurch	1	50N44	1W45	0:07:00
Chudleigh	2	50N36	3W38	0:14:32
Chulmleigh	1	50N55	3W52	0:15:28
Chunal	1	53N25	1W57	0:07:48
Church	1	53N45	2W24	0:09:36
Churchdown	1	51N53	2W10	0:08:40
Church Street	1	51N26	0E28	-0:01:52
Church Stretton	1	52N32	2W49	0:11:16
Churchtown	1	53N40	2W58	0:11:52
Cinderford	1	51N50	2W29	0:09:56
Cirencester	1	51N44	1W59	0:07:56
Clacton-on-Sea	1	51N48	1E09	-0:04:36
Clare	1	52N25	0E35	-0:02:20
Claremont	1	51N21	0W22	0:01:28
Claughton	1	54N06	2W40	0:10:40
Clay Cross	1	53N10	1W24	0:05:36
Claydon	2	52N06	1E07	-0:04:28
Claygate	1	51N22	0W20	0:01:20
Claygate Cross	1	51N16	0E19	-0:01:16
Clayton	1	53N47	1W52	0:07:28
Clayton-le-Moors	1	53N47	2W23	0:09:32
Clayton-le-Woods	1	53N41	2W38	0:10:32
Cleator Moor	1	54N31	3W30	0:14:00
Cleethorpes	1	53N34	0W02	0:00:08
Cleobury Mortimer	1	52N23	2W29	0:09:56
Clevedon	1	51N27	2W51	0:11:24
Cleveleys	1	53N53	3W03	0:12:12
Cley next the Sea	1	52N58	1E03	-0:04:12
Cliffe	1	51N28	0E30	-0:02:00
Cliffe Woods	1	51N26	0E30	-0:02:00
Clifton	1	53N46	2W49	0:11:16
Clitheroe	1	53N53	2W23	0:09:32
Clock Face	1	53N25	2W43	0:10:52
Clophill	1	52N05	0W30	0:02:00
Clough Foot	1	53N43	2W08	0:08:32
Clovelly	2	51N00	4W24	0:17:36
Clowne	1	53N18	1W16	0:05:04
Clun	1	52N26	3W00	0:12:00
Coalaston	1	53N18	1W28	0:05:52
Coalbrookdale	1	52N38	2W30	0:10:00
Coalpit Heath	1	51N32	2W28	0:09:52
Coalville	1	52S44	1W20	0:05:20
Cobham	1	51N23	0E24	-0:01:36
Cobham	1	51N20	0W25	0:01:40
Cock Clarks	1	51N42	0E37	-0:02:28
Cockerham	1	53N59	2W50	0:11:20
Cockermouth	1	54N40	3W21	0:13:24
Coddenham	2	52N09	1E07	-0:04:28
Codnor	1	53N03	1W23	0:05:32
Codsall	2	52N38	2W12	0:08:48
Coggeshall	1	51N52	0E41	-0:02:44
Colchester	2	51N54	0E54	-0:03:36
Cold Norton	1	51N40	0E40	-0:02:40
Coleby	1	53N14	0W33	0:02:12
Coleshill	1	51N39	0W38	0:02:32
Coleshill	1	52N30	1W42	0:06:48
Collingbourne Kingston	1	51N18	1W13	0:04:52
Colnbrook	1	51N29	0W31	0:02:04
Colne	1	53N52	2W09	0:08:36
Colney Heath	1	51N44	0W15	0:01:00
Colney Street	1	51N42	0W20	0:01:20
Colsterworth	1	52N48	0W37	0:02:28
Coltishall	2	52N44	1E22	-0:05:28
Colwell	1	55N04	2W04	0:08:16
Colyton	2	50N44	3W04	0:12:16
Combe Martin	2	51N13	4W02	0:16:08
Comberbach	1	53N17	2W32	0:10:08
Comberton	2	52N11	0E02	-0:00:08
Combs	1	53N18	1W57	0:07:48
Common Edge	1	53N47	3W02	0:12:08
Compstall	1	53N25	2W03	0:08:12
Compton	1	51N13	0W38	0:02:32
Congleton	1	53N10	2W13	0:08:52
Congresbury	1	51N23	2W48	0:11:12
Coningsby	1	53N07	0W10	0:00:40
Conisbrough	1	53N29	1W13	0:04:52
Coniston	1	54N22	3W05	0:12:20
Consett	1	54N51	1W49	0:07:16
Cookham	1	51N34	0W43	0:02:52
Cooksmill Green	2	51N44	0E22	-0:01:28
Cooling	1	51N27	0E32	-0:02:08
Coopersale Common	1	51N42	0E08	-0:00:32
Copplestone	2	50N49	3W45	0:15:00
Coppull	1	53N37	2W40	0:10:40
Copster Green	1	53N48	2W30	0:10:00
Corby	1	52N29	0W40	0:02:40
Corfe Castle	1	50N38	2W04	0:08:16
Cornforth	1	54N42	1W31	0:06:04
Cornholme	1	53N44	2W08	0:08:32
Cornwall	2	50N30	4W40	0:18:40
Corringham	1	51N31	0E28	-0:01:52
Corsham	2	51N26	2W11	0:08:44
Corton	2	52N32	1E44	-0:06:56
Coryton	1	51N31	0E31	-0:02:04
Cosby	1	52N33	1W11	0:04:44
Coseley	2	52N33	2W06	0:08:24
Costessey	2	52N40	1E11	-0:04:44
Cottam	1	53N47	2W46	0:11:04
Cottenham	2	52N18	0E09	-0:00:36
Cottingham (Haltemprice)	1	53N47	0W24	0:01:36
Coventry	1	52N25	1W30	0:06:00
Cowes	1	50N45	1W18	0:05:12
Cowley	2	51N43	1W12	0:04:48
Cowplain	2	50N54	1W01	0:04:04
Coxheath	1	51N14	0E30	-0:02:00
Cragg Vale	1	53N42	2W00	0:08:00
Cramlington	1	55N05	1W36	0:06:24
Cranage	1	53N12	2W22	0:09:28
Cranbrook	1	51N06	0E33	-0:02:12
Cranfield	1	52N05	0W35	0:02:20
Cranford	1	51N27	0E11	-0:00:44
Crank	1	53N29	2W45	0:11:00
Cranleigh	1	51N09	0W30	0:02:00
Craven Arms	1	52N26	2W50	0:11:20
Crawley	1	51N07	0W12	0:00:48
Crawshawbooth	1	53N43	2W17	0:09:08
Crayford	1	51N27	0E11	-0:00:44
Crays Hill	2	51N36	0E28	-0:01:52
Crediton	2	50N47	3W39	0:14:36
Creswell	1	53N16	1W12	0:04:48
Crewe	1	53N05	2W27	0:09:48
Crewkerne	1	50N53	2W48	0:11:12
Crick	1	52N21	1W07	0:04:28
Cricklade	1	51N39	1W51	0:07:24
Crockenhill	1	51N23	0E10	-0:00:40
Crockham Hill	1	51N14	0E04	-0:00:16
Croft	1	53N26	2W33	0:10:12
Croglin	1	54N49	2W39	0:10:36
Cromer	1	52N56	1E18	-0:05:12
Cronton	1	53N23	2W46	0:11:04
Crook	1	54N43	1W44	0:06:56
Crosby	1	53N30	3W02	0:12:08
Crossens	1	53N41	2W57	0:11:48
Croston	1	53N40	2W46	0:11:04
Crowborough	1	51N03	0E09	-0:00:36
Crowhurst	1	51N12	0W01	0:00:04
Crowland	1	52N41	0W11	0:00:44
Crowle	1	53N37	0W49	0:03:16
Crowthorne	1	51N23	0W49	0:03:16
Crowton	1	53N16	2W38	0:10:32
Croxley Green	1	51N39	0W27	0:01:48
Croyde	2	51N07	4W13	0:16:52
Croydon	1	51N23	0W06	0:00:24
Crudgington	1	52N46	2W33	0:10:12
Crystal Palace	1	51N25	0W04	0:00:16
Cuckfield	1	51N00	0W09	0:00:36
Cuckney	1	53N15	1W08	0:04:32
Cuddington	1	53N14	2W36	0:10:24
Cudham	1	51N19	0E05	-0:00:20
Cudworth	1	53N35	1W25	0:05:40
Cuffley	1	51N47	0W07	0:00:28
Culcheth	1	53N27	2W32	0:10:08
Cullompton	1	50N52	3W24	0:13:36
Culverstone Green	1	51N20	0E21	-0:01:24
Cumbria	1	54N30	3W00	0:12:00
Cumnor	2	51N44	1W20	0:05:20
Cumwhinton	1	54N52	2W51	0:11:24
Curry Rivel	1	51N02	2W52	0:11:28
Cuxton	1	51N22	0E27	-0:01:48
Dagenham	1	51N32	0E10	-0:00:40
Dalston	1	51N33	0W05	0:00:20
Dalton	1	53N34	2W46	0:11:04
Dalton-in-Furness	1	54N09	3W11	0:12:44
Damerham	1	50N57	1W52	0:07:28
Danbury	2	51N44	0E33	-0:02:12
Daresbury	1	53N21	2W38	0:10:32
Darlaston	2	52N34	2W02	0:08:08
Darlington	1	54N31	1W34	0:06:16
Dartford	1	51N27	0E14	-0:00:56
Dartmouth	2	50N21	3W35	0:14:20
Darton	1	53N36	1W32	0:06:08
Darwen	1	53N42	2W28	0:09:52
Datchet	1	51N29	0W34	0:02:16
Davenham	1	53N14	2W31	0:10:04
Daventry	1	52N16	1W09	0:04:36
Davyhulme	1	53N27	2W22	0:09:28
Dawley	1	52N40	2W28	0:09:52
Dawlish	2	50N35	3W28	0:13:52
Daws Heath	1	51N34	0E37	-0:02:28
Deal	1	51N14	1E24	-0:05:36
Deane	1	53N34	2W28	0:09:52
Dean Row	1	53N20	2W11	0:08:44
Debenham	1	52N13	1E11	-0:04:44
Deddington	1	51N59	1W19	0:05:16
Delabole	2	50N37	4W42	0:18:48
Delamere	1	53N13	2W39	0:10:36
Delph	1	53N34	2W01	0:08:04
Denby Dale	1	53N35	1W38	0:06:32
Denham	1	51N34	0W30	0:02:00
Denholme	1	53N48	1W54	0:07:36
Denshaw	1	53N35	2W02	0:08:08
Denton	1	53N27	2W07	0:08:28
Deptford	1	51N29	0W02	0:00:08
Derby	1	52N55	1W29	0:05:56
Derbyshire	1	53N00	1W33	0:06:12
Dersingham	1	52N51	0E30	-0:02:00
Desborough	1	52N27	0W49	0:03:16
Desford	1	52N39	1W17	0:05:08
Detling	1	51N18	0E34	-0:02:16
Devizes	2	51N22	1W59	0:07:56
Devon	1	50N45	3W50	0:15:20
Devonport	2	50N22	4W10	0:16:40
Dewsbury	1	53N42	1W37	0:06:28
Didcot	1	51N37	1W15	0:05:00
Diggle	1	53N34	1W59	0:07:56
Digmoor	1	53N32	2W45	0:11:00
Dinnington	1	53N22	1W12	0:04:48
Disley	1	53N21	2W02	0:08:08
Diss	1	52N23	1E07	-0:04:28
Distington	1	54N36	3W32	0:14:08
Ditton	1	53N22	2W45	0:11:00
Ditton	1	51N18	0E27	-0:01:48
Ditton Priors	1	52N30	2W35	0:10:20
Docking	1	52N55	0E38	-0:02:32
Doddinghurst	1	51N40	0E18	-0:01:12
Dolton	2	50N53	4W01	0:16:04
Doncaster	1	53N32	1W07	0:04:28
Donington	1	52N55	0W12	0:00:48
Donkey Town	1	51N20	0W39	0:02:36
Dorchester	1	51N39	1W10	0:04:40
Dorchester	5	50N43	2W26	0:09:44
Dordon	1	52N36	1W37	0:06:28
Dorking	1	51N14	0W20	0:01:20
Dorney	1	51N30	0W40	0:02:40
Dorridge	1	52N22	1W45	0:07:00
Dorset	5	50N47	2W20	0:09:20
Douvres → Dover	1	51N08	1E19	-0:05:16
Dove Holes	1	53N18	1W53	0:07:32
Dover	1	51N08	1E19	-0:05:16
Dovercourt	2	51N56	1E16	-0:05:04
Downham	2	52N26	0E15	-0:01:00
Downham	2	51N38	0E30	-0:02:00
Downham Market	1	52N36	0E23	-0:01:32
Downton	1	51N00	1W44	0:06:56
Driffield	1	54N00	0W27	0:01:48
Droitwich	1	52N16	2W09	0:08:36
Dronfield	1	53N19	1W27	0:05:48
Droylsden	1	53N29	2W10	0:08:40
Duddington	1	52N36	0W32	0:02:08
Dudley	2	52N30	2W05	0:08:20
Dukinfield	1	53N29	2W05	0:08:20
Dulverton	1	51N03	3W33	0:14:12
Dulwich	1	51N26	0W05	0:00:20
Dunchurch	1	52N20	1W16	0:05:04
Dunham-on-the-Hill	1	53N15	2W47	0:11:08
Dunham Town	1	53N23	2W24	0:09:36
Dunheved → Launceston	2	50N38	4W21	0:17:24
Dunk's Green	1	51N15	0E19	-0:01:16
Dunnockshaw	1	53N45	2W17	0:09:08
Dunsford	2	50N41	3W40	0:14:40
Dunstable	1	51N53	0W32	0:02:08
Dunster	1	51N12	3W27	0:13:48
Dunton Green	1	51N18	0E11	-0:00:44
Dunton Wayletts	1	51N35	0E24	-0:01:36
Durham	1	54N47	1W34	0:06:16
Durrington	1	51N13	1W45	0:07:00
Dursley	1	51N42	2W21	0:09:24
Duston	1	52N14	0W56	0:03:44
Dutton	1	53N19	2W38	0:10:32
Dymchurch	1	51N02	1E00	-0:04:00
Dymock	1	51N59	2W26	0:09:44
Ealing	1	51N31	0W20	0:01:20
Earby	1	53N56	2W08	0:08:32
Earcroft	1	53N43	2W29	0:09:56
Eardisley	1	52N08	2W59	0:11:56
Earlestown	1	53N27	2W39	0:10:36
Earls Colne	1	51N56	0E42	-0:02:48
Earl Shilton	1	52N35	1W20	0:05:20
Earl Soham	1	52N14	1E16	-0:05:04
Earsdon	1	55N03	1W29	0:05:56
Easington	1	54N47	1W19	0:05:16
Easingwold	1	54N07	1W11	0:04:44
East Barming	1	51N16	0E28	-0:01:52
Eastbourne	1	50N46	0E17	-0:01:08
Eastbury	1	51N37	0W25	0:01:40
Eastchurch	1	51N25	0E52	-0:03:28
East Clandon	1	51N15	0W29	0:01:56

East Dereham 1 52N41 0E56 -0:03:44
East Farleigh 1 51N15 0E29 -0:01:56
East Grinstead 1 51N08 0W01 0:00:04
Eastham 1 53N19 2W58 0:11:52
East Hanningfield
2 51N41 0E34 -0:02:16
East Harling 1 52N26 0E55 -0:03:40
East Hoathly 1 50N55 0E10 -0:00:40
East Horsley 1 51N15 0W26 0:01:44
East Hoyle 1 54N41 1W33 0:06:12
East Ilsley 1 51N32 1W17 0:05:08
Eastleigh 1 50N58 1W22 0:05:28
East Loof 2 50N22 4W27 0:17:48
East Malling 1 51N17 0E26 -0:01:44
East Markham 1 53N15 0W54 0:03:36
East Molesey 1 51N24 0W21 0:01:24
Easton 1 50N32 2W26 0:09:44
East Peckham 1 51N15 0E23 -0:01:32
East Retford 1 53N19 0W56 0:03:44
Eastry 1 51N15 1E18 -0:05:12
East Tilbury 1 51N28 0E26 -0:01:44
East Wittering 1 50N41 0W53 0:03:32
Eastwood 1 51N34 0E40 -0:02:40
Eastwood 1 53N43 2W03 0:08:12
Eastwood 1 53N01 1W18 0:05:12
Eaton Socon 1 52N13 0W18 0:01:12
Eccles 1 53N29 2W21 0:09:24
Eccles 1 51N19 0E29 -0:01:56
Ecclesfield 1 53N27 1W27 0:05:48
Eccleshall 1 52N52 2W15 0:09:00
Eccleston 1 53N27 2W47 0:11:08
Eccleston 1 53N39 2W44 0:10:56
Eckington 1 53N19 1W21 0:05:24
Edenbridge 1 51N12 0E04 -0:00:16
Edenfield 1 53N40 2W18 0:09:12
Edgworth 1 53N39 2W24 0:09:36
Edmondbyers 1 54N51 1W58 0:07:52
Edmonton 1 51N37 0W04 0:00:16
Edwinstowe 1 53N12 1W04 0:04:16
Effingham 1 51N16 0W24 0:01:36
Egerton 1 53N38 2W26 0:09:44
Egham 1 51N26 0W34 0:02:16
Egloskerry 2 50N39 4W27 0:17:48
Egremont 1 54N29 3W33 0:14:12
Egton 1 54N26 0W45 0:03:00
Elham 1 51N10 1E07 -0:04:28
Elland 1 53N41 1W50 0:07:20
Ellesmere 1 52N54 2W54 0:11:36
Ellesmere Park 1 53N29 2W20 0:09:20
Ellesmere Port 1 53N17 2W54 0:11:36
Ellington 1 55N13 1W34 0:06:16
Elm 1 52N38 0E10 -0:00:40
Elmswell 1 52N15 0E53 -0:03:32
Elstead 1 51N11 0W43 0:02:52
Elstree 1 51N39 0W16 0:01:04
Elton 1 53N16 2W49 0:11:16
Ely 2 52N24 0E16 -0:01:04
Embleton 1 55N30 1W37 0:06:28
Emneth 1 52N38 0E11 -0:00:44
Emsworth 1 50N51 0W56 0:03:44
Enderby 1 52N36 1W12 0:04:48
Enfield 1 51N40 0W05 0:00:20
Englefield Green 1 51N26 0W35 0:02:20
Ensworth 1 50N51 0W56 0:03:44
Enton 4 50N38 3W28 0:13:52
Epping 1 51N43 0E07 -0:00:28
Epping Green 1 51N45 0W07 0:00:28
Epping Green 1 51N44 0E05 -0:00:20
Epping Upland 1 51N43 0E06 -0:00:24
Epsom 1 51N20 0W16 0:01:04
Epworth 1 53N32 0W49 0:03:16
Escrick 1 53N53 1W02 0:04:08
Esher 1 51N23 0W22 0:01:28
Essendon 1 51N46 0W09 0:00:36
Essex 1 51N48 0E40 -0:02:40
Eston 1 54N34 1W07 0:04:28
Eton 1 51N31 0W37 0:02:28
Ettington 1 52N09 1W36 0:06:24
Euxton 1 53N40 2W41 0:10:44
Evercreech 1 51N09 2W30 0:10:00
Evesham 1 52N06 1W56 0:07:44
Ewell 1 51N21 0W15 0:01:00
Exeter 4 50N43 3W31 0:14:04
Exford 1 51N08 3W38 0:14:32
Exminster 4 50N41 3W29 0:13:56
Exmouth 2 50N37 3W25 0:13:40
Eyam 1 53N17 1W41 0:06:44
Eye 1 52N19 1E09 -0:04:36
Eye 1 52N35 0W10 0:00:40
Eyhorne Street 1 51N16 0E38 -0:02:32
Eynsford 1 51N22 0E13 -0:00:52
Eynsham 2 51N48 1W22 0:05:28
Eythorne 1 51N11 1E17 -0:05:08
Failsworth 1 53N31 2W09 0:08:36
Fairford 1 51N44 1W47 0:07:08
Fairlight 1 50N53 0E40 -0:02:40
Fairseat 1 51N20 0E20 -0:01:20
Fakenham 1 52N50 0E51 -0:03:24
Falmouth 2 50N08 5W04 0:20:16
Falstone 1 55N11 2W25 0:09:40
Fareham 2 50N51 1W10 0:04:40
Faringdon 1 51N40 1W35 0:06:20
Farington 1 53N43 2W42 0:10:48
Farleigh 1 51N19 0W02 0:00:08
Farley Green 1 51N12 0W29 0:01:56
Farnborough 1 51N17 0W46 0:03:04
Farncombe 1 51N12 0W36 0:02:24
Farnham 1 51N13 0W49 0:03:16
Farnham Common 1 51N33 0W37 0:02:28
Farnham Royal 1 51N32 0W37 0:02:28
Farningham 1 51N23 0E13 -0:00:52
Farnworth 1 53N33 2W24 0:09:36
Faversham 1 51N20 0E53 -0:03:32
Fawkham Green 1 51N22 0E17 -0:01:08
Fawley 1 50N49 1W20 0:05:20

Fearnhead 1 53N25 2W33 0:10:12
Featherstone 1 53N41 1W21 0:05:24
Felixstowe 2 51N58 1E20 -0:05:20
Felling 1 54N57 1W33 0:06:12
Felpham 1 50N47 0W39 0:02:36
Fen Ditton 2 52N13 0E10 -0:00:40
Feniscowles 1 53N43 2W32 0:10:08
Fenny Compton 1 52N09 1W20 0:05:20
Fenny Stratford 1 52N00 0W43 0:02:52
Ferndown 1 50N48 1W55 0:07:40
Fernilee 1 53N18 1W58 0:07:52
Ferryhill 1 54N41 1W33 0:06:12
Fetcham 1 51N17 0W22 0:01:28
Fiddlers Hamlet 1 51N41 0E08 -0:00:32
Filey 1 54N12 0W17 0:01:08
Filton 3 51N31 2W35 0:10:20
Fincham 1 52N37 0E30 -0:02:00
Finchley 1 51N36 0W10 0:00:40
Finedon 1 52N20 0W39 0:02:36
Finsbury 1 51N31 0W05 0:00:20
Firgrove 1 53N37 2W08 0:08:32
Fishbourne 1 50N44 1W12 0:04:48
Fishpool 1 53N35 2W17 0:09:08
Fittleworth 1 50N58 0W35 0:02:20
Flaunden 1 51N42 0W32 0:02:08
Fleet 1 51N16 0W50 0:03:20
Fleetwood 1 53N56 3W01 0:12:04
Flimby 1 54N41 3W31 0:14:04
Flitwick 1 52N00 0W29 0:01:56
Flodden 1 55N38 2W10 0:08:40
Fobbing 1 51N32 0E29 -0:01:56
Folkestone 1 51N05 1E11 -0:04:44
Folkingham 1 52N54 0W24 0:01:36
Fordingbridge 1 50N56 1W47 0:07:08
Forest Row 1 51N06 0E02 -0:00:08
Formby 1 53N34 3W05 0:12:20
Foster Street 1 51N46 0E09 -0:00:36
Fothergill 1 54N42 3W30 0:14:00
Foulsham 1 52N48 1E01 -0:04:04
Four Elms 1 51N13 0E06 -0:00:24
Fowey 2 50N20 4W38 0:18:32
Foxholes 1 54N08 0W28 0:01:52
Foxwist Green 1 53N12 2W34 0:10:16
Framlingham 1 52N13 1E21 -0:05:24
Frampton on Severn
1 51N46 2W22 0:09:28
Frankby 1 53N22 3W08 0:12:32
Freckleton 1 53N45 2W52 0:11:28
Fremington 2 51N04 4W07 0:16:28
Freshfield 1 53N34 3W04 0:12:16
Freshwater 1 50N40 1W30 0:06:00
Fridaythorpe 1 54N01 0W40 0:02:40
Friern Barnet 1 51N37 0W10 0:00:40
Frindsbury 1 51N24 0E30 -0:02:00
Frinsted 1 51N17 0E43 -0:02:52
Frinton-on-Sea 2 51N50 1E14 -0:04:56
Frizington 1 54N32 3W30 0:14:00
Frodsham 1 53N18 2W44 0:10:56
Frome 1 51N14 2W20 0:09:20
Fryerning 2 51N41 0E22 -0:01:28
Fulham 1 51N28 0W13 0:00:52
Fulmer 1 51N33 0W34 0:02:16
Fulwood 1 53N47 2W41 0:10:44
Fyfield 1 51N45 0E16 -0:01:04
Gainford 1 54N32 1W44 0:06:56
Gainsborough 1 53N24 0W46 0:03:04
Galgate 1 54N00 2W47 0:11:08
Galleyend 2 51N42 0E29 -0:01:56
Galleywood 2 51N42 0E28 -0:01:52
Garboldisham 1 52N24 0E56 -0:03:44
Garforth 1 53N48 1W22 0:05:28
Gargrave 1 53N59 2W06 0:08:24
Garsdale Head 1 54N19 2W20 0:09:20
Garstang 1 53N55 2W47 0:11:08
Garston 1 51N41 0W23 0:01:32
Garswood 1 53N29 2W40 0:10:40
Gateshead 1 54N58 1W37 0:06:28
Gathurst 1 53N34 2W42 0:10:48
Gatley 1 53N23 2W14 0:08:56
Gawsworth 1 53N13 2W10 0:08:40
Gayton 1 53N19 3W06 0:12:24
Gayton 1 52N45 0E34 -0:02:16
Gaywood 1 52N46 0E26 -0:01:44
Gee Cross 1 53N26 2W04 0:08:16
Gerrards Cross 1 51N35 0W34 0:02:16
Gidea Park 1 51N35 0E12 -0:00:48
Giggleswick 1 54N04 2W17 0:09:08
Gillingham 1 51N02 2W17 0:09:08
Gillingham 1 51N24 0E33 -0:02:12
Glastonbury 1 51N06 2W43 0:10:52
Glazebury 1 53N28 2W30 0:10:00
Glemsford 1 52N06 0E41 -0:02:44
Glenfield 1 52N39 1W12 0:04:48
Glossop 1 53N27 1W57 0:07:48
Gloucester 1 51N53 2W14 0:08:56
Glyndebourne 1 50N52 0E04 -0:00:16
Goathland 1 54N23 0W44 0:02:56
Godalming 1 51N11 0W37 0:02:28
Godmanchester 1 52N19 0W11 0:00:44
Godshill 1 50N38 1W14 0:04:56
Godstone 1 51N15 0W04 0:00:16
Goff's Oak 1 51N43 0W05 0:00:20
Golborne 1 53N29 2W36 0:10:24
Golcar 1 53N39 1W51 0:07:24
Golden Green 1 51N12 0E21 -0:01:24
Gomshall 1 51N13 0W27 0:01:48
Good Easter 2 51N47 0E21 -0:01:24
Goole 1 53N42 0W52 0:03:28
Goostrey 1 53N13 2W20 0:09:20
Goring 1 51N32 1W09 0:04:36
Goring-by-Sea 1 50N49 0W25 0:01:40
Gorleston on Sea 2 52N36 1E43 -0:06:52
Gosforth 1 55N01 1W37 0:06:28
Gosforth 1 54N26 3W27 0:13:48
Gosport 2 50N48 1W08 0:04:32

Goudhurst 1 51N07 0E28 -0:01:52
Grafty Green 1 51N12 0E41 -0:02:44
Grain 1 51N28 0E43 -0:02:52
Grange 1 53N23 3W09 0:12:36
Grange Hill 1 51N37 0E05 -0:00:20
Grange-over-Sands
1 54N12 2W55 0:11:40
Grantham 1 52N55 0W39 0:02:36
Grappenhall 1 53N22 2W32 0:10:08
Grasmere 1 54N28 3W02 0:12:08
Grasscroft 1 53N32 2W02 0:08:08
Grassington 1 54N04 4W59 0:19:56
Gravesend 1 51N27 0E24 -0:01:36
Grays 1 51N29 0E20 -0:01:20
Grayshott 1 51N11 0W45 0:03:00
Grays Thurrock 1 51N29 0E20 -0:01:20
Greasby 1 53N23 3W07 0:12:28
Great Altcar 1 53N33 3W01 0:12:04
Great Amwell 1 51N48 0W01 0:00:04
Great Baddow 2 51N43 0E29 -0:01:56
Great Barrow 1 53N12 2W48 0:11:12
Great Bookham 1 51N16 0W22 0:01:28
Great Braxted 1 51N48 0E42 -0:02:48
Great Budworth 1 53N18 2W30 0:10:00
Great Burstead 1 51N36 0E25 -0:01:40
Great Clifton 1 54N31 3W29 0:13:56
Great Crosby 1 53N29 3W01 0:12:04
Great Dunmow 1 51N53 0E22 -0:01:28
Great Gaddesden 1 51N47 0W30 0:02:00
Great Grimsby → Grimsby
1 53N35 0W05 0:00:20
Great Harwood 1 53N48 2W24 0:09:36
Great Malvern (Malvern)
1 52N07 2W19 0:09:16
Great Marton 1 53N48 3W02 0:12:08
Great Massingham 1 52N46 0E40 -0:02:40
Great Missenden 1 51N43 0W43 0:02:52
Great Oxney Green
2 51N44 0E25 -0:01:40
Great Parndon 1 51N45 0E05 -0:00:20
Great Sankey 1 53N23 2W39 0:10:36
Great Shelford 2 52N09 0E09 -0:00:36
Great Sutton 1 53N17 2W56 0:11:44
Great Torrington 2 50N57 4W08 0:16:32
Great Totham 1 51N47 0E43 -0:02:52
Great Waltham 2 51N48 0E28 -0:01:52
Great Warley 1 51N35 0E17 -0:01:08
Great Yarmouth 2 52N37 1E44 -0:06:56
Greenfield 1 53N32 2W01 0:08:04
Greenhithe 1 51N27 0E17 -0:01:08
Greenmount 1 53N37 2W20 0:09:20
Greenodd 1 54N14 3W04 0:12:16
Greenstead 1 51N42 0E14 -0:00:56
Green Street 1 51N40 0W16 0:01:04
Greenwich 1 51N29 0W00 0:00:00
Greetland 1 53N41 1W52 0:07:28
Grenoside 1 53N27 1W30 0:06:00
Greystoke 1 54N40 2W52 0:11:28
Grimeford Village
1 53N36 2W34 0:10:16
Grimsargh 1 53N48 2W38 0:10:32
Grimsby 1 53N35 0W05 0:00:20
Guildford 1 51N14 0W35 0:02:20
Guisborough 1 54N32 1W04 0:04:16
Guiseley 1 53N53 1W42 0:06:48
Gunnislake 2 50N31 4W12 0:16:48
Hacketts 1 51N45 0W05 0:00:20
Hackney 1 51N33 0W03 0:00:12
Haddenham 1 51N46 0W56 0:03:44
Haddenham 2 52N22 0E09 -0:00:36
Hadfield 1 53N28 1W58 0:07:52
Hadleigh 1 51N33 0E37 -0:02:28
Hadlow 1 51N14 0E20 -0:01:20
Hagley 1 52N26 2W08 0:08:32
Haigh 1 53N35 2W36 0:10:24
Hailey 1 51N46 0W01 0:00:04
Hailsham 1 50N52 0E16 -0:01:04
Halberton 1 50N55 3W25 0:13:40
Hale 1 53N23 2W21 0:09:24
Hale 1 53N20 2W48 0:11:12
Halebarns 1 53N22 2W19 0:09:16
Halesowen 1 52N26 2W05 0:08:20
Hale Street 1 51N13 0E24 -0:01:36
Halesworth 1 52N21 1E30 -0:06:00
Halewood 1 53N22 2W49 0:11:16
Halifax 1 53N44 1W52 0:07:28
Halling 1 51N21 0E27 -0:01:48
Halsall 1 53N35 2W57 0:11:48
Halstead 1 51N57 0E38 -0:02:32
Halstead 1 51N20 0E08 -0:00:32
Halton 1 53N20 2W42 0:10:48
Haltwhistle 1 54N58 2W27 0:09:48
Halwell 2 50N22 3W43 0:14:52
Hamble 1 50N52 1W19 0:05:16
Hambledon 1 50N56 1W04 0:04:16
Hammersmith 1 51N30 0W13 0:00:52
Hampshire 1 51N05 1W15 0:05:00
Hampstead 1 51N34 0W11 0:00:44
Handforth 1 53N21 2W13 0:08:52
Hants 1 51N05 1W15 0:05:00
Hapsford 1 53N16 2W48 0:11:12
Hapton 1 53N47 2W19 0:09:16
Harefield 1 51N36 0W29 0:01:56
Harlesdon 1 51N32 0W15 0:01:00
Harleston 1 52N24 1E18 -0:05:12
Harlow 1 51N47 0E08 -0:00:32
Harpenden 1 51N49 0W22 0:01:28
Harper Town 1 54N55 2W31 0:10:04
Harpur Hill 1 53N14 1W54 0:07:36
Harrietsham 1 51N15 0E41 -0:02:44
Harrington 1 54N37 3W34 0:14:16
Harrogate 1 54N00 1W33 0:06:12
Harrow 1 51N35 0W21 0:01:24
Hartford 1 53N15 2W33 0:10:12
Hartland 2 50N59 4W29 0:17:56

Hartlepool	1	54N42	1w11	0:04:44
Hartley	1	51N23	0E19	-0:01:16
Hartlip	1	51N21	0E39	-0:02:36
Hartshill	1	52N37	1w32	0:06:08
Harvel	1	51N21	0E22	-0:01:28
Harwell	1	51N37	1w18	0:05:12
Harwich	2	51N57	1E17	-0:05:08
Harwood	1	53N35	2w23	0:09:32
Haskayne	1	53N34	2w58	0:11:52
Hasketh Bank	1	53N43	2w51	0:11:24
Haslemere	1	51N06	0w43	0:02:52
Haslingden	1	53N43	2w18	0:09:12
Haslingden Grane	1	53N42	2w21	0:09:24
Haslington	1	53N06	2w24	0:09:36
Hastings	1	50N51	0E36	-0:02:24
Hastingwood	1	51N45	0E09	-0:00:36
Hatchmere	1	53N15	2w40	0:10:40
Hatfield	1	51N46	0w13	0:00:52
Hatfield Peverel	2	51N47	0E35	-0:02:20
Hatherleigh	2	50N49	4w04	0:16:16
Hathersage	1	53N19	1w38	0:06:32
Hatton	1	53N20	2w36	0:10:24
Haughton Green	1	53N27	2w06	0:08:24
Havant	2	50N51	0w59	0:03:56
Haverhill	1	52N05	0E26	-0:01:44
Haverigg	1	54N11	3w17	0:13:08
Havering's Grove	2	51N38	0E23	-0:01:32
Hawes	1	54N18	2w12	0:08:48
Hawkhurst	1	51N02	0E30	-0:02:00
Hawkwell	1	51N36	0E40	-0:02:40
Hawley	1	51N25	0E14	-0:00:56
Haydock	1	53N28	2w39	0:10:36
Haydon Bridge	1	54N58	2w14	0:08:56
Hayes	1	51N31	0w25	0:01:40
Hayfield	1	53N23	1w57	0:07:48
Haywards Heath	1	51N00	0w06	0:00:24
Hazel Grove	1	53N23	2w08	0:08:32
Heacham	1	52N55	0E30	-0:02:00
Headcorn	1	51N11	0E37	-0:02:28
Headington	2	51N45	1w13	0:04:52
Headley	1	51N07	0w50	0:03:20
Headley	1	51N17	0w16	0:01:04
Heald Green	1	53N22	2w14	0:08:56
Heanor	1	53N01	1w22	0:05:28
Heath End	1	51N22	1w09	0:04:36
Heathfield	1	50N59	0E17	-0:01:08
Heatley	1	53N24	2w27	0:09:48
Heaton Moor	1	53N25	2w11	0:08:44
Heaverham	1	51N18	0E15	-0:01:00
Heavitley	1	53N24	2w09	0:08:36
Hebburn	1	54N59	1w30	0:06:00
Hebden Bridge	1	53N45	2w00	0:08:00
Heckington	1	52N59	0w18	0:01:12
Hedgerley	1	51N35	0w36	0:02:24
Hednesford	1	52N43	2w00	0:08:00
Hedon	1	53N44	0w12	0:00:48
Hellifield	1	54N01	2w12	0:08:48
Helmshore	1	53N41	2w20	0:09:20
Helmsley	1	54N14	1w04	0:04:16
Helsby	1	53N16	2w46	0:11:04
Helston	2	50N05	5w16	0:21:04
Hemel Hempstead	1	51N46	0w28	0:01:52
Hempnall	1	52N30	1E19	-0:05:16
Hemsworth	1	53N38	1w21	0:05:24
Henbury	1	53N15	2w11	0:08:44
Hendon	1	51N35	0w14	0:00:56
Henfield	1	50N56	0w17	0:01:08
Henley-in-Arden	1	52N17	1w46	0:07:04
Henley-on-Thames	1	51N32	0w56	0:03:44
Henlow	1	52N02	0w18	0:01:12
Henstridge	1	50N59	2w24	0:09:36
Heptonstall	1	53N45	2w01	0:08:04
Hereford	1	52N04	2w43	0:10:52
Herne Bay	1	51N23	1E08	-0:04:32
Herongate	1	51N36	0E21	-0:01:24
Heronsgate	1	51N38	0w31	0:02:04
Hersham	1	51N22	0w23	0:01:32
Herstmon	1	50N53	0E20	-0:01:20
Herstmonceux	1	50N53	0E20	-0:01:20
Hertford	1	51N48	0w05	0:00:20
Hertfordshire	1	51N50	0w10	0:00:40
Hertingfordbury	1	51N48	0w06	0:00:24
Hesketh Bank	1	53N42	2w51	0:11:24
Heskin Green	1	53N38	2w42	0:10:48
Hessle	1	53N44	0w26	0:01:44
Heswall	1	53N20	3w06	0:12:24
Hetton-le-Hole	1	54N50	1w27	0:05:48
Hexham	1	54N58	2w06	0:08:24
Hextable	1	51N25	0E11	-0:00:44
Heybridge	1	51N44	0E41	-0:02:44
Heysham	1	54N02	2w54	0:11:36
Heywood	1	53N36	2w13	0:08:52
Hibaldstow	1	53N31	0w32	0:02:08
Higham Ferrers	1	52N18	0w36	0:02:24
Higham Upshire	1	51N26	0E28	-0:01:52
High Beach	1	51N39	0E02	-0:00:08
High Bentham	1	54N08	2w30	0:10:00
Highbridge	1	51N13	2w49	0:11:16
Higher Ballam	1	53N46	2w59	0:11:56
Higher Penwortham	1	53N45	2w44	0:10:56
Higher Walton	1	53N45	2w38	0:10:32
Higher Walton	1	53N22	2w37	0:10:28
Higher Whitley	1	53N19	2w35	0:10:20
High Halstow	1	51N27	0E34	-0:02:16
High Hesket	1	54N48	2w48	0:11:12
High Laver	1	51N45	0E13	-0:00:52
High Legh	1	53N21	2w27	0:09:48
High Ongar	1	51N43	0E16	-0:01:04
Hightown	1	53N32	3w04	0:12:16
Highworth	1	51N38	1w43	0:06:52
High Wycombe	1	51N38	0w46	0:03:04
Hildenborough	1	51N13	0E15	-0:01:00
Hinckley	1	52N33	1w21	0:05:24
Hindhead	1	51N07	0w44	0:02:56
Hindley	1	53N32	2w35	0:10:20
Hindley Green	1	53N31	2w32	0:10:08
Hindon	1	51N06	2w08	0:08:32
Histon	2	52N15	0E06	-0:00:24
Hitchin	1	51N57	0w17	0:01:08
Hockley	1	51N37	0E40	-0:02:40
Hoddesdon	1	51N46	0w01	0:00:04
Hoddlesden	1	53N42	2w26	0:09:44
Hodnet	1	52N51	2w35	0:10:20
Hoghton	1	53N44	2w35	0:10:20
Holbeach	1	52N49	0E01	-0:00:04
Holborn	1	51N31	0w07	0:00:28
Holland-on-Sea	1	51N48	1E13	-0:04:52
Hollingbourne	1	51N16	0E38	-0:02:32
Hollingworth	1	53N28	1w59	0:07:56
Hollins	1	53N34	2w17	0:09:08
Hollins Green	1	53N25	2w27	0:09:48
Holme	1	53N33	1w50	0:07:20
Holme Chapel	1	53N45	2w11	0:08:44
Holmeswood	1	53N39	2w52	0:11:28
Holmfirth	1	53N35	1w46	0:07:04
Holsworthy	2	50N49	4w21	0:17:24
Holywell Green	1	53N41	1w52	0:07:28
Honiton	1	50N48	3w13	0:12:52
Hoo	1	51N25	0E34	-0:02:16
Hook	2	51N17	0w58	0:03:52
Hooton	1	53N18	2w57	0:11:48
Horden	1	54N46	1w18	0:05:12
Horley	1	51N11	0w11	0:00:44
Horncastle	1	53N13	0w07	0:00:28
Horndean	1	50N55	1w00	0:04:00
Horndon on the Hill	1	51N31	0E25	-0:01:40
Horn Hill	1	51N37	0w32	0:02:08
Hornsea	1	53N55	0w10	0:00:40
Hornsey	1	51N33	0w06	0:00:24
Horrabridge	2	50N31	4w05	0:16:20
Horsell	1	51N19	0w34	0:02:16
Horsforth	1	53N51	1w39	0:06:36
Horsham	1	51N04	0w21	0:01:24
Horsham Saint Faith	2	52N41	1E16	-0:05:04
Horsley	1	51N16	0w26	0:01:44
Horsted Keynes	1	51N02	0w01	0:00:04
Horton	1	51N28	0w32	0:02:08
Horton in Ribblesdale	1	54N09	2w17	0:09:08
Horton Kirby	1	51N23	0E15	-0:01:00
Horwich	1	53N37	2w33	0:10:12
Hough Green	1	53N23	2w47	0:11:08
Houghton Green	1	53N25	2w34	0:10:16
Houghton-le-Spring	1	54N51	1w28	0:05:52
Houghton Regis	1	51N55	0w31	0:02:04
Hounslow	1	51N29	0w22	0:01:28
Houses of Parliament	1	51N30	0w07	0:00:28
Hove	1	50N49	0w10	0:00:40
Howden	1	53N45	0w52	0:03:28
Howe Green	2	51N42	0E32	-0:02:08
Hoylake	1	53N23	3w11	0:12:44
Hucclecote	1	51N51	2w11	0:08:44
Hucking	1	51N18	0E39	-0:02:36
Hucknall	1	53N02	1w11	0:04:44
Huddersfield	1	53N39	1w47	0:07:08
Hugh Town	2	49N55	6w17	0:25:08
Hull → Kingston upon Hull	1	53N45	0w20	0:01:20
Hullavington	1	51N33	2w09	0:08:36
Hullbridge	1	51N37	0E38	-0:02:32
Humberside	1	53N55	0w40	0:02:40
Huncoat	1	53N46	2w20	0:09:20
Hundred End	1	53N42	2w53	0:11:32
Hungerford	1	51N26	1w30	0:06:00
Hunstanton	1	52N57	0E30	-0:02:00
Huntingdon	1	52N20	0w12	0:00:48
Huntington	1	54N01	1w04	0:04:16
Hunton	1	51N13	0E28	-0:01:52
Hurdsfield	1	53N16	2w06	0:08:24
Hursley	1	51N02	1w24	0:05:36
Hurstbourne Tarrant	1	51N17	1w23	0:05:32
Hurstpierpoint	1	50N56	0w11	0:00:44
Huthwaite	1	53N09	1w17	0:05:08
Hutton	1	53N44	2w46	0:11:04
Hutton	1	51N38	0E22	-0:01:28
Huyton-with-Roby	1	53N25	2w52	0:11:28
Hyde	1	53N27	2w04	0:08:16
Hythe	1	51N05	1E05	-0:04:20
Hythe End	1	51N27	0w32	0:02:08
Ibstock	1	52N42	1w23	0:05:32
Idle Hill	1	51N15	0E08	-0:00:32
Ightham	1	51N17	0E17	-0:01:08
Ilchester	1	51N01	2w41	0:10:44
Ilford	1	51N33	0E05	-0:00:20
Ilfracombe	2	51N13	4w08	0:16:32
Ilkeston	1	52N59	1w18	0:05:12
Ilkley	1	53N55	1w50	0:07:20
Illingworth	1	53N45	1w54	0:07:36
Illminster	1	50N56	2w55	0:11:40
Immingham Dock	1	53N37	0w12	0:00:48
Ince	1	53N17	2w49	0:11:16
Ince Blundell	1	53N31	3w02	0:12:08
Ince-in-Makerfield	1	53N32	2w37	0:10:28
Ingatestone	2	51N41	0E22	-0:01:28
Ingleton	1	54N10	2w27	0:09:48
Ingrave	1	51N36	0E21	-0:01:24
Ipswich	2	52N04	1E10	-0:04:40
Irby	1	53N21	3w07	0:12:28
Irlam	1	53N28	2w25	0:09:40
Iron Bridge	1	52N38	2w29	0:09:56
Irthlingborough	1	52N20	0w37	0:02:28
Isleworth	1	51N28	0w20	0:01:20
Islington	1	51N33	0w06	0:00:24
Islip	2	51N50	1w14	0:04:56
Istead Rise	1	51N24	0E22	-0:01:28
Iver	1	51N31	0w30	0:02:00
Iver Heath	1	51N32	0w31	0:02:04
Ivybridge	1	50N23	3w56	0:15:44
Ivy Hatch	1	51N16	0E16	-0:01:04
Ixworth	1	52N18	0E50	-0:03:20
Jarrow	1	54N59	1w29	0:05:56
Jaywick	1	51N47	1E08	-0:04:32
Jordans	1	51N37	0w36	0:02:24
Kearsley	1	53N32	2w23	0:09:32
Keele	1	53N00	2w17	0:09:08
Kegworth	1	52N50	1w16	0:05:04
Keighley	1	53N52	1w54	0:07:36
Kelsall	1	53N13	2w43	0:10:52
Kelvedon	1	51N51	0E42	-0:02:48
Kelvedon Hatch	1	51N40	0E16	-0:01:04
Kempston	1	52N07	0w30	0:02:00
Kemsing	1	51N18	0E14	-0:00:56
Kendal	1	54N20	2w45	0:11:00
Kenilworth	1	52N21	1w34	0:06:16
Kennington	1	51N10	0E54	-0:03:36
Kensington	1	51N30	0w12	0:00:48
Kensington Palace	1	51N30	0w08	0:00:32
Kent	1	51N15	0E40	-0:02:40
Kenton	4	50N38	3w28	0:13:52
Kenyon	1	53N27	2w34	0:10:16
Kerridge	1	53N17	2w06	0:08:24
Kessingland	1	52N25	1E42	-0:06:48
Keswick	1	54N37	3w08	0:12:32
Kettering	1	52N24	0w44	0:02:56
Kettleshulme	1	53N19	2w01	0:08:04
Kettlewell	1	54N09	2w02	0:08:08
Keymer	1	50N55	0w08	0:00:32
Keynsham	3	51N26	2w30	0:10:00
Kibworth Beauchamp	1	52N32	1w00	0:04:00
Kidderminster	1	52N23	2w14	0:08:56
Kidlington	2	51N50	1w17	0:05:08
Kidsgrove	1	53N06	2w15	0:09:00
Kielder	1	55N14	2w35	0:10:20
Kilham	1	54N04	0w23	0:01:32
Kilkhampton	2	50N53	4w29	0:17:56
Kimbolton	1	52N18	0w24	0:01:36
Kineton	1	52N10	1w30	0:06:00
Kingsbridge	1	50N17	3w46	0:15:04
Kingsbury	1	52N35	1w40	0:06:40
Kingsclere	1	51N20	1w14	0:04:56
Kingsdown	1	51N11	1E25	-0:05:40
Kingskerswell	1	50N30	3w33	0:14:12
Kingsland	1	52N15	2w47	0:11:08
Kings Langley	1	51N43	0w28	0:01:52
Kingsley	1	53N01	1w59	0:07:56
Kingsley	1	53N16	2w40	0:10:40
King's Lynn	1	52N45	0E24	-0:01:36
King's Sutton	1	52N01	1w16	0:05:04
Kingsteignton	2	50N33	3w35	0:14:20
King Sterndale	1	53N15	1w52	0:07:28
Kingston	1	51N25	0w19	0:01:16
Kingston on Thames	1	51N25	0w19	0:01:16
Kingston upon Hull (Hull)	1	53N45	0w20	0:01:20
Kingswear	2	50N21	3w34	0:14:16
Kingswinford	2	52N29	2w10	0:08:40
Kingswood	1	51N17	0w13	0:00:52
Kingswood	2	51N27	2w22	0:09:28
King's Worthy	1	51N06	1w18	0:05:12
Kington	1	52N12	3w01	0:12:04
Kinnerley	1	52N47	2w59	0:11:56
Kinver	1	52N27	2w14	0:08:56
Kirbymoorside	1	54N16	0w55	0:03:40
Kirby Muxloe	1	52N38	1w13	0:04:52
Kirkbride	1	54N54	3w12	0:12:48
Kirkburton	1	53N37	1w42	0:06:48
Kirkby	1	53N29	2w54	0:11:36
Kirkby Lonsdale	1	54N13	2w36	0:10:24
Kirkby Malzeard	1	54N11	1w38	0:06:32
Kirkby Stephen	1	54N28	2w20	0:09:20
Kirkham	1	53N47	2w53	0:11:32
Kirkleyditch	1	53N18	2w12	0:08:48
Kirton	1	52N56	0w04	0:00:16
Kitt Green	1	53N33	2w41	0:10:44
Knaphill	1	51N19	0w37	0:02:28
Knaresborough	1	54N00	1w27	0:05:48
Knebworth	1	51N52	0w12	0:00:48
Knockholt	1	51N18	0E06	-0:00:24
Knockholt Pound	1	51N19	0E08	-0:00:32
Knolls Green	1	53N19	2w18	0:09:12
Knottingley	1	53N43	1w14	0:04:56
Knotty Green	1	51N37	0w39	0:02:36
Knowle	1	52N23	1w43	0:06:52
Knowsley	1	53N27	2w51	0:11:24
Knutsford	1	53N19	2w22	0:09:28
Lach Dennis	1	53N15	2w26	0:09:44
Laddingford	1	51N12	0E25	-0:01:40
Laindon	1	51N34	0E26	-0:01:44
Lakenheath	1	52N25	0E31	-0:02:04
Laleham	1	51N25	0w30	0:02:00
Lambeth	1	51N28	0w06	0:00:24
Lambourn	1	51N31	1w31	0:06:04
Lambourne End	1	51N38	0E08	-0:00:32
Lancashire	1	53N45	2w30	0:10:00
Lancaster	1	54N03	2w48	0:11:12
Lancing	1	50N50	0w19	0:01:16
Langdon Hills	1	51N34	0E25	-0:01:40
Langford	1	51N45	0E40	-0:02:40
Langho	1	53N48	2w27	0:09:48
Langley	1	53N15	2w05	0:08:20
Langley	1	51N30	0w33	0:02:12
Langley	1	51N14	0E35	-0:02:20
Langport	1	51N02	2w50	0:11:20
Lapford	1	50N55	3w47	0:15:08
Larkhill	1	51N12	1w50	0:07:20

Lasham	2	51N11	1W03	0:04:12
Lately Common	1	53N29	2W30	0:10:00
Latimer	1	51N41	0W33	0:02:12
Launceston	2	50N38	4W21	0:17:24
Lavendon	1	52N11	0W40	0:02:40
Lavenham	1	52N06	0E47	-0:03:08
Leadenham	1	53N05	0W34	0:02:16
Leaden Roding	1	51N48	0E19	-0:01:16
Leadgate	1	54N52	1W48	0:07:12
Leamington → Royal Leamington Spa	1	52N18	1W31	0:06:04
Leamington Spa → Royal Leamington Spa	1	52N18	1W31	0:06:04
Leatherhead	1	51N18	0W20	0:01:20
Lea Town	1	53N46	2W48	0:11:12
Lechlade	1	51N43	1W41	0:06:44
Ledbury	1	52N02	2W25	0:09:40
Ledsham	1	53N16	2W58	0:11:52
Leeds	1	53N50	1W35	0:06:20
Leedstown	2	50N10	5W22	0:21:28
Leek	1	53N06	2W01	0:08:04
Lee-on-the-Solent	2	50N47	1W12	0:04:48
Lees	1	53N32	2W04	0:08:16
Leicester	1	52N38	1W05	0:04:20
Leicestershire	1	52N46	0W53	0:03:32
Leigh	1	53N30	2W33	0:10:12
Leigh	1	51N12	0E13	-0:00:52
Leigh-on-Sea	1	51N33	0E38	-0:02:32
Leighton Buzzard	1	51N55	0W40	0:02:40
Leintwardine	1	52N23	2W51	0:11:24
Lelant	2	50N11	5W26	0:21:44
Lenham	1	51N14	0E43	-0:02:52
Leominster	1	52N14	2W45	0:11:00
Lesbury	1	55N24	1W36	0:06:24
Letchmore Heath	1	51N40	0W20	0:01:20
Letchworth	1	51N58	0W14	0:00:56
Lewes	1	50N52	0E01	-0:00:04
Lewisham	1	51N27	0W01	0:00:04
Leybourne	1	51N18	0E25	-0:01:40
Leyburn	1	54N19	1W49	0:07:16
Leyland	1	53N42	2W42	0:10:48
Leysdown-on-Sea	1	51N24	0E55	-0:03:40
Lichfield	1	52N42	1W48	0:07:12
Lifton	2	50N39	4W17	0:17:08
Lilleshall	1	52N44	2W21	0:09:24
Limbrick	1	53N38	2W36	0:10:24
Limefield	1	53N37	2W18	0:09:12
Limpsfield	1	51N16	0E01	-0:00:04
Lincoln	1	53N14	0W33	0:02:12
Lincolnshire	1	52N55	0W22	0:01:28
Lindfield	1	51N01	0W05	0:00:20
Linford	1	51N29	0E25	-0:01:40
Lingfield	1	51N11	0W01	0:00:04
Linslade	1	51N55	0W41	0:02:44
Linthwaite	1	53N37	1W51	0:07:24
Linton	1	51N13	0E31	-0:02:04
Linton	1	52N06	0E17	-0:01:08
Liphook	1	51N05	0W49	0:03:16
Liskeard	2	50N28	4W28	0:17:52
Liss	1	51N03	0W55	0:03:40
Litcham	1	52N44	0E47	-0:03:08
Litherland	1	53N28	2W59	0:11:56
Little Amwell	1	51N47	0W02	0:00:08
Little Baddow	2	51N44	0E35	-0:02:20
Little Berkhamsted	1	51N45	0W08	0:00:32
Littleborough	1	53N39	2W05	0:08:20
Little Burstead	1	51N36	0E24	-0:01:36
Little Chalfont	1	51N40	0W34	0:02:16
Little End	1	51N41	0E14	-0:00:56
Littlehampton	1	50N48	0W33	0:02:12
Little Hulton	1	53N32	2W25	0:09:40
Little Laver	1	51N46	0E14	-0:00:56
Little Leigh	1	53N17	2W35	0:10:20
Little Lever	1	53N34	2W22	0:09:28
Littleport	2	52N28	0E19	-0:01:16
Little Stanney	1	53N15	2W53	0:11:32
Little Sutton	1	53N17	2W57	0:11:48
Little Thurrock	1	51N28	0E21	-0:01:24
Littleton	1	51N24	0W28	0:01:52
Little Walshingham	1	52N54	0E51	-0:03:24
Little Waltham	2	51N47	0E29	-0:01:56
Little Warley	1	51N35	0E19	-0:01:16
Liverpool	1	53N25	2W55	0:11:40
Lizard	2	49N58	5W12	0:20:48
Loddon	1	52N32	1E29	-0:05:56
Loftus	1	54N33	0W53	0:03:32
London	1	51N30	0W10	0:00:40
London Colney	1	51N43	0W18	0:01:12
Londres → London	1	51N30	0W10	0:00:40
Longbenton	1	55N02	1W35	0:06:20
Long Buckby	1	52N19	1W04	0:04:16
Long Crendon	1	51N47	1W01	0:04:04
Long Ditton	1	51N23	0W20	0:01:20
Long Eaton	1	52N54	1W15	0:05:00
Longfield	1	51N24	0E18	-0:01:12
Longframlington	1	55N18	1W47	0:07:08
Longhorsley	1	55N15	1W46	0:07:04
Longhoughton	1	55N26	1W36	0:06:24
Long Melford	1	52N05	0E43	-0:02:52
Long Preston	1	54N02	2W15	0:09:00
Longridge	1	53N51	2W36	0:10:24
Long Sutton	1	52N47	0E08	-0:00:32
Longton	1	53N44	2W48	0:11:12
Longton	1	53N00	2W09	0:08:36
Longtown	1	55N01	2W58	0:11:52
Loose	1	51N14	0E31	-0:02:04
Lostock Gralam	1	53N16	2W28	0:09:52
Lostwithiel	2	50N25	4W40	0:18:40
Loughborough	1	52N47	1W11	0:04:44
Loughton	1	51N39	0E03	-0:00:12
Louth	1	53N22	0W01	0:00:04
Love Clough	1	53N44	2W17	0:09:08
Loves Green	2	51N43	0E24	-0:01:36
Lower Darwen	1	53N43	2W28	0:09:52
Lower Halstow	1	51N22	0E40	-0:02:40
Lower Higham	1	51N26	0E28	-0:01:52
Lower Nazeing	1	51N44	0E01	-0:00:04
Lower Peover	1	53N16	2W23	0:09:32
Lower Place	1	53N36	2W09	0:08:36
Lower Stoke	1	51N27	0E38	-0:02:32
Lower Whitley	1	53N18	2W35	0:10:20
Lowestoft	1	52N29	1E45	-0:07:00
Lowick	1	55N38	2W00	0:08:00
Lowton	1	53N28	2W35	0:10:20
Lowton Common	1	53N29	2W33	0:10:12
Luddenden	1	53N44	1W56	0:07:44
Luddesdown	1	51N22	0E24	-0:01:36
Ludgershall	1	51N16	1W37	0:06:28
Ludlow	1	52N22	2W43	0:10:52
Lumb	1	53N42	1W58	0:07:52
Lunt	1	53N31	2W59	0:11:56
Luton	1	51N22	0E32	-0:02:08
Luton	1	51N53	0W25	0:01:40
Lutterworth	1	52N28	1W10	0:04:40
Lydd	1	50N57	0E55	-0:03:40
Lydford	2	50N39	4W06	0:16:24
Lydgate	1	53N44	2W07	0:08:28
Lydham	1	52N31	2W58	0:11:52
Lydiate	1	53N32	2W57	0:11:48
Lydney	1	51N44	2W32	0:10:08
Lye Green	1	51N43	0W35	0:02:20
Lyme Regis	2	50N44	2W57	0:11:48
Lyminge	1	51N08	1E05	-0:04:20
Lymington	1	50N46	1W33	0:06:12
Lymm	1	53N23	2W29	0:09:56
Lympne	1	51N05	1E02	-0:04:08
Lyndhurst	1	50N52	1W34	0:06:16
Lyne	1	51N23	0W33	0:02:12
Lyneham	1	51N31	1W58	0:07:52
Lynemouth	1	55N12	1W31	0:06:04
Lynmouth	1	51N15	3W50	0:15:20
Lynton	1	51N15	3W50	0:15:20
Lytham Saint Anne's	1	53N45	2W57	0:11:48
Mablethorpe	1	53N21	0E15	-0:01:00
Macclesfield	1	53N16	2W07	0:08:28
Madeley	1	52N39	2W28	0:09:52
Madeley	1	52N59	2W20	0:09:20
Magdalen Laver	1	51N45	0E11	-0:00:44
Maghull	1	53N32	2W57	0:11:48
Maidenhead	1	51N32	0W44	0:02:56
Maiden Newton	1	50N46	2W35	0:10:20
Maidstone	1	51N17	0E32	-0:02:08
Maldon	1	51N45	0E40	-0:02:40
Malmesbury	1	51N36	2W06	0:08:24
Malpas	1	53N01	2W46	0:11:04
Maltby	1	53N26	1W11	0:04:44
Malton	1	54N08	0W48	0:03:12
Malvern	1	52N10	2W10	0:08:40
Malvern Link	1	52N08	2W18	0:09:12
Manchester	1	53N30	2W15	0:09:00
Manea	2	52N30	0E11	-0:00:44
Mangotsfield	3	51N28	2W28	0:09:52
Mankinholes	1	53N42	2W03	0:08:12
Manley	1	53N14	2W45	0:11:00
Manningtree	1	51N57	1E04	-0:04:16
Mansfield	1	53N09	1W11	0:04:44
Mansfield Woodhouse	1	53N11	1W12	0:04:48
Maple Cross	1	51N37	0W30	0:02:00
March	1	52N33	0E06	-0:00:24
Marfleet	1	53N45	0W17	0:01:08
Margaret Roding	1	51N47	0E19	-0:01:16
Margaretting	2	51N41	0E25	-0:01:40
Margate	2	51N24	1E24	-0:05:36
Market Bosworth	1	52N37	1W24	0:05:36
Market Deeping	1	52N41	0W19	0:01:16
Market Drayton	1	52N54	2W29	0:09:56
Market Harborough	1	52N29	0W55	0:03:40
Market Lavington	2	51N18	1W59	0:07:56
Market Rasen	1	53N24	0W21	0:01:24
Market Weighton	1	53N52	0W40	0:02:40
Marlborough	1	51N26	1W43	0:06:52
Marlow	1	51N35	0W48	0:03:12
Marlpit Hill	1	51N13	0E04	-0:00:16
Marnhull	1	50N58	2W18	0:09:12
Marple	1	53N24	2W03	0:08:12
Marsden	1	53N36	1W56	0:07:44
Marshfield	2	51N28	2W19	0:09:16
Marshside	1	53N40	2W58	0:11:52
Marske-by-the-Sea	1	54N36	1W01	0:04:04
Marston	1	53N16	2W30	0:10:00
Marthall	1	53N17	2W18	0:09:12
Martinscroft	1	53N24	2W31	0:10:04
Martock	1	50N59	2W46	0:11:04
Marton	1	53N12	2W13	0:08:52
Marylebone	1	53N34	2W38	0:10:32
Maryport	1	54N43	3W30	0:14:00
Masham	1	54N13	1W40	0:06:40
Mashbury	2	51N47	0E24	-0:01:36
Matching	1	51N47	0E13	-0:00:52
Matching Green	1	51N47	0E14	-0:00:56
Matching Tye	1	51N47	0E12	-0:00:48
Matlock	1	53N08	1W32	0:06:08
Mawdesley	1	53N38	2W46	0:11:04
Mawgan	2	50N06	5W06	0:20:24
Mayfield	1	53N01	1W45	0:07:00
Mayford	1	51N18	0W34	0:02:16
Measham	1	52N43	1W29	0:05:56
Medstead	2	51N08	1W04	0:04:16
Melbourn	1	52N05	0E01	-0:00:04
Melbourne	1	52N49	1W25	0:05:40
Melcombe Regis	5	50N38	2W28	0:09:52
Melksham	2	51N23	2W09	0:08:36
Melling	1	53N30	2W56	0:11:44
Mellor	1	53N46	2W32	0:10:08
Mellor Brook	1	53N47	2W33	0:10:12
Melmerby	1	54N44	2W35	0:10:20
Meltham	1	53N36	1W51	0:07:24
Melton Constable	1	52N53	1E01	-0:04:04
Melton Mowbray	1	52N46	0W53	0:03:32
Mendlesham	1	52N16	1E05	-0:04:20
Meopham	1	51N22	0E22	-0:01:28
Meopham Station	1	51N23	0E21	-0:01:24
Mepal	1	52N24	0E07	-0:00:28
Mere	1	51N06	2W16	0:09:04
Mere	1	53N20	2W25	0:09:40
Mere Brow	1	53N40	2W53	0:11:32
Mereclough	1	53N46	2W11	0:08:44
Mereworth	1	51N15	0E23	-0:01:32
Meriden	1	52N26	1W37	0:06:28
Merriott	1	50N54	2W48	0:11:12
Merseyside	1	53N29	2W59	0:11:56
Mersthaw	1	51N16	0W09	0:00:36
Merton	1	51N25	0W12	0:00:48
Methwold	1	52N31	0E33	-0:02:12
Mevagissey	2	50N16	4W48	0:19:12
Mexborough	1	53N30	1W17	0:05:08
Micheldever	1	51N09	1W15	0:05:00
Mickleham	1	51N16	0W19	0:01:16
Mickleover	1	52N24	1W34	0:06:16
Mickle Trafford	1	53N13	2W50	0:11:20
Middleham	1	54N17	1W49	0:07:16
Middlesbrough	1	54N35	1W14	0:04:56
Middlesex	1	51N29	0W22	0:01:28
Middleton	1	53N33	2W13	0:08:52
Middleton	1	53N45	1W32	0:06:08
Middleton	1	52N43	0E28	-0:01:52
Middleton in Teesdale	1	54N38	2W04	0:08:16
Middleton-on-the-Wolds	1	53N56	0W33	0:02:12
Middlewich	1	53N11	2W27	0:09:48
Midge Hall	1	53N42	2W45	0:11:00
Midgley	1	53N44	1W58	0:07:52
Midhurst	1	50N59	0W45	0:03:00
Midsomer Norton	2	51N18	2W28	0:09:52
Milborne Port	1	50N58	2W27	0:09:48
Mildenhall	1	52N21	0E30	-0:02:00
Milford	1	51N11	1W38	0:06:32
Milford-on-Sea	1	50N44	1W36	0:06:24
Millbrook	2	50N20	4W13	0:16:52
Mill Green	2	51N41	0E22	-0:01:28
Mill Hill	1	51N37	0W13	0:00:52
Millom	1	54N13	3W18	0:13:12
Milnrow	1	53N37	2W06	0:08:24
Milnthorpe	1	54N14	2W46	0:11:04
Milton Abbot	2	50N35	4W15	0:17:00
Milverton	1	51N02	3W16	0:13:04
Minchinhampton	1	51N42	2W10	0:08:40
Minehead	1	51N13	3W29	0:13:56
Minster	2	51N20	1E19	-0:05:16
Minster	1	51N26	0E49	-0:03:16
Minsterley	1	52N39	2W55	0:11:40
Mirfield	1	53N40	1W41	0:06:44
Misterton	1	53N27	0W51	0:03:24
Misterton	1	50N52	2W47	0:11:08
Mitcham	1	51N24	0W10	0:00:40
Mitcheldean	1	51N53	2W30	0:10:00
Mobberley	1	53N19	2W20	0:09:20
Modbury	1	50N21	3W53	0:15:32
Mollington	1	53N13	2W55	0:11:40
Monks Heath	1	53N16	2W14	0:08:56
Monmouth	1	51N49	2W43	0:10:52
Moore	1	53N21	2W38	0:10:32
Moorside	1	53N34	2W04	0:08:16
Morecambe	1	54N04	2W53	0:11:32
Moreton	1	51N44	0E14	-0:00:56
Moreton	1	53N24	3W07	0:12:28
Moretonhampstead	1	50N40	3W45	0:15:00
Moreton-in-Marsh	1	51N59	1W42	0:06:48
Morley	1	53N46	1W36	0:06:24
Morley Green	1	53N20	2W16	0:09:04
Morpeth	1	55N10	1W41	0:06:44
Morwenstow	2	50N54	4W33	0:18:12
Moss Bank	1	53N29	2W44	0:10:56
Mossley	1	53N32	2W02	0:08:08
Moss Side	1	53N46	2W57	0:11:48
Mottisfont	1	51N02	1W32	0:06:08
Mottram in Longdendale	1	53N27	2W01	0:08:04
Mouldsworth	1	53N14	2W44	0:10:56
Moulton	1	53N13	2W31	0:10:04
Mountnessing	1	51N39	0E21	-0:01:24
Mountsorrel	1	52N44	1W07	0:04:28
Much Dewchurch	1	51N59	2W46	0:11:04
Much Hoole	1	53N42	2W48	0:11:12
Much Wenlock	1	52N36	2W34	0:10:16
Mucking	1	51N30	0E26	-0:01:44
Mullion	2	50N01	5W15	0:21:00
Mundesley	1	52N53	1E26	-0:05:44
Mundon Hill	1	51N41	0E42	-0:02:48
Murton	1	54N49	1W24	0:05:36
Mytholm	1	53N44	2W01	0:08:04
Mytholmroyd	1	53N44	1W59	0:07:56
Nailsea	1	51N26	2W43	0:10:52
Nailsworth	1	51N42	2W14	0:08:56
Nantwich	1	53N04	2W32	0:10:08
Napton on the Hill	1	52N15	1W24	0:05:36
Naseby	1	52N25	0W58	0:03:52
Navestock	1	51N39	0E13	-0:00:52
Navestock Side	1	51N39	0E16	-0:01:04
Nayland	2	51N59	0E52	-0:03:28
Nazeing	1	51N44	0E03	-0:00:12
Needham Market	1	52N09	1E03	-0:04:12
Nelson	1	53N51	2W13	0:08:52
Ness	1	53N17	3W03	0:12:12
Neston	1	53N18	3W04	0:12:16
Nether Alderley	1	53N17	2W14	0:08:56

ENGLAND ANGLETERRE ANGLIA INGLATERRA

Netherton	1	53N30	2w58	0:11:52
Netley Marsh	1	50N53	1w21	0:05:24
Nettlebed	1	51N35	1w00	0:04:00
Nettleden	1	51N47	0w32	0:02:08
Nettlestead	1	51N15	0E25	-0:01:40
Nettlestead Green	1	51N14	0E25	-0:01:40
Nevendon	1	51N36	0E30	-0:02:00
New Alresford	1	51N06	1w10	0:04:40
Newark-upon-Trent	1	53N05	0w49	0:03:16
Newbiggin-by-the-Sea	1	55N11	1w30	0:06:00
New Brighton	1	53N26	3w03	0:12:12
Newburgh	1	53N35	2w47	0:11:08
Newburn	1	54N59	1w43	0:06:52
Newbury	1	51N25	1w20	0:05:20
Newbury Park	1	51N33	0E05	-0:00:20
Newby	1	54N20	0w28	0:01:52
Newby Bridge	1	54N16	2w58	0:11:52
Newcastle	1	52N26	3w06	0:12:24
Newcastle-under-Lyme	1	53N00	2w14	0:08:56
Newcastle upon Tyne	1	54N59	1w35	0:06:20
Newent	1	51N56	2w24	0:09:36
New Ferry	1	53N22	2w59	0:11:56
New Forest	1	50N53	1w35	0:06:20
Newgate Street	1	51N44	0w07	0:00:28
Newhall	1	52N48	1w34	0:06:16
Newhaven	1	50N47	0E03	-0:00:12
New Hey	1	53N36	2w06	0:08:24
New Holland	1	53N42	0w22	0:01:28
New Hythe	1	51N19	0E27	-0:01:48
Newington	1	51N05	1E08	-0:04:32
Newington	1	51N21	0E40	-0:02:40
New Lane	1	53N37	2w52	0:11:28
New Longton	1	53N44	2w45	0:11:00
Newlyn East	2	50N22	5w03	0:20:12
Newmarket	1	52N15	0E25	-0:01:40
New Mills	1	53N23	2w00	0:08:00
New Milton	1	50N44	1w40	0:06:40
Newnham	1	51N49	2w27	0:09:48
Newport	1	50N42	1w18	0:05:12
Newport	1	52N47	2w22	0:09:28
Newport Pagnell	1	52N05	0w44	0:02:56
Newquay	2	50N25	5w05	0:20:20
New Romney	1	50N59	0E57	-0:03:48
New Rossington	1	53N29	1w04	0:04:16
New Sarum → Salisbury	1	51N05	1w48	0:07:12
Newton	1	53N57	2w27	0:09:48
Newton	1	53N16	2w43	0:10:52
Newton Abbot	2	50N32	3w36	0:14:24
Newton Arlosh	1	54N53	3w15	0:13:00
Newton Aycliffe	1	54N36	1w32	0:06:08
Newton Ferrers	2	50N18	4w02	0:16:08
Newton Flotman	2	52N32	1E16	-0:05:04
Newton-le-Willows	1	53N28	2w37	0:10:28
Newtown	1	53N21	2w00	0:08:00
New Windsor → Windsor	1	51N29	0w38	0:02:32
Nine Ashes	1	51N42	0E18	-0:01:12
Ninfield	1	50N53	0E25	-0:01:40
Niton	1	50N35	1w16	0:05:04
Norden	1	53N38	2w13	0:08:52
Norfolk	1	52N35	1E00	-0:04:00
Norham	1	55N43	2w10	0:08:40
Norley	1	53N15	2w39	0:10:36
Normanton	1	53N41	1w27	0:05:48
Northallerton	1	54N20	1w26	0:05:44
Northam	2	51N02	4w12	0:16:48
Northampton	1	52N14	0w54	0:03:36
Northamptonshire	1	52N20	0w50	0:03:20
Northaw	1	51N42	0w09	0:00:36
North Benfleet	1	51N35	0E32	-0:02:08
Northchurch	1	51N46	0w36	0:02:24
Northfleet	1	51N27	0E21	-0:01:24
North Hill	2	50N34	4w25	0:17:40
North Hinksey	2	51N45	1w16	0:05:04
North Holmwood	1	51N13	0w20	0:01:20
Northleach	1	51N51	1w50	0:07:20
Northowram	1	53N44	1w50	0:07:20
North Petherton	1	51N06	3w01	0:12:04
North Seaton Colliery	1	55N11	1w32	0:06:08
North Somercotes	1	53N28	0E08	-0:00:32
North Sunderland	1	55N34	1w39	0:06:36
North Tawton	1	50N48	3w53	0:15:32
North Tidworth	1	51N16	1w40	0:06:40
Northumberland	1	55N15	2w05	0:08:20
North Walsham	1	52N50	1E24	-0:05:36
North Weald Bassett	1	51N43	0E10	-0:00:40
Northwich	1	53N16	2w32	0:10:08
Northwold	1	52N33	0E35	-0:02:20
Northwood	1	51N37	0w25	0:01:40
North Yorkshire	1	54N15	1w30	0:06:00
Norton	1	53N20	2w40	0:10:40
Norton	1	54N09	0w47	0:03:08
Norton Canes	1	52N41	1w59	0:07:56
Norton Fitzwarren	1	51N02	3w09	0:12:36
Norton Heath	1	51N43	0E19	-0:01:16
Norwich	2	52N38	1E18	-0:05:12
Nottingham	1	52N58	1w10	0:04:40
Nottinghamshire	1	53N00	1w00	0:04:00
Nounsley	1	51N46	0E36	-0:02:24
Nuneaton	1	52N32	1w28	0:05:52
Nutfield	1	51N14	0w07	0:00:28
Oadby	1	52N36	1w04	0:04:16
Oad Street	1	51N20	0E41	-0:02:44
Oakengates	1	52N42	2w28	0:09:52
Oakgrove	1	53N13	2w07	0:08:28
Oakham	1	52N40	0w43	0:02:52
Ockham	1	51N18	0w27	0:01:48
Odiham	2	51N15	0w57	0:03:48
Offham	1	51N17	0E23	-0:01:32
Okehampton	2	50N44	4w00	0:16:00
Oldbury	1	52N30	2w00	0:08:00
Old Fletton	1	52N33	0w15	0:01:00
Oldham	1	53N33	2w07	0:08:28
Old Windsor	1	51N28	0w35	0:02:20
Ollerton	1	53N12	1w00	0:04:00
Ollerton	1	53N17	2w20	0:09:20
Olney	1	52N09	0w42	0:02:48
Ombersley	1	52N17	2w13	0:08:52
Onslow Village	1	51N14	0w36	0:02:24
Orford	1	52N06	1E31	-0:06:04
Orford	1	53N25	2w35	0:10:20
Ormesby	1	54N33	1w11	0:04:44
Ormesby Saint Margaret	2	52N40	1E42	-0:06:48
Ormskirk	1	53N35	2w54	0:11:36
Orpington	1	51N23	0E06	-0:00:24
Orrell	1	53N32	2w43	0:10:52
Orsett	1	51N31	0E22	-0:01:28
Osbaldeston	1	53N47	2w32	0:10:08
Osmington	5	50N38	2w22	0:09:28
Ossett	1	53N41	1w35	0:06:20
Oswaldtwistle	1	53N43	2w26	0:09:44
Oswestry	1	52N52	3w04	0:12:16
Otford	1	51N19	0E12	-0:00:48
Otham	1	51N15	0E35	-0:02:20
Othery	1	51N05	2w53	0:11:32
Otley	1	53N54	1w41	0:06:44
Otterburn	1	55N14	2w10	0:08:40
Ottershaw	1	51N22	0w32	0:02:08
Ottery Saint Mary	1	50N45	3w17	0:13:08
Oulton Broad	2	52N31	1E42	-0:06:48
Oundle	1	52N29	0w29	0:01:56
Outlane	1	53N39	1w53	0:07:32
Outwell	1	52N37	0E14	-0:00:56
Outwood	1	53N42	1w30	0:06:00
Ovenden	1	53N44	1w53	0:07:32
Overseal	1	52N44	1w34	0:06:16
Overstrand	1	52N56	1E20	-0:05:20
Overton	1	51N15	1w15	0:05:00
Over Wallop	1	51N09	1w35	0:06:20
Oxford	2	51N46	1w15	0:05:00
Oxfordshire	1	51N39	1w10	0:04:40
Oxhey	1	51N39	0w23	0:01:32
Oxshott	1	51N20	0w21	0:01:24
Oxted	1	51N16	0w01	0:00:04
Paddington	1	51N32	0w12	0:00:48
Paddock Wood	1	51N11	0E23	-0:01:32
Padiham	1	53N49	2w19	0:09:16
Padstow	2	50N33	4w56	0:19:44
Paignton	2	50N26	3w34	0:14:16
Painswick	1	51N48	2w11	0:08:44
Pangbourne	1	51N29	1w05	0:04:20
Par	2	50N21	4w43	0:18:52
Parbold	1	53N36	2w46	0:11:04
Parkgate	1	53N18	3w05	0:12:20
Parkgate	1	53N16	2w20	0:09:20
Parkstone	5	50N47	2w20	0:09:20
Parliament	1	51N30	0w07	0:00:28
Partington	1	53N25	2w26	0:09:44
Parton	1	54N34	3w35	0:14:20
Patcham	1	50N52	0w08	0:00:32
Patchway	3	51N32	2w34	0:10:16
Pateley Bridge	1	54N05	1w45	0:07:00
Patrington	1	53N41	0w02	0:00:08
Patterdale	1	54N32	2w56	0:11:44
Peacehaven	1	50N47	0E01	-0:00:04
Peak Dale	1	53N17	1w52	0:07:28
Peak Forest	1	53N19	1w50	0:07:20
Pecket Well	1	53N46	2w00	0:08:00
Pegswood	1	55N11	1w38	0:06:32
Pemberton	1	53N32	2w41	0:10:44
Pembury	1	51N09	0E20	-0:01:20
Pendlebury	1	53N31	2w20	0:09:20
Penistone	1	53N32	1w37	0:06:28
Penketh	1	53N23	2w40	0:10:40
Penrith	1	54N40	2w44	0:10:56
Penryn	2	50N09	5w06	0:20:24
Pensby	1	53N21	3w06	0:12:24
Penshaw	1	54N53	1w29	0:05:56
Penzance	2	50N07	5w33	0:22:12
Peover Heath	1	53N15	2w19	0:09:16
Perivale	1	51N32	0w19	0:01:16
Perranporth	2	50N20	5w09	0:20:36
Pershore	1	52N07	2w05	0:08:20
Peterborough	1	52N35	0w15	0:01:00
Peterlee	1	54N46	1w19	0:05:16
Petersfield	1	51N00	0w56	0:03:44
Petworth	1	50N59	0w38	0:02:32
Pevensey	1	50N49	0E20	-0:01:20
Pewsey	1	51N21	1w46	0:07:04
Piccotts End	1	51N46	0w28	0:01:52
Pickering	1	54N14	0w46	0:03:04
Pickmere	1	53N17	2w28	0:09:52
Picton	1	53N14	2w51	0:11:24
Piddletrenthide	5	50N48	2w25	0:09:40
Pilgrims Hatch	1	51N38	0E17	-0:01:08
Pinfold	1	53N36	2w55	0:11:40
Pinhoe	4	50N44	3w27	0:13:48
Pinner	1	51N36	0w23	0:01:32
Pinxton	1	53N06	1w19	0:05:16
Pirbright	1	51N18	0w39	0:02:36
Pitch Place	1	51N16	0w36	0:02:24
Pitsea	1	51N34	0E31	-0:02:04
Plaistow	1	51N32	0E03	-0:00:12
Platt	1	51N17	0E20	-0:01:20
Plaxtol	1	51N15	0E18	-0:01:12
Pleasington	1	53N44	2w34	0:10:16
Plumley	1	53N17	2w25	0:09:40
Plymouth	2	50N23	4w10	0:16:40
Plympton	2	50N23	4w03	0:16:12
Plymstock	2	50N22	4w04	0:16:16
Pocklington	1	53N56	0w46	0:03:04
Polegate	1	50N49	0E15	-0:01:00
Pole Moor	1	53N39	1w54	0:07:36
Polesworth	1	52N37	1w36	0:06:24
Polperro	2	50N19	4w31	0:18:04
Polruan	2	50N19	4w36	0:18:24
Pontefract	1	53N42	1w18	0:05:12
Ponteland	1	55N03	1w44	0:06:56
Pontesbury	1	52N39	2w54	0:11:36
Poole	1	50N43	1w59	0:07:56
Poplar	1	51N31	0w10	0:00:40
Porlock	1	51N14	3w36	0:14:24
Port Chester	1	51N52	1w07	0:04:28
Port Isaac	2	50N35	4w49	0:19:16
Portishead	1	51N30	2w46	0:11:04
Portslade	1	50N50	0w11	0:00:44
Portsmouth	2	50N48	1w05	0:04:20
Port Sunlight	1	53N21	2w59	0:11:56
Potten End	1	51N46	0w31	0:02:04
Potter Heigham	1	52N44	1E33	-0:06:12
Potters Bar	1	51N42	0w11	0:00:44
Potter Street	1	51N46	0E08	-0:00:32
Potton	1	52N08	0w14	0:00:56
Pott Shrigley	1	53N19	2w05	0:08:20
Poulton-le-Fylde	1	53N51	2w59	0:11:56
Poundstock	2	50N46	4w33	0:18:12
Poyle	1	51N28	0w31	0:02:04
Poynton	1	53N21	2w07	0:08:28
Prenton	1	53N22	3w03	0:12:12
Prescot	1	53N26	2w48	0:11:12
Prestbury	1	53N17	2w09	0:08:36
Preston	1	53N46	0w12	0:00:48
Preston	1	53N46	2w42	0:10:48
Preston Brook	1	53N19	2w39	0:10:36
Prestwich	1	53N32	2w17	0:09:08
Princes Risborough	1	51N44	0w51	0:03:24
Princetown	2	50N33	4w00	0:16:00
Probus	2	50N17	4w57	0:19:48
Prudhoe	1	54N58	1w51	0:07:24
Puddington	1	53N15	3w00	0:12:00
Puddletown	5	50N45	2w21	0:09:24
Pudsey	1	53N48	1w40	0:06:40
Pulborough	1	50N58	0w30	0:02:00
Pulham Market	1	52N26	1E14	-0:04:56
Purfleet	1	51N29	0E15	-0:01:00
Purleigh	1	51N41	0E40	-0:02:40
Purley	1	51N20	0w07	0:00:28
Purton	1	51N36	1w52	0:07:28
Putney	1	51N28	0w13	0:00:52
Pyrford	1	51N19	0w30	0:02:00
Queenborough	1	51N26	0E45	-0:03:00
Queensbury	1	53N46	1w50	0:07:20
Quorndon	1	52N45	1w09	0:04:36
Raby	1	53N19	3w02	0:12:08
Radcliffe	1	53N34	2w20	0:09:20
Radcliffe-on-Trent	1	52N57	1w03	0:04:12
Radlett	1	51N42	0w20	0:01:20
Radstock	2	51N18	2w28	0:09:52
Rainford	1	53N30	2w48	0:11:12
Rainham	1	51N23	0E36	-0:02:24
Rainhill	1	53N26	2w46	0:11:04
Rainhill Stoops	1	53N24	2w45	0:11:00
Rainow	1	53N17	2w04	0:08:16
Rainworth	1	53N07	1w08	0:04:32
Rampside	1	54N05	3w10	0:12:40
Ramsbottom	1	53N40	2w19	0:09:16
Ramsden Bellhouse	2	51N37	0E29	-0:01:56
Ramsden Heath	2	51N38	0E28	-0:01:52
Ramsey	1	52N27	0w07	0:00:28
Ramsey	2	51N56	1E14	-0:04:56
Ramsgate	1	51N20	1E25	-0:05:40
Raunds	1	52N21	0w33	0:02:12
Ravenglass	1	54N21	3w24	0:13:36
Ravensthorpe	1	53N42	1w35	0:06:20
Rawmarsh	1	53N27	1w21	0:05:24
Rawreth	1	51N37	0E35	-0:02:20
Rawtenstall	1	53N42	2w18	0:09:12
Rayleigh	1	51N36	0E36	-0:02:24
Read	1	53N49	2w21	0:09:24
Reading	1	51N28	0w59	0:03:56
Redbourn	1	51N48	0w24	0:01:36
Redcar	1	54N37	1w04	0:04:16
Red Dial	1	54N48	3w10	0:12:40
Reddish	1	53N26	2w09	0:08:36
Redditch	1	52N19	1w56	0:07:44
Redhill	1	51N14	0w11	0:00:44
Redruth	2	50N13	5w14	0:20:56
Reepham	1	52N46	1E07	-0:04:28
Reigate	1	51N14	0w13	0:00:52
Rettendon	2	51N39	0E33	-0:02:12
Rettendon Place	1	51N38	0E34	-0:02:16
Rhodes	1	53N33	2w14	0:08:56
Ribbleton	1	53N46	2w40	0:10:40
Ribchester	1	53N49	2w32	0:10:08
Riccall	1	53N50	1w04	0:04:16
Richmond	1	54N24	1w44	0:06:56
Rickmansworth	1	51N39	0w29	0:01:56
Ridge	1	51N41	0w15	0:01:00
Rillington	1	54N09	0w42	0:02:48
Ringmer	1	50N53	0E04	-0:00:16
Ringwood	1	50N51	1w47	0:07:08
Ripley	1	51N18	0w29	0:01:56
Ripley	1	53N03	1w24	0:05:36
Ripon	1	54N08	1w31	0:06:04
Ripponden	1	53N41	1w57	0:07:48
Rishton	1	53N46	2w25	0:09:40
Rishworth	1	53N40	1w57	0:07:48
Riverhead	1	51N17	0E10	-0:00:40
Rivington	1	53N37	2w34	0:10:16
Roadhead	1	55N04	2w46	0:11:04

Robertsbridge	1	50N59	0E29	-0:01:56
Robin Hood's Bay	1	54N25	0W33	0:02:12
Roby	1	53N25	2W51	0:11:24
Roby Mill	1	53N34	2W44	0:10:56
Rochdale	1	53N38	2W09	0:08:36
Roche	2	50N24	4W48	0:19:12
Rochester	1	51N24	0E30	-0:02:00
Rochester	1	55N16	2W16	0:09:04
Rochford	1	51N36	0E43	-0:02:52
Rock Ferry	1	53N22	3W00	0:12:00
Romford	1	51N35	0E11	-0:00:44
Romiley	1	53N25	2W05	0:08:20
Romsey	1	50N59	1W30	0:06:00
Rookwood	1	50N58	1W22	0:05:28
Rossington	1	53N32	1W07	0:04:28
Ross-on-Wye	1	51N55	2W35	0:10:20
Rostherne	1	53N21	2W23	0:09:32
Rothbury	1	55N19	1W55	0:07:40
Rotherham	1	53N26	1W20	0:05:20
Rothwell	1	53N46	1W29	0:05:56
Rothwell	1	52N25	0W48	0:03:12
Rottingdean	1	50N48	0W04	0:00:16
Rowlands Gill	1	54N54	1W45	0:07:00
Rowley Regis	1	52N29	2W03	0:08:12
Roxwell	2	51N45	0E23	-0:01:32
Royal Leamington Spa	1	52N18	1W31	0:06:04
Royal Tunbridge Wells → Tunbridge Wells	1	51N08	0E16	-0:01:04
Roydon	1	51N46	0E03	-0:00:12
Royston	1	53N37	1W27	0:05:48
Royston	1	52N03	0W01	0:00:04
Royton	1	53N34	2W08	0:08:32
Rubery	1	52N24	2W00	0:08:00
Rufford	1	53N38	2W49	0:11:16
Rugby	1	52N23	1W15	0:05:00
Rugeley	1	52N46	1W55	0:07:40
Ruislip	1	51N34	0W25	0:01:40
Runcorn	1	53N20	2W44	0:10:56
Runnymede	1	51N24	0W32	0:02:08
Runwell	1	51N37	0E32	-0:02:08
Rushden	1	52N17	0W36	0:02:24
Rustington	1	50N48	0W31	0:02:04
Rutland	1	52N38	0W40	0:02:40
Ruyton-Eleven-Towns	1	52N48	2W54	0:11:36
Ryal Fold	1	53N41	2W30	0:10:00
Ryarsh	1	51N19	0E24	-0:01:36
Ryde	2	50N44	1W10	0:04:40
Rye	1	50N57	0E44	-0:02:56
Ryhope	1	54N52	1W21	0:05:24
Ryton	1	54N59	1W46	0:07:04
Ryton-on-Dunsmore	1	52N22	1W26	0:05:44
Saddleworth	1	53N33	1W59	0:07:56
Saffron Walden	1	52N01	0E15	-0:01:00
Saint Agnes	2	50N18	5W13	0:20:52
Saint Albans	1	51N46	0W21	0:01:24
Saint Anne's	1	53N45	3W02	0:12:08
Saint Austell	2	50N20	4W48	0:19:12
Saint Blazey	2	50N22	4W43	0:18:52
Saint Columb Major	2	50N26	5W03	0:20:12
Saint Dennis	2	50N23	4W53	0:19:32
Saint Germans	2	50N24	4W18	0:17:12
Saint Helens	2	50N42	1W06	0:04:24
Saint Helens	1	53N28	2W44	0:10:56
Saint Ives	1	52N20	0W05	0:00:20
Saint Ives	2	50N12	5W29	0:21:56
Saint Just	2	50N07	5W42	0:22:48
Saint Keverne	2	50N03	5W06	0:20:24
Saint Leonards	1	50N51	0E34	-0:02:16
Saint Margaret's at Cliffe	1	51N09	1E24	-0:05:36
Saint Mary Bourne	1	51N16	1W24	0:05:36
Saint Marylebone	1	51N31	0W09	0:00:36
Saint Mary's Bay	1	51N00	0E58	-0:03:52
Saint Mary's Hoo	1	51N28	0E36	-0:02:24
Saint Mawes	2	50N09	5W01	0:20:04
Saint Mawgan	2	50N28	4W58	0:19:52
Saint Merryn	2	50N31	4W58	0:19:52
Saint Neots	1	52N14	0W17	0:01:08
Saint Pancras	1	51N32	0W07	0:00:28
Saint Paul's Cathedral	1	51N31	0W06	0:00:24
Saint Tudy	2	50N33	4W43	0:18:52
Salcombe	1	50N13	3W47	0:15:08
Sale	1	53N26	2W19	0:09:16
Salesbury	1	53N47	2W30	0:10:00
Salford	1	53N28	2W18	0:09:12
Salfords	1	51N12	0W10	0:00:40
Salisbury	1	51N05	1W48	0:07:12
Salop	1	52N40	2W40	0:10:40
Saltash	2	50N24	4W12	0:16:48
Saltburn-by-the-Sea	1	54N35	0W58	0:03:52
Samlesbury	1	53N46	2W38	0:10:32
Samlesbury Bottoms	1	53N45	2W34	0:10:16
Sampford Peverell	1	50N56	3W22	0:13:28
Sandbach	1	53N09	2W22	0:09:28
Sandgate	1	51N05	1E08	-0:04:32
Sandhurst	1	51N19	0W48	0:03:12
Sandiway	1	53N14	2W36	0:10:24
Sandon	2	51N43	0E32	-0:02:08
Sandown	1	50N39	1W09	0:04:36
Sandridge	1	51N47	0W18	0:01:12
Sandringham	1	52N50	0E30	-0:02:00
Sandwich	1	51N17	1E20	-0:05:20
Sandy	1	52N08	0W18	0:01:12
Sarratt	1	51N41	0W29	0:01:56
Saughall	1	53N13	2W58	0:11:52
Sawbridgeworth	1	51N50	0E09	-0:00:36
Sawston	2	52N07	0E10	-0:00:40
Sawtry	1	52N27	0W17	0:01:08
Saxilby	1	53N17	0W40	0:02:40
Saxmundham	1	52N13	1E29	-0:05:56
Scalby	1	54N18	0W27	0:01:48
Scarborough	1	54N17	0W24	0:01:36
Scarisbrick	1	53N37	2W56	0:11:44
Scarth Hill	1	53N33	2W52	0:11:28
Scole	1	52N22	1E10	-0:04:40
Scremerston	1	55N44	1W59	0:07:56
Scrooby	1	53N25	1W01	0:04:04
Scunthorpe	1	53N36	0W38	0:02:32
Seacombe	1	53N25	3W01	0:12:04
Seaford	1	50N46	0E06	-0:00:24
Seaforth	1	53N28	3W01	0:12:04
Seaham	1	54N52	1W21	0:05:24
Seahouses	1	55N35	1W38	0:06:32
Seal	1	51N17	0E14	-0:00:56
Seascale	1	54N24	3W29	0:13:56
Seaton	1	53N54	0W14	0:00:56
Seaton	2	50N43	3W05	0:12:20
Seaton	1	54N41	3W33	0:14:12
Seaton Delaval	1	55N04	1W31	0:06:04
Sedbergh	1	54N20	2W31	0:10:04
Sedgefield	1	54N39	1W26	0:05:44
Sedgley	2	52N33	2W08	0:08:32
Seer Green	1	51N37	0W36	0:02:24
Sefton	1	53N30	2W58	0:11:52
Selborne	1	51N06	0W56	0:03:44
Selby	1	53N48	1W04	0:04:16
Selsey	1	50N44	0W48	0:03:12
Selston	1	53N04	1W20	0:05:20
Send	1	51N17	0W31	0:02:04
Sennen	2	50N04	5W42	0:22:48
Settle	1	54N04	2W16	0:09:04
Sevenoaks	1	51N16	0E12	-0:00:48
Sevenoaks Weald	1	51N14	0E12	-0:00:48
Shaftesbury	1	51N01	2W12	0:08:48
Shalford	1	51N13	0W34	0:02:16
Shanklin	1	50N38	1W10	0:04:40
Shap	1	54N32	2W41	0:10:44
Shaw	1	53N35	2W06	0:08:24
Shawbury	1	52N47	2W39	0:10:36
Shedfield	1	50N55	1W12	0:04:48
Sheerness	1	51N27	0E45	-0:03:00
Sheffield	1	53N23	1W30	0:06:00
Shefford	1	52N02	0W20	0:01:20
Shellow Bowells	1	51N45	0E20	-0:01:20
Shenfield	1	51N38	0E19	-0:01:16
Shenley	1	51N41	0W17	0:01:08
Shepperton	1	51N24	0W27	0:01:48
Shepshed	1	52N47	1W18	0:05:12
Shepton Mallet	1	51N12	2W33	0:10:12
Shepway	1	51N15	0E33	-0:02:12
Sherborne	1	50N57	2W31	0:10:04
Sherborne Saint John	2	51N18	1W07	0:04:28
Shere	1	51N13	0W28	0:01:52
Sheringham	1	52N57	1E12	-0:04:48
Shevington	1	53N34	2W42	0:10:48
Shevington Moor	1	53N35	2W41	0:10:44
Shibden Hall	1	53N44	1W51	0:07:24
Shifnal	1	52N40	2W21	0:09:24
Shilbottle	1	55N23	1W42	0:06:48
Shildon	1	54N38	1W39	0:06:36
Shillingstone	1	50N54	2W14	0:08:56
Shipbourne	1	51N15	0E17	-0:01:08
Shipdham	1	52N37	0E53	-0:03:32
Shipley	1	53N50	1W47	0:07:08
Shipston-on-Stour	1	52N04	1W37	0:06:28
Shirdley Hill	1	53N36	2W58	0:11:52
Shirebrook	1	53N12	1W13	0:04:52
Shirrell Heath	1	50N55	1W12	0:04:48
Shoeburyness	1	51N32	0E48	-0:03:12
Shoreditch	1	51N32	0W05	0:00:20
Shoreham	1	51N20	0E11	-0:00:44
Shoreham-by-Sea	1	50N49	0W16	0:01:04
Shorne	1	51N25	0E26	-0:01:44
Shotley Gate	2	51N58	1E15	-0:05:00
Shotton Colliery	1	54N44	1W20	0:05:20
Shotwick	1	53N14	2W59	0:11:56
Shrewsbury	1	52N43	2W45	0:11:00
Shrewton	1	51N12	1W55	0:07:40
Shrivenham	1	51N36	1W39	0:06:36
Shropshire	1	52N40	2W00	0:08:00
Sible Hedingham	1	51N58	0E35	-0:02:20
Sidcup	1	51N25	0E06	-0:00:24
Siddington	1	53N14	2W14	0:08:56
Sidmouth	1	50N41	3W15	0:13:00
Silloth	1	54N52	3W23	0:13:32
Silsden	1	53N55	1W55	0:07:40
Silverstone	1	52N05	1W02	0:04:08
Silverton	4	50N48	3W28	0:13:52
Simonsbath	1	51N09	3W45	0:15:00
Simonstone	1	53N48	2W20	0:09:20
Singleton	1	50N55	0W46	0:03:04
Singlewell or Ifield	1	51N25	0E23	-0:01:32
Sittingbourne	1	51N21	0E44	-0:02:56
Skegness	1	53N10	0E21	-0:01:24
Skelmersdale	1	53N33	2W48	0:11:12
Skelton	1	54N33	0W59	0:03:56
Skelton	1	54N43	2W51	0:11:24
Skipton	1	53N58	2W01	0:08:04
Slackhall	1	53N20	1W53	0:07:32
Slaithwaite	1	53N37	1W53	0:07:32
Slattocks	1	53N35	2W10	0:08:40
Sleaford	1	53N00	0W24	0:01:36
Sledmere	1	54N04	0W35	0:02:20
Slough	1	51N31	0W36	0:02:24
Smallbridge	1	53N38	2W08	0:08:32
Smethwick (Warley)	1	52N30	1W58	0:07:52
Smithfield	1	54N59	2W52	0:11:28
Snettisham	1	52N53	0E30	-0:02:00
Snodland	1	51N20	0E27	-0:01:48
Soham	2	52N20	0E20	-0:01:20
Solihull	1	52N25	1W45	0:07:00
Sollom	1	53N40	2W50	0:11:20
Somerset	1	51N08	3W00	0:12:00
Somersham	1	52N23	0E01	-0:00:04
Somerton	1	51N03	2W44	0:10:56
Sonning	1	51N29	0W55	0:03:40
Southam	1	52N15	1W23	0:05:32
Southampton	1	50N55	1W25	0:05:40
South Benfleet	1	51N33	0E34	-0:02:16
Southborough	1	51N10	0E15	-0:01:00
South Brent	1	50N25	3W50	0:15:20
South Cave	1	53N46	0W35	0:02:20
South Darenth	1	51N24	0E15	-0:01:00
Southend-on-Sea	1	51N33	0E43	-0:02:52
Southery	1	52N32	0E23	-0:01:32
South Farmbridge	1	51N38	0E41	-0:02:44
Southfleet	1	51N25	0E19	-0:01:16
Southgate	1	51N38	0W08	0:00:32
South Green	2	51N37	0E26	-0:01:44
South Hanningfield	2	51N39	0E31	-0:02:04
South Hayling	2	50N47	0W59	0:03:56
South Kirkby	1	53N34	1W20	0:05:20
South Mimms	1	51N42	0W14	0:00:56
Southminster	1	51N40	0E50	-0:03:20
South Molton	1	51N01	3W50	0:15:20
South Norwood	1	51N24	0W04	0:00:16
South Nutfield	1	51N14	0W08	0:00:32
South Ockendon	1	51N32	0E18	-0:01:12
Southowram	1	53N43	1W50	0:07:20
South Oxhey	1	51N38	0W23	0:01:32
South Petherton	1	50N58	2W49	0:11:16
Southport	1	53N39	3W01	0:12:04
South Sea	1	50N45	0W30	0:02:00
South Shields	1	55N00	1W25	0:05:40
Southwark	1	51N30	0W06	0:00:24
South Weald	1	51N37	0E16	-0:01:04
Southwick	1	50N50	0W13	0:00:52
Southwold	1	52N20	1E40	-0:06:40
South Woodham Ferrers	1	51N39	0E37	-0:02:28
South Yorkshire	1	53N30	1W15	0:05:00
South Zeal	1	50N44	3W54	0:15:36
Sowerby	1	53N42	1W56	0:07:44
Sowerby	1	54N13	1W21	0:05:24
Sowerby Bridge	1	53N43	1W54	0:07:36
Spalding	1	52N47	0W10	0:00:40
Sparkford	1	51N02	2W34	0:10:16
Sparrowpit	1	53N19	1W52	0:07:28
Spennymoor	1	54N42	1W35	0:06:20
Spondon	1	52N54	1W25	0:05:40
Stacksteads	1	53N41	2W13	0:08:52
Stafford	1	52N48	2W07	0:08:28
Staffordshire	1	52N50	2W00	0:08:00
Staines	1	51N26	0W31	0:02:04
Stainforth	1	53N36	1W01	0:04:04
Stainland	1	53N40	1W53	0:07:32
Stalbridge	1	50N58	2W23	0:09:32
Stalham	1	52N47	1E31	-0:06:04
Stalybridge	1	53N29	2W04	0:08:16
Stamford	1	52N39	0W29	0:01:56
Stamford Bridge	1	53N59	0W55	0:03:40
Stanborough	1	51N47	0W13	0:00:52
Standish	1	53N36	2W41	0:10:44
Standon	1	51N53	0E02	-0:00:08
Stanford le Hope	1	51N31	0E26	-0:01:44
Stanford Rivers	1	51N41	0E13	-0:00:52
Stanhope	1	54N45	2W01	0:08:04
Stanley	1	54N52	1W42	0:06:48
Stanlow	1	53N17	2W52	0:11:28
Stanmore	1	51N37	0W19	0:01:16
Stannington	1	55N06	1W40	0:06:40
Stanstead Abbots	1	51N47	0E01	-0:00:04
Stansted	1	51N20	0E18	-0:01:12
Stansted Mountfitchet	1	51N54	0E12	-0:00:48
Stanton	1	52N19	0E53	-0:03:32
Stanwell	1	51N27	0W29	0:01:56
Stanwell Moor	1	51N28	0W30	0:02:00
Stanwix	1	54N54	2W55	0:11:40
Stapleford	1	52N56	1W16	0:05:04
Stapleford Abbotts	1	51N38	0E10	-0:00:40
Stapleford Tawney	1	51N40	0E11	-0:00:44
Staplehurst	1	51N10	0E33	-0:02:12
Starcross	2	50N38	3W27	0:13:48
Staveley	1	53N16	1W20	0:05:20
Stepney	1	51N31	0W02	0:00:08
Stevenage	1	51N55	0W14	0:00:56
Steyning	1	50N53	0W20	0:01:20
Stock	2	51N40	0E27	-0:01:48
Stockbridge	1	51N07	1W29	0:05:56
Stockbury	1	51N20	0E39	-0:02:36
Stockport	1	53N25	2W10	0:08:40
Stocksbridge	1	53N27	1W34	0:06:16
Stockton Heath	1	53N22	2W35	0:10:20
Stockton-on-Tees	1	54N34	1W19	0:05:16
Stoke	1	51N27	0E37	-0:02:28
Stoke D'Abernon	1	51N19	0W23	0:01:32
Stoke Golding	1	52N34	1W24	0:05:36
Stokenchurch	1	51N40	0W55	0:03:40
Stoke Newington	1	51N34	0W05	0:00:20
Stoke-on-Trent	1	53N00	2W10	0:08:40
Stoke Poges	1	51N33	0W35	0:02:20
Stokesley	1	54N28	1W11	0:04:44
Stondon Massey	1	51N41	0E18	-0:01:12
Stone	1	51N27	0E16	-0:01:04
Stone	1	52N54	2W10	0:08:40
Stonehouse	1	51N45	2W17	0:09:08
Stoneleigh	1	52N21	1W31	0:06:04
Stony Stratford	1	52N04	0W52	0:03:28

Place		Lat	Long	Time
Storeton	1	53N21	3W03	0:12:12
Storrington	1	50N55	0W28	0:01:52
Stotfold	1	52N01	0W14	0:00:56
Stoughton	1	51N15	0W35	0:02:20
Stourbridge	1	52N27	2W09	0:08:36
Stourport-on-Severn	1	52N21	2W16	0:09:04
Stow Maries	1	51N40	0E39	-0:02:36
Stowmarket	1	52N11	1E00	-0:04:00
Stow-on-the-Wold	1	51N56	1W44	0:06:56
Stradbroke	1	52N19	1E16	-0:05:04
Stratford-upon-Avon	1	52N12	1W41	0:06:44
Stratton	2	50N50	4W31	0:18:04
Stratton Saint Margaret	1	51N35	1W45	0:07:00
Streatham	1	51N26	0W08	0:00:32
Street	1	51N07	2W42	0:10:48
Stretford	1	53N27	2W19	0:09:16
Stretton	1	53N21	2W35	0:10:20
Stretton	1	52N44	0W35	0:02:20
Strood	1	51N24	0E28	-0:01:52
Stroud	1	51N45	2W12	0:08:48
Stubbins	1	53N39	2W19	0:09:16
Studland	1	50N39	1W58	0:07:52
Studley	1	52N16	1W52	0:07:28
Sturminster Newton	1	50N50	2W19	0:09:16
Sturry	1	51N18	1E07	-0:04:28
Styal	1	53N21	2W15	0:09:00
Sudbury	1	52N02	0E44	-0:02:56
Sudburytown	1	52N02	0E44	-0:02:56
Suffolk	1	52N15	0E43	-0:02:52
Summer Bridge	1	54N03	1W41	0:06:44
Summerseat	1	53N38	2W19	0:09:16
Summit	1	53N40	2W05	0:08:20
Sunbury	1	51N25	0W26	0:01:44
Sunderland	1	54N55	1W23	0:05:32
Sundridge	1	51N17	0E18	-0:01:12
Sunningdale	1	51N24	0W38	0:02:32
Sunninghill	1	51N25	0W40	0:02:40
Surbiton	1	51N24	0W18	0:01:12
Surrey	1	51N10	0W20	0:01:20
Sussex	1	50N55	0E15	-0:01:00
Sutton	1	51N12	0W26	0:01:44
Sutton	1	52N23	0E07	-0:00:28
Sutton-at-Hone	1	51N25	0E14	-0:00:56
Sutton Bridge	1	52N46	0E12	-0:00:48
Sutton Coldfield	1	52N34	1W48	0:07:12
Sutton Courtenay	2	51N39	1W17	0:05:08
Sutton-in-Ashfield	1	53N08	1W15	0:05:00
Sutton Lane Ends	1	53N14	2W06	0:08:24
Sutton Leach	1	53N26	2W42	0:10:48
Sutton-on-Sea	1	53N19	0E17	-0:01:08
Sutton on Trent	1	53N10	0W49	0:03:16
Sutton Scotney	1	51N10	1W21	0:05:24
Sutton Valence	1	51N12	0E36	-0:02:24
Sutton Veny	1	51N11	2W08	0:08:32
Sutton Weaver	1	53N18	2W41	0:10:44
Swadlincote	1	52N47	1W33	0:06:12
Swaffham	1	52N39	0E41	-0:02:44
Swanage	1	50N37	1W58	0:07:52
Swanley	1	51N24	0E12	-0:00:48
Swanscombe	1	51N26	0E18	-0:01:12
Sway	1	50N47	1W37	0:06:28
Swindon	1	51N34	1W47	0:07:08
Swinton	1	53N31	2W20	0:09:20
Swinton	1	53N28	1W20	0:05:20
Sworton Heath	1	53N21	2W28	0:09:52
Syston	1	52N42	1W04	0:04:16
Tadcaster	1	53N53	1W16	0:05:04
Tadley	2	51N21	1W08	0:04:32
Tadworth	1	51N17	0W14	0:00:56
Tamerton Foliot	2	50N26	4W08	0:16:32
Tandridge	1	51N14	0W02	0:00:08
Tanworth	1	52N20	1W50	0:07:20
Tanworth-in-Arden	1	52N39	1W40	0:06:40
Tarbock Green	1	53N23	2W49	0:11:16
Tarleton	1	53N41	2W50	0:11:20
Tarlscough	1	53N37	2W52	0:11:28
Tarporley	1	53N09	2W40	0:10:40
Tarrant Hinton	1	50N53	2W05	0:08:20
Tatsfield	1	51N18	0E02	-0:00:08
Taunton	1	51N01	3W06	0:12:24
Tavistock	2	50N33	4W08	0:16:32
Tebay	1	54N26	2W35	0:10:20
Teddington	1	51N26	0W20	0:01:20
Teesside → Middlesbrough	1	54N35	1W14	0:04:56
Teignmouth	2	50N33	3W30	0:14:00
Templecombe	1	51N00	2W25	0:09:40
Temple Ewell	1	51N09	1E16	-0:05:04
Temple Sowerby	1	54N39	2W35	0:10:20
Tenbury Wells	1	52N19	2W35	0:10:20
Tenterden	1	51N05	0E42	-0:02:48
Terrington Saint Clement	1	52N45	0E18	-0:01:12
Teston	1	51N15	0E26	-0:01:44
Tetbury	1	51N39	2W10	0:08:40
Tettenhall	2	52N36	2W09	0:08:36
Tewkesbury	1	51N59	2W09	0:08:36
Teynham	1	51N20	0E50	-0:03:20
Thame	1	51N45	0W59	0:03:56
Thames	1	51N22	1E27	-0:05:48
Thames Ditton	1	51N23	0W21	0:01:24
Thames Haven	1	51N30	0E31	-0:02:04
Thatcham	1	51N25	1W15	0:05:00
Thatto Heath	1	53N26	2W45	0:11:00
Thaxted	1	51N57	0E20	-0:01:20
Theale	1	51N27	1W04	0:04:16
Thelwall	1	53N23	2W32	0:10:08
Thetford	1	52N25	0E45	-0:03:00
Theydon Bois	1	51N40	0E06	-0:00:24

Place		Lat	Long	Time
Thirsk	1	54N14	1W20	0:05:20
Thong	1	51N24	0E24	-0:01:36
Thormanby	1	54N10	1W14	0:04:56
Thornaby-on-Tees	1	54N34	1W18	0:05:12
Thornbury	1	51N37	2W32	0:10:08
Thorndon	1	52N17	1E08	-0:04:32
Thorne	1	53N37	0W58	0:03:52
Thorney	1	52N37	0W07	0:00:28
Thornton	1	53N53	3W02	0:12:08
Thornton	1	53N47	1W51	0:07:24
Thornton Dale	1	54N14	0W43	0:02:52
Thornton Hough	1	53N19	3W03	0:12:12
Thornton-le-Moors	1	53N16	2W50	0:11:20
Thornwood Common	1	51N43	0E08	-0:00:32
Thorpe	1	51N24	0W32	0:02:08
Thorpe-le-Soken	1	51N52	1E10	-0:04:40
Thorpe Saint Andrew	2	52N38	1E20	-0:05:20
Thrapston	1	52N24	0W32	0:02:08
Three Bridges	1	51N07	0W09	0:00:36
Threlkeld	1	54N38	3W03	0:12:12
Throckley	1	54N59	1W45	0:07:00
Thundersley	1	51N34	0E35	-0:02:20
Thurnham	1	51N17	0E36	-0:02:24
Thurnscoe	1	53N31	1W19	0:05:16
Thursby	1	54N51	3W03	0:12:12
Thurstaston	1	53N21	3W08	0:12:32
Ticehurst	1	51N03	0E25	-0:01:40
Tickhill	1	53N26	1W06	0:04:24
Tilbury	1	51N28	0E23	-0:01:32
Timperley	1	53N24	2W19	0:09:16
Tintagel	2	50N40	4W45	0:19:00
Tintwistle	1	53N28	1W58	0:07:52
Tipton	2	52N32	2W05	0:08:20
Tiptree	1	51N49	0E45	-0:03:00
Tisbury	1	51N04	2W03	0:08:12
Titchfield	1	50N51	1W13	0:04:52
Tiverton	1	50N55	3W29	0:13:56
Tockholes	1	53N42	2W31	0:10:04
Toddington	1	51N57	0W32	0:02:08
Todmorden	1	53N43	2W05	0:08:20
Tollesbury	1	51N46	0E50	-0:03:20
Tolpuddle	1	50N45	2W18	0:09:12
Tonbridge	1	51N12	0E16	-0:01:04
Toot Hill	1	51N42	0E12	-0:00:48
Top of Hebers	1	53N34	2W12	0:08:48
Toppings	1	53N37	2W25	0:09:40
Topsham	4	50N41	3W27	0:13:48
Torbay → Torquay	1	50N28	3W30	0:14:00
Torpoint	2	50N22	4W11	0:16:44
Torquay (Torbay)	1	50N28	3W30	0:14:00
Totnes	2	50N25	3W41	0:14:44
Tottenham	1	51N35	0W04	0:00:16
Tottington	1	53N37	2W20	0:09:20
Totton	1	50N56	1W29	0:05:56
Towcester	1	52N08	1W00	0:04:00
Tow Law	1	54N44	1W49	0:07:16
Toy's Hill	1	51N14	0E06	-0:00:24
Trafford Park	1	53N28	2W20	0:09:20
Tranmere	1	53N23	3W01	0:12:04
Treales	1	53N47	2W51	0:11:24
Triangle	1	53N42	1W56	0:07:44
Tring	1	51N48	0W40	0:02:40
Trottiscliffe	1	51N19	0E21	-0:01:24
Trowbridge	2	51N20	2W13	0:08:52
Truro	2	50N16	5W03	0:20:12
Tunbridge Wells	1	51N08	0E16	-0:01:04
Tunstall	1	53N05	2W13	0:08:52
Turton Bottoms	1	53N38	2W24	0:09:36
Tweedmouth	1	55N45	2W01	0:08:04
Twickenham	1	51N27	0W20	0:01:20
Twiss Green	1	53N27	2W32	0:10:08
Twyford	1	51N29	0W53	0:03:32
Twyford	1	51N01	1W19	0:05:16
Tyldesley	1	53N31	2W28	0:09:52
Tynemouth	1	55N01	1W24	0:05:36
Tytherington	1	53N17	2W08	0:08:32
Tywardreath	2	50N22	4W41	0:18:44
Uckfield	1	50N58	0E06	-0:00:24
Uffculme	1	50N54	3W20	0:13:20
Ulcombe	1	51N12	0E39	-0:02:36
Ulverston	1	54N12	3W06	0:12:24
Under River	1	51N15	0E14	-0:00:56
Upavon	1	51N18	1W49	0:07:16
Upchurch	1	51N23	0E39	-0:02:36
Up Holland	1	53N33	2W44	0:10:56
Upper End	1	53N17	1W52	0:07:28
Upper Tean	1	52N57	1W58	0:07:52
Uppingham	1	52N35	0W43	0:02:52
Upton	1	53N13	2W52	0:11:28
Upton	1	51N30	0W35	0:02:20
Upton upon Severn	1	52N04	2W13	0:08:52
Upwell	1	52N36	0E12	-0:00:48
Urmston	1	53N27	2W21	0:09:24
Uttoxeter	1	52N54	1W51	0:07:24
Uxbridge	1	51N33	0W29	0:01:56
Ventnor	1	50N36	1W11	0:04:44
Verwood	1	50N53	1W52	0:07:28
Veryan	2	50N13	4W54	0:19:36
Virginia Water	1	51N24	0W34	0:02:16
Waddesdon	1	51N51	0W56	0:03:44
Waddingham	1	53N27	0W31	0:02:04
Wadebridge	2	50N32	4W50	0:19:20
Wadhurst	1	51N04	0E21	-0:01:24
Wainfleet All Saints	1	53N07	0E14	-0:00:56
Wainscott	1	51N25	0E31	-0:02:04
Wainstalls	1	53N45	1W56	0:07:44
Wakefield	1	53N42	1W29	0:05:56
Walberswick	1	52N19	1E39	-0:06:36
Walderslade	1	51N21	0E32	-0:02:08
Walkden	1	53N32	2W24	0:09:36
Walk Mill	1	53N46	2W12	0:08:48

Place		Lat	Long	Time
Wallasey	1	53N26	3W03	0:12:12
Wallend	1	51N27	0E42	-0:02:48
Wallingford	1	51N37	1W08	0:04:32
Wallington	1	51N21	0W09	0:00:36
Wallmer Bridge	1	53N43	2W48	0:11:12
Wallsend	1	55N00	1W31	0:06:04
Wallsend-on-Tyne	1	55N00	1W31	0:06:04
Walmer	1	51N13	1E24	-0:05:36
Walmersley	1	53N37	2W18	0:09:12
Walpole Saint Peter	1	52N42	0E15	-0:01:00
Walsall	1	52N35	1W58	0:07:52
Walsden	1	53N42	2W06	0:08:24
Walsoken	1	52N41	0E12	-0:00:48
Waltham Abbey	1	51N42	0E01	-0:00:04
Waltham on the Wolds	1	52N49	0W49	0:03:16
Walthamstow	1	51N34	0W02	0:00:08
Walton	1	51N24	0W25	0:01:40
Walton	2	51N58	1E21	-0:05:24
Walton-le-Dale	1	53N45	2W39	0:10:36
Walton-on-Thames	1	51N24	0W25	0:01:40
Walton on the Hill	1	51N17	0W15	0:01:00
Walton-on-the-Naze	2	51N51	1E16	-0:05:04
Wanborough	1	51N33	1W42	0:06:48
Wandsworth	1	51N28	0W12	0:00:48
Wansbeck	1	55N08	1W35	0:06:20
Wantage	1	51N36	1W25	0:05:40
Warburton	1	53N24	2W27	0:09:48
Wardle	1	53N39	2W08	0:08:32
Ware	1	51N49	0W02	0:00:08
Wareham	1	50N41	2W07	0:08:28
Warkworth	1	55N21	1W36	0:06:24
Warland	1	53N41	2W05	0:08:20
Warley → Smethwick	1	52N30	1W58	0:07:52
Warlingham	1	51N19	0W04	0:00:16
Warlington	1	51N39	1W01	0:04:04
Warmington	1	52N08	1W24	0:05:36
Warminster	2	51N13	2W12	0:08:48
Warren	1	53N14	2W10	0:08:40
Warrington	1	53N24	2W37	0:10:28
Warsop	1	53N13	1W09	0:04:36
Warton	1	53N45	2W54	0:11:36
Warton	1	54N09	2W47	0:11:08
Warwick	1	52N17	1W34	0:06:16
Warwickshire	1	52N13	1W37	0:06:28
Washington	1	54N55	1W30	0:06:00
Watchet	1	51N12	3W20	0:13:20
Water	1	53N44	2W14	0:08:56
Waterbeach	2	52N16	0E11	-0:00:44
Waterend	1	51N47	0W30	0:02:00
Water End	1	53N41	2W15	0:09:00
Wateringbury	1	51N15	0E25	-0:01:40
Waterloo	1	53N28	3W02	0:12:08
Waterlooville	2	50N53	1W02	0:04:08
Watford	1	51N40	0W25	0:01:40
Wath upon Dearne	1	53N29	1W20	0:05:20
Watlington	1	51N37	1W00	0:04:00
Watton	1	52N35	0E48	-0:03:12
Wealdstone	1	51N36	0W20	0:01:20
Wearhead	1	54N45	2W13	0:08:52
Weaverham	1	53N16	2W35	0:10:20
Wedmore	1	51N14	2W49	0:11:16
Wednesbury	1	52N34	2W00	0:08:00
Wednesfield	2	52N36	2W04	0:08:16
Weedon Beck	1	52N14	1W05	0:04:20
Weeton	1	53N48	2W56	0:11:44
Welhamgreen	1	51N44	0W13	0:00:52
Wellesbourne	1	52N12	1W35	0:06:20
Well Hill	1	51N21	0E09	-0:00:36
Welling	1	51N28	0E07	-0:00:28
Wellingborough	1	52N19	0W42	0:02:48
Wellington	1	52N43	2W31	0:10:04
Wellington	1	50N59	3W14	0:12:56
Wells	1	51N13	2W39	0:10:36
Wells-next-the-Sea	1	52N58	0E51	-0:03:24
Welney	2	52N31	0E15	-0:01:00
Welwyn Garden City	1	51N50	0W13	0:00:52
Wem	1	52N51	2W44	0:10:56
Wembley	1	51N33	0W18	0:01:12
Wendover	1	51N46	0W46	0:03:04
Weobley	1	52N09	2W51	0:11:24
Wervin	1	53N15	2W52	0:11:28
Wesham	1	53N48	2W53	0:11:32
West Auckland	1	54N38	1W43	0:06:52
West Bergholt	2	51N55	0E51	-0:03:24
West Bridgford	1	52N56	1W08	0:04:32
West Bromwich	1	52N31	1W56	0:07:44
Westbury	2	51N16	2W11	0:08:44
Westbury	1	52N41	2W57	0:11:48
Westbury-on-Severn	1	51N50	2W24	0:09:36
West Clandon	1	51N15	0W30	0:02:00
Westcliff-on-Sea	1	51N32	0E41	-0:02:44
Westcott	1	51N13	0W22	0:01:28
West End	1	51N20	0W38	0:02:32
West End	1	51N44	0W04	0:00:16
Westerham	1	51N16	0E05	-0:00:20
West Farleigh	1	51N15	0E27	-0:01:48
Westfield	1	50N55	0E35	-0:02:20
Westgate-on-Sea	2	51N23	1E21	-0:05:24
West Ham	1	51N31	0E01	-0:00:04
West Hanningfield	2	51N40	0E30	-0:02:00
West Hartlepool	1	54N41	1W12	0:04:48
Westhead	1	53N34	2W51	0:11:24
West Horndon	1	51N34	0E21	-0:01:24
West Horsley	1	51N16	0W27	0:01:48
Westhoughton	1	53N33	2W32	0:10:08
West Humble	1	51N15	0W20	0:01:20

INGLATERRA ANGLIA ANGLETERRE ENGLAND

West Hyde	1	51N37	0W30	0:02:00
West Kingsdown	1	51N21	0E17	-0:01:08
West Kirby	1	53N22	3W10	0:12:40
Westleigh	1	53N30	2W31	0:10:04
West Looe	2	50N21	4W28	0:17:52
West Lulworth	1	50N38	2W15	0:09:00
West Malling	1	51N18	0E25	-0:01:40
West Meon	1	51N01	1W05	0:04:20
West Mersea	2	51N47	0E55	-0:03:40
Westminster	1	51N30	0W09	0:00:36
West Moors	1	50N49	1W55	0:07:40
West Norwood	1	51N26	0W06	0:00:24
Weston	1	53N19	2W44	0:10:56
Weston-Super-Mare	1	51N21	2W59	0:11:56
Weston upon Trent	1	52N45	2W02	0:08:08
West Peckham	1	51N15	0E22	-0:01:28
West Sussex	1	50N55	0E35	-0:02:20
West Thurrock	1	51N29	0E16	-0:01:04
West Tilbury	1	51N29	0E24	-0:01:36
Westward Ho!	2	51N02	4W15	0:17:00
West Wellow	1	50N58	1W35	0:06:20
West Wycombe	1	51N39	0W49	0:03:16
West Yorkshire	1	53N45	1W40	0:06:40
Wetherby	1	53N56	1W23	0:05:32
Wetwang	1	54N01	0W34	0:02:16
Weybridge	1	51N23	0W28	0:01:52
Weymouth	5	50N36	2W28	0:09:52
Whaley Bridge	1	53N20	1W59	0:07:56
Whalley	1	53N50	2W24	0:09:36
Whaplode	1	52N48	0W02	0:00:08
Wharles	1	53N49	2W50	0:11:20
Wheathampstead	1	51N49	0W17	0:01:08
Wheatley Hill	1	54N45	1W23	0:05:32
Wheelton	1	53N41	2W36	0:10:24
Whelpleyhill	1	51N44	0W33	0:02:12
Whiddon Down	1	50N43	3W51	0:15:24
Whiston	1	53N25	2W50	0:11:20
Whitby	1	54N29	0W37	0:02:28
Whitby	1	53N17	2W54	0:11:36
Whitchurch	1	51N52	2W39	0:10:36
Whitchurch	1	52N58	2W41	0:10:44
Whitchurch	1	51N53	0W51	0:03:24
Whitchurch	1	51N14	1W20	0:05:20
Whitechapel	1	51N31	0W04	0:00:16
Whitefield	1	53N33	2W18	0:09:12
Whitehaven	1	54N33	3W35	0:14:20
Whiteley Village	1	51N21	0W26	0:01:44
White Roding	1	51N48	0E16	-0:01:04
Whitley Bay	1	55N03	1W25	0:05:40
Whitley Row	1	51N15	0E09	-0:00:36
Whitstable	1	51N22	1E02	-0:04:08
Whittingham	1	55N24	1W54	0:07:36
Whittington	1	52N52	3W00	0:12:00
Whittle-le-Woods	1	53N41	2W38	0:10:32
Whittlesey	1	52N34	0W08	0:00:32
Whitwell	1	50N37	1W16	0:05:04
Whitwick	1	52N44	1W21	0:05:24
Whitworth	1	53N40	2W10	0:08:40
Wickford	2	51N38	0E31	-0:02:04
Wickham	2	50N54	1W10	0:04:40
Wickham Bishops	1	51N47	0E40	-0:02:40
Wickham Market	1	52N09	1E22	-0:05:28
Widecombe in the Moor	1	50N35	3W48	0:15:12
Widemouth Bay	2	50N47	4W32	0:18:08
Widford	2	51N43	0E27	-0:01:48
Widnes	1	53N22	2W44	0:10:56
Wigan	1	53N33	2W38	0:10:32
Wiggington	1	51N47	0W38	0:02:32
Wigglesworth	1	54N01	2W17	0:09:08
Wigmore	1	51N21	0E35	-0:02:20
Wigmore	1	52N19	2W51	0:11:24
Wigston Magna	1	52N36	1W05	0:04:20
Wigton	1	54N49	3W09	0:12:36
Wildboarclough	1	53N13	2W02	0:08:08
Willaston	1	53N18	3W00	0:12:00
Willenhall	2	52N36	2W02	0:08:08
Willerby	1	53N46	0W27	0:01:48
Willingale	1	51N44	0E19	-0:01:16
Willingdon	1	50N47	0E15	-0:01:00
Willingham	2	52N19	0E04	-0:00:16
Willington	1	54N43	1W41	0:06:44
Williton	1	51N10	3W20	0:13:20
Wilmington	1	51N26	0E12	-0:00:48
Wilmslow	1	53N20	2W15	0:09:00
Wilpshire	1	53N47	2W28	0:09:52
Wilshamstead	1	52N05	0W27	0:01:48
Wilton	1	51N05	1W52	0:07:28
Wiltshire	1	51N15	1W50	0:07:20
Wimbledon	1	51N25	0W12	0:00:48
Wimborne Minster	1	50N48	1W59	0:07:56
Wincanton	1	51N04	2W25	0:09:40
Wincham	1	53N16	2W29	0:09:56
Winchcombe	1	51N57	1W58	0:07:52
Winchelsea	1	50N55	0E42	-0:02:48
Winchester	1	51N04	1W19	0:05:16
Winchmore Hill	1	51N39	0W39	0:02:36
Windermere	1	54N23	2W54	0:11:36
Windlesham	1	51N22	0W40	0:02:40
Windsor	1	51N29	0W38	0:02:32
Windsor Castle	1	51N29	0W36	0:02:24
Wingates	1	53N34	2W32	0:10:08
Wingham	1	51N17	1E13	-0:04:52
Winsford	1	53N12	2W32	0:10:08
Winsford	1	51N06	3W33	0:14:12
Winshill	1	52N48	1W36	0:06:24
Winslow	1	51N57	0W54	0:03:36
Winterbourne Abbas	5	50N43	2W34	0:10:16
Winteron-on-Sea	2	52N43	1E42	-0:06:48
Winterton-on-Sea	2	52N43	1E42	-0:06:48
Winwick	1	53N26	2W36	0:10:24
Wisbech	1	52N40	0E10	-0:00:40
Witham	1	51N48	0E38	-0:02:32
Witheridge	1	50N55	3W42	0:14:48
Withernsea	1	53N44	0E02	-0:00:08
Withington Green	1	53N14	2W18	0:09:12
Withnell	1	53N42	2W34	0:10:16
Witley	1	51N09	0W38	0:02:32
Witney	1	51N48	1W29	0:05:56
Wiveliscombe	1	51N03	3W19	0:13:16
Wivenhoe	2	51N52	0E58	-0:03:52
Woburn Sands	1	52N01	0W39	0:02:36
Woking	1	51N20	0W34	0:02:16
Wokingham	1	51N25	0W51	0:03:24
Woldingham	1	51N17	0W02	0:00:08
Wolsingham	1	54N44	1W52	0:07:28
Wolverhampton	2	52N36	2W08	0:08:32
Wolverton	1	52N04	0W50	0:03:20
Wombwell	1	53N31	1W24	0:05:36
Wonersh	1	51N12	0W33	0:02:12
Woodbridge	1	52N06	1E19	-0:05:16
Woodbury	4	50N41	3W24	0:13:36
Woodchurch	1	51N05	0E46	-0:03:04
Woodford	1	53N21	2W10	0:08:40
Woodford Halse	1	52N10	1W12	0:04:48
Woodham	1	51N21	0W30	0:02:00
Woodham Ferrers	1	51N40	0E36	-0:02:24
Woodham Mortimer	1	51N43	0E37	-0:02:28
Woodham Walter	1	51N44	0E37	-0:02:28
Woodley	1	51N28	0W54	0:03:36
Woodmansey	1	53N50	0W29	0:01:56
Woodmansterne	1	51N19	0W10	0:00:40
Woodplumpton	1	53N48	2W47	0:11:08
Woodside	1	51N45	0W11	0:00:44
Woodstock	1	51N52	1W21	0:05:24
Wood Street	1	51N15	0W38	0:02:32
Wool	1	50N41	2W14	0:08:56
Woolacombe	2	51N10	4W13	0:16:52
Wooler	1	55N33	2W01	0:08:04
Woolpit	1	52N13	0E54	-0:03:36
Woolston	1	53N24	2W32	0:10:08
Woolwich	1	51N29	0E05	-0:00:20
Wootton Bassett	1	51N33	1W54	0:07:36
Wootton Wawen	1	52N16	1W47	0:07:08
Worcester	1	52N11	2W13	0:08:52
Workington	1	54N39	3W35	0:14:20
Worksop	1	53N18	1W07	0:04:28
Wormley	1	51N44	0W01	0:00:04
Wormshill	1	51N17	0E42	-0:02:48
Worplesdon	1	51N16	0W37	0:02:28
Worsley	1	53N30	2W23	0:09:32
Worsthorne	1	53N47	2W11	0:08:44
Worthen	1	52N38	3W00	0:12:00
Worthing	1	50N48	0W23	0:01:32
Wotton	1	51N13	0W23	0:01:32
Wotton-under-Edge	1	51N39	2W21	0:09:24
Wouldham	1	51N21	0E28	-0:01:52
Wragby	1	53N18	0W19	0:01:16
Wraysbury	1	51N27	0W33	0:02:12
Wrea Green	1	53N46	2W55	0:11:40
Wrentham	1	52N23	1E40	-0:06:40
Wrightington Bar	1	53N37	2W42	0:10:48
Writtle	2	51N44	0E26	-0:01:44
Wrotham	1	51N19	0E19	-0:01:16
Wrotham Heath	1	51N18	0E21	-0:01:24
Wroughton	1	51N31	1W46	0:07:04
Wroxham	2	52N42	1E24	-0:05:36
Wye	1	51N11	0E56	-0:03:44
Wyke Regis	5	50N36	2W29	0:09:56
Wymondham	1	52N34	1E07	-0:04:28
Yalding	1	51N13	0E26	-0:01:44
Yarcombe	2	50N52	3W05	0:12:20
Yarmouth	1	50N42	1W29	0:05:56
Yarmouth → Great Yarmouth	2	52N37	1E44	-0:06:56
Yate	1	51N32	2W25	0:09:40
Yatton	1	51N24	2W49	0:11:16
Yaxley	1	52N31	0W16	0:01:04
Yeadon	1	53N52	1W41	0:06:44
Yealmpton	1	50N21	3W59	0:15:56
Yelverton	2	50N30	4W05	0:16:20
Yeovil	1	50N57	2W39	0:10:36
Yetminster	1	50N53	2W33	0:10:12
York	1	53N58	1W05	0:04:20

GUINEA ECUATORIAL GUINÉE ÉQUATORIALE EQUATORIAL GUINEA

```
Time Table
Before  1/Jan/1912 LMT
Begin Standard     0W00
1/Jan/1912  0:00  0:00
Begin Standard    15E00
15/Dec/1963  0:00 -1:00
```

Acalayong	1N05	9E40	-0:38:40
Aconibe	1N18	10E56	-0:43:44
Acurenam	1N02	10E40	-0:42:40
Akurenan	1N02	10E40	-0:42:40
Amvamg	1N45	10E29	-0:41:56
Añisoc	1N51	10E46	-0:43:04
Asoc	1N26	11E18	-0:45:12
Ayamiken	2N07	10E01	-0:40:04
Basacato del Este	3N37	8E54	-0:35:36
Bata	1N51	9E45	-0:39:00
Cogo	1N05	9E42	-0:38:48
Concepción	3N23	8E46	-0:35:04
Corisco	0N54	9E20	-0:37:20
Ebebiyín	2N09	11E20	-0:45:20
Esong	2N09	10E58	-0:43:52
Etembue	1N17	9E25	-0:37:40
Evinayong	1N27	10E34	-0:42:16
Ipeia	0N54	9E20	-0:37:20
Kogo	1N05	9E42	-0:38:48
La Concepción	3N23	8E46	-0:35:04
Luba	3N27	8E33	-0:34:12
Malabo	3N45	8E47	-0:35:08
Mbini	1N35	9E37	-0:38:28
Midyobe	1N21	10E18	-0:41:12
Mikomeseng	2N08	10E37	-0:42:28
Mongomo	1N38	11E19	-0:45:16
Ncue	2N01	10E28	-0:41:52
Ndomayop	1N21	10E18	-0:41:12
Niefang	1N50	10E14	-0:40:56
Nsang	2N02	10E56	-0:43:44
Nsok	1N08	11E16	-0:45:04
Riaba	3N23	8E46	-0:35:04
Río Benito	1N35	9E37	-0:38:28
San Carlos	3N27	8E33	-0:34:12
Santa Isabel → Malabo	3N45	8E47	-0:35:08
Senye	1N34	9E50	-0:39:20
Utokota	17S50	20E22	-1:21:28
Utonde	1N56	9E49	-0:39:16

ETHIOPIA ETIOPÍA ABYSSINIA ÄTHIOPIEN YAITOPYA

Time Table # 1
Before 1/Jan/1870 LMT
Begin Standard 38E53
1/Jan/1870 0:00 -2:36
Begin Standard 38E50
1/Jan/1890 0:00 -2:35
Begin Standard 45E00
5/May/1936 0:00 -3:00
....

Time Table # 2
Before 1/Jan/1870 LMT
Begin Standard 37E30
1/Jan/1870 0:00 -2:30
Begin Standard 38E50
1/Jan/1890 0:00 -2:35
Begin Standard 45E00
5/May/1936 0:00 -3:00
....

Time Table # 3
Before 1/Jan/1870 LMT
Begin Standard 38E50
1/Jan/1870 0:00 -2:35
Begin Standard 45E00
5/May/1936 0:00 -3:00
....

Time Table # 4
Before 1/Jan/1870 LMT
Begin Standard 36E50
1/Jan/1870 0:00 -2:27
Begin Standard 38E50
1/Jan/1890 0:00 -2:35
Begin Standard 45E00
5/May/1936 0:00 -3:00
....

Time Table # 5
Before 1/Jan/1870 LMT
Begin Standard 42E08
1/Jan/1870 0:00 -2:49
Begin Standard 38E50
1/Jan/1890 0:00 -2:35
Begin Standard 45E00
5/May/1936 0:00 -3:00
....

Time Table # 6
Before 1/Jan/1870 LMT
Begin Standard 39E41
1/Jan/1870 0:00 -2:39
Begin Standard 38E50
1/Jan/1890 0:00 -2:35
Begin Standard 45E00
5/May/1936 0:00 -3:00

Place	TT	Lat	Long	Offset
Abardeb	4	16N06	37E03	-2:28:12
Abarra	4	5N23	39E58	-2:39:52
Abatimbo el Gumas	2	10N36	35E13	-2:20:52
Abelti	4	8N10	37E34	-2:30:16
Abiy Adi	1	13N26	39E05	-2:36:20
Abu Mendi	2	11N47	35E43	-2:22:52
Adaba	5	7N00	39E24	-2:37:36
Adailo	1	14N29	40E52	-2:43:28
Adami Tulu	3	7N52	38E42	-2:34:48
Adayto	1	14N25	40E53	-2:43:32
Addis Ababa → Adis Abeba	3	9N02	38E42	-2:34:48
Addis Alem	3	9N02	38E23	-2:33:32
Adi Arkay	2	13N27	37E57	-2:31:48
Adi Dairo	1	14N23	38E12	-2:32:48
Adi Daro	1	14N23	38E12	-2:32:48
Adigala	5	10N25	42E14	-2:48:56
Adigrat	1	14N17	39E28	-2:37:52
Adi Keyih	1	14N51	39E22	-2:37:28
Adi Kwala	1	14N38	38E50	-2:35:20
Adis Abeba (Addis Ababa)	3	9N02	38E42	-2:34:48
Adis Dera	3	10N15	38E50	-2:35:20
Adis Zemen	2	12N07	37E47	-2:31:08
Adi Ugri	1	14N53	38E49	-2:35:16
Adowa → Adwa	1	14N10	38E55	-2:35:40
Adwa	1	14N10	38E55	-2:35:40
Afdem	5	9N28	41E00	-2:44:00
Afodo	3	10N14	34E39	-2:18:36
Agaro	4	7N50	36E40	-2:26:40
Agere Hiywet	3	8N56	37E56	-2:31:44
Agordat → Akordat	1	15N33	37E53	-2:31:32
Agulaa	1	13N41	39E35	-2:38:20
Agulai	1	13N41	39E35	-2:38:20
Ajibar	6	10N52	38E40	-2:34:40
Akaki Beseka	3	8N52	38E47	-2:35:08
Akordat	1	15N33	37E53	-2:31:32
Aksum	1	14N08	38E43	-2:34:52
Akyel	2	12N33	37E04	-2:28:16
Alamata	6	12N25	39E33	-2:38:12
Alefa	2	11N57	36E52	-2:27:28
Aleta	2	11N57	36E52	-2:27:28
Algena	1	17N19	38E31	-2:34:04
Amarti	1	14N16	41E10	-2:44:40
Amba Maryam	6	11N26	39E17	-2:37:08
Amino	5	4N31	41E49	-2:47:16
Ankober	3	9N35	39E44	-2:38:56
Arafali	1	15N05	39E45	-2:39:00
Ara Terra	5	6N38	40E57	-2:43:48
Arawa	5	9N55	41E59	-2:47:56
Arba	5	9N01	40E23	-2:41:32
Arba Minch	4	6N02	37E33	-2:30:12
Arero	4	4N45	38E49	-2:35:16
Argedeb	5	6N10	41E10	-2:44:40
Arotali	1	15N02	39E43	-2:38:52
Aruaddin	1	16N15	38E43	-2:34:52
Arwadin	1	16N15	38E43	-2:34:52
Asale	1	14N22	40E32	-2:42:08
Asayita	6	11N33	41E30	-2:46:00
Asbe Teferi	5	9N02	40E58	-2:43:52
Aseb	1	13N00	42E45	-2:51:00
Asela	3	7N59	39E08	-2:36:32
Asendabo	3	9N50	37E33	-2:30:12
Asmara → Asmera	1	15N20	38E53	-2:35:32
Asmera	1	15N20	38E53	-2:35:32
Asosa	3	10N03	34E32	-2:18:08
Assab → Aseb	1	13N00	42E45	-2:51:00
Aual Edo	5	4N14	40E37	-2:42:28
Awal Edo	5	4N14	40E37	-2:42:28
Awara	5	5N30	40E00	-2:40:00
Aware	5	8N15	44E10	-2:56:40
Awasa	4	6N45	38E15	-2:33:00
Awash	3	8N59	40E10	-2:40:40
Aykota	1	15N12	37E05	-2:28:20
Aysha	5	10N46	42E37	-2:50:28
Azezo	2	12N35	37E28	-2:29:52
Babile	5	9N15	42E19	-2:49:16
Bachuma	4	6N48	35E53	-2:23:32
Baden	1	17N00	38E00	-2:32:00
Bahir Dar	2	11N35	37E28	-2:29:52
Bako	4	5N50	36E40	-2:26:40
Bambesi	3	9N45	34E38	-2:18:32
Barachit	1	14N39	39E27	-2:37:48
Bare	5	4N42	42E47	-2:51:08
Barentu	1	15N04	37E37	-2:30:28
Barge	4	6N14	36E58	-2:27:52
Bati	6	11N10	40E02	-2:40:08
Bedele	4	8N33	36E23	-2:25:32
Bedesa	5	8N54	40E47	-2:43:08
Bedeso	5	8N54	40E47	-2:43:08
Begi	3	9N20	34E29	-2:17:56
Beigi	3	9N20	34E29	-2:17:56
Bekoji	3	7N34	39E17	-2:37:08
Bentu Liben	3	8N40	38E28	-2:33:52
Berakit	1	14N39	39E27	-2:37:48
Bete Hor	6	11N37	39E02	-2:36:08
Betor	6	11N37	39E02	-2:36:08
Beylul	1	13N10	42E26	-2:49:44
Bichena	2	10N27	38E12	-2:32:48
Bike	5	9N30	41E18	-2:45:12
Bisha	1	15N28	37E34	-2:30:16
Biyo Keraba	5	10N22	42E37	-2:50:28
Biyo Weraba	5	8N52	42E14	-2:48:56
Bogol Manya	5	4N31	41E32	-2:46:08
Bogol Manyo	5	4N31	41E32	-2:46:08
Bolo	3	8N54	39E27	-2:37:48
Bolo Silase	3	8N54	39E27	-2:37:48
Boneya	4	5N44	37E45	-2:31:00
Bonga	4	7N17	36E15	-2:25:00
Bonneia	4	5N44	37E45	-2:31:00
Borale	5	9N10	42E35	-2:50:20
Bore	4	4N40	37E40	-2:30:40
Boreda	4	6N32	37E48	-2:31:12
Buccurale	5	4N31	42E01	-2:48:04
Bukrale	5	4N31	42E01	-2:48:04
Bulki	4	6N10	36E40	-2:26:40
Bure	4	8N15	35E09	-2:20:36
Burji	4	5N20	37E57	-2:31:48
Busi	5	5N28	44E25	-2:57:40
Busle	5	5N28	44E25	-2:57:40
Butajira	3	8N07	38E22	-2:33:28
Bute Giarti	4	4N33	37E45	-2:31:00
Bute Jarti	4	4N33	37E45	-2:31:00
Cara	4	5N52	37E12	-2:28:48
Chelelektu	4	6N00	38E09	-2:32:36
Chelga	2	12N30	37E04	-2:28:16
Cherelato	4	6N00	38E09	-2:32:36
Cheren → Keren	4	15N46	38E28	-2:33:52
Chitu	4	8N36	37E59	-2:31:56
Dabat	2	12N58	37E48	-2:31:12
Daga Medo	5	7N59	43E01	-2:52:04
Dangila	2	11N16	36E50	-2:27:20
Dangla	2	11N16	36E50	-2:27:20
Daror	5	8N14	44E42	-2:58:48
Dase → Dese	6	11N05	39E41	-2:38:44
Debre Birhan	3	9N40	39E33	-2:38:12
Debre Markos	2	10N20	37E45	-2:31:00
Debre May	2	11N19	37E30	-2:30:00
Debre Tabor	2	11N50	38E05	-2:32:20
Debre Zebit	6	11N50	38E40	-2:34:40
Debre Zeyit	3	8N45	38E59	-2:35:56
Debre Zeyt	3	8N45	38E59	-2:35:56
Dega Ahmedo	5	7N59	43E01	-2:52:04
Dega Werabe	5	8N08	45E22	-3:01:28
Degeh-Bur	5	8N13	43E34	-2:54:16
Degoma	2	12N28	37E37	-2:30:28
Dekemhare	1	15N05	39E02	-2:36:08
Dembecha	2	10N35	37E30	-2:30:00
Dembi	4	8N05	36E27	-2:25:48
Dembi Dolo	3	8N32	34E48	-2:19:12
Denan	5	6N30	43E30	-2:54:00
Deneba	3	9N50	39E09	-2:36:36
Dese	6	11N05	39E41	-2:38:44
Dibi	5	4N13	41E56	-2:47:44
Dibo	5	6N31	41E52	-2:47:28
Dihun	5	7N18	42E42	-2:50:48
Dikumbiya	1	14N47	37E28	-2:29:52
Dila	4	6N21	38E17	-2:33:08
Dima	4	6N16	36E20	-2:25:20
Dime	4	6N16	36E20	-2:25:20
Dire Dawa	5	9N37	41E52	-2:47:28
Dodola	3	7N02	39E07	-2:36:28
Dolo Bay	5	4N12	42E09	-2:48:36
Domo	5	7N54	46E52	-3:07:28
Dukambiya	1	14N47	37E28	-2:29:52
Ed	1	13N52	41E40	-2:46:40
El Der	5	5N07	43E10	-2:52:40
El Dere	5	5N07	43E10	-2:52:40
El Fud	5	7N20	42E50	-2:51:20
El Her	5	5N41	42E21	-2:49:24
El Kere	5	5N51	42E06	-2:48:24
El Kure	5	5N41	42E21	-2:49:24
El Leh	4	3N48	39E48	-2:39:12
El Niybo	4	4N32	39E59	-2:39:56
Erota	1	16N14	37E55	-2:31:40
Eroto	1	16N14	37E55	-2:31:40
Felhit	1	16N43	38E02	-2:32:08
Fenerwa	1	13N06	39E01	-2:36:04
Fiche	3	9N52	38E46	-2:35:04
Fik	5	8N10	42E18	-2:49:12
Filtu	5	5N07	40E39	-2:42:36
Finarwa	1	13N06	39E01	-2:36:04
Fitu	5	5N07	40E39	-2:42:36
Funan Gaba	4	4N25	37E57	-2:31:48
Funyan Goba	4	4N25	37E57	-2:31:48
Gambela	4	8N18	34E37	-2:18:28
Gebilu	5	10N35	41E28	-2:45:52
Geblelu	5	10N35	41E28	-2:45:52
Gecha	4	7N31	35E22	-2:21:28
Gedlegube	5	6N52	45E02	-3:00:08
Gedo	3	8N58	37E27	-2:29:48
Geladi	5	6N57	44E25	-2:57:40
Gelemso	5	8N48	40E35	-2:42:20
Geltsa	4	6N14	37E05	-2:28:20
Gerale	5	6N20	42E32	-2:50:08
Gerlogubi	5	6N52	45E02	-3:00:08
Gewane	5	10N10	40E39	-2:42:36
Gewani	5	10N10	40E39	-2:42:36
Gidami	3	9N58	34E37	-2:18:28
Gidda	3	9N34	35E23	-2:21:32
Gide	3	9N40	35E16	-2:21:04
Gidole	4	5N38	37E30	-2:30:00
Gimbi	3	9N10	35E42	-2:22:48
Ginir	5	7N07	40E46	-2:43:04
Giyon	3	8N30	38E00	-2:32:00
Goba	5	7N02	40E00	-2:40:00
Godere	5	5N05	43E50	-2:55:20
Gogeh	3	8N12	38E27	-2:33:48
Goma	4	8N27	36E52	-2:27:28
Gondar → Gonder	2	12N40	37E30	-2:30:00
Gonder	2	12N40	37E30	-2:30:00
Goradit	2	11N25	38E25	-2:33:40
Gore	4	8N08	35E33	-2:22:12
Gorgora	2	12N13	37E16	-2:29:04
Goro	5	6N56	40E32	-2:42:08
Gorrahei	5	6N37	44E20	-2:57:20
Guba	2	10N16	35E17	-2:21:08
Gulch	1	14N43	36E45	-2:27:00
Guleta	4	6N21	37E10	-2:28:40
Guna	3	8N19	39E51	-2:39:24
Guraferdo	4	6N50	35E06	-2:20:24
Gurgura	5	7N50	41E30	-2:46:00
Gusasale	5	6N30	43E00	-2:52:00
Hamer Koke	4	5N12	36E45	-2:27:00
Hamero Hadad	5	7N34	42E18	-2:49:12
Harar → Harer	5	9N18	42E08	-2:48:32
Harer	5	9N18	42E08	-2:48:32
Hareto	3	9N20	37E06	-2:28:24
Hargele	5	5N20	42E05	-2:48:20
Hawzen	1	13N56	39E28	-2:37:52
Hidilola	5	5N52	43E42	-2:54:48
Horakelifo	5	8N50	43E10	-2:52:40
Horanchia	4	6N35	38E46	-2:35:04
Hosaina	4	7N38	37E52	-2:31:28
Hula	4	6N29	38E34	-2:34:16
Hurso	5	9N38	41E38	-2:46:32
Huwun	5	4N23	40E08	-2:40:32
Idaga Hamus	1	14N12	39E48	-2:39:12
Ijaji	3	8N59	37E13	-2:28:52
Imi	5	6N28	42E18	-2:49:12
Inchini	3	8N48	37E43	-2:30:52
Inda Silase	1	14N05	38E20	-2:33:20
Injibara	2	11N00	36E59	-2:27:56
Jaba	4	6N17	35E12	-2:20:48
Jenya	4	4N12	37E32	-2:30:08
Jijiga	5	9N22	42E47	-2:51:08
Jima	4	7N36	36E50	-2:27:20
Jinjero	4	4N40	36E29	-2:25:56
Kachisi	3	9N39	37E50	-2:31:20
Kafta	2	13N56	37E13	-2:28:52
Kara	4	5N52	37E12	-2:28:48
Karkabet	1	16N13	37E30	-2:30:00
Kebri Dehar	5	6N47	44E17	-2:57:08
Kedada	4	5N20	36E00	-2:24:00
Kelafo	5	5N40	44E20	-2:57:20
Kelam	4	4N48	36E06	-2:24:24
Kela Met	1	16N04	38E43	-2:34:52
Kembolcha	6	11N02	39E43	-2:38:52
Keranyo	4	5N04	38E18	-2:33:12
Keren	1	15N46	38E28	-2:33:52
Kersa	5	9N28	41E53	-2:47:32
Kibre Mengist	4	5N52	39E00	-2:36:00
Kobo	6	12N11	39E33	-2:38:12
Kolme	4	5N17	37E22	-2:29:28
Koma	4	8N27	36E52	-2:27:28
Korahe	5	6N35	44E23	-2:57:32
Korbeta	1	13N03	39E43	-2:38:52
Korem	6	12N30	39E30	-2:38:00
Kosa	4	7N51	36E51	-2:27:24
Kunyo	5	6N17	42E33	-2:50:12
Kwiha	1	13N31	39E32	-2:38:08
Lalibela	6	12N02	39E02	-2:36:08
Lega Hida	5	7N56	41E04	-2:44:16
Lege Hida	5	7N56	41E04	-2:44:16
Lema Shilindi	5	4N55	42E02	-2:48:08
Loma	4	6N55	37E34	-2:30:16
Mai Aini	1	14N47	39E06	-2:36:24
Mai Mefales	1	14N59	38E16	-2:33:04
Maji	4	6N11	35E38	-2:22:32
Makalle → Mekele	1	13N33	39E30	-2:38:00
Massaua → Mesewa	1	15N38	39E28	-2:37:52
Massaua → Mitsiwa	1	15N38	39E28	-2:37:52
Massawa → Mesewa	1	15N38	39E28	-2:37:52
May Ayini	1	14N47	39E06	-2:36:24
Maychew	1	13N02	39E34	-2:38:16
May Nefalis	1	14N59	38E16	-2:33:04
Mechara	5	8N32	40E22	-2:41:28
Mega	4	4N07	38E16	-2:33:04
Megalo	5	6N55	41E48	-2:47:12
Mekdela	6	11N28	39E23	-2:37:32
Mekele	1	13N33	39E30	-2:38:00
Melka Teka	5	6N05	43E08	-2:52:32
Mena	5	6N25	39E51	-2:39:24
Mendi	3	9N50	35E06	-2:20:24
Merewa	4	7N40	37E00	-2:28:00
Mersa Fatma	1	14N55	40E20	-2:41:20

YAITOPYA ÄTHIOPIEN ABYSSINIA ETIOPÍA ETHIOPIA

Place	Zone	Lat	Long	Offset
Mesewa (Massaua)	1	15N38	39E28	-2:37:52
Mesfinto	2	13N20	37E19	-2:29:16
Meslo	5	6N27	39E50	-2:39:20
Metahara	3	8N54	39E55	-2:39:40
Metehara	3	8N54	39E55	-2:39:40
Metema	2	12N57	36E12	-2:24:48
Metu	4	8N20	35E36	-2:22:24
Mieso	5	9N15	40E48	-2:43:12
Mine	5	8N20	40E09	-2:40:36
Mitsiwa (Massawa)	1	15N38	39E28	-2:37:52
Mizan Teferi	4	6N53	35E28	-2:21:52
Mojo	3	8N38	39E07	-2:36:28
Molale	3	10N08	39E42	-2:38:48
Mota	2	11N02	37E52	-2:31:28
Moyale	4	3N30	39E07	-2:36:28
Muja	6	12N02	39E29	-2:37:56
Muke Arba	5	8N57	42E09	-2:48:36
Mustahil	5	5N12	44E17	-2:57:08
Nacchie	5	7N23	40E10	-2:40:40
Nakfa	1	16N43	38E32	-2:34:08
Namoruputh	4	4N34	35E57	-2:23:48
Nazeret	3	8N33	39E16	-2:37:04
Nazret	3	8N33	39E16	-2:37:04
Negele	4	5N20	39E36	-2:38:24
Nejo	3	9N30	35E30	-2:22:00
Nekemte	3	9N02	36E31	-2:26:04
Nigwar	2	13N53	36E32	-2:26:08
Nogara	2	13N53	36E32	-2:26:08
Nono	4	8N32	37E26	-2:29:44
Obbo	4	3N36	38E54	-2:35:36
Obo	4	3N46	38E50	-2:35:20
Obot	4	4N30	37E20	-2:29:20
Om Hajer	1	14N24	36E46	-2:27:04
Pertokar	1	16N59	37E28	-2:29:52
Ramo	5	6N42	41E23	-2:45:32
Remo	5	6N50	41E15	-2:45:00
Renda	1	14N30	39E53	-2:39:32
Rike	3	10N42	39E55	-2:39:40
Robe	3	7N52	39E38	-2:38:32
Robi	3	7N52	39E38	-2:38:32
Sala	1	16N58	37E27	-2:29:48
Samre	1	13N07	39E10	-2:36:40
Sasabeneh	5	7N55	43E39	-2:54:36
Sebderat	1	15N26	36E40	-2:26:40
Segag	5	7N40	42E50	-2:51:20
Segeg	5	7N40	42E50	-2:51:20
Seka	4	8N12	36E55	-2:27:40
Seke	3	9N56	38E19	-2:33:16
Sekota	6	12N38	39E03	-2:36:12
Sela Dingay	3	9N59	39E33	-2:38:12
Sendafa	3	9N07	39E00	-2:36:00
Serdo	6	11N58	41E18	-2:45:12
Seru	3	7N50	40E28	-2:41:52
Shambu	3	9N40	37E03	-2:28:12
Shasha	4	6N20	35E57	-2:23:48
Shashemene	1	7N12	38E43	-2:34:52
Shebele	5	9N43	42E43	-2:50:52
Shehojele	3	10N40	35E09	-2:20:36
Sheikh Hasan	2	12N04	35E53	-2:23:32
Shek Hasan	2	12N04	35E53	-2:23:32
Sherada	4	7N21	36E32	-2:26:08
Shewa Gimira	4	7N00	35E50	-2:23:20
Shilabo	5	6N05	44E48	-2:59:12
Sifani	6	12N16	40E21	-2:41:24
Sifeni	6	12N16	40E21	-2:41:24
Sire	3	9N00	36E55	-2:27:40
Sitona	1	14N28	37E27	-2:29:48
Sodo	4	6N52	37E47	-2:31:08
Suca	5	6N31	39E14	-2:36:56
Sulsul	5	5N06	44E55	-2:59:40
Sululta	3	9N10	38E48	-2:35:12
Suntu	4	8N06	36E57	-2:27:48
Supe	4	8N37	35E38	-2:22:32
Surar	5	7N27	40E57	-2:43:48
Surkole	3	10N25	34E38	-2:18:32
Suwa	1	14N17	41E06	-2:44:24
Tedesa	4	5N07	37E45	-2:31:00
Tendaho	6	11N48	40E52	-2:43:28
Tepi	4	7N10	35E23	-2:21:32
Teseney	1	15N07	36E41	-2:26:44
Tibe	3	9N03	37E08	-2:28:32
Ticho	3	7N50	39E32	-2:38:08
Tifi	4	6N15	37E00	-2:28:00
Tio	1	14N42	40E58	-2:43:52
Tiyo	1	14N42	40E58	-2:43:52
Togochale	5	9N33	43E18	-2:53:12
Tor	4	7N51	33E35	-2:14:20
Tori	4	7N51	33E35	-2:14:20
Trena	5	10N45	40E38	-2:42:32
Tsilmamo	4	6N01	35E17	-2:21:08
Wabera	5	6N26	40E42	-2:42:48
Waka	4	7N07	37E26	-2:29:44
Warder	5	6N58	45E20	-3:01:20
Webera	5	6N26	40E45	-2:43:00
Webera	3	9N39	39E03	-2:36:12
Weberi Bekera	3	9N39	39E03	-2:36:12
Weldiya	6	11N50	39E36	-2:38:24
Weldya	6	11N50	39E36	-2:38:24
Welkite	3	8N15	37E50	-2:31:20
Wendo	4	6N38	38E27	-2:33:48
Werder	5	6N58	45E20	-3:01:20
Were Ilu	6	10N37	39E28	-2:37:52
Wono	4	8N32	37E26	-2:29:44
Yabelo	4	4N54	38E05	-2:32:20
Yet	5	4N48	43E02	-2:52:08
Yifag	2	12N02	37E44	-2:30:56
Yirba Moda	4	6N12	38E42	-2:34:48
Yirba Muda	4	6N12	38E42	-2:34:48
Yirga Alem	4	6N52	38E22	-2:33:28
Yubdo	3	9N00	35E22	-2:21:28
Zala	4	6N28	37E20	-2:29:20
Zege	2	11N42	37E23	-2:29:32
Zeyse	4	5N46	37E22	-2:29:28
Zula	1	15N11	39E41	-2:38:44

FØROYAR FÄRÖER ÎLES FÉROÉ ISLAS FEROE FAEROE ISLANDS

Time Table

Before 11/Jan/1908 LMT

Begin Standard 0w00

Date	Time	Offset
11/Jan/1908	0:00	0:00
29/Mar/1981	1:00	-1:00
27/Sep/1981	2:00	0:00
28/Mar/1982	1:00	-1:00
26/Sep/1982	2:00	0:00
27/Mar/1983	1:00	-1:00
25/Sep/1983	2:00	0:00
25/Mar/1984	1:00	-1:00
30/Sep/1984	2:00	0:00
31/Mar/1985	1:00	-1:00
29/Sep/1985	2:00	0:00
30/Mar/1986	1:00	-1:00
28/Sep/1986	2:00	0:00
29/Mar/1987	1:00	-1:00
27/Sep/1987	2:00	0:00
27/Mar/1988	1:00	-1:00
25/Sep/1988	2:00	0:00
26/Mar/1989	1:00	-1:00
24/Sep/1989	2:00	0:00
25/Mar/1990	1:00	-1:00
30/Sep/1990	2:00	0:00
31/Mar/1991	1:00	-1:00
29/Sep/1991	2:00	0:00
29/Mar/1992	1:00	-1:00
27/Sep/1992	2:00	0:00
28/Mar/1993	1:00	-1:00
26/Sep/1993	2:00	0:00
27/Mar/1994	1:00	-1:00
25/Sep/1994	2:00	0:00
26/Mar/1995	1:00	-1:00
24/Sep/1995	2:00	0:00
31/Mar/1996	1:00	-1:00
29/Sep/1996	2:00	0:00
30/Mar/1997	1:00	-1:00
28/Sep/1997	2:00	0:00
29/Mar/1998	1:00	-1:00
27/Sep/1998	2:00	0:00
28/Mar/1999	1:00	-1:00
26/Sep/1999	2:00	0:00
26/Mar/2000	1:00	-1:00
24/Sep/2000	2:00	0:00

Place	Lat	Long	Offset
Thorshavn → Tőrshavn	62N01	6w46	0:27:04
Tőrshavn	62N01	6w46	0:27:04
Vaag	61N29	6w49	0:27:16

ISLAS MALVINAS FALKLAND-INSELN ÎLES FALKLAND FALKLAND ISLANDS

Time Table

Before 1/Jan/1890 LMT

Date	Time	Offset
Begin Standard		57w50
1/Jan/1890	0:00	3:51
Begin Standard		60w00
12/Mar/1912	0:00	4:00
26/Sep/1937	0:00	3:00
20/Mar/1938	0:00	4:00
25/Sep/1938	0:00	3:00
19/Mar/1939	0:00	4:00
1/Oct/1939	0:00	3:00
24/Mar/1940	0:00	4:00
29/Sep/1940	0:00	3:00
23/Mar/1941	0:00	4:00
28/Sep/1941	0:00	3:00
22/Mar/1942	0:00	4:00
27/Sep/1942	0:00	3:00
1/Jan/1943	0:00	4:00
Begin Standard		45w00
1/May/1983	0:00	3:00
25/Sep/1983	0:00	2:00
29/Apr/1984	0:00	3:00
16/Sep/1984	0:00	2:00
28/Apr/1985	0:00	3:00
Begin Standard		60w00
15/Sep/1985	0:00	3:00
20/Apr/1986	0:00	4:00
14/Sep/1986	0:00	3:00
19/Apr/1987	0:00	4:00
13/Sep/1987	0:00	3:00
17/Apr/1988	0:00	4:00
11/Sep/1988	0:00	3:00
16/Apr/1989	0:00	4:00
10/Sep/1989	0:00	3:00
22/Apr/1990	0:00	4:00
9/Sep/1990	0:00	3:00
21/Apr/1991	0:00	4:00

Place	Lat	Long	Offset
Darwin	51s50	58w58	3:55:52
Port Albemarle	52s11	60w26	4:01:44
Port Edgar	52s00	60w14	4:00:56
Port Louis	51s33	58w10	3:52:40
Port Stanley → Stanley	51s42	57w51	3:51:24
San Carlos	51s30	58w59	3:55:56
Stanley	51s42	57w51	3:51:24

FIJI FIDSCHI FIDJI

Time Table
Before 26/Oct/1915 LMT
Begin Standard 180E00

Date	Time	Offset
26/Oct/1915	0:00	-12:00

DIVISIONS

1. Kandavu
2. Lau Group
3. Ono-I-Lau
4. Rotuma
5. Taveuni
6. Vanua Levu
7. Vanua Mbalavu
8. Vita Levu

Place	Lat	Long	LMT
Kandavu Island 1	19S03	178E13	-11:52:52
Keiyasi 8	17S54	177E45	-11:51:00
Korolevu 8	18S13	177E44	-11:50:56
Korovou 8	17S57	178E21	-11:53:24
Lambasa 6	16S26	179E24	-11:57:36
Lau Group 2	18S20	178W30	11:54:00
Lautoka 8	17S37	177E27	-11:49:48
Levuka 8	17S41	178E50	-11:55:20
Lomaloma 7	17S17	178W59	11:55:56
Mba 8	17S33	177E41	-11:50:44
Mbua 6	16S48	178E37	-11:54:28
Mbutha 6	16S39	179E50	-11:59:20
Momi 8	17S55	177E17	-11:49:08
Nadi 8	17S48	177E25	-11:49:40
Nambouwalu 6	16S59	178E42	-11:54:48
Nandarivatu 8	17S34	177E58	-11:51:52
Nandi 8	17S48	177E25	-11:49:40
Nanduri 6	16S27	179E09	-11:56:36
Nausori 8	18S02	175E32	-11:42:08
Navua 8	18S14	178E10	-11:52:40
Ono-i-Lau Island 3	20S39	178W42	11:54:48
Rotuma Island 4	12S30	177E05	-11:48:20
Savusavu 6	16S16	179E21	-11:57:24
Singatoka 8	18S08	177E30	-11:50:00
Somosomo 5	16S46	179W58	11:59:52
Suva 8	18S08	178E25	-11:53:40
Taveuni Island 5	16S51	179W58	11:59:52
Tavua 8	17S27	177E51	-11:51:24
Vaileka 8	17S23	178E09	-11:52:36
Vanua Levu Island 6	16S33	179E15	-11:57:00
Vanua Mbalavu Island 7	17S40	178W57	11:55:48
Vatukoula 8	17S31	177E51	-11:51:24
Viti Levu Island 8	18S00	178E00	-11:52:00
Vunindawa 8	17S49	178E19	-11:53:16
Vunisea 1	19S03	178E09	-11:52:36
Vunisea Station 1	19S03	178E09	-11:52:36

FINLAND FINLANDIA FINLANDE FINNLAND SUOMI

Time Table
Before 31/May/1878 LMT
Begin Standard 24E58

Date	Time	Offset
31/May/1878	0:00	-1:40
Begin Standard 30E00		
1/May/1921	0:00	-2:00
3/Apr/1942	0:00	-3:00
3/Oct/1942	0:00	-2:00
29/Mar/1981	2:00	-3:00
27/Sep/1981	3:00	-2:00
28/Mar/1982	2:00	-3:00
26/Sep/1982	3:00	-2:00
27/Mar/1983	2:00	-3:00
25/Sep/1983	3:00	-2:00
25/Mar/1984	2:00	-3:00
30/Sep/1984	3:00	-2:00
31/Mar/1985	2:00	-3:00
29/Sep/1985	3:00	-2:00
30/Mar/1986	2:00	-3:00
28/Sep/1986	3:00	-2:00
29/Mar/1987	2:00	-3:00
27/Sep/1987	3:00	-2:00
27/Mar/1988	2:00	-3:00
25/Sep/1988	3:00	-2:00
26/Mar/1989	2:00	-3:00
24/Sep/1989	3:00	-2:00
25/Mar/1990	2:00	-3:00
30/Sep/1990	3:00	-2:00
31/Mar/1991	2:00	-3:00
29/Sep/1991	3:00	-2:00
29/Mar/1992	2:00	-3:00
27/Sep/1992	3:00	-2:00
28/Mar/1993	2:00	-3:00
26/Sep/1993	3:00	-2:00
27/Mar/1994	2:00	-3:00
25/Sep/1994	3:00	-2:00
26/Mar/1995	2:00	-3:00
24/Sep/1995	3:00	-2:00
31/Mar/1996	2:00	-3:00
29/Sep/1996	3:00	-2:00
30/Mar/1997	2:00	-3:00
28/Sep/1997	3:00	-2:00
29/Mar/1998	2:00	-3:00
27/Sep/1998	3:00	-2:00
28/Mar/1999	2:00	-3:00
26/Sep/1999	3:00	-2:00
26/Mar/2000	2:00	-3:00
24/Sep/2000	3:00	-2:00

Place	Lat	Long	LMT
Äänekoski	62N36	25E44	-1:42:56
Åbo → Turku	60N27	22E17	-1:29:08
Ähtäri	62N34	24E06	-1:36:24
Alahärmä	63N14	22E51	-1:31:24
Alajärvi	63N00	23E49	-1:35:16
Alastaro	60N56	22E55	-1:31:40
Alavieska	64N10	24E18	-1:37:12
Alavus	62N35	23E37	-1:34:28
Ämmänsaari	64N53	28E55	-1:55:40
Aulanko	61N02	24E27	-1:37:48
Aura	60N36	22E34	-1:30:16
Björköby	63N21	21E19	-1:25:16
Björneborg → Pori	61N29	21E47	-1:27:08
Bomarsund	60N13	20E15	-1:21:00
Borgå (Porvoo)	60N24	25E40	-1:42:40
Dalsbruk (Taalintehdas)	60N02	22E31	-1:30:04
Degerby	60N02	20E23	-1:21:32
Ekenäs (Taamisaari)	59N58	23E26	-1:33:44
Eno	62N48	30E09	-2:00:36
Enontekiö	68N23	23E38	-1:34:32
Esbo → Espoo	60N13	24E40	-1:38:40
Espoo (Esbo)	60N13	24E40	-1:38:40
Evijärvi	63N22	23E29	-1:33:56
Forsby	60N30	25E56	-1:43:44
Forssa	60N49	23E38	-1:34:32
Friitala	61N26	21E52	-1:27:28
Gamlakarleby → Kokkola	63N50	23E07	-1:32:28
Geta	60N23	19E50	-1:19:20
Grankulla (Kauniainen)	60N13	24E45	-1:39:00
Haapajärvi	63N45	25E20	-1:41:20
Haapamäki	62N15	24E28	-1:37:52
Haapavesi	64N08	25E22	-1:41:28
Hailuoto	65N00	24E43	-1:38:52
Hämeenkylä	60N16	24E47	-1:39:08
Hämeenlinna	61N00	24E27	-1:37:48
Hamina	60N34	27E12	-1:48:48
Hangö (Hanko)	59N50	22E57	-1:31:48
Hankasalmi	62N23	26E26	-1:45:44
Hanko → Hangö	59N50	22E57	-1:31:48
Harjavalta	61N19	22E08	-1:28:32
Hartola	61N35	26E01	-1:44:04
Haukipudas	65N11	25E21	-1:41:24
Haukivuori	62N01	27E13	-1:48:52
Heinävesi	62N26	28E36	-1:54:24
Heinola	61N13	26E02	-1:44:08
Helsingfors → Helsinki	60N10	24E58	-1:39:52
Helsinki (Helsingfors)	60N10	24E58	-1:39:52
Himanka	64N04	23E39	-1:34:36
Hinnerjoki	61N00	22E00	-1:28:00
Huittinen (Lauttakylä)	61N11	22E42	-1:30:48
Humppila	60N56	23E22	-1:33:28
Hyrynsalmi	64N40	28E32	-1:54:08
Hyvinge → Hyvinkää	60N38	24E52	-1:39:28
Hyvinkää	60N38	24E52	-1:39:28
Ii	65N19	25E22	-1:41:28
Iisalmi	63N34	27E11	-1:48:44
Iisvesi	62N40	27E02	-1:48:08
Iittala	61N04	24E10	-1:36:40
Ikaalinen	61N46	23E03	-1:32:12
Ilmajoki	62N44	22E34	-1:30:16
Ilomantsi	62N40	30E55	-2:03:40
Imatra	61N10	28E46	-1:55:04
Inari	68N54	27E01	-1:48:04
Inkeroinen	60N42	26E51	-1:47:24
Isojoki	62N07	21E58	-1:27:52
Isokyrö	63N00	22E19	-1:29:16
Ivalo	68N42	27E30	-1:50:00
Jakobstad (Pietarsaari)	63N40	22E42	-1:30:48
Jalasjärvi	62N30	22E45	-1:31:00
Jämsä	61N52	25E12	-1:40:48
Jämsänkoski	61N55	25E11	-1:40:44
Järvelä	60N52	25E17	-1:41:08
Järvenpää	60N28	25E06	-1:40:24
Jepua (Jeppo)	63N24	22E37	-1:30:28
Joensuu	62N36	29E46	-1:59:04
Jokioinen	60N49	23E28	-1:33:52
Joroinen	62N11	27E50	-1:51:20
Joutsa	61N44	26E07	-1:44:28
Joutseno	61N06	28E30	-1:54:00
Joutsijärvi	66N40	28E00	-1:52:00
Juankoski	63N04	28E21	-1:53:24
Jurva	62N41	21E59	-1:27:56
Juupajoki	61N47	24E27	-1:37:48
Juva	61N54	27E51	-1:51:24
Jyväskylä	62N14	25E44	-1:42:56
Kaavi	62N59	28E30	-1:54:00
Kajaani	64N14	27E41	-1:50:44
Kakisalmi	61N02	30E08	-2:00:32
Kalajoki	64N15	23E57	-1:35:48
Kälviä	63N52	23E26	-1:33:44
Kangasala	61N28	24E05	-1:36:20
Kangasniemi	61N59	26E38	-1:46:32
Kankaanpää	61N48	22E25	-1:29:40
Kannonkoski	62N58	25E15	-1:41:00
Kannus	63N54	23E54	-1:35:36
Karhula	60N31	26E57	-1:47:48
Karigasniemi	69N24	25E50	-1:43:20
Karis (Karjaa)	60N05	23E40	-1:34:40
Karjaa → Karis	60N05	23E40	-1:34:40
Karkkila	60N32	24E11	-1:36:44
Karkku	61N25	23E01	-1:32:04
Kärsämäki	63N58	25E46	-1:43:04
Karstula	62N52	24E47	-1:39:08
Karttula	62N53	26E58	-1:47:52
Karunki	66N02	24E01	-1:36:04
Kaskinen → Kaskö	62N23	21E13	-1:24:52
Kaskö (Kaskinen)	62N23	21E13	-1:24:52
Kastelholm	60N14	20E04	-1:20:16
Kauhajoki	62N26	22E11	-1:28:44
Kauhava	63N06	23E05	-1:32:20
Kauliranta	66N27	23E41	-1:34:44
Kauniainen → Grankulla	60N13	24E45	-1:39:00
Kausala	60N54	26E22	-1:45:28
Kaustinen	63N32	23E42	-1:34:48
Kauttua	61N06	22E10	-1:28:40
Keitele	63N11	26E22	-1:45:28
Kelloselkä	66N56	28E50	-1:55:20
Kelottijärvi	68N31	22E04	-1:28:16
Kemi	65N49	24E32	-1:38:08
Kemie	62N14	30E20	-2:01:20
Kemijärvi	66N40	27E25	-1:49:40
Kemiö → Kimito	60N10	22E45	-1:31:00
Kempele	64N55	25E30	-1:42:00
Kerava	60N24	25E07	-1:40:28
Kerimäki	61N55	29E17	-1:57:08
Kesälahti	61N54	29E50	-1:59:20
Kestilä	64N21	26E17	-1:45:08
Keuruu	62N16	24E42	-1:38:48
Kihniö	62N12	23E11	-1:32:44
Killinkoski	62N24	23E52	-1:35:28
Kilpisjärvi	69N03	20E48	-1:23:12
Kimito (Kemiö)	60N10	22E45	-1:31:00
Kinnula	63N22	24E58	-1:39:52
Kirkkonummi → Kyrkslätt	60N07	24E26	-1:37:44
Kitee	62N06	30E09	-2:00:36
Kittilä	67N40	24E54	-1:39:36
Kiuruvesi	63N39	26E37	-1:46:28
Kivijärvi	63N04	25E03	-1:40:12
Kokemäki	61N15	22E21	-1:29:24
Kokkola (Gamlakarleby)	63N50	23E07	-1:32:28
Kolari	67N20	23E48	-1:35:12
Kolho	62N08	24E31	-1:38:04
Konginkangas	62N46	25E48	-1:43:12
Kontiolahti	62N46	29E51	-1:59:24
Kontiomäki	64N21	28E09	-1:52:36
Korpilahti	62N01	25E33	-1:42:12
Korpo (Korppoo)	60N10	21E34	-1:26:16
Korsnäs	62N47	21E12	-1:24:48
Korso	60N21	25E06	-1:40:24
Koski	60N39	23E09	-1:32:36
Kotka	60N28	26E55	-1:47:40
Kouvola	60N52	26E42	-1:46:48
Kristiinankaupunki → Kristinestad	62N17	21E23	-1:25:32
Kristinestad (Kristiinankau-Punki)	62N17	21E23	-1:25:32
Kronoby (Kruunupyy)	63N43	23E02	-1:32:08
Kruunupyy → Kronoby	63N43	23E02	-1:32:08
Kuhmo	64N08	29E31	-1:58:04
Kuhmoinen	61N34	25E11	-1:40:44
Kuivaniemi	65N35	25E11	-1:40:44
Kukkola	65N59	24E04	-1:36:16
Kulju	61N23	23E46	-1:35:04
Kuopio	62N54	27E41	-1:50:44
Kuortane	62N48	23E30	-1:34:00

Place	Lat	Long	Time
Kurenalus	65N21	26E59	-1:47:56
Kurikka	62N37	22E25	-1:29:40
Kuru	61N52	23E44	-1:34:56
Kuttura	68N24	26E28	-1:45:52
Kuttusoja	67N46	28E50	-1:55:20
Kuusamo	65N58	29E11	-1:56:44
Kuusankoski	60N54	26E38	-1:46:32
Kyrkslätt (Kirkkonummi)	60N07	24E26	-1:37:44
Kyrö	60N42	22E45	-1:31:00
Kyröskoski	61N40	23E11	-1:32:44
Kyyjärvi	63N02	24E34	-1:38:16
Lahti	60N58	25E40	-1:42:40
Laihia	62N58	22E01	-1:28:04
Laitila	60N53	21E41	-1:26:44
Lammi	61N05	25E01	-1:40:04
Lampinsaari	64N25	25E09	-1:40:36
Långnäs	60N06	20E17	-1:21:08
Länkipohja	61N44	24E48	-1:39:12
Lapinjärvi (Lappträsk)	60N38	26E13	-1:44:52
Lapinlahti	63N22	27E24	-1:49:36
Lappajärvi	63N12	23E38	-1:34:32
Lappeenranta	61N04	28E11	-1:52:44
Lappfjärd (Lapväärtti)	62N15	21E32	-1:26:08
Lappi	61N06	21E50	-1:27:20
Lappträsk → Lapinjärvi	60N38	26E13	-1:44:52
Lapua	62N57	23E00	-1:32:00
Lapväärtti → Lappfjärd	62N15	21E32	-1:26:08
Laukaa	62N25	25E57	-1:43:48
Lauritsala	61N04	28E16	-1:53:04
Lauttakylä → Huittinen	61N11	22E42	-1:30:48
Lavia	61N36	22E36	-1:30:24
Lehtimäki	62N47	23E55	-1:35:40
Lempäälä	61N19	23E45	-1:35:00
Leppävirta	62N29	27E47	-1:51:08
Lestijärvi	63N32	24E39	-1:38:36
Lieksa	63N19	30E01	-2:00:04
Lillby	63N28	23E00	-1:32:00
Liminka	64N49	25E24	-1:41:36
Liperi	62N32	29E22	-1:57:28
Lohiniva	67N10	24E58	-1:39:52
Lohja	60N15	24E05	-1:36:20
Loimaa	60N51	23E03	-1:32:12
Lokka	67N49	27E44	-1:50:56
Loppi	60N43	24E27	-1:37:48
Loviisa → Lovisa	60N27	26E14	-1:44:56
Lovisa (Loviisa)	60N27	26E14	-1:44:56
Luhanka	61N47	25E42	-1:42:48
Maaninka	63N09	27E18	-1:49:12
Maarianhamina → Mariehamn	60N06	19E57	-1:19:48
Mänttä	62N02	24E38	-1:38:32
Mäntyharju	61N25	26E53	-1:47:32
Mäntyluoto	61N35	21E29	-1:25:56
Mariehamn	60N06	19E57	-1:19:48
Martinniemi	65N13	25E18	-1:41:12
Martti	67N28	28E28	-1:53:52
Masku	60N34	22E06	-1:28:24
Mätäsvaara	63N26	29E36	-1:58:24
Meltaus	66N54	25E22	-1:41:28
Merikarvia	61N51	21E30	-1:26:00
Mikkeli	61N41	27E15	-1:49:00
Muhola	63N20	25E05	-1:40:20
Muhos	64N48	25E59	-1:43:56
Multia	62N25	24E47	-1:39:08
Muonio	67N57	23E42	-1:34:48
Myllykoski	60N47	26E48	-1:47:12
Myllymäki	62N32	24E17	-1:37:08
Mynämäki	60N40	22E00	-1:28:00
Myrskylä (Mörskom)	60N40	25E51	-1:43:24
Naantali	60N27	22E02	-1:28:08
Närpes (Närpiö)	62N28	21E20	-1:25:20
Närpiö → Närpes	62N28	21E20	-1:25:20
Niinisalo	61N50	22E29	-1:29:56
Nilsiä	63N12	28E05	-1:52:20
Nivala	63N55	24E58	-1:39:52
Nokia	61N28	23E30	-1:34:00
Noormarkku	61N35	21E52	-1:27:28
Nurmes	63N33	29E07	-1:56:28
Nurmijärvi	60N28	24E48	-1:39:12
Nykarleby → Uusikaarlepyy	63N32	22E32	-1:30:08
Nyslott → Savonlinna	61N52	28E53	-1:55:32
Nystad → Uusikaupunki	60N48	21E25	-1:25:40
Oravainen → Oravais	63N18	22E23	-1:29:32
Oravais (Oravainen)	63N18	22E23	-1:29:32
Orimattila	60N48	25E45	-1:43:00
Oripää	60N51	22E41	-1:30:44
Orivesi	61N41	24E21	-1:37:24
Otanmäki	64N07	27E06	-1:48:24
Otava	61N39	27E04	-1:48:16
Oulainen	64N16	24E48	-1:39:12
Oulu	65N01	25E28	-1:41:52
Outokumpu	62N44	29E01	-1:56:04
övermark (Ylimarkku)	62N38	21E30	-1:26:00
Padasjoki	61N21	25E17	-1:41:08
Paimio	60N27	22E42	-1:30:48
Pälkäne	61N20	24E16	-1:37:04
Palojoensuu	68N17	23E05	-1:32:20
Paltamo	64N25	27E50	-1:51:20
Pankakoski	63N19	30E09	-2:00:36
Parainen → Pargas	60N18	22E18	-1:29:12
Pargas (Parainen)	60N18	22E18	-1:29:12
Parikkala	61N33	29E30	-1:58:00
Parkano	62N01	23E01	-1:32:04
Pehula	61N17	22E42	-1:30:48
Pelkosenniemi	67N07	27E30	-1:50:00
Pello	66N47	24E00	-1:36:00
Peräseinäjoki	62N34	23E04	-1:32:16
Perho	63N13	24E25	-1:37:40
Perniö	60N12	23E08	-1:32:32
Petäjävesi	62N15	25E12	-1:40:48
Petsamo	69N33	31E15	-2:05:00
Pieksämäki	62N18	27E08	-1:48:32
Pielavesi	63N14	26E45	-1:47:00
Pietarsaari → Jakobstad	63N40	22E42	-1:30:48
Pihlava	61N33	21E36	-1:26:24
Pihtipudas	63N23	25E34	-1:42:16
Piikkiö	60N26	22E31	-1:30:04
Piippola	64N10	25E58	-1:43:52
Pirttikylä → Pörtom	62N42	21E37	-1:26:28
Polvijärvi	62N51	29E22	-1:57:28
Pomarkku	61N42	22E00	-1:28:00
Pori	61N29	21E47	-1:27:08
Porkkala	59N59	24E26	-1:37:44
Porokylä	63N33	29E06	-1:56:24
Pörtom (Pirttikylä)	62N42	21E37	-1:26:28
Porvoo → Borgå	60N24	25E40	-1:42:40
Posio	66N06	28E09	-1:52:36
Puhos	62N05	29E54	-1:59:36
Pulkkila	64N16	25E52	-1:43:28
Punkalaidun	61N07	23E06	-1:32:24
Puolanka	64N52	27E40	-1:50:40
Puumala	61N32	28E11	-1:52:44
Pyhäjoki	64N28	24E14	-1:36:56
Pyhäsalmi	63N41	25E59	-1:43:56
Pyhäselkä	62N26	29E58	-1:59:52
Pyhtää (Pyttis)	60N29	26E32	-1:46:08
Pyttis → Pyhtää	60N29	26E32	-1:46:08
Raahe	64N41	24E29	-1:37:56
Rääkkylä	62N19	29E37	-1:58:28
Raja-Jooseppi	68N28	28E21	-1:53:24
Rajamäki	60N32	24E45	-1:39:00
Rantasalmi	62N04	28E18	-1:53:12
Rantsila	64N31	25E39	-1:42:36
Ranua	65N55	26E32	-1:46:08
Raseborg	59N59	23E39	-1:34:36
Rauma	61N08	21E30	-1:26:00
Rautalampi	62N38	26E50	-1:47:20
Rautavaara	63N29	28E18	-1:53:12
Reisjärvi	63N37	24E54	-1:39:36
Renko	60N54	24E17	-1:37:08
Reposaari	61N37	21E27	-1:25:48
Riihimäki	60N45	24E46	-1:39:04
Ristiina	61N30	27E16	-1:49:04
Ristijärvi	64N44	28E24	-1:53:36
Rovaniemi	66N34	25E48	-1:43:12
Ruokolahti	61N17	28E50	-1:55:20
Ruovesi	61N59	24E05	-1:36:20
Ruukki	64N40	25E06	-1:40:24
Saarijärvi	62N43	25E16	-1:41:04
Säkylä	61N02	22E20	-1:29:20
Salo	60N23	23E08	-1:32:32
Sankt Michel → Mikkeli	61N41	27E15	-1:49:00
Säräisniemi	64N27	26E47	-1:47:08
Sauvo	60N21	22E42	-1:30:48
Savitaipale	61N12	27E42	-1:50:48
Savonlinna	61N52	28E53	-1:55:32
Savonranta	62N11	29E12	-1:56:48
Säynätsalo	62N08	25E46	-1:43:04
Seinäjoki	62N47	22E50	-1:31:20
Sevettijärvi	69N26	28E38	-1:54:32
Sibbo	60N22	25E16	-1:41:04
Siilinjärvi	63N05	27E40	-1:50:40
Simpele	61N26	29E22	-1:57:28
Skaftung	62N07	21E22	-1:25:28
Sodankylä	67N29	26E32	-1:46:08
Soini	62N52	24E13	-1:36:52
Somero	60N37	23E32	-1:34:08
Sorsakoski	62N27	27E39	-1:50:36
Sotkamo	64N08	28E25	-1:53:40
Storby	60N13	19E34	-1:18:16
Sukeva	63N52	27E26	-1:49:44
Sulkava	61N47	28E23	-1:53:32
Suolahti	62N34	25E52	-1:43:28
Suomussalmi	64N53	29E05	-1:56:20
Suonenjoki	62N37	27E08	-1:48:32
Sysmä	61N30	25E41	-1:42:44
Taalintehdas → Dalsbruk	60N02	22E31	-1:30:04
Taavetti	60N55	27E34	-1:50:16
Taivalkoski	65N34	28E15	-1:53:00
Tammerfors → Tampere	61N30	23E45	-1:35:00
Tammisaari → Ekenäs	59N58	23E26	-1:33:44
Tampere	61N30	23E45	-1:35:00
Tannila	65N29	25E59	-1:43:56
Tavastehus → Hämeenlinna	61N00	24E27	-1:37:48
Teerijärvi → Terjärv	63N32	23E30	-1:34:00
Terjärv (Teerijärvi)	63N32	23E30	-1:34:00
Tervakoski	60N48	24E37	-1:38:28
Tervola	66N05	24E48	-1:39:12
Teuva	62N29	21E44	-1:26:56
Tiojala	61N10	23E52	-1:35:28
Toholampi	63N46	24E15	-1:37:00
Toijala	61N10	23E52	-1:35:28
Tornio	65N51	24E08	-1:36:32
Turenki	60N55	24E38	-1:38:32
Turku (Åbo)	60N27	22E17	-1:29:08
Tuupovaara	62N29	30E36	-2:02:24
Tuusniemi	62N49	28E30	-1:54:00
Uimaharju	62N55	30E15	-2:01:00
Uleåborg → Oulu	65N01	25E28	-1:41:52
Urjala	61N05	23E32	-1:34:08
Utajärvi	64N45	26E23	-1:45:32
Utsjoki	69N53	27E00	-1:48:00
Uusikaarlepyy (Nykarleby)	63N32	22E32	-1:30:08
Uusikaupunki (Nystad)	60N48	21E25	-1:25:40
Vaajakoski	62N16	25E54	-1:43:36
Vääksy	61N11	25E33	-1:42:12
Vaala	64N26	26E48	-1:47:12
Vaanta (Vanda)	60N16	25E03	-1:40:12
Vaasa (Vasa)	63N06	21E36	-1:26:24
Valkeakoski	61N16	24E02	-1:36:08
Valtimo	63N40	28E48	-1:55:12
Vammala	61N20	22E54	-1:31:36
Vanda → Vaanta	60N16	25E03	-1:40:12
Varkaus	62N19	27E55	-1:51:40
Varpaisjärvi	63N22	27E45	-1:51:00
Värtsilä	62N15	30E40	-2:02:40
Vasa → Vaasa	63N06	21E36	-1:26:24
Vesanto	62N56	26E25	-1:45:40
Vieremä	63N45	27E01	-1:48:04
Vierumäki	61N06	25E57	-1:43:48
Vihanti	64N29	25E00	-1:40:00
Vihti	60N25	24E20	-1:37:20
Viiala	61N13	23E47	-1:35:08
Viinijärvi	62N39	29E14	-1:56:56
Viitasaari	63N04	25E52	-1:43:28
Vikajärvi	66N37	26E12	-1:44:48
Villmanstrand → Lappeenranta	61N04	28E11	-1:52:44
Vilppula	62N01	24E31	-1:38:04
Vimpeli	63N09	23E48	-1:35:12
Virkkala	60N12	24E01	-1:36:04
Virojoki	60N35	27E42	-1:50:48
Virrat	62N14	23E47	-1:35:08
Virtaniemi	68N53	28E27	-1:53:48
Voikkaa	60N56	26E37	-1:46:28
Vörå (Vöyri)	63N09	22E15	-1:29:00
Vöyri → Vörå	63N09	22E15	-1:29:00
Vuohijärvi	61N05	26E48	-1:47:12
Vuoksenniska	61N13	28E49	-1:55:16
Vuotso	68N08	27E08	-1:48:32
Yläne	60N53	22E55	-1:31:40
Ylihärmä	63N09	22E47	-1:31:08
Ylimarkku → övermark	62N38	21E30	-1:26:00
Ylistaro	62N57	22E31	-1:30:04
Ylivieska	64N05	24E33	-1:38:12
Ylöjärvi	61N33	23E36	-1:34:24

FRANCE FRANKREICH FRANCIA

Time Table # 1
Before 15/Mar/1891 LMT
Begin Standard 2E20
15/Mar/1891 0:01 -0:09
Begin Standard 0W00
11/Mar/1911 0:00 0:00
14/Jun/1916 23:00 -1:00
1/Oct/1916 24:00 0:00
24/Mar/1917 23:00 -1:00
7/Oct/1917 24:00 0:00
9/Mar/1918 23:00 -1:00
6/Oct/1918 24:00 0:00
1/Mar/1919 23:00 -1:00
5/Oct/1919 24:00 0:00
14/Feb/1920 23:00 -1:00
23/Oct/1920 24:00 0:00
14/Mar/1921 23:00 -1:00
25/Oct/1921 24:00 0:00
25/Mar/1922 23:00 -1:00
7/Oct/1922 24:00 0:00
26/May/1923 23:00 -1:00
6/Oct/1923 24:00 0:00
29/Mar/1924 23:00 -1:00
4/Oct/1924 24:00 0:00
4/Apr/1925 23:00 -1:00
3/Oct/1925 24:00 0:00
17/Apr/1926 23:00 -1:00
2/Oct/1926 24:00 0:00
9/Apr/1927 23:00 -1:00
1/Oct/1927 24:00 0:00
14/Apr/1928 23:00 -1:00
6/Oct/1928 24:00 0:00
20/Apr/1929 23:00 -1:00
5/Oct/1929 24:00 0:00
12/Apr/1930 23:00 -1:00
4/Oct/1930 24:00 0:00
18/Apr/1931 23:00 -1:00
3/Oct/1931 24:00 0:00
2/Apr/1932 23:00 -1:00
1/Oct/1932 24:00 0:00
25/Mar/1933 23:00 -1:00
7/Oct/1933 24:00 0:00
7/Apr/1934 23:00 -1:00
6/Oct/1934 24:00 0:00
30/Mar/1935 23:00 -1:00
5/Oct/1935 24:00 0:00
18/Apr/1936 23:00 -1:00
3/Oct/1936 24:00 0:00
3/Apr/1937 23:00 -1:00
2/Oct/1937 24:00 0:00
26/Mar/1938 23:00 -1:00
1/Oct/1938 24:00 0:00
15/Apr/1939 23:00 -1:00
18/Nov/1939 24:00 0:00
25/Feb/1940 2:00 -1:00
4/May/1941 24:00 -2:00
6/Oct/1941 1:00 -1:00
8/Mar/1942 24:00 -2:00
2/Nov/1942 3:00 -1:00
29/Mar/1943 2:00 -2:00
4/Oct/1943 3:00 -1:00
3/Apr/1944 2:00 -2:00
8/Oct/1944 1:00 -1:00
2/Apr/1945 2:00 -2:00
Begin Standard 15E00
16/Sep/1945 3:00 -1:00
28/Mar/1976 2:00 -2:00
26/Sep/1976 3:00 -1:00
3/Apr/1977 2:00 -2:00
25/Sep/1977 3:00 -1:00
2/Apr/1978 2:00 -2:00
1/Oct/1978 3:00 -1:00
1/Apr/1979 2:00 -2:00
30/Sep/1979 3:00 -1:00
6/Apr/1980 2:00 -2:00
28/Sep/1980 3:00 -1:00
29/Mar/1981 2:00 -2:00
27/Sep/1981 3:00 -1:00
28/Mar/1982 2:00 -2:00
26/Sep/1982 3:00 -1:00
27/Mar/1983 2:00 -2:00
25/Sep/1983 3:00 -1:00
25/Mar/1984 2:00 -2:00
30/Sep/1984 3:00 -1:00
31/Mar/1985 2:00 -2:00
29/Sep/1985 3:00 -1:00
30/Mar/1986 2:00 -2:00
28/Sep/1986 3:00 -1:00
29/Mar/1987 2:00 -2:00
27/Sep/1987 3:00 -1:00
27/Mar/1988 2:00 -2:00
25/Sep/1988 3:00 -1:00
26/Mar/1989 2:00 -2:00
24/Sep/1989 3:00 -1:00
25/Mar/1990 2:00 -2:00
30/Sep/1990 3:00 -1:00
31/Mar/1991 2:00 -2:00
29/Sep/1991 3:00 -1:00
29/Mar/1992 2:00 -2:00
27/Sep/1992 3:00 -1:00
28/Mar/1993 2:00 -2:00
26/Sep/1993 3:00 -1:00
27/Mar/1994 2:00 -2:00
25/Sep/1994 3:00 -1:00
26/Mar/1995 2:00 -2:00
24/Sep/1995 3:00 -1:00
31/Mar/1996 2:00 -2:00
29/Sep/1996 3:00 -1:00
30/Mar/1997 2:00 -2:00
28/Sep/1997 3:00 -1:00
29/Mar/1998 2:00 -2:00
27/Sep/1998 3:00 -1:00
28/Mar/1999 2:00 -2:00
26/Sep/1999 3:00 -1:00
26/Mar/2000 2:00 -2:00
24/Sep/2000 3:00 -1:00
....
Time Table # 2
Before 1/Apr/1893 LMT
Begin Standard 15E00
1/Apr/1893 0:00 -1:00
30/Apr/1916 23:00 -2:00
1/Oct/1916 1:00 -1:00
16/Apr/1917 2:00 -2:00
17/Sep/1917 3:00 -1:00
15/Apr/1918 2:00 -2:00
16/Sep/1918 3:00 -1:00
Begin Standard 0W00
11/Nov/1918 0:00 0:00
1/Mar/1919 23:00 -1:00
5/Oct/1919 24:00 0:00
14/Feb/1920 23:00 -1:00
23/Oct/1920 24:00 0:00
14/Mar/1921 23:00 -1:00
25/Oct/1921 24:00 0:00
25/Mar/1922 23:00 -1:00
7/Oct/1922 24:00 0:00
26/May/1923 23:00 -1:00
6/Oct/1923 24:00 0:00
29/Mar/1924 23:00 -1:00
4/Oct/1924 24:00 0:00
4/Apr/1925 23:00 -1:00
3/Oct/1925 24:00 0:00
17/Apr/1926 23:00 -1:00
2/Oct/1926 24:00 0:00
9/Apr/1927 23:00 -1:00
1/Oct/1927 24:00 0:00
14/Apr/1928 23:00 -1:00
6/Oct/1928 24:00 0:00
20/Apr/1929 23:00 -1:00
5/Oct/1929 24:00 0:00
12/Apr/1930 23:00 -1:00
4/Oct/1930 24:00 0:00
18/Apr/1931 23:00 -1:00
3/Oct/1931 24:00 0:00
2/Apr/1932 23:00 -1:00
1/Oct/1932 24:00 0:00
25/Mar/1933 23:00 -1:00
7/Oct/1933 24:00 0:00
7/Apr/1934 23:00 -1:00
6/Oct/1934 24:00 0:00
30/Mar/1935 23:00 -1:00
5/Oct/1935 24:00 0:00
18/Apr/1936 23:00 -1:00
3/Oct/1936 24:00 0:00
3/Apr/1937 23:00 -1:00
2/Oct/1937 24:00 0:00
26/Mar/1938 23:00 -1:00
1/Oct/1938 24:00 0:00
15/Apr/1939 23:00 -1:00
18/Nov/1939 24:00 0:00
25/Feb/1940 2:00 -1:00
16/Jun/1940 0:00 -2:00
1/Nov/1942 3:00 -1:00
29/Mar/1943 2:00 -2:00
4/Oct/1943 3:00 -1:00
3/Apr/1944 2:00 -2:00
3/Oct/1944 3:00 -1:00
2/Apr/1945 2:00 -2:00
Begin Standard 15E00
16/Sep/1945 3:00 TT#1
....
Time Table # 3
Before 1/Apr/1893 LMT
Begin Standard 15E00
1/Apr/1893 0:00 TT#2
16/Jun/1940 0:00 -2:00
1/Nov/1942 3:00 -1:00
29/Mar/1943 2:00 -2:00
4/Oct/1943 3:00 -1:00
3/Apr/1944 2:00 -2:00
3/Oct/1944 3:00 -1:00
2/Apr/1945 2:00 -2:00
Begin Standard 15E00
16/Sep/1945 3:00 TT#1
....
Time Table # 4
Before 1/Apr/1893 LMT
Begin Standard 15E00
1/Apr/1893 0:00 TT#2
16/Jun/1940 0:00 -2:00
1/Nov/1942 3:00 -1:00
29/Mar/1943 2:00 -2:00
4/Oct/1943 3:00 -1:00
3/Apr/1944 2:00 -2:00
3/Oct/1944 3:00 -1:00
2/Apr/1945 2:00 -2:00
Begin Standard 15E00
16/Sep/1945 3:00 TT#1
....
Time Table # 5
Before 1/Apr/1893 LMT
Begin Standard 15E00
1/Apr/1893 0:00 TT#2
15/Jun/1940 0:00 -2:00
1/Nov/1942 3:00 -1:00
29/Mar/1943 2:00 -2:00
4/Oct/1943 3:00 -1:00
3/Apr/1944 2:00 -2:00
3/Oct/1944 3:00 -1:00
2/Apr/1945 2:00 -2:00
Begin Standard 15E00
16/Sep/1945 3:00 TT#1
....
Time Table # 6
Before 1/Apr/1893 LMT
Begin Standard 15E00
1/Apr/1893 0:00 TT#2
15/Jun/1940 0:00 -2:00
1/Nov/1942 3:00 -1:00
29/Mar/1943 2:00 -2:00
4/Oct/1943 3:00 -1:00
3/Apr/1944 2:00 -2:00
3/Oct/1944 3:00 -1:00
2/Apr/1945 2:00 -2:00
Begin Standard 15E00
16/Sep/1945 3:00 TT#1
....
Time Table # 7
Before 1/Apr/1893 LMT
Begin Standard 15E00
1/Apr/1893 0:00 TT#2
16/Jun/1940 0:00 -2:00
1/Nov/1942 3:00 -1:00
29/Mar/1943 2:00 -2:00
4/Oct/1943 3:00 -1:00
3/Apr/1944 2:00 -2:00
3/Oct/1944 3:00 -1:00
2/Apr/1945 2:00 -2:00
Begin Standard 15E00
16/Sep/1945 3:00 TT#1
....
Time Table # 8
Before 1/Apr/1893 LMT
Begin Standard 15E00
1/Apr/1893 0:00 TT#2
16/Jun/1940 0:00 -2:00
1/Nov/1942 3:00 -1:00
29/Mar/1943 2:00 -2:00
4/Oct/1943 3:00 -1:00
3/Apr/1944 2:00 -2:00
3/Oct/1944 3:00 -1:00
2/Apr/1945 2:00 -2:00
Begin Standard 15E00
16/Sep/1945 3:00 TT#1
....
Time Table # 9
Before 1/Apr/1893 LMT
Begin Standard 15E00
1/Apr/1893 0:00 TT#2
15/Jun/1940 0:00 -2:00
1/Nov/1942 3:00 -1:00
29/Mar/1943 2:00 -2:00
4/Oct/1943 3:00 -1:00
3/Apr/1944 2:00 -2:00
3/Oct/1944 3:00 -1:00
2/Apr/1945 2:00 -2:00
Begin Standard 15E00
16/Sep/1945 3:00 TT#1
....
Time Table # 10
Before 1/Apr/1893 LMT
Begin Standard 15E00
1/Apr/1893 0:00 TT#2
15/Jun/1940 0:00 -2:00
1/Nov/1942 3:00 -1:00
29/Mar/1943 2:00 -2:00
4/Oct/1943 3:00 -1:00
3/Apr/1944 2:00 -2:00
8/Oct/1944 1:00 -1:00
2/Apr/1945 2:00 -2:00
Begin Standard 15E00
16/Sep/1945 3:00 TT#1
....
Time Table # 11
Before 1/Apr/1893 LMT
Begin Standard 15E00
1/Apr/1893 0:00 TT#2
17/Jun/1940 0:00 -2:00
1/Nov/1942 3:00 -1:00
29/Mar/1943 2:00 -2:00
4/Oct/1943 3:00 -1:00
3/Apr/1944 2:00 -2:00
3/Oct/1944 3:00 -1:00
2/Apr/1945 2:00 -2:00
Begin Standard 15E00
16/Sep/1945 3:00 TT#1
....
Time Table # 12
Before 1/Apr/1893 LMT
Begin Standard 15E00
1/Apr/1893 0:00 TT#2
17/Jun/1940 0:00 -2:00
1/Nov/1942 3:00 -1:00
29/Mar/1943 2:00 -2:00
4/Oct/1943 3:00 -1:00
3/Apr/1944 2:00 -2:00
3/Oct/1944 3:00 -1:00
2/Apr/1945 2:00 -2:00
Begin Standard 15E00
16/Sep/1945 3:00 TT#1
....
Time Table # 13
Before 1/Apr/1893 LMT
Begin Standard 15E00
1/Apr/1893 0:00 TT#2
18/Jun/1940 0:00 -2:00
1/Nov/1942 3:00 -1:00
29/Mar/1943 2:00 -2:00
4/Oct/1943 3:00 -1:00
3/Apr/1944 2:00 -2:00
3/Oct/1944 3:00 -1:00
2/Apr/1945 2:00 -2:00
Begin Standard 15E00
16/Sep/1945 3:00 TT#1
....
Time Table # 14
Before 1/Apr/1893 LMT
Begin Standard 15E00
1/Apr/1893 0:00 TT#2
18/Jun/1940 0:00 -2:00
1/Nov/1942 3:00 -1:00
29/Mar/1943 2:00 -2:00
4/Oct/1943 3:00 -1:00
3/Apr/1944 2:00 -2:00
3/Oct/1944 3:00 -1:00
2/Apr/1945 2:00 -2:00
Begin Standard 15E00
16/Sep/1945 3:00 TT#1
....
Time Table # 15
Before 1/Apr/1893 LMT
Begin Standard 15E00
1/Apr/1893 0:00 TT#2
18/Jun/1940 0:00 -2:00
1/Nov/1942 3:00 -1:00
29/Mar/1943 2:00 -2:00
4/Oct/1943 3:00 -1:00
3/Apr/1944 2:00 -2:00
3/Oct/1944 3:00 -1:00
2/Apr/1945 2:00 -2:00
Begin Standard 15E00
16/Sep/1945 3:00 TT#1
....
Time Table # 16
Before 1/Apr/1893 LMT
Begin Standard 15E00
1/Apr/1893 0:00 TT#2
18/Jun/1940 0:00 -2:00
1/Nov/1942 3:00 -1:00
29/Mar/1943 2:00 -2:00
4/Oct/1943 3:00 -1:00
3/Apr/1944 2:00 -2:00
3/Oct/1944 3:00 -1:00
2/Apr/1945 2:00 -2:00
Begin Standard 15E00
16/Sep/1945 3:00 TT#1
....
Time Table # 17
Before 1/Apr/1893 LMT
Begin Standard 15E00
1/Apr/1893 0:00 TT#2
17/Jun/1940 0:00 -2:00
1/Nov/1942 3:00 -1:00
29/Mar/1943 2:00 -2:00
4/Oct/1943 3:00 -1:00
3/Apr/1944 2:00 -2:00
3/Oct/1944 3:00 -1:00
2/Apr/1945 2:00 -2:00
Begin Standard 15E00
16/Sep/1945 3:00 TT#1
....
Time Table # 18
Before 1/Apr/1893 LMT
Begin Standard 15E00
1/Apr/1893 0:00 TT#2
17/Jun/1940 0:00 -2:00
1/Nov/1942 3:00 -1:00
29/Mar/1943 2:00 -2:00
4/Oct/1943 3:00 -1:00
3/Apr/1944 2:00 -2:00
3/Oct/1944 3:00 -1:00
2/Apr/1945 2:00 -2:00
Begin Standard 15E00
16/Sep/1945 3:00 TT#1
....
Time Table # 19
Before 1/Apr/1893 LMT
Begin Standard 15E00
1/Apr/1893 0:00 TT#2
17/Jun/1940 0:00 -2:00
1/Nov/1942 3:00 -1:00
29/Mar/1943 2:00 -2:00
4/Oct/1943 3:00 -1:00
3/Apr/1944 2:00 -2:00
3/Oct/1944 3:00 -1:00
2/Apr/1945 2:00 -2:00
Begin Standard 15E00
16/Sep/1945 3:00 TT#1
....
Time Table # 20
Before 1/Apr/1893 LMT
Begin Standard 15E00
1/Apr/1893 0:00 TT#2
15/Jun/1940 0:00 -2:00
1/Nov/1942 3:00 -1:00
29/Mar/1943 2:00 -2:00
4/Oct/1943 3:00 -1:00
3/Apr/1944 2:00 -2:00
3/Oct/1944 3:00 -1:00
2/Apr/1945 2:00 -2:00
Begin Standard 15E00
16/Sep/1945 3:00 TT#1
....
Time Table # 21
Before 1/Apr/1893 LMT
Begin Standard 15E00
1/Apr/1893 0:00 TT#2
15/Jun/1940 0:00 -2:00
1/Nov/1942 3:00 -1:00
29/Mar/1943 2:00 -2:00
4/Oct/1943 3:00 -1:00
3/Apr/1944 2:00 -2:00
3/Oct/1944 3:00 -1:00
2/Apr/1945 2:00 -2:00
Begin Standard 15E00
16/Sep/1945 3:00 TT#1
....
Time Table # 22
Before 1/Apr/1893 LMT
Begin Standard 15E00
1/Apr/1893 0:00 TT#2
17/Jun/1940 0:00 -2:00
1/Nov/1942 3:00 -1:00
29/Mar/1943 2:00 -2:00
4/Oct/1943 3:00 -1:00
3/Apr/1944 2:00 -2:00
3/Oct/1944 3:00 -1:00
2/Apr/1945 2:00 -2:00
Begin Standard 15E00
16/Sep/1945 3:00 TT#1
....
Time Table # 23
Before 1/Apr/1893 LMT
Begin Standard 15E00
1/Apr/1893 0:00 TT#2
17/Jun/1940 0:00 -2:00
1/Nov/1942 3:00 -1:00
29/Mar/1943 2:00 -2:00
4/Oct/1943 3:00 -1:00
3/Apr/1944 2:00 -2:00
3/Oct/1944 3:00 -1:00
2/Apr/1945 2:00 -2:00
Begin Standard 15E00
16/Sep/1945 3:00 TT#1
....
Time Table # 24
Before 15/Mar/1891 LMT
Begin Standard 2E20
15/Mar/1891 0:01 TT#1
22/Jun/1940 0:00 -2:00
1/Nov/1942 3:00 -1:00
29/Mar/1943 2:00 -2:00
4/Oct/1943 3:00 -1:00
3/Apr/1944 2:00 TT#1
....
Time Table # 25
Before 15/Mar/1891 LMT
Begin Standard 2E20
15/Mar/1891 0:01 TT#1
20/Jun/1940 0:00 -2:00
1/Nov/1942 3:00 -1:00
29/Mar/1943 2:00 -2:00
4/Oct/1943 3:00 -1:00
3/Apr/1944 2:00 TT#1
....
Time Table # 26
Before 15/Mar/1891 LMT
Begin Standard 2E20
15/Mar/1891 0:01 TT#1
21/Jun/1940 0:00 -2:00
22/Jun/1940 0:00 TT#1
....
Time Table # 27
Before 15/Mar/1891 LMT
Begin Standard 2E20
15/Mar/1891 0:01 TT#1
20/Jun/1940 0:00 -2:00
22/Jun/1940 0:00 TT#1
....
Time Table # 28
Before 15/Mar/1891 LMT
Begin Standard 2E20
15/Mar/1891 0:01 TT#1
18/Jun/1940 0:00 -2:00
1/Nov/1942 3:00 -1:00
29/Mar/1943 2:00 -2:00
4/Oct/1943 3:00 -1:00
3/Apr/1944 2:00 TT#1
....
Time Table # 29
Before 15/Mar/1891 LMT
Begin Standard 2E20
15/Mar/1891 0:01 TT#1
18/Jun/1940 0:00 -2:00
22/Jun/1940 0:00 TT#1
....
Time Table # 30
Before 15/Mar/1891 LMT
Begin Standard 2E20
15/Mar/1891 0:01 TT#1
18/Jun/1940 0:00 -2:00
1/Nov/1942 3:00 -1:00
29/Mar/1943 2:00 -2:00
4/Oct/1943 3:00 -1:00
3/Apr/1944 2:00 -2:00
12/Sep/1944 0:00 TT#1
....
Time Table # 31
Before 15/Mar/1891 LMT
Begin Standard 2E20
15/Mar/1891 0:01 TT#1
20/Jun/1940 0:00 -2:00
1/Nov/1942 3:00 -1:00
29/Mar/1943 2:00 -2:00
4/Oct/1943 3:00 -1:00
3/Apr/1944 2:00 -2:00
11/Sep/1944 0:00 TT#1
....
Time Table # 32
Before 15/Mar/1891 LMT
Begin Standard 2E20
15/Mar/1891 0:01 TT#1
18/Jun/1940 0:00 -2:00
1/Nov/1942 3:00 -1:00
29/Mar/1943 2:00 -2:00
4/Oct/1943 3:00 -1:00
3/Apr/1944 2:00 -2:00
11/Sep/1944 0:00 TT#1
....
Time Table # 33
Before 15/Mar/1891 LMT
Begin Standard 2E20
15/Mar/1891 0:01 TT#1
22/Jun/1940 0:00 -2:00
1/Nov/1942 3:00 -1:00
29/Mar/1943 2:00 -2:00
4/Oct/1943 3:00 -1:00
3/Apr/1944 2:00 -2:00
3/Oct/1944 3:00 -1:00
2/Apr/1945 2:00 -2:00
9/May/1945 0:00 TT#1
....
Time Table # 34
Before 15/Mar/1891 LMT

Begin Standard 2E20
15/Mar/1891 0:01 TT#1
22/Jun/1940 0:00 -2:00
1/Nov/1942 3:00 -1:00
29/Mar/1943 2:00 -2:00
4/Oct/1943 3:00 -1:00
3/Apr/1944 2:00 -2:00
3/Oct/1944 3:00 -1:00
2/Apr/1945 2:00 -2:00
10/May/1945 0:00 TT#1
....

Time Table # 35
Before 15/Mar/1891 LMT
Begin Standard 2E20
15/Mar/1891 0:01 TT#1
22/Jun/1940 0:00 -2:00
1/Nov/1942 3:00 -1:00
29/Mar/1943 2:00 -2:00
4/Oct/1943 3:00 -1:00
3/Apr/1944 2:00 -2:00
6/Aug/1944 0:00 TT#1
....

Time Table # 36
Before 15/Mar/1891 LMT
Begin Standard 2E20
15/Mar/1891 0:01 TT#1
20/Jun/1940 0:00 -2:00
1/Nov/1942 3:00 -1:00
29/Mar/1943 2:00 -2:00
4/Oct/1943 3:00 -1:00
3/Apr/1944 2:00 -2:00
6/Aug/1944 0:00 TT#1
....

Time Table # 37
Before 15/Mar/1891 LMT
Begin Standard 2E20
15/Mar/1891 0:01 TT#1
20/Jun/1940 0:00 -2:00
1/Nov/1942 3:00 -1:00
29/Mar/1943 2:00 -2:00
4/Oct/1943 3:00 -1:00
3/Apr/1944 2:00 -2:00
18/Sep/1944 0:00 TT#1
....

Time Table # 38
Before 15/Mar/1891 LMT
Begin Standard 2E20
15/Mar/1891 0:01 TT#1
19/Jun/1940 0:00 -2:00
1/Nov/1942 3:00 -1:00
29/Mar/1943 2:00 -2:00
4/Oct/1943 3:00 -1:00
3/Apr/1944 2:00 -2:00
9/Aug/1944 0:00 TT#1
....

Time Table # 39
Before 15/Mar/1891 LMT
Begin Standard 2E20
15/Mar/1891 0:01 TT#1
19/Jun/1940 0:00 -2:00
1/Nov/1942 3:00 -1:00
29/Mar/1943 2:00 -2:00
4/Oct/1943 3:00 -1:00
3/Apr/1944 2:00 -2:00
10/Aug/1944 0:00 TT#1
....

Time Table # 40
Before 15/Mar/1891 LMT
Begin Standard 2E20
15/Mar/1891 0:01 TT#1
19/Jun/1940 0:00 -2:00
1/Nov/1942 3:00 -1:00
29/Mar/1943 2:00 -2:00
4/Oct/1943 3:00 -1:00
3/Apr/1944 2:00 -2:00
6/Aug/1944 0:00 TT#1
....

Time Table # 41
Before 15/Mar/1891 LMT
Begin Standard 2E20
15/Mar/1891 0:01 TT#1
19/Jun/1940 0:00 -2:00
1/Nov/1942 3:00 -1:00
29/Mar/1943 2:00 -2:00
4/Oct/1943 3:00 -1:00
3/Apr/1944 2:00 TT#1
....

Time Table # 42
Before 15/Mar/1891 LMT
Begin Standard 2E20
15/Mar/1891 0:01 TT#1
19/Jun/1940 0:00 -2:00
1/Nov/1942 3:00 -1:00
29/Mar/1943 2:00 -2:00
4/Oct/1943 3:00 -1:00
3/Apr/1944 2:00 -2:00
15/Aug/1944 0:00 TT#1
....

Time Table # 43
Before 15/Mar/1891 LMT
Begin Standard 2E20
15/Mar/1891 0:01 TT#1
18/Jun/1940 0:00 -2:00
1/Nov/1942 3:00 -1:00
29/Mar/1943 2:00 -2:00
4/Oct/1943 3:00 -1:00
3/Apr/1944 2:00 -2:00
15/Aug/1944 0:00 TT#1
....

Time Table # 44
Before 15/Mar/1891 LMT
Begin Standard 2E20
15/Mar/1891 0:01 TT#1
17/Jun/1940 0:00 -2:00
1/Nov/1942 3:00 -1:00
29/Mar/1943 2:00 -2:00
4/Oct/1943 3:00 -1:00
3/Apr/1944 2:00 -2:00
15/Aug/1944 0:00 TT#1
....

Time Table # 45
Before 15/Mar/1891 LMT
Begin Standard 2E20
15/Mar/1891 0:01 TT#1
17/Jun/1940 0:00 -2:00
1/Nov/1942 3:00 -1:00
29/Mar/1943 2:00 -2:00
4/Oct/1943 3:00 -1:00
3/Apr/1944 2:00 TT#1
....

Time Table # 46
Before 15/Mar/1891 LMT
Begin Standard 2E20
15/Mar/1891 0:01 TT#1
16/Jun/1940 0:00 -2:00
1/Nov/1942 3:00 -1:00
29/Mar/1943 2:00 -2:00
4/Oct/1943 3:00 -1:00
3/Apr/1944 2:00 TT#1
....

Time Table # 47
Before 15/Mar/1891 LMT
Begin Standard 2E20
15/Mar/1891 0:01 TT#1
18/Jun/1940 0:00 -2:00
1/Nov/1942 3:00 -1:00
29/Mar/1943 2:00 -2:00
4/Oct/1943 3:00 -1:00
3/Apr/1944 2:00 -2:00
10/Aug/1944 0:00 TT#1
....

Time Table # 48
Before 15/Mar/1891 LMT
Begin Standard 2E20
15/Mar/1891 0:01 TT#1
17/Jun/1940 0:00 -2:00
1/Nov/1942 3:00 -1:00
29/Mar/1943 2:00 -2:00
4/Oct/1943 3:00 -1:00
3/Apr/1944 2:00 -2:00
21/Aug/1944 0:00 TT#1
....

Time Table # 49
Before 15/Mar/1891 LMT
Begin Standard 2E20
15/Mar/1891 0:01 TT#1
17/Jun/1940 0:00 -2:00
1/Nov/1942 3:00 -1:00
29/Mar/1943 2:00 -2:00
4/Oct/1943 3:00 -1:00
3/Apr/1944 2:00 -2:00
12/Sep/1944 0:00 TT#1
....

Time Table # 50
Before 15/Mar/1891 LMT
Begin Standard 2E20
15/Mar/1891 0:01 TT#1
16/Jun/1940 0:00 -2:00
1/Nov/1942 3:00 -1:00
29/Mar/1943 2:00 -2:00
4/Oct/1943 3:00 -1:00
3/Apr/1944 2:00 -2:00
12/Sep/1944 0:00 TT#1
....

Time Table # 51
Before 15/Mar/1891 LMT
Begin Standard 2E20
15/Mar/1891 0:01 TT#1
17/Jun/1940 0:00 -2:00
1/Nov/1942 3:00 -1:00
29/Mar/1943 2:00 -2:00
4/Oct/1943 3:00 -1:00
3/Apr/1944 2:00 -2:00
18/Sep/1944 0:00 TT#1
....

Time Table # 52
Before 15/Mar/1891 LMT
Begin Standard 2E20
15/Mar/1891 0:01 TT#1
16/Jun/1940 0:00 -2:00
1/Nov/1942 3:00 -1:00
29/Mar/1943 2:00 -2:00
4/Oct/1943 3:00 -1:00
3/Apr/1944 2:00 -2:00
18/Sep/1944 0:00 TT#1
....

Time Table # 53
Before 15/Mar/1891 LMT
Begin Standard 2E20
15/Mar/1891 0:01 TT#1
18/Jun/1940 0:00 -2:00
1/Nov/1942 3:00 -1:00
29/Mar/1943 2:00 -2:00
4/Oct/1943 3:00 -1:00
3/Apr/1944 2:00 -2:00
18/Sep/1944 0:00 TT#1
....

Time Table # 54
Before 15/Mar/1891 LMT
Begin Standard 2E20
15/Mar/1891 0:01 TT#1
16/Jun/1940 0:00 -2:00
1/Nov/1942 3:00 -1:00
29/Mar/1943 2:00 -2:00
4/Oct/1943 3:00 -1:00
3/Apr/1944 2:00 -2:00
12/Sep/1944 0:00 TT#1
....

Time Table # 55
Before 15/Mar/1891 LMT
Begin Standard 2E20
15/Mar/1891 0:01 TT#1
16/Jun/1940 0:00 -2:00
1/Nov/1942 3:00 -1:00
29/Mar/1943 2:00 -2:00
4/Oct/1943 3:00 -1:00
3/Apr/1944 2:00 -2:00
11/Sep/1944 0:00 TT#1
....

Time Table # 56
Before 15/Mar/1891 LMT
Begin Standard 2E20
15/Mar/1891 0:01 TT#1
15/Jun/1940 0:00 -2:00
1/Nov/1942 3:00 -1:00
29/Mar/1943 2:00 -2:00
4/Oct/1943 3:00 -1:00
3/Apr/1944 2:00 -2:00
18/Sep/1944 0:00 TT#1
....

Time Table # 57
Before 15/Mar/1891 LMT
Begin Standard 2E20
15/Mar/1891 0:01 TT#1
16/Jun/1940 0:00 -2:00
1/Nov/1942 3:00 -1:00
29/Mar/1943 2:00 -2:00
4/Oct/1943 3:00 -1:00
3/Apr/1944 2:00 -2:00
30/Sep/1944 0:00 TT#1
....

Time Table # 58
Before 15/Mar/1891 LMT
Begin Standard 2E20
15/Mar/1891 0:01 TT#1
18/Jun/1940 0:00 -2:00
1/Nov/1942 3:00 -1:00
29/Mar/1943 2:00 -2:00
4/Oct/1943 3:00 -1:00
3/Apr/1944 2:00 -2:00
30/Sep/1944 0:00 TT#1
....

Time Table # 59
Before 15/Mar/1891 LMT
Begin Standard 2E20
15/Mar/1891 0:01 TT#1
16/Jun/1940 0:00 -2:00
1/Nov/1942 3:00 -1:00
29/Mar/1943 2:00 -2:00
4/Oct/1943 3:00 -1:00
3/Apr/1944 2:00 -2:00
30/Sep/1944 0:00 TT#1
....

Time Table # 60
Before 15/Mar/1891 LMT
Begin Standard 2E20
15/Mar/1891 0:01 TT#1
16/Jun/1940 0:00 -2:00
1/Nov/1942 3:00 -1:00
29/Mar/1943 2:00 -2:00
4/Oct/1943 3:00 -1:00
3/Apr/1944 2:00 -2:00
3/Oct/1944 3:00 -1:00
21/Nov/1944 0:00 TT#1
....

Time Table # 61
Before 15/Mar/1891 LMT
Begin Standard 2E20
15/Mar/1891 0:01 TT#1
14/Jun/1940 0:00 -2:00
1/Nov/1942 3:00 -1:00
29/Mar/1943 2:00 -2:00
4/Oct/1943 3:00 -1:00
3/Apr/1944 2:00 -2:00
25/Aug/1944 0:00 TT#1
....

Time Table # 62
Before 15/Mar/1891 LMT
Begin Standard 2E20
15/Mar/1891 0:01 TT#1
20/Jun/1940 0:00 -2:00
1/Nov/1942 3:00 -1:00
29/Mar/1943 2:00 -2:00
4/Oct/1943 3:00 -1:00
3/Apr/1944 2:00 -2:00
4/Aug/1944 0:00 TT#1
....

Time Table # 63
Before 15/Mar/1891 LMT
Begin Standard 2E20
15/Mar/1891 0:01 TT#1
19/Jun/1940 0:00 -2:00
1/Nov/1942 3:00 -1:00
29/Mar/1943 2:00 -2:00
4/Oct/1943 3:00 -1:00
3/Apr/1944 2:00 -2:00
4/Aug/1944 0:00 TT#1
....

Time Table # 64
Before 15/Mar/1891 LMT
Begin Standard 2E20
15/Mar/1891 0:01 TT#1
20/Jun/1940 0:00 -2:00
1/Nov/1942 3:00 -1:00
29/Mar/1943 2:00 -2:00
4/Oct/1943 3:00 -1:00
3/Apr/1944 2:00 -2:00
10/Aug/1944 0:00 TT#1
....

Time Table # 65
Before 15/Mar/1891 LMT
Begin Standard 2E20
15/Mar/1891 0:01 TT#1
18/Jun/1940 0:00 -2:00
1/Nov/1942 3:00 -1:00
29/Mar/1943 2:00 -2:00
4/Oct/1943 3:00 -1:00
3/Apr/1944 2:00 -2:00
5/Aug/1944 0:00 TT#1
....

Time Table # 66
Before 15/Mar/1891 LMT
Begin Standard 2E20
15/Mar/1891 0:01 TT#1
18/Jun/1940 0:00 -2:00
1/Nov/1942 3:00 -1:00
29/Mar/1943 2:00 -2:00
4/Oct/1943 3:00 -1:00
3/Apr/1944 2:00 -2:00
4/Aug/1944 0:00 TT#1
....

Time Table # 67
Before 15/Mar/1891 LMT
Begin Standard 2E20
15/Mar/1891 0:01 TT#1
19/Jun/1940 0:00 -2:00
1/Nov/1942 3:00 -1:00
29/Mar/1943 2:00 -2:00
4/Oct/1943 3:00 -1:00
3/Apr/1944 2:00 -2:00
29/Jul/1944 0:00 TT#1
....

Time Table # 68
Before 15/Mar/1891 LMT
Begin Standard 2E20
15/Mar/1891 0:01 TT#1
18/Jun/1940 0:00 -2:00
1/Nov/1942 3:00 -1:00
29/Mar/1943 2:00 -2:00
4/Oct/1943 3:00 -1:00
3/Apr/1944 2:00 -2:00
19/Aug/1944 0:00 TT#1
....

Time Table # 69
Before 15/Mar/1891 LMT
Begin Standard 2E20
15/Mar/1891 0:01 TT#1
18/Jun/1940 0:00 -2:00
1/Nov/1942 3:00 -1:00
29/Mar/1943 2:00 -2:00
4/Oct/1943 3:00 -1:00
3/Apr/1944 2:00 -2:00
23/Aug/1944 0:00 TT#1
....

Time Table # 70
Before 15/Mar/1891 LMT
Begin Standard 2E20
15/Mar/1891 0:01 TT#1
16/Jun/1940 0:00 -2:00
1/Nov/1942 3:00 -1:00
29/Mar/1943 2:00 -2:00
4/Oct/1943 3:00 -1:00
3/Apr/1944 2:00 -2:00
19/Aug/1944 0:00 TT#1
....

Time Table # 71
Before 15/Mar/1891 LMT
Begin Standard 2E20
15/Mar/1891 0:01 TT#1
17/Jun/1940 0:00 -2:00
1/Nov/1942 3:00 -1:00
29/Mar/1943 2:00 -2:00
4/Oct/1943 3:00 -1:00
3/Apr/1944 2:00 -2:00
19/Aug/1944 0:00 TT#1
....

Time Table # 72
Before 15/Mar/1891 LMT
Begin Standard 2E20
15/Mar/1891 0:01 TT#1
18/Jun/1940 0:00 -2:00
1/Nov/1942 3:00 -1:00
29/Mar/1943 2:00 -2:00
4/Oct/1943 3:00 -1:00
3/Apr/1944 2:00 -2:00
25/Aug/1944 0:00 TT#1
....

Time Table # 73
Before 15/Mar/1891 LMT
Begin Standard 2E20
15/Mar/1891 0:01 TT#1
16/Jun/1940 0:00 -2:00
1/Nov/1942 3:00 -1:00
29/Mar/1943 2:00 -2:00
4/Oct/1943 3:00 -1:00
3/Apr/1944 2:00 -2:00
24/Aug/1944 0:00 TT#1
....

Time Table # 74
Before 15/Mar/1891 LMT
Begin Standard 2E20
15/Mar/1891 0:01 TT#1
16/Jun/1940 0:00 -2:00
1/Nov/1942 3:00 -1:00
29/Mar/1943 2:00 -2:00
4/Oct/1943 3:00 -1:00
3/Apr/1944 2:00 -2:00
21/Aug/1944 0:00 TT#1
....

Time Table # 75
Before 15/Mar/1891 LMT
Begin Standard 2E20
15/Mar/1891 0:01 TT#1
17/Jun/1940 0:00 -2:00
1/Nov/1942 3:00 -1:00
29/Mar/1943 2:00 -2:00
4/Oct/1943 3:00 -1:00
3/Apr/1944 2:00 -2:00
22/Aug/1944 0:00 TT#1
....

Time Table # 76
Before 15/Mar/1891 LMT
Begin Standard 2E20
15/Mar/1891 0:01 TT#1
16/Jun/1940 0:00 -2:00
1/Nov/1942 3:00 -1:00
29/Mar/1943 2:00 -2:00
4/Oct/1943 3:00 -1:00
3/Apr/1944 2:00 -2:00
22/Aug/1944 0:00 TT#1
....

Time Table # 77
Before 15/Mar/1891 LMT
Begin Standard 2E20
15/Mar/1891 0:01 TT#1
16/Jun/1940 0:00 -2:00
1/Nov/1942 3:00 -1:00
29/Mar/1943 2:00 -2:00
4/Oct/1943 3:00 -1:00
3/Apr/1944 2:00 -2:00
28/Aug/1944 0:00 TT#1
....

Time Table # 78
Before 15/Mar/1891 LMT
Begin Standard 2E20
15/Mar/1891 0:01 TT#1
16/Jun/1940 0:00 -2:00
1/Nov/1942 3:00 -1:00
29/Mar/1943 2:00 -2:00
4/Oct/1943 3:00 -1:00
3/Apr/1944 2:00 -2:00
25/Aug/1944 0:00 TT#1
....

Time Table # 79
Before 15/Mar/1891 LMT
Begin Standard 2E20
15/Mar/1891 0:01 TT#1
14/Jun/1940 0:00 -2:00
1/Nov/1942 3:00 -1:00
29/Mar/1943 2:00 -2:00
4/Oct/1943 3:00 -1:00
3/Apr/1944 2:00 -2:00
24/Aug/1944 0:00 TT#1
....

Time Table # 80
Before 15/Mar/1891 LMT
Begin Standard 2E20
15/Mar/1891 0:01 TT#1
14/Jun/1940 0:00 -2:00
1/Nov/1942 3:00 -1:00
29/Mar/1943 2:00 -2:00
4/Oct/1943 3:00 -1:00
3/Apr/1944 2:00 -2:00
1/Sep/1944 0:00 TT#1
....

Time Table # 81
Before 15/Mar/1891 LMT
Begin Standard 2E20
15/Mar/1891 0:01 TT#1
14/Jun/1940 0:00 -2:00
1/Nov/1942 3:00 -1:00
29/Mar/1943 2:00 -2:00
4/Oct/1943 3:00 -1:00
3/Apr/1944 2:00 -2:00
29/Aug/1944 0:00 TT#1
....

Time Table # 82
Before 15/Mar/1891 LMT
Begin Standard 2E20
15/Mar/1891 0:01 TT#1
15/Jun/1940 0:00 -2:00
1/Nov/1942 3:00 -1:00
29/Mar/1943 2:00 -2:00
4/Oct/1943 3:00 -1:00
3/Apr/1944 2:00 -2:00
29/Aug/1944 0:00 TT#1
....

Time Table # 83
Before 15/Mar/1891 LMT
Begin Standard 2E20
15/Mar/1891 0:01 TT#1
12/Jun/1940 0:00 -2:00
1/Nov/1942 3:00 -1:00
29/Mar/1943 2:00 -2:00
4/Oct/1943 3:00 -1:00
3/Apr/1944 2:00 -2:00
30/Aug/1944 0:00 TT#1
....

Time Table # 84
Before 15/Mar/1891 LMT
Begin Standard 2E20
15/Mar/1891 0:01 TT#1
14/Jun/1940 0:00 -2:00
1/Nov/1942 3:00 -1:00
29/Mar/1943 2:00 -2:00
4/Oct/1943 3:00 -1:00
3/Apr/1944 2:00 -2:00
29/Aug/1944 0:00 TT#1
....

Time Table # 85
Before 15/Mar/1891 LMT
Begin Standard 2E20
15/Mar/1891 0:01 TT#1
15/Jun/1940 0:00 -2:00
1/Nov/1942 3:00 -1:00
29/Mar/1943 2:00 -2:00
4/Oct/1943 3:00 -1:00
3/Apr/1944 2:00 -2:00
28/Aug/1944 0:00 TT#1
....

Time Table # 86
Before 15/Mar/1891 LMT
Begin Standard 2E20
15/Mar/1891 0:01 TT#1
15/Jun/1940 0:00 -2:00

1/Nov/1942 3:00 -1:00
29/Mar/1943 2:00 -2:00
4/Oct/1943 3:00 -1:00
3/Apr/1944 2:00 -2:00
31/Aug/1944 0:00 TT#1
....
Time Table # 87
Before 15/Mar/1891 LMT
Begin Standard 2ε20
15/Mar/1891 0:01 TT#1
15/Jun/1940 0:00 -2:00
1/Nov/1942 3:00 -1:00
29/Mar/1943 2:00 -2:00
4/Oct/1943 3:00 -1:00
3/Apr/1944 2:00 -2:00
2/Sep/1944 0:00 TT#1
....
Time Table # 88
Before 15/Mar/1891 LMT
Begin Standard 2ε20
15/Mar/1891 0:01 TT#1
14/Jun/1940 0:00 -2:00
1/Nov/1942 3:00 -1:00
29/Mar/1943 2:00 -2:00
4/Oct/1943 3:00 -1:00
3/Apr/1944 2:00 -2:00
31/Aug/1944 0:00 TT#1
....
Time Table # 89
Before 15/Mar/1891 LMT
Begin Standard 2ε20
15/Mar/1891 0:01 TT#1
14/Jun/1940 0:00 -2:00
1/Nov/1942 3:00 -1:00
29/Mar/1943 2:00 -2:00
4/Oct/1943 3:00 -1:00
3/Apr/1944 2:00 -2:00
2/Sep/1944 0:00 TT#1
....
Time Table # 90
Before 15/Mar/1891 LMT
Begin Standard 2ε20
15/Mar/1891 0:01 TT#1
16/Jun/1940 0:00 -2:00
1/Nov/1942 3:00 -1:00
29/Mar/1943 2:00 -2:00
4/Oct/1943 3:00 -1:00
3/Apr/1944 2:00 -2:00
15/Sep/1944 0:00 TT#1
....
Time Table # 91
Before 15/Mar/1891 LMT
Begin Standard 2ε20
15/Mar/1891 0:01 TT#1
18/Jun/1940 0:00 -2:00
1/Nov/1942 3:00 -1:00
29/Mar/1943 2:00 -2:00
4/Oct/1943 3:00 -1:00
3/Apr/1944 2:00 -2:00
18/Sep/1944 0:00 TT#1
....
Time Table # 92
Before 15/Mar/1891 LMT
Begin Standard 2ε20
15/Mar/1891 0:01 TT#1
20/Jun/1940 0:00 -2:00
1/Nov/1942 3:00 -1:00
29/Mar/1943 2:00 -2:00
4/Oct/1943 3:00 -1:00
3/Apr/1944 2:00 -2:00
15/Sep/1944 0:00 TT#1
....
Time Table # 93
Before 15/Mar/1891 LMT
Begin Standard 2ε20
15/Mar/1891 0:01 TT#1
1/Nov/1914 0:00 -1:00
30/Apr/1916 23:00 -2:00
1/Oct/1916 1:00 -1:00
16/Apr/1917 2:00 -2:00
17/Sep/1917 3:00 -1:00
15/Apr/1918 2:00 -2:00
16/Sep/1918 3:00 -1:00
11/Nov/1918 0:00 0:00
1/Mar/1919 23:00 -1:00
5/Oct/1919 24:00 0:00
14/Feb/1920 23:00 -1:00
23/Oct/1920 24:00 0:00
14/Mar/1921 23:00 -1:00
25/Oct/1921 24:00 0:00
25/Mar/1922 23:00 -1:00
7/Oct/1922 24:00 0:00
26/May/1923 23:00 -1:00
6/Oct/1923 24:00 0:00
29/Mar/1924 23:00 -1:00
4/Oct/1924 24:00 0:00
4/Apr/1925 23:00 -1:00
3/Oct/1925 24:00 0:00
17/Apr/1926 23:00 -1:00
2/Oct/1926 24:00 0:00
9/Apr/1927 23:00 -1:00
1/Oct/1927 24:00 0:00
14/Apr/1928 23:00 -1:00
6/Oct/1928 24:00 0:00
20/Apr/1929 23:00 -1:00
5/Oct/1929 24:00 0:00
12/Apr/1930 23:00 -1:00
4/Oct/1930 24:00 0:00
18/Apr/1931 23:00 -1:00
3/Oct/1931 24:00 0:00
2/Apr/1932 23:00 -1:00
1/Oct/1932 24:00 0:00
25/Mar/1933 23:00 -1:00
7/Oct/1933 24:00 0:00
7/Apr/1934 23:00 -1:00
6/Oct/1934 24:00 0:00
30/Mar/1935 23:00 -1:00
5/Oct/1935 24:00 0:00
18/Apr/1936 23:00 -1:00
3/Oct/1936 24:00 0:00
3/Apr/1937 23:00 -1:00
2/Oct/1937 24:00 0:00
26/Mar/1938 23:00 -1:00
1/Oct/1938 24:00 0:00
15/Apr/1939 23:00 -1:00
18/Nov/1939 24:00 0:00
25/Feb/1940 2:00 -1:00
15/Jun/1940 0:00 -2:00
1/Nov/1942 3:00 -1:00
29/Mar/1943 2:00 -2:00
4/Oct/1943 3:00 -1:00
3/Apr/1944 2:00 -2:00
13/Sep/1944 0:00 TT#1
....
Time Table # 94
Before 15/Mar/1891 LMT
Begin Standard 2ε20
15/Mar/1891 0:01 TT#1
1/Nov/1914 0:00 -1:00
30/Apr/1916 23:00 -2:00
1/Oct/1916 1:00 -1:00
16/Apr/1917 2:00 -2:00
17/Sep/1917 3:00 -1:00
15/Apr/1918 2:00 -2:00
16/Sep/1918 3:00 -1:00
11/Nov/1918 0:00 0:00
1/Mar/1919 23:00 -1:00
5/Oct/1919 24:00 0:00
14/Feb/1920 23:00 -1:00
23/Oct/1920 24:00 0:00
14/Mar/1921 23:00 -1:00
25/Oct/1921 24:00 0:00
25/Mar/1922 23:00 -1:00
7/Oct/1922 24:00 0:00
26/May/1923 23:00 -1:00
6/Oct/1923 24:00 0:00
29/Mar/1924 23:00 -1:00
4/Oct/1924 24:00 0:00
4/Apr/1925 23:00 -1:00
3/Oct/1925 24:00 0:00
17/Apr/1926 23:00 -1:00
2/Oct/1926 24:00 0:00
9/Apr/1927 23:00 -1:00
1/Oct/1927 24:00 0:00
14/Apr/1928 23:00 -1:00
6/Oct/1928 24:00 0:00
20/Apr/1929 23:00 -1:00
5/Oct/1929 24:00 0:00
12/Apr/1930 23:00 -1:00
4/Oct/1930 24:00 0:00
18/Apr/1931 23:00 -1:00
3/Oct/1931 24:00 0:00
2/Apr/1932 23:00 -1:00
1/Oct/1932 24:00 0:00
25/Mar/1933 23:00 -1:00
7/Oct/1933 24:00 0:00
7/Apr/1934 23:00 -1:00
6/Oct/1934 24:00 0:00
30/Mar/1935 23:00 -1:00
5/Oct/1935 24:00 0:00
18/Apr/1936 23:00 -1:00
3/Oct/1936 24:00 0:00
3/Apr/1937 23:00 -1:00
2/Oct/1937 24:00 0:00
26/Mar/1938 23:00 -1:00
1/Oct/1938 24:00 0:00
15/Apr/1939 23:00 -1:00
18/Nov/1939 24:00 0:00
25/Feb/1940 2:00 -1:00
15/Jun/1940 0:00 -2:00
1/Nov/1942 3:00 -1:00
29/Mar/1943 2:00 -2:00
4/Oct/1943 3:00 -1:00
3/Apr/1944 2:00 -2:00
2/Sep/1944 0:00 TT#1
....
Time Table # 95
Before 15/Mar/1891 LMT
Begin Standard 2ε20
15/Mar/1891 0:01 TT#1
1/Nov/1914 0:00 -1:00
30/Apr/1916 23:00 -2:00
1/Oct/1916 1:00 -1:00
16/Apr/1917 2:00 -2:00
17/Sep/1917 3:00 -1:00
15/Apr/1918 2:00 -2:00
16/Sep/1918 3:00 -1:00
11/Nov/1918 0:00 0:00
1/Mar/1919 23:00 -1:00
5/Oct/1919 24:00 0:00
14/Feb/1920 23:00 -1:00
23/Oct/1920 24:00 0:00
14/Mar/1921 23:00 -1:00
25/Oct/1921 24:00 0:00
25/Mar/1922 23:00 -1:00
7/Oct/1922 24:00 0:00
26/May/1923 23:00 -1:00
6/Oct/1923 24:00 0:00
29/Mar/1924 23:00 -1:00
4/Oct/1924 24:00 0:00
4/Apr/1925 23:00 -1:00
3/Oct/1925 24:00 0:00
17/Apr/1926 23:00 -1:00
2/Oct/1926 24:00 0:00
9/Apr/1927 23:00 -1:00
1/Oct/1927 24:00 0:00
14/Apr/1928 23:00 -1:00
6/Oct/1928 24:00 0:00
20/Apr/1929 23:00 -1:00
5/Oct/1929 24:00 0:00
12/Apr/1930 23:00 -1:00
4/Oct/1930 24:00 0:00
18/Apr/1931 23:00 -1:00
3/Oct/1931 24:00 0:00
2/Apr/1932 23:00 -1:00
1/Oct/1932 24:00 0:00
25/Mar/1933 23:00 -1:00
7/Oct/1933 24:00 0:00
7/Apr/1934 23:00 -1:00
6/Oct/1934 24:00 0:00
30/Mar/1935 23:00 -1:00
5/Oct/1935 24:00 0:00
18/Apr/1936 23:00 -1:00
3/Oct/1936 24:00 0:00
3/Apr/1937 23:00 -1:00
2/Oct/1937 24:00 0:00
26/Mar/1938 23:00 -1:00
1/Oct/1938 24:00 0:00
15/Apr/1939 23:00 -1:00
18/Nov/1939 24:00 0:00
25/Feb/1940 2:00 -1:00
15/Jun/1940 0:00 -2:00
1/Nov/1942 3:00 -1:00
29/Mar/1943 2:00 -2:00
4/Oct/1943 3:00 -1:00
3/Apr/1944 2:00 -2:00
3/Sep/1944 0:00 TT#1
....
Time Table # 96
Before 15/Mar/1891 LMT
Begin Standard 2ε20
15/Mar/1891 0:01 TT#1
15/Jun/1940 0:00 -2:00
1/Nov/1942 3:00 -1:00
29/Mar/1943 2:00 -2:00
4/Oct/1943 3:00 -1:00
3/Apr/1944 2:00 -2:00
3/Sep/1944 0:00 TT#1
....
Time Table # 97
Before 15/Mar/1891 LMT
Begin Standard 2ε20
15/Mar/1891 0:01 TT#1
1/Nov/1914 0:00 -1:00
30/Apr/1916 23:00 -2:00
1/Oct/1916 1:00 -1:00
16/Apr/1917 2:00 -2:00
17/Sep/1917 3:00 -1:00
15/Apr/1918 2:00 -2:00
16/Sep/1918 3:00 -1:00
11/Nov/1918 0:00 0:00
1/Mar/1919 23:00 -1:00
5/Oct/1919 24:00 0:00
14/Feb/1920 23:00 -1:00
23/Oct/1920 24:00 0:00
14/Mar/1921 23:00 -1:00
25/Oct/1921 24:00 0:00
25/Mar/1922 23:00 -1:00
7/Oct/1922 24:00 0:00
26/May/1923 23:00 -1:00
6/Oct/1923 24:00 0:00
29/Mar/1924 23:00 -1:00
4/Oct/1924 24:00 0:00
4/Apr/1925 23:00 -1:00
3/Oct/1925 24:00 0:00
17/Apr/1926 23:00 -1:00
2/Oct/1926 24:00 0:00
9/Apr/1927 23:00 -1:00
1/Oct/1927 24:00 0:00
14/Apr/1928 23:00 -1:00
6/Oct/1928 24:00 0:00
20/Apr/1929 23:00 -1:00
5/Oct/1929 24:00 0:00
12/Apr/1930 23:00 -1:00
4/Oct/1930 24:00 0:00
18/Apr/1931 23:00 -1:00
3/Oct/1931 24:00 0:00
2/Apr/1932 23:00 -1:00
1/Oct/1932 24:00 0:00
25/Mar/1933 23:00 -1:00
7/Oct/1933 24:00 0:00
7/Apr/1934 23:00 -1:00
6/Oct/1934 24:00 0:00
30/Mar/1935 23:00 -1:00
5/Oct/1935 24:00 0:00
18/Apr/1936 23:00 -1:00
3/Oct/1936 24:00 0:00
3/Apr/1937 23:00 -1:00
2/Oct/1937 24:00 0:00
26/Mar/1938 23:00 -1:00
1/Oct/1938 24:00 0:00
15/Apr/1939 23:00 -1:00
18/Nov/1939 24:00 0:00
25/Feb/1940 2:00 -1:00
15/Jun/1940 0:00 -2:00
1/Nov/1942 3:00 -1:00
29/Mar/1943 2:00 -2:00
4/Oct/1943 3:00 -1:00
3/Apr/1944 2:00 -2:00
3/Sep/1944 0:00 TT#1
....
Time Table # 98
Before 15/Mar/1891 LMT
Begin Standard 2ε20
15/Mar/1891 0:01 TT#1
1/Nov/1914 0:00 -1:00
30/Apr/1916 23:00 -2:00
1/Oct/1916 1:00 -1:00
16/Apr/1917 2:00 -2:00
17/Sep/1917 3:00 -1:00
15/Apr/1918 2:00 -2:00
16/Sep/1918 3:00 -1:00
11/Nov/1918 0:00 0:00
1/Mar/1919 23:00 -1:00
5/Oct/1919 24:00 0:00
14/Feb/1920 23:00 -1:00
23/Oct/1920 24:00 0:00
14/Mar/1921 23:00 -1:00
25/Oct/1921 24:00 0:00
25/Mar/1922 23:00 -1:00
7/Oct/1922 24:00 0:00
26/May/1923 23:00 -1:00
6/Oct/1923 24:00 0:00
29/Mar/1924 23:00 -1:00
4/Oct/1924 24:00 0:00
4/Apr/1925 23:00 -1:00
3/Oct/1925 24:00 0:00
17/Apr/1926 23:00 -1:00
2/Oct/1926 24:00 0:00
9/Apr/1927 23:00 -1:00
1/Oct/1927 24:00 0:00
14/Apr/1928 23:00 -1:00
6/Oct/1928 24:00 0:00
20/Apr/1929 23:00 -1:00
5/Oct/1929 24:00 0:00
12/Apr/1930 23:00 -1:00
4/Oct/1930 24:00 0:00
18/Apr/1931 23:00 -1:00
3/Oct/1931 24:00 0:00
2/Apr/1932 23:00 -1:00
1/Oct/1932 24:00 0:00
25/Mar/1933 23:00 -1:00
7/Oct/1933 24:00 0:00
7/Apr/1934 23:00 -1:00
6/Oct/1934 24:00 0:00
30/Mar/1935 23:00 -1:00
5/Oct/1935 24:00 0:00
18/Apr/1936 23:00 -1:00
3/Oct/1936 24:00 0:00
3/Apr/1937 23:00 -1:00
2/Oct/1937 24:00 0:00
26/Mar/1938 23:00 -1:00
1/Oct/1938 24:00 0:00
15/Apr/1939 23:00 -1:00
18/Nov/1939 24:00 0:00
25/Feb/1940 2:00 -1:00
14/Jun/1940 0:00 -2:00
1/Nov/1942 3:00 -1:00
29/Mar/1943 2:00 -2:00
4/Oct/1943 3:00 -1:00
3/Apr/1944 2:00 -2:00
3/Sep/1944 0:00 TT#1
....
Time Table # 99
Before 15/Mar/1891 LMT
Begin Standard 2ε20
15/Mar/1891 0:01 TT#1
15/Jun/1940 0:00 -2:00
1/Nov/1942 3:00 -1:00
29/Mar/1943 2:00 -2:00
4/Oct/1943 3:00 -1:00
3/Apr/1944 2:00 -2:00
13/Sep/1944 0:00 TT#1
....
Time Table # 100
Before 15/Mar/1891 LMT
Begin Standard 2ε20
15/Mar/1891 0:01 TT#1
17/Jun/1940 0:00 -2:00
1/Nov/1942 3:00 -1:00
29/Mar/1943 2:00 -2:00
4/Oct/1943 3:00 -1:00
3/Apr/1944 2:00 -2:00
15/Sep/1944 0:00 TT#1
....
Time Table # 101
Before 15/Mar/1891 LMT
Begin Standard 2ε20
15/Mar/1891 0:01 TT#1
18/Jun/1940 0:00 -2:00
1/Nov/1942 3:00 -1:00
29/Mar/1943 2:00 -2:00
4/Oct/1943 3:00 -1:00
3/Apr/1944 2:00 -2:00
3/Oct/1944 3:00 -1:00
21/Nov/1944 0:00 TT#1
....
Time Table # 102
Before 15/Mar/1891 LMT
Begin Standard 2ε20
15/Mar/1891 0:01 TT#1
5/Jun/1940 0:00 -2:00
1/Nov/1942 3:00 -1:00
29/Mar/1943 2:00 -2:00
4/Oct/1943 3:00 -1:00
3/Apr/1944 2:00 -2:00
13/Sep/1944 0:00 TT#1
....
Time Table # 103
Before 15/Mar/1891 LMT
Begin Standard 2ε20
15/Mar/1891 0:01 TT#1
5/Jun/1940 0:00 -2:00
1/Nov/1942 3:00 -1:00
29/Mar/1943 2:00 -2:00
4/Oct/1943 3:00 -1:00
3/Apr/1944 2:00 -2:00
3/Sep/1944 0:00 TT#1
....
Time Table # 104
Before 15/Mar/1891 LMT
Begin Standard 2ε20
15/Mar/1891 0:01 TT#1
1/Nov/1914 0:00 -1:00
30/Apr/1916 23:00 -2:00
1/Oct/1916 1:00 -1:00
16/Apr/1917 2:00 -2:00
17/Sep/1917 3:00 -1:00
15/Apr/1918 2:00 -2:00
16/Sep/1918 3:00 -1:00
11/Nov/1918 0:00 0:00
1/Mar/1919 23:00 -1:00
5/Oct/1919 24:00 0:00
14/Feb/1920 23:00 -1:00
23/Oct/1920 24:00 0:00
14/Mar/1921 23:00 -1:00
25/Oct/1921 24:00 0:00
25/Mar/1922 23:00 -1:00
7/Oct/1922 24:00 0:00
26/May/1923 23:00 -1:00
6/Oct/1923 24:00 0:00
29/Mar/1924 23:00 -1:00
4/Oct/1924 24:00 0:00
4/Apr/1925 23:00 -1:00
3/Oct/1925 24:00 0:00
17/Apr/1926 23:00 -1:00
2/Oct/1926 24:00 0:00
9/Apr/1927 23:00 -1:00
1/Oct/1927 24:00 0:00
14/Apr/1928 23:00 -1:00
6/Oct/1928 24:00 0:00
20/Apr/1929 23:00 -1:00
5/Oct/1929 24:00 0:00
12/Apr/1930 23:00 -1:00
4/Oct/1930 24:00 0:00
18/Apr/1931 23:00 -1:00
3/Oct/1931 24:00 0:00
2/Apr/1932 23:00 -1:00
1/Oct/1932 24:00 0:00
25/Mar/1933 23:00 -1:00
7/Oct/1933 24:00 0:00
7/Apr/1934 23:00 -1:00
6/Oct/1934 24:00 0:00
30/Mar/1935 23:00 -1:00
5/Oct/1935 24:00 0:00
18/Apr/1936 23:00 -1:00
3/Oct/1936 24:00 0:00
3/Apr/1937 23:00 -1:00
2/Oct/1937 24:00 0:00
26/Mar/1938 23:00 -1:00
1/Oct/1938 24:00 0:00
15/Apr/1939 23:00 -1:00
18/Nov/1939 24:00 0:00
25/Feb/1940 2:00 -1:00
5/Jun/1940 0:00 -2:00
1/Nov/1942 3:00 -1:00
29/Mar/1943 2:00 -2:00
4/Oct/1943 3:00 -1:00
3/Apr/1944 2:00 -2:00
3/Sep/1944 0:00 TT#1
....
Time Table # 105
Before 15/Mar/1891 LMT
Begin Standard 2ε20
15/Mar/1891 0:01 TT#1
12/Jun/1940 0:00 -2:00
1/Nov/1942 3:00 -1:00
29/Mar/1943 2:00 -2:00
4/Oct/1943 3:00 -1:00
3/Apr/1944 2:00 -2:00
31/Aug/1944 0:00 TT#1
....
Time Table # 106
Before 15/Mar/1891 LMT
Begin Standard 2ε20
15/Mar/1891 0:01 TT#1
1/Nov/1914 0:00 -1:00
30/Apr/1916 23:00 -2:00
1/Oct/1916 1:00 -1:00
16/Apr/1917 2:00 -2:00
17/Sep/1917 3:00 -1:00
15/Apr/1918 2:00 -2:00
16/Sep/1918 3:00 -1:00
11/Nov/1918 0:00 0:00
1/Mar/1919 23:00 -1:00
5/Oct/1919 24:00 0:00
14/Feb/1920 23:00 -1:00
23/Oct/1920 24:00 0:00
14/Mar/1921 23:00 -1:00
25/Oct/1921 24:00 0:00
25/Mar/1922 23:00 -1:00
7/Oct/1922 24:00 0:00
26/May/1923 23:00 -1:00
6/Oct/1923 24:00 0:00
29/Mar/1924 23:00 -1:00
4/Oct/1924 24:00 0:00
4/Apr/1925 23:00 -1:00
3/Oct/1925 24:00 0:00
17/Apr/1926 23:00 -1:00
2/Oct/1926 24:00 0:00
9/Apr/1927 23:00 -1:00
1/Oct/1927 24:00 0:00
14/Apr/1928 23:00 -1:00
6/Oct/1928 24:00 0:00
20/Apr/1929 23:00 -1:00
5/Oct/1929 24:00 0:00
12/Apr/1930 23:00 -1:00
4/Oct/1930 24:00 0:00
18/Apr/1931 23:00 -1:00
3/Oct/1931 24:00 0:00
2/Apr/1932 23:00 -1:00
1/Oct/1932 24:00 0:00
25/Mar/1933 23:00 -1:00
7/Oct/1933 24:00 0:00
7/Apr/1934 23:00 -1:00
6/Oct/1934 24:00 0:00
30/Mar/1935 23:00 -1:00
5/Oct/1935 24:00 0:00
18/Apr/1936 23:00 -1:00
3/Oct/1936 24:00 0:00
3/Apr/1937 23:00 -1:00
2/Oct/1937 24:00 0:00
26/Mar/1938 23:00 -1:00
1/Oct/1938 24:00 0:00
15/Apr/1939 23:00 -1:00

18/Nov/1939 24:00 0:00
25/Feb/1940 2:00 -1:00
12/Jun/1940 0:00 -2:00
1/Nov/1942 3:00 -1:00
29/Mar/1943 2:00 -2:00
4/Oct/1943 3:00 -1:00
3/Apr/1944 2:00 -2:00
31/Aug/1944 0:00 TT#1
....

Time Table # 107
Before 15/Mar/1891 LMT
Begin Standard 2E20
15/Mar/1891 0:01 TT#1
1/Nov/1914 0:00 -1:00
30/Apr/1916 23:00 -2:00
1/Oct/1916 1:00 -1:00
16/Apr/1917 2:00 -2:00
17/Sep/1917 3:00 -1:00
15/Apr/1918 2:00 -2:00
16/Sep/1918 3:00 -1:00
11/Nov/1918 0:00 0:00
1/Mar/1919 23:00 -1:00
5/Oct/1919 24:00 0:00
14/Feb/1920 23:00 -1:00
23/Oct/1920 24:00 0:00
14/Mar/1921 23:00 -1:00
25/Oct/1921 24:00 0:00
25/Mar/1922 23:00 -1:00
7/Oct/1922 24:00 0:00
26/May/1923 23:00 -1:00
6/Oct/1923 24:00 0:00
29/Mar/1924 23:00 -1:00
4/Oct/1924 24:00 0:00
4/Apr/1925 23:00 -1:00
3/Oct/1925 24:00 0:00
17/Apr/1926 23:00 -1:00
2/Oct/1926 24:00 0:00
9/Apr/1927 23:00 -1:00
1/Oct/1927 24:00 0:00
14/Apr/1928 23:00 -1:00
6/Oct/1928 24:00 0:00
20/Apr/1929 23:00 -1:00
5/Oct/1929 24:00 0:00
12/Apr/1930 23:00 -1:00
4/Oct/1930 24:00 0:00
18/Apr/1931 23:00 -1:00
3/Oct/1931 24:00 0:00
2/Apr/1932 23:00 -1:00
1/Oct/1932 24:00 0:00
25/Mar/1933 23:00 -1:00
7/Oct/1933 24:00 0:00
7/Apr/1934 23:00 -1:00
6/Oct/1934 24:00 0:00
30/Mar/1935 23:00 -1:00
5/Oct/1935 24:00 0:00
18/Apr/1936 23:00 -1:00
3/Oct/1936 24:00 0:00
3/Apr/1937 23:00 -1:00
2/Oct/1937 24:00 0:00
26/Mar/1938 23:00 -1:00
1/Oct/1938 24:00 0:00
15/Apr/1939 23:00 -1:00
18/Nov/1939 24:00 0:00
25/Feb/1940 2:00 -1:00
12/Jun/1940 0:00 -2:00
1/Nov/1942 3:00 -1:00
29/Mar/1943 2:00 -2:00
4/Oct/1943 3:00 -1:00
3/Apr/1944 2:00 -2:00
30/Aug/1944 0:00 TT#1
....

Time Table # 108
Before 15/Mar/1891 LMT
Begin Standard 2E20
15/Mar/1891 0:01 TT#1
12/Jun/1940 0:00 -2:00
1/Nov/1942 3:00 -1:00
29/Mar/1943 2:00 -2:00
4/Oct/1943 3:00 -1:00
3/Apr/1944 2:00 -2:00
30/Aug/1944 0:00 TT#1
....

Time Table # 109
Before 15/Mar/1891 LMT
Begin Standard 2E20
15/Mar/1891 0:01 TT#1
1/Nov/1914 0:00 -1:00
30/Apr/1916 23:00 -2:00
1/Oct/1916 1:00 -1:00
16/Apr/1917 2:00 -2:00
17/Sep/1917 3:00 -1:00
15/Apr/1918 2:00 -2:00
16/Sep/1918 3:00 -1:00
11/Nov/1918 0:00 0:00
1/Mar/1919 23:00 -1:00
5/Oct/1919 24:00 0:00
14/Feb/1920 23:00 -1:00
23/Oct/1920 24:00 0:00
14/Mar/1921 23:00 -1:00
25/Oct/1921 24:00 0:00
25/Mar/1922 23:00 -1:00
7/Oct/1922 24:00 0:00
26/May/1923 23:00 -1:00
6/Oct/1923 24:00 0:00
29/Mar/1924 23:00 -1:00
4/Oct/1924 24:00 0:00
4/Apr/1925 23:00 -1:00
3/Oct/1925 24:00 0:00
17/Apr/1926 23:00 -1:00
2/Oct/1926 24:00 0:00
9/Apr/1927 23:00 -1:00
1/Oct/1927 24:00 0:00
14/Apr/1928 23:00 -1:00
6/Oct/1928 24:00 0:00
20/Apr/1929 23:00 -1:00
5/Oct/1929 24:00 0:00
12/Apr/1930 23:00 -1:00
4/Oct/1930 24:00 0:00
18/Apr/1931 23:00 -1:00
3/Oct/1931 24:00 0:00
2/Apr/1932 23:00 -1:00
1/Oct/1932 24:00 0:00
25/Mar/1933 23:00 -1:00
7/Oct/1933 24:00 0:00
7/Apr/1934 23:00 -1:00
6/Oct/1934 24:00 0:00
30/Mar/1935 23:00 -1:00
5/Oct/1935 24:00 0:00
18/Apr/1936 23:00 -1:00
3/Oct/1936 24:00 0:00
3/Apr/1937 23:00 -1:00
2/Oct/1937 24:00 0:00
26/Mar/1938 23:00 -1:00
1/Oct/1938 24:00 0:00
15/Apr/1939 23:00 -1:00
18/Nov/1939 24:00 0:00
25/Feb/1940 2:00 -1:00
12/Jun/1940 0:00 -2:00
1/Nov/1942 3:00 -1:00
29/Mar/1943 2:00 -2:00
4/Oct/1943 3:00 -1:00
3/Apr/1944 2:00 -2:00
1/Sep/1944 0:00 TT#1
....

Time Table # 110
Before 15/Mar/1891 LMT
Begin Standard 2E20
15/Mar/1891 0:01 TT#1
12/Jun/1940 0:00 -2:00
1/Nov/1942 3:00 -1:00
29/Mar/1943 2:00 -2:00
4/Oct/1943 3:00 -1:00
3/Apr/1944 2:00 -2:00
1/Sep/1944 0:00 TT#1
....

Time Table # 111
Before 15/Mar/1891 LMT
Begin Standard 2E20
15/Mar/1891 0:01 TT#1
1/Nov/1914 0:00 -1:00
30/Apr/1916 23:00 -2:00
1/Oct/1916 1:00 -1:00
16/Apr/1917 2:00 -2:00
17/Sep/1917 3:00 -1:00
15/Apr/1918 2:00 -2:00
16/Sep/1918 3:00 -1:00
11/Nov/1918 0:00 0:00
1/Mar/1919 23:00 -1:00
5/Oct/1919 24:00 0:00
14/Feb/1920 23:00 -1:00
23/Oct/1920 24:00 0:00
14/Mar/1921 23:00 -1:00
25/Oct/1921 24:00 0:00
25/Mar/1922 23:00 -1:00
7/Oct/1922 24:00 0:00
26/May/1923 23:00 -1:00
6/Oct/1923 24:00 0:00
29/Mar/1924 23:00 -1:00
4/Oct/1924 24:00 0:00
4/Apr/1925 23:00 -1:00
3/Oct/1925 24:00 0:00
17/Apr/1926 23:00 -1:00
2/Oct/1926 24:00 0:00
9/Apr/1927 23:00 -1:00
1/Oct/1927 24:00 0:00
14/Apr/1928 23:00 -1:00
6/Oct/1928 24:00 0:00
20/Apr/1929 23:00 -1:00
5/Oct/1929 24:00 0:00
12/Apr/1930 23:00 -1:00
4/Oct/1930 24:00 0:00
18/Apr/1931 23:00 -1:00
3/Oct/1931 24:00 0:00
2/Apr/1932 23:00 -1:00
1/Oct/1932 24:00 0:00
25/Mar/1933 23:00 -1:00
7/Oct/1933 24:00 0:00
7/Apr/1934 23:00 -1:00
6/Oct/1934 24:00 0:00
30/Mar/1935 23:00 -1:00
5/Oct/1935 24:00 0:00
18/Apr/1936 23:00 -1:00
3/Oct/1936 24:00 0:00
3/Apr/1937 23:00 -1:00
2/Oct/1937 24:00 0:00
26/Mar/1938 23:00 -1:00
1/Oct/1938 24:00 0:00
15/Apr/1939 23:00 -1:00
18/Nov/1939 24:00 0:00
25/Feb/1940 2:00 -1:00
5/Jun/1940 0:00 -2:00
1/Nov/1942 3:00 -1:00
29/Mar/1943 2:00 -2:00
4/Oct/1943 3:00 -1:00
3/Apr/1944 2:00 -2:00
31/Aug/1944 0:00 TT#1
....

Time Table # 112
Before 15/Mar/1891 LMT
Begin Standard 2E20
15/Mar/1891 0:01 TT#1
1/Nov/1914 0:00 -1:00
30/Apr/1916 23:00 -2:00
1/Oct/1916 1:00 -1:00
16/Apr/1917 2:00 -2:00
17/Sep/1917 3:00 -1:00
15/Apr/1918 2:00 -2:00
16/Sep/1918 3:00 -1:00
11/Nov/1918 0:00 0:00
1/Mar/1919 23:00 -1:00
5/Oct/1919 24:00 0:00
14/Feb/1920 23:00 -1:00
23/Oct/1920 24:00 0:00
14/Mar/1921 23:00 -1:00
25/Oct/1921 24:00 0:00
25/Mar/1922 23:00 -1:00
7/Oct/1922 24:00 0:00
26/May/1923 23:00 -1:00
6/Oct/1923 24:00 0:00
29/Mar/1924 23:00 -1:00
4/Oct/1924 24:00 0:00
4/Apr/1925 23:00 -1:00
3/Oct/1925 24:00 0:00
17/Apr/1926 23:00 -1:00
2/Oct/1926 24:00 0:00
9/Apr/1927 23:00 -1:00
1/Oct/1927 24:00 0:00
14/Apr/1928 23:00 -1:00
6/Oct/1928 24:00 0:00
20/Apr/1929 23:00 -1:00
5/Oct/1929 24:00 0:00
12/Apr/1930 23:00 -1:00
4/Oct/1930 24:00 0:00
18/Apr/1931 23:00 -1:00
3/Oct/1931 24:00 0:00
2/Apr/1932 23:00 -1:00
1/Oct/1932 24:00 0:00
25/Mar/1933 23:00 -1:00
7/Oct/1933 24:00 0:00
7/Apr/1934 23:00 -1:00
6/Oct/1934 24:00 0:00
30/Mar/1935 23:00 -1:00
5/Oct/1935 24:00 0:00
18/Apr/1936 23:00 -1:00
3/Oct/1936 24:00 0:00
3/Apr/1937 23:00 -1:00
2/Oct/1937 24:00 0:00
26/Mar/1938 23:00 -1:00
1/Oct/1938 24:00 0:00
15/Apr/1939 23:00 -1:00
18/Nov/1939 24:00 0:00
25/Feb/1940 2:00 -1:00
5/Jun/1940 0:00 -2:00
1/Nov/1942 3:00 -1:00
29/Mar/1943 2:00 -2:00
4/Oct/1943 3:00 -1:00
3/Apr/1944 2:00 -2:00
1/Sep/1944 0:00 TT#1
....

Time Table # 113
Before 15/Mar/1891 LMT
Begin Standard 2E20
15/Mar/1891 0:01 TT#1
12/Jun/1940 0:00 -2:00
1/Nov/1942 3:00 -1:00
29/Mar/1943 2:00 -2:00
4/Oct/1943 3:00 -1:00
3/Apr/1944 2:00 -2:00
1/Sep/1944 0:00 TT#1
....

Time Table # 114
Before 15/Mar/1891 LMT
Begin Standard 2E20
15/Mar/1891 0:01 TT#1
12/Jun/1940 0:00 -2:00
1/Nov/1942 3:00 -1:00
29/Mar/1943 2:00 -2:00
4/Oct/1943 3:00 -1:00
3/Apr/1944 2:00 -2:00
5/Sep/1944 0:00 TT#1
....

Time Table # 115
Before 15/Mar/1891 LMT
Begin Standard 2E20
15/Mar/1891 0:01 TT#1
9/Jun/1940 0:00 -2:00
1/Nov/1942 3:00 -1:00
29/Mar/1943 2:00 -2:00
4/Oct/1943 3:00 -1:00
3/Apr/1944 2:00 -2:00
5/Sep/1944 0:00 TT#1
....

Time Table # 116
Before 15/Mar/1891 LMT
Begin Standard 2E20
15/Mar/1891 0:01 TT#1
8/Jun/1940 0:00 -2:00
1/Nov/1942 3:00 -1:00
29/Mar/1943 2:00 -2:00
4/Oct/1943 3:00 -1:00
3/Apr/1944 2:00 -2:00
5/Sep/1944 0:00 TT#1
....

Time Table # 117
Before 15/Mar/1891 LMT
Begin Standard 2E20
15/Mar/1891 0:01 TT#1
1/Nov/1914 0:00 -1:00
30/Apr/1916 23:00 -2:00
1/Oct/1916 1:00 -1:00
16/Apr/1917 2:00 -2:00
17/Sep/1917 3:00 -1:00
15/Apr/1918 2:00 -2:00
16/Sep/1918 3:00 -1:00
11/Nov/1918 0:00 0:00
1/Mar/1919 23:00 -1:00
5/Oct/1919 24:00 0:00
14/Feb/1920 23:00 -1:00
23/Oct/1920 24:00 0:00
14/Mar/1921 23:00 -1:00
25/Oct/1921 24:00 0:00
25/Mar/1922 23:00 -1:00
7/Oct/1922 24:00 0:00
26/May/1923 23:00 -1:00
6/Oct/1923 24:00 0:00
29/Mar/1924 23:00 -1:00
4/Oct/1924 24:00 0:00
4/Apr/1925 23:00 -1:00
3/Oct/1925 24:00 0:00
17/Apr/1926 23:00 -1:00
2/Oct/1926 24:00 0:00
9/Apr/1927 23:00 -1:00
1/Oct/1927 24:00 0:00
14/Apr/1928 23:00 -1:00
6/Oct/1928 24:00 0:00
20/Apr/1929 23:00 -1:00
5/Oct/1929 24:00 0:00
12/Apr/1930 23:00 -1:00
4/Oct/1930 24:00 0:00
18/Apr/1931 23:00 -1:00
3/Oct/1931 24:00 0:00
2/Apr/1932 23:00 -1:00
1/Oct/1932 24:00 0:00
25/Mar/1933 23:00 -1:00
7/Oct/1933 24:00 0:00
7/Apr/1934 23:00 -1:00
6/Oct/1934 24:00 0:00
30/Mar/1935 23:00 -1:00
5/Oct/1935 24:00 0:00
18/Apr/1936 23:00 -1:00
3/Oct/1936 24:00 0:00
3/Apr/1937 23:00 -1:00
2/Oct/1937 24:00 0:00
26/Mar/1938 23:00 -1:00
1/Oct/1938 24:00 0:00
15/Apr/1939 23:00 -1:00
18/Nov/1939 24:00 0:00
25/Feb/1940 2:00 -1:00
5/Jun/1940 0:00 -2:00
1/Nov/1942 3:00 -1:00
29/Mar/1943 2:00 -2:00
4/Oct/1943 3:00 -1:00
3/Apr/1944 2:00 -2:00
5/Sep/1944 0:00 TT#1
....

Time Table # 118
Before 15/Mar/1891 LMT
Begin Standard 2E20
15/Mar/1891 0:01 TT#1
1/Nov/1914 0:00 -1:00
30/Apr/1916 23:00 -2:00
1/Oct/1916 1:00 -1:00
16/Apr/1917 2:00 -2:00
17/Sep/1917 3:00 -1:00
15/Apr/1918 2:00 -2:00
16/Sep/1918 3:00 -1:00
11/Nov/1918 0:00 0:00
1/Mar/1919 23:00 -1:00
5/Oct/1919 24:00 0:00
14/Feb/1920 23:00 -1:00
23/Oct/1920 24:00 0:00
14/Mar/1921 23:00 -1:00
25/Oct/1921 24:00 0:00
25/Mar/1922 23:00 -1:00
7/Oct/1922 24:00 0:00
26/May/1923 23:00 -1:00
6/Oct/1923 24:00 0:00
29/Mar/1924 23:00 -1:00
4/Oct/1924 24:00 0:00
4/Apr/1925 23:00 -1:00
3/Oct/1925 24:00 0:00
17/Apr/1926 23:00 -1:00
2/Oct/1926 24:00 0:00
9/Apr/1927 23:00 -1:00
1/Oct/1927 24:00 0:00
14/Apr/1928 23:00 -1:00
6/Oct/1928 24:00 0:00
20/Apr/1929 23:00 -1:00
5/Oct/1929 24:00 0:00
12/Apr/1930 23:00 -1:00
4/Oct/1930 24:00 0:00
18/Apr/1931 23:00 -1:00
3/Oct/1931 24:00 0:00
2/Apr/1932 23:00 -1:00
1/Oct/1932 24:00 0:00
25/Mar/1933 23:00 -1:00
7/Oct/1933 24:00 0:00
7/Apr/1934 23:00 -1:00
6/Oct/1934 24:00 0:00
30/Mar/1935 23:00 -1:00
5/Oct/1935 24:00 0:00
18/Apr/1936 23:00 -1:00
3/Oct/1936 24:00 0:00
3/Apr/1937 23:00 -1:00
2/Oct/1937 24:00 0:00
26/Mar/1938 23:00 -1:00
1/Oct/1938 24:00 0:00
15/Apr/1939 23:00 -1:00
18/Nov/1939 24:00 0:00
25/Feb/1940 2:00 -1:00
5/Jun/1940 0:00 -2:00
1/Nov/1942 3:00 -1:00
29/Mar/1943 2:00 -2:00
4/Oct/1943 3:00 -1:00
3/Apr/1944 2:00 -2:00
10/Sep/1944 0:00 TT#1
....

Time Table # 119
Before 15/Mar/1891 LMT
Begin Standard 2E20
15/Mar/1891 0:01 TT#1
9/Jun/1940 0:00 -2:00
1/Nov/1942 3:00 -1:00
29/Mar/1943 2:00 -2:00
4/Oct/1943 3:00 -1:00
3/Apr/1944 2:00 -2:00
1/Sep/1944 0:00 TT#1
....

Time Table # 120
Before 15/Mar/1891 LMT
Begin Standard 2E20
15/Mar/1891 0:01 TT#1
8/Jun/1940 0:00 -2:00
1/Nov/1942 3:00 -1:00
29/Mar/1943 2:00 -2:00
4/Oct/1943 3:00 -1:00
3/Apr/1944 2:00 -2:00
1/Sep/1944 0:00 TT#1
....

Time Table # 121
Before 15/Mar/1891 LMT
Begin Standard 2E20
15/Mar/1891 0:01 TT#1
5/Jun/1940 0:00 -2:00
1/Nov/1942 3:00 -1:00
29/Mar/1943 2:00 -2:00
4/Oct/1943 3:00 -1:00
3/Apr/1944 2:00 -2:00
1/Sep/1944 0:00 TT#1
....

Time Table # 122
Before 15/Mar/1891 LMT
Begin Standard 2E20
15/Mar/1891 0:01 TT#1
5/Jun/1940 0:00 -2:00
1/Nov/1942 3:00 -1:00
29/Mar/1943 2:00 -2:00
4/Oct/1943 3:00 -1:00
3/Apr/1944 2:00 -2:00
2/Sep/1944 0:00 TT#1
....

Time Table # 123
Before 15/Mar/1891 LMT
Begin Standard 2E20
15/Mar/1891 0:01 TT#1
1/Nov/1914 0:00 -1:00
30/Apr/1916 23:00 -2:00
1/Oct/1916 1:00 -1:00
16/Apr/1917 2:00 -2:00
17/Sep/1917 3:00 -1:00
15/Apr/1918 2:00 -2:00
16/Sep/1918 3:00 -1:00
11/Nov/1918 0:00 0:00
1/Mar/1919 23:00 -1:00
5/Oct/1919 24:00 0:00
14/Feb/1920 23:00 -1:00
23/Oct/1920 24:00 0:00
14/Mar/1921 23:00 -1:00
25/Oct/1921 24:00 0:00
25/Mar/1922 23:00 -1:00
7/Oct/1922 24:00 0:00
26/May/1923 23:00 -1:00
6/Oct/1923 24:00 0:00
29/Mar/1924 23:00 -1:00
4/Oct/1924 24:00 0:00
4/Apr/1925 23:00 -1:00
3/Oct/1925 24:00 0:00
17/Apr/1926 23:00 -1:00
2/Oct/1926 24:00 0:00
9/Apr/1927 23:00 -1:00
1/Oct/1927 24:00 0:00
14/Apr/1928 23:00 -1:00
6/Oct/1928 24:00 0:00
20/Apr/1929 23:00 -1:00
5/Oct/1929 24:00 0:00
12/Apr/1930 23:00 -1:00
4/Oct/1930 24:00 0:00
18/Apr/1931 23:00 -1:00
3/Oct/1931 24:00 0:00
2/Apr/1932 23:00 -1:00
1/Oct/1932 24:00 0:00
25/Mar/1933 23:00 -1:00
7/Oct/1933 24:00 0:00
7/Apr/1934 23:00 -1:00
6/Oct/1934 24:00 0:00
30/Mar/1935 23:00 -1:00
5/Oct/1935 24:00 0:00
18/Apr/1936 23:00 -1:00
3/Oct/1936 24:00 0:00
3/Apr/1937 23:00 -1:00
2/Oct/1937 24:00 0:00
26/Mar/1938 23:00 -1:00
1/Oct/1938 24:00 0:00
15/Apr/1939 23:00 -1:00
18/Nov/1939 24:00 0:00
25/Feb/1940 2:00 -1:00
5/Jun/1940 0:00 -2:00
1/Nov/1942 3:00 -1:00
29/Mar/1943 2:00 -2:00
4/Oct/1943 3:00 -1:00
3/Apr/1944 2:00 -2:00
2/Sep/1944 0:00 TT#1
....

Time Table # 124
Before 15/Mar/1891 LMT
Begin Standard 2E20
15/Mar/1891 0:01 TT#1
12/Jun/1940 0:00 -2:00
1/Nov/1942 3:00 -1:00
29/Mar/1943 2:00 -2:00
4/Oct/1943 3:00 -1:00
3/Apr/1944 2:00 -2:00
24/Aug/1944 0:00 TT#1
....

Time Table # 125
Before 15/Mar/1891 LMT
Begin Standard 2E20
15/Mar/1891 0:01 TT#1
12/Jun/1940 0:00 -2:00
1/Nov/1942 3:00 -1:00
29/Mar/1943 2:00 -2:00
4/Oct/1943 3:00 -1:00
3/Apr/1944 2:00 -2:00
25/Aug/1944 0:00 TT#1
....

Time Table # 126
Before 15/Mar/1891 LMT
Begin Standard 2E20
15/Mar/1891 0:01 TT#1
18/Jun/1940 0:00 -2:00
1/Nov/1942 3:00 -1:00
29/Mar/1943 2:00 -2:00
4/Oct/1943 3:00 -1:00
3/Apr/1944 2:00 -2:00
1/Sep/1944 0:00 TT#1
....
Time Table # 127
Before 15/Mar/1891 LMT
Begin Standard 2E20
15/Mar/1891 0:01 TT#1
14/Jun/1940 0:00 -2:00
1/Nov/1942 3:00 -1:00
29/Mar/1943 2:00 -2:00
4/Oct/1943 3:00 -1:00
3/Apr/1944 2:00 -2:00
1/Sep/1944 0:00 TT#1
....
Time Table # 128
Before 15/Mar/1891 LMT
Begin Standard 2E20
15/Mar/1891 0:01 TT#1
14/Jun/1940 0:00 -2:00
1/Nov/1942 3:00 -1:00
29/Mar/1943 2:00 -2:00
4/Oct/1943 3:00 -1:00
3/Apr/1944 2:00 -2:00
2/Sep/1944 0:00 TT#1
....
Time Table # 129
Before 15/Mar/1891 LMT
Begin Standard 2E20
15/Mar/1891 0:01 TT#1
18/Jun/1940 0:00 -2:00
1/Nov/1942 3:00 -1:00
29/Mar/1943 2:00 -2:00
4/Oct/1943 3:00 -1:00
3/Apr/1944 2:00 -2:00
2/Sep/1944 0:00 TT#1
....
Time Table # 130
Before 15/Mar/1891 LMT
Begin Standard 2E20
15/Mar/1891 0:01 TT#1
14/Jun/1940 0:00 -2:00
1/Nov/1942 3:00 -1:00
29/Mar/1943 2:00 -2:00
4/Oct/1943 3:00 -1:00
3/Apr/1944 2:00 -2:00
13/Sep/1944 0:00 TT#1
....
Time Table # 131
Before 15/Mar/1891 LMT
Begin Standard 2E20
15/Mar/1891 0:01 TT#1
12/Jun/1940 0:00 -2:00
1/Nov/1942 3:00 -1:00
29/Mar/1943 2:00 -2:00
4/Oct/1943 3:00 -1:00
3/Apr/1944 2:00 -2:00
2/Sep/1944 0:00 TT#1
....
Time Table # 132
Before 15/Mar/1891 LMT
Begin Standard 2E20
15/Mar/1891 0:01 TT#1
12/Jun/1940 0:00 -2:00
1/Nov/1942 3:00 -1:00
29/Mar/1943 2:00 -2:00
4/Oct/1943 3:00 -1:00
3/Apr/1944 2:00 -2:00
3/Sep/1944 0:00 TT#1
....
Time Table # 133
Before 15/Mar/1891 LMT
Begin Standard 2E20
15/Mar/1891 0:01 TT#1
8/Jun/1940 0:00 -2:00
1/Nov/1942 3:00 -1:00
29/Mar/1943 2:00 -2:00
4/Oct/1943 3:00 -1:00
3/Apr/1944 2:00 -2:00
3/Sep/1944 0:00 TT#1
....
Time Table # 134
Before 15/Mar/1891 LMT
Begin Standard 2E20
15/Mar/1891 0:01 TT#1
8/Jun/1940 0:00 -2:00
1/Nov/1942 3:00 -1:00
29/Mar/1943 2:00 -2:00
4/Oct/1943 3:00 -1:00
3/Apr/1944 2:00 -2:00
2/Sep/1944 0:00 TT#1
....
Time Table # 135
Before 15/Mar/1891 LMT
Begin Standard 2E20
15/Mar/1891 0:01 TT#1
5/Jun/1940 0:00 -2:00
1/Nov/1942 3:00 -1:00
29/Mar/1943 2:00 -2:00
4/Oct/1943 3:00 -1:00
3/Apr/1944 2:00 -2:00
3/Sep/1944 0:00 TT#1
....
Time Table # 136
Before 15/Mar/1891 LMT
Begin Standard 2E20
15/Mar/1891 0:01 TT#1
5/Jun/1940 0:00 -2:00
1/Nov/1942 3:00 -1:00
29/Mar/1943 2:00 -2:00
4/Oct/1943 3:00 -1:00
3/Apr/1944 2:00 -2:00
5/Sep/1944 0:00 TT#1
....
Time Table # 137
Before 15/Mar/1891 LMT
Begin Standard 2E20
15/Mar/1891 0:01 TT#1
5/Jun/1940 0:00 -2:00
1/Nov/1942 3:00 -1:00
29/Mar/1943 2:00 -2:00
4/Oct/1943 3:00 -1:00
3/Apr/1944 2:00 -2:00
8/Sep/1944 0:00 TT#1
....
Time Table # 138
Before 15/Mar/1891 LMT
Begin Standard 2E20
15/Mar/1891 0:01 TT#1
5/Jun/1940 0:00 -2:00
1/Nov/1942 3:00 -1:00
29/Mar/1943 2:00 -2:00
4/Oct/1943 3:00 -1:00
3/Apr/1944 2:00 -2:00
21/Sep/1944 0:00 TT#1
....
Time Table # 139
Before 15/Mar/1891 LMT
Begin Standard 2E20
15/Mar/1891 0:01 TT#1
5/Jun/1940 0:00 -2:00
1/Nov/1942 3:00 -1:00
29/Mar/1943 2:00 -2:00
4/Oct/1943 3:00 -1:00
3/Apr/1944 2:00 -2:00
30/Sep/1944 0:00 TT#1
....
Time Table # 140
Before 15/Mar/1891 LMT
Begin Standard 2E20
15/Mar/1891 0:01 TT#1
5/Jun/1940 0:00 -2:00
1/Nov/1942 3:00 -1:00
29/Mar/1943 2:00 -2:00
4/Oct/1943 3:00 -1:00
3/Apr/1944 2:00 -2:00
9/May/1944 0:00 TT#1
....
Time Table # 141
Before 15/Mar/1891 LMT
Begin Standard 2E20
15/Mar/1891 0:01 TT#1
1/Nov/1914 0:00 -1:00
30/Apr/1916 23:00 -2:00
1/Oct/1916 1:00 -1:00
16/Apr/1917 2:00 -2:00
17/Sep/1917 3:00 -1:00
15/Apr/1918 2:00 -2:00
16/Sep/1918 3:00 -1:00
11/Nov/1918 0:00 0:00
1/Mar/1919 23:00 -1:00
5/Oct/1919 24:00 0:00
14/Feb/1920 23:00 -1:00
23/Oct/1920 24:00 0:00
14/Mar/1921 23:00 -1:00
25/Oct/1921 24:00 0:00
25/Mar/1922 23:00 -1:00
7/Oct/1922 24:00 0:00
26/May/1923 23:00 -1:00
6/Oct/1923 24:00 0:00
29/Mar/1924 23:00 -1:00
4/Oct/1924 24:00 0:00
4/Apr/1925 23:00 -1:00
3/Oct/1925 24:00 0:00
17/Apr/1926 23:00 -1:00
2/Oct/1926 24:00 0:00
9/Apr/1927 23:00 -1:00
1/Oct/1927 24:00 0:00
14/Apr/1928 23:00 -1:00
6/Oct/1928 24:00 0:00
20/Apr/1929 23:00 -1:00
5/Oct/1929 24:00 0:00
12/Apr/1930 23:00 -1:00
4/Oct/1930 24:00 0:00
18/Apr/1931 23:00 -1:00
3/Oct/1931 24:00 0:00
2/Apr/1932 23:00 -1:00
1/Oct/1932 24:00 0:00
25/Mar/1933 23:00 -1:00
7/Oct/1933 24:00 0:00
7/Apr/1934 23:00 -1:00
6/Oct/1934 24:00 0:00
30/Mar/1935 23:00 -1:00
5/Oct/1935 24:00 0:00
18/Apr/1936 23:00 -1:00
3/Oct/1936 24:00 0:00
3/Apr/1937 23:00 -1:00
2/Oct/1937 24:00 0:00
26/Mar/1938 23:00 -1:00
1/Oct/1938 24:00 0:00
15/Apr/1939 23:00 -1:00
18/Nov/1939 24:00 0:00
25/Feb/1940 2:00 -1:00
5/Jun/1940 0:00 -2:00
1/Nov/1942 3:00 -1:00
29/Mar/1943 2:00 -2:00
4/Oct/1943 3:00 -1:00
3/Apr/1944 2:00 -2:00
8/Sep/1944 0:00 TT#1
....
Time Table # 142
Before 15/Mar/1891 LMT
Begin Standard 2E20
15/Mar/1891 0:01 TT#1
18/Jun/1940 0:00 -2:00
1/Nov/1942 3:00 -1:00
29/Mar/1943 2:00 -2:00
4/Oct/1943 3:00 -1:00
3/Apr/1944 2:00 -2:00
7/Jun/1944 0:00 TT#1
....
Time Table # 143
Before 15/Mar/1891 LMT
Begin Standard 2E20
15/Mar/1891 0:01 TT#1
18/Jun/1940 0:00 -2:00
1/Nov/1942 3:00 -1:00
29/Mar/1943 2:00 -2:00
4/Oct/1943 3:00 -1:00
3/Apr/1944 2:00 -2:00
9/Jun/1944 0:00 TT#1
....
Time Table # 144
Before 15/Mar/1891 LMT
Begin Standard 2E20
15/Mar/1891 0:01 TT#1
18/Jun/1940 0:00 -2:00
1/Nov/1942 3:00 -1:00
29/Mar/1943 2:00 -2:00
4/Oct/1943 3:00 -1:00
3/Apr/1944 2:00 -2:00
16/Jun/1944 0:00 TT#1
....
Time Table # 145
Before 15/Mar/1891 LMT
Begin Standard 2E20
15/Mar/1891 0:01 TT#1
18/Jun/1940 0:00 -2:00
1/Nov/1942 3:00 -1:00
29/Mar/1943 2:00 -2:00
4/Oct/1943 3:00 -1:00
3/Apr/1944 2:00 -2:00
27/Jun/1944 0:00 TT#1
....
Time Table # 146
Before 15/Mar/1891 LMT
Begin Standard 2E20
15/Mar/1891 0:01 TT#1
18/Jun/1940 0:00 -2:00
1/Nov/1942 3:00 -1:00
29/Mar/1943 2:00 -2:00
4/Oct/1943 3:00 -1:00
3/Apr/1944 2:00 -2:00
26/Jul/1944 0:00 TT#1
....
Time Table # 147
Before 15/Mar/1891 LMT
Begin Standard 2E20
15/Mar/1891 0:01 TT#1
18/Jun/1940 0:00 -2:00
1/Nov/1942 3:00 -1:00
29/Mar/1943 2:00 -2:00
4/Oct/1943 3:00 -1:00
3/Apr/1944 2:00 -2:00
10/Jul/1944 0:00 TT#1
....
Time Table # 148
Before 15/Mar/1891 LMT
Begin Standard 2E20
15/Mar/1891 0:01 TT#1
18/Jun/1940 0:00 -2:00
1/Nov/1942 3:00 -1:00
29/Mar/1943 2:00 -2:00
4/Oct/1943 3:00 -1:00
3/Apr/1944 2:00 -2:00
30/Jul/1944 0:00 TT#1
....
Time Table # 149
Before 15/Mar/1891 LMT
Begin Standard 2E20
15/Mar/1891 0:01 TT#1
19/Jun/1940 0:00 -2:00
1/Nov/1942 3:00 -1:00
29/Mar/1943 2:00 -2:00
4/Oct/1943 3:00 -1:00
3/Apr/1944 2:00 -2:00
30/Jul/1944 0:00 TT#1
....
Time Table # 150
Before 15/Mar/1891 LMT
Begin Standard 2E20
15/Mar/1891 0:01 TT#1
18/Jun/1940 0:00 -2:00
1/Nov/1942 3:00 -1:00
29/Mar/1943 2:00 -2:00
4/Oct/1943 3:00 -1:00
3/Apr/1944 2:00 -2:00
8/Jul/1944 0:00 TT#1
....
Time Table # 151
Before 15/Mar/1891 LMT
Begin Standard 2E20
15/Mar/1891 0:01 TT#1
18/Jun/1940 0:00 -2:00
1/Nov/1942 3:00 -1:00
29/Mar/1943 2:00 -2:00
4/Oct/1943 3:00 -1:00
3/Apr/1944 2:00 -2:00
19/Jun/1944 0:00 TT#1
....
Time Table # 152
Before 15/Mar/1891 LMT
Begin Standard 2E20
15/Mar/1891 0:01 TT#1
1/Nov/1914 0:00 -1:00
30/Apr/1916 23:00 -2:00
1/Oct/1916 1:00 -1:00
16/Apr/1917 2:00 -2:00
17/Sep/1917 3:00 -1:00
15/Apr/1918 2:00 -2:00
16/Sep/1918 3:00 -1:00
11/Nov/1918 0:00 0:00
1/Mar/1919 23:00 -1:00
5/Oct/1919 24:00 0:00
14/Feb/1920 23:00 -1:00
23/Oct/1920 24:00 0:00
14/Mar/1921 23:00 -1:00
25/Oct/1921 24:00 0:00
25/Mar/1922 23:00 -1:00
7/Oct/1922 24:00 0:00
26/May/1923 23:00 -1:00
6/Oct/1923 24:00 0:00
29/Mar/1924 23:00 -1:00
4/Oct/1924 24:00 0:00
4/Apr/1925 23:00 -1:00
3/Oct/1925 24:00 0:00
17/Apr/1926 23:00 -1:00
2/Oct/1926 24:00 0:00
9/Apr/1927 23:00 -1:00
1/Oct/1927 24:00 0:00
14/Apr/1928 23:00 -1:00
6/Oct/1928 24:00 0:00
20/Apr/1929 23:00 -1:00
5/Oct/1929 24:00 0:00
12/Apr/1930 23:00 -1:00
4/Oct/1930 24:00 0:00
18/Apr/1931 23:00 -1:00
3/Oct/1931 24:00 0:00
2/Apr/1932 23:00 -1:00
1/Oct/1932 24:00 0:00
25/Mar/1933 23:00 -1:00
7/Oct/1933 24:00 0:00
7/Apr/1934 23:00 -1:00
6/Oct/1934 24:00 0:00
30/Mar/1935 23:00 -1:00
5/Oct/1935 24:00 0:00
18/Apr/1936 23:00 -1:00
3/Oct/1936 24:00 0:00
3/Apr/1937 23:00 -1:00
2/Oct/1937 24:00 0:00
26/Mar/1938 23:00 -1:00
1/Oct/1938 24:00 0:00
15/Apr/1939 23:00 -1:00
18/Nov/1939 24:00 0:00
25/Feb/1940 2:00 -1:00
5/Jun/1940 0:00 -2:00
1/Nov/1942 3:00 -1:00
29/Mar/1943 2:00 -2:00
4/Oct/1943 3:00 -1:00
3/Apr/1944 2:00 -2:00
4/Sep/1944 0:00 TT#1
....
Time Table # 153
Before 15/Mar/1891 LMT
Begin Standard 2E20
15/Mar/1891 0:01 TT#1
1/Nov/1914 0:00 -1:00
30/Apr/1916 23:00 -2:00
1/Oct/1916 1:00 -1:00
16/Apr/1917 2:00 -2:00
17/Sep/1917 3:00 -1:00
15/Apr/1918 2:00 -2:00
16/Sep/1918 3:00 -1:00
11/Nov/1918 0:00 0:00
1/Mar/1919 23:00 -1:00
5/Oct/1919 24:00 0:00
14/Feb/1920 23:00 -1:00
23/Oct/1920 24:00 0:00
14/Mar/1921 23:00 -1:00
25/Oct/1921 24:00 0:00
25/Mar/1922 23:00 -1:00
7/Oct/1922 24:00 0:00
26/May/1923 23:00 -1:00
6/Oct/1923 24:00 0:00
29/Mar/1924 23:00 -1:00
4/Oct/1924 24:00 0:00
4/Apr/1925 23:00 -1:00
3/Oct/1925 24:00 0:00
17/Apr/1926 23:00 -1:00
2/Oct/1926 24:00 0:00
9/Apr/1927 23:00 -1:00
1/Oct/1927 24:00 0:00
14/Apr/1928 23:00 -1:00
6/Oct/1928 24:00 0:00
20/Apr/1929 23:00 -1:00
5/Oct/1929 24:00 0:00
12/Apr/1930 23:00 -1:00
4/Oct/1930 24:00 0:00
18/Apr/1931 23:00 -1:00
3/Oct/1931 24:00 0:00
2/Apr/1932 23:00 -1:00
1/Oct/1932 24:00 0:00
25/Mar/1933 23:00 -1:00
7/Oct/1933 24:00 0:00
7/Apr/1934 23:00 -1:00
6/Oct/1934 24:00 0:00
30/Mar/1935 23:00 -1:00
5/Oct/1935 24:00 0:00
18/Apr/1936 23:00 -1:00
3/Oct/1936 24:00 0:00
3/Apr/1937 23:00 -1:00
2/Oct/1937 24:00 0:00
26/Mar/1938 23:00 -1:00
1/Oct/1938 24:00 0:00
15/Apr/1939 23:00 -1:00
18/Nov/1939 24:00 0:00
25/Feb/1940 2:00 -1:00
5/Jun/1940 0:00 -2:00
1/Nov/1942 3:00 -1:00
29/Mar/1943 2:00 -2:00
4/Oct/1943 3:00 -1:00
3/Apr/1944 2:00 -2:00
4/Sep/1944 0:00 TT#1

Abbeville 135 50N06 1E50 -0:07:20
Ableiges 79 49N05 1E59 -0:07:56
Ablis 74 48N31 1E50 -0:07:20
Ablon sur Seine 61 48N43 2E25 -0:09:40
Abondance 1 46N17 6E44 -0:26:56
Abreschviller 14 48N38 7E06 -0:28:24
Abriès 1 44N47 6E56 -0:27:44
Abscon 117 50N20 3E18 -0:13:12
Achères 61 48N58 2E04 -0:08:16
Acheux en Amiénois
122 50N04 2E32 -0:10:08
Achicourt 123 50N16 2E46 -0:11:04
Adainville 70 48N43 1E39 -0:06:36
Agay 1 43N26 6E51 -0:27:24
Agde 1 43N19 3E28 -0:13:52
Agen 1 44N12 0E37 -0:02:28
Ahun 1 46N05 2E05 -0:08:20
Aignay le Duc 52 47N40 4E44 -0:18:56
Aigre 24 45N54 0E01 -0:00:04
Aiguebelette le Lac
1 45N32 5E49 -0:23:16
Aiguebelle 1 45N32 6E18 -0:25:12
Aigueperse 1 46N01 3E12 -0:12:48
Aigues Mortes 1 43N34 4E11 -0:16:44
Aigues Vives 1 43N44 4E10 -0:16:40
Aiguilles 1 44N47 6E52 -0:27:28
Aiguines 1 43N46 6E15 -0:25:00
Aigurande 1 46N26 1E50 -0:07:20
Ailefroide 1 44N53 6E27 -0:25:48
Aillant sur Tholon
46 47N52 3E21 -0:13:24
Ailly le Haut Clocher
122 50N05 2E00 -0:08:00
Ailly sur Noye 120 49N45 2E22 -0:09:28
Ailly sur Somme
121 49N55 2E12 -0:08:48
Aimargues 1 43N41 4E12 -0:16:48
Aime 1 45N33 6E39 -0:26:36
Aincourt 79 49N04 1E47 -0:07:08
Airaines 134 49N58 1E57 -0:07:48
Aire sur l'Adour 1 43N42 0W16 0:01:04
Aire sur la Lys
136 50N38 2E24 -0:09:36
Airvault 24 46N50 0W08 0:00:32
Aisey sur Seine 49 47N45 4E35 -0:18:20
Aïssey 55 47N16 6E20 -0:25:20
Aisy sur Armançon
49 47N39 4E13 -0:16:52
Aix en Othe 77 48N13 3E44 -0:14:56
Aix en Provence 1 43N32 5E26 -0:21:44
Aix les Bains 1 45N42 5E55 -0:23:40
Ajaccio 1 41N55 8E44 -0:34:56
Alban 1 43N54 2E28 -0:09:52
Albaron 1 43N37 4E28 -0:17:52
Albens 1 45N47 5E57 -0:23:48
Albert 122 50N00 2E39 -0:10:36
Albertville 1 45N41 6E23 -0:25:32
Albestroff 17 48N56 6E51 -0:27:24
Albi 1 43N56 2E09 -0:08:36

Alby 1 45N49 6E01 -0:24:04
Alençon 68 48N26 0E05 -0:00:20
Aléria 1 42N05 9E30 -0:38:00
Alès 1 44N08 4E05 -0:16:20
Alfortville 61 48N49 2E25 -0:09:40
Alise Sainte Reine 51 47N32 4E29 -0:17:56
Allaines 71 48N12 1E50 -0:07:20
Allanche 1 45N14 2E56 -0:11:44
Allauch 1 43N20 5E29 -0:21:56
Allègre 1 45N12 3E42 -0:14:48
Allemant 70 48N45 1E37 -0:06:28
Allemont 1 45N08 6E02 -0:24:08
Allevard 1 45N24 6E04 -0:24:16
Allibaudières 86 48N35 4E07 -0:16:28
Alligny en Morvan 45 47N12 4E10 -0:16:40
Allogny 25 47N13 2E19 -0:09:16
Allonnes 71 48N20 1E40 -0:06:40
Allos 1 44N14 6E38 -0:26:32
Almenêches 69 48N42 0E07 -0:00:28
Aloxe Corton 30 47N04 4E52 -0:19:28
Altkirch 4 47N37 7E15 -0:29:00
Amance 58 47N48 6E04 -0:24:16
Amancey 32 47N02 6E05 -0:24:20
Ambérieu en Bugey 27 45N57 5E21 -0:21:24
Ambert 1 45N33 3E45 -0:15:00
Ambleteuse 138 50N49 1E36 -0:06:24
Amboise 25 47N25 0E59 -0:03:56
Ambonnay 88 49N04 4E10 -0:16:40
Ambrières 40 48N24 0W38 0:02:32
Ambronay 27 46N00 5E21 -0:21:24
Amenucourt 79 49N06 1E39 -0:06:36
Amfreville la Campagne 73 49N13 0E57 -0:03:48
Amfreville les Champs 110 49N19 1E19 -0:05:16
Amiens 121 49N54 2E18 -0:09:12
Ammerschwihr 6 48N07 7E17 -0:29:08
Amphion les Bains 1 46N23 6E32 -0:26:08
Ampuis 1 45N29 4E49 -0:19:16
Ampus 1 43N36 6E23 -0:25:32
Ancenis 28 47N22 1W11 0:04:44
Ancerville 87 48N38 5E02 -0:20:08
Ancy le Franc 49 47N46 4E10 -0:16:40
Ancy sur Moselle 10 49N03 6E04 -0:24:16
Andance 1 45N14 4E47 -0:19:08
Andelot 57 48N15 5E18 -0:21:12
Andelot en Montagne 32 46N51 5E56 -0:23:44
Andelu 74 48N53 1E50 -0:07:20
Andeville 80 49N15 2E10 -0:08:40
Andlau au Val 15 48N23 7E25 -0:29:40
Andolsheim 6 48N04 7E25 -0:29:40
Andrésy 61 48N59 2E04 -0:08:16
Andrezel 77 48N37 2E49 -0:11:16
Andrézieux Bouthéon 1 45N32 4E16 -0:17:04
Anduze 1 44N03 3E59 -0:15:56
Anet 73 48N51 1E26 -0:05:44
Angers 28 47N28 0W33 0:02:12
Angerville 48 48N19 2E00 -0:08:00
Angervilliers 78 48N36 2E04 -0:08:16
Angevillers 10 49N23 6E02 -0:24:08
Anglure 77 48N35 3E49 -0:15:16
Angoulême 24 45N39 0E09 -0:00:36
Aniche 117 50N20 3E15 -0:13:00
Anizy le Château 111 49N30 3E27 -0:13:48
Annebault 129 49N15 0E04 -0:00:16
Annecy 1 45N54 6E07 -0:24:28
Annecy le Vieux 1 45N55 6E09 -0:24:36
Annemasse 1 46N12 6E15 -0:25:00
Annet sur Marne 61 48N56 2E43 -0:10:52
Annezin 136 50N32 2E37 -0:10:28
Annonay 1 45N14 4E40 -0:18:40
Annot 1 43N58 6E40 -0:26:40
Anse 27 45N56 4E43 -0:18:52
Ansouis 1 43N44 5E28 -0:21:52
Anthéor 1 43N26 6E53 -0:27:32
Antibes 1 43N35 7E07 -0:28:28
Antony 61 48N45 2E18 -0:09:12
Antraigues 1 44N43 4E21 -0:17:24
Antrain 63 48N27 1W29 0:05:56
Anvin 136 50N27 2E15 -0:09:00
Anzin 103 50N22 3E30 -0:14:00
Aoste 26 45N35 5E36 -0:22:24
Appoigny 46 47N53 3E32 -0:14:08
Apremont 27 46N13 5E40 -0:22:40
Apremont la Forêt 94 48N51 5E38 -0:22:32
Apt 1 43N53 5E24 -0:21:36
Arâches les Carroz 1 46N02 6E39 -0:26:36
Aramon 1 43N53 4E41 -0:18:44
Arbois 32 46N54 5E46 -0:23:04
Arbonne 77 48N25 2E34 -0:10:16
Arcachon 24 44N37 1W12 0:04:48
Arc en Barrois 52 47N57 5E00 -0:20:00
Arces 46 48N05 3E36 -0:14:24
Arc et Senans 32 47N02 5E46 -0:23:04
Arches 58 48N07 6E32 -0:26:08
Archiac 24 45N31 0W18 0:01:12
Arcis sur Aube 86 48N32 4E08 -0:16:32
Arc les Gray 30 47N27 5E35 -0:22:20
Arcueil 61 48N48 2E20 -0:09:20
Arcy sur Cure 45 47N36 3E45 -0:15:00
Ardenay sur Mérize 43 48N00 0E25 -0:01:40
Ardres 138 50N51 1E59 -0:07:56
Arèches 1 45N41 6E34 -0:26:16
Arès 24 44N46 1W08 0:04:32
Argelès Gazost 1 43N01 0E06 -0:00:24
Argelès sur Mer 1 42N33 3E01 -0:12:04
Argentan 69 48N45 0W01 0:00:04
Argentat 1 45N06 1E56 -0:07:44
Argenteuil 61 48N57 2E15 -0:09:00
Argentière 1 45N59 6E56 -0:27:44
Argentières 77 48N39 2E52 -0:11:28
Argenton Château 25 46N59 0W27 0:01:48
Argenton sur Creuse 1 46N35 1E31 -0:06:04
Argentré 65 48N05 0W39 0:02:36
Argent sur Sauldre 41 47N33 2E27 -0:09:48
Argoules 136 50N21 1E50 -0:07:20
Argueil 119 49N32 1E31 -0:06:04
Arinthod 27 46N23 5E34 -0:22:16
Arlanc 1 45N25 3E44 -0:14:56
Arles 1 43N40 4E38 -0:18:32
Arleux 117 50N17 3E06 -0:12:24
Arlod 27 46N06 5E49 -0:23:16
Armenonville les Gâtineaux 70 48N33 1E39 -0:06:36
Armentières 117 50N41 2E53 -0:11:32
Armoy 1 46N21 6E31 -0:26:04
Arnay le Duc 30 47N08 4E29 -0:17:56
Arnouville lès Gonesse 61 49N00 2E25 -0:09:40
Arnouville lès Mantes 74 48N55 1E44 -0:06:56
Arpajon 78 48N35 2E15 -0:09:00
Arques 137 50N44 2E17 -0:09:08
Arques la Bataille 131 49N53 1E08 -0:04:32
Arracourt 13 48N44 6E32 -0:26:08
Arras 123 50N17 2E47 -0:11:08
Ars On Ré 33 46N12 1W31 0:06:04
Ars sur Formans 27 45N59 4E49 -0:19:16
Ars sur Moselle 10 49N05 6E04 -0:24:16
Artemare 26 45N52 5E42 -0:22:48
Artenay 71 48N05 1E53 -0:07:32
Arthies 79 49N06 1E48 -0:07:12
Arthonnay 49 47N56 4E13 -0:16:52
Arvieux 1 44N46 6E44 -0:26:56
Arvillard 1 45N27 6E07 -0:24:28
Ascros 1 43N55 7E01 -0:28:04
Asnières (sur Seine) 61 48N55 2E17 -0:09:08
Aspach le Bas 2 47N46 7E09 -0:28:36
Aspres sur Buëch 1 44N31 5E45 -0:23:00
Asquins 45 47N29 3E45 -0:15:00
Astaffort 1 44N04 0E40 -0:02:40
Athies sur Laon 111 49N34 3E41 -0:14:44
Athis Mons 61 48N43 2E24 -0:09:36
Attainville 61 49N03 2E21 -0:09:24
Attichy 109 49N25 3E03 -0:12:12
Attigny 103 49N29 4E35 -0:18:20
Aubagne 1 43N17 5E34 -0:22:16
Aubenas 1 44N37 4E23 -0:17:32
Aubenton 103 49N50 4E12 -0:16:48
Aubepierre 77 48N38 2E53 -0:11:32
Aubergenville 74 48N58 1E51 -0:07:24
Auberive 52 47N47 5E03 -0:20:12
Aubervilliers 61 48N55 2E23 -0:09:32
Aubigny en Artois 135 50N21 2E35 -0:10:20
Aubigny sur Nère 41 47N29 2E26 -0:09:44
Aubin 1 44N32 2E14 -0:08:56
Auboué 97 49N13 5E59 -0:23:56
Aubrives 118 50N06 4E46 -0:19:04
Aubusson 1 45N57 2E11 -0:08:44
Auch 1 43N39 0E35 -0:02:20
Auchel 136 50N30 2E28 -0:09:52
Audenge 24 44N41 1W00 0:04:00
Audeux 30 47N16 5E53 -0:23:32
Audierne 35 48N01 4W32 0:18:08
Audincourt 60 47N29 6E50 -0:27:20
Audresselles 138 50N49 1E36 -0:06:24
Audruicq 138 50N53 2E05 -0:08:20
Audun le Roman 97 49N22 5E53 -0:23:32
Auffargis 74 48N42 1E53 -0:07:32
Auffay 131 49N43 1E06 -0:04:24
Aulnay 24 46N01 0W21 0:01:24
Aulnay sous Bois 61 48N57 2E31 -0:10:04
Aulnay sur Mauldre 74 48N56 1E51 -0:07:24
Aulnois sur Seille 100 48N52 6E19 -0:25:16
Aulnoye Aymeries 103 50N12 3E50 -0:15:20
Ault 133 50N06 1E27 -0:05:48
Aumale 120 49N46 1E45 -0:07:00
Aumetz 10 49N25 5E56 -0:23:44
Aumont Aubrac 1 44N43 3E17 -0:13:08
Auneau 71 48N27 1E46 -0:07:04
Auneuil 110 49N22 2E00 -0:08:00
Aups 1 43N37 6E14 -0:24:56
Auray 35 47N40 2W59 0:11:56
Aurillac 1 44N56 2E26 -0:09:44
Auriol 1 43N23 5E38 -0:22:32
Auron 1 44N14 6E56 -0:27:44
Auroux 1 44N45 3E44 -0:14:56
Aussois 1 45N14 6E45 -0:27:00
Auteuil 110 49N21 2E05 -0:08:20
Auteuil 74 48N50 1E49 -0:07:16
Autheuil 73 49N06 1E17 -0:05:08
Authon 1 44N14 6E08 -0:24:32
Authon du Perche 68 48N12 0E55 -0:03:40
Authon la Plaine 48 48N27 1E57 -0:07:48
Autrey lès Gray 53 47N29 5E30 -0:22:00
Autun 28 46N57 4E18 -0:17:12
Auve 89 49N02 4E42 -0:18:48
Auvernaux 78 48N32 2E30 -0:10:00
Auvers sur Oise 80 49N04 2E10 -0:08:40
Auxerre 46 47N48 3E34 -0:14:16
Auxi le Château 135 50N14 2E07 -0:08:28
Auxon 50 48N06 3E55 -0:15:40
Auxonne 30 47N12 5E23 -0:21:32
Auxy 28 46N57 4E24 -0:17:36
Auzances 1 46N02 2E30 -0:10:00
Avallon 45 47N29 3E54 -0:15:36
Avenas 27 46N12 4E37 -0:18:28
Avernes 79 49N05 1E52 -0:07:28
Avesnelles 103 50N07 3E57 -0:15:48
Avesnes 103 50N07 3E56 -0:15:44
Avesnes le Comte 122 50N17 2E32 -0:10:08
Avesnes lès Aubert 103 50N12 3E23 -0:13:32
Avesnes sur Helpe 103 50N07 3E56 -0:15:44
Avignon 1 43N57 4E49 -0:19:16
Avilley 55 47N26 6E16 -0:25:04
Avion 153 50N24 2E50 -0:11:20
Avioth 103 49N34 5E24 -0:21:36
Avize 88 48N58 4E01 -0:16:04
Avon 77 48N24 2E43 -0:10:52
Avoudrey 32 47N08 6E26 -0:25:44
Avrainville 78 48N34 2E15 -0:09:00
Avranches 63 48N41 1W22 0:05:28
Avrieux 1 45N13 6E43 -0:26:52
Avroult 137 50N38 2E09 -0:08:36
Axat 1 42N48 2E14 -0:08:56
Ax les Thermes 1 42N43 1E50 -0:07:20
Aÿ 84 49N03 4E00 -0:16:00
Azay le Rideau 24 47N16 0E28 -0:01:52
Azay sur Cher 25 47N21 0E51 -0:03:24
Azay sur Indre 24 47N12 0E57 -0:03:48
Azincourt 136 50N28 2E08 -0:08:32
Baccarat 101 48N27 6E45 -0:27:00
Bacqueville en Caux 131 49N47 1E00 -0:04:00
Badonviller 101 48N30 6E54 -0:27:36
Bâgé le Châtel 27 46N18 4E56 -0:19:44
Bagnères de Bigorre 1 43N04 0E09 -0:00:36
Bagnères de Luchon 1 42N47 0E36 -0:02:24
Bagneux 61 48N48 2E18 -0:09:12
Bagnolet 61 48N52 2E25 -0:09:40
Bagnols en Forêt 1 43N32 6E42 -0:26:48
Bagnols les Bains 1 44N30 3E40 -0:14:40
Bagnols sur Cèze 1 44N10 4E37 -0:18:28
Baigneux les Juifs 51 47N36 4E38 -0:18:32
Bailleau sous Gallardon 70 48N32 1E39 -0:06:36
Bailleul 136 50N44 2E44 -0:10:56
Bailly Romainvilliers 82 48N50 2E49 -0:11:16
Bain de Bretagne 36 47N50 1W41 0:06:44
Bains les Bains 58 48N00 6E16 -0:25:04
Bais 65 48N15 0W22 0:01:28
Balagny sur Thérain 110 49N18 2E20 -0:09:20
Balaruc le Vieux 1 43N27 3E41 -0:14:44
Balbigny 1 45N49 4E11 -0:16:44
Ballancourt 78 48N31 2E23 -0:09:32
Balleroy 144 49N11 0W50 0:03:20
Ballon 47 48N10 0E14 -0:00:56
Bandol 1 43N08 5E45 -0:23:00
Bannay 41 47N23 2E53 -0:11:32
Banon 1 44N02 5E38 -0:22:32
Bantheville 98 49N21 5E05 -0:20:20
Bapaume 117 50N06 2E51 -0:11:24
Barbentane 1 43N54 4E45 -0:19:00
Barbezieux 24 45N28 0W09 0:00:36
Barbizon 77 48N27 2E36 -0:10:24
Barcelonnette 1 44N23 6E39 -0:26:36
Barcillonnette 1 44N26 5E55 -0:23:40
Barcy 80 49N01 2E53 -0:11:32
Barentin 110 49N33 0E57 -0:03:48
Barfleur 145 49N40 1W15 0:05:00
Bargemon 1 43N37 6E32 -0:26:08
Barjac 1 44N18 4E21 -0:17:24
Barjols 1 43N33 6E00 -0:24:00
Bar le Duc 87 48N47 5E10 -0:20:40
Barles 1 44N16 6E16 -0:25:04
Barlin 135 50N27 2E37 -0:10:28
Barneville Carteret 151 49N23 1W47 0:07:08
Barr 15 48N24 7E27 -0:29:48
Barrême 1 43N57 6E22 -0:25:28
Barret le Bas 1 44N16 5E44 -0:22:56
Barst 17 49N04 6E50 -0:27:20
Bar sur Aube 85 48N14 4E43 -0:18:52
Bar sur Seine 50 48N07 4E22 -0:17:28
Bartenheim 8 47N38 7E28 -0:29:52
Bas en Basset 1 45N18 4E06 -0:16:24
Basse Yutz 10 49N21 6E11 -0:24:44
Bastelica 1 42N00 9E02 -0:36:08
Bastia 1 42N42 9E27 -0:37:48
Baud 35 47N52 3W01 0:12:04
Baume les Dames 55 47N21 6E22 -0:25:28
Bavans 55 47N29 6E44 -0:26:56
Bavay 152 50N18 3E47 -0:15:08
Bavilliers 60 47N37 6E50 -0:27:20
Bayel 85 48N12 4E47 -0:19:08
Bayeux 142 49N16 0W42 0:02:48
Bayon 91 48N29 6E19 -0:25:16
Bayonne 24 43N29 1W29 0:05:56
Bayons 1 44N20 6E10 -0:24:40

Bazainville	74	48N48	1E40	-0:06:40
Bazas	24	44N26	0W13	0:00:52
Bazeilles	102	49N40	4E59	-0:19:56
Bazemont	74	48N56	1E52	-0:07:28
Baziège	1	43N27	1E37	-0:06:28
Bazoches les Gallerandes	71	48N10	2E03	-0:08:12
Bazoches sur Hoëne	68	48N33	0E28	-0:01:52
Beaucaire	1	43N48	4E38	-0:18:32
Beauchamp	61	49N01	2E12	-0:08:48
Beaucourt	60	47N29	6E55	-0:27:40
Beaufort	27	46N34	5E26	-0:21:44
Beaufort	1	45N43	6E35	-0:26:20
Beaugency	44	47N47	1E38	-0:06:32
Beaujeu	27	46N09	4E36	-0:18:24
Beaulieu lès Loches	1	47N07	1E01	-0:04:04
Beaulieu sur Mer	1	43N42	7E20	-0:29:20
Beaumes de Venise	1	44N07	5E02	-0:20:08
Beaumesnil	72	49N01	0E43	-0:02:52
Beaumetz lès Loges	122	50N14	2E39	-0:10:36
Beaumont	145	49N40	1W51	0:07:24
Beaumont du Gâtinais	75	48N08	2E29	-0:09:56
Beaumont en Argonne	103	49N32	5E03	-0:20:12
Beaumont la Ronce	41	47N34	0E40	-0:02:40
Beaumont le Roger	72	49N05	0E47	-0:03:08
Beaumont sur Oise	80	49N08	2E17	-0:09:08
Beaumont sur Sarthe	47	48N13	0E08	-0:00:32
Beaune	30	47N02	4E50	-0:19:20
Beaune la Rolande	48	48N04	2E26	-0:09:44
Beaupréau	28	47N12	1W00	0:04:00
Beaurepaire	1	45N20	5E03	-0:20:12
Beaurepaire en Bresse	27	46N40	5E23	-0:21:32
Beaurières	1	44N35	5E33	-0:22:12
Beausoleil	1	43N45	7E26	-0:29:44
Beautor	112	49N39	3E20	-0:13:20
Beauvais	110	49N26	2E05	-0:08:20
Beauvais	48	48N32	2E03	-0:08:12
Beauval	122	50N06	2E20	-0:09:20
Beauvezer	1	44N09	6E36	-0:26:24
Beauville	1	44N17	0E52	-0:03:28
Beauvoir	77	48N39	2E52	-0:11:28
Beauvoir sur Mer	24	46N55	2W02	0:08:08
Beauvoir sur Niort	24	46N11	0W28	0:01:52
Bédarieux	1	43N37	3E09	-0:12:36
Bédarrides	1	44N02	4E54	-0:19:36
Bédoin	1	44N07	5E10	-0:20:40
Beglés	24	44N47	0W34	0:02:16
Béhoust	74	48N50	1E43	-0:06:52
Behren lès Forbach	19	49N10	6E57	-0:27:48
Beine Nauroy	89	49N15	4E13	-0:16:52
Bélâbre	1	46N33	1E09	-0:04:36
Bel Air	78	48N37	2E10	-0:08:40
Belfort	60	47N38	6E52	-0:27:28
Belgodere	1	42N35	9E01	-0:36:04
Belin	24	44N30	0W47	0:03:08
Bellac	1	46N07	1E02	-0:04:08
Belleau	83	49N06	3E18	-0:13:12
Belle Église	80	49N12	2E13	-0:08:52
Bellefontaine	31	46N33	6E04	-0:24:16
Bellefontaine	80	49N06	2E28	-0:09:52
Bellegarde	27	46N06	5E49	-0:23:16
Bellegarde	1	43N45	4E31	-0:18:04
Bellegarde du Loiret	48	47N59	2E26	-0:09:44
Belleherbe	55	47N16	6E40	-0:26:40
Bellême	68	48N22	0E34	-0:02:16
Bellencombre	110	49N42	1E14	-0:04:56
Bellevesvre	29	46N50	5E22	-0:21:28
Belleville	100	48N49	6E06	-0:24:24
Belleville sur Meuse	87	49N11	5E23	-0:21:32
Belleville sur Saône	27	46N06	4E45	-0:19:00
Bellevue	103	49N53	4E12	-0:16:48
Belley	26	45N46	5E41	-0:22:44
Belleydoux	27	46N15	5E46	-0:23:04
Bellicourt	103	49N57	3E14	-0:12:56
Belloy en France	61	49N05	2E22	-0:09:28
Belvès	1	44N47	1E00	-0:04:00
Belz	35	47N41	3W10	0:12:40
Bénestroff	17	48N55	6E45	-0:27:00
Beneuvre	52	47N42	4E57	-0:19:48
Bénévent l'Abbaye	1	46N07	1E38	-0:06:32
Benfeld	23	48N22	7E36	-0:30:24
Berck	137	50N24	1E34	-0:06:16
Berck sur Mer	137	50N24	1E36	-0:06:24
Bercu	117	50N31	3E17	-0:13:08
Bergerac	1	44N51	0E29	-0:01:56
Bergères lès Vertus	88	48N53	4E00	-0:16:00
Bergheim	7	48N12	7E22	-0:29:28
Bergnicourt	103	49N25	4E15	-0:17:00
Bergues	138	50N58	2E26	-0:09:44
Berlaimont	103	50N12	3E49	-0:15:16
Bernaville	135	50N08	2E10	-0:08:40
Bernay	72	49N06	0E36	-0:02:24
Berneval le Grand	131	49N57	1E12	-0:04:48
Berre des Alpes	1	43N50	7E19	-0:29:16
Berre l'Étang	1	43N28	5E11	-0:20:44
Berry au Bac	106	49N24	3E54	-0:15:36
Bertincourt	117	50N05	2E59	-0:11:56
Bertry	103	50N05	3E27	-0:13:48
Berville sur Mer	129	49N26	0E22	-0:01:28
Berzé la Ville	27	46N22	4E42	-0:18:48
Besançon	55	47N15	6E02	-0:24:08
Bessancourt	61	49N02	2E13	-0:08:52
Bessans	1	45N19	7E00	-0:28:00
Bessèges	1	44N17	4E06	-0:16:24
Bessé sur Braye	42	47N50	0E45	-0:03:00
Béthencourt sur Mer	135	50N05	1E30	-0:06:00
Béthisy Saint Pierre	80	49N18	2E49	-0:11:16
Bethoncourt	60	47N32	6E48	-0:27:12
Béthune	136	50N32	2E38	-0:10:32
Beton Bazoches	82	48N42	3E15	-0:13:00
Betz	80	49N09	2E57	-0:11:48
Beugneux	108	49N14	3E25	-0:13:40
Beuil	1	44N06	6E59	-0:27:56
Beure	55	47N12	6E00	-0:24:00
Beuvry	135	50N31	2E41	-0:10:44
Beuzeville	129	49N20	0E21	-0:01:24
Beynes	74	48N51	1E53	-0:07:32
Bèze	30	47N28	5E16	-0:21:04
Béziers	1	43N21	3E15	-0:13:00
Bezons	61	48N56	2E13	-0:08:52
Biache Saint Vaast	123	50N18	2E57	-0:11:48
Biarritz	24	43N29	1W34	0:06:16
Bierné	39	47N49	0W32	0:02:08
Biesles	52	48N05	5E18	-0:21:12
Bièvres	61	48N45	2E13	-0:08:52
Billiat	27	46N04	5E47	-0:23:08
Billom	1	45N44	3E21	-0:13:24
Billy Montigny	153	50N25	2E52	-0:11:28
Binas	44	47N54	1E28	-0:05:52
Bining	18	49N02	7E15	-0:29:00
Biot	1	43N38	7E06	-0:28:24
Biscarrosse	24	44N24	1W10	0:04:40
Bischheim	14	48N37	7E45	-0:31:00
Bischwiller	22	48N46	7E52	-0:31:28
Bitche	20	49N03	7E26	-0:29:44
Bitschwiller lès Thann	2	47N50	7E05	-0:28:20
Blain	35	47N29	1W46	0:07:04
Blainville sur l'Eau	91	48N33	6E24	-0:25:36
Blaisy Bas	51	47N22	4E44	-0:18:56
Blâmont	101	48N35	6E51	-0:27:24
Blamont	60	47N23	6E51	-0:27:24
Blancheface	78	48N32	2E06	-0:08:24
Blandy	77	48N34	2E47	-0:11:08
Blangy le Château	72	49N14	0E17	-0:01:08
Blangy sur Bresle	133	49N56	1E38	-0:06:32
Blanquefort	24	44N53	0W39	0:02:36
Blanzac	1	45N07	3E51	-0:15:24
Blanzy	25	46N42	4E23	-0:17:32
Blaye et Sainte Luce	24	45N08	0W39	0:02:36
Blendecques	137	50N43	2E16	-0:09:04
Bléneau	45	47N42	2E57	-0:11:48
Blénod lès Pont à Mousson	100	48N53	6E03	-0:24:12
Blénod lès Toul	90	48N36	5E50	-0:23:20
Blérancourt	109	49N31	3E09	-0:12:36
Bléré	25	47N20	1E00	-0:04:00
Blériot Plage	139	50N57	1E50	-0:07:20
Bletterans	29	46N45	5E27	-0:21:48
Bleury	74	48N31	1E45	-0:07:00
Bligny	108	49N11	3E52	-0:15:28
Bligny sur Ouche	30	47N06	4E40	-0:18:40
Blois	25	47N35	1E20	-0:05:20
Blonville sur Mer	129	49N19	0E02	-0:00:08
Blotzheim	8	47N36	7E29	-0:29:56
Bobigny	61	48N54	2E27	-0:09:48
Bocognano	1	42N05	9E03	-0:36:12
Boëge	1	46N13	6E25	-0:25:40
Boën sur Lignon	1	45N44	3E59	-0:15:56
Bogny sur Meuse	103	49N51	4E46	-0:19:04
Bohain en Vermandois	103	49N59	3E27	-0:13:48
Boinville en Mantois	74	48N56	1E46	-0:07:04
Boinvilliers	74	48N55	1E40	-0:06:40
Bois Colombes	61	48N55	2E16	-0:09:04
Bois d'Arcy	61	48N48	2E01	-0:08:04
Boisemont	80	49N01	2E00	-0:08:00
Bois Guillaume	127	49N28	1E08	-0:04:32
Bois le Roi	77	48N28	2E42	-0:10:48
Boissettes	77	48N31	2E37	-0:10:28
Boissise la Bertrand	78	48N32	2E35	-0:10:20
Boissy l'Aillerie	80	49N05	2E02	-0:08:08
Boissy Saint Léger	61	48N45	2E31	-0:10:04
Boissy sous Saint Yon	78	48N34	2E13	-0:08:52
Bolbec	127	49N34	0E29	-0:01:56
Bollène	1	44N17	4E45	-0:19:00
Bologne	56	48N12	5E08	-0:20:32
Bombon	77	48N34	2E52	-0:11:28
Bonboillon	30	47N20	5E42	-0:22:48
Bondoufle	78	48N37	2E23	-0:09:32
Bondues	141	50N42	3E06	-0:12:24
Bondy	61	48N54	2E28	-0:09:52
Bonifacio	1	41N23	9E10	-0:36:40
Bonnebosq	129	49N12	0E05	-0:00:20
Bonnelles	78	48N37	2E02	-0:08:08
Bonne sur Ménoge	1	46N10	6E20	-0:25:20
Bonnétable	43	48N11	0E26	-0:01:44
Bonneuil sur Marne	61	48N46	2E29	-0:09:56
Bonneval	71	48N11	1E24	-0:05:36
Bonneval sur Arc	1	45N22	7E03	-0:28:12
Bonnevaux	1	46N18	6E40	-0:26:40
Bonneville	1	46N05	6E25	-0:25:40
Bonnières	79	49N02	1E35	-0:06:20
Bonnieux	1	43N49	5E18	-0:21:12
Bonny sur Loire	41	47N34	2E50	-0:11:20
Bons	1	46N16	6E23	-0:25:32
Bonsecours	127	49N26	1E08	-0:04:32
Boos	127	49N23	1E12	-0:04:48
Bordeaux	24	44N50	0W34	0:02:16
Bormes les Mimosas	1	43N09	6E20	-0:25:20
Bort les Orgues	1	45N24	2E30	-0:10:00
Bouafle	74	48N58	1E54	-0:07:36
Bouaye	28	47N09	1W42	0:06:48
Bouchain	117	50N17	3E19	-0:13:16
Bouchoir	116	49N45	2E41	-0:10:44
Bouclans	55	47N14	6E15	-0:25:00
Boué	103	50N01	3E42	-0:14:48
Bouffémont	61	49N03	2E18	-0:09:12
Bouilly	77	48N12	4E00	-0:16:00
Boujailles	32	46N53	6E05	-0:24:20
Boulay Moselle	12	49N11	6E30	-0:26:00
Boulbon	1	43N52	4E41	-0:18:44
Bouligny	95	49N17	5E45	-0:23:00
Boullay les Troux	61	48N41	2E03	-0:08:12
Boulogne Billancourt	61	48N50	2E15	-0:09:00
Boulogne sur Gesse	1	43N18	0E39	-0:02:36
Boulogne sur Mer	138	50N43	1E37	-0:06:28
Bouloire	43	47N58	0E33	-0:02:12
Boulouris sur Mer	1	43N25	6E48	-0:27:12
Bouqueval	61	49N01	2E26	-0:09:44
Bouradière	1	43N58	5E19	-0:21:16
Bouray sur Juine	78	48N31	2E18	-0:09:12
Bourbon Lancy	25	46N38	3E46	-0:15:04
Bourbonne les Bains	58	47N57	5E45	-0:23:00
Bourbourg	137	50N57	2E12	-0:08:48
Bourdeaux	1	44N35	5E08	-0:20:32
Bourdonné	74	48N45	1E40	-0:06:40
Bourg Achard	127	49N21	0E49	-0:03:16
Bourganeuf	1	45N57	1E46	-0:07:04
Bourg Argental	1	45N18	4E33	-0:18:12
Bourg de Péage	1	45N02	5E03	-0:20:12
Bourg en Bresse	27	46N12	5E13	-0:20:52
Bourges	25	47N05	2E24	-0:09:36
Bourg la Reine	61	48N47	2E19	-0:09:16
Bourg Lastic	1	45N39	2E33	-0:10:12
Bourg lès Valence	1	44N57	4E53	-0:19:32
Bourgneuf	48	48N36	2E00	-0:08:00
Bourgneuf en Retz	24	47N02	1W57	0:07:48
Bourgogne	105	49N21	4E04	-0:16:16
Bourgoin Jallieu	26	45N35	5E17	-0:21:08
Bourg Saint Andéol	1	44N22	4E39	-0:18:36
Bourg Saint Maurice	1	45N37	6E46	-0:27:04
Bourgtheroulde	72	49N18	0E53	-0:03:32
Bourgueil	25	47N17	0E10	-0:00:40
Bourmont	57	48N12	5E35	-0:22:20
Bourneville	127	49N23	0E37	-0:02:28
Bourron Marlotte	75	48N20	2E42	-0:10:48
Bousbecque	141	50N46	3E05	-0:12:20
Boussac	1	46N21	2E13	-0:08:52
Bousse	10	49N17	6E12	-0:24:48
Boussières	32	47N09	5E54	-0:23:36
Boussois	152	50N17	4E03	-0:16:12
Boussy Saint Antoine	61	48N41	2E32	-0:10:08
Bouttencourt	133	49N56	1E38	-0:06:32
Bouvières	1	44N30	5E13	-0:20:52
Bouxières aux Dames	92	48N45	6E10	-0:24:40
Bouxwiller	21	48N49	7E29	-0:29:56
Bouyon	1	43N50	7E07	-0:28:28
Bouzonville	18	49N18	6E32	-0:26:08
Boves	121	49N51	2E23	-0:09:32
Bozel	1	45N27	6E39	-0:26:36
Bracieux	25	47N33	1E33	-0:06:12
Braine	107	49N20	3E32	-0:14:08
Brantôme	1	45N22	0E39	-0:02:36
Bray Dunes	138	51N05	2E31	-0:10:04
Bray sur Seine	77	48N25	3E14	-0:12:56
Bray sur Somme	122	49N56	2E43	-0:10:52
Brazey en Plaine	30	47N08	5E13	-0:20:52
Bréau	77	48N34	2E53	-0:11:32
Brécey	63	48N44	1W10	0:04:40
Brégy	80	49N05	2E52	-0:11:28
Bréhal	63	48N54	1W31	0:06:04
Breidenbach	20	49N08	7E25	-0:29:40
Breil sur Roya	1	43N56	7E30	-0:30:00
Brénod	27	46N04	5E36	-0:22:24
Bresles	110	49N25	2E15	-0:09:00
Bressuire	24	46N51	0W30	0:02:00
Brest	37	48N24	4W29	0:17:56
Bretenoux	1	44N55	1E50	-0:07:20

Breteuil 119 49N38 2E18 -0:09:12
Breteuil sur Iton 73 48N50 0E55 -0:03:40
Bréthencourt 74 48N30 1E55 -0:07:40
Brétigny sur Orge 78 48N37 2E19 -0:09:16
Breuil Bois Robert 74 48N57 1E43 -0:06:52
Breuillet 78 48N34 2E10 -0:08:40
Breuilpont 73 48N58 1E26 -0:05:44
Breux 78 48N34 2E11 -0:08:44
Brézins 1 45N21 5E19 -0:21:16
Brézolles 70 48N41 1E04 -0:04:16
Briançon 1 44N54 6E39 -0:26:36
Briare 41 47N38 2E44 -0:10:56
Briarres sur Essonne 48 48N14 2E25 -0:09:40
Bricquebec 151 49N28 1W38 0:06:32
Briec 35 48N06 4W00 0:16:00
Brie Comte Robert 61 48N41 2E37 -0:10:28
Brienne le Château 85 48N24 4E32 -0:18:08
Brienne sur Aisne 103 49N26 4E03 -0:16:12
Brienon sur Armançon 46 48N00 3E37 -0:14:28
Briey 97 49N15 5E56 -0:23:44
Brignoles 1 43N24 6E04 -0:24:16
Brignoud 1 45N15 5E54 -0:23:36
Briis sous Forges 78 48N38 2E07 -0:08:28
Brinon sur Beuvron 28 47N17 3E30 -0:14:00
Brionne 126 49N12 0E43 -0:02:52
Brion sur Ource 52 47N55 4E39 -0:18:36
Brioude 1 45N18 3E23 -0:13:32
Briouze 69 48N42 0W22 0:01:28
Brissac 1 43N52 3E42 -0:14:48
Brive la Gaillarde 1 45N10 1E32 -0:06:08
Brives Charensac 1 45N03 3E56 -0:15:44
Broglie 72 49N01 0E32 -0:02:08
Bron 27 45N44 4E55 -0:19:40
Broons 36 48N19 2W16 0:09:04
Brossac 24 45N20 0W03 0:00:12
Brou 68 48N13 1E11 -0:04:44
Brousseval 87 48N29 4E58 -0:19:52
Brou sur Chantereine 61 48N53 2E38 -0:10:32
Brouvelieures 101 48N14 6E44 -0:26:56
Brû 101 48N21 6E41 -0:26:44
Bruay en Artois 135 50N29 2E33 -0:10:12
Bruay sur l'Escaut 103 50N23 3E32 -0:14:08
Brue Auriac 1 43N32 5E57 -0:23:48
Brueil en Vexin 79 49N02 1E49 -0:07:16
Brumath 18 48N44 7E43 -0:30:52
Brunoy 61 48N42 2E30 -0:10:00
Brutelles 136 50N08 1E31 -0:06:04
Bruyères 101 48N12 6E43 -0:26:52
Bruyères le Châtel 78 48N36 2E11 -0:08:44
Buc 61 48N46 2E08 -0:08:32
Buchelay 74 48N59 1E40 -0:06:40
Buchy 119 49N35 1E22 -0:05:28
Bucquoy 122 50N08 2E42 -0:10:48
Bucy lès Pierrepont 103 49N39 3E54 -0:15:36
Bueil 73 48N56 1E27 -0:05:48
Bugeat 1 45N35 1E59 -0:07:56
Buhl 3 47N56 7E11 -0:28:44
Buis les Baronnies 1 44N16 5E16 -0:21:04
Bulgnéville 58 48N13 5E50 -0:23:20
Bullion 78 48N37 2E00 -0:08:00
Bully les Mines 153 50N26 2E43 -0:10:52
Burbure 136 50N32 2E28 -0:09:52
Burcin 1 45N26 5E26 -0:21:44
Burdeos → Bordeaux 24 44N50 0W34 0:02:16
Bures 61 48N57 1E58 -0:07:52
Bures sur Yvette 61 48N42 2E10 -0:08:40
Burey en Vaux 99 48N34 5E40 -0:22:40
Burzet 1 44N44 4E15 -0:17:00
Busigny 103 50N02 3E28 -0:13:52
Bussang 60 47N53 6E51 -0:27:24
Bussières 1 45N50 4E16 -0:17:04
Bussy Saint Georges 61 48N51 2E42 -0:10:48
Butten 21 48N58 7E13 -0:28:52
Buxy 25 46N43 4E41 -0:18:44
Buzançais 1 46N53 1E25 -0:05:40
Buzancy 98 49N25 4E57 -0:19:48
Cabourg 142 49N17 0W08 0:00:32
Cachan 61 48N48 2E20 -0:09:20
Cadenet 1 43N44 5E22 -0:21:28
Cadillac 24 44N38 0W19 0:01:16
Caen 147 49N11 0W21 0:01:24
Cagnes sur Mer 1 43N40 7E09 -0:28:36
Cahors 1 44N27 1E26 -0:05:44
Caille 1 43N46 6E44 -0:26:56
Cajarc 1 44N29 1E50 -0:07:20
Calacuccia 1 42N20 9E03 -0:36:12
Calais 139 50N57 1E50 -0:07:20
Callac 36 48N24 3W26 0:13:44
Callas 1 43N35 6E32 -0:26:08
Calonne Ricouart 136 50N29 2E29 -0:09:56
Caluire et Cuire 27 45N48 4E51 -0:19:24
Calvi 1 42N34 8E45 -0:35:00
Camarès 1 43N49 2E53 -0:11:32
Cambrai 117 50N10 3E14 -0:12:56
Cambremer 69 49N09 0E03 -0:00:12
Campagne lès Hesdin 136 50N24 1E52 -0:07:28
Canapville 129 49N19 0E08 -0:00:32
Cancale 64 48N41 1W51 0:07:24
Cancon 1 44N32 0E38 -0:02:32
Candé 38 47N34 1W02 0:04:08
Cannes 1 43N33 7E01 -0:28:04
Canteleu 127 49N27 1E02 -0:04:08
Cany Barville 131 49N47 0E38 -0:02:32
Captieux 24 44N18 0W16 0:01:04
Carbon Blanc 24 44N53 0W31 0:02:04
Carcassonne 1 43N13 2E21 -0:09:24
Carcès 1 43N28 6E11 -0:24:44
Carentan 143 49N18 1W14 0:04:56
Carhaix Plouguer 36 48N17 3W35 0:14:20
Carignan 102 49N38 5E10 -0:20:40
Carling 18 49N10 6E43 -0:26:52
Carmaux 1 44N03 2E09 -0:08:36
Carnetin 61 48N54 2E42 -0:10:48
Carnières 103 50N10 3E21 -0:13:24
Carnon Plage 1 43N32 3E59 -0:15:56
Carnoules 1 43N18 6E11 -0:24:44
Carpentras 1 44N03 5E03 -0:20:12
Carquefou 28 47N18 1W30 0:06:00
Carqueiranne 1 43N05 6E05 -0:24:20
Carrières sous Bois 61 48N57 2E07 -0:08:28
Carrières sous Poissy 61 48N57 2E03 -0:08:12
Carrières sur Seine 61 48N55 2E11 -0:08:44
Carro 1 43N20 5E02 -0:20:08
Carros 1 43N48 7E11 -0:28:44
Carrouges 68 48N34 0W09 0:00:36
Carry le Rouet 1 43N20 5E09 -0:20:36
Carvin 117 50N29 2E58 -0:11:52
Cassagnas 1 44N16 3E45 -0:15:00
Cassel 137 50N48 2E29 -0:09:56
Cassis 1 43N13 5E32 -0:22:08
Casteljaloux 1 44N19 0E05 -0:00:20
Castellane 1 43N51 6E31 -0:26:04
Castelmoron sur Lot 1 44N24 0E30 -0:02:00
Castelnaudary 1 43N19 1E57 -0:07:48
Castelnau Montratier 1 44N16 1E21 -0:05:24
Castelsarrasin 1 44N02 1E06 -0:04:24
Castets 24 43N53 1W09 0:04:36
Castillon la Bataille 24 44N51 0W03 0:00:12
Castres 1 43N36 2E15 -0:09:00
Castries 1 43N40 3E59 -0:15:56
Cattenom 12 49N25 6E15 -0:25:00
Catus 1 44N34 1E20 -0:05:20
Caudebec en Caux 127 49N32 0E44 -0:02:56
Caudebec lès Elbeuf 125 49N17 1E02 -0:04:08
Caudry 103 50N08 3E25 -0:13:40
Caumont sur Durance 1 43N54 4E57 -0:19:48
Caussade 1 44N10 1E32 -0:06:08
Cavaillon 1 43N50 5E02 -0:20:08
Cavalaire sur Mer 1 43N10 6E32 -0:26:08
Cavalière 1 43N09 6E26 -0:25:44
Cayeux sur Mer 136 50N11 1E29 -0:05:56
Caylus 1 44N14 1E46 -0:07:04
Cayres 1 44N55 3E48 -0:15:12
Cazères 1 43N13 1E05 -0:04:20
Celles sur Plaine 101 48N28 6E57 -0:27:48
Cellettes 25 47N32 1E23 -0:05:32
Cendras 1 44N09 4E04 -0:16:16
Censeau 32 46N49 6E04 -0:24:16
Cepoy 45 48N03 2E44 -0:10:56
Cercié 27 46N07 4E40 -0:18:40
Cerdon 27 46N05 5E28 -0:21:52
Cerdon 41 47N38 2E22 -0:09:28
Céreste 1 43N51 5E35 -0:22:20
Céret 1 42N29 2E45 -0:11:00
Cergy 80 49N02 2E04 -0:08:16
Cérilly 1 46N37 2E49 -0:11:16
Cerisiers 76 48N08 3E29 -0:13:56
Cernay 2 47N49 7E10 -0:28:40
Cernay la Ville 74 48N40 1E58 -0:07:52
Cerny en Laonnois 111 49N27 3E40 -0:14:40
Cervione 1 42N20 9E31 -0:38:04
Cesson 78 48N34 2E36 -0:10:24
Cevins 1 45N35 6E28 -0:25:52
Ceyzériat 27 46N10 5E19 -0:21:16
Chabanais 1 45N52 0E43 -0:02:52
Chabeuil 1 44N54 5E01 -0:20:04
Chablis 46 47N49 3E48 -0:15:12
Chabris 24 47N15 1E39 -0:06:36
Chagny 30 46N55 4E45 -0:19:00
Chahaignes 42 47N44 0E31 -0:02:04
Chaillé les Marais 24 46N24 1W01 0:04:04
Chailley 50 48N05 3E42 -0:14:48
Chailly en Bière 77 48N28 2E35 -0:10:20
Chalais 24 45N16 0E02 -0:00:08
Chalamont 27 46N00 5E10 -0:20:40
Chalampé 8 47N49 7E33 -0:30:12
Chaleine 74 48N36 1E43 -0:06:52
Châlette sur Loing 45 48N01 2E44 -0:10:56
Chalifert 82 48N53 2E46 -0:11:04
Chaligny 91 48N37 6E05 -0:24:20
Chalindrey 52 47N48 5E26 -0:21:44
Challans 24 46N51 1W53 0:07:32
Challes les Eaux 1 45N33 5E59 -0:23:56
Chalonnes sur Loire 28 47N21 0W46 0:03:04
Châlons sur Marne 88 48N57 4E22 -0:17:28
Chalon sur Saône 30 46N47 4E51 -0:19:24
Châlus 1 45N39 0E59 -0:03:56
Chamarande 78 48N31 2E13 -0:08:52
Chambéry 1 45N34 5E56 -0:23:44
Chambley Bussières 93 49N03 5E54 -0:23:36
Chambly 80 49N10 2E15 -0:09:00
Chambois 69 48N48 0E07 -0:00:28
Chambon sur Dolore 1 45N30 3E37 -0:14:28
Chambon sur Voueize 1 46N11 2E25 -0:09:40
Chambourcy 61 48N54 2E03 -0:08:12
Chambry 80 49N00 2E54 -0:11:36
Chamonix Mont Blanc 1 45N55 6E52 -0:27:28
Chamousset 1 45N33 6E12 -0:24:48
Chamoux sur Gelon 1 45N32 6E13 -0:24:52
Champagne 1 45N16 4E48 -0:19:12
Champagne en Valromay 26 45N54 5E41 -0:22:44
Champagne sur Seine 77 48N24 2E48 -0:11:12
Champagney 59 47N42 6E41 -0:26:44
Champagnole 31 46N45 5E55 -0:23:40
Champ Agny 1 45N27 6E42 -0:26:48
Champcueil 78 48N31 2E27 -0:09:48
Champdeniers 24 46N29 0W24 0:01:36
Champdeuil 77 48N37 2E44 -0:10:56
Champdor 27 46N01 5E36 -0:22:24
Champeaux 77 48N35 2E48 -0:11:12
Champeix 1 45N36 3E08 -0:12:32
Champier 1 45N27 5E17 -0:21:08
Champigneulles 92 48N44 6E10 -0:24:40
Champigny sur Marne 61 48N49 2E31 -0:10:04
Champlan 61 48N43 2E16 -0:09:04
Champlitte et le Prélot 53 47N37 5E31 -0:22:04
Champrond en Gâtine 68 48N24 1E05 -0:04:20
Champs 46 47N44 3E36 -0:14:24
Champs sur Marne 61 48N51 2E36 -0:10:24
Champvans 30 47N06 5E26 -0:21:44
Chamrousse 1 45N08 5E52 -0:23:28
Chanas 1 45N18 4E49 -0:19:16
Chanceaux 51 47N31 4E42 -0:18:48
Chanceaux sur Choisille 25 47N28 0E42 -0:02:48
Chanteloup 61 48N51 2E44 -0:10:56
Chanteloup les Vignes 61 48N59 2E02 -0:08:08
Chantilly 80 49N12 2E28 -0:09:52
Chantonnay 24 46N41 1W03 0:04:12
Chantraine 91 48N10 6E26 -0:25:44
Chantrans 32 47N03 6E09 -0:24:36
Chaource 49 48N04 4E08 -0:16:32
Chapareillan 1 45N28 5E58 -0:23:52
Chapeauroux 1 44N50 3E44 -0:14:56
Chapet 61 48N58 1E56 -0:07:44
Chaponval 80 49N04 2E09 -0:08:36
Charavines les Bains 1 45N26 5E31 -0:22:04
Charenton du Cher 1 46N44 2E38 -0:10:32
Charenton le Pont 61 48N49 2E25 -0:09:40
Charleville Mézières 103 49N46 4E43 -0:18:52
Charlieu 27 46N10 4E10 -0:16:40
Charly Sur Marne 83 48N58 3E17 -0:13:08
Charmentray 81 48N57 2E47 -0:11:08
Charmes 91 48N22 6E17 -0:25:08
Charmes sur Rhône 1 44N52 4E50 -0:19:20
Charmois l'Orgueilleux 58 48N06 6E16 -0:25:04
Charmont en Beauce 71 48N14 2E06 -0:08:24
Charnay lès Mâcon 27 46N18 4E47 -0:19:08
Charny 46 47N53 3E06 -0:12:24
Charny 81 48N58 2E46 -0:11:04
Charny sur Meuse 87 49N12 5E22 -0:21:28
Charolles 25 46N26 4E17 -0:17:08
Charquemont 55 47N13 6E49 -0:27:16
Charroux 24 46N09 0E24 -0:01:36
Chars 110 49N10 1E56 -0:07:44
Chartres 71 48N27 1E30 -0:06:00
Chartrettes 77 48N29 2E42 -0:10:48
Chasse sur Rhône 27 45N34 4E49 -0:19:16
Château Arnoux 1 44N06 6E00 -0:24:00
Châteaubriant 38 47N43 1W23 0:05:32
Château Chinon 28 47N04 3E56 -0:15:44
Château du Loir 42 47N42 0E25 -0:01:40
Châteaudun 71 48N05 1E20 -0:05:20
Châteaufort 61 48N44 2E06 -0:08:24
Château Gontier 38 47N50 0W42 0:02:48
Château Landon 75 48N09 2E42 -0:10:48
Château la Vallière 41 47N33 0E19 -0:01:16
Châteaulin 36 48N12 4W05 0:16:20

Châteaumeillant	1	46N34	2E12	-0:08:48
Châteauneuf	1	43N23	5E10	-0:20:40
Châteauneuf de Randon	1	44N39	3E40	-0:14:40
Châteauneuf du Pape	1	44N03	4E50	-0:19:20
Châteauneuf du Rhône	1	44N29	4E43	-0:18:52
Châteauneuf en Thymerais	70	48N35	1E15	-0:05:00
Châteauneuf sur Charente	24	45N36	0W03	0:00:12
Châteauneuf sur Loire	48	47N52	2E14	-0:08:56
Châteauneuf sur Sarthe	39	47N41	0W30	0:02:00
Châteauneuf Val de Bargis	28	47N17	3E14	-0:12:56
Château Porcien	103	49N32	4E15	-0:17:00
Château Queyras	1	44N45	6E47	-0:27:08
Châteauredon	1	44N01	6E13	-0:24:52
Châteaurenard	45	47N56	2E56	-0:11:44
Châteaurenard Provence	1	43N53	4E51	-0:19:24
Château Renault	41	47N35	0E55	-0:03:40
Châteauroux	1	46N49	1E42	-0:06:48
Château Salins	12	48N49	6E30	-0:26:00
Château Thierry	83	49N03	3E24	-0:13:36
Châteauvillain	52	48N02	4E55	-0:19:40
Châtel	1	46N17	6E50	-0:27:20
Châtel Censoir	45	47N31	3E38	-0:14:32
Châtellerault	24	46N49	0E33	-0:02:12
Châtel sur Moselle	91	48N18	6E24	-0:25:36
Châtelus Malvaleix	1	46N18	2E01	-0:08:04
Châtenay en France	61	49N04	2E27	-0:09:48
Châtenay Malabry	61	48N46	2E17	-0:09:08
Châtenois	58	48N18	5E50	-0:23:20
Châtenois	16	48N16	7E24	-0:29:36
Châtenois les Forges	60	47N34	6E51	-0:27:24
Châtillon	27	45N53	4E37	-0:18:28
Châtillon	61	48N48	2E17	-0:09:08
Châtillon Coligny	45	47N50	2E51	-0:11:24
Châtillon en Bazois	28	47N03	3E49	-0:15:16
Châtillon en Diois	1	44N41	5E28	-0:21:52
Châtillon la Borde	77	48N33	2E49	-0:11:16
Châtillon sur Chalaronne	27	46N07	4E58	-0:19:52
Châtillon sur Indre	1	46N59	1E11	-0:04:44
Châtillon sur Loire	41	47N35	2E45	-0:11:00
Châtillon sur Marne	84	49N06	3E45	-0:15:00
Châtillon sur Seine	52	47N51	4E33	-0:18:12
Chatonville	74	48N33	1E52	-0:07:28
Chatou	61	48N54	2E09	-0:08:36
Châtres	82	48N43	2E49	-0:11:16
Châttillon de Michaille	27	46N08	5E47	-0:23:08
Chauconin	81	48N58	2E51	-0:11:24
Chaudes Aigues	1	44N51	3E00	-0:12:00
Chauffayer	1	44N45	6E01	-0:24:04
Chaulnes	116	49N49	2E48	-0:11:12
Chaumergy	29	46N51	5E29	-0:21:56
Chaumes en Brie	82	48N40	2E51	-0:11:24
Chaumont	56	48N07	5E08	-0:20:32
Chaumont en Vexin	110	49N16	1E53	-0:07:32
Chaumont Porcien	103	49N39	4E15	-0:17:00
Chaumont sur Aire	87	48N56	5E15	-0:21:00
Chaumont sur Loire	25	47N29	1E11	-0:04:44
Chaumont sur Tharonne	41	47N37	1E54	-0:07:36
Chauny	112	49N37	3E13	-0:12:52
Chaussin	29	46N58	5E25	-0:21:40
Chauvigny	1	46N34	0E39	-0:02:36
Chauvirey le Châtel	53	47N47	5E45	-0:23:00
Chauvry	61	49N03	2E16	-0:09:04
Chavanges	86	48N31	4E34	-0:18:16
Chavenay	61	48N51	1E59	-0:07:56
Chaville	61	48N48	2E10	-0:08:40
Chazay d'Azergues	27	45N53	4E37	-0:18:28
Chazelles sur Lyon	1	45N38	4E23	-0:17:32
Chef Boutonne	24	46N07	0W04	0:00:16
Chelles	61	48N53	2E36	-0:10:24
Chemillé	25	47N13	0W44	0:02:56
Chemin	29	46N59	5E19	-0:21:16
Cheniménil	91	48N08	6E36	-0:26:24
Chennevières	80	49N00	2E07	-0:08:28
Chennevières lès Louvres	80	49N03	2E33	-0:10:12
Chenonceaux	25	47N20	1E04	-0:04:16
Chenôve	49	47N17	5E00	-0:20:00
Chens sur Léman	1	46N20	6E16	-0:25:04
Cheptainville	78	48N33	2E16	-0:09:04
Cherbourg	145	49N39	1W39	0:06:36
Chérence	79	49N05	1E41	-0:06:44
Chéroy	76	48N12	3E00	-0:12:00
Chessy	82	48N53	2E46	-0:11:04
Chevannes	78	48N32	2E27	-0:09:48
Chevenoz	1	46N20	6E39	-0:26:36
Cheverny	25	47N30	1E28	-0:05:52
Chevillon	87	48N32	5E08	-0:20:32
Chevilly Larue	61	48N46	2E21	-0:09:24
Chevreuse	61	48N42	2E03	-0:08:12
Chèvreville	80	49N07	2E51	-0:11:24
Chevry Cossigny	61	48N43	2E40	-0:10:40
Chilly Mazarin	61	48N42	2E19	-0:09:16
Chinon	24	47N10	0E15	-0:01:00
Chirens	1	45N25	5E33	-0:22:12
Chisseaux	25	47N20	1E05	-0:04:20
Choisel	61	48N41	2E01	-0:08:04
Choisy	1	45N59	6E03	-0:24:12
Choisy le Roi	61	48N46	2E25	-0:09:40
Cholet	25	47N04	0W53	0:03:32
Chomérac	1	44N42	4E39	-0:18:36
Chorges	1	44N33	6E17	-0:25:08
Cirey sur Vezouze	101	48N35	6E57	-0:27:48
Civray	24	46N09	0E18	-0:01:12
Cize	27	46N12	5E26	-0:21:44
Clairfontaine en Yvelines	74	48N37	1E55	-0:07:40
Clairmarais	137	50N46	2E18	-0:09:12
Clairvaux les Lacs	27	46N34	5E45	-0:23:00
Claix	1	45N07	5E40	-0:22:40
Clamart	61	48N48	2E16	-0:09:04
Clamecy	45	47N27	3E31	-0:14:04
Clans	1	44N00	7E09	-0:28:36
Claret	1	43N52	3E54	-0:15:36
Clary	103	50N05	3E24	-0:13:36
Claude	54	47N23	5E52	-0:23:28
Claye Souilly	61	48N57	2E42	-0:10:48
Clefmont	57	48N06	5E31	-0:22:04
Clelles	1	44N50	5E37	-0:22:28
Cléon d'Andran	1	44N37	4E56	-0:19:44
Clères	110	49N36	1E07	-0:04:28
Clermont	36	49N23	2E24	-0:09:36
Clermont en Argonne	87	49N06	5E04	-0:20:16
Clermont Ferrand	1	45N47	3E05	-0:12:20
Clerval	55	47N24	6E30	-0:26:00
Cléry Saint André	44	47N49	1E45	-0:07:00
Clichy	61	48N54	2E18	-0:09:12
Clichy sous Bois	61	48N55	2E33	-0:10:12
Clisson	24	47N05	1W17	0:05:08
Cloyes sur le Loir	44	48N00	1E14	-0:04:56
Cluny	27	46N26	4E39	-0:18:36
Cluses	1	46N04	6E36	-0:26:24
Coclois	86	48N28	4E20	-0:17:20
Cognac	24	45N42	0W20	0:01:20
Cognin	1	45N34	5E54	-0:23:36
Cogolin	1	43N15	6E32	-0:26:08
Coignières	74	48N45	1E55	-0:07:40
Colembert	137	50N45	1E50	-0:07:20
Coligny	27	46N23	5E21	-0:21:24
Collégien	61	48N50	2E40	-0:10:40
Collobrières	1	43N14	6E18	-0:25:12
Collonges	27	46N08	5E54	-0:23:36
Colmar	6	48N05	7E22	-0:29:28
Colmars	1	44N11	6E38	-0:26:32
Colombes	61	48N55	2E15	-0:09:00
Colombey les Belles	90	48N32	5E54	-0:23:36
Colombey les Deux Eglises	87	48N13	4E53	-0:19:32
Colonard Corubert	68	48N25	0E39	-0:02:36
Combeaufontaine	53	47N43	5E53	-0:23:32
Combles	117	50N01	2E52	-0:11:28
Combloux	1	45N54	6E39	-0:26:36
Combourg	62	48N25	1W45	0:07:00
Combres	68	48N19	1E04	-0:04:16
Combronde	1	45N59	3E05	-0:12:20
Combs la Ville	78	48N40	2E34	-0:10:16
Comines	141	50N46	3E01	-0:12:04
Commentry	1	46N17	2E44	-0:10:56
Commercy	94	48N45	5E35	-0:22:20
Compans	80	49N00	2E40	-0:10:40
Compiègne	113	49N25	2E50	-0:11:20
Comps sur Artuby	1	43N43	6E30	-0:26:00
Concarneau	35	47N52	3W55	0:15:40
Conches en Ouche	73	48N58	0E56	-0:03:44
Condat en Féniers	1	45N21	2E46	-0:11:04
Condé	40	48N51	0W33	0:02:12
Condécourt	79	49N02	1E57	-0:07:48
Condé en Brie	84	49N00	3E33	-0:14:12
Condé sur l'Escaut	117	50N27	3E35	-0:14:20
Condè sur Vesgre	74	48N45	1E40	-0:06:40
Condom	1	43N58	0E22	-0:01:28
Condrieu	1	45N27	4E46	-0:19:04
Conflans en Jarnisy	95	49N10	5E51	-0:23:24
Conflans Sainte Honorine	61	48N59	2E06	-0:08:24
Confolens	1	46N01	0E41	-0:02:44
Conliège	27	46N39	5E36	-0:22:24
Connaux	1	44N05	4E36	-0:18:24
Connerré	43	48N03	0E30	-0:02:00
Contes	1	43N49	7E19	-0:29:16
Contres	25	47N25	1E26	-0:05:44
Contrexéville	58	48N11	5E54	-0:23:36
Contrisson	87	48N48	4E57	-0:19:48
Conty	120	49N44	2E09	-0:08:36
Contz les Bains	12	49N27	6E21	-0:25:24
Corbeil Essonnes	78	48N36	2E29	-0:09:56
Corbenay	59	47N54	6E20	-0:25:20
Corbeny	106	49N28	3E49	-0:15:16
Corberon	30	47N01	4E59	-0:19:56
Corbie	122	49N55	2E30	-0:10:00
Corbigny	28	47N15	3E40	-0:14:40
Corcieux	101	48N10	6E53	-0:27:32
Cordes	1	44N04	1E57	-0:07:48
Corlay	36	48N19	3W03	0:12:12
Cormainville	71	48N08	1E36	-0:06:24
Cormatin	25	46N33	4E41	-0:18:44
Cormeilles	72	49N15	0E23	-0:01:32
Cormeilles en Parisis	61	48N59	2E12	-0:08:48
Cormery	25	47N16	0E51	-0:03:24
Cornas	1	44N58	4E51	-0:19:24
Corps	1	44N49	5E57	-0:23:48
Corte	1	42N18	9E08	-0:36:32
Cosne sur Loire	41	47N24	2E55	-0:11:40
Cossé le Vivien	38	47N57	0W55	0:03:40
Costaros	1	44N54	3E50	-0:15:20
Cotignac	1	43N32	6E09	-0:24:36
Coubert	77	48N40	2E42	-0:10:48
Coubron	61	48N55	2E35	-0:10:20
Couches les Mines	30	46N52	4E34	-0:18:16
Coucouron	1	44N48	3E58	-0:15:52
Coucy le Château Auffrique	112	49N31	3E19	-0:13:16
Coudekerque Branche	140	51N02	2E24	-0:09:36
Couhé	24	46N18	0E11	-0:00:44
Couilly Pont aux Dames	82	48N53	2E52	-0:11:28
Coulanges la Vineuse	45	47N42	3E35	-0:14:20
Coulanges sur Yonne	45	47N31	3E32	-0:14:08
Coulmier le Sec	51	47N45	4E29	-0:17:56
Coulogne	138	50N55	1E53	-0:07:32
Coulomby	137	50N42	2E00	-0:08:00
Coulommiers	82	48N49	3E05	-0:12:20
Coupvray	82	48N54	2E48	-0:11:12
Courbevoie	61	48N54	2E15	-0:09:00
Courbons	1	44N06	6E12	-0:24:48
Courçay	24	47N15	0E52	-0:03:28
Courcelle	61	48N42	2E06	-0:08:24
Courcelles	80	49N07	2E18	-0:09:12
Courcelles Chaussy	12	49N07	6E24	-0:25:36
Courcelles les Lens	117	50N25	3E01	-0:12:04
Courcelles sur Nied	12	49N04	6E18	-0:25:12
Courchevel	1	45N25	6E38	-0:26:32
Cour Cheverny	25	47N30	1E27	-0:05:48
Courçon	24	46N15	0W49	0:03:16
Courcouronnes	78	48N37	2E24	-0:09:36
Courdimanche	80	49N02	2E00	-0:08:00
Cour et Buis	1	45N26	5E00	-0:20:00
Courgent	74	48N54	1E40	-0:06:40
Courpière	1	45N45	3E33	-0:14:12
Courquetaine	82	48N41	2E45	-0:11:00
Courson les Carrières	45	47N36	3E30	-0:14:00
Courtacon	82	48N42	3E17	-0:13:08
Courtalain	44	48N05	1E09	-0:04:36
Courtenay	46	48N02	3E03	-0:12:12
Courthézon	1	44N05	4E53	-0:19:32
Courtisols	88	48N59	4E31	-0:18:04
Courtomer	68	48N38	0E22	-0:01:28
Courtomer	77	48N39	2E54	-0:11:36
Courtry	77	48N33	2E46	-0:11:04
Courtry	61	48N55	2E36	-0:10:24
Courville sur Eure	68	48N27	1E15	-0:05:00
Cousolre	152	50N15	4E09	-0:16:36
Coussegrey	50	47N57	4E01	-0:16:04
Coussey	57	48N25	5E41	-0:22:44
Coustellet	1	43N53	5E11	-0:20:44
Coutances	148	49N03	1W26	0:05:44
Coutevroult	82	48N52	2E51	-0:11:24
Coutras	24	45N02	0W08	0:00:32
Couture sur Loir	42	47N45	0E41	-0:02:44
Cozes	24	45N35	0W50	0:03:20
Craches	74	48N34	1E49	-0:07:16
Cramant	84	48N59	3E59	-0:15:56
Cran Gévrier	1	45N54	6E06	-0:24:24
Craon	38	47N51	0W57	0:03:48
Craonne	106	49N26	3E47	-0:15:08
Craponne	27	45N44	4E43	-0:18:52
Craponne	1	45N20	3E51	-0:15:24
Cravant	45	47N41	3E41	-0:14:44
Crêches sur Saône	27	46N15	4E47	-0:19:08
Crécy en Brie	82	48N51	2E55	-0:11:40
Crécy en Ponthieu	136	50N15	1E53	-0:07:32
Crécy sur Serre	112	49N42	3E37	-0:14:28
Crégy lès Meaux	81	48N58	2E52	-0:11:28
Créhange	12	49N03	6E35	-0:26:20
Creil	110	49N16	2E29	-0:09:56
Crémieu	26	45N43	5E15	-0:21:00
Crépieux la Pape	27	45N48	4E52	-0:19:28
Crépy en Laonnois	112	49N36	3E31	-0:14:04
Crépy en Valois	80	49N14	2E54	-0:11:36
Créquy	136	50N29	2E03	-0:08:12
Crespian	1	43N53	4E06	-0:16:24
Crespières	74	48N53	1E55	-0:07:40
Crespin	117	50N25	3E39	-0:14:36

Cressely 61 48N43 2E05 -0:08:20
Crest 1 44N44 5E02 -0:20:08
Créteil 61 48N48 2E28 -0:09:52
Creutzwald la Croix 18 49N12 6E41 -0:26:44
Crèvecœur en Auge 69 49N07 0E01 -0:00:04
Crèvecœur en Brie 82 48N45 2E55 -0:11:40
Crèvecœur le Grand 119 49N36 2E05 -0:08:20
Criel sur Mer 133 50N01 1E19 -0:05:16
Criquetot l'Esneval 128 49N39 0E16 -0:01:04
Crisenoy 77 48N36 2E45 -0:11:00
Croisilles 123 50N12 2E53 -0:11:32
Croissy Beaubourg 61 48N50 2E40 -0:10:40
Croissy sur Seine 61 48N53 2E09 -0:08:36
Croix 117 50N40 3E09 -0:12:36
Crolles 1 45N17 5E53 -0:23:32
Crosne 61 48N43 2E28 -0:09:52
Crotenay 27 46N45 5E49 -0:23:16
Crouy 107 49N24 3E22 -0:13:28
Crozon 37 48N15 4W29 0:17:56
Cruas 1 44N39 4E46 -0:19:04
Cruseilles 1 46N02 6E07 -0:24:28
Crusnes 10 49N26 5E55 -0:23:40
Cruzy le Châtel 49 47N51 4E12 -0:16:48
Cucuron 1 43N47 5E26 -0:21:44
Cuers 1 43N14 6E04 -0:24:16
Cuiseaux 27 46N30 5E24 -0:21:36
Cuisery 27 46N33 5E00 -0:20:00
Cuisy 80 49N01 2E46 -0:11:04
Culoz 26 45N51 5E47 -0:23:08
Cunlhat 1 45N38 3E35 -0:14:20
Cuperly 89 49N04 4E26 -0:17:44
Cussey sur l'Ognon 54 47N20 5E56 -0:23:44
Custines 100 48N48 6E09 -0:24:36
Cuvilly 114 49N33 2E42 -0:10:48
Cysoing 117 50N34 3E13 -0:12:52
Dabo 14 48N39 7E14 -0:28:56
Dambach la Ville 15 48N20 7E26 -0:29:44
Damelevières 91 48N33 6E23 -0:25:32
Damery 84 49N04 3E53 -0:15:32
Dammarie 71 48N21 1E30 -0:06:00
Dammarie lès Lys 77 48N31 2E39 -0:10:36
Dammartin en Goële 80 49N03 2E41 -0:10:44
Dammartin en Serve 74 48N54 1E37 -0:06:28
Dampierre 32 47N09 5E45 -0:23:00
Dampierre 61 48N42 1E59 -0:07:56
Dampierre en Burly 45 47N46 2E31 -0:10:04
Dampierre sur Linotte 54 47N31 6E14 -0:24:56
Dampierre sur Salon 30 47N33 5E41 -0:22:44
Dampmart 61 48N53 2E44 -0:10:56
Damprichard 60 47N15 6E53 -0:27:32
Damville 73 48N52 1E04 -0:04:16
Damvillers 98 49N20 5E24 -0:21:36
Danjoutin 60 47N37 6E52 -0:27:28
Dannemarie 60 47N38 7E08 -0:28:32
Daoulas 37 48N22 4W15 0:17:00
Darnétal 127 49N27 1E09 -0:04:36
Darney 58 48N05 6E03 -0:24:12
Davron 61 48N52 1E57 -0:07:48
Dax 24 43N43 1W03 0:04:12
Deauville 129 49N22 0E04 -0:00:16
Decazeville 1 44N34 2E15 -0:09:00
Déchy 117 50N21 3E07 -0:12:28
Decize 25 46N50 3E27 -0:13:48
Delle 60 47N30 7E00 -0:28:00
Delme 12 48N53 6E24 -0:25:36
Denain 103 50N20 3E23 -0:13:32
Denisy 74 48N33 1E56 -0:07:44
Dennemont 79 49N01 1E42 -0:06:48
Denouval 61 48N58 2E03 -0:08:12
Derval 35 47N40 1W40 0:06:40
Descartes 24 46N58 0E42 -0:02:48
Desvres 137 50N40 1E50 -0:07:20
Dettwiller 21 48N45 7E28 -0:29:52
Deuil la Barre 61 48N59 2E20 -0:09:20
Deville 118 49N53 4E42 -0:18:48
Déville lès Rouen 127 49N28 1E02 -0:04:08
Die 1 44N45 5E22 -0:21:28
Diedenhofen → Thionville 10 49N22 6E10 -0:24:40
Dieppe 131 49N56 1E05 -0:04:20
Dieue sur Meuse 87 49N04 5E25 -0:21:40
Dieulefit 1 44N31 5E04 -0:20:16
Dieulouard 100 48N51 6E04 -0:24:16
Dieuze 12 48N49 6E43 -0:26:52
Digne 1 44N06 6E14 -0:24:56
Digoin 25 46N29 3E59 -0:15:56
Dijon 49 47N19 5E01 -0:20:04
Dinan 62 48N27 2W02 0:08:08
Dinard 64 48N38 2W04 0:08:16
Dions 1 43N56 4E19 -0:17:16
Distroff 12 49N20 6E16 -0:25:04
Divion 135 50N28 2E30 -0:10:00
Divonne les Bains 27 46N22 6E08 -0:24:32
Dizy 84 49N04 3E58 -0:15:52
Dol de Bretagne 62 48N33 1W45 0:07:00
Dole 30 47N06 5E30 -0:22:00
Domart en Ponthieu 122 50N04 2E07 -0:08:28

Dombasle sur Meurthe 91 48N38 6E21 -0:25:24
Domène 1 45N12 5E50 -0:23:20
Domèvre en Haye 93 48N49 5E55 -0:23:40
Domfront 40 48N36 0W39 0:02:36
Dommartin lès Toul 93 48N40 5E54 -0:23:36
Dommartin Varimont 89 48N58 4E46 -0:19:04
Dommary Baroncourt 95 49N17 5E42 -0:22:48
Domont 61 49N02 2E20 -0:09:20
Dompaire 58 48N13 6E13 -0:24:52
Dompierre sur Besbre 25 46N31 3E41 -0:14:44
Domrémy la Pucelle 57 48N27 5E41 -0:22:44
Domvast 135 50N12 1E55 -0:07:40
Donchêry 103 49N42 4E52 -0:19:28
Donnemarie Dontilly 77 48N29 3E08 -0:12:32
Donzère 1 44N27 4E43 -0:18:52
Donzy 28 47N22 3E08 -0:12:32
Dordives 75 48N09 2E46 -0:11:04
Dormans 84 49N04 3E38 -0:14:32
Dornecy 45 47N26 3E35 -0:14:20
Dortan 27 46N19 5E40 -0:22:40
Douai 117 50N22 3E04 -0:12:16
Douarnenez 35 48N06 4W20 0:17:20
Doubs 32 46N56 6E21 -0:25:24
Douchy 46 47N57 3E03 -0:12:12
Douchy les Mines 103 50N18 3E23 -0:13:32
Doudeville 131 49N43 0E48 -0:03:12
Doulaincourt 99 48N19 5E12 -0:20:48
Doulevant le Château 87 48N23 4E55 -0:19:40
Doullens 122 50N09 2E21 -0:09:24
Dourdan 48 48N32 2E01 -0:08:04
Dourges 153 50N26 2E59 -0:11:56
Douvaine 1 46N19 6E18 -0:25:12
Douvres 142 49N17 0W23 0:01:32
Douvrin 117 50N31 2E50 -0:11:20
Douy la Ramée 80 49N04 2E53 -0:11:32
Douzy 102 49N40 5E03 -0:20:12
Draguignan 1 43N32 6E28 -0:25:52
Drancy 61 48N56 2E27 -0:09:48
Drap 1 43N45 7E19 -0:29:16
Draveil 61 48N41 2E25 -0:09:40
Dreux 70 48N44 1E22 -0:05:28
Drocourt 79 49N03 1E46 -0:07:04
Droué 44 48N02 1E05 -0:04:20
Droue sur Drouette 74 48N36 1E42 -0:06:48
Drulingen 21 48N52 7E11 -0:28:44
Drusenheim 22 48N46 7E57 -0:31:48
Druyes les Belles Fontaines 45 47N33 3E25 -0:13:40
Duclair 127 49N29 0E53 -0:03:32
Dugny 61 48N57 2E25 -0:09:40
Dugny sur Meuse 87 49N06 5E23 -0:21:32
Duingt 1 45N50 6E12 -0:24:48
Dunières 1 45N13 4E20 -0:17:20
Dunkerque 140 51N03 2E22 -0:09:28
Dunkirk → Dunkerque 140 51N03 2E22 -0:09:28
Dun le Palestel 1 46N17 1E48 -0:07:12
Dun sur Auron 1 46N53 2E34 -0:10:16
Dun sur Meuse 98 49N23 5E11 -0:20:44
Duras 1 44N41 0E11 -0:00:44
Eaubonne 61 49N00 2E17 -0:09:08
Eauze 1 43N52 0E06 -0:00:24
Echarcon 78 48N34 2E24 -0:09:36
Échauffour 69 48N44 0E23 -0:01:32
Échenoz la Méline 54 47N36 6E08 -0:24:32
Eckbolsheim 14 48N35 7E41 -0:30:44
Écommoy 39 47N50 0E16 -0:01:04
Écos 124 49N10 1E39 -0:06:36
Écouen 61 49N01 2E23 -0:09:32
Écouis 110 49N19 1E26 -0:05:44
Ecquevilly 74 48N57 1E55 -0:07:40
Écrosnes 74 48N33 1E44 -0:06:56
Écueillé 1 47N05 1E21 -0:05:24
Écuisses 25 46N45 4E32 -0:18:08
Écury sur Coole 88 48N54 4E20 -0:17:20
Égletons 1 45N24 2E03 -0:08:12
Égly 78 48N35 2E13 -0:08:52
Égreville 76 48N10 2E52 -0:11:28
Éguilles 1 43N34 5E22 -0:21:28
Eguisheim 6 48N03 7E18 -0:29:12
Einville au Jard 91 48N39 6E30 -0:26:00
Elancourt 61 48N47 1E58 -0:07:52
Elbeuf 125 49N17 1E00 -0:04:00
El Havre → Le Havre 130 49N30 0E08 -0:00:32
Élisabethville 74 48N58 1E51 -0:07:24
Elne 1 42N36 2E58 -0:11:52
Éloyes 101 48N06 6E37 -0:26:28
Elven 35 47N44 2W35 0:10:20
Émancé 74 48N35 1E44 -0:06:56
Embrun 1 44N34 6E30 -0:26:00
Embry 137 50N29 1E58 -0:07:52
Émerainville 61 48N49 2E37 -0:10:28
Enchenberg 20 49N01 7E20 -0:29:20
Enghien (Les Bains) 61 48N58 2E19 -0:09:16
Englefontaine 103 50N11 3E39 -0:14:36
Ennery 80 49N05 2E06 -0:08:24
Ensisheim 5 47N52 7E21 -0:29:24
Entraigues sur Sorgue 1 44N00 4E55 -0:19:40
Entrains sur Nohain 45 47N27 3E15 -0:13:00

Entraunes 1 44N11 6E45 -0:27:00
Entraygues 1 44N39 2E34 -0:10:16
Entrechaux 1 44N13 5E08 -0:20:32
Entremont le Vieux 1 45N26 5E53 -0:23:32
Entrevaux 1 43N57 6E49 -0:27:16
Envermeu 132 49N54 1E16 -0:05:04
Épernay 84 49N03 3E57 -0:15:48
Épernon 70 48N37 1E41 -0:06:44
Épiais lès Louvres 80 49N02 2E33 -0:10:12
Épinac les Mines 30 46N59 4E31 -0:18:04
Épinal 91 48N11 6E27 -0:25:48
Épinay sous Sénart 61 48N42 2E31 -0:10:04
Épinay sur Orge 78 48N40 2E20 -0:09:20
Épinay sur Seine 61 48N57 2E19 -0:09:16
Époisses 49 47N30 4E10 -0:16:40
Épône 74 48N57 1E49 -0:07:16
Eppeville 117 49N44 3E03 -0:12:12
Épuisay 42 47N54 0E56 -0:03:44
Équihen Plage 138 50N41 1E34 -0:06:16
Éragny 80 49N01 2E06 -0:08:24
Ermenonville 80 49N08 2E42 -0:10:48
Ermont 61 48N59 2E16 -0:09:04
Ernée 40 48N18 0W56 0:03:44
Erstein 23 48N26 7E40 -0:30:40
Ervy le Châtel 50 48N02 3E55 -0:15:40
Esbly 82 48N54 2E49 -0:11:16
Escaudain 103 50N20 3E21 -0:13:24
Eschau 23 48N29 7E43 -0:30:52
Espalion 1 44N31 2E46 -0:11:04
Espaly Saint Marcel 1 45N03 3E52 -0:15:28
Essarts 74 48N30 1E46 -0:07:04
Essoyes 51 48N04 4E32 -0:18:08
Estaires 136 50N38 2E43 -0:10:52
Estèng 1 44N14 6E45 -0:27:00
Esternay 82 48N44 3E34 -0:14:16
Estissac 77 48N16 3E49 -0:15:16
Estrasburgo → Strasbourg 14 48N35 7E45 -0:31:00
Estrées Saint Denis 110 49N26 2E39 -0:10:36
Étables 36 48N38 2W50 0:11:20
Étain 96 49N13 5E38 -0:22:32
Étampes 48 48N26 2E09 -0:08:36
Étaples 138 50N31 1E39 -0:06:36
Étiolles 78 48N38 2E29 -0:09:56
Étréchy 78 48N30 2E12 -0:08:48
Étrépagny 110 49N18 1E37 -0:06:28
Étretat 128 49N42 0E12 -0:00:48
Eu 133 50N03 1E25 -0:05:40
Eurville 87 48N35 5E02 -0:20:08
Euzet les Bains 1 44N04 4E14 -0:16:56
Ève 80 49N05 2E42 -0:10:48
Evecquemont 79 49N02 1E57 -0:07:48
Évian les Bains 1 46N23 6E35 -0:26:20
Evisa 1 42N15 8E47 -0:35:08
Évrange 10 49N30 6E12 -0:24:48
Évreux 73 49N01 1E09 -0:04:36
Evrieu 26 45N35 5E34 -0:22:16
Évry 78 48N38 2E27 -0:09:48
Évry les Châteaux 78 48N39 2E38 -0:10:32
Excenevex 1 46N21 6E21 -0:25:24
Exincourt 60 47N30 6E50 -0:27:20
Exmes 69 48N46 0E11 -0:00:44
Eygalières 1 43N45 4E57 -0:19:48
Eyguières 1 43N42 5E02 -0:20:08
Eymet 1 44N40 0E24 -0:01:36
Eymoutiers 1 45N44 1E44 -0:06:56
Ézanville 61 49N02 2E22 -0:09:28
Ézy sur Eure 73 48N52 1E25 -0:05:40
Fabrègues 1 43N33 3E46 -0:15:04
Faches Thumesnil 117 50N35 3E04 -0:12:16
Fagnières 88 48N58 4E19 -0:17:16
Fains les Sources 87 48N47 5E08 -0:20:32
Falaise 69 48N54 0W12 0:00:48
Falck 18 49N14 6E38 -0:26:32
Falicon 1 43N45 7E17 -0:29:08
Fameck 10 49N18 6E07 -0:24:28
Farcy 77 48N31 2E37 -0:10:28
Fargniers 112 49N39 3E19 -0:13:16
Farschviller 17 49N06 6E54 -0:27:36
Faucigny 1 46N07 6E22 -0:25:28
Faucogney 59 47N51 6E34 -0:26:16
Faucon de Barcelonnette 1 44N24 6E41 -0:26:44
Faulquemont 12 49N03 6E36 -0:26:24
Fauquembergues 137 50N36 2E05 -0:08:20
Fauville en Caux 127 49N39 0E35 -0:02:20
Faverges 1 45N45 6E18 -0:25:12
Faverney 58 47N46 6E06 -0:24:24
Favières 82 48N46 2E47 -0:11:08
Favrieux 74 48N57 1E39 -0:06:36
Fayence 1 43N37 6E41 -0:26:44
Fayl Billot 53 47N47 5E36 -0:22:24
Fay sur Lignon 1 44N59 4E14 -0:16:56
Fécamp 128 49N45 0E22 -0:01:28
Feignies 152 50N18 3E55 -0:15:40
Felletin 1 45N53 2E10 -0:08:40
Fénétrange 17 48N51 7E01 -0:28:04
Fépin 118 50N01 4E44 -0:18:56
Fère Champenoise 82 48N45 3E59 -0:15:56
Fère en Tardenois 108 49N12 3E31 -0:14:04
Ferney Voltaire 27 46N15 6E07 -0:24:28

Place	No.	Lat.	Long.	Time
Ferrière la Grande	152	50N15	4E00	-0:16:00
Ferrières	45	48N05	2E47	-0:11:08
Ferrières en Brie	61	48N49	2E43	-0:10:52
Feucherolles	61	48N52	1E58	-0:07:52
Feuquières en Vimeu	133	50N04	1E36	-0:06:24
Feurs	1	45N45	4E14	-0:16:56
Féy	10	49N02	6E06	-0:24:24
Feyzin	27	45N40	4E51	-0:19:24
Fienvillers	122	50N07	2E14	-0:08:56
Figeac	1	44N37	2E02	-0:08:08
Fins	117	50N02	3E03	-0:12:12
Firminy	1	45N23	4E18	-0:17:12
Fismes	108	49N18	3E41	-0:14:44
Fixin	49	47N15	4E58	-0:19:52
Fix Saint Geneys	1	45N08	3E40	-0:14:40
Flavigny sur Moselle	91	48N34	6E11	-0:24:44
Flavigny sur Ozerain	51	47N30	4E32	-0:18:08
Flavy le Martel	103	49N43	3E12	-0:12:48
Flers	40	48N45	0W34	0:02:16
Flers sur Noye	120	49N44	2E15	-0:09:00
Fleurance	1	43N50	0E40	-0:02:40
Fleurville	27	46N27	4E53	-0:19:32
Fleury les Aubrais	44	47N56	1E55	-0:07:40
Fleury Mérogis	78	48N38	2E22	-0:09:28
Fleury sur Andelle	110	49N22	1E22	-0:05:28
Flexanville	74	48N51	1E44	-0:06:56
Flines Lèz Râches	117	50N25	3E11	-0:12:44
Flins sur Seine	74	48N58	1E52	-0:07:28
Flirey	93	48N53	5E50	-0:23:20
Flixecourt	122	50N01	2E05	-0:08:20
Flize	103	49N42	4E46	-0:19:04
Flogny	50	47N57	3E52	-0:15:28
Floing	103	49N43	4E56	-0:19:44
Florac	1	44N19	3E36	-0:14:24
Florange	10	49N20	6E07	-0:24:28
Flosaille	26	45N39	5E18	-0:21:12
Flumet	1	45N49	6E30	-0:26:00
Foëcy	25	47N10	2E10	-0:08:40
Foix	1	42N58	1E36	-0:06:24
Folembray	112	49N33	3E17	-0:13:08
Follainville Dennemont	79	49N01	1E43	-0:06:52
Folschviller	17	49N04	6E41	-0:26:44
Foncine le Bas	31	46N38	6E03	-0:24:12
Fons Outre Gardon	1	43N54	4E11	-0:16:44
Fontaine	60	47N40	7E00	-0:28:00
Fontaine	1	45N11	5E40	-0:22:40
Fontainebleau	77	48N24	2E42	-0:10:48
Fontaine Française	53	47N31	5E22	-0:21:28
Fontaine le Dun	131	49N49	0E51	-0:03:24
Fontaine lès Dijon	49	47N21	5E01	-0:20:04
Fontaine lès Grès	77	48N25	3E54	-0:15:36
Fontaine lès Luxeuil	59	47N51	6E20	-0:25:20
Fontaines	30	46N51	4E46	-0:19:04
Fontaines sur Saône	27	45N50	4E51	-0:19:24
Fontan	1	44N00	7E33	-0:30:12
Fontenay aux Roses	61	48N47	2E17	-0:09:08
Fontenay en Parisis	61	49N03	2E27	-0:09:48
Fontenay le Comte	24	46N28	0W48	0:03:12
Fontenay le Fleury	61	48N49	2E03	-0:08:12
Fontenay lès Briis	78	48N37	2E09	-0:08:36
Fontenay le Vicomte	78	48N33	2E24	-0:09:36
Fontenay Saint Père	79	49N02	1E45	-0:07:00
Fontenay sous Bois	61	48N51	2E29	-0:09:56
Fontenay Trésigny	82	48N42	2E52	-0:11:28
Fontoy	10	49N21	6E00	-0:24:00
Fontvieille	1	43N43	4E43	-0:18:52
Forbach	19	49N11	6E54	-0:27:36
Forcalquier	1	43N58	5E47	-0:23:08
Forfry	80	49N03	2E51	-0:11:24
Forges les Bains	78	48N38	2E06	-0:08:24
Forges les Eaux	119	49N37	1E33	-0:06:12
Formerie	119	49N39	1E44	-0:06:56
Fort Mahon Plage	136	50N21	1E34	-0:06:16
Fossé	98	49N27	5E00	-0:20:00
Fosse Martin	80	49N05	2E54	-0:11:36
Fosses	80	49N06	2E29	-0:09:56
Fos sur Mer	1	43N26	4E57	-0:19:48
Foucarmont	133	49N51	1E34	-0:06:16
Fouesnant	35	47N54	4W01	0:16:04
Foug	93	48N41	5E47	-0:23:08
Fougères	65	48N21	1W12	0:04:48
Fougères sur Bièvre	25	47N27	1E21	-0:05:24
Fougerolles	59	47N53	6E24	-0:25:36
Fouju	77	48N35	2E47	-0:11:08
Foulain	52	48N02	5E13	-0:20:52
Fourmies	103	50N00	4E03	-0:16:12
Fourneaux	1	45N11	6E39	-0:26:36
Fourneaux	44	47N53	1E48	-0:07:12
Fourqueux	61	48N53	2E04	-0:08:16
Fours	28	46N49	3E43	-0:14:52
Fraisans	32	47N09	5E46	-0:23:04
Fraisse	1	45N23	4E15	-0:17:00
Fraize	7	48N11	7E00	-0:28:00
Franconville	61	48N59	2E14	-0:08:56
Francueil	25	47N19	1E05	-0:04:20
Frangy	27	46N01	5E56	-0:23:44
Franvillers	122	49N58	2E30	-0:10:00
Frasne	32	46N51	6E10	-0:24:40
Fréjus	1	43N26	6E44	-0:26:56
Frémainville	79	49N04	1E52	-0:07:28
Freneuse	79	49N03	1E36	-0:06:24
Frépillon	61	49N03	2E12	-0:08:48
Fresnes	61	48N45	2E19	-0:09:16
Fresne Saint Mamès	30	47N33	5E52	-0:23:28
Fresnes en Woëvre	96	49N08	5E39	-0:22:36
Fresnes sur Escaut	117	50N26	3E35	-0:14:20
Fresnes sur Marne	81	48N56	2E45	-0:11:00
Fresnoy Folny	133	49N53	1E26	-0:05:44
Fresnoy le Grand	103	49N57	3E25	-0:13:40
Fressenneville	133	50N04	1E34	-0:06:16
Fressin	136	50N27	2E03	-0:08:12
Fréteval	44	47N53	1E13	-0:04:52
Frétigney et Velloreille	54	47N29	5E56	-0:23:44
Fretin	117	50N33	3E08	-0:12:32
Frettes	53	47N41	5E34	-0:22:16
Frévent	135	50N16	2E17	-0:09:08
Froidmont Cohartille	112	49N41	3E42	-0:14:48
Froidos	87	49N03	5E07	-0:20:28
Froissy	119	49N34	2E13	-0:08:52
Fromelennes	118	50N08	4E52	-0:19:28
Fromentières	84	48N54	3E43	-0:14:52
Frontenard	30	46N55	5E10	-0:20:40
Frontenex Villard Rosset	1	45N38	6E19	-0:25:16
Frontignan	1	43N27	3E45	-0:15:00
Frouard	100	48N46	6E08	-0:24:32
Fruges	136	50N31	2E08	-0:08:32
Fumay	118	49N59	4E42	-0:18:48
Fumel	1	44N29	0E57	-0:03:48
Fures	1	45N19	5E30	-0:22:00
Fuveau	1	43N27	5E34	-0:22:16
Gacé	69	48N48	0E18	-0:01:12
Gagny	61	48N53	2E32	-0:10:08
Gaillac	1	43N54	1E55	-0:07:40
Gaillefontaine	119	49N39	1E37	-0:06:28
Gaillon	124	49N10	1E20	-0:05:20
Gaillon	79	49N02	1E54	-0:07:36
Gallardon	70	48N32	1E42	-0:06:48
Galluis	74	48N48	1E48	-0:07:12
Gamaches	133	49N59	1E33	-0:06:12
Gambais	74	48N46	1E40	-0:06:40
Gambaiseuil	74	48N45	1E44	-0:06:56
Gandrange	10	49N16	6E08	-0:24:32
Ganges	1	43N56	3E42	-0:14:48
Gannat	1	46N06	3E12	-0:12:48
Gap	1	44N34	6E05	-0:24:20
Garancières	74	48N49	1E46	-0:07:04
Garches	61	48N51	2E11	-0:08:44
Gardanne	1	43N27	5E28	-0:21:52
Gargenville	79	49N00	1E49	-0:07:16
Garges lès Gonesse	61	48N58	2E25	-0:09:40
Garlin	1	43N34	0W15	0:01:00
Garne	61	48N41	1E58	-0:07:52
Gas	70	48N34	1E40	-0:06:40
Gasny	79	49N05	1E36	-0:06:24
Gassin	1	43N13	6E35	-0:26:20
Gattières	1	43N46	7E11	-0:28:44
Gauchy	103	49N49	3E16	-0:13:04
Gavet	1	45N04	5E52	-0:23:28
Gazeran	74	48N38	1E46	-0:07:04
Gebweiler → Guebwiller	3	47N55	7E12	-0:28:48
Geispolsheim	14	48N31	7E39	-0:30:36
Gémenos	1	43N18	5E38	-0:22:32
Gençay	24	46N23	0E24	-0:01:36
Gendrey	30	47N12	5E41	-0:22:44
Génicourt	80	49N05	2E04	-0:08:16
Génicourt sur Meuse	87	49N02	5E26	-0:21:44
Génissiat	27	46N03	5E47	-0:23:08
Genlis	30	47N14	5E13	-0:20:52
Gennes	25	47N20	0W14	0:00:56
Gennevilliers	61	48N56	2E18	-0:09:12
Génolhac	1	44N21	3E57	-0:15:48
Gentilly	61	48N49	2E21	-0:09:24
Gentioux	1	45N47	1E59	-0:07:56
Gérardmer	101	48N04	6E53	-0:27:32
Gerbéviller	91	48N30	6E31	-0:26:04
Germay	99	48N25	5E21	-0:21:24
Gespunsart	102	49N49	4E50	-0:19:20
Gevrey Chambertin	49	47N14	4E57	-0:19:48
Gex	27	46N20	6E04	-0:24:16
Ghisonáccia	1	42N00	9E25	-0:37:40
Gien	41	47N42	2E38	-0:10:32
Giens	1	43N02	6E08	-0:24:32
Gièvres	25	47N16	1E40	-0:06:40
Giez	1	45N45	6E15	-0:25:00
Gif sur Yvette	61	48N42	2E08	-0:08:32
Gilette	1	43N51	7E10	-0:28:40
Gimont	1	43N38	0E53	-0:03:32
Giraumont	97	49N10	5E55	-0:23:40
Giromagny	59	47N45	6E50	-0:27:20
Giron	27	46N14	5E46	-0:23:04
Gironville sous les Côtes	94	48N48	5E40	-0:22:40
Gisors	110	49N17	1E47	-0:07:08
Giverny	79	49N04	1E32	-0:06:08
Givet	118	50N08	4E50	-0:19:20
Givors	1	45N35	4E46	-0:19:04
Givry	30	46N47	4E45	-0:19:00
Givry en Argonne	89	48N57	4E53	-0:19:32
Gizeux	25	47N24	0E12	-0:00:48
Glos la Ferrière	72	48N51	0E36	-0:02:24
Goderville	128	49N39	0E22	-0:01:28
Goetzenbruck	21	48N59	7E23	-0:29:32
Goldbey	91	48N12	6E26	-0:25:44
Golfe Juan	1	43N34	7E05	-0:28:20
Gometz la Ville	78	48N40	2E08	-0:08:32
Gometz le Châtel	61	48N41	2E08	-0:08:32
Gommécourt	79	49N05	1E36	-0:06:24
Goncelin	1	45N20	5E59	-0:23:56
Gondrecourt le Château	99	48N31	5E30	-0:22:00
Gondreville	93	48N42	5E58	-0:23:52
Gonesse	61	48N59	2E27	-0:09:48
Gonfaron	1	43N19	6E17	-0:25:08
Gordes	1	43N54	5E12	-0:20:48
Gorze	10	49N03	6E00	-0:24:00
Gouarec	36	48N13	3W11	0:12:44
Goudet	1	44N53	3E55	-0:15:40
Goumois	60	47N16	6E57	-0:27:48
Goupillières	74	48N53	1E46	-0:07:04
Gourdon	1	44N44	1E23	-0:05:32
Gourdon	1	43N43	6E59	-0:27:56
Gourin	35	48N08	3W36	0:14:24
Gournay en Bray	110	49N29	1E44	-0:06:56
Gournay sur Marne	61	48N52	2E34	-0:10:16
Goussainville	61	49N01	2E28	-0:09:52
Goussonville	74	48N55	1E46	-0:07:04
Graçay	1	47N08	1E51	-0:07:24
Gramat	1	44N47	1E43	-0:06:52
Grancey le Château	52	47N40	5E02	-0:20:08
Grand	57	48N23	5E29	-0:21:56
Grandchamp	53	47N43	5E27	-0:21:48
Grandchamp	70	48N43	1E37	-0:06:28
Grand Charmont	60	47N32	6E50	-0:27:20
Grand Couronne	127	49N21	1E00	-0:04:00
Grand Fort Philippe	138	51N00	2E06	-0:08:24
Grand Fougeray	35	47N44	1W44	0:06:56
Grand Gallargues	1	43N43	4E10	-0:16:40
Grandpré	89	49N20	4E52	-0:19:28
Grandrieu	1	44N47	3E38	-0:14:32
Grandvillars	60	47N33	6E58	-0:27:52
Grandvilliers	120	49N40	1E56	-0:07:44
Grâne	1	44N44	4E55	-0:19:40
Granges sur Vologne	101	48N09	6E47	-0:27:08
Granville	63	48N50	1W36	0:06:24
Grasse	1	43N40	6E55	-0:27:40
Gravelines	138	50N59	2E07	-0:08:28
Gravelotte	10	49N07	6E01	-0:24:04
Gravigny	73	49N03	1E10	-0:04:40
Gray	30	47N27	5E35	-0:22:20
Greffiers	74	48N37	1E51	-0:07:24
Grégy sur Yerre	78	48N40	2E37	-0:10:28
Grenay	153	50N27	2E44	-0:10:56
Grenoble	1	45N10	5E43	-0:22:52
Gréolières	1	43N48	6E57	-0:27:48
Gréoux les Bains	1	43N45	5E53	-0:23:32
Gresse en Vercors	1	44N54	5E34	-0:22:16
Gressey	74	48N50	1E37	-0:06:28
Gressy	61	48N58	2E41	-0:10:44
Grésy sur Aix	1	45N43	5E57	-0:23:48
Grésy sur Isère	1	45N36	6E15	-0:25:00
Gretz Armainvilliers	82	48N44	2E44	-0:10:56
Grez sur Loing	75	48N19	2E42	-0:10:48
Grignan	1	44N25	4E54	-0:19:36
Grignols	1	44N23	0W03	0:00:12
Grignon	61	48N51	1E57	-0:07:48
Grigny	1	45N37	4E47	-0:19:08
Grimaud	1	43N16	6E31	-0:26:04
Grisy Suisnes	61	48N41	2E40	-0:10:40
Groix	34	47N38	3W28	0:13:52
Groslay	61	48N59	2E21	-0:09:24
Grosrouvre	74	48N47	1E46	-0:07:04
Grostenquin	17	48N59	6E44	-0:26:56
Guebwiller (Gebweiler)	3	47N55	7E12	-0:28:48
Gué de Longroi	70	48N30	1E43	-0:06:52
Gué d'Hossus	118	49N57	4E32	-0:18:08
Guéherville	74	48N32	1E53	-0:07:32
Guéméné sur Scorff	35	48N04	3W12	0:12:48
Guer	35	47N54	2W07	0:08:28
Guérande	34	47N20	2W26	0:09:44
Guéret	1	46N10	1E52	-0:07:28
Guermantes	61	48N51	2E42	-0:10:48
Guernes	79	49N01	1E38	-0:06:32
Guerville	74	48N57	1E44	-0:06:56
Guichen	36	47N58	1W48	0:07:12
Guignes Rabutin	77	48N38	2E48	-0:11:12
Guilherand	1	44N56	4E52	-0:19:28
Guillaumes	1	44N05	6E51	-0:27:24
Guillestre	1	44N40	6E39	-0:26:36
Guillon	49	47N31	4E06	-0:16:24
Guilvinec	35	47N47	4W17	0:17:08
Guînes	138	50N52	1E52	-0:07:28

Place		Lat	Long	Time
Guingamp	36	48N33	3W11	0:12:44
Guiperreux	74	48N40	1E42	-0:06:48
Guiscard	117	49N39	3E03	-0:12:12
Guise	103	49N54	3E38	-0:14:32
Guitrancourt	79	49N01	1E47	-0:07:08
Guîtres	24	45N03	0W11	0:00:44
Guyancourt	61	48N46	2E04	-0:08:16
Gy	30	47N24	5E49	-0:23:16
Habère Poche	1	46N15	6E29	-0:25:56
Habsheim	8	47N44	7E25	-0:29:40
Hagetmau	1	43N40	0W35	0:02:20
Hagondange	10	49N15	6E10	-0:24:40
Haguenau	22	48N49	7E47	-0:31:08
Haillicourt	135	50N28	2E35	-0:10:20
Hallencourt	133	49N59	1E53	-0:07:32
Halluin	141	50N47	3E08	-0:12:32
Ham	117	49N45	3E04	-0:12:16
Hambach	18	49N04	7E02	-0:28:08
Hanches	70	48N36	1E39	-0:06:36
Han sur Nied	12	48N59	6E26	-0:25:44
Harbonnières	122	49N51	2E40	-0:10:40
Harcourt	72	49N10	0E48	-0:03:12
Hardelot Plage	138	50N38	1E35	-0:06:20
Hardricourt	79	49N01	1E54	-0:07:36
Harfleur	128	49N30	0E12	-0:00:48
Hargeville	74	48N53	1E45	-0:07:00
Harnes	153	50N27	2E54	-0:11:36
Haroué	91	48N28	6E11	-0:24:44
Haspres	103	50N15	3E25	-0:13:40
Hatten	22	48N54	7E59	-0:31:56
Hattstatt	6	48N01	7E17	-0:29:08
Haubourdin	117	50N36	2E59	-0:11:56
Haut Bout	74	48N32	1E55	-0:07:40
Hauteluce	1	45N45	6E35	-0:26:20
Hauterives	1	45N15	5E02	-0:20:08
Hauteville Lompnes	26	45N58	5E36	-0:22:24
Hautmont	152	50N15	3E56	-0:15:44
Hautvillers	84	49N05	3E57	-0:15:48
Havre → Le Havre	130	49N30	0E08	-0:00:32
Hayange	10	49N20	6E03	-0:24:12
Haybes	118	50N00	4E43	-0:18:52
Hazebrouck	137	50N43	2E32	-0:10:08
Hédé	62	48N18	1W48	0:07:12
Hégenheim	8	47N34	7E32	-0:30:08
Heiltz le Maurupt	88	48N48	4E49	-0:19:16
Hellemmes Lille	117	50N37	3E07	-0:12:28
Héming	14	48N42	6E57	-0:27:48
Hendaye	24	43N22	1W44	0:06:56
Hénin Beaumont	153	50N25	2E56	-0:11:44
Hennebont	34	47N48	3W17	0:13:08
Henrichemont	41	47N18	2E32	-0:10:08
Herbault	41	47N36	1E08	-0:04:32
Herbignac	35	47N27	2W19	0:09:16
Herblay	61	49N00	2E10	-0:08:40
Héricourt	59	47N35	6E45	-0:27:00
Hérimoncourt	60	47N26	6E53	-0:27:32
Hermeray	70	48N38	1E41	-0:06:44
Hermes	110	49N22	2E15	-0:09:00
Hermies	117	50N07	3E02	-0:12:08
Hérouville	80	49N06	2E08	-0:08:32
Herry	41	47N13	2E57	-0:11:48
Herserange	104	49N31	5E47	-0:23:08
Héry	1	45N46	6E28	-0:25:52
Héry	46	47N54	3E38	-0:14:32
Hesdin	136	50N22	2E02	-0:08:08
Hettange Grande	10	49N24	6E09	-0:24:36
Heuchin	136	50N28	2E16	-0:09:04
Heyrieux	26	45N38	5E03	-0:20:12
Hierges	118	50N06	4E44	-0:18:56
Hirsingue	4	47N35	7E15	-0:29:00
Hirson	103	49N55	4E05	-0:16:20
Hirtzfelden	9	47N55	7E27	-0:29:48
Hochfelden	18	48N45	7E34	-0:30:16
Hœrdt	22	48N42	7E47	-0:31:08
Hombourg Haut	17	49N08	6E46	-0:27:04
Homécourt	97	49N14	5E59	-0:23:56
Hondschoote	138	50N59	2E35	-0:10:20
Honfleur	129	49N25	0E14	-0:00:56
Honnecourt sur Escaut	117	50N02	3E12	-0:12:48
Horbourg	6	48N05	7E23	-0:29:32
Hornoy	133	49N51	1E54	-0:07:36
Hossegor	24	43N40	1W27	0:05:48
Houdain	135	50N27	2E32	-0:10:08
Houdan	73	48N47	1E36	-0:06:24
Houdelaincourt	99	48N33	5E28	-0:21:52
Houeillès	1	44N12	0E02	-0:00:08
Houilles	61	48N56	2E11	-0:08:44
Houplines	117	50N42	2E55	-0:11:40
Houx	70	48N34	1E37	-0:06:28
Hucqueliers	137	50N34	1E54	-0:07:36
Huelgoat	36	48N22	3W45	0:15:00
Huismes	24	47N14	0E15	-0:01:00
Huningue	8	47N36	7E35	-0:30:20
Hunspach	22	48N57	7E57	-0:31:48
Huriel	1	46N23	2E29	-0:09:56
Hussigny Godbrange	97	49N29	5E52	-0:23:28
Hyères	1	43N07	6E07	-0:24:28
Hyères Plage	1	43N06	6E10	-0:24:40
Igney	91	48N17	6E24	-0:25:36
Igny	61	48N45	2E14	-0:08:56
Ilay	27	46N37	5E53	-0:23:32
Illfurth	4	47N40	7E16	-0:29:04
Illhaeusern	7	48N11	7E26	-0:29:44
Illiers	68	48N18	1E15	-0:05:00
Illkirch Graffenstaden	14	48N32	7E43	-0:30:52
Illzach	4	47N47	7E20	-0:29:20
Ingersheim	6	48N06	7E18	-0:29:12
Ingwiller	21	48N52	7E29	-0:29:56
Irigny	27	45N40	4E49	-0:19:16
Isbergues	136	50N37	2E27	-0:09:48
Isdes	41	47N40	2E15	-0:09:00
Isigny	143	49N19	1W06	0:04:24
Isola	1	44N11	7E03	-0:28:12
Issigeac	1	44N44	0E36	-0:02:24
Issoire	1	45N33	3E15	-0:13:00
Issou	74	48N59	1E48	-0:07:12
Issoudun	1	46N57	2E00	-0:08:00
Is sur Tille	52	47N31	5E06	-0:20:24
Issy	61	48N49	2E17	-0:09:08
Issy les Moulineaux	61	48N49	2E17	-0:09:08
Istres	1	43N31	4E59	-0:19:56
Itteville	78	48N31	2E21	-0:09:24
Iverny	80	49N00	2E47	-0:11:08
Ivry la Bataille	73	48N53	1E28	-0:05:52
Ivry(sur Seine)	61	48N49	2E23	-0:09:32
Iwuy	117	50N14	3E19	-0:13:16
Izernore	27	46N13	5E33	-0:22:12
Jablines	81	48N55	2E46	-0:11:04
Jagny sous Bois	61	49N05	2E27	-0:09:48
Jallieu	26	45N35	5E16	-0:21:04
Jametz	98	49N26	5E23	-0:21:32
Janville	71	48N12	1E53	-0:07:32
Janville sur Juine	78	48N31	2E16	-0:09:04
Janvry	78	48N39	2E09	-0:08:36
Janzé	40	47N58	1W30	0:06:00
Jargeau	44	47N52	2E07	-0:08:28
Jarnac	24	45N41	0W10	0:00:40
Jarny	95	49N09	5E53	-0:23:32
Jarville la Malgrange	92	48N40	6E13	-0:24:52
Jassans Riottier	27	45N59	4E45	-0:19:00
Jausiers	1	44N25	6E44	-0:26:56
Jeumont	152	50N18	4E06	-0:16:24
Job	1	45N37	3E45	-0:15:00
Jœuf	10	49N14	6E01	-0:24:04
Joigny	46	47N59	3E24	-0:13:36
Joinville	87	48N27	5E08	-0:20:32
Joinville le Pont	61	48N49	2E28	-0:09:52
Jonquières	1	44N07	4E54	-0:19:36
Jonvilliers	70	48N34	1E42	-0:06:48
Jonzac	24	45N27	0W26	0:01:44
Josselin	35	47N57	2W33	0:10:12
Jossigny	82	48N50	2E45	-0:11:00
Jouarre	83	48N56	3E08	-0:12:32
Jouars Pontchartrain	74	48N47	1E54	-0:07:36
Joué lès Tours	25	47N21	0E40	-0:02:40
Jougne	32	46N46	6E24	-0:25:36
Jouques	1	43N38	5E38	-0:22:32
Jouy	70	48N31	1E33	-0:06:12
Jouy en Josas	61	48N46	2E10	-0:08:40
Jouy le Moutier	80	49N01	2E03	-0:08:12
Jouy le Potier	44	47N45	1E49	-0:07:16
Joyeuse	1	44N29	4E14	-0:16:56
Juan les Pins	1	43N34	7E06	-0:28:24
Jugon	36	48N25	2W20	0:09:20
Juillac	1	45N19	1E19	-0:05:16
Juilly	80	49N01	2E42	-0:10:48
Jujurieux	27	46N02	5E25	-0:21:40
Juliénas	27	46N14	4E43	-0:18:52
Jumeauville	74	48N55	1E47	-0:07:08
Jumièges	127	49N26	0E49	-0:03:16
Juniville	89	49N24	4E23	-0:17:32
Jussey	58	47N49	5E54	-0:23:36
Juvisy sur Orge	61	48N41	2E23	-0:09:32
Juzennecourt	56	48N11	4E59	-0:19:56
Juziers	79	49N00	1E51	-0:07:24
Kaltenhouse	22	48N48	7E50	-0:31:20
Kaysersberg	7	48N08	7E15	-0:29:00
Kédange sur Canner	12	49N19	6E20	-0:25:20
Kembs	8	47N41	7E30	-0:30:00
Kemper → Quimper	35	48N00	4W06	0:16:24
Keskastel	17	48N58	7E02	-0:28:08
Kingersheim	4	47N48	7E20	-0:29:20
Koenigsmacker	12	49N24	6E17	-0:25:08
La Balme de Sillingy	1	45N58	6E02	-0:24:08
La Balme les Grottes	26	45N51	5E20	-0:21:20
La Barre en Ouche	72	48N57	0E40	-0:02:40
La Bassée	136	50N32	2E48	-0:11:12
Labastide Murat	1	44N39	1E34	-0:06:16
La Bastide Puylaurent	1	44N36	3E54	-0:15:36
La Bâte	48	48N35	2E01	-0:08:04
La Baule	34	47N17	2W24	0:09:36
La Bazoche Gouet	68	48N08	0E59	-0:03:56
L'Abbé	74	48N34	1E50	-0:07:20
Labégude	1	44N39	4E22	-0:17:28
La Bégude Blanche	1	43N55	6E08	-0:24:32
La Bégude de Mazenc	1	44N32	4E56	-0:19:44
La Bérarde	1	44N56	6E18	-0:25:12
La Besace	103	49N34	4E58	-0:19:52
La Boissière	61	48N46	1E59	-0:07:56
La Boissière Ecole	70	48N41	1E39	-0:06:36
La Bollène Vésubie	1	43N59	7E20	-0:29:20
La Bonneville sur Iton	73	49N00	1E02	-0:04:08
La Borde	77	48N32	2E50	-0:11:20
Labouheyre	24	44N13	0W55	0:03:40
Labrède	24	44N41	0W31	0:02:04
La Bresse	101	48N00	6E53	-0:27:32
La Brigue	1	44N04	7E37	-0:30:28
La Brillanne	1	43N55	5E53	-0:23:32
Labrit	24	44N07	0W33	0:02:12
Labroye	136	50N17	1E59	-0:07:56
Labry	95	49N10	5E52	-0:23:28
La Cadière d'Azur	1	43N12	5E46	-0:23:04
Lacanau	24	44N59	1W05	0:04:20
La Canourgue	1	44N26	3E13	-0:12:52
La Capelle en Thiérache	103	49N58	3E55	-0:15:40
La Capelle lès Boulogne	137	50N44	1E42	-0:06:48
Lacapelle Marival	1	44N44	1E54	-0:07:36
Lacaune	1	43N43	2E42	-0:10:48
La Celle les Bordes	74	48N38	1E57	-0:07:48
La Celle Saint Cyr	46	47N58	3E18	-0:13:12
La Chaise Dieu	1	45N19	3E42	-0:14:48
La Chambre	1	45N22	6E18	-0:25:12
La Chapelle d'Angillon	41	47N22	2E26	-0:09:44
La Chapelle en Vercors	1	44N58	5E25	-0:21:40
La Chapelle Gauthier	77	48N33	2E54	-0:11:36
La Chapelle la Reine	75	48N19	2E35	-0:10:20
La Chapelle Saint Mesmin	44	47N53	1E50	-0:07:20
La Chapelle Vendômoise	41	47N40	1E15	-0:05:00
La Charité sur Loire	28	47N11	3E01	-0:12:04
La Chartre sur le Loir	42	47N44	0E35	-0:02:20
La Châtaigneraie	24	46N39	0W44	0:02:56
La Châtre	1	46N35	1E59	-0:07:56
La Ciotat	1	43N10	5E36	-0:22:24
La Clayette	27	46N18	4E19	-0:17:16
La Cluse	27	46N10	5E34	-0:22:16
La Cluse et Mijoux	32	46N53	6E23	-0:25:32
La Colle sur Loup	1	43N41	7E06	-0:28:24
La Condamine Châtelard	1	44N27	6E45	-0:27:00
Lacoste	1	43N50	5E18	-0:21:12
La Côte Saint André	1	45N23	5E15	-0:21:00
La Courneuve	61	48N56	2E23	-0:09:32
La Couronne	1	43N20	5E03	-0:20:12
La Courtine	1	45N42	2E16	-0:09:04
La Crau	1	43N09	6E04	-0:24:16
Lacroix Saint Ouen	80	49N21	2E47	-0:11:08
La Cure	31	46N28	6E05	-0:24:20
Ladon	45	48N00	2E32	-0:10:08
Lady	77	48N35	2E54	-0:11:36
Lafayette	26	45N35	5E04	-0:20:16
La Fère	112	49N40	3E22	-0:13:28
La Ferrière sur Risle	73	48N59	0E48	-0:03:12
La Ferté Alais	78	48N29	2E21	-0:09:24
La Ferté Bernard	68	48N11	0E40	-0:02:40
La Ferté Frênel	72	48N50	0E30	-0:02:00
La Ferté Gaucher	82	48N47	3E18	-0:13:12
La Ferté Macé	47	48N36	0W22	0:01:28
La Ferté Milon	108	49N10	3E07	-0:12:28
La Ferté Saint Aubin	44	47N43	1E56	-0:07:44
La Ferté sous Jouarre	83	48N57	3E08	-0:12:32
Laferté sur Amance	58	47N50	5E42	-0:22:48
La Ferté Vidame	70	48N37	0E55	-0:03:40
La Ferté Villeneuil	44	47N59	1E21	-0:05:24
Laffrey	1	45N02	5E46	-0:23:04
La Flèche	39	47N42	0W05	0:00:20
La Foux	1	43N16	6E35	-0:26:20
La Foux	1	44N17	6E34	-0:26:16
La Frette sur Seine	61	48N58	2E11	-0:08:44
Lafrimbolle	14	48N36	7E01	-0:28:04
La Garde	1	43N07	6E01	-0:24:04
La Garde Freinet	1	43N19	6E28	-0:25:52
La Garenne Colombes	61	48N55	2E15	-0:09:00
La Giettaz	1	45N52	6E30	-0:26:00
Lagnieu	27	45N54	5E21	-0:21:24
Lagny	61	48N52	2E43	-0:10:52
Lagny le Sec	80	49N05	2E45	-0:11:00
La Gorgue	136	50N38	2E42	-0:10:48
La Grand'Combe	1	44N13	4E02	-0:16:08
La Grave	1	45N03	6E18	-0:25:12
La Groise	103	50N05	3E41	-0:14:44
La Guêpière	74	48N35	1E50	-0:07:20
La Guerche de Bretagne	40	47N56	1W14	0:04:56
La Guerche sur L'Aubois	25	46N57	2E57	-0:11:48
Laguiole	1	44N41	2E51	-0:11:24
La Hauteville	70	48N42	1E37	-0:06:28
La Haye du Puits	150	49N18	1W33	0:06:12

La Häy les Roses 61 48N47 2E21 -0:09:24
La Houssaye en Brie 82 48N45 2E53 -0:11:32
La Hunière 74 48N36 1E52 -0:07:28
L'Aigle 72 48N45 0E38 -0:02:32
Laignes 49 47N50 4E22 -0:17:28
Lailly en Val 44 47N46 1E41 -0:06:44
Lainville 79 49N04 1E49 -0:07:16
Laissac 1 44N23 2E49 -0:11:16
Laissey 55 47N18 6E14 -0:24:56
La Jarrie 33 46N08 1W00 0:04:00
La Javie 1 44N10 6E21 -0:25:24
Lalbenque 1 44N20 1E33 -0:06:12
Lalevade d'Ardèche 1 44N39 4E19 -0:17:16
Lalinde 1 44N51 0E44 -0:02:56
La Londe 1 43N08 6E14 -0:24:56
La Loupe 68 48N28 1E01 -0:04:04
Lalouvesc 1 45N07 4E32 -0:18:08
L'Alpe d'Huez 1 45N06 6E04 -0:24:16
La Madeleine 117 50N39 3E04 -0:12:16
La Madrague 1 43N14 5E22 -0:21:28
La Mailleraye sur Seine 127 49N29 0E46 -0:03:04
Lamarche 57 48N04 5E47 -0:23:08
Lamarche sur Saône 30 47N16 5E23 -0:21:32
La Marolle en Sologne 41 47N35 1E47 -0:07:08
La Martre 1 43N46 6E36 -0:26:24
Lamastre 1 44N59 4E35 -0:18:20
Lamballe 36 48N28 2W31 0:10:04
Lambersart 117 50N39 3E02 -0:12:08
Lambesc 1 43N39 5E16 -0:21:04
La Membrolle sur Choisille 25 47N26 0E38 -0:02:32
La Mothe Achard 24 46N37 1W40 0:06:40
Lamotte Beuvron 41 47N36 2E01 -0:08:04
La Motte Chalançon 1 44N29 5E23 -0:21:32
La Motte du Caire 1 44N21 6E02 -0:24:08
Lamoura 27 46N24 5E58 -0:23:52
La Mure 1 44N54 5E47 -0:23:08
Lamure sur Azergues 27 46N04 4E30 -0:18:00
La Napoule 1 43N31 6E56 -0:27:44
Lanarce 1 44N44 4E00 -0:16:00
La Nartelle 1 43N19 6E39 -0:26:36
Lancey 1 45N14 5E53 -0:23:32
Lancin 27 45N43 5E24 -0:21:36
Landerneau 36 48N27 4W15 0:17:00
Landivisiau 36 48N31 4W04 0:16:16
Landos 1 44N51 3E50 -0:15:20
Landrecies 103 50N08 3E42 -0:14:48
Landres 95 49N19 5E48 -0:23:12
Landry 1 45N34 6E45 -0:27:00
Langeac 1 45N06 3E30 -0:14:00
Langeais 25 47N20 0E24 -0:01:36
Langogne 1 44N43 3E51 -0:15:24
Langon 24 44N33 0W15 0:01:00
Langres 52 47N52 5E20 -0:21:20
Lannemezan 1 43N08 0E23 -0:01:32
Lannilis 36 48N34 4W31 0:18:04
Lannion 36 48N44 3W28 0:13:52
Lans en Vercors 1 45N07 5E35 -0:22:20
Lanslebourg 1 45N17 6E52 -0:27:28
Lanslevillard 1 45N17 6E55 -0:27:40
Laon 111 49N34 3E40 -0:14:40
Lapalisse 33 46N15 3E38 -0:14:32
La Palud 1 43N47 6E20 -0:25:20
La Penne sur Huveaune 1 43N17 5E31 -0:22:04
La Pesse 27 46N18 5E51 -0:23:24
La Petite Pierre 21 48N52 7E19 -0:29:16
La Pomme 1 43N25 5E35 -0:22:20
Lapoutroie 7 48N09 7E10 -0:28:40
La Queue en Brie 61 48N47 2E35 -0:10:20
La Queue lès Yvelines 74 48N48 1E46 -0:07:04
Laragne Montéglin 1 44N19 5E49 -0:23:16
L'Arbresle 27 45N50 4E37 -0:18:28
Lardy 78 48N31 2E16 -0:09:04
La Réole 1 44N35 0W02 0:00:08
Largentière 1 44N32 4E18 -0:17:12
L'Argentière la Bessée 1 44N47 6E33 -0:26:12
La Ricamarie 1 45N24 4E22 -0:17:28
La Roche Bernard 35 47N31 2W18 0:09:12
La Roche de Rame 1 44N45 6E35 -0:26:20
La Roche des Arnauds 1 44N34 5E57 -0:23:48
La Roche en Brenil 49 47N22 4E10 -0:16:40
La Rochefoucauld 1 45N45 0E23 -0:01:32
La Roche Guyon 79 49N05 1E38 -0:06:32
La Rochelle 33 46N10 1W10 0:04:40
Laroche Saint Cydroine 46 47N58 3E31 -0:14:04
La Roche sur Foron 1 46N04 6E19 -0:25:16
La Roche sur Yon 24 46N40 1W26 0:05:44
La Rochette 1 45N28 6E07 -0:24:28
La Rochette 77 48N30 2E40 -0:10:40
Laroquebrou 1 44N58 2E11 -0:08:44
La Roquebrussanne 1 43N20 5E59 -0:23:56
La Route 82 48N48 2E47 -0:11:08
Larringes 1 46N22 6E35 -0:26:20
Laruns 1 42N59 0W25 0:01:40
La Salette Fallavaux 1 44N51 5E59 -0:23:56
Lasalle 1 44N03 3E51 -0:15:24
La Saulce 1 44N25 6E01 -0:24:04
La Sentinelle 103 50N21 3E29 -0:13:56
La Seyne 1 43N06 5E53 -0:23:32
La Seyne sur Mer 1 43N06 5E53 -0:23:32
Lassay 65 48N26 0W30 0:02:00
Lassigny 115 49N35 2E51 -0:11:24
Lassy 80 49N06 2E27 -0:09:48
La Suze 39 47N54 0E02 -0:00:08
La Teste de Buch 24 44N38 1W09 0:04:36
La Tour 1 43N57 7E11 -0:28:44
La Tour d'Aigues 1 43N44 5E33 -0:22:12
La Tour d'Auvergne 1 45N32 2E41 -0:10:44
La Tour du Pin 26 45N34 5E27 -0:21:48
La Tremblade 24 45N46 1W08 0:04:32
La Trimouille 1 46N28 1E02 -0:04:08
La Tronche 1 45N12 5E44 -0:22:56
La Tuilerie 78 48N34 2E08 -0:08:32
La Tuilière 1 44N11 5E32 -0:22:08
La Turbie 1 43N45 7E24 -0:29:36
Laudun 1 44N06 4E40 -0:18:40
Launois sur Vence 103 49N39 4E32 -0:18:08
Laurière 1 46N05 1E28 -0:05:52
Lautenbach 3 47N57 7E09 -0:28:36
Lauterbourg 22 48N59 8E11 -0:32:44
Lauzerte 1 44N15 1E08 -0:04:32
Lauzun 1 44N38 0E28 -0:01:52
La Vacherie 1 44N53 5E11 -0:20:44
Laval 65 48N04 0W46 0:03:04
La Valette du Var 1 43N08 5E59 -0:23:56
Lavardac 1 44N11 0E18 -0:01:12
Lavelanet 1 42N56 1E51 -0:07:24
Laventie 136 50N38 2E46 -0:11:04
Lavéra 1 43N23 5E02 -0:20:08
La Verpillière 1 45N38 5E09 -0:20:36
La Verrière 61 48N45 1E57 -0:07:48
La Ville du Bois 78 48N40 2E16 -0:09:04
La Villeneuve Saint Martin 79 49N04 1E58 -0:07:52
La Voulte sur Rhône 1 44N48 4E47 -0:19:08
Lavoûte sur Loire 1 45N07 3E54 -0:15:36
La Wantzenau 22 48N40 7E50 -0:31:20
Laxou 92 48N41 6E09 -0:24:36
Lay Saint Christophe 92 48N45 6E12 -0:24:48
Le Ban Saint Martin 11 49N07 6E09 -0:24:36
Le Bar sur le Loup 1 43N42 6E59 -0:27:56
Le Béage 1 44N51 4E07 -0:16:28
Le Beausset 1 43N12 5E48 -0:23:12
Le Bessat 1 45N22 4E31 -0:18:04
Le Biot 1 46N16 6E38 -0:26:32
Le Blanc 1 46N38 1E04 -0:04:16
Le Blanc Mesnil 61 48N56 2E28 -0:09:52
Le Bleymard 1 44N29 3E44 -0:14:56
Le Bois de Cise 135 50N05 1E26 -0:05:44
Le Bois Dieu 74 48N39 1E43 -0:06:52
Le Bois d'Oingt 27 45N55 4E35 -0:18:20
Le Boréon 1 44N07 7E17 -0:29:08
Le Boulay 74 48N47 1E40 -0:06:40
Le Bourg d'Oisans 1 45N03 6E02 -0:24:08
Le Bourget 61 48N56 2E26 -0:09:44
Le Bourget du Lac 1 45N39 5E52 -0:23:28
Le Broc 1 43N49 7E10 -0:28:40
Le Brugeron 1 45N43 3E43 -0:14:52
Le Brusc 1 43N04 5E48 -0:23:12
Le Bugue 1 44N55 0E56 -0:03:44
Le Camp du Castellet 1 43N15 5E45 -0:23:00
Le Cannet 1 43N34 7E01 -0:28:04
Le Cateau 103 50N06 3E33 -0:14:12
Le Catelet 117 50N00 3E15 -0:13:00
Le Châble 1 46N06 6E06 -0:24:24
L'Échalp 1 44N45 7E00 -0:28:00
Le Chambon Feugerolles 1 45N24 4E19 -0:17:16
Le Chambon sur Lignon 1 45N03 4E18 -0:17:12
Le Champ Renault 80 49N06 2E31 -0:10:04
Le Château d'Oléron 33 45N53 1W11 0:04:44
Le Châtelard 1 45N41 6E08 -0:24:32
Le Châtelet 1 46N39 2E17 -0:09:08
Le Châtelet en Brie 77 48N30 2E48 -0:11:12
Le Chêne Rogneux 74 48N46 1E46 -0:07:04
Le Chesnay 61 48N50 2E07 -0:08:28
Le Chesne 103 49N31 4E46 -0:19:04
Le Cheylard 1 44N54 4E25 -0:17:40
Le Conquet 36 48N22 4W46 0:19:04
Le Coudray Montceaux 78 48N34 2E31 -0:10:04
Le Coudray Saint Germer 119 49N25 1E50 -0:07:20
Le Creusot 28 46N48 4E26 -0:17:44
Le Croisic 34 47N18 2W31 0:10:04
Le Crotoy 136 50N13 1E37 -0:06:28
Le Deschaux 29 46N57 5E30 -0:22:00
Lédignan 1 43N59 4E06 -0:16:24
Le Donjon 27 46N21 3E48 -0:15:12
Le Dorat 1 46N13 1E05 -0:04:20
Le Faouët 35 48N02 3W29 0:13:56
Le Fayet 1 45N55 6E42 -0:26:48
Leforest 117 50N26 3E04 -0:12:16
Le Freney d'Oisans 1 45N02 6E07 -0:24:28
Le Grand Lucé 43 47N52 0E28 -0:01:52
Le Grand Quevilly 127 49N25 1E02 -0:04:08
Le Grand Serre 1 45N16 5E06 -0:20:24
Le Grau du Roi 1 43N32 4E08 -0:16:32
Le Gua 1 45N01 5E37 -0:22:28
Le Havre 130 49N30 0E08 -0:00:32
Le Hérie la Viéville 103 49N49 3E38 -0:14:32
Le Hohwald 15 48N24 7E20 -0:29:20
Le Houlme 127 49N31 1E02 -0:04:08
Le Kremlin Bicêtre 61 48N49 2E21 -0:09:24
Le Lac d'Issarlès 1 44N49 4E04 -0:16:16
Le Laus 1 44N31 6E09 -0:24:36
Le Lauzet Ubaye 1 44N26 6E26 -0:25:44
Le Lavandou 1 43N08 6E22 -0:25:28
Lélex 27 46N18 5E57 -0:23:48
Le Liège 24 47N13 1E06 -0:04:24
Le Lion d'Angers 39 47N38 0W43 0:02:52
Le Luc 1 43N23 6E19 -0:25:16
Le Lude 41 47N39 0E09 -0:00:36
Le Mans 39 48N00 0E12 -0:00:48
Le Markstein 3 47N56 7E02 -0:28:08
Le Mayet de Montagne 1 46N05 3E40 -0:14:40
Lembach 19 49N00 7E48 -0:31:12
Lemberg 20 49N00 7E23 -0:29:32
Le Mée sur Seine 77 48N32 2E38 -0:10:32
Le Mêle sur Sarthe 68 48N31 0E21 -0:01:24
Le Merlerault 69 48N42 0E18 -0:01:12
Le Mesle 74 48N43 1E41 -0:06:44
Le Mesnil Amelot 80 49N01 2E36 -0:10:24
Le Mesnil Aubry 61 49N03 2E24 -0:09:36
Le Mesnil le Roi 61 48N56 2E08 -0:08:32
Le Mesnil Saint Denis 61 48N45 1E58 -0:07:52
Le Mesnil sur Oger 88 48N57 4E01 -0:16:04
Le Monastier 1 44N56 4E00 -0:16:00
Le Monêtier les Bains 1 44N59 6E31 -0:26:04
Le Montet 1 46N25 3E03 -0:12:12
Le Moutier 74 48N50 1E42 -0:06:48
Le Muy 1 43N28 6E33 -0:26:12
Lencloître 24 46N49 0E20 -0:01:20
Le Neubourg 73 49N09 0E55 -0:03:40
Le Nouvion en Thiérache 103 50N01 3E47 -0:15:08
Lens 153 50N26 2E50 -0:11:20
Léon 24 43N53 1W18 0:05:12
Le Pailly 52 47N48 5E25 -0:21:40
Le Palais 35 47N21 3W09 0:12:36
Le Parcq 136 50N23 2E06 -0:08:24
Le Pâté 78 48N32 2E18 -0:09:12
Le Péage de Roussillon 1 45N22 4E48 -0:19:12
Le Pecq 61 48N54 2E07 -0:08:28
Le Pellerin 28 47N12 1W45 0:07:00
Le Perray en Yvelines 74 48N42 1E51 -0:07:24
Le Perreux sur Marne 61 48N51 2E30 -0:10:00
Le Petit Couronne 127 49N23 1E01 -0:04:04
Le Petit Quevilly 127 49N26 1E02 -0:04:08
Le Pin 61 48N55 2E38 -0:10:32
Le Pin au Haras 69 48N44 0E09 -0:00:36
L'Épine 88 48N58 4E28 -0:17:52
L'Épine 78 48N32 2E21 -0:09:24
Lépin le Lac 26 45N32 5E47 -0:23:08
Le Plessis aux Bois 80 49N00 2E46 -0:11:04
Le Plessis Belleville 80 49N06 2E46 -0:11:04
Le Plessis Bouchard 61 49N00 2E14 -0:08:56
Le Plessis Pâté 78 48N37 2E20 -0:09:20
Le Plessis Trévise 61 48N49 2E34 -0:10:16
Le Poët 1 44N17 5E53 -0:23:32
Le Pont de Beauvoisin 26 45N32 5E40 -0:22:40
Le Pont de Montvert 1 44N22 3E45 -0:15:00
Le Pontel 74 48N49 1E53 -0:07:32
Le Portel 138 50N42 1E34 -0:06:16
Le Port Marly 61 48N53 2E06 -0:08:24
Le Pouzin 1 44N45 4E45 -0:19:00
Le Pradet 1 43N06 6E01 -0:24:04
Le Pré Saint Gervais 61 48N53 2E25 -0:09:40
Le Puy 1 45N02 3E53 -0:15:32
Le Quesnoy 103 50N15 3E38 -0:14:32
Le Raincy 61 48N54 2E31 -0:10:04
Le Rayol Canadel sur Mer 1 43N10 6E28 -0:25:52
Léré 41 47N28 2E52 -0:11:28
Le Reposoir 1 46N00 6E33 -0:26:12
Lérouville 94 48N47 5E33 -0:22:12
Le Russey 32 47N10 6E44 -0:26:56

Les Abrets	26	45N32	5E35	-0:22:20
Les Aix d'Angillon	25	47N12	2E34	-0:10:16
Les Allues	1	45N26	6E33	-0:26:12
Les Alluets le Roi	74	48N55	1E55	-0:07:40
Les Andelys	110	49N15	1E25	-0:05:40
Le Sappey en Chartreuse	1	45N16	5E47	-0:23:08
Les Arcs	1	43N27	6E29	-0:25:56
Le Sauze	1	44N22	6E41	-0:26:44
Les Baux en Provence	1	43N45	4E48	-0:19:12
Les Bézards	45	47N48	2E44	-0:10:56
Les Bordes	74	48N39	1E58	-0:07:52
Les Bouchoux	27	46N18	5E49	-0:23:16
Les Bréviaires	74	48N42	1E49	-0:07:16
L'Escarène	1	43N50	7E21	-0:29:24
Les Chaises	74	48N39	1E42	-0:06:48
Les Chapieux	1	45N42	6E44	-0:26:56
Lesches	82	48N54	2E47	-0:11:08
Les Clayes sous Bois	61	48N49	1E59	-0:07:56
Les Contamines Montjoie	1	45N50	6E44	-0:26:56
Les Echarmeaux	27	46N10	4E27	-0:17:48
Les Échelles	1	45N26	5E45	-0:23:00
Les Essarts	24	46N46	1W14	0:04:56
Les Essarts le Roi	74	48N43	1E54	-0:07:36
Les Estables	1	44N54	4E10	-0:16:40
Les Étangs	12	49N09	6E23	-0:25:32
Les Fourgs	32	46N50	6E25	-0:25:40
Les Gâtines	61	48N48	1E58	-0:07:52
Les Gets	1	46N09	6E40	-0:26:40
Les Granges le Roi	48	48N30	2E01	-0:08:04
Les Halles	1	45N43	4E26	-0:17:44
Les Hautes Rivières	118	49N53	4E50	-0:19:20
Les Herbiers	25	46N52	1W01	0:04:04
Les Houches	1	45N53	6E48	-0:27:12
Lésigny	61	48N45	2E37	-0:10:28
Les Islettes	87	49N06	5E00	-0:20:00
Les Laumes	51	47N32	4E27	-0:17:48
Les Lecques	1	43N11	5E40	-0:22:40
Les Lilas	61	48N53	2E25	-0:09:40
Les Loges	78	48N34	2E03	-0:08:12
Les Loges en Josas	61	48N46	2E09	-0:08:36
Les Mées	1	44N02	5E59	-0:23:56
Les Mesnuls	74	48N45	1E50	-0:07:20
Les Molières	78	48N40	2E04	-0:08:16
Lesmont	86	48N26	4E25	-0:17:40
Les Mureaux	79	49N00	1E55	-0:07:40
Les Neyrolles	27	46N08	5E38	-0:22:32
Lesparre Médoc	24	45N18	0W56	0:03:44
Les Pavillons sous Bois	61	48N55	2E30	-0:10:00
Les Pieux	145	49N31	1W48	0:07:12
Les Planches en Montagne	31	46N40	6E01	-0:24:04
Les Praz de Chamonix	1	45N56	6E52	-0:27:28
Lesquin	117	50N35	3E07	-0:12:28
Les Riceys	49	47N59	4E22	-0:17:28
Les Roches l'Évêque	42	47N47	0E53	-0:03:32
Les Rousses	31	46N29	6E04	-0:24:16
Les Ruelles	70	48N40	1E37	-0:06:28
Les Sables d'Olonne	24	46N30	1W47	0:07:08
Les Salles sur Verdon	1	43N46	6E12	-0:24:48
Lessay	148	49N13	1W32	0:06:08
Les Scaffarels	1	43N57	6E41	-0:26:44
L'Estaque	1	43N22	5E20	-0:21:20
Les Thilliers en Vexin	124	49N14	1E36	-0:06:24
L'Estréchure	1	44N06	3E47	-0:15:08
Les Vans	1	44N24	4E08	-0:16:32
L'Étang la Ville	61	48N52	2E05	-0:08:20
Le Teil	1	44N33	4E41	-0:18:44
Le Temple	79	49N00	1E58	-0:07:52
Le Tertre Saint Denis	73	48N56	1E36	-0:06:24
Le Theil sur Huisne	68	48N16	0E42	-0:02:48
Le Thillot	60	47N53	6E46	-0:27:04
Le Tholy	101	48N05	6E45	-0:27:00
Le Thor	1	43N56	5E00	-0:20:00
Le Thoronet	1	43N27	6E18	-0:25:12
Le Touquet Paris Plage	138	50N31	1E35	-0:06:20
Le Touvet	1	45N21	5E57	-0:23:48
Le Trait	127	49N28	0E49	-0:03:16
Le Trayas	1	43N28	6E55	-0:27:40
Le Tremblay sur Mauldre	74	48N47	1E53	-0:07:32
Le Tréport	133	50N04	1E22	-0:05:28
Leudeville	78	48N34	2E20	-0:09:20
Leuglay	52	47N49	4E48	-0:19:12
Leuville sur Orge	78	48N37	2E16	-0:09:04
Le Val d'Ajol	58	47N55	6E29	-0:25:56
Le Val d'Albian	61	48N45	2E11	-0:08:44
Levallois Perret	61	48N54	2E18	-0:09:12
Le Val Saint Germain	78	48N34	2E04	-0:08:16
Levens	1	43N52	7E13	-0:28:52
Le Vésinet	61	48N54	2E08	-0:08:32
Levie	1	41N42	9E07	-0:36:28
Levier	32	46N57	6E08	-0:24:32
Le Vigan	1	43N59	3E35	-0:14:20
Lévis Saint Nom	61	48N43	1E58	-0:07:52
Levroux	1	46N59	1E37	-0:06:28
Lézat	27	46N30	5E56	-0:23:44
L'Hautil	80	49N00	2E01	-0:08:04
L'Hôpital	18	49N10	6E44	-0:26:56
L'Hôpital sous Rochefort	1	45N46	3E56	-0:15:44
Lhuis	26	45N45	5E32	-0:22:08
Liancourt	110	49N20	2E28	-0:09:52
Liart	103	49N46	4E20	-0:17:20
Libourne	24	44N55	0W14	0:00:56
Lichères Près Aigremont	45	47N43	3E51	-0:15:24
Lichtenberg	21	48N55	7E29	-0:29:56
Lièpvre	16	48N16	7E17	-0:29:08
Liernais	49	47N12	4E17	-0:17:08
Liesse	112	49N37	3E48	-0:15:12
Liessies	103	50N07	4E05	-0:16:20
Lieurey	126	49N14	0E29	-0:01:56
Lieusaint	78	48N38	2E33	-0:10:12
Liévin	153	50N25	2E46	-0:11:04
Liffol le Grand	57	48N19	5E35	-0:22:20
Liffré	66	48N13	1W30	0:06:00
Lignières	1	46N45	2E11	-0:08:44
Ligny en Barrois	87	48N41	5E20	-0:21:20
Ligny en Cambrésis	103	50N06	3E22	-0:13:28
Ligny le Châtel	46	47N54	3E45	-0:15:00
Ligny le Ribault	41	47N41	1E47	-0:07:08
Ligueil	24	47N03	0E49	-0:03:16
L'Île Bouchard	24	47N07	0E25	-0:01:40
L'Île Rousse	1	42N38	8E56	-0:35:44
Lille	117	50N38	3E04	-0:12:16
Lillebonne	127	49N31	0E33	-0:02:12
Lillers	136	50N34	2E29	-0:09:56
Limay	79	49N00	1E44	-0:06:56
Limoges	1	45N50	1E16	-0:05:04
Limoges Fourches	78	48N38	2E40	-0:10:40
Limogne	1	44N24	1E46	-0:07:04
Limonest	27	45N50	4E46	-0:19:04
Limours	78	48N39	2E05	-0:08:20
Limoux	1	43N04	2E14	-0:08:56
Linas	78	48N38	2E16	-0:09:04
Lingolsheim	14	48N34	7E41	-0:30:44
Linthal	3	47N56	7E08	-0:28:32
Liomer	133	49N51	1E49	-0:07:16
Lisieux	69	49N09	0E14	-0:00:56
L'Isle Adam	80	49N07	2E14	-0:08:56
L'Isle Jourdain	1	46N14	0E41	-0:02:44
L'Isle Jourdain	1	43N37	1E05	-0:04:20
L'Isle sur la Sorgue	1	43N55	5E03	-0:20:12
L'Isle sur le Doubs	55	47N27	6E35	-0:26:20
L'Isle sur Serein	49	47N35	4E00	-0:16:00
Lisses	78	48N36	2E26	-0:09:44
Lissy	77	48N38	2E42	-0:10:48
Livarot	69	49N01	0E09	-0:00:36
Liverdun	92	48N45	6E03	-0:24:12
Liverdy en Brie	82	48N42	2E47	-0:11:08
Livet et Gavet	1	45N06	5E56	-0:23:44
Livilliers	80	49N06	2E06	-0:08:24
Livron sur Drôme	1	44N46	4E51	-0:19:24
Livry Gargan	61	48N56	2E33	-0:10:12
Livry sur Seine	77	48N31	2E41	-0:10:44
Lizy sur Ourcq	83	49N01	3E02	-0:12:08
Loches	1	47N08	1E00	-0:04:00
Locminé	35	47N53	2W50	0:11:20
Locon	136	50N34	2E40	-0:10:40
Lodève	1	43N43	3E19	-0:13:16
Lods	32	47N03	6E15	-0:25:00
Lognes	61	48N50	2E38	-0:10:32
Loire	1	45N33	4E48	-0:19:12
Loisia	27	46N29	5E27	-0:21:48
Lomme	117	50N39	2E59	-0:11:56
Londinières	132	49N50	1E24	-0:05:36
Longchaumois	27	46N27	5E56	-0:23:44
Longchêne	78	48N38	2E00	-0:08:00
Longeau	52	47N46	5E18	-0:21:12
Longeville Lès Saint Avold	12	49N07	6E38	-0:26:32
Longjumeau	61	48N42	2E18	-0:09:12
Longlaville	104	49N32	5E47	-0:23:08
Longny au Perche	68	48N32	0E45	-0:03:00
Longperrier	80	49N03	2E40	-0:10:40
Longpont	107	49N16	3E13	-0:12:52
Longpré les Corps Saints	134	50N01	1E59	-0:07:56
Longué	25	47N23	0W06	0:00:24
Longueau	121	49N52	2E21	-0:09:24
Longuesse	79	49N04	1E56	-0:07:44
Longueville	77	48N31	3E15	-0:13:00
Longueville sur Scie	131	49N48	1E06	-0:04:24
Longuyon	97	49N26	5E36	-0:22:24
Longvic	49	47N17	5E04	-0:20:16
Longvilliers	48	48N35	2E00	-0:08:00
Longwy	104	49N31	5E46	-0:23:04
Lonny	103	49N49	4E35	-0:18:20
Lons le Saunier	27	46N40	5E33	-0:22:12
Loos	117	50N37	3E01	-0:12:04
Lorentzen	17	48N57	7E10	-0:28:40
Lorette	1	45N31	4E35	-0:18:20
Lorgues	1	43N29	6E22	-0:25:28
Lorient	34	47N45	3W22	0:13:28
Loriol sur Drôme	1	44N45	4E49	-0:19:16
L'Orme	70	48N39	1E41	-0:06:44
Lormes	45	47N17	3E49	-0:15:16
Lorquin	14	48N40	7E00	-0:28:00
Lorrez le Bocage	76	48N14	2E54	-0:11:36
Lorris	48	47N53	2E31	-0:10:04
Loubaresse	1	44N36	4E03	-0:16:12
Loudéac	36	48N10	2W45	0:11:00
Loudes	1	45N05	3E45	-0:15:00
Loudun	24	47N01	0E05	-0:00:20
Loué	39	48N00	0W09	0:00:36
Louhans	27	46N38	5E13	-0:20:52
Lourches	103	50N19	3E21	-0:13:24
Lourdes	1	43N06	0W03	0:00:12
Lourmarin	1	43N46	5E22	-0:21:28
Loury	71	48N00	2E05	-0:08:20
Louveciennes	61	48N52	2E07	-0:08:28
Louviers	124	49N13	1E10	-0:04:40
Louvigné du Désert	65	48N29	1W08	0:04:32
Louvres	61	49N02	2E30	-0:10:00
Louvroil	152	50N16	3E58	-0:15:52
Lubersac	1	45N27	1E24	-0:05:36
Lucenay l'Évêque	28	47N05	4E15	-0:17:00
Luc en Diois	1	44N37	5E27	-0:21:48
Lucéram	1	43N53	7E22	-0:29:28
Luché Pringé	41	47N42	0E05	-0:00:20
Luçon	24	46N27	1W10	0:04:40
Lugny	27	46N28	4E49	-0:19:16
Luisant	71	48N25	1E29	-0:05:56
Lumbres	137	50N42	2E08	-0:08:32
Lunel	1	43N41	4E08	-0:16:32
Luneray	131	49N50	0E55	-0:03:40
Lunéville	91	48N36	6E30	-0:26:00
Lure	59	47N41	6E30	-0:26:00
Lusignan	24	46N26	0E07	-0:00:28
Lusigny sur Barse	77	48N15	4E16	-0:17:04
Lus la Croix Haute	1	44N40	5E42	-0:22:48
Lussac les Châteaux	1	46N24	0E44	-0:02:56
Lussan	1	44N09	4E22	-0:17:28
Lutterbach	4	47N46	7E17	-0:29:08
Lutzelbourg	14	48N44	7E15	-0:29:00
Luxeuil les Bains	59	47N49	6E23	-0:25:32
Luzarches	80	49N07	2E25	-0:09:40
Luzy	28	46N48	3E58	-0:15:52
Lyon	27	45N45	4E51	-0:19:24
Lyons la Forêt	119	49N24	1E28	-0:05:52
Machault	89	49N21	4E30	-0:18:00
Machecoul	24	47N00	1W50	0:07:20
Machery	78	48N36	2E05	-0:08:20
Mâcon	27	46N18	4E50	-0:19:20
Maffliers	61	49N05	2E19	-0:09:16
Magnanville	74	48N58	1E41	-0:06:44
Magnières	91	48N27	6E34	-0:26:16
Magny en Vexin	79	49N09	1E47	-0:07:08
Magny le Hongre	82	48N52	2E49	-0:11:16
Magny les Hameaux	61	48N44	2E04	-0:08:16
Maîche	55	47N15	6E48	-0:27:12
Maignelay	114	49N33	2E31	-0:10:04
Maillane	1	43N50	4E47	-0:19:08
Mailley et Chazelot	54	47N32	6E03	-0:24:12
Maillezais	24	46N22	0W44	0:02:56
Mailly le Camp	86	48N40	4E13	-0:16:52
Mailly le Château	45	47N36	3E38	-0:14:32
Mailly Maillet	122	50N04	2E36	-0:10:24
Maincourt sur Yvette	61	48N43	1E58	-0:07:52
Maincy	77	48N33	2E42	-0:10:48
Mainguerin	74	48N32	1E51	-0:07:24
Maintenon	70	48N35	1E35	-0:06:20
Mainvilliers	71	48N27	1E28	-0:05:52
Maisons Alfort	61	48N48	2E26	-0:09:44
Maisons Laffitte	61	48N57	2E09	-0:08:36
Maisse	48	48N24	2E23	-0:09:32
Maizières lès Metz	11	49N13	6E09	-0:24:36
Maizières lès Vic	12	48N43	6E46	-0:27:04
Malakoff	61	48N49	2E19	-0:09:16
Malassis	78	48N38	2E03	-0:08:12
Malaucène	1	44N10	5E08	-0:20:32
Malaunay	127	49N32	1E02	-0:04:08
Malbuisson	32	46N48	6E18	-0:25:12
Malesherbes	48	48N18	2E25	-0:09:40
Malestroit	35	47N49	2W23	0:09:32
Mallemort	1	43N44	5E11	-0:20:44
Malnoue	61	48N50	2E36	-0:10:24
Malo les Bains	140	51N03	2E24	-0:09:36
Malzéville	92	48N43	6E12	-0:24:48
Mamers	68	48N21	0E23	-0:01:32
Mamirolle	55	47N12	6E10	-0:24:40
Mancieulles	97	49N17	5E53	-0:23:32
Mandelieu	1	43N33	6E56	-0:27:44
Mandeure	55	47N27	6E48	-0:27:12
Mandres les Roses	61	48N42	2E33	-0:10:12
Manosque	1	43N50	5E47	-0:23:08
Mansle	24	45N53	0E11	-0:00:44
Mantes la Jolie	74	48N59	1E43	-0:06:52
Manthelan	24	47N08	0E47	-0:03:08
Marainviller	91	48N35	6E36	-0:26:24
Marange Zondrange	12	49N07	6E32	-0:26:08
Marans	24	46N19	1W00	0:04:00
Maraye en Othe	77	48N10	3E51	-0:15:24
Marbache	100	48N48	6E05	-0:24:20
Marchais	48	48N31	2E03	-0:08:12
Marchaux	55	47N19	6E08	-0:24:32
Marchémoret	80	49N03	2E46	-0:11:04

Marchenoir	44	47N49	1E24	-0:05:36
Marchiennes	117	50N24	3E17	-0:13:08
Marcigny	27	46N17	4E02	-0:16:08
Marcillac Vallon	1	44N29	2E28	-0:09:52
Marcilloles	1	45N20	5E11	-0:20:44
Marcilly	80	49N02	2E53	-0:11:32
Marcilly la Campagne	73	48N50	1E13	-0:04:52
Marcilly le Hayer	77	48N21	3E38	-0:14:32
Marcilly sur Eure	73	48N49	1E21	-0:05:24
Marck	138	50N57	1E57	-0:07:48
Marckolsheim	23	48N10	7E33	-0:30:12
Marcoing	117	50N07	3E11	-0:12:44
Marcoussis	78	48N39	2E14	-0:08:56
Marcq	74	48N52	1E49	-0:07:16
Marcq en Baroeul	117	50N40	3E05	-0:12:20
Mareil en France	61	49N04	2E26	-0:09:44
Mareil le Guyon	74	48N47	1E51	-0:07:24
Mareil Marly	61	48N53	2E05	-0:08:20
Marennes	24	45N50	1W06	0:04:24
Mareuil en Brie	84	48N57	3E45	-0:15:00
Mareuil lès Meaux	81	48N56	2E52	-0:11:28
Mareuil sur Aÿ	84	49N03	4E02	-0:16:08
Mareuil sur Belle	1	45N28	0E28	-0:01:52
Marey sur Tille	52	47N35	5E03	-0:20:12
Margès	1	45N09	5E03	-0:20:12
Margny lès Compiègne	114	49N26	2E49	-0:11:16
Marguerittes	1	43N51	4E27	-0:17:48
Margut	102	49N35	5E16	-0:21:04
Marignane	1	43N25	5E13	-0:20:52
Marignier	1	46N06	6E31	-0:26:04
Marigny le Châtel	77	48N24	3E44	-0:14:56
Marigny l'église	45	47N22	3E56	-0:15:44
Marines	79	49N09	1E59	-0:07:56
Marle	103	49N44	3E46	-0:15:04
Marlenheim	14	48N37	7E30	-0:30:00
Marles en Brie	82	48N44	2E53	-0:11:32
Marles les Mines	136	50N30	2E31	-0:10:04
Marlieux	27	46N04	5E04	-0:20:16
Marly la Ville	80	49N05	2E30	-0:10:00
Marly le Roi	61	48N52	2E05	-0:08:20
Marmagne	28	46N50	4E21	-0:17:24
Marmande	1	44N30	0E10	-0:00:40
Marmoutier	18	48N41	7E23	-0:29:32
Marnay	30	47N17	5E46	-0:23:04
Marnaz	1	46N04	6E32	-0:26:08
Marolles en Brie	61	48N44	2E33	-0:10:12
Marolles en Hurepoix	78	48N34	2E18	-0:09:12
Marolles les Braults	68	48N15	0E19	-0:01:16
Maromme	127	49N28	1E02	-0:04:08
Marpent	152	50N18	4E05	-0:16:20
Marquion	117	50N13	3E05	-0:12:20
Marquise	138	50N49	1E42	-0:06:48
Marsac en Livradois	1	45N29	3E44	-0:14:56
Marsal	12	48N48	6E36	-0:26:24
Marsannay la Côte	49	47N16	4E59	-0:19:56
Marsanne	1	44N39	4E52	-0:19:28
Marseille	1	43N18	5E24	-0:21:36
Marseille en Beauvaisis	119	49N35	1E57	-0:07:48
Marsella → Marseille	1	43N18	5E24	-0:21:36
Marsillargues	1	43N40	4E11	-0:16:44
Mars la Tour	95	49N06	5E54	-0:23:36
Marson	88	48N55	4E32	-0:18:08
Martel	1	44N56	1E37	-0:06:28
Martignat	27	46N13	5E36	-0:22:24
Martigny les Bains	57	48N06	5E49	-0:23:16
Martigues	1	43N24	5E03	-0:20:12
Martin Église	131	49N54	1E09	-0:04:36
Marvejols	1	44N33	3E18	-0:13:12
Marville	97	49N27	5E27	-0:21:48
Masevaux	2	47N47	7E00	-0:28:00
Masnières	117	50N07	3E13	-0:12:52
Massay	1	47N09	2E00	-0:08:00
Masseube	1	43N26	0E35	-0:02:20
Massiac	1	45N15	3E12	-0:12:48
Massy	61	48N44	2E17	-0:09:08
Mas Thibert	1	43N34	4E44	-0:18:56
Matha	24	45N52	0W19	0:01:16
Matignon	62	48N36	2W18	0:09:12
Matour	27	46N18	4E29	-0:17:56
Maubeuge	152	50N17	3E58	-0:15:52
Mauchamps	78	48N32	2E12	-0:08:48
Maudétour en Vexin	79	49N06	1E47	-0:07:08
Mauguio	1	43N37	4E01	-0:16:04
Maulde	103	50N30	3E26	-0:13:44
Maule	74	48N55	1E51	-0:07:24
Mauléon	25	46N56	0W45	0:03:00
Maulette	74	48N48	1E37	-0:06:28
Maurecourt	80	49N00	2E04	-0:08:16
Maure de Bretagne	35	47N54	1W59	0:07:56
Mauregard	80	49N02	2E35	-0:10:20
Mauriac	1	45N13	2E20	-0:09:20
Mauron	36	48N06	2W18	0:09:12
Maurs	1	44N43	2E11	-0:08:44
Maussane	1	43N43	4E48	-0:19:12
Mauvezin	1	43N44	0E55	-0:03:40
Maxéville	92	48N43	6E10	-0:24:40
Mayenne	40	48N18	0W37	0:02:28
Mayet	42	47N46	0E17	-0:01:08
Mayres	1	44N40	4E07	-0:16:28
Mazamet	1	43N30	2E24	-0:09:36
Mazargues	1	43N15	5E24	-0:21:36
Meaux	81	48N57	2E52	-0:11:28
Médan	61	48N57	2E00	-0:08:00
Megève	1	45N52	6E37	-0:26:28
Mégevette	1	46N12	6E30	-0:26:00
Mehun sur Yévre	25	47N09	2E13	-0:08:52
Meillerie	1	46N24	6E43	-0:26:52
Mélisey	59	47N45	6E35	-0:26:20
Melle	24	46N13	0W09	0:00:36
Melun	77	48N32	2E40	-0:10:40
Menars	41	47N38	1E24	-0:05:36
Mende	1	44N30	3E30	-0:14:00
Ménéac	36	48N09	2W28	0:09:52
Ménil la Tour	93	48N46	5E52	-0:23:28
Mennecy	78	48N34	2E26	-0:09:44
Mennetou sur Cher	25	47N16	1E53	-0:07:32
Mens	1	44N49	5E45	-0:23:00
Menthon Saint Bernard	1	45N51	6E12	-0:24:48
Menton	1	43N47	7E30	-0:30:00
Mentone → Menton	1	43N47	7E30	-0:30:00
Menucourt	79	49N02	1E59	-0:07:56
Méounes lès Montrieux	1	43N17	5E58	-0:23:52
Mer	41	47N42	1E30	-0:06:00
Mercy le Bas	97	49N23	5E45	-0:23:00
Méré	74	48N47	1E49	-0:07:16
Méréville	48	48N19	2E05	-0:08:20
Méribel	1	45N25	6E34	-0:26:16
Méricourt	153	50N24	2E52	-0:11:28
Mériel	80	49N05	2E12	-0:08:48
Mérignac	24	44N50	0W42	0:02:48
Merlebach	17	49N09	6E48	-0:27:12
Merlimont Plage	137	50N28	1E35	-0:06:20
Mers les Bains	133	50N04	1E23	-0:05:32
Méru	80	49N14	2E08	-0:08:32
Mervans	29	46N48	5E11	-0:20:44
Merville	137	50N38	2E38	-0:10:32
Méry la Bataille	114	49N33	2E38	-0:10:32
Méry sur Oise	61	49N04	2E11	-0:08:44
Méry sur Seine	77	48N30	3E53	-0:15:32
Meslay du Maine	38	47N57	0W33	0:02:12
Meslay le Grenet	71	48N22	1E23	-0:05:32
Mesnil Val Plage	133	50N03	1E20	-0:05:20
Messy	61	48N58	2E42	-0:10:48
Métabief	32	46N47	6E21	-0:25:24
Mettray	25	47N27	0E39	-0:02:36
Metz	11	49N08	6E10	-0:24:40
Metzervisse	12	49N19	6E17	-0:25:08
Meudon	61	48N48	2E14	-0:08:56
Meulan	79	49N01	1E54	-0:07:36
Meung sur Loire	44	47N50	1E42	-0:06:48
Meursault	30	46N59	4E46	-0:19:04
Meuse	52	47N59	5E33	-0:22:12
Meximieux	27	45N54	5E12	-0:20:48
Meymac	1	45N32	2E09	-0:08:36
Meyrargues	1	43N38	5E32	-0:22:08
Meyrueis	1	44N10	3E26	-0:13:44
Mèze	1	43N25	3E36	-0:14:24
Mézel	1	43N59	6E12	-0:24:48
Mézières en Brenne	1	46N49	1E13	-0:04:52
Mézières sur Seine	74	48N58	1E48	-0:07:12
Mézilhac	1	44N48	4E21	-0:17:24
Mézin	1	44N03	0E16	-0:01:04
Mézy	79	49N00	1E53	-0:07:32
Miélan	1	43N26	0E19	-0:01:16
Migennes	46	47N58	3E31	-0:14:04
Mignovillard	32	46N48	6E08	-0:24:32
Mijoux	27	46N22	6E00	-0:24:00
Milhaud	1	43N47	4E18	-0:17:12
Millau	1	44N06	3E05	-0:12:20
Millemont	74	48N49	1E45	-0:07:00
Milly la Forêt	48	48N24	2E28	-0:09:52
Milly Lamartine	27	46N21	4E42	-0:18:48
Milon la Chapelle	61	48N44	2E03	-0:08:12
Mimizan	24	44N12	1W14	0:04:56
Mirabeau	1	43N42	5E39	-0:22:36
Miramar	1	43N30	6E57	-0:27:48
Miramas	1	43N35	5E00	-0:20:00
Mirambeau	24	45N23	0W34	0:02:16
Mirande	1	43N31	0E25	-0:01:40
Mirebeau sur Bèze	30	47N24	5E19	-0:21:16
Mirecourt	58	48N18	6E08	-0:24:32
Miribel	1	45N49	4E57	-0:19:48
Mitry le Neuf	61	48N57	2E36	-0:10:24
Mitry Mory	61	48N59	2E37	-0:10:28
Mittainville	70	48N40	1E39	-0:06:36
Modane	1	45N12	6E40	-0:26:40
Mohon	103	49N45	4E44	-0:18:56
Moirans	1	45N20	5E34	-0:22:16
Moirans en Montagne	27	46N26	5E44	-0:22:56
Moisdon	38	47N37	1W22	0:05:28
Moisenay	77	48N34	2E44	-0:10:56
Moissac	1	44N06	1E05	-0:04:20
Moisselles	61	49N03	2E20	-0:09:20
Moisson	79	49N05	1E40	-0:06:40
Moissy Cramayel	78	48N38	2E36	-0:10:24
Molières sur Cèze	1	44N15	4E09	-0:16:36
Molinges	27	46N21	5E46	-0:23:04
Molliens Vidame	120	49N53	2E01	-0:08:04
Moloy	52	47N32	4E55	-0:19:40
Molsheim	14	48N32	7E29	-0:29:56
Mommenheim	18	48N45	7E39	-0:30:36
Moncontour	36	48N21	2W39	0:10:36
Moncoutant	24	46N43	0W35	0:02:20
Mondoubleau	42	47N59	0E54	-0:03:36
Mondragon	1	44N14	4E43	-0:18:52
Monestier de Clermont	1	44N54	5E38	-0:22:32
Monflanquin	1	44N32	0E46	-0:03:04
Mon Idée	103	49N53	4E23	-0:17:32
Monistrol d'Allier	1	44N57	3E38	-0:14:32
Monistrol sur Loire	1	45N17	4E10	-0:16:40
Mons	1	43N41	6E43	-0:26:52
Monsols	27	46N13	4E31	-0:18:04
Montagrier	1	45N16	0E29	-0:01:56
Montaigu	25	46N59	1W19	0:05:16
Montaigut en Combraille	1	46N11	2E48	-0:11:12
Montainville	74	48N53	1E52	-0:07:28
Montalet le Bois	79	49N03	1E50	-0:07:20
Montalieu Vercieu	26	45N49	5E24	-0:21:36
Montargis	45	48N00	2E45	-0:11:00
Montataire	80	49N16	2E26	-0:09:44
Montauban	1	44N01	1E21	-0:05:24
Montauroux	1	43N37	6E46	-0:27:04
Montbard	51	47N37	4E20	-0:17:20
Montbarrey	32	47N01	5E39	-0:22:36
Montbazon	25	47N17	0E43	-0:02:52
Montbéliard	60	47N31	6E48	-0:27:12
Montbenoît	32	46N59	6E28	-0:25:52
Mont Bonvillers	97	49N20	5E51	-0:23:24
Montbozon	55	47N28	6E16	-0:25:04
Montbrison	1	45N36	4E03	-0:16:12
Montbron	1	45N40	0E30	-0:02:00
Montbronn	21	48N59	7E19	-0:29:16
Montceau les Mines	25	46N40	4E22	-0:17:28
Montcenis	25	46N47	4E23	-0:17:32
Montchanin	25	46N45	4E27	-0:17:48
Montchauvet	74	48N54	1E38	-0:06:32
Montcornet	103	49N41	4E01	-0:16:04
Mont de Marsan	24	43N53	0W30	0:02:00
Montdidier	115	49N39	2E34	-0:10:16
Montélimar	1	44N34	4E45	-0:19:00
Montendre	24	45N17	0W24	0:01:36
Montereau	45	47N51	2E34	-0:10:16
Montereau Faut Yonne	77	48N23	2E57	-0:11:48
Montereau sur le Jard	77	48N35	2E40	-0:10:40
Montesson	61	48N55	2E09	-0:08:36
Monteux	1	44N02	5E00	-0:20:00
Montévrain	82	48N53	2E45	-0:11:00
Montfaucon	1	45N10	4E18	-0:17:12
Montfaucon	89	49N17	5E08	-0:20:32
Montfermeil	61	48N54	2E34	-0:10:16
Montfleur	27	46N19	5E26	-0:21:44
Montfort	62	48N08	1W58	0:07:52
Montfort l'Amaury	74	48N47	1E49	-0:07:16
Montfort le Rotrou	43	48N03	0E25	-0:01:40
Montfort sur Risle	126	49N18	0E40	-0:02:40
Montfrin	1	43N53	4E36	-0:18:24
Montgé	80	49N02	2E45	-0:11:00
Montgenèvre	1	44N56	6E43	-0:26:52
Montgeron	61	48N42	2E27	-0:09:48
Montgeroult	80	49N05	2E00	-0:08:00
Montgesoye	32	47N05	6E12	-0:24:48
Montguyon	24	45N13	0W11	0:00:44
Monthermé	118	49N53	4E44	-0:18:56
Monthois	89	49N19	4E43	-0:18:52
Monthureux sur Saône	58	48N02	5E58	-0:23:52
Monthyon	80	49N00	2E50	-0:11:20
Montier en Der	86	48N29	4E46	-0:19:04
Montiers sur Saulx	87	48N32	5E16	-0:21:04
Montignac	1	45N04	1E10	-0:04:40
Montigny	101	48N31	6E48	-0:27:12
Montigny Devant Sassey	98	49N26	5E09	-0:20:36
Montigny le Bretonneux	61	48N46	2E02	-0:08:08
Montigny le Roi	57	48N00	5E30	-0:22:00
Montigny lès Cormeilles	61	48N59	2E12	-0:08:48
Montigny sur Aube	52	47N57	4E46	-0:19:04
Montivilliers	128	49N33	0E12	-0:00:48
Montjay la Tour	61	48N55	2E40	-0:10:40
Montlebon	32	47N02	6E37	-0:26:28
Montlhéry	78	48N38	2E16	-0:09:04
Montlignon	61	49N01	2E17	-0:09:08
Montlouet	70	48N31	1E43	-0:06:52
Mont Louis	1	42N31	2E07	-0:08:28
Montlouis sur Loire	25	47N23	0E50	-0:03:20
Montluçon	1	46N21	2E36	-0:10:24
Montluel	27	45N51	5E03	-0:20:12
Montmagny	61	48N58	2E21	-0:09:24
Montmédy	103	49N31	5E22	-0:21:28
Montmélian	1	45N30	6E04	-0:24:16
Montmerle sur Saône	27	46N05	4E46	-0:19:04
Montmin	1	45N48	6E16	-0:25:04

Place	Code	Lat.	Long.	Time
Montmirail	84	48N52	3E32	-0:14:08
Montmirail	43	48N06	0E48	-0:03:12
Montmirey le Château	30	47N13	5E32	-0:22:08
Montmoreau Saint Cybard	24	45N24	0E08	-0:00:32
Montmorillon	1	46N26	0E52	-0:03:28
Montmort	84	48N55	3E49	-0:15:16
Montoire sur le Loir	42	47N45	0E52	-0:03:28
Montpellier	1	43N36	3E53	-0:15:32
Montpezat sous Bauzon	1	44N43	4E12	-0:16:48
Mont Pichet	82	48N53	2E54	-0:11:36
Montpon Ménesterol	1	45N00	0E10	-0:00:40
Montpont en Bresse	27	46N33	5E09	-0:20:36
Montréal	49	47N32	4E02	-0:16:08
Montrésor	24	47N09	1E12	-0:04:48
Montret	27	46N41	5E07	-0:20:28
Montreuil	61	48N52	2E26	-0:09:44
Montreuil Bellay	25	47N08	0w09	0:00:36
Montreuil sous Bois	61	48N52	2E26	-0:09:44
Montreuil sur Mer	137	50N28	1E46	-0:07:04
Montrevel en Bresse	27	46N20	5E08	-0:20:32
Montrichard	25	47N21	1E11	-0:04:44
Montriond	1	46N12	6E41	-0:26:44
Montrond les Bains	1	45N38	4E14	-0:16:56
Montrouge	61	48N49	2E19	-0:09:16
Montry	82	48N53	2E50	-0:11:20
Monts	25	47N17	0E37	-0:02:28
Mont Saint Aignan	127	49N28	1E05	-0:04:20
Mont Saint Martin	104	49N32	5E47	-0:23:08
Mont Saint Vincent	25	46N38	4E29	-0:17:56
Montsauche	45	47N13	4E01	-0:16:04
Montsec	95	48N53	5E43	-0:22:52
Montsoult	61	49N04	2E19	-0:09:16
Mont sur Vaudrey	29	46N58	5E36	-0:22:24
Morainvilliers	61	48N56	1E56	-0:07:44
Morangis	61	48N42	2E20	-0:09:20
Morcenx	24	44N02	0w55	0:03:40
Morée	44	47N54	1E14	-0:04:56
Morestel	26	45N40	5E28	-0:21:52
Moret sur Loing	77	48N22	2E49	-0:11:16
Moreuil	120	49N46	2E29	-0:09:56
Morez	31	46N31	6E02	-0:24:08
Morhange	12	48N55	6E38	-0:26:32
Morienval	109	49N18	2E56	-0:11:44
Morlaix	36	48N35	3w50	0:15:20
Mormant	77	48N36	2E53	-0:11:32
Mormoiron	1	44N04	5E11	-0:20:44
Mornant	1	45N37	4E40	-0:18:40
Mornas	1	44N12	4E44	-0:18:56
Morsains	82	48N48	3E32	-0:14:08
Morsang sur Orge	78	48N40	2E21	-0:09:24
Morschwiller le Bas	4	47N45	7E16	-0:29:04
Mortagne	68	48N31	0E33	-0:02:12
Mortagne au Perche	68	48N31	0E33	-0:02:12
Mortagne sur Sèvre	25	47N00	0w57	0:03:48
Mortain	40	48N39	0w56	0:03:44
Morteau	32	47N04	6E37	-0:26:28
Mortefontaine	80	49N07	2E36	-0:10:24
Mortrée	68	48N38	0E05	-0:00:20
Morzine	1	46N11	6E43	-0:26:52
Mouans Sartoux	1	43N37	6E58	-0:27:52
Mouchard	32	46N58	5E48	-0:23:12
Moulin des Ponts	27	46N20	5E19	-0:21:16
Moulineaux	127	49N21	0E58	-0:03:52
Moulinet	1	43N57	7E25	-0:29:40
Moulins	25	46N34	3E20	-0:13:20
Moulins la Marche	68	48N39	0E29	-0:01:56
Mouriès	1	43N41	4E52	-0:19:28
Mourmelon le Grand	89	49N08	4E22	-0:17:28
Mousseaux sur Seine	79	49N03	1E39	-0:06:36
Moussey	12	48N40	6E47	-0:27:08
Moussy le Neuf	80	49N04	2E36	-0:10:24
Moussy le Vieux	80	49N03	2E38	-0:10:32
Moustiers Sainte Marie	1	43N51	6E13	-0:24:52
Mouthe	32	46N43	6E12	-0:24:48
Mouthier Haute Pierre	32	47N02	6E16	-0:25:04
Moûtiers	1	45N29	6E32	-0:26:08
Moutiers au Perche	68	48N29	0E51	-0:03:24
Mouy	80	49N19	2E19	-0:09:16
Mouzon	103	49N36	5E05	-0:20:20
Moydans	1	44N24	5E30	-0:22:00
Moÿ de l'Aisne	103	49N45	3E22	-0:13:28
Moyenmoutier	101	48N23	6E55	-0:27:40
Moyenneville	135	50N04	1E45	-0:07:00
Moyenvic	13	48N47	6E33	-0:26:12
Moyeuvre Grande	10	49N15	6E02	-0:24:08
Mugron	24	43N45	0w45	0:03:00
Muhlbach sur Munster	3	48N02	7E05	-0:28:20
Muides sur Loire	41	47N40	1E31	-0:06:04
Mülhausen → Mulhouse	4	47N45	7E20	-0:29:20
Mulhouse (Mülhausen)	4	47N45	7E20	-0:29:20
Mundolsheim	18	48N39	7E42	-0:30:48
Munster	3	48N03	7E08	-0:28:32
Munster	17	48N55	6E54	-0:27:36
Murat	1	45N07	2E52	-0:11:28
Mur de Barrez	1	44N51	2E39	-0:10:36
Muret	1	43N28	1E21	-0:05:24
Mussidan	1	45N02	0E22	-0:01:28
Mussy sur Seine	52	47N58	4E30	-0:18:00
Mutzig	14	48N32	7E28	-0:29:52
Muzillac	35	47N33	2w29	0:09:56
Najac	1	44N17	2E00	-0:08:00
Nampont Saint Martin	136	50N21	1E45	-0:07:00
Nancroix	1	45N32	6E46	-0:27:04
Nancy	92	48N41	6E12	-0:24:48
Nandy	78	48N35	2E34	-0:10:16
Nangis	77	48N33	3E00	-0:12:00
Nans les Pins	1	43N22	5E47	-0:23:08
Nant	1	44N01	3E18	-0:13:12
Nanterre	61	48N53	2E12	-0:08:48
Nantes	28	47N13	1w33	0:06:12
Nanteuil le Haudouin	80	49N08	2E48	-0:11:12
Nanteuil lès Meaux	81	48N56	2E54	-0:11:36
Nantouillet	80	49N00	2E42	-0:10:48
Nantua	27	46N09	5E37	-0:22:28
Naours	122	50N02	2E17	-0:09:08
Narbonne	1	43N11	3E00	-0:12:00
Nasbinals	1	44N40	3E03	-0:12:12
Naucelle	1	44N12	2E20	-0:09:20
Navenne	54	47N36	6E10	-0:24:40
Nâves Parmelan	1	45N56	6E11	-0:24:44
Neauphle le Château	74	48N49	1E54	-0:07:36
Neauphle le Vieux	74	48N49	1E52	-0:07:28
Nemours	75	48N16	2E42	-0:10:48
Nérac	1	44N08	0E20	-0:01:20
Néronde	1	45N50	4E14	-0:16:56
Nérondes	25	47N00	2E49	-0:11:16
Nerville la Forêt	61	49N05	2E17	-0:09:08
Nesle	116	49N46	2E55	-0:11:40
Nettancourt	87	48N52	4E57	-0:19:48
Neuf Brisach	23	48N01	7E32	-0:30:08
Neufchâteau	57	48N21	5E42	-0:22:48
Neufchâtel en Bray	120	49N44	1E27	-0:05:48
Neufchâtel sur Aisne	103	49N26	4E02	-0:16:08
Neufmanil	103	49N49	4E48	-0:19:12
Neuf Marché	119	49N25	1E43	-0:06:52
Neufmontiers lès Meaux	81	48N58	2E50	-0:11:20
Neuillé Pont Pierre	41	47N33	0E33	-0:02:12
Neuilly en Thelle	80	49N13	2E17	-0:09:08
Neuilly l'Évêque	52	47N55	5E26	-0:21:44
Neuilly Saint Front	108	49N10	3E16	-0:13:04
Neuilly sur Marne	61	48N51	2E32	-0:10:08
Neuilly sur Seine	61	48N53	2E16	-0:09:04
Neung sur Beuvron	25	47N32	1E48	-0:07:12
Neuve Chapelle	136	50N35	2E47	-0:11:08
Neuves Maisons	91	48N37	6E06	-0:24:24
Neuvic	1	45N23	2E16	-0:09:04
Neuville aux Bois	71	48N04	2E03	-0:08:12
Neuville de Poitou	24	46N41	0E15	-0:01:00
Neuville lès Dieppe	131	49N55	1E06	-0:04:24
Neuville sur Oise	80	49N01	2E04	-0:08:16
Neuville sur Saône	27	45N52	4E51	-0:19:24
Neuvy le Roi	41	47N36	0E36	-0:02:24
Neuvy sur Barangeon	41	47N19	2E15	-0:09:00
Neuvy sur Loire	41	47N31	2E53	-0:11:32
Neuwiller lès Saverne	21	48N49	7E24	-0:29:36
Névache	1	45N01	6E37	-0:26:28
Nevers	28	47N00	3E09	-0:12:36
Nexon	1	45N41	1E11	-0:04:44
Nice	1	43N42	7E15	-0:29:00
Niederbronn les Bains	20	48N57	7E38	-0:30:32
Nieppe	117	50N42	2E50	-0:11:20
Nîmes	1	43N50	4E21	-0:17:24
Niort	24	46N19	0w27	0:01:48
Nitry	45	47N40	3E53	-0:15:32
Nivillers	110	49N28	2E10	-0:08:40
Nizy le Comte	103	49N34	4E03	-0:16:12
Noailles	110	49N20	2E12	-0:08:48
Nocé	68	48N22	0E42	-0:02:48
Nods	32	47N06	6E20	-0:25:20
Nœux les Mines	135	50N29	2E40	-0:10:40
Nogaro	1	43N46	0w02	0:00:08
Nogent en Bassigny	52	48N02	5E21	-0:21:24
Nogent le Roi	70	48N39	1E32	-0:06:08
Nogent le Rotrou	68	48N19	0E50	-0:03:20
Nogent sur Marne	61	48N50	2E29	-0:09:56
Nogent sur Oise	80	49N16	2E28	-0:09:52
Nogent sur Seine	77	48N29	3E30	-0:14:00
Nogent sur Vernisson	45	47N51	2E45	-0:11:00
Noirétable	1	45N49	3E46	-0:15:04
Noirmoutier	35	47N00	2w14	0:08:56
Noiseau	61	48N47	2E33	-0:10:12
Noisiel	61	48N51	2E37	-0:10:28
Noisy le Grand	61	48N51	2E33	-0:10:12
Noisy le Roi	61	48N51	2E04	-0:08:16
Nolay	30	46N57	4E38	-0:18:32
Nomény	100	48N54	6E14	-0:24:56
Nomexy	91	48N18	6E23	-0:25:32
Nonancourt	70	48N46	1E12	-0:04:48
Nonant le Pin	69	48N42	0E13	-0:00:52
Nontron	1	45N32	0E40	-0:02:40
Nordausques	137	50N49	2E05	-0:08:20
Noroy le Bourg	54	47N37	6E18	-0:25:12
Norrent Fontes	136	50N35	2E24	-0:09:36
Nort sur Erdre	28	47N26	1w30	0:06:00
Notre Dame de Bellecombe	1	45N48	6E31	-0:26:04
Nouan le Fuzelier	41	47N32	2E02	-0:08:08
Nouans les Fontaines	1	47N08	1E18	-0:05:12
Nouvion en Ponthieu	136	50N12	1E47	-0:07:08
Nouvion sur Meuse	103	49N42	4E48	-0:19:12
Nouzonville	103	49N49	4E45	-0:19:00
Noves	1	43N52	4E54	-0:19:36
Novion Porcien	103	49N36	4E25	-0:17:40
Noyant	25	47N31	0E08	-0:00:32
Noyelles Sur Mer	135	50N11	1E43	-0:06:52
Noyers	49	47N42	4E00	-0:16:00
Noyon	115	49N35	3E00	-0:12:00
Nozay	35	47N34	1w38	0:06:32
Nozay	78	48N40	2E14	-0:08:56
Nozeroy	32	46N47	6E02	-0:24:08
Nuits Saint Georges	30	47N08	4E57	-0:19:48
Nuits sur Armançon	49	47N44	4E12	-0:16:48
Nyons	1	44N22	5E08	-0:20:32
Oberhaslach	14	48N33	7E20	-0:29:20
Obermodern	18	48N51	7E32	-0:30:08
Obernai	15	48N28	7E29	-0:29:56
Oberseebach	22	48N58	7E59	-0:31:56
Obersteinbach	19	49N02	7E41	-0:30:44
Oderen	3	47N55	6E59	-0:27:56
Offemont	60	47N40	6E53	-0:27:32
Offendorf	22	48N43	7E55	-0:31:40
Offranville	131	49N52	1E03	-0:04:12
Oignies	117	50N28	2E59	-0:11:56
Oinville sur Montcient	79	49N02	1E51	-0:07:24
Oisemont	133	49N57	1E46	-0:07:04
Oissel	127	49N20	1E06	-0:04:24
Oissery	80	49N04	2E49	-0:11:16
Olivet	44	47N52	1E54	-0:07:36
Ollainville	78	48N35	2E13	-0:08:52
Olliergues	1	45N40	3E38	-0:14:32
Ollioules	1	43N08	5E51	-0:23:24
Oloron Sainte Marie	1	43N12	0w36	0:02:24
Omont	103	49N36	4E44	-0:18:56
Onnaing	103	50N23	3E36	-0:14:24
Onzain	25	47N30	1E11	-0:04:44
Oost Cappel	138	50N55	2E36	-0:10:24
Oraison	1	43N55	5E55	-0:23:40
Orange	1	44N08	4E48	-0:19:12
Orbec en Auge	72	49N01	0E25	-0:01:40
Orbey	7	48N08	7E10	-0:28:40
Orbigny	24	47N12	1E14	-0:04:56
Orcemont	74	48N35	1E49	-0:07:16
Orchamps	32	47N09	5E40	-0:22:40
Orchies	117	50N28	3E14	-0:12:56
Orcières	1	44N41	6E20	-0:25:20
Orgelet	27	46N31	5E37	-0:22:28
Orgères en Beauce	71	48N09	1E42	-0:06:48
Orgerus	74	48N50	1E42	-0:06:48
Orgeval	61	48N55	1E59	-0:07:56
Orgnac l'Aven	1	44N19	4E27	-0:17:48
Orgon	1	43N47	5E02	-0:20:08
Origny en Thiérache	103	49N54	4E01	-0:16:04
Origny Sainte Benoite	103	49N50	3E30	-0:14:00
Orléans	44	47N55	1E54	-0:07:36
Orly	61	48N45	2E24	-0:09:36
Ornans	32	47N06	6E09	-0:24:36
Orphin	74	48N35	1E47	-0:07:08
Orpierre	1	44N19	5E41	-0:22:44
Orsan	1	44N08	4E40	-0:18:40
Orsay	61	48N48	2E11	-0:08:44
Orthez	1	43N29	0w46	0:03:04
Orvilliers	74	48N52	1E39	-0:06:36
Osmoy	74	48N52	1E43	-0:06:52
Osny	80	49N04	2E04	-0:08:16
Ostricourt	117	50N27	3E02	-0:12:08
Ostwald	14	48N33	7E43	-0:30:52
Othis	80	49N04	2E41	-0:10:44
Ouarville	71	48N21	1E46	-0:07:04
Oucques	44	47N49	1E18	-0:05:12
Ouistreham	142	49N17	0w15	0:01:00
Oulchy le Château	108	49N12	3E21	-0:13:24

Oulins 73 48N52 1E28 -0:05:52
Oullins 27 45N43 4E48 -0:19:12
Ourville en Caux 131 49N44 0E36 -0:02:24
Outarville 71 48N13 2E01 -0:08:04
Outreau 138 50N42 1E35 -0:06:20
Ouzouer le Marché 44 47N55 1E32 -0:06:08
Ouzouer sur Loire 48 47N46 2E29 -0:09:56
Oye et Pallet 32 46N51 6E20 -0:25:20
Oyonnax 27 46N15 5E40 -0:22:40
Ozoir la Ferrière 61 48N46 2E40 -0:10:40
Ozouer le Voulgis 82 48N40 2E47 -0:11:08
Pacy sur Eure 73 49N01 1E23 -0:05:32
Pagny sur Moselle 93 48N59 6E01 -0:24:04
Paimboeuf 35 47N17 2W02 0:08:08
Paimpol 36 48N46 3W03 0:12:12
Paladru 1 45N28 5E33 -0:22:12
Palaiseau 61 48N43 2E15 -0:09:00
Palavas les Flots 1 43N32 3E56 -0:15:44
Palinges 25 46N33 4E13 -0:16:52
Palluau 25 46N48 1W37 0:06:28
Pamiers 1 43N07 1E36 -0:06:24
Pange 12 49N05 6E22 -0:25:28
Panissières 1 45N47 4E20 -0:17:20
Pantin 61 48N54 2E24 -0:09:36
Paray le Monial 25 46N27 4E07 -0:16:28
Parentis en Born 24 44N21 1W05 0:04:20
Pargny sur Saulx 88 48N46 4E50 -0:19:20
Parigné l'Évêque 47 47N56 0E22 -0:01:28
Paris 61 48N52 2E20 -0:09:20
Parmain 80 49N07 2E12 -0:08:48
Parthenay 24 46N39 0W15 0:01:00
Pas en Artois 122 50N09 2E30 -0:10:00
Passy 1 45N55 6E41 -0:26:44
Patay 44 48N03 1E42 -0:06:48
Pau 1 43N18 0W22 0:01:28
Paulhan 1 43N32 3E27 -0:13:48
Pavilly 110 49N34 0E58 -0:03:52
Pecquencourt 117 50N23 3E13 -0:12:52
Pecqueuse 78 48N39 2E03 -0:08:12
Peïra Cava 1 43N56 7E22 -0:29:28
Peisey Nancroix 1 45N33 6E45 -0:27:00
Pélussin 1 45N25 4E41 -0:18:44
Penchard 81 48N59 2E52 -0:11:28
Penne d'Agenais 1 44N23 0E49 -0:03:16
Pennedepie 129 49N25 0E11 -0:00:44
Péone 1 44N07 6E54 -0:27:36
Perdreauville 74 48N58 1E38 -0:06:32
Périers 148 49N11 1W25 0:05:40
Périgueux 1 45N11 0E43 -0:02:52
Pernay 25 47N27 0E30 -0:02:00
Pernes les Fontaines 1 44N00 5E03 -0:20:12
Péronne 117 49N56 2E56 -0:11:44
Pérouges 27 45N54 5E11 -0:20:44
Perpignan 1 42N41 2E53 -0:11:32
Perriers sur Andelle 119 49N25 1E22 -0:05:28
Perrignier 1 46N18 6E27 -0:25:48
Perrigny 27 46N40 5E35 -0:22:20
Perros Guirec 36 48N49 3W27 0:13:48
Persan 108 49N09 2E16 -0:09:04
Perthes 86 48N39 4E49 -0:19:16
Pertuis 1 43N41 5E30 -0:22:00
Pervenchères 68 48N26 0E26 -0:01:44
Pesmes 30 47N17 5E34 -0:22:16
Pessac 24 44N48 0W38 0:02:32
Petite Synthe 138 51N01 2E19 -0:09:16
Petit Fort Philippe 138 51N00 2E07 -0:08:28
Peyrolles en Provence 1 43N39 5E35 -0:22:20
Peyruis 1 44N02 5E56 -0:23:44
Pézenas 1 43N27 3E25 -0:13:40
Pfaffenhoffen 18 48N51 7E37 -0:30:28
Pfastatt 4 47N47 7E18 -0:29:12
Phalempin 117 50N31 3E01 -0:12:04
Phalsbourg 21 48N46 7E16 -0:29:04
Piana 1 42N14 8E38 -0:34:32
Picquigny 121 49N57 2E09 -0:08:36
Piedicroce 1 42N23 9E23 -0:37:32
Piennes 95 49N19 5E47 -0:23:08
Pierre Buffière 1 45N42 1E21 -0:05:24
Pierreclos 27 46N20 4E41 -0:18:44
Pierre de Bresse 29 46N53 5E15 -0:21:00
Pierrefeu du Var 1 43N13 6E08 -0:24:32
Pierrefitte sur Aire 87 48N54 5E20 -0:21:20
Pierrefitte sur Sauldre 41 47N30 2E09 -0:08:36
Pierrefitte sur Seine 61 48N58 2E22 -0:09:28
Pierrefonds 109 49N21 2E59 -0:11:56
Pierrefontaine les Varans 55 47N13 6E33 -0:26:12
Pierrelatte 1 44N23 4E42 -0:18:48
Pierrelaye 61 49N01 2E09 -0:08:36
Pierry 84 49N01 3E56 -0:15:44
Pignans 1 43N18 6E13 -0:24:52
Pimelles 49 47N50 4E10 -0:16:40
Piney 77 48N22 4E20 -0:17:20
Pinsot 1 45N21 6E06 -0:24:24
Piolenc 1 44N11 4E46 -0:19:04
Pipriac 35 47N49 1W57 0:07:48
Pissos 24 44N19 0W47 0:03:08
Pithiviers 48 48N10 2E15 -0:09:00
Plage Sainte Cécile 138 50N34 1E35 -0:06:20
Plailly 80 49N06 2E35 -0:10:20
Plaisir 61 48N49 1E57 -0:07:48
Planches 69 48N42 0E22 -0:01:28
Plan d'Orgon 1 43N48 5E00 -0:20:00
Pléaux 1 45N08 2E14 -0:08:56
Pléneuf 36 48N36 2W33 0:10:12
Pleurs 82 48N41 3E52 -0:15:28
Pleyben 36 48N14 3W58 0:15:52
Ploërmel 35 47N56 2W24 0:09:36
Plombières les Bains 58 47N58 6E29 -0:25:56
Plombières lès Dijon 49 47N20 4E58 -0:19:52
Plouay 35 47N55 3W20 0:13:20
Ploudalmézeau 36 48N32 4W39 0:18:36
Plouescat 36 48N40 4W10 0:16:40
Plouguenast 36 48N17 2W43 0:10:52
Plouha 36 48N41 2W56 0:11:44
Pocé sur Cisse 25 47N26 0E59 -0:03:56
Podensac 24 44N39 0W22 0:01:28
Pogny 88 48N52 4E29 -0:17:56
Poigny la Forêt 74 48N41 1E45 -0:07:00
Poissons 99 48N25 5E13 -0:20:52
Poissy 61 48N56 2E03 -0:08:12
Poitiers 24 46N35 0E20 -0:01:20
Poix 120 49N47 1E59 -0:07:56
Poix Terron 103 49N39 4E39 -0:18:36
Polignac 1 45N04 3E52 -0:15:28
Poligny 32 46N50 5E43 -0:22:52
Pommard 30 47N01 4E47 -0:19:08
Pommera 122 50N10 2E26 -0:09:44
Pompey 100 48N46 6E07 -0:24:28
Pomponne 61 48N53 2E41 -0:10:44
Poncé sur le Loir 42 47N46 0E40 -0:02:40
Poncin 27 46N05 5E24 -0:21:36
Pons 24 45N35 0W33 0:02:12
Pontailler sur Saône 30 47N18 5E25 -0:21:40
Pont à Marcq 117 50N31 3E07 -0:12:28
Pont à Mousson 100 48N54 6E04 -0:24:16
Pontarlier 32 46N54 6E22 -0:25:28
Pontaubert 45 47N29 3E52 -0:15:28
Pont Audemer 126 49N21 0E31 -0:02:04
Pontault Combault 61 48N47 2E36 -0:10:24
Pontaumur 1 45N52 2E40 -0:10:40
Pont Aven 34 47N51 3W45 0:15:00
Pontcarré 61 48N48 2E42 -0:10:48
Pontcharra 1 45N26 6E01 -0:24:04
Pontchartrain 74 48N48 1E54 -0:07:36
Pontchâteau 35 47N26 2W05 0:08:20
Pont Croix 35 48N02 4W29 0:17:56
Pont d'Ain 27 46N03 5E20 -0:21:20
Pont de Chéruy 26 45N45 5E11 -0:20:44
Pont de l'Arche 110 49N18 1E10 -0:04:40
Pont de Pany 49 47N18 4E49 -0:19:16
Pont de Poitte 27 46N35 5E41 -0:22:44
Pont de Roide 55 47N23 6E46 -0:27:04
Pont de Ruan 24 47N15 0E35 -0:02:20
Pont de Salars 1 44N17 2E44 -0:10:56
Pont de Vaux 27 46N26 4E56 -0:19:44
Pont de Veyle 27 46N16 4E53 -0:19:32
Pont en Royans 1 45N04 5E21 -0:21:24
Pont Évêque 1 45N32 4E55 -0:19:40
Pontfaverger Moronvilliers 89 49N18 4E19 -0:17:16
Pontgibaud 1 45N50 2E52 -0:11:28
Ponthévrard 74 48N33 1E55 -0:07:40
Ponthierry 78 48N32 2E33 -0:10:12
Pontigny 46 47N55 3E43 -0:14:52
Pontivy 35 48N04 2W59 0:11:56
Pont l'Abbé 35 47N52 4W13 0:16:52
Pont lès Moulins 55 47N19 6E22 -0:25:28
Pont l'Évêque 72 49N18 0E11 -0:00:44
Pontlevoy 25 47N23 1E15 -0:05:00
Pontoise 80 49N03 2E06 -0:08:24
Pontorson 63 48N33 1W31 0:06:04
Pont Remy 134 50N03 1E55 -0:07:40
Pont Royal 1 43N43 5E11 -0:20:44
Pont Sainte Marie 77 48N19 4E06 -0:16:24
Pont Sainte Maxence 80 49N18 2E36 -0:10:24
Pont Saint Esprit 1 44N15 4E39 -0:18:36
Pont Saint Vincent 91 48N36 6E06 -0:24:24
Pont Scorff 34 47N50 3W24 0:13:36
Pont sur Yonne 76 48N17 3E12 -0:12:48
Pontvallain 42 47N45 0E12 -0:00:48
Porcelette 12 49N09 6E36 -0:26:24
Porcheville 74 48N58 1E47 -0:07:08
Pornic 35 47N07 2W06 0:08:24
Porquerolles 1 43N00 6E12 -0:24:48
Port Cros 1 43N00 6E23 -0:25:32
Port de Bouc 1 43N24 4E59 -0:19:56
Port en Bessin 142 49N21 0W45 0:03:00
Portes lès Valence 1 44N52 4E53 -0:19:32
Port Lesney 32 47N00 5E49 -0:23:16
Port Louis 34 47N43 3W21 0:13:24
Porto Vecchio 1 41N35 9E16 -0:37:04
Port Sainte Marie 1 44N15 0E24 -0:01:36
Port Saint Louis 1 43N23 4E48 -0:19:12
Port sur Saône 54 47N41 6E03 -0:24:12
Port Vendres 1 42N31 3E07 -0:12:28
Pouancé 38 47N44 1W11 0:04:44
Pouilly en Auxois 49 47N16 4E33 -0:18:12
Pouilly sur Loire 41 47N17 2E57 -0:11:48
Pouilly sur Meuse 103 49N32 5E07 -0:20:28
Pouru Saint Rémy 102 49N41 5E05 -0:20:20
Pourville sur Mer 131 49N55 1E02 -0:04:08
Pouxeux 58 48N06 6E34 -0:26:16
Pouzauges 24 46N47 0W50 0:03:20
Pradelles 1 44N46 3E53 -0:15:32
Prads 1 44N13 6E27 -0:25:48
Pralognan la Vanoise 1 45N23 6E43 -0:26:52
Prauthoy 52 47N40 5E17 -0:21:08
Praz sur Arly 1 45N50 6E34 -0:26:16
Précy sous Thil 49 47N23 4E19 -0:17:16
Précy sur Marne 81 48N56 2E47 -0:11:08
Précy sur Oise 80 49N12 2E22 -0:09:28
Pré en Pail 65 48N27 0W12 0:00:48
Prémery 28 47N10 3E20 -0:13:20
Prémontré 111 49N33 3E24 -0:13:36
Presles en Brie 82 48N43 2E45 -0:11:00
Priay 27 46N00 5E17 -0:21:08
Pringy 77 48N31 2E34 -0:10:16
Privas 1 44N44 4E36 -0:18:24
Propriano 1 41N40 8E55 -0:35:40
Provenchères sur Fave 16 48N19 7E05 -0:28:20
Provins 82 48N33 3E18 -0:13:12
Prunay le Temple 74 48N52 1E40 -0:06:40
Prunay sous Ablis 74 48N32 1E48 -0:07:12
Prunières 1 44N33 6E20 -0:25:20
Puget sur Argens 1 43N27 6E41 -0:26:44
Puget Théniers 1 43N57 6E54 -0:27:36
Puget Ville 1 43N17 6E08 -0:24:32
Puimoisson 1 43N52 6E08 -0:24:32
Puiseaux 48 48N12 2E28 -0:09:52
Puiseux en France 61 49N04 2E29 -0:09:56
Puiseux Pontoise 80 49N03 2E01 -0:08:04
Puisieux 122 50N07 2E42 -0:10:48
Pulversheim 5 47N51 7E18 -0:29:12
Pussay 48 48N21 2E00 -0:08:00
Puteaux 61 48N53 2E14 -0:08:56
Puttelange lès Farschviller 19 49N03 6E56 -0:27:44
Puylaurens 1 43N34 2E01 -0:08:04
Puy l'Évêque 1 44N30 1E08 -0:04:32
Puyloubier 1 43N31 5E41 -0:22:44
Quarré les Tombes 45 47N22 3E59 -0:15:56
Queige 1 45N43 6E28 -0:25:52
Quend 136 50N19 1E38 -0:06:32
Quend Plage 136 50N19 1E33 -0:06:12
Quesnoy 141 50N43 3E00 -0:12:00
Questembert 35 47N40 2W27 0:09:48
Quettehou 144 49N36 1W18 0:05:12
Quiberon 35 47N29 3W07 0:12:28
Quiberville 131 49N54 0E55 -0:03:40
Quiévy 103 50N10 3E25 -0:13:40
Quillan 1 42N52 2E11 -0:08:44
Quillebeuf sur Seine 126 49N29 0E31 -0:02:04
Quimper 35 48N00 4W06 0:16:24
Quimperlé 35 47N52 3W33 0:14:12
Quincampoix 110 49N32 1E11 -0:04:44
Quincy sous Sénart 78 48N40 2E33 -0:10:12
Quincy Voisins 82 48N54 2E53 -0:11:32
Quingey 32 47N06 5E53 -0:23:32
Quinson 1 43N42 6E02 -0:24:08
Quintin 36 48N24 2W55 0:11:40
Quissac 1 43N55 4E00 -0:16:00
Raismes 103 50N23 3E29 -0:13:56
Raizeux 70 48N37 1E41 -0:06:44
Ramatuelle 1 43N13 6E37 -0:26:28
Rambervillers 101 48N21 6E38 -0:26:32
Rambouillet 74 48N39 1E50 -0:07:20
Ramerupt 86 48N31 4E18 -0:17:12
Rampillon 77 48N33 3E04 -0:12:16
Randan 1 46N01 3E21 -0:13:24
Rantigny 110 49N20 2E26 -0:09:44
Raon l'Étape 101 48N24 6E51 -0:27:24
Raon sur Plaine 14 48N31 7E06 -0:28:24
Raucourt et Flaba 103 49N36 4E57 -0:19:48
Ravières 49 47N45 4E17 -0:17:08
Réalmont 1 43N47 2E12 -0:08:48
Réau 78 48N37 2E38 -0:10:32
Recey sur Ource 52 47N47 4E52 -0:19:28
Réchicourt le Château 12 48N40 6E51 -0:27:24
Recologne 30 47N16 5E50 -0:23:20
Redon 35 47N39 2W05 0:08:20
Regnéville 149 49N01 1W33 0:06:12
Réhon 97 49N30 5E45 -0:23:00
Reichshoffen 22 48N56 7E40 -0:30:40
Reignac sur Indre 24 47N13 0E55 -0:03:40
Reignier 1 46N08 6E16 -0:25:04
Reillanne 1 43N53 5E40 -0:22:40
Reims 105 49N15 4E02 -0:16:08
Rémalard 68 48N26 0E47 -0:03:08
Rémilly 12 49N01 6E24 -0:25:36
Remiremont 58 48N01 6E35 -0:26:20
Remollon 1 44N28 6E10 -0:24:40
Remoray 32 46N46 6E14 -0:24:56
Remoulins 1 43N56 4E34 -0:18:16
Rémuzat 1 44N24 5E21 -0:21:24

Place		Lat.	Long.	Time
Rennes	66	48N05	1W41	0:06:44
Renwez	103	49N50	4E36	-0:18:24
Réquista	1	44N02	2E32	-0:10:08
Ressons sur Matz	114	49N33	2E45	-0:11:00
Rethel	103	49N31	4E22	-0:17:28
Retiers	40	47N55	1W23	0:05:32
Retournac	1	45N12	4E02	-0:16:08
Revel	1	45N11	5E52	-0:23:28
Revest du Bion	1	44N05	5E33	-0:22:12
Revigny sur Ornain	87	48N50	4E59	-0:19:56
Revin	118	49N56	4E38	-0:18:32
Rezé	28	47N12	1W34	0:06:16
Rezonville	10	49N06	6E00	-0:24:00
Rheims → Reims	105	49N15	4E02	-0:16:08
Rhinau	23	48N19	7E42	-0:30:48
Rhodon	61	48N43	2E04	-0:08:16
Rians	1	43N37	5E45	-0:23:00
Ribeauvillé	7	48N12	7E19	-0:29:16
Ribécourt	113	49N31	2E55	-0:11:40
Ribemont	103	49N48	3E28	-0:13:52
Ribérac	1	45N15	0E20	-0:01:20
Ribiers	1	44N14	5E52	-0:23:28
Richebourg	74	48N49	1E38	-0:06:32
Richelieu	24	47N01	0E19	-0:01:16
Riedisheim	4	47N45	7E22	-0:29:28
Riez	1	43N49	6E06	-0:24:24
Rigney	55	47N23	6E11	-0:24:44
Rigny Ussé	24	47N15	0E18	-0:01:12
Rijssel → Lille	117	50N38	3E04	-0:12:16
Rillieux	27	45N49	4E54	-0:19:36
Rilly la Montagne	88	49N10	4E03	-0:16:12
Rimogne	103	49N50	4E33	-0:18:12
Rinxent	137	50N48	1E44	-0:06:56
Riom	1	45N54	3E07	-0:12:28
Riotord	1	45N14	4E24	-0:17:36
Rioz	54	47N25	6E04	-0:24:16
Riquewihr	7	48N10	7E18	-0:29:12
Riscle	1	43N40	0W05	0:00:20
Ris Orangis	78	48N39	2E25	-0:09:40
Rive de Gier	1	45N32	4E37	-0:18:28
Rives	1	45N21	5E30	-0:22:00
Rivesaltes	1	42N46	2E52	-0:11:28
Rixheim	8	47N46	7E24	-0:29:36
Roanne	27	46N02	4E04	-0:16:16
Robert Espagne	87	48N45	5E02	-0:20:08
Rochechouart	1	45N50	0E50	-0:03:20
Rochefort	33	45N57	0W58	0:03:52
Rochefort en Yvelines	74	48N35	1E59	-0:07:56
Rochefort Montagne	1	45N41	2E48	-0:11:12
Rochefort sur Nenon	30	47N07	5E34	-0:22:16
Roche la Molière	1	45N26	4E19	-0:17:16
Roche Lez Beaupré	55	47N17	6E07	-0:24:28
Rochemaure	1	44N35	4E42	-0:18:48
Rochetaillée	1	45N25	4E27	-0:17:48
Rocquencourt	61	48N50	2E07	-0:08:28
Rocroi	118	49N55	4E31	-0:18:04
Rodez	1	44N21	2E35	-0:10:20
Rogliano	1	42N57	9E25	-0:37:40
Rognac	1	43N29	5E14	-0:20:56
Rogny	45	47N45	2E53	-0:11:32
Rohrbach lès Bitche	18	49N03	7E16	-0:29:04
Roinville	48	48N32	2E03	-0:08:12
Roisel	117	49N57	3E06	-0:12:24
Roissy	61	48N47	2E39	-0:10:36
Roissy en France	61	49N00	2E31	-0:10:04
Rolampont	52	47N57	5E16	-0:21:04
Rolleboise	79	49N01	1E36	-0:06:24
Romagne sous Montfaucon	98	49N20	5E05	-0:20:20
Romainville	61	48N53	2E26	-0:09:44
Romans sur Isère	1	45N03	5E03	-0:20:12
Romenay	27	46N30	5E04	-0:20:16
Romilly sur Seine	77	48N31	3E43	-0:14:52
Romorantin Lanthenay	25	47N22	1E45	-0:07:00
Ronchamp	59	47N42	6E39	-0:26:36
Ronchin	117	50N36	3E06	-0:12:24
Roncq	141	50N45	3E07	-0:12:28
Roppe	60	47N40	6E55	-0:27:40
Roquebillière	1	44N01	7E18	-0:29:12
Roquebrune Cap Martin	1	43N46	7E28	-0:29:52
Roquebrune sur Argens	1	43N26	6E38	-0:26:32
Roquefort	1	44N02	0W19	0:01:16
Roquemaure	1	44N03	4E47	-0:19:08
Roquestéron	1	43N52	7E00	-0:28:00
Roquevaire	1	43N21	5E36	-0:22:24
Rosans	1	44N23	5E28	-0:21:52
Rosendaël	140	51N02	2E24	-0:09:36
Rosheim	14	48N30	7E28	-0:29:52
Rosières aux Salines	91	48N36	6E20	-0:25:20
Rosières en Santerre	116	49N49	2E43	-0:10:52
Rosny sous Bois	61	48N53	2E29	-0:09:56
Rosny sur Seine	79	49N00	1E38	-0:06:32
Rosporden	35	47N58	3W50	0:15:20
Roubaix	141	50N42	3E10	-0:12:40
Rouceux	57	48N22	5E41	-0:22:44
Rouen	127	49N26	1E05	-0:04:20
Rougé	36	47N47	1W27	0:05:48
Rougemont	55	47N29	6E21	-0:25:24
Rougemont le Château	60	47N44	6E58	-0:27:52
Rouillac	24	45N47	0W04	0:00:16
Rouillon	48	48N33	2E00	-0:08:00
Roulans	55	47N19	6E14	-0:24:56
Rousies	152	50N16	4E00	-0:16:00
Roussigny	78	48N39	2E06	-0:08:24
Roussillon	1	45N22	4E49	-0:19:16
Roussillon	1	43N54	5E17	-0:21:08
Roussy le Village	10	49N27	6E10	-0:24:40
Routot	127	49N23	0E44	-0:02:56
Rouvignies	103	50N20	3E26	-0:13:44
Rouvray	49	47N25	4E06	-0:16:24
Royan	24	45N37	1W01	0:04:04
Roybon	1	45N15	5E15	-0:21:00
Roye	116	49N42	2E48	-0:11:12
Rozay en Brie	82	48N41	2E58	-0:11:52
Rozoy sur Serre	103	49N43	4E08	-0:16:32
Rubelles	77	48N34	2E41	-0:10:44
Rue	136	50N16	1E40	-0:06:40
Rueil Malmaison	61	48N53	2E11	-0:08:44
Ruffec	24	46N01	0E12	-0:00:48
Ruffieu	27	46N00	5E40	-0:22:40
Ruffieux	26	45N51	5E50	-0:23:20
Rugles	73	48N49	0E42	-0:02:48
Rully	30	46N52	4E45	-0:19:00
Rumigny	103	49N48	4E16	-0:17:04
Rumilly	1	45N52	5E57	-0:23:48
Rumont	87	48N50	5E17	-0:21:08
Rungis	61	48N45	2E21	-0:09:24
Ruoms	1	44N27	4E21	-0:17:24
Rupt sur Moselle	60	47N56	6E40	-0:26:40
Ryes	142	49N19	0W37	0:02:28
Saales	15	48N21	7E07	-0:28:28
Sablé sur Sarthe	39	47N50	0W20	0:01:20
Sabres	24	44N09	0W44	0:02:56
Saché	24	47N14	0E33	-0:02:12
Sachy	102	49N40	5E08	-0:20:32
Saclay	61	48N44	2E10	-0:08:40
Sagy	79	49N03	1E57	-0:07:48
Saignon	1	43N52	5E26	-0:21:44
Saillans	1	44N42	5E11	-0:20:44
Sailly	79	49N02	1E48	-0:07:12
Sail sous Couzan	1	45N44	3E57	-0:15:48
Sainghin en Weppes	117	50N33	2E54	-0:11:36
Sains du Nord	103	50N06	4E00	-0:16:00
Sains en Gohelle	135	50N27	2E41	-0:10:44
Sains Richaumont	103	49N49	3E42	-0:14:48
Sainte Adresse	130	49N30	0E05	-0:00:20
Saint Affrique	1	43N57	2E53	-0:11:32
Sainte Agathe	1	45N49	3E37	-0:14:28
Sainte Agnès	1	43N48	7E28	-0:29:52
Saint Agrève	1	45N01	4E24	-0:17:36
Saint Aignan	24	47N16	1E23	-0:05:32
Saint Amand	88	48N49	4E36	-0:18:24
Saint Amand en Puisaye	45	47N31	3E04	-0:12:16
Saint Amand les Eaux	103	50N26	3E26	-0:13:44
Saint Amand Longpré	41	47N41	1E01	-0:04:04
Saint Amand Mont Rond	1	46N44	2E30	-0:10:00
Saint Amant Roche Savine	1	45N34	3E38	-0:14:32
Saint Amarin	3	47N53	7E01	-0:28:04
Saint Ambroix	1	44N15	4E11	-0:16:44
Saint Amour	27	46N26	5E21	-0:21:24
Saint André de l'Eure	73	48N54	1E17	-0:05:08
Saint André de Valborgne	1	44N09	3E41	-0:14:44
Saint André les Alpes	1	43N58	6E30	-0:26:00
Saint André les Vergers	77	48N17	4E03	-0:16:12
Saint Anthème	1	45N31	3E55	-0:15:40
Saint Antoine	1	45N10	5E13	-0:20:52
Saint Antonin	1	44N09	1E45	-0:07:00
Saint Arnoult en Yvelines	74	48N34	1E56	-0:07:44
Saint Astier	1	45N09	0E32	-0:02:08
Saint Auban	1	43N51	6E44	-0:26:56
Saint Aubin	30	47N02	5E20	-0:21:20
Saint Aubin	131	49N53	0E53	-0:03:32
Saint Aubin d'Aubigné	66	48N15	1W36	0:06:24
Saint Aubin lès Elbeuf	125	49N18	1E01	-0:04:04
Saint Aubin sur Aire	87	48N42	5E27	-0:21:48
Saint Aulaye	1	45N12	0E08	-0:00:32
Saint Avertin	25	47N22	0E44	-0:02:56
Saint Avold	17	49N06	6E42	-0:26:48
Saint Ay	44	47N51	1E45	-0:07:00
Saint Aygulf	1	43N23	6E44	-0:26:56
Saint Béat	1	42N55	0E42	-0:02:48
Saint Benoît	74	48N40	1E55	-0:07:40
Saint Benoît du Sault	1	46N27	1E23	-0:05:32
Saint Benoît en Woëvre	95	48N59	5E47	-0:23:08
Saint Béron	26	45N30	5E43	-0:22:52
Saint Blaise la Roche	15	48N24	7E10	-0:28:40
Saint Blin	57	48N16	5E25	-0:21:40
Saint Bonnet	1	44N41	6E05	-0:24:20
Saint Bonnet de Joux	25	46N29	4E27	-0:17:48
Saint Bonnet le Château	1	45N25	4E04	-0:16:16
Saint Bonnet le Froid	1	45N09	4E27	-0:17:48
Saint Brice sous Forêt	61	49N00	2E21	-0:09:24
Saint Brieuc	36	48N31	2W47	0:11:08
Saint Broing les Moines	52	47N41	4E50	-0:19:20
Saint Calais	42	47N55	0E45	-0:03:00
Saint Cannat	1	43N37	5E18	-0:21:12
Sainte Catherine de Fierbois	24	47N09	0E39	-0:02:36
Saint Céré	1	44N52	1E53	-0:07:32
Saint Cézaire sur Siagne	1	43N39	6E48	-0:27:12
Saint Chamas	1	43N33	5E02	-0:20:08
Saint Chamond	1	45N28	4E30	-0:18:00
Saint Chaptes	1	43N58	4E17	-0:17:08
Saint Chef	26	45N38	5E22	-0:21:28
Saint Chély d'Apcher	1	44N48	3E17	-0:13:08
Saint Chéron	78	48N33	2E07	-0:08:28
Saint Christophe en Bazelle	24	47N11	1E43	-0:06:52
Saint Ciers sur Gironde	24	45N18	0W37	0:02:28
Saint Clair sur Epte	124	49N12	1E41	-0:06:44
Saint Claud	1	45N53	0E23	-0:01:32
Saint Claude	27	46N23	5E52	-0:23:28
Saint Clément	91	48N32	6E36	-0:26:24
Saint Cloud	61	48N50	2E11	-0:08:44
Saint Colomban des Villards	1	45N18	6E14	-0:24:56
Sainte Colombe	52	47N52	4E32	-0:18:08
Saint Cosme en Vairais	68	48N16	0E28	-0:01:52
Sainte Croix aux Mines	16	48N16	7E13	-0:28:52
Sainte Croix Vallée Francaise	1	44N11	3E44	-0:14:56
Saint Cyprien	1	44N52	1E02	-0:04:08
Saint Cyr l'École	61	48N48	2E04	-0:08:16
Saint Cyr sous Dourdan	48	48N34	2E02	-0:08:08
Saint Cyr sur Loire	25	47N24	0E40	-0:02:40
Saint Cyr sur Mer	1	43N11	5E43	-0:22:52
Saint Dalmas de Tende	1	44N03	7E35	-0:30:20
Saint Denis	61	48N56	2E22	-0:09:28
Saint Denis de l'Hôtel	44	47N52	2E07	-0:08:28
Saint Denis en Bugey	27	45N57	5E20	-0:21:20
Saint Didier en Velay	1	45N18	4E17	-0:17:08
Saint Didier les Bains	1	44N00	5E07	-0:20:28
Saint Dié	101	48N17	6E57	-0:27:48
Saint Disdier	1	44N44	5E54	-0:23:36
Saint Dizier	87	48N38	4E57	-0:19:48
Saint Donat sur l'Herbasse	1	45N07	5E00	-0:20:00
Saint Dyé sur Loire	41	47N39	1E29	-0:05:56
Saint Égrève	1	45N14	5E41	-0:22:44
Sainte Enimie	1	44N22	3E26	-0:13:44
Saint Épain	24	47N08	0E32	-0:02:08
Saint Étienne	1	45N26	4E24	-0:17:36
Saint Étienne de Lugdarès	1	44N39	3E57	-0:15:48
Saint Étienne de Saint Geoirs	1	45N20	5E21	-0:21:24
Saint Étienne de Tinée	1	44N15	6E55	-0:27:40
Saint Étienne du Rouvray	127	49N23	1E06	-0:04:24
Saint Étienne en Dévoluy	1	44N42	5E56	-0:23:44
Saint Étienne le Laus	1	44N30	6E10	-0:24:40
Saint Étienne les Orgues	1	44N03	5E47	-0:23:08
Saint Étienne lès Remiremont	101	48N02	6E37	-0:26:28
Saint Evroult Notre Dame du Bois	72	48N48	0E28	-0:01:52
Saint Fargeau	45	47N38	3E04	-0:12:16
Saint Fargeau Ponthierry	78	48N33	2E32	-0:10:08
Saint Félicien	1	45N05	4E38	-0:18:32
Saint Félix	1	45N48	5E58	-0:23:52
Saint Firmin	1	44N47	6E02	-0:24:08
Saint Firmin sur Loire	41	47N37	2E44	-0:10:56
Saint Florentin	50	48N00	3E44	-0:14:56
Saint Florent sur Cher	1	46N59	2E15	-0:09:00
Saint Flour	1	45N02	3E05	-0:12:20
Saint Fons	27	45N42	4E52	-0:19:28
Sainte Foy la Grande	1	44N50	0E13	-0:00:52
Sainte Foy l'Argentière	1	45N42	4E28	-0:17:52
Sainte Foy lès Lyon	27	45N44	4E48	-0:19:12
Sainte Foy Tarentaise	1	45N35	6E53	-0:27:32

Saint François sur Bugeon 1 45N24 6E21 -0:25:24
Saint Front 1 44N59 4E08 -0:16:32
Saint Galmier 1 45N35 4E19 -0:17:16
Sainte Gauburge Sainte Colombe 69 48N42 0E26 -0:01:44
Saint Gaudens 1 43N07 0E44 -0:02:56
Saint Gaultier 1 46N38 1E25 -0:05:40
Saint Gély du Fesc 1 43N42 3E48 -0:15:12
Saint Genest Lerpt 1 45N27 4E20 -0:17:20
Saint Genest Malifaux 1 45N20 4E25 -0:17:40
Sainte Geneviève des Bois 78 48N38 2E20 -0:09:20
Saint Gengoux le National 25 46N37 4E39 -0:18:36
Saint Genis de Saintonge 24 45N29 0W34 0:02:16
Saint Genis Laval 27 45N41 4E48 -0:19:12
Saint Genis Pouilly 27 46N15 6E01 -0:24:04
Saint Genix sur Guiers 26 45N36 5E38 -0:22:32
Saint Geoire en Valdaine 1 45N27 5E38 -0:22:32
Saint Georges 13 48N40 6E56 -0:27:44
Saint Georges de Reneins 27 46N04 4E43 -0:18:52
Saint Georges en Couzan 1 45N42 3E56 -0:15:44
Saint Germain 61 48N54 2E05 -0:08:20
Saint Germain de Calberte 1 44N13 3E48 -0:15:12
Saint Germain de Joux 27 46N11 5E44 -0:22:56
Saint Germain des Champs 45 47N25 3E55 -0:15:40
Saint Germain du Bois 27 46N45 5E15 -0:21:00
Saint Germain du Plain 25 46N42 4E58 -0:19:52
Saint Germain en Laye 61 48N54 2E05 -0:08:20
Saint Germain Laval 1 45N50 4E01 -0:16:04
Saint Germain Laxis 77 48N35 2E43 -0:10:52
Saint Germain Lembron 1 45N28 3E14 -0:12:56
Saint Germain lès Arlay 27 46N46 5E34 -0:22:16
Saint Germain lès Corbeil 78 48N37 2E29 -0:09:56
Saint Germain l'Herm 1 45N28 3E33 -0:14:12
Saint Germain sur Morin 82 48N53 2E51 -0:11:24
Saint Germer de Fly 119 49N27 1E47 -0:07:08
Saint Gervais d'Auvergne 1 46N02 2E49 -0:11:16
Saint Gervais les Bains 1 45N54 6E43 -0:26:52
Saint Gervasy 1 43N53 4E29 -0:17:56
Saint Géry 1 44N29 1E35 -0:06:20
Saint Gilles 1 43N41 4E26 -0:17:44
Saint Gilles Croix de Vie 24 46N42 1W57 0:07:48
Saint Girons 1 42N59 1E09 -0:04:36
Saint Gobain 112 49N36 3E23 -0:13:32
Saint Gratien 61 48N58 2E17 -0:09:08
Saint Guénolé 35 47N49 4W20 0:17:20
Saint Héand 1 45N31 4E22 -0:17:28
Sainte Hermine 24 46N33 1W04 0:04:16
Saint Hilaire du Harcouët 62 48N35 1W06 0:04:24
Saint Hilarion 74 48N37 1E44 -0:06:56
Saint Hippolyte 55 47N19 6E49 -0:27:16
Saint Hippolyte 1 43N38 4E45 -0:19:00
Saint Hippolyte du Fort 1 43N58 3E51 -0:15:24
Saint Hubert le Roi 74 48N43 1E52 -0:07:28
Saint Jean aux Bois 109 49N21 2E55 -0:11:40
Saint Jean Cap Ferrat 1 43N41 7E20 -0:29:20
Saint Jean d'Angély 24 45N57 0W31 0:02:04
Saint Jean d'Assé 47 48N09 0E07 -0:00:28
Saint Jean de Bournay 1 45N29 5E08 -0:20:32
Saint Jean de Braye 44 47N54 1E58 -0:07:52
Saint Jean de Losne 30 47N06 5E15 -0:21:00
Saint Jean de Luz 24 43N23 1W40 0:06:40
Saint Jean de Maurienne 1 45N17 6E21 -0:25:24
Saint Jean de Monts 24 46N48 2W03 0:08:12
Saint Jean du Gard 1 44N06 3E53 -0:15:32
Saint Jean en Royans 1 45N01 5E18 -0:21:12
Saint Jean Pied de Port 24 43N10 1W14 0:04:56
Saint Jean Soleymieux 1 45N30 4E02 -0:16:08
Saint Jeoire 1 46N09 6E28 -0:25:52
Saint Jouin Bruneval 128 49N39 0E10 -0:00:40
Saint Julien 27 46N23 5E27 -0:21:48
Saint Julien Chapteuil 1 45N02 4E04 -0:16:16
Saint Julien du Sault 46 48N02 3E18 -0:13:12
Saint Julien du Verdon 1 43N55 6E32 -0:26:08
Saint Julien en Beauchêne 1 44N37 5E42 -0:22:48
Saint Julien en Born 24 44N04 1W14 0:04:56
Saint Julien en Genevois 1 46N08 6E05 -0:24:20
Saint Julien en Jarez 1 45N28 4E31 -0:18:04
Saint Julien les Villas 77 48N16 4E06 -0:16:24
Saint Julien Molin Molette 1 45N19 4E37 -0:18:28
Saint Junien 1 45N53 0E54 -0:03:36
Saint Just en Chaussée 114 49N30 2E26 -0:09:44
Saint Just en Chevalet 1 45N55 3E50 -0:15:20
Saint Just Malmont 1 45N20 4E19 -0:17:16
Saint Just sur Loire 1 45N29 4E16 -0:17:04
Saint Lambert 61 48N44 2E01 -0:08:04
Saint Laurent 91 48N09 6E27 -0:25:48
Saint Laurent Blangy 123 50N18 2E48 -0:11:12
Saint Laurent de Chamousset 1 45N44 4E28 -0:17:52
Saint Laurent du Pont 1 45N23 5E44 -0:22:56
Saint Laurent du Var 1 43N40 7E11 -0:28:44
Saint Laurent en Caux 131 49N45 0E53 -0:03:32
Saint Laurent en Grandvaux 27 46N35 5E57 -0:23:48
Saint Laurent et Benon 24 45N09 0W49 0:03:16
Saint Laurent les Bains 1 44N37 3E58 -0:15:52
Saint Laurent sur Saône 27 46N18 4E50 -0:19:20
Saint Léger en Yvelines 74 48N43 1E46 -0:07:04
Saint Léger sur Dheune 30 46N51 4E38 -0:18:32
Saint Léonard de Noblat 1 45N50 1E29 -0:05:56
Saint Leu d'Esserent 80 49N13 2E25 -0:09:40
Saint Leu la Forêt 61 49N01 2E15 -0:09:00
Saint Lô 146 49N07 1W05 0:04:20
Saint Louis 8 47N35 7E34 -0:30:16
Saint Loup sur Aujon 52 47N53 5E05 -0:20:20
Saint Loup sur Semouse 58 47N53 6E16 -0:25:04
Sainte Lucie 1 41N42 9E22 -0:37:28
Saint Lucien 70 48N39 1E38 -0:06:32
Saint Lupicin 27 46N24 5E47 -0:23:08
Sainte Magnance 45 47N27 4E04 -0:16:16
Saint Malo 64 48N39 2W01 0:08:04
Saint Mamert du Gard 1 43N53 4E12 -0:16:48
Saint Mammès 77 48N23 2E49 -0:11:16
Saint Mandé 61 48N50 2E25 -0:09:40
Saint Mandrier sur Mer 1 43N04 5E56 -0:23:44
Saint Marcel 30 46N47 4E54 -0:19:36
Saint Marcellin 1 45N09 5E19 -0:21:16
Saint Mard 80 49N02 2E42 -0:10:48
Sainte Marguerite sur Mer 131 49N55 0E57 -0:03:48
Sainte Marie aux Mines (Markirch) 16 48N15 7E11 -0:28:44
Saint Martin Boulogne 138 50N43 1E38 -0:06:32
Saint Martin d'Ardèche 1 44N18 4E35 -0:18:20
Saint Martin d'Auxigny 25 47N12 2E25 -0:09:40
Saint Martin de Belleville 1 45N23 6E30 -0:26:00
Saint Martin de Bossenay 77 48N26 3E41 -0:14:44
Saint Martin de Bréthencourt 74 48N31 1E56 -0:07:44
Saint Martin de Crau 1 43N38 4E49 -0:19:16
Saint Martin de Londres 1 43N47 3E44 -0:14:56
Saint Martin de Nigelles 70 48N37 1E37 -0:06:28
Saint Martin d'Entraunes 1 44N08 6E46 -0:27:04
Saint Martin des Champs 74 48N53 1E43 -0:06:52
Saint Martin de Valamas 1 44N56 4E22 -0:17:28
Saint Martin d'Hères 1 45N10 5E46 -0:23:04
Saint Martin du Puy 45 47N20 3E52 -0:15:28
Saint Martin du Tertre 61 49N06 2E21 -0:09:24
Saint Martin du Var 1 43N49 7E12 -0:28:48
Saint Martin en Bresse 30 46N49 5E04 -0:20:16
Saint Martin la Garenne 79 49N02 1E41 -0:06:44
Saint Martin la Plaine 1 45N32 4E36 -0:18:24
Saint Martin Vésubie 1 44N04 7E15 -0:29:00
Saint Mathieu 1 45N42 0E46 -0:03:04
Saint Maur des Fossés 61 48N48 2E30 -0:10:00
Sainte Maure de Touraine 24 47N07 0E37 -0:02:28
Saint Maurice 61 48N49 2E25 -0:09:40
Saint Maurice de Beynost 27 45N50 5E00 -0:20:00
Saint Maurice en Montagne 27 46N34 5E50 -0:23:20
Saint Maurice Montcouronne 78 48N35 2E07 -0:08:28
Saint Max 92 48N42 6E13 -0:24:52
Sainte Maxime 1 43N18 6E38 -0:26:32
Saint Maximin La Sainte Baume 1 43N27 5E52 -0:23:28
Saint Méen le Grand 36 48N11 2W12 0:08:48
Sainte Menehould 89 49N05 4E54 -0:19:36
Saint Menges 103 49N44 4E56 -0:19:44
Sainte Mère Église 143 49N25 1W19 0:05:16
Saint Méry 77 48N35 2E50 -0:11:20
Sainte Mesme 74 48N32 1E58 -0:07:52
Saint Mesmes 61 48N59 2E42 -0:10:48
Saint Michel 1 45N13 6E28 -0:25:52
Saint Michel 103 49N55 4E08 -0:16:32
Saint Michel sur Meurthe 101 48N19 6E54 -0:27:36
Saint Michel sur Orge 78 48N38 2E18 -0:09:12
Saint Mihiel 94 48N54 5E33 -0:22:12
Sainte Montaine 41 47N29 2E19 -0:09:16
Saint Nazaire 34 47N17 2W12 0:08:48
Saint Nazaire en Royans 1 45N04 5E15 -0:21:00
Saint Nazaire le Désert 1 44N34 5E17 -0:21:08
Saint Nicolas aux Bois 112 49N36 3E25 -0:13:40
Saint Nicolas d'Aliermont 132 49N53 1E13 -0:04:52
Saint Nicolas de Port 91 48N38 6E18 -0:25:12
Saint Nizier du Moucherotte 1 45N10 5E38 -0:22:32
Saint Nom la Bretèche 61 48N51 2E01 -0:08:04
Saint Omer 137 50N45 2E15 -0:09:00
Saint Ouen 134 50N02 2E03 -0:08:12
Saint Ouen 61 48N54 2E20 -0:09:20
Saint Ouen l'Aumône 80 49N03 2E06 -0:08:24
Saint Paterne 68 48N24 0E07 -0:00:28
Saint Pathus 80 49N04 2E48 -0:11:12
Saint Paul 1 43N42 7E07 -0:28:28
Saint Paul 1 44N31 6E45 -0:27:00
Saint Paul en Jarez 1 45N29 4E35 -0:18:20
Saint Paul et Valmalle 1 43N38 3E40 -0:14:40
Saint Paulien 1 45N08 3E49 -0:15:16
Saint Paul Trois Châteaux 1 44N21 4E46 -0:19:04
Saint Péravy la Colombe 44 48N00 1E42 -0:06:48
Saint Péray 1 44N57 4E50 -0:19:20
Saint Père 45 47N28 3E46 -0:15:04
Saint Pierre 1 45N40 3E45 -0:15:00
Saint Pierre d'Albigny 1 45N34 6E09 -0:24:36
Saint Pierre de Bœuf 1 45N22 4E45 -0:19:00
Saint Pierre de Chartreuse 1 45N20 5E49 -0:23:16
Saint Pierre des Corps 25 47N23 0E44 -0:02:56
Saint Pierre de Vacquière 1 43N52 4E13 -0:16:52
Saint Pierre du Vauvray 124 49N14 1E13 -0:04:52
Saint Pierre Église 145 49N40 1W24 0:05:36
Saint Pierre en Port 128 49N48 0E29 -0:01:56
Saint Pierre le Moûtier 25 46N48 3E07 -0:12:28
Saint Pierre lès Elbeuf 125 49N16 1E03 -0:04:12
Saint Pierreville 1 44N49 4E29 -0:17:56
Saint Pol de Léon 36 48N41 3W59 0:15:56
Saint Pol sur Mer 140 51N02 2E21 -0:09:24
Saint Pol sur Ternoise 135 50N23 2E20 -0:09:20
Saint Pons 1 43N29 2E46 -0:11:04
Saint Pourçain sur Sioule 1 46N19 3E17 -0:13:08
Saint Priest 27 45N42 4E57 -0:19:48
Saint Priest en Jarez 1 45N28 4E22 -0:17:28
Saint Prix 61 49N01 2E16 -0:09:04

Saint Quentin 103 49N51 3E17 -0:13:08
Saint Rambert d'Albon
1 45N17 4E49 -0:19:16
Saint Rambert en Bugey
27 45N57 5E26 -0:21:44
Saint Rambert sur Loire
1 45N30 4E15 -0:17:00
Saint Raphaël 1 43N25 6E46 -0:27:04
Saint Rémy 25 46N46 4E50 -0:19:20
Saint Rémy (lès Chevreuse)
61 48N42 2E05 -0:08:20
Saint Rémy de Provence
1 43N47 4E50 -0:19:20
Saint Rémy en Bouzemont
86 48N38 4E39 -0:18:36
Saint Rémy l'Honoré
74 48N45 1E53 -0:07:32
Saint Rémy sur Avre
70 48N46 1E15 -0:05:00
Saint Renan 37 48N26 4W37 0:18:28
Saint Révérien 28 47N13 3E30 -0:14:00
Saint Riquier 135 50N08 1E57 -0:07:48
Saint Romain de Colbosc
128 49N32 0E22 -0:01:28
Saint Romain le Puy
1 45N33 4E07 -0:16:28
Saint Romans 1 45N07 5E19 -0:21:16
Saintry sur Seine
78 48N36 2E30 -0:10:00
Saintes 24 45N45 0W38 0:02:32
Saint Saëns 110 49N40 1E17 -0:05:08
Saint Saturnin d'Apt
1 43N56 5E23 -0:21:32
Saint Sauveur 59 47N48 6E23 -0:25:32
Saint Sauveur 45 47N37 3E12 -0:12:48
Saint Sauveur sur Tinée
1 44N05 7E06 -0:28:24
Saint Savin 1 46N34 0E52 -0:03:28
Sainte Savine 77 48N18 4E03 -0:16:12
Saint Seine l'Abbaye
51 47N26 4E47 -0:19:08
Sainte Sigolène 1 45N14 4E15 -0:17:00
Saint Simon 103 49N45 3E10 -0:12:40
Saintes Maries de la Mer
1 43N27 4E26 -0:17:44
Saint Soupplets 80 49N02 2E48 -0:11:12
Saint Sulpice de Favières
78 48N33 2E11 -0:08:44
Saint Sulpice les Feuilles
1 46N19 1E22 -0:05:28
Sainte Suzanne 60 47N30 6E46 -0:27:04
Saint Symphorien
24 44N26 0W30 0:02:00
Saint Symphorien
74 48N31 1E46 -0:07:04
Saint Symphorien d'Ozon
1 45N38 4E52 -0:19:28
Saint Symphorien sur Coise
1 45N38 4E27 -0:17:48
Saint Thibault des Vignes
61 48N52 2E41 -0:10:44
Saint Trivier de Courtes
27 46N28 5E05 -0:20:20
Saint Trivier sur Moignans
27 46N04 4E54 -0:19:36
Saint Tropez 1 43N16 6E38 -0:26:32
Sainte Tulle 1 43N47 5E46 -0:23:04
Saint Uze 1 45N11 4E52 -0:19:28
Saint Valérien 76 48N11 3E06 -0:12:24
Saint Valéry en Caux
131 49N52 0E44 -0:02:56
Saint Valéry sur Somme
136 50N11 1E38 -0:06:32
Saint Vallier 25 46N38 4E22 -0:17:28
Saint Vallier 1 45N10 4E49 -0:19:16
Saint Vallier de Thiey
1 43N42 6E51 -0:27:24
Saint Varent 24 46N53 0W14 0:00:56
Saint Venant 136 50N37 2E33 -0:10:12
Saint Véran 1 44N42 6E52 -0:27:28
Saint Victoret 1 43N25 5E14 -0:20:56
Saint Vincent de Tyrosse
24 43N40 1W18 0:05:12
Saint Vit 30 47N11 5E49 -0:23:16
Saint Vivien de Médoc
24 45N26 1W02 0:04:08
Saint Vrain 78 48N33 2E20 -0:09:20
Saint Wandrille Rançon
127 49N32 0E46 -0:03:04
Saint Witz 80 49N05 2E34 -0:10:16
Saint Yrieix la Perche
1 45N31 1E12 -0:04:48
Saint Zacharie 1 43N23 5E43 -0:22:52
Salbris 41 47N26 2E03 -0:08:12
Salernes 1 43N33 6E14 -0:24:56
Salers 1 45N08 2E30 -0:10:00
Salies de Béarn 24 43N29 0W55 0:03:40
Salignac Eyvignes
1 44N59 1E19 -0:05:16
Salin de Giraud 1 43N25 4E44 -0:18:56
Salindres 1 44N10 4E10 -0:16:40
Salins les Bains
32 46N57 5E53 -0:23:32
Salins les Thermes
1 45N28 6E32 -0:26:08
Sallagriffon 1 43N53 6E54 -0:27:36
Sallanches 1 45N56 6E38 -0:26:32
Salles Curan 1 44N11 2E47 -0:11:08
Salles sous Bois 1 44N27 4E56 -0:19:44
Salon de Provence
1 43N38 5E06 -0:20:24
Salviac 1 44N41 1E16 -0:05:04
Samer 137 50N38 1E45 -0:07:00
Samoëns 1 46N05 6E44 -0:26:56
Sanary sur Mer 1 43N07 5E48 -0:23:12
Sancergues 25 47N09 2E55 -0:11:40
Sancerre 41 47N20 2E51 -0:11:24
Sancey le Grand 55 47N18 6E35 -0:26:20
Sancoins 25 46N50 2E55 -0:11:40
Sandrancourt 79 49N02 1E39 -0:06:36
Sangatte 138 50N56 1E45 -0:07:00
Sannois 61 48N58 2E15 -0:09:00
Santa Maria Siché
1 41N52 8E59 -0:35:56
Santenay 30 46N55 4E41 -0:18:44
Santeny 61 48N43 2E34 -0:10:16
Saorge 1 43N59 7E33 -0:30:12
Saou 1 44N39 5E04 -0:20:16
Sarcelles 61 49N00 2E23 -0:09:32
Sargé Lès le Mans
39 48N02 0E14 -0:00:56
Sarlat la Canéda 1 44N53 1E13 -0:04:52
Sarralbe 18 49N00 7E01 -0:28:04
Sarras 1 45N11 4E48 -0:19:12
Sarrebourg 14 48N44 7E03 -0:28:12
Sarreguemines 18 49N06 7E03 -0:28:12
Sarre Union 17 48N56 7E05 -0:28:20
Sartène 1 41N36 8E59 -0:35:56
Sartilly 63 48N45 1W27 0:05:48
Sartrouville 61 48N57 2E10 -0:08:40
Sarzeau 35 47N32 2W46 0:11:04
Sassenage 1 45N12 5E40 -0:22:40
Saudron 87 48N30 5E20 -0:21:20
Saujon 24 45N40 0W56 0:03:44
Saulieu 49 47N16 4E14 -0:16:56
Saulnot 55 47N34 6E38 -0:26:32
Sault de Vaucluse
1 44N05 5E25 -0:21:40
Sault lès Rethel
103 49N30 4E22 -0:17:28
Saulx de Vesoul 54 47N42 6E17 -0:25:08
Saulx les Chartreux
61 48N42 2E16 -0:09:04
Saulxures sur Moselotte
60 47N57 6E46 -0:27:04
Saumur 25 47N16 0W05 0:00:20
Sausset les Pins 1 43N20 5E07 -0:20:28
Saussy 52 47N28 4E57 -0:19:48
Sauvas 1 44N19 4E09 -0:16:36
Sauve 1 43N56 3E57 -0:15:48
Sauveterre 1 44N02 4E48 -0:19:12
Sauveterre de Béarn
24 43N24 0W56 0:03:44
Sauveterre de Guyenne
1 44N42 0W05 0:00:20
Savenay 35 47N22 1W57 0:07:48
Saverdun 1 43N14 1E35 -0:06:20
Saverne 18 48N44 7E22 -0:29:28
Savigny lès Beaune
30 47N04 4E49 -0:19:16
Savigny le Temple
78 48N35 2E35 -0:10:20
Savigny sur Braye
42 47N53 0E49 -0:03:16
Savigny sur Orge
78 48N40 2E21 -0:09:24
Savines 1 44N32 6E24 -0:25:36
Savonnières 25 47N21 0E33 -0:02:12
Saze 1 43N56 4E41 -0:18:44
Scaër 35 48N02 3W42 0:14:48
Sceaux 61 48N47 2E17 -0:09:08
Scey sur Saône et Saint Albin
53 47N40 5E58 -0:23:52
Schiltigheim 14 48N36 7E45 -0:31:00
Schirmeck 14 48N29 7E13 -0:28:52
Schleithal 22 48N59 8E02 -0:32:08
Schlettstadt → Sélestat
16 48N16 7E27 -0:29:48
Schweighouse sur Moder
18 48N49 7E44 -0:30:56
Schweyen 20 49N10 7E24 -0:29:36
Sciez 1 46N20 6E23 -0:25:32
Scionzier 1 46N03 6E34 -0:26:16
Séchault 89 49N16 4E44 -0:18:56
Seclin 117 50N33 3E02 -0:12:08
Sedan 103 49N42 4E57 -0:19:48
Séderon 1 44N12 5E32 -0:22:08
Sées 68 48N36 0E10 -0:00:40
Séez 1 45N37 6E48 -0:27:12
Segré 38 47N41 0W53 0:03:32
Seiches sur le Loir
28 47N35 0W22 0:01:28
Seignelay 46 47N54 3E36 -0:14:24
Seilhac 1 45N22 1E42 -0:06:48
Seillans 1 43N38 6E38 -0:26:32
Seine Port 78 48N33 2E33 -0:10:12
Sélestat (Schlettstadt)
16 48N16 7E27 -0:29:48
Selles sur Cher 24 47N16 1E33 -0:06:12
Sellières 29 46N50 5E34 -0:22:16
Selommes 44 47N45 1E12 -0:04:48
Seloncourt 60 47N28 6E52 -0:27:28
Selongey 52 47N35 5E10 -0:20:40
Seltz 22 48N53 8E06 -0:32:24
Sembadel 1 45N16 3E41 -0:14:44
Semblançay 25 47N30 0E35 -0:02:20
Semur en Auxois 49 47N29 4E20 -0:17:20
Senainville 70 48N30 1E37 -0:06:28
Sénas 1 43N45 5E05 -0:20:20
Sénez 1 43N55 6E24 -0:25:36
Senlis 80 49N12 2E35 -0:10:20
Senlisse 61 48N41 1E59 -0:07:56
Sennecey le Grand
25 46N39 4E52 -0:19:28
Sennevoy le Bas 49 47N48 4E17 -0:17:08
Senonches 70 48N33 1E02 -0:04:08
Senones 101 48N24 6E59 -0:27:56
Sens 76 48N12 3E17 -0:13:08
Sépeaux 46 47N57 3E14 -0:12:56
Seppois le Bas 60 47N33 7E10 -0:28:40
Septeuil 74 48N54 1E41 -0:06:44
Septvaux 111 49N34 3E23 -0:13:32
Sergines 77 48N20 3E15 -0:13:00
Sérifontaine 110 49N21 1E46 -0:07:04
Sérignan du Comtat
1 44N11 4E51 -0:19:24
Sermaise 78 48N32 2E05 -0:08:20
Sermaises 48 48N18 2E12 -0:08:48
Sermaize les Bains
87 48N47 4E55 -0:19:40
Sermizelles 45 47N32 3E48 -0:15:12
Serres 1 44N26 5E43 -0:22:52
Serrières 1 45N19 4E45 -0:19:00
Serris 82 48N51 2E47 -0:11:08
Servon 61 48N43 2E35 -0:10:20
Servoz 1 45N56 6E46 -0:27:04
Sessenheim 22 48N48 7E59 -0:31:56
Sète 1 43N24 3E41 -0:14:44
Seurre 30 47N00 5E09 -0:20:36
Sévérac le Château
1 44N19 3E04 -0:12:16
Sevran 61 48N56 2E32 -0:10:08
Sèvres 61 48N49 2E12 -0:08:48
Sévrier 1 45N52 6E08 -0:24:32
Sewen 2 47N48 6E54 -0:27:36
Seyches 1 44N33 0E18 -0:01:12
Seyne 1 44N21 6E21 -0:25:24
Seyssel 26 45N57 5E49 -0:23:16
Sézanne 82 48N43 3E43 -0:14:52
Siaugues Saint Romain
1 45N06 3E38 -0:14:32
Sierck les Bains
12 49N26 6E21 -0:25:24
Sigean 1 43N02 2E59 -0:11:56
Sigloy 48 47N50 2E14 -0:08:56
Signes 1 43N18 5E52 -0:23:28
Signy l'Abbaye 103 49N42 4E25 -0:17:40
Signy le Petit 103 49N54 4E17 -0:17:08
Sillé le Guillaume
47 48N12 0W08 0:00:32
Sillery 88 49N12 4E08 -0:16:32
Silly le Long 80 49N06 2E48 -0:11:12
Simiane 1 43N25 5E26 -0:21:44
Sin le Noble 117 50N22 3E07 -0:12:28
Sissonne 111 49N34 3E54 -0:15:36
Sisteron 1 44N12 5E56 -0:23:44
Sivry Courtry 77 48N32 2E45 -0:11:00
Sivry sur Meuse 89 49N19 5E16 -0:21:04
Six Fours la Plage
1 43N06 5E51 -0:23:24
Sizun 36 48N24 4W05 0:16:20
Sochaux 60 47N31 6E50 -0:27:20
Soignolles en Brie
77 48N39 2E42 -0:10:48
Soindres 74 48N57 1E40 -0:06:40
Soissons 107 49N22 3E20 -0:13:20
Soisy sous Montmorency
61 48N59 2E18 -0:09:12
Soisy sur Seine 78 48N39 2E27 -0:09:48
Solenzara 1 41N51 9E23 -0:37:32
Solers 77 48N40 2E43 -0:10:52
Solesmes 103 50N11 3E30 -0:14:00
Solgne 100 48N58 6E18 -0:25:12
Solignac sur Loire
1 44N58 3E53 -0:15:32
Soligny la Trappe
68 48N37 0E32 -0:02:08
Solliès Pont 1 43N11 6E03 -0:24:12
Solre le Château
103 50N10 4E05 -0:16:20
Solutré Pouilly 27 46N18 4E43 -0:18:52
Somain 117 50N22 3E17 -0:13:08
Sombernon 49 47N18 4E42 -0:18:48
Sommedieue 87 49N05 5E28 -0:21:52
Sommepy Tahure 89 49N15 4E33 -0:18:12
Sommesous 86 48N44 4E12 -0:16:48
Sompuis 86 48N41 4E23 -0:17:32
Sonchamp 74 48N35 1E53 -0:07:32
Songeons 119 49N33 1E52 -0:07:28
Sore 1 44N20 0W35 0:02:20
Sorgues 1 44N00 4E52 -0:19:28
Sospel 1 43N53 7E27 -0:29:48
Sotteville 127 49N25 1E06 -0:04:24
Souain Perthes lès Hurlus
89 49N11 4E32 -0:18:08
Souesmes 41 47N27 2E10 -0:08:40
Soufflenheim 22 48N50 7E58 -0:31:52
Souillac 1 44N54 1E29 -0:05:56
Souilly 87 49N01 5E17 -0:21:08
Soulac sur Mer 24 45N31 1W07 0:04:28
Soulaines Dhuys 85 48N22 4E44 -0:18:56
Soultzeren 3 48N04 7E06 -0:28:24
Soultz Haut Rhin 3 47N53 7E14 -0:28:56
Soultzmatt 3 47N58 7E14 -0:28:56
Soultz sous Forêts
22 48N56 7E53 -0:31:32
Souppes sur Loing
75 48N11 2E44 -0:10:56
Souvigny 1 46N32 3E11 -0:12:44
Souzy la Briche 78 48N32 2E09 -0:08:36
Soyons 1 44N53 4E51 -0:19:24
Spicheren 19 49N12 6E58 -0:27:52
Spincourt 97 49N20 5E40 -0:22:40
Stains 61 48N57 2E23 -0:09:32
Steenvoorde 137 50N48 2E35 -0:10:20
Steinbourg 21 48N46 7E25 -0:29:40
Stella Plage 137 50N29 1E35 -0:06:20
Stenay 98 49N29 5E11 -0:20:44
Stiring Wendel 19 49N12 6E56 -0:27:44
Strasbourg 14 48N35 7E45 -0:31:00
Strassburg → Strasbourg
14 48N35 7E45 -0:31:00
Sucy en Brie 61 48N46 2E32 -0:10:08
Suèvres 41 47N40 1E28 -0:05:52
Suippes 89 49N08 4E32 -0:18:08

Place	Code	Latitude	Longitude	Time
Sully sur Loire	48	47N46	2E22	-0:09:28
Sumène	1	43N59	3E43	-0:14:52
Sundhouse	23	48N15	7E36	-0:30:24
Surbourg	22	48N55	7E51	-0:31:24
Suresnes	61	48N52	2E14	-0:08:56
Surgères	24	46N07	0W45	0:03:00
Survilliers	80	49N06	2E33	-0:10:12
Sury le Comtal	1	45N32	4E10	-0:16:40
Sussey	49	47N13	4E22	-0:17:28
Suze la Rousse	1	44N17	4E51	-0:19:24
Syam	27	46N42	5E57	-0:23:48
Tacoignières	74	48N50	1E40	-0:06:40
Tain l'Hermitage	1	45N04	4E51	-0:19:24
Talant	49	47N19	5E00	-0:20:00
Tallard	1	44N28	6E03	-0:24:12
Talloires	1	45N51	6E13	-0:24:52
Talmas	122	50N02	2E20	-0:09:20
Talmont	24	46N28	1W37	0:06:28
Tancarville	126	49N29	0E28	-0:01:52
Taninges	1	46N07	6E36	-0:26:24
Tanlay	49	47N50	4E05	-0:16:20
Tannay	45	47N21	3E36	-0:14:24
Tantonville	91	48N28	6E08	-0:24:32
Tarare	27	45N54	4E26	-0:17:44
Tarascon	1	42N51	1E36	-0:06:24
Tarascon	1	43N48	4E40	-0:18:40
Tarbes	1	43N14	0E05	-0:00:20
Targon	1	44N44	0W16	0:01:04
Tartas	1	43N50	0W48	0:03:12
Tassin la Demi Lune	27	45N46	4E47	-0:19:08
Tauxigny	24	47N13	0E50	-0:03:20
Tavant	24	47N07	0E23	-0:01:32
Tavaux	30	47N02	5E24	-0:21:36
Tavernes	1	43N36	6E01	-0:24:04
Taverny	61	49N02	2E13	-0:08:52
Templeuve	117	50N32	3E10	-0:12:40
Tenay	26	45N55	5E30	-0:22:00
Tence	1	45N07	4E17	-0:17:08
Tencin	1	45N19	5E58	-0:23:52
Tende	1	44N05	7E36	-0:30:24
Tergnier	112	49N39	3E18	-0:13:12
Termignon	1	45N17	6E49	-0:27:16
Terrasson la Villedieu	1	45N08	1E18	-0:05:12
Tessancourt sur Aubette	79	49N02	1E55	-0:07:40
Tessy sur Vire	67	48N58	1W04	0:04:16
Téterchen	18	49N14	6E34	-0:26:16
Thann	2	47N49	7E05	-0:28:20
Thaon les Vosges	91	48N15	6E25	-0:25:40
Thémericourt	79	49N05	1E54	-0:07:36
Thénezay	24	46N43	0W02	0:00:08
Théoule sur Mer	1	43N31	6E57	-0:27:48
Thérouanne	136	50N38	2E15	-0:09:00
Theys	1	45N18	6E00	-0:24:00
Thiais	61	48N46	2E23	-0:09:32
Thiant	103	50N18	3E27	-0:13:48
Thiaucourt Regniéville	93	48N57	5E52	-0:23:28
Thiberville	72	49N08	0E27	-0:01:48
Thiéblemont Farémont	86	48N41	4E44	-0:18:56
Thiers	1	45N51	3E34	-0:14:16
Thierville sur Meuse	87	49N10	5E21	-0:21:24
Thieux	80	49N01	2E40	-0:10:40
Thilay	118	49N52	4E49	-0:19:16
Thines	1	44N29	4E03	-0:16:12
Thionville	10	49N22	6E10	-0:24:40
Thiron	68	48N19	0E59	-0:03:56
Thiverval Grignon	74	48N51	1E55	-0:07:40
Thiviers	1	45N25	0E56	-0:03:44
Thizy	27	46N02	4E19	-0:17:16
Thoirette	27	46N16	5E32	-0:22:08
Thoiry	74	48N52	1E48	-0:07:12
Thoissey	27	46N10	4E48	-0:19:12
Thollon	1	46N23	6E43	-0:26:52
Thônes	1	45N53	6E20	-0:25:20
Thonnance lès Joinville	87	48N27	5E10	-0:20:40
Thonon les Bains	1	46N22	6E29	-0:25:56
Thorame Haute	1	44N06	6E33	-0:26:12
Thorenc	1	43N48	6E49	-0:27:16
Thorens Glières	1	45N59	6E15	-0:25:00
Thorigny sur Marne	61	48N53	2E42	-0:10:48
Thorigny sur Oreuse	76	48N17	3E24	-0:13:36
Thouars	24	46N59	0W13	0:00:52
Thourotte	113	49N29	2E53	-0:11:32
Thueyts	1	44N41	4E13	-0:16:52
Thuilley aux Groseilles	90	48N34	5E58	-0:23:52
Thury Harcourt	40	48N59	0W29	0:01:56
Tigeaux	82	48N50	2E54	-0:11:36
Tigery	78	48N38	2E31	-0:10:04
Tignes	1	45N30	6E55	-0:27:40
Tigy	48	47N48	2E12	-0:08:48
Til Châtel	52	47N31	5E10	-0:20:40
Tillières sur Avre	70	48N46	1E04	-0:04:16
Tonnay Boutonne	1	45N58	0W42	0:02:48
Tonneins	1	44N23	0E19	-0:01:16
Tonnerre	49	47N51	3E58	-0:15:52
Torcy	61	48N51	2E39	-0:10:36
Torfou	78	48N32	2E14	-0:08:56
Tôtes	131	49N41	1E03	-0:04:12
Toucy	45	47N44	3E18	-0:13:12
Touët sur Var	1	43N57	7E00	-0:28:00
Toul	93	48N41	5E54	-0:23:36
Toulon	1	43N07	5E56	-0:23:44
Toulon sur Arroux	25	46N42	4E08	-0:16:32
Toulouse	1	43N36	1E26	-0:05:44
Touques	129	49N22	0E06	-0:00:24
Tourcoing	141	50N43	3E09	-0:12:36
Tournan en Brie	82	48N44	2E46	-0:11:04
Tournon	1	45N04	4E50	-0:19:20
Tournus	27	46N34	4E54	-0:19:36
Tourouvre	68	48N35	0E40	-0:02:40
Tourrette Levens	1	43N47	7E16	-0:29:04
Tours	25	47N23	0E41	-0:02:44
Tours sur Marne	88	49N03	4E07	-0:16:28
Tours sur Meymont	1	45N40	3E35	-0:14:20
Tourteron	103	49N32	4E39	-0:18:36
Tourves	1	43N24	5E56	-0:23:44
Toury	71	48N12	1E56	-0:07:44
Toussus le Noble	61	48N45	2E07	-0:08:28
Traînel	77	48N25	3E27	-0:13:48
Tramayes	27	46N18	4E36	-0:18:24
Trans en Provence	1	43N30	6E29	-0:25:56
Trappes	61	48N47	2E00	-0:08:00
Treffort	27	46N16	5E22	-0:21:28
Tréguier	36	48N47	3W14	0:12:56
Trélazé	28	47N27	0W28	0:01:52
Tremblay lès Gonesse	61	48N59	2E34	-0:10:16
Tressancourt	61	48N55	2E00	-0:08:00
Trets	1	43N27	5E41	-0:22:44
Trévoux	27	45N56	4E46	-0:19:04
Triaucourt en Argonne	87	48N59	5E04	-0:20:16
Tricot	115	49N34	2E35	-0:10:20
Triel sur Seine	61	48N59	2E00	-0:08:00
Trieux	10	49N20	5E56	-0:23:44
Trilbardou	81	48N57	2E48	-0:11:12
Trilport	81	48N57	2E57	-0:11:48
Troarn	143	49N11	0W11	0:00:44
Tronville en Barrois	87	48N43	5E17	-0:21:08
Troo	42	47N47	0E47	-0:03:08
Trouville sur Mer	129	49N22	0E05	-0:00:20
Troyes	77	48N18	4E05	-0:16:20
Truchtersheim	18	48N40	7E36	-0:30:24
Trun	69	48N51	0E02	-0:00:08
Tuffé	43	48N07	0E31	-0:02:04
Tulette	1	44N17	4E56	-0:19:44
Tulle	1	45N16	1E46	-0:07:04
Tullins	1	45N18	5E29	-0:21:56
Turckheim	6	48N05	7E17	-0:29:08
Turriers	1	44N24	6E10	-0:24:40
Ubaye	1	44N28	6E22	-0:25:28
Uchaud	1	43N45	4E16	-0:17:04
Uckange	10	49N18	6E09	-0:24:36
Ugine	1	45N45	6E25	-0:25:40
Unieux	1	45N24	4E16	-0:17:04
Uriage les Bains	1	45N09	5E50	-0:23:20
Us	79	49N06	1E58	-0:07:52
Ussel	1	45N33	2E18	-0:09:12
Usson en Forez	1	45N23	3E56	-0:15:44
Ustaritz	24	43N24	1W27	0:05:48
Utelle	1	43N55	7E15	-0:29:00
Uvernet	1	44N22	6E38	-0:26:32
Uzerche	1	45N26	1E34	-0:06:16
Uzès	1	44N01	4E25	-0:17:40
Vagney	101	48N01	6E43	-0:26:52
Vailly sur Aisne	111	49N25	3E31	-0:14:04
Vailly sur Sauldre	41	47N27	2E39	-0:10:36
Vaires sur Marne	61	48N52	2E39	-0:10:36
Vaison la Romaine	1	44N14	5E04	-0:20:16
Vaîte	30	47N35	5E44	-0:22:56
Valbonnais	1	44N54	5E54	-0:23:36
Valcivières	1	45N35	3E48	-0:15:12
Valdahon	32	47N09	6E21	-0:25:24
Valdeblore	1	44N04	7E12	-0:28:48
Val d'Isère	1	45N27	6E59	-0:27:56
Valdoie	60	47N40	6E51	-0:27:24
Valençay	1	47N09	1E34	-0:06:16
Valence	1	44N56	4E54	-0:19:36
Valenciennes	103	50N21	3E32	-0:14:08
Valensole	1	43N50	5E59	-0:23:56
Valentigney	60	47N28	6E50	-0:27:20
Valenton	61	48N45	2E28	-0:09:52
Valflaunès	1	43N48	3E52	-0:15:28
Valgorge	1	44N35	4E07	-0:16:28
Vallauris	1	43N35	7E03	-0:28:12
Valleraugue	1	44N05	3E38	-0:14:32
Valleroy	97	49N12	5E55	-0:23:40
Vallet	28	47N10	1W16	0:05:04
Vallières	1	45N54	5E56	-0:23:44
Valloire	1	45N10	6E26	-0:25:44
Vallon Pont d'Arc	1	44N24	4E24	-0:17:36
Vallorcine	1	46N02	6E56	-0:27:44
Vallouise	1	44N51	6E29	-0:25:56
Valmondois	80	49N06	2E12	-0:08:48
Valmont	128	49N44	0E31	-0:02:04
Valmy	89	49N05	4E46	-0:19:04
Valognes	144	49N31	1W28	0:05:52
Valréas	1	44N23	4E59	-0:19:56
Vals les Bains	1	44N40	4E22	-0:17:28
Vals Près le Puy	1	45N01	3E52	-0:15:28
Val Suzon	49	47N25	4E54	-0:19:36
Vanault les Dames	88	48N51	4E46	-0:19:04
Vandenesse	49	47N13	4E37	-0:18:28
Vanlay	46	48N02	4E01	-0:16:04
Vannes	35	47N39	2W46	0:11:04
Vannes sur Cosson	48	47N43	2E13	-0:08:52
Varades	28	47N23	1W02	0:04:08
Varages	1	43N36	5E58	-0:23:52
Varangéville	91	48N38	6E19	-0:25:16
Varces	1	45N05	5E41	-0:22:44
Varengeville sur Mer	131	49N55	0E59	-0:03:56
Varennes en Argonne	89	49N14	5E02	-0:20:08
Varennes Jarcy	61	48N41	2E34	-0:10:16
Varennes Saint Sauveur	27	46N29	5E15	-0:21:00
Varennes sur Allier	26	46N19	3E24	-0:13:36
Varennes sur Amance	58	47N54	5E37	-0:22:28
Vars	1	44N37	6E41	-0:26:44
Varzy	45	47N22	3E23	-0:13:32
Vassieux en Vercors	1	44N53	5E22	-0:21:28
Vassy	49	47N34	4E10	-0:16:40
Vatan	1	47N05	1E48	-0:07:12
Vaubecourt	87	48N56	5E07	-0:20:28
Vauclaix	28	47N14	3E49	-0:15:16
Vaucouleurs	99	48N36	5E40	-0:22:40
Vaucresson	61	48N50	2E09	-0:08:36
Vaudherland	61	49N00	2E29	-0:09:56
Vaudoy en Brie	77	48N41	3E05	-0:12:20
Vaufrey	60	47N21	6E55	-0:27:40
Vaugneray	1	45N44	4E39	-0:18:36
Vaugrigneuse	78	48N36	2E07	-0:08:28
Vauhallan	61	48N44	2E12	-0:08:48
Vaujours	61	48N56	2E35	-0:10:20
Vaulx en Velin	27	45N47	4E56	-0:19:44
Vauréal	80	49N02	2E02	-0:08:08
Vauvenargues	1	43N33	5E36	-0:22:24
Vauvert	1	43N42	4E17	-0:17:08
Vauvillers	58	47N55	6E06	-0:24:24
Vaux le Pénil	77	48N32	2E41	-0:10:44
Vaux Lès Saint Claude	27	46N22	5E44	-0:22:56
Vaux sous Aubigny	52	47N39	5E17	-0:21:08
Vaux sur Seine	79	49N00	1E58	-0:07:52
Vavincourt	87	48N49	5E13	-0:20:52
Vedène	1	43N59	4E54	-0:19:36
Veigné	25	47N17	0E44	-0:02:56
Vellechevreux et Courbenans	55	47N33	6E32	-0:26:08
Vémars	80	49N04	2E34	-0:10:16
Venaco	1	42N14	9E10	-0:36:40
Venanson	1	44N03	7E15	-0:29:00
Venant	48	48N30	2E06	-0:08:24
Venarey les Laumes	51	47N32	4E26	-0:17:44
Venasque	1	43N59	5E09	-0:20:36
Vence	1	43N43	7E07	-0:28:28
Vendargues	1	43N39	3E58	-0:15:52
Vendeuvre sur Barse	77	48N14	4E28	-0:17:52
Vendin lès Béthune	136	50N32	2E37	-0:10:28
Vendin le Vieil	117	50N28	2E52	-0:11:28
Vendôme	44	47N48	1E04	-0:04:16
Vénissieux	27	45N41	4E53	-0:19:32
Vénosc	1	44N59	6E07	-0:24:28
Verberie	80	49N19	2E44	-0:10:56
Vercel Villedieu le Camp	55	47N11	6E24	-0:25:36
Verclause	1	44N23	5E26	-0:21:44
Verdun	1	43N52	1E14	-0:04:56
Verdun	87	49N10	5E23	-0:21:32
Verdun sur le Doubs	30	46N54	5E01	-0:20:04
Véretz	25	47N22	0E48	-0:03:12
Vergons	1	43N55	6E35	-0:26:20
Vergt	1	45N02	0E43	-0:02:52
Vermand	117	49N52	3E09	-0:12:36
Vermenton	45	47N40	3E44	-0:14:56
Vernaison	27	45N39	4E49	-0:19:16
Verneuil	70	48N44	0E56	-0:03:44
Verneuil l'Étang	77	48N39	2E50	-0:11:20
Verneuil sur Avre	70	48N44	0E56	-0:03:44
Verneuil sur Seine	61	48N59	1E59	-0:07:56
Vernon	73	49N05	1E29	-0:05:56
Vernouillet	61	48N58	1E59	-0:07:56
Vernoux en Vivarais	1	44N54	4E39	-0:18:36
Verny	11	49N01	6E12	-0:24:48
Verrey sous Salmaise	51	47N26	4E40	-0:18:40
Verrières le Buisson	61	48N45	2E16	-0:09:04
Versailles	61	48N48	2E08	-0:08:32
Ver sur Launette	80	49N06	2E41	-0:10:44
Vert	74	48N57	1E41	-0:06:44
Verteillac	1	45N21	0E22	-0:01:28
Vert le Grand	78	48N34	2E22	-0:09:28
Vert le Petit	78	48N33	2E22	-0:09:28
Vertou	28	47N10	1W29	0:05:56
Vert Saint Denis	78	48N34	2E37	-0:10:28
Vertus	88	48N54	4E00	-0:16:00
Vervins	103	49N50	3E54	-0:15:36
Verzenay	88	49N10	4E09	-0:16:36
Verzy	88	49N09	4E10	-0:16:40
Vescovato	1	42N30	9E26	-0:37:44
Vesoul	54	47N38	6E10	-0:24:40
Vétheuil	79	49N04	1E42	-0:06:48

Place	Zone	Lat.	Long.	Time
Veules les Roses	131	49N52	0E48	-0:03:12
Veulettes sur Mer	131	49N51	0E36	-0:02:24
Veynes	1	44N32	5E49	-0:23:16
Veyrier	1	45N53	6E10	-0:24:40
Vézelay	45	47N28	3E44	-0:14:56
Vézelise	91	48N29	6E05	-0:24:20
Vézénobres	1	44N03	4E09	-0:16:36
Viarmes	80	49N08	2E22	-0:09:28
Vibraye	43	48N03	0E44	-0:02:56
Vic en Bigorre	1	43N23	0E03	-0:00:12
Vichy	26	46N08	3E26	-0:13:44
Vico	1	42N10	8E48	-0:35:12
Vicq	74	48N49	1E50	-0:07:20
Vic sur Aisne	109	49N24	3E07	-0:12:28
Vic sur Cère	1	44N59	2E37	-0:10:28
Vic sur Seille	13	48N47	6E32	-0:26:08
Vidauban	1	43N26	6E26	-0:25:44
Vielle Eglise en Yvelines	74	48N40	1E53	-0:07:32
Viels Maisons	84	48N54	3E24	-0:13:36
Vienne	1	45N31	4E52	-0:19:28
Vienne en Arthies	79	49N04	1E44	-0:06:56
Vienne le Château	89	49N11	4E53	-0:19:32
Vierzon	25	47N13	2E05	-0:08:20
Vieux Condé	117	50N27	3E34	-0:14:16
Vieux Ferette	4	47N30	7E18	-0:29:12
Vieux Thann	2	47N48	7E08	-0:28:32
Vif	1	45N03	5E40	-0:22:40
Vignacourt	122	50N01	2E12	-0:08:48
Vigneulles lès Hattonchâtel	95	48N59	5E43	-0:22:52
Vigneux sur Seine	61	48N42	2E25	-0:09:40
Vignory	56	48N17	5E06	-0:20:24
Vignot	94	48N46	5E36	-0:22:24
Vigny	79	49N05	1E56	-0:07:44
Vigy	12	49N12	6E18	-0:25:12
Vihiers	25	47N09	0W32	0:02:08
Villabé	78	48N35	2E27	-0:09:48
Villaines la Juhel	65	48N21	0W17	0:01:08
Villandraut	1	44N28	0W23	0:01:32
Villandry	25	47N20	0E31	-0:02:04
Villar d'Arène	1	45N02	6E20	-0:25:20
Villard Bonnot	1	45N14	5E53	-0:23:32
Villard de Lans	1	45N04	5E33	-0:22:12
Villaroche	78	48N37	2E39	-0:10:36
Villars Colmars	1	44N10	6E36	-0:26:24
Villars en Azois	52	48N04	4E45	-0:19:00
Villars les Dombes	27	46N00	5E01	-0:20:04
Villars sur Var	1	43N56	7E06	-0:28:24
Villé	16	48N20	7E18	-0:29:12
Villebon sur Yvette	61	48N42	2E15	-0:09:00
Villeconin	78	48N31	2E08	-0:08:32
Villecresnes	61	48N43	2E32	-0:10:08
Villecroze	1	43N35	6E16	-0:25:04
Ville d'Avray	61	48N50	2E11	-0:08:44
Villedieu	63	48N50	1W13	0:04:52
Ville en Tardenois	108	49N11	3E48	-0:15:12
Villefort	1	44N26	3E56	-0:15:44
Villefranche	27	45N59	4E43	-0:18:52
Villefranche de Rouergue	1	44N21	2E02	-0:08:08
Villefranche sur Cher	25	47N18	1E46	-0:07:04
Villefranche sur Mer	1	43N42	7E19	-0:29:16
Villejuif	61	48N48	2E22	-0:09:28
Villejust	61	48N41	2E14	-0:08:56
Villemaur sur Vanne	77	48N15	3E44	-0:14:56
Villemeux sur Eure	70	48N40	1E28	-0:05:52
Villemoisson sur Orge	78	48N40	2E19	-0:09:16
Villemomble	61	48N53	2E31	-0:10:04
Villenauxe la Grande	77	48N35	3E33	-0:14:12
Villeneuve d'Ascq	117	50N37	3E10	-0:12:40
Villeneuve d'Aveyron	1	44N26	2E02	-0:08:08
Villeneuve de Berg	1	44N33	4E30	-0:18:00
Villeneuve la Garenne	61	48N56	2E20	-0:09:20
Villeneuve la Guyard	77	48N20	3E04	-0:12:16
Villeneuve l'Archevêque	76	48N14	3E33	-0:14:12
Villeneuve le Comte	82	48N49	2E50	-0:11:20
Villeneuve le Roi	61	48N44	2E25	-0:09:40
Villeneuve lès Avignon	1	43N58	4E48	-0:19:12
Villeneuve lès Maguelonne	1	43N32	3E52	-0:15:28
Villeneuve Saint Denis	82	48N49	2E48	-0:11:12
Villeneuve Saint Georges	61	48N44	2E27	-0:09:48
Villeneuve sous Dammartin	80	49N02	2E39	-0:10:36
Villeneuve sur Lot	1	44N25	0E42	-0:02:48
Villeneuve sur Yonne	46	48N05	3E18	-0:13:12
Villennes sur Seine	61	48N56	2E00	-0:08:00
Villenoy	81	48N57	2E52	-0:11:28
Villeny	41	47N37	1E45	-0:07:00
Villeparisis	61	48N56	2E37	-0:10:28
Villepinte	61	48N58	2E32	-0:10:08
Villepreux	61	48N50	2E01	-0:08:04
Villequier	127	49N31	0E40	-0:02:40
Villeron	80	49N03	2E33	-0:10:12
Villeroy	81	48N59	2E47	-0:11:08
Villers Bocage	144	49N05	0W39	0:02:36
Villers Bocage	121	49N59	2E20	-0:09:20
Villers Bretonneux	122	49N52	2E31	-0:10:04
Villers Carbonnel	116	49N52	2E54	-0:11:36
Villers Cotterêts	109	49N15	3E05	-0:12:20
Villers en Arthies	79	49N05	1E44	-0:06:56
Villersexel	55	47N33	6E26	-0:25:44
Villers Farlay	32	47N00	5E45	-0:23:00
Villers le Lac	32	47N04	6E40	-0:26:40
Villers lès Nancy	92	48N40	6E09	-0:24:36
Villers lès Pots	30	47N13	5E21	-0:21:24
Villers Outréaux	103	50N02	3E18	-0:13:12
Villers Saint Paul	110	49N17	2E29	-0:09:56
Villers Semeuse	103	49N44	4E45	-0:19:00
Villerupt	10	49N28	5E56	-0:23:44
Villerville	129	49N24	0E08	-0:00:32
Villes sur Auzon	1	44N03	5E14	-0:20:56
Ville sur Tourbe	89	49N11	4E47	-0:19:08
Villeurbanne	27	45N46	4E53	-0:19:32
Villevaudé	61	48N55	2E39	-0:10:36
Villeziers	61	48N40	2E10	-0:08:40
Villiers Adam	61	49N04	2E14	-0:08:56
Villiers le Bâcle	61	48N44	2E08	-0:08:32
Villiers le Bel	61	49N00	2E23	-0:09:32
Villiers le Sec	61	49N04	2E23	-0:09:32
Villiers Saint Frédéric	74	48N49	1E54	-0:07:36
Villiers Saint Georges	82	48N39	3E25	-0:13:40
Villiers sur Marne	61	48N50	2E33	-0:10:12
Villiers sur Morin	82	48N52	2E53	-0:11:32
Vilosnes sur Meuse	98	49N20	5E14	-0:20:56
Vimoutiers	69	48N55	0E12	-0:00:48
Vimy	153	50N22	2E49	-0:11:16
Vinay	1	45N13	5E24	-0:21:36
Vincennes	61	48N51	2E26	-0:09:44
Vincey	91	48N20	6E20	-0:25:20
Vinon sur Verdon	1	43N43	5E48	-0:23:12
Viols le Fort	1	43N45	3E42	-0:14:48
Vire	40	48N50	0W53	0:03:32
Vireux Molhain	118	50N05	4E43	-0:18:52
Virieu	1	45N29	5E28	-0:21:52
Virieu le Grand	26	45N51	5E39	-0:22:36
Viroflay	61	48N48	2E10	-0:08:40
Vironvay	124	49N12	1E13	-0:04:52
Viry Châtillon	61	48N40	2E23	-0:09:32
Vis en Artois	123	50N15	2E56	-0:11:44
Vitré	40	48N08	1W12	0:04:48
Vitrey sur Mance	53	47N49	5E45	-0:23:00
Vitry en Artois	117	50N20	2E59	-0:11:56
Vitry la Ville	88	48N50	4E28	-0:17:52
Vitry le François	86	48N44	4E35	-0:18:20
Vitry(sur Seine)	61	48N48	2E24	-0:09:36
Vitteaux	51	47N24	4E32	-0:18:08
Vittel	58	48N12	5E57	-0:23:48
Viverols	1	45N26	3E53	-0:15:32
Viviers	1	44N29	4E41	-0:18:44
Viviers du Lac	1	45N39	5E54	-0:23:36
Vivonne	24	46N26	0E16	-0:01:04
Vizille	1	45N05	5E46	-0:23:04
Void	99	48N41	5E37	-0:22:28
Voiron	1	45N22	5E35	-0:22:20
Voise	71	48N24	1E43	-0:06:52
Voisenon	77	48N34	2E40	-0:10:40
Voisins le Bretonneux	61	48N45	2E03	-0:08:12
Voiteur	27	46N45	5E37	-0:22:28
Vollore Montagne	1	45N47	3E41	-0:14:44
Vollore Ville	1	45N47	3E36	-0:14:24
Volmerange les Mines	10	49N27	6E05	-0:24:20
Volmunster	20	49N07	7E21	-0:29:24
Volnay	30	47N00	4E47	-0:19:08
Volonne	1	44N07	6E01	-0:24:04
Volx	1	43N53	5E51	-0:23:24
Voreppe	1	45N18	5E38	-0:22:32
Vorey	1	45N11	3E54	-0:15:36
Vosves	77	48N31	2E36	-0:10:24
Voué	86	48N28	4E07	-0:16:28
Vougeot	49	47N10	4E58	-0:19:52
Vouillé	24	46N39	0E10	-0:00:40
Voujeaucourt	55	47N28	6E46	-0:27:04
Voulangis	82	48N51	2E54	-0:11:36
Voulx	76	48N17	2E58	-0:11:52
Voutenay sur Cure	45	47N33	3E47	-0:15:08
Vouvray	25	47N25	0E48	-0:03:12
Vouziers	89	49N24	4E42	-0:18:48
Voves	71	48N16	1E38	-0:06:32
Vrigne Meuse	103	49N42	4E51	-0:19:24
Vron	136	50N19	1E45	-0:07:00
Vuillafans	32	47N04	6E13	-0:24:52
Waldighoffen	4	47N33	7E19	-0:29:16
Walincourt	103	50N04	3E20	-0:13:20
Wallers	103	50N22	3E24	-0:13:36
Wangenbourg	14	48N37	7E19	-0:29:16
Warfusée Abancourt	122	49N52	2E35	-0:10:20
Warmeriville	89	49N21	4E13	-0:16:52
Wasquehal	117	50N40	3E09	-0:12:36
Wasselonne	14	48N38	7E27	-0:29:48
Wassigny	103	50N01	3E36	-0:14:24
Wassy	87	48N30	4E57	-0:19:48
Watten	137	50N50	2E13	-0:08:52
Wattignies	117	50N35	3E03	-0:12:12
Wattrelos	141	50N42	3E13	-0:12:52
Wavrin	117	50N34	2E55	-0:11:40
Waziers	117	50N23	3E07	-0:12:28
Westhoffen	14	48N36	7E26	-0:29:44
Weyersheim	22	48N43	7E48	-0:31:12
Wignehies	103	50N01	4E00	-0:16:00
Wildenstein	3	47N59	6E58	-0:27:52
Willer sur Thur	2	47N51	7E05	-0:28:20
Wimereux	138	50N46	1E37	-0:06:28
Wimmenau	21	48N55	7E25	-0:29:40
Wingen sur Moder	21	48N55	7E22	-0:29:28
Wingles	117	50N29	2E51	-0:11:24
Wintzenheim	6	48N04	7E17	-0:29:08
Wissant	138	50N53	1E40	-0:06:40
Wissembourg	19	49N02	7E57	-0:31:48
Wissous	61	48N44	2E20	-0:09:20
Witry lès Reims	105	49N18	4E07	-0:16:28
Wittelsheim	4	47N49	7E15	-0:29:00
Wittenheim	4	47N49	7E20	-0:29:20
Wizernes	137	50N43	2E14	-0:08:56
Woerth	22	48N56	7E45	-0:31:00
Woincourt	135	50N04	1E32	-0:06:08
Wormhoudt	137	50N53	2E28	-0:09:52
Wy Dit Joli Village	79	49N06	1E50	-0:07:20
Xertigny	58	48N03	6E24	-0:25:36
Yenne	26	45N42	5E46	-0:23:04
Yermenonville	70	48N33	1E37	-0:06:28
Yerres	61	48N43	2E30	-0:10:00
Yerville	131	49N40	0E54	-0:03:36
Ymeray	70	48N31	1E42	-0:06:48
Yport	128	49N44	0E19	-0:01:16
Yssingeaux	1	45N08	4E07	-0:16:28
Yvetot	127	49N37	0E46	-0:03:04
Yvette	74	48N43	1E55	-0:07:40
Yvoire	1	46N22	6E20	-0:25:20
Yzeron	1	45N42	4E35	-0:18:20
Zicavo	1	41N54	9E08	-0:36:32
Zillisheim	4	47N41	7E16	-0:29:04
Zinswiller	20	48N55	7E35	-0:30:20
Zonza	1	41N45	9E10	-0:36:40
Département 1	27	46N12	5E13	-0:20:52
Département 2	111	49N34	3E37	-0:14:28
Département 3	25	46N34	3E20	-0:13:20
Département 4	1	44N06	6E15	-0:25:00
Département 5	1	44N33	6E00	-0:24:00
Département 6	1	43N42	7E16	-0:29:04
Département 7	1	44N44	4E36	-0:18:24
Département 8	103	49N46	4E44	-0:18:56
Département 9	1	42N58	1E35	-0:06:20
Département 10	77	48N18	4E05	-0:16:20
Département 11	1	43N12	2E21	-0:09:24
Département 12	1	44N21	2E34	-0:10:16
Département 13	1	43N18	5E22	-0:21:28
Département 14	147	49N11	0W22	0:01:28
Département 15	1	44N56	2E26	-0:09:44
Département 16	1	45N39	0E10	-0:00:40
Département 17	24	46N09	1W10	0:04:40
Département 18	25	47N05	2E23	-0:09:32
Département 19	1	45N16	1E46	-0:07:04
Département 20	1	41N55	8E45	-0:35:00
Département 21	49	47N19	5E02	-0:20:08
Département 22	36	48N31	2W45	0:11:00
Département 23	1	46N17	1E52	-0:07:28
Département 24	1	45N11	0E44	-0:02:56
Département 25	55	47N15	6E02	-0:24:08
Département 26	1	44N56	4E54	-0:19:36
Département 27	73	49N01	1E11	-0:04:44
Département 28	71	48N27	1E30	-0:06:00
Département 29	35	48N00	4W06	0:16:24
Département 30	1	43N51	4E21	-0:17:24
Département 31	1	43N37	1E26	-0:05:44
Département 32	1	43N39	0E36	-0:02:24
Département 33	1	44N50	0W34	0:02:16
Département 34	1	43N37	3E53	-0:15:32
Département 35	66	48N07	1W40	0:06:40
Département 36	1	46N49	1E41	-0:06:44
Département 37	25	47N24	0E42	-0:02:48
Département 38	1	45N11	5E43	-0:22:52
Département 39	27	46N40	5E33	-0:22:12
Département 40	1	43N54	0W30	0:02:00
Département 41	25	47N35	1E20	-0:05:20
Département 42	1	45N26	4E23	-0:17:32
Département 43	1	45N03	3E53	-0:15:32
Département 44	28	47N13	1W35	0:06:20
Département 45	44	47N54	1E54	-0:07:36
Département 46	1	44N27	1E26	-0:05:44
Département 47	1	44N12	0E38	-0:02:32
Département 48	1	44N31	3E30	-0:14:00
Département 49	28	47N28	0W32	0:02:08
Département 50	146	49N07	1W05	0:04:20
Département 51	88	48N57	4E22	-0:17:28

FRANCE FRANKREICH FRANCIA

Name		Lat	Long	Offset
Département 52	56	48N07	5E08	-0:20:32
Département 53	65	48N04	0W45	0:03:00
Département 54	92	48N42	6E12	-0:24:48
Département 55	87	48N46	5E10	-0:20:40
Département 56	35	47N40	2W44	0:10:56
Département 57	11	49N07	6E11	-0:24:44
Département 58	28	46N59	3E09	-0:12:36
Département 59	117	50N39	3E05	-0:12:20
Département 60	110	49N26	2E05	-0:08:20
Département 61	68	48N26	0E05	-0:00:20
Département 62	123	50N18	2E46	-0:11:04
Département 63	1	45N47	3E05	-0:12:20
Département 64	1	43N18	0W22	0:01:28
Département 65	1	43N14	0E05	-0:00:20
Département 66	1	42N42	2E55	-0:11:40
Département 67	14	48N35	7E45	-0:31:00
Département 68	6	48N05	7E21	-0:29:24
Département 69	27	45N46	4E50	-0:19:20
Département 70	54	47N37	6E09	-0:24:36
Département 71	27	46N18	4E50	-0:19:20
Département 72	39	48N01	0E12	-0:00:48
Département 73	1	45N34	5E55	-0:23:40
Département 74	1	45N54	6E07	-0:24:28
Département 75	61	48N50	2E20	-0:09:20
Département 76	127	49N26	1E05	-0:04:20
Département 77	77	48N33	2E40	-0:10:40
Département 78	61	48N50	2E08	-0:08:32
Département 79	24	46N19	0W27	0:01:48
Département 80	121	49N54	2E18	-0:09:12
Département 81	1	43N55	2E08	-0:08:32
Département 82	1	44N01	1E20	-0:05:20
Département 83	1	43N32	6E28	-0:25:52
Département 84	1	43N57	4E50	-0:19:20
Département 85	24	46N40	1W25	0:05:40
Département 86	24	46N35	0E20	-0:01:20
Département 87	1	45N50	1E15	-0:05:00
Département 88	91	48N10	6E28	-0:25:52
Département 89	46	47N48	3E35	-0:14:20
Département 90	60	47N38	6E52	-0:27:28
Département 91	78	48N36	2E20	-0:09:20
Département 92	61	48N50	2E11	-0:08:44
Département 93	61	48N55	2E30	-0:10:00
Département 94	61	48N47	2E29	-0:09:56
Département 95	80	49N00	2E00	-0:08:00

FRENCH GUIANA GUAYANA FRANCESA GUYANE FRANÇAISE

Time Table
Before 1/Jul/1911 LMT
Begin Standard 60W00
1/Jul/1911 0:00 4:00
Begin Standard 45W00
1/Oct/1967 0:00 3:00

Name	Lat	Long	Offset
Caux	4N26	52W02	3:28:08
Cayenne	4N56	52W20	3:29:20
Forestière	5N13	54W20	3:37:20
Guisanbourg	4N25	51W56	3:27:44
Île du Diable (Devil's Island)	5N17	52W35	3:30:20
Iracoubo	5N29	53W13	3:32:52
Kaw	4N29	52W02	3:28:08
Kourou	5N09	52W39	3:30:36
Macouria	4N55	52W22	3:29:28
Mann	5N39	53W49	3:35:16
Matoury	4N51	52W20	3:29:20
Ouanary	4N13	51W40	3:26:40
Régina	4N19	52W08	3:28:32
Rémire	4N53	52W17	3:29:08
Roura	4N44	52W20	3:29:20
Saint Élie	4N50	53W17	3:33:08
Saint Georges	3N54	51W48	3:27:12
Saint Laurent du Maroni	5N30	54W02	3:36:08
Saül	3N37	53W12	3:32:48
Sinnamary	5N23	52W57	3:31:48

FRENCH POLYNESIA POLINESIA FRANCESA POLYNÉSIE FRANÇAISE

Time Table # 1
Before 1/Oct/1912 LMT
Begin Standard 135W00
1/Oct/1912 0:00 9:00

Time Table # 2
Before 1/Oct/1912 LMT
Begin Standard 142W30
1/Oct/1912 0:00 9:30

Time Table # 3
Before 1/Oct/1912 LMT
Begin Standard 150W00
1/Oct/1912 0:00 10:00

DIVISIONS

1. Ahunui Island
2. Amanu Island
3. Anaa Island
4. Australes, Îles
5. Bass, Îlots de
6. Bellingshausen Island
7. Bora-Bora Island
8. Désapointement, Îles du
9. Fakarava Island
10. Gambier, Îles
11. Hao Island
12. Haraiki Island
13. Hikueru Island
14. Hiva Oa Island
15. Kaukura Island
16. Makatea Island
17. Makemo Island
18. Manuhangi Island
19. Maria Island
20. Marquises, Îles (Marques
21. Marutea Island
22. Mataiva Island
23. Mehetia Island
24. Moorea Island
25. Mopelia Island
26. Nengonengo Island
27. Raevavae Island
28. Raiatea Island
29. Rapa Island
30. Raraka Island
31. Raroia Island
32. Ravahere Island
33. Rimatara Island
34. Roi Georges, Îles du
35. Rurutu Island
36. Scilly Island
37. Société, Îles de la
38. Tahaa Island
39. Tahiti Island
40. Tahuata Island
41. Takapoto Island
42. Tematangi Island
43. Tetiaroa Island
44. Tikei Island
45. Tupuai, Île
46. Vanavana Island

Name	Table	Lat	Long	Offset
Afaahiti 39	3	17S43	149W19	9:57:16
Afareaitu 24	3	17S33	149W47	9:59:08
Ahunui Island 1	3	19S39	140W25	9:21:40
Ahurei 29	3	27S36	144W18	9:37:12
Amanu Island 2	3	17S48	140W46	9:23:04
Anaa Island 3	3	17S25	145W30	9:42:00
Arue 39	3	17S32	149W32	9:58:08
Atimaono 39	3	17S46	149W28	9:57:52
Atu Ana 14	2	9S48	139W02	9:16:08
Atuona 14	2	9S48	139W02	9:16:08
Australes, Îles 4	3	23S00	150W00	10:00:00
Bass, Îlots de 5	3	27S55	143W26	9:33:44
Bellingshausen Island 6	3	15S48	154W33	10:18:12
Bora-Bora 7	3	16S30	151W45	10:07:00
Bora-Bora Island 7	3	16S30	151W45	10:07:00
Désappointement, Îles du 8	3	14S10	141W20	9:25:20
Faaone 39	3	17S40	149W18	9:57:12
Fakarava Island 9	3	16S20	145W37	9:42:28
Gambier, Îles 10	1	21S20	136W30	9:06:00
Haapiti 24	3	17S34	149W52	9:59:28
Haka Mui (Ua-Pou I) 20	2	9S23	140W00	9:20:00
Hana Teio 40	2	9S59	139W06	9:16:24
Hanatetena 40	2	9S58	139W04	9:16:16
Hana Tuuna 40	2	10S00	139W07	9:16:28
Hanaui 14	2	9S45	139W05	9:16:20
Hao Island 11	3	18S15	140W54	9:23:36
Haraiki Island 12	3	17S28	143W27	9:33:48
Hikueru Island 13	3	17S36	142W37	9:30:28
Hitiaa 39	3	17S36	149W18	9:57:12
Hiva Oa Island 14	2	9S45	139W00	9:16:00
Îles Australes 4	3	23S00	150W00	10:00:00
Îles de la Société 37	3	17S00	150W00	10:00:00
Îles du Désappointement 8	3	14S10	141W20	9:25:20
Îles du Roi Georges 34	3	14S32	145W08	9:40:32
Îles Gambier 10	1	21S20	136W30	9:06:00
Îles Marquises (Marquesas) 20	2	9S00	139W30	9:18:00
Île Tupuai 45	3	23S18	149W30	9:58:00
Îlots de Bass 5	3	27S55	143W26	9:33:44
Kaukura Island 15	3	15S45	146W42	9:46:48
Mahina 39	3	17S31	149W30	9:58:00
Makatea Island 16	3	15S50	148W15	9:53:00
Makemo Island 17	3	16S35	143W40	9:34:40
Manuhangi Island 18	3	19S12	141W16	9:25:04
Maraa 39	3	17S46	149W34	9:58:16
Marae 24	3	17S32	149W54	9:59:36
Maria Island 19	3	21S48	154W41	10:18:44
Marquesas 20	2	9S00	139W30	9:18:00
Marquises, Îles (Marquesas) 20	2	9S00	139W30	9:18:00
Marutea Island 21	3	17S00	143W10	9:32:40
Mataiea 39	3	17S45	149W23	9:57:32
Mataiva Island 22	3	14S53	148W40	9:54:40
Mataura 45	2	23S22	149W28	9:57:52
Mehetia Island 23	3	17S52	148W03	9:52:12

POLYNÉSIE FRANÇAISE — POLINESIA FRANCESA — FRENCH POLYNESIA

Place	Zone	Lat	Long	Offset
Moorea Island 24	3	17s32	149w40	9:58:40
Mopelia Island 25	3	16s50	153w55	10:15:40
Motopu 40	2	9s55	139w03	9:16:12
Nahoe 14	2	9s45	138w55	9:15:40
Nengonengo Island 26	3	18s47	141w48	9:27:12
Nutae 39	3	17s44	149w15	9:57:00
Paea 39	3	17s41	149w35	9:58:20
Paopao 24	3	17s31	149w49	9:59:16
Papara 39	3	17s44	149w21	9:57:24
Papeari 39	3	17s45	149w21	9:57:24
Papeete 39	3	17s32	149w34	9:58:16
Papenoo 39	3	17s30	149w25	9:57:40
Papetoai 24	3	17s29	149w52	9:59:28
Pirae 39	3	17s32	149w33	9:58:12
Pueu 39	3	17s44	149w13	9:56:52
Punaauia 39	3	17s38	149w36	9:58:24
Raevavae Island 27	3	23s52	147w40	9:50:40
Raiatea Island 28	3	16s50	151w25	10:05:40
Rapa Island 29	3	27s36	144w20	9:37:20
Raraka Island 30	3	16s10	144w54	9:39:36
Raroia Island 31	3	16s01	142w26	9:29:44
Ravahere Island 32	3	18s14	142w09	9:28:36
Rikitea 10	1	23s08	134w57	8:59:48
Rimatara Island 33	3	22s38	152w51	10:11:24
Roi Georges, îles du 34	3	14s32	145w08	9:40:32
Rotoava 9	3	16s02	145w36	9:42:24
Rurutu Island 35	3	22s26	151w20	10:05:20
Scilly Island 36	3	16s30	154w40	10:18:40
Société, îles de la 37	3	17s00	150w00	10:00:00
Tahaa Island 38	3	16s38	151w30	10:06:00
Tahiti Island 39	3	17s37	149w27	9:57:48
Tahuata Island 40	2	9s57	139w05	9:16:20
Taio Hae (Nuku Hiva I) 20	2	8s56	140w05	9:20:20
Takapoto Island 41	3	14s38	145w12	9:40:48
Tupuai, île 45	3	23s18	149w30	9:58:00
Taunoa 39	3	17s45	149w21	9:57:24
Tautira 39	3	17s44	149w09	9:56:36
Teahupoo 39	3	17s51	149w13	9:56:52
Teahupu 39	3	17s51	149w13	9:56:52
Temae 24	3	17s29	149w46	9:59:04
Tematangi Island 42	3	21s41	140w40	9:22:40
Tetiaroa Island 43	3	17s05	149w32	9:58:08
Tiarei 39	3	17s32	149w20	9:57:20
Tiarei 39	3	17s32	149w20	9:57:20
Tikei Island 44	3	14s58	144w32	9:38:08
Toanoano 39	3	17s51	149w13	9:56:52
Uturea 28	3	16s44	151w26	10:05:44
Vairao 39	3	17s47	149w17	9:57:08
Vaitahu 40	2	9s56	139w06	9:16:24
Vaitoto 39	3	17s46	149w07	9:56:28
Vanavana Island 46	2	20s47	139w09	9:16:36

GABÓN — GABOON — GABUN — GABON

Time Table
Before 1/Jan/1912 LMT
Begin Standard 15E00
1/Jan/1912 0:00 -1:00

Place	Lat	Long	Offset
Agouma	1s32	10E11	-0:40:44
Akiéni	1s11	13E53	-0:55:32
Akok	0N31	9E45	-0:39:00
Ancien Ekalla	1s27	14E00	-0:56:00
Ayémé	0N02	10E17	-0:41:08
Batoala	0N48	13E27	-0:53:48
Belinga	1N13	13E12	-0:52:48
Bifoum	0s22	10E23	-0:41:32
Bifoun	0s22	10E23	-0:41:32
Bitam	2N05	11E29	-0:45:56
Boléko	0N56	12E14	-0:48:56
Bongo	2s10	10E12	-0:40:48
Booué	0s06	11E56	-0:47:44
Bouggou	3s45	11E12	-0:44:48
Bougou	3s45	11E12	-0:44:48
Cocobeach	0N59	9E36	-0:38:24
Dendé	3s46	11E09	-0:44:36
Dimbou	1s29	11E52	-0:47:28
Diyanga	1s29	11E52	-0:47:28
Djiba	1s21	13E09	-0:52:36
Douigny	3s11	10E45	-0:43:00
Ebel	0N07	11E05	-0:44:20
Ekalla	1s27	14E00	-0:56:00
Ekwata	0s13	9E18	-0:37:12
Engong	0N36	10E06	-0:40:24
Equata	0s13	9E18	-0:37:12
Etéké	1s29	11E35	-0:46:20
Fougamou	1s13	10E36	-0:42:24
Franceville	1s38	13E35	-0:54:20
Gongoué	0s32	9E12	-0:36:48
Goumbou	3s11	10E45	-0:43:00
Guidouma	1s37	10E41	-0:42:44
Idemba	2s38	11E38	-0:46:32
Iguéla	1s55	9E19	-0:37:16
Kango	0N09	10E08	-0:40:32
Kombo	0s20	12E22	-0:49:28
Koula-Moutou	1s08	12E29	-0:49:56
Koumameyong	0N11	11E51	-0:47:24
Lalera	0N22	11E28	-0:45:52
Lambaréné	0s42	10E13	-0:40:52
Lara	0N22	11E28	-0:45:52
Lastoursville	0s49	12E42	-0:50:48
Lébamba	2s12	11E30	-0:46:00
Léconi	1s35	14E14	-0:56:56
Libreville	0N23	9E27	-0:37:48
Likokou	0s12	12E48	-0:51:12
Loanda	0s55	9E00	-0:36:00
Madjingo	1N22	14E04	-0:56:16
Makokou	0N34	12E52	-0:51:28
Malinga	2s25	12E14	-0:48:56
Mallémbé	3s32	10E53	-0:43:32
Mandji	1s36	10E26	-0:41:44
Mandji-Kili	1s36	10E26	-0:41:44
Mapfongui	1s15	12E59	-0:51:56
Massima	1s27	11E42	-0:46:48
Massima Camp	1s27	11E42	-0:46:48
Mayumba	3s25	10E39	-0:42:36
Mbigou	1s53	11E56	-0:47:44
Mbissa	0N41	10E59	-0:43:56
Médouneu	0N57	10E47	-0:43:08
Mekambo	1N01	13E56	-0:55:44
Mevang	0N07	11E05	-0:44:20
Mimongo	1s11	11E36	-0:46:24
Mintoum	0N27	12E16	-0:49:04
Minvoul	2N09	12E08	-0:48:32
Mitzic	0N47	11E34	-0:46:16
Moabi	2s15	11E00	-0:44:00
Moanda	1s34	13E11	-0:52:44
Momo	1N52	11E48	-0:47:12
Mouila	1s52	11E01	-0:44:04
Mourindi	2s32	10E48	-0:43:12
Mouyombi-Tali	2s32	10E48	-0:43:12
Mvadhi-Ousyé	1N13	13E12	-0:52:48
Mvam	0s13	9E39	-0:38:36
Nabigou	1s12	9E31	-0:38:04
Ndendé	2s23	11E23	-0:45:32
Ndindi	3s46	11E09	-0:44:36
Ndjolé	0s11	10E45	-0:43:00
Ndougou	1s39	9E40	-0:38:40
Nkolabona	1N14	11E43	-0:46:52
Ntoum	0N23	9E47	-0:39:08
Nzéla	1s25	12E39	-0:50:36
Okondja	0s41	13E47	-0:55:08
Omboué	1s34	9E15	-0:37:00
Omoy	1s21	13E09	-0:52:36
Owendo	0N17	9E30	-0:38:00
Oyan	0N02	10E17	-0:41:08
Oyem	1N37	11E35	-0:46:20
Paguilou	1s12	9E31	-0:38:04
Petit Loango	2s16	9E35	-0:38:20
Port-Gentil	0s43	8E47	-0:35:08
Sam	0N58	11E16	-0:45:04
Sette Cama	2s32	9E45	-0:39:00
Sindara	1s02	10E40	-0:42:40
Tandou Bougou	3s32	10E53	-0:43:32
Tchibanga	2s51	11E02	-0:44:08
Tsiga	1s32	10E11	-0:40:44
Yetsou	2s08	10E42	-0:42:48
Yetsou I	2s08	10E42	-0:42:48
Yombi	1s26	10E37	-0:42:28

GAMBIE — GAMBIA

Time Table
Before 1/Jan/1912 LMT
Begin Standard 16w39
1/Jan/1912 0:00 1:07
Begin Standard 15w00
1/Jan/1935 0:00 1:00
Begin Standard 0w00
1/Jan/1964 0:00 0:00

Place	Lat	Long	Offset
Banjul	13N28	16w39	1:06:36
Bansang	13N26	14w39	0:58:36
Barra	13N20	16w36	1:06:24
Basse Santa Su	13N19	14w13	0:56:52
Bathurst → Banjul	13N28	16w39	1:06:36
Bintang	13N10	16w08	1:04:32
Brikama	13N15	16w39	1:06:36
Fatoto	13N26	13w52	0:55:28
Georgetown	13N30	14w47	0:59:08
Kerewan	13N29	16w10	1:04:40
Kuntair	13N32	16w13	1:04:52
Kuntaur	13N40	14w48	0:59:12

GERMANY ALEMANIA ALLEMAGNE DEUTSCHLAND

Time Table # 1

Date	Time	Offset
Before 1/Apr/1893		LMT
Begin Standard		15E00
1/Apr/1893	0:00	-1:00
30/Apr/1916	23:00	-2:00
1/Oct/1916	1:00	-1:00
16/Apr/1917	2:00	-2:00
17/Sep/1917	3:00	-1:00
15/Apr/1918	2:00	-2:00
16/Sep/1918	3:00	-1:00
1/Apr/1940	2:00	-2:00
2/Nov/1942	3:00	-1:00
29/Mar/1943	2:00	-2:00
4/Oct/1943	3:00	-1:00
3/Apr/1944	2:00	-2:00
2/Oct/1944	3:00	-1:00
2/Apr/1945	2:00	-2:00
16/Sep/1945	2:00	-1:00
14/Apr/1946	2:00	-2:00
7/Oct/1946	2:00	-1:00
6/Apr/1947	3:00	-2:00
11/May/1947	3:00	-3:00
29/Jun/1947	3:00	-2:00
5/Oct/1947	3:00	-1:00
18/Apr/1948	2:00	-2:00
3/Oct/1948	3:00	-1:00
10/Apr/1949	2:00	-2:00
2/Oct/1949	3:00	-1:00
6/Apr/1980	2:00	-2:00
28/Sep/1980	3:00	-1:00
29/Mar/1981	2:00	-2:00
27/Sep/1981	3:00	-1:00
28/Mar/1982	2:00	-2:00
26/Sep/1982	3:00	-1:00
27/Mar/1983	2:00	-2:00
25/Sep/1983	3:00	-1:00
25/Mar/1984	2:00	-2:00
30/Sep/1984	3:00	-1:00
31/Mar/1985	2:00	-2:00
29/Sep/1985	3:00	-1:00
30/Mar/1986	2:00	-2:00
28/Sep/1986	3:00	-1:00
29/Mar/1987	2:00	-2:00
27/Sep/1987	3:00	-1:00
27/Mar/1988	2:00	-2:00
25/Sep/1988	3:00	-1:00
26/Mar/1989	2:00	-2:00
24/Sep/1989	3:00	-1:00
25/Mar/1990	2:00	-2:00
30/Sep/1990	3:00	-1:00
31/Mar/1991	2:00	-2:00
29/Sep/1991	3:00	-1:00
29/Mar/1992	2:00	-2:00
27/Sep/1992	3:00	-1:00
28/Mar/1993	2:00	-2:00
26/Sep/1993	3:00	-1:00
27/Mar/1994	2:00	-2:00
25/Sep/1994	3:00	-1:00
26/Mar/1995	2:00	-2:00
24/Sep/1995	3:00	-1:00
31/Mar/1996	2:00	-2:00
29/Sep/1996	3:00	-1:00
30/Mar/1997	2:00	-2:00
28/Sep/1997	3:00	-1:00
29/Mar/1998	2:00	-2:00
27/Sep/1998	3:00	-1:00
28/Mar/1999	2:00	-2:00
26/Sep/1999	3:00	-1:00
26/Mar/2000	2:00	-2:00
24/Sep/2000	3:00	-1:00

Time Table # 2

Date	Time	Offset
Before 1/Apr/1893		LMT
Begin Standard		15E00
1/Apr/1893	0:00	-1:00
30/Apr/1916	23:00	-2:00
1/Oct/1916	1:00	-1:00
16/Apr/1917	2:00	-2:00
17/Sep/1917	3:00	-1:00
15/Apr/1918	2:00	-2:00
16/Sep/1918	3:00	-1:00
1/Apr/1940	2:00	-2:00
2/Nov/1942	3:00	-1:00
29/Mar/1943	2:00	-2:00
4/Oct/1943	3:00	-1:00
3/Apr/1944	2:00	-2:00
2/Oct/1944	3:00	-1:00
2/Apr/1945	2:00	-2:00
24/May/1945	2:00	-3:00
24/Sep/1945	3:00	-2:00
18/Nov/1945	2:00	-1:00
14/Apr/1946	2:00	-2:00
7/Oct/1946	2:00	-1:00
6/Apr/1947	3:00	-2:00
11/May/1947	3:00	-3:00
29/Jun/1947	3:00	-2:00
5/Oct/1947	3:00	-1:00
18/Apr/1948	2:00	-2:00
3/Oct/1948	3:00	-1:00
10/Apr/1949	2:00	-2:00
2/Oct/1949	3:00	-1:00
6/Apr/1980	2:00	-2:00
28/Sep/1980	3:00	-1:00
29/Mar/1981	2:00	-2:00
27/Sep/1981	3:00	-1:00
28/Mar/1982	2:00	-2:00
26/Sep/1982	3:00	-1:00
27/Mar/1983	2:00	-2:00
25/Sep/1983	3:00	-1:00
25/Mar/1984	2:00	-2:00
30/Sep/1984	3:00	-1:00
31/Mar/1985	2:00	-2:00
29/Sep/1985	3:00	-1:00
30/Mar/1986	2:00	-2:00
28/Sep/1986	3:00	-1:00
29/Mar/1987	2:00	-2:00
27/Sep/1987	3:00	-1:00
27/Mar/1988	2:00	-2:00
25/Sep/1988	3:00	-1:00
26/Mar/1989	2:00	-2:00
24/Sep/1989	3:00	-1:00
25/Mar/1990	2:00	-2:00
30/Sep/1990	3:00	-1:00
31/Mar/1991	2:00	-2:00
29/Sep/1991	3:00	-1:00
29/Mar/1992	2:00	-2:00
27/Sep/1992	3:00	-1:00
28/Mar/1993	2:00	-2:00
26/Sep/1993	3:00	-1:00
27/Mar/1994	2:00	-2:00
25/Sep/1994	3:00	-1:00
26/Mar/1995	2:00	-2:00
24/Sep/1995	3:00	-1:00
31/Mar/1996	2:00	-2:00
29/Sep/1996	3:00	-1:00
30/Mar/1997	2:00	-2:00
28/Sep/1997	3:00	-1:00
29/Mar/1998	2:00	-2:00
27/Sep/1998	3:00	-1:00
28/Mar/1999	2:00	-2:00
26/Sep/1999	3:00	-1:00
26/Mar/2000	2:00	-2:00
24/Sep/2000	3:00	-1:00

Time Table # 3

Date	Time	Offset
Before 15/Mar/1891		LMT
Begin Standard		8E24
15/Mar/1891	0:00	-0:34
Begin Standard		15E00
1/Apr/1892	0:00	-1:00
30/Apr/1916	23:00	-2:00
1/Oct/1916	1:00	-1:00
16/Apr/1917	2:00	-2:00
17/Sep/1917	3:00	-1:00
15/Apr/1918	2:00	-2:00
16/Sep/1918	3:00	-1:00
1/Apr/1940	2:00	-2:00
2/Nov/1942	3:00	-1:00
29/Mar/1943	2:00	-2:00
4/Oct/1943	3:00	-1:00
3/Apr/1944	2:00	-2:00
2/Oct/1944	3:00	-1:00
2/Apr/1945	2:00	-2:00
16/Sep/1945	2:00	-1:00
14/Apr/1946	2:00	-2:00
7/Oct/1946	2:00	-1:00
6/Apr/1947	3:00	-2:00
11/May/1947	3:00	-3:00
29/Jun/1947	3:00	-2:00
5/Oct/1947	3:00	-1:00
18/Apr/1948	2:00	-2:00
3/Oct/1948	3:00	-1:00
10/Apr/1949	2:00	-2:00
2/Oct/1949	3:00	-1:00
6/Apr/1980	2:00	-2:00
28/Sep/1980	3:00	-1:00
29/Mar/1981	2:00	-2:00
27/Sep/1981	3:00	-1:00
28/Mar/1982	2:00	-2:00
26/Sep/1982	3:00	-1:00
27/Mar/1983	2:00	-2:00
25/Sep/1983	3:00	-1:00
25/Mar/1984	2:00	-2:00
30/Sep/1984	3:00	-1:00
31/Mar/1985	2:00	-2:00
29/Sep/1985	3:00	-1:00
30/Mar/1986	2:00	-2:00
28/Sep/1986	3:00	-1:00
29/Mar/1987	2:00	-2:00
27/Sep/1987	3:00	-1:00
27/Mar/1988	2:00	-2:00
25/Sep/1988	3:00	-1:00
26/Mar/1989	2:00	-2:00
24/Sep/1989	3:00	-1:00
25/Mar/1990	2:00	-2:00
30/Sep/1990	3:00	-1:00
31/Mar/1991	2:00	-2:00
29/Sep/1991	3:00	-1:00
29/Mar/1992	2:00	-2:00
27/Sep/1992	3:00	-1:00
28/Mar/1993	2:00	-2:00
26/Sep/1993	3:00	-1:00
27/Mar/1994	2:00	-2:00
25/Sep/1994	3:00	-1:00
26/Mar/1995	2:00	-2:00
24/Sep/1995	3:00	-1:00
31/Mar/1996	2:00	-2:00
29/Sep/1996	3:00	-1:00
30/Mar/1997	2:00	-2:00
28/Sep/1997	3:00	-1:00
29/Mar/1998	2:00	-2:00
27/Sep/1998	3:00	-1:00
28/Mar/1999	2:00	-2:00
26/Sep/1999	3:00	-1:00
26/Mar/2000	2:00	-2:00
24/Sep/2000	3:00	-1:00

Time Table # 4

Date	Time	Offset
Before 15/Mar/1891		LMT
Begin Standard		11E33
15/Mar/1891	0:00	-0:46
Begin Standard		15E00
1/Apr/1892	0:00	-1:00
30/Apr/1916	23:00	-2:00
1/Oct/1916	1:00	-1:00
16/Apr/1917	2:00	-2:00
17/Sep/1917	3:00	-1:00
15/Apr/1918	2:00	-2:00
16/Sep/1918	3:00	-1:00
1/Apr/1940	2:00	-2:00
2/Nov/1942	3:00	-1:00
29/Mar/1943	2:00	-2:00
4/Oct/1943	3:00	-1:00
3/Apr/1944	2:00	-2:00
2/Oct/1944	3:00	-1:00
2/Apr/1945	2:00	-2:00
16/Sep/1945	2:00	-1:00
14/Apr/1946	2:00	-2:00
7/Oct/1946	2:00	-1:00
6/Apr/1947	3:00	-2:00
11/May/1947	3:00	-3:00
29/Jun/1947	3:00	-2:00
5/Oct/1947	3:00	-1:00
18/Apr/1948	2:00	-2:00
3/Oct/1948	3:00	-1:00
10/Apr/1949	2:00	-2:00
2/Oct/1949	3:00	-1:00
6/Apr/1980	2:00	-2:00
28/Sep/1980	3:00	-1:00
29/Mar/1981	2:00	-2:00
27/Sep/1981	3:00	-1:00
28/Mar/1982	2:00	-2:00
26/Sep/1982	3:00	-1:00
27/Mar/1983	2:00	-2:00
25/Sep/1983	3:00	-1:00
25/Mar/1984	2:00	-2:00
30/Sep/1984	3:00	-1:00
31/Mar/1985	2:00	-2:00
29/Sep/1985	3:00	-1:00
30/Mar/1986	2:00	-2:00
28/Sep/1986	3:00	-1:00
29/Mar/1987	2:00	-2:00
27/Sep/1987	3:00	-1:00
27/Mar/1988	2:00	-2:00
25/Sep/1988	3:00	-1:00
26/Mar/1989	2:00	-2:00
24/Sep/1989	3:00	-1:00
25/Mar/1990	2:00	-2:00
30/Sep/1990	3:00	-1:00
31/Mar/1991	2:00	-2:00
29/Sep/1991	3:00	-1:00
29/Mar/1992	2:00	-2:00
27/Sep/1992	3:00	-1:00
28/Mar/1993	2:00	-2:00
26/Sep/1993	3:00	-1:00
27/Mar/1994	2:00	-2:00
25/Sep/1994	3:00	-1:00
26/Mar/1995	2:00	-2:00
24/Sep/1995	3:00	-1:00
31/Mar/1996	2:00	-2:00
29/Sep/1996	3:00	-1:00
30/Mar/1997	2:00	-2:00
28/Sep/1997	3:00	-1:00
29/Mar/1998	2:00	-2:00
27/Sep/1998	3:00	-1:00
28/Mar/1999	2:00	-2:00
26/Sep/1999	3:00	-1:00
26/Mar/2000	2:00	-2:00
24/Sep/2000	3:00	-1:00

Time Table # 5

Date	Time	Offset
Before 15/Mar/1891		LMT
Begin Standard		9E11
15/Mar/1891	0:00	-0:37
Begin Standard		15E00
1/Apr/1892	0:00	-1:00
30/Apr/1916	23:00	-2:00
1/Oct/1916	1:00	-1:00
16/Apr/1917	2:00	-2:00
17/Sep/1917	3:00	-1:00
15/Apr/1918	2:00	-2:00
16/Sep/1918	3:00	-1:00
1/Apr/1940	2:00	-2:00
2/Nov/1942	3:00	-1:00
29/Mar/1943	2:00	-2:00
4/Oct/1943	3:00	-1:00
3/Apr/1944	2:00	-2:00
2/Oct/1944	3:00	-1:00
2/Apr/1945	2:00	-2:00
16/Sep/1945	2:00	-1:00
14/Apr/1946	2:00	-2:00
7/Oct/1946	2:00	-1:00
6/Apr/1947	3:00	-2:00
11/May/1947	3:00	-3:00
29/Jun/1947	3:00	-2:00
5/Oct/1947	3:00	-1:00
18/Apr/1948	2:00	-2:00
3/Oct/1948	3:00	-1:00
10/Apr/1949	2:00	-2:00
2/Oct/1949	3:00	-1:00
6/Apr/1980	2:00	-2:00
28/Sep/1980	3:00	-1:00
29/Mar/1981	2:00	-2:00
27/Sep/1981	3:00	-1:00
28/Mar/1982	2:00	-2:00
26/Sep/1982	3:00	-1:00
27/Mar/1983	2:00	-2:00
25/Sep/1983	3:00	-1:00
25/Mar/1984	2:00	-2:00
30/Sep/1984	3:00	-1:00
31/Mar/1985	2:00	-2:00
29/Sep/1985	3:00	-1:00
30/Mar/1986	2:00	-2:00
28/Sep/1986	3:00	-1:00
29/Mar/1987	2:00	-2:00
27/Sep/1987	3:00	-1:00
27/Mar/1988	2:00	-2:00
25/Sep/1988	3:00	-1:00
26/Mar/1989	2:00	-2:00
24/Sep/1989	3:00	-1:00
25/Mar/1990	2:00	-2:00
30/Sep/1990	3:00	-1:00
31/Mar/1991	2:00	-2:00
29/Sep/1991	3:00	-1:00
29/Mar/1992	2:00	-2:00
27/Sep/1992	3:00	-1:00
28/Mar/1993	2:00	-2:00
26/Sep/1993	3:00	-1:00
27/Mar/1994	2:00	-2:00
25/Sep/1994	3:00	-1:00
26/Mar/1995	2:00	-2:00
24/Sep/1995	3:00	-1:00
31/Mar/1996	2:00	-2:00
29/Sep/1996	3:00	-1:00
30/Mar/1997	2:00	-2:00
28/Sep/1997	3:00	-1:00
29/Mar/1998	2:00	-2:00
27/Sep/1998	3:00	-1:00
28/Mar/1999	2:00	-2:00
26/Sep/1999	3:00	-1:00
26/Mar/2000	2:00	-2:00
24/Sep/2000	3:00	-1:00

Time Table # 6

Date	Time	Offset
Before 15/Mar/1891		LMT
Begin Standard		8E26
15/Mar/1891	0:00	-0:34
Begin Standard		15E00
1/Apr/1892	0:00	-1:00
30/Apr/1916	23:00	-2:00
1/Oct/1916	1:00	-1:00
16/Apr/1917	2:00	-2:00
17/Sep/1917	3:00	-1:00
15/Apr/1918	2:00	-2:00
16/Sep/1918	3:00	-1:00
Begin Standard		0W00
1/Jan/1919	23:00	0:00
1/Mar/1919	23:00	-1:00
5/Oct/1919	24:00	0:00
14/Feb/1920	23:00	-1:00
23/Oct/1920	24:00	0:00
14/Mar/1921	23:00	-1:00
25/Oct/1921	24:00	0:00
25/Mar/1922	23:00	-1:00
7/Oct/1922	24:00	0:00
10/Mar/1923	23:00	-1:00
6/Oct/1923	24:00	0:00
29/Mar/1924	23:00	-1:00
4/Oct/1924	24:00	0:00
4/Apr/1925	23:00	-1:00
3/Oct/1925	24:00	0:00
17/Apr/1926	23:00	-1:00
2/Oct/1926	24:00	0:00
Begin Standard		15E00
9/Apr/1927	23:00	-1:00
1/Apr/1940	2:00	-2:00
2/Nov/1942	3:00	-1:00
29/Mar/1943	2:00	-2:00
4/Oct/1943	3:00	-1:00
3/Apr/1944	2:00	-2:00
2/Oct/1944	3:00	-1:00
2/Apr/1945	2:00	-2:00
16/Sep/1945	2:00	-1:00
14/Apr/1946	2:00	-2:00
7/Oct/1946	2:00	-1:00
6/Apr/1947	3:00	-2:00
11/May/1947	3:00	-3:00
29/Jun/1947	3:00	-2:00
5/Oct/1947	3:00	-1:00
18/Apr/1948	2:00	-2:00
3/Oct/1948	3:00	-1:00
10/Apr/1949	2:00	-2:00
2/Oct/1949	3:00	-1:00
6/Apr/1980	2:00	-2:00
28/Sep/1980	3:00	-1:00
29/Mar/1981	2:00	-2:00
27/Sep/1981	3:00	-1:00
28/Mar/1982	2:00	-2:00
26/Sep/1982	3:00	-1:00
27/Mar/1983	2:00	-2:00
25/Sep/1983	3:00	-1:00
25/Mar/1984	2:00	-2:00
30/Sep/1984	3:00	-1:00
31/Mar/1985	2:00	-2:00
29/Sep/1985	3:00	-1:00
30/Mar/1986	2:00	-2:00
28/Sep/1986	3:00	-1:00
29/Mar/1987	2:00	-2:00
27/Sep/1987	3:00	-1:00
27/Mar/1988	2:00	-2:00
25/Sep/1988	3:00	-1:00
26/Mar/1989	2:00	-2:00
24/Sep/1989	3:00	-1:00
25/Mar/1990	2:00	-2:00
30/Sep/1990	3:00	-1:00
31/Mar/1991	2:00	-2:00
29/Sep/1991	3:00	-1:00
29/Mar/1992	2:00	-2:00
27/Sep/1992	3:00	-1:00
28/Mar/1993	2:00	-2:00
26/Sep/1993	3:00	-1:00
27/Mar/1994	2:00	-2:00
25/Sep/1994	3:00	-1:00
26/Mar/1995	2:00	-2:00
24/Sep/1995	3:00	-1:00
31/Mar/1996	2:00	-2:00
29/Sep/1996	3:00	-1:00
30/Mar/1997	2:00	-2:00
28/Sep/1997	3:00	-1:00
29/Mar/1998	2:00	-2:00
27/Sep/1998	3:00	-1:00
28/Mar/1999	2:00	-2:00
26/Sep/1999	3:00	-1:00
26/Mar/2000	2:00	-2:00
24/Sep/2000	3:00	-1:00

Time Table # 7

Date	Time	Offset
Before 1/Apr/1893		LMT
Begin Standard		15E00
1/Apr/1893	0:00	-1:00
30/Apr/1916	23:00	-2:00
1/Oct/1916	1:00	-1:00
16/Apr/1917	2:00	-2:00
17/Sep/1917	3:00	-1:00
15/Apr/1918	2:00	-2:00
16/Sep/1918	3:00	-1:00
Begin Standard		0W00
1/Jan/1919	23:00	0:00
1/Mar/1919	23:00	-1:00
5/Oct/1919	24:00	0:00
14/Feb/1920	23:00	-1:00
23/Oct/1920	24:00	0:00
14/Mar/1921	23:00	-1:00
25/Oct/1921	24:00	0:00
25/Mar/1922	23:00	-1:00
7/Oct/1922	24:00	0:00
10/Mar/1923	23:00	-1:00
6/Oct/1923	24:00	0:00
29/Mar/1924	23:00	-1:00
4/Oct/1924	24:00	0:00
4/Apr/1925	23:00	-1:00
3/Oct/1925	24:00	0:00
17/Apr/1926	23:00	-1:00
2/Oct/1926	24:00	0:00
Begin Standard		15E00
9/Apr/1927	23:00	-1:00
1/Apr/1940	2:00	-2:00
2/Nov/1942	3:00	-1:00
29/Mar/1943	2:00	-2:00
4/Oct/1943	3:00	-1:00
3/Apr/1944	2:00	-2:00
2/Oct/1944	3:00	-1:00
2/Apr/1945	2:00	-2:00
16/Sep/1945	2:00	-1:00
14/Apr/1946	2:00	-2:00
7/Oct/1946	2:00	-1:00
6/Apr/1947	3:00	-2:00
11/May/1947	3:00	-3:00
29/Jun/1947	3:00	-2:00
5/Oct/1947	3:00	-1:00
18/Apr/1948	2:00	-2:00
3/Oct/1948	3:00	-1:00
10/Apr/1949	2:00	-2:00
2/Oct/1949	3:00	-1:00
6/Apr/1980	2:00	-2:00
28/Sep/1980	3:00	-1:00
29/Mar/1981	2:00	-2:00
27/Sep/1981	3:00	-1:00
28/Mar/1982	2:00	-2:00
26/Sep/1982	3:00	-1:00
27/Mar/1983	2:00	-2:00
25/Sep/1983	3:00	-1:00
25/Mar/1984	2:00	-2:00
30/Sep/1984	3:00	-1:00
31/Mar/1985	2:00	-2:00
29/Sep/1985	3:00	-1:00
30/Mar/1986	2:00	-2:00
28/Sep/1986	3:00	-1:00
29/Mar/1987	2:00	-2:00
27/Sep/1987	3:00	-1:00
27/Mar/1988	2:00	-2:00
25/Sep/1988	3:00	-1:00
26/Mar/1989	2:00	-2:00
24/Sep/1989	3:00	-1:00
25/Mar/1990	2:00	-2:00
30/Sep/1990	3:00	-1:00
31/Mar/1991	2:00	-2:00
29/Sep/1991	3:00	-1:00
29/Mar/1992	2:00	-2:00
27/Sep/1992	3:00	-1:00
28/Mar/1993	2:00	-2:00
26/Sep/1993	3:00	-1:00
27/Mar/1994	2:00	-2:00
25/Sep/1994	3:00	-1:00
26/Mar/1995	2:00	-2:00
24/Sep/1995	3:00	-1:00
31/Mar/1996	2:00	-2:00
29/Sep/1996	3:00	-1:00
30/Mar/1997	2:00	-2:00
28/Sep/1997	3:00	-1:00
29/Mar/1998	2:00	-2:00
27/Sep/1998	3:00	-1:00
28/Mar/1999	2:00	-2:00
26/Sep/1999	3:00	-1:00
26/Mar/2000	2:00	-2:00
24/Sep/2000	3:00	-1:00

DIVISIONS

1. East Germany (DDR, GDR)
2. West Germany (BRD, FRG)

Aach 2 3 47N50 8E51 -0:35:24
Aach 2 4 47N31 9E58 -0:39:52
Aachen 2 7 50N47 6E05 -0:24:20
Aach im Allgäu 2
4 47N31 9E58 -0:39:52
Aach-Linz 2 3 47N54 9E11 -0:36:44
Aalen 2 5 48N50 10E05 -0:40:20
Abbach 2 4 48N55 12E00 -0:48:00
Abbehausen 2 1 53N29 8E26 -0:33:44
Abbensen 2 1 52N23 10E11 -0:40:44
Abenberg 2 4 49N14 10E57 -0:43:48
Abensberg 2 4 48N49 11E51 -0:47:24
Abtsgmünd 2 5 48N54 10E00 -0:40:00
Achern 2 3 48N37 8E04 -0:32:16
Achim 2 1 53N00 9E02 -0:36:08
Achterwehr 2 1 54N19 9E57 -0:39:48
Adelebsen 2 1 51N34 9E45 -0:39:00
Adelsheim 2 5 49N24 9E23 -0:37:32
Adelzhausen 2 4 48N21 11E08 -0:44:32
Adenau 2 6 50N23 6E55 -0:27:40
Adendorf 2 1 53N17 10E26 -0:41:44
Adenstedt 2 1 52N15 10E10 -0:40:40
Adorf 1 2 50N19 12E15 -0:49:00
Aerzen 2 1 52N03 9E16 -0:37:04
Afferde 2 1 52N06 9E25 -0:37:40
Afferde 2 1 51N34 7E39 -0:30:36
Affing 2 4 48N27 10E58 -0:43:52
Aglasterhausen 2
3 49N21 8E59 -0:35:56
Aham 2 4 48N32 12E28 -0:49:52
Ahaus 2 1 52N04 7E00 -0:28:00
Ahlbeck 1 2 53N40 14E11 -0:56:44
Ahlem 2 1 52N23 9E40 -0:38:40
Ahlen 2 1 51N46 7E53 -0:31:32
Ahlenberg 2 1 51N25 7E28 -0:29:52
Ahlhorn 2 1 52N54 8E14 -0:32:56
Ahlsdorf 1 2 51N32 11E28 -0:45:52
Ahrensbök 2 1 54N00 10E34 -0:42:16
Ahrensburg 2 1 53N40 10E14 -0:40:56
Ahrensdorf 1 2 52N10 14E05 -0:56:20
Ahrensdorf 1 2 52N19 13E12 -0:52:48
Ahrensfelde 1 2 52N35 13E35 -0:54:20
Aich 2 4 48N25 12E24 -0:49:36
Aichach 2 4 48N28 11E08 -0:44:32
Aicha vorm Wald 2
4 48N41 13E18 -0:53:12
Aichstetten 2 5 47N54 10E04 -0:40:16
Aidenbach 2 4 48N34 13E06 -0:52:24
Ailingen 2 5 47N41 9E29 -0:37:56
Ainring 2 4 47N48 12E56 -0:51:44
Aising 2 4 47N49 12E06 -0:48:24
Aislingen 2 4 48N30 10E27 -0:41:48
Aiterhofen 2 4 48N51 12E37 -0:50:28
Aitrach 2 5 47N56 10E05 -0:40:20
Aix-La-Chapelle → Aachen 2
7 50N47 6E05 -0:24:20
Aken 1 2 51N51 12E02 -0:48:08
Albachten 2 1 51N55 7E31 -0:30:04
Albbruck 2 3 47N35 8E07 -0:32:28
Albersloh 2 1 51N52 7E43 -0:30:52
Albertshof 1 2 52N42 13E40 -0:54:40
Alburg 2 4 48N52 12E32 -0:50:08
Aldenhoven 2 7 50N53 6E16 -0:25:04
Aldersbach 2 4 48N36 13E05 -0:52:20
Aldingen 2 3 48N05 8E41 -0:34:44
Alf 2 6 50N03 7E07 -0:28:28
Alfeld 2 1 51N59 9E50 -0:39:20
Alfeld 2 4 49N26 11E33 -0:46:12
Algermissen 2 1 52N15 9E58 -0:39:52
Alken 2 6 50N15 7E26 -0:29:44
Allagen 2 1 51N28 8E14 -0:32:56
Allendorf 2 1 51N02 8E38 -0:34:32
Allensbach 2 3 47N43 9E03 -0:36:12
Allersberg 2 4 49N15 11E15 -0:45:00
Allershausen 2 4 48N26 11E36 -0:46:24
Allmendingen 2 5 48N20 9E43 -0:38:52
Allstedt 1 2 51N24 11E23 -0:45:32
Alme 2 1 51N28 8E37 -0:34:28
Alpen 2 7 51N35 6E30 -0:26:00
Alpirsbach 2 3 48N21 8E23 -0:33:32
Alsdorf 2 7 50N53 6E10 -0:24:40
Alsenz 2 6 49N43 7E49 -0:31:16
Alsfeld 2 1 50N45 9E16 -0:37:04
Alsleben 1 2 51N42 11E41 -0:46:44
Alstätte 2 1 52N08 6E55 -0:27:40
Alswede 2 1 52N20 8E33 -0:34:12
Altastenberg 2 1 51N11 8E28 -0:33:52
Alt Buchhorst 1 2 52N26 13E51 -0:55:24
Altdöbern 1 2 51N39 14E02 -0:56:08
Altdorf 2 4 48N34 12E07 -0:48:28
Altdorf bei Nürnberg 2
4 49N23 11E21 -0:45:24
Altefähr 1 2 54N20 13E07 -0:52:28
Alteglofsheim 2 4 48N55 12E12 -0:48:48
Alte Grund 1 2 52N28 13E47 -0:55:08
Altena 2 1 51N17 7E40 -0:30:40
Altenahr 2 6 50N31 6E59 -0:27:56
Altenau 2 1 51N48 10E26 -0:41:44
Altenbeken 2 1 51N46 8E56 -0:35:44
Altenberg 1 2 50N46 13E45 -0:55:00
Altenberge 2 1 52N03 7E27 -0:29:48
Altenbruch 2 1 53N49 8E46 -0:35:04
Altenbüren 2 1 51N23 8E30 -0:34:00
Altenburg 1 2 50N59 12E26 -0:49:44
Altendorf 2 1 51N29 7E40 -0:30:40
Altendorf-Ulfkotte 2
1 51N38 7E00 -0:28:00
Altenerding 2 4 48N18 11E55 -0:47:40
Altenesch 2 1 53N08 8E37 -0:34:28
Altenhagen 1 2 53N45 13E06 -0:52:24
Altenhagen 2 1 52N03 8E38 -0:34:32
Altenhof 1 2 52N55 13E43 -0:54:52
Altenholz 2 1 54N24 10E07 -0:40:28
Altenkirchen 1 2 54N38 13E20 -0:53:20
Altenkirchen (Westerwald) 2
1 50N41 7E38 -0:30:32
Altenkrempe 2 1 54N08 10E49 -0:43:16
Altenkunstadt 2 4 50N07 11E14 -0:44:56
Altenmarkt 2 4 48N00 12E32 -0:50:08
Altenmarkt an der Alz 2
4 48N00 12E32 -0:50:08
Altenoythe 2 1 53N02 7E52 -0:31:28
Altenpleen 1 2 54N21 12E57 -0:51:48
Altenstadt an der Waldnaab 2
4 49N48 12E10 -0:48:40
Altensteig 2 3 48N35 8E37 -0:34:28
Altentreptow 1 2 53N42 13E14 -0:52:56
Altenvoerde 2 1 51N18 7E22 -0:29:28
Altenwalde 2 1 53N49 8E40 -0:34:40
Altenweddingen 1
2 52N00 11E31 -0:46:04
Altfraunhofen 2 4 48N27 12E10 -0:48:40
Altfriedland 1 2 52N38 14E12 -0:56:48
Altglashütten 2 3 47N51 8E06 -0:32:24
Altgruland 2 1 51N27 7E41 -0:30:44
Alt-Hartmannsdorf 1
2 52N21 13E50 -0:55:20
Alt Käbelich 1 2 53N29 13E29 -0:53:56
Altlandsberg 1 2 52N33 13E43 -0:54:52
Altlangerwisch 1
2 52N19 13E04 -0:52:16
Altlewin 1 2 52N42 14E16 -0:57:04
Altlüdersdorf 1 2 53N02 13E11 -0:52:44
Altlünen 2 1 51N38 7E31 -0:30:04
Altmannstein 2 4 48N54 11E39 -0:46:36
Altmittweida 1 2 50N58 12E57 -0:51:48
Altomünster 2 4 48N23 11E15 -0:45:00
Altona 2 1 53N34 9E48 -0:39:12
Altötting 2 4 48N13 12E40 -0:50:40
Altruppin 1 2 52N56 12E50 -0:51:20
Altshausen 2 5 47N56 9E32 -0:38:08
Alt Stahnsdorf 1
2 52N17 13E53 -0:55:32
Alt Töplitz 1 2 52N26 12E55 -0:51:40
Altusried 2 4 47N48 10E13 -0:40:52
Alzenau 2 4 50N05 9E04 -0:36:16
Alzey 2 6 49N45 8E07 -0:32:28
Amberg 2 4 49N27 11E52 -0:47:28
Amelinghausen 2 1 53N08 10E13 -0:40:52
Amelsbüren 2 1 51N53 7E37 -0:30:28
Amerang 2 4 48N00 12E18 -0:49:12
Amern 2 7 51N14 6E15 -0:25:00
Ammeloe 2 1 52N05 6E47 -0:27:08
Ammerthal 2 4 49N26 11E45 -0:47:00
Amöneburg 2 1 50N48 8E55 -0:35:40
Amorbach 2 4 49N39 9E13 -0:36:52
Ampermoching 2 4 48N18 11E29 -0:45:56
Ampfing 2 4 48N16 12E25 -0:49:40
Andernach 2 6 50N26 7E24 -0:29:36
Anderten 2 1 52N21 9E51 -0:39:24
Andisleben 1 2 51N04 10E56 -0:43:44
Angermund 2 1 51N20 6E47 -0:27:08
Angermünde 1 2 53N01 14E00 -0:56:00
Angern 1 2 52N21 11E44 -0:46:56
Anholt 2 1 51N52 6E27 -0:25:48
Anklam 1 2 53N51 13E41 -0:54:44
Ankum 2 1 52N32 7E52 -0:31:28
Annaberg-Buchholz 1
2 50N35 13E00 -0:52:00
Annaburg 1 2 51N44 13E03 -0:52:12
Annahütte 1 2 51N34 13E53 -0:55:32
Annweiler am Trifels 2
6 49N12 7E58 -0:31:52
Anrath 2 7 51N17 6E28 -0:25:52
Anröchte 2 1 51N33 8E19 -0:33:16
Ansbach 2 4 49N17 10E34 -0:42:16
Anschlag 2 1 51N10 7E29 -0:29:56
Anspach 2 1 50N17 8E29 -0:33:56
Apen 2 1 53N13 7E48 -0:31:12
Apensen 2 1 53N26 9E37 -0:38:28
Apolda 1 2 51N01 11E31 -0:46:04
Appelhülsen 2 1 51N54 7E25 -0:29:40
Appen 2 1 53N40 9E44 -0:38:56
Appenweier 2 3 48N32 7E58 -0:31:52
Archshofen 2 5 49N27 10E04 -0:40:16
Ardey 2 1 51N28 7E43 -0:30:52
Arenberg 2 1 50N22 7E39 -0:30:36
Arendsee 1 2 52N53 11E30 -0:46:00
Aresing 2 4 48N32 11E18 -0:45:12
Arnbach 2 4 48N20 11E21 -0:45:24
Arnbruck 2 4 49N08 13E00 -0:52:00
Arneburg 1 2 52N40 12E00 -0:48:00
Arnis 2 1 54N38 9E56 -0:39:44
Arnsberg 2 1 51N24 8E03 -0:32:12
Arnsberg 2 4 48N56 11E23 -0:45:32
Arnschwang 2 4 49N16 12E49 -0:51:16
Arnsdorf 1 2 51N05 13E59 -0:55:56
Arnstadt 1 2 50N50 10E57 -0:43:48
Arnstein 2 4 49N58 9E58 -0:39:52
Arnstorf 2 4 48N34 12E49 -0:51:16
Arolsen 2 1 51N23 9E01 -0:36:04
Arsbeck 2 7 51N08 6E12 -0:24:48
Artern 1 2 51N22 11E17 -0:45:08
Arth 2 4 48N35 12E04 -0:48:16
Artlenburg 2 1 53N22 10E29 -0:41:56
Arzfeld 2 6 50N05 6E16 -0:25:04
Asbeck 2 1 51N21 7E18 -0:29:12
Asberg 2 7 51N26 6E40 -0:26:40
Asch 2 4 47N57 10E49 -0:43:16
Aschaffenburg 2 4 49N59 9E09 -0:36:36
Ascheberg 2 1 54N08 10E20 -0:41:20
Ascheberg 2 1 51N47 7E37 -0:30:28
Aschendorf 2 1 53N04 7E22 -0:29:28
Aschersleben 1 2 51N45 11E27 -0:45:48
Asendorf 2 1 52N46 9E00 -0:36:00
Asperg 2 5 48N54 9E07 -0:36:28
Assel 2 1 53N41 9E25 -0:37:40
Asslar 2 1 50N35 8E28 -0:33:52
Assling 2 4 48N00 12E00 -0:48:00
Assmannshausen 2
1 49N59 7E52 -0:31:28
Athenstedt 1 2 51N56 10E55 -0:43:40
Atrop 2 7 51N24 6E43 -0:26:52
Attaching 2 4 48N23 11E46 -0:47:04
Attel 2 4 48N01 12E01 -0:48:04
Attendorn 2 1 51N07 7E54 -0:31:36
Attenhausen 2 4 47N59 10E20 -0:41:20
Attenkirchen 2 4 48N30 11E46 -0:47:04
Atzendorf 1 2 51N55 11E35 -0:46:20
Aub 2 4 49N33 10E04 -0:40:16
Aue 1 2 50N35 12E42 -0:50:48
Auerbach 1 2 50N41 12E54 -0:51:36
Auerbach 1 2 50N30 12E23 -0:49:32
Auerbach 2 4 48N48 13E06 -0:52:24
Auerbach in der Oberpfalz 2
4 49N42 11E38 -0:46:32
Auerswalde 1 2 50N54 12E55 -0:51:40
Auf dem Kreinberge 2
1 51N27 7E36 -0:30:24
Aufham 2 4 48N28 11E37 -0:46:28
Aufsess 2 4 49N54 11E13 -0:44:52
Augsburg 2 4 48N23 10E53 -0:43:32
Augustdorf 2 1 51N53 8E43 -0:34:52
Augustusburg 1 2 50N49 13E06 -0:52:24
Au in der Hallertau 2
4 48N33 11E45 -0:47:00
Aulendorf 2 5 47N57 9E38 -0:38:32
Auma 1 2 50N42 11E54 -0:47:36
Aumühle 2 1 53N31 10E19 -0:41:16
Aunkirchen 2 4 48N36 13E08 -0:52:32
Aurach 2 4 49N15 10E25 -0:41:40
Aurich 2 1 53N28 7E29 -0:29:56
Avenwedde 2 1 51N55 8E27 -0:33:48
Aying 2 4 47N58 11E46 -0:47:04
Baak 2 1 51N25 7E10 -0:28:40
Baal 2 7 51N02 6E17 -0:25:08
Babenhausen 2 4 48N09 10E15 -0:41:00
Babenhausen 2 1 49N57 8E56 -0:35:44
Bacharach 2 6 50N04 7E46 -0:31:04
Bachl 2 4 48N49 11E57 -0:47:48
Backnang 2 5 48N56 9E25 -0:37:40
Bad Abbach 2 4 48N56 12E03 -0:48:12
Bad Aibling 2 4 47N52 12E00 -0:48:00
Bad Bentheim 2 1 52N19 7E10 -0:28:40
Bad Bergzabern 2
6 49N07 8E00 -0:32:00
Bad Berka 1 2 50N54 11E17 -0:45:08
Bad Bertrich 2 6 50N04 7E02 -0:28:08
Bad Bibra 1 2 51N12 11E35 -0:46:20
Bad Blankenburg 1
2 50N41 11E16 -0:45:04
Bad Bramstedt 2 1 53N55 9E53 -0:39:32
Bad Breisig 2 6 50N31 7E18 -0:29:12
Bad Buchau 2 5 48N03 9E36 -0:38:24
Bad Cannstatt 5 48N48 9E12 -0:36:48
Bad Ditzenbach 2
5 48N35 9E41 -0:38:44
Bad Doberan 1 2 54N06 11E53 -0:47:32
Bad Dreibergen 2
1 53N12 8E01 -0:32:04
Bad Driburg 2 1 51N44 9E01 -0:36:04
Bad Düben 1 2 51N36 12E34 -0:50:16
Bad Dürkheim 2 6 49N28 8E10 -0:32:40
Bad Dürrenberg 1
2 51N18 12E04 -0:48:16
Bad Dürrheim 2 3 48N01 8E32 -0:34:08
Bad Eilsen 2 1 52N14 9E06 -0:36:24
Badel 1 2 52N44 11E19 -0:45:16
Bad Elster 1 2 50N17 12E14 -0:48:56
Bad Ems 2 1 50N20 7E43 -0:30:52
Baden 2 1 53N00 9E04 -0:36:16
Baden-Baden 2 3 48N46 8E14 -0:32:56
Badenweiler 2 3 47N48 7E40 -0:30:40
Badersleben 1 2 51N59 10E53 -0:43:32
Bad Essen 2 1 52N19 8E20 -0:33:20
Bad Frankenhausen 1
2 51N21 11E06 -0:44:24
Bad Freienwalde 1
2 52N47 14E01 -0:56:04
Bad Friedrichshall 2
5 49N14 9E11 -0:36:44
Bad Gandersheim 2
1 51N52 10E01 -0:40:04
Bad Godesberg 2 7 50N41 7E10 -0:28:40
Bad Gottleuba 1 2 50N51 13E56 -0:55:44
Bad Griesbach 2 3 48N27 8E14 -0:32:56
Bad Grund 2 1 51N48 10E14 -0:40:56
Bad Harzburg 2 1 51N53 10E33 -0:42:12
Bad Heilbrunn 2 4 47N45 11E28 -0:45:52
Bad Helmstedt 2 1 52N14 11E03 -0:44:12
Bad Hersfeld 2 1 50N52 9E42 -0:38:48
Bad Homburg vor der Höhe 2
1 50N13 8E37 -0:34:28
Bad Honnef am Rhein 2
1 50N39 7E13 -0:28:52
Bad Hönningen 2 1 50N31 7E19 -0:29:16
Bad Kissingen 2 4 50N12 10E04 -0:40:16
Bad Kleinen 1 2 53N46 11E28 -0:45:52
Bad Klosterlausnitz 1
2 50N55 11E52 -0:47:28
Bad Kohlgrub 2 4 47N40 11E03 -0:44:12
Bad König 2 1 49N45 9E01 -0:36:04
Bad Kösen 1 2 51N08 11E43 -0:46:52
Bad Köstritz 1 2 50N56 12E01 -0:48:04
Bad Kreuznach 2 6 49N52 7E51 -0:31:24
Bad Krozingen 2 3 47N55 7E43 -0:30:52
Bad Langensalza 1
2 51N06 10E38 -0:42:32
Bad Lauchstädt 1
2 51N23 11E52 -0:47:28
Bad Lausick 1 2 51N08 12E38 -0:50:32
Bad Lauterberg (im Harz) 2
1 51N38 10E28 -0:41:52

GERMANY ALEMANIA ALLEMAGNE DEUTSCHLAND

Bad Liebenstein 1 2 50N49 10E21 -0:41:24
Bad Liebenwerda 1 2 51N31 13E23 -0:53:32
Bad Liebenzell 2 5 48N46 8E44 -0:34:56
Bad Lippspringe 2 1 51N46 8E49 -0:35:16
Bad Meinberg 2 1 51N53 8E58 -0:35:52
Bad Mergentheim 2 5 49N30 9E46 -0:39:04
Bad Mingolsheim 2 3 49N14 8E39 -0:34:36
Bad Mukran 1 2 54N26 13E35 -0:54:20
Bad Münder 2 1 52N12 9E27 -0:37:48
Bad Münster am Stein 2 6 49N49 7E51 -0:31:24
Bad Münstereifel 2 7 50N33 6E46 -0:27:04
Bad Muskau 1 2 51N32 14E43 -0:58:52
Bad Nauheim 2 1 50N22 8E44 -0:34:56
Bad Nenndorf 2 1 52N20 9E22 -0:37:28
Bad Neuenahr-Ahrweiler 2 6 50N33 7E08 -0:28:32
Bad Neustadt an der Saale 2 4 50N19 10E13 -0:40:52
Bad Niedernau 2 5 48N27 8E53 -0:35:32
Bad Oeynhausen 2 1 52N12 8E48 -0:35:12
Bad Oldesloe 2 1 53N48 10E22 -0:41:28
Bad Orb 2 1 50N14 9E20 -0:37:20
Bad Peterstal 2 3 48N26 8E12 -0:32:48
Bad Pyrmont 2 1 51N59 9E15 -0:37:00
Bad Rappenau 2 3 49N14 9E06 -0:36:24
Bad Rehburg 2 1 52N26 9E13 -0:36:52
Bad Reichenhall 2 4 47N43 12E52 -0:51:28
Bad Rippoldsau 2 3 48N26 8E19 -0:33:16
Bad Rothenfelde 2 1 52N06 8E09 -0:32:36
Bad Saarow-Pieskow 1 2 52N17 14E03 -0:56:12
Bad Sachsa 2 1 51N36 10E32 -0:42:08
Bad Salzdetfurth 2 1 52N03 10E01 -0:40:04
Bad Salzig 2 6 50N12 7E38 -0:30:32
Bad Salzschlierf 2 1 50N37 9E29 -0:37:56
Bad Salzuflen 2 1 52N05 8E44 -0:34:56
Bad Salzungen 1 2 50N48 10E13 -0:40:52
Bad Sassendorf 2 1 51N35 8E10 -0:32:40
Bad Schandau 1 2 50N55 14E10 -0:56:40
Bad Schmiedeberg 1 2 51N41 12E44 -0:50:56
Bad Schwalbach 2 1 50N08 8E04 -0:32:16
Bad Schwartau 2 1 53N55 10E40 -0:42:40
Bad Segeberg 2 1 53N56 10E17 -0:41:08
Bad Soden 2 1 50N17 9E22 -0:37:28
Bad Soden 2 1 50N08 8E30 -0:34:00
Bad Sooden-Allendorf 2 1 51N16 9E58 -0:39:52
Bad Steben 2 4 50N22 11E38 -0:46:32
Bad Stuer 1 2 53N22 12E19 -0:49:16
Bad Suderode 1 2 51N44 11E07 -0:44:28
Bad Sulza 1 2 51N05 11E37 -0:46:28
Bad Sülze 1 2 54N06 12E38 -0:50:32
Bad Teinach 2 3 48N41 8E41 -0:34:44
Bad Tennstedt 1 2 51N09 10E50 -0:43:20
Bad Tölz 2 4 47N46 11E34 -0:46:16
Bad Vilbel 2 1 50N12 8E42 -0:34:48
Bad Waldsee 2 5 47N55 9E45 -0:39:00
Bad Westernkotten 2 1 51N38 8E21 -0:33:24
Bad Wiessee 2 4 47N43 11E43 -0:46:52
Bad Wildungen 2 1 51N07 9E07 -0:36:28
Bad Wilsnack 1 2 52N57 11E57 -0:47:48
Bad Wimpfen 2 5 49N14 9E09 -0:36:36
Bad Windsheim 2 4 49N31 10E25 -0:41:40
Bad Wörishofen 2 4 48N00 10E36 -0:42:24
Bad Wurzach 2 5 47N54 9E54 -0:39:36
Baerl 2 7 51N29 6E41 -0:26:44
Baesweiler 2 7 50N54 6E11 -0:24:44
Bagband 2 1 53N21 7E36 -0:30:24
Bahrdorf 2 1 52N23 11E00 -0:44:00
Baienfurt 2 5 47N49 9E38 -0:38:32
Baiersbronn 2 3 48N30 8E22 -0:33:28
Baiersdorf 2 4 49N39 11E01 -0:44:04
Bakum 2 1 52N45 8E11 -0:32:44
Balbini 2 4 49N18 12E26 -0:49:44
Balderschwang 2 4 47N28 10E06 -0:40:24
Balduinstein 2 1 50N20 7E58 -0:31:52
Balingen 2 5 48N16 8E51 -0:35:24
Ballenstedt 1 2 51N43 11E14 -0:44:56
Balve 2 1 51N20 7E51 -0:31:24
Bamberg 2 4 49N53 10E53 -0:43:32
Bannesdorf 2 1 54N28 11E13 -0:44:52
Bannewitz 1 2 51N00 13E43 -0:54:52
Banteln 2 1 52N04 9E44 -0:38:56
Barbis 2 1 51N37 10E25 -0:41:40
Barby 1 2 51N58 11E53 -0:47:32
Bardowick 2 1 53N18 10E23 -0:41:32
Barenburg 2 1 52N37 8E47 -0:35:08
Bärenklau 1 2 51N56 14E34 -0:58:16
Bärenstein 1 2 50N30 13E02 -0:52:08
Bärenstein 1 2 50N48 13E47 -0:55:08
Bargteheide 2 1 53N44 10E16 -0:41:04
Barkelsby 2 1 54N30 9E50 -0:39:20
Barleben 1 2 52N12 11E37 -0:46:28
Barmstedt 2 1 53N47 9E46 -0:39:04
Bärnau 2 4 49N49 12E26 -0:49:44
Barneberg 1 2 52N08 11E03 -0:44:12
Barnstorf 2 1 52N42 8E30 -0:34:00
Barntrup 2 1 51N59 9E06 -0:36:24
Barrien 2 1 52N56 8E49 -0:35:16
Barsinghausen 2 1 52N18 9E27 -0:37:48
Barssel 2 1 53N10 7E44 -0:30:56
Bartenstein 2 5 49N21 9E53 -0:39:32
Barth 1 2 54N22 12E43 -0:50:52
Baruth 1 2 52N03 13E30 -0:54:00
Barver 2 1 52N37 8E35 -0:34:20
Basdahl 2 1 53N26 8E59 -0:35:56
Basdorf 1 2 52N44 13E26 -0:53:44
Basdorf 2 1 51N12 8E58 -0:35:52
Bassen 2 1 53N04 9E04 -0:36:16
Bassenheim 2 6 50N21 7E27 -0:29:48
Bassum 2 1 52N51 8E43 -0:34:52
Battenberg 2 1 51N01 8E38 -0:34:32
Bauernschaft 2 7 51N34 6E33 -0:26:12
Baumberg 2 1 51N07 6E54 -0:27:36
Baumholder 2 6 49N37 7E20 -0:29:20
Baunach 2 4 49N59 10E50 -0:43:20
Baunatal 2 1 51N16 9E25 -0:37:40
Bausendorf 2 6 50N01 6E59 -0:27:56
Bausenhagen 2 1 51N31 7E48 -0:31:12
Bautzen 1 2 51N11 14E26 -0:57:44
Bayerisch Eisenstein 2 4 49N07 13E12 -0:52:48
Bayreuth 2 4 49N57 11E35 -0:46:20
Bayrischzell 2 4 47N40 12E00 -0:48:00
Bebenhausen 2 5 48N33 9E03 -0:36:12
Bebertal 1 2 52N15 11E18 -0:45:12
Bebra 2 1 50N58 9E47 -0:39:08
Bechhofen 2 4 49N09 10E33 -0:42:12
Becke 2 1 51N24 7E47 -0:31:08
Beckum 2 1 51N45 8E02 -0:32:08
Bedburdyck 2 7 51N07 6E34 -0:26:16
Bedburg 2 7 50N59 6E35 -0:26:20
Bedburg 2 1 51N03 8E23 -0:33:32
Bedburg-Hau 2 7 51N45 6E10 -0:24:40
Bederkesa 2 1 53N38 8E50 -0:35:20
Beedenbostel 2 1 52N38 10E16 -0:41:04
Beelen 2 1 51N55 8E07 -0:32:28
Beelitz 1 2 52N14 12E58 -0:51:52
Beendorf 1 2 52N14 11E05 -0:44:20
Beerfelden 2 1 49N34 8E58 -0:35:52
Beesenlaublingen 1 2 51N42 11E41 -0:46:44
Beeskow 1 2 52N10 14E14 -0:56:56
Beesten 2 1 52N26 7E30 -0:30:00
Beetzendorf 1 2 52N42 11E05 -0:44:20
Behringen 1 2 51N01 10E31 -0:42:04
Behringen 2 1 53N07 9E58 -0:39:52
Beierfeld 1 2 50N33 12E47 -0:51:08
Beiersdorf 1 2 52N42 13E47 -0:55:08
Beilngries 2 4 49N02 11E29 -0:45:56
Beilrode 1 2 51N35 13E03 -0:52:12
Beilstein 2 5 49N02 9E18 -0:37:12
Beilstein 2 1 50N36 8E14 -0:32:56
Beilstein 2 6 50N06 7E14 -0:28:56
Belecke 2 1 51N29 8E20 -0:33:20
Belgern 1 2 51N29 13E07 -0:52:28
Bellheim 2 6 49N11 8E16 -0:33:04
Bellnhausen 2 1 50N42 8E43 -0:34:52
Belzig 1 2 52N08 12E35 -0:50:20
Bendorf 2 1 50N25 7E34 -0:30:16
Benediktbeuern 2 4 47N42 11E25 -0:45:40
Benken 1 2 52N10 12E28 -0:49:52
Benndorf 1 2 51N34 11E29 -0:45:56
Benneckenstein 1 2 51N40 10E45 -0:43:00
Bennigsen 2 1 52N14 9E40 -0:38:40
Bennstedt 1 2 51N29 11E49 -0:47:16
Bensberg 2 1 50N58 7E09 -0:28:36
Bensdorf 1 2 52N24 12E20 -0:49:20
Bensersiel 2 1 53N40 7E34 -0:30:16
Benshausen 1 2 50N38 10E35 -0:42:20
Bensheim 2 1 49N41 8E37 -0:34:28
Bentheim 2 1 52N17 7E10 -0:28:40
Beratzhausen 2 4 49N06 11E48 -0:47:12
Berau 2 3 47N42 8E15 -0:33:00
Berching 2 4 49N07 11E27 -0:45:48
Berchtesgaden 2 4 47N38 13E01 -0:52:04
Berchum 2 1 51N23 7E32 -0:30:08
Berg 2 4 47N58 11E21 -0:45:24
Berga 1 2 50N45 12E10 -0:48:40
Berga 1 2 51N27 11E00 -0:44:00
Berge 1 2 53N15 11E50 -0:47:20
Berge 2 1 52N37 7E44 -0:30:56
Berge 2 1 51N21 7E22 -0:29:28
Bergen 2 4 47N48 12E35 -0:50:20
Bergen 2 1 52N53 10E58 -0:43:52
Bergen 2 1 52N48 9E58 -0:39:52
Bergen (auf Rügen) 1 2 54N25 13E26 -0:53:44
Bergerhof 2 1 51N12 7E21 -0:29:24
Bergfelde 1 2 52N40 13E19 -0:53:16
Berggiesshübel 1 2 50N52 13E57 -0:55:48
Bergham 2 4 49N12 12E17 -0:49:08
Berghausen 2 1 51N18 7E17 -0:29:08
Berghausen 2 1 51N07 6E55 -0:27:40
Bergheim 2 7 50N55 6E38 -0:26:32
Bergholz-Rehbrücke 1 2 52N20 13E05 -0:52:20
Bergisch-Born 2 1 51N09 7E15 -0:29:00
Bergisch Gladbach 2 1 50N59 7E07 -0:28:28
Bergkamen 2 1 51N38 7E38 -0:30:32
Bergneustadt 2 1 51N01 7E39 -0:30:36
Bergrheinfeld 2 4 50N00 10E10 -0:40:40
Bergtheim 2 4 49N54 10E04 -0:40:16
Bergwitz 1 2 51N48 12E35 -0:50:20
Beringhausen 2 1 51N24 8E46 -0:35:04
Berkheim 2 5 48N02 10E04 -0:40:16
Berlin 2 52N30 13E22 -0:53:28
Berlin (Ost) 1 2 52N32 13E25 -0:53:40
Berlin (West) 2 2 52N29 13E21 -0:53:24
Berlin-Schönberg 2 2 52N28 13E22 -0:53:28
Berlinchen 1 2 53N13 12E34 -0:50:16
Bernau am Chiemsee 2 4 47N48 12E22 -0:49:28
Bernau bei Berlin 1 2 52N40 13E35 -0:54:20
Bernbeuren 2 4 47N44 10E46 -0:43:04
Bernburg 1 2 51N48 11E44 -0:46:56
Berne 2 1 53N11 8E29 -0:33:56
Berneburg 2 1 51N04 9E53 -0:39:32
Bernkastel-Kues 2 6 49N55 7E04 -0:28:16
Bernried 2 4 47N52 11E17 -0:45:08
Bernried 2 4 49N19 12E33 -0:50:12
Bernrieth 2 4 49N34 12E17 -0:49:08
Bernsbach 1 2 50N34 12E46 -0:51:04
Bernsdorf 1 2 51N22 14E04 -0:56:16
Bernsfelden 2 5 49N34 9E53 -0:39:32
Bernstadt 1 2 51N03 14E50 -0:59:20
Bernstein 2 4 49N50 12E09 -0:48:36
Berolzheim 2 5 49N28 9E32 -0:38:08
Bersenbrück 2 1 52N33 7E56 -0:31:44
Berthelsdorf 1 2 51N05 14E13 -0:56:52
Bertkow 1 2 52N43 11E54 -0:47:36
Bertlich 2 1 51N37 7E04 -0:28:16
Besenfeld 2 3 48N35 8E25 -0:33:40
Besigheim 2 5 49N00 9E08 -0:36:32
Besse 2 1 51N13 9E23 -0:37:32
Besten 2 1 51N39 6E54 -0:27:36
Bestensee 1 2 52N15 13E37 -0:54:28
Betzdorf 2 1 50N47 7E53 -0:31:32
Betzenstein 2 4 49N41 11E25 -0:45:40
Beucha 1 2 51N19 12E34 -0:50:16
Beuel 2 1 50N38 7E14 -0:28:56
Beuron 2 3 48N03 8E58 -0:35:52
Bevensen 2 1 53N05 10E34 -0:42:16
Bevern 2 1 51N51 9E29 -0:37:56
Beverstedt 2 1 53N26 8E49 -0:35:16
Beverungen 2 1 51N39 9E22 -0:37:28
Biberach 2 3 48N20 8E02 -0:32:08
Biberach an der Riss 2 5 48N06 9E47 -0:39:08
Biberbach 2 4 48N31 10E48 -0:43:12
Biblis 2 1 49N41 8E27 -0:33:48
Bichl 2 4 47N43 11E24 -0:45:36
Bickenbach 2 1 49N45 8E37 -0:34:28
Biebelried 2 4 49N46 10E04 -0:40:16
Bieber 2 1 50N09 9E19 -0:37:16
Biedenkopf 2 1 50N55 8E32 -0:34:08
Biederitz 1 2 52N09 11E43 -0:46:52
Bielefeld 2 1 52N01 8E31 -0:34:04
Biemenhorst 2 1 51N49 6E36 -0:26:24
Bienenbüttel 2 1 53N08 10E29 -0:41:56
Biere 1 2 51N58 11E39 -0:46:36
Biesenthal 1 2 52N46 13E37 -0:54:28
Bietigheim 2 3 48N54 8E14 -0:32:56
Bietigheim 2 5 48N58 9E07 -0:36:28
Bigge 2 1 51N21 8E28 -0:33:52
Billerbeck 2 1 51N59 7E17 -0:29:08
Billigheim 2 3 49N21 9E15 -0:37:00
Billmerich 2 1 51N30 7E47 -0:31:08
Bilshausen 2 1 51N37 10E10 -0:40:40
Binau 2 3 49N22 9E04 -0:36:16
Bindlach 2 4 49N59 11E37 -0:46:28
Bindow 1 2 52N17 13E45 -0:55:00
Bingen 2 6 49N57 7E54 -0:31:36
Bingerbrück 2 6 49N58 7E53 -0:31:32
Binsheim 2 7 51N31 6E42 -0:26:48
Binz 1 2 54N24 13E36 -0:54:24
Birkenfeld 2 3 48N52 8E38 -0:34:32
Birkenfeld 2 4 49N51 9E42 -0:38:48
Birkenfeld 2 6 49N39 7E10 -0:28:40
Birkenwerder bei Berlin 1 2 52N41 13E16 -0:53:04
Birkesdorf 2 7 50N49 6E28 -0:25:52
Birkholz 1 2 52N38 13E34 -0:54:16
Birstein 2 1 50N21 9E19 -0:37:16
Birten 2 7 51N38 6E29 -0:25:56
Bischofsheim 2 4 50N24 10E01 -0:40:04
Bischofsheim 2 1 49N59 8E22 -0:33:28
Bischofswerda 1 2 51N07 14E10 -0:56:40
Bischofswiesen 2 4 47N39 12E57 -0:51:48
Bisingen 2 5 48N18 8E55 -0:35:40
Bislich 2 1 51N41 6E29 -0:25:56
Bismark 1 2 52N39 11E32 -0:46:08
Bispingen 2 1 53N05 10E00 -0:40:00
Bissendorf 2 1 52N31 9E45 -0:39:00
Bissingen 2 4 48N43 10E37 -0:42:28
Bisten 2 6 49N15 6E42 -0:26:48
Bitburg 2 6 49N58 6E31 -0:26:04
Bitterfeld 1 2 51N37 12E20 -0:49:20
Blaichach 2 4 47N34 10E15 -0:41:00
Blankenberg 2 1 50N45 7E22 -0:29:28
Blankenburg 1 2 51N48 10E58 -0:43:52
Blankenfelde 1 2 52N20 13E23 -0:53:32
Blankenhain 1 2 50N51 11E21 -0:45:24
Blankenheim 1 2 51N31 11E25 -0:45:40
Blankenheim 2 7 50N26 6E39 -0:26:36
Blankensee 1 2 52N14 13E08 -0:52:32
Blankenstein 2 1 51N24 7E14 -0:28:56
Blasheim 2 1 52N18 8E34 -0:34:16
Blatzheim 2 7 50N51 6E38 -0:26:32
Blaubeuren 2 5 48N24 9E47 -0:39:08
Blaufelden 2 5 49N18 9E58 -0:39:52
Bleckede 2 1 53N17 10E44 -0:42:56
Bleibach 2 3 48N07 8E01 -0:32:04
Bleicherode 1 2 51N26 10E34 -0:42:16
Bleidenstadt 2 1 50N08 8E08 -0:32:32
Blekendorf 2 1 54N16 10E38 -0:42:32
Blexen 2 1 53N32 8E32 -0:34:08
Bliersheim 2 7 51N23 6E43 -0:26:52

Place		Lat	Long	Time
Blieskastel 2	6	49N14	7E16	-0:29:04
Blomberg 2	1	51N56	9E05	-0:36:20
Blumberg 1	2	52N36	13E37	-0:54:28
Blumberg 2	3	47N50	8E31	-0:34:04
Bobbau 1	2	51N41	12E16	-0:49:04
Böbingen 2	5	48N49	9E54	-0:39:36
Bobingen 2	4	48N16	10E50	-0:43:20
Bobitz 1	2	53N47	11E20	-0:45:20
Böblingen 2	5	48N41	9E01	-0:36:04
Bocholt 2	1	51N50	6E36	-0:26:24
Bochum 2	1	51N28	7E13	-0:28:52
Bockel 2	1	53N12	9E17	-0:37:08
Bockenem 2	1	52N00	10E07	-0:40:28
Bockhorn 2	1	53N23	8E01	-0:32:04
Bockum 2	1	51N20	6E44	-0:26:56
Bockum-Hövel 2	1	51N42	7E46	-0:31:04
Bodenburg 2	1	52N01	10E01	-0:40:04
Bodenfelde 2	1	51N38	9E33	-0:38:12
Bodenheim 2	6	49N56	8E18	-0:33:12
Bodenmais 2	4	49N04	13E06	-0:52:24
Bodenteich 2	1	52N50	10E41	-0:42:44
Bodenwerder 2	1	51N59	9E31	-0:38:04
Bodenwöhr 2	4	49N16	12E19	-0:49:16
Bodstedt 1	2	54N22	12E37	-0:50:28
Boffzen 2	1	51N45	9E23	-0:37:32
Bogel 2	1	50N11	7E48	-0:31:12
Bogen 2	4	48N55	12E43	-0:50:52
Boges 2	1	50N11	7E48	-0:31:12
Böhlen 1	2	51N12	12E23	-0:49:32
Böhlitz-Ehrenberg 1	2	51N21	12E17	-0:49:08
Böhmenkirch 2	5	48N41	9E55	-0:39:40
Bohmte 2	1	52N22	8E19	-0:33:16
Bohsdorf 1	2	51N38	14E32	-0:58:08
Boitzenburg 1	2	53N15	13E37	-0:54:28
Boizenburg 1	2	53N22	10E43	-0:42:52
Bokel 2	1	53N23	8E46	-0:35:04
Böklund 2	1	54N36	9E34	-0:38:16
Boldekow 1	2	53N43	13E35	-0:54:20
Bölkenbusch 2	1	51N21	7E06	-0:28:24
Boll 2	5	48N38	9E37	-0:38:28
Bollendorf 2	6	49N51	6E22	-0:25:28
Bollensdorf 1	2	52N31	13E43	-0:54:52
Bollwerk 2	1	51N10	7E35	-0:30:20
Bömenzien 1	2	52N59	11E31	-0:46:04
Bomlitz 2	1	52N54	9E37	-0:38:28
Bommerholz 2	1	51N23	7E18	-0:29:12
Bondorf 2	5	48N31	8E49	-0:35:16
Bönen 2	1	51N36	7E44	-0:30:56
Bonn 2	7	50N44	7E05	-0:28:20
Bonndorf im Schwarzwald 2	3	47N49	8E20	-0:33:20
Bönninghardt 2	7	51N35	6E28	-0:25:52
Boock 1	2	53N29	14E15	-0:57:00
Boossen 1	2	52N22	14E29	-0:57:56
Bopfingen 2	5	48N51	10E21	-0:41:24
Boppard 2	6	50N14	7E35	-0:30:20
Borchen 2	1	51N39	8E44	-0:34:56
Bordesholm 2	1	54N11	10E01	-0:40:04
Borgentreich 2	1	51N34	9E14	-0:36:56
Börger 2	1	52N54	7E32	-0:30:08
Borghorst 2	1	52N07	7E23	-0:29:32
Borgsdorf 1	2	52N42	13E14	-0:52:56
Bork 2	1	51N40	7E30	-0:30:00
Borken 2	1	51N03	9E16	-0:37:04
Borken 2	1	51N51	6E51	-0:27:24
Borkenwirthe 2	1	51N53	6E50	-0:27:20
Borkum 2	1	53N35	6E40	-0:26:40
Born 1	2	54N23	12E31	-0:50:04
Born 1	2	52N22	11E28	-0:45:52
Born 1	2	45N22	12E31	-0:50:04
Borna 1	2	51N19	13E11	-0:52:44
Borna 1	2	51N07	12E30	-0:50:00
Bornheim 2	7	50N46	6E59	-0:27:56
Bornholte 2	1	51N52	8E29	-0:33:56
Bornhöved 2	1	54N04	10E16	-0:41:04
Börnicke 1	2	52N41	12E56	-0:51:44
Börnicke 1	2	52N40	13E38	-0:54:32
Bornsdorf 1	2	51N46	13E41	-0:54:44
Börry 2	1	52N01	9E27	-0:37:48
Borschemich 2	7	51N04	6E25	-0:25:40
Borsdorf 1	2	51N21	12E32	-0:50:08
Börssum 2	1	52N04	10E35	-0:42:20
Borstel 2	1	53N32	9E41	-0:38:44
Borstendorf 1	2	50N46	13E10	-0:52:40
Borth 2	7	51N36	6E33	-0:26:12
Bosau 2	1	54N06	10E25	-0:41:40
Bösel 2	1	53N00	7E58	-0:31:52
Bösingen 2	3	48N14	8E34	-0:34:16
Bösperde 2	1	51N28	7E46	-0:31:04
Bossdorf 1	2	51N59	12E40	-0:50:40
Bottrop 2	1	51N31	6E55	-0:27:40
Bötzingen 2	3	48N04	7E44	-0:30:56
Bötzow 1	2	52N39	13E08	-0:52:32
Bovenden 2	1	51N35	9E55	-0:39:40
Boxberg 2	5	49N29	9E38	-0:38:32
Brackenheim 2	5	49N05	9E03	-0:36:12
Brackwede 2	1	51N59	8E31	-0:34:04
Braderup 2	1	54N50	8E53	-0:35:32
Brake 2	1	53N19	8E28	-0:33:52
Brake 2	1	52N04	8E35	-0:34:20
Brake 2	1	52N01	8E55	-0:35:40
Brakel 2	1	51N43	9E10	-0:36:40
Bramey-Lenningsen 2	1	51N34	7E46	-0:31:04
Bramsche 2	1	52N24	7E58	-0:31:52
Bramstedt 2	1	53N22	8E41	-0:34:44
Brand 2	7	50N43	6E09	-0:24:36
Brandebourg → Brandenburg 1	2	52N24	12E32	-0:50:08
Brandenburg 1	2	52N24	12E32	-0:50:08
Brand-Erbisdorf 1	2	50N52	13E19	-0:53:16
Brandis 1	2	51N48	13E10	-0:52:40
Brandis 1	2	51N20	12E36	-0:50:24
Brannenburg 2	4	47N44	12E05	-0:48:20
Brassert 2	1	51N40	7E05	-0:28:20
Braubach 2	1	50N16	7E40	-0:30:40
Braunfels 2	1	50N31	8E23	-0:33:32
Braunlage 2	1	51N44	10E37	-0:42:28
Bräunlingen 2	3	47N55	8E26	-0:33:44
Braunsbedra 1	2	51N15	11E49	-0:47:16
Braunschweig 2	1	52N16	10E31	-0:42:04
Breckerfeld 2	1	51N16	7E28	-0:29:52
Breddin 1	2	52N52	12E13	-0:48:52
Bredenbeck 2	1	52N15	9E37	-0:38:28
Bredenbruch 2	1	51N21	7E45	-0:31:00
Bredenscheid-Stüter 2	1	51N22	7E11	-0:28:44
Bredereiche 1	2	53N08	13E14	-0:52:56
Bredstedt 2	1	54N37	8E59	-0:35:56
Brehna 1	2	51N33	12E12	-0:48:48
Breidenstein 2	1	50N55	8E28	-0:33:52
Breisach 2	3	48N01	7E40	-0:30:40
Breitbrunn 2	4	48N02	11E08	-0:44:32
Breitenbrunn 1	2	50N29	12E46	-0:51:04
Breitenfelde 2	1	53N36	10E38	-0:42:32
Breitengüssbach 2	4	49N58	10E53	-0:43:32
Breitenstein 1	2	51N37	10E56	-0:43:44
Breitenworbis 1	2	51N24	10E25	-0:41:40
Breitscheid 2	1	50N41	8E11	-0:32:44
Breitscheid 2	1	51N22	6E52	-0:27:28
Breitungen 1	2	50N45	10E20	-0:41:20
Breloh 2	1	53N01	10E04	-0:40:16
Brême → Bremen 2	1	53N04	8E49	-0:35:16
Bremelau 2	5	48N20	9E32	-0:38:08
Bremen 2	1	53N04	8E49	-0:35:16
Bremerhaven 2	1	53N33	8E34	-0:34:16
Bremervörde 2	1	53N29	9E08	-0:36:32
Bremke 2	1	51N15	8E12	-0:32:48
Bremke 2	1	52N07	9E06	-0:36:24
Brendlorenzen 2	4	50N20	10E13	-0:40:52
Brenz 2	5	48N33	10E17	-0:41:08
Bresewitz 1	2	54N24	12E40	-0:50:40
Bretnig 1	2	51N08	14E04	-0:56:16
Bretten 2	3	49N02	8E42	-0:34:48
Bricht 2	1	51N41	6E51	-0:27:24
Briese 1	2	52N42	13E18	-0:53:12
Brieselang 1	2	52N35	13E00	-0:52:00
Briesen 1	2	52N20	14E16	-0:57:04
Brieske 1	2	51N29	13E57	-0:55:48
Brieskow-Finkenheerd 1	2	52N16	14E35	-0:58:20
Briest 1	2	52N31	12E08	-0:48:32
Brilon 2	1	51N24	8E34	-0:34:16
Brinkum 2	1	53N00	8E47	-0:35:08
Britz 1	2	52N53	13E49	-0:55:16
Brochterbeck 2	1	52N13	7E44	-0:30:56
Brockenscheidt 2	1	51N38	7E25	-0:29:40
Brockhagen 2	1	51N59	8E20	-0:33:20
Brodenbach 2	6	50N14	7E26	-0:29:44
Broichweiden 2	7	50N49	6E09	-0:24:36
Broitzem 2	1	52N14	10E29	-0:41:56
Brokdorf 2	1	53N52	9E19	-0:37:16
Brome 2	1	52N36	10E56	-0:43:44
Bronkow 1	2	51N40	13E55	-0:55:40
Bronn 2	4	49N44	11E28	-0:45:52
Bronnzell 2	1	50N31	9E41	-0:38:44
Brotterode 1	2	50N49	10E26	-0:41:44
Bruchhausen 2	1	51N26	8E01	-0:32:04
Bruchhausen-Vilsen 2	1	52N50	9E00	-0:36:00
Bruchmühle 1	2	52N33	13E47	-0:55:08
Bruchsal 2	3	49N07	8E35	-0:34:20
Brück 1	2	52N12	12E46	-0:51:04
Brückenau 2	4	50N18	9E47	-0:39:08
Bruck in der Oberpfalz 2	4	49N15	12E18	-0:49:12
Bruckmühl 2	4	47N53	11E54	-0:47:36
Brüel 1	2	53N44	11E43	-0:46:52
Brügge 2	1	51N13	7E34	-0:30:16
Brüggen 2	7	51N14	6E11	-0:24:44
Brühl 2	7	50N48	6E54	-0:27:36
Brunau 1	2	52N45	11E28	-0:45:52
Brünen 2	1	51N43	6E39	-0:26:36
Brüninghausen 2	1	51N13	7E41	-0:30:44
Brünn 1	2	50N27	10E51	-0:43:24
Brunn 1	2	53N40	13E22	-0:53:28
Brunnen 2	4	48N38	11E18	-0:45:12
Brunow 1	2	52N44	13E52	-0:55:28
Brunsbüttel 2	1	53N54	9E07	-0:36:28
Brunsbüttelkoog 2	1	53N54	9E08	-0:36:32
Brunswick → Braunschweig 2	1	52N16	10E31	-0:42:04
Brusendorf 1	2	52N19	13E31	-0:54:04
Brüssow 1	2	53N24	14E07	-0:56:28
Bubenreuth 2	4	49N38	11E01	-0:44:04
Buchau 2	4	49N47	11E32	-0:46:08
Buchbach 2	4	48N19	12E17	-0:49:08
Büchen 2	1	53N29	10E36	-0:42:24
Buchen 2	3	49N32	9E17	-0:37:08
Buchenberg 2	4	47N42	10E14	-0:40:56
Büchenbeuren 2	6	49N55	7E16	-0:29:04
Buchholz 1	2	52N10	12E55	-0:51:40
Buchholz 1	2	52N35	13E47	-0:55:08
Buchholz 2	1	51N23	7E15	-0:29:00
Buchholz in der Nordheide 2	1	53N20	9E52	-0:39:28
Büchlberg 2	4	48N40	13E30	-0:54:00
Buchloe 2	4	48N02	10E44	-0:42:56
Bucholt 2	1	51N39	6E43	-0:26:52
Buchow-Karpzow 1	2	52N31	12E57	-0:51:48
Bückeburg 2	1	52N16	9E02	-0:36:08
Bücken 2	1	52N46	9E07	-0:36:28
Buckow 1	2	52N34	14E04	-0:56:16
Bückwitz 1	2	52N52	12E29	-0:49:56
Budberg 2	7	51N32	6E38	-0:26:32
Büdelsdorf 2	1	54N18	9E40	-0:38:40
Büderich 2	7	51N37	6E34	-0:26:16
Buderus 2	1	51N33	7E38	-0:30:32
Büdingen 2	1	50N17	9E07	-0:36:28
Bühl 2	3	48N42	8E08	-0:32:32
Bühlertal 2	3	48N41	8E10	-0:32:40
Buldern 2	1	51N52	7E22	-0:29:28
Bullay 2	6	50N03	7E08	-0:28:32
Bünde 2	1	52N12	8E35	-0:34:20
Bunde 2	1	53N11	7E16	-0:29:04
Bundenthal 2	6	49N06	7E48	-0:31:12
Bündheim 2	1	51N53	10E32	-0:42:08
Bünningstedt 2	1	53N41	10E13	-0:40:52
Burbach 2	1	50N45	8E05	-0:32:20
Büren 2	1	51N33	8E33	-0:34:12
Burg 1	2	51N49	14E08	-0:56:32
Burg 1	2	52N16	11E51	-0:47:24
Burg 2	1	50N42	8E19	-0:33:16
Burg 2	1	51N08	7E09	-0:28:36
Burgau 2	4	48N26	10E25	-0:41:40
Burg (auf Fehmarn) 2	1	54N26	11E12	-0:44:48
Burgbernheim 2	4	49N27	10E19	-0:41:16
Burgdorf 2	1	52N27	10E00	-0:40:00
Burgebrach 2	4	49N50	10E44	-0:42:56
Bürgel 1	2	50N56	11E45	-0:47:00
Burghausen 2	4	48N09	12E49	-0:51:16
Burgheim 2	4	48N42	11E01	-0:44:04
Burgjoss 2	1	50N12	9E29	-0:37:56
Burgkunstadt 2	4	50N08	11E14	-0:44:56
Burglengenfeld 2	4	49N13	12E03	-0:48:12
Burgsinn 2	4	50N09	9E38	-0:38:32
Burgstädt 1	2	50N55	12E49	-0:51:16
Burgstall 1	2	52N24	11E41	-0:46:44
Burg Stargard 1	2	53N29	13E18	-0:53:12
Burgsteinfurt 2	1	52N08	7E20	-0:29:20
Burgwindheim 2	4	49N49	10E35	-0:42:20
Burhave 2	1	53N34	8E21	-0:33:24
Burkau 1	2	51N10	14E10	-0:56:40
Burkhardtsdorf 1	2	50N44	12E55	-0:51:40
Burladingen 2	5	48N17	9E07	-0:36:28
Burow 1	2	53N46	13E16	-0:53:04
Burscheid 2	1	51N05	7E06	-0:28:24
Bürstadt 2	1	49N38	8E27	-0:33:48
Burtenbach 2	4	48N20	10E26	-0:41:44
Busdorf 2	1	54N29	9E32	-0:38:08
Büsingen 2	3	47N42	8E41	-0:34:44
Büsum 2	1	54N08	8E51	-0:35:24
Buttelstedt 1	2	51N05	11E20	-0:45:20
Büttgen 2	7	51N12	6E36	-0:26:24
Buttlar 1	2	50N45	9E57	-0:39:48
Buttstädt 1	2	51N07	11E25	-0:45:40
Butzbach 2	1	50N26	8E40	-0:34:40
Bützfleth 2	1	53N39	9E28	-0:37:52
Bützow 1	2	53N50	11E59	-0:47:56
Buxtehude 2	1	53N28	9E41	-0:38:44
Cadenberge 2	1	53N46	9E04	-0:36:16
Cainsdorf 1	2	50N41	12E29	-0:49:56
Calau 1	2	51N45	13E56	-0:55:44
Calbe 1	2	51N54	11E46	-0:47:04
Calle 2	1	51N20	8E13	-0:32:52
Calmbach 2	3	48N46	8E35	-0:34:20
Calvörde 1	2	52N23	11E17	-0:45:08
Calw 2	5	48N43	8E44	-0:34:56
Camberg 2	1	50N18	8E16	-0:33:04
Camburg 1	2	51N03	11E42	-0:46:48
Camin 1	2	53N27	10E58	-0:43:52
Canow 1	2	53N12	12E54	-0:51:36
Cappeln 2	1	52N48	8E07	-0:32:28
Cappenberg 2	1	51N39	7E32	-0:30:08
Caputh 1	2	52N21	13E00	-0:52:00
Carlsfeld 1	2	50N26	12E35	-0:50:20
Carmzow 1	2	53N23	14E02	-0:56:08
Casekow 1	2	53N12	14E12	-0:56:48
Castrop-Rauxel 2	1	51N34	7E18	-0:29:12
Cavertitz 1	2	51N23	13E08	-0:52:32
Celle 2	1	52N37	10E05	-0:40:20
Cham 2	4	49N13	12E41	-0:50:44
Cheine 1	2	52N52	11E04	-0:44:16
Chemnitz → Karl-Marx-Stadt 1	2	50N50	12E55	-0:51:40
Chursdorf 1	2	50N46	12E15	-0:49:00
Cismar 2	1	54N11	10E59	-0:43:56
Clarholz 2	1	51N54	8E11	-0:32:44
Claussnitz 1	2	50N56	12E53	-0:51:32
Clausthal-Zellerfeld 2	1	51N48	10E20	-0:41:20
Clenze 2	1	52N56	10E58	-0:43:52
Cleves → Kleve 2	7	51N48	6E09	-0:24:36
Clingen 1	2	51N14	10E55	-0:43:40
Cloppenburg 2	1	52N50	8E02	-0:32:08
Coblenz → Koblenz 2	6	50N21	7E35	-0:30:20
Coburg 2	4	50N15	10E58	-0:43:52
Cochem 2	6	50N11	7E09	-0:28:36
Cochstedt 1	2	51N53	11E24	-0:45:36
Coesfeld 2	1	51N56	7E10	-0:28:40
Cölbe 2	1	50N51	8E48	-0:35:12
Colbitz 1	2	52N19	11E36	-0:46:24
Colditz 1	2	51N07	12E48	-0:51:12
Colmnitz 1	2	50N54	13E31	-0:54:04
Cologne → Köln 2	7	50N56	6E59	-0:27:56
Colonia → Köln 2	7	50N56	6E59	-0:27:56
Constance → Konstanz 2	3	47N40	9E10	-0:36:40
Coppenbrügge 2	1	52N07	9E32	-0:38:08
Cossebaude 1	2	51N05	13E38	-0:54:32

Coswig 1	2	51N07	13E34	-0:54:16
Coswig 1	2	51N53	12E26	-0:49:44
Cottbus 1	2	51N45	14E19	-0:57:16
Crailsheim 2	5	49N08	10E04	-0:40:16
Crawinkel 1	2	50N47	10E47	-0:43:08
Creglingen 2	5	49N28	10E01	-0:40:04
Creussen 2	4	49N51	11E37	-0:46:28
Creuzburg 1	2	51N03	10E15	-0:41:00
Crimmitschau 1	2	50N49	12E23	-0:49:32
Crivitz 1	2	53N35	11E38	-0:46:32
Crossen 1	2	50N45	12E29	-0:49:56
Crottendorf 1	2	50N30	12E56	-0:51:44
Cunewalde 1	2	51N06	14E30	-0:58:00
Cuxhaven 2	1	53N52	8E42	-0:34:48
Daaden 2	1	50N44	7E58	-0:31:52
Dabendorf 1	2	52N14	13E26	-0:53:44
Dabringhausen 2	1	51N05	7E11	-0:28:44
Dachau 2	4	48N15	11E27	-0:45:48
Dahl 2	1	51N18	7E31	-0:30:04
Dahle 2	1	51N18	7E45	-0:31:00
Dahlem 2	7	50N23	6E33	-0:26:12
Dahlen 1	2	51N22	12E59	-0:51:56
Dahlenburg 2	1	53N11	10E44	-0:42:56
Dahlerau 2	1	51N13	7E19	-0:29:16
Dahlewitz 1	2	52N19	13E26	-0:53:44
Dahlhausen 1	2	53N03	12E20	-0:49:20
Dahlwitz-Hoppegarten 1	2	52N30	13E38	-0:54:32
Dahme 1	2	51N52	13E25	-0:53:40
Dahme 2	1	54N13	11E04	-0:44:16
Dahn 2	6	49N09	7E47	-0:31:08
Dähre 1	2	52N48	10E54	-0:43:36
Dalhausen 2	1	51N37	9E17	-0:37:08
Dallau 2	3	49N23	9E11	-0:36:44
Dallgow 1	2	52N32	13E05	-0:52:20
Dalum 2	1	52N35	7E14	-0:28:56
Dambeck 1	2	52N48	11E09	-0:44:36
Damm 2	1	51N40	6E48	-0:27:12
Damme 1	2	53N17	14E01	-0:56:04
Damme 2	1	52N30	8E08	-0:32:32
Danewitz 1	2	52N44	13E40	-0:54:40
Dänisch Nienhof 2	1	54N28	10E07	-0:40:28
Dankersen 2	1	52N17	8E58	-0:35:52
Dannenberg 2	1	53N06	11E05	-0:44:20
Dannenreich 1	2	52N19	13E45	-0:55:00
Dannenwalde 1	2	53N04	13E11	-0:52:44
Dannewerk 2	1	54N29	9E31	-0:38:04
Dardesheim 1	2	51N59	10E49	-0:43:16
Darfeld 2	1	52N01	7E16	-0:29:04
Dargun 1	2	53N54	12E51	-0:51:24
Darmstadt 2	1	49N53	8E40	-0:34:40
Darscheid 2	6	50N12	6E53	-0:27:32
Dasburg 2	6	50N03	6E07	-0:24:28
Dasing 2	4	48N23	11E03	-0:44:12
Dassel 2	1	51N48	9E41	-0:38:44
Dassow 1	2	53N50	10E59	-0:43:56
Dasswang 2	4	49N09	11E40	-0:46:40
Datteln 2	1	51N40	7E23	-0:29:32
Daun 2	6	50N11	6E50	-0:27:20
Dausenau 2	1	50N20	7E45	-0:31:00
Debstedt 2	1	53N37	8E38	-0:34:32
Dedeleben 1	2	52N03	10E25	-0:41:40
Dedelow 1	2	53N22	13E48	-0:55:12
Dedesdorf 2	1	53N27	8E30	-0:34:00
Degerndorf 2	4	47N44	12E06	-0:48:24
Deggendorf 2	4	48N51	12E59	-0:51:56
Deggingen 2	5	48N36	9E43	-0:38:52
Dehrn 2	1	50N25	8E05	-0:32:20
Deidesheim 2	6	49N24	8E11	-0:32:44
Deilinghofen 2	1	51N22	7E47	-0:31:08
Deining 2	4	49N13	11E32	-0:46:08
Delbrück 2	1	51N46	8E33	-0:34:12
Delitzsch 1	2	51N31	12E20	-0:49:20
Delligsen 2	1	51N57	9E48	-0:39:12
Dellwig 2	1	51N29	7E41	-0:30:44
Delmenhorst 2	1	53N03	8E38	-0:34:32
Delrath 2	7	51N08	6E47	-0:27:08
Demerthin 1	2	52N58	12E17	-0:49:08
Demitz-Thumitz 1	2	51N09	14E14	-0:56:56
Demmin 1	2	53N54	13E02	-0:52:08
Denkendorf 2	5	48N41	9E19	-0:37:16
Denkendorf 2	4	48N56	11E27	-0:45:48
Denkingen 2	3	47N53	9E19	-0:37:16
Denklingen 2	4	47N55	10E51	-0:43:24
Denklingen 2	1	50N55	7E39	-0:30:36
Denzlingen 2	3	48N04	7E52	-0:31:28
Derenburg 1	2	51N52	10E54	-0:43:36
Dermbach 1	2	50N43	10E06	-0:40:24
Derne 2	1	51N35	7E41	-0:30:44
Dersau 2	1	54N07	10E20	-0:41:20
Derschlag 2	1	51N00	7E37	-0:30:28
Dessau 1	2	51N50	12E14	-0:48:56
Dethlingen 2	1	52N57	10E07	-0:40:28
Detmold 2	1	51N56	8E52	-0:35:28
Dettelbach 2	4	49N48	10E09	-0:40:36
Dettingen an der Erms 2	5	48N32	9E20	-0:37:20
Deuben 1	2	51N06	12E04	-0:48:16
Deutsch-Neudorf 1	2	50N38	13E27	-0:53:48
Deutsch Wusterhausen 1	2	52N18	13E35	-0:54:20
Deutzen 1	2	51N06	12E26	-0:49:44
Dhünn 2	1	51N06	7E16	-0:29:04
Dibbersen 2	1	53N22	9E52	-0:39:28
Dieburg 2	1	49N54	8E50	-0:35:20
Diedersdorf 1	2	52N20	13E21	-0:53:24
Dielingen 2	1	52N26	8E20	-0:33:20
Diepenau 2	1	52N25	8E44	-0:34:56
Diepensee 1	2	52N22	13E31	-0:54:04
Diepholz 2	1	52N35	8E21	-0:33:24
Dierdorf 2	1	50N33	7E39	-0:30:36
Dierhagen 1	2	45N18	12E21	-0:49:24
Dieringhausen 2	1	50N59	7E31	-0:30:04
Diersfordt 2	1	51N42	6E33	-0:26:12
Diesdorf 1	2	52N45	10E52	-0:43:28
Dieskau 1	2	51N26	12E02	-0:48:08
Diessen 2	4	47N56	11E06	-0:44:24
Dietenheim 2	5	48N12	10E04	-0:40:16
Dietersburg 2	4	48N30	12E55	-0:51:40
Dietersdorf 2	4	50N13	10E49	-0:43:16
Dietfurt 2	4	48N57	10E56	-0:43:44
Dietfurt an der Altmühl 2	4	49N02	11E35	-0:46:20
Dietmannsried 2	4	47N49	10E17	-0:41:08
Dietzenbach 2	1	50N01	8E47	-0:35:08
Diez 2	1	50N22	8E01	-0:32:04
Dillenburg 2	1	50N44	8E17	-0:33:08
Dillingen 2	6	49N21	6E44	-0:26:56
Dillingen an der Donau 2	4	48N34	10E29	-0:41:56
Dingden 2	1	51N46	6E37	-0:26:28
Dingelsdorf 2	3	47N44	9E09	-0:36:36
Dingelstädt 1	2	51N18	10E19	-0:41:16
Dingelstedt 1	2	51N58	10E58	-0:43:52
Dinglingen 2	3	48N20	7E50	-0:31:20
Dingolfing 2	4	48N38	12E31	-0:50:04
Dinkelsbühl 2	4	49N04	10E19	-0:41:16
Dinkelscherben 2	4	48N21	10E35	-0:42:20
Dinklage 2	1	52N40	8E07	-0:32:28
Dinslaken 2	1	51N34	6E44	-0:26:56
Dinslakener Bruch 2	1	51N35	6E43	-0:26:52
Dippoldiswalde 1	2	50N54	13E40	-0:54:40
Dirnaich 2	4	48N27	12E30	-0:50:00
Dissen 2	1	52N07	8E12	-0:32:48
Disteln 2	1	51N36	7E09	-0:28:36
Ditfurt 1	2	51N50	11E11	-0:44:44
Ditzingen 2	5	48N49	9E03	-0:36:12
Ditzum 2	1	53N18	7E16	-0:29:04
Dobbertin 1	2	53N37	12E04	-0:48:16
Dobel 2	3	48N48	8E29	-0:33:56
Döbeln 1	2	51N07	13E07	-0:52:28
Döberitz 1	2	52N33	13E03	-0:52:12
Doberlug-Kirchhain 1	2	51N38	13E34	-0:54:16
Döbern 1	2	51N37	14E36	-0:58:24
Dobritz 1	2	52N01	12E13	-0:48:52
Dockweiler 2	6	50N15	6E46	-0:27:04
Dohna 1	2	50N57	13E51	-0:55:24
Dohrgaul 2	1	51N06	7E27	-0:29:48
Dolberg 2	1	51N42	7E55	-0:31:40
Dolgelin 1	2	52N29	14E24	-0:57:36
Döllbach 2	1	50N26	9E44	-0:38:56
Dolle 1	2	52N25	11E37	-0:46:28
Dollern 2	1	53N32	9E32	-0:38:08
Dollerup 2	1	54N46	9E40	-0:38:40
Döllnitz 1	2	51N24	12E01	-0:48:04
Dollnstein 2	4	48N52	11E04	-0:44:16
Döllstädt 1	2	51N05	10E49	-0:43:16
Dömitz 1	2	53N08	11E14	-0:44:56
Dommitzsch 1	2	51N38	12E53	-0:51:32
Donaueschingen 2	3	47N57	8E29	-0:33:56
Donaustauf 2	4	49N02	12E13	-0:48:52
Donauwörth 2	4	48N43	10E46	-0:43:04
Dönberg 2	1	51N18	7E10	-0:28:40
Donzdorf 2	5	48N41	9E48	-0:39:12
Dorchheim 2	1	50N30	8E04	-0:32:16
Dorfen 2	4	48N17	12E08	-0:48:32
Dorfmark 2	1	52N54	9E46	-0:39:04
Dormagen 2	7	51N05	6E50	-0:27:20
Dornap 2	1	51N15	7E04	-0:28:16
Dorndorf 1	2	50N50	10E05	-0:40:20
Dorndorf 1	2	51N00	11E40	-0:46:40
Dornhan 2	3	48N21	8E30	-0:34:00
Dornstadt 2	5	48N28	9E56	-0:39:44
Dornstetten 2	3	48N28	8E30	-0:34:00
Dornumersiel 2	1	53N40	7E28	-0:29:52
Dörpen 2	1	52N57	7E20	-0:29:20
Dorsten 2	1	51N39	6E58	-0:27:52
Dortmund 2	1	51N31	7E28	-0:29:52
Dorum 2	1	53N41	8E34	-0:34:16
Dörverden 2	1	52N51	9E13	-0:36:52
Dörzbach 2	5	49N23	9E42	-0:38:48
Drabenderhöhe 2	1	50N57	7E27	-0:29:48
Drakenburg 2	1	52N41	9E13	-0:36:52
Drangstedt 2	1	53N36	8E44	-0:34:56
Dransfeld 2	1	51N30	9E45	-0:39:00
Dranske 1	2	54N38	13E14	-0:52:56
Drebach 1	2	50N40	13E01	-0:52:04
Drebkau 1	2	51N39	14E13	-0:56:52
Dreihausen 2	1	50N43	8E50	-0:35:20
Drensteinfurt 2	1	51N48	7E44	-0:30:56
Dresde → Dresden 1	2	51N03	13E44	-0:54:56
Dresden 1	2	51N03	13E44	-0:54:56
Drevenack 2	1	51N40	6E45	-0:27:00
Drewer 2	1	51N40	7E07	-0:28:28
Drewitz 1	2	52N22	13E07	-0:52:28
Drewitz 1	2	52N12	12E10	-0:48:40
Dringenberg 2	1	51N40	9E02	-0:36:08
Drochtersen 2	1	53N42	9E23	-0:37:32
Drolshagen 2	1	51N01	7E46	-0:31:04
Dröschede 2	1	51N22	7E39	-0:30:36
Droyssig 1	2	51N02	12E01	-0:48:04
Ducherow 1	2	53N46	13E46	-0:55:04
Duderstadt 2	1	51N31	10E16	-0:41:04
Dudweiler 2	6	49N17	7E02	-0:28:08
Duhnen 2	1	53N53	8E38	-0:34:32
Duingen 2	1	52N00	9E42	-0:38:48
Duisburg 2	1	51N25	6E46	-0:27:04
Dülken 2	7	51N15	6E20	-0:25:20
Dülmen 2	1	51N51	7E16	-0:29:04
Dümpelfeld 2	6	50N27	6E56	-0:27:44
Dünzlau 2	4	48N47	11E20	-0:45:20
Durchholz 2	1	51N23	7E17	-0:29:08
Düren 2	7	50N48	6E28	-0:25:52
Durmersheim 2	3	48N56	8E16	-0:33:04
Dürnast 2	4	49N38	11E59	-0:47:56
Dürröhrsdorf 1	2	51N01	14E00	-0:56:00
Düshorn 2	1	52N49	9E37	-0:38:28
Düssel 2	1	51N16	7E03	-0:28:12
Düsseldorf 2	1	51N12	6E47	-0:27:08
Dusslingen 2	5	48N27	9E03	-0:36:12
Dyrotz 1	2	52N33	12E58	-0:51:52
East-Berlin → Berlin (Ost) 1	2	52N32	13E25	-0:53:40
Ebeleben 1	2	51N17	10E43	-0:42:52
Ebendorf 1	2	52N11	11E34	-0:46:16
Ebensfeld 2	4	50N04	10E58	-0:43:52
Eberbach 2	3	49N28	8E59	-0:35:56
Ebergötzen 2	1	51N34	10E06	-0:40:24
Ebermannstadt 2	4	49N43	11E13	-0:44:52
Ebern 2	4	50N05	10E47	-0:43:08
Ebersbach 1	2	51N00	14E35	-0:58:20
Ebersbach 2	5	48N43	9E31	-0:38:04
Ebersberg 2	4	48N05	11E58	-0:47:52
Ebersdorf 2	1	53N31	9E03	-0:36:12
Ebersdorf bei Coburg 2	4	50N13	11E04	-0:44:16
Eberswalde 1	2	52N50	13E49	-0:55:16
Ebingen 2	5	48N13	9E01	-0:36:04
Ebrach 2	4	49N50	10E29	-0:41:56
Ebstorf 2	1	53N01	10E25	-0:41:40
Eching 2	4	48N18	11E37	-0:46:28
Echterdingen 2	5	48N41	9E10	-0:36:40
Echternacherbrück 2	6	49N49	6E25	-0:25:40
Eckartsberga 1	2	51N07	11E34	-0:46:16
Eckenhagen 2	1	50N59	7E41	-0:30:44
Eckernförde 2	1	54N28	9E50	-0:39:20
Eckwarderhörne 2	1	53N31	8E14	-0:32:56
Edelsfeld 2	4	49N34	11E42	-0:46:48
Edelshausen 2	4	48N37	11E17	-0:45:08
Edemissen 2	1	52N23	10E16	-0:41:04
Edenkoben 2	6	49N17	8E07	-0:32:28
Edesheim 2	6	49N16	8E08	-0:32:32
Edewecht 2	1	53N07	8E02	-0:32:08
Ediger 2	6	50N06	7E09	-0:28:36
Effeltrich 2	4	49N40	11E06	-0:44:24
Efringen-Kirchen 2	3	47N49	7E35	-0:30:20
Egeln 1	2	51N56	11E25	-0:45:40
Egerpohl 2	1	51N07	7E27	-0:29:48
Egestorf 2	1	53N11	10E04	-0:40:16
Egestorf (am Süntel) 2	1	52N17	9E31	-0:38:04
Eggebek 2	1	54N37	9E22	-0:37:28
Eggenfelden 2	4	48N25	12E46	-0:51:04
Eggenstein 2	3	49N04	8E23	-0:33:32
Eggerscheid 2	1	51N19	6E53	-0:27:32
Eggersdorf 1	2	52N32	13E49	-0:55:16
Eggesin 1	2	53N41	14E05	-0:56:20
Egglham 2	4	48N32	13E04	-0:52:16
Ehingen 2	5	48N17	9E43	-0:38:52
Ehmen 2	1	52N24	10E41	-0:42:44
Ehra-Lessien 2	1	52N34	10E46	-0:43:04
Ehrang 2	6	49N49	6E41	-0:26:44
Ehrenfriedersdorf 1	2	50N38	12E58	-0:51:52
Ehreshoven 2	1	50N58	7E20	-0:29:20
Ehrhorn 2	1	53N10	9E53	-0:39:32
Ehringhausen 2	1	51N11	7E33	-0:30:12
Eibau 1	2	50N58	14E40	-0:58:40
Eibelshausen 2	1	50N49	8E20	-0:33:20
Eibelstadt 2	4	49N43	10E00	-0:40:00
Eibenstock 1	2	50N29	12E35	-0:50:20
Eicha 1	2	50N21	10E34	-0:42:16
Eiche 1	2	52N34	13E36	-0:54:24
Eiche 1	2	52N25	12E58	-0:51:52
Eichenbarleben 1	2	52N10	11E24	-0:45:36
Eichenbrandt 1	2	52N38	13E51	-0:55:24
Eichendorf 2	4	48N38	12E51	-0:51:24
Eichstädt 1	2	52N42	13E07	-0:52:28
Eichstätt 2	4	48N54	11E12	-0:44:48
Eichstetten 2	3	48N05	7E44	-0:30:56
Eichtersheim 2	3	49N14	8E46	-0:35:04
Eichwalde 1	2	52N22	13E37	-0:54:28
Eickelborn 2	1	51N39	8E13	-0:32:52
Eickerend 2	7	51N13	6E34	-0:26:16
Eicklingen 2	1	52N33	10E10	-0:40:40
Eifa 2	1	50N58	8E34	-0:34:16
Eigenrieden 1	2	51N11	10E22	-0:41:28
Eilenburg 1	2	51N27	12E37	-0:50:28
Eilsleben 1	2	52N09	11E13	-0:44:52
Eimbeckhausen 2	1	52N14	9E25	-0:37:40
Eimke 2	1	52N58	10E19	-0:41:16
Einbeck 2	1	51N49	9E52	-0:39:28
Einöd 2	6	49N16	7E19	-0:29:16
Einruhr 2	7	50N35	6E22	-0:25:28
Einsbach 2	4	48N16	11E16	-0:45:04
Einsiedel 1	2	50N46	12E58	-0:51:52
Eisenach 1	2	50N59	10E19	-0:41:16
Eisenberg 1	2	50N58	11E53	-0:47:32
Eisenberg 2	6	49N38	8E05	-0:32:20
Eisenhofen 2	4	48N21	11E17	-0:45:08
Eisenhüttenstadt 1	2	52N10	14E39	-0:58:36
Eisenschmitt 2	6	50N03	6E43	-0:26:52
Eiserfeld 2	1	50N50	7E59	-0:31:56
Eisern 2	1	50N50	8E02	-0:32:08
Eisfeld 1	2	50N26	10E54	-0:43:36
Eisleben 1	2	51N31	11E32	-0:46:08
Eislingen 2	5	48N42	9E42	-0:38:48
Eitorf 2	1	50N46	7E26	-0:29:44
Elberfeld 2	1	51N15	7E10	-0:28:40
Elbingerode 1	2	51N45	10E46	-0:43:04
Eldagsen 2	1	52N10	9E40	-0:38:40

Eldena 1 2 53N13 11E25 -0:45:40
Eldena 1 2 54N05 13E26 -0:53:44
Eldingen 2 1 52N41 10E21 -0:41:24
Elend 1 2 51N44 10E41 -0:42:44
Elfgen 2 7 51N05 6E32 -0:26:08
Elgershausen 2 1 51N16 9E22 -0:37:28
Elisabeth-Sophien-Koog 2 1 54N30 8E53 -0:35:32
Ellefeld 1 2 50N29 12E23 -0:49:32
Ellingen 2 4 49N04 10E58 -0:43:52
Ellrich 1 2 51N35 10E40 -0:42:40
Ellwangen 2 5 48N57 10E07 -0:40:28
Elm 2 1 53N31 9E12 -0:36:48
Elmpt 2 7 51N13 6E10 -0:24:40
Elmshorn 2 1 53N45 9E39 -0:38:36
Elmstein 2 6 49N21 7E56 -0:31:44
Elsdorf 2 7 50N54 6E34 -0:26:16
Elsdorf 2 1 53N14 9E20 -0:37:20
Elsen 2 1 51N44 8E39 -0:34:36
Elsey 2 1 51N22 7E34 -0:30:16
Elsfleth 2 1 53N14 8E28 -0:33:52
Elspe 2 1 51N09 8E04 -0:32:16
Elstal 1 2 52N32 12E59 -0:51:56
Elster 1 2 51N50 12E49 -0:51:16
Elsterberg 1 2 50N36 12E10 -0:48:40
Elsterwerda 1 2 51N28 13E31 -0:54:04
Elstra 1 2 51N13 14E08 -0:56:32
Elten 2 7 51N52 6E10 -0:24:40
Eltmann 2 4 49N58 10E40 -0:42:40
Eltville 2 1 50N02 8E07 -0:32:28
Elverdissen 2 1 52N05 8E38 -0:34:32
Elverlingsen 2 1 51N17 7E42 -0:30:48
Elxleben 1 2 51N02 10E56 -0:43:44
Elz 2 1 50N25 8E02 -0:32:08
Elzach 2 3 48N10 8E04 -0:32:16
Elze 2 1 52N35 9E44 -0:38:56
Elze 2 1 52N07 9E44 -0:38:56
Emden 2 1 53N22 7E12 -0:28:48
Emlichheim 2 1 52N36 6E50 -0:27:20
Emmendingen 2 3 48N07 7E50 -0:31:20
Emmerich 2 1 51N50 6E15 -0:25:00
Emmerstedt 2 1 52N15 10E58 -0:43:52
Empfingen 2 5 48N24 8E42 -0:34:48
Emsdetten 2 1 52N10 7E31 -0:30:04
Emskirchen 2 4 49N33 10E43 -0:42:52
Emstek 2 1 52N50 8E09 -0:32:36
Endingen 2 3 48N09 7E42 -0:30:48
Endorf in Oberbayern 2 4 47N54 12E18 -0:49:12
Engelsberg 2 4 49N19 11E38 -0:46:32
Engelsdorf 1 2 51N20 12E29 -0:49:56
Engelskirchen 2 1 50N59 7E24 -0:29:36
Engen 2 3 47N51 8E46 -0:35:04
Enger 2 1 52N08 8E34 -0:34:16
Engter 2 1 52N23 8E04 -0:32:16
Eningen unter Achalm 2 5 48N29 9E16 -0:37:04
Enkenbach 2 6 49N29 7E54 -0:31:36
Enkirch 2 6 49N59 7E07 -0:28:28
Ennepetal 2 1 51N18 7E22 -0:29:28
Enniger 2 1 51N50 7E56 -0:31:44
Ennigerloh 2 1 51N50 8E02 -0:32:08
Ennigloh 2 1 52N12 8E34 -0:34:16
Ensdorf 2 4 49N21 11E56 -0:47:44
Entringen 2 5 48N33 8E58 -0:35:52
Enzklösterle 2 3 48N40 8E28 -0:33:52
Enzweihingen 2 5 48N55 8E58 -0:35:52
Epe 2 1 52N11 7E02 -0:28:08
Eppendorf 1 2 50N48 13E14 -0:52:56
Eppingen 2 3 49N08 8E54 -0:35:36
Erbach 2 5 48N20 9E53 -0:39:32
Erbach 2 1 49N40 8E59 -0:35:56
Erbendorf 2 4 49N50 12E03 -0:48:12
Erbenheim 2 1 50N03 8E18 -0:33:12
Erdhausen 2 1 50N45 8E34 -0:34:16
Erding 2 4 48N18 11E54 -0:47:36
Erfde 2 1 54N19 9E19 -0:37:16
Erftstadt 2 7 50N48 6E46 -0:27:04
Erfurt 1 2 50N58 11E01 -0:44:04
Ergenzingen 2 5 48N29 8E48 -0:35:12
Ergolding 2 4 48N35 12E10 -0:48:40
Ergoldsbach 2 4 48N41 12E12 -0:48:48
Ergste 2 1 51N25 7E34 -0:30:16
Erichshagen 2 1 52N40 9E14 -0:36:56
Ering 2 4 48N18 13E09 -0:52:36
Erkelenz 2 7 51N05 6E19 -0:25:16
Erkheim 2 4 48N02 10E20 -0:41:20
Erkner 1 2 52N25 13E45 -0:55:00
Erkrath 2 1 51N13 6E55 -0:27:40
Erlangen 2 4 49N36 11E01 -0:44:04
Erlbach 1 2 50N18 12E22 -0:49:28
Ermsleben 1 2 51N44 11E21 -0:45:24
Erndtebrück 2 1 50N59 8E15 -0:33:00
Erp 2 7 50N46 6E43 -0:26:52
Ertingen 2 5 48N06 9E28 -0:37:52
Erwitte 2 1 51N37 8E20 -0:33:20
Erxleben 1 2 52N13 11E14 -0:44:56
Erzingen 2 3 47N39 8E25 -0:33:40
Esborn 2 1 51N23 7E20 -0:29:20
Eschach 2 5 47N44 9E36 -0:38:24
Eschebrügge 2 1 52N37 6E46 -0:27:04
Eschede 2 1 52N44 10E14 -0:40:56
Eschenau 2 4 49N34 11E12 -0:44:48
Eschenbach 2 4 49N45 11E49 -0:47:16
Eschenlohe 2 4 47N36 11E11 -0:44:44
Eschershausen 2 1 51N56 9E38 -0:38:32
Eschlkam 2 4 49N18 12E55 -0:51:40
Eschwege 2 1 51N11 10E04 -0:40:16
Eschweiler 2 7 50N49 6E16 -0:25:04
Esens 2 1 53N39 7E37 -0:30:28
Eslarn 2 4 49N35 12E32 -0:50:08
Eslohe 2 1 51N15 8E09 -0:32:36
Espasingen 2 3 47N49 9E00 -0:36:00
Espelkamp 2 1 52N25 8E36 -0:34:24
Espenhain 1 2 51N11 12E29 -0:49:56
Essen 2 1 51N28 7E01 -0:28:04
Essen 2 1 52N43 7E57 -0:31:48
Essenbach 2 4 48N37 12E13 -0:48:52
Essenberg 2 7 51N26 6E42 -0:26:48
Essig 2 7 50N40 6E54 -0:27:36
Essing 2 4 48N56 11E47 -0:47:08
Esslingen 2 5 48N45 9E16 -0:37:04
Esterwegen 2 1 52N59 7E38 -0:30:32
Ettal 2 4 47N34 11E05 -0:44:20
Ettenheim 2 3 48N15 7E49 -0:31:16
Ettlingen 2 3 48N56 8E24 -0:33:36
Ettringen 2 4 48N06 10E39 -0:42:36
Ettringen 2 6 50N21 7E13 -0:28:52
Euskirchen 2 7 50N39 6E47 -0:27:08
Eutin 2 1 54N08 10E37 -0:42:28
Eutingen 2 3 48N28 8E44 -0:34:56
Eutzsch 1 2 51N49 12E38 -0:50:32
Eveking 2 1 51N14 7E44 -0:30:56
Evenkamp 2 1 51N40 7E39 -0:30:36
Eversael 2 7 51N33 6E39 -0:26:36
Eversberg 2 1 51N21 8E20 -0:33:20
Eversen 2 1 52N45 10E02 -0:40:08
Everswinkel 2 1 51N55 7E50 -0:31:20
Evesen 2 1 52N17 8E59 -0:35:56
Evingsen 2 1 51N18 7E44 -0:30:56
Ewersbach 2 1 50N50 8E19 -0:33:16
Exing 2 4 48N38 12E37 -0:50:28
Exter 2 1 52N08 8E46 -0:35:04
Extertal 2 1 52N04 9E07 -0:36:28
Eystrup 2 1 52N46 9E13 -0:36:52
Eythra 1 2 51N14 12E17 -0:49:08
Fagel 2 1 54N27 9E31 -0:38:04
Fährdorf 1 2 53N58 11E28 -0:45:52
Fahrland 1 2 52N28 13E01 -0:52:04
Fahrnau 2 3 47N39 7E50 -0:31:20
Falkenau 1 2 50N51 13E07 -0:52:28
Falkenberg 1 2 52N48 13E58 -0:55:52
Falkenberg 1 2 51N35 13E14 -0:52:56
Falkenberg 2 4 49N52 12E14 -0:48:56
Falkenberg 2 4 48N28 12E43 -0:50:52
Falkenhagen 1 2 53N12 12E12 -0:48:48
Falkenhagen 1 2 52N26 14E19 -0:57:16
Falkenrehde 1 2 52N30 12E56 -0:51:44
Falkensee 1 2 52N33 13E04 -0:52:16
Falkenstein 1 2 50N29 12E22 -0:49:28
Falkenstein 2 4 49N06 12E30 -0:50:00
Falkenthal 1 2 52N54 13E17 -0:53:08
Fallersleben 2 1 52N25 10E43 -0:42:52
Fallingbostel 2 1 52N52 9E41 -0:38:44
Fambach 1 2 50N44 10E22 -0:41:28
Farchant 2 4 47N32 11E06 -0:44:24
Farnroda 1 2 50N56 10E23 -0:41:32
Fassberg 2 1 52N54 10E10 -0:40:40
Fehrbellin 1 2 52N49 12E46 -0:51:04
Feilitzsch 2 4 50N22 11E56 -0:47:44
Feilnbach 2 4 47N46 12E00 -0:48:00
Feldafing 2 4 47N57 11E17 -0:45:08
Feldberg 1 2 53N20 13E26 -0:53:44
Feldberg 2 3 47N51 8E02 -0:32:08
Feldhausen 2 1 51N37 6E59 -0:27:56
Feldkirchen 2 4 47N54 11E50 -0:47:20
Feldmark 2 1 51N41 6E38 -0:26:32
Feldstetten 2 5 48N28 9E37 -0:38:28
Fellbach 2 5 48N48 9E15 -0:37:00
Felsberg 2 1 51N08 9E25 -0:37:40
Ferbitz 1 2 52N30 13E01 -0:52:04
Ferch 1 2 52N19 12E56 -0:51:44
Ferchland 1 2 52N26 12E00 -0:48:00
Ferdinandshof 1 2 53N39 13E53 -0:55:32
Feucht 2 4 49N22 11E13 -0:44:52
Feuchtwangen 2 4 49N10 10E20 -0:41:20
Feudingen 2 1 50N56 8E19 -0:33:16
Feyen 2 6 49N44 6E38 -0:26:32
Fichtenau 1 2 52N27 13E42 -0:54:48
Finkenkrug 1 2 52N34 13E03 -0:52:12
Finnentrop 2 1 51N09 7E58 -0:31:52
Finow 1 2 52N50 13E43 -0:54:52
Finowfurt 1 2 52N51 13E41 -0:54:44
Finsterwalde 1 2 51N38 13E42 -0:54:48
Fintel 2 1 53N10 9E40 -0:38:40
Fischbach 2 6 49N44 7E23 -0:29:32
Fischbach 2 4 49N25 11E12 -0:44:48
Fischbachau 2 4 47N43 11E57 -0:47:48
Fischbeck 1 2 52N32 12E01 -0:48:04
Fischbeck 2 1 52N09 9E17 -0:37:08
Fischen 2 4 47N28 10E16 -0:41:04
Flachsmeer 2 1 53N07 7E28 -0:29:52
Fladungen 2 4 50N31 10E08 -0:40:32
Flammersfeld 2 1 50N38 7E32 -0:30:08
Flatow 1 2 52N44 12E57 -0:51:48
Flechtingen 1 2 52N20 11E14 -0:44:56
Fleckeby 2 1 54N29 9E41 -0:38:44
Flecken Zechlin 1 2 53N09 12E46 -0:51:04
Flehingen 2 3 49N05 8E46 -0:35:04
Flemsdorf 1 2 53N02 14E10 -0:56:40
Flensburg 2 1 54N47 9E26 -0:37:44
Flieden 2 1 50N25 9E33 -0:38:12
Flierich 2 1 51N35 7E48 -0:31:12
Flöha 1 2 50N51 13E04 -0:52:16
Flomborn 2 6 49N41 8E08 -0:32:32
Flörsheim 2 1 50N01 8E26 -0:33:44
Floss 2 4 49N44 12E17 -0:49:08
Flossenbürg 2 4 49N44 12E21 -0:49:24
Flüren 2 1 51N41 6E33 -0:26:12
Fockbek 2 1 54N18 9E36 -0:38:24
Folmhusen 2 1 53N10 7E28 -0:29:52
Forbach 2 3 48N41 8E21 -0:33:24
Forchheim 1 2 50N43 13E16 -0:53:04
Forchheim 2 4 49N43 11E04 -0:44:16
Förderstedt 1 2 51N54 11E38 -0:46:32
Forst 1 2 51N44 14E39 -0:58:36
Förste 2 1 51N44 10E10 -0:40:40
Forth 2 4 49N36 11E14 -0:44:56
Förtha 1 2 50N56 10E14 -0:40:56
Frammersbach 2 4 50N04 9E28 -0:37:52
Francfort-Sur-Main → Frankfurt am Main 1 50N07 8E40 -0:34:40
Frankenau 2 1 51N05 8E56 -0:35:44
Frankenbach 2 1 50N40 8E34 -0:34:16
Frankenberg 1 2 50N54 13E01 -0:52:04
Frankenberg-Eder 2 1 51N03 8E48 -0:35:12
Frankenheim 1 2 50N32 10E04 -0:40:16
Frankenstein 2 6 49N26 7E58 -0:31:52
Frankenthal 2 6 49N32 8E21 -0:33:24
Frankfurt am Main 2 1 50N07 8E40 -0:34:40
Frankfurt an der Oder 1 2 52N20 14E33 -0:58:12
Frankleben 1 2 51N18 11E56 -0:47:44
Franzburg 1 2 54N11 12E52 -0:51:28
Frasdorf 2 4 47N48 12E16 -0:49:04
Frauenstein 1 2 50N48 13E32 -0:54:08
Frauenwald 1 2 50N35 10E51 -0:43:24
Fraulautern 2 6 49N19 6E46 -0:27:04
Fraureuth 1 2 50N42 12E20 -0:49:20
Frechen 2 7 50N54 6E49 -0:27:16
Freckenhorst 2 1 51N55 7E58 -0:31:52
Fredeburg 2 1 51N11 8E18 -0:33:12
Freden 2 1 51N56 9E54 -0:39:36
Fredersdorf bei Berlin 1 2 52N31 13E44 -0:54:56
Freest 1 2 54N08 13E43 -0:54:52
Freiberg 1 2 50N54 13E20 -0:53:20
Freiburg an der Elbe 2 1 53N49 9E17 -0:37:08
Freiburg im Breisgau 2 3 47N59 7E51 -0:31:24
Freiendiez 2 1 50N23 8E02 -0:32:08
Freienfels 2 4 49N53 12E07 -0:48:28
Freienhufen 1 2 51N35 13E58 -0:55:52
Freihung 2 4 49N37 11E55 -0:47:40
Freilassing 2 4 47N50 12E59 -0:51:56
Freilingen 2 1 50N33 7E50 -0:31:20
Freinsheim 2 6 49N30 8E13 -0:32:52
Freisen 2 6 49N33 7E14 -0:28:56
Freising 2 4 48N23 11E44 -0:46:56
Freistett 2 3 48N41 7E56 -0:31:44
Freital 1 2 51N00 13E39 -0:54:36
Freiwalde 1 2 51N58 13E44 -0:54:56
Fremdingen 2 4 48N58 10E27 -0:41:48
Frensdorferhaar 2 1 52N25 7E03 -0:28:12
Freren 2 1 52N29 7E32 -0:30:08
Freudenberg 1 2 52N42 13E49 -0:55:16
Freudenberg 2 3 49N44 9E19 -0:37:16
Freudenberg 2 1 50N54 7E52 -0:31:28
Freudenstadt 2 3 48N28 8E25 -0:33:40
Freyburg 1 2 51N13 11E46 -0:47:04
Freyenstein 1 2 53N17 12E20 -0:49:20
Freystadt 2 4 49N12 11E20 -0:45:20
Freyung 2 4 48N48 13E33 -0:54:12
Frickhofen 2 1 50N30 8E07 -0:32:28
Fridingen an der Donau 2 3 48N01 8E56 -0:35:44
Fridolfing 2 4 48N00 12E49 -0:51:16
Friedberg 2 4 48N21 10E58 -0:43:52
Friedberg 2 1 50N20 8E45 -0:35:00
Friedeburg (/Saale) 1 2 51N37 11E44 -0:46:56
Friedenfels 2 4 49N53 11E17 -0:45:08
Friedersdorf 1 2 52N17 13E47 -0:55:08
Friedersdorf 1 2 51N01 14E34 -0:58:16
Friedersdorf 1 2 51N39 12E21 -0:49:24
Friedland 1 2 52N06 14E16 -0:57:04
Friedland 1 2 53N40 13E33 -0:54:12
Friedland 2 1 51N25 9E55 -0:39:40
Friedrichroda 1 2 50N52 10E34 -0:42:16
Friedrichsbrunn 1 2 51N41 11E02 -0:44:08
Friedrichsdorf 2 1 50N15 8E38 -0:34:32
Friedrichsfeld 2 1 51N38 6E39 -0:26:36
Friedrichshafen 2 5 47N39 9E28 -0:37:52
Friedrichshof 1 2 52N19 13E46 -0:55:04
Friedrichsruhe 1 2 53N31 11E45 -0:47:00
Friedrichstadt 2 1 54N22 9E05 -0:36:20
Friedrichsthal 1 2 52N48 13E16 -0:53:04
Friedrichswalde 1 2 53N02 13E42 -0:54:48
Frielendorf 2 1 50N58 9E19 -0:37:16
Friemersheim 2 7 51N23 6E42 -0:26:48
Friesack 1 2 52N44 12E34 -0:50:16
Friesenheim 2 3 48N22 7E53 -0:31:32
Friesenhofen 2 5 47N45 10E04 -0:40:16
Friesenried 2 4 47N52 10E31 -0:42:04
Friesoythe 2 1 53N01 7E51 -0:31:24
Fritzlar 2 1 51N08 9E16 -0:37:04
Frohburg 1 2 51N03 12E33 -0:50:12
Frohnhausen 2 1 51N29 7E48 -0:31:12
Frohse 1 2 52N02 11E43 -0:46:52
Froitzheim 2 7 50N42 6E34 -0:26:16
Frömern 2 1 51N30 7E44 -0:30:56
Frommern 2 5 48N15 8E52 -0:35:28
Fröndenberg 2 1 51N28 7E46 -0:31:04
Frönsberg 2 1 51N21 7E46 -0:31:04
Frontenhausen 2 4 48N33 12E32 -0:50:08
Frose 1 2 51N48 11E23 -0:45:32
Frotheim 2 1 52N21 8E40 -0:34:40
Füchtorf 2 1 52N03 8E02 -0:32:08
Fuhrberg 2 1 52N34 9E50 -0:39:20
Fuhrn 2 4 49N21 12E17 -0:49:08
Fulda 2 1 50N33 9E41 -0:38:44
Füramoos 2 5 48N00 9E53 -0:39:32

Fürstenau 2	1	51N50	9E19	-0:37:16
Fürstenau 2	1	52N31	7E40	-0:30:40
Fürstenberg 1	2	52N09	14E40	-0:58:40
Fürstenberg 2	1	51N44	9E24	-0:37:36
Fürstenberg/Havel 1	2	53N11	13E08	-0:52:32
Fürstenfeldbruck 2	4	48N10	11E15	-0:45:00
Fürstenhagen 2	1	51N12	9E41	-0:38:44
Fürstenstein 2	4	48N43	13E20	-0:53:20
Fürstenwalde 1	2	52N21	14E04	-0:56:16
Fürstenwerder 1	2	53N24	13E34	-0:54:16
Fürstenzell 2	4	48N32	13E19	-0:53:16
Fürth 2	4	49N28	10E59	-0:43:56
Fürth 2	1	49N39	8E47	-0:35:08
Furth im Wald 2	4	49N18	12E51	-0:51:24
Furtwangen 2	3	48N03	8E12	-0:32:48
Füssen 2	4	47N34	10E42	-0:42:48
Gablenz 1	2	51N41	14E31	-0:58:04
Gablingen 2	4	48N27	10E49	-0:43:16
Gadderbaum 2	1	52N00	8E31	-0:34:04
Gadebusch 1	2	53N42	11E07	-0:44:28
Gadernheim 2	1	49N43	8E44	-0:34:56
Gaggenau 2	3	48N48	8E19	-0:33:16
Gahlen 2	1	51N40	6E52	-0:27:28
Gaildorf 2	5	49N00	9E46	-0:39:04
Gaimersheim 2	4	48N49	11E22	-0:45:28
Gaisbeuren 2	5	47N54	9E43	-0:38:52
Galkhausen 2	1	51N05	6E58	-0:27:52
Gammertingen 2	5	48N15	9E13	-0:36:52
Ganacker 2	4	48N43	12E41	-0:50:44
Ganderkesee 2	1	53N02	8E32	-0:34:08
Gangelt 2	7	50N59	5E59	-0:23:56
Gangkofen 2	4	48N26	12E34	-0:50:16
Ganzlin 1	2	53N23	12E15	-0:49:00
Garbsen 2	1	52N25	9E34	-0:38:16
Garching 2	4	48N15	11E39	-0:46:36
Garching an der Alz 2	4	48N08	12E34	-0:50:16
Gardelegen 1	2	52N31	11E23	-0:45:32
Garding 2	1	54N20	8E46	-0:35:04
Garenfeld 2	1	51N24	7E31	-0:30:04
Gärmersdorf 2	4	49N26	11E54	-0:47:36
Garmisch-Partenkirchen 2	4	47N29	11E05	-0:44:20
Garrel 2	1	52N57	8E01	-0:32:04
Garstedt 2	1	53N41	9E58	-0:39:52
Gartow 2	1	53N02	11E29	-0:45:56
Gartrop-Bühl 2	1	51N40	6E49	-0:27:16
Gartz 1	2	53N12	14E23	-0:57:32
Garz 1	2	54N19	13E20	-0:53:20
Gatersleben 1	2	51N49	11E17	-0:45:08
Gau-Algesheim 2	6	49N57	8E01	-0:32:04
Gau-Odernheim 2	6	49N47	8E11	-0:32:44
Gauting 2	4	48N04	11E23	-0:45:32
Gebenbach 2	4	49N32	11E53	-0:47:32
Gebesee 1	2	51N07	10E56	-0:43:44
Gebra 1	2	51N24	10E35	-0:42:20
Gedern 2	1	50N25	9E12	-0:36:48
Geesthacht 2	1	53N26	10E22	-0:41:28
Gefell 1	2	50N26	11E52	-0:47:28
Gefrees 2	4	50N06	11E44	-0:46:56
Gehrden 2	1	52N18	9E36	-0:38:24
Gehren 1	2	50N39	10E59	-0:43:56
Geilenkirchen 2	7	50N57	6E07	-0:24:28
Geisa 1	2	50N43	9E57	-0:39:48
Geisecke 2	1	51N27	7E37	-0:30:28
Geiselhöring 2	4	48N50	12E23	-0:49:32
Geisenfeld 2	4	48N41	11E37	-0:46:28
Geisenhausen 2	4	48N28	12E15	-0:49:00
Geisenheim 2	1	49N59	7E58	-0:31:52
Geising 1	2	50N45	13E47	-0:55:08
Geisingen 2	3	47N55	8E38	-0:34:32
Geislingen an der Steige 2	5	48N36	9E50	-0:39:20
Geismar 2	1	51N31	9E57	-0:39:48
Geisweid 2	1	50N55	8E01	-0:32:04
Geithain 1	2	51N03	12E41	-0:50:44
Geldern 2	7	51N31	6E20	-0:25:20
Gelenau 1	2	50N42	12E58	-0:51:52
Gelnhausen 2	1	50N11	9E11	-0:36:44
Gelsdorf 2	6	50N35	7E02	-0:28:08
Gelsenkirchen 2	1	51N31	7E07	-0:28:28
Geltendorf 2	4	48N07	11E01	-0:44:04
Gelting 2	1	54N45	9E53	-0:39:32
Geltow 1	2	52N22	12E58	-0:51:52
Gemen 2	1	51N51	6E52	-0:27:28
Gemünd 2	7	50N34	6E30	-0:26:00
Gemünden 2	1	50N58	8E58	-0:35:52
Gemünden 2	6	49N54	7E28	-0:29:52
Gemünden 2	4	50N03	9E41	-0:38:44
Gengenbach 2	3	48N24	8E01	-0:32:04
Gennebreck 2	1	51N19	7E12	-0:28:48
Genshagen 1	2	52N19	13E19	-0:53:16
Gensingen 2	6	49N53	7E55	-0:31:40
Gensungen 2	1	51N08	9E26	-0:37:44
Genthin 1	2	52N24	12E09	-0:48:36
Georgensgmünd 2	4	49N11	11E00	-0:44:00
Georgenthal 1	2	50N49	10E40	-0:42:40
Georgsmarienhütte 2	1	52N12	8E02	-0:32:08
Gera 1	2	50N52	12E04	-0:48:16
Geraberg 1	2	50N43	10E50	-0:43:20
Gerabronn 2	5	49N15	9E55	-0:39:40
Gerblingerode 2	1	51N29	10E15	-0:41:00
Gerbstedt 1	2	51N38	11E37	-0:46:28
Gerchsheim 2	4	49N42	9E47	-0:39:08
Geretsried 2	4	47N51	11E28	-0:45:52
Geringswalde 1	2	51N04	12E54	-0:51:36
Gerlingen 2	5	48N48	9E03	-0:36:12
Germendorf 1	2	52N45	13E10	-0:52:40
Germersheim 2	6	49N13	8E22	-0:33:28
Gernrode 1	2	51N43	11E08	-0:44:32
Gernsbach 2	3	48N46	8E19	-0:33:16
Gernsheim 2	1	49N44	8E29	-0:33:56

Geroda 2	4	50N17	9E53	-0:39:32
Geroldsgrün 2	4	50N20	11E35	-0:46:20
Geroldstein 2	1	50N06	7E56	-0:31:44
Gerolfing 2	4	48N45	11E21	-0:45:24
Gerolsbach 2	4	48N30	11E22	-0:45:28
Gerolstein 2	6	50N13	6E40	-0:26:40
Gerolzhofen 2	4	49N54	10E21	-0:41:24
Gersdorf 1	2	50N45	12E42	-0:50:48
Gersfeld 2	1	50N27	9E55	-0:39:40
Gerstetten 2	4	48N37	10E01	-0:40:04
Gersthofen 2	4	48N25	10E53	-0:43:32
Gerstungen 1	2	50N58	10E04	-0:40:16
Gerwisch 1	2	52N10	11E44	-0:46:56
Gerzen 2	4	48N31	12E25	-0:49:40
Gescher 2	1	51N57	6E59	-0:27:56
Geschwenda 1	2	50N44	10E49	-0:43:16
Gesees 2	4	49N54	11E32	-0:46:08
Geseke 2	1	51N38	8E31	-0:34:04
Gessertshausen 2	4	48N20	10E44	-0:42:56
Gettorf 2	1	54N24	9E58	-0:39:52
Gevelsberg 2	1	51N19	7E20	-0:29:20
Geyer 1	2	50N37	12E55	-0:51:40
Giebelstadt 2	4	49N39	9E56	-0:39:44
Gieboldehausen 2	1	51N36	10E13	-0:40:52
Gielow 1	2	53N42	12E44	-0:50:56
Gielsdorf 1	2	52N36	13E52	-0:55:28
Giengen 2	5	48N37	10E14	-0:40:56
Gierath 2	7	51N07	6E33	-0:26:12
Gieselwerder 2	1	51N36	9E33	-0:38:12
Giessen 2	1	50N35	8E40	-0:34:40
Gifhorn 2	1	52N29	10E33	-0:42:12
Giflitz 2	1	51N09	9E07	-0:36:28
Gilching 2	4	48N07	11E17	-0:45:08
Gildehaus 2	1	52N18	7E06	-0:28:24
Gilserberg 2	1	50N57	9E04	-0:36:16
Gimborn 2	1	51N03	7E28	-0:29:52
Ginderich 2	7	51N39	6E32	-0:26:08
Gingst 1	2	54N27	13E16	-0:53:04
Gittelde 2	1	51N48	10E10	-0:40:40
Gladbach → Mönchengladbach 2	7	51N12	6E28	-0:25:52
Gladbeck 2	1	51N34	6E59	-0:27:56
Gladenbach 2	1	50N46	8E34	-0:34:16
Glandorf 2	1	52N05	7E59	-0:31:56
Glashütte 1	2	50N51	13E47	-0:55:08
Glashütte 2	1	53N41	10E02	-0:40:08
Glasow 1	2	52N20	13E28	-0:53:52
Glatten 2	3	48N26	8E31	-0:34:04
Glaubitz 1	2	51N19	13E22	-0:53:28
Glauchau 1	2	50N49	12E32	-0:50:08
Glehn 2	7	51N10	6E35	-0:26:20
Gleidingen 2	1	52N16	9E50	-0:39:20
Gleschendorf 2	1	54N02	10E40	-0:42:40
Glesien 1	2	51N27	12E13	-0:48:52
Gleussen 2	4	50N08	10E53	-0:43:32
Glienicke 1	2	52N13	14E05	-0:56:20
Glienicke 1	2	52N37	13E19	-0:53:16
Glinde 2	1	53N32	10E13	-0:40:52
Glindow 1	2	52N21	12E54	-0:51:36
Glonn 2	4	47N59	11E52	-0:47:28
Glowe 1	2	54N35	13E28	-0:53:52
Glöwen 1	2	52N55	12E05	-0:48:20
Glücksburg 2	1	54N50	9E33	-0:38:12
Glückstadt 2	1	53N47	9E25	-0:37:40
Gmund am Tegernsee 2	4	47N45	11E44	-0:46:56
Gnarrenburg 2	1	53N22	9E00	-0:36:00
Gnoien 1	2	53N58	12E42	-0:50:48
Goch 2	7	51N41	6E10	-0:24:40
Gochsheim 2	4	50N01	10E16	-0:41:04
Goddelau 2	1	49N50	8E30	-0:34:00
Godelheim 2	1	51N44	9E22	-0:37:28
Godramstein 2	6	49N12	8E05	-0:32:20
Godshorn 2	1	52N26	9E43	-0:38:52
Göggingen 2	4	48N20	10E52	-0:43:28
Gohfeld 2	1	52N12	8E45	-0:35:00
Göhl 2	1	54N17	10E56	-0:43:44
Gohr 2	7	51N06	6E43	-0:26:52
Göhrde 2	1	53N08	10E52	-0:43:28
Göhren 1	2	54N20	13E44	-0:54:56
Goldbeck 1	2	52N43	11E52	-0:47:28
Goldberg 1	2	53N35	12E05	-0:48:20
Goldenstedt 2	1	52N48	8E25	-0:33:40
Goldlauter 1	2	50N38	10E44	-0:42:56
Golm 1	2	52N24	12E57	-0:51:48
Gölsdorf 1	2	51N59	12E39	-0:50:36
Golssen 1	2	51N58	13E36	-0:54:24
Golzow 1	2	52N34	14E29	-0:57:56
Golzow 1	2	52N16	12E36	-0:50:24
Gomaringen 2	5	48N27	9E05	-0:36:20
Gommern 1	2	52N04	11E50	-0:47:20
Göppingen 2	5	48N42	9E40	-0:38:40
Görgeshausen 2	1	50N24	7E56	-0:31:44
Göritz 1	2	53N24	13E54	-0:55:36
Göritzhain 1	2	50N58	12E47	-0:51:08
Görke 1	2	53N51	13E38	-0:54:32
Görlitz 1	2	51N09	14E59	-0:59:56
Gorlosen 1	2	53N11	11E27	-0:45:48
Görmin 1	2	53N59	13E16	-0:53:04
Gornau 1	2	50N46	13E02	-0:52:08
Görsdorf 1	2	51N54	13E29	-0:53:56
Görwihl 2	3	47N39	8E04	-0:32:16
Görzig 1	2	51N40	12E00	-0:48:00
Görzke 1	2	52N10	12E22	-0:49:28
Gosberg 2	4	49N42	11E07	-0:44:28
Gosen 1	2	52N24	13E43	-0:54:52
Goslar 2	1	51N54	10E25	-0:41:40
Gossa 1	2	51N40	12E26	-0:49:44
Gössenheim 2	4	50N01	9E46	-0:39:04
Gössnitz 1	2	50N53	12E26	-0:49:44
Gössweinstein 2	4	49N46	11E20	-0:45:20
Gotha 1	2	50N57	10E41	-0:42:44
Gottenheim 2	3	48N03	7E44	-0:30:56

Götterswickerhamm 2	1	51N35	6E40	-0:26:40
Gottesbrücke 1	2	52N25	13E49	-0:55:16
Göttin 1	2	52N27	12E54	-0:51:36
Götting 2	4	47N52	11E56	-0:47:44
Göttingen 2	1	51N32	9E55	-0:39:40
Göttingen 2	1	50N52	8E46	-0:35:04
Gottmadingen 2	3	47N44	8E47	-0:35:08
Gottsbüren 2	1	51N35	9E30	-0:38:00
Gottsdorf 2	4	48N32	13E44	-0:54:56
Goyatz 1	2	52N01	14E09	-0:56:36
Graben 2	3	49N09	8E29	-0:33:56
Grabenstätt 2	4	47N51	12E32	-0:50:08
Grabow 1	2	53N16	11E34	-0:46:16
Gräfelfing 2	4	48N07	11E25	-0:45:40
Grafenau 2	4	48N52	13E25	-0:53:40
Gräfenberg 2	4	49N39	11E15	-0:45:00
Gräfenhainichen 1	2	51N44	12E27	-0:49:48
Gräfenroda 1	2	50N45	10E48	-0:43:12
Gräfenthal 1	2	50N31	11E18	-0:45:12
Gräfentonna 1	2	51N05	10E44	-0:42:56
Grafenwöhr 2	4	49N43	11E54	-0:47:36
Gräfinau-Angstedt 1	2	50N42	11E01	-0:44:04
Grafing bei München 2	4	48N02	11E59	-0:47:56
Gramschatz 2	4	49N56	9E58	-0:39:52
Gramzow 1	2	53N12	14E00	-0:56:00
Gransee 1	2	53N00	13E09	-0:52:36
Granzin 1	2	53N25	12E53	-0:51:32
Granzin 1	2	53N30	11E56	-0:47:44
Grasdorf 2	1	52N06	10E09	-0:40:36
Grasleben 2	1	52N18	11E01	-0:44:04
Grassau 2	4	47N47	12E27	-0:49:48
Graupa 1	2	51N00	13E54	-0:55:36
Grävenwiesbach 2	1	50N23	8E27	-0:33:48
Grebenhain 2	1	50N29	9E19	-0:37:16
Grebenstein 2	1	51N26	9E24	-0:37:36
Greding 2	4	49N03	11E21	-0:45:24
Greene 2	1	51N52	9E56	-0:39:44
Greetsiel 2	1	53N30	7E05	-0:28:20
Grefrath 2	7	51N20	6E20	-0:25:20
Grefrath 2	7	51N10	6E38	-0:26:32
Greifendorf 1	2	51N01	13E06	-0:52:24
Greiffenberg 1	2	53N05	13E58	-0:55:52
Greifswald 1	2	54N05	13E23	-0:53:32
Greinsheim 2	6	49N18	8E16	-0:33:04
Greiz 1	2	50N39	12E12	-0:48:48
Gremersdorf 2	1	54N20	10E55	-0:43:40
Greppin 1	2	51N39	12E18	-0:49:12
Gresenhorst 1	2	54N09	12E26	-0:49:44
Greussen 1	2	51N14	10E57	-0:43:48
Greven 2	1	52N05	7E36	-0:30:24
Grevenbroich 2	7	51N05	6E35	-0:26:20
Greven-Granzin 1	2	53N29	10E48	-0:43:12
Grevesmühlen 1	2	53N51	11E10	-0:44:40
Griesbach 2	4	48N36	12E35	-0:50:20
Griesbach im Rottal 2	4	48N28	13E11	-0:52:44
Griesen 2	4	47N29	10E56	-0:43:44
Griesheim 2	1	49N50	8E34	-0:34:16
Griessem 2	1	52N00	9E12	-0:36:48
Grillenburg 1	2	50N57	13E31	-0:54:04
Grimma 1	2	51N14	12E43	-0:50:52
Grimmen 1	2	54N07	13E02	-0:52:08
Gristow 1	2	54N10	13E20	-0:53:20
Gröben 1	2	52N17	13E10	-0:52:40
Gröbenzell 2	4	48N11	11E22	-0:45:28
Gröbzig 1	2	51N41	11E52	-0:47:28
Gröditsch 1	2	52N03	13E59	-0:55:56
Gröditz 1	2	51N24	13E27	-0:53:48
Grohnde 2	1	52N01	9E25	-0:37:40
Groitzsch 1	2	51N09	12E16	-0:49:04
Grömitz 2	1	54N09	10E58	-0:43:52
Gronau 2	1	52N13	7E00	-0:28:00
Gronau 2	1	52N05	9E46	-0:39:04
Grone 2	1	51N32	9E53	-0:39:32
Grönenbach 2	4	47N52	10E13	-0:40:52
Gröningen 1	2	51N56	11E13	-0:44:52
Grönwohld 2	1	53N39	10E25	-0:41:40
Grossaitingen 2	4	48N14	10E47	-0:43:08
Grossalmerode 2	1	51N15	9E46	-0:39:04
Grossalsleben 1	2	51N59	11E13	-0:44:52
Gross Ammensleben 1	2	52N14	11E31	-0:46:04
Grossauheim 2	1	50N06	8E56	-0:35:44
Gross-Beeren 1	2	52N21	13E18	-0:53:12
Gross Berkel 2	1	52N04	9E19	-0:37:16
Gross-Bieberau 2	1	49N48	8E49	-0:35:16
Grossbodungen 1	2	51N28	10E28	-0:41:52
Gross Börnecke 1	2	51N50	11E29	-0:45:56
Grossbothen 1	2	51N11	12E44	-0:50:56
Grossbottwar 2	5	49N00	9E17	-0:37:08
Grossbreitenbach 1	2	50N35	11E02	-0:44:08
Grossburgwedel 2	1	52N29	9E51	-0:39:24
Grossdeuben 1	2	51N14	12E23	-0:49:32
Grossdubrau 1	2	51N15	14E28	-0:57:52
Gross Düngen 2	1	52N06	10E01	-0:40:04
Grossebersdorf 1	2	50N47	11E57	-0:47:48
Grossenbrode 2	1	54N22	11E05	-0:44:20
Grossen-Buseck 2	1	50N36	8E47	-0:35:08
Grossengottern 1	2	51N09	10E34	-0:42:16
Grossengstingen 2	5	48N23	9E17	-0:37:08
Grossenhain 1	2	51N17	13E31	-0:54:04

Grossenheidorn 2 1 52N27 9E23 -0:37:32
Grossenkneten 2 1 52N56 8E16 -0:33:04
Grossen-Linden 2 1 50N31 8E39 -0:34:36
Grossenlüder 2 1 50N35 9E32 -0:38:08
Grossenritte 2 1 51N15 9E23 -0:37:32
Grossenwiehe 2 1 54N43 9E15 -0:37:00
Gross-Gerau 2 1 49N55 8E29 -0:33:56
Gross Gleidingen 2 1 52N14 10E25 -0:41:40
Gross Glienicke 1 2 52N28 13E07 -0:52:28
Grossgörschen 1 2 51N13 12E11 -0:48:44
Gross Grönau 2 1 53N46 10E44 -0:42:56
Grosshansdorf 2 1 53N40 10E17 -0:41:08
Grosshartmannsdorf 1 2 50N48 13E19 -0:53:16
Gross-Hehlen 2 1 52N39 10E03 -0:40:12
Grossheide 2 1 53N35 7E20 -0:29:20
Grosshennersdorf 1 2 50N59 14E47 -0:59:08
Grossholzleute 2 5 47N41 10E05 -0:40:20
Grosskayna 1 2 51N17 11E56 -0:47:44
Gross Kienitz 1 2 52N19 13E28 -0:53:52
Gross-Kollmar 2 1 53N44 9E30 -0:38:00
Grosskorbetha 1 2 51N16 12E01 -0:48:04
Gross Kreutz 1 2 52N24 12E46 -0:51:04
Grosslehna 1 2 51N18 12E10 -0:48:40
Gross Leine 1 2 52N00 14E03 -0:56:12
Grosslittgen 2 6 50N02 6E47 -0:27:08
Grossmachnow 1 2 52N16 13E28 -0:53:52
Grossmehring 2 4 48N46 11E32 -0:46:08
Gross Muckrow 1 2 52N04 14E26 -0:57:44
Grössnöbach 2 4 48N21 11E35 -0:46:20
Gross Oesingen 2 1 52N38 10E29 -0:41:56
Grossörner 1 2 51N37 11E29 -0:45:56
Grossostheim 2 4 49N55 9E04 -0:36:16
Grosspostwitz 1 2 51N07 14E26 -0:57:44
Grossquenstedt 1 2 51N56 11E07 -0:44:28
Grossräschen 1 2 51N35 14E00 -0:56:00
Gross Rhüden 2 1 51N56 10E07 -0:40:28
Grossrinderfeld 2 3 49N39 9E44 -0:38:56
Gross Rodensleben 1 2 52N08 11E25 -0:45:40
Grossröhrsdorf 1 2 51N08 14E01 -0:56:04
Gross Rosenburg 1 2 51N55 11E53 -0:47:32
Grossrückerswalde 1 2 50N38 13E07 -0:52:28
Grossrudestedt 1 2 51N05 11E06 -0:44:24
Grosssachsenheim 2 5 48N58 9E04 -0:36:16
Gross-Sarau 2 1 53N45 10E44 -0:42:56
Grossschirma 1 2 50N58 13E17 -0:53:08
Grossschönau 1 2 50N54 14E40 -0:58:40
Gross Schönebeck 1 2 52N54 13E32 -0:54:08
Gross-Schulzendorf 1 2 52N16 13E21 -0:53:24
Grosstimmern 2 1 49N52 8E50 -0:35:20
Gross-Umstadt 2 1 49N52 8E55 -0:35:40
Grosswell 2 4 47N41 11E18 -0:45:12
Gross Wittensee 2 1 54N24 9E46 -0:39:04
Gross Ziethen 1 2 52N44 13E01 -0:52:04
Gross Ziethen 1 2 52N24 13E27 -0:53:48
Grosszimmern 2 1 49N52 8E50 -0:35:20
Grube 1 2 52N26 12E57 -0:51:48
Grube 2 1 54N14 11E01 -0:44:04
Grubweg 2 4 48N35 13E29 -0:53:56
Gruiten 2 1 51N14 7E01 -0:28:04
Grüna 1 2 50N49 12E47 -0:51:08
Grünbach 1 2 50N26 12E22 -0:49:28
Grünberg 2 1 50N35 8E58 -0:35:52
Grünefeld 1 2 52N41 12E58 -0:51:52
Grünenplan 2 1 51N57 9E44 -0:38:56
Grünewald 1 2 51N24 14E00 -0:56:00
Grünewald 2 1 51N13 7E37 -0:30:28
Grünhain 1 2 50N35 12E48 -0:51:12
Grünhainichen 1 2 50N46 13E08 -0:52:32
Grünheide 1 2 52N25 13E49 -0:55:16
Grünsfeld 2 3 49N36 9E44 -0:38:56
Grünstadt 2 6 49N34 8E10 -0:32:40
Grüntal 1 2 52N45 13E44 -0:54:56
Grünwald 2 4 48N02 11E31 -0:46:04
Gschwend 2 5 48N56 9E44 -0:38:56
Gudensberg 2 1 51N10 9E22 -0:37:28
Gudow 2 1 53N33 10E46 -0:43:04
Güglingen 2 5 49N04 9E00 -0:36:00
Gummersbach 2 1 51N02 7E34 -0:30:16
Gundelfingen 2 3 48N03 7E52 -0:31:28
Gundelfingen 2 4 48N33 10E22 -0:41:28
Gundelsdorf 2 4 48N33 11E03 -0:44:12
Gundelsheim 2 5 49N17 9E09 -0:36:36
Gündlkoferau 2 4 48N31 12E02 -0:48:08
Güntersberge 1 2 51N38 10E59 -0:43:56
Guntersblum 2 6 49N47 8E21 -0:33:24
Günzburg 2 4 48N27 10E16 -0:41:04
Gunzenhausen 2 4 49N07 10E45 -0:43:00
Güsen 1 2 52N21 11E59 -0:47:56
Güsten 1 2 51N49 11E35 -0:46:20
Gustorf 2 7 51N04 6E34 -0:26:16
Güstrow 1 2 53N48 12E10 -0:48:40
Gutach 2 3 48N15 8E13 -0:32:52
Güterfelde 1 2 52N22 13E12 -0:52:48
Gütersloh 2 1 51N54 8E23 -0:33:32
Guttau 1 2 51N15 14E34 -0:58:16
Gützkow 1 2 53N56 13E24 -0:53:36
Guxhagen 2 1 51N12 9E28 -0:37:52
Haagen 2 3 47N38 7E40 -0:30:40
Haag in Oberbayern 2 4 48N10 12E11 -0:48:44
Haan 2 1 51N11 7E00 -0:28:00
Haar 2 4 48N06 11E44 -0:46:56
Haaren 2 1 51N34 8E44 -0:34:56
Haberskirchen 2 4 48N31 12E39 -0:50:36
Hachen 2 1 51N22 7E59 -0:31:56
Hachenburg 2 1 50N39 7E50 -0:31:20
Hachmühlen 2 1 52N10 9E28 -0:37:52
Hadamar 2 1 50N27 8E02 -0:32:08
Hadmersleben 1 2 51N59 11E18 -0:45:12
Haffen-Mehr 2 1 51N44 6E28 -0:25:52
Haffkrug-Scharbeutz 2 1 54N03 10E44 -0:42:56
Hagau 2 4 48N43 11E22 -0:45:28
Hage 2 1 53N36 7E17 -0:29:08
Hagen 2 1 51N22 7E28 -0:29:52
Hagen 2 1 52N34 9E26 -0:37:44
Hagen 2 1 52N12 7E59 -0:31:56
Hagenow 1 2 53N26 11E11 -0:44:44
Hagenwerder 1 2 51N04 14E58 -0:59:52
Hahlen 2 1 52N18 8E50 -0:35:20
Hahn 2 1 50N31 7E53 -0:31:32
Hahnbach 2 4 49N32 11E48 -0:47:12
Hahnenberg 2 1 51N12 7E24 -0:29:36
Hahnenklee-Bockswiese 2 1 51N51 10E20 -0:41:20
Hahnstätten 2 1 50N18 8E04 -0:32:16
Haidhof 2 4 49N50 11E39 -0:46:36
Haidmühle 2 4 48N50 13E46 -0:55:04
Haiger 2 1 50N44 8E13 -0:32:52
Haigerloch 2 5 48N22 8E48 -0:35:12
Hailing 2 4 48N45 12E33 -0:50:12
Haimhausen 2 4 48N19 11E34 -0:46:16
Haina 2 1 51N02 8E58 -0:35:52
Hainchen 2 1 50N51 8E12 -0:32:48
Hainewalde 1 2 50N54 14E41 -0:58:44
Hainichen 1 2 50N58 13E07 -0:52:28
Hainsbach 2 4 48N44 12E25 -0:49:40
Hainsberg 1 2 50N59 13E38 -0:54:32
Halbe 1 2 52N06 13E42 -0:54:48
Halberstadt 1 2 51N54 11E02 -0:44:08
Haldensleben 1 2 52N18 11E26 -0:45:44
Haldern 2 1 51N46 6E27 -0:25:48
Halfing 2 4 47N57 12E16 -0:49:04
Halingen 2 1 51N27 7E44 -0:30:56
Halle 1 2 51N29 11E58 -0:47:52
Halle 2 1 52N04 8E22 -0:33:28
Halle 2 1 51N59 9E33 -0:38:12
Hallenberg 2 1 51N06 8E37 -0:34:28
Hallstadt 2 4 49N55 10E52 -0:43:28
Halsbrücke 1 2 50N57 13E21 -0:53:24
Halstenbek 2 1 53N38 9E50 -0:39:20
Haltern 2 1 51N46 7E10 -0:28:40
Halver 2 1 51N11 7E30 -0:30:00
Hambergen 2 1 53N18 8E49 -0:35:16
Hambourg → Hamburg 2 1 53N33 9E59 -0:39:56
Hamburg 2 1 53N33 9E59 -0:39:56
Hamburgo → Hamburg 2 1 53N33 9E59 -0:39:56
Hämelerwald 2 1 52N22 10E05 -0:40:20
Hameln 2 1 52N06 9E21 -0:37:24
Hamersleben 1 2 52N04 11E05 -0:44:20
Hamm 2 1 51N41 7E49 -0:31:16
Hamm 2 1 51N43 7E10 -0:28:40
Hammelburg 2 4 50N07 9E53 -0:39:32
Hammerbrücke 1 2 50N26 12E25 -0:49:40
Hämmern 2 1 51N08 7E21 -0:29:24
Hamminkeln 2 1 51N44 6E35 -0:26:20
Hanau 2 1 50N08 8E55 -0:35:40
Handorf 2 1 51N59 7E41 -0:30:44
Handzell 2 4 48N34 11E04 -0:44:16
Hänigsen 2 1 52N29 10E05 -0:40:20
Hankensbüttel 2 1 52N44 10E36 -0:42:24
Hannover 2 1 52N24 9E44 -0:38:56
Hanover → Hannover 2 1 52N24 9E44 -0:38:56
Hanovre → Hannover 2 1 52N24 9E44 -0:38:56
Harbke 1 2 52N12 11E03 -0:44:12
Harburg 2 4 48N47 10E41 -0:42:44
Harburg-Wilhelmsburg 2 1 53N28 9E59 -0:39:56
Hardegsen 2 1 51N39 9E49 -0:39:16
Hardheim 2 3 49N36 9E28 -0:37:52
Hardt 2 1 51N07 6E58 -0:27:52
Haren 2 1 52N47 7E14 -0:28:56
Harlesiel 2 1 53N43 7E49 -0:31:16
Harlingerode 2 1 51N54 10E31 -0:42:04
Harpstedt 2 1 52N54 8E35 -0:34:20
Harrislee 2 1 54N48 9E22 -0:37:28
Harsefeld 2 1 53N27 9E30 -0:38:00
Harsewinkel 2 1 51N58 8E13 -0:32:52
Harsleben 1 2 51N52 11E05 -0:44:20
Harsum 2 1 52N12 9E57 -0:39:48
Hartenholm 2 1 53N54 10E03 -0:40:12
Hartenstein 1 2 50N39 12E40 -0:50:40
Hartha 1 2 51N05 12E58 -0:51:52
Hartmannsdorf 1 2 50N53 12E48 -0:51:12
Hartmannshain 2 1 50N28 9E16 -0:37:04
Harzgerode 1 2 51N38 11E08 -0:44:32
Hasbergen 2 1 52N14 7E57 -0:31:48
Hasbergen 2 1 53N05 8E40 -0:34:40
Haselünne 2 1 52N40 7E29 -0:29:56
Haslach im Kinzigtal 2 3 48N16 8E06 -0:32:24
Hassbergen 2 1 52N44 9E13 -0:36:52
Hassel 2 1 52N48 9E11 -0:36:44
Hasselbeck-Schwarzbach 2 1 51N16 6E53 -0:27:32
Hasselfelde 1 2 51N41 10E51 -0:43:24
Hassfurt 2 4 50N02 10E31 -0:42:04
Hassleben 1 2 53N13 13E41 -0:54:44
Hasslinghausen 2 1 51N20 7E17 -0:29:08
Hassloch 2 6 49N22 8E16 -0:33:04
Hatten 2 1 53N02 8E22 -0:33:28
Hattenhofen 2 4 48N13 11E07 -0:44:28
Hattingen 2 1 51N23 7E10 -0:28:40
Hattorf (am Harz) 2 1 51N39 10E14 -0:40:56
Hattstedt 2 1 54N31 9E01 -0:36:04
Haunersdorf 2 4 48N36 12E43 -0:50:52
Haunstetten 2 4 48N18 10E54 -0:43:36
Hausham 2 4 47N45 11E50 -0:47:20
Haussömmern 1 2 51N11 10E49 -0:43:16
Hauzenberg 2 4 48N39 13E38 -0:54:32
Havelberg 1 2 52N50 12E04 -0:48:16
Havixbeck 2 1 51N58 7E25 -0:29:40
Hechingen 2 5 48N21 8E58 -0:35:52
Hechthausen 2 1 53N38 9E14 -0:36:56
Heckelberg 1 2 52N44 13E50 -0:55:20
Hecklingen 1 2 51N51 11E32 -0:46:08
Hedemünden 2 1 51N23 9E46 -0:39:04
Hedersleben 1 2 51N51 11E15 -0:45:00
Heek 2 1 52N07 7E06 -0:28:24
Heepen 2 1 52N01 8E35 -0:34:20
Heeren-Werve 2 1 51N35 7E43 -0:30:52
Heeslingen 2 1 53N19 9E20 -0:37:20
Heessen 2 1 51N42 7E50 -0:31:20
Hehlen 2 1 51N59 9E28 -0:37:52
Heide 2 1 54N12 9E06 -0:36:24
Heideck 2 4 49N08 11E07 -0:44:28
Heidelberg 2 3 49N25 8E43 -0:34:52
Heidelsheim 2 3 49N06 8E38 -0:34:32
Heiden 2 1 51N59 8E50 -0:35:20
Heidenau 1 2 50N59 13E52 -0:55:28
Heidenau 2 1 53N19 9E39 -0:38:36
Heidenheim 2 4 49N01 10E44 -0:42:56
Heidenheim an der Brenz 2 5 48N40 10E08 -0:40:32
Heidenoldendorf 2 1 51N57 8E50 -0:35:20
Heigenbrücken 2 4 50N02 9E23 -0:37:32
Heikendorf 2 1 54N22 10E12 -0:40:48
Heil 2 1 51N38 7E35 -0:30:20
Heilbronn 2 5 49N08 9E13 -0:36:52
Heiligenberg 2 3 47N49 9E19 -0:37:16
Heiligendamm 1 2 54N08 11E50 -0:47:20
Heiligenhafen 2 1 54N22 10E58 -0:43:52
Heiligenhaus 2 1 51N19 6E59 -0:27:56
Heiligenstadt 1 2 51N23 10E09 -0:40:36
Heiligenstadt 2 4 49N51 11E10 -0:44:40
Heilsbronn 2 4 49N20 10E47 -0:43:08
Heimbach 2 7 50N38 6E28 -0:25:52
Heimbuchenthal 2 4 49N53 9E17 -0:37:08
Heimburg 1 2 51N49 10E54 -0:43:36
Heimenkirch 2 4 47N37 9E53 -0:39:32
Heimsheim 2 5 48N48 8E51 -0:35:24
Heinersdorf 1 2 52N27 14E13 -0:56:52
Heinersdorf 1 2 52N23 13E20 -0:53:20
Heining 2 4 48N35 13E24 -0:53:36
Heinrichshorst 1 2 52N20 11E42 -0:46:48
Heinsberg 2 7 51N03 6E05 -0:24:20
Heisfelde 2 1 53N15 7E26 -0:29:44
Heitersheim 2 3 47N53 7E40 -0:30:40
Helbra 1 2 51N33 11E29 -0:45:56
Heldburg 1 2 50N17 10E44 -0:42:56
Helden 2 1 51N07 7E56 -0:31:44
Heldenbergen 2 1 50N14 8E52 -0:35:28
Heldra 2 1 51N07 10E11 -0:40:44
Heldrungen 1 2 51N18 11E13 -0:44:52
Helenenberg 2 6 49N51 6E32 -0:26:08
Helfta 1 2 51N30 11E34 -0:46:16
Helgoland 2 1 54N12 7E53 -0:31:32
Hellenthal 2 7 50N29 6E26 -0:25:44
Hellern 2 1 52N15 7E58 -0:31:52
Hellersen 2 1 51N12 7E39 -0:30:36
Helmbrechts 2 4 50N14 11E43 -0:46:52
Helmstedt 2 1 52N13 11E00 -0:44:00
Hemau 2 4 49N03 11E47 -0:47:08
Hemeln 2 1 51N30 9E36 -0:38:24
Hemer 2 1 51N23 7E46 -0:31:04
Hemfurth-Edersee 2 1 51N10 9E02 -0:36:08
Hemmerde 2 1 51N33 7E48 -0:31:12
Hemmerden 2 7 51N07 6E36 -0:26:24
Hemmingen-Westerfeld 2 1 52N19 9E45 -0:39:00
Hemmoor 2 1 53N41 9E08 -0:36:32
Hengersberg 2 4 48N47 13E03 -0:52:12
Hengsen 2 1 51N29 7E38 -0:30:32
Henneberg 1 2 50N29 10E21 -0:41:24
Hennef 2 1 50N46 7E16 -0:29:04
Hennen 2 1 51N27 7E39 -0:30:36
Hennickendorf 1 2 52N30 13E51 -0:55:24
Hennigsdorf 1 2 52N38 13E12 -0:52:48
Henrichenburg 2 1 51N35 7E19 -0:29:16
Henstedt-Ulzburg 2 1 53N47 9E58 -0:39:52
Heppenheim an der Bergstrasse 2 1 49N39 8E38 -0:34:32
Herbede 2 1 51N25 7E16 -0:29:04
Herbern 2 1 51N44 7E39 -0:30:36
Herbertingen 2 5 48N04 9E26 -0:37:44
Herbolzheim 2 3 48N13 7E47 -0:31:08
Herborn 2 1 50N40 8E17 -0:33:08
Herbrechtingen 2 5 48N37 10E10 -0:40:40
Herbsleben 1 2 51N07 10E50 -0:43:20
Herbstein 2 1 50N34 9E20 -0:37:20
Herdecke 2 1 51N24 7E26 -0:29:44
Herdorf 2 1 50N46 7E56 -0:31:44
Herdringen 2 1 51N25 7E58 -0:31:52
Herford 2 1 52N06 8E40 -0:34:40

Place		Lat	Long	Time
Hergatz 2	4	47N39	9E50	-0:39:20
Hergisdorf 1	2	51N32	11E28	-0:45:52
Herhahn 2	7	50N33	6E26	-0:25:44
Heringen 1	2	51N27	10E52	-0:43:28
Heringsdorf 2	1	54N18	11E00	-0:44:00
Herleshausen 2	1	51N00	10E09	-0:40:36
Hermannsburg 2	1	52N50	10E05	-0:40:20
Hermannstein 2	1	50N35	8E29	-0:33:56
Hermeskeil 2	6	49N39	6E56	-0:27:44
Hermsdorf 1	2	50N54	11E52	-0:47:28
Herne 2	1	51N32	7E13	-0:28:52
Herongen 2	7	51N24	6E15	-0:25:00
Herpf 1	2	50N34	10E20	-0:41:20
Herrenalb 2	3	48N48	8E26	-0:33:44
Herrenberg 2	5	48N35	8E52	-0:35:28
Herrieden 2	4	49N14	10E30	-0:42:00
Herringen 2	1	51N40	7E44	-0:30:56
Herrlingen 2	5	48N25	9E53	-0:39:32
Herrnburg 1	2	53N47	10E45	-0:43:00
Herrnhut 1	2	51N01	14E44	-0:58:56
Herrsching am Ammersee 2	4	48N00	11E10	-0:44:40
Hersbruck 2	4	49N30	11E26	-0:45:44
Herschbach 2	1	50N34	7E44	-0:30:56
Herscheid 2	1	51N10	7E44	-0:30:56
Herten 2	1	51N35	7E07	-0:28:28
Hervest 2	1	51N40	7E01	-0:28:04
Herxheim 2	6	49N09	8E13	-0:32:52
Herzberg 1	2	52N54	12E58	-0:51:52
Herzberg 1	2	51N41	13E14	-0:52:56
Herzberg am Harz 2	1	51N39	10E20	-0:41:20
Herzebrock 2	1	51N53	8E14	-0:32:56
Herzfeld 2	1	51N40	8E08	-0:32:32
Herzfelde 1	2	52N29	13E50	-0:55:20
Herzhausen 2	1	51N11	8E53	-0:35:32
Herzogenaurach 2	4	49N34	10E53	-0:43:32
Herzsprung 1	2	53N04	12E28	-0:49:52
Hesel 2	1	53N18	7E35	-0:30:20
Hesepe 2	1	52N26	7E58	-0:31:52
Hesselte 2	1	52N25	7E22	-0:29:28
Hessen 1	2	52N02	10E15	-0:41:00
Hessenthal 2	4	49N55	9E17	-0:37:08
Hessisch Lichtenau 2	1	51N12	9E43	-0:38:52
Hessisch Oldendorf 2	1	52N10	9E15	-0:37:00
Hettenleidelheim 2	6	49N32	8E04	-0:32:16
Hettingen 2	5	48N13	9E14	-0:36:56
Hettstedt 1	2	51N38	11E30	-0:46:00
Hetzerath 2	6	49N52	6E49	-0:27:16
Heudeber 1	2	51N54	10E50	-0:43:20
Heustreu 2	4	50N21	10E15	-0:41:00
Heusweiler 2	6	49N20	6E55	-0:27:40
Heyerode 1	2	51N10	10E25	-0:41:40
Hiddenhausen 2	1	52N08	8E38	-0:34:32
Hiddesen 2	1	51N55	8E50	-0:35:20
Hiddinghausen 2	1	51N22	7E17	-0:29:08
Hienheim 2	4	48N52	11E46	-0:47:04
Hiesfeld 2	1	51N33	6E46	-0:27:04
Hilbersdorf 1	2	50N55	13E23	-0:53:32
Hilchenbach 2	1	51N00	8E06	-0:32:24
Hildburghausen 1	2	50N25	10E44	-0:42:56
Hilden 2	1	51N10	6E56	-0:27:44
Hilders 2	1	50N34	10E00	-0:40:00
Hildesheim 2	1	52N09	9E57	-0:39:48
Hilgen 2	1	51N06	7E09	-0:28:36
Hille 2	1	52N20	8E44	-0:34:56
Hillegossen 2	1	51N59	8E37	-0:34:28
Hillesheim 2	6	50N18	6E38	-0:26:32
Hillmersdorf 1	2	51N42	13E29	-0:53:56
Hilpotstein 2	4	49N12	11E12	-0:44:48
Hilter 2	1	52N08	8E08	-0:32:32
Hiltpolstein 2	4	49N40	11E19	-0:45:16
Hiltrup 2	1	51N54	7E38	-0:30:32
Himmelpforten 2	1	53N36	9E18	-0:37:12
Himmelsthür 2	1	52N09	9E55	-0:39:40
Hindelang 2	4	47N30	10E22	-0:41:28
Hinsbeck 2	7	51N21	6E17	-0:25:08
Hinte 2	1	53N25	7E11	-0:28:44
Hinterhermsdorf 1	2	50N55	14E22	-0:57:28
Hintersee 1	2	53N37	14E16	-0:57:04
Hintersee 2	4	47N36	12E50	-0:51:20
Hinterweidenthal 2	6	49N12	7E45	-0:31:00
Hinterzarten 2	3	47N54	8E06	-0:32:24
Hirsau 2	5	48N44	8E44	-0:34:56
Hirschaid 2	4	49N49	10E59	-0:43:56
Hirschau 2	4	49N33	11E57	-0:47:48
Hirschbach 1	2	50N33	10E44	-0:42:56
Hirschberg 1	2	50N24	11E49	-0:47:16
Hirschfeld 1	2	51N23	13E37	-0:54:28
Hirschfelde 1	2	50N57	14E53	-0:59:32
Hirschfelde 1	2	52N38	13E48	-0:55:12
Hirschhorn 2	3	49N27	8E53	-0:35:32
Hitzacker 2	1	53N09	11E02	-0:44:08
Höchberg 2	4	49N49	9E51	-0:39:24
Hochdahl 2	1	51N13	6E56	-0:27:44
Höchenschwand 2	3	47N44	8E10	-0:32:40
Hochheide 2	7	51N27	6E41	-0:26:44
Hochheim 2	1	50N01	8E20	-0:33:20
Hochkirch 1	2	51N09	14E34	-0:58:16
Hochneukirch 2	7	51N06	6E26	-0:25:44
Hochspeyer 2	6	49N26	7E54	-0:31:36
Höchst 2	1	49N48	8E59	-0:35:56
Höchstadt an der Aisch 2	4	49N42	10E44	-0:42:56
Höchstädt an der Donau 2	4	48N36	10E34	-0:42:16
Höchsten 2	1	51N27	7E29	-0:29:56
Höchstenbach 2	1	50N38	7E44	-0:30:56
Hockenheim 2	3	49N19	8E33	-0:34:12
Hockeroda 1	2	50N35	11E26	-0:45:44
Hodenhagen 2	1	52N46	9E35	-0:38:20
Hoeningen 2	7	51N05	6E41	-0:26:44
Hoerstgen 2	7	51N30	6E27	-0:25:48
Hof 2	4	50N18	11E55	-0:47:40
Hofeld 2	6	49N30	7E09	-0:28:36
Höfen 2	7	50N32	6E15	-0:25:00
Höfen 2	4	49N08	11E21	-0:45:24
Hoffnung 2	1	51N07	7E13	-0:28:52
Hofgeismar 2	1	51N30	9E22	-0:37:28
Hofheim 2	1	50N07	8E26	-0:33:44
Hofheim in Unterfranken 2	4	50N08	10E31	-0:42:04
Hofweier 2	3	48N25	7E55	-0:31:40
Hohebach 2	5	49N22	9E44	-0:38:56
Hohegeiss 2	1	51N40	10E40	-0:42:40
Hohenaschau 2	4	47N45	12E19	-0:49:16
Hohenberg 2	4	49N16	11E30	-0:46:00
Hohenbrunn 2	4	48N03	11E42	-0:46:48
Hohenbucko 1	2	51N46	13E28	-0:53:52
Hohendorf 1	2	54N01	13E44	-0:54:56
Hohenebra 1	2	51N18	10E49	-0:43:16
Hoheneggelsen 2	1	52N13	10E10	-0:40:40
Hohenfels 2	4	49N12	11E51	-0:47:24
Hohenfurch 2	4	47N51	10E54	-0:43:36
Hohengüstow 1	2	53N14	13E59	-0:55:56
Hohenhameln 2	1	52N15	10E03	-0:40:12
Hohenheide 2	1	51N29	7E47	-0:31:08
Hohenirlach 2	4	49N22	12E13	-0:48:52
Hohenkammer 2	4	48N25	11E32	-0:46:08
Hohenkirchen 1	2	50N51	10E41	-0:42:44
Hohenkirchen 1	2	53N51	11E17	-0:45:08
Hohenkirchen 2	1	51N23	9E29	-0:37:56
Hohenkirchen 2	1	53N39	7E55	-0:31:40
Hohenleipisch 1	2	51N30	13E34	-0:54:16
Hohenleuben 1	2	50N43	12E03	-0:48:12
Hohenlimburg 2	1	51N21	7E35	-0:30:20
Hohenlinden 2	4	48N09	12E00	-0:48:00
Hohenmölsen 1	2	51N09	12E06	-0:48:24
Hohen Neuendorf 1	2	52N40	13E16	-0:53:04
Hohenpolding 2	4	48N23	12E08	-0:48:32
Hohenseeden 1	2	52N19	12E01	-0:48:04
Hohenseefeld 1	2	51N53	13E18	-0:53:12
Hohenstaufen 2	5	48N44	9E43	-0:38:52
Hohenstein-Ernstthal 1	2	50N48	12E42	-0:50:48
Hohenthurm 1	2	51N31	12E05	-0:48:20
Hohenwart 2	4	48N36	11E23	-0:45:32
Hohenwarthe 1	2	52N13	11E42	-0:46:48
Hohenwutzen 1	2	52N51	14E07	-0:56:28
Hohenzethen 2	1	53N03	10E49	-0:43:16
Hoherlehme 1	2	52N19	13E37	-0:54:28
Höhn 2	1	50N37	8E00	-0:32:00
Hohndorf 1	2	50N45	12E40	-0:50:40
Hohne 2	1	52N35	10E22	-0:41:28
Hohnstein 1	2	50N59	14E10	-0:56:40
Hohwacht 2	1	54N19	10E41	-0:42:44
Hoisdorf 2	1	53N39	10E20	-0:41:20
Hoisten 2	7	51N08	6E42	-0:26:48
Holdenstedt 2	1	52N55	10E31	-0:42:04
Holdorf 2	1	52N35	8E07	-0:32:28
Hollage 2	1	52N20	7E58	-0:31:52
Holleben 1	2	51N26	11E53	-0:47:32
Hollenstedt 2	1	53N22	9E43	-0:38:52
Hollern 2	1	53N36	9E32	-0:38:08
Hollfeld 2	4	49N56	11E18	-0:45:12
Hollingstedt 2	1	54N27	9E19	-0:37:16
Holnstein 2	4	49N33	11E39	-0:46:36
Holsterhausen 2	1	51N41	6E57	-0:27:48
Holthausen 2	1	52N33	7E17	-0:29:08
Holthausen 2	1	51N23	7E13	-0:28:52
Holthusen 2	1	53N08	7E18	-0:29:12
Holtorf 2	1	52N40	9E13	-0:36:52
Holtwick 2	1	52N00	7E05	-0:28:20
Holzbüttgen 2	7	51N12	6E37	-0:26:28
Holzen 2	1	51N26	7E31	-0:30:04
Holzgerlingen 2	5	48N38	9E00	-0:36:00
Holzhausen 1	2	51N18	12E28	-0:49:52
Holzhausen 2	1	52N17	8E32	-0:34:08
Holzhausen 2	1	52N13	8E01	-0:32:04
Holzhausen 2	1	52N01	8E44	-0:34:56
Holzhausen an der Haide 2	1	50N13	7E55	-0:31:40
Holzheim 2	7	51N09	6E39	-0:26:36
Holzkirchen 2	4	47N52	11E42	-0:46:48
Holzminden 2	1	51N50	9E27	-0:37:48
Holzweissig 1	2	51N36	12E18	-0:49:12
Holzwickede 2	1	51N30	7E36	-0:30:24
Homberg 2	1	50N43	8E59	-0:35:56
Homberg 2	1	51N02	9E24	-0:37:36
Homberg 2	7	51N28	6E38	-0:26:32
Homberg 2	1	51N18	6E56	-0:27:44
Homburg 2	6	49N19	7E20	-0:29:20
Homburg → Bad Homburg vor der Höhe 2	1	50N13	8E37	-0:34:28
Hönebach 2	1	50N56	9E56	-0:39:44
Höngen 2	7	51N02	5E56	-0:23:44
Hönow 1	2	52N32	13E38	-0:54:32
Hoof 2	1	51N17	9E20	-0:37:20
Hoogstede 2	1	52N34	6E56	-0:27:44
Hooksiel 2	1	53N38	8E01	-0:32:04
Hoppegarten 1	2	52N31	13E40	-0:54:40
Hoppenrade 1	2	52N32	12E56	-0:51:44
Hopsten 2	1	52N23	7E36	-0:30:24
Horb am Neckar 2	3	48N26	8E41	-0:34:44
Hörbering 2	4	48N23	12E33	-0:50:12
Horka 1	2	51N16	14E56	-0:59:44
Horn 2	1	51N52	8E56	-0:35:44
Hornbach 2	6	49N11	7E22	-0:29:28
Hornberg 2	3	48N13	8E13	-0:32:52
Hornburg 2	1	52N01	10E36	-0:42:24
Horneburg 2	1	53N30	9E34	-0:38:16
Horneburg 2	1	51N38	7E18	-0:29:12
Hornhausen 1	2	52N02	11E10	-0:44:40
Hornow 1	2	51N38	14E31	-0:58:04
Hornstorf 1	2	53N54	11E32	-0:46:08
Horrem 2	7	51N06	6E48	-0:27:12
Hörsingen 1	2	52N16	11E09	-0:44:36
Horst 1	2	53N22	10E37	-0:42:28
Horst 2	1	53N48	9E37	-0:38:28
Hörstel 2	1	52N18	7E35	-0:30:20
Horstmar 2	1	52N05	7E17	-0:29:08
Horumersiel 2	1	53N41	8E00	-0:32:00
Hösbach 2	4	50N00	9E12	-0:36:48
Hösel 2	1	51N19	6E54	-0:27:36
Hosena 1	2	51N27	14E01	-0:56:04
Hötensleben 1	2	52N08	11E01	-0:44:04
Hötzum 2	1	52N13	10E37	-0:42:28
Hövelhof 2	1	51N49	8E40	-0:34:40
Höxter 2	1	51N46	9E23	-0:37:32
Hoya 2	1	52N48	9E08	-0:36:32
Hoyerswerda 1	2	51N26	14E14	-0:56:56
Hoym 1	2	51N47	11E19	-0:45:16
Hubbelrath 2	1	51N16	6E55	-0:27:40
Hückelhoven-Ratheim 2	7	51N04	6E10	-0:24:40
Hückeswagen 2	1	51N08	7E20	-0:29:20
Hude 2	1	53N07	8E27	-0:33:48
Hüffenhardt 2	3	49N18	9E04	-0:36:16
Hüfingen 2	3	47N55	8E29	-0:33:56
Hüinghausen 2	1	51N11	7E48	-0:31:12
Huldsessen 2	4	48N24	12E42	-0:50:48
Hüls 2	1	51N40	7E08	-0:28:32
Hüls 2	7	51N22	6E30	-0:26:00
Hülscheid 2	1	51N16	7E34	-0:30:16
Hümpfershausen 1	2	50N40	10E13	-0:40:52
Hundeluft 1	2	51N58	12E20	-0:49:20
Hünfeld 2	1	50N40	9E46	-0:39:04
Hungen 2	1	50N28	8E54	-0:35:36
Hunswinkel 2	1	51N05	7E48	-0:31:12
Hünxe 2	1	51N38	6E46	-0:27:04
Hürth 2	7	50N52	6E51	-0:27:24
Husum 2	1	54N28	9E03	-0:36:12
Hüttental 2	1	50N54	8E02	-0:32:08
Hütting 2	4	48N48	11E07	-0:44:28
Ibbenbüren 2	1	52N16	7E43	-0:30:52
Iburg 2	1	52N09	8E02	-0:32:08
Ichenhausen 2	4	48N22	10E18	-0:41:12
Ichenheim 2	3	48N26	7E49	-0:31:16
Ichtershausen 1	2	50N52	10E58	-0:43:52
Icking 2	4	47N57	11E25	-0:45:40
Idar-Oberstein 2	6	49N42	7E19	-0:29:16
Iden 1	2	52N46	11E55	-0:47:40
Idstedt 2	1	54N35	9E31	-0:38:04
Idstein 2	1	50N13	8E16	-0:33:04
Iffezheim 2	3	48N49	8E08	-0:32:32
Ifta 1	2	51N04	10E11	-0:40:44
Igel 2	6	49N42	6E32	-0:26:08
Igelsberg 2	3	48N32	8E26	-0:33:44
Igersheim 2	5	49N29	9E49	-0:39:16
Iggensbach 2	4	48N44	13E08	-0:52:32
Ihlienworth 2	1	53N44	8E55	-0:35:40
Ihmert 2	1	51N20	7E44	-0:30:56
Ihringen 2	3	48N02	7E39	-0:30:36
Ihringshausen 2	1	51N21	9E31	-0:38:04
Ihrlerstein 2	4	48N56	11E52	-0:47:28
Ilberstedt 1	2	51N48	11E40	-0:46:40
Ilfeld 1	2	51N34	10E47	-0:43:08
Illertissen 2	4	48N13	10E06	-0:40:24
Illingen 2	5	48N57	8E55	-0:35:40
Ilmenau 1	2	50N41	10E55	-0:43:40
Ilsenburg 1	2	51N52	10E40	-0:42:40
Ilshofen 2	5	49N10	9E55	-0:39:40
Ilten 2	1	52N21	9E55	-0:39:40
Ilverich 2	7	51N17	6E42	-0:26:48
Imgenbroich 2	7	50N34	6E16	-0:25:04
Immendingen 2	3	47N56	8E44	-0:34:56
Immenhausen 2	1	51N25	9E28	-0:37:52
Immensen 2	1	52N23	10E04	-0:40:16
Immenstaad 2	5	47N40	9E22	-0:37:28
Immenstadt 2	4	47N33	10E13	-0:40:52
Immigrath 2	1	51N06	6E57	-0:27:48
Impflingen 2	6	49N10	8E07	-0:32:28
In der Bredde 2	1	51N20	7E23	-0:29:32
Ingelfingen 2	5	49N18	9E39	-0:38:36
Ingelheim 2	6	49N59	8E05	-0:32:20
Ingolstadt 2	4	48N46	11E27	-0:45:48
Inning 2	4	48N05	11E09	-0:44:36
Inzell 2	4	47N46	12E44	-0:50:56
Iphofen 2	4	49N42	10E15	-0:41:00
Ippinghausen 2	1	51N17	9E08	-0:36:32
Irrel 2	6	49N51	6E28	-0:25:52
Irschenberg 2	4	47N50	11E55	-0:47:40
Irsee 2	4	47N54	10E34	-0:42:16
Isen 2	4	48N13	12E04	-0:48:16
Isenbüttel 2	1	52N26	10E34	-0:42:16
Iserlohn 2	1	51N22	7E41	-0:30:44
Ismaning 2	4	48N14	11E41	-0:46:44
Isny 2	5	47N41	10E02	-0:40:08
Ispringen 2	3	48N55	8E40	-0:34:40
Isselburg 2	1	51N51	6E28	-0:25:52
Isselhorst 2	1	51N57	8E24	-0:33:36
Issum 2	7	51N32	6E25	-0:25:40
Itzehoe 2	1	53N55	9E31	-0:38:04
Jabel 1	2	53N32	12E32	-0:50:08
Jachenau 2	4	47N36	11E25	-0:45:40
Jade 2	1	53N20	8E14	-0:32:56
Jagel 2	1	54N27	9E32	-0:38:08
Jagsthausen 2	5	49N19	9E28	-0:37:52
Jagstzell 2	5	49N02	10E05	-0:40:20
Jahnsdorf 1	2	50N44	12E51	-0:51:24
Jandelsbrunn 2	4	48N44	13E42	-0:54:48
Jarmen 1	2	53N55	13E20	-0:53:20
Jatznick 1	2	53N35	13E56	-0:55:44
Jävenitz 1	2	52N31	11E30	-0:46:00

Place		Lat.	Long.	Time
Jeber-Bergfrieden 1	2	51N59	12E20	-0:49:20
Jemgum 2	1	53N16	7E23	-0:29:32
Jena 1	2	50N56	11E35	-0:46:20
Jerichow 1	2	52N30	12E01	-0:48:04
Jerxheim 2	1	52N05	10E54	-0:43:36
Jeserig bei Wiesenburg 1	2	52N05	12E27	-0:49:48
Jessen 1	2	51N47	12E58	-0:51:52
Jessnitz 1	2	51N41	12E17	-0:49:08
Jestetten 2	3	47N39	8E34	-0:34:16
Jettingen 2	4	48N23	10E26	-0:41:44
Jever 2	1	53N34	7E54	-0:31:36
Joachimsthal 1	2	52N58	13E44	-0:54:56
Jocketa 1	2	50N33	12E10	-0:48:40
Johanngeorgenstadt 1	2	50N26	12E43	-0:50:52
Johanniskreuz 2	6	49N20	7E49	-0:31:16
Jöhstadt 1	2	50N30	13E05	-0:52:20
Jöllenbeck 2	1	52N11	8E45	-0:35:00
Jonsdorf 1	2	50N51	14E43	-0:58:52
Jördenstorf 1	2	53N52	12E37	-0:50:28
Jörlfeld 2	1	54N38	9E15	-0:37:00
Jossa 2	1	50N14	9E35	-0:38:20
Jüchen 2	7	51N06	6E30	-0:26:00
Juchhöh 1	2	50N24	11E52	-0:47:28
Jühnsdorf 1	2	52N18	13E23	-0:53:32
Juist 2	1	53N40	6E59	-0:27:56
Jülich 2	7	50N55	6E21	-0:25:24
Jütchendorf 1	2	52N16	13E10	-0:52:40
Jüterbog 1	2	51N59	13E04	-0:52:16
Kaarssen 1	2	53N12	11E02	-0:44:08
Kaarst 2	7	51N14	6E37	-0:26:28
Kablow 1	2	52N18	13E44	-0:54:56
Kablower Ziegelei 1	2	52N19	13E43	-0:54:52
Kahla 1	2	50N48	11E35	-0:46:20
Kahl am Main 2	4	50N04	9E00	-0:36:00
Kaisersesch 2	6	50N14	7E08	-0:28:32
Kaiserslautern 2	6	49N26	7E46	-0:31:04
Kaisheim 2	4	48N46	10E48	-0:43:12
Kalbe 1	2	52N40	11E25	-0:45:40
Kalkar 2	7	50N36	6E46	-0:27:04
Kalkhorst 1	2	53N58	11E02	-0:44:08
Kalkum 2	1	51N18	6E46	-0:27:04
Kall 2	7	50N32	6E32	-0:26:08
Kalletal 2	1	52N06	8E56	-0:35:44
Kallmünz 2	4	49N09	11E58	-0:47:52
Kaltenbrunn 2	4	49N39	11E57	-0:47:48
Kalteneber 1	2	51N19	10E08	-0:40:32
Kaltenkirchen 2	1	53N50	9E58	-0:39:52
Kaltennordheim 1	2	50N38	10E10	-0:40:40
Kaltensundheim 1	2	50N36	10E10	-0:40:40
Kalthof 2	1	51N26	7E40	-0:30:40
Kamen 2	1	51N35	7E40	-0:30:40
Kamenz 1	2	51N16	14E06	-0:56:24
Kamp 2	1	50N14	7E37	-0:30:28
Kamp-Lintfort 2	7	51N30	6E31	-0:26:04
Kamsdorf 1	2	50N38	11E28	-0:45:52
Kandel 2	6	49N05	8E11	-0:32:44
Kandern 2	3	47N43	7E40	-0:30:40
Kanin 1	2	52N17	12E50	-0:51:20
Kapellen 2	7	51N25	6E35	-0:26:20
Kapellen 2	7	51N34	6E22	-0:25:28
Kapellen 2	7	51N08	6E38	-0:26:32
Kappel 2	6	50N00	7E21	-0:29:24
Kappeln 2	1	54N40	9E56	-0:39:44
Karden 2	6	50N11	7E17	-0:29:08
Karl-Marx-Stadt (Chemnitz) 1	2	50N50	12E55	-0:51:40
Karlsfeld 2	4	48N13	11E28	-0:45:52
Karlshafen 2	1	51N38	9E27	-0:37:48
Karlshuld 2	4	48N41	11E18	-0:45:12
Karlsruhe 2	3	49N03	8E24	-0:33:36
Karlstadt 2	4	49N57	9E45	-0:39:00
Karnzow 1	2	52N59	12E26	-0:49:44
Karow 1	2	52N20	12E15	-0:49:00
Karow 1	2	53N32	12E15	-0:49:00
Karsdorf 1	2	51N17	11E39	-0:46:36
Karstädt 1	2	53N09	11E44	-0:46:56
Kartzow 1	2	52N29	12E58	-0:51:52
Kassel 2	1	51N19	9E29	-0:37:56
Kastellaun 2	6	50N04	7E26	-0:29:44
Kastl 2	4	49N22	11E42	-0:46:48
Kastorf 2	1	53N44	10E34	-0:42:16
Katerbow 1	2	52N59	12E39	-0:50:36
Kathlow 1	2	51N43	14E29	-0:57:56
Katlenburg-Duhm 2	1	51N41	10E06	-0:40:24
Katzenelnbogen 2	1	50N17	7E59	-0:31:56
Katzenfurt 2	1	50N37	8E21	-0:33:24
Katzhütte 1	2	50N33	11E03	-0:44:12
Kaub 2	1	50N05	7E46	-0:31:04
Kaufbeuren 2	4	47N53	10E37	-0:42:28
Kaufering 2	4	48N05	10E52	-0:43:28
Kaulsdorf 1	2	50N37	11E26	-0:45:44
Kayna 1	2	50N59	12E14	-0:48:56
Kehl 2	3	48N35	7E50	-0:31:20
Kehlen 2	5	47N41	9E33	-0:38:12
Kehrigk 1	2	52N09	13E55	-0:55:40
Kelberg 2	6	50N17	6E55	-0:27:40
Kelbra 1	2	51N26	11E02	-0:44:08
Kelheim 2	4	48N55	11E52	-0:47:28
Kelkheim 2	1	50N08	8E26	-0:33:44
Kellen 2	7	51N48	6E10	-0:24:40
Kellenhusen 2	1	54N11	11E03	-0:44:12
Kellinghusen 2	1	53N57	9E43	-0:38:52
Kellmünz 2	4	48N07	10E08	-0:40:32
Kelsterbach 2	1	50N04	8E32	-0:34:08
Kelzenberg 2	7	51N07	6E30	-0:26:00
Kemberg 1	2	51N46	12E38	-0:50:32
Kemnath 2	4	49N52	11E54	-0:47:36
Kemnitz 1	2	54N04	13E31	-0:54:04
Kempen 2	7	51N22	6E25	-0:25:40
Kempenich 2	6	50N25	7E07	-0:28:28
Kempten (Allgäu) 2	4	47N43	10E19	-0:41:16
Kenzingen 2	3	48N11	7E46	-0:31:04
Kerken 2	7	51N27	6E22	-0:25:28
Kerpen 2	7	50N52	6E41	-0:26:44
Kerstenhausen 2	1	51N04	9E13	-0:36:52
Kerzendorf 1	2	52N16	13E17	-0:53:08
Kesbern 2	1	51N20	7E42	-0:30:48
Kessebüren 2	1	51N31	7E43	-0:30:52
Kesselsdorf 1	2	51N02	13E35	-0:54:20
Ketsch 2	3	49N22	8E31	-0:34:04
Kettwig 2	1	51N22	6E56	-0:27:44
Ketzin 1	2	52N28	12E50	-0:51:20
Keula 1	2	51N20	10E31	-0:42:04
Kevelaer 2	7	51N35	6E15	-0:25:00
Kiefersfelden 2	4	47N37	12E11	-0:48:44
Kiekebusch 1	2	52N21	13E33	-0:54:12
Kiel 2	1	54N20	10E08	-0:40:32
Kienberg 1	2	52N40	12E54	-0:51:36
Kienitz 1	2	52N40	14E26	-0:57:44
Kierspe 2	1	51N08	7E35	-0:30:20
Kierspe-Bahnhof 2	1	51N08	7E37	-0:30:28
Kietz 1	2	52N34	14E36	-0:58:24
Kindelbrück 1	2	51N16	11E05	-0:44:20
Kinding 2	4	49N00	11E23	-0:45:32
Kippenheim 2	3	48N17	7E49	-0:31:16
Kipsdorf 1	2	50N47	13E32	-0:54:08
Kirchardt 2	3	49N12	8E59	-0:35:56
Kirchberg 1	2	50N37	12E32	-0:50:08
Kirchberg 2	5	49N12	9E58	-0:39:52
Kirchberg 2	6	49N56	7E24	-0:29:36
Kirchberg 2	4	48N54	13E11	-0:52:44
Kirchdorf 1	2	54N00	11E26	-0:45:44
Kirchdorf 2	1	52N36	8E49	-0:35:16
Kirchdorf im Wald 2	4	48N55	13E16	-0:53:04
Kircheib 2	1	50N42	7E28	-0:29:52
Kirchende 2	1	51N25	7E26	-0:29:44
Kirchenlaibach 2	4	49N53	11E46	-0:47:04
Kirchenlamitz 2	4	50N09	11E56	-0:47:44
Kirchenthumbach 2	4	49N45	11E43	-0:46:52
Kirchen-Wehbach 2	1	50N48	7E53	-0:31:32
Kirchhain 2	1	50N49	8E55	-0:35:40
Kirchham 2	4	48N21	13E16	-0:53:04
Kirchheiligen 1	2	51N11	10E42	-0:42:48
Kirchheimbolanden 2	6	49N40	8E00	-0:32:00
Kirchheim in Schwaben 2	4	48N10	10E30	-0:42:00
Kirchheim unter Teck 2	5	48N39	9E27	-0:37:48
Kirchhellen 2	1	51N36	6E55	-0:27:40
Kirchhofen 1	2	52N22	13E53	-0:55:32
Kirchhundem 2	1	51N05	8E05	-0:32:20
Kirchlinteln 2	1	52N56	9E19	-0:37:16
Kirchmöser 1	2	52N22	12E25	-0:49:40
Kirchohsen 2	1	52N03	9E23	-0:37:32
Kirchroth 2	4	48N57	12E33	-0:50:12
Kirchseeon 2	4	48N04	11E54	-0:47:36
Kirchveischede 2	1	51N05	7E59	-0:31:56
Kirchwalsede 2	1	53N01	9E23	-0:37:32
Kirchweyhe 2	1	52N59	8E52	-0:35:28
Kirchzarten 2	3	47N58	7E56	-0:31:44
Kirn 2	6	49N47	7E28	-0:29:52
Kirschau 1	2	51N04	14E27	-0:57:48
Kirtorf 2	1	50N46	9E06	-0:36:24
Kissing 2	4	48N18	10E59	-0:43:56
Kisslegg 2	5	47N47	9E53	-0:39:32
Kittendorf 1	2	53N37	12E54	-0:51:36
Kitzingen 2	4	49N44	10E09	-0:40:36
Kitzscher 1	2	51N09	12E33	-0:50:12
Kläden 1	2	52N38	11E39	-0:46:36
Klaffenbach 1	2	50N45	12E54	-0:51:36
Klais 2	4	47N29	11E14	-0:44:56
Klardorf 2	4	49N16	12E07	-0:48:28
Klausdorf 1	2	54N20	13E01	-0:52:04
Klausdorf 2	1	54N18	10E15	-0:41:00
Kleef 2	1	51N11	6E56	-0:27:44
Kleinbeeren 1	2	52N22	13E20	-0:53:20
Kleinbodungen 1	2	51N28	10E32	-0:42:08
Klein Bünzow 1	2	53N53	13E48	-0:55:12
Kleineichen 2	1	51N08	7E21	-0:29:24
Kleinenberg 2	1	51N35	8E58	-0:35:52
Kleinenbroich 2	7	51N12	6E35	-0:26:20
Kleinhammer 2	1	51N14	7E46	-0:31:04
Kleinhöbing 2	4	49N04	11E18	-0:45:12
Klein Kienitz 1	2	52N18	13E29	-0:53:56
Klein Lafferde 2	1	52N14	10E14	-0:40:56
Klein-Linden 2	1	50N34	8E38	-0:34:32
Kleinmachnow 1	2	52N24	13E15	-0:53:00
Klein Marzehns 1	2	52N01	12E37	-0:50:28
Kleinschönebeck 1	2	52N29	13E43	-0:54:52
Klein Stöckheim 2	1	52N12	10E31	-0:42:04
Klein Wanzleben 1	2	52N04	11E21	-0:45:24
Klein Ziethen 1	2	52N23	13E27	-0:53:48
Klenau 2	4	48N29	11E19	-0:45:16
Klettwitz 1	2	51N32	13E53	-0:55:32
Kleve 2	7	51N48	6E09	-0:24:36
Klietz 1	2	52N40	12E04	-0:48:16
Klingen 2	4	48N26	11E09	-0:44:36
Klingenberg 1	2	50N55	13E31	-0:54:04
Klingenberg am Main 2	4	49N47	9E11	-0:36:44
Klingenbrunn 2	4	48N56	13E19	-0:53:16
Klingenmünster 2	6	49N08	8E01	-0:32:04
Klingenthal 1	2	50N21	12E28	-0:49:52
Klink 1	2	53N29	12E37	-0:50:28
Klitten 1	2	51N20	14E36	-0:58:24
Klixbüll 2	1	54N48	8E53	-0:35:32
Klobbicke 1	2	52N46	13E48	-0:55:12
Kloster 1	2	54N35	13E06	-0:52:24
Klosterfelde 1	2	52N48	13E28	-0:53:52
Klostermansfeld 1	2	51N35	11E29	-0:45:56
Kloster Oesede 2	1	52N12	8E07	-0:32:28
Kloster Zinna 1	2	52N01	13E07	-0:52:28
Klötze 1	2	52N38	11E10	-0:44:40
Kluess 1	2	53N46	12E14	-0:48:56
Klüppelberg 2	1	51N06	7E28	-0:29:52
Klütz 1	2	53N58	11E10	-0:44:40
Knesebeck 2	1	52N41	10E42	-0:42:48
Knetzgau 2	4	50N00	10E33	-0:42:12
Kniebis 2	3	48N28	8E17	-0:33:08
Knittlingen 2	3	49N01	8E45	-0:35:00
Koblenz 2	6	50N21	7E35	-0:30:20
Koburg (Coburg) 2	4	50N15	10E58	-0:43:52
Kochel 2	4	47N39	11E22	-0:45:28
Kodersdorf 1	2	51N15	14E53	-0:59:32
Kofeld 2	5	47N44	9E41	-0:38:44
Köfering 2	4	48N56	12E12	-0:48:48
Kohlstädt 2	1	51N50	8E52	-0:35:28
Kohren-Sahlis 1	2	51N01	12E36	-0:50:24
Kolbermoor 2	4	47N51	12E04	-0:48:16
Kolenfeld 2	1	52N24	9E27	-0:37:48
Kolkwitz 1	2	51N45	14E15	-0:57:00
Kölleda 1	2	51N11	11E15	-0:45:00
Köln (Cologne) 2	7	50N56	6E59	-0:27:56
Kolochau 1	2	51N44	13E16	-0:53:04
Kolonie Stolp 1	2	52N28	13E46	-0:55:04
Kölsa 1	2	51N28	12E13	-0:48:52
Königheim 2	3	49N37	9E35	-0:38:20
Königsbach 2	3	48N58	8E36	-0:34:24
Königsberg 2	4	50N05	10E34	-0:42:16
Königsborn 2	1	51N33	7E41	-0:30:44
Königsbrück 1	2	51N16	13E54	-0:55:36
Königsbrunn 2	4	48N16	10E53	-0:43:32
Königsdorf 2	4	47N49	11E28	-0:45:52
Königsee 1	2	50N39	11E05	-0:44:20
Königsfeld im Schwarzwald 2	3	48N08	8E25	-0:33:40
Königshain 1	2	51N11	14E52	-0:59:28
Königshofen 2	3	49N32	9E44	-0:38:56
Königshofen im Grabfeld 2	4	50N18	10E29	-0:41:56
Königslutter 2	1	52N15	10E49	-0:43:16
Königssee 2	4	47N33	12E58	-0:51:52
Königstein 1	2	50N55	14E04	-0:56:16
Königstein 2	1	50N11	8E29	-0:33:56
Königstein 2	4	49N37	11E38	-0:46:32
Königswalde 1	2	50N33	13E02	-0:52:08
Königswartha 1	2	51N18	14E20	-0:57:20
Königswinter 2	1	50N40	7E11	-0:28:44
Königs Wusterhausen 1	2	52N18	13E37	-0:54:28
Könnern 1	2	51N40	11E46	-0:47:04
Konradsreuth 2	4	50N16	11E50	-0:47:20
Konstanz 2	3	47N40	9E10	-0:36:40
Konstein 2	4	48N50	11E04	-0:44:16
Konz 2	6	49N42	6E34	-0:26:16
Konzell 2	4	49N04	12E43	-0:50:52
Köpenick 1	2	52N26	13E35	-0:54:20
Köpernitz 1	2	53N04	12E56	-0:51:44
Kopperby 2	1	54N38	9E56	-0:39:44
Korbach 2	1	51N16	8E52	-0:35:28
Köritz 1	2	52N51	12E27	-0:49:48
Kornelimünster 2	7	50N43	6E11	-0:24:44
Körner 1	2	51N13	10E35	-0:42:20
Kornwestheim 2	5	48N52	9E11	-0:36:44
Korschenbroich 2	7	51N11	6E31	-0:26:04
Kösching 2	4	48N49	11E30	-0:46:00
Koserow 1	2	54N03	13E59	-0:55:56
Kossdorf 1	2	51N29	13E14	-0:52:56
Kösslarn 2	4	48N22	13E07	-0:52:28
Köthen 1	2	51N45	11E58	-0:47:52
Kötzting 2	4	49N11	12E52	-0:51:28
Krackow 1	2	53N20	14E16	-0:57:04
Kraftsdorf 1	2	50N52	11E55	-0:47:40
Kraiburg 2	4	48N10	12E26	-0:49:44
Krakow 1	2	53N39	12E16	-0:49:04
Kraksdorf 2	1	54N18	11E04	-0:44:16
Krampnitz 1	2	52N28	13E04	-0:52:16
Kranenburg 2	7	51N47	6E03	-0:24:12
Kranichfeld 1	2	50N51	11E12	-0:44:48
Krauchenwies 2	3	48N01	9E14	-0:36:56
Krauschwitz 1	2	51N31	14E41	-0:58:44
Krautheim 2	5	49N23	9E38	-0:38:32
Kreba 1	2	51N20	14E40	-0:58:40
Krefeld 2	7	51N20	6E34	-0:26:16
Kreiensen 2	1	51N51	9E58	-0:39:52
Kreischa 1	2	50N56	13E45	-0:55:00
Kremmen 1	2	52N45	13E01	-0:52:04
Krempe 2	1	53N50	9E29	-0:37:56
Krensitz 1	2	51N29	12E27	-0:49:48
Kressbronn 2	5	47N35	9E36	-0:38:24
Kreuth 2	4	47N38	11E44	-0:46:56
Kreuzberg 2	1	51N09	7E27	-0:29:48
Kreuznach → Bad Kreuznach 2	6	49N52	7E51	-0:31:24
Kreuztal 2	1	50N58	7E59	-0:31:56
Kreyenhagen 2	1	52N55	10E52	-0:43:28

Krögis 1	2	51N07	13E22	-0:53:28
Kröhstorf 2	4	48N37	12E57	-0:51:48
Krölpa 1	2	50N41	11E32	-0:46:08
Kronach 2	4	50N14	11E20	-0:45:20
Kronberg 2	1	50N10	8E30	-0:34:00
Kronshagen 2	1	54N20	10E05	-0:40:20
Kröpelin 1	2	54N04	11E48	-0:47:12
Kropp 2	1	54N24	9E31	-0:38:04
Kroppenstedt 1	2	51N56	11E18	-0:45:12
Kropstädt 1	2	51N58	12E44	-0:50:56
Kröslin 1	2	54N07	13E45	-0:55:00
Krossen 1	2	50N58	11E59	-0:47:56
Krostitz 1	2	51N28	12E27	-0:49:48
Kröv 2	6	49N59	7E05	-0:28:20
Kruckow 1	2	53N54	13E14	-0:52:56
Krudenburg 2	1	51N39	6E45	-0:27:00
Kruft 2	6	50N23	7E20	-0:29:20
Krugzell 2	4	47N47	10E16	-0:41:04
Krumbach 2	3	47N58	9E02	-0:36:08
Krumbach 2	4	48N14	10E22	-0:41:28
Krummenerl 2	1	51N05	7E45	-0:31:00
Krummensee 1	2	52N36	13E42	-0:54:48
Krün 2	4	47N30	11E16	-0:45:04
Kühbach 2	4	48N29	11E11	-0:44:44
Kühlungsborn 1	2	54N09	11E43	-0:46:52
Kühnhausen 1	2	51N02	10E58	-0:43:52
Kühren 1	2	51N20	12E50	-0:51:20
Kuhstedt 2	1	53N23	8E58	-0:35:52
Küllstedt 1	2	51N16	10E17	-0:41:08
Kulmbach 2	4	50N06	11E27	-0:45:48
Külsheim 2	3	49N40	9E31	-0:38:04
Kummerow 1	2	54N17	12E53	-0:51:32
Kümmersbruck 2	4	49N25	11E53	-0:47:32
Kunow 1	2	53N00	12E07	-0:48:28
Kunrau 1	2	52N35	11E01	-0:44:04
Künzelsau 2	5	49N16	9E41	-0:38:44
Künzing 2	4	48N40	13E05	-0:52:20
Kupferberg 2	1	51N09	7E27	-0:29:48
Kupfermühle 2	1	54N50	9E24	-0:37:36
Kupferzell 2	5	49N14	9E41	-0:38:44
Kuppenheim 2	3	48N49	8E15	-0:33:00
Küps 2	4	50N11	11E16	-0:45:04
Kusel 2	6	49N32	7E24	-0:29:36
Kusey 1	2	52N36	11E05	-0:44:20
Kutenholz 2	1	53N29	9E19	-0:37:16
Kyllburg 2	6	50N02	6E35	-0:26:20
Kyritz 1	2	52N56	12E23	-0:49:32
Laaber 2	4	49N04	11E53	-0:47:32
Laaberberg 2	4	48N46	12E01	-0:48:04
Laage 1	2	53N56	12E20	-0:49:20
Laase 2	1	53N04	11E18	-0:45:12
Laasphe 2	1	50N56	8E24	-0:33:36
Laatzen 2	1	52N19	9E47	-0:39:08
Laberweinting 2	4	48N48	12E19	-0:49:16
Laboe 2	1	54N24	10E15	-0:41:00
Lachendorf 2	1	52N37	10E14	-0:40:56
Ladbergen 2	1	52N08	7E44	-0:30:56
Ladeburg 1	2	52N42	13E35	-0:54:20
Laer 2	1	52N03	7E21	-0:29:24
Lage 2	1	51N59	8E48	-0:35:12
Lägerdorf 2	1	53N53	9E34	-0:38:16
Lähden 2	1	52N45	7E34	-0:30:16
Lahr 2	3	48N20	7E52	-0:31:28
Lahr Air Force Base 2	3	48N20	7E52	-0:31:28
Laichingen 2	5	48N29	9E41	-0:38:44
Lam 2	4	49N12	13E03	-0:52:12
Lambrecht 2	1	50N08	8E56	-0:35:44
Lampertheim 2	1	49N35	8E28	-0:33:52
Lamspringe 2	1	51N58	10E00	-0:40:00
Lamstedt 2	1	53N38	9E05	-0:36:20
Landau 2	6	49N12	8E07	-0:32:28
Landau an der Isar 2	4	48N40	12E43	-0:50:52
Landenhausen 2	1	50N36	9E28	-0:37:52
Landesbergen 2	1	52N33	9E07	-0:36:28
Landhausen 2	1	51N24	7E45	-0:31:00
Landkirchen 2	1	54N27	11E08	-0:44:32
Landsberg 1	2	51N31	12E10	-0:48:40
Landsberg am Lech 2	4	48N05	10E55	-0:43:40
Landshut 2	4	48N33	12E09	-0:48:36
Landstuhl 2	6	49N25	7E34	-0:30:16
Landweg 2	1	51N29	7E37	-0:30:28
Langburkersdorf 1	2	51N02	14E14	-0:56:56
Langebrück 1	2	51N07	13E50	-0:55:20
Langelsheim 2	1	51N56	10E19	-0:41:16
Langen 2	1	49N59	8E41	-0:34:44
Langen 2	1	53N36	8E35	-0:34:20
Langenargen 2	5	47N35	9E32	-0:38:08
Langenau 1	2	50N50	13E18	-0:53:12
Langenau 2	5	48N30	10E07	-0:40:28
Langenberg 2	1	51N21	7E09	-0:28:36
Langenberg 2	1	51N46	8E19	-0:33:16
Langenbernsdorf 1	2	50N45	12E19	-0:49:16
Langenbochum 2	1	51N37	7E07	-0:28:28
Langenbrücken 2	3	49N12	8E38	-0:34:32
Langenburg 2	5	49N15	9E50	-0:39:20
Langendorf 1	2	51N11	11E58	-0:47:52
Langeneichstädt 1	2	51N20	11E41	-0:46:44
Langenfeld 2	1	51N07	6E56	-0:27:44
Langenhagen 2	1	52N27	9E44	-0:38:56
Langenhessen 1	2	50N45	12E22	-0:49:28
Langenhorn 2	1	54N41	8E53	-0:35:32
Langenhorst 2	1	51N22	7E02	-0:28:08
Langennaundorf 1	2	51N36	13E20	-0:53:20
Langenneufnach 2	4	48N16	10E36	-0:42:24
Langenselbold 2	1	50N10	9E02	-0:36:08
Langensteinach 2	4	49N30	10E10	-0:40:40
Langenweddingen 1	2	52N02	11E31	-0:46:04
Langenwetzendorf 1	2	50N41	12E05	-0:48:20
Langenzenn 2	4	49N30	10E48	-0:43:12
Langeoog 2	1	53N45	7E29	-0:29:56
Langerwehe 2	7	50N49	6E22	-0:25:28
Langewiesen 1	2	50N40	10E58	-0:43:52
Langförden 2	1	52N47	8E14	-0:32:56
Lang-Göns 2	1	50N30	8E40	-0:34:40
Langquaid 2	4	48N49	12E03	-0:48:12
Langschede 2	1	51N29	7E43	-0:30:52
Langst-Kierst 2	7	51N18	6E43	-0:26:52
Langula 1	2	51N09	10E25	-0:41:40
Langwarden 2	1	53N36	8E19	-0:33:16
Langweid 2	4	48N29	10E51	-0:43:24
Langweiler 2	6	49N40	7E31	-0:30:04
Lassan 1	2	53N57	13E50	-0:55:20
Lastrup 2	1	52N48	7E52	-0:31:28
Lathen 2	1	52N52	7E19	-0:29:16
Laubach 2	1	50N33	8E59	-0:35:56
Laubenthal 2	4	48N59	11E03	-0:44:12
Laubusch 1	2	51N28	14E10	-0:56:40
Laubuseschbach 2	1	50N24	8E20	-0:33:20
Laucha 1	2	51N13	11E41	-0:46:44
Lauchhammer 1	2	51N30	13E47	-0:55:08
Lauchheim 2	5	48N52	10E14	-0:40:56
Lauda 2	3	49N34	9E41	-0:38:44
Lauenbrück 2	1	53N12	9E33	-0:38:12
Lauenburg 2	1	53N22	10E33	-0:42:12
Lauenförde 2	1	51N39	9E23	-0:37:32
Lauenstein 1	2	50N47	13E49	-0:55:16
Lauenstein 2	4	50N31	11E20	-0:45:20
Lauenstein 2	1	52N04	9E33	-0:38:12
Lauf an der Pegnitz 2	4	49N30	11E17	-0:45:08
Laufen 2	4	47N57	12E56	-0:51:44
Laufenburg (Baden) 2	3	47N35	8E04	-0:32:16
Lauffen am Neckar 2	5	49N05	9E10	-0:36:40
Lauingen 2	4	48N34	10E25	-0:41:40
Laupendahl 2	1	51N21	6E56	-0:27:44
Laupheim 2	5	48N14	9E52	-0:39:28
Laurenburg 2	1	50N20	7E54	-0:31:36
Lauscha 1	2	50N28	11E10	-0:44:40
Lauta 1	2	51N27	14E04	-0:56:16
Lautenthal 2	1	51N52	10E17	-0:41:08
Lauterbach 2	3	48N14	8E20	-0:33:20
Lauterbach 2	1	50N38	9E24	-0:37:36
Lauterbach 2	4	48N23	11E33	-0:46:12
Lauterecken 2	6	49N39	7E35	-0:30:20
Lauterhofen 2	4	49N22	11E37	-0:46:28
Lauter (Sachsen) 1	2	50N33	12E44	-0:50:56
Lebach 2	6	49N24	6E54	-0:27:36
Lebus 1	2	52N25	14E32	-0:58:08
Lechbruck 2	4	47N42	10E47	-0:43:08
Lechenich 2	7	50N48	6E46	-0:27:04
Leck 2	1	54N46	8E58	-0:35:52
Leegebruch 1	2	52N43	13E11	-0:52:44
Leer 2	1	53N14	7E26	-0:29:44
Leerhafe 2	1	53N32	7E47	-0:31:08
Leese 2	1	52N30	9E06	-0:36:24
Leeste 2	1	52N59	8E49	-0:35:16
Legau 2	4	47N51	10E07	-0:40:28
Legden 2	1	52N02	7E07	-0:28:28
Lehesten 1	2	50N29	11E28	-0:45:52
Lehnin 1	2	52N19	12E44	-0:50:56
Lehnitz 1	2	52N44	13E15	-0:53:00
Lehrbach 2	1	50N47	9E04	-0:36:16
Lehrberg 2	4	49N21	10E30	-0:42:00
Lehre 2	1	52N19	10E40	-0:42:40
Lehrte 2	1	52N22	9E59	-0:39:56
Leichlingen 2	1	51N06	7E01	-0:28:04
Leiferde 2	1	52N26	10E26	-0:41:44
Leimbach 1	2	51N36	11E28	-0:45:52
Leimstruth 2	1	50N59	8E19	-0:33:16
Leinburg 2	4	49N27	11E19	-0:45:16
Leinefelde 1	2	51N23	10E20	-0:41:20
Leinfelden 2	5	48N41	9E08	-0:36:32
Leipheim 2	4	48N27	10E13	-0:40:52
Leipzig 1	2	51N19	12E20	-0:49:20
Leisnig 1	2	51N09	12E56	-0:51:44
Leitzkau 1	2	52N03	11E57	-0:47:48
Lembeck 2	1	51N45	7E00	-0:28:00
Lembruch 2	1	52N31	8E22	-0:33:28
Lemförde 2	1	52N28	8E22	-0:33:28
Lemgo 2	1	52N02	8E54	-0:35:36
Lemke 2	1	52N39	9E09	-0:36:36
Lendringsen 2	1	51N24	7E49	-0:31:16
Lengede 2	1	52N12	10E18	-0:41:12
Lengefeld 1	2	50N43	13E11	-0:52:44
Lengelscheid 2	1	51N08	7E40	-0:30:40
Lengenfeld 1	2	51N13	10E13	-0:40:52
Lengenfeld 1	2	50N34	12E22	-0:49:28
Lengerich 2	1	52N11	7E50	-0:31:20
Lengerich 2	1	52N33	7E32	-0:30:08
Lenggries 2	4	47N41	11E34	-0:46:16
Lennep 2	1	51N11	7E15	-0:29:00
Lensahn 2	1	54N13	10E52	-0:43:28
Lenting 2	4	48N48	11E28	-0:45:52
Lenzen 1	2	53N05	11E28	-0:45:52
Lenzinghausen 2	1	52N07	8E28	-0:33:52
Lenzkirch 2	3	47N52	8E12	-0:32:48
Leonberg 2	5	48N48	9E01	-0:36:04
Leonbronn 2	3	49N03	8E53	-0:35:32
Leopoldshagen 1	2	53N46	13E53	-0:55:32
Leppin 1	2	52N53	11E34	-0:46:16
Lerche 2	1	51N37	7E43	-0:30:52
Letmathe 2	1	51N22	7E37	-0:30:28
Letschin 1	2	52N39	14E21	-0:57:24
Letter 2	1	52N24	9E38	-0:38:32
Letzlingen 1	2	52N26	11E29	-0:45:56
Leubnitz 1	2	50N43	12E21	-0:49:24
Leubsdorf 1	2	50N48	13E08	-0:52:32
Leuchtenberg 2	4	49N36	12E15	-0:49:00
Leuna 1	2	51N19	12E01	-0:48:04
Leupoldsgrün 2	4	50N17	11E47	-0:47:08
Leupoldstein 2	4	49N42	11E23	-0:45:32
Leutenberg 1	2	50N34	11E28	-0:45:52
Leutersdorf 1	2	50N57	14E40	-0:58:40
Leutershausen 2	4	49N18	10E24	-0:41:36
Leutesdorf 2	1	50N27	7E23	-0:29:32
Leutkirch 2	5	47N49	10E01	-0:40:04
Leverkusen 2	1	51N03	6E59	-0:27:56
Levern 2	1	52N22	8E26	-0:33:44
Liblar 2	7	50N49	6E49	-0:27:16
Lich 2	1	50N33	8E50	-0:35:20
Lichte 1	2	50N31	11E10	-0:44:40
Lichtenau 2	3	48N43	8E01	-0:32:04
Lichtenberg 1	2	50N50	13E25	-0:53:40
Lichtenberg 2	4	50N23	11E40	-0:46:40
Lichtendorf 2	1	51N28	7E37	-0:30:28
Lichtenfels 2	4	50N09	11E04	-0:44:16
Lichtensee 1	2	51N23	13E22	-0:53:28
Lichtenstein 1	2	50N45	12E37	-0:50:28
Lichtentanne 1	2	50N42	12E25	-0:49:40
Liebenau 2	1	52N36	9E05	-0:36:20
Liebenburg 2	1	52N01	10E26	-0:41:44
Liebenwalde 1	2	52N52	13E23	-0:53:32
Lieberhausen 2	1	51N03	7E40	-0:30:40
Lieberose 1	2	51N59	14E17	-0:57:08
Liebertwolkwitz 1	2	51N17	12E28	-0:49:52
Liebstadt 1	2	50N52	13E51	-0:55:24
Liedberg 2	7	51N10	6E32	-0:26:08
Lienen 2	1	52N09	7E58	-0:31:52
Liepe 1	2	53N58	13E56	-0:55:44
Liesborn 2	1	51N43	8E15	-0:33:00
Lieskau 1	2	51N37	13E48	-0:55:12
Lietzow 1	2	54N29	13E30	-0:54:00
Lilienthal 2	1	53N08	8E55	-0:35:40
Limbach-Oberfrohna 1	2	50N51	12E45	-0:51:00
Limburg an der Lahn 2	1	50N23	8E04	-0:32:16
Limburgerhof 2	6	49N25	8E24	-0:33:36
Lindau 1	2	52N02	12E06	-0:48:24
Lindau 2	1	54N36	9E47	-0:39:08
Lindau 2	4	47N33	9E41	-0:38:44
Lindau 2	1	51N39	10E07	-0:40:28
Lindenberg 1	2	53N02	12E07	-0:48:28
Lindenberg 1	2	52N36	13E31	-0:54:04
Lindenberg 1	2	52N12	14E07	-0:56:28
Lindenberg im Allgäu 2	4	47N36	9E53	-0:39:32
Lindenfels 2	1	49N41	8E47	-0:35:08
Lindenthal 1	2	51N24	12E20	-0:49:20
Linderhausen 2	1	51N18	7E17	-0:29:08
Lindern 2	1	52N50	7E46	-0:31:04
Lindhorst 2	1	52N21	9E17	-0:37:08
Lindkirchen 2	4	48N40	11E47	-0:47:08
Lindlar 2	1	51N01	7E23	-0:29:32
Lindow 1	2	52N58	13E00	-0:52:00
Lingen 2	1	52N31	7E19	-0:29:16
Linkenheim 2	3	49N07	8E24	-0:33:36
Linnich 2	7	50N59	6E16	-0:25:04
Linow 1	2	53N06	12E49	-0:51:16
Lintorf 2	1	51N20	6E49	-0:27:16
Linum 1	2	52N46	12E53	-0:51:32
Linz 2	1	50N34	7E17	-0:29:08
Lippborg 2	1	51N40	8E02	-0:32:08
Lipperode 2	1	51N41	8E22	-0:33:28
Lippoldsberg 2	1	51N37	9E33	-0:38:12
Lippstadt 2	1	51N40	8E19	-0:33:16
Lissberg 2	1	50N22	9E05	-0:36:20
Lissingen 2	6	50N14	6E38	-0:26:32
Löbau 1	2	51N05	14E40	-0:58:40
Löbejün 1	2	51N38	11E53	-0:47:32
Lobenstein 1	2	50N26	11E38	-0:46:32
Löbnitz 1	2	51N35	12E28	-0:49:52
Löbnitz 1	2	54N17	12E43	-0:50:52
Lobstädt 1	2	51N08	12E29	-0:49:56
Loburg 1	2	52N07	12E05	-0:48:20
Loccum 2	1	52N27	9E08	-0:36:32
Lochau 2	4	49N55	11E59	-0:47:56
Löcknitz 1	2	53N27	14E12	-0:56:48
Lodenau 1	2	51N24	14E57	-0:59:48
Löderburg 1	2	51N52	11E32	-0:46:08
Löffingen 2	3	47N53	8E20	-0:33:20
Loga 2	1	53N14	7E29	-0:29:56
Lohberg 2	1	51N35	6E46	-0:27:04
Lohfelden 2	1	51N16	9E32	-0:38:08
Lohheide 2	7	51N30	6E40	-0:26:40
Lohlbach 2	1	51N04	8E58	-0:35:52
Lohma 2	4	49N37	12E26	-0:49:44
Lohmar 2	1	50N50	7E13	-0:28:52
Löhme 1	2	52N37	13E40	-0:54:40
Lohme 1	2	54N35	13E37	-0:54:28
Lohmen 1	2	50N59	13E59	-0:55:56
Lohmen 1	2	53N41	12E05	-0:48:20
Lohmühle 2	7	51N31	6E40	-0:26:40
Löhne 2	1	52N11	8E41	-0:34:44
Lohne 2	1	52N42	8E12	-0:32:48
Löhnen 2	1	51N36	6E39	-0:26:36
Lohr am Main 2	1	50N00	9E34	-0:38:16
Lohsa 1	2	51N23	14E24	-0:57:36
Loitz 1	2	53N58	13E07	-0:52:28
Lollar 2	1	50N39	8E42	-0:34:48
Lommatzsch 1	2	51N12	13E18	-0:53:12
Longkamp 2	6	49N53	7E07	-0:28:28
Löningen 2	1	52N44	7E46	-0:31:04
Lönnewitz 1	2	51N34	13E11	-0:52:44
Loose 2	1	54N31	9E53	-0:39:32
Lorch 2	5	48N49	9E40	-0:38:40
Lorch 2	1	50N02	7E48	-0:31:12
Lorchhausen 2	1	50N03	7E47	-0:31:08
Lörrach 2	3	47N37	7E40	-0:30:40

Place		Lat	Long	Time
Lorsch 2	1	49N39	8E34	-0:34:16
Lorup 2	1	52N55	7E38	-0:30:32
Löschenrod 2	1	50N30	9E41	-0:38:44
Losheim 2	6	49N30	6E44	-0:26:56
Lossa 1	2	51N13	11E25	-0:45:40
Lossburg 2	3	48N25	8E27	-0:33:48
Lössel 2	1	51N21	7E39	-0:30:36
Lössnitz 1	2	50N37	12E43	-0:50:52
Lottstetten 2	3	47N38	8E34	-0:34:16
Löwenberg 1	2	52N54	13E08	-0:52:32
Löwenbruch 1	2	52N18	13E19	-0:53:16
Löwenstein 2	5	49N06	9E22	-0:37:28
Loxstedt 2	1	53N28	8E38	-0:34:32
Loxten 2	1	52N03	8E08	-0:32:32
Lübars 1	2	52N39	12E02	-0:48:08
Lübars 1	2	52N10	12E09	-0:48:36
Lübbecke 2	1	52N18	8E36	-0:34:24
Lübben 1	2	51N56	13E53	-0:55:32
Lübbenau 1	2	51N52	13E57	-0:55:48
Lübbow 2	1	52N54	11E10	-0:44:40
Lübeck 2	1	53N52	10E40	-0:42:40
Lübesse 1	2	53N29	11E28	-0:45:52
Lubmin 1	2	54N08	13E37	-0:54:28
Lübtheen 1	2	53N18	11E04	-0:44:16
Lübz 1	2	53N27	12E01	-0:48:04
Lüchow 2	1	52N58	11E10	-0:44:40
Lüchtringen 2	1	51N47	9E25	-0:37:40
Lucka 1	2	51N06	12E20	-0:49:20
Luckau 1	2	51N51	13E43	-0:54:52
Luckenwalde 1	2	52N05	13E10	-0:52:40
Lüdenscheid 2	1	51N13	7E38	-0:30:32
Lüderitz 1	2	52N30	11E44	-0:46:56
Lüdersdorf 1	2	53N47	10E46	-0:43:04
Lüdinghausen 2	1	51N46	7E26	-0:29:44
Ludwag 2	4	49N57	11E05	-0:44:20
Ludwigsburg 2	5	48N53	9E11	-0:36:44
Ludwigsfelde 1	2	52N17	13E16	-0:53:04
Ludwigshafen 2	6	49N29	8E26	-0:33:44
Ludwigshafen am Bodensee 2	3	47N49	9E03	-0:36:12
Ludwigslust 1	2	53N19	11E30	-0:46:00
Ludwigsstadt 2	4	50N30	11E23	-0:45:32
Lugau 1	2	50N44	12E44	-0:50:56
Lügde 2	1	51N57	9E15	-0:37:00
Luhe 2	4	49N35	12E09	-0:48:36
Lühmannsdorf 1	2	54N00	13E38	-0:54:32
Luisenthal 1	2	50N47	10E43	-0:42:52
Lunden 2	1	54N20	9E01	-0:36:04
Lüneburg 2	1	53N15	10E23	-0:41:32
Lünen 2	1	51N36	7E32	-0:30:08
Lünern 2	1	51N33	7E46	-0:31:04
Lunzenau 1	2	50N58	12E45	-0:51:00
Lupberg 2	4	49N09	11E45	-0:47:00
Luppa 1	2	51N20	12E57	-0:51:48
Lüstringen 2	1	52N16	8E08	-0:32:32
Luthe 2	1	52N26	9E28	-0:37:52
Lütjenburg 2	1	54N17	10E35	-0:42:20
Lütjensee 2	1	53N39	10E22	-0:41:28
Lutter am Barenberge 2	1	51N59	10E16	-0:41:04
Lützel 2	1	50N58	8E10	-0:32:40
Lützen 1	2	51N15	12E08	-0:48:32
Lutzerath 2	6	50N07	7E00	-0:28:00
Lützow 1	2	53N40	11E11	-0:44:44
Lützschena 1	2	51N23	12E16	-0:49:04
Lychen 1	2	53N12	13E19	-0:53:16
Maasholm 2	1	54N41	9E59	-0:39:56
Machern 1	2	51N21	12E37	-0:50:28
Mackenrode 1	2	51N33	10E33	-0:42:12
Magdeborn 1	2	51N14	12E26	-0:49:44
Magdeburg 1	2	52N07	11E38	-0:46:32
Magdeburgo → Magdeburg 1	2	52N07	11E38	-0:46:32
Mahlberg 2	3	48N17	7E48	-0:31:12
Mahlow 1	2	52N22	13E24	-0:53:36
Mahlsdorf 1	2	52N47	11E13	-0:44:52
Mähring 2	4	49N55	12E32	-0:50:08
Maikammer 2	5	49N18	9E07	-0:36:28
Mainau 2	3	47N42	9E11	-0:36:44
Mainburg 2	4	48N38	11E47	-0:47:08
Mainhardt 2	5	49N04	9E33	-0:38:12
Mainleus 2	4	50N06	11E22	-0:45:28
Mainz 2	1	50N01	8E16	-0:33:04
Maisach 2	4	48N13	11E16	-0:45:04
Malchin 1	2	53N44	12E46	-0:51:04
Malching 2	4	48N19	13E12	-0:52:48
Malchow 1	2	53N28	12E25	-0:49:40
Malente 2	1	54N10	10E33	-0:42:12
Malgersdorf 2	4	48N32	12E45	-0:51:00
Mallersdrof 2	4	48N47	12E16	-0:49:04
Malsch 2	3	48N53	8E19	-0:33:16
Mammendorf 2	4	48N12	11E09	-0:44:36
Manching 2	4	48N43	11E30	-0:46:00
Manderscheid 2	6	50N05	6E49	-0:27:16
Manebach 1	2	50N41	10E51	-0:43:24
Mangolding 2	4	48N57	12E13	-0:48:52
Mannheim 2	3	49N29	8E29	-0:33:56
Mansfeld 1	2	51N35	11E27	-0:45:48
Mantel 2	4	49N39	12E03	-0:48:12
Marbach 1	2	51N02	13E13	-0:52:52
Marbach 2	1	50N37	9E43	-0:38:52
Marbach am Neckar 2	5	48N56	9E14	-0:36:56
Marbeck 2	1	51N49	6E52	-0:27:28
Marburg an der Lahn 2	1	50N49	8E46	-0:35:04
Marching 2	4	48N49	11E43	-0:46:52
Marienbaum 2	7	51N41	6E22	-0:25:28
Marienberg 1	2	50N39	13E10	-0:52:40
Marienberg 2	1	50N39	7E57	-0:31:48
Marienborn 1	2	52N12	11E08	-0:44:32
Marienhafe 2	1	53N31	7E16	-0:29:04
Marienheide 2	1	51N05	7E32	-0:30:08
Mariental 2	1	52N16	10E59	-0:43:56
Markdorf 2	5	47N43	9E23	-0:37:32
Markendorf 1	2	51N59	13E10	-0:52:40
Markgröningen 2	5	48N54	9E05	-0:36:20
Märkisch Buchholz 1	2	52N07	13E46	-0:55:04
Markkleeberg 1	2	51N17	12E23	-0:49:32
Markneukirchen 1	2	50N18	12E19	-0:49:16
Markoldendorf 2	1	51N48	9E46	-0:39:04
Markranstädt 1	2	51N18	12E13	-0:48:52
Marksuhl 1	2	50N55	10E11	-0:40:44
Markt Bibart 2	4	49N39	10E26	-0:41:44
Marktbreit 2	4	49N40	10E08	-0:40:32
Markt Erlbach 2	4	49N29	10E38	-0:42:32
Marktheidenfeld 2	4	49N50	9E36	-0:38:24
Markt Indersdorf 2	4	48N22	11E23	-0:45:32
Marktl 2	4	48N15	12E51	-0:51:24
Marktleugast 2	4	50N10	11E38	-0:46:32
Marktleuthen 2	4	50N08	12E00	-0:48:00
Marktoberdorf 2	4	47N47	10E37	-0:42:28
Marktredwitz 2	4	50N00	12E06	-0:48:24
Markt Rettenbach 2	4	47N57	10E23	-0:41:32
Marktschellenberg 2	4	47N42	13E02	-0:52:08
Markt Schwaben 2	4	48N11	11E51	-0:47:24
Marl 2	1	51N38	7E05	-0:28:20
Marlow 1	2	54N09	12E34	-0:50:16
Marne 2	1	53N57	9E00	-0:36:00
Marnitz 1	2	53N19	11E56	-0:47:44
Maroldsweisach 2	4	50N12	10E39	-0:42:36
Marquardt 1	2	52N27	12E57	-0:51:48
Marquartstein 2	4	47N45	12E28	-0:49:52
Martfeld 2	1	52N52	9E04	-0:36:16
Martinsbuch 2	4	48N45	12E25	-0:49:40
Martinshaun 2	4	48N40	12E13	-0:48:52
Martinstein 2	6	49N48	7E32	-0:30:08
Martinsthal 2	1	50N03	8E07	-0:32:28
Marwitz 1	2	52N41	13E09	-0:52:36
Marxhagen 1	2	53N37	12E36	-0:50:24
Marzahna 1	2	52N00	12E46	-0:51:04
Marzahne 1	2	52N31	12E31	-0:50:04
Maschen 2	1	53N24	10E02	-0:40:08
Massen 2	1	51N32	7E38	-0:30:32
Materborn 2	7	51N46	6E06	-0:24:24
Maulbach 2	1	50N43	9E04	-0:36:16
Maulbronn 2	3	49N00	8E49	-0:35:16
Mauth 2	4	48N53	13E35	-0:54:20
Maxhütte Haidhof 2	4	49N12	12E05	-0:48:20
Mayen 2	6	50N19	7E13	-0:28:52
Mayence → Mainz 2	1	50N01	8E16	-0:33:04
Mechernich 2	7	50N35	6E38	-0:26:32
Meckelfeld 2	1	53N25	10E01	-0:40:04
Meckenbeuren 2	5	47N42	9E34	-0:38:16
Meckenheim 2	7	50N37	7E07	-0:28:28
Meckesheim 2	3	49N19	8E49	-0:35:16
Meckinghoven 2	1	51N37	7E19	-0:29:16
Mecklenburg 1	2	53N47	11E28	-0:45:52
Medebach 2	1	51N12	8E42	-0:34:48
Medow 1	2	53N50	13E32	-0:54:08
Meerane 1	2	50N51	12E28	-0:49:52
Meerbeck 2	7	51N28	6E39	-0:26:36
Meerbusch 2	7	51N15	6E42	-0:26:48
Meersburg 2	3	47N41	9E16	-0:37:04
Mehlem 2	7	50N39	7E11	-0:28:44
Mehlteuer 1	2	50N32	12E02	-0:48:08
Mehr 2	1	51N43	6E29	-0:25:56
Mehring 2	6	49N48	6E49	-0:27:16
Mehrow 1	2	52N34	13E37	-0:54:28
Mehrum 2	1	51N35	6E37	-0:26:28
Meide 2	1	51N11	6E55	-0:27:40
Meiersberg 2	1	51N17	6E57	-0:27:48
Meihern 2	4	49N00	11E38	-0:46:32
Meila 1	2	51N09	13E13	-0:52:52
Meine 2	1	52N23	10E32	-0:42:08
Meinerzhagen 2	1	51N06	7E38	-0:30:32
Meiningen 1	2	50N34	10E25	-0:41:40
Meisburg 2	6	50N06	6E41	-0:26:44
Meisenheim 2	6	49N42	7E40	-0:30:40
Meissen 1	2	51N10	13E28	-0:53:52
Meissendorf 2	1	52N43	9E50	-0:39:20
Meitingen 2	4	48N32	10E50	-0:43:20
Melaune 1	2	51N11	14E44	-0:58:56
Meldorf 2	1	54N05	9E05	-0:36:20
Melle 2	1	52N12	8E20	-0:33:20
Melleck 2	4	47N40	12E45	-0:51:00
Mellendorf 2	1	52N33	9E43	-0:38:52
Mellingen 1	2	50N56	11E23	-0:45:32
Mellrichstadt 2	4	50N26	10E18	-0:41:12
Melsungen 2	1	51N08	9E32	-0:38:08
Memmelsdorf 2	4	49N56	10E57	-0:43:48
Memmingen 2	4	47N59	10E11	-0:40:44
Mengede 2	1	51N34	7E23	-0:29:32
Menden 2	1	51N26	7E47	-0:31:08
Mendorf 2	4	48N52	11E36	-0:46:24
Mengen 2	3	48N03	9E20	-0:37:20
Mengeringhausen 2	1	51N22	8E59	-0:35:56
Mengersgereuth-Hämmern 1	2	50N24	11E07	-0:44:28
Mennighüffen 2	1	52N13	8E43	-0:34:52
Menslage 2	1	52N41	7E49	-0:31:16
Menteroda 1	2	51N18	10E33	-0:42:12
Menzelen 2	7	51N37	6E32	-0:26:08
Menzelerheide 2	7	51N37	6E31	-0:26:04
Menzenschwand 2	3	47N49	8E04	-0:32:16
Meppen 2	1	52N41	7E17	-0:29:08
Mering 2	4	48N16	10E59	-0:43:56
Merkendorf 2	4	49N12	10E42	-0:42:48
Merklingen 2	5	48N30	9E44	-0:38:56
Merseburg 1	2	51N21	11E59	-0:47:56
Mertingen 2	4	48N39	10E47	-0:43:08
Merxleben 1	2	51N07	10E40	-0:42:40
Merzdorf 1	2	51N23	14E32	-0:58:08
Merzhausen 2	3	47N58	7E49	-0:31:16
Merzig 2	6	49N27	6E36	-0:26:24
Meschede 2	1	51N20	8E17	-0:33:08
Messdorf 1	2	52N43	11E33	-0:46:12
Messkirch 2	3	47N59	9E07	-0:36:28
Messtetten 2	5	48N11	8E58	-0:35:52
Mestlin 1	2	53N35	11E56	-0:47:44
Mesum 2	1	52N13	7E29	-0:29:56
Metelen 2	1	52N08	7E12	-0:28:48
Methler 2	1	51N35	7E37	-0:30:28
Metschow 1	2	53N49	12E58	-0:51:52
Metten 2	4	48N52	12E55	-0:51:40
Mettendorf 2	6	49N57	6E19	-0:25:16
Mettingen 2	1	52N18	7E46	-0:31:04
Mettlach 2	6	49N30	6E36	-0:26:24
Mettmann 2	1	51N15	6E58	-0:27:52
Metzingen 2	5	48N32	9E17	-0:37:08
Metzkausen 2	1	51N16	6E57	-0:27:48
Meuselwitz 1	2	51N02	12E17	-0:49:08
Meyenburg 1	2	53N18	12E14	-0:48:56
Michelau 2	4	50N10	11E06	-0:44:24
Michelfeld 2	4	49N42	11E35	-0:46:20
Michelsneukirchen 2	4	49N08	12E33	-0:50:12
Michelstadt 2	1	49N41	9E00	-0:36:00
Michendorf 1	2	52N18	13E01	-0:52:04
Midlum 2	1	53N43	8E37	-0:34:28
Miersdorf 1	2	52N20	13E37	-0:54:28
Miesau 2	6	49N24	7E26	-0:29:44
Miesbach 2	4	47N47	11E50	-0:47:20
Mieste 1	2	52N28	11E11	-0:44:44
Miesterhorst 1	2	52N27	11E09	-0:44:36
Mihla 1	2	51N04	10E20	-0:41:20
Mildenau 1	2	50N35	13E04	-0:52:16
Milmersdorf 1	2	53N06	13E38	-0:54:32
Milow 1	2	53N11	11E32	-0:46:08
Milow 1	2	52N31	12E18	-0:49:12
Milspe 2	1	51N18	7E21	-0:29:24
Miltach 2	4	49N09	12E46	-0:51:04
Miltenberg 2	4	49N42	9E15	-0:37:00
Miltitz 1	2	51N19	12E16	-0:49:04
Miltzow 1	2	54N12	13E13	-0:52:52
Mindelheim 2	4	48N03	10E29	-0:41:56
Minden 2	1	52N17	8E55	-0:35:40
Minsen 2	1	53N42	7E58	-0:31:52
Mintard 2	1	51N22	6E54	-0:27:36
Minzow 1	2	53N23	12E30	-0:50:00
Mirow 1	2	53N16	12E49	-0:51:16
Misburg 2	1	52N23	9E51	-0:39:24
Mistelbach 2	4	49N55	11E31	-0:46:04
Mistelgau 2	4	49N55	11E28	-0:45:52
Mittelberg 2	4	47N38	10E25	-0:41:40
Mittelfischach 2	5	49N02	9E52	-0:39:28
Mittelsaida 1	2	50N46	13E18	-0:53:12
Mittelstetten 2	4	48N15	11E06	-0:44:24
Mittenwald 2	4	47N27	11E15	-0:45:00
Mittenwalde 1	2	53N11	13E39	-0:54:36
Mittenwalde 1	2	52N16	13E32	-0:54:08
Mitterskirchen 2	4	48N21	12E44	-0:50:56
Mitterteich 2	4	49N57	12E15	-0:49:00
Mittweida 1	2	50N59	12E59	-0:51:56
Mitwitz 2	4	50N15	11E12	-0:44:48
Möckern 1	2	52N08	11E57	-0:47:48
Möckmühl 2	5	49N19	9E22	-0:37:28
Mockrehna 1	2	51N30	12E49	-0:51:16
Möderath 2	7	50N53	6E43	-0:26:52
Moers 2	7	51N27	6E37	-0:26:28
Möhlau 1	2	51N44	12E21	-0:49:24
Mohorn 1	2	51N00	13E28	-0:53:52
Möhringen 2	3	47N57	8E46	-0:35:04
Molbergen 2	1	52N51	7E55	-0:31:40
Mölkau 1	2	51N20	12E26	-0:49:44
Möllen 2	1	51N35	6E42	-0:26:48
Möllenbeck 1	2	53N17	11E44	-0:46:56
Möllenbeck 1	2	53N23	13E20	-0:53:20
Mölln 2	1	53N37	10E41	-0:42:44
Mönchengladbach 2	7	51N12	6E28	-0:25:52
Mönchröden 2	4	50N18	11E03	-0:44:12
Mönchweiler 2	3	48N06	8E25	-0:33:40
Mondfeld 2	3	49N47	9E25	-0:37:40
Monheim 2	4	48N50	10E51	-0:43:24
Monheim 2	1	51N05	6E52	-0:27:28
Mönkebude 1	2	53N46	13E57	-0:55:48
Monschau 2	7	50N33	6E14	-0:24:56
Mönsheim 2	5	48N52	8E52	-0:35:28
Monsheim 2	6	49N38	8E12	-0:32:48
Montabaur 2	1	50N26	7E50	-0:31:20
Moorburg 2	1	53N17	7E53	-0:31:32
Moordorf 2	1	53N28	7E23	-0:29:32
Moorrege 2	1	53N40	9E39	-0:38:36
Moorriem 2	1	53N15	8E19	-0:33:16
Moorsburg an der Isar 2	4	48N29	11E57	-0:47:48
Moosburg 2	4	48N29	11E57	-0:47:48
Moosham 2	4	48N56	12E16	-0:49:04
Morbach 2	6	49N48	7E07	-0:28:28
Mörfelden 2	1	49N58	8E34	-0:34:16
Moringen 2	1	51N42	9E52	-0:39:28
Morles 2	1	50N38	9E51	-0:39:24
Morsbach 2	1	50N52	7E43	-0:30:52
Mörsch 2	3	48N58	8E17	-0:33:08
Mosbach 2	3	49N21	9E08	-0:36:32
Mosel 1	2	50N47	12E28	-0:49:52
Mössingen 2	5	48N24	9E03	-0:36:12
Möttingen 2	4	48N48	10E35	-0:42:20
Much 2	1	50N54	7E25	-0:29:40
Mücheln 1	2	51N18	11E48	-0:47:12
Mücka 1	2	51N18	14E40	-0:58:40

Mücke 2 1 50N38 9E03 -0:36:12
Mudau 2 3 49N32 9E11 -0:36:44
Müden 2 1 52N52 10E07 -0:40:28
Müden 2 1 52N31 10E22 -0:41:28
Mudersbach 2 1 50N49 7E56 -0:31:44
Mügeln 1 2 51N14 13E02 -0:52:08
Muggendorf 2 4 49N48 11E16 -0:45:04
Mühlacker 2 3 48N57 8E50 -0:35:20
Mühlau 1 2 50N54 12E45 -0:51:00
Mühlberg 1 2 51N26 13E13 -0:52:52
Mühldorf am Inn 2 4 48N15 12E32 -0:50:08
Mühlenbeck 1 2 52N40 13E22 -0:53:28
Mühlen Eichsen 1 2 53N45 11E15 -0:45:00
Mühlenrahmede 2 1 51N16 7E40 -0:30:40
Mühlhausen 2 1 51N33 7E44 -0:30:56
Mühlhausen 1 2 51N12 10E27 -0:41:48
Mühlhausen im Täle 2 5 48N34 9E39 -0:38:36
Mühlheim 2 6 49N54 7E01 -0:28:04
Mühlheim 2 1 50N07 8E50 -0:35:20
Mühlheim an der Donau 2 3 48N01 8E53 -0:35:32
Mühltroff 1 2 50N32 11E55 -0:47:40
Mühringen 2 5 48N25 8E46 -0:35:04
Mulda 1 2 50N48 13E25 -0:53:40
Muldenstein 1 2 51N40 12E19 -0:49:16
Mülheim an der Ruhr 2 1 51N24 6E54 -0:27:36
Müllenbach 2 6 50N19 6E55 -0:27:40
Müllheim 2 3 47N48 7E38 -0:30:32
Müllrose 1 2 52N14 14E25 -0:57:40
Münchberg 2 4 50N11 11E47 -0:47:08
Müncheberg 1 2 52N30 14E08 -0:56:32
Münchehofe 1 2 52N30 13E40 -0:54:40
München 2 4 48N08 11E34 -0:46:16
Münchenbernsdorf 1 2 50N49 11E56 -0:47:44
München-Gladbach → Mönchengladbach 2 7 51N12 6E28 -0:25:52
Münchhausen 2 1 50N57 8E43 -0:34:52
Münchnerau 2 4 48N32 12E05 -0:48:20
Münden 2 1 51N25 9E39 -0:38:36
Munderkingen 2 5 48N14 9E38 -0:38:32
Mündheim 2 6 49N29 8E27 -0:33:48
Munich → München 2 4 48N08 11E34 -0:46:16
Münnerstadt 2 4 50N15 10E11 -0:40:44
Münsing 2 4 47N54 11E22 -0:45:28
Münsingen 2 5 48N25 9E29 -0:37:56
Münster 2 1 51N57 7E37 -0:30:28
Munster 2 1 52N59 10E05 -0:40:20
Münstermaifeld 2 6 50N15 7E22 -0:29:28
Münzenberg 2 1 50N27 8E46 -0:35:04
Murchin 1 2 53N54 13E44 -0:54:56
Murg 2 3 47N33 8E01 -0:32:04
Murnau 2 4 47N40 11E12 -0:44:48
Murrhardt 2 5 48N59 9E34 -0:38:16
Müsch 2 6 50N23 6E49 -0:27:16
Muschwitz 1 2 51N11 12E07 -0:48:28
Mussum 2 1 51N48 6E34 -0:26:16
Mutterstadt 2 6 49N26 8E21 -0:33:24
Mutzschen 1 2 51N16 12E53 -0:51:32
Mylau 1 2 50N37 12E16 -0:49:04
Nabburg 2 4 49N28 12E11 -0:48:44
Nachrodt-Wiblingwerde 2 1 51N19 7E37 -0:30:28
Nachterstedt 1 2 51N49 11E20 -0:45:20
Nagold 2 5 48N33 8E43 -0:34:52
Nahmer 2 1 51N20 7E35 -0:30:20
Naila 2 4 50N19 11E42 -0:46:48
Nandlstadt 2 4 48N32 11E48 -0:47:12
Nassau 1 2 50N46 13E32 -0:54:08
Nassau 2 1 50N19 7E47 -0:31:08
Nassenfels 2 4 48N48 11E16 -0:45:04
Nassenheide 1 2 52N49 13E12 -0:52:48
Nastätten 2 1 50N12 7E51 -0:31:24
Natorp 2 1 51N30 7E38 -0:30:32
Natternberg 2 4 48N50 12E55 -0:51:40
Nattwerder 1 2 52N26 12E56 -0:51:44
Natzungen 2 1 51N36 9E14 -0:36:56
Nauen 1 2 52N36 12E52 -0:51:28
Naumburg 1 2 51N09 11E48 -0:47:12
Naumburg 2 1 51N15 9E10 -0:36:40
Naundorf 1 2 50N56 13E25 -0:53:40
Naunhof 1 2 51N16 12E35 -0:50:20
Nauroth 2 1 50N42 7E52 -0:31:28
Nebra 1 2 51N17 11E34 -0:46:16
Neckarailfingen 2 5 48N36 9E16 -0:37:04
Neckarbischofsheim 2 3 49N17 8E57 -0:35:48
Neckarelz 2 3 49N20 9E06 -0:36:24
Neckargemünd 2 3 49N23 8E47 -0:35:08
Neckarsteinach 2 3 49N25 8E53 -0:35:32
Neckarsulm 2 5 49N12 9E13 -0:36:52
Neckartenzlingen 2 5 48N35 9E14 -0:36:56
Nedlitz 1 2 52N04 12E14 -0:48:56
Neermoor 2 1 53N18 7E26 -0:29:44
Neersen 2 7 51N15 6E29 -0:25:56
Neetze 2 1 53N15 10E39 -0:42:36
Negast 1 2 54N15 13E01 -0:52:04
Negenborn 2 1 51N53 9E34 -0:38:16
Neheim-Hüsten 2 1 51N27 7E57 -0:31:48
Neimen 2 1 51N29 7E48 -0:31:12
Neindorf 2 1 52N20 10E50 -0:43:20
Neinstedt 1 2 51N45 11E05 -0:44:20
Nellingen 2 5 48N33 9E47 -0:39:08
Nellingen 2 5 48N44 9E18 -0:37:12
Nenndorf 2 1 53N23 9E53 -0:39:32
Neppermin 1 2 53N56 14E02 -0:56:08
Nerchau 1 2 51N16 12E47 -0:51:08
Nerenstetten 2 5 48N31 10E06 -0:40:24
Neresheim 2 5 48N45 10E15 -0:41:00
Nersingen 2 4 48N25 10E07 -0:40:28
Nesselwang 2 4 47N37 10E30 -0:42:00
Nessmersiel 2 1 53N40 7E21 -0:29:24
Netra 2 1 51N06 10E05 -0:40:20
Nette 2 1 52N02 10E05 -0:40:20
Nettelstedt 2 1 52N18 8E41 -0:34:44
Nettetal 2 7 51N18 6E16 -0:25:04
Netzschkau 1 2 50N36 12E14 -0:48:56
Neualbenreuth 2 4 49N59 12E27 -0:49:48
Neuastenberg 2 1 51N10 8E29 -0:33:56
Neubeckum 2 1 51N48 8E01 -0:32:04
Neubrandenburg 1 2 53N33 13E15 -0:53:00
Neu Büddenstedt 2 1 52N10 10E31 -0:42:04
Neubukow 1 2 54N02 11E40 -0:46:40
Neuburg am Inn 2 4 48N30 13E27 -0:53:48
Neuburg an der Donau 2 4 48N44 11E11 -0:44:44
Neudenau 2 5 49N17 9E16 -0:37:04
Neudietendorf 1 2 50N55 10E55 -0:43:40
Neudorf 1 2 50N29 12E58 -0:51:52
Neudorf 2 3 49N10 8E29 -0:33:56
Neuemühle 1 2 52N18 13E39 -0:54:36
Neuenbürg 2 3 48N50 8E35 -0:34:20
Neuenburg 2 3 47N49 7E35 -0:30:20
Neuenburg 2 1 53N23 7E57 -0:31:48
Neuendettelsau 2 4 49N17 10E47 -0:43:08
Neuendorf 1 2 54N31 13E05 -0:52:20
Neuenhagen bei Berlin 1 2 52N32 13E41 -0:54:44
Neuenhaus 2 1 52N30 6E59 -0:27:56
Neuenhoven 2 7 51N08 6E31 -0:26:04
Neuenkirchen 1 2 54N32 13E20 -0:53:20
Neuenkirchen 2 1 52N30 8E04 -0:32:16
Neuenkirchen 2 1 51N50 8E26 -0:33:44
Neuenkirchen 2 1 53N14 8E31 -0:34:04
Neuenkirchen 2 1 53N02 9E42 -0:38:48
Neuenkirchen 2 1 52N14 7E22 -0:29:28
Neuenkirchen 2 1 53N46 8E53 -0:35:32
Neuenrade 2 1 51N17 7E47 -0:31:08
Neuensalz 1 2 50N30 12E13 -0:48:52
Neuenstadt am Kocher 2 5 49N14 9E20 -0:37:20
Neuenwalde 2 1 53N40 8E40 -0:34:40
Neuerburg 2 6 50N00 6E17 -0:25:08
Neu Fahrland 1 2 52N26 13E03 -0:52:12
Neufahrn bei Freising 2 4 48N19 11E40 -0:46:40
Neufahrn in Niederbayern 2 4 48N44 12E11 -0:48:44
Neuffen 2 5 48N33 9E22 -0:37:28
Neugersdorf 1 2 50N59 14E36 -0:58:24
Neuglobsow 1 2 53N09 13E02 -0:52:08
Neuharlingersiel 2 1 53N42 7E42 -0:30:48
Neu-Hartmannsdorf 1 2 52N22 13E51 -0:55:24
Neuhaus 1 2 50N30 11E08 -0:44:32
Neuhaus 1 2 53N17 10E55 -0:43:40
Neuhaus 2 3 47N48 8E34 -0:34:16
Neuhaus an der Oste 2 1 53N48 9E02 -0:36:08
Neuhausen 1 2 50N41 13E28 -0:53:52
Neuhausen 2 3 47N58 8E55 -0:35:40
Neuhausen auf den Fildern 2 5 48N41 9E16 -0:37:04
Neuhaus im Solling 2 1 51N45 9E31 -0:38:04
Neuhaus-Schierschnitz 1 2 50N19 11E14 -0:44:56
Neuhof 2 1 50N27 9E40 -0:38:40
Neuhof an der Zenn 2 4 49N27 10E38 -0:42:32
Neu-Isenburg 2 1 50N03 8E41 -0:34:44
Neukalen 1 2 53N49 12E47 -0:51:08
Neu Kaliss 1 2 53N10 11E17 -0:45:08
Neukieritzsch 1 2 51N10 12E25 -0:49:40
Neukirch 1 2 51N17 13E58 -0:55:52
Neukirch 1 2 51N05 14E20 -0:57:20
Neukirch 2 5 47N39 9E41 -0:38:44
Neukirchen 1 2 51N05 12E32 -0:50:08
Neukirchen 1 2 50N47 12E22 -0:49:28
Neukirchen 1 2 50N46 12E52 -0:51:28
Neukirchen 2 1 54N52 8E44 -0:34:56
Neukirchen 2 1 50N46 9E41 -0:38:44
Neukirchen 2 6 49N29 6E50 -0:27:20
Neukirchen 2 1 54N19 11E01 -0:44:04
Neukirchen 2 4 49N05 11E45 -0:47:00
Neukirchen 2 7 51N07 6E41 -0:26:44
Neukirchen bei Sulzbach-Rosenberg 2 4 49N32 11E38 -0:46:32
Neukirchen-Vluyn 2 7 51N27 6E33 -0:26:12
Neukloster 1 2 53N52 11E41 -0:46:44
Neulangerwisch 1 2 52N19 13E04 -0:52:16
Neulienken 1 2 53N27 14E22 -0:57:28
Neu Lübbenau 1 2 52N04 13E53 -0:55:32
Neulussheim 2 3 49N17 8E31 -0:34:04
Neumagen 2 6 49N51 6E53 -0:27:32
Neumark 1 2 50N39 12E21 -0:49:24
Neumarkt in der Oberpfalz 2 4 49N16 11E28 -0:45:52
Neumarkt-Sankt Veit 2 4 48N22 12E30 -0:50:00
Neumühle 2 4 49N28 11E50 -0:47:20
Neumünster 2 1 54N04 9E59 -0:39:56
Neunburg vorm Wald 2 4 49N21 12E24 -0:49:36
Neundorf 1 2 51N49 11E34 -0:46:16
Neunkirchen 2 1 50N32 8E06 -0:32:24
Neunkirchen/Saar 2 6 49N20 7E10 -0:28:40
Neunkirchen am Brand 2 4 49N37 11E08 -0:44:32
Neunkirchen am Potzberg 2 6 49N30 7E29 -0:29:56
Neuötting 2 4 48N14 12E42 -0:50:48
Neupetershain 1 2 51N36 14E09 -0:56:36
Neuravensburg 2 5 47N38 9E46 -0:39:04
Neuruppin 1 2 52N55 12E48 -0:51:12
Neusalza-Spremberg 1 2 51N02 14E32 -0:58:08
Neuseddin 1 2 52N18 12E59 -0:51:56
Neusorg 2 4 49N56 11E58 -0:47:52
Neuss 2 7 51N12 6E41 -0:26:44
Neustadt 1 2 52N52 12E25 -0:49:40
Neustadt 1 2 51N01 14E13 -0:56:52
Neustadt 1 2 50N44 11E44 -0:46:56
Neustadt 2 1 50N51 9E07 -0:36:28
Neustadt am Rübenberge 2 1 52N30 9E28 -0:37:52
Neustadt an der Aisch 2 4 49N34 10E37 -0:42:28
Neustadt an der Donau 2 4 48N48 11E46 -0:47:04
Neustadt an der Waldnaab 2 4 49N44 12E11 -0:48:44
Neustadt an der Weinstrasse 2 6 49N21 8E08 -0:32:32
Neustadt bei Coburg 2 4 50N19 11E07 -0:44:28
Neustadt-Glewe 1 2 53N25 11E36 -0:46:24
Neustadt in Holstein 2 1 54N06 10E48 -0:43:12
Neustrelitz 1 2 53N21 13E04 -0:52:16
Neu Töplitz 1 2 52N27 12E54 -0:51:36
Neutraubling 2 4 48N59 12E12 -0:48:48
Neutrebbin 1 2 52N40 14E13 -0:56:52
Neu-Ulm 2 4 48N23 10E01 -0:40:04
Neuwied 2 1 50N25 7E27 -0:29:48
Neuwirtshaus 2 4 50N11 9E50 -0:39:20
Neu Wulmstorf 2 1 53N28 9E48 -0:39:12
Neuzelle 1 2 52N05 14E38 -0:58:32
Neu Zittau 1 2 52N23 13E44 -0:54:56
Neviges 2 1 51N19 7E05 -0:28:20
New Uosenow 1 2 53N47 13E46 -0:55:04
Neye 2 1 51N07 7E22 -0:29:28
Nidda 2 1 50N24 9E00 -0:36:00
Nideggen 2 7 50N47 6E29 -0:25:56
Niebüll 2 1 54N48 8E50 -0:35:20
Niederaschau 2 4 47N47 12E19 -0:49:16
Niederau 1 2 51N10 13E32 -0:54:08
Niederaula 2 1 50N48 9E36 -0:38:24
Niederbobritzsch 1 2 50N54 13E26 -0:53:44
Niederbonsfeld 2 1 51N23 7E08 -0:28:32
Niederdonk 2 7 51N14 6E41 -0:26:44
Niederelfringhausen 2 1 51N21 7E10 -0:28:40
Niederfinow 1 2 52N50 13E55 -0:55:40
Niederfrohna 1 2 50N53 12E43 -0:50:52
Niederhaverbeck 2 1 53N09 9E54 -0:39:36
Niederheimbach 2 6 50N02 7E48 -0:31:12
Niederhohne 2 1 51N13 10E06 -0:40:24
Niederkrüchten 2 7 51N12 6E13 -0:24:52
Nieder-Lahnstein 2 1 50N19 7E36 -0:30:24
Niederlehme 1 2 52N19 13E39 -0:54:36
Niedermarsberg 2 1 51N28 8E50 -0:35:20
Niedermarschacht 2 1 53N25 10E21 -0:41:24
Nieder-Mörlen 2 1 50N23 8E43 -0:34:52
Niederndodeleben 1 2 52N08 11E30 -0:46:00
Nieder-Neuendorf 1 2 52N37 13E12 -0:52:48
Niedernhall 2 5 49N17 9E36 -0:38:24
Niedernwöhren 2 1 52N21 9E08 -0:36:32
Niederoderwitz 1 2 50N57 14E44 -0:58:56
Nieder-Ohmen 2 1 50N38 9E02 -0:36:08
Nieder-Olm 2 6 49N55 8E11 -0:32:44
Niederorschel 1 2 51N22 10E25 -0:41:40
Niedersachswerfen 1 2 51N33 10E46 -0:43:04
Niederselters 2 1 50N20 8E14 -0:32:56
Niedersonthofen 2 4 47N38 10E13 -0:40:52
Niederstetten 2 5 49N24 9E55 -0:39:40
Niederstotzingen 2 5 48N32 10E14 -0:40:56
Niederwalgern 2 1 50N44 8E41 -0:34:44
Niederwiesa 1 2 50N51 13E01 -0:52:04
Nieder-Wöllstadt 2 1 50N16 8E46 -0:35:04
Niederwürschnitz 1 2 50N43 12E45 -0:51:00
Nieheim 2 1 51N48 9E06 -0:36:24
Niemegk 1 2 52N04 12E41 -0:50:44
Nienberge 2 1 52N00 7E34 -0:30:16
Nienborg-Wigbold 2 1 52N08 7E06 -0:28:24
Nienburg 1 2 51N50 11E46 -0:47:04
Nienburg 2 1 52N38 9E13 -0:36:52
Niendorf 2 1 53N59 10E50 -0:43:20
Nienhagen 1 2 51N57 11E09 -0:44:36
Nienhagen 2 1 52N33 10E05 -0:40:20

Nierst 2 7 51N19 6E43 -0:26:52
Nierstein 2 6 49N52 8E20 -0:33:20
Niesky 1 2 51N17 14E49 -0:59:16
Nievenheim 2 7 51N07 6E46 -0:27:04
Nittenau 2 4 49N12 12E16 -0:49:04
Nittendorf 2 4 49N02 11E58 -0:47:52
Nobitz 1 2 50N58 12E29 -0:49:56
Nochten 1 2 51N26 14E36 -0:58:24
Noer 2 1 54N27 10E00 -0:40:00
Nonnenhorn 2 4 47N34 9E36 -0:38:24
Nonnevitz 1 2 54N39 13E17 -0:53:08
Nonnweiler 2 6 49N36 6E58 -0:27:52
Nordbögge 2 1 51N37 7E44 -0:30:56
Norddeich 2 1 53N37 7E09 -0:28:36
Norden 2 1 53N36 7E12 -0:28:48
Nordendorf 2 4 48N36 10E50 -0:43:20
Nordenham 2 1 53N29 8E28 -0:33:52
Norderney 2 1 53N42 7E08 -0:28:32
Norderstapel 2 1 54N21 9E14 -0:36:56
Norderstedt 2 1 53N43 10E00 -0:40:00
Nordgermersleben 1
2 52N13 11E20 -0:45:20
Nordhalben 2 4 50N22 11E30 -0:46:00
Nordhausen 1 2 51N30 10E47 -0:43:08
Nordheim von der Rhön 2
4 50N28 10E11 -0:40:44
Nordhorn 2 1 52N27 7E05 -0:28:20
Nordkirchen 2 1 51N44 7E31 -0:30:04
Nördlingen 2 4 48N51 10E30 -0:42:00
Nordstemmen 2 1 52N09 9E46 -0:39:04
Nordwalde 2 1 52N05 7E28 -0:29:52
Noremberg → Nürnberg 2
4 49N27 11E04 -0:44:16
Norf 2 7 51N09 6E43 -0:26:52
Nörten-Hardenberg 2
1 51N38 9E56 -0:39:44
Northeim 2 1 51N42 10E00 -0:40:00
Nortorf 2 1 53N55 9E16 -0:37:04
Nossen 1 2 51N03 13E17 -0:53:08
Nottleben 1 2 50N58 10E50 -0:43:20
Nottuln 2 1 51N55 7E22 -0:29:28
Nudow 1 2 52N20 13E10 -0:52:40
Nünchritz 1 2 51N18 13E23 -0:53:32
Nürburg 2 6 50N21 6E57 -0:27:48
Nuremberg → Nürnberg 2
4 49N27 11E04 -0:44:16
Nürnberg 2 4 49N27 11E04 -0:44:16
Nürtingen 2 5 48N38 9E20 -0:37:20
Nusplingen 2 5 48N08 8E53 -0:35:32
Ober-Abtsteinach 2
1 49N33 8E47 -0:35:08
Oberalteich 2 4 48N55 12E40 -0:50:40
Oberammergau 2 4 47N35 11E04 -0:44:16
Oberau 2 4 47N33 11E08 -0:44:32
Oberaudorf 2 4 47N39 12E10 -0:48:40
Oberbauer 2 1 51N17 7E26 -0:29:44
Oberbieber 2 1 50N28 7E29 -0:29:56
Oberbonsfeld 2 1 51N22 7E08 -0:28:32
Oberbrügge 2 1 51N11 7E34 -0:30:16
Obercunnersdorf 1
2 51N02 14E40 -0:58:40
Oberdolling 2 4 48N50 11E35 -0:46:20
Oberdorla 1 2 51N10 10E25 -0:41:40
Oberelfringhausen 2
1 51N20 7E11 -0:28:44
Obergeis 2 1 50N54 9E35 -0:38:20
Obergünzburg 2 4 47N51 10E25 -0:41:40
Obergurig 1 2 51N07 14E24 -0:57:36
Oberhaan 2 1 51N13 7E02 -0:28:08
Oberhaching 2 4 48N02 11E37 -0:46:28
Oberharmersbach 2
3 48N22 8E07 -0:32:28
Oberhausen 2 1 51N28 6E50 -0:27:20
Oberhof 1 2 50N41 10E44 -0:42:56
Oberhollerau 2 4 48N41 12E27 -0:49:48
Oberjettingen 2 5 48N34 8E46 -0:35:04
Oberjoch 2 4 47N31 10E23 -0:41:32
Oberkaufungen 2 1 51N17 9E38 -0:38:32
Oberkirch 2 3 48N31 8E05 -0:32:20
Oberkirchen 2 1 51N09 8E22 -0:33:28
Oberkochen 2 5 48N47 10E06 -0:40:24
Oberkotzau 2 4 50N16 11E56 -0:47:44
Oberlungwitz 1 2 50N47 12E44 -0:50:56
Obermarchtal 2 5 48N14 9E34 -0:38:16
Obermeiser 2 1 51N26 9E19 -0:37:16
Obermoschel 2 6 49N44 7E46 -0:31:04
Obermünstertal 2
3 47N52 7E49 -0:31:16
Obernbeck 2 1 52N12 8E41 -0:34:44
Obernburg am Main 2
4 49N50 9E08 -0:36:32
Oberndorf 2 1 53N45 9E08 -0:36:32
Oberndorf am Neckar 2
3 48N18 8E34 -0:34:16
Obernhausen 2 1 50N29 9E56 -0:39:44
Obernkirchen 2 1 52N16 9E07 -0:36:28
Obernsees 2 4 49N55 11E23 -0:45:32
Obernzell 2 4 48N34 13E39 -0:54:36
Oberoderwitz 1 2 50N58 14E42 -0:58:48
Oberpleis 2 1 50N43 7E16 -0:29:04
Ober-Ramstadt 2 1 49N49 8E44 -0:34:56
Oberried 2 4 49N06 13E03 -0:52:12
Oberröblingen 1 2 51N26 11E18 -0:45:12
Ober-Roden 2 1 49N59 8E50 -0:35:20
Oberscheidental 2
3 49N30 9E09 -0:36:36
Oberscheinfeld 2
4 49N42 10E26 -0:41:44
Oberscheld 2 1 50N44 8E20 -0:33:20
Oberschleissheim 2
4 48N15 11E34 -0:46:16
Obersickte 2 1 52N13 10E38 -0:42:32
Oberspier 1 2 51N19 10E51 -0:43:24
Oberstadtfeld 2 6 50N10 6E46 -0:27:04
Oberstaufen 2 4 47N33 10E01 -0:40:04

Oberstdorf 2 4 47N24 10E16 -0:41:04
Oberstreu 2 4 50N24 10E17 -0:41:08
Obersuhl 2 1 50N56 10E02 -0:40:08
Obertheres 2 4 50N01 10E26 -0:41:44
Obertraubling 2 4 48N58 12E10 -0:48:40
Obertürken 2 4 48N19 12E50 -0:51:20
Oberursel 2 1 50N11 8E35 -0:34:20
Oberviechtach 2 4 49N28 12E25 -0:49:40
Oberweissbach 1 2 50N35 11E08 -0:44:32
Oberweissenbrunn 2
4 50N24 9E57 -0:39:48
Oberwengern 2 1 51N23 7E22 -0:29:28
Oberwesel 2 6 50N06 7E43 -0:30:52
Oberwiesenthal 1
2 50N25 12E59 -0:51:56
Ober-Wilden 2 1 50N48 8E05 -0:32:20
Oberwolfach 2 3 48N19 8E12 -0:32:48
Obgruiten 2 1 51N13 7E01 -0:28:04
Obhausen 1 2 51N23 11E39 -0:46:36
Obing 2 4 48N00 12E24 -0:49:36
Obrighoven-Lackhausen 2
1 51N40 6E38 -0:26:32
Ochsenfurt 2 4 49N40 10E03 -0:40:12
Ochsenhausen 2 5 48N04 9E56 -0:39:44
Ochtendung 2 6 50N21 7E23 -0:29:32
Ochtrup 2 1 52N13 7E11 -0:28:44
Ockholm 2 1 54N40 8E49 -0:35:16
Odelzhausen 2 4 48N19 11E12 -0:44:48
Odenthal 2 1 51N02 7E07 -0:28:28
Oderberg 1 2 52N52 14E02 -0:56:08
Oebisfelde 1 2 52N25 10E59 -0:43:56
Oederan 1 2 50N52 13E09 -0:52:36
Oeding 2 1 51N56 6E49 -0:27:16
Oedt 2 7 51N19 6E22 -0:25:28
Oelde 2 1 51N49 8E08 -0:32:32
Oelsig 1 2 51N41 13E22 -0:53:28
Oelsnitz 1 2 50N24 12E10 -0:48:40
Oelsnitz 1 2 50N43 12E41 -0:50:44
Oer-Erkenschwick 2
1 51N39 7E15 -0:29:00
Oerlinghausen 2 1 51N57 8E39 -0:34:36
Oermten 2 7 51N29 6E27 -0:25:48
Oesede 2 1 52N12 8E04 -0:32:16
Oeslau 2 4 50N17 11E01 -0:44:04
Oestrich 2 1 51N22 7E38 -0:30:32
Oestrum 2 7 51N25 6E40 -0:26:40
Oettingen in Bayern 2
4 48N57 10E36 -0:42:24
Oeventrop 2 1 51N23 8E08 -0:32:32
Oeversee 2 1 54N42 9E26 -0:37:44
Offenbach 2 1 50N08 8E47 -0:35:08
Offenburg 2 3 48N28 7E57 -0:31:48
Offingen 2 4 48N29 10E21 -0:41:24
Öflingen 2 3 47N35 7E55 -0:31:40
Oggersheim 2 6 49N29 8E22 -0:33:28
Ogrosen 1 2 51N42 14E02 -0:56:08
Ohorn 1 2 51N10 14E02 -0:56:08
Ohrdruf 1 2 50N50 10E44 -0:42:56
Öhringen 2 5 49N12 9E29 -0:37:56
Ohrnberg 2 5 49N15 9E27 -0:37:48
Ohu 2 4 48N36 12E14 -0:48:56
Oker 2 1 51N54 10E29 -0:41:56
Olbernhau 1 2 50N39 13E20 -0:53:20
Olbersdorf 1 2 50N52 14E46 -0:59:04
Olbersleben 1 2 51N09 11E20 -0:45:20
Oldenbrok 2 1 53N17 8E23 -0:33:32
Oldenburg 2 1 53N08 8E13 -0:32:52
Oldenburg in Holstein 2
1 54N17 10E52 -0:43:28
Oldendorf 2 1 53N35 9E14 -0:36:56
Oldenstadt 2 1 52N58 10E35 -0:42:20
Oldenswort 2 1 54N22 8E56 -0:35:44
Oldersum 2 1 53N20 7E20 -0:29:20
Oldisleben 1 2 51N18 11E10 -0:44:40
Olfen 2 1 51N42 7E23 -0:29:32
Olpe 2 1 51N02 7E52 -0:31:28
Olsberg 2 1 51N21 8E29 -0:33:56
Olvenstedt 1 2 52N09 11E34 -0:46:16
Onstmettingen 2 5 48N17 9E00 -0:36:00
Oos 2 3 48N47 8E11 -0:32:44
Opherdicke 2 1 51N29 7E38 -0:30:32
Opladen 2 1 51N04 7E00 -0:28:00
Oppach 1 2 51N03 14E30 -0:58:00
Oppelhain 1 2 51N33 13E35 -0:54:20
Oppenau 2 3 48N28 8E10 -0:32:40
Oppenheim 2 6 49N51 8E21 -0:33:24
Oranienbaum 1 2 51N48 12E24 -0:49:36
Oranienburg 1 2 52N45 13E14 -0:52:56
Orken 2 7 51N06 6E34 -0:26:16
Orlamünde 1 2 50N47 11E31 -0:46:04
Orsoy 2 7 51N31 6E41 -0:26:44
Ortenberg 2 3 48N27 7E58 -0:31:52
Ortenberg 2 1 50N21 9E02 -0:36:08
Ortenburg 2 4 48N33 13E14 -0:52:56
Orth 2 1 54N27 11E03 -0:44:12
Ortrand 1 2 51N22 13E45 -0:55:00
Oschatz 1 2 51N17 13E07 -0:52:28
Oschersleben 1 2 52N01 11E13 -0:44:52
Osnabrück 2 1 52N16 8E02 -0:32:08
Ossenberg 2 7 51N34 6E35 -0:26:20
Ossling 1 2 51N21 14E09 -0:56:36
Ossum-Bösinghoven 2
7 51N18 6E39 -0:26:36
Ost-Berlin → Berlin (Ost) 1
2 52N32 13E25 -0:53:40
Ostbevern 2 1 52N02 7E50 -0:31:20
Ostbüren 2 1 51N31 7E46 -0:31:04
Ostenfelde 2 1 51N52 8E04 -0:32:16
Osterath 2 7 51N16 6E37 -0:26:28
Osterbönen 2 1 51N37 7E48 -0:31:12
Osterburg 1 2 52N47 11E44 -0:46:56
Osterburken 2 5 49N26 9E26 -0:37:44
Ostercappeln 2 1 52N20 8E13 -0:32:52
Osterfeld 1 2 51N05 11E56 -0:47:44
Osterhofen 2 4 48N42 13E01 -0:52:04

Osterholz-Scharmbeck 2
1 53N14 8E47 -0:35:08
Osternienburg 1 2 51N48 12E01 -0:48:04
Osterode 2 1 51N44 10E11 -0:40:44
Osterrönfeld 2 1 54N17 9E41 -0:38:44
Osterwick 2 1 52N01 7E13 -0:28:52
Osterwieck 1 2 51N58 10E42 -0:42:48
Ostfeld 2 1 51N40 7E45 -0:31:00
Ostgrossefehn 2 1 53N24 7E36 -0:30:24
Ostheim vor der Rhön 2
4 50N27 10E14 -0:40:56
Osthofen 2 6 49N42 8E19 -0:33:16
Ostrach 2 5 47N57 9E23 -0:37:32
Ostrau 1 2 51N12 13E09 -0:52:36
Ostrhauderfehn 2
1 53N08 7E37 -0:30:28
Östrich 2 1 51N40 6E55 -0:27:40
Östringen 2 3 49N13 8E43 -0:34:52
Ostritz 1 2 51N01 14E56 -0:59:44
Ostseebad Ahrenshoop 1
2 54N23 12E25 -0:49:40
Ostseebad Boltenhagen 1
2 54N00 11E12 -0:44:48
Ostseebad Dierhagen 1
2 54N17 12E22 -0:49:28
Ostseebad Graal-Müritz 1
2 54N15 12E12 -0:48:48
Ostseebad Nienhagen 1
2 54N09 11E58 -0:47:52
Ostseebad Rerik 1
2 54N06 11E37 -0:46:28
Ostseebad Wustrow 1
2 54N21 12E23 -0:49:32
Ost-Sümmern 2 1 51N26 7E44 -0:30:56
Othfresen 2 1 52N00 10E23 -0:41:32
Ottbergen 2 1 51N42 9E18 -0:37:12
Ottendorf-Okrilla 1
2 51N11 13E50 -0:55:20
Ottenhöfen 2 3 48N34 8E09 -0:32:36
Otterberg 2 6 49N30 7E46 -0:31:04
Otterhöfen 2 3 48N33 8E12 -0:32:48
Otterndorf 2 1 53N48 8E53 -0:35:32
Ottersberg 2 1 53N06 9E08 -0:36:32
Ottleben 1 2 52N05 11E07 -0:44:28
Ottmarsbocholt 2
1 51N49 7E32 -0:30:08
Ottobeuren 2 4 47N56 10E18 -0:41:12
Ottobrunn 2 4 48N04 11E40 -0:46:40
Ottoschwanden 2 3 48N12 7E52 -0:31:28
Ottweiler 2 6 49N24 7E09 -0:28:36
Ovelgönne 2 1 53N20 8E25 -0:33:40
Overath 2 1 50N55 7E14 -0:28:56
Overberge 2 1 51N37 7E41 -0:30:44
Owen 2 5 48N35 9E27 -0:37:48
Oy 2 4 47N38 10E28 -0:41:52
Oybin 1 2 50N50 14E44 -0:58:56
Oyten 2 1 53N04 9E01 -0:36:04
Paaren 1 2 52N39 12E59 -0:51:56
Paderborn 2 1 51N43 8E45 -0:35:00
Pampow 1 2 53N32 14E15 -0:57:00
Pang 2 4 47N49 12E05 -0:48:20
Panker 2 1 54N20 10E34 -0:42:16
Pansfelde 1 2 51N39 11E16 -0:45:04
Papenburg 2 1 53N05 7E23 -0:29:32
Pappenheim 1 2 50N47 10E27 -0:41:48
Pappenheim 2 4 48N56 10E58 -0:43:52
Parchen 1 2 52N21 12E05 -0:48:20
Parchim 1 2 53N25 11E51 -0:47:24
Parey 1 2 52N22 11E59 -0:47:56
Parkstein 2 4 49N44 12E04 -0:48:16
Parkstetten 2 4 48N55 12E36 -0:50:24
Parsberg 2 4 49N09 11E43 -0:46:52
Parsdorf 2 4 48N09 11E47 -0:47:08
Pasewalk 1 2 53N30 14E00 -0:56:00
Pasing 2 4 48N08 11E27 -0:45:48
Passau 2 4 48N35 13E28 -0:53:52
Passow 1 2 53N08 14E06 -0:56:24
Patersdorf 2 4 49N01 12E59 -0:51:56
Pattensen 2 1 52N15 9E46 -0:39:04
Pattscheid 2 1 51N05 7E03 -0:28:12
Patzig 1 2 54N28 13E24 -0:53:36
Paulinenaue 1 2 52N40 12E43 -0:50:52
Paulushofen 2 4 49N01 11E30 -0:46:00
Pausa 1 2 50N35 12E00 -0:48:00
Pausin 1 2 52N38 13E03 -0:52:12
Päwesin 1 2 52N31 12E42 -0:50:48
Peckeloh 2 1 52N01 8E07 -0:32:28
Peckelsheim 2 1 51N36 9E07 -0:36:28
Peenemünde 1 2 54N08 13E46 -0:55:04
Pegau 1 2 51N10 12E14 -0:48:56
Pegnitz 2 4 49N45 11E33 -0:46:12
Peine 2 1 52N19 10E13 -0:40:52
Peissenberg 2 4 47N48 11E04 -0:44:16
Peiting 2 4 47N47 10E55 -0:43:40
Peitz 1 2 51N51 14E24 -0:57:36
Pelkum 2 1 51N40 7E24 -0:29:36
Pelkum 2 1 51N39 7E45 -0:31:00
Pellingen 2 6 49N40 6E40 -0:26:40
Pelsin 1 2 53N48 13E40 -0:54:40
Pemfling 2 4 49N16 12E37 -0:50:28
Penig 1 2 50N56 12E41 -0:50:44
Penkun 1 2 53N17 14E14 -0:56:56
Penzberg 2 4 47N45 11E23 -0:45:32
Penzlin 1 2 53N30 13E05 -0:52:20
Perl 2 6 49N28 6E36 -0:26:24
Perleberg 1 2 53N04 11E51 -0:47:24
Perwenitz 1 2 52N40 13E01 -0:52:04
Pesch 2 7 51N11 6E32 -0:26:08
Pessin 1 2 52N38 12E40 -0:50:40
Petersberg 2 1 50N33 9E43 -0:38:52
Petersdorf 2 1 54N29 11E04 -0:44:16
Petersdorf 2 4 48N31 11E02 -0:44:08
Petershagen 1 2 52N24 14E20 -0:57:20
Petershagen 2 1 52N23 8E58 -0:35:52

GERMANY ALEMANIA ALLEMAGNE DEUTSCHLAND

Petershagen bei Berlin 1
2 52N31 13E46 -0:55:04
Petershausen 2 4 48N24 11E28 -0:45:52
Peterskirchen 2 4 48N05 12E29 -0:49:56
Petkus 1 2 51N59 13E21 -0:53:24
Petzow 1 2 52N21 12E56 -0:51:44
Pewsum 2 1 53N26 7E05 -0:28:20
Pfaffenhausen 2 4 48N07 10E27 -0:41:48
Pfaffenhofen an der Ilm 2
4 48N31 11E30 -0:46:00
Pfalzdorf 2 7 51N42 6E11 -0:24:44
Pfalzel 2 6 49N47 6E41 -0:26:44
Pfarrkirchen 2 4 48N27 12E56 -0:51:44
Pfarrweisach 2 4 50N09 10E44 -0:42:56
Pfatter 2 4 48N58 12E23 -0:49:32
Pfeddersheim 2 6 49N38 8E16 -0:33:04
Pfeffenhausen 2 4 48N40 11E58 -0:47:52
Pforzen 2 4 47N55 10E37 -0:42:28
Pforzheim 2 3 48N54 8E42 -0:34:48
Pfreimd 2 4 49N30 12E11 -0:48:44
Pfronten 2 4 47N34 10E33 -0:42:12
Pfuhl 2 4 48N24 10E02 -0:40:08
Pfullendorf 2 3 47N55 9E15 -0:37:00
Pfullingen 2 5 48N28 9E13 -0:36:52
Pfungstadt 2 1 49N48 8E36 -0:34:24
Pfünz 2 4 48N53 11E16 -0:45:04
Philippsreut 2 4 48N52 13E41 -0:54:44
Philippsthal 1 2 52N20 13E09 -0:52:36
Piding 2 4 47N46 12E55 -0:51:40
Pilsum 2 1 53N29 7E04 -0:28:16
Pinneberg 2 1 53N40 9E47 -0:39:08
Pirk 1 2 50N25 12E04 -0:48:16
Pirmasens 2 6 49N12 7E36 -0:30:24
Pirna 1 2 50N58 13E56 -0:55:44
Planegg 2 4 48N06 11E25 -0:45:40
Plankenfels 2 4 49N53 11E20 -0:45:20
Plattling 2 4 48N47 12E53 -0:51:32
Plau 1 2 53N27 12E16 -0:49:04
Plaue 1 2 52N24 12E25 -0:49:40
Plaue 1 2 50N47 10E54 -0:43:36
Plauen 1 2 50N30 12E08 -0:48:32
Pleinfeld 2 4 49N06 10E59 -0:43:56
Pleissa 1 2 50N50 12E46 -0:51:04
Pless 2 4 48N05 10E08 -0:40:32
Plessa 1 2 51N28 13E37 -0:54:28
Plettenberg 2 1 51N13 7E52 -0:31:28
Pleystein 2 4 49N39 12E25 -0:49:40
Pliening 2 4 48N12 11E48 -0:47:12
Pliezhausen 2 5 48N33 9E12 -0:36:48
Plochingen 2 5 48N42 9E25 -0:37:40
Plön 2 1 54N09 10E25 -0:41:40
Plötz 1 2 51N38 11E56 -0:47:44
Pobershau 1 2 50N38 13E13 -0:52:52
Pockau 1 2 50N40 13E27 -0:53:48
Pöcking 2 4 47N58 11E17 -0:45:08
Pocking 2 4 48N24 13E19 -0:53:16
Poggendorf 1 2 54N03 13E07 -0:52:28
Pöhla 1 2 50N31 12E49 -0:51:16
Pöhlde 2 1 51N37 10E18 -0:41:12
Pohl-Göns 2 1 50N28 8E39 -0:34:36
Poing 2 4 48N10 11E49 -0:47:16
Polch 2 6 50N18 7E18 -0:29:12
Pollanten 2 4 49N09 11E28 -0:45:52
Polleben 1 2 51N34 11E36 -0:46:24
Pollenfeld 2 4 48N57 11E12 -0:44:48
Polling 2 4 47N48 11E09 -0:44:36
Polsum 2 1 51N37 7E03 -0:28:12
Pölzig 1 2 50N57 12E11 -0:48:44
Pomellen 1 2 53N20 14E23 -0:57:32
Pommersfelden 2 4 49N46 10E49 -0:43:16
Pomssen 1 2 51N14 12E37 -0:50:28
Pondorf 2 4 48N57 11E34 -0:46:16
Pönitz 2 1 54N03 10E40 -0:42:40
Ponitz 1 2 50N51 12E25 -0:49:40
Poppenhausen 2 4 50N06 10E08 -0:40:32
Pörnbach 2 4 48N37 11E28 -0:45:52
Porta Westfalica 2
1 52N14 8E55 -0:35:40
Porz 2 1 50N53 7E03 -0:28:12
Poseritz 1 2 54N18 13E16 -0:53:04
Pösing 2 4 49N14 12E33 -0:50:12
Possendorf 1 2 50N57 13E42 -0:54:48
Pössneck 1 2 50N42 11E37 -0:46:28
Postau 2 4 48N39 12E20 -0:49:20
Postbauer 2 4 49N19 11E21 -0:45:24
Pötenitz 1 2 53N57 10E58 -0:43:52
Potsdam 1 2 52N24 13E04 -0:52:16
Potshausen 2 1 53N11 7E37 -0:30:28
Pottenstein 2 4 49N46 11E25 -0:45:40
Pöttmes 2 4 48N35 11E06 -0:44:24
Pouch 1 2 51N37 12E24 -0:49:36
Poxau 2 4 48N34 12E33 -0:50:12
Prackenbach 2 4 49N06 12E50 -0:51:20
Pramort 1 2 54N26 12E55 -0:51:40
Pratau 1 2 51N50 12E38 -0:50:32
Preetz 2 1 54N14 10E16 -0:41:04
Premnitz 1 2 52N32 12E19 -0:49:16
Prenzlau 1 2 53N19 13E52 -0:55:28
Prerow 1 2 54N26 12E35 -0:50:20
Pressath 2 4 49N46 11E56 -0:47:44
Pressel 1 2 51N34 12E41 -0:50:44
Prettin 1 2 51N39 12E55 -0:51:40
Pretzfeld 2 4 49N45 11E11 -0:44:44
Pretzier 1 2 52N49 11E15 -0:45:00
Pretzsch 1 2 51N42 12E48 -0:51:12
Preussisch-Oldendorf 2
1 52N18 8E30 -0:34:00
Preussisch-Ströhen 2
1 52N29 8E40 -0:34:40
Prien am Chiemsee 2
4 47N51 12E20 -0:49:20
Prieros 1 2 52N13 13E46 -0:55:04
Priestewitz 1 2 51N15 13E30 -0:54:00
Primstal 2 6 49N32 6E58 -0:27:52
Priort 1 2 52N31 12E58 -0:51:52

Pritzerbe 1 2 52N30 12E27 -0:49:48
Pritzier 1 2 53N22 11E04 -0:44:16
Pritzwalk 1 2 53N09 12E10 -0:48:40
Probstzella 1 2 50N32 11E22 -0:45:28
Profen 1 2 51N07 12E13 -0:48:52
Pronsfeld 2 6 50N10 6E20 -0:25:20
Prösen 1 2 51N25 13E30 -0:54:00
Prosigk 1 2 51N42 12E03 -0:48:12
Prötzel 1 2 52N38 13E59 -0:55:56
Prüm 2 6 50N12 6E25 -0:25:40
Prunn 2 4 48N57 11E44 -0:46:56
Prutting 2 4 47N53 12E11 -0:48:44
Puchhausen 2 4 48N45 12E30 -0:50:00
Puchheim 2 4 48N09 11E20 -0:45:20
Puffendorf 2 7 50N56 6E13 -0:24:52
Pulheim 2 7 51N00 6E47 -0:27:08
Pullach im Isarta 2
4 48N03 11E31 -0:46:04
Pulsen 1 2 51N23 13E26 -0:53:44
Pulsnitz 1 2 51N11 14E01 -0:56:04
Pünderich 2 6 50N02 7E08 -0:28:32
Putbus 1 2 54N21 13E28 -0:53:52
Putgarten 1 2 54N40 13E25 -0:53:40
Putlitz 1 2 53N15 12E02 -0:48:08
Pütt 2 1 51N11 6E59 -0:27:56
Puttgarden 2 1 54N30 11E13 -0:44:52
Püttlingen 2 6 49N17 6E53 -0:27:32
Putzkau 1 2 51N06 14E13 -0:56:52
Quadrath-Ichendorf 2
7 50N56 6E41 -0:26:44
Quakenbrück 2 1 52N40 7E57 -0:31:48
Quedlinburg 1 2 51N48 11E09 -0:44:36
Quelle 2 1 52N00 8E29 -0:33:56
Quellendorf 1 2 51N45 12E07 -0:48:28
Querenhorst 2 1 52N20 10E57 -0:43:48
Querfurt 1 2 51N23 11E36 -0:46:24
Quickborn 2 1 53N44 9E53 -0:39:32
Rabenau 1 2 50N57 13E38 -0:54:32
Radeberg 1 2 51N07 13E55 -0:55:40
Radebeul 1 2 51N06 13E40 -0:54:40
Radeburg 1 2 51N13 13E43 -0:54:52
Radegast 1 2 51N39 12E05 -0:48:20
Radevormwald 2 1 51N12 7E21 -0:29:24
Radiumbad Brambach 1
2 50N13 12E19 -0:49:16
Radldorf 2 4 48N53 12E27 -0:49:48
Radolfzell 2 3 47N44 8E58 -0:35:52
Raesfeld 2 1 51N46 6E50 -0:27:20
Rägelin 1 2 53N01 12E38 -0:50:32
Ragewitz 1 2 51N14 12E51 -0:51:24
Ragow 1 2 52N17 13E33 -0:54:12
Raguhn 1 2 51N42 12E17 -0:49:08
Rahden 2 1 52N26 8E36 -0:34:24
Rahm 2 7 51N26 6E26 -0:25:44
Rain 2 4 48N41 10E55 -0:43:40
Raisdorf 2 1 54N17 10E16 -0:41:04
Raitenbuch 2 4 49N01 11E08 -0:44:32
Ramrath 2 7 51N06 6E41 -0:26:44
Ramsau 2 4 47N36 12E54 -0:51:36
Ramsbeck 2 1 51N18 8E24 -0:33:36
Ramsdorf 2 1 51N54 6E55 -0:27:40
Ramsloh 2 1 53N06 7E40 -0:30:40
Ramstein 2 6 49N27 7E33 -0:30:12
Rangsdorf 1 2 52N17 13E25 -0:53:40
Ranis 1 2 50N39 11E34 -0:46:16
Ransbach 2 4 49N19 11E45 -0:47:00
Ranstadt 2 1 50N21 8E59 -0:35:56
Rantzau 2 1 54N15 10E30 -0:42:00
Raschau 1 2 50N32 12E50 -0:51:20
Rasdorf 2 1 50N43 9E53 -0:39:32
Rastatt 2 3 48N51 8E12 -0:32:48
Rastede 2 1 53N15 8E11 -0:32:44
Rastenberg 1 2 51N10 11E25 -0:45:40
Rastorf 2 1 54N16 10E19 -0:41:16
Ratekau 2 1 53N57 10E44 -0:42:56
Rathebur 1 2 53N44 13E46 -0:55:04
Ratheim 2 7 51N04 6E10 -0:24:40
Rathenow 1 2 52N36 12E20 -0:49:20
Rathmecke 2 1 51N15 7E38 -0:30:32
Rathstock 1 2 52N31 14E32 -0:58:08
Ratingen 2 1 51N18 6E51 -0:27:24
Ratisbon → Regensburg 2
4 49N01 12E06 -0:48:24
Ratzeburg 2 1 53N42 10E46 -0:43:04
Rätzlingen 1 2 52N23 11E08 -0:44:32
Rauen 1 2 52N20 14E01 -0:56:04
Rauenstein 1 2 50N24 11E03 -0:44:12
Raumünzach 2 3 48N38 8E21 -0:33:24
Raunheim 2 1 50N01 8E28 -0:33:52
Rauschenberg 2 1 50N53 8E55 -0:35:40
Ravensburg 2 5 47N47 9E37 -0:38:28
Rayen 2 7 51N28 6E32 -0:26:08
Rechberghausen 2
5 48N44 9E38 -0:38:32
Rechlin 1 2 53N21 12E43 -0:50:52
Recke 2 1 52N22 7E43 -0:30:52
Recklinghausen 2
1 51N36 7E13 -0:28:52
Redefin 1 2 53N21 11E11 -0:44:44
Redlin 1 2 53N22 12E01 -0:48:04
Rees 2 1 51N45 6E23 -0:25:32
Reetz 1 2 53N11 11E52 -0:47:28
Regen 2 4 48N59 13E07 -0:52:28
Regensburg 2 4 49N01 12E06 -0:48:24
Regenstauf 2 4 49N08 12E08 -0:48:32
Regis-Breitingen 1
2 51N05 12E26 -0:49:44
Reh 2 1 51N22 7E33 -0:30:12
Rehau 2 4 50N15 12E02 -0:48:08
Rehberg 1 2 52N43 12E10 -0:48:40
Rehburg 2 1 52N28 9E13 -0:36:52
Rehden 2 1 52N37 8E29 -0:33:56
Rehe 2 1 50N38 8E07 -0:32:28
Rehefeld-Zaunhaus 1
2 50N43 13E42 -0:54:48

Rehfelde 1 2 52N30 13E54 -0:55:36
Rehme 2 1 52N12 8E49 -0:35:16
Rehna 1 2 53N47 11E03 -0:44:12
Reichelsheim 2 1 49N43 8E50 -0:35:20
Reichenau 2 3 47N41 9E03 -0:36:12
Reichenbach 1 2 51N08 14E48 -0:59:12
Reichenbach 1 2 50N37 12E18 -0:49:12
Reichenhofen 2 5 47N50 9E58 -0:39:52
Reichensachsen 2
1 51N09 9E59 -0:39:56
Reichertshausen 2
4 48N28 11E31 -0:46:04
Reichertsheim 2 4 48N12 12E17 -0:49:08
Reichertshofen 2
4 48N40 11E28 -0:45:52
Reinbek 2 1 53N31 10E14 -0:40:56
Reinberg 1 2 54N12 13E15 -0:53:00
Reinfeld 2 1 53N49 10E28 -0:41:52
Reinhardtsdorf 1
2 50N53 14E11 -0:56:44
Reinheim 2 1 49N49 8E50 -0:35:20
Reinsdorf 1 2 50N42 12E33 -0:50:12
Reinsdorf 1 2 51N54 12E37 -0:50:28
Reinstorf 1 2 53N50 11E38 -0:46:32
Reischach 2 4 48N17 12E44 -0:50:56
Reit im Winkl 2 4 47N40 12E28 -0:49:52
Reitmehring 2 4 48N03 12E12 -0:48:48
Reitzenhain 1 2 50N33 13E13 -0:52:52
Reken 2 1 51N50 7E02 -0:28:08
Rellingen 2 1 53N39 9E49 -0:39:16
Remagen 2 6 50N34 7E13 -0:28:52
Remels 2 1 53N18 7E44 -0:30:56
Remptendorf 1 2 50N31 11E39 -0:46:36
Remscheid 2 1 51N11 7E11 -0:28:44
Remsfeld 2 1 51N00 9E29 -0:37:56
Renchen 2 3 48N35 8E01 -0:32:04
Rendsburg 2 1 54N18 9E40 -0:38:40
Rengsdorf 2 1 50N30 7E29 -0:29:56
Rennau 2 1 52N17 10E55 -0:43:40
Rennerod 2 1 50N36 8E04 -0:32:16
Rennertshofen 2 4 48N45 11E02 -0:44:08
Renningen 2 5 48N46 8E56 -0:35:44
Rentweinsdorf 2 4 50N04 10E47 -0:43:08
Rethem 2 1 52N45 9E23 -0:37:32
Rettenberg 2 4 47N35 10E17 -0:41:08
Rettin 2 1 54N06 10E53 -0:43:32
Retzow 1 2 52N37 12E41 -0:50:44
Reuden 1 2 52N04 12E18 -0:49:12
Reusrath 2 1 51N06 6E57 -0:27:48
Reuterstadt Stavenhagen 1
2 53N42 12E53 -0:51:32
Reutlingen 2 5 48N29 9E11 -0:36:44
Rhade 2 1 53N19 9E07 -0:36:28
Rhaunen 2 6 49N52 7E20 -0:29:20
Rheda-Wiedenbrück 2
1 51N50 8E18 -0:33:12
Rhede 2 1 53N03 7E16 -0:29:04
Rhede 2 7 51N50 6E11 -0:24:44
Rheinbach 2 7 50N37 6E57 -0:27:48
Rheinberg 2 7 51N33 6E35 -0:26:20
Rheinbischofsheim 2
3 48N39 7E55 -0:31:40
Rheinböllen 2 6 50N00 7E40 -0:30:40
Rheinbrohl 2 1 50N30 7E19 -0:29:16
Rheindürkheim 2 6 49N42 8E21 -0:33:24
Rheine 2 1 52N17 7E26 -0:29:44
Rheinen 2 1 51N27 7E38 -0:30:32
Rheinfelden 2 3 47N33 7E47 -0:31:08
Rheinhausen 2 7 51N24 6E44 -0:26:56
Rheinkamp 2 1 51N30 6E37 -0:26:28
Rheinsberg 1 2 53N06 12E53 -0:51:32
Rheinzabern 2 6 49N07 8E16 -0:33:04
Rhens 2 6 50N17 7E37 -0:30:28
Rheurdt 2 7 51N28 6E28 -0:25:52
Rheydt 2 7 51N10 6E25 -0:25:40
Rhinow 1 2 52N45 12E20 -0:49:20
Rhoden 2 1 51N28 9E00 -0:36:00
Rhodt 2 6 49N16 8E07 -0:32:28
Ribnitz-Damgarten 1
2 54N15 12E28 -0:49:52
Richrath 2 1 51N08 6E56 -0:27:44
Richtenberg 1 2 54N12 12E53 -0:51:32
Rickling 2 1 54N01 10E13 -0:40:52
Riedelbach 2 1 50N18 8E23 -0:33:32
Rieden 2 4 49N19 11E57 -0:47:48
Riedenburg 2 4 48N58 11E41 -0:46:44
Rieder 1 2 51N44 11E10 -0:44:40
Riedern 2 4 49N40 9E23 -0:37:32
Riedlingen 2 5 48N09 9E28 -0:37:52
Riegel 2 3 48N09 7E45 -0:31:00
Rielasingen 2 3 47N44 8E50 -0:35:20
Rieneck 2 4 50N05 9E38 -0:38:32
Riesa 1 2 51N18 13E17 -0:53:08
Rieseby 2 1 54N32 9E48 -0:39:12
Riesenbeck 2 1 52N16 7E37 -0:30:28
Riestedt 1 2 51N29 11E21 -0:45:24
Rietberg 2 1 51N47 8E25 -0:33:40
Rietschen 1 2 51N23 14E47 -0:59:08
Rimpar 2 4 49N51 9E57 -0:39:48
Rinchnach 2 4 48N57 13E12 -0:52:48
Ringenwalde 1 2 53N03 13E42 -0:54:48
Rinkerode 2 1 51N50 7E41 -0:30:44
Rinnthal 2 6 49N13 7E55 -0:31:40
Rinteln 2 1 52N11 9E04 -0:36:16
Rischenau 2 1 51N53 9E17 -0:37:08
Risstissen 2 5 48N16 9E49 -0:39:16
Risum-Lindholm 2
1 54N45 8E53 -0:35:32
Ritterhude 2 1 53N11 8E45 -0:35:00
Rittersgrün 1 2 50N29 12E47 -0:51:08
Ritzleben 1 2 52N50 11E21 -0:45:24
Röbel 1 2 53N23 12E35 -0:50:20
Röblingen 1 2 51N28 11E40 -0:46:40
Rochlitz 1 2 51N03 12E47 -0:51:08
Rockenhausen 2 6 49N38 7E49 -0:31:16

Rockensüss 2	1	51N03	9E50	-0:39:20
Rodach 2	4	50N20	10E46	-0:43:04
Rodalben 2	6	49N14	7E38	-0:30:32
Rodenberg 2	1	52N18	9E21	-0:37:24
Rodenkirchen 2	7	50N54	6E59	-0:27:56
Rodenkirchen 2	1	53N24	8E26	-0:33:44
Röderau 1	2	51N19	13E19	-0:53:16
Rodewisch 1	2	50N32	12E24	-0:49:36
Rodheim-Bieber 2	1	50N37	8E35	-0:34:20
Roding 2	4	49N12	12E32	-0:50:08
Roetgen 2	7	50N39	6E12	-0:24:48
Rogäsen 1	2	52N19	12E20	-0:49:20
Rogätz 1	2	52N19	11E46	-0:47:04
Rohdenhaus 2	1	51N18	7E01	-0:28:04
Rohr 2	4	48N46	11E58	-0:47:52
Rohrbeck 1	2	52N32	13E02	-0:52:08
Rohrberg 1	2	52N42	11E02	-0:44:08
Rohrbrunn 2	4	49N54	9E23	-0:37:32
Röhrenfurth 2	1	51N09	9E32	-0:38:08
Röhrsdorf 1	2	50N51	12E50	-0:51:20
Roitzsch 1	2	51N34	12E16	-0:49:04
Roklum 2	1	52N04	10E44	-0:42:56
Römhild 1	2	50N24	10E32	-0:42:08
Rommerskirchen 2	7	51N02	6E40	-0:26:40
Romrod 2	1	50N43	9E13	-0:36:52
Ronneburg 1	2	50N51	12E10	-0:48:40
Ronnenberg 2	1	52N20	9E40	-0:38:40
Rönsahl 2	1	51N07	7E30	-0:30:00
Rosbach 2	1	50N48	7E37	-0:30:28
Rosdorf 2	1	51N30	9E53	-0:39:32
Rosellen 2	7	51N08	6E43	-0:26:52
Rosellerheide 2	7	51N07	6E44	-0:26:56
Rosenfeld 2	5	48N17	8E43	-0:34:52
Rosenheim 2	4	47N51	12E07	-0:48:28
Rosenthal 1	2	50N51	14E04	-0:56:16
Rosenthal 2	1	50N58	8E52	-0:35:28
Rositz 1	2	51N01	12E22	-0:49:28
Roskow 1	2	52N28	12E42	-0:50:48
Rösrath 2	1	50N54	7E11	-0:28:44
Rossach 2	4	50N09	10E56	-0:43:44
Rossau 1	2	52N47	11E38	-0:46:32
Rossbach 1	2	51N15	11E53	-0:47:32
Rossdorf 2	1	49N51	8E45	-0:35:00
Rosshaupten 2	4	47N39	10E43	-0:42:52
Rossla 1	2	51N28	11E04	-0:44:16
Rosslau 1	2	51N53	12E14	-0:48:56
Rossleben 1	2	51N17	11E25	-0:45:40
Rosstal 2	4	49N25	10E52	-0:43:28
Rosswein 1	2	51N03	13E10	-0:52:40
Rostock 1	2	54N05	12E07	-0:48:28
Rot am See 2	5	49N15	10E01	-0:40:04
Rotberg 1	2	52N21	13E31	-0:54:04
Rotenburg 2	1	53N06	9E24	-0:37:36
Rotenburg an der Fulda 2	1	51N00	9E45	-0:39:00
Roth 2	1	50N46	7E42	-0:30:48
Rötha 1	2	51N12	12E25	-0:49:40
Roth bei Nürnberg 2	4	49N15	11E06	-0:44:24
Rothemühl 1	2	53N36	13E49	-0:55:16
Rothemühle 2	1	50N57	7E49	-0:31:16
Röthenbach 2	4	47N37	9E59	-0:39:56
Röthenbach an der Pegnitz 2	4	49N29	11E15	-0:45:00
Rothenburg 1	2	51N20	14E58	-0:59:52
Rothenburg ob der Tauber 2	4	49N23	10E10	-0:40:40
Rothenkirchen 1	2	50N33	12E30	-0:50:00
Rothenschirmbach 1	2	51N27	11E33	-0:46:12
Rothenstadt 2	4	49N38	12E09	-0:48:36
Rott 2	4	47N54	10E59	-0:43:56
Rottach-Egern 2	4	47N41	11E46	-0:47:04
Rott am Inn 2	4	47N59	12E07	-0:48:28
Röttenbach 2	4	49N09	11E02	-0:44:08
Rottenbach-Tremersdorf 2	4	50N21	10E56	-0:43:44
Rottenbuch 2	4	47N44	10E58	-0:43:52
Rottenburg am Neckar 2	5	48N28	8E56	-0:35:44
Rottenburg an der Laaber 2	4	48N42	12E02	-0:48:08
Rotthalmünster 2	4	48N21	13E12	-0:52:48
Röttingen 2	4	49N30	9E58	-0:39:52
Rottleberode 1	2	51N31	10E57	-0:43:48
Rottum 2	1	51N36	7E42	-0:30:48
Rottweil 2	3	48N10	8E37	-0:34:28
Rötz 2	4	49N21	12E32	-0:50:08
Rövershagen 1	2	54N10	12E15	-0:49:00
Roxel 2	1	51N57	7E32	-0:30:08
Rübeland 1	2	51N45	10E50	-0:43:20
Rüdersdorf 1	2	52N29	13E47	-0:55:08
Rüdesheim am Rheim 2	1	49N59	7E56	-0:31:44
Rüdnitz 1	2	52N43	13E37	-0:54:28
Rudolstadt 1	2	50N43	11E20	-0:45:20
Rüggeberg 2	1	51N16	7E22	-0:29:28
Ruhla 1	2	50N53	10E22	-0:41:28
Ruhland 1	2	51N27	13E52	-0:55:28
Ruhlsdorf 1	2	52N23	13E16	-0:53:04
Ruhmannsfelden 2	4	48N59	12E59	-0:51:56
Ruhpolding 2	4	47N45	12E38	-0:50:32
Ruhstorf an der Rott 2	4	48N26	13E20	-0:53:20
Ruit 2	5	48N43	9E14	-0:36:56
Rulle 2	1	52N20	8E04	-0:32:16
Rumeln-Kaldenhausen 2	7	51N23	6E40	-0:26:40
Rummenohl 2	1	51N17	7E32	-0:30:08
Ründeroth 2	1	50N59	7E28	-0:29:52
Runkel 2	1	50N24	8E10	-0:32:40
Rünthe 2	1	51N39	7E39	-0:30:36
Ruppertenrod 2	1	50N37	9E05	-0:36:20
Rurberg 2	7	50N37	6E22	-0:25:28
Russee 2	1	54N18	10E04	-0:40:16
Rüsselsheim 2	1	50N00	8E25	-0:33:40
Rust 2	3	48N16	7E43	-0:30:52
Rütenbrock 2	1	52N50	7E10	-0:28:40
Rüthen 2	1	51N29	8E25	-0:33:40
Ruwer 2	6	49N47	6E43	-0:26:52
Saal 1	2	54N19	12E29	-0:49:56
Saal an der Donau 2	4	48N54	11E56	-0:47:44
Saal an der Saale 2	4	50N19	10E21	-0:41:24
Saalburg 1	2	50N30	11E43	-0:46:52
Saaldorf 1	2	50N27	11E41	-0:46:44
Saalfeld 1	2	50N39	11E22	-0:45:28
Saarbrücken 2	6	49N14	6E59	-0:27:56
Saarburg 2	6	49N36	6E33	-0:26:12
Saarelouis → Saarlouis 2	6	49N21	6E45	-0:27:00
Saarlautern → Saarlouis 2	6	49N21	6E45	-0:27:00
Saarlouis 2	6	49N21	6E45	-0:27:00
Saarmund 1	2	52N19	13E07	-0:52:28
Sachrang 2	4	47N41	12E15	-0:49:00
Sachsenbrunn 1	2	50N27	10E56	-0:43:44
Sachsenhagen 2	1	52N24	9E16	-0:37:04
Sachsenhausen 1	2	52N47	13E14	-0:52:56
Sachsenhausen 2	1	51N15	9E00	-0:36:00
Säckingen 2	3	47N33	7E56	-0:31:44
Sadelkow 1	2	53N36	13E26	-0:53:44
Saerbeck 2	1	52N10	7E38	-0:30:32
Sagard 1	2	54N31	13E33	-0:54:12
Sahlenburg 2	1	53N52	8E38	-0:34:32
Salching 2	4	48N49	12E34	-0:50:16
Salem 2	3	47N46	9E16	-0:37:04
Sallgast 1	2	51N35	13E51	-0:55:24
Salmünster 2	1	50N16	9E22	-0:37:28
Salzberg 2	4	47N38	13E02	-0:52:08
Salzbergen 2	1	52N19	7E20	-0:29:20
Salzgitter 2	1	52N10	10E25	-0:41:40
Salzhausen 2	1	53N13	10E09	-0:40:36
Salzhemmendorf 2	1	52N04	9E35	-0:38:20
Salzkotten 2	1	51N40	8E36	-0:34:24
Salzmünde 1	2	51N31	11E49	-0:47:16
Salzwedel 1	2	52N51	11E09	-0:44:36
Samtens 1	2	54N21	13E17	-0:53:08
Sand 2	3	48N32	7E55	-0:31:40
Sandau 1	2	52N47	12E02	-0:48:08
Sandbochum 2	1	51N40	7E41	-0:30:44
Sande 2	1	51N45	8E39	-0:34:36
Sande 2	1	53N30	8E01	-0:32:04
Sandersdorf 1	2	51N37	12E15	-0:49:00
Sandersdorf 2	4	48N54	11E37	-0:46:28
Sandersleben 1	2	51N40	11E34	-0:46:16
Sandesneben 2	1	53N41	10E30	-0:42:00
Sandhorst 2	1	53N29	7E29	-0:29:56
Sandizell 2	4	48N35	11E11	-0:44:44
Sandkrug 1	2	52N53	13E52	-0:55:28
Sandstedt 2	1	53N21	8E31	-0:34:04
Sangerhausen 1	2	51N28	11E17	-0:45:08
Sanitz 1	2	54N04	12E22	-0:49:28
Sankt Andreasberg 2	1	51N43	10E31	-0:42:04
Sankt Blasien 2	3	47N46	8E07	-0:32:28
Sankt Egidien 1	2	50N47	12E36	-0:50:24
Sankt Georgen 2	3	48N07	8E20	-0:33:20
Sankt Georgen 2	3	47N59	7E47	-0:31:08
Sankt Goar 2	6	50N09	7E43	-0:30:52
Sankt Goarshausen 2	1	50N09	7E44	-0:30:56
Sankt Hubert 2	7	51N23	6E26	-0:25:44
Sankt Ingbert 2	6	49N17	7E06	-0:28:24
Sankt Mang 2	4	47N44	10E21	-0:41:24
Sankt Märgen 2	3	48N00	8E05	-0:32:20
Sankt Mauritz 2	1	51N57	7E39	-0:30:36
Sankt Oswald 2	4	48N54	13E25	-0:53:40
Sankt Peter 2	1	54N18	8E38	-0:34:32
Sankt Peter 2	3	48N01	8E01	-0:32:04
Sankt Wendel 2	6	49N28	7E10	-0:28:40
Sanspareil 2	4	49N59	11E19	-0:45:16
Sarnow 1	2	53N45	13E37	-0:54:28
Sarrebruck → Saarbrücken 2	6	49N14	6E59	-0:27:56
Sarstedt 2	1	52N14	9E51	-0:39:24
Sasbach 2	3	48N08	7E37	-0:30:28
Sassenberg 2	1	51N59	8E02	-0:32:08
Sassnitz 1	2	54N31	13E38	-0:54:32
Satow 1	2	53N59	11E51	-0:47:24
Satrup 2	1	54N41	9E35	-0:38:20
Satzkorn 1	2	52N29	12E59	-0:51:56
Sauerlach 2	4	47N58	11E38	-0:46:32
Saulgau 2	5	48N01	9E30	-0:38:00
Saulgrub 2	4	47N40	11E01	-0:44:04
Sayda 1	2	50N43	13E25	-0:53:40
Schaephuysen 2	7	51N26	6E29	-0:25:56
Schafstädt 1	2	51N23	11E46	-0:47:04
Schäftlarn 2	4	47N59	11E28	-0:45:52
Schale 2	1	52N26	7E37	-0:30:28
Schalkau 1	2	50N24	11E00	-0:44:00
Schalksmühle 2	1	51N14	7E31	-0:30:04
Schandelah 2	1	52N16	10E41	-0:42:44
Schapbach 2	3	48N22	8E17	-0:33:08
Schapen 2	1	52N24	7E33	-0:30:12
Schaprode 1	2	54N31	13E10	-0:52:40
Scharl 2	1	51N06	7E40	-0:30:40
Scharrel 2	1	53N04	7E42	-0:30:48
Scharzfeld 2	1	51N37	10E22	-0:41:28
Scheessel 2	1	53N10	9E29	-0:37:56
Scheibenberg 1	2	50N32	12E55	-0:51:40
Scheidegg 2	4	47N35	9E51	-0:39:24
Scheinfeld 2	4	49N40	10E27	-0:41:48
Schelklingen 2	5	48N22	9E44	-0:38:56
Schenefeld 2	1	53N36	9E49	-0:39:16
Schenkendorf 1	2	52N16	13E35	-0:54:20
Schenkenhorst 1	2	52N20	13E12	-0:52:48
Schenklengsfeld 2	1	50N49	9E50	-0:39:20
Schepsdorf-Lohne 2	1	52N30	7E16	-0:29:04
Scherfede 2	1	51N32	9E02	-0:36:08
Scherlebeck 2	1	51N37	7E08	-0:28:32
Schermbeck 2	1	51N41	6E52	-0:27:28
Schesslitz 2	4	49N59	11E01	-0:44:04
Schieder 2	1	51N55	9E09	-0:36:36
Schiefbahn 2	7	51N14	6E31	-0:26:04
Schierke 1	2	51N46	10E40	-0:42:40
Schierling 2	4	48N50	12E08	-0:48:32
Schiessen 2	4	48N18	10E14	-0:40:56
Schiffdorf 2	1	53N32	8E39	-0:34:36
Schifferstadt 2	6	49N23	8E22	-0:33:28
Schildau 1	2	51N27	12E56	-0:51:44
Schildow 1	2	52N38	13E23	-0:53:32
Schillingsfürst 2	4	49N17	10E15	-0:41:00
Schillingstedt 1	2	51N14	11E11	-0:44:44
Schiltach 2	3	48N17	8E20	-0:33:20
Schimborn 2	4	50N03	9E11	-0:36:44
Schipkau 1	2	51N31	13E53	-0:55:32
Schirgiswalde 1	2	51N05	14E27	-0:57:48
Schirnding 2	4	50N05	12E13	-0:48:52
Schkeuditz 1	2	51N24	12E13	-0:48:52
Schkölen 1	2	51N02	11E49	-0:47:16
Schkopau 1	2	51N23	11E59	-0:47:56
Schladen 2	1	52N01	10E32	-0:42:08
Schlangen 2	1	51N49	8E50	-0:35:20
Schlangenbad 2	1	50N05	8E05	-0:32:20
Schlanstedt 1	2	52N00	11E02	-0:44:08
Schleiden 2	7	50N31	6E28	-0:25:52
Schleife 1	2	51N32	14E32	-0:58:08
Schleiz 1	2	50N34	11E49	-0:47:16
Schlema 1	2	50N40	12E40	-0:50:40
Schlepzig 1	2	52N01	13E53	-0:55:32
Schleswig 2	1	54N31	9E33	-0:38:12
Schlettau 1	2	50N33	12E56	-0:51:44
Schleusingen 1	2	50N31	10E45	-0:43:00
Schlieben 1	2	51N43	13E23	-0:53:32
Schliengen 2	3	47N46	7E35	-0:30:20
Schliersee 2	4	47N44	11E51	-0:47:24
Schlitz 2	1	50N40	9E33	-0:38:12
Schloss Holte 2	1	51N52	8E35	-0:34:20
Schloss Neuhaus 2	1	51N44	8E43	-0:34:52
Schlossvippach 1	2	51N06	11E08	-0:44:32
Schloss Zeil 2	5	47N52	10E00	-0:40:00
Schlotheim 1	2	51N14	10E39	-0:42:36
Schluchsee 2	3	47N49	8E10	-0:32:40
Schlüchtern 2	1	50N20	9E31	-0:38:04
Schlüsselburg 2	1	52N29	9E04	-0:36:16
Schlüsselfeld 2	4	49N45	10E37	-0:42:28
Schmalfeld 2	1	53N52	9E58	-0:39:52
Schmalkalden 1	2	50N43	10E26	-0:41:44
Schmallenberg 2	1	51N09	8E17	-0:33:08
Schmalnau 2	1	50N27	9E47	-0:39:08
Schmannewitz 1	2	51N24	12E58	-0:51:52
Schmarsau 2	1	52N54	11E21	-0:45:24
Schmelz 2	6	49N27	6E51	-0:27:24
Schmidmühlen 2	4	49N16	11E56	-0:47:44
Schmidt 2	7	50N39	6E25	-0:25:40
Schmiedeberg 1	2	50N50	13E40	-0:54:40
Schmiedefeld 1	2	50N37	10E49	-0:43:16
Schmilka 1	2	50N53	14E14	-0:56:56
Schmölln 1	2	50N53	12E20	-0:49:20
Schnabelwaid 2	4	49N49	11E35	-0:46:20
Schnackenburg 2	1	53N02	11E32	-0:46:08
Schnait 2	5	48N47	9E23	-0:37:32
Schnaitsee 2	4	48N04	12E22	-0:49:28
Schnaittach 2	4	49N31	11E19	-0:45:16
Schnaittenbach 2	4	49N33	12E01	-0:48:04
Schnakenbek 2	1	53N23	10E30	-0:42:00
Schneeberg 1	2	50N36	12E38	-0:50:32
Schneverdingen 2	1	53N07	9E47	-0:39:08
Schney 2	4	50N10	11E04	-0:44:16
Schobüll 2	1	54N30	9E00	-0:36:00
Scholen 2	1	52N44	8E46	-0:35:04
Schollene 1	2	52N41	12E13	-0:48:52
Schöller 2	1	51N14	7E01	-0:28:04
Schöllkrippen 2	4	50N05	9E14	-0:36:56
Schöllnach 2	4	48N45	13E11	-0:52:44
Schömberg 2	5	48N13	8E46	-0:35:04
Schömberg 2	5	48N47	8E38	-0:34:32
Schonach 2	3	48N08	8E11	-0:32:44
Schönaich 2	5	48N39	9E03	-0:36:12
Schönau 2	4	47N37	12E59	-0:51:56
Schönau 2	3	49N26	8E49	-0:35:16
Schönau 2	3	47N47	7E53	-0:31:32
Schönbeck 1	2	53N34	13E34	-0:54:16
Schönberg 1	2	53N50	11E38	-0:46:32
Schönberg 2	1	54N23	10E22	-0:41:28
Schönberg 2	4	48N50	13E20	-0:53:20
Schönberg 1	2	50N31	11E57	-0:47:48
Schönberg 1	2	50N11	12E19	-0:49:16
Schönberger Strand 2	1	54N25	10E24	-0:41:36
Schönbrunn 2	4	48N33	12E12	-0:48:48
Schönbrunn 1	2	50N32	10E53	-0:43:32
Schönebeck 1	2	52N01	11E44	-0:46:56
Schönebeck 1	2	53N03	12E13	-0:48:52
Schöneck 1	2	50N23	12E20	-0:49:20
Schönecken 2	6	50N09	6E27	-0:25:48
Schönefeld 1	2	52N23	13E30	-0:54:00
Schöneiche 1	2	52N28	13E41	-0:54:44
Schönerlinde 1	2	52N39	13E27	-0:53:48
Schönewalde 1	2	51N49	13E13	-0:52:52

Schönfeld 1 2 52N41 13E44 -0:54:56
Schönficht 2 4 49N49 12E15 -0:49:00
Schönfliess 1 2 52N39 13E20 -0:53:20
Schongau 2 4 47N49 10E54 -0:43:36
Schönhagen 2 1 54N38 10E01 -0:40:04
Schönhagen 2 1 51N41 9E33 -0:38:12
Schönhaid 2 4 49N54 12E12 -0:48:48
Schönhausen 1 2 52N35 12E02 -0:48:08
Schönhausen 2 1 51N37 7E38 -0:30:32
Schönheide 1 2 50N30 12E31 -0:50:04
Schönholthausen 2 1 51N11 8E00 -0:32:00
Schöningen 2 1 52N08 10E58 -0:43:52
Schönkirchen 2 1 54N20 10E15 -0:41:00
Schönmünzach 2 3 48N36 8E22 -0:33:28
Schönningstedt 2 1 53N32 10E15 -0:41:00
Schönow 1 2 52N40 13E32 -0:54:08
Schönsee 2 4 49N31 12E33 -0:50:12
Schönthal 2 4 49N21 12E36 -0:50:24
Schonungen 2 4 50N03 10E18 -0:41:12
Schönwald 2 3 48N06 8E11 -0:32:44
Schönwalde 1 2 52N40 13E26 -0:53:44
Schönwalde 1 2 52N37 13E07 -0:52:28
Schönwalde 2 1 54N11 10E45 -0:43:00
Schopfheim 2 3 47N39 7E49 -0:31:16
Schopfloch 2 4 49N07 10E18 -0:41:12
Schopp 2 6 49N21 7E41 -0:30:44
Schöppenstedt 2 1 52N08 10E46 -0:43:04
Schöppingen 2 1 52N05 7E14 -0:28:56
Schorfheide 1 2 52N56 13E43 -0:54:52
Schorndorf 2 5 48N48 9E31 -0:38:04
Schortens 2 1 53N31 7E56 -0:31:44
Schötmar 2 1 52N04 8E45 -0:35:00
Schotten 2 1 50N30 9E07 -0:36:28
Schramberg 2 3 48N13 8E23 -0:33:32
Schraplau 1 2 51N26 11E40 -0:46:40
Schrobenhausen 2 4 48N33 11E17 -0:45:08
Schrozberg 2 5 49N20 9E59 -0:39:56
Schulenburg 2 1 52N12 9E47 -0:39:08
Schulzendorf 1 2 52N22 13E35 -0:54:20
Schulzenhöhe 1 2 52N29 13E47 -0:55:08
Schussenried 2 5 48N00 9E40 -0:38:40
Schüttorf 2 1 52N19 7E13 -0:28:52
Schwaan 1 2 53N56 12E06 -0:48:24
Schwabach 2 4 49N20 11E01 -0:44:04
Schwäbisch Gmünd 2 5 48N48 9E47 -0:39:08
Schwäbisch Hall 2 5 49N07 9E44 -0:38:56
Schwabmünchen 2 4 48N11 10E45 -0:43:00
Schwabstedt 2 1 54N23 9E11 -0:36:44
Schwafheim 2 7 51N25 6E39 -0:26:36
Schwagstorf 2 1 52N31 7E45 -0:31:00
Schwaigern 2 5 49N08 9E03 -0:36:12
Schwalenberg 2 1 51N52 9E11 -0:36:44
Schwalmtal 2 7 51N13 6E16 -0:25:04
Schwandorf in Bayern 2 4 49N20 12E08 -0:48:32
Schwanebeck 1 2 52N37 13E32 -0:54:08
Schwanebeck 1 2 51N58 11E07 -0:44:28
Schwanewede 2 1 53N14 8E35 -0:34:20
Schwangau 2 4 47N35 10E44 -0:42:56
Schwante 1 2 52N44 13E05 -0:52:20
Schwarme 2 1 52N54 9E01 -0:36:04
Schwarmstedt 2 1 52N40 9E37 -0:38:28
Schwarza 1 2 50N38 10E32 -0:42:08
Schwarza 1 2 50N41 11E19 -0:45:16
Schwarzach 2 4 48N55 12E49 -0:51:16
Schwarzbach 2 4 47N46 12E55 -0:51:40
Schwarzburg 1 2 50N38 11E12 -0:44:48
Schwarzenbach am Wald 2 4 50N17 11E37 -0:46:28
Schwarzenbach an der Saale 2 4 50N13 11E56 -0:47:44
Schwarzenbek 2 1 53N30 10E29 -0:41:56
Schwarzenberg 1 2 50N32 12E47 -0:51:08
Schwarzenberg 2 7 51N24 6E42 -0:26:48
Schwarzenborn 2 1 50N37 9E58 -0:39:52
Schwarzenbruck 2 4 49N21 11E14 -0:44:56
Schwarzenfeld 2 4 49N23 12E08 -0:48:32
Schwarze Pumpe 1 2 51N32 14E20 -0:57:20
Schwarzheide 1 2 51N29 13E51 -0:55:24
Schwedeneck 2 1 54N27 10E05 -0:40:20
Schwedt 1 2 53N03 14E17 -0:57:08
Schweez 1 2 53N53 12E24 -0:49:36
Schweflinghausen 2 1 51N16 7E25 -0:29:40
Schwegenheim 2 6 49N16 8E20 -0:33:20
Schwei 2 1 53N24 8E21 -0:33:24
Schweich 2 6 49N49 6E45 -0:27:00
Schweighausen 2 3 48N13 7E57 -0:31:48
Schweinfurt 2 4 50N03 10E14 -0:40:56
Schweinitz 1 2 51N48 13E01 -0:52:04
Schweinrich 1 2 53N10 12E37 -0:50:28
Schwelm 2 1 51N17 7E17 -0:29:08
Schwendi 2 5 48N10 9E58 -0:39:52
Schwenke 2 1 51N11 7E26 -0:29:44
Schwepnitz 1 2 51N20 13E57 -0:55:48
Schwerin 1 2 53N38 11E25 -0:45:40
Schwerte 2 1 51N26 7E34 -0:30:16
Schwetzingen 2 3 49N23 8E34 -0:34:16
Schwieberdingen 2 5 48N52 9E04 -0:36:16
Schwitten 2 1 51N27 7E48 -0:31:12
Sebnitz 1 2 50N58 14E16 -0:57:04
Seckach 2 3 49N26 9E20 -0:37:20
Seddin 1 2 52N16 13E01 -0:52:04
Sedlitz 1 2 51N33 14E03 -0:56:12
Seebad Ahlbeck 1 2 53N56 14E11 -0:56:44
Seebad Bansin 1 2 53N57 14E07 -0:56:28
Seebad Heringsdorf 1 2 53N56 14E08 -0:56:32
Seeberg 1 2 52N33 13E41 -0:54:44
Seebruck 2 4 47N56 12E28 -0:49:52
Seebrugg 2 3 47N49 8E13 -0:32:52
Seeburg 1 2 52N31 13E07 -0:52:28
Seefeld 1 2 52N37 13E40 -0:54:40
Seefeld 2 1 53N27 8E21 -0:33:24
Seeg 2 4 47N38 10E36 -0:42:24
Seegatterl 2 4 47N39 12E32 -0:50:08
Seehausen 1 2 52N06 11E17 -0:45:08
Seehausen 1 2 52N53 11E45 -0:47:00
Seehof 1 2 52N24 13E17 -0:53:08
Seelbach 2 3 48N18 7E56 -0:31:44
Seelingstädt 1 2 50N46 12E14 -0:48:56
Seelow 1 2 52N32 14E23 -0:57:32
Seelze 2 1 52N24 9E35 -0:38:20
Seeon 2 4 47N58 12E26 -0:49:44
Seerhausen 1 2 51N16 13E15 -0:53:00
Seesen 2 1 51N53 10E10 -0:40:40
Seeshaupt 2 4 47N49 11E18 -0:45:12
Seevetal 2 1 53N23 9E59 -0:39:56
Seffern 2 6 50N04 6E30 -0:26:00
Sehma 1 2 50N32 13E00 -0:52:00
Sehnde 2 1 52N18 9E57 -0:39:48
Seiffen 1 2 50N39 13E26 -0:53:44
Seifhennersdorf 1 2 50N56 14E36 -0:58:24
Selb 2 4 50N10 12E08 -0:48:32
Selbach 2 6 49N32 7E02 -0:28:08
Selbitz 2 4 50N19 11E44 -0:46:56
Selchow 1 2 52N21 13E28 -0:53:52
Selent 2 1 54N17 10E26 -0:41:44
Seligenporten 2 4 49N16 11E19 -0:45:16
Seligenstadt 2 1 50N02 8E58 -0:35:52
Seligenthal 1 2 50N45 10E28 -0:41:52
Sellin 1 2 54N22 13E41 -0:54:44
Selm 2 1 51N42 7E28 -0:29:52
Selmigerheide 2 1 51N38 7E47 -0:31:08
Selmsdorf 1 2 53N48 10E50 -0:43:20
Selsingen 2 1 53N22 9E13 -0:36:52
Selters 2 1 50N32 7E44 -0:30:56
Senden 2 4 48N19 10E03 -0:40:12
Senden 2 1 51N51 7E29 -0:29:56
Sendenhorst 2 1 51N50 7E49 -0:31:16
Senftenberg 1 2 51N31 14E00 -0:56:00
Sengwarden 2 1 53N35 8E02 -0:32:08
Senne I 2 1 51N57 8E31 -0:34:04
Senne II → Sennestadt 2 1 51N59 8E37 -0:34:28
Sennestadt (Senne II) 2 1 51N59 8E37 -0:34:28
Senzig 1 2 52N17 13E39 -0:54:36
Seppenrade 2 1 51N46 7E23 -0:29:32
Seuversholz 2 4 48N57 11E11 -0:44:44
Sevelen 2 7 51N29 6E25 -0:25:40
Sewekow 1 2 53N15 12E39 -0:50:36
Seybothernreuth 2 4 49N54 11E43 -0:46:52
Seyda 1 2 51N53 12E53 -0:51:32
Sickingmühle 2 1 51N42 7E07 -0:28:28
Siddinghausen 2 1 51N32 7E48 -0:31:12
Siebenlehn 1 2 51N01 13E18 -0:53:12
Sieber 2 1 51N42 10E25 -0:41:40
Siedenbollentin 1 2 53N44 13E23 -0:53:32
Siedenburg 2 1 52N41 8E56 -0:35:44
Siegburg 2 1 50N47 7E12 -0:28:48
Siegen 2 1 50N52 8E02 -0:32:08
Siegenburg 2 4 48N45 11E51 -0:47:24
Sieglar 2 1 50N48 7E08 -0:28:32
Siegsdorf 2 4 47N46 12E39 -0:50:36
Sielbeck 2 1 54N11 10E37 -0:42:28
Sielenbach 2 4 48N24 11E10 -0:44:40
Sierksdorf 2 1 54N04 10E46 -0:43:04
Siersleben 1 2 51N36 11E32 -0:46:08
Siethen 1 2 52N17 13E13 -0:52:52
Sietow 1 2 53N26 12E35 -0:50:20
Sigl 2 4 49N37 11E45 -0:47:00
Sigmaringen 2 3 48N05 9E13 -0:36:52
Sigmaringendorf 2 3 48N04 9E15 -0:37:00
Sigras 2 4 49N36 11E43 -0:46:52
Sillenstede 2 1 53N34 7E59 -0:31:56
Silschede 2 1 51N21 7E19 -0:29:16
Simbach 2 4 48N34 12E45 -0:51:00
Simbach am Inn 2 4 48N16 13E01 -0:52:04
Simmelsdorf 2 4 49N36 11E21 -0:45:24
Simmerath 2 7 50N36 6E18 -0:25:12
Simmerberg 2 4 47N35 9E56 -0:39:44
Simmern 2 6 49N59 7E31 -0:30:04
Sindelfingen 2 5 48N42 9E00 -0:36:00
Singen (Hohentwiel) 2 3 47N46 8E50 -0:35:20
Sinnersdorf 2 7 51N01 6E49 -0:27:16
Sinsen 2 1 51N40 7E11 -0:28:44
Sinsheim 2 3 49N15 8E53 -0:35:32
Sinspelt 2 6 49N58 6E19 -0:25:16
Sinzig 2 6 50N32 7E15 -0:29:00
Sinzing 2 4 49N00 12E02 -0:48:08
Sipplingen 2 3 47N47 9E05 -0:36:20
Sistig 2 7 50N29 6E30 -0:26:00
Sittensen 2 1 53N17 9E30 -0:38:00
Skaby 1 2 52N19 13E51 -0:55:24
Sobernheim 2 6 49N47 7E38 -0:30:32
Södel 2 1 50N23 8E48 -0:35:12
Soest 2 1 51N34 8E07 -0:32:28
Sögel 2 1 52N50 7E31 -0:30:04
Sohland 1 2 51N02 14E25 -0:57:40
Söhlde 2 1 52N11 10E14 -0:40:56
Solingen 2 1 51N10 7E05 -0:28:20
Söllingen 2 1 52N05 10E55 -0:43:40
Sollstedt 1 2 51N25 10E31 -0:42:04
Solnhofen 2 4 48N53 10E59 -0:43:56
Soltau 2 1 52N59 9E49 -0:39:16
Somborn 2 1 50N08 9E07 -0:36:28
Sommerberg 2 1 51N27 7E32 -0:30:08
Sömmerda 1 2 51N10 11E07 -0:44:28
Sommersdorf 1 2 53N17 14E11 -0:56:44
Sondershausen 1 2 51N22 10E52 -0:43:28
Sonneberg 1 2 50N22 11E10 -0:44:40
Sonnefeld 2 4 50N13 11E08 -0:44:32
Sonnen 2 4 48N41 13E43 -0:54:52
Sonnewalde 1 2 51N42 13E38 -0:54:32
Sonsbeck 2 7 51N37 6E22 -0:25:28
Sontheim 2 5 49N07 9E11 -0:36:44
Sonthofen 2 4 47N31 10E17 -0:41:08
Sontra 2 1 51N04 9E56 -0:39:44
Sörup 2 1 54N43 9E40 -0:38:40
Sosa 1 2 50N30 12E39 -0:50:36
Sottrum 2 1 53N06 9E14 -0:36:56
Spaden 2 1 53N34 8E38 -0:34:32
Spahl 1 2 50N39 9E55 -0:39:40
Spaichingen 2 5 48N04 8E44 -0:34:56
Spalt 2 4 49N10 10E55 -0:43:40
Spandau 2 2 52N32 13E14 -0:52:56
Spangenberg 2 1 51N07 9E40 -0:38:40
Sparneck 2 4 50N09 11E50 -0:47:20
Spechtsbrunn 1 2 50N30 11E14 -0:44:56
Speinshart 2 4 49N47 11E49 -0:47:16
Spellen 2 1 51N37 6E37 -0:26:28
Spenge 2 1 52N08 8E28 -0:33:52
Sperenberg 1 2 52N08 13E22 -0:53:28
Spexard 2 1 51N52 8E24 -0:33:36
Speyer 2 6 49N19 8E26 -0:33:44
Spiegelau 2 4 48N55 13E22 -0:53:28
Spieka 2 1 53N45 8E35 -0:34:20
Spires → Speyer 2 6 49N19 8E26 -0:33:44
Spornitz 1 2 53N24 11E43 -0:46:52
Spreenhagen 1 2 52N20 13E52 -0:55:28
Spremberg 1 2 51N34 14E22 -0:57:28
Sprendlingen 2 1 50N01 8E41 -0:34:44
Sprendlingen 2 6 49N51 7E59 -0:31:56
Springe 2 1 52N12 9E32 -0:38:08
Sprockhövel 2 1 51N22 7E15 -0:29:00
Sprötze 2 1 53N18 9E49 -0:39:16
Sputendorf 1 2 52N20 13E13 -0:52:52
Stade 2 1 53N36 9E28 -0:37:52
Staden 2 1 50N20 8E54 -0:35:36
Stadt Allendorf 2 1 50N50 9E01 -0:36:04
Stadtbergen 2 4 48N22 10E50 -0:43:20
Stadthagen 2 1 52N19 9E13 -0:36:52
Stadtilm 1 2 50N47 11E05 -0:44:20
Städtische Rahmede 2 1 51N17 7E40 -0:30:40
Stadtkyll 2 6 50N21 6E32 -0:26:08
Stadtlauringen 2 4 50N11 10E22 -0:41:28
Stadtlengsfeld 1 2 50N47 10E07 -0:40:28
Stadtlohn 2 1 51N59 6E55 -0:27:40
Stadtoldendorf 2 1 51N53 9E37 -0:38:28
Stadtprozelten 2 4 49N47 9E25 -0:37:40
Stadtroda 1 2 50N51 11E44 -0:46:56
Stadtsteinach 2 4 50N09 11E30 -0:46:00
Stadt Wehlen 1 2 50N58 14E02 -0:56:08
Stadum 2 1 54N44 9E03 -0:36:12
Staffelde 1 2 52N44 13E00 -0:52:00
Staffelstein 2 4 50N06 11E00 -0:44:00
Stahlbrode 1 2 54N14 13E17 -0:53:08
Stahle 2 1 51N50 9E25 -0:37:40
Stahnsdorf 1 2 52N23 13E13 -0:52:52
Stahringen 2 3 47N47 8E58 -0:35:52
Stallwang 2 4 49N03 12E40 -0:50:40
Stammbach 2 4 50N09 11E41 -0:46:44
Stammham 2 4 48N15 12E53 -0:51:32
Stammheim 2 5 48N41 8E46 -0:35:04
Stapelburg 1 2 51N53 10E40 -0:42:40
Stapelfeld 2 1 53N36 10E13 -0:40:52
Starnberg 2 4 48N00 11E20 -0:45:20
Stassfurt 1 2 51N51 11E34 -0:46:16
Staufen 2 3 47N53 7E44 -0:30:56
Staufenberg 2 1 50N40 8E43 -0:34:52
Stechow 1 2 52N38 12E28 -0:49:52
Stederdorf 2 1 52N21 10E15 -0:41:00
Stedten 1 2 51N26 11E41 -0:46:44
Stegelitz 1 2 53N08 13E51 -0:55:24
Steigra 1 2 51N18 11E39 -0:46:36
Steimbke 2 1 52N40 9E22 -0:37:28
Stein 2 4 47N59 12E32 -0:50:08
Steina 1 2 51N12 14E01 -0:56:04
Steinach 1 2 50N25 11E10 -0:44:40
Steinach 2 3 48N18 8E04 -0:32:16
Steinau 2 1 50N23 9E27 -0:37:48
Steinbach 2 3 48N43 8E10 -0:32:40
Steinbach 2 4 50N01 9E36 -0:38:24
Steinbach-Hallenberg 1 2 50N42 10E34 -0:42:16
Stein bei Nürnberg 2 4 49N25 11E01 -0:44:04
Steinberg 2 4 48N34 12E35 -0:50:20
Steinen 2 3 47N38 7E44 -0:30:56
Steinfeld 1 2 50N22 10E44 -0:42:56
Steinfeld 2 1 52N35 8E12 -0:32:48
Steinforth 2 7 51N09 6E32 -0:26:08
Steingaden 2 4 47N42 10E51 -0:43:24
Steinhagen 1 2 54N13 12E59 -0:51:56
Steinhagen 2 1 52N00 8E24 -0:33:36
Steinheid 1 2 50N28 11E04 -0:44:16
Steinheim 2 4 48N01 10E09 -0:40:36
Steinheim 2 5 48N58 9E16 -0:37:04
Steinheim 2 1 50N06 8E55 -0:35:40
Steinheim 2 1 51N52 9E05 -0:36:20
Steinhöfel 1 2 52N24 14E10 -0:56:40
Steinhöring 2 4 48N05 12E02 -0:48:08

Steinhude 2 1 52N27 9E21 -0:37:24
Steinloge 2 1 52N54 8E19 -0:33:16
Stein-Neukirch 2 1 50N41 8E03 -0:32:12
Steinpleis 1 2 50N43 12E23 -0:49:32
Steinsdorf 1 2 52N02 14E40 -0:58:40
Steinwiesen 2 4 50N17 11E28 -0:45:52
Stelle 2 1 53N23 10E06 -0:40:24
Stendal 1 2 52N36 11E51 -0:47:24
Stenden 2 7 51N25 6E27 -0:25:48
Stentrop 2 1 51N30 7E49 -0:31:16
Stephanskirchen 2 4 47N51 12E11 -0:48:44
Sternberg 1 2 53N43 11E49 -0:47:16
Sterup 2 1 54N44 9E44 -0:38:56
Stetten am kalten Markt 2 5 48N07 9E04 -0:36:16
Steyerberg 2 1 52N34 9E01 -0:36:04
Stiege 1 2 51N40 10E53 -0:43:32
Stockach 2 3 47N51 9E00 -0:36:00
Stockelsdorf 2 1 53N54 10E38 -0:42:32
Stöcken 2 1 53N00 10E40 -0:42:40
Stockheim 2 1 50N19 9E01 -0:36:04
Stöckheim bei Braunschweig 2 1 52N12 10E31 -0:42:04
Stockstadt 2 1 49N48 8E28 -0:33:52
Stockum 2 1 51N40 7E42 -0:30:48
Stockum 2 1 51N32 7E47 -0:31:08
Stockum 2 1 51N36 6E39 -0:26:36
Stolberg 1 2 51N34 10E57 -0:43:48
Stolberg 2 7 50N46 6E13 -0:24:52
Stollberg 1 2 50N42 12E47 -0:51:08
Stolpe 1 2 52N40 13E16 -0:53:04
Stolpen 1 2 51N05 14E04 -0:56:16
Stolzenau 2 1 52N31 9E04 -0:36:16
Storkow 1 2 53N19 14E17 -0:57:08
Storkow 1 2 52N15 13E56 -0:55:44
Stössen 1 2 51N06 11E55 -0:47:40
Stotternheim 1 2 51N03 11E02 -0:44:08
Straach 1 2 51N57 12E35 -0:50:20
Straberg 2 7 51N05 6E45 -0:27:00
Straelen 2 7 51N27 6E16 -0:25:04
Stralsund 1 2 54N19 13E05 -0:52:20
Strande 2 1 54N26 10E12 -0:40:48
Strasburg 1 2 53N30 13E44 -0:54:56
Strassgiech 2 4 49N58 11E00 -0:44:00
Strasskirchen 2 4 48N50 12E43 -0:50:52
Straubing 2 4 48N53 12E34 -0:50:16
Strauch 2 1 51N09 6E56 -0:27:44
Straupitz 1 2 51N54 14E07 -0:56:28
Strausberg 1 2 52N35 13E53 -0:55:32
Strausberg-Vorstadt 1 2 52N32 13E51 -0:55:24
Straussberg 1 2 51N23 10E44 -0:42:56
Straussfurt 1 2 51N09 10E59 -0:43:56
Strehla 1 2 51N21 13E13 -0:52:52
Streitberg 2 4 49N49 11E13 -0:44:52
Strelitzalt 1 2 53N20 13E05 -0:52:20
Strickherdicke 2 1 51N29 7E43 -0:30:52
Ströhen 2 1 52N32 8E41 -0:34:44
Stromberg 2 6 49N57 7E46 -0:31:04
Stromberg 2 1 51N48 8E12 -0:32:48
Strömkendorf 1 2 53N58 11E29 -0:45:56
Strücklingen 2 1 53N07 7E40 -0:30:40
Strullendorf 2 4 49N50 10E59 -0:43:56
Strümp 2 7 51N17 6E40 -0:26:40
Stübbecken 2 1 51N23 7E36 -0:30:24
Stubbenfelde 1 2 54N02 14E01 -0:56:04
Stubbenkammer 1 2 54N35 13E40 -0:54:40
Stühlingen 2 3 47N44 8E26 -0:33:44
Stuhr 2 1 53N01 8E45 -0:35:00
Stukenbrock 2 1 51N54 8E39 -0:34:36
Stülpe 1 2 52N02 13E19 -0:53:16
Stumpf 2 1 51N06 7E13 -0:28:52
Stumsdorf 1 2 51N37 12E03 -0:48:12
Stuppach 2 5 49N27 9E44 -0:38:56
Stürzelberg 2 7 51N08 6E49 -0:27:16
Stuttgart 2 5 48N46 9E11 -0:36:44
Stützengrün 1 2 50N32 12E31 -0:50:04
Stützerbach 1 2 50N38 10E51 -0:43:24
Süchteln 2 7 51N17 6E22 -0:25:28
Süderbrarup 2 1 54N38 9E46 -0:39:04
Süderlügum 2 1 54N52 8E55 -0:35:40
Südkamen 2 1 51N35 7E39 -0:30:36
Südlengern 2 1 52N11 8E38 -0:34:32
Sudweyhe 2 1 52N59 8E53 -0:35:32
Suhl 1 2 50N37 10E41 -0:42:44
Suhlendorf 2 1 52N55 10E46 -0:43:04
Sülfeld 2 1 53N48 10E14 -0:40:56
Sulingen 2 1 52N41 8E47 -0:35:08
Sulz 2 3 48N18 7E51 -0:31:24
Sulz am Neckar 2 3 48N21 8E37 -0:34:28
Sulzbach 2 6 49N18 7E07 -0:28:28
Sulzbach am Kocher 2 5 48N58 9E50 -0:39:20
Sulzbach-Rosenberg 2 4 49N30 11E45 -0:47:00
Sulzbrunn 2 4 47N41 10E20 -0:41:20
Sulzburg 2 3 47N50 7E42 -0:30:48
Sülze 2 1 52N46 10E02 -0:40:08
Sümmern 2 1 51N25 7E43 -0:30:52
Summt 1 2 52N41 13E22 -0:53:28
Sünching 2 4 48N53 12E21 -0:49:24
Sundern 2 1 51N20 8E00 -0:32:00
Sünderup 2 1 54N46 9E27 -0:37:48
Sundhausen 1 2 50N56 10E40 -0:42:40
Sundwig 2 1 51N23 7E47 -0:31:08
Süpplingen 2 1 52N14 10E54 -0:43:36
Surendorf 2 1 54N28 10E04 -0:40:16
Surwold 2 1 53N00 7E30 -0:30:00
Süsel 2 1 54N04 10E43 -0:42:52
Süssen 2 5 48N41 9E45 -0:39:00
Suttrop 2 1 51N27 8E22 -0:33:28

Syke 2 1 52N54 8E49 -0:35:16
Tabarz 1 2 50N52 10E31 -0:42:04
Tacherting 2 4 48N05 12E34 -0:50:16
Tailfingen 2 5 48N15 9E01 -0:36:04
Tambach-Dietharz 1 2 50N48 10E36 -0:42:24
Tangerhütte 1 2 52N26 11E48 -0:47:12
Tangermünde 1 2 52N32 11E58 -0:47:52
Tann 2 1 50N38 10E01 -0:40:04
Tanna 1 2 50N30 11E51 -0:47:24
Tanne 1 2 51N41 10E42 -0:42:48
Tannenbergsthal 1 2 50N26 12E27 -0:49:48
Tännesberg 2 4 49N32 12E20 -0:49:20
Tannhausen 2 5 48N59 10E21 -0:41:24
Tarmstedt 2 1 53N13 9E04 -0:36:16
Tarnewitz 1 2 53N58 11E14 -0:44:56
Tarp 2 1 54N40 9E23 -0:37:32
Tassdorf 1 2 52N30 13E47 -0:55:08
Tauberbischofsheim 2 3 49N37 9E40 -0:38:40
Taucha 1 2 51N23 12E30 -0:50:00
Taufkirchen 2 4 48N21 12E08 -0:48:32
Taura 1 2 50N55 12E50 -0:51:20
Tecklenburg 2 1 52N13 7E48 -0:31:12
Tegernsee 2 4 47N43 11E45 -0:47:00
Teichröda 1 2 50N45 11E18 -0:45:12
Teichwolframsdorf 1 2 50N43 12E14 -0:48:56
Teisendorf 2 4 47N51 12E49 -0:51:16
Teisnach 2 4 49N02 13E00 -0:52:00
Telgte 2 1 51N59 7E47 -0:31:08
Teltow 1 2 52N23 13E16 -0:53:04
Tempelfelde 1 2 52N43 13E43 -0:54:52
Templin 1 2 53N07 13E30 -0:54:00
Tengen 2 3 47N49 8E40 -0:34:40
Tennenbronn 2 3 48N11 8E20 -0:33:20
Tente 2 1 51N07 7E11 -0:28:44
Termsdorf 1 2 52N16 13E07 -0:52:28
Terpe 1 2 51N32 14E19 -0:57:16
Teschendorf 1 2 52N51 13E10 -0:52:40
Tesperhude 2 1 53N24 10E26 -0:41:44
Tessin 1 2 54N01 12E28 -0:49:52
Teterow 1 2 53N46 12E34 -0:50:16
Tettau 2 4 50N28 11E15 -0:45:00
Tettens 2 1 53N38 7E53 -0:31:32
Tettnang 2 5 47N40 9E35 -0:38:20
Teublitz 2 4 49N13 12E05 -0:48:20
Teuchern 1 2 51N07 12E01 -0:48:04
Teunz 2 4 49N29 12E23 -0:49:32
Teupitz 1 2 52N08 13E36 -0:54:24
Teuschnitz 2 4 50N24 11E23 -0:45:32
Teutleben 1 2 50N57 10E33 -0:42:12
Teutschenthal 1 2 51N27 11E46 -0:47:04
Thal 1 2 50N55 10E23 -0:41:32
Thale 1 2 51N45 11E02 -0:44:08
Thalfang 2 6 49N45 6E59 -0:27:56
Thalheim 1 2 50N42 12E51 -0:51:24
Thalheim 2 4 49N28 11E33 -0:46:12
Thalitter 2 1 51N13 8E53 -0:35:32
Thallwitz 1 2 51N26 12E40 -0:50:40
Thalmässing 2 4 49N05 11E13 -0:44:52
Thambach 2 4 48N25 12E32 -0:50:08
Thannhausen 2 4 48N17 10E28 -0:41:52
Tharandt 1 2 50N59 13E35 -0:54:20
Thedinghausen 2 1 52N58 9E01 -0:36:04
Theessen 1 2 52N14 12E02 -0:48:08
Theissen 1 2 51N05 12E06 -0:48:24
Themar 1 2 50N30 10E37 -0:42:28
Theuern 2 4 49N22 11E55 -0:47:40
Thiendorf 1 2 51N17 13E44 -0:54:56
Thier 2 1 51N05 7E22 -0:29:28
Thierhaupten 2 4 48N34 10E54 -0:43:36
Thiersheim 2 4 50N04 12E07 -0:48:28
Thiessow 1 2 54N16 13E43 -0:54:52
Tholey 2 6 49N29 7E02 -0:28:08
Thum 1 2 50N40 12E57 -0:51:48
Thumby 2 1 54N35 9E54 -0:39:36
Thüngen 2 4 49N56 9E51 -0:39:24
Thürkow 1 2 53N50 12E33 -0:50:12
Tiefenbach 2 4 49N26 12E35 -0:50:20
Tiefenbroich 2 1 51N18 6E49 -0:27:16
Tiefensee 1 2 52N41 13E50 -0:55:20
Tiengen 2 3 47N38 8E16 -0:33:04
Tietzow 1 2 52N43 12E56 -0:51:44
Timmendorfer Strand 2 1 54N00 10E46 -0:43:04
Tirschenreuth 2 4 49N53 12E21 -0:49:24
Titisee-Neustadt 2 3 47N54 8E13 -0:32:52
Titting 2 4 49N00 11E13 -0:44:52
Tittling 2 4 48N44 13E23 -0:53:32
Tittmoning 2 4 48N04 12E46 -0:51:04
Titz 2 7 51N01 6E25 -0:25:40
Todtenhausen 2 1 52N20 8E56 -0:35:44
Todtmoos 2 3 47N44 8E00 -0:32:00
Todtmoos Au 2 3 47N42 7E58 -0:31:52
Todtnau 2 3 47N50 7E56 -0:31:44
Töging am Inn 2 4 48N15 12E35 -0:50:20
Tönisberg 2 7 51N25 6E30 -0:26:00
Tönisheide 2 1 51N19 7E03 -0:28:12
Tönisvort 2 7 51N19 6E29 -0:25:56
Tönning 2 1 54N19 8E56 -0:35:44
Tönsholt 2 1 51N38 6E58 -0:27:52
Töpchin 1 2 52N10 13E34 -0:54:16
Töpen 2 4 50N23 11E52 -0:47:28
Torgau 1 2 51N34 13E00 -0:52:00
Torgelow 1 2 53N37 14E00 -0:56:00
Tornesch 2 1 53N41 9E43 -0:38:52
Tossens 2 1 53N34 8E16 -0:33:04
Tostedt 2 1 53N17 9E42 -0:38:48
Traben-Trarbach 2 6 49N57 7E06 -0:28:24
Trappenkamp 2 1 54N03 10E16 -0:41:04
Trasching 2 4 49N09 12E28 -0:49:52

Trassem 2 6 49N34 6E31 -0:26:04
Trasslberg 2 4 49N29 11E50 -0:47:20
Trauchgau 2 4 47N38 10E49 -0:43:16
Traunreut 2 4 47N56 12E35 -0:50:20
Traunstein 2 4 47N52 12E38 -0:50:32
Traunwalchen 2 4 47N56 12E36 -0:50:24
Trautenstein 1 2 51N41 10E43 -0:42:52
Trebatsch 1 2 52N05 14E09 -0:56:36
Trebbin 1 2 52N13 13E13 -0:52:52
Trebel 2 1 52N59 11E20 -0:45:20
Trebitz 1 2 51N45 12E44 -0:50:56
Trebsen 1 2 51N17 12E45 -0:51:00
Treffurt 1 2 51N08 10E14 -0:40:56
Treia 2 1 54N30 9E17 -0:37:08
Treis 2 6 50N10 7E17 -0:29:08
Tremsbüttel 2 1 53N44 10E18 -0:41:12
Trendelburg 2 1 51N34 9E25 -0:37:40
Trent 1 2 54N31 13E15 -0:53:00
Treuchtlingen 2 4 48N57 10E54 -0:43:36
Treuen 1 2 50N32 12E18 -0:49:12
Treuenbrietzen 1 2 52N06 12E52 -0:51:28
Trèves → Trier 2 6 49N45 6E38 -0:26:32
Treysa 2 1 50N55 9E11 -0:36:44
Triberg 2 3 48N08 8E13 -0:32:52
Tribsees 1 2 54N05 12E45 -0:51:00
Triebes 1 2 50N41 12E01 -0:48:04
Trieching 2 4 48N45 12E40 -0:50:40
Triepkendorf 1 2 53N17 13E20 -0:53:20
Trier 2 6 49N45 6E38 -0:26:32
Triftern 2 4 48N24 13E01 -0:52:04
Triglitz 1 2 53N12 12E05 -0:48:20
Triptis 1 2 50N44 11E52 -0:47:28
Trittau 2 1 53N37 10E25 -0:41:40
Trittenheim 2 6 49N49 6E54 -0:27:36
Trochtelfingen 2 5 48N18 9E14 -0:36:56
Tröglitz 1 2 51N04 12E11 -0:48:44
Troisdorf 2 1 50N49 7E08 -0:28:32
Trossingen 2 3 48N04 8E38 -0:34:32
Trostberg 2 4 48N01 12E32 -0:50:08
Trusetal 1 2 50N47 10E25 -0:41:40
Tschernitz 1 2 51N35 14E37 -0:58:28
Tübingen 2 5 48N31 9E02 -0:36:08
Tucheim 1 2 52N17 12E11 -0:48:44
Tüchen 1 2 53N04 12E05 -0:48:20
Tündern 2 1 52N04 9E22 -0:37:28
Tuntenhausen 2 4 47N56 12E01 -0:48:04
Türkheim 2 4 48N03 10E38 -0:42:32
Tüssling 2 4 48N13 12E36 -0:50:24
Tuttlingen 2 3 47N59 8E49 -0:35:16
Tutzing 2 4 47N54 11E17 -0:45:08
Twist 2 1 52N38 7E03 -0:28:12
Twistringen 2 1 52N48 8E38 -0:34:32
Übach-Palenberg 2 7 50N55 6E07 -0:24:28
Überlingen 2 3 47N46 9E10 -0:36:40
Übersee 2 4 47N49 12E28 -0:49:52
Uchte 2 1 52N30 8E54 -0:35:36
Uchtspringe 1 2 52N32 11E36 -0:46:24
Uckro 1 2 51N51 13E37 -0:54:28
Uder 1 2 51N22 10E05 -0:40:20
Uebigau 1 2 51N35 13E18 -0:53:12
Ueckeritz 1 2 54N00 14E02 -0:56:08
Ueckermünde 1 2 53N44 14E03 -0:56:12
Uedem 2 7 51N40 6E16 -0:25:04
Uehlfeld 2 4 49N40 10E43 -0:42:52
Uelsen 2 1 52N30 6E53 -0:27:32
Uelzen 2 1 52N58 10E33 -0:42:12
Uelzen 2 1 51N33 7E44 -0:30:56
Uetersen 2 1 53N41 9E39 -0:38:36
Uettingen 2 4 49N48 9E43 -0:38:52
Uetz 1 2 52N28 12E56 -0:51:44
Uetze 2 1 52N28 10E11 -0:40:44
Uffenheim 2 4 49N32 10E14 -0:40:56
Uhingen 2 5 48N42 9E35 -0:38:20
Ühlingen 2 3 47N43 8E19 -0:33:16
Uhlstädt 1 2 50N44 11E28 -0:45:52
Uhyst 1 2 51N11 14E13 -0:56:52
Uhyst 1 2 51N24 14E30 -0:58:00
Ulm 2 5 48N24 10E00 -0:40:00
Ulmeu-Meisereich 2 6 50N13 6E58 -0:27:52
Ulrichstein 2 1 50N34 9E11 -0:36:44
Ummanz 1 2 54N28 13E10 -0:52:40
Ummeln 2 1 51N58 8E27 -0:33:48
Ummendorf 1 2 52N09 11E11 -0:44:44
Umpferstedt 1 2 50N59 11E25 -0:45:40
Undersdorf 2 6 50N09 6E49 -0:27:16
Unkel 2 1 50N35 7E13 -0:28:52
Unna 2 1 51N32 7E41 -0:30:44
Unseburg 1 2 51N56 11E30 -0:46:00
Unsleben 2 4 50N22 10E15 -0:41:00
Unterbach 2 1 51N12 6E54 -0:27:36
Unterelchingen 2 4 48N27 10E07 -0:40:28
Unterföhring 2 4 48N12 11E38 -0:46:32
Untergermaringen 2 4 47N56 10E40 -0:42:40
Unterglottertal 2 3 48N03 7E56 -0:31:44
Untergriesbach 2 4 48N35 13E40 -0:54:40
Untergröningen 2 5 48N55 9E53 -0:39:32
Untergrüne 2 1 51N22 7E39 -0:30:36
Unterhaching 2 4 48N04 11E38 -0:46:32
Unterhausen 2 5 48N26 9E16 -0:37:04
Unterjettenberg 2 4 47N41 12E49 -0:51:16
Unterlüss 2 1 52N50 10E17 -0:41:08
Untermünkheim 2 5 49N09 9E44 -0:38:56
Untermünstertal 2 3 47N51 7E46 -0:31:04

Unterneuses 2	4	50N05	10E58	-0:43:52
Unteröwisheim 2	3	49N08	8E40	-0:34:40
Unterschwaningen 2	4	49N04	10E37	-0:42:28
Unterthingau 2	4	47N46	10E31	-0:42:04
Unteruhldingen 2	3	47N43	9E14	-0:36:56
Unterweissbach 1	2	50N37	11E10	-0:44:40
Unterwellenborn 1	2	50N39	11E26	-0:45:44
Unterwössen 2	4	47N44	12E27	-0:49:48
Upgant-Schott 2	1	53N30	7E16	-0:29:04
Uphusen 2	1	53N01	8E58	-0:35:52
Urach 2	5	48N29	9E23	-0:37:32
Urbach 2	1	50N53	7E05	-0:28:20
Ursensollen 2	4	49N24	11E46	-0:47:04
Urspring 2	5	48N33	9E53	-0:39:32
Ürzig 2	6	49N59	7E01	-0:28:04
Usadel 1	2	53N26	13E11	-0:52:44
Usedom 1	2	53N52	13E55	-0:55:40
Usingen 2	1	50N20	8E32	-0:34:08
Uslar 2	1	51N39	9E38	-0:38:32
Utersum 2	1	54N43	8E24	-0:33:36
Utfort 2	7	51N28	6E38	-0:26:32
Uttenweiler 2	5	48N09	9E36	-0:38:24
Ütterlingsen 2	1	51N15	7E45	-0:31:00
Utting 2	4	48N02	11E05	-0:44:20
Vacha 1	2	50N50	10E01	-0:40:04
Vaihingen an der Enz 2	5	48N56	8E58	-0:35:52
Vaihingen auf den Fildern 2	5	48N44	9E07	-0:36:28
Valbert 2	1	51N07	7E44	-0:30:56
Valdorf 2	1	52N09	8E51	-0:35:24
Valepp 2	4	47N37	11E53	-0:47:32
Vallendar 2	1	50N24	7E37	-0:30:28
Varel 2	1	53N22	8E10	-0:32:40
Vechelde 2	1	52N16	10E22	-0:41:28
Vechta 2	1	52N43	8E16	-0:33:04
Veckerhagen 2	1	51N30	9E35	-0:38:20
Veen 2	7	51N37	6E27	-0:25:48
Veert 2	7	51N33	6E17	-0:25:08
Vehlefanz 1	2	52N43	13E06	-0:52:24
Veilsdorf 1	2	50N24	10E48	-0:43:12
Veitsbronn 2	4	49N31	10E53	-0:43:32
Veitshöchheim 2	4	49N50	9E52	-0:39:28
Velbert 2	1	51N20	7E02	-0:28:08
Velburg 2	4	49N14	11E41	-0:46:44
Velden 2	4	49N37	11E31	-0:46:04
Velden 2	4	48N19	12E16	-0:49:04
Velen 2	1	51N53	6E59	-0:27:56
Velgast 1	2	54N16	12E48	-0:51:12
Vellahn 2	1	53N24	10E58	-0:43:52
Vellberg 2	5	49N05	9E53	-0:39:32
Vellmar 2	1	51N21	9E28	-0:37:52
Velmede 2	1	51N21	8E22	-0:33:28
Velpke 2	1	52N24	10E56	-0:43:44
Velten 1	2	52N41	13E10	-0:52:40
Veltheim 2	1	52N11	8E58	-0:35:52
Verden 2	1	52N55	9E13	-0:36:52
Veringenstadt 2	5	48N11	9E12	-0:36:48
Verl (Senne I) 2	1	51N53	8E31	-0:34:04
Verne 2	1	51N41	8E34	-0:34:16
Versmold 2	1	52N02	8E09	-0:32:36
Vetschau 1	2	51N47	14E04	-0:56:16
Victorbur 2	1	53N29	7E20	-0:29:20
Viecht 2	4	48N30	12E04	-0:48:16
Viechtach 2	4	49N05	12E53	-0:51:32
Viehhausen 2	4	48N59	11E58	-0:47:52
Vielank 1	2	53N15	11E08	-0:44:32
Vienenburg 2	1	51N57	10E34	-0:42:16
Viereck 1	2	53N32	14E02	-0:56:08
Viernau 1	2	50N40	10E32	-0:42:08
Viernheim 2	1	49N32	8E34	-0:34:16
Vierraden 1	2	53N06	14E17	-0:57:08
Viersen 2	7	51N15	6E23	-0:25:32
Viesecke 1	2	53N01	12E01	-0:48:04
Vieselbach 1	2	51N00	11E08	-0:44:32
Vietgest 1	2	53N45	12E20	-0:49:20
Villigst 2	1	51N26	7E35	-0:30:20
Villingen-Schwenningen 2	3	48N04	8E28	-0:33:52
Vilmnitz 1	2	54N21	13E31	-0:54:04
Vilsbiburg 2	4	48N27	12E12	-0:48:48
Vilseck 2	4	49N37	11E48	-0:47:12
Vilsheim 2	4	48N27	12E07	-0:48:28
Vilshofen 2	4	48N39	13E12	-0:52:48
Vilzing 2	4	49N11	12E41	-0:50:44
Vinnhorst 2	1	52N25	9E43	-0:38:52
Vinnum 2	1	51N41	7E24	-0:29:36
Vinzelberg 1	2	52N33	11E40	-0:46:40
Vipperow 1	2	53N19	12E41	-0:50:44
Virneburg 2	6	50N20	7E04	-0:28:16
Visbek 2	1	52N48	8E19	-0:33:16
Visselhövede 2	1	52N59	9E35	-0:38:20
Vitte 1	2	54N34	13E06	-0:52:24
Vlatten 2	7	50N39	6E32	-0:26:08
Vlotho 2	1	52N10	8E51	-0:35:24
Vluyn 2	7	51N26	6E32	-0:26:08
Voerde 2	1	51N35	6E41	-0:26:44
Voerde 2	1	51N18	7E24	-0:29:36
Voesch 2	7	51N24	6E26	-0:25:44
Vogelsang 1	2	53N43	14E09	-0:56:36
Vogelsang 2	7	50N35	6E27	-0:25:48
Vohburg an der Donau 2	4	48N46	11E37	-0:46:28
Vohenstrauss 2	4	49N37	12E21	-0:49:24
Vöhringen 2	3	48N02	8E18	-0:33:12
Vöhringen 2	4	48N16	10E04	-0:40:16
Vöhringen 2	5	48N20	8E40	-0:34:40
Vöhrum 2	1	52N20	10E10	-0:40:40
Volkach 2	4	49N52	10E13	-0:40:52
Völklingen 2	6	49N15	6E50	-0:27:20
Volkmarsen 2	1	51N24	9E07	-0:36:28
Völksen 2	1	52N13	9E37	-0:38:28
Vollersode 2	1	53N18	8E56	-0:35:44
Vollme 2	1	51N10	7E36	-0:30:24
Volmarstein 2	1	51N22	7E23	-0:29:32
Völpke 1	2	52N08	11E09	-0:44:36
Vorbach 2	4	49N49	11E45	-0:47:00
Vörden 2	1	52N28	8E05	-0:32:20
Vorderriss 2	4	47N33	11E26	-0:45:44
Vorhelm 2	1	51N48	7E56	-0:31:44
Vormholz 2	1	51N24	7E18	-0:29:12
Vornbach 2	4	48N29	13E27	-0:53:48
Vorra 2	4	49N33	11E30	-0:46:00
Vorsfelde 2	1	52N26	10E49	-0:43:16
Vorst 2	7	51N18	6E25	-0:25:40
Voslapp 2	1	53N36	8E05	-0:32:20
Voxtrup 2	1	52N14	8E07	-0:32:28
Vreden 2	1	52N02	6E52	-0:27:28
Waabs 2	1	54N32	9E58	-0:39:52
Waakirchen 2	4	47N46	11E40	-0:46:40
Waal 2	4	48N00	10E46	-0:43:04
Wabern 2	1	51N06	9E20	-0:37:20
Wachenheim 2	6	49N26	8E10	-0:32:40
Wachenzell 2	4	48N58	11E14	-0:44:56
Wachtendonk 2	7	51N24	6E20	-0:25:20
Wächtersbach 2	1	50N15	9E17	-0:37:08
Wackersdorf 2	4	49N19	12E11	-0:48:44
Wadern 2	6	49N32	6E53	-0:27:32
Wadersloh 2	1	51N44	8E15	-0:33:00
Wagenfeld-Hasslingen 2	1	52N33	8E34	-0:34:16
Waging am See 2	4	47N56	12E43	-0:50:52
Wahlen 2	1	49N37	8E51	-0:35:24
Wahlstedt 2	1	53N57	10E12	-0:40:48
Wahn 2	1	50N52	7E05	-0:28:20
Wahrenbrück 1	2	51N33	13E22	-0:53:28
Wahrenholz 2	1	52N36	10E36	-0:42:24
Waiblingen 2	5	48N50	9E19	-0:37:16
Waibstadt 2	3	49N18	8E54	-0:35:36
Waischenfeld 2	4	49N51	11E21	-0:45:24
Walbeck 2	7	51N30	6E15	-0:25:00
Walchensee 2	4	47N35	11E19	-0:45:16
Walda 2	4	48N37	11E06	-0:44:24
Waldangelloch 2	3	49N12	8E47	-0:35:08
Waldböckelheim 2	6	49N49	7E43	-0:30:52
Waldbröl 2	1	50N53	7E37	-0:30:28
Waldburg 2	5	47N45	9E43	-0:38:52
Waldeck 2	1	51N12	9E04	-0:36:16
Waldeck 2	4	49N52	11E57	-0:47:48
Waldenbuch 2	5	48N38	9E07	-0:36:28
Waldenburg 1	2	50N52	12E36	-0:50:24
Waldenburg 2	5	49N11	9E38	-0:38:32
Waldershof 2	4	49N59	12E04	-0:48:16
Waldfischbach 2	6	49N17	7E40	-0:30:40
Waldheim 1	2	51N04	13E01	-0:52:04
Waldkappel 2	1	51N08	9E52	-0:39:28
Waldkirch 2	3	48N05	7E57	-0:31:48
Waldkirchen 2	4	48N44	13E37	-0:54:28
Waldkraiburg 2	4	48N12	12E28	-0:49:52
Waldmünchen 2	4	49N23	12E43	-0:50:52
Waldsassen 2	4	50N00	12E18	-0:49:12
Waldshut 2	3	47N37	8E13	-0:32:52
Waldthurn 2	4	49N40	12E20	-0:49:20
Walheim 2	7	50N42	6E10	-0:24:40
Walkenried 2	1	51N35	10E37	-0:42:28
Wallach 2	7	51N35	6E34	-0:26:16
Wallau 2	1	50N56	8E28	-0:33:52
Walldorf 1	2	50N36	10E23	-0:41:32
Walldorf 2	3	49N18	8E38	-0:34:32
Walldürn 2	3	49N35	9E22	-0:37:28
Wallenfels 2	4	50N16	11E28	-0:45:52
Wallersdorf 2	4	48N44	12E45	-0:51:00
Wallerstein 2	4	48N53	10E28	-0:41:52
Wallgau 2	4	47N31	11E16	-0:45:04
Wallmerod 2	1	50N29	7E56	-0:31:44
Wallsbüll 2	1	54N47	9E14	-0:36:56
Wallstawe 1	2	52N47	11E01	-0:44:04
Walschleben 1	2	51N04	10E56	-0:43:44
Walsrode 2	1	52N52	9E35	-0:38:20
Walsum 2	1	51N32	6E41	-0:26:44
Waltenhofen 2	4	47N40	10E17	-0:41:08
Waltersdorf 1	2	50N52	14E38	-0:58:32
Waltersdorf 1	2	52N22	13E35	-0:54:20
Waltershausen 1	2	50N53	10E33	-0:42:12
Waltershofen 2	5	47N46	9E55	-0:39:40
Waltrop 2	1	51N37	7E23	-0:29:32
Walze 2	1	51N16	7E31	-0:30:04
Wanderup 2	1	54N41	9E20	-0:37:20
Wandhofen 2	1	51N26	7E33	-0:30:12
Wandlitz 1	2	52N45	13E26	-0:53:44
Wanfried 2	1	51N10	10E10	-0:40:40
Wangels 2	1	54N16	10E45	-0:43:00
Wangen 2	4	48N01	11E24	-0:45:36
Wangen im Allgäu 2	5	47N41	9E50	-0:39:20
Wangersen 2	1	53N22	9E25	-0:37:40
Wankendorf 2	1	54N07	10E13	-0:40:52
Wankum 2	7	51N24	6E20	-0:25:20
Wanna 2	1	53N44	8E46	-0:35:04
Wanne-Eickel 2	1	51N32	7E09	-0:28:36
Wansdorf 1	2	52N38	13E05	-0:52:20
Wansleben 1	2	51N27	11E45	-0:47:00
Wanzleben 1	2	52N03	11E26	-0:45:44
Warburg 2	1	51N29	9E08	-0:36:32
Wardenburg 2	1	53N04	8E11	-0:32:44
Warder 2	1	53N59	10E22	-0:41:28
Wardt 2	7	51N41	6E25	-0:25:40
Waren 1	2	53N31	12E40	-0:50:40
Warendorf 2	1	51N57	7E59	-0:31:56
Warin 1	2	53N48	11E42	-0:46:48
Warmensteinach 2	4	49N59	11E47	-0:47:08
Warnemünde 1	2	54N10	12E04	-0:48:16
Warngau 2	4	47N50	11E41	-0:46:44
Warnkenhagen 1	2	54N00	11E04	-0:44:16
Warrenzin 1	2	53N54	12E57	-0:51:48
Warsingsfehn 2	1	53N20	7E28	-0:29:52
Warstein 2	1	51N26	8E21	-0:33:24
Wartburg 1	2	50N58	10E18	-0:41:12
Wartenberg 2	4	48N24	11E59	-0:47:56
Wartin 1	2	53N15	14E09	-0:56:36
Warza 1	2	51N00	10E41	-0:42:44
Wäschenbeuren 2	5	48N46	9E41	-0:38:44
Wassenberg 2	7	51N06	6E08	-0:24:32
Wasseralfingen 2	5	48N52	10E06	-0:40:24
Wasserburg am Inn 2	4	48N04	12E13	-0:48:52
Wasserkurl 2	1	51N33	7E38	-0:30:32
Wasserleben 1	2	51N55	10E44	-0:42:56
Wassertrüdingen 2	4	49N02	10E35	-0:42:20
Wassmannsdorf 1	2	52N22	13E28	-0:53:52
Wasungen 1	2	50N40	10E22	-0:41:28
Wathlingen 2	1	52N32	10E09	-0:40:36
Wattenscheid 2	1	51N29	7E08	-0:28:32
Waxweiler 2	6	50N05	6E22	-0:25:28
Webau 1	2	51N10	12E04	-0:48:16
Webling 2	4	48N17	11E25	-0:45:40
Wechmar 1	2	50N53	10E47	-0:43:08
Wechselburg 1	2	51N00	12E47	-0:51:08
Weddinghofen 2	1	51N36	7E37	-0:30:28
Wedel 2	1	53N35	9E41	-0:38:44
Weende 2	1	51N33	9E55	-0:39:40
Weener 2	1	53N10	7E21	-0:29:24
Weesby 2	1	54N50	9E08	-0:36:32
Weesow 1	2	52N39	13E43	-0:54:52
Weetfeld 2	1	51N38	7E49	-0:31:16
Weeze 2	7	51N37	6E12	-0:24:48
Wefensleben 1	2	52N11	11E09	-0:44:36
Weferlingen 1	2	52N19	11E02	-0:44:08
Wegberg 2	7	51N08	6E16	-0:25:04
Wegeleben 1	2	51N53	11E10	-0:44:40
Wegendorf 1	2	52N36	13E45	-0:55:00
Wegenstedt 1	2	52N23	11E11	-0:44:44
Wegeringhausen 2	1	51N02	7E45	-0:31:00
Wegscheid 2	4	48N36	13E48	-0:55:12
Wehdel 2	1	53N30	8E48	-0:35:12
Wehingen 2	5	48N08	8E47	-0:35:08
Wehr 2	3	47N37	7E54	-0:31:36
Wehrsdorf 1	2	51N03	14E22	-0:57:28
Weichshofen 2	4	48N43	12E26	-0:49:44
Weida 1	2	50N45	12E04	-0:48:16
Weidenberg 2	4	49N57	11E43	-0:46:52
Weiden in der Oberpfalz 2	4	49N41	12E10	-0:48:40
Weidenstetten 2	5	48N33	9E59	-0:39:56
Weidhausen 2	4	50N12	11E08	-0:44:32
Weiding 2	4	49N16	12E46	-0:51:04
Weihmichl 2	4	48N36	12E03	-0:48:12
Weikersheim 2	5	49N29	9E54	-0:39:36
Weil am Rhein 2	3	47N37	7E38	-0:30:32
Weilbach 2	1	50N03	8E26	-0:33:44
Weilburg 2	1	50N29	8E15	-0:33:00
Weil der Stadt 2	5	48N45	8E52	-0:35:28
Weiler 2	4	47N36	9E55	-0:39:40
Weilerbach 2	6	49N29	7E37	-0:30:28
Weilerswist 2	7	50N45	6E50	-0:27:20
Weilheim 2	4	47N50	11E08	-0:44:32
Weilheim an der Teck 2	5	48N37	9E32	-0:38:08
Weilmünster 2	1	50N26	8E22	-0:33:28
Weimar 1	2	50N59	11E19	-0:45:16
Weimar 2	1	51N22	9E23	-0:37:32
Weinböhla 1	2	51N10	13E34	-0:54:16
Weingarten 2	5	47N48	9E38	-0:38:32
Weingarten 2	3	49N05	8E31	-0:34:04
Weinheim 2	3	49N33	8E39	-0:34:36
Weinsberg 2	5	49N10	9E17	-0:37:08
Weischlitz 1	2	50N26	12E02	-0:48:08
Weisendorf 2	4	49N37	10E49	-0:43:16
Weismain 2	4	50N05	11E14	-0:44:56
Weissach 2	4	47N41	11E45	-0:47:00
Weissach 2	5	48N50	8E55	-0:35:40
Weissenberg 1	2	51N11	14E40	-0:58:40
Weissenborn 1	2	50N52	13E25	-0:53:40
Weissenbrunn 2	4	50N12	11E20	-0:45:20
Weissenburg in Bayern 2	4	49N01	10E58	-0:43:52
Weissenfels 1	2	51N12	11E58	-0:47:52
Weissenhorn 2	4	48N18	10E09	-0:40:36
Weissensee 1	2	51N11	11E04	-0:44:16
Weissenstadt 2	4	50N06	11E53	-0:47:32
Weissenstein 2	5	48N42	9E53	-0:39:32
Weissenthurm 2	6	50N24	7E27	-0:29:48
Weissig 1	2	51N05	13E52	-0:55:28
Weisswasser 1	2	51N30	14E38	-0:58:32
Weisweiler 2	7	50N50	6E19	-0:25:16
Weitendorf 1	2	53N54	12E16	-0:49:04
Weitin 1	2	53N34	13E12	-0:52:48
Weitnau 2	4	47N38	10E07	-0:40:28
Weitzgrund 1	2	52N11	12E32	-0:50:08
Weixdorf 1	2	51N09	13E48	-0:55:12
Welden 2	4	48N27	10E40	-0:42:40
Wellaune 1	2	51N34	12E33	-0:50:12
Wellerode 2	1	51N14	9E34	-0:38:16
Wellheim 2	4	48N48	11E06	-0:44:24
Welmen 2	1	51N39	6E41	-0:26:44
Welschbillig 2	6	49N51	6E34	-0:26:16
Welsickendorf 1	2	51N54	13E08	-0:52:32
Welsleben 1	2	52N00	11E38	-0:46:32
Weltenburg 2	4	48N54	11E50	-0:47:20
Welzheim 2	5	48N53	9E38	-0:38:32
Welzow 1	2	51N34	14E10	-0:56:40
Wemding 2	4	48N52	10E43	-0:42:52
Wemmetsweiler 2	6	49N22	7E05	-0:28:20
Wendelsheim 2	6	49N46	7E59	-0:31:56

Wendelstein 2 4 49N21 11E08 -0:44:32
Wenden 2 1 52N19 10E30 -0:42:00
Wendisch Rietz 1
2 52N13 14E01 -0:56:04
Wendish Baggendorf 1
2 54N04 12E56 -0:51:44
Wendlingen am Neckar 2
5 48N40 9E23 -0:37:32
Weng 2 4 48N40 12E23 -0:49:32
Wengen 2 4 47N41 10E09 -0:40:36
Wengern 2 1 51N24 7E21 -0:29:24
Wennigsen 2 1 52N16 9E34 -0:38:16
Wensickendorf 1 2 52N45 13E23 -0:53:32
Wentorf 2 1 53N30 10E15 -0:41:00
Wenzenbach 2 4 49N05 12E12 -0:48:48
Werbellin 1 2 52N53 13E41 -0:54:44
Werben 1 2 52N52 11E58 -0:47:52
Werdau 1 2 50N44 12E22 -0:49:28
Werder 1 2 52N23 12E56 -0:51:44
Werdohl 2 1 51N15 7E45 -0:31:00
Werkel 2 1 51N09 9E18 -0:37:12
Werl 2 1 51N33 7E54 -0:31:36
Werlaburgdorf 2 1 52N04 10E31 -0:42:04
Werl-Aspe 2 1 52N04 8E43 -0:34:52
Werleshausen 2 1 51N19 9E54 -0:39:36
Werlte 2 1 52N51 7E41 -0:30:44
Wermelskirchen 2
1 51N08 7E13 -0:28:52
Wermsdorf 1 2 51N17 12E56 -0:51:44
Wernau 2 5 48N41 9E25 -0:37:40
Wernberg 2 4 49N32 12E10 -0:48:40
Werne an der Lippe 2
1 51N40 7E38 -0:30:32
Werneck 2 4 49N59 10E05 -0:40:20
Werneuchen 1 2 52N38 13E44 -0:54:56
Wernigerode 1 2 51N50 10E47 -0:43:08
Wernitz 1 2 52N34 12E55 -0:51:40
Wernsdorf 1 2 52N22 13E43 -0:54:52
Wernshausen 1 2 50N43 10E21 -0:41:24
Werries 2 1 51N41 7E53 -0:31:32
Werschweiler 2 6 49N27 7E13 -0:28:52
Wersen 2 1 52N18 7E56 -0:31:44
Wertach 2 4 47N36 10E25 -0:41:40
Wertheim 2 3 49N46 9E31 -0:38:04
Werther 1 2 51N29 10E46 -0:43:04
Werther 2 1 52N04 8E24 -0:33:36
Wertingen 2 4 48N34 10E41 -0:42:44
Weseke 2 1 51N54 6E51 -0:27:24
Wesel 2 1 51N40 6E38 -0:26:32
Wesenberg 1 2 53N17 12E58 -0:51:52
Wesendahl 1 2 52N36 13E49 -0:55:16
Wesendorf 2 1 52N35 10E31 -0:42:04
Wesermünde 2 1 53N32 8E33 -0:34:12
Wesseling 2 7 50N49 6E58 -0:27:52
Wessobrunn 2 4 47N52 11E01 -0:44:04
Wessum 2 1 52N05 6E58 -0:27:52
West-Berlin → Berlin (West) 2
2 52N29 13E21 -0:53:24
Westbevern 2 1 52N01 7E47 -0:31:08
Westende 2 1 51N25 7E24 -0:29:36
Westenholz 2 1 51N45 8E28 -0:33:52
Westerbönen 2 1 51N36 7E46 -0:31:04
Westerburg 2 1 50N33 7E58 -0:31:52
Westercelle 2 1 52N36 10E05 -0:40:20
Westeregeln 1 2 51N57 11E23 -0:45:32
Westerhausen 1 2 51N48 11E03 -0:44:12
Westerholt 2 1 51N36 7E05 -0:28:20
Westerkappeln 2 1 52N18 7E52 -0:31:28
Westerland 2 1 54N54 8E18 -0:33:12
Westerstede 2 1 53N15 7E55 -0:31:40
Westhausen 2 5 48N53 10E11 -0:40:44
Westheim 2 5 49N03 9E44 -0:38:56
Westhemmerde 2 1 51N33 7E47 -0:31:08
Westhofen 2 1 51N25 7E31 -0:30:04
Westick 2 1 51N35 7E38 -0:30:32
Westig 2 1 51N22 7E45 -0:31:00
Westkirchen 2 1 51N53 8E02 -0:32:08
Westönnen 2 1 51N33 7E58 -0:31:52
Westrhauderfehn 2
1 53N08 7E34 -0:30:16
Wethau 1 2 51N08 11E52 -0:47:28
Wethmar 2 1 51N37 7E33 -0:30:12
Wetten 2 7 51N34 6E17 -0:25:08
Wetter 2 1 50N54 8E43 -0:34:52
Wetter 2 1 51N23 7E23 -0:29:32
Wettin 1 2 51N35 11E48 -0:47:12
Wettringen 2 1 52N12 7E19 -0:29:16
Wetzlar 2 1 50N33 8E29 -0:33:56
Wevelinghoven 2 7 51N06 6E37 -0:26:28
Wewelsfleth 2 1 53N50 9E24 -0:37:36
Wewer 2 1 51N41 8E42 -0:34:48
Weyarn 2 4 47N51 11E48 -0:47:12
Weyhausen 2 1 52N47 10E23 -0:41:32
Wickede 2 1 51N29 7E52 -0:31:28
Wickrath 2 7 51N07 6E24 -0:25:36
Widdern 2 5 49N19 9E25 -0:37:40
Wiebelskirchen 2
6 49N22 7E11 -0:28:44
Wieck 1 2 54N06 13E26 -0:53:44
Wieda 2 1 51N38 10E34 -0:42:16
Wiederitzsch 1 2 51N24 12E22 -0:49:28
Wiefelstede 2 1 53N15 8E07 -0:32:28
Wiehe 1 2 51N16 11E25 -0:45:40
Wiehl 2 1 50N57 7E31 -0:30:04
Wiek 1 2 54N37 13E17 -0:53:08
Wienhausen 2 1 52N35 10E11 -0:40:44
Wiepke 1 2 52N36 11E20 -0:45:20
Wieren 2 1 52N53 10E39 -0:42:36
Wiesa 1 2 50N36 13E01 -0:52:04
Wiesau 2 4 49N55 12E11 -0:48:44
Wiesbaden 2 1 50N05 8E14 -0:32:56
Wiesede 2 1 53N27 7E46 -0:31:04
Wiesenburg 1 2 52N07 12E26 -0:49:44
Wiesenfeld 1 2 51N16 10E06 -0:40:24
Wiesenfelden 2 4 49N02 12E32 -0:50:08
Wiesensteig 2 5 48N34 9E37 -0:38:28
Wiesental 2 3 49N14 8E31 -0:34:04
Wiesentheid 2 4 49N47 10E20 -0:41:20
Wiesloch 2 3 49N17 8E42 -0:34:48
Wiesmoor 2 1 53N25 7E43 -0:30:52
Wietmarschen 2 1 52N31 7E07 -0:28:28
Wietze 2 1 52N39 9E50 -0:39:20
Wietzen 2 1 52N43 9E04 -0:36:16
Wiggensbach 2 4 47N44 10E14 -0:40:56
Wildau 1 2 52N19 13E38 -0:54:32
Wildbad im Schwarzwald 2
3 48N45 8E32 -0:34:08
Wildberg 1 2 52N52 12E37 -0:50:28
Wildberg 2 5 48N37 8E44 -0:34:56
Wildemann 2 1 51N49 10E17 -0:41:08
Wildenbruch 1 2 52N17 13E04 -0:52:16
Wildenfels 1 2 50N40 12E35 -0:50:20
Wildenranna 2 4 48N35 13E44 -0:54:56
Wildenthal 1 2 50N27 12E37 -0:50:28
Wildeshausen 2 1 52N54 8E26 -0:33:44
Wildflecken 2 4 50N23 9E54 -0:39:36
Wilferdingen 2 3 48N56 8E35 -0:34:20
Wilgersdorf 2 1 50N49 8E09 -0:32:36
Wilhelm-Pieck-Stadt Guben 1
2 51N57 14E43 -0:58:52
Wilhelmshaven 2 1 53N31 8E08 -0:32:32
Wilhelmshorst 1 2 52N19 13E03 -0:52:12
Wilkau-Hasslau 1
2 50N40 12E31 -0:50:04
Willebadessen 2 1 51N37 9E02 -0:36:08
Willerswalde 1 2 54N07 13E08 -0:52:32
Willich 2 7 51N16 6E33 -0:26:12
Willingen 2 1 51N17 8E37 -0:34:28
Willmersdorf 1 2 52N40 13E41 -0:54:44
Wilsdruff 1 2 51N05 13E32 -0:54:08
Wilster 2 1 53N55 9E22 -0:37:28
Wilthen 1 2 51N06 14E24 -0:57:36
Wimmelburg 1 2 51N31 11E30 -0:46:00
Windecken 2 1 50N13 8E52 -0:35:28
Windischeschenbach 2
4 49N48 12E09 -0:48:36
Windorf 2 4 48N37 13E13 -0:52:52
Windsbach 2 4 49N14 10E50 -0:43:20
Wingst 2 1 53N43 9E03 -0:36:12
Winhöring 2 4 48N16 12E39 -0:50:36
Winnekendonk 2 7 51N36 6E17 -0:25:08
Winnenden 2 5 48N53 9E24 -0:37:36
Winningen 1 2 51N49 11E26 -0:45:44
Winningen 2 6 50N18 7E31 -0:30:04
Winnweiler 2 6 49N34 7E51 -0:31:24
Winsen 2 1 52N41 9E54 -0:39:36
Winsen 2 1 53N22 10E12 -0:40:48
Winterberg 2 1 51N11 8E32 -0:34:08
Winterberg 2 1 51N17 7E18 -0:29:12
Winterfeld 1 2 52N44 11E14 -0:44:56
Winterlingen 2 5 48N11 9E07 -0:36:28
Wintersdorf 1 2 51N03 12E21 -0:49:24
Winzenberg 2 1 51N06 7E38 -0:30:32
Winzer 2 4 48N44 13E04 -0:52:16
Winzermark 2 1 51N23 7E08 -0:28:32
Wipperdorf 1 2 51N28 10E42 -0:42:48
Wipperfeld 2 1 51N05 7E19 -0:29:16
Wipperfürth 2 1 51N07 7E23 -0:29:32
Wippra 1 2 51N34 11E16 -0:45:04
Wischhafen 2 1 53N46 9E19 -0:37:16
Wismar 1 2 53N53 11E28 -0:45:52
Wissen 2 1 50N47 7E43 -0:30:52
Wissmar 2 1 50N38 8E41 -0:34:44
Witten 2 1 51N26 7E20 -0:29:20
Wittenberg 1 2 51N52 12E39 -0:50:36
Wittenberge 1 2 53N00 11E44 -0:46:56
Wittenburg 1 2 53N31 11E04 -0:44:16
Wittgensdorf 1 2 50N53 12E52 -0:51:28
Wittichenau 1 2 51N23 14E14 -0:56:56
Wittingen 2 1 52N43 10E44 -0:42:56
Wittislingen 2 4 48N37 10E25 -0:41:40
Wittlaer 2 1 51N19 6E44 -0:26:56
Wittlich 2 6 49N59 6E53 -0:27:32
Wittmar 2 1 52N07 10E38 -0:42:32
Wittmund 2 1 53N34 7E47 -0:31:08
Wittstock 1 2 53N10 12E29 -0:49:56
Witzenhausen 2 1 51N20 9E51 -0:39:24
Witzhelden 2 1 51N07 7E06 -0:28:24
Wöbbelin 1 2 53N24 11E30 -0:46:00
Wohlde 2 1 54N24 9E17 -0:37:08
Wolbeck 2 1 51N55 7E43 -0:30:52
Woldegk 1 2 53N27 13E35 -0:54:20
Wolfach 2 3 48N17 8E13 -0:32:52
Wolfegg 2 5 47N49 9E47 -0:39:08
Wolfen 1 2 51N40 12E16 -0:49:04
Wolfenbüttel 2 1 52N10 10E32 -0:42:08
Wolfertschwenden 2
4 47N53 10E16 -0:41:04
Wolfhagen 2 1 51N19 9E10 -0:36:40
Wölfis 1 2 50N48 10E46 -0:43:04
Wolframs-Eschenbach 2
4 49N14 10E43 -0:42:52
Wolfratshausen 2
4 47N54 11E25 -0:45:40
Wolfsburg 2 1 52N25 10E47 -0:43:08
Wolfskehlen 2 1 49N51 8E30 -0:34:00
Wolfstein 2 6 49N35 7E36 -0:30:24
Wolgast 1 2 54N03 13E46 -0:55:04
Wolkenstein 1 2 50N39 13E04 -0:52:16
Wölkisch 1 2 51N13 13E21 -0:53:24
Wolkramshausen 1
2 51N25 10E44 -0:42:56
Wöllstein 2 6 49N49 7E58 -0:31:52
Wolmirsleben 1 2 51N57 11E29 -0:45:56
Wolmirstedt 1 2 52N15 11E37 -0:46:28
Wolnzach 2 4 48N36 11E37 -0:46:28
Wolterdingen 2 1 53N02 9E50 -0:39:20
Woltersdorf 1 2 52N24 12E22 -0:49:28
Woltersdorf 1 2 52N26 13E45 -0:55:00
Worbis 1 2 51N25 10E21 -0:41:24
Wörlitz 1 2 51N50 12E25 -0:49:40
Worms 2 6 49N38 8E22 -0:33:28
Worpswede 2 1 53N13 8E56 -0:35:44
Wörrstadt 2 6 49N50 8E07 -0:32:28
Wörth 2 4 49N48 9E09 -0:36:36
Worth 2 1 51N13 7E39 -0:30:36
Wörth am Rhein 2
6 49N03 8E16 -0:33:04
Wörth an der Donau 2
4 49N00 12E25 -0:49:40
Wredenhagen 1 2 53N17 12E31 -0:50:04
Wremen 2 1 53N39 8E30 -0:34:00
Wriezen 1 2 52N43 14E08 -0:56:32
Wulfen 2 1 51N43 7E00 -0:28:00
Wülfrath 2 1 51N17 7E02 -0:28:08
Wulfsen 2 1 53N18 10E08 -0:40:32
Wulfsode 2 1 53N04 10E13 -0:40:52
Wulften 2 1 51N40 10E10 -0:40:40
Wüllen 2 1 52N04 6E58 -0:27:52
Wünnenberg 2 1 51N31 8E42 -0:34:48
Wünschendorf 1 2 50N48 12E05 -0:48:20
Wünsdorf 1 2 52N10 13E28 -0:53:52
Wunstorf 2 1 52N25 9E26 -0:37:44
Wuppertal 2 1 51N16 7E11 -0:28:44
Wurgwitz 1 2 51N01 13E37 -0:54:28
Wurmannsquick 2 4 48N21 12E47 -0:51:08
Würselen 2 7 50N49 6E08 -0:24:32
Wurzbach 1 2 50N28 11E32 -0:46:08
Würzburg 2 4 49N48 9E56 -0:39:44
Wurzen 1 2 51N22 12E44 -0:50:56
Wust 1 2 52N33 12E07 -0:48:28
Wüsten 2 1 52N06 8E47 -0:35:08
Wüstensachsen 2 1 50N30 10E00 -0:40:00
Wusterhausen 1 2 52N54 12E28 -0:49:52
Wusterhusen 1 2 54N07 13E37 -0:54:28
Wustermark 1 2 52N33 12E56 -0:51:44
Wüstermarke 1 2 51N49 13E36 -0:54:24
Wusterwitz 1 2 52N22 12E18 -0:49:12
Wüsting 2 1 53N07 8E20 -0:33:20
Wustrow 1 2 54N05 11E34 -0:46:16
Wustrow 2 1 52N55 11E07 -0:44:28
Wyhl 2 3 48N09 7E39 -0:30:36
Wyk 2 1 54N42 8E34 -0:34:16
Xanten 2 7 51N39 6E26 -0:25:44
Zaberfeld 2 3 49N03 8E55 -0:35:40
Zahna 1 2 51N54 12E47 -0:51:08
Zahrensdorf 1 2 53N45 11E40 -0:46:40
Zangenstein 2 4 49N24 12E19 -0:49:16
Zapfendorf 2 4 50N01 10E56 -0:43:44
Zarrentin 1 2 53N35 10E55 -0:43:40
Zarten 2 3 47N58 7E56 -0:31:44
Zaschendorf 1 2 53N42 11E37 -0:46:28
Zaschwitz 1 2 51N10 13E02 -0:52:08
Zasenbeck 2 1 52N40 10E51 -0:43:24
Zauchwitz 1 2 52N12 13E02 -0:52:08
Zechlinerhütte 1
2 53N09 12E51 -0:51:24
Zeesen 1 2 52N16 13E38 -0:54:32
Zeestow 1 2 52N34 12E58 -0:51:52
Zehdenick 1 2 52N59 13E20 -0:53:20
Zehlendorf 1 2 52N47 13E23 -0:53:32
Zeil 2 4 50N01 10E35 -0:42:20
Zeithain 1 2 51N19 13E19 -0:53:16
Zeitlarn 2 4 49N05 12E06 -0:48:24
Zeitz 1 2 51N03 12E08 -0:48:32
Zell 2 3 47N42 7E51 -0:31:24
Zell 2 6 50N01 7E10 -0:28:40
Zella-Mehlis 1 2 50N39 10E39 -0:42:36
Zell am Harmersbach 2
3 48N21 8E04 -0:32:16
Zellingen 2 4 49N53 9E43 -0:38:52
Zemmer 2 6 49N53 6E41 -0:26:44
Zempin 1 2 54N04 13E57 -0:55:48
Zepernick 1 2 52N39 13E32 -0:54:08
Zerbst 1 2 51N58 12E04 -0:48:16
Zerf 2 6 49N36 6E41 -0:26:44
Zernsdorf 1 2 52N18 13E41 -0:54:44
Zetel 2 1 53N25 7E58 -0:31:52
Zeulenroda 1 2 50N39 11E58 -0:47:52
Zeuthen 1 2 52N20 13E37 -0:54:28
Zeven 2 1 53N18 9E16 -0:37:04
Zickhusen 1 2 53N45 11E25 -0:45:40
Ziegelroda 1 2 51N20 11E28 -0:45:52
Ziegendorf 1 2 53N18 11E49 -0:47:16
Ziegenhain 2 1 50N55 9E15 -0:37:00
Ziegenhals 1 2 52N21 13E40 -0:54:40
Ziegenrück 1 2 50N37 11E38 -0:46:32
Ziemetshausen 2 4 48N18 10E31 -0:42:04
Zierenberg 2 1 51N22 9E18 -0:37:12
Ziesar 1 2 52N16 12E17 -0:49:08
Ziesendorf 1 2 54N00 12E02 -0:48:08
Ziethen 1 2 53N53 13E40 -0:54:40
Zilly 1 2 51N56 10E49 -0:43:16
Ziltendorf 1 2 52N12 14E37 -0:58:28
Zingst 1 2 54N26 12E41 -0:50:44
Zinnowitz 1 2 54N04 13E55 -0:55:40
Zinnwald-Georgenfeld 1
2 50N44 13E46 -0:55:04
Zipsendorf 1 2 51N02 12E16 -0:49:04
Zirchow 1 2 53N53 14E08 -0:56:32
Zirndorf 2 4 49N26 10E58 -0:43:52
Zittau 1 2 50N54 14E47 -0:59:08
Zöblitz 1 2 50N39 13E14 -0:52:56
Zollhaus 2 1 50N17 8E04 -0:32:16
Zolling 2 4 48N27 11E46 -0:47:04
Zons 2 7 51N07 6E50 -0:27:20
Zörbig 1 2 51N37 12E07 -0:48:28
Zorge 2 1 51N38 10E38 -0:42:32
Zorneding 2 4 48N05 11E49 -0:47:16
Zöschen 1 2 51N21 12E07 -0:48:28
Zossen 1 2 52N13 13E27 -0:53:48
Zscherndorf 1 2 51N36 12E15 -0:49:00
Zschopau 1 2 50N44 13E04 -0:52:16
Zschorlau 1 2 50N34 12E38 -0:50:32
Zschornewitz 1 2 51N43 12E25 -0:49:40

GERMANY ALEMANIA ALLEMAGNE DEUTSCHLAND

Place	Zone	Lat	Long	Offset
Zschortau 1	2	51N28	12E21	-0:49:24
Zuchering 2	4	48N43	11E24	-0:45:36
Zudar 1	2	54N15	13E20	-0:53:20
Zühlsdorf 1	2	52N44	13E24	-0:53:36
Zülpich 2	7	50N41	6E39	-0:26:36
Zusmarshausen 2	4	48N24	10E35	-0:42:20
Züssow 1	2	53N59	13E32	-0:54:08
Zützen 1	2	51N57	13E38	-0:54:32
Zweibrücken 2	6	49N15	7E21	-0:29:24
Zweifall 2	7	50N43	6E15	-0:25:00
Zwenkau 1	2	51N13	12E19	-0:49:16
Zwesten 2	1	51N03	9E10	-0:36:40
Zwickau 1	2	50N44	12E29	-0:49:56
Zwiefalten 2	5	48N14	9E28	-0:37:52
Zwiefaltendorf 2	5	48N13	9E31	-0:38:04
Zwiesel 2	4	49N01	13E14	-0:52:56
Zwillbrock 2	1	52N04	6E42	-0:26:48
Zwingenberg 2	3	49N25	9E02	-0:36:08
Zwingenberg 2	1	49N43	8E37	-0:34:28
Zwischenahn 2	1	53N11	8E00	-0:32:00
Zwochau 1	2	51N28	12E16	-0:49:04
Zwönitz 1	2	50N38	12E49	-0:51:16
Zwota 1	2	50N21	12E25	-0:49:40

GHANA GOLD COAST GANA GHANA

Time Table
Before 1/Jan/1918 LMT
Begin Standard 0w00
1/Jan/1918 0:00 0:00

Date	Time	Offset
1/Sep/1936	0:00	-0:20
31/Dec/1936	0:00	0:00
1/Sep/1937	0:00	-0:20
31/Dec/1937	0:00	0:00
1/Sep/1938	0:00	-0:20
31/Dec/1938	0:00	0:00
1/Sep/1939	0:00	-0:20
31/Dec/1939	0:00	0:00
1/Sep/1940	0:00	-0:20
31/Dec/1940	0:00	0:00
1/Sep/1941	0:00	-0:20
31/Dec/1941	0:00	0:00
1/Sep/1942	0:00	-0:20
31/Dec/1942	0:00	0:00

Place	Lat	Long	Offset
Abodom	5N32	0w49	0:03:16
Aboso	5N22	1w56	0:07:44
Accra	5N33	0w13	0:00:52
Achiasi	5N52	1w00	0:04:00
Ada	5N47	0E24	-0:01:36
Aflao	6N05	1E08	-0:04:32
Agogo	6N47	1w04	0:04:16
Akkra → Accra	5N33	0w13	0:00:52
Akrofuom	6N07	1w39	0:06:36
Akumadan	7N24	1w57	0:07:48
Akuse	6N06	0E08	-0:00:32
Akwatia	6N04	0w49	0:03:16
Anloga	5N47	0E50	-0:03:20
Apam	5N17	0w44	0:02:56
Asafo	6N11	0w28	0:01:52
Asamankese	5N52	0w42	0:02:48
Asankrangwa	5N48	2w26	0:09:44
Ashanti	6N55	0E32	-0:02:08
Asikuma	5N35	1w00	0:04:00
Atebubu	7N45	0w59	0:03:56
Awaso	6N14	2w16	0:09:04
Axim	4N52	2w14	0:08:56
Bamboi	8N10	2w02	0:08:08
Bawku	11N05	0w14	0:00:56
Bechem	7N05	2w02	0:08:08
Begoro	6N23	0w23	0:01:32
Bekwai	6N27	1w35	0:06:20
Berekum	7N27	2w37	0:10:28
Bibiani	6N28	2w20	0:09:20
Bimbila	8N51	0E04	-0:00:16
Bogoso	5N34	2w01	0:08:04
Bole	9N02	2w29	0:09:56
Bolgatanga	10N46	0w52	0:03:28
Bompata	6N38	1w04	0:04:16
Cape Coast	5N05	1w15	0:05:00
Chereponi	10N09	0E17	-0:01:08
Daboya	9N32	1w23	0:05:32
Damongo	9N05	1w49	0:07:16
Doninga	10N37	1w26	0:05:44
Dormaa Ahenkro	7N17	2w53	0:11:32
Du	10N30	0w59	0:03:56
Duayaw Nkwanta	7N10	2w06	0:08:24
Dunkwa	5N58	1w46	0:07:04
Dunkwa	5N22	1w12	0:04:48
Dzodze	6N14	1E00	-0:04:00
Effiakuma	5N06	1w39	0:06:36
Efiduasi	6N51	1w24	0:05:36
Ejura	7N23	1w22	0:05:28
Elmina	5N05	1w21	0:05:24
Enchi	5N49	2w49	0:11:16
Esiama	4N56	2w21	0:09:24
Fian	10N23	2w29	0:09:56
Foso	5N42	1w17	0:05:08
Funsi	10N17	1w58	0:07:52
Ga	9N47	2w30	0:10:00
Gambaga	10N32	0w26	0:01:44
Garu	10N51	0w11	0:00:44
Gawso	6N48	2w31	0:10:04
Gushiago	9N55	0w12	0:00:48
Half Assini	5N03	2w53	0:11:32
Hamale	10N59	2w44	0:10:56
Han	10N41	2w27	0:09:48
Ho	6N35	0E30	-0:02:00
Hohoe	7N09	0E28	-0:01:52
Huni Valley	5N28	1w55	0:07:40
Jasikan	7N24	0E28	-0:01:52
Jinjini	7N26	2w39	0:10:36
Kade	6N05	0w50	0:03:20
Karni	10N40	2w37	0:10:28
Kedjebi	8N12	0E25	-0:01:40
Keta	5N55	1E00	-0:04:00
Kete Krachi	7N46	0w03	0:00:12
Kibi	6N10	0w33	0:02:12
Kintampo	8N03	1w43	0:06:52
Koforidua	6N03	0w17	0:01:08
Komenda	5N03	1w29	0:05:56
Konongo	6N37	1w11	0:04:44
Kpandae	8N28	0w01	0:00:04
Kpandu	7N00	0E18	-0:01:12
Kpong	6N09	0E04	-0:00:16
Kumasi	6N41	1w35	0:06:20
Kwesimintim	4N54	1w47	0:07:08
Larabanga	9N13	1w51	0:07:24
Larteh Aheneasi	5N56	0E04	-0:00:16
Lawra	10N39	2w52	0:11:28
Maluwe	8N40	2w17	0:09:08
Mampong	7N04	1w24	0:05:36
Maso	7N14	2w53	0:11:32
Mim	6N54	2w34	0:10:16
Morno	8N41	1w31	0:06:04
Mpraeso	6N35	0w44	0:02:56
Nandom	10N51	2w45	0:11:00
Nasia	10N09	0w48	0:03:12
Navrongo	10N54	1w06	0:04:24
Nkawkaw	6N33	0w47	0:03:08
Nsaba	5N39	0w45	0:03:00
Nsawam	5N50	0w20	0:01:20
Nsuta	5N17	1w58	0:07:52
Nyakrom	5N37	0w48	0:03:12
Obuasi	6N14	1w39	0:06:36
Oda	5N55	0w59	0:03:56
Paga	10N58	1w06	0:04:24
Pong Tamale	9N41	0w49	0:03:16
Prampram	5N42	0E07	-0:00:28
Prang	7N59	0w53	0:03:32
Prestea	5N27	2w08	0:08:32
Pwalagu	10N35	0w50	0:03:20
Salaga	8N33	0w31	0:02:04
Saltpond	5N12	1w04	0:04:16
Samreboi	5N36	2w34	0:10:16
Savelugu	9N37	0w49	0:03:16
Sawla	9N17	2w25	0:09:40
Sekondi-Takoradi	4N59	1w43	0:06:52
Sekpiegu	9N33	0w02	0:00:08
Sogakofe	6N00	0E36	-0:02:24
Suhum	6N05	0w27	0:01:48
Sunyani	7N20	2w20	0:09:20
Swedru	5N32	0w43	0:02:52
Tafo	6N13	0w22	0:01:28
Takoradi → Sekondi-Takoradi	4N59	1w43	0:06:52
Tale	9N26	1w07	0:04:28
Tamale	9N25	0w50	0:03:20
Tamale Port → Yapei	9N10	1w10	0:04:40
Tappo	10N12	2w38	0:10:32
Tarkwa	5N19	1w59	0:07:56
Techiman	7N35	1w56	0:07:44
Techimentia	7N11	2w02	0:08:08
Tefle	5N59	0E35	-0:02:20
Tema	5N38	0E01	-0:00:04
Tepa	7N00	2w10	0:08:40
Teshi	5N35	0w05	0:00:20
Tumu	10N52	1w59	0:07:56
Wa	10N04	2w29	0:09:56
Walembele	10N30	1w58	0:07:52
Walewale	10N21	0w48	0:03:12
Wenchi	7N42	2w07	0:08:28
Wiasi	10N21	1w20	0:05:20
Wiawso	6N12	2w29	0:09:56
Winneba	5N25	0w36	0:02:24
Yala	10N07	1w52	0:07:28
Yapei (Tamale Port)	9N10	1w10	0:04:40
Yeji	8N13	0w39	0:02:36
Yendi	9N26	0w01	0:00:04
Zabzugu	9N17	0E22	-0:01:28
Zebila	10N56	0w29	0:01:56
Zuarungu	10N47	0w48	0:03:12

GIBRALTAR

GIBRALTAR

Time Table

Date	Time	Offset
Before 1/Jan/1880	LMT	
Begin Standard		0w00
1/Jan/1880	0:00	0:00
21/May/1916	2:00	-1:00
1/Oct/1916	3:00	0:00
8/Apr/1917	2:00	-1:00
17/Sep/1917	3:00	0:00
24/Mar/1918	2:00	-1:00
30/Sep/1918	3:00	0:00
30/Mar/1919	2:00	-1:00
29/Sep/1919	3:00	0:00
28/Mar/1920	2:00	-1:00
25/Oct/1920	3:00	0:00
3/Apr/1921	2:00	-1:00
3/Oct/1921	3:00	0:00
26/Mar/1922	2:00	-1:00
8/Oct/1922	3:00	0:00
22/Apr/1923	2:00	-1:00
16/Sep/1923	3:00	0:00
13/Apr/1924	2:00	-1:00
21/Sep/1924	3:00	0:00
19/Apr/1925	2:00	-1:00
4/Oct/1925	3:00	0:00
18/Apr/1926	2:00	-1:00
3/Oct/1926	3:00	0:00
10/Apr/1927	2:00	-1:00
2/Oct/1927	3:00	0:00
22/Apr/1928	2:00	-1:00
7/Oct/1928	3:00	0:00
21/Apr/1929	2:00	-1:00
6/Oct/1929	3:00	0:00
13/Apr/1930	2:00	-1:00
5/Oct/1930	3:00	0:00
19/Apr/1931	2:00	-1:00
4/Oct/1931	3:00	0:00
17/Apr/1932	2:00	-1:00
2/Oct/1932	3:00	0:00
9/Apr/1933	2:00	-1:00
8/Oct/1933	3:00	0:00
22/Apr/1934	2:00	-1:00
7/Oct/1934	3:00	0:00
14/Apr/1935	2:00	-1:00
6/Oct/1935	3:00	0:00
19/Apr/1936	2:00	-1:00
4/Oct/1936	3:00	0:00
18/Apr/1937	2:00	-1:00
3/Oct/1937	3:00	0:00
10/Apr/1938	2:00	-1:00
2/Oct/1938	3:00	0:00
16/Apr/1939	2:00	-1:00
19/Nov/1939	3:00	0:00
25/Feb/1940	2:00	-1:00
4/May/1941	2:00	-2:00
10/Aug/1941	3:00	-1:00
5/Apr/1942	2:00	-2:00
9/Aug/1942	3:00	-1:00
4/Apr/1943	2:00	-2:00
15/Aug/1943	3:00	-1:00
2/Apr/1944	2:00	-2:00
17/Sep/1944	3:00	-1:00
2/Apr/1945	2:00	-2:00
15/Jul/1945	3:00	-1:00
7/Oct/1945	3:00	0:00
14/Apr/1946	2:00	-1:00
6/Oct/1946	3:00	0:00
16/Mar/1947	2:00	-1:00
13/Apr/1947	2:00	-2:00
10/Aug/1947	3:00	-1:00
2/Nov/1947	3:00	0:00
14/Mar/1948	2:00	-1:00
31/Oct/1948	3:00	0:00
3/Apr/1949	2:00	-1:00
30/Oct/1949	3:00	0:00
16/Apr/1950	2:00	-1:00
22/Oct/1950	3:00	0:00
15/Apr/1951	2:00	-1:00
21/Oct/1951	3:00	0:00
20/Apr/1952	2:00	-1:00
26/Oct/1952	3:00	0:00
19/Apr/1953	2:00	-1:00
4/Oct/1953	3:00	0:00
11/Apr/1954	2:00	-1:00
3/Oct/1954	3:00	0:00
17/Apr/1955	2:00	-1:00
2/Oct/1955	3:00	0:00
22/Apr/1956	2:00	-1:00
7/Oct/1956	2:00	0:00
Begin Standard		15E00
14/Apr/1957	2:00	-1:00
28/Mar/1982	2:00	-2:00
26/Sep/1982	3:00	-1:00
27/Mar/1983	2:00	-2:00
25/Sep/1983	3:00	-1:00
25/Mar/1984	2:00	-2:00
30/Sep/1984	3:00	-1:00
31/Mar/1985	2:00	-2:00
29/Sep/1985	3:00	-1:00
30/Mar/1986	2:00	-2:00
28/Sep/1986	3:00	-1:00
29/Mar/1987	2:00	-2:00
27/Sep/1987	3:00	-1:00
27/Mar/1988	2:00	-2:00
25/Sep/1988	3:00	-1:00
26/Mar/1989	2:00	-2:00
24/Sep/1989	3:00	-1:00
25/Mar/1990	2:00	-2:00
30/Sep/1990	3:00	-1:00
31/Mar/1991	2:00	-2:00
29/Sep/1991	3:00	-1:00
29/Mar/1992	2:00	-2:00
27/Sep/1992	3:00	-1:00
28/Mar/1993	2:00	-2:00
26/Sep/1993	3:00	-1:00
27/Mar/1994	2:00	-2:00
25/Sep/1994	3:00	-1:00
26/Mar/1995	2:00	-2:00
24/Sep/1995	3:00	-1:00
31/Mar/1996	2:00	-2:00
29/Sep/1996	3:00	-1:00
30/Mar/1997	2:00	-2:00
28/Sep/1997	3:00	-1:00
29/Mar/1998	2:00	-2:00
27/Sep/1998	3:00	-1:00
28/Mar/1999	2:00	-2:00
26/Sep/1999	3:00	-1:00
26/Mar/2000	2:00	-2:00
24/Sep/2000	3:00	-1:00

Place	Latitude	Longitude	LMT offset
Gibraltar	36N08	5W21	0:21:24

ELLÁS GRIECHENLAND GRÈCE GRECIA GREECE

Time Table

Date	Time	Offset
Before 14/Sep/1895	LMT	
Begin Standard		23E43
14/Sep/1895	0:00	-1:35
Begin Standard		30E00
28/Jul/1916	0:01	-2:00
7/Jul/1932	0:00	-3:00
1/Sep/1932	0:00	-2:00
7/Apr/1941	0:00	-3:00
Begin Standard		15E00
30/Apr/1941	0:00	-2:00
2/Nov/1942	3:00	-1:00
30/Mar/1943	0:00	-2:00
4/Oct/1943	0:00	-1:00
Begin Standard		30E00
4/Apr/1944	0:00	-2:00
1/Jul/1952	0:00	-3:00
2/Nov/1952	0:00	-2:00
12/Apr/1975	0:00	-3:00
26/Nov/1975	1:00	-2:00
11/Apr/1976	2:00	-3:00
10/Oct/1976	3:00	-2:00
3/Apr/1977	2:00	-3:00
26/Sep/1977	3:00	-2:00
2/Apr/1978	2:00	-3:00
24/Sep/1978	4:00	-2:00
1/Apr/1979	9:00	-3:00
29/Sep/1979	1:00	-2:00
6/Apr/1980	0:00	-3:00
28/Sep/1980	0:00	-2:00
29/Mar/1981	2:00	-3:00
27/Sep/1981	3:00	-2:00
28/Mar/1982	2:00	-3:00
26/Sep/1982	3:00	-2:00
27/Mar/1983	2:00	-3:00
25/Sep/1983	3:00	-2:00
25/Mar/1984	2:00	-3:00
30/Sep/1984	3:00	-2:00
31/Mar/1985	2:00	-3:00
29/Sep/1985	3:00	-2:00
30/Mar/1986	2:00	-3:00
28/Sep/1986	3:00	-2:00
29/Mar/1987	2:00	-3:00
27/Sep/1987	3:00	-2:00
27/Mar/1988	2:00	-3:00
25/Sep/1988	3:00	-2:00
26/Mar/1989	2:00	-3:00
24/Sep/1989	3:00	-2:00
25/Mar/1990	2:00	-3:00
30/Sep/1990	3:00	-2:00
31/Mar/1991	2:00	-3:00
29/Sep/1991	3:00	-2:00
29/Mar/1992	2:00	-3:00
27/Sep/1992	3:00	-2:00
28/Mar/1993	2:00	-3:00
26/Sep/1993	3:00	-2:00
27/Mar/1994	2:00	-3:00
25/Sep/1994	3:00	-2:00
26/Mar/1995	2:00	-3:00
24/Sep/1995	3:00	-2:00
31/Mar/1996	2:00	-3:00
29/Sep/1996	3:00	-2:00
30/Mar/1997	2:00	-3:00
28/Sep/1997	3:00	-2:00
29/Mar/1998	2:00	-3:00
27/Sep/1998	3:00	-2:00
28/Mar/1999	2:00	-3:00
26/Sep/1999	3:00	-2:00
26/Mar/2000	2:00	-3:00
24/Sep/2000	3:00	-2:00

Place	Latitude	Longitude	LMT offset
Aegina (Aíyina) Island	37N46	23E26	-1:33:44
Afándou	36N17	28E10	-1:52:40
Agrínion	38N37	21E24	-1:25:36
Aiándion	37N55	23E28	-1:33:52
Aígina	37N44	23E27	-1:33:48
Aígion	38N15	22E05	-1:28:20
Aitolikón	38N27	21E22	-1:25:28
Aiyáleo	37N59	23E41	-1:34:44
Aíyina	37N44	23E27	-1:33:48
Aíyina (Aegina) Island	37N46	23E26	-1:33:44
Aiyínion	40N30	22E33	-1:30:12
Aíyion	38N15	22E05	-1:28:20
Akharnaí	38N05	23E44	-1:34:56
Alexandroúpolis	40N50	25E52	-1:43:28
Alistráti	41N04	23E57	-1:35:48
Alivérion	38N24	24E02	-1:36:08
Almirós	39N11	22E46	-1:31:04
Alónnisos	39N08	23E50	-1:35:20
Amaliás	37N49	21E23	-1:25:32
Amaroúsion	38N03	23E49	-1:35:16
Ambelákia	37N57	23E32	-1:34:08
Amfíklia	38N38	22E35	-1:30:20
Amfilokhía	38N51	21E10	-1:24:40
Ámfissa	38N31	22E24	-1:29:36
Amorgós	36N50	25E54	-1:43:36
Amorgós Island	36N50	25E59	-1:43:56
Ámphissa	38N31	22E24	-1:29:36
Anáfi Island	36N21	25E50	-1:43:20
Andikíthira Island	35N52	23E18	-1:33:12
Andimákhia	36N48	27E07	-1:48:28
Ándissa	39N14	25E59	-1:43:56
Ándros	37N50	24E57	-1:39:48
Áno Liósia	38N05	23E42	-1:34:48
Apolakkiá	36N06	27E50	-1:51:20
Arákhova	38N29	22E35	-1:30:20
Arápis	37N59	23E32	-1:34:08
Áratos	41N05	25E33	-1:42:12
Árgos	37N39	22E44	-1:30:56
Árgos Orestikón	40N28	21E16	-1:25:04
Argostólion	38N10	20E30	-1:22:00
Aridhaía	40N59	22E03	-1:28:12
Arkansa	35N28	27E08	-1:48:32
Arkhangélos	36N12	28E08	-1:52:32
Armenistís	37N36	26E08	-1:44:32
Arnaía	40N29	23E35	-1:34:20
Árnissa	40N48	21E50	-1:27:20
Árta	39N09	20E59	-1:23:56
Artemón	36N59	24E43	-1:38:52
Aryiroúpolis	37N54	23E45	-1:35:00
Asprópirgos	38N04	23E35	-1:34:20
Astakós	38N32	21E05	-1:24:20
Astipálaia	36N30	26E30	-1:46:00
Astipálaia Island	36N35	26E25	-1:45:40
Atalándi	38N39	23E00	-1:32:00
Atenas → Athínai	37N58	23E43	-1:34:52
Athen → Athínai	37N58	23E43	-1:34:52
Athènes → Athínai	37N58	23E43	-1:34:52
Athens → Athínai	37N58	23E43	-1:34:52
Athínai (Athens)	37N58	23E43	-1:34:52
Ayía Marína	37N09	26E52	-1:47:28
Ayía Paraskeví	39N15	26E16	-1:45:04
Ayiássos	39N05	26E23	-1:45:32
Ayía Varvára	37N59	23E39	-1:34:36
Áyioi Anáryiroi	38N02	23E43	-1:34:52
Áyios Dhimítrios	37N56	23E44	-1:34:56
Áyios Ioánnis Réndis	37N58	23E40	-1:34:40
Áyios Kírikos	37N37	26E14	-1:44:56
Áyios Nikólaos	35N11	25E42	-1:42:48
Candía → Iráklion	35N20	25E09	-1:40:36
Canea → Khaniá	35N31	24E02	-1:36:08
Ceos (Kea) Island	37N34	24E22	-1:37:28
Cefalonia (Kefallinía) Island	38N15	20E35	-1:22:20
Chalcis → Khalkís	38N28	23E36	-1:34:24
Chios (Khíos) Island	38N22	26E00	-1:44:00
Chios → Khíos	38N22	26E08	-1:44:32
Corfu (Kérkira) Island	39N40	19E42	-1:18:48
Corfu → Kérkira	39N36	19E56	-1:19:44
Corinth → Kórinthos	37N56	22E56	-1:31:44
Crete (Kríti) Island	35N29	24E42	-1:38:48
Cyclades (Kikládhes) Island	37N30	25E00	-1:40:00
Cythera (Kíthira) Island	36N20	22E58	-1:31:52
Delos (Dhílos) Island	37N26	25E16	-1:41:04
Dháfni	37N48	22E01	-1:28:04
Dheskáti	39N55	21E49	-1:27:16
Dhiavolítsion	37N18	21E58	-1:27:52
Dhidhimótikhon	41N21	26E30	-1:46:00
Dhílos (Delos) Island	37N26	25E16	-1:41:04
Dhimitsána	37N37	22E03	-1:28:12
Dhiónisos	38N06	23E53	-1:35:32
Dhodhekánisos (Dodecanese) Islands	36N30	27E00	-1:48:00
Áyios Evstrátios Island	39N30	25E00	-1:40:00
Dhoxáton	41N05	24E14	-1:36:56
Dhrapetsóna	37N57	23E37	-1:34:28
Dráma	41N09	24E08	-1:36:32
Drosiá	38N07	23E52	-1:35:28
Edessa → Édhessa	40N48	22E03	-1:28:12
Édhessa	40N48	22E03	-1:28:12
Ekáli	38N07	23E50	-1:35:20
Ekhínos	41N17	24E59	-1:39:56
Elaía	39N35	20E20	-1:21:20
Elassón	39N54	22E11	-1:28:44
Eleusis → Elevsís	38N02	23E32	-1:34:08
Elevsís	38N02	23E32	-1:34:08
Elevtheroúpolis	40N55	24E16	-1:37:04
Ellinikón	37N53	23E44	-1:34:56
Epanomí	40N26	22E56	-1:31:44
Eráklion	35N20	25E09	-1:40:36
Eressós	39N18	25E51	-1:43:24
Erétria	38N24	23E48	-1:35:12
Erithraí	38N13	23E19	-1:33:16
Ermoúpolis	37N26	24E56	-1:39:44
Evstrátios Island	39N30	25E00	-1:40:00
Euboea (Évvoia) Island	38N34	23E50	-1:35:20
Évvoia (Euboea) Island	38N34	23E50	-1:35:20
Fársala	39N18	22E23	-1:29:32
Férrai	40N54	26E10	-1:44:40
Filiatrá	37N10	21E35	-1:26:20
Fiskárdhon	38N27	20E35	-1:22:20
Flórina	40N47	21E24	-1:25:36
Galátsion	38N01	23E45	-1:35:00
Galaxídhion	38N22	22E23	-1:29:32
Gargaliánoi	37N04	21E39	-1:26:36
Gastoúni	37N51	21E16	-1:25:04
Gávrion	37N52	24E46	-1:39:04
Glífa	38N57	22E58	-1:31:52
Glifádha	37N52	23E45	-1:35:00
Gouménissa	40N57	22E27	-1:29:48
Grevená	40N05	21E25	-1:25:40
Hydra (Ídhra) Island	37N20	23E32	-1:34:08
Ídhra	37N20	23E29	-1:33:56
Ierápetra	35N00	25E45	-1:43:00
Ierisós	40N24	23E52	-1:35:28
Igoumenítsa	39N30	20E16	-1:21:04
Ikaría Island	37N46	26E20	-1:45:20
Ilioúpolis	37N56	23E45	-1:35:00
Imittós	37N57	23E45	-1:35:00
Ioánnina	39N40	20E50	-1:23:20
Ionian (Iónioi Nísoi) Islands	38N30	20E30	-1:22:00
Íos	36N44	25E17	-1:41:08
Iráklion	35N20	25E09	-1:40:36

GREECE GRECIA GRÈCE GRIECHENLAND ELLÁS

Place	Lat.	Long.	Time
Iráklion	38N04	23E46	-1:35:04
Istiaía	38N57	23E09	-1:32:36
Itéa	38N26	22E24	-1:29:36
Itháki	38N23	20E42	-1:22:48
Itháki (Ithaca) Island	38N24	20E42	-1:22:48
Janina → Ioánnina	39N40	20E50	-1:23:20
Kaisarianí	37N58	23E47	-1:35:08
Kalabáka	39N42	21E43	-1:26:52
Kalámai	37N04	22E07	-1:28:28
Kalamákion	37N55	23E43	-1:34:52
Kalamariá	40N35	22E58	-1:31:52
Kalampáka	39N42	21E39	-1:26:36
Kalavárdha	36N20	27E57	-1:51:48
Kalávrita	38N01	22E06	-1:28:24
Kaleme	37N04	22E07	-1:28:28
Kálimnos	36N57	26E59	-1:47:56
Kallithéa	37N57	23E42	-1:34:48
Kalpáki	39N55	20E20	-1:21:20
Karavás	36N21	22E57	-1:31:48
Kardhámaina	36N47	27E09	-1:48:36
Kardhámila	38N32	26E05	-1:44:20
Kardhítsa	39N21	21E55	-1:27:40
Kariaí	40N16	24E15	-1:37:00
Káristos	38N00	24E24	-1:37:36
Karlovásion	37N48	26E44	-1:46:56
Kárpathos	35N30	27E14	-1:48:56
Kárpathos Island	35N40	27E10	-1:48:40
Karpenísion	38N55	21E40	-1:26:40
Karyaí	40N16	24E15	-1:37:00
Kásos Island	35N22	26E56	-1:47:44
Kastanéai	41N38	26E28	-1:45:52
Kastellorizo	36N07	29E35	-1:58:20
Kastoría	40N31	21E15	-1:25:00
Kastron	39N52	25E04	-1:40:16
Kateríni	40N16	22E30	-1:30:00
Káto Akhaïa	38N09	21E32	-1:26:08
Katoúna	38N47	21E07	-1:24:28
Kattaviá	35N57	27E46	-1:51:04
Kavālla	40N56	24E25	-1:37:40
Kéa	37N38	24E21	-1:37:24
Kéa (Ceos) Island	37N34	24E22	-1:37:28
Kédhron	39N13	22E03	-1:28:12
Kefallinía (Cefalonia) Island	38N15	20E35	-1:22:20
Kéfalos	36N45	27E00	-1:48:00
Keratéa	37N48	23E59	-1:35:56
Keratsínion	37N58	23E37	-1:34:28
Kerion	37N40	20E48	-1:23:12
Kérkira (Corfu)	39N36	19E56	-1:19:44
Kérkira (Corfu) Island	39N40	19E42	-1:18:48
Khaïdhárion	37N33	22E53	-1:31:32
Khalándrion	38N01	23E48	-1:35:12
Khalkís	38N28	23E36	-1:34:24
Khaniá	35N31	24E02	-1:36:08
Khíos	38N22	26E08	-1:44:32
Khíos (Chios) Island	38N22	26E00	-1:44:00
Kholargós	38N00	23E48	-1:35:12
Khóra	37N04	21E43	-1:26:52
Khóra Sfakíon	35N12	24E09	-1:36:36
Khrisoúpolis	40N58	24E42	-1:38:48
Khryson	38N28	22E27	-1:29:48
Kifisiá	38N04	23E48	-1:35:12
Kilkís	41N00	22E53	-1:31:32
Killíni	37N55	21E09	-1:24:36
Kími	38N37	24E06	-1:36:24
Kiparissía	37N14	21E40	-1:26:40
Kissamos	35N30	23E38	-1:34:32
Kíthira	36N09	23E00	-1:32:00
Kíthira (Cythera) Island	36N20	22E58	-1:31:52
Kíthnos	37N26	24E26	-1:37:44
Kíthnos Island	37N25	24E28	-1:37:52
Komotiní	41N08	25E25	-1:41:40
Kónitsa	40N02	20E45	-1:23:00
Koos	36N53	27E18	-1:49:12
Koridhallós	37N59	23E39	-1:34:36
Kórinthos (Corinth)	37N56	22E56	-1:31:44
Koróni	36N48	21E56	-1:27:44
Koropíon	37N54	23E53	-1:35:32
Kos	36N53	27E18	-1:49:12
Kozáni	40N18	21E47	-1:27:08
Kranídhion	37N22	23E10	-1:32:40
Kría Vrísi	40N41	22E18	-1:29:12
Kríti (Crete) Island	35N29	24E42	-1:38:48
Kikládhes (Cyclades) Islands	37N30	25E00	-1:40:00
Kos Island	36N50	27E10	-1:48:40
Ládhi	41N27	26E17	-1:45:08
Lamía	38N54	22E26	-1:29:44
Langadhás	40N45	23E04	-1:32:16
Langádhia	37N41	22E02	-1:28:08
Lárisa	39N38	22E25	-1:29:40
Lávara	41N16	26E22	-1:45:28
Lávrion	37N44	24E04	-1:36:16
Lekhainá	37N56	21E17	-1:25:08
Lemnos (Límnos) Island	39N54	25E21	-1:41:24
Leondárion	37N59	23E51	-1:35:24
Leonídhion	37N10	22E52	-1:31:28
Lepanto → Návpaktos	38N23	21E50	-1:27:20
Lesbos (Lésvos) Island	39N10	26E20	-1:45:20
Levádhia	38N25	22E54	-1:31:36
Levkás	38N50	20E41	-1:22:44
Levkás (Leucas) Island	38N39	20E27	-1:21:48
Levkímmi	39N25	20E04	-1:20:16
Liapádhes	39N40	19E44	-1:18:56
Linariá	37N24	24E57	-1:39:48
Líndhos	36N06	28E04	-1:52:16
Litókhoron	40N06	22E30	-1:30:00
Livanátai	38N42	23E03	-1:32:12
Lixoúrion	38N12	20E26	-1:21:44
Loutrá Aidhipsoú	38N51	23E02	-1:32:08
Loutrópirgos	38N02	23E28	-1:33:52
Magoúla	38N04	23E32	-1:34:08
Mándra	38N04	23E30	-1:34:00
Marathón	38N10	23E58	-1:35:52
Markópoulon	37N54	23E54	-1:35:36
Megálon Khoríon	36N27	27E21	-1:49:24
Megalópolis	37N24	22E08	-1:28:32
Mégara	38N01	23E21	-1:33:24
Meligalás	37N13	21E59	-1:27:56
Melíssia	38N03	23E50	-1:35:20
Melívoia	39N45	22E48	-1:31:12
Mesolóngion	38N21	21E17	-1:25:08
Messíni	37N04	22E00	-1:28:00
Mestá	38N15	25E55	-1:43:40
Methóni	36N50	21E43	-1:26:52
Métsovon	39N46	21E11	-1:24:44
Míkonos	37N26	25E20	-1:41:20
Míkonos Island	37N29	25E25	-1:41:40
Melos (Mílos) Island	36N41	24E15	-1:37:00
Miléai	39N20	23E09	-1:32:36
Mílos	36N45	24E27	-1:37:48
Mírina	39N52	25E04	-1:40:16
Missolonghi → Mesolóngion	38N21	21E17	-1:25:08
Míthimna	39N22	26E10	-1:44:40
Mitilíni	39N06	26E32	-1:46:08
Moláoi	36N48	22E52	-1:31:28
Monemvasía	36N41	23E03	-1:32:12
Moskháton	37N57	23E41	-1:34:44
Moúdhros	39N52	25E16	-1:41:04
Mouzákion	39N26	21E40	-1:26:40
Mytilene → Mitilíni	39N06	26E32	-1:46:08
Náousa	40N37	22E05	-1:28:20
Náfpaktos	38N23	21E50	-1:27:20
Navarino → Pílos	36N55	21E43	-1:26:52
Návpaktos	38N23	21E50	-1:27:20
Návplion	37N34	22E48	-1:31:12
Náxos	37N06	25E23	-1:41:32
Náxos Island	37N02	25E35	-1:42:20
Néa Erithraía	38N05	23E49	-1:35:16
Néa Filadhélfia	38N02	23E44	-1:34:56
Néa Ionía	38N02	23E45	-1:35:00
Néa Khalkidhón	38N02	23E43	-1:34:52
Néa Liósia	38N02	23E42	-1:34:48
Néa Pendéli	38N04	23E52	-1:35:28
Néa Péramos	38N00	23E26	-1:33:44
Neápolis	36N30	23E04	-1:32:16
Neápolis	35N15	25E37	-1:42:28
Néa Psará	38N23	23E48	-1:35:12
Néa Smírni	37N57	23E43	-1:34:52
Néon Fáliron	37N57	23E40	-1:34:40
Néon Karlovásion	37N48	26E44	-1:46:56
Néon Psikhikón	38N00	23E47	-1:35:08
Nerákion	38N01	23E27	-1:33:48
Nigríta	40N55	23E30	-1:34:00
Níkaia	37N58	23E39	-1:34:36
Northern Sporadhes Islands	39N20	24E00	-1:36:00
Ólimbos	35N44	27E11	-1:48:44
Orestiás	41N30	26E31	-1:46:04
Palanía	37N57	23E51	-1:35:24
Pákhi	37N59	23E22	-1:33:28
Palaiá Epídhavros	37N38	23E09	-1:32:36
Palaiá Psará	38N46	25E36	-1:42:24
Palaiokhóra	35N14	23E41	-1:34:44
Palaión Fáliron	37N55	23E41	-1:34:44
Palamás	39N28	22E05	-1:28:20
Pallíni	38N00	23E53	-1:35:32
Paloúkia	37N58	23E31	-1:34:04
Panayía	39N56	25E20	-1:41:20
Pánormos	37N38	25E02	-1:40:08
Paralía Asproпírgos	38N02	23E35	-1:34:20
Paramithiá	39N28	20E30	-1:22:00
Párga	39N17	20E23	-1:21:32
Páros	37N04	25E08	-1:40:32
Páros Island	37N08	25E12	-1:40:48
Pátmos Island	37N20	26E33	-1:46:12
Pátrai	38N15	21E44	-1:26:56
Patras → Pátrai	38N15	21E44	-1:26:56
Paxoí Island	39N12	20E12	-1:20:48
Pendéli	38N03	23E52	-1:35:28
Péplos	40N58	26E16	-1:45:04
Pérama	37N58	23E34	-1:34:16
Peristérion	38N01	23E42	-1:34:48
Pessáni	41N05	26E06	-1:44:24
Petroúpolis	38N03	23E41	-1:34:44
Pigádhia	35N31	27E12	-1:48:48
Pílos	36N55	21E43	-1:26:52
Piraeus → Piraiévs	37N57	23E38	-1:34:32
Piraiévs (Piraeus)	37N57	23E38	-1:34:32
Pírgos	37N41	21E28	-1:25:52
Plomárion	38N59	26E22	-1:45:28
Pogonianí	40N00	20E25	-1:21:40
Polígiros	40N23	23E27	-1:33:48
Políkastron	41N00	22E34	-1:30:16
Polikhnítos	39N05	26E11	-1:44:44
Políyiros	40N23	23E27	-1:33:48
Porto Lago	37N09	26E51	-1:47:24
Préveza	38N57	20E44	-1:22:56
Prosotsáni	41N10	23E59	-1:35:56
Psakhná	38N35	23E38	-1:34:32
Psará Island	38N35	25E37	-1:42:28
Psárion	37N20	21E51	-1:27:24
Pserimos	36N56	27E09	-1:48:36
Psikhikón	38N01	23E46	-1:35:04
Ptolemaís	40N31	21E41	-1:26:44
Pylos → Pílos	36N55	21E43	-1:26:52
Pyrgos → Pírgos	37N41	21E28	-1:25:52
Réthimnon	35N22	24E29	-1:37:56
Rhodes (Ródhos) Island	36N10	28E00	-1:52:00
Rhodes → Ródhos	36N26	28E13	-1:52:52
Ródhos (Rhodes)	36N26	28E13	-1:52:52
Salamís	37N59	23E28	-1:33:52
Salamís Island	37N54	23E26	-1:33:44
Salonika → Thessaloníki	40N38	22E56	-1:31:44
Sámos	37N45	27E00	-1:48:00
Sámos Island	37N48	26E44	-1:46:56
Samothráki	40N28	25E31	-1:42:04
Samothráki (Samothrace) Island	40N30	25E32	-1:42:08
Sápai	41N02	25E41	-1:42:44
Selínia	37N56	23E32	-1:34:08
Sérifos	37N09	24E31	-1:38:04
Sérrai	41N05	23E32	-1:34:08
Sérvia	40N11	22E00	-1:28:00
Siátista	40N16	21E33	-1:26:12
Sidhirókastron	41N14	23E22	-1:33:28
Sífnos (Siphnos) Island	36N59	24E40	-1:38:40
Sikéai	36N46	22E56	-1:31:44
Sikiá	40N02	23E56	-1:35:44
Síkinos	25N07	26E43	-1:46:52
Sími	36N36	27E50	-1:51:20
Sími Island	36N35	27E52	-1:51:28
Síros → Ermoúpolis	37N26	24E56	-1:39:44
Síros Island	37N26	24E54	-1:39:36
Sithoniá	35N12	26E07	-1:44:28
Skála Oropoú	38N20	23E46	-1:35:04
Skaramagás	38N01	23E36	-1:34:24
Skíathos	39N10	23E29	-1:33:56
Skíathos Island	39N10	23E29	-1:33:56
Skíros	38N53	24E33	-1:38:12
Skíros Island	38N53	24E32	-1:38:08
Skópelos	39N07	23E43	-1:34:52
Skópelos Island	39N10	23E40	-1:34:40
Sofádhes	39N20	22E06	-1:28:24
Sokhós	40N49	23E21	-1:33:24
Souflíón	41N12	26E18	-1:45:12
Sparta → Spárti	37N05	22E27	-1:29:48
Spárti (Sparta)	37N05	22E27	-1:29:48
Spáta	38N00	21E31	-1:26:04
Stenón	37N58	22E20	-1:29:20
Stilís	38N55	22E36	-1:30:24
Táyros	37N58	23E42	-1:34:48
Thásos	40N47	24E42	-1:38:48
Thásos Island	40N41	24E47	-1:39:08
Theólogos	40N39	24E41	-1:38:44
Thesprotikón	39N15	20E47	-1:23:08
Thessaloníki (Salonika)	40N38	22E56	-1:31:44
Thessalonique → Thessaloníki	40N38	22E56	-1:31:44
Thíra	36N25	25E26	-1:41:44
Thívai (Thebes)	38N21	23E19	-1:33:16
Tílos Island	36N25	27E25	-1:49:40
Timbákion	35N04	24E46	-1:39:04
Tínos	37N32	25E10	-1:40:40
Tínos Island	37N38	25E10	-1:40:40
Tírnavos	39N45	22E17	-1:29:08
Triánda	36N24	28E10	-1:52:40
Tríkala	39N34	21E46	-1:27:04
Trípolis	37N31	22E21	-1:29:24
Vasiliká	40N28	23E08	-1:32:32
Vathí	37N45	26E59	-1:47:56
Velestínon	39N23	22E45	-1:31:00
Véroia	40N31	22E12	-1:28:48
Víron	37N57	23E45	-1:35:00
Volissós	38N29	25E58	-1:43:52
Vólos	39N21	22E56	-1:31:44
Vrilíssia	38N02	23E50	-1:35:20
Vrondádhes	38N24	26E08	-1:44:32
Xánthi	41N08	24E53	-1:39:32
Xilókastron	38N05	22E38	-1:30:32
Yanina → Ioánnina	39N40	20E50	-1:23:20
Yerolimín	36N28	22E24	-1:29:36
Yiannitsá	40N48	22E25	-1:29:40
Yíthion	36N45	22E34	-1:30:16
Zákas	40N02	21E16	-1:25:04
Zákinthos	37N47	20E53	-1:23:32
Zante (Zákinthos)	37N52	20E44	-1:22:56
Zográfos	37N59	23E46	-1:35:04

GRØNLAND KALÂDLIT NUNÂT GROENLAND GROENLANDIA GREENLAND

Time Table # 1		
Before 28/Jul/1916 LMT		
Begin Standard	45w00	
28/Jul/1916	0:00	3:00
6/Apr/1980	2:00	2:00
28/Sep/1980	3:00	3:00
29/Mar/1981	2:00	2:00
27/Sep/1981	3:00	3:00
28/Mar/1982	2:00	2:00
26/Sep/1982	3:00	3:00
27/Mar/1983	2:00	2:00
25/Sep/1983	3:00	3:00
25/Mar/1984	2:00	2:00
30/Sep/1984	3:00	3:00
31/Mar/1985	2:00	2:00
29/Sep/1985	3:00	3:00
30/Mar/1986	2:00	2:00
28/Sep/1986	3:00	3:00
29/Mar/1987	2:00	2:00
27/Sep/1987	3:00	3:00
27/Mar/1988	2:00	2:00
25/Sep/1988	3:00	3:00
26/Mar/1989	2:00	2:00
24/Sep/1989	3:00	3:00
25/Mar/1990	2:00	2:00
30/Sep/1990	3:00	3:00
31/Mar/1991	2:00	2:00
29/Sep/1991	3:00	3:00
29/Mar/1992	2:00	2:00
27/Sep/1992	3:00	3:00
28/Mar/1993	2:00	2:00
26/Sep/1993	3:00	3:00
27/Mar/1994	2:00	2:00
25/Sep/1994	3:00	3:00
26/Mar/1995	2:00	2:00
24/Sep/1995	3:00	3:00
31/Mar/1996	2:00	2:00
29/Sep/1996	3:00	3:00
30/Mar/1997	2:00	2:00
28/Sep/1997	3:00	3:00
29/Mar/1998	2:00	2:00
27/Sep/1998	3:00	3:00
28/Mar/1999	2:00	2:00
26/Sep/1999	3:00	3:00
26/Mar/2000	2:00	2:00
24/Sep/2000	3:00	3:00
....		
Time Table # 2		
Before 28/Jul/1916 LMT		
Begin Standard	60w00	
28/Jul/1916	0:00	4:00
....		
Time Table # 3		
Before 28/Jul/1916 LMT		
Begin Standard	30w00	
28/Jul/1916	0:00	2:00
6/Apr/1980	2:00	1:00
28/Sep/1980	3:00	2:00
Begin Standard	15w00	
29/Mar/1981	0:00	1:00
29/Mar/1981	2:00	0:00
27/Sep/1981	3:00	1:00
28/Mar/1982	2:00	0:00
26/Sep/1982	3:00	1:00
27/Mar/1983	2:00	0:00
25/Sep/1983	3:00	1:00
25/Mar/1984	2:00	0:00
30/Sep/1984	3:00	1:00
31/Mar/1985	2:00	0:00
29/Sep/1985	3:00	1:00
30/Mar/1986	2:00	0:00
28/Sep/1986	3:00	1:00
29/Mar/1987	2:00	0:00
27/Sep/1987	3:00	1:00
27/Mar/1988	2:00	0:00
25/Sep/1988	3:00	1:00
26/Mar/1989	2:00	0:00
24/Sep/1989	3:00	1:00
25/Mar/1990	2:00	0:00
30/Sep/1990	3:00	1:00
31/Mar/1991	2:00	0:00
29/Sep/1991	3:00	1:00
29/Mar/1992	2:00	0:00
27/Sep/1992	3:00	1:00
28/Mar/1993	2:00	0:00
26/Sep/1993	3:00	1:00
27/Mar/1994	2:00	0:00
25/Sep/1994	3:00	1:00
26/Mar/1995	2:00	0:00
24/Sep/1995	3:00	1:00
31/Mar/1996	2:00	0:00
29/Sep/1996	3:00	1:00
30/Mar/1997	2:00	0:00
28/Sep/1997	3:00	1:00
29/Mar/1998	2:00	0:00
27/Sep/1998	3:00	1:00
28/Mar/1999	2:00	0:00
26/Sep/1999	3:00	1:00
26/Mar/2000	2:00	0:00
24/Sep/2000	3:00	1:00

Place	TT	Lat	Long	Offset
Angmagssalik	1	65N36	37w41	2:30:44
Christianshåb	1	68N50	51w12	3:24:48
Egedesminde	1	68N42	52w45	3:31:00
Etah	2	78N19	72w38	4:50:32
Frederikshåb	1	62N00	49w43	3:18:52
Godhavn	1	69N15	53w33	3:34:12
Godthåb → Nuuk	1	64N11	51w44	3:26:56
Holsteinsborg	1	66N55	53w40	3:34:40
Itseqqortoormiit	3	70N30	22w15	1:29:00
Ivigtut	1	61N12	48w10	3:12:40
Jakobshavn	1	69N13	51w06	3:24:24
Julianehåb	1	60N43	46w01	3:04:04
Kap York	2	76N34	68w47	4:35:08
Lievely	1	69N15	53w33	3:34:12
Narssag	1	60N54	46w00	3:04:00
Nuuk	1	64N11	51w44	3:26:56
Qutdligssat	1	70N04	53w01	3:32:04
Ritenbenk	1	69N46	51w19	3:25:16
Scoresby Sound	3	70N30	22w15	1:29:00
Sisimut	1	66N55	53w40	3:34:40
Søndre Strømfjord	1	66N59	50w40	3:22:40
Sukkertoppen	1	65N25	52w53	3:31:32
Thule	2	76N34	68w47	4:35:08
Umanak	1	70N40	52w07	3:28:28
Upernavik	1	72N47	56w10	3:44:40

GRANADA CONCEPCIÓN GRENADA

Time Table		
Before 1/Jul/1911 LMT		
Begin Standard	60w00	
1/Jul/1911	0:00	4:00

Place	Lat	Long	Offset
Baillies Bacolet	12N02	61w41	4:06:44
Charlotte Town (Gouyave)	12N10	61w44	4:06:56
Gouyave → Charlotte Town	12N10	61w44	4:06:56
Grand Roy	12N08	61w45	4:07:00
Grenville	12N07	61w37	4:06:28
Marquis	12N06	61w37	4:06:28
Saint George's	12N03	61w45	4:07:00
Sauteurs	12N14	61w38	4:06:32
Tivoli	12N10	61w37	4:06:28
Victoria	12N12	61w42	4:06:48

GUADALUPE GUADELOUPE

Time Table		
Before 8/Jun/1911 LMT		
Begin Standard	60w00	
8/Jun/1911	0:00	4:00

Place	Lat	Long	Offset
Anse Bertrand	16N29	61w31	4:06:04
Baie Mahault	16N16	61w35	4:06:20
Baillif	16N01	61w45	4:07:00
Basse-Terre	16N00	61w44	4:06:56
Bouillante	16N06	61w45	4:07:00
Bourg	15N52	61w36	4:06:24
Capesterre	16N03	61w34	4:06:16
Capesterre	15N54	61w13	4:04:52
Deshaies	16N18	61w48	4:07:12
Gourbeyre	16N00	61w42	4:06:48
Goyave	16N08	61w34	4:06:16
Grand Bourg	15N53	61w19	4:05:16
Grande Anse	16N18	61w04	4:04:16
Gustavia	17N54	62w51	4:11:24
Lamentin	16N16	61w38	4:06:32
Le Gosier	16N12	61w30	4:06:00
Le Moule	16N20	61w21	4:05:24
Les Abymes	16N16	61w31	4:06:04
Marigot	18N04	63w06	4:12:24
Morne à l'Eau	16N21	61w31	4:06:04
Petit Bourg	16N12	61w36	4:06:24
Petit Canal	16N23	61w29	4:05:56
Pointe à Pitre	16N14	61w32	4:06:08
Pointe Noire	16N14	61w47	4:07:08
Port Louis	16N25	61w32	4:06:08
Sainte Anne	16N14	61w23	4:05:32
Saint Claude	16N02	61w42	4:06:48
Saint François	16N15	61w17	4:05:08
Saint Louis	15N57	61w19	4:05:16
Sainte Rose	16N20	61w42	4:06:48
Terre De Bas	15N51	61w39	4:06:36
Terre De Haut	15N58	61w35	4:06:20
Trois Rivières	15N59	61w39	4:06:36
Vieux Fort	15N57	61w43	4:06:52
Vieux Habitants	16N04	61w46	4:07:04

GUAM

GUAHAN

GUAM

Time Table

Before	1/Jan/1901	LMT
Begin	Standard	150E00
1/Jan/1901	0:00	-10:00

Place	Latitude	Longitude	Offset
Agana	13N28	144E45	-9:39:00
Agana Heights	13N28	144E45	-9:39:00
Apra Harbor	13N27	144E38	-9:38:32
Agat	13N24	144E39	-9:38:36
Asan	13N28	144E43	-9:38:52
Barrigada	13N28	144E48	-9:39:12
Dededo	13N31	144E49	-9:39:16
Fafalog	13N37	144E51	-9:39:24
Inarajan	13N16	144E45	-9:39:00
Malolos	13N18	144E46	-9:39:04
Merizo	13N16	144E40	-9:38:40
Piti	13N28	144E41	-9:38:44
Sinajana	13N28	144E45	-9:39:00
Talofofo	13N21	144E45	-9:39:00
Tamuning	13N29	144E46	-9:39:04
Timoneng	13N29	144E46	-9:39:04
Umatac	13N18	144E39	-9:38:36
Yona	13N25	144E47	-9:39:08

GUATEMALA

GUATEMALA

Time Table

Before	5/Oct/1918	LMT
Begin	Standard	90W00
5/Oct/1918	0:00	6:00
25/Nov/1973	0:00	5:00
24/Feb/1974	0:00	6:00
21/May/1983	0:00	5:00
22/Sep/1983	0:00	6:00

Place	Latitude	Longitude	Offset
Almolonga	14N49	91W30	6:06:00
Amatitlán	14N29	90W37	6:02:28
Antigua Guatemala	14N34	90W44	6:02:56
Asunción Mita	14N20	89W43	5:58:52
Barberena	14N18	90W22	6:01:28
Barillas	15N48	91W18	6:05:12
Barrita Vieja	13N55	90W54	6:03:36
Buena Vista	13N49	90W19	6:01:16
Cahabón	15N34	89W49	5:59:16
Chahal	15N45	89W34	5:58:16
Chajul	15N30	91W02	6:04:08
Champerico	14N18	91W55	6:07:40
Chichicastenango	14N56	91W07	6:04:28
Chimaltenango	14N40	90W49	6:03:16
Chiquimula	14N48	89W33	5:58:12
Chiquimulilla	14N05	90W23	6:01:32
Chisec	15N49	90W17	6:01:08
Chuntuquí	17N31	90W09	6:00:36
Ciudad Tecún Umán	14N40	92W09	6:08:36
Ciudad Vieja	14N31	90W46	6:03:04
Coatepeque	14N42	91W52	6:07:28
Cobán	15N29	90W19	6:01:16
Comalapa	14N44	90W53	6:03:32
Concepción	15N37	91W41	6:06:44
Cuajiniquilapa	14N16	90W17	6:01:08
Cuilapa	14N17	90W18	6:01:12
Cuilco	15N24	91W58	6:07:52
Dolores	16N31	89W25	5:57:40
El Adelanto	14N10	89W50	5:59:20
El Cedral	16N26	90W03	6:00:12
El Encanto	17N17	89W34	5:58:16
El Estor	15N32	89W21	5:57:24
El Manchón	14N23	92W02	6:08:08
El Progreso	14N51	90W04	6:00:16
El Progreso	14N21	89W51	5:59:24
Escuintla	14N18	90W47	6:03:08
Esquipulas	14N34	89W21	5:57:24
Flores	16N56	89W53	5:59:32
Gualán	15N08	89W22	5:57:28
Guatemala	14N38	90W31	6:02:04
Guazacapán	14N04	90W25	6:01:40
Huehuetenango	15N20	91W28	6:05:52
Ixchiguán	15N12	91W53	6:07:32
Izabal	15N24	89W08	5:56:32
Iztapa	13N56	90W43	6:02:52
Jacaltenango	15N40	91W44	6:06:56
Jalapa	14N38	89W59	5:59:56
Jocotán	14N49	89W23	5:57:32
Jutiapa	14N17	89W54	5:59:36
La Florida	16N33	90W27	6:01:48
La Gomera	14N05	91W03	6:04:12
La Libertad	16N47	90W07	6:00:28
Lanquín	15N34	89W58	5:59:52
Lívingston	15N50	88W45	5:55:00
Los Amates	15N16	89W06	5:56:24
Masagua	14N12	90W51	6:03:24
Mazatenango	14N32	91W30	6:06:00
Morales	15N29	88W49	5:55:16
Morazán	14N56	90W09	6:00:36
Nebaj	15N24	91W08	6:04:32
Nueva Venecia	14N03	91W33	6:06:12
Ocós	14N31	92W11	6:08:44
Palín	14N24	90W42	6:02:48
Panzós	15N24	89W40	5:58:40
Pasaco	13N59	90W12	6:00:48
Patulul	14N25	91W10	6:04:40
Patzicía	14N38	90W56	6:03:44
Patzún	14N41	91W01	6:04:04
Piedras Negras	17N11	91W15	6:05:00
Poptún	16N21	89W26	5:57:44
Progreso	14N51	90W04	6:00:16
Puerto Barrios	15N43	88W36	5:54:24
Puerto de San José	13N55	90W49	6:03:16
Quezaltenango	14N50	91W31	6:06:04
Quezaltepeque	14N38	89W27	5:57:48
Rabinal	15N06	90W27	6:01:48
Retalhuleu	14N32	91W41	6:06:44
Salamá	15N06	90W16	6:01:04
Salcajá	14N53	91W27	6:05:48
San Andrés Sajcabajá	15N13	90W55	6:03:40
San Antonio Suchitepéquez	14N32	91W25	6:05:40
San Benito	16N55	89W54	5:59:36
San Cristóbal Totonicapán	14N55	91W26	6:05:44
San Cristóbal Verapaz	15N23	90W24	6:01:36
San Jerónimo	15N03	90W12	6:00:48
San Juan	15N52	88W53	5:55:32
San Juan Cotzal	15N26	91W01	6:04:04
San Juan Sacatepéquez	14N43	90W39	6:02:36
San Luis	16N14	89W27	5:57:48
San Luis Jilotepeque	14N39	89W44	5:58:56
San Marcos	14N58	91W48	6:07:12
San Mateo Ixtatán	15N50	91W29	6:05:56
San Miguel Ixtahuacán	15N15	91W45	6:07:00
San Pedro Ayampuc	14N47	90W27	6:01:48
San Pedro Carchá	15N29	90W16	6:01:04
San Pedro Pinula	14N40	89W51	5:59:24
San Pedro Sacatepéquez	14N58	91W46	6:07:04
San Sebastián	14N34	91W39	6:06:36
Santa Cruz del Quiché	15N02	91W08	6:04:32
Santa Eulalia	15N45	91W29	6:05:56
Santa Lucía Cotzumalguapa	14N20	91W01	6:04:04
Santa Marta	13N58	91W18	6:05:12
Santiago Atitlán	14N38	91W14	6:04:56
Sayaxché	16N31	90W10	6:00:40
Senahú	15N24	89W50	5:59:20
Sololá	14N46	91W11	6:04:44
Tacaná	15N14	92W05	6:08:20
Taxisco	14N04	90W28	6:01:52
Tecpán Guatemala	14N46	91W00	6:04:00
Tiquisate	14N17	91W22	6:05:28
Totonicapán	14N55	91W22	6:05:28
Villa Nueva	14N31	90W35	6:02:20
Zacapa	14N58	89W32	5:58:08
Zacualpa	15N05	90W50	6:03:20

GUERNESEY GUERNSEY

Time Table	14/Apr/1935 2:00 -1:00	15/Apr/1951 2:00 -1:00	19/Mar/1967 2:00 -1:00	31/Mar/1985 1:00 -1:00
Before 1/Jan/1880 LMT	6/Oct/1935 3:00 0:00	21/Oct/1951 3:00 0:00	29/Oct/1967 3:00 0:00	27/Oct/1985 2:00 0:00
Begin Standard 0W00	19/Apr/1936 2:00 -1:00	20/Apr/1952 2:00 -1:00	Begin Standard 15E00	30/Mar/1986 1:00 -1:00
1/Jan/1880 0:00 0:00	4/Oct/1936 3:00 0:00	26/Oct/1952 3:00 0:00	18/Feb/1968 2:00 -1:00	26/Oct/1986 2:00 0:00
3/Apr/1921 2:00 -1:00	18/Apr/1937 2:00 -1:00	19/Apr/1953 2:00 -1:00	Begin Standard 0W00	29/Mar/1987 1:00 -1:00
3/Oct/1921 3:00 0:00	3/Oct/1937 3:00 0:00	4/Oct/1953 3:00 0:00	31/Oct/1971 3:00 0:00	25/Oct/1987 2:00 0:00
26/Mar/1922 2:00 -1:00	10/Apr/1938 2:00 -1:00	11/Apr/1954 2:00 -1:00	19/Mar/1972 2:00 -1:00	27/Mar/1988 1:00 -1:00
8/Oct/1922 3:00 0:00	2/Oct/1938 3:00 0:00	3/Oct/1954 3:00 0:00	29/Oct/1972 3:00 0:00	23/Oct/1988 2:00 0:00
22/Apr/1923 2:00 -1:00	16/Apr/1939 2:00 -1:00	17/Apr/1955 2:00 -1:00	18/Mar/1973 2:00 -1:00	26/Mar/1989 1:00 -1:00
16/Sep/1923 3:00 0:00	19/Nov/1939 3:00 0:00	2/Oct/1955 3:00 0:00	28/Oct/1973 3:00 0:00	29/Oct/1989 2:00 0:00
13/Apr/1924 2:00 -1:00	25/Feb/1940 2:00 -1:00	22/Apr/1956 2:00 -1:00	17/Mar/1974 2:00 -1:00	25/Mar/1990 1:00 -1:00
21/Sep/1924 3:00 0:00	30/Jun/1940 0:00 -2:00	7/Oct/1956 3:00 0:00	27/Oct/1974 3:00 0:00	28/Oct/1990 2:00 0:00
19/Apr/1925 2:00 -1:00	1/Nov/1942 3:00 -1:00	14/Apr/1957 2:00 -1:00	16/Mar/1975 2:00 -1:00	31/Mar/1991 1:00 -1:00
4/Oct/1925 3:00 0:00	29/Mar/1943 2:00 -2:00	6/Oct/1957 3:00 0:00	26/Oct/1975 3:00 0:00	27/Oct/1991 2:00 0:00
18/Apr/1926 2:00 -1:00	4/Oct/1943 3:00 -1:00	20/Apr/1958 2:00 -1:00	21/Mar/1976 2:00 -1:00	29/Mar/1992 1:00 -1:00
3/Oct/1926 3:00 0:00	3/Apr/1944 2:00 -2:00	5/Oct/1958 3:00 0:00	24/Oct/1976 3:00 0:00	25/Oct/1992 2:00 0:00
10/Apr/1927 2:00 -1:00	3/Oct/1944 3:00 -1:00	19/Apr/1959 2:00 -1:00	20/Mar/1977 2:00 -1:00	28/Mar/1993 1:00 -1:00
2/Oct/1927 3:00 0:00	2/Apr/1945 2:00 -2:00	4/Oct/1959 3:00 0:00	23/Oct/1977 3:00 0:00	24/Oct/1993 2:00 0:00
22/Apr/1928 2:00 -1:00	15/Jul/1945 3:00 -1:00	10/Apr/1960 2:00 -1:00	19/Mar/1978 2:00 -1:00	27/Mar/1994 1:00 -1:00
7/Oct/1928 3:00 0:00	7/Oct/1945 3:00 0:00	2/Oct/1960 3:00 0:00	29/Oct/1978 3:00 0:00	23/Oct/1994 2:00 0:00
21/Apr/1929 2:00 -1:00	14/Apr/1946 2:00 -1:00	26/Mar/1961 2:00 -1:00	18/Mar/1979 2:00 -1:00	26/Mar/1995 1:00 -1:00
6/Oct/1929 3:00 0:00	6/Oct/1946 3:00 0:00	29/Oct/1961 3:00 0:00	28/Oct/1979 3:00 0:00	29/Oct/1995 2:00 0:00
13/Apr/1930 2:00 -1:00	16/Mar/1947 2:00 -1:00	25/Mar/1962 2:00 -1:00	16/Mar/1980 2:00 -1:00	31/Mar/1996 1:00 -1:00
5/Oct/1930 3:00 0:00	13/Apr/1947 2:00 -2:00	28/Oct/1962 3:00 0:00	26/Oct/1980 3:00 0:00	27/Oct/1996 2:00 0:00
19/Apr/1931 2:00 -1:00	10/Aug/1947 3:00 -1:00	31/Mar/1963 2:00 -1:00	29/Mar/1981 1:00 -1:00	30/Mar/1997 1:00 -1:00
4/Oct/1931 3:00 0:00	2/Nov/1947 3:00 0:00	27/Oct/1963 3:00 0:00	25/Oct/1981 2:00 0:00	26/Oct/1997 2:00 0:00
17/Apr/1932 2:00 -1:00	14/Mar/1948 2:00 -1:00	22/Mar/1964 2:00 -1:00	28/Mar/1982 1:00 -1:00	29/Mar/1998 1:00 -1:00
2/Oct/1932 3:00 0:00	31/Oct/1948 3:00 0:00	25/Oct/1964 3:00 0:00	24/Oct/1982 2:00 0:00	25/Oct/1998 2:00 0:00
9/Apr/1933 2:00 -1:00	3/Apr/1949 2:00 -1:00	21/Mar/1965 2:00 -1:00	27/Mar/1983 1:00 -1:00	28/Mar/1999 1:00 -1:00
8/Oct/1933 3:00 0:00	30/Oct/1949 3:00 0:00	24/Oct/1965 3:00 0:00	23/Oct/1983 2:00 0:00	24/Oct/1999 2:00 0:00
22/Apr/1934 2:00 -1:00	16/Apr/1950 2:00 -1:00	20/Mar/1966 2:00 -1:00	25/Mar/1984 1:00 -1:00	26/Mar/2000 1:00 -1:00
7/Oct/1934 3:00 0:00	22/Oct/1950 3:00 0:00	23/Oct/1966 3:00 0:00	28/Oct/1984 2:00 0:00	29/Oct/2000 2:00 0:00

Castel	49N28	2W34	0:10:16
Saint Anne	49N42	2W12	0:08:48
Saint Peter Port	49N27	2W32	0:10:08
Saint Sampson	49N29	2W31	0:10:04
Torteval	49N27	2W38	0:10:32
Vale	49N29	2W31	0:10:04

GUINÉE FRENCH GUINEA GUINEA

Time Table
Before 1/Jan/1912 LMT
Begin Standard 0W00
1/Jan/1912 0:00 0:00
Begin Standard 15W00
26/Feb/1934 0:00 1:00
Begin Standard 0W00
1/Jan/1960 0:00 0:00

Bafelé	10N09	10W08	0:40:32
Baléya	9N15	10W29	0:41:56
Bembou Sambayabé	10N55	13W44	0:54:56
Beyla	8N41	8W37	0:34:28
Bissikrima	10N51	10W56	0:43:44
Boffa	10N10	14W02	0:56:08
Bofosso	8N40	9W42	0:38:48
Bohodou	9N46	9W04	0:36:16
Boké	10N56	14W18	0:57:12
Boola	8N22	8W43	0:34:52
Conakry	9N31	13W43	0:54:52
Coyah	9N43	13W23	0:53:32
Dabola	10N45	11W07	0:44:28
Dalaba	10N42	12W15	0:49:00
Dalabani	10N28	9W27	0:37:48
Dalao	11N29	13W40	0:54:40
Danea	11N27	13W12	0:52:48
Diabakania	10N38	10W58	0:43:52
Diecke	7N21	8W58	0:35:52
Dinguiraye	11N18	10W43	0:42:52
Dubréka	9N48	13W31	0:54:04
Fabala	9N44	9W05	0:36:20
Faranah	10N02	10W44	0:42:56
Fodécontea	10N50	14W22	0:57:28
Forécariah	9N26	13W06	0:52:24
Foula Mori	12N10	13W51	0:55:24
Fria	10N05	13W32	0:54:08
Friguia	12N03	10W56	0:43:44
Gaoual	11N45	13W12	0:52:48
Gouéké	8N02	8W43	0:34:52
Guéckédou	8N33	10W09	0:40:36
Irié	8N17	9W11	0:36:44
Kaba	10N09	11W40	0:46:40
Kabot	10N48	14W57	0:59:48
Kalankalan	10N07	8W54	0:35:36
Kankan	10N23	9W18	0:37:12
Kérouané	9N16	9W01	0:36:04
Kifaya	12N10	13W04	0:52:16
Kindia	10N04	12W51	0:51:24
Kintinian	11N36	9W23	0:37:32
Kissidougou	9N11	10W06	0:40:24
Kolenté	10N06	12W37	0:50:28
Konfara	11N55	8W50	0:35:20
Konsankoro	9N02	9W00	0:36:00
Koossa	9N32	8W32	0:34:08
Koubia	11N35	11W54	0:47:36
Koumbia	11N48	13W30	0:54:00
Koumbouma	10N24	12W56	0:51:44
Koundara	12N29	13W18	0:53:12
Kouroussa	10N39	9W53	0:39:32
Labé	11N19	12W17	0:49:08
Lola	7N48	8W32	0:34:08
Macenta	8N33	9W28	0:37:52
Mali	12N05	12W18	0:49:12
Mamou	10N23	12W05	0:48:20
Mandiana	10N38	8W41	0:34:44
Minianko	9N58	8W22	0:33:28
Moribaya	9N53	9W33	0:38:12
Niagassola	12N19	9W07	0:36:28
Niandan Koro	11N05	9W15	0:37:00
Nianforando	9N32	10W31	0:42:04
Nionsamoridougou	8N43	8W50	0:35:20
Nzébéla	8N05	9W06	0:36:24
Nzérékoré	7N45	8W49	0:35:16
Oualto	9N01	10W06	0:40:24
Parahi	11N09	13W07	0:52:28
Péla	7N37	9W07	0:36:28
Pita	11N05	12W24	0:49:36
Saraya	10N46	10W24	0:41:36
Siguiri	11N25	9W10	0:36:40
Sissela	10N49	10W37	0:42:28
Takabara	11N50	11W30	0:46:00
Tamba Dabatou	11N48	10W40	0:42:40
Télimélé	10N54	13W02	0:52:08
Timbo	10N38	11W50	0:47:20
Tindila	10N16	8W15	0:33:00
Tintioulé	10N13	9W12	0:36:48
Tiriro	10N27	8W39	0:34:36
Tombadonkéa	11N00	14W23	0:57:32
Tougué	11N27	11W41	0:46:44
Victoria	10N50	14W33	0:58:12
Wassou	10N02	13W39	0:54:36
Yambéring	11N49	12W21	0:49:24
Yayouta	8N11	8W30	0:34:00
Yende Millimou	8N53	10W11	0:40:44
Yomou	7N34	9W16	0:37:04
Youkounkoun	12N32	13W08	0:52:32

GUINEA-BISSAU

GUINA-BISSAU

PORTUGUESE GUINEA

GUINÉE-BISSAU

Time Table
Before 26/May/1911 LMT
Begin Standard 15w00
26/May/1911 0:00 1:00
Begin Standard 0w00
1/Jan/1975 0:00 0:00

Place	Lat	Long	Offset
Bafatá	12N10	14w40	0:58:40
Barro	12N24	15w30	1:02:00
Bissau	11N51	15w35	1:02:20
Bissorã	12N14	15w31	1:02:04
Bolama	11N35	15w28	1:01:52
Buba	11N36	14w55	0:59:40
Bubaque	11N17	15w50	1:03:20
Cacheu	12N16	16w10	1:04:40
Cacine	11N08	14w57	0:59:48
Catió	11N13	15w10	1:00:40
Eticoga	11N09	16w08	1:04:32
Farim	12N27	15w17	1:01:08
Fulacunda	11N44	15w03	1:00:12
Madina do Boé	11N45	14w13	0:56:52
Mansabá	12N18	15w15	1:01:00
Mansôa	12N10	14w36	0:58:24
Nova Lamego	12N19	14w11	0:56:44
São Domingos	12N22	16w08	1:04:32
São João	11N32	15w26	1:01:44
Teixeira Pinto	12N10	13w55	0:55:40
Xitole	11N43	14w50	0:59:20

GUYANA

GUAYANA

BRITISH GUIANA

GUYANE

Time Table
Before 1/Mar/1915 LMT
Begin Standard 56w15
1/Mar/1915 0:00 3:45
Begin Standard 45w00
31/Jul/1975 0:00 3:00

Place	Lat	Long	Offset
Anna Regina	7N16	58w30	3:54:00
Bartica	6N24	58w37	3:54:28
Bush Lot	6N12	57w16	3:49:04
Buxton	6N47	58w02	3:52:08
Charity	7N24	58w36	3:54:24
Dadanawa	2N50	59w30	3:58:00
Enmore	6N46	57w59	3:51:56
Enterprise	6N56	58w24	3:53:36
Fort Wellington	6N24	57w36	3:50:24
Georgetown	6N48	58w10	3:52:40
Holmia	4N58	59w35	3:58:20
Hyde Park	6N30	58w16	3:53:04
Isherton	2N19	59w22	3:57:28
Issano	5N49	59w25	3:57:40
Lethem	3N23	59w48	3:59:12
Mabaruma	8N12	59w47	3:59:08
Mackenzie	6N00	58w17	3:53:08
Mahaicony Village	6N36	57w48	3:51:12
Marlborough	7N29	58w38	3:54:32
Matthews Ridge	7N30	60w10	4:00:40
Morawhanna	8N16	59w45	3:59:00
New Amsterdam	6N15	57w31	3:50:04
Orinduik	4N42	60w01	4:00:04
Parika	6N52	58w25	3:53:40
Potaro Landing	5N23	59w08	3:56:32
Queenstown	7N12	58w29	3:53:56
Rockstone	5N59	58w33	3:54:12
Rose Hall	6N16	57w21	3:49:24
Rosignol	6N17	57w32	3:50:08
Saint Ignatius	3N20	59w47	3:59:08
Skeldon	5N53	57w08	3:48:32
Spring Garden	6N59	58w31	3:54:04
Suddie	7N07	58w29	3:53:56
Taruma	2N02	58w22	3:53:28
Tumatumari	5N22	59w00	3:56:00
Vreed en Hoop	6N48	58w11	3:52:44
Wismar	6N00	58w18	3:53:12

HAITI

HAITÍ

HAÏTI

Time Table
Before 1/Jan/1890 LMT
Begin Standard 72w20
1/Jan/1890 0:00 4:49
Begin Standard 75w00
24/Jan/1917 12:00 5:00

Date	Time	Offset
8/May/1983	0:00	4:00
30/Oct/1983	0:00	5:00
29/Apr/1984	0:00	4:00
28/Oct/1984	0:00	5:00
28/Apr/1985	0:00	4:00
27/Oct/1985	0:00	5:00
27/Apr/1986	0:00	4:00
26/Oct/1986	0:00	5:00
26/Apr/1987	0:00	4:00
26/Oct/1987	0:00	5:00
3/Apr/1988	2:00	4:00
30/Oct/1988	2:00	5:00
2/Apr/1989	2:00	4:00
29/Oct/1989	2:00	5:00
1/Apr/1990	2:00	4:00
28/Oct/1990	2:00	5:00
7/Apr/1991	2:00	4:00
27/Oct/1991	2:00	5:00
5/Apr/1992	2:00	4:00
25/Oct/1992	2:00	5:00
4/Apr/1993	2:00	4:00
31/Oct/1993	2:00	5:00
3/Apr/1994	2:00	4:00
30/Oct/1994	2:00	5:00
2/Apr/1995	2:00	4:00
29/Oct/1995	2:00	5:00
7/Apr/1996	2:00	4:00
27/Oct/1996	2:00	5:00
6/Apr/1997	2:00	4:00
26/Oct/1997	2:00	5:00
5/Apr/1998	2:00	4:00
25/Oct/1998	2:00	5:00
4/Apr/1999	2:00	4:00
31/Oct/1999	2:00	5:00
2/Apr/2000	2:00	4:00
29/Oct/2000	2:00	5:00

Place	Lat	Long	Offset
Anse-à-Veau	18N40	73w21	4:53:24
Anse-d'Hainault	18N30	74w27	4:57:48
Aquin	18N17	73w24	4:53:36
Aux Cayes → Les Cayes	18N12	73w45	4:55:00
Cap-Haïtien	19N45	72w12	4:48:48
Cayes → Les Cayes	18N12	73w45	4:55:00
Coteaux	18N12	74w02	4:56:08
Derac	19N39	71w49	4:47:16
Gonaïves	19N27	72w41	4:50:44
Hinche	19N09	72w01	4:48:04
Jacmel	18N14	72w32	4:50:08
Jérémie	18N39	74w07	4:56:28
Le Cap → Cap-Haïtien	19N45	72w12	4:48:48
Le Limbe	19N44	72w22	4:49:28
Le Mole Saint Nicholas	19N49	73w23	4:53:32
Léogâne	18N31	72w38	4:50:32
Les Cayes	18N12	73w45	4:55:00
Los Coteaux	18N12	74w02	4:56:08
Pétionville	18N31	72w17	4:49:08
Petit-Goâve	18N26	72w52	4:51:28
Port-au-Prince	18N32	72w20	4:49:20
Port-de-Paix	19N57	72w50	4:51:20
Saint-Marc	19N07	72w42	4:50:48
Trou-du-Nord	19N38	72w01	4:48:04
Verrettes	19N03	72w28	4:49:52

HONDURAS

Time Table		
Before 1/Jan/1921 LMT		
Begin Standard		90W00
1/Jan/1921	0:00	6:00
3/May/1987	0:00	5:00
27/Sep/1987	0:00	6:00
1/May/1988	0:00	5:00
25/Sep/1988	0:00	6:00

Place	Lat	Long	Time
Ajuterique	14N20	87W43	5:50:52
Alianza	13N31	87W44	5:50:56
Amapala	13N17	87W40	5:50:40
Arada	14N48	88W18	5:53:12
Azacualpa	14N27	86W09	5:44:36
Azacualpa	15N19	88W33	5:54:12
Balfate	15N48	86W25	5:45:40
Baracoa	15N43	87W52	5:51:28
Brus Laguna	15N47	84W35	5:38:20
Camacosni	14N57	85W08	5:40:32
Campamento	14N33	86W42	5:46:48
Catacamas	14N54	85W56	5:43:44
Cedros	14N35	87W08	5:48:32
Chamelecón	15N24	88W01	5:52:04
Choloma	15N34	87W56	5:51:44
Choluteca	13N18	87W12	5:48:48
Cofradía	15N24	88W09	5:52:36
Colorado	15N47	87W19	5:49:16
Comayagua	14N25	87W37	5:50:28
Copán	14N50	89W09	5:56:36
Corozal	15N48	86W43	5:46:52
Corquín	14N34	88W52	5:55:28
Cuyamel	15N38	88W12	5:52:48
Danlí	14N00	86W35	5:46:20
Dulce Nombre de Culmí	15N09	85W37	5:42:28
El Corpus	13N16	87W03	5:48:12
El Negrito	15N16	87W41	5:50:44
El Paraíso	13N51	86W34	5:46:16
El Progreso	15N21	87W49	5:51:16
El Triunfo	15N46	87W26	5:49:44
El Triunfo	13N06	87W00	5:48:00
Florida	15N01	88W50	5:55:20
Goascorán	13N36	87W45	5:51:00
Gracias	14N35	88W35	5:54:20
Guaimaca	14N32	86W51	5:47:24
Guanaja	16N27	85W54	5:43:36
Guanpata	15N01	85W02	5:40:08
Guarizama	14N55	86W20	5:45:20
Guayape	14N45	86W52	5:47:28
Güinope	13N51	86W55	5:47:40
Intibucá	14N16	88W10	5:52:40
Iriona	15N57	85W11	5:40:44
Jacaleapa	14N00	86W40	5:46:40
Jesús de Otoro	14N26	87W59	5:51:56
Jocón	15N17	86W58	5:47:52
Juticalpa	14N42	86W15	5:45:00
Jutiquile	14N45	86W08	5:44:32
La Ceiba	15N47	86W50	5:47:20
La Esperanza	14N20	88W10	5:52:40
La Libertad	14N43	87W36	5:50:24
La Lima	15N24	87W56	5:51:44
La Masica	15N37	87W07	5:48:28
Langue	13N37	87W39	5:50:36
La Paz	14N16	87W40	5:50:40
Las Vegas	14N49	88W06	5:52:24
Lima Nueva	15N23	87W56	5:51:44
Limón	15N52	85W33	5:42:12
Macuelizo	15N18	88W31	5:54:04
Manguilile	15N03	86W49	5:47:16
Marcala	14N07	88W00	5:52:00
Mezapa	15N33	87W23	5:49:32
Minas de Oro	14N46	87W20	5:49:20
Morazán	15N17	87W34	5:50:16
Nacaome	13N31	87W30	5:50:00
Naranjito	14N57	88W41	5:54:44
Nueva Ocotepeque	14N24	89W13	5:56:52
Ocotepeque	14N24	89W13	5:56:52
Olanchito	15N30	86W35	5:46:20
Orica	14N41	86W56	5:47:44
Orocuina	13N26	87W06	5:48:24
Paya	15N37	85W17	5:41:08
Pespire	13N35	87W22	5:49:28
Potrerillos	15N11	87W58	5:51:52
Progreso	15N21	87W49	5:51:16
Puerto Castilla	16N01	86W01	5:44:04
Puerto Cortés	15N48	87W56	5:51:44
Puerto Delón	14N22	85W53	5:43:32
Puerto Lempira	15N13	83W47	5:35:08
Roatán	16N18	86W35	5:46:20
Sabanagrande	13N50	87W15	5:49:00
Salamá	14N50	86W36	5:46:24
San Esteban	15N17	85W52	5:43:28
San Francisco	13N41	88W07	5:52:28
San Francisco de la Paz	14N55	86W14	5:44:56
San Ignacio	14N38	87W02	5:48:08
San José	14N54	88W44	5:54:56
San Juan de Flores	14N15	87W02	5:48:08
San Lorenzo	13N25	87W27	5:49:48
San Marcos	14N24	88W56	5:55:44
San Marcos	15N17	88W23	5:53:32
San Marcos de Colón	13N26	86W48	5:47:12
San Nicolás	15N00	88W45	5:55:00
San Pedro Sula	15N27	88W02	5:52:08
San Sebastián	14N24	88W42	5:54:48
Santa Bárbara	14N53	88W14	5:52:56
Santa Fé	15N55	86W05	5:44:20
Santa Rita	15N09	87W53	5:51:32
Santa Rosa de Aguán	15N57	85W43	5:42:52
Santa Rosa (de Copán)	14N47	88W46	5:55:04
Siguatepeque	14N32	87W49	5:51:16
Sonaguera	15N38	86W20	5:45:20
Taulabé	14N38	87W59	5:51:56
Tegucigalpa	14N06	87W13	5:48:52
Tela	15N44	87W27	5:49:48
Tocoa	15N41	86W03	5:44:12
Trinidad	14N57	88W45	5:55:00
Trujillo	15N55	86W00	5:44:00
Utila	16N06	86W54	5:47:36
Valencia	14N47	85W18	5:41:12
Villa de San Antonio	14N16	87W36	5:50:24
Villa de San Francisco	14N10	86W58	5:47:52
Villanueva	15N17	88W00	5:52:00
Yoro	15N09	87W07	5:48:28
Yuscarán	13N55	86W51	5:47:24

HONG-KONG HONGKONG HONG KONG

Time Table		
Before 30/Oct/1904 LMT		
Begin Standard		120E00
30/Oct/1904	0:00	-8:00
20/Apr/1946	3:30	-9:00
1/Dec/1946	3:30	-8:00
13/Apr/1947	3:30	-9:00
30/Dec/1947	3:30	-8:00
2/May/1948	3:30	-9:00
31/Oct/1948	3:30	-8:00
3/Apr/1949	3:30	-9:00
30/Oct/1949	3:30	-8:00
2/Apr/1950	3:30	-9:00
29/Oct/1950	3:30	-8:00
1/Apr/1951	3:30	-9:00
28/Oct/1951	3:30	-8:00
6/Apr/1952	3:30	-9:00
25/Oct/1952	3:30	-8:00
5/Apr/1953	3:30	-9:00
1/Nov/1953	3:30	-8:00
21/Mar/1954	3:30	-9:00
31/Oct/1954	3:30	-8:00
20/Mar/1955	3:30	-9:00
6/Nov/1955	3:30	-8:00
18/Mar/1956	3:30	-9:00
4/Nov/1956	3:30	-8:00
24/Mar/1957	3:30	-9:00
3/Nov/1957	3:30	-8:00
23/Mar/1958	3:30	-9:00
2/Nov/1958	3:30	-8:00
22/Mar/1959	3:30	-9:00
1/Nov/1959	3:30	-8:00
20/Mar/1960	3:30	-9:00
6/Nov/1960	3:30	-8:00
19/Mar/1961	3:30	-9:00
5/Nov/1961	3:30	-8:00
18/Mar/1962	3:30	-9:00
4/Nov/1962	3:30	-8:00
24/Mar/1963	3:30	-9:00
3/Nov/1963	3:30	-8:00
22/Mar/1964	3:30	-9:00
1/Nov/1964	3:30	-8:00
18/Apr/1965	3:30	-9:00
17/Oct/1965	3:30	-8:00
17/Apr/1966	3:30	-9:00
16/Oct/1966	3:30	-8:00
16/Apr/1967	3:30	-9:00
22/Oct/1967	3:30	-8:00
21/Apr/1968	3:30	-9:00
20/Oct/1968	3:30	-8:00
20/Apr/1969	3:30	-9:00
19/Oct/1969	3:30	-8:00
19/Apr/1970	3:30	-9:00
18/Oct/1970	3:30	-8:00
18/Apr/1971	3:30	-9:00
17/Oct/1971	3:30	-8:00
16/Apr/1972	3:30	-9:00
22/Oct/1972	3:30	-8:00
22/Apr/1973	3:30	-9:00
21/Oct/1973	2:20	-8:00
30/Dec/1973	3:30	-9:00
20/Oct/1974	3:30	-8:00
20/Apr/1975	3:30	-9:00
19/Oct/1975	3:30	-8:00
18/Apr/1976	3:30	-9:00
17/Oct/1976	3:30	-8:00
17/Apr/1977	3:30	-9:00
16/Oct/1977	3:30	-8:00
13/May/1979	3:30	-9:00
21/Oct/1979	3:30	-8:00
11/May/1980	3:30	-9:00
19/Oct/1980	3:30	-8:00

Place	Lat	Long	Time
Aberdeen (Xianggangzi)	22N15	114E09	-7:36:36
Chek Kang	22N26	114E21	-7:37:24
Cheung Shue Tan	22N26	114E12	-7:36:48
Chinese University	22N26	114E12	-7:36:48
Chuen Lung	22N24	114E06	-7:36:24
Chung Hau	22N16	114E00	-7:36:00
Hang Hau Town	22N19	114E16	-7:37:04
Ho Chung	22N22	114E14	-7:36:56
Hok So Wan	22N13	114E14	-7:36:56
Hong Kong → Victoria	22N17	114E09	-7:36:36
Ho Pui	22N25	114E03	-7:36:12
Jiulong → Kowloon	22N18	114E10	-7:36:40
Kam Tin	22N27	114E03	-7:36:12
Kaolun → Kowloon	22N18	114E10	-7:36:40
Kowloon (Jiulong)	22N18	114E10	-7:36:40
Kowloon City	22N19	114E11	-7:36:44
Kwun Tong	22N19	114E12	-7:36:48
Lam Uk Wei	22N26	114E22	-7:37:28
Long Ke	22N23	114E22	-7:37:28
Ma Liu Shui	22N25	114E12	-7:36:48
Ma On Shan Tsuen	22N24	114E14	-7:36:56
Mong Tung Hang	22N20	114E02	-7:36:08
Mui Wo	22N16	113E59	-7:35:56
New Kowloon (Xinjiulong)	22N20	114E10	-7:36:40
Ngau Tau Kok → Kwun Tong	22N19	114E12	-7:36:48
North Point	22N17	114E12	-7:36:48
Pak Kong	22N23	114E15	-7:37:00
Ping Shan	22N27	114E00	-7:36:00
Rennie's Mill	22N18	114E15	-7:37:00
Sai Keng	22N26	114E16	-7:37:04
Sai Kung	22N23	114E15	-7:37:00
Sha Tin	22N23	114E11	-7:36:44
Shek Kong	22N26	114E06	-7:36:24
Siu Lek Yuen	22N23	114E12	-7:36:48
Stanley	22N13	114E12	-7:36:48
Tai Hang	22N17	114E11	-7:36:44
Tai Lam Chung	22N22	114E01	-7:36:04
Tai Long	22N25	114E22	-7:37:28
Tai Long	22N13	113E59	-7:35:56
Tai Mong Tsai	22N24	114E18	-7:37:12
Tai O	22N15	113E51	-7:35:24
Tai Po Tsai	22N21	114E15	-7:37:00
Tai Shui Hang	22N25	14E13	-0:56:52
Tai Tong	22N25	114E01	-7:36:04
Tai Wan	22N10	114E15	-7:37:00
Tai Wan Tau	22N18	114E17	-7:37:08
Ting Kau	22N22	114E05	-7:36:20
Tin Sam	22N22	114E11	-7:36:44
Tsuen Wan (Quanwan)	22N22	114E07	-7:36:28
Tuen Mun	22N24	113E58	-7:35:52
Tung O	22N12	114E08	-7:36:32
Victoria (Xianggang)	22N17	114E09	-7:36:36
Wong Ka Wai	22N24	113E58	-7:35:52
Xianggang → Victoria	22N17	114E09	-7:36:36
Yau Tong	22N18	114E13	-7:36:52
Yi Pak	22N19	114E00	-7:36:00
Yuen Long	22N26	114E02	-7:36:08
Yung Shue Wan	22N14	114E06	-7:36:24

HUNGARY HUNGRÍA HONGRIE UNGARN MAGYARORSZÁG

Time Table

Before 1/Oct/1890 LMT

Begin Standard 15E00

Date	Time	Offset
1/Oct/1890	0:00	-1:00
30/Apr/1916	23:00	-2:00
1/Oct/1916	1:00	-1:00
16/Apr/1917	3:00	-2:00
17/Sep/1917	3:00	-1:00
1/Apr/1918	3:00	-2:00
29/Sep/1918	3:00	-1:00
15/Apr/1919	3:00	-2:00
15/Sep/1919	3:00	-1:00
5/Apr/1920	3:00	-2:00
30/Sep/1920	3:00	-1:00
6/Apr/1941	2:00	-2:00
2/Nov/1942	3:00	-1:00
29/Mar/1943	2:00	-2:00
4/Oct/1943	3:00	-1:00
3/Apr/1944	2:00	-2:00
2/Oct/1944	3:00	-1:00
1/May/1945	23:00	-2:00
3/Nov/1945	0:00	-1:00
31/Mar/1946	2:00	-2:00
7/Oct/1946	3:00	-1:00
6/Apr/1947	2:00	-2:00
5/Oct/1947	3:00	-1:00
4/Apr/1948	2:00	-2:00
3/Oct/1948	3:00	-1:00
10/Apr/1949	2:00	-2:00
2/Oct/1949	3:00	-1:00
17/Apr/1950	2:00	-2:00
23/Oct/1950	2:00	-1:00
23/May/1954	0:00	-2:00
3/Oct/1954	0:00	-1:00
23/May/1955	0:00	-2:00
3/Oct/1955	0:00	-1:00
3/Jun/1956	0:00	-2:00
30/Sep/1956	0:00	-1:00
2/Jun/1957	1:00	-2:00
29/Sep/1957	3:00	-1:00
6/Apr/1980	1:00	-2:00
28/Sep/1980	3:00	-1:00
29/Mar/1981	2:00	-2:00
27/Sep/1981	3:00	-1:00
28/Mar/1982	2:00	-2:00
26/Sep/1982	3:00	-1:00
27/Mar/1983	2:00	-2:00
25/Sep/1983	3:00	-1:00
25/Mar/1984	2:00	-2:00
30/Sep/1984	3:00	-1:00
31/Mar/1985	2:00	-2:00
29/Sep/1985	3:00	-1:00
30/Mar/1986	2:00	-2:00
28/Sep/1986	3:00	-1:00
29/Mar/1987	2:00	-2:00
27/Sep/1987	3:00	-1:00
27/Mar/1988	2:00	-2:00
25/Sep/1988	3:00	-1:00
26/Mar/1989	2:00	-2:00
24/Sep/1989	3:00	-1:00
25/Mar/1990	2:00	-2:00
30/Sep/1990	3:00	-1:00
31/Mar/1991	2:00	-2:00
29/Sep/1991	3:00	-1:00
29/Mar/1992	2:00	-2:00
27/Sep/1992	3:00	-1:00
28/Mar/1993	2:00	-2:00
26/Sep/1993	3:00	-1:00
27/Mar/1994	2:00	-2:00
25/Sep/1994	3:00	-1:00
26/Mar/1995	2:00	-2:00
24/Sep/1995	3:00	-1:00
31/Mar/1996	2:00	-2:00
29/Sep/1996	3:00	-1:00
30/Mar/1997	2:00	-2:00
28/Sep/1997	3:00	-1:00
29/Mar/1998	2:00	-2:00
27/Sep/1998	3:00	-1:00
28/Mar/1999	2:00	-2:00
26/Sep/1999	3:00	-1:00
26/Mar/2000	2:00	-2:00
24/Sep/2000	3:00	-1:00

Place	Lat	Long	Offset
Abony	47N11	20E01	-1:20:04
Ajka	47N07	17E34	-1:10:16
Albertirsa	47N15	19E38	-1:18:32
Alsónémedi	47N19	19E10	-1:16:40
Aszód	47N39	19E31	-1:18:04
Bácsalmás	46N08	19E20	-1:17:20
Baja	46N11	18E57	-1:15:48
Bajánsenye	46N48	16E23	-1:05:32
Bak	46N43	16E51	-1:07:24
Balassagyarmat	48N05	19E18	-1:17:12
Barcs	45N58	17E28	-1:09:52
Bátaszék	46N12	18E44	-1:14:56
Battonya	46N17	21E01	-1:24:04
Becsehely	46N27	16E48	-1:07:12
Békés	46N46	21E08	-1:24:32
Békéscsaba	46N41	21E06	-1:24:24
Beregszasz	48N13	22E38	-1:30:32
Berettyóújfalu	47N14	21E32	-1:26:08
Bicske	47N29	18E37	-1:14:28
Bóly	45N58	18E32	-1:14:08
Bonyhád	46N19	18E32	-1:14:08
Budakalász	47N37	19E03	-1:16:12
Budakeszi	47N31	18E56	-1:15:44
Budaörs	47N27	18E58	-1:15:52
Budapest	47N30	19E05	-1:16:20
Bük	47N23	16E45	-1:07:00
Cegléd	47N10	19E48	-1:19:12
Celldömölk	47N16	17E09	-1:08:36
Csobánka	47N38	18E58	-1:15:52
Csomád	47N40	19E15	-1:17:00
Csömör	47N33	19E14	-1:16:56
Csongrád	46N43	20E09	-1:20:36
Csorna	47N37	17E16	-1:09:04
Csurgó	46N16	17E06	-1:08:24
Debrecen	47N32	21E38	-1:26:32
Decs	46N17	18E46	-1:15:04
Derecske	47N21	21E34	-1:26:16
Dévaványa	47N02	20E58	-1:23:52
Devecser	47N06	17E26	-1:09:44
Diósd	47N25	18E57	-1:15:48
Dombóvár	46N23	18E08	-1:12:32
Dombrád	48N14	21E56	-1:27:44
Dorog	47N43	18E44	-1:14:56
Dunaföldvár	46N48	18E55	-1:15:40
Dunaharaszti	47N21	19E05	-1:16:20
Dunakeszi	47N38	19E08	-1:16:32
Dunaújváros	46N58	18E57	-1:15:48
Ecser	47N27	19E20	-1:17:20
Edelény	48N18	20E44	-1:22:56
Eger	47N54	20E23	-1:21:32
Emőd	47N56	20E49	-1:23:16
Encs	48N20	21E08	-1:24:32
Érd	47N23	18E56	-1:15:44
Ersekujvar	47N59	18E10	-1:12:40
Esztergom	47N48	18E45	-1:15:00
Fadd	46N28	18E50	-1:15:20
Fehérgyarmat	47N58	22E32	-1:30:08
Felsogalla	47N32	18E27	-1:13:48
Fót	47N37	19E12	-1:16:48
Fünfkirchen → Pécs	46N05	18E13	-1:12:52
Gödöllő	47N36	19E22	-1:17:28
Gran → Esztergom	47N48	18E45	-1:15:00
Gyál	47N23	19E14	-1:16:56
Gyoma	46N56	20E50	-1:23:20
Gyöngyös	47N47	19E56	-1:19:44
Győr	47N42	17E38	-1:10:32
Gyula	46N39	21E17	-1:25:08
Hajdúböszörmény	47N41	21E30	-1:26:00
Hajdúnánás	47N51	21E26	-1:25:44
Hajdúszoboszló	47N27	21E24	-1:25:36
Hatvan	47N40	19E41	-1:18:44
Heves	47N36	20E17	-1:21:08
Hódmezővásárhely	46N25	20E20	-1:21:20
Igal	46N31	17E55	-1:11:40
Izsák	46N48	19E22	-1:17:28
Jánoshalma	46N18	19E20	-1:17:20
Jánosháza	47N08	17E10	-1:08:40
Jászapáti	47N31	20E09	-1:20:36
Jászberény	47N30	19E55	-1:19:40
Kalocsa	46N32	18E59	-1:15:56
Kaposvár	46N22	17E47	-1:11:08
Kapuvár	47N36	17E02	-1:08:08
Karcag	47N19	20E56	-1:23:44
Kazincbarcika	48N16	20E37	-1:22:28
Kecel	46N32	19E16	-1:17:04
Kecskemét	46N54	19E42	-1:18:48
Kerepes	47N34	19E18	-1:17:12
Keszthely	46N46	17E15	-1:09:00
Kisbér	47N30	18E02	-1:12:08
Kiskőrös	46N38	19E17	-1:17:08
Kiskunfélegyháza	46N43	19E52	-1:19:28
Kiskunhalas	46N26	19E30	-1:18:00
Kiskunmajsa	46N30	19E45	-1:19:00
Kistarcsa	47N33	19E16	-1:17:04
Kisújszállás	47N13	20E46	-1:23:04
Kisvárda	48N13	22E05	-1:28:20
Komárom	47N44	18E08	-1:12:32
Komló	46N12	18E16	-1:13:04
Körmend	47N01	16E37	-1:06:28
Kőszeg	47N23	16E33	-1:06:12
Kunhegyes	47N22	20E38	-1:22:32
Kunszentmárton	46N51	20E18	-1:21:12
Lajosmizse	47N02	19E34	-1:18:16
Lenti	46N37	16E33	-1:06:12
Letenye	46N26	16E43	-1:06:52
Losonc	48N20	19E41	-1:18:44
Lovászi	46N33	16E34	-1:06:16
Lövő	47N30	16E47	-1:07:08
Maglód	47N27	19E21	-1:17:24
Makó	46N13	20E29	-1:21:56
Marcali	46N35	17E25	-1:09:40
Mátészalka	47N57	22E19	-1:29:16
Mélykút	46N13	19E24	-1:17:36
Mernye	46N30	17E50	-1:11:20
Mezőberény	46N50	21E02	-1:24:08
Mezőcsát	47N49	20E55	-1:23:40
Mezőkovácsháza	46N25	20E55	-1:23:40
Mezőkövesd	47N50	20E34	-1:22:16
Mezőtúr	47N00	20E38	-1:22:32
Miskolc	48N06	20E47	-1:23:08
Mogyoród	47N36	19E15	-1:17:00
Mohács	45N59	18E42	-1:14:48
Monor	47N21	19E27	-1:17:48
Mór	47N23	18E12	-1:12:48
Mórahalom	46N13	19E54	-1:19:36
Mosonmagyaróvár	47N51	17E17	-1:09:08
Mosonszentjános	47N47	17E08	-1:08:32
Munkacs	48N26	22E43	-1:30:52
Nagyatád	46N14	17E22	-1:09:28
Nagybajom	46N23	17E31	-1:10:04
Nagycenk	47N36	16E42	-1:06:48
Nagyecsed	47N52	22E24	-1:29:36
Nagykálló	47N53	21E51	-1:27:24
Nagykanizsa	46N27	17E00	-1:08:00
Nagykáta	47N25	19E45	-1:19:00
Nagykőrös	47N02	19E43	-1:18:52
Nagytarcsa	47N32	19E17	-1:17:08
Nova	46N41	16E41	-1:06:44
Nyíradony	47N41	21E55	-1:27:40
Nyírbátor	47N50	22E08	-1:28:32
Nyíregyháza	47N59	21E43	-1:26:52
Ödenburg → Sopron	47N41	16E36	-1:06:24
Őriszentpéter	46N51	16E25	-1:05:40
Orosháza	46N34	20E40	-1:22:40
Oroszlány	47N30	18E19	-1:13:16
Ózd	48N14	20E18	-1:21:12
Paks	46N39	18E53	-1:15:32
Pápa	47N19	17E28	-1:09:52
Parád	47N55	20E02	-1:20:08
Pásztó	47N55	19E42	-1:18:48
Pécel	47N29	19E21	-1:17:24
Pécs	46N05	18E13	-1:12:52
Pétervására	48N01	20E06	-1:20:24
Pilisborosjenő	47N36	19E00	-1:16:00
Polgár	47N52	21E08	-1:24:32
Pomáz	47N39	19E02	-1:16:08
Püspökladány	47N19	21E07	-1:24:28
Raab → Győr	47N42	17E38	-1:10:32
Rábahidvég	47N04	16E45	-1:07:00
Ráckeve	47N10	18E56	-1:15:44
Rajka	48N02	17E11	-1:08:44
Rakamaz	48N08	21E30	-1:26:00
Rédics	46N36	16E30	-1:06:00
Rimaszombat	48N23	20E02	-1:20:08
Rum	47N08	16E51	-1:07:24
Sajószentpéter	48N13	20E44	-1:22:56
Salgótarján	48N07	19E48	-1:19:12
Sárbogárd	46N53	18E38	-1:14:32
Sarkad	46N44	21E23	-1:25:32
Sármellék	46N44	17E10	-1:08:40
Sárospatak	48N19	21E34	-1:26:16
Sárvár	47N15	16E57	-1:07:48
Sásd	46N15	18E06	-1:12:24
Siklos	45N51	18E19	-1:13:16
Sátoraljaújhely	48N24	21E39	-1:26:36
Siófok	46N54	18E04	-1:12:16
Solt	46N48	19E00	-1:16:00
Solymár	47N36	18E56	-1:15:44
Sopron	47N41	16E36	-1:06:24
Steinamanger → Szombathely	47N14	16E38	-1:06:32
Stuhlweissenburg → Székesfehérvár	47N12	18E25	-1:13:40
Sümeg	46N59	17E17	-1:09:08
Szada	47N38	19E19	-1:17:16
Szarvas	46N52	20E34	-1:22:16
Százhalombatta	47N20	18E56	-1:15:44
Szécsény	48N06	19E31	-1:18:04
Szeged	46N15	20E09	-1:20:36
Szeghalom	47N01	21E11	-1:24:44
Székesfehérvár	47N12	18E25	-1:13:40
Szekszárd	46N21	18E42	-1:14:48
Szentendre	47N40	19E05	-1:16:20
Szentes	46N39	20E16	-1:21:04
Szentgotthárd	46N57	16E17	-1:05:08
Szerencs	48N09	21E13	-1:24:52
Szigethalom	47N20	19E00	-1:16:00
Szigetszentmiklós	47N21	19E03	-1:16:12
Szigetvar	46N03	17E49	-1:11:16
Szob	47N50	18E52	-1:15:28
Szolnok	47N10	20E12	-1:20:48
Szombathely	47N14	16E38	-1:06:32
Taksony	47N20	19E04	-1:16:16
Tamási	46N38	18E18	-1:13:12
Tapolca	46N53	17E27	-1:09:48
Tata	47N39	18E18	-1:13:12
Tatabánya	47N34	18E26	-1:13:44
Tésa	48N02	18E51	-1:15:24
Tiszaföldvár	46N59	20E15	-1:21:00
Tiszafüred	47N37	20E46	-1:23:04
Tiszavasvári	47N58	21E22	-1:25:28
Tököl	47N19	18E58	-1:15:52
Tolna	46N26	18E46	-1:15:04
Törökszentmiklós	47N11	20E25	-1:21:40
Túrkeve	47N06	20E45	-1:23:00
Újfehértó	47N48	21E40	-1:26:40
Ujpest	47N35	19E07	-1:16:28
Üllő	47N23	19E21	-1:17:24
Ungvar	48N37	22E19	-1:29:16
Üröm	47N36	19E01	-1:16:04
Vác	47N47	19E08	-1:16:32
Várpalota	47N12	18E09	-1:12:36
Vasvár	47N03	16E49	-1:07:16
Vát	47N17	16E47	-1:07:08
Vecsés	47N25	19E16	-1:17:04
Veresegyház	47N39	19E17	-1:17:08
Veszprém	47N06	17E55	-1:11:40
Vésztő	46N55	21E16	-1:25:04
Waitzen → Vác	47N47	19E08	-1:16:32
Záhony	48N25	22E11	-1:28:44
Zalaegerszeg	46N51	16E51	-1:07:24
Zalalövő	46N51	16E35	-1:06:20
Zalaszentgrót	46N59	17E02	-1:08:08

ÍSLAND ISLAND ISLANDE ISLANDIA ICELAND

Time Table		
Before 1/Jan/1837 LMT		
Begin Standard		21w57
1/Jan/1837	0:00	1:28
Begin Standard		15w00
1/Jan/1908	0:00	1:00
20/Feb/1917	2:00	0:00
25/Oct/1917	2:00	1:00
20/Feb/1918	2:00	0:00
15/Nov/1918	2:00	1:00
19/Feb/1919	2:00	0:00
15/Nov/1919	2:00	1:00
19/Mar/1921	2:00	0:00
22/Jun/1921	2:00	1:00
1/Mar/1941	2:00	0:00
2/Jul/1941	2:00	1:00
7/Mar/1942	2:00	0:00
2/Jul/1942	2:00	1:00
7/Mar/1943	2:00	0:00
24/Oct/1943	2:00	1:00
5/Mar/1944	2:00	0:00
22/Oct/1944	2:00	1:00
4/Mar/1945	2:00	0:00
28/Oct/1945	2:00	1:00
3/Mar/1946	2:00	0:00
27/Oct/1946	2:00	1:00
6/Apr/1947	2:00	0:00
26/Oct/1947	2:00	1:00
4/Apr/1948	2:00	0:00
24/Oct/1948	2:00	1:00
3/Apr/1949	2:00	0:00
30/Oct/1949	2:00	1:00
2/Apr/1950	2:00	0:00
22/Oct/1950	2:00	1:00
1/Apr/1951	2:00	0:00
28/Oct/1951	2:00	1:00
6/Apr/1952	2:00	0:00
26/Oct/1952	2:00	1:00
5/Apr/1953	2:00	0:00
26/Oct/1953	2:00	1:00
4/Apr/1954	2:00	0:00
24/Oct/1954	2:00	1:00
3/Apr/1955	2:00	0:00
23/Oct/1955	2:00	1:00
1/Apr/1956	2:00	0:00
28/Oct/1956	2:00	1:00
7/Apr/1957	2:00	0:00
27/Oct/1957	2:00	1:00
6/Apr/1958	2:00	0:00
26/Oct/1958	2:00	1:00
5/Apr/1959	2:00	0:00
25/Oct/1959	2:00	1:00
3/Apr/1960	2:00	0:00
23/Oct/1960	2:00	1:00
2/Apr/1961	2:00	0:00
22/Oct/1961	2:00	1:00
1/Apr/1962	2:00	0:00
28/Oct/1962	2:00	1:00
7/Apr/1963	1:00	0:00
27/Oct/1963	2:00	1:00
5/Apr/1964	1:00	0:00
25/Oct/1964	2:00	1:00
4/Apr/1965	1:00	0:00
24/Oct/1965	2:00	1:00
3/Apr/1966	1:00	0:00
23/Oct/1966	2:00	1:00
2/Apr/1967	1:00	0:00
29/Oct/1967	2:00	1:00
7/Apr/1968	1:00	0:00
Begin Standard		0w00
27/Oct/1968	2:00	0:00

Place	Lat	Long	Offset
Akranes	64N18	22w02	1:28:08
Akureyri	65N44	18w08	1:12:32
Bakkafjörđur	66N04	14w45	0:59:00
Bakkagerđi	65N32	13w48	0:55:12
Blönduós	65N39	20w15	1:21:00
Borđeyri	65N15	21w10	1:24:40
Borgarnes	64N35	21w53	1:27:32
Búđardalur	65N10	21w42	1:26:48
Búđir	64N56	13w58	0:55:52
Dalvík	65N59	18w32	1:14:08
Djúpivogur	64N40	14w10	0:56:40
Egilsstađir	65N16	14w18	0:57:12
Eskifjörđur	65N04	13w59	0:55:56
Eyrarbakki	63N53	21w05	1:24:20
Fagurhólsmýri	63N54	16w38	1:06:32
Flatey	65N19	23w07	1:32:28
Flateyri	65N59	23w42	1:34:48
Grímsstađir	65N40	16w01	1:04:04
Grindavík	63N52	22w27	1:29:48
Hafnarfjörđur	64N03	21w56	1:27:44
Hof	64N34	14w39	0:58:36
Höfđakaupstađur	65N50	20w19	1:21:16
Höfn	64N17	15w10	1:00:40
Hólmavík	65N43	21w43	1:26:52
Húsavík	66N04	17w18	1:09:12
Hveragerđi	64N03	21w10	1:24:40
Hvolsvöllur	63N45	20w10	1:20:40
Ísafjörđur	66N08	23w13	1:32:52
Kálfafell	63N58	17w40	1:10:40
Keflavík	64N02	22w36	1:30:24
Kirkjubæjarklaustur	63N47	18w04	1:12:16
Kópasker	66N20	16w24	1:05:36
Kópavogur	64N06	21w50	1:27:20
Neskaupstađur	65N10	13w43	0:54:52
Ólafsfjörđur	66N06	18w38	1:14:32
Ólafsvík	64N54	23w43	1:34:52
Peykjahliđ	65N40	16w50	1:07:20
Raufarhöfn	66N30	15w57	1:03:48
Reykjavík	64N09	21w51	1:27:24
Sauđárkrókur	65N46	19w41	1:18:44
Selfoss	63N56	20w57	1:23:48
Seyđisfjörđur	65N16	14w00	0:56:00
Siglufjörđur	66N10	18w56	1:15:44
Skarđ	64N03	19w50	1:19:20
Skinnastađur	66N07	16w24	1:05:36
Stykkishólmur	65N06	22w48	1:31:12
Thingvellir	64N17	21w07	1:24:28
Thorlákshöfn	63N53	21w18	1:25:12
Thórshöfn	66N13	15w17	1:01:08
Vatneyri	65N38	23w57	1:35:48
Vestmannaeyjar	63N26	20w12	1:20:48
Vík	63N25	19w00	1:16:00
Vopnafjörđur	65N47	14w44	0:58:56

BHĀRAT INDIEN INDE INDIA

Time Table # 1		
Before 18/Jul/1911 LMT		
Begin Standard		82E30
18/Jul/1911	0:00	-5:30
1/Sep/1942	0:00	-6:30
15/Oct/1945	0:00	-5:30

Time Table # 2		
Before 1/Jan/1880 LMT		
Begin Standard		80E15
1/Jan/1880	0:00	-5:21
Begin Standard		82E30
1/Jan/1907	0:00	-5:30
1/Sep/1942	0:00	-6:30
15/Oct/1945	0:00	-5:30

Time Table # 3		
Before 1/Jan/1880 LMT		
Begin Standard		88E20
1/Jan/1880	0:00	-5:53
Begin Standard		97E30
1/Oct/1941	0:00	-6:30
Begin Standard		82E30
15/May/1942	0:00	-5:30
1/Sep/1942	0:00	-6:30
1/Sep/1947	0:00	-5:30

Time Table # 4		
Before 1/Nov/1941 LMT		
Begin Standard		97E30
1/Nov/1941	0:00	-6:30
Begin Standard		82E30
15/May/1942	0:00	-5:30
1/Sep/1942	0:00	-6:30
15/Oct/1945	0:00	-5:30

Time Table # 5		
Before 1/Dec/1941 LMT		
Begin Standard		97E30
1/Dec/1941	0:00	-6:30
Begin Standard		82E30
15/May/1942	0:00	-5:30
1/Sep/1942	0:00	-6:30
15/Oct/1945	0:00	-5:30

Place	TT	Lat	Long	Offset
Abhayāpuri	4	26N20	90E40	-6:02:40
Abohar	2	30N09	74E11	-4:56:44
Abring	2	33N42	76E35	-5:06:20
Abu Road	2	24N29	72E47	-4:51:08
Achalpur	2	21N16	77E31	-5:10:04
Achhībal	2	33N41	75E14	-5:00:56
Achhnera	2	27N11	77E46	-5:11:04
Adai	2	19N01	73E08	-4:52:32
Ādampur	2	31N26	75E43	-5:02:52
Adauli	2	19N06	73E02	-4:52:08
Adayar (Adyar)	2	13N01	80E15	-5:21:00
Addanki	2	15N49	80E01	-5:20:04
Adhāta	3	22N52	88E32	-5:54:08
Ādilābād	2	19N40	78E32	-5:14:08
Ādoni	2	15N38	77E17	-5:09:08
Ādra	3	23N30	86E40	-5:46:40
Afaspida	2	19N08	73E04	-4:52:16
Afzalgarh	2	29N24	78E41	-5:14:44
Agāhpur	2	28N34	77E22	-5:09:28
Agar	2	23N42	76E01	-5:04:04
Agartala	4	23N49	91E16	-6:05:04
Agasan	2	19N11	73E04	-4:52:16
Agia	4	26N05	90E32	-6:02:08
Āgra	2	27N11	78E01	-5:12:04
Ahmadābād	2	23N02	72E37	-4:50:28
Ahmadgarh	2	30N41	75E50	-5:03:20
Ahmadnagar	2	19N05	74E44	-4:58:56
Ahmadpur	2	23N31	77E13	-5:08:52
Ahmadpur	3	23N50	87E42	-5:50:48
Ahmedabad → Ahmadābād	2	23N02	72E37	-4:50:28
Ahraura	2	25N01	83E01	-5:32:04
Aijal	4	23N44	92E43	-6:10:52
Ajanta	2	20N32	75E45	-5:03:00
Ajmer	2	26N27	74E38	-4:58:32
Ajnāla	2	31N51	74E48	-4:59:12
Akalkot	2	17N32	76E13	-5:04:52
Akaltara	2	22N01	82E26	-5:29:44
Akbarpur	5	24N39	83E58	-5:35:52
Akbarpur	2	26N25	82E33	-5:30:12
Akhnūr	2	32N54	74E44	-4:58:56
Ākna	3	22N59	88E21	-5:53:24
Akodia	2	23N23	76E36	-5:06:24
Akola	2	20N44	77E00	-5:08:00
Akot	2	21N11	77E04	-5:08:16
Akurli	2	19N01	73E08	-4:52:32
Alampur	3	22N25	88E08	-5:52:32
Alampur	2	15N54	78E11	-5:12:44
Aland	2	17N34	76E34	-5:06:16
Alandur	2	13N02	80E15	-5:21:00
Alāwalpur	2	31N26	75E39	-5:02:36
Alībāg	2	18N39	72E54	-4:51:36
Alīganj	2	28N07	80E36	-5:22:24
Alīganj	2	27N30	79E11	-5:16:44
Alīgarh	2	27N53	78E05	-5:12:20
Ālipur	3	22N43	88E12	-5:52:48
Alipur	3	22N55	88E11	-5:52:44
Alīpur Duār	3	26N29	89E44	-5:58:56
Āli Rājpur	2	22N19	74E21	-4:57:24
Allāhābād	2	25N27	81E51	-5:27:24
Allāhbās	2	28N31	77E25	-5:09:40
Allāh Durg	2	18N01	77E46	-5:11:04
Allāhwardipur	2	28N33	77E26	-5:09:44
Alleppey	2	9N29	76E19	-5:05:16
Allinagaram	2	10N02	77E30	-5:10:00
Allur	2	14N11	80E05	-5:20:20
Almora	2	29N37	79E40	-5:18:40
Along	4	28N12	94E52	-6:19:28
Alur	2	15N24	77E16	-5:09:04
Alwar	2	27N34	76E36	-5:06:24
Alwaye	2	10N07	76E21	-5:05:24
Amalāpuram	2	16N35	82E01	-5:28:04
Amalner	2	21N03	75E04	-5:00:16
Amānganj	2	24N26	80E02	-5:20:08
Amarda	2	21N47	87E08	-5:48:32
Amarkantak	2	22N40	81E45	-5:27:00
Amarpātan	2	24N19	80E59	-5:23:56
Amarwāra	2	22N18	79E10	-5:16:40
Amausi	2	26N46	80E51	-5:23:24
Ambāh	2	26N43	78E14	-5:12:56
Ambājogāi	2	18N44	76E23	-5:05:32
Ambāla	2	30N21	76E50	-5:07:20
Ambarnāth	2	19N11	73E10	-4:52:40
Ambāsamudram	2	8N42	77E28	-5:09:52
Amber	2	26N59	75E52	-5:03:28
Ambikānagar	5	22N57	86E46	-5:47:04
Ambikāpur	2	23N07	83E12	-5:32:48
Amboshe	2	19N09	73E08	-4:52:32
Āmbūr	2	12N47	78E42	-5:14:48
Āmdānga	3	22N49	88E31	-5:54:04
Amili	4	28N26	95E52	-6:23:28
Amitha	3	22N35	88E00	-5:52:00
Amla	2	21N56	78E07	-5:12:28
Āmlāgora	3	22N50	87E20	-5:49:20
Amloh	2	30N37	76E14	-5:04:56
Amnān	3	22N56	88E18	-5:53:12
Amrabad	2	16N23	78E48	-5:15:12
Amraoti → Amrāvati	2	20N56	77E45	-5:11:00
Amrāvati	2	20N56	77E45	-5:11:00
Amreli	2	21N37	71E14	-4:44:56
Āmreswar	3	22N28	88E34	-5:54:16
Amritsar	2	31N35	74E53	-4:59:32
Amroha	2	28N55	78E28	-5:13:52
Amta	3	22N35	88E01	-5:52:04
Āmtala	3	23N55	88E27	-5:53:48
Anakāpalle	2	17N41	83E01	-5:32:04
Anamalai	2	10N35	76E56	-5:07:44
Ānand	2	22N34	72E56	-4:51:44
Anandanagar	3	22N51	88E16	-5:53:04
Anandapur	3	22N34	87E25	-5:49:40
Anandpur	2	31N15	76E30	-5:06:00
Anantapur	2	14N41	77E36	-5:10:24
Anantnāg (Islāmābād)	2	33N44	75E09	-5:00:36
Anāra	5	23N28	86E33	-5:46:12
Andāl	2	17N53	78E03	-5:12:12
Andāl	3	23N36	87E12	-5:48:48
Angul	2	20N51	85E06	-5:40:24
Anjad	2	22N02	75E03	-5:00:12
Anjangaon	2	21N10	77E18	-5:09:12
Anjār	2	23N08	70E01	-4:40:04
Anklesvar	2	21N36	73E00	-4:52:00
Anūpgarh	2	29N11	73E13	-4:52:52
Anūpshahr	2	28N22	78E16	-5:13:04
Ānūr	3	22N55	87E39	-5:50:36
Aonla	2	28N17	79E09	-5:16:36
Arāmbāgh	3	22N53	87E47	-5:51:08
Arang	2	21N12	81E58	-5:27:52
Ārani	2	12N40	79E17	-5:17:08
Arantāngi	2	10N10	78E59	-5:15:56
Arāpānja	3	22N26	88E28	-5:53:52
Arāria	2	26N08	87E24	-5:49:36
Ārbālia	3	22N41	88E47	-5:55:08
Arcot	2	12N54	79E20	-5:17:20
Ārgoal	3	21N58	87E38	-5:50:32
Ārgur	3	22N48	88E13	-5:52:52
Ariah	5	23N33	86E20	-5:45:20
Ariyalūr	2	11N08	79E05	-5:16:20
Arki	2	31N09	76E58	-5:07:52
Arkonam	2	13N06	79E40	-5:18:40
Armori	2	20N28	79E59	-5:19:56
Ārmūr	2	18N48	78E17	-5:13:08
Aroali	3	24N03	87E56	-5:51:44
Arrah	5	25N34	84E40	-5:38:40
Ārsāpota	3	22N55	88E18	-5:53:12
Arsikere	2	13N20	76E15	-5:05:00
Arthal	2	33N16	76E11	-5:04:44
Arthala	2	28N40	77E24	-5:09:36
Arumuganeri	2	8N34	78E07	-5:12:28
Aruppukkottai	2	9N31	78E06	-5:12:24
Arvi	2	20N59	78E14	-5:12:56
Arwal	5	25N15	84E41	-5:38:44
Asanbāni	2	24N07	87E27	-5:49:48
Asanbani	5	22N43	86E20	-5:45:20
Asansol	3	23N41	86E59	-5:47:56
Asansol	2	24N14	87E17	-5:49:08
Asati	3	22N29	88E14	-5:52:56
Ashoknagar	2	24N34	77E43	-5:10:52

Name		Lat.	Long.	Time
Ashta	2	23N01	76E43	-5:06:52
Ashta	2	16N57	74E24	-4:57:36
Asifabad	2	19N23	79E21	-5:17:24
Aska	2	19N36	84E39	-5:38:36
Aswatthaberia	3	22N26	88E32	-5:54:08
Atāri	2	31N36	74E35	-4:58:20
Ataur	2	28N43	77E24	-5:09:36
Ateli	2	28N06	76E17	-5:05:08
Atghara	3	22N37	88E27	-5:53:48
Athni	2	16N44	75E04	-5:00:16
Atirāmpattinam	2	10N21	79E24	-5:17:36
Atmakūr	2	18N46	78E38	-5:14:32
Atmakūr	2	14N37	79E40	-5:18:40
Atmakūr	2	15N53	78E35	-5:14:20
Atpur	3	22N50	88E23	-5:53:32
Atrauli	2	28N02	78E17	-5:13:08
Atta	2	28N34	77E20	-5:09:20
Attingal	2	8N41	76E50	-5:07:20
Āttūr	2	11N36	78E37	-5:14:28
Atzalpur	2	28N43	77E21	-5:09:24
Auagrām	3	23N31	87E41	-5:50:44
Auraiya	2	26N28	79E31	-5:18:04
Aurangābād	5	24N45	84E22	-5:37:28
Aurangābād	2	19N53	75E20	-5:01:20
Āyān	3	22N43	88E09	-5:52:36
Ayodhya	2	26N48	82E12	-5:28:48
Azamgarh	2	26N04	83E11	-5:32:44
Azhikode	2	11N59	75E21	-5:01:24
Azimganj	3	24N14	88E15	-5:53:00
Babīna	2	25N15	78E28	-5:13:52
Bābu Bheri	3	22N51	88E14	-5:52:56
Bābūpur	2	28N30	76E59	-5:07:56
Bābupur	2	24N01	87E10	-5:48:40
Bacheli	2	18N40	81E16	-5:25:04
Badagara	2	11N36	75E35	-5:02:20
Badakasira	2	13N58	77E14	-5:08:56
Bādāmi	2	15N55	75E41	-5:02:44
Bādāmpahār	2	22N06	86E06	-5:44:24
Badanganj	3	22N54	87E33	-5:50:12
Badgom	2	34N01	74E43	-4:58:52
Bādinan	3	22N54	88E14	-5:52:56
Bādkulla	3	23N17	88E32	-5:54:08
Badnera	2	20N52	77E44	-5:10:56
Badrīnāth	2	30N44	79E29	-5:17:56
Bādshāhpur	2	25N47	82E49	-5:31:16
Bāduria	3	22N44	88E47	-5:55:08
Badvel	2	14N45	79E03	-5:16:12
Bagaha	5	27N06	84E05	-5:36:20
Bāgalkot	2	16N11	75E42	-5:02:48
Bagasra	2	21N29	70E57	-4:43:48
Bāgda	5	23N13	86E41	-5:46:44
Bagdaha	3	23N13	88E53	-5:55:32
Bagdanga	3	24N02	88E32	-5:54:08
Bāgevādi	2	16N35	75E58	-5:03:52
Baghdobā	3	22N08	87E54	-5:51:36
Bāghmundi	3	23N12	86E03	-5:44:12
Bāghpat	2	28N57	77E13	-5:08:52
Bāgli	2	22N39	76E21	-5:05:24
Bāgnān	3	22N28	87E59	-5:51:56
Bagodar	5	24N05	85E52	-5:43:28
Bagrakote	3	26N40	88E30	-5:54:00
Bāguiati	3	22N36	88E26	-5:53:44
Bagula	3	23N19	88E39	-5:54:36
Bāh	2	26N53	78E36	-5:14:24
Bahādurgarh	2	28N41	76E56	-5:07:44
Bāhādurpur	3	23N25	88E28	-5:53:52
Baharāgora	5	22N17	86E43	-5:46:52
Baheri	2	28N47	79E30	-5:18:00
Bahjoi	2	28N24	78E37	-5:14:28
Bahl	2	28N38	75E38	-5:02:32
Bahlolpur	2	28N37	77E24	-5:09:36
Bahraich	2	27N35	81E36	-5:26:24
Baidyabāti	3	22N47	88E20	-5:53:20
Baidyanāth	5	24N29	86E42	-5:46:48
Baihar	2	22N06	80E33	-5:22:12
Baijala	3	22N51	88E16	-5:53:04
Baijnāth	2	29N55	79E37	-5:18:28
Baikunthapur	2	23N15	82E33	-5:30:12
Baikunthapur	3	22N59	88E13	-5:52:52
Bail Hongal	2	15N49	74E52	-4:59:28
Bainchi	3	23N07	88E14	-5:52:56
Bainchipota	3	22N52	88E16	-5:53:04
Baisingga	2	21N39	86E54	-5:47:36
Baita	3	22N27	88E11	-5:52:44
Baital	3	22N57	87E28	-5:49:52
Bājengdoba	4	25N54	90E31	-6:02:04
Bajghera	2	28N32	77E01	-5:08:04
Bakaruma	2	22N32	83E25	-5:33:40
Bakaspur	5	23N00	85E00	-5:40:00
Bakhra	3	22N24	88E11	-5:52:44
Bakhri	5	25N35	86E16	-5:45:04
Bakhtiyārpur	5	25N28	85E31	-5:42:04
Bakkeswar	3	22N25	88E22	-5:53:28
Bakloh	2	32N28	75E55	-5:03:40
Baladbandh	3	22N52	88E07	-5:52:28
Bālāghāt	2	21N48	80E11	-5:20:44
Bālandi	3	22N58	88E32	-5:54:08
Balāngīr	2	20N43	83E29	-5:33:56
Bālāpur	2	20N40	76E46	-5:07:04
Balarāmbāti	3	22N48	88E13	-5:52:52
Balarāmpota	3	22N31	88E08	-5:52:32
Balarāmpur	3	23N07	86E13	-5:44:52
Bālārampuram	2	8N26	77E03	-5:08:12
Balasore	2	21N30	86E56	-5:47:44
Bale	2	19N08	73E06	-4:52:24
Bali	2	25N50	74E05	-4:56:20
Bāliāpāl	2	21N40	87E17	-5:49:08
Bāli Chak	3	22N22	87E33	-5:50:12
Bālidiha	2	21N58	86E38	-5:46:32
Bālighai	3	21N52	87E35	-5:50:20
Bālihāti	3	22N44	88E19	-5:53:16
Balipada	4	26N09	92E09	-6:08:36
Balkonda	2	19N05	78E20	-5:13:20
Ballabgarh	2	28N21	77E19	-5:09:16
Ballabhpur	3	22N44	88E21	-5:53:24
Ballālpur	2	19N50	79E22	-5:17:28
Ballia	2	25N45	84E10	-5:36:40
Bālly	3	22N38	88E21	-5:53:24
Ballyganj	3	22N40	88E07	-5:52:28
Baloda Bāzār	2	21N40	82E10	-5:28:40
Bālotra	2	25N50	72E14	-4:48:56
Balrāmpur	3	23N06	86E13	-5:44:52
Balrāmpur	2	27N26	82E11	-5:28:44
Bālughāta	3	22N05	88E01	-5:52:04
Bāluhāti	3	22N39	88E16	-5:53:04
Bālurghāt	3	25N13	88E46	-5:55:04
Bāmangāchi	3	22N46	88E31	-5:54:04
Bāmangawān	5	24N14	86E49	-5:47:16
Bāmanghāra	3	22N31	88E28	-5:53:52
Bāmanhat	3	26N03	89E33	-5:58:12
Bāmanmura	3	22N42	88E31	-5:54:04
Bambāvi	2	18N58	73E03	-4:52:12
Bananga	4	6N56	93E54	-6:15:36
Banaras → Vārānasi	2	25N20	83E00	-5:32:00
Banarhat	3	26N44	89E03	-5:56:12
Banda	2	24N03	78E57	-5:15:48
Bānda	2	25N29	80E20	-5:21:20
Bandar → Machilīpatnam	2	16N10	81E08	-5:24:32
Bāndel	3	22N56	88E22	-5:53:28
Bāndikūi	2	27N03	76E34	-5:06:16
Bandipur	3	22N44	88E26	-5:53:44
Bandipur	3	22N51	88E10	-5:52:40
Bandipura	2	34N25	74E39	-4:58:36
Bandoyan	3	22N53	86E31	-5:46:04
Bānduān	5	22N53	86E31	-5:46:04
Banehra	2	28N44	77E23	-5:09:32
Banga	2	31N11	75E59	-5:03:56
Bangalore	2	12N59	77E35	-5:10:20
Bangalur → Bangalore	2	12N59	77E35	-5:10:20
Banganapalle	2	15N19	78E17	-5:13:08
Bangaon	3	23N04	88E49	-5:55:16
Bangārapet	2	12N58	78E12	-5:12:48
Bāngriposi	5	22N10	86E32	-5:46:08
Bānka	5	24N53	86E55	-5:47:40
Bānkādāba	3	22N58	87E21	-5:49:24
Bānkipur	3	22N48	88E14	-5:52:56
Bānkura	3	23N15	87E04	-5:48:16
Bānmankhi Bazar	2	25N53	87E11	-5:48:44
Banpās	3	23N24	87E45	-5:51:00
Banpura	3	22N27	87E22	-5:49:28
Bānsbāria	3	22N58	88E24	-5:53:36
Bānsda	2	20N45	73E22	-4:53:28
Bānsi	2	27N11	82E56	-5:31:44
Bansihari	3	25N24	88E26	-5:53:44
Bānskupi	5	24N10	86E41	-5:46:44
Banstala	3	22N32	88E25	-5:53:40
Bānswāra	2	23N33	74E27	-4:57:48
Bāntra	3	22N35	88E19	-5:53:16
Bāntva	2	21N29	70E05	-4:40:20
Banūr	2	30N34	76E43	-5:06:52
Bāp	2	27N23	72E21	-4:49:24
Bāpatla	2	15N54	80E28	-5:21:52
Bara	3	22N43	88E31	-5:54:04
Bara	3	22N46	88E17	-5:53:08
Bāra	2	25N13	87E22	-5:49:28
Bara Bāngurda	5	22N57	86E24	-5:45:36
Bāra Banki	2	26N55	81E12	-5:24:48
Barābhūm	5	23N02	86E22	-5:45:28
Baragaon → Nālanda	5	25N07	85E25	-5:41:40
Barahabhum	3	23N01	86E22	-5:45:28
Baraily	2	23N00	78E14	-5:12:56
Bāra Jamda	5	22N09	85E23	-5:41:32
Bara Jorda	5	23N10	86E50	-5:47:20
Barākar	5	24N07	86E14	-5:44:56
Bara Khunta	2	21N43	86E38	-5:46:32
Barākot	2	21N33	85E01	-5:40:04
Barāl	3	22N27	88E22	-5:53:28
Barām	5	22N57	86E18	-5:45:12
Barāmāria	2	21N42	87E04	-5:48:16
Bārāmati	2	18N09	74E35	-4:58:20
Bāramūla	2	34N12	74E21	-4:57:24
Bārān	2	25N06	76E31	-5:06:04
Baranagar	3	22N38	88E22	-5:53:28
Barapeta	4	26N20	91E03	-6:04:12
Barasāhi	2	21N43	86E44	-5:46:56
Barasarenga	3	22N48	87E00	-5:48:00
Bārāsat	3	22N43	88E29	-5:53:56
Bārasat	3	22N51	88E22	-5:53:28
Baratolia	5	22N25	86E37	-5:46:28
Baraula	2	28N34	77E22	-5:09:28
Baraut	2	29N06	77E16	-5:09:04
Bar Bigha	5	25N13	85E44	-5:42:56
Barbil	2	22N06	85E20	-5:41:20
Bardoli	2	21N07	73E07	-4:52:28
Bareilly	2	28N21	79E25	-5:17:40
Barengapāra	4	25N14	90E14	-6:00:56
Bareta	2	29N52	75E42	-5:02:48
Bargāchia	3	22N39	88E07	-5:52:28
Bargāchia	3	22N48	88E27	-5:53:48
Bargarh	2	21N20	83E37	-5:34:28
Bārh	5	25N29	85E43	-5:42:52
Barharwa	5	24N52	87E47	-5:51:08
Barhi	5	24N18	85E25	-5:41:40
Barhiya	5	25N17	86E02	-5:44:08
Bāri	2	23N03	78E05	-5:12:20
Bāri	2	26N39	77E36	-5:10:24
Baripāda	2	21N56	86E43	-5:46:52
Bari Sādri	2	24N25	74E28	-4:57:52
Barjora	3	23N26	87E17	-5:49:08
Barka Kāna	5	23N37	85E29	-5:41:56
Barki Saraiya	5	24N10	85E53	-5:43:32
Barkuhi	2	22N13	78E42	-5:14:48
Barmer	2	25N45	71E23	-4:45:32
Barnagar	2	23N03	75E22	-5:01:28
Barnāla	2	30N23	75E33	-5:02:12
Baroda	2	22N18	73E12	-4:52:48
Baroda	2	25N30	76E39	-5:06:36
Barpathār	4	26N17	93E53	-6:15:32
Barpeta	4	26N19	91E00	-6:04:00
Barrackpore	3	22N46	88E21	-5:53:24
Barrackpore Cantonment	3	22N46	88E22	-5:53:28
Bārsi	2	18N14	75E42	-5:02:48
Bartala	3	22N33	88E16	-5:53:04
Bāruipāra	3	22N46	88E14	-5:52:56
Bāruipur	3	22N21	88E27	-5:53:48
Bāruni	5	25N29	85E59	-5:43:56
Barwa	5	23N51	86E26	-5:45:44
Barwāh	2	22N16	76E03	-5:04:12
Barwāni	2	22N02	74E54	-4:59:36
Barwa Sāgar	2	25N23	78E44	-5:14:56
Basanti	3	22N12	88E42	-5:54:48
Basavakalyān	2	17N52	76E57	-5:07:48
Basi	2	30N36	76E50	-5:07:20
Basi	2	30N41	76E24	-5:05:36
Basīrhāt	3	22N40	88E53	-5:55:32
Basiya	5	22N52	84E53	-5:39:32
Basmat	2	19N19	77E10	-5:08:40
Bāsoda	2	23N51	77E56	-5:11:44
Basoli	2	32N30	75E49	-5:03:16
Basta	2	21N41	87E03	-5:48:12
Basti	2	26N48	82E43	-5:30:52
Basubāti	3	22N47	88E12	-5:52:48
Bāsudebpur	3	22N49	88E25	-5:53:40
Bāsudebpur	3	21N49	87E38	-5:50:32
Baswa	3	24N08	87E52	-5:51:28
Batāla	2	31N48	75E12	-5:00:48
Batanagar	3	22N31	88E15	-5:53:00
Batiāgarh	2	24N07	79E21	-5:17:24
Batoti	2	33N06	75E19	-5:01:16
Baudh	2	20N50	84E19	-5:37:16
Bāuria	3	22N29	88E10	-5:52:40
Bāwal	2	28N05	76E35	-5:06:20
Bāwāli	3	22N25	88E12	-5:52:48
Bayāna	2	26N54	77E17	-5:09:08
Beās	2	31N31	75E17	-5:01:08
Beāwar	2	26N06	74E19	-4:57:16
Bedi	2	22N30	70E02	-4:40:08
Begamganj	2	23N36	78E20	-5:13:20
Begusarai	5	25N25	86E08	-5:44:32
Behāla	3	22N31	88E19	-5:53:16
Behrāmpur	2	28N38	77E24	-5:09:36
Bela	2	25N56	81E59	-5:27:56
Belampalli	2	19N02	79E30	-5:18:00
Belapurpāda	2	19N01	73E02	-4:52:08
Belbunia	3	23N17	87E09	-5:48:36
Belda	3	22N05	87E21	-5:49:24
Beldānga	3	23N56	88E15	-5:53:00
Belgaum	2	15N52	74E31	-4:58:04
Belhar	5	24N55	86E36	-5:46:24
Beliābera	5	22N17	86E57	-5:47:48
Beliātor	3	23N20	87E13	-5:48:52
Bellary	2	15N09	76E56	-5:07:44
Belmuri	3	22N57	88E09	-5:52:36
Belpāda	2	19N02	73E03	-4:52:12
Belur	3	22N38	88E18	-5:53:12
Belūr	2	13N10	75E52	-5:03:28
Benagaria	5	24N11	87E37	-5:50:28
Benares → Vārānasi	2	25N20	83E00	-5:32:00
Bengābād	5	24N18	86E21	-5:45:24
Beohāri	2	24N03	81E23	-5:25:32
Beonta	3	22N31	88E31	-5:54:04
Berābāria	3	22N52	88E34	-5:54:16
Berāberi	3	22N51	88E12	-5:52:48
Beraberi	3	22N46	88E27	-5:53:48
Berāsi	2	23N36	81E51	-5:27:24
Berasia	2	23N38	77E26	-5:09:44
Berhampore	3	24N06	88E15	-5:53:00
Berhampur	2	19N19	84E47	-5:39:08
Beri	2	28N42	76E35	-5:06:20
Bermo	5	23N47	85E57	-5:43:48
Besani	2	24N08	80E17	-5:21:08
Betā	3	22N55	88E14	-5:52:56
Betnoti	2	21N44	86E51	-5:47:24
Bettiah	5	26N48	84E30	-5:38:00
Betūl	2	21N55	77E54	-5:11:36
Bewār	2	27N13	79E18	-5:17:12
Beypore	2	11N11	75E49	-5:03:16
Bezwada → Vijayawāda	2	16N31	80E37	-5:22:28
Bhabānipur	3	22N56	88E13	-5:52:52
Bhabānipur	3	22N57	88E27	-5:53:48
Bhābta	3	23N59	88E15	-5:53:00
Bhabua	2	25N03	83E37	-5:34:28
Bhadarwah	2	32N59	75E43	-5:02:52
Bhadaur	2	30N29	75E19	-5:01:16
Bhadohi	2	25N25	82E34	-5:30:16
Bhādra	2	29N07	75E10	-5:00:40
Bhadrāchalam	2	17N40	80E53	-5:23:32
Bhadrakal	3	22N15	88E24	-5:53:36
Bhadrakh	2	21N04	86E30	-5:46:00
Bhadrāvati	2	13N52	75E43	-5:02:52
Bhadreswar	3	22N50	88E21	-5:53:24
Bhādua	3	22N41	88E12	-5:52:48
Bhagaiya	2	25N12	87E29	-5:49:56
Bhāgalpur	5	25N15	87E00	-5:48:00
Bhagirathpur	3	24N05	88E29	-5:53:56
Bhagwānpur	3	22N07	87E45	-5:51:00
Bhainsa	2	19N10	77E59	-5:11:56
Bhaironghāti	2	31N01	78E53	-5:15:32
Bhaisa	2	19N06	77E58	-5:11:52
Bhal	2	19N11	73E08	-4:52:32
Bhālki	2	18N02	77E13	-5:08:52
Bhandāra	2	21N10	79E39	-5:18:36
Bhandārdaha	3	22N37	88E13	-5:52:52
Bhānder	2	25N44	78E45	-5:15:00
Bhāngar	3	22N31	88E37	-5:54:28
Bhānvad	2	21N56	69E47	-4:39:08
Bharatpur	2	27N13	77E29	-5:09:56
Bharatpur	3	23N53	88E05	-5:52:20

Name		Lat.	Long.	Time
Bharthana	2	26N45	79E14	-5:16:56
Bhātāpāra	2	21N44	81E56	-5:27:44
Bhātār	3	23N25	87E54	-5:51:36
Bhatewar	2	24N38	74E00	-4:56:00
Bhatinda	2	30N12	74E57	-4:59:48
Bhatkal	2	13N58	74E34	-4:58:16
Bhātpāra	3	22N52	88E24	-5:53:36
Bhātpur	3	22N43	88E25	-5:53:40
Bhattiprolu	2	16N06	80E47	-5:23:08
Bhātua	3	22N57	88E22	-5:53:28
Bhaunagar	2	21N46	72E09	-4:48:36
Bhaunja	2	28N40	77E25	-5:09:40
Bhavāni	2	11N27	77E41	-5:10:44
Bhawānīgarh	2	30N16	76E02	-5:04:08
Bhawāni Mandi	2	24N25	75E50	-5:03:20
Bhawānipatna	2	19N54	83E10	-5:32:40
Bhedia	3	23N36	87E42	-5:50:48
Bhendkhal	2	18N53	72E59	-4:51:56
Bhīkampur	2	28N45	77E27	-5:09:48
Bhikangaon	2	21N52	75E57	-5:03:48
Bhiknathori	5	27N30	84E38	-5:38:32
Bhilai	2	21N13	81E26	-5:25:44
Bhilainagar → Bhilai	2	21N13	81E26	-5:25:44
Bhīlwāra	2	25N21	74E38	-4:58:32
Bhīmavaram	2	16N32	81E32	-5:26:08
Bhimnagar	5	26N30	86E57	-5:47:48
Bhīmpur	3	22N37	87E08	-5:48:32
Bhimpur	3	22N46	88E08	-5:52:32
Bhind	2	26N34	78E48	-5:15:12
Bhinga	2	27N43	81E56	-5:27:44
Bhīnmāl	2	25N00	72E15	-4:49:00
Bhiwandi	2	19N18	73E04	-4:52:16
Bhiwāni	2	28N47	76E08	-5:04:32
Bhoāgāchi	3	22N57	88E20	-5:53:20
Bhojudih	5	23N38	86E27	-5:45:48
Bhokardan	2	20N16	75E46	-5:03:04
Bhongaon	2	27N15	79E11	-5:16:44
Bhongīr	2	17N31	78E53	-5:15:32
Bhonrāsa	2	22N59	76E12	-5:04:48
Bhopāl	2	23N16	77E24	-5:09:36
Bhopar	2	19N12	73E05	-4:52:20
Bhopura	2	28N42	77E20	-5:09:20
Bhowali	2	29N23	79E31	-5:18:04
Bhuāpur	2	28N43	77E26	-5:09:44
Bhuban	2	20N53	85E50	-5:43:20
Bhubaneswar	2	20N14	85E50	-5:43:20
Bhucho	2	30N13	75E06	-5:00:24
Bhuj	2	23N16	69E40	-4:38:40
Bhunarheri	2	30N13	76E27	-5:05:48
Bhusāwal	2	21N03	75E46	-5:03:04
Bhutali	2	19N07	73E04	-4:52:16
Biaora	2	23N55	76E54	-5:07:36
Bichhia	2	22N27	80E42	-5:22:48
Bīdar	2	17N54	77E33	-5:10:12
Bidhūna	2	26N49	79E31	-5:18:04
Bidyādharpur	3	22N50	88E24	-5:53:36
Bīhar	5	25N11	85E31	-5:42:04
Bihārīganj	5	25N44	86E59	-5:47:56
Bihta	5	25N33	84E52	-5:39:28
Bijainagar	2	25N56	74E38	-4:58:32
Bijaipura	2	24N46	77E48	-5:11:12
Bījāpur	2	18N48	80E49	-5:23:16
Bijāpur	2	16N50	75E42	-5:02:48
Bijāwar	2	24N38	79E30	-5:18:00
Bījbiāra	2	33N48	75E06	-5:00:24
Bijeypur	2	26N03	77E22	-5:09:28
Bijna	3	22N55	88E27	-5:53:48
Bijni	4	26N31	90E40	-6:02:40
Bijnor	2	29N22	78E08	-5:12:32
Bijpur	3	22N56	88E26	-5:53:44
Bīkaner	2	28N01	73E18	-4:53:12
Bilāra	2	26N10	73E42	-4:54:48
Bilāri	2	28N38	78E48	-5:15:12
Bilāsipāra	4	26N14	90E14	-6:00:56
Bilaspur	2	28N53	79E16	-5:17:04
Bilāspur	2	22N05	82E09	-5:28:36
Bilāspur	2	31N20	76E45	-5:07:00
Bilgrām	2	27N11	80E02	-5:20:08
Bilimora	2	20N45	72E57	-4:51:48
Bilsārā	3	23N05	88E10	-5:52:40
Bilsi	2	28N08	78E55	-5:15:40
Bīna-Etāwa	2	24N11	78E11	-5:12:44
Bindki	2	26N02	80E36	-5:22:24
Binpur	5	22N36	86E55	-5:47:40
Bīr	2	18N59	75E46	-5:03:04
Bira	3	22N47	88E34	-5:54:16
Birati	3	22N39	88E27	-5:53:48
Bīrbhūm	3	23N55	87E32	-5:50:08
Birgi	5	22N42	86E41	-5:46:44
Birmitrapur	2	22N24	84E46	-5:39:04
Birnagar	3	23N14	88E33	-5:54:12
Birsilpur	2	28N10	72E15	-4:49:00
Birūr	2	13N37	75E58	-5:03:52
Bisāi	5	22N10	86E24	-5:45:36
Bīsalpur	2	28N18	79E48	-5:19:12
Bishenpur	4	24N38	93E46	-6:15:04
Bishnāh	2	32N37	74E52	-4:59:28
Bishnath	4	26N37	93E10	-6:12:40
Bishnupur	3	22N23	88E16	-5:53:04
Bishnupur	3	23N05	87E19	-5:49:16
Bishnupur	3	22N37	88E31	-5:54:04
Bisrakh	2	28N34	77E26	-5:09:44
Bisrāmpur	5	24N15	83E56	-5:35:44
Biswān	2	27N30	81E00	-5:24:00
Bobbili	2	18N34	83E22	-5:33:28
Bodāi	3	22N48	88E29	-5:53:56
Bodhan	2	18N40	77E54	-5:11:36
Bodināyakkanūr	2	10N01	77E21	-5:09:24
Bokad	2	18N53	72E58	-4:51:52
Bokāro	5	23N51	86E02	-5:44:08
Bolpur	3	23N40	87E43	-5:50:52
Bombay	2	18N58	72E50	-4:51:20
Bomdila	4	27N15	92E25	-6:09:40
Bonaigarh	2	21N50	84E57	-5:39:48
Bongaigaon	4	26N28	90E34	-6:02:16
Bonsari	2	19N04	73E02	-4:52:08
Boram	3	23N29	86E14	-5:44:56
Borsad	2	22N25	72E54	-4:51:36
Bosna	3	22N37	88E30	-5:54:00
Boso	3	22N58	88E08	-5:52:32
Botād	2	22N10	71E40	-4:46:40
Brahmapur	3	22N28	88E22	-5:53:28
Brāhmaur	2	32N27	76E32	-5:06:08
Broach	2	21N42	72E58	-4:51:52
Budaun	2	28N03	79E07	-5:16:28
Buddh Gaya	5	24N42	84E59	-5:39:56
Budge Budge	3	22N27	88E10	-5:52:40
Budhamghat	5	25N57	87E02	-5:48:08
Budhlāda	2	29N56	75E34	-5:02:16
Bukkapatnam	2	14N11	77E47	-5:11:08
Bulandshahr	2	28N24	77E51	-5:11:24
Buldāna	2	20N32	76E11	-5:04:44
Bulsār	2	20N38	72E56	-4:51:44
Būndi	2	25N27	75E39	-5:02:36
Būndu	5	23N11	85E35	-5:42:20
Bungtlang	4	22N20	92E46	-6:11:04
Burda	2	25N50	77E35	-5:10:20
Burdul	2	19N07	73E07	-4:52:28
Burdwān	3	23N15	87E51	-5:51:24
Burhānpur	2	21N18	76E14	-5:04:56
Burhar	2	23N13	81E32	-5:26:08
Būriya	2	30N09	77E21	-5:09:24
Burnpur	5	23N40	86E57	-5:47:48
Buxar	5	25N35	83E59	-5:35:56
Byadgi	2	14N41	75E29	-5:01:56
Calcutta	3	22N32	88E22	-5:53:28
Calicut	2	11N15	75E46	-5:03:04
Cambay	2	22N18	72E37	-4:50:28
Cannanore	2	11N51	75E22	-5:01:28
Canning Port	3	22N20	88E40	-5:54:40
Cape Comorin → Kanniyākumāri	2	8N05	77E34	-5:10:16
Cassimbazar	3	24N07	88E16	-5:53:04
Cawnpore → Kānpur	2	26N28	80E21	-5:21:24
Chābi	2	22N49	80E41	-5:22:44
Chāchora	2	24N10	76E59	-5:07:56
Chaibāsā	5	22N34	85E49	-5:43:16
Chainpur	5	23N08	84E15	-5:37:00
Chaital	3	22N31	88E47	-5:55:08
Chakāltor	5	23N14	86E22	-5:45:28
Chakdaha	3	22N20	88E20	-5:53:20
Chākdaha	3	23N05	88E31	-5:54:04
Chākia	5	26N25	85E03	-5:40:12
Chakradharpur	5	22N42	85E38	-5:42:32
Chakrāta	2	30N42	77E51	-5:11:24
Chākulia	5	22N29	86E43	-5:46:52
Chal	2	19N06	73E08	-4:52:32
Chālisgaon	2	20N28	75E01	-5:00:04
Challakere	2	14N19	76E39	-5:06:36
Chāmārpāra	3	22N35	88E08	-5:52:32
Chamba	2	32N34	76E08	-5:04:32
Chamoli	2	30N24	79E21	-5:17:24
Chāmpa	2	22N03	82E39	-5:30:36
Champādānga	3	22N50	87E58	-5:51:52
Chāmpahāti	3	22N23	88E29	-5:53:56
Champapur	5	24N02	86E31	-5:46:04
Champāwat	2	29N20	80E06	-5:20:24
Champdāni	3	22N48	88E21	-5:53:24
Chāmpua	2	22N05	85E40	-5:42:40
Chāmrāil	3	22N38	88E18	-5:53:12
Chāmrājnagar Rāmasamudram	2	11N55	76E57	-5:07:48
Chānanwāla	2	30N22	73E57	-4:55:48
Chānasma	2	23N43	72E07	-4:48:28
Chāndābila	2	22N05	87E00	-5:48:00
Chanda → Chandrapur	2	19N57	79E18	-5:17:12
Chandan Chauki	2	28N33	80E47	-5:23:08
Chandankiāri	5	23N34	86E22	-5:45:28
Chandannagar	3	22N51	88E21	-5:53:24
Chandausi	2	28N27	78E46	-5:15:04
Chanderi	2	24N43	78E08	-5:12:32
Chandernagore → Chandannagar	3	22N51	88E21	-5:53:24
Chandīgarh	2	30N44	76E55	-5:07:40
Chāndil	5	22N58	86E03	-5:44:12
Chanditala	3	22N41	88E16	-5:53:04
Chandla	2	25N05	80E12	-5:20:48
Chāndpara	3	22N58	88E47	-5:55:08
Chāndpur	2	29N09	78E16	-5:13:04
Chāndra	3	22N28	87E09	-5:48:36
Chandrakona	3	22N44	87E31	-5:50:04
Chandrakona Road	3	22N44	87E21	-5:49:24
Chandrapur	2	19N57	79E18	-5:17:12
Chandrupatla	2	18N34	80E23	-5:21:32
Chāndvad	2	20N20	74E15	-4:57:00
Changanācheri	2	9N28	76E33	-5:06:12
Channagiri	2	14N02	75E56	-5:03:44
Channapatna	2	12N39	77E13	-5:08:52
Chanumla	4	8N19	93E05	-6:12:20
Chāparmukh	4	26N12	92E32	-6:10:08
Chāpra	3	23N32	88E33	-5:54:12
Chāpra	5	25N46	84E45	-5:39:00
Charanpur	3	23N45	87E02	-5:48:08
Charduār	4	26N52	92E46	-6:11:04
Charkhāri	2	25N24	79E45	-5:19:00
Charkhi Dādri	2	28N37	76E16	-5:05:04
Chās	5	23N38	86E10	-5:44:40
Chatra	3	22N46	88E20	-5:53:20
Chatra	5	24N13	84E52	-5:39:28
Chatrapur	2	19N21	84E59	-5:39:56
Chātsu	2	26N36	75E57	-5:03:48
Chaubaria	3	22N59	88E40	-5:54:40
Chaukhandi	2	28N37	77E24	-5:09:36
Chaumua	3	22N39	88E33	-5:54:12
Chaupāran	5	24N23	85E15	-5:41:00
Chavakkad	2	10N32	76E06	-5:04:24
Chelyāma	5	23N37	86E33	-5:46:12
Chengannur	2	9N20	76E38	-5:06:32
Chengele	4	28N47	96E16	-6:25:04
Cherrapunji	4	25N18	91E42	-6:06:48
Chetput	2	12N28	79E21	-5:17:24
Chhabra	2	24N40	76E50	-5:07:20
Chhachhrauli	2	30N15	77E22	-5:09:28
Chhajārsi	2	28N38	77E23	-5:09:32
Chhalera Bāngar	2	28N33	77E20	-5:09:20
Chhatarpur	2	24N55	79E36	-5:18:24
Chhatarpur	5	24N23	84E11	-5:36:44
Chhātna	5	23N18	86E58	-5:47:52
Chheharta	2	31N38	74E48	-4:59:12
Chhibrāmau	2	27N09	79E31	-5:18:04
Chhināmor	3	22N48	88E18	-5:53:12
Chhindwāra	2	22N04	78E56	-5:15:44
Chhiruti	3	24N01	88E11	-5:52:44
Chhitauni	5	27N09	83E58	-5:35:52
Chhota-Chhindwāra	2	23N03	79E29	-5:17:56
Chhota Udepur	2	22N19	74E01	-4:56:04
Chicholi	2	22N01	77E40	-5:10:40
Chichra	5	22N19	86E53	-5:47:32
Chidambaram	2	11N24	79E42	-5:18:48
Chik Ballāpur	2	13N28	77E44	-5:10:56
Chikhli	2	20N21	76E15	-5:05:00
Chikmagalūr	2	13N19	75E47	-5:03:08
Chiknāyakanhalli	2	13N26	76E37	-5:06:28
Chikodi	2	16N26	74E36	-4:58:24
Chilakalūrupet	2	16N05	80E10	-5:20:40
Chilpi	2	22N15	81E33	-5:26:12
Chincholi	2	19N10	73E08	-4:52:32
Chineni	2	33N02	75E17	-5:01:08
Chingleput	2	12N42	79E59	-5:19:56
Chīni	2	31N32	78E15	-5:13:00
Chinnur	2	19N07	79E43	-5:18:52
Chinpāi	3	23N50	87E28	-5:49:52
Chinsura	3	22N53	88E27	-5:53:48
Chintāmani	2	13N24	78E04	-5:12:16
Chiplūn	2	17N32	73E31	-4:54:04
Chirad	2	19N09	73E07	-4:52:28
Chīrāla	2	15N49	80E21	-5:21:24
Chirāwa	2	28N15	75E38	-5:02:32
Chīrgaon	2	25N35	78E49	-5:15:16
Chirki	5	24N03	86E09	-5:44:36
Chirle	2	18N56	73E02	-4:52:08
Chirmiri Colliery	2	23N12	82E21	-5:29:24
Chītāpur	2	17N07	77E05	-5:08:20
Chitarda	2	21N50	86E57	-5:47:48
Chitorgarh	2	24N53	74E38	-4:58:32
Chitradurga	2	14N14	76E24	-5:05:36
Chitrakūt Dham	2	25N11	80E52	-5:23:28
Chitrasāli	3	22N52	88E09	-5:52:36
Chittaranjan	5	23N52	86E52	-5:47:28
Chittoor	2	13N12	79E07	-5:16:28
Chittūr	2	10N42	76E45	-5:07:00
Chityal	2	17N15	79E11	-5:16:44
Choāli	3	22N24	88E24	-5:53:36
Chodavaram	2	17N50	82E57	-5:31:48
Chohtan	2	25N29	71E04	-4:44:16
Chomu	2	27N10	75E44	-5:02:56
Chonkham	4	27N48	96E02	-6:24:08
Chopan	2	24N31	83E02	-5:32:08
Chopda	2	21N15	75E18	-5:01:12
Chopra	3	26N20	88E19	-5:53:16
Chora Saādatpur	2	28N36	77E21	-5:09:24
Chotila	2	22N25	71E11	-4:44:44
Chunār	2	25N08	82E54	-5:31:36
Churachandpur	4	24N20	93E40	-6:14:40
Churu	2	28N18	74E57	-4:59:48
Chushul	2	33N36	78E39	-5:14:36
Cochin	2	9N58	76E14	-5:04:56
Coimbatore	2	11N00	76E58	-5:07:52
Colgong	2	25N16	87E13	-5:48:52
Colonelganj	2	27N08	81E42	-5:26:48
Conjeeveram → Kānchipuram	2	12N50	79E43	-5:18:52
Contai	3	21N47	87E45	-5:51:00
Cooch Behār	3	26N19	89E26	-5:57:44
Coondapoor	2	13N38	74E42	-4:58:48
Coonoor	2	11N21	76E49	-5:07:16
Cuddalore	2	11N45	79E45	-5:19:00
Cuddapah	2	14N28	78E49	-5:15:16
Cumbum	2	15N34	79E09	-5:16:36
Cuttack	2	20N30	85E50	-5:43:20
Dabhoi	2	22N11	73E26	-4:53:44
Dābhol	2	17N36	73E10	-4:52:40
Dabra	2	25N54	78E20	-5:13:20
Dadon	2	27N57	78E28	-5:13:52
Dādpur	3	22N54	88E31	-5:54:04
Dādpur	3	22N42	88E33	-5:54:12
Dādri	2	28N34	77E33	-5:10:12
Dagshai	2	30N53	77E03	-5:08:12
Dahijuri	5	22N31	86E59	-5:47:56
Dainhāt	3	23N37	88E04	-5:52:16
Dakaur	2	24N48	87E54	-5:51:36
Dākoānk	4	7N02	93E43	-6:14:52
Dakshingram	3	24N03	87E48	-5:51:12
Dalgomai	4	26N06	90E47	-6:03:08
Dalhousie	2	32N32	75E59	-5:03:56
Dālkola	5	25N52	87E51	-5:51:24
Dalli Rajhāra	2	20N35	81E04	-5:24:16
Dalmau	2	26N04	81E02	-5:24:08
Dalsingh Sarai	5	25N40	85E50	-5:43:20
Dalsingpara	3	26N47	89E22	-5:57:28
Daltonganj	5	24N02	84E04	-5:36:16
Damān	1	20N25	72E51	-4:51:24
Damoh	2	23N50	79E27	-5:17:48
Damotapāda	2	19N03	73E04	-4:52:16
Dānāpur	5	25N38	85E03	-5:40:12
Dandeli	2	15N15	74E37	-4:58:28
Dānga	3	22N47	88E28	-5:53:52
Dangādiha	2	21N30	86E19	-5:45:16

Dāntan 3 21N57 87E16 -5:49:04
Dantewāra 2 18N54 81E21 -5:25:24
Daosa 2 26N53 76E20 -5:05:20
Daranga 4 26N51 91E26 -6:05:44
Darave 2 19N02 73E01 -4:52:04
Darbhanga 5 26N10 85E54 -5:43:36
Darjeeling 3 27N02 88E16 -5:53:04
Darodih 5 23N14 86E27 -5:45:48
Darsi 2 15N50 79E44 -5:18:56
Dārwha 2 20N19 77E46 -5:11:04
Daryābād 2 26N53 81E33 -5:26:12
Daryāpur 2 20N56 77E20 -5:09:20
Dasāda 2 23N19 71E50 -4:47:20
Daspalla 2 20N21 84E51 -5:39:24
Dasūya 2 31N49 75E38 -5:02:32
Datia 2 25N40 78E28 -5:13:52
Dativli 2 19N11 73E03 -4:52:12
Dātra 3 22N58 88E16 -5:53:04
Dattapukur 3 22N45 88E33 -5:54:12
Dattapulia 3 23N14 88E43 -5:54:52
Daudnagar 5 25N02 84E24 -5:37:36
Daulatabad 3 24N08 88E22 -5:53:28
Daulatpur 3 22N26 88E18 -5:53:12
Daule 2 19N10 73E03 -4:52:12
Daund 2 18N28 74E36 -4:58:24
Dāvangere 2 14N28 75E55 -5:03:40
Dayghar 2 19N09 73E03 -4:52:12
Debagrām 3 23N41 88E18 -5:53:12
Debānāndapur 3 22N56 88E22 -5:53:28
Debipur 3 24N14 88E38 -5:54:32
Debogram 3 23N40 88E17 -5:53:08
Debra 3 22N24 87E33 -5:50:12
Dechu 2 26N47 72E20 -4:49:20
Dediāpāda 2 21N38 73E35 -4:54:20
Deeg 2 27N28 77E20 -5:09:20
Deesa 2 24N15 72E10 -4:48:40
Deganga 3 22N40 88E39 -5:54:36
Deharda 2 21N40 87E25 -5:49:40
Dehej 2 21N42 72E35 -4:50:20
Dehra Dūn 2 30N19 78E02 -5:12:08
Dehri 5 24N52 84E11 -5:36:44
Dehu 2 18N35 73W51 4:55:24
Delhi 2 28N40 77E13 -5:08:52
Delhi Cantonment
2 28N36 77E08 -5:08:32
Denkanikota 2 12N32 77E48 -5:11:12
Deoband 2 29N42 77E41 -5:10:44
Deocha 3 24N03 87E35 -5:50:20
Deogarh 2 24N33 78E15 -5:13:00
Deogarh 2 21N32 84E44 -5:38:56
Deogarh 2 25N32 73E54 -4:55:36
Deoghar 5 24N29 86E42 -5:46:48
Deolāli 2 19N57 73E50 -4:55:20
Deoli 2 22N03 86E49 -5:47:16
Deoli 2 25N45 75E23 -5:01:32
Deori 2 23N08 78E41 -5:14:44
Deoria 2 26N31 83E47 -5:35:08
Deori Khās 2 23N24 79E01 -5:16:04
Deosil 2 23N42 82E15 -5:29:00
Depāl 3 21N44 87E33 -5:50:12
Depāra 3 22N53 88E34 -5:54:16
Dera Gopipur 2 31N54 76E13 -5:04:52
Dera Nānak 2 32N02 75E01 -5:00:04
Dergaon 4 26N42 93E58 -6:15:52
Deshnoke 2 27N48 73E21 -4:53:24
Deūlgaon Rāja 2 20N01 76E02 -5:04:08
Deulpur 3 22N36 88E10 -5:52:40
Deulti 3 22N26 87E56 -5:51:44
Devakottai 2 9N57 78E49 -5:15:16
Devaprayāg 2 30N09 78E37 -5:14:28
Devarkonda 2 16N42 78E58 -5:15:52
Devgad Bāria 2 22N42 73E54 -4:55:36
Devīkot 2 26N42 71E12 -4:44:48
Dewās 2 22N58 76E04 -5:04:16
Dhādkā 5 22N47 86E30 -5:46:00
Dhāka 5 26N41 85E10 -5:40:40
Dhākauli 2 24N45 77E51 -5:11:24
Dhampur 2 29N19 78E31 -5:14:04
Dhamtari 2 20N41 81E34 -5:26:16
Dhanaula 2 30N17 75E35 -5:02:20
Dhanaura 2 28N58 78E15 -5:13:00
Dhānbād 5 23N48 86E27 -5:45:48
Dhandhuka 2 22N22 71E59 -4:47:56
Dhanera 5 23N25 86E39 -5:46:36
Dhang 5 26N42 85E20 -5:41:20
Dhaniakhāli 3 22N58 88E06 -5:52:24
Dhansar 2 19N07 73E05 -4:52:20
Dhanushkodi 2 9N11 79E24 -5:17:36
Dhānyahānā 3 22N48 88E11 -5:52:44
Dhār 2 22N36 75E18 -5:01:12
Dharampur 2 20N32 73E11 -4:52:44
Dharangaon 2 21N01 75E16 -5:01:04
Dhārāpuram 2 10N44 77E31 -5:10:04
Dhāri 2 21N20 71E01 -4:44:04
Dhārīwāl 2 31N57 75E19 -5:01:16
Dharmābād 2 18N54 77E51 -5:11:24
Dharmapuri 2 12N08 78E10 -5:12:40
Dharmavaram 2 14N26 77E43 -5:10:52
Dharmjaygarh 2 22N28 83E13 -5:32:52
Dharmkot 2 30N57 75E14 -5:00:56
Dharmsāla 2 32N13 76E19 -5:05:16
Dhārni 2 21N33 76E53 -5:07:32
Dhārwār 2 15N28 75E01 -5:00:04
Dhātrigrām 3 23N15 88E20 -5:53:20
Dhenkānāl 2 20N40 85E36 -5:42:24
Dhokra 3 22N40 88E34 -5:54:16
Dholka 2 22N43 72E28 -4:49:52
Dholpur 2 26N42 77E54 -5:11:36
Dhone 2 15N25 77E53 -5:11:32
Dhorāji 2 21N44 70E27 -4:41:48
Dhosha 3 22N15 88E33 -5:54:12
Dhowa 5 24N03 86E54 -5:47:36
Dhrāngadhra 2 22N59 71E28 -4:45:52
Dhrol 2 22N34 70E25 -4:41:40
Dhubri 4 26N02 89E58 -5:59:52

Dhulāgarh 3 22N35 88E11 -5:52:44
Dhule 2 20N54 74E47 -4:59:08
Dhulia → Dhule 2 20N54 74E47 -4:59:08
Dhuliān 3 24N41 87E58 -5:51:52
Dhupgāri 3 26N36 89E01 -5:56:04
Dhūri 2 30N22 75E52 -5:03:28
Diamond Harbour 3 22N12 88E12 -5:52:48
Dibai 2 28N13 78E15 -5:13:00
Dibrugarh 4 27N29 94E54 -6:19:36
Dīdwāna 2 27N24 74E34 -4:58:16
Dīg 2 27N28 77E20 -5:09:20
Digambarpur 3 21N57 88E22 -5:53:28
Digboi 4 27N23 95E38 -6:22:32
Dighipāra 3 21N58 88E17 -5:53:08
Dighode 2 18N54 73E02 -4:52:08
Dighra 3 22N47 88E32 -5:54:08
Dīglūr 2 18N33 77E36 -5:10:24
Dīgnagar 3 23N27 87E41 -5:50:44
Digra 3 22N50 88E20 -5:53:20
Digras 2 20N07 77E43 -5:10:52
Dilerpur 3 22N51 88E10 -5:52:40
Dimāpur 4 25N54 93E44 -6:14:56
Dīnānagar 2 32N09 75E28 -5:01:52
Dinapur 5 25N38 85E05 -5:40:20
Dindigul 2 10N21 77E57 -5:11:48
Dindori 2 22N57 81E05 -5:24:20
Dīnhāta 3 26N08 89E28 -5:57:52
Diodār 2 24N06 71E47 -4:47:08
Diphu 4 25N50 93E20 -6:13:20
Dirangdzong 4 27N14 92E18 -6:09:12
Dishergarh 5 23N41 86E50 -5:47:20
Diu 1 20N42 70E59 -4:43:56
Dīva 2 19N09 72E59 -4:51:56
Dive 2 19N11 73E02 -4:52:08
Djabalpur → Jabalpur
2 23N10 79E57 -5:19:48
Djaipur → Jaipur
2 26N55 75E49 -5:03:16
Djamschedpur → Jamshedpur
5 22N48 86E11 -5:44:44
Doda 2 33N08 75E34 -5:02:16
Dod Ballāpur 2 13N18 77E32 -5:10:08
Dogāchia 3 22N58 88E31 -5:54:04
Dogadda 2 29N48 78E37 -5:14:28
Dohad 2 22N50 74E16 -4:57:04
Dohhi 5 24N32 84E54 -5:39:36
Dohrīghāt 2 26N16 83E31 -5:34:04
Domariāganj 2 27N13 82E40 -5:30:40
Domohani 3 26N35 88E48 -5:55:12
Dondaicha 2 21N20 74E34 -4:58:16
Dongargarh 2 21N12 80E44 -5:22:56
Doraha 2 30N49 76E01 -5:04:04
Drās 2 34N27 75E46 -5:03:04
Dubi Bheri 3 22N53 88E17 -5:53:08
Dubra 5 23N32 86E31 -5:46:04
Dubrājpur 3 23N48 87E23 -5:49:32
Dūdhi 2 24N13 83E15 -5:33:00
Dudhnai 4 25N59 90E44 -6:02:56
Dudoda 2 18N00 78E56 -5:15:44
Duff Dunbar 2 32N15 77E12 -5:08:48
Dumaria 5 24N24 84E25 -5:37:40
Dum-Dum 3 22N35 88E24 -5:53:36
Dumjor 3 22N38 88E13 -5:52:52
Dumka 2 24N16 87E15 -5:49:00
Dumra 5 26N34 85E31 -5:42:04
Dumraon 5 25N33 84E09 -5:36:36
Dumuria 5 22N11 86E20 -5:45:20
Dundāhera 2 28N38 77E26 -5:09:44
Dūngarpur 2 23N50 73E43 -4:54:52
Durg 2 21N11 81E17 -5:25:08
Durgāpur 3 23N29 87E20 -5:49:20
Durlabhpur 3 22N47 88E29 -5:53:56
Dwarbasini 3 22N59 88E14 -5:52:56
Dwārka 2 22N14 68E58 -4:35:52
Dwarli 2 19N12 73E08 -4:52:32
Egra 3 21N54 87E32 -5:50:08
Eirauli 2 19N10 72E59 -4:51:56
Eksāra 3 22N38 88E17 -5:53:08
Elamanchili 2 17N33 82E52 -5:31:28
Ellichpur → Achalpur
2 21N16 77E31 -5:10:04
Ellora 2 20N01 75E10 -5:00:40
Ellore → Elūru 2 16N42 81E06 -5:24:24
Elura → Ellora 2 20N01 75E10 -5:00:40
Elūru 2 16N42 81E06 -5:24:24
Emmiganūru 2 15N44 77E29 -5:09:56
English Bāzār 3 25N00 88E09 -5:52:36
Ernākulam 2 9N59 76E17 -5:05:08
Erode 2 11N21 77E44 -5:10:56
Eruar 3 23N28 87E52 -5:51:28
Etah 2 27N38 78E40 -5:14:40
Etāwah 2 25N32 76E22 -5:05:28
Etāwah 2 26N46 79E02 -5:16:08
Faizābād 2 26N47 82E08 -5:28:32
Fakirganj 4 25N58 90E02 -6:00:08
Fālākāta 3 26N32 89E12 -5:56:48
Falta 3 22N17 88E07 -5:52:28
Farīdābād 2 28N26 77E19 -5:09:16
Farīdkot 2 30N40 74E45 -4:59:00
Farīdnagar 2 28N46 77E37 -5:10:28
Farīdpur 2 28N13 79E33 -5:18:12
Farrakka 3 24N50 87E53 -5:51:32
Farrukhābād 2 27N24 79E34 -5:18:16
Farrukhnagar 2 28N43 77E23 -5:09:32
Farrukhnagar 2 28N27 76E49 -5:07:16
Fatehābād 2 29N31 75E27 -5:01:48
Fatehābād 2 27N01 78E19 -5:13:16
Fatehgarh 2 24N48 76E58 -5:07:52
Fatehgarh 2 27N22 79E38 -5:18:32
Fatehgarh Chūriān
2 31N52 74E58 -4:59:52
Fatehpur 2 25N56 80E48 -5:23:12
Fatehpur 2 27N10 81E13 -5:24:52
Fatehpur 3 22N17 88E14 -5:52:56
Fatehpur 3 24N05 87E44 -5:50:56

Fatehpur 2 27N59 74E57 -4:59:48
Fatehpur Sīkri 2 27N06 77E40 -5:10:40
Fatwā 5 25N31 85E19 -5:41:16
Fāzilka 2 30N24 74E02 -4:56:08
Ferokh 2 11N11 75E51 -5:03:24
Ferozepore → Fīrozpur
2 30N55 74E36 -4:58:24
Fīrozābād 2 27N09 78E25 -5:13:40
Fīrozpur 2 30N55 74E36 -4:58:24
Firozpur Jhirka 2 27N48 76E57 -5:07:48
Forbesganj 2 26N18 87E15 -5:49:00
Funde 2 18N54 72E58 -4:51:52
Fyzabad 2 26N46 82E08 -5:28:32
Gadag 2 15N25 75E37 -5:02:28
Gādarwāra 2 22N55 78E47 -5:15:08
Gadwāl 2 16N14 77E48 -5:11:12
Gagret 2 31N40 76E04 -5:04:16
Gaighāta 3 22N56 88E44 -5:54:56
Gajā 3 22N52 88E10 -5:52:40
Gajendragarh 2 15N44 75E59 -5:03:56
Gājol 3 25N13 88E12 -5:52:48
Gaj Singhpur 2 29N40 73E27 -4:53:48
Galgalia 3 26N33 88E10 -5:52:40
Galsi 3 23N20 87E42 -5:50:48
Gāndarbal 2 34N14 74E47 -4:59:08
Gānde 5 24N10 86E26 -5:45:44
Gandevi 2 20N49 72E59 -4:51:56
Gangādharpur 3 22N36 88E11 -5:52:44
Gangājalghāti 3 23N25 87E07 -5:48:28
Ganganagar → Sri Gangānagar
2 29N55 73E53 -4:55:32
Gangāpur 2 19N41 75E01 -5:00:04
Gangāpur 2 25N13 74E16 -4:57:04
Gangāpur 2 26N29 76E43 -5:06:52
Gāngārāmpur 3 25N24 88E31 -5:54:04
Ganga Sāgar 3 21N38 88E05 -5:52:20
Gangāwati 2 15N26 76E32 -5:06:08
Gangdhār 2 23N57 75E37 -5:02:28
Gāngnāpur 3 23N09 88E38 -5:54:32
Gangoh 2 29N46 77E15 -5:09:00
Gangotri 2 30N56 79E02 -5:16:08
Gangtok 3 27N20 88E37 -5:54:28
Ganj Dundwara 2 27N44 78E57 -5:15:48
Gapālnagar 3 22N49 88E08 -5:52:32
Garānberia 3 22N24 88E34 -5:54:16
Garautha 2 25N34 79E18 -5:17:12
Garden Reach 3 22N33 88E17 -5:53:08
Garhākota 2 23N46 79E09 -5:16:36
Garhbeta 3 22N51 87E19 -5:49:16
Garhdīwāla 2 31N44 75E45 -5:03:00
Garhi Jasaya 2 28N46 77E16 -5:09:04
Garhi Katiya 2 28N45 77E16 -5:09:04
Garhi Malehra 2 25N02 79E40 -5:18:40
Garhmuktesar 2 28N48 78E06 -5:12:24
Garhshankar 2 31N13 76E08 -5:04:32
Gariya 3 22N28 88E23 -5:53:32
Gārji 3 22N15 88E19 -5:53:16
Garohills 4 25N30 90E30 -6:02:00
Garubhāsa 4 26N33 90E22 -6:01:28
Gārulia 3 22N49 88E22 -5:53:28
Garwa 5 24N11 83E49 -5:35:16
Gauhāti 4 26N11 91E44 -6:06:56
Gaura Barhaj 2 26N17 83E44 -5:34:56
Gaurela 2 22N45 81E54 -5:27:36
Gaurhāti 3 22N46 87E48 -5:51:12
Gauribidanūr 2 13N37 77E31 -5:10:04
Gauri Phanta 2 28N41 80E33 -5:22:12
Gauripur 4 26N05 89E58 -5:59:52
Gāvanpāda 2 18N57 73E01 -4:52:04
Gawān 5 24N37 85E55 -5:43:40
Gaya 5 24N47 85E00 -5:40:00
Gejah 2 28N31 77E23 -5:09:32
Geonkhāli 3 22N12 88E03 -5:52:12
Geria Nij 5 23N56 86E55 -5:47:40
Gethaoli 2 19N08 73E01 -4:52:04
Ghafe 2 19N05 73E07 -4:52:28
Ghāgra 5 23N17 84E33 -5:38:12
Ghairatganj 2 23N24 78E13 -5:12:52
Ghansoli 2 19N08 72E59 -4:51:56
Ghārāpuri 2 18N54 72E56 -4:51:44
Gharaunda 2 29N33 76E58 -5:07:52
Gharghoda 2 22N10 83E21 -5:33:24
Ghātāl 3 22N40 87E43 -5:50:52
Ghatampur 3 22N54 88E10 -5:52:40
Ghātsīla 5 22N36 86E29 -5:45:56
Ghāziābād 2 28N40 77E26 -5:09:44
Ghazipur 3 22N36 88E34 -5:54:16
Ghāzīpur 2 25N35 83E34 -5:34:16
Ghesar 2 19N09 73E05 -4:52:20
Ghorāsahan 5 26N50 85E08 -5:40:32
Ghoshpur 3 22N23 88E29 -5:53:56
Ghushuri 3 22N37 88E22 -5:53:28
Giddalūr 2 15N21 78E55 -5:15:40
Giddarbāha 2 30N12 74E40 -4:58:40
Giddhaur 5 24N51 86E20 -5:45:20
Gidhni 5 22N29 86E51 -5:47:24
Giridih 5 24N11 86E18 -5:45:12
Goālpāra 4 26N10 90E37 -6:02:28
Goāltor 3 22N43 87E10 -5:48:40
Gobardānga 3 22N53 88E45 -5:55:00
Gobindapur 3 22N23 88E25 -5:53:40
Gobindapur 3 22N55 88E12 -5:52:48
Gobindapur 3 23N16 87E58 -5:51:52
Gobindgarh 2 30N41 76E18 -5:05:12
Gobindpur 5 23N50 86E31 -5:46:04
Godadharpur 3 24N00 87E42 -5:50:48
Godda 2 24N50 87E13 -5:48:52
Godhra 2 22N45 73E38 -4:54:32
Gogha 2 21N41 72E17 -4:49:08
Gohad 2 26N26 78E27 -5:13:48
Gohāna 2 29N08 76E42 -5:06:48
Gohpur 4 26N53 93E38 -6:14:32
Goichran 2 31N04 78E07 -5:12:28
Gokāk 2 16N10 74E50 -4:59:20
Gokarna 3 24N03 88E07 -5:52:28

Golabāri	3	22N36	88E20	-5:53:20
Golāghāt	4	26N31	93E58	-6:15:52
Gola Gokaran Nath	2	28N05	80E28	-5:21:52
Golconda	2	17N23	78E27	-5:13:48
Golden Rock	2	10N48	78E44	-5:14:56
Gomoh	5	23N52	86E10	-5:44:40
Gompa	2	35N02	77E20	-5:09:20
Gonda	2	27N08	81E56	-5:27:44
Gondal	2	21N58	70E48	-4:43:12
Gondia	2	21N27	80E12	-5:20:48
Goniānamandi	2	30N19	74E54	-4:59:36
Gooty	2	15N07	77E38	-5:10:32
Gopālganj	5	26N28	84E26	-5:37:44
Gopālnagar	3	23N03	88E45	-5:55:00
Gopālnagar	3	22N50	88E14	-5:52:56
Gopālpur	3	22N38	88E27	-5:53:48
Gopīballabhpur	5	22N13	86E54	-5:47:36
Gopichettipālaiyam	2	11N28	77E27	-5:09:48
Gopinagar	3	22N50	88E07	-5:52:28
Gorakhpur	2	26N45	83E22	-5:33:28
Goras	2	25N32	76E56	-5:07:44
Goria	3	22N24	88E29	-5:53:56
Gosāba	3	22N10	88E48	-5:55:12
Govardhan	2	27N30	77E28	-5:09:52
Govindgarh	2	24N23	81E18	-5:25:12
Govindpur	5	23N51	86E34	-5:46:16
Goyerkāta	3	26N42	89E02	-5:56:08
Gua	5	22N12	85E23	-5:41:32
Gubbi	2	13N19	76E56	-5:07:44
Gūdalūr	2	11N30	76E30	-5:06:00
Gūdalūr	2	9N41	77E16	-5:09:04
Gudivāda	2	16N27	80E59	-5:23:56
Gudiyāttam	2	12N57	78E52	-5:15:28
Gūdūr	2	14N08	79E51	-5:19:24
Gulaothi	2	28N36	77E47	-5:11:08
Gulbarga	2	17N20	76E50	-5:07:20
Guledagudda	2	16N03	75E48	-5:03:12
Gulmarg	2	34N03	74E23	-4:57:32
Gumla	5	23N03	84E33	-5:38:12
Guna	2	24N39	77E19	-5:09:16
Gundlupet	2	11N48	76E41	-5:06:44
Gunjrauliya	5	26N35	84E34	-5:38:16
Guntakal	2	15N10	77E23	-5:09:32
Guntūr	2	16N18	80E27	-5:21:48
Gunupur	2	19N05	83E49	-5:35:16
Gurais	2	34N38	74E50	-4:59:20
Gurdāspur	2	32N02	75E31	-5:02:04
Gurgaon	2	28N28	77E02	-5:08:08
Gūrha	2	14N14	74E50	-4:59:20
Gursarai	2	25N37	79E11	-5:16:44
Guru Har Sahāi	2	30N43	74E25	-4:57:40
Guruzala	2	16N32	79E38	-5:18:32
Guskhara	3	23N30	87E45	-5:51:00
Gustia	3	22N59	88E26	-5:53:44
Gwalior	2	26N13	78E10	-5:12:40
Habibpur	3	25N00	88E20	-5:53:20
Hābra	3	22N50	88E38	-5:54:32
Hachi	4	27N46	94E01	-6:16:04
Hāflong	4	25N11	93E02	-6:12:08
Hāhipur	3	22N47	88E10	-5:52:40
Haibatpur	2	28N37	77E26	-5:09:44
Haidargarh	2	26N37	81E22	-5:25:28
Haiderabad → Hyderābād	2	17N23	78E29	-5:13:56
Hailākāndi	4	24N41	92E34	-6:10:16
Hājīpur	5	25N41	85E13	-5:40:52
Hājīpur	3	22N49	87E38	-5:50:32
Hajipur	3	22N57	88E19	-5:53:16
Haldībāri	3	26N20	88E46	-5:55:04
Haldwāni	2	29N13	79E31	-5:18:04
Hālisahar	3	22N56	88E25	-5:53:40
Haliyāl	2	15N20	74E46	-4:59:04
Hamīrpur	2	25N57	80E09	-5:20:36
Hamīrpur	2	31N41	76E31	-5:06:04
Handawor	2	34N24	74E17	-4:57:08
Hānle	2	32N48	79E00	-5:16:00
Hānsdiha	2	24N36	87E05	-5:48:20
Hansi	2	32N27	77E50	-5:11:20
Hānsi	2	29N06	75E58	-5:03:52
Hansia	3	22N48	88E24	-5:53:36
Hānskhāli	3	23N21	88E37	-5:54:28
Hapoli	4	27N43	93E50	-6:15:20
Hāpur	2	28N43	77E47	-5:11:08
Hārāt	3	22N53	88E11	-5:52:44
Harbāti	3	22N55	88E33	-5:54:12
Harda	2	22N20	77E06	-5:08:24
Hardoi	2	27N25	80E07	-5:20:28
Hardwār	2	29N58	78E10	-5:12:40
Hariāna	2	31N38	75E51	-5:03:24
Harihar	2	14N31	75E48	-5:03:12
Hariharpāra	3	24N02	88E27	-5:53:48
Harike	2	31N10	74E57	-4:59:48
Harinagab	5	27N09	84E19	-5:37:16
Haripād	2	9N18	76E28	-5:05:52
Haripāl	3	22N49	88E07	-5:52:28
Haripur	2	24N18	87E05	-5:48:20
Haripur	3	22N56	88E14	-5:52:56
Haripur	3	22N42	88E10	-5:52:40
Harnai	2	17N48	73E06	-4:52:24
Harnātānr	5	27N19	84E01	-5:36:04
Harola	2	28N36	77E19	-5:09:16
Harpālpur	2	25N17	79E20	-5:17:20
Harpanahalli	2	14N48	75E59	-5:03:56
Harrai	2	22N37	79E13	-5:16:52
Harsūd	2	22N06	76E44	-5:06:56
Harūr	2	12N04	78E30	-5:14:00
Hasanparti	2	18N04	79E32	-5:18:08
Hasanpur	2	28N43	78E17	-5:13:08
Hāsnābād	3	22N35	88E55	-5:55:40
Hasnācha	3	22N26	88E09	-5:52:36
Hassan	2	13N00	76E05	-5:04:20
Hāthras	2	27N36	78E03	-5:12:12
Hātiāra	3	22N37	88E27	-5:53:48
Hātisāla	3	22N33	88E32	-5:54:08
Hatkori	5	24N11	85E02	-5:40:08
Hāt Pīplia	2	22N46	76E18	-5:05:12
Hatta	2	24N07	79E36	-5:18:24
Hāudullāpur	3	22N25	88E33	-5:54:12
Hāveri	2	14N48	75E24	-5:01:36
Hazāribāgh	5	23N59	85E21	-5:41:24
Hedutne	2	19N10	73E06	-4:52:24
Herbertabad	4	11N43	92E37	-6:10:28
Hesadi	5	22N45	85E20	-5:41:20
Himatnagar	2	23N36	72E57	-4:51:48
Hindaun	2	26N43	77E01	-5:08:04
Hindu Malkot	2	30N09	73E55	-4:55:40
Hindupur	2	13N49	77E29	-5:09:56
Hinganghāt	2	20N34	78E50	-5:15:20
Hingoli	2	19N43	77E09	-5:08:36
Hīrākud	2	21N31	83E57	-5:35:48
Hīrāpur	2	24N22	79E13	-5:16:52
Hiriyūr	2	13N58	76E36	-5:06:24
Hisābpur	3	22N51	88E32	-5:54:08
Hisār	2	29N10	75E43	-5:02:52
Hisua	5	24N50	85E25	-5:41:40
Hodal	2	27N54	77E22	-5:09:28
Hojāi	4	26N00	92E51	-6:11:24
Holalkere	2	14N02	76E11	-5:04:44
Hole Narsipur	2	12N47	76E15	-5:05:00
Homnābād	2	17N46	77E08	-5:08:32
Honāvar	2	14N17	74E27	-4:57:48
Hooghly-Chinsura	3	22N54	88E24	-5:53:36
Hoshangābād	2	22N45	77E43	-5:10:52
Hoshiārpur	2	31N32	75E54	-5:03:36
Hoshiarpur	2	28N35	77E22	-5:09:28
Hospet	2	15N16	76E24	-5:05:36
Hostigrām	3	22N26	88E31	-5:54:04
Hosūr	2	12N43	77E49	-5:11:16
Howrah	3	22N35	88E20	-5:53:20
Hubli	2	15N21	75E10	-5:00:40
Hunsūr	2	12N18	76E17	-5:05:08
Hura	5	23N18	86E39	-5:46:36
Hurshi	3	24N17	88E28	-5:53:52
Husainābād	5	24N32	84E01	-5:36:04
Husainīwāla	2	30N59	74E34	-4:58:16
Huzurabad	2	18N13	79E22	-5:17:28
Huzurnagar	2	16N53	79E55	-5:19:40
Hyderābād	2	17N23	78E29	-5:13:56
Hydernagar	5	24N35	84E00	-5:36:00
Ichak	5	24N05	85E25	-5:41:40
Ichalkaranji	2	16N42	74E28	-4:57:52
Ichāpur	3	22N50	88E24	-5:53:36
Ichchāpuram	2	19N07	84E42	-5:38:48
Ichhāwar	2	23N01	77E01	-5:08:04
Idāppādi	2	11N35	77E51	-5:11:24
Idar	2	23N50	73E00	-4:52:00
Igatpuri	2	19N42	73E33	-4:54:12
Ikra	3	23N42	87E07	-5:48:28
Ilaiyānkudi	2	9N38	78E38	-5:14:32
Ilām Bāzār	3	23N38	87E32	-5:50:08
Ilkal	2	15N58	76E08	-5:04:32
Imphāl	4	24N49	93E57	-6:15:48
Indas	3	23N10	87E39	-5:50:36
Indi	2	17N10	75E58	-5:03:52
Indore	2	22N43	75E50	-5:03:20
Indpur	5	23N10	86E56	-5:47:44
Indur → Indore	2	22N43	75E50	-5:03:20
Irinjālakuda	2	10N20	76E14	-5:04:56
Isāgarh	2	24N50	77E53	-5:11:32
Īsānagar	2	27N54	81E13	-5:24:52
Islāmābād → Anantnāg	2	33N44	75E09	-5:00:36
Islāmpur	5	25N09	85E12	-5:40:48
Islāmpur	3	26N16	88E12	-5:52:48
Islāmpur	3	21N43	87E39	-5:50:36
Islāmpur	3	24N09	88E28	-5:53:52
Itārsi	2	22N37	77E45	-5:11:00
Itimādpur	2	27N15	78E12	-5:12:48
Itwa	2	27N20	82E42	-5:30:48
Jabalpur	2	23N10	79E57	-5:19:48
Jadcherla	2	16N46	78E12	-5:12:48
Jāfarābād	2	20N52	71E22	-4:45:28
Jagādhri	2	30N10	77E18	-5:09:12
Jagalūr	2	14N32	76E21	-5:05:24
Jagannāthpūr	3	22N43	88E19	-5:53:16
Jagatnagar	3	22N47	88E13	-5:52:52
Jagatsingpur	2	20N16	86E10	-5:44:40
Jagdalpur	2	19N04	82E02	-5:28:08
Jagdīspur	5	25N29	84E25	-5:37:40
Jaggayyapeta	2	16N54	80E06	-5:20:24
Jagraon	2	30N47	75E29	-5:01:56
Jagtiāl	2	18N48	78E56	-5:15:44
Jāguli	3	22N56	88E32	-5:54:08
Jāgulia	3	22N44	88E32	-5:54:08
Jahānābād	5	25N13	84E59	-5:39:56
Jahāngīrābād	2	28N25	78E06	-5:12:24
Jaijōn	2	31N21	76E09	-5:04:36
Jainti	3	26N42	89E36	-5:58:24
Jaipur	2	26N55	75E49	-5:03:16
Jāis	2	26N15	81E32	-5:26:08
Jaisalmer	2	26N55	70E54	-4:43:36
Jaito	2	30N28	74E53	-4:59:32
Jājpur	2	20N51	86E20	-5:45:20
Jākhal	2	29N48	75E50	-5:03:20
Jakhāu	2	23N13	68E43	-4:34:52
Jalālābād	2	27N43	79E40	-5:18:40
Jalālābād	2	30N37	74E15	-4:57:00
Jalālpur	2	26N19	82E44	-5:30:56
Jalangi	3	24N08	88E42	-5:54:48
Jālaun	2	26N09	79E21	-5:17:24
Jalda	3	21N56	87E30	-5:50:00
Jalesar	2	27N29	78E19	-5:13:16
Jaleswar	2	21N49	87E13	-5:48:52
Jālgaon	2	21N01	75E34	-5:02:16
Jālgaon	2	21N03	76E32	-5:06:08
Jālna	2	19N50	75E53	-5:03:32
Jālor	2	25N21	72E37	-4:50:28
Jalpaiguri	3	26N31	88E44	-5:54:56
Jāmālbāti	3	22N51	88E08	-5:52:32
Jamālpur	3	23N03	88E00	-5:52:00
Jamālpur	5	25N18	86E30	-5:46:00
Jamālpurganj	3	23N04	87E59	-5:51:56
Jāmbād	5	22N42	86E35	-5:46:20
Jambusar	2	22N03	72E48	-4:51:12
Jamjodhpur	2	21N54	70E01	-4:40:04
Jamkhandi	2	16N31	75E18	-5:01:12
Jammalamadugu	2	14N50	78E24	-5:13:36
Jammu	2	32N42	74E52	-4:59:28
Jāmnagar	2	22N28	70E04	-4:40:16
Jamnotri	2	31N01	78E27	-5:13:48
Jāmpur	3	22N56	88E12	-5:52:48
Jamshedpur	5	22N48	86E11	-5:44:44
Jāmtāra	5	23N57	86E48	-5:47:12
Jamuāni	2	21N57	86E14	-5:44:56
Jamūi	5	24N55	86E13	-5:44:52
Jāmuria	3	23N44	87E02	-5:48:08
Janāi	3	22N43	88E16	-5:53:04
Jandiāla	2	31N36	75E03	-5:00:12
Jangaon	2	17N43	79E11	-5:16:44
Jangipāra	3	22N45	88E04	-5:52:16
Jangipur	3	24N28	88E04	-5:52:16
Janka	3	21N52	87E56	-5:51:44
Jankāpur	3	21N54	87E23	-5:49:32
Jānsath	2	29N20	77E51	-5:11:24
Jaora	2	23N38	75E08	-5:00:32
Japla	5	24N33	84E01	-5:36:04
Jaridih	5	23N38	86E04	-5:44:16
Jarwa	2	27N39	82E31	-5:30:04
Jasai	2	18N56	73E01	-4:52:04
Jasdan	2	22N02	71E12	-4:44:48
Jashpurnagar	2	22N54	84E09	-5:36:36
Jasidih	5	24N31	86E39	-5:46:36
Jaskhar	2	18N54	72E59	-4:51:56
Jaspur	2	29N17	78E49	-5:15:16
Jasra	2	25N17	81E48	-5:27:12
Jaswantnagar	2	26N53	78E55	-5:15:40
Jatni	2	20N10	85E42	-5:42:48
Jaugrām	3	23N06	88E05	-5:52:20
Jauli	2	28N44	77E21	-5:09:24
Jaunpur	2	25N44	82E41	-5:30:44
Jawāla Mukhi	2	31N53	76E19	-5:05:16
Jayamkondachola-Puram	2	11N13	79E22	-5:17:28
Jaynagar	5	26N35	86E09	-5:44:36
Jaynagar Majilpur	3	22N11	88E25	-5:53:40
Jaypur	3	23N03	87E27	-5:49:48
Jejur	3	22N53	88E08	-5:52:32
Jetpur	2	21N44	70E37	-4:42:28
Jeypore	4	27N15	95E26	-6:21:44
Jeypore	2	18N51	82E35	-5:30:20
Jhābua	2	22N46	74E36	-4:58:24
Jhāhtipahāri	5	23N22	86E54	-5:47:36
Jhajha	5	24N46	86E22	-5:45:28
Jhajjar	2	28N37	76E39	-5:06:36
Jhālawār	2	24N36	76E09	-5:04:36
Jhalida	3	23N22	85E58	-5:43:52
Jhālod	2	23N06	74E09	-4:56:36
Jhālrapātan	2	24N33	76E10	-5:04:40
Jhānsi	2	25N26	78E35	-5:14:20
Jhārgrām	3	22N27	86E59	-5:47:56
Jharia	5	23N45	86E24	-5:45:36
Jhārpokhariā	5	22N10	86E38	-5:46:32
Jhārsuguda	2	21N51	84E02	-5:36:08
Jhenkāri	3	22N46	88E18	-5:53:12
Jhikra	3	22N37	87E55	-5:51:40
Jhilimili	5	22N49	86E37	-5:46:28
Jhinkpāni	5	22N25	85E47	-5:43:08
Jhūnjhunu	2	28N08	75E24	-5:01:36
Jiaganj	3	24N14	88E16	-5:53:04
Jīnd	2	29N19	76E19	-5:05:16
Jobat	2	22N25	74E34	-4:58:16
Jodhpur	2	26N17	73E02	-4:52:08
Jodiya	2	22N42	70E18	-4:41:12
Jogbani	2	26N25	87E15	-5:49:00
Jogindarnagar	2	31N59	76E46	-5:07:04
Joka	3	22N27	88E18	-5:53:12
Jolārpettai	2	12N34	78E35	-5:14:20
Jora	2	26N20	77E49	-5:11:16
Jorhāt	4	26N45	94E13	-6:16:52
Joshīmath	2	30N34	79E34	-5:18:16
Jowai	4	25N27	92E12	-6:08:48
Jubbulpore → Jabalpur	2	23N10	79E57	-5:19:48
Jui	2	19N01	73E05	-4:52:20
Julāna	2	29N08	76E25	-5:05:40
Jullundur	2	31N19	75E34	-5:02:16
Junāgadh	2	21N31	70E28	-4:41:52
Junnar	2	19N12	73E53	-4:55:32
Jutogh	2	31N06	77E07	-5:08:28
Kachhwa	2	25N13	82E43	-5:30:52
Kadaiyanallūr	2	9N05	77E21	-5:09:24
Kadi	2	23N18	72E20	-4:49:20
Kādīpur	2	26N10	82E23	-5:29:32
Kadiri	2	14N07	78E10	-5:12:40
Kadūr	2	13N34	76E01	-5:04:04
Kagaznagar	2	19N18	79E50	-5:19:20
Kailāshahar	4	24N20	92E01	-6:08:04
Kaimganj	2	27N34	79E21	-5:17:24
Kaintragarh	2	20N43	84E32	-5:38:08
Kairābani	2	24N08	87E02	-5:48:08
Kairāna	2	29N24	77E12	-5:08:48
Kaisarganj	2	27N15	81E33	-5:26:12
Kaithal	2	29N48	76E23	-5:05:32
Kājlāgarh	3	22N02	87E47	-5:51:08
Kakana	4	9N07	92E49	-6:11:16
Kākdwīp	3	21N53	88E11	-5:52:44
Kakhra	3	21N38	87E27	-5:49:48
Kākināda	2	16N56	82E13	-5:28:52
Kakrāla	2	28N33	77E25	-5:09:40
Kāksa	3	23N28	87E28	-5:49:52
Kālahasti	2	13N45	79E43	-5:18:52

Kalamboli 2 19N01 73E06 -4:52:24
Kālānwāli 2 29N51 74E57 -4:59:48
Kalchini 3 26N43 89E26 -5:57:44
Kalhe 2 18N52 73E06 -4:52:24
Kāliganj 3 23N44 88E14 -5:52:56
Kālikāpur 3 22N29 88E32 -5:54:08
Kālikāpur 5 22N37 86E17 -5:45:08
Kālimpong 3 27N04 88E29 -5:53:56
Kālinagar 3 22N26 88E51 -5:55:24
Kālipur 3 22N41 88E17 -5:53:08
Kāliyāganj 3 25N38 88E19 -5:53:16
Kālka 2 30N50 76E56 -5:07:44
Kalkutta → Calcutta
3 22N32 88E22 -5:53:28
Kallakkurichchi 2 11N44 78E58 -5:15:52
Kālna 3 23N13 88E22 -5:53:28
Kālol 2 23N15 72E29 -4:49:56
Kālol 2 22N36 73E27 -4:53:48
Kālpi 2 26N07 79E44 -5:18:56
Kālundri 2 18N59 73E08 -4:52:32
Kalwa 2 19N12 72E59 -4:51:56
Kalyān 2 19N15 73E09 -4:52:36
Kalyāndrug 2 14N33 77E06 -5:08:24
Kāman 2 27N39 77E16 -5:09:04
Kamareddi 2 18N28 78E22 -5:13:28
Kāmāreddi 2 18N19 78E21 -5:13:24
Kāmārhāti 3 22N40 88E22 -5:53:28
Kāmārkunda 3 22N49 88E13 -5:52:52
Kambam 2 9N44 77E18 -5:09:12
Kāmdebpur 3 22N47 88E30 -5:54:00
Kāmdebpur 3 22N54 88E20 -5:53:20
Kamku 4 27N30 96E30 -6:26:00
Kāmpa 3 22N56 88E28 -5:53:52
Kampil 2 27N37 79E17 -5:17:08
Kampli 2 15N24 76E37 -5:06:28
Kāmthi 2 21N14 79E12 -5:16:48
Kanakapura 2 12N33 77E25 -5:09:40
Kanaudi 2 23N36 81E23 -5:25:32
Kānchipuram 2 12N50 79E43 -5:18:52
Kānchrāpāra 3 22N57 88E28 -5:53:52
Kandāghat 2 30N59 77E07 -5:08:28
Kāndhla 2 29N19 77E16 -5:09:04
Kāndi 3 23N57 88E02 -5:52:08
Kandkurt 2 18N53 77E56 -5:11:44
Kāndra 3 23N44 87E58 -5:51:52
Kandukūr 2 15N13 79E55 -5:19:40
Kāngpokpi 4 25N08 93E58 -6:15:52
Kāngra 2 32N06 76E16 -5:05:04
Kanhangad 2 12N19 75E04 -5:00:16
Kanigiri 2 15N24 79E31 -5:18:04
Kanina 2 28N20 76E19 -5:05:16
Kānker 2 20N17 81E29 -5:25:56
Kannad 2 20N16 75E08 -5:00:32
Kannauj 2 27N04 79E55 -5:19:40
Kanniyākumāri 2 8N05 77E34 -5:10:16
Kannod 2 22N40 76E44 -5:06:56
Kanpoli 2 19N04 73E09 -4:52:36
Kānpur 2 26N28 80E21 -5:21:24
Kānsāripāra 3 22N56 88E14 -5:52:56
Kantābānji 2 20N29 82E55 -5:31:40
Kantalvi 2 18N54 73E03 -4:52:12
Kāntāphor 2 22N35 76E34 -5:06:16
Kānth 2 29N04 78E38 -5:14:32
Kanti 5 26N13 85E21 -5:41:24
Kapadvanj 2 23N01 73E04 -4:52:16
Kaptipada 2 21N31 86E32 -5:46:08
Kapūrthala 2 31N23 75E23 -5:01:32
Karād 2 17N17 74E12 -4:56:48
Karagola Road 2 25N29 87E23 -5:49:32
Karaia 2 25N54 78E01 -5:12:04
Kāraikkudi 2 10N04 78E47 -5:15:08
Kāranja 2 20N29 77E29 -5:09:56
Karanjia 2 21N47 85E58 -5:43:52
Karauli 2 26N30 77E01 -5:08:04
Karave 2 19N01 73E01 -4:52:04
Karea 3 22N42 88E33 -5:54:12
Kareli 2 22N55 79E04 -5:16:16
Karen 4 12N51 92E53 -6:11:32
Karera 2 28N41 77E23 -5:09:32
Kargil 2 34N34 76E06 -5:04:24
Karhal 2 27N01 78E57 -5:15:48
Kārikāl 2 10N55 79E50 -5:19:20
Karīmganj 4 24N50 92E30 -6:10:00
Karīmnagar 2 18N26 79E09 -5:16:36
Karīmpur 3 23N58 88E37 -5:54:28
Kārkal 2 13N12 74E59 -4:59:56
Karmāla 2 18N25 75E12 -5:00:48
Karmatānr 5 24N05 86E42 -5:46:48
Karnāl 2 29N41 76E59 -5:07:56
Karon 5 24N07 86E44 -5:46:56
Kartārpur 2 31N27 75E30 -5:02:00
Karūr 2 10N57 78E05 -5:12:20
Kārwār 2 14N48 74E08 -4:56:32
Karwi 2 25N12 80E54 -5:23:36
Kāsaragod 2 12N30 75E00 -5:00:00
Kasauli 2 30N55 76E57 -5:07:48
Kasba 5 25N51 87E33 -5:50:12
Kasbagoas 3 24N11 88E30 -5:54:00
Kasba Kamarda 2 21N46 87E21 -5:49:24
Kasba Mirgoda 3 21N42 87E28 -5:49:52
Kasba Nārāyangarh
3 22N10 87E23 -5:49:32
Kasba Patāspur 2 22N02 87E32 -5:50:08
Kāsganj 2 27N49 78E39 -5:14:36
Kashīpur 2 29N13 78E57 -5:15:48
Kāshipur 5 23N26 86E40 -5:46:40
Kasia 2 26N45 83E55 -5:35:40
Kasiāri 3 22N08 87E14 -5:48:56
Kāsimpur 3 22N46 88E31 -5:54:04
Kāsināthpur 3 22N35 88E31 -5:54:04
Kāsipur 3 22N25 88E10 -5:52:40
Katai 2 19N10 73E05 -4:52:20
Katangi 2 23N27 79E47 -5:19:08
Katanimara 3 22N17 87E11 -5:48:44
Katarniān Ghāt 2 28N20 81E09 -5:24:36
Katghora 2 22N30 82E33 -5:30:12
Kāthgodām 2 29N16 79E32 -5:18:08
Kathiār 5 25N32 87E35 -5:50:20
Kathla 2 31N59 76E47 -5:07:08
Kathor 2 21N18 72E56 -4:51:44
Kathua 2 32N22 75E31 -5:02:04
Katihār 5 25N32 87E35 -5:50:20
Katni → Murwāra 2 23N51 80E24 -5:21:36
Kātol 2 21N16 78E35 -5:14:20
Katra 2 32N59 74E57 -4:59:48
Kātrās 5 23N48 86E17 -5:45:08
Kāttuputtūr 2 10N59 78E14 -5:12:56
Kātūria 5 24N44 86E43 -5:46:52
Kātwa 3 23N39 88E08 -5:52:32
Kauriāla Ghāt 2 28N23 81E02 -5:24:08
Kausa 2 19N10 73E02 -4:52:08
Kāvali 2 14N55 79E59 -5:19:56
Kawardha 2 22N01 81E15 -5:25:00
Kāyalpattinam 2 8N34 78E07 -5:12:28
Kāyamba 3 22N41 88E32 -5:54:08
Kayankulam 2 9N11 76E30 -5:06:00
Kāzipāra 3 22N43 88E31 -5:54:04
Kedarnath 2 30N44 79E04 -5:16:16
Kekpāra 5 22N27 86E35 -5:46:20
Kekri 2 25N58 75E09 -5:00:36
Kenda 5 23N12 86E32 -5:46:08
Kendai 2 22N45 82E37 -5:30:28
Kendghāta 2 24N05 87E10 -5:48:40
Kendrāpāra 2 20N30 86E25 -5:45:40
Kendua 3 22N34 88E10 -5:52:40
Keonchi 2 22N38 81E47 -5:27:08
Keonjhargarh 2 21N38 85E35 -5:42:20
Keshod 2 21N18 70E15 -4:41:00
Kespur 3 22N35 87E29 -5:49:56
Khādar 2 28N33 77E22 -5:09:28
Khadki (Kirkee) 2 18N34 73E52 -4:55:28
Khagaria 5 25N30 86E29 -5:45:56
Khāgrāmuri 3 22N26 88E14 -5:52:56
Khair 2 27N57 77E50 -5:11:20
Khairābād 2 27N32 80E45 -5:23:00
Khairāgarh 2 21N25 80E58 -5:23:52
Khairbani 2 24N14 87E05 -5:48:20
Khairna 2 19N06 73E01 -4:52:04
Khajrāho 2 24N50 79E58 -5:19:52
Khājuri 3 21N52 87E58 -5:51:52
Khajuria 3 24N58 87E55 -5:51:40
Khalatse 2 34N20 76E49 -5:07:16
Khālsar 2 34N31 77E41 -5:10:44
Khambhāliya 2 22N12 69E39 -4:38:36
Khāmgaon 2 20N41 76E34 -5:06:16
Khammam 2 17N15 80E09 -5:20:36
Khāna 3 23N20 87E44 -5:50:56
Khānākul 3 22N43 87E51 -5:51:24
Khandaghosh 3 23N13 87E41 -5:50:44
Khandela 2 27N36 75E30 -5:02:00
Khandwa 2 21N50 76E20 -5:05:20
Khānkurda 3 22N00 87E25 -5:49:40
Khanna 2 30N42 76E13 -5:04:52
Khānpur 3 22N40 88E16 -5:53:04
Kharagdiha 5 24N25 86E10 -5:44:40
Kharagpur 3 22N20 87E20 -5:49:20
Kharagpur 5 25N07 86E33 -5:46:12
Kharar 3 22N42 87E41 -5:50:44
Kharar 2 30N45 76E39 -5:06:36
Khardah 3 22N44 88E22 -5:53:28
Khārghar 2 19N03 73E04 -4:52:16
Khargon 2 21N49 75E36 -5:02:24
Khariār Road 2 20N54 82E31 -5:30:04
Kharri 3 22N55 88E14 -5:52:56
Kharsāwān 5 22N48 85E50 -5:43:20
Kharsia 2 21N58 83E07 -5:32:28
Khāsbāti 3 22N55 88E25 -5:53:40
Khatauli 2 29N17 77E43 -5:10:52
Khātegaon 2 22N36 76E55 -5:07:40
Khātra 3 22N59 86E51 -5:47:24
Khāvda 2 23N51 69E43 -4:38:52
Khayerpur 3 22N35 88E33 -5:54:12
Khayrasole 3 23N48 87E16 -5:49:04
Kheardaha 3 22N29 88E28 -5:53:52
Khed 2 17N43 73E23 -4:53:32
Khefapur 2 28N30 77E05 -5:08:20
Khejurdaha 3 22N59 88E10 -5:52:40
Khem Karan 2 31N09 74E34 -4:58:16
Khenyen 3 22N59 88E19 -5:53:16
Kheri 2 27N54 80E48 -5:23:12
Kherli 2 27N12 77E02 -5:08:08
Kherwāra 2 23N59 73E35 -4:54:20
Khetia 2 21N40 74E35 -4:58:20
Khilchipur 2 24N02 76E34 -5:06:16
Khilkāpur 3 22N46 88E29 -5:53:56
Khirpai 3 22N42 87E37 -5:50:28
Khoni 2 19N10 73E07 -4:52:28
Khorel 3 22N42 88E19 -5:53:16
Khoru 3 22N51 88E31 -5:54:04
Khowai 4 24N06 91E38 -6:06:32
Khowāng 4 27N16 94E53 -6:19:32
Khunti 5 23N05 85E17 -5:41:08
Khurai 2 24N03 78E19 -5:13:16
Khurda 2 20N11 85E37 -5:42:28
Khurigāchi 3 22N49 88E20 -5:53:20
Khurja 2 28N15 77E51 -5:11:24
Kibar 2 32N20 78E01 -5:12:04
Kīlakarai 2 9N14 78E47 -5:15:08
Kilikollūr 2 8N54 76E39 -5:06:36
Kinaūni 2 28N39 77E23 -5:09:32
Kinchara 3 22N53 88E32 -5:54:08
Kiranpur 3 23N46 87E53 -5:51:32
Kīratpur 2 29N31 78E12 -5:12:48
Kirkee → Khadki 2 18N34 73E52 -4:55:28
Kirnāhar 3 23N45 87E52 -5:51:28
Kishanganj 3 26N07 87E56 -5:51:44
Kishangarh 2 26N34 74E52 -4:59:28
Kishangarh 2 27N52 70E34 -4:42:16
Kishtwār 2 33N19 75E46 -5:03:04
Kisoripur 3 22N05 88E34 -5:54:16
Kiul 5 25N09 86E06 -5:44:24
Kizhake Chālakudi
2 10N18 76E20 -5:05:20
Knargram 3 24N01 87E59 -5:51:56
Kochugaon 4 26N34 90E04 -6:00:16
Kodad 2 17N00 79E58 -5:19:52
Kodaikānal 2 10N14 77E29 -5:09:56
Kodarma 5 24N28 85E36 -5:42:24
Kodinār 2 20N47 70E42 -4:42:48
Koduru 2 14N53 78E08 -5:12:32
Kohīma 4 25N40 94E07 -6:16:28
Kohir 2 17N35 77E40 -5:10:40
Koihoa 4 8N12 93E29 -6:13:56
Koil-Aligarh → Alīgarh
2 27N53 78E05 -5:12:20
Koilkanda 2 16N45 77E50 -5:11:20
Koilkuntla 2 15N14 78E19 -5:13:16
Kokpāra Narsinghgarh
5 22N31 86E33 -5:46:12
Kokrajhar 4 26N24 90E16 -6:01:04
Kolachel 2 8N10 77E15 -5:09:00
Kolār 2 13N08 78E08 -5:12:32
Kolāras 2 25N14 77E36 -5:10:24
Kolār Gold Fields
2 12N55 78E17 -5:13:08
Kolāyat 2 27N50 72E57 -4:51:48
Kolebira 5 22N43 84E42 -5:38:48
Kolhāpur 2 16N42 74E13 -4:56:52
Kolhāpur 2 16N06 78E16 -5:13:04
Kollegāl 2 12N09 77E07 -5:08:28
Kolora 3 22N55 88E22 -5:53:28
Kolosib 4 24N14 92E42 -6:10:48
Komdhārā 3 22N53 88E14 -5:52:56
Kona 3 22N37 88E18 -5:53:12
Konārak 2 19N54 86E07 -5:44:28
Konch 2 25N59 79E09 -5:16:36
Kondagaon 2 19N36 81E40 -5:26:40
Konnagar 3 22N42 88E22 -5:53:28
Konnur 2 16N12 74E45 -4:59:00
Kopāganj 2 26N01 83E34 -5:34:16
Kopargaon 2 19N53 74E29 -4:57:56
Koparkhairna 2 19N06 72E59 -4:51:56
Koparpāda 2 19N02 73E04 -4:52:16
Koppal 2 15N21 76E09 -5:04:36
Kopri 2 19N11 72E58 -4:51:52
Korangal 2 17N08 77E36 -5:10:24
Koraput 2 18N49 82E43 -5:30:52
Koratla 2 18N49 78E43 -5:14:52
Korba 2 22N21 82E41 -5:30:44
Korwai 2 24N08 78E03 -5:12:12
Kosgi 2 17N00 77E43 -5:10:52
Kosi 2 27N48 77E26 -5:09:44
Kosigi 2 15N51 77E16 -5:09:04
Kota 2 22N18 82E02 -5:28:08
Kota 2 25N11 75E50 -5:03:20
Kotagiri 2 11N26 76E53 -5:07:32
Kotālpur 3 23N02 87E36 -5:50:24
Kotdwāra 2 29N45 78E32 -5:14:08
Kot Fateh 2 30N07 75E05 -5:00:20
Kot Kapūra 2 30N35 74E54 -4:59:36
Kotla 2 32N15 76E02 -5:04:08
Kot Pūtli 2 27N43 76E12 -5:04:48
Kotra 3 22N46 88E34 -5:54:16
Kotra 2 24N22 73E10 -4:52:40
Kotrung → Uttarpara-Kotrung
3 22N40 88E21 -5:53:24
Kottagūdem 2 17N33 80E38 -5:22:32
Kottayam 2 9N35 76E31 -5:06:04
Kottūr 2 10N32 76E59 -5:07:56
Kottūru 2 14N49 76E13 -5:04:52
Kovilpatti 2 9N10 77E52 -5:11:28
Kovūr 2 14N29 79E59 -5:19:56
Kovvur 2 17N01 81E44 -5:26:56
Kowār 5 24N13 86E11 -5:44:44
Koyambattur → Coimbatore
2 11N00 76E58 -5:07:52
Kozhikode → Calicut
2 11N15 75E46 -5:03:04
Krishnachaadrapur
2 21N50 86E49 -5:47:16
Krishnagiri 2 12N32 78E14 -5:12:56
Krishnamāti 3 22N40 88E32 -5:54:08
Krishnanagar 3 23N13 87E33 -5:50:12
Krishnanagar 3 23N24 88E30 -5:54:00
Krishnapur 3 22N36 88E26 -5:53:44
Krishnarājpet 2 12N40 76E30 -5:06:00
Krishnarāmpur 3 22N43 88E14 -5:52:56
Kuchaiburi 2 22N16 86E10 -5:44:40
Kuchāman 2 27N09 74E52 -4:59:28
Kūd 2 33N05 75E17 -5:01:08
Kuilāpāl 5 22N50 86E38 -5:46:32
Kukshi 2 22N12 74E45 -4:59:00
Kulasekharapatnam
2 8N24 78E03 -5:12:12
Kulgam 2 33N39 75E01 -5:00:04
Kulpahār 2 25N19 79E39 -5:18:36
Kulpi 3 22N06 88E15 -5:53:00
Kulti 3 23N44 86E51 -5:47:24
Kultikri 3 22N10 87E09 -5:48:36
Kulu 2 31N58 77E06 -5:08:24
Kumārapālaiyam 2 11N28 77E43 -5:10:52
Kumarganj 3 22N59 87E44 -5:50:56
Kumārgrām 4 26N37 89E50 -5:59:20
Kumbakonam 2 10N58 79E23 -5:17:32
Kumedpur 3 25N26 87E50 -5:51:20
Kumrābād 2 24N10 87E16 -5:49:04
Kumta 2 14N25 74E24 -4:57:36
Kundahit 2 23N58 87E10 -5:48:40
Kundam 2 23N13 80E21 -5:21:24
Kundara 2 8N57 76E41 -5:06:44
Kundla 2 21N20 71E18 -4:45:12
Kunkuri 2 22N45 83E57 -5:35:48
Kunnamkulam 2 10N39 76E05 -5:04:20
Kunnan 4 23N57 93E20 -6:13:20
Kuppam 2 12N44 78E23 -5:13:32

Kūrāli 2 30N50 76E35 -5:06:20
Kurāon 2 24N59 82E05 -5:28:20
Kurauli 2 27N24 78E59 -5:15:56
Kurduvādi 2 18N05 75E26 -5:01:44
Kuriasol 2 22N06 86E39 -5:46:36
Kurinjippadi 2 11N34 79E36 -5:18:24
Kurnool 2 15N50 78E03 -5:12:12
Kursela 2 25N27 87E15 -5:49:00
Kurseong 3 26N53 88E17 -5:53:08
Kurukshetra 2 29N59 76E51 -5:07:24
Kushālgarh 2 23N10 74E27 -4:57:48
Kusria 3 22N58 88E14 -5:52:56
Kusthalia 3 23N29 87E03 -5:48:12
Kusumba 3 22N27 88E24 -5:53:36
Kutiyāna 2 21N38 69E59 -4:39:56
Kuyāli 5 22N31 86E11 -5:44:44
Lābpur 3 23N50 87E49 -5:51:16
Lachhmangarh 2 27N49 75E02 -5:00:08
Ladhurka 5 23N22 86E32 -5:46:08
Lādnun 2 27N39 74E23 -4:57:32
Lādwa 2 29N59 77E03 -5:08:12
Lahār 2 26N12 78E57 -5:15:48
Lāharpur 2 27N43 80E54 -5:23:36
Laheria Sarai 5 26N07 85E54 -5:43:36
Lākheri 2 25N40 76E10 -5:04:40
Lakhīmpur 2 27N57 80E46 -5:23:04
Lakhīmpur 4 27N14 94E15 -6:17:00
Lakhipur 4 24N48 93E01 -6:12:04
Lakhipur 4 26N02 90E18 -6:01:12
Lakhnādon 2 22N36 79E36 -5:18:24
Lakhpat 2 23N49 68E47 -4:35:08
Laknau → Lucknow
2 26N51 80E55 -5:23:40
Lakshamannāth 2 21N51 87E13 -5:48:52
Lakshmanpur 3 22N38 88E16 -5:53:04
Lakshmeshwar 2 15N08 75E28 -5:01:52
Lakshmikantapur 3 22N07 88E20 -5:53:20
Lakshmisāgar 5 22N55 87E01 -5:48:04
Lālganj 5 25N52 85E11 -5:40:44
Lālgarh 3 22N35 87E03 -5:48:12
Lalitpur 2 24N41 78E25 -5:13:40
Lālpur 2 22N12 69E58 -4:39:52
Lālsot 2 26N34 76E20 -5:05:20
Lāmta 2 22N08 80E07 -5:20:28
Langting 4 25N30 93E07 -6:12:28
Lansdowne 2 29N50 78E41 -5:14:44
Lashkar → Gwalior
2 26N13 78E10 -5:12:40
Lātehār 5 23N45 84E30 -5:38:00
Lāthi 2 21N43 71E23 -4:45:32
Lātūr 2 18N24 76E35 -5:06:20
Laungowāl 2 30N13 75E41 -5:02:44
Lauriya Nandangarh
5 26N59 84E24 -5:37:36
Ledo 4 27N18 95E44 -6:22:56
Leh 2 34N10 77E35 -5:10:20
Lehra Gāga 2 29N55 75E49 -5:03:16
Liluāh 3 22N35 88E23 -5:53:32
Limbdi 2 22N34 71E48 -4:47:12
Lingapur 2 19N03 78E08 -5:12:32
Litipāra 5 24N42 87E37 -5:50:28
Lodhāsuli 3 22N19 87E03 -5:48:12
Lohārdaga 5 23N26 84E41 -5:38:44
Lohāru 2 28N27 75E49 -5:03:16
Lohiān 2 31N10 75E11 -5:00:44
Lonāvale 2 18N45 73E25 -4:53:40
Loni 2 28N45 77E17 -5:09:08
Lowāda 3 22N27 87E37 -5:50:28
Luckeesarai 5 25N11 86E05 -5:44:20
Lucknow 2 26N51 80E55 -5:23:40
Ludhiāna 2 30N54 75E51 -5:03:24
Lumding 4 25N43 93E13 -6:12:52
Lūnāvāda 2 23N08 73E37 -4:54:28
Lungleh 4 22N53 92E44 -6:10:56
Lūni 2 26N00 73E00 -4:52:00
Māchalpur 2 24N08 76E18 -5:05:12
Mācherla 2 16N29 79E26 -5:17:44
Machhīwara 2 30N55 76E12 -5:04:48
Machhlīshahr 2 25N41 82E25 -5:29:40
Machilīpatnam (Bandar)
2 16N10 81E08 -5:24:32
Madanapalle 2 13N33 78E30 -5:14:00
Madanpur 3 22N40 88E32 -5:54:08
Mādāri Hāt 3 26N42 89E17 -5:57:08
Mādārpur 3 22N54 88E27 -5:53:48
Madgaon (Margao)
1 15N18 73E57 -4:55:48
Madhepura 5 25N57 86E51 -5:47:24
Madhipura 5 25N55 86E47 -5:47:08
Mādhopur 2 32N22 75E36 -5:02:24
Mādhopur 2 24N18 86E37 -5:46:28
Madhra 2 16N54 80E25 -5:21:40
Madhubani 5 26N22 86E05 -5:44:20
Madhudaha 3 22N31 88E25 -5:53:40
Madhugiri 2 13N40 77E12 -5:08:48
Madhupar 5 22N54 86E28 -5:45:52
Madhupur 5 24N16 86E39 -5:46:36
Madhyamgrām 3 22N42 88E27 -5:53:48
Madnur 2 18N31 77E37 -5:10:28
Madras 2 13N05 80E17 -5:21:08
Madurai 2 9N56 78E07 -5:12:28
Madura → Madurai
2 9N56 78E07 -5:12:28
Madurāntakam 2 12N31 79E54 -5:19:36
Magara 3 22N34 87E34 -5:50:16
Magra 3 22N59 88E22 -5:53:28
Magra Hāt 3 22N14 88E23 -5:53:32
Mahābaleshwar 2 17N55 73E40 -4:54:40
Mahābalipuram 2 12N37 80E12 -5:20:48
Mahād 2 18N05 73E25 -4:53:40
Mahājan 2 28N47 73E50 -4:55:20
Mahālandi 3 24N04 88E07 -5:52:28
Maham 2 28N59 76E18 -5:05:12
Mahānadpati 3 23N00 88E16 -5:53:04
Mahape 2 19N07 73E01 -4:52:04
Mahārājganj 5 26N07 84E29 -5:37:56
Mahārājganj 2 27N09 83E34 -5:34:16
Mahārājpur 2 25N01 79E44 -5:18:56
Mahārājpur 2 28N39 77E20 -5:09:20
Mahāsamund 2 21N06 82E06 -5:28:24
Mahbūbābād 2 17N37 80E01 -5:20:04
Mahbūbnagar 2 16N44 77E59 -5:11:56
Mahe 2 11N42 75E32 -5:02:08
Mahendraganj 4 25N20 89E45 -5:59:00
Mahendragarh 2 28N17 76E09 -5:04:36
Mahesgādi 3 22N39 88E33 -5:54:12
Maheshmunda 5 24N13 86E24 -5:45:36
Maheshtala 3 22N30 88E15 -5:53:00
Maheshwar 5 26N32 84E28 -5:37:52
Maheshwar 2 22N11 75E35 -5:02:20
Mahgawān 2 26N29 78E37 -5:14:28
Mahiāri 3 22N35 88E14 -5:52:56
Māhikpur 3 22N32 88E14 -5:52:56
Mahīshādal 3 22N11 87E59 -5:51:56
Mahishdānga 3 22N54 88E11 -5:52:44
Mahmūdābād 2 27N18 81E07 -5:24:28
Mahmudpur 3 22N41 88E09 -5:52:36
Mahmūdpur 2 28N46 77E22 -5:09:28
Mahoba 2 25N17 79E52 -5:19:28
Mahroni 2 24N35 78E43 -5:14:52
Mahulia 5 22N39 86E24 -5:45:36
Mahuva 2 21N05 71E48 -4:47:12
Mahwah 2 27N03 76E56 -5:07:44
Maihar 2 24N16 80E45 -5:23:00
Mailāni 2 28N17 80E21 -5:21:24
Maināguri 3 26N34 88E49 -5:55:16
Mainpuri 2 27N14 79E01 -5:16:04
Mairabāri 4 26N28 92E26 -6:09:44
Majītha 2 31N46 74E57 -4:59:48
Majnan 3 22N59 88E09 -5:52:36
Māju 3 22N37 88E05 -5:52:20
Makanapur 2 28N38 77E21 -5:09:24
Mākhālpur 3 22N56 88E10 -5:52:40
Makhdūmnagar 2 26N28 82E46 -5:31:04
Makrai 2 22N04 77E06 -5:08:24
Makrāna 2 27N03 74E43 -4:58:52
Maksudangarh 2 24N03 77E15 -5:09:00
Māl 3 26N52 88E44 -5:54:56
Mālancha 3 22N55 88E26 -5:53:44
Mālandighi 3 23N33 87E24 -5:49:36
Malaut 2 30N13 74E29 -4:57:56
Malavalli 2 12N23 77E05 -5:08:20
Malcompeth → Mahābaleshwar
2 17N55 73E40 -4:54:40
Mālda 3 25N02 88E09 -5:52:36
Mālegaon 2 20N33 74E32 -4:58:08
Malehra 2 24N34 79E19 -5:17:16
Māler Kotla 2 30N31 75E53 -5:03:32
Malighati 3 22N33 87E40 -5:50:40
Malīhābād 2 26N55 80E43 -5:22:52
Malīpara 3 22N57 88E14 -5:52:56
Māliya 2 23N05 70E46 -4:43:04
Malkāpur 2 20N53 76E12 -5:04:48
Malkapuram 2 17N42 83E16 -5:33:04
Malpe 2 13N21 74E43 -4:58:52
Mālpura 2 26N17 75E23 -5:01:32
Maluti 3 24N09 87E41 -5:50:44
Mālvan 2 16N04 73E28 -4:53:52
Man 2 33N51 78E32 -5:14:08
Manāli 2 32N16 77E10 -5:08:40
Manappārai 2 10N36 78E25 -5:13:40
Manāwar 2 22N14 75E05 -5:00:20
Mānbāzār 5 23N04 86E39 -5:46:36
Mancherāl 2 18N52 79E26 -5:17:44
Manda 2 22N06 86E14 -5:44:56
Mandalkia 3 22N43 88E08 -5:52:32
Mandapeta 2 16N52 81E56 -5:27:44
Mandapur 3 23N00 88E29 -5:53:56
Mandasor 2 24N04 75E04 -5:00:16
Mandāwar 2 29N30 78E08 -5:12:32
Mandi 2 31N43 76E55 -5:07:40
Mandi Dabwāli 2 29N58 74E42 -4:58:48
Mandla 2 22N36 80E23 -5:21:32
Māndrā 3 22N55 88E07 -5:52:28
Māndu 2 22N22 75E23 -5:01:32
Māndvi 2 22N50 69E22 -4:37:28
Māndvi 2 21N15 73E18 -4:53:12
Mandya 2 12N33 76E54 -5:07:36
Manendragarh 2 23N13 82E13 -5:28:52
Mangal 3 23N31 87E55 -5:51:40
Mangalagiri 2 16N26 80E33 -5:22:12
Mangaldai 4 26N26 92E02 -6:08:08
Mangalkot 3 23N33 87E54 -5:51:36
Mangalore 2 12N52 74E53 -4:59:32
Mangalvedha 2 17N31 75E28 -5:01:52
Mangawān 2 24N41 81E33 -5:26:12
Manglagiri 2 16N26 80E36 -5:22:24
Manglaur 2 29N48 77E52 -5:11:28
Māngrol 2 21N07 70E07 -4:40:28
Mangrūl Pīr 2 20N19 77E21 -5:09:24
Manihari 5 25N21 87E38 -5:50:32
Manikanāli 3 23N19 87E03 -5:48:12
Mānikpur 2 25N04 81E07 -5:24:28
Mani Majra 2 30N43 76E50 -5:07:20
Manjeri 2 11N07 76E07 -5:04:28
Manjeshwara 2 12N42 74E53 -4:59:32
Mānkundu 3 22N50 88E22 -5:53:28
Mānkur 3 23N20 87E33 -5:50:12
Mānkur 3 22N30 87E54 -5:51:36
Manmād 2 20N15 74E27 -4:57:48
Mannārgudi 2 10N40 79E26 -5:17:44
Manoharpur 3 21N59 87E18 -5:49:12
Manoharpur 5 22N23 85E12 -5:40:48
Mānpur 2 23N46 81E08 -5:24:32
Mānpur 2 20N22 80E43 -5:22:52
Mānsa 2 29N59 75E23 -5:01:32
Mānsa 2 23N26 72E40 -4:50:40
Mānsinhapur 3 22N39 88E09 -5:52:36
Manteswar 3 23N26 88E06 -5:52:24
Māntri 2 21N39 86E49 -5:47:16
Manulia 5 22N39 86E30 -5:46:00
Mānushmuria 5 22N22 86E47 -5:47:08
Mānwat 2 19N18 76E30 -5:06:00
Mara 4 28N11 94E06 -6:16:24
Mārahra 2 27N44 78E35 -5:14:20
Maram 4 25N25 94E06 -6:16:24
Margao → Madgaon
1 15N18 73E57 -4:55:48
Mārgherita 4 27N17 95E41 -6:22:44
Mariāhu 2 25N37 82E37 -5:30:28
Mariāni 4 26N40 94E20 -6:17:20
Mārkāpur 2 15N44 79E17 -5:17:08
Mārwār 2 25N44 73E36 -4:54:24
Masānjor 2 24N07 87E19 -5:49:16
Masina 3 22N55 88E32 -5:54:08
Masulipatam → Machilīpatnam
2 16N10 81E08 -5:24:32
Mātābhānga 3 26N20 89E13 -5:56:52
Māthle 3 22N35 88E14 -5:52:56
Mathura 2 10N57 78E27 -5:13:48
Mathura 2 27N30 77E41 -5:10:44
Mathurai → Madurai
2 9N56 78E07 -5:12:28
Matiakhola 5 23N16 86E56 -5:47:44
Mātiāli 3 26N56 88E49 -5:55:16
Mattāncheri 2 9N59 76E16 -5:05:04
Mau 2 25N17 81E23 -5:25:32
Mau Aimma 2 25N42 81E55 -5:27:40
Maudaha 2 25N41 80E07 -5:20:28
Mauganj 2 24N41 81E53 -5:27:32
Maunath Bhanjan 2 25N57 83E33 -5:34:12
Maur 2 30N05 75E15 -5:01:00
Mau Rānīpur 2 25N15 79E08 -5:16:32
Māvelikara 2 9N16 76E33 -5:06:12
Mawāna 2 29N06 77E55 -5:11:40
Mawi 2 28N39 77E25 -5:09:40
Māyāpur 3 22N27 88E08 -5:52:32
Mayna 3 22N14 87E47 -5:51:08
Māyūram 2 11N06 79E40 -5:18:40
Medak 2 18N02 78E16 -5:13:04
Meerut 2 28N59 77E42 -5:10:48
Mehekar 2 20N09 76E34 -5:06:16
Mehidpur 2 23N49 75E40 -5:02:40
Mehnagar 2 25N53 83E07 -5:32:28
Mehndāwal 2 26N59 83E07 -5:32:28
Mehsāna 2 23N36 72E24 -4:49:36
Mejia 3 23N34 87E06 -5:48:24
Mekhliganj 3 26N21 88E55 -5:55:40
Melappālaiyam 2 8N42 77E43 -5:10:52
Mele 3 22N49 88E09 -5:52:36
Melūr 2 10N03 78E20 -5:13:20
Memāri 3 23N12 88E07 -5:52:28
Meola Āgri 2 28N42 77E23 -5:09:32
Mercāra 2 12N25 75E44 -5:02:56
Meria 3 22N59 88E20 -5:53:20
Merta 2 26N39 74E02 -4:56:08
Merta Road 2 26N43 73E55 -4:55:40
Metagācha 3 22N38 88E31 -5:54:04
Mettuppālaiyam 2 11N18 76E57 -5:07:48
Mettūr 2 11N48 77E48 -5:11:12
Mhasvād 2 17N38 74E47 -4:59:08
Mhow 2 22N33 75E46 -5:03:04
Miājlar 2 26N15 70E23 -4:41:32
Miāni 2 21N51 69E23 -4:37:32
Midnapore 3 22N26 87E20 -5:49:20
Minutang 4 28N13 96E32 -6:26:08
Mipi 4 28N57 95E48 -6:23:12
Miraj 2 16N50 74E38 -4:58:32
Mirij Guda 2 16N53 79E33 -5:18:12
Mirzāpur 2 25N09 82E35 -5:30:20
Mirzāpur 3 22N50 88E24 -5:53:36
Misrikh 2 27N27 80E31 -5:22:04
Mithapur 2 22N25 69E00 -4:36:00
Modāsa 2 23N28 73E18 -4:53:12
Moga 2 30N48 75E10 -5:00:40
Mohana 2 25N54 77E45 -5:11:00
Mohania 5 25N11 83E37 -5:34:28
Mohanpur 3 21N51 87E26 -5:49:44
Mohanpur 2 28N44 77E10 -5:08:40
Mokameh 5 25N24 85E55 -5:43:40
Mokokchūng 4 26N20 94E32 -6:18:08
Monghyr 5 25N23 86E28 -5:45:52
Mora 2 18N54 72E56 -4:51:44
Morādābād 2 28N50 78E47 -5:15:08
Morena 2 26N30 78E09 -5:12:36
Morna 2 28N35 77E22 -5:09:28
Morsi 2 21N21 78E00 -5:12:00
Mort 2 28N43 77E25 -5:09:40
Morta 2 28N44 77E27 -5:09:48
Morvi 2 22N49 70E50 -4:43:20
Moth 2 25N43 78E57 -5:15:48
Motīhāri 5 26N39 84E55 -5:39:40
Mubārakpur 2 26N05 83E18 -5:33:12
Mudhol 2 16N21 75E17 -5:01:08
Mudhol 2 19N00 77E52 -5:11:28
Mughalsarai 2 25N18 83E07 -5:32:28
Muhamdi 2 27N57 80E13 -5:20:52
Muhammadābād 2 26N02 83E23 -5:33:32
Mukandwara 2 24N49 75E59 -5:03:56
Mukeriān 2 31N57 75E37 -5:02:28
Muktsar 2 30N29 74E31 -4:58:04
Mūl 2 20N04 79E40 -5:18:40
Mulbāgal 2 13N10 78E24 -5:13:36
Mūlki 2 13N06 74E48 -4:59:12
Multai 2 21N46 78E15 -5:13:00
Munābāo 2 25N45 70E17 -4:41:08
Mundra 2 22N51 69E44 -4:38:56
Mungaoli 2 24N25 78E06 -5:12:24
Mungeli 2 22N04 81E41 -5:26:44
Mungod 2 17N06 79E00 -5:16:00
Mungra Badshāhpur
2 25N40 82E11 -5:28:44
Munsarpur 3 24N18 88E26 -5:53:44
Murādnagar 2 28N47 77E30 -5:10:00
Murāgācha 3 23N32 88E24 -5:53:36

Murarai	3	24N27	87E52	-5:51:28
Muratpur	3	22N59	88E27	-5:53:48
Mūrinda	2	30N47	76E29	-5:05:56
Murkong Selek	4	27N49	95E16	-6:21:04
Murliganj	5	25N54	86E59	-5:47:56
Murshidābād	3	24N11	88E16	-5:53:04
Murtajāpur	2	20N44	77E23	-5:09:32
Murud	2	18N19	72E58	-4:51:52
Murwāra	2	23N51	80E24	-5:21:36
Musar	3	22N54	88E14	-5:52:56
Mushābani	5	22N31	86E27	-5:45:48
Muskira	2	25N40	79E48	-5:19:12
Mussoorie	2	30N27	78E05	-5:12:20
Muttra → Mathura	2	27N30	77E41	-5:10:44
Muttukuru	2	14N17	80E08	-5:20:32
Muttyāluppettai	2	11N57	79E50	-5:19:20
Mūvattupula	2	9N58	76E35	-5:06:20
Muzaffarnagar	2	29N28	77E41	-5:10:44
Muzaffarpur	5	26N07	85E24	-5:41:36
Mysore	2	12N18	76E39	-5:06:36
Nabābpur	3	22N42	88E12	-5:52:48
Nabadwīp	3	23N25	88E22	-5:53:28
Nabagram	3	24N12	88E06	-5:52:24
Nabasta	3	23N15	88E01	-5:52:04
Nābha	2	30N22	76E09	-5:04:36
Nāchinda	3	21N53	87E46	-5:51:04
Nāchna	2	27N30	71E43	-4:46:52
Nachuge	4	10N45	92E22	-6:09:28
Nadābhānga	3	22N24	88E14	-5:52:56
Nadaul	5	25N15	85E00	-5:40:00
Nadbai	2	27N14	77E12	-5:08:48
Nadia	3	23N24	88E56	-5:55:44
Nadiād	2	22N42	72E52	-4:51:28
Naenwa	2	25N46	75E51	-5:03:24
Nagachoti	4	26N00	94E20	-6:17:20
Nāgappattinam	2	10N46	79E50	-5:19:20
Nagar	2	27N26	77E06	-5:08:24
Nagar	2	32N07	77E10	-5:08:40
Nagari	2	13N20	79E33	-5:18:12
Nagari Hills	2	13N40	79E50	-5:19:20
Nagarkata	3	26N52	88E55	-5:55:40
Nagar Kurnool	2	16N30	78E19	-5:13:16
Nagar Untāri	2	24N17	83E30	-5:34:00
Nāgaur	2	27N12	73E44	-4:54:56
Nāgda	2	23N27	75E25	-5:01:40
Nāgercoil	2	8N10	77E26	-5:09:44
Nagīna	2	29N27	78E27	-5:13:48
Nagla	2	28N31	77E22	-5:09:28
Nāgod	2	24N34	80E36	-5:22:24
Nāgpur	2	21N09	79E06	-5:16:24
Nāgrākata	3	26N54	88E55	-5:55:40
Nagrota	2	32N03	76E05	-5:04:20
Nāhan	2	30N33	77E18	-5:09:12
Naihāti	3	22N54	88E25	-5:53:40
Naini Tāl	2	29N23	79E27	-5:17:48
Nainpur	2	22N26	80E07	-5:20:28
Najībābād	2	29N38	78E20	-5:13:20
Nākāsipāra	3	23N35	88E21	-5:53:24
Nakhola	4	26N07	92E11	-6:08:44
Nakhtarana	2	23N20	69E15	-4:37:00
Nakodar	2	31N07	75E29	-5:01:56
Nakūr	2	29N55	77E18	-5:09:12
Nālāgarh	2	31N03	76E43	-5:06:52
Nālanda	5	25N07	85E25	-5:41:40
Nalbāri	4	26N25	91E26	-6:05:44
Nāldera	2	31N11	77E11	-5:08:44
Nalgonda	2	17N03	79E16	-5:17:04
Nalhāti	3	24N18	87E49	-5:51:16
Nālikul	3	22N49	88E11	-5:52:44
Nāmakkal	2	11N14	78E10	-5:12:40
Nāmkhāna	3	21N46	88E14	-5:52:56
Nāndāha	3	22N50	88E17	-5:53:08
Nānded	2	19N09	77E20	-5:09:20
Nāndgaon	2	18N58	73E08	-4:52:32
Nāndgaon	2	20N19	74E39	-4:58:36
Nandigrām	3	22N01	87E58	-5:51:52
Nandikotkūr	2	15N52	78E16	-5:13:04
Nāndūra	2	20N50	76E27	-5:05:48
Nandurbār	2	21N22	74E15	-4:57:00
Nandyāl	2	15N29	78E29	-5:13:56
Nangi	3	22N31	88E13	-5:52:52
Nanjangūd	2	12N06	76E42	-5:06:48
Nanoshi	2	18N56	73E05	-4:52:20
Nānpāra	2	27N52	81E30	-5:26:00
Nānūr	3	23N42	87E52	-5:51:28
Naoābād	3	22N28	88E27	-5:53:48
Naopukuria	3	22N55	88E16	-5:53:04
Naraini	2	25N11	80E29	-5:21:56
Narainpur	5	24N03	86E36	-5:46:24
Narasannapeta	2	18N25	84E03	-5:36:12
Narasapur	2	16N27	81E40	-5:26:40
Narasaraopet	2	16N15	80E04	-5:20:16
Nārāyanpāra	3	22N54	88E19	-5:53:16
Nārāyanpet	2	16N44	77E30	-5:10:00
Nārāyanpur	3	22N29	88E34	-5:54:16
Narendranagar	2	30N10	78E18	-5:13:12
Nargund	2	15N43	75E23	-5:01:32
Narhan	2	19N08	73E07	-4:52:28
Nārkanda	2	31N16	77E27	-5:09:48
Narkatiāganj	5	27N06	84E28	-5:37:52
Nārnaul	2	28N03	76E06	-5:04:24
Narsapur	2	16N26	81E45	-5:27:00
Narsimhapur	2	22N57	79E12	-5:16:48
Narsinghgarh	2	23N42	77E06	-5:08:24
Narsīpatnam	2	17N40	82E37	-5:30:28
Narwāna	2	29N37	76E07	-5:04:28
Nāsik	2	19N59	73E48	-4:55:12
Nasīrābād	2	26N18	74E44	-4:58:56
Nāsriganj	5	25N03	84E20	-5:37:20
Nastauli	2	28N43	77E22	-5:09:28
Nātāgarh	3	22N42	88E25	-5:53:40
Nāthdwāra	2	24N56	73E49	-4:55:16
Nattam	2	10N14	78E14	-5:12:56
Naude	2	19N03	73E06	-4:52:24
Naugachhia	2	25N24	87E06	-5:48:24
Naushahra	2	33N09	74E14	-4:56:56
Nautanwa	2	27N26	83E25	-5:33:40
Navibandar	2	21N26	69E48	-4:39:12
Navsāri	2	20N51	72E55	-4:51:40
Nawābganj	2	26N56	81E13	-5:24:52
Nawābganj	2	28N33	79E38	-5:18:32
Nawābganj	2	26N52	82E08	-5:28:32
Nawāda	5	24N53	85E32	-5:42:08
Nawalgarh	2	27N51	75E16	-5:01:04
Nawapārā	3	23N29	88E15	-5:53:00
Nawāpāra	2	20N58	81E51	-5:27:24
Nawāshahr	2	31N07	76E08	-5:04:32
Nayābās	2	28N35	77E19	-5:09:16
Nayāgarh	3	20N08	85E06	-5:40:24
Nayāgrām	2	22N02	87E11	-5:48:44
Nayāpāra	2	21N35	87E01	-5:48:04
Nāzira	4	26N55	94E44	-6:18:56
Negapatam → Nāgappattinam	2	10N46	79E50	-5:19:20
Nellikuppam	2	11N46	79E41	-5:18:44
Nellore	2	14N26	79E58	-5:19:52
Nemam	2	8N27	77E01	-5:08:04
Nepa Nagar	2	21N28	76E23	-5:05:32
Nerul	2	19N02	73E01	-4:52:04
Netarhāt	5	23N29	84E16	-5:37:04
Neu-Delhi → New Delhi	2	28N36	77E12	-5:08:48
Nevali	2	19N01	73E07	-4:52:28
Newabāgam	3	22N48	88E24	-5:53:36
New Delhi	2	28N36	77E12	-5:08:48
Neyyāttinkara	2	8N24	77E05	-5:08:20
Nibria	3	22N36	88E16	-5:53:04
Nidadavole	2	16N55	81E40	-5:26:40
Nigan	3	23N30	87E59	-5:51:56
Nighāsan	2	28N14	80E52	-5:23:28
Nihtaur	2	29N20	78E23	-5:13:32
Nileshwar	2	12N15	75E06	-5:00:24
Nilgani	3	22N46	88E26	-5:53:44
Nīlgiri	2	21N28	86E46	-5:47:04
Nīmach	2	24N28	74E52	-4:59:28
Nīmbahera	2	24N37	74E41	-4:58:44
Nīm Ka Thāna	2	27N44	75E48	-5:03:12
Nimta	3	22N40	88E25	-5:53:40
Nipāni	2	16N24	74E23	-4:57:32
Nirmal	2	19N06	78E21	-5:13:24
Nirmali	5	26N19	86E35	-5:46:20
Nirsa	5	23N47	86E43	-5:46:52
Nischintāpur	3	22N26	88E22	-5:53:28
Nitalas	2	19N06	73E08	-4:52:32
Nithāri	2	28N35	77E21	-5:09:24
Nizāmābād	2	15N54	80E43	-5:22:52
Nizāmābād	2	18N40	78E07	-5:12:28
Nizamghāt	4	28N16	95E42	-6:22:48
Noābād	3	22N34	88E31	-5:54:04
Noamundi	5	22N09	85E32	-5:42:08
Nohar	2	29N11	74E46	-4:59:04
Nohjhīl	2	27N51	77E39	-5:10:36
Nohta	2	23N40	79E34	-5:18:16
Nokha	2	27N35	73E29	-4:53:56
Nongpoh	4	25N54	91E53	-6:07:32
Nongstoin	4	25N31	91E16	-6:05:04
North Barrackpore	3	22N46	88E22	-5:53:28
North Dum-Dum	3	22N38	88E23	-5:53:32
North Lakhimpur	4	27N14	94E07	-6:16:28
North Vijayapuri	2	16N52	79E35	-5:18:20
Nova Goa → Panaji	1	15N29	73E50	-4:55:20
Nowgong	2	25N04	79E27	-5:17:48
Nowgong	4	26N21	92E40	-6:10:40
Nowrangapur	2	19N14	82E33	-5:30:12
Nūh	2	28N07	77E01	-5:08:04
Nūrmahal	2	31N06	75E36	-5:02:24
Nurpur	3	22N13	88E05	-5:52:20
Nūrpur	2	31N10	76E29	-5:05:56
Nūrpur	2	32N18	75E54	-5:03:36
Nūzvīd	2	16N47	80E51	-5:23:24
Nyoma	2	33N11	78E38	-5:14:32
Nyuri	4	27N42	92E13	-6:08:52
Onchāi	3	22N57	88E19	-5:53:16
Onda	3	23N08	87E12	-5:48:48
Ongole	2	15N31	80E04	-5:20:16
Ootacamund	2	11N24	76E42	-5:06:48
Orai	2	25N59	79E28	-5:17:52
Orchha	2	25N21	78E39	-5:14:36
Osiān	2	26N43	72E55	-4:51:40
Osmānābād	2	18N33	79E15	-5:17:00
Osmānābād	2	18N10	76E02	-5:04:08
Owe	2	19N04	73E04	-4:52:16
Pachamba	5	24N12	86E16	-5:45:04
Pachmarhi	2	22N28	78E26	-5:13:44
Pachor	2	23N42	76E44	-5:06:56
Pāchora	2	20N40	75E21	-5:01:24
Padam	2	33N28	76E53	-5:07:32
Padampur	2	20N59	83E04	-5:32:16
Padeghar	2	18N58	73E03	-4:52:12
Padghe	2	19N03	73E07	-4:52:28
Padle	2	19N09	73E03	-4:52:12
Padmanābhapuram	2	8N14	77E20	-5:09:20
Pādra	2	22N14	73E05	-4:52:20
Padrauna	2	26N55	83E59	-5:35:56
Pagote	2	18N54	72E59	-4:51:56
Pahāsu	2	28N11	78E03	-5:12:12
Pahlād Garhi	2	28N40	77E21	-5:09:24
Pahlgām	2	34N02	75E20	-5:01:20
Paikar	3	24N24	87E55	-5:51:40
Pail	2	30N43	76E03	-5:04:12
Pākāla	2	13N28	79E07	-5:16:28
Pakaur	5	24N38	87E51	-5:51:24
Palai	2	9N44	76E41	-5:06:44
Pālakollu	2	16N32	81E44	-5:26:56
Palamau	5	23N52	84E17	-5:37:08
Pālampur	2	32N07	76E32	-5:06:08
Pālanpur	2	24N10	72E26	-4:49:44
Palāshdānga	3	23N24	87E22	-5:49:28
Palāstha	3	23N51	87E03	-5:48:12
Pālayankottai	2	8N43	77E44	-5:10:56
Palel	4	24N27	94E02	-6:16:08
Pālghāt	2	10N47	76E39	-5:06:36
Pāli	2	25N46	73E20	-4:53:20
Pali	2	25N51	76E33	-5:06:12
Paliganj	5	25N22	84E45	-5:39:00
Pālitāna	2	21N31	71E50	-4:47:20
Pālkonda	2	18N36	83E45	-5:35:00
Palkot	5	22N52	84E41	-5:38:44
Pallu	2	28N56	74E13	-4:56:52
Palma	3	23N18	86E25	-5:45:40
Palmaner	2	13N14	78E48	-5:15:12
Palni	2	10N28	77E32	-5:10:08
Pālsit	3	23N12	88E03	-5:52:12
Palwal	2	28N09	77E20	-5:09:20
Pāmpur	2	34N01	74E56	-4:59:44
Panāgar	2	23N18	79E59	-5:19:56
Panaji (Panjim)	1	15N29	73E50	-4:55:20
Pānākua	3	22N23	88E21	-5:53:24
Panakudi	2	8N19	77E36	-5:10:24
Pānchāl	3	23N15	87E18	-5:49:12
Panchgachia	5	25N55	86E24	-5:45:36
Pānchghara	3	22N44	88E16	-5:53:04
Panchgram	3	24N12	88E01	-5:52:04
Panchla	3	22N32	88E09	-5:52:36
Pānchur	3	22N32	88E16	-5:53:04
Pānchuria	3	22N33	88E29	-5:53:56
Pandalāyini	2	11N28	75E43	-5:02:52
Pandaria	2	22N14	81E25	-5:25:40
Pandaveswar	3	23N43	87E17	-5:49:08
Pāndharkawada	2	20N01	78E32	-5:14:08
Pandharpur	2	17N40	75E20	-5:01:20
Pāndhurna	2	21N36	78E31	-5:14:04
Pandua	3	25N08	88E10	-5:52:40
Pandua	3	23N05	88E17	-5:53:08
Pandud	3	23N04	88E17	-5:53:08
Pānihāti	3	22N42	88E22	-5:53:28
Panīpat	2	29N23	76E58	-5:07:52
Panje	2	18N54	72E57	-4:51:48
Panjim → Panaji	1	15N29	73E50	-4:55:20
Panna	2	24N43	80E12	-5:20:48
Panruti	2	11N46	79E33	-5:18:12
Pānskura	3	22N25	87E42	-5:50:48
Pānuria	5	23N49	86E58	-5:47:52
Panvel	2	18N59	73E06	-4:52:24
Panwāri	2	25N27	79E29	-5:17:56
Paonta	2	30N27	77E37	-5:10:28
Paramagudi	2	9N33	78E36	-5:14:24
Parāsia	2	22N12	78E46	-5:15:04
Parasida	3	23N46	87E20	-5:49:20
Parasnāth	5	23N59	86E02	-5:44:08
Parbhani	2	19N16	76E47	-5:07:08
Pārdi	2	20N31	72E57	-4:51:48
Pārgaon	2	18N59	73E05	-4:52:20
Parkasam	2	15N30	80E06	-5:20:24
Parlākimidi	2	18N46	84E05	-5:36:20
Pārola	2	20N53	75E07	-5:00:28
Parorā	3	22N48	88E09	-5:52:36
Parsad	2	24N11	73E42	-4:54:48
Partābpur	2	23N29	83E13	-5:32:52
Partāppur	2	21N48	86E44	-5:46:56
Parthala	2	28N36	77E24	-5:09:36
Parūr	2	10N09	76E14	-5:04:56
Pārvatīpuram	2	18N47	83E26	-5:33:44
Pasān	2	22N51	82E12	-5:28:48
Pasaunda	2	28N42	77E21	-5:09:24
Pāsighāt	4	28N04	95E20	-6:21:20
Pātāchārkuchi	4	26N31	91E16	-6:05:04
Pātan	2	23N50	72E07	-4:48:28
Pātan	2	23N18	79E42	-5:18:48
Pataudi	2	28N19	76E47	-5:07:08
Pathalgaon	2	22N34	83E28	-5:33:52
Pathānkot	2	32N17	75E39	-5:02:36
Pātharghāra	3	22N34	88E35	-5:54:20
Patharia	2	23N54	79E12	-5:16:48
Patiāla	2	30N19	76E24	-5:05:36
Pātihāl	3	22N39	88E08	-5:52:32
Patipāda	2	19N04	73E05	-4:52:20
Pātiram	3	25N19	88E45	-5:55:00
Patna	3	21N56	87E52	-5:51:28
Pātna	3	22N59	88E18	-5:53:12
Patna	5	25N36	85E07	-5:40:28
Patnāgarh	2	20N43	83E09	-5:32:36
Pātnoli	2	18N57	73E05	-4:52:20
Pātrasāer	3	23N13	87E31	-5:50:04
Pattancheru	2	17N36	78E20	-5:13:20
Patti	2	25N55	82E12	-5:28:48
Patti	2	31N17	74E51	-4:59:24
Pattikonda	2	15N21	77E33	-5:10:12
Pattukkottai	2	10N26	79E19	-5:17:16
Pātul	3	22N45	88E10	-5:52:40
Pātuli	3	23N33	88E15	-5:53:00
Pātūr	2	20N27	76E56	-5:07:44
Patwāri	2	28N35	77E27	-5:09:48
Pāunān	3	22N57	88E17	-5:53:08
Pauni	2	20N47	79E38	-5:18:32
Pauri	2	25N32	77E21	-5:09:24
Pauri	2	30N09	78E47	-5:15:08
Pavne	2	19N05	73E01	-4:52:04
Pawāyan	2	28N04	80E06	-5:20:24
Payāgpur	2	27N25	81E48	-5:27:12
Paylampur	3	22N47	88E16	-5:53:04
Pazanji	2	10N41	76E04	-5:04:16
Pedana	2	16N16	81E10	-5:24:40
Pedapalli	2	18N40	79E25	-5:17:40
Peddāpuram	2	17N05	82E08	-5:28:32
Pedong	3	27N15	88E35	-5:54:20
Pehowa	2	29N59	76E35	-5:06:20
Pendhar	2	19N04	73E06	-4:52:24
Penugonda	2	16N40	81E44	-5:26:56
Penukonda	2	14N05	77E35	-5:10:20
Perambalūr	2	11N14	78E53	-5:15:32

Place		Lat.	Long.	Time
Peranāmbattu	2	12N56	78E43	-5:14:52
Periyakulam	2	10N07	77E33	-5:10:12
Petlād	2	22N28	72E48	-4:51:12
Petua	3	22N25	88E27	-5:53:48
Phagwāra	2	31N14	75E46	-5:03:04
Phalodi	2	27N08	72E22	-4:49:28
Phaltan	2	17N59	74E26	-4:57:44
Phalti	3	22N46	88E34	-5:54:16
Pharenda	2	27N06	83E17	-5:33:08
Phillaur	2	31N01	75E47	-5:03:08
Phinga	3	22N41	88E25	-5:53:40
Phulbari	3	21N52	88E08	-5:52:32
Phulkusma	5	22N43	86E52	-5:47:28
Phūlpur	2	25N33	82E06	-5:28:24
Phurphura	3	22N44	88E08	-5:52:32
Pichhor	2	25N58	78E24	-5:13:36
Pichor	2	25N11	78E11	-5:12:44
Pihāni	2	27N38	80E12	-5:20:48
Pilamedu	2	11N01	77E01	-5:08:04
Pīlībhīt	2	28N38	79E48	-5:19:12
Pilkhua	2	28N43	77E39	-5:10:36
Pindwāra	2	24N48	73E04	-4:52:16
Pipalkoti	2	30N26	79E27	-5:17:48
Pīpār	2	26N23	73E32	-4:54:08
Piparia	2	22N45	78E21	-5:13:24
Pīpar Road	2	26N27	73E27	-4:53:48
Piplūn	3	23N21	88E07	-5:52:28
Pipri	2	23N58	82E40	-5:30:40
Pirakata	3	22N34	87E11	-5:48:44
Pisarve	2	19N06	73E05	-4:52:20
Pithāpuram	2	17N07	82E16	-5:29:04
Pithoragarh	2	29N35	80E13	-5:20:52
Plassey	3	23N47	88E15	-5:53:00
Podile	2	15N36	79E39	-5:18:36
Pokaran	2	26N55	71E55	-4:47:40
Pokharia	5	23N55	86E37	-5:46:28
Polavaram	2	17N33	81E37	-5:26:28
Polba	3	22N57	88E18	-5:53:12
Pollāchi	2	10N40	77E01	-5:08:04
Polūr	2	12N30	79E08	-5:16:32
Pondicherry	2	11N56	79E53	-5:19:32
Ponnāni	2	10N46	75E54	-5:03:36
Ponnūru Nidubrolu	2	16N04	80E34	-5:22:16
Ponpāj	3	22N56	88E15	-5:53:00
Poona → Pune	2	18N32	73E52	-4:55:28
Porādiha	2	21N33	86E26	-5:45:44
Porbandar	2	21N38	69E36	-4:38:24
Port Blair	4	11N40	92E45	-6:11:00
Port Canning	3	22N18	88E40	-5:54:40
Port Cornwallis	4	13N18	93E05	-6:12:20
Porto Novo	2	11N29	79E46	-5:19:04
Pratāpgarh	2	24N02	74E47	-4:59:08
Proddatūr	2	14N44	78E33	-5:14:12
Pudukkottai	2	10N23	78E49	-5:15:16
Puinān	3	22N56	88E13	-5:52:52
Pukhrāyān	2	26N14	79E51	-5:19:24
Pulbari	3	26N19	89E26	-5:57:44
Pulga	2	31N59	77E26	-5:09:44
Pulgaon	2	20N44	78E20	-5:13:20
Pulicat	2	13N25	80E19	-5:21:16
Pulivendla	2	14N25	78E16	-5:13:04
Puliyangudi	2	9N10	77E25	-5:09:40
Pūnch	2	33N46	74E06	-4:56:24
Puncha	5	23N10	86E39	-5:46:36
Pūndri	2	29N45	76E33	-5:06:12
Pune (Poona)	2	18N32	73E52	-4:55:28
Punganūru	2	13N22	78E35	-5:14:20
Purandarpur	3	23N51	87E36	-5:50:24
Pūranpur	2	28N31	80E09	-5:20:36
Purbashthāli	3	23N28	88E21	-5:53:24
Puri	2	19N48	85E51	-5:43:24
Purli	2	18N51	76E32	-5:06:08
Purnea	2	25N47	87E31	-5:50:04
Purūlia	3	23N20	86E22	-5:45:28
Pusa	5	25N59	85E41	-5:42:44
Pusad	2	19N54	77E35	-5:10:20
Pushkar	2	26N30	74E33	-4:58:12
Puttaparthy	2	14N15	77E45	-5:11:00
Puttūr	2	13N27	79E33	-5:18:12
Pyapali	2	15N14	77E47	-5:11:08
Qādiān	2	31N49	75E23	-5:01:32
Qāzigund	2	33N38	75E09	-5:00:36
Qizil Jilga	2	35N21	78E52	-5:15:28
Qizil Langar	2	35N13	77E59	-5:11:56
Quilon	2	8N53	76E36	-5:06:24
Rabkavi Banhatti	2	16N28	75E06	-5:00:24
Radaur	2	30N02	77E09	-5:08:36
Rādhānagar	3	23N09	87E19	-5:49:16
Rādhānagar	3	22N27	88E28	-5:53:52
Rādhanpur	2	23N50	71E36	-4:46:24
Rāe Bareli	2	26N13	81E14	-5:24:56
Raghabpur	3	22N25	88E21	-5:53:24
Rāghogarh	2	24N27	77E12	-5:08:48
Raghumāthbāri	3	22N22	87E47	-5:51:08
Raghunāthpur	3	23N33	86E40	-5:46:40
Rahatgaon	2	22N15	77E14	-5:08:56
Rāhatgarh	2	23N47	78E22	-5:13:28
Rahimatpur	2	17N36	74E12	-4:56:48
Rāhon	2	31N03	76E07	-5:04:28
Rāichūr	2	16N12	77E22	-5:09:28
Rāidighi	3	22N00	88E26	-5:53:44
Raiganj	3	25N37	88E07	-5:52:28
Raigarh	2	21N54	83E24	-5:33:36
Raigarh	3	25N37	88E07	-5:52:28
Rāikot	2	30N39	75E36	-5:02:24
Raipur	2	30N19	78E06	-5:12:24
Raipur	5	22N48	86E57	-5:47:48
Raipur	2	28N32	77E20	-5:09:20
Raipur	3	22N24	88E09	-5:52:36
Raipur	2	21N14	81E38	-5:26:32
Rairākhol	2	21N04	84E21	-5:37:24
Raisen	2	23N20	77E48	-5:11:12
Raisinghnagar	2	29N32	73E27	-4:53:48
Rājābhāt Khāwa	3	26N37	89E32	-5:58:08
Rājābhita	5	23N52	86E20	-5:45:20
Rājahmundry	2	16N59	81E47	-5:27:08
Rājākhera	2	26N55	78E11	-5:12:44
Rājaldesar	2	28N02	74E28	-4:57:52
Rājāluka	5	22N09	86E38	-5:46:32
Rājampet	2	14N11	79E10	-5:16:40
Rājapālaiyam	2	9N27	77E34	-5:10:16
Rājāpur	2	25N23	81E09	-5:24:36
Rājāpur	3	22N39	88E11	-5:52:44
Rājāpur	2	16N40	73E31	-4:54:04
Rājauri	2	33N23	74E18	-4:57:12
Rājbāri	3	22N25	88E48	-5:55:12
Rāj Gāngpur	2	22N11	84E36	-5:38:24
Rājgarh	2	23N56	76E58	-5:07:52
Rājgarh	2	28N38	75E23	-5:01:32
Rājgarh	2	27N14	76E38	-5:06:32
Rājgīr	5	25N02	85E25	-5:41:40
Rājhāt	3	22N56	88E21	-5:53:24
Rājibpur	3	22N49	88E34	-5:54:16
Rājkot	2	22N18	70E47	-4:43:08
Rājmahāl	5	25N03	87E50	-5:51:20
Rājnagar	3	23N57	87E19	-5:49:16
Rāj-Nāndgaon	2	21N06	81E02	-5:24:08
Rājpīpla	2	21N47	73E34	-4:54:16
Rājpur	3	22N25	88E25	-5:53:40
Rājpur	2	28N44	77E22	-5:09:28
Rājpur	2	21N56	75E08	-5:00:32
Rājpura	2	30N29	76E36	-5:06:24
Rajula	2	21N03	71E26	-4:45:44
Ramachandrapuram	2	16N51	82E01	-5:28:04
Ramalkotta	2	15N35	78E02	-5:12:08
Raman	2	29N58	74E58	-4:59:52
Rāmanagaram	2	12N43	77E18	-5:09:12
Rāmanāthapuram	2	9N23	78E50	-5:15:20
Ramānāthpur	3	22N41	88E14	-5:52:56
Ramanbāti	3	22N47	88E08	-5:52:32
Rāmānuj Ganj	5	23N48	83E42	-5:34:48
Rāmban	2	33N15	75E15	-5:01:00
Rām Dās	2	31N58	74E54	-4:59:36
Rāmdurg	2	15N57	75E18	-5:01:12
Rāmeswaram	2	9N17	79E18	-5:17:12
Rāmgarh	2	27N15	75E11	-5:00:44
Rāmgarh	5	23N38	85E31	-5:42:04
Rāmgarh	2	24N34	87E15	-5:49:00
Rāmgarh	3	22N42	87E04	-5:48:16
Rāmgarh	2	27N22	70E30	-4:42:00
Rāmjībanpur	3	22N50	87E37	-5:50:28
Rāmkānāli	5	23N35	86E45	-5:47:00
Rāmnagar	2	29N24	79E07	-5:16:28
Rāmnagar	2	32N49	75E19	-5:01:16
Rāmnagar	3	21N41	87E33	-5:50:12
Rāmnagar	3	22N23	88E19	-5:53:16
Rāmnagar	2	25N17	83E02	-5:32:08
Rāmoswaram	2	9N17	79E18	-5:17:12
Rāmpur	2	28N49	79E02	-5:16:08
Rāmpur	2	29N49	77E27	-5:09:48
Rāmpur	2	31N27	77E38	-5:10:32
Rāmpura	2	24N28	75E26	-5:01:44
Rāmpura Phūl	2	30N17	75E14	-5:00:56
Rāmpur Hāt	3	24N10	87E47	-5:51:08
Rāmsāgar	3	23N05	87E17	-5:49:08
Rāmshai	3	26N44	88E51	-5:55:24
Rāmtek	2	21N24	79E20	-5:17:20
Ranagar	3	23N05	87E55	-5:51:40
Rānāghāt	3	23N11	88E35	-5:54:20
Ranbīrsinghpura	2	32N38	74E44	-4:58:56
Rānchī	5	23N21	85E20	-5:41:20
Rānder	2	21N14	72E47	-4:51:08
Rāner	2	28N53	73E17	-4:53:08
Rāneswar	2	24N02	87E25	-5:49:40
Rangia	4	26N28	91E38	-6:06:32
Rangpo	3	27N11	88E32	-5:54:08
Rānibāndh	5	22N52	86E47	-5:47:08
Rānībennur	2	14N37	75E37	-5:02:28
Rānīganj	3	23N37	87E08	-5:48:32
Rānīkhet	2	29N39	79E25	-5:17:40
Raninagar	3	26N33	88E36	-5:54:24
Rānipet	2	12N56	79E20	-5:17:20
Rāniwāra	2	24N45	72E13	-4:48:52
Rānsai	2	18N53	73E05	-4:52:20
Rānvād	2	18N53	72E55	-4:51:40
Rāpar	2	23N34	70E38	-4:42:32
Rāribahāl	2	24N05	87E21	-5:49:24
Rāsipuram	2	11N28	78E10	-5:12:40
Raskunda	3	22N48	87E26	-5:49:44
Rasra	2	25N51	83E51	-5:35:24
Rasulpur	2	28N37	77E22	-5:09:28
Ratangarh	2	28N05	74E36	-4:58:24
Ratanpur	3	22N50	88E14	-5:52:56
Ratanpur	3	23N07	87E04	-5:48:16
Rāth	2	25N35	79E34	-5:18:16
Ratlām	2	23N19	75E04	-5:00:16
Ratnāgiri	2	16N59	73E18	-4:53:12
Raurkela	2	22N13	84E53	-5:39:32
Rāutara	3	22N51	88E28	-5:53:52
Ravalgaon	2	20N38	74E25	-4:57:40
Rāver	2	21N15	76E02	-5:04:08
Raxaul	5	26N59	84E51	-5:39:24
Rāyachoti	2	14N03	78E45	-5:15:00
Rāyadrug	2	14N42	76E52	-5:07:28
Rāyagada	2	19N10	83E25	-5:33:40
Rāyana	3	23N05	87E54	-5:51:36
Rāyna	3	23N05	87E54	-5:51:36
Rāypur	3	22N25	88E31	-5:54:04
Rehli	2	23N38	79E05	-5:16:20
Rehti	2	22N44	77E26	-5:09:44
Rejinagar	3	23N53	88E15	-5:53:00
Rekjoāti	3	22N37	88E28	-5:53:52
Remuna	2	21N33	86E54	-5:47:36
Reni	2	28N41	75E02	-5:00:08
Repalle	2	16N02	80E53	-5:23:32
Repur	2	14N12	79E36	-5:18:24
Revelganj	5	25N47	84E40	-5:38:40
Rewa	2	24N32	81E18	-5:25:12
Rewāri	2	28N11	76E37	-5:06:28
Riāng	4	27N32	92E56	-6:11:44
Riāsi	2	33N05	74E50	-4:59:20
Rīngus	2	27N21	75E34	-5:02:16
Rishīkesh	2	30N07	78E42	-5:14:48
Rishra	3	22N43	88E21	-5:53:24
Riu	4	28N19	95E03	-6:20:12
Robertsganj	2	24N42	83E04	-5:32:16
Rohinjan	2	19N06	73E04	-4:52:16
Rohtak	2	28N54	76E34	-5:06:16
Rohtasgarh	5	24N36	83E52	-5:35:28
Roorkee	2	29N52	77E53	-5:11:32
Rourkela → Raurkela	5	22N13	84E53	-5:39:32
Rudauli	2	26N45	81E45	-5:27:00
Rukni	5	23N33	86E33	-5:46:12
Rūpar	2	30N59	76E31	-5:06:04
Rusera	5	25N45	86E02	-5:44:08
Russa	3	22N29	88E21	-5:53:24
Russellkonda	2	19N56	84E35	-5:38:20
Sabalgarh	2	26N15	77E24	-5:09:36
Sābang	3	22N11	87E36	-5:50:24
Sabathu	2	30N59	76E59	-5:07:56
Sabe	2	19N11	73E02	-4:52:08
Sadābād	2	27N27	78E03	-5:12:12
Sādarpur	2	28N33	77E21	-5:09:24
Sadaseopet	2	17N44	77E58	-5:11:52
Sādhaura	2	30N23	77E13	-5:08:52
Sadiya	4	27N50	95E40	-6:22:40
Sādri	2	25N11	73E26	-4:53:44
Sadulgarh	2	29N35	74E19	-4:57:16
Sadulpur	2	28N38	75E24	-5:01:36
Safidon	2	29N25	76E40	-5:06:40
Sagaon	2	19N12	73E06	-4:52:24
Sāgar	2	14N10	75E02	-5:00:08
Sāgar	2	23N50	78E43	-5:14:52
Sāgardīghi	3	24N17	88E06	-5:52:24
Sagauli	5	26N47	84E48	-5:39:12
Saguna	3	22N59	88E29	-5:53:56
Sāgwāra	2	23N41	74E01	-4:56:04
Sahāranpur	2	29N58	77E33	-5:10:12
Saharsa	5	25N53	86E36	-5:46:24
Sahaswān	2	28N05	78E45	-5:15:00
Sāhibabad	2	28N40	77E22	-5:09:28
Sāhibganj	5	25N15	87E39	-5:50:36
Saidpur	2	25N33	83E11	-5:32:44
Sainthia	3	23N57	87E40	-5:50:40
Sakleshpur	2	12N58	75E47	-5:03:08
Sākoli	2	21N05	79E59	-5:19:56
Sakri	2	20N59	74E19	-4:57:16
Sakti	2	22N02	82E58	-5:31:52
Saktipur	3	23N52	88E11	-5:52:44
Salāya	2	22N19	69E35	-4:38:20
Sālbani	3	22N38	87E20	-5:49:20
Salem	2	11N39	78E10	-5:12:40
Salkhia	3	22N35	88E21	-5:53:24
Sāltora	5	23N32	86E56	-5:47:44
Salūmbar	2	24N08	74E03	-4:56:12
Sālūr	2	18N32	83E13	-5:32:52
Sam	2	26N50	70E31	-4:42:04
Sāmalkot	2	17N03	82E11	-5:28:44
Samāna	2	30N09	76E12	-5:04:48
Samāstipur	5	25N51	85E47	-5:43:08
Sāmba	2	32N34	75E07	-5:00:28
Sambalpur	2	21N27	83E58	-5:35:52
Sambhal	2	28N35	78E33	-5:14:12
Sāmbhar	2	26N55	75E12	-5:00:48
Samdari	2	25N49	72E35	-4:50:20
Samrāla	2	30N51	76E11	-5:04:44
Samthar	2	25N51	78E55	-5:15:40
Samūdragarh	3	23N21	88E20	-5:53:20
Sānand	2	22N59	72E23	-4:49:32
Sanaur	2	30N18	76E27	-5:05:48
Sanāwad	2	22N11	76E04	-5:04:16
Sānchi	2	23N29	77E44	-5:10:56
Sandeshkhali	3	22N22	88E53	-5:55:32
Sāndi	2	27N18	79E57	-5:19:48
Sandīla	2	27N05	80E31	-5:22:04
Sangamner	2	19N34	74E13	-4:56:52
Sangāreddipet	2	17N38	78E07	-5:12:28
Sangat	2	30N05	74E50	-4:59:20
Sāngli	2	16N52	74E34	-4:58:16
Sāngola	2	17N26	75E12	-5:00:48
Sangrūr	2	30N14	75E50	-5:03:20
Sāngurli	2	18N56	73E07	-4:52:28
Sankaranayinārkovil	2	9N10	77E33	-5:10:12
Sankarpur	3	22N51	88E27	-5:53:48
Sankeshwar	2	16N16	74E29	-4:57:56
Sankheda	2	22N10	73E35	-4:54:20
Sānkrāil	3	22N34	88E14	-5:52:56
Sanpāda	2	19N04	73E01	-4:52:04
Santaldih	3	23N38	86E33	-5:46:12
Sāntalpur	2	23N45	71E10	-4:44:40
Sāntipur	3	23N15	88E26	-5:53:44
Santoshpur	3	22N40	88E10	-5:52:40
Saoner	2	21N23	78E54	-5:15:36
Sapatgrām	4	26N20	90E08	-6:00:32
Saraikela	5	22N43	85E57	-5:43:48
Saraipali	2	21N20	83E00	-5:32:00
Sārangarh	2	21N36	83E05	-5:32:20
Sārangpur	2	23N34	76E28	-5:05:52
Sarath	5	24N14	86E50	-5:47:20
Sardārpur	2	22N39	74E59	-4:59:56
Sardārshahr	2	28N26	74E29	-4:57:56
Sardhana	2	29N09	77E37	-5:10:28
Sardiha	3	22N22	87E09	-5:48:36
Sārenga	3	22N31	88E13	-5:52:52
Sārenga	3	22N46	87E02	-5:48:08
Sarsol	2	19N02	73E01	-4:52:04
Sarsuna	3	22N28	88E18	-5:53:12
Sasarām	5	24N57	84E02	-5:36:08
Sāsni	2	27N43	78E05	-5:12:20
Saspul Gompa	2	34N15	77E09	-5:08:36

Place	Code	Latitude	Longitude	Time
Satāna	2	20N35	74E12	-4:56:48
Sātāra	2	17N41	73E59	-4:55:56
Sātbāria	3	22N25	88E33	-5:54:12
Sātgāchia	3	23N16	88E08	-5:52:32
Sātghara	3	22N44	88E21	-5:53:24
Satna	2	24N35	80E50	-5:23:20
Sattānkulam	2	8N27	77E56	-5:11:44
Sattenapalle	2	16N24	80E11	-5:20:44
Sātuli	3	22N33	88E34	-5:54:16
Satyamangalam	2	11N31	77E15	-5:09:00
Saugor → Sāgar	2	23N50	78E43	-5:14:52
Saundatti	2	15N47	75E07	-5:00:28
Sausar	2	21N39	78E47	-5:15:08
Sāvantvādi	2	15N54	73E49	-4:55:16
Savanūr	2	14N58	75E21	-5:01:24
Sawai Mādhopur	2	25N59	76E22	-5:05:28
Secunderabad	2	17N27	78E33	-5:14:12
Sehāni Kalān	2	28N41	77E25	-5:09:40
Sehāni Khurd	2	28N42	77E25	-5:09:40
Sehāra Bāzār	3	23N06	87E49	-5:51:16
Sehore	2	23N12	77E05	-5:08:20
Selghar	2	18N57	73E02	-4:52:08
Semaria	2	24N16	79E54	-5:19:36
Semli Kalān	2	24N10	76E39	-5:06:36
Sendamangalam	2	11N18	78E14	-5:12:56
Sendhwa	2	21N41	75E06	-5:00:24
Sendurjana	2	21N32	78E17	-5:13:08
Seohāra	2	29N13	78E35	-5:14:20
Seoni	2	22N05	79E32	-5:18:08
Seoni Mālwa	2	22N27	77E28	-5:09:52
Seorīnārāyan	2	21N44	82E35	-5:30:20
Serampore	3	22N45	88E21	-5:53:24
Seringapatam	2	12N25	76E42	-5:06:48
Sevagram	2	20N45	78E30	-5:14:00
Shāhābād	2	19N01	73E02	-4:52:08
Shāhābād	2	17N08	76E56	-5:07:44
Shāhābād	2	27N39	79E57	-5:19:48
Shāhābād	2	30N10	76E53	-5:07:32
Shāhāda	2	21N28	74E18	-4:57:12
Shāhdara	2	28N30	77E25	-5:09:40
Shahdol	2	23N20	81E21	-5:25:24
Shāhganj	2	26N03	82E41	-5:30:44
Shāhgarh	2	24N19	79E08	-5:16:32
Shāhgarh	2	27N07	69E54	-4:39:36
Shāhjahānpur	2	27N53	79E55	-5:19:40
Shāhpur	2	16N42	76E50	-5:07:20
Shāhpura	2	27N23	75E58	-5:03:52
Shāhpura	2	25N38	74E56	-4:59:44
Shāhpura	2	23N11	80E42	-5:22:48
Shaikhpura	5	25N09	85E51	-5:43:24
Shājāpur	2	23N26	76E16	-5:05:04
Shakarpura	2	28N46	77E21	-5:09:24
Shām Churasi	2	31N30	75E45	-5:03:00
Shāmli	2	29N27	77E19	-5:09:16
Shamsābād	2	17N13	78E42	-5:14:48
Shamsābād	2	27N01	78E08	-5:12:32
Shamsher	2	28N44	77E24	-5:09:36
Shamsi	3	25N16	88E01	-5:52:04
Shantipur	3	23N14	88E29	-5:53:56
Sharafābād	2	28N36	77E23	-5:09:32
Sheakhala	3	22N46	88E10	-5:52:40
Shegaon	2	20N47	76E41	-5:06:44
Shencottah	2	8N58	77E16	-5:09:04
Sheo	2	26N11	71E15	-4:45:00
Sheoganj	2	25N09	73E04	-4:52:16
Sheopur	2	25N40	76E42	-5:06:48
Shertallai	2	9N42	76E20	-5:05:20
Shet Bandar	2	18N58	72E56	-4:51:44
Sheva	2	18N56	72E57	-4:51:48
Sheva Nhava	2	18N58	72E58	-4:51:52
Shikārpur	2	28N17	78E01	-5:12:04
Shikārpur	2	14N16	75E21	-5:01:24
Shikohābād	2	27N06	78E36	-5:14:24
Shil	2	19N09	73E03	-4:52:12
Shillong	4	25N34	91E53	-6:07:32
Shimoga	2	13N55	75E34	-5:02:16
Shirākol	3	22N18	88E16	-5:53:04
Shiraone	2	19N03	73E01	-4:52:04
Shirpur	2	21N21	74E53	-4:59:32
Shivpuri	2	25N26	77E39	-5:10:36
Sholāpur	2	17N41	75E55	-5:03:40
Sholinghur	2	13N07	79E25	-5:17:40
Shoranūr	2	10N46	76E17	-5:05:08
Shorāpur	2	16N31	76E45	-5:07:00
Shujālpur	2	23N24	76E43	-5:06:52
Shupīyan	2	33N43	74E50	-4:59:20
Shyamdih	5	23N47	86E56	-5:47:44
Shyampur	3	22N17	88E01	-5:52:04
Shyok	2	34N11	78E08	-5:12:32
Sialkot	2	32N29	74E33	-4:58:12
Sialsūk	4	23N24	92E45	-6:11:00
Sibpur	3	22N24	88E33	-5:54:12
Sibpur	3	22N34	88E19	-5:53:16
Sibsāgar	4	26N59	94E38	-6:18:32
Siddhavattam	2	14N28	79E01	-5:16:04
Siddipet	2	18N06	78E51	-5:15:24
Sidhauli	2	27N17	80E50	-5:23:20
Sidhi	2	24N25	81E53	-5:27:32
Sidhpur	2	23N55	72E23	-4:49:32
Sidlaghatta	2	13N23	77E52	-5:11:28
Sidli	4	26N33	90E28	-6:01:52
Sihor	2	21N42	71E58	-4:47:52
Sihorā	2	23N29	80E07	-5:20:28
Sikandarābād	2	28N27	77E42	-5:10:48
Sikandarpur	2	28N42	77E21	-5:09:24
Sikandarpur	3	22N57	88E12	-5:52:48
Sikandra	5	24N57	86E02	-5:44:08
Sikandra Rao	2	27N42	78E24	-5:13:36
Sīkar	2	27N37	75E09	-5:00:36
Sikarpur	3	22N36	88E32	-5:54:08
Sikkim	3	27N35	88E35	-5:54:20
Sikrod	2	28N43	77E11	-5:08:44
Silchar	4	24N49	92E48	-6:11:12
Silda	3	22N37	86E49	-5:47:16
Silghāt	4	26N37	92E56	-6:11:44
Silīgurī	3	26N42	88E26	-5:53:44
Silkāripāra	5	24N14	87E28	-5:49:52
Silphuh	5	23N44	86E22	-5:45:28
Silvassa	2	20N17	73E00	-4:52:00
Simaltala	5	24N43	86E33	-5:46:12
Simaria	5	24N04	84E56	-5:39:44
Simdega	5	22N37	84E31	-5:38:04
Simla	2	31N06	77E10	-5:08:40
Simla	3	22N47	88E16	-5:53:04
Simla	3	22N54	88E22	-5:53:28
Simlāpāl	3	22N55	87E05	-5:48:20
Simlipālgarh	2	21N51	86E23	-5:45:32
Simurāli	3	23N03	88E30	-5:54:00
Sindari	2	25N35	71E55	-4:47:40
Sindhnūr	2	15N47	76E46	-5:07:04
Sindri	5	23N45	86E42	-5:46:48
Singānallūr	2	11N00	77E01	-5:08:04
Singe	3	22N57	88E26	-5:53:44
Singhi	3	23N37	87E48	-5:51:12
Singing	4	28N53	94E47	-6:19:08
Singing	4	28N59	94E50	-6:19:20
Singpāra	3	22N40	88E31	-5:54:04
Singrāmau	2	25N57	82E23	-5:29:32
Singur	3	22N49	88E14	-5:52:56
Sinnar	2	19N51	74E00	-4:56:00
Sīra	2	13N45	76E54	-5:07:36
Sirāmpur	5	24N08	86E20	-5:45:20
Sirhind	2	30N39	76E23	-5:05:32
Sirkābād	5	23N16	86E12	-5:44:48
Sirmaur	2	24N51	81E23	-5:25:32
Sir Muttra	2	26N31	77E22	-5:09:28
Sirohi	2	24N54	72E51	-4:51:24
Sironj	2	24N06	77E42	-5:10:48
Sirpur	2	19N32	79E21	-5:17:24
Sirsa	2	29N32	75E01	-5:00:04
Sirsa	5	22N14	86E38	-5:46:32
Sirsāganj	2	27N03	78E42	-5:14:48
Sirsi	2	14N37	74E51	-4:59:24
Sirsilla	2	18N23	78E50	-5:15:20
Sisaiya Thana	2	27N35	81E20	-5:25:20
Sitalkuchi	3	26N10	89E11	-5:56:44
Sītāmarhi	5	26N36	85E29	-5:41:56
Sītāpur	2	27N34	80E41	-5:22:44
Sitārāmpur	5	23N43	86E53	-5:47:32
Sitarampuram	2	15N11	79E10	-5:16:40
Sivaganga	2	9N52	78E29	-5:13:56
Sivakāsi	2	9N27	77E49	-5:11:16
Sivok	3	26N53	88E25	-5:53:40
Siwān	5	26N13	84E22	-5:37:28
Siwāni	2	28N55	75E37	-5:02:28
Siyāna	2	28N38	78E03	-5:12:12
Sodpur	3	22N39	88E23	-5:53:32
Sohāgpur	2	23N19	81E21	-5:25:24
Sohāgpur	2	22N42	78E12	-5:12:48
Soharkha	2	28N35	77E24	-5:09:36
Sohna	2	28N15	77E04	-5:08:16
Sojat	2	25N55	73E40	-4:54:40
Sojitra	2	22N33	72E43	-4:50:52
Solangāri	3	22N36	88E27	-5:53:48
Solon	2	30N55	77E07	-5:08:28
Sompeta	2	18N56	84E36	-5:38:24
Sonahula	5	25N05	87E09	-5:48:36
Sonāmarg	2	34N18	75E18	-5:01:12
Sonāmukhi	3	23N18	87E25	-5:49:40
Sonāmura	4	23N29	91E17	-6:05:08
Sonari	2	18N52	72E59	-4:51:56
Sonārpur	3	22N26	88E25	-5:53:40
Sonātikri	3	22N57	88E20	-5:53:20
Sonepur	5	25N42	85E13	-5:40:52
Sonepur	2	20N50	83E55	-5:35:40
Sonīpat	2	28N59	77E01	-5:08:04
Sonkach	2	22N59	76E21	-5:05:24
Sonnagar	5	24N50	84E15	-5:37:00
Sonwān	2	27N40	81E45	-5:27:00
Sopur	2	34N18	74E28	-4:57:52
Sorada	2	19N45	84E26	-5:37:44
Sorbhog	4	26N30	90E52	-6:03:28
Soro	2	21N17	86E40	-5:46:40
Soron	2	27N53	78E45	-5:15:00
South Dum-Dum	3	22N37	88E25	-5:53:40
South Salmara	4	25N55	90E01	-6:00:04
South Suburban → Behāla	3	22N31	88E19	-5:53:16
South Vijayapuri	2	16N49	79E33	-5:18:12
Soyet	2	24N12	76E10	-5:04:40
Sri Dūngargarh	2	28N05	74E00	-4:56:00
Sri Gangānagar	2	29N55	73E53	-4:55:32
Sri Hargobindpur	2	31N41	75E39	-5:02:36
Sri Hari Kota	2	13N45	80E15	-5:21:00
Srīkākulam	2	18N18	83E54	-5:35:36
Sri Karanpur	2	29N50	73E27	-4:53:48
Sri Mohangarh	2	27N17	71E14	-4:44:56
Srīnagar	2	30N13	78E47	-5:15:08
Srīnagar	2	34N05	74E49	-4:59:16
Srirāmpur	3	22N49	88E29	-5:53:56
Srīrangam	2	10N52	78E41	-5:14:44
Sri Sailam	2	16N02	78E56	-5:15:44
Srīvardhan	2	18N02	73E01	-4:52:04
Srīvilliputtūr	2	9N31	77E38	-5:10:32
Suār	2	29N02	79E03	-5:16:12
Suātala	2	23N09	79E02	-5:16:08
Subarnapur	3	22N58	88E34	-5:54:16
Subhepur	2	28N45	77E16	-5:09:04
Subipur	3	22N54	88E08	-5:52:32
Suchetgarh	3	32N34	74E40	-4:58:40
Sudarsan	3	22N59	88E17	-5:53:08
Sugandha	3	22N54	88E20	-5:53:20
Sugauli Bazar	5	26N46	84E44	-5:38:56
Sūjāngarh	2	27N42	74E28	-4:57:52
Sukchar	3	22N42	88E22	-5:53:28
Suklāra	5	23N11	86E21	-5:45:24
Sultānpur	2	26N16	82E04	-5:28:16
Sultānpur	2	31N13	75E11	-5:00:44
Sūlūru	2	13N42	80E01	-5:20:04
Sumdo	2	35N01	78E41	-5:14:44
Sumnal	2	35N45	78E40	-5:14:40
Sunām	2	30N08	75E48	-5:03:12
Sundargarh	2	22N07	84E02	-5:36:08
Sundarnagar	2	31N32	76E53	-5:07:32
Supaul	5	26N07	86E36	-5:46:24
Sūpkhār	2	22N12	80E56	-5:23:44
Supur	5	23N01	86E52	-5:47:28
Surat	2	21N10	72E50	-4:51:20
Sūratgarh	2	29N19	73E54	-4:55:36
Surendranagar	2	22N42	71E41	-4:46:44
Sūri (Bīrbhūm)	3	23N55	87E32	-5:50:08
Suria	3	22N51	88E33	-5:54:12
Suriāpet	2	17N09	79E37	-5:18:28
Suryapet	2	17N10	79E39	-5:18:36
Sutāhāta	3	22N08	88E07	-5:52:28
Sutak	2	33N12	77E28	-5:09:52
Suthiāna	2	28N31	77E26	-5:09:44
Swarupnagar	3	22N49	88E52	-5:55:28
Syāmpur	3	22N18	88E02	-5:52:08
Syampur	3	22N29	88E13	-5:52:52
Tādepallegūdem	2	16N50	81E30	-5:26:00
Tādpatri	2	14N55	78E01	-5:12:04
Tājpur	3	22N44	88E16	-5:53:04
Tajpur	5	25N51	85E41	-5:42:44
Tajpur	2	29N10	78E29	-5:13:56
Takapalle	2	15N55	79E16	-5:17:04
Takhatpur	2	22N09	81E52	-5:27:28
Tāki	3	22N36	88E55	-5:55:40
Takipur	3	24N19	87E58	-5:51:52
Tāla	2	23N43	81E02	-5:24:08
Talāja	2	21N21	72E03	-4:48:12
Tālāla	2	21N02	70E32	-4:42:08
Tālbāndh	2	22N03	86E20	-5:45:20
Tālcher	2	20N57	85E13	-5:40:52
Tāldāngra	3	23N02	87E06	-5:48:24
Tālīkota	2	16N29	76E19	-5:05:16
Taliparamba	2	12N03	75E21	-5:01:24
Tal Lah	3	22N19	87E18	-5:49:12
Taloda	2	21N34	74E13	-4:56:52
Taloje Budrukh	2	19N05	73E05	-4:52:20
Tālsa	3	22N49	88E33	-5:54:12
Talwandi Bhāi	2	30N51	74E56	-4:59:44
Tāmbaram	2	12N55	80E07	-5:20:28
Tamkuhi	2	26N41	84E11	-5:36:44
Tamlūk	3	22N18	87E55	-5:51:40
Tāmma	4	25N11	93E42	-6:14:48
Tāmna	5	23N15	86E21	-5:45:24
Tanakpur	2	29N05	80E07	-5:20:28
Tānda	2	28N59	78E56	-5:15:44
Tānda	2	26N33	82E39	-5:30:36
Tandor	2	19N10	79E22	-5:17:28
Tāndūr	2	17N14	77E35	-5:10:20
Tāngi	2	19N56	85E24	-5:41:36
Tangla	4	26N30	92E00	-6:08:00
Tangmarg	2	34N02	74E26	-4:57:44
Tangtse	2	34N02	78E11	-5:12:44
Tanjore → Thanjāvūr	2	10N48	79E09	-5:16:36
Tāntipāra	3	23N54	87E22	-5:49:28
Tanuku	2	16N45	81E42	-5:26:48
Tanūr	2	10N58	75E52	-5:03:28
Tapa	2	30N19	75E21	-5:01:24
Tapasi	3	23N40	87E08	-5:48:32
Tappal	2	28N03	77E35	-5:10:20
Taraia	5	26N05	84E53	-5:39:32
Tārakeswar	3	22N54	88E02	-5:52:08
Tāratanr	5	23N58	86E29	-5:45:56
Tārdah	3	22N27	88E31	-5:54:04
Targa	2	22N27	84E40	-5:38:40
Tarikere	2	13N43	75E49	-5:03:16
Tarn Tāran	2	31N27	74E55	-4:59:40
Tāsgaon	2	17N02	74E36	-4:58:24
Tasrār Sharīf	2	33N52	74E46	-4:59:04
Tawang	4	27N33	91E48	-6:07:12
Taxpur	4	26N37	92E58	-6:11:52
Teghra	5	25N29	85E57	-5:43:48
Tehata	3	23N43	88E32	-5:54:08
Tehri	2	30N23	78E29	-5:13:56
Tejpur	4	26N37	92E50	-6:11:20
Teju	4	27N55	96E11	-6:24:44
Tekāri	5	24N56	84E50	-5:39:20
Tekkali	2	18N37	84E14	-5:36:56
Tela	2	28N44	77E20	-5:09:20
Tellicherry	2	11N45	75E32	-5:02:08
Tenāli	2	16N15	80E35	-5:22:20
Tengra	3	22N48	88E32	-5:54:08
Tenkāsi	2	8N58	77E18	-5:09:12
Tentulia	3	22N50	88E28	-5:53:52
Terdal	2	16N30	75E03	-5:00:12
Tezpur	4	26N38	92E48	-6:11:12
Thākurdwāra	2	29N12	78E51	-5:15:24
Thākurdwāri	3	22N34	88E28	-5:53:52
Thākurpukur	3	22N28	88E19	-5:53:16
Thākurvādi	2	18N54	73E04	-4:52:16
Thāna	2	19N12	72E58	-4:51:52
Thāna Ghāzi	2	27N25	76E19	-5:05:16
Thāna Kasba	2	25N13	77E20	-5:09:20
Thānesar	2	29N59	76E49	-5:07:16
Thanjāvūr	2	10N48	79E09	-5:16:36
Tharād	2	24N24	71E38	-4:46:32
Then	2	32N26	75E44	-5:02:56
Theog	2	31N07	77E21	-5:09:24
Tīkamgarh	2	24N44	78E50	-5:15:20
Tilhar	2	27N59	79E44	-5:18:56
Tiluria	3	23N34	86E59	-5:47:56
Timarni Muafi	2	22N22	77E22	-5:09:28
Tindis	2	21N35	86E44	-5:46:56
Tindivanam	2	12N15	79E39	-5:18:36
Tinsukia	4	27N30	95E22	-6:21:28
Tiptūr	2	13N16	76E29	-5:05:56
Tirodi	2	21N41	79E42	-5:18:48
Tīrthahalli	2	13N42	75E14	-5:00:56

Tiruchchirāppalli	2	10N49	78E41	-5:14:44
Tiruchendūr	2	8N29	78E07	-5:12:28
Tiruchengodu	2	11N23	77E56	-5:11:44
Tirukkalukkunram	2	12N37	80E04	-5:20:16
Tirukkoyilūr	2	11N57	79E12	-5:16:48
Tirumangalam	2	9N50	77E59	-5:11:56
Tirunelveli	2	8N44	77E42	-5:10:48
Tirupati	2	13N39	79E25	-5:17:40
Tirupparangunram	2	9N53	78E05	-5:12:20
Tiruppattūr	2	12N30	78E34	-5:14:16
Tiruppattūr	2	10N08	78E37	-5:14:28
Tiruppur	2	11N06	77E21	-5:09:24
Tirūr	2	10N54	75E55	-5:03:40
Tiruttani	2	13N11	79E38	-5:18:32
Tirutturaippūndi	2	10N32	79E39	-5:18:36
Tiruvalla	2	9N23	76E34	-5:06:16
Tiruvallūr	2	13N09	79E55	-5:19:40
Tiruvālūr	2	10N46	79E39	-5:18:36
Tiruvanmiyur	2	12N55	80E15	-5:21:00
Tiruvannāmalai	2	12N13	79E04	-5:16:16
Tiruvettipuram	2	12N40	79E33	-5:18:12
Tiruvottiyūr	2	13N09	80E18	-5:21:12
Tiruvur	2	17N06	80E38	-5:22:32
Tisaiyanvilai	2	8N20	77E53	-5:11:32
Titāgarh	3	22N45	88E22	-5:53:28
Tithwal	2	34N24	73E47	-4:55:08
Titlagarh	2	20N18	83E09	-5:32:36
Tiuni	2	30N57	77E51	-5:11:24
Toda Bhīm	2	26N55	76E49	-5:07:16
Toda Rai Singh	2	26N01	75E29	-5:01:56
Tohāna	2	29N42	75E54	-5:03:36
Tondhre	2	19N05	73E08	-4:52:32
Tondi	2	9N44	79E01	-5:16:04
Tonk	2	26N10	75E47	-5:03:08
Topchānchi	5	23N54	86E12	-5:44:48
Totānāla	3	22N05	87E40	-5:50:40
Tranquebar	2	11N02	79E51	-5:19:24
Tribeni	3	22N59	88E24	-5:53:36
Trichinopoly → Tiruchchirāppalli	2	10N49	78E41	-5:14:44
Trichūr	2	10N31	76E13	-5:04:52
Trivandrum	2	8N29	76E55	-5:07:40
Tufānganj	3	26N19	89E40	-5:58:40
Tumkūr	2	13N21	77E05	-5:08:20
Tumsar	2	21N23	79E44	-5:18:56
Tundi	5	23N58	86E25	-5:45:40
Tūndla	2	27N12	78E17	-5:13:08
Tuni	2	17N21	82E33	-5:30:12
Tura	4	25N31	90E13	-6:00:52
Turaiyūr	2	11N10	78E37	-5:14:28
Turambhe	2	19N04	73E01	-4:52:04
Turtipār	2	26N10	83E54	-5:35:36
Tuticorin	2	8N47	78E08	-5:12:32
Ubaidullāhganj	2	22N59	77E36	-5:10:24
Uchāna	2	29N28	76E10	-5:04:40
Udaipur	2	24N35	73E41	-4:54:44
Udala	2	21N35	86E34	-5:46:16
Udalguri	4	26N46	92E08	-6:08:32
Udamalpet	2	10N35	77E15	-5:09:00
Udankudi	2	8N26	78E01	-5:12:04
Udayagiri	2	14N54	79E18	-5:17:12
Udgīr	2	18N23	77E07	-5:08:28
Udhampur	2	32N56	75E08	-5:00:32
Udipi	2	13N21	74E45	-4:59:00
Ujhāni	2	28N01	79E01	-5:16:04
Ujjain	2	23N11	75E46	-5:03:04
Ukhra	3	23N39	87E14	-5:48:56
Ukhrul	4	25N07	94E22	-6:17:28
Ula	3	22N43	88E33	-5:54:12
Ulhāsnagar	2	19N13	73E07	-4:52:28
Ulubāria	3	22N28	88E06	-5:52:24
Uludāngar	3	22N51	88E31	-5:54:04
Ulva	2	18N59	73E02	-4:52:08
Umaria	2	23N32	80E50	-5:23:20
Umaria	2	23N48	80E56	-5:23:44
Umbargaon	2	20N12	72E45	-4:51:00
Umbroli	2	19N11	73E06	-4:52:24
Umrer	2	20N51	79E20	-5:17:20
Umreth	2	22N42	73E07	-4:52:28
Una	2	31N29	76E17	-5:05:08
Una	2	20N49	71E02	-4:44:08
Unao	2	25N35	78E36	-5:14:24
Unchahra	2	24N23	80E47	-5:23:08
Unjha	2	23N48	72E24	-4:49:36
Unnāo	2	26N32	80E30	-5:22:00
Upleta	2	21N44	70E17	-4:41:08
Upshi	2	33N50	77E49	-5:11:16
Uran	2	18N52	72E56	-4:51:44
Uravakonda	2	14N57	77E16	-5:09:04
Uri	2	34N05	74E02	-4:56:08
Urma	5	23N10	86E15	-5:45:00
Urmar Tanda	2	31N42	75E38	-5:02:32
Urun-Islāmpur	2	17N03	74E16	-4:57:04
Utraula	2	27N19	82E25	-5:29:40
Uttamapālaiyam	2	9N48	77E20	-5:09:20
Uttarkāshi	2	30N44	78E27	-5:13:48
Uttarpara-Kotrung	3	22N40	88E21	-5:53:24
Vādi	2	18N56	73E06	-4:52:24
Vadnagar	2	23N47	72E38	-4:50:32
Vaijāpur	2	19N55	74E44	-4:58:56
Vaikam	2	9N46	76E24	-5:05:36
Vaklan	2	19N07	73E06	-4:52:24
Valap	2	19N03	73E08	-4:52:32
Vala Ull	2	19N02	73E07	-4:52:28
Valparai	2	10N22	76E58	-5:07:52
Vandavāsi	2	12N30	79E37	-5:18:28
Vāniyambādi	2	12N41	78E37	-5:14:28
Vanthali	2	21N29	70E20	-4:41:20
Vārānasi (Benares)	2	25N20	83E00	-5:32:00
Varkallai	2	8N40	76E50	-5:07:20
Vasai (Bassein)	2	19N21	72E48	-4:51:12
Vasar	2	19N11	73E09	-4:52:36
Vāshi	2	19N04	72E59	-4:51:56
Vattalkundu	2	10N10	77E46	-5:11:04
Vayalpao	2	13N38	78E40	-5:14:40
Vedāranniyam	2	10N22	79E51	-5:19:24
Velapāda	2	18N59	73E04	-4:52:16
Vellore	2	12N56	79E08	-5:16:32
Velpura	2	16N53	81E38	-5:26:32
Vempalle	2	14N22	78E28	-5:13:52
Vengurla	2	15N52	73E38	-4:54:32
Venkatagiri	2	13N58	79E35	-5:18:20
Venkatagiri Kota	2	13N00	78E34	-5:14:16
Venkatpuram	2	18N17	80E36	-5:22:24
Venukonda	2	16N04	79E47	-5:19:08
Verāval	2	20N54	70E22	-4:41:28
Vetapālem	2	15N47	80E19	-5:21:16
Vettaikkāranpudūr	2	10N34	76E56	-5:07:44
Vidisha	2	23N32	77E49	-5:11:16
Vijāpur	2	23N34	72E45	-4:51:00
Vijayapuri	2	16N52	79E35	-5:18:20
Vijayawāda	2	16N31	80E37	-5:22:28
Vikārābad	2	17N20	77E54	-5:11:36
Vikramasingapuram	2	8N43	77E24	-5:09:36
Villupuram	2	11N56	79E29	-5:17:56
Viramgām	2	23N07	72E02	-4:48:08
Vīrarājendrapet	2	12N12	75E48	-5:03:12
Virudunagar	2	9N36	77E58	-5:11:52
Vishākhapatnam	2	17N42	83E18	-5:33:12
Visnagar	2	23N42	72E33	-4:50:12
Vite	2	17N17	74E33	-4:58:12
Vizagapatam → Vishākhapatnam	2	17N42	83E18	-5:33:12
Vizianagaram	2	18N07	83E25	-5:33:40
Vriddhāchalam	2	11N30	79E20	-5:17:20
Vrindāvan	2	27N35	77E42	-5:10:48
Vuyyūru	2	16N22	80E51	-5:23:24
Vyāra	2	21N07	73E24	-4:53:36
Wai	2	17N56	73E54	-4:55:36
Waidhān	2	24N04	82E20	-5:29:20
Wālājāpet	2	12N56	79E23	-5:17:32
Wani	2	20N04	78E57	-5:15:48
Wānkāner	2	22N37	70E56	-4:43:44
Wanparti	2	16N22	78E04	-5:12:16
Wāpi	2	20N22	72E54	-4:51:36
Warangal	2	18N00	79E35	-5:18:20
Wārāseoni	2	21N45	80E02	-5:20:08
Wardha	2	20N45	78E37	-5:14:28
Wāris Alīganj	5	25N01	85E38	-5:42:32
Warud	2	21N28	78E16	-5:13:04
Wāshim	2	20N06	77E09	-5:08:36
Wati	4	28N02	96E59	-6:27:56
Weir	2	27N01	77E11	-5:08:44
Wokha	4	26N06	94E16	-6:17:04
Yādgīr	2	16N46	77E08	-5:08:32
Yallareddi	2	18N13	78E00	-5:12:00
Yamunānagar	2	30N07	77E18	-5:09:12
Yanam	2	16N44	82E13	-5:28:52
Yāval	2	21N10	75E42	-5:02:48
Yavatmāl	2	20N24	78E08	-5:12:32
Yellandu	2	17N36	80E20	-5:21:20
Yeola	2	20N02	74E29	-4:57:56
Yeshvi	2	18N55	73E03	-4:52:12
Zahirābād	2	17N41	77E37	-5:10:28
Zaidpur	2	26N50	81E20	-5:25:20
Zeyādah Kot	3	22N27	88E20	-5:53:20
Zira	2	30N58	74E59	-4:59:56
Zirāpur	2	24N01	76E22	-5:05:28
Ziro	4	27N38	93E42	-6:14:48

INDONESIA INDONÉSIE INDONESIEN NETHERLANDS EAST INDIES INDONÉSIA

Time Table # 1
Before 10/Aug/1867 LMT
Begin Standard 106E48
10/Aug/1867 0:00 -7:07
Begin Standard 110E00
1/Jan/1924 0:13 -7:20
Begin Standard 112E30
1/Nov/1932 0:00 -7:30
Begin Standard 135E00
23/Mar/1942 0:00 -9:00
Begin Standard 112E30
1/Aug/1945 0:00 -7:30
Begin Standard 120E00
1/May/1948 0:00 -8:00
Begin Standard 112E30
1/May/1950 0:00 -7:30
Begin Standard 105E00
1/Jan/1964 0:00 -7:00
....

Time Table # 2
Before 10/Jun/1872 LMT
Begin Standard 106E48
10/Jun/1872 0:00 -7:07
Begin Standard 110E00
1/Jan/1924 0:13 -7:20
Begin Standard 112E30
1/Nov/1932 0:00 -7:30
Begin Standard 135E00
23/Mar/1942 0:00 -9:00
Begin Standard 112E30
1/Aug/1945 0:00 -7:30
Begin Standard 120E00
1/May/1948 0:00 -8:00
Begin Standard 112E30
1/May/1950 0:00 -7:30
Begin Standard 105E00
1/Jan/1964 0:00 -7:00
....

Time Table # 3
Before 2/May/1879 LMT
Begin Standard 106E48
2/May/1879 0:00 -7:07
Begin Standard 110E00
1/Jan/1924 0:13 -7:20
Begin Standard 112E30
1/Nov/1932 0:00 -7:30
Begin Standard 135E00
23/Mar/1942 0:00 -9:00
Begin Standard 112E30
1/Aug/1945 0:00 -7:30
Begin Standard 120E00
1/May/1948 0:00 -8:00
Begin Standard 112E30
1/May/1950 0:00 -7:30
Begin Standard 105E00
1/Jan/1964 0:00 -7:00
....

Time Table # 4
Before 21/Mar/1882 LMT
Begin Standard 106E48
21/Mar/1882 0:00 -7:07
Begin Standard 110E00
1/Jan/1924 0:13 -7:20
Begin Standard 112E30
1/Nov/1932 0:00 -7:30
Begin Standard 135E00
23/Mar/1942 0:00 -9:00
Begin Standard 112E30
1/Aug/1945 0:00 -7:30
Begin Standard 120E00
1/May/1948 0:00 -8:00
Begin Standard 112E30
1/May/1950 0:00 -7:30
Begin Standard 105E00
1/Jan/1964 0:00 -7:00
....

Time Table # 5
Before 2/Jul/1883 LMT
Begin Standard 106E48
2/Jul/1883 0:00 -7:07
Begin Standard 110E00
1/Jan/1924 0:13 -7:20
Begin Standard 112E30
1/Nov/1932 0:00 -7:30
Begin Standard 135E00
23/Mar/1942 0:00 -9:00
Begin Standard 112E30
1/Aug/1945 0:00 -7:30
Begin Standard 120E00
1/May/1948 0:00 -8:00
Begin Standard 112E30
1/May/1950 0:00 -7:30
Begin Standard 105E00
1/Jan/1964 0:00 -7:00
....

Time Table # 6
Before 15/Mar/1884 LMT
Begin Standard 106E48
15/Mar/1884 0:00 -7:07
Begin Standard 110E00
1/Jan/1924 0:13 -7:20
Begin Standard 112E30
1/Nov/1932 0:00 -7:30
Begin Standard 135E00
23/Mar/1942 0:00 -9:00
Begin Standard 112E30
1/Aug/1945 0:00 -7:30
Begin Standard 120E00
1/May/1948 0:00 -8:00
Begin Standard 112E30
1/May/1950 0:00 -7:30
Begin Standard 105E00
1/Jan/1964 0:00 -7:00
....

Time Table # 7
Before 19/Apr/1884 LMT
Begin Standard 106E48
19/Apr/1884 0:00 -7:07
Begin Standard 110E00
1/Jan/1924 0:13 -7:20
Begin Standard 112E30
1/Nov/1932 0:00 -7:30
Begin Standard 135E00
23/Mar/1942 0:00 -9:00
Begin Standard 112E30
1/Aug/1945 0:00 -7:30
Begin Standard 120E00
1/May/1948 0:00 -8:00
Begin Standard 112E30
1/May/1950 0:00 -7:30
Begin Standard 105E00
1/Jan/1964 0:00 -7:00
....

Time Table # 8
Before 17/May/1884 LMT
Begin Standard 106E48
17/May/1884 0:00 -7:07
Begin Standard 110E00
1/Jan/1924 0:13 -7:20
Begin Standard 112E30
1/Nov/1932 0:00 -7:30
Begin Standard 135E00
23/Mar/1942 0:00 -9:00
Begin Standard 112E30
1/Aug/1945 0:00 -7:30
Begin Standard 120E00
1/May/1948 0:00 -8:00
Begin Standard 112E30
1/May/1950 0:00 -7:30
Begin Standard 105E00
1/Jan/1964 0:00 -7:00
....

Time Table # 9
Before 24/May/1884 LMT
Begin Standard 106E48
24/May/1884 0:00 -7:07
Begin Standard 110E00
1/Jan/1924 0:13 -7:20
Begin Standard 112E30
1/Nov/1932 0:00 -7:30
Begin Standard 135E00
23/Mar/1942 0:00 -9:00
Begin Standard 112E30
1/Aug/1945 0:00 -7:30
Begin Standard 120E00
1/May/1948 0:00 -8:00
Begin Standard 112E30
1/May/1950 0:00 -7:30
Begin Standard 105E00
1/Jan/1964 0:00 -7:00
....

Time Table # 10
Before 31/Mar/1887 LMT
Begin Standard 106E48
31/Mar/1887 0:00 -7:07
Begin Standard 110E00
1/Jan/1924 0:13 -7:20
Begin Standard 112E30
1/Nov/1932 0:00 -7:30
Begin Standard 135E00
23/Mar/1942 0:00 -9:00
Begin Standard 112E30
1/Aug/1945 0:00 -7:30
Begin Standard 120E00
1/May/1948 0:00 -8:00
Begin Standard 112E30
1/May/1950 0:00 -7:30
Begin Standard 105E00
1/Jan/1964 0:00 -7:00
....

Time Table # 11
Before 20/Jul/1887 LMT
Begin Standard 106E48
20/Jul/1887 0:00 -7:07
Begin Standard 110E00
1/Jan/1924 0:13 -7:20
Begin Standard 112E30
1/Nov/1932 0:00 -7:30
Begin Standard 135E00
23/Mar/1942 0:00 -9:00
Begin Standard 112E30
1/Aug/1945 0:00 -7:30
Begin Standard 120E00
1/May/1948 0:00 -8:00
Begin Standard 112E30
1/May/1950 0:00 -7:30
Begin Standard 105E00
1/Jan/1964 0:00 -7:00
....

Time Table # 12
Before 1/Apr/1889 LMT
Begin Standard 106E48
1/Apr/1889 0:00 -7:07
Begin Standard 110E00
1/Jan/1924 0:13 -7:20
Begin Standard 112E30
1/Nov/1932 0:00 -7:30
Begin Standard 135E00
23/Mar/1942 0:00 -9:00
Begin Standard 112E30
1/Aug/1945 0:00 -7:30
Begin Standard 120E00
1/May/1948 0:00 -8:00
Begin Standard 112E30
1/May/1950 0:00 -7:30
Begin Standard 105E00
1/Jan/1964 0:00 -7:00
....

Time Table # 13
Before 14/Aug/1889 LMT
Begin Standard 106E48
14/Aug/1889 0:00 -7:07
Begin Standard 110E00
1/Jan/1924 0:13 -7:20
Begin Standard 112E30
1/Nov/1932 0:00 -7:30
Begin Standard 135E00
23/Mar/1942 0:00 -9:00
Begin Standard 112E30
1/Aug/1945 0:00 -7:30
Begin Standard 120E00
1/May/1948 0:00 -8:00
Begin Standard 112E30
1/May/1950 0:00 -7:30
Begin Standard 105E00
1/Jan/1964 0:00 -7:00
....

Time Table # 14
Before 1/Oct/1889 LMT
Begin Standard 106E48
1/Oct/1889 0:00 -7:07
Begin Standard 110E00
1/Jan/1924 0:13 -7:20
Begin Standard 112E30
1/Nov/1932 0:00 -7:30
Begin Standard 135E00
23/Mar/1942 0:00 -9:00
Begin Standard 112E30
1/Aug/1945 0:00 -7:30
Begin Standard 120E00
1/May/1948 0:00 -8:00
Begin Standard 112E30
1/May/1950 0:00 -7:30
Begin Standard 105E00
1/Jan/1964 0:00 -7:00
....

Time Table # 15
Before 21/Jun/1891 LMT
Begin Standard 106E48
21/Jun/1891 0:00 -7:07
Begin Standard 110E00
1/Jan/1924 0:13 -7:20
Begin Standard 112E30
1/Nov/1932 0:00 -7:30
Begin Standard 135E00
23/Mar/1942 0:00 -9:00
Begin Standard 112E30
1/Aug/1945 0:00 -7:30
Begin Standard 120E00
1/May/1948 0:00 -8:00
Begin Standard 112E30
1/May/1950 0:00 -7:30
Begin Standard 105E00
1/Jan/1964 0:00 -7:00
....

Time Table # 16
Before 16/Sep/1893 LMT
Begin Standard 106E48
16/Sep/1893 0:00 -7:07
Begin Standard 110E00
1/Jan/1924 0:13 -7:20
Begin Standard 112E30
1/Nov/1932 0:00 -7:30
Begin Standard 135E00
23/Mar/1942 0:00 -9:00
Begin Standard 112E30
1/Aug/1945 0:00 -7:30
Begin Standard 120E00
1/May/1948 0:00 -8:00
Begin Standard 112E30
1/May/1950 0:00 -7:30
Begin Standard 105E00
1/Jan/1964 0:00 -7:00
....

Time Table # 17
Before 13/Sep/1894 LMT
Begin Standard 106E48
13/Sep/1894 0:00 -7:07
Begin Standard 110E00
1/Jan/1924 0:13 -7:20
Begin Standard 112E30
1/Nov/1932 0:00 -7:30
Begin Standard 135E00
23/Mar/1942 0:00 -9:00
Begin Standard 112E30
1/Aug/1945 0:00 -7:30
Begin Standard 120E00
1/May/1948 0:00 -8:00
Begin Standard 112E30
1/May/1950 0:00 -7:30
Begin Standard 105E00
1/Jan/1964 0:00 -7:00
....

Time Table # 18
Before 16/Jul/1896 LMT
Begin Standard 106E48
16/Jul/1896 0:00 -7:07
Begin Standard 110E00
1/Jan/1924 0:13 -7:20
Begin Standard 112E30
1/Nov/1932 0:00 -7:30
Begin Standard 135E00
23/Mar/1942 0:00 -9:00
Begin Standard 112E30
1/Aug/1945 0:00 -7:30
Begin Standard 120E00
1/May/1948 0:00 -8:00
Begin Standard 112E30
1/May/1950 0:00 -7:30
Begin Standard 105E00
1/Jan/1964 0:00 -7:00
....

Time Table # 19
Before 5/Dec/1896 LMT
Begin Standard 106E48
5/Dec/1896 0:00 -7:07
Begin Standard 110E00
1/Jan/1924 0:13 -7:20
Begin Standard 112E30
1/Nov/1932 0:00 -7:30
Begin Standard 135E00
23/Mar/1942 0:00 -9:00
Begin Standard 112E30
1/Aug/1945 0:00 -7:30
Begin Standard 120E00
1/May/1948 0:00 -8:00
Begin Standard 112E30
1/May/1950 0:00 -7:30
Begin Standard 105E00
1/Jan/1964 0:00 -7:00
....

Time Table # 20
Before 1/May/1897 LMT
Begin Standard 106E48
1/May/1897 0:00 -7:07
Begin Standard 110E00
1/Jan/1924 0:13 -7:20
Begin Standard 112E30
1/Nov/1932 0:00 -7:30
Begin Standard 135E00
23/Mar/1942 0:00 -9:00
Begin Standard 112E30
1/Aug/1945 0:00 -7:30
Begin Standard 120E00
1/May/1948 0:00 -8:00
Begin Standard 112E30
1/May/1950 0:00 -7:30
Begin Standard 105E00
1/Jan/1964 0:00 -7:00
....

Time Table # 21
Before 2/May/1897 LMT
Begin Standard 106E48
2/May/1897 0:00 -7:07
Begin Standard 110E00
1/Jan/1924 0:13 -7:20
Begin Standard 112E30
1/Nov/1932 0:00 -7:30
Begin Standard 135E00
23/Mar/1942 0:00 -9:00
Begin Standard 112E30
1/Aug/1945 0:00 -7:30
Begin Standard 120E00
1/May/1948 0:00 -8:00
Begin Standard 112E30
1/May/1950 0:00 -7:30
Begin Standard 105E00
1/Jan/1964 0:00 -7:00
....

Time Table # 22
Before 20/Jul/1897 LMT
Begin Standard 106E48
20/Jul/1897 0:00 -7:07
Begin Standard 110E00
1/Jan/1924 0:13 -7:20
Begin Standard 112E30
1/Nov/1932 0:00 -7:30
Begin Standard 135E00
23/Mar/1942 0:00 -9:00
Begin Standard 112E30
1/Aug/1945 0:00 -7:30
Begin Standard 120E00
1/May/1948 0:00 -8:00
Begin Standard 112E30
1/May/1950 0:00 -7:30
Begin Standard 105E00
1/Jan/1964 0:00 -7:00
....

Time Table # 23
Before 15/Nov/1897 LMT
Begin Standard 106E48
15/Nov/1897 0:00 -7:07
Begin Standard 110E00
1/Jan/1924 0:13 -7:20
Begin Standard 112E30
1/Nov/1932 0:00 -7:30
Begin Standard 135E00
23/Mar/1942 0:00 -9:00
Begin Standard 112E30
1/Aug/1945 0:00 -7:30
Begin Standard 120E00
1/May/1948 0:00 -8:00
Begin Standard 112E30
1/May/1950 0:00 -7:30
Begin Standard 105E00
1/Jan/1964 0:00 -7:00
....

Time Table # 24
Before 12/Jan/1898 LMT
Begin Standard 106E48
12/Jan/1898 0:00 -7:07
Begin Standard 110E00
1/Jan/1924 0:13 -7:20
Begin Standard 112E30
1/Nov/1932 0:00 -7:30
Begin Standard 135E00
23/Mar/1942 0:00 -9:00
Begin Standard 112E30
1/Aug/1945 0:00 -7:30
Begin Standard 120E00
1/May/1948 0:00 -8:00
Begin Standard 112E30
1/May/1950 0:00 -7:30
Begin Standard 105E00
1/Jan/1964 0:00 -7:00
....

Time Table # 25
Before 20/Mar/1898 LMT
Begin Standard 106E48
20/Mar/1898 0:00 -7:07
Begin Standard 110E00
1/Jan/1924 0:13 -7:20
Begin Standard 112E30
1/Nov/1932 0:00 -7:30
Begin Standard 135E00
23/Mar/1942 0:00 -9:00
Begin Standard 112E30
1/Aug/1945 0:00 -7:30
Begin Standard 120E00
1/May/1948 0:00 -8:00
Begin Standard 112E30
1/May/1950 0:00 -7:30
Begin Standard 105E00
1/Jan/1964 0:00 -7:00
....

Time Table # 26
Before 23/Jun/1898 LMT
Begin Standard 106E48
23/Jun/1898 0:00 -7:07
Begin Standard 110E00
1/Jan/1924 0:13 -7:20
Begin Standard 112E30
1/Nov/1932 0:00 -7:30
Begin Standard 135E00
23/Mar/1942 0:00 -9:00
Begin Standard 112E30
1/Aug/1945 0:00 -7:30
Begin Standard 120E00
1/May/1948 0:00 -8:00
Begin Standard 112E30
1/May/1950 0:00 -7:30
Begin Standard 105E00
1/Jan/1964 0:00 -7:00
....

Time Table # 27
Before 1/Jul/1898 LMT
Begin Standard 106E48
1/Jul/1898 0:00 -7:07
Begin Standard 110E00
1/Jan/1924 0:13 -7:20
Begin Standard 112E30
1/Nov/1932 0:00 -7:30
Begin Standard 135E00
23/Mar/1942 0:00 -9:00
Begin Standard 112E30
1/Aug/1945 0:00 -7:30
Begin Standard 120E00
1/May/1948 0:00 -8:00
Begin Standard 112E30
1/May/1950 0:00 -7:30
Begin Standard 105E00
1/Jan/1964 0:00 -7:00
....

Time Table # 28
Before 2/Jan/1899 LMT
Begin Standard 106E48
2/Jan/1899 0:00 -7:07
Begin Standard 110E00
1/Jan/1924 0:13 -7:20
Begin Standard 112E30
1/Nov/1932 0:00 -7:30
Begin Standard 135E00
23/Mar/1942 0:00 -9:00
Begin Standard 112E30
1/Aug/1945 0:00 -7:30
Begin Standard 120E00
1/May/1948 0:00 -8:00
Begin Standard 112E30
1/May/1950 0:00 -7:30
Begin Standard 105E00
1/Jan/1964 0:00 -7:00
....

Time Table # 29
Before 1/Feb/1899 LMT
Begin Standard 106E48
1/Feb/1899 0:00 -7:07
Begin Standard 110E00
1/Jan/1924 0:13 -7:20
Begin Standard 112E30
1/Nov/1932 0:00 -7:30
Begin Standard 135E00
23/Mar/1942 0:00 -9:00
Begin Standard 112E30
1/Aug/1945 0:00 -7:30
Begin Standard 120E00
1/May/1948 0:00 -8:00
Begin Standard 112E30
1/May/1950 0:00 -7:30
Begin Standard 105E00
1/Jan/1964 0:00 -7:00
....

Time Table # 30
Before 1/Oct/1899 LMT
Begin Standard 106E48
1/Oct/1899 0:00 -7:07
Begin Standard 110E00
1/Jan/1924 0:13 -7:20
Begin Standard 112E30
1/Nov/1932 0:00 -7:30
Begin Standard 135E00
23/Mar/1942 0:00 -9:00
Begin Standard 112E30
1/Aug/1945 0:00 -7:30
Begin Standard 120E00
1/May/1948 0:00 -8:00
Begin Standard 112E30
1/May/1950 0:00 -7:30
Begin Standard 105E00
1/Jan/1964 0:00 -7:00
....

Time Table # 31
Before 1/May/1900 LMT
Begin Standard 106E48
1/May/1900 0:00 -7:07
Begin Standard 110E00

```
1/Jan/1924 0:13 -7:20
Begin Standard 112E30
1/Nov/1932 0:00 -7:30
Begin Standard 135E00
23/Mar/1942 0:00 -9:00
Begin Standard 112E30
1/Aug/1945 0:00 -7:30
Begin Standard 120E00
1/May/1948 0:00 -8:00
Begin Standard 112E30
1/May/1950 0:00 -7:30
Begin Standard 105E00
1/Jan/1964 0:00 -7:00
......................
Time Table # 32
Before 1/Jul/1900 LMT
Begin Standard 106E48
1/Jul/1900 0:00 -7:07
Begin Standard 110E00
1/Jan/1924 0:13 -7:20
Begin Standard 112E30
1/Nov/1932 0:00 -7:30
Begin Standard 135E00
23/Mar/1942 0:00 -9:00
Begin Standard 112E30
1/Aug/1945 0:00 -7:30
Begin Standard 120E00
1/May/1948 0:00 -8:00
Begin Standard 112E30
1/May/1950 0:00 -7:30
Begin Standard 105E00
1/Jan/1964 0:00 -7:00
......................
Time Table # 33
Before 15/Jun/1902 LMT
Begin Standard 106E48
15/Jun/1902 0:00 -7:07
Begin Standard 110E00
1/Jan/1924 0:13 -7:20
Begin Standard 112E30
1/Nov/1932 0:00 -7:30
Begin Standard 135E00
23/Mar/1942 0:00 -9:00
Begin Standard 112E30
1/Aug/1945 0:00 -7:30
Begin Standard 120E00
1/May/1948 0:00 -8:00
Begin Standard 112E30
1/May/1950 0:00 -7:30
Begin Standard 105E00
1/Jan/1964 0:00 -7:00
......................
Time Table # 34
Before 27/Dec/1902 LMT
Begin Standard 106E48
27/Dec/1902 0:00 -7:07
Begin Standard 110E00
1/Jan/1924 0:13 -7:20
Begin Standard 112E30
1/Nov/1932 0:00 -7:30
Begin Standard 135E00
23/Mar/1942 0:00 -9:00
Begin Standard 112E30
1/Aug/1945 0:00 -7:30
Begin Standard 120E00
1/May/1948 0:00 -8:00
Begin Standard 112E30
1/May/1950 0:00 -7:30
Begin Standard 105E00
1/Jan/1964 0:00 -7:00
......................
Time Table # 35
Before 18/Jun/1906 LMT
Begin Standard 106E48
18/Jun/1906 0:00 -7:07
Begin Standard 110E00
1/Jan/1924 0:13 -7:20
Begin Standard 112E30
1/Nov/1932 0:00 -7:30
Begin Standard 135E00
23/Mar/1942 0:00 -9:00
Begin Standard 112E30
1/Aug/1945 0:00 -7:30
Begin Standard 120E00
1/May/1948 0:00 -8:00
Begin Standard 112E30
1/May/1950 0:00 -7:30
Begin Standard 105E00
1/Jan/1964 0:00 -7:00
......................
Time Table # 36
Before 1/May/1908 LMT
Begin Standard 106E48
1/May/1908 0:00 -7:07
Begin Standard 110E00
1/Jan/1924 0:13 -7:20
Begin Standard 112E30
1/Nov/1932 0:00 -7:30
Begin Standard 135E00
23/Mar/1942 0:00 -9:00
Begin Standard 112E30
1/Aug/1945 0:00 -7:30
Begin Standard 120E00
1/May/1948 0:00 -8:00
Begin Standard 112E30
1/May/1950 0:00 -7:30
Begin Standard 105E00
1/Jan/1964 0:00 -7:00
......................
Time Table # 37
Before 16/May/1878 LMT
Begin Standard 112E45
16/May/1878 0:00 -7:31
Begin Standard 106E48
1/May/1908 0:00 -7:07
Begin Standard 110E00
1/Jan/1924 0:13 -7:20
Begin Standard 112E30
1/Nov/1932 0:00 -7:30
Begin Standard 135E00
19/Mar/1942 0:00 -9:00
Begin Standard 112E30
1/Aug/1945 0:00 -7:30
Begin Standard 120E00
1/May/1948 0:00 -8:00
Begin Standard 112E30
1/May/1950 0:00 -7:30
Begin Standard 105E00
1/Jan/1964 0:00 -7:00
......................
Time Table # 38
Before 1/Nov/1878 LMT
Begin Standard 112E45
1/Nov/1878 0:00 -7:31
Begin Standard 106E48
1/May/1908 0:00 -7:07
Begin Standard 110E00
1/Jan/1924 0:13 -7:20
Begin Standard 112E30
1/Nov/1932 0:00 -7:30
Begin Standard 135E00
19/Mar/1942 0:00 -9:00
Begin Standard 112E30
1/Aug/1945 0:00 -7:30
Begin Standard 120E00
1/May/1948 0:00 -8:00
Begin Standard 112E30
1/May/1950 0:00 -7:30
Begin Standard 105E00
1/Jan/1964 0:00 -7:00
......................
Time Table # 39
Before 1/May/1879 LMT
Begin Standard 112E45
1/May/1879 0:00 -7:31
Begin Standard 106E48
1/May/1908 0:00 -7:07
Begin Standard 110E00
1/Jan/1924 0:13 -7:20
Begin Standard 112E30
1/Nov/1932 0:00 -7:30
Begin Standard 135E00
19/Mar/1942 0:00 -9:00
Begin Standard 112E30
1/Aug/1945 0:00 -7:30
Begin Standard 120E00
1/May/1948 0:00 -8:00
Begin Standard 112E30
1/May/1950 0:00 -7:30
Begin Standard 105E00
1/Jan/1964 0:00 -7:00
......................
Time Table # 40
Before 20/Jul/1879 LMT
Begin Standard 112E45
20/Jul/1879 0:00 -7:31
Begin Standard 106E48
1/May/1908 0:00 -7:07
Begin Standard 110E00
1/Jan/1924 0:13 -7:20
Begin Standard 112E30
1/Nov/1932 0:00 -7:30
Begin Standard 135E00
19/Mar/1942 0:00 -9:00
Begin Standard 112E30
1/Aug/1945 0:00 -7:30
Begin Standard 120E00
1/May/1948 0:00 -8:00
Begin Standard 112E30
1/May/1950 0:00 -7:30
Begin Standard 105E00
1/Jan/1964 0:00 -7:00
......................
Time Table # 41
Before 1/Oct/1879 LMT
Begin Standard 112E45
1/Oct/1879 0:00 -7:31
Begin Standard 106E48
1/May/1908 0:00 -7:07
Begin Standard 110E00
1/Jan/1924 0:13 -7:20
Begin Standard 112E30
1/Nov/1932 0:00 -7:30
Begin Standard 135E00
19/Mar/1942 0:00 -9:00
Begin Standard 112E30
1/Aug/1945 0:00 -7:30
Begin Standard 120E00
1/May/1948 0:00 -8:00
Begin Standard 112E30
1/May/1950 0:00 -7:30
Begin Standard 105E00
1/Jan/1964 0:00 -7:00
......................
Time Table # 42
Before 16/Oct/1880 LMT
Begin Standard 112E45
16/Oct/1880 0:00 -7:31
Begin Standard 106E48
1/May/1908 0:00 -7:07
Begin Standard 110E00
1/Jan/1924 0:13 -7:20
Begin Standard 112E30
1/Nov/1932 0:00 -7:30
Begin Standard 135E00
19/Mar/1942 0:00 -9:00
Begin Standard 112E30
1/Aug/1945 0:00 -7:30
Begin Standard 120E00
1/May/1948 0:00 -8:00
Begin Standard 112E30
1/May/1950 0:00 -7:30
Begin Standard 105E00
1/Jan/1964 0:00 -7:00
......................
Time Table # 43
Before 25/Jun/1881 LMT
Begin Standard 112E45
25/Jun/1881 0:00 -7:31
Begin Standard 106E48
1/May/1908 0:00 -7:07
Begin Standard 110E00
1/Jan/1924 0:13 -7:20
Begin Standard 112E30
1/Nov/1932 0:00 -7:30
Begin Standard 135E00
19/Mar/1942 0:00 -9:00
Begin Standard 112E30
1/Aug/1945 0:00 -7:30
Begin Standard 120E00
1/May/1948 0:00 -8:00
Begin Standard 112E30
1/May/1950 0:00 -7:30
Begin Standard 105E00
1/Jan/1964 0:00 -7:00
......................
Time Table # 44
Before 13/Aug/1881 LMT
Begin Standard 112E45
13/Aug/1881 0:00 -7:31
Begin Standard 106E48
1/May/1908 0:00 -7:07
Begin Standard 110E00
1/Jan/1924 0:13 -7:20
Begin Standard 112E30
1/Nov/1932 0:00 -7:30
Begin Standard 135E00
19/Mar/1942 0:00 -9:00
Begin Standard 112E30
1/Aug/1945 0:00 -7:30
Begin Standard 120E00
1/May/1948 0:00 -8:00
Begin Standard 112E30
1/May/1950 0:00 -7:30
Begin Standard 105E00
1/Jan/1964 0:00 -7:00
......................
Time Table # 45
Before 1/Oct/1881 LMT
Begin Standard 112E45
1/Oct/1881 0:00 -7:31
Begin Standard 106E48
1/May/1908 0:00 -7:07
Begin Standard 110E00
1/Jan/1924 0:13 -7:20
Begin Standard 112E30
1/Nov/1932 0:00 -7:30
Begin Standard 135E00
19/Mar/1942 0:00 -9:00
Begin Standard 112E30
1/Aug/1945 0:00 -7:30
Begin Standard 120E00
1/May/1948 0:00 -8:00
Begin Standard 112E30
1/May/1950 0:00 -7:30
Begin Standard 105E00
1/Jan/1964 0:00 -7:00
......................
Time Table # 46
Before 2/Jun/1883 LMT
Begin Standard 112E45
2/Jun/1883 0:00 -7:31
Begin Standard 106E48
1/May/1908 0:00 -7:07
Begin Standard 110E00
1/Jan/1924 0:13 -7:20
Begin Standard 112E30
1/Nov/1932 0:00 -7:30
Begin Standard 135E00
19/Mar/1942 0:00 -9:00
Begin Standard 112E30
1/Aug/1945 0:00 -7:30
Begin Standard 120E00
1/May/1948 0:00 -8:00
Begin Standard 112E30
1/May/1950 0:00 -7:30
Begin Standard 105E00
1/Jan/1964 0:00 -7:00
......................
Time Table # 47
Before 3/May/1884 LMT
Begin Standard 112E45
3/May/1884 0:00 -7:31
Begin Standard 106E48
1/May/1908 0:00 -7:07
Begin Standard 110E00
1/Jan/1924 0:13 -7:20
Begin Standard 112E30
1/Nov/1932 0:00 -7:30
Begin Standard 135E00
19/Mar/1942 0:00 -9:00
Begin Standard 112E30
1/Aug/1945 0:00 -7:30
Begin Standard 120E00
1/May/1948 0:00 -8:00
Begin Standard 112E30
1/May/1950 0:00 -7:30
Begin Standard 105E00
1/Jan/1964 0:00 -7:00
......................
Time Table # 48
Before 16/Jun/1884 LMT
Begin Standard 112E45
16/Jun/1884 0:00 -7:31
Begin Standard 106E48
1/May/1908 0:00 -7:07
Begin Standard 110E00
1/Jan/1924 0:13 -7:20
Begin Standard 112E30
1/Nov/1932 0:00 -7:30
Begin Standard 135E00
19/Mar/1942 0:00 -9:00
Begin Standard 112E30
1/Aug/1945 0:00 -7:30
Begin Standard 120E00
1/May/1948 0:00 -8:00
Begin Standard 112E30
1/May/1950 0:00 -7:30
Begin Standard 105E00
1/Jan/1964 0:00 -7:00
......................
Time Table # 49
Before 16/May/1887 LMT
Begin Standard 112E45
16/May/1887 0:00 -7:31
Begin Standard 106E48
1/May/1908 0:00 -7:07
Begin Standard 110E00
1/Jan/1924 0:13 -7:20
Begin Standard 112E30
1/Nov/1932 0:00 -7:30
Begin Standard 135E00
19/Mar/1942 0:00 -9:00
Begin Standard 112E30
1/Aug/1945 0:00 -7:30
Begin Standard 120E00
1/May/1948 0:00 -8:00
Begin Standard 112E30
1/May/1950 0:00 -7:30
Begin Standard 105E00
1/Jan/1964 0:00 -7:00
......................
Time Table # 50
Before 1/Jul/1892 LMT
Begin Standard 112E45
1/Jul/1892 0:00 -7:31
Begin Standard 106E48
1/May/1908 0:00 -7:07
Begin Standard 110E00
1/Jan/1924 0:13 -7:20
Begin Standard 112E30
1/Nov/1932 0:00 -7:30
Begin Standard 135E00
19/Mar/1942 0:00 -9:00
Begin Standard 112E30
1/Aug/1945 0:00 -7:30
Begin Standard 120E00
1/May/1948 0:00 -8:00
Begin Standard 112E30
1/May/1950 0:00 -7:30
Begin Standard 105E00
1/Jan/1964 0:00 -7:00
......................
Time Table # 51
Before 5/Jan/1896 LMT
Begin Standard 112E45
5/Jan/1896 0:00 -7:31
Begin Standard 106E48
1/May/1908 0:00 -7:07
Begin Standard 110E00
1/Jan/1924 0:13 -7:20
Begin Standard 112E30
1/Nov/1932 0:00 -7:30
Begin Standard 135E00
19/Mar/1942 0:00 -9:00
Begin Standard 112E30
1/Aug/1945 0:00 -7:30
Begin Standard 120E00
1/May/1948 0:00 -8:00
Begin Standard 112E30
1/May/1950 0:00 -7:30
Begin Standard 105E00
1/Jan/1964 0:00 -7:00
......................
Time Table # 52
Before 1/Jun/1897 LMT
Begin Standard 112E45
1/Jun/1897 0:00 -7:31
Begin Standard 106E48
1/May/1908 0:00 -7:07
Begin Standard 110E00
1/Jan/1924 0:13 -7:20
Begin Standard 112E30
1/Nov/1932 0:00 -7:30
Begin Standard 135E00
19/Mar/1942 0:00 -9:00
Begin Standard 112E30
1/Aug/1945 0:00 -7:30
Begin Standard 120E00
1/May/1948 0:00 -8:00
Begin Standard 112E30
1/May/1950 0:00 -7:30
Begin Standard 105E00
1/Jan/1964 0:00 -7:00
......................
Time Table # 53
Before 1/Dec/1898 LMT
Begin Standard 112E45
1/Dec/1898 0:00 -7:31
Begin Standard 106E48
1/May/1908 0:00 -7:07
Begin Standard 110E00
1/Jan/1924 0:13 -7:20
Begin Standard 112E30
1/Nov/1932 0:00 -7:30
Begin Standard 135E00
19/Mar/1942 0:00 -9:00
Begin Standard 112E30
1/Aug/1945 0:00 -7:30
Begin Standard 120E00
1/May/1948 0:00 -8:00
Begin Standard 112E30
1/May/1950 0:00 -7:30
Begin Standard 105E00
1/Jan/1964 0:00 -7:00
......................
Time Table # 54
Before 1/Apr/1900 LMT
Begin Standard 112E45
1/Apr/1900 0:00 -7:31
Begin Standard 106E48
1/May/1908 0:00 -7:07
Begin Standard 110E00
1/Jan/1924 0:13 -7:20
Begin Standard 112E30
1/Nov/1932 0:00 -7:30
Begin Standard 135E00
19/Mar/1942 0:00 -9:00
Begin Standard 112E30
1/Aug/1945 0:00 -7:30
Begin Standard 120E00
1/May/1948 0:00 -8:00
Begin Standard 112E30
1/May/1950 0:00 -7:30
Begin Standard 105E00
1/Jan/1964 0:00 -7:00
......................
Time Table # 55
Before 15/Aug/1900 LMT
Begin Standard 112E45
15/Aug/1900 0:00 -7:31
Begin Standard 106E48
1/May/1908 0:00 -7:07
Begin Standard 110E00
1/Jan/1924 0:13 -7:20
Begin Standard 112E30
1/Nov/1932 0:00 -7:30
Begin Standard 135E00
19/Mar/1942 0:00 -9:00
Begin Standard 112E30
1/Aug/1945 0:00 -7:30
Begin Standard 120E00
1/May/1948 0:00 -8:00
Begin Standard 112E30
1/May/1950 0:00 -7:30
Begin Standard 105E00
1/Jan/1964 0:00 -7:00
......................
Time Table # 56
Before 1/Mar/1902 LMT
Begin Standard 112E45
1/Mar/1902 0:00 -7:31
Begin Standard 106E48
1/May/1908 0:00 -7:07
Begin Standard 110E00
1/Jan/1924 0:13 -7:20
Begin Standard 112E30
1/Nov/1932 0:00 -7:30
Begin Standard 135E00
19/Mar/1942 0:00 -9:00
Begin Standard 112E30
1/Aug/1945 0:00 -7:30
Begin Standard 120E00
1/May/1948 0:00 -8:00
Begin Standard 112E30
1/May/1950 0:00 -7:30
Begin Standard 105E00
1/Jan/1964 0:00 -7:00
......................
Time Table # 57
Before 1/Jun/1902 LMT
Begin Standard 112E45
1/Jun/1902 0:00 -7:31
Begin Standard 106E48
1/May/1908 0:00 -7:07
Begin Standard 110E00
1/Jan/1924 0:13 -7:20
Begin Standard 112E30
1/Nov/1932 0:00 -7:30
Begin Standard 135E00
19/Mar/1942 0:00 -9:00
Begin Standard 112E30
1/Aug/1945 0:00 -7:30
Begin Standard 120E00
1/May/1948 0:00 -8:00
Begin Standard 112E30
1/May/1950 0:00 -7:30
Begin Standard 105E00
1/Jan/1964 0:00 -7:00
......................
Time Table # 58
Before 10/Sep/1902 LMT
Begin Standard 112E45
10/Sep/1902 0:00 -7:31
Begin Standard 106E48
1/May/1908 0:00 -7:07
Begin Standard 110E00
1/Jan/1924 0:13 -7:20
Begin Standard 112E30
1/Nov/1932 0:00 -7:30
Begin Standard 135E00
19/Mar/1942 0:00 -9:00
Begin Standard 112E30
1/Aug/1945 0:00 -7:30
Begin Standard 120E00
1/May/1948 0:00 -8:00
Begin Standard 112E30
1/May/1950 0:00 -7:30
Begin Standard 105E00
1/Jan/1964 0:00 -7:00
......................
Time Table # 59
Before 1/May/1908 LMT
Begin Standard 112E45
1/May/1908 0:00 -7:31
```

INDONESIA INDONÉSIE INDONESIEN NETHERLANDS EAST INDIES INDONÉSIA

Begin Standard 106E48
1/May/1908 0:00 -7:07
Begin Standard 110E00
1/Jan/1924 0:13 -7:20
Begin Standard 112E30
1/Nov/1932 0:00 -7:30
Begin Standard 135E00
19/Mar/1942 0:00 -9:00
Begin Standard 112E30
1/Aug/1945 0:00 -7:30
Begin Standard 120E00
1/May/1948 0:00 -8:00
Begin Standard 112E30
1/May/1950 0:00 -7:30
Begin Standard 105E00
1/Jan/1964 0:00 -7:00
....
Time Table # 60
Before 1/Nov/1932 LMT
Begin Standard 112E45
1/Nov/1932 0:00 -7:31
Begin Standard 106E48
1/May/1908 0:00 -7:07
Begin Standard 110E00
1/Jan/1924 0:13 -7:20
Begin Standard 112E30
1/Nov/1932 0:00 -7:30
Begin Standard 135E00
19/Mar/1942 0:00 -9:00
Begin Standard 112E30
1/Aug/1945 0:00 -7:30
Begin Standard 120E00
1/May/1948 0:00 -8:00
Begin Standard 112E30
1/May/1950 0:00 -7:30
Begin Standard 105E00
1/Jan/1964 0:00 -7:00
....
Time Table # 61
Before 1/Apr/1918 LMT
Begin Standard 100E21
1/Apr/1918 0:00 -6:41
Begin Standard 97E30
1/Nov/1932 0:00 -6:30
Begin Standard 135E00
14/Mar/1942 0:00 -9:00
Begin Standard 97E30
1/Aug/1945 0:00 -6:30
Begin Standard 105E00
1/May/1948 0:00 -7:00
Begin Standard 97E30
1/May/1950 0:00 -6:30
Begin Standard 105E00
1/Jan/1964 0:00 -7:00
....
Time Table # 62
Before 1/Apr/1918 LMT
Begin Standard 100E21
1/Apr/1918 0:00 -6:41
Begin Standard 105E00
1/Nov/1932 0:00 -7:00
Begin Standard 135E00
25/Feb/1942 0:00 -9:00
Begin Standard 105E00
1/Aug/1945 0:00 -7:00
....
Time Table # 63
Before 1/Apr/1918 LMT
Begin Standard 100E21
1/Apr/1918 0:00 -6:41
Begin Standard 105E00
1/Nov/1932 0:00 -7:00
Begin Standard 135E00
19/Feb/1942 0:00 -9:00
Begin Standard 105E00
1/Aug/1945 0:00 -7:00
....
Time Table # 64
Before 1/Apr/1918 LMT
Begin Standard 100E21
1/Apr/1918 0:00 -6:41
Begin Standard 105E00
1/Nov/1932 0:00 -7:00
Begin Standard 135E00
30/Jan/1942 0:00 -9:00
Begin Standard 105E00
1/Aug/1945 0:00 -7:00
Begin Standard 97E30
1/May/1950 0:00 -6:30
Begin Standard 105E00
1/Jan/1964 0:00 -7:00
....
Time Table # 65
Before 1/Nov/1932 LMT
Begin Standard 100E21
1/Nov/1932 0:00 -6:41
Begin Standard 105E00
1/Nov/1932 0:00 -7:00
Begin Standard 135E00
30/Jan/1942 0:00 -9:00
Begin Standard 105E00
1/Aug/1945 0:00 -7:00
Begin Standard 97E30
1/May/1950 0:00 -6:30
Begin Standard 105E00
1/Jan/1964 0:00 -7:00
....
Time Table # 66
Before 1/Apr/1918 LMT
Begin Standard 100E21
1/Apr/1918 0:00 -6:41
Begin Standard 97E30
1/Nov/1932 0:00 -6:30
Begin Standard 135E00
28/Mar/1942 0:00 -9:00
Begin Standard 97E30
1/Aug/1945 0:00 -6:30
Begin Standard 105E00
1/May/1948 0:00 -7:00
Begin Standard 97E30
1/May/1950 0:00 -6:30
Begin Standard 105E00
1/Jan/1964 0:00 -7:00
....
Time Table # 67
Before 1/Nov/1932 LMT
Begin Standard 105E00
1/Nov/1932 0:00 -7:00
Begin Standard 135E00
30/Apr/1942 0:00 -9:00
Begin Standard 105E00
1/Aug/1945 0:00 -7:00
....
Time Table # 68
Before 1/Nov/1932 LMT
Begin Standard 97E30
1/Nov/1932 0:00 -6:30
Begin Standard 135E00
30/Apr/1942 0:00 -9:00
Begin Standard 97E30
1/Aug/1945 0:00 -6:30
Begin Standard 105E00
1/May/1948 0:00 -7:00
Begin Standard 97E30
1/May/1950 0:00 -6:30
Begin Standard 105E00
1/Jan/1964 0:00 -7:00
....
Time Table # 69
Before 1/Nov/1932 LMT
Begin Standard 97E30
1/Nov/1932 0:00 -6:30
Begin Standard 135E00
22/Apr/1942 0:00 -9:00
Begin Standard 97E30
1/Aug/1945 0:00 -6:30
Begin Standard 105E00
1/May/1948 0:00 -7:00
Begin Standard 97E30
1/May/1950 0:00 -6:30
Begin Standard 105E00
1/Jan/1964 0:00 -7:00
....
Time Table # 70
Before 1/Nov/1932 LMT
Begin Standard 105E00
1/Nov/1932 0:00 -7:00
Begin Standard 135E00
10/Apr/1942 0:00 -9:00
Begin Standard 105E00
1/Aug/1945 0:00 -7:00
....
Time Table # 71
Before 1/May/1908 LMT
Begin Standard 109E15
1/May/1908 0:00 -7:17
Begin Standard 112E30
1/Nov/1932 0:00 -7:30
Begin Standard 135E00
29/Jan/1942 0:00 -9:00
Begin Standard 112E30
1/Aug/1945 0:00 -7:30
Begin Standard 120E00
1/May/1948 0:00 -8:00
Begin Standard 112E30
1/May/1950 0:00 -7:30
Begin Standard 120E00
1/Jan/1964 0:00 -8:00
....
Time Table # 72
Before 1/May/1908 LMT
Begin Standard 109E15
1/May/1908 0:00 -7:17
Begin Standard 112E30
1/Nov/1932 0:00 -7:30
Begin Standard 135E00
6/Feb/1942 0:00 -9:00
Begin Standard 112E30
1/Aug/1945 0:00 -7:30
Begin Standard 120E00
1/May/1948 0:00 -8:00
Begin Standard 112E30
1/May/1950 0:00 -7:30
Begin Standard 120E00
1/Jan/1964 0:00 -8:00
....
Time Table # 73
Before 1/May/1908 LMT
Begin Standard 109E15
1/May/1908 0:00 -7:17
Begin Standard 112E30
1/Nov/1932 0:00 -7:30
Begin Standard 135E00
13/Feb/1942 0:00 -9:00
Begin Standard 112E30
1/Aug/1945 0:00 -7:30
Begin Standard 120E00
1/May/1948 0:00 -8:00
Begin Standard 112E30
1/May/1950 0:00 -7:30
Begin Standard 120E00
1/Jan/1964 0:00 -8:00
....
Time Table # 74
Before 1/May/1908 LMT
Begin Standard 109E15
1/May/1908 0:00 -7:17
Begin Standard 112E30
1/Nov/1932 0:00 -7:30
Begin Standard 135E00
24/Jan/1942 0:00 -9:00
Begin Standard 112E30
1/Aug/1945 0:00 -7:30
Begin Standard 120E00
1/May/1948 0:00 -8:00
Begin Standard 112E30
1/May/1950 0:00 -7:30
Begin Standard 120E00
1/Jan/1964 0:00 -8:00
....
Time Table # 75
Before 1/Nov/1932 LMT
Begin Standard 135E00
1/Nov/1932 0:00 -9:00
Begin Standard 142E30
1/May/1950 0:00 -9:30
Begin Standard 135E00
1/Jan/1964 0:00 -9:00
....
Time Table # 76
Before 1/Nov/1932 LMT
Begin Standard 135E00
1/Nov/1932 0:00 -9:00
Begin Standard 142E30
1/Feb/1949 0:00 -9:30
Begin Standard 135E00
1/Jan/1964 0:00 -9:00
....
Time Table # 77
Before 1/Nov/1932 LMT
Begin Standard 135E00
1/Nov/1932 0:00 -9:00
Begin Standard 142E30
1/May/1950 0:00 -9:30
Begin Standard 135E00
1/Jan/1964 0:00 -9:00
....
Time Table # 78
Before 1/Nov/1932 LMT
Begin Standard 127E30
1/Nov/1932 0:00 -8:30
Begin Standard 135E00
10/May/1942 0:00 -9:00
Begin Standard 127E30
1/Aug/1945 0:00 -8:30
Begin Standard 135E00
1/May/1948 0:00 -9:00
Begin Standard 127E30
1/May/1950 0:00 -8:30
Begin Standard 135E00
1/Jan/1964 0:00 -9:00
....
Time Table # 79
Before 1/Nov/1932 LMT
Begin Standard 127E30
1/Nov/1932 0:00 -8:30
Begin Standard 135E00
21/Feb/1942 0:00 -9:00
Begin Standard 127E30
1/Aug/1945 0:00 -8:30
Begin Standard 135E00
1/Feb/1949 0:00 -9:00
Begin Standard 127E30
1/May/1950 0:00 -8:30
Begin Standard 135E00
1/Jan/1964 0:00 -9:00
....
Time Table # 80
Before 1/Nov/1932 LMT
Begin Standard 127E30
1/Nov/1932 0:00 -8:30
Begin Standard 135E00
2/Feb/1942 0:00 -9:00
Begin Standard 127E30
1/Aug/1945 0:00 -8:30
Begin Standard 135E00
1/May/1948 0:00 -9:00
Begin Standard 127E30
1/May/1950 0:00 -8:30
Begin Standard 135E00
1/Jan/1964 0:00 -9:00
....
Time Table # 81
Before 1/Nov/1932 LMT
Begin Standard 112E30
1/Nov/1932 0:00 -7:30
Begin Standard 135E00
25/Feb/1942 0:00 -9:00
Begin Standard 112E30
1/Aug/1945 0:00 -7:30
Begin Standard 120E00
1/May/1948 0:00 -8:00
Begin Standard 112E30
1/May/1950 0:00 -7:30
Begin Standard 120E00
1/Jan/1964 0:00 -8:00
....
Time Table # 82
Before 1/Nov/1932 LMT
Begin Standard 105E00
1/Nov/1932 0:00 -7:00
Begin Standard 135E00
30/Apr/1942 0:00 -9:00
Begin Standard 105E00
10/Aug/1945 0:00 -7:00
....
Time Table # 83
Before 1/Jan/1920 LMT
Begin Standard 119E30
1/Jan/1920 0:00 -7:58
Begin Standard 120E00
1/Nov/1932 0:00 -8:00
Begin Standard 135E00
9/Feb/1942 0:00 -9:00
Begin Standard 120E00
1/Aug/1945 0:00 -8:00
....
Time Table # 84
Before 1/Jan/1920 LMT
Begin Standard 125E00
1/Jan/1920 0:00 -8:20
Begin Standard 120E00
1/Nov/1932 0:00 -8:00
Begin Standard 135E00
12/Jan/1942 0:00 -9:00
Begin Standard 120E00
1/Aug/1945 0:00 -8:00
....
Time Table # 85
Before 1/Nov/1932 LMT
Begin Standard 127E30
1/Nov/1932 0:00 -8:30
Begin Standard 135E00
12/Jan/1942 0:00 -9:00
Begin Standard 127E30
1/Aug/1945 0:00 -8:30
Begin Standard 120E00
1/May/1848 0:00 -8:00
....
Time Table # 86
Before 1/Jan/1920 LMT
Begin Standard 119E30
1/Jan/1920 0:00 -7:58
Begin Standard 120E00
1/Nov/1932 0:00 -8:00
Begin Standard 135E00
12/Jan/1942 0:00 -9:00
Begin Standard 120E00
1/Aug/1945 0:00 -8:00
....
Time Table # 87
Before 1/Nov/1932 LMT
Begin Standard 112E30
1/Nov/1932 0:00 -7:30
Begin Standard 135E00
13/May/1942 0:00 -9:00
Begin Standard 112E30
1/Aug/1945 0:00 -7:30
Begin Standard 120E00
1/May/1948 0:00 -8:00
Begin Standard 112E30
1/May/1950 0:00 -7:30
Begin Standard 120E00
1/Jan/1964 0:00 -8:00
....
Time Table # 88
Before 1/Nov/1932 LMT
Begin Standard 120E00
1/Nov/1932 0:00 -8:00
Begin Standard 135E00
13/May/1942 0:00 -9:00
Begin Standard 120E00
1/Aug/1945 0:00 -8:00
....
Time Table # 89
Before 1/Nov/1932 LMT
Begin Standard 120E00
1/Nov/1932 0:00 -8:00
Begin Standard 135E00
13/May/1942 0:00 -9:00
Begin Standard 120E00
1/Aug/1945 0:00 -8:00
Begin Standard 135E00
1/Feb/1949 0:00 -9:00
Begin Standard 120E00
1/May/1950 0:00 -8:00
....
Time Table # 90
Before 1/Jan/1912 LMT
Begin Standard 120E00
1/Jan/1912 0:00 -8:00
Begin Standard 135E00
21/Feb/1942 23:00 -9:00
Begin Standard 120E00
3/May/1976 0:00 -8:00
....
Time Table # 91
Before 1/Jan/1912 LMT
Begin Standard 120E00
1/Jan/1912 0:00 -8:00
Begin Standard 135E00
12/Mar/1943 23:00 -9:00
Begin Standard 120E00
3/May/1976 0:00 -8:00
....
Time Table # 92
Before 1/Nov/1932 LMT
Begin Standard 135E00
1/Nov/1932 0:00 -9:00
Begin Standard 142E30
1/Jan/1944 0:00 -9:30
Begin Standard 135E00
1/Jan/1964 0:00 -9:00
....
Time Table # 93
Before 1/Nov/1932 LMT
Begin Standard 127E30
1/Nov/1932 0:00 -8:30
Begin Standard 135E00
8/May/1942 0:00 -9:00
Begin Standard 127E30
1/Aug/1945 0:00 -8:30
Begin Standard 135E00
1/May/1948 0:00 -9:00
Begin Standard 127E30
1/May/1950 0:00 -8:30
Begin Standard 135E00
1/Jan/1964 0:00 -9:00

DIVISIONS

1. Bali
2. Bangka
3. Belitung
4. Borneo (Kalimantan)
5. Buru
6. Flores
7. Halmahera
8. Jawa (Java)
9. Kabaena
10. Kepulauan Alor (Pulau Alor)
11. Kepulauan Anambas
12. Kepulauan Aru
13. Kepulauan Banda
14. Kepulauan Banggai
15. Kepulauan Batu
16. Kepulauan Bowokan
17. Kepulauan Bunguran Selatan
18. Kepulauan Bunguran Utara
19. Kepulauan Kai
20. Kepulauan Kangean
21. Kepulauan Leti
22. Kepulauan Lingga
23. Kepulauan Mentawai
24. Kepulauan Sangihe
25. Kepulauan Schouten
26. Kepulauan Tanimbar
27. Kepulauan Togian
28. Kepulauan Tukangbesi
29. Lombok
30. Madura
31. Maluku
32. Muna
33. New Guinea (Irian Jaya)
34. Pulau Adonara
35. Pulau Babar
36. Pulau Bacan
37. Pulau Bawean
38. Pulau Bengkalis
39. Pulau Bintan
40. Pulau Butung
41. Pulau Damar
42. Pulau Enggano
43. Pulau Kalao
44. Pulau Kundur
45. Pulau Laut
46. Pulau Lomblen
47. Pulau Misool
48. Pulau Nias
49. Pulau Obi
50. Pulau Padang
51. Pulau Pantar
52. Pulau Rangsang
53. Pulau Rupat
54. Pulau Sebangka
55. Pulau Seleyar (Salayar)
56. Pulau Siberut
57. Pulau Simeulue
58. Pulau Singkep
59. Pulau Tanahjampea
60. Pulau Tebingtinggi
61. Pulau Waigeo
62. Pulau Wowoni
63. Pulau Yapen
64. Salawati
65. Seram (Ceram)
66. Sulawesi (Celebes)
67. Sumatera (Sumatra)
68. Sumba
69. Sumbawa
70. Timor (Timur)

Adaut 26	93	8S08	131E07	-8:44:28
Adiwerna 8	26	6S56	109E07	-7:16:28
Adua 47	75	1S55	129E50	-8:39:20
Aekhumbang 67	66	1N59	99E11	-6:36:44
Afia 48	69	1N25	97E30	-6:30:00
Afulu 48	69	1N20	97E14	-6:28:56
Agats 33	92	5S33	138E08	-9:12:32
Aimere 6	88	8S50	120E52	-8:03:28
Airbangis 67	66	0N12	99E23	-6:37:32
Airdikit 67	63	2S40	101E15	-6:45:00
Airgegas 2	70	2S42	106E25	-7:05:40
Airhaji 67	66	1S57	100E53	-6:43:32
Airjamban 67	64	1N13	101E14	-6:44:56
Airmolek 67	64	0S22	102E17	-6:49:08
Airtenang 67	63	3S08	101E43	-6:46:52
Airterjun 67	64	1N20	100E27	-6:41:48
Ajibarang 8	18	7S25	109E04	-7:16:16
Alahanpanjang 67	66	1S05	100E47	-6:43:08
Alas 69	88	8S32	117E00	-7:48:00
Alasan 16	84	1S45	123E19	-8:13:16
Aluedua 67	61	4N47	97E47	-6:31:08
Amahai 65	93	3S20	128E55	-8:35:40
Ambarawa 8	36	7S15	110E24	-7:21:36
Amboina → Ambon 65	93	3S43	128E12	-8:32:48
Ambon 65	80	3S43	128E12	-8:32:48
Ambulu 8	59	8S21	113E36	-7:34:24
Ambuntentimur 30	59	6S54	113E45	-7:35:00
Amburambur 29	87	8S15	116E18	-7:45:12
Ampana 66	86	0S51	121E32	-8:06:08
Ampang 69	88	8S47	118E00	-7:52:00
Ampel 8	36	7S27	110E32	-7:22:08
Amuntai 4	73	2S26	115E15	-7:41:00
Amurang 66	84	1N11	124E35	-8:18:20
Anabanua 66	83	3S57	120E04	-8:00:16
Angar 65	93	3S39	130E50	-8:43:20
Ansudu 33	92	2S08	139E20	-9:17:20
Ansus 63	76	1S44	135E49	-9:03:16
Anyer-Kidul 8	36	6S04	105E53	-7:03:32
Arandai 33	92	2S10	133E01	-8:52:04
Arjasa 20	60	6S51	115E16	-7:41:04
Arjawinangun 8	36	6S39	108E24	-7:13:36
Arosbaya 30	59	6S56	112E51	-7:31:24
Arwala 31	79	7S41	126E49	-8:27:16
Arzo 33	92	2S56	140E47	-9:23:08
Asembagus 8	59	7S45	114E14	-7:36:56
Atambua 70	89	9S07	124E54	-8:19:36
Atapupu 70	89	9S00	124E51	-8:19:24
Atkri 47	75	1S44	130E04	-8:40:16
Auponhia 31	78	1S56	125E29	-8:21:56
Awang 29	87	8S54	116E24	-7:45:36
Baa 70	89	10S43	123E03	-8:12:12
Baah 68	88	10S28	121E59	-8:07:56
Babat 67	63	2S45	103E38	-6:54:32
Babat 8	55	7S06	112E10	-7:28:40
Babelijamun 33	92	2S04	137E43	-9:10:52
Babo 33	92	2S33	133E25	-8:53:40
Bade 33	92	7S10	139E35	-9:18:20
Bagansiapi-Api 67	64	2N09	100E49	-6:43:16
Bagansinembah 67	64	1N46	100E29	-6:41:56
Bagansitukang 67	66	2N38	100E15	-6:41:00
Bahumbelu 66	86	2S13	121E41	-8:06:44
Baing 68	88	10S14	120E34	-8:02:16
Bajawa (Badjawa) 6	88	8S47	120E59	-8:03:56
Bajo 66	86	0N27	120E48	-8:03:12
Bajo 69	88	8S35	119E01	-7:56:04
Bajulmati 8	59	7S56	114E23	-7:37:32
Bake 23	68	3S03	100E16	-6:41:04
Bakem 2	70	1S58	105E54	-7:03:36
Bakumpai 4	73	1S26	113E05	-7:32:20
Bakungan 67	66	2N56	97E30	-6:30:00
Balaikarangan 4	71	0N50	110E26	-7:21:44
Balaiselasa 67	66	1S48	100E50	-6:43:20
Balaisepuah 4	73	0N27	111E13	-7:24:52
Balapulang 8	36	7S03	109E05	-7:16:20
Balaraja 8	36	6S12	106E27	-7:05:48
Balatan 12	77	6S05	134E45	-8:59:00
Balaurin 46	89	8S15	123E43	-8:14:52
Balige 67	66	2N20	99E04	-6:36:16
Balikpapan 4	74	1S17	116E50	-7:47:20
Balimbing 67	62	5S55	104E34	-6:58:16
Balong 8	59	7S57	111E26	-7:25:44
Bamol 33	92	7S38	138E37	-9:14:28
Bancahsaga 67	64	0N49	101E07	-6:44:28
Banda Aceh (Kutaraja) 67	61	5N34	95E20	-6:21:20
Banda Elat 19	77	5S39	132E59	-8:51:56
Bandanaira 13	93	4S32	129E54	-8:39:36
Bandar 8	36	7S02	109E47	-7:19:08
Bandardurian 67	66	2N21	99E44	-6:38:56
Bandarpulau 67	66	2N41	99E31	-6:38:04
Bandung (Bandoeng) 8	8	6S54	107E36	-7:10:24
Banggai (Luwuk) 14	84	1S34	123E30	-8:14:00
Bangil 8	38	7S36	112E47	-7:31:08
Bangkalan 30	59	7S02	112E44	-7:30:56
Bangkinang 67	64	0N21	101E02	-6:44:08
Bangkir 66	86	0N48	120E14	-8:00:56
Bangko 67	64	2S05	102E17	-6:49:08
Bangkulua 69	88	8S41	118E13	-7:52:52
Bangsri 8	36	6S30	110E45	-7:23:00
Bangunpurba 67	66	3N23	98E50	-6:35:20
Baniara 67	66	2N31	98E39	-6:34:36
Banjar 8	36	7S22	108E32	-7:14:08
Banjarmasin 4	73	3S20	114E35	-7:38:20
Banjarnegara 8	36	7S23	109E41	-7:18:44
Banjoemas → Banyumas 8	11	7S31	109E17	-7:17:08
Bantaian 67	64	1N56	100E54	-6:43:36
Bantarkawung 8	36	7S13	108E55	-7:15:40
Banten 8	32	6S03	106E09	-7:04:36
Bantul 8	2	7S54	110E20	-7:21:20
Banyumas 8	11	7S32	109E17	-7:17:08
Banyuwangi 8	58	8S12	114E21	-7:37:24
Banyuwedang 1	60	8S08	114E36	-7:38:24
Barabai 4	73	2S35	115E23	-7:41:32
Barangbarang 55	83	6S24	120E28	-8:01:52
Barapasi 33	92	2S07	137E00	-9:08:00
Barate 70	89	9S54	123E38	-8:14:32
Barhau 42	67	5S19	102E10	-6:48:40
Barma 33	92	1S54	133E00	-8:52:00
Barus 67	66	2N00	98E24	-6:33:36
Basiano 14	84	1S16	122E50	-8:11:20
Batakan 4	73	4S05	114E38	-7:38:32
Batang 8	24	6S55	109E45	-7:19:00
Batangbatangdaya 30	59	6S56	113E59	-7:35:56
Batangtoru 67	66	1N29	99E03	-6:36:12
Batu 8	40	7S52	112E31	-7:30:04
Batu-Batu 66	83	4S09	119E52	-7:59:28
Batubetumpang 2	70	2S53	106E09	-7:04:36
Batui 66	86	1S17	122E33	-8:10:12
Batuidu 70	89	10S38	123E25	-8:13:40
Batukelau 4	73	0N48	115E01	-7:40:04
Batulicin 4	73	3S27	116E00	-7:44:00
Batumelinggang 67	66	3N50	98E25	-6:33:40
Batupanjang 53	64	1N43	101E31	-6:46:04
Batuputih 4	72	1N24	118E29	-7:53:56
Baturaja 67	62	4S08	104E10	-6:56:40
Baturetno 8	36	7S59	110E56	-7:23:44
Baturotok 69	88	8S42	117E10	-7:48:40
Baturusa 2	70	2S02	106E07	-7:04:28
Batusangkar 67	66	0S27	100E35	-6:42:20
Batutinggi 4	73	1S55	113E19	-7:33:16
Baubau 40	83	5S28	122E38	-8:10:32
Baun 70	89	10S18	123E43	-8:14:52
Bawang 8	36	7S06	109E55	-7:19:40
Bawean 37	81	5S45	112E37	-7:30:28
Bayan 29	87	8S16	116E26	-7:45:44
Bayat 67	63	2S06	103E38	-6:54:32
Bayeuen 67	61	4N36	97E53	-6:31:32
Bayunglencir 67	63	2S03	103E41	-6:54:44
Bedinggong 2	70	2S42	106E13	-7:04:52
Bekancan 67	66	3N18	98E24	-6:33:36
Bekasi 8	10	6S14	106E59	-7:07:56
Belambanganumpu 67	62	4S54	105E03	-7:00:12
Belang 66	84	0N57	124E47	-8:19:08
Belawan 67	66	3N47	98E41	-6:34:44
Belinyu 2	70	1S38	105E46	-7:03:04
Benculuk 8	59	8S26	114E13	-7:36:52
Bengara 4	72	3N11	117E12	-7:48:48
Bengkalis 38	65	1N28	102E07	-6:48:28
Bengkayang 4	71	0N50	109E29	-7:17:56
Bengkulu (Benkoelen) 67	63	3S48	102E16	-6:49:04
Bengoi 65	93	3S01	130E12	-8:40:48
Benoa 1	60	8S46	115E13	-7:40:52
Benteng (Salayar) 55	83	6S08	120E27	-8:01:48
Beringin 67	63	3S41	104E18	-6:57:12
Besikama 70	89	9S36	124E57	-8:19:48
Besitang 67	66	4N02	98E12	-6:32:48
Besuki 8	59	7S45	113E41	-7:34:44
Betano 70	91	9S10	125E43	-8:22:52
Betung 67	63	2S50	104E14	-6:56:56
Betung 67	64	1S52	103E16	-6:53:04
Bikeru 66	83	5S15	120E07	-8:00:28
Bilato 66	84	0N32	122E38	-8:10:32
Bima 69	88	8S28	118E43	-7:54:52
Binanga 67	66	1N24	99E46	-6:39:04
Binjai 67	66	3N36	98E30	-6:34:00
Binjai 18	82	3N45	108E12	-7:12:48
Binjohara 67	66	2N12	98E12	-6:32:48
Bintauna 66	84	0N53	123E33	-8:14:12
Bintuhan 67	62	4S48	103E22	-6:53:28
Birab 33	92	6S12	138E25	-9:13:40
Bireuen 67	61	5N12	96E41	-6:26:44
Birufu 33	92	5S52	138E24	-9:13:36
Bitung 66	84	1N27	125E11	-8:20:44
Blangkejeren 67	66	3N59	97E20	-6:29:20
Blangpidie 67	66	3N45	96E51	-6:27:24
Blega 30	59	7S08	113E03	-7:32:12
Blitar 8	48	8S06	112E09	-7:28:36
Blongas 29	87	8S53	116E02	-7:44:08
Blora 8	17	6S57	111E25	-7:25:40
Boawai 6	88	8S46	121E10	-8:04:40
Boba 6	88	8S57	121E04	-8:04:16
Bobotsari 8	36	7S18	109E22	-7:17:28
Bogor 8	36	6S35	106E47	-7:07:08
Bohorok 67	66	3N30	98E12	-6:32:48
Boja 8	3	7S06	110E16	-7:21:04
Bojonegoro 8	57	7S09	111E52	-7:27:28
Bokong 70	89	9S58	124E04	-8:16:16
Bolaang Mongondow 66	84	0N56	124E10	-8:16:40
Bonai 67	64	1N16	100E52	-6:43:28
Bonandolok 67	66	1N47	98E48	-6:35:12
Bondowoso 8	59	7S55	113E49	-7:35:16
Bone 32	83	4S46	122E52	-8:11:28
Bonebone 66	83	2S36	120E33	-8:02:12
Bonelipu 40	83	4S50	123E11	-8:12:44
Bonelohe 55	83	5S48	120E27	-8:01:48
Boneogeh 43	83	7S16	120E48	-8:03:12
Bone → Watampone 66	83	4S32	120E20	-8:01:20
Bongka 66	86	0S58	121E27	-8:05:48
Bonjol 67	66	0S01	100E13	-6:40:52
Bonoi 33	92	1S51	137E48	-9:11:12
Bontang 4	72	0N08	117E30	-7:50:00
Bonthain 66	83	5S32	119E56	-7:59:44
Boroko 66	84	0N55	123E16	-8:13:04
Bosnik 25	76	1S10	136E14	-9:04:56
Boyoali 8	36	7S32	110E35	-7:22:20
Brebes 8	23	6S53	109E03	-7:16:12
Buapinang 66	83	4S46	121E34	-8:06:16
Buatan 67	64	0N44	101E51	-6:47:24
Buguba 33	92	3S41	137E30	-9:10:00
Bukitbatu 67	64	1N27	102E00	-6:48:00
Bukittinggi 67	66	0S19	100E22	-6:41:28
Bula 65	93	3S06	130E30	-8:42:00

Place			Lat.	Long.	Time
Buluduku	67	66	2N20	98E14	-6:32:56
Bulukumba	66	83	5S33	120E11	-8:00:44
Bululawang	8	51	8S05	112E38	-7:30:32
Bulupayung	67	66	1N38	99E11	-6:36:44
Bumbulan	66	84	0N29	122E04	-8:08:16
Bumiayu	8	36	7S15	109E00	-7:16:00
Bumijawa	8	36	7S10	109E07	-7:16:28
Bungamas	67	63	3S42	102E23	-6:49:32
Bungbulang	8	36	7S27	107E35	-7:10:20
Bungegep	33	92	7S48	139E52	-9:19:28
Bungku	66	86	2S33	121E58	-8:07:52
Bunguran Selatan	17	82	2N45	109E00	-7:16:00
Bunguran Utara	18	82	4N40	108E00	-7:12:00
Bunta	66	86	0S48	122E10	-8:08:40
Buntok	4	73	1S42	114E48	-7:39:12
Bunut	4	73	0N46	112E30	-7:30:00
Buol	66	86	1N10	121E26	-8:05:44
Bupul	33	92	7S31	140E52	-9:23:28
Butong	4	73	1S06	114E50	-7:39:20
Calang	67	61	4N38	95E34	-6:22:16
Camba	66	83	4S54	119E50	-7:59:20
Camplong	70	89	10S02	123E55	-8:15:40
Caruban	8	50	7S33	111E39	-7:26:36
Cenrana	66	83	3S18	118E50	-7:55:20
Cepu	8	36	7S09	111E35	-7:26:20
Cerenti	67	64	0S30	101E52	-6:47:28
Cereweh	69	88	8S52	116E51	-7:47:24
Cheribon → Cirebon	8	20	6S44	108E34	-7:14:16
Ciamis	8	36	7S20	108E21	-7:13:24
Ciandur	8	35	6S24	105E59	-7:03:56
Cianjur	8	36	6S49	107E08	-7:08:32
Ciawi	8	36	7S10	108E09	-7:12:36
Ciawi	8	36	6S40	106E50	-7:07:20
Ciawigebang	8	36	6S58	108E34	-7:14:16
Cibadak	8	36	6S53	106E46	-7:07:04
Cibaliung	8	36	6S46	105E51	-7:03:24
Cibatu	8	13	7S06	107E59	-7:11:56
Cibeber	8	36	6S56	107E07	-7:08:28
Cibinong	8	36	6S27	106E51	-7:07:24
Cicalengka	8	36	6S59	107E50	-7:11:20
Cicurug	8	36	6S47	106E47	-7:07:08
Cihara	8	36	6S52	106E06	-7:04:24
Cijulang	8	36	7S44	108E27	-7:13:48
Cikajang	8	36	7S22	107E47	-7:11:08
Cikalong-Kulon	8	36	6S42	107E12	-7:08:48
Cikampek	8	36	6S24	107E27	-7:09:48
Cikarang	8	25	6S15	107E09	-7:08:36
Cikatomas	8	36	7S37	108E15	-7:13:00
Cilacap	8	36	7S44	109E00	-7:16:00
Cilamaya	8	36	6S15	107E35	-7:10:20
Ciledug	8	36	6S54	108E44	-7:14:56
Cilegon	8	32	6S01	106E03	-7:04:12
Cililin	8	36	6S56	107E26	-7:09:44
Cilimus	8	20	6S52	108E29	-7:13:56
Cimahi	8	8	6S53	107E32	-7:10:08
Cimalaka	8	36	6S49	107E56	-7:11:44
Cimpu	66	83	3S25	120E22	-8:01:28
Ciomas	8	32	6S12	106E01	-7:04:04
Ciparay	8	36	7S03	107E43	-7:10:52
Cipatujah	8	36	7S45	108E00	-7:12:00
Ciranjang	8	36	6S49	107E14	-7:08:56
Cirebon	8	20	6S44	108E34	-7:14:16
Ciruas	8	32	6S06	106E13	-7:04:52
Cisarua	8	36	6S40	106E59	-7:07:56
Cisolok	8	36	6S57	106E26	-7:05:44
Ciwidey	8	36	7S06	107E27	-7:09:48
Comal	8	29	6S55	109E31	-7:18:04
Cubadak	67	66	0N19	100E00	-6:40:00
Cukas	58	67	0S25	104E18	-6:57:12
Curug	8	28	6S15	106E33	-7:06:12
Curup	67	63	3S28	102E32	-6:50:08
Daludalu	67	64	1N05	100E15	-6:41:00
Damaraja	8	36	6S55	108E05	-7:12:20
Dampelas → Sabang	66	86	0N11	119E51	-7:59:24
Dampit	8	59	8S13	112E45	-7:31:00
Danai	67	64	0N29	103E26	-6:53:44
Danompari	4	73	0N09	115E02	-7:40:08
Darap	4	73	1S13	112E03	-7:28:12
Datagenoyang	4	73	2N03	115E10	-7:40:40
Datumakuta	4	72	2N32	117E51	-7:51:24
Dayu	4	73	1S59	115E04	-7:40:16
Delanggu	8	9	7S37	110E41	-7:22:44
Delitua	67	66	3N30	98E41	-6:34:44
Demak	8	5	6S53	110E38	-7:22:32
Demta	33	92	2S20	140E08	-9:20:32
Dendang	3	70	3S05	107E54	-7:11:36
Denpasar	1	60	8S39	115E13	-7:40:52
Depok	8	36	6S24	106E50	-7:07:20
Dili	70	90	8S33	125E35	-8:22:20
Dima	48	69	1N21	97E25	-6:29:40
Djailolo → Jailolo	7	93	1N05	127E30	-8:30:00
Djakarta → Jakarta	8	1	6S10	106E48	-7:07:12
Djokjakarta → Yogyakarta	8	2	7S48	110E22	-7:21:28
Djokja → Yogyakarta	8	2	7S48	110E22	-7:21:28
Dobo	12	77	5S46	134E13	-8:56:52
Doka	12	77	6S39	134E15	-8:57:00
Dolokparibuan	67	66	3N01	98E39	-6:34:36
Dompu	69	88	8S32	118E28	-7:53:52
Donggala	66	86	0S40	119E44	-7:58:56
Donggi	66	86	1S33	122E15	-8:09:00
Dongi	66	86	2S02	121E28	-8:05:52
Dongkalang	66	86	0N10	120E06	-8:00:24
Doro	8	24	7S02	109E41	-7:18:44
Dorokempo	69	88	8S33	118E15	-7:53:00
Doromata	69	88	8S46	118E13	-7:52:52
Dosi	12	77	5S56	134E34	-8:58:16
Driorejo	8	37	7S21	112E37	-7:30:28
Dumai	67	64	1N41	101E27	-6:45:48
Dumaring	4	72	1N36	118E12	-7:52:48
Dumoga-Kecil	66	84	0N31	123E55	-8:15:40
Duriansebatang	4	71	0S47	109E56	-7:19:44
Ekas	29	87	8S53	116E27	-7:45:48
Eliase	26	93	8S21	130E47	-8:43:08
Enaratoli	33	92	3S55	136E21	-9:05:24
Ende	6	88	8S50	121E39	-8:06:36
Enrekang	66	83	3S34	119E47	-7:59:08
Fakfak	33	92	2S55	132E18	-8:49:12
Fort de Kock	67	66	0S10	100E22	-6:41:28
Galela	7	93	1N50	127E50	-8:31:20
Galis	30	59	7S08	113E33	-7:34:12
Galugur	67	66	2N34	99E39	-6:38:36
Gampongbatak	67	61	4N48	97E39	-6:30:36
Gani	7	93	0S47	128E13	-8:32:52
Gantung	3	70	2S58	108E09	-7:12:36
Garut	8	13	7S13	107E54	-7:11:36
Gedongdalem	67	62	5S04	105E25	-7:01:40
Gedongtataan	67	62	5S23	105E05	-7:00:20
Geliting	6	88	8S39	122E18	-8:09:12
Gemolong	8	36	7S24	110E50	-7:23:20
Gending	8	47	7S48	113E18	-7:33:12
Genteng	8	59	8S22	114E09	-7:36:36
Genting	67	66	3N42	98E10	-6:32:40
Genyem	33	92	2S46	140E12	-9:20:48
Geser	65	93	3S53	130E54	-8:43:36
Gesi	8	36	7S20	111E01	-7:24:04
Geudubang	67	61	4N54	97E23	-6:29:32
Geumpang	67	61	4N48	96E09	-6:24:36
Gianyar	1	60	8S32	115E20	-7:41:20
Gilimanuk	1	60	8S10	114E26	-7:37:44
Gimpu	66	86	1S36	120E02	-8:00:08
Godo	69	88	8S33	118E40	-7:54:40
Godong	8	12	7S02	110E46	-7:23:04
Gomogomo	12	77	6S40	134E43	-8:58:52
Gondang	8	36	7S24	111E06	-7:24:24
Goreda	33	92	3S39	134E58	-8:59:52
Gorontalo	66	84	0N33	123E03	-8:12:12
Grajagan	8	59	8S35	114E13	-7:36:52
Gratitunon	8	59	7S43	113E00	-7:32:00
Gresik	67	63	2S18	103E57	-6:55:48
Gresik	8	37	7S09	112E38	-7:30:32
Grisee → Gresik	8	37	7S09	112E38	-7:30:32
Grobogan	8	12	7S01	110E55	-7:23:40
Grokgak	1	60	8S11	114E47	-7:39:08
Gubug	8	15	7S03	110E40	-7:22:40
Gulukguluk	30	59	7S04	113E40	-7:34:40
Gundik	8	12	7S12	110E54	-7:23:36
Guntingsaga	67	66	2N33	99E39	-6:38:36
Guntung	67	64	1N38	101E34	-6:46:16
Gunungkencana	8	36	6S34	106E04	-7:04:16
Gunungmegang	67	63	3S27	103E52	-6:55:28
Gunungsahilan	67	64	0N06	101E18	-6:45:12
Gunungsitoli	48	69	1N17	97E37	-6:30:28
Gunungtua	67	66	1N30	99E37	-6:38:28
Gyebu	33	92	3S03	133E51	-8:55:24
Hanjalipan	4	73	2S15	112E47	-7:31:08
Har	19	77	5S20	133E10	-8:52:40
Hariarapitu	67	66	2N33	98E35	-6:34:20
Haya	65	93	3S27	129E33	-8:38:12
Hila	31	79	7S35	127E24	-8:29:36
Hilialawa	48	69	0N44	97E54	-6:31:36
Hiligeo	48	69	1N22	97E10	-6:28:40
Hiliotaluwa	48	69	0N44	97E53	-6:31:32
Hollandia → Jayapura	33	92	2S32	140E42	-9:22:48
Hulim	67	66	1N12	99E31	-6:38:04
Hutanopan	67	66	0N41	99E42	-6:38:48
Huu	69	88	8S48	118E25	-7:53:40
Ibonma	33	92	3S28	133E28	-8:53:52
Idi	67	61	4N57	97E46	-6:31:04
Idi-Cut	67	61	4N59	97E42	-6:30:48
Ilwaki	31	79	7S56	126E26	-8:25:44
Imogiri	8	2	7S55	110E23	-7:21:32
Inanwatan	33	92	2S08	132E10	-8:48:40
Indramayu	8	36	6S20	108E19	-7:13:16
Indrapuri	67	61	5N26	95E27	-6:21:48
Inobonto	66	84	0N52	123E57	-8:15:48
Intu	4	73	0S15	115E21	-7:41:24
Ipuh	67	63	3S00	101E30	-6:46:00
Irmauw	26	93	7S25	131E42	-8:46:48
Isak	67	61	4N28	96E55	-6:27:40
Ismu	66	84	0N40	122E51	-8:11:24
Jabung	67	62	5S29	105E40	-7:02:40
Jailolo	7	93	1N05	127E30	-8:30:00
Jakarta	8	1	6S10	106E48	-7:07:12
Jakenan	8	7	6S45	111E11	-7:24:44
Jambi	67	64	1S42	103E34	-6:54:16
Jampang-Kulon	8	36	7S16	106E37	-7:06:28
Jangeru	4	74	2S20	116E29	-7:45:56
Jangong	67	61	4N23	96E48	-6:27:12
Janlohong	4	72	2N15	117E03	-7:48:12
Japero → Yapero	33	92	4S59	137E11	-9:08:44
Jasinga	8	36	6S29	106E27	-7:05:48
Jatibarang	8	36	6S28	108E17	-7:13:08
Jatilawang	8	11	7S32	109E06	-7:16:24
Jatiroto	8	59	8S07	113E21	-7:33:24
Jatisrono	8	36	7S49	111E07	-7:24:28
Jatiwangi	8	36	6S44	108E15	-7:13:00
Jawi	4	71	0S48	109E16	-7:17:04
Jayapura (Sukarnapura)	33	92	2S32	140E42	-9:22:48
Jebus	2	70	1S44	105E29	-7:01:56
Jember	8	52	8S10	113E42	-7:34:48
Jeneponto	66	83	5S41	119E42	-7:58:48
Jenu	4	71	0S36	109E52	-7:19:28
Jepara	8	36	6S35	110E39	-7:22:36
Jernih	67	61	4N25	97E43	-6:30:52
Jeunieb	67	61	5N10	96E29	-6:25:56
Jimbaran	1	60	8S46	115E11	-7:40:44
Jojogan	8	59	6S58	111E46	-7:27:04
Jombang	8	43	7S33	112E14	-7:28:56
Jonggol	8	36	6S28	107E03	-7:08:12
Jorong	4	73	3S58	114E56	-7:39:44
Jumapolo	8	36	7S42	111E00	-7:24:00
Juring	12	77	6S26	134E20	-8:57:20
Juwana	8	7	6S42	111E09	-7:24:36
Juwangi	8	15	7S10	110E45	-7:23:00
Kabali	66	86	1S42	121E54	-8:07:36
Kabanjahe	67	66	3N06	98E30	-6:34:00
Kabinu	4	72	4N00	116E05	-7:44:20
Kabir	51	89	8S17	124E13	-8:16:52
Kadipaten	8	36	6S46	108E10	-7:12:40
Kai	33	92	2S15	136E32	-9:06:08
Kai Beab	33	92	7S29	139E40	-9:18:40
Kaimana	33	92	3S39	133E45	-8:55:00
Kaioba	32	83	5S20	122E37	-8:10:28
Kairatu	65	93	3S21	128E22	-8:33:28
Kaiwatu	21	93	8S07	127E49	-8:31:16
Kajang	66	83	5S20	120E21	-8:01:24
Kajen	8	36	7S02	109E34	-7:18:16
Kalabahi	10	89	8S13	124E31	-8:18:04
Kalakepen	67	66	2N45	97E50	-6:31:20
Kalampising	4	72	3N44	116E42	-7:46:48
Kalasin	4	73	0N12	114E16	-7:37:04
Kalianda	67	62	5S45	105E38	-7:02:32
Kalianget	30	59	7S03	113E56	-7:35:44
Kalijati	8	36	6S32	107E40	-7:10:40
Kalisat	8	57	8S08	113E48	-7:35:12
Kaliwiro	8	36	7S27	109E51	-7:19:24
Kaliwungu	8	3	6S57	110E14	-7:20:56
Kalolio	27	86	0S11	121E38	-8:06:32
Kaloran	8	36	7S15	110E15	-7:21:00
Kamal	30	59	7S10	112E42	-7:30:48
Kambang	67	66	1S42	100E42	-6:42:48
Kambu	69	88	8S23	118E20	-7:53:20
Kampungbaru	67	64	1S12	102E57	-6:51:48
Kampung Sailolof	64	92	1S15	130E46	-8:43:04
Kananggar	68	88	10S03	120E22	-8:01:28
Kandang	67	66	3N03	97E20	-6:29:20
Kandangan	4	73	2S47	115E16	-7:41:04
Kandanghaur	8	36	6S21	108E06	-7:12:24
Kansyat	33	92	2S15	138E51	-9:15:24
Kapan	70	89	9S44	124E17	-8:17:08
Karambu	45	73	3S51	116E04	-7:44:16
Karangagung	67	63	2S22	104E27	-6:57:48
Karangampel	8	36	6S28	108E27	-7:13:48
Karangasem	1	60	8S27	115E37	-7:42:28
Karangbinangun	8	54	7S01	112E30	-7:30:00
Karangbolong	8	36	7S45	109E28	-7:17:52
Karanggede	8	36	7S22	110E37	-7:22:28
Karangkobar	8	36	7S16	109E44	-7:18:56
Karangnunggal	8	36	7S38	108E06	-7:12:24
Karangpandan	8	36	7S37	111E04	-7:24:16
Karangsembung	8	20	6S51	108E39	-7:14:36
Karosa	66	83	1S48	119E20	-7:57:20
Kartosuro	8	9	7S33	110E44	-7:22:56
Karufa	33	92	3S50	133E27	-8:53:48
Karuni	68	88	9S26	119E19	-7:57:16
Kasimbar	66	86	0S09	120E00	-8:00:00
Kasungan	4	73	1S58	113E24	-7:33:36
Kawali	8	36	7S11	108E22	-7:13:28
Kawe	33	92	7S50	138E14	-9:12:56
Kawinda	69	88	8S07	118E04	-7:52:16
Kayaapu	42	67	5S26	102E24	-6:49:36
Kayeli	5	78	3S23	127E06	-8:28:24
Kayen	8	7	6S54	110E59	-7:23:56
Kayuagung	67	63	3S24	104E50	-6:59:20
Kayumas	8	59	7S50	114E08	-7:36:32
Kebanyartimur	30	59	7S09	112E52	-7:31:28
Kebumen	8	36	7S40	109E39	-7:18:36
Kedawung	8	20	6S42	108E31	-7:14:04
Kediri	8	44	7S49	112E01	-7:28:04
Kedungdung	30	59	7S06	113E15	-7:33:00
Kedungjati	8	15	7S10	110E37	-7:22:28
Kedungwuni	8	24	6S58	109E39	-7:18:36
Kefamenanu	70	89	9S27	124E29	-8:17:56
Kelantan	67	64	0N51	101E40	-6:46:40
Kelapa	2	70	1S52	105E42	-7:02:48
Kelolokan	4	72	1N08	117E54	-7:51:36
Kema	66	84	1N23	125E04	-8:20:16
Kembani	14	84	1S34	122E54	-8:11:36
Kendal	8	21	6S55	110E12	-7:20:48
Kendari	66	83	3S57	122E35	-8:10:20
Kendawangan	4	71	2S32	110E12	-7:20:48
Kepahiang	67	63	3S39	102E34	-6:50:16
Kepanjen	8	51	8S07	112E34	-7:30:16
Kepi	33	92	6S32	139E19	-9:17:16
Kepo	2	70	2S56	106E33	-7:06:12
Kerandin	22	67	0S12	104E46	-6:59:04
Keritang	67	64	0S51	102E39	-6:50:36

Place		Lat.	Long.	Time
Kertamulia 4	71	0S23	109E09	-7:16:36
Kertosono 8	43	7S35	112E06	-7:28:24
Ketapang 30	59	6S54	113E17	-7:33:08
Ketapang 67	62	5S44	105E48	-7:03:12
Ketapang 4	71	1S52	109E59	-7:19:56
Ketaun 67	63	3S23	101E49	-6:47:16
Keudemane 67	61	5N15	96E55	-6:27:40
Keudepasi 67	66	4N18	95E56	-6:23:44
Keudeteunom 67	61	4N27	95E48	-6:23:12
Keudeunga 67	61	5N01	95E22	-6:21:28
Kilo 69	88	8S21	118E24	-7:53:36
Kimaam 33	92	7S58	138E53	-9:15:32
Kinara 33	92	2S16	132E44	-8:50:56
Kindadal 14	84	1S35	123E11	-8:12:44
Kintamani 1	60	8S14	115E19	-7:41:16
Kintap 4	73	3S51	115E13	-7:40:52
Kisaran 67	66	2N59	99E37	-6:38:28
Klakah 8	59	7S59	113E15	-7:33:00
Klamono 33	92	1S08	131E30	-8:46:00
Klaten 8	36	7S42	110E35	-7:22:20
Kluang 67	63	2S41	103E54	-6:55:36
Klungkung 1	60	8S32	115E24	-7:41:36
Kluwang 46	89	8S31	123E17	-8:13:08
Koba 2	70	2S29	106E24	-7:05:36
Koepang → Kupang 70	89	10S10	123E35	-8:14:20
Koetaradja → Banda Aceh 67	61	5N34	95E20	-6:21:20
Kokas 33	92	2S42	132E26	-8:49:44
Kokonau 33	92	4S43	136E26	-9:05:44
Kola 12	77	5S26	134E29	-8:57:56
Kolaka 66	83	4S03	121E36	-8:06:24
Kolbano 70	89	10S02	124E31	-8:18:04
Kolono 66	83	4S18	122E41	-8:10:44
Kolonodale 66	83	2S00	121E19	-8:05:16
Komfane 12	77	5S39	134E44	-8:58:56
Komodo 6	88	8S35	119E30	-7:58:00
Kompot 66	84	0N24	124E10	-8:16:40
Konto 8	59	7S46	112E19	-7:29:16
Kopang 29	87	8S39	116E21	-7:45:24
Korido 25	76	0S50	135E35	-9:02:20
Korim 25	76	0S54	136E02	-9:04:08
Kotaagung 67	62	5S30	104E38	-6:58:32
Kotabaharu 4	73	0S48	111E33	-7:26:12
Kotabangun 4	72	0S16	116E35	-7:46:20
Kotabaru 67	66	1S08	101E43	-6:46:52
Kotabaru 45	73	3S14	116E13	-7:44:52
Kotabaru → Jayapura 33	92	2S32	140E42	-9:22:48
Kotabumi 67	62	4S50	104E54	-6:59:36
Kotabunan 66	84	0N49	124E38	-8:18:32
Kotadabok 58	67	0S30	104E33	-6:58:12
Kotamobagu 66	84	0N46	124E19	-8:17:16
Kotapinang 67	66	1N53	100E05	-6:40:20
Kotatengah 67	64	1N05	100E33	-6:42:12
Kotawaringin 4	73	2S29	111E25	-7:25:40
Kowa 33	92	7S53	140E32	-9:22:08
Kowangge 69	88	8S16	118E32	-7:54:08
Kragan 8	36	6S42	111E37	-7:26:28
Kraksaan 8	59	7S46	113E25	-7:33:40
Krapuh 67	66	3N39	98E10	-6:32:40
Krawang 8	25	6S19	107E17	-7:09:08
Kretek 8	36	7S59	110E19	-7:21:16
Krian 8	42	7S24	112E35	-7:30:20
Kroya 8	11	7S38	109E14	-7:16:56
Kruenggeukueh 67	61	5N15	97E02	-6:28:08
Kruengluak 67	66	2N50	97E45	-6:31:00
Krui 67	62	5S11	103E56	-6:55:44
Krumasye 33	92	1S40	133E09	-8:52:36
Kuala 67	66	3N32	98E24	-6:33:36
Kuala 11	82	2N55	105E48	-7:03:12
Kualabee 67	61	4N24	96E03	-6:24:12
Kualacenako 67	64	0S28	102E40	-6:50:40
Kualakapuas 4	73	3S01	114E21	-7:37:24
Kualakeriau 4	73	0N50	113E20	-7:33:20
Kualakurun 4	73	1S07	113E53	-7:35:32
Kualalangsa 67	61	4N32	98E01	-6:32:04
Kualamanjual 4	73	1S25	112E00	-7:28:00
Kualapesaguan 4	71	2S01	110E08	-7:20:32
Kualasimpang 67	66	4N17	98E03	-6:32:12
Kuandang 66	84	0N52	122E55	-8:11:40
Kubu 1	60	8S16	115E35	-7:42:20
Kubumesaai 4	73	1N31	115E06	-7:40:24
Kubutambahan 1	60	8S05	115E10	-7:40:40
Kudap 50	65	1N17	102E26	-6:49:44
Kudene 12	77	6S14	134E39	-8:58:36
Kudus 8	6	6S48	110E50	-7:23:20
Kumai 4	73	2S44	111E43	-7:26:52
Kumai 4	73	3S23	112E33	-7:30:12
Kumbe 33	92	8S21	140E13	-9:20:52
Kuningan 8	36	6S59	108E29	-7:13:56
Kupang 70	89	10S10	123E35	-8:14:20
Kutabaru 67	64	0S44	102E56	-6:51:44
Kutabuloh 67	66	3N28	97E04	-6:28:16
Kutacane 67	66	3N30	97E48	-6:31:12
Kutanibong 67	66	3N53	96E22	-6:25:28
Kutaradja → Banda Aceh 67	61	5N34	95E20	-6:21:20
Kutasawang 67	61	5N08	96E54	-6:27:36
Kutoarjo 8	11	7S43	109E54	-7:19:36
Kwatisore 33	92	3S15	134E57	-8:59:48
Labuha 36	93	0S37	127E29	-8:29:56
Labuhan 8	35	6S22	105E50	-7:03:20
Labuhanbajo 6	88	8S29	119E54	-7:59:36
Labuhanbatu 67	66	2N12	100E12	-6:40:48
Labuhanbilik 67	66	2N31	100E10	-6:40:40
Labuhanhaji 29	87	8S42	116E34	-7:46:16
Labuhanhaji 67	66	3N33	97E00	-6:28:00
Labuhanmarege 59	83	7S06	120E40	-8:02:40
Labuhanmaringgai 67	62	5S21	105E48	-7:03:12
Labuhanpandan 29	87	8S23	116E43	-7:46:52
Labuhanruku 67	66	3N13	99E35	-6:38:20
Labuhanwaiharu 67	62	5S44	104E26	-6:57:44
Labu Kananga 69	88	8S08	117E47	-7:51:08
Ladara 48	69	1N27	97E29	-6:29:56
Lageuen 67	61	4N44	95E31	-6:22:04
Laham 4	73	0N22	115E24	-7:41:36
Lahat 67	62	3S48	103E32	-6:54:08
Lahewa 48	69	1N24	97E11	-6:28:44
Lais 66	86	0N47	120E27	-8:01:48
Lais 67	63	3S32	102E03	-6:48:12
Laiwui 49	93	1S22	127E40	-8:30:40
Lalindi 68	88	10S12	120E10	-8:00:40
Laloa 66	83	4S50	121E54	-8:07:36
Lamdessar-Timur 26	93	7S12	131E58	-8:47:52
Lammeulo 67	61	5N15	95E56	-6:23:44
Lamongan 8	54	7S07	112E25	-7:29:40
Langara 62	83	4S02	123E00	-8:12:00
Langgam 67	64	0N15	101E43	-6:46:52
Langgapayung 67	66	1N43	99E59	-6:39:56
Langsa 67	61	4N28	97E58	-6:31:52
Laosolu 67	66	3N11	98E02	-6:32:08
Lape 69	88	8S39	117E37	-7:50:28
Larantuka 6	88	8S21	122E59	-8:11:56
Larat 26	93	7S09	131E45	-8:47:00
Lariang 66	83	1S26	119E17	-7:57:08
Larona 66	83	2S45	121E20	-8:05:20
Lasan 4	73	1N14	115E13	-7:40:52
Lasem 8	31	6S42	111E26	-7:25:44
Lasolo 66	83	3S29	122E04	-8:08:16
Latuna 51	89	8S23	124E06	-8:16:24
Lautem 70	91	8S24	126E22	-8:25:28
Lawang 8	39	7S49	112E42	-7:30:48
Lawatu 66	83	2S53	120E18	-8:01:12
Lawele 40	83	5S13	122E57	-8:11:48
Laweueng 67	61	5N31	95E52	-6:23:28
Lawowa 40	83	4S26	122E56	-8:11:44
Lebongtandai 67	63	3S01	101E54	-6:47:36
Leça 70	91	8S45	126E34	-8:26:16
Ledo 4	71	1N02	109E36	-7:18:24
Lekitobi 31	78	1S58	124E33	-8:18:12
Leles 8	13	7S07	107E53	-7:11:32
Lelewau 66	83	3S02	121E05	-8:04:20
Lelingluang 26	93	7S09	131E43	-8:46:52
Lelintah 47	75	2S03	130E16	-8:41:04
Lelogama 70	89	9S44	123E57	-8:15:48
Lemahabang 8	36	6S17	107E27	-7:09:48
Lembak 4	72	0N52	117E32	-7:50:08
Lembang 8	8	6S49	107E36	-7:10:24
Lemoro 66	86	1S25	121E05	-8:04:20
Lempe 66	86	1S40	120E14	-8:00:56
Lemutan 4	73	3N03	115E49	-7:43:16
Lenangguar 69	88	8S44	117E24	-7:49:36
Lengkong 8	45	7S32	112E04	-7:28:16
Lenmalu 47	75	1S44	130E13	-8:40:52
Lereh 33	92	3S08	139E54	-9:19:36
Letong 11	82	2N58	105E42	-7:02:48
Leuwiliang 8	36	6S34	106E37	-7:06:28
Lewapaku 68	88	9S43	119E55	-7:59:40
Lewoleba 46	89	8S23	123E24	-8:13:36
Lhokkruet 67	61	4N52	95E24	-6:21:36
Lhoknga 67	61	5N29	95E15	-6:21:00
Lhokseumawe 67	61	5N10	97E08	-6:28:32
Lhoksukon 67	61	5N03	97E19	-6:29:16
Liang 65	80	3S30	128E19	-8:33:16
Liangbuaya 4	72	0N05	116E46	-7:47:04
Liburung 66	83	3S55	120E09	-8:00:36
Liki 67	66	1S36	101E11	-6:44:44
Likupang 66	84	1N41	125E04	-8:20:16
Limapuluh 67	66	3N10	99E26	-6:37:44
Limas 54	67	0N14	104E31	-6:58:04
Limboto 66	84	0N37	122E57	-8:11:48
Liopa 31	79	7S40	126E00	-8:24:00
Lipatkain 67	64	0S01	101E13	-6:44:52
Liwa 67	62	5S04	104E06	-6:56:24
Lobo 33	92	3S45	134E05	-8:56:20
Lodoyo 8	48	8S10	112E13	-7:28:52
Lombagin 66	84	0N55	124E04	-8:16:16
Lombok 29	87	8S30	116E40	-7:46:40
Longbangun 4	73	0N36	115E11	-7:40:44
Longbeleh 4	72	0N16	116E11	-7:44:44
Longguntur 4	73	0N13	112E12	-7:28:48
Longiram 4	73	0S02	115E38	-7:42:32
Longnawan 4	73	1N54	114E53	-7:39:32
Longsegah 4	72	2N15	116E42	-7:46:48
Longwai 4	72	0N42	116E39	-7:46:36
Losarang 8	36	6S24	108E10	-7:12:40
Lotak 4	73	0S11	115E54	-7:43:36
Luaha-Sibuha 15	79	0S31	98E28	-6:33:52
Luan Balu 57	69	2N38	96E13	-6:24:52
Lubu 66	86	0S46	122E30	-8:10:00
Lubukambacang 67	64	0S37	101E25	-6:45:40
Lubukbatang 67	62	4S03	104E12	-6:56:48
Lubukbertubung 67	64	0N02	102E08	-6:48:32
Lubuklinggau 67	63	3S18	102E52	-6:51:28
Lubukpakam 67	66	3N33	98E52	-6:35:28
Lubuksikaping 67	66	0N08	100E10	-6:40:40
Lumajang 8	59	8S08	113E13	-7:32:52
Lumbanganjang 67	66	2N22	98E43	-6:34:52
Lumbangaraga 67	66	1N53	99E04	-6:36:16
Lumbanlobu 67	66	2N31	99E08	-6:36:32
Lumbis 4	72	4N18	116E15	-7:45:00
Lumu 66	83	2S11	119E09	-7:56:36
Lunyuk 69	88	8S57	117E14	-7:48:56
Luwuk 66	86	0S56	122E47	-8:11:08
Luwuk → Banggai 14	84	1S34	123E30	-8:14:00
Mabau 4	73	2S14	111E54	-7:27:36
Madiun (Madioen) 8	50	7S37	111E31	-7:26:04
Magelang 8	27	7S28	110E13	-7:20:52
Magetan 8	59	7S39	111E20	-7:25:20
Majalengka 8	36	6S50	108E13	-7:12:52
Majenang 8	36	7S18	108E45	-7:15:00
Majene 66	83	3S33	118E57	-7:55:48
Makale 66	83	3S06	119E51	-7:59:24
Makasar → Ujung Pandang 66	83	5S07	119E24	-7:57:36
Maki 33	92	3S11	134E14	-8:56:56
Malamala 66	83	3S21	120E55	-8:03:40
Malang 8	40	7S59	112E37	-7:30:28
Malik 33	92	0S34	123E14	-8:12:56
Malili 66	83	2S38	121E06	-8:04:24
Malinau 4	72	3N35	116E38	-7:46:32
Malingping 8	36	6S46	106E01	-7:04:04
Malino 66	83	5S15	119E51	-7:59:24
Malunda 66	83	3S00	118E50	-7:55:20
Mamasa 66	83	2S56	119E22	-7:57:28
Mamehaktebo 4	73	0N08	115E32	-7:42:08
Mamuju 66	83	2S41	118E54	-7:55:36
Manado 66	84	1N29	124E51	-8:19:24
Manatang 10	89	8S26	124E28	-8:17:52
Mandiangin 67	64	2S01	102E58	-6:51:52
Manggar 3	70	2S53	108E16	-7:13:04
Manggeng 67	66	3N36	96E55	-6:27:40
Manggonggri 33	92	3S30	133E19	-8:53:16
Mangkutana 66	83	2S24	120E48	-8:03:12
Mangsang 67	63	2S10	104E00	-6:56:00
Manna 67	62	4S27	102E55	-6:51:40
Manokwari 33	92	0S52	134E05	-8:56:20
Mantok 14	84	1S09	123E14	-8:12:56
Maospati 8	50	7S36	111E26	-7:25:44
Mapaga 66	86	0S06	119E48	-7:59:12
Mapan 4	73	2S21	111E10	-7:24:40
Mapane 66	86	1S24	120E40	-8:02:40
Mapi 33	92	7S07	139E23	-9:17:32
Mapida 66	86	0S33	119E46	-7:59:04
Marabahan 4	73	3S00	114E45	-7:39:00
Marek 66	83	4S48	120E21	-8:01:24
Mariar 33	92	2S48	132E50	-8:51:20
Marintu 4	71	0N34	110E00	-7:20:00
Marisa 66	84	0N28	121E56	-8:07:44
Marlasi 12	77	5S30	134E38	-8:58:32
Maros 66	83	5S00	119E34	-7:58:16
Martapura 67	62	4S19	104E22	-6:57:28
Martapura 4	73	3S25	114E51	-7:39:24
Masamba 66	83	2S32	120E20	-8:01:20
Masapun 31	79	7S47	126E38	-8:26:32
Masaran 8	9	7S28	110E55	-7:23:40
Masihi 67	66	2N47	99E40	-6:38:40
Masin 33	92	6S15	139E19	-9:17:16
Mata 6	88	8S12	122E56	-8:11:44
Matan 4	71	1S52	110E00	-7:20:00
Mataram 29	87	8S35	116E07	-7:44:28
Matobe 23	68	2S42	100E11	-6:40:44
Matua 4	71	2S59	110E45	-7:23:00
Maubara 70	91	8S37	125E12	-8:20:48
Mauk 8	28	6S04	106E30	-7:06:00
Maumere 6	88	8S37	122E14	-8:08:56
Mawasangka 32	83	5S17	122E18	-8:09:12
Mayung 60	65	0N46	103E03	-6:52:12
Mborong 6	88	8S49	120E37	-8:02:28
Medan 67	66	3N35	98E40	-6:34:40
Medang 53	64	2N06	101E38	-6:46:32
Meester Cornelis 8	1	6S12	106E51	-7:07:24
Mega 33	92	0S41	131E53	-8:47:32
Mehakit 4	73	2S51	115E57	-7:43:48
Meliau 4	71	0S08	110E18	-7:21:12
Melolo 68	88	9S53	120E40	-8:02:40
Memala 4	73	1S44	112E36	-7:30:24
Membalong 3	70	3S09	107E38	-7:10:32
Memboro 68	88	9S22	119E32	-7:58:08
Mempawah 4	71	0N22	108E58	-7:15:52
Menado → Manado 66	84	1N29	124E51	-8:19:24
Menate 4	73	0S14	113E02	-7:32:08
Mendawai 4	73	2S59	113E16	-7:33:04
Mendaya 1	60	8S23	114E42	-7:38:48
Mendung 67	64	0N31	103E13	-6:52:52
Menes 8	35	6S23	105E55	-7:03:40
Menggala 67	62	4S28	105E17	-7:01:08
Meno 33	92	3S52	135E31	-9:02:04
Merah 4	72	0N50	116E48	-7:47:12
Merakurak 8	59	6S53	111E59	-7:27:56
Meranggau 4	71	0S12	110E17	-7:21:08
Merauke 33	92	8S28	140E20	-9:21:20
Merbau 60	65	1N07	102E33	-6:50:12
Meskum 38	65	1N34	102E01	-6:48:04
Metro 67	62	5S05	105E20	-7:01:20
Meulaboh 67	66	4N09	96E08	-6:24:32
Meureudu 67	61	5N16	96E16	-6:25:04

Meyanodas 26	93	7S38	131E38	-8:46:32
Minas 67	64	0N50	101E29	-6:45:56
Mindiptana 33	92	5S45	140E42	-9:22:48
Modowi 33	92	4S05	134E39	-8:58:36
Mojoagung 8	42	7S34	112E21	-7:29:24
Mojokerto 8	42	7S28	112E26	-7:29:44
Mojosari 8	42	7S31	112E33	-7:30:12
Molibagu 66	84	0N23	123E59	-8:15:56
Mombum 33	92	8S23	138E51	-9:15:24
Mondeodo 66	83	3S33	122E12	-8:08:48
Monse 62	83	4S07	123E15	-8:13:00
Monterado 4	71	0N45	109E08	-7:16:32
Morowali 66	86	1S52	121E30	-8:06:00
Moutong 66	86	0N28	121E13	-8:04:52
Mranggen 8	1	7S01	110E31	-7:22:04
Mualang 4	73	0N42	111E18	-7:25:12
Muaraaman 67	63	3S07	102E12	-6:48:48
Muaraancalung 4	72	0N27	116E41	-7:46:44
Muarabeliti 67	63	3S15	103E02	-6:52:08
Muarabenangin 4	73	0S58	115E19	-7:41:16
Muarabinuangeun 8	36	6S50	105E53	-7:03:32
Muarabulian 67	64	1S43	103E15	-6:53:00
Muarabungo 67	64	1S28	102E07	-6:48:28
Muaradua 67	62	4S32	104E05	-6:56:20
Muaraenim 67	63	3S39	103E48	-6:55:12
Muaragusung 4	72	1N35	117E17	-7:49:08
Muarajuloi 4	73	0S12	114E03	-7:36:12
Muarakaman 4	72	0S09	116E43	-7:46:52
Muarakelingi 67	63	3S05	103E14	-6:52:56
Muarakumpe 67	64	1S24	104E00	-6:56:00
Muaralabuh 67	66	1S29	101E03	-6:44:12
Muaralakitan 67	63	2S51	103E19	-6:53:16
Muaralasan 4	72	1N48	117E12	-7:48:48
Muaralembu 67	64	0S24	101E21	-6:45:24
Muaramawai 4	72	0N37	116E49	-7:47:16
Muarapangean 4	72	2N38	116E41	-7:46:44
Muarapantai 67	64	0S45	101E43	-6:46:52
Muarapayang 4	73	1S32	115E48	-7:43:12
Muararupit 67	63	2S44	102E54	-6:51:36
Muarasabak 67	64	1S08	103E51	-6:55:24
Muarasiberut 56	69	1S36	99E11	-6:36:44
Muarasipongi 67	66	0N37	99E51	-6:39:24
Muaratebo 67	64	1S30	102E26	-6:49:44
Muarateladang 67	63	2S50	103E58	-6:55:52
Muaratembesi 67	64	1S42	103E07	-6:52:28
Muaratewe 4	73	0S57	114E53	-7:39:32
Muaratuhup 4	73	0S37	114E50	-7:39:20
Muaratunan 4	74	1S24	116E39	-7:46:36
Muarawahau 4	72	1N02	116E52	-7:47:28
Mukomuko 67	63	2S35	101E07	-6:44:28
Mukusaki 6	88	8S33	121E37	-8:06:28
Muncar 8	59	8S26	114E20	-7:37:20
Munte 66	86	0N30	119E55	-7:59:40
Muntok 2	70	2S04	105E11	-7:00:44
Murana 33	92	3S33	133E49	-8:55:16
Muting 33	92	7S23	140E20	-9:21:20
Muturi 33	92	2S06	133E43	-8:54:52
Nabire 33	92	3S22	135E29	-9:01:56
Nahabuan 4	73	0N49	114E05	-7:36:20
Naikliu 70	89	9S30	123E50	-8:15:20
Naivos 57	69	2N30	96E10	-6:24:40
Namber 33	92	1S04	134E49	-8:59:16
Nameh 4	72	2N34	116E21	-7:45:24
Namlea 5	78	3S18	127E06	-8:28:24
Namo 66	86	1S24	119E57	-7:59:48
Nangabadau 4	73	1N02	111E54	-7:27:36
Nangahale 6	88	8S34	122E32	-8:10:08
Nangakelawit 4	73	0N23	112E26	-7:29:44
Nangalangki 4	73	1S15	111E40	-7:26:40
Nangamau 4	73	0S06	111E55	-7:27:40
Nangamuntatai 4	73	0S22	112E23	-7:29:32
Nangaobat 4	73	0N57	113E13	-7:32:52
Nangapinoh 4	73	0S20	111E44	-7:26:56
Nangaraun 4	73	0N38	113E11	-7:32:44
Nangatayap 4	71	1S32	110E34	-7:22:16
Nanggulan 8	11	7S46	110E12	-7:20:48
Napaku 4	73	2N32	115E58	-7:43:52
Napido 25	76	0S41	135E23	-9:01:32
Napu 68	88	9S24	119E56	-7:59:44
Natal 67	66	0N33	99E07	-6:36:28
Ndona 6	88	8S46	121E45	-8:07:00
Negara 4	73	2S37	115E06	-7:40:24
Negara 1	60	8S22	114E37	-7:38:28
Negeribatin 67	62	4S35	104E32	-6:58:08
Nembrala 70	89	10S53	122E50	-8:11:20
Neuheum 67	61	5N34	95E32	-6:22:08
Ngabang 4	71	0N23	109E57	-7:19:48
Ngadirojo 8	59	8S13	111E19	-7:25:16
Ngalipaeng 24	85	3N24	125E37	-8:22:28
Nganjuk 8	45	7S36	111E55	-7:27:40
Ngawen 8	17	7S00	111E18	-7:25:12
Ngawi 8	59	7S24	111E26	-7:25:44
Ngebel 8	59	7S46	111E37	-7:26:28
Ngimbang 8	59	7S17	112E12	-7:28:48
Ngoro 8	59	7S41	112E16	-7:29:04
Ngunut 8	48	8S06	112E01	-7:28:04
Nikiniki 70	89	9S49	124E28	-8:17:52
Nime 33	92	4S45	136E32	-9:06:08
Nita 6	88	8S40	122E11	-8:08:44
Nitibe 70	89	9S19	124E12	-8:16:48
Nova Anadia 70	91	8S56	125E52	-8:23:28
Nova Sagres 70	91	8S24	127E15	-8:29:00
Ocussi 70	89	9S12	124E21	-8:17:24
Oholtom 19	77	5S56	132E41	-8:50:44
Okaba 33	92	8S06	139E42	-9:18:48
Omatena 68	88	9S53	119E47	-7:59:08
Onolimbu 48	69	1N05	97E53	-6:31:32
Oreng 67	66	4N03	97E28	-6:29:52
Pabean 20	60	6S50	115E19	-7:41:16
Paca 6	88	8S29	120E11	-8:00:44
Pacet 8	36	6S45	107E03	-7:08:12
Paciran 8	59	6S52	112E20	-7:29:20
Pacitan 8	59	8S12	111E07	-7:24:28
Padang 67	66	0S57	100E21	-6:41:24
Padang 4	71	1S39	108E55	-7:15:40
Padang 11	82	2N59	105E40	-7:02:40
Padang 55	83	6S11	120E26	-8:01:44
Padangbetuah 67	63	3S39	102E13	-6:48:52
Padangpanjang 67	66	0S27	100E25	-6:41:40
Padangsidempuan 67	66	1N22	99E16	-6:37:04
Padangtiji 67	61	5N22	95E50	-6:23:20
Padas 8	59	7S25	111E32	-7:26:08
Pagadenbaru 8	36	6S28	107E48	-7:11:12
Pagaralam 67	62	4S01	103E16	-6:53:04
Pagaran Tonga 67	66	1N14	99E46	-6:39:04
Pagatan 4	73	3S36	115E56	-7:43:44
Pagerdewa 67	63	3S46	105E18	-7:01:12
Painan 67	66	1S21	100E34	-6:42:16
Paiton 8	59	7S43	113E30	-7:34:00
Pakanbaru 67	64	0N32	101E27	-6:45:48
Palangkaraya 4	73	2S16	113E56	-7:35:44
Paleleh 66	86	1N04	121E57	-8:07:48
Palembang 67	63	2S55	104E45	-6:59:00
Palima 66	83	4S20	120E22	-8:01:28
Palimanan 8	20	6S42	108E26	-7:13:44
Paloh 4	71	1N43	109E18	-7:17:12
Palopo 66	83	3S00	120E12	-8:00:48
Palu 66	86	0S53	119E53	-7:59:32
Pamaluan 4	74	1S04	116E39	-7:46:36
Pamangkat 4	71	1N10	108E58	-7:15:52
Pamanukan 8	36	6S16	107E49	-7:11:16
Pamarayan 8	30	6S16	106E17	-7:05:08
Pamekasan 30	59	7S10	113E28	-7:33:52
Pamenang 67	64	2S07	102E31	-6:50:04
Pameungpeuk 8	36	7S38	107E43	-7:10:52
Pamotan 8	31	6S46	111E29	-7:25:56
Pampanua 66	83	4S14	120E08	-8:00:32
Panahan 4	73	1S44	111E49	-7:27:16
Panarukan 8	41	7S42	113E56	-7:35:44
Pandakan 8	38	7S39	112E41	-7:30:44
Pandeglang 8	30	6S18	106E06	-7:04:24
Pangandaran 8	36	7S41	108E39	-7:14:36
Pangian 66	83	1S06	119E24	-7:57:36
Pangkah 8	23	6S58	109E10	-7:16:40
Pangkajene 66	83	4S50	119E32	-7:58:08
Pangkalanberandan 67	66	4N01	98E17	-6:33:08
Pangkalanbuun 4	73	2S41	111E37	-7:26:28
Pangkalansusu 67	66	4N06	98E14	-6:32:56
Pangkalpinang 2	70	2S08	106E08	-7:04:32
Pangkatan 67	66	2N09	100E00	-6:40:00
Pangururan 67	66	2N37	98E42	-6:34:48
Panjang 67	62	5S28	105E18	-7:01:12
Panji 67	66	2N34	97E50	-6:31:20
Panopah 4	73	1S56	111E11	-7:24:44
Pantonlabu 67	61	5N08	97E28	-6:29:52
Panyabungan 67	66	0N51	99E33	-6:38:12
Papalia 28	83	5S58	124E01	-8:16:04
Papar 8	44	7S41	112E04	-7:28:16
Parado 69	88	8S45	118E36	-7:54:24
Parakan 8	36	7S17	110E06	-7:20:24
Parara 66	83	2S37	120E07	-8:00:28
Parbakalan 67	66	2N38	98E27	-6:33:48
Parburuan 67	66	1N52	99E55	-6:39:40
Pardomuan 67	66	2N06	98E20	-6:33:20
Pare 8	59	7S46	112E11	-7:28:44
Parepare 66	83	4S01	119E38	-7:58:32
Pargarutan 67	66	1N28	99E20	-6:37:20
Parhebangan 67	66	2N15	98E45	-6:35:00
Pariaman 67	66	0S38	100E08	-6:40:32
Parigi 8	36	6S12	106E22	-7:05:28
Parigi 66	86	0S48	120E10	-8:00:40
Parit 67	63	3S10	104E38	-6:58:32
Pariti 70	89	10S01	123E43	-8:14:52
Parsoburan 67	66	2N19	99E20	-6:37:20
Parung 8	36	6S25	106E42	-7:06:48
Pasangkayu 66	83	1S10	119E20	-7:57:20
Pasarbantal 67	63	2S45	101E20	-6:45:20
Pasarseluma 67	62	4S09	102E32	-6:50:08
Pasarwajo 40	83	5S29	122E50	-8:11:20
Pasirganting 67	66	2S02	100E53	-6:43:32
Pasirian 8	59	8S13	113E06	-7:32:24
Pasirpengarayan 67	64	0N51	100E16	-6:41:04
Pasuruan 8	49	7S38	112E54	-7:31:36
Pati 8	7	6S45	111E01	-7:24:04
Pati 4	73	0S33	111E19	-7:25:16
Pauh 67	64	2S08	102E48	-6:51:12
Payadapu 67	66	3N05	97E23	-6:29:32
Payakumbuh 67	66	0S14	100E38	-6:42:32
Payangan 1	60	8S26	115E15	-7:41:00
Payeti 68	88	9S41	120E20	-8:01:20
Pecangakan 8	36	6S41	110E42	-7:22:48
Pecatu 1	60	8S50	115E07	-7:40:28
Pekalongan 8	24	6S53	109E40	-7:18:40
Pekanheran 67	64	0S21	102E26	-6:49:44
Pelabuhandagaung 67	64	1S08	103E05	-6:52:20
Pelabuhanratu 8	36	6S59	106E33	-7:06:12
Pelaihari 4	73	3S48	114E45	-7:39:00
Pelalawan 67	64	0N27	102E05	-6:48:20
Pemalang 8	29	6S54	109E22	-7:17:28
Pematang 67	64	0S12	102E04	-6:48:16
Pematangsiantar 67	66	2N57	99E03	-6:36:12
Pematangtanahjawa 67	66	2N53	99E12	-6:36:48
Pembuang 4	73	2S34	112E19	-7:29:16
Pendang 4	73	1S28	114E51	-7:39:24
Pendeng 67	66	4N06	97E36	-6:30:24
Pendolo 66	86	2S05	120E42	-8:02:48
Pendopo 67	63	3S17	103E52	-6:55:28
Penebel 1	60	8S25	115E09	-7:40:36
Pengastulan 1	60	8S11	114E55	-7:39:40
Peninjai 67	64	1S26	101E50	-6:47:20
Penuba 58	67	0S20	104E28	-6:57:52
Penuguan 67	63	2S27	104E31	-6:58:04
Perabumulih 67	63	3S27	104E15	-6:57:00
Perigiraja 67	64	0S16	103E30	-6:54:00
Peudada 67	61	5N12	96E35	-6:26:20
Peureulak 67	61	4N48	97E53	-6:31:32
Pinrang 66	83	3S48	119E38	-7:58:32
Pionierbivak 33	92	2S16	138E02	-9:12:08
Piru 65	93	3S04	128E12	-8:32:48
Pising 9	83	5S05	121E54	-8:07:36
Plampang 69	88	8S48	117E48	-7:51:12
Plered 8	34	6S38	107E23	-7:09:32
Plumbon 8	20	6S42	108E28	-7:13:52
Podi 66	86	1S08	121E16	-8:05:04
Poh 66	86	0S46	122E49	-8:11:16
Poleang 66	83	4S42	121E46	-8:07:04
Polewali 66	83	3S25	119E20	-7:57:20
Pono 12	77	6S22	134E36	-8:58:24
Ponorogo 8	59	7S52	111E27	-7:25:48
Pontianak 4	71	0S02	109E20	-7:17:20
Popoh 8	59	8S15	111E48	-7:27:12
Porong 8	42	7S32	112E41	-7:30:44
Porsea 67	66	2N27	99E09	-6:36:36
Poso (Posso) 66	86	1S23	120E44	-8:02:56
Pota 6	88	8S20	120E46	-8:03:04
Praikalogu 68	88	9S45	119E25	-7:57:40
Prajekan 8	41	7S47	113E59	-7:35:56
Prambanan 8	2	7S45	110E30	-7:22:00
Prapat 67	66	2N40	98E56	-6:35:44
Praya 29	87	8S42	116E17	-7:45:08
Prembun 8	11	7S43	109E48	-7:19:12
Pringgabaja 29	87	8S34	116E37	-7:46:28
Probolinggo 8	47	7S45	113E13	-7:32:52
Pujon 8	59	7S50	112E28	-7:29:52
Pujun 4	73	1S20	114E20	-7:37:20
Pujut 67	64	1N25	100E39	-6:42:36
Pulangpisau 4	73	2S46	114E14	-7:36:56
Pulaukida 67	63	2S44	102E34	-6:50:16
Pulaukijang 67	64	0S42	103E12	-6:52:48
Pulaumerak 8	36	5S56	106E00	-7:04:00
Pulautelo 15	79	0N03	98E16	-6:33:04
Punan 4	72	3N24	116E16	-7:45:04
Punan 4	73	1N20	115E34	-7:42:16
Punung 8	59	8S08	111E01	-7:24:04
Puper 61	75	0S10	131E18	-8:45:12
Purba 67	66	2N54	98E42	-6:34:48
Purbolinggo 8	32	7S24	109E22	-7:17:28
Purukcahu 4	73	0S35	114E35	-7:38:20
Purwakarta 8	34	6S34	107E26	-7:09:44
Purwantoro 8	36	7S51	111E15	-7:25:00
Purwareja 8	36	7S28	109E25	-7:17:40
Purwodadi 8	12	7S05	110E54	-7:23:36
Purwodadi 8	11	7S49	110E00	-7:20:00
Purwokerto 8	18	7S25	109E14	-7:16:56
Purworejo 8	17	7S43	110E01	-7:20:04
Putussibau 4	73	0N50	112E56	-7:31:44
Raba 69	88	8S27	118E46	-7:55:04
Rabal 12	77	6S22	134E52	-8:59:28
Raha 32	83	4S51	122E43	-8:10:52
Rajabasa 67	62	5S25	104E24	-6:57:36
Rajik 2	70	2S36	105E56	-7:03:44
Rakwa 33	92	2S42	134E30	-8:58:00
Rambipuji 8	52	8S13	113E36	-7:34:24
Rancabali 8	36	7S08	107E21	-7:09:24
Rancah 8	36	7S12	108E30	-7:14:00
Randowaya 63	76	1S52	136E31	-9:06:04
Randublatung 8	36	7S12	111E23	-7:25:32
Randudongkal 8	36	7S06	109E19	-7:17:16
Raneue 67	61	5N03	95E20	-6:21:20
Rangantemiang 4	73	0S35	113E19	-7:33:16
Rangkasbitung 8	30	6S21	106E15	-7:05:00
Ransiki 33	92	1S30	134E10	-8:56:40
Rantau 4	73	2S56	115E09	-7:40:36
Rantaukampar 67	64	1N24	100E59	-6:43:56
Rantaupanjang 67	64	1S51	102E19	-6:49:16
Rantaupanjang 67	64	1S16	101E49	-6:47:16

INDONÉSIA NETHERLANDS EAST INDIES INDONESIEN INDONÉSIE INDONESIA

Rantaupanjang 67	64	0N58	99E13	-6:36:52
Rantauprapat 67	66	2N06	99E50	-6:39:20
Rantepao 66	83	2S59	119E54	-7:59:36
Rapang 66	83	3S50	119E48	-7:59:12
Rasawi 33	92	2S04	134E01	-8:56:04
Ratahan 66	84	1N04	124E48	-8:19:12
Rau 67	66	0N34	100E01	-6:40:04
Raya 4	72	1N05	118E32	-7:54:08
Rebi 12	77	6S23	134E06	-8:56:24
Rembang 8	33	6S42	111E20	-7:25:20
Rengasdengklok 8	25	6S09	107E17	-7:09:08
Rengat 67	64	0S24	102E33	-6:50:12
Rengel 8	56	7S04	112E00	-7:28:00
Rengkang 4	73	1N07	112E10	-7:28:40
Reo 6	88	8S19	120E30	-8:02:00
Reungeut 67	61	4N34	96E22	-6:25:28
Rigaih 67	61	4N40	95E34	-6:22:16
Rinca 6	88	8S37	119E48	-7:59:12
Rogojampi 8	58	8S19	114E17	-7:37:08
Rokan 67	64	0N34	100E25	-6:41:40
Rongkop 8	36	8S10	110E45	-7:23:00
Ropang 69	88	8S52	117E29	-7:49:56
Rumaat 19	77	5S49	132E48	-8:51:12
Rumahtinggih 33	92	6S23	140E17	-9:21:08
Rundeng 67	66	2N39	97E52	-6:31:28
Ruteng 6	88	8S36	120E27	-8:01:48
Sabal 66	86	0S59	123E14	-8:12:56
Sabang 67	61	5N55	95E19	-6:21:16
Sabang (Dampelas) 66	86	0N11	119E51	-7:59:24
Sagalaherang 8	36	6S40	107E39	-7:10:36
Sagaranten 8	36	7S13	106E52	-7:07:28
Sagu 34	89	8S15	123E13	-8:12:52
Sajam 33	92	0S53	132E41	-8:50:44
Sajen 8	59	7S40	112E31	-7:30:04
Salaman 8	27	7S35	110E08	-7:20:32
Salatiga 8	36	7S19	110E30	-7:22:00
Salimbatu 4	72	2N57	117E21	-7:49:24
Salipolo 66	83	3S45	119E29	-7:57:56
Samalanga 67	61	5N13	96E22	-6:25:28
Samarinda 4	72	0S30	117E09	-7:48:36
Sambas 4	71	1N20	109E15	-7:17:00
Samboja 4	74	1S02	117E02	-7:48:08
Sampaga 66	83	2S19	119E07	-7:56:28
Sampalan 1	60	8S41	115E34	-7:42:16
Sampanahan 4	74	2S38	116E11	-7:44:44
Sampang 30	59	7S12	113E14	-7:32:56
Sampit 4	73	2S32	112E57	-7:31:48
Sampolawa 40	83	5S36	122E43	-8:10:52
Samu 4	73	2S01	115E57	-7:43:48
Sanana 31	78	2S04	125E58	-8:23:52
Sandai 4	71	1S15	110E31	-7:22:04
Sangasanga-Dalam 4	72	0S40	117E14	-7:48:56
Sanggau 4	71	0N08	110E36	-7:22:24
Sanggi 67	62	5S27	104E30	-6:58:00
Sanggona 66	83	3S52	121E46	-8:07:04
Sangkapura 37	81	5S52	112E40	-7:30:40
Sangkulirang 4	72	0N59	117E58	-7:51:52
Santan 4	72	0S03	117E28	-7:49:52
Santigi 66	86	1N20	120E54	-8:03:36
Saonek 61	75	0S28	130E47	-8:43:08
Sape 69	88	8S34	118E59	-7:55:56
Sapulu 30	59	6S54	112E57	-7:31:48
Sapuran 8	36	7S28	109E58	-7:19:52
Sarmi 33	92	1S51	138E44	-9:14:56
Saroako 66	83	2S31	121E22	-8:05:28
Sarolangun 67	64	2S18	102E42	-6:50:48
Sasak 67	66	0S01	99E42	-6:38:48
Satui 4	73	3S47	115E27	-7:41:48
Saumlaki 26	93	7S57	131E19	-8:45:16
Sausu 66	86	1S00	120E30	-8:02:00
Sawah 4	73	2N23	115E14	-7:40:56
Sawahlunto 67	66	0S40	100E47	-6:43:08
Sawai 65	93	2S58	129E09	-8:36:36
Sawan 1	60	8S08	115E11	-7:40:44
Sawang 44	67	0N45	103E21	-6:53:24
Seba 68	88	10S29	121E50	-8:07:20
Sebakung 4	74	1S37	116E26	-7:45:44
Sebanga 67	64	1N24	101E10	-6:44:40
Seberida 67	64	0S43	102E31	-6:50:04
Sebuku 4	72	4N03	116E56	-7:47:44
Secang 8	27	7S23	110E15	-7:21:00
Sedah 70	89	10S46	123E12	-8:12:48
Sedayu 8	59	6S59	112E33	-7:30:12
Segeri 66	83	4S39	119E33	-7:58:12
Seguntur 4	72	1N54	117E47	-7:51:08
Sejaka 45	73	3S34	116E12	-7:44:48
Sejorong 69	88	9S02	116E48	-7:47:12
Sekadau 4	71	0S01	110E54	-7:23:36
Sekayu 67	63	2S51	103E51	-6:55:24
Sekeladi 67	63	2S38	102E14	-6:48:56
Sekima 4	73	1S41	111E31	-7:26:04
Selatpanjang 60	65	1N00	102E43	-6:50:52
Selemadeg 1	60	8S29	115E02	-7:40:08
Selimbau 4	73	0N37	112E08	-7:28:32
Selong 29	87	8S39	116E32	-7:46:08
Semanu 8	36	8S00	110E39	-7:22:36
Semarang 8	1	6S58	110E25	-7:21:40
Semitau 4	73	0N33	111E58	-7:27:52
Sempol 8	59	8S01	114E08	-7:36:32
Semuda 4	73	2S51	112E58	-7:31:52
Senamaninik 67	64	0N45	100E47	-6:43:08
Senduruhan 4	71	1S00	110E46	-7:23:04
Sengkamang 67	64	0N42	101E55	-6:47:40
Sentolo 8	11	7S50	110E13	-7:20:52
Sepahat 67	64	1N34	101E53	-6:47:32
Sepasu 4	72	0N43	117E35	-7:50:20
Serang 8	32	6S07	106E09	-7:04:36
Serengka 4	71	1S40	110E40	-7:22:40
Seribudolok 67	66	2N51	99E04	-6:36:16
Seribudolok 67	66	2N56	98E37	-6:34:28
Serui 63	76	1S53	136E14	-9:04:56
Seruwai 67	61	4N21	98E10	-6:32:40
Serwaru 21	93	8S10	127E42	-8:30:48
Sesayap-Lama 4	72	3N36	117E03	-7:48:12
Sesibu 4	72	4N02	116E33	-7:46:12
Seulimeum 67	61	5N22	95E35	-6:22:20
Sia 12	77	6S49	134E19	-8:57:16
Siabu 67	66	1N01	99E29	-6:37:56
Siaksriinderapura 67	64	0N46	102E04	-6:48:16
Sialang 67	66	1N31	99E27	-6:37:48
Sibigo 57	69	2N51	95E55	-6:23:40
Siboa 66	86	0N30	120E02	-8:00:08
Sibolga 67	66	1N45	98E48	-6:35:12
Siborang 67	66	1N08	99E26	-6:37:44
Siborongborong 67	66	2N13	98E59	-6:35:56
Sidareja 8	36	7S29	108E47	-7:15:08
Sidas 4	71	0N24	109E46	-7:19:04
Sidenreng 66	83	4S03	119E38	-7:58:32
Sidikalang 67	66	2N45	98E19	-6:33:16
Sidoan 66	86	0N16	120E12	-8:00:48
Sidoarjo 8	42	7S27	112E43	-7:30:52
Sifahandra 48	69	1N29	97E25	-6:29:40
Si Galangang 67	66	1N15	99E20	-6:37:20
Sigep 56	69	1S02	98E49	-6:35:16
Sigli 67	61	5N23	95E57	-6:23:48
Sihepeng 67	66	1N06	99E27	-6:37:48
Sijunjung 67	66	0S42	100E58	-6:43:52
Sika 6	88	8S45	122E12	-8:08:48
Sikeli 9	83	5S16	121E48	-8:07:12
Sikijang 67	61	4N22	98E02	-6:32:08
Sikutu 66	86	0N53	120E37	-8:02:28
Silalahi 67	66	2N48	98E32	-6:34:08
Silat 4	73	0N21	111E47	-7:27:08
Silaut 67	63	2S22	101E08	-6:44:32
Silogui 56	69	1S14	99E00	-6:36:00
Siluas 4	71	1N17	109E51	-7:19:24
Silvicola 70	91	8S39	126E59	-8:27:56
Simangumban 67	66	1N42	99E10	-6:36:40
Simpang 4	71	1S03	110E06	-7:20:24
Simpang 67	64	0N09	103E15	-6:53:00
Simpang 67	64	1S16	104E05	-6:56:20
Simpangkawat 67	66	2N55	99E43	-6:38:52
Simpangtiga 67	66	2N23	99E47	-6:39:08
Simpangulim 67	61	5N06	97E32	-6:30:08
Sinabang 57	69	2N29	96E23	-6:25:32
Sindangbarang 8	36	7S27	107E08	-7:08:32
Singaparna 8	19	7S21	108E06	-7:12:24
Singaraja (Singardja) 1	60	8S07	115E06	-7:40:24
Singkang 66	83	4S08	120E01	-8:00:04
Singkawang 4	71	0N54	109E00	-7:16:00
Singkil 67	66	2N17	97E49	-6:31:16
Singkuang 67	66	1N03	98E56	-6:35:44
Sinjai 66	83	5S07	120E15	-8:01:00
Sintang 4	73	0N04	111E30	-7:26:00
Sintong 67	64	1N31	100E58	-6:43:52
Sipirok 67	66	1N37	99E16	-6:37:04
Sipot 67	61	4N31	96E02	-6:24:08
Sipupus 67	66	1N25	99E31	-6:38:04
Sirombu 48	69	0N57	97E25	-6:29:40
Situbondo 8	41	7S42	114E00	-7:36:00
Siulakderas 67	66	1S55	101E18	-6:45:12
Siumbatu 66	86	2S45	122E03	-8:08:12
Slaung 8	59	8S02	111E24	-7:25:36
Slawi 8	23	6S59	109E08	-7:16:32
Sleman 8	2	7S42	110E20	-7:21:20
Soasiu → Tidore 7	93	0N40	127E26	-8:29:44
Soe 70	89	9S52	124E17	-8:17:08
Soembawa Besar 69	88	8S30	117E26	-7:49:44
Soerabaja → Surabaya 8	37	7S15	112E45	-7:31:00
Soerakarta 8	9	7S35	110E50	-7:23:20
Solok 67	66	0S48	100E39	-6:42:36
Solo → Surakarta 8	9	7S35	110E50	-7:23:20
Sonar 33	92	2S33	133E00	-8:52:00
Sondi 67	66	2N58	98E52	-6:35:28
Sorido 25	76	1S09	136E03	-9:04:12
Sorong 33	92	0S53	131E15	-8:45:00
Sosok 4	71	0N17	110E14	-7:20:56
Sowek 25	76	0S49	135E30	-9:02:00
Sragen 8	36	7S26	111E02	-7:24:08
Stagen 45	73	3S18	116E10	-7:44:40
Steenkool 33	92	2S07	133E32	-8:54:08
Subah 8	36	6S58	109E52	-7:19:28
Subang 8	36	6S34	107E45	-7:11:00
Sukabihanawa 70	89	9S30	124E57	-8:19:48
Sukabumi 8	4	6S55	106E56	-7:07:44
Sukadana 4	71	1S15	109E57	-7:19:48
Sukadana 67	62	5S05	105E33	-7:02:12
Sukamandi 8	36	6S20	107E39	-7:10:36
Sukamara 4	73	2S43	111E11	-7:24:44
Sukanegara 8	36	7S06	107E07	-7:08:28
Sukapura 8	59	7S52	113E03	-7:32:12
Sukaraja 8	19	7S27	108E12	-7:12:48
Sukaraja 8	18	7S27	109E17	-7:17:08
Sukaraja 4	71	2S21	110E37	-7:22:28
Sukodadi 8	55	7S06	112E19	-7:29:16
Sukoharjo 8	9	7S41	110E50	-7:23:20
Sulang 8	31	6S48	111E23	-7:25:32
Suliki 67	66	0S06	100E27	-6:41:48
Sumalata 66	84	0N59	122E30	-8:10:00
Sumbawa Besar 69	88	8S30	117E26	-7:49:44
Sumedang 8	36	6S52	107E55	-7:11:40
Sumenep 30	59	7S01	113E52	-7:35:28
Sumpangbinangae 66	83	4S24	119E36	-7:58:24
Sumpiuh 8	11	7S37	109E21	-7:17:24
Sungaianyar 4	74	2S55	116E18	-7:45:12
Sungaibamban 67	66	3N26	99E09	-6:36:36
Sungaibatu 4	71	0N48	110E45	-7:23:00
Sungaibuntu 8	36	6S03	107E24	-7:09:36
Sungaidareh 67	66	0S58	101E30	-6:46:00
Sungaigerong 67	63	2S59	104E52	-6:59:28
Sungaiguntung 67	64	0N18	103E37	-6:54:28
Sungaikakap 4	71	0S04	109E10	-7:16:40
Sungailangsat 67	66	0S52	101E18	-6:45:12
Sungailiat 2	70	1S51	106E08	-7:04:32
Sungailimau 67	66	0S31	100E03	-6:40:12
Sungaimanasip 67	64	1N49	100E54	-6:43:36
Sungainipah 67	66	0N57	98E57	-6:35:48
Sungaipenuh 67	64	2S05	101E23	-6:45:32
Sungaipenyu 4	71	0N16	109E04	-7:16:16
Sungaipinang 4	73	0S48	114E04	-7:36:16
Sungairampah 67	66	3N29	99E09	-6:36:36
Sungairotan 67	64	1S39	102E51	-6:51:24
Sungairotan 67	63	3S06	104E18	-6:57:12
Sungaisalak 67	64	0S27	102E59	-6:51:56
Sungaiselan 2	70	2S24	105E59	-7:03:56
Sungaitampang 67	66	2N20	100E07	-6:40:28
Sungaitiram 4	72	0S47	117E12	-7:48:48
Sunggumimasa 66	83	5S12	119E27	-7:57:48
Sungsang 67	63	2S22	104E56	-6:59:44
Surabaya 8	37	7S15	112E45	-7:31:00
Surakarta 8	9	7S35	110E50	-7:23:20
Suramana 66	83	0S50	119E33	-7:58:12
Surodadi 8	29	6S53	109E15	-7:17:00
Surulangun 67	62	2S37	102E45	-6:51:00
Susoh 67	66	3N43	96E50	-6:27:20
Tabanan 1	60	8S32	115E08	-7:40:32
Taduno 16	84	1S55	123E05	-8:12:20
Tafermaar 12	77	6S51	134E06	-8:56:24
Tahuna 24	85	3N37	125E29	-8:21:56
Tais 67	62	4S06	102E34	-6:50:16
Takalar 66	83	5S28	119E24	-7:57:36
Takingeun 67	61	4N38	96E50	-6:27:20
Talaga 31	78	2S11	125E53	-8:23:32
Talangbatu 67	62	4S06	105E29	-7:01:56
Talangbetutu 67	63	2S53	104E41	-6:58:44
Talangpadang 67	62	5S21	104E11	-6:56:44
Talangrimbo 67	63	3S29	105E25	-7:01:40
Taliwang 69	88	8S44	116E52	-7:47:28
Talok 4	72	1N03	118E48	-7:55:12
Talu 67	66	0N14	99E59	-6:39:56
Taludaa 66	84	0N20	123E28	-8:13:52
Taluk 67	64	0S32	101E35	-6:46:20
Talukpambang 38	65	1N29	102E33	-6:50:12
Tamalea 66	83	2S29	119E19	-7:57:16
Taman 8	42	7S25	112E41	-7:30:44
Tamanan 8	59	8S01	113E49	-7:35:16
Tamanusi 66	86	1S48	121E18	-8:05:12
Tamarome 33	92	2S54	133E38	-8:54:32
Tambak 37	81	5S45	112E37	-7:30:28
Tambakboyo 8	59	6S48	111E50	-7:27:20
Tambakrejo 8	59	7S16	111E36	-7:26:24
Tambalan 4	73	3N08	115E34	-7:42:16
Tambangsawah 67	63	3S02	102E11	-6:48:44
Tambea 66	83	4S12	121E36	-8:06:24
Tamboli 66	83	3S57	121E20	-8:05:20
Tambu 66	86	0S02	119E52	-7:59:28
Tamenuen 33	92	6S27	139E48	-9:19:12
Tampang 67	62	5S54	104E43	-6:58:52
Tanahgrogot 4	74	1S55	116E12	-7:44:48
Tanahmerah 4	72	3N41	117E31	-7:50:04
Tanahmerah 33	92	6S05	140E17	-9:21:08
Tanahputih 67	64	1N41	101E03	-6:44:12
Tandjoengpandan 3	70	2S45	107E39	-7:10:36
Tandun 67	64	0N36	100E38	-6:42:32
Tanete 66	83	4S32	119E36	-7:58:24
Tangerang 8	28	6S11	106E37	-7:06:28
Tanggul 8	59	8S10	113E26	-7:33:44
Tangkahan 4	73	1S36	113E52	-7:35:28
Tanglad 1	60	8S47	115E35	-7:42:20
Tangse 67	61	5N01	95E55	-6:23:40
Tanjoengpandan 3	70	2S45	107E39	-7:10:36
Tanjung 29	87	8S21	116E09	-7:44:36

INDONESIA INDONÉSIE INDONESIEN NETHERLANDS EAST INDIES INDONÉSIA

Tanjung 4	73	2S11	115E23	-7:41:32
Tanjung 8	36	6S52	108E52	-7:15:28
Tanjungbalai 67	66	2N58	99E48	-6:39:12
Tanjungbatu 67	64	0N38	103E26	-6:53:44
Tanjungbatu 4	72	0N45	117E26	-7:49:44
Tanjungbatu 4	72	2N17	118E05	-7:52:20
Tanjungenim 67	63	3S45	103E48	-6:55:12
Tanjungkarang 67	62	5S25	105E16	-7:01:04
Tanjunglabu 2	70	2S57	106E54	-7:07:36
Tanjungmedan 67	64	1N26	100E34	-6:42:16
Tanjungmengedar 67	66	2N39	100E01	-6:40:04
Tanjungpandan 3	70	2S45	107E39	-7:10:36
Tanjungpinang 39	67	0N55	104E27	-6:57:48
Tanjungpura 67	66	3N54	98E26	-6:33:44
Tanjungpusu 4	73	0S01	113E30	-7:34:00
Tanjungraja 67	63	3S21	104E40	-6:58:40
Tanjungredep 4	72	2N09	117E29	-7:49:56
Tanjungselor 4	72	2N51	117E22	-7:49:28
Tanjungslamat 67	66	3N49	98E20	-6:33:20
Tanjunguban 39	67	1N03	104E14	-6:56:56
Tapaktuan 67	66	3N16	97E11	-6:28:44
Tapan 67	66	2S10	101E04	-6:44:16
Taraju 8	36	7S27	107E59	-7:11:56
Tarakan 4	72	3N18	117E38	-7:50:32
Taramana 10	89	8S10	124E51	-8:19:24
Taratakbuluh 67	64	0N23	101E27	-6:45:48
Taring 67	66	3N50	97E33	-6:30:12
Tarutung 67	66	2N01	98E58	-6:35:52
Tasikmalaya 8	16	7S20	108E12	-7:12:48
Tawaeli 66	86	0S43	119E51	-7:59:24
Tayan 4	71	0S02	110E07	-7:20:28
Tayu 8	36	6S32	111E02	-7:24:08
Teba 33	92	1S29	137E54	-9:11:36
Tebingbulan 67	63	3S03	103E44	-6:54:56
Tebingtinggi 67	66	3N20	99E09	-6:36:36
Tebingtinggi 67	64	0N36	101E36	-6:46:24
Tebingtinggi 67	63	3S36	103E05	-6:52:20
Tegal 8	26	6S52	109E08	-7:16:32
Tegalombo 8	59	8S04	111E17	-7:25:08
Tegineneng 67	62	5S12	105E10	-7:00:40
Tehoru 65	93	3S23	129E30	-8:38:00
Tejakula 1	60	8S08	115E20	-7:41:20
Teku 66	86	0S46	123E26	-8:13:44
Telaga-Kulon 8	36	6S58	108E18	-7:13:12
Telegapulang 4	73	2S55	112E25	-7:29:40
Teloekbetoeng → Telukbetung 67	62	5S27	105E16	-7:01:04
Telukbatang 4	71	1S00	109E46	-7:19:04
Telukbayur 67	66	1S00	100E22	-6:41:28
Telukbayur 4	72	2N09	117E24	-7:49:36
Telukbetung 67	62	5S27	105E16	-7:01:04
Telukbrombang 67	64	2N03	100E52	-6:43:28
Telukbutun 18	82	4N13	108E12	-7:12:48
Telukdalem 48	69	0N34	97E49	-6:31:16
Teluklanjut 67	64	0N09	103E29	-6:53:56
Teluklecah 53	64	1N51	101E44	-6:46:56
Telukmerbau 67	64	2N04	100E38	-6:42:32
Teluksamak 52	65	0N52	103E03	-6:52:12
Temangga 4	73	0N27	111E21	-7:25:24
Temanggung 8	36	7S18	110E10	-7:20:40
Tembilahan 67	64	0S19	103E09	-6:52:36
Teminabuan 33	92	1S26	132E01	-8:48:04
Tempilang 2	70	2S07	105E40	-7:02:40
Tempino 67	64	1S44	103E29	-6:53:56
Tenggarong 4	72	0S24	116E58	-7:47:52
Tentena 66	86	1S47	120E39	-8:02:36
Tepa 35	93	7S52	129E31	-8:38:04
Terampa 11	82	3N14	106E14	-7:04:56
Teratak 4	71	0S46	110E32	-7:22:08
Ternate 7	93	0N48	127E24	-8:29:36
Terujak 67	61	4N23	97E31	-6:30:04
Teureubangan Cut 67	66	3N12	97E18	-6:29:12
Tewah 4	73	1S05	113E42	-7:34:48
Tianyar 1	60	8S12	115E30	-7:42:00
Tidore 7	93	0N40	127E26	-8:29:44
Tiku 67	66	0S24	99E56	-6:39:44
Tilamuta 66	84	0N30	122E20	-8:09:20
Tilomar 70	91	9S21	125E08	-8:20:32
Timun 44	67	0N47	103E21	-6:53:24
Tinambung 66	83	3S31	119E01	-7:56:04
Tinompo 66	86	2S09	121E17	-8:05:08
Tioro 32	83	4S41	122E36	-8:10:24
Tiwuronto 6	88	8S48	120E09	-8:00:36
Tjimahi (Cimahi) 8	8	6S53	107E32	-7:10:08
Tobelo 7	93	1N44	128E01	-8:32:04
Tobelombang 66	86	0S57	122E00	-8:08:00
Tobo 65	93	3S34	130E11	-8:40:44
Toboali 2	70	3S00	106E30	-7:06:00
Toboli 66	86	0S43	120E05	-8:00:20
Todeli 31	78	1S40	124E29	-8:17:56
Togian 27	86	0S11	121E38	-8:06:32
Toili 66	86	1S27	122E24	-8:09:36
Tojo 66	86	1S17	121E11	-8:04:44
Tokala 66	86	1S47	121E43	-8:06:52
Tokolimbu 66	83	2S48	121E34	-8:06:16
Tokung 4	73	0S18	114E28	-7:37:52
Tolala 66	83	2S56	121E06	-8:04:24
Tolang 67	66	1N56	99E26	-6:37:44
Tolitoli 66	86	1N02	120E49	-8:03:16
Tomini 66	86	0N30	120E32	-8:02:08
Tomohon 66	84	1N19	124E49	-8:19:16
Tompo 66	86	0N56	120E20	-8:01:20
Tondano 66	84	1N19	124E54	-8:19:36
Tongas 8	47	7S44	113E06	-7:32:24
Toribulu 66	86	0S19	120E01	-8:00:04
Torjun 30	59	7S10	113E13	-7:32:52
Torobuku 66	83	4S25	122E26	-8:09:44
Torue 66	86	0S58	120E18	-8:01:12
Tosari 8	59	7S53	112E54	-7:31:36
Tossi 68	88	9S35	118E57	-7:55:48
Towari 66	83	4S36	121E29	-8:05:56
Toyapakeh 1	60	8S41	115E29	-7:41:56
Trenggalek 8	46	8S03	111E43	-7:26:52
Tretet 67	61	4N40	96E51	-6:27:24
Trumon 67	66	2N49	97E38	-6:30:32
Tual 19	77	5S40	132E45	-8:51:00
Tuanan 4	73	2S07	114E24	-7:37:36
Tuban 8	59	6S54	112E03	-7:28:12
Tudameda 70	89	10S52	122E55	-8:11:40
Tulungagung 8	46	8S04	111E54	-7:27:36
Tulungselapan 67	63	3S15	105E19	-7:01:16
Tum 65	93	3S38	130E23	-8:41:32
Tumpang 8	40	8S00	112E46	-7:31:04
Turen 8	59	8S10	112E41	-7:30:44
Tutuala 70	91	8S24	127E15	-8:29:00
Uebonti 66	86	0S55	121E38	-8:06:32
Ujongtankayji 67	66	3N32	97E13	-6:28:52
Ujung 59	83	7S04	120E46	-8:03:04
Ujungbatu 67	64	0N43	100E31	-6:42:04
Ujungberung 8	8	6S55	107E42	-7:10:48
Ujunggading 67	66	0N16	99E33	-6:38:12
Ujunggenteng 8	36	7S22	106E24	-7:05:36
Ujunglamuru 66	83	4S40	119E58	-7:59:52
Ujung Pandang (Makasar) 66	83	5S07	119E24	-7:57:36
Ukui 67	64	0S09	102E11	-6:48:44
Ulakmedan 67	66	2N43	99E38	-6:38:32
Ulu 24	85	2N45	125E24	-8:21:36
Ungaran 8	1	7S07	110E24	-7:21:36
Utan 69	88	8S24	117E07	-7:48:28
Uwak 67	61	4N23	97E07	-6:28:28
Vila Armindo Monteiro 70	91	9S02	125E22	-8:21:28
Vila de Manabuto 70	91	8S30	126E01	-8:24:04
Vila General Carmona 70	91	8S43	125E34	-8:22:16
Vila Nova de Malaca 70	91	8S22	126E54	-8:27:36
Vila Salazar 70	91	8S27	126E27	-8:25:48
Viquique 70	91	8S52	126E22	-8:25:28
Wahai 65	93	2S48	129E30	-8:38:00
Wai 49	93	1S42	127E59	-8:31:56
Waibakul 68	88	9S36	119E35	-7:58:20
Waibeem 33	92	0S28	132E58	-8:51:52
Waikabubak 68	88	9S38	119E25	-7:57:40
Waikelo 68	88	9S24	119E14	-7:56:56
Waimangura 68	88	9S30	119E14	-7:56:56
Waingapu 68	88	9S39	120E16	-8:01:04
Waiwo 64	92	0S56	131E03	-8:44:12
Waiya 65	93	3S13	128E55	-8:35:40
Wakajabi 12	77	5S38	134E24	-8:57:36
Wakre 61	75	0S19	131E09	-8:44:36
Walia 33	92	3S47	138E32	-9:14:08
Wamsasi 5	78	3S33	126E10	-8:24:40
Wanapiri 33	92	4S33	135E59	-9:03:56
Wanau 33	92	1S22	132E42	-8:50:48
Wandai 33	92	3S41	136E41	-9:06:44
Wangal 12	77	6S10	134E12	-8:56:48
Wariap 33	92	1S34	134E11	-8:56:44
Warilau 12	77	5S24	134E30	-8:58:00
Warkopi 33	92	1S08	134E07	-8:56:28
Warmandi 33	92	0S22	132E39	-8:50:36
Waru 65	93	3S24	130E40	-8:42:40
Wasian 33	92	1S54	133E17	-8:53:08
Wasior 33	92	2S43	134E30	-8:58:00
Watampone (Bone) 66	83	4S32	120E20	-8:01:20
Watansoppeng 66	83	4S21	119E53	-7:59:32
Wates 8	44	7S55	112E07	-7:28:28
Wates 8	22	7S51	110E10	-7:20:40
Wates 67	64	1N00	100E16	-6:41:04
Watlaar 19	77	5S28	133E07	-8:52:28
Watudirang 6	88	8S40	122E34	-8:10:16
Watukancoa 66	86	1S36	121E48	-8:07:12
Wayabula 7	93	2N17	128E12	-8:32:48
Weda 7	93	0N21	127E52	-8:31:28
Weleri 8	36	6S58	110E04	-7:20:16
Wendesi 33	92	2S25	134E13	-8:56:52
Weri 33	92	3S12	132E38	-8:50:32
Werwaru 21	93	8S13	128E11	-8:32:44
Wesiri 31	79	7S35	126E38	-8:26:32
Widodaren 8	59	7S25	111E14	-7:24:56
Wirosari 8	14	7S05	111E05	-7:24:20
Wlingi 8	59	8S05	112E19	-7:29:16
Wolowaru 6	88	8S46	121E54	-8:07:36
Wonggarasi 66	84	0N33	121E36	-8:06:24
Wonogiri 8	36	7S49	110E55	-7:23:40
Wonokromo 8	53	7S18	112E44	-7:30:56
Wonosari 8	36	7S58	110E35	-7:22:20
Wonosegoro 8	15	7S18	110E39	-7:22:36
Wonosobo 8	36	7S22	109E54	-7:19:36
Wonreli 31	79	8S05	127E09	-8:28:36
Wosimi 33	92	2S54	134E31	-8:58:04
Wosu 66	86	2S21	121E50	-8:07:20
Wotu 66	83	2S35	120E48	-8:03:12
Wuluhan 8	59	8S21	113E33	-7:34:12
Wulur 41	93	7S09	128E39	-8:34:36
Wurong 33	92	6S07	140E47	-9:23:08
Wuryantoro 8	36	7S54	110E51	-7:23:24
Yakarta → Jakarta 8	1	6S10	106E48	-7:07:12
Yapakopra 33	92	4S24	135E05	-9:00:20
Yapero 33	92	4S59	137E11	-9:08:44
Yaratuar 33	92	2S58	134E40	-8:58:40
Yetti 33	92	3S00	140E53	-9:23:32
Yobi 63	76	1S42	136E27	-9:05:48
Yobi 33	92	1S43	138E04	-9:12:16
Yogyakarta 8	2	7S48	110E22	-7:21:28
Yosowilangun 8	59	8S15	113E18	-7:33:12

IRAN IRÁN PERSIA ĪRĀN

Time Table
Before 1/Jan/1916 LMT
Begin Standard 51E26
1/Jan/1916 0:00 -3:26
Begin Standard 52E30
1/Jan/1946 0:00 -3:30
Begin Standard 60E00
1/Nov/1977 0:00 -4:00
21/Mar/1978 0:00 -5:00
21/Oct/1978 0:00 -4:00
Begin Standard 52E30
1/Jan/1979 0:00 -3:30
21/Mar/1979 0:00 -4:30
19/Sep/1979 0:00 -3:30
21/Mar/1980 0:00 -4:30
23/Sep/1980 0:00 -3:30

Ābādān	30N20	48E16	-3:13:04
Ābādeh	31N10	52E37	-3:30:28
Abarqū	31N08	53E17	-3:33:08
'Abbāsābād	35N44	51E25	-3:25:40
Ābdānān	32N58	47E26	-3:09:44
Abhar	36N09	49E13	-3:16:52
Āghā Jārī	30N42	49E50	-3:19:20
Ahar	38N28	47E04	-3:08:16
Aḥmadābād-E Sarjām	35N51	59E36	-3:58:24
Aḥmadī	27N56	56E42	-3:46:48
Ahram	28N52	51E16	-3:25:04
Ahvāz	31N19	48E42	-3:14:48
'Ajab Shīr	37N28	45E54	-3:03:36
Akbarābād	35N41	51E21	-3:25:24
Ālājūjeh	38N57	46E41	-3:06:44
'Alīābād	36N57	54E59	-3:39:56
Alīgūdarz	33N24	49E41	-3:18:44
Alī Seyyed	32N09	59E52	-3:59:28
'Alī Shāh 'Avaẓ	35N39	51E04	-3:24:16
Alīshārī	39N02	47E15	-3:09:00
Amīrābād	36N04	54E10	-3:36:40
Āmol	36N23	52E20	-3:29:20
Anār	30N53	55E18	-3:41:12

Place	Latitude	Longitude	Time
Anārak	33N20	53E42	-3:34:48
Andīmeshk	32N27	48E21	-3:13:24
Angohrān	26N35	57E54	-3:51:36
Āqbolāgh	38N54	44E32	-2:58:08
Aq Qal'Eh	37N01	54E30	-3:38:00
'Arabābād	33N02	57E41	-3:50:44
Arāk	34N05	49E41	-3:18:44
Ārān	34N04	51E29	-3:25:56
Ardabīl	38N15	48E18	-3:13:12
Ardakān	30N16	52E01	-3:28:04
Ardakān	32N19	53E59	-3:35:56
Ardal	31N59	50E39	-3:22:36
Ardestān	33N22	52E23	-3:29:32
Arsenjān	29N56	53E18	-3:33:12
Asadābād	34N47	48E07	-3:12:28
Aslan-Sara	39N02	48E16	-3:13:04
Āstāneh	37N17	49E59	-3:19:56
Āstāneh	33N53	49E22	-3:17:28
Āstārā	38N26	48E52	-3:15:28
Āvej	35N34	49E13	-3:16:52
Awīn	35N48	51E24	-3:25:36
Āzādshahr	37N07	55E16	-3:41:04
Āzar Shahr	37N45	45E59	-3:03:56
Bābol	36N34	52E42	-3:30:48
Bābol Sar	36N43	52E39	-3:30:36
Bād	33N41	52E01	-3:28:04
Bāfq	31N35	55E24	-3:41:36
Bāft	29N14	56E38	-3:46:32
Bāgh-E Malek	31N32	49E55	-3:19:40
Bāghīn	30N12	36E48	-2:27:12
Bahār	34N54	48E26	-3:13:44
Bāhū Kalāt	25N43	61E25	-4:05:40
Bājgīrān	37N36	58E24	-3:53:36
Bakhtaran (Kermānshāh)	34N19	47E04	-3:08:16
Baladeh	36N12	51E48	-3:27:12
Bām	36N58	57E59	-3:51:56
Bam	29N06	58E21	-3:53:24
Bampūr	27N12	60E27	-4:01:48
Bandān	31N23	60E44	-4:02:56
Bandar 'Abbās	27N11	56E17	-3:45:08
Bandar-E Anzalī (Bandar-E Pahlavī)	37N28	49E27	-3:17:48
Bandar-E Chārak	26N43	54E16	-3:37:04
Bandar-E Deylam	30N04	50E10	-3:20:40
Bandar-E Gaz	36N47	53E59	-3:35:56
Bandar-E Khomeynī (Bandar-E Shāhpū	30N25	49E05	-3:16:20
Bandar-E Lengeh	26N33	54E53	-3:39:32
Bandar-E Māh Shahr	30N33	49E12	-3:16:48
Bandar-E Moghūyeh	26N35	54E31	-3:38:04
Bandar-E Rīg	29N29	50E38	-3:22:32
Bandar-E Torkman	36N56	54E06	-3:36:24
Bāneh	35N59	45E53	-3:03:32
Bardeskan	35N12	57E58	-3:51:52
Barin	39N13	44E28	-2:57:52
Bāsa'īdū	26N39	55E17	-3:41:08
Bastak	27N14	54E22	-3:37:28
Basṭām	36N29	55E04	-3:40:16
Bazmān	27N49	60E12	-4:00:48
Behbehān	30N35	50E14	-3:20:56
Behshahr	36N43	53E34	-3:34:16
Bejestān	34N31	58E10	-3:52:40
Benāb	37N20	46E04	-3:04:16
Bent	26N17	59E31	-3:58:04
Bīdokht	34N21	58E46	-3:55:04
Bījār	35N52	47E36	-3:10:24
Bījenābād	27N55	58E03	-3:52:12
Bīrjand	32N53	59E13	-3:56:52
Bojnūrd	37N28	57E19	-3:49:16
Borāzjān	29N16	51E12	-3:24:48
Borūjen	31N59	51E18	-3:25:12
Borūjerd	33N54	48E46	-3:15:04
Boshrūyeh	33N53	57E26	-3:49:44
Bostān	31N43	47E59	-3:11:56
Bowkān	36N31	46E12	-3:04:48
Būshehr	28N59	50E50	-3:23:20
Chādegān	32N46	50E39	-3:22:36
Chāhak	33N17	58E54	-3:55:36
Chāh Bahār	25N18	60E37	-4:02:28
Chālūs	36N38	51E26	-3:25:44
Chanārān	36N39	59E06	-3:56:24
Charām	30N45	50E44	-3:22:56
Chāt	37N59	55E16	-3:41:04
Chelvand	38N18	48E50	-3:15:20
Damāvand	35N43	52E04	-3:28:16
Dāmghān	39N09	54E22	-3:37:28
Dārāb	28N45	54E34	-3:38:16
Darakeh	35N48	51E23	-3:25:32
Dārān	32N59	50E24	-3:21:36
Darband	35N49	51E26	-3:25:44
Darkhazīneh	31N54	48E59	-3:15:56
Darreh Gaz	37N27	59E07	-3:56:28
Dasht-e Āzādegān (Sūsangerd)	31N34	48E11	-3:12:44
Dastgardān	34N19	56E51	-3:47:24
Dastjerd	34N33	50E15	-3:21:00
Dāvar Panāh	27N21	62E21	-4:09:24
Dāvarzan	36N23	56E50	-3:47:20
Deh Bārez	27N26	57E12	-3:48:48
Deh Bīd	30N38	53E13	-3:32:52
Dehdez	31N43	50E17	-3:21:08
Dehgolān	35N17	47E25	-3:09:40
Deh Kord	33N49	48E53	-3:15:32
Dehlorān	32N41	47E16	-3:09:04
Deh Salm	31N12	59E19	-3:57:16
Delījān	33N59	50E40	-3:22:40
Deyhūk	33N17	57E30	-3:50:00
Deyyer	27N50	51E55	-3:27:40
Dezfūl	32N23	48E24	-3:13:36
Dez Gerd	30N45	51E57	-3:27:48
Dīvāndarreh	35N55	47E02	-3:08:08
Dowlatābād	28N18	56E40	-3:46:40
Dowlatābād	35N37	51E27	-3:25:48
Dow Rūd	33N28	49E04	-3:16:16
Dowsārī	28N25	57E59	-3:51:56
Dūlāb	35N37	51E27	-3:25:48
Dūruḥ	32N17	60E30	-4:02:00
Emāmshahr (Shāhrūd)	36N25	55E01	-3:40:04
Eqlīd	30N55	52E39	-3:30:36
Eṣfahān (Isfahan)	32N40	51E38	-3:26:32
Eslāmābād	34N06	46E31	-3:06:04
Esmā'īlābād	28N48	56E39	-3:46:36
Eṣṭahbānāt	29N08	54E04	-3:36:16
Evaz	27N46	53E59	-3:35:56
Eyvānakī	35N20	52E04	-3:28:16
Fahraj	28N58	58E52	-3:55:28
Falāvarjān	32N33	51E30	-3:26:00
Faraḥābād	35N42	51E30	-3:26:00
Farazād	35N47	51E21	-3:25:24
Farīmān	35N43	59E53	-3:59:32
Farmahīn	34N30	49E41	-3:18:44
Farrāshband	28N53	52E06	-3:28:24
Fasā	28N56	53E42	-3:34:48
Fedeshk	32N45	58E50	-3:55:20
Ferdows	34N00	58E09	-3:52:36
Feyẕābād	35N01	58E46	-3:55:04
Fīrūzābād	28N50	52E36	-3:30:24
Fīrūz Bahram	35N38	51E15	-3:25:00
Fīrūz Kūh	35N45	52E47	-3:31:08
Fowman	37N13	49E19	-3:17:16
Fūlād Maḥalleh	36N02	53E44	-3:34:56
Fūrg	28N18	55E13	-3:40:52
Gābrīk	25N44	58E28	-3:53:52
Gachsārān	30N12	50E47	-3:23:08
Galeh Dār	27N38	52E42	-3:30:48
Galūgāh-E Āsīyeh	34N01	59E55	-3:59:40
Garmsar	35N20	52E13	-3:28:52
Gatvand	32N15	48E50	-3:15:20
Gāv Koshī	28N38	57E12	-3:48:48
Germī	39N01	48E03	-3:12:12
Gevān	26N03	57E17	-3:49:08
Gīlān-E Gharb	34N08	45E55	-3:03:40
Golāshkerd	27N59	57E16	-3:49:04
Golpāyegān	33N27	50E18	-3:21:12
Gomīshān	37N04	54E06	-3:36:24
Gonābād	34N20	58E42	-3:54:48
Gonbad-E Qābūs	37N17	55E17	-3:41:08
Gorgān	36N50	54E29	-3:37:56
Gowk	29N51	57E44	-3:50:56
Haft Gel	31N27	49E27	-3:17:48
Hamadān	34N48	48E30	-3:14:00
Harsīn	34N16	47E35	-3:10:20
Ḥasanābād	35N44	51E19	-3:25:16
Ḥasanābād-E Khāleṣeh	35N37	51E12	-3:24:48
Ḥasan Kīādeh	37N24	49E58	-3:19:52
Ḥasharūd	37N30	47E16	-3:09:04
Hashtpar	37N48	48E55	-3:15:40
Ḥāsīn-E Bozorg	39N23	44E42	-2:58:48
Ḥavīq	38N10	48E54	-3:15:36
Hendījān	30N14	49E43	-3:18:52
Herowābād	37N37	48E32	-3:14:08
Hesarak	35N47	51E19	-3:25:16
Homāyūnshahr	32N41	51E31	-3:26:04
Ḥoseynābād	35N33	47E08	-3:08:32
Ḥoseynīyeh-Ye Khodā-Dād	32N42	48E14	-3:12:56
Hoveyzeh	31N27	48E04	-3:12:16
Hūmedān	25N24	59E39	-3:58:36
Hūrand	38N51	47E22	-3:09:28
Igdir	39N20	47E30	-3:10:00
Īlām	33N38	46E26	-3:05:44
Īrānshahr	27N13	60E41	-4:02:44
Isfahan → Eṣfahān	32N40	51E38	-3:26:32
Īzad Khvāst	31N31	52E07	-3:28:28
Īzeh	31N50	49E50	-3:19:20
Ja'Farābād	35N43	50E43	-3:22:52
Jahrom	28N31	53E33	-3:34:12
Jājarm	36N58	56E27	-3:45:48
Jandaq	34N02	54E26	-3:37:44
Jāsk	25N38	57E46	-3:51:04
Joghatāy	36N36	57E01	-3:48:04
Jolfā	38N57	45E38	-3:02:32
Jūyom	28N10	53E52	-3:35:28
Kabūd Gonbad	37N00	59E45	-3:59:00
Kabūd Rāhang	35N12	48E44	-3:14:56
Kadkan	35N35	58E50	-3:55:20
Kahnūj	27N58	57E45	-3:51:00
Kākī	28N19	51E34	-3:26:16
Kalasarv	39N11	48E03	-3:12:12
Kaleybar	38N47	47E02	-3:08:08
Kamīzgān	38N58	47E44	-3:10:56
Kan	35N45	51E16	-3:25:04
Kangān	27N50	52E03	-3:28:12
Kangāvar	34N30	47E58	-3:11:52
Karaj	35N48	50E59	-3:23:56
Kārīz	34N49	60E47	-4:03:08
Kārkīn Dar	25N47	59E15	-3:57:00
Kāshān	33N59	51E29	-3:25:56
Kāshmar	35N12	58E27	-3:53:48
Kāzerūn	29N37	51E38	-3:26:32
Kazvin → Qazvīn	36N16	50E00	-3:20:00
Kerend	34N16	46E15	-3:05:00
Kermān	30N17	57E05	-3:48:20
Kermānshāh	34N19	47E04	-3:08:16
Khāneh Khvodī	36N05	56E04	-3:44:16
Kharānaq	32N20	54E39	-3:38:36
Khāsh	28N14	61E14	-4:04:56
Khīyāv	38N24	47E40	-3:10:40
Khomām	37N22	49E40	-3:18:40
Khomeyn	33N38	50E04	-3:20:16
Khorramābād	33N30	48E20	-3:13:20
Khorram Daraq	36N26	48E36	-3:14:24
Khorramshahr	30N25	48E11	-3:12:44
Khūr	32N57	58E26	-3:53:44
Khurramshahr → Khorramshahr	30N25	48E11	-3:12:44
Khūsf	32N46	58E53	-3:55:32
Khvāf	34N33	60E08	-4:00:32
Khvor	33N47	55E03	-3:40:12
Khvormūj	28N39	51E23	-3:25:32
Khvoy	38N33	44E58	-2:59:52
Kīshar Bāla	35N49	51E13	-3:24:52
Kom → Qom	34N39	50E54	-3:23:36
Kord Kūy	36N48	54E07	-3:36:28
Kūhdasht	33N32	47E36	-3:10:24
Kūhpāyeh	32N43	52E26	-3:29:44
Lādīz	28N56	61E19	-4:05:16
Lāhījān	37N12	50E01	-3:20:04
Langarūd	37N11	50E10	-3:20:40
Lār	27N41	54E17	-3:37:08
Lārī	38N30	47E49	-3:11:16
Lashkarak	35N49	51E36	-3:26:24
Lāsjerd	35N24	53E04	-3:32:16
Loṭfābād	37N32	59E20	-3:57:20
Mahābād	36N45	45E43	-3:02:52
Maḥallāt	33N55	50E27	-3:21:48
Maḥmūdābād	36N38	52E15	-3:29:00
Mākū	39N17	44E31	-2:58:04
Malāyer	34N17	48E50	-3:15:20
Malek Kandī	37N09	46E06	-3:04:24
Manūjān	27N24	57E32	-3:50:08
Marāgheh	37N23	46E13	-3:04:52
Mārākand	38N52	45E14	-3:00:56
Marand	38N26	45E46	-3:03:04
Marāveh Tappeh	37N55	55E57	-3:43:48
Margam	39N09	44E57	-2:59:48
Marīvān	35N31	46E10	-3:04:40
Marv Dasht	29N50	52E40	-3:30:40
Mashhad	36N18	59E36	-3:58:24
Mashīz	29N56	56E37	-3:46:28
Masjed Soleymān	31N58	49E18	-3:17:12
Maskūtān	26N51	59E49	-3:59:16
Māsūleh	37N10	48E59	-3:15:56
Mayāmey	36N24	55E42	-3:42:48
Māzhān	32N35	59E01	-3:56:04
Mazīnān	36N18	56E46	-3:47:04
Mehrābād	36N53	47E55	-3:11:40
Mehrābād	35N40	51E20	-3:25:20
Mehrān	33N07	46E10	-3:04:40
Mehrīz	31N35	54E28	-3:37:52
Mesgarābād	35N37	51E31	-3:26:04
Meshed → Mashhad	36N18	59E36	-3:58:24
Meymeh	33N27	51E10	-3:24:40
Mīānābād	37N02	57E27	-3:49:48
Mīāndowāb	36N58	46E06	-3:04:24
Mīāneh	37N26	47E42	-3:10:48
Mīghān	31N49	59E28	-3:57:52
Mīnāb	27N09	57E05	-3:48:20
Mīrjāveh	29N01	61E28	-4:05:52
Moḥammadābād	30N53	61E28	-4:05:52
Molkābād	34N32	52E35	-3:30:20
Mūrcheh Khvort	33N06	51E30	-3:26:00
Nahāvand	34N12	48E22	-3:13:28
Nā'īn	32N52	53E05	-3:32:20
Najafābād	32N37	51E21	-3:25:24
Namīn	38N25	48E30	-3:14:00
Naqadeh	36N57	45E23	-3:01:32
Naṣrābād	34N08	51E26	-3:25:44
Naṭanz	33N21	51E40	-3:26:40
Nāy Band	32N20	57E34	-3:50:16
Nāy Band	27N23	52E38	-3:30:32
Nehbandān	31N32	60E02	-4:00:08
Nematābād	35N38	51E21	-3:25:24
Neyrīz	29N12	54E19	-3:37:16
Neyshābūr	36N12	58E50	-3:55:20
Nīkshahr	26N13	60E12	-4:00:48
Nīr	38N02	47E59	-3:11:56
Noṣratābād	29N54	59E59	-3:59:56
Nowbarān	35N08	48E42	-3:14:48
Nowfel low Shātow	34N23	50E32	-3:22:08
Ōrūmīyeh (Reẓā'īyeh)	37N33	45E04	-3:00:16
Oshnovīyeh	37N02	45E06	-3:00:24
Oshtorīnān	34N01	48E38	-3:14:32
Oskū	37N55	46E06	-3:04:24
Ozgol	35N47	51E30	-3:26:00
Pahlavī → Bandar-E Anzalī	37N28	49E27	-3:17:48
Pahlevi → Bandar-E Anzalī	37N28	49E27	-3:17:48
Pāveh	35N03	46E22	-3:05:28
Pīrān Shahr	36N41	45E08	-3:00:32
Polān	25N35	61E12	-4:04:48
Pol-E Safīd	36N06	53E01	-3:32:04
Qāderābād	30N17	53E16	-3:33:04
Qā'emshahr	36N28	52E53	-3:31:32
Qamṣar	33N45	51E26	-3:25:44
Qareh Ẕīā' od Dīn	38N54	45E02	-3:00:08
Qaṣa-E Qand	26N12	60E45	-4:03:00
Qāsemābād	35N46	51E31	-3:26:04
Qaṣr-E Fīrūzeh	35N40	51E32	-3:26:08
Qaṣr-E Shīrīn	34N31	45E35	-3:02:20
Qāyen	33N44	59E11	-3:56:44
Qazvīn	36N16	50E00	-3:20:00
Qeshm	26N58	56E16	-3:45:04
Qeydār	36N07	48E35	-3:14:20
Qezel Qeshlāq	39N08	45E21	-3:01:24
Qolhak	35N47	51E26	-3:25:44
Qom	34N39	50E54	-3:23:36
Qorveh	35N10	47E48	-3:11:12
Qoṭbābād	28N42	53E34	-3:34:16
Qoṭūr	38N28	44E25	-2:57:40
Qūchān	37N06	58E30	-3:54:00
Qūshchī	37N59	45E03	-3:00:12
Qūyjāq-E-Bālā	39N16	47E07	-3:08:28
Rafsanjān	30N24	56E01	-3:44:04
Rakhneh	31N39	59E13	-3:56:52
Rāmhormoz	31N16	49E36	-3:18:24
Rāmsar	36N53	50E41	-3:22:44
Rāmshīr	30N54	49E24	-3:17:36
Rasht	37N16	49E36	-3:18:24

IRAN　IRÁN　PERSIA　ĪRĀN

Place	Lat	Long	Offset
Rāsk	26N13	61E25	-4:05:40
Ravānsar	34N43	46E40	-3:06:40
Rāvar	31N15	56E53	-3:47:32
Rāyen	29N34	57E26	-3:49:44
Razan	35N23	49E02	-3:16:08
Remeshk	26N50	58E49	-3:55:16
Rey	35N35	51E25	-3:25:40
Reẓā'īyeh → Orūmīyeh	37N33	45E04	-3:00:16
Reẓvāndeh	37N33	49E09	-3:16:36
Rīgān	28N37	58E58	-3:55:52
Rī Shahr	28N55	50E50	-3:23:20
Rīvash	35N26	58E26	-3:53:44
Rīz	32N23	51E20	-3:25:20
Rīzaīyeh	37N34	45E04	-3:00:16
Robāṭ	30N04	54E49	-3:39:16
Robāṭ Karīm	35N28	51E05	-3:24:20
Rūdbār	36N48	49E24	-3:17:36
Rūdbar	33N35	47E00	-3:08:00
Rūd Sar	37N08	50E18	-3:21:12
Sa'ādatābād	30N06	53E08	-3:32:32
Sabzevār	36N13	57E42	-3:50:48
Sa'Dābād	29N23	51E07	-3:24:28
Ṣafarābād	38N59	47E27	-3:09:48
Ṣafīābād	36N45	57E58	-3:51:52
Ṣafīdābeh	30N56	60E35	-4:02:20
Ṣaḥneh	34N29	47E41	-3:10:44
Sa'īdābād	35N40	51E11	-3:24:44
Sā'īn Dezh	36N40	46E33	-3:06:12
Salmās	38N11	44E47	-2:59:08
Sāmen	34N12	48E42	-3:14:48
Sanandaj	35N19	47E00	-3:08:00
Sang Bast	35N59	59E46	-3:59:04
Saqqez	36N14	46E16	-3:05:04
Sarāb	37N56	47E32	-3:10:08
Sarakhs	36N32	61E11	-4:04:44
Sarāvān	27N15	62E40	-4:10:40
Sarāyān	33N51	58E31	-3:54:04
Sarbāz	26N39	61E15	-4:05:00
Sardaq	34N48	58E07	-3:52:28
Sar Dasht	36N09	45E28	-3:01:52
Sar Dasht	32N32	48E52	-3:15:28
Sar-E Pol-E Ẕahāb	34N28	45E52	-3:03:28
Sārī	36N34	53E04	-3:32:16
Sarvestān	29N16	53E13	-3:32:52
Sāveh	35N01	50E20	-3:21:20
Selvānā	37N25	44E51	-2:59:24
Semnān	35N33	53E24	-3:33:36
Ṣeydābād	34N51	50E36	-3:22:24
Shabestar	38N11	45E42	-3:02:48
Shādegān	30N40	48E38	-3:14:32
Shaft	37N12	49E24	-3:17:36
Shāhābād	37N32	56E54	-3:47:36
Shāhābād	35N49	51E29	-3:25:56
Shahr-E Bābak	30N07	55E09	-3:40:36
Shahreẓā	32N01	51E52	-3:27:28
Shahr Kord	32N19	50E50	-3:23:20
Shākhen	33N22	59E32	-3:58:08
Shamīl	27N30	56E53	-3:47:32
Sharafkhāneh	38N11	45E29	-3:01:56
Shīrāz	29N37	52E33	-3:30:12
Shīrvān	37N24	57E55	-3:51:40
Shūrāb	33N43	56E29	-3:45:56
Shūrāb	28N09	60E18	-4:01:12
Shūsf	31N48	60E01	-4:00:04
Shūsh	32N11	48E15	-3:13:00
Shūshtar	32N03	48E51	-3:15:24
Sīrdān	36N39	49E12	-3:16:48
Solṭānābād	36N23	58E02	-3:52:08
Solṭānīyeh	36N26	48E48	-3:15:12
Sonqor	34N47	47E36	-3:10:24
Ṣūfīān	38N17	45E59	-3:03:56
Sūhānak	35N48	51E32	-3:26:08
Sūldeh	36N34	52E01	-3:28:04
Sūlgan	35N49	51E15	-3:25:00
Sulṭanatābād	35N46	51E28	-3:25:52
Sūmār	33N52	45E39	-3:02:36
Sūrak	25N43	58E48	-3:55:12
Sūrān	27N18	62E04	-4:08:16
Surkh Hisār	35N43	51E33	-3:26:12
Sūrmaq	31N03	52E48	-3:31:12
Sūsangerd	31N34	48E11	-3:12:44
Ṭabas	33N36	56E54	-3:47:36
Ṭabas	32N48	60E14	-4:00:56
Tabrīz	38N05	46E18	-3:05:12
Taft	31N45	54E14	-3:36:56
Ṭāherī	27N42	52E21	-3:29:24
Tajrīsh	35N48	51E25	-3:25:40
Takāb	36N24	47E07	-3:08:28
Tākestān	36N04	49E43	-3:18:52
Tal-E Khosravī	30N37	51E35	-3:26:20
Talish-Mikeyli	39N23	48E22	-3:13:28
Tankābon	36N49	50E53	-3:23:32
Tarasht	35N42	51E21	-3:25:24
Tarkhowrān	34N41	50E00	-3:20:00
Ṭayyebāt	34N44	60E45	-4:03:00
Teheran → Tehrān	35N40	51E26	-3:25:44
Tehrān	35N40	51E26	-3:25:44
Tonekābon	36N49	50E53	-3:23:32
Torbat-E Ḥeydarīyeh	35N16	59E13	-3:56:52
Torbat-E Jām	35N14	60E36	-4:02:24
Torkamān	37N35	47E23	-3:09:32
Towlī	39N11	47E32	-3:10:08
Turkmān Deh	35N40	51E36	-3:26:24
Tūysarkān	34N33	48E27	-3:13:48
Urmia → Reẓā'īyeh	37N33	45E04	-3:00:16
Vanak	35N45	51E23	-3:25:32
Varāmīn	35N20	51E39	-3:26:36
Ward	35N48	51E10	-3:24:40
Wasfanārd	35N39	51E21	-3:25:24
Yaftābād	35N39	51E19	-3:25:16
Yazd	31N53	54E25	-3:37:40
Yezd → Yazd	31N53	54E25	-3:37:40
Yūsofābād	35N44	51E25	-3:25:40
Zābol	31N02	61E30	-4:06:00
Zābolī	27N07	61E40	-4:06:40
Zāgheh	33N30	48E42	-3:14:48
Zāhedān	29N30	60E52	-4:03:28
Zanjān	36N40	48E29	-3:13:56
Zarand	30N48	56E35	-3:46:20
Zarand-E Kohneh	35N17	50E00	-3:22:00
Zarnān	35N41	51E09	-3:24:36
Zarqān	29N46	52E43	-3:30:52
Zeyveh	39N07	47E42	-3:10:48
Zūrābād	38N49	44E35	-2:58:20

IRAQ　IRAK　AL-'IRĀQ

Time Table

Before 1/Jan/1890 LMT
Begin Standard 44E24

Date	Time	Offset
1/Jan/1890	0:00	-2:58

Begin Standard 45E00

Date	Time	Offset
1/Jan/1918	0:00	-3:00
1/May/1982	0:00	-4:00
1/Oct/1982	0:00	-3:00
31/Mar/1983	0:00	-4:00
1/Oct/1983	0:00	-3:00
1/Apr/1984	0:00	-4:00
1/Oct/1984	0:00	-3:00
1/Apr/1985	0:00	-4:00
29/Sep/1985	2:00	-3:00
30/Mar/1986	1:00	-4:00
28/Sep/1986	2:00	-3:00
29/Mar/1987	1:00	-4:00
27/Sep/1987	2:00	-3:00
27/Mar/1988	1:00	-4:00
25/Sep/1988	2:00	-3:00
26/Mar/1989	1:00	-4:00
24/Sep/1989	2:00	-3:00
25/Mar/1990	1:00	-4:00
30/Sep/1990	2:00	-3:00
31/Mar/1991	1:00	-4:00
29/Sep/1991	2:00	-3:00
29/Mar/1992	1:00	-4:00
27/Sep/1992	2:00	-3:00
28/Mar/1993	1:00	-4:00
26/Sep/1993	2:00	-3:00
27/Mar/1994	1:00	-4:00
25/Sep/1994	2:00	-3:00
26/Mar/1995	1:00	-4:00
24/Sep/1995	2:00	-3:00
31/Mar/1996	1:00	-4:00
29/Sep/1996	2:00	-3:00
30/Mar/1997	1:00	-4:00
28/Sep/1997	2:00	-3:00
29/Mar/1998	1:00	-4:00
27/Sep/1998	2:00	-3:00
28/Mar/1999	1:00	-4:00
26/Sep/1999	2:00	-3:00
26/Mar/2000	1:00	-4:00
24/Sep/2000	2:00	-3:00

Place	Lat	Long	Offset
Abū al-Khaṣīb	30N27	47E59	-3:11:56
Ad-Dīwānīyah	31N59	44E56	-2:59:44
'Afak	32N04	45E15	-3:01:00
Al-'Amādīyah	37N06	43E29	-2:53:56
Al-'Amārah	31N50	47E09	-3:08:36
Al-Baṣrah (Basra)	30N30	47E47	-3:11:08
Al-Baṭḥā'	31N06	45E53	-3:03:32
Al-Fallūjah	33N20	43E46	-2:55:04
Al-Fāw	29N58	48E29	-3:13:56
Al-Ḥadīthah	34N07	42E23	-2:49:32
Al-Ḥaḍr	35N35	42E44	-2:50:56
Al-Ḥalfāyah	31N49	47E26	-3:09:44
Al-Ḥayy	32N10	46E03	-3:04:12
Al-Ḥillah	32N29	44E25	-2:57:40
Al-Hindīyah	32N33	44E13	-2:56:52
'Alī al-Gharbī	32N27	46E41	-3:06:44
Al-Kāẓimīyah	33N22	44E20	-2:57:20
Al-Khālis	33N49	44E32	-2:58:08
Al-Kifl	32N14	44E22	-2:57:28
Al-Kūfah	32N02	44E24	-2:57:36
Al-Kūt	32N25	45E49	-3:03:16
Al-Ma'ānīyah	30N44	43E00	-2:52:00
Al-Mawṣil (Mosul)	36N20	43E08	-2:52:32
Al-Musayyib	32N47	44E18	-2:57:12
Al-Qā'im	34N21	41E07	-2:44:28
Al-Qurnah	31N00	47E26	-3:09:44
Āltūn Kūprī	35N45	44E09	-2:56:36
Amārah	31N50	47E09	-3:08:36
'Ānah	34N28	41E56	-2:47:44
An-Najaf	31N59	44E20	-2:57:20
An-Nāṣirīyah	31N02	46E16	-3:05:04
'Aqrah	36N45	43E54	-2:55:36
Arbīl	36N11	44E01	-2:56:04
Ar-Ramādī	33N25	43E17	-2:53:08
Ar-Rumaythah	31N32	45E12	-3:00:48
Ar-Ruṭbah	33N02	40E17	-2:41:08
Ash-Shabakah	30N49	43E39	-2:54:36
Ash-Sharqāṭ	35N27	43E16	-2:53:04
Ash-Shaṭrah	31N25	46E10	-3:04:40
Ash-Shināfīyah	31N35	44E39	-2:58:36
As-Sa'Dīyah	34N11	45E07	-3:00:28
As-Salmān	30N30	44E32	-2:58:08
As-Samāwah	31N18	45E17	-3:01:08
As-Sulaymānīyah	35N33	45E26	-3:01:44
Az-Zubayr	30N23	47E43	-3:10:52
Babil (Babylon)	32N33	44E26	-2:57:44
Babylon	32N33	44E26	-2:57:44
Bagdad → Baghdād	33N21	44E25	-2:57:40
Baghdād	33N21	44E25	-2:57:40
Balad	34N01	44E09	-2:56:36
Ba'Qūbah	33N45	44E38	-2:58:32
Basra → Al-Baṣrah	30N30	47E47	-3:11:08
Dahūk	36N52	43E00	-2:52:00
Habaniya	33N23	43E34	-2:54:16
Ḥalabjah	35N10	45E59	-3:03:56
Ḥillah	32N30	44E25	-2:57:40
Hīt	33N38	42E49	-2:51:16
Irbīl	36N11	44E01	-2:56:04
Jadīdah	34N01	42E28	-2:49:52
Kadhimain → Al-Kāẓimīyah	33N22	44E20	-2:57:20
Karbalā'	32N36	44E02	-2:56:08
Kerbela → Karbalā'	32N36	44E02	-2:56:08
Khān al-Baghdādī	33N51	42E33	-2:50:12
Khānaqīn	34N21	45E22	-3:01:28
Kibāsī	30N34	47E50	-3:11:20
Kifrī	34N42	44E58	-2:59:52
Kirkūk	35N28	44E28	-2:57:52
Kut-al-Imara	32N30	45E50	-3:03:20
Kūysanjaq	36N05	44E38	-2:58:32
Mandalī	33N45	45E32	-3:02:08
Mosul → Al-Mawṣil	36N20	43E08	-2:52:32
Nāṣirīyah	31N02	46E16	-3:05:04
Nukhayb	32N02	42E15	-2:49:00
Qal'At Ṣāliḥ	31N31	47E16	-3:09:04
Qal'At Sukkar	31N51	46E05	-3:04:20
Ramadi	34N12	43E54	-2:55:36
Rāniyah	36N15	44E53	-2:59:32
Rāwah	34N28	41E55	-2:47:40
Rāwāndūz	36N37	44E31	-2:58:04
Ṣafwān	30N07	47E43	-3:10:52
Sāmarrā'	34N12	43E52	-2:55:28
Shahraban	33N58	44E59	-2:59:56
Shaykh Sa'D	32N34	46E17	-3:05:08
Shithāthah	32N33	43E29	-2:53:56
Sinjār	36N19	41E52	-2:47:28
Sulaymānīyah	35N33	45E26	-3:01:44
Sūq ash-Shuyūkh	30N53	46E28	-3:05:52
Tall 'Afar	36N22	42E27	-2:49:48
Tall Kayf	36N29	43E08	-2:52:32
Ṭaqṭaq	35N53	44E35	-2:58:20
Ṭāwūq	35N08	44E27	-2:57:48
Tikrīt	34N36	43E42	-2:54:48
Tudmur	34N32	38E15	-2:33:00
Tukayyid	29N47	45E36	-3:02:24
Ṭūz Khurmātū	34N53	44E38	-2:58:32
Zākhū	37N08	42E41	-2:50:44

EIRE — IRLAND — IRLANDE — IRLANDA — IRELAND

Time Table		
Before 1/Jan/1880	LMT	
Begin Standard		6w15
1/Jan/1880	0:00	0:25
21/May/1916	2:00	-0:35
Begin Standard		0w00
1/Oct/1916	2:00	-1:00
1/Oct/1916	3:00	0:00
8/Apr/1917	2:00	-1:00
17/Sep/1917	3:00	0:00
24/Mar/1918	2:00	-1:00
30/Sep/1918	3:00	0:00
30/Mar/1919	2:00	-1:00
29/Sep/1919	3:00	0:00
28/Mar/1920	2:00	-1:00
25/Oct/1920	3:00	0:00
3/Apr/1921	2:00	-1:00
3/Oct/1921	3:00	0:00
26/Mar/1922	2:00	-1:00
8/Oct/1922	3:00	0:00
22/Apr/1923	2:00	-1:00
16/Sep/1923	3:00	0:00
13/Apr/1924	2:00	-1:00
21/Sep/1924	3:00	0:00
19/Apr/1925	2:00	-1:00
4/Oct/1925	3:00	0:00
18/Apr/1926	2:00	-1:00
3/Oct/1926	3:00	0:00
10/Apr/1927	2:00	-1:00
2/Oct/1927	3:00	0:00
22/Apr/1928	2:00	-1:00
7/Oct/1928	3:00	0:00
21/Apr/1929	2:00	-1:00
6/Oct/1929	3:00	0:00
13/Apr/1930	2:00	-1:00
5/Oct/1930	3:00	0:00
19/Apr/1931	2:00	-1:00
4/Oct/1931	3:00	0:00
17/Apr/1932	2:00	-1:00
2/Oct/1932	3:00	0:00
9/Apr/1933	2:00	-1:00
8/Oct/1933	3:00	0:00
22/Apr/1934	2:00	-1:00
7/Oct/1934	3:00	0:00
14/Apr/1935	2:00	-1:00
6/Oct/1935	3:00	0:00
19/Apr/1936	2:00	-1:00
4/Oct/1936	3:00	0:00
18/Apr/1937	2:00	-1:00
3/Oct/1937	3:00	0:00
10/Apr/1938	2:00	-1:00
2/Oct/1938	3:00	0:00
16/Apr/1939	2:00	-1:00
19/Nov/1939	3:00	0:00
25/Feb/1940	2:00	-1:00
6/Oct/1946	2:00	0:00
16/Mar/1947	2:00	-1:00
2/Nov/1947	2:00	0:00
18/Apr/1948	2:00	-1:00
31/Oct/1948	3:00	0:00
3/Apr/1949	2:00	-1:00
30/Oct/1949	3:00	0:00
16/Apr/1950	2:00	-1:00
22/Oct/1950	3:00	0:00
15/Apr/1951	2:00	-1:00
21/Oct/1951	3:00	0:00
20/Apr/1952	2:00	-1:00
26/Oct/1952	3:00	0:00
19/Apr/1953	2:00	-1:00
4/Oct/1953	3:00	0:00
11/Apr/1954	2:00	-1:00
3/Oct/1954	3:00	0:00
17/Apr/1955	2:00	-1:00
2/Oct/1955	3:00	0:00
22/Apr/1956	2:00	-1:00
7/Oct/1956	3:00	0:00
14/Apr/1957	2:00	-1:00
6/Oct/1957	3:00	0:00
20/Apr/1958	2:00	-1:00
5/Oct/1958	3:00	0:00
19/Apr/1959	2:00	-1:00
4/Oct/1959	3:00	0:00
10/Apr/1960	2:00	-1:00
2/Oct/1960	3:00	0:00
26/Mar/1961	2:00	-1:00
29/Oct/1961	3:00	0:00
25/Mar/1962	2:00	-1:00
28/Oct/1962	3:00	0:00
31/Mar/1963	2:00	-1:00
27/Oct/1963	3:00	0:00
22/Mar/1964	2:00	-1:00
25/Oct/1964	3:00	0:00
21/Mar/1965	2:00	-1:00
24/Oct/1965	3:00	0:00
20/Mar/1966	2:00	-1:00
23/Oct/1966	3:00	0:00
19/Mar/1967	2:00	-1:00
29/Oct/1967	3:00	0:00
Begin Standard		15E00
18/Feb/1968	2:00	-1:00
Begin Standard		0w00
31/Oct/1971	2:00	0:00
19/Mar/1972	2:00	-1:00
29/Oct/1972	3:00	0:00
18/Mar/1973	2:00	-1:00
28/Oct/1973	3:00	0:00
17/Mar/1974	2:00	-1:00
27/Oct/1974	3:00	0:00
16/Mar/1975	2:00	-1:00
26/Oct/1975	3:00	0:00
21/Mar/1976	2:00	-1:00
24/Oct/1976	3:00	0:00
20/Mar/1977	2:00	-1:00
23/Oct/1977	3:00	0:00
19/Mar/1978	2:00	-1:00
29/Oct/1978	3:00	0:00
18/Mar/1979	2:00	-1:00
28/Oct/1979	3:00	0:00
16/Mar/1980	2:00	-1:00
26/Oct/1980	3:00	0:00
29/Mar/1981	1:00	-1:00
25/Oct/1981	3:00	0:00
28/Mar/1982	1:00	-1:00
24/Oct/1982	2:00	0:00
27/Mar/1983	1:00	-1:00
23/Oct/1983	2:00	0:00
25/Mar/1984	1:00	-1:00
28/Oct/1984	2:00	0:00
31/Mar/1985	1:00	-1:00
27/Oct/1985	2:00	0:00
30/Mar/1986	1:00	-1:00
26/Oct/1986	2:00	0:00
29/Mar/1987	1:00	-1:00
25/Oct/1987	2:00	0:00
27/Mar/1988	1:00	-1:00
23/Oct/1988	2:00	0:00
26/Mar/1989	1:00	-1:00
29/Oct/1989	2:00	0:00
25/Mar/1990	1:00	-1:00
28/Oct/1990	2:00	0:00
31/Mar/1991	1:00	-1:00
27/Oct/1991	2:00	0:00
29/Mar/1992	1:00	-1:00
25/Oct/1992	2:00	0:00
28/Mar/1993	1:00	-1:00
24/Oct/1993	2:00	0:00
27/Mar/1994	1:00	-1:00
23/Oct/1994	2:00	0:00
26/Mar/1995	1:00	-1:00
29/Oct/1995	2:00	0:00
31/Mar/1996	1:00	-1:00
27/Oct/1996	2:00	0:00
30/Mar/1997	1:00	-1:00
26/Oct/1997	2:00	0:00
29/Mar/1998	1:00	-1:00
25/Oct/1998	2:00	0:00
28/Mar/1999	1:00	-1:00
24/Oct/1999	2:00	0:00
26/Mar/2000	1:00	-1:00
29/Oct/2000	2:00	0:00

Place	Lat	Long	Time
Abbeydorney	52N19	9w41	0:38:44
Abbeyfeale	52N24	9w18	0:37:12
Abbeyleix	52N55	7w20	0:29:20
Achill	53N56	9w54	0:39:36
Achill Sound	53N55	9w58	0:39:52
Adare	52N34	8w48	0:35:12
Adrigole	51N40	9w42	0:38:48
Aghleam	54N08	10w07	0:40:28
Ahascragh	53N24	8w20	0:33:20
Allihies	51N38	10w03	0:40:12
Annagassan	53N53	6w20	0:25:20
Annestown	52N07	7w16	0:29:04
An Uaimh → Navan	53N39	6w41	0:26:44
Ardagh	52N28	9w04	0:36:16
Ardara	54N46	8E25	-0:33:40
Ardee	53N52	6w33	0:26:12
Ardgroom	51N42	9w52	0:39:28
Ardmore	51N57	7w43	0:30:52
Ardnaree	54N06	9w08	0:36:32
Arklow	52N48	6w09	0:24:36
Arvagh	53N55	7w34	0:30:16
Ashbourne	53N31	6w24	0:25:36
Askeaton	52N36	8w58	0:35:52
Athboy	53N37	6w55	0:27:40
Athea	52N28	9w17	0:37:08
Athenry	53N18	8w45	0:35:00
Athleague	53N34	8w15	0:33:00
Athlone	53N25	7w56	0:31:44
Āth Luain → Athlone	53N25	7w56	0:31:44
Athy	53N00	7w00	0:28:00
Attymon	53N19	8w35	0:34:20
Aughrim	52N51	6w17	0:25:08
Baile Ātha Cliath → Dublin	53N20	6w15	0:25:00
Bailieborough	53N54	6w59	0:27:56
Balbriggan	53N37	6w11	0:24:44
Baldoyle	53N24	6w08	0:24:32
Balla	53N48	9w09	0:36:36
Ballagh	52N35	7w59	0:31:56
Ballaghaderreen	53N55	8w36	0:34:24
Ballina	54N07	9w09	0:36:36
Ballina	52N49	8w26	0:33:44
Ballinakill	52N53	7w18	0:29:12
Ballinalack	53N37	7w28	0:29:52
Ballinascarty	51N40	8w51	0:35:24
Ballinasloe	53N20	8w13	0:32:52
Ballindine	53N39	8w59	0:35:56
Ballineen	51N44	8w56	0:35:44
Ballingarry	52N29	8w52	0:35:28
Ballingeary	51N49	9w13	0:36:52
Ballinrobe	53N37	9w13	0:36:52
Ballintra	54N35	8w08	0:32:32
Ballybay	54N08	6w54	0:27:36
Ballybofey	54N48	7w47	0:31:08
Ballybunion	52N31	9w40	0:38:40
Ballycanew	52N36	6w19	0:25:16
Ballycastle	54N16	9w23	0:37:32
Ballyconneely	53N26	10w02	0:40:08
Ballyconnell	54N07	7w35	0:30:20
Ballycotton	51N50	8w01	0:32:04
Ballycroy	54N01	9w51	0:39:24
Ballyduff	52N27	9w40	0:38:40
Ballyduff	52N09	8w03	0:32:12
Ballyferriter	52N09	10w26	0:41:44
Ballygar	53N32	8w20	0:33:20
Ballygorman	55N22	7w21	0:29:24
Ballyhaise	54N03	7w19	0:29:16
Ballyhaunis	53N46	8w46	0:35:04
Ballyjamesduff	53N52	7w12	0:28:48
Ballylongford	52N33	9w28	0:37:52
Ballymacoda	51N57	7w54	0:31:36
Ballymahon	53N34	7w45	0:31:00
Ballymakeery (Ballyvourney)	51N55	9w09	0:36:36
Ballymoe	53N42	8w29	0:33:56
Ballymote	54N06	8w31	0:34:04
Ballymurray	53N35	8w08	0:32:32
Ballyneety	52N35	8w33	0:34:12
Ballynoe	52N03	8w05	0:32:20
Ballyragget	52N47	7w20	0:29:20
Ballysadare	54N13	8w31	0:34:04
Ballyshannon	54N30	8w11	0:32:44
Ballyvaughan	53N07	9w07	0:36:28
Ballyvourney → Ballymakeery	51N55	9w09	0:36:36
Baltimore	51N29	9w22	0:37:28
Baltinglass	52N55	6w41	0:26:44
Banagher	53N11	7w59	0:31:56
Bandon	51N45	8w45	0:35:00
Bangor Erris	54N09	9w45	0:39:00
Bansha	52N28	8w04	0:32:16
Banteer	52N07	8w54	0:35:36
Bantry	51N41	9w27	0:37:48
Bellahy	53N58	8w48	0:35:12
Belmullet	54N14	10w00	0:40:00
Beltra	54N13	8w37	0:34:28
Belturbet	54N06	7w28	0:29:52
Bennettsbridge	52N36	7w12	0:28:48
Birr	53N05	7w54	0:31:36
Blackrock	53N18	6w10	0:24:40
Blackwater	52N26	6w21	0:25:24
Blarney	51N56	8w34	0:34:16
Blessington	53N10	6w32	0:26:08
Borris	52N35	6w06	0:24:24
Borrisokane	52N59	8w07	0:32:28
Borrisoleigh	52N45	7w57	0:31:48
Boyle	53N58	8w18	0:33:12
Bray	53N12	6w06	0:24:24
Brí Chualann → Bray	53N12	6w06	0:24:24
Brittas	53N14	6w27	0:25:48
Bruff	52N29	8w33	0:34:12
Bruree	52N26	8w36	0:34:24
Bunclody	52N38	6w40	0:26:40
Buncrana	55N08	7w27	0:29:48
Bundoran	54N28	8w17	0:33:08
Bunnahowen	54N11	9w54	0:39:36
Butlers Bridge	54N02	7w22	0:29:28
Buttevant	52N14	8w40	0:34:40
Caher	52N21	7w56	0:31:44
Caherdaniel	51N45	10w05	0:40:20
Cahirciveen	51N57	10w13	0:40:52
Callan	52N33	7w23	0:29:32
Caltra	53N26	8w25	0:33:40
Cappamore	52N37	8w20	0:33:20
Cappoquin	52N08	7w50	0:31:20
Carlow	52N50	6w55	0:27:40
Carndonagh	55N15	7w15	0:29:00
Carnew	52N43	6w30	0:26:00
Carrickart	55N10	7w47	0:31:08
Carrickmacross	53N58	6w43	0:26:52
Carrick-On-Shannon	53N57	8w05	0:32:20
Carrick-On-Suir	52N21	7w25	0:29:40
Carrigahorig	53N04	8w09	0:32:36
Carrigaline	51N48	8w24	0:33:36
Carrigallen	53N59	7w39	0:30:36
Cashel	52N31	7w53	0:31:32
Cashel	53N25	9w48	0:39:12
Castlebar	53N52	9w17	0:37:08
Castlebellingham	53N54	6w23	0:25:32
Castleblayney	54N07	6w44	0:26:56
Castlecomer	52N48	7w12	0:28:48
Castledermot	52N55	6w50	0:27:20
Castlefin	54N47	7w35	0:30:20
Castleisland	52N14	9w27	0:37:48
Castlemaine	52N09	9w43	0:38:52
Castlemartyr	51N55	8w03	0:32:12
Castlepollard	53N40	7w17	0:29:08
Castlerea	53N46	8w29	0:33:56
Castletown	53N26	7w38	0:30:32
Castletown Bearhaven → CastletownBere	51N39	9w55	0:39:40
Castletown Bere (Castletown Bearhaven)	51N39	9w55	0:39:40
Castletownroche	52N10	8w28	0:33:52
Castletownshend	51N32	9w11	0:36:44
Cavan	54N00	7w21	0:29:24
Ceanannus Mór	53N44	6w53	0:27:32
Ceatharlach → Carlow	52N50	6w55	0:27:40
Charlestown	53N57	8w49	0:35:16
Cill Āirne → Killarney	52N03	9w30	0:38:00
Cill Choinnigh → Kilkenny	52N39	7w15	0:29:00
Clane	53N18	6w41	0:26:44
Clara	53N20	7w36	0:30:24
Clarecastle	52N49	8w57	0:35:48
Claregalway	53N21	8w57	0:35:48
Claremorris	53N44	9w00	0:36:00
Clashmore	52N00	7w48	0:31:12
Cleggan	53N33	10w09	0:40:36
Clifden	53N29	10w01	0:40:04
Cloghan	54N51	7w56	0:31:44
Cloghan	53N13	7w53	0:31:32
Cloghane	52N13	10w12	0:40:48
Clogheen	52N16	8w00	0:32:00
Cloghjordan	52N57	8w02	0:32:08
Clonakilty	51N37	8w54	0:35:36
Clondalkin	53N19	6w24	0:25:36
Clonee	53N25	6w26	0:25:44
Clones	54N11	7w15	0:29:00
Clonfert	53N14	8w05	0:32:20
Clonmany	55N14	7w25	0:29:40
Clonmel	52N21	7w42	0:30:48
Clonroche	52N27	6w43	0:26:52
Cloone	53N57	7w46	0:31:04
Cloyne	51N51	8w08	0:32:32
Cluain Meala → Clonmel	52N21	7w42	0:30:48
Coachford	51N53	8w48	0:35:12
Cobh	51N51	8w17	0:33:08
Collon	53N47	6w29	0:25:56
Collooney	54N11	8w29	0:33:56
Cong	53N32	9w19	0:37:16
Coolaney	54N11	8w29	0:33:56
Cootehill	54N04	7w05	0:28:20
Corcaigh → Cork	51N54	8w28	0:33:52
Cork	51N54	8w28	0:33:52
Corofin	52N56	9w03	0:36:12
Costelloe	53N17	9w32	0:38:08
Courtmacsherry	51N38	8w43	0:34:52
Courtown Harbour	52N38	6w13	0:24:52
Craughwell	53N13	8w43	0:34:52
Cregganbaun	53N42	9w51	0:39:24
Crookstown	51N50	8w50	0:35:20
Croom	52N31	8w42	0:34:48
Crosshaven	51N48	8w17	0:33:08
Crossmolina	54N06	9w20	0:37:20
Crusheen	52N58	8w53	0:35:32
Culdaff	55N18	7w11	0:28:44
Curreeney	52N43	8w08	0:32:32
Daingean	53N18	7w17	0:29:08
Dalkey	53N16	6w06	0:24:24
Delvin	53N36	7w05	0:28:20
Derrybrien	53N04	8w36	0:34:24
Dingle	52N08	10w15	0:41:00
Donegal	54N39	8w07	0:32:28
Doneraile	52N13	8w35	0:34:20
Donoughmore	51N57	8w45	0:35:00
Dooagh	53N59	10w09	0:40:36
Doonbeg	52N44	9w32	0:38:08
Drimoleague	51N38	9w14	0:36:56
Drogheda	53N43	6w21	0:25:24
Droichead Ātha → Drogheda	53N43	6w21	0:25:24
Droichead Nua	53N11	6w48	0:27:12
Dromahair	54N14	8w19	0:33:16
Dromcollliher	52N20	8w54	0:35:36
Dromod	53N51	7w55	0:31:40
Dromore West	54N15	8w53	0:35:32
Drumcliffe	54N20	8w30	0:34:00
Drumlish	53N48	7w46	0:31:04
Drumshanbo	54N02	8w02	0:32:08
Dublin (Baile Ātha Cliath)	53N20	6w15	0:25:00
Dugort	54N01	10w01	0:40:04
Duleek	53N39	6w25	0:25:40

IRELAND IRLANDA IRLANDE IRLAND EIRE

Duncormick 52N14 6w39 0:26:36
Dundalk 54N01 6w25 0:25:40
Dún Dealgan → Dundalk 54N01 6w25 0:25:40
Dundrum 53N17 6w15 0:25:00
Dunfanaghy 55N11 7w59 0:31:56
Dungarvan 52N05 7w37 0:30:28
Dungloe 54N57 8w22 0:33:28
Dunkerrin 52N55 7w55 0:31:40
Dunkineely 54N38 8w23 0:33:32
Dún Laoghaire 53N17 6w08 0:24:32
Dunlavin 53N02 6w41 0:26:44
Dunleary → Dún Laoghaire 53N17 6w08 0:24:32
Dunleer 53N50 6w24 0:25:36
Dunmanway 51N43 9w06 0:36:24
Dunmore 53N36 8w46 0:35:04
Dunmore East 52N09 7w00 0:28:00
Durris 51N36 9w31 0:38:04
Durrow 52N50 7w22 0:29:28
Easky 54N18 8w58 0:35:52
Edenderry 53N21 7w35 0:30:20
Edgeworthstown 53N42 7w36 0:30:24
Elphin 53N51 8w12 0:32:48
Emyvale 54N20 6w59 0:27:56
Ennis 52N50 8w59 0:35:56
Enniscorthy 52N30 6w34 0:26:16
Ennistymon 52N57 9w15 0:37:00
Eyrecourt 53N11 8w07 0:32:28
Fahan 55N05 7w28 0:29:52
Ferbane 53N15 7w49 0:31:16
Fermoy 52N08 8w16 0:33:04
Ferns 52N35 6w31 0:26:04
Fethard 52N27 7w41 0:30:44
Fintown 54N52 8w08 0:32:32
Foxford 53N58 9w08 0:36:32
Foynes 52N37 9w06 0:36:24
Freemount 52N16 8w53 0:35:32
Frenchpark 53N52 8w26 0:33:44
Freshford 52N43 7w24 0:29:36
Gaillimh → Galway 53N16 9w03 0:36:12
Galway 53N16 9w03 0:36:12
Glasson 53N28 7w52 0:31:28
Glenamaddy 53N37 8w35 0:34:20
Glenamoy 54N14 9w42 0:38:48
Glenbeigh 52N02 9w58 0:39:52
Glencolumbkille 54N43 8E45 -0:35:00
Glendowan 54N58 7w57 0:31:48
Glenealy 52N57 6w11 0:24:44
Glenfarne 54N17 7w59 0:31:56
Glengarriff 51N45 9w33 0:38:12
Glenties 54N47 8w17 0:33:08
Glenville 52N03 8w26 0:33:44
Glin 52N34 9w17 0:37:08
Golden 52N29 7w58 0:31:52
Goleen 51N28 9w43 0:38:52
Gorey 52N40 6w18 0:25:12
Gort 53N04 8w50 0:35:20
Gortahork 55N08 8w09 0:32:36
Granard 53N47 7w30 0:30:00
Greencastle 55N12 6w59 0:27:56
Grenagh 52N00 8w37 0:34:28
Greystones 53N09 6w04 0:24:16
Gweedore 55N03 8w14 0:32:56
Gweesalla 54N07 9w54 0:39:36
Hacketstown 52N52 6w33 0:26:12
Headford 53N28 9w05 0:36:20
Hollywood 53N06 6w35 0:26:20
Holycross 52N38 7w52 0:31:28
Hospital 52N29 8w25 0:33:40
Howth 53N23 6w04 0:24:16
Inch 52N08 9w59 0:39:56
Inistioge 52N29 7w04 0:28:16
Inniscrone 54N12 9w06 0:36:24
Jamestown 53N55 8w02 0:32:08
Kanturk 52N10 8w55 0:35:40
Kells → Ceanannus Mór 53N44 6w53 0:27:32
Kenmare 51N53 9w35 0:38:20
Kilbaha 52N33 9w52 0:39:28
Kilbeggan 53N22 7w29 0:29:56
Kilcar 54N38 8w35 0:34:20
Kilchreest 53N10 8w38 0:34:32
Kilcolgan 53N13 8w52 0:35:28
Kilconnell 53N20 8w25 0:33:40
Kilcormac 53N10 7w43 0:30:52
Kilcullen 53N08 6w45 0:27:00
Kildare 53N10 6w55 0:27:40
Kildorrery 52N14 8w26 0:33:44
Kildysart 52N41 9w06 0:36:24
Kilfenora 52N59 9w13 0:36:52
Kilfinane 52N21 8w28 0:33:52
Kilgarvan 51N45 9w26 0:37:44
Kilkee 52N41 9w38 0:38:32
Kilkelly 53N53 8w51 0:35:24
Kilkenny 52N39 7w15 0:29:00
Kilkerrin 53N33 8w34 0:34:16
Kilkieran 53N19 9w43 0:38:52
Killadoon 53N42 9w56 0:39:44
Killala 54N13 9w13 0:36:52
Killaloe 52N48 8w27 0:33:48
Killarney 52N03 9w30 0:38:00
Killashandra 54N00 7w32 0:30:08
Killavally 53N45 9w23 0:37:32
Killenaule 52N34 7w40 0:30:40
Killimor 53N10 8w17 0:33:08
Killorglin 52N06 9w47 0:39:08
Killucan 53N31 7w07 0:28:28
Killybegs 54N38 8w27 0:33:48
Kilmacthomas 52N12 7w25 0:29:40
Kilmaine 53N34 9w09 0:36:36
Kilmallock 52N23 8w34 0:34:16
Kilnaleck 53N52 7w19 0:29:16
Kilrush 52N39 9w30 0:38:00
Kiltealy 52N34 6w45 0:27:00
Kiltimagh 53N51 9w01 0:36:04
Kiltoom 53N28 8w01 0:32:04
Kingscourt 53N53 6w48 0:27:12
Kingstown → Dún Laoghaire 53N17 6w08 0:24:32
Kinnegad 53N26 7w05 0:28:20
Kinsale 51N42 8w32 0:34:08
Kinvara 53N08 8w55 0:35:40
Knoc 52N38 9w20 0:37:20
Knocklong 52N26 8w24 0:33:36
Laghy 54N37 8w05 0:32:20
Leenaun 53N36 9w45 0:39:00
Leighlinbridge 52N44 6w59 0:27:56
Leitrim 54N00 8w04 0:32:16
Letterfrack 53N33 10w00 0:40:00
Letterkenny 54N57 7w44 0:30:56
Lettermullen 53N13 9w42 0:38:48
Lifford 54N50 7w29 0:29:56
Limerick 52N40 8w38 0:34:32
Liscarney 53N43 9w35 0:38:20
Lisdoonvarna 53N01 9w15 0:37:00
Lismore 52N08 7w55 0:31:40
Listowel 52N27 9w29 0:37:56
Loch Garman → Wexford 52N20 6w27 0:25:48
Longford 53N44 7w47 0:31:08
Loughrea 53N12 8w34 0:34:16
Louisburgh 53N46 9w51 0:39:24
Louth 53N37 6w53 0:27:32
Louth 53N57 6w33 0:26:12
Lucan 53N22 6w27 0:25:48
Luimneach → Limerick 52N40 8w38 0:34:32
Lusk 53N32 6w10 0:24:40
Lyracrumpane 52N20 9w30 0:38:00
Maam Cross 53N27 9w31 0:38:04
Maas 54N50 8w22 0:33:28
Macroom 51N54 8w57 0:35:48
Malahide 57N27 6w09 0:24:36
Malin 55N18 7w15 0:29:00
Malin Beg 54N40 8E48 -0:35:12
Mallaranny 53N54 9w49 0:39:16
Mallow 52N08 8w39 0:34:36
Manorhamilton 54N18 8w10 0:32:40
Maryborough → Portlaoighise 53N02 7w17 0:29:08
Maynooth 53N23 6w35 0:26:20
Midleton 51N55 8w10 0:32:40
Millford 55N07 7w43 0:30:52
Millstreet 52N03 9w04 0:36:16
Miltown Malbay 52N50 9w23 0:37:32
Mitchelstown 52N16 8w16 0:33:04
Moate 53N24 7w58 0:31:52
Mohill 53N54 7w52 0:31:28
Monaghan 54N15 6w58 0:27:52
Monamolin 52N33 6w20 0:25:20
Monasterevin 53N07 7w02 0:28:08
Moneygall 52N53 7w57 0:31:48
Monivea 53N23 8w43 0:34:52
Mount Bellew Bridge 53N28 8w29 0:33:56
Mountmellick 53N07 7w20 0:29:20
Mountrath 53N00 7w27 0:29:48
Moville 55N11 7w03 0:28:12
Moycullen 53N21 9w09 0:36:36
Muine Bheag 52N41 6w58 0:27:52
Mullagh 53N49 6w57 0:27:48
Mullinahone 52N30 7w30 0:30:00
Mullinavat 52N21 7w10 0:28:40
Mullingar 53N32 7w20 0:29:20
Naas 53N13 6w39 0:26:36
Navan 53N39 6w41 0:26:44
Nenagh 52N52 8w12 0:32:48
Newbridge → Droichead Nua 53N11 6w48 0:27:12
Newcastle 52N16 7w48 0:31:12
Newcastle West 52N27 9w03 0:36:12
Newcestown 51N47 8w51 0:35:24
New Inn 52N26 7w53 0:31:32
Newmarket 52N13 9w00 0:36:00
Newmarket-On-Fergus 52N45 8w53 0:35:32
Newport 53N53 9w34 0:38:16
Newport 52N42 8w24 0:33:36
New Ross 52N24 6w56 0:27:44
Newtown Forbes 53N46 7w50 0:31:20
Oldcastle 53N46 7w10 0:28:40
Oranmore 53N16 8w54 0:35:36
Oughterard 53N25 9w17 0:37:08
Pallas Green 52N33 8w22 0:33:28
Pallaskenry 52N39 8w52 0:35:28
Partree 53N41 9w19 0:37:16
Passage East 52N13 6w59 0:27:56
Passage West 51N52 8w20 0:33:20
Paulstown 52N41 7w01 0:28:04
Pembroke 53N19 6w12 0:24:48
Pettigo 54N33 7w50 0:31:20
Portacloy 54N19 9w48 0:39:12
Portarlington 53N10 7w11 0:28:44
Port Láirghe → Waterford 52N15 7w06 0:28:24
Portlaoighise 53N02 7w17 0:29:08
Portlaw 52N17 7w19 0:29:16
Portsalon 55N13 7w37 0:30:28
Portumna 53N06 8w13 0:32:52
Queenstown → Cobh 51N51 8w17 0:33:08
Quilty 52N47 9w26 0:37:44
Raphoe 54N52 7w36 0:30:24
Rathangan 53N12 6w59 0:27:56
Rathcormack 52N54 8w17 0:33:08
Rathdowney 52N50 7w34 0:30:16
Rathdrum 52N56 6w13 0:24:52
Rathmines 53N19 6w15 0:25:00
Rathkeale 52N32 8w56 0:35:44
Ráth Luirc 52N21 8w41 0:34:44
Rathmelton 55N02 7w38 0:30:32
Rathmore 52N03 9w13 0:36:52
Rathmullen 55N06 7w33 0:30:12
Rathnew 53N00 6w05 0:24:20
Rathowen 53N40 7w31 0:30:04
Ringville 52N02 7w34 0:30:16
Robertstown 53N15 6w59 0:27:56
Rochfort Bridge 53N23 7w17 0:29:08
Rockcorry 54N07 7w01 0:28:04
Roscommon 53N38 8w11 0:32:44
Roscrea 52N57 7w47 0:31:08
Ros Mhic Treoin → New Ross 52N24 6w56 0:27:44
Rosscarbery 51N35 9w01 0:36:04
Rosses Point 54N18 8w33 0:34:12
Rosslare 52N17 6w23 0:25:32
Rosslare Harbour 52N15 6w22 0:25:28
Roundstone 53N23 9w53 0:39:32
Roundwood 53N04 6w13 0:24:52
Rush 53N32 6w06 0:24:24
Scarriff 52N55 8w31 0:34:04
Scartaglin 52N10 9w26 0:37:44
Schull 51N32 9w33 0:38:12
Shercock 54N00 6w54 0:27:36
Shillelagh 52N45 6w32 0:26:08
Shrule 53N30 9w08 0:36:32
Silvermines 52N47 8w13 0:32:52
Skibbereen 51N33 9w15 0:37:00
Skreen 54N15 8w45 0:35:00
Sligeach → Sligo 54N17 8w28 0:33:52
Sligo 54N17 8w28 0:33:52
Stradbally 53N00 7w08 0:28:32
Stradone 53N58 7w14 0:28:56
Strandhill 54N17 8w36 0:34:24
Stranorlar 54N48 7w46 0:31:04
Strokestown 53N47 8w08 0:32:32
Summerhill 53N29 6w44 0:26:56
Swanlinbar 54N10 7w42 0:30:48
Swinford 53N57 8w57 0:35:48
Swords 53N28 6w13 0:24:52
Taghmon 52N18 6w39 0:26:36
Tallaght 53N26 6w21 0:25:24
Tallow 52N05 8w00 0:32:00
Tarbert 52N32 9w23 0:37:32
Templemore 52N48 7w50 0:31:20
Thomastown 52N31 7w08 0:28:32
Thurles 52N41 7w49 0:31:16
Timahoe 53N20 6w49 0:27:16
Tinahely 52N47 7w26 0:29:44
Tipperary 52N29 8w10 0:32:40
Tobercurry 54N03 8w43 0:34:52
Toomevara 52N50 8w02 0:32:08
Toormakeady 53N39 9w24 0:37:36
Traighlí → Tralee 52N16 9w42 0:38:48
Tralee 52N16 9w42 0:38:48
Tramore 52N10 7w10 0:28:40
Trim 53N34 6w47 0:27:08
Tuam 53N31 8w50 0:35:20
Tulla 52N52 8w45 0:35:00
Tullamore 53N16 7w30 0:30:00
Tullow 52N48 6w44 0:26:56
Tulsk 53N47 8w16 0:33:04
Tynagh 53N09 8w22 0:33:28
Tyrrellspass 53N23 7w22 0:29:28
Urlingford 52N42 7w35 0:30:20
Ventry 52N08 10w22 0:41:28
Virginia 53N49 7w04 0:28:16
Waterford 52N15 7w06 0:28:24
Watergrasshill 52N01 8w21 0:33:24
Waterville 51N49 10w13 0:40:52
Westport 53N48 9w32 0:38:08
Wexford 52N20 6w27 0:25:48
Whitegate 51N50 8w14 0:32:56
Wicklow 52N59 6w03 0:24:12
Woodford 53N03 8w23 0:33:32
Youghal 51N51 7w50 0:31:20

IRLANDA DEL NORTE NORD IRLAND IRLANDE DU NORD IRELAND, NORTHERN

Time Table		
Before 1/Jan/1880 LMT		
Begin Standard		5w55
1/Jan/1880	0:00	0:24
Begin Standard		0w00
21/May/1916	2:00	0:00
3/Apr/1921	2:00	-1:00
3/Oct/1921	3:00	0:00
26/Mar/1922	2:00	-1:00
8/Oct/1922	3:00	0:00
22/Apr/1923	2:00	-1:00
16/Sep/1923	3:00	0:00
13/Apr/1924	2:00	-1:00
21/Sep/1924	3:00	0:00
19/Apr/1925	2:00	-1:00
4/Oct/1925	3:00	0:00
18/Apr/1926	2:00	-1:00
3/Oct/1926	3:00	0:00
10/Apr/1927	2:00	-1:00
2/Oct/1927	3:00	0:00
22/Apr/1928	2:00	-1:00
7/Oct/1928	3:00	0:00
21/Apr/1929	2:00	-1:00
6/Oct/1929	3:00	0:00
13/Apr/1930	2:00	-1:00
5/Oct/1930	3:00	0:00
19/Apr/1931	2:00	-1:00
4/Oct/1931	3:00	0:00
17/Apr/1932	2:00	-1:00
2/Oct/1932	3:00	0:00
9/Apr/1933	2:00	-1:00
8/Oct/1933	3:00	0:00
22/Apr/1934	2:00	-1:00
7/Oct/1934	3:00	0:00
14/Apr/1935	2:00	-1:00
6/Oct/1935	3:00	0:00
19/Apr/1936	2:00	-1:00
4/Oct/1936	3:00	0:00
18/Apr/1937	2:00	-1:00
3/Oct/1937	3:00	0:00
10/Apr/1938	2:00	-1:00
2/Oct/1938	3:00	0:00
16/Apr/1939	2:00	-1:00
24/Jul/1945	2:00	0:00
14/Apr/1946	2:00	-1:00
6/Oct/1946	3:00	0:00
16/Mar/1947	2:00	-1:00
2/Nov/1947	3:00	0:00
14/Mar/1948	2:00	-1:00
31/Oct/1948	3:00	0:00
3/Apr/1949	2:00	-1:00
30/Oct/1949	3:00	0:00
16/Apr/1950	2:00	-1:00
22/Oct/1950	3:00	0:00
15/Apr/1951	2:00	-1:00
21/Oct/1951	3:00	0:00
20/Apr/1952	2:00	-1:00
26/Oct/1952	3:00	0:00
19/Apr/1953	2:00	-1:00
4/Oct/1953	3:00	0:00
11/Apr/1954	2:00	-1:00
3/Oct/1954	3:00	0:00
17/Apr/1955	2:00	-1:00
2/Oct/1955	3:00	0:00
22/Apr/1956	2:00	-1:00
7/Oct/1956	3:00	0:00
14/Apr/1957	2:00	-1:00
6/Oct/1957	3:00	0:00
20/Apr/1958	2:00	-1:00
5/Oct/1958	3:00	0:00
19/Apr/1959	2:00	-1:00
4/Oct/1959	3:00	0:00
10/Apr/1960	2:00	-1:00
2/Oct/1960	3:00	0:00
26/Mar/1961	2:00	-1:00
29/Oct/1961	3:00	0:00
25/Mar/1962	2:00	-1:00
28/Oct/1962	3:00	0:00
31/Mar/1963	2:00	-1:00
27/Oct/1963	3:00	0:00
22/Mar/1964	2:00	-1:00
25/Oct/1964	3:00	0:00
21/Mar/1965	2:00	-1:00
24/Oct/1965	3:00	0:00
20/Mar/1966	2:00	-1:00
23/Oct/1966	3:00	0:00
19/Mar/1967	2:00	-1:00
29/Oct/1967	3:00	0:00
Begin Standard		15E00
18/Feb/1968	2:00	-1:00
Begin Standard		0w00
31/Oct/1971	2:00	0:00
19/Mar/1972	2:00	-1:00
29/Oct/1972	3:00	0:00
18/Mar/1973	2:00	-1:00
28/Oct/1973	3:00	0:00
17/Mar/1974	2:00	-1:00
27/Oct/1974	3:00	0:00
16/Mar/1975	2:00	-1:00
26/Oct/1975	3:00	0:00
21/Mar/1976	2:00	-1:00
24/Oct/1976	3:00	0:00
20/Mar/1977	2:00	-1:00
23/Oct/1977	3:00	0:00
19/Mar/1978	2:00	-1:00
29/Oct/1978	3:00	0:00
18/Mar/1979	2:00	-1:00
28/Oct/1979	3:00	0:00
16/Mar/1980	2:00	-1:00
26/Oct/1980	3:00	0:00
29/Mar/1981	1:00	-1:00
25/Oct/1981	2:00	0:00
28/Mar/1982	1:00	-1:00
24/Oct/1982	2:00	0:00
27/Mar/1983	1:00	-1:00
23/Oct/1983	2:00	0:00
25/Mar/1984	1:00	-1:00
28/Oct/1984	2:00	0:00
31/Mar/1985	1:00	-1:00
27/Oct/1985	2:00	0:00
30/Mar/1986	1:00	-1:00
26/Oct/1986	2:00	0:00
29/Mar/1987	1:00	-1:00
25/Oct/1987	2:00	0:00
27/Mar/1988	1:00	-1:00
23/Oct/1988	2:00	0:00
26/Mar/1989	1:00	-1:00
29/Oct/1989	2:00	0:00
25/Mar/1990	1:00	-1:00
28/Oct/1990	2:00	0:00
31/Mar/1991	1:00	-1:00
27/Oct/1991	2:00	0:00
29/Mar/1992	1:00	-1:00
25/Oct/1992	2:00	0:00
28/Mar/1993	1:00	-1:00
24/Oct/1993	2:00	0:00
27/Mar/1994	1:00	-1:00
23/Oct/1994	2:00	0:00
26/Mar/1995	1:00	-1:00
29/Oct/1995	2:00	0:00
31/Mar/1996	1:00	-1:00
27/Oct/1996	2:00	0:00
30/Mar/1997	1:00	-1:00
26/Oct/1997	2:00	0:00
29/Mar/1998	1:00	-1:00
25/Oct/1998	2:00	0:00
28/Mar/1999	1:00	-1:00
24/Oct/1999	2:00	0:00
26/Mar/2000	1:00	-1:00
29/Oct/2000	2:00	0:00

Place	Lat	Long	Time
Antrim	54N43	6w13	0:24:52
Ardglass	54N16	5w36	0:22:24
Armagh	54N21	6w39	0:26:36
Augher	54N26	7w09	0:28:36
Aughnacloy	54N25	6w58	0:27:52
Ballintoy	55N14	6w21	0:25:24
Ballybogy	55N07	6w34	0:26:16
Ballycastle	55N12	6w15	0:25:00
Ballyclare	54N46	6w01	0:24:04
Ballygawley	54N28	7w02	0:28:08
Ballyhalbert	54N30	5w28	0:21:52
Ballymena	54N52	6w17	0:25:08
Ballymoney	55N04	6w31	0:26:04
Ballynahinch	54N24	5w54	0:23:36
Ballyvoy	55N12	6w11	0:24:44
Ballywalter	54N33	5w30	0:22:00
Banbridge	54N21	6w16	0:25:04
Bangor	54N40	5w40	0:22:40
Belcoo	54N17	7w52	0:31:28
Belfast	54N35	5w55	0:23:40
Belleek	54N28	8w06	0:32:24
Brookeborough	54N19	7w24	0:29:36
Broughshane	54N54	6w12	0:24:48
Bushmills	55N12	6w32	0:26:08
Carncastle	54N54	5w53	0:23:32
Carnlough	54N59	5w59	0:23:56
Carrickfergus	54N43	5w49	0:23:16
Castledawson	54N47	6w33	0:26:12
Castlederg	54N42	7w36	0:30:24
Castlereagh	54N33	5w48	0:23:12
Castlewellan	54N16	5w57	0:23:48
Claudy	54N54	7w09	0:28:36
Clogher	54N25	7w12	0:28:48
Clough	54N17	5w50	0:23:20
Coalisland	54N32	6w42	0:26:48
Coleraine	55N08	6w40	0:26:40
Comber	54N33	5w45	0:23:00
Cookstown	54N39	6w45	0:27:00
Crossgar	54N24	5w45	0:23:00
Crossmaglen	54N05	6w37	0:26:28
Crumlin	54N37	6w14	0:24:56
Cushendall	55N06	6w04	0:24:16
Cushendun	55N08	6w02	0:24:08
Derry → Londonderry	55N00	7w19	0:29:16
Derrykeevan	55N08	6w29	0:25:56
Donaghadee	54N39	5w33	0:22:12
Donaghmore	54N32	6w49	0:27:16
Downpatrick	54N20	5w43	0:22:52
Draperstown	54N48	6w47	0:27:08
Dromara	54N23	6w01	0:24:04
Dromore	54N25	6w09	0:24:36
Drumquin	54N37	7w30	0:30:00
Dundrum	54N16	5w51	0:23:24
Dungannon	54N31	6w46	0:27:04
Dungiven	54N55	6w55	0:27:40
Dunloy	55N01	6w25	0:25:40
Dunmurry	54N33	6w01	0:24:04
Dunnamanagh	54N52	7w18	0:29:12
Eden	54N43	5w47	0:23:08
Ederny	54N32	7w39	0:30:36
Eglinton	55N01	7w11	0:28:44
Enniskillen	54N21	7w38	0:30:32
Fintona	54N30	7w19	0:29:16
Finvoy	55N00	6w30	0:26:00
Fivemiletown	54N23	7w18	0:29:12
Garrison	54N25	8w05	0:32:20
Gilford	54N23	6w22	0:25:28
Glenarm	54N58	5w57	0:23:48
Glenavy	54N35	6w13	0:24:52
Greenisland	54N42	5w52	0:23:28
Greyabbey	54N32	5w30	0:22:00
Hillsborough	54N28	6w05	0:24:20
Hilltown	54N12	6w08	0:24:32
Holywood	54N38	5w49	0:23:16
Irvinestown	54N28	7w38	0:30:32
Katesbridge	54N17	6w08	0:24:32
Keady	54N15	6w42	0:26:48
Kesh	54N32	7w43	0:30:52
Kilkeel	54N04	6w00	0:24:00
Killeter	54N40	7w41	0:30:44
Killough	54N16	5w39	0:22:36
Killyleagh	54N24	5w39	0:22:36
Kircubbin	54N24	5w28	0:21:52
Lack	54N33	7w35	0:30:20
Larne	54N51	5w49	0:23:16
Limavady	55N03	6w57	0:27:48
Lisburn	54N31	6w03	0:24:12
Lisnaskea	54N15	7w27	0:29:48
Londonderry	55N00	7w19	0:29:16
Lurgan	54N28	6w20	0:25:20
Macosquin	55N06	6w43	0:26:52
Maghera	54N51	6w40	0:26:40
Magherafelt	54N45	6w36	0:26:24
Markethill	54N18	6w31	0:26:04
Middletown	54N18	6w50	0:27:20
Moira	54N30	6w17	0:25:08
Moneymore	54N42	6w41	0:26:44
Moy	54N27	6w42	0:26:48
Newcastle	54N12	5w54	0:23:36
Newry	54N11	6w20	0:25:20
Newtownabbey	54N36	5w54	0:23:36
Newtownards	54N36	5w41	0:22:44
Newtownbutler	54N12	7w23	0:29:32
Newtown Crommelin	54N59	6w13	0:24:52
Newtownhamilton	54N11	6w35	0:26:20
Newtownstewart	54N43	7w24	0:29:36
North Down Cbangor	54N40	5w40	0:22:40
Omagh	54N36	7w18	0:29:12
Parkmore	55N02	6w06	0:24:24
Plumbridge	54N46	7w15	0:29:00
Pomeroy	54N36	6w56	0:27:44
Portadown	54N26	6w27	0:25:48
Portaferry	54N23	5w33	0:22:12
Portglenone	54N53	6w27	0:25:48
Portrush	55N12	6w40	0:26:40
Portstewart	55N11	6w43	0:26:52
Poyntzpass	54N18	6w23	0:25:32
Randalstown	54N45	6w18	0:25:12
Rathfriland	54N14	6w10	0:24:40
Rosslea	54N14	7w11	0:28:44
Rostrevor	54N06	6w12	0:24:48
Saintfield	54N28	5w47	0:23:08
Sixmilecross	54N34	7w08	0:28:32
Stewartstown	54N35	6w41	0:26:44
Strabane	54N49	7w27	0:29:48
Strangford	54N22	5w34	0:22:16
Tandragee	54N21	6w25	0:25:40
Toomebridge	54N45	6w27	0:25:48
Trillick	54N27	7w30	0:30:00
Warrenpoint	54N06	6w15	0:25:00
Whitehead	54N46	5w43	0:22:52

ISRAEL | ISRAËL | PALESTINE | YISRA'EL

Time Table # 1

Date	Time	Offset
Before 1/Oct/1900 LMT		
Begin Standard 30E00		
1/Oct/1900	0:00	-2:00
10/May/1957	0:00	-3:00
1/Oct/1957	0:00	-2:00
1/May/1958	0:00	-3:00
1/Oct/1958	0:00	-2:00
1/May/1959	1:00	-3:00
30/Sep/1959	3:00	-2:00
1/May/1960	1:00	-3:00
30/Sep/1960	3:00	-2:00
1/May/1961	1:00	-3:00
30/Sep/1961	3:00	-2:00
1/May/1962	1:00	-3:00
30/Sep/1962	3:00	-2:00
1/May/1963	1:00	-3:00
30/Sep/1963	3:00	-2:00
1/May/1964	1:00	-3:00
30/Sep/1964	3:00	-2:00
1/May/1965	1:00	-3:00
30/Sep/1965	3:00	-2:00
1/May/1966	1:00	-3:00
1/Oct/1966	3:00	-2:00
1/May/1967	0:00	-3:00
30/Jun/1967	0:00	-2:00
7/Jul/1974	0:00	-3:00
13/Oct/1974	0:00	-2:00
20/Apr/1975	0:00	-3:00
31/Aug/1975	0:00	-2:00
14/Apr/1985	0:00	-3:00
15/Sep/1985	0:00	-2:00
18/May/1986	0:00	-3:00
7/Sep/1986	0:00	-2:00
15/Apr/1987	0:00	-3:00
13/Sep/1987	0:00	-2:00
9/Apr/1988	0:00	-3:00
3/Sep/1988	0:00	-2:00
29/Apr/1989	0:00	-3:00
2/Sep/1989	0:00	-2:00
25/Mar/1990	0:00	-3:00
26/Aug/1990	0:00	-2:00
10/Mar/1991	0:00	-3:00
1/Sep/1991	0:00	-2:00

....

Time Table # 2

Date	Time	Offset
Before 1/Jan/1920 LMT		
Begin Standard 30E00		
1/Jan/1920	0:00	-2:00
18/Apr/1920	2:00	-3:00
3/Oct/1920	2:00	-2:00
17/Apr/1921	2:00	-3:00
2/Oct/1921	2:00	-2:00
16/Apr/1922	2:00	-3:00
1/Oct/1922	2:00	-2:00
15/Apr/1923	2:00	-3:00
7/Oct/1923	2:00	-2:00
29/Apr/1962	2:00	-3:00
1/Oct/1962	2:00	-2:00
1/May/1963	2:00	-3:00
30/Sep/1963	2:00	-2:00
1/May/1964	2:00	-3:00
1/Oct/1964	2:00	-2:00
1/May/1965	2:00	-3:00
30/Sep/1965	2:00	-2:00
24/Apr/1966	2:00	-3:00
1/Oct/1966	2:00	-2:00
1/May/1967	2:00	-3:00
1/Jul/1967	0:00	-2:00
7/Jul/1974	0:00	-3:00
13/Oct/1974	0:00	-2:00
20/Apr/1975	0:00	-3:00
31/Aug/1975	0:00	-2:00
14/Apr/1985	0:00	-3:00
15/Sep/1985	0:00	-2:00
18/May/1986	0:00	-3:00
7/Sep/1986	0:00	-2:00
15/Apr/1987	0:00	-3:00
13/Sep/1987	0:00	-2:00
9/Apr/1988	0:00	-3:00
3/Sep/1988	0:00	-2:00
29/Apr/1989	0:00	-3:00
2/Sep/1989	0:00	-2:00
25/Mar/1990	0:00	-3:00
26/Aug/1990	0:00	-2:00
10/Mar/1991	0:00	-3:00
1/Sep/1991	0:00	-2:00

....

Time Table # 3

Date	Time	Offset
Before 1/Jan/1880 LMT		
Begin Standard 35E10		
1/Jan/1880	0:00	-2:21
Begin Standard 30E00		
1/Jan/1918	0:00	-2:00
1/Jun/1940	0:00	-3:00
1/Nov/1942	0:00	-2:00
1/Apr/1943	2:00	-3:00
1/Nov/1943	0:00	-2:00
1/Apr/1944	0:00	-3:00
1/Nov/1944	0:00	-2:00
16/Apr/1945	0:00	-3:00
1/Nov/1945	2:00	-2:00
16/Apr/1946	2:00	-3:00
1/Nov/1946	0:00	-2:00
23/May/1948	0:00	-4:00
1/Sep/1948	0:00	-3:00
1/Nov/1948	2:00	-2:00
1/May/1949	0:00	-3:00
1/Nov/1949	2:00	-2:00
16/Apr/1950	0:00	-3:00
15/Sep/1950	3:00	-2:00
1/Apr/1951	0:00	-3:00
11/Nov/1951	3:00	-2:00
20/Apr/1952	2:00	-3:00
19/Oct/1952	3:00	-2:00
12/Apr/1953	2:00	-3:00
13/Sep/1953	3:00	-2:00
13/Jun/1954	0:00	-3:00
12/Sep/1954	0:00	-2:00
11/Jun/1955	2:00	-3:00
11/Sep/1955	0:00	-2:00
3/Jun/1956	0:00	-3:00
30/Sep/1956	3:00	-2:00
29/Apr/1957	2:00	-3:00
22/Sep/1957	0:00	-2:00
7/Jul/1974	0:00	-3:00
13/Oct/1974	0:00	-2:00
20/Apr/1975	0:00	-3:00
31/Aug/1975	0:00	-2:00
14/Apr/1985	0:00	-3:00
15/Sep/1985	0:00	-2:00
18/May/1986	0:00	-3:00
7/Sep/1986	0:00	-2:00
15/Apr/1987	0:00	-3:00
13/Sep/1987	0:00	-2:00
9/Apr/1988	0:00	-3:00
3/Sep/1988	0:00	-2:00
29/Apr/1989	0:00	-3:00
2/Sep/1989	0:00	-2:00
25/Mar/1990	0:00	-3:00
26/Aug/1990	0:00	-2:00
10/Mar/1991	0:00	-3:00
1/Sep/1991	0:00	-2:00

....

Time Table # 4

Date	Time	Offset
Before 1/Jan/1880 LMT		
Begin Standard 35E10		
1/Jan/1880	0:00	-2:21
Begin Standard 30E00		
1/Jan/1918	0:00	-2:00
1/Jun/1940	0:00	-3:00
1/Nov/1942	0:00	-2:00
1/Apr/1943	2:00	-3:00
1/Nov/1943	0:00	-2:00
1/Apr/1944	0:00	-3:00
1/Nov/1944	0:00	-2:00
16/Apr/1945	0:00	-3:00
1/Nov/1945	2:00	-2:00
16/Apr/1946	2:00	-3:00
1/Nov/1946	0:00	-2:00
7/Jul/1974	0:00	-3:00
13/Oct/1974	0:00	-2:00
20/Apr/1975	0:00	-3:00
31/Aug/1975	0:00	-2:00
14/Apr/1985	0:00	-3:00
15/Sep/1985	0:00	-2:00
18/May/1986	0:00	-3:00
7/Sep/1986	0:00	-2:00
15/Apr/1987	0:00	-3:00
13/Sep/1987	0:00	-2:00
9/Apr/1988	0:00	-3:00
3/Sep/1988	0:00	-2:00
29/Apr/1989	0:00	-3:00
2/Sep/1989	0:00	-2:00
25/Mar/1990	0:00	-3:00
26/Aug/1990	0:00	-2:00
10/Mar/1991	0:00	-3:00
1/Sep/1991	0:00	-2:00

DIVISIONS

1. Israel (before 1967)
2. Gaza Strip (annexed 1967)
3. Golan Heights (annexed 1967)
4. West Bank (annexed 1967)

Place	Table	Lat	Long	Offset
Abū Ghaush 1	3	31N48	35E06	-2:20:24
Abū Qashash 4	4	31N57	35E11	-2:20:44
Acre → 'Akko 1	3	32N55	35E05	-2:20:20
Afiqim 1	3	32N40	35E35	-2:22:20
'Afula 1	3	32N36	35E17	-2:21:08
'Afula 'Illit 1	3	32N38	35E20	-2:21:20
'Akko (Acre) 1	3	32N55	35E05	-2:20:20
Al-'Āl 3	2	32N48	35E44	-2:22:56
Al-'Aqabah 4	4	29N31	35E00	-2:20:00
Al-Bīrah 4	4	31N54	35E13	-2:20:52
Al-Faluje 1	3	31N37	34E44	-2:18:56
Al-Khalīl (Hebron) 4	4	31N32	35E06	-2:20:24
Al-Khushnīyah 3	2	33N00	35E48	-2:23:12
Allone Abba 1	3	32N44	35E10	-2:20:40
Almagor 1	3	32N55	35E36	-2:22:24
Al-Majdal 1	3	31N45	34E35	-2:18:20
Al-Quds → Yerushalayim 1	3	31N46	35E14	-2:20:56
Al Yāmūn 4	4	32N29	35E14	-2:20:56
Al Yehudiya 1	3	32N02	34E53	-2:19:32
'Anabtā 4	4	32N19	35E07	-2:20:28
'Anātā 4	4	31N49	35E16	-2:21:04
An-Nazlah 2	1	31N32	34E29	-2:17:56
'Arad 1	3	31N15	35E13	-2:20:52
Arbel 1	3	32N49	35E29	-2:21:56
Arīḥā (Jericho) 4	4	31N52	35E27	-2:21:48
Ashdod 1	3	31N49	34E40	-2:18:40
Ashdot Ya'Aqov 1	3	32N40	35E35	-2:22:20
Ashmura 1	3	33N03	35E39	-2:22:36
Ashqelon 1	3	31N40	34E35	-2:18:20
As-Samū' 4	4	31N24	35E04	-2:20:16
'Atlit 1	3	32N41	34E56	-2:19:44
'Attīl 4	4	32N22	35E04	-2:20:16
Azor 1	3	32N01	34E48	-2:19:12
Az-Zabābidah 4	4	32N23	35E20	-2:21:20
Az-Ẓāhirīyah 4	4	31N25	34E58	-2:19:52
'Azzūn 4	4	32N11	35E03	-2:20:12
Bahjī 1	3	32N56	35E06	-2:20:24
Banī Suhaylah 2	1	31N20	34E20	-2:17:20
Bāniyās 3	2	33N15	35E41	-2:22:44
Bāqa el Gharbiyya 1	3	32N25	35E03	-2:20:12
Bat Yam 1	3	32N01	34E45	-2:19:00
Bayt Ḥānūm 2	1	31N32	34E33	-2:18:12
Bayt Jālā 4	4	31N43	35E11	-2:20:44
Bayt Laḥm (Bethlehem) 4	4	31N43	35E12	-2:20:48
Bayt Sāḥūr 4	4	31N42	35E13	-2:20:52
Bayt Sīrā 4	4	31N53	35E03	-2:20:12
Be'er Menuḥa 1	3	30N19	35E08	-2:20:32
Be'er Ora 1	3	29N43	34E59	-2:19:56
Beersheba → Be'er Sheva' 1	3	31N14	34E47	-2:19:08
Be'er Sheva' (Beersheba) 1	3	31N14	34E47	-2:19:08
Be'er Toviyya 1	3	31N44	34E44	-2:18:56
Be'er Ya'Agov 1	3	31N56	34E50	-2:19:20
Beisan 1	3	32N30	35E30	-2:22:00
Beit Jibran → Bet Guvrin 1	3	31N36	34E54	-2:19:36
Bene Beraq 1	3	32N05	34E50	-2:19:20
Bene Berit 1	3	32N35	35E26	-2:21:44
Bene Re'em 1	3	31N46	34E47	-2:19:08
Beror Ḥayil 1	3	31N33	34E38	-2:18:32
Bet Alfa 1	3	32N31	35E26	-2:21:44
Bet Dagan 1	3	32N00	34E50	-2:19:20
Bet Guvrin 1	3	31N36	34E54	-2:19:36
Bet Ha'Arava 4	4	31N48	35E32	-2:22:08
Bet HaShitta 1	3	32N33	35E26	-2:21:44
Bethlehem → Bayt Laḥm 4	4	31N43	35E12	-2:20:48
Bet Sh'ean 1	3	32N30	35E30	-2:22:00
Bet Shemesh 1	3	31N45	35E00	-2:20:00
Beẓet 1	3	33N05	35E08	-2:20:32
Biddiyā 4	4	32N07	35E05	-2:20:20
Binyamina 1	3	32N31	34E57	-2:19:48
Bnei Braq → Bene Beraq 1	3	32N05	34E50	-2:19:20
Buṭayḥah 3	2	32N56	35E53	-2:23:32
Dabbūrīya 1	3	32N41	35E22	-2:21:28
Dafna 1	3	33N14	35E38	-2:22:32
Dāliyat el Karmel 1	3	32N42	35E03	-2:20:12
Daliyya 1	3	32N35	35E04	-2:20:16
Dan 1	3	33N14	35E39	-2:22:36
Dayr al-Balaḥ 2	1	31N25	34E21	-2:17:24
Dayr al-Ghuṣūn 4	4	32N21	35E05	-2:20:20
Dayr Dibwān 4	4	31N55	35E16	-2:21:04
Dayr Sharaf 4	4	32N15	35E11	-2:20:44
Deganya 1	3	32N42	35E35	-2:22:20
Deir el Asad 1	3	32N56	35E16	-2:21:04
Dimona 1	3	31N04	35E02	-2:20:08
Dor 1	3	32N37	34E55	-2:19:40
Dūrā 4	4	31N30	35E02	-2:20:08
Elat 1	3	29N33	34E57	-2:19:48
El Faluje 1	3	31N37	34E44	-2:18:56
El Majdal 1	3	31N45	34E35	-2:18:20
'En Dor 1	3	32N39	35E25	-2:21:40
'En Gedi 1	3	31N27	35E23	-2:21:32
'En Gev 1	3	32N47	35E38	-2:22:32
'En Ḥarod 1	3	32N33	35E23	-2:21:32
'En HaShofet 1	3	32N35	35E06	-2:20:24
'En Netafim 1	3	29N35	34E53	-2:19:32
'En Yahav 1	3	30N38	35E11	-2:20:44
Erez 1	3	31N34	34E34	-2:18:16
Eshta'ol 1	3	31N47	35E00	-2:20:00
Eṭ Ṭaiyiba 1	3	32N16	35E01	-2:20:04
Eṭ Ṭīra 1	3	32N14	34E57	-2:19:48
Even Yehuda 1	3	32N16	34E53	-2:19:32
'Evron 1	3	32N59	35E06	-2:20:24
Faqqū'Ah 4	4	32N30	35E24	-2:21:36
Fīq 3	2	32N47	35E42	-2:22:48
Gat 1	3	31N37	34E47	-2:19:08
Ga'Ton 1	3	33N00	35E13	-2:20:52
Gedera 1	3	31N49	34E46	-2:19:04
Gesher HaZiw 1	3	33N02	35E06	-2:20:24
Gezer 1	3	31N52	34E55	-2:19:40
Ghazzah (Gaza) 2	1	31N30	34E28	-2:17:52
Ginnosar 1	3	32N51	35E31	-2:22:04
Giv'Atayim 1	3	32N04	34E48	-2:19:12
Giv'At Brenner 1	3	31N52	34E48	-2:19:12
Gonen 1	3	33N08	35E39	-2:22:36
Ḥadera 1	3	32N26	34E55	-2:19:40
HaGosherim 1	3	33N13	35E37	-2:22:28
Haifa → Ḥefa 1	3	32N49	34E59	-2:19:56
Ḥalḥūl 4	4	31N35	35E07	-2:20:28
Ḥanita 1	3	33N05	35E10	-2:20:40
HaOn 1	3	32N43	35E38	-2:22:32
Ḥaẓerim 1	3	31N14	34E43	-2:18:52
Ḥaẓor 1	3	32N59	35E33	-2:22:12
Hebron → Al-Khalīl 4	4	31N32	35E06	-2:20:24
Ḥefa (Haifa) 1	3	32N49	34E59	-2:19:56
Ḥeleẓ 1	3	31N35	34E40	-2:18:40
Herzliyya 1	3	32N10	34E51	-2:19:24
Hod HaSharon 1	3	32N09	34E53	-2:19:32
Ḥolon 1	3	32N01	34E46	-2:19:04
Ḥulda 1	3	31N50	34E53	-2:19:32
Ḥuwwārah 4	4	32N09	35E15	-2:21:00
Īdnah 4	4	31N34	34E59	-2:19:56
Iksāl 1	3	32N41	35E19	-2:21:16
'Isfiyā 1	3	32N43	35E04	-2:20:16
Jabālyah 2	1	31N32	34E29	-2:17:56
Jaffa, Tel Aviv- → Tel Aviv-Yafo 1	3	32N04	34E46	-2:19:04
Jaffa → Tel Aviv-Yafo 1	3	32N04	34E46	-2:19:04
Janīn 4	4	32N28	35E18	-2:21:12
Jatt (Tel Gat) 1	3	32N24	35E02	-2:20:08
Jemmain 4	4	32N08	35E27	-2:21:48
Jericho → Arīḥā 4	4	31N52	35E27	-2:21:48
Jerusalem → Yerushalayim 1	3	31N46	35E14	-2:20:56
Jīsh (Gush Ḥalav) 1	3	33N02	35E27	-2:21:48
Juwayzah 3	2	33N02	35E51	-2:23:24
Kabberi 1	3	33N01	35E09	-2:20:36
Kafr Kannā 1	3	32N45	35E20	-2:21:20
Kafr Naffākh 3	2	33N04	35E44	-2:22:56
Kafr Yāsīf 1	3	32N57	35E10	-2:20:40
Kaisariye 1	3	32N30	34E54	-2:19:36
Karkur 1	3	32N28	35E00	-2:20:00
Karmi'el 1	3	32N55	35E18	-2:21:12
Karmiyya 1	3	31N36	34E33	-2:18:12
Kefar 'Azza 1	3	31N29	34E32	-2:18:08
Kefar Blum 1	3	33N10	35E36	-2:22:24
Kefar 'Eqron 1	3	31N51	34E49	-2:19:16
Kefar Sava 1	3	32N10	34E54	-2:19:36
Kefar Shammay 1	3	32N57	35E27	-2:21:48
Kefar Syrkin 1	3	32N04	34E56	-2:19:44
Kefar Szold 1	3	33N11	35E39	-2:22:36
Kefar Vitkin 1	3	34N23	34E53	-2:19:32
Kefar Warburg 1	3	31N43	34E44	-2:18:56
Kerem Maharal 1	3	32N39	34E59	-2:19:56
Khān Yūnus 2	1	31N21	34E19	-2:17:16
Kharbatā 4	4	31N57	35E04	-2:20:16
Khirbat Abū Qashṭah 2	1	31N16	34E16	-2:17:04
Khisfīn 3	2	32N51	35E49	-2:23:16
Kifār 'Aṣyūn 4	4	31N39	35E08	-2:20:32
Kinneret 1	3	32N43	35E33	-2:22:12
Kokhav 1	3	31N38	34E40	-2:18:40
Lakhish 1	3	31N34	34E51	-2:19:24
Liman 1	3	33N03	35E06	-2:20:24
Lod (Lydda) 1	3	31N58	34E54	-2:19:36
Lydda → Lod 1	3	31N58	34E54	-2:19:36
Ma'Alot-Tarshiḥa 1	3	33N01	35E17	-2:21:08
Ma'Barot 1	3	32N22	34E54	-2:19:36
Magen 1	3	31N18	34E26	-2:17:44
Maghār 1	3	32N53	35E24	-2:21:36
Majd el Kurūm 1	3	32N55	35E15	-2:21:00
Makhfar al-Quwayrah 4	4	29N48	35E19	-2:21:16
Manṣūrah 3	2	33N08	35E48	-2:23:12
Mas'Adah (Cæsarea Philippi) 3	2	33N14	35E45	-2:23:00
Mash'abbe Sade 1	3	31N00	34E47	-2:19:08
Mashhad 1	3	32N44	35E19	-2:21:16
Maythalūn 4	4	32N21	35E16	-2:21:04
Mazra'ih 1	3	32N59	35E06	-2:20:24

Name		Lat.	Long.	Time
Merẖavya 1	3	32N36	35E19	-2:21:16
Meron 1	3	32N59	35E26	-2:21:44
Metulla 1	3	33N16	35E35	-2:22:20
Migdal 1	3	32N50	35E30	-2:22:00
Migdal Ha‘Emeq 1	3	32N41	35E15	-2:21:00
Mishmar HaNegev 1	3	31N21	34E43	-2:18:52
Mishmar HaYarden 1	3	33N00	35E36	-2:22:24
Miẕpe Ramon 1	3	30N36	34E48	-2:19:12
Montefiore 1	3	31N47	35E11	-2:20:44
Moẕa 1	3	31N47	35E09	-2:20:36
Mughr 3	2	33N05	35E43	-2:22:52
Mukhmās 4	4	31N52	35E17	-2:21:08
Muṣmuṣ 1	3	32N32	35E09	-2:20:36
Nābulus 4	4	32N13	35E16	-2:21:04
Nahalal 1	3	32N41	35E12	-2:20:48
Naẖal ‘Oz 1	3	31N28	34E30	-2:18:00
Nahariyya 1	3	33N00	35E05	-2:20:20
Naḥf 1	3	32N56	35E19	-2:21:16
Nazareth → Naẕerat 1	3	32N42	35E18	-2:21:12
Naẕerat (Nazareth) 1	3	32N42	35E18	-2:21:12
Naẕerat ‘Illit 1	3	32N42	35E19	-2:21:16
Negba 1	3	31N40	34E41	-2:18:44
Nein 1	3	32N38	35E21	-2:21:24
Nesher 1	3	32N46	35E03	-2:20:12
Nes Ẕiyyona 1	3	31N55	34E48	-2:19:12
Netanya 1	3	32N20	34E51	-2:19:24
Nīfī Ya‘Qūb 4	4	31N50	35E14	-2:20:56
Nir‘Am 1	3	31N31	34E35	-2:18:20
Nirim 1	3	31N20	34E24	-2:17:36
Niẕẕanim 1	3	31N43	34E38	-2:18:32
Nordiyya 1	3	32N19	34E54	-2:19:36
Ofaqim 1	3	31N17	34E37	-2:18:28
Or ‘Aqiva 1	3	32N30	34E55	-2:19:40
Or Yehuda 1	3	32N01	34E51	-2:19:24
Palmaẖim 1	3	31N56	34E42	-2:18:48
Pardes H̱anna 1	3	32N28	34E58	-2:19:52
Peqi‘In H̱adasha 1	3	32N59	35E20	-2:21:20
Petaẖ Tiqwa 1	3	32N05	34E53	-2:19:32
Qabātiyah 4	4	32N25	35E17	-2:21:08
Qalqilīya 4	4	32N11	34E58	-2:19:52
Qan‘Abah 3	2	33N08	35E40	-2:22:40
Qeẕi‘Ot 1	3	30N53	34E27	-2:17:48
Qibyā 4	4	31N59	35E01	-2:20:04
Qiryat 1	3	32N49	35E06	-2:20:24
Qiryat ‘Anavim 1	3	31N48	35E07	-2:20:28
Qiryat Bialik 1	3	32N50	35E05	-2:20:20
Qiryat Binyamin 1	3	32N48	35E05	-2:20:20
Qiryat Gat 1	3	31N36	34E46	-2:19:04
Qiryat H̱ayyim 1	3	32N49	35E04	-2:20:16
Qiryat Mal'akhi 1	3	31N44	34E44	-2:18:56
Qiryat Motzkin 1	3	32N50	35E04	-2:20:16
Qiryat Ono 1	3	32N04	34E51	-2:19:24
Qiryat Shemona 1	3	33N13	35E34	-2:22:16
Qiryat Tiv‘On 1	3	32N43	35E08	-2:20:32
Qiryat Yam 1	3	32N51	35E04	-2:20:16
Ra‘Ananna 1	3	32N11	34E53	-2:19:32
Rafaḥ 2	1	31N18	34E15	-2:17:00
Rama 1	3	32N56	35E22	-2:21:28
Rām Allāh 4	4	31N54	35E12	-2:20:48
Ramat Gan 1	3	32N05	34E49	-2:19:16
Ramat HaSharon 1	3	32N09	34E50	-2:19:20
Ramat HaShofet 1	3	32N37	35E06	-2:20:24
Ramat Yoẖanan 1	3	32N47	35E07	-2:20:28
Ramla 1	3	31N55	34E52	-2:19:28
Reẖovot 1	3	31N54	34E49	-2:19:16
Rishon leẔiyyon 1	3	31N58	34E48	-2:19:12
Rishpon 1	3	32N12	34E49	-2:19:16
Rosh Ha‘Ayin 1	3	32N06	34E57	-2:19:48
Rosh Pinna 1	3	32N58	35E32	-2:22:08
Ruẖama 1	3	31N30	34E42	-2:18:48
Sa‘Ad 1	3	31N28	34E32	-2:18:08
Sabasṭīyah (Samaria) 4	4	32N17	35E12	-2:20:48
Safad → Ẕefat 1	3	32N58	35E30	-2:22:00
Sa‘īr 4	4	31N35	35E09	-2:20:36
Sakhnīn 1	3	32N52	35E17	-2:21:08
Ṣānūr 4	4	32N21	35E15	-2:21:00
Sasa 1	3	33N02	35E24	-2:21:36
Sdud 1	3	31N45	34E39	-2:18:36
Sebustie → Sabasṭīyah 4	4	32N17	35E12	-2:20:48
Sede Boqer 1	3	30N52	34E47	-2:19:08
Sederot 1	3	31N31	34E35	-2:18:20
Sedom 1	3	31N04	35E24	-2:21:36
Sedot Yam 1	3	32N29	34E53	-2:19:32
Seffurie → Ẕippori 1	3	32N45	35E17	-2:21:08
Sepphoris → Ẕippori 1	3	32N45	35E17	-2:21:08
Sha‘Alvim 1	3	31N52	34E59	-2:19:56
Sha‘Ar HaGolan 1	3	32N41	35E36	-2:22:24
Sha‘Ar Menashe 1	3	32N27	35E01	-2:20:04
Shafir 1	3	31N42	34E44	-2:18:56
Shave Ẕiyyon 1	3	32N59	35E05	-2:20:20
Shechem → Nābulus 1	3	32N13	35E16	-2:21:04
Shefar‘Am 1	3	32N48	35E10	-2:20:40
Shevut ‘Am 1	3	32N19	34E55	-2:19:40
Shomera 1	3	33N05	35E17	-2:21:08
Shuwaykah 4	4	32N20	35E02	-2:20:08
Sīlat aẓ-Ẓahr 4	4	32N19	35E11	-2:20:44
Tabariye → Teverya 1	3	32N47	35E32	-2:22:08
Tamra 1	3	32N51	35E12	-2:20:48
Tantura → Dor 1	3	32N37	34E55	-2:19:40
Tarqūmiyah 4	4	31N35	35E01	-2:20:04
Tarshiha (Tershiha) 1	3	33N05	35E16	-2:21:04
Tel Aviv 1	3	32N04	34E46	-2:19:04
Tel Aviv-Yafo 1	3	32N04	34E46	-2:19:04
Telhum 1	3	32N53	35E33	-2:22:12
Tel Mond 1	3	32N15	34E56	-2:19:44
Tequma 1	3	31N27	34E35	-2:18:20
Teverya (Tiberias) 1	3	32N47	35E32	-2:22:08
Tiberias → Teverya 1	3	32N47	35E32	-2:22:08
Tirat Karmel 1	3	32N46	34E58	-2:19:52
Tirat Ẕevi 1	3	32N25	35E32	-2:22:08
Ṭūbās 4	4	32N19	35E22	-2:21:28
Ṭūlkarm 4	4	32N19	35E02	-2:20:08
Ümm el Faḥm 1	3	32N31	35E09	-2:20:36
Ya‘Bad 4	4	32N27	35E10	-2:20:40
Yad Mordekhay 1	3	31N35	34E34	-2:18:16
Yāfā 1	3	32N41	35E17	-2:21:08
Yafo → Tel Aviv-Yafo 1	3	32N04	34E46	-2:19:04
Yagur 1	3	32N44	35E04	-2:20:16
Yaṭṭah 4	4	31N27	35E05	-2:20:20
Yavne 1	3	31N53	34E45	-2:19:00
Yebnah 1	3	31N52	34E45	-2:19:00
Yehud 1	3	32N02	34E53	-2:19:32
Yeroẖam 1	3	31N00	34E55	-2:19:40
Yerushalayim (Al-Quds) (Jerusalem) 1	3	31N46	35E14	-2:20:56
Yesud HaMa‘Ala 1	3	33N03	35E36	-2:22:24
Yirkā 1	3	32N57	35E13	-2:20:52
Yizre‘El 1	3	32N33	35E20	-2:21:20
Yoqne‘Am 1	3	32N39	35E07	-2:20:28
Yotvata 1	3	29N53	35E03	-2:20:12
Ẕefat (Safad) 1	3	32N58	35E30	-2:22:00
Zikhron Ya‘Aqov 1	3	32N34	34E57	-2:19:48
Ẕippori 1	3	32N45	35E17	-2:21:08
Zohar 1	3	31N36	34E42	-2:18:48

Time Table # 1
Before 22/Sep/1866 LMT
Begin Standard 12E29
22/Sep/1866 0:00 -0:50
Begin Standard 15E00
1/Nov/1893 0:00 -1:00
3/Jun/1916 24:00 -2:00
30/Sep/1916 24:00 -1:00
31/Mar/1917 24:00 -2:00
29/Sep/1917 24:00 -1:00
9/Mar/1918 24:00 -2:00
5/Oct/1918 24:00 -1:00
1/Mar/1919 24:00 -2:00
4/Oct/1919 24:00 -1:00
20/Mar/1920 24:00 -2:00
18/Sep/1920 24:00 -1:00
14/Jun/1940 24:00 -2:00
2/Nov/1942 3:00 -1:00
29/Mar/1943 2:00 -2:00
4/Oct/1943 3:00 -1:00
3/Apr/1944 2:00 -2:00
2/Oct/1944 3:00 -1:00
2/Apr/1945 2:00 -2:00
16/Sep/1945 24:00 -1:00
17/Mar/1946 2:00 -2:00
6/Oct/1946 3:00 -1:00
16/Mar/1947 0:00 -2:00
5/Oct/1947 1:00 -1:00
29/Feb/1948 2:00 -2:00
3/Oct/1948 3:00 -1:00
22/May/1966 0:00 -2:00
24/Sep/1966 24:00 -1:00
28/May/1967 0:00 -2:00
23/Sep/1967 24:00 -1:00
26/May/1968 0:00 -2:00
21/Sep/1968 24:00 -1:00
1/Jun/1969 0:00 -2:00
27/Sep/1969 24:00 -1:00
31/May/1970 0:00 -2:00
27/Sep/1970 0:00 -1:00
23/May/1971 0:00 -2:00
26/Sep/1971 1:00 -1:00
28/May/1972 0:00 -2:00
1/Oct/1972 0:00 -1:00
3/Jun/1973 0:00 -2:00
30/Sep/1973 0:00 -1:00
26/May/1974 0:00 -2:00
29/Sep/1974 0:00 -1:00
1/Jun/1975 0:00 -2:00
28/Sep/1975 1:00 -1:00
30/May/1976 0:00 -2:00
26/Sep/1976 1:00 -1:00
22/May/1977 0:00 -2:00
25/Sep/1977 1:00 -1:00
28/May/1978 0:00 -2:00
1/Oct/1978 1:00 -1:00
27/May/1979 0:00 -2:00
30/Sep/1979 1:00 -1:00
6/Apr/1980 2:00 -2:00
28/Sep/1980 3:00 -1:00
29/Mar/1981 2:00 -2:00
27/Sep/1981 3:00 -1:00
28/Mar/1982 2:00 -2:00
26/Sep/1982 3:00 -1:00
27/Mar/1983 2:00 -2:00
25/Sep/1983 3:00 -1:00
25/Mar/1984 2:00 -2:00
30/Sep/1984 3:00 -1:00
31/Mar/1985 2:00 -2:00
29/Sep/1985 3:00 -1:00
30/Mar/1986 2:00 -2:00
28/Sep/1986 3:00 -1:00
29/Mar/1987 2:00 -2:00
27/Sep/1987 3:00 -1:00
27/Mar/1988 2:00 -2:00
25/Sep/1988 3:00 -1:00
26/Mar/1989 2:00 -2:00
24/Sep/1989 3:00 -1:00
25/Mar/1990 2:00 -2:00
30/Sep/1990 3:00 -1:00
31/Mar/1991 2:00 -2:00
29/Sep/1991 3:00 -1:00
29/Mar/1992 2:00 -2:00
27/Sep/1992 3:00 -1:00
28/Mar/1993 2:00 -2:00
26/Sep/1993 3:00 -1:00
27/Mar/1994 2:00 -2:00
25/Sep/1994 3:00 -1:00
26/Mar/1995 2:00 -2:00
24/Sep/1995 3:00 -1:00
31/Mar/1996 2:00 -2:00
29/Sep/1996 3:00 -1:00
30/Mar/1997 2:00 -2:00
28/Sep/1997 3:00 -1:00
29/Mar/1998 2:00 -2:00
27/Sep/1998 3:00 -1:00
28/Mar/1999 2:00 -2:00
26/Sep/1999 3:00 -1:00
26/Mar/2000 2:00 -2:00
24/Sep/2000 3:00 -1:00
....

Time Table # 2
Before 22/Sep/1866 LMT
Begin Standard 12E29
22/Sep/1866 0:00 -0:50
Begin Standard 15E00
1/Nov/1893 0:00 -1:00
3/Jun/1916 24:00 -2:00
30/Sep/1916 24:00 -1:00
31/Mar/1917 24:00 -2:00
29/Sep/1917 24:00 -1:00
9/Mar/1918 24:00 -2:00
5/Oct/1918 24:00 -1:00
1/Mar/1919 24:00 -2:00
4/Oct/1919 24:00 -1:00
20/Mar/1920 24:00 -2:00
18/Sep/1920 24:00 -1:00
14/Jun/1940 24:00 -2:00
2/Nov/1942 3:00 -1:00
29/Mar/1943 2:00 -2:00
4/Oct/1943 3:00 -1:00
2/Apr/1945 2:00 -2:00
16/Sep/1945 24:00 -1:00
17/Mar/1946 2:00 -2:00
6/Oct/1946 3:00 -1:00
16/Mar/1947 0:00 -2:00
5/Oct/1947 1:00 -1:00
29/Feb/1948 2:00 -2:00
3/Oct/1948 3:00 -1:00
22/May/1966 0:00 -2:00
24/Sep/1966 24:00 -1:00
28/May/1967 0:00 -2:00
23/Sep/1967 24:00 -1:00
26/May/1968 0:00 -2:00
21/Sep/1968 24:00 -1:00
1/Jun/1969 0:00 -2:00
27/Sep/1969 24:00 -1:00
31/May/1970 0:00 -2:00
27/Sep/1970 0:00 -1:00
23/May/1971 0:00 -2:00
26/Sep/1971 1:00 -1:00
28/May/1972 0:00 -2:00
1/Oct/1972 0:00 -1:00
3/Jun/1973 0:00 -2:00
30/Sep/1973 0:00 -1:00
26/May/1974 0:00 -2:00
29/Sep/1974 0:00 -1:00
1/Jun/1975 0:00 -2:00
28/Sep/1975 1:00 -1:00
30/May/1976 0:00 -2:00
26/Sep/1976 1:00 -1:00
22/May/1977 0:00 -2:00
25/Sep/1977 1:00 -1:00
28/May/1978 0:00 -2:00
1/Oct/1978 1:00 -1:00
27/May/1979 0:00 -2:00
30/Sep/1979 1:00 -1:00
6/Apr/1980 2:00 -2:00
28/Sep/1980 3:00 -1:00
29/Mar/1981 2:00 -2:00
27/Sep/1981 3:00 -1:00
28/Mar/1982 2:00 -2:00
26/Sep/1982 3:00 -1:00
27/Mar/1983 2:00 -2:00
25/Sep/1983 3:00 -1:00
25/Mar/1984 2:00 -2:00
30/Sep/1984 3:00 -1:00
31/Mar/1985 2:00 -2:00
29/Sep/1985 3:00 -1:00
30/Mar/1986 2:00 -2:00
28/Sep/1986 3:00 -1:00
29/Mar/1987 2:00 -2:00
27/Sep/1987 3:00 -1:00
27/Mar/1988 2:00 -2:00
25/Sep/1988 3:00 -1:00
26/Mar/1989 2:00 -2:00
24/Sep/1989 3:00 -1:00
25/Mar/1990 2:00 -2:00
30/Sep/1990 3:00 -1:00
31/Mar/1991 2:00 -2:00
29/Sep/1991 3:00 -1:00
29/Mar/1992 2:00 -2:00
27/Sep/1992 3:00 -1:00
28/Mar/1993 2:00 -2:00
26/Sep/1993 3:00 -1:00
27/Mar/1994 2:00 -2:00
25/Sep/1994 3:00 -1:00
26/Mar/1995 2:00 -2:00
24/Sep/1995 3:00 -1:00
31/Mar/1996 2:00 -2:00
29/Sep/1996 3:00 -1:00
30/Mar/1997 2:00 -2:00
28/Sep/1997 3:00 -1:00
29/Mar/1998 2:00 -2:00
27/Sep/1998 3:00 -1:00
28/Mar/1999 2:00 -2:00
26/Sep/1999 3:00 -1:00
26/Mar/2000 2:00 -2:00
24/Sep/2000 3:00 -1:00
....

Time Table # 3
Before 22/Sep/1866 LMT
Begin Standard 13E22
22/Sep/1866 0:00 -0:53
Begin Standard 15E00
1/Nov/1893 0:00 -1:00
3/Jun/1916 24:00 -2:00
30/Sep/1916 24:00 -1:00
31/Mar/1917 24:00 -2:00
29/Sep/1917 24:00 -1:00
9/Mar/1918 24:00 -2:00
5/Oct/1918 24:00 -1:00
1/Mar/1919 24:00 -2:00
4/Oct/1919 24:00 -1:00
20/Mar/1920 24:00 -2:00
18/Sep/1920 24:00 -1:00
14/Jun/1940 24:00 -2:00
2/Nov/1942 3:00 -1:00
29/Mar/1943 2:00 -2:00
4/Oct/1943 3:00 -1:00
2/Apr/1945 2:00 -2:00
16/Sep/1945 24:00 -1:00
17/Mar/1946 2:00 -2:00
6/Oct/1946 3:00 -1:00
16/Mar/1947 0:00 -2:00
5/Oct/1947 1:00 -1:00
29/Feb/1948 2:00 -2:00
3/Oct/1948 3:00 -1:00
22/May/1966 0:00 -2:00
24/Sep/1966 24:00 -1:00
28/May/1967 0:00 -2:00
23/Sep/1967 24:00 -1:00
26/May/1968 0:00 -2:00
21/Sep/1968 24:00 -1:00
1/Jun/1969 0:00 -2:00
27/Sep/1969 24:00 -1:00
31/May/1970 0:00 -2:00
27/Sep/1970 0:00 -1:00
23/May/1971 0:00 -2:00
26/Sep/1971 1:00 -1:00
28/May/1972 0:00 -2:00
1/Oct/1972 0:00 -1:00
3/Jun/1973 0:00 -2:00
30/Sep/1973 0:00 -1:00
26/May/1974 0:00 -2:00
29/Sep/1974 0:00 -1:00
1/Jun/1975 0:00 -2:00
28/Sep/1975 1:00 -1:00
30/May/1976 0:00 -2:00
26/Sep/1976 1:00 -1:00
22/May/1977 0:00 -2:00
25/Sep/1977 1:00 -1:00
28/May/1978 0:00 -2:00
1/Oct/1978 1:00 -1:00
27/May/1979 0:00 -2:00
30/Sep/1979 1:00 -1:00
6/Apr/1980 2:00 -2:00
28/Sep/1980 3:00 -1:00
29/Mar/1981 2:00 -2:00
27/Sep/1981 3:00 -1:00
28/Mar/1982 2:00 -2:00
26/Sep/1982 3:00 -1:00
27/Mar/1983 2:00 -2:00
25/Sep/1983 3:00 -1:00
25/Mar/1984 2:00 -2:00
30/Sep/1984 3:00 -1:00
31/Mar/1985 2:00 -2:00
29/Sep/1985 3:00 -1:00
30/Mar/1986 2:00 -2:00
28/Sep/1986 3:00 -1:00
29/Mar/1987 2:00 -2:00
27/Sep/1987 3:00 -1:00
27/Mar/1988 2:00 -2:00
25/Sep/1988 3:00 -1:00
26/Mar/1989 2:00 -2:00
24/Sep/1989 3:00 -1:00
25/Mar/1990 2:00 -2:00
30/Sep/1990 3:00 -1:00
31/Mar/1991 2:00 -2:00
29/Sep/1991 3:00 -1:00
29/Mar/1992 2:00 -2:00
27/Sep/1992 3:00 -1:00
28/Mar/1993 2:00 -2:00
26/Sep/1993 3:00 -1:00
27/Mar/1994 2:00 -2:00
25/Sep/1994 3:00 -1:00
26/Mar/1995 2:00 -2:00
24/Sep/1995 3:00 -1:00
31/Mar/1996 2:00 -2:00
29/Sep/1996 3:00 -1:00
30/Mar/1997 2:00 -2:00
28/Sep/1997 3:00 -1:00
29/Mar/1998 2:00 -2:00
27/Sep/1998 3:00 -1:00
28/Mar/1999 2:00 -2:00
26/Sep/1999 3:00 -1:00
26/Mar/2000 2:00 -2:00
24/Sep/2000 3:00 -1:00
....

Time Table # 4
Before 22/Sep/1866 LMT
Begin Standard 9E08
22/Sep/1866 0:00 -0:37
Begin Standard 15E00
1/Nov/1893 0:00 -1:00
3/Jun/1916 24:00 -2:00
30/Sep/1916 24:00 -1:00
31/Mar/1917 24:00 -2:00
29/Sep/1917 24:00 -1:00
9/Mar/1918 24:00 -2:00
5/Oct/1918 24:00 -1:00
1/Mar/1919 24:00 -2:00
4/Oct/1919 24:00 -1:00
20/Mar/1920 24:00 -2:00
18/Sep/1920 24:00 -1:00
14/Jun/1940 24:00 -2:00
2/Nov/1942 3:00 -1:00
29/Mar/1943 2:00 -2:00
4/Oct/1943 3:00 -1:00
2/Apr/1945 2:00 -2:00
16/Sep/1945 24:00 -1:00
17/Mar/1946 2:00 -2:00
6/Oct/1946 3:00 -1:00
16/Mar/1947 0:00 -2:00
5/Oct/1947 1:00 -1:00
29/Feb/1948 2:00 -2:00
3/Oct/1948 3:00 -1:00
22/May/1966 0:00 -2:00
24/Sep/1966 24:00 -1:00
28/May/1967 0:00 -2:00
23/Sep/1967 24:00 -1:00
26/May/1968 0:00 -2:00
21/Sep/1968 24:00 -1:00
1/Jun/1969 0:00 -2:00
27/Sep/1969 24:00 -1:00
31/May/1970 0:00 -2:00
27/Sep/1970 0:00 -1:00
23/May/1971 0:00 -2:00
26/Sep/1971 1:00 -1:00
28/May/1972 0:00 -2:00
1/Oct/1972 0:00 -1:00
3/Jun/1973 0:00 -2:00
30/Sep/1973 0:00 -1:00
26/May/1974 0:00 -2:00
29/Sep/1974 0:00 -1:00
1/Jun/1975 0:00 -2:00
28/Sep/1975 1:00 -1:00
30/May/1976 0:00 -2:00
26/Sep/1976 1:00 -1:00
22/May/1977 0:00 -2:00
25/Sep/1977 1:00 -1:00
28/May/1978 0:00 -2:00
1/Oct/1978 1:00 -1:00
27/May/1979 0:00 -2:00
30/Sep/1979 1:00 -1:00
6/Apr/1980 2:00 -2:00
28/Sep/1980 3:00 -1:00
29/Mar/1981 2:00 -2:00
27/Sep/1981 3:00 -1:00
28/Mar/1982 2:00 -2:00
26/Sep/1982 3:00 -1:00
27/Mar/1983 2:00 -2:00
25/Sep/1983 3:00 -1:00
25/Mar/1984 2:00 -2:00
30/Sep/1984 3:00 -1:00
31/Mar/1985 2:00 -2:00
29/Sep/1985 3:00 -1:00
30/Mar/1986 2:00 -2:00
28/Sep/1986 3:00 -1:00
29/Mar/1987 2:00 -2:00
27/Sep/1987 3:00 -1:00
27/Mar/1988 2:00 -2:00
25/Sep/1988 3:00 -1:00
26/Mar/1989 2:00 -2:00
24/Sep/1989 3:00 -1:00
25/Mar/1990 2:00 -2:00
30/Sep/1990 3:00 -1:00
31/Mar/1991 2:00 -2:00
29/Sep/1991 3:00 -1:00
29/Mar/1992 2:00 -2:00
27/Sep/1992 3:00 -1:00
28/Mar/1993 2:00 -2:00
26/Sep/1993 3:00 -1:00
27/Mar/1994 2:00 -2:00
25/Sep/1994 3:00 -1:00
26/Mar/1995 2:00 -2:00
24/Sep/1995 3:00 -1:00
31/Mar/1996 2:00 -2:00
29/Sep/1996 3:00 -1:00
30/Mar/1997 2:00 -2:00
28/Sep/1997 3:00 -1:00
29/Mar/1998 2:00 -2:00
27/Sep/1998 3:00 -1:00
28/Mar/1999 2:00 -2:00
26/Sep/1999 3:00 -1:00
26/Mar/2000 2:00 -2:00
24/Sep/2000 3:00 -1:00

Abano Terme 1 45N21 11E47 -0:47:08
Abbadia San Salvatore 1 42N53 11E41 -0:46:44
Abbasanta 4 40N08 8E49 -0:35:16
Abbiategrasso 1 45N24 8E54 -0:35:36
Abetone 1 44N08 10E40 -0:42:40
Abriola 2 40N30 15E49 -1:03:16
Acate 3 37N02 14E28 -0:57:52
Accadia 2 41N10 15E10 -1:00:40
Acceglio 1 44N28 7E00 -0:28:00
Accettura 2 40N29 16E09 -1:04:36
Acciano 1 42N10 13E43 -0:54:52
Accumoli 1 42N42 13E15 -0:53:00
Acerenza 2 40N48 15E57 -1:03:48
Acerno 2 40N44 15E03 -1:00:12
Acerra 2 40N57 14E22 -0:57:28
Aci Castello 3 37N33 15E08 -1:00:32
Aci Catena 3 37N36 15E08 -1:00:32
Acireale 3 37N37 15E10 -1:00:40
Aci Sant'Antonio 3 37N36 15E07 -1:00:28
Acquacalda 3 38N31 14E57 -0:59:48
Acqualagna 1 43N37 12E40 -0:50:40
Acquanegra sul Chiese 1 45N10 10E26 -0:41:44
Acquapendente 1 42N44 11E52 -0:47:28
Acquappesa 2 39N29 15E57 -1:03:48
Acquasanta Terme 1 42N46 13E24 -0:53:36
Acquasparta 1 42N41 12E33 -0:50:12
Acquaviva delle Fonti 2 40N54 16E50 -1:07:20
Acquaviva Platani 3 37N34 13E42 -0:54:48
Acqui Terme 1 44N41 8E28 -0:33:52
Acri 2 39N29 16E23 -1:05:32
Acuto 1 41N47 13E10 -0:52:40
Adelfia 2 41N00 16E52 -1:07:28
Adrano 3 37N40 14E50 -0:59:20
Adria 1 45N03 12E03 -0:48:12
Adro 1 45N37 9E57 -0:39:48
Affi 1 45N33 10E46 -0:43:04
Afragola 2 40N55 14E18 -0:57:12
Africo 2 38N04 15E59 -1:03:56
Agazzano 1 44N57 9E31 -0:38:04
Aggius 4 40N46 9E04 -0:36:16
Agira 3 37N39 14E31 -0:58:04
Agliana 1 43N54 11E00 -0:44:00
Agliano 1 44N47 8E15 -0:33:00
Aglientu 4 41N05 9E07 -0:36:28
Agna 1 45N10 11E58 -0:47:52
Agnadello 1 45N26 9E33 -0:38:12
Agnone 1 41N48 14E22 -0:57:28
Agordo 1 46N17 12E02 -0:48:08
Agrate Brianza 1 45N34 9E21 -0:37:24
Agripoli 2 40N21 15E00 -1:00:00
Agugliano 1 43N32 13E23 -0:53:32
Aidomaggiore 4 40N10 8E51 -0:35:24
Aidone 3 37N25 14E27 -0:57:48
Aiello Calabro 2 39N07 16E10 -1:04:40
Airasca 1 44N55 7E29 -0:29:56
Airola 2 41N04 14E33 -0:58:12
Airole 1 43N52 7E33 -0:30:12
Airuno 1 45N45 9E25 -0:37:40
Ala 1 45N45 11E00 -0:44:00
Alà dei Sardi 4 40N39 9E20 -0:37:20
Ala di Stura 1 45N19 7E19 -0:29:16
Alagna Valsesia 1 45N51 7E56 -0:31:44
Alano di Piave 1 45N55 11E52 -0:47:28
Alassio 1 44N00 8E10 -0:32:40
Alatri 1 41N43 13E21 -0:53:24
Alba 1 44N42 8E02 -0:32:08
Albacina 1 43N21 13E01 -0:52:04
Albairate 1 45N25 8E56 -0:35:44
Albanella 2 40N30 15E08 -1:00:32
Albano di Lucania 2 40N35 16E02 -1:04:08
Albano Laziale 1 41N44 12E39 -0:50:36
Albaredo d'Adige 1 45N19 11E16 -0:45:04
Albenga 1 44N03 8E13 -0:32:52
Alberobello 2 40N47 17E15 -1:09:00
Alberona 2 41N26 15E07 -1:00:28
Albettone 1 45N21 11E35 -0:46:20
Albiate 1 45N39 9E15 -0:37:00
Albidona 2 39N55 16E28 -1:05:52
Albignasego 1 45N21 11E52 -0:47:28
Albinea 1 44N37 10E36 -0:42:24
Albino 1 45N46 9E47 -0:39:08
Albisola Marina 1 44N19 8E30 -0:34:00
Albisola Superiore 1 44N20 8E31 -0:34:04
Albizzate 1 45N43 8E44 -0:34:56
Albuzzano 1 45N11 9E16 -0:37:04
Alcamo 3 37N59 12E58 -0:51:52
Alcara li Fusi 3 38N01 14E42 -0:58:48

Aldino 1 46N23 11E20 -0:45:20
Ales 4 39N46 8E49 -0:35:16
Alessandria 1 44N54 8E37 -0:34:28
Alessandria del Carretto 2 39N57 16E23 -1:05:32
Alessandria della Rocca 3 37N34 13E27 -0:53:48
Alessano 2 39N53 18E20 -1:13:20
Alezio 2 40N04 18E03 -1:12:12
Alfedena 1 41N44 14E02 -0:56:08
Alfianello 1 45N16 10E10 -0:40:40
Alfonsine 1 44N30 12E03 -0:48:12
Alghero 4 40N33 8E19 -0:33:16
Alì 3 38N02 15E25 -1:01:40
Alia 3 37N47 13E43 -0:54:52
Aliano 2 40N19 16E14 -1:04:56
Alice Superiore 1 45N28 7E47 -0:31:08
Alife 2 41N20 14E20 -0:57:20
Alimena 3 37N42 14E07 -0:56:28
Aliminusa 3 37N52 13E47 -0:55:08
Alì Terme 3 38N01 15E26 -1:01:44
Alleghe 1 46N24 12E01 -0:48:04
Allerona 1 42N49 11E58 -0:47:52
Alliste 2 39N57 18E05 -1:12:20
Allumiere 1 42N09 11E54 -0:47:36
Almenno San Salvatore 1 45N45 9E35 -0:38:20
Alpignano 1 45N06 7E31 -0:30:04
Alseno 1 44N54 9E59 -0:39:56
Altamura 2 40N50 16E33 -1:06:12
Altare 1 44N20 8E20 -0:33:20
Altavilla Irpina 2 41N00 14E47 -0:59:08
Altavilla Milicia 3 38N02 13E32 -0:54:08
Altavilla Silentina 2 40N32 15E08 -1:00:32
Altofonte 3 38N03 13E18 -0:53:12
Altomonte 2 39N42 16E08 -1:04:32
Alvito 1 41N41 13E45 -0:55:00
Alzano Lombardo 1 45N44 9E43 -0:38:52
Amalfi 2 40N38 14E36 -0:58:24
Amandola 1 42N59 13E21 -0:53:24
Amantea 2 39N08 16E05 -1:04:20
Amatrice 1 42N38 13E17 -0:53:08
Ameglia 1 44N04 9E57 -0:39:48
Amelia 1 42N33 12E25 -0:49:40
Amendolara 2 39N57 16E35 -1:06:20
Amorosi 2 41N12 14E28 -0:57:52
Ampezzo 1 46N25 12E48 -0:51:12
Anacapri 2 40N33 14E13 -0:56:52
Anagni 1 41N44 13E09 -0:52:36
Ancarano 1 42N50 13E44 -0:54:56
Ancona 1 43N38 13E30 -0:54:00
Andalo 1 46N10 11E00 -0:44:00
Andora 1 43N59 8E08 -0:32:32
Andorno Micca 1 45N37 8E03 -0:32:12
Andrate 1 45N32 7E53 -0:31:32
Andretta 2 40N56 15E19 -1:01:16
Andria 2 41N13 16E18 -1:05:12
Anfo 1 45N46 10E29 -0:41:56
Angera 1 45N46 8E35 -0:34:20
Anghiari 1 43N32 12E03 -0:48:12
Angri 2 40N44 14E34 -0:58:16
Angrogna 1 44N50 7E13 -0:28:52
Anguillara Sabazia 1 42N05 12E16 -0:49:04
Anguillara Veneta 1 45N08 11E53 -0:47:32
Annicco 1 45N14 9E52 -0:39:28
Anoia 2 38N27 16E05 -1:04:20
Antegnate 1 45N29 9E47 -0:39:08
Anterselva di Sopra 1 46N52 12E08 -0:48:32
Antey-Saint-André 1 45N48 7E36 -0:30:24
Antignano 1 43N30 10E19 -0:41:16
Antillo 3 37N58 15E15 -1:01:00
Antrodoco 1 42N25 13E05 -0:52:20
Antronapiana 1 46N03 8E07 -0:32:28
Anversa degli Abruzzi 1 41N59 13E48 -0:55:12
Anzano di Puglia 2 41N07 15E17 -1:01:08
Anzi 2 40N31 15E55 -1:03:40
Anzio 2 41N27 12E37 -0:50:28
Anzola dell'Emilia 1 44N33 11E11 -0:44:44
Aosta 1 45N44 7E20 -0:29:20
Apecchio 1 43N33 12E25 -0:49:40
Apice 2 41N07 14E56 -0:59:44
Appiano (Eppan) 1 46N28 11E15 -0:45:00
Appiano Gentile 1 45N44 8E59 -0:35:56
Apricena 2 41N47 15E27 -1:01:48
Aprigliano 2 39N14 16E20 -1:05:20
Aprilia 2 41N36 12E39 -0:50:36
Aquila degli Abruzzi 1 42N24 13E24 -0:53:36
Aquileia 1 45N46 13E22 -0:53:28
Aquilonia (S.M.) 2 41N00 15E29 -1:01:56
Aquino 2 41N30 13E42 -0:54:48
Arabba 1 46N30 11E52 -0:47:28
Aradeo 2 40N08 18E08 -1:12:32
Aragona 3 37N24 13E37 -0:54:28
Arbatax 4 39N56 9E42 -0:38:48
Arborea 4 39N46 8E35 -0:34:20
Arbus 4 39N32 8E36 -0:34:24
Arcade 1 45N47 12E13 -0:48:52
Arce 2 41N35 13E34 -0:54:16
Arcevia 1 43N30 12E56 -0:51:44
Archi 1 42N05 14E23 -0:57:32
Arcidosso 1 42N52 11E33 -0:46:12
Arcille 1 42N48 11E15 -0:45:00
Arcinazzo Romano 1 41N48 13E12 -0:52:48
Arcisate 1 45N54 8E52 -0:35:28
Arco 1 45N55 10E53 -0:43:32
Arcola 1 44N07 9E54 -0:39:36
Arconate 1 45N32 8E51 -0:35:24
Arcore 1 45N38 9E19 -0:37:16
Ardara 4 40N37 8E48 -0:35:12
Ardea 2 41N36 12E33 -0:50:12
Ardenno 1 46N10 9E39 -0:38:36
Ardenza 1 43N31 10E19 -0:41:16
Ardore 2 38N11 16E10 -1:04:40
Arena 2 38N34 16E13 -1:04:52
Arenzano 1 44N24 8E41 -0:34:44
Arese 1 45N33 9E05 -0:36:20
Arezzo 1 43N25 11E53 -0:47:32
Argegno 1 45N56 9E08 -0:36:32
Argenta 1 44N37 11E50 -0:47:20
Argentera 1 44N24 6E57 -0:27:48
Argentiera 4 40N44 8E09 -0:32:36
Ariano Irpino 2 41N09 15E05 -1:00:20
Ariano nel Polesine 1 44N56 12E07 -0:48:28
Ariccia 1 41N43 12E40 -0:50:40
Arienzo 2 41N01 14E30 -0:58:00
Aritzo 4 39N57 9E12 -0:36:48
Arluno 1 45N30 8E56 -0:35:44
Arma di Taggia 1 43N50 7E51 -0:31:24
Armeno 1 45N49 8E26 -0:33:44
Armento 2 40N18 16E04 -1:04:16
Arnaccio 1 43N40 10E17 -0:41:08
Arnaz 1 45N38 7E43 -0:30:52
Arni 1 44N04 10E15 -0:41:00
Arona 1 45N46 8E34 -0:34:16
Arpaia 2 41N02 14E33 -0:58:12
Arpino 2 41N39 13E36 -0:54:24
Arquà Petrarca 1 45N16 11E43 -0:46:52
Arquà Polesine 1 45N01 11E45 -0:47:00
Arquata del Tronto 1 42N46 13E18 -0:53:12
Arquata Scrivia 1 44N41 8E53 -0:35:32
Arsiè 1 45N59 11E45 -0:47:00
Arsiero 1 45N48 11E21 -0:45:24
Arsoli 1 42N02 13E01 -0:52:04
Arta Terme 1 46N28 13E01 -0:52:04
Artegna 1 46N14 13E09 -0:52:36
Artèn 1 46N00 11E50 -0:47:20
Arvier 1 45N42 7E11 -0:28:44
Arzachena 4 41N05 9E23 -0:37:32
Arzana 4 39N55 9E31 -0:38:04
Arzano 2 40N55 14E16 -0:57:04
Arzignano 1 45N31 11E20 -0:45:20
Ascea 2 40N08 15E11 -1:00:44
Asciano 1 43N14 11E33 -0:46:12
Ascoli Piceno 1 42N51 13E34 -0:54:16
Ascoli Satriano 2 41N12 15E34 -1:02:16
Asiago 1 45N52 11E30 -0:46:00
Asola 1 45N13 10E24 -0:41:36
Asolo 1 45N48 11E54 -0:47:36
Assago 1 45N24 9E08 -0:36:32
Assemini 4 39N17 9E00 -0:36:00
Assergi 1 42N25 13E30 -0:54:00
Assisi 1 43N04 12E37 -0:50:28
Asso 1 45N52 9E16 -0:37:04
Assoro 3 37N37 14E25 -0:57:40
Asti 1 44N54 8E12 -0:32:48
Asuni 4 39N52 8E56 -0:35:44
Ateleta 1 41N51 14E12 -0:56:48
Atella 2 40N52 15E39 -1:02:36
Atena Lucana 2 40N27 15E33 -1:02:12
Atessa 1 42N04 14E27 -0:57:48
Atina 2 41N37 13E48 -0:55:12
Atri 1 42N35 13E58 -0:55:52
Atripalda 2 40N55 14E50 -0:59:20
Attigliano 1 42N31 12E17 -0:49:08
Attimis 1 46N11 13E16 -0:53:04
Auer → Ora 1 46N21 11E18 -0:45:12
Augusta 3 37N13 15E13 -1:00:52
Auletta 2 40N34 15E25 -1:01:40
Aulla 1 44N12 9E58 -0:39:52
Aurisina 1 45N45 13E41 -0:54:44
Auronzo di Cadore 1 46N33 12E26 -0:49:44
Avelengo 1 46N38 11E13 -0:44:52
Avella 2 40N58 14E36 -0:58:24
Avellino 2 40N54 14E47 -0:59:08
Aversa 2 40N58 14E12 -0:56:48
Avetrana 2 40N21 17E43 -1:10:52
Avezzano 1 42N02 13E25 -0:53:40
Aviano 1 46N04 12E36 -0:50:24
Avigliana 1 45N05 7E23 -0:29:32
Avigliano 2 40N44 15E44 -1:02:56
Avio 1 45N44 10E56 -0:43:44
Avola 3 36N54 15E08 -1:00:32
Ayas 1 45N50 7E41 -0:30:44
Azzanello 1 45N18 9E55 -0:39:40
Azzano Decimo 1 45N53 12E43 -0:50:52
Baceno 1 46N16 8E19 -0:33:16
Bacoli 2 40N48 14E05 -0:56:20
Badalucco 1 43N55 7E51 -0:31:24
Badia (Abtei) 1 46N37 11E54 -0:47:36
Badia a Prataglia 1 43N47 11E52 -0:47:28
Badia Calavena 1 45N34 11E09 -0:44:36
Badia Polesine 1 45N05 11E29 -0:45:56
Badia Tedalda 1 43N42 12E11 -0:48:44
Badolato 2 38N34 16E31 -1:06:04
Bagheria 3 38N05 13E30 -0:54:00
Bagnacavallo 1 44N25 12E00 -0:48:00
Bagnaia 1 42N25 12E09 -0:48:36
Bagnara Calabra 2 38N18 15E49 -1:03:16
Bagnara di Romagna 1 44N23 11E49 -0:47:16
Bagnasco 1 44N18 8E02 -0:32:08
Bagni Acque Albule 1 41N57 12E43 -0:50:52
Bagni del Masino 1 46N15 9E36 -0:38:24
Bagni di Lucca 1 44N01 10E35 -0:42:20
Bagni di Rabbi 1 46N24 10E48 -0:43:12
Bagno a Ripoli 1 43N45 11E19 -0:45:16
Bagno di Romagna 1 43N50 11E57 -0:47:48
Bagnoli del Trigno 1 41N42 14E27 -0:57:48
Bagnoli di Sopra 1 45N11 11E53 -0:47:32
Bagnoli Irpino 2 40N50 15E04 -1:00:16
Bagnolo in Piano 1 44N46 10E40 -0:42:40
Bagnolo Mella 1 45N26 10E10 -0:40:40
Bagnone 1 44N19 10E00 -0:40:00
Bagnoregio 1 42N37 12E05 -0:48:20
Bagno Vignoni 1 43N02 11E39 -0:46:36
Bagolino 1 45N49 10E28 -0:41:52
Baia 2 40N49 14E04 -0:56:16
Baiano 2 40N57 14E37 -0:58:28
Baiardo 1 43N54 7E43 -0:30:52
Balangero 1 45N16 7E31 -0:30:04
Baldichieri d'asti 1 44N54 8E07 -0:32:28
Balestrate 3 38N03 13E00 -0:52:00
Ballao 4 39N33 9E22 -0:37:28
Ballata 3 37N58 12E41 -0:50:44
Ballino 1 45N58 10E48 -0:43:12
Balme 1 45N18 7E13 -0:28:52
Balsorano 1 41N49 13E34 -0:54:16
Balvano 2 40N39 15E31 -1:02:04
Balzola 1 45N11 8E24 -0:33:36
Banari 4 40N34 8E42 -0:34:48
Banzi 2 40N52 16E01 -1:04:04
Baradili 4 39N43 8E54 -0:35:36
Baragiano 2 40N41 15E35 -1:02:20
Baranello 2 41N32 14E34 -0:58:16
Barano d'Ischia 2 40N42 13E55 -0:55:40
Barbarano Vicentino 1 45N24 11E32 -0:46:08
Barbarasco 1 44N14 9E56 -0:39:44
Barberino di Mugello 1 44N00 11E15 -0:45:00
Barberino Val d'Elsa 1 43N32 11E10 -0:44:40
Barcellona Pozzo di Gotto 3 38N09 15E13 -1:00:52
Barcis 1 46N11 12E33 -0:50:12
Bard 1 45N36 7E45 -0:31:00
Bardi 1 44N38 9E44 -0:38:56
Bardolino 1 45N33 10E43 -0:42:52
Bardonecchia 1 45N05 6E42 -0:26:48
Bareggio 1 45N29 9E00 -0:36:00
Barga 1 44N04 10E29 -0:41:56
Bargagli 1 44N27 9E05 -0:36:20
Barge 1 44N43 7E20 -0:29:20
Barghe 1 45N41 10E24 -0:41:36
Bari 2 41N07 16E52 -1:07:28
Baricella 1 44N39 11E32 -0:46:08
Barigazzo 1 44N16 10E39 -0:42:36
Barile 2 40N57 15E40 -1:02:40
Bari Sardo 4 39N50 9E38 -0:38:32
Barisciano 1 42N19 13E35 -0:54:20
Barlassina 1 45N39 9E08 -0:36:32
Barletta 2 41N19 16E17 -1:05:08
Baronissi 2 40N44 14E45 -0:59:00
Barrafranca 3 37N22 14E12 -0:56:48
Barrali 4 39N28 9E06 -0:36:24
Barrea 1 41N45 13E59 -0:55:56
Barumini 4 39N42 9E00 -0:36:00
Barzio 1 45N57 9E27 -0:37:48
Basaluzzo 1 44N46 8E42 -0:34:48
Baschi 1 42N40 12E13 -0:48:52
Baselga di Pinè 1 46N08 11E14 -0:44:56
Baselice 2 41N24 14E58 -0:59:52
Basicò 3 38N04 15E04 -1:00:16
Basiliano 1 46N01 13E06 -0:52:24
Basovizza 1 45N38 13E52 -0:55:28
Bassano del Grappa 1 45N46 11E44 -0:46:56
Bassignana 1 45N00 8E44 -0:34:56
Bastia 1 43N04 12E33 -0:50:12
Bastiglia 1 44N43 11E00 -0:44:00
Battaglia Terme 1 45N17 11E47 -0:47:08
Battipaglia 2 40N37 14E58 -0:59:52
Battuello 1 45N27 8E56 -0:35:44
Baucina 3 37N55 13E32 -0:54:08
Baunei 4 40N02 9E40 -0:38:40
Bavari 1 44N26 9E01 -0:36:04
Baveno 1 45N55 8E30 -0:34:00
Bazzano 1 44N30 11E05 -0:44:20
Bedonia 1 44N30 9E38 -0:38:32
Beinette 1 44N22 7E39 -0:30:36
Belcastro 2 39N02 16E47 -1:07:08
Belfiore 1 45N23 11E12 -0:44:48
Belforte del Chienti 1 43N10 13E14 -0:52:56
Belgioioso 1 45N10 9E19 -0:37:16
Bella 2 40N45 15E32 -1:02:08
Bellagio 1 45N59 9E15 -0:37:00
Bellano 1 46N03 9E18 -0:37:12
Bellaria 1 44N09 12E28 -0:49:52
Bellariva 2 41N55 15E58 -1:03:52
Bellinzago Novarese 1 45N34 8E38 -0:34:32
Bellosguardo 2 40N25 15E19 -1:01:16
Belluno 1 46N09 12E13 -0:48:52
Belmonte Calabro 2 39N09 16E05 -1:04:20
Belmonte Mezzagno 3 38N02 13E23 -0:53:32
Belpasso 3 37N35 14E58 -0:59:52

Place	Zone	Lat	Long	Time
Belvedere	1	45N44	13E23	-0:53:32
Belvedere di Spinello	2	39N12	16E53	-1:07:32
Belvedere Marittimo	2	39N37	15E52	-1:03:28
Belvedere Ostrense	1	43N34	13E09	-0:52:36
Benetutti	4	40N27	9E10	-0:36:40
Bene Vagienna	1	44N33	7E50	-0:31:20
Benevento	2	41N08	14E45	-0:59:00
Berbenno di Valtellina	1	46N10	9E44	-0:38:56
Berceto	1	44N31	9E59	-0:39:56
Berchidda	4	40N47	9E10	-0:36:40
Bereguardo	1	45N15	9E01	-0:36:04
Bergamo	1	45N41	9E43	-0:38:52
Bergantino	1	45N05	11E15	-0:45:00
Bernalda	2	40N24	16E41	-1:06:44
Bernate	1	45N29	8E49	-0:35:16
Berra	1	44N59	11E58	-0:47:52
Bertinoro	1	44N09	12E08	-0:48:32
Besana in Brianza	1	45N42	9E17	-0:37:08
Besozzo	1	45N51	8E39	-0:34:36
Bettola	1	44N47	9E36	-0:38:24
Bettona	1	43N01	12E29	-0:49:56
Bevagna	1	42N56	12E36	-0:50:24
Beverino	1	44N14	9E47	-0:39:08
Bezzecca	1	45N55	10E43	-0:42:52
Biacesa	1	45N56	10E47	-0:43:08
Biadene	1	45N47	12E04	-0:48:16
Biancavilla	3	37N38	14E52	-0:59:28
Bianchi	2	39N06	16E24	-1:05:36
Bianco	2	38N05	16E09	-1:04:36
Bianzè	1	45N18	8E07	-0:32:28
Biassono	1	45N37	9E16	-0:37:04
Bibbiano	1	44N40	10E28	-0:41:52
Bibbiena	1	43N42	11E49	-0:47:16
Bibbona	1	43N16	10E35	-0:42:20
Bibione	1	45N38	13E00	-0:52:00
Biccari	2	41N24	15E11	-1:00:44
Bidoni	4	40N07	8E56	-0:35:44
Biella	1	45N34	8E03	-0:32:12
Bienno	1	45N56	10E18	-0:41:12
Bientina	1	43N42	10E37	-0:42:28
Binasco	1	45N20	9E06	-0:36:24
Bionaz	1	45N52	7E25	-0:29:40
Birgi Vecchi	3	37N53	12E29	-0:49:56
Bisaccia	2	41N01	15E22	-1:01:28
Bisacquino	3	37N42	13E15	-0:53:00
Bisceglie	2	41N14	16E31	-1:06:04
Bisignano	2	39N31	16E17	-1:05:08
Bitetto	2	41N02	16E45	-1:07:00
Bitonto	2	41N06	16E42	-1:06:48
Bitritto	2	41N03	16E50	-1:07:20
Bitti	4	40N29	9E23	-0:37:32
Bivona	3	37N37	13E26	-0:53:44
Bivongi	2	38N28	16E27	-1:05:48
Blevio	1	45N50	9E05	-0:36:20
Boara Pisani	1	45N08	11E47	-0:47:08
Boara Polesine	1	45N07	11E48	-0:47:12
Boario Terme	1	45N54	10E10	-0:40:40
Bobbio	1	44N46	9E23	-0:37:32
Bobbio Pellice	1	44N48	7E07	-0:28:28
Boccaleone	1	44N39	11E48	-0:47:12
Bocchigliero	2	39N25	16E45	-1:07:00
Boccon	1	45N19	11E39	-0:46:36
Bocconi	1	44N01	11E46	-0:47:04
Boden → Fleres	1	46N58	11E21	-0:45:24
Boffalora	1	45N28	8E50	-0:35:20
Bogliasco	1	44N23	9E04	-0:36:16
Bognanco Fonti	1	46N07	8E12	-0:32:48
Boiano	2	41N29	14E29	-0:57:56
Bolladello	1	45N41	8E50	-0:35:20
Bollate	1	45N33	9E07	-0:36:28
Bologna	1	44N29	11E20	-0:45:20
Bologne → Bologna	1	44N29	11E20	-0:45:20
Bolognetta	3	37N58	13E27	-0:53:48
Bolognola	1	42N59	13E14	-0:52:56
Bolonia → Bologna	1	44N29	11E20	-0:45:20
Bolótana	4	40N20	8E57	-0:35:48
Bolsena	1	42N39	11E59	-0:47:56
Bolzaneto	1	44N27	8E54	-0:35:36
Bolzano (Bozen)	1	46N31	11E22	-0:45:28
Bomba	1	42N02	14E22	-0:57:28
Bompensiere	3	37N28	13E47	-0:55:08
Bompietro	3	37N44	14E06	-0:56:24
Bonarcardo	4	40N06	8E39	-0:34:36
Bonassola	1	44N11	9E35	-0:38:20
Bondeno	1	44N53	11E25	-0:45:40
Bonefro	2	41N42	14E56	-0:59:44
Bonifati	2	39N35	15E54	-1:03:36
Bonito	2	41N06	15E00	-1:00:00
Bonnanaro	4	40N32	8E45	-0:35:00
Bono	4	40N25	9E02	-0:36:08
Bonorva	4	40N25	8E46	-0:35:04
Borca di Cadore	1	46N26	12E13	-0:48:52
Bordighera	1	43N46	7E39	-0:30:36
Bore	1	44N43	9E47	-0:39:08
Borello	1	44N03	12E11	-0:48:44
Borello	1	41N55	14E18	-0:57:12
Boretto	1	44N54	10E33	-0:42:12
Borgata Costiera	3	37N43	12E39	-0:50:36
Borgetto	3	38N03	13E08	-0:52:32
Borghetto	1	45N41	10E56	-0:43:44
Borghetto di Vara	1	44N13	9E43	-0:38:52
Borghetto Lodigiano	1	45N13	9E30	-0:38:00
Borghetto Santo Spirito	1	44N06	8E14	-0:32:56
Borgia	2	38N49	16E30	-1:06:00
Borgio-Verezzi	1	44N10	8E18	-0:33:12
Borgo	1	46N03	11E27	-0:45:48
Borgo alla Collina	1	43N45	11E43	-0:46:52
Borgo a Mozzano	1	43N59	10E33	-0:42:12
Borgo Cerreto	1	42N49	12E54	-0:51:36
Borgo d'Ale	1	45N21	8E03	-0:32:12
Borgoforte	1	45N03	10E45	-0:43:00
Borgofranco d'Ivrea	1	45N30	7E51	-0:31:24
Borgolavezzaro	1	45N19	8E42	-0:34:48
Borgomanero	1	45N42	8E28	-0:33:52
Borgomaro	1	43N58	7E56	-0:31:44
Borgonovo Val Tidone	1	45N01	9E26	-0:37:44
Borgo Pace	1	43N39	12E17	-0:49:08
Borgoricco	1	45N32	11E58	-0:47:52
Borgorose	1	42N11	13E13	-0:52:52
Borgo San Dalmazzo	1	44N20	7E30	-0:30:00
Borgo San Giacomo	1	45N21	9E58	-0:39:52
Borgo San Lorenzo	1	43N57	11E23	-0:45:32
Borgosatollo	1	45N28	10E14	-0:40:56
Borgosesia	1	45N43	8E16	-0:33:04
Borgo Ticino	1	45N41	8E36	-0:34:24
Borgo Tossignano	1	44N16	11E35	-0:46:20
Borgo Val di Taro	1	44N29	9E46	-0:39:04
Borgo Vercelli	1	45N21	8E28	-0:33:52
Bormio	1	46N28	10E22	-0:41:28
Borno	1	45N56	10E12	-0:40:48
Borore	4	40N13	8E48	-0:35:12
Borriana	1	45N30	8E02	-0:32:08
Borsano	1	45N35	8E51	-0:35:24
Bortigali	4	40N17	8E50	-0:35:20
Bortigiadas	4	40N53	9E02	-0:36:08
Borzonasca	1	44N25	9E23	-0:37:32
Bosa	4	40N18	8E30	-0:34:00
Bosco	1	44N53	12E14	-0:48:56
Bosco	1	43N08	12E28	-0:49:52
Bosco Chiesanuova	1	45N37	11E02	-0:44:08
Bosco Marengo	1	44N49	8E41	-0:34:44
Boscotrecase	2	40N46	14E28	-0:57:52
Bossolasco	1	44N32	8E02	-0:32:08
Botricello	2	38N56	16E51	-1:07:24
Bova	2	38N00	15E56	-1:03:44
Bovalino Marina	2	38N10	16E11	-1:04:44
Bova Marina	2	37N56	15E55	-1:03:40
Bovegno	1	45N48	10E16	-0:41:04
Boves	1	44N19	7E33	-0:30:12
Boville Ernica	2	41N38	13E28	-0:53:52
Bovino	2	41N15	15E20	-1:01:20
Bovisio Masciago	1	45N37	9E09	-0:36:36
Bovolenta	1	45N16	11E56	-0:47:44
Bovolone	1	45N15	11E07	-0:44:28
Bozen → Bolzano	1	46N31	11E22	-0:45:28
Bozzolo	1	45N06	10E29	-0:41:56
Bra	1	44N42	7E51	-0:31:24
Bracciano	1	42N06	12E10	-0:48:40
Bracigliano	2	40N49	14E42	-0:58:48
Braies (Prags)	1	46N42	12E08	-0:48:32
Brancaleone Marina	2	37N58	16E06	-1:04:24
Brandizzo	1	45N11	7E51	-0:31:24
Branzi	1	46N00	9E46	-0:39:04
Bratto	1	45N55	10E04	-0:40:16
Breganze	1	45N42	11E34	-0:46:16
Breguzzo	1	46N00	10E42	-0:42:48
Brembio	1	45N13	9E34	-0:38:16
Brennero (Brenner)	1	47N00	11E30	-0:46:00
Breno	1	45N57	10E18	-0:41:12
Brentino	1	45N40	10E55	-0:43:40
Brentonico	1	45N49	10E57	-0:43:48
Brescello	1	44N54	10E31	-0:42:04
Brescia	1	45N33	13E15	-0:53:00
Bressanone (Brixen)	1	46N43	11E39	-0:46:36
Bresso	1	45N32	9E11	-0:36:44
Breuil-Cervinia	1	45N56	7E38	-0:30:32
Briatico	2	38N43	16E02	-1:04:08
Bribano	1	46N06	12E05	-0:48:20
Bricherasio	1	44N49	7E18	-0:29:12
Brienno	1	45N55	9E07	-0:36:28
Brienza	2	40N29	15E37	-1:02:28
Brindisi	2	40N38	17E56	-1:11:44
Brindisi Montagna	2	40N37	15E57	-1:03:48
Brisighella	1	44N13	11E46	-0:47:04
Brivio	1	45N44	9E27	-0:37:48
Brolo	3	38N09	14E50	-0:59:20
Broni	1	45N04	9E16	-0:37:04
Bronte	3	37N47	14E50	-0:59:20
Bronzolo (Branzoll)	1	46N24	11E19	-0:45:16
Brossasco	1	44N34	7E21	-0:29:24
Brosso	1	45N30	7E48	-0:31:12
Brozzo	1	45N43	10E14	-0:40:56
Brugherio	1	45N33	9E18	-0:37:12
Brugnato	1	44N14	9E43	-0:38:52
Brunate	1	45N49	9E06	-0:36:24
Brunico (Bruneck)	1	46N48	11E56	-0:47:44
Brusasco	1	45N09	8E04	-0:32:16
Brusson	1	45N45	7E44	-0:30:56
Bruzzano Zeffirio	2	38N02	16E05	-1:04:20
Buccheri	3	37N08	14E51	-0:59:24
Bucchianico	1	42N18	14E11	-0:56:44
Buccinasco	1	45N24	9E07	-0:36:28
Buccino	2	40N37	15E23	-1:01:32
Bucine	1	43N29	11E37	-0:46:28
Buddusò	4	40N35	9E15	-0:37:00
Budoni	4	40N43	9E42	-0:38:48
Budrio	1	44N32	11E32	-0:46:08
Buggerru	4	39N24	8E24	-0:33:36
Bultei	4	40N27	9E03	-0:36:12
Buonalbergo	2	41N13	14E59	-0:59:56
Buonconvento	1	43N08	11E29	-0:45:56
Burcei	4	39N21	9E21	-0:37:24
Burgio	3	37N36	13E17	-0:53:08
Burgos	4	40N23	8E59	-0:35:56
Burgstall → Postal	1	46N36	11E11	-0:44:44
Burgusio (Burgeis)	1	46N42	10E31	-0:42:04
Buronzo	1	45N29	8E16	-0:33:04
Busachi	4	40N02	8E54	-0:35:36
Busalla	1	44N34	8E57	-0:35:48
Busana	1	44N22	10E19	-0:41:16
Busca	1	44N31	7E29	-0:29:56
Buscate	1	45N32	8E49	-0:35:16
Busche	1	46N02	11E59	-0:47:56
Buseto Palizzolo	3	38N01	12E43	-0:50:52
Bussana	1	43N49	7E51	-0:31:24
Busseto	1	44N59	10E02	-0:40:08
Bussi sul Tirino	1	42N12	13E49	-0:55:16
Bussolengo	1	45N28	10E51	-0:43:24
Bussoleno	1	45N08	7E09	-0:28:36
Busto Arsizio	1	45N37	8E51	-0:35:24
Busto Garolfo	1	45N33	8E53	-0:35:32
Butera	3	37N11	14E11	-0:56:44
Buti	1	43N44	10E35	-0:42:20
Buttapietra	1	45N20	11E00	-0:44:00
Buttrio	1	46N01	13E20	-0:53:20
Cabiate	1	45N40	9E10	-0:36:40
Cabras	4	39N56	8E32	-0:34:08
Caccamo	3	37N56	13E40	-0:54:40
Caccuri	2	39N14	16E47	-1:07:08
Cadeo	1	44N58	9E48	-0:39:12
Cadipietra (Steinhaus)	1	46N59	11E59	-0:47:56
Cadoneghe	1	45N26	11E55	-0:47:40
Caerano di San Marco	1	45N47	12E00	-0:48:00
Caggiano	2	40N34	15E29	-1:01:56
Cagli	1	43N33	12E39	-0:50:36
Cagliari	4	39N13	9E07	-0:36:28
Cagnano Varano	2	41N49	15E47	-1:03:08
Caiazzo	2	41N11	14E22	-0:57:28
Caino	1	45N38	10E18	-0:41:12
Cairano	2	40N54	15E22	-1:01:28
Cairo Montenotte	1	44N24	8E16	-0:33:04
Calabernardo	3	36N52	15E08	-1:00:32
Calabritto	2	40N47	15E13	-1:00:52
Cala d'Oliva	4	41N05	8E20	-0:33:20
Cala Gonone	4	40N18	9E38	-0:38:32
Calalzo di Cadore	1	46N27	12E23	-0:49:32
Calamonaci	3	37N31	13E17	-0:53:08
Calangianus	4	40N56	9E11	-0:36:44
Calanna	2	38N11	15E43	-1:02:52
Calascibetta	3	37N35	14E16	-0:57:04
Calasetta	4	39N07	8E22	-0:33:28
Calatabiano	3	37N49	15E14	-1:00:56
Calatafimi	3	37N55	12E52	-0:51:28
Calavino	1	46N03	10E59	-0:43:56
Calciano	2	40N35	16E11	-1:04:44
Calcinaia	1	43N41	10E37	-0:42:28
Calcinato	1	45N27	10E24	-0:41:36
Calcio	1	45N30	9E50	-0:39:20
Caldaro (Kaltern)	1	46N25	11E14	-0:44:56
Caldarola	1	43N08	13E13	-0:52:52
Caldè	1	45N57	8E38	-0:34:32
Caldes	1	46N22	10E56	-0:43:44
Caldiero	1	45N22	11E11	-0:44:44
Caldonazzo	1	45N59	11E16	-0:45:04
Calenzano	1	43N51	11E09	-0:44:36
Calimera	2	40N15	18E17	-1:13:08
Calitri	2	40N54	15E27	-1:01:48
Calizzano	1	44N14	8E07	-0:32:28
Calliano	1	45N56	11E05	-0:44:20
Calliano	1	45N00	8E15	-0:33:00
Calmazzo	1	43N40	12E46	-0:51:04
Calolziocorte	1	45N48	9E26	-0:37:44
Caloveto	2	39N30	16E45	-1:07:00
Caltabellotta	3	37N34	13E13	-0:52:52
Caltagirone	3	37N14	14E31	-0:58:04
Caltanissetta	3	37N29	14E04	-0:56:16
Caltavuturo	3	37N49	13E53	-0:55:32
Caluso	1	45N18	7E53	-0:31:32
Calvello	2	40N28	15E51	-1:03:24
Calvera	2	40N09	16E09	-1:04:36
Calvi dell'Umbria	1	42N24	12E34	-0:50:16
Calvisano	1	45N20	10E20	-0:41:20
Camaiore	1	43N56	10E18	-0:41:12
Camarda	1	42N23	13E29	-0:53:56
Camastra	3	37N15	13E47	-0:55:08
Cambiano	1	44N58	7E47	-0:31:08
Camerano	1	43N32	13E33	-0:54:12
Cameri	1	45N30	8E39	-0:34:36
Camerino	1	43N08	13E04	-0:52:16
Camerota	2	40N02	15E23	-1:01:32
Camisano Vicentino	1	45N31	11E43	-0:46:52
Cammarata	3	37N38	13E38	-0:54:32
Camogli	1	44N21	9E09	-0:36:36
Campagna	2	40N40	15E08	-1:00:32
Campagna Lupia	1	45N21	12E06	-0:48:24

Place		Lat	Long	Time
Campagnano di Roma	1	42N08	12E23	-0:49:32
Campagnatico	1	42N53	11E16	-0:45:04
Campana	2	39N24	16E50	-1:07:20
Camparada	1	45N39	9E19	-0:37:16
Campegine	1	44N45	10E32	-0:42:08
Campello Monti	1	45N56	8E15	-0:33:00
Campi Bisenzio	1	43N49	11E08	-0:44:32
Campiglia dei Fosci	1	43N27	11E03	-0:44:12
Campiglia Marittima	1	43N03	10E37	-0:42:28
Campione del Garda	1	45N45	10E45	-0:43:00
Campi Salentina	2	40N24	18E01	-1:12:04
Campitello	1	46N28	11E44	-0:46:56
Campli	1	42N43	13E41	-0:54:44
Campobasso	2	41N34	14E39	-0:58:36
Campobello di Licata	3	37N15	13E55	-0:55:40
Campobello di Mazara	3	37N38	12E45	-0:51:00
Campo Catino	1	41N48	13E20	-0:53:20
Campodarsego	1	45N30	11E54	-0:47:36
Campo di Giove	1	42N01	14E03	-0:56:12
Campo di Trens (Trens)	1	46N52	11E29	-0:45:56
Campodolcino	1	46N24	9E21	-0:37:24
Campofelice di Fitalia	3	37N50	13E29	-0:53:56
Campofelice di Roccella	3	37N59	13E53	-0:55:32
Campofiorito	3	37N45	13E16	-0:53:04
Campoformido	1	46N01	13E09	-0:52:36
Campofranco	3	37N30	13E43	-0:54:52
Campogalliano	1	44N41	10E50	-0:43:20
Campolaro	1	45N55	10E20	-0:41:20
Campolasta (Astfeld)	1	46N40	11E22	-0:45:28
Campolieto	2	41N38	14E46	-0:59:04
Campo Ligure	1	44N32	8E42	-0:34:48
Campomarino	2	41N57	15E02	-1:00:08
Campomorone	1	44N30	8E53	-0:35:32
Campora	2	40N19	15E17	-1:01:08
Camporeale	3	37N54	13E06	-0:52:24
Camporgiano	1	44N09	10E20	-0:41:20
Camposampiero	1	45N34	11E56	-0:47:44
Camposanto	1	44N47	11E08	-0:44:32
Campotosto	1	42N33	13E22	-0:53:28
Campo Tures (Sand in Taufers)	1	46N55	11E57	-0:47:48
Campovalano	1	42N44	13E40	-0:54:40
Camucia	1	43N16	11E58	-0:47:52
Canale	1	44N48	8E00	-0:32:00
Canaro	1	44N56	11E40	-0:46:40
Canazei	1	46N28	11E46	-0:47:04
Cancellara	2	40N44	15E56	-1:03:44
Cancello e Arnone	2	41N04	14E03	-0:56:12
Canda	1	45N03	11E30	-0:46:00
Candela	2	41N08	15E31	-1:02:04
Candelo	1	45N33	8E07	-0:32:28
Candia Canavese	1	45N20	7E53	-0:31:32
Candia Lomellina	1	45N11	8E36	-0:34:24
Canegrate	1	45N34	8E56	-0:35:44
Canelli	1	44N43	8E17	-0:33:08
Caneva	1	45N58	12E26	-0:49:44
Canicattì	3	37N21	13E51	-0:55:24
Canicattini Bagni	3	37N02	15E04	-1:00:16
Canino	1	42N28	11E45	-0:47:00
Canna	2	40N05	16E30	-1:06:00
Cannara	1	43N00	12E35	-0:50:20
Cannero-Riviera	1	46N01	8E41	-0:34:44
Canneto	1	43N12	10E44	-0:42:56
Canneto	3	38N29	14E58	-0:59:52
Canneto sull'Oglio	1	45N09	10E25	-0:41:40
Cannobio	1	46N04	8E42	-0:34:48
Canosa di Puglia	2	41N13	16E04	-1:04:16
Cantalupo in Sabina	1	42N18	12E39	-0:50:36
Cantalupo nel Sannio	2	41N31	14E24	-0:57:36
Cantiano	1	43N28	12E38	-0:50:32
Cantoira	1	45N21	7E23	-0:29:32
Cantù	1	45N44	9E08	-0:36:32
Canzo	1	45N51	9E16	-0:37:04
Caorle	1	45N36	12E53	-0:51:32
Caorso	1	45N03	9E52	-0:39:28
Capaccio	2	40N25	15E05	-1:00:20
Capaci	3	38N10	13E14	-0:52:56
Capalbio	1	42N27	11E25	-0:45:40
Capannoli	1	43N35	10E41	-0:42:44
Capannori	1	43N50	10E34	-0:42:16
Capestrano	1	42N16	13E46	-0:55:04
Capistrano	2	38N41	16E17	-1:05:08
Capistrello	1	41N57	13E23	-0:53:32
Capizzi	3	37N51	14E29	-0:57:56
Capodimonte	1	42N33	11E55	-0:47:40
Capo di Ponte	1	46N02	10E21	-0:41:24
Capo d'Orlando	3	38N10	14E53	-0:59:32
Capoliveri	1	42N45	10E22	-0:41:28
Caposele	2	40N49	15E13	-1:00:52
Capostrada	1	43N57	10E54	-0:43:36
Capoterra	4	39N11	8E58	-0:35:52
Cappelle	1	42N03	13E22	-0:53:28
Cappelle sul Tavo	1	42N28	14E06	-0:56:24
Capracotta	1	41N50	14E16	-0:57:04
Capraia	1	43N03	9E50	-0:39:20
Capranica	1	42N15	12E11	-0:48:44
Caprarola	1	42N19	12E14	-0:48:56

Place		Lat	Long	Time
Caprese Michelangelo	1	43N39	11E59	-0:47:56
Capri	2	40N33	14E14	-0:56:56
Capriati a Volturno	2	41N28	14E08	-0:56:32
Capri Leone	3	38N05	14E44	-0:58:56
Caprino Veronese	1	45N36	10E47	-0:43:08
Capua	2	41N06	14E12	-0:56:48
Capurso	2	41N03	16E55	-1:07:40
Caraffa di Catanzaro	2	38N53	16E29	-1:05:56
Caraglio	1	44N25	7E26	-0:29:44
Caramagna-Piemonte	1	44N46	7E44	-0:30:56
Caramanico Terme	1	42N09	14E00	-0:56:00
Carano	1	46N16	11E27	-0:45:48
Carasco	1	44N21	9E21	-0:37:24
Carate Brianza	1	45N41	9E14	-0:36:56
Caravaggio	1	45N30	9E38	-0:38:32
Carbonare	1	45N56	11E13	-0:44:52
Carbone	2	40N09	16E05	-1:04:20
Carbonia	4	39N10	8E31	-0:34:04
Carbonin	1	46N37	12E13	-0:48:52
Carcare	1	44N21	8E18	-0:33:12
Cardinale	2	38N38	16E23	-1:05:32
Cardito	2	40N57	14E18	-0:57:12
Careri	2	38N10	16E07	-1:04:28
Caresana	1	45N13	8E30	-0:34:00
Cariati	2	39N30	16E56	-1:07:44
Carife	2	41N01	15E12	-1:00:48
Carignano	1	43N49	12E56	-0:51:44
Carignano	1	44N55	7E40	-0:30:40
Carini	3	38N08	13E11	-0:52:44
Carinola	2	41N11	13E58	-0:55:52
Carisolo	1	46N10	10E45	-0:43:00
Carlentini	3	37N16	15E01	-1:00:04
Carloforte	4	39N08	8E18	-0:33:12
Carlopoli	2	39N03	16E27	-1:05:48
Carmagnola	1	44N51	7E43	-0:30:52
Carmiano	2	40N21	18E03	-1:12:12
Carmignano di Brenta	1	45N38	11E42	-0:46:48
Carnia	1	46N22	13E08	-0:52:32
Carolei	2	39N15	16E13	-1:04:52
Carona	1	46N01	9E47	-0:39:08
Caronia	3	38N01	14E26	-0:57:44
Caronno Pertusella	1	45N36	9E03	-0:36:12
Carosino	2	40N27	17E23	-1:09:32
Carovigno	2	40N42	17E39	-1:10:36
Carovilli	1	41N43	14E17	-0:57:08
Carpaneto Piacentino	1	44N55	9E47	-0:39:08
Carpanzano	2	39N09	16E18	-1:05:12
Carpegna	1	43N47	12E20	-0:49:20
Carpenedolo	1	45N22	10E26	-0:41:44
Carpi	1	44N47	10E53	-0:43:32
Carpignano Sesia	1	45N32	8E25	-0:33:40
Carpineti	1	44N28	10E31	-0:42:04
Carpineto Romano	2	41N36	13E05	-0:52:20
Carpino	2	41N51	15E51	-1:03:24
Carpinone	2	41N35	14E19	-0:57:16
Carrara	1	44N05	10E06	-0:40:24
Carrodano	1	44N14	9E39	-0:38:36
Carrù	1	44N29	7E52	-0:31:28
Carsoli	1	42N06	13E05	-0:52:20
Cartura	1	45N16	11E50	-0:47:20
Casabona	2	39N15	16E57	-1:07:48
Casacalenda	2	41N44	14E51	-0:59:24
Casalanguida	1	42N03	14E30	-0:58:00
Casalattico	2	41N37	13E43	-0:54:52
Casalbordino	1	42N09	14E35	-0:58:20
Casalbuono	2	40N13	15E41	-1:02:44
Casalbuttano	1	45N15	9E58	-0:39:52
Casal di Principe	2	41N00	14E08	-0:56:32
Casalecchio di Reno	1	44N28	11E16	-0:45:04
Casale Monferrato	1	45N08	8E27	-0:33:48
Casale sul Sile	1	45N36	12E19	-0:49:16
Casaletto Spartano	2	40N09	15E37	-1:02:28
Casalmaggiore	1	44N59	10E26	-0:41:44
Casalmorano	1	45N17	9E54	-0:39:36
Casalnuovo Monterotaro	2	41N37	15E06	-1:00:24
Casalpusterlengo	1	45N11	9E39	-0:38:36
Casal Velino	2	40N11	15E06	-1:00:24
Casalvieri	2	41N38	13E43	-0:54:52
Casamassima	2	40N57	16E55	-1:07:40
Casamicciola Terme	2	40N45	13E54	-0:55:36
Casarano	2	40N00	18E10	-1:12:40
Casarsa della Delizia	1	45N57	12E50	-0:51:20
Cascia	1	42N43	13E01	-0:52:04
Casciana Terme	1	43N31	10E32	-0:42:08
Cascina	1	43N41	10E33	-0:42:12
Casei Gerola	1	45N00	8E55	-0:35:40
Casella	1	44N32	9E00	-0:36:00
Caselle in Pittari	2	40N10	15E33	-1:02:12
Caselle Torinese	1	45N10	7E39	-0:30:36
Casenove	1	42N58	12E50	-0:51:20
Casenuove	1	45N38	8E42	-0:34:48
Caserta	2	41N04	14E20	-0:57:20
Casina	1	44N30	10E30	-0:42:00

Place		Lat	Long	Time
Casola in Lunigiana	1	44N14	10E10	-0:40:40
Casole d'Elsa	1	43N20	11E02	-0:44:08
Casoli	1	42N07	14E18	-0:57:12
Casorate Primo	1	45N19	9E01	-0:36:04
Casorate Sempione	1	45N40	8E44	-0:34:56
Casorezzo	1	45N31	8E54	-0:35:36
Casoria	2	40N54	14E17	-0:57:08
Caspoggio	1	46N16	9E52	-0:39:28
Cassano allo Ionio	2	39N47	16E20	-1:05:20
Cassano d'Adda	1	45N32	9E31	-0:38:04
Cassano delle Murge	2	40N53	16E46	-1:07:04
Cassano Magnago	1	45N41	8E50	-0:35:20
Cassaro	3	37N07	14E56	-0:59:44
Cassine	1	44N45	8E31	-0:34:04
Cassinetta di Lugagnano	1	45N25	8E54	-0:35:36
Cassino	2	41N30	13E49	-0:55:16
Cassio	1	44N35	10E02	-0:40:08
Cassolnovo	1	45N22	8E48	-0:35:12
Cassone	1	45N44	10E46	-0:43:04
Castagnaro	1	45N07	11E24	-0:45:36
Castagneto Carducci	1	43N10	10E36	-0:42:24
Castano Primo	1	45N33	8E47	-0:35:08
Casteggio	1	45N00	9E07	-0:36:28
Castel Baronia	2	41N03	15E11	-1:00:44
Castel Bolognese	1	44N19	11E48	-0:47:12
Castelbuono	3	37N56	14E05	-0:56:20
Castelcivita	2	40N30	15E15	-1:01:00
Casteldaccia	3	38N03	13E32	-0:54:08
Castel d'Ario	1	45N11	10E58	-0:43:52
Casteldarne (Ehrenburg)	1	46N48	11E50	-0:47:20
Casteldelfino	1	44N35	7E04	-0:28:16
Castel del Monte	1	42N22	13E43	-0:54:52
Castel del Piano	1	42N53	11E32	-0:46:08
Castel del Rio	1	44N12	11E30	-0:46:00
Castel di Ieri	1	42N06	13E44	-0:54:56
Castel di Lucio	3	37N53	14E19	-0:57:16
Castel di Iudica	3	37N30	14E38	-0:58:32
Castel di Sangro	1	41N47	14E06	-0:56:24
Castel di Tora	1	42N13	12E58	-0:51:52
Castelfidardo	1	43N28	13E33	-0:54:12
Castelfiorentino	1	43N36	10E58	-0:43:52
Castelfondo	1	46N27	11E07	-0:44:28
Castelforte	2	41N18	13E49	-0:55:16
Castelfranco di Sotto	1	43N42	10E45	-0:43:00
Castelfranco Emilia	1	44N37	11E03	-0:44:12
Castelfranco in Miscano	2	41N18	15E05	-1:00:20
Castelfranco Veneto	1	45N40	11E55	-0:47:40
Castel Frentano	1	42N12	14E22	-0:57:28
Castel Gandolfo	1	41N45	12E39	-0:50:36
Castel Giorgio	1	42N42	11E59	-0:47:56
Castelgrande	2	40N47	15E26	-1:01:44
Castellabate	2	40N17	14E57	-0:59:48
Castell'Alfero	1	44N59	8E13	-0:32:52
Castellalto	1	42N40	13E49	-0:55:16
Castellammare del Golfo	3	38N01	12E53	-0:51:32
Castellammare di Stabia	2	40N42	14E29	-0:57:56
Castellamonte	1	45N23	7E42	-0:30:48
Castellana Grotte	2	40N53	17E11	-1:08:44
Castellana Sicula	3	37N47	14E02	-0:56:08
Castellaneta	2	40N37	16E57	-1:07:48
Castellanza	1	45N37	8E54	-0:35:36
Castellarano	1	44N30	10E44	-0:42:56
Castell'Arquato	1	44N51	9E52	-0:39:28
Castell'Azzara	1	42N46	11E42	-0:46:48
Castellazzo Bormida	1	44N51	8E34	-0:34:16
Castelleone	1	45N18	9E46	-0:39:04
Castelletto	1	45N30	8E48	-0:35:12
Castelletto di Brenzone	1	45N41	10E45	-0:43:00
Castelli	1	42N29	13E43	-0:54:52
Castellina in Chianti	1	43N28	11E17	-0:45:08
Castellina Marittima	1	43N25	10E35	-0:42:20
Castello d'Annone	1	44N53	8E19	-0:33:16
Castello di Fiemme	1	46N17	11E26	-0:45:44
Castello Lavazzo	1	46N17	12E18	-0:49:12
Castello Tesino	1	46N04	11E38	-0:46:32
Castellucchio	1	45N09	10E39	-0:42:36
Castelluccio	2	40N00	15E58	-1:03:52
Castell'Umberto	3	38N05	14E48	-0:59:12
Castelluzzo	3	38N06	12E44	-0:50:56
Castel Madama	1	41N58	12E52	-0:51:28
Castel Maggiore	1	44N34	11E22	-0:45:28
Castelmagno	1	44N24	7E13	-0:28:52
Castelmassa	1	45N01	11E18	-0:45:12
Castelmauro	2	41N50	14E43	-0:58:52
Castelmezzano	2	40N32	16E03	-1:04:12
Castelnovo di Sotto	1	44N49	10E34	-0:42:16

Place	Zone	Lat	Long	Time
Castelnovo ne'Monti	1	44N26	10E24	-0:41:36
Castelnuovo	1	45N26	10E47	-0:43:08
Castelnuovo Berardenga	1	43N21	11E30	-0:46:00
Castelnuovo dell'Abate	1	43N00	11E31	-0:46:04
Castelnuovo della Daunia	2	41N35	15E07	-1:00:28
Castelnuovo di Garfagnana	1	44N06	10E24	-0:41:36
Castelnuovo di Porto	1	42N07	12E30	-0:50:00
Castelnuovo di Val di Cecina	1	43N12	10E59	-0:43:56
Castelnuovo Don Bosco	1	45N03	7E58	-0:31:52
Castelnuovo Nigra	1	45N26	7E41	-0:30:44
Castelnuovo Rangone	1	44N33	10E56	-0:43:44
Castelnuovo Scrivia	1	44N59	8E53	-0:35:32
Castel Pagano	2	41N24	14E48	-0:59:12
Castelraimondo	1	43N12	13E04	-0:52:16
Castel San Gimignano	1	43N24	11E00	-0:44:00
Castel San Giorgio	2	40N47	14E42	-0:58:48
Castel San Giovanni	1	45N04	9E26	-0:37:44
Castel San Lorenzo	2	40N25	15E14	-1:00:56
Castel San Pietro	1	44N24	11E35	-0:46:20
Castel Sant'Elia	1	42N15	12E22	-0:49:28
Castelsaraceno	2	40N10	16E00	-1:04:00
Castelsardo	4	40N55	8E43	-0:34:52
Castelsilano	2	39N16	16E46	-1:07:04
Casteltermini	3	37N32	13E39	-0:54:36
Castelvecchio Subequo	1	42N08	13E44	-0:54:56
Castelvetere in Val Fortore	2	41N27	14E56	-0:59:44
Castelvetrano	3	37N41	12E47	-0:51:08
Castelvetro di Modena	1	44N30	10E57	-0:43:48
Castelvetro Piacentino	1	45N05	9E59	-0:39:56
Castel Viscardo	1	42N45	12E00	-0:48:00
Castel Volturno	1	44N13	11E37	-0:46:28
Castel Volturno	2	41N02	13E56	-0:55:44
Castenaso	1	44N30	11E28	-0:45:52
Castenedolo	1	45N28	10E18	-0:41:12
Castiglioncello	1	43N24	10E24	-0:41:36
Castiglione Chiavarese	1	44N16	9E31	-0:38:04
Castiglione d'Adda	1	45N13	9E41	-0:38:44
Castiglione dei Pepoli	1	44N08	11E09	-0:44:36
Castiglione del Lago	1	43N07	12E03	-0:48:12
Castiglione della Pescaia	1	42N46	10E53	-0:43:32
Castiglione delle Stiviere	1	45N23	10E29	-0:41:56
Castiglione del Pepoli	1	44N08	11E09	-0:44:36
Castiglione di Sicilia	3	37N53	15E07	-1:00:28
Castiglione d'Orcia	1	43N00	11E37	-0:46:28
Castiglione d'Ossola	1	46N03	8E13	-0:32:52
Castiglione Messer Marino	1	41N52	14E27	-0:57:48
Castiglione Olona	1	45N46	8E52	-0:35:28
Castiglion Fibocchi	1	43N32	11E46	-0:47:04
Castiglion Fiorentino	1	43N20	11E55	-0:47:40
Castione della Presolana	1	45N54	10E04	-0:40:16
Castions di Strada	1	45N54	13E11	-0:52:44
Castorano	1	42N54	13E43	-0:54:52
Castro	1	45N48	10E04	-0:40:16
Castrocaro	1	44N10	11E57	-0:47:48
Castrocielo	2	41N32	13E42	-0:54:48
Castro dei Volsci	2	41N30	13E24	-0:53:36
Castrofilippo	3	37N21	13E46	-0:55:04
Castrogiovanni	3	37N33	14E17	-0:57:08
Castronuovo di Sant'Andrea	2	40N11	16E11	-1:04:44
Castronuovo di Sicilia	3	37N41	13E36	-0:54:24
Castropignano	2	41N37	14E33	-0:58:12
Castroreale	3	38N06	15E12	-1:00:48
Castrovillari	2	39N49	16E13	-1:04:52
Catania	3	37N30	15E06	-1:00:24
Catanzaro	2	38N54	16E26	-1:05:44
Catanzaro Lido	2	38N49	16E36	-1:06:24
Catenanuova	3	37N34	14E41	-0:58:44
Catignano	1	42N21	13E57	-0:55:48
Cattolica	1	43N58	12E44	-0:50:56
Cattolica Eraclea	3	37N26	13E24	-0:53:36
Caulonia	2	38N23	16E25	-1:05:40
Cava de' Tirreni	2	40N42	14E42	-0:58:48
Cavaglià	1	45N24	8E05	-0:32:20
Cavalese	1	46N17	11E27	-0:45:48
Cavallermaggiore	1	44N43	7E41	-0:30:44
Cava Manara	1	45N08	9E07	-0:36:28
Cavarzere	1	45N08	12E05	-0:48:20
Cavaso del Tomba	1	45N51	11E52	-0:47:28
Cave	1	41N49	12E56	-0:51:44
Cave del Predil	1	46N26	13E34	-0:54:16
Cavedine	1	45N59	10E59	-0:43:56
Cavernago	1	45N38	9E46	-0:39:04
Cavezzo	1	44N50	11E02	-0:44:08
Cavi	1	44N17	9E22	-0:37:28
Cavour	1	44N47	7E22	-0:29:28
Cavriago	1	44N42	10E31	-0:42:04
Cavriana	1	45N21	10E36	-0:42:24
Ceccano	2	41N34	13E20	-0:53:20
Cecina	1	43N19	10E31	-0:42:04
Cedegolo	1	46N05	10E21	-0:41:24
Cefalà Diana	3	37N54	13E28	-0:53:52
Cefalù	3	38N02	14E01	-0:56:04
Ceglie Messapico	2	40N39	17E31	-1:10:04
Celano	1	42N05	13E33	-0:54:12
Celenza sul Trigno	1	41N52	14E35	-0:58:20
Celenza Valfortore	2	41N34	14E58	-0:59:52
Celico	2	39N19	16E20	-1:05:20
Celle Ligure	1	44N20	8E33	-0:34:12
Cellino Attanasio	1	42N36	13E52	-0:55:28
Cellino San Marco	2	40N28	17E58	-1:11:52
Cembra	1	46N10	11E13	-0:44:52
Cencenighe	1	46N21	11E58	-0:47:52
Cene	1	45N47	9E49	-0:39:16
Centallo	1	44N30	7E35	-0:30:20
Centeno	1	42N48	11E49	-0:47:16
Cento	1	44N43	11E17	-0:45:08
Centola	2	40N04	15E19	-1:01:16
Centuripe	3	37N37	14E44	-0:58:56
Ceprano	2	41N33	13E31	-0:54:04
Ceraino	1	45N35	10E50	-0:43:20
Cerami	3	37N49	14E30	-0:58:00
Cerano	1	45N25	8E47	-0:35:08
Ceraso	2	40N11	15E15	-1:01:00
Cerchiara di Calabria	2	39N51	16E23	-1:05:32
Cercola	2	40N51	14E21	-0:57:24
Cerda	3	37N54	13E49	-0:55:16
Cerea	1	45N12	11E13	-0:44:52
Cereglio	1	44N18	11E04	-0:44:16
Ceres	1	45N19	7E23	-0:29:32
Ceresole Reale	1	45N26	7E15	-0:29:00
Ceriale	1	44N06	8E14	-0:32:56
Ceriana	1	43N53	7E46	-0:31:04
Ceriano	1	45N38	9E05	-0:36:20
Cerignola	2	41N16	15E54	-1:03:36
Cerisano	2	39N16	16E11	-1:04:44
Cermignano	1	42N35	13E47	-0:55:08
Cernobbio	1	45N50	9E04	-0:36:16
Cernusco sul Naviglio	1	45N31	9E19	-0:37:16
Cerreto d'Esi	1	43N19	12E59	-0:51:56
Cerreto Guidi	1	43N45	10E53	-0:43:32
Cerreto Sannita	2	41N17	14E33	-0:58:12
Cerrina	1	45N07	8E13	-0:32:52
Cerro	1	45N54	8E36	-0:34:24
Cersosimo	2	40N03	16E21	-1:05:24
Certaldo	1	43N33	11E02	-0:44:08
Certosa (Karthaus)	1	46N42	10E54	-0:43:36
Certosa di Pavia	1	45N15	9E09	-0:36:36
Cervarezza	1	44N23	10E20	-0:41:20
Cervaro	2	41N29	13E54	-0:55:36
Cerveteri	1	42N00	12E06	-0:48:24
Cervia	1	44N15	12E22	-0:49:28
Cervignano del Friuli	1	45N49	13E20	-0:53:20
Cervinara	2	41N01	14E37	-0:58:28
Cervo	1	43N55	8E07	-0:32:28
Cesana Torinese	1	44N57	6E47	-0:27:08
Cesano	1	42N07	12E21	-0:49:24
Cesano	1	43N45	13E10	-0:52:40
Cesano Boscone	1	45N27	9E06	-0:36:24
Cesano Maderno	1	45N38	9E08	-0:36:32
Cesarò	3	37N50	14E43	-0:58:52
Cesate	1	45N36	9E05	-0:36:20
Cesena	1	44N08	12E15	-0:49:00
Cesenatico	1	44N12	12E24	-0:49:36
Cesiomaggiore	1	46N05	11E59	-0:47:56
Cessalto	1	45N42	12E36	-0:50:24
Cetara	2	40N39	14E42	-0:58:48
Cetona	1	42N58	11E54	-0:47:36
Cetraro	2	39N31	15E56	-1:03:44
Ceva	1	44N23	8E02	-0:32:08
Chamois	1	45N50	7E37	-0:30:28
Champdepraz	1	45N41	7E39	-0:30:36
Champoluc	1	45N50	7E44	-0:30:56
Châtillon	1	45N45	7E37	-0:30:28
Cherasco	1	44N39	7E51	-0:31:24
Chialamberto	1	45N22	7E21	-0:29:24
Chiampo	1	45N33	11E17	-0:45:08
Chianciano Terme	1	43N03	11E50	-0:47:20
Chianni	1	43N29	10E38	-0:42:32
Chiaramonte Gulfi	3	37N02	14E42	-0:58:48
Chiaramonti	4	40N45	8E49	-0:35:16
Chiaravalle	1	43N36	13E19	-0:53:16
Chiaravalle Centrale	2	38N41	16E25	-1:05:40
Chiareggio	1	46N19	9E47	-0:39:08
Chiari	1	45N32	9E56	-0:39:44
Chiaromonte	2	40N07	16E13	-1:04:52
Chiavari	1	44N19	9E19	-0:37:16
Chiavenna	1	46N19	9E24	-0:37:36
Chienes (Kiens)	1	46N48	11E50	-0:47:20
Chieri	1	45N01	7E49	-0:31:16
Chiesa in Valmalenco	1	46N16	9E51	-0:39:24
Chieti	1	42N21	14E10	-0:56:40
Chieuti	2	41N51	15E10	-1:00:40
Chignolo Po	1	45N09	9E29	-0:37:56
Chilivani	4	40N36	8E56	-0:35:44
Chioggia	1	45N13	12E17	-0:49:08
Chiomonte	1	45N07	6E59	-0:27:56
Chiuduno	1	45N40	9E51	-0:39:24
Chiuppano	1	45N46	11E28	-0:45:52
Chiuro	1	46N10	9E59	-0:39:56
Chiusa (Klausen)	1	46N38	11E34	-0:46:16
Chiusa di Pesio	1	44N19	7E40	-0:30:40
Chiusa di San Michele	1	45N06	7E19	-0:29:16
Chiusaforte	1	46N24	13E18	-0:53:12
Chiusa Sclafani	3	37N41	13E16	-0:53:04
Chiusi	1	43N01	11E57	-0:47:48
Chivasso	1	45N11	7E53	-0:31:32
Ciago	1	46N12	12E46	-0:51:04
Ciampino	1	41N48	12E36	-0:50:24
Cianciana	3	37N31	13E26	-0:53:44
Ciano d'Enza	1	44N36	10E24	-0:41:36
Ciavolo	3	37N46	12E33	-0:50:12
Cibiana	1	46N23	12E17	-0:49:08
Cicagna	1	44N25	9E14	-0:36:56
Cicala	2	39N01	16E29	-1:05:56
Cicciano	2	40N58	14E32	-0:58:08
Cigliano	1	45N18	8E01	-0:32:04
Cilavegna	1	45N19	8E44	-0:34:56
Cimabanche (Schluderbach)	1	46N37	12E11	-0:48:44
Cima Gogna	1	46N31	12E28	-0:49:52
Ciminna	3	37N54	13E34	-0:54:16
Cimitile	2	40N56	14E31	-0:58:04
Cimolais	1	46N17	12E26	-0:49:44
Cingoli	1	43N22	13E13	-0:52:52
Cinigiano	1	42N53	11E24	-0:45:36
Cinisello Balsamo	1	45N33	9E13	-0:36:52
Cinisi	3	38N09	13E06	-0:52:24
Cinquefrondi	2	38N25	16E06	-1:04:24
Cinto Euganeo	1	45N16	11E40	-0:46:40
Cireglio	1	43N59	10E51	-0:43:24
Ciriè	1	45N14	7E36	-0:30:24
Cirigliano	2	40N24	16E10	-1:04:40
Cirò	2	39N23	17E04	-1:08:16
Cirò Marina	2	39N22	17E08	-1:08:32
Cisano	1	45N32	10E43	-0:42:52
Cislago	1	45N39	8E58	-0:35:52
Cisliano	1	45N27	8E59	-0:35:56
Cismon del Grappa	1	45N55	11E44	-0:46:56
Cison di Valmarino	1	45N58	12E10	-0:48:40
Cisterna di Latina	2	41N35	12E49	-0:51:16
Cisternino	2	40N44	17E25	-1:09:40
Cittadella	1	45N39	11E47	-0:47:08
Città della Pieve	1	42N57	12E00	-0:48:00
Città di Castello	1	43N27	12E14	-0:48:56
Cittaducale	1	42N23	12E57	-0:51:48
Cittanova	2	38N21	16E05	-1:04:20
Cittareale	1	42N37	13E10	-0:52:40
Città Sant'Angelo	1	42N31	14E03	-0:56:12
Civate	1	45N50	9E21	-0:37:24
Civenna	1	45N56	9E16	-0:37:04
Civezzano	1	46N05	11E11	-0:44:44
Cividale del Friuli	1	46N06	13E25	-0:53:40
Cividate al Piano	1	45N33	9E50	-0:39:20
Cividate Camuno	1	45N57	10E17	-0:41:08
Civita	2	39N49	16E18	-1:05:12
Civitacampomarano	2	41N47	14E41	-0:58:44
Civita Castellana	1	42N17	12E25	-0:49:40
Civita di Bagno	1	42N18	13E26	-0:53:44
Civitanova Alta	1	43N19	13E40	-0:54:40
Civitanova del Sannio	1	41N40	14E24	-0:57:36
Civitanova Marche	1	43N18	13E44	-0:54:56
Civitaquana	1	42N19	13E54	-0:55:36
Civitavecchia	1	42N06	11E48	-0:47:12
Civitella del Tronto	1	42N46	13E40	-0:54:40
Civitella di Romagna	1	44N00	11E56	-0:47:44
Civitella in Val di Chiana	1	43N25	11E43	-0:46:52
Civitella Marittima	1	43N00	11E17	-0:45:08
Civitella Roveto	1	41N54	13E25	-0:53:40
Cles	1	46N22	11E02	-0:44:08
Clusone	1	45N53	9E57	-0:39:48
Coazze	1	45N03	7E18	-0:29:12
Coccaglio	1	45N34	9E58	-0:39:52
Cocconato	1	45N05	8E02	-0:32:08
Codaruina	4	40N56	8E49	-0:35:16
Codigoro	1	44N49	12E08	-0:48:32
Codogno	1	45N09	9E42	-0:38:48
Codroipo	1	45N58	12E59	-0:51:56

Place	Zone	Lat	Long	Time
Codrongianos	4	40N39	8E41	-0:34:44
Coggiola	1	45N41	8E11	-0:32:44
Cogliate	1	45N39	9E05	-0:36:20
Cogne	1	45N37	7E21	-0:29:24
Cogoleto	1	44N23	8E39	-0:34:36
Cogollo del Cengio	1	45N47	11E25	-0:45:40
Cogolo	1	46N21	10E41	-0:42:44
Coldrano	1	46N38	10E50	-0:43:20
Colfiorito	1	43N02	12E55	-0:51:40
Colico	1	46N08	9E22	-0:37:28
Collagna	1	44N21	10E16	-0:41:04
Collalbo (Klobenstein)	1	46N32	11E28	-0:45:52
Collalto Sabino	1	42N08	13E02	-0:52:08
Collarmele	1	42N03	13E38	-0:54:32
Collazzone	1	42N54	12E26	-0:49:44
Collecchio	1	44N45	10E13	-0:40:52
Collecorvino	1	42N27	14E01	-0:56:04
Colle di Tora	1	42N13	12E57	-0:51:48
Colle di Val d'Elsa	1	43N25	11E07	-0:44:28
Colleferro	1	41N44	12E59	-0:51:56
Collegno	1	45N05	7E34	-0:30:16
Colle Isarco (Gossensass)	1	46N56	11E26	-0:45:44
Collepardo	1	41N46	13E22	-0:53:28
Collepasso	2	40N04	18E10	-1:12:40
Collepietro	1	42N13	13E46	-0:55:04
Collesalvetti	1	43N35	10E28	-0:41:52
Colle Sannita	2	41N22	14E50	-0:59:20
Collesano	3	37N55	13E56	-0:55:44
Colletorto	2	41N40	14E58	-0:59:52
Colliano	2	40N43	15E17	-1:01:08
Colli a Volturno	2	41N36	14E06	-0:56:24
Colli del Tronto	1	42N52	13E44	-0:54:56
Colli di Monte Bove	1	42N06	13E09	-0:52:36
Collio	1	45N48	10E20	-0:41:20
Colobraro	2	40N11	16E25	-1:05:40
Cologna Veneta	1	45N18	11E23	-0:45:32
Cologno al Serio	1	45N37	9E42	-0:38:48
Cologno Monzese	1	45N32	9E17	-0:37:08
Colonna	1	41N50	12E45	-0:51:00
Colonnata	1	44N05	10E10	-0:40:40
Colorno	1	44N56	10E23	-0:41:32
Colosimi	2	39N07	16E24	-1:05:36
Comacchio	1	44N42	12E11	-0:48:44
Comeglians	1	46N31	12E52	-0:51:28
Comelico Superiore	1	46N35	12E30	-0:50:00
Comiso	3	36N56	14E36	-0:58:24
Comitini	3	37N24	13E39	-0:54:36
Como	1	45N47	9E05	-0:36:20
Comunanza	1	42N57	13E25	-0:53:40
Conco	1	45N48	11E36	-0:46:24
Concordia sulla Secchia	1	44N55	10E59	-0:43:56
Concorezzo	1	45N35	9E20	-0:37:20
Condino	1	45N53	10E36	-0:42:24
Condove	1	45N07	7E18	-0:29:12
Conegliano	1	45N53	12E18	-0:49:12
Configni	1	42N25	12E38	-0:50:32
Conflenti	2	39N04	16E17	-1:05:08
Consandolo	1	44N39	11E46	-0:47:04
Conselice	1	44N31	11E49	-0:47:16
Conselve	1	45N14	11E52	-0:47:28
Consuma	1	43N47	11E35	-0:46:20
Contarina	1	45N00	12E13	-0:48:52
Contigliano	1	42N24	12E46	-0:51:04
Contursi	2	40N39	15E14	-1:00:56
Conversano	2	40N58	17E08	-1:08:32
Copertino	2	40N16	18E03	-1:12:12
Copparo	1	44N54	11E49	-0:47:16
Corato	2	41N09	16E25	-1:05:40
Corbeolona	1	45N10	9E22	-0:37:28
Corbetta	1	45N28	8E55	-0:35:40
Corbola	1	45N00	12E05	-0:48:20
Corciano	1	43N08	12E17	-0:49:08
Cordenons	1	45N59	12E42	-0:50:48
Cordignano	1	45N57	12E25	-0:49:40
Coreglia Antelminelli	1	44N04	10E31	-0:42:04
Corese Terra	1	42N10	12E42	-0:50:48
Cori	2	41N39	12E55	-0:51:40
Corigliano Calabro	2	39N36	16E31	-1:06:04
Corigliano d'Otranto	2	40N09	18E15	-1:13:00
Corinaldo	1	43N39	13E03	-0:52:12
Corleone	3	37N49	13E18	-0:53:12
Corleto Perticara	2	40N23	16E03	-1:04:12
Cormano	1	45N33	9E10	-0:36:40
Cormons	1	45N58	13E28	-0:53:52
Corna	1	45N53	10E10	-0:40:40
Cornaredo	1	45N30	9E02	-0:36:08
Cornedo Vicentino	1	45N37	11E20	-0:45:20
Corniglia	1	44N07	9E42	-0:38:48
Cornuda	1	45N50	12E00	-0:48:00
Correggio	1	44N46	10E47	-0:43:08
Correzzana	1	45N40	9E18	-0:37:12
Corridonia	1	43N15	13E30	-0:54:00
Corropoli	1	42N49	13E50	-0:55:20
Corsano	2	39N53	18E22	-1:13:28
Corsico	1	45N26	9E07	-0:36:28
Cortaccia (Kurtatsch)	1	46N19	11E13	-0:44:52
Cortale	2	38N50	16E25	-1:05:40
Cortemaggiore	1	44N59	9E56	-0:39:44
Cortemilia	1	44N35	8E12	-0:32:48
Cortina d'Ampezzo	1	46N32	12E08	-0:48:32
Cortona	1	43N16	11E59	-0:47:56
Corvara in Badia	1	46N33	11E52	-0:47:28
Cosenza	2	39N17	16E15	-1:05:00
Cossato	1	45N34	8E10	-0:32:40
Cossoine	4	40N27	8E43	-0:34:52
Costacciaro	1	43N21	12E42	-0:50:48
Costa di Rovigo	1	45N03	11E42	-0:46:48
Costigliole d'Asti	1	44N47	8E11	-0:32:44
Costigliole Saluzzo	1	44N34	7E29	-0:29:56
Cotignola	1	44N23	11E56	-0:47:44
Cotronei	2	39N09	16E47	-1:07:08
Cottanello	1	42N24	12E41	-0:50:44
Courmayeur	1	45N47	6E58	-0:27:52
Covigliaio	1	44N08	11E18	-0:45:12
Craco	2	40N23	16E26	-1:05:44
Crema	1	45N22	9E41	-0:38:44
Cremia	1	46N05	9E16	-0:37:04
Cremona	1	45N07	10E02	-0:40:08
Crescentino	1	45N11	8E06	-0:32:24
Crespano del Grappa	1	45N49	11E50	-0:47:20
Crespino	1	44N59	11E53	-0:47:32
Crevacuore	1	45N41	8E15	-0:33:00
Crevalcore	1	44N43	11E09	-0:44:36
Crevoladossola	1	46N09	8E18	-0:33:12
Crichi	2	38N57	16E38	-1:06:32
Crispiano	2	40N36	17E14	-1:08:56
Crocefieschi	1	44N35	9E01	-0:36:04
Crocetta del Montello	1	45N50	12E02	-0:48:08
Cropalati	2	39N31	16E43	-1:06:52
Cropani	2	38N58	16E47	-1:07:08
Crosia	2	39N34	16E46	-1:07:04
Crotone	2	39N05	17E07	-1:08:28
Crucoli	2	39N25	17E00	-1:08:00
Cuccaro Vetere	2	40N09	15E18	-1:01:12
Cuggiono	1	45N31	8E49	-0:35:16
Cuglieri	4	40N11	8E34	-0:34:16
Cumiana	1	44N59	7E22	-0:29:28
Cuneo	1	44N23	7E32	-0:30:08
Cuorgnè	1	45N23	7E39	-0:30:36
Cupello	2	42N04	14E40	-0:58:40
Cupra Marittima	1	43N01	13E51	-0:55:24
Cupramontana	1	43N27	13E07	-0:52:28
Curinga	2	38N49	16E19	-1:05:16
Curon Venosta (Graun)	1	46N49	10E32	-0:42:08
Cursi	2	40N09	18E18	-1:13:12
Curtarolo	1	45N31	11E50	-0:47:20
Cusago	1	45N27	9E02	-0:36:08
Cusano Milanino	1	45N33	9E11	-0:36:44
Cusano Mutri	2	41N20	14E30	-0:58:00
Custonaci	3	38N04	12E41	-0:50:44
Cutro	2	39N02	16E59	-1:07:56
Cutrofiano	2	40N07	18E12	-1:12:48
Cuzzago	1	46N00	8E22	-0:33:28
Dairago	1	45N34	8E52	-0:35:28
Dalmine	1	45N39	9E36	-0:38:24
Darfo	1	45N53	10E11	-0:40:44
Darzo	1	45N51	10E33	-0:42:12
Dattilo	3	37N58	12E39	-0:50:36
Davoli	2	38N39	16E29	-1:05:56
Decimomannu	4	39N19	8E58	-0:35:52
Decimoputzu	4	39N20	8E55	-0:35:40
Decollatura	2	39N03	16E21	-1:05:24
Dego	1	44N27	8E19	-0:33:16
Deiva Marina	1	44N13	9E30	-0:38:00
Delia	3	37N21	13E55	-0:55:40
Delianuova	2	38N14	15E55	-1:03:40
Deliceto	2	41N13	15E23	-1:01:32
Dello	1	45N25	10E04	-0:40:16
Demonte	1	44N19	7E17	-0:29:08
Dermulo	1	46N20	11E04	-0:44:16
Deruta	1	42N59	12E25	-0:49:40
Desenzano del Garda	1	45N28	10E32	-0:42:08
Desio	1	45N37	9E13	-0:36:52
Desulo	4	40N01	9E14	-0:36:56
Dezzo di Scalve	1	45N59	10E05	-0:40:20
Diamante	2	39N41	15E49	-1:03:16
Diano Marina	1	43N54	8E05	-0:32:20
Dicomano	1	43N53	11E31	-0:46:04
Dignano	1	46N05	12E56	-0:51:44
Dimaro	1	46N20	10E52	-0:43:28
Dinami	2	38N31	16E09	-1:04:36
Dipignano	2	39N15	16E15	-1:05:00
Diso	2	40N00	18E23	-1:13:32
Divignano	1	45N40	8E36	-0:34:24
Dobbiaco (Toblach)	1	46N44	12E14	-0:48:56
Doganella	2	41N34	12E56	-0:51:44
Dogliani	1	44N32	7E56	-0:31:44
Dogna	1	46N27	13E19	-0:53:16
Dolceacqua	1	43N51	7E37	-0:30:28
Dolianova	4	39N22	9E10	-0:36:40
Dolo	1	45N25	12E05	-0:48:20
Domanico	2	39N13	16E12	-1:04:48
Domaso	1	46N09	9E19	-0:37:16
Domegge di Cadore	1	46N27	12E25	-0:49:40
Domodossola	1	46N07	8E17	-0:33:08
Domus de Maria	4	38N57	8E52	-0:35:28
Domusnovas	4	39N19	8E39	-0:34:36
Donada	1	45N02	12E12	-0:48:48
Dongo	1	46N07	9E17	-0:37:08
Donnalucata	3	36N45	14E38	-0:58:32
Donnaz	1	45N36	7E46	-0:31:04
Dorgali	4	40N17	9E35	-0:38:20
Dorno	1	45N09	8E57	-0:35:48
Dovadola	1	44N07	11E53	-0:47:32
Dozza	1	44N22	11E37	-0:46:28
Dragoni	2	41N16	14E18	-0:57:12
Drena	1	45N58	10E56	-0:43:44
Dro	1	45N58	10E54	-0:43:36
Dronero	1	44N28	7E22	-0:29:28
Dualchi	4	40N13	8E54	-0:35:36
Dubino	1	46N09	9E27	-0:37:48
Dueville	1	45N38	11E32	-0:46:08
Duino	1	45N46	13E36	-0:54:24
Eboli	2	40N37	15E04	-1:00:16
Edolo	1	46N11	10E20	-0:41:20
Egna (Neumarkt)	1	46N19	11E16	-0:45:04
El Faro	4	40N36	8E13	-0:32:52
Elmas	4	39N16	9E03	-0:36:12
Empoli	1	43N43	10E57	-0:43:48
Endine	1	45N46	9E59	-0:39:56
Endine Gaiano	1	45N48	9E59	-0:39:56
Enemonzo	1	46N25	12E53	-0:51:32
Enna	3	37N34	14E16	-0:57:04
Entracque	1	44N14	7E24	-0:29:36
Entrèves	1	45N49	6E57	-0:27:48
Episcopia	2	40N04	16E06	-1:04:24
Equi Terme	1	44N09	10E10	-0:40:40
Eraclea	1	45N35	12E40	-0:50:40
Erba	1	45N48	9E15	-0:37:00
Erchie	2	40N26	17E44	-1:10:56
Ercolano	2	40N48	14E21	-0:57:24
Erice	3	38N02	12E35	-0:50:20
Erli	1	44N08	8E06	-0:32:24
Erto	1	46N16	12E22	-0:49:28
Escalaplano	4	39N37	9E21	-0:37:24
Esine	1	45N55	10E15	-0:41:00
Esperia	2	41N23	13E41	-0:54:44
Este	1	45N14	11E39	-0:46:36
Etroubles	1	45N49	7E14	-0:28:56
Fabbrico	1	44N52	10E50	-0:43:20
Fabriano	1	43N20	12E54	-0:51:36
Fabrica di Roma	1	42N20	12E18	-0:49:12
Fabrizia	2	38N29	16E18	-1:05:12
Fadalto	1	46N05	12E20	-0:49:20
Faedis	1	46N10	13E20	-0:53:20
Faenza	1	44N17	11E53	-0:47:32
Fagnano Castello	2	39N34	16E03	-1:04:12
Fagnano Olona	1	45N40	8E52	-0:35:28
Fahrn → Varna	1	46N44	11E38	-0:46:32
Falcade	1	46N21	11E51	-0:47:24
Falconara Albanese	2	39N16	16E05	-1:04:20
Falconara Alta	1	43N37	13E24	-0:53:36
Falconara Marittima	1	43N37	13E24	-0:53:36
Falcone	3	38N07	15E05	-1:00:20
Falerna	2	39N00	16E10	-1:04:40
Falerone	1	43N06	13E28	-0:53:52
Fanano	1	44N12	10E47	-0:43:08
Fano	1	43N50	13E01	-0:52:04
Fara in Sabina	1	42N12	12E43	-0:50:52
Fara Novarese	1	45N33	8E27	-0:33:48
Farini d'Olmo	1	44N43	9E34	-0:38:16
Farra d'Isonzo	1	45N56	12E31	-0:50:04
Fasano	2	40N50	17E22	-1:09:28
Fauglia	1	43N34	10E31	-0:42:04
Favara	3	37N19	13E39	-0:54:36
Favignana	3	37N56	12E20	-0:49:20
Felino	1	44N42	10E15	-0:41:00
Felizzano	1	44N54	8E26	-0:33:44
Feltre	1	46N01	11E54	-0:47:36
Fenestrelle	1	45N02	7E03	-0:28:12
Fenis	1	45N44	7E29	-0:29:56
Ferentillo	1	42N37	12E47	-0:51:08
Ferentino	1	41N42	13E15	-0:53:00
Ferla	3	37N07	14E56	-0:59:44
Fermignano	1	43N40	12E39	-0:50:36
Fermo	1	43N09	13E43	-0:54:52
Ferno	1	45N37	8E45	-0:35:00
Feroleto Antico	2	38N58	16E23	-1:05:32
Feroleto della Chiesa	2	38N28	16E04	-1:04:16
Ferrandina	2	40N29	16E28	-1:05:52
Ferrara	1	44N50	11E35	-0:46:20
Ferrazzano	2	41N32	14E40	-0:58:40
Ferrera Erbognone	1	45N07	8E52	-0:35:28
Ferriere	1	44N38	9E30	-0:38:00
Ferruzzano	2	38N02	16E05	-1:04:20
Fiamignano	1	42N16	13E07	-0:52:28
Fiano	1	45N13	7E31	-0:30:04
Fiavè	1	46N00	10E50	-0:43:20
Ficarazzi	3	38N05	13E28	-0:53:52
Ficarolo	1	44N57	11E26	-0:45:44
Ficarra	3	38N06	14E50	-0:59:20
Ficulle	1	42N50	12E04	-0:48:16
Fidenza	1	44N52	10E03	-0:40:12
Fiè (Völs)	1	46N31	11E30	-0:46:00
Fiera di Primiero	1	46N10	11E49	-0:47:16
Fiesole	1	43N48	11E17	-0:45:08
Fiesso d'Artico	1	45N24	12E02	-0:48:08
Fiesso Umbertiano	1	44N56	11E36	-0:46:24
Figline Valdarno	1	43N37	11E28	-0:45:52
Filadelfia	2	38N48	16E18	-1:05:12
Filandari	2	38N37	16E02	-1:04:08
Filettino	1	41N53	13E19	-0:53:16
Filiano	2	40N49	15E42	-1:02:48
Filogaso	2	38N41	16E14	-1:04:56
Filottrano	1	43N26	13E21	-0:53:24
Finale Emilia	1	44N50	11E17	-0:45:08
Finale Ligure	1	44N10	8E20	-0:33:20
Fiorano Modenese	1	44N32	10E49	-0:43:16
Fiorenzuola d'Arda	1	44N56	9E55	-0:39:40

Fiorenzuola di Focara	1	43N57	12E48	-0:51:12
Firenze (Florence)	1	43N46	11E15	-0:45:00
Firenzuola	1	44N07	11E23	-0:45:32
Firmo	2	39N43	16E10	-1:04:40
Fiuggi	1	41N48	13E13	-0:52:52
Fiumalbo	1	44N11	10E39	-0:42:36
Fiumedinisi	3	38N02	15E23	-1:01:32
Fiumefreddo Bruzio	2	39N14	16E04	-1:04:16
Fiumefreddo di Sicilia	3	37N47	15E12	-1:00:48
Fiumesino	1	43N38	13E22	-0:53:28
Fiume Veneto	1	45N56	12E44	-0:50:56
Fiumicino	1	41N46	12E14	-0:48:56
Fivizzano	1	44N14	10E08	-0:40:32
Fleres (Boden)	1	46N58	11E21	-0:45:24
Florence → Firenze	1	43N46	11E15	-0:45:00
Florencia → Firenze	1	43N46	11E15	-0:45:00
Florenz → Firenze	1	43N46	11E15	-0:45:00
Floresta	3	37N59	14E55	-0:59:40
Floridia	3	37N05	15E09	-1:00:36
Flumeri	2	41N05	15E09	-1:00:36
Fluminimaggiore	4	39N26	8E30	-0:34:00
Fobello	1	45N53	8E10	-0:32:40
Foggia	2	41N27	15E34	-1:02:16
Foglianise	2	41N10	14E40	-0:58:40
Foglizzo	1	45N16	7E49	-0:31:16
Foiano della Chiana	1	43N15	11E49	-0:47:16
Foiano di Val Fortore	2	41N21	14E59	-0:59:56
Folgaria	1	45N55	11E10	-0:44:40
Foligno	1	42N57	12E42	-0:50:48
Follina	1	45N57	12E07	-0:48:28
Follonica	1	42N55	10E45	-0:43:00
Fondachelli	3	37N58	15E11	-1:00:44
Fondi	2	41N21	13E25	-0:53:40
Fondo	1	46N26	11E08	-0:44:32
Fonni	4	40N07	9E15	-0:37:00
Fontanafredda	1	45N58	12E34	-0:50:16
Fontanarosa	2	41N01	15E01	-1:00:04
Fontanelice	1	44N15	11E33	-0:46:12
Fontanella	1	45N27	9E48	-0:39:12
Fontanellato	1	44N53	10E10	-0:40:40
Fontanetto Po	1	45N12	8E11	-0:32:44
Fontanigorda	1	44N33	9E19	-0:37:16
Fonte	1	41N46	13E13	-0:52:52
Fonte	1	45N47	11E53	-0:47:32
Fonte Blanda	1	42N34	11E10	-0:44:40
Fontespina	1	43N17	13E45	-0:55:00
Fontevivo	1	44N51	10E10	-0:40:40
Fonzaso	1	46N01	11E48	-0:47:12
Foppolo	1	46N03	9E45	-0:39:00
Fordongianus	4	39N59	8E48	-0:35:12
Forenza	2	40N51	15E51	-1:03:24
Forgaria	1	46N13	12E58	-0:51:52
Forino	2	40N52	14E44	-0:58:56
Forlì	1	44N13	12E03	-0:48:12
Forlimpopoli	1	44N11	12E07	-0:48:28
Formazza	1	46N22	8E26	-0:33:44
Formia	2	41N15	13E37	-0:54:28
Formigine	1	44N34	10E51	-0:43:24
Formignana	1	44N50	11E51	-0:47:24
Fornelli	4	41N00	8E14	-0:32:56
Forni Avoltri	1	46N35	12E46	-0:51:04
Forni di sopra	1	46N25	12E35	-0:50:20
Forni di sotto	1	46N23	12E40	-0:50:40
Forni di Val d'Astico	1	45N51	11E22	-0:45:28
Forno	1	46N21	11E37	-0:46:28
Forno Alpi Graie	1	45N22	7E13	-0:28:52
Forno di Zoldo	1	46N21	12E11	-0:48:44
Fornovo di Taro	1	44N42	10E06	-0:40:24
Forte dei Marmi	1	43N57	10E10	-0:40:40
Fortezza (Franzensfeste)	1	46N47	11E37	-0:46:28
Forza d'Agrò	3	37N55	15E20	-1:01:20
Fosdinovo	1	44N08	10E01	-0:40:04
Fossacesia	1	42N15	14E29	-0:57:56
Fossacesia Marina	1	42N15	14E30	-0:58:00
Fossano	1	44N33	7E43	-0:30:52
Fossato di Vico	1	43N18	12E46	-0:51:04
Fossombrone	1	43N41	12E48	-0:51:12
Foza	1	45N54	11E38	-0:46:32
Frabosa Soprana	1	44N17	7E48	-0:31:12
Fragagnano	2	40N26	17E28	-1:09:52
Fragneto Monforte	2	41N15	14E46	-0:59:04
Francavilla al Mare	1	42N25	14E17	-0:57:08
Francavilla Angitola	2	38N46	16E16	-1:05:04
Francavilla d'Ete	1	43N11	13E32	-0:54:08
Francavilla di Sicilia	3	37N54	15E08	-1:00:32
Francavilla Fontana	2	40N31	17E35	-1:10:20
Francavilla in Sinni	2	40N05	16E12	-1:04:48
Francavilla Marittima	2	39N49	16E23	-1:05:32
Francofonte	3	37N14	14E53	-0:59:32
Francolise	2	41N11	14E03	-0:56:12
Franzensfeste → Fortezza	1	46N47	11E37	-0:46:28
Frascati	1	41N48	12E41	-0:50:44
Frascineto	2	39N50	16E16	-1:05:04
Frassinoro	1	44N18	10E34	-0:42:16
Frattamaggiore	2	40N57	14E16	-0:57:04
Frattócchie	1	41N46	12E37	-0:50:28
Frazzanò	3	38N04	14E44	-0:58:56
Frigento	2	41N01	15E06	-1:00:24
Frignano	2	41N00	14E10	-0:56:40
Frosinone	2	41N38	13E19	-0:53:16
Frosolone	2	41N36	14E27	-0:57:48
Fubine	1	44N58	8E26	-0:33:44
Fucecchio	1	43N44	10E48	-0:43:12
Fucine	1	46N18	10E44	-0:42:56
Fulgatore	3	37N57	12E42	-0:50:48
Furci Siculo	3	37N57	15E23	-1:01:32
Furnari	3	38N07	15E08	-1:00:32
Furtei	4	39N34	8E57	-0:35:48
Fuscaldo	2	39N25	16E02	-1:04:08
Fusignano	1	44N28	11E57	-0:47:48
Fusine in Valromana	1	46N30	13E39	-0:54:36
Gabicce Mare	1	43N58	12E46	-0:51:04
Gabria	1	45N52	13E34	-0:54:16
Gaby	1	45N43	7E53	-0:31:32
Gaeta	2	41N12	13E35	-0:54:20
Gaggi	3	37N51	15E13	-1:00:52
Gaggiano	1	45N24	9E02	-0:36:08
Gagliano Castelferrato	3	37N43	14E32	-0:58:08
Gagliano del Capo	2	39N50	18E22	-1:13:28
Gaiarine	1	45N52	12E29	-0:49:56
Gaiole in Chianti	1	43N28	11E26	-0:45:44
Gais	1	46N50	11E57	-0:47:48
Galatina	2	40N10	18E10	-1:12:40
Galatone	2	40N09	18E04	-1:12:16
Galatro	2	38N28	16E06	-1:04:24
Galeata	1	44N00	11E55	-0:47:40
Gallarate	1	45N40	8E47	-0:35:08
Galliate	1	45N29	8E42	-0:34:48
Gallicano	1	44N04	10E26	-0:41:44
Gallicano nel Lazio	1	41N52	12E49	-0:51:16
Gallicchio	2	40N17	16E08	-1:04:32
Gallico	2	38N10	15E41	-1:02:44
Galliera Veneta	1	45N39	11E49	-0:47:16
Gallio	1	45N53	11E33	-0:46:12
Gallipoli	2	40N03	17E58	-1:11:52
Gallivaggio	1	46N21	9E21	-0:37:24
Galtelli	4	40N23	9E37	-0:38:28
Gambara	1	45N15	10E18	-0:41:12
Gambarie	2	38N10	15E50	-1:03:20
Gambassi	1	43N32	10E57	-0:43:48
Gambatesa	2	41N30	14E54	-0:59:36
Gambellara	1	45N28	11E20	-0:45:20
Gambolò	1	45N15	8E51	-0:35:24
Gandino	1	45N49	9E54	-0:39:36
Gangi	3	37N41	14E10	-0:56:40
Garaguso	2	40N33	16E14	-1:04:56
Garbagna	1	45N23	8E39	-0:34:36
Garbagnate Milanese	1	45N35	9E05	-0:36:20
Garda	1	45N34	10E42	-0:42:48
Gardolo	1	46N07	11E05	-0:44:20
Gardone Riviera	1	45N37	10E34	-0:42:16
Gardone Val Trompia	1	45N41	10E11	-0:40:44
Garessio	1	44N12	8E02	-0:32:08
Gargazzone (Gargazon)	1	46N35	11E12	-0:44:48
Gargnano	1	45N41	10E40	-0:42:40
Garlasco	1	45N12	8E55	-0:35:40
Garlate	1	45N49	9E23	-0:37:32
Garzeno	1	46N08	9E15	-0:37:00
Gasperina	2	38N44	16E30	-1:06:00
Gassino Torinese	1	45N08	7E49	-0:31:16
Gattinara	1	45N37	8E22	-0:33:28
Gattorna	1	44N26	9E11	-0:36:44
Gavardo	1	45N35	10E26	-0:41:44
Gavello	1	45N01	11E55	-0:47:40
Gavi	1	44N41	8E49	-0:35:16
Gavinana	1	44N05	10E45	-0:43:00
Gavirate	1	45N50	8E43	-0:34:52
Gavoi	4	40N10	9E12	-0:36:48
Gavorrano	1	42N55	10E54	-0:43:36
Gazoldo degli Ippoliti	1	45N12	10E35	-0:42:20
Gazzada	1	45N47	8E51	-0:35:24
Gazzaniga	1	45N48	9E50	-0:39:20
Gazzuolo	1	45N04	10E35	-0:42:20
Gela	3	37N04	14E15	-0:57:00
Gemona del Friuli	1	46N16	13E09	-0:52:36
Gemonio	1	45N53	8E40	-0:34:40
Genazzano	1	41N50	12E58	-0:51:52
Gênes → Genova	1	44N25	8E57	-0:35:48
Genga	1	43N26	12E56	-0:51:44
Genoa → Genova	1	44N25	8E57	-0:35:48
Genola	1	44N35	7E39	-0:30:36
Genova (Genoa)	1	44N25	8E57	-0:35:48
Genua → Genova	1	44N25	8E57	-0:35:48
Genzano di Lucania	2	40N51	16E02	-1:04:08
Genzano di Roma	1	41N42	12E41	-0:50:44
Gerace	2	38N16	16E13	-1:04:52
Geraci Siculo	3	37N51	14E09	-0:56:36
Gerenzano	1	45N38	9E00	-0:36:00
Germagnano	1	45N15	7E28	-0:29:52
Gerola Alta	1	46N03	9E32	-0:38:08
Gessopalena	1	42N03	14E16	-0:57:04
Gesualdo	2	41N00	15E04	-1:00:16
Ghedi	1	45N24	10E16	-0:41:04
Ghemme	1	45N37	8E25	-0:33:40
Ghigo	1	44N53	7E03	-0:28:12
Ghilarza	4	40N07	8E50	-0:35:20
Giano dell'Umbria	1	42N50	12E35	-0:50:20
Giardinello	3	38N05	13E09	-0:52:36
Giardinetto	2	41N19	15E24	-1:01:36
Giardini	3	37N50	15E17	-1:01:08
Giarratana	3	37N03	14E48	-0:59:12
Giarre	3	37N43	15E11	-1:00:44
Giaveno	1	45N02	7E21	-0:29:24
Giazza	1	45N39	11E07	-0:44:28
Giba	4	39N04	8E38	-0:34:32
Gibellina	3	37N47	12E58	-0:51:52
Giffone	2	38N27	16E10	-1:04:40
Giffoni Valle Piana	2	40N44	14E56	-0:59:44
Giglio Castello	1	42N22	10E54	-0:43:36
Gigliola	1	44N51	12E14	-0:48:56
Giglio Porto	1	42N22	10E55	-0:43:40
Gignod	1	45N46	7E17	-0:29:08
Gimigliano	2	38N58	16E32	-1:06:08
Ginosa	2	40N35	16E46	-1:07:04
Ginostra	3	38N47	15E11	-1:00:44
Gioi	2	40N17	15E13	-1:00:52
Gioia dei Marsi	1	41N57	13E42	-0:54:48
Gioia del Colle	2	40N48	16E56	-1:07:44
Gioia Tauro	2	38N26	15E54	-1:03:36
Gioia Vecchio	1	41N54	13E44	-0:54:56
Gioiosa Ionica	2	38N20	16E18	-1:05:12
Gioiosa Marea	3	38N10	14E54	-0:59:36
Giovinazzo	2	41N11	16E40	-1:06:40
Girgenti → Agrigento	3	37N18	13E35	-0:54:20
Girifalco	2	38N49	16E25	-1:05:40
Gissi	1	42N01	14E33	-0:58:12
Giugliano in Campania	2	40N56	14E12	-0:56:48
Giuliana	3	37N40	13E14	-0:52:56
Giulianova	1	42N45	13E57	-0:55:48
Giussano	1	45N42	9E14	-0:36:56
Gizzeria	2	38N59	16E12	-1:04:48
Glorenza (Glurns)	1	46N40	10E33	-0:42:12
Godega di Sant'Urbano	1	45N56	12E24	-0:49:36
Godrano	3	37N54	13E26	-0:53:44
Goglio	1	46N18	8E16	-0:33:04
Goito	1	45N15	10E40	-0:42:40
Golfo Aranci	4	40N59	9E38	-0:38:32
Gomagoi	1	46N35	10E32	-0:42:08
Gonars	1	45N53	13E13	-0:52:52
Goni	4	39N34	9E17	-0:37:08
Gonnesa	4	39N16	8E28	-0:33:52
Gonnosfanadiga	4	39N29	8E39	-0:34:36
Gonnostramatza	4	39N41	8E50	-0:35:20
Gonzaga	1	44N57	10E49	-0:43:16
Gorgoglione	2	40N23	16E09	-1:04:36
Gorgonzola	1	45N32	9E24	-0:37:36
Gorica → Gorizia	1	45N57	13E38	-0:54:32
Gorizia	1	45N57	13E38	-0:54:32
Gorlago	1	45N40	9E49	-0:39:16
Gorla Maggiore	1	45N40	8E53	-0:35:32
Gorla Minore	1	45N39	8E54	-0:35:36
Goro	1	44N51	12E18	-0:49:12
Görz → Gorizia	1	45N57	13E38	-0:54:32
Gosaldo	1	46N13	11E58	-0:47:52
Gossensass → Colle Isarco	1	46N56	11E26	-0:45:44
Gossolengo	1	44N59	9E37	-0:38:28
Gottolengo	1	45N17	10E16	-0:41:04
Gozzano	1	45N45	8E26	-0:33:44
Gradara	1	43N57	12E46	-0:51:04
Gradisca d'Isonzo	1	45N53	13E30	-0:54:00
Grado	1	45N40	13E23	-0:53:32
Gradoli	1	42N39	11E51	-0:47:24
Graffignano	1	42N34	12E12	-0:48:48
Graglia	1	45N33	7E59	-0:31:56
Gragnano	2	40N41	14E31	-0:58:04
Gragnano Trebbiense	1	45N01	9E34	-0:38:16
Grammichele	3	37N13	14E38	-0:58:32
Granaglione	1	44N07	10E58	-0:43:52
Granarolo dell'Emilia	1	44N33	11E27	-0:45:48
Granatello	3	37N53	12E32	-0:50:08
Grandola	1	46N02	9E13	-0:36:52
Graniti	3	37N53	15E14	-1:00:56
Granitola Torretta	3	37N34	12E40	-0:50:40
Grantorto	1	45N36	11E43	-0:46:52
Grassano	2	40N38	16E18	-1:05:12
Graun → Curon Venosta	1	46N49	10E32	-0:42:08
Gravedona	1	46N09	9E18	-0:37:12
Gravellona-Toce	1	45N55	8E26	-0:33:44
Gravina in Puglia	2	40N49	16E25	-1:05:40
Greggio	1	45N27	8E23	-0:33:32
Gressoney-La-Trinité	1	45N50	7E49	-0:31:16
Gressoney-Saint-Jean	1	45N47	7E49	-0:31:16
Greve	1	43N35	11E19	-0:45:16
Grezzana	1	45N31	11E01	-0:44:04
Grignano	1	45N42	13E43	-0:54:52
Grignasco	1	45N41	8E20	-0:33:20
Grigno	1	46N01	11E38	-0:46:32
Grimaldi	2	39N08	16E14	-1:04:56
Grisolia	2	39N43	15E51	-1:03:24
Grizzana	1	44N15	11E09	-0:44:36
Gromo	1	45N58	9E56	-0:39:44
Gropello Cairoli	1	45N11	9E00	-0:36:00
Groscavallo	1	45N22	7E15	-0:29:00
Grosio	1	46N18	10E16	-0:41:04

Grosotto	1	46N17	10E15	-0:41:00
Grosseto	1	42N46	11E08	-0:44:32
Grottaferrata	1	41N47	12E40	-0:50:40
Grottaglie	2	40N32	17E26	-1:09:44
Grottaminarda	2	41N04	15E02	-1:00:08
Grottammare	1	42N59	13E52	-0:55:28
Grotte	3	37N24	13E42	-0:54:48
Grotte di Castro	1	42N40	11E52	-0:47:28
Grotteria	2	38N22	16E17	-1:05:08
Grottole	2	40N36	16E23	-1:05:32
Grugliasco	1	45N04	7E35	-0:30:20
Grumello del Monte	1	45N38	9E52	-0:39:28
Grumento Nova	2	40N17	15E53	-1:03:32
Grumo Appula	2	41N01	16E42	-1:06:48
Guagnano	2	40N24	17E57	-1:11:48
Gualdo Tadino	1	43N14	12E47	-0:51:08
Gualtieri	1	44N54	10E38	-0:42:32
Guarcino	1	41N48	13E19	-0:53:16
Guardavalle	2	38N30	16E30	-1:06:00
Guardea	1	42N37	12E18	-0:49:12
Guardiagrele	1	42N11	14E13	-0:56:52
Guardia Lombardi	2	40N57	15E12	-1:00:48
Guardia Sanframondi	2	41N15	14E36	-0:58:24
Guasila	4	39N34	9E03	-0:36:12
Guastalla	1	44N55	10E39	-0:42:36
Gubbio	1	43N21	12E35	-0:50:20
Guglionesi	2	41N55	14E55	-0:59:40
Guidizzolo	1	45N19	10E35	-0:42:20
Guidonia	1	42N01	12E45	-0:51:00
Guiglia	1	44N26	10E58	-0:43:52
Guspini	4	39N32	8E37	-0:34:28
Gussago	1	45N35	10E09	-0:40:36
Gussola	1	45N00	10E20	-0:41:20
Iato	3	37N58	13E07	-0:52:28
Idro	1	45N44	10E29	-0:41:56
Ielsi	2	41N30	14E48	-0:59:12
Ienne	1	41N53	13E10	-0:52:40
Ierzu	4	39N47	9E31	-0:38:04
Iesi	1	43N31	13E14	-0:52:56
Iesolo	1	45N32	12E38	-0:50:32
Igea Marina	1	44N08	12E29	-0:49:56
Iglesias	4	39N19	8E32	-0:34:08
Il Catalano	4	39N53	8E17	-0:33:08
Illasi	1	45N28	11E10	-0:44:40
Imola	1	44N21	11E42	-0:46:48
Imperia	1	43N53	8E03	-0:32:12
Imperiale	2	40N07	16E35	-1:06:20
Impruneta	1	43N41	11E15	-0:45:00
Incisa in Val d'Arno	1	43N40	11E27	-0:45:48
Incudine	1	46N14	10E22	-0:41:28
Induno Olona	1	45N52	8E51	-0:35:24
Innichen → San Candido	1	46N44	12E17	-0:49:08
Introbio	1	45N57	9E27	-0:37:48
Introdacqua	1	42N00	13E54	-0:55:36
Inveruno	1	45N31	8E51	-0:35:24
Inzago	1	45N32	9E29	-0:37:56
Ioppolo	2	38N35	15E53	-1:03:32
Ioppolo Giancaxio	3	37N23	13E33	-0:54:12
Irsina	2	40N45	16E15	-1:05:00
Ischia	2	40N44	13E57	-0:55:48
Ischia di Castro	1	42N33	11E45	-0:47:00
Ischitella	2	41N54	15E54	-1:03:36
Iselle	1	46N12	8E12	-0:32:48
Iseo	1	45N39	10E03	-0:40:12
Isernia	2	41N36	14E14	-0:56:56
Isili	4	39N44	9E06	-0:36:24
Isola d'Asti	1	44N50	8E11	-0:32:44
Isola del Cantone	1	44N39	8E57	-0:35:48
Isola del Gran Sasso d'Italia	1	42N30	13E40	-0:54:40
Isola della Scala	1	45N16	11E00	-0:44:00
Isola del Liri	1	41N41	13E34	-0:54:16
Isola di Capo Rizzuto	2	38N58	17E06	-1:08:24
Isola Dovarese	1	45N10	10E18	-0:41:12
Isola Vicentina	1	45N38	11E25	-0:45:40
Isoletta	2	41N30	13E34	-0:54:16
Isorella	1	45N18	10E19	-0:41:16
Ispani	2	40N08	15E34	-1:02:16
Ispica	3	36N47	14E55	-0:59:40
Ispra	1	45N49	8E37	-0:34:28
Issime	1	45N41	7E51	-0:31:24
Issogne	1	45N39	7E41	-0:30:44
Istrana	1	45N41	12E07	-0:48:28
Itri	2	41N17	13E32	-0:54:08
Ittiri	4	40N36	8E34	-0:34:16
Ivrea	1	45N28	7E52	-0:31:28
Jesi → Iesi	1	43N31	13E14	-0:52:56
Khamma	3	36N47	12E02	-0:48:08
Kiens → Chienes	1	46N48	11E50	-0:47:20
Kurtatsch → Cortaccia	1	46N19	11E13	-0:44:52
Laas → Lasa	1	46N37	10E42	-0:42:48
Labico	1	41N47	12E53	-0:51:32
Lacchiarella	1	45N19	9E08	-0:36:32
Lacco Ameno	2	40N45	13E54	-0:55:36
Lacedonia	2	41N03	15E25	-1:01:40
Laces (Latsch)	1	46N37	10E52	-0:43:28
Laconi	4	39N51	9E03	-0:36:12
Ladispoli	1	41N56	12E05	-0:48:20
La Foce	1	44N08	9E47	-0:39:08
Lago	2	39N10	16E09	-1:04:36
Lago di Como	1	46N00	9E20	-0:37:20
Lagonegro	2	40N07	15E46	-1:03:04
Lagosanto	1	44N46	12E08	-0:48:32
Lagundo	1	46N41	11E08	-0:44:32
Laigueglia	1	43N58	8E09	-0:32:36
Lainate	1	45N34	9E02	-0:36:08
Laino Borgo	2	39N57	15E59	-1:03:56
Laives (Leifers)	1	46N26	11E20	-0:45:20
La Lima	1	44N04	10E46	-0:43:04
La Maddalena	4	41N13	9E24	-0:37:36
Lama dei Peligni	1	42N02	14E11	-0:56:44
Lama Mocogno	1	44N18	10E45	-0:43:00
Lampedusa	3	35N30	12E56	-0:51:44
Lana	1	46N37	11E09	-0:44:36
Lanciano	1	42N14	14E23	-0:57:32
Landriano	1	45N19	9E15	-0:37:00
Landro (Höhlenstein)	1	46N39	12E14	-0:48:56
Langhirano	1	44N37	10E16	-0:41:04
Lantsch → Laces	1	46N37	10E52	-0:43:28
Lanusei	4	39N53	9E32	-0:38:08
Lanuvio	1	41N40	12E42	-0:50:48
Lanzada	1	46N15	9E51	-0:39:24
Lanzo Torinese	1	45N16	7E28	-0:29:52
Lappago (Lappach)	1	46N55	11E48	-0:47:12
L'Aquila	1	42N22	13E22	-0:53:28
Lardaro	1	45N58	10E39	-0:42:36
Larderello	1	43N14	10E53	-0:43:32
Lari	1	43N34	10E35	-0:42:20
Larino	2	41N48	14E54	-0:59:36
Lasa (Laas)	1	46N37	10E42	-0:42:48
La Salle	1	45N45	7E04	-0:28:16
Lascari	3	38N00	13E56	-0:55:44
La Siligata	1	43N56	12E45	-0:51:00
La Spezia	1	44N07	9E50	-0:39:20
Lastra a Signa	1	43N46	11E06	-0:44:24
Latera	1	42N38	11E50	-0:47:20
Laterina	1	43N31	11E43	-0:46:52
Laterza	2	40N37	16E48	-1:07:12
La Thuile	1	45N43	6E57	-0:27:48
Latiano	2	40N33	17E43	-1:10:52
Latina	2	41N28	12E52	-0:51:28
Latisana	1	45N47	13E00	-0:52:00
Latronico	2	40N05	16E01	-1:04:04
Lattarico	2	39N28	16E08	-1:04:32
Laureana di Borrello	2	38N30	16E05	-1:04:20
Laurenzana	2	40N28	15E58	-1:03:52
Lauria	2	40N02	15E50	-1:03:20
Laurino	2	40N20	15E20	-1:01:20
Laurito	2	40N10	15E24	-1:01:36
Lavagna	1	44N18	9E20	-0:37:20
Lavarone	1	45N56	11E15	-0:45:00
Lavello	2	41N03	15E48	-1:03:12
Laveno	1	45N55	8E37	-0:34:28
Lavenone	1	45N44	10E26	-0:41:44
Lavezzola	1	44N34	11E52	-0:47:28
Laviano	2	40N47	15E18	-1:01:12
La Villa	1	46N36	11E54	-0:47:36
Lavinio Lido di Enea	2	41N30	12E05	-0:48:20
Lavis	1	46N08	11E07	-0:44:28
Lazise	1	45N30	10E44	-0:42:56
Lazzaro	2	37N58	15E40	-1:02:40
Lazzate	1	45N40	9E05	-0:36:20
Lecce	2	40N23	18E11	-1:12:44
Lecce nei Marsi	1	41N56	13E41	-0:54:44
Lecco	1	45N51	9E23	-0:37:32
Leffe	1	45N48	9E53	-0:39:32
Le Focette	1	43N55	10E13	-0:40:52
Leghorn → Livorno	1	43N33	10E19	-0:41:16
Legnago	1	45N11	11E18	-0:45:12
Legnano	1	45N36	8E54	-0:35:36
Lemie	1	45N14	7E17	-0:29:08
Lendinara	1	45N05	11E36	-0:46:24
Leno	1	45N22	10E13	-0:40:52
Lenola	2	41N24	13E28	-0:53:52
Lentate sul Seveso	1	45N41	9E07	-0:36:28
Lentini	3	37N17	15E00	-1:00:00
Leonessa	1	42N34	12E58	-0:51:52
Leonforte	3	37N38	14E23	-0:57:32
Le Piastre	1	44N00	10E50	-0:43:20
Leporano	2	40N23	17E20	-1:09:20
Lercara Friddi	3	37N45	13E36	-0:54:24
Lerici	1	44N04	9E55	-0:39:40
Lesa	1	45N50	8E34	-0:34:16
Lesignano de'Bagni	1	44N39	10E18	-0:41:12
Lesina	2	41N52	15E21	-1:01:24
Lesmo	1	45N39	9E18	-0:37:12
Letino	2	41N26	14E17	-0:57:08
Leuca	2	39N48	18E21	-1:13:24
Levanto	1	44N10	9E38	-0:38:32
Levanzo	3	37N59	12E20	-0:49:20
Leverano	2	40N17	18E00	-1:12:00
Levico	1	46N01	11E18	-0:45:12
Lezzeno	1	45N56	9E11	-0:36:44
Librizzi	3	38N06	14E57	-0:59:48
Licata	3	37N06	13E56	-0:55:44
Licciana Nardi	1	44N16	10E02	-0:40:08
Licodia Eubea	3	37N09	14E42	-0:58:48
Lido	1	45N25	12E22	-0:49:28
Lido di Camaiore	1	43N54	10E13	-0:40:52
Lido di Iesolo	1	45N30	12E39	-0:50:36
Lido di Metaponto	2	40N22	16E50	-1:07:20
Lido di Pomposa	1	44N45	12E14	-0:48:56
Lido di Siponto	2	41N37	15E55	-1:03:40
Lierna	1	45N57	9E18	-0:37:12
Lignano Pineta	1	45N40	13E07	-0:52:28
Lignano Sabbiadoro	1	45N42	13E09	-0:52:36
Limbadi	2	38N33	15E58	-1:03:52
Limbiate	1	45N36	9E07	-0:36:28
Limena	1	45N29	11E50	-0:47:20
Limina	3	37N56	15E17	-1:01:08
Limone Piemonte	1	44N12	7E34	-0:30:16
Limone sul Garda	1	45N49	10E47	-0:43:08
Linguaglossa	3	37N50	15E08	-1:00:32
Linosa	3	35N51	12E52	-0:51:28
Lioni	2	40N52	15E11	-1:00:44
Lipari	3	38N28	14E57	-0:59:48
Liscia	4	41N11	9E19	-0:37:16
Lissone	1	45N37	9E14	-0:36:56
Littoria	2	41N28	12E54	-0:51:36
Livergnano	1	44N19	11E21	-0:45:24
Livigno	1	46N32	10E04	-0:40:16
Livorno (Leghorn)	1	43N33	10E19	-0:41:16
Livorno Ferraris	1	45N17	8E05	-0:32:20
Livourne → Livorno	1	43N33	10E19	-0:41:16
Lizzana	1	45N51	11E03	-0:44:12
Lizzanello	2	40N18	18E13	-1:12:52
Lizzano	2	40N23	17E27	-1:09:48
Lizzano in Belvedere	1	44N10	10E53	-0:43:32
Loano	1	44N08	8E15	-0:33:00
Locana	1	45N25	7E27	-0:29:48
Locate Triulzi	1	45N21	9E13	-0:36:52
Loceri	4	39N51	9E35	-0:38:20
Locorotondo	2	40N45	17E20	-1:09:20
Locri	2	38N14	16E16	-1:05:04
Lodè	4	40N35	9E32	-0:38:08
Lodi	1	45N19	9E30	-0:38:00
Lodi Vecchio	1	45N18	9E24	-0:37:36
Lodrone	1	45N50	10E32	-0:42:08
Loiano	1	44N16	11E19	-0:45:16
Lomazzo	1	45N42	9E02	-0:36:08
Lomello	1	45N07	8E47	-0:35:08
Lonate Pozzolo	1	45N36	8E45	-0:35:00
Lonato	1	45N27	10E29	-0:41:56
Longare	1	45N29	11E36	-0:46:24
Longarone	1	46N16	12E18	-0:49:12
Longi	3	38N01	14E45	-0:59:00
Longobucco	2	39N27	16E37	-1:06:28
Lonigo	1	45N23	11E23	-0:45:32
Lorenzago di Cadore	1	46N29	12E28	-0:49:52
Loreo	1	45N04	12E11	-0:48:44
Loreto	1	43N26	13E36	-0:54:24
Loreto Aprutino	1	42N26	13E59	-0:55:56
Loretto → Loreto	1	43N26	13E36	-0:54:24
Loro Ciuffenna	1	43N35	11E38	-0:46:32
Lorsica	1	44N26	9E16	-0:37:04
Lotzorai	4	39N58	9E39	-0:38:36
Lovere	1	45N49	10E04	-0:40:16
Lovero	1	46N14	10E14	-0:40:56
Lozzo di Cadore	1	46N29	12E27	-0:49:48
Lu	1	45N00	8E29	-0:33:56
Lucca	1	43N50	10E29	-0:41:56
Lucca Sicula	3	37N35	13E18	-0:53:12
Lucera	2	41N30	15E20	-1:01:20
Lucito	2	41N44	14E41	-0:58:44
Luco dei Marsi	1	41N58	13E28	-0:53:52
Lugagnano Val d'Arda	1	44N49	9E50	-0:39:20
Lugnano in Teverina	1	42N34	12E20	-0:49:20
Lugo	1	44N25	11E54	-0:47:36
Luino	1	46N00	8E44	-0:34:56
Lula	4	40N28	9E29	-0:37:56
Lunamatrona	4	39N39	8E54	-0:35:36
Lunano	1	43N44	12E26	-0:49:44
Lungavilla	1	45N02	9E04	-0:36:16
Lungro	2	39N44	16E07	-1:04:28
Luogosanto	4	41N03	9E13	-0:36:52
Lurisia	1	44N18	7E42	-0:30:48
Luserna San Giovanni	1	44N48	7E15	-0:29:00
Lusiana	1	45N47	11E34	-0:46:16
Lutago (Luttach)	1	46N57	11E55	-0:47:40
Luttach → Lutago	1	46N57	11E55	-0:47:40
Luzzara	1	44N58	10E41	-0:42:44
Luzzi	2	39N27	16E17	-1:05:08
Macchiagodena	2	41N33	14E24	-0:57:36
Macerata	1	43N18	13E27	-0:53:48
Macerata Feltria	1	43N48	12E26	-0:49:44
Macherio	1	45N38	9E16	-0:37:04
Macomer	4	40N16	8E47	-0:35:08
Macugnaga	1	45N58	7E58	-0:31:52
Maddaloni	2	41N02	14E22	-0:57:28
Maderno	1	45N38	10E35	-0:42:20
Madonna (Unserfrau)	1	46N43	10E52	-0:43:28
Madonna dell'Olmo	1	44N25	7E32	-0:30:08
Madonna di Campiglio	1	46N14	10E49	-0:43:16
Madonna di Tirano	1	46N13	10E09	-0:40:36
Maenza	2	41N31	13E11	-0:52:44
Magenta	1	45N28	8E53	-0:35:32
Magione	1	43N08	12E12	-0:48:48
Magisano	2	39N01	16E27	-1:05:48
Magliano dei Marsi	1	42N05	13E22	-0:53:28
Magliano in Toscana	1	42N36	11E17	-0:45:08
Magliano Sabina	1	42N22	12E29	-0:49:56
Maglie	2	40N07	18E19	-1:13:16

ITALY ITALIE ITALIEN ITALIA

Place	Zone	Lat	Long	Time
Magnago	1	45N35	8E48	-0:35:12
Magrè (Margreid)	1	46N17	11E12	-0:44:48
Maiano	1	46N11	13E04	-0:52:16
Maida	2	38N51	16E22	-1:05:28
Maierato	2	38N42	16E11	-1:04:44
Mailand → Milano	1	45N28	9E12	-0:36:48
Maiolati Spontini	1	43N28	13E06	-0:52:24
Maiori	2	40N39	14E38	-0:58:32
Malalbergo	1	44N43	11E32	-0:46:08
Malamocco	1	45N22	12E20	-0:49:20
Malborghetto Valbruna	1	46N30	13E26	-0:53:44
Malcesine	1	45N46	10E48	-0:43:12
Malcontenta	1	45N25	12E13	-0:48:52
Male	1	46N21	10E55	-0:43:40
Malegno	1	45N56	10E14	-0:40:56
Malegno	1	46N40	11E08	-0:44:32
Maleo	1	45N10	9E46	-0:39:04
Malesco	1	46N08	8E30	-0:34:00
Maletto	3	37N49	14E52	-0:59:28
Malfa	3	38N35	14E50	-0:59:20
Malles Venosta (Mals)	1	46N41	10E32	-0:42:08
Malnate	1	45N48	8E53	-0:35:32
Malo	1	45N39	11E24	-0:45:36
Malonno	1	46N07	10E18	-0:41:12
Mals → Malles Venosta	1	46N41	10E32	-0:42:08
Malvaglio	1	45N31	8E47	-0:35:08
Malvagna	3	37N55	15E04	-1:00:16
Malvito	2	39N36	16E03	-1:04:12
Mammola	2	38N22	16E15	-1:05:00
Mamoiada	4	40N13	9E17	-0:37:08
Manciano	1	42N35	11E31	-0:46:04
Mandanici	3	38N00	15E19	-1:01:16
Mandas	4	39N38	9E07	-0:36:28
Mandatoriccio	2	39N28	16E50	-1:07:20
Mandello del Lario	1	45N54	9E19	-0:37:16
Mandriole	1	44N33	12E14	-0:48:56
Manduria	2	40N24	17E38	-1:10:32
Manerbio	1	45N21	10E08	-0:40:32
Manfredonia	2	41N38	15E55	-1:03:40
Mangone	2	39N12	16E20	-1:05:20
Maniago	1	46N10	12E43	-0:50:52
Mannu	4	39N18	8E58	-0:35:52
Manoppello	1	42N15	14E03	-0:56:12
Manta	1	44N37	7E29	-0:29:56
Mantova	1	45N09	10E48	-0:43:12
Mantua → Mantova	1	45N09	10E48	-0:43:12
Manzano	1	45N59	13E23	-0:53:32
Manziana	1	42N08	12E08	-0:48:32
Maracalagonis	4	39N17	9E13	-0:36:52
Maranello	1	44N32	10E52	-0:43:28
Marano	1	45N38	8E38	-0:34:32
Marano di Napoli	2	40N54	14E11	-0:56:44
Marano Lagunare	1	45N46	13E10	-0:52:40
Marano sul Panaro	1	44N27	10E58	-0:43:52
Marano Vicentino	1	45N41	11E25	-0:45:40
Maratea	2	39N59	15E45	-1:03:00
Marausa	3	37N56	12E30	-0:50:00
Marcallo con Casone	1	45N29	8E52	-0:35:28
Marcaria	1	45N07	10E32	-0:42:08
Marcedusa	2	39N02	16E50	-1:07:20
Marcellina	1	42N01	12E48	-0:51:12
Marchesato	2	39N07	16E58	-1:07:52
Marciana	1	42N47	10E10	-0:40:40
Marciana Marina	1	42N48	10E12	-0:40:48
Marcianise	2	41N02	14E17	-0:57:08
Marciano della Chiana	1	43N18	11E47	-0:47:08
Marco	1	45N51	11E01	-0:44:04
Marene	1	44N39	7E44	-0:30:56
Marettimo	3	37N58	12E04	-0:48:16
Margherita di Savoia	2	41N23	16E09	-1:04:36
Margone	1	45N13	7E11	-0:28:44
Margreid → Magrè	1	46N17	11E12	-0:44:48
Mariano Comense	1	45N42	9E11	-0:36:44
Mariano del Friuli	1	45N55	13E27	-0:53:48
Marianopoli	3	37N36	13E55	-0:55:40
Marigliano	2	40N56	14E27	-0:57:48
Marina di Andora	1	43N57	8E08	-0:32:32
Marina di Campo	1	42N44	10E14	-0:40:56
Marina di Caronia	3	38N02	14E28	-0:57:52
Marina di Carrara	1	44N02	10E02	-0:40:08
Marina di Cecina	1	43N18	10E29	-0:41:56
Marina di Gioiosa Ionica	2	38N18	16E20	-1:05:20
Marina di Grosseto	1	42N43	10E59	-0:43:56
Marina di Massa	1	44N00	10E06	-0:40:24
Marina di Minturno	2	41N16	13E45	-0:55:00
Marina di Orosei	4	40N22	9E43	-0:38:52
Marina di Pietrasanta	1	43N56	10E12	-0:40:48
Marina di Pisa	1	43N40	10E16	-0:41:04
Marina di Ragusa	3	36N47	14E33	-0:58:12
Marina di Ravenna	1	44N29	12E17	-0:49:08
Marinella	3	37N35	12E50	-0:51:20
Marineo	3	37N57	13E25	-0:53:40
Marino	1	41N46	12E39	-0:50:36
Marmirolo	1	45N13	10E45	-0:43:00
Marmore	1	42N33	12E43	-0:50:52
Marnate	1	45N38	8E54	-0:35:36
Marone	1	45N44	10E05	-0:40:20
Marostica	1	45N45	11E39	-0:46:36
Marotta	1	43N46	13E08	-0:52:32
Marradi	1	44N04	11E37	-0:46:28
Marrubiu	4	39N45	8E38	-0:34:32
Marsala	3	37N48	12E26	-0:49:44
Marsciano	1	42N54	12E20	-0:49:20
Marsico Nuovo	2	40N25	15E44	-1:02:56
Marsico Vetere	2	40N23	15E49	-1:03:16
Marta	1	42N32	11E55	-0:47:40
Martano	2	40N12	18E18	-1:13:12
Martello	1	46N34	10E47	-0:43:08
Martignacco	1	46N05	13E08	-0:52:32
Martina Franca	2	40N42	17E21	-1:09:24
Martinengo	1	45N34	9E46	-0:39:04
Martis	4	40N47	8E49	-0:35:16
Maruggio	2	40N19	17E34	-1:10:16
Marzabotto	1	44N20	11E12	-0:44:48
Marzolara	1	44N38	10E10	-0:40:40
Mascali	3	37N45	15E12	-1:00:48
Mascalucia	3	37N34	15E03	-1:00:12
Maschito	2	40N54	15E50	-1:03:20
Maser	1	45N48	11E59	-0:47:56
Maserada sul Piave	1	45N45	12E17	-0:49:08
Masone	1	44N30	8E42	-0:34:48
Massa	1	44N01	10E09	-0:40:36
Massa Fermana	1	43N09	13E28	-0:53:52
Massa Fiscaglia	1	44N48	12E01	-0:48:04
Massafra	2	40N35	17E07	-1:08:28
Massa Lombarda	1	44N27	11E49	-0:47:16
Massa Lubrense	2	40N36	14E20	-0:57:20
Massa Marittima	1	43N03	10E53	-0:43:32
Massa Martana	1	42N46	12E31	-0:50:04
Massarosa	1	43N52	10E20	-0:41:20
Massello	1	44N57	7E04	-0:28:16
Matelica	1	43N15	13E00	-0:52:00
Matera	2	40N40	16E37	-1:06:28
Mathi	1	45N15	7E32	-0:30:08
Matino	2	40N02	18E08	-1:12:32
Mattarana	1	44N15	9E37	-0:38:28
Mattarello	1	46N00	11E07	-0:44:28
Mattinata	2	41N42	16E03	-1:04:12
Mazara del Vallo	3	37N39	12E35	-0:50:20
Mazzarino	3	37N18	14E13	-0:56:52
Mazzarrà Sant'andrea	3	38N05	15E08	-1:00:32
Mazzin	1	46N27	11E42	-0:46:48
Meana Sardo	4	39N57	9E04	-0:36:16
Meda	1	45N40	9E09	-0:36:36
Mede	1	45N06	8E44	-0:34:56
Medesano	1	44N45	10E08	-0:40:32
Medicina	1	44N28	11E38	-0:46:32
Medolla	1	44N51	11E04	-0:44:16
Meina	1	45N47	8E32	-0:34:08
Mel	1	46N04	12E05	-0:48:20
Melara	1	45N03	11E11	-0:44:44
Meldola	1	44N07	12E05	-0:48:20
Mele	1	44N27	8E45	-0:35:00
Melegnano	1	45N21	9E19	-0:37:16
Melendugno	2	40N16	18E20	-1:13:20
Melfi	2	41N00	15E39	-1:02:36
Melicuccà	2	38N18	15E53	-1:03:32
Melilli	3	37N11	15E07	-1:00:28
Melissa	2	39N18	17E01	-1:08:04
Melissano	2	39N58	18E07	-1:12:28
Melito di Porto Salvo	2	37N55	15E47	-1:03:08
Melzo	1	45N30	9E25	-0:37:40
Menaggio	1	46N01	9E14	-0:36:56
Mendatica	1	44N05	7E49	-0:31:16
Menfi	3	37N36	12E58	-0:51:52
Mentana	1	42N02	12E38	-0:50:32
Meolo	1	45N37	12E27	-0:49:48
Meran → Merano	1	46N40	11E09	-0:44:36
Merano (Meran)	1	46N40	11E09	-0:44:36
Merate	1	45N42	9E25	-0:37:40
Mercatale	1	43N15	12E08	-0:48:32
Mercato San Severino	2	40N47	14E46	-0:59:04
Mercato Saraceno	1	43N57	12E12	-0:48:48
Mercogliano	2	40N55	14E44	-0:58:56
Mergozzo	1	45N58	8E26	-0:33:44
Merlara	1	45N10	11E26	-0:45:44
Mesagne	2	40N33	17E49	-1:11:16
Mese	1	46N17	9E21	-0:37:24
Mesero	1	45N30	8E51	-0:35:24
Mesola	1	44N55	12E14	-0:48:56
Mesoraca	2	39N05	16E48	-1:07:12
Messina	3	38N11	15E34	-1:02:16
Mestre	1	45N29	12E15	-0:49:00
Mestrino	1	45N26	11E45	-0:47:00
Meta	2	40N39	14E24	-0:57:36
Metaurilia	1	43N49	13E03	-0:52:12
Mezzana	1	46N19	10E48	-0:43:12
Mezzano	1	46N09	11E48	-0:47:12
Mezzenile	1	45N17	7E23	-0:29:32
Mezzocorona	1	46N13	11E07	-0:44:28
Mezzoiuso	3	37N52	13E28	-0:53:52
Mezzoldo	1	46N01	9E40	-0:38:40
Mezzolombardo	1	46N13	11E05	-0:44:20
Mezzomerico	1	45N37	8E36	-0:34:24
Miane	1	45N57	12E06	-0:48:24
Migliarino	1	44N46	11E56	-0:47:44
Migliaro	1	44N48	11E58	-0:47:52
Miglionico	2	40N34	16E30	-1:06:00
Mignano Monte Lungo	2	41N23	13E58	-0:55:52
Milan → Milano	1	45N28	9E12	-0:36:48
Milano (Milan)	1	45N28	9E12	-0:36:48
Milano Marittima	1	44N16	12E21	-0:49:24
Milazzo	3	38N13	15E14	-1:00:56
Milena	3	37N28	13E44	-0:54:56
Mileto	2	38N36	16E04	-1:04:16
Milis	4	40N03	8E38	-0:34:32
Militello in Val di Catania	3	37N16	14E48	-0:59:12
Militello Rosmarino	3	38N03	14E41	-0:58:44
Millesimo	1	44N22	8E12	-0:32:48
Mineo	3	37N16	14E42	-0:58:48
Minerbe	1	45N14	11E20	-0:45:20
Minerbio	1	44N37	11E29	-0:45:56
Minervino Murge	2	41N05	16E05	-1:04:20
Minturno	2	41N15	13E45	-0:55:00
Mioglia	1	44N29	8E25	-0:33:40
Mira	1	45N26	12E08	-0:48:32
Mirabella Eclano	2	41N02	14E59	-0:59:56
Mirabella Imbaccari	3	37N19	14E27	-0:57:48
Mirabello Monferrato	1	45N02	8E31	-0:34:04
Miramare	1	44N02	12E38	-0:50:32
Mirandola	1	44N53	11E04	-0:44:16
Mirano	1	45N30	12E07	-0:48:28
Mirto	3	38N05	14E45	-0:59:00
Mis	1	46N12	11E57	-0:47:48
Misano Adriatico	1	43N57	12E39	-0:50:36
Miseno	2	40N47	14E05	-0:56:20
Misilmeri	3	38N02	13E27	-0:53:48
Misinto	1	45N40	9E05	-0:36:20
Missanello	2	40N17	16E10	-1:04:40
Misterbianco	3	37N31	15E00	-1:00:00
Mistretta	3	37N56	14E22	-0:57:28
Misurina	1	46N35	12E15	-0:49:00
Modena	1	44N40	10E55	-0:43:40
Modica	3	36N52	14E46	-0:59:04
Modigliana	1	44N09	11E47	-0:47:08
Modugno	2	41N05	16E47	-1:07:08
Moena	1	46N22	11E39	-0:46:36
Moggio Udinese	1	46N25	13E12	-0:52:48
Moglia	1	44N56	10E55	-0:43:40
Mogliano Veneto	1	45N33	12E14	-0:48:56
Mogorella	4	39N52	8E51	-0:35:24
Mogoro	4	39N41	8E47	-0:35:08
Moiano	2	40N39	14E28	-0:57:52
Moiano	2	41N05	14E32	-0:58:08
Moio Alcantara	3	37N54	15E03	-1:00:12
Mola di Bari	2	41N04	17E05	-1:08:20
Molaretto	1	45N10	7E00	-0:28:00
Molfetta	2	41N12	16E36	-1:06:24
Molina di Ledro	1	45N56	10E46	-0:43:04
Molinara	2	41N18	14E54	-0:59:36
Molinella	1	44N37	11E40	-0:46:40
Molini di Tures (Mühlen)	1	46N54	11E56	-0:47:44
Moliterno	2	40N14	50E52	-3:23:28
Mollaro	1	46N16	11E05	-0:44:20
Mollia	1	45N49	8E02	-0:32:08
Molochio	2	38N18	16E02	-1:04:08
Mombaruzzo	1	44N46	8E27	-0:33:48
Monasterace	2	38N27	16E33	-1:06:12
Monasterolo di Savigliano	1	44N40	7E37	-0:30:28
Monastir	4	39N23	9E02	-0:36:08
Moncalieri	1	45N00	7E41	-0:30:44
Moncalvo	1	45N03	8E16	-0:33:04
Mondaino	1	43N51	12E41	-0:50:44
Mondavio	1	43N40	12E58	-0:51:52
Mondello	3	38N13	13E20	-0:53:20
Mondolfo	1	43N45	13E06	-0:52:24
Mondovì	1	44N23	7E49	-0:31:16
Mondragone	2	41N07	13E53	-0:55:32
Moneglia	1	44N14	9E30	-0:38:00
Monesiglio	1	44N28	8E07	-0:32:28
Monfalcone	1	45N49	13E32	-0:54:08
Monforte San Giorgio	3	38N09	15E23	-1:01:32
Monghidoro	1	44N13	11E19	-0:45:16
Mongiana	2	38N31	16E19	-1:05:16
Mongiuffi	3	37N55	15E17	-1:01:08
Mongrando	1	45N31	8E00	-0:32:00
Monguelfo (Welsberg)	1	46N45	12E06	-0:48:24
Monopoli	2	40N57	17E19	-1:09:16
Monreale	3	38N05	13E17	-0:53:08
Monselice	1	45N14	11E45	-0:47:00
Monserrato	4	39N15	9E08	-0:36:32
Monsummano Terme	1	43N52	10E49	-0:43:16
Montà	1	44N48	7E57	-0:31:48
Montagano	2	41N39	14E40	-0:58:40
Montagnana	1	45N14	11E28	-0:45:52
Montagnareale	3	38N07	14E57	-0:59:48
Montaione	1	43N33	10E55	-0:43:40
Montalbano Elicona	3	38N02	15E01	-1:00:04
Montalbano Ionico	2	40N17	16E34	-1:06:16
Montalcino	1	43N03	11E29	-0:45:56
Montaldo di Cosola	1	44N40	9E11	-0:36:44
Montale	1	43N56	11E01	-0:44:04
Montallegro	3	37N23	13E21	-0:53:24
Montalto delle Marche	1	42N59	13E36	-0:54:24

Montalto di Castro 1 42N21 11E37 -0:46:28
Montalto Ligure 1 43N56 7E51 -0:31:24
Montalto Uffugo 2 39N25 16E10 -1:04:40
Montanaro 1 45N14 7E51 -0:31:24
Montano Antilia 2 40N10 15E22 -1:01:28
Montazzoli 1 41N57 14E26 -0:57:44
Montebello 1 45N00 9E06 -0:36:24
Montebello Iónico 2 37N59 15E45 -1:03:00
Montebello Vicentino 1 45N27 11E23 -0:45:32
Montebelluna 1 45N47 12E03 -0:48:12
Montebruno 1 44N31 9E15 -0:37:00
Montecalvo Irpino 2 41N11 15E02 -1:00:08
Monte Campatri 1 41N48 12E44 -0:50:56
Montecarotto 1 43N31 13E04 -0:52:16
Montecassiano 1 43N21 13E26 -0:53:44
Montecastrilli 1 42N39 12E29 -0:49:56
Montecatini Terme 1 43N53 10E46 -0:43:04
Monte Cavallo 1 42N59 13E00 -0:52:00
Montecchio 1 43N51 12E46 -0:51:04
Montecchio Emilia 1 44N42 10E27 -0:41:48
Montecchio Maggiore 1 45N30 11E24 -0:45:36
Montecelio 1 42N01 12E44 -0:50:56
Montechiaro d'Asti 1 45N01 8E07 -0:32:28
Montechiarugolo 1 44N42 10E25 -0:41:40
Monteciccardo 1 43N49 12E48 -0:51:12
Montecilfone 2 41N54 14E50 -0:59:20
Montecorice 2 40N14 14E59 -0:59:56
Montecorvino Pugliano 2 40N41 14E57 -0:59:48
Montecorvino Rovella 2 40N42 14E59 -0:59:56
Montecosaro 1 43N19 13E37 -0:54:28
Montecreto 1 44N14 10E41 -0:42:44
Montedinove 1 42N58 13E35 -0:54:20
Monte di Procida 2 40N48 14E03 -0:56:12
Montedoro 3 37N27 13E49 -0:55:16
Montefalcione 2 40N58 14E53 -0:59:32
Montefalco 1 42N54 12E39 -0:50:36
Montefalcone di Val Fortore 2 41N20 15E00 -1:00:00
Montefano 1 43N25 13E26 -0:53:44
Montefiascone 1 42N32 12E02 -0:48:08
Montefiorino 1 44N22 10E37 -0:42:28
Monteforte d'Alpone 1 45N25 11E17 -0:45:08
Monteforte Irpino 2 40N54 14E42 -0:58:48
Montegallo 1 42N50 13E19 -0:53:16
Montegiordano 2 40N02 16E32 -1:06:08
Montegiorgio 1 43N08 13E32 -0:54:08
Montegranaro 1 43N14 13E38 -0:54:32
Monte Grimano 1 43N52 12E29 -0:49:56
Montegrotto Terme 1 45N19 11E46 -0:47:04
Monteiasi 2 40N30 17E23 -1:09:32
Monteleone di Puglia 2 41N10 15E15 -1:01:00
Monteleone di Spoleto 1 42N39 12E58 -0:51:52
Monteleone Rocco Doria 4 40N29 8E34 -0:34:16
Monteleone Sabino 1 42N14 12E51 -0:51:24
Montelepre 3 38N05 13E10 -0:52:40
Montella 2 40N51 15E01 -1:00:04
Montelungo 1 44N24 9E54 -0:39:36
Montelupo Fiorentino 1 43N44 11E01 -0:44:04
Montemaggiore Belsito 3 37N51 13E46 -0:55:04
Montemagno 1 44N59 8E20 -0:33:20
Montemarano 2 40N55 15E00 -1:00:00
Montemarciano 1 43N38 13E19 -0:53:16
Montemesola 2 40N34 17E20 -1:09:20
Montemiletto 2 41N01 14E54 -0:59:36
Montemilone 2 41N02 15E38 -1:02:32
Montemurro 2 40N18 15E59 -1:03:56
Montenero 1 43N30 10E21 -0:41:24
Montenero di Bisaccia 2 41N57 14E47 -0:59:08
Monteodorisio 1 42N05 14E39 -0:58:36
Montepescali 1 42N53 11E05 -0:44:20
Monteporzio 1 43N42 13E03 -0:52:12
Monte Porzio Catone 1 41N49 12E43 -0:50:52
Monteprandone 1 42N55 13E50 -0:55:20
Montepulciano 1 43N05 11E47 -0:47:08
Monterchi 1 43N29 12E07 -0:48:28
Montereale 1 42N31 13E15 -0:53:00
Montereale Valcellina 1 46N10 12E39 -0:50:36
Monteriggioni 1 43N23 11E13 -0:44:52
Monte Romano 1 42N16 11E54 -0:47:36
Monteroni d'Arbia 1 43N14 11E25 -0:45:40
Monteroni di Lecce 2 40N19 18E06 -1:12:24
Monterosso al Mare 1 44N09 9E39 -0:38:36
Monterosso Almo 3 37N05 14E46 -0:59:04
Monterosso Calabro 2 38N43 16E17 -1:05:08
Monterotondo 1 42N03 12E37 -0:50:28
Monterotondo Marittimo 1 43N09 10E51 -0:43:24
Monterubbiano 1 43N05 13E43 -0:54:52
Monte San Biagio 2 41N21 13E21 -0:53:24
Monte San Giovanni Campano 2 41N38 13E31 -0:54:04
Montesano 2 40N16 15E43 -1:02:52
Montesano sulla Marcellana 2 40N16 15E42 -1:02:48
Monte San Savino 1 43N20 11E43 -0:46:52
Monte Santa Maria Tiberina 1 43N26 12E09 -0:48:36
Monte Sant'Angelo 2 41N42 15E57 -1:03:48
Montesarchio 2 41N04 14E38 -0:58:32
Montescaglioso 2 40N33 16E40 -1:06:40
Montescudaio 1 43N18 10E40 -0:42:40
Montese 1 44N16 10E56 -0:43:44
Montesilvano 1 42N29 14E08 -0:56:32
Montespertoli 1 43N38 11E04 -0:44:16
Montespluga 1 46N30 9E21 -0:37:24
Montevago 3 37N42 12E58 -0:51:52
Montevarchi 1 43N31 11E34 -0:46:16
Monteverde 2 41N00 15E32 -1:02:08
Montezemolo 1 44N22 8E08 -0:32:32
Monti 4 40N49 9E19 -0:37:16
Monticelli d'Ongina 1 45N05 9E56 -0:39:44
Monticello Conte Otto 1 45N35 11E35 -0:46:20
Montichiari 1 45N25 10E23 -0:41:32
Monticiano 1 43N08 11E11 -0:44:44
Montieri 1 43N08 11E01 -0:44:04
Montjovet 1 45N43 7E40 -0:30:40
Montodine 1 45N17 9E42 -0:38:48
Montoggio 1 44N31 9E03 -0:36:12
Montone 1 43N22 12E20 -0:49:20
Montopoli in Val d'Arno 1 43N40 10E45 -0:43:00
Montorio al Vomano 1 42N35 13E38 -0:54:32
Montorio nei Frentani 2 41N46 14E55 -0:59:40
Montorio Veronese 1 45N27 11E04 -0:44:16
Montresta 4 40N22 8E30 -0:34:00
Monza 1 45N35 9E16 -0:37:04
Moos → Moso 1 46N41 12E23 -0:49:32
Moos → Moso in Passiria 1 46N50 11E10 -0:44:40
Moraduccio 1 44N10 11E29 -0:45:56
Morano Calabro 2 39N50 16E08 -1:04:32
Morano sul Po 1 45N10 8E22 -0:33:28
Morbegno 1 46N08 9E34 -0:38:16
Morciano di Romagna 1 43N55 12E38 -0:50:32
Morcone 2 41N20 14E40 -0:58:40
Mores 4 40N33 8E50 -0:35:20
Moretta 1 44N46 7E32 -0:30:08
Morgex 1 45N45 7E02 -0:28:08
Morgongiori 4 39N45 8E46 -0:35:04
Mori 1 45N51 10E59 -0:43:56
Morigerati 2 40N08 15E33 -1:02:12
Morino 1 41N53 13E25 -0:53:40
Mormanno 2 39N53 16E00 -1:04:00
Morro d'Oro 1 42N39 13E54 -0:55:36
Morrone del Sannio 2 41N43 14E47 -0:59:08
Mortara 1 45N15 8E44 -0:34:56
Mortegliano 1 45N57 13E10 -0:52:40
Mortola Inferiore 1 43N47 7E33 -0:30:12
Mosciano Sant'Angelo 1 42N45 13E53 -0:55:32
Moscufo 1 42N25 14E03 -0:56:12
Moso (Moos) 1 46N41 12E23 -0:49:32
Moso in Passiria (Moos) 1 46N50 11E10 -0:44:40
Mosso Santa Maria 1 45N38 8E08 -0:32:32
Mostizzolo 1 46N24 11E01 -0:44:04
Motrone 1 43N54 10E12 -0:40:48
Motta 1 45N36 11E29 -0:45:56
Motta Camastra 3 37N54 15E10 -1:00:40
Motta d'Affermo 3 37N59 14E18 -0:57:12
Motta di Livenza 1 45N47 12E36 -0:50:24
Mottafollone 2 39N39 16E04 -1:04:16
Motta Montecorvino 2 41N30 15E07 -1:00:28
Motta San Giovanni 2 38N00 15E41 -1:02:44
Motta Sant'Anastasia 3 37N31 14E58 -0:59:52
Motta Visconti 1 45N17 8E59 -0:35:56
Mottola 2 40N38 17E03 -1:08:12
Mozzanica 1 45N29 9E41 -0:38:44
Mozzano 1 42N50 13E31 -0:54:04
Mozzate 1 45N41 8E57 -0:35:48
Muccia 1 43N05 13E02 -0:52:08
Muggia 1 45N36 13E46 -0:55:04
Muggio 1 45N36 9E14 -0:36:56
Mühlen → Molini de Tures 1 46N54 11E56 -0:47:44
Mulazzo 1 44N19 9E53 -0:39:32
Mules (Mauls) 1 46N51 11E31 -0:46:04
Muoro 4 40N20 9E20 -0:37:20
Muravera 4 39N25 9E34 -0:38:16
Murisengo 1 45N05 8E08 -0:32:32
Murlo 1 43N09 11E23 -0:45:32
Muro Lucano 2 40N45 15E29 -1:01:56
Mussomeli 3 37N35 13E45 -0:55:00
Muzzana del Turgnano 1 45N49 13E08 -0:52:32
Nago 1 45N53 10E53 -0:43:32
Nalles (Nals) 1 46N32 11E12 -0:44:48
Naples → Napoli 2 40N51 14E17 -0:57:08
Napola 3 37N59 12E38 -0:50:32
Nápoles → Napoli 2 40N51 14E17 -0:57:08
Napoli (Naples) 2 40N51 14E17 -0:57:08
Narcao 4 39N10 8E40 -0:34:40
Nardò 2 40N11 18E02 -1:12:08
Narni 1 42N31 12E31 -0:50:04
Narzole 1 44N35 7E52 -0:31:28
Naso 3 38N07 14E47 -0:59:08
Naturno (Naturns) 1 46N39 11E00 -0:44:00
Nave 1 45N35 10E17 -0:41:08
Neapel → Napoli 2 40N51 14E17 -0:57:08
Neirone 1 44N27 9E11 -0:36:44
Nembro 1 45N45 9E45 -0:39:00
Nemi 1 41N43 12E43 -0:50:52
Nemoli 2 40N04 15E48 -1:03:12
Neoneli 4 40N04 8E57 -0:35:48
Nepi 1 42N14 12E21 -0:49:24
Nereto 1 42N49 13E49 -0:55:16
Nerito 1 42N32 13E28 -0:53:52
Nervi 1 44N23 9E02 -0:36:08
Nerviano 1 45N33 8E58 -0:35:52
Nesso 1 45N55 9E08 -0:36:32
Nettuno 2 41N27 12E39 -0:50:36
Neviano 2 40N06 18E06 -1:12:24
Neviano degli Arduini 1 44N35 10E19 -0:41:16
Nibbiano 1 44N54 9E19 -0:37:16
Nicastro 2 38N59 16E20 -1:05:20
Nichelino 1 44N59 7E38 -0:30:32
Nicolosi 3 37N37 15E01 -1:00:04
Nicosia 3 37N45 14E24 -0:57:36
Nicotera 2 38N34 15E57 -1:03:48
Nimis 1 46N12 13E16 -0:53:04
Niscemi 3 37N09 14E23 -0:57:32
Nissoria 3 37N39 14E27 -0:57:48
Nizza Monferrato 1 44N46 8E21 -0:33:24
Noale 1 45N32 12E04 -0:48:16
Noasca 1 45N27 7E19 -0:29:16
Nocera Inferiore 2 40N44 14E38 -0:58:32
Nocera Superiore 2 40N44 14E40 -0:58:40
Nocera Tirinese 2 39N02 16E09 -1:04:36
Nocera Umbra 1 43N05 12E47 -0:51:08
Noceto 1 44N48 10E11 -0:40:44
Noci 2 40N48 17E08 -1:08:32
Nociglia 2 40N02 18E20 -1:13:20
Noepoli 2 40N05 16E20 -1:05:20
Nogara 1 45N11 11E04 -0:44:16
Noicattaro 2 41N02 16E59 -1:07:56
Nola 2 40N55 14E33 -0:58:12
Nole 1 45N15 7E35 -0:30:20
Noli 1 44N12 8E26 -0:33:44
Nonantola 1 44N41 11E02 -0:44:08
None 1 44N56 7E32 -0:30:08
Norcia 1 42N48 13E05 -0:52:20
Norma 2 41N35 12E58 -0:51:52
Nosate 1 45N33 8E43 -0:34:52
Noto 3 36N53 15E04 -1:00:16
Novafeltria 1 43N53 12E17 -0:49:08
Novalesa 1 45N11 7E01 -0:28:04
Nova Milanese 1 45N35 9E12 -0:36:48
Nova Ponente (Deutschnofen) 1 46N25 11E25 -0:45:40
Novara 1 45N28 8E38 -0:34:32
Novara di Sicilia 3 38N01 15E08 -1:00:32
Nova Siri 2 40N09 16E32 -1:06:08
Novate Mezzola 1 46N15 9E27 -0:37:48
Novate Milanese 1 45N32 9E08 -0:36:32
Nove 1 45N43 11E40 -0:46:40
Novellara 1 44N51 10E44 -0:42:56
Noventa di Piave 1 45N39 12E31 -0:50:04
Noventa Padovana 1 45N24 11E58 -0:47:52
Noventa Vicentina 1 45N17 11E32 -0:46:08
Novi di Modena 1 44N54 10E54 -0:43:36
Novi Ligure 1 44N46 8E47 -0:35:08
Novoli 2 40N23 18E03 -1:12:12
Nozza 1 45N42 10E23 -0:41:32
Nucetto 1 44N20 8E04 -0:32:16
Nulvi 4 40N47 8E45 -0:35:00
Numana 1 43N31 13E37 -0:54:28
Nuoro 4 40N19 9E20 -0:37:20
Nurallao 4 39N47 9E05 -0:36:20
Nuraminis 4 39N26 9E01 -0:36:04
Nurri 4 39N43 9E14 -0:36:56
Nus 1 45N45 7E28 -0:29:52
Nusco 2 40N53 15E05 -1:00:20
Nuxis 4 39N09 8E44 -0:34:56
Occhieppo Inferiore 1 45N33 8E01 -0:32:04
Occhiobello 1 44N55 11E35 -0:46:20
Occimiano 1 45N03 8E30 -0:34:00
Oderzo 1 45N47 12E29 -0:49:56
Offanengo 1 45N22 9E44 -0:38:56
Offida 1 42N56 13E41 -0:54:44
Ogliastro Cilento 2 40N21 15E03 -1:00:12
Olbia 4 40N55 9E31 -0:38:04
Oleggio 1 45N36 8E38 -0:34:32
Olevano Romano 1 41N52 13E02 -0:52:08
Olevano sul Tusciano 2 40N40 15E01 -1:00:04
Olgiata 1 42N02 12E22 -0:49:28
Olgiate Comasco 1 45N48 8E58 -0:35:52
Olgiate Olona 1 45N38 8E53 -0:35:32
Olginate 1 45N48 9E24 -0:37:36
Oliena 4 40N16 9E24 -0:37:36

Oliveri	3	38N07	15E03	-1:00:12
Oliveto Citra	2	40N41	15E14	-1:00:56
Oliveto Lucano	2	40N32	16E11	-1:04:44
Ollomont	1	45N50	7E22	-0:29:28
Olmedo	4	40N39	8E23	-0:33:32
Olmo al Brembo	1	45N58	9E39	-0:38:36
Oltre il Colle	1	45N54	9E46	-0:39:04
Olzai	4	40N11	9E09	-0:36:36
Omegna	1	45N53	8E24	-0:33:36
Oneglia	1	43N53	8E02	-0:32:08
Onifai	4	40N24	9E39	-0:38:36
Oniferi	4	40N16	9E10	-0:36:40
Onno	1	45N55	9E17	-0:37:08
Opi	1	41N47	13E50	-0:55:20
Oppido Lucano	2	40N47	16E00	-1:04:00
Oppido Mamertina	2	38N16	16E00	-1:04:00
Oppio	1	44N03	10E50	-0:43:20
Ora (Auer)	1	46N21	11E18	-0:45:12
Orani	4	40N15	9E11	-0:36:44
Orbassano	1	45N01	7E32	-0:30:08
Orbetello	1	42N27	11E13	-0:44:52
Orgiano	1	45N21	11E28	-0:45:52
Orgosolo	4	40N12	9E21	-0:37:24
Oria	2	40N30	17E38	-1:10:32
Oricola	1	42N02	13E02	-0:52:08
Origgio	1	45N36	9E01	-0:36:04
Oriolo	2	40N03	16E27	-1:05:48
Oristano	4	39N54	8E36	-0:34:24
Ormea	1	44N09	7E54	-0:31:36
Ornavasso	1	45N58	8E24	-0:33:36
Orosei	4	40N23	9E42	-0:38:48
Orotelli	4	40N18	9E07	-0:36:28
Orsago	1	45N56	12E25	-0:49:40
Orsara di Puglia	2	41N17	15E16	-1:01:04
Orsogna	1	42N13	14E17	-0:57:08
Orsomarso	2	39N48	15E55	-1:03:40
Orta Nova	2	41N19	15E42	-1:02:48
Orta San Giulio	1	45N48	8E25	-0:33:40
Orte	1	42N27	12E23	-0:49:32
Ortisei (Sankt Ulrich)	1	46N34	11E40	-0:46:40
Ortona	1	42N21	14E24	-0:57:36
Ortovero	1	44N03	8E07	-0:32:28
Ortueri	4	40N02	8E59	-0:35:56
Orune	4	40N24	9E22	-0:37:28
Orvieto	1	42N43	12E07	-0:48:28
Orvinio	1	42N08	12E56	-0:51:44
Orzinuovi	1	45N24	9E55	-0:39:40
Oschiri	4	40N43	9E06	-0:36:24
Osiglia	1	44N17	8E12	-0:32:48
Osilo	4	40N45	8E40	-0:34:40
Osimo	1	43N29	13E29	-0:53:56
Osini	4	39N50	9E29	-0:37:56
Osio Sotto	1	45N36	9E35	-0:38:20
Osoppo	1	46N15	13E05	-0:52:20
Ospedaletti	1	43N48	7E43	-0:30:52
Ospedaletto	1	46N17	13E07	-0:52:28
Ospedaletto	1	46N03	11E33	-0:46:12
Ospitale di Cadore	1	46N20	12E19	-0:49:16
Ospitaletto	1	45N33	10E04	-0:40:16
Ossi	4	40N40	8E35	-0:34:20
Ossona	1	45N30	8E54	-0:35:36
Ostellato	1	44N45	11E56	-0:47:44
Ostiano	1	45N13	10E15	-0:41:00
Ostiglia	1	45N04	11E08	-0:44:32
Ostra	1	43N37	13E09	-0:52:36
Ostra Vetere	1	43N36	13E03	-0:52:12
Ostuni	2	40N44	17E35	-1:10:20
Otranto	2	40N09	18E30	-1:14:00
Otricoli	1	42N25	12E29	-0:49:56
Ottana	4	40N14	9E02	-0:36:08
Ottati	2	40N28	15E19	-1:01:16
Ottaviano	2	40N51	14E28	-0:57:52
Ottobiano	1	45N09	8E50	-0:35:20
Ottone	1	44N37	9E20	-0:37:20
Oulx	1	45N02	6E50	-0:27:20
Ovada	1	44N38	8E38	-0:34:32
Ovaro	1	46N29	12E52	-0:51:28
Oviglio	1	44N52	8E29	-0:33:56
Ovindoli	1	42N08	13E31	-0:54:04
Ozieri	4	40N35	9E00	-0:36:00
Pabillonis	4	39N35	8E43	-0:34:52
Paceco	3	37N59	12E33	-0:50:12
Pachino	3	36N43	15E05	-1:00:20
Paderno Dugnano	1	45N34	9E10	-0:36:40
Paderno Ponchielli	1	45N14	9E55	-0:39:40
Padola	1	46N36	12E28	-0:49:52
Padoue → Padova	1	45N25	11E53	-0:47:32
Padova	1	45N25	11E53	-0:47:32
Padria	4	40N24	8E38	-0:34:32
Padua → Padova	1	45N25	11E53	-0:47:32
Padula	2	40N20	15E39	-1:02:36
Paduli	2	41N10	14E53	-0:59:32
Paesana	1	44N41	7E16	-0:29:04
Paese	1	45N40	12E10	-0:48:40
Pagani	2	40N45	14E37	-0:58:28
Paganica	1	42N21	13E28	-0:53:52
Paganico	1	42N56	11E16	-0:45:04
Pagliara	3	37N59	15E22	-1:01:28
Paglieta	1	42N10	14E30	-0:58:00
Paisco	1	46N04	10E17	-0:41:08
Palagano	1	44N20	10E39	-0:42:36
Palagianello	2	40N37	16E58	-1:07:52
Palagiano	2	40N35	17E02	-1:08:08
Palagonia	3	37N19	14E45	-0:59:00
Palaia	1	43N36	10E46	-0:43:04
Palanzano	1	44N26	10E11	-0:40:44
Palata	2	41N53	14E47	-0:59:08
Palau	4	41N11	9E23	-0:37:32
Palazzo Adriano	3	37N41	13E23	-0:53:32
Palazzolo Acreide	3	37N04	14E54	-0:59:36
Palazzolo dello Stella	1	45N48	13E05	-0:52:20
Palazzolo sull'Oglio	1	45N36	9E53	-0:39:32
Palazzolo Vercellese	1	45N11	8E14	-0:32:56
Palazzo San Gervasio	2	40N56	16E00	-1:04:00
Palazzuolo sul Senio	1	44N07	11E33	-0:46:12
Palena	1	41N59	14E08	-0:56:32
Palermo	3	38N07	13E22	-0:53:28
Palestrina	1	41N50	12E53	-0:51:32
Paliano	1	41N48	13E03	-0:52:12
Palinuro	2	40N02	15E17	-1:01:08
Palizzi	2	37N58	15E59	-1:03:56
Pallagorio	2	39N18	16E54	-1:07:36
Palma Campania	2	40N52	14E33	-0:58:12
Palma di Montechiaro	3	37N11	13E46	-0:55:04
Palmanova	1	45N54	13E19	-0:53:16
Palmi	2	38N21	15E51	-1:03:24
Palmoli	1	41N56	14E32	-0:58:08
Palo	1	41N56	12E06	-0:48:24
Palo del Colle	2	41N03	16E42	-1:06:48
Palombara Sabina	1	42N04	12E46	-0:51:04
Palomonte	2	40N40	15E17	-1:01:08
Palù del Fersina	1	46N08	11E21	-0:45:24
Paludi	2	39N32	16E41	-1:06:44
Paluzza	1	46N32	13E01	-0:52:04
Pamparato	1	44N17	7E55	-0:31:40
Pancalieri	1	44N50	7E35	-0:30:20
Pandino	1	45N24	9E33	-0:38:12
Paneveggio	1	46N18	11E44	-0:46:56
Panni	2	41N13	15E16	-1:01:04
Pantelleria	3	36N50	11E57	-0:47:48
Paola	2	39N22	16E03	-1:04:12
Papasidero	2	39N52	15E54	-1:03:36
Papozze	1	44N59	12E02	-0:48:08
Parabiago	1	45N33	8E57	-0:35:48
Parabita	2	40N03	18E08	-1:12:32
Parapayè	1	45N55	7E32	-0:30:08
Paratico	1	45N39	9E57	-0:39:48
Parcines (Partschins)	1	46N41	11E04	-0:44:16
Parma	1	44N48	10E20	-0:41:20
Partanna	3	37N43	12E53	-0:51:32
Partinico	3	38N03	13E07	-0:52:28
Partschins → Parcines	1	46N41	11E04	-0:44:16
Pasian di Prato	1	46N03	13E11	-0:52:44
Pasiano di Pordenone	1	45N51	12E37	-0:50:28
Passignano sul Trasimeno	1	43N11	12E08	-0:48:32
Passo Corese	1	42N09	12E39	-0:50:36
Passopisciaro	3	37N52	15E02	-1:00:08
Pastrengo	1	45N29	10E48	-0:43:12
Paternò	3	37N34	14E54	-0:59:36
Pattada	4	40N35	9E06	-0:36:24
Patti	3	38N08	14E58	-0:59:52
Paularo	1	46N32	13E07	-0:52:28
Paulilatino	4	40N05	8E46	-0:35:04
Paullo	1	45N25	9E24	-0:37:36
Pausania	4	40N55	9E06	-0:36:24
Pavia	1	45N10	9E10	-0:36:40
Pavia di Udine	1	45N59	13E17	-0:53:08
Pavona	1	41N43	12E37	-0:50:28
Pavullo nel Frignano	1	44N20	10E50	-0:43:20
Peccioli	1	43N33	10E43	-0:42:52
Pedaso	1	43N06	13E50	-0:55:20
Pederobba	1	45N53	11E58	-0:47:52
Pedesina	1	46N05	9E33	-0:38:12
Pegli	1	44N26	8E48	-0:35:12
Pegolotte	1	45N12	12E02	-0:48:08
Peio	1	46N22	10E40	-0:42:40
Pelago	1	43N46	11E30	-0:46:00
Pellaro	2	38N01	15E39	-1:02:36
Pellegrino Parmense	1	44N44	9E55	-0:39:40
Pennabilli	1	43N49	12E16	-0:49:04
Penne	1	42N27	13E55	-0:55:40
Pennes (Pens)	1	46N47	11E25	-0:45:40
Pens → Pennes	1	46N47	11E25	-0:45:40
Perarolo di Cadore	1	46N24	12E21	-0:49:24
Perdasdefogu	4	39N41	9E26	-0:37:44
Perdifumo	2	40N16	15E01	-1:00:04
Perfugas	4	40N50	8E53	-0:35:32
Pergine Valdarno	1	43N28	11E41	-0:46:44
Pergine Valsugana	1	46N04	11E14	-0:44:56
Pergola	1	43N34	12E50	-0:51:20
Peri	1	45N39	10E54	-0:43:36
Perinaldo	1	43N52	7E40	-0:30:40
Perito	2	40N18	15E09	-1:00:36
Pernate	1	45N27	8E41	-0:34:44
Pero	1	45N31	9E05	-0:36:20
Perosa Argentina	1	44N58	7E10	-0:28:40
Peroulaz	1	45N42	7E19	-0:29:16
Perrero	1	44N56	7E05	-0:28:20
Perugia	1	43N08	12E22	-0:49:28
Pesaro	1	43N54	12E55	-0:51:40
Pescaglia	1	43N58	10E25	-0:41:40
Pescantina	1	45N29	10E51	-0:43:24
Pescara	1	42N28	14E13	-0:56:52
Pescasseroli	1	41N48	13E47	-0:55:08
Peschici	2	41N57	16E01	-1:04:04
Peschiera del Garda	1	45N26	10E42	-0:42:48
Pescia	1	43N54	10E41	-0:42:44
Pescina	1	42N02	13E39	-0:54:36
Pescocostanzo	1	41N53	14E04	-0:56:16
Pescolanciano	1	41N41	14E20	-0:57:20
Pescopagano	2	40N50	15E24	-1:01:36
Pescorocchiano	1	42N12	13E09	-0:52:36
Pesco Sannita	2	41N14	14E49	-0:59:16
Pessinetto	1	45N17	7E24	-0:29:36
Petilia Policastro	2	39N07	16E47	-1:07:08
Petralia Soprana	3	37N47	14E06	-0:56:24
Petralia Sottana	3	37N48	14E05	-0:56:20
Petrella Salto	1	42N18	13E04	-0:52:16
Petrella Tifernina	2	41N41	14E42	-0:58:48
Petronà	2	39N03	16E45	-1:07:00
Petrosino	3	37N43	12E29	-0:49:56
Pettineo	3	37N58	14E17	-0:57:08
Peveragno	1	44N20	7E37	-0:30:28
Pezzana	1	45N16	8E29	-0:33:56
Piacenza	1	45N01	9E40	-0:38:40
Piadena	1	45N08	10E22	-0:41:28
Piaggine	2	40N21	15E23	-1:01:32
Piana Crixia	1	44N29	8E18	-0:33:12
Piana degli Albanesi	3	38N00	13E17	-0:53:08
Piancastagnaio	1	42N51	11E41	-0:46:44
Pian di Sco	1	43N38	11E33	-0:46:12
Pianella	1	42N24	14E02	-0:56:08
Pianello Val Tidone	1	44N57	9E24	-0:37:36
Pianezza	1	45N06	7E33	-0:30:12
Piano	1	45N46	11E08	-0:44:32
Piano d'Arta	1	46N29	13E01	-0:52:04
Piano del Voglio	1	44N10	11E13	-0:44:52
Pianoro	1	44N22	11E20	-0:45:20
Pianosinatico	1	44N07	10E44	-0:42:56
Piazza Armerina	3	37N23	14E22	-0:57:28
Piazzola sul Brenta	1	45N32	11E47	-0:47:08
Piccione	1	43N11	12E31	-0:50:04
Picerno	2	40N38	15E38	-1:02:32
Picinisco	2	41N39	13E52	-0:55:28
Pico	2	41N27	13E34	-0:54:16
Piedicavallo	1	45N42	7E57	-0:31:48
Piediluco	1	42N32	12E45	-0:51:00
Piedimonte Etneo	3	37N48	15E12	-1:00:48
Piedimonte Matese	2	41N21	14E22	-0:57:28
Piedimonte San Germano	2	41N30	13E45	-0:55:00
Piedimulera	1	46N01	8E16	-0:33:04
Piè di Ripa	1	43N15	13E29	-0:53:56
Piegaro	1	42N58	12E05	-0:48:20
Pienza	1	43N04	11E41	-0:46:44
Pietrabbondante	1	41N45	14E23	-0:57:32
Pietracamela	1	42N31	13E33	-0:54:12
Pietracatella	2	41N35	14E52	-0:59:28
Pietragalla	2	40N45	15E53	-1:03:32
Pietra Ligure	1	44N09	8E17	-0:33:08
Pietralunga	1	43N26	12E26	-0:49:44
Pietramala	1	44N10	11E20	-0:45:20
Pietramelara	2	41N16	14E11	-0:56:44
Pietramontecorvino	2	41N32	15E07	-1:00:28
Pietrapaola	2	39N29	16E49	-1:07:16
Pietrapertosa	2	40N31	16E04	-1:04:16
Pietraperzia	3	37N25	14E08	-0:56:32
Pietrasanta	1	43N57	10E14	-0:40:56
Pietrelcina	2	41N12	14E51	-0:59:24
Pieve	1	45N46	10E45	-0:43:00
Pieve d'Alpago	1	46N10	12E21	-0:49:24
Pieve del Cairo	1	45N03	8E48	-0:35:12
Pieve di Cadore	1	46N26	12E22	-0:49:28
Pieve di Cento	1	44N43	11E18	-0:45:12
Pieve di Soligo	1	45N53	12E10	-0:48:40
Pieve di Teco	1	44N03	7E56	-0:31:44
Pieve Fosciana	1	44N08	10E25	-0:41:40
Pievepelago	1	44N12	10E37	-0:42:28
Pieve Porto Morone	1	45N07	9E26	-0:37:44
Pieve Santo Stefano	1	43N40	12E02	-0:48:08
Piglio	1	41N49	13E08	-0:52:32
Pigna	1	43N56	7E40	-0:30:40
Pignataro Maggiore	2	41N11	14E10	-0:56:40
Pignola	2	40N34	15E47	-1:03:08
Pila	1	45N41	7E18	-0:29:12
Pinerolo	1	44N53	7E21	-0:29:24
Pineto	1	42N36	14E04	-0:56:16
Pinocchio	1	43N35	13E30	-0:54:00
Pinzano al Tagliamento	1	46N11	12E57	-0:51:48
Piobbico	1	43N35	12E31	-0:50:04
Piombino	1	42N55	10E32	-0:42:08
Pioppo	3	38N03	13E14	-0:52:56
Pioraco	1	43N11	12E59	-0:51:56
Piove di Sacco	1	45N18	12E02	-0:48:08
Piovene-Rocchette	1	45N45	11E25	-0:45:40
Piraino	3	38N10	14E52	-0:59:28
Pisa	1	43N43	10E23	-0:41:32
Pisciotta	2	40N06	15E14	-1:00:56
Pisogne	1	45N48	10E06	-0:40:24
Pisticci	2	40N23	16E34	-1:06:16
Pistoia	1	43N55	10E54	-0:43:36
Piteglio	1	44N01	10E46	-0:43:04
Pitigliano	1	42N38	11E40	-0:46:40

Piverone 1 45N27 8E00 -0:32:00
Pizzighettone 1 45N11 9E47 -0:39:08
Pizzo 2 38N44 16E10 -1:04:40
Pizzoferrato 1 41N55 14E14 -0:56:56
Pizzoli 1 42N26 13E18 -0:53:12
Pizzone 1 41N40 14E02 -0:56:08
Placanica 2 38N25 16E27 -1:05:48
Platì 2 38N13 16E03 -1:04:12
Ploaghe 4 40N40 8E45 -0:35:00
Pocol 1 46N31 12E07 -0:48:28
Podenzano 1 44N57 9E41 -0:38:44
Poetto 4 39N12 9E10 -0:36:40
Poggiardo 2 40N03 18E23 -1:13:32
Poggibonsi 1 43N28 11E09 -0:44:36
Poggio 1 44N30 10E00 -0:40:00
Poggio Berni 1 44N02 12E24 -0:49:36
Poggio Bustone 1 42N30 12E53 -0:51:32
Poggio Imperiale 2 41N49 15E22 -1:01:28
Poggiomarino 2 40N48 14E32 -0:58:08
Poggio Mirteto 1 42N16 12E41 -0:50:44
Poggio Moiano 1 42N12 12E53 -0:51:32
Poggioreale 3 37N47 13E01 -0:52:04
Poggio Renatico 1 44N46 11E29 -0:45:56
Poggiorsini 2 40N55 16E15 -1:05:00
Poggio Rusco 1 44N59 11E07 -0:44:28
Poggio Sannita 1 41N47 14E25 -0:57:40
Pogliano 1 45N32 8E59 -0:35:56
Poirino 1 44N55 7E51 -0:31:24
Polesella 1 44N58 11E45 -0:47:00
Polesine Parmense 1 45N01 10E04 -0:40:16
Polia 2 38N45 16E19 -1:05:16
Policastro Bussentino 2 40N09 15E32 -1:02:08
Policoro 2 40N13 16E41 -1:06:44
Polignano a Mare 2 41N00 17E13 -1:08:52
Polistena 2 38N25 16E05 -1:04:20
Polizzi Generosa 3 37N49 14E00 -0:56:00
Polla 2 40N30 15E30 -1:02:00
Pollenza 1 43N16 13E21 -0:53:24
Pollica 2 40N11 15E03 -1:00:12
Pollina 3 37N59 14E09 -0:56:36
Pollutri 1 42N08 14E35 -0:58:20
Polverigi 1 43N31 13E23 -0:53:32
Pomarance 1 43N18 10E52 -0:43:28
Pomarico 2 40N31 16E33 -1:06:12
Pombia 1 45N39 8E38 -0:34:32
Pomezia 1 41N40 12E30 -0:50:00
Pomigliano d'Arco 2 40N54 14E23 -0:57:32
Pompei 2 40N45 14E30 -0:58:00
Pomposa 1 44N49 12E11 -0:48:44
Ponsacco 1 43N37 10E38 -0:42:32
Pont 1 45N34 7E07 -0:28:28
Pontassieve 1 43N46 11E26 -0:45:44
Pont Canavese 1 45N25 7E36 -0:30:24
Ponte a Elsa 1 43N41 10E54 -0:43:36
Ponte a Moriano 1 43N54 10E31 -0:42:04
Pontebba 1 46N30 13E18 -0:53:12
Ponte Caffaro 1 45N50 10E32 -0:42:08
Pontecagnano 2 40N39 14E52 -0:59:28
Pontecchio Marconi 1 44N25 11E15 -0:45:00
Pontecchio Polesine 1 45N01 11E49 -0:47:16
Pontecorvo 2 41N27 13E40 -0:54:40
Pontecurone 1 44N57 8E56 -0:35:44
Ponte d'Arbia 1 43N10 11E28 -0:45:52
Ponte delle Arche 1 46N02 10E52 -0:43:28
Ponte dell'Olio 1 44N52 9E39 -0:38:36
Pontedera 1 43N40 10E38 -0:42:32
Ponte di Barbarano 1 45N23 11E34 -0:46:16
Ponte di Legno 1 46N16 10E31 -0:42:04
Ponte di Nava 1 44N08 7E53 -0:31:32
Ponte di Piave 1 45N43 12E28 -0:49:52
Ponte Gardena (Waidbruck) 1 46N36 11E32 -0:46:08
Ponte Ghiereto 1 43N59 11E15 -0:45:00
Pontegrande 1 45N59 8E09 -0:32:36
Ponte in Valtellina 1 46N12 9E59 -0:39:56
Pontelagoscuro 1 44N53 11E36 -0:46:24
Pontelandolfo 2 41N17 14E41 -0:58:44
Pontelongo 1 45N15 12E02 -0:48:08
Ponte nell'Alpi 1 46N11 12E16 -0:49:04
Ponte Nuovo 1 43N01 12E28 -0:49:52
Pontenure 1 44N59 9E47 -0:39:08
Pontepetri 1 44N02 10E53 -0:43:32
Pontericcioli 1 43N26 12E38 -0:50:32
Ponte Rocchetta 1 46N14 11E04 -0:44:16
Ponte San Giovanni 1 43N05 12E26 -0:49:44
Ponte San Pietro 1 45N42 9E35 -0:38:20
Ponte Selva 1 45N52 9E54 -0:39:36
Pontestura 1 45N08 8E20 -0:33:20
Ponte*Trèdici Archi* 2 41N31 14E56 -0:59:44
Pontevico 1 45N16 10E05 -0:40:20
Pontida 1 45N43 9E30 -0:38:00
Pontinia 2 41N24 13E02 -0:52:08
Pontremoli 1 44N22 9E53 -0:39:32
Pont-Saint-Martin 1 45N36 7E48 -0:31:12
Ponza 2 40N54 12E58 -0:51:52
Ponzòne 1 44N35 8E27 -0:33:48
Popoli 1 42N10 13E50 -0:55:20
Poppi 1 43N43 11E46 -0:47:04
Populonia 1 42N59 10E29 -0:41:56
Porcia 1 45N57 12E36 -0:50:24
Pordenone 1 45N57 12E39 -0:50:36
Porlezza 1 46N03 9E07 -0:36:28
Pornassio 1 44N04 7E52 -0:31:28
Porretta Terme 1 44N09 10E59 -0:43:56
Port'Ercole 1 42N23 11E12 -0:44:48
Portici 2 40N49 14E20 -0:57:20
Portico di Romagna 1 44N01 11E47 -0:47:08
Portigliola 2 38N14 16E13 -1:04:52
Porto Azzurro 1 42N46 10E24 -0:41:36
Porto Ceresio 1 45N54 8E55 -0:35:40
Porto d'Ascoli 1 42N55 13E53 -0:55:32
Porto di Potenza Picena 1 43N21 13E42 -0:54:48
Porto Empedocle 3 37N17 13E32 -0:54:08
Portoferraio 1 42N49 10E19 -0:41:16
Portofino 1 44N18 9E12 -0:36:48
Porto Garibaldi 1 44N41 12E14 -0:48:56
Portogruaro 1 45N47 12E50 -0:51:20
Portomaggiore 1 44N42 11E48 -0:47:12
Porto Maurizio 1 43N52 8E01 -0:32:04
Portopalo 3 36N41 15E08 -1:00:32
Porto Palo 3 37N34 12E54 -0:51:36
Porto Recanati 1 43N26 13E40 -0:54:40
Porto San Giorgio 1 43N11 13E48 -0:55:12
Porto Sant'Elpidio 1 43N15 13E45 -0:55:00
Porto Santo Stefano 1 42N26 11E07 -0:44:28
Portoscuso 4 39N12 8E23 -0:33:32
Porto Tolle 1 44N56 12E22 -0:49:28
Porto Torres 4 40N50 8E24 -0:33:36
Porto Valtravaglia 1 45N58 8E41 -0:34:44
Portovenere 1 44N03 9E51 -0:39:24
Posada 4 40N38 9E43 -0:38:52
Posaro 1 43N55 12E55 -0:51:40
Poscara 1 42N28 14E13 -0:56:52
Posina 1 45N47 11E15 -0:45:00
Positano 2 40N38 14E29 -0:57:56
Possagno 1 45N51 11E51 -0:47:24
Posta 1 42N31 13E06 -0:52:24
Postal (Burgstall) 1 46N36 11E11 -0:44:44
Postiglione 2 40N33 15E13 -1:00:52
Potenza 2 40N38 15E49 -1:03:16
Potenza Picena 1 43N22 13E37 -0:54:28
Poviglio 1 44N51 10E32 -0:42:08
Pozzallo 3 36N43 14E51 -0:59:24
Pozzolo Formigaro 1 44N48 8E47 -0:35:08
Pozzomaggiore 4 40N24 8E39 -0:34:36
Pozzuoli 2 40N49 14E07 -0:56:28
Pozzuolo del Friuli 1 45N59 13E12 -0:52:48
Pradleves 1 44N25 7E17 -0:29:08
Pragelato 1 45N01 6E57 -0:27:48
Praia a Mare 2 39N54 15E47 -1:03:08
Praino 2 40N37 14E32 -0:58:08
Pralboino 1 45N16 10E13 -0:40:52
Prali 1 44N54 7E03 -0:28:12
Pranzo 1 45N55 10E48 -0:43:12
Praraye 1 45N55 7E32 -0:30:08
Pratella 2 41N24 14E11 -0:56:44
Prato 1 43N53 11E06 -0:44:24
Prato allo Stelvio 1 46N37 10E35 -0:42:20
Pratola Peligna 1 42N06 13E52 -0:55:28
Pratola Serra 2 40N59 14E51 -0:59:24
Pratolino 1 43N52 11E18 -0:45:12
Prazzo 1 44N29 7E03 -0:28:12
Preci 1 42N53 13E02 -0:52:08
Predappio 1 44N06 11E58 -0:47:52
Predazzo 1 46N19 11E36 -0:46:24
Predoi (Prettau) 1 47N02 12E06 -0:48:24
Predore 1 45N40 10E01 -0:40:04
Pregnana 1 45N31 9E00 -0:36:00
Premana 1 46N03 9E25 -0:37:40
Premosello 1 46N00 8E20 -0:33:20
Pré-Saint-Didier 1 45N46 6E59 -0:27:56
Preseglie 1 45N40 10E24 -0:41:36
Presicce 2 39N54 18E16 -1:13:04
Pressana 1 45N17 11E24 -0:45:36
Prettau → Predoi 1 47N02 12E06 -0:48:24
Primolano 1 45N58 11E42 -0:46:48
Priolo Gargallo 3 37N09 15E11 -1:00:44
Priverno 2 41N28 13E11 -0:52:44
Prizzi 3 37N43 13E26 -0:53:44
Procchio 1 42N47 10E15 -0:41:00
Procida 2 40N46 14E02 -0:56:08
Promitorio 1 42N03 12E39 -0:50:36
Pula 4 39N01 9E00 -0:36:00
Pulfero 1 46N11 13E29 -0:53:56
Puliciano 1 43N23 11E51 -0:47:24
Pulsano 2 40N23 17E22 -1:09:28
Putifigari 4 40N34 8E27 -0:33:48
Putignano 2 40N51 17E07 -1:08:28
Putzu Idu 4 40N02 8E25 -0:33:40
Quarrata 1 43N51 10E58 -0:43:52
Quartu Sant'elena 4 39N14 9E11 -0:36:44
Quercianella 1 43N27 10E22 -0:41:28
Quero 1 45N55 11E56 -0:47:44
Quinzano d'Oglio 1 45N19 10E00 -0:40:00
Quistello 1 45N00 10E59 -0:43:56
Racale 2 39N57 18E06 -1:12:24
Racalmuto 3 37N24 13E44 -0:54:56
Racconigi 1 44N46 7E46 -0:31:04
Raccuia 3 38N03 14E54 -0:59:36
Racines 1 46N52 11E18 -0:45:12
Radda in Chianti 1 43N29 11E22 -0:45:28
Raddusa 3 37N28 14E32 -0:58:08
Radicofani 1 42N54 11E46 -0:47:04
Radicondoli 1 43N16 11E02 -0:44:08
Raffadali 3 37N24 13E32 -0:54:08
Ragada 1 46N10 10E38 -0:42:32
Ragusa 3 36N55 14E44 -0:58:56
Raiano 1 42N06 13E49 -0:55:16
Rains → Riva di Tures 1 46N57 12E04 -0:48:16
Ramacca 3 37N23 14E42 -0:58:48
Randazzo 3 37N53 14E57 -0:59:48
Rapallo 1 44N21 9E14 -0:36:56
Rapolano Terme 1 43N17 11E36 -0:46:24
Rapolla 2 40N58 15E41 -1:02:44
Rapone 2 40N51 15E30 -1:02:00
Rasen-Antholz → Anterselva di Sopra 1 46N52 12E08 -0:48:32
Rasun di sopra 1 46N48 12E03 -0:48:12
Rasun di sotto 1 46N47 12E02 -0:48:08
Rasura 1 46N06 9E33 -0:38:12
Ravanusa 3 37N16 13E58 -0:55:52
Ravarano 1 44N35 10E04 -0:40:16
Ravarino 1 44N44 11E06 -0:44:24
Ravascletto 1 46N32 12E57 -0:51:48
Ravenna 1 44N25 12E12 -0:48:48
Rayello 2 40N39 14E37 -0:58:28
Realmonte 3 37N18 13E28 -0:53:52
Reana del Roiale 1 46N12 13E13 -0:52:52
Recanati 1 43N24 13E32 -0:54:08
Recco 1 44N22 9E09 -0:36:36
Recoaro Terme 1 45N42 11E13 -0:44:52
Regalbuto 3 37N39 14E38 -0:58:32
Reggello 1 43N41 11E32 -0:46:08
Reggio di Calabria 2 38N06 15E39 -1:02:36
Reggiolo 1 44N55 10E48 -0:43:12
Reggio nell'Emilia 1 44N43 10E36 -0:42:24
Reitano 3 37N58 14E20 -0:57:20
Rende 2 39N19 16E11 -1:04:44
Rescalda 1 45N38 8E56 -0:35:44
Rescaldina 1 45N37 8E57 -0:35:48
Resiutta 1 46N23 13E13 -0:52:52
Resuttano 3 37N41 14E02 -0:56:08
Revere 1 45N03 11E08 -0:44:32
Revò 1 46N23 11E03 -0:44:12
Rezzato 1 45N31 10E19 -0:41:16
Rezzoaglio 1 44N32 9E23 -0:37:32
Rezzonico 1 46N04 9E16 -0:37:04
Rhêmes-Notre-Dame 1 45N34 7E07 -0:28:28
Rho 1 45N32 9E02 -0:36:08
Riace 2 38N25 16E29 -1:05:56
Ribera 3 37N30 13E16 -0:53:04
Ricadi 2 38N37 15E52 -1:03:28
Riccia 2 41N29 14E50 -0:59:20
Riccione 1 43N59 12E39 -0:50:36
Ridanna (Ridnaun) 1 46N55 11E15 -0:45:00
Ridnaun → Ridanna 1 46N55 11E15 -0:45:00
Riese Pio X 1 45N44 11E55 -0:47:40
Riesi 3 37N17 14E05 -0:56:20
Rieti 1 42N24 12E51 -0:51:24
Rifiano (Riffian) 1 46N42 11E11 -0:44:44
Rignano Flaminio 1 42N12 12E29 -0:49:56
Rignano Garganico 2 41N40 15E35 -1:02:20
Rignano sull'Arno 1 43N43 11E27 -0:45:48
Rilievo 3 37N55 12E33 -0:50:12
Rima San Giuseppe 1 45N52 8E00 -0:32:00
Rimini 1 44N04 12E34 -0:50:16
Riola 1 44N16 11E04 -0:44:16
Riola Sardo 4 39N59 8E32 -0:34:08
Riolo Terme 1 44N16 11E43 -0:46:52
Riomaggiore 1 44N06 9E44 -0:38:56
Rio Marina 1 42N49 10E25 -0:41:40
Rionero in Vulture 2 40N56 15E41 -1:02:44
Rionero Sannitico 1 41N42 14E08 -0:56:32
Rio Saliceto 1 44N49 10E49 -0:43:16
Rioveggio 1 44N17 11E14 -0:44:56
Ripacandida 2 40N55 15E43 -1:02:52
Ripatransone 1 43N00 13E46 -0:55:04
Riposto 3 37N44 15E12 -1:00:48
Riva 1 45N53 10E50 -0:43:20
Riva del Sole 1 42N46 10E52 -0:43:28
Riva di Tures (Rain) 1 46N57 12E04 -0:48:16
Rivanazzano 1 44N56 9E01 -0:36:04
Rivarolo Canavese 1 45N19 7E43 -0:30:52
Rivarolo Mantovano 1 45N04 10E26 -0:41:44
Riva Trigoso 1 44N16 9E26 -0:37:44
Rive d'Arcano 1 46N08 13E02 -0:52:08
Rivello 2 40N04 15E45 -1:03:00
Rivergaro 1 44N55 9E36 -0:38:24
Rivignano 1 45N52 13E03 -0:52:12
Rivisondoli 1 41N52 14E04 -0:56:16
Rivoli 1 45N04 7E31 -0:30:04
Rivolta d'Adda 1 45N28 9E31 -0:38:04
Rivoltella 1 45N27 10E33 -0:42:12
Rizziconi 2 38N25 15E57 -1:03:48
Roana 1 45N52 11E28 -0:45:52
Robbio 1 45N17 8E35 -0:34:20

Robecchetto con Induno
1 45N32 8E46 -0:35:04
Robecco d'Oglio 1 45N15 10E04 -0:40:16
Robecco sul Naviglio
1 45N26 8E53 -0:35:32
Roccabernarda 2 39N08 16E52 -1:07:28
Roccacasale 1 42N07 13E53 -0:55:32
Roccadaspide 2 40N26 15E12 -1:00:48
Rocca di Cambio 1 42N14 13E29 -0:53:56
Rocca di Mezzo 1 42N12 13E31 -0:54:04
Rocca di Neto 2 39N11 17E00 -1:08:00
Rocca di Papa 1 41N46 12E42 -0:50:48
Roccafluvione 1 42N51 13E29 -0:53:56
Roccagloriosa 2 40N06 15E26 -1:01:44
Roccalbegna 1 42N47 11E30 -0:46:00
Roccalumera 3 37N58 15E24 -1:01:36
Rocca Massima 1 41N41 12E55 -0:51:40
Roccamena 3 37N50 13E09 -0:52:36
Roccamonfina 2 41N17 13E59 -0:55:56
Roccanova 2 40N13 16E12 -1:04:48
Roccapalumba 3 37N48 13E39 -0:54:36
Rocca Pia 1 41N56 13E59 -0:55:56
Rocca Pietore 1 46N26 11E59 -0:47:56
Roccaprebalza 1 44N31 9E57 -0:39:48
Rocca Priora 1 41N48 12E45 -0:51:00
Roccaraso 1 41N51 14E05 -0:56:20
Rocca San Casciano
1 44N03 11E50 -0:47:20
Rocca Santa Maria
1 42N41 13E30 -0:54:00
Roccasecca 2 41N33 13E40 -0:54:40
Roccasecca dei Volsci
2 41N29 13E13 -0:52:52
Roccastrada 1 43N00 11E10 -0:44:40
Roccavione 1 44N19 7E29 -0:29:56
Roccavivara 1 41N50 14E36 -0:58:24
Roccella Ionica 2 38N19 16E24 -1:05:36
Roccella Valdemone
3 37N56 15E00 -1:00:00
Rocchetta Sant'Antonio
2 41N06 15E27 -1:01:48
Rodi Garganico 2 41N55 15E53 -1:03:32
Rofrano 2 40N12 15E25 -1:01:40
Roggiano Gravina
2 39N37 16E09 -1:04:36
Roghudi 2 38N03 15E55 -1:03:40
Rogliano 2 39N11 16E20 -1:05:20
Rom → Roma 1 41N54 12E29 -0:49:56
Roma (Rome) 1 41N54 12E29 -0:49:56
Romagnano Sesia 1 45N38 8E23 -0:33:32
Romano di Lombardia
1 45N31 9E45 -0:39:00
Romans d'Isonzo 1 45N53 13E26 -0:53:44
Rome → Roma 1 41N54 12E29 -0:49:56
Romeno 1 46N24 11E07 -0:44:28
Romentino 1 45N28 8E42 -0:34:48
Rometta 3 38N10 15E25 -1:01:40
Romitorio 1 42N01 12E39 -0:50:36
Roncade 1 45N38 12E22 -0:49:28
Roncegno 1 46N03 11E25 -0:45:40
Ronchi dei Legionari
1 45N50 13E30 -0:54:00
Ronchis 1 45N49 13E00 -0:52:00
Ronciglione 1 42N17 12E13 -0:48:52
Ronco Canavese 1 45N30 7E32 -0:30:08
Roncofreddo 1 44N02 12E20 -0:49:20
Roncone 1 45N59 10E40 -0:42:40
Ronco Scrivia 1 44N37 8E59 -0:35:56
Rondissone 1 45N15 7E58 -0:31:52
Roreto Chisone 1 44N59 7E06 -0:28:24
Rosà 1 45N43 11E45 -0:47:00
Rosarno 2 38N29 15E59 -1:03:56
Rosazza 1 45N41 7E58 -0:31:52
Rosciolo 1 42N07 13E20 -0:53:20
Rose 2 39N24 16E17 -1:05:08
Roseto Capo Spulico
2 39N59 16E36 -1:06:24
Roseto degli Abruzzi
1 42N41 14E01 -0:56:04
Roseto Valfortore
2 41N22 15E06 -1:00:24
Rosignano Marittimo
1 43N24 10E28 -0:41:52
Rosignano Solvay
1 43N23 10E26 -0:41:44
Rosolina 1 45N05 12E15 -0:49:00
Rosolini 3 36N49 14E57 -0:59:48
Rossano 2 39N35 16E39 -1:06:36
Rossiglione 1 44N34 8E40 -0:34:40
Rotonda 2 39N57 16E02 -1:04:08
Rotondella 2 40N10 16E32 -1:06:08
Rottofreno 1 45N03 9E34 -0:38:16
Rovasenda 1 45N32 8E19 -0:33:16
Rovato 1 45N34 10E00 -0:40:00
Rovegno 1 44N35 9E17 -0:37:08
Rovellasca 1 45N40 9E03 -0:36:12
Rovello Porro 1 45N39 9E02 -0:36:08
Roverbella 1 45N16 10E46 -0:43:04
Rovere 1 42N10 13E31 -0:54:04
Roverè della Luna
1 46N15 11E10 -0:44:40
Rovereto 1 45N53 11E02 -0:44:08
Roverè Veronese 1 45N36 11E03 -0:44:12
Roviano 1 42N01 13E00 -0:52:00
Rovigo 1 45N04 11E47 -0:47:08
Rubiana 1 45N08 7E23 -0:29:32
Rubiera 1 44N39 10E45 -0:43:00
Ruda 1 45N50 13E24 -0:53:36
Ruffano 2 39N59 18E15 -1:13:00
Rufina 1 43N49 11E29 -0:45:56
Ruoti 2 40N43 15E41 -1:02:44
Russi 1 44N22 12E02 -0:48:08
Rutigliano 2 41N01 17E00 -1:08:00
Rutino 2 40N18 15E04 -1:00:16
Ruvo del Monte 2 40N51 15E32 -1:02:08
Ruvo di Puglia 2 41N07 16E29 -1:05:56
Sabaudia 2 41N18 13E01 -0:52:04
Sabbioneta 1 45N00 10E39 -0:42:36
Sacile 1 45N57 12E30 -0:50:00
Sadali 4 39N49 9E16 -0:37:04
Sagrado 1 45N52 13E29 -0:53:56
Saint-Pierre 1 45N42 7E14 -0:28:56
Saint-Rhémy 1 45N50 7E11 -0:28:44
Sala Baganza 1 44N43 10E14 -0:40:56
Sala Consilina 2 40N24 15E36 -1:02:24
Salandra 2 40N31 16E19 -1:05:16
Salaparuta 3 37N47 13E00 -0:52:00
Salara 1 44N59 11E25 -0:45:40
Sale 1 44N59 8E48 -0:35:12
Sale Marasino 1 45N43 10E06 -0:40:24
Salemi 3 37N49 12E48 -0:51:12
Salento 2 40N15 15E11 -1:00:44
Salerno 2 40N41 14E47 -0:59:08
Salice Salentino
2 40N23 17E58 -1:11:52
Salice Terme 1 44N55 9E01 -0:36:04
Saline di Volterra
1 43N22 10E49 -0:43:16
Salò 1 45N36 10E31 -0:42:04
Salorno (Salurn)
1 46N14 11E13 -0:44:52
Salsomaggiore Terme
1 44N49 9E59 -0:39:56
Saltara 1 43N45 12E54 -0:51:36
Saludecio 1 43N52 12E40 -0:50:40
Saluggia 1 45N14 8E00 -0:32:00
Salurn → Salorno
1 46N14 11E13 -0:44:52
Salussola 1 45N27 8E07 -0:32:28
Saluzzo 1 44N39 7E29 -0:29:56
Salve 2 39N51 18E17 -1:13:08
Salza Irpina 2 40N55 14E53 -0:59:32
Samarate 1 45N38 8E47 -0:35:08
Samassi 4 39N29 8E54 -0:35:36
Sambiase 2 38N58 16E17 -1:05:08
Sambuca di Sicilia
3 37N39 13E07 -0:52:28
Sambuca Pistoiese
1 44N06 11E00 -0:44:00
Sammichele di Bari
2 40N53 16E57 -1:07:48
Samolaco 1 46N15 9E21 -0:37:24
Sampéyre 1 44N34 7E11 -0:28:44
Sampieri 3 36N43 14E44 -0:58:56
Samugheo 4 39N57 8E56 -0:35:44
San Antonio Ticino
1 45N35 8E46 -0:35:04
San Bartolomeo in Galdo
2 41N24 15E01 -1:00:04
San Basilio 4 39N32 9E11 -0:36:44
San Benedetto del Tronto
1 42N57 13E53 -0:55:32
San Benedetto in Alpe
1 43N59 11E41 -0:46:44
San Benedetto Po
1 45N02 10E55 -0:43:40
San Benigno Canavese
1 45N13 7E46 -0:31:04
San Biagio 1 44N35 11E52 -0:47:28
San Biagio di Callalta
1 45N41 12E22 -0:49:28
San Biagio Platani
3 37N31 13E32 -0:54:08
San Biagio Saracinisco
2 41N37 13E55 -0:55:40
San Bonifacio 1 45N24 11E16 -0:45:04
San Bovio 1 45N28 9E19 -0:37:16
San Buono 1 41N59 14E34 -0:58:16
San Calogero 2 38N34 16E01 -1:04:04
San Candido (Innichen)
1 46N44 12E17 -0:49:08
San Casciano dei Bagni
1 42N52 11E53 -0:47:32
San Casciano in Val di Pesa
1 43N39 11E11 -0:44:44
San Cataldo 2 40N23 18E17 -1:13:08
San Cataldo 3 37N29 13E59 -0:55:56
San Cesario di Lecce
2 40N18 18E10 -1:12:40
San Cesario sul Panaro
1 44N34 11E02 -0:44:08
San Chirico Raparo
2 40N11 16E05 -1:04:20
San Cipirello 3 37N58 13E10 -0:52:40
San Cipriano Picentino
2 40N43 14E52 -0:59:28
San Colombano al Lambro
1 45N11 9E29 -0:37:56
San Cono 3 37N17 14E22 -0:57:28
San Cosmo Albanese
2 39N35 16E25 -1:05:40
San Costantino Albanese
2 40N02 16E18 -1:05:12
San Damiano d'Asti
1 44N50 8E04 -0:32:16
San Damiano Macra
1 44N29 7E16 -0:29:04
San Daniele del Friuli
1 46N09 13E00 -0:52:00
San Demetrio Corone
2 39N34 16E22 -1:05:28
San Demetrio ne'Vestini
1 42N17 13E34 -0:54:16
San Donaci 2 40N27 17E55 -1:11:40
San Donà di Piave
1 45N38 12E34 -0:50:16
San Donato di Lecce
2 40N15 18E10 -1:12:40
San Donato di Ninea
2 39N42 16E03 -1:04:12
San Donato Milanese
1 45N24 9E16 -0:37:04
San Donato Val di Comino
1 41N42 13E49 -0:55:16
San Dorligo della Valle
1 45N36 13E51 -0:55:24
Sandrigo 1 45N39 11E36 -0:46:24
San Fele 2 40N49 15E32 -1:02:08
San Felice (Sankt Felix)
1 46N30 11E08 -0:44:32
San Felice Circeo
2 41N14 13E05 -0:52:20
San Felice sul Panaro
1 44N50 11E08 -0:44:32
San Ferdinando di Puglia
2 41N18 16E04 -1:04:16
San Fili 2 39N20 16E09 -1:04:36
San Filippo del Mela
3 38N10 15E17 -1:01:08
San Floriano 1 46N02 12E18 -0:49:12
San Fratello 3 38N01 14E36 -0:58:24
San Gavino Monreale
4 39N33 8E47 -0:35:08
San Gemini 1 42N37 12E33 -0:50:12
San Genesio Atesino
1 46N32 11E20 -0:45:20
San Germano Vercellese
1 45N21 8E15 -0:33:00
San Giacomo (Sankt Jakob in Pfitsch)
1 46N57 11E36 -0:46:24
San Giacomo Filippo
1 46N20 9E21 -0:37:24
San Gimignano 1 43N28 11E02 -0:44:08
San Ginesio 1 43N06 13E19 -0:53:16
San Giorgio Canavese
1 45N20 7E48 -0:31:12
San Giorgio della Richinvelda
1 46N03 12E52 -0:51:28
San Giorgio del Sannio
2 41N04 14E51 -0:59:24
San Giorgio di Lomellina
1 45N10 8E47 -0:35:08
San Giorgio di Nogaro
1 45N50 13E13 -0:52:52
San Giorgio di Piano
1 44N39 11E22 -0:45:28
San Giorgio Ionico
2 40N27 17E23 -1:09:32
San Giorgio la Molara
2 41N16 14E55 -0:59:40
San Giorgio Lucano
2 40N07 16E23 -1:05:32
San Giorgio Monferrato
1 45N07 8E23 -0:33:32
San Giorgio Morgeto
2 38N23 16E06 -1:04:24
San Giorgio Piacentino
1 44N57 9E44 -0:38:56
San Giorgio su Legnano
1 45N34 8E55 -0:35:40
San Giovanni (Sankt Johann)
1 46N38 11E44 -0:46:56
San Giovanni al Timavo (Sankt Johann in
1 46N58 11E57 -0:47:48
San Giovanni a Piro
2 40N03 15E27 -1:01:48
San Giovanni-Bianco
1 45N52 9E39 -0:38:36
San Giovanni d'Asso
1 43N09 11E35 -0:46:20
San Giovanni Gemini
3 37N38 13E39 -0:54:36
San Giovanni Ilarione
1 45N30 11E15 -0:45:00
San Giovanni in Croce
1 45N05 10E22 -0:41:28
San Giovanni in Fiore
2 39N15 16E42 -1:06:48
San Giovanni in Persiceto
1 44N38 11E11 -0:44:44
San Giovanni la Punta
3 37N35 15E07 -1:00:28
San Giovanni Lupatoto
1 45N23 11E03 -0:44:12
San Giovanni Rotondo
2 41N42 15E44 -1:02:56
San Giovanni Suergiu
4 39N07 8E31 -0:34:04
San Giovanni Valdarno
1 43N34 11E32 -0:46:08
San Giuliano Milanese
1 45N24 9E17 -0:37:08
San Giuliano Terme
1 43N46 10E26 -0:41:44
San Giuseppe 1 44N22 8E18 -0:33:12
San Giuseppe 3 37N58 13E11 -0:52:44
San Giuseppe Vesuviano
2 40N50 14E30 -0:58:00
San Giustino 1 43N33 12E10 -0:48:40
San Giusto Canavese
1 45N19 7E49 -0:31:16
San Godenzo 1 43N55 11E37 -0:46:28
San Gregorio 1 42N19 13E29 -0:53:56
San Gregorio Magno
2 40N39 15E24 -1:01:36
Sanguinetto 1 45N11 11E09 -0:44:36
Sankt Gertraud → Santa Gertrude
1 46N29 10E53 -0:43:32
Sankt Jakob → San Giacomo
1 46N57 11E36 -0:46:24
Sankt Johann → San Giovanni
1 46N38 11E44 -0:46:56
Sankt Leonhard → San Leonardo
1 46N49 11E15 -0:45:00

Sankt Lorenzen → San Lorenzo di Sebato 1 46N47 11E54 -0:47:36
Sankt Martin in Gsies → San Martino in 1 46N49 12E14 -0:48:56
Sankt Niklaus → San Nicolò d'Ultimo 1 46N30 10E55 -0:43:40
Sankt Ulrich → Ortisei 1 46N34 11E40 -0:46:40
Sankt Wallburg → Santa Valburga 1 46N33 11E00 -0:44:00
San Lazzaro di Savena 1 44N28 11E25 -0:45:40
San Leo 1 43N54 12E21 -0:49:24
San Leonardo (Sankt Leonhard) 1 46N49 11E15 -0:45:00
San Leone 3 37N16 13E35 -0:54:20
San Lorenzo 2 38N01 15E50 -1:03:20
San Lorenzo Bellizzi 2 39N53 16E20 -1:05:20
San Lorenzo del Vallo 2 39N40 16E18 -1:05:12
San Lorenzo di Sebato (Sankt Lorenzen) 1 46N47 11E54 -0:47:36
San Lorenzo in Campo 1 43N36 12E56 -0:51:44
San Lorenzo Nuovo 1 42N41 11E54 -0:47:36
San Luca 2 38N09 16E04 -1:04:16
Sanluri 4 39N34 8E54 -0:35:36
San Macario 1 45N36 8E47 -0:35:08
San Mamete 1 46N02 9E04 -0:36:16
San Mango d'aquino 2 39N03 16E11 -1:04:44
San Marcello Pistoiese 1 44N03 10E47 -0:43:08
San Marco Argentano 2 39N33 16E07 -1:04:28
San Marco dei Cavoti 2 41N18 14E53 -0:59:32
San Marco in Lamis 2 41N43 15E38 -1:02:32
San Marco la Catola 2 41N31 15E00 -1:00:00
San Martino (Sankt Martin) 1 46N47 11E13 -0:44:52
San Martino 1 45N27 8E47 -0:35:08
San Martino Buon Albergo 1 45N25 11E05 -0:44:20
San Martino d'agri 2 40N14 16E04 -1:04:16
San Martino di Castrozza 1 46N16 11E48 -0:47:12
San Martino di Lupari 1 45N39 11E51 -0:47:24
San Martino in Badia (Saint Martin) 1 46N41 11E52 -0:47:28
San Martino in Casies (Sankt Martin in 1 46N49 12E14 -0:48:56
San Martino in Rio 1 44N44 10E48 -0:43:12
San Martino Valle Caudina 2 41N01 14E39 -0:58:36
San Marzano di San Giuseppe 2 40N27 17E30 -1:10:00
San Marzano sul Sarno 2 40N46 14E35 -0:58:20
San Mauro Castelverde 3 37N55 14E11 -0:56:44
San Mauro Forte 2 40N29 16E15 -1:05:00
San Mauro la Bruca 2 40N07 15E17 -1:01:08
San Mauro Marchesato 2 39N06 16E56 -1:07:44
San Mauro Torinese 1 45N06 7E46 -0:31:04
San Menaio 2 41N56 15E58 -1:03:52
San Michele all'Adige 1 46N12 11E08 -0:44:32
San Michele al Tagliamento 1 45N46 12E59 -0:51:56
San Michele di Ganzaria 3 37N17 14E26 -0:57:44
San Michele Mondovì 1 44N23 7E54 -0:31:36
San Michele Salentino 2 40N38 17E37 -1:10:28
San Miniato 1 43N41 10E51 -0:43:24
Sannazzaro de'Burgondi 1 45N06 8E54 -0:35:36
Sannicandro di Bari 2 41N00 16E48 -1:07:12
Sannicandro Garganico 2 41N50 15E34 -1:02:16
Sannicola 2 40N05 18E04 -1:12:16
San Nicola Arcella 2 39N51 15E48 -1:03:12
San Nicola da Crissa 2 38N40 16E17 -1:05:08
San Nicolò di Comelico 1 46N35 12E31 -0:50:04
San Nicolò d'Ultimo (Sankt Nikolaus) 1 46N30 10E55 -0:43:40
San Nicolò Ferrarese 1 44N42 11E42 -0:46:48
San Nicolò Gerrei 4 39N30 9E18 -0:37:12
San Pancrazio Salentino 2 40N25 17E50 -1:11:20
San Paolo 1 46N29 11E15 -0:45:00
San Paolo di Civitate 2 41N44 15E15 -1:01:00
San Pellegrino Terme 1 45N50 9E40 -0:38:40
San Piero a Grado 1 43N41 10E21 -0:41:24
San Piero in Bagno 1 43N51 11E58 -0:47:52
San Pietro (Sankt Peter) 1 47N01 12E03 -0:48:12
San Pietro a Maida 2 38N50 16E20 -1:05:20
San Pietro di Cadore 1 46N34 12E35 -0:50:20
San Pietro in Casale 1 44N42 11E24 -0:45:36
San Pietro in Gu 1 45N37 11E40 -0:46:40
San Pietro in Guarano 2 39N20 16E19 -1:05:16
San Pietro in Palazzi 1 43N20 10E30 -0:42:00
San Pietro Vara 1 44N20 9E35 -0:38:20
San Pietro Vernotico 2 40N29 18E00 -1:12:00
San Polo d'Enza 1 44N38 10E26 -0:41:44
San Quirico d'Orcia 1 43N03 11E36 -0:46:24
San Remo 1 43N49 7E46 -0:31:04
San Roberto 2 38N18 15E44 -1:02:56
San Rufo 2 40N26 15E28 -1:01:52
San Salvatore Monferrato 1 44N59 8E34 -0:34:16
San Salvatore Telesino 2 41N14 14E30 -0:58:00
San Salvo 2 42N03 14E44 -0:58:56
San Sebastiano Curone 1 44N47 9E04 -0:36:16
San Secondo Parmense 1 44N55 10E14 -0:40:56
Sansepolcro 1 43N34 12E08 -0:48:32
San Severino Lucano 2 40N01 16E08 -1:04:32
San Severino Marche 1 43N13 13E10 -0:52:40
San Severo 2 41N41 15E23 -1:01:32
San Sigismondo (Sankt Sigmund) 1 46N49 11E46 -0:47:04
San Sosti 2 39N40 16E02 -1:04:08
San Sperate 4 39N21 9E00 -0:36:00
San Stefano Ticino 1 45N29 8E55 -0:35:40
Santa Caterina di Pittinuri 4 40N06 8E30 -0:34:00
Santa Caterina Valfurva 1 46N25 10E29 -0:41:56
Santa Caterina Villarmosa 3 37N35 14E02 -0:56:08
Santa Cesarea Terme 2 40N02 18E29 -1:13:56
Santa Cristina 1 46N34 11E43 -0:46:52
Santa Cristina d'aspromonte 2 38N15 15E58 -1:03:52
Santa Croce 1 46N05 12E18 -0:49:12
Santa Croce Camerina 3 36N50 14E31 -0:58:04
Santa Croce del Sannio 2 41N23 14E43 -0:58:52
Santa Croce di Magliano 2 41N42 14E59 -0:59:56
Santadi 4 39N05 8E43 -0:34:52
Santa Domenica Talao 2 39N49 15E51 -1:03:24
Santa Domenica Vittoria 3 37N55 14E58 -0:59:52
Santa Elisabetta 3 37N26 13E33 -0:54:12
Santa Fiora 1 42N50 11E35 -0:46:20
Santa Flavia 3 38N05 13E31 -0:54:04
Sant'Agata Bolognese 1 44N40 11E08 -0:44:32
Sant'Agata de'Goti 2 41N05 14E30 -0:58:00
Sant'Agata del Bianco 2 38N05 16E05 -1:04:20
Sant'Agata di Militello 3 38N04 14E38 -0:58:32
Sant'Agata di Puglia 2 41N09 15E23 -1:01:32
Sant'Agata Feltria 1 43N52 12E12 -0:48:48
Sant'Agata sul Santerno 1 44N26 11E51 -0:47:24
Santa Gertrude (Sankt Gertraud) 1 46N29 10E53 -0:43:32
Sant'Agostino 1 44N48 11E23 -0:45:32
Sant'Alberto 1 44N32 12E09 -0:48:36
Sant'Alfio 3 37N44 15E08 -1:00:32
Santa Luce 1 43N28 10E34 -0:42:16
Santa Lucia 1 46N28 10E21 -0:41:24
Santa Lucia del Mela 3 38N09 15E17 -1:01:08
Santa Lucia di Piave 1 45N51 12E17 -0:49:08
Santa Margherita di Belice 3 37N41 13E01 -0:52:04
Santa Margherita Ligure 1 44N20 9E12 -0:36:48
Santa Maria a Monte 1 43N42 10E42 -0:42:48
Santa Maria a Vico 2 41N02 14E29 -0:57:56
Santa Maria Capua Vetere 2 41N05 14E15 -0:57:00
Santa Maria degli Angeli 1 43N03 12E34 -0:50:16
Santa Maria del Cedro 2 39N45 15E50 -1:03:20
Santa Maria della Versa 1 44N59 9E18 -0:37:12
Santa Maria di Licodia 3 37N37 14E53 -0:59:32
Santa Maria Maggiore 1 46N08 8E28 -0:33:52
Santa Maria Nuova 1 43N29 13E18 -0:53:12
Santa Marinella 1 42N02 11E51 -0:47:24
Sant'Ambrogio 1 45N31 10E50 -0:43:20
Sant'Anastasia 2 40N52 14E24 -0:57:36
Sant'Andrea Frius 4 39N29 9E10 -0:36:40
Sant'Angelo dei Lombardi 2 40N56 15E11 -1:00:44
Sant'Angelo in Vado 1 43N40 12E25 -0:49:40
Sant'Angelo Lodigiano 1 45N14 9E24 -0:37:36
Sant'Angelo Muxard 3 37N28 13E32 -0:54:08
Sant'Angelo Romano 1 42N02 12E42 -0:50:48
Santa Ninfa 3 37N46 12E53 -0:51:32
Sant'Antimo 2 40N56 14E14 -0:56:56
Sant'Antioco 4 39N04 8E27 -0:33:48
Sant'Antonio Abate 2 40N43 14E32 -0:58:08
Sant'Antonio di Santadi 4 39N43 8E29 -0:33:56
Sant'Antonio Morignone 1 46N24 10E21 -0:41:24
Sant'Arcangelo 2 40N15 16E17 -1:05:08
Santarcangelo di Romagna 1 44N04 12E27 -0:49:48
Sant'Arcangelo Trimonte 2 41N10 14E56 -0:59:44
Sant'Arsenio 2 40N28 15E29 -1:01:56
Santa Severa 1 42N02 11E57 -0:47:48
Santa Severina 2 39N09 16E55 -1:07:40
Santa Sofia 1 43N57 11E54 -0:47:36
Santa Teresa di Riva 3 37N57 15E22 -1:01:28
Santa Teresa Gallura 4 41N14 9E11 -0:36:44
Santa Valburga (Sankt Wallburg) 1 46N33 11E00 -0:44:00
Santa Venerina 3 37N41 15E08 -1:00:32
Santa Vittoria in Matenano 1 43N01 13E29 -0:53:56
Sant'Egidio alla Vibrata 1 42N49 13E42 -0:54:48
Sant'Elena 1 45N12 11E43 -0:46:52
Sant'Elia a Pianisi 2 41N38 14E52 -0:59:28
Sant'Elia Fiumerapido 2 41N32 13E52 -0:55:28
Sant'Elpidio a Mare 1 43N14 13E41 -0:54:44
Santena 1 44N57 7E45 -0:31:00
San Teodoro 3 37N51 14E42 -0:58:48
San Teodoro 4 40N46 9E39 -0:38:36
Santermo in Colle 2 40N48 16E45 -1:07:00
Sant'Eufemia a Maiella 1 42N07 14E02 -0:56:08
Sant'Eufemia d'Aspromonte 2 38N16 15E52 -1:03:28
Sant'Eufemia Lamezia 2 38N55 16E15 -1:05:00
Santhià 1 45N22 8E10 -0:32:40
Santi Filippo e Giacomo 3 37N51 12E31 -0:50:04
Sant'Ilario d'Enza 1 44N46 10E27 -0:41:48
Sant'Olcese 1 44N30 8E58 -0:35:52
San Tommaso 1 42N11 13E58 -0:55:52
Sant'Omobono Imagna 1 45N48 9E32 -0:38:08
Sant'Oreste 1 42N14 12E32 -0:50:08
Santorso 1 45N44 11E23 -0:45:32
Santo Stefano Belbo 1 44N43 8E14 -0:32:56
Santo Stefano d'Aveto 1 44N35 9E27 -0:37:48
Santo Stefano di Cadore 1 46N33 12E32 -0:50:08
Santo Stefano di Camastra 3 38N01 14E21 -0:57:24
Santo Stefano di Magra 1 44N10 9E55 -0:39:40
Santo Stefano Quisquina 3 37N37 13E29 -0:53:56
Santo Stino di Livenza 1 45N44 12E41 -0:50:44
Santu Lussurgiu 4 40N08 8E39 -0:34:36
San Valentino in Abruzzo Citeriore 1 42N14 13E59 -0:55:56
San Valentino Torio 2 40N48 14E36 -0:58:24
San Venanzo 1 42N52 12E16 -0:49:04
San Vendemiano 1 45N54 12E20 -0:49:20
San Vigilio 1 45N34 10E41 -0:42:44
San Vincenzo 1 43N06 10E32 -0:42:08
San Vito 4 39N26 9E32 -0:38:08
San Vito al Tagliamento 1 45N54 12E52 -0:51:28
San Vito Chietino 1 42N18 14E27 -0:57:48
San Vito dei Normanni 2 40N39 17E42 -1:10:48
San Vito lo Capo 3 38N10 12E45 -0:51:00
San Vito Romano 1 41N53 12E59 -0:51:56
San Vito sullo Ionio 2 38N43 16E25 -1:05:40
Sanza 2 40N15 15E33 -1:02:12

San Zeno di Montagna
1 45N37 10E43 -0:42:52
Saonara 1 45N22 11E59 -0:47:56
Saponara 3 38N11 15E26 -1:01:44
Sappada 1 46N34 12E41 -0:50:44
Sapri 2 40N04 15E38 -1:02:32
Saracena 2 39N46 16E09 -1:04:36
Sarche di Calavino
1 46N03 10E57 -0:43:48
Sardagna 1 46N03 11E06 -0:44:24
Sardara 4 39N37 8E49 -0:35:16
Sarentino (Sarnthein)
1 46N38 11E21 -0:45:24
Sarezzo 1 45N39 10E12 -0:40:48
Sarnano 1 43N02 13E18 -0:53:12
Sarnico 1 45N40 9E57 -0:39:48
Sarno 2 40N49 14E37 -0:58:28
Sarnthein → Sarentino
1 46N38 11E21 -0:45:24
Saronno 1 45N38 9E02 -0:36:08
Sarre 1 45N43 7E15 -0:29:00
Sarroch 4 39N04 9E00 -0:36:00
Sarsina 1 43N55 12E08 -0:48:32
Sarteano 1 42N59 11E52 -0:47:28
Sartirana Lomellina
1 45N07 8E39 -0:34:36
Sarzana 1 44N07 9E58 -0:39:52
Sassano 2 40N20 15E33 -1:02:12
Sassari 4 40N43 8E34 -0:34:16
Sassello 1 44N29 8E30 -0:34:00
Sassocorvaro 1 43N47 12E30 -0:50:00
Sasso di Castalda
2 40N30 15E40 -1:02:40
Sassoferrato 1 43N26 12E51 -0:51:24
Sasso Marconi 1 44N24 11E15 -0:45:00
Sassuolo 1 44N33 10E47 -0:43:08
Satriano di Lucania
2 40N33 15E33 -1:02:12
Sauze di Cesana 1 44N56 6E51 -0:27:24
Sauze d'Oulx 1 45N02 6E52 -0:27:28
Sava 2 40N24 17E34 -1:10:16
Savelli 2 39N19 16E47 -1:07:08
Saviano 2 40N54 14E30 -0:58:00
Savigliano 1 44N38 7E40 -0:30:40
Savignano Irpino
2 41N14 15E11 -1:00:44
Savignano sul Panaro
1 44N29 11E02 -0:44:08
Savignano sul Rubicone
1 44N05 12E24 -0:49:36
Savignone 1 44N34 8E58 -0:35:52
Savio 1 44N18 12E18 -0:49:12
Saviore dell'Adamello
1 46N05 10E24 -0:41:36
Savona 1 44N17 8E30 -0:34:00
Scafati 2 40N45 14E31 -0:58:04
Scala Coeli 2 39N27 16E53 -1:07:32
Scalea 2 39N49 15E48 -1:03:12
Scaletta Zanclea
3 38N03 15E28 -1:01:52
Scandale 2 39N07 16E57 -1:07:48
Scandiano 1 44N36 10E43 -0:42:52
Scandicci 1 43N45 11E11 -0:44:44
Scanno 1 41N54 13E53 -0:55:32
Scansano 1 42N41 11E20 -0:45:20
Scarlino 1 42N54 10E51 -0:43:24
Scarperia 1 44N00 11E21 -0:45:24
Scauri 2 41N15 13E42 -0:54:48
Scauri 3 36N45 11E58 -0:47:52
Scena 1 46N41 11E12 -0:44:48
Scerni 1 42N07 14E34 -0:58:16
Schabs → Sciaves
1 46N46 11E40 -0:46:40
Scheggia 1 43N24 12E40 -0:50:40
Scheggino 1 42N43 12E50 -0:51:20
Schilpario 1 46N01 10E09 -0:40:36
Schio 1 45N43 11E21 -0:45:24
Schlanders → Silandro
1 46N38 10E46 -0:43:04
Schluderns → Sluderno
1 46N40 10E35 -0:42:20
Sciacca 3 37N31 13E03 -0:52:12
Sciara 3 37N55 13E45 -0:55:00
Sciaves (Schabs)
1 46N46 11E40 -0:46:40
Scicli 3 36N47 14E42 -0:58:48
Scigliano 2 39N08 16E19 -1:05:16
Scilla 2 38N15 15E44 -1:02:56
Sclafani Bagni 3 37N49 13E51 -0:55:24
Scopello 1 45N46 8E06 -0:32:24
Scordia 3 37N18 14E51 -0:59:24
Scorrano 1 42N35 13E49 -0:55:16
Scorrano 2 40N05 18E18 -1:13:12
Scorzè 1 45N34 12E06 -0:48:24
Scurcola Marsicana
1 42N03 13E20 -0:53:20
Sedico 1 46N06 12E06 -0:48:24
Sedilo 4 40N10 8E55 -0:35:40
Sedini 4 40N51 8E49 -0:35:16
Sedriano 1 45N29 8E58 -0:35:52
Sedrina 1 45N47 9E38 -0:38:32
Seggiano 1 42N56 11E33 -0:46:12
Segni 1 41N41 13E01 -0:52:04
Segrate 1 45N29 9E19 -0:37:16
Selargius 4 39N16 9E10 -0:36:40
Selegas 4 39N34 9E06 -0:36:24
Sella 1 46N00 11E25 -0:45:40
Sella di Corno 1 42N21 13E14 -0:52:56
Sellano 1 42N54 12E55 -0:51:40
Sellero 1 46N03 10E20 -0:41:20
Sellia Marina 2 38N55 16E45 -1:07:00
Selva 1 46N33 11E46 -0:47:04
Selva di Cadore 1 46N27 12E02 -0:48:08
Selvino 1 45N48 9E45 -0:39:00
Seminara 2 38N20 15E52 -1:03:28
Senago 1 45N35 9E07 -0:36:28
Senale 1 46N31 11E06 -0:44:24
Seneghe 4 40N05 8E36 -0:34:24
Senerchia 2 40N44 15E12 -1:00:48
Senigallia 1 43N43 13E13 -0:52:52
Senise 2 40N09 16E18 -1:05:12
Sennori 4 40N47 8E35 -0:34:20
Senorbì 4 39N32 9E08 -0:36:32
Sepino 2 41N24 14E37 -0:58:28
Sequals 1 46N10 12E50 -0:51:20
Serapo 2 41N13 13E34 -0:54:16
Seravalle Sesia 1 45N41 8E19 -0:33:16
Seravezza 1 43N59 10E13 -0:40:52
Seregno 1 45N39 9E12 -0:36:48
Seren del Grappa
1 45N59 11E51 -0:47:24
Seriate 1 45N41 9E43 -0:38:52
Serino 2 40N51 14E52 -0:59:28
Sermide 1 45N00 11E18 -0:45:12
Sermoneta 2 41N33 12E59 -0:51:56
Serracapriola 2 41N48 15E09 -1:00:36
Serrada 1 45N53 11E09 -0:44:36
Serra d'aiello 2 39N05 16E08 -1:04:32
Serra de'Conti 1 43N33 13E02 -0:52:08
Serradifalco 3 37N27 13E53 -0:55:32
Serramanna 4 39N25 8E55 -0:35:40
Serramazzoni 1 44N25 10E47 -0:43:08
Serrara 2 40N42 13E54 -0:55:36
Serra San Bruno 2 38N35 16E20 -1:05:20
Serra San Quirico
1 43N27 13E01 -0:52:04
Serrastretta 2 39N01 16E25 -1:05:40
Serravalle 1 43N57 12E30 -0:50:00
Serravalle 1 42N47 13E01 -0:52:04
Serravalle all'Adige
1 45N49 11E01 -0:44:04
Serravalle Pistoiese
1 43N54 10E49 -0:43:16
Serravalle Scrivia
1 44N43 8E51 -0:35:24
Serre 2 40N35 15E11 -1:00:44
Serrenti 4 39N29 8E58 -0:35:52
Serri 4 39N42 9E08 -0:36:32
Sersale 2 39N01 16E44 -1:06:56
Servigliano 1 43N05 13E29 -0:53:56
Sessa Aurunca 2 41N14 13E56 -0:55:44
Sesta Godano 1 44N17 9E40 -0:38:40
Sestino 1 43N42 12E18 -0:49:12
Sesto (Sexten) 1 46N42 12E21 -0:49:24
Sesto Calende 1 45N44 8E38 -0:34:32
Sesto Fiorentino
1 43N50 11E12 -0:44:48
Sestola 1 44N14 10E46 -0:43:04
Sesto San Giovanni
1 45N32 9E14 -0:36:56
Sestriere 1 44N57 6E53 -0:27:32
Sestri Levante 1 44N16 9E24 -0:37:36
Sestri Ponente 1 44N25 8E51 -0:35:24
Sestu 4 39N18 9E05 -0:36:20
Settimo Milanese
1 45N29 9E03 -0:36:12
Settimo San Pietro
4 39N17 9E11 -0:36:44
Settimo Torinese
1 45N09 7E46 -0:31:04
Settimo Vittone 1 45N33 7E50 -0:31:20
Settingiano 2 38N55 16E31 -1:06:04
Seui 4 39N50 9E19 -0:37:16
Seulo 4 39N52 9E14 -0:36:56
Seveso 1 45N39 9E09 -0:36:36
Sexten → Sesto 1 46N42 12E21 -0:49:24
Sezze 2 41N30 13E03 -0:52:12
Sgurgola 1 41N40 13E09 -0:52:36
Siamanna 4 39N55 8E46 -0:35:04
Sicignano degli Alburni
2 40N34 15E18 -1:01:12
Siculiana 3 37N20 13E25 -0:53:40
Siderno 2 38N16 16E18 -1:05:12
Siena 1 43N19 11E21 -0:45:24
Sienna → Siena 1 43N19 11E21 -0:45:24
Sigillo 1 43N20 12E44 -0:50:56
Signa 1 43N47 11E05 -0:44:20
Silandro (Schlanders)
1 46N38 10E46 -0:43:04
Silanus 4 40N17 8E53 -0:35:32
Siliqua 4 39N18 8E48 -0:35:12
Silvano d'Orba 1 44N41 8E40 -0:34:40
Silvi 1 42N34 14E05 -0:56:20
Simaxis 4 39N56 8E41 -0:34:44
Simbario 2 38N37 16E20 -1:05:20
Sinagra 3 38N05 14E51 -0:59:24
Sinalunga 1 43N12 11E44 -0:46:56
Sindia 4 40N18 8E39 -0:34:36
Siniscola 4 40N34 9E41 -0:38:44
Sinnai 4 39N18 9E12 -0:36:48
Siracusa (Syracuse)
3 37N04 15E18 -1:01:12
Sirmione 1 45N30 10E36 -0:42:24
Sirolo 1 43N32 13E37 -0:54:28
Siurgus Donigala
4 39N35 9E12 -0:36:48
Siusi (Seis) 1 46N32 11E34 -0:46:16
Siziano 1 45N20 9E12 -0:36:48
Sluderno (Schluderns)
1 46N40 10E35 -0:42:20
Soave 1 45N25 11E15 -0:45:00
Socchieve 1 46N25 12E52 -0:51:28
Sogliano al Rubicone
1 44N00 12E18 -0:49:12
Solarino 3 37N06 15E07 -1:00:28
Solaro 1 45N37 9E05 -0:36:20
Solbiate Arno 1 45N42 8E48 -0:35:12
Solbiate Olona 1 45N39 8E53 -0:35:32
Solero 1 44N55 8E30 -0:34:00
Solferino 1 45N23 10E34 -0:42:16
Soliera 1 44N45 10E55 -0:43:40
Solofra 2 40N50 14E51 -0:59:24
Solopaca 2 41N11 14E33 -0:58:12
Somma 1 42N40 12E44 -0:50:56
Somma 1 45N41 8E42 -0:34:48
Sommacampagna 1 45N24 10E50 -0:43:20
Somma Lombardo 1 45N41 8E42 -0:34:48
Sommariva del Bosco
1 44N46 7E47 -0:31:08
Sommatino 3 37N20 13E59 -0:55:56
Somma Vesuviana 2 40N52 14E26 -0:57:44
Somplago 1 46N21 13E04 -0:52:16
Soncino 1 45N24 9E52 -0:39:28
Sondalo 1 46N20 10E19 -0:41:16
Sondrio 1 46N10 9E52 -0:39:28
Sonico 1 46N10 10E21 -0:41:24
Sonnino 2 41N25 13E14 -0:52:56
Soprabolzano 1 46N32 11E24 -0:45:36
Sora 1 41N43 13E37 -0:54:28
Soraga 1 46N22 11E39 -0:46:36
Soragna 1 44N56 10E07 -0:40:28
Sorano 1 42N41 11E43 -0:46:52
Sorbolo 1 44N51 10E28 -0:41:52
Sordevolo 1 45N34 7E59 -0:31:56
Soresina 1 45N17 9E51 -0:39:24
Sorgono 4 40N01 9E06 -0:36:24
Sori 1 44N22 9E06 -0:36:24
Soriano Calabro 2 38N36 16E14 -1:04:56
Soriano nel Cimino
1 42N25 12E14 -0:48:56
Sorico 1 46N10 9E22 -0:37:28
Sorrento 2 40N37 14E22 -0:57:28
Sorso 4 40N48 8E34 -0:34:16
Sortino 3 37N09 15E02 -1:00:08
Sospirolo 1 46N09 12E04 -0:48:16
Sottomarina 1 45N13 12E17 -0:49:08
Soverato 2 38N41 16E33 -1:06:12
Sovere 1 45N49 10E01 -0:40:04
Soveria Mannelli
2 39N05 16E22 -1:05:28
Sovicille 1 43N17 11E13 -0:44:52
Sovico 1 45N39 9E16 -0:37:04
Sozzago 1 45N24 8E43 -0:34:52
Spadafora 3 38N13 15E22 -1:01:28
Spello 1 42N59 12E40 -0:50:40
Sperlonga 2 41N15 13E26 -0:53:44
Spezia → La Spezia
1 44N07 9E50 -0:39:20
Spezzano Albanese
2 39N40 16E19 -1:05:16
Spezzano della Sila
2 39N18 16E20 -1:05:20
Spiazzo 1 46N07 10E40 -0:42:40
Spilamberto 1 44N32 11E01 -0:44:04
Spilimbergo 1 46N07 12E54 -0:51:36
Spilinga 2 38N37 15E54 -1:03:36
Spinazzola 2 40N58 16E06 -1:04:24
Spindoli 1 43N12 12E54 -0:51:36
Spinea 1 45N29 12E10 -0:48:40
Spinetta Marengo
1 44N53 8E41 -0:34:44
Spinoso 2 40N16 15E58 -1:03:52
Spoleto 1 42N44 12E44 -0:50:56
Spoltore 1 42N27 14E08 -0:56:32
Spondigna 1 46N38 10E37 -0:42:28
Spotorno 1 44N14 8E25 -0:33:40
Spresiano 1 45N46 12E16 -0:49:04
Squillace 2 38N47 16E31 -1:06:04
Squinzano 2 40N26 18E03 -1:12:12
Staletti 2 38N46 16E32 -1:06:08
Stanghella 1 45N08 11E45 -0:47:00
Staranzano 1 45N49 13E30 -0:54:00
Stazzema 1 43N59 10E19 -0:41:16
Stella 1 44N24 8E30 -0:34:00
Stenico 1 46N03 10E51 -0:43:24
Sterzing → Vipiteno
1 46N54 11E26 -0:45:44
Stezzano 1 45N38 9E39 -0:38:36
Stia 1 43N48 11E42 -0:46:48
Stigliano 2 40N24 16E14 -1:04:56
Stilo 2 38N29 16E28 -1:05:52
Stimigliano 1 42N18 12E34 -0:50:16
Stintino 4 40N56 8E13 -0:32:52
Stornara 2 41N17 15E46 -1:03:04
Stornarella 2 41N15 15E44 -1:02:56
Storo 1 45N51 10E35 -0:42:20
Stra 1 45N25 12E00 -0:48:00
Stradella 1 45N05 9E18 -0:37:12
Strambino 1 45N23 7E53 -0:31:32
Stravignano 1 43N05 12E49 -0:51:16
Strembo 1 46N09 10E44 -0:42:56
Stresa 1 45N53 8E32 -0:34:08
Strigno 1 46N04 11E31 -0:46:04
Strongoli 2 39N15 17E03 -1:08:12
Stroppiana 1 45N14 8E27 -0:33:48
Sturla 1 44N24 8E59 -0:35:56
Subbiano 1 43N34 11E52 -0:47:28
Subiaco 1 41N55 13E06 -0:52:24
Sulmona 1 42N03 13E55 -0:55:40
Sulzano 1 45N41 10E05 -0:40:20
Suni 4 40N17 8E33 -0:34:12
Supersano 2 40N01 18E14 -1:12:56
Supino 2 41N37 13E14 -0:52:56
Surbo 2 40N24 18E08 -1:12:32
Susa 1 45N08 7E03 -0:28:12
Susegana 1 45N51 12E15 -0:49:00
Sutera 3 37N31 13E44 -0:54:56
Sutri 1 42N14 12E13 -0:48:52
Sutrio 1 46N31 12E59 -0:51:56
Suvereto 1 43N05 10E40 -0:42:40
Suzzara 1 45N00 10E45 -0:43:00
Syracuse → Siracusa
3 37N04 15E18 -1:01:12
Tabiano Terme 1 44N48 10E21 -0:41:24
Taceno 1 46N02 9E21 -0:37:24

Place	Zone	Lat.	Long.	Time
Tadasuni	4	40N06	8E53	-0:35:32
Taggia	1	43N52	7E51	-0:31:24
Tagliacozzo	1	42N04	13E14	-0:52:56
Taglio di Po	1	45N00	12E12	-0:48:48
Tai	1	46N25	12E20	-0:49:20
Taibon Agordino	1	46N18	12E00	-0:48:00
Taio	1	46N20	11E04	-0:44:16
Talamone	1	42N33	11E08	-0:44:32
Talana	4	40N02	9E30	-0:38:00
Taormina	3	37N51	15E17	-1:01:08
Taranta Peligna	1	42N01	14E10	-0:56:40
Taranto	2	40N28	17E15	-1:09:00
Tarcento	1	46N13	13E13	-0:52:52
Tarquinia	1	42N15	11E45	-0:47:00
Tarvisio	1	46N30	13E35	-0:54:20
Tarzo	1	45N58	12E14	-0:48:56
Taurasi	2	41N00	14E57	-0:59:48
Taurianova	2	38N21	16E01	-1:04:04
Taurisano	2	39N57	18E13	-1:12:52
Tavarnelle Val di Pesa	1	43N33	11E10	-0:44:40
Taverna	2	39N01	16E35	-1:06:20
Tavernelle	1	43N00	12E09	-0:48:36
Tavernelle	1	44N18	10E04	-0:40:16
Tavernole sul Mella	1	45N45	10E14	-0:40:56
Taviano	2	39N59	18E05	-1:12:20
Teano	2	41N15	14E04	-0:56:16
Teggiano	2	40N23	15E32	-1:02:08
Teglio	1	46N10	10E04	-0:40:16
Telese	2	41N13	14E32	-0:58:08
Telti	4	40N52	9E21	-0:37:24
Tempio Pausania	4	40N54	9E06	-0:36:24
Temù	1	46N15	10E28	-0:41:52
Tenno	1	45N55	10E49	-0:43:16
Teolo	1	45N21	11E40	-0:46:40
Teor	1	45N51	13E03	-0:52:12
Teora	2	40N51	15E15	-1:01:00
Teramo	1	42N39	13E42	-0:54:48
Terlago	1	46N06	11E02	-0:44:08
Terlano	1	46N32	11E15	-0:45:00
Terlizzi	2	41N08	16E32	-1:06:08
Terme del Brennero (Brennerbad)	1	46N58	11E29	-0:45:56
Terme di Stigliano	1	42N09	12E01	-0:48:04
Terme di Suio	2	41N18	13E51	-0:55:24
Terme di Valdieri	1	44N12	7E16	-0:29:04
Termeno (Tramin)	1	46N20	11E14	-0:44:56
Termini Imerese	3	37N59	13E42	-0:54:48
Termoli	2	42N00	15E00	-1:00:00
Terni	1	42N34	12E37	-0:50:28
Terontola	1	43N13	12E02	-0:48:08
Terracina	2	41N17	13E15	-0:53:00
Terra del Sole	1	44N11	11E57	-0:47:48
Terralba	4	39N43	8E39	-0:34:36
Terranova da Sibari	2	39N39	16E20	-1:05:20
Terranova di Pollino	2	39N59	16E18	-1:05:12
Terranova di Sicilia → Gela	3	37N04	14E15	-0:57:00
Terranuova Bracciolini	1	43N33	11E35	-0:46:20
Terrasini	3	38N09	13E05	-0:52:20
Terravecchia	2	39N29	16E58	-1:07:52
Tertenia	4	39N42	9E34	-0:38:16
Terzigno	2	40N48	14E29	-0:57:56
Tesero	1	46N17	11E31	-0:46:04
Tesimo (Tisens)	1	46N34	11E10	-0:44:40
Teulada	4	38N58	8E46	-0:35:04
Thiene	1	45N42	11E29	-0:45:56
Thiesi	4	40N31	8E43	-0:34:52
Tiana	4	40N04	9E08	-0:36:32
Tiarno	1	45N53	10E40	-0:42:40
Tignale	1	45N44	10E44	-0:42:56
Timau	1	46N35	13E00	-0:52:00
Timavo San Giovanni	1	45N48	13E37	-0:54:28
Tione di Trento	1	46N02	10E43	-0:42:52
Tirano	1	46N13	10E10	-0:40:40
Tires (Tiers)	1	46N28	11E31	-0:46:04
Tirolo (Tirol)	1	46N42	11E10	-0:44:40
Tirrenia	1	43N38	10E17	-0:41:08
Tito	2	40N35	15E40	-1:02:40
Tivoli	1	41N58	12E48	-0:51:12
Toano	1	44N23	10E34	-0:42:16
Toblach → Dobbiaco	1	46N44	12E14	-0:48:56
Todi	1	42N47	12E24	-0:49:36
Tolentino	1	43N12	13E17	-0:53:08
Tolfa	1	42N09	11E56	-0:47:44
Tolmezzo	1	46N24	13E01	-0:52:04
Tolve	2	40N42	16E01	-1:04:04
Tombolo	1	45N38	11E50	-0:47:20
Ton	1	46N15	11E04	-0:44:16
Tonadico	1	46N11	11E50	-0:47:20
Tonara	4	40N02	9E10	-0:36:40
Torano Castello	2	39N30	16E08	-1:04:32
Torbole	1	45N52	10E52	-0:43:28
Torchiarolo	2	40N29	18E03	-1:12:12
Torino (Turin)	1	45N03	7E40	-0:30:40
Torino di Sangro Marina	1	42N11	14E32	-0:58:08
Toritto	2	41N00	16E41	-1:06:44
Tormini	1	45N36	10E29	-0:41:56
Tornareccio	1	42N02	14E24	-0:57:36
Tornimparte	1	42N17	13E18	-0:53:12
Torpè	4	40N38	9E40	-0:38:40
Torraca	2	40N07	15E38	-1:02:32
Torre Annunziata	2	40N45	14E27	-0:57:48
Torrebelvicino	1	45N43	11E18	-0:45:12
Torre Beretti	1	45N04	8E40	-0:34:40
Torrebruna	1	41N52	14E33	-0:58:12
Torre del Greco	2	40N47	14E22	-0:57:28
Torre del Lago Puccini	1	43N50	10E17	-0:41:08
Torre de'Passeri	1	42N14	13E56	-0:55:44
Torre di Mosto	1	45N41	12E43	-0:50:52
Torre di Santa Maria	1	46N14	9E51	-0:39:24
Torregrotta	3	38N11	15E21	-1:01:24
Torremaggiore	2	41N41	15E17	-1:01:08
Torrenieri	1	43N05	11E33	-0:46:12
Torre Orsaia	2	40N08	15E28	-1:01:52
Torre Pedrera	1	44N06	12E31	-0:50:04
Torre Pellice	1	44N49	7E13	-0:28:52
Torre Santa Susanna	2	40N28	17E44	-1:10:56
Torretta	3	38N08	13E14	-0:52:56
Torrette di Fano	1	43N47	13E07	-0:52:28
Torricella	2	40N21	17E29	-1:09:56
Torricella in Sabina	1	42N16	12E52	-0:51:28
Torricella Peligna	1	42N01	14E15	-0:57:00
Torricella Sicura	1	42N39	13E39	-0:54:36
Torriglia	1	44N31	9E10	-0:36:40
Torrita di Siena	1	43N10	11E46	-0:47:04
Tortolì	4	39N55	9E39	-0:38:36
Tortona	1	44N54	8E52	-0:35:28
Tortora	2	39N56	15E48	-1:03:12
Tortoreto	1	42N48	13E55	-0:55:40
Tortorici	3	38N02	14E49	-0:59:16
Toscolano	1	45N38	10E37	-0:42:28
Tosi	1	43N45	11E31	-0:46:04
Tossicia	1	42N33	13E39	-0:54:36
Trabia	3	37N59	13E39	-0:54:36
Tradate	1	45N43	8E54	-0:35:36
Trafoi	1	46N33	10E31	-0:42:04
Tramatza	4	40N00	8E39	-0:34:36
Tramin → Termeno	1	46N20	11E14	-0:44:56
Tramonti di sopra	1	46N18	12E47	-0:51:08
Tramutola	2	40N19	15E47	-1:03:08
Trani	2	41N17	16E26	-1:05:44
Traona	1	46N09	9E31	-0:38:04
Trapani	3	38N01	12E29	-0:49:56
Trappeto	3	38N04	13E03	-0:52:12
Trasacco	1	41N57	13E32	-0:54:08
Tratalias	4	39N06	8E34	-0:34:16
Travagliato	1	45N31	10E05	-0:40:20
Travedona	1	45N48	8E40	-0:34:40
Traversella	1	45N30	7E45	-0:31:00
Traversetolo	1	44N38	10E23	-0:41:32
Trebisacce	2	39N52	16E32	-1:06:08
Trecastagni	3	37N37	15E05	-1:00:20
Trecate	1	45N26	8E44	-0:34:56
Trecchina	2	40N02	15E46	-1:03:04
Trecenta	1	45N02	11E28	-0:45:52
Tregnago	1	45N31	11E10	-0:44:40
Treia	1	43N19	13E19	-0:53:16
Tremezzo	1	45N59	9E15	-0:37:00
Trent → Trento	1	46N04	11E08	-0:44:32
Trento	1	46N04	11E08	-0:44:32
Trentola-Ducenta	2	40N59	14E10	-0:56:40
Trepalade	1	45N34	12E24	-0:49:36
Trepuzzi	2	40N24	18E05	-1:12:20
Trequanda	1	43N11	11E40	-0:46:40
Trescore Balneario	1	45N41	9E50	-0:39:20
Tresenda	1	46N10	10E05	-0:40:20
Tresnuraghes	4	40N15	8E31	-0:34:04
Trevi	1	42N52	12E45	-0:51:00
Treviglio	1	45N31	9E35	-0:38:20
Trevignano Romano	1	42N09	12E15	-0:49:00
Treviso	1	45N40	12E15	-0:49:00
Trezzano	1	45N25	9E04	-0:36:16
Trezzo sull'Adda	1	45N36	9E31	-0:38:04
Triana	1	42N47	11E33	-0:46:12
Tricarico	2	40N37	16E09	-1:04:36
Tricase	2	39N56	18E22	-1:13:28
Tricesimo	1	46N10	13E13	-0:52:52
Trichiana	1	46N05	12E07	-0:48:28
Trient → Trento	1	46N04	11E08	-0:44:32
Trieste (Triest)	1	45N40	13E46	-0:55:04
Triggiano	2	41N04	16E55	-1:07:40
Trinità	1	44N30	7E45	-0:31:00
Trinità d'agultu	4	40N59	8E54	-0:35:36
Trinitapoli	2	41N21	16E05	-1:04:20
Trino	1	45N12	8E18	-0:33:12
Triora	1	43N59	7E46	-0:31:04
Tripi	3	38N03	15E06	-1:00:24
Triponzo	1	42N50	12E56	-0:51:44
Triuggio	1	45N40	9E16	-0:37:04
Trivento	1	41N47	14E33	-0:58:12
Trivero	1	45N40	8E10	-0:32:40
Trivigno	2	40N35	15E59	-1:03:56
Trofarello	1	44N59	7E44	-0:30:56
Troia	2	41N22	15E18	-1:01:12
Troina	3	37N47	14E36	-0:58:24
Tromello	1	45N12	8E52	-0:35:28
Tronzano Vercellese	1	45N21	8E10	-0:32:40
Tropea	2	38N41	15E54	-1:03:36
Trst → Trieste	1	45N40	13E46	-0:55:04
Tubre	1	46N39	10E27	-0:41:48
Tuenno	1	46N20	11E01	-0:44:04
Tufo	2	41N00	14E47	-0:59:08
Tuglie	2	40N04	18E05	-1:12:20
Tula	4	40N44	8E59	-0:35:56
Turate	1	45N39	9E00	-0:36:00
Turbigo	1	45N32	8E44	-0:34:56
Turi	2	40N55	17E01	-1:08:04
Turin → Torino	1	45N03	7E40	-0:30:40
Turriaco	1	45N49	13E26	-0:53:44
Tursi	2	40N15	16E28	-1:05:52
Tusa	3	37N59	14E14	-0:56:56
Tuscania	1	42N25	11E52	-0:47:28
Uboldo	1	45N37	9E00	-0:36:00
Ucria	3	38N03	14E53	-0:59:32
Udine	1	46N03	13E14	-0:52:56
Ugento	2	39N56	18E10	-1:12:40
Uggiano la Chiesa	2	40N06	18E27	-1:13:48
Ugovizza	1	46N31	13E29	-0:53:56
Umbertide	1	43N18	12E20	-0:49:20
Umbriatico	2	39N21	16E55	-1:07:40
Unserfrau → Madonna	1	46N43	10E52	-0:43:28
Uras	4	39N42	8E42	-0:34:48
Urbania	1	43N40	12E31	-0:50:04
Urbe	1	44N29	8E36	-0:34:24
Urbino	1	43N43	12E38	-0:50:32
Urbisaglia	1	43N12	13E23	-0:53:32
Urgnano	1	45N35	9E41	-0:38:44
Uri	4	40N38	8E29	-0:33:56
Urzulei	4	40N06	9E30	-0:38:00
Uscio	1	44N25	9E10	-0:36:40
Usellus	4	39N48	8E51	-0:35:24
Usini	4	40N40	8E32	-0:34:08
Usmate Velate	1	45N39	9E21	-0:37:24
Ussassai	4	39N49	9E23	-0:37:32
Usseglio	1	45N14	7E13	-0:28:52
Ustica	3	38N42	13E11	-0:52:44
Uta	4	39N17	8E57	-0:35:48
Vado Ligure	1	44N17	8E27	-0:33:48
Vaglia	1	43N54	11E17	-0:45:08
Vaglio Basilicata	2	40N40	15E55	-1:03:40
Vaiano	1	43N58	11E07	-0:44:28
Vairano Scalo	2	41N20	14E08	-0:56:32
Valbondione	1	46N02	10E00	-0:40:00
Valchiusella	1	45N32	7E42	-0:30:48
Valdagno	1	45N39	11E18	-0:45:12
Valderice	3	38N03	12E38	-0:50:32
Valdieri	1	44N17	7E24	-0:29:36
Valdobbiadene	1	45N54	12E00	-0:48:00
Valdurna (Durnholz)	1	46N44	11E26	-0:45:44
Valeggio sul Mincio	1	45N21	10E44	-0:42:56
Valentano	1	42N34	11E49	-0:47:16
Valenza	1	45N01	8E38	-0:34:32
Valenzano	2	41N02	16E53	-1:07:32
Valfabbrica	1	43N09	12E36	-0:50:24
Valfurva	1	46N27	10E25	-0:41:40
Valgrisanche	1	45N38	7E04	-0:28:16
Valguarnera Caropepe	3	37N30	14E23	-0:57:32
Vallarsa	1	45N47	11E07	-0:44:28
Vallata	2	41N02	15E15	-1:01:00
Valle	1	46N04	10E25	-0:41:40
Valle Castellana	1	42N44	13E29	-0:53:56
Vallecorsa	2	41N27	13E24	-0:53:36
Valle di Cadore	1	46N24	12E20	-0:49:20
Valle di Sotto	1	46N25	10E21	-0:41:24
Valledolmo	3	37N45	13E49	-0:55:16
Vallefiorita	2	38N46	16E27	-1:05:48
Valle Lomellina	1	45N09	8E40	-0:34:40
Vallelunga Pratameno	3	37N41	13E50	-0:55:20
Valle Mosso	1	45N38	8E09	-0:32:36
Vallepietra	1	41N55	13E14	-0:52:56
Vallerotonda	2	41N33	13E55	-0:55:40
Valli del Pasubio	1	45N41	11E15	-0:45:00
Vallio	1	45N38	10E23	-0:41:32
Vallo della Lucania	2	40N14	15E17	-1:01:08
Vallombrosa	1	43N44	11E32	-0:46:08
Valmontone	1	41N46	12E57	-0:51:48
Valprato Soana	1	45N31	7E33	-0:30:12
Valsinni	2	40N10	16E26	-1:05:44
Valstagna	1	45N51	11E39	-0:46:36
Valtorta	1	45N59	9E32	-0:38:08
Valtournanche	1	45N53	7E37	-0:30:28
Valvasone	1	45N59	12E52	-0:51:28
Vandoies (Vintl)	1	46N49	11E43	-0:46:52
Vanzaghello	1	45N35	8E47	-0:35:08
Vanzago	1	45N32	9E00	-0:36:00
Vaprio d'Adda	1	45N35	9E31	-0:38:04
Varallo	1	45N49	8E15	-0:33:00
Varallo	1	45N40	8E38	-0:34:32
Varano de'Melegari	1	44N41	10E01	-0:40:04
Varapodio	2	38N19	15E59	-1:03:56
Varazze	1	44N22	8E34	-0:34:16
Varedo	1	45N36	9E09	-0:36:36
Varenna	1	46N01	9E17	-0:37:08
Varese	1	45N48	8E48	-0:35:12
Varese Ligure	1	44N22	9E37	-0:38:28
Varigotti	1	44N11	8E24	-0:33:36
Varna (Vahrn)	1	46N44	11E38	-0:46:32
Varsi	1	44N40	9E51	-0:39:24
Varzi	1	44N49	9E12	-0:36:48
Varzo	1	46N12	8E15	-0:33:00
Vas	1	45N56	11E56	-0:47:44
Vasto	2	42N07	14E42	-0:58:48

ITALY ITALIE ITALIEN ITALIA

Place	Zone	Lat	Long	Offset
Vatican (Cité du)	1	41N54	12E27	-0:49:48
Vatican City	1	41N54	12E27	-0:49:48
Vatikanstadt	1	41N54	12E27	-0:49:48
Vazzola	1	45N50	12E23	-0:49:32
Vecchiano	1	43N47	10E23	-0:41:32
Vedano al Lambro	1	45N37	9E16	-0:37:04
Vedano Olona	1	45N46	8E53	-0:35:32
Vedelago	1	45N41	12E01	-0:48:04
Vedeseta	1	45N53	9E32	-0:38:08
Veglie	2	40N20	17E58	-1:11:52
Vellano	1	43N57	10E43	-0:42:52
Velletri	1	41N41	12E47	-0:51:08
Velo d'Astico	1	45N43	11E23	-0:45:32
Velva	1	44N16	9E33	-0:38:12
Venafro	2	41N29	14E02	-0:56:08
Venalzio	1	45N09	7E01	-0:28:04
Venaria	1	45N08	7E38	-0:30:32
Venasca	1	44N33	7E24	-0:29:36
Venecia → Venezia	1	45N27	12E21	-0:49:24
Venedig → Venezia	1	45N27	12E21	-0:49:24
Venezia (Venice)	1	45N27	12E21	-0:49:24
Venice → Venezia	1	45N27	12E21	-0:49:24
Venise → Venezia	1	45N27	12E21	-0:49:24
Venosa	2	40N57	15E49	-1:03:16
Venticano	2	41N05	14E50	-0:59:20
Ventimiglia	1	43N47	7E36	-0:30:24
Ventimiglia di Sicilia	3	37N55	13E34	-0:54:16
Ventotene	2	40N48	13E26	-0:53:44
Venturina	1	43N02	10E36	-0:42:24
Venzone	1	46N20	13E09	-0:52:36
Verano Brianza	1	45N41	9E14	-0:36:56
Verbania	1	45N56	8E33	-0:34:12
Verbicaro	2	39N45	15E55	-1:03:40
Vercelli	1	45N19	8E25	-0:33:40
Verdello	1	45N36	9E37	-0:38:28
Vergato	1	44N17	11E07	-0:44:28
Verghereto	1	43N47	12E00	-0:48:00
Vergiate	1	45N43	8E42	-0:34:48
Vermezzo	1	45N24	8E59	-0:35:56
Vermiglio	1	46N18	10E42	-0:42:48
Vernante	1	44N15	7E32	-0:30:08
Vernazza	1	44N08	9E41	-0:38:44
Vernio	1	44N03	11E09	-0:44:36
Vernole	2	40N17	18E18	-1:13:12
Verolanuova	1	45N19	10E04	-0:40:16
Verolavecchia	1	45N19	10E03	-0:40:12
Veroli	1	41N41	13E25	-0:53:40
Verona	1	45N27	11E00	-0:44:00
Verrès	1	45N40	7E42	-0:30:48
Vertova	1	45N48	9E50	-0:39:20
Verucchio	1	43N59	12E25	-0:49:40
Verzegnis	1	46N25	12E59	-0:51:56
Verzino	2	39N19	16E51	-1:07:24
Verzuolo	1	44N36	7E29	-0:29:56
Vescovato	1	45N10	10E10	-0:40:40
Vespolate	1	45N21	8E40	-0:34:40
Vestone	1	45N42	10E24	-0:41:36
Vestreno	1	46N06	9E18	-0:37:12
Vesuvius	2	40N49	14E26	-0:57:44
Vetralla	1	42N19	12E03	-0:48:12
Vetriolo	1	46N02	11E18	-0:45:12
Vetto	1	44N29	10E20	-0:41:20
Vetulonia	1	42N51	10E58	-0:43:52
Vezza d'Oglio	1	46N14	10E24	-0:41:36
Vezzano	1	46N05	11E00	-0:44:00
Vezzano Ligure	1	44N09	9E52	-0:39:28
Viadana	1	44N56	10E31	-0:42:04
Viareggio	1	43N52	10E14	-0:40:56
Vibo Valentia	2	38N40	16E06	-1:04:24
Vicarello	1	42N10	12E12	-0:48:48
Vicari	3	37N49	13E34	-0:54:16
Vicchio	1	43N56	11E28	-0:45:52
Vicenza	1	45N33	11E33	-0:46:12
Vico Canavese	1	45N30	7E47	-0:31:08
Vico del Gargano	2	41N54	15E57	-1:03:48
Vico Equense	2	40N40	14E25	-0:57:40
Vicoforte	1	44N21	7E54	-0:31:36
Vicopisano	1	43N42	10E35	-0:42:20
Vicovaro	1	42N01	12E54	-0:51:36
Vieste	2	41N53	16E10	-1:04:40
Vietri di Potenza	2	40N36	15E30	-1:02:00
Vietri sul Mare	2	40N40	14E44	-0:58:56
Vigarano Mainarda	1	44N50	11E30	-0:46:00
Vigatto	1	44N43	10E20	-0:41:20
Vigevano	1	45N19	8E51	-0:35:24
Viggianello	2	39N58	16E05	-1:04:20
Viggiano	2	40N20	15E54	-1:03:36
Viggiù	1	45N52	8E54	-0:35:36
Vignale	1	45N01	8E24	-0:33:36
Vignanello	1	42N23	12E17	-0:49:08
Vignola	1	44N29	11E00	-0:44:00
Vigodarzere	1	45N27	11E53	-0:47:32
Vigo di Fassa	1	46N25	11E40	-0:46:40
Vigolzone	1	44N55	9E40	-0:38:40
Vigone	1	44N51	7E30	-0:30:00
Vigonovo	1	45N23	12E00	-0:48:00
Vigo-Rendena	1	46N05	10E43	-0:42:52
Viguzzolo	1	44N54	8E55	-0:35:40
Villabassa (Niederdorf)	1	46N44	12E10	-0:48:40
Villabate	3	38N04	13E26	-0:53:44
Villa Castelli	2	40N35	17E28	-1:09:52
Villacidro	4	39N27	8E44	-0:34:56
Villa Cortese	1	45N34	8E53	-0:35:32
Villadeati	1	45N04	8E10	-0:32:40
Villa di Chiavenna	1	46N20	9E29	-0:37:56
Villadose	1	45N04	11E53	-0:47:32
Villadossola	1	46N04	8E16	-0:33:04
Villafranca d'Asti	1	44N55	8E02	-0:32:08
Villafranca di Verona	1	45N21	10E50	-0:43:20
Villafranca in Lunigiana	1	44N17	9E57	-0:39:48
Villafranca Piemonte	1	44N47	7E33	-0:30:12
Villafranca Sicula	3	37N35	13E17	-0:53:08
Villafranca Tirrena	3	38N14	15E26	-1:01:44
Villafrati	3	37N54	13E29	-0:53:56
Villagrande Strisaili	4	39N58	9E30	-0:38:00
Villa Grazia	3	38N09	13E10	-0:52:40
Villa Lagarina	1	45N55	11E01	-0:44:04
Villalago	1	41N56	13E50	-0:55:20
Villalba	3	37N39	13E50	-0:55:20
Villalvernia	1	44N49	8E51	-0:35:24
Villamar	4	39N37	8E59	-0:35:56
Villamarzana	1	45N01	11E41	-0:46:44
Villamassargia	4	39N16	8E38	-0:34:32
Villa Minozzo	1	44N22	10E28	-0:41:52
Villanova d'Asti	1	44N57	7E56	-0:31:44
Villanova Mondovì	1	44N21	7E45	-0:31:00
Villanova Monferrato	1	45N11	8E28	-0:33:52
Villanova Monteleone	4	40N30	8E28	-0:33:52
Villanova sull'Arda	1	45N01	10E00	-0:40:00
Villanova Tulo	4	39N47	9E13	-0:36:52
Villa Opicina	1	45N40	13E49	-0:55:16
Villa Ottone (Uttenheim)	1	46N52	11E57	-0:47:48
Villapiana	2	39N51	16E28	-1:05:52
Villapiana Lido	2	39N48	16E29	-1:05:56
Villa Potenza	1	43N19	13E25	-0:53:40
Villaputzu	4	39N26	9E34	-0:38:16
Villarosa	3	37N35	14E10	-0:56:40
Villar Pellice	1	44N48	7E09	-0:28:36
Villar Perosa	1	44N56	7E15	-0:29:00
Villa San Giovanni	2	38N13	15E38	-1:02:32
Villasanta	1	45N37	9E18	-0:37:12
Villa Santa Maria	1	41N57	14E21	-0:57:24
Villa Santina	1	46N24	12E55	-0:51:40
Villasimius	4	39N08	9E31	-0:38:04
Villasor	4	39N23	8E56	-0:35:44
Villa Vallelonga	1	41N52	13E37	-0:54:28
Villaverla	1	45N39	11E29	-0:45:56
Villa Vomano	1	42N37	13E46	-0:55:04
Villeneuve	1	45N42	7E14	-0:28:56
Villetta Barrea	1	41N47	13E56	-0:55:44
Villorba	1	45N44	12E14	-0:48:56
Villotta	1	45N52	12E45	-0:51:00
Vimercate	1	45N37	9E22	-0:37:28
Vimodrone	1	45N31	9E17	-0:37:08
Vinadio	1	44N18	7E10	-0:28:40
Vinchiaturo	2	41N29	14E35	-0:58:20
Vinci	1	43N47	10E55	-0:43:40
Vinovo	1	44N57	7E38	-0:30:32
Vipiteno (Sterzing)	1	46N54	11E26	-0:45:44
Virgilio	1	45N07	10E47	-0:43:08
Viserba	1	44N05	12E32	-0:50:08
Visso	1	42N56	13E05	-0:52:20
Vita	3	37N52	12E49	-0:51:16
Viterbo	1	42N25	12E06	-0:48:24
Vittoria	3	36N57	14E32	-0:58:08
Vittorio Veneto	1	45N59	12E18	-0:49:12
Vitulano	2	41N10	14E38	-0:58:32
Viù	1	45N14	7E22	-0:29:28
Vizzini	3	37N09	14E46	-0:59:04
Vizzola	1	45N38	8E42	-0:34:48
Vobarno	1	45N39	10E30	-0:42:00
Vodo	1	46N25	12E14	-0:48:56
Voghera	1	44N59	9E01	-0:36:04
Vogogna	1	46N01	8E17	-0:33:08
Volano	1	45N55	11E03	-0:44:12
Volpago del Montello	1	45N47	12E07	-0:48:28
Volpedo	1	44N53	8E59	-0:35:56
Volpiano	1	45N12	7E46	-0:31:04
Völs → Fiè	1	46N31	11E30	-0:46:00
Voltaggio	1	44N37	8E50	-0:35:20
Voltago	1	46N16	12E00	-0:48:00
Volta Mantovana	1	45N19	10E39	-0:42:36
Volterra	1	43N24	10E51	-0:43:24
Voltri	1	44N26	8E45	-0:35:00
Volturara Appula	2	41N30	15E03	-1:00:12
Volturara Irpina	2	40N53	14E55	-0:59:40
Volturino	2	41N28	15E07	-1:00:28
Waidbruck → Ponte Gardena	1	46N36	11E32	-0:46:08
Welsberg → Monguelfo	1	46N45	12E06	-0:48:24
Zafferana Etnea	3	37N41	15E06	-1:00:24
Zagarise	2	39N00	16E39	-1:06:36
Zagarolo	1	41N50	12E50	-0:51:20
Zambrone	2	38N42	15E59	-1:03:56
Zelo Surrigone	1	45N23	8E59	-0:35:56
Zenna	1	46N06	8E45	-0:35:00
Zenson di Piave	1	45N41	12E29	-0:49:56
Zeri	1	44N21	9E46	-0:39:04
Zevio	1	45N22	11E08	-0:44:32
Ziano	1	46N17	11E34	-0:46:16
Zimella	1	45N20	11E22	-0:45:28
Zoagli	1	44N20	9E16	-0:37:04
Zocca	1	44N21	10E59	-0:43:56
Zogno	1	45N48	9E40	-0:38:40
Zola Predosa	1	44N29	11E12	-0:44:48
Zoldo Alto	1	46N22	12E06	-0:48:24
Zuccarello	1	44N07	8E07	-0:32:28
Zuel	1	46N31	12E08	-0:48:32
Zungri	2	38N39	15E59	-1:03:56

IVORY COAST COSTA DE MARFIL ELFENBEINKÜSTE CÔTE D'IVOIRE

Time Table
Before 1/Jan/1912 LMT
Begin Standard 0W00
1/Jan/1912 0:00 0:00

Place	Lat	Long	Offset
Abengourou	6N44	3W29	0:13:56
Abidjan	5N19	4W02	0:16:08
Aboisso	5N28	3W12	0:12:48
Adiaké	5N16	3W17	0:13:08
Adzopé	6N06	3W52	0:15:28
Afféry	6N19	3W57	0:15:48
Agboville	5N56	4W13	0:16:52
Agnibilékrou	7N08	3W12	0:12:48
Akoupé	6N23	3W54	0:15:36
Ananda	7N17	4W16	0:17:04
Anyama	5N30	4W03	0:16:12
Arra	6N40	3W58	0:15:52
Arrah	6N40	3W58	0:15:52
Ayamé	5N37	3W11	0:12:44
Bako	9N09	7W37	0:30:28
Bangolo	7N01	7W29	0:29:56
Béoumi	7N40	5W34	0:22:16
Biankouma	7N44	7W37	0:30:28
Bingerville	5N21	3W54	0:15:36
Bin-Houyé	6N47	8W19	0:33:16
Bocanda	7N04	4W30	0:18:00
Bondoukou	8N02	2W48	0:11:12
Bongouanou	6N39	4W12	0:16:48
Bonoua	5N16	3W36	0:14:24
Borotou	8N44	7W30	0:30:00
Botro	7N51	5W19	0:21:16
Bouaflé	6N59	5W45	0:23:00
Bouaké	7N41	5W02	0:20:08
Bouandougou	8N13	5W40	0:22:40
Bouna	9N16	3W00	0:12:00
Boundiali	9N31	6W29	0:25:56
Brobo	7N43	4W42	0:18:48
Buyo	6N16	7W03	0:28:12
Bwandougou	8N13	5W40	0:22:40
Dabakala	8N22	4W26	0:17:44
Dabou	5N19	4W23	0:17:32
Daloa	6N53	6W27	0:25:48
Danané	7N16	8W09	0:32:36
Daoukro	7N03	3W58	0:15:52

CÔTE D'IVOIRE — ELFENBEINKÜSTE — COSTA DE MARFIL — IVORY COAST

Place	Lat	Long	Time
Diabo	7N47	5w11	0:20:44
Dianra	8N45	6w14	0:24:56
Diaouala	10N07	5w28	0:21:52
Diawala	10N07	5w28	0:21:52
Dikodougou	9N04	5w46	0:23:04
Dimbokro	6N39	4w42	0:18:48
Divo	5N50	5w22	0:21:28
Duékoué	6N45	7w21	0:29:24
Ferkéssédougou	9N36	5w12	0:20:48
Fresco	5N05	5w34	0:22:16
Gagnoa	6N08	5w56	0:23:44
Ganwé	8N11	7w51	0:31:24
Gbon	9N50	6w27	0:25:48
Gohitafla	7N30	5w53	0:23:32
Goulia	10N01	7w11	0:28:44
Grabo	4N55	7w30	0:30:00
Grand Aféri	6N19	3w57	0:15:48
Grand-Bassam	5N12	3w44	0:14:56
Grand-Lahou	5N08	5w01	0:20:04
Grand Morié	5N59	4w08	0:16:32
Gregbe	6N48	6w43	0:26:52
Guéyo	5N49	6w36	0:26:24
Guibéroua	6N14	6w10	0:24:40
Guiglo	6N33	7w29	0:29:56
Guitri	5N31	5w14	0:20:56
Guitry	5N31	5w14	0:20:56
Issia	6N29	6w35	0:26:20
Jacqueville	5N12	4w25	0:17:40
Kani	8N29	6w36	0:26:24
Katiola	8N08	5w06	0:20:24
Kokolopozo	5N08	6w05	0:24:20
Kolia	9N46	6w28	0:25:52
Konan	8N21	8w00	0:32:00
Kong	9N09	4w37	0:18:28
Korhogo	9N27	5w38	0:22:32
Koro	8N34	7w28	0:29:52
Kotouba	8N41	3w12	0:12:48
Kouassi-Datékro	7N49	3w31	0:14:04
Koun	7N29	3w15	0:13:00
Koun-Fao	7N29	3w15	0:13:00
Kouto	9N53	6w25	0:25:40
Koutouba	8N41	3w12	0:12:48
Lakota	5N51	5w41	0:22:44
Logoualé	7N07	7w33	0:30:12
Madam	7N58	3w32	0:14:08
Madinani	9N37	6w57	0:27:48
Maminigui	7N24	5w50	0:23:20
Man	7N24	7w33	0:30:12
Manignan	10N00	7w50	0:31:20
Maninian	10N00	7w50	0:31:20
Mankono	8N04	6w12	0:24:48
Mbahiakro	7N27	4w20	0:17:20
Mbatto	6N28	4w22	0:17:28
M'bengué	10N00	5w54	0:23:36
Mbingué	10N00	5w54	0:23:36
Napiéolédougou	9N18	5w35	0:22:20
Nassian	8N27	3w29	0:13:56
Ndouci	5N52	4w46	0:19:04
Niakaramandougou	8N40	5w17	0:21:08
Niélé	10N12	5w38	0:22:32
Nielle	10N12	5w38	0:22:32
Odienné	9N30	7w34	0:30:16
Ouangolodougou	9N58	5w09	0:20:36
Ouaninou	8N11	7w51	0:31:24
Ouellé	7N18	4w01	0:16:04
Ouergayo	6N19	5w56	0:23:44
Oumé	6N23	5w25	0:21:40
Ouragahio	6N19	5w56	0:23:44
Pakouabo	7N10	5w48	0:23:12
Port-Bouët	5N15	3w58	0:15:52
Prikro	7N39	3w59	0:15:56
Sakasso	7N27	5w18	0:21:12
Sakassou	7N27	5w18	0:21:12
Sanhala	10N03	6w51	0:27:24
San Pédro	4N44	6w37	0:26:28
Sassandra	4N58	6w05	0:24:20
Ségélo-Koro	9N25	7w09	0:28:36
Séguéla	7N57	6w40	0:26:40
Séguélon	9N25	7w09	0:28:36
Sianhala	10N03	6w51	0:27:24
Sifié	7N59	6w55	0:27:40
Sikensi	5N40	4w34	0:18:16
Sikinssi	5N40	4w34	0:18:16
Sinfra	6N37	5w55	0:23:40
Sirasso	9N16	6w06	0:24:24
Soubré	5N47	6w36	0:26:24
Souroukaha	8N13	5w08	0:20:32
Tabou	4N25	7w21	0:29:24
Tafiré	9N04	5w10	0:20:40
Taï	5N52	7w27	0:29:48
Tanda	7N48	3w10	0:12:40
Téhini	9N36	3w40	0:14:40
Tengréla	10N29	6w24	0:25:36
Tiassalé	5N54	4w50	0:19:20
Tiébissou	7N10	5w13	0:20:52
Tiémé	9N33	7w19	0:29:16
Tiénigbé	8N11	5w43	0:22:52
Tiénigboué	8N11	5w43	0:22:52
Tienko	10N14	7w29	0:29:56
Tingréla	10N29	6w24	0:25:36
Tioroniaradougou	9N21	5w38	0:22:32
Touba	8N17	7w41	0:30:44
Toulépleu	6N35	8w25	0:33:40
Toumodi	6N33	5w01	0:20:04
Tyémé	9N33	7w19	0:29:16
Tyoronyaradougou	9N21	5w38	0:22:32
Vavoua	7N23	6w29	0:25:56
Yamoussoukro	6N49	5w17	0:21:08
Zouan-Hounien	6N55	8w13	0:32:52
Zuénoula	7N26	6w03	0:24:12

JAMAÏQUE — JAMAIKA — JAMAICA

Time Table
Before 1/Jan/1890 LMT
Begin Standard 76w48
1/Jan/1890 0:00 5:07
Begin Standard 75w00
1/Feb/1912 0:00 5:00

Date	Time	Offset
6/Jan/1974	2:00	4:00
27/Oct/1974	2:00	5:00
23/Feb/1975	2:00	4:00
26/Oct/1975	2:00	5:00
25/Apr/1976	2:00	4:00
31/Oct/1976	2:00	5:00
24/Apr/1977	2:00	4:00
30/Oct/1977	2:00	5:00
30/Apr/1978	2:00	4:00
29/Oct/1978	2:00	5:00
29/Apr/1979	2:00	4:00
28/Oct/1979	2:00	5:00
27/Apr/1980	2:00	4:00
26/Oct/1980	2:00	5:00
26/Apr/1981	2:00	4:00
25/Oct/1981	2:00	5:00
25/Apr/1982	2:00	4:00
31/Oct/1982	2:00	5:00
24/Apr/1983	2:00	4:00
30/Oct/1983	2:00	5:00

Place	Lat	Long	Time
Albert Town	18N17	77w33	5:10:12
Alligator Pond	17N52	77w34	5:10:16
Annotto Bay	18N16	76w46	5:07:04
Black River	18N01	77w51	5:11:24
Browns Town	18N24	77w22	5:09:28
Chapelton	18N05	77w16	5:09:04
Christiana	18N10	77w29	5:09:56
Clark's Town	18N25	77w34	5:10:16
Duncans	18N28	77w32	5:10:08
Ewarton	18N11	77w05	5:08:20
Falmouth	18N30	77w39	5:10:36
Four Paths	17N58	77w18	5:09:12
Frankfield	18N09	77w22	5:09:28
Kingston	18N00	76w48	5:07:12
Linstead	18N08	77w02	5:08:08
Lionel Town	17N48	77w14	5:08:56
Little London	18N15	78w13	5:12:52
Lucea	18N27	78w10	5:12:40
Manchioneal	18N02	76w17	5:05:08
Mandeville	18N02	77w30	5:10:00
May Pen	17N58	77w14	5:08:56
Montego Bay	18N28	77w55	5:11:40
Montpelier	18N22	77w56	5:11:44
Morant Bay	17N53	76w25	5:05:40
Ocho Rios	18N25	77w07	5:08:28
Old Harbour	17N56	77w07	5:08:28
Port Antonio	18N11	76w28	5:05:52
Port Maria	18N22	76w54	5:07:36
Port Morant	17N54	76w19	5:05:16
Port Royal	17N56	76w51	5:07:24
Porus	18N02	77w25	5:09:40
Saint Ann's Bay	18N26	77w08	5:08:32
Savanna-la-Mar	18N13	78w08	5:12:32
Spanish Town	17N59	76w57	5:07:48
Whithorn	18N15	78w02	5:12:08
Williamsfield	17N56	77w46	5:11:04

NIHON — JAPON — NIPPON — JAPÓN — JAPAN

Time Table # 1
Before 1/Jan/1896 LMT
Begin Standard 135E00
1/Jan/1896 0:00 -9:00
....

Time Table # 2
Before 1/Jan/1896 LMT
Begin Standard 135E00
1/Jan/1896 0:00 -9:00
2/May/1948 2:00 -10:00
11/Sep/1948 2:00 -9:00
3/Apr/1949 2:00 -10:00
10/Sep/1949 2:00 -9:00
7/May/1950 2:00 -10:00
9/Sep/1950 2:00 -9:00
6/May/1951 2:00 -10:00
8/Sep/1951 2:00 -9:00
....

Time Table # 3
Before 1/Jan/1896 LMT
Begin Standard 120E00
1/Jan/1896 0:00 -8:00

Place	Table	Lat	Long	Time
Abashiri	1	44N01	144E17	-9:37:08
Abiko	1	35N52	140E03	-9:20:12
Abu	1	34N30	131E28	-8:45:52
Abuta	1	42N33	140E46	-9:23:04
Achi	1	35N27	137E45	-9:11:00
Ada	1	26N44	128E19	-8:33:16
Adogawa	1	35N20	136E02	-9:04:08
Agatsuma	1	36N34	138E50	-9:15:20
Agawa	1	33N34	133E10	-8:52:40
Agematsu	1	35N47	137E42	-9:10:48
Ageo	1	35N58	139E36	-9:18:24
Ago	1	34N20	136E51	-9:07:24
Agui	1	34N55	136E55	-9:07:40
Aha	1	26N43	128E17	-8:33:08
Aikawa	1	38N02	138E15	-9:13:00
Aikawa	1	35N32	139E17	-9:17:08
Aimi	1	35N22	133E22	-8:53:28
Aimoto	1	34N59	135E10	-9:00:40
Aio	1	34N00	131E26	-8:45:44
Aioi	1	34N48	134E28	-8:57:52
Aizu-Bange	1	37N34	139E49	-9:19:16
Aizu-Wakamatsu	1	37N30	139E56	-9:19:44
Aji	1	34N23	134E08	-8:56:32
Ajigasawa	1	40N47	140E12	-9:20:48
Ajimu	1	33N26	131E21	-8:45:24
Ajisu	1	34N00	131E22	-8:45:28
Akabane	1	34N37	137E12	-9:08:48
Akabira	1	43N34	142E03	-9:28:12
Akabori	1	36N22	139E14	-9:16:56
Akagi	1	36N33	139E03	-9:16:12
Akagi	1	35N00	132E43	-8:50:52
Akan	1	43N06	144E10	-9:36:40
Akaoka	1	33N32	133E43	-8:54:52
Akasaki	1	35N31	133E38	-8:54:32
Akashi	1	34N38	134E59	-8:59:56
Akashina	1	36N21	137E56	-9:11:44
Akechi	1	35N18	137E23	-9:09:32
Akehama	1	33N19	132E26	-8:49:44
Akeno	1	36N15	140E02	-9:20:08
Akeno	1	35N46	138E26	-9:13:44
Aki	1	33N30	133E54	-8:55:36
Aki	1	33N28	131E43	-8:46:52
Akishima	1	35N41	139E22	-9:17:28
Akita	1	39N43	140E07	-9:20:28
Akitsu	1	34N19	132E50	-8:51:20
Akitsu	1	34N56	135E06	-9:00:24
Akiyama	1	35N34	139E05	-9:16:20
Akkeshi	1	43N02	144E51	-9:39:24
Akō	1	34N45	134E24	-8:57:36
Akune	1	32N01	130E11	-8:40:44
Amagasaki	1	34N43	135E25	-9:01:40
Amagase	1	33N15	131E02	-8:44:08
Amagi	1	33N25	130E39	-8:42:36
Amagi-Yugashima	1	34N53	138E56	-9:15:44
Amano	1	34N26	135E33	-9:02:12
Amarume	1	38N50	139E55	-9:19:40
Amatsu-Kominato	1	35N07	140E10	-9:20:40
Ami	1	36N02	140E14	-9:20:56
Amino	1	35N41	135E02	-9:00:08
Amitori	3	24N18	123E41	-8:14:44
Anabuki	1	34N02	134E11	-8:56:44

Place		Lat.	Long.	Time
Anamizu	1	37N14	136E54	-9:07:36
Anan	1	35N19	137E49	-9:11:16
Anan	1	33N55	134E39	-8:58:36
Ando	1	34N37	135E46	-9:03:04
Anegasaki	1	35N28	140E02	-9:20:08
Angyō	1	35N51	139E46	-9:19:04
Anjō	1	34N57	137E05	-9:08:20
Annaka	1	36N19	138E54	-9:15:36
Anō	1	34N46	136E27	-9:05:48
Aogaki	1	35N14	135E00	-9:00:00
Aomori	1	40N49	140E45	-9:23:00
Aoya	1	35N31	133E59	-8:55:56
Aoyama	1	34N40	136E11	-9:04:44
Arai	1	37N01	138E15	-9:13:00
Arai	1	34N41	137E34	-9:10:16
Arakawa	1	35N57	139E02	-9:16:08
Arakawa	1	26N39	128E15	-8:33:00
Arao	1	32N57	130E28	-8:41:52
Arida	1	34N05	135E07	-9:00:28
Arikawa	1	32N59	129E07	-8:36:28
Arume	1	26N36	128E07	-8:32:28
Asa	1	34N33	132E26	-8:49:44
Asaba	1	34N42	137E56	-9:11:44
Asahi	1	35N14	137E22	-9:09:28
Asahi	1	35N43	140E39	-9:22:36
Asahi	1	35N59	136E07	-9:04:28
Asahi	1	36N05	137E21	-9:09:24
Asahi	1	36N14	140E31	-9:22:04
Asahi	1	35N02	136E40	-9:06:40
Asahi	1	36N07	137E52	-9:11:28
Asahi	1	36N57	137E34	-9:10:16
Asahi	1	34N59	133E50	-8:55:20
Asahi	1	34N51	132E16	-8:49:04
Asahi	1	34N17	131E28	-8:45:52
Asahigawa → Asahikawa	1	43N46	142E22	-9:29:28
Asahikawa	1	43N46	142E22	-9:29:28
Asaka	1	35N48	139E36	-9:18:24
Asakawa	1	37N05	140E25	-9:21:40
Asako	1	35N14	134E48	-8:59:12
Asakura	1	33N23	130E44	-8:42:56
Asashina	1	36N16	138E25	-9:13:40
Ashibe	1	33N48	129E46	-8:39:04
Ashibetsu	1	43N31	142E11	-9:28:44
Ashikaga	1	36N20	139E27	-9:17:48
Ashio	1	36N38	139E27	-9:17:48
Ashiya	1	33N53	130E40	-8:42:40
Ashiya	1	34N43	135E17	-9:01:08
Ashiya Air Force Base	2	33N53	130E40	-8:42:40
Ashiyasu	1	35N38	138E23	-9:13:32
Ashiyoro	1	43N15	143E30	-9:34:00
Asō	1	35N59	140E29	-9:21:56
Aso	1	32N58	131E02	-8:44:08
Asuka	1	34N28	135E50	-9:03:20
Asuke	1	35N08	137E19	-9:09:16
Asuwa	1	36N01	136E16	-9:05:04
Atami	1	35N05	139E04	-9:16:16
Atō	1	34N24	131E43	-8:46:52
Atsugi	1	35N27	139E22	-9:17:28
Atsugi Naval Air Station (US)	2	35N27	139E27	-9:17:48
Atsumi	1	38N37	139E35	-9:18:20
Atsumi	1	34N37	137E07	-9:08:28
Atsuta	1	26N17	127E49	-8:31:16
Awa	1	34N04	134E12	-8:56:48
Awa	1	26N36	127E56	-8:31:44
Awaji	1	34N35	135E01	-9:00:04
Awano	1	36N31	139E41	-9:18:44
Awara	1	36N13	136E12	-9:04:48
Ayabe	1	35N18	135E15	-9:01:00
Ayase	1	35N26	139E26	-9:17:44
Azai	1	35N26	136E18	-9:05:12
Azama	1	26N11	127E49	-8:31:16
Azuchi	1	35N09	136E08	-9:04:32
Azuma	1	35N56	140E28	-9:21:52
Azuma	1	36N36	138E20	-9:13:20
Azumazaka	1	34N26	135E39	-9:02:36
Azumi	1	36N11	137E47	-9:11:08
Batō	1	36N44	140E10	-9:20:40
Beppu	1	33N17	131E30	-8:46:00
Besshiyama	1	33N50	133E23	-8:53:32
Bessho	1	34N27	135E31	-9:02:04
Betsukai	1	43N23	145E17	-9:41:08
Bibai	1	43N19	141E52	-9:27:28
Biei	1	43N35	142E28	-9:29:52
Bifuka	1	44N29	142E21	-9:29:24
Bihoro	1	43N49	144E07	-9:36:28
Bijōki	1	35N49	139E39	-9:18:36
Bisai	1	35N16	136E44	-9:06:56
Bise	1	26N42	127E54	-8:31:36
Bisei	1	34N41	133E33	-8:54:12
Bitchū	1	34N47	133E27	-8:53:48
Bizen	1	34N44	134E09	-8:56:36
Bōfu → Hōfu	1	34N03	131E34	-8:46:16
Boppu	1	33N15	131E28	-8:45:52
Bubai	1	35N40	139E29	-9:17:56
Bungo-Takada	1	33N33	131E27	-8:45:48
Bushi	1	35N50	139E22	-9:17:28
Buzen	1	33N37	131E08	-8:44:32
Cheshi	1	35N42	140E51	-9:23:24
Chiba	1	35N36	140E07	-9:20:28
Chichibu	1	35N59	139E05	-9:16:20
Chigasaki	1	35N19	139E24	-9:17:36
Chihaya-Akasaka	1	34N24	135E38	-9:02:32
Chikugo	1	33N12	130E30	-8:42:00
Chikura	1	34N57	139E57	-9:19:48
Chikusa	1	35N09	134E26	-8:57:44
Chikushino	1	33N29	130E31	-8:42:04
Chin	1	26N26	127E55	-8:31:40
Chinā	1	26N24	127E46	-8:31:04
Chinen	1	26N09	127E49	-8:31:16
Chino	1	35N59	138E09	-9:12:36
Chiryū	1	35N00	137E02	-9:08:08
Chita	1	35N00	136E51	-9:07:24
Chitose	1	42N49	141E39	-9:26:36
Chiyoda	1	36N12	139E26	-9:17:44
Chiyoda	1	36N11	140E14	-9:20:56
Chiyoda	1	34N41	132E32	-8:50:08
Chizu	1	35N16	134E14	-8:56:56
Chōfu	1	35N39	139E33	-9:18:12
Chōnan	1	35N24	140E14	-9:20:56
Chōshi	1	35N44	140E50	-9:23:20
Chūō	1	35N00	133E58	-8:55:52
Chūta	1	26N32	127E58	-8:31:52
Chūzu	1	35N06	136E00	-9:04:00
Daian	1	35N05	136E33	-9:06:12
Daiei	1	35N29	133E45	-8:55:00
Daigo	1	36N46	140E21	-9:21:24
Daimon	1	36N44	137E03	-9:08:12
Daimon	1	35N53	139E44	-9:18:56
Daishin	1	37N12	140E15	-9:21:00
Daitō	1	34N42	135E38	-9:02:32
Daitō	1	35N19	132E58	-8:51:52
Daiwa	1	34N32	132E57	-8:51:48
Daiwa	1	34N57	132E39	-8:50:36
Date	1	42N27	140E51	-9:23:24
Dejima	1	36N05	140E20	-9:21:20
Doi	1	33N57	133E26	-8:53:44
Dōjō	1	35N51	139E37	-9:18:28
Dōshi	1	35N32	139E02	-9:16:08
Ebetsu	1	43N07	141E34	-9:26:16
Ebina	1	35N26	139E25	-9:17:40
Ebino	1	32N03	130E50	-8:43:20
Echigawa	1	35N10	136E12	-9:04:48
Echizen	1	35N54	136E00	-9:04:00
Edosaki	1	35N57	140E19	-9:21:16
Eigenji	1	35N04	136E18	-9:05:12
Eiheiji	1	36N05	136E20	-9:05:20
Embetsu	1	44N44	141E47	-9:27:08
Emukae	1	33N18	129E38	-8:38:32
Ena	1	35N27	137E25	-9:09:40
Endō	1	35N23	139E27	-9:17:48
Engaru	1	44N03	143E31	-9:34:04
Eniwa	1	42N45	141E33	-9:26:12
Enzan	1	35N42	138E44	-9:14:56
Erimo	1	42N01	143E09	-9:32:36
Esashi	1	41N52	140E07	-9:20:28
Esashi	1	39N12	141E09	-9:24:36
Esashi	1	44N56	142E35	-9:30:20
Etajima	1	34N15	132E30	-8:50:00
Fuchū	1	35N40	139E29	-9:17:56
Fuchū	1	36N39	137E10	-9:08:40
Fuchū	1	34N24	132E30	-8:50:00
Fuchū	1	34N34	133E14	-8:52:56
Fuji	1	35N09	138E39	-9:14:36
Fujiidera	1	34N34	135E36	-9:02:24
Fujikawa	1	35N08	138E37	-9:14:28
Fujikubo	1	35N50	139E32	-9:18:08
Fujimi	1	36N27	139E05	-9:16:20
Fujimi	1	35N55	138E15	-9:13:00
Fujimi	1	35N51	139E33	-9:18:12
Fujino	1	35N37	139E10	-9:16:40
Fujinomiya	1	35N12	138E38	-9:14:32
Fujioka	1	35N12	137E12	-9:08:48
Fujioka	1	36N15	139E05	-9:16:20
Fujioka	1	36N15	139E39	-9:18:36
Fujisawa	1	35N21	139E29	-9:17:56
Fujiseiko	1	35N17	136E42	-9:06:48
Fujishiro	1	35N55	140E07	-9:20:28
Fujiwara	1	35N09	136E30	-9:06:00
Fujiwara	1	36N51	139E44	-9:18:56
Fuji-Yoshida	1	35N29	138E48	-9:15:12
Fukagawa	1	43N43	142E03	-9:28:12
Fukami	1	35N28	139E28	-9:17:52
Fukaya	1	36N12	139E17	-9:17:08
Fukiage	1	36N06	139E27	-9:17:48
Fukube	1	35N33	134E18	-8:57:12
Fukuchiyama	1	35N18	135E07	-9:00:28
Fukude	1	34N40	137E53	-9:11:32
Fukue	1	32N41	128E50	-8:35:20
Fukui	1	36N04	136E13	-9:04:52
Fukui	1	34N51	135E34	-9:02:16
Fukuma	1	33N46	130E28	-8:41:52
Fukumitsu	1	36N33	136E52	-9:07:28
Fukuno	1	36N35	136E55	-9:07:40
Fukuoka	1	35N34	137E27	-9:09:48
Fukuoka	1	36N42	136E56	-9:07:44
Fukuoka	1	33N35	130E24	-8:41:36
Fukuroi	1	34N45	137E55	-9:11:40
Fukushima	1	37N45	140E28	-9:21:52
Fukushima	1	41N29	140E15	-9:21:00
Fukusumi	1	34N37	135E56	-9:03:44
Fukuyama	1	34N29	133E22	-8:53:28
Fukuzaki	1	34N57	134E45	-8:59:00
Fumahashi	1	36N42	137E19	-9:09:16
Funabashi	1	35N42	139E59	-9:19:56
Funagawa → Oga	1	39N53	139E51	-9:19:24
Funakuyā	3	24N30	124E17	-8:17:08
Funaoka	1	35N23	134E14	-8:56:56
Funasaka	1	34N48	135E17	-9:01:08
Funo	1	34N53	132E47	-8:51:08
Furano	1	43N21	142E24	-9:29:36
Furudono	1	37N05	140E34	-9:22:16
Furukawa	1	38N34	140E58	-9:23:52
Furukawa	1	36N14	137E11	-9:08:44
Furuyakami	1	35N55	139E32	-9:18:08
Fuse	1	35N53	140E00	-9:20:00
Fuse → Higashiōsaka	1	34N39	135E35	-9:02:20
Fusō	1	35N21	136E55	-9:07:40
Fussa	1	35N45	139E20	-9:17:20
Futaba	1	35N41	138E30	-9:14:00
Futamata → Tenryū	1	34N52	137E49	-9:11:16
Futami	1	33N41	132E38	-8:50:32
Futami	1	34N30	136E47	-9:07:08
Futtsu	1	35N19	139E49	-9:19:16
Futtsu	1	35N13	139E52	-9:19:28
Gamagōri	1	34N50	137E14	-9:08:56
Gamō	1	35N52	139E48	-9:19:12
Gamō	1	35N03	136E11	-9:04:44
Geihoku	1	34N44	132E17	-8:49:08
Geinō	1	34N48	136E25	-9:05:40
Geisei	1	33N31	133E49	-8:55:16
Genaibashi	1	35N21	140E04	-9:20:16
Genkai	1	33N51	130E30	-8:42:00
Gero	1	35N48	137E14	-9:08:56
Gifu	1	35N25	136E45	-9:07:00
Gihu → Gifu	1	35N25	136E45	-9:07:00
Ginowan	1	26N17	127E46	-8:31:04
Ginoza	1	26N28	127E57	-8:31:48
Gobō	1	33N53	135E10	-9:00:40
Gōdo	1	35N25	136E36	-9:06:24
Gōdo	1	35N51	139E44	-9:18:56
Gohoku	1	33N39	133E21	-8:53:24
Gojō	1	34N21	135E42	-9:02:48
Gojōme	1	39N56	140E07	-9:20:28
Gōkōmutsumi	1	35N48	139E59	-9:19:56
Gōnoura	1	33N45	129E41	-8:38:44
Gose	1	34N27	135E44	-9:02:56
Gosen	1	37N44	139E11	-9:16:44
Goshiki	1	34N24	134E47	-8:59:08
Goshogawara	1	40N48	140E27	-9:21:48
Gotemba	1	35N18	138E56	-9:15:44
Gotō Islands	1	32N50	129E00	-8:36:00
Gotō-rettō	1	32N50	129E00	-8:36:00
Gōtsu	1	35N00	132E14	-8:48:56
Gozen-Yama	1	36N32	140E20	-9:21:20
Gunma	1	36N24	139E00	-9:16:00
Gushichan	1	26N07	127E45	-8:31:00
Gushikami	1	26N07	127E45	-8:31:00
Gushikawa	1	26N21	127E52	-8:31:28
Guskube	3	24N45	125E26	-8:21:44
Gyōda	1	36N08	139E28	-9:17:52
Habikino	1	34N33	135E37	-9:02:28
Haboro	1	44N22	141E42	-9:26:48
Habu	1	34N27	135E24	-9:01:36
Habutaki	1	34N25	135E26	-9:01:44
Hachijō	1	34N37	135E48	-9:03:12
Hachiman	1	35N45	136E57	-9:07:48
Hachiman → Ōmi-Hachiman	1	35N08	136E06	-9:04:24
Hachinohe	1	40N30	141E29	-9:25:56
Hachiōji	1	35N39	139E20	-9:17:20
Hadano	1	35N22	139E14	-9:16:56
Haga	1	36N32	140E04	-9:20:16
Haga	1	35N09	134E33	-8:58:12
Hagi	1	34N24	131E25	-8:45:40
Hagitani	1	34N54	135E35	-9:02:20
Hagiwara	1	35N52	137E12	-9:08:48
Haibara	1	34N32	135E57	-9:03:48
Haibara	1	34N44	138E13	-9:12:52
Haijima	1	35N42	139E21	-9:17:24
Haimi	3	24N15	123E52	-8:15:28
Hakata	1	34N12	133E07	-8:52:28
Haki	1	33N20	130E50	-8:43:20
Hakodate	1	41N45	140E43	-9:22:52
Hakone	1	35N12	139E06	-9:16:24
Hakuba	1	36N42	137E52	-9:11:28
Hakui	1	36N53	136E47	-9:07:08
Hakusan	1	34N38	136E21	-9:05:24
Hakushū	1	35N48	138E20	-9:13:20
Hakuta	1	35N21	133E17	-8:53:08
Hamada	1	34N53	132E05	-8:48:20
Hamakita	1	34N48	137E47	-9:11:08
Hamamatsu	1	34N42	137E44	-9:10:56
Hamanaka	1	43N05	145E10	-9:40:40
Hamano	1	35N33	140E08	-9:20:32
Hamaoka	1	34N39	138E08	-9:12:32
Hamasaka	1	35N37	134E27	-8:57:48
Hama-Tombetsu	1	45N07	142E23	-9:29:32
Hamura	1	35N45	139E19	-9:17:16
Hanamaki	1	39N23	141E07	-9:24:28
Hanawa	1	36N57	140E25	-9:21:40
Hanawa	1	35N13	139E53	-9:19:32
Hanchō	1	34N49	135E27	-9:01:48
Handa	1	34N53	136E56	-9:07:44
Handa	1	34N02	134E02	-8:56:08
Hannō	1	35N51	139E19	-9:17:16
Hanoura	1	33N57	134E38	-8:58:32
Hanyū	1	36N10	139E32	-9:18:08
Hara	1	35N58	138E14	-9:12:56
Hara	1	35N50	139E46	-9:19:04
Harajuku	1	35N54	139E21	-9:17:24
Haramachi	1	37N38	140E58	-9:23:52
Haramachida	1	35N33	139E27	-9:17:48
Harigabessho	1	34N37	135E58	-9:03:52
Harima	1	34N42	134E53	-8:59:32
Harue	1	36N08	136E14	-9:04:56
Haruna	1	36N23	138E53	-9:15:32
Haruno	1	34N57	137E53	-9:11:32
Haruno	1	33N30	133E30	-8:54:00
Hasaki	1	35N44	140E50	-9:23:20
Hase	1	35N47	138E06	-9:12:24
Hase	1	34N32	135E54	-9:03:36
Hashima	1	35N19	136E42	-9:06:48
Hashimoto	1	34N19	135E37	-9:02:28
Hashimoto	1	34N26	135E23	-9:01:32
Hasuda	1	35N59	139E40	-9:18:40
Hasumi	1	34N52	132E37	-8:50:28
Hata	1	36N11	137E51	-9:11:24
Hatashō	1	35N10	136E15	-9:05:00
Hatinoe → Hachinohe	1	40N30	141E29	-9:25:56
Hatiozi → Hachiōji	1	35N39	139E20	-9:17:20
Hatogaya	1	35N50	139E44	-9:18:56
Hatoyama	1	35N59	139E20	-9:17:20
Hatsukaichi	1	34N21	132E20	-8:49:20
Hatsutomi	1	35N46	140E01	-9:20:04
Hattori	1	34N46	135E27	-9:01:48
Hattori	1	34N52	135E36	-9:02:24
Hayakawa	1	35N25	138E22	-9:13:28

Hayama	1	35N16	139E35	-9:18:20
Hayama	1	33N26	133E13	-8:52:52
Hayashima	1	34N36	133E50	-8:55:20
Hazu	1	34N47	137E08	-9:08:32
Heanna	1	26N19	127E54	-8:31:36
Heda	1	34N58	138E46	-9:15:04
Hedo	1	26N51	128E16	-8:33:04
Heguri	1	34N38	135E42	-9:02:48
Heiwa	1	35N12	136E44	-9:06:56
Hekinan	1	34N51	136E58	-9:07:52
Hentona	1	26N45	128E10	-8:32:40
Hida → Hita	1	33N19	130E56	-8:43:44
Hidaka	1	35N28	134E47	-8:59:08
Hidaka	1	33N55	135E09	-9:00:36
Hidaka	1	35N54	139E21	-9:17:24
Higashi	1	26N38	128E09	-8:32:36
Higashibetsuin	1	34N56	135E34	-9:02:16
Higashihiroshima	1	34N26	132E42	-8:50:48
Higashiichiki	1	31N40	130E20	-8:41:20
Higashiiyayama	1	33N52	133E54	-8:55:36
Higashiizu	1	34N48	139E04	-9:16:16
Higashikurume	1	35N45	139E32	-9:18:08
Higashimatsuyama	1	36N02	139E24	-9:17:36
Higashimonzen	1	35N56	139E40	-9:18:40
Higashimurayama	1	35N46	139E29	-9:17:56
Higashinakano	1	35N38	139E25	-9:17:40
Higashine	1	38N26	140E24	-9:21:36
Higashinose	1	34N55	135E30	-9:02:00
Higashiōsaka	1	34N39	135E35	-9:02:20
Higashishirakawa	1	35N39	137E19	-9:09:16
Higashitsuno	1	33N23	133E02	-8:52:08
Higashiura	1	34N59	136E58	-9:07:52
Higashiyamato	1	35N44	139E26	-9:17:44
Higashiyoshino	1	34N24	135E58	-9:03:52
Hiji	1	33N22	131E32	-8:46:08
Hijikawa	1	33N27	132E41	-8:50:44
Hikami	1	35N10	135E02	-9:00:08
Hikari	1	33N58	131E56	-8:47:44
Hikari	1	35N39	140E30	-9:22:00
Hikarigaoka	1	35N50	139E58	-9:19:52
Hikawa	1	35N25	132E50	-8:51:20
Hiketa	1	34N13	134E24	-8:57:36
Hikigawa	1	33N34	135E27	-9:01:48
Hikimi	1	34N34	132E01	-8:48:04
Hikiura	1	34N33	134E58	-8:59:52
Hikone	1	35N15	136E15	-9:05:00
Himeji	1	34N49	134E42	-8:58:48
Himi	1	36N51	136E59	-9:07:56
Hinase	1	34N44	134E16	-8:57:04
Hino	1	35N14	133E27	-8:53:48
Hino	1	35N00	136E15	-9:05:00
Hino	1	35N41	139E24	-9:17:36
Hinode	1	35N45	139E14	-9:16:56
Hinoemata	1	37N01	139E23	-9:17:32
Hinohara	1	35N43	139E09	-9:16:36
Hinokage	1	32N39	131E24	-8:45:36
Hirado	1	33N22	129E33	-8:38:12
Hiraizumi	1	38N59	141E07	-9:24:28
Hirakata	1	35N56	139E33	-9:18:12
Hirakata	1	34N48	135E38	-9:02:32
Hirakawa	1	34N52	135E47	-9:03:08
Hirakubo	3	24N35	124E19	-8:17:16
Hirano	3	24N35	124E19	-8:17:16
Hirao	1	33N56	132E04	-8:48:16
Hiraoka → Higashiōsaka	1	34N39	135E35	-9:02:20
Hirara	3	24N48	125E17	-8:21:08
Hirata	1	35N15	136E38	-9:06:32
Hirata	1	35N26	132E49	-8:51:16
Hiratsuka	1	35N19	139E21	-9:17:24
Hiraya	1	35N19	137E37	-9:10:28
Hirokawa	1	33N15	130E32	-8:42:08
Hirokawa	1	34N01	135E11	-9:00:44
Hiromi	1	33N15	132E41	-8:50:44
Hiroo	1	42N17	143E19	-9:33:16
Hirooka	1	35N15	140E04	-9:20:16
Hirosaki	1	40N35	140E28	-9:21:52
Hiroschima → Hiroshima	1	34N24	132E27	-8:49:48
Hirose	1	35N22	133E10	-8:52:40
Hiroshima	1	34N24	132E27	-8:49:48
Hirosima → Hiroshima	1	34N24	132E27	-8:49:48
Hirota	1	34N45	135E21	-9:01:24
Hirukawa	1	35N31	137E23	-9:09:32
Hisai	1	34N40	136E28	-9:05:52
Hisai	1	34N25	135E28	-9:01:52
Hita	1	33N19	130E56	-8:43:44
Hitachi	1	36N36	140E39	-9:22:36
Hitachi-ōta	1	36N32	140E31	-9:22:04
Hitati → Hitachi	1	36N36	140E39	-9:22:36
Hitokura	1	34N55	135E25	-9:01:40
Hitoyoshi	1	32N13	130E45	-8:43:00
Hiwa	1	34N59	132E59	-8:51:56
Hiwasa	1	33N44	134E32	-8:58:08
Hiyoshi	1	35N53	137E45	-9:11:00
Hiyoshi	1	33N20	132E48	-8:51:12
Hiyoshi	1	35N09	135E31	-9:02:04
Hizaonna	1	26N24	127E50	-8:31:20
Hōfu	1	34N03	131E34	-8:46:16
Hōhoku	1	34N17	130E57	-8:43:48
Hōjō	1	33N58	132E46	-8:51:04
Hōjō	1	34N54	134E56	-8:59:44
Hōjō → Kasai	1	34N56	134E50	-8:59:20
Hōkōji	1	34N52	135E07	-9:00:28
Hokota	1	36N09	140E31	-9:22:04
Hokubo	1	34N57	133E38	-8:54:32
Hokudan	1	34N32	134E56	-8:59:44
Hokusei	1	35N09	136E31	-9:06:04
Hommura	1	34N22	139E15	-9:17:00

Honai	1	33N30	132E25	-8:49:40
Honami	1	33N36	130E42	-8:42:48
Honbetsu	1	43N07	143E37	-9:34:28
Hondo	1	32N27	130E12	-8:40:48
Hongawa	1	33N43	133E19	-8:53:16
Hongō	1	34N24	132E59	-8:51:56
Hongō	1	34N17	132E02	-8:48:08
Hongyōtoku	1	35N41	139E55	-9:19:40
Honjō	1	39N23	140E03	-9:20:12
Honjō	1	36N24	138E01	-9:12:04
Honjō	1	36N14	139E11	-9:16:44
Hon-Kawane	1	35N07	138E09	-9:12:36
Horado	1	35N36	136E50	-9:07:20
Hōrai	1	34N56	137E34	-9:10:16
Horigane	1	35N50	139E27	-9:17:48
Horinouchi	1	37N14	138E56	-9:15:44
Hosoe	1	34N49	137E39	-9:10:36
Hota	1	35N08	139E51	-9:19:24
Hotaka	1	36N20	137E53	-9:11:32
Hōya	1	35N43	139E34	-9:18:16
Hozumi	1	35N24	136E41	-9:06:44
Hukui → Fukui	1	36N04	136E13	-9:04:52
Hukuoka → Fukuoka	1	33N35	130E24	-8:41:36
Hukusima → Fukushima	1	37N45	140E28	-9:21:52
Hukuyama → Fukuyama	1	34N29	133E22	-8:53:28
Hunabasi → Funabashi	1	35N42	139E59	-9:19:56
Huse → Higashiōsaka	1	34N39	135E35	-9:02:20
Huzisawa → Fujisawa	1	35N21	139E29	-9:17:56
Hyakuna	1	26N08	127E48	-8:31:12
Hyūga	1	32N25	131E38	-8:46:32
Ibara	1	34N36	133E28	-8:53:52
Ibaraki	1	36N17	140E26	-9:21:44
Ibaraki	1	34N49	135E34	-9:02:16
Ibaruma	3	24N30	124E17	-8:17:08
Ibigawa	1	35N29	136E34	-9:06:16
Ibu	1	26N45	128E19	-8:33:16
Ibuki	1	35N24	136E23	-9:05:32
Ibusuki	1	31N16	130E39	-8:42:36
Ichiba	1	34N05	134E17	-8:57:08
Ichihara	1	35N31	140E05	-9:20:20
Ichikai	1	36N32	140E06	-9:20:24
Ichikawa	1	35N44	139E55	-9:19:40
Ichikawa	1	34N59	134E46	-8:59:04
Ichikawa-Daimon	1	35N34	138E30	-9:14:00
Ichinohe	1	40N13	141E17	-9:25:08
Ichinomiya	1	34N41	137E26	-9:09:44
Ichinomiya	1	35N18	136E48	-9:07:12
Ichinomiya	1	35N22	140E22	-9:21:28
Ichinomiya	1	35N39	138E41	-9:14:44
Ichinomiya	1	34N28	134E51	-8:59:24
Ichinomiya	1	35N06	134E35	-8:58:20
Ichinomiya	1	32N57	131E07	-8:44:28
Ichinomoto	1	34N37	135E50	-9:03:20
Ichinose	1	34N53	135E10	-9:00:40
Ichinoseki	1	38N55	141E08	-9:24:32
Ichiu	1	33N57	134E04	-8:56:16
Ide	1	34N47	135E49	-9:03:16
Ie	1	26N42	127E48	-8:31:12
Ieshima	1	34N40	134E32	-8:58:08
Iga	1	34N49	136E13	-9:04:52
Iida	1	35N31	137E50	-9:11:20
Iijima	1	35N40	137E56	-9:11:44
Iinan	1	34N27	136E24	-9:05:36
Iioka	1	35N42	140E43	-9:22:52
Iitaka	1	34N26	136E21	-9:05:24
Iiyama	1	36N51	138E22	-9:13:28
Iizuka	1	33N38	130E41	-8:42:44
Ijira	1	35N31	136E44	-9:06:56
Ikaho	1	36N30	138E55	-9:15:40
Ikaruga	1	34N36	135E44	-9:02:56
Ikawa	1	35N13	138E15	-9:13:00
Ikazaki	1	33N32	132E39	-8:50:36
Ikeda	1	35N53	136E21	-9:05:24
Ikeda	1	35N26	136E34	-9:06:16
Ikeda	1	36N25	137E53	-9:11:32
Ikeda	1	34N49	135E25	-9:01:40
Ikeda	1	34N01	133E48	-8:55:12
Ikeda	1	42N55	143E27	-9:33:48
Ikegawa	1	33N36	133E11	-8:52:44
Ikeura	1	34N30	135E25	-9:01:40
Ikoma	1	34N41	135E42	-9:02:48
Ikuno	1	35N10	134E48	-8:59:12
Ikusaka	1	36N25	137E56	-9:11:44
Ikuta	1	35N36	137E32	-9:10:08
Imabari	1	34N03	133E00	-8:52:00
Imadomi	1	35N28	140E06	-9:20:24
Imaichi	1	36N43	139E41	-9:18:44
Imajō	1	35N46	136E12	-9:04:48
Imajuku	1	35N58	139E21	-9:17:24
Imaki	1	34N24	135E46	-9:03:04
Imari	1	33N16	129E53	-8:39:32
Imazu	1	35N24	136E02	-9:04:08
Ina	1	35N59	139E38	-9:18:32
Ina	1	37N10	139E32	-9:18:08
Ina	1	35N59	140E03	-9:20:12
Ina	1	35N50	137E57	-9:11:48
Inaba	1	34N26	135E27	-9:01:48
Inabe	1	35N07	136E33	-9:06:12
Inabu	1	35N13	137E30	-9:10:00
Inada	1	34N54	135E08	-9:00:32
Inagawa	1	34N53	135E22	-9:01:28
Inage	1	35N38	140E05	-9:20:20
Inagi	1	35N38	139E30	-9:18:00
Inami	1	34N45	134E54	-8:59:36
Inami	1	33N48	135E13	-9:00:52
Inami	1	36N33	136E58	-9:07:52
Inasa	1	34N50	137E40	-9:10:40
Inatsuki	1	33N36	130E43	-8:42:52

Inazawa	1	35N15	136E47	-9:07:08
Inba	1	35N46	140E14	-9:20:56
Ine	1	35N39	135E17	-9:01:08
Innoshima	1	34N17	133E11	-8:52:44
Ino	1	33N33	133E26	-8:53:44
Inoue	1	34N48	135E03	-9:00:12
Inukai	1	33N04	131E38	-8:46:32
Inuyama	1	35N23	136E56	-9:07:44
Inzai	1	35N50	140E09	-9:20:36
Irabu	3	24N50	125E09	-8:20:36
Iriyamazu	1	35N16	139E39	-9:18:36
Iruma	1	35N50	139E24	-9:17:36
Isahaya	1	32N50	130E03	-8:40:12
Isawa	1	35N39	138E38	-9:14:32
Ise (Uji-Yamada)	1	34N29	136E42	-9:06:48
Isehara	1	35N24	139E18	-9:17:12
Isesaki	1	36N19	139E12	-9:16:48
Isezaki → Isesaki	1	36N19	139E12	-9:16:48
Ishibashi	1	36N26	139E52	-9:19:28
Ishibe	1	35N00	136E04	-9:04:16
Ishigaki	3	24N20	124E09	-8:16:36
Ishige	1	36N07	139E58	-9:19:52
Ishii	1	34N04	134E26	-8:57:44
Ishikawa	1	37N09	140E27	-9:21:48
Ishikawa	1	26N25	127E50	-8:31:20
Ishiki	1	34N48	137E01	-9:08:04
Ishikiri	1	34N41	135E39	-9:02:36
Ishinomaki	1	38N25	141E18	-9:25:12
Ishioka	1	36N11	140E16	-9:21:04
Ishiyama	1	34N58	135E55	-9:03:40
Isobe	1	34N22	136E49	-9:07:16
Isumi	1	35N17	140E19	-9:21:16
Itako	1	35N56	140E33	-9:22:12
Itakura	1	36N13	139E36	-9:18:24
Itakura	1	37N03	138E18	-9:13:12
Itami	1	34N46	135E25	-9:01:40
Itano	1	34N07	134E28	-8:57:52
Itikawa → Ichikawa	1	35N44	139E55	-9:19:40
Itinomiya → Ichinomiya	1	35N18	136E48	-9:07:12
Itō	1	34N58	139E05	-9:16:20
Itoigawa	1	37N02	137E51	-9:11:24
Itoman	1	26N08	127E40	-8:30:40
Itsukaichi	1	35N44	139E13	-9:16:52
Itsukaichi	1	34N24	132E22	-8:49:28
Itsuki	1	32N24	130E50	-8:43:20
Itsuwa	1	32N30	130E10	-8:40:40
Iwade	1	34N15	135E19	-9:01:16
Iwafune	1	36N19	139E40	-9:18:40
Iwafune	1	34N44	135E54	-9:03:36
Iwagi	1	34N15	133E09	-8:52:36
Iwai	1	36N03	139E54	-9:19:36
Iwaizumi	1	39N50	141E48	-9:27:12
Iwaki (Taira)	1	37N03	140E55	-9:23:40
Iwakuni	1	34N09	132E11	-8:48:44
Iwakura	1	35N17	136E52	-9:07:28
Iwama	1	36N18	140E16	-9:21:04
Iwami	1	34N53	132E26	-8:49:44
Iwami	1	35N35	134E20	-8:57:20
Iwamizawa	1	43N12	141E46	-9:27:04
Iwamura	1	35N22	137E26	-9:09:44
Iwanai	1	42N58	140E30	-9:22:00
Iwanuma	1	38N06	140E52	-9:23:28
Iwase	1	36N21	140E06	-9:20:24
Iwase	1	35N17	139E52	-9:19:28
Iwata	1	34N42	137E48	-9:11:12
Iwataki	1	35N34	135E09	-9:00:36
Iwatsuki	1	35N57	139E42	-9:18:48
Iwaya	1	34N35	135E02	-9:00:08
Iwaya → Awaji	1	34N35	135E01	-9:00:04
Iwayama	1	34N52	135E52	-9:03:28
Iwazono	1	34N45	135E19	-9:01:16
Iyo	1	33N46	132E42	-8:50:48
Iyo-Mishima	1	33N58	133E33	-8:54:12
Izuhara	1	34N12	129E17	-8:37:08
Izumi	1	34N55	134E55	-8:59:40
Izumi	1	38N20	140E53	-9:23:32
Izumi	1	32N05	130E22	-8:41:28
Izumi	1	35N54	136E40	-9:06:40
Izumi	1	34N29	135E26	-9:01:44
Izumi-ōtsu	1	34N30	135E24	-9:01:36
Izumi-Sano	1	34N25	135E19	-9:01:16
Izumizaki	1	37N09	140E17	-9:21:08
Izumo	1	35N22	132E46	-8:51:04
Izu-Nagaoka	1	35N02	138E56	-9:15:44
Izushi	1	35N28	134E52	-8:59:28
Izuwara	1	34N53	135E32	-9:02:08
Jajichi	1	26N47	128E13	-8:32:52
Jinseki	1	34N48	133E11	-8:52:44
Jiō	1	34N58	135E28	-9:01:52
Joetsu	1	37N06	138E15	-9:13:00
Jōgawara	1	35N42	139E22	-9:17:28
Jōge	1	34N42	133E07	-8:52:28
Jōhana	1	36N31	136E54	-9:07:36
Jōhen	1	32N57	132E35	-8:50:20
Jōhoku	1	36N28	140E22	-9:21:28
Jōjima	1	33N15	130E26	-8:41:44
Jōyō	1	34N51	135E47	-9:03:08
Jūō	1	36N40	140E41	-9:22:44
Jūshiyama	1	35N06	136E46	-9:07:04
Kabira	3	24N27	124E08	-8:16:32
Kabira	1	26N42	127E48	-8:31:12
Kadena	1	26N22	127E45	-8:31:00
Kadogawa	1	32N28	131E39	-8:46:36
Kaga	1	36N18	136E18	-9:05:12
Kagami	1	33N37	133E26	-8:53:44
Kagamigahara	1	35N24	136E54	-9:07:36
Kagamino	1	35N05	133E56	-8:55:44
Kagawa	1	34N15	134E02	-8:56:08
Kagoshima	1	31N36	130E33	-8:42:12
Kahoku	1	33N39	133E47	-8:55:08
Kahoku	1	33N06	130E41	-8:42:44

Name		Lat.	Long.	Time
Kaibara	1	35N08	135E05	-9:00:20
Kaida	1	35N56	137E36	-9:10:24
Kaidori	1	35N37	139E27	-9:17:48
Kaifu	1	33N35	134E21	-8:57:24
Kainan	1	33N36	134E22	-8:57:28
Kainan	1	34N09	135E12	-9:00:48
Kaita	1	34N20	132E32	-8:50:08
Kaizu	1	35N13	136E38	-9:06:32
Kaizuka	1	34N27	135E21	-9:01:24
Kajikazawa	1	35N33	138E27	-9:13:48
Kajiki	1	31N44	130E40	-8:42:40
Kake	1	34N36	132E19	-8:49:16
Kakegawa	1	34N46	138E01	-9:12:04
Kakeya	1	35N11	132E49	-8:51:16
Kakinoki	1	34N26	131E52	-8:47:28
Kakizaki	1	37N15	138E25	-9:13:40
Kakogawa	1	34N46	134E51	-8:59:24
Kakuda	1	37N58	140E47	-9:23:08
Kakunodate	1	39N35	140E34	-9:22:16
Kamae	1	32N48	131E56	-8:47:44
Kamagaya	1	35N45	140E01	-9:20:04
Kamaishi	1	39N16	141E53	-9:27:32
Kamakura	1	35N19	139E33	-9:18:12
Kambara	1	35N07	138E36	-9:14:24
Kameda	1	37N52	139E07	-9:16:28
Kameoka	1	35N00	135E35	-9:02:20
Kameyama	1	34N51	136E27	-9:05:48
Kami	1	35N05	134E53	-8:59:32
Kamiasō	1	35N35	139E30	-9:18:00
Kamifukuoka	1	35N52	139E32	-9:18:08
Kamigōri	1	34N52	134E22	-8:57:28
Kamiichi	1	36N42	137E22	-9:09:28
Kamiishihara	1	35N39	139E32	-9:18:08
Kamiiso	1	41N49	140E39	-9:22:36
Kamiita	1	34N07	134E24	-8:57:36
Kamikatsu	1	33N53	134E24	-8:57:36
Kamikawa	1	43N51	142E46	-9:31:04
Kamikawa	1	36N13	139E07	-9:16:28
Kamikume	1	34N55	135E03	-9:00:12
Kamimaki	1	34N34	135E43	-9:02:52
Kamimizo	1	35N33	139E22	-9:17:28
Kaminaka	1	35N28	135E51	-9:03:24
Kaminaka	1	33N48	134E22	-8:57:28
Kaminoho	1	35N37	137E03	-9:08:12
Kaminokawa	1	36N26	139E55	-9:19:40
Kaminokuni	1	41N48	140E06	-9:20:24
Kaminoseki	1	33N49	132E07	-8:48:28
Kaminoyama	1	38N09	140E17	-9:21:08
Kamioka	1	36N16	137E18	-9:09:12
Kamioyamada	1	35N35	139E24	-9:17:36
Kamisato	1	36N15	139E09	-9:16:36
Kamishii	1	36N04	136E24	-9:05:36
Kamishinden	1	34N49	135E30	-9:02:00
Kamisunagawa	1	43N30	142E00	-9:28:00
Kamitaira	1	36N24	136E54	-9:07:36
Kamitakara	1	36N17	137E22	-9:09:28
Kamitakino	1	34N57	134E59	-8:59:56
Kamitomi	1	35N49	139E31	-9:18:04
Kamitonda	1	33N43	135E27	-9:01:48
Kamitsuruma	1	35N31	139E25	-9:17:40
Kamitsushima	1	34N50	129E28	-8:37:52
Kamiura	1	33N03	131E55	-8:47:40
Kamiyahagi	1	35N18	137E29	-9:09:56
Kamiyama	1	33N58	134E23	-8:57:32
Kamiyamada	1	36N28	138E09	-9:12:36
Kamiyugi	1	35N37	139E23	-9:17:32
Kamo	1	34N45	135E52	-9:03:28
Kamo	1	35N10	134E04	-8:56:16
Kamo	1	35N20	132E55	-8:51:40
Kamo	1	34N55	135E13	-9:00:52
Kamo	1	37N39	139E03	-9:16:12
Kamo	1	34N50	138E46	-9:15:04
Kamogata	1	34N32	133E35	-8:54:20
Kamogawa	1	35N06	140E06	-9:20:24
Kamogawa	1	34N51	133E49	-8:55:16
Kamojima	1	34N04	134E21	-8:57:24
Kamoto	1	33N00	130E45	-8:43:00
Kanada	1	33N41	130E47	-8:43:08
Kanae	1	35N30	137E49	-9:11:16
Kanagi	1	34N53	132E11	-8:48:44
Kanai	1	35N35	139E28	-9:17:52
Kanamori	1	35N32	139E28	-9:17:52
Kanan	1	34N29	135E38	-9:02:32
Kanaoka	1	34N33	135E32	-9:02:08
Kanasagō	1	36N33	140E28	-9:21:52
Kanaya	1	35N10	139E50	-9:19:20
Kanaya	1	34N49	138E08	-9:12:32
Kanaya	1	34N04	135E15	-9:01:00
Kanayama	1	35N39	137E09	-9:08:36
Kanazawa	1	36N34	136E39	-9:06:36
Kanazu	1	36N13	136E14	-9:04:56
Kanda	1	33N47	130E59	-8:43:56
Kaneda	1	35N28	139E22	-9:17:28
Kaneyama	1	35N28	137E06	-9:08:24
Kani	1	35N22	137E04	-9:08:16
Kanie	1	35N08	136E48	-9:07:12
Kanna	1	26N28	127E57	-8:31:48
Kannabe	1	34N32	133E23	-8:53:32
Kannami	1	35N05	138E57	-9:15:48
Kano	1	34N14	131E49	-8:47:16
Kanonji	1	34N07	133E39	-8:54:36
Kanoya	1	31N23	130E51	-8:43:24
Kanra	1	36N13	138E55	-9:15:40
Kanuma	1	36N33	139E44	-9:18:56
Karakuni	1	34N28	135E28	-9:01:52
Karasu	1	34N39	136E32	-9:06:08
Karasuyama	1	36N39	140E09	-9:20:36
Karatsu	1	33N26	129E58	-8:39:52
Karimata	3	24N54	125E17	-8:21:08
Kariya	1	34N59	136E59	-9:07:56
Karuizawa	1	36N21	138E38	-9:14:32
Karumai	1	40N19	141E28	-9:25:52
Kasagi	1	34N45	135E56	-9:03:44
Kasahara	1	35N17	137E09	-9:08:36
Kasahata	1	35N54	139E25	-9:17:40
Kasai	1	34N56	134E50	-8:59:20
Kasakake	1	36N23	139E17	-9:17:08
Kasama	1	36N23	140E16	-9:21:04
Kasamatsu	1	35N22	136E46	-9:07:04
Kasaoka	1	34N30	133E30	-8:54:00
Kaseda	1	31N25	130E19	-8:41:16
Kashiba	1	34N33	135E42	-9:02:48
Kashihara	1	34N30	135E46	-9:03:04
Kashima	1	33N07	130E06	-8:40:24
Kashima	1	35N58	140E38	-9:22:32
Kashima	1	36N58	136E55	-9:07:40
Kashima	1	35N30	133E01	-8:52:04
Kashimo	1	35N43	137E23	-9:09:32
Kashiwa	1	35N52	139E59	-9:19:56
Kashiwara	1	34N35	135E37	-9:02:28
Kashiwazaki	1	37N22	138E33	-9:14:12
Kashiwazaki	1	35N56	139E42	-9:18:48
Kasiwa → Kashiwa	1	35N52	139E59	-9:19:56
Kasuga	1	35N10	135E06	-9:00:24
Kasuga	1	35N28	136E29	-9:05:56
Kasuga	1	33N32	130E27	-8:41:48
Kasugai	1	35N14	136E58	-9:07:52
Kasugai	1	35N39	138E39	-9:14:36
Kasukabe	1	35N58	139E45	-9:19:00
Kasukawa	1	36N24	139E13	-9:16:52
Kasumi	1	35N38	134E38	-8:58:32
Katakura	1	34N29	135E31	-9:02:04
Katano	1	34N47	135E40	-9:02:40
Kataoka	1	35N03	135E58	-9:03:52
Katase	1	35N19	139E29	-9:17:56
Katashina	1	36N46	139E14	-9:16:56
Katayama	1	35N46	139E34	-9:18:16
Katsunuma	1	35N39	138E44	-9:14:56
Katsuragi	1	34N15	135E30	-9:02:00
Katsuta	1	36N24	140E30	-9:22:00
Katsuta	1	35N04	134E11	-8:56:44
Katsuura	1	35N08	140E18	-9:21:12
Katsuura	1	33N56	134E30	-8:58:00
Katsuyama	1	36N03	136E30	-9:06:00
Katsuyama	1	35N05	133E41	-8:54:44
Kawaba	1	36N41	139E07	-9:16:28
Kawabe	1	35N29	137E04	-9:08:16
Kawabe	1	33N55	135E11	-9:00:44
Kawachi	1	36N24	136E38	-9:06:32
Kawachi	1	36N37	139E56	-9:19:44
Kawachi-Nagano	1	34N27	135E34	-9:02:16
Kawage	1	34N47	136E33	-9:06:12
Kawagoe	1	35N55	139E29	-9:17:56
Kawaguchi	1	35N48	139E43	-9:18:52
Kawaguchiko	1	35N30	138E46	-9:15:04
Kawahara	1	35N24	134E12	-8:56:48
Kawai	1	36N18	137E07	-9:08:28
Kawai	1	34N35	135E45	-9:03:00
Kawajiri	1	34N14	132E42	-8:50:48
Kawakami	1	35N17	133E39	-8:54:36
Kawakami	1	35N58	138E35	-9:14:20
Kawakami	1	34N44	133E29	-8:53:56
Kawakubo	1	34N54	135E38	-9:02:32
Kawamata	1	37N39	140E36	-9:22:24
Kawamoto	1	36N09	139E17	-9:17:08
Kawamoto	1	34N59	132E30	-8:50:00
Kawane	1	34N57	138E05	-9:12:20
Kawanishi	1	34N49	135E24	-9:01:36
Kawanishi	1	34N35	135E47	-9:03:08
Kawanoe	1	34N01	133E34	-8:54:16
Kawara	1	33N40	130E51	-8:43:24
Kawara	1	34N59	135E18	-9:01:12
Kawarai	1	35N25	140E05	-9:20:20
Kawasaki	1	35N32	139E43	-9:18:52
Kawasaki	1	33N35	130E49	-8:43:16
Kawashima	1	34N04	134E19	-8:57:16
Kawashima	1	35N21	136E50	-9:07:20
Kawashima	1	35N59	139E30	-9:18:00
Kawatana	1	33N04	129E52	-8:39:28
Kawauchi	1	33N48	132E55	-8:51:40
Kawazu	1	34N44	138E59	-9:15:56
Kaya	1	35N30	135E06	-9:00:24
Kayō	1	34N51	133E42	-8:54:48
Kayō	1	26N33	128E07	-8:32:28
Kazo	1	36N07	139E36	-9:18:24
Kazuno	1	40N11	140E47	-9:23:08
Keihoku	1	35N09	135E38	-9:02:32
Kesennuma	1	38N54	141E35	-9:26:20
Ketaka	1	35N30	134E03	-8:56:12
Kichijōji	1	35N42	139E35	-9:18:20
Kii-Nagashima	1	34N12	136E20	-9:05:20
Kijimadaira	1	36N51	138E24	-9:13:36
Kijoka	1	26N42	128E09	-8:32:36
Kikuchi	1	32N59	130E49	-8:43:16
Kikugawa	1	34N45	138E05	-9:12:20
Kikugawa	1	34N07	131E02	-8:44:08
Kikuka	1	33N02	130E46	-8:43:04
Kikuma	1	34N03	132E53	-8:51:32
Kikuna	1	35N10	139E40	-9:18:40
Kikusui	1	32N58	130E36	-8:42:24
Kimitsu	1	35N20	139E54	-9:19:36
Kin	1	26N26	127E55	-8:31:40
Kinasa	1	36N42	138E01	-9:12:04
Kinoe	1	34N14	132E55	-8:51:40
Kinomoto	1	35N30	136E13	-9:04:52
Kinosaki	1	35N37	134E49	-8:59:16
Kioto → Kyōto	1	35N00	135E45	-9:03:00
Kira	1	34N49	137E05	-9:08:20
Kiryū	1	36N24	139E20	-9:17:20
Kisa	1	34N43	132E59	-8:51:56
Kisai	1	36N06	139E35	-9:18:20
Kisaichi	1	34N46	135E42	-9:02:48
Kisakata	1	39N13	139E54	-9:19:36
Kisarazu	1	35N23	139E55	-9:19:40
Kisawa	1	33N49	134E18	-8:57:12
Kishigawa	1	34N13	135E20	-9:01:20
Kishimoto	1	35N23	133E25	-8:53:40
Kishiwada	1	34N28	135E22	-9:01:28
Kisiwada → Kishiwada	1	34N28	135E22	-9:01:28
Kiso	1	35N34	139E26	-9:17:44
Kiso	1	35N56	137E47	-9:11:08
Kisofukushima	1	35N51	137E42	-9:10:48
Kisogawa	1	35N20	136E47	-9:07:08
Kisozaki	1	35N04	136E44	-9:06:56
Kisuki	1	35N17	132E54	-8:51:36
Kitaaiki	1	36N04	138E34	-9:14:16
Kitagata	1	35N26	136E41	-9:06:44
Kitagawa	1	33N27	134E03	-8:56:12
Kitaibaraki	1	36N48	140E45	-9:23:00
Kitairiso	1	35N50	139E26	-9:17:44
Kitajima	1	34N05	134E35	-8:58:20
Kitakami	1	39N18	141E07	-9:24:28
Kitakata	1	37N39	139E52	-9:19:28
Kitakyuschu → Kitakyūshū	1	33N53	130E50	-8:43:20
Kitakyūshū	1	33N53	130E50	-8:43:20
Kitami	1	43N48	143E54	-9:35:36
Kitamoto	1	36N02	139E32	-9:18:08
Kitano	1	35N47	139E26	-9:17:44
Kitano	1	33N20	130E35	-8:42:20
Kitanoshinden	1	35N48	139E26	-9:17:44
Kitatachibana	1	36N29	139E03	-9:16:12
Kitatajima	1	35N56	139E30	-9:18:00
Kitatawara	1	34N44	135E42	-9:02:48
Kitaura	1	36N04	140E32	-9:22:08
Kitō	1	33N46	134E12	-8:56:48
Kitō	1	34N42	138E03	-9:12:12
Kitsuki	1	33N25	131E37	-8:46:28
Kitsuregawa	1	36N43	140E01	-9:20:04
Kiyama	1	33N25	130E32	-8:42:08
Kiyan	1	26N05	127E40	-8:30:40
Kiyokawa	1	35N29	139E17	-9:17:08
Kiyomi	1	36N07	137E11	-9:08:44
Kiyosawa	1	35N03	138E15	-9:13:00
Kiyose	1	35N47	139E32	-9:18:08
Kiyosu	1	35N13	136E50	-9:07:20
Kiyotani	1	34N52	134E59	-8:59:56
Kizu	1	34N44	135E49	-9:03:16
Kizuki	1	35N34	139E40	-9:18:40
Kizuri	1	34N39	135E34	-9:02:16
Kobayashi	1	31N59	130E59	-8:43:56
Kōbe	1	34N41	135E10	-9:00:40
Kobuchizawa	1	35N52	138E19	-9:13:16
Kōchi	1	33N33	133E33	-8:54:12
Kochinda	1	26N08	127E43	-8:30:52
Kōda	1	34N42	132E45	-8:51:00
Kōda	1	34N52	137E10	-9:08:40
Kodaira	1	35N44	139E29	-9:17:56
Kodama	1	36N11	139E08	-9:16:32
Kōfu	1	35N17	133E30	-8:54:00
Kōfu	1	35N39	138E35	-9:14:20
Koga	1	33N40	130E30	-8:42:00
Koga	1	36N11	139E43	-9:18:52
Kogane	1	35N50	139E56	-9:19:44
Koganei	1	35N42	139E32	-9:18:08
Kōge	1	35N24	134E15	-8:57:00
Kohoku	1	35N26	136E15	-9:05:00
Kohu → Kōfu	1	35N39	138E35	-9:14:20
Koide	1	37N13	138E57	-9:15:48
Kōka	1	34N54	136E13	-9:04:52
Kokawa	1	34N16	135E24	-9:01:36
Kokinu	1	35N59	139E59	-9:19:56
Kokonoe	1	33N10	131E10	-8:44:40
Kokubu	1	31N44	130E46	-8:43:04
Kokubunji	1	34N18	133E58	-8:55:52
Kokufu	1	35N28	134E16	-8:57:04
Kokura	1	33N52	130E52	-8:43:28
Komae	1	35N38	139E35	-9:18:20
Komagane	1	35N43	137E55	-9:11:40
Komaki	1	35N17	136E55	-9:07:40
Komatsu	1	33N53	133E07	-8:52:28
Komatsu	1	36N24	136E27	-9:05:48
Komatsushima	1	34N00	134E35	-8:58:20
Komenoi	1	35N55	140E01	-9:20:04
Komi	3	24N19	123E54	-8:15:36
Kominato → Amatsu-Kominato	1	35N07	140E10	-9:20:40
Komono	1	35N00	136E31	-9:06:04
Komoro	1	36N19	138E26	-9:13:44
Kōnan	1	34N56	136E11	-9:04:44
Kōnan	1	35N20	136E53	-9:07:32
Konkō	1	34N32	133E37	-8:54:28
Kōno	1	35N49	136E04	-9:04:16
Kōnoike	1	34N42	135E37	-9:02:28
Kōnosu	1	36N03	139E31	-9:18:04
Kōnu	1	34N42	133E05	-8:52:20
Kōra	1	35N12	136E15	-9:05:00
Kōri	1	34N47	135E39	-9:02:36
Kōriyama	1	37N24	140E23	-9:21:32
Kōriyama → Yamato-Kōriyama	1	34N38	135E47	-9:03:08
Koromo → Toyota	1	35N05	137E09	-9:08:36
Kōryō	1	34N33	135E45	-9:03:00
Kosai	1	34N43	137E33	-9:10:12
Kosaka	1	40N19	140E44	-9:22:56
Kose	1	34N25	135E46	-9:03:04
Koshigaya	1	35N54	139E48	-9:19:12
Koshigoe	1	35N18	139E30	-9:18:00
Koshino	1	36N02	136E01	-9:04:04
Kōshoku	1	36N32	138E06	-9:12:24
Kosuge	1	35N45	138E57	-9:15:48
Kosugi	1	36N43	137E06	-9:08:24
Kotake	1	33N41	130E43	-8:42:52
Koti → Kōchi	1	33N33	133E33	-8:54:12
Kotō	1	35N08	136E14	-9:04:56
Kotohira	1	34N11	133E49	-8:55:16
Kotonami	1	34N10	133E56	-8:55:44
Koumi	1	36N05	138E29	-9:13:56
Kōya	1	34N12	135E35	-9:02:20
Koyadaira	1	33N56	134E13	-8:56:52
Kōyaguchi	1	34N18	135E33	-9:02:12

Place		Lat	Long	Time
Koza	1	26N20	127E50	-8:31:20
Kozakai	1	34N48	137E22	-9:09:28
Kōzaki	1	35N54	140E24	-9:21:36
Kōzan	1	34N35	133E03	-8:52:12
Kozuka	1	35N09	139E57	-9:19:48
Kōzuki	1	34N59	134E20	-8:57:20
Kozuya	1	34N52	135E45	-9:03:00
Kubiki	1	37N11	138E20	-9:13:20
Kubokawa	1	33N12	133E08	-8:52:32
Kubura	3	24N27	122E57	-8:11:48
Kuchiwa	1	34N53	132E55	-8:51:40
Kudamatsu	1	34N00	131E52	-8:47:28
Kudoyama	1	34N17	135E34	-9:02:16
Kuga	1	34N05	132E05	-8:48:20
Kuguno	1	36N03	137E16	-9:09:04
Kuji	1	40N11	141E46	-9:27:04
Kujirai	1	35N56	139E27	-9:17:48
Kujū	1	33N01	131E18	-8:45:12
Kujūkuri	1	35N32	140E25	-9:21:40
Kuki	1	36N04	139E40	-9:18:40
Kuma	1	33N39	132E54	-8:51:36
Kumagaya	1	36N08	139E23	-9:17:32
Kumaishi	1	42N08	139E59	-9:19:56
Kumamoto	1	32N48	130E43	-8:42:52
Kumano	1	34N20	132E34	-8:50:16
Kumano	1	33N54	136E05	-9:04:20
Kumatori	1	34N24	135E22	-9:01:28
Kume	1	35N03	133E54	-8:55:36
Kumenan	1	34N56	133E58	-8:55:52
Kumihama	1	35N36	134E55	-8:59:40
Kumiyama	1	34N53	135E45	-9:03:00
Kuni	1	36N35	138E38	-9:14:32
Kunigami	1	26N45	128E10	-8:32:40
Kunimi	1	33N41	131E36	-8:46:24
Kunisaki	1	33N33	131E45	-8:47:00
Kurabuchi	1	36N25	138E48	-9:15:12
Kurahashi	1	34N06	132E30	-8:50:00
Kurakaki	1	34N59	135E28	-9:01:52
Kuranami	1	35N27	140E00	-9:20:00
Kurashiki	1	34N35	133E46	-8:55:04
Kurasiki → Kurashiki	1	34N35	133E46	-8:55:04
Kurate	1	33N47	130E41	-8:42:44
Kurayoshi	1	35N26	133E49	-8:55:16
Kure	1	34N14	132E34	-8:50:16
Kurihama	1	35N13	139E43	-9:18:52
Kurihashi	1	36N08	139E42	-9:18:48
Kurimoto	1	35N49	140E30	-9:22:00
Kuriyama	1	43N03	141E47	-9:27:08
Kuriyama	1	36N52	139E37	-9:18:28
Kurobane	1	36N51	140E07	-9:20:28
Kurobe	1	36N51	137E26	-9:09:44
Kurodashō	1	35N01	135E00	-9:00:00
Kurogi	1	33N12	130E40	-8:42:40
Kurohone	1	36N30	139E17	-9:17:08
Kuroishi	1	40N38	140E36	-9:22:24
Kuroiso	1	36N58	140E03	-9:20:12
Kurose	1	34N19	132E40	-8:50:40
Kurosu	1	35N51	139E23	-9:17:32
Kuroya	1	35N55	139E44	-9:18:56
Kurume	1	33N19	130E31	-8:42:04
Kusabe	1	34N31	135E29	-9:01:56
Kusatsu	1	36N37	138E36	-9:14:24
Kusatsu	1	35N00	135E57	-9:03:48
Kuse	1	35N04	133E45	-8:55:00
Kushi	1	26N31	128E01	-8:32:04
Kushigata	1	35N36	138E28	-9:13:52
Kushihiki	1	35N55	139E36	-9:18:24
Kushikino	1	31N44	130E16	-8:41:04
Kushima	1	31N29	131E14	-8:44:56
Kushimoto	1	33N28	135E47	-9:03:08
Kushira	1	34N28	135E43	-9:02:52
Kushiro	1	42N58	144E23	-9:37:32
Kusiro → Kushiro	1	42N58	144E23	-9:37:32
Kusu	1	33N16	131E09	-8:44:36
Kusu	1	34N55	136E38	-9:06:32
Kusunoki	1	34N03	131E15	-8:45:00
Kutchan	1	42N54	140E45	-9:23:00
Kutsuki	1	35N21	135E55	-9:03:40
Kuwabara	1	34N53	135E15	-9:01:00
Kuwana	1	35N04	136E42	-9:06:48
Kuze	1	35N33	136E30	-9:06:00
Kuzuha	1	34N52	135E41	-9:02:44
Kuzuu	1	36N24	139E37	-9:18:28
Kyonan	1	35N07	139E50	-9:19:20
Kyōto	1	35N00	135E45	-9:03:00
Kyōwa	1	36N19	140E03	-9:20:12
Kyūhōji	1	34N38	135E35	-9:02:20
Kyūshū	1	33N00	131E00	-8:44:00
Kyūshū Island	1	33N00	131E00	-8:44:00
Mabashi	1	35N49	139E55	-9:19:40
Mabi	1	34N38	133E41	-8:54:44
Mabuni	1	26N05	127E43	-8:30:52
Machida	1	35N32	139E27	-9:17:48
Maebaru	1	33N33	130E12	-8:40:48
Maebashi	1	36N23	139E04	-9:16:16
Maeda	1	34N55	135E08	-9:00:32
Maginu	1	35N35	139E36	-9:18:24
Maihara	1	35N19	136E17	-9:05:08
Maisaka	1	34N41	137E37	-9:10:28
Maitani	1	34N49	135E22	-9:01:28
Maizuru	1	35N28	135E24	-9:01:36
Makabe	1	36N16	140E06	-9:20:24
Maki	1	34N52	135E04	-9:00:16
Maki	1	37N45	138E53	-9:15:32
Makino	1	35N28	136E05	-9:04:20
Makioka	1	35N45	138E43	-9:14:52
Mako	1	23N55	119E32	-7:58:08
Makuhari	1	35N39	140E03	-9:20:12
Makurazaki	1	31N16	130E19	-8:41:16
Mamba	1	36N07	138E55	-9:15:40
Manazuru	1	35N09	139E08	-9:16:32
Manganji	1	35N40	139E26	-9:17:44
Mannō	1	34N11	133E51	-8:55:24
Marugame	1	34N17	133E47	-8:55:08
Maruko	1	36N19	138E16	-9:13:04
Maruoka	1	36N09	136E16	-9:05:04
Maruyama	1	35N01	139E58	-9:19:52
Masaki	1	35N13	140E02	-9:20:08
Masaki	1	33N47	132E42	-8:50:48
Mashike	1	43N51	141E31	-9:26:04
Mashiko	1	36N28	140E06	-9:20:24
Masuda	1	34N40	131E51	-8:47:24
Masuho	1	35N34	138E28	-9:13:52
Matama	1	33N36	131E28	-8:45:52
Matsubara	1	34N34	135E33	-9:02:12
Matsubushi	1	35N55	139E49	-9:19:16
Matsuda	1	35N21	139E09	-9:16:36
Matsudai	1	37N08	138E37	-9:14:28
Matsudo	1	35N47	139E54	-9:19:36
Matsue	1	35N28	133E04	-8:52:16
Matsugasaki	1	35N53	139E58	-9:19:52
Matsuida	1	36N19	138E48	-9:15:12
Matsukawa	1	35N36	137E55	-9:11:40
Matsukawa	1	36N25	137E51	-9:11:24
Matsumae	1	41N26	140E07	-9:20:28
Matsumoto	1	36N14	137E58	-9:11:52
Matsuno	1	33N13	132E42	-8:50:48
Matsunoyama	1	37N05	138E37	-9:14:28
Matsuo	1	35N38	140E28	-9:21:52
Matsuōji	1	35N08	140E01	-9:20:04
Matsuoka	1	36N05	136E18	-9:05:12
Matsusaka	1	34N34	136E32	-9:06:08
Matsushima	1	38N22	141E04	-9:24:16
Matsutō	1	36N31	136E34	-9:06:16
Matsuura	1	33N22	129E42	-8:38:48
Matsuyama	1	33N50	132E45	-8:51:00
Matsuzaki	1	34N45	138E47	-9:15:08
Matudo → Matsudo	1	35N47	139E54	-9:19:36
Matue → Matsue	1	35N28	133E04	-8:52:16
Matumoto → Matsumoto	1	36N14	137E58	-9:11:52
Matuzaka → Matsusaka	1	34N34	136E32	-9:06:08
Maze	1	35N52	137E10	-9:08:40
Meiwa	1	34N33	136E39	-9:06:36
Menuma	1	36N13	139E23	-9:17:32
Miasa	1	36N34	137E53	-9:11:32
Mibu	1	36N25	139E48	-9:19:12
Midori	1	34N43	132E37	-8:50:28
Mie	1	32N58	131E35	-8:46:20
Mihama	1	33N54	135E08	-9:00:32
Mihama	1	34N46	136E54	-9:07:36
Mihama	1	35N36	135E56	-9:03:44
Mihara	1	34N32	135E34	-9:02:16
Mihara	1	34N24	133E05	-8:52:20
Mihara	1	34N17	134E46	-8:59:04
Miho	1	36N00	140E18	-9:21:12
Mihonoseki	1	35N34	133E19	-8:53:16
Mikame	1	33N25	132E27	-8:49:48
Mikasa	1	43N14	141E53	-9:27:32
Mikata	1	35N33	135E55	-9:03:40
Mikawa	1	33N37	132E58	-8:51:52
Mikawa	1	36N29	136E29	-9:05:56
Mikazuki	1	34N58	134E27	-8:57:48
Miki	1	34N17	134E05	-8:56:20
Miki	1	34N48	134E59	-8:59:56
Mikkabi	1	34N48	137E33	-9:10:12
Mikkaichi	1	34N26	135E35	-9:02:20
Mikuni	1	36N13	136E09	-9:04:36
Mima	1	33N17	132E36	-8:50:24
Mimasaka	1	35N00	134E10	-8:56:40
Mimmaya	1	41N12	140E26	-9:21:44
Minabe	1	33N46	135E19	-9:01:16
Minabegawa	1	33N47	135E20	-9:01:20
Minakami	1	36N46	138E58	-9:15:52
Minakuchi	1	34N58	136E10	-9:04:40
Minamata	1	32N13	130E24	-8:41:36
Minami	1	35N39	136E57	-9:07:48
Minamiaiki	1	36N02	138E33	-9:14:12
Minamiashigara	1	35N19	139E07	-9:16:28
Minamichita	1	34N44	136E52	-9:07:28
Minamiizu	1	34N39	138E50	-9:15:20
Minamimaki	1	36N00	138E30	-9:14:00
Minaminasu	1	36N39	140E06	-9:20:24
Minamishinano	1	35N19	137E56	-9:11:44
Minano	1	36N04	139E06	-9:16:24
Mine	1	34N10	131E13	-8:44:52
Mine	1	33N17	130E26	-8:41:44
Mineyama	1	35N37	135E04	-9:00:16
Minō	1	34N50	135E30	-9:02:00
Mino	1	35N32	136E55	-9:07:40
Minobu	1	35N22	138E26	-9:13:44
Mino-Kamo	1	35N26	137E01	-9:08:04
Minori	1	36N14	140E21	-9:21:24
Minoshō	1	34N39	135E49	-9:03:16
Minowa	1	35N55	137E59	-9:11:56
Mirasaka	1	34N46	132E58	-8:51:52
Misaka	1	35N38	138E40	-9:14:40
Misaki	1	34N19	135E09	-9:00:36
Misaki	1	35N18	140E22	-9:21:28
Misaki	1	33N23	132E07	-8:48:28
Misaki → Miura	1	35N08	139E37	-9:18:28
Misakubo	1	35N09	137E52	-9:11:28
Misasa	1	35N24	133E54	-8:55:36
Misasagi → Fujiidera	1	34N34	135E36	-9:02:24
Misato	1	34N43	136E24	-9:05:36
Misato	1	36N15	137E54	-9:11:36
Misato	1	34N09	135E22	-9:01:28
Misato	1	35N50	139E53	-9:19:32
Misato	1	36N23	138E57	-9:15:48
Misawa	1	40N41	141E24	-9:25:36
Mishima	1	35N07	138E55	-9:15:40
Mishima → Settsu	1	34N46	135E33	-9:02:12
Mishō	1	32N57	132E34	-8:50:16
Misugi	1	34N33	136E16	-9:05:04
Misumi	1	34N22	131E15	-8:45:00
Misumi	1	32N37	130E27	-8:41:48
Misumi	1	34N46	131E58	-8:47:52
Mitaka	1	35N40	139E33	-9:18:12
Mitake	1	35N51	137E37	-9:10:28
Mitake	1	35N25	137E08	-9:08:32
Mito	1	36N22	140E28	-9:21:52
Mito	1	34N40	131E59	-8:47:56
Mitō	1	34N13	131E21	-8:45:24
Mito	1	35N10	139E37	-9:18:28
Mito	1	34N49	137E19	-9:09:16
Mitomi	1	35N47	138E44	-9:14:56
Mitoya	1	35N17	132E52	-8:51:28
Mitsu	1	34N48	133E56	-8:55:44
Mitsu	1	34N47	134E33	-8:58:12
Mitsubori	1	35N56	139E56	-9:19:44
Mitsue	1	34N29	136E10	-9:04:40
Mitsugi	1	34N30	133E09	-8:52:36
Mitsukaidō	1	36N01	139E59	-9:19:56
Mitsuke	1	37N32	138E56	-9:15:44
Mitsuzaku	1	35N25	140E00	-9:20:00
Miura	1	35N08	139E37	-9:18:28
Miwa	1	34N31	135E51	-9:03:24
Miwa	1	35N11	136E47	-9:07:08
Miwa	1	36N39	140E18	-9:21:12
Miwa	1	35N12	135E14	-9:00:56
Miwa	1	34N13	132E06	-8:48:24
Miwa	1	34N39	132E51	-8:51:24
Miya	1	36N05	137E15	-9:09:00
Miyagawa	1	34N22	136E21	-9:05:24
Miyagawa	1	36N19	137E09	-9:08:36
Miyahara	1	35N56	139E37	-9:18:28
Miyajima	1	34N18	132E19	-8:49:16
Miyake	1	34N35	135E47	-9:03:08
Miyako	1	39N38	141E57	-9:27:48
Miyakonojō	1	31N44	131E04	-8:44:16
Miyama	1	36N00	136E22	-9:05:28
Miyama	1	35N33	136E45	-9:07:00
Miyama	1	35N16	135E33	-9:02:12
Miyama	1	33N59	135E22	-9:01:28
Miyama	1	34N06	136E14	-9:04:56
Miyanojō	1	31N54	130E27	-8:41:48
Miyara	3	24N20	124E14	-8:16:56
Miyata	1	33N44	130E40	-8:42:40
Miyazaki	1	35N56	136E05	-9:04:20
Miyazaki	1	31N54	131E26	-8:45:44
Miyazu	1	35N32	135E11	-9:00:44
Miyoshi	1	35N50	139E31	-9:18:04
Miyoshi	1	33N57	133E03	-8:52:12
Miyoshi	1	34N48	132E51	-8:51:24
Miyoshi	1	34N02	133E52	-8:55:28
Miyota	1	36N18	138E30	-9:14:00
Mizoguchi	1	35N21	133E26	-8:53:44
Mizonokuchi	1	35N36	139E37	-9:18:28
Mizonuma	1	35N48	139E36	-9:18:24
Mizuho	1	34N51	132E31	-8:50:04
Mizuho	1	35N46	139E21	-9:17:24
Mizuho	1	35N10	135E22	-9:01:28
Mizukaidō → Mitsukaidō	1	36N01	139E59	-9:19:56
Mizuko	1	35N50	139E34	-9:18:16
Mizumaki	1	33N51	130E42	-8:42:48
Mizunami	1	35N22	137E15	-9:09:00
Mizusawa	1	39N08	141E08	-9:24:32
Mizutori	1	34N47	135E45	-9:03:00
Mobara	1	35N25	140E18	-9:21:12
Mochigase	1	35N20	134E12	-8:56:48
Mochizuki	1	36N16	138E22	-9:13:28
Moji	1	33N55	130E58	-8:43:52
Mōka	1	36N26	140E01	-9:20:04
Mombetsu	1	44N21	143E22	-9:33:28
Momozaka	1	34N51	135E02	-9:00:08
Monobe	1	33N42	133E53	-8:55:32
Monzen	1	37N17	136E46	-9:07:04
Mori	1	34N32	135E00	-9:00:00
Mori	1	42N06	140E35	-9:22:20
Mori	1	34N50	137E56	-9:11:44
Moriguchi	1	34N44	135E34	-9:02:16
Morioka	1	39N42	141E09	-9:24:36
Moriya	1	35N56	140E00	-9:20:00
Moriyama	1	35N04	135E59	-9:03:56
Moroyama	1	35N56	139E19	-9:17:16
Motegi	1	36N32	140E11	-9:20:44
Motobu	1	26N39	127E54	-8:31:36
Motosu	1	35N29	136E40	-9:06:40
Motoyama	1	33N45	133E35	-8:54:20
Mozu	1	34N34	135E29	-9:01:56
Mugegawa	1	35N31	136E51	-9:07:24
Mugi	1	35N34	137E01	-9:08:04
Mugi	1	33N40	134E25	-8:57:40
Muikaichi	1	34N21	131E56	-8:47:44
Muikamachi	1	37N04	138E53	-9:15:32
Mukaishima	1	34N20	133E10	-8:52:40
Mukawa	1	35N47	138E23	-9:13:32
Mukō	1	34N56	135E42	-9:02:48
Munakata	1	33N50	130E35	-8:42:20
Murakami	1	38N14	139E29	-9:17:56
Muraoka	1	35N28	134E35	-8:58:20
Murayama	1	38N28	140E22	-9:21:28
Mure	1	36N45	138E14	-9:12:56
Murō	1	34N34	136E02	-9:04:08
Muroran	1	42N18	140E59	-9:23:56
Muroto	1	33N18	134E09	-8:56:36
Musashi	1	33N30	131E43	-8:46:52
Musashi → Iruma	1	35N50	139E24	-9:17:36
Musashimurayama	1	35N45	139E23	-9:17:32
Musashino	1	35N42	139E34	-9:18:16
Mutsu	1	41N17	141E10	-9:24:40
Mutsuai	1	35N08	139E38	-9:18:32
Mutsumi	1	34N26	131E34	-8:46:16
Myōgata	1	35N51	137E02	-9:08:08
Myōgi	1	36N17	138E49	-9:15:16
Myōkō	1	36N56	138E13	-9:12:52

Place	Zone	Lat	Long	Time
Myōkō-Kōgen	1	36N52	138E12	-9:12:48
Nabari	1	34N37	136E05	-9:04:20
Nachi-Katsuura	1	33N30	135E55	-9:03:40
Nadachi	1	37N09	138E06	-9:12:24
Nadasaki	1	34N32	133E52	-8:55:28
Naga	1	34N16	135E26	-9:01:44
Nagahama	1	35N23	136E16	-9:05:04
Nagahama	1	33N36	132E29	-8:49:56
Nagai	1	38N06	140E02	-9:20:08
Nagai	1	35N12	139E37	-9:18:28
Nagano	1	36N39	138E11	-9:12:44
Naganohara	1	36N33	138E38	-9:14:32
Nagao	1	34N16	134E10	-8:56:40
Nagao	1	34N50	135E43	-9:02:52
Nagaoka	1	37N27	138E51	-9:15:24
Nagaokakyō	1	34N55	135E42	-9:02:48
Nagara	1	34N26	135E44	-9:02:56
Nagareyama	1	35N51	139E54	-9:19:36
Nagasaka	1	35N49	138E22	-9:13:28
Nagasaki	1	32N48	129E55	-8:39:40
Nagasawa	1	35N12	139E41	-9:18:44
Nagashima	1	35N05	136E42	-9:06:48
Nagasu	1	32N56	130E27	-8:41:48
Nagasu → Usa	1	33N31	131E22	-8:45:28
Nagataki	1	34N23	135E20	-9:01:20
Nagato	1	36N15	138E16	-9:13:04
Nagato	1	34N21	131E10	-8:44:40
Nagawa	1	36N05	137E41	-9:10:44
Nagi	1	35N07	134E11	-8:56:44
Nagiso	1	35N36	137E37	-9:10:28
Nago	1	26N35	127E59	-8:31:56
Nagoja → Nagoya	1	35N10	136E55	-9:07:40
Nagoya	1	35N10	136E55	-9:07:40
Naguri	1	35N53	139E11	-9:16:44
Naha	1	26N13	127E40	-8:30:40
Nahari	1	33N25	134E01	-8:56:04
Najio	1	34N50	135E18	-9:01:12
Naka	1	35N49	140E03	-9:20:12
Naka	1	34N50	135E48	-9:03:12
Naka	1	34N42	135E45	-9:03:00
Naka	1	36N27	140E30	-9:22:00
Naka	1	35N02	134E55	-8:59:40
Nakagami	1	35N49	139E21	-9:17:24
Nakagawa	1	35N38	137E56	-9:11:44
Nakagō	1	36N58	138E14	-9:12:56
Nakagusuku	1	26N15	127E49	-8:31:16
Nakaheji	1	33N47	135E31	-9:02:04
Nakai	1	35N20	139E14	-9:16:56
Nakaizu	1	34N57	139E00	-9:16:00
Nakajima	1	33N58	132E07	-8:48:28
Nakajima	1	35N26	139E56	-9:19:44
Nakajima	1	35N18	139E58	-9:19:52
Nakajima	1	37N07	136E51	-9:07:24
Nakajō	1	36N36	138E02	-9:12:08
Nakajō	1	38N03	139E24	-9:17:36
Nakakawane	1	35N03	138E05	-9:12:20
Nakama	1	33N50	130E43	-8:42:52
Nakaminato	1	36N21	140E36	-9:22:24
Nakamura	1	32N59	132E56	-8:51:44
Nakano	1	35N20	139E54	-9:19:36
Nakano	1	34N58	135E58	-9:03:52
Nakano	1	36N45	138E22	-9:13:28
Nakanojō	1	36N35	138E51	-9:15:24
Nakaosu	1	26N37	128E02	-8:32:08
Nakashibetsu	1	43N33	144E59	-9:39:56
Nakatō	1	35N45	139E24	-9:17:36
Nakatomi	1	35N49	139E30	-9:18:00
Nakatomi	1	35N28	138E26	-9:13:44
Nakatosa	1	33N20	133E14	-8:52:56
Nakatsu	1	33N57	135E18	-9:01:12
Nakatsu	1	35N30	139E20	-9:17:20
Nakatsu	1	33N34	131E13	-8:44:52
Nakatsue	1	33N08	130E56	-8:43:44
Nakatsugawa	1	35N29	137E30	-9:10:00
Nakauchigami	1	34N56	135E10	-9:00:40
Nakayama	1	35N31	133E35	-8:54:20
Nakayama	1	33N38	132E42	-8:50:48
Nakazato	1	37N03	138E42	-9:14:48
Nakazato	1	36N05	138E50	-9:15:20
Nakazuma	1	35N58	139E35	-9:18:20
Namegawa	1	36N04	139E22	-9:17:28
Namerikawa	1	36N46	137E20	-9:09:20
Namiai	1	35N22	137E41	-9:10:44
Namie	1	37N29	141E00	-9:24:00
Nanao	1	37N03	136E58	-9:07:52
Nanatsuka	1	36N44	136E41	-9:06:44
Nanbu	1	35N17	138E27	-9:13:48
Nandan	1	34N15	134E43	-8:58:52
Nangō	1	37N13	139E33	-9:18:12
Nangō	1	31N32	131E23	-8:45:32
Nanjō	1	35N50	136E13	-9:04:52
Nankan	1	33N03	130E32	-8:42:08
Nankoku	1	33N39	133E44	-8:54:56
Nanmoku	1	36N10	138E44	-9:14:56
Nannō	1	35N13	136E36	-9:06:24
Nansei	1	34N22	136E41	-9:06:44
Nanto	1	34N20	136E31	-9:06:04
Nan-Yō	1	38N03	140E10	-9:20:40
Naoetsu	1	37N11	138E15	-9:13:00
Naoiri	1	33N04	131E23	-8:45:32
Naoshima	1	34N27	133E59	-8:55:56
Nara	1	34N41	135E50	-9:03:20
Narakawa	1	35N59	137E50	-9:11:20
Narao	1	32N50	129E04	-8:36:16
Narashino	1	35N41	140E02	-9:20:08
Nariai	1	34N53	135E38	-9:02:32
Narita	1	35N47	140E19	-9:21:16
Nariwa	1	34N47	133E33	-8:54:12
Naru	1	32N49	128E56	-8:35:44
Naruko	1	38N44	140E43	-9:22:52
Naruo	1	34N43	135E23	-9:01:32
Narusawa	1	35N29	138E41	-9:14:44
Naruto	1	34N11	134E37	-8:58:28
Narutō	1	35N36	140E25	-9:21:40
Nase → Naze	1	28N23	129E30	-8:38:00
Nasu	1	37N01	140E07	-9:20:28
Natashō	1	35N24	135E38	-9:02:32
Natori	1	38N08	140E55	-9:23:40
Nawa	1	35N30	133E30	-8:54:00
Nawa → Naha	1	26N13	127E40	-8:30:40
Nayoro	1	44N21	142E28	-9:29:52
Naze	1	28N23	129E30	-8:38:00
Ne	1	35N47	140E03	-9:20:12
Neagari	1	36N27	136E27	-9:05:48
Neba	1	35N15	137E35	-9:10:20
Negishi	1	35N51	139E23	-9:17:32
Nemuro	1	43N20	145E35	-9:42:20
Neo	1	35N38	136E37	-9:06:28
Neyagawa	1	34N46	135E38	-9:02:32
Nichihara	1	34N33	131E50	-8:47:20
Nichinan	1	35N09	133E16	-8:53:04
Nichinan	1	31N36	131E23	-8:45:32
Nihommatsu	1	37N35	140E26	-9:21:44
Niigata	1	37N55	139E03	-9:16:12
Niihama	1	33N58	133E16	-8:53:04
Niihari	1	36N07	140E09	-9:20:36
Niiharu	1	36N41	138E55	-9:15:40
Niimi	1	34N59	133E28	-8:53:52
Niitsu	1	37N48	139E07	-9:16:28
Niiza	1	35N48	139E34	-9:18:16
Nikkō	1	36N45	139E37	-9:18:28
Nima	1	35N09	132E24	-8:49:36
Ninohe	1	40N16	141E18	-9:25:12
Ninomiya	1	36N22	139E58	-9:19:52
Ninomiya	1	35N18	139E16	-9:17:04
Nio	1	34N12	133E39	-8:54:36
Nirasaki	1	35N42	138E27	-9:13:48
Nirayama	1	35N03	138E57	-9:15:48
Nishiazai	1	35N31	136E10	-9:04:40
Nishibetsuin	1	34N58	135E31	-9:02:04
Nishigō	1	37N09	140E10	-9:20:40
Nishiiyayama	1	33N53	133E49	-8:55:16
Nishiizu	1	34N46	138E47	-9:15:08
Nishikata	1	36N28	139E45	-9:19:00
Nishikatsura	1	35N31	138E51	-9:15:24
Nishiki	1	34N16	131E57	-8:47:48
Nishikiori	1	34N29	135E34	-9:02:16
Nishinasuno	1	36N53	139E59	-9:19:56
Nishinomiya	1	34N43	135E20	-9:01:20
Nishinoomote	1	30N44	131E00	-8:44:00
Nishio	1	34N52	137E03	-9:08:12
Nishitosa	1	33N09	132E47	-8:51:08
Nishiwaki	1	34N59	134E58	-8:59:52
Nisinomiya → Nishinomiya	1	34N43	135E20	-9:01:20
Nisshin	1	35N08	137E02	-9:08:08
Nita	1	35N12	133E01	-8:52:04
Nitta	1	36N17	139E18	-9:17:12
Niyodo	1	33N32	133E08	-8:52:32
Nō	1	37N06	137E59	-9:11:56
Nobeoka	1	32N35	131E40	-8:46:40
Nobidome	1	35N48	139E35	-9:18:20
Noboribetsu	1	42N27	141E11	-9:24:44
Noborito	1	35N37	139E34	-9:18:16
Noda	1	35N56	139E52	-9:19:28
Nodagawa	1	35N31	135E06	-9:00:24
Nodera	1	34N45	134E56	-8:59:44
Nogami	1	36N07	139E07	-9:16:28
Nōgata	1	33N44	130E44	-8:42:56
Nogi	1	36N14	139E44	-9:18:56
Nogisaki	1	35N57	139E58	-9:19:52
Noheji	1	40N52	141E08	-9:24:32
Noichi	1	33N33	133E42	-8:54:48
Nokami	1	34N15	135E20	-9:01:20
Nōke	1	34N26	135E29	-9:01:56
Nomozaki	1	32N35	129E45	-8:39:00
Nomura	1	33N22	132E38	-8:50:32
Nonoichi	1	36N32	136E37	-9:06:28
Nosaka	1	35N39	140E34	-9:22:16
Nose	1	34N58	135E24	-9:01:36
Noshiro	1	40N12	140E02	-9:20:08
Noto	1	37N18	137E09	-9:08:36
Notogawa	1	35N10	136E10	-9:04:40
Noto-Jima	1	37N08	137E00	-9:08:00
Notsu	1	33N02	131E42	-8:46:48
Notsuharu	1	33N09	131E32	-8:46:08
Nozawa-Onsen	1	36N55	138E27	-9:13:48
Nozuta	1	35N35	139E27	-9:17:48
Nukata	1	34N55	137E17	-9:09:08
Numakuma	1	34N23	133E20	-8:53:20
Numata	1	36N38	139E03	-9:16:12
Numata	1	34N27	132E24	-8:49:36
Numata	1	43N48	141E57	-9:27:48
Numazu	1	35N06	138E52	-9:15:28
Nyūkawa	1	36N10	137E19	-9:09:16
Nyūzen	1	36N56	137E30	-9:10:00
Ōamishirasato	1	35N31	140E19	-9:21:16
Ōana	1	35N45	140E04	-9:20:16
Ōarai	1	36N18	140E34	-9:22:16
Obama	1	35N30	135E45	-9:03:00
Obama	1	32N43	130E13	-8:40:52
Obanazawa	1	38N36	140E24	-9:21:36
Obata	1	34N30	136E40	-9:06:40
Obihiro	1	42N55	143E12	-9:32:48
Obira	1	44N00	141E35	-9:26:20
Ōbu	1	35N00	136E58	-9:07:52
Obuse	1	36N42	138E19	-9:13:16
Ōchi	1	35N04	132E36	-8:50:24
Ōchi	1	34N16	134E18	-8:57:12
Ochi	1	33N32	133E15	-8:53:00
Ochiai	1	35N01	133E45	-8:55:00
Ōda	1	35N11	132E30	-8:50:00
Oda	1	33N34	132E48	-8:51:12
Ōdai	1	34N24	136E25	-9:05:40
Odaka	1	37N34	141E00	-9:24:00
Ōdate	1	40N16	140E34	-9:22:16
Odawara	1	35N15	139E10	-9:16:40
Ōe	1	35N23	135E09	-9:00:36
Ōfukuroshinden	1	35N53	139E27	-9:17:48
Ōfuna	1	35N21	139E32	-9:18:08
Ōfunato	1	39N04	141E43	-9:26:52
Oga	1	39N53	139E51	-9:19:24
Ōgaki	1	34N06	132E30	-8:50:00
Ōgaki	1	35N21	136E37	-9:06:28
Ogano	1	36N01	139E00	-9:16:00
Ogasa	1	34N41	138E06	-9:12:24
Ōgata	1	33N01	133E01	-8:52:04
Ogata	1	32N58	131E29	-8:45:56
Ōgata	1	37N13	138E20	-9:13:20
Ogatsu	1	38N31	141E28	-9:25:52
Ogawa	1	36N10	140E21	-9:21:24
Ogawa	1	36N37	137E58	-9:11:52
Ogawa	1	36N03	139E16	-9:17:04
Ogawa	1	36N45	140E08	-9:20:32
Ogawa	1	35N44	139E28	-9:17:52
Ogawa	1	32N35	130E41	-8:42:52
Ōgimi	1	26N42	128E07	-8:32:28
Ōgo	1	36N25	139E10	-9:16:40
Ogōri	1	33N22	130E32	-8:42:08
Ogōri	1	34N06	131E24	-8:45:36
Ogose	1	35N58	139E18	-9:17:12
Ōguchi	1	35N20	136E55	-9:07:40
Oguni	1	38N04	139E45	-9:19:00
Oguni	1	33N07	131E04	-8:44:16
Ōhara	1	35N15	140E23	-9:21:32
Ōhara	1	35N07	134E20	-8:57:20
Ōhata	1	41N24	141E10	-9:24:40
Ōhatake	1	35N57	139E46	-9:19:04
Ōhira	1	36N20	139E42	-9:18:48
Ōhito	1	35N01	138E56	-9:15:44
Ōho	1	36N08	140E06	-9:20:24
Ōhori	1	35N20	139E52	-9:19:28
Ōi	1	35N28	135E37	-9:02:28
Ōi	1	35N51	139E30	-9:18:00
Ōigawa	1	34N48	138E17	-9:13:08
Ōiso	1	35N18	139E19	-9:17:16
Ōiso	1	34N33	135E01	-9:00:04
Ōita	1	33N14	131E36	-8:46:24
Ōiwa	1	34N53	135E33	-9:02:12
Ōizumi	1	36N15	139E25	-9:17:40
Ōizumi	1	35N52	138E23	-9:13:32
Ōji	1	34N35	135E42	-9:02:48
Ōjima	1	36N15	139E20	-9:17:20
Ojiya	1	37N18	138E48	-9:15:12
Okabe	1	36N12	139E15	-9:17:00
Okabe	1	34N55	138E17	-9:13:08
Okagaki	1	33N50	130E38	-8:42:32
Okamoto	1	34N59	135E58	-9:03:52
Okasaki	1	34N46	135E52	-9:03:28
Ōkawa	1	33N47	133E26	-8:53:44
Ōkawa	1	33N12	130E23	-8:41:32
Ōkawa	1	35N05	138E15	-9:13:00
Ōkawachi	1	35N04	134E45	-8:59:00
Ōkawado	1	35N56	139E50	-9:19:20
Okaya	1	36N03	138E03	-9:12:12
Okayama	1	34N39	133E55	-8:55:40
Okazaki	1	34N57	137E10	-9:08:40
Okegawa	1	36N00	139E35	-9:18:20
Okinawa	1	26N20	127E50	-8:31:20
Oku	1	34N40	134E05	-8:56:20
Oku	1	26N50	128E17	-8:33:08
Ōkubo	1	35N21	139E56	-9:19:44
Ōkubo	1	34N41	134E57	-8:59:48
Ōkuchi	1	32N04	130E37	-8:42:28
Okuchi	1	36N17	136E39	-9:06:36
Okushiri	1	42N10	139E31	-9:18:04
Okutsu	1	35N14	133E56	-8:55:44
Ōkuwa	1	35N41	137E40	-9:10:40
Ōma	1	41N32	140E55	-9:23:40
Ōmachi	1	36N30	137E52	-9:11:28
Ōmachi	1	34N28	135E25	-9:01:40
Omaezaki	1	34N35	138E13	-9:12:52
Ōmagari	1	39N27	140E29	-9:21:56
Ōmagi	1	35N52	139E42	-9:18:48
Ōmama	1	36N26	139E17	-9:17:08
Ōme	1	35N47	139E15	-9:17:00
Ōmi	1	37N01	137E48	-9:11:12
Ōmi	1	35N20	136E24	-9:05:36
Omi	1	36N27	138E03	-9:12:12
Omigawa	1	35N51	140E37	-9:22:28
Ōmi-Hachiman	1	35N08	136E06	-9:04:24
Ōminato → Mutsu	1	41N17	141E10	-9:24:40
Ōmino	1	34N32	135E33	-9:02:12
Ōmiya	1	35N54	139E38	-9:18:32
Ōmiya	1	35N35	135E06	-9:00:24
Ōmiya	1	36N33	140E25	-9:21:40
Omogo	1	33N41	133E02	-8:52:08
Omotegō	1	37N03	140E18	-9:21:12
Ōmu	1	44N34	142E58	-9:31:52
Ōmuda → Ōmuta	1	33N02	130E27	-8:41:48
Ōmura	1	32N54	129E57	-8:39:48
Ōmuro	1	35N54	139E58	-9:19:52
Ōmuta	1	33N02	130E27	-8:41:48
Onagawa	1	38N26	141E27	-9:25:48
Onahama	1	36N57	140E54	-9:23:36
Ōnari	1	35N55	139E37	-9:18:28
Ondo	1	34N11	132E32	-8:50:08
Onishi	1	36N09	139E04	-9:16:16
Onji	1	34N37	135E38	-9:02:32
Onjuku	1	35N11	140E22	-9:21:28
Onna	1	26N30	127E51	-8:31:24
Ōno	1	33N02	131E30	-8:46:00
Ono	1	34N57	135E14	-9:00:56
Ōno	1	35N59	136E29	-9:05:56
Ōno	1	35N28	136E38	-9:06:32
Ōno	1	34N18	132E17	-8:49:08
Ono	1	34N51	134E56	-8:59:44
Onoda	1	33N59	131E11	-8:44:44
Onogami	1	36N33	138E56	-9:15:44
Ōnohara	1	34N05	133E40	-8:54:40
Ōnojō	1	33N32	130E28	-8:41:52
Ōnomi	1	33N21	133E09	-8:52:36
Onomichi	1	34N25	133E12	-8:52:48

Name		Lat.	Long.	Time
Onsen	1	35N33	134E29	-8:57:56
Ōnuma	1	35N32	139E25	-9:17:40
Ōoka	1	36N30	137E59	-9:11:56
Ōra	1	26N33	128E02	-8:32:08
Oroku	1	26N12	127E39	-8:30:36
Ōsa	1	35N05	133E34	-8:54:16
Ōsaka	1	34N40	135E30	-9:02:00
Ōsawano	1	36N34	137E12	-9:08:48
Oshamambe	1	42N30	140E22	-9:21:28
Oshika	1	38N16	141E32	-9:26:08
Ōshika	1	35N34	138E02	-9:12:08
Ōshima	1	33N03	129E33	-8:38:12
Ōshima	1	37N07	138E30	-9:14:00
Ōshima	1	34N45	139E22	-9:17:28
Ōshima	1	33N55	132E15	-8:49:00
Ōshima	1	34N45	139E21	-9:17:24
Oshimizu	1	36N49	136E46	-9:07:04
Oshino	1	35N28	138E51	-9:15:24
Ōsuka	1	34N41	137E59	-9:11:56
Ōsumi	1	34N50	135E45	-9:03:00
Ōta	1	36N18	139E22	-9:17:28
Ōta	1	33N31	131E33	-8:46:12
Ota	1	35N58	136E04	-9:04:16
Ōtake	1	34N12	132E13	-8:48:52
Ōtaki	1	35N48	137E33	-9:10:12
Ōtaki	1	35N57	138E56	-9:15:44
Ōtaki	1	35N17	140E15	-9:21:00
Otari	1	36N46	137E54	-9:11:36
Otaru	1	43N13	141E00	-9:24:00
Ōtawara	1	36N52	140E02	-9:20:08
Ōtō	1	33N41	135E35	-9:02:20
Ōtomi	3	24N19	123E54	-8:15:36
Ōtori-Kita	1	34N33	135E27	-9:01:48
Otowa	1	34N51	137E18	-9:09:12
Ōtoyo	1	33N46	133E40	-8:54:40
Ōtsu	1	35N16	139E42	-9:18:48
Ōtsu	1	35N00	135E52	-9:03:28
Ōtsuchi	1	39N21	141E54	-9:27:36
Ōtsuki	1	35N36	138E57	-9:15:48
Otu → Ōtsu	1	35N00	135E52	-9:03:28
Ōuda	1	34N28	135E56	-9:03:44
Ōwada	1	35N49	139E33	-9:18:12
Owariashi	1	35N12	137E02	-9:08:08
Owase	1	34N04	136E12	-9:04:48
Ōya	1	35N20	134E40	-8:58:40
Oyabe	1	36N40	136E52	-9:07:28
Oyama	1	36N18	139E48	-9:19:12
Ōyama	1	36N36	137E18	-9:09:12
Oyama	1	35N36	139E22	-9:17:28
Oyama	1	35N21	139E00	-9:16:00
Ōyamada	1	34N46	136E13	-9:04:52
Ōyamazaki	1	34N54	135E42	-9:02:48
Ōyano	1	32N35	130E26	-8:41:44
Ōyodo	1	34N23	135E48	-9:03:12
Ozaki	1	35N59	139E51	-9:19:24
Ōzu	1	33N30	132E33	-8:50:12
Ōzu	1	32N52	130E52	-8:43:28
Rausu	1	44N01	145E12	-9:40:48
Reihoku	1	32N31	130E02	-8:40:08
Rikuzen-Takata	1	39N01	141E38	-9:26:32
Rittō	1	35N01	136E00	-9:04:00
Rokugō	1	35N29	138E27	-9:13:48
Rokusei	1	36N58	136E52	-9:07:28
Rubeshibe	1	43N47	143E38	-9:34:32
Rumoi	1	43N56	141E39	-9:26:36
Ryō	1	34N44	135E55	-9:03:40
Ryōkami	1	36N00	138E58	-9:15:52
Ryōke	1	35N58	139E33	-9:18:12
Ryōnan	1	33N15	133E55	-8:55:40
Ryōtsu	1	38N05	138E26	-9:13:44
Ryūgasaki	1	35N54	140E11	-9:20:44
Ryūjin	1	33N53	135E29	-9:01:56
Ryūō	1	35N39	138E30	-9:14:00
Ryūō	1	35N04	136E07	-9:04:28
Ryūsen	1	34N28	135E37	-9:02:28
Ryūyō	1	34N40	137E48	-9:11:12
Sabae	1	35N57	136E11	-9:04:44
Sada	1	35N15	132E43	-8:50:52
Sadamitsu	1	34N02	134E04	-8:56:16
Sadowara	1	32N02	131E26	-8:45:44
Saeki	1	34N51	134E06	-8:56:24
Saeki	1	34N22	132E11	-8:48:44
Saeki → Saiki	1	32N57	131E54	-8:47:36
Saga	1	33N05	133E06	-8:52:24
Saga	1	33N15	130E18	-8:41:12
Sagae	1	38N22	140E17	-9:21:08
Sagamihara	1	35N34	139E23	-9:17:32
Sagamiko	1	35N37	139E12	-9:16:48
Saganoseki	1	33N15	131E53	-8:47:32
Sagara	1	34N41	138E12	-9:12:48
Saidaiji	1	34N39	134E02	-8:56:08
Saido	1	35N52	139E41	-9:18:44
Saigawa	1	33N39	130E57	-8:43:48
Saigō	1	36N12	133E20	-8:53:20
Saihaku	1	35N20	133E20	-8:53:20
Saijō	1	33N55	133E11	-8:52:44
Saiki	1	32N57	131E54	-8:47:36
Saita	1	34N08	133E49	-8:55:16
Saito	1	32N06	131E24	-8:45:36
Sakado	1	35N57	139E24	-9:17:36
Sakae	1	36N58	138E35	-9:14:20
Sakae	1	35N50	140E15	-9:21:00
Sakahogi	1	35N26	136E59	-9:07:56
Sakai	1	36N06	139E48	-9:19:12
Sakai	1	34N35	135E28	-9:01:52
Sakai	1	35N25	139E22	-9:17:28
Sakai	1	36N10	136E14	-9:04:56
Sakai	1	36N16	139E15	-9:17:00
Sakaide	1	34N19	133E52	-8:55:28
Sakaigawa	1	35N35	138E37	-9:14:28
Sakaiminato	1	35N33	133E15	-8:53:00
Sakaki	1	36N28	138E11	-9:12:44
Sakakita	1	36N25	138E01	-9:12:04
Sakashita	1	35N34	137E32	-9:10:08
Sakata	1	38N55	139E50	-9:19:20
Sakauchi	1	35N36	136E25	-9:05:40
Sakawa	1	33N30	133E17	-8:53:08
Sakito	1	33N02	129E32	-8:38:08
Sako	1	34N53	135E47	-9:03:08
Saku	1	36N13	138E29	-9:13:56
Sakugi	1	34N52	132E43	-8:50:52
Sakuma	1	35N05	137E48	-9:11:12
Sakura	1	35N43	140E14	-9:20:56
Sakurae	1	34N57	132E20	-8:49:20
Sakurai	1	34N30	135E51	-9:03:24
Sakutō	1	35N01	134E14	-8:56:56
Samani	1	42N07	142E56	-9:31:44
Samegawa	1	37N02	140E31	-9:22:04
Samukawa	1	35N22	139E23	-9:17:32
Sanada	1	36N27	138E20	-9:13:20
Sanagōchi	1	33N59	134E28	-8:57:52
Sanbu	1	35N39	140E23	-9:21:32
Sanda	1	35N28	139E21	-9:17:24
Sanda	1	34N53	135E14	-9:00:56
Sango	1	34N36	135E42	-9:02:48
Sanjō	1	37N37	138E57	-9:15:48
Sanmaiden	1	34N34	135E51	-9:03:24
Sannan	1	35N04	135E02	-9:00:08
Sannohe	1	40N22	141E15	-9:25:00
Sano	1	36N19	139E35	-9:18:20
Santō	1	35N19	134E53	-8:59:32
Santō	1	35N21	136E22	-9:05:28
Sanuki	1	35N16	139E53	-9:19:32
Sanwa	1	34N42	133E15	-8:53:00
Sanwa	1	36N12	139E49	-9:19:16
Sanwa	1	37N07	138E21	-9:13:24
Sanyō	1	34N02	131E10	-8:44:40
Sanyō	1	34N45	134E01	-8:56:04
Saori	1	35N11	136E44	-9:06:56
Sapporo	1	43N03	141E21	-9:25:24
Sarufutsu	1	45N16	142E12	-9:28:48
Sasaguri	1	33N37	130E32	-8:42:08
Sasao	1	34N57	135E20	-9:01:20
Sasayama	1	35N04	135E13	-9:00:52
Sasebo	1	33N10	129E43	-8:38:52
Sashiki	1	26N10	127E47	-8:31:08
Sashima	1	36N08	139E51	-9:19:24
Sasiki	1	26N10	127E47	-8:31:08
Satomi	1	36N43	140E30	-9:22:00
Satte	1	36N04	139E43	-9:18:52
Sawada	3	24N50	125E09	-8:20:36
Sawara	1	35N53	140E30	-9:22:00
Sawata	1	38N00	138E16	-9:13:04
Sayama	1	35N51	139E24	-9:17:36
Sayama	1	34N31	135E34	-9:02:16
Sayō	1	35N00	134E22	-8:57:28
Saza	1	33N14	129E39	-8:38:36
Schisuoka → Shizuoka	1	34N58	138E23	-9:13:32
Seidan	1	34N19	134E45	-8:59:00
Seika	1	34N46	135E48	-9:03:12
Seinaiji	1	35N30	137E42	-9:10:48
Seiwa	1	34N29	136E30	-9:06:00
Seki	1	35N29	136E55	-9:07:40
Seki	1	34N51	136E24	-9:05:36
Sekigahara	1	35N22	136E28	-9:05:52
Sekigane	1	35N22	133E46	-8:55:04
Sekijō	1	36N14	139E55	-9:19:40
Sekinomiya	1	35N22	134E38	-8:58:32
Sekiya	1	34N27	135E42	-9:02:48
Sekiyado	1	36N06	139E47	-9:19:08
Sendai	1	31N49	130E18	-8:41:12
Sendai	1	38N15	140E53	-9:23:32
Sennan	1	34N22	135E17	-9:01:08
Senriyama	1	34N47	135E30	-9:02:00
Sera	1	34N36	133E03	-8:52:12
Seta	1	34N58	135E55	-9:03:40
Setaka	1	33N09	130E28	-8:41:52
Setana	1	42N26	139E51	-9:19:24
Seto	1	35N14	137E06	-9:08:24
Seto	1	33N27	132E15	-8:49:00
Seto	1	34N44	134E02	-8:56:08
Setoda	1	34N18	133E05	-8:52:20
Setouchi	1	28N10	129E15	-8:37:00
Settsu	1	34N46	135E33	-9:02:12
Shari	1	43N55	144E50	-9:39:20
Shibakawa	1	35N13	138E33	-9:14:12
Shibasaki	1	35N39	139E34	-9:18:16
Shibata	1	37N57	139E20	-9:17:20
Shibayama	1	35N41	140E25	-9:21:40
Shibecha	1	43N17	144E36	-9:38:24
Shibetsu	1	43N40	145E08	-9:40:32
Shibetsu	1	44N10	142E23	-9:29:32
Shibukawa	1	36N29	139E00	-9:16:00
Shibushi	1	31N28	131E07	-8:44:28
Shichisō	1	35N33	137E07	-9:08:28
Shido	1	34N19	134E10	-8:56:40
Shiga	1	36N20	137E59	-9:11:56
Shiga	1	35N09	135E55	-9:03:40
Shigaraki	1	34N52	136E03	-9:04:12
Shigenobu	1	33N48	132E50	-8:51:20
Shiida	1	33N39	131E04	-8:44:16
Shijōnawate	1	34N45	135E39	-9:02:36
Shika	1	37N01	136E47	-9:07:08
Shikano	1	35N28	134E04	-8:56:16
Shikatsu	1	35N14	136E53	-9:07:32
Shiki	1	35N49	139E35	-9:18:20
Shiki	1	35N50	139E35	-9:18:20
Shikishima	1	35N41	138E32	-9:14:08
Shikoma	1	35N11	139E56	-9:19:44
Shima	1	34N13	136E51	-9:07:24
Shima	1	34N59	135E20	-9:01:20
Shimabara	1	32N47	130E22	-8:41:28
Shimada	1	34N49	138E11	-9:12:44
Shimada	1	35N59	139E25	-9:17:40
Shimagahara	1	34N46	136E03	-9:04:12
Shimamoto	1	34N53	135E40	-9:02:40
Shimizu	1	35N01	138E29	-9:13:56
Shimizu	1	34N05	135E26	-9:01:44
Shimizu	1	43N01	142E53	-9:31:32
Shimizu	1	36N02	136E09	-9:04:36
Shimizu → Tosa-Shimizu	1	32N46	132E57	-8:51:48
Shimminato	1	36N47	137E04	-9:08:16
Shimobe	1	35N27	138E29	-9:13:56
Shimoda	1	34N40	138E57	-9:15:48
Shimodate	1	36N18	139E59	-9:19:56
Shimofusa	1	35N52	140E21	-9:21:24
Shimogawara	1	35N56	139E21	-9:17:24
Shimogōri	1	35N21	140E03	-9:20:12
Shimohōya	1	35N45	139E34	-9:18:16
Shimoichi	1	34N22	135E47	-9:03:08
Shimoji	3	24N45	125E16	-8:21:04
Shimojō	1	35N24	137E47	-9:11:08
Shimokawa	1	44N18	142E39	-9:30:36
Shimomatsu	1	34N27	135E23	-9:01:32
Shimomizo	1	35N31	139E23	-9:17:32
Shimoniikura	1	35N47	139E38	-9:18:32
Shimonita	1	36N13	138E47	-9:15:08
Shimonoseki	1	33N57	130E57	-8:43:48
Shimookudomi	1	35N53	139E26	-9:17:44
Shimosakamoto	1	35N03	135E53	-9:03:32
Shimosuwa	1	36N04	138E05	-9:12:20
Shimotajiri	1	34N57	135E28	-9:01:52
Shimotomi	1	35N50	139E29	-9:17:56
Shimotsu	1	34N10	135E08	-9:00:32
Shimotsuchidana	1	35N24	139E27	-9:17:48
Shimotsui	1	34N26	133E47	-8:55:08
Shimotsuma	1	36N11	139E58	-9:19:52
Shimotsuruma	1	35N29	139E28	-9:17:52
Shimoya	1	35N23	139E21	-9:17:24
Shimoyama	1	35N02	137E19	-9:09:16
Shimoyugi	1	35N38	139E23	-9:17:32
Shinano	1	36N48	138E13	-9:12:52
Shindo	1	35N21	139E21	-9:17:24
Shingo	1	34N59	133E23	-8:53:32
Shingū	1	34N55	134E33	-8:58:12
Shingū	1	33N44	135E59	-9:03:56
Shinichi	1	34N33	133E16	-8:53:04
Shinji	1	35N24	132E54	-8:51:36
Shinjō	1	34N30	135E44	-9:02:56
Shinjō	1	38N46	140E18	-9:21:12
Shinjuku	1	35N41	139E42	-9:18:48
Shinkawa	1	35N09	136E50	-9:07:20
Shinmachi	1	36N16	139E07	-9:16:28
Shinnayō	1	34N04	131E47	-8:47:08
Shinshiro	1	34N54	137E30	-9:10:00
Shinshū-Shinmachi	1	36N34	138E01	-9:12:04
Shintone	1	35N50	140E20	-9:21:20
Shio	1	36N52	136E48	-9:07:12
Shiobara	1	36N58	139E49	-9:19:16
Shiogama	1	38N19	141E01	-9:24:04
Shiojiri	1	36N06	137E58	-9:11:52
Shiokawa	3	24N40	124E41	-8:18:44
Shionoe	1	34N10	134E05	-8:56:20
Shioya	1	36N46	139E51	-9:19:24
Shiozawa	1	37N02	138E51	-9:15:24
Shippō	1	35N10	136E48	-9:07:12
Shirahama	1	33N40	135E20	-9:01:20
Shirahama	1	34N54	139E54	-9:19:36
Shirakawa	1	35N35	137E12	-9:08:48
Shirakawa	1	36N16	136E54	-9:07:36
Shirakawa	1	37N07	140E13	-9:20:52
Shirako	1	35N26	140E23	-9:21:32
Shiramine	1	36N10	136E37	-9:06:28
Shirane	1	35N38	138E28	-9:13:52
Shiranuka	1	42N57	144E05	-9:36:20
Shiraoi	1	42N33	141E21	-9:25:24
Shiraoka	1	36N01	139E40	-9:18:40
Shirasawa	1	36N40	139E08	-9:16:32
Shiroi	1	35N48	140E04	-9:20:16
Shiroishi	1	38N00	140E37	-9:22:28
Shirokawa	1	33N23	132E46	-8:51:04
Shirone	1	37N46	139E01	-9:16:04
Shirotori	1	34N15	134E20	-8:57:20
Shirotori	1	35N53	136E52	-9:07:28
Shiroyama	1	35N35	139E19	-9:17:16
Shishikui	1	33N34	134E18	-8:57:12
Shisui	1	35N43	140E16	-9:21:04
Shitara	1	35N05	137E35	-9:10:20
Shizugawa	1	38N40	141E27	-9:25:48
Shizunai	1	42N20	142E22	-9:29:28
Shizuoka	1	34N58	138E23	-9:13:32
Shōbara	1	34N51	133E01	-8:52:04
Shōboku	1	35N06	134E07	-8:56:28
Shōdai	1	34N51	135E42	-9:02:48
Shōdo-shima	1	34N30	134E17	-8:57:08
Shōdo-shima Island	1	34N30	134E17	-8:57:08
Shōgawa	1	36N34	136E59	-9:07:56
Shōkawa	1	36N02	136E57	-9:07:48
Shōmonoseki	1	33N58	130E55	-8:43:40
Shōnai	1	33N11	131E26	-8:45:44
Shōnan	1	35N50	140E02	-9:20:08
Shōō	1	35N02	134E08	-8:56:32
Shōwa	1	34N43	133E39	-8:54:36
Shōwa	1	36N37	139E04	-9:16:16
Shūhō	1	34N13	131E18	-8:45:12
Shuri	1	26N13	127E43	-8:30:52
Shūtō	1	34N05	132E05	-8:48:20
Shuya	1	26N40	128E06	-8:32:24
Shuzenji	1	34N58	138E56	-9:15:44
Simizu → Shimizu	1	35N01	138E29	-9:13:56
Simonoseki → Shimonoseki	1	33N57	130E57	-8:43:48
Sizuoka → Shizuoka	1	34N58	138E23	-9:13:32
Sobue	1	35N15	136E43	-9:06:52
Sodegaura	1	35N26	139E57	-9:19:48
Soeda	1	33N34	130E52	-8:43:28
Sōja	1	34N40	133E45	-8:55:00
Sōka	1	35N49	139E48	-9:19:12

JAPAN JAPÓN NIPPON JAPON NIHON

Place		Lat.	Long.	Time
Sōma	1	37N48	140E57	-9:23:48
Sono	1	34N48	135E55	-9:03:40
Sonobe	1	35N06	135E28	-9:01:52
Sue	1	33N35	130E30	-8:42:00
Sugano	1	35N44	139E56	-9:19:44
Sugito	1	36N02	139E44	-9:18:56
Suifu	1	36N37	140E29	-9:21:56
Suita	1	34N45	135E32	-9:02:08
Sukagawa	1	37N17	140E23	-9:21:32
Sukematsu	1	34N31	135E26	-9:01:44
Sukumo	1	32N56	132E44	-8:50:56
Sumoto	1	34N21	134E54	-8:59:36
Sunagawa	1	43N29	141E55	-9:27:40
Sunami	1	35N25	136E40	-9:06:40
Sunashinden	1	35N53	139E30	-9:18:00
Suneori	1	35N56	139E24	-9:17:36
Susa	1	34N37	131E36	-8:46:24
Susaki	1	33N22	133E17	-8:53:08
Susami	1	33N33	135E30	-9:02:00
Susono	1	35N09	138E54	-9:15:36
Susu	1	26N47	128E19	-8:33:16
Sutama	1	35N47	138E25	-9:13:40
Suttsu	1	42N48	140E14	-9:20:56
Suwa	1	36N02	138E08	-9:12:32
Suzaka	1	36N39	138E19	-9:13:16
Suzu	1	37N25	137E17	-9:09:08
Suzuka	1	34N51	136E35	-9:06:20
Suzuki	1	35N43	139E31	-9:18:04
Syukunoshō	1	34N50	135E32	-9:02:08
Tabayama	1	35N47	138E55	-9:15:40
Tabuse	1	33N57	132E03	-8:48:12
Tachibana	1	33N54	132E17	-8:49:08
Tachibana	1	33N11	130E36	-8:42:24
Tachikawa	1	35N42	139E25	-9:17:40
Tachikawa Air Force Base	2	35N43	139E25	-9:17:40
Tadain	1	34N52	135E24	-9:01:36
Tadami	1	37N21	139E19	-9:17:16
Tado	1	35N08	136E38	-9:06:32
Tadotsu	1	34N16	133E45	-8:55:00
Taga	1	34N49	135E49	-9:03:16
Taga	1	35N13	136E17	-9:05:08
Tagajō	1	38N20	141E00	-9:24:00
Tagawa	1	33N38	130E49	-8:43:16
Tahara	1	34N40	137E16	-9:09:04
Tai	1	34N31	135E26	-9:01:44
Taiei	1	35N49	140E25	-9:21:40
Taiho	1	26N39	128E07	-8:32:28
Taima	1	34N30	135E42	-9:02:48
Tainaka	1	34N36	135E37	-9:02:28
Taira	1	26N38	128E09	-8:32:36
Taira	1	36N26	136E57	-9:07:48
Taira → Iwaki	1	37N03	140E55	-9:23:40
Taisha	1	35N24	132E40	-8:50:40
Taisha → Izumo	1	35N22	132E46	-8:51:04
Taishi	1	34N31	135E39	-9:02:36
Taishi	1	34N50	134E33	-8:58:12
Taishō	1	33N12	132E58	-8:51:52
Tajima	1	37N12	139E46	-9:19:04
Tajimi	1	35N19	137E08	-9:08:32
Tajiri	1	34N24	135E18	-9:01:12
Takachiho	1	32N42	131E18	-8:45:12
Takada → Bungo-Takada	1	33N33	131E27	-8:45:48
Takada → Yamato-Takada	1	34N31	135E45	-9:03:00
Takagi	1	35N56	139E35	-9:18:20
Takahagi	1	36N43	140E43	-9:22:52
Takahama	1	37N00	136E46	-9:07:04
Takahama	1	35N29	135E33	-9:02:12
Takahama	1	34N55	136E59	-9:07:56
Takahashi	1	34N47	133E37	-8:54:28
Takaishi	1	34N32	135E26	-9:01:44
Takamatsu	1	34N20	134E03	-8:56:12
Takamatsu	1	36N46	136E43	-9:06:52
Takamiya	1	34N47	132E44	-8:50:56
Takamori	1	35N33	137E53	-9:11:32
Takanabe	1	32N08	131E30	-8:46:00
Takane	1	35N50	138E25	-9:13:40
Takanezawa	1	36N37	139E59	-9:19:56
Takano	1	35N02	132E55	-8:51:40
Takanosu	1	40N13	140E22	-9:21:28
Takaoka	1	36N45	137E01	-9:08:04
Takasago	1	34N45	134E48	-8:59:12
Takasaki	1	36N20	139E01	-9:16:04
Takase	1	34N10	133E45	-8:55:00
Takashima	1	35N18	136E01	-9:04:04
Takashima	1	32N39	129E45	-8:39:00
Takashippu	1	26N24	127E44	-8:30:56
Takasu	1	35N57	136E53	-9:07:32
Takata	1	33N06	130E28	-8:41:52
Takata → Joetsu	1	37N06	138E15	-9:13:00
Takata → Rikuzen-Takata	1	39N01	141E38	-9:26:32
Takatō	1	35N50	138E04	-9:12:16
Takatomi	1	35N29	136E47	-9:07:08
Takatori	1	34N27	135E48	-9:03:12
Takatsuki	1	34N51	135E37	-9:02:28
Takatsuki	1	35N28	136E14	-9:04:56
Takayama	1	34N45	135E44	-9:02:56
Takayama	1	36N08	137E15	-9:09:00
Takayama	1	36N37	138E57	-9:15:48
Takayama	1	36N40	138E21	-9:13:24
Takayanagi	1	35N25	139E57	-9:19:48
Takayanagi	1	37N13	138E38	-9:14:32
Takefu	1	35N54	136E10	-9:04:40
Takehara	1	34N21	132E55	-8:51:40
Takeo	1	33N12	130E01	-8:40:04
Takeoka	1	35N12	139E51	-9:19:24
Takeshi	1	36N17	138E14	-9:12:56
Taketa	1	32N58	131E24	-8:45:36
Taketoyo	1	34N51	136E55	-9:07:40
Taki	1	35N16	132E38	-8:50:32
Taki	1	34N30	136E33	-9:06:12
Takikawa	1	43N33	141E54	-9:27:36
Takino	1	34N56	134E58	-8:59:52
Tako	1	35N44	140E28	-9:21:52
Taku	1	33N17	130E08	-8:40:32
Takuma	1	34N13	133E40	-8:54:40
Tama	1	35N37	139E27	-9:17:48
Tamagawa	1	34N01	132E56	-8:51:44
Tamagawa	1	37N12	140E24	-9:21:36
Tamaki	1	34N29	136E38	-9:06:32
Tamamura	1	36N18	139E07	-9:16:28
Tamana	1	32N55	130E33	-8:42:12
Tamano	1	34N30	133E56	-8:55:44
Tamashima	1	34N32	133E40	-8:54:40
Tamatsukuri	1	36N06	140E25	-9:21:40
Tamayu	1	35N25	133E01	-8:52:04
Tamba	1	35N09	135E25	-9:01:40
Tambara	1	33N54	133E04	-8:52:16
Tamura	1	35N22	139E22	-9:17:28
Tanabe	1	33N44	135E22	-9:01:28
Tanabe	1	34N49	135E46	-9:03:04
Tanagura	1	37N02	140E23	-9:21:32
Tanashi	1	35N44	139E33	-9:18:12
Tancha	3	26N28	121E50	-8:07:20
Taneichi	1	40N26	141E43	-9:26:52
Tango	1	35N44	135E06	-9:00:24
Tanigumi	1	35N31	136E36	-9:06:24
Tannan	1	35N05	135E10	-9:00:40
Tano	1	34N57	135E36	-9:02:24
Tano	1	33N26	134E00	-8:56:00
Tantō	1	35N29	135E00	-9:00:00
Tanuma	1	36N22	139E35	-9:18:20
Tanushimaru	1	33N21	130E41	-8:42:44
Tarama	3	24N40	124E41	-8:18:44
Tarui	1	35N22	136E32	-9:06:08
Tarumizu	1	31N29	130E42	-8:42:48
Tatebayashi	1	36N15	139E32	-9:18:08
Tateiwa	1	37N05	139E32	-9:18:08
Tateshina	1	36N16	138E19	-9:13:16
Tateyama	1	34N59	139E52	-9:19:28
Tateyama	1	36N40	137E19	-9:09:16
Tatikawa → Tachikawa	1	35N42	139E25	-9:17:40
Tatomi	1	35N36	138E31	-9:14:04
Tatsuno	1	35N59	137E59	-9:11:56
Tatsuno	1	34N52	134E33	-8:58:12
Tatsunokuchi	1	36N27	136E35	-9:06:20
Tatsuruhama	1	37N04	136E53	-9:07:32
Tatsuyama	1	34N58	137E49	-9:11:16
Tawara	1	34N27	135E57	-9:03:48
Tawarada	1	35N19	140E04	-9:20:16
Tawaramoto	1	34N33	135E48	-9:03:12
Tendō	1	38N21	140E22	-9:21:28
Tenri	1	34N36	135E51	-9:03:24
Tenryū	1	35N16	137E51	-9:11:24
Tenryū	1	34N52	137E49	-9:11:16
Teradomari	1	37N38	138E46	-9:15:04
Terai	1	36N26	136E30	-9:06:00
Teshikaga	1	43N29	144E28	-9:37:52
Teshio	1	44N53	141E44	-9:26:56
Tessei	1	34N56	133E20	-8:53:20
Tetsuta	1	34N56	133E28	-8:53:52
Tiba → Chiba	1	35N36	140E07	-9:20:28
Tigasaki → Chigasaki	1	35N19	139E24	-9:17:36
Toba	1	34N29	136E51	-9:07:24
Tobata → Kitakyūshū	1	33N53	130E50	-8:43:20
Tobe	1	33N44	132E47	-8:51:08
Tōbetsu	1	43N13	141E31	-9:26:04
Tōbu	1	36N21	138E20	-9:13:20
Tochigi	1	36N23	139E44	-9:18:56
Tochio	1	37N28	139E00	-9:16:00
Toda	1	35N48	139E41	-9:18:44
Todoromi	1	34N53	135E28	-9:01:52
Tōei	1	35N04	137E41	-9:10:44
Toga	1	36N27	137E02	-9:08:08
Togakushi	1	36N44	138E05	-9:12:20
Tōgane	1	35N33	140E22	-9:21:28
Togauchi	1	34N34	132E13	-8:48:52
Togi	1	37N08	136E44	-9:06:56
Tōgō	1	35N05	137E03	-9:08:12
Tōgō	1	35N28	133E53	-8:55:32
Toguchi	1	26N39	127E54	-8:31:36
Togura	1	36N29	138E09	-9:12:36
Tōhaku	1	35N30	133E40	-8:54:40
Toi	1	34N54	138E47	-9:15:08
Tōin	1	35N05	136E35	-9:06:20
Tōjō	1	34N53	133E16	-8:53:04
Tōjō	1	34N55	135E04	-9:00:16
Tōkagi	1	35N42	139E56	-9:19:44
Tōkai	1	36N27	140E34	-9:22:16
Tōkai	1	35N00	136E53	-9:07:32
Tōkamachi	1	37N08	138E46	-9:15:04
Toki	1	35N21	137E11	-9:08:44
Tokio → Tōkyō	1	35N42	139E46	-9:19:04
Tokiwadaira	1	35N48	139E57	-9:19:48
Tokoname	1	34N53	136E51	-9:07:24
Tokorozawa	1	35N47	139E28	-9:17:52
Tokuji	1	34N11	131E40	-8:46:40
Tokura	1	34N58	135E18	-9:01:12
Tokushima	1	34N04	134E34	-8:58:16
Tokuyama	1	35N42	136E29	-9:05:56
Tokuyama	1	34N03	131E49	-8:47:16
Tōkyō	1	35N42	139E46	-9:19:04
Tomakomai	1	42N38	141E36	-9:26:24
Tomioka	1	36N15	138E54	-9:15:36
Tomisato	1	35N44	140E19	-9:21:16
Tomiura	1	35N03	139E50	-9:19:20
Tomiyama	1	35N11	137E48	-9:11:12
Tomiyama	1	35N05	139E51	-9:19:24
Tomizawa	1	35N14	138E29	-9:13:56
Tomobe	1	36N20	140E20	-9:21:20
Tomori	1	26N08	127E44	-8:30:56
Tonami	1	36N38	136E54	-9:07:36
Tonbara	1	35N05	132E47	-8:51:08
Tonda	1	34N50	135E36	-9:02:24
Tondabayashi	1	34N30	135E36	-9:02:24
Tone	1	36N42	139E13	-9:16:52
Tone	1	35N51	140E09	-9:20:36
Tōno	1	39N19	141E32	-9:26:08
Tonogaya	1	35N46	139E22	-9:17:28
Tōnoshō	1	35N49	140E42	-9:22:48
Tonoshō	1	34N29	134E11	-8:56:44
Torahime	1	35N25	136E16	-9:05:04
Toride	1	35N53	140E04	-9:20:16
Torigoe	1	36N21	136E36	-9:06:24
Toriido	1	34N25	135E43	-9:02:52
Toriya	1	36N59	136E54	-9:07:36
Tosa	1	33N29	133E25	-8:53:40
Tosa-Shimizu	1	32N46	132E57	-8:51:48
Tosayama	1	33N38	133E32	-8:54:08
Tosa-Yamada	1	33N36	133E41	-8:54:44
Tosu	1	33N22	130E31	-8:42:04
Tottori	1	35N30	134E14	-8:56:56
Tōwa	1	33N13	132E53	-8:51:32
Towada	1	40N37	141E13	-9:24:52
Toyama	1	36N41	137E13	-9:08:52
Tōyō	1	33N30	134E16	-8:57:04
Tōyo	1	33N55	133E05	-8:52:20
Toyoake	1	35N03	137E01	-9:08:04
Toyoda	1	34N45	137E49	-9:11:16
Toyoda	1	35N39	139E23	-9:17:32
Toyofuta	1	35N53	139E57	-9:19:48
Toyohama	1	34N04	133E38	-8:54:32
Toyohara	3	24N15	123E48	-8:15:12
Toyohashi	1	34N46	137E23	-9:09:32
Toyohira	1	34N40	132E24	-8:49:36
Toyokawa	1	34N49	137E24	-9:09:36
Toyonaka	1	34N47	135E28	-9:01:52
Toyonaka	1	34N09	133E42	-8:54:48
Toyone	1	35N09	137E43	-9:10:52
Toyono	1	36N43	138E16	-9:13:04
Toyooka	1	34N50	137E52	-9:11:28
Toyooka	1	35N32	134E50	-8:59:20
Toyooka	1	35N11	139E58	-9:19:52
Toyooka	1	35N33	137E54	-9:11:36
Toyosaka	1	37N56	139E13	-9:16:52
Toyosaka	1	34N34	132E50	-8:51:20
Toyosato	1	36N06	140E02	-9:20:08
Toyoshina	1	36N18	137E54	-9:11:36
Toyota	1	35N05	137E09	-9:08:36
Toyota	1	36N46	138E19	-9:13:16
Toyota	1	34N12	131E04	-8:44:16
Toyotomi	1	35N34	138E33	-9:14:12
Toyotsu	1	33N40	130E58	-8:43:52
Toyoura	1	34N08	130E58	-8:43:52
Tsu	1	34N43	136E31	-9:06:04
Tsubame	1	37N39	138E56	-9:15:44
Tsubata	1	36N40	136E44	-9:06:56
Tsuchiura	1	36N05	140E12	-9:20:48
Tsuchiyama	1	34N56	136E17	-9:05:08
Tsuda	1	34N49	135E43	-9:02:52
Tsuda	1	34N17	134E15	-8:57:00
Tsuge	1	34N37	135E57	-9:03:48
Tsugu	1	35N10	137E37	-9:10:28
Tsuha	1	26N14	127E47	-8:31:08
Tsuiki	1	33N40	131E03	-8:44:12
Tsujidō	1	35N20	139E27	-9:17:48
Tsukahara	1	35N18	139E58	-9:19:52
Tsukechi	1	35N38	137E26	-9:09:44
Tsukigase	1	34N42	136E02	-9:04:08
Tsukiyono	1	36N41	138E59	-9:15:56
Tsukuba	1	36N13	140E06	-9:20:24
Tsukude	1	34N59	137E25	-9:09:40
Tsukui	1	35N35	139E16	-9:17:04
Tsukumi	1	33N04	131E52	-8:47:28
Tsumagoi	1	36N31	138E32	-9:14:08
Tsuna	1	34N26	134E54	-8:59:36
Tsunan	1	37N01	138E39	-9:14:36
Tsuru	1	35N33	138E55	-9:15:40
Tsuruga	1	35N39	136E04	-9:04:16
Tsurugashima	1	35N56	139E24	-9:17:36
Tsurugi	1	36N27	136E38	-9:06:32
Tsuruhara	1	34N26	135E20	-9:01:20
Tsuruma	1	35N51	139E33	-9:18:12
Tsuruoka	1	38N44	139E50	-9:19:20
Tsushima	1	33N05	132E30	-8:50:00
Tsushima	1	35N10	136E43	-9:06:52
Tsuwano	1	34N28	131E46	-8:47:04
Tsuyama	1	35N03	134E00	-8:56:00
Tsuyazaki	1	33N47	130E28	-8:41:52
Tu → Tsu	1	34N43	136E31	-9:06:04
Ube	1	33N56	131E15	-8:45:00
Uchihara	1	36N22	140E21	-9:21:24
Uchihata	1	34N25	135E27	-9:01:48
Uchiko	1	33N33	132E39	-8:50:36
Uchinada	1	36N39	136E39	-9:06:36
Uchinomi	1	34N30	134E20	-8:57:20
Uchinoura	1	31N16	131E05	-8:44:20
Uchiumi	1	33N01	132E30	-8:50:00
Udono	1	33N44	136E01	-9:04:04
Uebaru	3	24N25	123E46	-8:15:04
Ueda	1	36N24	138E16	-9:13:04
Uegō	1	35N13	139E56	-9:19:44
Ueharu	3	24N25	123E46	-8:15:04
Ueno	1	34N45	136E08	-9:04:32
Ueno	1	34N53	135E14	-9:00:56
Ueno	1	36N05	138E47	-9:15:08
Uenohara	1	35N37	139E07	-9:16:28
Uenoshiba	1	34N33	135E28	-9:01:52
Ugimi	1	26N42	128E07	-8:32:28
Uji	1	34N53	135E48	-9:03:12
Ujiie	1	36N41	139E58	-9:19:52
Uji-Tawara	1	34N51	135E31	-9:02:04
Uji-Yamada → Ise	1	34N29	136E42	-9:06:48
Uka	1	26N48	128E14	-8:32:56
Ukiha	1	33N19	130E47	-8:43:08
Uku	1	26N50	128E17	-8:33:08
Umaji	1	33N33	134E03	-8:56:12

Umaze	1	34N57	135E03	-9:00:12
Umedani	1	34N44	135E51	-9:03:24
Umi	1	33N34	130E30	-8:42:00
Unakami	1	35N46	140E45	-9:23:00
Unazuki	1	36N49	137E35	-9:10:20
Unoke	1	36N43	136E42	-9:06:48
Unten	1	26N41	128E00	-8:32:00
Uozu	1	36N48	137E24	-9:09:36
Uraga	1	35N15	139E43	-9:18:52
Uragawara	1	37N09	138E26	-9:13:44
Urahoro	1	42N48	143E39	-9:34:36
Urakawa	1	42N09	142E47	-9:31:08
Urasaki	1	26N40	127E53	-8:31:32
Urasoe	1	26N15	127E43	-8:30:52
Urawa	1	35N51	139E39	-9:18:36
Urayasu	1	35N39	139E54	-9:19:36
Ureshino	1	33N06	129E59	-8:39:56
Ureshino	1	34N37	136E29	-9:05:56
Urizura	1	36N30	140E27	-9:21:48
Urugi	1	35N16	137E42	-9:10:48
Usa	1	33N31	131E22	-8:45:28
Ushibuka	1	32N11	130E01	-8:40:04
Ushiku	1	35N58	140E08	-9:20:32
Ushimado	1	34N37	134E10	-8:56:40
Usuda	1	36N12	138E29	-9:13:56
Usui	1	33N34	130E42	-8:42:48
Usuki	1	33N08	131E49	-8:47:16
Utano	1	34N28	135E59	-9:03:56
Utashinai	1	43N31	142E03	-9:28:12
Uto	1	32N41	130E40	-8:42:40
Utsumi	1	34N21	133E17	-8:53:08
Utsunomiya	1	36N33	139E52	-9:19:28
Utunomiya → Utsunomiya				
	1	36N33	139E52	-9:19:28
Uwa	1	33N20	132E30	-8:50:00
Uwajima	1	33N13	132E34	-8:50:16
Uyama	1	34N50	135E41	-9:02:44
Wachi	1	35N15	135E24	-9:01:36
Wada	1	35N12	139E38	-9:18:32
Wada	1	34N33	135E55	-9:03:40
Wada	1	35N02	140E01	-9:20:04
Wada	1	36N12	138E13	-9:12:52
Wadayama	1	35N19	134E52	-8:59:28
Wajiki	1	33N51	134E30	-8:58:00
Wajima	1	37N24	136E54	-9:07:36
Wakakusa	1	35N36	138E29	-9:13:56
Wakamatsu	1	33N55	130E48	-8:43:12
Wakamatsu → Aizu-Wakamatsu				
	1	37N30	139E56	-9:19:44
Wakamiya	1	33N44	130E37	-8:42:28
Wakasa	1	35N20	134E24	-8:57:36
Wakayama	1	34N13	135E11	-9:00:44
Wakayanagi	1	38N46	141E08	-9:24:32
Wake	1	34N48	134E08	-8:56:32
Waki	1	34N04	134E09	-8:56:36
Wakkanai	1	45N25	141E40	-9:26:40
Wakō	1	35N47	139E37	-9:18:28
Wanouchi	1	35N17	136E38	-9:06:32
Wara	1	35N45	137E05	-9:08:20
Warabi	1	35N49	139E41	-9:18:44
Warumi	3	24N45	125E26	-8:21:44
Washimiya	1	36N06	139E40	-9:18:40
Watarai	1	34N26	136E37	-9:06:28
Wazuka	1	34N47	135E55	-9:03:40
Yabakei	1	33N27	131E07	-8:44:28
Yabe	1	33N09	130E49	-8:43:16
Yabu	1	35N22	134E47	-8:59:08
Yabu	1	26N36	127E57	-8:31:48
Yabuki	1	37N12	140E19	-9:21:16
Yachimata	1	35N39	140E19	-9:21:16
Yachiyo	1	35N43	140E07	-9:20:28
Yachiyo	1	36N10	139E53	-9:19:32
Yagi	1	35N04	135E32	-9:02:08
Yahata → Kitakyūshū				
	1	33N53	130E50	-8:43:20
Yaho	1	35N41	139E27	-9:17:48
Yaita	1	36N48	139E56	-9:19:44
Yaita	1	35N57	140E03	-9:20:12
Yaizu	1	34N52	138E20	-9:13:20
Yakage	1	34N37	133E35	-8:54:20
Yakuendai	1	35N43	140E03	-9:20:12
Yakumo	1	42N15	140E16	-9:21:04
Yakuno	1	35N19	135E00	-9:00:00
Yamada	1	26N26	127E47	-8:31:08
Yamada	1	34N31	135E39	-9:02:36
Yamada	1	39N28	141E57	-9:27:48
Yamada	1	35N49	140E36	-9:22:24
Yamada	1	36N34	137E05	-9:08:20
Yamada	1	33N33	130E47	-8:43:08
Yamada → Tosa-Yamada				
	1	33N36	133E41	-8:54:44
Yamaga	1	33N01	130E41	-8:42:44
Yamaga	1	33N27	131E30	-8:46:00
Yamagata	1	36N38	140E24	-9:21:36
Yamagata	1	36N10	137E52	-9:11:28
Yamagata	1	38N15	140E20	-9:21:20
Yamagawa	1	31N12	130E39	-8:42:36
Yamaguchi	1	34N10	131E29	-8:45:56
Yamaguchi	1	34N50	135E15	-9:01:00
Yamaguchi	1	35N33	137E33	-9:10:12
Yamakawa	1	34N04	134E15	-8:57:00
Yamakita	1	35N21	139E05	-9:16:20
Yamakuni	1	33N24	131E02	-8:44:08
Yamamoto	1	34N07	133E44	-8:54:56
Yamamoto	1	34N38	135E38	-9:02:32
Yamanaka	1	36N15	136E22	-9:05:28
Yamanakako	1	35N24	138E52	-9:15:28
Yamanashi	1	35N40	138E40	-9:14:40
Yamanouchi	1	36N44	138E25	-9:13:40
Yamasaki	1	35N00	134E33	-8:58:12
Yamashiro	1	33N57	133E45	-8:55:00
Yamashiro	1	34N45	135E49	-9:03:16
Yamate	1	34N30	135E27	-9:01:48
Yamato	1	37N10	138E56	-9:15:44
Yamato	1	33N08	130E26	-8:41:44
Yamato	1	35N48	136E54	-9:07:36
Yamato	1	35N29	139E29	-9:17:56
Yamato-Kōriyama				
	1	34N38	135E47	-9:03:08
Yamato-Takada	1	34N31	135E45	-9:03:00
Yamatsuri	1	36N52	140E25	-9:21:40
Yamazaki	1	35N56	139E54	-9:19:36
Yame	1	33N28	130E34	-8:42:16
Yanadani	1	33N32	133E01	-8:52:04
Yanagawa	1	33N10	130E24	-8:41:36
Yanagi	1	34N25	135E56	-9:03:44
Yanagimoto	1	34N34	135E51	-9:03:24
Yanahara	1	34N55	134E05	-8:56:20
Yanai	1	33N58	132E07	-8:48:28
Yanaka	1	35N24	140E01	-9:20:04
Yao	1	34N37	135E36	-9:02:24
Yaotsu	1	35N28	137E09	-9:08:36
Yasaka	1	35N39	135E07	-9:00:28
Yasaka	1	34N46	132E04	-8:48:16
Yasato	1	36N14	140E12	-9:20:48
Yashio	1	35N49	139E51	-9:19:24
Yashiro	1	34N55	134E58	-8:59:52
Yasu	1	35N03	136E01	-9:04:04
Yasu	1	33N32	133E45	-8:55:00
Yasuda	1	33N26	133E59	-8:55:56
Yasugi	1	35N26	133E15	-8:53:00
Yasuoka	1	35N22	137E50	-9:11:20
Yasuura	1	34N17	132E45	-8:51:00
Yasuzuka	1	37N08	138E28	-9:13:52
Yatabe	1	36N02	140E04	-9:20:16
Yatomi	1	35N06	136E43	-9:06:52
Yatsuka	1	35N17	133E42	-8:54:48
Yatsuo	1	36N34	137E08	-9:08:32
Yatsushiro	1	32N30	130E36	-8:42:24
Yatusiro → Yatsushiro				
	1	32N30	130E36	-8:42:24
Yawahara	1	35N59	140E01	-9:20:04
Yawata	1	34N52	135E42	-9:02:48
Yawata	1	35N32	140E08	-9:20:32
Yawatahama	1	33N27	132E24	-8:49:36
Yawata → Kitakyūshū				
	1	33N53	130E50	-8:43:20
Yōda	1	35N24	139E25	-9:17:40
Yodoe	1	35N28	133E26	-8:53:44
Yogo	1	35N33	136E12	-9:04:48
Yoichi	1	43N12	140E41	-9:22:44
Yōka	1	35N24	134E46	-8:59:04
Yōkaichi	1	35N06	136E12	-9:04:48
Yōkaichiba	1	35N42	140E33	-9:22:12
Yokawa	1	34N52	135E06	-9:00:24
Yokohama	1	35N27	139E39	-9:18:36
Yokonuma	1	35N58	139E27	-9:17:48
Yokoshiba	1	35N40	140E28	-9:21:52
Yokosuka	1	35N18	139E40	-9:18:40
Yokosuka Naval Base (US)				
	2	35N17	139E41	-9:18:44
Yokota	1	35N23	140E01	-9:20:04
Yokota	1	34N40	135E55	-9:03:40
Yokota	1	35N10	133E06	-8:52:24
Yokota Air Force Base (US)				
	2	35N45	139E21	-9:17:24
Yokote	1	39N18	140E34	-9:22:16
Yonabaru	1	26N12	127E45	-8:31:00
Yonago	1	35N26	133E20	-8:53:20
Yonaguni	3	24N27	122E57	-8:11:48
Yonaha	3	24N45	125E16	-8:21:04
Yonezawa	1	37N55	140E07	-9:20:28
Yono	1	35N53	139E38	-9:18:32
Yorii	1	36N07	139E12	-9:16:48
Yorishima	1	34N29	133E35	-8:54:20
Yōrō	1	35N18	136E33	-9:06:12
Yoshida	1	34N40	132E42	-8:50:48
Yoshida	1	35N10	132E51	-8:51:24
Yoshida	1	36N02	139E02	-9:16:08
Yoshida	1	34N46	138E15	-9:13:00
Yoshida	1	33N16	132E33	-8:50:12
Yoshii	1	34N55	134E06	-8:56:24
Yoshii	1	34N53	135E03	-9:00:12
Yoshii	1	36N15	138E59	-9:15:56
Yoshii	1	33N20	130E45	-8:43:00
Yoshii	1	34N38	133E26	-8:53:44
Yoshikawa	1	34N55	135E28	-9:01:52
Yoshikawa	1	37N13	138E25	-9:13:40
Yoshikawa	1	35N53	139E51	-9:19:24
Yoshimi	1	36N02	139E27	-9:17:48
Yoshino	1	34N06	134E23	-8:57:32
Yoshino	1	34N21	135E51	-9:03:24
Yoshinodani	1	36N17	136E39	-9:06:36
Yoshioka	1	36N27	139E01	-9:16:04
Yoshiumi	1	34N09	133E03	-8:52:12
Yoshiwa	1	34N29	132E09	-8:48:36
Yotsukaidō	1	35N39	140E10	-9:20:40
Yū	1	34N02	132E13	-8:48:52
Yuasa	1	34N02	135E11	-9:00:44
Yubara	1	35N12	133E45	-8:55:00
Yūbari	1	43N04	141E59	-9:27:56
Yūbetsu	1	44N14	143E37	-9:34:28
Yuda	1	39N20	140E50	-9:23:20
Yufuin	1	33N15	131E20	-8:45:20
Yugawara	1	35N09	139E04	-9:16:16
Yuge	1	34N15	133E12	-8:52:48
Yui	1	35N06	138E34	-9:14:16
Yuki	1	33N46	134E36	-8:58:24
Yūki	1	36N18	139E53	-9:19:32
Yuki	1	34N29	132E16	-8:49:04
Yuki	1	34N46	133E17	-8:53:08
Yukuhashi	1	33N44	130E59	-8:43:56
Yumesaki	1	34N58	134E42	-8:58:48
Yuna	1	26N46	128E12	-8:32:48
Yunotani	1	37N14	139E01	-9:16:04
Yunotsu	1	35N05	132E21	-8:49:24
Yura	1	34N17	134E57	-8:59:48
Yusuhara	1	33N23	132E55	-8:51:40
Yūtō	1	34N42	137E38	-9:10:32
Yuza	1	39N01	139E54	-9:19:36
Yuzawa	1	36N56	138E49	-9:15:16
Yuzawa	1	39N10	140E30	-9:22:00
Zaimokuza	1	35N18	139E33	-9:18:12
Zama	1	35N29	139E24	-9:17:36
Zama-Iriya	1	35N29	139E24	-9:17:36
Zentsūji	1	34N14	133E47	-8:55:08
Zeze	1	35N00	135E54	-9:03:36
Zushi	1	35N18	139E35	-9:18:20

JERSEY

Time Table

Date	Time	Offset
Before 1/Jan/1880	LMT	
Begin Standard		0W00
1/Jan/1880	0:00	0:00
3/Apr/1921	2:00	-1:00
3/Oct/1921	3:00	0:00
26/Mar/1922	2:00	-1:00
8/Oct/1922	3:00	0:00
22/Apr/1923	2:00	-1:00
16/Sep/1923	3:00	0:00
13/Apr/1924	2:00	-1:00
21/Sep/1924	3:00	0:00
19/Apr/1925	2:00	-1:00
4/Oct/1925	3:00	0:00
18/Apr/1926	2:00	-1:00
3/Oct/1926	3:00	0:00
10/Apr/1927	2:00	-1:00
2/Oct/1927	3:00	0:00
22/Apr/1928	2:00	-1:00
7/Oct/1928	3:00	0:00
21/Apr/1929	2:00	-1:00
6/Oct/1929	3:00	0:00
13/Apr/1930	2:00	-1:00
5/Oct/1930	3:00	0:00
19/Apr/1931	2:00	-1:00
4/Oct/1931	3:00	0:00
17/Apr/1932	2:00	-1:00
2/Oct/1932	3:00	0:00
9/Apr/1933	2:00	-1:00
8/Oct/1933	3:00	0:00
22/Apr/1934	2:00	-1:00
7/Oct/1934	3:00	0:00
14/Apr/1935	2:00	-1:00
6/Oct/1935	3:00	0:00
19/Apr/1936	2:00	-1:00
4/Oct/1936	3:00	0:00
18/Apr/1937	2:00	-1:00
3/Oct/1937	3:00	0:00
10/Apr/1938	2:00	-1:00
2/Oct/1938	3:00	0:00
16/Apr/1939	2:00	-1:00
19/Nov/1939	3:00	0:00
25/Feb/1940	2:00	-1:00
30/Jun/1940	0:00	-2:00
1/Nov/1942	3:00	-1:00
29/Mar/1943	2:00	-2:00
4/Oct/1943	3:00	-1:00
3/Apr/1944	2:00	-2:00
3/Oct/1944	3:00	-1:00
2/Apr/1945	2:00	-2:00
15/Jul/1945	3:00	-1:00
7/Oct/1945	3:00	0:00
14/Apr/1946	2:00	-1:00
6/Oct/1946	3:00	0:00
16/Mar/1947	2:00	-1:00
13/Apr/1947	2:00	-2:00
10/Aug/1947	3:00	-1:00
2/Nov/1947	3:00	0:00
14/Mar/1948	2:00	-1:00
31/Oct/1948	3:00	0:00
3/Apr/1949	2:00	-1:00
30/Oct/1949	3:00	0:00
16/Apr/1950	2:00	-1:00
22/Oct/1950	3:00	0:00
15/Apr/1951	2:00	-1:00
21/Oct/1951	3:00	0:00
20/Apr/1952	2:00	-1:00
26/Oct/1952	3:00	0:00
19/Apr/1953	2:00	-1:00
4/Oct/1953	3:00	0:00
11/Apr/1954	2:00	-1:00
3/Oct/1954	3:00	0:00
17/Apr/1955	2:00	-1:00
2/Oct/1955	3:00	0:00
22/Apr/1956	2:00	-1:00
7/Oct/1956	3:00	0:00
14/Apr/1957	2:00	-1:00
6/Oct/1957	3:00	0:00
20/Apr/1958	2:00	-1:00
5/Oct/1958	3:00	0:00
19/Apr/1959	2:00	-1:00
4/Oct/1959	3:00	0:00
10/Apr/1960	2:00	-1:00
2/Oct/1960	3:00	0:00
26/Mar/1961	2:00	-1:00
29/Oct/1961	3:00	0:00
25/Mar/1962	2:00	-1:00
28/Oct/1962	3:00	0:00
31/Mar/1963	2:00	-1:00
27/Oct/1963	3:00	0:00
22/Mar/1964	2:00	-1:00
25/Oct/1964	3:00	0:00
21/Mar/1965	2:00	-1:00
24/Oct/1965	3:00	0:00
20/Mar/1966	2:00	-1:00
23/Oct/1966	3:00	0:00
19/Mar/1967	2:00	-1:00
29/Oct/1967	3:00	0:00
Begin Standard		15E00
18/Feb/1968	2:00	-1:00
Begin Standard		0W00
31/Oct/1971	3:00	0:00
19/Mar/1972	2:00	-1:00
29/Oct/1972	3:00	0:00
18/Mar/1973	2:00	-1:00
28/Oct/1973	3:00	0:00
17/Mar/1974	2:00	-1:00
27/Oct/1974	3:00	0:00
16/Mar/1975	2:00	-1:00
26/Oct/1975	3:00	0:00
21/Mar/1976	2:00	-1:00
24/Oct/1976	3:00	0:00
20/Mar/1977	2:00	-1:00
23/Oct/1977	3:00	0:00
19/Mar/1978	2:00	-1:00
29/Oct/1978	3:00	0:00
18/Mar/1979	2:00	-1:00
28/Oct/1979	3:00	0:00
16/Mar/1980	2:00	-1:00
26/Oct/1980	3:00	0:00
29/Mar/1981	1:00	-1:00
25/Oct/1981	2:00	0:00
28/Mar/1982	1:00	-1:00
24/Oct/1982	2:00	0:00
27/Mar/1983	1:00	-1:00
23/Oct/1983	2:00	0:00
25/Mar/1984	1:00	-1:00
28/Oct/1984	2:00	0:00
31/Mar/1985	1:00	-1:00
27/Oct/1985	2:00	0:00
30/Mar/1986	1:00	-1:00
26/Oct/1986	2:00	0:00
29/Mar/1987	1:00	-1:00
25/Oct/1987	2:00	0:00
27/Mar/1988	1:00	-1:00
23/Oct/1988	2:00	0:00
26/Mar/1989	1:00	-1:00
29/Oct/1989	2:00	0:00
25/Mar/1990	1:00	-1:00
28/Oct/1990	2:00	0:00
31/Mar/1991	1:00	-1:00
27/Oct/1991	2:00	0:00
29/Mar/1992	1:00	-1:00
25/Oct/1992	2:00	0:00
28/Mar/1993	1:00	-1:00
24/Oct/1993	2:00	0:00
27/Mar/1994	1:00	-1:00
23/Oct/1994	2:00	0:00
26/Mar/1995	1:00	-1:00
29/Oct/1995	2:00	0:00
31/Mar/1996	1:00	-1:00
27/Oct/1996	2:00	0:00
30/Mar/1997	1:00	-1:00
26/Oct/1997	2:00	0:00
29/Mar/1998	1:00	-1:00
25/Oct/1998	2:00	0:00
28/Mar/1999	1:00	-1:00
24/Oct/1999	2:00	0:00
26/Mar/2000	1:00	-1:00
29/Oct/2000	2:00	0:00

Place	Latitude	Longitude	Offset
Gorey	49N12	2W02	0:08:08
Rozel	49N14	2W03	0:08:12
Saint Aubin	49N11	2W10	0:08:40
Saint Helier	49N12	2W37	0:10:28
Saint John	49N15	2W08	0:08:32
Saint Saviour	49N11	2W06	0:08:24

JORDAN

JORDANIA — JORDANIEN — TRANSJORDAN — AL-URDUNN

Time Table # 1

Date	Time	Offset
Before 1/Jan/1931	LMT	
Begin Standard		30E00
1/Jan/1931	0:00	-2:00
6/Jun/1973	0:00	-3:00
1/Oct/1973	0:00	-2:00
1/May/1974	0:00	-3:00
1/Oct/1974	0:00	-2:00
1/May/1975	0:00	-3:00
1/Oct/1975	0:00	-2:00
1/May/1976	0:00	-3:00
1/Nov/1976	0:00	-2:00
1/May/1977	0:00	-3:00
1/Oct/1977	0:00	-2:00
30/Apr/1978	0:00	-3:00
30/Sep/1978	0:00	-2:00
1/Apr/1985	0:00	-3:00
1/Oct/1985	0:00	-2:00
4/Apr/1986	0:00	-3:00
3/Oct/1986	0:00	-2:00
3/Apr/1987	0:00	-3:00
2/Oct/1987	0:00	-2:00
1/Apr/1988	0:00	-3:00
7/Oct/1988	0:00	-2:00
8/May/1989	0:00	-3:00
6/Oct/1989	0:00	-2:00
27/Apr/1990	0:00	-3:00
5/Oct/1990	0:00	-2:00
19/Apr/1991	0:00	-3:00
27/Sep/1991	0:00	-2:00
3/Apr/1992	0:00	-3:00
2/Oct/1992	0:00	-2:00
2/Apr/1993	0:00	-3:00
1/Oct/1993	0:00	-2:00
1/Apr/1994	0:00	-3:00
7/Oct/1994	0:00	-2:00
7/Apr/1995	0:00	-3:00
6/Oct/1995	0:00	-2:00
5/Apr/1996	0:00	-3:00
4/Oct/1996	0:00	-2:00
4/Apr/1997	0:00	-3:00
3/Oct/1997	0:00	-2:00
3/Apr/1998	0:00	-3:00
2/Oct/1998	0:00	-2:00
2/Apr/1999	0:00	-3:00
1/Oct/1999	0:00	-2:00
7/Apr/2000	0:00	-3:00
6/Oct/2000	0:00	-2:00

....

Time Table # 2

Date	Time	Offset
Before 1/Jan/1880	LMT	
Begin Standard		35E10
1/Jan/1880	0:00	-2:21
Begin Standard		30E00
1/Jan/1918	0:00	-2:00
1/Jun/1940	0:00	-3:00
1/Nov/1942	0:00	-2:00
1/Apr/1943	2:00	-3:00
1/Nov/1943	0:00	-2:00
1/Apr/1944	0:00	-3:00
1/Nov/1944	0:00	-2:00
16/Apr/1945	0:00	-3:00
1/Nov/1945	2:00	-2:00
16/Apr/1946	2:00	-3:00
1/Nov/1946	0:00	-2:00
7/Jul/1974	0:00	-3:00
13/Oct/1974	0:00	-2:00
20/Apr/1975	0:00	-3:00
31/Aug/1975	0:00	-2:00
14/Apr/1985	0:00	-3:00
15/Sep/1985	0:00	-2:00
18/May/1986	0:00	-3:00
7/Sep/1986	0:00	-2:00
15/Apr/1987	0:00	-3:00
13/Sep/1987	0:00	-2:00
9/Apr/1988	0:00	-3:00
3/Sep/1988	0:00	-2:00
29/Apr/1989	0:00	-3:00
2/Sep/1989	0:00	-2:00
25/Mar/1990	0:00	-3:00
26/Aug/1990	0:00	-2:00
10/Mar/1991	0:00	-3:00
1/Sep/1991	0:00	-2:00

DIVISIONS

1. Jordan
2. West Bank (Israel, since 1967)

Place	Div.	Latitude	Longitude	Offset
Abū Qashash 2	2	31N57	35E11	-2:20:44
‘Ajlūn 1	1	32N20	35E45	-2:23:00
Al-‘Adasīyah 1	1	32N40	35E37	-2:22:28
Al-‘Aqabah 2	2	29N31	35E00	-2:20:00
Al-Bārīḥah 1	1	32N34	35E50	-2:23:20
Al-Bīrah 2	2	31N54	35E13	-2:20:52
Al-Buwayḍah 1	1	32N28	36E04	-2:24:16
Al-Ḥiṣn 1	1	32N29	35E52	-2:23:28
Al-İfranj 1	1	31N11	35E41	-2:22:44
Al-‘Irāq 1	1	31N05	35E39	-2:22:36
Al-Jafr 1	1	30N18	36E13	-2:24:52
Al-Judayyidah 1	1	31N32	35E39	-2:22:36
Al-Judayyidah 1	1	31N15	35E49	-2:23:16
Al-Karak 1	1	31N11	35E42	-2:22:48
Al-Khalīl (Hebron) 2	2	31N32	35E06	-2:20:24
Al-Khirbah as-Samrā’ 1	1	32N11	36E10	-2:24:40
Al-Khuraybah 1	1	32N40	35E52	-2:23:28
Al-Madwar 1	1	32N17	36E00	-2:24:00
Al-Mafraq 1	1	32N21	36E12	-2:24:48
Al-Mazār 1	1	31N04	35E42	-2:22:48
Al-Mazra‘Ah 1	1	31N16	35E31	-2:22:04
Al-Qaṣr 1	1	31N19	35E45	-2:23:00
Al-Qiṣfah 1	1	32N38	35E52	-2:23:28
Al Yāmūn 2	2	32N29	35E14	-2:20:56
‘Ammān 1	1	31N57	35E56	-2:23:44
‘Anabtā 2	2	32N19	35E07	-2:20:28
‘Anātā 2	2	31N49	35E16	-2:21:04
‘Anjarah 1	1	32N18	35E45	-2:23:00
Arīḥā 1	1	31N25	35E47	-2:23:08
Arīḥā (Jericho) 2	2	31N52	35E27	-2:21:48
Ar-Rabbah 1	1	31N16	35E44	-2:22:56
Ar-Ramthā 1	1	32N34	36E00	-2:24:00
Ar-Rummān 1	1	32N10	35E50	-2:23:20
Aṣfar al-Maḥaṭṭah 1	1	30N11	35E46	-2:23:04
Ash-Shāgūr 1	1	31N50	35E39	-2:22:36
Ash-Shajarah 1	1	32N39	35E56	-2:23:44
Ash-Shawbak 1	1	30N32	35E34	-2:22:16
Aṣ-Ṣāfī 1	1	31N02	35E28	-2:21:52
As-Salṭ 1	1	32N03	35E44	-2:22:56
As-Samū‘ 2	2	31N24	35E04	-2:20:16
Aṣ-Ṣarīḥ 1	1	32N30	35E54	-2:23:36
As-Simākīyah 1	1	31N18	35E48	-2:23:12
As-Sukhnah 1	1	32N08	36E04	-2:24:16
Ath-Thanīyah 1	1	31N10	35E43	-2:22:52
Aṭ-Ṭafīlah 1	1	30N50	35E36	-2:22:24
Aṭ-Ṭayyibah 1	1	32N33	35E43	-2:22:52
‘Attīl 2	2	32N22	35E04	-2:20:16
Aṭ-Ṭunayb 1	1	31N48	35E57	-2:23:48
Ayl 1	1	30N13	35E32	-2:22:08
Az-Zabābidah 2	2	32N23	35E20	-2:21:20
Aẓ-Ẓāhirīyah 2	2	31N25	34E58	-2:19:52
Az-Zarqā’ 1	1	32N05	36E06	-2:24:24
‘Azzūn 2	2	32N11	35E03	-2:20:12
Bā’ir 1	1	30N46	36E41	-2:26:44
Bal‘Amā 1	1	32N14	36E05	-2:24:20
Basṭah 1	1	30N14	35E32	-2:22:08
Batīr 1	1	31N16	35E42	-2:22:48
Bayt Jālā 2	2	31N43	35E11	-2:20:44
Bayt Laḥm (Bethlehem) 2	2	31N43	35E12	-2:20:48
Bayt Sāḥūr 2	2	31N42	35E13	-2:20:52
Bayt Sīrā 2	2	31N53	35E03	-2:20:12
Bet Ha‘Arava 2	2	31N48	35E32	-2:22:08
Bethlehem → Bayt Laḥm 2	2	31N43	35E12	-2:20:48
Biddiyā 2	2	32N07	35E05	-2:20:20
Dāmiyā 1	1	32N06	35E33	-2:22:12
Dayr Abū Sa‘īd 1	1	32N30	35E41	-2:22:44
Dayr al-Ghuṣūn 2	2	32N21	35E05	-2:20:20
Dayr ‘Allā 1	1	32N12	35E37	-2:22:28
Dayr Dibwān 2	2	31N55	35E16	-2:21:04
Dayr Sharaf 2	2	32N15	35E11	-2:20:44
Dhībān 1	1	31N30	35E47	-2:23:08
Dūrā 2	2	31N30	35E02	-2:20:08
Faqqū‘Ah 2	2	32N30	35E24	-2:21:36
Ḥalḥūl 2	2	31N35	35E07	-2:20:28
Ḥartā 1	1	32N42	35E51	-2:23:24
Ḥawwārah 1	1	32N32	35E54	-2:23:36
Hebron → Al-Khalīl 2	2	31N32	35E06	-2:20:24
Ḥisbān 1	1	31N48	35E48	-2:23:12
Ḥuwwārah 2	2	32N09	35E15	-2:21:00
İdnah 2	2	31N34	34E59	-2:19:56
Irbid 1	1	32N33	35E51	-2:23:24
Janīn 2	2	32N28	35E18	-2:21:12
Jarash 1	1	32N17	35E54	-2:23:36
Jericho → Arīḥā 2	2	31N52	35E27	-2:21:48
Kathrabbā 1	1	31N08	35E37	-2:22:28
Kharbatā 2	2	31N57	35E04	-2:20:16
Khirbat Umm as-Surab 1	1	32N26	36E19	-2:25:16
Kifār ‘Aṣyūn 2	2	31N39	35E08	-2:20:32
Kufrinjah 1	1	32N18	35E42	-2:22:48
Kurayyimah 1	1	32N16	35E36	-2:22:24
Jurf ad-Darāwīsh 1	1	30N42	35E52	-2:23:28
Ma‘ān 1	1	30N12	35E44	-2:22:56
Ma’dabā 1	1	31N43	35E48	-2:23:12
Maḥaṭṭat Abū al-Lasan 1	1	30N05	35E31	-2:22:04
Maḥaṭṭat Abū Jirdhān 1	1	30N20	35E46	-2:23:04
Maḥaṭṭat Abū Ṭarafah 1	1	30N00	35E56	-2:23:44
Maḥaṭṭat al-Furayfirah 1	1	30N54	35E59	-2:23:56
Maḥaṭṭat al-Ḥasā 1	1	30N49	35E59	-2:23:56
Maḥaṭṭat al-Jīzah 1	1	31N43	35E58	-2:23:52

AL-URDUNN TRANSJORDAN JORDANIEN JORDANIA JORDAN

Name	Zone	Lat.	Long.	Time
Maḥaṭṭat al-Manzil 1	1	31N03	36E01	-2:24:04
Maḥaṭṭat al-Qaṣr 1	1	31N54	35E56	-2:23:44
Maḥaṭṭat al-Qaṭrānah 1	1	31N15	36E03	-2:24:12
Maḥaṭṭat 'Aqabat Ḥijāzīyah	1	29N44	35E52	-2:23:28
Maḥaṭṭat ash-Shīdīyah 1	1	29N56	35E56	-2:23:44
Maḥaṭṭat as-Suwāqah 1	1	31N22	36E07	-2:24:28
Maḥaṭṭat Ḍab'Ah 1	1	31N36	36E04	-2:24:16
Maḥaṭṭat Faṣṣū'Ah 1	1	29N46	35E54	-2:23:36
Maḥaṭṭat Jurf ad-Darāwīsh 1	1	30N42	35E52	-2:23:28
Maḥaṭṭat Muṣawwal 1	1	30N05	35E52	-2:23:28
Maḥaṭṭat Samnah 1	1	30N09	35E39	-2:22:36
Maḥaṭṭat 'Unayzah 1	1	30N29	35E48	-2:23:12
Mā'īn 1	1	31N41	35E44	-2:22:56
Makhfar al-Quwayrah 2	2	29N48	35E19	-2:21:16
Manjā 1	1	31N45	35E51	-2:23:24
Mārkā 1	1	31N59	35E59	-2:23:56
Maythalūn 2	2	32N21	35E16	-2:21:04
Mukāwir 1	1	31N34	35E38	-2:22:32
Mukhmās 2	2	31N52	35E17	-2:21:08
Mu'tah 1	1	31N06	35E42	-2:22:48
Nābulus 2	2	32N13	35E16	-2:21:04
Natl 1	1	31N39	35E52	-2:23:28
Nā'ūr 1	1	31N53	35E50	-2:23:20
Nīfī Ya'Qūb 2	2	31N50	35E14	-2:20:56
Nijil 1	1	30N31	35E33	-2:22:12
Qabātiyah 2	2	32N25	35E17	-2:21:08
Qalqilīya 2	2	32N11	34E58	-2:19:52
Qibyā 2	2	31N59	35E01	-2:20:04
Rākīn 1	1	31N14	35E42	-2:22:48
Rām Allāh 2	2	31N54	35E12	-2:20:48
Ra's an-Naqb 1	1	30N00	35E29	-2:21:56
Riḥāb 1	1	32N19	36E06	-2:24:24
Rujm aṣ-Ṣakhrī 1	1	31N02	35E43	-2:22:52
Sabasṭīyah (Samaria) 2	2	32N17	35E12	-2:20:48
Ṣabḥā 1	1	32N20	36E30	-2:26:00
Ṣaḥāb 1	1	31N53	36E00	-2:24:00
Saḥam 1	1	32N42	35E47	-2:23:08
Sa'īr 2	2	31N35	35E09	-2:20:36
Sākib 1	1	32N17	35E49	-2:23:16
Samā 1	1	32N28	36E14	-2:24:56
Ṣānūr 2	2	32N21	35E15	-2:21:00
Shammākh 1	1	30N30	35E30	-2:22:00
Shūnat Nimrīn 1	1	31N54	35E37	-2:22:28
Shuwaykah 2	2	32N20	35E02	-2:20:08
Sīlat aẓ-Ẓahr 2	2	32N19	35E11	-2:20:44
Sūf 1	1	32N19	35E50	-2:23:20
Ṣuwayliḥ 1	1	32N02	35E50	-2:23:20
Tarqūmiyah 2	2	31N35	35E01	-2:20:04
Ṭūbās 2	2	32N19	35E22	-2:21:28
Ṭūlkarm 2	2	32N19	35E02	-2:20:08
Turf ad-Darāwīsh 1	1	30N42	35E52	-2:23:28
Udhruḥ 1	1	30N20	35E36	-2:22:24
Umm al-Qiṭṭayn 1	1	32N19	36E38	-2:26:32
Umm Ḥamāṭ 1	1	31N02	35E46	-2:23:04
Umm Qusayr 1	1	31N40	35E53	-2:23:32
Wādī as-Sīr 1	1	31N57	35E49	-2:23:16
Wādī Mūsā 1	1	30N19	35E29	-2:21:56
Waqqāṣ 1	1	32N33	35E36	-2:22:24
Ya'Bad 2	2	32N27	35E10	-2:20:40
Yaṭṭah 2	2	31N27	35E05	-2:20:20
Zuwayzā 1	1	31N42	35E55	-2:23:40

KÂMPŬCHEA CAMBODIA KAMPUCHEA

Time Table
Before 9/Jun/1906 LMT
Begin Standard 106E35
9/Jun/1906 0:00 -7:06
Begin Standard 105E00
11/Mar/1911 0:01 -7:00
Begin Standard 120E00
1/May/1912 0:00 -8:00
Begin Standard 105E00
1/May/1931 0:00 -7:00

Name	Lat.	Long.	Time
Ângk Tasaôm	11N01	104E41	-6:58:44
Ânlóng Vêng	14N14	104E05	-6:56:20
Auke	9N52	106E03	-7:04:12
Bâ Kêv	13N42	107E12	-7:08:48
Bătdâmbâng	13N06	103E12	-6:52:48
Battambang → Bătdâmbâng	13N06	103E12	-6:52:48
Bœng Lvea	12N36	105E34	-7:02:16
Chhêb Kândal	13N45	105E24	-7:01:36
Chŏâm Khsant	14N13	104E56	-6:59:44
Chŏng Kal	13N57	103E35	-6:54:20
Kâmchay Méa	11N35	105E40	-7:02:40
Kâmpóng Cham	12N00	105E27	-7:01:48
Kâmpóng Chhnăng	12N15	104E40	-6:58:40
Kâmpóng Kântuŏt	11N26	104E49	-6:59:16
Kâmpóng Saôm	10N38	103E30	-6:54:00
Kâmpóng Thum	12N42	104E54	-6:59:36
Kâmpóng Trâlach	11N54	104E47	-6:59:08
Kâmpôt	10N37	104E11	-6:56:44
Kbal Dâmrei	14N07	105E21	-7:01:24
Khŭm Bathéay	11N59	104E57	-6:59:48
Krâchéh	12N29	106E01	-7:04:04
Krâkôr	12N32	104E12	-6:56:48
Krŏng Kaôh Kŏng	11N37	102E59	-6:51:56
Krŏng Kêb	10N29	104E19	-6:57:16
Léach	12N21	103E46	-6:55:04
Lumphăt	13N30	106E59	-7:07:56
Mémót	11N49	106E11	-7:04:44
Moung Roessei	12N46	103E27	-6:53:48
Ŏdŏngk	11N48	104E45	-6:59:00
Pailĭn	12N51	102E36	-6:50:24
Paôy Pêt	13N39	102E33	-6:50:12
Phnom Penh → Phnum Pénh	11N33	104E55	-6:59:40
Phnum Pénh	11N33	104E55	-6:59:40
Phnum Tbêng Méanchey	13N49	104E58	-6:59:52
Phsar Réam	10N30	103E37	-6:54:28
Phumĭ Bâ Khăm	13N51	107E22	-7:09:28
Phumĭ Banam	11N19	105E18	-7:01:12
Phumĭ Béng	13N05	104E18	-6:57:12
Phumĭ Châmbák	11N14	104E49	-6:59:16
Phumĭ Chângho Ândêng	12N39	104E35	-6:58:20
Phumĭ Chhuk	10N50	104E28	-6:57:52
Phumĭ Chruŏy Slêng	13N14	105E57	-7:03:48
Phumĭ Dăk Dăm	12N20	107E21	-7:09:24
Phumĭ Kâmpóng Srâlau	14N05	105E46	-7:03:04
Phumĭ Kâmpóng Trâbâk	13N06	105E14	-7:00:56
Phumĭ Kântuŏt Sâmraông	14N12	104E37	-6:58:28
Phumĭ Kaôh Kért	13N47	104E32	-6:58:08
Phumĭ Kaôh Kŏng	11N26	103E11	-6:52:44
Phumĭ Khpôb	11N02	105E12	-7:00:48
Phumĭ Krêk	11N46	105E56	-7:03:44
Phumĭ Lvéa Kraôm	13N21	102E54	-6:51:36
Phumĭ Moŭng	13N45	103E33	-6:54:12
Phumĭ Narŭng	13N53	105E34	-7:02:16
Phumĭ Phnum Srâlau	11N03	103E42	-6:54:48
Phumĭ Prêk Kák	12N15	105E32	-7:02:08
Phumĭ Prêk Sândêk	11N51	105E22	-7:01:28
Phumĭ Prey Toch	12N54	103E23	-6:53:32
Phumĭ Puŏk Chăs	13N26	103E44	-6:54:56
Phumĭ Rôluŏs Chăs	13N19	104E00	-6:56:00
Phumĭ Sâmraông	14N11	103E31	-6:54:04
Phumĭ Spœ Tbong	12N20	105E19	-7:01:16
Phumĭ Srê Kôkir	13N08	106E04	-7:04:16
Phumĭ Srê Rônéam	12N16	106E25	-7:05:40
Phumĭ Tbêng	13N35	104E55	-6:59:40
Phumĭ Thalabârĭvăt	13N33	105E57	-7:03:48
Phumĭ Thmâ Pôk	13N57	103E04	-6:52:16
Phumĭ Tnaôt	12N56	104E34	-6:58:16
Phumĭ Tœk Choŭ	13N36	103E24	-6:53:36
Pônley	12N26	104E27	-6:57:48
Poŭthĭsăt	12N32	103E55	-6:55:40
Prĕk Poŭthĭ	11N51	105E07	-7:00:28
Prey Lvéa	11N10	104E57	-6:59:48
Prey Nób	10N38	103E47	-6:55:08
Prey Vêng	11N29	105E19	-7:01:16
Pursat → Poŭthĭsăt	12N32	103E55	-6:55:40
Sâmbor	12N46	105E58	-7:03:52
Sândăn	12N42	106E01	-7:04:04
Senmonorom	12N27	107E12	-7:08:48
Siĕmpang	14N07	106E23	-7:05:32
Siĕmréab	13N22	103E51	-6:55:24
Sihanoukville → Kâmpóng Saôm	10N38	103E30	-6:54:00
Sisŏphŏn	13N35	102E59	-6:51:56
Skón	12N04	105E04	-7:00:16
Snay Pôl	11N40	105E13	-7:00:52
Snuŏl	12N04	106E26	-7:05:44
Spóng	13N27	105E34	-7:02:16
Srê Âmbĕl	11N07	103E46	-6:55:04
Srê Khtŭm	12N10	106E52	-7:07:28
Srê Moăt	13N18	107E10	-7:08:40
Stœng Tréng	13N31	105E58	-7:03:52
Svay Chék	13N48	102E58	-6:51:52
Svay Riĕng	11N05	105E48	-7:03:12
Takêv	10N59	104E47	-6:59:08
Trêng	12N49	102E54	-6:51:36
Tuk Méas	10N40	104E34	-6:58:16
Udon (Udonp)	11N48	104E47	-6:59:08
Virôchey	13N59	106E49	-7:07:16

KENYA

KENIA

```
    Time Table
Before  1/Jul/1928 LMT
Begin Standard    45E00
1/Jul/1928  0:00 -3:00
Begin Standard    37E30
1/Jan/1930  0:00 -2:30
Begin Standard    41E15
1/Jan/1940  0:00 -2:45
Begin Standard    45E00
1/Jan/1960  0:00 -3:00
```

Place	Lat	Long	Offset
Alanga Arba	0N07	40E25	-2:41:40
Archer's Post	0N39	37E41	-2:30:44
Athi River	1S27	36E59	-2:27:56
Bakitabu	1S29	35E34	-2:22:16
Baragoi	1N47	36E47	-2:27:08
Baringo	0N28	35E58	-2:23:52
Buna	2N47	39E31	-2:38:04
Bungoma	0N34	34E34	-2:18:16
Bura	3S30	38E18	-2:33:12
Bura	1S06	39E57	-2:39:48
Butere	0N13	34E30	-2:18:00
Chemagal	0S41	35E07	-2:20:28
Choba	2N26	38E03	-2:32:12
Dagoretti	1S18	36E46	-2:27:04
Dif	0N59	40E57	-2:43:48
Eldoret	0N31	35E17	-2:21:08
El Roba	3N57	40E01	-2:40:04
El Wak	2N49	40E56	-2:43:44
Emali	2S05	37E38	-2:30:32
Embu	0S32	37E27	-2:29:48
Fort Hall	0S43	37E09	-2:28:36
Garba Tula	0N32	38E31	-2:34:04
Garissa	0S28	39E38	-2:38:32
Garsen	2S16	40E07	-2:40:28
Gasi	4S25	39E30	-2:38:00
Gazi	4S25	39E30	-2:38:00
Gilgil	0S30	36E19	-2:25:16
Habaswein	1N01	39E29	-2:37:56
Higlet	1S04	40E19	-2:41:16
Hola	1S29	40E02	-2:40:08
Homa Bay	0S31	34E27	-2:17:48
Ijara	1S36	40E31	-2:42:04
Ileret	4N19	36E13	-2:24:52
Isiolo	0N21	37E35	-2:30:20
Kajiado	1S51	36E47	-2:27:08
Kakamega	0N17	34E45	-2:19:00
Kakuma	3N43	34E52	-2:19:28
Kaningo	0S49	38E32	-2:34:08
Kapenguria	1N04	35E07	-2:20:28
Kapsabet	0N12	35E06	-2:20:24
Karpedo	1N10	36E06	-2:24:24
Karungu	0S51	34E09	-2:16:36
Kendu Bay	0S22	34E39	-2:18:36
Kericho	0S22	35E17	-2:21:08
Kiambu	1S10	36E50	-2:27:20
Kiboko	2S15	37E42	-2:30:48
Kibwezi	2S25	37E58	-2:31:52
Kijabe	0S56	36E34	-2:26:16
Kilifi	3S38	39E51	-2:39:24
Kinango	4S08	39E19	-2:37:16
Kipini	2S32	40E31	-2:42:04
Kisii	0S41	34E46	-2:19:04
Kisumu	0S06	34E45	-2:19:00
Kitale	1N01	35E00	-2:20:00
Kitui	1S22	38E01	-2:32:04
Kiunga	1S45	41E29	-2:45:56
Kolbio	1S10	41E15	-2:45:00
Konza	1S45	37E07	-2:28:28
Kuchelebai	1N29	35E01	-2:20:04
Kundi	1S08	40E41	-2:42:44
Kwale	4S11	39E27	-2:37:48
Kyebaiwa	0N33	34E48	-2:19:12
Laisamis	1N36	37E48	-2:31:12
Lamu	2S16	40E54	-2:43:36
Lare	0N20	37E56	-2:31:44
Leseru	0N35	35E10	-2:20:40
Liboi	0N24	40E57	-2:43:48
Limuru	1S06	36E39	-2:26:36
Lodwar	3N07	35E36	-2:22:24
Logumukum	0N27	36E05	-2:24:20
Lokichar	2N23	35E39	-2:22:36
Lokichokio	4N12	34E21	-2:17:24
Lokitaung	4N16	35E45	-2:23:00
Lumbwa	0S12	35E28	-2:21:52
Machakos	1S31	37E16	-2:29:04
Mackinnon Road	3S44	39E03	-2:36:12
Mado Gashi	0N44	39E10	-2:36:40
Magadi	1S54	36E17	-2:25:08
Makindu	2S17	37E49	-2:31:16
Maktau	3S24	38E08	-2:32:32
Malindi	3S13	40E07	-2:40:28
Mambrui	3S07	40E09	-2:40:36
Mandera	3N56	41E52	-2:47:28
Manyani	3S05	38E30	-2:34:00
Maralal	1N06	36E42	-2:26:48
Mararui	1S56	41E18	-2:45:12
Mariakani	3S52	39E28	-2:37:52
Marsabit	2N20	37E59	-2:31:56
Maungu	3S33	38E45	-2:35:00
Merti	1N04	38E40	-2:34:40
Meru	0N03	37E39	-2:30:36
Mikinduri	0N07	37E50	-2:31:20
Mkunumbi	2S18	40E42	-2:42:48
Mohoru	1S01	34E07	-2:16:28
Mombasa	4S03	39E40	-2:38:40
Moyale	3N32	39E03	-2:36:12
Mtito Andei	2S41	38E10	-2:32:40
Mukutan	0N38	36E16	-2:25:04
Mumias	0N20	34E29	-2:17:56
Murang'a	0S43	37E09	-2:28:36
Mutha	1S48	38E26	-2:33:44
Muvukoni	0S24	38E14	-2:32:56
Mwereni	4S20	39E08	-2:36:32
Mwingi	0S56	38E04	-2:32:16
Nairobi	1S17	36E49	-2:27:16
Naivasha	0S43	36E26	-2:25:44
Nakuru	0S17	36E04	-2:24:16
Namanga	2S33	36E46	-2:27:04
Namuruputh	4N34	35E57	-2:23:48
Nanyuki	0N01	37E04	-2:28:16
Narok	1S05	35E52	-2:23:28
Ngong	1S22	36E39	-2:26:36
Ngorengore	1S02	35E30	-2:22:00
North Horr	3N19	37E04	-2:28:16
Nyahururu Falls	0N02	36E22	-2:25:28
Nyeri	0S25	36E57	-2:27:48
Parkitapo	1S29	35E34	-2:22:16
Pate	2S08	41E00	-2:44:00
Rabai	3S58	39E37	-2:38:28
Ramu	3N56	41E13	-2:44:52
Rongai	0S10	35E51	-2:23:24
Rumuruti	0N16	36E32	-2:26:08
Sabarei	4N20	36E55	-2:27:40
Saka	0S09	39E20	-2:37:20
Sarim	0S23	40E58	-2:43:52
Sericho	2N30	40E10	-2:40:40
Shimoni	4S39	39E23	-2:37:32
Simba	2S10	37E36	-2:30:24
Solai	0N02	36E09	-2:24:36
South Horr	2N06	36E55	-2:27:40
Suna	1S05	34E26	-2:17:44
Takaungu	3S41	39E51	-2:39:24
Tangulbei	0N48	36E17	-2:25:08
Taveta	3S24	37E41	-2:30:44
Thika	1S03	37E05	-2:28:20
Thomson's Falls	0N02	36E22	-2:25:28
Timau	0N05	37E14	-2:28:56
Todenyang	4N32	35E56	-2:23:44
Tsavo	2S59	38E28	-2:33:52
Vanga	4S39	39E13	-2:36:52
Voi	3S23	38E34	-2:34:16
Wajir	1N45	40E04	-2:40:16
Wamba	0N59	37E19	-2:29:16
Wange	2S00	40E55	-2:43:40
Wangi	2S00	40E55	-2:43:40
Witu	2S23	40E26	-2:41:44

KIRIBATI

GILBERT ISLANDS

```
    Time Table # 1
Before  1/Jan/1901 LMT
Begin Standard   180E00
1/Jan/1901  0:00 -12:00
........................

    Time Table # 2
Before  1/Jan/1901 LMT
Begin Standard   180W00
1/Jan/1901  0:00  12:00
Begin Standard   165W00
1/Oct/1979  0:00  11:00
........................

    Time Table # 3
Before  1/Jan/1901 LMT
Begin Standard   160W00
1/Jan/1901  0:00  10:40
Begin Standard   150W00
1/Oct/1979  0:00  10:00
```

DIVISIONS

1. Abemama Island
2. Arorae Island
3. Banaba Island
4. Beru Island
5. Birnie Island
6. Canton Island
7. Caroline Atoll
8. Christmas Island (Kiritimati)
9. Enderbury Island
10. Fanning Island
11. Filippo Reef
12. Flint Island
13. Gardner Island
14. Hull Island
15. Kuria Island
16. Makin Island
17. Malden Island
18. Merlin Seamount
19. Nikunau Island
20. Nonouti Island
21. Onotoa Island
22. Phoenix Island
23. Starbuck Island
24. Sydney Island
25. Tabiteuea Island
26. Tamana Island
27. Tapeteuea Island
28. Tarawa Island
29. Vostok Island
30. Washington Island

```
Abaokoro 28        1  1N29 173E02-11:32:08
Abemama Island 1
                   1  0N21 173E51-11:35:24
Apaiang 28         1  1N58 172E53-11:31:32
Arorae Island 2
                   1  3S38 176E49-11:47:16
Bairiki 28         1  1N20 173E01-11:32:04
Banaba Island 3
                   1  0S52 169E35-11:18:20
Banraeaba 28       1  1N20 173E02-11:32:08
Banreaba 28        1  1N20 173E02-11:32:08
Beru Island 4      1  1S20 176E00-11:44:00
Betio 28           1  1N21 172E56-11:31:44
Bikenibeu 28       1  1N21 173E07-11:32:28
Birnie Island 5
                   2  3S35 171W31 11:26:04
Bonriki 28         1  1N23 173E09-11:32:36
Buakonikai 3       1  0S52 169E36-11:18:24
Buariki 28         1  1N36 172E58-11:31:52
Canton Island 6
                   2  2S50 171W41 11:26:44
Caroline Atoll 7
                   3  9S58 150W13 10:00:52
Christmas Island → Kiritimati 8
                   3  1N52 157W20 10:29:20
Eita 28            1  1N21 173E05-11:32:20
Enderbury Island 9
                   2  3S08 171W05 11:24:20
Fanning Island 10
                   3  3N52 159W20 10:37:20
Filippo Reef 11
                   3  5S30 151W50 10:07:20
Flint Island 12
                   3 11S26 151W48 10:07:12
Gardner Island 13
                   2  4S40 174W32 11:38:08
Hull Island 14 2  4S29 172W10 11:28:40
Kiritimati (Christmas Island) 8
                   3  1N52 157W20 10:29:20
Kuria Island 15
                   2  0N14 173W25 11:33:40
London 8           3  1N58 157W28 10:29:52
Main Camp 8        3  2N01 157W25 10:29:40
Makin Island 16
                   1  3N07 172E48-11:31:12
Malden Island 17
                   3  4S03 154W59 10:19:56
Maranenuka 28      1  1N29 173E02-11:32:08
Merlin Seamount 18
                   3  8S20 150W25 10:01:40
Nabeina 28         1  1N26 173E05-11:32:20
Nikunau Island 19
                   1  1S23 176E26-11:45:44
```

GILBERT ISLANDS — KIRIBATI

Place	Zone	Latitude	Longitude	Offset
Nonouti Island 20	2	0s40	174w21	11:37:24
Northside 6	2	2s47	171w43	11:26:52
Nuatabu 28	1	1N33	172E59	-11:31:56
Ocean Island (Banaba) 3	1	0s52	169E35	-11:18:20
Onotoa Island 21	1	1s52	175E34	-11:42:16
Ooma 3	1	0s53	169E36	-11:18:24
Paris 8	3	1N56	157w29	10:29:56
Phoenix Island 22	2	3s43	170w43	11:22:52
Poland 8	3	1N59	157w32	10:30:08
Puakonikai 3	1	0s52	169E36	-11:18:24
Southside 6	2	2s49	171w43	11:26:52
Starbuck Island 23	3	5s37	155w53	10:23:32
Sydney Island 24	2	4s27	171w15	11:25:00
Tabiang 3	1	0s52	169E35	-11:18:20
Tabiang 28	1	1N26	173E06	-11:32:24
Tabiteuea 28	1	1N25	173E07	-11:32:28
Tabiteuea Island 25	1	1s20	174E50	-11:39:20
Tamana Island 26	1	2s29	175E59	-11:43:56
Tapeteuea Island 27	1	1s29	175E11	-11:40:44
Tapiwa 3	1	0s52	169E35	-11:18:20
Taratai 28	1	1N32	173E00	-11:32:00
Tarawa Island 28	1	1N25	173E00	-11:32:00
Taritai 28	1	1N32	173E00	-11:32:00
Tearinibai 28	1	1N35	172E58	-11:31:52
Vostok Island 29	3	10s06	152w23	10:09:32
Washington Island 30	3	4N43	160w24	10:41:36

C.M.I.K. NORDKOREA CORÉE DU NORD COREA DEL NORTE KOREA, NORTH

Time Table
Before 1/Jan/1890 LMT
Begin Standard 127E30
1/Jan/1890 0:00 -8:30
Begin Standard 135E00
1/Dec/1904 0:00 -9:00
Begin Standard 127E30
1/Jan/1928 0:00 -8:30
Begin Standard 135E00
1/Jan/1932 0:00 -9:00
Begin Standard 120E00
21/Mar/1954 0:00 -8:00
Begin Standard 135E00
10/Aug/1961 0:01 -9:00

Place	Latitude	Longitude	Offset
Anbyŏn	39N03	127E32	-8:30:08
Andong-Ni	39N28	127E27	-8:29:48
Anju	39N36	125E40	-8:22:40
Aoji	42N31	130E23	-8:41:32
Chaeryŏng	38N24	125E36	-8:22:24
Ch'angdo	38N30	127E40	-8:30:40
Ch'ang-Dong	39N03	126E34	-8:26:16
Changhŭng-Ni	40N24	128E19	-8:33:16
Changjin-ŭp	40N23	127E15	-8:29:00
Changnyŏn-Ni	38N37	125E16	-8:21:04
Ch'angp'yŏng-Dong	41N27	127E31	-8:30:04
Changyŏn	38N15	125E06	-8:20:24
Chasŏng	41N27	126E37	-8:26:28
Chasŏngganggu	41N34	126E36	-8:26:24
Chigyŏng	39N51	127E26	-8:29:44
Chinnampo → Namp'o	38N45	125E23	-8:21:32
Ch'ŏlsan	39N46	124E40	-8:18:40
Ch'ŏngdan	37N58	125E56	-8:23:44
Ch'ŏngjin	41N47	129E50	-8:39:20
Chŏngju	39N41	125E13	-8:20:52
Ch'ŏngsong	41N47	129E48	-8:39:12
Ch'ŏnma	40N03	125E01	-8:20:04
Ch'ŏnsu-Ri	41N43	128E45	-8:35:00
Ch'osan	40N50	125E47	-8:23:08
Chosanch'am	40N22	126E11	-8:24:44
Ch'owŏn-Ni	39N40	127E17	-8:29:08
Chunggang-Ni	40N52	127E20	-8:29:20
Chunghwa	38N52	125E47	-8:23:08
Chungp'yŏngjang	41N11	128E03	-8:32:12
Chungsam-Ni	38N34	127E09	-8:28:36
Chŭngsan	39N06	125E22	-8:21:28
Ch'wiya-Ri	38N03	125E32	-8:22:08
Gensan → Wŏnsan	39N09	127E25	-8:29:40
Haeju	38N02	125E42	-8:22:48
Haengyŏng-Ni	42N33	129E56	-8:39:44
Hagal	40N23	127E15	-8:29:00
Hahyŏn-Ni	38N33	127E57	-8:31:48
Hamhŭng	39N54	127E32	-8:30:08
Hamjong-Ni	38N59	125E17	-8:21:08
Hanam-Ni	38N23	126E43	-8:26:52
Happ'o-Ri	40N40	127E49	-8:31:16
Hapsu	41N13	128E51	-8:35:24
Heijō → P'yŏngyang	39N01	125E45	-8:23:00
Hoeryŏng	42N27	129E44	-8:38:56
Hoeyang	38N43	127E36	-8:30:24
Honggun	40N46	128E27	-8:33:48
Hongwŏn	40N02	127E57	-8:31:48
Huch'ang	41N25	127E03	-8:28:12
Hŭich'ŏn	40N10	126E17	-8:25:08
Hŭngin-Ni	39N03	126E26	-8:25:44
Hŭngnam	39N50	127E38	-8:30:32
Hun-Yung	42N53	130E12	-8:40:48
Hwach'ŏn-Ni	39N01	126E02	-8:24:08
Hwanggong-Ni	40N03	129E27	-8:37:48
Hwangju	38N42	125E46	-8:23:04
Hyesan	41N23	128E12	-8:32:48
Ich'on	38N30	126E50	-8:27:20
Ijin	42N05	130E08	-8:40:32
Imokt'an	38N50	126E41	-8:26:44
Inp'ung-Dong	41N25	126E34	-8:26:16
Insan-Ni	41N01	127E21	-8:29:24
Isan-Ni	40N46	128E55	-8:35:40
Iwŏn	40N19	128E39	-8:34:36
Kach'ang-Ni	38N24	126E11	-8:24:44
Kaech'ŏn	39N42	125E53	-8:23:32
Kaesŏng	37N59	126E33	-8:26:12
Kaijo → Kaesŏng	37N59	126E33	-8:26:12
Kamsu-Ri	38N03	125E54	-8:23:36
Kangdong	39N09	126E05	-8:24:20
Kanggup'o	41N07	127E31	-8:30:04
Kanggye	40N58	126E34	-8:26:16
Kangsŏ	38N58	125E26	-8:21:44
Kankō → Hamhŭng	39N54	127E32	-8:30:08
Kapsan	41N04	128E19	-8:33:16
Kasan-Dong	41N18	126E55	-8:27:40
Kilchu	40N58	129E20	-8:37:20
Kimch'aek (Sŏngjin)	40N41	129E12	-8:36:48
Kimhwa	38N26	127E36	-8:30:24
Koch'am-Ni	41N06	129E23	-8:37:32
Koin-Ni	40N28	126E22	-8:25:28
Kojŏ	38N57	127E51	-8:31:24
Kokku	40N22	128E44	-8:34:56
Koksan	38N46	126E40	-8:26:40
Komusan	42N08	129E41	-8:38:44
Konan → Hŭngnam	39N50	127E38	-8:30:32
Kosan	38N52	127E24	-8:29:36
Kowŏn	39N26	127E14	-8:28:56
Kuch'ang-Ni	40N09	124E46	-8:19:04
Kujang	39N52	126E01	-8:24:04
Kujŏng-Ni	37N53	125E54	-8:23:36
Kŭmch'ŏn	38N10	126E29	-8:25:56
Kŭmsan-Ni	37N55	125E41	-8:22:44
Kusŏng	39N59	125E15	-8:21:00
Kyŏmip'o → Songnim	38N44	125E38	-8:22:32
Kyŏngsŏng	41N35	129E36	-8:38:24
Kyŏngwŏn	42N48	130E09	-8:40:36
Maengsan	39N40	126E30	-8:26:00
Majŏn-Ni	39N06	127E07	-8:28:28
Monggŭmp'o	38N09	124E47	-8:19:08
Mugo-Ri	38N58	126E31	-8:26:04
Muksi-Ri	39N52	125E54	-8:23:36
Munam-Ni	38N41	126E54	-8:27:36
Munch'ŏn	39N16	127E15	-8:29:00
Musan	42N14	129E13	-8:36:52
Najin	42N15	130E18	-8:41:12
Namho-Ri	38N07	125E10	-8:20:40
Namp'o	38N45	125E23	-8:21:32
Namsanyŏng-Ni	38N59	127E26	-8:29:44
Namsi	39N54	124E36	-8:18:24
Namyang	42N57	129E53	-8:39:32
Nanam	41N43	129E41	-8:38:44
Nogangjin	39N30	125E23	-8:21:32
Nuch'ŏn-Ni	38N14	126E16	-8:25:04
Ŏdaejin	41N34	129E40	-8:38:40
Ŏgu-Dong	38N57	126E56	-8:27:44
Okkang-Ni	40N18	124E42	-8:18:48
Oktong-Ni	38N27	127E07	-8:28:28
Ŏmyŏnbo	41N16	127E36	-8:30:24
Onch'ŏn-Dong	40N51	129E07	-8:36:28
Ongjin	37N57	125E21	-8:21:24
Oro	40N02	127E26	-8:29:44
Osich'ŏn-Ni	41N25	128E16	-8:33:04
Pakch'ŏn	39N45	125E35	-8:22:20
P'anmunjŏm	37N57	126E40	-8:26:40
P'anp'yŏng-Ni	40N28	125E49	-8:23:16
P'ihyŏn	40N01	124E37	-8:18:28
Pjöngjang → P'yŏngyang	39N01	125E45	-8:23:00
Ponghyŏn	37N49	125E36	-8:22:24
Pŏptong	38N59	127E05	-8:28:20
Pugŏ-Ri	42N01	129E59	-8:39:56
Pukch'ang	39N36	126E17	-8:25:08
Pukchin	40N10	125E43	-8:22:52
Pukch'ŏng	40N15	128E20	-8:33:20
P'ungsan	38N28	125E01	-8:20:04
P'ungsong-Ni	39N56	127E11	-8:28:44
Pusŏng-Ni	40N19	127E19	-8:29:16
Puyun-Dong	41N55	129E30	-8:38:00
Pyŏlch'ang-Ni	39N17	126E26	-8:25:44
P'yŏnggang	38N26	127E16	-8:29:04
P'yŏngyang	39N01	125E45	-8:23:00
Pyŏrha-Ri	40N48	126E32	-8:26:08
Rashin → Najin	42N15	130E18	-8:41:12
Sainjang	39N15	125E51	-8:23:24
Sakchu	40N23	125E01	-8:20:04
Samho	39N56	127E53	-8:31:32
Samsu	41N19	127E59	-8:31:56
Sangnyŏng-Ni	38N14	126E54	-8:27:36
Sap'o-Ri	40N49	129E31	-8:38:04
Sariwŏn	38N31	125E44	-8:22:56
Sehyŏn-Ni	38N20	127E41	-8:30:44
Seishin → Ch'ŏngjin	41N47	129E50	-8:39:20
Sep'o	38N39	127E22	-8:29:28
Shingishū → Sinŭiju	40N05	124E24	-8:17:36
Simp'o-Ri	38N36	127E41	-8:30:44
Sinanju	39N36	125E36	-8:22:24
Sinbokchang	41N01	128E54	-8:35:36
Sinch'ang	40N07	128E28	-8:33:52
Sinch'ang	40N19	125E27	-8:21:48
Sinch'ŏn	38N22	125E28	-8:21:52
Sin'gye	38N36	126E30	-8:26:00
Sinhŭng	40N11	127E34	-8:30:16
Sinjang-Ni	39N04	127E46	-8:31:04
Sinmak	38N25	126E14	-8:24:56
Sinp'a	41N24	127E46	-8:31:04
Sinp'o	40N03	128E12	-8:32:48
Sinsang	39N38	127E25	-8:29:40
Sinsi-Ri	39N59	124E58	-8:19:52
Sinŭiju	40N05	124E24	-8:17:36
Sinŭp	39N54	126E47	-8:27:08
Sinwŏn-Ni	38N13	125E44	-8:22:56
Sŏam	38N01	126E43	-8:26:52
Sŏhŭng	38N27	126E10	-8:24:40
Sŏkp'o-Ri	37N46	125E27	-8:21:48
Soksa-Ri	40N40	127E17	-8:29:08
Sŏman	41N20	128E54	-8:35:36
Sŏnch'ŏn	39N48	124E55	-8:19:40
Sŏngbyŏn-Ni	38N03	125E18	-8:21:12
Songhwa	38N21	125E08	-8:20:32
Sŏngjang-Ni	41N02	126E50	-8:27:20
Sŏngjin → Kimch'aek	40N41	129E12	-8:36:48
Sŏngnae-Ri	39N28	126E59	-8:27:56
Sŏng-Ni	39N38	127E06	-8:28:24
Songnim	38N44	125E38	-8:22:32
Sŏsura	42N16	130E37	-8:42:28
Suan	38N42	126E22	-8:25:28
Sukch'ŏn	39N24	125E38	-8:22:32
Sunan	39N13	125E41	-8:22:44
Sunch'ŏn	39N26	125E54	-8:23:36
Sup'ung	40N27	124E57	-8:19:48
Suwon-Dong	41N54	129E43	-8:38:52
Taedong	39N05	125E31	-8:22:04
Taegwan	40N13	125E12	-8:20:48
Taehŭng	40N06	126E56	-8:27:44
Taejujŏm	38N24	127E58	-8:31:52
Taeryanghwa	41N14	129E42	-8:38:48
T'agyŏng-Ni	38N04	126E03	-8:24:12
Tanch'ŏn	40N27	128E54	-8:35:36
Toandonggu	40N33	127E35	-8:30:20
T'oejo	39N54	127E46	-8:31:04
T'ohyŏn-Ni	39N53	124E52	-8:19:28
Tŏkch'ŏn	39N46	126E19	-8:25:16
Tŏkhŭng-Ni	40N02	127E08	-8:28:32
T'ongch'ŏn	38N54	127E54	-8:31:36
T'osan	38N18	126E43	-8:26:52

KOREA, NORTH   COREA DEL NORTE   CORÉE DU NORD   NORDKOREA   C.M.I.K.

Place	Lat	Long	Time
Tuji-Ri	41N31	127E12	-8:28:48
Uha-Dong	40N41	125E38	-8:22:32
Ŭiju	40N12	124E32	-8:18:08
Ŭnch'ŏn	38N34	125E26	-8:21:44
Unggi	42N20	130E24	-8:41:36
Ŭnp'a	38N26	125E45	-8:23:00
Ŭnsan	39N25	126E01	-8:24:04
Ŭpchŏ-Ri	37N53	125E09	-8:20:36
Wŏnjang-Ni	39N05	125E32	-8:22:08
Wŏnsan	39N09	127E25	-8:29:40
Wŏrun-Dong	39N36	125E20	-8:21:20
Yangp'yŏng-Ni	40N53	127E58	-8:31:52
Yankdŏk	39N14	126E41	-8:26:44
Yŏnan	37N55	126E10	-8:24:40
Yongamp'o	39N55	124E24	-8:17:36
Yŏngan	41N15	129E30	-8:38:00
Yŏngbyŏn	39N49	125E48	-8:23:12
Yongch'ŏn	39N59	124E28	-8:17:52
Yongch'ŏn-Dong	41N18	129E40	-8:38:40
Yonggangonch'ŏn	38N53	125E14	-8:20:56
Yonghŭng	39N32	127E13	-8:28:52
Yŏngmi-Dong	39N40	125E31	-8:22:04
Yongsan-Ni	38N52	125E56	-8:23:44
Yongwŏn-Ni	40N41	128E42	-8:34:48
Yŏngyn	39N18	125E34	-8:22:16
Yongyŏn-Ni	40N44	126E09	-8:24:36
Yop'o-Ri	38N50	125E33	-8:22:12
Yul-Li	38N52	126E13	-8:24:52
Yuwŏnjin	40N18	126E37	-8:26:28
Yuyŏn-Ni	38N42	127E10	-8:28:40

KOREA, SOUTH   COREA DEL SUR   CORÉE DU SUD   TAEHAN-MIN'GUK

Time Table
Before 1/Jan/1890 LMT
Begin Standard 127E30
1/Jan/1890 0:00 -8:30
Begin Standard 135E00
1/Dec/1904 0:00 -9:00
Begin Standard 127E30
1/Jan/1928 0:00 -8:30
Begin Standard 135E00
1/Jan/1932 0:00 -9:00
Begin Standard 120E00
21/Mar/1954 0:00 -8:00
15/May/1960 0:00 -9:00
13/Sep/1960 0:00 -8:00
Begin Standard 127E30
10/Aug/1961 0:01 -8:30
Begin Standard 135E00
1/Oct/1968 0:00 -9:00
10/May/1987 0:00 -10:00
11/Oct/1987 0:00 -9:00
8/May/1988 0:00 -10:00
9/Oct/1988 0:00 -9:00

Place	Lat	Long	Time
Ahwa-Ri	35N54	129E02	-8:36:08
Andong	36N35	128E44	-8:34:56
Anhŭng	36N41	126E10	-8:24:40
Ansŏng	37N02	127E16	-8:29:04
Anŭi	35N38	127E48	-8:31:12
Anyang	37N23	126E55	-8:27:40
Busan → Pusan	35N06	129E03	-8:36:12
Changdan	37N56	126E45	-8:27:00
Changgi-Li	37N35	126E44	-8:26:56
Changgi-Ri	37N38	126E41	-8:26:44
Changgye-Ri	34N33	126E49	-8:27:16
Changhang	36N01	126E40	-8:26:40
Changhowŏn	37N08	127E39	-8:30:36
Changhŭng	34N41	126E52	-8:27:28
Changmong-Ni	34N58	128E41	-8:34:44
Ch'angnyŏng	35N33	128E29	-8:33:56
Changsŏng	35N20	126E49	-8:27:16
Changsu	35N40	127E32	-8:30:08
Chech'on	37N08	128E12	-8:32:48
Cheju	33N31	126E32	-8:26:08
Chemulpo → Inch'ŏn	37N28	126E38	-8:26:32
Cheonan → Ch'ŏnan	36N48	127E09	-8:28:36
Cheongju → Ch'ŏngju	36N39	127E31	-8:30:04
Chinan	35N48	127E25	-8:29:40
Chinch'ŏn	36N52	127E26	-8:29:44
Chindo	34N28	126E15	-8:25:00
Chindong	35N07	128E29	-8:33:56
Chinhae	35N09	128E40	-8:34:40
Chinju	35N11	128E05	-8:32:20
Chisep'o	34N50	128E42	-8:34:48
Choch'iwŏn	36N37	127E18	-8:29:12
Ch'ŏnan	36N48	127E09	-8:28:36
Ch'ŏngdo	35N38	128E43	-8:34:52
Ch'ŏngha	36N13	129E20	-8:37:20
Ch'onghak-Ni	37N43	127E05	-8:28:20
Ch'ŏngju	36N39	127E31	-8:30:04
Ch'ŏngsan	36N22	127E46	-8:31:04
Chŏngsŏn	37N22	128E38	-8:34:32
Chŏngŭp	35N36	126E51	-8:27:24
Ch'ŏngyang	36N27	126E48	-8:27:12
Chŏnju	35N49	127E08	-8:28:32
Chŏnŭi	36N42	127E11	-8:28:44
Ch'ŏrwŏn	38N16	127E12	-8:28:48
Chugyo-Ri	37N39	126E50	-8:27:20
Chulp'o	35N37	126E40	-8:26:40
Chumunjin	37N54	128E49	-8:35:16
Chuncheon → Ch'unch'ŏn	37N52	127E43	-8:30:52
Ch'unch'ŏn	37N52	127E43	-8:30:52
Ch'ungju	36N58	127E58	-8:31:52
Ch'ungmu	34N51	128E25	-8:33:40
Ch'unyang	36N56	128E54	-8:35:36
Daegu → Taegu	35N52	128E35	-8:34:20
Daejeon → Taejŏn	36N20	127E26	-8:29:44
Euijeongbu → Ŭijŏngbu	37N44	127E03	-8:28:12
Fusan → Pusan	35N06	129E03	-8:36:12
Gangneung → Kangnŭng	37N45	128E54	-8:35:36
Gimcheon → Kimch'ŏn	36N07	128E05	-8:32:20
Gunsan → Kunsan	35N58	126E41	-8:26:44
Gwangju → Kwangju	35N09	126E54	-8:27:36
Gyeongju → Kyŏngju	35N51	129E14	-8:36:56
Hadong	35N05	127E44	-8:30:56
Haenam	34N34	126E35	-8:26:20
Haman	35N15	128E24	-8:33:36
Hamp'yŏng	35N05	126E30	-8:26:00
Hamyang	35N32	127E42	-8:30:48
Hayang	35N55	128E47	-8:35:08
Hongch'ŏn	37N42	127E52	-8:31:28
Hongsŏng	36N36	126E39	-8:26:36
Hŭngho-Ri	37N14	127E44	-8:30:56
Hwach'ŏn	38N06	127E41	-8:30:44
Hyŏn-Ni	37N57	128E20	-8:33:20
Hyŏpch'ŏn	35N35	128E08	-8:32:32
Ich'ŏn	37N17	127E27	-8:29:48
Ilsan-Ni	37N41	126E46	-8:27:04
Imp'a	35N59	126E49	-8:27:16
Imsil	35N37	127E15	-8:29:00
Imwŏn-Ni	37N15	129E20	-8:37:20
Inch'ŏn	37N28	126E38	-8:26:32
Inje	38N05	128E09	-8:32:36
Intschön → Inch'ŏn	37N28	126E38	-8:26:32
Iri	35N56	126E57	-8:27:48
Iyang	34N53	127E01	-8:28:04
Jeju → Cheju	33N31	126E32	-8:26:08
Jeonju → Chŏnju	35N49	127E08	-8:28:32
Jinhae → Chinhae	35N09	128E40	-8:34:40
Jinju → Chinju	35N11	128E05	-8:32:20
Jinsen → Inch'ŏn	37N28	126E38	-8:26:32
Kach'i-Ri	34N27	126E08	-8:24:32
Kaedo-Ri	34N35	127E39	-8:30:36
Kagyo-Ri	34N25	126E48	-8:27:12
Kahyŏn-Ni	37N32	126E44	-8:26:56
Kamp'o	35N48	129E29	-8:37:56
Kanggyŏng	36N10	127E00	-8:28:00
Kanghwa	37N45	126E30	-8:26:00
Kangjin	34N39	126E45	-8:27:00
Kangnŭng	37N45	128E54	-8:35:36
Kangsŏ-Ri	38N06	126E58	-8:27:52
Kansŏng	38N22	128E29	-8:33:56
Kaŭl-Li	37N58	124E37	-8:18:28
Keijō → Sŏul	37N33	126E58	-8:27:52
Kiltu-Ri	34N35	127E20	-8:29:20
Kimch'ŏn	36N07	128E05	-8:32:20
Kimhae	35N14	128E52	-8:35:28
Kimje	35N48	126E52	-8:27:28
Kimp'o	37N37	126E43	-8:26:52
Kŏch'ang	35N26	126E42	-8:26:48
Kŏch'ang	35N41	127E55	-8:31:40
Kohŭng	34N37	127E16	-8:29:04
Koksŏng	35N17	127E17	-8:29:08
Kongju	36N27	127E07	-8:28:28
Koryŏng	35N44	128E15	-8:33:00
Koshu → Kwangju	35N09	126E54	-8:27:36
Kosŏng	34N58	128E18	-8:33:12
Koyang-Ni	37N42	126E56	-8:27:44
Kudongho	35N31	126E29	-8:25:56
Kŭmhwa	38N17	127E28	-8:29:52
Kŭmsan	36N07	127E30	-8:30:00
Kunsan	35N58	126E41	-8:26:44
Kunwi	36N15	128E34	-8:34:16
Kup'abal	37N37	126E54	-8:27:36
Kuryongp'o	35N59	129E32	-8:38:08
Kusan-Ni	37N43	128E49	-8:35:16
Kusung	36N18	128E55	-8:35:40
Kwangju	35N09	126E54	-8:27:36
Kwangyang	34N59	127E34	-8:30:16
Kwansan-Ni	37N43	126E51	-8:27:24
Kyoha-Ri	37N46	126E46	-8:27:04
Kyohyŏn-Ni	37N43	126E58	-8:27:52
Kyŏngju	35N51	129E14	-8:36:56
Kyŏngsan	35N48	128E43	-8:34:52
Kyŏngsŏng → Sŏul	37N33	126E58	-8:27:52
Maegye-Ri	34N45	126E18	-8:25:12
Majŏn-Ni	37N36	126E41	-8:26:44
Makok-Ni	37N43	126E38	-8:26:32
Man'gyŏng	35N52	126E48	-8:27:12
Masan	35N11	128E32	-8:34:08
Miryang	35N31	128E44	-8:34:56
Mokp'o	34N48	126E22	-8:25:28
Mongbyŏn-Ni	37N40.	126E44	-8:26:56
Moppo → Mokp'o	34N48	126E22	-8:25:28
Muan	34N58	126E26	-8:25:44
Mujang-Ni	35N26	126E32	-8:26:08
Muju	36N02	127E40	-8:30:40
Mukho	37N33	129E06	-8:36:24
Munbong-Ni	37N43	126E49	-8:27:16
Mun'gyŏng	36N44	128E07	-8:32:28
Munhye-Ri	38N10	127E19	-8:29:16
Munpal-Li	37N45	126E43	-8:26:52
Munsan	37N51	126E48	-8:27:12
Mup'ungjang	35N58	127E49	-8:31:16
Nae-Dong	37N16	126E27	-8:25:48
Naju	35N03	126E43	-8:26:52
Namch'ang	35N26	129E16	-8:37:04
Namhae	34N50	127E54	-8:31:36
Namji-Ri	35N23	128E29	-8:33:56
Namwŏn	35N25	127E21	-8:29:24
Namyang	37N14	126E44	-8:26:56
Nawŏn-Ni	36N25	126E40	-8:26:40
Nonsan	36N12	127E05	-8:28:20
Noryang	34N56	127E52	-8:31:28
Okch'ŏn	36N20	127E34	-8:30:16
Ŏnyang	35N34	129E07	-8:36:28
Ŏran-Ni	34N22	126E29	-8:25:56
Osan	37N11	127E04	-8:28:16
Osu-Ri	35N31	127E18	-8:29:12
Paedun	35N03	128E21	-8:33:24
Pangŏjin	35N29	129E26	-8:37:44
Paranjang	37N08	126E55	-8:27:40
P'ohang	36N03	129E20	-8:37:20
Pŏlgyo	34N52	127E21	-8:29:24
Pŏpsŏng	35N22	126E27	-8:25:48
Posŏng	34N47	127E04	-8:28:16
Poŭn	36N29	127E43	-8:30:52
Puan	35N45	126E44	-8:26:56
Pugong-Ni	37N43	126E58	-8:27:52
Pukch'ŏn	36N13	126E45	-8:27:00
P'ungam-Ni	37N43	128E11	-8:32:44
Pup'yŏng	37N30	126E43	-8:26:52
Pusan	35N06	129E03	-8:36:12
Puyŏ	36N18	126E54	-8:27:36
P'yŏngch'ang	37N23	128E22	-8:33:28
P'yŏngdong-Ni	37N10	128E02	-8:32:08
P'yonghae	36N46	129E28	-8:37:52
P'yŏngt'aek	37N00	127E05	-8:28:20
Ryeosu → Yŏsu	34N46	127E44	-8:30:56
Samch'ŏk	37N27	129E10	-8:36:40
Samch'ŏnp'o	34N57	128E03	-8:32:12
Samga	35N25	128E05	-8:32:20
Samnangjin	35N23	128E50	-8:35:20
Samnye	35N55	127E05	-8:28:20
Sanch'ŏng	35N26	127E54	-8:31:36
Sangju	36N26	128E09	-8:32:36
Sapta-Ri	37N43	126E44	-8:26:56
Seoul → Sŏul	37N33	126E58	-8:27:52
Seúl → Sŏul	37N33	126E58	-8:27:52
Sinch'ŏn-Ni	37N27	126E48	-8:27:12
Sindŏk	36N47	126E10	-8:24:40
Sin'kok-Ni	37N37	126E46	-8:27:04
Sinnyŏng	36N04	128E46	-8:35:04
Sinŭp	37N54	127E12	-8:28:48
Sŏch'ŏn	36N05	126E41	-8:26:44
Sogcho → Sokch'o	38N12	128E36	-8:34:24
Sŏhwa-Ri	38N15	128E13	-8:32:52
Soka	37N30	126E48	-8:27:12
Sokch'o	38N12	128E36	-8:34:24
Songjŏng	35N10	126E46	-8:27:04
Sŏngju	35N55	128E16	-8:33:04
Sŏngnam-Si	37N26	127E08	-8:28:32
Sŏngsa-Ri	37N38	126E52	-8:27:28
Songu-Ri	37N49	127E09	-8:28:36
Sŏnsan	36N16	128E17	-8:33:08
Sŏp'yŏng-Ni	35N01	127E24	-8:29:36
Sosa	37N29	126E47	-8:27:08
Sŏsan	36N47	126E26	-8:25:44
Sŏul (Seoul)	37N33	126E58	-8:27:52
Sunch'ang	35N23	127E07	-8:28:28
Sunch'ŏn	34N57	127E28	-8:29:52
Suwŏn	37N17	127E01	-8:28:04
Tabu-Dong	36N03	128E31	-8:34:04
T'aean	36N46	126E16	-8:25:04
Taech'ŏn	36N22	126E34	-8:26:16
Taegu	35N52	128E35	-8:34:20
Taehwajŏn	37N36	126E52	-8:27:28
T'aein	35N40	126E55	-8:27:40
Taejin	36N34	129E24	-8:37:36
Taejŏn	36N20	127E26	-8:29:44
Taiden → Taejŏn	36N20	127E26	-8:29:44
Taikyu → Taegu	35N52	128E35	-8:34:20
Tamyang	35N21	126E58	-8:27:52
Tangjin	36N54	126E37	-8:26:28
Tang-Ni	34N12	126E52	-8:27:28
Tanyang	36N57	128E21	-8:33:24
Todang-Ni	37N37	126E50	-8:27:20
Tongho-Ri	35N49	127E54	-8:31:36
Tongmang-Ni	37N37	126E26	-8:25:44
Tongnae	35N12	129E05	-8:36:20
Tongsan-Ni	37N38	126E53	-8:27:32
Ŭijŏngbu	37N44	127E03	-8:28:12
Ŭisŏng	36N22	128E41	-8:34:44

TAEHAN-MIN'GUK — CORÉE DU SUD — COREA DEL SUR — KOREA, SOUTH

Place	Lat	Long	Time
Ulchin	36N59	129E23	-8:37:32
Ulsan	35N34	129E19	-8:37:16
Ŭmsŏng	36N56	127E41	-8:30:44
Ungch'ŏn	35N07	128E44	-8:34:56
Usuyŏng	34N35	126E18	-8:25:12
Waegwan	35N58	128E24	-8:33:36
Wando	34N18	126E47	-8:27:08
Wanggil-Li	37N36	126E39	-8:26:36
Wŏndong-Ni	34N23	126E40	-8:26:40
Wŏnju	37N22	127E58	-8:31:52
Yanggong-Ni	37N39	126E37	-8:26:28
Yanggu	38N06	127E59	-8:31:56
Yangp'yŏng	37N30	127E29	-8:29:56
Yangsan	35N21	129E03	-8:36:12
Yangyang	38N04	128E36	-8:34:24
Yech'ŏn	36N40	128E26	-8:33:44
Yesan	36N41	126E50	-8:27:20
Yŏju	37N18	127E37	-8:30:28
Yŏngam	34N48	126E40	-8:26:40
Yŏngch'ŏn	35N58	128E56	-8:35:44
Yŏngdŏk	36N26	129E23	-8:37:32
Yŏngdong	36N10	127E48	-8:31:12
Yonggi	36N24	128E24	-8:33:36
Yŏngju	36N50	128E37	-8:34:28
Yŏngsanp'o	34N58	126E44	-8:26:56
Yŏngwŏl	37N12	128E28	-8:33:52
Yŏngyang	36N40	129E07	-8:36:28
Yŏnhŭi-Ri	37N33	126E41	-8:26:44
Yŏsu	34N46	127E44	-8:30:56
Yŏyang-Ni	37N30	128E43	-8:34:52

AL-KUWAYT — KOWEÏT — KUWAIT

Time Table

Before	1/Jan/1950	LMT
Begin Standard		45E00
1/Jan/1950	0:00	-3:00

Place	Lat	Long	Time
Al-Jahrah	29N20	47E40	-3:10:40
Al-Kuwayt	29N20	47E59	-3:11:56
Mīnā' al-Aḥmadī	29N04	48E08	-3:12:32
Wafrah	28N33	48E02	-3:12:08

LAO — LAOS

Time Table

Before	9/Jun/1906	LMT
Begin Standard		106E35
9/Jun/1906	0:00	-7:06
Begin Standard		105E00
11/Mar/1911	0:01	-7:00
Begin Standard		120E00
1/May/1912	0:00	-8:00
Begin Standard		105E00
1/May/1931	0:00	-7:00

Place	Lat	Long	Time
Attapu	14N48	106E50	-7:07:20
Ban Ban	19N38	103E34	-6:54:16
Ban Bonèng	17N58	104E35	-6:58:20
Ban Bouang-Nom	15N47	106E47	-7:07:08
Ban Bungxai	15N42	106E14	-7:04:56
Ban Chak	14N17	105E25	-7:01:40
Ban Cha La	17N11	106E05	-7:04:20
Ban Dangtai	17N06	104E57	-6:59:48
Ban Donhiang	18N05	101E48	-6:47:12
Ban Dônko	16N12	106E17	-7:05:08
Ban Gnômmarat Kèo	17N36	105E10	-7:00:40
Ban Hatgnao	14N40	106E35	-7:06:20
Ban Hatkiang	18N11	102E40	-6:50:40
Ban Hèt	14N44	107E29	-7:09:56
Ban Hin Heup	18N38	102E20	-6:49:20
Ban Hong Muang	17N04	105E12	-7:00:48
Ban Houayxay	20N18	100E26	-6:41:44
Ban Katèp	16N48	105E52	-7:03:28
Ban Kavak	17N18	105E37	-7:02:28
Ban Kèngkabao	16N48	104E45	-6:59:00
Ban Kèngkok	16N26	105E12	-7:00:48
Ban Kèngtangan	16N05	105E22	-7:01:28
Ban Khamphô	14N38	106E17	-7:05:08
Ban Kheun	20N13	101E07	-6:44:28
Ban Mit	18N51	101E55	-6:47:40
Ban Muangngat	19N05	104E04	-6:56:16
Ban Nadou	15N51	105E38	-7:02:32
Ban Nagnom	17N02	105E44	-7:02:56
Ban Nahin	18N14	104E13	-6:56:52
Ban Nakala	16N17	105E11	-7:00:44
Ban Nalan	15N50	106E04	-7:04:16
Ban Nalè	18N42	101E34	-6:46:16
Ban Namcha	19N09	102E53	-6:51:32
Ban Namnga	20N22	102E19	-6:49:16
Ban Nam Tao	17N50	101E15	-6:45:00
Ban Naxon	18N12	103E05	-6:52:20
Ban Naxouang	18N25	104E29	-6:57:56
Ban Ngam	20N11	104E53	-6:59:32
Ban Pakha	14N38	107E24	-7:09:36
Ban Pakkhop	19N49	100E36	-6:42:24
Ban Pakneun	19N14	101E50	-6:47:20
Ban Phon	15N25	106E42	-7:06:48
Ban Phông Pho	14N36	105E52	-7:03:28
Ban Phya	21N35	102E55	-6:51:40
Ban Sa-Ang	17N26	105E44	-7:02:56
Ban Samang	19N43	102E36	-6:50:24
Ban Sam Pong	18N32	102E47	-6:51:08
Ban San Xieng La	19N27	102E26	-6:49:44
Ban Signo	17N51	105E04	-7:00:16
Ban Songkhon	17N58	105E10	-7:00:40
Ban Sôppheung	18N33	104E17	-6:57:08
Ban Teung	17N54	105E29	-7:01:56
Ban Thabôk	18N22	103E12	-6:52:48
Ban Thanoun	19N50	101E29	-6:45:56
Ban Thapayi	16N19	105E41	-7:02:44
Ban Thieng	19N08	102E12	-6:48:48
Ban Tian Sa	18N43	103E14	-6:52:56
Ban Van Hom	18N44	104E01	-6:56:04
Ban Vat	16N54	106E25	-7:05:40
Ban Xènkhalôk	19N42	101E54	-6:47:36
Ban Xot	18N11	104E05	-6:56:20
Borikhan	18N33	103E43	-6:54:52
Boun Nua	21N38	101E54	-6:47:36
Champasak	14N53	105E52	-7:03:28
Houamuang	20N09	103E38	-6:54:32
Khamkeut	18N15	104E43	-6:58:52
Khangkhai	19N28	103E15	-6:53:00
Louang Namtha	20N57	101E25	-6:45:40
Louangphrabang	19N52	102E08	-6:48:32
Luang Prabang → Louangphrabang	19N52	102E08	-6:48:32
Mahaxai	17N25	105E12	-7:00:48
Mounlapamôk	14N20	105E52	-7:03:28
Muang Bèng	20N22	101E44	-6:46:56
Muang Hay	21N03	101E49	-6:47:16
Muang Hinboun	17N35	104E36	-6:58:24
Muang Hôngsa	19N43	101E20	-6:45:20
Muang Houn	20N09	101E27	-6:45:48
Muang Hounxianghoung	21N37	102E18	-6:49:12
Muang Huang	18N45	103E42	-6:54:48
Muang Khammouan	17N24	104E48	-6:59:12
Muang Khao	19N47	103E29	-6:53:56
Muang Khi	18N27	101E46	-6:47:04
Muang Không	14N07	105E51	-7:03:24
Muang Khôngxédôn	15N34	105E49	-7:03:16
Muang Khoua	21N05	102E31	-6:50:04
Muang La	20N52	102E07	-6:48:28
Muang Liap	18N29	101E40	-6:46:40
Muang Long	20N57	100E48	-6:43:12
Muang Meung	20N43	100E28	-6:41:52
Muang Ngoy	20N43	102E41	-6:50:44
Muang Nong	16N22	106E30	-7:06:00
Muang Ou Nua	22N18	101E48	-6:47:12
Muang Ou Tai	22N07	101E48	-6:47:12
Muang Pakbèng	19N54	101E08	-6:44:32
Muang Pak-Lay	18N12	101E25	-6:45:40
Muang Paktha	20N06	100E36	-6:42:24
Muang Pakxan	18N22	103E39	-6:54:36
Muang Peun	20N13	103E52	-6:55:28
Muang Phalan	16N39	105E34	-7:02:16
Muang Phiang	19N06	101E32	-6:46:08
Muang Phônthong	15N05	105E39	-7:02:36
Muang Phoun	19N07	102E43	-6:50:52
Muang Sing	21N11	101E09	-6:44:36
Muang Soum	18N45	102E36	-6:50:24
Muang Souvannakhili	15N23	105E49	-7:03:16
Muang Souy	19N33	102E52	-6:51:28
Muang Sung	20N19	102E27	-6:49:48
Muang Thadua	19N26	101E50	-6:47:20
Muang Thatèng	15N26	106E23	-7:05:32
Muang Thathôm	19N00	103E36	-6:54:24
Muang Va	21N53	102E19	-6:49:16
Muang Vangviang	18N56	102E27	-6:49:48
Muang Vapi	15N40	105E55	-7:03:40
Muang Xaignabouri	19N15	101E45	-6:47:00
Muang Xamtong	19N51	103E51	-6:55:24
Muang Xay	20N42	101E59	-6:47:56
Muang Xépôn	16N41	106E14	-7:04:56
Muang Xon	20N27	103E19	-6:53:16
Muang Yo	21N31	101E51	-6:47:24
Muang You	19N49	102E50	-6:51:20
Muong Het	20N49	104E01	-6:56:04
Muong Saiapoun	18N24	101E31	-6:46:04
Napè	18N18	105E06	-7:00:24
Ngay Nua	21N50	101E54	-6:47:36
Nong Hèt	19N29	103E59	-6:55:56
Pak Ban	21N14	102E28	-6:49:52
Pak Sane → Muang Pakxan	18N22	103E39	-6:54:36
Pakxé	15N07	105E47	-7:03:08
Phôngsali	21N41	102E06	-6:48:24
Sam Nua	20N25	104E02	-6:56:08
Saravan	15N43	106E25	-7:05:40
Savannakhét	16N33	104E45	-6:59:00
Sépone → Muang Xépôn	16N41	106E14	-7:04:56
Sop Hao	20N33	104E27	-6:57:48
Sop Pong	22N04	102E03	-6:48:12
Thakhek → Muang Khammouan	17N24	104E48	-6:59:12
Tourakom	18N26	102E32	-6:50:08
Viangchan (Vientiane)	17N58	102E36	-6:50:24
Viangphoukha	20N41	101E04	-6:44:16
Vientiane → Viangchan	17N58	102E36	-6:50:24
Xam Nua	20N25	104E02	-6:56:08
Xénô	16N35	104E50	-6:59:20
Xiangkhoang	19N20	103E22	-6:53:28

LEBANON — LÍBANO — LIBAN — LIBANON — AL-LUBNĀN

Time Table		
Before	1/Jan/1880	LMT
Begin Standard		30E00
1/Jan/1880	0:00	-2:00
28/Mar/1920	0:00	-3:00
25/Oct/1920	0:00	-2:00
3/Apr/1921	0:00	-3:00
3/Oct/1921	0:00	-2:00
26/Mar/1922	0:00	-3:00
8/Oct/1922	0:00	-2:00
22/Apr/1923	0:00	-3:00
16/Sep/1923	0:00	-2:00
1/May/1957	0:00	-3:00
1/Oct/1957	0:00	-2:00
1/May/1958	0:00	-3:00
1/Oct/1958	0:00	-2:00
1/May/1959	0:00	-3:00
1/Oct/1959	0:00	-2:00
1/May/1960	0:00	-3:00
1/Oct/1960	0:00	-2:00
1/May/1961	0:00	-3:00
1/Oct/1961	0:00	-2:00
22/Jun/1972	0:00	-3:00
1/Oct/1972	0:00	-2:00
1/May/1973	0:00	-3:00
1/Oct/1973	0:00	-2:00
1/May/1974	0:00	-3:00
1/Oct/1974	0:00	-2:00
1/May/1975	0:00	-3:00
1/Oct/1975	0:00	-2:00
1/May/1976	0:00	-3:00
1/Oct/1976	0:00	-2:00
1/May/1977	0:00	-3:00
1/Oct/1977	0:00	-2:00
30/Apr/1978	0:00	-3:00
30/Sep/1978	0:00	-2:00
1/May/1984	0:00	-3:00
15/Oct/1984	0:00	-2:00
1/May/1985	0:00	-3:00
16/Oct/1985	0:00	-2:00
1/May/1986	0:00	-3:00
16/Oct/1986	0:00	-2:00
1/May/1987	0:00	-3:00
16/Oct/1987	0:00	-2:00
1/Jun/1988	0:00	-3:00
1/Nov/1988	0:00	-2:00
10/May/1989	0:00	-3:00
16/Oct/1989	0:00	-2:00
1/May/1990	0:00	-3:00
16/Oct/1990	0:00	-2:00
1/May/1991	0:00	-3:00
16/Oct/1991	0:00	-2:00
1/May/1992	0:00	-3:00
16/Oct/1992	0:00	-2:00
1/May/1993	0:00	-3:00
16/Oct/1993	0:00	-2:00
1/May/1994	0:00	-3:00
16/Oct/1994	0:00	-2:00
1/May/1995	0:00	-3:00
16/Oct/1995	0:00	-2:00
1/May/1996	0:00	-3:00
16/Oct/1996	0:00	-2:00
1/May/1997	0:00	-3:00
16/Oct/1997	0:00	-2:00
1/May/1998	0:00	-3:00
16/Oct/1998	0:00	-2:00
1/May/1999	0:00	-3:00
16/Oct/1999	0:00	-2:00
1/May/2000	0:00	-3:00
16/Oct/2000	0:00	-2:00

Place	Lat.	Long.	Time
Ad-Dāmūr	33N44	35E27	-2:21:48
Ad-Duwayr	33N23	35E25	-2:21:40
'Ajaltūn	33N58	35E41	-2:22:44
Al-'Atīqah	33N42	35E27	-2:21:48
'Ālayh	33N48	35E36	-2:22:24
Al-Batrūn	34N15	35E39	-2:22:36
Al-Furzul	33N52	35E56	-2:23:44
Al-Ghāzīyah	33N31	35E22	-2:21:28
'Alī an-Nahrī	33N51	36E01	-2:24:04
Al-Khiyām	33N19	35E36	-2:22:24
Al-Kufayr	33N26	35E44	-2:22:56
Al-Labwah	34N12	36E21	-2:25:24
Al-Mīnā'	34N27	35E49	-2:23:16
Al-Mu'Allaqah	33N50	35E54	-2:23:36
Al-Mutayn	33N54	35E44	-2:22:56
Al-Qir'Awn	33N34	35E43	-2:22:52
Amyūn	34N18	35E49	-2:23:16
An-Nabaṭīyah at-Taḥtā	33N23	35E29	-2:21:56
An-Nabī Shīt	33N52	36E07	-2:24:28
An-Nāqūrah	33N07	35E08	-2:20:32
Anṣār	33N23	35E21	-2:21:24
Anṭilyās	33N55	35E35	-2:22:20
Ash-Shīyāḥ	33N51	35E30	-2:22:00
Ash-Shuwayfāt	33N49	35E31	-2:22:04
Ash-Shuwayr	33N55	35E43	-2:22:52
Aṣ-Ṣarafand	33N27	35E18	-2:21:12
'Aytā al-Fakhkhār	33N38	35E54	-2:23:36
'Aytanīt	33N34	35E40	-2:22:40
Az-Zrārīyah	33N21	35E20	-2:21:20
B'Abdā	33N50	35E32	-2:22:08
B'Abdāt	33N53	35E40	-2:22:40
Ba'Labakk	34N00	36E12	-2:24:48
B'Aqlīn	33N41	35E33	-2:22:12
Barjā	33N39	35E26	-2:21:44
Barr Ilyās	33N46	35E54	-2:23:36
'Bayh	33N44	35E31	-2:22:04
Bayrūt (Beirut)	33N53	35E30	-2:22:00
Bayt ad-Dīn	33N42	35E35	-2:22:20
Bayt Mirī	33N52	35E36	-2:22:24
Beirut → Bayrūt	33N53	35E30	-2:22:00
Beyrouth → Bayrūt	33N53	35E30	-2:22:00
Bikfayyā	33N55	35E41	-2:22:44
Bint Jubayl	33N07	35E26	-2:21:44
Biskintā	33N57	35E48	-2:23:12
Bkāsīn	33N34	35E35	-2:22:20
Bsharrī	34N15	36E01	-2:24:04
Byblos → Jubayl	34N07	35E39	-2:22:36
Dayr al-'Ashā'ir	33N32	36E01	-2:24:04
Dūmā	34N12	35E50	-2:23:20
Furn ash-Shubbāk	33N52	35E31	-2:22:04
Gharīfah	33N38	35E33	-2:22:12
Ghazīr	34N01	35E40	-2:22:40
Ghazzah	33N40	35E49	-2:23:16
Ḥabbūsh	33N24	35E29	-2:21:56
Ḥalbā	34N33	36E05	-2:24:20
Ḥammānā	33N49	35E44	-2:22:56
Ḥārat Ḥurayk	33N51	35E30	-2:22:00
Ḥāṣbayyā	33N24	35E41	-2:22:44
Ḥawsh Mūsá	33N43	35E56	-2:23:44
Jazzīn	33N32	35E34	-2:22:16
Jbā'	33N29	35E31	-2:22:04
Jubayl (Byblos)	34N07	35E39	-2:22:36
Jubb Jannīn	33N37	35E47	-2:23:08
Jūn	33N35	35E27	-2:21:48
Jūniyah	33N59	35E38	-2:22:32
Jwayyā	33N14	35E19	-2:21:16
Kafr Ḥūnah	33N29	35E35	-2:22:20
Kafr Nabrakh	33N42	35E38	-2:22:32
Kafr Shīmā	33N49	35E32	-2:22:08
Khirbat Qanāfār	33N38	35E43	-2:22:52
Ma'āṣir ash-Shūf	33N40	35E40	-2:22:40
Maghdūshah	33N31	35E23	-2:21:32
Maḥaṭṭat Bḥamdūn	33N48	35E39	-2:22:36
Majdal 'Anjar	33N42	35E54	-2:23:36
Ma'Rakah	33N16	35E18	-2:21:12
Marj 'Uyūn	33N22	35E35	-2:22:20
Mār Yūsuf	33N53	35E33	-2:22:12
Mashgharah	33N32	35E39	-2:22:36
Qabb Ilyās	33N48	35E49	-2:23:16
Qānā	33N13	35E18	-2:21:12
Qarṭabā	34N06	35E51	-2:23:24
Raḥbah	34N30	36E09	-2:24:36
Ra's Ba'Labakk	34N15	36E25	-2:25:40
Rāshayyā	33N30	35E51	-2:23:24
Rishmayyā	33N44	35E36	-2:22:24
Rīyāq	33N51	36E00	-2:24:00
Rumaysh	33N05	35E22	-2:21:28
Ṣaghbīn	33N37	35E42	-2:22:48
Ṣaydā (Sidon)	33N33	35E22	-2:21:28
Shab'ā	33N21	35E45	-2:23:00
Shaqrā	33N12	35E28	-2:21:52
Shḥīm	33N37	35E29	-2:21:56
Sidon → Ṣaydā	33N33	35E22	-2:21:28
Sīr aḍ-Ḍinnīyah	34N23	36E02	-2:24:08
Ṣūr (Tyre)	33N16	35E11	-2:20:44
Taḥwīṭat an-Nahr	33N52	35E31	-2:22:04
Ṭarābulus (Tripoli)	34N26	35E51	-2:23:24
Tibnīn	33N12	35E25	-2:21:40
Tripoli → Ṭarābulus	34N26	35E51	-2:23:24
Tyre → Ṣūr	33N16	35E11	-2:20:44
Yanṭā	33N36	35E57	-2:23:48
Yāṭar	33N09	35E20	-2:21:20
Zaḥlah	33N51	35E53	-2:23:32
Zghartā	34N24	35E54	-2:23:36
Zibdīn	33N22	35E28	-2:21:52
Zūq Mīkhā'īl	33N58	35E37	-2:22:28

LESOTHO — BASUTOLAND — LESOTHO

Time Table		
Before	1/Mar/1903	LMT
Begin Standard		30E00
1/Mar/1903	0:00	-2:00
19/Sep/1943	2:00	-3:00
19/Mar/1944	2:00	-2:00

Place	Lat.	Long.	Time
Butha Buthe	28S45	28E15	-1:53:00
Joel	28S42	28E21	-1:53:24
Leribe	28S58	28E00	-1:52:00
Mafeteng	29S51	27E15	-1:49:00
Marakabei	29S32	28E09	-1:52:36
Maseru	29S28	27E30	-1:50:00
Matsieng	29S36	27E32	-1:50:08
Mohale's Hoek	30S07	27E26	-1:49:44
Mokhotlong	29S22	29E02	-1:56:08
Morija	29S34	27E31	-1:50:04
Mount Moorosi	30S16	27E53	-1:51:32
Pitseng	28S58	28E16	-1:53:04
Qacha's Nek	30S06	28E42	-1:54:48
Quthing	30S30	27E36	-1:50:24
Roma	29S27	27E45	-1:51:00
Sehlaba-Thebe	29S53	29E05	-1:56:20
Sekake	29S58	28E27	-1:53:48
Sekake's	29S58	28E27	-1:53:48
Teyateyaneng	29S07	27E34	-1:50:16

LIBERIA — LIBÉRIA

Time Table		
Before	1/Jan/1882	LMT
Begin Standard		10W47
1/Jan/1882	0:00	0:43
Begin Standard		11W00
1/Mar/1919	0:00	0:44
Begin Standard		0W00
1/May/1972	0:00	0:00

Place	Lat.	Long.	Time
Bahn	7N05	8W45	0:35:00
Bellé Yella	7N22	10W00	0:40:00
Bendaja	7N10	11W15	0:45:00
Bentol	6N26	10W36	0:42:24
Bopolu	7N03	10W32	0:42:08
Brewerville	6N26	10W47	0:43:08
Buchanan	5N57	10W02	0:40:08
Camp King	4N55	7W58	0:31:52
Careysburg	6N30	10W32	0:42:08
Duabo	5N40	8W05	0:32:20
Edina	6N01	10W10	0:40:40
Ganta	7N15	8W59	0:35:56
Gbanka	7N00	9W29	0:37:56
Grand Bassa	5N52	10W57	0:43:48
Grand Cess	4N36	8W10	0:32:40
Greenville	5N01	9W03	0:36:12
Harper	4N25	7W43	0:30:52
Howeke	4N50	7W45	0:31:00

LIBÉRIA LIBERIA

Place	Lat	Long	Offset
Jedepo	5N16	8W20	0:33:20
Juarzon	5N20	8W52	0:35:28
Kakata	6N35	10W19	0:41:16
Kolahun	8N24	10W02	0:40:08
Marshall	6N10	10W23	0:41:32
Monrovia	6N18	10W47	0:43:08
Nana Kru	4N50	8W44	0:34:56
Nyaake	4N52	7W37	0:30:28
Paluke	5N02	8W06	0:32:24
Pleebo	4N35	7W40	0:30:40
River Cess	5N28	9W32	0:38:08
Robertsfield	6N15	10W24	0:41:36
Robertsport	6N45	11W22	0:45:28
Ross Port	4N58	8W57	0:35:48
Sagleipie	7N00	8W52	0:35:28
Salala	6N40	10W05	0:40:20
Samuel Alfred Ross Port	4N58	8W57	0:35:48
Sanniquellie	7N22	8W43	0:34:52
Sastown	4N40	8W26	0:33:44
Sehnkwehn	5N13	9W12	0:36:48
Sino	5N01	9W04	0:36:16
Tapeta	6N29	8W51	0:35:24
Tappi	6N29	8W54	0:35:36
Tchien	6N04	8W08	0:32:32
Timbo	5N37	9W43	0:38:52
Vaitown	6N52	10W52	0:43:28
Voinjama	8N25	9W45	0:39:00
White Plains	6N29	10W43	0:42:52
Zorzor	7N46	9W28	0:37:52

LĪBIYĀ LIBYEN LIBYE LIBIA LIBYA

Time Table		
Before 1/Jan/1920	LMT	
Begin Standard	15E00	
1/Jan/1920	0:00	-1:00
14/Oct/1951	2:00	-2:00
1/Jan/1952	0:00	-1:00
9/Oct/1953	2:00	-2:00
1/Jan/1954	0:00	-1:00
30/Sep/1955	0:00	-2:00
1/Jan/1956	0:00	-1:00
Begin Standard	30E00	
1/Jan/1959	0:00	-2:00
Begin Standard	15E00	
1/Jan/1982	0:00	-1:00
1/Apr/1982	0:00	-2:00
1/Oct/1982	0:00	-1:00
1/Apr/1983	0:00	-2:00
1/Oct/1983	0:00	-1:00
1/Apr/1984	0:00	-2:00
1/Oct/1984	0:00	-1:00
6/Apr/1985	0:00	-2:00
1/Oct/1985	0:00	-1:00
4/Apr/1986	0:00	-2:00
3/Oct/1986	0:00	-1:00
1/Apr/1987	0:00	-2:00
1/Oct/1987	0:00	-1:00
1/Apr/1988	0:00	-2:00
1/Oct/1988	0:00	-1:00
1/Apr/1989	0:00	-2:00
1/Oct/1989	0:00	-1:00
4/May/1990	0:00	-2:00
1/Oct/1990	0:00	-1:00

Place	Lat	Long	Offset
Adrī	27N32	13E14	-0:52:56
Ajdābiyah	30N48	20E14	-1:20:56
Al-Abyār	32N11	20E36	-1:22:24
Al-Apollonia → Marsā Sūsah	32N54	21E58	-1:27:52
Al-'Azīzīyah	32N32	13E01	-0:52:04
Al-Bardia → Bardīyah	31N46	25E06	-1:40:24
Al-Barkāt	24N54	10E11	-0:40:44
Al-Bayḍā (Beida)	28N22	18E55	-1:15:40
Al-Bu'ayrāt	31N24	15E44	-1:02:56
Al-Bunbah	32N24	23E08	-1:32:32
Al-Fuqahā'	27N50	16E22	-1:05:28
Al-Ḥufrah	29N10	18E02	-1:12:08
Al-'Irq	29N02	21E33	-1:26:12
Al-Jaghbūb	29N45	24E31	-1:38:04
Al-Jawf	24N11	23E19	-1:33:16
Al-Jawsh	32N00	11E40	-0:46:40
Al-Khums (Homs)	32N39	14E16	-0:57:04
Al-Makīlī	32N09	22E17	-1:29:08
Al-Marj	32N30	20E54	-1:23:36
Al-Qaddāḥīyah	31N22	15E14	-1:00:56
Al-Qaryah ash-Sharqīyah	30N24	13E36	-0:54:24
Al-Qaṣabāt	32N35	14E03	-0:56:12
Al-Qaṭrūn	24N56	14E38	-0:58:32
Al-'Uqaylah	30N16	19E12	-1:16:48
Amal	29N25	21E10	-1:24:40
An-Nawfalīyah	30N47	17E50	-1:11:20
As-Sulṭān	31N07	17E10	-1:08:40
At-Tāj	24N13	23E18	-1:33:12
At-Tamīmī	32N20	23E04	-1:32:16
Awbārī	26N35	12E46	-0:51:04
Awjilah	29N09	21E15	-1:25:00
'Ayn al-Ghazālah	32N10	23E20	-1:33:20
Az-Zāwiyah	32N45	12E44	-0:50:56
Az-Zuwaytīnah	30N58	20E07	-1:20:28
Banghāzī	32N07	20E04	-1:20:16
Banīnah	32N05	20E16	-1:21:04
Banī Walīd	31N45	14E01	-0:56:04
Barce → Al-Marj	32N30	20E54	-1:23:36
Bardīyah	31N46	25E06	-1:40:24
Beida → Zāwiyat al-Bayḍā'	32N46	21E43	-1:26:52
Bengasi → Banghāzī	32N07	20E04	-1:20:16
Benghazi → Banghāzī	32N07	20E04	-1:20:16
Beni Ulid → Qaṣr Banī Walīd	31N45	14E01	-0:56:04
Bin Ghashīr	32N41	13E11	-0:52:44
Birāk	27N32	14E16	-0:57:04
Bi'r al-Uzam	31N54	23E58	-1:35:52
Brach	27N32	14E16	-0:57:04
Bū al-Ḥīḍān	28N10	19E18	-1:17:12
Bu'ayrāt al-ḥasūn	31N24	15E44	-1:02:56
Burayk	26N33	13E08	-0:52:32
Buzaymah	24N55	22E02	-1:28:08
Daf'	28N03	19E57	-1:19:48
Dahra	29N34	17E50	-1:11:20
Daraj	30N09	10E26	-0:41:44
Darnah (Derna)	32N46	22E39	-1:30:36
Dirj	30N09	10E26	-0:41:44
Dulaym	25N58	14E03	-0:56:12
El-Azizia → Al-'Azīzīyah	32N32	13E01	-0:52:04
El-Beida → Zāwiyat al-Bayḍā'	32N46	21E43	-1:26:52
El-Gusbat → Al-Qaṣabāt	32N35	14E03	-0:56:12
Emgayet	29N04	12E58	-0:51:52
Facha	29N27	17E18	-1:09:12
Feuet	24N57	10E04	-0:40:16
Funduq Bin Ghashīr	32N41	13E11	-0:52:44
Gadamos → Ghudāmis	30N08	9E30	-0:38:00
Garian → Gharyān	32N10	13E01	-0:52:04
Ghadāmis	30N08	9E30	-0:38:00
Ghaddūwah	26N26	14E18	-0:57:12
Gharyān (Garian)	32N10	13E01	-0:52:04
Ghāt	24N58	10E11	-0:40:44
Ghudāmis	30N08	9E30	-0:38:00
Goddua	26N26	14E18	-0:57:12
Homs → Al-Khums	32N39	14E16	-0:57:04
Hūn	29N07	15E56	-1:03:44
Jabal	28N36	19E58	-1:19:52
Jādū	31N57	12E01	-0:48:04
Jālū	29N02	21E32	-1:26:08
Jardas al-'Abīd	32N19	20E56	-1:23:44
Jarmah	26N33	13E04	-0:52:16
Khuff	28N20	18E48	-1:15:12
Kiklah	32N05	12E41	-0:50:44
Kotla	28N33	18E58	-1:15:52
Lukk	32N01	24E45	-1:39:00
Mabrūk	29N50	17E10	-1:08:40
Madinat al-Abyār	32N11	20E36	-1:22:24
Madrūsah	24N48	14E32	-0:58:08
Ma'Fan	25N55	14E29	-0:57:56
Marādah	29N14	19E13	-1:16:52
Marāwah	32N29	21E25	-1:25:40
Marsā al-Burayqah	30N25	19E34	-1:18:16
Marsā Sūsah	32N54	21E58	-1:27:52
Martūbah	32N35	22E46	-1:31:04
Marzūq	25N55	13E55	-0:55:40
Misrātah	32N23	15E06	-1:00:24
Mizdah	31N26	12E59	-0:51:56
Musaid	31N35	25E03	-1:40:12
Nafoora	29N20	21E20	-1:25:20
Nāfūrah	29N20	21E20	-1:25:20
Nālūt	31N52	10E59	-0:43:56
Ora	28N33	19E24	-1:17:36
Qamīnis	31N39	20E03	-1:20:12
Qaryat al-Qaddāḥīyah	31N22	15E14	-1:00:56
Qaryat al-Zuwaytīnah	30N58	20E07	-1:20:28
Qaṣr al-Burayqah	30N25	19E34	-1:18:16
Qaṣr al Qarābūllī	32N45	13E43	-0:54:52
Qaṣr al-Qarahbullī	32N45	13E43	-0:54:52
Qaṣr aṣ-Ṣaḥabi	30N01	20E48	-1:23:12
Qaṣr Banī Walīd	31N45	14E01	-0:56:04
Qaṣr Bū-Hādī	31N03	16E40	-1:06:40
Rāqūbah	29N04	19E08	-1:16:32
Ra's al-Unūf	30N31	18E34	-1:14:16
Sabhā	27N03	14E26	-0:57:44
Sabhah	27N03	14E26	-0:57:44
Ṣabrātah	32N47	12E29	-0:49:56
Samah	28N12	19E09	-1:16:36
Samnū	27N17	14E53	-0:59:32
Sardalas	25N46	10E34	-0:42:16
Sarīr	27N36	22E32	-1:30:08
Sawknah	29N04	15E47	-1:03:08
Sciuēref	29N53	14E08	-0:56:32
Shaḥḥāt	32N49	21E52	-1:27:28
Sīnāwan	31N02	10E36	-0:42:24
Sīnāwin	31N02	10E36	-0:42:24
Sirte	31N11	16E36	-1:06:24
Sliten → Ẓlītan	32N28	14E34	-0:58:16
Soluch → Sulūq	31N39	20E15	-1:21:00
Sulunṭah	32N36	21E43	-1:26:52
Sulūq	31N39	20E15	-1:21:00
Sūsah	32N54	21E58	-1:27:52
Taghrīfat	29N12	17E22	-1:09:28
Tajarḥī	24N21	14E28	-0:57:52
Tājūrā'	32N53	13E21	-0:53:24
Takartibah	26N32	13E15	-0:53:00
Tamanhint	27N13	14E36	-0:58:24
Ṭarābulus (Tripoli)	32N54	13E11	-0:52:44
Tarāghin	25N59	14E26	-0:57:44
Tarbū	26N02	15E10	-1:00:40
Tarhūnah	32N26	13E38	-0:54:32
Tasāwah	25N58	13E30	-0:54:00
Tāwurghā'	32N02	15E09	-1:00:36
Tījī	32N01	11E22	-0:45:28
Tmassah	26N22	15E47	-1:03:08
Tmīsān	27N32	13E19	-0:53:16
Tobruk → Ṭubruq	32N05	23E59	-1:35:56
Trāghan	25N59	14E26	-0:57:44
Tripolis → Ṭarābulus	32N54	13E11	-0:52:44
Tripoli → Ṭarābulus	32N54	13E11	-0:52:44
Ṭubruq (Tobruk)	32N05	23E59	-1:35:56
Tūkrah	32N32	20E34	-1:22:16
Ṭulmaythah	32N43	20E57	-1:23:48
Tummo	22N40	14E10	-0:56:40
Umm Al-'Abīd	27N31	15E02	-1:00:08
Umm al-Arānib	26N08	14E45	-0:59:00
Waddān	29N10	16E08	-1:04:32
Waha	28N16	19E54	-1:19:36
Wanzarīk	27N31	13E29	-0:53:56
Wāw al-Kabīr	25N20	16E43	-1:06:52
Wāzin	31N57	10E40	-0:42:40
Yafran	32N04	12E31	-0:50:04
Zalṭan	32N57	11E52	-0:47:28
Zaqqūṭ	28N29	19E37	-1:18:28
Zawīlah	26N10	15E07	-1:00:28
Zāwiyat al-Bayḍā' (Beida)	32N46	21E43	-1:26:52
Zāwiyat al-Mukhaylā	32N09	22E17	-1:29:08
Zāwiyat Masūs	31N33	21E03	-1:24:12
Zillah	28N33	17E35	-1:10:20
Ẓlītan	32N28	14E34	-0:58:16
Zuwārah	32N56	12E06	-0:48:24

LIECHTENSTEIN

LIECHTENSTEIN

Time Table
Before 1/Jun/1894 LMT
Begin Standard 15E00

Date	Time	Offset
1/Jun/1894	0:00	-1:00
29/Mar/1981	2:00	-2:00
27/Sep/1981	3:00	-1:00
28/Mar/1982	2:00	-2:00
26/Sep/1982	3:00	-1:00
27/Mar/1983	2:00	-2:00
25/Sep/1983	3:00	-1:00
25/Mar/1984	2:00	-2:00
30/Sep/1984	3:00	-1:00
31/Mar/1985	2:00	-2:00
29/Sep/1985	3:00	-1:00
30/Mar/1986	2:00	-2:00
28/Sep/1986	3:00	-1:00
29/Mar/1987	2:00	-2:00
27/Sep/1987	3:00	-1:00
27/Mar/1988	2:00	-2:00
25/Sep/1988	3:00	-1:00
26/Mar/1989	2:00	-2:00
24/Sep/1989	3:00	-1:00
25/Mar/1990	2:00	-2:00
30/Sep/1990	3:00	-1:00
31/Mar/1991	2:00	-2:00
29/Sep/1991	3:00	-1:00
29/Mar/1992	2:00	-2:00
27/Sep/1992	3:00	-1:00
28/Mar/1993	2:00	-2:00
26/Sep/1993	3:00	-1:00
27/Mar/1994	2:00	-2:00
25/Sep/1994	3:00	-1:00
26/Mar/1995	2:00	-2:00
24/Sep/1995	3:00	-1:00
31/Mar/1996	2:00	-2:00
29/Sep/1996	3:00	-1:00
30/Mar/1997	2:00	-2:00
28/Sep/1997	3:00	-1:00
29/Mar/1998	2:00	-2:00
27/Sep/1998	3:00	-1:00
28/Mar/1999	2:00	-2:00
26/Sep/1999	3:00	-1:00
26/Mar/2000	2:00	-2:00
24/Sep/2000	3:00	-1:00

Place	Latitude	Longitude	Offset
Balzers	47N04	9E30	-0:38:00
Eschen	47N13	9E31	-0:38:04
Malbun	47N35	9E33	-0:38:12
Nendeln	47N12	9E32	-0:38:08
Ruggel	47N15	9E32	-0:38:08
Schaan	47N10	9E31	-0:38:04
Triesen	47N06	9E31	-0:38:04
Vaduz	47N09	9E31	-0:38:04

LUXEMBOURG

LUXEMBURG

LUXEMBURGO

Time Table
Before 1/Jun/1904 LMT
Begin Standard 15E00

Date	Time	Offset
1/Jun/1904	0:00	-1:00
14/May/1916	23:00	-2:00
1/Oct/1916	1:00	-1:00
28/Apr/1917	23:00	-2:00
17/Sep/1917	1:00	-1:00
15/Apr/1918	2:00	-2:00
16/Sep/1918	3:00	-1:00
Begin Standard		0W00
25/Nov/1918	1:00	0:00
1/Mar/1919	23:00	-1:00
5/Oct/1919	3:00	0:00
14/Feb/1920	23:00	-1:00
23/Oct/1920	2:00	0:00
14/Mar/1921	23:00	-1:00
26/Oct/1921	2:00	0:00
25/Mar/1922	23:00	-1:00
8/Oct/1922	1:00	0:00
21/Apr/1923	23:00	-1:00
7/Oct/1923	2:00	0:00
29/Mar/1924	23:00	-1:00
5/Oct/1924	1:00	0:00
4/Apr/1925	23:00	-1:00
4/Oct/1925	1:00	0:00
17/Apr/1926	23:00	-1:00
3/Oct/1926	1:00	0:00
9/Apr/1927	23:00	-1:00
2/Oct/1927	1:00	0:00
14/Apr/1928	23:00	-1:00
7/Oct/1928	1:00	0:00
20/Apr/1929	23:00	-1:00
6/Oct/1929	3:00	0:00
13/Apr/1930	2:00	-1:00
5/Oct/1930	3:00	0:00
19/Apr/1931	2:00	-1:00
4/Oct/1931	3:00	0:00
3/Apr/1932	2:00	-1:00
2/Oct/1932	3:00	0:00
26/Mar/1933	2:00	-1:00
8/Oct/1933	3:00	0:00
8/Apr/1934	2:00	-1:00
7/Oct/1934	3:00	0:00
31/Mar/1935	2:00	-1:00
6/Oct/1935	3:00	0:00
19/Apr/1936	2:00	-1:00
4/Oct/1936	3:00	0:00
4/Apr/1937	2:00	-1:00
3/Oct/1937	3:00	0:00
27/Mar/1938	2:00	-1:00
2/Oct/1938	3:00	0:00
16/Apr/1939	2:00	-1:00
19/Nov/1939	3:00	0:00
Begin Standard		15E00
14/May/1940	3:00	-2:00
2/Nov/1942	3:00	-1:00
29/Mar/1943	2:00	-2:00
4/Oct/1943	3:00	-1:00
3/Apr/1944	2:00	-2:00
18/Sep/1944	3:00	-1:00
2/Apr/1945	2:00	-2:00
16/Sep/1945	3:00	-1:00
19/May/1946	2:00	-2:00
7/Oct/1946	2:00	-1:00
3/Apr/1977	2:00	-2:00
25/Sep/1977	3:00	-1:00
2/Apr/1978	2:00	-2:00
1/Oct/1978	3:00	-1:00
1/Apr/1979	2:00	-2:00
30/Sep/1979	3:00	-1:00
6/Apr/1980	2:00	-2:00
28/Sep/1980	3:00	-1:00
29/Mar/1981	2:00	-2:00
27/Sep/1981	3:00	-1:00
28/Mar/1982	2:00	-2:00
26/Sep/1982	3:00	-1:00
27/Mar/1983	2:00	-2:00
25/Sep/1983	3:00	-1:00
25/Mar/1984	2:00	-2:00
30/Sep/1984	3:00	-1:00
31/Mar/1985	2:00	-2:00
29/Sep/1985	3:00	-1:00
30/Mar/1986	2:00	-2:00
28/Sep/1986	3:00	-1:00
29/Mar/1987	2:00	-2:00
27/Sep/1987	3:00	-1:00
27/Mar/1988	2:00	-2:00
25/Sep/1988	3:00	-1:00
26/Mar/1989	2:00	-2:00
24/Sep/1989	3:00	-1:00
25/Mar/1990	2:00	-2:00
30/Sep/1990	3:00	-1:00
31/Mar/1991	2:00	-2:00
29/Sep/1991	3:00	-1:00
29/Mar/1992	2:00	-2:00
27/Sep/1992	3:00	-1:00
28/Mar/1993	2:00	-2:00
26/Sep/1993	3:00	-1:00
27/Mar/1994	2:00	-2:00
25/Sep/1994	3:00	-1:00
26/Mar/1995	2:00	-2:00
24/Sep/1995	3:00	-1:00
31/Mar/1996	2:00	-2:00
29/Sep/1996	3:00	-1:00
30/Mar/1997	2:00	-2:00
28/Sep/1997	3:00	-1:00
29/Mar/1998	2:00	-2:00
27/Sep/1998	3:00	-1:00
28/Mar/1999	2:00	-2:00
26/Sep/1999	3:00	-1:00
26/Mar/2000	2:00	-2:00
24/Sep/2000	3:00	-1:00

Place	Latitude	Longitude	Offset
Asembourg	49N43	6E02	-0:24:08
Beaufort	49N51	6E18	-0:25:12
Berdorf	49N50	6E21	-0:25:24
Berg	49N49	6E05	-0:24:20
Bettembourg	49N32	6E02	-0:24:08
Boulaide	49N54	5E49	-0:23:16
Bourscheid	49N55	6E04	-0:24:16
Capellen	49N38	5E59	-0:23:56
Clervaux	50N04	6E01	-0:24:04
Consdorf	49N46	6E20	-0:25:20
Diekirch	49N53	6E10	-0:24:40
Differdange	49N32	5E52	-0:23:28
Dudelange	49N28	6E05	-0:24:20
Echternach	49N48	6E26	-0:25:44
Esch-Sur-Alzette	49N30	5E59	-0:23:56
Esch-Sur-Sûre	49N55	5E55	-0:23:40
Ettelbruck	49N52	6E05	-0:24:20
Frisange	49N32	6E12	-0:24:48
Grauinster	49N45	6E18	-0:25:12
Grevenmacher	49N42	6E20	-0:25:20
Heiderscheid	49N53	5E54	-0:23:36
Hesperange	49N34	6E09	-0:24:36
Hosingen	50N01	6E05	-0:24:20
Junglinster	49N43	6E15	-0:25:00
Larochette	49N47	6E15	-0:25:00
Luxembourg	49N36	6E09	-0:24:36
Mersch	49N46	6E06	-0:24:24
Mondorf-Les-Bains	49N31	6E16	-0:25:04
Niederanven	49N39	6E16	-0:25:04
Pétange	49N34	5E52	-0:23:28
Redange	49N46	5E54	-0:23:36
Reisdorf	49N53	6E15	-0:25:00
Remich	49N33	6E22	-0:25:28
Rumelange	49N28	6E02	-0:24:08
Saeul	49N44	5E59	-0:23:56
Sandweiler	49N37	6E13	-0:24:52
Steinfort	49N40	5E55	-0:23:40
Troisvierges	50N08	6E00	-0:24:00
Useldange	49N47	5E59	-0:23:56
Vianden	49N57	6E11	-0:24:44
Waldbillig	49N47	6E18	-0:25:12
Wasserbillig	49N44	6E30	-0:26:00
Wemperhardt	50N09	6E05	-0:24:20
Wiltz	49N48	5E55	-0:23:40

MACAO

MACAU

Time Table
Before 1/Jan/1912 LMT
Begin Standard 120E00

Date	Time	Offset
1/Jan/1912	0:00	-8:00
19/Mar/1961	3:30	-9:00
5/Nov/1961	3:30	-8:00
18/Mar/1962	3:30	-9:00
4/Nov/1962	3:30	-8:00
17/Mar/1963	0:00	-9:00
3/Nov/1963	3:30	-8:00
22/Mar/1964	3:30	-9:00
1/Nov/1964	3:30	-8:00
21/Mar/1965	0:00	-9:00
31/Oct/1965	0:00	-8:00
17/Apr/1966	3:30	-9:00
16/Oct/1966	3:30	-8:00
16/Apr/1967	3:30	-9:00
22/Oct/1967	3:30	-8:00
21/Apr/1968	3:30	-9:00
20/Oct/1968	3:30	-8:00
20/Apr/1969	3:30	-9:00
19/Oct/1969	3:30	-8:00
19/Apr/1970	3:30	-9:00
18/Oct/1970	3:30	-8:00
18/Apr/1971	3:30	-9:00
17/Oct/1971	3:30	-8:00
16/Apr/1972	0:00	-9:00
15/Oct/1972	0:00	-8:00
15/Apr/1973	0:00	-9:00
21/Oct/1973	0:00	-8:00
21/Apr/1974	0:00	-9:00
20/Oct/1974	0:00	-8:00
20/Apr/1975	3:30	-9:00
19/Oct/1975	3:30	-8:00
18/Apr/1976	3:30	-9:00
17/Oct/1976	3:30	-8:00
17/Apr/1977	3:30	-9:00
16/Oct/1977	3:30	-8:00
16/Apr/1978	0:00	-9:00
15/Oct/1978	0:00	-8:00
15/Apr/1979	0:00	-9:00
21/Oct/1979	0:00	-8:00
20/Apr/1980	0:00	-9:00
19/Oct/1980	0:00	-8:00

Place	Latitude	Longitude	Offset
Aomen → Macau	22N14	113E35	-7:34:20
Macau	22N14	113E35	-7:34:20

Time Table
Before 1/Jul/1911 LMT
Begin Standard 45E00
1/Jul/1911 0:00 -3:00
27/Feb/1954 23:00 -4:00
29/May/1954 24:00 -3:00

Place	Lat	Long	Offset
Alakamisy	21S19	47E14	-3:08:56
Alarobia Vohiposa	20S59	47E09	-3:08:36
Ambahikily	21S36	43E41	-2:54:44
Ambahita	24S01	45E16	-3:01:04
Ambakaka	24S10	46E17	-3:05:08
Ambalabe	18S24	49E10	-3:16:40
Ambalanjanakomby	16S42	47E05	-3:08:20
Ambalavao	21S50	46E56	-3:07:44
Ambanja	13S41	48E27	-3:13:48
Ambararata	15S03	48E33	-3:14:12
Ambarijeby	14S56	47E41	-3:10:44
Ambato	13S24	48E29	-3:13:56
Ambato Boeni	16S28	46E43	-3:06:52
Ambato Boeny	16S28	46E43	-3:06:52
Ambatofinandrahana	20S33	46E48	-3:07:12
Ambatolampy	19S23	47E25	-3:09:40
Ambatomainty	17S41	45E40	-3:02:40
Ambatomanoina	18S18	47E37	-3:10:28
Ambatondrazaka	17S50	48E25	-3:13:40
Ambatosoratra	17S34	48E32	-3:14:08
Ambenja	15S17	46E58	-3:07:52
Ambevongo	15S27	47E27	-3:09:48
Ambilobe	13S12	49E04	-3:16:16
Ambinanindrano	20S20	48E19	-3:13:16
Ambinanitelo	15S21	49E35	-3:18:20
Ambinanyndrano	20S20	48E19	-3:13:16
Ambinanytelo	15S21	49E35	-3:18:20
Ambinda	16S25	45E52	-3:03:28
Ambivy	21S31	44E02	-2:56:08
Amboahangy	24S15	46E22	-3:05:28
Amboasary	25S02	46E23	-3:05:32
Amboasary	18S26	48E16	-3:13:04
Ambodifototra	16S59	49E52	-3:19:28
Ambodilazana	18S06	49E10	-3:16:40
Ambodiriana	17S55	49E18	-3:17:12
Ambohibary	19S20	46E17	-3:05:08
Ambohidratrimo	18S50	47E26	-3:09:44
Ambohidray	18S36	48E18	-3:13:12
Ambohimahamasina	21S56	47E11	-3:08:44
Ambohimahasoa	21S07	47E13	-3:08:52
Ambohimanga du Sud	20S52	47E36	-3:10:24
Ambohimitombo	20S43	47E26	-3:09:44
Ambondro	25S13	45E44	-3:02:56
Ambositra	20S31	47E15	-3:09:00
Ambovombe	25S11	46E05	-3:04:20
Ampanavoana	15S41	50E22	-3:21:28
Ampanihy	24S42	44E45	-2:59:00
Amparafaravola	17S35	48E13	-3:12:52
Amparihy	23S57	47E20	-3:09:20
Amparihy	16S40	44E49	-2:59:16
Ampasibe	22S56	46E58	-3:07:52
Ampasinambo	20S31	48E00	-3:12:00
Ampisikina	12S57	49E49	-3:19:16
Ampitsikinana	12S57	49E49	-3:19:16
Ampombiantambo	12S42	48E57	-3:15:48
Ampotaka	25S03	44E41	-2:58:44
Ampoza	22S20	44E44	-2:58:56
Analalava	14S38	47E45	-3:11:00
Analapatsy	25S10	46E42	-3:06:48
Analapetsa	25S10	46E42	-3:06:48
Analavoka	22S33	46E30	-3:06:00
Andaingo	18S12	48E17	-3:13:08
Andapa	14S39	49E39	-3:18:36
Andevoranto	18S57	49E06	-3:16:24
Andilamena	17S01	48E35	-3:14:20
Andramaimbo	12S13	49E11	-3:16:44
Andramasina	19S11	47E35	-3:10:20
Andranopasy	21S17	43E44	-2:54:56
Andranovory	23S08	44E10	-2:56:40
Andriamena	17S26	47E30	-3:10:00
Andriandampy	22S45	45E41	-3:02:44
Andriba	17S36	46E55	-3:07:40
Androka	25S02	44E05	-2:56:20
Anivorano	18S44	48E58	-3:15:52
Anivorano Nord	12S44	49E13	-3:16:52
Anjavimihavana	12S32	49E16	-3:17:04
Anjiabe	12S07	49E20	-3:17:20
Anjozorobe	18S24	47E52	-3:11:28
Ankaramena	21S57	46E39	-3:06:36
Ankarimbelo	22S08	47E20	-3:09:20
Ankasakasa	16S21	44E52	-2:59:28
Ankavandra	18S46	45E18	-3:01:12
Ankazoabo	22S18	44E31	-2:58:04
Ankazobe	18S21	47E07	-3:08:28
Ankazomiriotra	19S38	46E32	-3:06:08
Ankiabe	13S13	48E56	-3:15:44
Ankilimalinika	22S58	43E45	-2:55:00
Ankilizato	20S25	45E01	-3:00:04
Ankisabe	19S17	46E29	-3:05:56
Ankororoka	25S30	45E11	-3:00:44
Anorotsangana	13S56	47E55	-3:11:40
Anosibe	19S26	48E13	-3:12:52
Antalaha	14S53	50E16	-3:21:04
Antambohobe	22S20	46E47	-3:07:08
Antanambao Manampotsy	19S29	48E34	-3:14:16
Antanambe	16S26	49E52	-3:19:28
Antananarivo	18S55	47E31	-3:10:04
Antanetibe	18S27	46E42	-3:06:48
Antanifotsy	19S39	47E19	-3:09:16
Antanimieva	22S12	43E44	-2:54:56
Antanimora	24S49	45E40	-3:02:40
Antetikireja	14S42	47E29	-3:09:56
Antevamena	21S02	44E08	-2:56:32
Antoetra	20S46	47E20	-3:09:20
Antonibe	15S07	47E24	-3:09:36
Antsakabary	15S03	48E56	-3:15:44
Antsalova	18S40	44E37	-2:58:28
Antsenavolo	21S24	48E03	-3:12:12
Antsiafabositra	17S18	46E57	-3:07:48
Antsirabe	14S00	49E59	-3:19:56
Antsirabe	15S57	48E58	-3:15:52
Antsirabe	19S51	47E02	-3:08:08
Antsiranana	12S16	49E17	-3:17:08
Antsirane → Diégo-Suarez	12S16	49E17	-3:17:08
Antsohihy	14S52	47E59	-3:11:56
Arivonimamo	19S01	47E15	-3:09:00
Bandabe	15S31	49E04	-3:16:16
Basibasy	22S10	43E40	-2:54:40
Bealanana	14S33	48E44	-3:14:56
Bebao	17S22	44E33	-2:58:12
Befandriana	22S06	43E54	-2:55:36
Befandriana	15S16	48E32	-3:14:08
Befandriana Atsimo	22S06	43E54	-2:55:36
Befasy	20S33	44E23	-2:57:32
Befotaka	13S15	48E16	-3:13:04
Befotaka	14S32	48E01	-3:12:04
Befotaka	23S49	46E59	-3:07:56
Befotaka	21S29	44E44	-2:58:56
Bekily	24S13	45E19	-3:01:16
Bekisopa	21S40	45E54	-3:03:36
Bekitro	24S33	45E18	-3:01:12
Bekodoka	16S58	45E07	-3:00:28
Bekopaka	19S09	44E48	-2:59:12
Belavenona	24S50	47E04	-3:08:16
Belo	19S42	44E33	-2:58:12
Beloha	25S10	45E03	-3:00:12
Belo-Sur-Mer	20S44	44E00	-2:56:00
Bemarivo	16S56	44E21	-2:57:24
Bemarivo	21S45	44E45	-2:59:00
Bemavo	21S37	45E24	-3:01:36
Bemolanga	17S44	45E06	-3:00:24
Benenitra	23S27	45E05	-3:00:20
Beraketa	24S11	45E42	-3:02:48
Beraketa	23S07	44E25	-2:57:40
Beramanja	13S13	48E56	-3:15:44
Beravina	18S10	45E14	-3:00:56
Berevo	19S44	44E58	-2:59:52
Berevo	17S14	44E17	-2:57:08
Beroroha	21S41	45E10	-3:00:40
Besalampy	16S45	44E30	-2:58:00
Betafo	19S50	46E51	-3:07:24
Betioky	23S42	44E22	-2:57:28
Betioky	22S27	43E44	-2:54:56
Betroka	23S16	46E06	-3:04:24
Betsiboka	21S31	44E28	-2:57:52
Bevoalavo	25S13	45E26	-3:01:44
Bezaha	23S30	44E31	-2:58:04
Brickaville	18S49	49E04	-3:16:16
Daraina	13S12	49E40	-3:18:40
Didy	18S07	48E32	-3:14:08
Diégo-Suarez	12S16	49E17	-3:17:08
Doany	14S22	49E31	-3:18:04
Ejeda	24S20	44E31	-2:58:04
Esira	24S20	46E42	-3:06:48
Etrotroka	22S53	47E36	-3:10:24
Fanambana	13S34	50E00	-3:20:00
Fandriana	20S14	47E23	-3:09:32
Fanjakana	21S10	46E53	-3:07:32
Faradofay	25S02	47E00	-3:08:00
Farafangana	22S49	47E50	-3:11:20
Farahalana	14S26	50E10	-3:20:40
Faratsiho	19S24	46E57	-3:07:48
Faux-Cap	25S33	45E32	-3:02:08
Fénérive	17S22	49E25	-3:17:40
Fenoarivo	21S43	46E24	-3:05:36
Fenoarivo	20S52	46E53	-3:07:32
Fenoarivo	18S26	46E34	-3:06:16
Fenoarivo Atsinanana	17S22	49E25	-3:17:40
Fianarantsoa	21S26	47E05	-3:08:20
Fiantsonana	19S09	46E12	-3:04:48
Fierenana	18S29	48E24	-3:13:36
Fihaonana	18S36	47E12	-3:08:48
Folakara	18S20	45E02	-3:00:08
Fort-Carnot	21S53	47E28	-3:09:52
Fort-Dauphin	25S02	47E00	-3:08:00
Fotadrevo	24S03	45E01	-3:00:04
Foulpointe	17S41	49E31	-3:18:04
Hell-Ville	13S25	48E16	-3:13:04
Iakora	23S06	46E40	-3:06:40
Ifanadiana	21S19	47E39	-3:10:36
Ihorombe	23S00	47E33	-3:10:12
Ihosy	22S24	46E08	-3:04:32
Ikalamavony	21S09	46E35	-3:06:20
Ilaka	20S20	47E09	-3:08:36
Ilaka	19S33	48E52	-3:15:28
Imanombo	24S26	45E49	-3:03:16
Imerimandroso	17S23	48E38	-3:14:32
Isoanala	23S50	45E44	-3:02:56
Itampolo	24S41	43E57	-2:55:48
Itandrano	21S47	45E17	-3:01:08
Ivahona	23S27	46E10	-3:04:40
Ivato	20S37	47E12	-3:08:48
Ivohibe	22S29	46E52	-3:07:28
Ivondro	24S47	46E52	-3:07:28
Jangany	23S14	45E27	-3:01:48
Janjina	20S30	45E50	-3:03:20
Kandreho	17S29	46E06	-3:04:24
Karianga	22S22	47E26	-3:09:44
Katsepe	15S45	46E15	-3:05:00
Kiangara	17S58	47E02	-3:08:08
Kilimavony	23S48	43E41	-2:54:44
Kiranomena	18S17	46E03	-3:04:12
Lambomakondro	22S41	44E44	-2:58:56
Lavanono	25S24	44E55	-2:59:40
Lavaraty	23S16	46E59	-3:07:56
Lazarivo	23S54	44E59	-2:59:56
Loky	12S47	49E39	-3:18:36
Madirobe	16S04	46E15	-3:05:00
Madirovalo	16S26	46E30	-3:06:00
Maevatanana	16S56	46E49	-3:07:16
Mahabe	17S05	45E20	-3:01:20
Mahabo	20S23	44E40	-2:58:40
Mahabo	23S40	46E08	-3:04:32
Mahajanga	15S43	46E19	-3:05:16
Mahanoro	19S54	48E48	-3:15:12
Mahasoa	22S12	46E06	-3:04:24
Mahasolo	19S07	46E22	-3:05:28
Mahatsinjo	21S26	45E51	-3:03:24
Maintirano	18S03	44E01	-2:56:04
Majunga	15S43	46E19	-3:05:16
Malaimbandy	20S20	45E36	-3:02:24
Mampikony	16S06	47E38	-3:10:32
Manakara	22S08	48E01	-3:12:04
Manambato	13S14	49E54	-3:19:36
Manambato	13S43	49E07	-3:16:28
Manambolosy	16S02	49E40	-3:18:40
Manampatrana	21S40	47E35	-3:10:20
Mananara	16S10	49E46	-3:19:04
Manandaza	19S19	45E23	-3:01:32
Mananjary	21S13	48E20	-3:13:20
Manantenina	24S17	47E19	-3:09:16
Manapatrana	21S40	47E35	-3:10:20
Manaravolo	23S59	45E39	-3:02:36
Mandabe	20S55	45E49	-3:03:16
Mandabe	21S03	44E55	-2:59:40
Mandoto	19S34	46E17	-3:05:08
Mandritsara	15S50	48E49	-3:15:16
Mandronarivo	21S07	45E38	-3:02:32
Manera	22S55	44E20	-2:57:20
Mangaoka	12S19	49E07	-3:16:28
Mangindrano	14S17	48E58	-3:15:52
Manja	21S26	44E20	-2:57:20
Manjakandriana	18S55	47E47	-3:11:08
Manombo	22S57	43E28	-2:53:52
Marerano	21S23	44E52	-2:59:28
Mariarano	15S29	46E42	-3:06:48
Maroala	15S23	47E59	-3:11:56
Maroantsetra	15S26	49E44	-3:18:56
Marofandilia	20S07	44E34	-2:58:16
Marolambo	20S02	48E07	-3:12:28
Maromandia	14S13	48E08	-3:12:32
Maroseranana	18S32	48E51	-3:15:24
Marotandrano	16S10	48E50	-3:15:20
Marotolana	14S01	48E37	-3:14:28
Marovato	16S28	48E25	-3:13:40
Marovato	15S48	48E05	-3:12:20
Marovato	13S59	48E36	-3:14:24
Marovoay	16S06	46E39	-3:06:36
Marovoay Nord	16S57	44E34	-2:58:16
Masoala	15S59	50E10	-3:20:40
Masoarivo	19S03	44E19	-2:57:16
Masomeloka	20S17	48E37	-3:14:28
Miandrivazo	19S31	45E28	-3:01:52
Miarinarivo	16S38	48E15	-3:13:00
Miarinarivo	18S57	46E55	-3:07:40
Miarinavaratra	20S13	47E31	-3:10:04
Midongy Nord	20S45	46E13	-3:04:52
Midongy Sud	23S35	47E01	-3:08:04
Milanoa	13S35	49E47	-3:19:08
Mitsinjo	16S01	45E52	-3:03:28
Morafenobe	17S49	44E55	-2:59:40
Moramanga	18S56	48E12	-3:12:48
Morombe	21S45	43E22	-2:53:28
Morondava	20S17	44E17	-2:57:08
Nosy Varika	20S35	48E32	-3:14:08
Port-Bergé	15S33	47E40	-3:10:40
Port Choiseul	15S24	49E51	-3:19:24
Poste Ramartina	19S38	45E58	-3:03:52
Ranohira	22S29	45E24	-3:01:36
Ranomafana	18S57	48E50	-3:15:20
Ranomafana	24S36	46E58	-3:07:52
Ranomena	23S25	47E17	-3:09:08
Ranopiso	25S03	46E40	-3:06:40
Ranotsara Nord	22S48	46E36	-3:06:24
Rantabe	15S42	49E39	-3:18:36
Sahana Ambodipont	14S37	50E11	-3:20:44
Sahasinaka	21S49	47E49	-3:11:16
Saint-Augustin	23S33	43E46	-2:55:04
Sakaraha	22S55	44E32	-2:58:08
Sambava	14S16	50E10	-3:20:40
Sitampiky	16S41	46E06	-3:04:24
Soahanina	18S42	44E13	-2:56:52
Soahany	18S42	44E13	-2:56:52
Soalala	16S06	45E20	-3:01:20
Soalara	23S36	43E44	-2:54:56
Soalary	23S36	43E44	-2:54:56
Soaloka	18S32	45E15	-3:01:00
Soamanonga	23S52	44E47	-2:59:08
Soanierana Ivongo	16S55	49E35	-3:18:20
Soanindrariny	19S54	47E14	-3:08:56
Soavina	20S23	46E56	-3:07:44
Soavinandriana	19S09	46E45	-3:07:00

MADAGASCAR MADAGASKAR MALAGASY REPUBLIC MADAGASIKARA

Place	Lat	Long	Offset
Solila	21S25	46E37	-3:06:28
Tamatave	18S10	49E23	-3:17:32
Tambohorano	17S30	43E58	-2:55:52
Tananarive → Antananarivo	18S55	47E31	-3:10:04
Tangainony	22S42	47E45	-3:11:00
Toamasina	18S10	49E23	-3:17:32
Toliara	23S21	43E40	-2:54:40
Tolongoina	21S33	47E31	-3:10:04
Tongobory	23S32	44E20	-2:57:20
Trangahy	19S07	44E43	-2:58:52
Tranoroa	24S42	45E04	-3:00:16
Tritriva	22S46	46E07	-3:04:28
Tsarabaria	13S46	49E58	-3:19:52
Tsaramandroso	16S22	47E02	-3:08:08
Tsaratanana	16S47	47E39	-3:10:36
Tsianaloka	18S08	44E50	-2:59:20
Tsihombe	25S18	45E29	-3:01:56
Tsimilofo	24S59	45E10	-3:00:40
Tsinjoarivo	19S37	47E40	-3:10:40
Tsinjomitondraka	15S36	47E08	-3:08:32
Tsiroanomandidy	18S46	46E02	-3:04:08
Tsitondroina	21S19	46E00	-3:04:00
Tsivory	24S04	46E05	-3:04:20
Tuléar	23S21	43E40	-2:54:40
Vangaindrano	23S21	47E36	-3:10:24
Vatomandry	19S20	48E59	-3:15:56
Vavatenina	17S28	49E12	-3:16:48
Vohémar	13S21	50E02	-3:20:08
Vohibinany	18S49	49E04	-3:16:16
Vohilava	21S04	48E00	-3:12:00
Vohimarina	13S21	50E02	-3:20:08
Vohipeno	22S22	47E51	-3:11:24
Vohitsora	23S54	44E17	-2:57:08
Vondrozo	22S49	47E20	-3:09:20
Zazafotsy	22S13	46E26	-3:05:44

MALAWI NYASALAND MALAWI

Time Table
Before 1/Mar/1903 LMT
Begin Standard 30E00
1/Mar/1903 0:00 -2:00

Place	Lat	Long	Offset
Bakile	13S58	35E15	-2:21:00
Balaka	14S59	34E57	-2:19:48
Bana	12S25	34E08	-2:16:32
Bandawe	11S57	34E10	-2:16:40
Benga	13S19	34E16	-2:17:04
Blantyre	15S47	35E00	-2:20:00
Bolero	10S59	33E45	-2:15:00
Chamama	12S55	33E43	-2:14:52
Chikwawa	16S03	34E48	-2:19:12
Chilumba	10S28	34E12	-2:16:48
Chiluvya	12S18	34E01	-2:16:04
Chinteche	11S52	34E09	-2:16:36
Chintembwe	13S25	33E59	-2:15:56
Chintheche	11S52	34E09	-2:16:36
Chipoka	14S00	34E31	-2:18:04
Chiradzulu	15S42	35E10	-2:20:40
Chiromo	16S33	35E08	-2:20:32
Chisenga	9S56	33E26	-2:13:44
Chitipa	9S43	33E16	-2:13:04
Cholo	16S10	35E10	-2:20:40
Dedza	14S22	34E20	-2:17:20
Domasi	15S18	35E20	-2:21:20
Dowa	13S40	33E58	-2:15:52
Ekwendeni	11S23	33E50	-2:15:20
Fort Hill → Chitipa	9S43	33E16	-2:13:04
Fort Johnston → Mangoche	14S28	35E16	-2:21:04
Fort Maguire	13S08	34E52	-2:19:28
Karonga	9S56	33E56	-2:15:44
Kasungu	13S01	33E30	-2:14:00
Kasupe	15S10	35E15	-2:21:00
Katete	12S17	33E39	-2:14:36
Kota Kota → Nkhota Kota	12S57	34E17	-2:17:08
Lilongwe	13S59	33E44	-2:14:56
Limbe	15S49	35E03	-2:20:12
Livingstonia	10S36	34E07	-2:16:28
Liwonde	14S52	35E28	-2:21:52
Mchinji	13S41	32E55	-2:11:40
Mangoche	14S28	35E16	-2:21:04
Mangochi	14S28	35E16	-2:21:04
Matope	15S20	34E59	-2:19:56
Monkey Bay	14S05	34E55	-2:19:40
Mpimbe	15S18	35E04	-2:20:16
Mponela	13S21	33E43	-2:14:52
Mtakataka	14S12	34E32	-2:18:08
Mulanje	16S03	35E31	-2:22:04
Mvela	14S46	35E16	-2:21:04
Mwanza	15S37	34E31	-2:18:04
Mzimba	11S52	33E34	-2:14:16
Mzuzu	11S27	33E55	-2:15:40
Namwera	14S22	35E30	-2:22:00
Ncheu	14S49	34E38	-2:18:32
Neno	15S24	34E39	-2:18:36
Nkhata Bay	11S33	34E18	-2:17:12
Nkhota Kota	12S57	34E17	-2:17:08
Nsanje	16S55	35E12	-2:20:48
Ntcheu	14S49	34E38	-2:18:32
Ntchisi	13S19	33E58	-2:15:52
Nyungwe	10S16	34E07	-2:16:28
Port Herald	16S54	35E16	-2:21:04
Rumphi	11S01	33E52	-2:15:28
Salima	13S47	34E26	-2:17:44
Thyolo	16S10	35E10	-2:20:40
Usisya	11S09	34E11	-2:16:44
Zomba	15S23	35E18	-2:21:12

MALAYSIA MALAISIE MALASIA

Time Table # 1
Before 1/Oct/1904 LMT
Begin Standard 120E00
1/Oct/1904 0:00 -8:00
....
Time Table # 2
Before 1/Jan/1880 LMT
Begin Standard 103E51
1/Jan/1880 0:00 -6:55
Begin Standard 105E00
1/Jun/1905 0:00 -7:00
Begin Standard 110E00
1/Jan/1933 0:00 -7:20
Begin Standard 135E00
15/Feb/1942 0:00 -9:00
Begin Standard 110E00
2/Sep/1945 0:00 -7:20
Begin Standard 112E30
1/Jan/1950 0:00 -7:30
Begin Standard 120E00
1/May/1982 0:00 -8:00
....
Time Table # 3
Before 1/Mar/1926 LMT
Begin Standard 112E30
1/Mar/1926 0:00 -7:30
Begin Standard 120E00
1/Jan/1933 0:00 -8:00
14/Sep/1935 0:00 -8:20
14/Dec/1935 0:00 -8:00
14/Sep/1936 0:00 -8:20
14/Dec/1936 0:00 -8:00
14/Sep/1937 0:00 -8:20
14/Dec/1937 0:00 -8:00
14/Sep/1938 0:00 -8:20
14/Dec/1938 0:00 -8:00
14/Sep/1939 0:00 -8:20
14/Dec/1939 0:00 -8:00
14/Sep/1940 0:00 -8:20
14/Dec/1940 0:00 -8:00
14/Sep/1941 0:00 -8:20
14/Dec/1941 0:00 -8:00
Begin Standard 135E00
1/Jan/1942 0:00 -9:00
Begin Standard 120E00
2/Sep/1945 0:00 -8:00

DIVISIONS

1. Malaya
2. Sarawak
3. Labuan

Place	Div.	TT	Lat	Long	Offset
Abai	2	3	5N41	118E23	-7:53:32
Adjan	2	3	2N11	113E12	-7:32:48
Ajil	1	2	5N05	103E05	-6:52:20
Alor Gajah	1	2	2N23	102E13	-6:48:52
Alor Setar	1	2	6N07	100E22	-6:41:28
Alor Star → Alor Setar	1	2	6N07	100E22	-6:41:28
Arau	1	2	6N26	100E16	-6:41:04
Asahan	1	2	2N23	102E33	-6:50:12
Ayer Baloi	1	2	1N35	103E20	-6:53:20
Ayer Hitam	1	2	1N55	103E11	-6:52:44
Ayer Hitam	1	2	2N56	102E24	-6:49:36
Ayer Jerneh	1	2	4N24	103E24	-6:53:36
Ayer Kuning Selatan	1	2	2N30	102E28	-6:49:52
Bachok	1	2	6N04	102E24	-6:49:36
Bagan Datoh	1	2	3N59	100E47	-6:43:08
Bagan Serai	1	2	5N01	100E32	-6:42:08
Bahau	1	2	2N49	102E25	-6:49:40
Bakap	1	2	4N26	101E04	-6:44:16
Baling	1	2	5N40	100E55	-6:43:40
Balingian	2	3	2N55	112E32	-7:30:08
Bandar Baharu	1	2	5N08	100E30	-6:42:00
Bandar Maharani	1	2	2N03	103E33	-6:54:12
Bandar Penggaram → Batu Pahat	1	2	1N51	102E56	-6:51:44
Banting	1	2	2N49	101E30	-6:46:00
Bareo	2	3	3N45	115E27	-7:41:48
Batang Berjuntai	1	2	3N23	101E25	-6:45:40
Batang Kali	1	2	3N28	101E38	-6:46:32
Batu Arang	1	2	3N19	101E28	-6:45:52
Batu Caves	1	2	3N14	101E40	-6:46:40
Batu Enam	1	2	2N35	102E43	-6:50:52
Batu Gajah	1	2	4N28	101E03	-6:44:12
Batu Laut	1	2	2N41	101E31	-6:46:04
Batu Pahat (Bandar Penggaram)	1	2	1N51	102E56	-6:51:44
Batu Rakit	1	2	5N27	103E03	-6:52:12
Bau	2	3	1N25	110E08	-7:20:32
Beaufort	2	3	5N20	115E45	-7:43:00
Bedong	1	2	5N44	100E31	-6:42:04
Bekok	1	2	2N18	103E08	-6:52:32
Belaga	2	3	2N42	113E47	-7:35:08
Beluran	2	3	5N54	117E33	-7:50:12
Bemban	1	2	2N16	102E23	-6:49:32
Benta	1	2	4N01	101E58	-6:47:52
Bentong	1	2	3N32	101E55	-6:47:40
Benut	1	2	1N38	103E16	-6:53:04
Beroga	1	2	2N56	101E55	-6:47:40
Bertam	1	2	5N09	102E03	-6:48:12
Beruas	1	2	4N30	100E47	-6:43:08
Beserah	1	2	3N52	103E22	-6:53:28
Betang Melaka	1	2	2N28	102E25	-6:49:40
Betong	2	3	1N24	111E31	-7:26:04
Bidor	1	2	4N07	101E17	-6:45:08
Bintulu	2	3	3N10	113E02	-7:32:08
Bongon	2	3	6N35	116E52	-7:47:28
Bukit Betong	1	2	4N15	101E56	-6:47:44
Bukit Fraser	1	2	3N43	101E45	-6:47:00
Bukit Kachi	1	2	6N24	100E32	-6:42:08
Bukit Mertajam	1	2	5N22	100E28	-6:41:52
Bukit Serok	1	2	2N55	102E50	-6:51:20
Butterworth	1	2	5N25	100E24	-6:41:36
Cameron Highlands	1	2	4N29	101E27	-6:45:48
Chabang Tiga	1	2	5N19	103E08	-6:52:32
Changlun	1	2	6N26	100E26	-6:41:44
Chegar Perah	1	2	4N25	101E56	-6:47:44
Chemor	1	2	4N43	101E07	-6:44:28
Chenderiang	1	2	4N16	101E14	-6:44:56
Chodoi	1	2	2N50	101E27	-6:45:48
Chukai	1	2	4N15	103E25	-6:53:40
Dabong	1	2	5N23	102E01	-6:48:04
Dalat	2	3	2N44	111E56	-7:27:44
Degong	1	2	4N05	101E08	-6:44:32

Durian Tipus 1 2 3N07 102E13 -6:48:52
Gambang 1 2 3N43 103E06 -6:52:24
Gemas 1 2 2N35 102E37 -6:50:28
Genuang 1 2 2N29 102E53 -6:51:32
George Town (Pinang) 1
2 5N25 100E20 -6:41:20
Gerik 1 2 5N25 101E08 -6:44:32
Gopeng 1 2 4N28 101E10 -6:44:40
Gua Musang 1 2 4N53 101E58 -6:47:52
Guar Chempedak 1
2 5N52 100E28 -6:41:52
Gurun 1 2 5N49 100E29 -6:41:56
Gusi 2 3 6N07 117E08 -7:48:32
Hutan Melintang 1
2 3N53 100E56 -6:43:44
Igan 2 3 2N49 111E43 -7:26:52
Ipoh 1 2 4N35 101E05 -6:44:20
Jabi 1 2 2N32 102E48 -6:51:12
Jasin 1 2 2N19 102E26 -6:49:44
Jemaluang 1 2 2N17 103E52 -6:55:28
Jendarata 1 2 3N55 100E57 -6:43:48
Jeniang 1 2 5N49 100E38 -6:42:32
Jeransang 1 2 3N52 102E22 -6:49:28
Jerantut 1 2 3N56 102E22 -6:49:28
Jerteh 1 2 5N45 102E30 -6:50:00
Jesselton → Kota Kinabalu 2
3 5N59 116E04 -7:44:16
Jitra 1 2 6N16 100E25 -6:41:40
Johol 1 2 2N36 102E16 -6:49:04
Johor Baharu 1 2 1N28 103E45 -6:55:00
Kajang 1 2 2N59 101E47 -6:47:08
Kalabakan 2 3 4N25 117E29 -7:49:56
Kampar 1 2 4N18 101E09 -6:44:36
Kampong Ayer Puteh 1
2 4N16 103E12 -6:52:48
Kampong Baharu 1
2 3N43 103E17 -6:53:08
Kampong Benta 1
2 3N32 103E22 -6:53:28
Kampong Buloh 1
2 5N32 102E45 -6:51:00
Kampong Chenor 1
2 3N29 102E36 -6:50:24
Kampong Dong 1 2 3N54 101E54 -6:47:36
Kampong Guchil 1
2 5N33 102E14 -6:48:56
Kampong Jabor 1
2 3N57 103E20 -6:53:20
Kampong Jerangau 1
2 4N51 103E12 -6:52:48
Kampong Kandang 1
2 2N11 102E18 -6:49:12
Kampong Kenyam 1
2 4N31 102E28 -6:49:52
Kampong Kuala Kemaman 1
2 4N14 103E27 -6:53:48
Kampong Lamir 1
2 3N36 103E21 -6:53:24
Kampong Lawa 1 2 5N40 101E42 -6:46:48
Kampong Mengkarak 1
2 3N19 102E27 -6:49:48
Kampong Merang 1
2 5N32 102E57 -6:51:48
Kampong Nuri 1 2 5N02 102E23 -6:49:32
Kampong Penarek 1
2 5N37 102E48 -6:51:12
Kampong Raja 1 2 5N48 102E35 -6:50:20
Kampong Renggong 1
2 4N33 102E35 -6:50:20
Kampong Sebuyau 2
3 1N31 110E56 -7:23:44
Kampong Sekendi 1
2 3N43 100E56 -6:43:44
Kampong Surau 1
2 5N49 100E54 -6:43:36
Kampong Tanjong Batu 1
2 3N12 103E27 -6:53:48
Kampong Tebing Runtoh 1
2 1N26 103E40 -6:54:40
Kampong Ulu Chalok 1
2 5N26 102E50 -6:51:20
Kangar 1 2 6N26 100E12 -6:40:48
Kangkar Lenggor 1
2 2N16 103E44 -6:54:56
Kangkar Teberau 1
2 1N32 103E45 -6:55:00
Kanowit 2 3 2N06 112E09 -7:28:36
Kapit 2 3 2N01 112E56 -7:31:44
Karak 1 2 3N24 102E02 -6:48:08
Kejaman 2 3 2N39 113E45 -7:35:00
Kelanang 1 2 2N48 101E26 -6:45:44
Kelang 1 2 3N02 101E27 -6:45:48
Keluang 1 2 2N02 103E19 -6:53:16
Kemasik 1 2 4N25 103E27 -6:53:48
Kemayan 1 2 3N08 102E22 -6:49:28
Kemubu 1 2 5N18 102E01 -6:48:04
Keningau 2 3 5N20 116E10 -7:44:40
Kepala Batas 1 2 5N31 100E26 -6:41:44
Kerling 1 2 3N35 101E36 -6:46:24
Keroh 1 2 5N43 101E00 -6:44:00
Kerteh 1 2 4N31 103E27 -6:53:48
Kijal 1 2 4N21 103E29 -6:53:56
Klagan 2 3 5N58 117E27 -7:49:48
Klang → Kelang 1
2 3N02 101E27 -6:45:48
Kodiang 1 2 6N24 100E18 -6:41:12
Kota 1 2 5N35 100E23 -6:41:32
Kota 1 2 2N31 102E10 -6:48:40
Kota Baharu 1 2 6N08 102E15 -6:49:00
Kota Kinabalu (Jesselton) 2
3 5N59 116E04 -7:44:16
Kota Sarang Semut 1
2 5N59 100E24 -6:41:36
Kota Tinggi 1 2 1N44 103E54 -6:55:36
Kuah 1 2 6N19 99E51 -6:39:24

Kuala Berang 1 2 5N04 103E01 -6:52:04
Kuala Dungun 1 2 4N47 103E26 -6:53:44
Kuala Kangsar 1
2 4N46 100E56 -6:43:44
Kuala Kedah 1 2 6N06 100E18 -6:41:12
Kuala Kelawang 1
2 2N56 102E05 -6:48:20
Kuala Kerai 1 2 5N32 102E12 -6:48:48
Kuala Kerau 1 2 3N43 102E22 -6:49:28
Kuala Ketil 1 2 5N36 100E39 -6:42:36
Kuala Kubu Baharu 1
2 3N34 101E39 -6:46:36
Kuala Kurau 1 2 5N01 100E26 -6:41:44
Kuala Lipis 1 2 4N11 102E03 -6:48:12
Kuala Lumpur 1 2 3N10 101E42 -6:46:48
Kuala Nerang 1 2 6N15 100E36 -6:42:24
Kuala Pilah 1 2 2N44 102E15 -6:49:00
Kuala Selangor 1
2 3N21 101E15 -6:45:00
Kuala Terengganu 1
2 5N20 103E08 -6:52:32
Kuamut 2 3 5N13 117E30 -7:50:00
Kuantan 1 2 3N48 103E20 -6:53:20
Kubu Gajah 1 2 5N10 100E41 -6:42:44
Kuching 2 3 1N33 110E20 -7:21:20
Kudat 2 3 6N53 116E50 -7:47:20
Kukup 1 2 1N19 103E27 -6:53:48
Kulai 1 2 1N40 103E36 -6:54:24
Kulim 1 2 5N22 100E34 -6:42:16
Labis 1 2 2N23 103E02 -6:52:08
Labuan 3 1 5N17 115E15 -7:41:00
Ladang Jagor 1 2 4N42 101E35 -6:46:20
Lahad Datu 2 3 5N02 118E19 -7:53:16
Lahat 1 2 4N33 101E02 -6:44:08
Lamag 2 3 5N29 117E49 -7:51:16
Lanas 2 3 5N20 116E30 -7:46:00
Lanchang 1 2 3N30 102E11 -6:48:44
Lawin 1 2 5N18 101E04 -6:44:16
Layang Layang 1
2 1N49 103E29 -6:53:56
Lekir 1 2 4N07 100E44 -6:42:56
Lenga 1 2 2N17 102E49 -6:51:16
Limbang 2 3 4N45 115E00 -7:40:00
Lio Matoh 2 3 3N10 115E14 -7:40:56
Litang 2 3 5N20 118E31 -7:54:04
Lombong 1 2 1N48 103E51 -6:55:24
Long Akah 2 3 3N19 114E47 -7:39:08
Long Belepai 2 3 2N45 114E04 -7:36:16
Long Lama 2 3 3N46 114E24 -7:37:36
Long Teru 2 3 3N52 114E15 -7:37:00
Lubok China 1 2 2N27 102E04 -6:48:16
Lumut 1 2 4N14 100E38 -6:42:32
Lutong 2 3 4N28 114E00 -7:36:00
Machang 1 2 5N46 102E13 -6:48:52
Malaka → Melaka 1
2 2N12 102E15 -6:49:00
Malim Nawar 1 2 4N21 101E07 -6:44:28
Manek Urai 1 2 5N23 102E14 -6:48:56
Manong 1 2 4N36 100E53 -6:43:32
Mantin 1 2 2N49 101E54 -6:47:36
Maran 1 2 3N35 102E46 -6:51:04
Marang 1 2 5N12 103E13 -6:52:52
Marudi 2 3 4N11 114E19 -7:37:16
Masai 1 2 1N29 103E53 -6:55:32
Masjid Tanah 1 2 2N21 102E07 -6:48:28
Matang 1 2 4N49 100E41 -6:42:44
Matu 2 3 2N41 111E32 -7:26:08
Mawai 1 2 1N52 103E57 -6:55:48
Melaka 1 2 2N12 102E15 -6:49:00
Melalap 2 3 5N14 116E00 -7:44:00
Meluan 2 3 1N52 111E56 -7:27:44
Mengkibol 1 2 1N58 103E20 -6:53:20
Mengkuang 1 2 3N11 102E24 -6:49:36
Mentekab 1 2 3N29 102E21 -6:49:24
Merapoh 1 2 4N41 101E59 -6:47:56
Merotai Besar 2
3 4N26 117E46 -7:51:04
Mersing 1 2 2N26 103E50 -6:55:20
Miri 2 3 4N23 113E59 -7:35:56
Morib 1 2 2N45 101E26 -6:45:44
Mostyn 2 3 4N40 118E11 -7:52:44
Muar (Bandar Maharani) 1
2 2N02 102E34 -6:50:16
Mukah 2 3 2N54 112E06 -7:28:24
Nenasi 1 2 3N08 103E27 -6:53:48
Niah 2 3 3N52 113E44 -7:34:56
Nibong Tebal 1 2 5N10 100E29 -6:41:56
Niyor 1 2 2N05 103E17 -6:53:08
Nyalas 1 2 2N26 102E28 -6:49:52
Oya 2 3 2N52 111E53 -7:27:32
Padang Besar 1 2 6N40 100E19 -6:41:16
Padang Endau 1 2 2N40 103E37 -6:54:28
Padang Tungku 1
2 4N14 101E59 -6:47:56
Pahi 1 2 5N28 102E13 -6:48:52
Paka 1 2 4N39 103E26 -6:53:44
Paloh 2 3 2N25 111E15 -7:25:00
Paloh 1 2 2N11 103E12 -6:52:48
Panchor 1 2 2N10 102E43 -6:50:52
Pandan 2 3 3N09 113E22 -7:33:28
Pandasan 2 3 6N28 116E32 -7:46:08
Papar 2 3 5N44 115E56 -7:43:44
Parit Bunga 1 2 2N04 102E33 -6:50:12
Parit Buntar 1 2 5N07 100E30 -6:42:00
Parit Jawa 1 2 1N57 102E39 -6:50:36
Pasir Gudang 1 2 1N27 103E53 -6:55:32
Pasir Mas 1 2 6N02 102E08 -6:48:32
Pasir Puteh 1 2 5N50 102E24 -6:49:36
Pasir Puteh 1 2 1N26 103E56 -6:55:44
Paya Besar 1 2 3N47 103E16 -6:53:04
Pedas 1 2 2N37 102E04 -6:48:16
Pekan 1 2 3N30 103E25 -6:53:40
Pelabuhan Kelang 1
2 3N00 101E24 -6:45:36
Pelawan 1 2 2N47 102E55 -6:51:40

Penang → George Town 1
2 5N25 100E20 -6:41:20
Pengkalan Baharu 1
2 4N28 100E38 -6:42:32
Pensiangan 2 3 4N33 116E19 -7:45:16
Peringat 1 2 6N02 102E17 -6:49:08
Petaling Jaya 1
2 3N05 101E39 -6:46:36
Petoh 1 2 2N53 103E15 -6:53:00
Pinang → George Town 1
2 5N25 100E20 -6:41:20
Pinangah 2 3 5N12 116E50 -7:47:20
Pintasan 2 3 5N26 117E43 -7:50:52
Pokok Sena 1 2 6N10 100E32 -6:42:08
Pondok Tanjong 1
2 5N00 100E44 -6:42:56
Pontian Kechil 1
2 1N29 103E23 -6:53:32
Port Dickson 1 2 2N31 101E48 -6:47:12
Port Swettenhamg 1
2 3N00 101E23 -6:45:32
Port Weld 1 2 4N50 100E38 -6:42:32
Prai → Kota 1 2 5N35 100E23 -6:41:32
Pusa 2 3 1N36 111E17 -7:25:08
Ranau 2 3 5N58 116E41 -7:46:44
Rantau 1 2 2N35 101E58 -6:47:52
Raub 1 2 3N48 101E52 -6:47:28
Rawang 1 2 3N19 101E35 -6:46:20
Redang Panjang 1
2 5N07 100E47 -6:43:08
Rembau 1 2 2N35 102E06 -6:48:24
Rembia 1 2 2N20 102E13 -6:48:52
Rengam 1 2 1N53 103E24 -6:53:36
Rengit 1 2 1N41 103E09 -6:52:36
Ringlet 1 2 4N25 101E23 -6:45:32
Rompin 1 2 2N42 102E31 -6:50:04
Rompin 1 2 2N48 103E29 -6:53:56
Sabak Bernam 1 2 3N46 100E59 -6:43:56
Sandakan 2 3 5N50 118E07 -7:52:28
Saratok 2 3 1N44 111E20 -7:25:20
Sarikei 2 3 2N07 111E31 -7:26:04
Segamat 1 2 2N30 102E49 -6:51:16
Sekudai 1 2 1N32 103E40 -6:54:40
Selama 1 2 5N13 100E42 -6:42:48
Selim 1 2 3N51 101E29 -6:45:56
Selim River 1 2 3N50 101E24 -6:45:36
Semanggol 1 2 4N57 100E38 -6:42:32
Sematan 2 3 1N48 109E46 -7:19:04
Semenyih 1 2 2N57 101E51 -6:47:24
Semporna 2 3 4N28 118E36 -7:54:24
Senai 1 2 1N36 103E39 -6:54:36
Senaja 2 3 6N45 117E03 -7:48:12
Senggarang 1 2 1N45 103E03 -6:52:12
Sepang 1 2 2N42 101E45 -6:47:00
Seremban 1 2 2N43 101E56 -6:47:44
Serian 2 3 1N10 110E34 -7:22:16
Setapak 1 2 3N11 101E42 -6:46:48
Sibu 2 3 2N18 111E49 -7:27:16
Sibuti 2 3 4N03 113E48 -7:35:12
Sik 1 2 5N49 100E44 -6:42:56
Sikuati 2 3 6N53 116E40 -7:46:40
Simanggang 2 3 1N15 111E26 -7:25:44
Simpang Empat 1
2 6N20 100E11 -6:40:44
Simpang Rengam 1
2 1N50 103E19 -6:53:16
Simunjan 2 3 1N23 110E45 -7:23:00
Sipitang 2 3 5N05 115E33 -7:42:12
Song 2 3 2N01 112E33 -7:30:12
Suai 2 3 3N48 113E38 -7:34:32
Sukau 2 3 5N32 118E17 -7:53:08
Sundar 2 3 4N54 115E12 -7:40:48
Sungai Bayor 1 2 5N15 100E47 -6:43:08
Sungai Lembing 1
2 3N55 103E02 -6:52:08
Sungai Petani 1
2 5N39 100E30 -6:42:00
Sungai Siput 1 2 4N49 101E04 -6:44:16
Sungkai 1 2 4N00 101E19 -6:45:16
Susui 2 3 4N56 116E41 -7:46:44
Taiping 1 2 4N51 100E44 -6:42:56
Tambunan 2 3 5N40 116E22 -7:45:28
Tampin 1 2 2N28 102E14 -6:48:56
Tanah Merah 1 2 5N48 102E09 -6:48:36
Tanah Merah 1 2 2N36 101E48 -6:47:12
Tangkak 1 2 2N16 102E33 -6:50:12
Tanjong Dawai 1
2 5N41 100E22 -6:41:28
Tanjong Malim 1
2 3N41 101E31 -6:46:04
Tapah 1 2 4N11 101E16 -6:45:04
Tapah Road 1 2 4N10 101E12 -6:44:48
Tawau 2 3 4N15 117E54 -7:51:36
Tebakang 2 3 1N06 110E30 -7:22:00
Telaga 2 3 6N51 117E03 -7:48:12
Telok Anson 1 2 4N02 101E01 -6:44:04
Telok Datok 1 2 2N49 101E31 -6:46:04
Temangan Baharu 1
2 5N42 102E09 -6:48:36
Tembeling 1 2 4N04 102E19 -6:49:16
Temengor 1 2 5N19 101E22 -6:45:28
Temerloh 1 2 3N27 102E25 -6:49:40
Tenghilan 2 3 6N14 116E19 -7:45:16
Tenom 2 3 5N08 115E57 -7:43:48
Teranum 1 2 3N44 101E49 -6:47:16
Teras 1 2 3N45 101E49 -6:47:16
Teriang 1 2 3N14 102E25 -6:49:40
Terolak 1 2 3N53 101E23 -6:45:32
Terong 1 2 4N43 100E44 -6:42:56
Titi Karangan 1
2 5N31 100E37 -6:42:28
Tokai 1 2 6N01 100E24 -6:41:36
Tomani 2 3 4N50 115E55 -7:43:40
Tuaran 2 3 6N11 116E14 -7:44:56
Tubau 2 3 3N08 113E42 -7:34:48

MALAYSIA — MALAISIE — MALASIA

Place		Lat	Long	LMT
Tumpat 1	2	6N12	102E10	-6:48:40
Tungku 2	3	5N01	118E53	-7:55:32
Tunjang 1	2	6N16	100E21	-6:41:24
Ulu Tiram 1	2	1N36	103E49	-6:55:16
Ulu Yam 1	2	3N27	101E38	-6:46:32
Umbai 1	2	2N10	102E20	-6:49:20
Victoria 3	1	5N17	115E15	-7:41:00
Weston 2	3	5N13	115E36	-7:42:24
Yan 1	2	5N48	100E22	-6:41:28
Yong Peng 1	2	2N01	103E04	-6:52:16

MALDIVES — MALEDIVEN — MALDIVAS

Time Table
Before 1/Jan/1880 LMT
Begin Standard 73E30
1/Jan/1880 0:00 -4:54
Begin Standard 75E00
1/Jan/1960 0:00 -5:00

Place	Lat	Long	LMT
Male	4N10	73E30	-4:54:00

MALI — FRENCH SUDAN — MALÍ

Time Table # 1
Before 1/Jan/1912 LMT
Begin Standard 0w00
1/Jan/1912 0:00 0:00
....

Time Table # 2
Before 1/Jan/1912 LMT
Begin Standard 0w00
1/Jan/1912 0:00 0:00
Begin Standard 15w00
26/Feb/1934 0:00 1:00
Begin Standard 0w00
20/Jun/1960 0:00 0:00

Place		Lat	Long	LMT
Aguelhok	1	19N28	0E52	-0:03:28
Akor	2	14N53	6w58	0:27:52
Ambidédi	2	14N35	11w47	0:47:08
Andéranboukane	1	15N26	3E02	-0:12:08
Anefis I-N-Darane	1	18N03	0E36	-0:02:24
Ansongo	1	15N40	0E30	-0:02:00
Aourou	2	14N57	11w35	0:46:20
Araouane	1	18N54	3w33	0:14:12
Badogo	2	11N02	8w13	0:32:52
Badoumbé	2	13N38	10w13	0:40:52
Bafing Makana	2	12N33	10w15	0:41:00
Bafoulabé	2	13N48	10w50	0:43:20
Baï	2	13N38	3w22	0:13:28
Ballé	2	15N20	8w35	0:34:20
Bamako	2	12N39	8w00	0:32:00
Bamba	1	17N02	1w24	0:05:36
Bambara Maoundé	1	15N51	2w47	0:11:08
Banamba	2	13N33	7w27	0:29:48
Bandiagara	1	14N21	3w37	0:14:28
Bankas	1	14N04	3w31	0:14:04
Barouéli	2	13N04	6w50	0:27:20
Bénéna	2	13N07	4w22	0:17:28
Bla	2	12N57	5w46	0:23:04
Boré	1	15N08	3w29	0:13:56
Boron	2	14N01	7w30	0:30:00
Bougouni	2	11N25	7w29	0:29:56
Bouloulí	2	15N34	9w21	0:37:24
Boumboum	1	15N01	1w42	0:06:48
Boura	2	12N25	4w33	0:18:12
Bourem	1	16N57	0w21	0:01:24
Dénié	2	11N14	7w29	0:29:56
Diafarabé	1	14N09	5w01	0:20:04
Dialassagou	2	13N45	3w37	0:14:28
Diangounté Kamara	2	14N33	9w31	0:38:04
Didiéni	2	13N53	8w06	0:32:24
Diéma	2	14N32	9w12	0:36:48
Dilly	2	15N01	7w40	0:30:40
Dindanko	2	14N08	9w30	0:38:00
Dinguira	2	14N11	11w16	0:45:04
Dioïla	2	12N29	6w48	0:27:12
Dioumanténé	2	10N32	5w55	0:23:40
Diounganí	1	14N19	2w44	0:10:56
Dioura	1	14N50	5w15	0:21:00
Diré	1	16N16	3w24	0:13:36
Djénné	2	13N54	4w33	0:18:12
Djibrouïa	2	13N13	11w14	0:44:56
Doro	1	16N09	0w51	0:03:24
Doubabougou	2	14N13	7w59	0:31:56
Douentza	1	15N00	2w57	0:11:48
Doumanaba	2	11N40	5w56	0:23:44
Douna	1	14N39	1w44	0:06:56
Doura	2	13N14	5w55	0:23:40
Dyero	2	12N50	6w30	0:26:00
Fafa	1	15N20	0E43	-0:02:52
Faladyé	2	13N08	8w20	0:33:20
Faléa	2	12N16	11w17	0:45:08
Fana	2	12N47	6w57	0:27:48
Fassa	2	13N26	8w15	0:33:00
Foré	2	13N08	10w42	0:42:48
Foulalaba	2	10N41	7w22	0:29:28
Galougo	2	13N50	11w04	0:44:16
Gangafani	1	14N23	2w24	0:09:36
Gao	1	16N16	0w03	0:00:12
Gargouna	1	15N56	0E13	-0:00:52
Gatié Loumo	1	15N28	4w37	0:18:28
Goan	2	13N14	5w09	0:20:36
Gossi	1	15N49	1w17	0:05:08
Goumbou	2	14N59	7w27	0:29:48
Goundam	1	16N25	3w40	0:14:40
Gourbassi	2	13N24	11w38	0:46:32
Gourma Rharous	1	16N53	1w55	0:07:40
Hamdallay Timbou	2	12N03	10w37	0:42:28
Hombori	1	15N17	1w42	0:06:48
Kadiana	2	10N45	6w30	0:26:00
Kadiolo	2	10N33	5w46	0:23:04
Kalana	2	10N47	8w12	0:32:48
Kali	2	12N10	11w29	0:45:56
Kangaba	2	11N56	8w25	0:33:40
Kangaré	2	11N35	8w10	0:32:40
Kankéla	2	10N50	6w40	0:26:40
Kara	2	12N56	6w15	0:25:00
Karangana	2	12N13	5w02	0:20:08
Karou	1	15N07	0E39	-0:02:36
Katélé	2	10N38	5w37	0:22:28
Kati	2	12N44	8w04	0:32:16
Kayes	2	14N27	11w26	0:45:44
Ké Macina	2	13N58	5w22	0:21:28
Kemparana	2	12N50	4w56	0:19:44
Kéniéba	2	12N50	11w14	0:44:56
Kersinyane	2	15N24	10w10	0:40:40
Kidal	1	18N26	1E24	-0:05:36
Kirane	2	15N25	10w14	0:40:56
Kita	2	13N03	9w29	0:37:56
Kogoni	2	14N44	6w02	0:24:08
Kolokani	2	13N35	8w02	0:32:08
Kolondiéba	2	11N05	6w54	0:27:36
Kona	1	14N57	3w53	0:15:32
Koniakari	2	14N34	10w54	0:43:36
Korienzé	1	15N24	3w47	0:15:08
Koro	1	14N04	3w05	0:12:20
Korodougou	2	12N26	6w17	0:25:08
Koualé	2	11N24	7w01	0:28:04
Koulikoro	2	12N53	7w33	0:30:12
Koulouguidi	2	13N27	11w03	0:44:12
Koumankou Markala	2	12N06	6w08	0:24:32
Kouragué	2	12N18	10w02	0:40:08
Kouroukoto	2	12N35	10w05	0:40:20
Kourounínkoto	2	13N52	9w35	0:38:20
Koury	2	12N11	4w48	0:19:12
Koussané	2	14N53	11w14	0:44:56
Koussili	2	13N30	11w38	0:46:32
Koutiala	2	12N23	5w28	0:21:52
Labbezanga	1	14N57	0E42	-0:02:48
Lakamané	2	14N31	9w55	0:39:40
Léré	1	15N43	4w55	0:19:40
Madina	2	13N24	8w51	0:35:24
Madougou	1	14N24	3w05	0:12:20
Mahina	2	13N46	10w51	0:43:24
Manankoro	2	10N28	7w27	0:29:48
Manimpé	2	14N09	5w31	0:22:04
Mansara	2	13N20	4w39	0:18:36
Marana	2	14N38	11w55	0:47:40
Markala	2	13N41	6w05	0:24:20
Ménaka	1	15N55	2E24	-0:09:36
Molodo	2	14N14	6w02	0:24:08
Mondoro	1	14N40	1w57	0:07:48
Mopti	1	14N30	4w12	0:16:48
Mourdiah	2	14N28	7w28	0:29:52
Mpessoba	2	12N40	5w43	0:22:52
Nampala	2	15N17	5w33	0:22:12
Nangola	2	12N40	6w36	0:26:24
Nara	2	15N10	7w17	0:29:08
Négala	2	12N52	8w27	0:33:48
Ngouma	1	15N38	3w22	0:13:28
Niafounké	1	15N56	4w00	0:16:00
Niéna	2	11N26	6w21	0:25:24
Niga	2	13N38	5w27	0:21:48
Ningari	1	14N40	3w16	0:13:04
Niono	2	14N15	6w00	0:24:00
Nioro du Sahel	2	15N15	9w35	0:38:20
Nossombougou	2	13N06	7w56	0:31:44
Nyamina	2	13N19	6w59	0:27:56
Ouani	1	16N46	0w17	0:01:08
Ouenkoro	2	13N23	3w50	0:15:20
Ouolossébougou	2	12N00	7w55	0:31:40
Râs el Mâ	1	16N37	4w28	0:17:52
Sadiola	2	13N53	11w42	0:46:48
Sah	1	15N38	4w03	0:16:12
Saï	2	13N50	5w00	0:20:00
San	2	13N18	4w54	0:19:36
Sandaré	2	14N42	10w18	0:41:12
Sanga	1	14N28	3w19	0:13:16
Sanso	2	11N43	6w51	0:27:24
Santiguila	2	12N42	7w26	0:29:44
Saraféré	1	15N50	3w42	0:14:48
Sarro	2	13N43	5w15	0:21:00
Satadougou	2	12N21	10w07	0:40:28
Sébékoro	2	12N57	8w59	0:35:56
Séféto	2	14N08	9w49	0:39:16
Ségou	2	13N27	6w16	0:25:04
Séguéla	2	14N07	6w44	0:26:56
Sénou	2	12N31	6w56	0:27:44
Séro	2	14N48	11w04	0:44:16
Sévaré	1	14N32	4w06	0:16:24
Siby	2	12N23	8w20	0:33:20
Sido	2	11N40	7w36	0:30:24
Sikasso	2	11N19	5w40	0:22:40
Sitakili	2	13N07	11w14	0:44:56
Sokolo	2	14N44	6w08	0:24:32
Tamani	2	13N20	6w50	0:27:20
Taoudenni	1	22N40	4w00	0:16:00
Taoussa	1	16N55	0w35	0:02:20
Ténenkou	1	14N28	4w55	0:19:40
Tessalit	1	20N12	1E00	-0:04:00
Timbuktu → Tombouctou	1	16N46	3w01	0:12:04
Timétrine	1	19N27	0w26	0:01:44
Toba	2	11N52	7w28	0:29:52

MALÍ — FRENCH SUDAN — MALI

Place	Zone	Lat	Long	Offset
Tombouctou (Timbuktu)	1	16N46	3w01	0:12:04
Tominian	2	13N17	4w35	0:18:20
Tondibi	1	16N39	0w14	0:00:56
Tondidji	2	13N06	10w20	0:41:20
Toukoto	2	13N27	9w53	0:39:32
Yanfolila	2	11N11	8w09	0:32:36
Yélimané	2	15N08	10w34	0:42:16
Yoro	1	14N17	2w08	0:08:32
Yorosso	2	12N22	4w47	0:19:08
Zangasso	2	12N09	5w37	0:22:28
Zantiébougou	2	11N24	7w15	0:29:00
Zégoua	2	10N30	5w40	0:22:40

MALTE — MELITA — MALTA

Time Table
Before 2/Nov/1893 LMT
Begin Standard 15E00

Date	Time	Offset
2/Nov/1893	0:00	-1:00
3/Jun/1916	24:00	-2:00
30/Sep/1916	24:00	-1:00
31/Mar/1917	24:00	-2:00
29/Sep/1917	24:00	-1:00
9/Mar/1918	24:00	-2:00
5/Oct/1918	24:00	-1:00
1/Mar/1919	24:00	-2:00
4/Oct/1919	24:00	-1:00
20/Mar/1920	24:00	-2:00
18/Sep/1920	24:00	-1:00
14/Jun/1940	24:00	-2:00
2/Nov/1942	3:00	-1:00
29/Mar/1943	2:00	-2:00
4/Oct/1943	3:00	-1:00
2/Apr/1945	2:00	-2:00
16/Sep/1945	24:00	-1:00
17/Mar/1946	2:00	-2:00
6/Oct/1946	3:00	-1:00
16/Mar/1947	0:00	-2:00
5/Oct/1947	1:00	-1:00
29/Feb/1948	2:00	-2:00
3/Oct/1948	3:00	-1:00
22/May/1966	0:00	-2:00
24/Sep/1966	24:00	-1:00
28/May/1967	0:00	-2:00
23/Sep/1967	24:00	-1:00
26/May/1968	0:00	-2:00
21/Sep/1968	24:00	-1:00
1/Jun/1969	0:00	-2:00
27/Sep/1969	24:00	-1:00
31/May/1970	0:00	-2:00
27/Sep/1970	0:00	-1:00
23/May/1971	0:00	-2:00
26/Sep/1971	1:00	-1:00
28/May/1972	0:00	-2:00
1/Oct/1972	0:00	-1:00
31/Mar/1973	0:00	-2:00
29/Sep/1973	1:00	-1:00
21/Apr/1974	0:00	-2:00
16/Sep/1974	1:00	-1:00
20/Apr/1975	2:00	-2:00
21/Sep/1975	2:00	-1:00
18/Apr/1976	2:00	-2:00
19/Sep/1976	3:00	-1:00
17/Apr/1977	2:00	-2:00
18/Sep/1977	3:00	-1:00
16/Apr/1978	2:00	-2:00
17/Sep/1978	3:00	-1:00
15/Apr/1979	2:00	-2:00
16/Sep/1979	3:00	-1:00
31/Mar/1980	2:00	-2:00
21/Sep/1980	2:00	-1:00
29/Mar/1981	2:00	-2:00
27/Sep/1981	3:00	-1:00
28/Mar/1982	2:00	-2:00
26/Sep/1982	3:00	-1:00
27/Mar/1983	2:00	-2:00
25/Sep/1983	3:00	-1:00
25/Mar/1984	2:00	-2:00
30/Sep/1984	3:00	-1:00
31/Mar/1985	2:00	-2:00
29/Sep/1985	3:00	-1:00
30/Mar/1986	2:00	-2:00
28/Sep/1986	3:00	-1:00
29/Mar/1987	2:00	-2:00
27/Sep/1987	3:00	-1:00
27/Mar/1988	2:00	-2:00
25/Sep/1988	3:00	-1:00
26/Mar/1989	2:00	-2:00
24/Sep/1989	3:00	-1:00
25/Mar/1990	2:00	-2:00
30/Sep/1990	3:00	-1:00
31/Mar/1991	2:00	-2:00
29/Sep/1991	3:00	-1:00
29/Mar/1992	2:00	-2:00
27/Sep/1992	3:00	-1:00
28/Mar/1993	2:00	-2:00
26/Sep/1993	3:00	-1:00
27/Mar/1994	2:00	-2:00
25/Sep/1994	3:00	-1:00
26/Mar/1995	2:00	-2:00
24/Sep/1995	3:00	-1:00
31/Mar/1996	2:00	-2:00
29/Sep/1996	3:00	-1:00
30/Mar/1997	2:00	-2:00
28/Sep/1997	3:00	-1:00
29/Mar/1998	2:00	-2:00
27/Sep/1998	3:00	-1:00
28/Mar/1999	2:00	-2:00
26/Sep/1999	3:00	-1:00
26/Mar/2000	2:00	-2:00
24/Sep/2000	3:00	-1:00

Place	Lat	Long	Offset
Birżebbuġa	35N49	14E32	-0:58:08
Citta Vecchia	35N53	14E24	-0:57:36
La Valette → Valletta	35N54	14E31	-0:58:04
Medina	35N53	14E24	-0:57:36
Notabile	35N53	14E24	-0:57:36
Rabat	35N52	14E25	-0:57:40
Rabat (Victoria)	36N02	14E14	-0:56:56
Valette, La → Valletta	35N54	14E31	-0:58:04
Valletta	35N54	14E31	-0:58:04
Vecchia	35N53	14E24	-0:57:36
Zeitun	35N51	14E32	-0:58:08

ISLA DE MAN — MONAPIA — INSEL MAN — ÎLE DE MAN — MAN, ISLE OF

Time Table
Before 1/Jan/1848 LMT
Begin Standard 0W00

Date	Time	Offset
1/Jan/1848	0:00	0:00
3/Apr/1921	2:00	-1:00
3/Oct/1921	3:00	0:00
26/Mar/1922	2:00	-1:00
8/Oct/1922	3:00	0:00
22/Apr/1923	2:00	-1:00
16/Sep/1923	3:00	0:00
13/Apr/1924	2:00	-1:00
21/Sep/1924	3:00	0:00
19/Apr/1925	2:00	-1:00
4/Oct/1925	3:00	0:00
18/Apr/1926	2:00	-1:00
3/Oct/1926	3:00	0:00
10/Apr/1927	2:00	-1:00
2/Oct/1927	3:00	0:00
22/Apr/1928	2:00	-1:00
7/Oct/1928	3:00	0:00
21/Apr/1929	2:00	-1:00
6/Oct/1929	3:00	0:00
13/Apr/1930	2:00	-1:00
5/Oct/1930	3:00	0:00
19/Apr/1931	2:00	-1:00
4/Oct/1931	3:00	0:00
17/Apr/1932	2:00	-1:00
2/Oct/1932	3:00	0:00
9/Apr/1933	2:00	-1:00
8/Oct/1933	3:00	0:00
22/Apr/1934	2:00	-1:00
7/Oct/1934	3:00	0:00
14/Apr/1935	2:00	-1:00
6/Oct/1935	3:00	0:00
19/Apr/1936	2:00	-1:00
4/Oct/1936	3:00	0:00
18/Apr/1937	2:00	-1:00
3/Oct/1937	3:00	0:00
10/Apr/1938	2:00	-1:00
2/Oct/1938	3:00	0:00
16/Apr/1939	2:00	-1:00
19/Nov/1939	3:00	0:00
25/Feb/1940	2:00	-1:00
4/May/1941	2:00	-2:00
10/Aug/1941	3:00	-1:00
5/Apr/1942	2:00	-2:00
9/Aug/1942	3:00	-1:00
4/Apr/1943	2:00	-2:00
15/Aug/1943	3:00	-1:00
2/Apr/1944	2:00	-2:00
17/Sep/1944	3:00	-1:00
2/Apr/1945	2:00	-2:00
15/Jul/1945	3:00	-1:00
7/Oct/1945	3:00	0:00
14/Apr/1946	2:00	-1:00
6/Oct/1946	3:00	0:00
16/Mar/1947	2:00	-1:00
13/Apr/1947	2:00	-2:00
10/Aug/1947	3:00	-1:00
2/Nov/1947	3:00	0:00
14/Mar/1948	2:00	-1:00
31/Oct/1948	3:00	0:00
3/Apr/1949	2:00	-1:00
30/Oct/1949	3:00	0:00
16/Apr/1950	2:00	-1:00
22/Oct/1950	3:00	0:00
15/Apr/1951	2:00	-1:00
21/Oct/1951	3:00	0:00
20/Apr/1952	2:00	-1:00
26/Oct/1952	3:00	0:00
19/Apr/1953	2:00	-1:00
4/Oct/1953	3:00	0:00
11/Apr/1954	2:00	-1:00
3/Oct/1954	3:00	0:00
17/Apr/1955	2:00	-1:00
2/Oct/1955	3:00	0:00
22/Apr/1956	2:00	-1:00
7/Oct/1956	3:00	0:00
14/Apr/1957	2:00	-1:00
6/Oct/1957	3:00	0:00
20/Apr/1958	2:00	-1:00
5/Oct/1958	3:00	0:00
19/Apr/1959	2:00	-1:00
4/Oct/1959	3:00	0:00
10/Apr/1960	2:00	-1:00
2/Oct/1960	3:00	0:00
26/Mar/1961	2:00	-1:00
29/Oct/1961	3:00	0:00
25/Mar/1962	2:00	-1:00
28/Oct/1962	3:00	0:00
31/Mar/1963	2:00	-1:00
27/Oct/1963	3:00	0:00
22/Mar/1964	2:00	-1:00
25/Oct/1964	3:00	0:00
21/Mar/1965	2:00	-1:00
24/Oct/1965	3:00	0:00
20/Mar/1966	2:00	-1:00
23/Oct/1966	3:00	0:00
19/Mar/1967	2:00	-1:00
29/Oct/1967	3:00	0:00
Begin Standard	15E00	
18/Feb/1968	2:00	-1:00
Begin Standard	0W00	
31/Oct/1971	3:00	0:00
19/Mar/1972	2:00	-1:00
29/Oct/1972	3:00	0:00
18/Mar/1973	2:00	-1:00
28/Oct/1973	3:00	0:00
17/Mar/1974	2:00	-1:00
27/Oct/1974	3:00	0:00
16/Mar/1975	2:00	-1:00
26/Oct/1975	3:00	0:00
21/Mar/1976	2:00	-1:00
24/Oct/1976	3:00	0:00
20/Mar/1977	2:00	-1:00
23/Oct/1977	3:00	0:00
19/Mar/1978	2:00	-1:00
29/Oct/1978	3:00	0:00
18/Mar/1979	2:00	-1:00
28/Oct/1979	3:00	0:00
16/Mar/1980	2:00	-1:00
26/Oct/1980	3:00	0:00
29/Mar/1981	1:00	-1:00
25/Oct/1981	2:00	0:00
28/Mar/1982	1:00	-1:00
24/Oct/1982	2:00	0:00
27/Mar/1983	1:00	-1:00
23/Oct/1983	2:00	0:00
25/Mar/1984	1:00	-1:00
28/Oct/1984	2:00	0:00
31/Mar/1985	1:00	-1:00
27/Oct/1985	2:00	0:00
30/Mar/1986	1:00	-1:00
26/Oct/1986	2:00	0:00
29/Mar/1987	1:00	-1:00
25/Oct/1987	2:00	0:00
27/Mar/1988	1:00	-1:00
23/Oct/1988	2:00	0:00
26/Mar/1989	1:00	-1:00
29/Oct/1989	2:00	0:00
25/Mar/1990	1:00	-1:00
28/Oct/1990	2:00	0:00
31/Mar/1991	1:00	-1:00
27/Oct/1991	2:00	0:00
29/Mar/1992	1:00	-1:00
25/Oct/1992	2:00	0:00
28/Mar/1993	1:00	-1:00
24/Oct/1993	2:00	0:00
27/Mar/1994	1:00	-1:00
23/Oct/1994	2:00	0:00
26/Mar/1995	1:00	-1:00
29/Oct/1995	2:00	0:00
31/Mar/1996	1:00	-1:00
27/Oct/1996	2:00	0:00
30/Mar/1997	1:00	-1:00
26/Oct/1997	2:00	0:00
29/Mar/1998	1:00	-1:00
25/Oct/1998	2:00	0:00
28/Mar/1999	1:00	-1:00
24/Oct/1999	2:00	0:00
26/Mar/2000	1:00	-1:00
29/Oct/2000	2:00	0:00

Place	Lat	Long	Offset
Ballaugh	54N20	4w32	0:18:08
Bride	54N22	4w22	0:17:28
Castletown	54N04	4w40	0:18:40
Douglas	54N09	4w28	0:17:52
Laxey	54N14	4w23	0:17:32
Peel	54N13	4w40	0:18:40
Port Erin	54N06	4w44	0:18:56
Ramsey	54N20	4w21	0:17:24

MARTINIQUE — MARTINICA

Time Table		
Before 1/Jan/1890		LMT
Begin Standard		61w05
1/Jan/1890	0:00	4:04
Begin Standard		60w00
1/May/1911	0:00	4:00
6/Apr/1980	0:00	3:00
28/Sep/1980	0:00	4:00

Place	Lat	Long	Time
Basse-Pointe	14N52	61w07	4:04:28
Bellefontaine	14N40	61w10	4:04:40
Case-Pilote	14N38	61w08	4:04:32
Carbet	14N43	61w11	4:04:44
Diamant	14N29	61w02	4:04:08
Ducos	14N34	60w58	4:03:52
Fort-de-France	14N36	61w05	4:04:20
Grand' Rivière	14N52	61w11	4:04:44
Gros-Morne	14N43	61w01	4:04:04
Lamentin	14N37	61w01	4:04:04
La Trinité	14N44	60w58	4:03:52
Le Carbet	14N43	61w11	4:04:44
Le Diamant	14N29	61w02	4:04:08
Le François	14N37	60w54	4:03:36
Le Lamentin	14N37	61w01	4:04:04
Le Lorrain	14N50	61w04	4:04:16
Le Marin	14N28	60w53	4:03:32
Le Prêcheur	14N48	61w14	4:04:56
Le Robert	14N41	60w57	4:03:48
Le Saint-Esprit	14N34	60w57	4:03:48
Les Anses-d'Arlets	14N29	61w05	4:04:20
Le Vauclin	14N33	60w51	4:03:24
Marin	14N28	60w53	4:03:32
Morne-Rouge	14N46	61w08	4:04:32
Rivière-Pilote	14N29	60w54	4:03:36
Rivière-Salée	14N32	60w59	4:03:56
Sainte-Anne	14N26	60w53	4:03:32
Saint-Esprit	14N34	60w57	4:03:48
Saint-Joseph	14N40	61w03	4:04:12
Sainte-Luce	14N28	60w56	4:03:44
Sainte-Marie	14N47	61w00	4:04:00
Saint-Pierre	14N45	61w11	4:04:44
Trinité	14N44	60w58	4:03:52
Trois-Îlets	14N32	61w02	4:04:08

MAURITANIA — MAURETANIEN — MAURITANIE

Time Table		
Before 1/Jan/1912		LMT
Begin Standard		0w00
1/Jan/1912	0:00	0:00
Begin Standard		15w00
26/Feb/1934	0:00	1:00
Begin Standard		0w00
28/Nov/1960	0:00	0:00

Place	Lat	Long	Time
Aïn ben Tili	26N00	9w32	0:38:08
Akjoujt	19N45	14w23	0:57:32
Aleg	17N03	13w55	0:55:40
Arhrîjît	18N24	9w15	0:37:00
Artémou	15N31	12w16	0:49:04
Atar	20N31	13w03	0:52:12
'Ayoûn el 'Atroûs	16N40	9w37	0:38:28
Baediam	15N03	11w51	0:47:24
Bassikounou	15N52	5w57	0:23:48
Bir Mogreïn (Fort-Trinquet)	25N14	11w35	0:46:20
Bogué	16N35	14w16	0:57:04
Bouly	15N19	11w48	0:47:12
Boumdeit	17N26	9w50	0:39:20
Boutilimit	17N33	14w42	0:58:48
Cansado	20N51	17w02	1:08:08
Chinguetti	20N27	12w22	0:49:28
Fdérik	22N41	12w43	0:50:52
Fort-Gourand → Fdérik	22N41	12w43	0:50:52
Fort-Trinquet → Bir Mogreïn	25N14	11w35	0:46:20
Kaédi	16N09	13w30	0:54:00
Kankossa	15N56	11w31	0:46:04
Kiffa	16N37	11w24	0:45:36
Ksar el Barka	18N24	12w13	0:48:52
Maghama	15N31	12w51	0:51:24
Mal	16N58	13w23	0:53:32
Mbout	16N02	12w35	0:50:20
Mederdra	16N55	15w39	1:02:36
Moudjéria	17N53	12w20	0:49:20
Mouit	16N35	13w05	0:52:20
Néma	16N37	7w15	0:29:00
Nouadhibou	20N54	17w04	1:08:16
Nouakchott	18N06	15w57	1:03:48
Nouamrhar	19N22	16w31	1:06:04
Ouadane	20N56	11w37	0:46:28
Oualâta	17N18	7w02	0:28:08
Podor	16N40	15w00	1:00:00
Port-Étienne → Nouadhibou	20N54	17w04	1:08:16
Rosso	16N30	15w49	1:03:16
Sélibaby	15N10	12w11	0:48:44
Sivé	15N42	13w12	0:52:48
Tamchaket	17N15	10w40	0:42:40
Tîchît	18N28	9w30	0:38:00
Tidjikdja	18N33	11w25	0:45:40
Timbédra	16N15	8w10	0:32:40
Zouîrât	22N42	12w30	0:50:00

MAURITIUS — MAURICE — ÎLE DE FRANCE — MAURICIO

Time Table		
Before 1/Jan/1907		LMT
Begin Standard		60E00
1/Jan/1907	0:00	-4:00

Place	Lat	Long	Time
Curepipe	20s19	57E31	-3:50:04
Mahébourg	20s24	57E42	-3:50:48
Port Louis	20s10	57E30	-3:50:00
Rivière du Rempart	20s06	57E41	-3:50:44
Rose Hill	20s14	57E27	-3:49:48
Royal Alfred Observatory	20s06	57E33	-3:50:12
Triolet	20s03	57E32	-3:50:08
Vacoas	20s18	57E29	-3:49:56

MAYOTTE — MAYOTTE

Time Table		
Before 1/Jul/1911		LMT
Begin Standard		45E00
1/Jul/1911	0:00	-3:00

Place	Lat	Long	Time
Bandeli	12s55	45E13	-3:00:52
Boeni	12s55	45E06	-3:00:24
Chingoni	12s48	45E08	-3:00:32
Dzaoudzi	12s47	45E17	-3:01:08
Mamoutzou	12s47	45E14	-3:00:56

Time Table # 1
Before 1/Jan/1922 LMT
Begin Standard 90w00
1/Jan/1922 0:23 6:00
....
Time Table # 2
Before 1/Jan/1922 LMT
Begin Standard 105w00
1/Jan/1922 0:23 7:00
Begin Standard 90w00
10/Jun/1927 23:00 6:00
Begin Standard 105w00
15/Nov/1930 0:00 7:00
Begin Standard 90w00
1/May/1931 23:00 6:00
....
Time Table # 3
Before 1/Jan/1922 LMT
Begin Standard 120w00
1/Jan/1922 0:23 8:00
Begin Standard 105w00
10/Jun/1927 23:00 7:00
Begin Standard 120w00
16/Nov/1930 0:00 8:00
Begin Standard 105w00
1/Apr/1942 0:00 7:00
Begin Standard 120w00
14/Jan/1949 0:00 8:00
30/Apr/1950 2:00 7:00
24/Sep/1950 2:00 8:00
29/Apr/1951 2:00 7:00
30/Sep/1951 2:00 8:00
27/Apr/1952 2:00 7:00
28/Sep/1952 2:00 8:00
26/Apr/1953 2:00 7:00
27/Sep/1953 2:00 8:00
25/Apr/1954 2:00 7:00
26/Sep/1954 2:00 8:00
24/Apr/1955 2:00 7:00
25/Sep/1955 2:00 8:00
29/Apr/1956 2:00 7:00
30/Sep/1956 2:00 8:00
28/Apr/1957 2:00 7:00
29/Sep/1957 2:00 8:00
27/Apr/1958 2:00 7:00
28/Sep/1958 2:00 8:00
26/Apr/1959 2:00 7:00
27/Sep/1959 2:00 8:00
24/Apr/1960 2:00 7:00
25/Sep/1960 2:00 8:00
30/Apr/1961 2:00 7:00
24/Sep/1961 2:00 8:00
29/Apr/1962 2:00 7:00
28/Oct/1962 2:00 8:00
28/Apr/1963 2:00 7:00
27/Oct/1963 2:00 8:00
26/Apr/1964 2:00 7:00
25/Oct/1964 2:00 8:00
25/Apr/1965 2:00 7:00
31/Oct/1965 2:00 8:00
24/Apr/1966 2:00 7:00
30/Oct/1966 2:00 8:00
30/Apr/1967 2:00 7:00
29/Oct/1967 2:00 8:00
28/Apr/1968 2:00 7:00
27/Oct/1968 2:00 8:00
27/Apr/1969 2:00 7:00
26/Oct/1969 2:00 8:00
26/Apr/1970 2:00 7:00
25/Oct/1970 2:00 8:00
25/Apr/1971 2:00 7:00
31/Oct/1971 2:00 8:00
30/Apr/1972 2:00 7:00
29/Oct/1972 2:00 8:00
29/Apr/1973 2:00 7:00
28/Oct/1973 2:00 8:00
6/Jan/1974 2:00 7:00
27/Oct/1974 2:00 8:00
23/Feb/1975 2:00 7:00
26/Oct/1975 2:00 8:00
25/Apr/1976 2:00 7:00
31/Oct/1976 2:00 8:00
24/Apr/1977 2:00 7:00
30/Oct/1977 2:00 8:00
30/Apr/1978 2:00 7:00
29/Oct/1978 2:00 8:00
29/Apr/1979 2:00 7:00
28/Oct/1979 2:00 8:00
27/Apr/1980 2:00 7:00
26/Oct/1980 2:00 8:00
26/Apr/1981 2:00 7:00
25/Oct/1981 2:00 8:00
25/Apr/1982 2:00 7:00
31/Oct/1982 2:00 8:00
24/Apr/1983 2:00 7:00
30/Oct/1983 2:00 8:00
29/Apr/1984 2:00 7:00
28/Oct/1984 2:00 8:00
28/Apr/1985 2:00 7:00
27/Oct/1985 2:00 8:00
27/Apr/1986 2:00 7:00
26/Oct/1986 2:00 8:00
5/Apr/1987 2:00 7:00
25/Oct/1987 2:00 8:00
3/Apr/1988 2:00 7:00
30/Oct/1988 2:00 8:00
2/Apr/1989 2:00 7:00
29/Oct/1989 2:00 8:00
1/Apr/1990 2:00 7:00
28/Oct/1990 2:00 8:00
7/Apr/1991 2:00 7:00
27/Oct/1991 2:00 8:00
5/Apr/1992 2:00 7:00
25/Oct/1992 2:00 8:00
4/Apr/1993 2:00 7:00
31/Oct/1993 2:00 8:00
3/Apr/1994 2:00 7:00
30/Oct/1994 2:00 8:00
2/Apr/1995 2:00 7:00
29/Oct/1995 2:00 8:00
7/Apr/1996 2:00 7:00
27/Oct/1996 2:00 8:00
6/Apr/1997 2:00 7:00
26/Oct/1997 2:00 8:00
5/Apr/1998 2:00 7:00
25/Oct/1998 2:00 8:00
4/Apr/1999 2:00 7:00
31/Oct/1999 2:00 8:00
2/Apr/2000 2:00 7:00
29/Oct/2000 2:00 8:00
....
Time Table # 4
Before 1/Jan/1922 LMT
Begin Standard 120w00
1/Jan/1922 0:23 8:00
Begin Standard 105w00
10/Jun/1927 23:00 7:00
Begin Standard 120w00
16/Nov/1930 0:00 8:00
Begin Standard 105w00
1/Apr/1942 0:00 7:00
Begin Standard 120w00
14/Jan/1949 0:00 8:00
....
Time Table # 5
Before 1/Jan/1922 LMT
Begin Standard 105w00
1/Jan/1922 0:23 7:00
Begin Standard 90w00
10/Jun/1927 23:00 6:00
Begin Standard 105w00
15/Nov/1930 0:00 7:00
Begin Standard 90w00
1/May/1931 23:00 6:00
Begin Standard 105w00
1/Oct/1931 0:00 7:00
Begin Standard 90w00
30/Mar/1932 23:00 6:00
....
Time Table # 6
Before 1/Jan/1922 LMT
Begin Standard 105w00
1/Jan/1922 0:23 7:00
Begin Standard 90w00
10/Jun/1927 23:00 6:00
Begin Standard 105w00
15/Nov/1930 0:00 7:00
Begin Standard 90w00
1/May/1931 23:00 6:00
Begin Standard 105w00
1/Oct/1931 0:00 7:00
Begin Standard 90w00
30/Mar/1932 23:00 6:00
5/Feb/1939 0:00 5:00
25/Jun/1939 0:00 6:00
9/Dec/1940 0:00 5:00
1/Apr/1941 0:00 6:00
16/Dec/1943 0:00 5:00
1/May/1944 0:00 6:00
12/Feb/1950 0:00 5:00
30/Jul/1950 0:00 6:00
....
Time Table # 7
Before 1/Jan/1922 LMT
Begin Standard 105w00
1/Jan/1922 0:23 7:00
Begin Standard 90w00
10/Jun/1927 23:00 6:00
Begin Standard 105w00
15/Nov/1930 0:00 7:00
Begin Standard 90w00
1/May/1931 23:00 6:00
Begin Standard 105w00
1/Oct/1931 0:00 7:00
Begin Standard 90w00
30/Mar/1932 23:00 6:00
Begin Standard 105w00
1/Apr/1942 0:00 7:00
Begin Standard 120w00
14/Jan/1949 0:00 8:00
Begin Standard 105w00
1/Jan/1970 0:00 7:00
....
Time Table # 8
Before 1/Jan/1922 LMT
Begin Standard 120w00
1/Jan/1922 0:23 8:00
Begin Standard 105w00
10/Jun/1927 23:00 7:00
Begin Standard 120w00
15/Nov/1930 0:00 8:00
Begin Standard 105w00
1/Apr/1942 0:00 7:00
Begin Standard 120w00
14/Jan/1949 0:00 8:00
Begin Standard 105w00
1/Jan/1970 0:00 7:00

DIVISIONS

1. Aguascalientes
2. Baja California Norte
3. Baja California Sur
4. Campeche
5. Chiapas
6. Chihuahua
7. Coahuila
8. Coalima
9. District Federal
10. Durango
11. Guanajuato
12. Guerrero
13. Hidalgo
14. Jalisco
15. México
16. Michoacán
17. Morelos
18. Nayarit
19. Nuevo León
20. Oaxaca
21. Puebla
22. Querétaro
23. Quintana Roo
24. San Luis Potosí
25. Sinaloa
26. Sonora
27. Tabasco
28. Tamaulipas
29. Tlaxcala
30. Veracruz
31. Yucatán
32. Zacatecas

Abasolo 10 5 25N18 104w40 6:58:40
Abasolo 28 1 24N04 98w22 6:33:28
Abasolo 2 3 32N39 115w21 7:41:24
Abasolo 11 5 20N27 101w32 6:46:08
Abasolo 7 5 27N12 101w24 6:45:36
Abasolo 19 5 25N57 100w24 6:41:36
Abasolo del Valle 30 1 17N44 95w29 6:21:56
Acacio 10 5 24N50 102w44 6:50:56
Acajete 21 5 19N06 97w57 6:31:48
Acala 5 1 16N34 92w48 6:11:12
Acámbaro 11 5 20N02 100w44 6:42:56
Acaponeta 18 7 22N30 105w22 7:01:28
Acapulco (de Juárez) 12 5 16N51 99w55 6:39:40
Acatic 14 5 20N47 102w53 6:51:32
Acatlán 13 5 20N09 98w27 6:33:48
Acatlán de Juárez 14 5 20N26 103w38 6:54:32
Acatlán de Osorio 21 5 18N12 98w03 6:32:12
Acatlán (de Pérez Figueroa) 20 1 18N32 96w37 6:26:28
Acatzingo (de Hidalgo) 21 5 18N59 97w47 6:31:08
Acayucan 30 1 17N57 94w55 6:19:40
Acebuches 7 5 28N15 102w43 6:50:52
Aconchi 26 7 29N50 110w12 7:20:48
Actopan 13 5 20N16 98w56 6:35:44
Acuitzio del Canje 16 5 19N29 101w20 6:45:20
Adolfo Ruíz Cortines 25 7 25N40 108w40 7:14:40
Agostitlán 16 5 19N33 100w41 6:42:44
Agricola Oriental 9 6 19N24 99w03 6:36:12
Agua Caliente 10 5 23N20 105w20 7:01:20
Agua Caliente de Chínipas 6 5 27N27 108w32 7:14:08
Agua Caliente Grande de Gastelum 25 7 26N31 108w22 7:13:28
Agua Dulce 27 1 18N08 94w08 6:16:32
Agua Escondida 14 5 19N08 103w27 6:53:48
Agualeguas 19 5 26N18 99w34 6:38:16
Aguapepito 25 7 24N33 107w39 7:10:36
Agua Prieta 26 7 31N18 109w34 7:18:16
Aguaruto 25 7 24N47 107w29 7:09:56
Aguascalientes 1 2 21N53 102w18 6:49:12
Aguascalientes 2 4 32N18 115w10 7:40:40
Agua Zarca 10 5 23N10 104w28 6:57:52
Agua Zarca 26 7 31N10 110w59 7:23:56
Aguililla 16 5 18N44 102w44 6:50:56
Agujita 7 5 27N53 101w09 6:44:36
Ahuacatlán 18 7 21N03 104w29 6:57:56
Ahuacatlán 21 5 20N00 97w52 6:31:28
Ahuacuotzingo 12 5 17N42 98w56 6:35:44
Ahualulco de Mercado 14 5 20N42 103w59 6:55:56
Ahuijullo 14 5 19N05 103w05 6:52:20
Ahumada 2 3 32N30 115w30 7:42:00
Ajalpan 21 5 18N22 97w15 6:29:00
Ajijic 14 5 20N18 103w17 6:53:08
Ajoya 25 7 24N04 106w22 7:05:28
Ajuchitlán del Progreso 12 5 18N09 100w29 6:41:56
Ajusco 2 4 31N35 116w25 7:45:40
Alamillo 26 7 31N02 110w35 7:22:20
Alamo 30 1 20N55 97w41 6:30:44
Alamos 26 7 27N01 108w56 7:15:44
Alamos 19 5 26N25 100w25 6:41:40
Alaquines 24 5 22N08 99w36 6:38:24
Albarradas 20 1 16N50 96w15 6:25:00
Alcihuatl 14 5 19N55 104w34 6:58:16
Alcomunga 21 5 18N25 97w02 6:28:08
Aldama 6 5 28N51 105w54 7:03:36
Aldama 28 1 22N55 98w04 6:32:16
Alfredo M. Terrazas 24 5 21N28 98w51 6:35:24
Allende 19 5 25N17 100w01 6:40:04
Allende 7 5 28N20 100w51 6:43:24
Allende 30 1 18N09 94w16 6:17:04
Altamira 28 1 22N24 97w55 6:31:40
Altamirano 28 1 25N55 97w47 6:31:08
Altar 26 7 30N43 111w44 7:26:56
Altata 25 7 24N38 107w55 7:11:40
Alto Lucero 30 1 19N37 96w43 6:26:52
Altotonga 30 1 19N46 97w14 6:28:56
Alvarado 30 1 18N46 95w46 6:23:04
Álvaro Obregón 16 5 19N50 101w05 6:44:20
Amadores 28 1 22N51 99w43 6:38:52
Amatenango de la Frontera 5 1 15N26 92w07 6:08:28
Amatitán 14 5 20N50 103w43 6:54:52
Amatlán de Cañas 18 7 20N52 104w27 6:57:48
Amatlán de los Reyes 30 1 18N50 96w55 6:27:40
Ameca 14 5 20N33 104w02 6:56:08
Amecameca (de Juárez) 15 5 19N07 98w46 6:35:04
Amixtlán 21 5 20N03 97w48 6:31:12
Amozoc 21 5 19N02 98w03 6:32:12
Amusgos 20 1 16N39 98w06 6:32:24
Anáhuac 6 5 28N25 106w40 7:06:40
Anáhuac 28 1 25N48 97w45 6:31:00
Ancón 24 5 22N35 101w11 6:44:44
Angamacutiro (de la Unión) 16 5 20N10 101w41 6:46:44
Angangueo 16 5 19N37 100w18 6:41:12
Angel Albino Corzo 5 1 16N10 93w15 6:13:00
Angel R. Cabada 30 1 18N35 95w26 6:21:44
Angostura 25 7 25N22 108w11 7:12:44
Antiguo Morelos 28 1 22N33 99w05 6:36:20
Antonio Amaro 10 5 24N16 104w01 6:56:04
Antonio Escobedo 14 5 20N46 103w57 6:55:48
Apam 13 5 19N43 98w25 6:33:40
Apango 12 5 17N44 99w20 6:37:20
Apaseo el Grande 11 5 20N33 100w41 6:42:44
Apatzingán (de la Constitución) 16 5 19N05 102w21 6:49:24
Apaxtla de Castrejón 12 5 18N09 99w52 6:39:28
Apipilulco 12 5 18N11 99w41 6:38:44
Apizaco 29 5 19N25 98w09 6:32:36
Apizolaya 32 5 24N50 102w15 6:49:00
Apo 16 5 19N25 102w25 6:49:40
Aporo 16 5 19N41 100w25 6:41:40
Apozolco 18 7 21N22 104w00 6:56:00
Aquila 16 5 18N36 103w30 6:54:00
Aquiles Serdán 6 5 28N36 105w53 7:03:32
Aramberri 19 5 24N06 99w49 6:39:16
Arandas 14 5 20N42 102w21 6:49:24
Arcelia 12 5 18N17 100w16 6:41:04
Arío de Rosales 16 5 19N12 101w43 6:46:52
Arista 5 1 15N56 93w48 6:15:12
Arista 24 5 22N39 100w50 6:43:20
Arizpe 26 7 30N20 110w10 7:20:40
Armería 8 5 18N56 103w58 6:55:52
Arriaga 5 1 16N14 93w54 6:15:36
Arroyo Frío 12 5 17N26 100w35 6:42:20
Arteaga 16 5 18N28 102w25 6:49:40
Ascensión 6 5 31N06 107w59 7:11:56
Ascensión 19 5 24N20 99w55 6:39:40
Asunción Nochixtlán 20 1 17N28 97w14 6:28:56

Atemajac de Brizuela 14
5 20N11 103w42 6:54:48
Atemajac del Valle 14
5 20N45 103w22 6:53:28
Atenango del Río 12
5 18N05 99w06 6:36:24
Atencingo 21 5 18N30 98w36 6:34:24
Atenguillo 14 5 20N25 104w31 6:58:04
Atenquique 14 5 19N31 103w30 6:54:00
Atil 26 7 30N50 111w35 7:26:20
Atlacomulco de Fabela 15
5 19N48 99w53 6:39:32
Atlixco 21 5 18N54 98w26 6:33:44
Atotonilco 10 5 23N35 104w20 6:57:20
Atotonilco de los Martínez 32
5 24N15 102w45 6:51:00
Atotonilco de Tula 13
5 20N00 99w13 6:36:52
Atotonilco el Alto 14
5 20N33 102w31 6:50:04
Atoyac 14 5 20N01 103w32 6:54:08
Atoyac de Alvarez 12
5 17N12 100w26 6:41:44
Atzacán 30 1 18N54 97w05 6:28:20
Autlán de Navarro 14
5 19N46 104w22 6:57:28
Axochiapan 17 5 18N30 98w46 6:35:04
Ayo el Chico 14
5 20N32 102w21 6:49:24
Ayoquezco 20 1 16N41 96w50 6:27:20
Ayutla 14 5 20N07 104w22 6:57:28
Ayutla (de los Libres) 12
5 16N54 99w13 6:36:52
Azcapotzalco 9 6 19N28 99w14 6:36:56
Azoyú 12 5 16N43 98w44 6:34:56
Bacerac 26 7 30N18 108w50 7:15:20
Bachíniva 6 5 28N45 107w15 7:09:00
Bacoachi 26 7 30N38 109w56 7:19:44
Bácum 26 7 27N33 110w05 7:20:20
Badiraguato 25 7 25N22 107w31 7:10:04
Bahía Kino 26 7 28N50 111w55 7:27:40
Baja California 2
4 32N18 115w12 7:40:48
Baján 7 5 26N32 101w15 6:45:00
Bajos del Balsamar 12
5 17N34 100w48 6:43:12
Banderas 6 5 31N01 105w35 7:02:20
Banderilla 30 1 19N36 96w56 6:27:44
Bañón 32 5 23N11 102w29 6:49:56
Barcelona 10 5 26N12 103w25 6:53:40
Barranco Azul 6
5 29N21 104w17 6:57:08
Barranco de Guadalupe 6
5 30N02 104w44 6:58:56
Batuc 26 7 29N15 109w44 7:18:56
Bavispe 26 7 30N24 108w50 7:15:20
Becal 4 1 20N27 90w02 6:00:08
Belén del Refugio 14
5 21N31 102w25 6:49:40
Benito Juárez 16
5 19N14 100w28 6:41:52
Benito Juárez 27
1 17N50 92w32 6:10:08
Benjamín Hill 26
7 30N10 111w10 7:24:40
Bermejillo 10 5 25N53 103w37 6:54:28
Berriozábal 5 1 16N48 93w16 6:13:04
Boca del Río 30
1 19N06 96w06 6:24:24
Bochil 5 1 16N59 92w55 6:11:40
Bolaños 14 5 21N41 103w47 6:55:08
Bolonchén de Rejón 4
1 20N00 89w49 5:59:16
Boquilla del Refugio 7
5 25N33 102w28 6:49:52
Boquillas del Carmen 7
5 29N17 102w53 6:51:32
Briseñas de Matamoros 16
5 20N16 102w33 6:50:12
Brittingham 10 5 25N45 103w24 6:53:36
Buenaventura 6 5 29N51 107w29 7:09:56
Buena Vista 2 3 32N32 116w44 7:46:56
Buenavista 32 5 22N30 103w10 6:52:40
Buenavista de Cuéllar 12
5 18N27 99w25 6:37:40
Buenavista Revolución Mexicana 5
1 16N03 93w04 6:12:16
Buenavista Tomatlán 16
5 19N12 102w36 6:50:24
Buen Día 10 5 26N21 104w32 6:58:08
Burgos 28 1 24N57 98w47 6:35:08
Bustamante 19 5 26N33 100w30 6:42:00
Bustamante 28 1 23N26 99w47 6:39:08
Cabo San Lucas 3
8 22N53 109w54 7:19:36
Cabrel 14 5 20N06 105w14 7:00:56
Cacahoatán 5 1 14N59 92w10 6:08:40
Cacaluta 14 5 20N03 104w52 6:59:28
Cadereyta Jiménez 19
5 25N36 100w00 6:40:00
Calabacillas 28
1 23N13 99w45 6:39:00
Calera Víctor Rosales 32
5 22N57 102w42 6:50:48
Caliente Race Track 2
3 32N32 117w00 7:48:00
Calihualá 20 1 17N35 98w10 6:32:40
Calnalí 13 5 20N55 98w35 6:34:20
Calpan 21 5 19N06 98w27 6:33:48
Calpulalpan 29 5 19N35 98w35 6:34:20
Calvillo 1 2 21N51 102w43 6:50:52
Camacho 32 5 24N25 102w18 6:49:12
Campeche 4 1 19N51 90w32 6:02:08
Campo Morado 12
5 17N35 100w05 6:40:20

Canachal 25 7 24N04 107w05 7:08:20
Cañada de Caracheo 11
5 20N22 100w57 6:43:48
Canalejas 15 5 19N57 99w39 6:38:36
Cananea 26 7 30N57 110w18 7:21:12
Canatlán 10 5 24N31 104w47 6:59:08
Cancún 23 1 21N05 86w46 5:47:04
Candela 7 5 26N50 100w40 6:42:40
Candelaria Loxicha 20
1 15N54 96w31 6:26:04
Cándido Aguilar 28
1 25N30 98w02 6:32:08
Cañitas de Felipe Pescador 32
5 23N36 102w43 6:50:52
Cantabria 16 5 19N50 101w44 6:46:56
Caobanal 27 1 17N37 93w22 6:13:28
Carácuaro de Morelos 16
5 18N46 101w02 6:44:08
Carbó 26 7 29N42 110w58 7:23:52
Cárdenas 24 5 22N00 99w40 6:38:40
Cárdenas 27 1 17N59 93w22 6:13:28
Carichic 6 5 27N56 107w03 7:08:12
Carmen → Ciudad del Carmen 4
1 18N38 91w50 6:07:20
Carrillo 6 5 26N54 103w55 6:55:40
Carrillo Puerto 16
5 19N08 102w42 6:50:48
Carrillo Puerto 18
7 21N09 104w52 6:59:28
Casas 28 1 23N44 98w45 6:35:00
Casimiro Castillo 14
5 19N38 104w28 6:57:52
Castillo Velasco 20
1 16N45 96w35 6:26:20
Catemaco 30 1 18N25 95w07 6:20:28
Catorce 24 5 23N42 100w54 6:43:36
Ceballos 10 5 23N23 104w50 6:59:20
Ceceda 10 5 26N04 103w25 6:53:40
Cedral 24 5 23N48 100w44 6:42:56
Cedros 32 5 24N41 101w47 6:47:08
Celaya 11 5 20N31 100w49 6:43:16
Celestún 31 1 20N52 90w24 6:01:36
Centinela 7 5 28N47 100w34 6:42:16
Cerano 11 5 20N07 101w23 6:45:32
Cerralvo 19 5 26N06 99w37 6:38:28
Cerritos 24 5 22N26 100w17 6:41:08
Cerro Azul 30 1 21N12 97w44 6:30:56
Cerro Prieto 2 4 32N27 115w17 7:41:08
Chacaltianguis 30
1 18N20 95w50 6:23:20
Chahuites 20 1 16N17 94w11 6:16:44
Chalcatongo de Hidalgo 20
1 17N02 97w35 6:30:20
Chalchihuites 32
5 23N29 103w53 6:55:32
Chalco (de Díaz Covarrubias) 15
5 19N16 98w54 6:35:36
Chalihuey 32 5 22N43 104w04 6:56:16
Chamela 14 5 19N32 105w05 7:00:20
Champotón 4 1 19N21 90w43 6:02:52
Chapala 14 5 20N18 103w12 6:52:48
Chapo 6 5 29N17 104w20 6:57:20
Chapultepec 2 3 31N50 116w38 7:46:32
Chapultepec 2 3 32N22 115w05 7:40:20
Charapán 16 5 19N41 102w06 6:48:24
Charcas 24 5 23N08 101w07 6:44:28
Charcos de Figueroa 7
5 27N45 102w11 6:48:44
Charcos de Risa 7
5 26N15 103w10 6:52:40
Charo 16 5 19N45 101w03 6:44:12
Chavinda 16 5 20N01 102w27 6:49:48
Chazumba 20 1 18N12 97w40 6:30:40
Chemax 31 1 20N39 87w56 5:51:44
Cherán 16 5 19N41 101w57 6:47:48
Chetumal 23 1 18N30 88w18 5:53:12
Chiapa de Corzo 5
1 16N42 93w00 6:12:00
Chiautla de Tapia 21
5 18N17 98w36 6:34:24
Chiautzingo 21 5 19N12 98w28 6:33:52
Chichén Itzá 31
1 20N40 88w34 5:54:16
Chichigapa 30 1 17N47 94w25 6:17:40
Chichihualco 12
5 17N41 99w39 6:38:36
Chichimilá 31 1 20N37 88w13 5:52:52
Chicomuselo 5 1 15N46 92w16 6:09:04
Chicontepec 30 1 20N58 98w10 6:32:40
Chicorato 25 7 26N02 107w54 7:11:36
Chicualoque 30 1 20N23 97w39 6:30:36
Chicxulub 31 1 21N08 89w31 5:58:04
Chietla 21 5 18N31 98w35 6:34:20
Chignahuapan 21
5 19N50 98w02 6:32:08
Chihuahua 6 5 28N38 106w05 7:04:20
Chikindzonot 31
1 20N20 88w29 5:53:56
Chila 16 5 18N55 102w28 6:49:52
Chilacachapa 12
5 18N17 99w43 6:38:52
Chilapa de Alvarez 12
5 17N36 99w10 6:36:40
Chilapa de Díaz 20
1 17N31 97w41 6:30:44
Chilchota 16 5 19N51 102w08 6:48:32
Chilón 5 1 17N14 92w25 6:09:40
Chilpancingo (de los Bravos) 12
5 17N33 99w30 6:38:00
Chimaltitán 32 5 21N33 103w50 6:55:20
China 19 5 25N42 99w14 6:36:56
Chinitos 25 7 25N01 107w54 7:11:36
Chiquihuitlán de Juárez 20
1 17N59 96w48 6:27:12
Choapan 20 1 17N20 95w57 6:23:48

Chocamán 30 1 18N59 97w01 6:28:04
Choix 25 7 26N43 108w17 7:13:08
Cholula (de Rivadabia) 21
5 19N04 98w18 6:33:12
Chuhuichupa 6 5 29N38 108w22 7:13:28
Chunhuás 23 1 19N12 88w55 5:55:40
Chupaderos 32 5 23N50 102w20 6:49:20
Churintzio 16 5 20N09 102w04 6:48:16
Churumuco 16 5 18N37 101w38 6:46:32
Cibuta 26 7 31N04 110w54 7:23:36
Ciénega de Flores 19
5 25N57 100w11 6:40:44
Cihuatlán 14 5 19N14 104w35 6:58:20
Cinco de Mayo 10
5 25N46 104w19 6:57:16
Cintalapa de Figueroa 5
1 16N44 93w43 6:14:52
Ciudad 10 5 23N44 105w42 7:02:48
Ciudad Acuña 7 5 29N18 100w55 6:43:40
Ciudad Altamirano 12
5 18N20 100w40 6:42:40
Ciudad Anáhuac 19
5 27N14 100w09 6:40:36
Ciudad Camargo 6
5 27N40 105w10 7:00:40
Ciudad Camargo 28
1 26N19 98w50 6:35:20
Ciudad Chetumal 23
1 18N30 88w18 5:53:12
Ciudad del Carmen 4
1 18N38 91w50 6:07:20
Ciudad del Maíz 24
5 22N24 99w36 6:38:24
Ciudad de México (Mexico City) 9
6 19N24 99w09 6:36:36
Ciudad de Naucalpan de Juárez 15
5 19N28 99w14 6:36:56
Ciudad de Valles 24
5 21N59 99w01 6:36:04
Ciudad de Villaldama 19
5 26N30 100w26 6:41:44
Ciudad Guerrero 6
5 28N33 107w30 7:10:00
Ciudad Guzmán 14
5 19N41 103w29 6:53:56
Ciudad Hidalgo 16
5 19N41 100w34 6:42:16
Ciudad Hidalgo 5
1 14N41 92w09 6:08:36
Ciudad Ixtepec 20
1 16N34 95w06 6:20:24
Ciudad Jiménez 6
5 27N08 104w55 6:59:40
Ciudad Juárez 6
5 31N44 106w29 7:05:56
Ciudad Lerdo 10
5 25N32 103w32 6:54:08
Ciudad López Mateos 15
5 19N33 99w15 6:37:00
Ciudad Madero 28
1 22N16 97w50 6:31:20
Ciudad Mante 28
1 22N44 98w57 6:35:48
Ciudad Manuel Doblado 11
5 20N44 101w56 6:47:44
Ciudad Melchor Múzquiz 7
5 27N53 101w31 6:46:04
Ciudad Mendoza 30
1 18N48 97w11 6:28:44
Ciudad Mier 28 1 26N26 99w09 6:36:36
Ciudad Miguel Alemán 28
1 26N23 99w01 6:36:04
Ciudad Morelos 2
4 32N38 114w52 7:39:28
Ciudad Obregón 26
7 27N29 109w56 7:19:44
Ciudad Ocampo 28
1 22N50 99w20 6:37:20
Ciudad Sahagún 13
5 19N47 98w33 6:34:12
Ciudad Santos 24
5 21N36 98w58 6:35:52
Ciudad Serdán 21
5 18N59 97w27 6:29:48
Ciudad Victoria 2
4 32N20 115w06 7:40:24
Ciudad Victoria 28
1 23N44 99w08 6:36:32
Cloete 7 5 27N55 101w10 6:44:40
Coacalco de Berriozábal 15
5 19N37 99w05 6:36:20
Coacoyole 10 5 24N31 106w34 7:06:16
Coacuilco 13 5 21N07 98w35 6:34:20
Coahuayana 16 5 18N44 103w41 6:54:44
Coahuayutla de Guerrero 12
5 18N19 101w49 6:47:16
Coahuila 26 7 32N12 114w59 7:39:56
Coalcomán de Matamoros 16
5 18N47 103w09 6:52:36
Coapilla 5 1 17N08 93w10 6:12:40
Coatepec 30 1 19N27 96w58 6:27:52
Coatepec de Harinas 15
5 18N54 99w43 6:38:52
Coatzacoalcos 30
1 18N09 94w25 6:17:40
Coatzintla 30 1 20N29 97w27 6:29:48
Cocotitlán 15 5 19N14 98w52 6:35:28
Cocula 12 5 18N14 99w40 6:38:40
Cocula 14 5 20N23 103w50 6:55:20
Coeneo (de la Libertad) 16
5 19N49 101w35 6:46:20
Coixtlahuaca 20
1 17N43 97w19 6:29:16
Cojumatlán de Régules 16
5 20N07 102w50 6:51:20

Colima 8 5 19N14 103W43 6:54:52
Colima 2 4 32N25 115W05 7:40:20
Colmeneros 12 5 18N06 101W40 6:46:40
Colombia 19 5 27N42 99W45 6:39:00
Colonet 2 4 31N05 116W10 7:44:40
Colonia Cristóbal Obregón 1 16N20 93W30 6:14:00
Colonia Guadalupe 2 4 32N04 116W37 7:46:28
Colonia Morelos 26 7 30N50 109W10 7:16:40
Colonia Progreso 2 3 32N35 115W37 7:42:28
Colonia Progreso 32 5 23N48 103W18 6:53:12
Colorado de Abajo 19 5 26N28 99W54 6:39:36
Colorines 15 5 19N07 100W12 6:40:48
Colotlán 14 5 22N06 103W16 6:53:04
Colotlipa 12 5 17N25 99W09 6:36:36
Comala 8 5 19N19 103W45 6:55:00
Comalcalco 27 1 18N16 93W13 6:12:52
Comales 28 1 26N10 98W56 6:35:44
Comanja de Corona 14 5 21N19 101W42 6:46:48
Comitán (de Domínguez) 5 1 16N15 92W08 6:08:32
Comondú 3 8 26N03 111W46 7:27:04
Comonfort 11 5 20N43 100W46 6:43:04
Compostela 18 7 21N15 104W53 6:59:32
Concepción de Buenos Aires 14 5 19N58 103W16 6:53:04
Concepcion del Oro 32 5 24N38 101W25 6:45:40
Concordia 7 5 25N47 103W07 6:52:28
Concordia 25 7 23N17 106W04 7:04:16
Congregación Cuauhtémoc 28 1 22N38 98W08 6:32:32
Congregación Ignacio Zaragoza 28 1 23N15 98W50 6:35:20
Conitaca 25 7 24N10 106W43 7:06:52
Copainalá 5 1 17N05 93W12 6:12:48
Copala 12 5 16N37 98W58 6:35:52
Copalillo 12 5 18N02 99W07 6:36:28
Copalquín 10 5 25N29 107W00 7:08:00
Copanatoyac 12 5 17N15 98W45 6:35:00
Copándaro de Galeana 16 5 19N53 101W13 6:44:52
Coquimatlán 8 5 19N12 103W48 6:55:12
Córdoba 30 1 18N53 96W56 6:27:44
Corerepe 25 7 25N40 108W40 7:14:40
Coronado 24 5 22N55 100W56 6:43:44
Corongoros 14 5 19N17 102W48 6:51:12
Corralitos 6 5 26N57 104W39 6:58:36
Cortazar 11 5 20N29 100W56 6:43:44
Cosamaloapan (de Carpio) 30 1 18N22 95W48 6:23:12
Coscomatepec (de Bravo) 30 1 19N04 97W02 6:28:08
Cosoleacaque 30 1 18N00 94W37 6:18:28
Costa Rica 26 7 28N55 111W36 7:26:24
Cotija de la Paz 16 5 19N49 102W43 6:50:52
Coxquihui 30 1 20N11 97W35 6:30:20
Coyoacán 9 6 19N20 99W10 6:36:40
Coyame 6 5 29N28 105W06 7:00:24
Coyotepec 15 5 19N46 99W12 6:36:48
Coyuca de Benítez 12 5 17N02 100W04 6:40:16
Coyuca de Catalán 12 5 18N20 100W39 6:42:36
Coyutla 30 1 20N15 97W39 6:30:36
Cozoyoapan 12 5 16N46 98W15 6:33:00
Cozumel 23 1 20N31 86W55 5:47:40
Creel 6 5 27N45 107W38 7:10:32
Cruces 6 5 29N26 107W24 7:09:36
Cruillas 28 1 24N45 98W31 6:34:04
Cruz de Elorza 19 5 23N49 100W29 6:41:56
Cruz Grande 12 5 16N44 99W08 6:36:32
Cuacnopalan 21 5 18N49 97W30 6:30:00
Cuajinicuilapa 12 5 16N28 98W25 6:33:40
Cuapiaxtla 29 5 19N18 97W46 6:31:04
Cuatro Ciénegas (de Carranza) 7 5 26N59 102W05 6:48:20
Cuauhtémoc 6 5 28N25 106W52 7:07:28
Cuauhtémoc 8 5 19N20 103W36 6:54:24
Cuautepec (de Hinojosa) 13 5 20N02 98W18 6:33:12
Cuautitlán 14 5 19N26 104W23 6:57:32
Cuautitlán (de Romero Rubio) 15 5 19N40 99W11 6:36:44
Cuautla 14 5 20N11 104W21 6:57:24
Cuautla Morelos 17 5 18N48 98W57 6:35:48
Cucharas 18 7 22N52 105W19 7:01:16
Cucurpe 26 7 30N20 110W43 7:22:52
Cuencamé (de Ceniceros) 10 5 24N53 103W42 6:54:48
Cuerámaro 11 5 20N37 101W43 6:46:52
Cuernavaca 17 5 18N55 99W15 6:37:00
Cuetzala del Progreso 12 5 18N07 99W50 6:39:20
Cuetzalan del Progreso 21 5 20N02 97W31 6:30:04
Cuichapa 30 1 17N59 94W15 6:17:00
Cuitláhuac 30 1 18N49 96W43 6:26:52
Cuitzeo del Porvenir 16 5 19N59 101W09 6:44:36
Cuitzmala 14 5 19N23 104W59 6:59:56
Culiacán 25 7 24N48 107W24 7:09:36
Culiacancito 25 7 24N50 107W32 7:10:08
Cumeral Nuevo 26 7 30N54 110W51 7:23:24
Cumpas 26 7 30N02 109W48 7:19:12
Cumuripa 26 7 28N08 109W53 7:19:32
Cuquío 14 5 20N55 103W02 6:52:08
Curimeo 16 5 20N01 101W42 6:46:48
Cusihuiriáchic 6 5 28N14 106W50 7:07:20
Cutzamala de Pinzón 12 5 18N28 100W34 6:42:16
Cutzio 16 5 18N39 100W54 6:43:36
Degollado 14 5 20N28 102W09 6:48:36
Delicias 6 5 28N13 105W28 7:01:52
Delta 2 4 32N22 115W12 7:40:48
Derrame 10 5 26N19 104W23 6:57:32
Dieciocho de Marzo 28 1 25N38 97W50 6:31:20
Diez de Octubre 10 5 24N44 104W39 6:58:36
Dinamita 10 5 25N43 103W38 6:54:32
Doce de Octubre 28 1 25N38 97W47 6:31:08
Doctor Arroyo 19 5 23N40 100W11 6:40:44
Doctor Coss 19 5 25N55 99W11 6:36:44
Doctor González 19 5 25N52 99W57 6:39:48
Dolores 6 5 28N53 108W27 7:13:48
Dolores 7 5 26N20 101W29 6:45:56
Dolores Hidalgo 11 5 21N10 100W56 6:43:44
Don Martín 7 5 27N32 100W37 6:42:28
Dos Arroyos 12 5 17N02 99W40 6:38:40
Dulce Grande 24 5 22N59 102W14 6:48:56
Durango 10 5 24N02 104W40 6:58:40
Dzemul 31 1 21N12 89W18 5:57:12
Dzibalchén 4 1 19N31 89W45 5:59:00
Dzilam González 31 1 21N17 88W56 5:55:44
Dzitás 31 1 20N51 88W31 5:54:04
Dzitbalché 4 1 20N19 90W03 6:00:12
Ebano 24 5 22N13 98W22 6:33:28
Ecatepec de Morelos 15 5 19N35 99W04 6:36:16
Ecuandureo 16 5 20N10 102W11 6:48:44
Ejutla de Crespo 20 1 16N34 96W44 6:26:56
El Álamo 2 4 31N34 116W02 7:44:08
El Álamo 7 5 27N32 100W52 6:43:28
El Álamo 19 5 26N29 99W46 6:39:04
El Arco 2 4 28N00 113W25 7:33:40
El Arenal 14 5 20N47 103W42 6:54:48
El Avión 25 7 24N08 106W59 7:07:56
El Barreal 6 5 31N17 107W10 7:08:40
El Barril 24 5 23N02 102W08 6:48:32
El Barrio 20 1 16N48 95W15 6:21:00
El Bosque 5 1 17N04 92W44 6:10:56
El Capomo 18 7 21N17 105W13 7:00:52
El Carmen 5 1 15N35 93W05 6:12:20
El Carmen 21 5 19N19 97W40 6:30:40
El Carricito 7 5 28N24 103W23 6:53:32
El Carrizal 28 1 23N00 97W50 6:31:20
El Carrizo 6 5 29N58 105W16 7:01:04
El Casco 10 5 25N34 104W35 6:58:20
El Cedrito 7 5 29N11 101W59 6:47:56
El Centinela 2 3 32N38 115W40 7:42:40
El Chamal 28 1 23N56 97W54 6:31:36
El Chante 14 5 19N41 104W10 6:56:40
El Charco Largo 28 1 24N10 97W58 6:31:52
El Ciprés 2 4 31N50 116W38 7:46:32
El Coacoyul 12 5 17N37 101W26 6:45:44
El Consuelo 26 7 31N02 111W53 7:27:32
El Coyote 26 7 30N50 112W40 7:30:40
El Cozón 26 7 31N18 112W29 7:29:56
El Cuidado 32 5 22N20 103W07 6:52:28
El Dátil 26 7 30N07 112W15 7:29:00
El Depósito 30 1 17N44 94W23 6:17:32
El Descanso 2 4 32N12 116W55 7:47:40
El Desemboque 26 7 30N30 112W59 7:31:56
El Dorado 25 7 24N17 107W21 7:09:24
El Estribo 24 5 22N16 99W07 6:36:28
El Fuerte 25 7 26N25 108W39 7:14:36
El Golfo de Santa Clara 26 7 31N42 114W30 7:38:00
El Grullo 14 5 19N48 104W13 6:56:52
El Guaje 7 5 27N52 103W18 6:53:12
El Higo 30 1 21N46 98W28 6:33:52
El Jaralito 10 5 26N07 104W10 6:56:40
El Limón 12 5 18N05 101W59 6:47:56
El Limón 14 5 19N49 104W11 6:56:44
El Limón de Talleaché 25 7 24N16 107W04 7:08:16
El Lucero 10 5 25N53 103W25 6:53:40
El Maneadero 2 4 31N45 116W35 7:46:20
El Meco 24 5 22N35 99W20 6:37:20
El Médano 3 8 24N25 111W30 7:26:00
El Mimbre 7 5 25N40 102W20 6:49:20
El Molinito 15 5 19N27 99W15 6:37:00
El Moral 7 5 28N51 100W39 6:42:36
El Mulato 6 5 29N22 104W10 6:56:40
El Naranjo 28 1 22N30 98W38 6:34:32
El Pacayal 5 1 15N37 92W02 6:08:08
El Paraíso 12 5 17N25 100W15 6:41:00
El Peñuelo 19 5 24N34 100W46 6:43:04
El Placer 25 7 23N33 106W10 7:04:40
El Platanillo 12 5 18N28 101W52 6:47:28
El Plomo 26 7 31N15 112W04 7:28:16
El Porvenir 6 5 31N15 105W51 7:03:24
El Porvenir 2 4 32N05 116W38 7:46:32
El Porvenir 5 1 15N44 93W22 6:13:28
El Porvenir 6 5 27N33 104W57 6:59:48
El Potosí 19 5 24N51 100W19 6:41:16
El Potrero 19 5 26N23 100W27 6:41:48
El Quelite 25 7 23N32 106W28 7:05:52
El Ranchito 16 5 18N40 103W41 6:54:44
El Remolino 30 1 17N39 94W13 6:16:52
El Remolino 7 5 28N44 101W07 6:44:28
El Roble 25 7 23N32 106W14 7:04:56
El Rucio 32 5 23N23 102W05 6:48:20
El Sahuaro 26 7 31N05 112W55 7:31:40
El Salto 10 5 23N47 105W22 7:01:28
El Salto 14 5 20N32 103W11 6:52:44
El Sauz 6 5 29N02 106W16 7:05:04
El Sauzal 2 4 31N54 116W41 7:46:44
El Sueco 6 5 29N54 106W24 7:05:36
El Tanque 19 5 26N28 99W38 6:38:32
El Tapextle 10 5 23N52 105W33 7:02:12
El Terrero 16 5 18N58 102W28 6:49:52
El Timbiriche 16 5 18N38 101W31 6:46:04
El Triunfo 3 8 23N47 110W08 7:20:32
El Tuito 14 5 20N19 105W22 7:01:28
El Verde 25 7 23N21 106W09 7:04:36
El Zapotal 5 1 15N27 93W10 6:12:40
El Zapotán 16 5 18N41 103W39 6:54:36
El Zapote de Calabacillas 6 5 25N42 106W32 7:06:08
Emiliano Zapata 5 1 17N45 91W46 6:07:04
Empalme 26 7 27N58 110W51 7:23:24
Empalme Escobedo 11 5 20N41 100W44 6:42:56
Empalme Purísima 10 5 23N55 105W05 7:00:20
Encarnación de Díaz 14 5 21N31 102W14 6:48:56
Enchilayas 26 7 30N50 112W50 7:31:20
Encinas 7 5 25N40 101W08 6:44:32
Encrucijada 27 1 18N18 93W29 6:13:56
Enmedio 6 5 29N04 103W29 6:53:56
Ensenada 2 4 31N52 116W37 7:46:28
Ermita de los Correa 32 5 22N54 103W01 6:52:04
Escalón 6 5 26N45 104W20 6:57:20
Escárcega de Matamoros 4 1 18N37 90W43 6:02:52
Escobedo 7 5 27N13 101W21 6:45:24
Escuinapa (de Hidalgo) 25 7 22N51 105W48 7:03:12
Escuintla 5 1 15N20 92W38 6:10:32
Esmeralda 10 5 25N40 103W30 6:54:00
Esperanza 26 7 27N35 109W56 7:19:44
Esperanza 21 5 18N52 97W24 6:29:36
Espinal 20 1 16N29 95W03 6:20:12
Espinazo 7 5 26N16 101W06 6:44:24
Espinos de Judío 14 5 19N52 104W35 6:58:20
Espita 31 1 21N01 88W19 5:53:16
Estancia de los López 18 7 20N53 104W31 6:58:04
Etchojoa 26 7 26N55 109W38 7:18:32
Etchoropo 26 7 26N41 109W40 7:18:40
Etzatlán 14 5 20N46 104W05 6:56:20
Felipe Carrillo Puerto 23 1 19N35 88W03 5:52:12
Félix Gómez 26 7 29N50 111W30 7:26:00
Félix U. Gómez 6 5 30N35 105W50 7:03:20
Fernández Leal 6 5 30N51 108W17 7:13:08
Filisola 30 1 17N50 94W19 6:17:16
Filomeno Mata 30 1 20N12 97W42 6:30:48
Finisterre 7 5 25N59 103W15 6:53:00
Fortín de las Flores 30 1 18N54 97W00 6:28:00
Fracción del Refugio 24 5 21N57 100W02 6:40:08
Francisco González Villarreal 28 1 25N22 97W53 6:31:32
Francisco I. Madero 7 5 25N45 103W21 6:53:24
Francisco I. Madero 10 5 24N32 104W22 6:57:28
Francisco I. Madero 5 1 16N50 93W50 6:15:20
Francisco I. Madero 18 7 21N36 104W49 6:59:16
Francisco Primo Verdad 14 5 21N48 101W55 6:47:40
Francisco Zarco 2 4 32N06 116W30 7:46:00
Fresnillo 32 5 23N10 102W53 6:51:32
Frontera 27 1 18N32 92W38 6:10:32
Fronteras 26 7 30N56 109W31 7:18:04
Fuente 7 5 28N40 100W32 6:42:08
Fundición de Avalos 6 5 28N35 106W00 7:04:00
Gabriel Zamora 16 5 19N05 102W05 6:48:20
Galeana 6 5 30N07 107W38 7:10:32
Galeana 19 5 24N50 100W04 6:40:16
Gámbara 16 5 18N55 102W05 6:48:20
García 6 5 29N59 108W20 7:13:20
García de la Cadena 32 5 21N09 103W28 6:53:52
Garza Ayala 19 5 26N29 100W02 6:40:08
General Bravo 19 5 25N48 99W10 6:36:40
General Cepeda 7 5 25N23 101W27 6:45:48
General Escobedo 10 5 25N30 105W15 7:01:00
General Escobedo 19 5 25N49 100W20 6:41:20

General Panfilo Natera 32 5 22N40 102w06 6:48:24
General Terán 19 5 25N16 99w41 6:38:44
General Treviño 19 5 26N14 99w29 6:37:56
General Zuazua 19 5 25N54 100w07 6:40:28
Germán 28 1 25N10 97w54 6:31:36
Gómez Farías 6 5 29N18 107w40 7:10:40
Gómez Farías 14 5 19N47 103w29 6:53:56
Gómez Palacio 10 5 25N34 103w30 6:54:00
González Ortega 2 3 32N40 115w23 7:41:32
Guachinango 14 5 20N32 104w24 6:57:36
Guachochic 6 5 26N51 107w05 7:08:20
Guadalajara 14 5 20N40 103w20 6:53:20
Guadalcázar 24 5 22N37 100w24 6:41:36
Guadalupe 5 1 16N16 91w27 6:05:48
Guadalupe 19 5 25N41 100w15 6:41:00
Guadalupe 32 5 22N45 102w31 6:50:04
Guadalupe 7 5 28N09 100w36 6:42:24
Guadalupe (Bravos) 6 5 31N23 106w07 7:04:28
Guadalupe de Ramírez 20 1 17N45 98w10 6:32:40
Guadalupe Garzarón 32 5 24N35 101w15 6:45:00
Guadalupe Victoria 10 5 24N27 104w07 6:56:28
Guadalupe Victoria 21 5 19N17 97w21 6:29:24
Guadalupe Victoria 7 5 27N47 101w04 6:44:16
Guamúchil 25 7 23N55 106w05 7:04:20
Guanaceví 10 5 25N56 105w57 7:03:48
Guanajuato 11 5 21N01 101w15 6:45:00
Guardado de Abajo 28 1 26N22 98w57 6:35:48
Guasave 25 7 25N34 108w27 7:13:48
Guayabo 25 7 26N00 107w26 7:09:44
Guayabo Colorado 16 5 19N02 101w35 6:46:20
Guayameo 12 5 18N12 101w19 6:45:16
Guaycora 26 7 28N50 109w21 7:17:24
Guaymas 26 7 27N56 110w54 7:23:36
Guazapares 6 5 27N22 108w15 7:13:00
Guazárachic 6 5 26N57 106w43 7:06:52
Güemes 28 1 23N56 99w00 6:36:00
Guerrero 7 5 28N20 100w23 6:41:32
Guichicovi 20 1 16N58 95w06 6:20:24
Gustavo Madero 9 6 19N29 99w08 6:36:32
Gutiérrez Zamora 30 1 20N27 97w05 6:28:20
Guzmán 6 5 31N13 107w27 7:09:48
Guzmán → Ciudad Guzmán 14 5 19N41 103w29 6:53:56
Halachó 31 1 20N29 90w05 6:00:20
Hecelchakán 4 1 20N10 90w08 6:00:32
Hechiceros 6 5 28N33 103w38 6:54:32
Hermanas 7 5 27N13 101w14 6:44:56
Hermosillo 26 7 29N04 110w58 7:23:52
Hermosillo 2 4 32N30 114w59 7:39:56
Hernández 24 5 23N01 102w01 6:48:04
Heroica Caborca 26 7 30N37 112w06 7:28:24
Heroica Nogales 26 7 31N20 110w56 7:23:44
Hidalgo 7 5 27N47 99w52 6:39:28
Hidalgo 19 5 25N59 100w27 6:41:48
Hidalgo 28 1 24N15 99w26 6:37:44
Hidalgo 32 5 23N10 103w13 6:52:52
Hidalgo del Parral 6 5 26N56 105w40 7:02:40
Hidalgo Yalalag 20 1 17N11 96w11 6:24:44
Higuera Blanca 14 5 19N42 105w10 7:00:40
Higuera de Zaragoza 25 7 25N59 109w16 7:17:04
Higuera Gorda 18 7 22N04 104w29 6:57:56
Higueras 19 5 25N58 100w01 6:40:04
Hipólito 7 5 25N41 101w26 6:45:44
Hopelchén 4 1 19N46 89w51 5:59:24
Hostotipaquillo 14 5 21N04 104w04 6:56:16
Huajimic 18 7 21N42 104w20 6:57:20
Huajintepec 12 5 16N36 98w14 6:32:56
Huajuapan de León 20 1 17N48 97w46 6:31:04
Hualahuises 19 5 24N53 99w41 6:38:44
Huamantla 29 5 19N19 97w56 6:31:44
Huamuxtitlán 12 5 17N49 98w34 6:34:16
Huandacareo 16 5 19N59 101w17 6:45:08
Huaniqueo (de Morales) 16 5 19N54 101w26 6:45:44
Huásabas 26 7 29N47 109w18 7:17:12
Huasamota 10 5 22N30 104w30 6:58:00
Huatabampo 26 7 26N50 109w38 7:18:32
Huatusco de Chicuellar 30 1 19N09 96w57 6:27:48
Huauchinango 21 5 20N11 98w03 6:32:12
Huautla 13 5 21N02 98w17 6:33:08
Huautla de Jiménez 20 1 18N08 96w51 6:27:24
Huazolotitlán 20 1 16N17 97w56 6:31:44
Huehuetán 5 1 15N01 92w22 6:09:28
Huehuetlán el Chico 21 5 18N21 98w42 6:34:48
Huejúcar 14 5 22N21 103w13 6:52:52
Huejuquilla el Alto 14 5 22N36 103w52 6:55:28
Huejutla de Reyes 13 5 21N08 98w25 6:33:40
Huetamo de Núñez 16 5 18N35 100w53 6:43:32
Hueyapan 17 5 18N52 98w40 6:34:40
Hueyapan de Ocampo 30 1 18N07 95w09 6:20:36
Huichapan 13 5 20N23 99w39 6:38:36
Huimanguillo 27 1 17N51 93w23 6:13:32
Huisachal 7 5 26N47 101w07 6:44:28
Huistepec 12 5 16N39 98w20 6:33:20
Huitiupan 5 1 17N13 92w39 6:10:36
Huitzitlán 21 5 19N58 97w41 6:30:44
Huitzuco de los Figueroa 12 5 18N18 99w21 6:37:24
Huixtla 5 1 15N09 92w28 6:09:52
Huizache 24 5 22N55 100w25 6:41:40
Hunucmá 31 1 21N01 89w52 5:59:28
Icamole 19 5 25N55 100w43 6:42:52
Ignacio de la Llave 30 1 18N43 95w59 6:23:56
Ignacio Zaragoza 6 5 29N35 107w30 7:10:00
Ignacio Zaragoza 32 5 23N55 103w42 6:54:48
Iguala 12 5 18N21 99w32 6:38:08
Illatenco 12 5 16N58 98w40 6:34:40
Illescas 24 5 23N13 102w07 6:48:28
Imuris 26 7 30N47 110w52 7:23:28
Indaparapeo 16 5 19N47 100w58 6:43:52
Indé 10 5 25N54 105w13 7:00:52
Inmaculadita 26 7 29N55 111w48 7:27:12
Irámuco 11 5 19N57 100w55 6:43:40
Irapuato 11 5 20N41 101w21 6:45:24
Isla 30 1 18N01 95w30 6:22:00
Isla Mujeres 23 1 21N12 86w43 5:46:52
Iturbide 4 1 19N40 89w37 5:58:28
Ixhuatlán del Café 30 1 19N04 96w59 6:27:56
Ixmiquilpan 13 5 20N29 99w14 6:36:56
Ixtacalco 9 6 19N23 99w08 6:36:32
Ixtaltepec 20 1 16N30 95w03 6:20:12
Ixtapalapa 9 6 19N21 99w05 6:36:20
Ixtapan de la Sal 15 5 18N50 99w41 6:38:44
Ixtlahuacán del Río 14 5 20N52 103w15 6:53:00
Ixtlán 16 5 20N11 102w24 6:49:36
Ixtlán de Juárez 20 1 17N20 96w29 6:25:56
Ixtlán del Río 18 7 21N02 104w22 6:57:28
Izúcar de Matamoros 21 5 18N36 98w28 6:33:52
Jaboncillos 7 5 28N57 102w39 6:50:36
Jacala de Ledesma 13 5 21N01 99w11 6:36:44
Jacona de Plancarte 16 5 19N57 102w16 6:49:04
Jala 18 7 21N05 104w26 6:57:44
Jalacingo 30 1 19N48 97w18 6:29:12
Jalapa 27 1 17N43 92w49 6:11:16
Jalapa de Díaz 20 1 18N04 96w32 6:26:08
Jalapa Enríquez 30 1 19N32 96w55 6:27:40
Jalcocotán 18 7 21N28 105w07 7:00:28
Jalea de Catalán 12 5 17N26 99w51 6:39:24
Jalisco 18 7 21N27 104w54 6:59:36
Jalostotitlán 14 5 21N12 102w28 6:49:52
Jalpa 27 5 21N38 102w58 6:51:52
Jalpa de Méndez 27 1 18N08 93w05 6:12:20
Jalpan 22 5 21N14 99w29 6:37:56
Jaltenango de la Paz 5 1 15N55 92w43 6:10:52
Jáltipan 30 1 17N58 94w42 6:18:48
Jaltocán 13 5 21N09 98w32 6:34:08
Jamay 14 5 20N18 102w43 6:50:52
Jamiltepec 20 1 16N17 97w49 6:31:16
Janos 6 5 30N54 108w10 7:12:40
Jantetelco 17 5 18N42 98w46 6:35:04
Jaral del Progreso 11 5 20N22 101w04 6:44:16
Jaumave 28 1 23N25 99w23 6:37:32
Jerécuaro 11 5 20N09 100w31 6:42:04
Jerez de García Salinas 32 5 22N39 103w00 6:52:00
Jesús Carranza 30 1 17N26 95w02 6:20:08
Jesús María 25 7 25N06 107w28 7:09:52
Jesús María 1 2 21N58 102w21 6:49:24
Jilotepec de Abasolo 15 5 19N58 99w32 6:38:08
Jilotlán de los Dolores 14 5 19N14 102w59 6:51:56
Jiménez 7 5 29N02 100w41 6:42:44
Jiménez del Teúl 32 5 23N10 104w05 6:56:20
Jiquilpan de Juárez 16 5 19N59 102w43 6:50:52
Jiquipilas 5 1 16N40 93w39 6:14:36
Jiquipilco 15 5 19N32 99w36 6:38:24
Jitotol 5 1 17N02 92w52 6:11:28
Jocotepec 14 5 20N18 103w26 6:53:44
Jocotitlán 15 5 19N42 99w48 6:39:12
Jocuixtita 25 7 24N15 106w16 7:05:04
Jojutla 17 5 18N37 99w11 6:36:44
Jonacatepec 17 5 18N41 98w48 6:35:12
Jonuta 27 1 18N05 92w08 6:08:32
Joquicingo 15 5 19N03 99w33 6:38:12
José Cardel 30 1 19N22 96w22 6:25:28
Juanacatlán 14 5 20N31 103w10 6:52:40
Juan Aldama 32 5 24N19 103w21 6:53:24
Juan Díaz Covarrubias 30 1 18N07 95w09 6:20:36
Juan Eugenio 7 5 25N10 103w20 6:53:20
Juanita 30 1 17N47 95w09 6:20:36
Juan Rodríguez Clara 30 1 18N00 95w25 6:21:40
Juárez 7 5 27N37 100w44 6:42:56
Juárez → Ciudad Juárez 6 5 31N44 106w29 7:05:56
Juárez 5 1 17N39 93w10 6:12:40
Juchipila 32 5 21N25 103w07 6:52:28
Juchitán (de Zaragoza) 20 1 16N26 95w01 6:20:04
Juchitepec 15 5 19N06 98w53 6:35:32
Juchitlán 14 5 20N05 104w07 6:56:28
Juile 30 1 17N45 94w59 6:19:56
Julimes 6 5 28N25 105w27 7:01:48
Jungapeo 16 5 19N27 100w29 6:41:56
Juquila 20 1 16N14 97w18 6:29:12
Juxtlahuaca 20 1 17N20 98w01 6:32:04
Kantunilkín 23 1 21N06 87w29 5:49:56
La Aldea 11 5 20N54 101w29 6:45:56
La Azufrosa 7 5 28N14 100w50 6:43:20
La Babía 7 5 28N34 102w04 6:48:16
La Barca 14 5 20N17 102w34 6:50:16
La Boca 28 1 23N56 99w17 6:37:08
La Cadena 10 5 25N53 104w12 6:56:48
La Campana 25 7 22N45 105w35 7:02:20
La Cañada 22 5 20N37 100w19 6:41:16
La Candelaria 6 5 31N07 106w29 7:05:56
La Capilla 20 1 18N30 96w40 6:26:40
La Capilla 28 1 23N59 98w25 6:33:40
La Casita 10 5 23N43 104w46 6:59:04
La Ciénega 20 1 16N54 96w46 6:27:04
La Colmena 15 5 19N36 99w18 6:37:12
La Colorada 26 7 28N41 110w25 7:21:40
La Concepción 16 5 18N15 102w27 6:49:48
La Cruz 7 5 28N33 100w48 6:43:12
La Cuchilla 16 5 18N54 103w19 6:53:16
La Cuesta 14 5 20N10 104w51 6:59:24
La Encarnacion 28 1 23N23 98w01 6:32:04
La Escondida 28 1 25N40 98w18 6:33:12
La Escondida 19 5 26N17 99w46 6:39:04
La Esmeralda 7 5 27N17 103w39 6:54:36
La Esperanza 10 5 26N46 104w00 6:56:00
La Esperanza 26 7 32N06 114w47 7:39:08
La Estancia 12 5 18N05 101w25 6:45:40
La Garita 14 5 19N43 103w10 6:52:40
Lagos de Moreno 14 5 21N21 101w55 6:47:40
Laguna de Jaco 6 5 27N50 104w00 6:56:00
Lagunillas 24 5 21N34 99w35 6:38:20
La Huacana 16 5 18N58 101w49 6:47:16
La Huerta 14 5 19N28 104w39 6:58:36
La Jarita 7 5 28N03 103w20 6:53:20
Lajas 10 5 23N07 105w07 7:00:28
La Joya 26 7 32N08 114w01 7:36:04
La Joya 7 5 26N26 101w08 6:44:32
La Junta 6 5 28N28 107w20 7:09:20
La Lajilla 19 5 26N47 99w37 6:38:28
La Leona 7 5 25N52 101w05 6:44:20
La Loma 25 7 22N53 105w51 7:03:24
La Luz 28 1 25N52 97w37 6:30:28
Lamadrid 7 5 27N05 101w50 6:47:20
La Mancha 7 5 24N52 102w47 6:51:08
La Maroma 7 5 28N34 100w45 6:43:00
La Mira 16 5 18N02 102w19 6:49:16
La Misión 2 4 32N05 116w50 7:47:20
La Moncada 11 5 20N16 100w48 6:43:12
La Mutua 24 5 22N23 99w18 6:37:12
La Palma 12 5 17N05 99w29 6:37:56
La Palma 16 5 20N09 102w46 6:51:04
La Palma 32 5 22N49 103w57 6:55:48
La Palmita 19 5 25N57 99w18 6:37:12
La Parota 12 5 18N20 101w08 6:44:32
La Parota 16 5 18N19 103w02 6:52:08
La Parotita 16 5 19N07 101w15 6:45:00
La Paz 3 8 24N10 110w18 7:21:12
La Paz 24 5 23N41 100w43 6:42:52
La Perla 6 5 28N18 104w38 6:58:32
La Pesca 28 1 23N46 97w47 6:31:08
La Piedad (Cavadas) 16 5 20N21 102w00 6:48:00
La Pimienta 24 5 21N28 99w01 6:36:04
La Purísima 3 8 26N10 112w04 7:28:16
La Reforma 25 7 25N06 108w05 7:12:20
La Rumorosa 2 4 32N34 116w06 7:44:24
La Salada 12 5 18N01 101w58 6:47:52
La Sauceda 7 5 28N26 100w38 6:42:32
Las Auras 28 1 26N25 99w20 6:37:20
Las Blancas 28 1 25N42 97w35 6:30:20
Las Casas → San Cristóbal de las Casa 5 1 16N45 92w38 6:10:32
Las Choapas 27 1 17N55 94w05 6:16:20
Las Chorreras 6 5 28N50 105w18 7:01:12
Las Cidras 16 5 19N15 101w08 6:44:32
Las Colimas 28 1 25N21 98w40 6:34:40

Las Cruces 16 5 18N45 102w16 6:49:04
Las Cuevas 7 5 29N38 101w19 6:45:16
Las Delicias 5 1 15N58 91w50 6:07:20
Las Escobas 2 4 30N33 115w56 7:43:44
Las Flores 27 1 18N22 93w10 6:12:40
Las Guayabas 28 1 24N00 97w45 6:31:00
Las Higueras 25 7 23N41 106w06 7:04:24
Las Iglesias 7 5 27N35 101w21 6:45:24
Las Margaritas 5 1 16N19 91w59 6:07:56
Las Mesas 12 5 17N00 99w30 6:38:00
Las Nieves 10 5 26N24 105w22 7:01:28
Las Peñas 16 5 18N03 102w30 6:50:00
Las Rosas 5 1 16N24 92w23 6:09:32
Las Truchas 16 5 17N55 102w12 6:48:48
Las Varas 6 5 29N29 108w01 7:12:04
Las Varas 18 7 21N10 105w10 7:00:40
Las Vigas 30 1 19N38 97w05 6:28:20
La Tapona 24 5 22N48 100w38 6:42:32
La Unión 12 5 17N58 101w49 6:47:16
La Venada 28 1 25N50 97w30 6:30:00
La Ventura 7 5 24N38 100w54 6:43:36
La Yesca 18 7 21N19 104w02 6:56:08
La Zarca 10 5 25N50 104w44 6:58:56
Lazaro Cárdenas 7 5 25N23 103w10 6:52:40
Leona Vicario 2 4 32N10 115w10 7:40:40
León (de los Aldamas) 11 5 21N07 101w40 6:46:40
León Guzmán 10 5 25N31 103w34 6:54:16
Lerdo → Ciudad Lerdo 10 5 25N32 103w32 6:54:08
Lerdo de Tejada 30 1 18N37 95w31 6:22:04
Ligui 3 8 25N43 111w16 7:25:04
Limón de Ramos 25 7 24N43 107w08 7:08:32
Linares 19 5 24N52 99w34 6:38:16
Llano Colorado 2 4 31N38 115w55 7:43:40
Llano Grande 14 5 20N28 105w37 7:02:28
Llera 28 1 23N19 99w01 6:36:04
Lobatos 32 5 22N49 103w24 6:53:36
Lobos 14 5 20N29 105w03 7:00:12
Loma Blanca 6 5 31N35 106w17 7:05:08
Loma Bonita 20 1 18N07 95w53 6:23:32
Loma Linda 15 5 19N28 99w14 6:36:56
Lomas Alegres 27 1 17N38 92w36 6:10:24
Lomas del Real 28 1 22N30 97w54 6:31:36
Lomas de Monreal 26 7 31N17 110w56 7:23:44
López Collada 26 7 31N45 113w55 7:35:40
Loreto 3 8 26N01 111w21 7:25:24
Loreto 32 5 22N16 101w58 6:47:52
Los Alamos 7 5 28N40 103w30 6:54:00
Los Aldamas 19 5 26N03 99w11 6:36:44
Los Altos 28 1 26N14 98w28 6:33:52
Los Amates 16 5 18N08 102w15 6:49:00
Los Burros 3 8 25N03 110w50 7:23:20
Los Ebanos 28 1 24N40 97w45 6:31:00
Los Garzas 19 5 26N23 99w46 6:39:04
Los Guerras 28 1 26N25 99w05 6:36:20
Los Haros 32 5 22N46 102w57 6:51:48
Los Herreras 10 5 25N10 105w31 7:02:04
Los Herreras 19 5 25N55 99w24 6:37:36
Los López 28 1 26N15 99w05 6:36:20
Los Metates 25 7 23N46 106w02 7:04:08
Los Mochis 25 7 25N45 108w57 7:15:48
Los Nogales 19 5 26N16 99w43 6:38:52
Los Placeres 12 5 18N13 100w54 6:43:36
Los Ramones 19 5 25N42 99w37 6:38:28
Los Reyes de Salgado 16 5 19N35 102w29 6:49:56
Los Reyes la Paz 15 5 19N21 98w58 6:35:52
Los Rodríguez 7 5 27N11 101w21 6:45:24
Los Tres Palos 28 1 24N33 98w18 6:33:12
Los Vidrios 26 7 31N59 113w28 7:33:52
Lucero 6 5 30N49 106w30 7:06:00
Luis Moya 32 5 22N25 102w15 6:49:00
Macedonio Alcalá 20 1 17N52 96w02 6:24:08
Maclovio Herrera 6 5 29N05 105w08 7:00:32
Macuspana 27 1 17N46 92w36 6:10:24
Madera 6 5 29N12 108w07 7:12:28
Magdalena 14 5 20N55 103w57 6:55:48
Magdalena de Kino 26 7 30N38 110w57 7:23:48
Magdalena Peñasco 20 1 17N14 97w34 6:30:16
Magdalena Tequisistlán 20 1 16N22 95w15 6:21:00
Magiscatzin 28 1 22N48 98w42 6:34:48
Maijoma 6 5 28N55 104w21 6:57:24
Malinaltepec 12 5 17N03 98w40 6:34:40
Malpaso 32 5 22N37 102w46 6:51:04
Maltrata 30 1 18N48 97w16 6:29:04
Mamulique 19 5 26N08 100w20 6:41:20
Manuel 28 1 22N44 98w19 6:33:16
Manuel Benavides 6 5 29N05 103w55 6:55:40
Manuel M. Diéguez 14 5 19N34 102w55 6:51:40
Manzanillo 8 5 19N03 104w20 6:57:20
Mapastepec 5 1 15N26 92w54 6:11:36
Mapimí 10 5 25N49 103w51 6:55:24
Maravatío de Ocampo 16 5 19N54 100w27 6:41:48
Maravillas 6 5 27N22 104w29 6:57:56
Marín 19 5 25N52 100w03 6:40:12
Martínez de la Torre 30 1 20N04 97w03 6:28:12
Mascota 14 5 20N32 104w49 6:59:16
Matamoros 28 1 25N53 97w30 6:30:00
Matamoros de la Laguna 7 5 25N32 103w15 6:53:00
Matanzas 14 5 21N37 101w38 6:46:32
Mata Ortiz 6 5 30N08 108w03 7:12:12
Matehuala 24 5 23N39 100w39 6:42:36
Matías Romero 20 1 16N53 95w02 6:20:08
Matlapa 24 5 21N20 98w50 6:35:20
Maxcanú 31 1 20N35 89w59 5:59:56
Mazamitla 14 5 19N55 103w02 6:52:08
Mazatlán 25 7 23N13 106w25 7:05:40
Mazatlán de Flores 20 1 18N02 96w54 6:27:36
Mecatán 18 7 21N32 105w08 7:00:32
Mecatlán 30 1 20N13 97w41 6:30:44
Mecoacán 27 1 18N23 93w07 6:12:28
Melchor Ocampo 19 5 26N03 99w33 6:38:12
Meoqui 6 5 28N17 105w29 7:01:56
Mérida 31 1 20N58 89w37 5:58:28
Mérida 2 4 32N39 114w58 7:39:52
Mesa del Nayar 18 7 22N16 104w35 6:58:20
Mesa de Santa Rita 25 7 23N04 105w31 7:02:04
Mesillas 25 7 23N14 106w03 7:04:12
Mesillas 32 5 23N33 103w35 6:54:20
Metepec 15 5 19N15 99w36 6:38:24
Metepec 21 5 18N56 98w28 6:33:52
Metlatonoc 12 5 17N11 98w20 6:33:20
Metztitlán 13 5 20N37 98w46 6:35:04
Mexicali 2 3 32N40 115w29 7:41:56
Mexico City → Ciudad de México 9 6 19N24 99w09 6:36:36
Mexiko → Ciudad de México 9 6 19N24 99w09 6:36:36
Mexticacán 14 5 21N13 102w43 6:50:52
Mezquital 10 5 23N29 104w23 6:57:32
Mezquital del Oro 32 5 21N10 103w23 6:53:32
Mezquitic 14 5 22N23 103w41 6:54:44
Miacatlán 17 5 18N46 99w22 6:37:28
Miahuatlán de Porfirio Díaz 20 1 16N20 96w36 6:26:24
Michoacán 2 4 32N28 115w20 7:41:20
Michoacanejo 14 5 21N33 102w36 6:50:24
Mier y Noriega 19 5 23N25 100w07 6:40:28
Miguel Auza 10 5 24N18 103w25 6:53:40
Mina 19 5 26N01 100w32 6:42:08
Minas de Barroterán 7 5 27N40 101w20 6:45:20
Minatitlán 30 1 17N59 94w31 6:18:04
Mineral del Monte 13 5 20N08 98w40 6:34:40
Mineral del Oro 15 5 19N48 100w08 6:40:32
Miquihuana 28 1 23N34 99w47 6:39:08
Misantla 30 1 19N56 96w50 6:27:20
Mixquiahuala 13 5 20N14 99w13 6:36:52
Mixtán 20 1 17N55 95w51 6:23:24
Mixtlán 14 5 20N26 104w25 6:57:40
Mochitlán 12 5 17N30 99w18 6:37:12
Mocorito 25 7 25N29 107w55 7:11:40
Moctezuma 26 7 29N48 109w42 7:18:48
Moctezuma 24 5 22N45 101w05 6:44:20
Momax 32 5 21N56 103w19 6:53:16
Monclova 7 5 26N54 101w25 6:45:40
Monte Escobedo 32 5 22N18 103w35 6:54:20
Montemorelos 19 5 25N12 99w49 6:39:16
Monterrey 19 5 25N40 100w19 6:41:16
Monterrey 5 1 16N05 93w23 6:13:32
Morelia 16 5 19N42 101w07 6:44:28
Morelos 6 5 26N42 107w40 7:10:40
Morelos 32 5 22N53 102w37 6:50:28
Morelos 7 5 28N25 100w53 6:43:32
Moroleón 11 5 20N08 101w12 6:44:48
Morro de Mazatán 20 1 16N07 95w27 6:21:48
Motozintla de Mendoza 5 1 15N22 92w14 6:08:56
Móvano 7 5 26N42 103w39 6:54:36
Moyahua 32 5 21N16 103w10 6:52:40
Mulatos 26 7 28N39 108w51 7:15:24
Mulegé 3 8 26N53 112w01 7:28:04
Multé 27 1 17N41 91w24 6:05:36
Muna 31 1 20N29 89w43 5:58:52
Nabogame 6 5 26N14 106w57 7:07:48
Nacajuca 27 1 18N08 93w01 6:12:04
Nacastillo 14 5 19N35 104w55 6:59:40
Naco 26 7 31N20 109w56 7:19:44
Nácori Chico 26 7 29N39 109w01 7:16:04
Nacozari (de García) 26 7 30N24 109w39 7:18:36
Nahuatzén 16 5 19N42 101w50 6:47:20
Naicá 6 5 27N53 105w31 7:02:04
Nanacamilpa 29 5 19N29 98w33 6:34:12
Nanchital 30 1 18N04 94w24 6:17:36
Naolinco de Victoria 30 1 19N39 96w51 6:27:24
Naranjos 30 1 21N21 97w41 6:30:44
Naucalpan → Ciudad de N. de Juárez 15 5 19N28 99w14 6:36:56
Nautla 30 1 20N13 96w47 6:27:08
Nava 7 5 28N25 100w46 6:43:04
Navidad 14 5 20N35 104w42 6:58:48
Navojoa 26 7 27N06 109w26 7:17:44
Navolato 25 7 24N47 107w42 7:10:48
Nayarit 2 4 32N20 115w19 7:41:16
Nazas 10 5 25N14 104w08 6:56:32
Nejapa de Madero 20 1 16N37 95w59 6:23:56
Nicolás Bravo 27 1 18N21 93w10 6:12:40
Nieves 32 5 24N00 103w01 6:52:04
Niltepec 20 1 16N34 94w37 6:18:28
Nochistlán 32 5 21N22 102w51 6:51:24
Nocupétaro 16 5 18N48 101w04 6:44:16
Nogales 26 7 31N20 110w56 7:23:44
Nogales 30 1 18N49 97w10 6:28:40
Nombre de Dios 6 5 28N41 106w05 7:04:20
Nombre de Dios 10 5 23N51 104w14 6:56:56
Nonoava 6 5 27N28 106w44 7:06:56
Nopaltepec 30 1 18N17 95w59 6:23:56
Norogachic 6 5 27N15 107w07 7:08:28
Nueva Atzacoalco 9 6 19N28 99w03 6:36:12
Nueva Casas Grandes 6 5 30N25 107w55 7:11:40
Nueva Ciudad Guerrero 28 1 26N35 99w15 6:37:00
Nueva Cuadrilla 12 5 18N04 101w33 6:46:12
Nueva Italia de Ruiz 16 5 19N01 102w06 6:48:24
Nueva Rosita 7 5 27N57 101w13 6:44:52
Nuevo Camarón 19 5 27N05 99w55 6:39:40
Nuevo Laredo 28 1 27N30 99w31 6:38:04
Nuevo Léon 2 4 32N20 115w12 7:40:48
Nuevo Morelos 30 1 17N31 95w02 6:20:08
Nuevo Necaxa 21 5 20N13 98w00 6:32:00
Nuevo Poblado el Oro 7 5 26N50 101w19 6:45:16
Nuevo Primero de Mayo 28 1 26N01 98w02 6:32:08
Nuevo Progreso 4 1 18N38 92w18 6:09:12
Nuevo Saucillo 6 5 27N20 104w54 6:59:36
Numarán 16 5 20N15 101w56 6:47:44
Nunkiní 4 1 20N20 90w11 6:00:44
Nurí 26 7 28N02 109w22 7:17:28
Oaxaca (de Juárez) 20 1 17N03 96w43 6:26:52
Ocampo 6 5 28N11 108w23 7:13:32
Ocampo 7 5 27N20 102w21 6:49:24
Ocampo 11 5 21N39 101w30 6:46:00
Ocotepec 5 1 17N13 93w09 6:12:36
Ocotlán 14 5 20N21 102w46 6:51:04
Ocotlán de Morelos 20 1 16N48 96w40 6:26:40
Ocoyoacac 15 5 19N16 99w26 6:37:44
Ocozingo 5 1 16N54 92w07 6:08:28
Ocozocoautla (de Espinosa) 5 1 16N46 93w22 6:13:28
Ocuilán de Arteaga 15 5 18N58 99w25 6:37:40
Ojinaga 6 5 29N34 104w25 6:57:40
Ojitlán 20 1 18N04 96w23 6:25:32
Ojocaliente 32 5 22N34 102w15 6:49:00
Ojo de Agua de Alférez 28 1 22N51 99w42 6:38:48
Ojo de la Casa 6 5 31N23 106w32 7:06:08
Ojuelos de Jalisco 14 5 21N52 101w35 6:46:20
Olinalá 12 5 17N50 98w51 6:35:24
Oluta 30 1 17N55 94w54 6:19:36
Ometepec 12 5 16N41 98w25 6:33:40
Opopeo 16 5 19N24 101w36 6:46:24
Oriental 21 5 19N22 97w37 6:30:28
Orizaba 30 1 18N51 97w06 6:28:24
Oropeo 16 5 18N50 101w48 6:47:12
Ortiz 26 7 28N17 110w43 7:22:52
Ostuacán 5 1 17N25 93w18 6:13:12
Ostula 16 5 18N30 103w28 6:53:52
Otatitlán 30 1 18N12 96w02 6:24:08
Oteapan 30 1 18N00 94w39 6:18:36
Otinapa 10 5 24N11 105w02 7:00:08
Oyameles 21 5 19N43 97w32 6:30:08
Ozuluama 30 1 21N40 97w51 6:31:24
Ozumba de Alzate 15 5 19N03 98w48 6:35:12
Pabellon de Arteaga 1 2 22N10 102w21 6:49:24
Pachuca (de Soto) 13 5 20N07 98w44 6:34:56
Pahuatlán de Valle 21 5 20N17 98w09 6:32:36
Pajacuarán 16 5 20N07 102w34 6:50:16
Pajapan 30 1 18N15 94w42 6:18:48
Palau 7 5 27N54 101w26 6:45:44
Palenque 5 1 17N31 91w58 6:07:52
Palestina 7 5 29N10 100w55 6:43:40
Palizada 4 1 18N15 92w05 6:08:20

Palma Pegada 24 5 22N42 101w48 6:47:12
Palmar de Sepúlveda 25 7 25N43 107w55 7:11:40
Palmarito (Tochapan) 21 5 18N54 97w37 6:30:28
Palmira 7 5 28N58 100w47 6:43:08
Palo Alto 19 5 26N32 99w45 6:39:00
Palo Blanco 7 5 26N45 101w32 6:46:08
Palomas 6 5 31N44 107w37 7:10:28
Palomas 6 5 28N43 103w45 6:55:00
Panabá 31 1 21N17 88w16 5:53:04
Panindícuaro 16 5 19N59 101w46 6:47:04
Pánuco 30 1 22N03 98w10 6:32:40
Papanoa 12 5 17N21 101w02 6:44:08
Papantla (de Olarte) 30 1 20N27 97w19 6:29:16
Paracho (de Verduzco) 16 5 19N39 102w04 6:48:16
Parácuaro 11 5 20N09 100w46 6:43:04
Paraíso 27 1 18N24 93w14 6:12:56
Paraíso Novillero 30 1 18N16 95w59 6:23:56
Parás 19 5 26N30 99w31 6:38:04
Paredón 7 5 25N56 100w58 6:43:52
Parral → Hidalgo del Parral 6 5 26N56 105w40 7:02:40
Parras de la Fuente 7 5 25N25 102w11 6:48:44
Paso del Macho 30 1 18N58 96w43 6:26:52
Paso del Toro 30 1 19N02 96w07 6:24:28
Paso de Ovejas 30 1 19N17 96w26 6:25:44
Paso de San Antonio 6 5 29N05 103w55 6:55:40
Paso Hondo 5 1 15N49 92w02 6:08:08
Paso Real de Sarabia 20 1 17N03 95w01 6:20:04
Patamban 16 5 19N48 102w18 6:49:12
Pátzcuaro 16 5 19N31 101w36 6:46:24
Pedernales 16 5 19N08 101w28 6:45:52
Pedriceña 10 5 25N06 103w47 6:55:08
Pegueros 14 5 20N57 102w40 6:50:40
Pejelagartero 27 1 18N04 93w45 6:15:00
Penjamillo (de Degollado) 16 5 20N06 101w54 6:47:36
Pénjamo 11 5 20N26 101w44 6:46:56
Peñoles 10 5 25N39 104w30 6:58:00
Peñón Blanco 10 5 24N47 104w02 6:56:08
Peotillos 24 5 22N30 100w37 6:42:28
Peribán de Ramos 16 5 19N32 102w28 6:49:52
Pericos 25 7 25N03 107w42 7:10:48
Perote 30 1 19N34 97w14 6:28:56
Pesquería 19 5 25N47 100w03 6:40:12
Petalcingo 5 1 17N17 92w27 6:09:48
Petatlán 12 5 17N31 101w16 6:45:04
Petlalcingo 21 5 18N05 97w54 6:31:36
Peto 31 1 20N08 88w55 5:55:40
Pichátaro 16 5 19N30 101w46 6:47:04
Pichucalco 5 1 17N31 93w09 6:12:36
Pico de Oro 27 1 18N01 93w37 6:14:28
Piedra Blanca 7 5 29N05 102w19 6:49:16
Piedras Negras 7 5 28N42 100w31 6:42:04
Pihuamo 14 5 19N15 103w23 6:53:32
Pijijiapan 5 1 15N42 93w14 6:12:56
Pilares 6 5 30N24 104w52 6:59:28
Pinos 32 5 22N18 101w34 6:46:16
Pinotepa de Don Luis 20 1 16N25 97w55 6:31:40
Pinotepa Nacional 20 1 16N19 98w01 6:32:04
Pitillal del Norte 14 5 20N40 105w01 7:00:04
Pitiquito 26 7 30N42 112w02 7:28:08
Placeres de Picacho 25 7 23N11 105w42 7:02:48
Platón Sánchez 30 1 21N17 98w22 6:33:28
Playa Azul 16 5 17N59 102w24 6:49:36
Playa del Carmen 23 1 20N36 87w06 5:48:24
Playa Vicente 30 1 17N50 95w49 6:23:16
Pluma Hidalgo 20 1 15N55 96w25 6:25:40
Pochutla 20 1 15N44 96w28 6:25:52
Pomaro 16 5 18N20 103w18 6:53:12
Poncitlán 14 5 20N22 102w55 6:51:40
Portezuelo 14 5 20N25 102w31 6:50:04
Pótam 26 7 27N36 110w23 7:21:32
Potrero de Gallegos 32 5 22N38 103w41 6:54:44
Potrero del Llano 6 5 29N12 104w28 6:57:52
Potrero Grande 10 5 24N59 106w26 7:05:44
Poza Grande 3 8 25N50 112w05 7:28:20
Poza Rica de Hidalgo 30 1 20N33 97w27 6:29:48
Pozos 11 5 21N14 100w29 6:41:56
Primero de Mayo 7 5 27N12 101w15 6:45:00
Progreso 31 1 21N17 89w40 5:58:40
Progreso 7 5 27N28 100w59 6:43:56
Progreso Industrial 15 5 19N38 99w21 6:37:24
Providencia 7 5 27N06 103w32 6:54:08
Puebla (de Zaragoza) 21 5 19N03 98w12 6:32:48
Pueblo Nuevo 11 5 20N31 101w22 6:45:28
Pueblo Viejo 12 5 17N33 100w05 6:40:20
Pueblo Viejo 30 1 17N24 93w47 6:15:08
Puente de Camotlán 18 7 21N32 104w12 6:56:48
Puente de Ixtla 17 5 18N37 99w20 6:37:20
Puente Negro 7 5 27N55 101w01 6:44:04
Puerto Ángel 20 1 15N40 96w29 6:25:56
Puerto de San Juan de Dios 24 5 22N19 99w33 6:38:12
Puerto Escondido 20 1 15N50 97w10 6:28:40
Puerto Juárez 23 1 21N11 86w49 5:47:16
Puerto Libertad 26 7 29N55 112w43 7:30:52
Puerto Morelos 23 1 20N50 86w52 5:47:28
Puerto Peñasco 26 7 31N20 113w33 7:34:12
Puerto Vallarta 14 5 20N37 105w15 7:01:00
Punta Prieta 2 4 28N58 114w17 7:37:08
Purépero 16 5 19N55 102w01 6:48:04
Purificación 14 5 19N43 104w38 6:58:32
Purísima 10 5 25N25 105w26 7:01:44
Purísima 7 5 29N09 100w46 6:43:04
Purísima de Bustos 11 5 21N02 101w52 6:47:28
Puruándiro 16 5 20N05 101w30 6:46:00
Puruarán 16 5 19N06 101w32 6:46:08
Putla de Guerrero 20 1 17N02 97w56 6:31:44
Quecholac 21 5 18N57 97w40 6:30:40
Quechultenango 12 5 17N25 99w13 6:36:52
Querétaro 22 5 20N36 100w23 6:41:32
Querobabi 26 7 30N03 111w01 7:24:04
Quilá 25 7 24N23 107w13 7:08:52
Quimichis 18 7 22N21 105w32 7:02:08
Quiroga 16 5 19N40 101w32 6:46:08
Ramírez 7 5 27N20 100w58 6:43:52
Ramírez 28 1 25N57 97w46 6:31:04
Ramos 24 5 22N50 101w55 6:47:40
Ramos Arizpe 7 5 25N33 100w58 6:43:52
Rancho Nuevo 28 1 23N12 97w48 6:31:12
Rancho Nuevo 19 5 26N22 99w54 6:39:36
Rayón 26 7 29N43 110w35 7:22:20
Rayón 5 1 17N12 93w00 6:12:00
Rayón 24 5 21N51 99w40 6:38:40
Rayones 19 5 25N01 100w05 6:40:20
Real del Castillo 2 4 31N58 116w19 7:45:16
Reata 7 5 26N08 101w05 6:44:20
Reforma de Pineda 20 1 16N24 94w28 6:17:52
Repueblo de Oriente 19 5 25N51 99w39 6:38:36
Resurrección 21 5 19N06 98w07 6:32:28
Reynosa 28 1 26N07 98w18 6:33:12
Ricardo Flores Magón 6 5 29N58 106w58 7:07:52
Rinconada 19 5 25N42 100w43 6:42:52
Rincón de Romos 1 2 22N14 102w18 6:49:12
Rincón de Tamayo 11 5 20N25 100w45 6:43:00
Río Balsas 12 5 17N59 99w47 6:39:08
Río Blanco (Tenango de Río Blanco) 30 1 18N50 97w09 6:28:36
Río Bravo 28 1 25N59 98w06 6:32:24
Río Bravo 7 5 28N17 100w55 6:43:40
Río de las Playas 30 1 17N51 94w02 6:16:08
Río Grande 20 1 15N59 97w27 6:29:48
Río Grande 32 5 23N50 103w02 6:52:08
Río Hondo 15 5 19N25 99w16 6:37:04
Río Lagartos 31 1 21N36 88w10 5:52:40
Rioverde 24 5 21N56 99w59 6:39:56
Rodeo 10 5 25N11 104w34 6:58:16
Rodríguez 19 5 27N10 100w01 6:40:04
Romita 11 5 20N52 101w31 6:46:04
Rosales 6 5 28N12 105w33 7:02:12
Rosamorada 18 7 22N08 105w12 7:00:48
Rosario 2 4 30N01 115w40 7:42:40
Rosario 25 7 23N00 105w52 7:03:28
Rosarito 2 3 32N20 117w02 7:48:08
Rosarito 3 8 26N27 111w38 7:26:32
Rosarito Beach 2 3 32N20 117w02 7:48:08
Rosas 10 5 26N09 103w27 6:53:48
Ruiz 18 7 21N57 105w09 7:00:36
Sabancuy 4 1 18N58 91w11 6:04:44
Sabanilla 7 5 25N08 101w44 6:46:56
Sabinas 7 5 27N51 101w07 6:44:28
Sabinas Hidalgo 19 5 26N30 100w10 6:40:40
Sahuaripa 26 7 29N03 109w14 7:16:56
Sahuayo 16 5 20N04 102w43 6:50:52
Saín Alto 32 5 23N35 103w15 6:53:00
Salamanca 11 5 20N34 101w12 6:44:48
Salina Cruz 20 1 16N10 95w12 6:20:48
Salinas de Hidalgo 24 5 22N38 101w43 6:46:52
Salinas del Rey 7 5 27N38 102w24 6:49:36
Salinas Victoria 19 5 25N53 100w19 6:41:16
Saltillo 7 5 25N25 101w00 6:44:00
Salvatierra 11 5 20N13 100w53 6:43:32
Samalayuca 6 5 31N21 106w28 7:05:52
San Agustín Atenango 20 1 17N38 97w59 6:31:56
San Agustín Loxicha 20 1 16N01 96w38 6:26:32
San Agustín Oapan 12 5 17N58 99w27 6:37:48
San Agustín Tlaxiaca 13 5 20N07 98w53 6:35:32
San Alberto 7 5 27N30 101w20 6:45:20
San Andrés 3 8 27N14 114w14 7:36:56
San Andrés Cohamiata 14 5 22N12 104w03 6:56:12
San Andrés Tuxtla 30 1 18N27 95w13 6:20:52
San Antonio de Bravo 6 5 30N10 104w42 6:58:48
San Antonio de las Alazanas 7 5 25N16 100w36 6:42:24
San Antonio de Padua 10 5 22N35 104w30 6:58:00
San Antonio Eloxochitlán 20 1 18N11 96w52 6:27:28
San Antonio Nogalar 28 1 23N04 98w22 6:33:28
San Antonio Zomeyucan 15 5 19N27 99w16 6:37:04
San Bartolomé Ayautla 20 1 18N02 96w40 6:26:40
San Bartolo Morelos 15 5 19N41 99w29 6:37:56
San Bernardo 10 5 25N59 105w33 7:02:12
San Blas 25 7 26N05 108w46 7:15:04
San Blas 18 7 21N31 105w16 7:01:04
San Blas Atempa 20 1 16N16 95w10 6:20:40
San Buenaventura 7 5 27N05 101w32 6:46:08
San Carlos 7 5 29N01 100w51 6:43:24
San Carlos 28 1 24N35 98w56 6:35:44
Sánchez Magallanes 27 1 18N14 93w52 6:15:28
San Ciro de Acosta 24 5 21N38 99w49 6:39:16
San Cosme Xalostoc 29 5 19N24 98w03 6:32:12
San Cristóbal de la Barranca 14 5 21N03 103w26 6:53:44
San Cristóbal de las Casas 5 1 16N45 92w38 6:10:32
San Diego de la Unión 11 5 21N28 100w52 6:43:28
San Felipe 2 4 31N00 114w52 7:39:28
San Felipe 11 5 21N29 101w13 6:44:52
San Felipe Aztatán 18 7 22N23 105w24 7:01:36
San Felipe Nuevo Mercurio 32 5 24N22 102w06 6:48:24
San Fermín 10 5 26N20 104w49 6:59:16
San Fernando 28 1 24N50 98w10 6:32:40
San Fernando 5 1 16N52 93w13 6:12:52
San Fernando 7 5 28N32 100w54 6:43:36
San Fernando 26 7 31N16 110w36 7:22:24
San Francisco de Arriba 7 5 26N15 102w50 6:51:20
San Francisco de Borja 6 5 27N53 106w41 7:06:44
San Francisco de Horizonte 10 5 25N56 103w26 6:53:44
San Francisco del Mar 20 1 16N14 94w39 6:18:36
San Francisco del Oro 6 5 26N52 105w51 7:03:24
San Francisco del Rincón 11 5 21N01 101w51 6:47:24
San Francisco Ixhuatán 20 1 16N22 94w29 6:17:56
San Francisco Tlalcilalcalpa 11 5 19N18 99w46 6:39:04
San Gabriel Chilac 21 5 18N19 97w21 6:29:24
San Ignacio 3 8 27N27 112w51 7:31:24
San Ignacio 24 5 23N12 100w12 6:40:48
San Ignacio 25 7 23N55 106w25 7:05:40
San Isidro 24 5 21N55 100w15 6:41:00
San Isidro 6 5 31N31 106w18 7:05:12
San Jacinto 10 5 25N29 103w44 6:54:56
San Javier 19 5 26N16 99w27 6:37:48
San Jerónimo de Juárez 12 5 17N08 100w28 6:41:52
San José 26 7 27N32 110w09 7:20:36
San José 7 5 28N16 100w15 6:41:00
San José Ayuquila 20 1 17N58 97w57 6:31:48
San José de Aura 7 5 27N34 101w23 6:45:32
San José de Gracia 14 5 20N40 102w35 6:50:20
San José de la Parilla 10 5 23N44 104w07 6:56:28
San José de la Popa 19 5 26N10 100w47 6:43:08
San José de las Flores 20 1 17N20 95w24 6:21:36

San José del Cabo 3 8 23N03 109w41 7:18:44
San José de Llanetes 32 5 22N55 103w16 6:53:04
San José de Lourdes 32 5 23N18 103w01 6:52:04
San José de Raíces 19 5 24N35 100w14 6:40:56
San José Iturbide 11 5 21N00 100w23 6:41:32
San Juan 7 5 27N47 103w57 6:55:48
San Juan 6 5 29N34 104w36 6:58:24
San Juan Bautista 7 5 26N58 101w24 6:45:36
San Juan Bautista Cuicatlán 20 1 17N48 96w58 6:27:52
San Juan Colorado 20 1 16N32 97w55 6:31:40
San Juan de Abajo 18 7 20N48 105w13 7:00:52
San Juan de Guadalupe 10 5 24N38 102w44 6:50:56
San Juan de la Vega 11 5 20N38 100w46 6:43:04
San Juan de los Lagos 14 5 21N15 102w18 6:49:12
San Juan del Río 10 5 24N47 104w27 6:57:48
San Juan del Río 22 5 20N23 100w00 6:40:00
San Juan del Salado 24 5 23N18 101w56 6:47:44
San Juan de Sabinas 7 5 27N55 101w18 6:45:12
San Juan Evangelista 30 1 17N54 95w08 6:20:32
San Juan Ixcaquixtla 21 5 18N27 97w49 6:31:16
San Juan Lachao 20 1 16N14 97w09 6:28:36
San Juan Mazatlán 20 1 17N02 95w25 6:21:40
San Juan Peyotán 18 7 22N24 104w21 6:57:24
San Juan Quiahije 20 1 16N17 97w20 6:29:20
San Juan Sayultepec 20 1 17N27 97w17 6:29:08
San Judas 24 5 23N15 100w52 6:43:28
San Julián 14 5 21N01 102w10 6:48:40
San Leonardo 6 5 27N28 104w55 6:59:40
San Lorenzo 7 5 25N32 102w11 6:48:44
San Lorenzo 28 1 25N37 97w35 6:30:20
San Lucas 3 8 22N53 109w54 7:19:36
San Lucas 32 5 24N13 103w04 6:52:16
San Luis Acatlán 12 5 16N48 98w45 6:35:00
San Luis de la Loma 12 5 17N18 100w55 6:43:40
San Luis de la Paz 11 5 21N18 100w31 6:42:04
San Luis del Cordero 10 5 25N26 104w18 6:57:12
San Luis Gonzaga 3 8 24N55 111w16 7:25:04
San Luis Potosí 24 5 22N09 100w59 6:43:56
San Luis Río Colorado 26 7 32N29 114w48 7:39:12
San Luis Soyatlán 14 5 20N12 103w18 6:53:12
San Manuel 27 1 17N37 93w24 6:13:36
San Marcos 12 5 16N48 99w21 6:37:24
San Marcos 13 5 20N02 99w20 6:37:20
San Marcos 14 5 20N47 104w11 6:56:44
San Marcos Arteaga 20 1 17N45 97w58 6:31:52
San Martín de Bolaños 14 5 21N29 103w58 6:55:52
San Martín (de las Pirámides) 15 5 19N42 98w50 6:35:20
San Martín de las Vacas 7 5 25N30 101w20 6:45:20
San Martín Hidalgo 14 5 20N27 103w57 6:55:48
San Martín Peras 20 1 17N19 98w15 6:33:00
San Mateo 32 5 22N59 103w30 6:54:00
San Mateo Atenco 15 5 19N16 99w32 6:38:08
San Mateo del Mar 20 1 16N12 95w00 6:20:00
San Miguel 28 1 23N23 98w10 6:32:40
San Miguel Canoa 21 5 19N09 98w05 6:32:20
San Miguel Chimalapa 20 1 16N43 94w41 6:18:44
San Miguel de Allende 11 5 20N55 100w45 6:43:00
San Miguel de Cruces 10 5 24N25 105w51 7:03:24
San Miguel el Alto 14 5 21N01 102w21 6:49:24
San Miguel Octopan 11 5 20N34 100w44 6:42:56
San Miguel (o San Graciano) 7 5 29N10 101w28 6:45:52
San Miguel Talea de Castro 20 1 17N22 96w15 6:25:00
San Miguel Tenango 20 1 16N16 95w36 6:22:24
San Miguel Totolapan 12 5 18N08 100w23 6:41:32
San Nicolás 12 5 16N26 98w32 6:34:08
San Nicolas 16 5 19N05 101w07 6:44:28
San Nicolás de los Garzas 19 5 25N45 100w18 6:41:12
San Pablo Autopan 15 5 19N21 99w40 6:38:40
San Pablo Balleza 6 5 26N57 106w21 7:05:24
San Pablo Huitzo 20 1 17N15 96w52 6:27:28
San Pablo Huixtepec 20 1 16N50 96w46 6:27:04
San Pablo Villa de Mitla 20 1 16N55 96w24 6:25:36
San Pedro Apóstol 20 1 16N44 96w44 6:26:56
San Pedro de la Cueva 26 7 29N18 109w44 7:18:56
San Pedro de las Colonias 7 5 25N45 102w59 6:51:56
San Pedro del Gallo 10 5 25N33 104w18 6:57:12
San Pedro El Alto 20 1 16N01 96w28 6:25:52
San Pedro Huamelula 20 1 16N02 95w40 6:22:40
San Pedro Jicayán 20 1 16N25 97w59 6:31:56
San Pedro Juchatengo 20 1 16N21 97w06 6:28:24
San Pedro Mixtepec 20 1 16N00 97w07 6:28:28
San Pedro Piedra Gorda 32 5 22N27 102w21 6:49:24
San Pedro Tapanatepec 20 1 16N21 94w12 6:16:48
San Pedro Xalostoc 15 5 19N32 99w05 6:36:20
San Rafael 19 5 25N01 100w33 6:42:12
San Rafael 26 7 28N34 111w42 7:26:48
San Rafael 30 1 20N12 96w51 6:27:24
San Rafael de Arriba 2 4 31N05 116w05 7:44:20
San Rafael de las Tortillas 28 1 26N49 99w32 6:38:08
San Salvador el Seco 21 5 19N08 97w39 6:30:36
San Sebastián 5 21N26 102w21 6:49:24
San Sebastián 14 5 20N47 104w51 6:59:24
San Sebastián 7 22N10 104w19 6:57:16
San Simon 2 4 30N30 115w58 7:43:52
Santa Ana 19 5 24N04 100w30 6:42:00
Santa Ana 26 7 30N33 111w07 7:24:28
Santa Ana 27 1 18N15 93w28 6:13:52
Santa Ana 29 5 19N19 98w11 6:32:44
Santa Ana Pacueco 11 5 20N22 102w00 6:48:00
Santa Anita 14 5 20N33 103w27 6:53:48
Santa Apolonia 28 1 25N38 97w59 6:31:56
Santa Bárbara 6 5 26N48 105w49 7:03:16
Santa Bárbara 16 5 18N52 101w07 6:44:28
Santa Catarina 19 5 25N41 100w28 6:41:52
Santa Catarina 2 4 31N37 115w48 7:43:12
Santa Catarina 16 5 19N18 101w10 6:44:40
Santa Catarina Yosonotú 20 1 16N59 97w39 6:30:36
Santa Clara 6 5 29N17 107w01 7:08:04
Santa Clara 16 5 19N41 102w30 6:50:00
Santa Clara Coatitla 15 5 19N34 99w04 6:36:16
Santa Cruz 28 1 23N05 97w50 6:31:20
Santa Cruz 26 7 31N14 110w35 7:22:20
Santa Cruz de Bravo 23 1 19N35 88w02 5:52:08
Santa Cruz de Juventino Rosas 11 5 20N39 101w00 6:44:00
Santa Cruz Tacache Mina 20 1 17N51 98w07 6:32:28
Santa Elena 7 5 27N28 102w33 6:50:12
Santa Elena 16 5 18N39 101w34 6:46:16
Santa Elena 6 5 27N59 103w56 6:55:44
Santa Gertrudis 28 1 26N09 98w44 6:34:56
Santa Inés Ahuatempan 21 5 18N25 98w01 6:32:04
Santa Inés Zacatelco 29 5 19N13 98w14 6:32:56
Santa María 7 5 28N02 101w38 6:46:32
Santa María Ajoloapan 15 5 19N58 99w03 6:36:12
Santa María Chimalapa 20 1 16N55 94w41 6:18:44
Santa María Colotepec 20 1 15N53 96w55 6:27:40
Santa María del Oro 10 5 25N56 105w22 7:01:28
Santa María de los Ángeles 14 5 22N11 103w14 6:52:56
Santa María del Refugio 24 5 23N44 101w14 6:44:56
Santa María del Río 24 5 21N48 100w45 6:43:00
Santa María del Valle 14 5 20N54 102w22 6:49:28
Santa María Jalapa (del Marqués) 1 16N30 95w28 6:21:52
Santa María Magdalena (Cahuacán) 15 5 19N38 99w25 6:37:40
Santa María Tulpetlac 15 5 19N34 99w03 6:36:12
Santa María Zoquitlán 20 1 16N33 96w23 6:25:32
Santa Mónica 7 5 28N12 100w37 6:42:28
Santander Jiménez 28 1 24N13 98w28 6:33:52
Santa Rita 7 5 27N29 100w33 6:42:12
Santa Rita del Rucio 24 5 23N04 100w19 6:41:16
Santa Rosa 2 4 31N59 116w45 7:47:00
Santa Rosa 15 5 19N41 100w02 6:40:08
Santa Rosa 18 7 22N18 104w24 6:57:36
Santa Rosa Jáuregui 22 5 20N44 100w27 6:41:48
Santa Rosalía 3 8 27N19 112w17 7:29:08
Santa Rosalía 28 1 26N08 98w59 6:35:56
Santa Teresa 18 7 22N28 104w44 6:58:56
Santa Teresa 6 5 29N34 104w39 6:58:36
Santa Teresa 26 7 30N52 111w33 7:26:12
Santiago 3 8 23N28 109w43 7:18:52
Santiago 19 5 25N25 100w09 6:40:36
Santiago Apóstol 20 1 16N49 96w42 6:26:48
Santiago de la Peña 30 1 20N57 97w24 6:29:36
Santiago Ixcuintla 18 7 21N49 105w13 7:00:52
Santiago Ixtayutla 20 1 16N33 97w39 6:30:36
Santiago Lachiguirí 20 1 16N41 95w32 6:22:08
Santiago Maravatío 11 5 20N10 101w00 6:44:00
Santiago Papasquiaro 10 5 25N03 105w25 7:01:40
Santiago Tulantepec 13 5 20N02 98w22 6:33:28
Santiago Tutla 20 1 17N10 95w26 6:21:44
Santiago Tuxtla 30 1 18N28 95w18 6:21:12
Santiago Yaveo 20 1 17N19 95w42 6:22:48
Santiago Zacatepec 20 1 17N11 95w51 6:23:24
Santo Domingo 3 8 25N32 112w02 7:28:08
Santo Domingo 24 5 23N20 101w44 6:46:56
Santo Domingo 7 5 25N38 101w05 6:44:20
Santo Domingo 10 5 25N48 104w28 6:57:52
Santo Domingo Nuxaá 20 1 17N08 97w02 6:28:08
Santo Domingo Teojomulco 20 1 16N36 97w14 6:28:56
Santo Tomás 2 4 31N33 116w24 7:45:36
Santo Tomás Ocotepec 20 1 17N08 97w46 6:31:04
San Vicente 2 4 31N20 116w15 7:45:00
San Vicente Tancuayalab 24 5 21N44 98w34 6:34:16
Sarabia 11 5 20N31 101w05 6:44:20
Sáric 26 7 31N08 111w23 7:25:32
Sasabe 26 7 31N27 111w31 7:26:04
Saucillo 6 5 28N01 105w17 7:01:08
Sauzal 6 5 31N37 106w18 7:05:12
Sayula 26 7 29N22 111w33 7:26:12
Sayula 14 5 19N52 103w37 6:54:28
Sayula de Alemán 30 1 17N52 94w57 6:19:48
Senecú 6 5 31N43 106w23 7:05:32
Seybaplaya 4 1 19N39 90w40 6:02:40
Sierra Mojada 7 5 27N17 103w42 6:54:48
Sifón Villanueva 19 5 27N17 100w17 6:41:08
Silacayoapan 20 1 17N30 98w09 6:32:36
Silao 11 5 20N56 101w26 6:45:44
Simojovel de Allende 5 1 17N12 92w38 6:10:32
Socoltenango 5 1 16N13 92w15 6:09:00
Sola de Vega 20 1 16N31 96w59 6:27:56
Soledad de Doblado 30 1 19N03 96w25 6:25:40
Soledad Díez Gutiérrez 24 5 22N12 100w57 6:43:48
Soliseño 28 1 26N01 97w48 6:31:12
Sombrerete 32 5 23N38 103w39 6:54:36
Sombreretillo 19 5 26N19 99w58 6:39:52
Sonoita 26 7 31N51 112w50 7:31:20
Soto la Marina 28 1 23N46 98w13 6:32:52
Suaqui Grande 26 7 28N24 109w54 7:19:36
Suchiapa 5 1 16N37 93w05 6:12:20
Súchil 10 5 23N38 103w55 6:55:40
Suchilquitongo 20 1 17N15 96w53 6:27:32
Suchitlán 8 5 19N22 103w43 6:54:52
Tabasco 2 4 32N35 114w55 7:39:40
Tacámbaro de Codallos 16 5 19N14 101w28 6:45:52
Tacotalpa 27 1 17N36 92w49 6:11:16
Tacubaya 6 5 28N20 104w34 6:58:16
Tajitos 26 7 30N58 112w18 7:29:12
Tala 14 5 20N40 103w42 6:54:48
Talia 7 5 25N44 102w26 6:49:44

Talpa de Allende 14 5 20N23 104w51 6:59:24
Tamapatz 24 5 21N35 99w09 6:36:36
Tamazula 10 5 24N57 106w57 7:07:48
Tamazula de Gordiano 14 5 19N38 103w15 6:53:00
Tamazulapan (del Progreso) 20 1 17N41 97w34 6:30:16
Tamazunchale 24 5 21N16 98w47 6:35:08
Tameapa 25 7 25N39 107w22 7:09:28
Tamiahua 30 1 21N16 97w27 6:29:48
Tampico 28 1 22N13 97w51 6:31:24
Tamuín 24 5 21N59 98w45 6:35:00
Tancítaro 16 5 19N20 102w22 6:49:28
Tangamandapio 16 5 19N57 102w26 6:49:44
Tangancícuaro (de Arista) 16 5 19N54 102w08 6:48:32
Tanhuato 16 5 20N17 102w20 6:49:20
Tanque de Dolores 24 5 23N40 101w10 6:44:40
Tantoyuca 30 1 21N21 98w14 6:32:56
Tapachula 5 1 14N54 92w17 6:09:08
Tapalpa 14 5 19N57 103w46 6:55:04
Tapilula 5 1 17N14 93w02 6:12:08
Tarandacuao 11 5 19N59 100w32 6:42:08
Tarimoro 11 5 20N17 100w45 6:43:00
Tastiota 26 7 28N22 111w23 7:25:32
Tatahuicapan 30 1 18N14 94w45 6:19:00
Taxco de Alarcón 12 5 18N33 99w36 6:38:24
Tayoltita 10 5 24N05 105w56 7:03:44
Teacapán 25 7 22N33 105w45 7:03:00
Teapa 27 1 17N33 92w57 6:11:48
Tecalitlán 14 5 19N26 103w15 6:53:00
Tecamachalco 21 5 18N53 97w44 6:30:56
Tecate 2 3 32N34 116w38 7:46:32
Tecolotlán 14 5 20N13 104w03 6:56:12
Tecomán 8 5 18N55 103w53 6:55:32
Tecomaxtlahuaca 20 1 17N21 98w02 6:32:08
Tecominoacán 27 1 17N53 93w37 6:14:28
Tecozautla 13 5 20N32 99w38 6:38:32
Tecpan de Galeana 12 5 17N15 100w41 6:42:44
Tecpatán 5 1 17N08 93w18 6:13:12
Tecuala 18 7 22N23 105w27 7:01:48
Tehuacán 21 5 18N27 97w23 6:29:32
Tehuantepec 16 5 18N41 103w17 6:53:08
Tehuantepec 20 1 16N20 95w14 6:20:56
Tehuipango 30 1 18N31 97w04 6:28:16
Tehuitzingo 21 5 18N21 98w17 6:33:08
Teita 20 1 17N05 97w25 6:29:40
Teitipac 20 1 16N54 96w34 6:26:16
Tejamén 10 5 24N48 105w07 7:00:28
Tejupilco de Hidalgo 15 5 18N54 100w09 6:40:36
Tekax de Álvaro Obregón 31 1 20N12 89w17 5:57:08
Telixtlahuaca 20 1 17N18 96w54 6:27:36
Teloloapan 12 5 18N21 99w51 6:39:24
Temalacacingo 12 5 17N52 98w41 6:34:44
Temascal 10 5 23N24 104w14 6:56:56
Temascal 20 1 18N15 96w20 6:25:20
Temastián 14 5 21N53 103w28 6:53:52
Temax 31 1 21N09 88w56 5:55:44
Temixco 17 5 18N50 99w14 6:36:56
Temoaya 15 5 19N28 99w35 6:38:20
Temósachic 6 5 28N57 107w51 7:11:24
Tempoal 30 1 21N31 98w23 6:33:32
Tenabo 4 1 20N03 90w14 6:00:56
Tenamaxtlán 14 5 20N13 104w10 6:56:40
Tenancingo (de Degollado) 15 5 18N58 99w36 6:38:24
Tenango del Valle 15 5 19N07 99w33 6:38:12
Tenango de Río Blanco 30 1 18N50 97w09 6:28:36
Tenexpa 12 5 17N11 100w43 6:42:52
Tenextepango 17 5 18N43 98w57 6:35:48
Tenosique de Pino Suárez 27 1 17N29 91w26 6:05:44
Teocaltiche 14 5 21N26 102w35 6:50:20
Teocelo 30 1 19N23 96w58 6:27:52
Teocuitatlán de Corona 14 5 20N07 103w24 6:53:36
Teocuitlapa 12 5 17N22 98w58 6:35:52
Teotitlán del Camino 20 1 18N08 97w05 6:28:20
Teotitlán del Valle 20 1 17N02 96w30 6:26:00
Tepalcatepec 16 5 19N11 102w51 6:51:24
Tepalcingo 17 5 18N36 98w51 6:35:24
Tepatepec 13 5 20N14 99w05 6:36:20
Tepatitlán (de Morelos) 14 5 20N49 102w44 6:50:56
Tepatlaxco (de Hidalgo) 21 5 19N04 97w58 6:31:52
Tepeaca 21 5 18N58 97w54 6:31:36
Tepeapulco 13 5 19N47 98w33 6:34:12
Tepechitlán 32 5 21N40 103w20 6:53:20
Tepecoacuilco (de Trujano) 12 5 18N18 99w29 6:37:56
Tepeguaje 28 1 23N30 97w50 6:31:20
Tepeguaje 19 5 25N40 99w50 6:39:20
Tepehuanes 10 5 25N21 105w44 7:02:56
Tepeji del Río 15 5 19N54 99w21 6:37:24
Tepelmeme (de Morelos) 20 1 17N51 97w21 6:29:24
Tepetixtla 12 5 17N13 100w08 6:40:32
Tepetlixpa 15 5 19N02 98w49 6:35:16
Tepic 18 7 21N30 104w54 6:59:36
Teposcolula 20 1 17N31 97w29 6:29:56
Tepuzhuacán 14 5 20N53 104w33 6:58:12
Tequila 14 5 20N54 103w47 6:55:08
Tequisquiac 15 5 19N55 99w09 6:36:36
Terán 5 1 16N45 93w10 6:12:40
Tetla 29 5 19N26 98w06 6:32:24
Teúl de González Ortega 32 5 21N28 103w29 6:53:56
Texcaltitlán 15 5 18N54 99w55 6:39:40
Texcoco (de Mora) 15 5 19N31 98w53 6:35:32
Texistepec 30 1 17N53 94w47 6:19:08
Teziutlán 21 5 19N49 97w21 6:29:24
Tezoatlán (de Segura y Luna) 20 1 17N42 97w49 6:31:16
Ticul 31 1 20N24 89w32 5:58:08
Tierra Blanca 30 1 18N25 96w20 6:25:20
Tierra Blanca 6 5 27N12 104w53 6:59:32
Tierra Colorada 12 5 17N10 99w35 6:38:20
Tierra Colorada 27 1 17N56 92w39 6:10:36
Tierra Nueva 27 1 17N47 93w28 6:13:52
Tierras Coloradas 18 7 22N24 104w35 6:58:20
Tihuatlán 30 1 20N43 97w32 6:30:08
Tijuana 2 3 32N32 117w01 7:48:04
Tilzapotla 17 5 18N29 99w16 6:37:04
Timilpan 15 5 19N52 99w45 6:39:00
Tingambato 16 5 19N30 101w52 6:47:28
Tingüindín 16 5 19N45 102w29 6:49:56
Tiquicheo 16 5 18N53 100w44 6:42:56
Tiradero 27 1 17N47 91w10 6:04:40
Tixtla (de Guerrero) 12 5 17N35 99w26 6:37:44
Tizapán el Alto 14 5 20N10 103w04 6:52:16
Tizayuca 13 5 19N50 98w59 6:35:56
Tizimín 31 1 21N10 88w10 5:52:40
Tizoc 7 5 25N41 101w59 6:47:56
Tlachichuca 21 5 19N06 97w25 6:29:40
Tlacoapa 12 5 17N09 98w52 6:35:28
Tlacolula (de Matamoros) 20 1 16N57 96w29 6:25:56
Tlacotalpan 30 1 18N37 95w40 6:22:40
Tlacotepec 12 5 17N46 99w59 6:39:56
Tlacuitapa 14 5 21N14 102w12 6:48:48
Tlahualilo de Zaragoza 10 5 26N07 103w27 6:53:48
Tlahuelilpa de Ocampo 13 5 20N08 99w14 6:36:56
Tlahuitoltepec 20 1 17N04 95w59 6:23:56
Tlajomulco de Zúñiga 14 5 20N28 103w27 6:53:48
Tlalchapa 12 5 18N24 100w28 6:41:52
Tlalcozotitlán 12 5 17N54 99w15 6:37:00
Tlalixtac de Cabrera 20 1 17N04 96w39 6:26:36
Tlalixtaquilla 12 5 17N21 98w28 6:33:52
Tlalnepantla 15 5 19N33 99w12 6:36:48
Tlalpujahua 16 5 19N48 100w10 6:40:40
Tlaltenango de Sánchez Román 32 5 21N47 103w19 6:53:16
Tlapa 12 5 17N33 98w33 6:34:12
Tlalpan 9 6 19N17 99w11 6:36:44
Tlapacoyan 30 1 19N58 97w13 6:28:52
Tlapehuala 12 5 18N13 100w31 6:42:04
Tlaquepaque 14 5 20N39 103w19 6:53:16
Tlatlauqui 21 5 19N51 97w29 6:29:56
Tlaxcala (de Xicoténcatl) 29 5 19N19 98w14 6:32:56
Tlaxcoapan 13 5 20N05 99w13 6:36:52
Tlaxco (de Morelos) 29 5 19N37 98w07 6:32:28
Tlaxiaco 20 1 17N16 97w41 6:30:44
Tlaxmalac 12 5 18N21 99w25 6:37:40
Tlazazalca 16 5 19N58 102w04 6:48:16
Toahayaná 25 7 26N08 107w44 7:10:56
Tochimilco 21 5 18N54 98w34 6:34:16
Todos Santos 3 8 23N27 110w13 7:20:52
Tolimán 14 5 19N36 103w55 6:55:40
Tolimán 22 5 20N55 99w56 6:39:44
Toluca (de Lerdo) 15 5 19N17 99w40 6:38:40
Tomatlán 14 5 19N56 105w15 7:01:00
Tonalá 5 1 16N04 93w45 6:15:00
Tonalá 14 5 20N37 103w14 6:52:56
Tonatico 15 5 18N47 99w41 6:38:44
Tónichi 26 7 28N35 109w34 7:18:16
Tonila 14 5 19N26 103w31 6:54:04
Topia 10 5 25N13 106w34 7:06:16
Topolobampo 25 7 25N36 109w03 7:16:12
Torín 26 7 27N34 110w14 7:20:56
Torreón 7 5 25N33 103w26 6:53:44
Totatiche 14 5 21N56 103w27 6:53:48
Tototlán 14 5 20N33 102w48 6:51:12
Trancoso 32 5 22N44 102w22 6:49:28
Tres Picos 5 1 15N52 93w32 6:14:08
Tres Valles 30 1 18N15 96w08 6:24:32
Trincheras 26 7 30N24 111w32 7:26:08
Trincheras 7 5 25N37 101w55 6:47:40
Trinitaria 5 1 16N07 92w03 6:08:12
Triunfo de Madero 5 1 16N52 93w48 6:15:12
Tubutama 26 7 30N53 111w29 7:25:56
Tuitán 14 5 21N08 103w48 6:55:12
Tula 28 1 23N00 99w43 6:38:52
Tula de Allende 13 5 20N03 99w21 6:37:24
Tulancingo 13 5 20N05 98w22 6:33:28
Tulcingo de Valle 21 5 18N03 98w26 6:33:44
Tulillo 32 5 22N30 104w05 6:56:20
Tultepec 15 5 19N41 99w08 6:36:32
Tultitlán de Mariano Escobedo 15 5 19N39 99w09 6:36:36
Tulum 23 1 20N13 87w28 5:49:52
Tumbiscatio de Ruiz 16 5 18N31 102w21 6:49:24
Tunkás 31 1 20N54 88w45 5:55:00
Tututepec 20 1 16N09 97w38 6:30:32
Tuxpan 14 5 19N33 103w24 6:53:36
Tuxpan 14 7 21N37 104w07 6:56:28
Tuxpan 16 5 19N34 100w28 6:41:52
Tuxpan 18 7 21N57 105w18 7:01:12
Tuxpan de Rodríguez Cano 30 1 20N57 97w24 6:29:36
Tuxtepec 20 1 18N06 96w07 6:24:28
Tuxtla Chico 5 1 14N57 92w10 6:08:40
Tuxtla Gutiérrez 5 1 16N45 93w07 6:12:28
Tuzamapan 30 1 19N24 96w51 6:27:24
Tzimol 5 1 16N16 92w16 6:09:04
Tzucacab 31 1 20N04 89w03 5:56:12
Umán 31 1 20N53 89w45 5:59:00
Uña de Gato 19 5 25N58 99w41 6:38:44
Unión de San Antonio 14 5 21N06 101w58 6:47:52
Unión de Tula 14 5 19N58 104w16 6:57:04
Unión Hidalgo 20 1 16N28 94w50 6:19:20
Ures 26 7 29N26 110w24 7:21:36
Uriangato 11 5 20N09 101w11 6:44:44
Urique 6 5 27N13 107w55 7:11:40
Uruapan 2 4 31N38 116w15 7:45:00
Uruapan (del Progreso) 16 5 19N25 102w04 6:48:16
Usmajac 14 5 19N52 103w34 6:54:16
Uxmal 31 1 20N22 89w46 5:59:04
Vado de Cedillos 6 5 31N05 105w50 7:03:20
Vado de Piedra 6 5 29N50 104w40 6:58:40
Vado Hondo 26 7 31N09 111w22 7:25:28
Valadeces 28 1 26N14 98w40 6:34:40
Valladares 7 5 26N53 100w37 6:42:28
Valladolid 31 1 20N41 88w12 5:52:48
Vallecillo 19 5 26N40 99w58 6:39:52
Valle de Bravo 15 5 19N11 100w08 6:40:32
Valle de Guadalupe 14 5 21N00 102w37 6:50:28
Valle de Juárez 14 5 19N53 102w51 6:51:24
Valle de Olivos 6 5 27N12 106w17 7:05:08
Valle de San José 28 1 23N20 98w24 6:33:36
Valle de Santiago 11 5 20N23 101w12 6:44:48
Valle de Zaragoza 6 5 27N28 105w49 7:03:16
Valle Hermoso 28 1 25N39 97w52 6:31:28
Valle Redondo 2 4 32N31 116w46 7:47:04
Valles → Ciudad de Valles 24 5 21N59 99w01 6:36:04
Valparaíso 32 5 22N46 103w34 6:54:16
Valtierrilla 11 5 20N32 101w08 6:44:32
Vanegas 24 5 23N51 100w52 6:43:28
Velardeña 10 5 25N04 103w44 6:54:56
Venado 24 5 22N56 101w05 6:44:20
Venustiano Carranza 5 1 16N21 92w33 6:10:12
Venustiano Carranza 14 5 19N44 103w47 6:55:08
Veracruz 2 4 32N25 115w05 7:40:20
Veracruz (Llave) 30 1 19N12 96w08 6:24:32
Vergel 10 5 25N39 103w32 6:54:08
Vicente Guerrero 2 4 30N45 116w00 7:44:00
Vicente Guerrero 27 1 18N24 92w53 6:11:32
Vicente Guerrero 29 5 19N08 98w10 6:32:40
Victoria → Ciudad Victoria 28 1 23N44 99w08 6:36:32
Victoria de Durango → Durango 10 5 24N02 104w40 6:58:40
Victor Manuel Bueno 28 1 24N20 98w58 6:35:52
Viesca 7 5 25N21 102w48 6:51:12
Villa Acuña → Ciudad Acuña 7 5 29N18 100w55 6:43:40
Villa Ahumada 6 5 30N37 106w31 7:06:04
Villa Alta 20 1 17N21 96w09 6:24:36
Villa Colón 22 5 20N48 100w03 6:40:12
Villa Corona 14 5 20N25 103w41 6:54:44

Villa Cuauhtémoc 15	5	19N24	99w34	6:38:16
Villa Cuauhtémoc 30	1	22N11	97w50	6:31:20
Villa de Apaseo el Alto 11	5	20N27	100w37	6:42:28
Villa de Arriaga 24	5	21N54	101w23	6:45:32
Villa de Comaltitlán 5	1	15N13	92w35	6:10:20
Villa de Cos 32	5	23N17	102w21	6:49:24
Villa de García 19	5	25N49	100w35	6:42:20
Villa de Guadalupe 24	5	23N22	100w46	6:43:04
Villa del Pueblito 22	5	20N32	100w27	6:41:48
Villa de Méndez 28	1	25N07	98w34	6:34:16
Villa de Reyes 24	5	21N48	100w56	6:43:44
Villa Escalante 16	5	19N24	101w39	6:46:36
Villa Flores 5	1	16N14	93w14	6:12:56
Villa Frontera 7	5	26N56	101w27	6:45:48
Villa García 32	5	22N10	101w57	6:47:48
Villa González 28	1	22N50	98w27	6:33:48
Villa González Ortega 32	5	22N30	101w55	6:47:40
Villagrán 28	1	24N29	99w29	6:37:56
Villagrán 11	5	20N31	100w59	6:43:56
Villa Guerrero 14	5	21N59	103w36	6:54:24
Villa Guerrero 15	5	18N52	99w39	6:38:36
Villahermosa 27	1	17N59	92w55	6:11:40
Villa Hidalgo 2	4	30N59	116w10	7:44:40
Villa Hidalgo 14	5	21N40	102w36	6:50:24
Villa Hidalgo 18	7	21N44	105w15	7:01:00
Villa Jiménez 16	5	19N55	101w35	6:46:20
Villa Juárez 26	7	27N10	109w50	7:19:20
Villa Juárez 24	5	22N20	100w17	6:41:08
Villa López 6	5	27N00	105w02	7:00:08
Villa Madero 16	5	19N24	101w16	6:45:04
Villa Mainero 28	1	24N32	99w38	6:38:32
Villa Morelos 16	5	20N00	101w25	6:45:40
Villanueva 32	5	22N31	102w53	6:51:32
Villa Obregón 14	5	21N07	102w42	6:50:48
Villa Obregón 9	6	19N21	99w11	6:36:44
Villa Orestes Pereyra 10	5	26N31	105w40	7:02:40
Villarreales 19	5	26N07	100w20	6:41:20
Villa Unión 7	5	28N15	100w43	6:42:52
Villa Unión 10	5	23N58	104w02	6:56:08
Villa Unión 25	7	23N12	106w14	7:04:56
Villa Vicente Guerrero 10	5	23N45	103w59	6:55:56
Villa Victoria 16	5	18N47	103w24	6:53:36
Virulento 6	5	28N52	104w21	6:57:24
Vista Hermosa 14	5	19N38	103w22	6:53:28
Vista Hermosa 16	5	20N16	102w29	6:49:56
Walamo 25	7	23N07	106w15	7:05:00
Xadani 20	1	15N56	96w04	6:24:16
Xalpatláhuac 12	5	17N01	99w18	6:37:12
Xaltianguis 12	5	17N04	99w50	6:39:20
X-Can 31	1	20N50	87w43	5:50:52
Xico 30	1	19N25	97w00	6:28:00
Xicoténcatl 28	1	23N00	98w56	6:35:44
Xicotepec de Juárez 21	5	20N17	97w57	6:31:48
Xilitla 24	5	21N20	98w58	6:35:52
Xkalak 23	1	18N16	87w50	5:51:20
Xochapa 30	1	17N39	95w46	6:23:04
Xochimilco 9	6	19N15	99w08	6:36:32
Xochipala 12	5	17N48	99w39	6:38:36
Xochistlahuaca 12	5	16N47	98w15	6:33:00
Xochitlán 21	5	19N59	97w36	6:30:24
Xoxocotla 17	5	18N41	99w15	6:37:00
Yago 18	7	21N50	105w04	7:00:16
Yahualica 14	5	21N08	102w51	6:51:24
Yanga 30	1	18N50	96w48	6:27:12
Yaqui 26	7	27N19	110w01	7:20:04
Yautepec 17	5	18N53	99w04	6:36:16
Yavaros 26	7	26N42	109w31	7:18:04
Yecapixtla 17	5	18N53	98w52	6:35:28
Yécora 26	7	28N20	108w58	7:15:52
Yepachic 6	5	28N26	108w23	7:13:32
Yurécuaro 16	5	20N20	102w18	6:49:12
Yuriria 11	5	20N12	101w09	6:44:36
Zaachila 20	1	16N57	96w45	6:27:00
Zacapoaxtla 21	5	19N53	97w35	6:30:20
Zacapu 16	5	19N50	101w43	6:46:52
Zacatecas 32	5	22N47	102w35	6:50:20
Zacatepec 17	5	18N39	99w12	6:36:48
Zacatlán 21	5	19N56	97w58	6:31:52
Zacatongo 14	5	20N49	104w33	6:58:12
Zacoalco de Torres 14	5	20N14	103w35	6:54:20
Zacpa 14	5	21N38	102w58	6:51:52
Zacualpan 18	7	21N15	105w10	7:00:40
Zacualpan 30	1	20N28	98w22	6:33:28
Zacualtipán 13	5	20N39	98w36	6:34:24
Zamora de Hidalgo 16	5	19N59	102w16	6:49:04
Zanatepec 20	1	16N29	94w21	6:17:24
Zapopan 14	5	20N43	103w24	6:53:36
Zapotiltic 14	5	19N37	103w26	6:53:44
Zapotitlán 14	5	19N31	103w44	6:54:56
Zapotitlán Tablas 12	5	17N25	98w45	6:35:00
Zapotlanejo 14	5	20N38	103w04	6:52:16
Zaragoza 6	5	31N39	106w20	7:05:20
Zaragoza 7	5	28N29	100w55	6:43:40
Zaragoza 19	5	23N58	99w46	6:39:04
Zaragoza 21	5	19N46	97w33	6:30:12
Zaragoza 24	5	22N02	100w44	6:42:56
Zempoala 30	1	19N24	96w24	6:25:36
Zicapa 12	5	17N57	99w02	6:36:08
Zihuatanejo 12	5	17N38	101w33	6:46:12
Zimapán 13	5	20N45	99w21	6:37:24
Zimatlán de Alvarez 20	1	16N52	96w47	6:27:08
Zinacatepec 21	5	18N20	97w15	6:29:00
Zinapécuaro (de Figueroa) 16	5	19N52	100w49	6:43:16
Zirándaro 12	5	18N27	100w59	6:43:56
Zitácuaro 16	5	19N24	100w22	6:41:28
Zitlala 12	5	17N38	99w05	6:36:20
Zitlaltepec 29	5	19N12	97w54	6:31:36
Zumpango 15	5	19N48	99w06	6:36:24
Zumpango del Río 12	5	17N39	99w30	6:38:00

MIDWAY ISLANDS MIDWAY ISLANDS

Time Table
Before 1/Jan/1901 LMT
Begin Standard 165w00
1/Jan/1901 0:00 11:00

Eastern Island	28N12	177w20	11:49:20
Middle Ground	28N15	177w25	11:49:40
Midway Islands	28N13	177w22	11:49:28
Midway Naval Station	28N13	177w26	11:49:44
North Breakers	28N14	177w25	11:49:40
Sand Island	28N12	177w23	11:49:32
Sand Islet	28N16	177w23	11:49:32

MÓNACO MONACO

Time Table
Before 15/Mar/1891 LMT
Begin Standard 2E20
15/Mar/1891 0:01 -0:09
Begin Standard 0w00

11/Mar/1911	0:00	0:00
14/Jun/1916	23:00	-1:00
1/Oct/1916	24:00	0:00
24/Mar/1917	23:00	-1:00
7/Oct/1917	24:00	0:00
9/Mar/1918	23:00	-1:00
6/Oct/1918	24:00	0:00
1/Mar/1919	23:00	-1:00
5/Oct/1919	24:00	0:00
14/Feb/1920	23:00	-1:00
23/Oct/1920	24:00	0:00
14/Mar/1921	23:00	-1:00
25/Oct/1921	24:00	0:00
25/Mar/1922	23:00	-1:00
7/Oct/1922	24:00	0:00
26/May/1923	23:00	-1:00
6/Oct/1923	24:00	0:00
29/Mar/1924	23:00	-1:00
4/Oct/1924	24:00	0:00
4/Apr/1925	23:00	-1:00
3/Oct/1925	24:00	0:00
17/Apr/1926	23:00	-1:00
2/Oct/1926	24:00	0:00
9/Apr/1927	23:00	-1:00
1/Oct/1927	24:00	0:00
14/Apr/1928	23:00	-1:00
6/Oct/1928	24:00	0:00
20/Apr/1929	23:00	-1:00
5/Oct/1929	24:00	0:00
12/Apr/1930	23:00	-1:00
4/Oct/1930	24:00	0:00
18/Apr/1931	23:00	-1:00
3/Oct/1931	24:00	0:00
2/Apr/1932	23:00	-1:00
1/Oct/1932	24:00	0:00
25/Mar/1933	23:00	-1:00
7/Oct/1933	24:00	0:00
7/Apr/1934	23:00	-1:00
6/Oct/1934	24:00	0:00
30/Mar/1935	23:00	-1:00
5/Oct/1935	24:00	0:00
18/Apr/1936	23:00	-1:00
3/Oct/1936	24:00	0:00
3/Apr/1937	23:00	-1:00
2/Oct/1937	24:00	0:00
26/Mar/1938	23:00	-1:00
1/Oct/1938	24:00	0:00
15/Apr/1939	23:00	-1:00
18/Nov/1939	24:00	0:00
25/Feb/1940	2:00	-1:00
4/May/1941	24:00	-2:00
6/Oct/1941	1:00	-1:00
8/Mar/1942	24:00	-2:00
2/Nov/1942	3:00	-1:00
29/Mar/1943	2:00	-2:00
4/Oct/1943	3:00	-1:00
3/Apr/1944	2:00	-2:00
8/Oct/1944	1:00	-1:00
2/Apr/1945	2:00	-2:00
Begin Standard		1E00
16/Sep/1945	3:00	-1:00
28/Mar/1976	2:00	-2:00
26/Sep/1976	3:00	-1:00
3/Apr/1977	2:00	-2:00
25/Sep/1977	3:00	-1:00
2/Apr/1978	2:00	-2:00
1/Oct/1978	3:00	-1:00
1/Apr/1979	2:00	-2:00
30/Sep/1979	3:00	-1:00
6/Apr/1980	2:00	-2:00
28/Sep/1980	3:00	-1:00
29/Mar/1981	2:00	-2:00
27/Sep/1981	3:00	-1:00
28/Mar/1982	2:00	-2:00
26/Sep/1982	3:00	-1:00
27/Mar/1983	2:00	-2:00
25/Sep/1983	3:00	-1:00
25/Mar/1984	2:00	-2:00
30/Sep/1984	3:00	-1:00
31/Mar/1985	2:00	-2:00
29/Sep/1985	3:00	-1:00
30/Mar/1986	2:00	-2:00
28/Sep/1986	3:00	-1:00
29/Mar/1987	2:00	-2:00
27/Sep/1987	3:00	-1:00
27/Mar/1988	2:00	-2:00
25/Sep/1988	3:00	-1:00
26/Mar/1989	2:00	-2:00
24/Sep/1989	3:00	-1:00
25/Mar/1990	2:00	-2:00
30/Sep/1990	3:00	-1:00
31/Mar/1991	2:00	-2:00
29/Sep/1991	3:00	-1:00
29/Mar/1992	2:00	-2:00
27/Sep/1992	3:00	-1:00
28/Mar/1993	2:00	-2:00
26/Sep/1993	3:00	-1:00
27/Mar/1994	2:00	-2:00
25/Sep/1994	3:00	-1:00
26/Mar/1995	2:00	-2:00
24/Sep/1995	3:00	-1:00
31/Mar/1996	2:00	-2:00
29/Sep/1996	3:00	-1:00
30/Mar/1997	2:00	-2:00
28/Sep/1997	3:00	-1:00
29/Mar/1998	2:00	-2:00
27/Sep/1998	3:00	-1:00
28/Mar/1999	2:00	-2:00
26/Sep/1999	3:00	-1:00
26/Mar/2000	2:00	-2:00
24/Sep/2000	3:00	-1:00

Monaco	43N42	7E23	-0:29:32
Monte Carlo	43N45	7E25	-0:29:40

MONGOLIA MONGOLIE MONGOLEI MONGOL ARD ULS

Time Table # 1

Date	Time	Offset
Before 1/Aug/1905	LMT	
Begin Standard	90E00	
1/Aug/1905	0:00	-6:00
Begin Standard	105E00	
1/Jan/1978	0:00	-7:00
1/Apr/1983	0:00	-8:00
1/Oct/1983	0:00	-7:00
1/Apr/1984	0:00	-8:00
1/Oct/1984	0:00	-7:00
31/Mar/1985	1:00	-8:00
29/Sep/1985	2:00	-7:00
30/Mar/1986	1:00	-8:00
28/Sep/1986	2:00	-7:00
29/Mar/1987	1:00	-8:00
27/Sep/1987	2:00	-7:00
27/Mar/1988	1:00	-8:00
25/Sep/1988	2:00	-7:00
26/Mar/1989	1:00	-8:00
24/Sep/1989	2:00	-7:00
25/Mar/1990	1:00	-8:00
30/Sep/1990	2:00	-7:00
31/Mar/1991	1:00	-8:00
29/Sep/1991	2:00	-7:00
29/Mar/1992	1:00	-8:00
27/Sep/1992	2:00	-7:00
28/Mar/1993	1:00	-8:00
26/Sep/1993	2:00	-7:00
27/Mar/1994	1:00	-8:00
25/Sep/1994	2:00	-7:00
26/Mar/1995	1:00	-8:00
24/Sep/1995	2:00	-7:00
31/Mar/1996	1:00	-8:00
29/Sep/1996	2:00	-7:00
30/Mar/1997	1:00	-8:00
28/Sep/1997	2:00	-7:00
29/Mar/1998	1:00	-8:00
27/Sep/1998	2:00	-7:00
28/Mar/1999	1:00	-8:00
26/Sep/1999	2:00	-7:00
26/Mar/2000	1:00	-8:00
24/Sep/2000	2:00	-7:00

Time Table # 2

Date	Time	Offset
Before 1/Aug/1905	LMT	
Begin Standard	105E00	
1/Aug/1905	0:00	-7:00
Begin Standard	120E00	
1/Jan/1978	0:00	-8:00
1/Apr/1983	0:00	-9:00
1/Oct/1983	0:00	-8:00
1/Apr/1984	0:00	-9:00
1/Oct/1984	0:00	-8:00
31/Mar/1985	1:00	-9:00
29/Sep/1985	2:00	-8:00
30/Mar/1986	1:00	-9:00
28/Sep/1986	2:00	-8:00
29/Mar/1987	1:00	-9:00
27/Sep/1987	2:00	-8:00
27/Mar/1988	1:00	-9:00
25/Sep/1988	2:00	-8:00
26/Mar/1989	1:00	-9:00
24/Sep/1989	2:00	-8:00
25/Mar/1990	1:00	-9:00
30/Sep/1990	2:00	-8:00
31/Mar/1991	1:00	-9:00
29/Sep/1991	2:00	-8:00
29/Mar/1992	1:00	-9:00
27/Sep/1992	2:00	-8:00
28/Mar/1993	1:00	-9:00
26/Sep/1993	2:00	-8:00
27/Mar/1994	1:00	-9:00
25/Sep/1994	2:00	-8:00
26/Mar/1995	1:00	-9:00
24/Sep/1995	2:00	-8:00
31/Mar/1996	1:00	-9:00
29/Sep/1996	2:00	-8:00
30/Mar/1997	1:00	-9:00
28/Sep/1997	2:00	-8:00
29/Mar/1998	1:00	-9:00
27/Sep/1998	2:00	-8:00
28/Mar/1999	1:00	-9:00
26/Sep/1999	2:00	-8:00
26/Mar/2000	1:00	-9:00
24/Sep/2000	2:00	-8:00

Time Table # 3

Date	Time	Offset
Before 1/Aug/1905	LMT	
Begin Standard	105E00	
1/Aug/1905	0:00	-7:00
Begin Standard	120E00	
1/Jan/1978	0:00	-8:00
Begin Standard	135E00	
1/Apr/1983	0:00	-10:00
1/Oct/1983	0:00	-9:00
1/Apr/1984	0:00	-10:00
1/Oct/1984	0:00	-9:00
31/Mar/1985	1:00	-10:00
29/Sep/1985	2:00	-9:00
30/Mar/1986	1:00	-10:00
28/Sep/1986	2:00	-9:00
29/Mar/1987	1:00	-10:00
27/Sep/1987	2:00	-9:00
27/Mar/1988	1:00	-10:00
25/Sep/1988	2:00	-9:00
26/Mar/1989	1:00	-10:00
24/Sep/1989	2:00	-9:00
25/Mar/1990	1:00	-10:00
30/Sep/1990	2:00	-9:00
31/Mar/1991	1:00	-10:00
29/Sep/1991	2:00	-9:00
29/Mar/1992	1:00	-10:00
27/Sep/1992	2:00	-9:00
28/Mar/1993	1:00	-10:00
26/Sep/1993	2:00	-9:00
27/Mar/1994	1:00	-10:00
25/Sep/1994	2:00	-9:00
26/Mar/1995	1:00	-10:00
24/Sep/1995	2:00	-9:00
31/Mar/1996	1:00	-10:00
29/Sep/1996	2:00	-9:00
30/Mar/1997	1:00	-10:00
28/Sep/1997	2:00	-9:00
29/Mar/1998	1:00	-10:00
27/Sep/1998	2:00	-9:00
28/Mar/1999	1:00	-10:00
26/Sep/1999	2:00	-9:00
26/Mar/2000	1:00	-10:00
24/Sep/2000	2:00	-9:00

Place	TT	Lat	Long	Offset
Agaruut	2	43N10	109E26	-7:17:44
Ak-Aral	1	49N10	90E57	-6:03:48
Altaj (Jesönbulag)	1	46N20	96E18	-6:25:12
Altaj	1	48N18	89E35	-5:58:20
Altanbulag	2	50N19	106E30	-7:06:00
Altanbulag	2	47N41	106E22	-7:05:28
Altancögc	1	49N03	90E27	-6:01:48
Altan-Cögor	1	49N03	90E27	-6:01:48
Altanširee	2	45N35	110E27	-7:21:48
Arvajcheer	2	46N15	102E48	-6:51:12
Baacagaan	2	45N35	99E27	-6:37:48
Bajan-Adraga	2	48N32	111E03	-7:24:12
Bajan Agt	2	49N02	102E05	-6:48:20
Bajancagaan	2	45N00	98E59	-6:35:56
Bajan Chajrchan	1	49N18	96E20	-6:25:20
Bajanchongor	2	46N08	100E43	-6:42:52
Bajancogt	2	45N54	106E10	-7:04:40
Bajandalaj	2	43N28	103E28	-6:53:52
Bajandelger	2	47N44	108E07	-7:12:28
Bajandelger	3	45N40	112E20	-7:29:20
Bajan Dün	3	49N13	113E23	-7:33:32
Bajandžargalan	2	45N40	107E59	-7:11:56
Bajan Dzürch	2	50N12	98E58	-6:35:52
Bajan-Enger	1	48N25	90E50	-6:03:20
Bajango	2	48N55	106E06	-7:04:24
Bajangov'	2	44N44	100E24	-6:41:36
Bajanleg	2	44N33	100E50	-6:43:20
Bajannuur	1	48N54	91E14	-6:04:56
Bajan-Öndör	2	44N47	98E39	-6:34:36
Bajan-Ovoo	2	47N47	112E05	-7:28:20
Bajan-Ovoo	2	42N57	106E07	-7:04:28
Bajan Tümen	3	48N04	114E24	-7:37:36
Bajan Uul	2	47N40	101E30	-6:46:00
Bajan Uul	3	49N10	112E50	-7:31:20
Bajan Uul	1	49N41	96E20	-6:25:20
Baruun Bajan-Ulaan	2	45N10	101E24	-6:45:36
Baruun-Urt	3	46N42	113E15	-7:33:00
Batcengel	2	47N47	101E58	-6:47:52
Batnorov	2	47N55	111E30	-7:26:00
Bat Sûmber	2	48N29	106E42	-7:06:48
Beger	1	45N42	97E10	-6:28:40
Bičigt	1	47N06	95E05	-6:20:20
Binder	2	48N35	110E36	-7:22:24
Böchmörön	1	49N40	90E20	-6:01:20
Bogd	2	45N11	100E43	-6:42:52
Bugat	1	48N59	90E10	-6:00:40
Bugat	2	47N55	101E16	-6:45:04
Bujant	1	48N33	89E34	-5:58:16
Bujant	1	48N10	91E55	-6:07:40
Bujant-Ovoo	2	44N58	107E05	-7:08:20
Bulgan	1	46N53	91E05	-6:04:20
Bulgan	2	48N45	103E34	-6:54:16
Bulgan	2	44N05	103E32	-6:54:08
Bureg Changaj	2	48N14	103E57	-6:55:48
Büren	1	47N13	95E54	-6:23:36
Büren Chaan	2	49N29	99E14	-6:36:56
Cachir	2	48N06	98E52	-6:35:28
Cagaan Chajrchan	1	49N25	94E15	-6:17:00
Cagaangol	1	48N57	89E07	-5:56:28
Cagaannuur	1	49N32	89E42	-5:58:48
Cagaannuur	2	50N20	105E03	-7:00:12
Cagaan-Ovoo	2	45N51	105E17	-7:01:08
Cagaan Uul	2	49N28	98E30	-6:34:00
Cagaan Üür	2	50N32	101E30	-6:46:00
Čandman'	1	45N20	97E59	-6:31:56
Candman'	1	50N02	92E03	-6:08:12
Čarüngol	2	49N14	106E29	-7:05:56
Cecer Chaan → Öndörchaan	2	47N19	110E39	-7:22:36
Cecerleg	2	48N52	101E14	-6:44:56
Cecerleg	2	47N30	101E27	-6:45:48
Cecerleg	2	49N30	97E36	-6:30:24
Ceel	1	45N36	95E51	-6:23:24
Cenchermandal	2	47N37	109E05	-7:16:20
Cengel	1	48N56	89E10	-5:56:40
Chajrchan	2	48N35	101E56	-6:47:44
Chajrchandulaan	2	45N57	102E03	-6:48:12
Chalchgol	3	48N11	114E54	-7:39:36
Chaliun	2	48N50	103E59	-6:55:56
Chanbogd	2	43N12	107E10	-7:08:40
Chanch	2	51N30	100E40	-6:42:40
Chanchongor	2	43N50	104E25	-6:57:40
Chandman'	1	50N02	92E03	-6:08:12
Changaj	2	47N52	99E28	-6:37:52
Changal	2	49N19	104E24	-6:57:36
Char-Ajrag	2	45N49	109E17	-7:17:08
Chatanbulag	2	43N09	109E08	-7:16:32
Chatgal	2	50N26	100E09	-6:40:36
Chentij	2	48N05	109E45	-7:19:00
Chišig Öndör	2	48N19	103E25	-6:53:40
Chjargas	1	49N32	93E48	-6:15:12
Chöchmor't	1	47N21	94E33	-6:18:12
Chölönbujr	3	47N55	112E57	-7:31:48
Chongor	3	45N59	112E45	-7:31:00
Chovd	1	49N16	90E30	-6:02:00
Chovd	1	48N08	91E23	-6:05:32
Chovd	1	48N01	91E38	-6:06:32
Chovd	2	44N42	102E24	-6:49:36
Chövsgöl	2	43N36	109E39	-7:18:36
Chudzirt	1	47N05	91E10	-6:04:40
Chuld	2	45N04	105E35	-7:02:20
Chürmen	2	43N20	104E05	-6:56:20
Chutag	2	49N23	102E43	-6:50:52
Chutag Uul	2	43N23	110E13	-7:20:52
Cogt	1	45N20	96E38	-6:26:32
Cogtoandman'	2	45N50	104E28	-6:57:52
Cogt-Ovoo	2	44N25	105E20	-7:01:20
Čojbalsan	3	48N25	114E52	-7:39:28
Čojbalsan	3	48N04	114E30	-7:38:00
Čuluunchoroot	3	49N41	114E15	-7:37:00
Čuluut	2	45N48	107E05	-7:08:20
Dadal	2	49N01	111E37	-7:26:28
Dalajchöl	1	47N59	90E47	-6:03:08
Dalan Dzadgad	2	43N37	104E29	-6:57:56
Dalandžargalan	2	45N55	109E05	-7:16:20
Darchan	2	49N29	105E55	-7:03:40
Dariganga	3	45N18	113E52	-7:35:28
Dariv	1	46N57	93E38	-6:14:32
Daš Balbar	3	49N31	114E21	-7:37:24
Dašinčilen	2	47N51	104E03	-6:56:12
Davst	1	50N36	92E28	-6:09:52
Delgerchangaj	2	45N15	104E50	-6:59:20
Delgerchet	2	45N52	110E26	-7:21:44
Delgercogt	2	46N08	106E23	-7:05:32
Delgerech	2	45N48	111E12	-7:24:48
Delüün	1	47N42	90E59	-6:03:56
Dörvöldžin	1	48N08	93E58	-6:15:52
Duut	1	47N30	91E40	-6:06:40
Dzaamar	2	48N10	104E50	-6:59:20
Dzachuj	1	44N59	96E37	-6:26:28
Džargalant → Chovd	1	48N01	91E39	-6:06:36
Džargalant	2	48N40	100E43	-6:42:52
Džargalant	3	46N57	115E15	-7:41:00
Džargalant	2	48N33	99E20	-6:37:20
Džargaltchaan	2	47N28	109E30	-7:18:00
Dzavchan	1	48N48	93E07	-6:12:28
Dzavchan Mandal	1	48N19	95E07	-6:20:28
Džavchlant → Uliastaj	1	47N45	96E49	-6:27:16
Džinst	2	45N24	100E35	-6:42:20
Dzürch	2	48N55	100E10	-6:40:40
Dzüün Changaj	1	49N17	95E14	-6:20:56
Džüün Charaa	2	48N52	106E28	-7:05:52
Dzüün Gov	1	49N55	93E47	-6:15:08
Dzuunmod	2	47N45	106E55	-7:07:40
Erdene	2	47N48	107E55	-7:11:40
Erdene	2	44N15	111E14	-7:24:56
Erdene	1	45N08	97E45	-6:31:00
Erdene Bulgan	2	50N07	101E35	-6:46:20
Erdenebüren	1	48N26	91E27	-6:05:48
Erdenedalaj	2	46N02	104E55	-6:59:40
Erdene Mandal	2	48N30	101E21	-6:45:24
Galt	2	48N46	99E53	-6:39:32
Galuut	3	48N33	113E12	-7:32:48
Gučin-Us	2	45N27	102E25	-6:49:40
Günnarijn	2	45N38	102E01	-6:48:04
Gurvanbulag	2	47N38	103E31	-6:54:04
Gurvansajchan	2	45N32	107E00	-7:08:00
Gurvantes	2	43N26	101E36	-6:46:24
Hantaj	2	49N31	103E13	-6:52:52
Hudžirt	1	47N05	91E10	-6:04:40
Ichbulag	3	45N21	113E10	-7:32:40
Ichdžargalan	2	45N31	108E48	-7:15:12
Ichtamir	2	47N30	100E52	-6:43:28
Ich Uul	1	48N33	98E40	-6:34:40
Ich Uul	2	49N27	101E27	-6:45:48
Ider	1	48N13	97E23	-6:29:32
Idermeg	2	47N40	111E05	-7:24:20
Jaruu	1	48N08	96E45	-6:27:00
Jeröö	2	49N45	106E40	-7:06:40
Jesönbulag → Altaj	1	46N20	96E18	-6:25:12
Lün	2	47N24	102E52	-6:51:28
Lün	2	47N52	105E15	-7:01:00
Luus	2	45N30	105E45	-7:03:00
Malčin	1	49N44	93E18	-6:13:12
Mandach	2	44N28	108E11	-7:12:44
Mandalgov'	2	45N45	106E12	-7:04:48
Mandal-Ovoo	2	44N35	104E05	-6:56:20
Manlaj	2	44N07	106E50	-7:07:20
Matad	3	46N58	115E18	-7:41:12
Mjangad	1	48N15	91E57	-6:07:48
Mogod	2	48N24	103E00	-6:52:00
Möngön Mor't	2	48N11	108E29	-7:13:56
Mörön	2	48N15	100E23	-6:41:32
Mörön	2	47N24	110E16	-7:21:04
Mörön	2	49N38	100E10	-6:40:40
Nalajch	2	47N45	107E16	-7:09:04
Naran	1	48N34	98E17	-6:33:08
Naranbulag	1	49N22	92E33	-6:10:12
Narijnteel	2	45N57	101E29	-6:45:56
Nogoonnuur	1	49N33	90E17	-6:01:08
Nojon	2	43N10	102E07	-6:48:28
Nomgon	2	45N26	105E08	-7:00:32
Nomgon	2	42N50	105E07	-7:00:28
Norovlin	2	48N40	112E00	-7:28:00
Ojgor	1	49N10	89E17	-5:57:08
Öldzijt	2	48N07	102E34	-6:50:16
Öldzijt	2	45N18	106E12	-7:04:48
Ölgij	1	48N56	89E57	-5:59:48
Ölgij	1	48N59	92E01	-6:08:04
Ömnödelger	2	47N52	109E55	-7:19:40
Ömnögov'	1	49N06	91E43	-6:06:52
Öndörchaan	2	47N19	110E39	-7:22:36
Öndör Changaj	1	49N20	94E50	-6:19:20
Öndör-Önc	2	45N51	103E11	-6:52:44
Öndöršireet	2	47N27	104E50	-6:59:20
Öndör Ulaan	2	48N03	100E30	-6:42:00
Ongon	3	45N21	113E09	-7:32:36
Onon	3	49N08	112E38	-7:30:32
Orchon	2	49N09	105E21	-7:01:24
Orchon Tuul	2	48N58	104E59	-6:59:56
Otgon	1	47N11	97E33	-6:30:12
Rašaant	2	49N07	101E25	-6:45:40
Rinčinlchümbe	2	51N07	99E40	-6:38:40
Šaamar	2	50N08	106E10	-7:04:40
Sagil	1	50N20	91E40	-6:06:40
Sagsaj	1	48N54	89E37	-5:58:28
Sajchan	2	48N40	102E39	-6:50:36
Sajchandulaan	2	44N40	109E01	-7:16:04
Sajchan-Ovoo	2	45N27	103E54	-6:55:36
Sajnšand	2	44N52	110E09	-7:20:36
Selenge	2	49N25	103E59	-6:55:56
Sevrej	2	43N35	102E12	-6:48:48
Šine Ider	2	48N56	99E33	-6:38:12
Songino	1	48N54	95E54	-6:23:36
Süchbaatar	2	50N15	106E12	-7:04:48
Sulincheer	2	42N41	109E20	-7:17:20
Sümber	2	46N21	108E20	-7:13:20
Tamsagbulag	3	47N14	117E21	-7:49:24
Tarialan	1	49N47	91E55	-6:07:40
Tariat	2	48N06	99E32	-6:38:08
Telmen	1	48N38	97E37	-6:30:28
Tes	1	50N27	93E30	-6:14:00
Tešig	2	49N56	102E34	-6:50:16
Tögrög	1	45N46	94E48	-6:19:12
Tögrög	2	45N32	102E59	-6:51:56
Tolbonuur	1	48N25	90E17	-6:01:08
Tömör Bulag	2	49N16	100E15	-6:41:00
Toson Cengel	1	48N47	98E15	-6:33:00
Türgen	1	50N04	91E36	-6:06:24
Ugtaal Cajdam	2	48N17	105E25	-7:01:40
Ulaanbaatar	2	47N55	106E53	-7:07:32
Ulaanbadrach	2	44N07	110E11	-7:20:44
Ulaanchus	1	49N02	89E23	-5:57:32
Ulaangom	1	49N58	92E02	-6:08:08
Ulan Bator → Ulaan Baatar	2	47N55	106E53	-7:07:32
Uliast	1	48N57	91E17	-6:05:08
Uliastaj (Džavchlant)	1	47N45	96E49	-6:27:16

MONGOL ARD ULS — MONGOLEI — MONGOLIE — MONGOLIA

Place	Div	Lat	Long	Offset
Un't	2	49N07	102E50	-6:51:20
Urga → Ulaan Baatar	2	47N55	106E53	-7:07:32
Urgamal	1	48N29	94E20	-6:17:20

MONTSERRAT — MONTSERRAT

Time Table
Before 1/Jul/1911 LMT
Begin Standard 60w00
1/Jul/1911 0:01 4:00

Place	Lat	Long	Offset
Plymouth	16N42	62w13	4:08:52
Salem	16N45	62w15	4:09:00

AL-MAGREB — MAROKKO — MAROC — MARRUECOS — MOROCCO

Time Table # 1
Before 26/Oct/1913 LMT
Begin Standard 0w00
26/Oct/1913 0:00 0:00
12/Sep/1939 0:00 -1:00
19/Nov/1939 0:00 0:00
25/Feb/1940 0:00 -1:00
18/Nov/1945 0:00 0:00
11/Jun/1950 0:00 -1:00
29/Oct/1950 0:00 0:00
3/Jun/1967 12:00 -1:00
1/Oct/1967 0:00 0:00
24/Jun/1974 0:00 -1:00
1/Sep/1974 0:00 0:00
1/May/1976 0:00 -1:00
1/Aug/1976 0:00 0:00
1/May/1977 0:00 -1:00
28/Sep/1977 0:00 0:00
1/Jun/1978 0:00 -1:00
4/Aug/1978 0:00 0:00
Begin Standard 15E00
16/Mar/1984 0:00 -1:00
Begin Standard 0w00
1/Jan/1986 0:00 0:00
....

Time Table # 2
Before 26/Oct/1917 LMT
Begin Standard 0w00
26/Oct/1917 0:00 0:00
6/May/1918 23:00 -1:00
7/Oct/1918 23:00 0:00
16/Apr/1924 23:00 -1:00
4/Oct/1924 23:00 0:00
17/Apr/1926 23:00 -1:00
2/Oct/1926 23:00 0:00
9/Apr/1927 23:00 -1:00
1/Oct/1927 23:00 0:00
14/Apr/1928 23:00 -1:00
6/Oct/1928 23:00 0:00
3/Jun/1967 12:00 -1:00
1/Oct/1967 0:00 0:00
24/Jun/1974 0:00 -1:00
1/Sep/1974 0:00 0:00
1/May/1976 0:00 -1:00
1/Aug/1976 0:00 0:00
1/May/1977 0:00 -1:00
28/Sep/1977 0:00 0:00
1/Jun/1978 0:00 -1:00
4/Aug/1978 0:00 0:00
Begin Standard 15E00
16/Mar/1984 0:00 -1:00
Begin Standard 0w00
1/Jan/1986 0:00 0:00
....

Time Table # 3
Before 1/Jan/1931 LMT
Begin Standard 0w00
1/Jan/1931 0:00 0:00
24/Jun/1974 0:00 -1:00
1/Sep/1974 0:00 0:00
1/May/1976 0:00 -1:00
1/Aug/1976 0:00 0:00
1/May/1977 0:00 -1:00
28/Sep/1977 0:00 0:00
1/Jun/1978 0:00 -1:00
4/Aug/1978 0:00 0:00
Begin Standard 15E00
16/Mar/1984 0:00 -1:00
Begin Standard 0w00
1/Jan/1986 0:00 0:00
....

Time Table # 4
Before 1/Jan/1934 LMT
Begin Standard 15w00
1/Jan/1934 0:00 1:00
Begin Standard 0w00
14/Apr/1976 0:00 0:00
....

Time Table # 5
Before 1/Jan/1901 LMT
Begin Standard 0w00
1/Jan/1901 0:00 0:00
6/May/1918 23:00 -1:00
7/Oct/1918 23:00 0:00
16/Apr/1924 23:00 -1:00
4/Oct/1924 23:00 0:00
17/Apr/1926 23:00 -1:00
2/Oct/1926 23:00 0:00
9/Apr/1927 23:00 -1:00
1/Oct/1927 23:00 0:00
14/Apr/1928 23:00 -1:00
6/Oct/1928 23:00 0:00
3/Jun/1967 12:00 -1:00
1/Oct/1967 0:00 0:00
24/Jun/1974 0:00 -1:00
1/Sep/1974 0:00 0:00
1/May/1976 0:00 -1:00
1/Aug/1976 0:00 0:00
1/May/1977 0:00 -1:00
28/Sep/1977 0:00 0:00
1/Jun/1978 0:00 -1:00
4/Aug/1978 0:00 0:00
Begin Standard 15E00
16/Mar/1984 0:00 -1:00
30/Mar/1986 2:00 -2:00
28/Sep/1986 3:00 -1:00
29/Mar/1987 2:00 -2:00
27/Sep/1987 3:00 -1:00
27/Mar/1988 2:00 -2:00
25/Sep/1988 3:00 -1:00
26/Mar/1989 2:00 -2:00
24/Sep/1989 3:00 -1:00
25/Mar/1990 2:00 -2:00
30/Sep/1990 3:00 -1:00
31/Mar/1991 2:00 -2:00
29/Sep/1991 3:00 -1:00
29/Mar/1992 2:00 -2:00
27/Sep/1992 3:00 -1:00
28/Mar/1993 2:00 -2:00
26/Sep/1993 3:00 -1:00
27/Mar/1994 2:00 -2:00
25/Sep/1994 3:00 -1:00
26/Mar/1995 2:00 -2:00
24/Sep/1995 3:00 -1:00
31/Mar/1996 2:00 -2:00
29/Sep/1996 3:00 -1:00
30/Mar/1997 2:00 -2:00
28/Sep/1997 3:00 -1:00
29/Mar/1998 2:00 -2:00
27/Sep/1998 3:00 -1:00
28/Mar/1999 2:00 -2:00
26/Sep/1999 3:00 -1:00
26/Mar/2000 2:00 -2:00
24/Sep/2000 3:00 -1:00

DIVISIONS

1. Morocco
2. Tangier (since 1956)
3. Sidi Ifni (since 1969)
4. Western Sahara (since 1976)
5. Spanish Morocco

Place	Div	Lat	Long	Offset
Aaiun → El Aaiún 4	4	27N09	13w12	0:52:48
Aazanèn 1	1	35N13	3w10	0:12:40
Agadir 1	1	30N26	9w36	0:38:24
Ahfir 1	1	34N57	2w17	0:09:08
Aït-Melloul 1	1	30N21	9w31	0:38:04
Aït-Ourir 1	1	31N38	7w42	0:30:48
Ait Youssef ou Ali 1	1	35N13	3w55	0:15:40
Aiún → El Aaiún 4	4	27N09	13w12	0:52:48
Akka 1	1	29N22	8w14	0:32:56
Aknoul 1	1	34N43	3w49	0:15:16
Alcazarquivir → Er-Rachidia 1	1	31N58	4w25	0:17:40
Alcazarquivir → Ksar-El-Kebir 1	1	35N01	5w54	0:23:36
Al Hajeb 1	1	33N43	5w13	0:20:52
Al-Hoceima 1	1	35N15	3w55	0:15:40
Amerzgane 1	1	31N00	7w10	0:28:40
Amizmiz 1	1	31N14	8w14	0:32:56
Arbaoua 1	1	34N54	5w56	0:23:44
Asilah 1	1	35N32	6w00	0:24:00
Asni 1	1	31N14	7w55	0:31:40
Assa 1	1	28N34	9w27	0:37:48
Azemmour 1	1	33N20	8w25	0:33:40
Azilal 1	1	31N58	6w34	0:26:16
Azrou 1	1	33N27	5w14	0:20:56
Bab-Taza 1	1	35N03	5w14	0:20:56
Benahmed 1	1	33N07	7w17	0:29:08
Benguerir 1	1	32N14	7w57	0:31:48
Beni-Mellal 1	1	32N22	6w29	0:25:56
Ben-Slimane 1	1	33N41	7w10	0:28:40
Berguent 1	1	34N03	2w02	0:08:08
Berkane 1	1	34N59	2w20	0:09:20
Berrechid 1	1	33N17	7w35	0:30:20
Bine-El-Ouidane 1	1	32N07	6w26	0:25:44
Bou Ahmed 1	1	35N25	5w00	0:20:00
Bou Anane 1	1	32N03	3w03	0:12:12
Bou Arfa 1	1	32N30	1w59	0:07:56
Boudenib 1	1	31N57	4w38	0:18:32
Boudnib 1	1	31N57	4w38	0:18:32
Bou Izakarn 1	1	29N09	9w44	0:38:56
Boujad 1	1	32N48	6w26	0:25:44
Boulmane 1	1	33N22	4w45	0:19:00
Boumalne 1	1	31N32	5w27	0:21:48
Casablanca (Dar-El-Beida) 1	1	33N39	7w35	0:30:20
Ceuta 5	5	35N53	5w19	0:21:16
Chaouen 1	1	35N10	5w16	0:21:04
Chechaouene 1	1	35N10	5w16	0:21:04
Chemaïa 1	1	31N30	8w47	0:35:08
Chemaïa 1	1	32N05	8w37	0:34:28
Dakhla 4	4	23N43	15w57	1:03:48
Dar-Beni-Kriche-Bahri 1	1	35N30	5w20	0:21:20
Dardara 1	1	35N08	5w15	0:21:00
Dar-El-Beida → Casablanca 1	1	33N39	7w35	0:30:20
Dar-Ould-Zidouh 1	1	32N22	6w49	0:27:16
Demnat 1	1	31N44	6w59	0:27:56
Demnate 1	1	31N44	6w59	0:27:56
El Aaiún 4	4	27N09	13w12	0:52:48
El-Borj 1	1	35N43	5w40	0:22:40
El-Borouj 1	1	32N30	7w10	0:28:40
El-Hajeb 1	1	33N43	5w13	0:20:52
El-Jadida (Mazagan) 1	1	33N16	8w30	0:34:00
El-Jebha 1	1	35N13	4w38	0:18:32
El-Kelâa-Des-Srarhna 1	1	32N02	7w23	0:29:32
Erfoud 1	1	31N28	4w10	0:16:40
Er-Rachidia 1	1	31N58	4w25	0:17:40
Essaouira (Mogador) 1	1	31N30	9w47	0:39:08
Fedala → Mohammedia 1	1	33N44	7w24	0:29:36
Fès 1	1	34N05	4w57	0:19:48
Fez → Fès 1	1	34N05	4w57	0:19:48
Figuig 1	1	32N10	1w15	0:05:00
Fkih-Ben-Salah 1	1	32N32	6w40	0:26:40
Foum-El-Hassane 1	1	28N59	8w55	0:35:40
Foum-El-Hisn 1	1	28N59	8w55	0:35:40
Foum-Zguid 1	1	30N04	6w54	0:27:36
Goulimime 1	1	28N56	10w04	0:40:16
Goulmima 1	1	31N02	5w00	0:20:00
Guelta Zemmur 4	4	25N15	12w20	0:49:20
Güera 4	4	20N48	17w08	1:08:32
Guercif 1	1	34N15	3w21	0:13:24
Hausa 4	4	27N06	10w55	0:43:40
Imi-N'tanout 1	1	31N10	8w50	0:35:20
Infrane 1	1	33N28	5w03	0:20:12
Jerada 1	1	34N17	2w13	0:08:52
Karia-Ba-Mohammed 1	1	34N19	5w10	0:20:40
Kasba-Tadla 1	1	32N34	6w18	0:25:12
Kenitra 1	1	34N16	6w40	0:26:40
Ketama 1	1	34N50	4w37	0:18:28
Khemisset 1	1	33N50	6w03	0:24:12
Khenifra 1	1	33N00	5w40	0:22:40
Khouribga 1	1	32N54	6w57	0:27:48
Ksar-El-Kebir 1	1	35N01	5w54	0:23:36
Ksar-Es-Seghir 1	1	35N50	5w32	0:22:08
Ksar-Es-Souk 1	1	31N58	4w25	0:17:40
Larache 1	1	35N12	6w10	0:24:40
Louis Gentil → Youssoufia 1	1	32N16	8w33	0:34:12
Mahbés 4	4	27N13	9w44	0:38:56
Marrakech 1	1	31N38	8w00	0:32:00
Martil 1	1	35N37	5w17	0:21:08
Mazagan → El-Jadida 1	1	33N16	8w30	0:34:00
Mechra Safsaf 1	1	34N52	2w36	0:10:24
Meknès 1	1	33N53	5w37	0:22:28
Melilla 5	5	35N19	2w58	0:11:52

MOROCCO MARRUECOS MAROC MAROKKO AL-MAGREB

Place	Zone	Lat	Long	LMT
Mesied 4	4	26N36	13W00	0:52:00
Mestasa 1	1	35N07	4W25	0:17:40
Midar 1	1	34N58	3W30	0:14:00
Midelt 1	1	32N41	4W43	0:18:52
Mogador → Essaouira 1	1	31N30	9W47	0:39:08
Mohammedia (Fedala) 1	1	33N44	7W24	0:29:36
Mokrisset 1	1	34N59	5W20	0:21:20
Moulay-Bou-Selham 1	1	34N53	6W15	0:25:00
Moulay-Idriss 1	1	34N02	5W27	0:21:48
Nador 1	1	35N12	2W55	0:11:40
Oualidia 1	1	32N44	9W08	0:36:32
Ouarzazate 1	1	30N57	6W50	0:27:20
Oudjda → Oujda 1	1	34N41	1W45	0:07:00
Oued-Zem 1	1	32N55	6W33	0:26:12
Ouezzane 1	1	34N52	5W35	0:22:20
Oujda 1	1	34N41	1W45	0:07:00
Ounara 1	1	31N33	9W28	0:37:52
Port-Lyautey → Kenitra 1	1	34N16	6W40	0:26:40
Rabat 1	1	34N02	6W51	0:27:24
Regaïa 1	1	35N38	5W46	0:23:04
Restinga 1	1	35N42	5W23	0:21:32
Rissani 1	1	31N23	4W09	0:16:36
Rommani 1	1	34N34	6W37	0:26:28
Safi 1	1	32N20	9W17	0:37:08
Saïdia 1	1	35N04	2W15	0:09:00
Salé 1	1	34N04	6W50	0:27:20
Sefrou 1	1	33N50	4W50	0:19:20
Segangane 1	1	35N09	3W00	0:12:00
Selouane 1	1	35N04	2W58	0:11:52
Semara 4	4	26N44	11W41	0:46:44
Settat 1	1	33N04	7W37	0:30:28
Sidi-Bennour 1	1	32N30	8W30	0:34:00
Sidi Ifni 3	3	29N24	10W12	0:40:48
Sidi-Kacem 1	1	34N15	5W39	0:22:36
Sidi-Slimane 1	1	34N15	5W49	0:23:16
Sidi-Smaïl 1	1	32N49	8W30	0:34:00
Smara → Semara 4	4	26N44	11W41	0:46:44
Souk-El-Arba-Des-Beni-Hassan 1	1	35N16	5W20	0:21:20
Souk-El-Arba-Du-Rharb 1	1	34N43	6W01	0:24:04
Souk-Khemis-Du-Sahel 1	1	35N17	6W05	0:24:20
Souk Larbat Gharb 1	1	34N43	6W01	0:24:04
Tafraout 1	1	29N40	8W58	0:35:52
Tafraoute 1	1	29N40	8W58	0:35:52
Tagounit 1	1	29N58	5W36	0:22:24
Tahala 1	1	34N04	4W20	0:17:20
Tahanaoute 1	1	31N24	7W54	0:31:36
Tahnaout 1	1	31N24	7W54	0:31:36
Taliouine 1	1	30N36	7W49	0:31:16
Tamanar 1	1	31N00	9W35	0:38:20
Tamelelt 1	1	31N50	7W29	0:29:56
Tamri 1	1	30N43	9W43	0:38:52
Tanger (Tangier) 2	2	35N48	5W45	0:23:00
Tangier → Tanger 2	2	35N48	5W45	0:23:00
Tan-Tan 1	1	28N26	11W06	0:44:24
Taounate 1	1	34N25	4W39	0:18:36
Taourirt 1	1	34N25	2W53	0:11:32
Tarfaya 1	1	27N58	12W55	0:51:40
Targuist 1	1	34N57	4W18	0:17:12
Tarhjicht 1	1	29N05	9W24	0:37:36
Tarhjijt 1	1	29N05	9W24	0:37:36
Taroudant 1	1	30N31	8W55	0:35:40
Tata 1	1	29N44	7W56	0:31:44
Taza 1	1	34N16	4W01	0:16:04
Tazenakht 1	1	30N35	7W12	0:28:48
Tendrara 1	1	33N04	1W59	0:07:56
Tétouan 1	1	35N34	5W23	0:21:32
Tichla 4	4	21N35	14W58	0:59:52
Tiglit 1	1	28N31	10W15	0:41:00
Tinrhir 1	1	31N28	5W30	0:22:00
Tiznit 1	1	29N43	9W44	0:38:56
Torres de Alcalá 1	1	35N10	4W16	0:17:04
Villa Cisneros 4	4	23N40	15W55	1:03:40
Xauen → Chechaouene 1	1	35N10	5W16	0:21:04
Youssoufia 1	1	32N16	8W33	0:34:12
Zagora 1	1	30N22	5W50	0:23:20
Zaouia Bouhamed 1	1	35N25	5W00	0:20:00

MOZAMBIQUE MOSAMBIK PORTUGUESE EAST AFRICA MOÇAMBIQUE

Time Table
Before 1/Mar/1903 LMT
Begin Standard 30E00
1/Mar/1903 0:00 -2:00

Place	Lat	Long	LMT
Alto Ligonha	15S30	38E20	-2:33:20
Alto Molócuè	15S38	37E42	-2:30:48
Ancuabe	12S58	39E54	-2:39:36
António Enes	16S14	39E58	-2:39:52
Augusto Cardoso	12S44	34E50	-2:19:20
Balama	13S20	38E30	-2:34:00
Bandula	19S02	33E07	-2:12:28
Bartolomeu Dias	21S10	35E09	-2:20:36
Beira	19S49	34E52	-2:19:28
Bela Vista	26S20	32E40	-2:10:40
Belém	14S13	35E58	-2:23:52
Boila	16S10	39E50	-2:39:20
Campo	17S44	36E21	-2:25:24
Casula	15S25	33E40	-2:14:40
Cataxa	15S58	33E12	-2:12:48
Catembe	26S00	32E33	-2:10:12
Catuane	26S48	32E18	-2:09:12
Catur	13S45	35E30	-2:22:00
Chalaua	16S06	39E11	-2:36:44
Chamba	12S07	36E57	-2:27:48
Changalane	26S16	32E13	-2:08:52
Changara	16S54	33E14	-2:12:56
Chemba	17S08	34E52	-2:19:28
Chibabava	20S19	33E39	-2:14:36
Chibuto	24S44	33E33	-2:14:12
Chicoa	15S37	32E24	-2:09:36
Chicomo	24S31	34E17	-2:17:08
Chidenguele	24S54	34E13	-2:16:52
Chigubo	22S50	33E34	-2:14:16
Chinde	18S37	36E24	-2:25:36
Chingune	20S38	34E55	-2:19:40
Chinizíua	19S00	35E09	-2:20:36
Chioco	16S25	32E50	-2:11:20
Chipera	15S28	32E30	-2:10:00
Chirape	21S18	33E33	-2:14:12
Chofombo	14S35	31E50	-2:07:20
Chongoene	25S00	33E47	-2:15:08
Cóbuè	12S04	34E50	-2:19:20
Cometela	21S51	34E29	-2:17:56
Conceição	18S45	36E10	-2:24:40
Covane	21S22	33E56	-2:15:44
Derre	16S56	36E11	-2:24:44
Diaca	11S30	39E59	-2:39:56
Divinhe	20S40	34E49	-2:19:16
Doa	16S44	34E32	-2:18:08
Dombe	19S59	33E25	-2:13:40
Dona Ana	17S25	35E07	-2:20:28
Dondo	19S36	34E44	-2:18:56
Entre-Rios	14S57	37E20	-2:29:20
Errego	16S02	37E14	-2:28:56
Espungabera	20S29	32E48	-2:11:12
Fingoè	15S12	31E50	-2:07:20
Fumane	24S29	33E58	-2:15:52
Funhalouro	23S03	34E25	-2:17:40
Furancungo	14S55	33E35	-2:14:20
Gogoi	20S17	33E08	-2:12:32
Gondola	19S10	33E40	-2:14:40
Goonda	19S51	34E00	-2:16:00
Homoíne	23S52	35E09	-2:20:36
Ibo	12S20	40E35	-2:42:20
Inhaca	26S01	32E58	-2:11:52
Inhafenga	20S35	33E53	-2:15:32
Inhambane	23S51	35E29	-2:21:56
Inhaminga	18S24	35E00	-2:20:00
Inharrime	24S29	35E01	-2:20:04
Inhassoro	21S33	35E11	-2:20:44
Itóculo	14S42	40E18	-2:41:12
Jangamo	24S06	35E21	-2:21:24
João Belo	25S02	33E34	-2:14:16
Jofane	21S17	34E16	-2:17:04
Lacerdónia	18S01	35E30	-2:22:00
Larde	16S28	39E43	-2:38:52
Lichinga	13S18	35E14	-2:20:56
Lourenço Marques → Maputo	25S58	32E35	-2:10:20
Luabo	18S30	36E10	-2:24:40
Lugela	16S25	36E43	-2:26:52
Lugenda	12S30	37E43	-2:30:52
Luido	21S31	34E41	-2:18:44
Lumbo	15S00	40E44	-2:42:56
Lúrio	13S35	40E30	-2:42:00
Maave	21S03	34E47	-2:19:08
Mabalane	23S37	32E31	-2:10:04
Mabote	22S03	34E09	-2:16:36
Machaíla	22S15	32E55	-2:11:40
Machanga	20S58	34E59	-2:19:56
Machava	25S54	32E29	-2:09:56
Machaze	20S51	33E26	-2:13:44
Machece	19S17	35E33	-2:22:12
Macia	25S03	33E10	-2:12:40
Macossa	17S52	33E56	-2:15:44
Macovane	21S28	35E04	-2:20:16
Macuze	17S42	37E11	-2:28:44
Màgoé	15S48	31E43	-2:06:52
Magude	25S02	32E40	-2:10:40
Mandié	16S30	33E30	-2:14:00
Mandimba	14S21	35E39	-2:22:36
Manhiça	25S24	32E48	-2:11:12
Maniamba	12S43	35E00	-2:20:00
Manjacaze	24S44	33E53	-2:15:32
Mapai	25S51	31E58	-2:07:52
Mapinhane	22S19	35E03	-2:20:12
Mapulanguene	24S29	32E06	-2:08:24
Maputo (Lourenço Marques)	25S58	32E35	-2:10:20
Marromeu	18S20	35E56	-2:23:44
Marrupa	13S08	37E30	-2:30:00
Massangena	21S32	32E57	-2:11:48
Massara	18S20	34E09	-2:16:36
Massinga	23S20	35E25	-2:21:40
Massingir	23S51	32E04	-2:08:16
Matola	25S59	32E29	-2:09:56
Matola-Rio	25S58	32E26	-2:09:44
Matuba	24S27	32E55	-2:11:40
Matuto	14S46	35E59	-2:23:56
Maúa	13S51	37E10	-2:28:40
Mau-é-Ele	24S21	34E07	-2:16:28
Mavanza	22S43	35E08	-2:20:32
Mavita	19S33	33E10	-2:12:40
Mavonde	18S32	33E02	-2:12:08
Maxixe	23S51	35E21	-2:21:24
Mazoco	11S40	35E48	-2:23:12
Mecanhelas	15S12	35E54	-2:23:36
Meconta	14S49	39E50	-2:39:20
Mecubúri	14S39	38E54	-2:35:36
Mecúfi	13S17	40E30	-2:42:00
Mecula	12S04	37E40	-2:30:40
Meloco	13S25	39E08	-2:36:32
Meluco	12S36	39E38	-2:38:32
Memba	14S11	40E30	-2:42:00
Mesa	13S00	39E33	-2:38:12
Metarica	14S20	36E48	-2:27:12
Metuge	12S58	40E20	-2:41:20
Micaúne	18S18	36E35	-2:26:20
Milepa	11S43	36E20	-2:25:20
Miramar	23S50	35E34	-2:22:16
Miranda	12S30	35E28	-2:21:52
Moamba	25S35	32E13	-2:08:52
Moatize	16S08	33E45	-2:15:00
Moçambique	15S03	40E42	-2:42:48
Mocímboa da Praia	11S20	40E21	-2:41:24
Mocímboa do Rovuma	11S20	39E18	-2:37:12
Mocoduene	23S40	35E10	-2:20:40
Mocuba	16S50	36E59	-2:27:56
Mocubúri	14S39	38E54	-2:35:36
Mogincual	15S35	40E25	-2:41:40
Molumbo	15S27	30E15	-2:01:00
Moma	16S44	39E14	-2:36:56
Monapo	14S57	40E17	-2:41:08
Monguè	16S22	35E35	-2:22:20
Montepuez	13S07	39E00	-2:36:00
Mopeia Velha	17S59	35E44	-2:22:56
Morrumbala	17S22	35E36	-2:22:24
Morrumbene	23S39	35E20	-2:21:20
Mossuril	14S58	40E42	-2:42:48
Motaze	24S48	32E52	-2:11:28
Mozambique → Moçambique	15S03	40E42	-2:42:48
Mualama	16S53	38E17	-2:33:08
Muanza	18S59	34E48	-2:19:12
Mucacata	13S20	39E59	-2:39:56
Mucubela	16S55	37E52	-2:31:28
Mucumbura	16S09	31E31	-2:06:04
Mucupia	18S01	36E48	-2:27:12
Mueda	11S39	39E33	-2:38:12
Mugazine	26S07	32E30	-2:10:00
Muhula	13S53	39E30	-2:38:00
Muite	14S02	39E00	-2:36:00
Mulanje	16S03	35E45	-2:23:00
Mulevala	16S30	37E30	-2:30:00
Mungári	17S12	33E31	-2:14:04
Munhamade	16S37	36E58	-2:27:52
Murrébuè	13S02	40E30	-2:42:00
Murrupula	15S27	38E47	-2:35:08
Mutanda	21S02	33E31	-2:14:04
Nacala	14S34	40E41	-2:42:44
Nacala-Velha	14S32	40E37	-2:42:28
Nalázi	24S03	33E20	-2:13:20
Namaacha	25S58	32E05	-2:08:20
Namacurra	17S29	37E01	-2:28:04
Namapa	13S43	39E50	-2:39:20
Namarrói	15S58	36E55	-2:27:40
Nametil	15S43	39E21	-2:37:24
Nampuecha	13S59	40E18	-2:41:12
Nampula	15S07	39E15	-2:37:00
Nangade	11S05	39E36	-2:38:24
Nantuego	11S21	38E24	-2:33:36
Nantulo	12S17	39E03	-2:36:12

MOÇAMBIQUE PORTUGUESE EAST AFRICA MOSAMBIK MOZAMBIQUE

Place	Lat	Long	Offset
Negomano	11s27	38E31	-2:34:04
Netia	14s48	39E59	-2:39:56
Nhacoongo	24s18	35E14	-2:20:56
Nhamacolomo	18s05	34E26	-2:17:44
Nipepe	14s01	37E55	-2:31:40
Nova Freixo	14s49	36E33	-2:26:12
Nova Lusitânia	19s54	34E35	-2:18:20
Nova Mambone	20s59	35E01	-2:20:04
Nova Nabúri	16s46	38E57	-2:35:48
Nova Sofala	20s09	34E42	-2:18:48
Olivença	11s47	35E13	-2:20:52
Pafúri	22s27	31E21	-2:05:24
Palma	10s46	40E29	-2:41:56
Panda	24s02	34E45	-2:19:00
Pebane	17s10	38E08	-2:32:32
Pomene	22s53	35E33	-2:22:12
Ponte do Púngoè	19s30	34E32	-2:18:08
Porto Amélia	12s58	40E30	-2:42:00
Quedas	19s30	33E29	-2:13:56
Quelimane	17s53	36E51	-2:27:24
Quinga	15s49	40E15	-2:41:00
Quionga	10s37	40E30	-2:42:00
Quissanga	12s25	40E29	-2:41:56
Quissico	24s42	34E44	-2:18:56
Quiterajo	11s48	40E25	-2:41:40
Révia	13s23	36E31	-2:26:04
Ribauè	14s57	38E17	-2:33:08
Rio das Pedras	23s12	35E23	-2:21:32
Rotanda	19s33	32E50	-2:11:20
Salamanga	26s28	32E39	-2:10:36
Santaca	26s36	32E32	-2:10:08
Sena	17s27	35E00	-2:20:00
Tambara	16s45	34E15	-2:17:00
Tembuè	14s52	32E58	-2:11:52
Tete	16s13	33E35	-2:14:20
Tsangano	15s08	34E32	-2:18:08
Uampochane	26s23	32E41	-2:10:44
Unango	12s50	35E20	-2:21:20
Valadim	12s22	36E10	-2:24:40
Vandúzi	18s57	33E16	-2:13:04
Vila Alferes Chamusca	24s29	33E00	-2:12:00
Vila Cabral	13s18	35E14	-2:20:56
Vila Caldas Xavier	15s59	34E12	-2:16:48
Vila Coutinho	14s37	34E19	-2:17:16
Vila da Maganja	17s18	37E30	-2:30:00
Vila de Manica	18s56	32E53	-2:11:32
Vila Fontes	17s50	35E21	-2:21:24
Vila Gamito	14s12	33E00	-2:12:00
Vila Gomes da Costa	24s19	33E38	-2:14:32
Vila Gouveia	18s03	33E11	-2:12:44
Vila Junqueiro	15s25	36E58	-2:27:52
Vila Luísa	25s44	32E40	-2:10:40
Vila Machado	19s18	34E11	-2:16:44
Vilanculos	22s01	35E19	-2:21:16
Vila Paiva de Andrada	18s44	34E03	-2:16:12
Vila Pery	19s08	33E29	-2:13:56
Vila Trigo de Morais	24s36	33E00	-2:12:00
Vila Vasco da Gama	14s54	32E14	-2:08:56
Xinavane	25s02	32E47	-2:11:08
Zâmbuè	15s10	30E50	-2:03:20
Zitundo	26s45	32E50	-2:11:20
Zóbuè	15s38	34E26	-2:17:44
Zumbo	15s36	30E25	-2:01:40
Zune	18s59	35E18	-2:21:12

NAMIBIE SUIDWES-AFRIKA SOUTH-WEST AFRICA NAMIBIA

Time Table

Before 8/Feb/1892		LMT
Begin Standard		22E30
8/Feb/1892	0:00	-1:30
Begin Standard		30E00
1/Mar/1903	0:00	-2:00
20/Sep/1942	2:00	-3:00
21/Mar/1943	2:00	-2:00

Place	Lat	Long	Offset
Aminuis	23s43	19E21	-1:17:24
Anabib	18s08	12E30	-0:50:00
Andara	18s03	21E27	-1:25:48
Arandis	22s24	15E00	-1:00:00
Aranos	24s09	19E09	-1:16:36
Ariamsvlei	28s08	19E50	-1:19:20
Aroab	26s47	19E40	-1:18:40
Asab	25s29	17E59	-1:11:56
Aub	26s33	19E08	-1:16:32
Aus	26s40	16E15	-1:05:00
Berseba	26s00	17E46	-1:11:04
Bethanien	26s32	17E11	-1:08:44
Bogenfels	27s23	15E22	-1:01:28
Brakwater	22s24	17E06	-1:08:24
Buitepos	22s18	19E57	-1:19:48
Chefuzwe	17s38	24E30	-1:38:00
Dabegabis	28s07	18E36	-1:14:24
Daberas	25s38	18E29	-1:13:56
Davignab	27s32	19E48	-1:19:12
Dordabis	22s52	17E38	-1:10:32
Ebony	22s05	15E15	-1:01:00
Elim	17s48	15E31	-1:02:04
Enana	17s29	16E19	-1:05:16
Endola	17s37	15E50	-1:03:20
Epokiro	21s41	19E08	-1:16:32
Epukiro	21s41	19E08	-1:16:32
Erongo	21s44	15E53	-1:03:32
Erundu	20s36	16E25	-1:05:40
Fransfontein	20s12	15E01	-1:00:04
Garub	26s33	16E00	-1:04:00
Gawachab	27s03	17E50	-1:11:20
Gibeon	25s09	17E43	-1:10:52
Goageb	26s44	17E15	-1:09:00
Gobabis	22s30	18E58	-1:15:52
Gochas	24s55	18E55	-1:15:40
Goreeis	20s00	15E45	-1:03:00
Grootfontein	19s32	18E05	-1:12:20
Grünau	27s47	18E23	-1:13:32
Guibes	26s41	16E42	-1:06:48
Haalenberg	26s52	15E30	-1:02:00
Hamrivier	28s08	19E18	-1:17:12
Haribes	24s20	17E40	-1:10:40
Haris	22s48	16E52	-1:07:28
Helmeringhausen	25s54	16E57	-1:07:48
Hentiesbaai	22s08	14E18	-0:57:12
Hochfeld	21s28	17E58	-1:11:52
Holoog	27s22	17E55	-1:11:40
Kalkfeld	20s53	16E11	-1:04:44
Kalkrand	24s03	17E33	-1:10:12
Kamanjab	19s35	14E51	-0:59:24
Kangongo	17s57	21E02	-1:24:08
Kanovlei	19s10	19E23	-1:17:32
Kanus	27s54	18E40	-1:14:40
Kaoko Otavi	18s14	13E40	-0:54:40
Kapps	22s22	17E52	-1:11:28
Karakuwisa	18s56	19E40	-1:18:40
Karasburg	28s00	18E43	-1:14:52
Karibib	21s58	15E51	-1:03:24
Karukuwisa	18s56	19E40	-1:18:40
Keetmanshoop	26s36	18E08	-1:12:32
Klein-Karas	27s32	18E06	-1:12:24
Kiries West	26s34	19E00	-1:16:00
Kiriis West	26s34	19E00	-1:16:00
Kitwitwi	17s25	18E25	-1:13:40
Klipdam	27s35	19E56	-1:19:44
Knolvlei	19s10	19E23	-1:17:32
Kochena	27s00	18E50	-1:15:20
Koes	25s59	19E08	-1:16:32
Kolmanskop	26s40	15E12	-1:00:48
Kranzberg	21s55	15E43	-1:02:52
Kuring Kuru	17s38	18E35	-1:14:20
Lekkerwater	23s38	17E14	-1:08:56
Leonardville	23s29	18E49	-1:15:16
Linyanti	18s04	24E01	-1:36:04
Lüderitz	26s38	15E10	-1:00:40
Lupala	17s50	19E06	-1:16:24
Maltahöhe	24s50	17E00	-1:08:00
Mariental	24s36	17E59	-1:11:56
Maroelaboom	19s15	18E53	-1:15:32
Momanga	18s12	21E42	-1:26:48
Mupini	17s50	19E40	-1:18:40
Namutoni	18s49	16E55	-1:07:40
Naos	22s46	16E42	-1:06:48
Narubis	27s10	19E05	-1:16:20
Narubis	26s55	18E35	-1:14:20
Nieuwefontein	28s01	19E06	-1:16:24
Nomtsas	24s22	16E47	-1:07:08
Noordoewer	28s45	17E37	-1:10:28
Nossob	22s18	17E10	-1:08:40
Nyangana	18s00	20E41	-1:22:44
Ohopoho	18s03	13E45	-0:55:00
Okahandja	21s59	16E58	-1:07:52
Okaputa	20s09	16E56	-1:07:44
Okaukuejo	19s10	15E54	-1:03:36
Okombahe	21s23	15E22	-1:01:28
Olukonda	18s03	16E00	-1:04:00
Omaruru	21s28	15E56	-1:03:44
Ombombo	18s43	13E53	-0:55:32
Omitara	22s18	18E01	-1:12:04
Ondangua	17s55	16E00	-1:04:00
Orangemouth → Oranjemund	28s38	16E24	-1:05:36
Oranjemund	28s38	16E24	-1:05:36
Oshigambo	17s47	16E05	-1:04:20
Oshikango	17s25	15E56	-1:03:44
Osire	20s59	17E19	-1:09:16
Otavi	19s39	17E20	-1:09:20
Otjikondo	19s50	15E23	-1:01:32
Otjimbingue	22s19	16E10	-1:04:40
Otjinene	21s13	18E42	-1:14:48
Otjituuo	19s40	18E32	-1:14:08
Otjiwarongo	20s29	16E36	-1:06:24
Otjiwero	17s59	13E22	-0:53:28
Otju	18s15	13E18	-0:53:12
Outjo	20s08	16E08	-1:04:32
Platveld	19s58	17E07	-1:08:28
Pomona	27s09	15E18	-1:01:12
Purros	18s38	12E59	-0:51:56
Rehoboth	23s18	17E03	-1:08:12
Rietfontein	21s58	20E58	-1:23:52
Rössing	22s31	14E52	-0:59:28
Runtu	17s52	19E43	-1:18:52
Salzbrunn	24s23	18E00	-1:12:00
Sambusu	17s50	19E20	-1:17:20
Seeheim	26s50	17E45	-1:11:00
Seeis	22s29	17E39	-1:10:36
Sendlingsdrift	28s12	16E53	-1:07:32
Sesfontein	19s07	13E39	-0:54:36
Sikerete	19s03	20E50	-1:23:20
Sikosi	17s59	23E19	-1:33:16
Simkwe	19s41	20E30	-1:22:00
Singalamwe	17s41	23E23	-1:33:32
Sorris Sorris	20s57	14E50	-0:59:20
Stampriet	24s20	18E28	-1:13:52
Steinhausen	21s49	18E20	-1:13:20
Sukses	21s01	16E52	-1:07:28
Swakopmund	22s41	14E34	-0:58:16
Tondoro	17s45	18E50	-1:15:20
Tränental	27s09	19E33	-1:18:12
Trekkopje	22s18	14E53	-0:59:32
Tsaraxaibis	27s25	19E22	-1:17:28
Tsaukaib	26s37	15E31	-1:02:04
Tses	25s58	18E08	-1:12:32
Tshandi	17s42	14E50	-0:59:20
Tshimhaka	17s20	13E51	-0:55:24
Tsintsabis	18s45	17E51	-1:11:24
Tsobis	19s27	17E30	-1:10:00
Tsumeb	19s13	17E42	-1:10:48
Tsumis Park	23s43	17E28	-1:09:52
Tuguwa	17s25	18E25	-1:13:40
Uchab	19s47	17E42	-1:10:48
Uhlenhorst	23s45	17E55	-1:11:40
Uis	21s08	14E49	-0:59:16
Ukamas	28s02	19E45	-1:19:00
Usakos	22s01	15E32	-1:02:08
Utapi	17s31	15E08	-1:00:32
Utokota	17s50	20E22	-1:21:28
Warmbad	28s29	18E41	-1:14:44
Waterberg	20s28	17E13	-1:08:52
Welwitschia	20s21	14E57	-0:59:48
Wilhelmstal	21s54	16E19	-1:05:16
Windhoek	22s34	17E06	-1:08:24
Witbooisvlei	25s04	18E27	-1:13:48
Witvlei	22s23	18E32	-1:14:08
Witzputz	27s25	17E43	-1:10:52
Zaniasand	23s28	18E26	-1:13:44

NAURU

PLEASANT ISLAND

Time Table
Before 15/Jan/1921 LMT
Begin Standard 172E30
15/Jan/1921 0:00 -11:30
Begin Standard 135E00
15/Mar/1942 0:00 -9:00
Begin Standard 172E30
15/Aug/1944 0:00 -11:30
Begin Standard 180E00
1/May/1979 0:00 -12:00

Place	Latitude	Longitude	Offset
Anabar	0S30	166E57	-11:07:48
Government Station	0S32	166E55	-11:07:40
Ijuh	0S30	166E57	-11:07:48
Ijuw	0S30	166E57	-11:07:48
Settlement	0S32	166E56	-11:07:44
Uaboe	0S31	166E55	-11:07:40
Waboe	0S31	166E55	-11:07:40
Yangor	0S31	166E54	-11:07:36

NEPAL

NÉPAL

NEPĀL

Time Table
Before 1/Jan/1920 LMT
Begin Standard 82E30
1/Jan/1920 0:00 -5:30
Begin Standard 86E15
1/Jan/1986 0:00 -5:45

Place	Latitude	Longitude	Offset
Amlekhganj	27N17	84E59	-5:39:56
Bāglung	28N16	83E36	-5:34:24
Bahādurganj	27N32	82E50	-5:31:20
Bairia	27N00	85E23	-5:41:32
Baitadi	29N32	80E26	-5:21:44
Bandīpur	27N56	84E25	-5:37:40
Bardīa	28N18	81E22	-5:25:28
Bhādgāon → Bhaktapur	27N42	85E27	-5:41:48
Bhairawa	27N31	83E24	-5:33:36
Bhaktapur	27N42	85E27	-5:41:48
Bhatgaon → Bhaktapur	27N42	85E27	-5:41:48
Bhīmphedi	27N32	85E07	-5:40:28
Bhojpur	27N10	87E03	-5:48:12
Bijauri	28N06	82E20	-5:29:20
Bilauri	28N41	80E21	-5:21:24
Birātnagar	26N29	87E17	-5:49:08
Bīrganj	27N00	84E52	-5:39:28
Burāthum	28N04	84E50	-5:39:20
Butwal	27N42	83E27	-5:33:48
Chautāra	27N46	85E42	-5:42:48
Chisapani	27N34	85E08	-5:40:32
Dailekh	28N50	81E44	-5:26:56
Dandeldhura	29N18	80E35	-5:22:20
Dhāding	27N52	84E55	-5:39:40
Dhangarhi	28N41	80E36	-5:22:24
Dhankuta	26N59	87E20	-5:49:20
Dharān Bāzār	26N49	87E17	-5:49:08
Dhulikhel	27N37	85E33	-5:42:12
Dingla	27N21	87E08	-5:48:32
Gurkha	28N00	84E37	-5:38:28
Hanumānnagar	26N30	86E51	-5:47:24
Hariharpur Garhi	27N19	85E29	-5:41:56
Ilām	26N55	87E56	-5:51:44
Jājarkot	28N42	82E12	-5:28:48
Jaleshwar	26N38	85E48	-5:43:12
Jhāpa	26N29	87E51	-5:51:24
Jhawāni	27N35	84E31	-5:38:04
Jumla	29N17	82E10	-5:28:40
Kadarbana	26N46	85E20	-5:41:20
Kalaiya	27N02	85E00	-5:40:00
Kāndrāng Garhi	27N43	84E47	-5:39:08
Kapilavastu	27N28	83E16	-5:33:04
Kathmandu	27N43	85E19	-5:41:16
Kātmāndu → Kathmandu	27N43	85E19	-5:41:16
Kewāre	27N57	83E47	-5:35:08
Kodari	27N56	85E56	-5:43:44
Kumbher	28N16	81E24	-5:25:36
Kunchha	28N08	84E20	-5:37:20
Kusma	28N14	83E41	-5:34:44
Lalitpur	27N41	85E20	-5:41:20
Makaising	27N53	84E41	-5:38:44
Makwānpur Garhi	27N25	85E08	-5:40:32
Malangwa	26N52	85E34	-5:42:16
Mānebhanjyāng	27N12	86E26	-5:45:44
Mustāng	29N11	83E58	-5:35:52
Nawākot	27N55	85E10	-5:40:40
Nepālganj	28N03	81E37	-5:26:28
Nuwākot	28N08	83E53	-5:35:32
Okhaldhunga	27N19	86E30	-5:46:00
Parāsi	27N32	83E40	-5:34:40
Patan → Lalitpur	27N41	85E20	-5:41:20
Piuthān	28N06	82E54	-5:31:36
Pokhara	28N14	83E59	-5:35:56
Rāmechhāp	27N20	86E05	-5:44:20
Riri Bāzār	27N57	83E26	-5:33:44
Sallyāna	28N22	82E10	-5:28:40
Silgarhi-Doti	29N16	80E59	-5:23:56
Simikot	29N58	81E50	-5:27:20
Sindhūli Garhi	27N16	85E58	-5:43:52
Sirha	26N39	86E12	-5:44:48
Tālkot	29N37	81E19	-5:25:16
Tanhu	28N02	84E20	-5:37:20
Tānsing	27N52	83E33	-5:34:12
Tāplejung	27N21	87E40	-5:50:40
Taulihawa	27N32	83E03	-5:32:12
Tehrthum	27N07	87E32	-5:50:08
Thānkot	27N41	85E11	-5:40:44
Udaypur	26N56	86E31	-5:46:04
Upardāng Garhi	27N46	84E34	-5:38:16

Time Table # 1
Before 1/May/1892 LMT
Begin Standard 4E53
1/May/1892 0:00 -0:20
30/Apr/1916 24:00 -1:20
1/Oct/1916 0:00 -0:20
16/Apr/1917 2:00 -1:20
17/Sep/1917 3:00 -0:20
1/Apr/1918 2:00 -1:20
30/Sep/1918 3:00 -0:20
7/Apr/1919 2:00 -1:20
29/Sep/1919 3:00 -0:20
5/Apr/1920 2:00 -1:20
27/Sep/1920 3:00 -0:20
4/Apr/1921 2:00 -1:20
26/Sep/1921 3:00 -0:20
26/Mar/1922 2:00 -1:20
8/Oct/1922 3:00 -0:20
1/Jun/1923 2:00 -1:20
7/Oct/1923 3:00 -0:20
30/Mar/1924 2:00 -1:20
5/Oct/1924 3:00 -0:20
5/Jun/1925 2:00 -1:20
4/Oct/1925 3:00 -0:20
15/May/1926 2:00 -1:20
3/Oct/1926 3:00 -0:20
15/May/1927 2:00 -1:20
2/Oct/1927 3:00 -0:20
15/May/1928 2:00 -1:20
7/Oct/1928 3:00 -0:20
15/May/1929 2:00 -1:20
6/Oct/1929 3:00 -0:20
15/May/1930 2:00 -1:20
5/Oct/1930 3:00 -0:20
15/May/1931 2:00 -1:20
4/Oct/1931 3:00 -0:20
22/May/1932 2:00 -1:20
2/Oct/1932 3:00 -0:20
15/May/1933 2:00 -1:20
8/Oct/1933 3:00 -0:20
15/May/1934 2:00 -1:20
7/Oct/1934 3:00 -0:20
15/May/1935 2:00 -1:20
6/Oct/1935 3:00 -0:20
15/May/1936 2:00 -1:20
4/Oct/1936 3:00 -0:20
22/May/1937 2:00 -1:20
Begin Standard 5E00
1/Jul/1937 0:00 -1:20
3/Oct/1937 3:00 -0:20
15/May/1938 2:00 -1:20
2/Oct/1938 3:00 -0:20
15/May/1939 2:00 -1:20
8/Oct/1939 3:00 -0:20
16/May/1940 0:40 -1:20
Begin Standard 15E00
16/May/1940 2:00 -2:00
2/Nov/1942 3:00 -1:00
29/Mar/1943 2:00 -2:00
4/Oct/1943 3:00 -1:00
3/Apr/1944 2:00 -2:00
2/Oct/1944 3:00 -1:00
2/Apr/1945 2:00 -2:00
20/May/1945 0:00 -1:00
3/Apr/1977 2:00 -2:00
25/Sep/1977 3:00 -1:00
2/Apr/1978 2:00 -2:00
1/Oct/1978 3:00 -1:00
1/Apr/1979 2:00 -2:00
30/Sep/1979 3:00 -1:00
6/Apr/1980 2:00 -2:00
28/Sep/1980 3:00 -1:00
29/Mar/1981 2:00 -2:00
27/Sep/1981 3:00 -1:00
28/Mar/1982 2:00 -2:00
26/Sep/1982 3:00 -1:00
27/Mar/1983 2:00 -2:00
25/Sep/1983 3:00 -1:00
25/Mar/1984 2:00 -2:00
30/Sep/1984 3:00 -1:00
31/Mar/1985 2:00 -2:00
29/Sep/1985 3:00 -1:00
30/Mar/1986 2:00 -2:00
28/Sep/1986 3:00 -1:00
29/Mar/1987 2:00 -2:00
27/Sep/1987 3:00 -1:00
27/Mar/1988 2:00 -2:00
25/Sep/1988 3:00 -1:00
26/Mar/1989 2:00 -2:00
24/Sep/1989 3:00 -1:00
25/Mar/1990 2:00 -2:00
30/Sep/1990 3:00 -1:00
31/Mar/1991 2:00 -2:00
29/Sep/1991 3:00 -1:00
29/Mar/1992 2:00 -2:00
27/Sep/1992 3:00 -1:00
28/Mar/1993 2:00 -2:00
26/Sep/1993 3:00 -1:00
27/Mar/1994 2:00 -2:00
25/Sep/1994 3:00 -1:00
26/Mar/1995 2:00 -2:00
24/Sep/1995 3:00 -1:00
31/Mar/1996 2:00 -2:00
29/Sep/1996 3:00 -1:00
30/Mar/1997 2:00 -2:00
28/Sep/1997 3:00 -1:00
29/Mar/1998 2:00 -2:00
27/Sep/1998 3:00 -1:00
28/Mar/1999 2:00 -2:00
26/Sep/1999 3:00 -1:00
26/Mar/2000 2:00 -2:00
24/Sep/2000 3:00 -1:00
....

Time Table # 2
Before 1/May/1892 LMT
Begin Standard 4E53
1/May/1892 0:00 -0:20
16/Apr/1917 2:00 TT#1
....

Time Table # 3
Before 1/May/1892 LMT
Begin Standard 4E53
1/May/1892 0:00 -0:20
30/Apr/1916 24:00 -1:20
1/Oct/1916 0:00 -0:20
16/Apr/1917 2:00 -1:20
17/Sep/1917 3:00 -0:20
1/Apr/1918 2:00 -1:20
30/Sep/1918 3:00 -0:20
7/Apr/1919 2:00 -1:20
29/Sep/1919 3:00 -0:20
5/Apr/1920 2:00 -1:20
27/Sep/1920 3:00 -0:20
4/Apr/1921 2:00 -1:20
26/Sep/1921 3:00 -0:20
26/Mar/1922 2:00 -1:20
8/Oct/1922 3:00 -0:20
1/Jun/1923 2:00 -1:20
7/Oct/1923 3:00 -0:20
30/Mar/1924 2:00 -1:20
5/Oct/1924 3:00 -0:20
5/Jun/1925 2:00 -1:20
4/Oct/1925 3:00 -0:20
15/May/1926 2:00 -1:20
3/Oct/1926 3:00 -0:20
15/May/1927 2:00 -1:20
2/Oct/1927 3:00 -0:20
15/May/1928 2:00 -1:20
7/Oct/1928 3:00 -0:20
15/May/1929 2:00 -1:20
6/Oct/1929 3:00 -0:20
15/May/1930 2:00 -1:20
5/Oct/1930 3:00 -0:20
15/May/1931 2:00 -1:20
4/Oct/1931 3:00 -0:20
22/May/1932 2:00 -1:20
2/Oct/1932 3:00 -0:20
15/May/1933 2:00 -1:20
8/Oct/1933 3:00 -0:20
15/May/1934 2:00 -1:20
7/Oct/1934 3:00 -0:20
15/May/1935 2:00 -1:20
6/Oct/1935 3:00 -0:20
15/May/1936 2:00 -1:20
4/Oct/1936 3:00 -0:20
22/May/1937 2:00 -1:20
Begin Standard 5E00
1/Jul/1937 0:00 -1:20
3/Oct/1937 3:00 -0:20
15/May/1938 2:00 -1:20
2/Oct/1938 3:00 -0:20
15/May/1939 2:00 -1:20
8/Oct/1939 3:00 -0:20
16/May/1940 0:40 -1:20
Begin Standard 15E00
16/May/1940 2:00 -2:00
2/Nov/1942 3:00 -1:00
29/Mar/1943 2:00 -2:00
4/Oct/1943 3:00 -1:00
3/Apr/1944 2:00 -2:00
20/Sep/1944 14:00 -1:00
3/Apr/1977 2:00 TT#1
....

Time Table # 4
Before 1/May/1892 LMT
Begin Standard 4E53
1/May/1892 0:00 -0:20
30/Apr/1916 24:00 -1:20
1/Oct/1916 0:00 -0:20
16/Apr/1917 2:00 -1:20
17/Sep/1917 3:00 -0:20
1/Apr/1918 2:00 -1:20
30/Sep/1918 3:00 -0:20
7/Apr/1919 2:00 -1:20
29/Sep/1919 3:00 -0:20
5/Apr/1920 2:00 -1:20
27/Sep/1920 3:00 -0:20
4/Apr/1921 2:00 -1:20
26/Sep/1921 3:00 -0:20
26/Mar/1922 2:00 -1:20
8/Oct/1922 3:00 -0:20
1/Jun/1923 2:00 -1:20
7/Oct/1923 3:00 -0:20
30/Mar/1924 2:00 -1:20
5/Oct/1924 3:00 -0:20
5/Jun/1925 2:00 -1:20
4/Oct/1925 3:00 -0:20
15/May/1926 2:00 -1:20
3/Oct/1926 3:00 -0:20
15/May/1927 2:00 -1:20
2/Oct/1927 3:00 -0:20
15/May/1928 2:00 -1:20
7/Oct/1928 3:00 -0:20
15/May/1929 2:00 -1:20
6/Oct/1929 3:00 -0:20
15/May/1930 2:00 -1:20
5/Oct/1930 3:00 -0:20
15/May/1931 2:00 -1:20
4/Oct/1931 3:00 -0:20
22/May/1932 2:00 -1:20
2/Oct/1932 3:00 -0:20
15/May/1933 2:00 -1:20
8/Oct/1933 3:00 -0:20
15/May/1934 2:00 -1:20
7/Oct/1934 3:00 -0:20
15/May/1935 2:00 -1:20
6/Oct/1935 3:00 -0:20
15/May/1936 2:00 -1:20
4/Oct/1936 3:00 -0:20
22/May/1937 2:00 -1:20
Begin Standard 5E00
1/Jul/1937 0:00 -1:20
3/Oct/1937 3:00 -0:20
15/May/1938 2:00 -1:20
2/Oct/1938 3:00 -0:20
15/May/1939 2:00 -1:20
8/Oct/1939 3:00 -0:20
16/May/1940 0:40 -1:20
Begin Standard 15E00
16/May/1940 2:00 -2:00
2/Nov/1942 3:00 -1:00
29/Mar/1943 2:00 -2:00
4/Oct/1943 3:00 -1:00
3/Apr/1944 2:00 -2:00
21/Sep/1944 3:00 -1:00
3/Apr/1977 2:00 TT#1
....

Time Table # 5
Before 1/May/1892 LMT
Begin Standard 4E53
1/May/1892 0:00 -0:20
30/Apr/1916 24:00 -1:20
1/Oct/1916 0:00 -0:20
16/Apr/1917 2:00 -1:20
17/Sep/1917 3:00 -0:20
1/Apr/1918 2:00 -1:20
30/Sep/1918 3:00 -0:20
7/Apr/1919 2:00 -1:20
29/Sep/1919 3:00 -0:20
5/Apr/1920 2:00 -1:20
27/Sep/1920 3:00 -0:20
4/Apr/1921 2:00 -1:20
26/Sep/1921 3:00 -0:20
26/Mar/1922 2:00 -1:20
8/Oct/1922 3:00 -0:20
1/Jun/1923 2:00 -1:20
7/Oct/1923 3:00 -0:20
30/Mar/1924 2:00 -1:20
5/Oct/1924 3:00 -0:20
5/Jun/1925 2:00 -1:20
4/Oct/1925 3:00 -0:20
15/May/1926 2:00 -1:20
3/Oct/1926 3:00 -0:20
15/May/1927 2:00 -1:20
2/Oct/1927 3:00 -0:20
15/May/1928 2:00 -1:20
7/Oct/1928 3:00 -0:20
15/May/1929 2:00 -1:20
6/Oct/1929 3:00 -0:20
15/May/1930 2:00 -1:20
5/Oct/1930 3:00 -0:20
15/May/1931 2:00 -1:20
4/Oct/1931 3:00 -0:20
22/May/1932 2:00 -1:20
2/Oct/1932 3:00 -0:20
15/May/1933 2:00 -1:20
8/Oct/1933 3:00 -0:20
15/May/1934 2:00 -1:20
7/Oct/1934 3:00 -0:20
15/May/1935 2:00 -1:20
6/Oct/1935 3:00 -0:20
15/May/1936 2:00 -1:20
4/Oct/1936 3:00 -0:20
22/May/1937 2:00 -1:20
Begin Standard 5E00
1/Jul/1937 0:00 -1:20
3/Oct/1937 3:00 -0:20
15/May/1938 2:00 -1:20
2/Oct/1938 3:00 -0:20
15/May/1939 2:00 -1:20
8/Oct/1939 3:00 -0:20
16/May/1940 0:40 -1:20
Begin Standard 15E00
16/May/1940 2:00 -2:00
2/Nov/1942 3:00 -1:00
29/Mar/1943 2:00 -2:00
4/Oct/1943 3:00 -1:00
3/Apr/1944 2:00 -2:00
26/Sep/1944 0:00 -1:00
3/Apr/1977 2:00 TT#1
....

Time Table # 6
Before 1/May/1892 LMT
Begin Standard 4E53
1/May/1892 0:00 -0:20
30/Apr/1916 24:00 -1:20
1/Oct/1916 0:00 -0:20
16/Apr/1917 2:00 -1:20
17/Sep/1917 3:00 -0:20
1/Apr/1918 2:00 -1:20
30/Sep/1918 3:00 -0:20
7/Apr/1919 2:00 -1:20
29/Sep/1919 3:00 -0:20
5/Apr/1920 2:00 -1:20
27/Sep/1920 3:00 -0:20
4/Apr/1921 2:00 -1:20
26/Sep/1921 3:00 -0:20
26/Mar/1922 2:00 -1:20
8/Oct/1922 3:00 -0:20
1/Jun/1923 2:00 -1:20
7/Oct/1923 3:00 -0:20
30/Mar/1924 2:00 -1:20
5/Oct/1924 3:00 -0:20
5/Jun/1925 2:00 -1:20
4/Oct/1925 3:00 -0:20
15/May/1926 2:00 -1:20
3/Oct/1926 3:00 -0:20
15/May/1927 2:00 -1:20
2/Oct/1927 3:00 -0:20
15/May/1928 2:00 -1:20
7/Oct/1928 3:00 -0:20
15/May/1929 2:00 -1:20
6/Oct/1929 3:00 -0:20
15/May/1930 2:00 -1:20
5/Oct/1930 3:00 -0:20
15/May/1931 2:00 -1:20
4/Oct/1931 3:00 -0:20
22/May/1932 2:00 -1:20
2/Oct/1932 3:00 -0:20
15/May/1933 2:00 -1:20
8/Oct/1933 3:00 -0:20
15/May/1934 2:00 -1:20
7/Oct/1934 3:00 -0:20
15/May/1935 2:00 -1:20
6/Oct/1935 3:00 -0:20
15/May/1936 2:00 -1:20
4/Oct/1936 3:00 -0:20
22/May/1937 2:00 -1:20
Begin Standard 5E00
1/Jul/1937 0:00 -1:20
3/Oct/1937 3:00 -0:20
15/May/1938 2:00 -1:20
2/Oct/1938 3:00 -0:20
15/May/1939 2:00 -1:20
8/Oct/1939 3:00 -0:20
16/May/1940 0:40 -1:20
Begin Standard 15E00
16/May/1940 2:00 -2:00
2/Nov/1942 3:00 -1:00
29/Mar/1943 2:00 -2:00
4/Oct/1943 3:00 -1:00
3/Apr/1944 2:00 -2:00
19/Sep/1944 3:00 -1:00
3/Apr/1977 2:00 TT#1
....

Time Table # 7
Before 1/May/1892 LMT
Begin Standard 4E53
1/May/1892 0:00 -0:20
30/Apr/1916 24:00 -1:20
1/Oct/1916 0:00 -0:20
16/Apr/1917 2:00 -1:20
17/Sep/1917 3:00 -0:20
1/Apr/1918 2:00 -1:20
30/Sep/1918 3:00 -0:20
7/Apr/1919 2:00 -1:20
29/Sep/1919 3:00 -0:20
5/Apr/1920 2:00 -1:20
27/Sep/1920 3:00 -0:20
4/Apr/1921 2:00 -1:20
26/Sep/1921 3:00 -0:20
26/Mar/1922 2:00 -1:20
8/Oct/1922 3:00 -0:20
1/Jun/1923 2:00 -1:20
7/Oct/1923 3:00 -0:20
30/Mar/1924 2:00 -1:20
5/Oct/1924 3:00 -0:20
5/Jun/1925 2:00 -1:20
4/Oct/1925 3:00 -0:20
15/May/1926 2:00 -1:20
3/Oct/1926 3:00 -0:20
15/May/1927 2:00 -1:20
2/Oct/1927 3:00 -0:20
15/May/1928 2:00 -1:20
7/Oct/1928 3:00 -0:20
15/May/1929 2:00 -1:20
6/Oct/1929 3:00 -0:20
15/May/1930 2:00 -1:20
5/Oct/1930 3:00 -0:20
15/May/1931 2:00 -1:20
4/Oct/1931 3:00 -0:20
22/May/1932 2:00 -1:20
2/Oct/1932 3:00 -0:20
15/May/1933 2:00 -1:20
8/Oct/1933 3:00 -0:20
15/May/1934 2:00 -1:20
7/Oct/1934 3:00 -0:20
15/May/1935 2:00 -1:20
6/Oct/1935 3:00 -0:20
15/May/1936 2:00 -1:20
4/Oct/1936 3:00 -0:20
22/May/1937 2:00 -1:20
Begin Standard 5E00
1/Jul/1937 0:00 -1:20
3/Oct/1937 3:00 -0:20
15/May/1938 2:00 -1:20
2/Oct/1938 3:00 -0:20
15/May/1939 2:00 -1:20
8/Oct/1939 3:00 -0:20
16/May/1940 0:40 -1:20
Begin Standard 15E00
16/May/1940 2:00 -2:00
2/Nov/1942 3:00 -1:00
29/Mar/1943 2:00 -2:00
4/Oct/1943 3:00 -1:00
3/Apr/1944 2:00 -2:00
19/Sep/1944 21:00 -1:00
3/Apr/1977 2:00 TT#1
....

Time Table # 8
Before 1/May/1892 LMT
Begin Standard 4E53
1/May/1892 0:00 -0:20
30/Apr/1916 24:00 -1:20
1/Oct/1916 0:00 -0:20
16/Apr/1917 2:00 -1:20
17/Sep/1917 3:00 -0:20
1/Apr/1918 2:00 -1:20
30/Sep/1918 3:00 -0:20
7/Apr/1919 2:00 -1:20
29/Sep/1919 3:00 -0:20
5/Apr/1920 2:00 -1:20
27/Sep/1920 3:00 -0:20
4/Apr/1921 2:00 -1:20
26/Sep/1921 3:00 -0:20
26/Mar/1922 2:00 -1:20
8/Oct/1922 3:00 -0:20
1/Jun/1923 2:00 -1:20
7/Oct/1923 3:00 -0:20
30/Mar/1924 2:00 -1:20
5/Oct/1924 3:00 -0:20
5/Jun/1925 2:00 -1:20
4/Oct/1925 3:00 -0:20
15/May/1926 2:00 -1:20
3/Oct/1926 3:00 -0:20
15/May/1927 2:00 -1:20
2/Oct/1927 3:00 -0:20
15/May/1928 2:00 -1:20
7/Oct/1928 3:00 -0:20
15/May/1929 2:00 -1:20
6/Oct/1929 3:00 -0:20
15/May/1930 2:00 -1:20
5/Oct/1930 3:00 -0:20
15/May/1931 2:00 -1:20
4/Oct/1931 3:00 -0:20
22/May/1932 2:00 -1:20
2/Oct/1932 3:00 -0:20
15/May/1933 2:00 -1:20
8/Oct/1933 3:00 -0:20
15/May/1934 2:00 -1:20
7/Oct/1934 3:00 -0:20
15/May/1935 2:00 -1:20
6/Oct/1935 3:00 -0:20
15/May/1936 2:00 -1:20
4/Oct/1936 3:00 -0:20
22/May/1937 2:00 -1:20
Begin Standard 5E00
1/Jul/1937 0:00 -1:20
3/Oct/1937 3:00 -0:20
15/May/1938 2:00 -1:20
2/Oct/1938 3:00 -0:20
15/May/1939 2:00 -1:20
8/Oct/1939 3:00 -0:20
16/May/1940 0:40 -1:20
Begin Standard 15E00
16/May/1940 2:00 -2:00
2/Nov/1942 3:00 -1:00
29/Mar/1943 2:00 -2:00
4/Oct/1943 3:00 -1:00
3/Apr/1944 2:00 -2:00
22/Sep/1944 0:00 -1:00
3/Apr/1977 2:00 TT#1
....

Time Table # 9
Before 1/May/1892 LMT
Begin Standard 4E53
1/May/1892 0:00 -0:20
30/Apr/1916 24:00 -1:20
1/Oct/1916 0:00 -0:20
16/Apr/1917 2:00 -1:20
17/Sep/1917 3:00 -0:20
1/Apr/1918 2:00 -1:20
30/Sep/1918 3:00 -0:20
7/Apr/1919 2:00 -1:20
29/Sep/1919 3:00 -0:20
5/Apr/1920 2:00 -1:20
27/Sep/1920 3:00 -0:20
4/Apr/1921 2:00 -1:20
26/Sep/1921 3:00 -0:20
26/Mar/1922 2:00 -1:20
8/Oct/1922 3:00 -0:20
1/Jun/1923 2:00 -1:20
7/Oct/1923 3:00 -0:20
30/Mar/1924 2:00 -1:20
5/Oct/1924 3:00 -0:20
5/Jun/1925 2:00 -1:20
4/Oct/1925 3:00 -0:20
15/May/1926 2:00 -1:20
3/Oct/1926 3:00 -0:20
15/May/1927 2:00 -1:20
2/Oct/1927 3:00 -0:20
15/May/1928 2:00 -1:20
7/Oct/1928 3:00 -0:20
15/May/1929 2:00 -1:20
6/Oct/1929 3:00 -0:20
15/May/1930 2:00 -1:20
5/Oct/1930 3:00 -0:20
15/May/1931 2:00 -1:20
4/Oct/1931 3:00 -0:20
22/May/1932 2:00 -1:20
2/Oct/1932 3:00 -0:20
15/May/1933 2:00 -1:20
8/Oct/1933 3:00 -0:20
15/May/1934 2:00 -1:20
7/Oct/1934 3:00 -0:20
15/May/1935 2:00 -1:20
6/Oct/1935 3:00 -0:20
15/May/1936 2:00 -1:20
4/Oct/1936 3:00 -0:20
22/May/1937 2:00 -1:20
Begin Standard 5E00
1/Jul/1937 0:00 -1:20
3/Oct/1937 3:00 -0:20
15/May/1938 2:00 -1:20
2/Oct/1938 3:00 -0:20
15/May/1939 2:00 -1:20
8/Oct/1939 3:00 -0:20
16/May/1940 0:40 -1:20
Begin Standard 15E00
16/May/1940 2:00 -2:00
2/Nov/1942 3:00 -1:00
29/Mar/1943 2:00 -2:00
4/Oct/1943 3:00 -1:00
3/Apr/1944 2:00 -2:00
2/Oct/1944 3:00 -1:00
2/Apr/1945 2:00 -2:00
6/May/1945 8:00 -1:00
3/Apr/1977 2:00 TT#1

NETHERLANDS PAÍSES BAJOS PAYS-BAS NIEDERLANDE NEDERLAND

Place		Lat.	Long.	Time
Aalsmeer	1	52N16	4E45	-0:19:00
Aalst	1	51N23	5E29	-0:21:56
Aalten	1	51N56	6E35	-0:26:20
Aardenburg	1	51N16	3E27	-0:13:48
Aarle-Rixtel	1	51N31	5E38	-0:22:32
Abcoude	1	52N16	4E58	-0:19:52
Achthuizen	1	51N42	4E16	-0:17:04
Aduard	1	53N15	6E26	-0:25:44
Akersloot	1	52N34	4E44	-0:18:56
Akkerwoude	1	53N17	5E58	-0:23:52
Akkrum	1	53N03	5E50	-0:23:20
Alblasserdam	1	51N52	4E40	-0:18:40
Alkmaar	1	52N37	4E44	-0:18:56
Almelo	1	52N21	6E39	-0:26:36
Alphen aan den Rijn	1	52N07	4E40	-0:18:40
Amby	1	50N53	5E44	-0:22:56
America	1	51N26	5E59	-0:23:56
Amerongen	1	52N00	5E27	-0:21:48
Amersfoort	1	52N09	5E24	-0:21:36
Amstelveen	1	52N18	4E51	-0:19:24
Amsterdam	1	52N22	4E54	-0:19:36
Andijk	1	52N45	5E12	-0:20:48
Angeren	1	51N55	5E58	-0:23:52
Apeldoorn	1	52N13	5E58	-0:23:52
Appingedam	1	53N18	6E52	-0:27:28
Arcen	1	51N29	6E11	-0:24:44
Arnemuiden	1	51N30	3E41	-0:14:44
Arnhem	1	51N59	5E55	-0:23:40
Assen	1	52N59	6E34	-0:26:16
Assendelft	1	52N27	4E45	-0:19:00
Asten	1	51N24	5E45	-0:23:00
Austerlitz	1	52N05	5E19	-0:21:16
Axel	1	51N16	3E55	-0:15:40
Baarle-Nassau	1	51N27	4E53	-0:19:32
Baarlo	1	51N20	6E05	-0:24:20
Baarn	1	52N13	5E16	-0:21:04
Badhoevedorp	1	52N21	4E46	-0:19:04
Bakkeveen	1	53N05	6E15	-0:25:00
Balk	1	52N54	5E34	-0:22:16
Balkbrug	1	52N36	6E24	-0:25:36
Barendrecht	1	51N51	4E32	-0:18:08
Barneveld	1	52N08	5E35	-0:22:20
Bedum	1	53N17	6E36	-0:26:24
Beek	1	50N56	5E49	-0:23:16
Beek	1	51N51	5E54	-0:23:36
Beek	1	51N32	5E38	-0:22:32
Beerta	1	53N10	7E05	-0:28:20
Beetsterzwaag	1	53N03	6E05	-0:24:20
Beilen	1	52N52	6E31	-0:26:04
Belfeld	1	51N19	6E06	-0:24:24
Bellingwolde	1	53N07	7E09	-0:28:36
Bemmel	1	51N54	5E54	-0:23:36
Bennekom	1	52N00	5E40	-0:22:40
Bergambacht	1	51N56	4E46	-0:19:04
Bergeijk	1	51N19	5E22	-0:21:28
Bergen	1	52N40	4E41	-0:18:44
Bergen aan Zee	1	52N38	4E37	-0:18:28
Bergen op Zoom	1	51N30	4E17	-0:17:08
Berghem	1	51N46	5E34	-0:22:16
Bergum	1	53N11	5E59	-0:23:56
Berlicum	1	51N42	5E23	-0:21:32
Berlikum	1	53N15	5E39	-0:22:36
Best	1	51N31	5E24	-0:21:36
Beverwijk	1	52N28	4E40	-0:18:40
Bilthoven	1	52N07	5E17	-0:21:08
Bladel	1	51N23	5E13	-0:20:52
Blaricum	1	52N16	5E15	-0:21:00
Blerick	1	51N23	6E10	-0:24:40
Bloemendaal	1	52N24	4E37	-0:18:28
Blokzijl	1	52N44	5E57	-0:23:48
Bocholtz	1	50N49	6E00	-0:24:00
Bodegraven	1	52N05	4E45	-0:19:00
Boekelo	1	52N13	6E47	-0:27:08
Bolsward	1	53N03	5E31	-0:22:04
Borculo	1	52N07	6E31	-0:26:04
Borger	1	52N55	6E46	-0:27:04
Borne	1	52N18	6E45	-0:27:00
Boskoop	1	52N04	4E35	-0:18:20
Bourtange	1	53N00	7E11	-0:28:44
Bovenkarspel	1	52N42	5E15	-0:21:00
Boxmeer	1	51N39	5E57	-0:23:48
Boxtel	1	51N35	5E20	-0:21:20
Bozum	1	53N05	5E42	-0:22:48
Breda	1	51N35	4E46	-0:19:04
Breskens	1	51N24	3E34	-0:14:16
Breukelen	1	52N10	5E00	-0:20:00
Brielle	1	51N54	4E10	-0:16:40
Broek (op Langendijk)	1	52N40	4E48	-0:19:12
Brouwershaven	1	51N44	3E54	-0:15:36
Bruinisse	1	51N40	4E06	-0:16:24
Brummen	1	52N05	6E09	-0:24:36
Brunssum	1	50N56	5E59	-0:23:56
Budel	1	51N17	5E35	-0:22:20
Buinen	1	52N55	6E50	-0:27:20
Buitenpost	1	53N15	6E09	-0:24:36
Bunde	1	50N54	5E45	-0:23:00
Bunnik	1	52N04	5E12	-0:20:48
Bunschoten	1	52N14	5E22	-0:21:28
Bussum	1	52N16	5E10	-0:20:40
Cadzand	1	51N22	3E25	-0:13:40
Callantsoog	1	52N49	4E41	-0:18:44
Capelle (aan de IJssel)	1	51N55	4E35	-0:18:20
Castricum	1	52N33	4E39	-0:18:36
Chaam	1	51N31	4E52	-0:19:28
Coevorden	1	52N40	6E45	-0:27:00
Colijnsplaat	1	51N36	3E51	-0:15:24
Creil	1	52N45	5E40	-0:22:40
Culemborg	1	51N56	5E13	-0:20:52
Cuyk	1	51N44	5E52	-0:23:28
Dalfsen	1	52N30	6E16	-0:25:04
De Bilt	1	52N06	5E10	-0:20:40
De Cocksdorp	1	53N08	4E52	-0:19:28
Dedemsvaart	1	52N36	6E28	-0:25:52
De Koog	1	53N05	4E45	-0:19:00
De Krim	1	52N38	6E38	-0:26:32
Delft	1	52N00	4E21	-0:17:24
Delfzijl	1	53N19	6E46	-0:27:04
De Lier	1	51N57	4E15	-0:17:00
Den Burg	1	53N03	4E48	-0:19:12
Denekamp	1	52N23	7E00	-0:28:00
Den Haag → 's-Gravenhage	1	52N06	4E18	-0:17:12
Den Helder	1	52N54	4E45	-0:19:00
Den Oever	1	52N56	5E02	-0:20:08
De Rijp	1	52N34	4E50	-0:19:20
De Steeg	1	52N02	6E04	-0:24:16
Deurne	1	51N28	5E47	-0:23:08
Deventer	1	52N15	6E10	-0:24:40
Didam	1	51N56	6E08	-0:24:32
Diemen	1	52N20	4E58	-0:19:52
Diepenheim	1	52N12	6E33	-0:26:12
Diepenveen	1	52N18	6E08	-0:24:32
Dieren	1	52N03	6E06	-0:24:24
Diever	1	52N52	6E19	-0:25:16
Dinteloord	1	51N37	4E22	-0:17:28
Dinxperlo	1	51N52	6E29	-0:25:56
Dirkshorn	1	52N45	4E45	-0:19:00
Dirksland	1	51N44	4E06	-0:16:24
Doesburg	1	52N01	6E09	-0:24:36
Doetinchem	1	51N58	6E17	-0:25:08
Dokkum	1	53N19	6E00	-0:24:00
Domburg	1	51N34	3E30	-0:14:00
Dongen	1	51N37	4E56	-0:19:44
Donk	1	51N33	5E37	-0:22:28
Doorn	1	52N03	5E21	-0:21:24
Dordrecht	1	51N49	4E40	-0:18:40
Dort → Dordrecht	1	51N49	4E40	-0:18:40
Drachten	1	53N06	6E05	-0:24:20
Driebergen	1	52N03	5E16	-0:21:04
Dronrijp	1	53N11	5E38	-0:22:32
Drunen	1	51N42	5E08	-0:20:32
Druten	1	51N54	5E36	-0:22:24
Dubbeldam	1	51N47	4E42	-0:18:48
Dwingeloo	1	52N50	6E21	-0:25:24
Echt	1	51N06	5E52	-0:23:28
Edam	1	52N31	5E03	-0:20:12
Ede	1	52N03	5E40	-0:22:40
Eede	1	51N15	3E28	-0:13:52
Eefde	1	52N10	6E14	-0:24:56
Eelde	1	53N07	6E35	-0:26:20
Eerbeek	1	52N07	6E04	-0:24:16
Eersel	1	51N22	5E19	-0:21:16
Eexta	1	53N10	6E59	-0:27:56
Egmond aan Zee	1	52N36	4E37	-0:18:28
Egmond-Binnen	1	52N35	4E39	-0:18:36
Eibergen	1	52N06	6E39	-0:26:36
Eijsden	1	50N47	5E43	-0:22:52
Eindhoven	3	51N26	5E28	-0:21:52
Elburg	1	52N26	5E50	-0:23:20
Ellewoutsdijk	1	51N24	3E49	-0:15:16
Elsloo	1	50N56	5E46	-0:23:04
Elspeet	1	52N17	5E46	-0:23:04
Elst	1	51N55	5E50	-0:23:20
Emmeloord	1	52N43	5E45	-0:23:00
Emmen	1	52N47	7E00	-0:28:00
Emmer-Compascuum	1	52N48	7E02	-0:28:08
Emmer-Erfscheidenveen	1	52N48	7E01	-0:28:04
Enkhuizen	1	52N42	5E17	-0:21:08
Ens	1	52N38	5E50	-0:23:20
Enschede	1	52N12	6E53	-0:27:32
Enter	1	52N18	6E34	-0:26:16
Epe	1	52N21	6E00	-0:24:00
Erica	1	52N43	6E55	-0:27:40
Ermelo	1	52N17	5E37	-0:22:28
Etten-Leur	1	51N34	4E38	-0:18:32
Eursinge	1	52N46	6E28	-0:25:52
Exloërmond	1	52N54	6E57	-0:27:48
Fijnaart	1	51N37	4E31	-0:18:04
Finsterwolde	1	53N12	7E04	-0:28:16
Flushing → Vlissingen	1	51N26	3E35	-0:14:20
Franeker	1	53N11	5E32	-0:22:08
Gaanderen	1	51N56	6E21	-0:25:24
Gasselte	1	52N57	6E46	-0:27:04
Geertruidenberg	1	51N43	4E52	-0:19:28
Geldermalsen	1	51N53	5E17	-0:21:08
Geldrop	1	51N25	5E33	-0:22:12
Geleen	1	50N58	5E52	-0:23:28
Gemert	1	51N34	5E40	-0:22:40
Gendringen	1	51N52	6E22	-0:25:28
Gendt	1	51N53	5E59	-0:23:56
Genemuiden	1	52N37	6E07	-0:24:28
Gennep	1	51N42	5E58	-0:23:52
Gieten	1	53N00	6E46	-0:27:04
Giethoorn	1	52N43	6E05	-0:24:20
Gilze	1	51N33	4E57	-0:19:48
Glanerbrug	1	52N13	6E58	-0:27:52
Goes	1	51N30	3E54	-0:15:36
Goirle	1	51N32	5E04	-0:20:16
Goor	1	52N14	6E35	-0:26:20
Gorinchem	1	51N50	5E00	-0:20:00
Gorredijk	1	53N00	6E05	-0:24:20
Gouda	1	52N01	4E43	-0:18:52
Goudswaard	1	51N47	4E16	-0:17:04
Graauw	1	51N20	4E05	-0:16:20
Grave	1	51N45	5E44	-0:22:56
Grijpskerk	1	53N15	6E18	-0:25:12
Groede	1	51N23	3E30	-0:14:00
Groenlo	1	52N03	6E38	-0:26:32
Groesbeek	1	51N47	5E55	-0:23:40
Groningen	1	53N13	6E33	-0:26:12
Grootebroek	1	52N43	5E13	-0:20:52
Grouw	1	53N05	5E45	-0:23:00
Gulpen	1	50N48	5E54	-0:23:36
Haag → 's-Gravenhage	1	52N06	4E18	-0:17:12
Haaksbergen	1	52N09	6E44	-0:26:56
Haamstede	1	51N43	3E45	-0:15:00
Haaren	1	51N36	5E12	-0:20:48
Haarlem	1	52N23	4E38	-0:18:32
Halsteren	1	51N32	4E16	-0:17:04
Hansweert	1	51N26	4E00	-0:16:00
Hapert	1	51N23	5E15	-0:21:00
Hardegarijp	1	53N13	5E56	-0:23:44
Hardenberg	1	52N34	6E37	-0:26:28
Harderwijk	1	52N21	5E36	-0:22:24
Haren	1	53N10	6E35	-0:26:20
Harkema-Opeinde	1	53N11	6E08	-0:24:32
Harlingen	1	53N10	5E24	-0:21:36
Harmelen	1	52N05	4E58	-0:19:52
Harskamp	1	52N07	5E45	-0:23:00
Hasselt	1	52N35	6E05	-0:24:20
Hattem	1	52N28	6E04	-0:24:16
Haulerwijk	1	53N04	6E20	-0:25:20
Haye, La → 's-Gravenhage	1	52N06	4E18	-0:17:12
Hedel	1	51N45	5E15	-0:21:00
Heel	1	51N11	5E53	-0:23:32
Heemskerk	1	52N31	4E40	-0:18:40
Heemstede	1	52N21	4E37	-0:18:28
Heer	1	50N50	5E44	-0:22:56
Heerde	1	52N23	6E03	-0:24:12
Heerenveen	1	52N57	5E55	-0:23:40
Heerlen	4	50N54	5E59	-0:23:56
Heesch	1	51N44	5E32	-0:22:08
Heeze	1	51N24	5E35	-0:22:20
Heiloo	1	52N36	4E43	-0:18:52
Heino	1	52N26	6E14	-0:24:56
Hellendoorn	1	52N24	6E26	-0:25:44
Hellevoetsluis	1	51N49	4E08	-0:16:32
Helmond	5	51N29	5E40	-0:22:40
Helvoirt	1	51N38	5E13	-0:20:52
Hengelo	1	52N15	6E45	-0:27:00
Hillegom	1	52N18	4E35	-0:18:20
Hilvarenbeek	1	51N29	5E09	-0:20:36
Hilversum	1	52N14	5E10	-0:20:40
Hindeloopen	1	52N56	5E24	-0:21:36
Hippolytushoef	1	52N54	4E57	-0:19:48
Hoedekenskerke	1	51N25	3E55	-0:15:40
Hoek van Holland	1	51N59	4E09	-0:16:36
Hoensbroek	1	50N55	5E55	-0:23:40
Hollum	1	53N26	5E37	-0:22:28
Holsloot	1	52N44	6E48	-0:27:12
Holten	1	52N17	6E25	-0:25:40
Holwerd	1	53N22	5E54	-0:23:36
Hoogerheide	1	51N25	4E20	-0:17:20
Hoogeveen	1	52N43	6E29	-0:25:56
Hoogezand	1	53N09	6E47	-0:27:08
Hoogkerk	1	53N13	6E30	-0:26:00
Hoogvliet	1	51N52	4E21	-0:17:24
Hoorn	1	52N38	5E04	-0:20:16
Horst	1	51N27	6E04	-0:24:16
Huisduinen	1	52N56	4E44	-0:18:56
Huissen	1	51N57	5E56	-0:23:44
Huizen	1	52N17	5E14	-0:20:56
Hulst	1	51N17	4E03	-0:16:12
Hummelo	1	52N00	6E14	-0:24:56
IJmuiden	1	52N27	4E36	-0:18:24
IJsselmuiden	1	52N34	5E56	-0:23:44
IJsselstein	1	52N02	5E03	-0:20:12
IJzendijke	1	51N19	3E38	-0:14:32
Irnsum	1	53N05	5E47	-0:23:08
Ittersum	1	52N28	6E07	-0:24:28
Joure	1	52N57	5E47	-0:23:08
Jutphaas	1	52N03	5E05	-0:20:20
Kaatsheuvel	1	51N40	5E02	-0:20:08
Kamerik	1	52N06	4E54	-0:19:36
Kampen	1	52N33	5E54	-0:23:36
Kapelle	1	51N28	3E58	-0:15:52
Katwijk aan de Rijn	1	52N11	4E26	-0:17:44
Katwijk aan Zee	1	52N13	4E24	-0:17:36
Kerkdriel	1	51N46	5E20	-0:21:20
Kerkrade (-Holz)	1	50N52	6E04	-0:24:16
Klaaswaal	1	51N46	4E26	-0:17:44
Klazienaveen	1	52N44	7E00	-0:28:00
Kloosterveen	1	52N59	6E33	-0:26:12
Kloosterzande	1	51N22	4E02	-0:16:08
Klundert	1	51N40	4E32	-0:18:08
Kollum	1	53N16	6E09	-0:24:36
Koog (aan de Zaan)	1	52N27	4E49	-0:19:16
Kootwijk	1	52N12	5E45	-0:23:00
Kortgene	1	51N34	3E48	-0:15:12
Krabbendijke	1	51N26	4E07	-0:16:28
Krimpen aan de IJssel	1	51N54	4E35	-0:18:20
Krommenie	1	52N29	4E45	-0:19:00
Kruiningen	1	51N27	4E02	-0:16:08
Kruisland	1	51N34	4E24	-0:17:36
Kuinre	1	52N47	5E50	-0:23:20
Lage Zwaluwe	1	51N43	4E41	-0:18:44
La Haye → 's-Gravenhage	1	52N06	4E18	-0:17:12
Landsmeer	1	52N26	4E52	-0:19:28
Langweer	1	52N57	5E43	-0:22:52
Laren	1	52N15	5E14	-0:20:56
Leek	1	53N09	6E24	-0:25:36
Leende	1	51N21	5E33	-0:22:12
Leerdam	1	51N54	5E05	-0:20:20
Leersum	1	52N01	5E26	-0:21:44
Leeuwarden	1	53N12	5E46	-0:23:04
Leiden	1	52N09	4E30	-0:18:00
Leiderdorp	1	52N09	4E32	-0:18:08
Leidschendam	1	52N05	4E24	-0:17:36
Lelystad	1	52N31	5E27	-0:21:48
Lemele	1	52N27	6E25	-0:25:40
Lemmer	1	52N50	5E42	-0:22:48
Lewedorp	1	51N30	3E45	-0:15:00
Leyden → Leiden	1	52N09	4E30	-0:18:00
Lichtenvoorde	1	51N59	6E34	-0:26:16

Place		Lat.	Long.	Time
Lieshout	1	51N32	5E35	-0:22:20
Limmen	1	52N34	4E41	-0:18:44
Linne	1	51N10	5E57	-0:23:48
Lisse	1	52N15	4E33	-0:18:12
Lochem	1	52N09	6E25	-0:25:40
Loenen	1	52N07	6E01	-0:24:04
Loon op Zand	1	51N38	5E04	-0:20:16
Lopik	1	51N58	4E56	-0:19:44
Loppersum	1	53N19	6E45	-0:27:00
Losser	1	52N15	7E00	-0:28:00
Lunteren	1	52N05	5E37	-0:22:28
Maarssen	1	52N08	5E08	-0:20:32
Maasbracht	6	51N08	5E53	-0:23:32
Maasdam	1	51N47	4E32	-0:18:08
Maasniel	1	51N13	6E01	-0:24:04
Maassluis	1	51N55	4E15	-0:17:00
Maastricht	1	50N52	5E43	-0:22:52
Made	1	51N41	4E46	-0:19:04
Makkum	1	53N04	5E24	-0:21:36
Markelo	1	52N14	6E30	-0:26:00
Marknesse	1	52N43	5E52	-0:23:28
Marssum	1	53N12	5E42	-0:22:48
Marum	1	53N08	6E16	-0:25:04
Medemblik	1	52N46	5E06	-0:20:24
Meerkerk	1	51N45	5E00	-0:20:00
Meerseen	1	50N53	5E45	-0:23:00
Meijel	1	51N21	5E53	-0:23:32
Menaldum	1	53N12	5E39	-0:22:36
Meppel	1	52N42	6E11	-0:24:44
Middelburg	1	51N30	3E37	-0:14:28
Middelharnis	1	51N45	4E11	-0:16:44
Middelstum	1	53N20	6E38	-0:26:32
Middenbeemster	1	52N33	4E55	-0:19:40
Middenmeer	1	52N47	5E00	-0:20:00
Midsland	1	53N22	5E16	-0:21:04
Midwolda	1	53N12	7E00	-0:28:00
Mierlo	1	51N27	5E37	-0:22:28
Mijdrecht	1	52N13	4E52	-0:19:28
Mill	1	51N41	5E47	-0:23:08
Millingen aan de Rijn	1	51N52	6E02	-0:24:08
Minnertsga	1	53N15	5E35	-0:22:20
Moerdijk	1	51N43	4E38	-0:18:32
Moergestel	1	51N33	5E11	-0:20:44
Monnickendam	1	52N27	5E02	-0:20:08
Monster	1	52N02	4E10	-0:16:40
Montfoort	1	52N03	4E57	-0:19:48
Mook	1	51N45	5E54	-0:23:36
Moordrecht	1	51N59	4E40	-0:18:40
Muiden	1	52N19	5E04	-0:20:16
Muntendam	1	53N07	6E53	-0:27:32
Murmerwoude	1	53N16	6E00	-0:24:00
Musselkanaal	1	52N56	7E00	-0:28:00
Naaldwijk	1	52N00	4E12	-0:16:48
Naarden	1	52N17	5E09	-0:20:36
Nagele	1	52N37	5E44	-0:22:56
Nederweert	1	51N17	5E45	-0:23:00
Neede	1	52N08	6E36	-0:26:24
Nes	1	53N04	5E51	-0:23:24
Nes	1	53N26	5E45	-0:23:00
Nieuw-Amsterdam	1	52N44	6E51	-0:27:24
Nieuw-Buinen	1	52N57	6E55	-0:27:40
Nieuwe-Niedorp	1	52N45	4E54	-0:19:36
Nieuwe-Pekela	1	53N04	6E58	-0:27:52
Nieuweschans	1	53N11	7E12	-0:28:48
Nieuwkoop	1	52N08	4E47	-0:19:08
Nieuwolda	1	53N14	6E59	-0:27:56
Nieuw-Schoonebeek	1	52N38	6E59	-0:27:56
Nieuw-Vennep	1	52N16	4E38	-0:18:32
Nieuw-Weerdinge	1	52N52	6E59	-0:27:56
Nijkerk	1	52N13	5E30	-0:22:00
Nijmegen	1	51N50	5E50	-0:23:20
Nijverdal	1	52N22	6E27	-0:25:48
Nispen	1	51N29	4E28	-0:17:52
Nistelrode	1	51N43	5E33	-0:22:12
Noordhorn	1	53N16	6E24	-0:25:36
Noord-Scharwoude	1	52N43	4E47	-0:19:08
Noordwijk aan Zee	1	52N14	4E26	-0:17:44
Noordwijk-Binnen	1	52N13	4E27	-0:17:48
Noordwijkerhout	1	52N15	4E30	-0:18:00
Noordwolde	1	52N54	6E09	-0:24:36
Norg	1	53N04	6E27	-0:25:48
Nuenen	1	51N29	5E33	-0:22:12
Numansdorp	1	51N44	4E26	-0:17:44
Nunspeet	1	52N23	5E46	-0:23:04
Nuth	1	50N55	5E54	-0:23:36
Obdam	1	52N41	4E41	-0:18:44
Obergum	1	53N20	6E31	-0:26:04
Odoorn	1	52N51	6E51	-0:27:24
Oegstgeest	1	52N10	4E29	-0:17:56
Oirschot	1	51N30	5E18	-0:21:12
Oisterwijk	1	51N35	5E12	-0:20:48
Oldebroek	1	52N26	5E54	-0:23:36
Oldenzaal	1	52N19	6E56	-0:27:44
Olst	1	52N20	6E06	-0:24:24
Ommen	1	52N32	6E25	-0:25:40
Onderdijk	1	52N45	5E07	-0:20:28
Onstwedde	1	53N02	7E02	-0:28:08
Oostburg	1	51N20	3E30	-0:14:00
Oosterbeek	1	52N00	5E50	-0:23:20
Oosterend	1	53N05	4E52	-0:19:28
Oosterhout	1	51N38	4E51	-0:19:24
Oosterwolde	1	52N59	6E17	-0:25:08
Oosthuizen	1	52N35	5E00	-0:20:00
Oostmahorn	1	53N24	6E09	-0:24:36
Oost-Souburg	1	51N27	3E35	-0:14:20
Oost-Vlieland	1	53N17	5E04	-0:20:16
Oostvoorne	1	51N55	4E06	-0:16:24
Ootmarsum	1	52N25	6E54	-0:27:36
Opheusden	1	51N56	5E38	-0:22:32
Opmeer	1	52N43	4E56	-0:19:44
Oppenhuizen	1	53N00	5E42	-0:22:48
Oranje	1	52N55	6E28	-0:25:52
Oss	1	51N46	5E31	-0:22:04
Ossendrecht	1	51N24	4E19	-0:17:16
Otterlo	1	52N06	5E45	-0:23:00
Oud-Beijerland	1	51N49	4E25	-0:17:40
Ouddorp	1	51N18	3E56	-0:15:44
Oudenbosch	1	51N35	4E31	-0:18:04
Oude-Pekela	1	53N04	6E58	-0:27:52
Oudeschild	1	53N02	4E50	-0:19:20
Oude-Tonge	1	51N41	4E12	-0:16:48
Oudewater	1	52N02	4E52	-0:19:28
Oud-Gastel	1	51N35	4E27	-0:17:48
Oud-Loosdrecht	1	52N13	5E04	-0:20:16
Overdinkel	1	52N14	7E01	-0:28:04
Overloon	1	51N35	5E57	-0:23:48
Panningen	1	51N20	5E59	-0:23:56
Papendrecht	1	51N50	4E40	-0:18:40
Paterswolde	1	53N08	6E35	-0:26:20
Peij	1	51N06	5E53	-0:23:32
Petten	1	52N45	4E39	-0:18:36
Pieterburen	1	53N24	6E27	-0:25:48
Pijnacker	1	52N02	4E27	-0:17:48
Poeldijk	1	52N01	4E12	-0:16:48
Posterholt	1	51N07	6E03	-0:24:12
Prinsenbeek	1	51N36	4E42	-0:18:48
Purmerend	1	52N31	4E57	-0:19:48
Putte	1	51N22	4E23	-0:17:32
Putten	1	52N15	5E36	-0:22:24
Raalte	1	52N24	6E16	-0:25:04
Raamsdonksveer	1	51N42	4E56	-0:19:44
Renesse	1	51N44	3E46	-0:15:04
Renkum	1	51N58	5E45	-0:23:00
Reusel	1	51N21	5E22	-0:21:28
Reuver	1	51N17	6E05	-0:24:20
Rheden	1	52N01	6E02	-0:24:08
Rhenen	1	51N57	5E34	-0:22:16
Ridderkerk	1	51N52	4E36	-0:18:24
Rijen	1	51N35	4E55	-0:19:40
Rijksdorp	1	52N09	4E25	-0:17:40
Rijnsburg	1	52N12	4E27	-0:17:48
Rijssen	1	52N18	6E30	-0:26:00
Rijswijk	1	52N04	4E20	-0:17:20
Rinsumageest	1	53N18	5E57	-0:23:48
Rockanje	1	51N53	4E05	-0:16:20
Roden	1	53N07	6E26	-0:25:44
Roelofarendsveen	1	52N12	4E38	-0:18:32
Roermond	1	51N12	6E00	-0:24:00
Rolde	1	52N58	6E38	-0:26:32
Roodeschool	1	53N25	6E45	-0:27:00
Roordahuizum	1	53N06	5E46	-0:23:04
Roosendaal	1	51N32	4E28	-0:17:52
Rosmalen	1	51N43	5E22	-0:21:28
Rotterdam	1	51N55	4E28	-0:17:52
Rouveen	1	52N36	6E11	-0:24:44
Rucphen	1	51N32	4E34	-0:18:16
Ruinen	1	52N46	6E22	-0:25:28
Ruurlo	1	52N05	6E26	-0:25:44
Santpoort	1	52N25	4E38	-0:18:32
Sappemeer	1	53N09	6E50	-0:27:20
Sassenheim	1	52N13	4E31	-0:18:04
Sas van Gent	7	51N14	3E47	-0:15:08
Schagen	1	52N46	4E47	-0:19:08
Schermerhorn	1	52N36	4E52	-0:19:28
Scherpenzeel	1	52N05	5E30	-0:22:00
Scheveningen	1	52N06	4E16	-0:17:04
Schiedam	1	51N55	4E24	-0:17:36
Schiermonnikoog	1	53N24	6E10	-0:24:40
Schijndel	1	51N37	5E25	-0:21:40
Schildwolde	1	53N14	6E49	-0:27:16
Schimmert	1	50N55	5E50	-0:23:20
Schinveld	1	50N57	5E59	-0:23:56
Schoondijke	1	51N21	3E32	-0:14:08
Schoonebeek	1	52N29	6E52	-0:27:28
Schoonhoven	1	51N56	4E51	-0:19:24
Schoorl	1	52N42	4E41	-0:18:44
Serooskerke	1	51N42	3E50	-0:15:20
's-Gravendeel	1	51N46	4E37	-0:18:28
's-Gravenhage (The Hague)	1	52N06	4E18	-0:17:12
's-Gravenzande	1	52N00	4E10	-0:16:40
's-Heerenberg	1	51N53	6E15	-0:25:00
's-Heerenhoek	1	51N27	3E46	-0:15:04
's-Hertogenbosch	1	51N41	5E19	-0:21:16
Siddeburen	1	53N25	6E52	-0:27:28
Sijbekarspel	1	52N43	4E59	-0:19:56
Silvolde	1	51N54	6E53	-0:27:32
Sint Annaland	1	51N36	4E06	-0:16:24
Sint Annaparochie	1	53N16	5E39	-0:22:36
Sint Anthonis	1	51N37	5E52	-0:23:28
Sint Maarten	1	52N46	4E44	-0:18:56
Sint Maartensdijk	1	51N33	4E05	-0:16:20
Sint Michielsgestel	1	51N38	5E21	-0:21:24
Sint-Oedenrode	1	51N34	5E27	-0:21:48
Sint Pancras	1	52N39	4E46	-0:19:04
Sint Willebrord	1	51N33	4E35	-0:18:20
Sittard	8	51N00	5E53	-0:23:32
Sleen	1	52N46	6E48	-0:27:12
Sliedrecht	1	51N49	4E45	-0:19:00
Slikkerveer	1	51N53	4E37	-0:18:28
Slochteren	1	53N12	6E47	-0:27:08
Sloten	1	52N54	5E38	-0:22:32
Sluis	1	51N18	3E24	-0:13:36
Sluiskil	1	51N16	3E50	-0:15:20
Smilde	1	52N56	5E27	-0:21:48
Sneek	1	53N02	5E40	-0:22:40
Soest	1	52N09	5E18	-0:21:12
Soestdijk	1	52N11	5E18	-0:21:12
Soesterberg	1	52N07	5E17	-0:21:08
Someren	1	51N24	5E44	-0:22:56
Sommelsdijk	1	51N45	4E09	-0:16:36
Son	1	51N31	5E30	-0:22:00
Spakenburg	1	52N15	5E23	-0:21:32
Spijkenisse	1	51N21	4E20	-0:17:20
Stad-Delden	1	52N16	6E42	-0:26:48
Stadskanaal	1	53N00	6E55	-0:27:40
Staphorst	2	52N37	6E12	-0:24:48
Staveren	1	52N53	5E22	-0:21:28
Stedum	1	53N18	6E41	-0:26:44
Steenbergen	1	51N35	4E19	-0:17:16
Steenderen	1	52N04	6E11	-0:24:44
Steenwijk	1	52N47	6E08	-0:24:32
Stein	1	50N57	5E46	-0:23:04
Stiens	1	53N15	5E45	-0:23:00
Strijen	1	51N45	4E33	-0:18:12
Surhuisterveen	1	53N10	6E10	-0:24:40
Susteren	1	51N04	5E51	-0:23:24
Swalmen	1	51N15	6E02	-0:24:08
Tegelen	1	51N21	6E09	-0:24:36
Ter Apel	1	52N53	7E04	-0:28:16
Terborg	1	51N55	6E21	-0:25:24
Terhorne	1	53N02	5E46	-0:23:04
Terneuzen	1	51N20	3E50	-0:15:20
Terwolde	1	52N16	6E06	-0:24:24
't Harde	1	52N25	5E53	-0:23:32
The Hague → 's-Gravenhage	1	52N06	4E18	-0:17:12
Tholen	2	51N32	4E12	-0:16:48
Thorn	1	51N10	5E50	-0:23:20
Tiel	1	51N54	5E25	-0:21:40
Tilburg	1	51N34	5E05	-0:20:20
Tolbert	1	53N10	6E21	-0:25:24
Tubbergen	1	52N25	6E46	-0:27:04
Tweede Exloërmond	1	52N55	6E58	-0:27:52
Twello	1	52N14	6E06	-0:24:24
Uddel	1	52N15	5E46	-0:23:04
Uden	1	51N40	5E36	-0:22:24
Udenhout	1	51N37	5E08	-0:20:32
Uitgeest	1	52N32	4E43	-0:18:52
Uithoorn	1	52N14	4E50	-0:19:20
Uithuizen	1	53N24	6E40	-0:26:40
Uithuizermeeden	1	53N24	6E42	-0:26:48
Ulft	1	51N54	6E23	-0:25:32
Ulrum	1	53N22	6E20	-0:25:20
Ulvenhout	1	51N34	4E48	-0:19:12
Ureterp	1	53N05	6E10	-0:24:40
Urk	1	52N39	5E36	-0:22:24
Utrecht	1	52N05	5E08	-0:20:32
Vaals	1	50N56	6E01	-0:24:04
Vaassen	1	52N17	5E57	-0:23:48
Valkenburg	1	50N52	5E50	-0:23:20
Valkenswaard	1	51N21	5E28	-0:21:52
Valthermond	1	52N53	6E59	-0:27:56
Valzon	1	52N28	4E39	-0:18:36
Varsseveld	1	51N57	6E28	-0:25:52
Veendam	1	53N06	6E58	-0:27:52
Veenendaal	1	52N02	5E34	-0:22:16
Veenhuizen	1	53N03	6E24	-0:25:36
Veenoord	1	52N43	6E50	-0:27:20
Veere	1	51N34	3E40	-0:14:40
Veghel	1	51N37	5E33	-0:22:12
Veldhoven	1	51N24	5E24	-0:21:36
Velp	1	52N00	5E59	-0:23:56
Velsen	1	52N27	4E39	-0:18:36
Venlo	1	51N24	6E10	-0:24:40
Venraij	1	51N32	5E59	-0:23:56
Vianen	1	52N00	5E05	-0:20:20
Vierhouten	1	52N20	5E50	-0:23:20
Vinkeveen	1	52N13	4E54	-0:19:36
Vlaardingen	1	51N54	4E21	-0:17:24
Vledder	1	52N52	6E12	-0:24:48
Vleuten	1	52N05	5E02	-0:20:08
Vlijmen	1	51N42	5E15	-0:21:00
Vlissingen (Flushing)	1	51N26	3E35	-0:14:20
Vlodrop	1	51N08	6E05	-0:24:20
Vogelenzang	1	52N19	4E35	-0:18:20
Volendam	1	52N30	5E04	-0:20:16
Volkel	1	51N38	5E40	-0:22:40
Vollenhove	1	52N41	5E58	-0:23:52
Voorburg	1	52N05	4E23	-0:17:32
Voorschoten	1	52N07	4E27	-0:17:48
Voorst	1	52N10	6E09	-0:24:36
Voorthuizen	1	52N12	5E35	-0:22:20
Vorden	1	52N07	6E18	-0:25:12
Vreeswijk	1	52N01	5E05	-0:20:20
Vries	1	53N04	6E35	-0:26:20
Vriezenveen	1	52N25	6E38	-0:26:32
Vroomshoop	1	52N27	6E34	-0:26:16
Vught	1	51N40	5E17	-0:21:08
Waalre	1	51N24	5E26	-0:21:44
Waalwijk	1	51N42	5E04	-0:20:16
Waddinxveen	1	52N03	4E40	-0:18:40
Wagenborgen	1	53N15	6E56	-0:27:44
Wageningen	1	51N58	5E40	-0:22:40
Walsoorden	1	51N23	4E02	-0:16:08
Wamel	1	51N53	5E28	-0:21:52
Warffum	1	53N23	6E34	-0:26:16
Warga	1	53N08	5E51	-0:23:24
Warmenhuizen	1	52N43	4E44	-0:18:56
Warns	1	52N52	5E25	-0:21:40
Warnsveld	1	52N08	6E13	-0:24:52
Wassenaar	1	52N07	4E24	-0:17:36
Wateringen	1	52N02	4E16	-0:17:04
Waubach	1	50N55	6E03	-0:24:12
Weert	8	51N15	5E43	-0:22:52
Weesp	1	52N17	5E02	-0:20:08
Well	1	51N34	6E06	-0:24:24
Wemeldinge	1	51N31	4E00	-0:16:00
Werkendam	1	51N49	4E53	-0:19:32
Wervershoof	1	52N44	5E09	-0:20:36
Westenschouwen	1	51N41	3E42	-0:14:48
Westerblokker	1	52N39	5E08	-0:20:32
Westerbork	1	52N51	6E37	-0:26:28
Westkapelle	1	51N32	3E27	-0:13:48
West-Terschelling	1	53N21	5E13	-0:20:52
Wezep	1	52N27	6E00	-0:24:00

NETHERLANDS PAÍSES BAJOS PAYS-BAS NIEDERLANDE NEDERLAND

Place	TT	Lat	Long	LMT
Wierden	1	52N22	6E35	-0:26:20
Wieringerwerf	1	52N51	5E02	-0:20:08
Wijchen	1	51N48	5E43	-0:22:52
Wijhe	1	52N24	6E07	-0:24:28
Wijk aan Zee	1	52N29	4E35	-0:18:20
Wijk bij Duurstede	1	51N58	5E20	-0:21:20
Wildervank	1	53N04	6E51	-0:27:24
Wilhelminaoord	1	52N53	6E10	-0:24:40
Willemsoord	1	52N49	6E05	-0:24:20
Willemstad	1	51N42	4E26	-0:17:44
Winschoten	1	53N08	7E02	-0:28:08
Winsum	1	53N19	6E31	-0:26:04
Winterswijk	1	51N58	6E44	-0:26:56
Wissenkerke	1	51N35	3E45	-0:15:00
Woensdrecht	1	51N26	4E18	-0:17:12
Woerden	1	52N05	4E54	-0:19:36
Wognum	1	52N41	5E01	-0:20:04
Wolvega	1	52N53	6E00	-0:24:00
Wommels	1	53N06	5E36	-0:22:24
Workum	1	52N57	5E26	-0:21:44
Wormerveer	1	52N28	4E46	-0:19:04
Woudenberg	1	52N05	5E25	-0:21:40
Woudrichem	1	51N49	5E00	-0:20:00
Woudsend	1	52N56	5E36	-0:22:24
Wouw	1	51N32	4E24	-0:17:36
Yerseke	1	51N29	4E02	-0:16:08
Zaandam	1	52N26	4E49	-0:19:16
Zaltbommel	9	51N48	5E15	-0:21:00
Zandvoort	1	52N22	4E32	-0:18:08
Zeeland	1	51N42	5E40	-0:22:40
Zeist	1	52N05	5E15	-0:21:00
Zevenaar	1	51N56	6E05	-0:24:20
Zevenbergen	1	51N38	4E36	-0:18:24
Zevenbergschen Hoek	1	51N41	4E40	-0:18:40
Zierikzee	1	51N38	3E55	-0:15:40
Zoetermeer	1	52N03	4E30	-0:18:00
Zoutelande	1	51N30	3E30	-0:14:00
Zoutkamp	1	53N20	6E18	-0:25:12
Zuid-Beijerland	1	51N45	4E22	-0:17:28
Zuidbroek	1	53N10	6E52	-0:27:28
Zuidhorn	1	53N14	6E24	-0:25:36
Zuidland	1	51N48	4E15	-0:17:00
Zuidlaren	1	53N05	6E41	-0:26:44
Zuidwolde	1	53N15	6E35	-0:26:20
Zundert	1	51N28	4E40	-0:18:40
Zurich	1	53N06	5E23	-0:21:32
Zutphen	1	52N08	6E12	-0:24:48
Zwaag	1	52N40	5E05	-0:20:20
Zwaagwesteinde	1	53N15	6E04	-0:24:16
Zwanenburg	1	52N23	4E45	-0:19:00
Zwartemeer	1	52N43	7E03	-0:28:12
Zwartsluis	1	52N37	6E04	-0:24:16
Zwijndrecht	1	51N49	4E39	-0:18:36
Zwolle	1	52N30	6E05	-0:24:20

NETHERLANDS ANTILLES CURAÇAO NEDERLANDSE ANTILLEN

Time Table # 1
Before 2/Mar/1912 LMT
Begin Standard 60w00
2/Mar/1912 0:00 4:00
....

Time Table # 2
Before 2/Feb/1912 LMT
Begin Standard 68w17
2/Feb/1912 0:00 4:33
Begin Standard 60w00
1/Jan/1965 0:00 4:00
....

Time Table # 3
Before 12/Feb/1912 LMT
Begin Standard 67w30
12/Feb/1912 0:00 4:30
Begin Standard 60w00
1/Jan/1965 0:00 4:00

DIVISIONS

1. Aruba Island
2. Bonaire Island
3. Curaçao Island
4. Saba Island
5. Sint Maarten Island

Place	TT	Lat	Long	LMT
Aruba Island 1	3	12N30	68w58	4:35:52
Bonaire Island 2	3	12N10	68w15	4:33:00
Bottom 4	1	17N37	63w14	4:12:56
Bushiribana 1	3	12N33	69w58	4:39:52
Curaçao Island 3	3	12N11	69w00	4:36:00
Hato 3	3	12N12	68w57	4:35:48
Kralendijk 2	2	12N10	68w17	4:33:08
New Port 3	3	12N03	68w49	4:35:16
Oranjestad 1	3	12N33	70w06	4:40:24
Philipsburg 5	1	17N59	63w10	4:12:40
Rincon 2	2	12N15	68w20	4:33:20
Saba Island 4	3	17N38	63w10	4:12:40
Saint Martin Island 5	3	18N04	63w04	4:12:16
Sint Kruis 3	3	12N18	69w08	4:36:32
Sint Maarten Island 5	3	18N04	63w04	4:12:16
Sint Nicolaas 1	3	12N27	69w52	4:39:28
Willemstad 3	3	12N06	68w56	4:35:44

NEW CALEDONIA NUEVA CALEDONIA NEUKALEDONIEN NOUVELLE-CALÉDONIE

Time Table
Before 13/Jan/1912 LMT
Begin Standard 165E00
13/Jan/1912 0:00 -11:00
4/Dec/1977 0:00 -12:00
27/Feb/1978 0:00 -11:00
3/Dec/1978 0:00 -12:00
27/Feb/1979 0:00 -11:00

DIVISIONS

1. Chesterfield, Îles
2. Hunter Island
3. Lifou, Île
4. Mare, Île
5. New Caledonia Island
6. Pins, Îles des
7. Uvea, Île

Place	Lat	Long	LMT
Aoumou 5	21s24	165E50	-11:03:20
Bouloupari 5	21s52	166E04	-11:04:16
Bourail 5	21s34	165E30	-11:02:00
Bourake Airport 5	21s56	166E00	-11:04:00
Canala 5	21s32	165E57	-11:03:48
Chépénéhé 3	20s47	167E09	-11:08:36
Chesterfield, Îles 1	19s30	158E00	-10:32:00
Cuamoea 6	22s35	167E28	-11:09:52
Goro 5	22s16	167E02	-11:08:08
Hienghène 5	20s41	164E56	-10:59:44
Houaïlou 5	21s17	165E38	-11:02:32
Hunter Island 2	22s24	172E03	-11:28:12
Kaala-Gomen 5	20s40	164E25	-10:57:40
Kanala 5	21s52	165E58	-11:03:52
Koné 5	21s04	164E52	-10:59:28
Koumac 5	20s33	164E17	-10:57:08
Kuto 6	22s40	167E27	-11:09:48
La Foa 5	21s43	165E50	-11:03:20
Lifou, Île 3	20s53	167E13	-11:08:52
Loyalty Islands	21s00	167E00	-11:08:00
Loyauté, Îles	21s00	167E00	-11:08:00
Maré, Île 4	21s30	168E00	-11:12:00
Moindou 5	21s42	165E41	-11:02:44
Mont Dore 5	22s16	166E34	-11:06:16
Mou 3	21s05	165E26	-11:01:44
Mouly 7	20s42	166E25	-11:05:40
Muli 7	20s42	166E25	-11:05:40
Nakéty 5	21s33	166E03	-11:04:12
New Caledonia Island 5	21s30	165E30	-11:02:00
Nouméa 5	22s16	166E27	-11:05:48
Ouaco 5	20s50	164E29	-10:57:56
Paagoumène 5	20s29	164E11	-10:56:44
Païta 5	22s08	166E22	-11:05:28
Pam 5	20s16	164E19	-10:57:16
Pins, Îles des 6	22s37	167E30	-11:10:00
Ponérihouen 5	21s05	165E24	-11:01:36
Pouembout 5	21s08	164E53	-10:59:32
Poum 5	20s14	164E02	-10:56:08
Poume 5	20s14	164E02	-10:56:08
Poya 5	21s19	165E07	-11:00:28
Rho 4	21s22	167E50	-11:11:20
Rô 4	21s22	167E50	-11:11:20
Saint-Joseph 7	20s27	166E36	-11:06:24
Tadine 4	21s33	167E52	-11:11:28
Tadinou 4	21s33	167E52	-11:11:28
Thio 5	21s37	166E14	-11:04:56
Tiéti 5	20s57	165E19	-11:01:16
Touho 5	20s47	165E14	-11:00:56
Uegoa 5	20s20	164E25	-10:57:40
Uvéa 7	20s27	166E36	-11:06:24
Uvéa, Île 7	20s30	166E35	-11:06:20
Uves 5	19s40	163E40	-10:54:40
Vao 6	22s39	167E32	-11:10:08
Voh 5	20s58	164E42	-10:58:48
Wailu 5	21s16	165E38	-11:02:32
Yaté 5	22s09	166E57	-11:07:48

NUEVA ZELANDA NEUSEELAND NOUVELLE-ZÉLANDE NEW ZEALAND

Time Table				
Before 1/Jan/1868 LMT	29/Apr/1934 2:00 -11:30	26/Oct/1975 2:00 -13:00	4/Mar/1984 2:00 -12:00	4/Oct/1992 2:00 -13:00
Begin Standard 172E30	30/Sep/1934 2:00 -12:00	7/Mar/1976 2:00 -12:00	28/Oct/1984 2:00 -13:00	21/Mar/1993 2:00 -12:00
1/Jan/1868 0:00 -11:30	28/Apr/1935 2:00 -11:30	24/Oct/1976 2:00 -13:00	3/Mar/1985 2:00 -12:00	3/Oct/1993 2:00 -13:00
6/Nov/1927 2:00 -12:30	29/Sep/1935 2:00 -12:00	6/Mar/1977 2:00 -12:00	27/Oct/1985 2:00 -13:00	20/Mar/1994 2:00 -12:00
4/Mar/1928 2:00 -11:30	26/Apr/1936 2:00 -11:30	30/Oct/1977 2:00 -13:00	2/Mar/1986 2:00 -12:00	2/Oct/1994 2:00 -13:00
14/Oct/1928 2:00 -12:00	27/Sep/1936 2:00 -12:00	5/Mar/1978 2:00 -12:00	19/Oct/1986 2:00 -13:00	19/Mar/1995 2:00 -12:00
17/Mar/1929 2:00 -11:30	25/Apr/1937 2:00 -11:30	29/Oct/1978 2:00 -13:00	1/Mar/1987 2:00 -12:00	1/Oct/1995 2:00 -13:00
13/Oct/1929 2:00 -12:00	26/Sep/1937 2:00 -12:00	4/Mar/1979 2:00 -12:00	25/Oct/1987 2:00 -13:00	17/Mar/1996 2:00 -12:00
16/Mar/1930 2:00 -11:30	24/Apr/1938 2:00 -11:30	28/Oct/1979 2:00 -13:00	6/Mar/1988 2:00 -12:00	6/Oct/1996 2:00 -13:00
12/Oct/1930 2:00 -12:00	25/Sep/1938 2:00 -12:00	2/Mar/1980 2:00 -12:00	30/Oct/1988 2:00 -13:00	16/Mar/1997 2:00 -12:00
15/Mar/1931 2:00 -11:30	30/Apr/1939 2:00 -11:30	26/Oct/1980 2:00 -13:00	5/Mar/1989 2:00 -12:00	5/Oct/1997 2:00 -13:00
11/Oct/1931 2:00 -12:00	24/Sep/1939 2:00 -12:00	1/Mar/1981 2:00 -12:00	8/Oct/1989 2:00 -13:00	15/Mar/1998 2:00 -12:00
20/Mar/1932 2:00 -11:30	28/Apr/1940 2:00 -11:30	25/Oct/1981 2:00 -13:00	18/Mar/1990 2:00 -12:00	4/Oct/1998 2:00 -13:00
9/Oct/1932 2:00 -12:00	Begin Standard 180E00	7/Mar/1982 2:00 -12:00	7/Oct/1990 2:00 -13:00	21/Mar/1999 2:00 -12:00
19/Mar/1933 2:00 -11:30	29/Sep/1940 2:00 -12:00	31/Oct/1982 2:00 -13:00	17/Mar/1991 2:00 -12:00	3/Oct/1999 2:00 -13:00
8/Oct/1933 2:00 -12:00	3/Nov/1974 2:00 -13:00	6/Mar/1983 2:00 -12:00	6/Oct/1991 2:00 -13:00	19/Mar/2000 2:00 -12:00
	23/Feb/1975 2:00 -12:00	30/Oct/1983 2:00 -13:00	15/Mar/1992 2:00 -12:00	

Place	Lat	Long / Offset
Ahaura	42s21	171E32-11:26:08
Ahipara	35s10	173E10-11:32:40
Akaroa	43s48	172E58-11:31:52
Albany	36s43	174E42-11:38:48
Albury	44s14	170E52-11:23:28
Alexandra	45s15	169E24-11:17:36
Amberley	43s10	172E44-11:30:56
Apiti	39s58	175E53-11:43:32
Arapuni	38s04	175E39-11:42:36
Aria	38s33	174E59-11:39:56
Arrowtown	44s56	168E50-11:15:20
Arthur's Pass	42s57	171E34-11:26:16
Ashburton	43s55	171E45-11:27:00
Ashhurst	40s18	175E45-11:43:00
Athol	45s31	168E35-11:14:20
Auckland	36s52	174E46-11:39:04
Awakino	38s39	174E38-11:38:32
Awanui	35s03	173E15-11:33:00
Balclutha	46s14	169E44-11:18:56
Balfour	45s50	168E35-11:14:20
Bay View	39s25	176E53-11:47:32
Beaumont	45s49	169E32-11:18:08
Belfast	43s27	172E38-11:30:32
Birchwood	45s56	167E52-11:11:28
Blenheim	41s31	173E57-11:35:48
Bluff	46s36	168E20-11:13:20
Brighton	45s57	170E20-11:21:20
Broadwood	35s16	173E23-11:33:32
Bruce Bay	43s35	169E41-11:18:44
Brunner	42s27	171E19-11:25:16
Bulls	40s10	175E23-11:41:32
Cambridge	37s53	175E28-11:41:52
Canvastown	41s18	173E40-11:34:40
Carterton	41s02	175E31-11:42:04
Castlecliff	39s57	174E59-11:39:56
Castlepoint	40s54	176E13-11:44:52
Cave	44s19	170E57-11:23:48
Chalmers	45s49	170E37-11:22:28
Charleston	41s54	171E26-11:25:44
Cheviot	42s49	173E16-11:33:04
Christchurch	43s32	172E38-11:30:32
Clarence	42s10	173E56-11:35:44
Clinton	46s12	169E22-11:17:28
Clive	39s35	176E55-11:47:40
Clyde	45s11	169E19-11:17:16
Coal Creek Flat	45s29	169E18-11:17:12
Coalgate	43s29	171E58-11:27:52
Collingwood	40s40	172E41-11:30:44
Colville	36s38	175E28-11:41:52
Coromandel	36s46	175E30-11:42:00
Cromwell	45s03	169E12-11:16:48
Cronadun	42s02	171E52-11:27:28
Culverden	42s46	172E51-11:31:24
Cust	43s19	172E22-11:29:28
Dannevirke	40s12	176E07-11:44:28
Dargaville	35s56	173E53-11:35:32
Denniston	41s44	171E48-11:27:12
Devonport	36s49	174E48-11:39:12
Dipton	45s54	168E22-11:13:28
Domett	42s51	173E13-11:32:52
Donnellys Crossing	35s43	173E37-11:34:28
Drummond	46s09	168E09-11:12:36
Dunback	45s23	170E38-11:22:32
Dunedin	45s52	170E30-11:22:00
Dunsandel	43s40	172E11-11:28:44
Duntroon	44s52	170E41-11:22:44
Eastbourne	41s18	174E54-11:39:36
East Coast Bays	36s45	174E46-11:39:04
Edendale	46s19	168E47-11:15:08
Edgecumbe	37s59	176E50-11:47:20
Edievale	45s48	169E22-11:17:28
Eketahuna	40s39	175E42-11:42:48
Eltham	39s26	174E18-11:37:12
Enfield	45s03	170E52-11:23:28
Erua	39s14	175E24-11:41:36
Eskdale	39s24	176E50-11:47:20
Fairlie	44s06	170E50-11:23:20
Featherston	41s07	175E20-11:41:20
Feilding	40s13	175E34-11:42:16
Fortrose	46s34	168E48-11:15:12
Fox Glacier	43s28	170E00-11:20:00
Foxton	40s28	175E18-11:41:12
Foxton Beach	40s28	175E13-11:40:52
Franz Josef Glacier	43s24	170E11-11:20:44
Frasertown	38s58	177E24-11:49:36
French Pass	40s56	173E50-11:35:20
Galatea	38s25	176E45-11:47:00
Geraldine	44s05	171E14-11:24:56
Gisborne	38s40	178E01-11:52:04
Glen Afton	37s37	175E02-11:40:08
Glenavy	44s55	171E06-11:24:24
Glenhope	41s39	172E39-11:30:36
Glenorchy	44s51	168E23-11:13:32
Gordonton	37s40	175E18-11:41:12
Gore	46s06	168E58-11:15:52
Granity	41s38	171E51-11:27:24
Green Island	45s54	170E26-11:21:44
Greerton	37s43	176E08-11:44:32
Greymouth	42s28	171E12-11:24:48
Greytown	41s05	175E27-11:41:48
Haast	43s53	169E03-11:16:12
Halcombe	40s09	175E30-11:42:00
Half-Moon Bay	46s54	168E08-11:12:32
Hamilton	37s47	175E17-11:41:08
Hampden	45s19	170E49-11:23:16
Hangatiki	38s15	175E10-11:40:40
Hanmer Springs	42s31	172E49-11:31:16
Harewood	43s29	172E35-11:30:20
Harihari	43s09	170E33-11:22:12
Hastings	39s38	176E51-11:47:24
Havelock	41s17	173E46-11:35:04
Havelock North	39s40	176E53-11:47:32
Hawarden	42s56	172E38-11:30:32
Hawera	39s35	174E17-11:37:08
Hector	41s36	171E53-11:27:32
Helensville	36s40	174E28-11:37:52
Herbert	45s14	170E47-11:23:08
Herekino	35s15	173E13-11:32:52
Heriot	45s50	169E16-11:17:04
Hermitage	43s44	170E06-11:20:24
Hexton	38s37	177E58-11:51:52
Hicks Bay	37s36	178E18-11:53:12
Hikurangi	35s36	174E18-11:37:12
Hikutaia	37s17	175E39-11:42:36
Hinds	44s00	171E34-11:26:16
Hokitika	42s43	170E58-11:23:52
Hornby	43s33	172E32-11:30:08
Horotiu	37s43	175E12-11:40:48
Horrelville	43s20	172E20-11:29:20
Hunterville	39s56	175E34-11:42:16
Huntly	37s33	175E10-11:40:40
Hyde	45s18	170E15-11:21:00
Ikamatua	42s16	171E41-11:26:44
Inangahua Junction	41s51	171E57-11:27:48
Inglewood	39s09	174E12-11:36:48
Invercargill	46s24	168E21-11:13:24
Johnsonville	41s14	174E47-11:39:08
Kaeo	35s06	173E47-11:35:08
Kaiapoi	43s23	172E40-11:30:40
Kaihu	35s46	173E42-11:34:48
Kai-Iwi	39s51	174E56-11:39:44
Kaikohe	35s25	173E48-11:35:12
Kaikoura	42s25	173E41-11:34:44
Kaitaia	35s07	173E16-11:33:04
Kaitangata	46s18	169E51-11:19:24
Kaiwaka	36s10	174E27-11:37:48
Kaka Point	46s23	169E47-11:19:08
Kakaramea	39s43	174E27-11:37:48
Kakatahi	39s41	175E20-11:41:20
Kamo	35s41	174E19-11:37:16
Kaniere	42s45	171E00-11:24:00
Kaponga	39s26	174E09-11:36:36
Karamea	41s15	172E07-11:28:28
Katikati	37s33	175E55-11:43:40
Kaukapakapa	36s37	174E30-11:38:00
Kawakawa	35s23	174E04-11:36:16
Kawerau	38s03	176E43-11:46:52
Kawhia	38s04	174E49-11:39:16
Kekerengu	42s00	174E01-11:36:04
Kerikeri	35s13	173E58-11:35:52
Kihikihi	38s02	175E21-11:41:24
Kimbolton	40s03	175E47-11:43:08
Kingston	45s20	168E42-11:14:48
Kinleith	38s16	175E54-11:43:36
Kirwee	43s30	172E13-11:28:52
Kohukohu	35s21	173E32-11:34:08
Kohuratahi	39s06	174E46-11:39:04
Kowhitirangi	42s52	171E01-11:24:04
Kumara	42s38	171E11-11:24:44
Kuripapango	39s23	176E21-11:45:24
Kurow	44s44	170E28-11:21:52
Kutarere	38s03	177E09-11:48:36
Lake Coleridge	43s22	171E32-11:26:08
Lake Paringa	43s43	169E29-11:17:56
Lake Pukaki	44s11	170E09-11:20:36
Lake Tekapo	44s01	170E30-11:22:00
Lawrence	45s55	169E41-11:18:44
Leeston	43s46	172E18-11:29:12
Leigh	36s17	174E49-11:39:16
Lepperton	39s04	174E13-11:36:52
Levin	40s37	175E17-11:41:08
Lincoln	43s39	172E29-11:29:56
Linton	40s26	175E33-11:42:12
Little River	43s46	172E47-11:31:08
Lower Hutt	41s13	174E55-11:39:40
Lumsden	45s44	168E27-11:13:48
Lyttelton	43s35	172E42-11:30:48
Maheno	45s10	170E50-11:23:20
Makarewa	46s20	168E21-11:13:24
Maketu	37s46	176E27-11:45:48
Makikihi	44s38	171E09-11:24:36
Makotuku	40s07	176E14-11:44:56
Mamaku	38s06	176E05-11:44:20
Manaia	39s33	174E08-11:36:32
Manakau	40s43	175E13-11:40:52
Manapouri	45s34	167E36-11:10:24
Mandeville	46s00	168E49-11:15:16
Mangakino	38s22	175E47-11:43:08
Mangamahu	39s49	175E22-11:41:28
Mangapehi	38s31	175E18-11:41:12
Mangaweka	39s48	175E47-11:43:08
Mangonui	34s59	173E32-11:34:08
Manukau	37s02	174E54-11:39:36
Manunui	38s53	175E20-11:41:20
Manutahi	39s40	174E24-11:37:36
Manutuke	38s41	177E55-11:51:40
Martinborough	41s13	175E28-11:41:52
Marton	40s05	175E23-11:41:32
Maruia	42s11	172E13-11:28:52
Masterton	40s57	175E40-11:42:40
Matakana	36s21	174E43-11:38:52
Matamata	37s49	175E47-11:43:08
Matangi	37s49	175E25-11:41:40
Matapu	39s29	174E14-11:36:56
Matata	37s53	176E45-11:47:00
Mataura	46s11	168E52-11:15:28
Matawai	38s21	177E32-11:50:08
Matiere	38s45	175E06-11:40:24
Maungatapere	35s45	174E12-11:36:48
Maungaturoto	36s06	174E22-11:37:28
Mauriceville	40s47	175E42-11:42:48
Mayfield	43s49	171E25-11:25:40
Mercer	37s16	175E03-11:40:12
Methven	43s38	171E39-11:26:36
Middlemarch	45s31	170E07-11:20:28
Milford Sound	44s40	167E54-11:11:36
Millers Flat	45s40	169E25-11:17:40
Milton	46s07	169E58-11:19:52
Moawhango	39s35	175E52-11:43:28
Moerewa	35s23	174E02-11:36:08
Mohaka	39s07	177E11-11:48:44
Mokai	38s32	175E54-11:43:36
Mokau	38s41	174E37-11:38:28
Morrinsville	37s39	175E32-11:42:08
Morven	44s50	171E07-11:24:28
Mosgiel	45s53	170E21-11:21:24
Mossburn	45s40	168E15-11:13:00
Motueka	41s07	173E00-11:32:00
Mount Maunganui	37s37	176E11-11:44:44
Mount Roskill	36s55	174E45-11:39:00
Mount Somers	43s43	171E24-11:25:36
Mount Wellington	36s54	174E51-11:39:24
Moutohora	38s17	177E32-11:50:08
Murchison	41s48	172E20-11:29:20
Muriwai	38s46	177E55-11:51:40
Murupara	38s28	176E42-11:46:48
Napier	39s29	176E55-11:47:40
Naseby	45s02	170E09-11:20:36
Nelson	41s17	173E17-11:33:08
New Brighton	43s31	172E44-11:30:56
New Plymouth	39s04	174E05-11:36:20
Ngahere	42s24	171E27-11:25:48
Ngapara	44s57	170E45-11:23:00
Ngaruawahia	37s40	175E09-11:40:36
Ngatea	37s17	175E30-11:42:00
Ngongotaha	38s05	176E12-11:44:48
Nightcaps	45s58	168E02-11:12:08
Normanby	39s32	174E17-11:37:08
Norsewood	40s04	176E13-11:44:52
Nuhaka	39s03	177E45-11:51:00
Oakura	39s07	173E57-11:35:48
Oamaru	45s06	170E58-11:23:52
Oaro	42s31	173E30-11:34:00
Ohai	45s55	167E57-11:11:48
Ohakune	39s25	175E24-11:41:36
Ohaupo	37s55	175E19-11:41:16
Ohingaiti	39s52	175E43-11:42:52
Ohura	38s50	174E59-11:39:56
Okahukura	38s47	175E13-11:40:52
Okaihau	35s19	173E47-11:35:08
Okarito	43s14	170E11-11:20:44
Okato	39s12	173E53-11:35:32
Omakau	45s05	169E36-11:18:24
Omarama	44s29	169E58-11:19:52
Ongaonga	39s55	176E25-11:45:40
Ongarue	38s43	175E17-11:41:08
Opotiki	38s00	177E17-11:49:08
Opua	35s19	174E07-11:36:28
Opunake	39s27	173E51-11:35:24
Orawia	46s03	167E49-11:11:16
Orepuki	46s17	167E44-11:10:56
Orewa	36s34	174E42-11:38:48

NEW ZEALAND NOUVELLE-ZÉLANDE NEUSEELAND NUEVA ZELANDA

Orini 37s34 175e18-11:41:12
Oruanui 38s35 176e02-11:44:08
Otahuhu 36s57 174e51-11:39:24
Otaki 40s45 175e09-11:40:36
Otane 39s53 176e38-11:46:32
Otatara 46s26 168e18-11:13:12
Otautau 46s09 168e00-11:12:00
Otematata 44s37 170e16-11:21:04
Otira 42s50 171e33-11:26:12
Otorohanga 38s11 175e12-11:40:48
Owaka 46s27 169e40-11:18:40
Owen River 41s39 172e27-11:29:48
Owhango 39s00 175e23-11:41:32
Oxford 43s18 172e11-11:28:44
Paekakariki 40s59 174e57-11:39:48
Paengaroa 37s49 176e25-11:45:40
Paeroa 37s23 175e40-11:42:40
Pahiatua 40s27 175e50-11:43:20
Pakipaki 39s41 176e48-11:47:12
Palmerston 45s29 170e43-11:22:52
Palmerston North 40s21 175e37-11:42:28
Papakura 37s04 174e57-11:39:48
Paparoa 36s06 174e14-11:36:56
Papatoetoe 36s58 174e52-11:39:28
Paraparaumu 40s55 175e01-11:40:04
Paraparaumu Beach 40s54 174e59-11:39:56
Paremata 41s07 174e52-11:39:28
Pareora 44s30 171e12-11:24:48
Parnassus 42s43 173e18-11:33:12
Patea 39s45 174e28-11:37:52
Patearoa 45s16 170e03-11:20:12
Patumahoe 37s11 174e50-11:39:20
Petone 41s13 174e52-11:39:28
Picton 41s18 174e01-11:36:04
Pihama 39s30 173e56-11:35:44
Piopio 38s28 175e01-11:40:04
Pipiriki 39s29 175e03-11:40:12
Pirongia 38s00 175e12-11:40:48
Pleasant Point 44s16 171e08-11:24:32
Plimmerton 41s05 174e52-11:39:28
Pongaroa 40s33 176e11-11:44:44
Porangahau 40s18 176e37-11:46:28
Porirua 41s08 174e51-11:39:24
Port Chalmers 45s49 170e37-11:22:28
Port Fitzroy 36s10 175e21-11:41:24
Portland 35s48 174e19-11:37:16
Pukekohe 37s12 174e55-11:39:40
Pukeuri Junction 45s02 171e02-11:24:08
Putaruru 38s03 175e47-11:43:08
Putorino 39s08 177e00-11:48:00
Queenstown 45s02 168e40-11:14:40
Raetihi 39s26 175e17-11:41:08
Raglan 37s48 174e53-11:39:32
Rahotu 39s20 173e48-11:35:12
Rakaia 43s45 172e01-11:28:04
Ranfurly 45s08 170e06-11:20:24
Rangiora 43s18 172e36-11:30:24
Rangitukia 37s46 178e27-11:53:48
Raurimu 39s07 175e24-11:41:36
Rawene 35s24 173e30-11:34:00
Reefton 42s07 171e52-11:27:28
Renwick 41s30 173e50-11:35:20
Reporoa 38s26 176e21-11:45:24
Riccarton 43s32 172e36-11:30:24
Richmond 41s20 173e11-11:32:44
Riversdale 45s54 168e45-11:15:00
Riverton 46s21 168e01-11:12:04
Riwaka 41s05 173e00-11:32:00
Roa 42s21 171e23-11:25:32
Rockville 40s44 172e38-11:30:32
Rolleston 43s35 172e23-11:29:32
Rongotea 40s18 175e25-11:41:40
Ross 42s54 170e49-11:23:16
Rotherham 42s42 172e57-11:31:48
Rotomanu 42s39 171e32-11:26:08
Rotorua 38s09 176e15-11:45:00
Rotowaro 37s36 175e05-11:40:20
Roxburgh 45s32 169e19-11:17:16
Ruatahuna 38s33 176e57-11:47:48
Ruatapu 42s48 170e53-11:23:32
Ruatoria 37s53 178e20-11:53:20
Ruawai 36s08 174e02-11:36:08
Runanga 42s24 171e16-11:25:04
Russell 35s16 174e07-11:36:28
Saint Kilda 45s54 170e30-11:22:00
Sanson 40s13 175e25-11:41:40
Scargill 42s56 172e57-11:31:48
Seddon 41s40 174e05-11:36:20
Seddonville 41s33 171e59-11:27:56
Sefton 43s15 172e40-11:30:40
Shannon 40s33 175e25-11:41:40
Sheffield 43s23 172e01-11:28:04
Silverdale 36s37 174e40-11:38:40
Southbridge 43s49 172e15-11:29:00
Southbrook 43s20 172e36-11:30:24
Springburn 43s40 171e28-11:25:52
Spring Creek 41s28 173e58-11:35:52
Springfield 43s20 171e55-11:27:40
Springs Junction 42s19 172e11-11:28:44
Stratford 39s20 174e17-11:37:08
Studholme Junction 44s44 171e08-11:24:32
Tahakopa 46s31 169e23-11:17:32
Taheke 35s27 173e39-11:34:36
Taihape 39s40 175e48-11:43:12
Taitapu 43s40 172e33-11:30:12
Takaka 40s51 172e48-11:31:12
Takapau 40s02 176e21-11:45:24
Takapuna 36s47 174e47-11:39:08
Taneatua 38s04 177e01-11:48:04
Tangowahine 35s52 173e56-11:35:44
Tapanui 45s57 169e16-11:17:04
Tapawera 41s24 172e49-11:31:16
Taradale 39s32 176e51-11:47:24
Tarawera 39s02 176e35-11:46:20
Tariki 39s14 174e15-11:37:00
Tarras 44s50 169e25-11:17:40
Taumarunui 38s52 175e17-11:41:08
Taupiri 37s37 175e11-11:40:44
Taupo 38s41 176e05-11:44:20
Tauranga 37s42 176e10-11:44:40
Tawa 41s10 174e51-11:39:24
Te Anau 45s25 167e43-11:10:52
Te Araroa 37s38 178e22-11:53:28
Te Aroha 37s33 175e43-11:42:52
Te Awamutu 38s01 175e19-11:41:16
Te Hapua 34s31 172e54-11:31:36
Te Haroto 39s08 176e36-11:46:24
Te Kaha 37s44 177e41-11:50:44
Te Kao 34s39 172e57-11:31:48
Te Karaka 38s28 177e52-11:51:28
Te Kauwhata 37s24 175e09-11:40:36
Te Kopuru 36s02 173e56-11:35:44
Te Kuiti 38s20 175e10-11:40:40
Temuka 44s15 171e17-11:25:08
Te Pohue 39s15 176e41-11:46:44
Te Puia 38s04 178e18-11:53:12
Te Puke 37s47 176e20-11:45:20
Te Rehunga 40s13 176e01-11:44:04
Te Teko 38s02 176e48-11:47:12
Te Whaiti 38s35 176e47-11:47:08
Thames 37s08 175e33-11:42:12
Thornbury 46s17 168e06-11:12:24
Tikitiki 37s48 178e24-11:53:36
Tikokino 39s49 176e27-11:45:48
Timaru 44s24 171e15-11:25:00
Tinui 40s53 176e04-11:44:16
Tinwald 43s55 171e43-11:26:52
Tirau 37s59 175e45-11:43:00
Tokaanu 38s58 175e46-11:43:04
Tokanui 46s34 168e56-11:15:44
Toko 39s20 174e24-11:37:36
Tokomaru 40s28 175e30-11:42:00
Tokomaru Bay 38s08 178e18-11:53:12
Tokoroa 38s14 175e52-11:43:28
Tolaga Bay 38s22 178e18-11:53:12
Towai 35s29 174e08-11:36:32
Tuakau 37s16 174e57-11:39:48
Tuamarina 41s26 173e57-11:35:48
Tuapeka Mouth 46s01 169e31-11:18:04
Tuatapere 46s08 167e41-11:10:44
Turakina 40s02 175e13-11:40:52
Turangi 39s00 175e49-11:43:16
Turua 37s14 175e34-11:42:16
Upper Hutt 41s08 175e04-11:40:16
Upper Moutere 41s16 173e00-11:32:00
Upper Takaka 41s02 172e50-11:31:20
Urenui 39s00 174e23-11:37:32
Uruti 38s57 174e32-11:38:08
Waharoa 37s46 175e46-11:43:04
Waiau 42s39 173e03-11:32:12
Waihao Downs 44s48 170e55-11:23:40
Waihi 37s24 175e51-11:43:24
Waihola 46s02 170e06-11:20:24
Waikaia 45s44 168e51-11:15:24
Waikanae 40s53 175e04-11:40:16
Waikari 42s58 172e41-11:30:44
Waikino 37s25 175e46-11:43:04
Waikouaiti 45s36 170e41-11:22:44
Waimahaka 46s31 168e49-11:15:16
Waimamaku 35s33 173e29-11:33:56
Waimana 38s09 177e05-11:48:20
Waimangaroa 41s43 171e46-11:27:04
Waimarama 39s48 176e59-11:47:56
Waimate 44s44 171e02-11:24:08
Wainuiomata 41s16 174e57-11:39:48
Waiohau 38s14 176e51-11:47:24
Waiotira 35s56 174e12-11:36:48
Waiouru 39s29 175e40-11:42:40
Waipahi 46s07 169e15-11:17:00
Waipaoa 38s32 177e54-11:51:36
Waipara 43s04 172e45-11:31:00
Waipawa 39s56 176e36-11:46:24
Waipiata 45s11 170e10-11:20:40
Waipiro 38s01 178e20-11:53:20
Waipu 35s59 174e27-11:37:48
Waipukurau 40s00 176e34-11:46:16
Wairakei 38s38 176e06-11:44:24
Wairau Valley 41s34 173e32-11:34:08
Wairio 46s00 168e02-11:12:08
Wairoa 39s02 177e25-11:49:40
Waitahanui 38s47 176e05-11:44:20
Waitahuna 45s59 169e46-11:19:04
Waitakaruru 37s15 175e23-11:41:32
Waitara 39s00 174e13-11:36:52
Waitarere 40s33 175e12-11:40:48
Waitati 45s45 170e34-11:22:16
Waitoa 37s37 175e38-11:42:32
Waitotara 39s48 174e44-11:38:56
Waiuku 37s15 174e45-11:39:00
Waiuta 42s18 171e49-11:27:16
Waiwera South 46s13 169e30-11:18:00
Wakefield 41s24 173e03-11:32:12
Wanaka 44s42 169e09-11:16:36
Wanganui 39s56 175e03-11:40:12
Wanstead 40s08 176e32-11:46:08
Ward 41s50 174e08-11:36:32
Warkworth 36s24 174e40-11:38:40
Warrington 45s43 170e35-11:22:20
Washdyke 44s21 171e14-11:24:56
Waverley 39s46 174e38-11:38:32
Wellington 41s18 174e47-11:39:08
Wellsford 36s17 174e31-11:38:04
West Harbour 45s51 170e35-11:22:20
Westport 41s45 171e36-11:26:24
Whakatane 37s58 177e00-11:48:00
Whangamata 37s12 175e52-11:43:28
Whangamomona 39s09 174e44-11:38:56
Whangara 38s34 178e13-11:52:52
Whangarei 35s43 174e19-11:37:16
Whataroa 43s17 170e25-11:21:40
Whatatutu 38s23 177e50-11:51:20
Whitianga 36s50 175e42-11:42:48
Winchester 44s12 171e17-11:25:08
Winton 46s09 168e20-11:13:20
Woodlands 46s22 168e33-11:14:12
Woodville 40s20 175e52-11:43:28
Wyndham 46s20 168e51-11:15:24

NICARAGUA NICARAGUA

Time Table
Before 1/Jan/1890 LMT
Begin Standard 86w18
1/Jan/1890 0:00 5:45
Begin Standard 90w00
23/Jun/1934 0:00 6:00
Begin Standard 75w00
1/May/1973 0:00 5:00
Begin Standard 90w00
16/Feb/1975 0:00 6:00
18/Mar/1979 0:00 5:00
25/Jun/1979 0:00 6:00
16/Mar/1980 0:00 5:00
23/Jun/1980 0:00 6:00

Acoyapa 11n58 85w10 5:40:40
Alta Gracia 11n34 85w35 5:42:20
Barra de Río Grande 12n54 83w32 5:34:08
Barra Punta Gorda 11n31 83w47 5:35:08
Belén 11n30 85w53 5:43:32
Bilwaskarma 14n45 83w53 5:35:32
Bluefields 12n00 83w45 5:35:00
Boaco 12n28 85w40 5:42:40
Bocay 14n19 85w10 5:40:40
Bonanza 14n01 84w35 5:38:20

NICARAGUA

NICARAGUA

Place	Lat	Long	Time
Cabo Gracias a Dios	14N59	83W10	5:32:40
Camoapa	12N23	85W31	5:42:04
Cárdenas	11N12	85W31	5:42:04
Chichigalpa	12N34	87W02	5:48:08
Chinandega	12N37	87W09	5:48:36
Cinco Pinos	13N14	86W52	5:47:28
Ciudad Darío	12N43	86W08	5:44:32
Comalapa	12N17	85W31	5:42:04
Condega	13N21	86W24	5:45:36
Corinto	12N29	87W10	5:48:40
Diriamba	11N51	86W14	5:44:56
Diriomo	11N52	86W03	5:44:12
El Bluff	11N59	83W40	5:34:40
El Castillo	11N01	84W24	5:37:36
El Jícaro	13N43	86W08	5:44:32
El Sauce	12N53	86W32	5:46:08
El Viejo	12N40	87W10	5:48:40
Esquipulas	12N40	85W47	5:43:08
Estelí	13N05	86W23	5:45:32
Granada	11N56	85W57	5:43:48
Greytown → San Juan del Norte	10N55	83W42	5:34:48
Jalapa	13N55	86W08	5:44:32
Jinotega	13N06	86W00	5:44:00
Jinotepe	11N51	86W12	5:44:48
Juigalpa	12N05	85W24	5:41:36
La Cruz de Río Grande	13N06	84W10	5:36:40
La Libertad	12N13	85W10	5:40:40
La Paz Centro	12N20	86W41	5:46:44
Larreynaga	12N40	86W34	5:46:16
Las Torres	13N28	85W48	5:43:12
La Trinidad	12N58	86W14	5:44:56
León	12N26	86W53	5:47:32
Malpaisillo	12N35	86W41	5:46:44
Managua	12N09	86W17	5:45:08
Masachapa	11N47	86W31	5:46:04
Masatepe	11N55	86W09	5:44:36
Masaya	11N58	86W06	5:44:24
Matagalpa	12N55	85W55	5:43:40
Mateare	12N14	86W26	5:45:44
Matiguás	12N50	85W28	5:41:52
Mina el Limón	12N45	86W44	5:46:56
Moyogalpa	11N32	85W42	5:42:48
Muelle de los Bueyes	12N04	84W32	5:38:08
Muy Muy	12N46	85W38	5:42:32
Nagarote	12N16	86W34	5:46:16
Nandaime	11N46	86W03	5:44:12
Nindirí	12N00	86W08	5:44:32
Ocotal	13N38	86W29	5:45:56
Prinzapolka	13N24	83W34	5:34:16
Pueblo Nuevo	13N23	86W29	5:45:56
Puerto Cabezas	14N02	83W23	5:33:32
Puerto Morazán	12N51	87W11	5:48:44
Puerto Morrito	11N37	85W05	5:40:20
Puerto Somoza	12N12	86W46	5:47:04
Quilalí	13N34	86W02	5:44:08
Raiti	14N35	85W02	5:40:08
Rama	12N09	84W15	5:37:00
Rivas	11N26	85W50	5:43:20
Rosita	13N53	84W24	5:37:36
San Carlos	11N07	84W47	5:39:08
San Dionisio	12N45	85W51	5:43:24
San Franciscó del Carnicero	12N30	86W18	5:45:12
San Isidro	12N56	86W12	5:44:48
San Jorge	11N27	85W48	5:43:12
San José de Achuapa	13N03	86W35	5:46:20
San Juan de Limay	13N10	86W37	5:46:28
San Juan del Norte	10N55	83W42	5:34:48
San Juan del Sur	11N15	85W52	5:43:28
San Lorenzo	12N23	85W40	5:42:40
San Miguelito	11N24	84W54	5:39:36
San Pedro del Norte	13N04	84W33	5:38:12
San Rafael del Norte	13N12	86W06	5:44:24
San Rafael del Sur	11N51	86W27	5:45:48
San Sebastián de Yalí	13N18	86W11	5:44:44
Santo Domingo	12N16	85W05	5:40:20
Santo Tomás	12N04	85W05	5:40:20
Santo Tomás de Nance	13N11	86W56	5:47:44
San Ubaldo	11N51	85W20	5:41:20
Sébaco	12N51	86W06	5:44:24
Siuna	13N44	84W46	5:39:04
Somotillo	13N02	86W55	5:47:40
Somoto	13N28	86W35	5:46:20
Telpaneca	13N32	86W17	5:45:08
Tipitapa	12N12	86W06	5:44:24
Tisma	12N05	86W01	5:44:04
Tungla	13N18	84W26	5:37:44
Villa el Carmen	11N59	86W31	5:46:04
Villanueva	12N58	86W49	5:47:16
Villa Somoza	12N03	84W59	5:39:56
Waspam	14N44	83W58	5:35:52
Wounta	13N33	83W32	5:34:08
Yablis	14N10	83W49	5:35:16

NIGER

NIGER

Time Table # 1
Before 1/Jan/1912 LMT
Begin Standard 15E00
1/Jan/1912 0:00 -1:00
....
1/Jan/1912 0:00 1:00
1/Jan/1960 0:00 -1:00

Time Table # 2
Before 1/Jan/1912 LMT
Begin Standard 15W00
Begin Standard 0W00
26/Feb/1934 0:00 0:00
Begin Standard 15E00
....

Time Table # 3
Before 1/Jan/1912 LMT
Begin Standard 0W00
1/Jan/1912 0:00 0:00
Begin Standard 15E00
1/Jan/1960 0:00 -1:00

Place	Table	Lat	Long	Offset
Abala	2	14N56	3E26	-0:13:44
Abalak	3	15N27	6E17	-0:25:08
Achénouma	1	19N08	12E55	-0:51:40
Adébour	1	13N20	11E54	-0:47:36
Agadem	1	16N50	13E17	-0:53:08
Agadez	1	16N58	7E59	-0:31:56
Aguié	1	13N30	7E47	-0:31:08
Alkamari	1	13N24	11E07	-0:44:28
Aney	1	19N24	12E56	-0:51:44
Aouderas	1	17N37	8E26	-0:33:44
Arlit	1	19N00	7E38	-0:30:32
Assodé	1	18N26	8E28	-0:33:52
Ayorou	2	14N44	0E55	-0:03:40
Badéguichéri	3	14N31	5E22	-0:21:28
Badifa	2	13N12	3E47	-0:15:08
Bagaroua	3	14N38	4E21	-0:17:24
Baléyara	2	13N47	2E57	-0:11:48
Bani Bangou	2	15N03	2E42	-0:10:48
Bankilaré	2	14N35	0E44	-0:02:56
Bayzo	3	13N52	4E45	-0:19:00
Béla Bérim	1	15N59	13E12	-0:52:48
Bilma	1	18N41	12E56	-0:51:44
Birni Ngaouré	2	13N05	2E54	-0:11:36
Birni Nkonni	3	13N48	5E15	-0:21:00
Bonkoukou	2	14N01	3E13	-0:12:52
Bossé Bangou	2	13N21	1E18	-0:05:12
Bosso	1	13N42	13E19	-0:53:16
Boumba	2	12N25	2E51	-0:11:24
Boureïmi	2	13N10	3E44	-0:14:56
Bouza	3	14N25	6E02	-0:24:08
Chirfa	1	20N57	12E21	-0:49:24
Dabnou	3	14N09	5E22	-0:21:28
Dakoro	1	14N31	6E46	-0:27:04
Dakouraoua	3	13N58	6E15	-0:25:00
Dargol	2	13N55	1E15	-0:05:00
Dietkorom	1	13N41	12E03	-0:48:12
Diffa	1	13N19	12E37	-0:50:28
Dillia Téfidinga	1	15N16	12E06	-0:48:24
Dioundiou	2	12N37	3E33	-0:14:12
Dirkou	1	19N01	12E53	-0:51:32
Djado	1	21N01	12E18	-0:49:12
Dogondoutchi	2	13N38	4E02	-0:16:08
Doguéraoua	3	13N58	5E35	-0:22:20
Dosso	2	13N03	3E12	-0:12:48
Dungas	1	13N04	9E20	-0:37:20
Fachi	1	18N06	11E34	-0:46:16
Falmey	2	12N36	2E51	-0:11:24
Farié Haoussa	2	13N48	1E38	-0:06:32
Filingué	2	14N21	3E19	-0:13:16
Foulatari	1	13N41	12E03	-0:48:12
Gangara	1	13N33	7E14	-0:28:56
Gangara	1	14N36	8E30	-0:34:00
Garoua	1	13N53	13E11	-0:52:44
Garoumélé	1	14N07	12E58	-0:51:52
Gaya	2	11N53	3E27	-0:13:48
Gazaoua	1	13N32	7E55	-0:31:40
Gothèye	2	13N52	1E34	-0:06:16
Goudoumaria	1	13N42	11E10	-0:44:40
Gouré	1	13N58	10E18	-0:41:12
Guidigri	1	13N40	9E51	-0:39:24
Guidimouni	1	13N42	9E30	-0:38:00
Hamdilaye	2	13N34	2E24	-0:09:36
Iferouâne	1	19N04	8E24	-0:33:36
Illéla	3	14N28	5E15	-0:21:00
I-N-Gall	1	16N47	6E56	-0:27:44
Kantché	1	13N33	8E28	-0:33:52
Karguéri	1	13N27	10E25	-0:41:40
Karma	2	13N40	1E49	-0:07:16
Kawara Débé	2	12N20	3E26	-0:13:44
Keïta	3	14N46	5E46	-0:23:04
Kirtachi Seybou	2	12N48	2E29	-0:09:56
Kolo	2	13N14	2E20	-0:09:20
Koré Mayroua	2	13N18	3E55	-0:15:40
Loga	2	13N37	3E14	-0:12:56
Madama	1	21N58	13E39	-0:54:36
Madaoua	3	14N06	6E01	-0:24:04
Magaria	1	13N00	8E54	-0:35:36
Maïné-Soroa	1	13N12	12E02	-0:48:08
Mallaoua	1	13N02	9E36	-0:38:24
Mandaoua Gadaoulé	1	14N14	11E01	-0:44:04
Maradi	1	13N29	7E06	-0:28:24
Matameye	1	13N26	8E28	-0:33:52
Mayahi	1	13N58	7E40	-0:30:40
May Jirgui	1	13N44	8E08	-0:32:32
Mir	1	14N05	11E59	-0:47:56
Mirria	1	13N43	9E07	-0:36:28
Nguigmi	1	14N15	13E07	-0:52:28
Niamey	2	13N31	2E07	-0:08:28
Ouallam	2	14N19	2E05	-0:08:20
Ouatcha	1	13N22	9E18	-0:37:12
Sabonkafi	1	14N38	8E45	-0:35:00
Sakoyra	2	14N17	1E24	-0:05:36
Sara	1	20N46	12E28	-0:49:52
Satoou	1	13N38	6E58	-0:27:52
Say	2	13N07	2E21	-0:09:24
Séguédine	1	20N12	12E59	-0:51:56
Simiri	2	14N08	2E08	-0:08:32
Tabla	2	13N46	3E01	-0:12:04
Tahoua	3	14N54	5E16	-0:21:04
Tamaské	3	14N49	5E39	-0:22:36
Tânout	1	14N58	8E53	-0:35:32
Tarka	1	14N37	7E55	-0:31:40
Tassara	3	16N48	5E39	-0:22:36
Tchin Tabaraden	3	15N58	5E50	-0:23:20
Tchin-Tabâradene	3	15N58	5E50	-0:23:20
Téra	2	14N01	0E45	-0:03:00
Tessaoua	1	13N45	7E59	-0:31:56
Tibiri	2	13N06	4E00	-0:16:00
Tibiri	1	13N34	7E04	-0:28:16
Tillaberi	2	14N13	1E27	-0:05:48
Tillabéry	2	14N13	1E27	-0:05:48
Tillia	3	16N08	4E47	-0:19:08
Tondi Kiwindi	2	14N28	2E02	-0:08:08
Torodi	2	13N18	1E40	-0:06:40
Toubori	1	13N59	12E18	-0:49:12
Toumfafi	3	15N02	5E38	-0:22:32
Yamia	1	13N24	10E18	-0:41:12
Yari	1	13N59	12E18	-0:49:12
Yatakala	2	14N48	0E22	-0:01:28
Yéni	2	13N26	2E59	-0:11:56
Zinder	1	13N48	8E59	-0:35:56

Time Table
Before 1/Sep/1919 LMT
Begin Standard 15E00
1/Sep/1919 0:00 -1:00

Aba	5N06	7E21	-0:29:24
Abaji	8N28	6E57	-0:27:48
Abak	4N57	7E47	-0:31:08
Abakaliki	6N21	8E06	-0:32:24
Abeokuta	7N10	3E26	-0:13:44
Abong	6N59	10E44	-0:42:56
Abonnema	4N43	6E47	-0:27:08
Abraka	5N50	6E05	-0:24:20
Abuja	9N12	7E11	-0:28:44
Ado-Ekiti	7N38	5E12	-0:20:48
Ado-Odo	6N36	2E56	-0:11:44
Afikpo	5N53	7E56	-0:31:44
Agaie	9N03	6E18	-0:25:12
Agbaja	7N58	6E38	-0:26:32
Agbede	6N40	3E29	-0:13:56
Agboju	6N28	3E17	-0:13:08
Agbor	6N18	6E11	-0:24:44
Agege	6N37	3E20	-0:13:20
Agidingbi	6N38	3E21	-0:13:24
Agwarra	10N42	4E35	-0:18:20
Ahoada	5N05	6E38	-0:26:32
Ajaokuta	7N28	6E39	-0:26:36
Ajasse	8N17	4E48	-0:19:12
Ajasso	5N52	8E52	-0:35:28
Ajegunle	6N36	3E17	-0:13:08
Aketu-Oja	6N41	3E23	-0:13:32
Akiode	6N38	3E21	-0:13:24
Akitan	6N39	3E16	-0:13:04
Akitipa	8N17	6E16	-0:25:04
Ako	10N17	10E58	-0:43:52
Akowonjo	6N37	3E19	-0:13:16
Aku	6N42	7E20	-0:29:20
Akure	7N15	5E12	-0:20:48
Akwanga	8N55	8E23	-0:33:32
Alagbado	6N41	3E18	-0:13:12
Alaguntan	6N26	3E30	-0:14:00
Alawa	10N20	6E39	-0:26:36
Aliade	7N16	8E28	-0:33:52
Amagunze	6N20	7E40	-0:30:40
Amper	9N20	9E43	-0:38:52
Amuwo	6N28	3E18	-0:13:12
Anchau	10N59	8E23	-0:33:32
Anka	12N07	5E55	-0:23:40
Ankpa	7N23	7E37	-0:30:28
Argungu	12N45	4E31	-0:18:04
Arida	6N34	3E16	-0:13:04
Arochukwu	5N23	7E55	-0:31:40
Arufu	7N50	9E14	-0:36:56
Asaba	6N12	6E44	-0:26:56
Askira	10N39	12E55	-0:51:40
Ason	6N34	3E31	-0:14:04
Auchi	7N02	6E14	-0:24:56
Auna	10N12	4E45	-0:19:00
Auno	11N50	12E53	-0:51:32
Awe	8N09	9E07	-0:36:28
Awgu	5N51	7E23	-0:29:32
Awka	6N12	7E05	-0:28:20
Ayangba	7N30	7E08	-0:28:32
Azara	8N21	9E12	-0:36:48
Azare	11N40	10E11	-0:40:44
Babana	10N26	3E50	-0:15:20
Babura	12N46	9E01	-0:36:04
Badagri	6N27	2E55	-0:11:40
Badeggi	9N05	6E08	-0:24:32
Bagoni	7N53	10E43	-0:42:52
Bakori	11N34	7E27	-0:29:48
Bale-Akiosi	6N41	3E21	-0:13:24
Bama	11N30	13E41	-0:54:44
Bara	10N22	10E44	-0:42:56
Baro	8N37	6E25	-0:25:40
Bauchi	10N19	9E50	-0:39:20
Baure	12N50	8E45	-0:35:00
Bebeji	11N40	8E19	-0:33:16
Belel	9N38	13E12	-0:52:48
Bena	11N18	5E55	-0:23:40
Bende	5N36	7E39	-0:30:36
Beni	10N27	10E24	-0:41:36
Benin City	6N19	5E41	-0:22:44
Benisheikh	11N49	12E29	-0:49:56
Besse	11N15	4E30	-0:18:00
Bida	12N20	13E25	-0:53:40
Bida	9N05	6E01	-0:24:04
Biliri	9N52	11E13	-0:44:52
Bin Yauri	10N47	4E50	-0:19:20
Birnin Gwari	11N01	6E48	-0:27:12
Birnin Kebbi	12N32	4E12	-0:16:48
Birnin Kudu	11N27	9E30	-0:38:00
Bissaula	7N00	10E27	-0:41:48
Biu	10N35	12E13	-0:48:52
Bode Sadu	9N00	4E47	-0:19:08
Boi	9N34	9E27	-0:37:48
Boju	7N25	7E52	-0:31:28
Boju Ega	7N24	8E04	-0:32:16
Bokani	9N26	5E13	-0:20:52
Bonny	4N27	7E10	-0:28:40
Bopo	7N37	7E52	-0:31:28
Bori	4N42	7E21	-0:29:24
Brass	4N19	6E14	-0:24:56
Buga	8N30	7E21	-0:29:24
Bukuru	9N48	8E51	-0:35:24
Bunga	11N04	9E38	-0:38:32
Bununu Dass	10N00	9E31	-0:38:04
Bunza	12N08	4E00	-0:16:00
Burutu	5N21	5E31	-0:22:04
Bussa	10N15	4E33	-0:18:12
Calabar	4N57	8E19	-0:33:16
Chafe	11N56	6E55	-0:27:40
Cheranchi	12N40	7E42	-0:30:48
Coker	6N29	3E20	-0:13:20
Dabai	11N31	5E11	-0:20:44
Dadiya	9N37	11E26	-0:45:44
Dakingari	11N37	4E01	-0:16:04
Damaturu	11N45	11E58	-0:47:52
Dambarta	12N26	8E31	-0:34:04
Dan Dume	11N27	7E10	-0:28:40
Dange	12N52	5E21	-0:21:24
Dan Gora	11N30	8E09	-0:32:36
Dan Gulbi	11N38	6E16	-0:25:04
Danja	11N21	7E31	-0:30:04
Dankama	13N20	7E44	-0:30:56
Dapchi	12N28	11E32	-0:46:08
Darazo	11N00	10E24	-0:41:36
Daura	13N02	8E21	-0:33:24
Dawaki	12N06	8E20	-0:33:20
Deba	10N20	11E54	-0:47:36
Degema	4N45	6E47	-0:27:08
Dekina	7N39	7E02	-0:28:08
Dikwa	12N02	13E56	-0:55:44
Dindima	10N18	10E12	-0:40:48
Dosara	12N32	6E09	-0:24:36
Duku	10N49	10E46	-0:43:04
Duku	11N10	4E55	-0:19:40
Dumboa	11N10	12E45	-0:51:00
Dutsen Wai	10N50	8E12	-0:32:48
Eban	9N44	4E56	-0:19:44
Ebute-Ikorodu	6N37	3E30	-0:14:00
Ede	7N44	4E27	-0:17:48
Effon-Alaiye	7N40	4E56	-0:19:44
Egbe	6N33	3E17	-0:13:08
Egbe	8N16	5E31	-0:22:04
Eha-Amufu	6N40	7E46	-0:31:04
Ejigbo	6N33	3E18	-0:13:12
Ejigbo	7N55	4E19	-0:17:16
Eket	4N39	7E56	-0:31:44
Eko → Lagos	6N27	3E24	-0:13:36
Ekpoma	6N46	6E08	-0:24:32
Elele	5N07	6E48	-0:27:12
Elepete	6N41	3E28	-0:13:52
Emuren	6N40	3E31	-0:14:04
Enugu	6N27	7E27	-0:29:48
Epe	6N37	3E59	-0:15:56
Eregun	6N36	3E22	-0:13:28
Erunkan	6N37	3E24	-0:13:36
Ewu	6N33	3E19	-0:13:16
Faggo	11N23	9E57	-0:39:48
Fiditi	7N45	3E53	-0:15:32
Fika	11N17	11E18	-0:45:12
Fogolawa	12N19	8E41	-0:34:44
Fokku	11N40	4E31	-0:18:04
Forcados	5N22	5E24	-0:21:36
Funtua	11N31	7E17	-0:29:08
Gabai	11N05	11E39	-0:46:36
Gagarawa	12N25	9E32	-0:38:08
Gajiram	12N30	13E12	-0:52:48
Gamawa	12N08	10E32	-0:42:08
Gandi	12N55	5E49	-0:23:16
Gandole	8N26	11E34	-0:46:16
Ganwo	11N13	4E42	-0:18:48
Garkida	10N25	12E36	-0:50:24
Garko	11N38	8E48	-0:35:12
Gashaka	7N21	11E27	-0:45:48
Gashua	12N54	11E00	-0:44:00
Gassol	8N32	10E28	-0:41:52
Gawu	9N14	6E52	-0:27:28
Gaya	11N53	9E02	-0:36:08
Gbogbo	6N36	3E31	-0:14:04
Gboko	7N20	8E57	-0:35:48
Gbongan	7N29	4E21	-0:17:24
Geidam	12N57	11E57	-0:47:48
Giro	11N06	4E46	-0:19:04
Gombe	10N19	11E02	-0:44:08
Gombi	10N10	12E45	-0:51:00
Goniri	11N30	12E20	-0:49:20
Gorgoram	12N38	10E43	-0:42:52
Goronyo	13N29	5E39	-0:22:36
Gubio	12N29	12E48	-0:51:12
Gujba	11N30	11E55	-0:47:40
Gumel	12N39	9E22	-0:37:28
Gummi	12N09	5E09	-0:20:36
Gusau	12N12	6E40	-0:26:40
Gwadabawa	13N20	5E15	-0:21:00
Gwagwada	10N14	7E14	-0:28:56
Gwanara	8N55	3E09	-0:12:36
Gwandu	12N30	4E41	-0:18:44
Gwarzo	11N56	7E56	-0:31:44
Gwasero	9N29	3E30	-0:14:00
Hadejia	12N30	9E59	-0:39:56
Hausa	6N37	3E21	-0:13:24
Ibadan	7N17	3E30	-0:14:00
Ibese	6N33	3E29	-0:13:56
Ibeto	10N29	5E09	-0:20:36
Ibi	8N12	9E45	-0:39:00
Idah	7N07	6E43	-0:26:52
Idimu	6N35	3E17	-0:13:08
Idomogu	6N43	3E30	-0:14:00
Ifako	6N39	3E20	-0:13:20
Ife	7N30	4E30	-0:18:00
Ifon	6N58	5E45	-0:23:00
Igana	7N59	3E14	-0:12:56
Iganna	7N59	3E14	-0:12:56
Igarra	7N18	6E07	-0:24:28
Igaun	6N42	3E23	-0:13:32
Igbaja	8N23	4E52	-0:19:28
Igbobi	6N32	3E22	-0:13:28
Igboho	8N51	3E45	-0:15:00
Igbologun	6N25	3E20	-0:13:20
Igbo-Ora	7N26	3E17	-0:13:08
Igbor	7N27	8E34	-0:34:16
Igumale	6N49	7E59	-0:31:56
Ihiala	5N51	6E51	-0:27:24
Ihugh	7N02	9E00	-0:36:00
Ijaiye	6N40	3E18	-0:13:12
Ijebu-Igbo	6N56	4E01	-0:16:04
Ijebu-Ode	6N50	3E56	-0:15:44
Ijesa-Tedo	6N30	3E19	-0:13:16
Iju Junction	6N40	3E19	-0:13:16
Ikang	4N50	8E32	-0:34:08
Ikara	11N12	8E15	-0:33:00
Ikare	7N32	5E45	-0:23:00
Ikeja	6N36	3E21	-0:13:24
Ikerre	7N31	5E14	-0:20:56
Ikire	7N23	4E12	-0:16:48
Ikirun	7N55	4E41	-0:18:44
Ikole	7N49	5E30	-0:22:00
Ikom	5N58	8E42	-0:34:48
Ikorodu	6N37	3E31	-0:14:04
Ikot Ekpene	5N12	7E40	-0:30:40
Ikuata	6N25	3E22	-0:13:28
Ila	8N01	4E55	-0:19:40
Ilara	6N42	3E27	-0:13:48
Ilaro	6N53	3E03	-0:12:12
Ilawe	7N37	5E06	-0:20:24
Ilesha	7N38	4E45	-0:19:00
Ilesha	8N56	3E25	-0:13:40
Ilobu	7N51	4E30	-0:18:00
Ilora	7N45	3E50	-0:15:20
Ilorin	8N30	4E32	-0:18:08
Imore	6N26	3E17	-0:13:08
Imoro	6N43	3E30	-0:14:00
Imute	6N42	3E29	-0:13:56
Inisa	7N52	4E20	-0:17:20
Inshar	8N49	9E40	-0:38:40
Iperu	6N52	3E38	-0:14:32
Irrua	6N46	6E14	-0:24:56
Isa	13N14	6E24	-0:25:36
Isagatedo	6N32	3E20	-0:13:20
Isanlu Makutu	8N17	5E46	-0:23:04
Isara	6N59	3E41	-0:14:44
Isasi	6N40	3E23	-0:13:32
Iseri	6N39	3E23	-0:13:32
Iseri-Oke	6N38	3E23	-0:13:32
Iseri-Osun	6N31	3E17	-0:13:08
Iseyin	7N58	3E36	-0:14:24
Isheri-Olofin	6N35	3E17	-0:13:08
Ishua	7N24	5E57	-0:23:48
Isolo	6N32	3E19	-0:13:16
Isunba	6N27	3E17	-0:13:08
Itaki	6N43	3E17	-0:13:08
Itire	6N31	3E21	-0:13:24
Ivorogbo	5N30	6E21	-0:25:24
Iwo	7N38	4E11	-0:16:44
Jada	8N46	12E09	-0:48:36
Jaredi	12N46	5E05	-0:20:20
Jebba	9N08	4E50	-0:19:20
Jega	12N15	4E23	-0:17:32
Jemaa	9N27	8E23	-0:33:32
Jibiya	13N05	7E12	-0:28:48
Jos	9N55	8E53	-0:35:32
Kabba	7N50	6E03	-0:24:12
Kachia	9N53	7E58	-0:31:52
Kado	7N39	9E44	-0:38:56
Kaduna	10N33	7E27	-0:29:48
Kafanchan	9N36	8E17	-0:33:08
Kafin	9N30	7E04	-0:28:16
Kafin Madaki	10N41	9E46	-0:39:04
Kagarko	9N29	7E41	-0:30:44
Kaiama	9N37	3E58	-0:15:52
Kajuru	10N21	7E40	-0:30:40
Kala	12N05	14E27	-0:57:48
Kamba	11N53	3E36	-0:14:24
Kano	12N00	8E30	-0:34:00
Kaoje	11N14	4E07	-0:16:28
Karaye	11N48	8E02	-0:32:08
Kataeregi	9N22	6E17	-0:25:08
Katsina	13N00	7E32	-0:30:08
Kaugama	12N28	9E44	-0:38:56
Kaura Namoda	12N35	6E35	-0:26:20
Kauru	10N33	8E12	-0:32:48
Kebbe	12N08	4E44	-0:18:56
Keffi	8N51	7E52	-0:31:28
Keffin Hausa	12N15	9E58	-0:39:52
Kende	11N30	4E12	-0:16:48
Kishi	9N05	3E52	-0:15:28
Kogin Baba	7N55	11E30	-0:46:00
Koko	11N26	4E32	-0:18:08
Konduga	11N39	13E24	-0:53:36
Kontagora	10N24	5E28	-0:21:52
Koton-Karifi	8N08	6E48	-0:27:12
Kotonkoro	11N02	5E58	-0:23:52
Kukawa	12N56	13E35	-0:54:20
Kumo	10N03	11E13	-0:44:52
Kungana	7N50	10E42	-0:42:48
Kunya	12N14	8E34	-0:34:16
Kushaka	10N32	6E48	-0:27:12
Kusherki	10N33	6E28	-0:25:52
Kuta	9N52	6E43	-0:26:52
Kwale	5N46	6E26	-0:25:44
Kwali	8N56	7E00	-0:28:00
Kware	13N12	5E14	-0:20:56
Kwiello	11N16	7E00	-0:28:00
Kwolla	9N00	9E15	-0:37:00
Lafia	8N30	8E30	-0:34:00
Lafiagi	8N52	5E25	-0:21:40
Lagos	6N27	3E24	-0:13:36

NIGÉRIA — NIGERIA

Place	Lat	Long	Offset
Lambe	6N42	3E21	-0:13:24
Lame	10N23	9E13	-0:36:52
Lankoviri	9N00	11E25	-0:45:40
Lantewa	12N16	11E44	-0:46:56
Lapai	9N06	6E45	-0:27:00
Lau	9N13	11E17	-0:45:08
Lema	12N57	4E14	-0:16:56
Lere	9N43	9E21	-0:37:24
Loko	8N02	7E49	-0:31:16
Lokoja	7N47	6E45	-0:27:00
Losi	6N40	3E31	-0:14:04
Magboro	6N43	3E24	-0:13:36
Magumeri	12N08	12E50	-0:51:20
Maguru	12N28	6E35	-0:26:20
Maiduguri	11N51	13E10	-0:52:40
Maigatari	12N46	9E27	-0:37:48
Makurdi	7N45	8E32	-0:34:08
Malumfashi	11N47	7E37	-0:30:28
Marte	12N22	13E51	-0:55:24
Maru	12N22	6E22	-0:25:28
Masba	11N30	13E00	-0:52:00
Mashi	13N00	7E54	-0:31:36
Maska	11N20	7E20	-0:29:20
Masu	12N10	13E19	-0:53:16
Matsena	13N05	10E05	-0:40:20
Mayo Faran	8N57	12E04	-0:48:16
Mayo Ndaga	6N54	11E25	-0:45:40
Mberubu	6N10	7E38	-0:30:32
Mebisere	6N42	3E31	-0:14:04
Meran	6N38	3E16	-0:13:04
Meringa	10N44	12E09	-0:48:36
Michika	10N38	13E24	-0:53:36
Minna	9N37	6E33	-0:26:12
Moba	6N27	3E28	-0:13:52
Mofoluku	6N33	3E20	-0:13:20
Mokwa	9N20	5E02	-0:20:08
Monguno	12N40	13E38	-0:54:32
Moriki	12N52	6E30	-0:26:00
Mubi	10N18	13E20	-0:53:20
Muri	9N11	10E53	-0:43:32
Mushin	6N32	3E22	-0:13:28
Mutum Biyu	8N38	10E46	-0:43:04
Nabordo	10N10	9E20	-0:37:20
Nafada	11N08	11E20	-0:45:20
Nasarawa	8N30	7E40	-0:30:40
Nembe	4N35	6E26	-0:25:44
Ngala	12N20	14E10	-0:56:40
Ngamdu	11N48	12E18	-0:49:12
Ngetera	12N31	12E38	-0:50:32
Ngurore	9N18	12E14	-0:48:56
Nguru	12N52	10E27	-0:41:48
Nike	6N26	7E29	-0:29:56
Ningi	11N04	9E32	-0:38:08
Nnewi	6N00	6E59	-0:27:56
Nsukka	6N52	7E24	-0:29:36
Oban	5N17	8E35	-0:34:20
Obi	8N22	8E46	-0:35:04
Obiaruku	5N51	6E09	-0:24:36
Obubra	6N05	8E21	-0:33:24
Obudu	6N40	9E09	-0:36:36
Offa	8N09	4E44	-0:18:56
Ofin	6N33	3E30	-0:14:00
Ogbomosho	8N08	4E15	-0:17:00
Ogijo	6N42	3E31	-0:14:04
Ogoja	6N40	8E48	-0:35:12
Ogoyo	6N26	3E29	-0:13:56
Ogudu	6N34	3E24	-0:13:36
Ogunlogun	6N41	3E28	-0:13:52
Oguta	5N44	6E44	-0:26:56
Ogwashi-Uku	6N10	6E31	-0:26:04
Ojota	6N35	3E23	-0:13:32
Oju	6N53	8E26	-0:33:44
Oka	7N29	5E49	-0:23:16
Oke-Aro	6N41	3E19	-0:13:16
Oke-Igbo	7N09	4E43	-0:18:52
Okene	7N33	6E15	-0:25:00
Oke-Ode	8N33	5E02	-0:20:08
Oke Ogbe	6N24	3E23	-0:13:32
Okitipupa	6N29	4E46	-0:19:04
Okrika	4N47	7E04	-0:28:16
Okundi	6N22	8E44	-0:34:56
Okuta	9N14	3E15	-0:13:00
Okwoga	7N01	7E50	-0:31:20
Olasore	6N40	3E17	-0:13:08
Olute	6N28	3E16	-0:13:04
Oluwo	6N42	3E18	-0:13:12
Omoko	5N20	6E39	-0:26:36
Omole	6N38	3E22	-0:13:28
Omu-Aran	8N09	5E07	-0:20:28
Ondo	7N04	4E47	-0:19:08
Onitsha	6N09	6E47	-0:27:08
Opeilu	6N42	3E18	-0:13:12
Opobo	4N34	7E27	-0:29:48
Opobo Town	4N30	7E30	-0:30:00
Ore	6N44	4E52	-0:19:28
Orlu	5N47	7E02	-0:28:08
Oron	4N48	8E14	-0:32:56
Oruba	6N35	3E25	-0:13:40
Oshodi	6N34	3E21	-0:13:24
Oshogbo	7N47	4E34	-0:18:16
Osi	8N08	5E14	-0:20:56
Osorun	6N33	3E29	-0:13:56
Otta	6N42	3E10	-0:12:40
Otu	8N14	3E24	-0:13:36
Otukpa	7N09	7E41	-0:30:44
Otun	6N42	3E22	-0:13:28
Oturkpo	7N14	8E08	-0:32:32
Owerri	5N29	7E02	-0:28:08
Owo	7N15	5E37	-0:22:28
Oworonsoki	6N33	3E24	-0:13:36
Oyo	7N51	3E56	-0:15:44
Ozubulu	5N57	6E51	-0:27:24
Pambegua	10N40	8E19	-0:33:16
Pambeguwa	10N40	8E19	-0:33:16
Pankshin	9N20	9E24	-0:37:36
Panyam	9N25	9E13	-0:36:52
Pategi	8N44	5E44	-0:22:56
Pindiga	9N59	10E54	-0:43:36
Port Harcourt	4N43	7E05	-0:28:20
Potiskum	11N43	11E05	-0:44:20
Rigacikun	10N40	7E28	-0:29:52
Rijau	11N07	5E14	-0:20:56
Rimi	12N58	7E43	-0:30:52
Ringim	12N08	9E10	-0:36:40
Sapele	5N54	5E41	-0:22:44
Saya	9N28	3E11	-0:12:44
Shagamu	6N51	3E39	-0:14:36
Shaki	8N39	3E25	-0:13:40
Share	8N50	4E56	-0:19:44
Shellen	9N54	12E00	-0:48:00
Shendam	8N53	9E32	-0:38:08
Shogunle	6N35	3E21	-0:13:24
Shomolu	6N32	3E23	-0:13:32
Siluko	6N31	5E09	-0:20:36
Sokoto	13N04	5E16	-0:21:04
Song	9N50	12E38	-0:50:32
Suya	9N28	3E11	-0:12:44
Takum	7N17	9E59	-0:39:56
Talata Mafara	12N35	6E04	-0:24:16
Tegina	10N05	6E14	-0:24:56
Tissa	7N26	10E16	-0:41:04
Toungo	8N07	12E03	-0:48:12
Tula	9N50	11E28	-0:45:52
Tunga	8N00	9E19	-0:37:16
Ubiaja	6N38	6E21	-0:25:24
Udi	6N19	7E25	-0:29:40
Udubo	11N57	10E38	-0:42:32
Ugep	5N50	8E05	-0:32:20
Ughelli	5N29	5E59	-0:23:56
Umuahia	5N33	7E29	-0:29:56
Uromi	6N44	6E18	-0:25:12
Usoro	5N34	6E13	-0:24:52
Uyo	5N03	7E56	-0:31:44
Vom	9N41	8E42	-0:34:48
Wamba	8N58	8E36	-0:34:24
Warri	5N31	5E45	-0:23:00
Wasagu	11N25	5E49	-0:23:16
Wase	9N06	9E59	-0:39:56
Wawa	9N55	4E25	-0:17:40
Weto	7N57	7E50	-0:31:20
Wukari	7N51	9E47	-0:39:08
Wurno	13N17	5E24	-0:21:36
Wushishi	9N46	6E07	-0:24:28
Yandev	7N20	9E01	-0:36:04
Yashi	12N23	7E54	-0:31:36
Yashikera	9N46	3E28	-0:13:52
Yasku	12N20	12E30	-0:50:00
Yelwa	10N51	4E46	-0:19:04
Yenagoa	4N55	6E19	-0:25:16
Yola	9N12	12E29	-0:49:56
Yuli	9N42	10E17	-0:41:08
Zalanga	10N37	10E10	-0:40:40
Zalau	10N20	9E00	-0:36:00
Zari	13N04	12E43	-0:50:52
Zaria	11N07	7E44	-0:30:56
Zungeru	9N48	6E09	-0:24:36
Zungur	9N58	9E47	-0:39:08
Zurmi	12N46	6E48	-0:27:12
Zuru	11N27	5E12	-0:20:48

SAVAGE ISLAND — NIUE

Time Table
Before 1/Jan/1901 LMT
Begin Standard 170w00
1/Jan/1901 0:00 11:20
Begin Standard 172w30
1/Jan/1951 0:00 11:30
Begin Standard 165w00
1/Oct/1978 0:00 11:00

Place	Lat	Long	Offset
Alofi	19s01	169w55	11:19:40
Avatele	19s06	169w55	11:19:40
Hakupu	19s06	169w50	11:19:20
Hikutivake	18s56	169w53	11:19:32
Lakepa	18s59	169w48	11:19:12
Liku	19s02	169w47	11:19:08
Makefu	18s59	169w55	11:19:40
Mamakula	18s57	169w54	11:19:36
Motutapu	19s02	169w52	11:19:28
Mutalau	18s56	169w50	11:19:20
Namakula	18s57	169w54	11:19:36
Tamakautoga	19s05	169w55	11:19:40
Tamakautonga	19s05	169w55	11:19:40
Toi	18s57	169w51	11:19:24
Tuapa	18s57	169w54	11:19:36
Tufukia	19s02	169w56	11:19:44

NORFOLK ISLAND ÎLES NORFOLK NORFOLK-INSEL ISLAS NORFOLK

Time Table		
Before 1/Jan/1901	LMT	
Begin Standard	168E00	
1/Jan/1901	0:00	-11:12
Begin Standard	172E30	
1/Jan/1951	0:00	-11:30

Place	Lat	Long	Offset
Anson Bay	29S01	167E55	-11:11:40
Captain Cook Monument	29S00	167E56	-11:11:44
Kingston	29S03	167E58	-11:11:52
Melanesian Mission Station	29S02	167E55	-11:11:40
Nepean Island	29S04	167E58	-11:11:52
Norfolk Island	29S02	167E57	-11:11:48
Norfolk Island Aerodrome	29S03	167E56	-11:11:44
Rocky Point	29S03	167E55	-11:11:40
Steele's Point	29S02	168E00	-11:12:00

NORWAY NORUEGA NORVÈGE NORWEGEN NORGE

Time Table		
Before 1/Jan/1895	LMT	
Begin Standard	15E00	
1/Jan/1895	0:00	-1:00
22/May/1916	1:00	-2:00
30/Sep/1916	3:00	-1:00
10/Aug/1940	23:00	-2:00
2/Nov/1942	3:00	-1:00
29/Mar/1943	2:00	-2:00
4/Oct/1943	3:00	-1:00
3/Apr/1944	2:00	-2:00
2/Oct/1944	3:00	-1:00
2/Apr/1945	2:00	-2:00
1/Oct/1945	3:00	-1:00
15/Mar/1959	2:00	-2:00
20/Sep/1959	3:00	-1:00
20/Mar/1960	2:00	-2:00
18/Sep/1960	3:00	-1:00
19/Mar/1961	2:00	-2:00
17/Sep/1961	3:00	-1:00
18/Mar/1962	2:00	-2:00
16/Sep/1962	3:00	-1:00
17/Mar/1963	2:00	-2:00
15/Sep/1963	3:00	-1:00
15/Mar/1964	2:00	-2:00
20/Sep/1964	3:00	-1:00
25/Apr/1965	2:00	-2:00
19/Sep/1965	3:00	-1:00
6/Apr/1980	2:00	-2:00
28/Sep/1980	3:00	-1:00
29/Mar/1981	2:00	-2:00
27/Sep/1981	3:00	-1:00
28/Mar/1982	2:00	-2:00
26/Sep/1982	3:00	-1:00
27/Mar/1983	2:00	-2:00
25/Sep/1983	3:00	-1:00
25/Mar/1984	2:00	-2:00
30/Sep/1984	3:00	-1:00
31/Mar/1985	2:00	-2:00
29/Sep/1985	3:00	-1:00
30/Mar/1986	2:00	-2:00
28/Sep/1986	3:00	-1:00
29/Mar/1987	2:00	-2:00
27/Sep/1987	3:00	-1:00
27/Mar/1988	2:00	-2:00
25/Sep/1988	3:00	-1:00
26/Mar/1989	2:00	-2:00
24/Sep/1989	3:00	-1:00
25/Mar/1990	2:00	-2:00
30/Sep/1990	3:00	-1:00
31/Mar/1991	2:00	-2:00
29/Sep/1991	3:00	-1:00
29/Mar/1992	2:00	-2:00
27/Sep/1992	3:00	-1:00
28/Mar/1993	2:00	-2:00
26/Sep/1993	3:00	-1:00
27/Mar/1994	2:00	-2:00
25/Sep/1994	3:00	-1:00
26/Mar/1995	2:00	-2:00
24/Sep/1995	3:00	-1:00
31/Mar/1996	2:00	-2:00
29/Sep/1996	3:00	-1:00
30/Mar/1997	2:00	-2:00
28/Sep/1997	3:00	-1:00
29/Mar/1998	2:00	-2:00
27/Sep/1998	3:00	-1:00
28/Mar/1999	2:00	-2:00
26/Sep/1999	3:00	-1:00
26/Mar/2000	2:00	-2:00
24/Sep/2000	3:00	-1:00

Place	Lat	Long	Offset
Aalesund → Ålesund	62N28	6E09	-0:24:36
Åfjord	63N58	10E12	-0:40:48
Aga	60N18	6E36	-0:26:24
Åkrehamn	59N16	5E11	-0:20:44
Ål	60N38	8E34	-0:34:16
Ålesund	62N28	6E09	-0:24:36
Ålgård	58N46	5E51	-0:23:24
Alta	69N55	23E12	-1:32:48
Alvdal	62N07	10E39	-0:42:36
Ålvik	60N26	6E26	-0:25:44
Åmli	58N47	8E30	-0:34:00
Åmot	59N35	8E00	-0:32:00
Åmot	59N54	9E54	-0:39:36
Åndalsnes	62N34	7E42	-0:30:48
Andenes	69N16	16E08	-1:04:32
Årdalstangen	61N14	7E43	-0:30:52
Arendal	58N27	8E48	-0:35:12
Årnes	60N09	11E28	-0:45:52
Ås	59N40	10E48	-0:43:12
Åsen	63N36	11E03	-0:44:12
Åsgårdstrand	59N21	10E28	-0:41:52
Asker	59N50	10E26	-0:41:44
Askim	59N35	11E10	-0:44:40
Askvoll	61N21	5E04	-0:20:16
Atnosen	61N44	10E49	-0:43:16
Atrå	59N59	8E45	-0:35:00
Aulestad	61N13	10E17	-0:41:08
Aurdal	60N56	9E24	-0:37:36
Aure	63N16	8E32	-0:34:08
Aurlandsvangen	60N54	7E11	-0:28:44
Austnes	62N38	6E16	-0:25:04
Austråt	63N43	9E45	-0:39:00
Avaldsnes	59N21	5E16	-0:21:04
Bagn	60N49	9E34	-0:38:16
Balestrand	61N12	6E32	-0:26:08
Ballangen	68N20	16E50	-1:07:20
Bardu	68N52	18E21	-1:13:24
Bardufoss	69N04	18E30	-1:14:00
Berg	69N26	17E15	-1:09:00
Bergen	60N23	5E20	-0:21:20
Berkåk	62N50	10E00	-0:40:00
Berlevåg	70N51	29E06	-1:56:24
Bessheim	61N31	8E51	-0:35:24
Bindal	65N06	12E30	-0:50:00
Birkeland	58N20	8E14	-0:32:56
Bismo	61N53	8E16	-0:33:04
Bjørkelangen	59N53	11E34	-0:46:16
Bø	68N37	14E33	-0:58:12
Bø	59N25	9E04	-0:36:16
Bodø	67N17	14E23	-0:57:32
Bognes	68N10	16E00	-1:04:00
Bøvågen	60N40	4E58	-0:19:52
Bøverdal	61N43	8E21	-0:33:24
Brandbu	60N28	10E30	-0:42:00
Brandvold	68N49	18E10	-1:12:40
Brattvåg	62N36	6E27	-0:25:48
Brekken	62N39	11E53	-0:47:32
Brekstad	63N41	9E41	-0:38:44
Brevik	59N04	9E42	-0:38:48
Brønnøysund	65N30	12E10	-0:48:40
Brumunddal	60N53	10E56	-0:43:44
Brunkeberg	59N26	8E29	-0:33:56
Bryne	58N44	5E39	-0:22:36
Bud	62N55	6E55	-0:27:40
Bugøynes	69N58	29E39	-1:58:36
Burfjord	69N56	22E00	-1:28:00
Bygdin	61N20	8E48	-0:35:12
Byglandsfjord	58N41	7E48	-0:31:12
Bykle	59N21	7E20	-0:29:20
Christiania → Oslo	59N55	10E45	-0:43:00
Dale	60N35	5E49	-0:23:16
Dalen	59N27	8E00	-0:32:00
Dokka	60N50	10E05	-0:40:20
Dombås	62N05	9E08	-0:36:32
Dovre	61N59	9E15	-0:37:00
Drammen	59N44	10E15	-0:41:00
Drøbak	59N39	10E39	-0:42:36
Dyrnesvågen	63N26	7E51	-0:31:24
Egersund	58N27	6E00	-0:24:00
Eide	62N55	7E26	-0:29:44
Eidfjord	60N28	7E05	-0:28:20
Eidsvåg	60N27	5E21	-0:21:24
Eidsvåg	62N47	8E03	-0:32:12
Eidsvoll	60N19	11E14	-0:44:56
Eina	60N38	10E36	-0:42:24
Elverum	60N53	11E34	-0:46:16
Engjan	63N09	8E32	-0:34:08
Espevær	59N36	5E10	-0:20:40
Etne	59N40	5E56	-0:23:44
Evje	58N36	7E51	-0:31:24
Eydehavn	58N31	8E53	-0:35:32
Fåberg	61N10	10E24	-0:41:36
Fagernes	60N59	9E15	-0:37:00
Fannrem	63N16	9E50	-0:39:20
Farsund	58N05	6E48	-0:27:12
Fauske	67N15	15E24	-1:01:36
Fåvang	61N27	10E11	-0:40:44
Fedje	60N47	4E42	-0:18:48
Femundsenden	61N55	11E55	-0:47:40
Fetsund	59N56	11E10	-0:44:40
Fevik	58N23	8E42	-0:34:48
Finnsnes	69N14	17E59	-1:11:56
Finse	60N36	7E30	-0:30:00
Flåm	60N50	7E07	-0:28:28
Flekkefjord	58N17	6E41	-0:26:44
Flisa	60N34	12E06	-0:48:24
Florø	61N36	5E00	-0:20:00
Florvåg	60N25	5E14	-0:20:56
Follafoss	63N59	11E06	-0:44:24
Folldal	62N08	10E03	-0:40:12
Follebu	61N14	10E17	-0:41:08
Førde	59N36	5E29	-0:21:56
Førde	61N27	5E52	-0:23:28
Fosnavåg	62N21	5E39	-0:22:36
Fredrikstad	59N13	10E57	-0:43:48
Gardermoen	60N13	11E06	-0:44:24
Geilo	60N31	8E12	-0:32:48
Geiranger	62N06	7E12	-0:28:48
Gjøvik	60N48	10E42	-0:42:48
Gol	60N42	8E57	-0:35:48
Granvin	60N33	6E43	-0:26:52
Greåker	59N16	11E02	-0:44:08
Grimstad	58N20	8E36	-0:34:24
Grip	63N14	7E37	-0:30:28
Grong	64N28	12E18	-0:49:12
Gudvangen	60N52	6E50	-0:27:20
Gulsvik	60N23	9E35	-0:38:20
Halden	59N09	11E23	-0:45:32
Hamar	60N48	11E06	-0:44:24
Hammerfest	70N40	23E42	-1:34:48
Hamningberg	70N31	30E37	-2:02:28
Hanke	59N12	10E47	-0:43:08
Hareid	62N22	6E02	-0:24:08
Harstad	68N46	16E30	-1:06:00
Hauge	58N18	6E15	-0:25:00
Haugesund	59N25	5E18	-0:21:12
Haukeligrend	59N45	7E31	-0:30:04
Hedal	60N37	9E42	-0:38:48
Hegra	63N28	11E07	-0:44:28
Heimdal	63N21	10E22	-0:41:28
Hell	63N26	10E54	-0:43:36
Hellesylt	62N05	6E54	-0:27:36
Hemsedal	60N52	8E34	-0:34:16
Hermansverk	61N11	6E51	-0:27:24
Hjelmelandsvågen	59N14	6E11	-0:24:44
Hokksund	59N47	9E59	-0:39:56
Holmen	60N40	10E22	-0:41:28
Holmenkollen	59N58	10E40	-0:42:40
Holmestrand	59N29	10E18	-0:41:12
Holmsbu	59N33	10E27	-0:41:48
Hommersåk	58N58	5E42	-0:22:48
Hønefoss	60N10	10E18	-0:41:12
Honningsvåg	70N59	25E59	-1:43:56
Hornindal	61N58	6E31	-0:26:04
Horten	59N25	10E30	-0:42:00
Høyanger	61N13	6E05	-0:24:20
Hundorp	61N33	9E54	-0:39:36
Hvittingfoss	59N29	10E01	-0:40:04
Hylestad	59N05	7E32	-0:30:08
Jessheim	60N09	11E11	-0:44:44
Jevnaker	60N15	10E28	-0:41:52
Jordet	61N25	12E09	-0:48:36
Jørpeland	59N01	6E03	-0:24:12
Kalvåg	61N46	4E53	-0:19:32
Kapp	60N42	10E52	-0:43:28
Karasjok	69N27	25E30	-1:42:00
Kaupanger	61N11	7E14	-0:28:56
Kautokeino	69N00	23E02	-1:32:08
Kinn	61N36	4E45	-0:19:00
Kinsarvik	60N23	6E43	-0:26:52
Kirkenær	60N28	12E03	-0:48:12
Kirkenes	69N40	30E03	-2:00:12
Kløfta	60N04	11E09	-0:44:36
Knaben gruver	58N39	7E04	-0:28:16
Kolbotn	59N49	10E48	-0:43:12
Kolvereid	64N51	11E32	-0:46:08
Kongsberg	59N39	9E39	-0:38:36
Kongsvinger	60N12	12E00	-0:48:00
Kongsvoll	62N18	9E37	-0:38:28
Kopervik	59N17	5E18	-0:21:12
Koppang	61N34	11E04	-0:44:16
Kopperå	63N24	11E51	-0:47:24
Kornsjø	58N57	11E39	-0:46:36
Kragerø	58N52	9E25	-0:37:40
Kristiania → Oslo	59N55	10E45	-0:43:00
Kristiansand	58N10	8E00	-0:32:00
Kristiansund	63N07	7E45	-0:31:00
Kroken	65N22	14E20	-0:57:20
Kunes	70N21	26E31	-1:46:04
Kvam	61N40	9E42	-0:38:48
Kvanndal	60N29	6E36	-0:26:24
Kyrksæterøra	63N17	9E06	-0:36:24
Lærdalsøyri	61N06	7E29	-0:29:56
Lakselv	70N04	24E56	-1:39:44
Langesund	59N00	9E45	-0:39:00
Langevåg	62N27	6E12	-0:24:48
Larvik	59N04	10E00	-0:40:00
Lavik	61N06	5E30	-0:22:00
Lebesby	70N34	26E59	-1:47:56
Leikanger	61N10	6E52	-0:27:28
Leirvik	59N45	5E30	-0:22:00
Leksvik	63N40	10E37	-0:42:28
Lesjaskog	62N15	8E22	-0:33:28
Levanger	63N45	11E18	-0:45:12
Liknes	58N19	6E59	-0:27:56
Lillehammer	61N08	10E30	-0:42:00
Lillesand	58N15	8E24	-0:33:36
Lillestrøm	59N57	11E05	-0:44:20
Ljan	59N51	10E48	-0:43:12
Loen	61N52	6E52	-0:27:28

NORGE NORWEGEN NORVÈGE NORUEGA NORWAY

Place	Lat	Long	Offset
Lofthus	60N20	6E40	-0:26:40
Løken	59N48	11E29	-0:45:56
Løkken verk	63N08	9E42	-0:38:48
Lom	61N50	8E33	-0:34:12
Lomi	67N05	16E09	-1:04:36
Longyearbyen	78N00	16E00	-1:04:00
Lønsdal	66N44	15E28	-1:01:52
Løten	60N49	11E19	-0:45:16
Luster	61N26	7E24	-0:29:36
Lyngdal	58N08	7E05	-0:28:20
Lyngen	69N34	20E10	-1:20:40
Lyngør	58N38	9E10	-0:36:40
Lysaker	59N54	10E36	-0:42:24
Magnor	59N57	12E12	-0:48:48
Malm	64N04	11E13	-0:44:52
Måløy	61N56	5E07	-0:20:28
Mandal	58N02	7E27	-0:29:48
Melhus	63N17	10E16	-0:41:04
Meråker	63N26	11E45	-0:47:00
Mjøndalen	59N45	10E01	-0:40:04
Mo	66N15	14E08	-0:56:32
Moelv	60N56	10E42	-0:42:48
Moi	58N28	6E32	-0:26:08
Molde	62N44	7E11	-0:28:44
Mosby	58N14	7E54	-0:31:36
Mosjøen	65N50	13E10	-0:52:40
Moss	59N26	10E42	-0:42:48
Mysen	59N33	11E20	-0:45:20
Nærbø	58N40	5E39	-0:22:36
Namsos	64N29	11E30	-0:46:00
Narvik	68N26	17E25	-1:09:40
Naustdal	61N31	5E43	-0:22:52
Nedstrand	59N21	5E51	-0:23:24
Nes	60N34	9E59	-0:39:56
Nesbyen	60N34	9E09	-0:36:36
Nesna	66N12	13E02	-0:52:08
Nesttun	60N19	5E20	-0:21:20
Nevlunghamn	58N58	9E52	-0:39:28
Nittedal	60N04	10E53	-0:43:32
Nordfjordeid	61N54	6E00	-0:24:00
Nordfold	67N46	15E12	-1:00:48
Nordkjosbotn	69N13	19E30	-1:18:00
Nordreisa	69N46	21E03	-1:24:12
Nore	60N10	9E01	-0:36:04
Norheimsund	60N22	6E08	-0:24:32
Notodden	59N34	9E17	-0:37:08
Nybergsund	61N15	12E19	-0:49:16
Odda	60N04	6E33	-0:26:12
Olden	61N50	6E49	-0:27:16
Ølen	59N36	5E48	-0:23:12
Ona	62N52	6E34	-0:26:16
Oppdal	62N36	9E40	-0:38:40
Ørje	59N29	11E39	-0:46:36
Orkanger	63N19	9E52	-0:39:28
Ornes	61N18	7E22	-0:29:28
Ørsta	62N12	6E09	-0:24:36
Os	62N30	11E12	-0:44:48
Osen	64N17	10E30	-0:42:00
Oslo	59N55	10E45	-0:43:00
Osøyra	60N11	5E28	-0:21:52
Østby	61N15	12E32	-0:50:08
Otnes	61N45	11E14	-0:44:56
Otta	61N46	9E32	-0:38:08
Overhalla	64N30	11E57	-0:47:48
Øvre Årdal	61N19	7E48	-0:31:12
Øvre Rendal	61N53	11E05	-0:44:20
Øystese	60N23	6E13	-0:24:52
Polmak	70N04	28E00	-1:52:00
Porsgrunn	59N09	9E40	-0:38:40
Preststranda	59N06	9E04	-0:36:16
Råde	59N21	10E51	-0:43:24
Rakkestad	59N26	11E21	-0:45:24
Råkvåg	63N46	10E05	-0:40:20
Raufoss	60N43	10E37	-0:42:28
Rena	61N08	11E22	-0:45:28
Repvåg	70N45	25E41	-1:42:44
Rindal	63N03	9E13	-0:36:52
Ringebu	61N31	10E10	-0:40:40
Risør	58N43	9E14	-0:36:56
Rjukan	59N52	8E34	-0:34:16
Roa	60N17	10E37	-0:42:28
Rødberg	60N16	8E58	-0:35:52
Rødven	62N38	7E33	-0:30:12
Røldal	59N49	6E48	-0:27:12
Røn	61N03	9E03	-0:36:12
Røros	62N35	11E20	-0:45:20
Rosendal	59N59	6E01	-0:24:04
Roverud	60N15	12E03	-0:48:12
Rubbestadneset	59N49	5E17	-0:21:08
Ryfoss	61N09	8E49	-0:35:16
Rygge	59N23	10E43	-0:42:52
Rygnestad	59N16	7E29	-0:29:56
Sand	59N29	6E15	-0:25:00
Sandane	61N46	6E13	-0:24:52
Sandefjord	59N08	10E14	-0:40:56
Sandnes	58N51	5E44	-0:22:56
Sandvika	59N54	10E31	-0:42:04
Sarpsborg	59N17	11E07	-0:44:28
Sauda	59N39	6E20	-0:25:20
Selbu	63N13	11E02	-0:44:08
Selje	62N03	5E22	-0:21:28
Seljord	59N29	8E37	-0:34:28
Sinnes	58N56	6E50	-0:27:20
Sira	58N25	6E38	-0:26:32
Sirevåg	58N30	5E47	-0:23:08
Sistranda	63N43	8E50	-0:35:20
Sjøholt	62N29	6E48	-0:27:12
Skaidi	70N25	24E30	-1:38:00
Skånevik	59N44	5E59	-0:23:56
Skarnes	60N15	11E41	-0:46:44
Skaugum	59N51	10E26	-0:41:44
Skei	61N38	6E30	-0:26:00
Skeikampen	61N20	10E07	-0:40:28
Ski	59N43	10E50	-0:43:20
Skibotn	69N24	20E16	-1:21:04
Skien	59N12	9E36	-0:38:24
Skjeberg	59N14	11E12	-0:44:48
Skoganvarre	69N47	25E06	-1:40:24
Skotfoss	59N12	9E30	-0:38:00
Skotterud	59N59	12E07	-0:48:28
Skreia	60N39	10E56	-0:43:44
Skudeneshavn	59N09	5E17	-0:21:08
Søgne	58N05	7E49	-0:31:16
Sokna	60N14	9E54	-0:39:36
Sola	58N53	5E36	-0:22:24
Solheim	60N53	5E27	-0:21:48
Son	59N31	10E42	-0:42:48
Songe	58N41	9E00	-0:36:00
Sørfold	67N28	15E22	-1:01:28
Sørli	64N15	13E45	-0:55:00
Sortland	68N40	15E20	-1:01:20
Søvik	62N33	6E18	-0:25:12
Spitzbergen	78N00	20E00	-1:20:00
Spjelkavik	62N28	6E23	-0:25:32
Stalheim	60N50	6E40	-0:26:40
Stange	60N43	11E11	-0:44:44
Stavanger	58N58	5E45	-0:23:00
Stavern	59N00	10E02	-0:40:08
Steinkjer	64N01	11E30	-0:46:00
Steinshamn	62N47	6E29	-0:25:56
Stiklestad	63N48	11E33	-0:46:12
Stjørdalshalsen	63N28	10E56	-0:43:44
Støren	63N02	10E18	-0:41:12
Storvarts gruve	62N38	11E31	-0:46:04
Stranda	62N19	6E54	-0:27:36
Straumen	63N52	11E18	-0:45:12
Stryn	61N55	6E47	-0:27:08
Stugudal	62N54	11E52	-0:47:28
Sunde	59N50	5E43	-0:22:52
Sunndalsøra	62N40	8E33	-0:34:12
Surnadalsøra	62N59	8E39	-0:34:36
Svalbard	78N00	20E00	-1:20:00
Svelgen	61N47	5E15	-0:21:00
Svelvik	59N37	10E24	-0:41:36
Svindal	58N30	7E28	-0:29:52
Svolvær	68N14	14E34	-0:58:16
Svorkmo	63N10	9E45	-0:39:00
Svullrya	60N25	12E24	-0:49:36
Sykkylven	62N24	6E35	-0:26:20
Tana	70N28	28E18	-1:53:12
Tau	59N04	5E54	-0:23:36
Telavåg	60N16	4E49	-0:19:16
Tingvoll	62N54	8E12	-0:32:48
Tinnoset	59N43	9E02	-0:36:08
Titran	63N40	8E18	-0:33:12
Tofte	59N33	10E34	-0:42:16
Tolga	62N25	11E00	-0:44:00
Tomra	62N35	6E56	-0:27:44
Tønsberg	59N17	10E25	-0:41:40
Tonstad	58N40	6E43	-0:26:52
Torpo	60N40	8E43	-0:34:52
Tretten	61N19	10E19	-0:41:16
Tromsø	69N40	18E58	-1:15:52
Trondheim	63N25	10E25	-0:41:40
Trysil	61N19	12E16	-0:49:04
Tvedestrand	58N37	8E55	-0:35:40
Tveitsund	59N01	8E32	-0:34:08
Tydal	63N04	11E34	-0:46:16
Tynset	62N17	10E47	-0:43:08
Tysse	60N22	5E45	-0:23:00
Tyssedal	60N07	6E34	-0:26:16
Ulefoss	59N17	9E16	-0:37:04
Ulsteinvik	62N20	5E53	-0:23:32
Uskedal	59N56	5E52	-0:23:28
Ustaoset	60N30	8E04	-0:32:16
Utsira	59N18	4E54	-0:19:36
Uvdal	60N16	8E44	-0:34:56
Vadheim	61N13	5E49	-0:23:16
Vadsø	70N05	29E46	-1:59:04
Vågåmo	61N53	9E06	-0:36:24
Vaksdal	60N29	5E44	-0:22:56
Våler	60N40	11E50	-0:47:20
Valldal	62N20	7E21	-0:29:24
Vangsnes	61N11	6E38	-0:26:32
Vardø	70N21	31E02	-2:04:08
Vennesla	58N17	7E59	-0:31:56
Verdalsøra	63N48	11E29	-0:45:56
Vestbygd	58N06	6E35	-0:26:20
Vevelstad	65N43	12E30	-0:50:00
Vigeland	58N05	7E18	-0:29:12
Vigrestad	58N34	5E42	-0:22:48
Vikersund	59N59	10E02	-0:40:08
Vikna	64N57	10E58	-0:43:52
Viksøyri	61N05	6E35	-0:26:20
Vinstra	61N36	9E45	-0:39:00
Volda	62N09	6E06	-0:24:24
Voss	60N39	6E26	-0:25:44
Vrådal	59N20	8E25	-0:33:40
Ydstebøhavn	59N08	5E15	-0:21:00
Ytre Arna	60N26	5E30	-0:22:00

'UMĀN MUSCAT AND OMAN OMÁN OMAN

Time Table
Before 1/Jan/1920 LMT
Begin Standard 60E00
1/Jan/1920 0:00 -4:00

Place	Lat	Long	Offset
Ādam	22N24	57E32	-3:50:08
Al-Ghurayfah	24N00	56E29	-3:45:56
Al-Jawārah	18N55	57E17	-3:49:08
Al-Khābūrah	23N59	57E08	-3:48:32
Al-Khaṣab	26N12	56E15	-3:45:00
Al-Qābil	23N57	55E48	-3:43:12
Al-Qurayyāt	23N17	58E55	-3:55:40
As-Sīb	23N41	58E11	-3:52:44
Ḍank	23N33	56E17	-3:45:08
Fins	22N56	59E13	-3:56:52
'Ibrī	23N14	56E30	-3:46:00
Izkī	22N56	57E46	-3:51:04
Kalbā'	25N03	56E21	-3:45:24
Kumzār	26N20	56E25	-3:45:40
Maskin	23N35	56E39	-3:46:36
Masqaṭ (Muscat)	23N37	58E35	-3:54:20
Maṭraḥ	23N38	58E34	-3:54:16
Mirbāṭ	17N00	54E45	-3:39:00
Muscat → Masqaṭ	23N37	58E35	-3:54:20
Nazwā	22N56	57E32	-3:50:08
Ṣalālah	17N00	54E06	-3:36:24
Sarūr	23N22	58E07	-3:52:28
Shināṣ	24N46	56E28	-3:45:52
Ṣuḥār	24N22	56E45	-3:47:00
Ṣūr	22N35	59E31	-3:58:04
Tan'Am	23N09	56E29	-3:45:56
Ṭīwī	22N49	59E16	-3:57:04

PACIFIC ISLANDS TRUST TERR — MARSHALLS, CAROLINES, MARIANAS, PALAUS

Time Table # 1
Before 1/Jan/1901 LMT
Begin Standard 165E00
1/Jan/1901 0:00 -11:00
....
Time Table # 2
Before 1/Jan/1901 LMT
Begin Standard 135E00
1/Jan/1901 0:00 -9:00
....
Time Table # 3
Before 1/Jan/1901 LMT
Begin Standard 135E00
1/Jan/1901 0:00 -9:00
Begin Standard 150E00
1/Oct/1969 0:00 -10:00
....
Time Table # 4
Before 1/Jan/1901 LMT
Begin Standard 165E00
1/Jan/1901 0:00 -11:00
Begin Standard 180E00
1/Oct/1969 0:00 -12:00
....
Time Table # 5
Before 1/Jan/1901 LMT
Begin Standard 150E00
1/Jan/1901 0:00 -10:00
Begin Standard 165E00
1/Oct/1978 0:00 -11:00
....
Time Table # 6
Before 1/Jan/1901 LMT
Begin Standard 165E00
1/Jan/1901 0:00 -11:00
Begin Standard 180W00
1/Oct/1969 0:00 12:00

DIVISIONS

1. Agrihan Island
2. Alamagan Island
3. Anatahan Island
4. Arno Island
5. Asuncion Island
6. Bikar Island
7. Bikini Island
8. Dalap Island
9. Eauripik Island
10. Ebon Island
11. Engebi Island
12. Eniwetok Island
13. Fais Island
14. Falalu Island
15. Farallon de Pajaros Island
16. Gaferut Island
17. Guguan Island
18. Helen Island
19. Ifalik Island
20. Jaluit Island
21. Kapingamarangi Island
22. Kili Island
23. Kusaie Island
24. Kwajalein Island
25. Lae Island
26. Lamotrek Island
27. Lib Island
28. Losap Island
29. Majuro Island
30. Maloelap Island
31. Maug Islands
32. Menschikoo Island
33. Merir Island
34. Mili Island
35. Mokil Island
36. Murilo Island
37. Namoi Islands
38. Namoluk Island
39. Namonuito Island
40. Namorik Island
41. Namu Island
42. Ngatik Island
43. Ngulu Island
44. Nukuoro Island
45. Olimarao Island
46. Oroluk Island
47. Pagan Island
48. Pakin Island
49. Palau Islands
50. Pikelot Island
51. Pingelap Island
52. Ponape Island
53. Pulap Island
54. Pulo Anna Island
55. Pulusuk Island
56. Rongelap Island
57. Rota Island
58. Saipan Island
59. Sonsorol Islands
60. Sorol Island
61. Taongi Island
62. Taroa Island
63. Tinian Island
64. Tobi Island
65. Tol Island
66. Truk Islands
67. Ujae Island
68. Ujelang Island
69. Ulithi Island
70. Ulul Island
71. Utirik Island
72. Woleai Island
73. Wotho Island
74. Wotje Island
75. Yap Island

Agrihan Island 1 3 18N46 145E40 -9:42:40
Aiyon 49 2 7N43 134E37 -8:58:28
Alamagan Island 2 3 17N36 145E50 -9:43:20
Anatahan Island 3 3 16N22 145E40 -9:42:40
Angaur Island 49 2 6N54 134E09 -8:56:36
Anipaj 52 1 6N50 158E19-10:33:16
Anipen 52 1 6N49 158E14-10:32:56
Arno Island 4 4 7N05 171E41-11:26:44
Asuncion Island 5 3 19N40 145E24 -9:41:36
Auak 52 1 6N58 158E16-10:33:04
Aumar 52 1 6N57 158E10-10:32:40
Babelthuap Island 49 2 7N30 134E36 -8:58:24
Bikar Island 6 4 12N15 170E06-11:20:24
Bikini Island 7 4 11N35 165E23-11:01:32
Caroline Islands 3 8N00 147E00 -9:48:00
Chalan Kanoa 58 3 15N08 145E43 -9:42:52
Charan Kanoa 58 3 15N08 145E43 -9:42:52
Chittoin 10 4 4N35 168E42-11:14:48
Colonia 75 3 9N31 138E08 -9:12:32
Dalap Island 8 4 7N05 171E23-11:25:32
Eauripik Island 9 3 6N42 143E03 -9:32:12
Ebon Island 10 4 4N35 168E44-11:14:56
Engebi Island 11 4 11N40 162E15-10:49:00
Eniwetok Island 12 4 11N30 162E15-10:49:00
Eten Anchorage 66 5 7N22 151E54-10:07:36
Faal 75 3 9N37 138E10 -9:12:40
Fais Island 13 3 9N46 140E31 -9:22:04
Falalu Island 14 5 7N38 151E41-10:06:44
Farallon de Pajaros Island 15 3 30N32 144E54 -9:39:36
Gachpar 75 3 9N33 138E10 -9:12:40
Gaferut Island 16 3 9N14 145E23 -9:41:32
Gagil 75 3 9N33 138E10 -9:12:40
Garapan 58 3 15N12 145E43 -9:42:52
Goikul 49 2 7N22 134E36 -8:58:24
Gorror 75 3 9N27 138E04 -9:12:16
Guguan Island 17 3 17N19 145E51 -9:43:24
Gurror 75 3 9N27 138E04 -9:12:16
Helen Island 18 2 2N58 131E49 -8:47:16
Ifalik Island 19 3 7N15 144E27 -9:37:48
Ipat 52 1 6N58 158E12-10:32:48
Jaluit Island 20 4 6N00 169E35-11:18:20
Jelatak 52 1 6N56 158E17-10:33:08
Kanif 75 3 9N31 138E05 -9:12:20
Kanifay 75 3 9N31 138E05 -9:12:20
Kapingamarangi Island 21 5 1N04 154E46-10:19:04
Keklau 49 2 7N35 134E39 -8:58:36
Kili Island 22 4 5N39 169E04-11:16:16
Kloulklubed 49 2 7N02 134E15 -8:57:00
Kolonia 52 1 6N58 158E13-10:32:52
Koror 49 2 7N20 134E29 -8:57:56
Kusaie Island 23 4 5N19 162E59-10:51:56
Kwajalein Island 24 6 9N05 167E20-11:09:20
Lae Island 25 4 8N56 166E14-11:04:56
Lamotrek Island 26 3 7N30 146E20 -9:45:20
Lib Island 27 4 8N19 167E25-11:09:40
Losap Island 28 5 6N54 152E44-10:10:56
Lot 52 1 6N49 158E18-10:33:12
Lukop 52 1 6N54 158E19-10:33:16
Majijo 52 1 6N55 158E19-10:33:16
Majuro Island 29 4 7N09 171E12-11:24:48
Malakal 49 2 7N19 134E28 -8:57:52
Maloelap Island 30 4 8N45 171E03-11:24:12
Mariana Islands 3 16N00 145E30 -9:42:00
Mariana Ridge 3 17N00 146E00 -9:44:00
Marshall Islands 4 9N00 168E00-11:12:00
Maug Islands 31 3 20N01 145E13 -9:40:52
Mechol 75 3 9N37 138E10 -9:12:40
Meilap 52 1 6N54 158E09-10:32:36
Meitik 52 1 6N57 158E14-10:32:56
Melekeiok 49 2 7N29 134E38 -8:58:32
Melekeok 49 2 7N29 134E38 -8:58:32
Menschikoo Island 32 4 8N44 167E29-11:09:56
Meqruur 75 3 9N31 138E09 -9:12:36
Merir Island 33 2 4N19 132E19 -8:49:16
Mesa 66 5 7N21 151E51-10:07:24
Metalanim 52 1 6N53 158E16-10:33:04
Meyungs 49 2 7N20 134E27 -8:57:48
Mili Island 34 4 6N08 171E55-11:27:40
Mokil Island 35 4 6N40 159E47-10:39:08
Mukeru 49 2 7N25 134E30 -8:58:00
Murilo Island 36 5 8N40 152E11-10:08:44
Namoi Islands 37 5 5N27 153E40-10:14:40
Namoluk Island 38 5 5N55 153E08-10:12:32
Namonuito Island 39 5 8N46 150E02-10:00:08
Namorik Island 40 4 5N36 168E07-11:12:28
Namu Island 41 4 8N00 168E10-11:12:40
Ngaramasch 49 2 6N54 134E08 -8:56:32
Ngardmau 49 2 7N37 134E35 -8:58:20
Ngatik Island 42 1 5N51 157E16-10:29:04
Ngerkeel 49 2 7N25 134E30 -8:58:00
Ngermechau 49 2 7N35 134E39 -8:58:36
Ngetbong 49 2 7N37 134E35 -8:58:20
Ngulu Island 43 3 8N27 137E29 -9:09:56
Nif 75 3 9N28 138E04 -9:12:16
Nukan 66 5 7N23 151E53-10:07:32
Nukuoro Island 44 5 3N51 154E58-10:19:52
Okau 75 3 9N32 138E06 -9:12:24
Olimarao Island 45 3 7N41 145E52 -9:43:28
Ollei 49 2 7N43 134E37 -8:58:28
Omin 75 3 9N36 138E10 -9:12:40
Oroluk Island 46 1 7N32 155E18-10:21:12
Pagan Island 47 3 18N07 145E46 -9:43:04
Pakin Island 48 1 7N04 157E48-10:31:12
Palau Islands 49 2 7N30 134E30 -8:58:00
Pikelot Island 50 3 8N05 147E38 -9:50:32
Pingelap Island 51 4 6N13 160E42-10:42:48
Pok 52 1 6N49 158E12-10:32:48
Ponape 52 1 6N58 158E13-10:32:52
Ponape Island 52 1 6N55 158E15-10:33:00
Pulap Island 53 5 7N35 149E24 -9:57:36
Pulo Anna Island 54 2 4N40 131E58 -8:47:52
Pulusuk Island 55 5 6N42 149E19 -9:57:16
Reu 52 1 6N49 158E16-10:33:04
Roi 52 1 6N56 158E17-10:33:08
Rongelap Island 56 4 11N20 166E50-11:07:20
Ronkiti 52 1 6N49 158E10-10:32:40
Rota Island 57 3 14N10 145E12 -9:40:48
Runu 75 3 9N35 138E09 -9:12:36
Saipan 49 2 6N54 134E08 -8:56:32
Saipan Island 58 3 15N12 145E45 -9:43:00
San Antonio 58 3 15N08 145E43 -9:42:52
San Jose 58 3 15N09 145E43 -9:42:52
San Roque 58 3 15N15 145E47 -9:43:08
Sapou 66 5 7N18 151E53-10:07:32
Senyavin Islands 1 6N55 158E00-10:32:00
Sonsorol Islands 59 2 5N20 132E13 -8:48:52
Sorol Island 60 3 8N08 140E23 -9:21:32
Sunharon 63 3 14N57 145E36 -9:42:24
Tabunifi 75 3 9N28 138E05 -9:12:20
Tamoroi 52 1 6N51 158E19-10:33:16
Tanapag 58 3 15N14 145E45 -9:43:00
Taongi Island 61 4 14N37 168E58-11:15:52
Taroa Island 62 4 8N43 171E14-11:24:56
Tinian 63 3 14N58 145E38 -9:42:32
Tinian Island 63 3 15N00 145E38 -9:42:32
Tobi Island 64 2 3N00 131E10 -8:44:40
Tol Island 65 5 7N22 151E37-10:06:28
Tomara 52 1 6N54 158E10-10:32:32
Tomil 75 3 9N31 138E09 -9:12:36
Tomorolong 52 1 6N51 158E10-10:32:40
Truk Islands 66 5 7N25 151E47-10:07:08
Ujae Island 67 4 9N05 165E40-11:02:40
Ujelang Island 68 4 9N49 160E58-10:43:52
Ulithi Island 69 3 9N58 139E40 -9:18:40
Ulul Island 70 5 8N35 149E40 -9:58:40
Utirik Island 71 4 11N15 169E48-11:19:12
Woleai Island 72 3 7N21 143E52 -9:35:28
Wotho Island 73 4 10N06 165E59-11:03:56
Wotje Island 74 4 9N27 170E02-11:20:08
Yap Island 75 3 9N31 138E06 -9:12:24

```
     Time Table
  Before  1/Jan/1907 LMT
  Begin Standard    82E30
  1/Jan/1907  0:00 -5:30
  1/Sep/1942  0:00 -6:30
15/Oct/1945  0:00 -5:30
  Begin Standard    75E00
30/Sep/1951  0:00 -5:00
```

Abbottābād	34N09	73E13	-4:52:52
Abdul Hakīm	30N33	72E07	-4:48:28
Ahmadpur East	29N09	71E16	-4:45:04
Ahmadpur Siāl	30N41	71E46	-4:47:04
Ahmad Wāl	29N25	65E56	-4:23:44
Akālgarh	32N16	73E49	-4:55:16
Akora	34N00	72E08	-4:48:32
Aliabād	36N18	74E37	-4:58:28
Alīpur	29N23	70E55	-4:43:40
Alīpur Janūbi	30N13	71E18	-4:45:12
Allāhābād	28N57	70E53	-4:43:32
Amāngarh	34N00	71E55	-4:47:40
Amb	34N19	72E51	-4:51:24
Amīr Chāh	29N13	62E28	-4:09:52
Amrūka	30N19	73E53	-4:55:32
Ārifwāla	30N17	73E04	-4:52:16
Ashewat	31N22	68E32	-4:34:08
Asrāni	29N31	72E07	-4:48:28
Astor	35N22	74E51	-4:59:24
Athārān Hazāri	31N11	72E06	-4:48:24
Attock	33N54	72E15	-4:49:00
Badal Khān Goth	26N31	67E06	-4:28:24
Baddomalhi	31N59	74E40	-4:58:40
Badhāna	31N28	74E37	-4:58:28
Badīn	24N39	68E50	-4:35:20
Bādrāh	27N20	68E01	-4:32:04
Baffa	34N26	73E13	-4:52:52
Bāgh	33N59	73E47	-4:55:08
Bahāwalnagar	29N59	73E16	-4:53:04
Bahāwalpur	29N24	71E41	-4:46:44
Bālākot	34N33	73E21	-4:53:24
Baltit	36N20	74E40	-4:58:40
Bānda Dāūd Shāh	33N16	71E11	-4:44:44
Bāndhi	26N35	68E18	-4:33:12
Bannu	32N59	70E36	-4:42:24
Bārkhān	29N54	69E31	-4:38:04
Basāl	33N33	72E15	-4:49:00
Basīrpur	30N35	73E50	-4:55:20
Bazdār	26N21	65E03	-4:20:12
Bela	26N14	66E19	-4:25:16
Bellpat	28N59	68E00	-4:32:00
Bhāg	29N02	67E49	-4:31:16
Bhāi Pheru	31N12	73E57	-4:55:48
Bhakkar	31N38	71E04	-4:44:16
Bhalwāl	32N16	72E54	-4:51:36
Bhaun	32N52	72E45	-4:51:00
Bhera	32N29	72E55	-4:51:40
Bhimbar	32N59	74E04	-4:56:16
Bībi Nāni	29N42	67E23	-4:29:32
Bijbān Chāh	26N54	64E42	-4:18:48
Bostān	30N26	67E02	-4:28:08
Bunji	35N40	74E36	-4:58:24
Burzil	34N52	75E07	-5:00:28
Campbellpore	33N46	72E22	-4:49:28
Chāchro	25N07	70E15	-4:41:00
Chāgai	29N18	64E42	-4:18:48
Chak Amru	32N22	75E11	-5:00:44
Chak Jhumra	31N34	73E11	-4:52:44
Chakwāl	32N56	72E52	-4:51:28
Chalt	36N15	74E20	-4:57:20
Chaman	30N55	66E27	-4:25:48
Chamburi Kalāt	26N09	64E43	-4:18:52
Chanuwāla	32N44	73E08	-4:52:32
Chārsadda	34N09	71E44	-4:46:56
Chawinda	32N21	74E42	-4:58:48
Cherāt	33N49	71E53	-4:47:32
Chhab	33N14	71E54	-4:47:36
Chīchāwatni	30N32	72E42	-4:50:48
Chilam	35N03	75E07	-5:00:28
Chilās	35N26	74E05	-4:56:20
Chiniot	31N43	72E59	-4:51:56
Chinjan	30N34	67E58	-4:31:52
Chishtiān Mandi	29N48	72E52	-4:51:28
Chitrāl	35N51	71E47	-4:47:08
Chūhar Kāna	31N45	73E48	-4:55:12
Chūnd	31N26	72E16	-4:49:04
Chūniān	30N58	73E59	-4:55:56
Chushālgarh	33N30	71E54	-4:47:36
Dādhar	29N28	67E39	-4:30:36
Dādu	26N44	67E47	-4:31:08
Dāira Dīn Panāh	30N34	70E56	-4:43:44
Dājal	29N33	70E23	-4:41:32
Dālbandin	28N53	64E25	-4:17:40
Dandot	32N39	72E58	-4:51:52
Darāban	31N44	70E20	-4:41:20
Darband	34N20	72E52	-4:51:28
Dargai	34N11	71E53	-4:47:32
Darkhāna	30N39	72E11	-4:48:44
Darya Khān	31N48	71E06	-4:44:24
Dās	35N05	75E05	-5:00:20
Daska	32N20	74E21	-4:57:24
Dāūd Khel	32N53	71E34	-4:46:16
Daulatpur	26N30	67E58	-4:31:52
Daultāla	33N12	73E09	-4:52:36
Dera Bugti	29N02	69E09	-4:36:36
Dera Ghāzi Khān	30N03	70E38	-4:42:32
Dera Ismāīl Khān	31N50	70E54	-4:43:36
Dera Nawāb	29N06	71E16	-4:45:04
Derāwar Fort	28N46	71E20	-4:45:20
Dhabān Singh	31N44	73E34	-4:54:16
Dhudiāl	33N04	72E58	-4:51:52
Digri	25N10	69E07	-4:36:28
Dinga	25N26	67E10	-4:28:40
Dinga	32N38	73E43	-4:54:52
Dīpālpur	30N40	73E39	-4:54:36
Diplo	24N28	69E35	-4:38:20
Dīr	35N12	71E53	-4:47:32
Dokri	27N23	68E06	-4:32:24
Duki	30N09	68E34	-4:34:16
Dunyāpur	29N48	71E44	-4:46:56
Dureji	25N53	67E18	-4:29:12
Eminābād	32N02	74E16	-4:57:04
Faisalabad (Lyallpur)	31N25	73E05	-4:52:20
Fanepura	31N29	72E54	-4:51:36
Fatehjang	33N34	72E39	-4:50:36
Fatehpur	31N09	71E13	-4:44:52
Fāzilpur	29N18	70E27	-4:41:48
Fort Abbās	29N12	72E52	-4:51:28
Fort Sandeman	31N20	69E27	-4:37:48
Gadra	25N40	70E37	-4:42:28
Gākuch	36N10	73E45	-4:55:00
Gamboli	29N50	68E26	-4:33:44
Ganda Singhwāla	31N02	74E31	-4:58:04
Gandāva	28N37	67E29	-4:29:56
Garhi Khairo	28N04	67E59	-4:31:56
Garhi Habibullāh Khan	34N24	73E23	-4:53:32
Ghakhar	32N18	74E09	-4:56:36
Gharībwāl	32N41	73E10	-4:52:40
Gharo	24N44	67E35	-4:30:20
Ghazlūna	31N24	67E49	-4:31:16
Ghazni Khel	32N33	70E44	-4:42:56
Ghotki	28N01	69E19	-4:37:16
Gilgit	35N55	74E18	-4:57:12
Godar	28N10	63E14	-4:12:56
Gojra	31N09	72E41	-4:50:44
Golra	33N42	72E58	-4:51:52
Gor	35N32	74E31	-4:58:04
Gugera	30N58	73E19	-4:53:16
Gūjar Khān	33N16	73E19	-4:53:16
Gujrānwāla	32N26	74E33	-4:58:12
Gujrāt	32N34	74E05	-4:56:20
Gul Imām	32N16	70E32	-4:42:08
Gulistān	30N36	66E35	-4:26:20
Gupis	36N14	73E26	-4:53:44
Guru	29N34	66E43	-4:26:52
Gwādar	25N07	62E19	-4:09:16
Gwāl Haidarzai	30N44	68E48	-4:35:12
Hab Nadi Chowki	25N01	66E53	-4:27:32
Hadāli	32N18	72E12	-4:48:48
Hāfizābād	32N04	73E41	-4:54:44
Haiderabad → Hyderābād	25N22	68E22	-4:33:28
Hāla	25N49	68E25	-4:33:40
Hangu	33N32	71E04	-4:44:16
Harappa	30N38	72E52	-4:51:28
Harappa Road	30N36	72E55	-4:51:40
Harīpur	33N59	72E56	-4:51:44
Harnai	30N06	67E56	-4:31:44
Hārūnābād	29N37	73E08	-4:52:32
Hasan Abdāl	33N49	72E41	-4:50:44
Hāsilpur	29N43	72E33	-4:50:12
Hathāla	32N03	70E34	-4:42:16
Haveli	30N27	73E42	-4:54:48
Haveliān	34N03	73E10	-4:52:40
Hazro	33N54	72E29	-4:49:56
Hindubāgh	30N49	67E45	-4:31:00
Hirok Sāmi	26N02	63E25	-4:13:40
Hoshāb	26N01	63E56	-4:15:44
Hundewāli	31N55	72E38	-4:50:32
Hurmāgai	28N18	64E26	-4:17:44
Hyderābād	25N22	68E22	-4:33:28
Īsa Khel	32N41	71E17	-4:45:08
Ishkumān	36N32	73E49	-4:55:16
Islāmābād	33N42	73E10	-4:52:40
Islāmkot	24N42	70E11	-4:40:44
Ispikān	26N14	62E12	-4:08:48
Jabbi	33N08	72E38	-4:50:32
Jabori	34N36	73E16	-4:53:04
Jacobābād	28N17	68E26	-4:33:44
Jāgan	28N05	68E30	-4:34:00
Jahānābād	32N11	72E29	-4:49:56
Jahāngīra	33N58	72E13	-4:48:52
Jahānia	30N02	71E49	-4:47:16
Jajjha	28N45	70E34	-4:42:16
Jalālpur	32N38	74E12	-4:56:48
Jalālpur Pīrwāla	29N30	71E13	-4:44:52
Jamesābād	25N17	69E15	-4:37:00
Jāmpur	29N39	70E36	-4:42:24
Jand	33N26	72E01	-4:48:04
Jarānwāla	31N20	73E26	-4:53:44
Jassar	32N06	74E57	-4:59:48
Jāti	24N21	68E16	-4:33:04
Jatoi Janūbi	29N31	70E51	-4:43:24
Jebri	27N18	65E44	-4:22:56
Jhal	28N17	67E27	-4:29:48
Jhal Jhao	26N18	65E35	-4:22:20
Jhang Maghiāna	31N16	72E19	-4:49:16
Jhānsi Post	33N52	71E24	-4:45:36
Jhawāriān	32N22	72E38	-4:50:32
Jhelum	32N56	73E44	-4:54:56
Jhok Rind	31N27	70E26	-4:41:44
Jīwani	25N03	61E45	-4:07:00
Johi	26N41	67E37	-4:30:28
Jungshāhi	24N51	67E46	-4:31:04
Jun Kharchanai	36N52	75E01	-5:00:04
Kabīr Kili	33N11	71E19	-4:45:16
Kabīrwāla	30N24	71E52	-4:47:28
Kāgān	34N47	73E32	-4:54:08
Kāhna	31N22	74E22	-4:57:28
Kahror Pakka	29N37	71E55	-4:47:40
Kahūta	33N35	73E23	-4:53:32
Kālābagh	32N58	71E34	-4:46:16
Kalām	35N32	72E35	-4:50:20
Kalāt	29N02	66E35	-4:26:20
Kalchās	29N21	69E42	-4:38:48
Kallar Kahār	32N47	72E42	-4:50:48
Kalri	31N39	72E33	-4:50:12
Kalūr Kot	32N09	71E16	-4:45:04
Kamālia	30N44	72E39	-4:50:36
Kambar	27N36	68E00	-4:32:00
Kāmoke	31N58	74E13	-4:56:52
Kandāhu	27N33	69E24	-4:37:36
Kandhkot	28N14	69E11	-4:36:44
Kandiāro	27N04	68E13	-4:32:52
Kandrāch	25N29	65E29	-4:21:56
Kanganpur	30N46	74E08	-4:56:32
Kappar	25N19	62E42	-4:10:48
Karāchi	24N52	67E03	-4:28:12
Karatschi → Karāchi	24N52	67E03	-4:28:12
Karor	31N13	70E57	-4:43:48
Kashmor	28N26	69E35	-4:38:20
Kasūr	31N07	74E27	-4:57:48
Kātlang	34N22	72E05	-4:48:20
Keti Bandar	24N08	67E27	-4:29:48
Khairpur	27N32	68E46	-4:35:04
Khairpur	29N35	72E14	-4:48:56
Khānewāl	30N18	71E56	-4:47:44
Khāngāh Dogrān	31N50	73E37	-4:54:28
Khāngarh	28N22	71E43	-4:46:52
Khāngarh	29N55	71E10	-4:44:40
Khānozai	30N37	67E19	-4:29:16
Khānpur	28N39	70E39	-4:42:36
Khapalu	35N10	76E20	-5:05:20
Kharak	33N07	71E06	-4:44:24
Khārān	28N35	65E25	-4:21:40
Khāriān	32N49	73E52	-4:55:28
Khaur	33N16	72E28	-4:49:52
Khewāri	26N36	68E52	-4:35:28
Khewra	32N39	73E01	-4:52:04
Khipro	25N50	69E22	-4:37:28
Khudiān	30N59	74E17	-4:57:08
Khurli	28N59	65E52	-4:23:28
Khushāb	32N18	72E21	-4:49:24
Khuzdār	27N48	66E37	-4:26:28
Kingri	30N27	69E49	-4:39:16
Kinjar Khās	29N55	70E58	-4:43:52
Kohak	25N44	62E33	-4:10:12
Kohāt	33N35	71E26	-4:45:44
Kot Addu	30N28	70E58	-4:43:52
Kot Chutta	29N53	70E39	-4:42:36
Kotli	33N31	73E55	-4:55:40
Kot Mūmin	32N11	73E02	-4:52:08
Kot Rādha Kishan	31N10	74E06	-4:56:24
Kotri	25N22	68E18	-4:33:12
Kotri Allahrakhio	24N24	67E50	-4:31:20
Kot Sultān	30N46	70E56	-4:43:44
Kulāchi	31N56	70E27	-4:41:48
Kundiān	32N27	71E28	-4:45:52
Kunjāh	32N32	73E59	-4:55:56
Kurram	30N06	66E31	-4:26:04
Lāhor	34N03	72E22	-4:49:28
Lahor → Lahore	31N35	74E18	-4:57:12
Lahore	31N35	74E18	-4:57:12
Lahri	29N11	68E13	-4:32:52
Lakaband	31N00	69E30	-4:38:00
Lakki	32N36	70E55	-4:43:40
Lāla Mūsa	32N42	73E58	-4:55:52
Lāliān	31N49	72E48	-4:51:12
Landi Kotal	34N06	71E09	-4:44:36
Lārkāna	27N33	68E13	-4:32:52
Lasht	36N48	73E01	-4:52:04
Latambar	33N07	70E52	-4:43:28
Lawrencepur	33N50	72E30	-4:50:00
Lehtar	33N42	73E26	-4:53:44
Leiah	30N58	70E56	-4:43:44
Liāquatpur	28N56	70E57	-4:43:48
Liāri	25N41	66E29	-4:25:56
Lillah Bharwanah	32N34	72E45	-4:51:00
Lodhrān	29N32	71E38	-4:46:32
Loe Āgra	34N35	71E43	-4:46:52
Lora	33N53	73E17	-4:53:08
Loralai	30N22	68E36	-4:34:24
Luddan	29N54	72E34	-4:50:16
Luliāni	31N15	74E25	-4:57:40
Lyallpur → Faisalabad	31N25	73E05	-4:52:20
McLeodganj	30N15	73E42	-4:54:48
McLeodganj Road	30N09	73E44	-4:54:56
Mailsi	29N48	72E11	-4:48:44
Makhad	33N08	71E44	-4:46:56
Malākand	34N34	71E56	-4:47:44
Malakwāl	32N34	73E13	-4:52:52
Mānānwala	31N35	73E41	-4:54:44
Mand	26N07	62E03	-4:08:12
Mandi Bahāuddīn	32N35	73E30	-4:54:00
Mandi Būrewāla	30N09	72E41	-4:50:44
Mandi Sādiqganj	30N10	73E44	-4:54:56
Mandra	33N22	73E14	-4:52:56
Mangla	33N07	73E39	-4:54:36

PAKISTAN PAQUISTÁN WEST PAKISTAN PĀKISTĀN

Place	Lat	Long	Offset
Mankera	31N23	71E26	-4:45:44
Mānsar	33N54	72E19	-4:49:16
Mānsehra	34N20	73E12	-4:52:48
Mānzai	30N07	68E52	-4:35:28
Manzil	29N15	63E05	-4:12:20
Mardān	34N12	72E02	-4:48:08
Mashki Chāh	29N01	62E27	-4:09:48
Mastūj	36N17	72E31	-4:50:04
Mastung	29N48	66E51	-4:27:24
Matanni	33N48	71E34	-4:46:16
Matiāri	25N36	68E27	-4:33:48
Mātli	25N02	68E39	-4:34:36
Mehar	27N11	67E49	-4:31:16
Mekhtar	30N28	69E22	-4:37:28
Miān Channūn	30N27	72E22	-4:49:28
Miāni	32N32	73E04	-4:52:16
Miānwāli	32N35	71E33	-4:46:12
Minchinābād	30N10	73E34	-4:54:16
Mingāora	34N47	72E22	-4:49:28
Minimarg	34N47	75E05	-5:00:20
Mīram Shāh	33N01	70E04	-4:40:16
Mīrān	31N24	70E43	-4:42:52
Mīrpur	33N11	73E46	-4:55:04
Mīrpur Batoro	24N44	68E16	-4:33:04
Mīrpur Bībīwāri	28N32	67E44	-4:30:56
Mīrpur Khās	25N32	69E00	-4:36:00
Mīrpur Sakro	24N33	67E37	-4:30:28
Misgār	36N47	74E47	-4:59:08
Mitha Tiwāna	32N15	72E07	-4:48:28
Mithi	24N44	69E48	-4:39:12
Mochh	32N45	71E31	-4:46:04
Montgomery → Sāhiwāl	30N40	73E06	-4:52:24
Moro	26N40	68E00	-4:32:00
Mowshera	34N01	71E59	-4:47:56
Multān	30N11	71E29	-4:45:56
Murgha Faqīrzai	30N11	67E48	-4:31:12
Murgha Kibzai	30N44	69E25	-4:37:40
Murīdke	31N48	74E16	-4:57:04
Murree	33N54	73E24	-4:53:36
Mūsa Khel	32N38	71E44	-4:46:56
Mūsa Khel Bāzār	30N52	69E49	-4:39:16
Mūsāzai	30N23	66E32	-4:26:08
Muzaffarābād	34N22	73E28	-4:53:52
Muzaffargarh	30N04	71E12	-4:44:48
Nāg	27N24	65E08	-4:20:32
Nagar Pārkar	24N22	70E45	-4:43:00
Nagrai	34N23	72E41	-4:50:44
Nahakki	34N25	71E20	-4:45:20
Nāka Khārari	25N15	66E44	-4:26:56
Nankāna Sāhib	31N27	73E42	-4:54:48
Naokot	24N51	69E27	-4:37:48
Nārang	31N54	74E31	-4:58:04
Nārowāl	32N07	73E25	-4:53:40
Nasīrābād	28N23	68E24	-4:33:36
Nathia Gali	34N04	73E24	-4:53:36
Nauroz Kalāt	28N47	65E38	-4:22:32
Naushahro Fīroz	26N50	68E07	-4:32:28
Nawābshāh	26N15	68E25	-4:33:40
Nawa Kot	28N20	71E22	-4:45:28
Nawān Kot	31N06	71E32	-4:46:08
Nawāshahr	34N10	73E16	-4:53:04
Nirwāno	26N22	62E43	-4:10:52
Nok Kundi	28N46	62E46	-4:11:04
Nowshera	34N01	71E59	-4:47:56
Nūrpur	31N53	71E54	-4:47:36
Nushki	29N33	66E01	-4:24:04
Oghi	34N31	73E01	-4:52:04
Okāra	30N49	73E27	-4:53:48
Ormāra	25N12	64E38	-4:18:32
Pabbi	34N01	71E47	-4:47:08
Pail	32N38	72E27	-4:49:48
Pākpattan	30N21	73E24	-4:53:36
Panjgūr	26N58	64E06	-4:16:24
Panjpāi	29N55	66E30	-4:26:00
Pārachinār	33N54	70E06	-4:40:24
Pasni	25N16	63E28	-4:13:52
Pasrūr	32N16	74E40	-4:58:40
Pattoki	31N01	73E51	-4:55:24
Peshāwar	34N01	71E33	-4:46:12
Peshmāl	35N26	72E36	-4:50:24
Pezu	32N19	70E44	-4:42:56
Phālia	32N26	73E35	-4:54:20
Phariāro	27N12	68E59	-4:35:56
Phularwān	32N22	73E00	-4:52:00
Phulra	34N20	73E03	-4:52:12
Pidarak	25N51	63E14	-4:12:56
Piffgal	36N10	73E10	-4:52:40
Pind Dādan Khān	32N35	73E03	-4:52:12
Pindi Bhattiān	31N54	73E16	-4:53:04
Pindi Gheb	33N14	72E16	-4:49:04
Piplān	32N17	71E21	-4:45:24
Pīr Jo Goth	27N36	68E37	-4:34:28
Pīr Mahal	30N46	72E26	-4:49:44
Pishīn	30N35	67E00	-4:28:00
Qamr-Ud-Dīn Kārez	31N39	68E25	-4:33:40
Qāsimwāla	30N09	73E50	-4:55:20
Qila Abdullāh	30N43	66E38	-4:26:32
Qila Dīdār Singh	32N08	74E01	-4:56:04
Qila Lādgasht	27N54	62E57	-4:11:48
Qila Saifullāh	30N43	68E21	-4:33:24
Qila Sobha Singh	32N14	74E46	-4:59:04
Quetta	30N12	67E00	-4:28:00
Rahīm ki Bāzār	24N19	69E09	-4:36:36
Rahīmyār Khān	28N25	70E18	-4:41:12
Rāhwāli	32N15	74E10	-4:56:40
Rāiwind	31N15	74E13	-4:56:52
Rāja Jang	31N13	74E16	-4:57:04
Rājanpur	29N06	70E19	-4:41:16
Rakhni	30N03	69E55	-4:39:40
Rangpur	30N31	71E34	-4:46:16
Rasūl	32N42	73E34	-4:54:16
Rasūlnagar	32N20	73E47	-4:55:08
Ratodero	27N48	68E18	-4:33:12
Rattu	35N08	74E48	-4:59:12
Rāwala Kot	33N52	73E46	-4:55:04
Rāwalpindi	33N36	73E04	-4:52:16
Regiwar	25N57	65E44	-4:22:56
Renāla Khurd	30N53	73E36	-4:54:24
Risālpur Cantonment	34N04	72E00	-4:48:00
Rohri	27N41	68E54	-4:35:36
Rungāni	26N38	65E43	-4:22:52
Rustam	34N21	72E17	-4:49:08
Sadda	33N42	70E20	-4:41:20
Sādiqābad	28N18	70E08	-4:40:32
Sāhiwāl (Montgomery)	30N40	73E06	-4:52:24
Sāhiwāl	31N58	72E20	-4:49:20
Saidu	34N45	72E21	-4:49:24
Saindak	29N17	61E34	-4:06:16
Sakesar	32N33	71E56	-4:47:44
Sakhi Sarwar	29N59	70E18	-4:41:12
Sakrand	26N08	68E16	-4:33:04
Salāmbek	28N18	65E09	-4:20:36
Samasata	29N21	71E33	-4:46:12
Samawāri	28N34	66E46	-4:27:04
Sambāza	31N49	69E20	-4:37:20
Sambriāl	32N28	74E21	-4:57:24
Samundri	31N04	72E58	-4:51:52
Sanāwān	30N19	70E59	-4:43:56
Sanghar	26N02	68E57	-4:35:48
Sāngla	31N43	73E23	-4:53:32
Sanjāwi	30N17	68E21	-4:33:24
Sarāi Naurang	32N50	70E47	-4:43:08
Sardār Chāh	27N58	64E50	-4:19:20
Sargodha	32N05	72E40	-4:50:40
Sehwān	26N26	67E52	-4:31:28
Shabqadar	34N13	71E34	-4:46:16
Shāhbandar	24N10	67E54	-4:31:36
Shāhbāz Kalāt	26N42	63E58	-4:15:52
Shāhdādkot	27N51	67E54	-4:31:36
Shāhdādpur	25N56	68E37	-4:34:28
Shāhdara	31N38	74E18	-4:57:12
Shāh Kot	31N34	73E29	-4:53:56
Shāhpur	28N43	68E25	-4:33:40
Shāhpur	32N17	72E26	-4:49:44
Shāhpur Chākar	26N09	68E39	-4:34:36
Shaighālu	31N11	68E49	-4:35:16
Shakardarra	33N14	71E30	-4:46:00
Shakargarh	32N16	75E10	-5:00:40
Sharan Jogīzai	31N02	68E33	-4:34:12
Sharqpur	31N28	74E06	-4:56:24
Shekhūpura	31N42	73E59	-4:55:56
Sher Qila	36N06	74E03	-4:56:12
Sher Shāh	30N06	71E21	-4:45:24
Shikārpur	27N57	68E38	-4:34:32
Shināwari	33N32	70E48	-4:43:12
Shorkot	30N50	72E04	-4:48:16
Shorkot Road	30N47	72E15	-4:49:00
Shujāābād	29N53	71E18	-4:45:12
Siālkot	32N30	74E31	-4:58:04
Siari	34N56	76E44	-5:06:56
Sibi	29N33	67E53	-4:31:32
Sillānwāli	31N50	72E33	-4:50:12
Singal	36N06	73E53	-4:55:32
Skārdu	35N18	75E37	-5:02:28
Sodhra	32N28	74E11	-4:56:44
Sonmiāni	25N26	66E36	-4:26:24
Sūi	28N37	69E19	-4:37:16
Sujāwal	24N36	68E05	-4:32:20
Sukkur	27N42	68E52	-4:35:28
Sulaimān Khel	33N41	71E01	-4:44:04
Suntsar	25N31	62E00	-4:08:00
Sūrāb	28N29	66E16	-4:25:04
Surtanāhu	26N22	70E00	-4:40:00
Swābi	34N07	72E28	-4:49:52
Takht-I-Bhāi	34N17	71E56	-4:47:44
Tāl	34N55	72E13	-4:48:52
Talagang	32N55	72E25	-4:49:40
Talamba	30N32	72E14	-4:48:56
Talhār	24N53	68E49	-4:35:16
Tānda	32N42	74E22	-4:57:28
Tāndliānwāla	31N02	73E08	-4:52:32
Tando Ādam	25N46	68E40	-4:34:40
Tando Allāhyār	25N28	68E43	-4:34:52
Tando Bāgo	24N47	68E58	-4:35:52
Tando Muhammad Khān	25N08	68E32	-4:34:08
Tangi	34N18	71E40	-4:46:40
Tānk	32N13	70E23	-4:41:32
Tarbela	34N08	72E49	-4:51:16
Tatta	24N45	67E55	-4:31:40
Taunsa	30N42	70E39	-4:42:36
Taxila	33N44	72E49	-4:51:16
Teru	36N11	72E45	-4:51:00
Thak	30N32	70E13	-4:40:52
Thal	33N22	70E33	-4:42:12
Thāna	28N55	63E45	-4:15:00
Thānedārwāla	32N36	71E07	-4:44:28
Thāno Bula Khān	25N22	67E50	-4:31:20
Thul	28N14	68E46	-4:35:04
Toba Tek Singh	30N58	72E29	-4:49:56
Toi Sar	31N06	69E54	-4:39:36
Tolti	35N02	76E06	-5:04:24
Trand	34N38	72E59	-4:51:56
Triman	29N38	69E05	-4:36:20
Turbat	25N59	63E04	-4:12:16
Ubauro	28N10	69E44	-4:38:56
Uch	29N14	71E03	-4:44:12
Umarkot	25N22	69E44	-4:38:56
Uthal	25N48	66E37	-4:26:28
Utmānzai	34N11	71E46	-4:47:04
Vihāri	30N02	72E21	-4:49:24
Vihowa	31N08	70E30	-4:42:00
Wad	27N21	66E22	-4:25:28
Wāgah	31N36	74E33	-4:58:12
Wah	33N48	72E42	-4:50:48
Wārāh	27N27	67E48	-4:31:12
Warburton	31N33	73E50	-4:55:20
Warcha	32N25	71E59	-4:47:56
Warsak	34N10	71E25	-4:45:40
Wasāwewāla	30N28	73E40	-4:54:40
Wāshuk	27N44	64E48	-4:19:12
Wazīrābād	32N27	74E07	-4:56:28
Yakmach	28N45	63E51	-4:15:24
Yārik	32N06	70E47	-4:43:08
Yāsīn	33N57	72E30	-4:50:00
Yazmān	29N08	71E45	-4:47:00
Zafarwāl	32N21	74E54	-4:59:36
Zāwa	28N04	66E23	-4:25:32
Ziārat	30N23	67E43	-4:30:52

PANAMA PANAMÁ

Time Table
Before 1/Jan/1890 LMT
Begin Standard 79w54
1/Jan/1890 0:00 5:20
Begin Standard 75w00
22/Apr/1908 0:00 5:00

Place	Lat	Long	Offset
Aguadulce	8N15	80w33	5:22:12
Alligandí	9N14	78w01	5:12:04
Alanje	8N24	82w33	5:30:12
Albrook Field	8N58	79w34	5:18:16
Almirante	9N18	82w24	5:29:36
Ancon	8N58	79w33	5:18:12
Antón	8N24	80w16	5:21:04
Aspinwall → Colón	9N22	79w54	5:19:36
Atalaya	8N03	80w56	5:23:44
Bajo Boquete	8N47	82w26	5:29:44
Balboa	8N57	79w34	5:18:16
Balboa Heights	8N57	79w33	5:18:12
Bastimentos	9N21	82w12	5:28:48
Bejuco	8N36	79w53	5:19:32
Boca del Monte	8N21	82w07	5:28:28
Bocas del Toro	9N20	82w15	5:29:00
Boquerón	8N30	82w34	5:30:16
Cabecera de Dupí	8N22	81w54	5:27:36
Calobre	8N19	80w51	5:23:24
Cañazas	8N19	81w13	5:24:52
Capira	8N45	79w53	5:19:32
Chame	8N35	79w53	5:19:32
Chepo	9N10	79w06	5:16:24
Chichica	8N22	81w40	5:26:40
Chimán	8N42	78w37	5:14:28
Chiriquí	8N24	82w19	5:29:16
Chiriquí Grande	8N57	82w07	5:28:28
Chitré	7N58	80w26	5:21:44
Colón	9N22	79w54	5:19:36
Cocosolo	9N23	79w53	5:19:32
Concepción	8N31	82w37	5:30:28
Corozal	8N59	79w34	5:18:16
Cristóbal	9N21	79w55	5:19:40

PANAMÁ — PANAMA

Cusapin	9N11	81w54	5:27:36
Darien	9N08	79w46	5:19:04
David	8N26	82w26	5:29:44
Divalá	8N25	82w43	5:30:52
Dolega	8N34	82w25	5:29:40
El Real	8N08	77w43	5:10:52
El Valle	8N36	80w08	5:20:32
Escobal	9N09	79w58	5:19:52
Fort Amador	8N57	79w33	5:18:12
Fort Clayton	9N00	79w35	5:18:20
Fort Davis	9N17	79w55	5:19:40
Fort Randolph	9N23	79w53	5:19:32
Fort Sherman	9N22	79w57	5:19:48
France Field	9N21	79w53	5:19:32
Gamboa	9N07	79w42	5:18:48
Garachiné	8N04	78w22	5:13:28
Gatun	9N16	79w56	5:19:44
Guabito	9N30	82w37	5:30:28
Gualaca	8N32	82w18	5:29:12
Guararé	7N49	80w17	5:21:08
Hato del Volcán	8N46	82w38	5:30:32
Horconcitos	8N19	82w10	5:28:40
Jaqué	7N31	78w10	5:12:40
La Arena	7N58	80w28	5:21:52
La Chorrera	8N53	79w47	5:19:08
La Concepción	8N31	82w37	5:30:28
La Mesa	8N09	81w11	5:24:44
La Palma	8N25	78w09	5:12:36
La Palma	7N42	80w12	5:20:48
La Pintada	8N36	80w27	5:21:48
Las Lajas	8N15	81w52	5:27:28
Las Palmas	8N08	81w27	5:25:48
Las Tablas	7N46	80w17	5:21:08
Lídice	8N45	79w54	5:19:36
Los Santos	7N56	80w25	5:21:40
Luzon	9N25	82w32	5:30:08
Mandinga	9N27	79w04	5:16:16
Margarita	9N20	79w45	5:19:00
Miguel de la Borda	9N09	80w19	5:21:16
Mindi	9N18	79w55	5:19:40
Monagrillo	7N59	80w26	5:21:44
Montijo	7N59	81w03	5:24:12
Mount Hope	9N20	79w54	5:19:36
Mulatupo	8N57	77w45	5:11:00
Natá	8N20	80w31	5:22:04
Nombre de Dios	9N35	79w28	5:17:52
Nuevo Chagres	9N14	80w05	5:20:20
Ocú	7N57	80w47	5:23:08
Olá	8N25	80w39	5:22:36
Pacora	9N05	79w17	5:17:08
Palmas Bellas	9N14	80w05	5:20:20
Palo Seco Leper Colony	8N54	79w34	5:18:16
Panamá	8N58	79w32	5:18:08
Paraiso	9N02	79w38	5:18:32
Pedasí	7N32	80w02	5:20:08
Pedregal	8N22	82w26	5:29:44
Pedro Miguel	9N01	79w36	5:18:24
Peña Blanca	8N27	81w40	5:26:40
Penonomé	8N31	80w22	5:21:28
Pesé	7N54	80w37	5:22:28
Piedra Roja	8N38	81w48	5:27:12
Playon Grande	9N21	78w20	5:13:20
Plaza Caisan	8N46	82w45	5:31:00
Pocrí	8N16	80w33	5:22:12
Portobelo	9N33	79w39	5:18:36
Potrerillos Arriba	8N41	82w30	5:30:00
Puerto Armuelles	8N17	82w52	5:31:28
Puerto Pilón	9N22	79w48	5:19:12
Rainbow City	9N21	79w53	5:19:32
Red Tank	9N01	79w36	5:18:24
Remedios	8N14	81w51	5:27:24
Río de Jesús	7N59	81w10	5:24:40
Río Grande	8N37	81w17	5:25:08
Río Hato	8N23	80w10	5:20:40
San Andrés	8N36	82w44	5:30:56
San Carlos	8N29	79w57	5:19:48
San Francisco	8N15	80w58	5:23:52
San Miguel	8N27	78w56	5:15:44
Santa Catalina	8N47	81w20	5:25:20
Santa Fe	8N31	81w05	5:24:20
Santa María	8N07	80w40	5:22:40
Santiago	8N06	80w59	5:23:56
Soná	8N01	81w19	5:25:16
Summit	9N04	79w39	5:18:36
Taboga	8N48	79w33	5:18:12
Tolé	8N14	81w41	5:26:44
Tonosí	7N24	80w27	5:21:48
Tranquilla	8N30	80w14	5:20:56
Ustupo Yantupo	9N27	78w34	5:14:16
Yaviza	8N11	77w41	5:10:44

PAPUA NUEVA GUINEA — PAPUA NOUVELLE-GUINÉE — PAPUA NEW GUINEA

Time Table # 1
Before 1/Jan/1880 LMT
Begin Standard 147E08
1/Jan/1880 0:00 -9:49
Begin Standard 150E00
1/Jan/1895 0:00 -10:00
....
Time Table # 2
Before 1/Jan/1880 LMT
Begin Standard 147E08
1/Jan/1880 0:00 -9:49
Begin Standard 150E00
1/Jan/1895 0:00 -10:00
Begin Standard 135E00
15/Mar/1942 0:00 -9:00
Begin Standard 150E00
2/Sep/1945 0:00 -10:00
....
Time Table # 3
Before 1/Jan/1880 LMT
Begin Standard 147E08
1/Jan/1880 0:00 -9:49
Begin Standard 150E00
1/Jan/1895 0:00 -10:00
Begin Standard 135E00
15/Mar/1942 0:00 -9:00
Begin Standard 150E00
15/Sep/1943 0:00 -10:00
....
Time Table # 4
Before 1/Jan/1880 LMT
Begin Standard 147E08
1/Jan/1880 0:00 -9:49
Begin Standard 150E00
1/Jan/1895 0:00 -10:00
Begin Standard 135E00
15/Mar/1942 0:00 -9:00
Begin Standard 150E00
1/Nov/1943 0:00 -10:00

DIVISIONS

1. Bismark Islands
2. Bougainville
3. d'Entrecasteaux Islands
4. Feni Islands
5. Green Islands
6. Hermit Islands
7. Kaniet Islands
8. Lihir Islands
9. Louisiade Islands
10. Manus Island
11. Mussau Island
12. New Britain
13. New Guinea
14. New Hanover Island
15. New Ireland
16. Ninigo Islands
17. Nuguria Islands
18. Nukumanu Islands
19. Rossel Island
20. Tabar Islands
21. Tagula Island
22. Tanga Islands
23. Tauu Islands
24. Trobriand Island
25. Woodlark Island
26. Wuvulu Island

Abau 13	1	10s11	148E42	-9:54:48
Ailo 12	4	4s50	151E40	-10:06:40
Aiome 13	3	5s10	144E45	-9:39:00
Aisega 12	4	5s44	148E21	-9:53:24
Aitape 13	3	3s08	142E21	-9:29:24
Alexishafen 13	1	5s06	145E48	-9:43:12
Amaimon 13	3	5s10	145E25	-9:41:40
Amau 13	1	10s02	148E34	-9:54:16
Ambunti 13	3	4s14	142E50	-9:31:20
Amele 13	3	5s16	145E42	-9:42:48
Amun 2	4	5s57	154E45	-10:19:00
Angoram 13	3	4s04	144E04	-9:36:16
Annanberg 13	3	4s55	144E40	-9:38:40
Arona 13	1	6s20	146E00	-9:44:00
Atemble 13	3	5s05	144E45	-9:39:00
Aworro 13	1	7s45	143E10	-9:32:40
Awul 12	4	6s00	151E00	-10:04:00
Baimuru 13	1	7s30	144E49	-9:39:16
Bainyik 13	3	3s40	143E00	-9:32:00
Baiyer River 13	1	5s35	144E10	-9:36:40
Balimo 13	1	8s03	142E56	-9:31:44
Baniara 13	3	9s46	149E53	-9:59:32
Banz 13	1	5s47	144E37	-9:38:28
Beara 13	1	7s30	144E50	-9:39:20
Beipa'a 13	1	8s30	146E35	-9:46:20
Birribi 13	1	9s31	147E27	-9:49:48
Bisianumu 13	1	9s25	147E25	-9:49:40
Bismark Islands 1	3	5s00	150E00	-10:00:00
Bogadjim 13	3	5s25	145E45	-9:43:00
Bogia 13	3	4s15	144E55	-9:39:40
Bonagai 25	1	9s06	152E42	-10:10:48
Bonatui 2	4	5s14	154E34	-10:18:16
Boru 13	1	10s14	148E50	-9:55:20
Bosman 13	3	4s10	144E40	-9:38:40
Bougainville 2	4	6s00	155E00	-10:20:00
Bua 13	3	6s45	147E35	-9:50:20
Bubia 13	3	6s40	146E55	-9:47:40
Buin 2	4	6s50	155E44	-10:22:56
Bulldog 13	3	7s45	146E25	-9:45:40
Bulolo 13	3	7s10	146E40	-9:46:40
Buna 13	3	8s40	148E25	-9:53:40
Bunai 10	4	2s11	147E14	-9:48:56
Bundi 13	1	5s40	145E15	-9:41:00
Bwagaoia 9	1	10s41	152E51	-10:11:24
Dagua 13	3	3s25	143E20	-9:33:20
Dahuni 13	1	10s31	149E55	-9:59:40
Daru 13	1	9s04	143E21	-9:33:24
Dein 13	3	5s30	146E10	-9:44:40
d'Entrecasteaux Islands 3	3	9s30	150E40	-10:02:40
Dios 2	4	5s33	154E58	-10:19:52
Dogura 13	1	10s05	150E05	-10:00:20
Dreikikir 13	3	3s35	142E45	-9:31:00
Dumpu 13	3	5s50	145E45	-9:43:00
Emagan 15	4	1s17	149E33	-9:58:12
Epo 13	1	8s40	146E30	-9:46:00
Erap 13	3	6s35	146E40	-9:46:40
Erave 13	1	6s40	143E50	-9:35:20
Esa-Ala 3	3	9s44	150E49	-10:03:16
Feni Islands 4	3	4s05	153E42	-10:14:48
Finschhafen 13	3	6s35	147E50	-9:51:20
Gagan 2	4	5s14	154E37	-10:18:28
Gaima 13	1	8s20	142E55	-9:31:40
Garaina 13	3	7s50	147E10	-9:48:40
Gasmata 12	4	6s17	150E20	-10:01:20
Gehua 13	1	10s20	150E25	-10:01:40
Gesoa 13	1	8s25	143E35	-9:34:20
Gona 13	3	8s37	148E17	-9:53:08
Goroka 13	1	6s05	145E25	-9:41:40
Green Islands 5	3	4s30	154E10	-10:16:40
Green River 13	3	3s55	141E10	-9:24:40
Guaugurina 13	1	10s37	150E28	-10:01:52
Gubam 13	1	8s40	141E55	-9:27:40
Gurewaia 3	1	9s39	151E03	-10:04:12
Henganofi 13	1	6s15	145E35	-9:42:20
Hermit Islands 6	3	1s30	145E05	-9:40:20
Hisiu 13	1	9s05	146E45	-9:47:00
Hoskins 12	4	5s27	150E30	-10:02:00
Ihu 13	1	7s55	145E25	-9:41:40
Ilop 13	1	2s54	141E13	-9:24:52
Inaporok 13	1	8s15	141E55	-9:27:40
Inauaia 13	1	8s40	146E35	-9:46:20
Inus 2	1	5s42	155E08	-10:20:32
Ioma 13	3	8s20	147E50	-9:51:20
Josephstaal 13	3	4s44	145E01	-9:40:04
Kaiapit 13	1	6s15	146E15	-9:45:00
Kainantu 13	1	6s15	145E55	-9:43:40
Kairuku 13	1	8s50	146E35	-9:46:20
Kakasa 13	3	9s20	148E45	-9:55:00
Kalo 13	1	10s00	147E45	-9:51:00
Kanam 15	4	3s25	152E10	-10:08:40
Kandrian 12	4	6s15	149E35	-9:58:20
Kaniet Islands 7	3	0s53	145E30	-9:42:00
Kapogere 13	1	9s50	147E45	-9:51:00
Karau 13	3	3s45	144E20	-9:37:20
Karema 13	1	9s12	147E14	-9:48:56
Kaukauai 2	4	6s52	155E36	-10:22:24
Kaunun 2	4	5s40	154E44	-10:18:56
Kaup 13	3	3s50	144E00	-9:36:00
Kavieng 15	4	2s35	150E50	-10:03:20
Kawin 15	4	2s45	150E45	-10:03:00
Kelaua Harbor 10	4	2s06	147E17	-9:49:08
Kembul 12	4	5s55	150E40	-10:02:40
Keravat 12	4	4s19	152E01	-10:08:04
Kerema 13	1	8s00	145E45	-9:43:00
Kerowagi 13	1	5s50	144E50	-9:39:20
Kiberi 13	1	7s25	143E48	-9:35:12
Kido 13	1	9s15	146E55	-9:47:40
Kieta 2	4	6s13	155E38	-10:22:32
Kikori 13	1	7s25	144E15	-9:37:00
Kila Kila 13	1	9s30	147E10	-9:48:40
Kiunga 13	1	6s10	141E15	-9:25:00
Kokoda 13	3	8s52	147E45	-9:51:00
Kokopo 12	4	4s20	152E15	-10:09:00
Kompiam 13	1	5s20	143E55	-9:35:40
Korapun 12	4	5s25	152E00	-10:08:00
Koroba 13	1	5s40	142E45	-9:31:00
Kui 13	3	7s30	147E15	-9:49:00
Kukipi 13	1	8s10	146E05	-9:44:20
Kulumadau 25	1	9s03	152E43	-10:10:52
Kundiawa 13	1	6s00	145E00	-9:40:00
Kundima 13	3	4s14	143E52	-9:35:28
Kurum 13	3	4s45	145E55	-9:43:40
Kwada 13	1	6s09	141E53	-9:27:32
Lae 13	3	6s45	147E00	-9:48:00
Laiagam 13	1	5s30	143E20	-9:33:20
Laloki 13	1	9s25	147E15	-9:49:00
Lambu 15	4	3s09	151E41	-10:06:44
Lamogai 12	4	5s50	149E20	-9:57:20
Lau 12	4	5s50	151E20	-10:05:20
Laua 2	4	5s30	154E55	-10:19:40
Leitre 13	3	2s50	141E40	-9:26:40

PAPUA NEW GUINEA — PAPUA NOUVELLE-GUINÉE — PAPUA NUEVA GUINEA

Lemankoa 2 4 5s02 154E35-10:18:20
Lemanmanu Mission 2 4 5s02 154E35-10:18:20
Lihir Islands 8 3 3s05 152E35-10:10:20
Linden Harbor (Lindenhafen) 12 4 6s18 150E27-10:01:48
Logia 15 4 2s55 151E27-10:05:48
Lorengau 10 4 2s00 147E15 -9:49:00
Losuia 24 1 8s32 151E04-10:04:16
Louisiade Islands 9 1 11s00 153E00-10:12:00
Mabaduan 13 1 9s16 142E44 -9:30:56
Madang 13 3 5s15 145E50 -9:43:20
Maipa 13 1 8s21 146E33 -9:46:12
Malala 13 3 5s15 147E10 -9:48:40
Malom 15 4 3s10 151E50-10:07:20
Mamagota 2 4 6s46 155E24-10:21:36
Mamaregu 2 4 6s32 155E12-10:20:48
Mangai 15 4 2s45 151E05-10:04:20
Manus Island 10 4 2s00 147E00 -9:48:00
Maprik 13 3 3s40 143E05 -9:32:20
Maragini 13 3 3s33 141E34 -9:26:16
Mare 13 1 9s10 141E40 -9:26:40
Marienberg 13 3 3s55 144E15 -9:37:00
Marua 13 3 9s30 149E20 -9:57:20
Marui 13 3 4s05 143E00 -9:32:00
Matong 12 4 5s35 151E45-10:07:00
Mava 13 1 6s50 141E25 -9:25:40
Medino 13 3 9s40 149E40 -9:58:40
Mendi 13 1 6s10 143E40 -9:34:40
Menyamya 13 1 7s10 146E00 -9:44:00
Merai 12 4 4s50 152E20-10:09:20
Minj 13 1 5s54 144E39 -9:38:36
Miriyama 13 3 3s57 141E45 -9:27:00
Morobe 13 3 7s45 147E35 -9:50:20
Mount Hagen 13 1 5s50 144E15 -9:37:00
Mumeng 13 3 7s00 146E35 -9:46:20
Musara 13 1 10s00 149E50 -9:59:20
Mussau Island 11 3 1s30 149E40 -9:58:40
Namatanai (Nomatanai) 15 4 3s40 152E25-10:09:40
Nambling 12 4 5s10 152E00-10:08:00
Nanu 13 1 8s50 142E40 -9:30:40
New Britain 12 4 6s00 150E00-10:00:00
New Guinea 13 1 6s00 140E00 -9:20:00
New Hanover Island 14 4 2s30 150E15-10:01:00
New Ireland 15 4 2s20 152E00-10:08:00
Ninigo Islands 16 3 1s15 144E15 -9:37:00
Nugima 14 4 2s27 150E14-10:00:56
Nuguria Islands 17 3 3s20 154E45-10:19:00
Nukuhu 12 4 5s35 149E25 -9:57:40
Nukumanu Islands 18 3 4s30 159E30-10:38:00
Oriomo 13 1 8s50 143E15 -9:33:00
Otibanda 13 3 7s15 146E30 -9:46:00
Pabarabuk 13 1 6s05 144E05 -9:36:20
Patusi 10 4 2s10 147E10 -9:48:40
Paup 13 3 3s15 142E35 -9:30:20
Pomio 12 4 5s30 151E30-10:06:00
Pongani 13 3 9s05 148E35 -9:54:20
Popondetta 13 3 8s46 148E14 -9:52:56
Port Moresby 13 1 9s30 147E10 -9:48:40
Puto 2 4 5s41 154E43-10:18:52
Rabaul 12 2 4s12 152E12-10:08:48
Rigo 13 1 9s47 147E34 -9:50:16
Rossel Island 19 1 11s21 154E09-10:16:36
Rouku 13 1 8s40 141E35 -9:26:20
Ruango 12 4 5s35 150E10-10:00:40
Safia 13 3 9s35 148E40 -9:54:40
Sag Sag 12 4 5s35 148E20 -9:53:20
Saidor 13 3 5s35 146E30 -9:46:00
Salamaoa 13 3 7s02 147E06 -9:48:24
Samarai 13 1 10s37 150E40-10:02:40
Samo 15 4 3s58 152E51-10:11:24
Sebidiro 13 1 9s00 142E15 -9:29:00
Segera 13 1 8s15 143E30 -9:34:00
Singorkai 13 3 5s55 146E55 -9:47:40
Sipul 12 4 5s50 148E45 -9:55:00
Sissano 13 3 3s00 142E05 -9:28:20
Sohano 2 4 5s27 154E40-10:18:40
Suain 13 3 3s20 142E55 -9:31:40
Sulu 12 4 5s25 151E00-10:04:00
Suri 13 1 7s10 143E55 -9:35:40
Suru 13 1 6s50 144E45 -9:39:00
Tabar Islands 20 3 2s55 152E05-10:08:20
Tage 13 1 6s20 143E20 -9:33:20
Tagula Island 21 1 11s30 153E30-10:14:00
Taki 2 4 6s29 155E50-10:23:20
Talasea 12 4 5s20 150E05-10:00:20
Tanga Islands 22 3 3s30 153E15-10:13:00
Tapini 13 1 8s20 147E00 -9:48:00
Tarara 2 4 6s02 155E24-10:21:36
Tari 13 1 5s50 143E00 -9:32:00
Taron 15 4 4s25 153E05-10:12:20
Taskul 14 4 2s35 150E25-10:01:40
Tauu Islands 23 3 4s45 157E00-10:28:00
Telefomin 13 1 5s10 141E35 -9:26:20
Terarama 13 1 8s00 141E50 -9:27:20
Tirio 13 1 8s25 143E00 -9:32:00
Torokina 2 4 6s14 155E03-10:20:12
Trobriand Island 24 1 8s35 151E05-10:04:20
Tufi 13 3 9s05 149E20 -9:57:20
Tupuseleia 13 1 9s33 147E18 -9:49:12
Ubai 12 4 5s40 150E40-10:02:40
Ulamona 12 4 5s00 151E15-10:05:00
Ulingan 13 3 4s30 145E25 -9:41:40
Umbukul 14 4 2s30 150E00-10:00:00
Vanimo 13 3 2s40 141E20 -9:25:20
Vito 2 4 6s02 155E24-10:21:36
Wabag 13 1 5s30 143E40 -9:34:40
Wakis 12 4 6s13 150E17-10:01:08
Waku 12 4 6s05 149E05 -9:56:20
Wakunai 2 4 5s52 155E13-10:20:52
Wanigela 13 3 9s22 149E10 -9:56:40
Wapenamanda 13 1 5s35 143E55 -9:35:40
Wasu 13 3 6s00 147E15 -9:49:00
Wasum 12 4 6s05 149E20 -9:57:20
Wat Wat 12 4 4s29 152E21-10:09:24
Wau 13 3 7s20 146E45 -9:47:00
Weam 13 1 8s40 141E08 -9:24:32
Wewak 13 3 3s35 143E40 -9:34:40
Woodlark Island 25 1 9s05 152E50-10:11:20
Wuruf 13 3 6s43 146E25 -9:45:40
Wuvulu Island 26 3 1s45 142E50 -9:31:20
Yarmu 13 3 4s18 142E17 -9:29:08
Jaba 2 4 6s32 155E12-10:20:48

PARAGUAY — PARAGUAY

Time Table
Before 1/Jan/1890 LMT
Begin Standard 57w41
1/Jan/1890 0:00 3:51
Begin Standard 60w00
10/Oct/1931 0:00 4:00
Begin Standard 45w00
1/Oct/1972 0:00 3:00
Begin Standard 60w00
1/Apr/1974 0:00 4:00
1/Oct/1975 0:00 3:00
1/Mar/1976 0:00 4:00
1/Oct/1976 0:00 3:00
1/Mar/1977 0:00 4:00
1/Oct/1977 0:00 3:00
1/Mar/1978 0:00 4:00
1/Oct/1978 0:00 3:00
1/Apr/1980 0:00 4:00
1/Oct/1980 0:00 3:00
1/Apr/1981 0:00 4:00
1/Oct/1981 0:00 3:00
1/Apr/1982 0:00 4:00
1/Oct/1982 0:00 3:00
1/Apr/1983 0:00 4:00
1/Oct/1983 0:00 3:00
1/Apr/1984 0:00 4:00
1/Oct/1984 0:00 3:00
1/Apr/1985 0:00 4:00
1/Oct/1985 0:00 3:00
1/Apr/1986 0:00 4:00
1/Oct/1986 0:00 3:00
1/Apr/1987 0:00 4:00
1/Oct/1987 0:00 3:00
1/Apr/1988 0:00 4:00
1/Oct/1988 0:00 3:00
1/Apr/1989 0:00 4:00
22/Oct/1989 0:00 3:00
1/Apr/1990 0:00 4:00
1/Oct/1990 0:00 3:00
1/Apr/1991 0:00 4:00
1/Oct/1991 0:00 3:00
1/Apr/1992 0:00 4:00
1/Oct/1992 0:00 3:00
1/Apr/1993 0:00 4:00
1/Oct/1993 0:00 3:00
1/Apr/1994 0:00 4:00
1/Oct/1994 0:00 3:00
1/Apr/1995 0:00 4:00
1/Oct/1995 0:00 3:00
1/Apr/1996 0:00 4:00
1/Oct/1996 0:00 3:00
1/Apr/1997 0:00 4:00
1/Oct/1997 0:00 3:00
1/Apr/1998 0:00 4:00
1/Oct/1998 0:00 3:00
1/Apr/1999 0:00 4:00
1/Oct/1999 0:00 3:00
1/Apr/2000 0:00 4:00

Abaí 26s01 55w57 3:43:48
Acahay 25s55 57w09 3:48:36
Alberdi 26s10 58w09 3:52:36
Antequera 24s08 57w07 3:48:28
Areguá 25s18 57w25 3:49:40
Arroyos y Esteros 25s04 57w06 3:48:24
Asunción 25s16 57w40 3:50:40
Belén 23s30 57w06 3:48:24
Bella Vista 22s08 56w31 3:46:04
Benjamín Aceval 24s58 57w34 3:50:16
Buena Vista 26s08 56w03 3:44:12
Caacupé 25s23 57w09 3:48:36
Caaguazú 25s26 56w02 3:44:08
Caapucú 26s13 57w12 3:48:48
Caazapá 26s09 56w24 3:45:36
Capitán Bado 23s16 55w32 3:42:08
Capitán Meza 26s55 55w15 3:41:00
Caraguatay 25s14 56w52 3:47:28
Carapeguá 25s48 57w14 3:48:56
Carayaó 25s10 56w26 3:45:44
Carreria 21s59 58w35 3:54:20
Concepción 23s25 57w17 3:49:08
Coronel Bogado 27s11 56w18 3:45:12
Coronel Oviedo 25s25 56w27 3:45:48
Curuguaty 24s31 55w42 3:42:48
Doctor Cecilio Báez 25s03 56w19 3:45:16
Doctor Pedro P. Peña 22s26 62w22 4:09:28
Domingo M. Irala 25s54 54w43 3:38:52
Encarnación 27s20 55w54 3:43:36
Fernando de la Mora 25s19 57w36 3:50:24
Fortín Ayacucho 19s58 59w47 3:59:08
Fortín Coroneles Sanchez 19s20 59w58 3:59:52
Fortín Florida 20s45 59w17 3:57:08
Fortín Garrapatal 21s27 61w30 4:06:00
Fortín Teniente Montanía 22s04 59w57 3:59:48
Fuerte Olimpo 21s02 57w54 3:51:36
General Aquino 24s26 56w42 3:46:48
General Elizardo Aquino 26s53 56w17 3:45:08
General Eugenio A. Garay 25s55 56w11 3:44:44
General Eugenio A. Garay 20s31 62w08 4:08:32
Hernandarias 25s22 54w45 3:39:00
Hohenau 27s05 55w45 3:43:00
Horqueta 23s24 56w53 3:47:32
Humaitá 27s03 58w33 3:54:12
Itá 25s29 57w21 3:49:24
Itacurubí del Rosario 24s29 56w41 3:46:44
Itaquyry 24s56 55w13 3:40:52
Iturbe 26s01 56w30 3:46:00
Jesús 27s03 55w47 3:43:08
Juan de Mena 24s55 56w44 3:46:56
La Esmeralda 22s13 62w38 4:10:32
Lima 23s54 56w20 3:45:20
Loreto 23s16 57w11 3:48:44
Mariscal Estigarribia 22s02 60w38 4:02:32
Mayor Pablo Lagerenza 19s58 60w45 4:03:00
Ñacunday 26s01 54w46 3:39:04
Nueva Germania 23s54 56w45 3:47:00
Paraguarí 25s38 57w09 3:48:36
Paso de Patria 27s13 58w35 3:54:20
Pedro Juan Caballero 22s34 55w37 3:42:28
Pilar 26s52 58w23 3:53:32
Piribebuy 25s29 57w03 3:48:12
Pozo Colorado 23s28 58w51 3:55:24
Puerto Adela 24s33 54w22 3:37:28
Puerto Bahía Negra 20s15 58w12 3:52:48
Puerto Casado 22s20 57w55 3:51:40
Puerto Fonciere 22s29 57w48 3:51:12
Puerto Guaraní 21s18 57w55 3:51:40
Puerto Leda 20s41 58w02 3:52:08
Puerto Mihanovich 20s52 57w59 3:51:56
Puerto Pinasco 22s43 57w50 3:51:20
Puerto Presidente Stroessner 25s30 54w36 3:38:24
Puerto Sastre 22s06 57w59 3:51:56
Puerto Ybapobó 23s42 57w12 3:48:48
Quiindy 25s58 57w16 3:49:04
Quyquyó 26s14 57w01 3:48:04
Quyyndy 25s58 57w16 3:49:04
Rosario 24s27 57w03 3:48:12
Saltos del Guaira 24s03 54w17 3:37:08
San Carlos 22s16 57w18 3:49:12
San Estanislao 24s39 56w26 3:45:44
San Ignacio 26s52 57w03 3:48:12
San Joaquín 24s57 56w07 3:44:28
San José 25s33 56w45 3:47:00
San Juan Bautista 26s38 57w10 3:48:40
San Juan Nepomuceno 26s06 55w58 3:43:52
San Lázaro 22s10 57w55 3:51:40
San Pedro 24s07 56w59 3:47:56
San Pedro del Paraná 26s46 56w15 3:45:00
Santa Rosa 26s52 56w49 3:47:16
Santa Rosa 21s46 61w43 4:06:52
Santiago 27s09 56w47 3:47:08
Siracuas 21s03 61w46 4:07:04
Tacuatí 23s27 56w35 3:46:20
Tavaí 26s07 55w32 3:42:08
Unión 24s48 56w33 3:46:12
Villa Florida 26s23 57w09 3:48:36
Villa Hayes 25s06 57w34 3:50:16
Villa Oliva 26s01 57w53 3:51:32

Place	Lat	Long	Time
Villarrica	25s45	56w26	3:45:44
Villeta	25s29	57w35	3:50:20
Ybycuí	26s01	57w03	3:48:12
Yegros	26s24	56w25	3:45:40
Ygatimí	24s05	55w30	3:42:00
Yhú	24s59	55w59	3:43:56
Ypacaraí	25s23	57w16	3:49:04
Ypé Jhu	23s54	55w20	3:41:20
Yuty	26s32	56w18	3:45:12

PERÚ PÉROU PERU

Time Table
Before 1/Jan/1890 LMT
Begin Standard 77w09
1/Jan/1890 0:00 5:09
Begin Standard 75w00
28/Jul/1908 0:00 5:00
1/Jan/1938 0:00 4:00
1/Apr/1938 0:00 5:00
25/Sep/1938 0:00 4:00
26/Mar/1939 0:00 5:00
24/Sep/1939 0:00 4:00
24/Mar/1940 0:00 5:00
1/Jan/1987 0:00 4:00
1/Apr/1987 0:00 5:00
1/Jan/1990 0:00 4:00
1/Apr/1990 0:00 5:00

Place	Lat	Long	Time
Abancay	13s35	72w55	4:51:40
Acarí	15s26	74w37	4:58:28
Acobamba	12s48	74w34	4:58:16
Acolla	11s44	75w34	5:02:16
Acomayo	13s55	71w41	4:46:44
Acomayo	9s46	76w05	5:04:20
Acoria	12s37	74w53	4:59:32
Acuracay	5s35	74w10	4:56:40
Aija	9s46	77w38	5:10:32
Alca	15s08	72w46	4:51:04
Ambar	10s44	77w16	5:09:04
Ambo	10s07	76w10	5:04:40
Ananea	14s42	69w33	4:38:12
Ancón	11s47	77w11	5:08:44
Andahuaylas	13s39	73w23	4:53:32
Andamarca	11s46	74w44	4:58:56
Andaray	15s49	72w50	4:51:20
Andoas	2s50	76w30	5:06:00
Anta	13s29	72w09	4:48:36
Antabamba	14s19	72w55	4:51:40
Aplao	16s05	72w31	4:50:04
Arequipa	16s24	71w33	4:46:12
Ascope	7s43	79w07	5:16:28
Atalaya	10s44	73w45	4:55:00
Atico	16s14	73w39	4:54:36
Atocongo	12s08	76w56	5:07:44
Aucará	14s15	74w05	4:56:20
Ayabaca	4s38	79w43	5:18:52
Ayacucho	13s07	74w13	4:56:52
Ayaviri	14s52	70w35	4:42:20
Ayo	15s41	72w16	4:49:04
Azángaro	14s55	70w13	4:40:52
Aznapuquio	11s59	77w04	5:08:16
Bagua	5s40	78w31	5:14:04
Bambamarca	6s41	78w32	5:14:08
Baños	10s05	76w45	5:07:00
Barbadillo	12s02	76w56	5:07:44
Barranca	10s45	77w46	5:11:04
Barranca	4s50	76w42	5:06:48
Barranco	12s09	77w02	5:08:08
Barrio Obrero Industrial	12s04	77w04	5:08:16
Bayóvar	5s50	81w03	5:24:12
Bellavista	4s54	80w42	5:22:48
Bellavista	7s04	76w35	5:06:20
Bellavista	12s04	77w08	5:08:32
Bocanegra	12s01	77w07	5:08:28
Bolívar	7s18	77w48	5:11:12
Bolognesi	6s35	73w10	4:52:40
Borja	4s26	77w33	5:10:12
Breña	12s04	77w04	5:08:16
Buldibuyo	8s07	77w22	5:09:28
Caballococha	3s54	70w32	4:42:08
Cabana	8s24	78w02	5:12:08
Cabanaconde	15s37	71w59	4:47:56
Cacra	12s48	75w48	5:03:12
Cailloma	15s12	71w46	4:47:04
Cajabamba	7s37	78w03	5:12:12
Cajacay	10s10	77w26	5:09:44
Cajamarca	7s10	78w31	5:14:04
Cajatambo	10s29	77w02	5:08:08
Calca	13s20	71w57	4:47:48
Callanmarca	12s52	74w38	4:58:32
Callao	12s04	77w09	5:08:36
Calzada	6s02	77w02	5:08:08
Camaná	16s37	72w42	4:50:48
Camporredondo	6s07	78w21	5:13:24
Canchaque	5s24	79w36	5:18:24
Candarave	17s16	70w15	4:41:00
Cangallo	13s33	74w12	4:56:48
Canta	11s25	76w38	5:06:32
Canto Grande	11s59	77w01	5:08:04
Caraibamba	14s24	73w09	4:52:36
Caras	9s03	77w45	5:11:00
Caravelí	15s46	73w22	4:53:28
Carhuamayo	10s55	76w02	5:04:08
Carhuanca	13s45	73w48	4:55:12
Carhuás	9s16	77w38	5:10:32
Carumas	16s49	70w43	4:42:52
Casma	9s28	78w19	5:13:16
Castilla	5s12	80w38	5:22:32
Castrovirreyna	13s16	75w19	5:01:16
Catacaos	5s16	80w41	5:22:44
Cayna	10s11	76w20	5:05:20
Ccapi	13s52	72w05	4:48:20
Celendín	6s52	78w09	5:12:36
Cerro Azul	13s02	76w30	5:06:00
Cerro de Pasco	10s41	76w16	5:05:04
Chacanilla	6s13	77w51	5:11:24
Chacarilla	12s02	77w01	5:08:04
Chacayán	10s24	76w25	5:05:40
Chachas	15s30	72w16	4:49:04
Chacra Cerro	11s55	77w04	5:08:16
Chala	15s52	74w16	4:57:04
Chalhuanca	14s17	73w15	4:53:00
Chama	12s08	77w00	5:08:00
Chancay	11s35	77w16	5:09:04
Chapimarca	13s58	73w04	4:52:16
Charcana	15s15	73w04	4:52:16
Chasuta	6s35	76w11	5:04:44
Chaullay	12s57	72w39	4:50:36
Chavarría	12s01	77w05	5:08:20
Chaviña	14s59	73w50	4:55:20
Chepén	7s13	79w27	5:17:48
Chiclayo	6s46	79w51	5:19:24
Chilca	12s32	76w44	5:06:56
Chilete	7s14	78w51	5:15:24
Chillón	11s55	77w05	5:08:20
Chimbote	9s05	78w36	5:14:24
Chincha Alta	13s27	76w08	5:04:32
Chincheros	13s27	73w44	4:54:56
Chipao	14s15	73w57	4:55:48
Chiquián	10s09	77w11	5:08:44
Chiquintirca	13s09	73w41	4:54:44
Chirinos	5s16	78w52	5:15:28
Chivay	15s40	71w35	4:46:20
Chocope	7s47	79w13	5:16:52
Chongos Bajo	12s07	75w16	5:01:04
Chongoyape	6s39	79w24	5:17:36
Chorrillos	12s10	77w02	5:08:08
Chosica	11s54	76w42	5:06:48
Chota	6s33	78w39	5:14:36
Chucuito	15s53	69w53	4:39:32
Chulucanas	5s06	80w10	5:20:40
Chumpi	15s06	73w46	4:55:04
Chupaca	12s04	75w19	5:01:16
Chuquibamba	15s50	72w39	4:50:36
Chuquibambilla	14s07	72w43	4:50:52
Chuquitanta	11s58	77w06	5:08:24
Churcampa	12s42	74w24	4:57:36
Coayllo	12s44	76w28	5:05:52
Cocachacra	17s06	71w46	4:47:04
Colca	12s18	75w13	5:00:52
Colcamar	6s16	77w55	5:11:40
Collique Alto	11s55	77w03	5:08:12
Colta	15s10	73w18	4:53:12
Comas	11s46	75w02	5:00:08
Comas	11s57	77w04	5:08:16
Concepción	11s55	75w17	5:01:08
Concordia	4s30	74w55	4:59:40
Conderilla Señor	12s02	77w05	5:08:20
Contamana	7s15	74w54	4:59:36
Contumaza	7s22	78w49	5:15:16
Coracora	15s02	73w47	4:55:08
Córdova	14s04	75w03	5:00:12
Corire	16s14	72w28	4:49:52
Coris	9s50	77w45	5:11:00
Corongo	8s35	77w55	5:11:40
Cospán	7s26	78w33	5:14:12
Cotabambas	13s45	72w21	4:49:24
Cotahuasi	15s12	72w56	4:51:44
Crucero	14s21	70w00	4:40:00
Cuajone	17s00	70w43	4:42:52
Cusco → Cuzco	13s31	71w59	4:47:56
Cutervo	6s22	78w51	5:15:24
Cuzco	13s31	71w59	4:47:56
El Alto	4s18	81w07	5:24:28
El Carmen	13s30	76w04	5:04:16
Espinar	14s47	71w29	4:45:56
Eten	6s54	79w52	5:19:28
Ferreñafe	6s38	79w45	5:19:00
Flores	12s01	77w01	5:08:04
Florida	5s50	77w55	5:11:40
Frías	4s52	79w57	5:19:48
Ganso Azul	8s51	74w44	4:58:56
Gorgor	10s35	77w02	5:08:08
Granado	12s04	76w57	5:07:48
Guadalupe	7s15	79w29	5:17:56
Haquira	14s13	72w11	4:48:44
Huacaña	14s02	74w02	4:56:08
Huachipa	12s00	76w56	5:07:44
Huacho	11s07	77w37	5:10:28
Huachón	10s40	75w57	5:03:48
Huachos	13s12	75w31	5:02:04
Huacrachuco	8s39	77w05	5:08:20
Huaillati	14s05	72w31	4:50:04
Hualgayoc	6s46	78w37	5:14:28
Hualla	13s44	73w55	4:55:40
Huallanca	8s49	77w52	5:11:28
Huallanca	9s51	76w56	5:07:44
Huamachuco	7s48	78w04	5:12:16
Huamanquiquia	13s44	74w15	4:57:00
Huambo	15s44	72w07	4:48:28
Huambos	6s28	78w58	5:15:52
Huancabamba	10s21	75w32	5:02:08
Huancabamba	5s14	79w28	5:17:52
Huancané	15s12	69w46	4:39:04
Huancapi	13s41	74w04	4:56:16
Huancarama	13s39	73w05	4:52:20
Huancarqui	16s06	72w29	4:49:56
Huancavelica	12s46	75w02	5:00:08
Huancaybamba	9s05	76w50	5:07:20
Huancayo	12s04	75w14	5:00:56
Huando	12s29	74w58	4:59:52
Huanta	12s56	74w15	4:57:00
Huántar	9s26	77w15	5:09:00
Huánuco	9s55	76w14	5:04:56
Huaral	11s30	77w12	5:08:48
Huarás	9s32	77w32	5:10:08
Huari	9s20	77w14	5:08:56
Huariaca	10s27	76w07	5:04:28
Huaribamba	12s16	74w57	4:59:48
Huarmey	10s04	78w10	5:12:40
Huarochirí	12s09	76w14	5:04:56
Huarocondo	13s25	72w13	4:48:52
Huaura	11s04	77w36	5:10:24
Huayllay	11s01	76w21	5:05:24
Huaytará	13s36	75w22	5:01:28
Huicungo	7s17	76w48	5:07:12
Ica	14s04	75w42	5:02:48
Ilabaya	17s25	70w31	4:42:04
Illimo	6s28	79w51	5:19:24
Ilo	17s38	71w20	4:45:20
Imperial	13s04	76w21	5:05:24
Iñapari	10s57	69w35	4:38:20
Infantas	11s57	77w04	5:08:16
Intuto	3s39	74w44	4:58:56
Iquitos	3s46	73w15	4:53:00
Jaén	5s42	78w47	5:15:08
Jaqui	15s30	74w26	4:57:44
Jauja	11s48	75w30	5:02:00
Jayanca	6s24	79w50	5:19:20
Jeberos	5s17	76w13	5:04:52
Jepelacio	6s07	76w57	5:07:48
Jesús María	12s04	77w04	5:08:16
Juan Guerra	6s35	76w21	5:05:24
Juanjuí	7s11	76w45	5:07:00
Juli	16s13	69w27	4:37:48
Juliaca	15s30	70w08	4:40:32
Jumbilla	5s54	77w45	5:11:00
Junín	11s10	76w00	5:04:00
La Calera	12s12	76w54	5:07:36
Lagunas	5s14	75w38	5:02:32
La Huaca	4s54	80w57	5:23:48
La Jalca	6s29	77w43	5:10:52
La Joya	16s44	71w51	4:47:24
Lamas	6s25	76w35	5:06:20
Lambayeque	6s42	79w55	5:19:40
Lambrama	13s52	72w46	4:51:04
La Merced	11s03	75w19	5:01:16
La Molina	12s05	76w57	5:07:48
Lampa	15s21	70w22	4:41:28
Lamud	6s09	77w55	5:11:40
Lancones	4s35	80w30	5:22:00
La Oroya	11s32	75w54	5:03:36
La Perla	12s05	77w08	5:08:32
La Punta	12s05	77w11	5:08:44
Laramate	14s15	74w52	4:59:28
Laraos	12s17	75w50	5:03:20
Lares	13s04	72w05	4:48:20
Lari	15s37	71w46	4:47:04
La Rinconada	12s05	76w57	5:07:48
Las Lomas	4s40	80w15	5:21:00
La Unión	9s46	76w48	5:07:12
La Unión	5s24	80w45	5:23:00
La Victoria	12s04	77w02	5:08:08
Lima	12s03	77w03	5:08:12
Limbani	14s08	69w42	4:38:48
Lince	12s06	77w03	5:08:12
Lircay	12s56	74w43	4:58:52
Llata	9s25	76w47	5:07:08
Llusco	14s21	72w07	4:48:28
Lobitos	4s26	81w17	5:25:08
Locroja	12s41	74w26	4:57:44
Locumba	17s36	70w46	4:43:04
Lomas	15s34	74w50	4:59:20
Lucanas	14s36	74w15	4:57:00
Lurigancho	12s02	77w01	5:08:04
Lurín	12s17	76w52	5:07:28
Machupicchu	13s07	72w34	4:50:16
Macusani	14s05	70w26	4:41:44
Magdalena	6s21	77w49	5:11:16
Magdalena Nueva	12s06	77w05	5:08:20

PERU PÉROU PERÚ

Place	Lat	Long	Time
Mala	12s39	76w38	5:06:32
Mamara	14s14	72w35	4:50:20
Máncora	4s06	81w05	5:24:20
Manu	12s15	70w50	4:43:20
Mara	14s06	72w07	4:48:28
Marangani	14s22	71w10	4:44:40
Maras	13s20	72w09	4:48:36
Marcaconga	13s59	71w34	4:46:16
Marcona	15s03	75w01	5:00:04
Margos	10s04	76w26	5:05:44
Márquez	11s57	77w08	5:08:32
Masisea	8s36	74w19	4:57:16
Matará	7s16	78w16	5:13:04
Matarani	17s00	72w06	4:48:24
Matasango	12s05	76w58	5:07:52
Matucana	11s51	76w24	5:05:36
Mendoza	6s20	77w24	5:09:36
Mendoza	12s06	76w59	5:07:56
Miraflores	12s07	77w02	5:08:08
Mayobamba	6s03	76w58	5:07:52
Mollendo	17s02	72w01	4:48:04
Mollepata	13s31	72w32	4:50:08
Monsefú	6s52	79w52	5:19:28
Monzón	9s10	76w23	5:05:32
Moquegua	17s12	70w56	4:43:44
Morales	6s28	76w28	5:05:52
Morococha	11s37	76w09	5:04:36
Morropón	5s15	80w00	5:20:00
Motupe	6s09	79w44	5:18:56
Moya	12s24	75w10	5:00:40
Moyobamba	6s03	76w58	5:07:52
Naranjal	11s58	77w06	5:08:24
Ñaupe	5s36	79w54	5:19:36
Nauta	4s32	73w33	4:54:12
Nazca	14s50	74w57	4:59:48
Negritos	4s38	81w19	5:25:16
Nepeña	9s10	78w23	5:13:32
Nievería	11s59	76w55	5:07:40
Ocallí	6s09	78w18	5:13:12
Ocoña	16s26	73w07	4:52:28
Ocongate	13s38	71w24	4:45:36
Ocros	10s24	77w24	5:09:36
Ollantaytambo	13s16	72w16	4:49:04
Olmos	5s59	79w46	5:19:04
Omaguas	4s08	73w15	4:53:00
Omas	12s31	76w17	5:05:08
Omate	16s41	70w59	4:43:56
Oquendo	11s58	77w08	5:08:32
Orcotuna	11s58	75w20	5:01:20
Orellana	6s54	75w04	5:00:16
Otuzco	7s54	78w35	5:14:20
Oxapampa	10s34	75w24	5:01:36
Oyón	10s39	76w47	5:07:08
Oyotún	6s51	79w19	5:17:16
Pacarán	12s52	76w03	5:04:12
Pacaraos	11s11	76w44	5:06:56
Pacasmayo	7s24	79w34	5:18:16
Pachacamac	12s14	76w53	5:07:32
Pachiza	7s16	76w46	5:07:04
Pacllón	10s18	77w07	5:08:28
Paico	14s02	73w39	4:54:36
Paiján	7s44	79w19	5:17:16
Paita	5s06	81w07	5:24:28
Palca	11s21	75w31	5:02:04
Palcamayo	11s18	75w46	5:03:04
Pallasca	8s15	78w01	5:12:04
Palomares	12s00	77w01	5:08:04
Palpa	14s32	75w11	5:00:44
Pampacolca	15s43	72w33	4:50:12
Pampas	12s24	74w54	4:59:36
Panao	9s49	76w00	5:04:00
Paramonga	10s40	77w50	5:11:20
Paras	13s30	74w35	4:58:20
Paruro	13s46	71w51	4:47:24
Pataz	7s44	77w37	5:10:28
Pativilca	10s42	77w47	5:11:08
Paucarbamba	12s25	74w36	4:58:24
Paucarpata	16s26	71w30	4:46:00
Paucartambo	13s18	71w40	4:46:40
Pausa	15s16	73w20	4:53:20
Pebas	3s20	71w49	4:47:16
Pedreros	12s01	76w57	5:07:48
Picota	6s55	76w20	5:05:20
Pimentel	6s50	79w57	5:19:48
Pisco	13s42	76w13	5:04:52
Pitumarca	13s59	71w25	4:45:40
Piura	5s12	80w38	5:22:32
Pomabamba	8s50	77w28	5:09:52
Pomacanchi	14s02	71w34	4:46:16
Pomata	16s16	69w18	4:37:12
Pozuzo	10s04	75w32	5:02:08
Pro	11s57	77w05	5:08:20
Pucallpa	8s23	74w32	4:58:08
Pueblo Libre	12s05	77w04	5:08:16
Puerto Bermúdez	10s20	74w54	4:59:36
Puerto Chicama	7s42	79w27	5:17:48
Puerto Maldonado	12s36	69w11	4:36:44
Puerto Portillo	9s46	72w45	4:51:00
Puerto Supe	10s49	77w45	5:11:00
Puerto Victoria	9s54	74w58	4:59:52
Puica	15s04	72w42	4:50:48
Pullo	15s14	73w50	4:55:20
Puno	15s50	70w02	4:40:08
Punta de Bombón	17s11	71w48	4:47:12
Punta Moreno	7s36	78w54	5:15:36
Puquio	14s42	74w08	4:56:32
Puruchuca	12s04	76w57	5:07:48
Putina	14s55	69w52	4:39:28
Querecotillo	4s50	80w40	5:22:40
Querobamba	13s52	73w50	4:55:20
Quiches	8s25	77w27	5:09:48
Quillabamba	12s49	72w43	4:50:52
Quimpitirique	12s15	73w52	4:55:28
Quincemil	13s16	70w38	4:42:32
Quinches	12s13	76w05	5:04:20
Quiruvilca	8s00	78w19	5:13:16
Quivilla	9s32	76w41	5:06:44
Recuay	9s43	77w28	5:09:52
Repartición	12s00	77w04	5:08:16
Requena	4s58	73w50	4:55:20
Reventazón	6s10	80w58	5:23:52
Rímac	12s03	77w03	5:08:12
Rioja	6s05	77w09	5:08:36
Sacanche	7s05	76w44	5:06:56
Salamanca	15s31	72w50	4:51:20
Salamanca	12s05	77w00	5:08:00
Salas	6s16	79w37	5:18:28
Salaverry	8s14	78w58	5:15:52
Saña	6s55	79w35	5:18:20
San Agustín	12s02	77w07	5:08:28
San Antonio	6s22	76w21	5:05:24
San Benito	7s26	78w56	5:15:44
San Damián	12s02	76w24	5:05:36
Sandia	14s17	69w26	4:37:44
San Felipe de Vichayal	4s52	81w05	5:24:20
San Isidro	12s07	77w03	5:08:12
San José de los Molinos	13s57	75w41	5:02:44
San José de Sisa	6s37	76w39	5:06:36
San Juan	15s21	75w10	5:00:40
San Miguel	13s01	73w58	4:55:52
San Miguel	12s06	77w07	5:08:28
San Miguel de Pallaques	7s00	78w51	5:15:24
San Nicolás	15s13	75w12	5:00:48
San Pedro de Lloc	7s26	79w31	5:18:04
San Ramón	11s08	75w20	5:01:20
Santa	8s59	78w36	5:14:24
Santa Clarita	12s00	77w01	5:08:04
Santa Clotilde	2s34	73w44	4:54:56
Santa Cruz	6s37	78w57	5:15:48
Santa Isabel de Sihuas	16s20	72w06	4:48:24
Santa María	11s59	77w00	5:08:00
Santa Rosa	12s00	77w06	5:08:24
Santa Rosita	12s03	76w59	5:07:56
Santiago	14s11	75w44	5:02:56
Santiago de Cao	7s58	79w15	5:17:00
Santiago de Chocorvos	13s50	75w16	5:01:04
Santiago de Chuco	8s09	78w11	5:12:44
Santo Tomás	6s36	77w48	5:11:12
Santo Tomás	14s29	72w06	4:48:24
San Vicente de Cañete	13s05	76w24	5:05:36
Sapallanga	12s09	75w11	5:00:44
Saposoa	6s56	76w48	5:07:12
Saquena	4s40	73w31	4:54:04
Satipo	11s16	74w37	4:58:28
Sauce	6s44	76w10	5:04:40
Sayán	11s08	77w12	5:08:48
Sechura	5s33	80w51	5:23:24
Sicuani	14s16	71w13	4:44:52
Sihaus	8s34	77w37	5:10:28
Simbal	7s58	78w49	5:15:16
Sitabamba	8s02	77w44	5:10:56
Sócota	6s18	78w44	5:14:56
Soras	14s07	73w37	4:54:28
Soraya	14s10	73w19	4:53:16
Sullana	4s53	80w41	5:22:44
Sumbay	15s58	71w23	4:45:32
Surco	12s09	77w01	5:08:04
Surquillo	12s07	77w02	5:08:08
Suyo	4s30	80w00	5:20:00
Tabalosos	6s21	76w41	5:06:44
Tacna	18s01	70w15	4:41:00
Talara	4s34	81w17	5:25:08
Tambo	12s56	74w01	4:56:04
Tambo Grande	4s56	80w21	5:21:24
Tamshiyacu	4s05	72w58	4:51:52
Tarapoto	6s30	76w25	5:05:40
Tarata	17s28	70w02	4:40:08
Tarma	11s25	75w42	5:02:48
Tarqui	1s35	75w15	5:01:00
Tauripampa	12s35	76w07	5:04:28
Taurisma	15s10	72w51	4:51:24
Tayabamba	8s17	77w18	5:09:12
Tebes	12s07	77w00	5:08:00
Tingo de Saposoa	7s07	76w38	5:06:32
Tingo María	9s09	75w56	5:03:44
Toraya	14s03	73w18	4:53:12
Totos	13s31	74w30	4:58:00
Trujillo	8s07	79w02	5:16:08
Tumbes	3s34	80w28	5:21:52
Uchiza	8s29	76w23	5:05:32
Ulcumayo	11s01	75w55	5:03:40
Urcos	13s42	71w38	4:46:32
Urubamba	13s18	72w07	4:48:28
Viñac	12s56	75w47	5:03:08
Vinchos	13s16	74w21	4:57:24
Virú	8s25	78w45	5:15:00
Vista Alegre	12s09	77w00	5:08:00
Vitarte	12s02	76w56	5:07:44
Vitor	16s26	71w49	4:47:16
Yambrasbamba	5s45	77w54	5:11:36
Yanahuara	16s24	71w33	4:46:12
Yanaoca	14s13	71w26	4:45:44
Yanque	15s39	71w39	4:46:36
Yauca	15s40	74w32	4:58:08
Yauli	11s41	76w06	5:04:24
Yauyos	12s24	75w57	5:03:48
Yungay	9s09	77w44	5:10:56
Yura	16s11	71w40	4:46:40
Yurimaguas	5s54	76w05	5:04:20
Zarumilla	3s30	80w16	5:21:04
Zorritos	3s40	80w40	5:22:40

PHILIPPINES FILIPINAS PHILIPPINEN PILIPINAS

Time Table
Before 11/May/1899 LMT
Begin Standard 120E00

Date	Time	Offset
11/May/1899	0:00	-8:00
1/Nov/1936	0:00	-9:00
1/Feb/1937	0:00	-8:00
1/May/1942	0:00	-9:00
1/Nov/1944	0:00	-8:00
12/Apr/1954	0:00	-9:00
1/Jul/1954	0:00	-8:00
22/Mar/1978	0:00	-9:00
21/Sep/1978	0:00	-8:00

Place	Lat	Long	Time
Aborlan	9N26	118E33	-7:54:12
Abucay	14N45	120E30	-8:02:00
Abulug	18N27	121E27	-8:05:48
Abuyog	10N45	125E01	-8:20:04
Agcawayan	13N46	120E16	-8:01:04
Agno	16N07	119E48	-7:59:12
Agoo	16N20	120E22	-8:01:28
Agutaya	11N09	120E56	-8:03:44
Ajuy	11N10	123E01	-8:12:04
Alaminos	16N10	119E59	-7:59:56
Alangalang	11N12	124E51	-8:19:24
Albuera	10N55	124E42	-8:18:48
Alcala	17N54	121E39	-8:06:36
Alcantara	12N16	122E03	-8:08:12
Alicia	16N45	121E42	-8:06:48
Alicia	7N30	122E55	-8:11:40
Alimodian	10N49	122E26	-8:09:44
Allacapan	18N15	121E35	-8:06:20
Allen	12N30	124E17	-8:17:08
Alubijid	8N35	124E29	-8:17:56
Ambil	13N49	120E20	-8:01:20
Amutag	12N23	123E16	-8:13:04
Anao-Aon	9N47	125E25	-8:21:40
Anda	16N17	119E57	-7:59:48
Angat	14N56	121E02	-8:04:08
Angeles	15N09	120E35	-8:02:20
Angono	14N31	121E09	-8:04:36
Antipolo	14N35	121E10	-8:04:40
Aparri	18N22	121E39	-8:06:36
Araceli	10N33	119E59	-7:59:56

Arayat	15N10	120E46	-8:03:04
Argao	9N52	123E36	-8:14:24
Aringay	16N26	120E21	-8:01:24
Aritao	16N18	121E02	-8:04:08
Aroroy	12N31	123E24	-8:13:36
Arteche	12N17	125E22	-8:21:28
Astorga	6N54	125E27	-8:21:48
Asturias	10N34	123E43	-8:14:52
Atimonan	14N00	121E55	-8:07:40
Ayuñgon	9N51	123E08	-8:12:32
Baao	13N27	123E22	-8:13:28
Babak	7N08	125E41	-8:22:44
Babuyan	10N00	118E54	-7:55:36
Bacacay	13N18	123E47	-8:15:08
Bacao	10N27	119E48	-7:59:12
Bacarra	18N15	120E35	-8:02:20
Bachauan	12N28	122E06	-8:08:24
Bachawan	12N28	122E06	-8:08:24
Bacolod	10N40	122E57	-8:11:48
Bacon	13N03	124E03	-8:16:12
Bacoor	14N28	120E56	-8:03:44
Bacuag	9N37	125E38	-8:22:32
Bacungan	9N56	118E42	-7:54:48
Bacuyangan	9N39	122E27	-8:09:48
Bagabag	16N37	121E15	-8:05:00
Bagac	14N36	120E23	-8:01:32
Bagamanoc	13N57	124E17	-8:17:08
Bagañga	7N35	126E34	-8:26:16
Baggao	17N56	121E46	-8:07:04
Bagñon	13N44	122E50	-8:11:20
Bago	10N32	122E50	-8:11:20
Baguio	16N25	120E36	-8:02:24
Bagumbayan	14N28	121E03	-8:04:12
Bahi	13N53	123E38	-8:14:32
Bais	9N35	123E07	-8:12:28
Bakar	7N09	125E42	-8:22:48
Balabac	7N59	117E04	-7:48:16
Balamban	10N30	123E42	-8:14:48
Balanga	14N41	120E32	-8:02:08
Balangiga	11N07	125E23	-8:21:32
Balatan	13N20	123E10	-8:12:40
Balayan	13N57	120E44	-8:02:56
Baleno	12N28	123E30	-8:14:00
Baler	15N46	121E34	-8:06:16
Baliangao	8N40	123E36	-8:14:24
Balibago	13N37	121E18	-8:05:12
Balimbing	5N05	119E58	-7:59:52
Balindong (Watu)	7N55	124E12	-8:16:48
Balingasag	8N45	124E47	-8:19:08
Baliuag	14N57	120E54	-8:03:36
Ballesteros	18N25	121E31	-8:06:04
Balud	12N02	123E12	-8:12:48
Bamban	15N17	120E34	-8:02:16
Bambang	16N23	121E06	-8:04:24
Banago	7N30	124E07	-8:16:28
Banaue	16N55	121E04	-8:04:16
Banga	11N38	122E20	-8:09:20
Bañgad	12N10	123E24	-8:13:36
Bangon	13N44	122E50	-8:11:20
Bangued	17N36	120E37	-8:02:28
Bangui	18N32	120E46	-8:03:04
Bani	16N11	119E52	-7:59:28
Bantayan	11N10	123E43	-8:14:52
Banton (Jones)	12N57	122E05	-8:08:20
Baon	6N47	126E05	-8:24:20
Baras	13N40	124E22	-8:17:28
Barcelona	12N52	124E09	-8:16:36
Barili	10N06	123E30	-8:14:00
Barobo	8N33	126E07	-8:24:28
Barotac Nuevo	10N54	122E42	-8:10:48
Barotac Viejo	11N03	122E51	-8:11:24
Barugo	11N20	124E44	-8:18:56
Basco	20N27	121E58	-8:07:52
Basey	11N17	125E04	-8:20:16
Basilan → Isabela	6N42	121E58	-8:07:52
Batac	18N05	120E35	-8:02:20
Batad	11N25	123E06	-8:12:24
Batan	11N35	122E30	-8:10:00
Batangas	13N45	121E03	-8:04:12
Bato	10N20	124E47	-8:19:08
Bato	13N36	124E18	-8:17:12
Batuan	12N25	123E47	-8:15:08
Bauan	13N48	121E01	-8:04:04
Bauang	16N31	120E20	-8:01:20
Bayag	18N16	121E02	-8:04:08
Bayambang	15N49	120E27	-8:01:48
Bayanbayanan	14N39	121E06	-8:04:24
Bayang	7N48	124E12	-8:16:48
Bayawan	9N22	122E48	-8:11:12
Baybay	10N41	124E48	-8:19:12
Bayombong	16N29	121E09	-8:04:36
Beri	12N41	124E22	-8:17:28
Binalbagan	10N12	122E50	-8:11:20
Binalonan	16N03	120E36	-8:02:24
Binangonan	14N28	121E11	-8:04:44
Binga	10N45	119E19	-7:57:16
Biri	12N41	124E22	-8:17:28
Bislig	8N13	126E19	-8:25:16
Bitadton	11N30	122E05	-8:08:20
Boac	13N27	121E50	-8:07:20
Bobon	12N32	124E34	-8:18:16
Bogo	11N03	124E00	-8:16:00
Bohon	18N30	120E35	-8:02:20
Bojelebung	6N31	122E11	-8:08:44
Bokod	16N30	120E50	-8:03:20
Bolinao	16N23	119E54	-7:59:36
Boljoon	9N38	123E29	-8:13:56
Bonawon	9N08	122E55	-8:11:40
Bongabon	15N38	121E08	-8:04:32
Bongabong	12N45	121E29	-8:05:56
Bonggaw	5N02	119E46	-7:59:04
Bonifacio	8N03	123E37	-8:14:28
Bontoc	17N05	120E58	-8:03:52
Borongan	11N37	125E26	-8:21:44
Boston	7N52	126E22	-8:25:28
Botolan	15N17	120E01	-8:00:04
Brooke's Point	8N47	117E50	-7:51:20
Buayan	6N07	125E15	-8:21:00
Buenavista	8N59	125E24	-8:21:36
Buenavista	13N15	121E57	-8:07:48
Buenavista	10N04	118E49	-7:55:16
Buenavista	7N15	122E16	-8:09:04
Bugallon	15N57	120E13	-8:00:52
Bugasong	11N03	122E04	-8:08:16
Buguey	18N17	121E50	-8:07:20
Buhi	13N26	123E31	-8:14:04
Bulalacao	12N20	121E20	-8:05:20
Bulan	12N40	123E52	-8:15:28
Bulan	6N44	124E47	-8:19:08
Buldon	7N33	124E25	-8:17:40
Buliluyan	8N20	117E12	-7:48:48
Buluan	6N44	124E47	-8:19:08
Bulusan	12N45	124E08	-8:16:32
Bunawan	8N12	125E57	-8:23:48
Burauen	10N58	124E53	-8:19:32
Burdeos	14N51	121E58	-8:07:52
Burgos	16N04	119E52	-7:59:28
Burgos	15N30	120E24	-8:01:36
Buruanga	11N51	121E53	-8:07:32
Busuanga	12N10	119E55	-7:59:40
Butag	12N38	123E56	-8:15:44
Butuan	8N57	125E33	-8:22:12
Cabadbaran	9N10	125E38	-8:22:32
Cabagan	17N26	121E46	-8:07:04
Cabalian	10N16	125E10	-8:20:40
Cabanatuan	15N29	120E58	-8:03:52
Cabangan	15N10	120E03	-8:00:12
Cabiao	15N15	120E51	-8:03:24
Cabucgayan	11N29	124E34	-8:18:16
Cabugao	17N48	120E27	-8:01:48
Cadiz	10N57	123E18	-8:13:12
Cagayancillo	9N34	121E12	-8:04:48
Cagayan de Oro	8N29	124E39	-8:18:36
Cagayan de Sulu	7N01	118E30	-7:54:00
Cagwait	8N55	126E18	-8:25:12
Caibiran	11N34	124E35	-8:18:20
Calabanga	13N42	123E12	-8:12:48
Calaca	13N56	120E49	-8:03:16
Calamba	14N13	121E10	-8:04:40
Calamba	8N35	123E39	-8:14:36
Calamba	10N11	123E17	-8:13:08
Calapan	13N25	121E10	-8:04:40
Calape	9N54	123E52	-8:15:28
Calatagan	13N50	120E38	-8:02:32
Calauan	14N09	121E19	-8:05:16
Calayan	19N16	121E28	-8:05:52
Calbayog	12N04	124E36	-8:18:24
Calbiga	11N38	125E01	-8:20:04
Calinog	11N07	122E32	-8:10:08
Calintaan	12N35	120E56	-8:03:44
Callang	17N02	121E38	-8:06:32
Calolbon	13N36	124E06	-8:16:24
Caloocan	14N39	120E58	-8:03:52
Calubian	11N27	124E26	-8:17:44
Camiling	15N42	120E24	-8:01:36
Candelaria	15N38	119E56	-7:59:44
Candijay	9N49	124E30	-8:18:00
Candon	17N12	120E27	-8:01:48
Canicanian	14N46	122E01	-8:08:04
Canipaan	8N35	117E16	-7:49:04
Canlaon	10N22	123E12	-8:12:48
Capalonga	14N20	122E30	-8:10:00
Capas	15N20	120E35	-8:02:20
Capiz → Roxas	11N35	122E45	-8:11:00
Capul	12N25	124E11	-8:16:44
Caraga	7N20	126E34	-8:26:16
Caramay	10N11	119E14	-7:56:56
Caramoan	13N46	123E52	-8:15:28
Caramoran	13N59	124E08	-8:16:32
Carcar	10N06	123E38	-8:14:32
Caridad	10N50	124E45	-8:19:00
Caridad	14N29	120E53	-8:03:32
Carigara	11N18	124E41	-8:18:44
Carles	11N34	123E08	-8:12:32
Carmen	8N59	125E17	-8:21:08
Carmen	9N50	124E12	-8:16:48
Carmen	10N35	124E01	-8:16:04
Carmen	12N37	122E07	-8:08:28
Carmona	14N19	121E03	-8:04:12
Carranglan	15N58	121E04	-8:04:16
Carrascal	9N22	125E56	-8:23:44
Caruray	10N20	119E00	-7:56:00
Casiguran	16N17	122E07	-8:08:28
Casiguran	12N52	124E00	-8:16:00
Cataingan	12N00	124E00	-8:16:00
Catanauan	13N36	122E19	-8:09:16
Catarman	9N08	124E40	-8:18:40
Catarman	12N30	124E38	-8:18:32
Catbalogan	11N46	124E53	-8:19:32
Cateel	7N48	126E27	-8:25:48
Catubig	12N24	125E03	-8:20:12
Cauayan	16N56	121E46	-8:07:04
Cauayan	9N58	122E37	-8:10:28
Cavite	14N29	120E55	-8:03:40
Cawayan	11N56	123E46	-8:15:04
Cayapoñga	5N48	125E33	-8:22:12
Cebu	10N18	123E54	-8:15:36
Cervantes	16N59	120E44	-8:02:56
Clarin	9N58	124E01	-8:16:04
Clark Air Force Base	15N11	120E32	-8:02:08
Claver	9N35	125E44	-8:22:56
Claveria	18N37	121E05	-8:04:20
Claveria	8N38	124E55	-8:19:40
Compostela	7N40	126E02	-8:24:08
Concepcion	11N13	123E06	-8:12:24
Concepcion	10N42	123E03	-8:12:12
Concepcion	12N24	122E06	-8:08:24
Concepcion	15N19	120E39	-8:02:36
Conner	17N48	121E19	-8:05:16
Cordon	16N40	121E28	-8:05:52
Coron	12N00	120E12	-8:00:48
Corregidor	14N23	120E35	-8:02:20
Cortes	9N17	126E11	-8:24:44
Cotabato	7N13	124E15	-8:17:00
Cuambog	7N20	125E52	-8:23:28
Culaba	11N40	124E32	-8:18:08
Culaman	5N58	125E40	-8:22:40
Culasi	11N26	122E03	-8:08:12
Culasi	10N43	125E43	-8:22:52
Culasian	8N51	117E29	-7:49:56
Culion	11N53	120E01	-8:00:04
Curuan	7N13	122E14	-8:08:56
Cuyapo	15N46	120E40	-8:02:40
Cuyo	10N51	121E00	-8:04:00
Daanbantayan	11N14	124E00	-8:16:00
Dadiangas → General Santos	6N07	125E11	-8:20:44
Daet	14N05	122E55	-8:11:40
Dagupan	16N03	120E20	-8:01:20
Dalaguete	9N46	123E32	-8:14:08
Danao	10N32	124E02	-8:16:08
Danao	12N29	122E39	-8:10:36
Dansalan	8N00	124E18	-8:17:12
Dao	10N31	121E57	-8:07:48
Dapa	9N46	126E03	-8:24:12
Dapdap	14N14	122E15	-8:09:00
Dapitan	8N39	123E25	-8:13:40
Daraga	11N54	123E52	-8:15:28
Daraga	13N10	123E43	-8:14:52
Dasol	15N59	119E52	-7:59:28
Datu Piang	7N01	124E30	-8:18:00
Dauin	9N12	123E16	-8:13:04
Davao	7N04	125E36	-8:22:24
Davila	18N29	120E35	-8:02:20
Del Gallego	13N56	122E36	-8:10:24
Despujols	12N31	122E01	-8:08:04
Diculom	7N54	122E14	-8:08:56
Diffun	16N34	121E33	-8:06:12
Digos	6N45	125E20	-8:21:20
Dimasalang	12N12	123E51	-8:15:24
Dimataling	7N32	123E22	-8:13:28
Dinagat	9N59	125E35	-8:22:20
Dinalupihan	14N52	120E28	-8:01:52
Dinas	7N38	123E20	-8:13:20
Dingras	18N06	120E42	-8:02:48
Dipaculao	15N51	121E32	-8:06:08
Dipolog	8N35	123E20	-8:13:20
Donsol	12N54	123E36	-8:14:24
Dulag	10N57	125E02	-8:20:08
Dumaguete	9N18	123E18	-8:13:12
Dumalag	11N18	122E37	-8:10:28
Dumalinao	7N49	123E23	-8:13:32
Dumangas	10N49	122E42	-8:10:48
Dumanjug	10N04	123E26	-8:13:44
Dupax	16N17	121E05	-8:04:20
Echague	16N42	121E40	-8:06:40
El Nido	11N11	119E23	-7:57:32
El Salvador	8N34	124E32	-8:18:08
Enrile	17N34	121E42	-8:06:48
Erenas	12N25	124E19	-8:17:16
Escalante	10N50	123E33	-8:14:12
Esperanza	8N43	125E36	-8:22:24
Esperanza	11N44	124E03	-8:16:12
Estancia	11N28	123E09	-8:12:36
Fabrica	10N54	123E23	-8:13:32
Faire	17N53	121E34	-8:06:16
Gabaldon	15N28	121E19	-8:05:16
Gamay	12N23	125E18	-8:21:12
Ganassi	7N49	124E06	-8:16:24
Gapan	15N19	120E57	-8:03:48
Garchitorena	13N52	123E40	-8:14:40
Garcia Hernandez	9N37	124E18	-8:17:12
Gasan	13N19	121E51	-8:07:24
General Luna	9N47	126E09	-8:24:36
General MacArthur (Pambuhan Sur)	11N15	125E32	-8:22:08
General Santos (Dadiangas)	6N07	125E11	-8:20:44
General Tinio	15N21	121E03	-8:04:12
Gerona	15N36	120E36	-8:02:24
Getulio	10N45	122E40	-8:10:40
Gigmoto	13N47	124E23	-8:17:32
Gingoog	8N50	125E07	-8:20:28
Giporlos	11N07	125E27	-8:21:48
Glan	5N49	125E10	-8:20:40
Goa	13N42	123E29	-8:13:56
Gonzaga	18N16	122E00	-8:08:00
Governor Generoso	6N39	126E05	-8:24:20
Granada	10N40	123E02	-8:12:08
Guagua	14N58	120E38	-8:02:32
Gubat	12N55	124E07	-8:16:28
Guihulngan	10N07	123E16	-8:13:04
Guijalo	13N44	123E52	-8:15:28
Guimba	15N40	120E46	-8:03:04
Guimbal	10N40	122E19	-8:09:16
Guinayang	14N42	121E08	-8:04:32
Guinayangan	13N54	122E27	-8:09:48
Guindulman	9N46	124E29	-8:17:56
Guinobatan	13N11	123E36	-8:14:24
Guiong	6N25	122E01	-8:08:04
Guisijan	11N05	122E03	-8:08:12
Guiuan	11N02	125E43	-8:22:52
Gumaca	13N55	122E06	-8:08:24
Gumahang	12N35	123E16	-8:13:04
Hagonoy	14N50	120E44	-8:02:56
Hernani	11N20	125E37	-8:22:28
Hibaiyo	10N16	123E20	-8:13:20
Hilongos	10N23	124E45	-8:19:00
Himamaylan	10N06	122E52	-8:11:28
Hinabangan	11N42	125E04	-8:20:16
Hinatuan	8N23	126E20	-8:25:20
Hindang	10N26	124E44	-8:18:56

Hingatungan	10N35	125E11	-8:20:44
Hinigaran	10N17	122E51	-8:11:24
Hinoba-An	9N35	122E28	-8:09:52
Hinundayan	10N21	125E15	-8:21:00
Iba	15N20	119E58	-7:59:52
Ibajay	11N49	122E10	-8:08:40
Idio	11N37	122E06	-8:08:24
Iguig	17N45	121E44	-8:06:56
Ilagan	17N10	121E54	-8:07:36
Iligan	8N14	124E14	-8:16:56
Ilijan	13N38	121E04	-8:04:16
Ilin	12N15	121E02	-8:04:08
Ilocos Norte	18N10	120E45	-8:03:00
Ilocos Sur	17N05	120E35	-8:02:20
Iloilo	10N42	122E34	-8:10:16
Impasugong	8N19	125E00	-8:20:00
Inagawan	9N33	118E39	-7:54:36
Indanan	5N58	120E59	-8:03:56
Infanta	15N50	119E55	-7:59:40
Infanta	14N45	121E39	-8:06:36
Initao	8N30	124E18	-8:17:12
Ipil	7N47	122E35	-8:10:20
Iraan	9N04	117E42	-7:50:48
Iriga	13N25	123E25	-8:13:40
Irosin	12N42	124E02	-8:16:08
Isabel	10N56	124E26	-8:17:44
Isabela	10N12	122E59	-8:11:56
Isabela (Basilan)	6N42	121E58	-8:07:52
Isulan	6N34	124E37	-8:18:28
Jabonga	9N20	125E32	-8:22:08
Jalajala	14N21	121E19	-8:05:16
Janiuay	10N58	122E30	-8:10:00
Jaro	11N11	124E47	-8:19:08
Jaro	10N43	122E33	-8:10:12
Jasaan	8N39	124E45	-8:19:00
Jerusalim (Talusan)	7N26	122E49	-8:11:16
Jetafe	10N09	124E09	-8:16:36
Jiabong	11N46	124E57	-8:19:48
Jimenez	8N20	123E50	-8:15:20
Jolo	6N03	121E00	-8:04:00
Jones	16N33	121E42	-8:06:48
Jordan	10N40	122E35	-8:10:20
Jose Abad Santos	5N38	125E27	-8:21:48
Jose Panganiban	14N17	122E41	-8:10:44
Jovellar	13N04	123E36	-8:14:24
Juagdan	10N00	124E35	-8:18:20
Kabacan	7N08	124E49	-8:19:16
Kabankalan	9N59	122E49	-8:11:16
Kabasalan	7N48	122E45	-8:11:00
Kabayan	16N37	120E51	-8:03:24
Kalaong	6N04	124E28	-8:17:52
Kalibo	11N43	122E22	-8:09:28
Kanemi	6N55	123E58	-8:15:52
Kapalong	7N35	125E42	-8:22:48
Kapangan	16N35	120E35	-8:02:20
Kapatagan	7N52	123E44	-8:14:56
Karomatan	7N46	123E44	-8:14:56
Katipunan	8N31	123E17	-8:13:08
Kauswagan	8N11	124E05	-8:16:20
Kawayan	11N41	124E21	-8:17:24
Kawit	14N27	120E54	-8:03:36
Kayapa	16N22	120E53	-8:03:32
Kiamba	5N59	124E37	-8:18:28
Kibawe	7N34	125E00	-8:20:00
Kidapawan	7N01	125E03	-8:20:12
Kinogitan	9N00	124E48	-8:19:12
Kling	5N58	124E42	-8:18:48
Kolambugan	8N07	123E55	-8:15:40
Koronadal	6N30	124E51	-8:19:24
Kumalarang	7N44	123E08	-8:12:32
Labason	8N04	122E31	-8:10:04
Labo	14N09	122E51	-8:11:24
La Carlota	10N25	122E55	-8:11:40
La Castellana	10N20	123E03	-8:12:12
Lagay	14N06	122E12	-8:08:48
Lagayan	17N43	120E42	-8:02:48
Lagonglong	8N48	124E47	-8:19:08
Lagonoy	13N44	123E31	-8:14:04
Lais	6N20	125E39	-8:22:36
Laiya	13N40	121E24	-8:05:36
Lala	7N59	123E46	-8:15:04
Lambunao	11N03	122E29	-8:09:56
Lamitan	6N39	122E08	-8:08:32
Landang Gua	6N58	122E15	-8:09:00
Lanuza	9N14	126E04	-8:24:16
Laoag	18N12	120E36	-8:02:24
Laoang	12N34	125E00	-8:20:00
La Paz	8N19	125E43	-8:22:52
Lapu-Lapu (Opon)	10N19	123E57	-8:15:48
Lapuyan	7N36	123E12	-8:12:48
Larap	14N18	122E39	-8:10:36
Larena	9N15	123E35	-8:14:20
Las Navas	12N21	125E02	-8:20:08
Las Piñas	14N29	120E59	-8:03:56
La Trinidad	16N28	120E35	-8:02:20
La Union	6N42	126E05	-8:24:20
Laur	15N35	121E11	-8:04:44
Lavezares	12N32	124E20	-8:17:20
Lawa	6N12	125E41	-8:22:44
Lazi	9N08	123E38	-8:14:32
Lebak	6N32	124E03	-8:16:12
Legaspi → Legazpi	13N08	123E44	-8:14:56
Legazpi	13N08	123E44	-8:14:56
Lemery	13N53	120E55	-8:03:40
Leon	10N47	122E23	-8:09:32
Leyte	11N23	124E29	-8:17:56
Lianga	8N38	126E06	-8:24:24
Libagon	10N18	125E03	-8:20:12
Libona	8N20	124E44	-8:18:56
Ligao	13N14	123E32	-8:14:08
Ligao	6N17	124E09	-8:16:36
Lilio	14N08	121E26	-8:05:44
Liloan	10N09	125E07	-8:20:28
Liloy	8N08	122E40	-8:10:40
Limay	14N34	120E36	-8:02:24
Lingayen	16N01	120E14	-8:00:56
Lingig	8N02	126E24	-8:25:36
Lipa	13N57	121E10	-8:04:40
Llorente	11N25	125E33	-8:22:12
Loay	9N36	124E01	-8:16:04
Lobo	13N39	121E13	-8:04:52
Locsin	13N09	123E43	-8:14:52
Looc	12N16	121E59	-8:07:56
Loon	9N48	123E47	-8:15:08
Loreto	8N12	125E45	-8:23:00
Loreto	10N21	125E34	-8:22:16
Lubang	13N52	120E07	-8:00:28
Lubao	14N56	120E36	-8:02:24
Lubuagan	17N21	121E10	-8:04:40
Lucban	14N06	121E33	-8:06:12
Lucena	13N56	121E37	-8:06:28
Lumban	14N18	121E27	-8:05:48
Luna	16N51	120E23	-8:01:32
Luna	18N18	121E21	-8:05:24
Lupao	15N53	120E54	-8:03:36
Lupon	6N54	126E00	-8:24:00
Lutao	10N00	124E04	-8:16:16
Ma-Ao	10N29	122E59	-8:11:56
Maasin	10N08	124E50	-8:19:20
Macalaya	12N53	123E46	-8:15:04
Macalelon	13N45	122E08	-8:08:32
MacArthur	10N50	125E00	-8:20:00
Macrohon	10N05	124E56	-8:19:44
Maddela	16N21	121E41	-8:06:44
Madrid	9N15	126E00	-8:24:00
Madridejos	11N18	123E44	-8:14:56
Magallanes	12N50	123E50	-8:15:20
Magdiwang	12N30	122E31	-8:10:04
Magonoy	6N54	124E33	-8:18:12
Magsaysay (Linugos)	9N01	125E11	-8:20:44
Magsingal	17N41	120E25	-8:01:40
Mahinog	9N09	124E47	-8:19:08
Maimbung	5N56	121E02	-8:04:08
Mainit	9N32	125E32	-8:22:08
Makati	14N34	121E02	-8:04:08
Makilala	6N55	125E05	-8:20:20
Malabang	7N38	124E03	-8:16:12
Malabon	14N39	120E57	-8:03:48
Malabuyoc	9N39	123E19	-8:13:16
Malalag	6N36	125E24	-8:21:36
Malambunga	9N02	117E38	-7:50:32
Malangas	7N37	123E01	-8:12:04
Malasiqui	15N55	120E25	-8:01:40
Malayal	7N12	121E57	-8:07:48
Malaybalay	8N09	125E05	-8:20:20
Malimono	9N34	125E25	-8:21:40
Malita	6N25	125E36	-8:22:24
Malitbog	10N10	125E00	-8:20:00
Mallig	17N08	121E41	-8:06:44
Malna	8N08	124E27	-8:17:48
Malolos	14N51	120E49	-8:03:16
Maluso	6N33	121E53	-8:07:32
Mambajao	9N15	124E43	-8:18:52
Mambalot	8N51	117E55	-7:51:40
Mamburao	13N14	120E35	-8:02:20
Mananao	13N30	120E34	-8:02:16
Manaoag	16N03	120E29	-8:01:56
Manapla	10N58	123E07	-8:12:28
Manaul	12N27	121E25	-8:05:40
Manay	7N13	126E32	-8:26:08
Mandaluyong	14N35	121E02	-8:04:08
Mandaon	12N14	123E17	-8:13:08
Mandaue	10N20	123E56	-8:15:44
Mangagoy	8N11	126E21	-8:25:24
Mangatarem	15N47	120E17	-8:01:08
Manicahan	7N01	122E12	-8:08:48
Manila	14N35	121E00	-8:04:00
Manille → Manila	14N35	121E00	-8:04:00
Manjuyod	9N41	123E09	-8:12:36
Manolo Fortich (Maluko)	8N25	124E58	-8:19:52
Mansalay	12N31	121E26	-8:05:44
Manticao	8N24	124E17	-8:17:08
Manukan	8N31	123E06	-8:12:24
Marabut	11N07	125E13	-8:20:52
Maramag	7N46	125E00	-8:20:00
Marangas	8N40	117E38	-7:50:32
Marawi	8N01	124E18	-8:17:12
Margosatubig	7N34	123E10	-8:12:40
Maria	9N12	123E39	-8:14:36
Marihatag	8N48	126E18	-8:25:12
Marikina	14N38	121E06	-8:04:24
Mariveles	14N26	120E29	-8:01:56
Masaguisi	12N41	121E32	-8:06:08
Masbate	12N22	123E36	-8:14:24
Masinloc	15N32	119E57	-7:59:48
Matag-Ob	11N07	124E29	-8:17:56
Mati	6N57	126E13	-8:24:52
Matnog	12N35	124E05	-8:16:20
Matuog	9N55	123E09	-8:12:36
Mauban	14N12	121E44	-8:06:56
Mayantoc	15N37	120E23	-8:01:32
Maydolong	11N30	125E30	-8:22:00
Mayoyao	16N59	121E14	-8:04:56
Medellin	11N08	123E58	-8:15:52
Medina	8N55	125E01	-8:20:04
Mendez-Nuñez	14N08	120E54	-8:03:36
Mercedes	14N07	123E01	-8:12:04
Merida	10N55	124E32	-8:18:08
Meycauayan	14N44	120E58	-8:03:52
Miagao	10N39	122E14	-8:08:56
Miarayon	8N04	124E50	-8:19:20
Midsayap	7N12	124E32	-8:18:08
Milagros	12N13	123E30	-8:14:00
Milbuk	6N10	124E16	-8:17:04
Misamis	8N09	123E51	-8:15:24
M'Lang	6N55	124E53	-8:19:32
Moalboal	9N56	123E23	-8:13:32
Molundo	7N56	124E23	-8:17:32
Moncada	15N44	120E34	-8:02:16
Mondragon	12N31	124E45	-8:19:00
Monkayo	7N50	126E03	-8:24:12
Morong	14N41	120E16	-8:01:04
Motiong	11N47	125E00	-8:20:00
Muñoz	15N43	120E54	-8:03:36
Murcia	10N36	123E02	-8:12:08
Nabas	11N50	122E05	-8:08:20
Nabua	13N24	123E22	-8:13:28
Nabunturan	7N35	125E58	-8:23:52
Naci	6N19	124E46	-8:19:04
Naci	14N19	120E46	-8:03:04
Naga	13N37	123E11	-8:12:44
Naga	10N13	123E45	-8:15:00
Nagas	13N06	123E18	-8:13:12
Nagcarlan	14N08	121E25	-8:05:40
Nagiba	13N41	120E53	-8:03:32
Naguilian	17N01	121E50	-8:07:20
Naic	14N19	120E46	-8:03:04
Nampicuan	15N44	120E38	-8:02:32
Narvacan	17N25	120E28	-8:01:52
Nasugbu	14N05	120E38	-8:02:32
Naujan	13N20	121E18	-8:05:12
Naval	11N34	124E23	-8:17:32
Navotas	14N39	120E57	-8:03:48
New Washington	11N39	122E26	-8:09:44
Norala	6N28	124E38	-8:18:32
Norzagaray	14N54	121E02	-8:04:08
Numancia	9N52	125E58	-8:23:52
Oas	13N16	123E30	-8:14:00
Obando	14N43	120E56	-8:03:44
Odiongan	12N24	121E59	-8:07:56
Olivo	10N52	123E53	-8:15:32
Olongapo	14N50	120E16	-8:01:04
Olutanga (Suba Nipa)	7N26	122E54	-8:11:36
Opol	8N31	124E34	-8:18:16
Opon → Lapu-Lapu	10N19	123E57	-8:15:48
Oquendo	12N08	124E32	-8:18:08
Orani	14N49	120E32	-8:02:08
Oras	12N09	125E26	-8:21:44
Orion	14N37	120E34	-8:02:16
Ormoc	11N00	124E37	-8:18:28
Oroquieta	8N29	123E48	-8:15:12
Oslob	9N31	123E26	-8:13:44
Osmeña	10N11	125E31	-8:22:04
Oton	10N42	122E29	-8:09:56
Ozamiz	8N08	123E50	-8:15:20
Padada	6N42	125E22	-8:21:28
Padre Burgos	10N02	125E01	-8:20:04
Paete	14N23	121E29	-8:05:56
Pagadian	7N49	123E25	-8:13:40
Pagalungan	7N04	124E41	-8:18:44
Pagbilao	13N58	121E41	-8:06:44
Pagsangahan	13N13	122E33	-8:10:12
Pagsanjan	14N15	121E25	-8:05:40
Pagudpud	18N34	120E47	-8:03:08
Palanas	12N09	123E55	-8:15:40
Palapag	12N33	125E07	-8:20:28
Palauig	15N26	119E54	-7:59:36
Palayan	15N33	121E06	-8:04:24
Palimbang	6N12	124E12	-8:16:48
Palo	11N10	124E59	-8:19:56
Palompon	11N03	124E23	-8:17:32
Paluan	13N25	120E28	-8:01:52
Pambuhan	13N59	123E05	-8:12:20
Pambujan	12N34	124E56	-8:19:44
Panabo	7N19	125E42	-8:22:48
Panacan	9N16	118E25	-7:53:40
Pandan	11N43	122E06	-8:08:24
Pandan	14N03	124E10	-8:16:40
Panganiran	13N02	123E26	-8:13:44
Pangantocan	7N50	124E49	-8:19:16
Panganuran	7N24	122E03	-8:08:12
Pangasinan	16N00	120E20	-8:01:20
Panglao	9N35	123E45	-8:15:00
Pangubatan	6N57	125E47	-8:23:08
Panguiranan	12N04	123E19	-8:13:16
Pangutaran	6N18	120E35	-8:02:20
Pangyan	5N42	125E17	-8:21:08
Paniqui	15N40	120E35	-8:02:20
Panitian	9N05	118E05	-7:52:20
Pantabañgan	15N50	121E09	-8:04:36
Panukulan	14N56	121E49	-8:07:16
Paracale	14N17	122E48	-8:11:12
Parañaque	14N30	120E59	-8:03:56
Parang	7N23	124E16	-8:17:04
Parang	5N55	120E54	-8:03:36
Parasan	8N05	123E33	-8:14:12
Parubcan	13N43	123E45	-8:15:00
Pasacao	13N31	123E03	-8:12:12
Pasay	14N33	121E00	-8:04:00
Pasig	14N33	121E05	-8:04:20
Passi	11N06	122E39	-8:10:36
Pasuquin	18N20	120E37	-8:02:28
Pata	5N51	121E10	-8:04:40
Pateros	14N33	121E04	-8:04:16
Patikul	6N04	121E06	-8:04:24
Patnoñgon	10N55	122E00	-8:08:00
Piat	17N48	121E29	-8:05:56
Pigkawagan	7N12	124E32	-8:18:08
Pilar	11N29	123E00	-8:12:00
Pilar	9N52	126E06	-8:24:24
Pili	13N33	123E16	-8:13:04
Pinamalayan	13N02	121E29	-8:05:56
Pinamungajan	10N16	123E35	-8:14:20
Pintuyan	9N57	125E15	-8:21:00
Pinukpuk	17N35	121E22	-8:05:28
Pio V. Corpus (Limbujan)	11N53	124E03	-8:16:12
Pitogo	10N08	124E33	-8:18:12
Placer	11N52	123E55	-8:15:40

PILIPINAS — PHILIPPINEN — FILIPINAS — PHILIPPINES

Place	Lat	Long	Time
Placer	9N39	125E36	-8:22:24
Plaridel	10N32	124E46	-8:19:04
Plaridel	8N37	123E43	-8:14:52
Pola	13N09	121E26	-8:05:44
Polangui	13N17	123E29	-8:13:56
Polillo	14N43	121E56	-8:07:44
Polo	14N42	120E57	-8:03:48
Pontevedra	10N22	122E52	-8:11:28
Poona-Bayabo (Gata)	7N51	124E22	-8:17:28
Pototan	10N55	122E40	-8:10:40
President Roxas	11N26	122E56	-8:11:44
Prieto Diaz	13N02	124E12	-8:16:48
Prosperidad	8N34	125E52	-8:23:28
Puerto Princesa	9N44	118E44	-7:54:56
Puerto Princesa	10N06	125E29	-8:21:56
Pulupandan	10N31	122E48	-8:11:12
Pundaguitan	6N22	126E10	-8:24:40
Punta Flecha	7N23	123E25	-8:13:40
Quezon	15N34	120E49	-8:03:16
Quezon	14N01	122E11	-8:08:44
Quezon City	14N38	121E03	-8:04:12
Ragay	13N49	122E47	-8:11:08
Rapu-Rapu	13N11	124E08	-8:16:32
Real	14N40	121E36	-8:06:24
Rio Tuba	8N30	117E25	-7:49:40
Rizal	15N43	121E06	-8:04:24
Rizal → Pasay	14N33	121E00	-8:04:00
Romblon	12N35	122E15	-8:09:00
Rosales	15N54	120E38	-8:02:32
Rosario	13N51	121E12	-8:04:48
Rosario	16N14	120E29	-8:01:56
Roxas (Capiz)	11N35	122E45	-8:11:00
Roxas	17N08	121E36	-8:06:24
Roxas	12N35	121E31	-8:06:04
Roxas	10N20	119E21	-7:57:24
Sablayan	12N50	120E46	-8:03:04
Sadanga	17N09	121E02	-8:04:08
Sagay	10N56	123E26	-8:13:44
Salay	8N52	124E47	-8:19:08
Salcedo	11N09	125E40	-8:22:40
Salug	8N07	122E47	-8:11:08
Salvador	7N54	123E50	-8:15:20
Samal (Peñaplata)	7N05	125E42	-8:22:48
Samboan	9N32	123E18	-8:13:12
San Agustin	16N30	121E45	-8:07:00
San Agustin	12N25	120E59	-8:03:56
San Antonio	12N25	124E17	-8:17:08
San Antonio	14N57	120E05	-8:00:20
San Carlos	10N30	123E25	-8:13:40
San Carlos	15N55	120E20	-8:01:20
San Dionisio	11N16	123E06	-8:12:24
San Emilio	17N14	120E37	-8:02:28
San Fabian	16N05	120E25	-8:01:40
San Felipe	15N04	120E04	-8:00:16
San Fernando	16N37	120E19	-8:01:16
San Fernando	12N30	123E46	-8:15:04
San Fernando	15N01	120E41	-8:02:44
San Francisco	8N30	125E56	-8:23:44
San Francisco	10N04	125E09	-8:20:36
San Isidro	11N24	124E21	-8:17:24
San Jacinto	12N34	123E44	-8:14:56
San Joaquin	10N35	122E08	-8:08:32
San Jose	10N45	121E56	-8:07:44
San Jose	15N48	121E00	-8:04:00
San Jose	12N27	121E03	-8:04:12
San Jose de Buan	12N02	125E01	-8:20:04
San Juan	13N50	121E24	-8:05:36
San Juan	16N40	120E20	-8:01:20
San Juan	8N25	126E20	-8:25:20
San Juan del Monte	14N36	121E02	-8:04:08
San Julian	11N45	125E27	-8:21:48
San Manuel	16N04	120E40	-8:02:40
San Marcelino	14N58	120E09	-8:00:36
San Mateo	14N42	121E07	-8:04:28
San Miguel	15N09	120E59	-8:03:56
San Narciso	13N34	122E34	-8:10:16
San Narciso	15N01	120E05	-8:00:20
San Nicolas	18N09	120E38	-8:02:32
San Nicolas	16N04	120E46	-8:03:04
San Pablo	14N04	121E19	-8:05:16
San Pablo	7N40	123E27	-8:13:48
San Pascual	13N08	122E59	-8:11:56
San Policarpio	12N11	125E30	-8:22:00
San Quintin	16N00	120E50	-8:03:20
San Ramon	13N16	124E05	-8:16:20
San Remigio	11N05	123E56	-8:15:44
San Roque	14N29	120E54	-8:03:36
Santa	17N29	120E26	-8:01:44
Santa Barbara	10N50	122E31	-8:10:04
Santa Catalina	9N20	122E51	-8:11:24
Santa Cruz	6N50	125E25	-8:21:40
Santa Cruz	14N17	121E25	-8:05:40
Santa Cruz	13N29	122E02	-8:08:08
Santa Cruz	13N04	120E43	-8:02:52
Santa Cruz	15N46	119E55	-7:59:40
Santa Cruz (Tubajon)	10N19	125E33	-8:22:12
Santa Fe	11N09	123E47	-8:15:08
Santa Fe	16N10	120E57	-8:03:48
Santa Fe	12N10	122E00	-8:08:00
Santa Josefa	8N02	125E57	-8:23:48
Santa Maria	14N49	120E58	-8:03:52
Santa Maria	17N22	120E29	-8:01:56
Santander	9N25	123E20	-8:13:20
Santa Rita	11N27	124E56	-8:19:44
Santiago	16N41	121E33	-8:06:12
Santo Tomas	7N29	125E38	-8:22:32
Sapao	10N01	126E02	-8:24:08
Sara	11N16	123E01	-8:12:04
Sariaya	13N58	121E32	-8:06:08
Siasi	5N33	120E49	-8:03:16
Siaton	9N04	123E02	-8:12:08
Sibalom	10N47	122E01	-8:08:04
Sierra-Bullones	9N51	124E20	-8:17:20
Silang	14N14	120E58	-8:03:52
Silay	10N48	122E58	-8:11:52
Sindangan	8N14	123E00	-8:12:00
Siniloan	14N25	121E27	-8:05:48
Siocon	7N42	122E08	-8:08:32
Sipalay	9N45	122E24	-8:09:36
Sipocot	13N46	122E58	-8:11:52
Siraway	7N34	122E08	-8:08:32
Siruma	14N00	123E15	-8:13:00
Sison	9N40	125E31	-8:22:04
Si Tangkay	4N40	119E24	-7:57:36
Socorro	9N37	125E58	-8:23:52
Sogod	10N45	124E00	-8:16:00
Sogod	10N23	124E59	-8:19:56
Solano	16N31	121E11	-8:04:44
Sorsogon	12N58	124E00	-8:16:00
South Ubian	5N11	120E30	-8:02:00
Sual	16N04	120E05	-8:00:20
Subic	14N53	120E14	-8:00:56
Subic Bay	14N45	120E13	-8:00:52
Sugbay	7N31	123E19	-8:13:16
Sugod	12N03	124E09	-8:16:36
Sulat	11N49	125E27	-8:21:48
Sultan sa Barongis	6N46	124E38	-8:18:32
Sumilao	8N18	124E57	-8:19:48
Surigao	9N45	125E30	-8:22:00
Tabaco	13N23	123E44	-8:14:56
Tabango	11N19	124E22	-8:17:28
Tabogon	10N57	124E02	-8:16:08
Tabuelan	10N49	123E52	-8:15:28
Tabuk	17N24	121E25	-8:05:40
Tacloban	11N15	125E00	-8:20:00
Taclobo	12N20	122E34	-8:10:16
Tacurong	6N42	124E42	-8:18:48
Taft	11N54	125E25	-8:21:40
Tagabukid	7N00	126E21	-8:25:24
Tagana-An	9N42	125E35	-8:22:20
Tagaytay	14N06	120E56	-8:03:44
Tagbilaran	9N39	123E51	-8:15:24
Tagilaran	9N39	123E51	-8:15:24
Tagig	14N32	121E04	-8:04:16
Tago	9N02	126E13	-8:24:52
Tagoloan	8N32	124E45	-8:19:00
Tagudin	16N56	120E27	-8:01:48
Tagum	7N28	125E48	-8:23:12
Talacogon	8N28	125E46	-8:23:04
Talakag	8N16	124E37	-8:18:28
Talavera	15N35	120E55	-8:03:40
Talayan	6N55	124E24	-8:17:36
Talibon	10N09	124E19	-8:17:16
Talisay	14N08	122E55	-8:11:40
Talisay	10N44	122E58	-8:11:52
Talisayan	9N00	124E55	-8:19:40
Tambler	6N03	125E09	-8:20:36
Tamparan	8N27	117E13	-7:48:52
Tanauan	11N07	125E01	-8:20:04
Tanauan	14N05	121E09	-8:04:36
Tanay	14N30	121E17	-8:05:08
Tandag	9N04	126E12	-8:24:48
Tandubas	5N10	120E20	-8:01:20
Tangub	8N03	123E44	-8:14:56
Tanjay	9N31	123E09	-8:12:36
Tanza	14N24	120E51	-8:03:24
Tapaz	11N16	122E32	-8:10:08
Tarangnan	11N54	124E45	-8:19:00
Tarlac	15N29	120E35	-8:02:20
Tayabas	14N01	121E35	-8:06:20
Taytay	10N49	119E31	-7:58:04
Taytay	14N34	121E08	-8:04:32
Tayug	16N02	120E45	-8:03:00
Teneguiban	11N22	119E30	-7:58:00
Ternate	14N17	120E43	-8:02:52
Tiaong	13N57	121E19	-8:05:16
Tibiao	11N17	122E02	-8:08:08
Tiblawan	6N29	126E06	-8:24:24
Tigbauan	10N41	122E22	-8:09:28
Tinalmud	13N36	122E53	-8:11:32
Tinambac	13N49	123E19	-8:13:16
Tingloy	13N40	120E52	-8:03:28
Tiniguiban	11N22	119E30	-7:58:00
Tinitian	10N04	119E12	-7:56:48
Tipas	14N33	121E00	-8:04:00
Tiwi	13N27	123E41	-8:14:44
Toboso	10N43	123E31	-8:14:04
Togoron	12N35	123E37	-8:14:28
Toledo	10N23	123E38	-8:14:32
Torrijos	13N19	122E05	-8:08:20
Trece Martires	14N16	120E50	-8:03:20
Tubli	13N56	124E09	-8:16:36
Tubod	8N03	123E48	-8:15:12
Tuburan	10N44	123w49	8:15:16
Tuburan	6N39	122E16	-8:09:04
Tudela	8N15	123E50	-8:15:20
Tuguegarao	17N37	121E44	-8:06:56
Tukuran	7N51	123E35	-8:14:20
Tumarbong	10N23	119E27	-7:57:48
Tumauini	17N17	121E49	-8:07:16
Tupi	6N19	124E57	-8:19:48
Tupilac	7N40	122E30	-8:10:00
Ubay	10N03	124E28	-8:17:52
Umingan	15N56	120E50	-8:03:20
Unisan	13N51	121E59	-8:07:56
Upi	6N57	124E09	-8:16:36
Urdaneta	15N59	120E34	-8:02:16
Uson	12N13	123E47	-8:15:08
Valderrama	11N00	122E08	-8:08:32
Valencia	7N57	125E03	-8:20:12
Valenzuela	14N42	120E58	-8:03:52
Vallehermoso	10N20	123E19	-8:13:16
Victoria	13N12	121E15	-8:05:00
Victoria	15N35	120E41	-8:02:44
Victorias	10N54	123E05	-8:12:20
Vigan	17N34	120E23	-8:01:32
Villaba	11N13	124E23	-8:17:32
Villalon	11N31	124E22	-8:17:28
Villareal	11N34	124E56	-8:19:44
Villasis	15N54	120E35	-8:02:20
Virac	13N35	124E15	-8:17:00
Virac	16N22	120E39	-8:02:36
Vitali	7N22	122E18	-8:09:12
Zamboanga	6N54	122E04	-8:08:16
Zamboanguita	9N06	123E12	-8:12:48
Zumarraga	11N38	124E50	-8:19:20

PITCAIRN — PITCAIRN

Time Table
Before 1/Jan/1901 LMT
Begin Standard 127w30
1/Jan/1901 0:00 8:30

Place	Lat	Long	Time
Adamstown	25s04	130w05	8:40:20
Bounty Bay	25s04	130w05	8:40:20
Henderson Island	24s22	128w19	8:33:16
Pitcairn Island	25s04	130w06	8:40:24
Point Christian	25s04	130w07	8:40:28
Saint Paul's Point	25s04	130w05	8:40:20
The Rope	25s04	130w05	8:40:20
Young's Rock	25s03	130w07	8:40:28

POLAND POLONIA POLOGNE POLEN POLSKA

Time Table # 1

Date	Time	Offset
Before	1/Apr/1893	LMT
Begin Standard		15E00
1/Apr/1893	0:00	-1:00
30/Apr/1916	23:00	-2:00
1/Oct/1916	1:00	-1:00
16/Apr/1917	2:00	-2:00
17/Sep/1917	3:00	-1:00
15/Apr/1918	2:00	-2:00
16/Sep/1918	3:00	-1:00
1/Apr/1940	2:00	-2:00
2/Nov/1942	3:00	-1:00
29/Mar/1943	2:00	-2:00
4/Oct/1943	3:00	-1:00
3/Apr/1944	2:00	-2:00
4/Oct/1944	2:00	-1:00
28/Apr/1945	24:00	-2:00
31/Oct/1945	24:00	-1:00
13/Apr/1946	24:00	-2:00
6/Sep/1946	24:00	-1:00
4/May/1947	0:00	-2:00
5/Oct/1947	0:00	-1:00
18/Apr/1948	0:00	-2:00
3/Oct/1948	0:00	-1:00
2/Jun/1957	1:00	-2:00
29/Sep/1957	2:00	-1:00
30/Mar/1958	1:00	-2:00
28/Sep/1958	2:00	-1:00
31/May/1959	1:00	-2:00
4/Oct/1959	2:00	-1:00
3/Apr/1960	1:00	-2:00
2/Oct/1960	2:00	-1:00
28/May/1961	1:00	-2:00
1/Oct/1961	2:00	-1:00
27/May/1962	1:00	-2:00
30/Sep/1962	2:00	-1:00
26/May/1963	1:00	-2:00
29/Sep/1963	2:00	-1:00
31/May/1964	1:00	-2:00
27/Sep/1964	2:00	-1:00
3/Apr/1977	1:00	-2:00
25/Sep/1977	2:00	-1:00
2/Apr/1978	1:00	-2:00
1/Oct/1978	2:00	-1:00
1/Apr/1979	1:00	-2:00
30/Sep/1979	2:00	-1:00
6/Apr/1980	1:00	-2:00
28/Sep/1980	2:00	-1:00
29/Mar/1981	1:00	-2:00
27/Sep/1981	2:00	-1:00
28/Mar/1982	1:00	-2:00
26/Sep/1982	2:00	-1:00
27/Mar/1983	1:00	-2:00
25/Sep/1983	2:00	-1:00
25/Mar/1984	1:00	-2:00
30/Sep/1984	2:00	-1:00
31/Mar/1985	1:00	-2:00
29/Sep/1985	2:00	-1:00
30/Mar/1986	1:00	-2:00
28/Sep/1986	2:00	-1:00
29/Mar/1987	1:00	-2:00
27/Sep/1987	2:00	-1:00
27/Mar/1988	1:00	-2:00
25/Sep/1988	2:00	-1:00
26/Mar/1989	1:00	-2:00
24/Sep/1989	2:00	-1:00
25/Mar/1990	1:00	-2:00
30/Sep/1990	2:00	-1:00
31/Mar/1991	1:00	-2:00
29/Sep/1991	2:00	-1:00
29/Mar/1992	1:00	-2:00
27/Sep/1992	2:00	-1:00
28/Mar/1993	1:00	-2:00
26/Sep/1993	2:00	-1:00
27/Mar/1994	1:00	-2:00
25/Sep/1994	2:00	-1:00
26/Mar/1995	1:00	-2:00
24/Sep/1995	2:00	-1:00
31/Mar/1996	1:00	-2:00
29/Sep/1996	2:00	-1:00
30/Mar/1997	1:00	-2:00
28/Sep/1997	2:00	-1:00
29/Mar/1998	1:00	-2:00
27/Sep/1998	2:00	-1:00
28/Mar/1999	1:00	-2:00
26/Sep/1999	2:00	-1:00
26/Mar/2000	1:00	-2:00
24/Sep/2000	2:00	-1:00

Time Table # 2

Date	Time	Offset
Before	1/Apr/1893	LMT
Begin Standard		15E00
1/Apr/1893	0:00	-1:00
30/Apr/1916	23:00	-2:00
1/Oct/1916	1:00	-1:00
16/Apr/1917	2:00	-2:00
17/Sep/1917	3:00	-1:00
15/Apr/1918	2:00	-2:00
Begin Standard		30E00
16/Sep/1918	3:00	-2:00
15/Apr/1919	2:00	-3:00
16/Sep/1919	3:00	-2:00
Begin Standard		15E00
1/Jun/1922	0:00	-1:00
23/Jun/1940	2:00	-2:00
2/Nov/1942	3:00	-1:00
29/Mar/1943	2:00	-2:00
4/Oct/1943	3:00	-1:00
3/Apr/1944	2:00	-2:00
4/Oct/1944	2:00	-1:00
28/Apr/1945	24:00	-2:00
31/Oct/1945	24:00	-1:00
13/Apr/1946	24:00	-2:00
6/Sep/1946	24:00	-1:00
4/May/1947	0:00	-2:00
5/Oct/1947	0:00	-1:00
18/Apr/1948	0:00	-2:00
3/Oct/1948	0:00	-1:00
2/Jun/1957	1:00	-2:00
29/Sep/1957	2:00	-1:00
30/Mar/1958	1:00	-2:00
28/Sep/1958	2:00	-1:00
31/May/1959	1:00	-2:00
4/Oct/1959	2:00	-1:00
3/Apr/1960	1:00	-2:00
2/Oct/1960	2:00	-1:00
28/May/1961	1:00	-2:00
1/Oct/1961	2:00	-1:00
27/May/1962	1:00	-2:00
30/Sep/1962	2:00	-1:00
26/May/1963	1:00	-2:00
29/Sep/1963	2:00	-1:00
31/May/1964	1:00	-2:00
27/Sep/1964	2:00	-1:00
3/Apr/1977	1:00	-2:00
25/Sep/1977	2:00	-1:00
2/Apr/1978	1:00	-2:00
1/Oct/1978	2:00	-1:00
1/Apr/1979	1:00	-2:00
30/Sep/1979	2:00	-1:00
6/Apr/1980	1:00	-2:00
28/Sep/1980	2:00	-1:00
29/Mar/1981	1:00	-2:00
27/Sep/1981	2:00	-1:00
28/Mar/1982	1:00	-2:00
26/Sep/1982	2:00	-1:00
27/Mar/1983	1:00	-2:00
25/Sep/1983	2:00	-1:00
25/Mar/1984	1:00	-2:00
30/Sep/1984	2:00	-1:00
31/Mar/1985	1:00	-2:00
29/Sep/1985	2:00	-1:00
30/Mar/1986	1:00	-2:00
28/Sep/1986	2:00	-1:00
29/Mar/1987	1:00	-2:00
27/Sep/1987	2:00	-1:00
27/Mar/1988	1:00	-2:00
25/Sep/1988	2:00	-1:00
26/Mar/1989	1:00	-2:00
24/Sep/1989	2:00	-1:00
25/Mar/1990	1:00	-2:00
30/Sep/1990	2:00	-1:00
31/Mar/1991	1:00	-2:00
29/Sep/1991	2:00	-1:00
29/Mar/1992	1:00	-2:00
27/Sep/1992	2:00	-1:00
28/Mar/1993	1:00	-2:00
26/Sep/1993	2:00	-1:00
27/Mar/1994	1:00	-2:00
25/Sep/1994	2:00	-1:00
26/Mar/1995	1:00	-2:00
24/Sep/1995	2:00	-1:00
31/Mar/1996	1:00	-2:00
29/Sep/1996	2:00	-1:00
30/Mar/1997	1:00	-2:00
28/Sep/1997	2:00	-1:00
29/Mar/1998	1:00	-2:00
27/Sep/1998	2:00	-1:00
28/Mar/1999	1:00	-2:00
26/Sep/1999	2:00	-1:00
26/Mar/2000	1:00	-2:00
24/Sep/2000	2:00	-1:00

Time Table # 3

Date	Time	Offset
Before	1/Jan/1880	LMT
Begin Standard		21E00
1/Jan/1880	0:00	-1:24
Begin Standard		15E00
5/Aug/1915	0:00	-1:00
30/Apr/1916	23:00	-2:00
1/Oct/1916	1:00	-1:00
16/Apr/1917	2:00	-2:00
17/Sep/1917	3:00	-1:00
15/Apr/1918	2:00	-2:00
Begin Standard		30E00
16/Sep/1918	3:00	-2:00
15/Apr/1919	2:00	-3:00
16/Sep/1919	3:00	-2:00
Begin Standard		15E00
1/Jun/1922	0:00	-1:00
23/Jun/1940	2:00	-2:00
2/Nov/1942	3:00	-1:00
29/Mar/1943	2:00	-2:00
4/Oct/1943	3:00	-1:00
3/Apr/1944	2:00	-2:00
4/Oct/1944	2:00	-1:00
28/Apr/1945	24:00	-2:00
31/Oct/1945	24:00	-1:00
13/Apr/1946	24:00	-2:00
6/Sep/1946	24:00	-1:00
4/May/1947	0:00	-2:00
5/Oct/1947	0:00	-1:00
18/Apr/1948	0:00	-2:00
3/Oct/1948	0:00	-1:00
2/Jun/1957	1:00	-2:00
29/Sep/1957	2:00	-1:00
30/Mar/1958	1:00	-2:00
28/Sep/1958	2:00	-1:00
31/May/1959	1:00	-2:00
4/Oct/1959	2:00	-1:00
3/Apr/1960	1:00	-2:00
2/Oct/1960	2:00	-1:00
28/May/1961	1:00	-2:00
1/Oct/1961	2:00	-1:00
27/May/1962	1:00	-2:00
30/Sep/1962	2:00	-1:00
26/May/1963	1:00	-2:00
29/Sep/1963	2:00	-1:00
31/May/1964	1:00	-2:00
27/Sep/1964	2:00	-1:00
3/Apr/1977	1:00	-2:00
25/Sep/1977	2:00	-1:00
2/Apr/1978	1:00	-2:00
1/Oct/1978	2:00	-1:00
1/Apr/1979	1:00	-2:00
30/Sep/1979	2:00	-1:00
6/Apr/1980	1:00	-2:00
28/Sep/1980	2:00	-1:00
29/Mar/1981	1:00	-2:00
27/Sep/1981	2:00	-1:00
28/Mar/1982	1:00	-2:00
26/Sep/1982	2:00	-1:00
27/Mar/1983	1:00	-2:00
25/Sep/1983	2:00	-1:00
25/Mar/1984	1:00	-2:00
30/Sep/1984	2:00	-1:00
31/Mar/1985	1:00	-2:00
29/Sep/1985	2:00	-1:00
30/Mar/1986	1:00	-2:00
28/Sep/1986	2:00	-1:00
29/Mar/1987	1:00	-2:00
27/Sep/1987	2:00	-1:00
27/Mar/1988	1:00	-2:00
25/Sep/1988	2:00	-1:00
26/Mar/1989	1:00	-2:00
24/Sep/1989	2:00	-1:00
25/Mar/1990	1:00	-2:00
30/Sep/1990	2:00	-1:00
31/Mar/1991	1:00	-2:00
29/Sep/1991	2:00	-1:00
29/Mar/1992	1:00	-2:00
27/Sep/1992	2:00	-1:00
28/Mar/1993	1:00	-2:00
26/Sep/1993	2:00	-1:00
27/Mar/1994	1:00	-2:00
25/Sep/1994	2:00	-1:00
26/Mar/1995	1:00	-2:00
24/Sep/1995	2:00	-1:00
31/Mar/1996	1:00	-2:00
29/Sep/1996	2:00	-1:00
30/Mar/1997	1:00	-2:00
28/Sep/1997	2:00	-1:00
29/Mar/1998	1:00	-2:00
27/Sep/1998	2:00	-1:00
28/Mar/1999	1:00	-2:00
26/Sep/1999	2:00	-1:00
26/Mar/2000	1:00	-2:00
24/Sep/2000	2:00	-1:00

Time Table # 4

Date	Time	Offset
Before	1/Jan/1880	LMT
Begin Standard		30E15
1/Jan/1880	0:00	-2:01
Begin Standard		15E00
5/Aug/1915	0:00	-1:00
30/Apr/1916	23:00	-2:00
1/Oct/1916	1:00	-1:00
16/Apr/1917	2:00	-2:00
17/Sep/1917	3:00	-1:00
15/Apr/1918	2:00	-2:00
Begin Standard		30E00
16/Sep/1918	3:00	-2:00
15/Apr/1919	2:00	-3:00
16/Sep/1919	3:00	-2:00
Begin Standard		15E00
1/Jun/1922	0:00	-1:00
23/Jun/1940	2:00	-2:00
2/Nov/1942	3:00	-1:00
29/Mar/1943	2:00	-2:00
4/Oct/1943	3:00	-1:00
3/Apr/1944	2:00	-2:00
4/Oct/1944	2:00	-1:00
28/Apr/1945	24:00	-2:00
31/Oct/1945	24:00	-1:00
13/Apr/1946	24:00	-2:00
6/Sep/1946	24:00	-1:00
4/May/1947	0:00	-2:00
5/Oct/1947	0:00	-1:00
18/Apr/1948	0:00	-2:00
3/Oct/1948	0:00	-1:00
2/Jun/1957	1:00	-2:00
29/Sep/1957	2:00	-1:00
30/Mar/1958	1:00	-2:00
28/Sep/1958	2:00	-1:00
31/May/1959	1:00	-2:00
4/Oct/1959	2:00	-1:00
3/Apr/1960	1:00	-2:00
2/Oct/1960	2:00	-1:00
28/May/1961	1:00	-2:00
1/Oct/1961	2:00	-1:00
27/May/1962	1:00	-2:00
30/Sep/1962	2:00	-1:00
26/May/1963	1:00	-2:00
29/Sep/1963	2:00	-1:00
31/May/1964	1:00	-2:00
27/Sep/1964	2:00	-1:00
3/Apr/1977	1:00	-2:00
25/Sep/1977	2:00	-1:00
2/Apr/1978	1:00	-2:00
1/Oct/1978	2:00	-1:00
1/Apr/1979	1:00	-2:00
30/Sep/1979	2:00	-1:00
6/Apr/1980	1:00	-2:00
28/Sep/1980	2:00	-1:00
29/Mar/1981	1:00	-2:00
27/Sep/1981	2:00	-1:00
28/Mar/1982	1:00	-2:00
26/Sep/1982	2:00	-1:00
27/Mar/1983	1:00	-2:00
25/Sep/1983	2:00	-1:00
25/Mar/1984	1:00	-2:00
30/Sep/1984	2:00	-1:00
31/Mar/1985	1:00	-2:00
29/Sep/1985	2:00	-1:00
30/Mar/1986	1:00	-2:00
28/Sep/1986	2:00	-1:00
29/Mar/1987	1:00	-2:00
27/Sep/1987	2:00	-1:00
27/Mar/1988	1:00	-2:00
25/Sep/1988	2:00	-1:00
26/Mar/1989	1:00	-2:00
24/Sep/1989	2:00	-1:00
25/Mar/1990	1:00	-2:00
30/Sep/1990	2:00	-1:00
31/Mar/1991	1:00	-2:00
29/Sep/1991	2:00	-1:00
29/Mar/1992	1:00	-2:00
27/Sep/1992	2:00	-1:00
28/Mar/1993	1:00	-2:00
26/Sep/1993	2:00	-1:00
27/Mar/1994	1:00	-2:00
25/Sep/1994	2:00	-1:00
26/Mar/1995	1:00	-2:00
24/Sep/1995	2:00	-1:00
31/Mar/1996	1:00	-2:00
29/Sep/1996	2:00	-1:00
30/Mar/1997	1:00	-2:00
28/Sep/1997	2:00	-1:00
29/Mar/1998	1:00	-2:00
27/Sep/1998	2:00	-1:00
28/Mar/1999	1:00	-2:00
26/Sep/1999	2:00	-1:00
26/Mar/2000	1:00	-2:00
24/Sep/2000	2:00	-1:00

DIVISIONS

1. German (Prussian) before 1944
2. Austrian before 1918
3. German (Prussian) before 1918
4. "Congress" P, Russian before 1918
5. "Russian" P, Russian before 1918
6. Gdańsk (Danzig), Ind. before 1939

Place	TT	Lat	Long	Offset
Adamów 4	3	51N45	22E17	-1:29:08
Aleksandrów Kujawski 3	2	52N52	18E42	-1:14:48
Aleksandrów Łódzki 4	3	51N49	19E19	-1:17:16
Allenstein → Olsztyn 1	1	53N48	20E29	-1:21:56
Andreashütte → Zawadzkie 3	2	50N37	18E29	-1:13:56
Andrychów 2	2	49N52	19E21	-1:17:24
Angerburg → Węgorzewo 1	1	54N14	21E44	-1:26:56
Annopol 4	3	50N54	21E52	-1:27:28
Arys → Orzysz 1	1	53N49	21E56	-1:27:44
Augustów 4	3	53N51	22E59	-1:31:56
Auschwitz → Oświęcim 1	1	50N03	19E12	-1:16:48
Babimost 1	1	52N10	15E51	-1:03:24
Baborów 1	1	50N09	17E59	-1:11:56
Bad Polzin → Połczyn Zdrój 1	1	53N46	16E06	-1:04:24
Bad Warmbrunn → Cieplice Śląskie-Zd 1	1	50N52	15E41	-1:02:44
Baldenburg → Biały Bór 1	1	53N54	16E51	-1:07:24
Banie 1	1	53N08	14E38	-0:58:32
Baranów Sandomierski 2	2	50N30	21E33	-1:26:12
Barcin 3	2	52N52	17E57	-1:11:48
Barczewo 1	1	53N50	20E42	-1:22:48
Barlinek 1	1	53N00	15E12	-1:00:48
Barnówko 1	1	52N48	14E45	-0:59:00
Bartoszyce 1	1	54N16	20E49	-1:23:16
Bärwalde → Mieszkowice 1	1	52N46	14E30	-0:58:00
Barwice 1	1	53N45	16E22	-1:05:28
Bełchatów 4	3	51N22	19E21	-1:17:24
Belgard → Białogard 1	1	54N01	16E00	-1:04:00
Bełżec 2	2	50N24	23E26	-1:33:44
Bełżyce 4	3	51N11	22E18	-1:29:12
Bernstadt → Bierutów 1	1	51N08	17E32	-1:10:08
Bernstein → Pełczyce 1	1	53N03	15E18	-1:01:12
Beuthen → Bytom 1	1	50N22	18E54	-1:15:36
Biała 1	1	50N23	17E40	-1:10:40
Biała Piska 1	1	53N37	22E04	-1:28:16
Biała Podlaska 4	3	52N02	23E06	-1:32:24
Biała Rawska 4	3	51N49	20E29	-1:21:56
Białobrzegi 4	3	51N40	20E57	-1:23:48
Białogard 1	1	54N01	16E00	-1:04:00
Biały Bór 1	1	53N54	16E51	-1:07:24
Białystok 5	4	53N09	23E09	-1:32:36
Biecz 2	2	49N44	21E14	-1:24:56
Bielawa 1	1	50N41	16E38	-1:06:32
Bielin 1	1	52N47	14E28	-0:57:52
Bielsk 4	3	52N40	19E49	-1:19:16
Bielsko-Biała 2	2	49N49	19E02	-1:16:08
Bielsk Podlaski 5	4	52N47	23E12	-1:32:48
Bieruń Stary 1	1	50N06	19E06	-1:16:24
Bierutów 1	1	51N08	17E32	-1:10:08
Biłgoraj 4	3	50N34	22E43	-1:30:52
Bischofsburg → Biskupiec 1	1	53N52	20E58	-1:23:52
Bischofstal → Ujazd 1	1	50N24	18E22	-1:13:28
Bischofstein → Bisztynek 1	1	54N06	20E55	-1:23:40
Biskupiec 1	1	53N52	20E58	-1:23:52
Bisztynek 1	1	54N06	20E55	-1:23:40
Błaszki 4	3	51N39	18E27	-1:13:48
Błażowa 2	2	49N54	22E05	-1:28:20
Bobolice 1	1	53N57	16E36	-1:06:24
Bochnia 2	2	49N58	20E26	-1:21:44
Boczów 1	1	52N19	14E58	-0:59:52
Bodzentyn 4	3	50N56	20E57	-1:23:48
Bogatynia 1	1	50N53	15E00	-1:00:00
Bojadła 1	1	51N57	15E50	-1:03:20
Bolesławiec 1	1	51N16	15E34	-1:02:16
Boleszkowice 1	1	52N44	14E36	-0:58:24
Borzyszkowy 1	1	54N03	17E22	-1:09:28
Boyadel → Bojadła 1	1	51N57	15E50	-1:03:20
Braniewo 1	1	54N24	19E50	-1:19:20
Brańsk 4	3	52N45	22E51	-1:31:24
Braunsberg → Braniewo 1	1	54N24	19E50	-1:19:20

Breslau → Wrocław 1
1 51N06 17E00 -1:08:00
Brieg → Brzeg 1 1 50N52 17E27 -1:09:48
Brodnica 3 2 53N16 19E23 -1:17:32
Brody 1 1 51N45 14E45 -0:59:00
Brok 4 3 52N43 21E52 -1:27:28
Bromberg → Bydgoszcz 3
2 53N08 18E00 -1:12:00
Brusy 3 2 53N53 17E45 -1:11:00
Brwinów 4 3 52N09 20E43 -1:22:52
Brzeg 1 1 50N52 17E27 -1:09:48
Brześć Kujawski 4
3 52N37 18E55 -1:15:40
Brzesko 2 2 49N59 20E36 -1:22:24
Brzeszcze 2 2 49N59 19E08 -1:16:32
Brzeziny 4 3 51N48 19E46 -1:19:04
Brzozów 2 2 49N42 22E02 -1:28:08
Bublitz → Bobolice 1
1 53N57 16E36 -1:06:24
Buk 3 2 52N22 16E31 -1:06:04
Busko Zdrój 4 3 50N28 20E44 -1:22:56
Bütow → Bytów 1 1 54N11 17E30 -1:10:00
Bychawa 4 3 51N01 22E32 -1:30:08
Byczyna 1 1 51N07 18E11 -1:12:44
Bydgoszcz 3 2 53N08 18E00 -1:12:00
Bystrzyca Kłodzka 1
1 50N18 16E38 -1:06:32
Bytom (Beuthen) 1
1 50N22 18E54 -1:15:36
Bytów 1 1 54N11 17E30 -1:10:00
Cammin → Kamień Pomorski 1
1 53N58 14E46 -0:59:04
Cedynia 1 1 52N50 14E14 -0:56:56
Chęciny 4 3 50N48 20E28 -1:21:52
Chełm 4 3 51N10 23E28 -1:33:52
Chełmno 3 2 53N22 18E26 -1:13:44
Chełmża 3 2 53N12 18E37 -1:14:28
Chmielnik 4 3 50N37 20E46 -1:23:04
Chocianów 1 1 51N25 15E55 -1:03:40
Chociwel 1 1 53N28 15E19 -1:01:16
Chodecz 4 3 52N24 19E01 -1:16:04
Chodzież 3 2 52N59 16E56 -1:07:44
Chojna 1 1 52N58 14E28 -0:57:52
Chojnice 3 2 53N42 17E34 -1:10:16
Chojnów 1 1 51N17 15E56 -1:03:44
Choroszcz 5 4 53N09 22E59 -1:31:56
Chorzele 4 3 53N16 20E55 -1:23:40
Chorzow 1 1 50N19 18E57 -1:15:48
Choszczno 1 1 53N10 15E26 -1:01:44
Christburg → Dzierzgoń 1
1 53N56 19E21 -1:17:24
Chrzanów 2 2 50N09 19E24 -1:17:36
Ciechanów 4 3 52N53 20E38 -1:22:32
Ciechanowiec 4 3 52N42 22E31 -1:30:04
Ciechocinek 4 3 52N52 18E49 -1:15:16
Cieplice Śląskie-Zdrój 1
1 50N52 15E41 -1:02:44
Cieszanów 2 2 50N16 23E08 -1:32:32
Cieszyn 2 2 49N45 18E38 -1:14:32
Ćmielów 4 3 50N53 21E31 -1:26:04
Cosel → Koźle 1 1 50N20 18E08 -1:12:32
Cracovie → Kraków 2
2 50N03 19E58 -1:19:52
Crossen → Krosno Odrzańskie 1
1 52N04 15E05 -1:00:20
Cybinka 1 1 52N12 14E48 -0:59:12
Czaplinek 1 1 53N34 16E14 -1:04:56
Czarna Białostocka 5
4 53N19 23E16 -1:33:04
Czarna Woda 3 2 53N51 18E06 -1:12:24
Czarne 1 1 53N42 16E57 -1:07:48
Czarnków 3 2 52N55 16E34 -1:06:16
Czechowice-Dziedzice 2
2 49N54 19E00 -1:16:00
Czempiń 3 2 52N10 16E47 -1:07:08
Czerniejewo 3 2 52N26 17E30 -1:10:00
Czersk 3 2 53N48 18E00 -1:12:00
Czerwieńsk 1 1 52N01 15E25 -1:01:40
Częstochowa 4 3 50N49 19E06 -1:16:24
Człopa 1 1 53N06 16E08 -1:04:32
Człuchów 1 1 53N41 17E21 -1:09:24
Czudec 2 2 49N57 21E50 -1:27:20
Daber → Dobra 1 1 53N35 15E18 -1:01:12
Dąbie 4 3 52N06 18E49 -1:15:16
Dąbrowa Białostocka 5
4 53N39 23E20 -1:33:20
Dąbrowa Tarnowska 2
2 50N11 21E00 -1:24:00
Daleszyce 4 3 50N48 20E48 -1:23:12
Danzig → Gdańsk 6
2 54N23 18E40 -1:14:40
Darłowo 1 1 54N26 16E23 -1:05:32
Dębica 2 2 50N04 21E24 -1:25:36
Dęblin 4 3 51N35 21E50 -1:27:20
Dębno 1 1 52N45 14E40 -0:58:40
Debrzno 1 1 53N33 17E14 -1:08:56
Deutsch Eylau → Iława 1
1 53N37 19E33 -1:18:12
Deutsch Krone → Wałcz 1
1 53N17 16E28 -1:05:52
Dievenow → Dziwnów 1
1 54N03 14E45 -0:59:00
Dirschau → Tczew 3
2 54N06 18E47 -1:15:08
Dobczyce 2 2 49N54 20E06 -1:20:24
Dobiegniew 1 1 52N59 15E47 -1:03:08
Dobra 4 3 51N54 18E37 -1:14:28
Dobra 1 1 53N35 15E18 -1:01:12
Dobre Miasto 1 1 53N59 20E25 -1:21:40
Dobrodzień 1 1 50N44 18E27 -1:13:48
Dobrzany 1 1 53N22 15E25 -1:01:40
Dobrzyń nad Wisłą 4
3 52N38 19E20 -1:17:20
Dolsk 3 2 52N00 17E03 -1:08:12

Dramburg → Drawsko Pomorskie 1
1 53N32 15E48 -1:03:12
Drawno 1 1 53N13 15E45 -1:03:00
Drawsko Pomorskie 1
1 53N32 15E48 -1:03:12
Drezdenko 1 1 52N51 15E50 -1:03:20
Driesen → Drezdenko 1
1 52N51 15E50 -1:03:20
Drohiczyn 4 3 52N24 22E41 -1:30:44
Drossen → Ośno 1
1 52N28 14E50 -0:59:20
Drzewica 4 3 51N27 20E28 -1:21:52
Drzewice 1 1 52N38 14E38 -0:58:32
Dukla 2 2 49N34 21E41 -1:26:44
Dynów 2 2 49N49 22E14 -1:28:56
Działdowo 3 2 53N15 20E10 -1:20:40
Działoszyce 4 3 50N22 20E21 -1:21:24
Dzierzgoń 1 1 53N56 19E21 -1:17:24
Dzierżoniów (Reichenbach) 1
1 50N44 16E39 -1:06:36
Dziwnów 1 1 54N03 14E45 -0:59:00
Elbing → Elbląg 1
1 54N10 19E25 -1:17:40
Elbląg (Elbing) 1
1 54N10 19E25 -1:17:40
Ełk 1 1 53N50 22E22 -1:29:28
Falkenberg → Niemodlin 1
1 50N39 17E37 -1:10:28
Falkenburg → Złocieniec 1
1 53N33 16E01 -1:04:04
Festenberg → Twardogóra 1
1 51N22 17E28 -1:09:52
Flatow → Złotów 1
1 53N22 17E02 -1:08:08
Frampol 4 3 50N41 22E40 -1:30:40
Frankenstein → Ząbkowice Śląskie 1
1 50N36 16E53 -1:07:32
Frauenburg → Frombork 1
1 54N22 19E41 -1:18:44
Freiburg → Świebodzice 1
1 50N52 16E19 -1:05:16
Freienwalde in Pommern → Chociwel 1
1 53N28 15E19 -1:01:16
Freistadt → Kożuchów 1
1 51N45 15E35 -1:02:20
Freiwaldau → Gozdnica 1
1 51N26 15E06 -1:00:24
Friedeberg in der Neumark → Strzelce Kr
1 52N53 15E32 -1:02:08
Friedland → Mieroszów 1
1 50N41 16E10 -1:04:40
Frombork 1 1 54N22 19E41 -1:18:44
Fürstenfelde → Boleszkowice 1
1 52N44 14E36 -0:58:24
Gąbin 4 3 52N25 19E44 -1:18:56
Gardno 1 1 53N15 14E38 -0:58:32
Garwolin 4 3 51N54 21E37 -1:26:28
Gassen → Jasień 1
1 51N46 15E01 -1:00:04
Gdańsk (Danzig) 6
2 54N23 18E40 -1:14:40
Gdynia 3 2 54N32 18E33 -1:14:12
Gehlenburg → Biała Piska 1
1 53N37 22E04 -1:28:16
Giesebitz → Izbica 1
1 54N42 17E26 -1:09:44
Giżycko 1 1 54N03 21E47 -1:27:08
Glatz → Kłodzko 1
1 50N27 16E39 -1:06:36
Gleiwitz → Gliwice 1
1 50N17 18E40 -1:14:40
Gliwice (Gleiwitz) 1
1 50N17 18E40 -1:14:40
Glogau → Głogów 1
1 51N40 16E05 -1:04:20
Głogów 1 1 51N40 16E05 -1:04:20
Głogów 2 2 50N10 21E58 -1:27:52
Głogówek 1 1 50N22 17E51 -1:11:24
Głowno 4 3 51N58 19E44 -1:18:56
Głubczyce 1 1 50N13 17E49 -1:11:16
Głuchołazy 1 1 50N20 17E22 -1:09:28
Gnesen → Gniezno 3
2 52N31 17E37 -1:10:28
Gniew 3 2 53N51 18E49 -1:15:16
Gniewkowo 3 2 52N54 18E25 -1:13:40
Gniezno 3 2 52N31 17E37 -1:10:28
Gogolin 1 1 50N30 18E02 -1:12:08
Gołańcz 3 2 52N57 17E18 -1:09:12
Golczewo 1 1 53N49 14E59 -0:59:56
Gołdap 1 1 54N19 22E19 -1:29:16
Goldberg → Złotoryja 1
1 51N08 15E55 -1:03:40
Goleniów 1 1 53N36 14E50 -0:59:20
Golina 4 3 52N16 18E05 -1:12:20
Gollnow → Goleniów 1
1 53N36 14E50 -0:59:20
Golub-Dobrzyń 3 2 53N08 19E02 -1:16:08
Goniądz 4 3 53N30 22E45 -1:31:00
Góra 1 1 51N40 16E33 -1:06:12
Góra Kalwaria 4 3 51N59 21E12 -1:24:48
Gorlice 2 2 49N40 21E10 -1:24:40
Górowo Iławeckie 1
1 54N17 20E30 -1:22:00
Górzno 3 2 53N13 19E38 -1:18:32
Gorzów Śląski 4 3 51N02 18E24 -1:13:36
Gorzów Wielkopolski (Landsberg an War)
1 52N44 15E15 -1:01:00
Górzyca 1 1 52N29 14E40 -0:58:40
Gostyń 3 2 51N53 17E00 -1:08:00
Gostynin 4 3 52N26 19E29 -1:17:56
Gozdnica 1 1 51N26 15E06 -1:00:24
Gozdowice 1 1 52N45 14E18 -0:57:12
Grabowiec 4 3 50N50 23E33 -1:34:12
Grabów nad Prosną 3
2 51N31 18E06 -1:12:24

Grajewo 4 3 53N39 22E27 -1:29:48
Graudenz → Grudziądz 3
2 53N29 18E45 -1:15:00
Greifenberg → Gryfice 1
1 53N56 15E12 -1:00:48
Greifenhagen → Gryfino 1
1 53N12 14E30 -0:58:00
Grodków 1 1 50N43 17E22 -1:09:28
Grodzisk Mazowiecki 4
3 52N07 20E37 -1:22:28
Grodzisk (wielkopolski) 3
2 52N14 16E22 -1:05:28
Grójec 4 3 51N52 20E52 -1:23:28
Gross Möllen → Mielno 1
1 54N16 16E01 -1:04:04
Gross Strehlitz → Strzelce Opolskie 1
1 50N31 18E19 -1:13:16
Gross Wartenberg → Syców 3
2 51N19 17E43 -1:10:52
Grottkau → Grodków 1
1 50N43 17E22 -1:09:28
Grudziądz 3 2 53N29 18E45 -1:15:00
Grünberg → Zielona Góra 1
1 51N56 15E31 -1:02:04
Grybów 2 2 49N38 20E56 -1:23:44
Gryfice 1 1 53N56 15E12 -1:00:48
Gryfino 1 1 53N12 14E30 -0:58:00
Gubin 1 1 51N56 14E45 -0:59:00
Guhrau → Góra 1 1 51N40 16E33 -1:06:12
Guttentag → Dobrodzień 1
1 50N44 18E27 -1:13:48
Guttstadt → Dobre Miasto 1
1 53N59 20E25 -1:21:40
Habelschwerdt → Bystrzyca Kłodzka 1
1 50N18 16E38 -1:06:32
Hajnówka 5 4 52N45 23E36 -1:34:24
Halbau → Iłowa 1
1 51N30 15E12 -1:00:48
Hammermühle → Kępice 1
1 54N15 16E52 -1:07:28
Hammerstein → Czarne 1
1 53N42 16E57 -1:07:48
Haynau → Chojnów 1
1 51N17 15E56 -1:03:44
Heilsberg → Lidzbark Warmiński 1
1 54N09 20E35 -1:22:20
Hel 3 2 54N37 18E48 -1:15:12
Herrnstadt → Wąsosz 1
1 51N34 16E42 -1:06:48
Heyderbreck → Kędzierzyn 1
1 50N20 18E12 -1:12:48
Hindenburg → Zabrze 1
1 50N18 18E46 -1:15:04
Hirschberg → Jelenia Góra 1
1 50N55 15E46 -1:03:04
Hohensalza → Inowrocław 3
2 52N48 18E15 -1:13:00
Hohenstein → Olsztynek 1
1 53N36 20E17 -1:21:08
Hrubieszów 4 3 50N49 23E55 -1:35:40
Iława 1 1 53N37 19E33 -1:18:12
Iłowa 1 1 51N30 15E12 -1:00:48
Iłża 4 3 51N11 21E14 -1:24:56
Inowrocław 3 2 52N48 18E15 -1:13:00
Ińsko 1 1 53N27 15E33 -1:02:12
Izbica 4 3 50N54 23E09 -1:32:36
Izbica 1 1 54N42 17E26 -1:09:44
Jabłonka 2 2 49N29 19E41 -1:18:44
Jabłonowo 3 2 53N24 19E09 -1:16:36
Jakobshagen → Dobrzany 1
1 53N22 15E25 -1:01:40
Janikowo 3 2 52N45 18E07 -1:12:28
Janowiec Wielkopolski 3
2 52N46 17E31 -1:10:04
Janów Lubelski 4
3 50N43 22E24 -1:29:36
Jarocin 3 2 51N59 17E31 -1:10:04
Jarosław 2 2 50N02 22E42 -1:30:48
Jasień 1 1 51N46 15E01 -1:00:04
Jasienica 1 1 53N37 14E32 -0:58:08
Jasło 2 2 49N45 21E29 -1:25:56
Jastarnia 3 2 54N43 18E40 -1:14:40
Jastrow → Jastrowie 1
1 53N26 16E49 -1:07:16
Jastrowie 1 1 53N26 16E49 -1:07:16
Jauer → Jawor 1 1 51N03 16E11 -1:04:44
Jawor 1 1 51N03 16E11 -1:04:44
Jaworzno 1 1 50N13 19E15 -1:17:00
Jędrzejów 4 3 50N39 20E18 -1:21:12
Jedwabne 4 3 53N17 22E19 -1:29:16
Jelenia Góra (Hirschberg) 1
1 50N55 15E46 -1:03:04
Jeziorany 1 1 53N58 20E46 -1:23:04
Johannisburg → Pisz 1
1 53N38 21E49 -1:27:16
Jordanów 2 2 49N40 19E50 -1:19:20
Józefów 4 3 52N09 21E12 -1:24:48
Jutrosin 3 2 51N40 17E10 -1:08:40
Kalety 3 2 50N34 18E54 -1:15:36
Kalisch → Kalisz 4
3 51N46 18E06 -1:12:24
Kalisz 4 3 51N46 18E06 -1:12:24
Kalisz Pomorski 1
1 53N19 15E54 -1:03:36
Kallies → Kalisz Pomorski 1
1 53N19 15E54 -1:03:36
Kałuszyn 4 3 52N13 21E49 -1:27:16
Kalwaria Zebrzydowska 2
2 49N52 19E41 -1:18:44
Kamień Krajeński 3
2 53N33 17E32 -1:10:08
Kamienna Góra 1 1 50N47 16E01 -1:04:04
Kamień Pomorski 1
1 53N58 14E46 -0:59:04
Kamieńsk 4 3 51N12 19E30 -1:18:00

Kańczuga 2   2 49N59 22E24 -1:29:36
Kanth → Kąty Wrocławskie 1
  1 51N02 16E46 -1:07:04
Karczew 4   3 52N06 21E15 -1:25:00
Karlino 1   1 54N03 15E51 -1:03:24
Karsin 3   2 53N54 17E56 -1:11:44
Kartuzy 3   2 54N20 18E12 -1:12:48
Katowice 1   1 50N16 19E00 -1:16:00
Katscher → Kietrz 1
  1 50N05 18E01 -1:12:04
Kattowitz → Katowice 1
  1 50N16 19E00 -1:16:00
Kąty Wrocławskie 1
  1 51N02 16E46 -1:07:04
Kauffung → Wojcieszów 1
  1 50N58 15E56 -1:03:44
Kazimierza Wielka 4
  3 50N16 20E30 -1:22:00
Kazimierz Dolny 4
  3 51N20 21E58 -1:27:52
Kcynia 3   2 53N00 17E30 -1:10:00
Kędzierzyn 1   1 50N20 18E12 -1:12:48
Kępice 1   1 54N15 16E52 -1:07:28
Kępno 3   2 51N17 17E59 -1:11:56
Kętrzyn (Rastenburg) 1
  1 54N06 21E23 -1:25:32
Kęty 2   2 49N53 19E13 -1:16:52
Kielce 4   3 50N52 20E37 -1:22:28
Kietrz 1   1 50N05 18E01 -1:12:04
Kikorze 1   1 53N39 15E01 -1:00:04
Kłecko 3   2 52N38 17E26 -1:09:44
Kleczew 4   3 52N23 18E10 -1:12:40
Kłobuck 4   3 50N55 18E57 -1:15:48
Kłodawa 4   3 52N16 18E55 -1:15:40
Kłodzko 1   1 50N27 16E39 -1:06:36
Kłomnice 4   3 50N56 19E21 -1:17:24
Kluczbork 1   1 50N59 18E13 -1:12:52
Knyszyn 5   4 53N19 22E55 -1:31:40
Kobylanka 1   1 53N19 14E50 -0:59:20
Kobylin 3   2 51N43 17E13 -1:08:52
Kock 4   3 51N39 22E27 -1:29:48
Kohlfurt → Węgliniec 1
  1 51N17 15E13 -1:00:52
Kolberg → Kołobrzeg 1
  1 54N12 15E33 -1:02:12
Kolbuszowa 2   2 50N15 21E47 -1:27:08
Kołczewo 1   1 53N58 14E38 -0:58:32
Kolno 4   3 53N25 21E56 -1:27:44
Koło 4   3 52N12 18E38 -1:14:32
Kołobrzeg 1   1 54N12 15E33 -1:02:12
Koluszki 4   3 51N44 19E49 -1:19:16
Koniecpol 4   3 50N48 19E41 -1:18:44
Königsberg → Chojna 1
  1 52N58 14E28 -0:57:52
Konin 4   3 52N13 18E16 -1:13:04
Końskie 4   3 51N12 20E26 -1:21:44
Konstadt → Wołczyn 1
  1 51N01 18E03 -1:12:12
Konstantynów Łódzki 4
  3 51N45 19E20 -1:17:20
Kopice 1   1 53N44 14E32 -0:58:08
Körlin → Karlino 1
  1 54N03 15E51 -1:03:24
Kórnik 3   2 52N17 17E04 -1:08:16
Koronowo 3   2 53N19 17E57 -1:11:48
Korschen → Korsze 1
  1 54N10 21E09 -1:24:36
Korsze 1   1 54N10 21E09 -1:24:36
Kościan 3   2 52N06 16E38 -1:06:32
Kościerzyna 3   2 54N08 18E00 -1:12:00
Köslin → Koszalin 1
  1 54N12 16E09 -1:04:36
Kostrzyn 1   1 52N37 14E39 -0:58:36
Koszalin (Köslin) 1
  1 54N12 16E09 -1:04:36
Koszyce 4   3 50N11 20E35 -1:22:20
Kotzenau → Chocianów 1
  1 51N25 15E55 -1:03:40
Kowal 4   3 52N32 19E09 -1:16:36
Kowalewo Pomorskie 3
  2 53N10 18E53 -1:15:32
Koziegłowy 4   3 50N36 19E09 -1:16:36
Kozienice 4   3 51N35 21E33 -1:26:12
Koźle 1   1 50N20 18E08 -1:12:32
Koźmin 3   2 51N50 17E28 -1:09:52
Kożuchów 1   1 51N45 15E35 -1:02:20
Krajenka 1   1 53N19 17E00 -1:08:00
Krajnik Dolny 1   1 53N05 14E25 -0:57:40
Krakau → Kraków 2
  2 50N03 19E58 -1:19:52
Kraków 2   2 50N03 19E58 -1:19:52
Krapkowice 1   1 50N29 17E56 -1:11:44
Krappitz → Krapkowice 1
  1 50N29 17E56 -1:11:44
Kraśnik 4   3 50N56 22E13 -1:28:52
Kraśnik Fabryczny 4
  3 50N58 22E12 -1:28:48
Krasnobród 4   3 50N33 23E13 -1:32:52
Krasnosielc 4   3 53N03 21E10 -1:24:40
Krasnystaw 4   3 50N59 23E10 -1:32:40
Kreuz an der Ostbahn → Krzyż 1
  1 52N54 16E01 -1:04:04
Kreuzburg → Kluczbork 1
  1 50N59 18E13 -1:12:52
Krobia 3   2 51N47 16E58 -1:07:52
Krojanke → Krajenka 1
  1 53N19 17E00 -1:08:00
Krokowa 3   2 54N48 18E11 -1:12:44
Krościenko 2   2 49N27 20E26 -1:21:44
Krośniewice 4   3 52N16 19E10 -1:16:40
Krosno 2   2 49N42 21E46 -1:27:04
Krosno Odrzańskie 1
  1 52N04 15E05 -1:00:20
Krotoszyn 3   2 51N42 17E26 -1:09:44
Kruszwica 3   2 52N41 18E19 -1:13:16

Krynica 2   2 49N25 20E56 -1:23:44
Krzepice 4   3 50N58 18E44 -1:14:56
Krzeszowice 2   2 50N09 19E39 -1:18:36
Krzeszyce 1   1 52N36 15E01 -1:00:04
Krzywiń 3   2 51N58 16E49 -1:07:16
Krzyż 1   1 52N54 16E01 -1:04:04
Książ Wielkopolski 3
  2 52N05 17E14 -1:08:56
Kunowice 1   1 52N20 14E50 -0:59:20
Küstrin → Kostrzyn 1
  1 52N37 14E39 -0:58:36
Kutno 4   3 52N15 19E23 -1:17:32
Kwidzyn 3   2 53N45 18E56 -1:15:44
Labes → Łobez 1   1 53N39 15E36 -1:02:24
Łabiszyn 3   2 52N57 17E55 -1:11:40
Lähn → Wleń 1   1 51N01 15E40 -1:02:40
Łańcut 2   2 50N05 22E13 -1:28:52
Landeck in Westpreussen → Lędyczek 1
  1 53N33 16E58 -1:07:52
Landsberg an der Warthe → Gorzów W. 1
  1 52N44 15E15 -1:01:00
Landsberg in Oberschlesien → Gorzów S 4
  3 51N02 18E24 -1:13:36
Landsberg in Ostpreussen → Górowo I. 1
  1 54N17 20E30 -1:22:00
Langenbielau → Bielawa 1
  1 50N41 16E38 -1:06:32
Łapy 4   3 53N00 22E53 -1:31:32
Łasin 3   2 53N32 19E05 -1:16:20
Łask 4   3 51N36 19E07 -1:16:28
Łaskarzew 4   3 51N48 21E35 -1:26:20
Latowicz 4   3 52N02 21E48 -1:27:12
Lauban → Lubań 1
  1 51N08 15E18 -1:01:12
Lauenburg → Lębork 1
  1 54N33 17E44 -1:10:56
Łeba 1   1 54N47 17E33 -1:10:12
Lębork 1   1 54N33 17E44 -1:10:56
Łęczna 4   3 51N19 22E52 -1:31:28
Łęczyca 4   3 52N04 19E13 -1:16:52
Lędyczek 1   1 53N33 16E58 -1:07:52
Legionowo 4   3 52N25 20E56 -1:23:44
Legnica (Liegnitz) 1
  1 51N13 16E09 -1:04:36
Łęknice 1   1 51N35 14E45 -0:59:00
Lemierzyce 1   1 52N35 14E56 -0:59:44
Leobschütz → Głubczyce 1
  1 50N13 17E49 -1:11:16
Lesko 2   2 49N29 22E21 -1:29:24
Leśna 1   1 51N02 15E16 -1:01:04
Leszno 3   2 51N51 16E35 -1:06:20
Lewin Brzeski 1   1 50N46 17E37 -1:10:28
Leżajsk 2   2 50N16 22E24 -1:29:36
Lidzbark 3   2 53N17 19E49 -1:19:16
Lidzbark Warmiński 1
  1 54N09 20E35 -1:22:20
Liebenthal → Lubomierz 1
  1 51N01 15E30 -1:02:00
Liegnitz → Legnica 1
  1 51N13 16E09 -1:04:36
Limanowa 2   2 49N43 20E26 -1:21:44
Lipiany 1   1 53N00 14E59 -0:59:56
Lipno 4   3 52N51 19E10 -1:16:40
Lipsko 4   3 51N09 21E39 -1:26:36
Litzmannstadt → Łódź 4
  3 51N46 19E30 -1:18:00
Łobez 1   1 53N39 15E36 -1:02:24
Łobżenica 3   2 53N16 17E15 -1:09:00
Lodsch → Łódź 4   3 51N46 19E30 -1:18:00
Łódź 4   3 51N46 19E30 -1:18:00
Łomazy 4   3 51N55 23E10 -1:32:40
Łomża 4   3 53N11 22E05 -1:28:20
Łopuszno 4   3 50N57 20E15 -1:21:00
Łosice 4   3 52N14 22E43 -1:30:52
Lötzen → Giżycko 1
  1 54N03 21E47 -1:27:08
Löwen → Lewin Brzeski 1
  1 50N46 17E37 -1:10:28
Löwenberg → Lwówek Śląski 1
  1 51N07 15E35 -1:02:20
Łowicz 4   3 52N07 19E56 -1:19:44
Lubaczów 2   2 50N10 23E07 -1:32:28
Lubań 1   1 51N08 15E18 -1:01:12
Lubanowo 1   1 53N09 14E36 -0:58:24
Lubartów 4   3 51N28 22E38 -1:30:32
Lubawa 1   1 53N30 19E45 -1:19:00
Lüben → Lubin 1   1 51N24 16E13 -1:04:52
Lubień Kujawski 4
  3 52N25 19E10 -1:16:40
Lubin 1   1 51N24 16E13 -1:04:52
Lubin 1   1 53N50 14E25 -0:57:40
Lublin 4   3 51N15 22E35 -1:30:20
Lubliniec 3   2 50N40 18E41 -1:14:44
Lubomierz 1   1 51N01 15E30 -1:02:00
Luboń 3   2 52N23 16E54 -1:07:36
Lubraniec 4   3 52N33 18E50 -1:15:20
Lubsko 1   1 51N46 14E59 -0:59:56
Łuków 4   3 51N56 22E23 -1:29:32
Łupawa 1   1 54N26 17E24 -1:09:36
Lupow → Łupawa 1
  1 54N26 17E24 -1:09:36
Lwówek 3   2 52N28 16E10 -1:04:40
Lwówek Śląski 1   1 51N07 15E35 -1:02:20
Lyck → Ełk 1   1 53N50 22E22 -1:29:28
Maków Mazowiecki 4
  3 52N52 21E06 -1:24:24
Maków Podhalański 2
  2 49N44 19E41 -1:18:44
Malapane → Ozimek 1
  1 50N41 18E13 -1:12:52
Malbork 1   1 54N02 19E01 -1:16:04
Malczyce 1   1 51N14 16E29 -1:05:56
Mallwitz → Małowice 1
  1 51N34 15E27 -1:01:48
Małowice 1   1 51N34 15E27 -1:01:48

Maltsch → Malczyce 1
  1 51N14 16E29 -1:05:56
Margonin 3   2 52N59 17E05 -1:08:20
Marienburg → Malbork 1
  1 54N02 19E01 -1:16:04
Märkisch Friedland → Mirosławiec 1
  1 53N21 16E05 -1:04:20
Marklissa → Leśna 1
  1 51N02 15E16 -1:01:04
Maszewo 1   1 53N29 15E02 -1:00:08
Maszewo 1   1 52N06 14E55 -0:59:40
Mehlsack → Pieniężno 1
  1 54N15 20E08 -1:20:32
Meseritz → Międzyrzecz 1
  1 52N28 15E35 -1:02:20
Miasteczko Krajeńskie 3
  2 53N06 17E01 -1:08:04
Miastko 1   1 54N01 17E00 -1:08:00
Michów 4   3 51N32 22E19 -1:29:16
Miechów 4   3 50N23 20E01 -1:20:04
Międzybórz 3   2 51N24 17E40 -1:10:40
Międzychód 1   1 52N36 15E55 -1:03:40
Międzylesie 1   1 50N10 16E40 -1:06:40
Międzyrzec Podlaski 4
  3 52N00 22E47 -1:31:08
Międzyrzecz 1   1 52N28 15E35 -1:02:20
Międzyzdroje 1   1 53N55 14E28 -0:57:52
Miejska Górka 3   2 51N40 16E58 -1:07:52
Mielec 2   2 50N18 21E25 -1:25:40
Mielno 1   1 54N16 16E01 -1:04:04
Mieroszów 1   1 50N41 16E10 -1:04:40
Mieszkowice 1   1 52N46 14E30 -0:58:00
Mikołajki 1   1 53N49 21E36 -1:26:24
Mikołów 1   1 50N11 18E55 -1:15:40
Mikstat 3   2 51N32 17E59 -1:11:56
Milicz 1   1 51N32 17E17 -1:09:08
Militsch → Milicz 1
  1 51N32 17E17 -1:09:08
Miłosław 3   2 52N13 17E29 -1:09:56
Mińsk Mazowiecki 4
  3 52N11 21E34 -1:26:16
Mirosławiec 1   1 53N21 16E05 -1:04:20
Mitteldorf → Międzychód 1
  1 52N36 15E55 -1:03:40
Mittwalde → Międzylesie 1
  1 50N10 16E40 -1:06:40
Mława 4   3 53N06 20E23 -1:21:32
Mogielnica 4   3 51N42 20E43 -1:22:52
Mogilno 3   2 52N40 17E58 -1:11:52
Mohrungen → Morąg 1
  1 53N56 19E56 -1:19:44
Mońki 5   4 53N24 22E49 -1:31:16
Morąg 1   1 53N56 19E56 -1:19:44
Mordy 4   3 52N13 22E31 -1:30:04
Moryń 1   1 52N49 14E13 -0:56:52
Mosina 3   2 52N16 16E51 -1:07:24
Mrągowo 1   1 53N52 21E19 -1:25:16
Mrocza 3   2 53N14 17E36 -1:10:24
Mszana Dolna 2   2 49N42 20E05 -1:20:20
Mszczonów 4   3 51N58 20E31 -1:22:04
Münsterberg → Ziębice 1
  1 50N37 17E00 -1:08:00
Murowana Goślina 3
  2 52N35 17E01 -1:08:04
Muszyna 2   2 49N21 20E54 -1:23:36
Myślenice 2   2 49N51 19E56 -1:19:44
Myślibórz 1   1 52N55 14E52 -0:59:28
Mysłowice 1   1 50N15 19E07 -1:16:28
Myszków 4   3 50N36 19E20 -1:17:20
Myszyniec 4   3 53N24 21E21 -1:25:24
Nagłowice 4   3 50N41 20E06 -1:20:24
Nakło nad Notecią 3
  2 53N08 17E35 -1:10:20
Nałęczów 4   3 51N18 22E11 -1:28:44
Namslau → Namysłów 1
  1 51N05 17E42 -1:10:48
Namysłów 1   1 51N05 17E42 -1:10:48
Narol 2   2 50N22 23E21 -1:33:24
Nasielsk 4   3 52N36 20E48 -1:23:12
Naumburg am Queiss → Nowogrodziec 1
  1 51N12 15E25 -1:01:40
Neidenburg → Nidzica 1
  1 53N22 20E26 -1:21:44
Neu Bentschen → Zbąszynek 1
  1 52N15 15E50 -1:03:20
Neudamm → Dębno 1
  1 52N45 14E40 -0:58:40
Neumarkt → Środa Śląska 1
  1 51N10 16E36 -1:06:24
Neumittelwalde → Międzybórz 3
  2 51N24 17E40 -1:10:40
Neurode → Nowa Ruda 1
  1 50N35 16E31 -1:06:04
Neusalz → Nowa Sól 1
  1 51N48 15E44 -1:02:56
Neusandetz 2   2 49N38 20E42 -1:22:48
Neustädtel → Nowe Miasteczko 1
  1 51N42 15E45 -1:03:00
Neustadt in Oberschlesien → Prudnik 1
  1 50N19 17E34 -1:10:16
Neustettin → Szczecinek 1
  1 53N43 16E42 -1:06:48
Neuteich → Nowy Staw 6
  1 54N09 19E00 -1:16:00
Neuwarp → Nowe Warpno 1
  1 53N44 14E16 -0:57:04
Neuwedell → Drawno 1
  1 53N13 15E45 -1:03:00
Nidzica 1   1 53N22 20E26 -1:21:44
Niedersee → Ruciane-Nida 1
  1 53N39 21E35 -1:26:20
Niemodlin 1   1 50N39 17E37 -1:10:28
Niepołomice 2   2 50N03 20E13 -1:20:52
Nieszawa 4   3 52N50 18E55 -1:15:40

Nikolaiken → Mikołajki 1 1 53N49 21E36 -1:26:24
Nörenberg → Ińsko 1 1 53N27 15E33 -1:02:12
Nowa Dęba 2 2 50N26 21E46 -1:27:04
Nowa Ruda 1 1 50N35 16E31 -1:06:04
Nowa Sól (Neusalz) 1 1 51N48 15E44 -1:02:56
Nowe 3 2 53N40 18E43 -1:14:52
Nowe Miasteczko 1 1 51N42 15E45 -1:03:00
Nowe Miasto Lubawskie 3 2 53N27 19E35 -1:18:20
Nowe Miasto nad Pilicą 4 3 51N38 20E35 -1:22:20
Nowe Warpno 1 1 53N44 14E16 -0:57:04
Nowogard 1 1 53N40 15E08 -1:00:32
Nowogród 4 3 53N15 21E53 -1:27:32
Nowogrodziec 1 1 51N12 15E25 -1:01:40
Nowy Dwór Gdański 6 1 54N13 19E06 -1:16:24
Nowy Dwór Mazowiecki 4 3 52N26 20E43 -1:22:52
Nowy Sącz 2 2 49N38 20E42 -1:22:48
Nowy Staw 6 1 54N09 19E00 -1:16:00
Nowy Targ 2 2 49N29 20E02 -1:20:08
Nowy Tomyśl 3 2 52N20 16E07 -1:04:28
Nysa 1 1 50N29 17E20 -1:09:20
Oberglogau → Głogówek 1 1 50N22 17E51 -1:11:24
Oborniki 3 2 52N39 16E51 -1:07:24
Obryta 1 1 53N13 14E59 -0:59:56
Odolanów 3 2 51N35 17E39 -1:10:36
Odra Port 1 1 53N52 14E14 -0:56:56
Odrzywół 4 3 51N32 20E33 -1:22:12
Oels → Oleśnica 1 1 51N13 17E23 -1:09:32
Ognica 1 1 53N07 14E27 -0:57:48
Ogrodzieniec 4 3 50N27 19E31 -1:18:04
Ohlau → Oława 1 1 50N57 17E17 -1:09:08
Okonek 1 1 53N33 16E50 -1:07:20
Oława 1 1 50N57 17E17 -1:09:08
Olecko 1 1 54N03 22E30 -1:30:00
Oleśnica 1 1 51N13 17E23 -1:09:32
Olesno 1 1 50N53 18E25 -1:13:40
Olsztyn (Allenstein) 1 1 53N48 20E29 -1:21:56
Olsztynek 1 1 53N36 20E17 -1:21:08
Opalenica 3 2 52N19 16E23 -1:05:32
Opatów 4 3 50N49 21E26 -1:25:44
Opoczno 4 3 51N23 20E17 -1:21:08
Opole (Oppeln) 1 1 50N41 17E55 -1:11:40
Opole Lubelskie 4 3 51N09 21E58 -1:27:52
Oppeln → Opole 1 1 50N41 17E55 -1:11:40
Orneta 1 1 54N08 20E08 -1:20:32
Ortelsburg → Szczytno 1 1 53N34 21E00 -1:24:00
Orzysz 1 1 53N49 21E56 -1:27:44
Osiek 4 3 50N31 21E28 -1:25:52
Osinów Dolny 1 1 52N48 14E10 -0:56:40
Ośno 1 1 52N28 14E50 -0:59:20
Osterode → Ostróda 1 1 53N43 19E59 -1:19:56
Ostróda 1 1 53N43 19E59 -1:19:56
Ostrołęka 4 3 53N06 21E34 -1:26:16
Ostroróg 3 2 52N39 16E27 -1:05:48
Ostrowiec Świętokrzyski 4 3 50N57 21E23 -1:25:32
Ostrów Lubelski 4 3 51N30 22E52 -1:31:28
Ostrów Mazowiecka 4 3 52N49 21E54 -1:27:36
Ostrów Wielkopolski 3 2 51N39 17E49 -1:11:16
Ostrzeszów 3 2 51N25 17E57 -1:11:48
Oświęcim 1 1 50N03 19E12 -1:16:48
Otmuchów 1 1 50N28 17E10 -1:08:40
Ottmachau → Otmuchów 1 1 50N28 17E10 -1:08:40
Otwock 4 3 52N07 21E16 -1:25:04
Ozimek 1 1 50N41 18E13 -1:12:52
Ozorków 4 3 51N58 19E19 -1:17:16
Pabianice 4 3 51N40 19E22 -1:17:28
Paczkow 1 1 50N27 17E00 -1:08:00
Pajęczno 4 3 51N09 19E00 -1:16:00
Pakość 3 2 52N49 18E05 -1:12:20
Parchwitz → Prochowice 1 1 51N17 16E22 -1:05:28
Parczew 4 3 51N39 22E54 -1:31:36
Pasłęk 1 1 54N05 19E39 -1:18:36
Peiskretscham → Pyskowice 1 1 50N24 18E38 -1:14:32
Pełczyce 1 1 53N03 15E18 -1:01:12
Pelplin 3 2 53N56 18E42 -1:14:48
Penzig → Pieńsk 1 1 51N15 15E03 -1:00:12
Pförten → Brody 1 1 51N45 14E45 -0:59:00
Piaseczno 4 3 52N05 21E01 -1:24:04
Piaski 4 3 51N08 22E51 -1:31:24
Pieniężno 1 1 54N15 20E08 -1:20:32
Pieńsk 1 1 51N15 15E03 -1:00:12
Piła (Schneidemühl) 1 1 53N10 16E44 -1:06:56
Pilawa 4 3 51N58 21E31 -1:26:04
Pilzno 2 2 49N59 21E17 -1:25:08
Pińczów 4 3 50N32 20E35 -1:22:20
Pionki 4 3 51N30 21E27 -1:25:48
Piotrków Trybunalski 4 3 51N25 19E42 -1:18:48
Pisz 1 1 53N38 21E49 -1:27:16

Pitschen → Byczyna 1 1 51N07 18E11 -1:12:44
Piwniczna 2 2 49N27 20E42 -1:22:48
Plathe → Płoty 1 1 53N49 15E16 -1:01:04
Pless → Pszczyna 1 1 49N59 18E57 -1:15:48
Pleszew 3 2 51N54 17E48 -1:11:12
Płock 4 3 52N33 19E43 -1:18:52
Płońsk 4 3 52N38 20E23 -1:21:32
Płoty 1 1 53N49 15E16 -1:01:04
Pniewy 3 2 52N31 16E15 -1:05:00
Poddębice 4 3 51N53 18E58 -1:15:52
Polanów 1 1 54N08 16E39 -1:06:36
Połczyn Zdrój 1 1 53N46 16E06 -1:04:24
Police 1 1 53N35 14E33 -0:58:12
Pölitz → Police 1 1 53N35 14E33 -0:58:12
Pollnow → Polanów 1 1 54N08 16E39 -1:06:36
Poniatowa 4 3 51N11 22E05 -1:28:20
Poniec 3 2 51N47 16E50 -1:07:20
Posen → Poznań 3 2 52N25 16E55 -1:07:40
Poznań 3 2 52N25 16E55 -1:07:40
Prabuty 1 1 53N46 19E10 -1:16:40
Praga 4 3 52N16 21E02 -1:24:08
Praszka 4 3 51N04 18E26 -1:13:44
Preussisch Friedland → Debrzno 1 1 53N33 17E14 -1:08:56
Preussisch Holland → Pasłęk 1 1 54N05 19E39 -1:18:36
Preussisch Königsdorf → Olesno 1 1 50N53 18E25 -1:13:40
Primkenau → Przemków 1 1 51N32 15E48 -1:03:12
Prochowice 1 1 51N17 16E22 -1:05:28
Prostken → Prostki 1 1 53N43 22E26 -1:29:44
Prostki 1 1 53N43 22E26 -1:29:44
Proszowice 4 3 50N12 20E18 -1:21:12
Prudnik 1 1 50N19 17E34 -1:10:16
Pruszków 4 3 52N11 20E48 -1:23:12
Przasnysz 4 3 53N01 20E55 -1:23:40
Przedbórz 4 3 51N06 19E53 -1:19:32
Przemków 1 1 51N32 15E48 -1:03:12
Przemocze 1 1 53N27 14E55 -0:59:40
Przemyśl 2 2 49N47 22E47 -1:31:08
Przeworsk 2 2 50N05 22E29 -1:29:56
Przewóz 1 1 51N29 14E59 -0:59:56
Przybiernów 1 1 53N46 14E46 -0:59:04
Przysucha 4 3 51N22 20E38 -1:22:32
Pszczyna 1 1 49N59 18E57 -1:15:48
Pszów 1 1 50N03 18E24 -1:13:36
Puck 3 2 54N44 18E27 -1:13:48
Puławy 4 3 51N25 21E57 -1:27:48
Pułtusk 4 3 52N43 21E05 -1:24:20
Puszczykowo 3 2 52N17 16E52 -1:07:28
Pyritz → Pyrzyce 1 1 53N10 14E55 -0:59:40
Pyrzyce 1 1 53N10 14E55 -0:59:40
Pyskowice 1 1 50N24 18E38 -1:14:32
Pyzdry 3 2 52N11 17E41 -1:10:44
Rabka 2 2 49N36 19E56 -1:19:44
Raciąż 4 3 52N47 20E06 -1:20:24
Racibórz (Ratibor) 1 1 50N06 18E13 -1:12:52
Radom 4 3 51N25 21E10 -1:24:40
Radomicko 1 1 52N10 14E58 -0:59:52
Radomsko 4 3 51N05 19E25 -1:17:40
Radomyśl Wielki 2 2 50N12 21E16 -1:25:04
Radymno 2 2 49N57 22E48 -1:31:12
Radziejów 4 3 52N38 18E32 -1:14:08
Radzyń Chełmiński 3 2 53N24 18E56 -1:15:44
Radzyń Podlaski 4 3 51N48 22E38 -1:30:32
Rajgród 4 3 53N44 22E42 -1:30:48
Rakoniewice 3 2 52N10 16E16 -1:05:04
Rastenburg → Kętrzyn 1 1 54N06 21E23 -1:25:32
Ratibor → Racibórz 1 1 50N06 18E13 -1:12:52
Ratzebuhr → Okonek 1 1 53N33 16E50 -1:07:20
Rawa Mazowiecka 4 3 51N46 20E16 -1:21:04
Rawicz 3 2 51N37 16E52 -1:07:28
Recz 1 1 53N16 15E33 -1:02:12
Reda 3 2 54N37 18E21 -1:13:24
Reetz in der Neumark → Recz 1 1 53N16 15E33 -1:02:12
Reichenau → Bogatynia 1 1 50N53 15E00 -1:00:00
Reichenbach → Dzierżoniów 1 1 50N44 16E39 -1:06:36
Rejowiec Fabryczny 4 3 51N08 23E13 -1:32:52
Reppen → Rzepin 1 1 52N22 14E50 -0:59:20
Resko 1 1 53N47 15E25 -1:01:40
Rhein → Ryn 1 1 53N56 21E33 -1:26:12
Riesenburg → Prabuty 1 1 53N46 19E10 -1:16:40
Rogoźno 3 2 52N46 17E00 -1:08:00
Ropczyce 2 2 50N03 21E37 -1:26:28
Rosenberg → Susz 1 1 53N44 19E20 -1:17:20
Rothenburg an der Oder → Czerwieńsk 1 1 52N01 15E25 -1:01:40
Rów 1 1 52N58 14E45 -0:59:00
Różan 4 3 52N53 21E25 -1:25:40
Rożnów 2 2 49N46 20E42 -1:22:48
Ruciane-Nida 1 1 53N39 21E35 -1:26:20

Ruda Śląska 1 1 50N18 18E51 -1:15:24
Rudnik 2 2 50N28 22E15 -1:29:00
Rügenwalde → Darłowo 1 1 54N26 16E23 -1:05:32
Rumia 3 2 54N35 18E25 -1:13:40
Rummelsburg → Miastko 1 1 54N01 17E00 -1:08:00
Rybnik 1 1 50N06 18E32 -1:14:08
Rychwał 4 3 52N05 18E09 -1:12:36
Rydzyna 3 2 51N48 16E40 -1:06:40
Ryki 4 3 51N39 21E56 -1:27:44
Rymanów 2 2 49N34 21E53 -1:27:32
Ryn 1 1 53N56 21E33 -1:26:12
Rypin 4 3 53N05 19E25 -1:17:40
Rzepin 1 1 52N22 14E50 -0:59:20
Rzeszów 2 2 50N03 22E00 -1:28:00
Sagan → Żagań 1 1 51N37 15E19 -1:01:16
Sandomierz 4 3 50N41 21E45 -1:27:00
Sanok 2 2 49N34 22E13 -1:28:52
Sarbinowo 1 1 52N40 14E40 -0:58:40
Sarnowa 3 2 51N38 16E54 -1:07:36
Schippenbeil → Sępopol 1 1 54N15 21E00 -1:24:00
Schivelbein → Świdwin 1 1 53N47 15E47 -1:03:08
Schlichtingsheim → Szlichtyngowa 1 1 51N43 16E15 -1:05:00
Schlochau → Człuchów 1 1 53N41 17E21 -1:09:24
Schloppe → Człopa 1 1 53N06 16E08 -1:04:32
Schneidemühl → Piła 1 1 53N10 16E44 -1:06:56
Schönau → Świerzawa 1 1 51N01 15E54 -1:03:36
Schönlanke → Trzcianka 1 1 53N03 16E28 -1:05:52
Schützenbruch → Kalety 3 2 50N34 18E54 -1:15:36
Schweidnitz → Świdnica 1 1 50N51 16E29 -1:05:56
Schwerin an der Warthe → Skwierzyna 1 1 52N36 15E30 -1:02:00
Schwiebus → Świebodzin 1 1 52N15 15E32 -1:02:08
Ścinawa 1 1 51N25 16E27 -1:05:48
Sędziszów 2 2 50N04 21E41 -1:26:44
Seeburg → Jeziorany 1 1 53N58 20E46 -1:23:04
Sejny 4 3 54N07 23E20 -1:33:20
Sensburg → Mrągowo 1 1 53N52 21E19 -1:25:16
Sępólno Krajeńskie 3 2 53N28 17E32 -1:10:08
Sępopol 1 1 54N15 21E00 -1:24:00
Serock 4 3 52N31 21E03 -1:24:12
Sianów 1 1 54N15 16E16 -1:05:04
Siedlce 4 3 52N11 22E16 -1:29:04
Siemianowice Śląskie 1 1 50N19 19E01 -1:16:04
Siemiatycze 5 4 52N26 22E53 -1:31:32
Sieniawa 2 2 50N11 22E36 -1:30:24
Sieradz 4 3 51N36 18E45 -1:15:00
Sieraków 3 2 52N39 16E04 -1:04:16
Sierpc 4 3 52N52 19E41 -1:18:44
Skalbmierz 4 3 50N19 20E25 -1:21:40
Skarszewy 3 2 54N05 18E27 -1:13:48
Skaryszew 4 3 51N19 21E15 -1:25:00
Skarżysko-Kamienna 4 3 51N08 20E53 -1:23:32
Skawina 2 2 49N59 19E49 -1:19:16
Skierniewice 4 3 51N58 20E08 -1:20:32
Skoki 3 2 52N41 17E10 -1:08:40
Skolwin 1 1 53N32 14E35 -0:58:20
Skórcz 3 2 53N48 18E32 -1:14:08
Skwierzyna 1 1 52N36 15E30 -1:02:00
Sława 3 2 51N53 16E04 -1:04:16
Sławno 1 1 54N22 16E40 -1:06:40
Ślesin 4 3 52N23 18E19 -1:13:16
Słomniki 4 3 50N15 20E06 -1:20:24
Słońsk 1 1 52N35 14E50 -0:59:20
Słubice 1 1 52N20 14E32 -0:58:08
Słupca 3 2 52N19 17E52 -1:11:28
Słupsk (Stolp) 1 1 54N28 17E01 -1:08:04
Śmigiel 3 2 52N01 16E32 -1:06:08
Sobótka 1 1 50N55 16E45 -1:07:00
Sochaczew 4 3 52N14 20E14 -1:20:56
Sokółka 5 4 53N25 23E31 -1:34:04
Sokołów 2 2 50N14 22E07 -1:28:28
Sokołów Podlaski 4 3 52N25 22E15 -1:29:00
Soldin → Myślibórz 1 1 52N55 14E52 -0:59:28
Solec Kujawski 3 2 53N06 18E14 -1:12:56
Sommerfeld → Lubsko 1 1 51N46 14E59 -0:59:56
Sompolno 4 3 52N24 18E31 -1:14:04
Sopot 3 2 54N28 18E34 -1:14:16
Sorau → Żary 1 1 51N38 15E09 -1:00:36
Sosnowiec 1 1 50N18 19E08 -1:16:32
Sprottau → Szprotawa 1 1 51N34 15E33 -1:02:12
Śrem 3 2 52N08 17E01 -1:08:04
Środa Śląska 1 1 51N10 16E36 -1:06:24
Środa Wielkopolski 3 2 52N14 17E17 -1:09:08
Stalinogród → Katowice 1 1 50N16 19E00 -1:16:00
Stalowa Wola 2 2 50N35 22E02 -1:28:08
Stąporków 4 3 51N09 20E34 -1:22:16
Starachowice 4 3 51N03 21E04 -1:24:16
Stare Czarnowo 1 1 53N16 14E45 -0:59:00

Stargard Szczeciński (Stargard in Pomm
1 53N20 15E02 -1:00:08
Starogard Gdański 3
2 53N59 18E33 -1:14:12
Starosiedle 1 1 51N50 14E50 -0:59:20
Stary Sącz 2 2 49N34 20E38 -1:22:32
Staszów 4 3 50N34 21E20 -1:25:20
Stawiski 4 3 53N23 22E09 -1:28:36
Stawiszyn 4 3 51N55 18E07 -1:12:28
Steinau → Ścinawa 1
1 51N25 16E27 -1:05:48
Stepnica 1 1 53N40 14E36 -0:58:24
Sterdyń 4 3 52N35 22E18 -1:29:12
Sternberg in der Neumark → Torzym 1
1 52N20 15E04 -1:00:16
Stęszew 3 2 52N18 16E42 -1:06:48
Stettin → Szczecin 1
1 53N24 14E32 -0:58:08
Stoczek Łukowski 4
3 51N58 21E58 -1:27:52
Stolp → Słupsk 1
1 54N28 17E01 -1:08:04
Stolpmünde → Ustka 1
1 54N35 16E50 -1:07:20
Stopnica 4 3 50N27 20E57 -1:23:48
Strehlen → Strzelin 1
1 50N47 17E03 -1:08:12
Striegau → Strzegom 1
1 50N57 16E21 -1:05:24
Stryków 4 3 51N55 19E37 -1:18:28
Strzegom 1 1 50N57 16E21 -1:05:24
Strzegowo-Osada 4
3 52N55 20E18 -1:21:12
Strzelce Krajeńskie 1
1 52N53 15E32 -1:02:08
Strzelce Opolskie 1
1 50N31 18E19 -1:13:16
Strzelin 1 1 50N47 17E03 -1:08:12
Strzelno 3 2 52N38 18E11 -1:12:44
Strzyżów 2 2 49N52 21E47 -1:27:08
Stuhm → Sztum 1 1 53N56 19E01 -1:16:04
Sucha (beskidzka) 2
2 49N44 19E36 -1:18:24
Suchań 1 1 53N17 15E19 -1:01:16
Suchedniów 4 3 51N03 20E51 -1:23:24
Sulechów 1 1 52N06 15E37 -1:02:28
Sulęcin 1 1 52N26 15E08 -1:00:32
Sulejów 4 3 51N22 19E53 -1:19:32
Sulejówek 4 3 52N14 21E17 -1:25:08
Supraśl 5 4 53N13 23E20 -1:33:20
Suraż 4 3 52N58 22E58 -1:31:52
Susz 1 1 53N44 19E20 -1:17:20
Suwałki 4 3 54N07 22E56 -1:31:44
Swarzędz 3 2 52N26 17E05 -1:08:20
Świdnica (Schweidnitz) 1
1 50N51 16E29 -1:05:56
Świdnik 4 3 51N14 22E41 -1:30:44
Świdwin 1 1 53N47 15E47 -1:03:08
Świebodzice 1 1 50N52 16E19 -1:05:16
Świebodzin 1 1 52N15 15E32 -1:02:08
Świecie 3 2 53N25 18E28 -1:13:52
Świerzawa 1 1 51N01 15E54 -1:03:36
Świerzno 1 1 53N57 14E59 -0:59:56
Święta 1 1 53N35 14E36 -0:58:24
Swinemünde → Świnoujście 1
1 53N53 14E14 -0:56:56
Świnoujście (Swinemünde) 1
1 53N53 14E14 -0:56:56
Syców 3 2 51N19 17E43 -1:10:52
Szamocin 3 2 53N02 17E08 -1:08:32
Szamotuły 3 2 52N37 16E35 -1:06:20
Szczawnica 2 2 49N26 20E30 -1:22:00
Szczecin (Stettin) 1
1 53N24 14E32 -0:58:08
Szczecinek (Neustettin) 1
1 53N43 16E42 -1:06:48
Szczekociny 4 3 50N38 19E50 -1:19:20
Szczuczyn 4 3 53N34 22E18 -1:29:12
Szczytno 1 1 53N34 21E00 -1:24:00
Szlichtyngowa 1 1 51N43 16E15 -1:05:00
Szprotawa 1 1 51N34 15E33 -1:02:12
Sztum 1 1 53N56 19E01 -1:16:04
Szubin 3 2 53N00 17E44 -1:10:56
Szydłowiec 4 3 51N14 20E51 -1:23:24
Szypliszki 4 3 54N15 23E05 -1:32:20
Tarnobrzeg 2 2 50N35 21E41 -1:26:44
Tarnogród 4 3 50N23 22E45 -1:31:00
Tarnów 2 2 50N01 21E00 -1:24:00
Tarnów 1 1 52N47 14E58 -0:59:52
Tarnowskie Góry 1
1 50N27 18E52 -1:15:28
Tczew 3 2 54N06 18E47 -1:15:08
Tempelburg → Czaplinek 1
1 53N34 16E14 -1:04:56
Terespol 4 3 52N05 23E36 -1:34:24
Teuplitz → Tuplice 1
1 51N41 14E50 -0:59:20
Thorn → Toruń 3 2 53N02 18E35 -1:14:20
Tiegenhof → Nowy Dwór Gdański 6
1 54N13 19E06 -1:16:24

Tirschtiegel → Trzciel 1
1 52N23 15E52 -1:03:28
Tłuszcz 4 3 52N26 21E26 -1:25:44
Tolkmicko 1 1 54N20 19E31 -1:18:04
Tomaszów Lubelski 4
3 50N28 23E25 -1:33:40
Tomaszów Mazowiecki 4
3 51N32 20E01 -1:20:04
Toruń 3 2 53N02 18E35 -1:14:20
Torzym 1 1 52N20 15E04 -1:00:16
Tost → Toszek 1 1 50N28 18E32 -1:14:08
Toszek 1 1 50N28 18E32 -1:14:08
Trachenberg → Żmigród 1
1 51N29 16E55 -1:07:40
Treblinka 4 3 52N39 22E03 -1:28:12
Trebnitz → Trzebnica 1
1 51N19 17E03 -1:08:12
Treptow an der Rega → Trzebiatów 1
1 54N04 15E14 -1:00:56
Treuburg → Olecko 1
1 54N03 22E30 -1:30:00
Trzcianka 1 1 53N03 16E28 -1:05:52
Trzciel 1 1 52N23 15E52 -1:03:28
Trzcińsko-Zdrój 1
1 52N58 14E35 -0:58:20
Trzebiatów 1 1 54N04 15E14 -1:00:56
Trzebiel 1 1 51N37 14E50 -0:59:20
Trzebież 1 1 53N42 14E31 -0:58:04
Trzebinia 2 2 50N10 19E18 -1:17:12
Trzebnica 1 1 51N19 17E03 -1:08:12
Trzemeszno 3 2 52N35 17E50 -1:11:20
Trzęsacz 1 1 54N05 14E58 -0:59:52
Tschenstochau → Częstochowa 4
3 50N49 19E06 -1:16:24
Tuchola 3 2 53N35 17E50 -1:11:20
Tuchów 2 2 49N54 21E03 -1:24:12
Tuczna 4 3 51N54 23E26 -1:33:44
Tuliszków 4 3 52N05 18E17 -1:13:08
Tuplice 1 1 51N41 14E50 -0:59:20
Turek 4 3 52N02 18E30 -1:14:00
Turobin 4 3 50N50 22E45 -1:31:00
Tuszyn 4 3 51N37 19E34 -1:18:16
Twardogóra 1 1 51N22 17E28 -1:09:52
Tychy 1 1 50N09 18E59 -1:15:56
Tyczyn 2 2 49N58 22E02 -1:28:08
Ujazd 1 1 50N24 18E22 -1:13:28
Ujście 1 1 53N04 16E43 -1:06:52
Ulanów 4 3 50N30 22E16 -1:29:04
Ułazów 2 2 50N17 23E00 -1:32:00
Uniejów 4 3 51N58 18E49 -1:15:16
Urad 1 1 52N15 14E45 -0:59:00
Ursus 4 3 52N12 20E53 -1:23:32
Ustka 1 1 54N35 16E50 -1:07:20
Ustroń 2 2 49N43 18E49 -1:15:16
Ustrzyki Dolne 2
2 49N26 22E37 -1:30:28
Varsovie → Warszawa 4
3 52N15 21E00 -1:24:00
Vietz → Witnica 1
1 52N40 14E55 -0:59:40
Wąbrzeźno 3 2 53N17 18E57 -1:15:48
Wadowice 2 2 49N53 19E30 -1:18:00
Wągrowiec 3 2 52N49 17E11 -1:08:44
Wałbrzych (Waldenburg) 1
1 50N46 16E17 -1:05:08
Wałcz 1 1 53N17 16E28 -1:05:52
Waldenburg → Wałbrzych 1
1 50N46 16E17 -1:05:08
Wangerin → Węgorzyno 1
1 53N32 15E33 -1:02:12
Wansen → Wiązów 1
1 50N49 17E11 -1:08:44
Warka 4 3 51N47 21E10 -1:24:40
Warsaw → Warszawa 4
3 52N15 21E00 -1:24:00
Warschau → Warszawa 4
3 52N15 21E00 -1:24:00
Warszawa (Warsaw) 4
3 52N15 21E00 -1:24:00
Warta 4 3 51N42 18E38 -1:14:32
Wasilków 5 4 53N12 23E12 -1:32:48
Wąsosz 1 1 51N34 16E42 -1:06:48
Węgliniec 1 1 51N17 15E13 -1:00:52
Węgorzewo 1 1 54N14 21E44 -1:26:56
Węgorzyno 1 1 53N32 15E33 -1:02:12
Węgrów 4 3 52N25 22E01 -1:28:04
Wejherowo 3 2 54N37 18E15 -1:13:00
Wiązów 1 1 50N49 17E11 -1:08:44
Widuchowa 1 1 53N10 14E25 -0:57:40
Więcbork 3 2 53N22 17E30 -1:10:00
Wieleń 1 1 52N54 16E10 -1:04:40
Wielichowo 3 2 52N08 16E21 -1:05:24
Wieliczka 2 2 49N59 20E04 -1:20:16
Wieluń 4 3 51N14 18E34 -1:14:16
Wieruszów 3 2 51N18 18E08 -1:12:32
Wisła 2 2 49N40 18E52 -1:15:28
Wisznice 4 3 51N48 23E12 -1:32:48
Witkowo 3 2 52N27 17E47 -1:11:08
Witnica 1 1 52N40 14E55 -0:59:40
Wiżajny 4 3 54N23 22E51 -1:31:24

Władysławowo 3 2 54N49 18E25 -1:13:40
Wleń 1 1 51N01 15E40 -1:02:40
Włocławek 4 3 52N39 19E02 -1:16:08
Włodawa 4 3 51N34 23E32 -1:34:08
Włoszczowa 4 3 50N52 19E59 -1:19:56
Wodzisław Śląski 1
1 50N00 18E28 -1:13:52
Wohlau → Wołów 1
1 51N21 16E39 -1:06:36
Wojcieszów 1 1 50N58 15E56 -1:03:44
Wolbrom 4 3 50N24 19E46 -1:19:04
Wołczyn 1 1 51N01 18E03 -1:12:12
Woldenburg → Dobiegniew 1
1 52N59 15E47 -1:03:08
Wolin 1 1 53N50 14E35 -0:58:20
Wołomin 4 3 52N21 21E14 -1:24:56
Wołów 1 1 51N21 16E39 -1:06:36
Wolsztyn 3 2 52N08 16E06 -1:04:24
Wormditt → Orneta 1
1 54N08 20E08 -1:20:32
Woźniki 4 3 50N36 19E03 -1:16:12
Wrocław (Breslau) 1
1 51N06 17E00 -1:08:00
Wronki 3 2 52N43 16E23 -1:05:32
Września 3 2 52N20 17E34 -1:10:16
Wschowa 1 1 51N48 16E19 -1:05:16
Wyrzysk 3 2 53N10 17E15 -1:09:00
Wyśmierzyce 4 3 51N38 20E49 -1:23:16
Wysoka 3 2 53N11 17E05 -1:08:20

Wysokie Mazowieckie 4
3 52N56 22E32 -1:30:08
Wyszków 4 3 52N36 21E28 -1:25:52
Wyszogród 4 3 52N23 20E11 -1:20:44
Ząbkowice Śląskie 1
1 50N36 16E53 -1:07:32
Zabłudów 5 4 53N01 23E20 -1:33:20
Żabno 2 2 50N09 20E53 -1:23:32
Zabrze 1 1 50N18 18E46 -1:15:04
Zachan → Suchań 1
1 53N17 15E19 -1:01:16
Żagań 1 1 51N37 15E19 -1:01:16
Zagórów 4 3 52N11 17E55 -1:11:40
Zagórz 2 2 49N31 22E17 -1:29:08
Zakliczyn 2 2 49N51 20E48 -1:23:12
Zaklików 4 3 50N47 22E06 -1:28:24
Zakopane 3 2 49N19 19E57 -1:19:48
Zakroczym 4 3 52N26 20E37 -1:22:28
Zambrów 4 3 53N00 22E15 -1:29:00
Zamch 4 3 50N20 23E00 -1:32:00
Zamość 4 3 50N44 23E15 -1:33:00
Żarki 4 3 50N38 19E22 -1:17:28
Żary (Sorau) 1 1 51N38 15E09 -1:00:36
Zasieki 1 1 51N43 14E43 -0:58:52
Zawadzkie 3 2 50N37 18E29 -1:13:56
Zawichost 4 3 50N49 21E52 -1:27:28
Zawiercie 4 3 50N30 19E25 -1:17:40
Zbąszyń 1 1 52N16 15E55 -1:03:40
Zbąszynek 1 1 52N15 15E50 -1:03:20
Zduńska Wola 4 3 51N36 18E57 -1:15:48
Zduny 3 2 51N39 17E24 -1:09:36
Zehden → Cedynia 1
1 52N50 14E14 -0:56:56
Żelechów 4 3 51N49 21E54 -1:27:36
Zelów 4 3 51N28 19E13 -1:16:52
Żerków 3 2 52N05 17E34 -1:10:16
Zgierz 4 3 51N52 19E25 -1:17:40
Zgorzelec 1 1 51N12 15E01 -1:00:04
Ziębice 1 1 50N37 17E00 -1:08:00
Ziegenhals → Głuchołazy 1
1 50N20 17E22 -1:09:28
Ziegenort → Trzebież 1
1 53N42 14E31 -0:58:04
Zielenzig → Sulęcin 1
1 52N26 15E08 -1:00:32
Zielona Góra (Grünberg) 1
1 51N56 15E31 -1:02:04
Złocieniec 1 1 53N33 16E01 -1:04:04
Złoczew 4 3 51N25 18E36 -1:14:24
Złotoryja 1 1 51N08 15E55 -1:03:40
Złotów 1 1 53N22 17E02 -1:08:08
Żmigród 1 1 51N29 16E55 -1:07:40
Żnin 3 2 52N52 17E43 -1:10:52
Żółkiewka 4 3 50N55 22E51 -1:31:24
Zoppot → Sopot 3
2 54N28 18E34 -1:14:16
Zopten am Berge → Sobótka 1
1 50N55 16E45 -1:07:00
Żukowo 3 2 54N21 18E22 -1:13:28
Zulkiew 2 2 50N04 20E00 -1:20:00
Züllichau → Sulechów 1
1 52N06 15E37 -1:02:28
Züls → Biała 1 1 50N23 17E40 -1:10:40
Żuromin 4 3 53N04 19E55 -1:19:40
Zwierzyniec 4 3 50N37 22E58 -1:31:52
Zwoleń 4 3 51N22 21E35 -1:26:20
Żychlin 4 3 52N15 19E39 -1:18:36
Żyrardów 4 3 52N04 20E25 -1:21:40
Żyrzyn 4 3 51N30 22E07 -1:28:28
Żywiec 2 2 49N41 19E12 -1:16:48

Time Table # 1

Date	Time	Offset
Before 1/Jan/1884		LMT
Begin Standard		9w08
1/Jan/1884	0:00	0:37
Begin Standard		0w00
24/May/1911	0:00	0:00
17/Jun/1916	23:00	-1:00
1/Nov/1916	1:00	0:00
28/Feb/1917	23:00	-1:00
14/Oct/1917	24:00	0:00
1/Mar/1918	23:00	-1:00
14/Oct/1918	24:00	0:00
28/Feb/1919	23:00	-1:00
14/Oct/1919	24:00	0:00
29/Feb/1920	23:00	-1:00
14/Oct/1920	24:00	0:00
28/Feb/1921	23:00	-1:00
14/Oct/1921	24:00	0:00
16/Apr/1924	23:00	-1:00
14/Oct/1924	24:00	0:00
17/Apr/1926	23:00	-1:00
2/Oct/1926	24:00	0:00
9/Apr/1927	23:00	-1:00
1/Oct/1927	24:00	0:00
14/Apr/1928	23:00	-1:00
6/Oct/1928	24:00	0:00
20/Apr/1929	23:00	-1:00
5/Oct/1929	24:00	0:00
18/Apr/1931	23:00	-1:00
3/Oct/1931	24:00	0:00
2/Apr/1932	23:00	-1:00
1/Oct/1932	24:00	0:00
7/Apr/1934	23:00	-1:00
6/Oct/1934	24:00	0:00
30/Apr/1935	23:00	-1:00
5/Oct/1935	24:00	0:00
18/Apr/1936	23:00	-1:00
3/Oct/1936	24:00	0:00
3/Apr/1937	23:00	-1:00
2/Oct/1937	24:00	0:00
26/Mar/1938	23:00	-1:00
1/Oct/1938	24:00	0:00
15/Apr/1939	23:00	-1:00
18/Nov/1939	24:00	0:00
24/Feb/1940	23:00	-1:00
7/Oct/1940	24:00	0:00
5/Apr/1941	23:00	-1:00
5/Oct/1941	24:00	0:00
14/Mar/1942	23:00	-1:00
25/Apr/1942	23:00	-2:00
15/Aug/1942	24:00	-1:00
24/Oct/1942	24:00	0:00
13/Mar/1943	23:00	-1:00
17/Apr/1943	23:00	-2:00
28/Aug/1943	24:00	-1:00
30/Oct/1943	24:00	0:00
11/Mar/1944	23:00	-1:00
22/Apr/1944	23:00	-2:00
26/Aug/1944	24:00	-1:00
28/Oct/1944	24:00	0:00
10/Mar/1945	23:00	-1:00
21/Apr/1945	23:00	-2:00
25/Aug/1945	24:00	-1:00
27/Oct/1945	24:00	0:00
6/Apr/1946	23:00	-1:00
5/Oct/1946	24:00	0:00
6/Apr/1947	2:00	-1:00
5/Oct/1947	3:00	0:00
4/Apr/1948	2:00	-1:00
3/Oct/1948	3:00	0:00
3/Apr/1949	2:00	-1:00
2/Oct/1949	3:00	0:00
2/Apr/1950	2:00	-1:00
1/Oct/1950	3:00	0:00
1/Apr/1951	2:00	-1:00
7/Oct/1951	3:00	0:00
6/Apr/1952	2:00	-1:00
5/Oct/1952	3:00	0:00
5/Apr/1953	2:00	-1:00
4/Oct/1953	3:00	0:00
4/Apr/1954	2:00	-1:00
3/Oct/1954	3:00	0:00
3/Apr/1955	2:00	-1:00
2/Oct/1955	3:00	0:00
1/Apr/1956	2:00	-1:00
7/Oct/1956	3:00	0:00
7/Apr/1957	2:00	-1:00
6/Oct/1957	3:00	0:00
6/Apr/1958	2:00	-1:00
5/Oct/1958	3:00	0:00
5/Apr/1959	2:00	-1:00
4/Oct/1959	3:00	0:00
3/Apr/1960	2:00	-1:00
2/Oct/1960	3:00	0:00
2/Apr/1961	2:00	-1:00
1/Oct/1961	3:00	0:00
1/Apr/1962	2:00	-1:00
7/Oct/1962	3:00	0:00
7/Apr/1963	2:00	-1:00
6/Oct/1963	3:00	0:00
5/Apr/1964	2:00	-1:00
4/Oct/1964	3:00	0:00
4/Apr/1965	2:00	-1:00
3/Oct/1965	3:00	0:00
Begin Standard		15E00
3/Apr/1966	2:00	-1:00
Begin Standard		0w00
26/Sep/1976	1:00	0:00
27/Mar/1977	0:00	-1:00
25/Sep/1977	1:00	0:00
2/Apr/1978	0:00	-1:00
1/Oct/1978	1:00	0:00
1/Apr/1979	0:00	-1:00
30/Sep/1979	2:00	0:00
30/Mar/1980	0:00	-1:00
28/Sep/1980	2:00	0:00
29/Mar/1981	1:00	-1:00
27/Sep/1981	2:00	0:00
28/Mar/1982	1:00	-1:00
26/Sep/1982	2:00	0:00
27/Mar/1983	2:00	-1:00
25/Sep/1983	2:00	0:00
25/Mar/1984	1:00	-1:00
30/Sep/1984	2:00	0:00
31/Mar/1985	1:00	-1:00
29/Sep/1985	2:00	0:00
30/Mar/1986	1:00	-1:00
28/Sep/1986	2:00	0:00
29/Mar/1987	1:00	-1:00
27/Sep/1987	2:00	0:00
27/Mar/1988	1:00	-1:00
25/Sep/1988	2:00	0:00
26/Mar/1989	1:00	-1:00
24/Sep/1989	2:00	0:00
25/Mar/1990	1:00	-1:00
30/Sep/1990	2:00	0:00
31/Mar/1991	1:00	-1:00
29/Sep/1991	2:00	0:00
29/Mar/1992	1:00	-1:00
27/Sep/1992	2:00	0:00
28/Mar/1993	1:00	-1:00
26/Sep/1993	2:00	0:00
27/Mar/1994	1:00	-1:00
25/Sep/1994	2:00	0:00
26/Mar/1995	1:00	-1:00
24/Sep/1995	2:00	0:00
31/Mar/1996	1:00	-1:00
29/Sep/1996	2:00	0:00
30/Mar/1997	1:00	-1:00
28/Sep/1997	2:00	0:00
29/Mar/1998	1:00	-1:00
27/Sep/1998	2:00	0:00
28/Mar/1999	1:00	-1:00
26/Sep/1999	2:00	0:00
26/Mar/2000	1:00	-1:00
24/Sep/2000	2:00	0:00

Time Table # 2

Date	Time	Offset
Before 1/Jan/1884		LMT
Begin Standard		28w38
1/Jan/1884	0:00	1:55
Begin Standard		30w00
24/May/1911	0:00	2:00
17/Jun/1916	23:00	1:00
1/Nov/1916	1:00	2:00
28/Feb/1917	23:00	1:00
14/Oct/1917	24:00	2:00
1/Mar/1918	23:00	1:00
14/Oct/1918	24:00	2:00
28/Feb/1919	23:00	1:00
14/Oct/1919	24:00	2:00
29/Feb/1920	23:00	1:00
14/Oct/1920	24:00	2:00
28/Feb/1921	23:00	1:00
14/Oct/1921	24:00	2:00
16/Apr/1924	23:00	1:00
14/Oct/1924	24:00	2:00
17/Apr/1926	23:00	1:00
2/Oct/1926	24:00	2:00
9/Apr/1927	23:00	1:00
1/Oct/1927	24:00	2:00
14/Apr/1928	23:00	1:00
6/Oct/1928	24:00	2:00
20/Apr/1929	23:00	1:00
5/Oct/1929	24:00	2:00
18/Apr/1931	23:00	1:00
3/Oct/1931	24:00	2:00
2/Apr/1932	23:00	1:00
1/Oct/1932	24:00	2:00
7/Apr/1934	23:00	1:00
6/Oct/1934	24:00	2:00
30/Apr/1935	23:00	1:00
5/Oct/1935	24:00	2:00
18/Apr/1936	23:00	1:00
3/Oct/1936	24:00	2:00
3/Apr/1937	23:00	1:00
2/Oct/1937	24:00	2:00
26/Mar/1938	23:00	1:00
1/Oct/1938	24:00	2:00
15/Apr/1939	23:00	1:00
18/Nov/1939	24:00	2:00
24/Feb/1940	23:00	1:00
7/Oct/1940	24:00	2:00
5/Apr/1941	23:00	1:00
5/Oct/1941	24:00	2:00
14/Mar/1942	23:00	1:00
25/Apr/1942	23:00	0:00
15/Aug/1942	24:00	1:00
24/Oct/1942	24:00	2:00
13/Mar/1943	23:00	1:00
17/Apr/1943	23:00	0:00
28/Aug/1943	24:00	1:00
30/Oct/1943	24:00	2:00
11/Mar/1944	23:00	1:00
22/Apr/1944	23:00	0:00
26/Aug/1944	24:00	1:00
28/Oct/1944	24:00	2:00
10/Mar/1945	23:00	1:00
21/Apr/1945	23:00	0:00
25/Aug/1945	24:00	1:00
27/Oct/1945	24:00	2:00
6/Apr/1946	23:00	1:00
5/Oct/1946	24:00	2:00
6/Apr/1947	2:00	1:00
5/Oct/1947	3:00	2:00
4/Apr/1948	2:00	1:00
3/Oct/1948	3:00	2:00
3/Apr/1949	2:00	1:00
2/Oct/1949	3:00	2:00
2/Apr/1950	2:00	1:00
1/Oct/1950	3:00	2:00
1/Apr/1951	2:00	1:00
7/Oct/1951	3:00	2:00
6/Apr/1952	2:00	1:00
5/Oct/1952	3:00	2:00
5/Apr/1953	2:00	1:00
4/Oct/1953	3:00	2:00
4/Apr/1954	2:00	1:00
3/Oct/1954	3:00	2:00
3/Apr/1955	2:00	1:00
2/Oct/1955	3:00	2:00
1/Apr/1956	2:00	1:00
7/Oct/1956	3:00	2:00
7/Apr/1957	2:00	1:00
6/Oct/1957	3:00	2:00
6/Apr/1958	2:00	1:00
5/Oct/1958	3:00	2:00
5/Apr/1959	2:00	1:00
4/Oct/1959	3:00	2:00
3/Apr/1960	2:00	1:00
2/Oct/1960	3:00	2:00
2/Apr/1961	2:00	1:00
1/Oct/1961	3:00	2:00
1/Apr/1962	2:00	1:00
7/Oct/1962	3:00	2:00
7/Apr/1963	2:00	1:00
6/Oct/1963	3:00	2:00
5/Apr/1964	2:00	1:00
4/Oct/1964	3:00	2:00
4/Apr/1965	2:00	1:00
3/Oct/1965	3:00	2:00
Begin Standard		15w00
3/Apr/1966	2:00	1:00
27/Mar/1977	0:00	0:00
25/Sep/1977	1:00	1:00
2/Apr/1978	0:00	0:00
1/Oct/1978	1:00	1:00
1/Apr/1979	0:00	0:00
30/Sep/1979	2:00	1:00
30/Mar/1980	0:00	0:00
28/Sep/1980	2:00	1:00
29/Mar/1981	1:00	0:00
27/Sep/1981	2:00	1:00
28/Mar/1982	1:00	0:00
26/Sep/1982	2:00	1:00
27/Mar/1983	2:00	0:00
25/Sep/1983	2:00	1:00
25/Mar/1984	1:00	0:00
30/Sep/1984	2:00	1:00
31/Mar/1985	1:00	0:00
29/Sep/1985	2:00	1:00
30/Mar/1986	1:00	0:00
28/Sep/1986	2:00	1:00
29/Mar/1987	1:00	0:00
27/Sep/1987	2:00	1:00
27/Mar/1988	1:00	0:00
25/Sep/1988	2:00	1:00
26/Mar/1989	1:00	0:00
24/Sep/1989	2:00	1:00
25/Mar/1990	1:00	0:00
30/Sep/1990	2:00	1:00
31/Mar/1991	1:00	0:00
29/Sep/1991	2:00	1:00
29/Mar/1992	1:00	0:00
27/Sep/1992	2:00	1:00
28/Mar/1993	1:00	0:00
26/Sep/1993	2:00	1:00
27/Mar/1994	1:00	0:00
25/Sep/1994	2:00	1:00
26/Mar/1995	1:00	0:00
24/Sep/1995	2:00	1:00
31/Mar/1996	1:00	0:00
29/Sep/1996	2:00	1:00
30/Mar/1997	1:00	0:00
28/Sep/1997	2:00	1:00
29/Mar/1998	1:00	0:00
27/Sep/1998	2:00	1:00
28/Mar/1999	1:00	0:00
26/Sep/1999	2:00	1:00
26/Mar/2000	1:00	0:00
24/Sep/2000	2:00	1:00

Time Table # 3

Date	Time	Offset
Before 1/Jan/1884		LMT
Begin Standard		16w54
1/Jan/1884	0:00	1:08
Begin Standard		15w00
24/May/1911	0:00	1:00
17/Jun/1916	23:00	0:00
1/Nov/1916	1:00	1:00
28/Feb/1917	23:00	0:00
14/Oct/1917	24:00	1:00
1/Mar/1918	23:00	0:00
14/Oct/1918	24:00	1:00
28/Feb/1919	23:00	0:00
14/Oct/1919	24:00	1:00
29/Feb/1920	23:00	0:00
14/Oct/1920	24:00	1:00
28/Feb/1921	23:00	0:00
14/Oct/1921	24:00	1:00
16/Apr/1924	23:00	0:00
14/Oct/1924	24:00	1:00
17/Apr/1926	23:00	0:00
2/Oct/1926	24:00	1:00
9/Apr/1927	23:00	0:00
1/Oct/1927	24:00	1:00
14/Apr/1928	23:00	0:00
6/Oct/1928	24:00	1:00
20/Apr/1929	23:00	0:00
5/Oct/1929	24:00	1:00
18/Apr/1931	23:00	0:00
3/Oct/1931	24:00	1:00
2/Apr/1932	23:00	0:00
1/Oct/1932	24:00	1:00
7/Apr/1934	23:00	0:00
6/Oct/1934	24:00	1:00
30/Apr/1935	23:00	0:00
5/Oct/1935	24:00	1:00
18/Apr/1936	23:00	0:00
3/Oct/1936	24:00	1:00
3/Apr/1937	23:00	0:00
2/Oct/1937	24:00	1:00
26/Mar/1938	23:00	0:00
1/Oct/1938	24:00	1:00
15/Apr/1939	23:00	0:00
18/Nov/1939	24:00	1:00
24/Feb/1940	23:00	0:00
7/Oct/1940	24:00	1:00
5/Apr/1941	23:00	0:00
5/Oct/1941	24:00	1:00
14/Mar/1942	23:00	0:00
25/Apr/1942	23:00	-1:00
15/Aug/1942	24:00	0:00
24/Oct/1942	24:00	1:00
13/Mar/1943	23:00	0:00
17/Apr/1943	23:00	-1:00
28/Aug/1943	24:00	0:00
30/Oct/1943	24:00	1:00
11/Mar/1944	23:00	0:00
22/Apr/1944	23:00	-1:00
26/Aug/1944	24:00	0:00
28/Oct/1944	24:00	1:00
10/Mar/1945	23:00	0:00
21/Apr/1945	23:00	-1:00
25/Aug/1945	24:00	0:00
27/Oct/1945	24:00	1:00
6/Apr/1946	23:00	0:00
5/Oct/1946	24:00	1:00
6/Apr/1947	2:00	0:00
5/Oct/1947	3:00	1:00
4/Apr/1948	2:00	0:00
3/Oct/1948	3:00	1:00
3/Apr/1949	2:00	0:00
2/Oct/1949	3:00	1:00
2/Apr/1950	2:00	0:00
1/Oct/1950	3:00	1:00
1/Apr/1951	2:00	0:00
7/Oct/1951	3:00	1:00
6/Apr/1952	2:00	0:00
5/Oct/1952	3:00	1:00
5/Apr/1953	2:00	0:00
4/Oct/1953	3:00	1:00
4/Apr/1954	2:00	0:00
3/Oct/1954	3:00	1:00
3/Apr/1955	2:00	0:00
2/Oct/1955	3:00	1:00
1/Apr/1956	2:00	0:00
7/Oct/1956	3:00	1:00
7/Apr/1957	2:00	0:00
6/Oct/1957	3:00	1:00
6/Apr/1958	2:00	0:00
5/Oct/1958	3:00	1:00
5/Apr/1959	2:00	0:00
4/Oct/1959	3:00	1:00
3/Apr/1960	2:00	0:00
2/Oct/1960	3:00	1:00
2/Apr/1961	2:00	0:00
1/Oct/1961	3:00	1:00
1/Apr/1962	2:00	0:00
7/Oct/1962	3:00	1:00
7/Apr/1963	2:00	0:00
6/Oct/1963	3:00	1:00
5/Apr/1964	2:00	0:00
4/Oct/1964	3:00	1:00
4/Apr/1965	2:00	0:00
3/Oct/1965	3:00	1:00
Begin Standard		0w00
3/Apr/1966	2:00	0:00
27/Mar/1977	0:00	-1:00
25/Sep/1977	1:00	0:00
2/Apr/1978	0:00	-1:00
1/Oct/1978	1:00	0:00
1/Apr/1979	0:00	-1:00
30/Sep/1979	2:00	0:00
30/Mar/1980	0:00	-1:00
28/Sep/1980	2:00	0:00
29/Mar/1981	1:00	-1:00
27/Sep/1981	2:00	0:00
28/Mar/1982	1:00	-1:00
26/Sep/1982	2:00	0:00
27/Mar/1983	2:00	-1:00
25/Sep/1983	2:00	0:00
25/Mar/1984	1:00	-1:00
30/Sep/1984	2:00	0:00
31/Mar/1985	1:00	-1:00
29/Sep/1985	2:00	0:00
30/Mar/1986	1:00	-1:00
28/Sep/1986	2:00	0:00
29/Mar/1987	1:00	-1:00
27/Sep/1987	2:00	0:00
27/Mar/1988	1:00	-1:00
25/Sep/1988	2:00	0:00
26/Mar/1989	1:00	-1:00
24/Sep/1989	2:00	0:00
25/Mar/1990	1:00	-1:00
30/Sep/1990	2:00	0:00
31/Mar/1991	1:00	-1:00
29/Sep/1991	2:00	0:00
29/Mar/1992	1:00	-1:00
27/Sep/1992	2:00	0:00
28/Mar/1993	1:00	-1:00
26/Sep/1993	2:00	0:00
27/Mar/1994	1:00	-1:00
25/Sep/1994	2:00	0:00
26/Mar/1995	1:00	-1:00
24/Sep/1995	2:00	0:00
31/Mar/1996	1:00	-1:00
29/Sep/1996	2:00	0:00
30/Mar/1997	1:00	-1:00
28/Sep/1997	2:00	0:00
29/Mar/1998	1:00	-1:00
27/Sep/1998	2:00	0:00
28/Mar/1999	1:00	-1:00
26/Sep/1999	2:00	0:00
26/Mar/2000	1:00	-1:00
24/Sep/2000	2:00	0:00

DIVISIONS

1. Mainland Portugal
2. Azores
3. Madeira Islands

Place	Div.	Lat.	Long.	Offset
Abóbada 1	1	38N43	9w20	0:37:20
Abrantes 1	1	39N28	8w12	0:32:48
Abrunheira 1	1	38N46	9w21	0:37:24
A-Da-Beja 1	1	38N47	9w14	0:36:56
Agualva-Cacém 1	1	38N46	9w18	0:37:12
Águeda 1	1	40N34	8w27	0:33:48
Albarraque 1	1	38N46	9w21	0:37:24
Albergaria-A-Velha 1	1	40N42	8w29	0:33:56
Albogas 1	1	38N51	9w15	0:37:00
Albufeira 1	1	37N05	8w15	0:33:00
Alcabideche 1	1	38N44	9w24	0:37:36
Alcácer do Sal 1	1	38N22	8w30	0:34:00
Alcains 1	1	39N55	7w27	0:29:48
Alcobaça 1	1	39N33	8w59	0:35:56
Alcochete 1	1	38N45	8w58	0:35:52
Alcoitão 1	1	38N44	9w24	0:37:36
Alcoutim 1	1	37N28	7w28	0:29:52
Aldeia de Paio Pires 1	1	38N38	9w05	0:36:20
Aldeia Nova de Santo Bento 1	1	37N55	7w25	0:29:40
Algés 1	1	38N42	9w13	0:36:52
Alguierão-Mem Martins 1	1	38N48	9w20	0:37:20
Alhos Vedros 1	1	38N39	9w02	0:36:08
Aljezur 1	1	37N19	8w48	0:35:12
Aljustrel 1	1	37N52	8w10	0:32:40
Almada 1	1	38N41	9w09	0:36:36
Almargem do Bispo 1	1	38N51	9w16	0:37:04
Almeida 1	1	40N43	6w54	0:27:36
Almeirim 1	1	39N12	8w38	0:34:32
Almoçageme 1	1	38N48	9w28	0:37:52
Almodôvar 1	1	37N31	8w04	0:32:16
Alpiarça 1	1	39N15	8w35	0:34:20

Place	Zone	Lat	Long	Time
Alter do Chão 1	1	39N12	7w40	0:30:40
Alvaiázere 1	1	39N49	8w23	0:33:32
Alvarinhos 1	1	38N54	9w22	0:37:28
Alverca 1	1	38N54	9w02	0:36:08
Alvito 1	1	38N15	7w59	0:31:56
Amadora 1	1	38N45	9w14	0:36:56
Amareleja 1	1	38N12	7w14	0:28:56
Amares 1	1	41N38	8w21	0:33:24
Amora 1	1	38N37	9w07	0:36:28
Angra do Heroísmo 2	2	38N39	27w13	1:48:52
Apelação 1	1	38N49	9w08	0:36:32
Arco de Baúlhe 1	1	41N29	7w58	0:31:52
Areeiro 1	1	38N39	9w12	0:36:48
Areia 1	1	38N43	9w08	0:36:32
Arneiro dos Marinheiros 1	1	38N51	9w25	0:37:40
Arrentela 1	1	38N38	9w06	0:36:24
Arronches 1	1	39N07	7w17	0:29:08
Atalaia 1	1	38N42	8w55	0:35:40
Aveiro 1	1	40N38	8w39	0:34:36
Aviz 1	1	39N03	7w53	0:31:32
Azambuja 1	1	39N04	8w52	0:35:28
Azenhas do Mar 1	1	38N50	9w28	0:37:52
Azoia 1	1	38N46	9w29	0:37:56
Azores 2	2	37N44	25w40	1:42:40
Baratã 1	1	38N48	9w19	0:37:16
Barcarena 1	1	38N44	9w17	0:37:08
Barcelos 1	1	41N32	8w37	0:34:28
Barranco do Velho 1	1	37N14	7w56	0:31:44
Barrancos 1	1	38N08	6w59	0:27:56
Barreiro 1	1	38N40	9w04	0:36:16
Batalha 1	1	39N39	8w50	0:35:20
Beja 1	1	38N01	7w52	0:31:28
Belas 1	1	38N47	9w16	0:37:04
Belmonte 1	1	40N21	7w21	0:29:24
Benavente 1	1	38N59	8w48	0:35:12
Bombarral 1	1	39N16	9w09	0:36:36
Borba 1	1	38N48	7w27	0:29:48
Boticas 1	1	41N41	7w40	0:30:40
Braga 1	1	41N33	8w26	0:33:44
Bragança 1	1	41N49	6w45	0:27:00
Bucelas 1	1	38N54	9w07	0:36:28
Cabeço de Montachique 1	1	38N54	9w11	0:36:44
Cacilhas 1	1	38N41	9w09	0:36:36
Caldas da Rainha 1	1	39N24	9w08	0:36:32
Calhota 3	3	32N44	17w12	1:08:48
Caminha 1	1	41N52	8w50	0:35:20
Campo Maior 1	1	39N01	7w04	0:28:16
Caneças 1	1	38N49	9w14	0:36:56
Cantanhede 1	1	40N21	8w36	0:34:24
Cantribana 1	1	38N53	9w25	0:37:40
Caparica 1	1	38N40	9w12	0:36:48
Carcavelos 1	1	38N41	9w20	0:37:20
Carcavelos 1	1	38N53	9w14	0:36:56
Carnaxide 1	1	38N43	9w15	0:37:00
Cartaxo 1	1	39N09	8w47	0:35:08
Casainhos 1	1	38N53	9w10	0:36:40
Cascais 1	1	38N42	9w25	0:37:40
Castanheira de Pêra 1	1	40N00	8w13	0:32:52
Castelo Branco 1	1	39N49	7w30	0:30:00
Castro Daire 1	1	40N54	7w56	0:31:44
Castro Marim 1	1	37N13	7w26	0:29:44
Castro Verde 1	1	37N42	8w05	0:32:20
Caxias 1	1	38N42	9w16	0:37:04
Celorico da Beira 1	1	40N38	7w23	0:29:32
Chamusca 1	1	39N21	8w29	0:33:56
Charneca 1	1	38N44	9w27	0:37:48
Chaves 1	1	41N44	7w28	0:29:52
Cheleiros 1	1	38N53	9w20	0:37:20
Cintra → Sintra 1	1	38N48	9w23	0:37:32
Coimbra 1	1	40N12	8w25	0:33:40
Colares 1	1	38N48	9w27	0:37:48
Constânzia 1	1	39N28	8w20	0:33:20
Corroios 1	1	38N38	9w09	0:36:36
Coruche 1	1	38N57	8w31	0:34:04
Costa de Caparica 1	1	38N38	9w14	0:36:56
Cova da Piedade 1	1	38N40	9w10	0:36:40
Covilhã 1	1	40N17	7w30	0:30:00
Covões 1	1	38N50	9w20	0:37:20
Cuba 1	1	38N10	7w53	0:31:32
Elvas 1	1	38N53	7w10	0:28:40
Entroncamento 1	1	39N28	8w28	0:33:52
Ericeira 1	1	38N59	9w25	0:37:40
Ermidas 1	1	38N00	8w23	0:33:32
Espinho 1	1	41N00	8w39	0:34:36
Esposende 1	1	41N32	8w47	0:35:08
Estarreja 1	1	40N45	8w34	0:34:16
Estoril 1	1	38N42	9w23	0:37:32
Estremoz 1	1	38N51	7w35	0:30:20
Évora 1	1	38N34	7w54	0:31:36
Fafe 1	1	41N27	8w10	0:32:40
Fanhões 1	1	38N53	9w09	0:36:36
Faro 1	1	37N01	7w56	0:31:44
Fátima 1	1	39N37	8w39	0:34:36
Ferreira do Alentejo 1	1	38N03	8w07	0:32:28
Figueira da Foz 1	1	40N09	8w52	0:35:28
Foguetetro 1	1	38N37	9w07	0:36:28
Fontanelas 1	1	38N51	9w26	0:37:44
Forte de Magoito 1	1	38N52	9w27	0:37:48
Foz Giraldo 1	1	40N00	7w43	0:30:52
Freixial 1	1	38N54	9w09	0:36:36
Frielas 1	1	38N49	9w09	0:36:36
Funchal 3	3	32N38	16w54	1:07:36
Fundão 1	1	40N08	7w30	0:30:00
Galamares 1	1	38N48	9w25	0:37:40
Góis 1	1	40N09	8w07	0:32:28
Gondomar 1	1	41N09	8w32	0:34:08
Gouveia 1	1	38N50	9w26	0:37:44
Grândola 1	1	38N10	8w34	0:34:16
Granja 1	1	38N51	9w06	0:36:24
Guarda 1	1	40N32	7w16	0:29:04
Guimarães 1	1	41N27	8w18	0:33:12
Horta 2	2	38N32	28w38	1:54:32
Idanha-A-Nova 1	1	39N55	7w14	0:28:56
Ilhavo 1	1	40N36	8w40	0:34:40
Janas 1	1	38N49	9w26	0:37:44
Lagos 1	1	37N06	8w40	0:34:40
Lamego 1	1	41N06	7w49	0:31:16
Leião 1	1	38N44	9w18	0:37:12
Leiria 1	1	39N45	8w48	0:35:12
Linda-A-Velha 1	1	38N43	9w14	0:36:56
Linhó 1	1	38N46	9w23	0:37:32
Lisboa (Lisbon) 1	1	38N43	9w08	0:36:32
Lisbon → Lisboa 1	1	38N43	9w08	0:36:32
Lisbonne → Lisboa 1	1	38N43	9w08	0:36:32
Lissabon → Lisboa 1	1	38N43	9w08	0:36:32
Loulé 1	1	37N08	8w02	0:32:08
Lourel de Baixo 1	1	38N49	9w22	0:37:28
Loures 1	1	38N50	9w10	0:36:40
Lourinhã 1	1	39N14	9w19	0:37:16
Lourosa 1	1	40N19	7w56	0:31:44
Lousã 1	1	40N07	8w15	0:33:00
Lousa 1	1	38N53	9w12	0:36:48
Macão 1	1	39N33	8w00	0:32:00
Macedo de Cavaleiros 1	1	41N32	6w58	0:27:52
Maceira 1	1	38N52	9w19	0:37:16
Machico 3	3	32N42	16w46	1:07:04
Madeira 3	3	32N38	16w54	1:07:36
Mafra 1	1	38N56	9w20	0:37:20
Magoito 1	1	38N52	9w26	0:37:44
Maia 1	1	41N14	8w37	0:34:28
Malveira 1	1	38N45	9w27	0:37:48
Mangualde 1	1	40N36	7w46	0:31:04
Manique de Baixo 1	1	38N44	9w22	0:37:28
Marinha Grande 1	1	39N45	8w56	0:35:44
Matosinhos 1	1	41N11	8w42	0:34:48
Mealhada 1	1	40N22	8w27	0:33:48
Meda 1	1	40N58	7w16	0:29:04
Melgaço 1	1	42N07	8w16	0:33:04
Mercês 1	1	38N47	9w19	0:37:16
Mértola 1	1	37N38	7w40	0:30:40
Mira 1	1	40N26	8w44	0:34:56
Miranda do Douro 1	1	41N30	6w16	0:25:04
Mirandela 1	1	41N29	7w11	0:28:44
Mogadouro 1	1	41N20	6w39	0:26:36
Moita 1	1	38N39	8w59	0:35:56
Moncão 1	1	42N05	8w29	0:33:56
Monchique 1	1	37N19	8w33	0:34:12
Monforte 1	1	39N03	7w26	0:29:44
Montalegre 1	1	41N49	7w48	0:31:12
Montargil 1	1	39N05	8w10	0:32:40
Monte Estoril 1	1	38N42	9w24	0:37:36
Montelavar 1	1	38N51	9w20	0:37:20
Montemor 1	1	38N49	9w12	0:36:48
Montemor-O-Novo 1	1	38N39	8w13	0:32:52
Montemor-O-Velho 1	1	40N10	8w41	0:34:44
Montijo 1	1	38N42	8w58	0:35:52
Mora 1	1	38N56	8w10	0:32:40
Moscavide 1	1	38N47	9w06	0:36:24
Moura 1	1	38N08	7w27	0:29:48
Mucifal 1	1	38N48	9w26	0:37:44
Murča 1	1	41N24	7w27	0:29:48
Murtal 1	1	38N42	9w22	0:37:28
Murtosa 1	1	40N44	8w38	0:34:32
Nafarros 1	1	38N49	9w25	0:37:40
Nazaré 1	1	39N36	9w04	0:36:16
Negrais 1	1	38N53	9w17	0:37:08
Nisa 1	1	39N31	7w39	0:30:36
Odemira 1	1	37N36	8w38	0:34:32
Odivelas 1	1	38N47	9w11	0:36:44
Odrinhas 1	1	38N53	9w22	0:37:28
Oeiras 1	1	38N41	9w21	0:37:24
Olhão 1	1	37N02	8w50	0:35:20
Olival Basto 1	1	38N47	9w10	0:36:40
Oporto → Porto 1	1	41N11	8w36	0:34:24
Ourique 1	1	37N39	8w13	0:32:52
Ovar 1	1	40N52	8w38	0:34:32
Paço de Arcos 1	1	38N42	9w17	0:37:08
Palhais 1	1	38N37	9w03	0:36:12
Pancas 1	1	38N48	8w55	0:35:40
Parede 1	1	38N41	9w21	0:37:24
Pedras Salgadas 1	1	41N32	7w36	0:30:24
Pedrógão Grande 1	1	39N55	8w09	0:32:36
Penafiel 1	1	41N12	8w17	0:33:08
Penedono 1	1	40N59	7w24	0:29:36
Penela 1	1	40N02	8w23	0:33:32
Peniche 1	1	39N21	9w23	0:37:32
Pero Pinheiro 1	1	38N51	9w20	0:37:20
Peso da Régua 1	1	41N10	7w47	0:31:08
Pinhal Novo 1	1	38N38	8w55	0:35:40
Pinheiro de Loures 1	1	38N50	9w12	0:36:48
Pinhel 1	1	40N46	7w04	0:28:16
Pinteus 1	1	38N52	9w09	0:36:36
Pombal 1	1	39N55	8w38	0:34:32
Ponta Delgada 2	2	37N44	25w40	1:42:40
Pontão 1	1	39N55	8w22	0:33:28
Ponte da Barca 1	1	41N48	8w25	0:33:40
Ponte de Sor 1	1	39N15	8w01	0:32:04
Ponte do Lima 1	1	41N46	8w35	0:34:20
Portalegre 1	1	39N17	7w26	0:29:44
Portel 1	1	38N18	7w42	0:30:48
Portimão 1	1	37N08	8w32	0:34:08
Porto 1	1	41N11	8w36	0:34:24
Pôrto de Mós 1	1	39N36	8w39	0:34:36
Porto Salvo 1	1	38N43	9w18	0:37:12
Porto Santo 3	3	33N03	16w19	1:05:16
Povoação 2	2	37N45	25w15	1:41:00
Póvoa de Santa Iria 1	1	38N52	9w04	0:36:16
Póvoa de Santo Adrião 1	1	38N48	9w10	0:36:40
Póvoa de Varzim 1	1	41N23	8w46	0:35:04
Praia da Cruz Quebrada 1	1	38N42	9w14	0:36:56
Praia das Maçãs 1	1	38N50	9w28	0:37:52
Praia da Vitória 2	2	38N44	27w04	1:48:16
Proença-A-Nova 1	1	39N45	7w55	0:31:40
Queluz 1	1	38N45	9w15	0:37:00
Ranholas 1	1	38N47	9w22	0:37:28
Redondo 1	1	38N39	7w33	0:30:12
Reguengos de Monsaraz 1	1	38N25	7w32	0:30:08
Ribeira Grande 2	2	37N49	25w31	1:42:04
Rio de Mouro 1	1	38N46	9w20	0:37:20
Rosairinho 1	1	38N40	9w01	0:36:04
Sabugal 1	1	40N21	7w05	0:28:20
Sabugo 1	1	38N49	9w18	0:37:12
Sacavém 1	1	38N47	9w06	0:36:24
Sacotes 1	1	38N48	9w20	0:37:20
Sagres 1	1	37N00	8w56	0:35:44
Salvaterra de Magos 1	1	39N01	8w48	0:35:12
Samouco 1	1	38N43	9w00	0:36:00
Santa Comba Dão 1	1	40N24	8w08	0:32:32
Santa Cruz da Graciosa 2	2	39N05	28w01	1:52:04
Santa Cruz das Flores 2	2	39N27	31w07	2:04:28
Santa Iria de Azóia 1	1	38N51	9w05	0:36:20
Santa Luzia 1	1	37N44	8w24	0:33:36
Santa Luzia (Pico) 2	1	38N33	28w24	1:53:36
Santarém 1	1	39N14	8w41	0:34:44
Santiago do Cacém 1	1	38N01	8w42	0:34:48
Santo António da Charneca 1	1	38N37	9w02	0:36:08
Santo Tirso 1	1	41N21	8w28	0:33:52
São Brás de Alportel 1	1	37N09	7w53	0:31:32
São João da Madeira 1	1	40N54	8w30	0:34:00
São João das Lampas 1	1	38N52	9w24	0:37:36
São Julião da Barra 1	1	38N40	9w21	0:37:24
São Julião do Tojal 1	1	38N51	9w08	0:36:32
São Mateus 2	2	38N26	28w27	1:53:48
São Pedro do Estoril 1	1	38N42	9w22	0:37:28
São Pedro do Sul 1	1	40N45	8w04	0:32:16
Sarilhos Grandes 1	1	38N41	8w58	0:35:52
Sarilhos Pequenos 1	1	38N41	8w59	0:35:56
Sátão 1	1	40N44	7w44	0:30:56
Segura 1	1	39N50	6w59	0:27:56
Seia 1	1	40N25	7w42	0:30:48
Seixal 1	1	38N38	9w06	0:36:24
Serpa 1	1	37N56	7w36	0:30:24
Sertã 1	1	39N48	8w06	0:32:24
Setúbal 1	1	38N32	8w54	0:35:36
Sezimbra 1	1	38N26	9w06	0:36:24
Silves 1	1	37N11	8w26	0:33:44
Sines 1	1	37N57	8w52	0:35:28
Sinfães 1	1	41N04	8w05	0:32:20
Sintra 1	1	38N48	9w23	0:37:32
Sao Vicente 3	3	32N47	17w03	1:08:12
Sobrado 1	1	41N02	8w16	0:33:04
Soure 1	1	40N03	8w38	0:34:32
Sousel 1	1	38N57	7w40	0:30:40
Tabuaço 1	1	41N07	7w34	0:30:16
Tarouca 1	1	41N00	7w40	0:30:40
Tavira 1	1	37N07	7w39	0:30:36
Terrugem 1	1	38N51	9w20	0:37:20
Tires 1	1	38N43	9w21	0:37:24
Tomar 1	1	39N36	8w25	0:33:40
Torrão 1	1	38N18	8w13	0:32:52
Torre de Moncorvo 1	1	41N10	7w03	0:28:12
Torres Novas 1	1	39N29	8w32	0:34:08
Torres Vedras 1	1	39N06	9w16	0:37:04
Trafaria 1	1	38N40	9w14	0:36:56
Trajouce 1	1	38N44	9w20	0:37:20

PORTUGAL — LUSITANIA — PORTUGAL

Place		Lat	Long	Time
Trancoso 1	1	40N47	7w21	0:29:24
Ulgueira 1	1	38N47	9w28	0:37:52
Unhos 1	1	38N50	9w07	0:36:28
Vale de Lobos 1	1	38N49	9w17	0:37:08
Valença 1	1	42N02	8w38	0:34:32
Valongo 1	1	41N11	8w30	0:34:00
Varzea de Sintra 1	1	38N49	9w24	0:37:36
Velas 2	2	38N41	28w13	1:52:52
Venda Nova 1	1	41N40	7w58	0:31:52
Vendas Novas 1	1	38N41	8w28	0:33:52
Vialonga 1	1	38N52	9w05	0:36:20
Viana do Alentejo 1	1	38N20	8w00	0:32:00
Viana do Castelo 1	1	41N42	8w50	0:35:20
Vidigueira 1	1	38N13	7w48	0:31:12
Vieira do Minho 1	1	41N39	8w09	0:32:36
Vila das Velas (San Jorge) 2	1	38N41	28w13	1:52:52
Vila de Rei 1	1	39N40	8w09	0:32:36
Vila de Topo (San Jorge) 2	1	38N33	27w47	1:51:08
Vila do Bispo 1	1	37N05	8w55	0:35:40
Vila do Conde 1	1	41N21	8w45	0:35:00
Vila do Porto 2	2	36N56	25w09	1:40:36
Vila Flor 1	1	41N18	7w09	0:28:36
Vila Franca de Campo (San Miguel) 2	1	37N42	25w53	1:43:32
Vila Franca de Xira 1	1	38N57	8w59	0:35:56
Vila Nova de Famalicão 1	1	41N25	8w32	0:34:08
Vila Nova de Foz Côa 1	1	41N05	7w12	0:28:48
Vila Nova de Gaia 1	1	41N08	8w37	0:34:28
Vila Novo de Ourém 1	1	39N39	8w35	0:34:20
Vila Real 1	1	41N18	7w45	0:31:00
Vila Real de Santo Antônio 1	1	37N12	7w25	0:29:40
Vilar Formoso 1	1	40N37	6w50	0:27:20
Vila Velha de Rôdão 1	1	39N38	7w40	0:30:40
Vila Verde 1	1	41N39	8w26	0:33:44
Vila Verde 1	1	38N50	9w22	0:37:28
Vila Viçosa 1	1	38N47	8w13	0:32:52
Vinhais 1	1	41N50	7w00	0:28:00
Viseu 1	1	40N39	7w55	0:31:40
Zambujal 1	1	38N52	9w07	0:36:28

PUERTO RICO — PORTO RICO — PUERTO RICO

Time Table

Before 28/Mar/1899 LMT

Begin	Standard	60w00
28/Mar/1899	12:00	4:00
3/May/1942	0:00	3:00
30/Sep/1945	2:00	4:00

DIVISIONS

1. Aguadilla
2. Arecibo
3. Bayamon
4. Buayama
5. Humacao
6. Mayaguez
7. Ponce
8. San Juan

Place	Lat	Long	Time
Adjuntas 6	18N10	66w43	4:26:52
Aguada 1	18N23	67w11	4:28:44
Aguadilla 1	18N26	67w09	4:28:36
Aguas Buenas 4	18N15	66w06	4:24:24
Aibonito 7	18N08	66w16	4:25:04
Anasco 6	18N17	67w08	4:28:32
Arecibo 2	18N28	66w43	4:26:52
Arenal 4	17N59	66w19	4:25:16
Arroyo 4	17N58	66w04	4:24:16
Asomante 2	18N23	66w36	4:26:24
Bahomamey 1	18N20	66w59	4:27:56
Barceloneta 2	18N27	66w32	4:26:08
Barinas 6	18N01	66w51	4:27:24
Barranquitas 4	18N11	66w18	4:25:12
Bayamón 3	18N24	66w09	4:24:36
Boca Chica 7	17N59	66w32	4:26:08
Boqueroen 6	18N02	67w10	4:28:40
Botijas 7	18N15	66w22	4:25:28
Cabo Rojo 6	18N05	67w09	4:28:36
Caguas 4	18N14	66w02	4:24:08
Camuy 1	18N29	66w51	4:27:24
Canovanas 3	18N23	65w54	4:23:36
Carolina 3	18N23	65w57	4:23:48
Catano 8	18N27	66w07	4:24:28
Cayey 4	18N07	66w10	4:24:40
Ceiba 5	18N16	65w39	4:22:36
Central Aguirre 4	17N57	66w13	4:24:52
Centro Puntas 1	18N22	67w16	4:29:04
Charco Hondo 2	18N25	66w43	4:26:52
Ciales 2	18N20	66w28	4:25:52
Cidra 4	18N11	66w10	4:24:40
Coamo 7	18N05	66w22	4:25:28
Collores 7	18N12	66w37	4:26:28
Colonia Providencia 4	17N59	66w00	4:24:00
Comereo 4	18N13	66w14	4:24:56
Comerio 4	18N13	66w14	4:24:56
Coqui 4	17N59	66w14	4:24:56
Corcega 1	18N19	67w15	4:29:00
Corozal 3	18N21	66w17	4:25:08
Coto Laurel 7	18N03	66w33	4:26:12
Culebra 5	18N18	65w18	4:21:12
Daguao 5	18N14	65w41	4:22:44
Dewey 5	18N18	65w18	4:21:12
Domingo Ruiz 2	18N27	66w41	4:26:44
Dorado 2	18N28	66w16	4:25:04
Dos Bocas 2	18N20	66w40	4:26:40
El Campamento 2	18N22	66w28	4:25:52
El Coto 2	18N28	66w44	4:26:56
El Faro 6	18N00	66w47	4:27:08
El Minao 3	18N22	66w05	4:24:20
El Polvorin 2	18N26	66w17	4:25:08
Ensenada 6	17N58	66w56	4:27:44
Esperanza	18N06	65w28	4:21:52
Fajardo 5	18N20	65w39	4:22:36
Feliciano 1	18N28	67w08	4:28:32
Florida 2	18N22	66w34	4:26:16
Florida 5	18N14	65w47	4:23:08
Guaenica 6	17N59	66w55	4:27:40
Guanabana 6	18N01	67w07	4:28:28
Guanica 6	17N58	66w55	4:27:40
Guayama 4	17N59	66w07	4:24:28
Guayanilla 6	18N01	66w47	4:27:08
Guaynabo 3	18N22	66w07	4:24:28
Gurabo 5	18N16	65w58	4:23:52
Hatillo 1	18N29	66w49	4:27:16
Hato Rey 3	18N25	66w03	4:24:12
Hormigueros 6	18N09	67w08	4:28:32
Humacao 5	18N09	65w50	4:23:20
Indiera Alta 6	18N09	66w53	4:27:32
Isabel Segunda	18N09	65w27	4:21:48
Isabela 1	18N30	67w01	4:28:04
Jayuga 7	18N14	66w36	4:26:24
Jayuya 7	18N13	66w36	4:26:24
Jobos 4	17N58	66w10	4:24:40
Joyuda 6	18N07	67w11	4:28:44
Juana Diaz 7	18N03	66w31	4:26:04
Juncos 5	18N14	65w55	4:23:40
La Cuesta 2	18N25	66w49	4:27:16
La Esperanza 3	18N22	66w07	4:24:28
Lajas 6	18N03	67w04	4:28:16
Lares 6	18N18	66w53	4:27:32
Las Arenas 6	18N02	67w09	4:28:36
Las Flores 7	18N03	66w22	4:25:28
Las Mareas 4	17N56	66w09	4:24:36
Las Marias 6	18N15	67w00	4:28:00
Las Palmas 4	17N59	66w02	4:24:08
Las Piedras 5	18N11	65w52	4:23:28
Las Pinas 5	18N15	65w55	4:23:40
Las Vegas 6	18N11	67w02	4:28:08
Loiza Aldea	18N26	65w53	4:23:32
Los Llanos 7	18N03	66w24	4:25:36
Los Rabanos 6	18N11	66w50	4:27:20
Luquillo 5	18N22	65w43	4:22:52
Machuchal 6	18N03	66w56	4:27:44
Mamayes 5	18N22	65w46	4:23:04
Manati 2	18N26	66w29	4:25:56
Mani 6	18N15	67w10	4:28:40
Maricao 6	18N11	66w59	4:27:56
Maunabo 4	18N01	65w54	4:23:36
Mayagüez 6	18N12	67w09	4:28:36
Moca 1	18N24	67w07	4:28:28
Montebello 2	18N22	66w31	4:26:04
Mora 1	18N28	67w02	4:28:08
Morovis 2	18N20	66w24	4:25:36
Naguabo 5	18N13	65w44	4:22:56
Naranjito 3	18N18	66w15	4:25:00
Orocovis 7	18N14	66w23	4:25:32
Palmarejo 6	18N03	67w05	4:28:20
Palmer 5	18N22	65w46	4:23:04
Palo Blanco 2	18N26	66w39	4:26:36
Palo Seco 8	18N28	66w09	4:24:36
Parguera 6	17N59	67w03	4:28:12
Paso Seco 7	17N59	66w23	4:25:32
Pastillo 7	17N59	66w29	4:25:56
Patillas 4	18N00	66w01	4:24:04
Peñuelas 6	18N03	66w43	4:26:52
Perchas 6	18N19	66w59	4:27:56
Playa de Fajardo 5	18N20	65w38	4:22:32
Playa de Guayanes 5	18N04	65w49	4:23:16
Playa de Guayanilla 6	18N01	66w46	4:27:04
Playa De Humacao 5	18N10	65w45	4:23:00
Playa de Naguabo 5	18N12	65w43	4:22:52
Playa de Ponce 7	17N59	66w37	4:26:28
Poblado Cerro Gordo 2	18N29	66w20	4:25:20
Poblado Jacuaguas 7	18N03	66w32	4:26:08
Poblado Mediania Alta	18N26	65w50	4:23:20
Poblados Abalos 6	18N11	67w09	4:28:36
Poblado Santana 2	18N27	66w40	4:26:40
Ponce 7	18N01	66w37	4:26:28
Pueblito de Ponce 1	18N26	66w58	4:27:52
Pueblo Nuevo 1	18N28	66w51	4:27:24
Puerto Real 6	18N05	67w11	4:28:44
Punta Santiago 5	18N10	65w45	4:23:00
Quebrada Seca 5	18N14	65w40	4:22:40
Quebradillas 1	18N29	66w56	4:27:44
Rincon 1	18N20	67w15	4:29:00
Rio Canias 7	18N03	66w26	4:25:44
Rio Grande	18N23	65w50	4:23:20
Rio Jueyes 7	18N01	66w20	4:25:20
Rio Piedras 3	18N24	66w03	4:24:12
Rosario 6	18N10	67w05	4:28:20
Sabana 5	18N20	65w44	4:22:56
Sabana Grande 6	18N05	66w58	4:27:52
Sabana Llana 6	18N02	66w15	4:25:00
Saint Just 3	18N23	66w00	4:24:00
Salinas 4	17N59	66w18	4:25:12
San Antonio 1	18N30	67w07	4:28:28
San Felipe 4	17N58	66w13	4:24:52
San German 6	18N05	67w03	4:28:12
San Juan 8	18N28	66w07	4:24:28
San Lorenzo 5	18N11	65w58	4:23:52
San Sebastian 1	18N20	66w59	4:27:56
Santa Isabel 7	17N58	66w24	4:25:36
Santa Maria	18N09	65w26	4:21:44
San Turce 8	18N27	66w05	4:24:20
Soroco 5	18N22	65w38	4:22:32
Tablones 5	18N15	65w45	4:23:00
Toa Alta 3	18N23	66w15	4:25:00
Toa Baja 3	18N27	66w15	4:25:00
Trujillo Alto 3	18N22	66w01	4:24:04
Utuado 2	18N16	66w42	4:26:48
Vega Alta 2	18N25	66w20	4:25:20
Vega Baja 2	18N27	66w23	4:25:32
Vertedero 6	18N05	66w15	4:25:00
Victoria 1	18N25	67w10	4:28:40
Vieques	18N09	65w27	4:21:48
Villalba 7	18N08	66w30	4:26:00
Villa Perez 6	18N12	66w47	4:27:08
Yabucoa 5	18N03	65w53	4:23:32
Yauco 6	18N02	66w51	4:27:24

QATAR KATAR QAṬAR

Time Table

Before 1/Jan/1920		LMT
Begin Standard		60E00
1/Jan/1920	0:00	-4:00
Begin Standard		45E00
1/Jun/1972	0:00	-3:00

Place	Lat	Long	Offset
Ad-Dawḥah (Doha)	25N17	51E32	-3:26:08
Al-Wakrah	25N10	51E36	-3:26:24
Doha → Ad-Dawḥah	25N17	51E32	-3:26:08
Dukhān	25N25	50E48	-3:23:12
Musay'īd	24N59	51E32	-3:26:08

REUNION REUNIÓN BOURBON BONAPARTE RÉUNION

Time Table

Before 1/Jun/1911		LMT
Begin Standard		60E00
1/Jun/1911	0:00	-4:00

Place	Lat	Long	Offset
Le Port	20s55	55E18	-3:41:12
Pointe-Des-Galets → Le Port	20s55	55E18	-3:41:12
Port → Le Port	20s55	55E18	-3:41:12
Saint-André	20s57	55E39	-3:42:36
Saint-Benoît	21s02	55E43	-3:42:52
Saint-Denis	20s52	55E28	-3:41:52
Saint-Joseph	21s22	55E36	-3:42:24
Saint-Louis	21s16	55E25	-3:41:40
Saint-Paul	21s00	55E16	-3:41:04
Saint-Pierre	21s19	55E29	-3:41:56

ROMANIA RUMANIA ROUMANIE RUMÄNIEN ROMÂNIA

Time Table

Before 1/Oct/1891		LMT
Begin Standard		26E06
1/Oct/1891	0:00	-1:44
Begin Standard		30E00
24/Jul/1931	0:00	-2:00
21/May/1932	24:00	-3:00
2/Oct/1932	1:00	-2:00
1/Apr/1933	24:00	-3:00
1/Oct/1933	1:00	-2:00
7/Apr/1934	24:00	-3:00
7/Oct/1934	1:00	-2:00
6/Apr/1935	24:00	-3:00
6/Oct/1935	1:00	-2:00
4/Apr/1936	24:00	-3:00
4/Oct/1936	1:00	-2:00
3/Apr/1937	24:00	-3:00
3/Oct/1937	1:00	-2:00
2/Apr/1938	24:00	-3:00
2/Oct/1938	1:00	-2:00
1/Apr/1939	24:00	-3:00
7/Oct/1939	1:00	-2:00
27/May/1979	0:00	-3:00
30/Sep/1979	0:00	-2:00
5/Apr/1980	23:00	-3:00
28/Sep/1980	1:00	-2:00
29/Mar/1981	2:00	-3:00
27/Sep/1981	3:00	-2:00
28/Mar/1982	2:00	-3:00
26/Sep/1982	3:00	-2:00
27/Mar/1983	2:00	-3:00
25/Sep/1983	3:00	-2:00
25/Mar/1984	2:00	-3:00
30/Sep/1984	3:00	-2:00
31/Mar/1985	2:00	-3:00
29/Sep/1985	3:00	-2:00
30/Mar/1986	2:00	-3:00
28/Sep/1986	3:00	-2:00
29/Mar/1987	2:00	-3:00
27/Sep/1987	3:00	-2:00
27/Mar/1988	2:00	-3:00
25/Sep/1988	3:00	-2:00
26/Mar/1989	2:00	-3:00
24/Sep/1989	3:00	-2:00
25/Mar/1990	2:00	-3:00
30/Sep/1990	3:00	-2:00
31/Mar/1991	2:00	-3:00
29/Sep/1991	3:00	-2:00
29/Mar/1992	2:00	-3:00
27/Sep/1992	3:00	-2:00
28/Mar/1993	2:00	-3:00
26/Sep/1993	3:00	-2:00
27/Mar/1994	2:00	-3:00
25/Sep/1994	3:00	-2:00
26/Mar/1995	2:00	-3:00
24/Sep/1995	3:00	-2:00
31/Mar/1996	2:00	-3:00
29/Sep/1996	3:00	-2:00
30/Mar/1997	2:00	-3:00
28/Sep/1997	3:00	-2:00
29/Mar/1998	2:00	-3:00
27/Sep/1998	3:00	-2:00
28/Mar/1999	2:00	-3:00
26/Sep/1999	3:00	-2:00
26/Mar/2000	2:00	-3:00
24/Sep/2000	3:00	-2:00

Place	Lat	Long	Offset
Abrud	46N17	23E04	-1:32:16
Acîş	47N33	22E47	-1:31:08
Adamclisi	44N05	27E57	-1:51:48
Adjud	46N04	27E11	-1:48:44
Agnita	45N59	24E38	-1:38:32
Aiud	46N19	23E44	-1:34:56
Alba-Iulia	46N04	23E35	-1:34:20
Aleşd	47N04	22E24	-1:29:36
Alexandria	43N58	25E20	-1:41:20
Amărăştii-De-Jos	43N59	24E10	-1:36:40
Anina	45N05	21E51	-1:27:24
Arad	46N11	21E20	-1:25:20
Armeniş	45N12	22E19	-1:29:16
Azuga	45N27	25E33	-1:42:12
Babadag	44N54	28E43	-1:54:52
Bacău	46N34	26E55	-1:47:40
Baia-De-Aramă	45N00	22E49	-1:31:16
Baia-Mare	47N40	23E35	-1:34:20
Baia Sprie	47N40	23E42	-1:34:48
Băile Govora	45N05	24E11	-1:36:44
Băile Herculane	44N54	22E25	-1:29:40
Băile Olăneşti	45N11	24E16	-1:37:04
Băileşti	44N02	23E21	-1:33:24
Balaci	44N21	24E55	-1:39:40
Bălceşti	44N37	23E56	-1:35:44
Balş	44N21	24E06	-1:36:24
Băneasa	44N04	27E42	-1:50:48
Baraolt	46N05	25E36	-1:42:24
Bârlad → Bîrlad	46N14	27E40	-1:50:40
Basarabi	44N10	28E24	-1:53:36
Beceni	45N23	26E46	-1:47:04
Bechet	43N46	23E58	-1:35:52
Beclean	47N11	24E10	-1:36:40
Beiuş	46N40	22E21	-1:29:24
Bereşti	46N06	27E53	-1:51:32
Bicaz	46N54	26E05	-1:44:20
Bîrca	43N58	23E37	-1:34:28
Bîrlad	46N14	27E40	-1:50:40
Bistreţ	43N54	23E30	-1:34:00
Bistriţa	47N08	24E30	-1:38:00
Blaj	46N11	23E55	-1:35:40
Borş	47N07	21E49	-1:27:16
Borşa	46N56	23E40	-1:34:40
Borşa	47N39	24E40	-1:38:40
Botoşani	47N45	26E40	-1:46:40
Botoşaniţa	47N53	26E07	-1:44:28
Bozovici	44N55	21E59	-1:27:56
Brad	46N08	22E47	-1:31:08
Brăila	45N16	27E58	-1:51:52
Braşov	45N39	25E37	-1:42:28
Brassó → Braşov	45N39	25E37	-1:42:28
Bratca	46N56	22E37	-1:30:28
Breaza	45N11	25E40	-1:42:40
Bucarest → Bucureşti	44N26	26E06	-1:44:24
Bucharest → Bucureşti	44N26	26E06	-1:44:24
Bucureşti (Bucharest)	44N26	26E06	-1:44:24
Budeşti	44N14	26E28	-1:45:52
Buhuşi	46N43	26E41	-1:46:44
Bukarest → Bucureşti	44N26	26E06	-1:44:24
Burila Mare	44N27	22E34	-1:30:16
Buşteni	45N25	25E32	-1:42:08
Buzău	45N09	26E49	-1:47:16
Buziaş	45N39	21E36	-1:26:24
Căciulaţi	44N38	26E10	-1:44:40
Calafat	43N59	22E56	-1:31:44
Călăraşi	44N11	27E20	-1:49:20
Călimăneşti	45N14	24E20	-1:37:20
Călugăreni	44N07	26E01	-1:44:04
Caracal	44N07	24E21	-1:37:24
Caransebeş	45N25	22E13	-1:28:52
Carei	47N42	22E28	-1:29:52
Casimcea	44N43	28E23	-1:53:32
Căzăneşti	44N37	27E01	-1:48:04
Cehu-Silvaniei	47N25	23E11	-1:32:44
Cermei	46N33	21E51	-1:27:24
Cerna	45N04	28E18	-1:53:12
Cernavodă	44N21	28E01	-1:52:04
Cetate	44N06	23E03	-1:32:12
Chişineu-Criş	46N31	21E31	-1:26:04
Cîmpeni	46N22	23E03	-1:32:12
Cîmpia Turzii	46N33	23E54	-1:35:36
Cîmpina	45N08	25E44	-1:42:56
Cîmpulung	45N16	25E03	-1:40:12
Cîmpulung Moldovenesc	47N31	25E34	-1:42:16
Ciocăneşti	44N12	27E04	-1:48:16
Cîrlibaba	47N35	25E07	-1:40:28
Cisnădie	45N43	24E09	-1:36:36
Cluj	46N47	23E36	-1:34:24
Cobadin	44N04	28E13	-1:52:52
Codăeşti	46N52	27E46	-1:51:04
Codlea	45N42	25E27	-1:41:48
Coloneşti	46N34	27E18	-1:49:12
Comana	43N54	28E19	-1:53:16
Comăneşti	46N25	26E26	-1:45:44
Comloşu Mare	45N54	20E38	-1:22:32
Constanţa	44N11	28E39	-1:54:36
Corabia	43N46	24E30	-1:38:00
Corbu	44N29	24E43	-1:38:52
Corund	46N28	25E11	-1:40:44
Corzu	44N28	23E10	-1:32:40
Costeşti	44N40	24E53	-1:39:32
Covasna	45N51	26E11	-1:44:44
Craiova	44N19	23E48	-1:35:12
Crasna	45N36	26E08	-1:44:32
Crasna	46N31	27E51	-1:51:24
Crîngeni	44N01	24E47	-1:39:08
Cristuru-Secuiesc	46N17	25E02	-1:40:08
Crucea	44N32	28E14	-1:52:56
Cugir	45N50	23E22	-1:33:28
Curcani	44N12	26E35	-1:46:20
Curtea-De-Argeş	45N08	24E41	-1:38:44
Daia	44N00	25E59	-1:43:56
Dămieneşti	46N44	26E59	-1:47:56
Darabani	48N11	26E35	-1:46:20
Deda	46N57	24E53	-1:39:32
Dej	47N09	23E52	-1:35:28
Deta	45N24	21E13	-1:24:52
Deva	45N53	22E55	-1:31:40
Dobroteasa	44N47	24E23	-1:37:32
Domneşti	44N25	25E56	-1:43:44
Dorohoi	47N57	26E24	-1:45:36
Dragalina	44N26	27E20	-1:49:20
Drăgăneşti-Olt	44N10	24E32	-1:38:08
Drăgăneşti-Vlaşca	44N06	25E36	-1:42:24
Drăgăşani	44N40	24E16	-1:37:04
Drobeta-Turnu-Severin	44N38	22E39	-1:30:36
Dr. Petru Groza	46N32	22E28	-1:29:52
Dumbrăveni	46N14	24E35	-1:38:20
Dunavăţu-De-Sus	44N59	29E13	-1:56:52
Eforie	44N06	28E38	-1:54:32
Ezeriş	45N24	21E53	-1:27:32
Făgăraş	45N51	24E58	-1:39:52
Făget	45N51	22E10	-1:28:40
Fălciu	46N18	28E08	-1:52:32
Fălticeni	47N28	26E18	-1:45:12
Făurei	45N06	27E14	-1:48:56
Feteşti	44N23	27E50	-1:51:20
Filiaşi	44N33	23E31	-1:34:04

Focşani	45N41	27E11	-1:48:44
Foeni	45N30	20E53	-1:23:32
Frumuşiţa	45N40	28E04	-1:52:16
Furculeşti	43N52	25E09	-1:40:36
Găeşti	44N43	25E19	-1:41:16
Galaţi	45N26	28E03	-1:52:12
Galatz → Galaţi	45N26	28E03	-1:52:12
Gătaia	45N26	21E26	-1:25:44
Gheorghe Gheorghiu-Dej	46N14	26E44	-1:46:56
Gheorgheni	46N43	25E36	-1:42:24
Gherla	47N02	23E55	-1:35:40
Gîrbovu	44N44	23E21	-1:33:24
Giurgiu	43N53	25E57	-1:43:48
Glodeanu-Silíştea	44N50	26E48	-1:47:12
Gorgota	44N47	26E05	-1:44:20
Gorgova	45N11	29E10	-1:56:40
Grosswardein → Oradea	47N03	21E57	-1:27:48
Gruia	44N16	22E42	-1:30:48
Gurahonţ	46N16	22E21	-1:29:24
Gura Humorului	47N33	25E54	-1:43:36
Gyulafehérvár → Alba-Iulia	46N04	23E35	-1:34:20
Haţeg	45N37	22E57	-1:31:48
Hermannstadt → Sibiu	45N48	24E09	-1:36:36
Hîrlău	47N25	26E54	-1:47:36
Hîrşova	44N41	27E57	-1:51:48
Holod	46N47	22E08	-1:28:32
Horezu	45N08	23E59	-1:35:56
Hotarele	44N10	26E22	-1:45:28
Huedin	46N52	23E02	-1:32:08
Hunedoara	45N45	22E54	-1:31:36
Huşi	46N40	28E04	-1:52:16
Iaşi	47N10	27E35	-1:50:20
Iazu	44N44	27E25	-1:49:40
Ibăneşti	48N04	26E22	-1:45:28
Ilia	45N56	22E39	-1:30:36
Independenţa	43N58	28E05	-1:52:20
Ineu	46N26	21E49	-1:27:16
Isaccea	45N16	28E28	-1:53:52
Işalniţa	44N24	23E44	-1:34:56
Jassy → Iaşi	47N10	27E35	-1:50:20
Jebel	45N33	21E14	-1:24:56
Jimbolia	45N47	20E43	-1:22:52
Karlsburg → Alba-Iulia	46N04	23E35	-1:34:20
Klausenburg → Cluj	46N47	23E36	-1:34:24
Kolozsvár → Cluj	46N47	23E36	-1:34:24
Kronstadt → Braşov	45N39	25E37	-1:42:28
Lăpuş	47N30	24E01	-1:36:04
Leu	44N11	24E00	-1:36:00
Lichitiseni	46N23	27E17	-1:49:08
Lieşti	45N38	27E32	-1:50:08
Lipova	46N05	21E40	-1:26:40
Livada	47N52	23E07	-1:32:28
Luduş	46N29	24E05	-1:36:20
Lugoj	45N41	21E54	-1:27:36
Lugos → Lugoj	45N41	21E54	-1:27:36
Lupeni	45N22	23E13	-1:32:52
Măcin	45N15	28E08	-1:52:32
Malu Mare	44N15	23E51	-1:35:24
Mamaia	44N15	28E37	-1:54:28
Mangalia	43N50	28E35	-1:54:20
Mărăşeşti	45N52	27E14	-1:48:56
Marghita	47N21	22E21	-1:29:24
Marosvásárhely → Tîrgu Mureş	46N33	24E33	-1:38:12
Mărtineşti	45N30	27E18	-1:49:12
Medgidia	44N15	28E16	-1:53:04
Medgyes → Mediaş	46N10	24E21	-1:37:24
Mediaş	46N10	24E21	-1:37:24
Mehadia	44N55	22E22	-1:29:28
Miercurea-Ciuc	46N22	25E48	-1:43:12
Miersig	46N53	21E51	-1:27:24
Mihăeşti	45N07	25E00	-1:40:00
Mihai Viteazu	44N39	28E41	-1:54:44
Mînăstirea	44N13	26E54	-1:47:36
Mironeasa	46N58	27E25	-1:49:40
Mizil	45N00	26E26	-1:45:44
Moineşti	46N28	26E29	-1:45:56
Moldova-Nouă	44N44	21E40	-1:26:40
Moreni	45N00	25E39	-1:42:36
Motru	44N50	23E00	-1:32:00
Murgeni	46N12	28E01	-1:52:04
Nădlac	46N10	20E45	-1:23:00
Nagybánya → Baia-Mare	47N40	23E35	-1:34:20
Nagyvarad → Oradea	47N03	21E57	-1:27:48
Năsăud	47N17	24E24	-1:37:36
Negreşti	46N50	27E27	-1:49:48
Negreşti-Oaş	47N52	23E25	-1:33:40
Negru-Vodă	43N50	28E12	-1:52:48
Neumarkt → Tîrgu-Secuiesc	46N00	26E08	-1:44:32
Neumarkt → Tîrgu Mureş	46N33	24E33	-1:38:12
Nicolae Bălcescu	47N34	26E52	-1:47:28
Nucet	46N28	22E35	-1:30:20
Oancea	45N55	28E06	-1:52:24
Ocna Mureş	46N23	23E51	-1:35:24
Odobeşti	45N45	27E04	-1:48:16
Odorheiu Secuiesc	46N18	25E18	-1:41:12
Olteni	44N10	25E18	-1:41:12
Olteniţa	44N05	26E39	-1:46:36
Oradea	47N03	21E57	-1:27:48
Orăştie	45N50	23E12	-1:32:48
Oraşul Stalin → Braşov	45N39	25E37	-1:42:28
Oraviţa	45N02	21E41	-1:26:44
Orşova	44N42	22E24	-1:29:36
Osica de Jos	44N15	24E17	-1:37:08
Ostrov	44N06	27E22	-1:49:28
Padea	44N01	23E52	-1:35:28
Panciu	45N55	27E05	-1:48:20
Paşcani	47N15	26E44	-1:46:56
Pătîrlagele	45N19	26E22	-1:45:28
Pecica	46N10	21E05	-1:24:20
Periprava	45N24	29E32	-1:58:08
Petrila	45N27	23E25	-1:33:40
Petroşani	45N25	23E22	-1:33:28
Petrozsény → Petroşani	45N25	23E22	-1:33:28
Piatra-Neamţ	46N56	26E22	-1:45:28
Piatra Olt	44N24	24E16	-1:37:04
Pişchia	45N55	21E20	-1:25:20
Pişcolt	47N35	22E18	-1:29:12
Piteşti	44N52	24E52	-1:39:28
Ploeşti → Ploieşti	44N56	26E02	-1:44:08
Ploieşti	44N56	26E02	-1:44:08
Podu Turcului	46N12	27E23	-1:49:32
Pogoanele	44N54	27E00	-1:48:00
Poiana Mare	43N55	23E04	-1:32:16
Pomi	47N42	23E19	-1:33:16
Popeşti	47N14	22E25	-1:29:40
Popeşti-Leordeni	44N23	26E10	-1:44:40
Popricani	47N18	27E31	-1:50:04
Predeal	45N30	25E35	-1:42:20
Predeşti	44N21	23E36	-1:34:24
Pucioasa	45N04	25E26	-1:41:44
Puieşti	46N25	27E33	-1:50:12
Pungeşti	46N42	27E20	-1:49:20
Răcari	44N38	25E45	-1:43:00
Rădăuţi	47N51	25E55	-1:43:40
Rădineşti	44N48	23E46	-1:35:04
Rast	43N53	23E17	-1:33:08
Răsvani	44N25	26E53	-1:47:32
Războeni	47N05	26E32	-1:46:08
Reghin	46N47	24E42	-1:38:48
Reşiţa	45N17	21E53	-1:27:32
Reviga	44N42	27E06	-1:48:24
Rîmnicu-Sărat	45N23	27E03	-1:48:12
Rîmnicu-Vîlcea	45N06	24E22	-1:37:28
Rîşnov	45N36	25E28	-1:41:52
Roman	46N55	26E56	-1:47:44
Roşiori-De-Vede	44N07	25E00	-1:40:00
Roznov	46N50	26E31	-1:46:04
Rupea	46N02	25E13	-1:40:52
Săcele	45N37	25E42	-1:42:48
Săcueni	47N21	22E06	-1:28:24
Şagu	46N03	21E17	-1:25:08
Şalard	47N13	22E03	-1:28:12
Salcia	43N57	24E56	-1:39:44
Salonta	46N48	21E40	-1:26:40
Sărmaşu	46N46	24E11	-1:36:44
Satu Mare	47N48	22E53	-1:31:32
Săveni	47N57	26E52	-1:47:28
Săvîrşin	46N01	22E14	-1:28:56
Scărişoara	44N00	24E35	-1:38:20
Schässburg → Sighişoara	46N13	24E48	-1:39:12
Sebeş	45N58	23E34	-1:34:16
Sebiş	46N23	22E08	-1:28:32
Şegarcea	44N06	23E45	-1:35:00
Segesvár → Sighişoara	46N13	24E48	-1:39:12
Sfîntu-Gheorghe	45N52	25E47	-1:43:08
Sibiu	45N48	24E09	-1:36:36
Sighetul Marmaţiei	47N56	23E54	-1:35:36
Sighişoara	46N13	24E48	-1:39:12
Simeria	45N51	23E01	-1:32:04
Şimleul Silvaniei	47N14	22E48	-1:31:12
Sinaia	45N21	25E33	-1:42:12
Sînnicolau Mare	46N05	20E38	-1:22:32
Sîntana	46N21	21E30	-1:26:00
Siret	47N57	26E04	-1:44:16
Slănic	45N15	25E57	-1:43:48
Slănic Moldova	46N13	26E26	-1:45:44
Slatina	44N26	24E22	-1:37:28
Slobozia	44N34	27E23	-1:49:32
Slobozia	43N51	25E54	-1:43:36
Solacolu	44N23	26E34	-1:46:16
Solca	47N42	25E50	-1:43:20
Şomcuta-Mare	47N31	23E29	-1:33:56
Sovata	46N35	25E04	-1:40:16
Stalin → Braşov	45N39	25E37	-1:42:28
Ştefan Vodă	44N19	27E19	-1:49:16
Strehaia	44N37	23E12	-1:32:48
Suceava	47N39	26E19	-1:45:16
Sulina	45N09	29E40	-1:58:40
Surduleşti	44N23	24E57	-1:39:48
Szatmárnémeti → Satu Mare	47N48	22E53	-1:31:32
Ţăndărei	44N38	27E40	-1:50:40
Târgu-Mureş → Tîrgu Mureş	46N33	24E33	-1:38:12
Tarna Mare	47N29	26E20	-1:45:20
Tarna Mare	48N04	23E12	-1:32:48
Tăşnad	47N29	22E35	-1:30:20
Teaca	46N55	24E31	-1:38:04
Techirghiol	44N03	28E36	-1:54:24
Tecuci	45N50	27E26	-1:49:44
Temesvár → Timişoara	45N45	21E13	-1:24:52
Timişoara	45N45	21E13	-1:24:52
Tîrgovişte	44N56	25E27	-1:41:48
Tîrgu Bujor	45N52	27E54	-1:51:36
Tîrgu-Cărbuneşti	44N58	23E31	-1:34:04
Tîrgu-Frumos	47N13	27E00	-1:48:00
Tîrgu-Jiu	45N02	23E17	-1:33:08
Tîrgu-Lăpuş	47N27	23E52	-1:35:28
Tîrgu Mureş	46N33	24E33	-1:38:12
Tîrgu-Neamţ	47N12	26E22	-1:45:28
Tîrgu-Ocna	46N15	26E37	-1:46:28
Tîrgu-Secuiesc	46N00	26E08	-1:44:32
Tîrgusor	44N28	28E25	-1:53:40
Tîrnăveni	46N20	24E17	-1:37:08
Titu	44N41	25E32	-1:42:08
Topliţa	46N55	25E21	-1:41:24
Topolog	44N53	28E22	-1:53:28
Topolovăţu Mare	45N46	21E37	-1:26:28
Torda → Turda	46N34	23E47	-1:35:08
Truşeşti	47N46	27E01	-1:48:04
Tulcea	45N11	28E48	-1:55:12
Turda	46N34	23E47	-1:35:08
Turnu-Măgurele	43N45	24E53	-1:39:32
Turnu-Severin → Drobeta-Turnu-Severin	44N38	22E39	-1:30:36
Ulma	47N53	25E18	-1:41:12
Ulmeni	45N04	26E39	-1:46:36
Urlaţi	44N59	26E14	-1:44:56
Urziceni	44N43	26E38	-1:46:32
Vădeni	45N22	27E56	-1:51:44
Valea lui Mihai	47N31	22E09	-1:28:36
Vălenii-De-Munte	45N12	26E03	-1:44:12
Vaşcău	46N28	22E28	-1:29:52
Vasile Roaită	44N03	28E38	-1:54:32
Vaslui	46N38	27E44	-1:50:56
Vaţa de Jos	46N10	22E35	-1:30:20
Vatra Dornei	47N21	25E21	-1:41:24
Vedea	44N47	24E37	-1:38:28
Vetrişoaia	46N26	28E13	-1:52:52
Victoria	45N45	24E41	-1:38:44
Videle	44N16	25E31	-1:42:04
Vidra	44N16	26E11	-1:44:44
Vidra	45N55	26E54	-1:47:36
Vînju Mare	44N26	22E52	-1:31:28
Vintilă Vodă	45N28	26E44	-1:46:56
Vîrfurile	46N19	22E31	-1:30:04
Vîrtopu	44N12	23E21	-1:33:24
Vişeu de Sus	47N44	24E22	-1:37:28
Vlădeni	47N25	27E20	-1:49:20
Voineşti	47N05	27E26	-1:49:44
Vulcan	45N23	23E17	-1:33:08
Yassy → Iaşi	47N10	27E35	-1:50:20
Zăbalţ	46N01	21E55	-1:27:40
Zalău	47N11	23E03	-1:32:12
Zărneşti	45N34	25E19	-1:41:16
Zerind	46N37	21E31	-1:26:04
Zimbor	47N00	23E16	-1:33:04
Zimnicea	43N39	25E21	-1:41:24

RWANDA — RUANDA

Time Table
Before 1/Jun/1935 LMT
Begin Standard 30E00
1/Jun/1935 0:00 -2:00

Place	Lat	Long	Offset
Bunyambili	2s21	29E25	-1:57:40
Butare	2s36	29E44	-1:58:56
Byumba	1s35	30E04	-2:00:16
Cyangugu	2s29	28E54	-1:55:36
Gahini	1s50	30E30	-2:02:00
Gikongoro	2s29	29E34	-1:58:16
Gisenyi	1s42	29E15	-1:57:00
Gishyita	2s11	29E18	-1:57:12
Gitarama	2s07	29E45	-1:59:00
Kagitumba	1s04	30E27	-2:01:48
Kibungo	2s10	30E32	-2:02:08
Kibuye	2s03	29E21	-1:57:24
Kigali	1s57	30E04	-2:00:16
Kiziguro	1s46	30E23	-2:01:32
Murambi	1s46	30E23	-2:01:32
Ngoma	2s11	29E18	-1:57:12
Nyanza	2s21	29E45	-1:59:00
Ruhengeri	1s30	29E38	-1:58:32
Rwamagana	1s57	30E34	-2:02:16

SAINT HELENA — SANTA ELENA — SANKT HELENA — SAINTE-HÉLÈNE

Time Table
Before 1/Jan/1890 LMT
Begin Standard 1w26
1/Jan/1890 0:00 0:06
Begin Standard 0w00
1/Jan/1951 0:00 0:00

Place	Lat	Long	Offset
Jamestown	15s55	5w42	0:22:48
Longwood	15s57	5w40	0:22:40

SAINT KITTS-NEVIS — SAINT-CHRISTOPHE-NEVIS — SANTA CHRISTÓBAL-NEVIS

Time Table
Before 2/Mar/1912 LMT
Begin Standard 60w00
2/Mar/1912 0:00 4:00

Place	Lat	Long	Offset
Basseterre	17N18	62w43	4:10:52
Charles Fort Leper Asylum	17N21	62w50	4:11:20
Charlestown	17N08	62w37	4:10:28
Newcastle	17N13	62w34	4:10:16
Sandy Point	17N22	62w50	4:11:20
Tabernacle	17N23	64w46	4:19:04
Zion Hill	17N09	62w32	4:10:08

SAINT LUCIA — SAINTE-LUCIE — SANTA LUCIA — SANTA LUCÍA

Time Table
Before 1/Jan/1890 LMT
Begin Standard 61w00
1/Jan/1890 0:00 4:04
Begin Standard 60w00
1/Jan/1912 0:00 4:00

Place	Lat	Long	Offset
Anse La Raye	13N57	61w03	4:04:12
Canaries	13N55	61w04	4:04:16
Castries	14N01	61w00	4:04:00
Choiseul	13N47	61w03	4:04:12
Dennery	13N55	60w54	4:03:36
Desruisseaux	13N47	60w56	4:03:44
Gros Islet	14N05	60w58	4:03:52
Laborie	13N45	61w00	4:04:00
Micoud	13N50	60w54	4:03:36
Soufrière	13N52	61w04	4:04:16
Vieux Fort	13N44	60w57	4:03:48

SAINT PIERRE AND MIQUELON — SAN PEDRO Y MIQUELÓN

Time Table
Before 15/May/1911 LMT
Begin Standard 60w00
15/May/1911 0:00 4:00
Begin Standard 45w00
1/May/1980 0:00 3:00
5/Apr/1987 2:00 2:00

Date	Time	Offset
25/Oct/1987	2:00	3:00
3/Apr/1988	2:00	2:00
30/Oct/1988	2:00	3:00
2/Apr/1989	2:00	2:00
29/Oct/1989	2:00	3:00
1/Apr/1990	2:00	2:00
28/Oct/1990	2:00	3:00
7/Apr/1991	2:00	2:00
27/Oct/1991	2:00	3:00
5/Apr/1992	2:00	2:00
25/Oct/1992	2:00	3:00
4/Apr/1993	2:00	2:00
31/Oct/1993	2:00	3:00
3/Apr/1994	2:00	2:00
30/Oct/1994	2:00	3:00
2/Apr/1995	2:00	2:00
29/Oct/1995	2:00	3:00
7/Apr/1996	2:00	2:00
27/Oct/1996	2:00	3:00
6/Apr/1997	2:00	2:00
26/Oct/1997	2:00	3:00
5/Apr/1998	2:00	2:00
25/Oct/1998	2:00	3:00
4/Apr/1999	2:00	2:00
31/Oct/1999	2:00	3:00
2/Apr/2000	2:00	2:00
29/Oct/2000	2:00	3:00

SAN PEDRO Y MIQUELÓN — SAINT PIERRE AND MIQUELON

Place	Lat	Long	Time
Langlade Island	46N50	56w20	3:45:20
Miquelon Island	47N03	56w20	3:45:20
Saint-Pierre	46N40	56w10	3:44:40
Saint-Pierre Island	46N47	56w11	3:44:44

SAN VICENTE — SANKT VINCENT — SAINT VINCENT AND GRENADINES

Time Table

Before 1/Jan/1890 LMT

Begin Standard 61w14

1/Jan/1890 0:00 4:05

Begin Standard 60w00

1/Jan/1912 0:00 4:00

DIVISIONS

1. Bequia Island
2. Canouan Island
3. Carriacou Island
4. Saint Vincent Island

Place	Lat	Long	Time
Barrouallie 4	13N14	61w17	4:05:08
Bequia Island 1	13N01	61w13	4:04:52
Calliaqua 4	13N08	61w12	4:04:48
Canouan Island 2	12N43	61w20	4:05:20
Carriacou Island 3	12N30	61w27	4:05:48
Chateaubelair 4	13N17	61w15	4:05:00
Cheltenham 2	12N53	61w11	4:04:44
Dumfries 3	12N28	61w27	4:05:48
Fancy 4	13N22	61w11	4:04:44
Georgetown 4	13N16	61w08	4:04:32
Hillsboro 3	12N29	61w28	4:05:52
Kingstown 4	13N09	61w14	4:04:56
Layou 4	13N12	61w17	4:05:08
Port Elizabeth 1	13N03	61w13	4:04:52
Wallibou 4	13N19	61w15	4:05:00

SAMOA AMERICANA — SAMOA AMÉRICAINES — SAMOA, AMERICAN

Time Table

Before 1/Jan/1911 LMT

Begin Standard 172w30

1/Jan/1911 0:00 11:30

Begin Standard 165w00

1/Jan/1950 0:00 11:00

DIVISIONS

1. Manua Islands
2. Tutuila
3. Ofu

Place	Lat	Long	Time
Aloafao 3	14s10	169w43	11:18:52
Alofau 2	14s16	170w36	11:22:24
Amanave 2	14s19	170w49	11:23:16
Anua 2	14s16	170w40	11:22:40
Aoloau 2	14s18	170w46	11:23:04
Aua 2	14s16	170w40	11:22:40
Fagaitua 2	14s16	170w37	11:22:28
Fagasa 2	14s17	170w43	11:22:52
Fagatogo 2	14s17	170w41	11:22:44
Faleasao 1	14s13	169w32	11:18:08
Fitiuta 1	14s13	169w27	11:17:48
Futiga 2	14s21	170w45	11:23:00
Laulii 2	14s17	170w39	11:22:36
Leone 2	14s20	170w47	11:23:08
Luma 1	14s14	169w32	11:18:08
Maia 1	14s13	169w28	11:17:52
Manua Islands 1	14s14	169w32	11:18:08
Nuuuli 2	14s18	170w42	11:22:48
Nu'uuli 2	14s18	170w42	11:22:48
Ofu 3	14s10	169w42	11:18:48
Ofu Island 3	14s10	169w42	11:18:48
Olosega 1	14s11	169w39	11:18:36
Pago Pago 2	14s16	170w42	11:22:48
Siufaga 1	14s14	169w32	11:18:08
Si'ufage 1	14s14	169w32	11:18:08
Tatuila Island 2	14s16	170w42	11:22:48
Tau 1	14s14	169w32	11:18:08
Tau Island 1	14s14	169w32	11:18:08
Tula 2	14s15	170w34	11:22:16
U S Naval Station 2	14s17	170w41	11:22:44
Utulei 2	14s17	170w40	11:22:40
Vailoatai 2	14s22	170w47	11:23:08
Vaitogi 2	14s21	170w44	11:22:56
Vatia 2	14s15	170w40	11:22:40

SAMOA OCCIDENTAL — WESTSAMOA — SAMOA-OCCIDENTALE — SAMOA, WESTERN

Time Table

Before 1/Jan/1911 LMT

Begin Standard 172w30

1/Jan/1911 0:00 11:30

Begin Standard 165w00

1/Jan/1950 0:00 11:00

DIVISIONS

1. Savai'i
2. Upolu

Place	Lat	Long	Time
Aopo 1	13s29	172w30	11:30:00
A'opo 1	13s29	172w30	11:30:00
Apia 2	13s50	171w44	11:26:56
Fagamalo 1	13s25	172w21	11:29:24
Fealalili 2	14s01	171w41	11:26:44
Falelatai 2	13s55	171w59	11:27:56
Falelima 1	13s32	172w41	11:30:44
Falevai 2	13s55	171w59	11:27:56
Leulumoega 2	13s49	171w55	11:27:40
Lotofaga 2	13s59	171w50	11:27:20
Matautu 2	13s57	171w56	11:27:44
Matāutu 2	13s57	171w56	11:27:44
Matavai 1	13s28	172w35	11:30:20
Poutasi 2	14s01	171w41	11:26:44
Puapua 1	13s34	172w09	11:28:36
Pu'upu'a 1	13s34	172w09	11:28:36
Safetu 1	13s26	172w24	11:29:36
Safutolafai 1	13s40	172w08	11:28:32
Salailua 1	13s41	172w34	11:30:16
Sala'ilua 1	13s41	172w34	11:30:16
Salani 2	14s00	171w33	11:26:12
Salelologa 1	13s44	172w10	11:28:40
Saluafata 2	13s51	171w35	11:26:20
Sataua 1	13s28	172w40	11:30:40
Savai'i Island 1	13s38	172w26	11:29:44
Taga 1	13s46	172w28	11:29:52
Tiavea 2	13s57	171w24	11:25:36
Ti'avea 2	13s57	171w24	11:25:36
Tuasivi 1	13s40	172w07	11:28:28
Upolu Island 2	13s50	171w44	11:26:56

SAN MARINO

SAINT-MARIN

Time Table		
Before 22/Sep/1866		LMT
Begin Standard		12E29
22/Sep/1866	0:00	-0:50
Begin Standard		15E00
1/Nov/1893	0:00	-1:00
3/Jun/1916	24:00	-2:00
30/Sep/1916	24:00	-1:00
31/Mar/1917	24:00	-2:00
29/Sep/1917	24:00	-1:00
9/Mar/1918	24:00	-2:00
5/Oct/1918	24:00	-1:00
1/Mar/1919	24:00	-2:00
4/Oct/1919	24:00	-1:00
20/Mar/1920	24:00	-2:00
18/Sep/1920	24:00	-1:00
14/Jun/1940	24:00	-2:00
2/Nov/1942	3:00	-1:00
29/Mar/1943	2:00	-2:00
4/Oct/1943	3:00	-1:00
3/Apr/1944	2:00	-2:00
2/Oct/1944	3:00	-1:00
2/Apr/1945	2:00	-2:00
16/Sep/1945	24:00	-1:00
17/Mar/1946	2:00	-2:00
6/Oct/1946	3:00	-1:00
16/Mar/1947	0:00	-2:00
5/Oct/1947	1:00	-1:00
29/Feb/1948	2:00	-2:00
3/Oct/1948	3:00	-1:00
22/May/1966	0:00	-2:00
24/Sep/1966	24:00	-1:00
28/May/1967	0:00	-2:00
23/Sep/1967	24:00	-1:00
26/May/1968	0:00	-2:00
21/Sep/1968	24:00	-1:00
1/Jun/1969	0:00	-2:00
27/Sep/1969	24:00	-1:00
31/May/1970	0:00	-2:00
27/Sep/1970	0:00	-1:00
23/May/1971	0:00	-2:00
26/Sep/1971	1:00	-1:00
28/May/1972	0:00	-2:00
1/Oct/1972	0:00	-1:00
3/Jun/1973	0:00	-2:00
30/Sep/1973	0:00	-1:00
26/May/1974	0:00	-2:00
29/Sep/1974	0:00	-1:00
1/Jun/1975	0:00	-2:00
28/Sep/1975	1:00	-1:00
30/May/1976	0:00	-2:00
26/Sep/1976	1:00	-1:00
22/May/1977	0:00	-2:00
25/Sep/1977	1:00	-1:00
28/May/1978	0:00	-2:00
1/Oct/1978	1:00	-1:00
27/May/1979	0:00	-2:00
30/Sep/1979	1:00	-1:00
6/Apr/1980	2:00	-2:00
28/Sep/1980	3:00	-1:00
29/Mar/1981	2:00	-2:00
27/Sep/1981	3:00	-1:00
28/Mar/1982	2:00	-2:00
26/Sep/1982	3:00	-1:00
27/Mar/1983	2:00	-2:00
25/Sep/1983	3:00	-1:00
25/Mar/1984	2:00	-2:00
30/Sep/1984	3:00	-1:00
31/Mar/1985	2:00	-2:00
29/Sep/1985	3:00	-1:00
30/Mar/1986	2:00	-2:00
28/Sep/1986	3:00	-1:00
29/Mar/1987	2:00	-2:00
27/Sep/1987	3:00	-1:00
27/Mar/1988	2:00	-2:00
25/Sep/1988	3:00	-1:00
26/Mar/1989	2:00	-2:00
24/Sep/1989	3:00	-1:00
25/Mar/1990	2:00	-2:00
30/Sep/1990	3:00	-1:00
31/Mar/1991	2:00	-2:00
29/Sep/1991	3:00	-1:00
29/Mar/1992	2:00	-2:00
27/Sep/1992	3:00	-1:00
28/Mar/1993	2:00	-2:00
26/Sep/1993	3:00	-1:00
27/Mar/1994	2:00	-2:00
25/Sep/1994	3:00	-1:00
26/Mar/1995	2:00	-2:00
24/Sep/1995	3:00	-1:00
31/Mar/1996	2:00	-2:00
29/Sep/1996	3:00	-1:00
30/Mar/1997	2:00	-2:00
28/Sep/1997	3:00	-1:00
29/Mar/1998	2:00	-2:00
27/Sep/1998	3:00	-1:00
28/Mar/1999	2:00	-2:00
26/Sep/1999	3:00	-1:00
26/Mar/2000	2:00	-2:00
24/Sep/2000	3:00	-1:00

Place	Latitude	Longitude	Offset
Acquaviva	43N57	12E25	-0:49:40
San Marino	43N55	12E28	-0:49:52

SAO TOME AND PRINCIPE

SÃO TOMÉ Y PRINCIPE

SÃO TOMÉ E PRÍNCIPE

Time Table		
Before 1/Jan/1884		LMT
Begin Standard		9W08
1/Jan/1884	0:00	0:37
Begin Standard		0W00
1/Jan/1912	0:00	0:00

Place	Latitude	Longitude	Offset
Porto Alegre	0N02	6E32	-0:26:08
Príncipe Island	1N37	7E25	-0:29:40
Santo Antônio	1N39	7E26	-0:29:44
São Tomé	0N20	6E44	-0:26:56
São Tomé Island	0N12	6E39	-0:26:36

SAUDI ARABIA

ARABIA SAUDITA

AL-‘ARABĪYAH AS-SA‘ŪDĪYAH

Time Table # 1		
Before 1/Jan/1950		LMT
Begin Standard		45E00
1/Jan/1950	0:00	-3:00
....		

Time Table # 2		
Before 1/Jan/1950		LMT
Begin Standard		60E00
1/Jan/1950	0:00	-4:00
Begin Standard		45E00
1/May/1968	0:00	-3:00

Place	Table	Latitude	Longitude	Offset
Abā as-Su’ūd	1	17N29	44E08	-2:56:32
Abhā	1	18N13	42E30	-2:50:00
Abū an-Na’am	1	25N15	38E51	-2:35:24
Abū ‘Arīsh	1	16N57	42E50	-2:51:20
Abū Rubayq	1	23N44	39E42	-2:38:48
Abyār ‘Alī	1	24N25	39E32	-2:38:08
Ad-Dafīnah	1	23N18	41E58	-2:47:52
Ad-Dammām	2	26N26	50E07	-3:20:28
Ad-Dār al-Ḥamrā’	1	27N19	37E44	-2:30:56
Ad-Darb	1	17N43	42E15	-2:49:00
Ad-Dawādimī	1	24N28	44E18	-2:57:12
Ad-Dilam	1	23N59	47E12	-3:08:48
Ad-Dūqah	1	19N36	40E54	-2:43:36
Ad-Duwayd	1	30N15	42E17	-2:49:08
‘Afīf	1	23N55	42E56	-2:51:44
Āl-‘Ābis	1	18N04	43E10	-2:52:40
Al-Aflāj	1	22N15	46E50	-3:07:20
Al-‘Awsajīyah	1	26N49	41E41	-2:46:44
Al-Barrah	1	24N55	45E52	-3:03:28
Al-Bid‘	1	28N25	35E04	-2:20:16
Al-Bi’r	1	28N50	36E19	-2:25:16
Al-Bi’r al-Jadīd	1	26N01	38E29	-2:33:56
Al-Birk	1	18N13	41E33	-2:46:12
Al-Ghāṭ	1	26N00	45E03	-3:00:12
Al-Ghazālah	1	26N48	41E19	-2:45:16
Al-Ḥadīthah	1	31N30	37E09	-2:28:36
Al-Ḥamrā’	1	23N57	38E52	-2:35:28
Al-Ḥarīq	1	23N37	46E31	-3:06:04
Al-Ḥawṭah	1	23N27	46E46	-3:07:04
Al-Ḥayyānīyah	1	28N38	42E45	-2:51:00
Al-Hufūf	2	25N22	49E34	-3:18:16
Al-Ḥulwah	1	23N27	46E47	-3:07:08
Al-Ḥuwayyiṭ	1	25N36	40E23	-2:41:32
Al-Jalāmīd	1	31N20	39E56	-2:39:44
Al-Jawf	1	29N50	39E52	-2:39:28
Al-Kahfah	1	27N04	43E02	-2:52:08
Al-Khabrā’	1	25N59	43E39	-2:54:36
Al-Khubar	2	26N17	50E12	-3:20:48
Al-Khurmah	1	21N54	42E03	-2:48:12
Al-Lidām	1	20N29	44E50	-2:59:20
Al-Līth	1	20N09	40E16	-2:41:04
Al-Madīnah (Medina)	1	24N28	39E36	-2:38:24
Al-Maqnāh	1	28N24	34E45	-2:19:00
Al-Midhnab	1	25N54	44E14	-2:56:56
Al-Mubarraz	1	22N17	46E44	-3:06:56
Al-Mubarraz	2	25N55	49E36	-3:18:24
Al-Mudawwarah	1	29N19	36E01	-2:24:04
Al-Musayjid	1	24N05	39E06	-2:36:24
Al-Muwassam	1	16N25	42E20	-2:49:20
Al-Muwayh	1	22N45	41E36	-2:46:24
Al-Muwayliḥ	1	27N41	35E27	-2:21:48
Al-Qaḍīmah	1	22N21	39E09	-2:36:36
Al-Qaḥmah	1	18N00	41E41	-2:46:44
Al-Qalībah	1	28N32	37E42	-2:30:48
Al-Qārah	1	29N52	40E15	-2:41:00
Al-Qaṭīf	2	26N33	50E00	-3:20:00
Al-Qayṣūmah	1	28N16	46E03	-3:04:12
Al-Qunfudhah	1	19N08	41E05	-2:44:20
Al-Quway‘īyah	1	24N03	45E15	-3:01:00
Al-‘Ubaylah	1	21N59	50E57	-3:23:48
Al-‘Ulā	1	26N37	37E52	-2:31:28
Al-‘Uqayr	2	25N39	50E12	-3:20:48
Al-‘Uyaynah	1	24N54	46E23	-3:05:32
Al-Wajh	1	26N15	36E26	-2:25:44
Al-Yamāmah → As-Sulaymānīyah	1	24N09	47E19	-3:09:16
An-Nafī	1	24N57	43E42	-2:54:48
Anṣāb	1	29N11	44E43	-2:58:52
‘Ar‘Ar	1	13N53	44E50	-2:59:20
Ar-Rabaḍ	1	23N11	39E32	-2:38:08
Ar-Rass	1	25N52	43E28	-2:53:52
Ar-Rawḍah	1	26N05	40E37	-2:42:28
Ar-Rimāh	1	25N34	47E09	-3:08:36
Ar-Riyāḍ (Riyadh)	1	24N38	46E43	-3:06:52
Ash-Shaqrā’	1	25N15	45E15	-3:01:00
Ash-Sharmah	1	28N01	35E18	-2:21:12
Ash-Shufayyah	1	23N50	39E08	-2:36:32
Ash-Shuqayq	1	17N43	42E01	-2:48:04
Ash-Shurayf	1	25N43	39E14	-2:36:56
Aṣ-Ṣabyā	1	17N09	42E37	-2:50:28
As-Sidr	1	23N27	39E45	-2:39:00
As-Sulaymānīyah	1	24N09	47E19	-3:09:16
As-Sulaymī	1	26N17	41E21	-2:45:24
As-Sulayyil	1	20N27	45E34	-3:02:16
Aṭ-Ṭā’if	1	21N16	40E24	-2:41:36
Aṭ-Ṭurayf	1	31N44	38E33	-2:34:12
Aṭ-Ṭuwayyah	1	27N36	41E13	-2:44:52
‘Ayn Dār	2	25N59	49E23	-3:17:32
‘Aynūnah	1	28N05	35E08	-2:20:32
Aẓ-Ẓahrān (Dhahran)	2	26N18	50E08	-3:20:32
Az-Zilfī	1	26N18	44E48	-2:59:12
Badanah	1	30N59	41E02	-2:44:08
Badr Ḥunayn	1	23N44	38E46	-2:35:04
Baḥrah	1	21N24	39E29	-2:37:56
Bi’r Naṣīf	1	24N51	39E11	-2:36:44
Buqayq	2	25N56	49E40	-3:18:40
Buraydah	1	26N20	43E59	-2:55:56
Dahabān	1	21N55	39E04	-2:36:16
Dawqah	1	19N36	40E54	-2:43:36
Dhahran → Aẓ-Ẓahrān	2	26N18	50E08	-3:20:32
Ḍirs	1	18N32	42E05	-2:48:20
Djedda → Jiddah	1	21N30	39E12	-2:36:48
Dschidda → Jiddah	1	21N30	39E12	-2:36:48
Er-Riad → Ar-Riyāḍ	1	24N38	46E43	-3:06:52
Fayd	1	27N07	42E27	-2:49:48
Ghurayrah	1	18N37	42E41	-2:50:44
Hadīyah	1	25N34	38E41	-2:34:44
Ḥafīrat al-‘Aydā	1	26N26	39E10	-2:36:40
Ḥā’il	1	27N33	41E42	-2:46:48
Ḥamḍah	1	19N02	43E36	-2:54:24
Ḥamdānah	1	19N58	40E35	-2:42:20
Ḥanak	1	25N33	36E56	-2:27:44
Ḥaql	1	29N18	34E57	-2:19:48
Ḥaraḍ	1	24N08	49E05	-3:16:20
Hofuf → Al-Hufūf	2	25N22	49E34	-3:18:16
Ḥuraymilā	1	25N08	46E08	-3:04:32
Jalājil	1	25N41	45E28	-3:01:52
Jarad	1	18N59	41E24	-2:45:36
Jiddah	1	21N30	39E12	-2:36:48

AL-'ARABĪYAH AS-SA'ŪDĪYAH ARABIA SAUDITA SAUDI ARABIA

Jīzān	1	16N54	42E29	-2:49:56
Jubbah	1	28N02	40E56	-2:43:44
Juddah → Jiddah	1	21N30	39E12	-2:36:48
Juḥā	1	16N41	42E54	-2:51:36
Kāf	1	31N24	37E24	-2:29:36
Khamīs Mushayṭ	1	18N18	42E44	-2:50:56
Khaybar	1	25N42	39E31	-2:38:04
Khuff	1	24N57	44E42	-2:58:48
Kulākh	1	21N18	40E41	-2:42:44
La Meca → Makkah	1	21N27	39E49	-2:39:16
La Mecque → Makkah	1	21N27	39E49	-2:39:16
Lawqah	1	29N49	42E45	-2:51:00
Laylā	1	22N17	46E45	-3:07:00
Līnah	1	28N42	43E48	-2:55:12
Madā'in Ṣāliḥ	1	26N48	37E53	-2:31:32
Madrakah	1	21N59	39E59	-2:39:56
Mahd adh-Dhahab	1	23N30	40E52	-2:43:28
Majma'Ah	1	25N54	45E20	-3:01:20
Makkah (Mecca)	1	21N27	39E49	-2:39:16
Ma'Qalā'	1	26N31	47E19	-3:09:16
Mastābah	1	20N49	39E20	-2:37:20
Mastūrah	1	23N06	38E50	-2:35:20

Meca, La → Makkah	1	21N27	39E49	-2:39:16
Mecca → Makkah	1	21N27	39E49	-2:39:16
Mecque, La → Makkah	1	21N27	39E49	-2:39:16
Medina → Al-Madīnah	1	24N28	39E36	-2:38:24
Mekka → Makkah	1	21N27	39E49	-2:39:16
Minā	1	21N25	39E52	-2:39:28
Munā	1	21N25	39E52	-2:39:28
Qafarah	1	23N59	45E11	-3:00:44
Qal'At al-Akhḍar	1	28N06	37E07	-2:28:28
Qal'At al-Mu'Aẓẓam	1	27N43	37E27	-2:29:48
Qal'At Bīshah	1	20N01	42E36	-2:50:24
Qanā	1	27N47	41E25	-2:45:40
Qasr Abā as-Sa'ūd	1	17N29	44E08	-2:56:32
Qīzān	1	16N54	42E29	-2:49:56
Qulbān al-'Īsāwīyah	1	30N38	37E53	-2:31:32
Rābigh	1	22N48	39E01	-2:36:04
Rafḥā'	1	29N42	43E30	-2:54:00

Ra'īs	1	23N34	38E36	-2:34:24
Rawḥah	1	19N28	41E48	-2:47:12
Riyadh → Ar-Riyāḍ	1	24N38	46E43	-3:06:52
Ṣabyā	1	17N09	42E37	-2:50:28
Sakākah	1	29N59	40E06	-2:40:24
Ṣufaynah	1	23N09	40E32	-2:42:08
Sūq Suwayq	1	24N23	38E27	-2:33:48
Tabūk	1	28N23	36E35	-2:26:20
Taif → Aṭ-Ṭā'if	1	21N16	40E24	-2:41:36
Taymā'	1	27N38	38E29	-2:33:56
Thādiq	1	25N18	45E52	-3:03:28
Turabah	1	21N13	41E39	-2:46:36
Umm al-Birak	1	23N25	39E13	-2:36:52
Umm al-Khashab	1	17N21	42E32	-2:50:08
Umm Lajj	1	25N04	37E13	-2:28:52
'Unayzah	1	26N06	43E56	-2:55:44
'Usfān	1	21N55	39E21	-2:37:24
'Ushayrah	1	21N46	40E38	-2:42:32
Yanbu'	1	24N05	38E03	-2:32:12
Ẓahrān	1	17N40	43E30	-2:54:00
Ẓibā'	1	27N21	35E40	-2:22:40
Ẓurayghiṭ	1	26N29	40E33	-2:42:12

ESCOCIA CALEDONIA SCHOTTLAND ÉCOSSE SCOTLAND

Time Table
Before 30/Jan/1848 LMT
Begin Standard 0W00

30/Jan/1848	0:00	0:00
21/May/1916	2:00	-1:00
1/Oct/1916	3:00	0:00
8/Apr/1917	2:00	-1:00
17/Sep/1917	3:00	0:00
24/Mar/1918	2:00	-1:00
30/Sep/1918	3:00	0:00
30/Mar/1919	2:00	-1:00
29/Sep/1919	3:00	0:00
28/Mar/1920	2:00	-1:00
25/Oct/1920	3:00	0:00
3/Apr/1921	2:00	-1:00
3/Oct/1921	3:00	0:00
26/Mar/1922	2:00	-1:00
8/Oct/1922	3:00	0:00
22/Apr/1923	2:00	-1:00
16/Sep/1923	3:00	0:00
13/Apr/1924	2:00	-1:00
21/Sep/1924	3:00	0:00
19/Apr/1925	2:00	-1:00
4/Oct/1925	3:00	0:00
18/Apr/1926	2:00	-1:00
3/Oct/1926	3:00	0:00
10/Apr/1927	2:00	-1:00
2/Oct/1927	3:00	0:00
22/Apr/1928	2:00	-1:00
7/Oct/1928	3:00	0:00
21/Apr/1929	2:00	-1:00
6/Oct/1929	3:00	0:00
13/Apr/1930	2:00	-1:00
5/Oct/1930	3:00	0:00
19/Apr/1931	2:00	-1:00
4/Oct/1931	3:00	0:00
17/Apr/1932	2:00	-1:00
2/Oct/1932	3:00	0:00
9/Apr/1933	2:00	-1:00
8/Oct/1933	3:00	0:00
22/Apr/1934	2:00	-1:00
7/Oct/1934	3:00	0:00
14/Apr/1935	2:00	-1:00
6/Oct/1935	3:00	0:00
19/Apr/1936	2:00	-1:00
4/Oct/1936	3:00	0:00
18/Apr/1937	2:00	-1:00
3/Oct/1937	3:00	0:00
10/Apr/1938	2:00	-1:00
2/Oct/1938	3:00	0:00
16/Apr/1939	2:00	-1:00
19/Nov/1939	3:00	0:00
25/Feb/1940	2:00	-1:00
4/May/1941	2:00	-2:00
10/Aug/1941	3:00	-1:00
5/Apr/1942	2:00	-2:00
9/Aug/1942	3:00	-1:00
4/Apr/1943	2:00	-2:00
15/Aug/1943	3:00	-1:00
2/Apr/1944	2:00	-2:00
17/Sep/1944	3:00	-1:00
2/Apr/1945	2:00	-2:00
15/Jul/1945	3:00	-1:00
7/Oct/1945	3:00	0:00
14/Apr/1946	2:00	-1:00
6/Oct/1946	3:00	0:00
16/Mar/1947	2:00	-1:00
13/Apr/1947	2:00	-2:00
10/Aug/1947	3:00	-1:00
2/Nov/1947	3:00	0:00
14/Mar/1948	2:00	-1:00
31/Oct/1948	3:00	0:00
3/Apr/1949	2:00	-1:00
30/Oct/1949	3:00	0:00
16/Apr/1950	2:00	-1:00
22/Oct/1950	3:00	0:00
15/Apr/1951	2:00	-1:00
21/Oct/1951	3:00	0:00
20/Apr/1952	2:00	-1:00
26/Oct/1952	3:00	0:00
19/Apr/1953	2:00	-1:00
4/Oct/1953	3:00	0:00
11/Apr/1954	2:00	-1:00
3/Oct/1954	3:00	0:00
17/Apr/1955	2:00	-1:00
2/Oct/1955	3:00	0:00
22/Apr/1956	2:00	-1:00
7/Oct/1956	3:00	0:00
14/Apr/1957	2:00	-1:00
6/Oct/1957	3:00	0:00
20/Apr/1958	2:00	-1:00
5/Oct/1958	3:00	0:00
19/Apr/1959	2:00	-1:00
4/Oct/1959	3:00	0:00
10/Apr/1960	2:00	-1:00
2/Oct/1960	3:00	0:00
26/Mar/1961	2:00	-1:00
29/Oct/1961	3:00	0:00
25/Mar/1962	2:00	-1:00
28/Oct/1962	3:00	0:00
31/Mar/1963	2:00	-1:00
27/Oct/1963	3:00	0:00
22/Mar/1964	2:00	-1:00
25/Oct/1964	3:00	0:00
21/Mar/1965	2:00	-1:00
24/Oct/1965	3:00	0:00
20/Mar/1966	2:00	-1:00
23/Oct/1966	3:00	0:00
19/Mar/1967	2:00	-1:00
29/Oct/1967	3:00	0:00
Begin Standard		15E00
18/Feb/1968	2:00	-1:00
Begin Standard		0W00
31/Oct/1971	2:00	0:00
19/Mar/1972	2:00	-1:00
29/Oct/1972	3:00	0:00
18/Mar/1973	2:00	-1:00
28/Oct/1973	3:00	0:00
17/Mar/1974	2:00	-1:00
27/Oct/1974	3:00	0:00
16/Mar/1975	2:00	-1:00
26/Oct/1975	3:00	0:00
21/Mar/1976	2:00	-1:00
24/Oct/1976	3:00	0:00
20/Mar/1977	2:00	-1:00
23/Oct/1977	3:00	0:00
19/Mar/1978	2:00	-1:00
29/Oct/1978	3:00	0:00
18/Mar/1979	2:00	-1:00
28/Oct/1979	3:00	0:00
16/Mar/1980	2:00	-1:00
26/Oct/1980	3:00	0:00
29/Mar/1981	1:00	-1:00
25/Oct/1981	2:00	0:00
28/Mar/1982	1:00	-1:00
24/Oct/1982	2:00	0:00
27/Mar/1983	1:00	-1:00
23/Oct/1983	2:00	0:00
25/Mar/1984	1:00	-1:00
28/Oct/1984	2:00	0:00
31/Mar/1985	1:00	-1:00
27/Oct/1985	2:00	0:00
30/Mar/1986	1:00	-1:00
26/Oct/1986	2:00	0:00
29/Mar/1987	1:00	-1:00
25/Oct/1987	2:00	0:00
27/Mar/1988	1:00	-1:00
23/Oct/1988	2:00	0:00
26/Mar/1989	1:00	-1:00
29/Oct/1989	2:00	0:00
25/Mar/1990	1:00	-1:00
28/Oct/1990	2:00	0:00
31/Mar/1991	1:00	-1:00
27/Oct/1991	2:00	0:00
29/Mar/1992	1:00	-1:00
25/Oct/1992	2:00	0:00
28/Mar/1993	1:00	-1:00
24/Oct/1993	2:00	0:00
27/Mar/1994	1:00	-1:00
23/Oct/1994	2:00	0:00
26/Mar/1995	1:00	-1:00
29/Oct/1995	2:00	0:00
31/Mar/1996	1:00	-1:00
27/Oct/1996	2:00	0:00
30/Mar/1997	1:00	-1:00
26/Oct/1997	2:00	0:00
29/Mar/1998	1:00	-1:00
25/Oct/1998	2:00	0:00
28/Mar/1999	1:00	-1:00
24/Oct/1999	2:00	0:00
26/Mar/2000	1:00	-1:00
29/Oct/2000	2:00	0:00

Aberchirder	57N33	2W38	0:10:32
Aberdeen	57N10	2W04	0:08:16
Aberdour	56N03	3W19	0:13:16
Aberfeldy	56N37	3W54	0:15:36
Aberfoyle	56N11	4W23	0:17:32
Aberlour	57N28	3W14	0:12:56
Abernethy	56N20	3W19	0:13:16
Aberuthven	56N19	3W39	0:14:36
Aboyne	57N05	2W50	0:11:20
Abriachan	57N22	4W24	0:17:36
Acharacle	56N44	5W47	0:23:08
Achavanich	58N22	3W24	0:13:36
Achnasaul	56N58	4W59	0:19:56
Achnasheen	57N35	5W06	0:20:24
Achosnich	56N45	6W06	0:24:24
Advie	57N23	3W27	0:13:48
Airdrie	55N52	3W59	0:15:56
Airor	57N04	5W46	0:23:04
Aith	60N16	1W23	0:05:32
Alexandria	55N59	4W36	0:18:24
Alford	57N13	2W42	0:10:48
Alloa	56N07	3W49	0:15:16
Alness	57N41	4W15	0:17:00
Altnaharra	58N16	4W27	0:17:48
Alva	56N09	3W48	0:15:12
Alyth	56N37	3W13	0:12:52
Amulree	56N30	3W47	0:15:08
Ancrum	55N31	2W35	0:10:20
Annan	54N59	3W16	0:13:04
Anstruther	56N13	2W42	0:10:48
Applecross	57N25	5W49	0:23:16
Arbroath	56N34	2W35	0:10:20
Ardarroch	57N25	5W38	0:22:32
Ardbeg	55N39	6W05	0:24:20
Ardcharnich	57N51	5W05	0:20:20
Ardentinny	56N03	4W55	0:19:40
Ardfern	56N10	5W32	0:22:08
Ardlui	56N18	4W43	0:18:52
Ardlussa	56N02	5W47	0:23:08
Ardmolich	56N49	5W41	0:22:44
Ardrishaig	56N01	5W27	0:21:48
Ardrossan	55N39	4W49	0:19:16
Ardtalnaig	56N31	4W06	0:16:24
Arinagour	56N37	6W31	0:26:04
Arisaig	56N51	5W51	0:23:24
Armadale	55N54	3W42	0:14:48
Arrochar	56N12	4W44	0:18:56
Auchenblae	56N54	2W26	0:09:44
Auchencairn	54N51	3W53	0:15:32
Auchinleck	55N28	4W17	0:17:08
Auchterarder	56N18	3W43	0:14:52
Auchterderran	56N09	3W16	0:13:04
Auchtermuchty	56N17	3W15	0:13:00
Auldearn	57N34	3W49	0:15:16
Aultbea	57N50	5W35	0:22:20
Aviemore	57N12	3W50	0:15:20
Ayr	55N28	4W38	0:18:32
Badenyon	57N15	3W05	0:12:20
Balallan	58N05	6W35	0:26:20
Balfour	59N01	2W55	0:11:40
Balfron	56N04	4W20	0:17:20
Ballachulish	56N40	5W10	0:20:40
Ballantrae	55N06	5W00	0:20:00
Ballater	57N03	3W03	0:12:12
Ballinluig	56N38	3W39	0:14:36
Balloch	57N29	4W07	0:16:28
Balmerino	56N24	3W02	0:12:08
Balmoral Castle	57N02	3W13	0:12:52
Balnacra	57N28	5W23	0:21:32
Baltasound	60N45	0W52	0:03:28
Balvicar	56N14	5W38	0:22:32
Banchory	57N30	2W30	0:10:00
Banff	57N40	2W33	0:10:12
Bankfoot	56N30	3W30	0:14:00
Bannockburn	56N06	3W55	0:15:40
Barrhead	55N48	4W24	0:17:36
Barrhill	55N07	4W46	0:19:04
Barvas	58N22	6W32	0:26:08
Bathgate	55N55	3W39	0:14:36
Bayble	58N12	6W13	0:24:52
Bayhead	57N33	7W24	0:29:36
Bearsden	55N56	4W20	0:17:20
Beattock	55N18	3W28	0:13:52
Beauly	57N29	4W29	0:17:56
Beith	55N45	4W38	0:18:32
Bellshill	55N49	4W01	0:16:04
Bernisdale	57N27	6W24	0:25:36
Berriedale	58N11	3W29	0:13:56
Bettyhill	58N32	4W14	0:16:56
Biggar	55N38	3W32	0:14:08
Blackburn	57N12	2W18	0:09:12
Blackford	56N15	3W46	0:15:04
Blacklunans	56N44	3W22	0:13:28
Blackwaterfoot	55N30	5W19	0:21:16
Blair Atholl	56N46	3W51	0:15:24
Blairgowrie	56N36	3W21	0:13:24
Blyth Bridge	55N42	3W24	0:13:36
Boarhills	56N19	2W42	0:10:48
Boath	57N44	4W23	0:17:32
Boat of Garten	57N20	3W44	0:14:56
Boddam	57N28	1W47	0:07:08
Boddam	59N55	1W17	0:05:08
Bonarbridge	53N33	4W21	0:17:24
Bonawe	56N26	5W13	0:20:52
Bonchester Bridge	55N24	2W40	0:10:40
Bo'ness	56N01	3W37	0:14:28
Bonhill	55N59	4W34	0:18:16
Bonnyrigg	55N52	3W08	0:12:32
Borrowstounness	56N01	3W36	0:14:24
Borve	56N58	7W32	0:30:08
Bowmore	55N45	6W17	0:25:08
Braco	56N15	3W53	0:15:32
Brae	60N23	1W21	0:05:24
Braemar	57N01	3W23	0:13:32
Bragar	58N24	6W40	0:26:40
Brechin	56N44	2W40	0:10:40
Brenish	58N08	7W08	0:28:32

SCOTLAND ÉCOSSE SCHOTTLAND CALEDONIA ESCOCIA

Bridgend	56N48	2w45	0:11:00
Bridgend	55N48	6w16	0:25:04
Bridge of Allan	56N09	3w57	0:15:48
Bridge of Gaur	56N41	4w27	0:17:48
Bridge of Orchy	56N30	4w46	0:19:04
Bridge of Weir	55N52	4w35	0:18:20
Brig o' Turk	56N13	4w22	0:17:28
Brinyan	59N07	2w59	0:11:56
Broadford	57N14	5w54	0:23:36
Brochel	57N26	6w01	0:24:04
Brodick	55N35	5w09	0:20:36
Brora	58N01	3w51	0:15:24
Brough	58N39	3w20	0:13:20
Broughton	55N37	3w25	0:13:40
Broughtown	59N15	2w36	0:10:24
Broughty Ferry	56N28	2w53	0:11:32
Buckhaven	56N11	3w03	0:12:12
Buckie	57N40	2w58	0:11:52
Bunessan	56N19	6w14	0:24:56
Burghead	57N42	3w30	0:14:00
Burnhaven	57N29	1w47	0:07:08
Burnmouth	55N50	2w04	0:08:16
Burntisland	56N03	3w15	0:13:00
Burravoe	60N32	1w28	0:05:52
Burwick	58N44	2w57	0:11:48
Cairndow	56N15	4w56	0:19:44
Cairnryan	54N58	5w02	0:20:08
Callander	56N15	4w14	0:16:56
Callanish	58N12	6w43	0:26:52
Cambuslang	55N49	4w10	0:16:40
Campbelltown	57N34	4w02	0:16:08
Campbeltown	55N26	5w36	0:22:24
Cannich	57N21	4w46	0:19:04
Canonbie	55N05	2w57	0:11:48
Cappercleuch	55N29	3w12	0:12:48
Carbost	57N18	6w22	0:25:28
Cargill	56N30	3w22	0:13:28
Carinish	57N31	7w18	0:29:12
Carloway	58N17	6w48	0:27:12
Carluke	55N45	3w51	0:15:24
Carnoustie	56N30	2w44	0:10:56
Carnwath	55N43	3w38	0:14:32
Carradale	55N35	5w28	0:21:52
Carrbridge	57N17	3w49	0:15:16
Carronbridge	55N16	3w48	0:15:12
Carsaig	56N17	6w00	0:24:00
Carstairs	55N42	3w42	0:14:48
Castlebay	56N57	7w28	0:29:52
Castle Douglas	54N57	3w56	0:15:44
Castletown	58N35	3w23	0:13:32
Catlodge	57N00	4w15	0:17:00
Catrine	55N30	4w20	0:17:20
Caulkerbush	54N54	3w40	0:14:40
Cawdor	57N31	3w56	0:15:44
Chirnside	55N48	2w13	0:08:52
Clachan	55N45	5w34	0:22:16
Clackmannan	56N06	3w46	0:15:04
Cladich	56N21	5w05	0:20:20
Claonaig	55N46	5w22	0:21:28
Clova	56N50	3w06	0:12:24
Clydebank	55N54	4w24	0:17:36
Coalburn	55N36	3w54	0:15:36
Coatbridge	55N52	4w01	0:16:04
Cock Bridge	57N09	3w14	0:12:56
Cockburnspath	55N56	2w21	0:09:24
Cockenzie	55N58	2w58	0:11:52
Coldbackie	58N31	4w23	0:17:32
Coldingham	55N53	2w10	0:08:40
Coldstream	55N39	2w15	0:09:00
Collieston	57N21	1w56	0:07:44
Colmonell	55N08	4w55	0:19:40
Comrie	56N22	4w00	0:16:00
Connel Park	55N23	4w12	0:16:48
Cornhill	57N36	2w42	0:10:48
Corran	56N43	5w14	0:20:56
Corsock	55N04	3w57	0:15:48
Cortachy	56N43	2w58	0:11:52
Coupar Angus	56N33	3w17	0:13:08
Cove	57N51	5w42	0:22:48
Cowdenbeath	56N07	3w21	0:13:24
Craighouse	55N51	5w57	0:23:48
Craignure	56N28	5w42	0:22:48
Crail	56N16	2w38	0:10:32
Crathie	57N02	3w12	0:12:48
Crawford	55N28	3w40	0:14:40
Creagan	56N33	5w17	0:21:08
Creagorry	57N26	7w19	0:29:16
Creetown	54N54	4w23	0:17:32
Crianlarich	56N23	4w36	0:18:24
Crieff	56N23	3w52	0:15:28
Crinan	56N05	5w35	0:22:20
Croachy	57N19	4w14	0:16:56
Crocketford	55N02	3w50	0:15:20
Croggan	56N22	5w42	0:22:48
Croick	57N53	4w35	0:18:20
Cromarty	57N40	4w02	0:16:08
Cromore	58N09	6w29	0:25:56
Crook of Alves	57N38	3w27	0:13:48
Crossbost	58N08	6w23	0:25:32
Crosshill	55N19	4w39	0:18:36
Croy	57N31	4w02	0:16:08
Cruden Bay	57N25	1w50	0:07:20
Cullen	57N41	2w49	0:11:16
Cullicudden	57N39	4w13	0:16:52
Culrain	57N55	4w24	0:17:36
Cults	57N07	2w10	0:08:40
Cumbernauld	55N58	3w59	0:15:56
Cuminestown	57N32	2w20	0:09:20
Cumnock	55N27	4w16	0:17:04
Cupar	56N19	3w01	0:12:04
Currie	55N54	3w20	0:13:20
Dairsie	56N20	2w56	0:11:44
Dalry	55N43	4w43	0:18:52
Dalbeattie	54N56	3w49	0:15:16
Dalhalvaig	58N28	3w54	0:15:36

Dalkeith	55N54	3w04	0:12:16
Dallas	57N33	3w28	0:13:52
Dalmally	56N24	4w58	0:19:52
Dalmellington	55N19	4w24	0:17:36
Dalnaspidal	56N50	4w14	0:16:56
Dalry	55N43	4w44	0:18:56
Dalry	55N07	4w10	0:16:40
Dalwhinnie	56N56	4w14	0:16:56
Darvel	55N37	4w18	0:17:12
Davington	55N18	3w12	0:12:48
Daviot	57N25	4w08	0:16:32
Dell	58N30	6w20	0:25:20
Denny	56N02	3w55	0:15:40
Diabaig	57N34	5w40	0:22:40
Dingwall	57N35	4w29	0:17:56
Dinnet	57N03	2w54	0:11:36
Dollar	56N09	3w40	0:14:40
Dores	57N22	4w15	0:17:00
Dornie	57N17	5w31	0:22:04
Dornoch	57N52	4w02	0:16:08
Douglas	55N33	3w51	0:15:24
Doune	56N12	4w05	0:16:20
Dowally	56N36	3w37	0:14:28
Drimnin	56N36	6w00	0:24:00
Drumbeg	58N14	5w12	0:20:48
Drummore	54N42	4w54	0:19:36
Drymen	56N04	4w27	0:17:48
Dufftown	57N26	3w08	0:12:32
Duirinish	57N19	5w41	0:22:44
Dulnain Bridge	57N16	3w41	0:14:44
Dumbarton	55N57	4w35	0:18:20
Dumfries	55N04	3w37	0:14:28
Dunbar	56N00	2w31	0:10:04
Dunbeath	58N15	3w25	0:13:40
Dunblane	56N12	3w59	0:15:56
Duncon	55N57	4w56	0:19:44
Dundee	56N28	3w00	0:12:00
Dunfermline	56N04	3w29	0:13:56
Dunkeld	56N34	3w35	0:14:20
Dunlop	55N43	4w32	0:18:08
Dunnet	58N31	3w20	0:13:20
Dunoon	55N57	4w56	0:19:44
Duns	55N47	2w20	0:09:20
Dunvegan	57N26	6w35	0:26:20
Durness	58N33	4w45	0:19:00
Dyce	57N12	2w11	0:08:44
Dyke	57N36	3w41	0:14:44
Dysart	56N08	3w08	0:12:32
Eaglesfield	55N03	3w12	0:12:48
Eaglesham	55N44	4w18	0:17:12
Earlish	57N34	6w23	0:25:32
Earlston	55N39	2w40	0:10:40
East Calder	55N54	3w27	0:13:48
East Kilbride	55N46	4w10	0:16:40
East Linton	55N59	2w39	0:10:36
Eastriggs	54N59	3w10	0:12:40
Ecclefechan	55N03	3w17	0:13:08
Echt	57N08	2w26	0:09:44
Edderton	57N50	4w10	0:16:40
Eddleston	55N43	3w13	0:12:52
Edimbourg → Edinburgh	55N57	3w13	0:12:52
Edimburgo → Edinburgh	55N57	3w13	0:12:52
Edinburgh	55N57	3w13	0:12:52
Edzell	56N48	2w39	0:10:36
Eishken	58N01	6w32	0:26:08
Elgin	57N39	3w20	0:13:20
Elgol	57N09	6w06	0:24:24
Ellon	57N22	2w05	0:08:20
Embo	57N54	3w59	0:15:56
Eriboll	58N28	4w41	0:18:44
Errogie	57N16	4w22	0:17:28
Evanton	57N40	4w20	0:17:20
Eyemouth	55N52	2w06	0:08:24
Fairlie	55N46	4w51	0:19:24
Falkirk	56N00	3w48	0:15:12
Falkland	56N15	3w12	0:12:48
Farr	57N21	4w12	0:16:48
Fauldhouse	55N50	3w37	0:14:28
Fetterangus	57N33	2w01	0:08:04
Fettercairn	56N51	2w34	0:10:16
Findhorn	57N39	3w36	0:14:24
Five Penny Borve	58N25	6w25	0:25:40
Fochabers	57N37	3w05	0:12:20
Ford	56N10	5w26	0:21:44
Forfar	56N38	2w54	0:11:36
Forres	57N37	3w38	0:14:32
Fort Augustus	57N09	4w41	0:18:44
Fortevoit	56N20	3w32	0:14:08
Forth	55N47	3w41	0:14:44
Fortrose	57N34	4w09	0:16:36
Fort William	56N49	5w07	0:20:28
Foss	56N41	3w58	0:15:52
Foveran	57N18	2w02	0:08:08
Foyers	57N14	4w29	0:17:56
Fraserburgh	57N42	2w00	0:08:00
Freswick	58N35	3w05	0:12:20
Friockheim	56N38	2w38	0:10:32
Furnace	56N09	5w10	0:20:40
Fyvie	57N25	2w23	0:09:32
Gairloch	57N42	5w40	0:22:40
Galashiels	55N37	2w49	0:11:16
Galston	55N36	4w24	0:17:36
Garelochhead	56N05	4w50	0:19:20
Garinin	58N21	6w50	0:27:20
Garlieston	54N48	4w22	0:17:28
Garmouth	57N40	3w07	0:12:28
Garros	57N37	6w11	0:24:44
Garve	57N37	4w42	0:18:48
Gatehouse of Fleet	54N53	4w11	0:16:44
Gifford	55N54	2w45	0:11:00
Girvan	55N15	4w51	0:19:24
Glamis	56N36	3w00	0:12:00
Glasgow	55N53	4w15	0:17:00

Glenelg	57N13	5w38	0:22:32
Glenfarg	56N16	3w24	0:13:36
Glenfinnan	56N52	5w27	0:21:48
Glenluce	54N53	4w49	0:19:16
Glenrothes	56N12	3w10	0:12:40
Golspie	57N58	3w58	0:15:52
Gordon	55N41	2w34	0:10:16
Gorebridge	55N51	3w02	0:12:08
Gourock	55N58	4w49	0:19:16
Grandtully	56N39	3w46	0:15:04
Grangemouth	56N02	3w45	0:15:00
Granton	55N59	3w14	0:12:56
Grantown on Spey	57N20	3w58	0:15:52
Grantshouse	55N53	2w19	0:09:16
Greenlaw	55N43	2w28	0:09:52
Greenock	55N57	4w45	0:19:00
Gretna Green	54N59	3w04	0:12:16
Grongemouth	56N01	3w44	0:14:56
Gruting	60N14	1w30	0:06:00
Guildtown	56N28	3w24	0:13:36
Gullane	56N02	2w50	0:11:20
Gutcher	60N40	1w00	0:04:00
Haddington	55N58	2w47	0:11:08
Halkirk	58N30	3w30	0:14:00
Hamilton	55N47	4w03	0:16:12
Haroldswick	60N41	0w50	0:03:20
Harrietfield	56N25	3w39	0:14:36
Harris	56N59	6w20	0:25:20
Hatton	57N25	1w54	0:07:36
Haugh of Urr	54N58	3w52	0:15:28
Hawick	55N25	2w47	0:11:08
Helensburgh	56N01	4w44	0:18:56
Helmsdale	58N07	3w40	0:14:40
Hill of Fearn	57N45	3w56	0:15:44
Hillswick	60N28	1w30	0:06:00
Hollandstoun	59N21	2w16	0:09:04
Hopeman	57N42	3w25	0:13:40
Howmore	57N18	7w23	0:29:32
Hunter's Quay	55N58	4w55	0:19:40
Huntly	57N27	2w47	0:11:08
Hurlford	55N36	4w28	0:17:52
Hurliness	58N47	3w15	0:13:00
Inchbare	56N47	2w38	0:10:32
Inchnadamph	58N09	4w59	0:19:56
Inchture	56N26	3w10	0:12:40
Innellan	55N54	4w57	0:19:48
Innerleithen	55N38	3w05	0:12:20
Insch	57N21	2w37	0:10:28
Inver	57N49	3w55	0:15:40
Inveraray	56N13	5w05	0:20:20
Inverarity	56N35	2w53	0:11:32
Inverbervie	56N51	2w17	0:09:08
Inverdruie	57N10	3w48	0:15:12
Invergarry	57N02	4w47	0:19:08
Invergordon	57N42	4w10	0:16:40
Inverkeilor	56N38	2w32	0:10:08
Inverkeithing	56N02	3w25	0:13:40
Inverkeithny	57N30	2w37	0:10:28
Invermoriston	57N13	4w38	0:18:32
Inverness	57N27	4w15	0:17:00
Inveruglas	56N15	4w43	0:18:52
Inverurie	57N17	2w23	0:09:32
Irvine	55N37	4w40	0:18:40
Isbister	60N36	1w19	0:05:16
Islivig	58N05	7w11	0:28:44
Janetstown	58N16	3w22	0:13:28
Jedburgh	55N29	2w34	0:10:16
John O'groats	58N38	3w05	0:12:20
Johnshaven	56N47	2w20	0:09:20
Johnstone	55N50	4w31	0:18:04
Kames	55N54	5w15	0:21:00
Keig	57N15	2w39	0:10:36
Keith	57N32	2w57	0:11:48
Kelso	55N36	2w25	0:09:40
Kenmore	56N34	3w59	0:15:56
Kentallen	56N39	5w15	0:21:00
Kilbarchan	55N50	4w33	0:18:12
Kilbirnie	55N46	4w41	0:18:44
Kilbride	57N05	7w27	0:29:48
Kilchoan	56N42	6w06	0:24:24
Kilchrenan	56N21	5w11	0:20:44
Kildonan	58N10	3w51	0:15:24
Kildrummy	57N14	2w52	0:11:28
Killearn	56N03	4w22	0:17:28
Killilan	57N19	5w25	0:21:40
Killin	56N28	4w19	0:17:16
Kilmacolm	55N54	4w38	0:18:32
Kilmallie	56N47	5w07	0:20:28
Kilmaluag	57N41	6w17	0:25:08
Kilmarnock	55N36	4w30	0:18:00
Kilmartin	56N07	5w29	0:21:56
Kilmaurs	55N39	4w32	0:18:08
Kilmelford	56N16	5w29	0:21:56
Kilninver	56N20	5w31	0:22:04
Kilrenny	56N14	2w41	0:10:44
Kilsyth	55N59	4w04	0:16:16
Kilwinning	55N40	4w42	0:18:48
Kinbrace	58N15	3w56	0:15:44
Kinbuck	56N13	3w57	0:15:48
Kincardine	56N04	3w44	0:14:56
Kincraig	57N08	3w55	0:15:40
Kinfauns	56N22	3w21	0:13:24
Kingarth	55N46	5w03	0:20:12
Kingsbarns	56N18	2w39	0:10:36
Kingshouse	56N21	4w19	0:17:16
Kingussie	57N05	4w03	0:16:12
Kinldchleven	56N42	4w58	0:19:52
Kinlochbervie	58N28	5w03	0:20:12
Kinlochell	56N51	5w20	0:21:20
Kinlochewe	57N36	5w20	0:21:20
Kinloch Hourn	57N06	5w22	0:21:28
Kinloch Rannoch	56N42	4w11	0:16:44
Kinross	56N13	3w27	0:13:48
Kintore	57N13	2w21	0:09:24
Kippen	56N08	4w11	0:16:44

ESCOCIA CALEDONIA SCHOTTLAND ÉCOSSE SCOTLAND

Place	Lat.	Long.	Time
Kirkabister	60N07	1w08	0:04:32
Kirkcaldy	56N07	3w10	0:12:40
Kirkcolm	54N58	5w05	0:20:20
Kirkconnel	55N23	4w00	0:16:00
Kirkcudbright	54N50	4w03	0:16:12
Kirkhill	57N28	4w26	0:17:44
Kirkintilloch	55N57	4w10	0:16:40
Kirkliston	55N58	3w25	0:13:40
Kirkmichael	56N43	3w29	0:13:56
Kirkstile	55N12	3w00	0:12:00
Kirkton of Culsalmond	57N23	2w34	0:10:16
Kirkton of Glenisla	56N44	3w17	0:13:08
Kirktown of Auchterless	57N27	2w28	0:09:52
Kirkwall	58N59	2w58	0:11:52
Kirriemuir	56N41	3w01	0:12:04
Kirton of Largo	56N13	2w55	0:11:40
Knock	57N33	2w45	0:11:00
Kyleakin	57N16	5w44	0:22:56
Kyle of Lochalsh	57N17	5w43	0:22:52
Kylerhea	57N14	5w41	0:22:44
Kylestrome	58N16	5w02	0:20:08
Ladybank	56N16	3w08	0:12:32
Laggan	57N02	4w16	0:17:04
Laide	57N52	5w32	0:22:08
Lair	57N29	5w20	0:21:20
Lairg	58N01	4w25	0:17:40
Lamlash	55N32	5w08	0:20:32
Lanark	55N41	3w46	0:15:04
Langholm	55N09	3w00	0:12:00
Largoward	56N15	2w51	0:11:24
Largs	55N48	4w52	0:19:28
Larkhall	55N45	3w59	0:15:56
Lasswade	55N53	3w08	0:12:32
Lauder	55N43	2w45	0:11:00
Laurencekirk	56N50	2w29	0:09:56
Laxay	58N09	6w35	0:26:20
Leadburn	55N47	3w14	0:12:56
Leadhills	55N25	3w47	0:15:08
Leith	55N59	3w10	0:12:40
Lennoxtown	55N59	4w12	0:16:48
Lerwick	60N09	1w09	0:04:36
Leslie	56N12	3w13	0:12:52
Lesmahagow	55N39	3w55	0:15:40
Leuchars	56N23	2w53	0:11:32
Leven	56N12	3w00	0:12:00
Leverburgh	57N45	7w00	0:28:00
Lhanbryde	57N37	3w13	0:12:52
Lincluden	55N05	3w38	0:14:32
Linlithgow	55N59	3w37	0:14:28
Littlemill	57N32	3w49	0:15:16
Livingston	55N53	3w32	0:14:08
Loanhead	55N53	3w09	0:12:36
Lochailort	56N53	5w40	0:22:40
Lochaline	56N32	5w47	0:23:08
Lochboisdale	57N09	7w19	0:29:16
Lochcarron	57N24	5w30	0:22:00
Lochdonhead	56N26	5w41	0:22:44
Lochearnhead	56N23	4w17	0:17:08
Lochgair	56N03	5w20	0:21:20
Lochgelly	56N08	3w19	0:13:16
Lochgilphead	56N03	5w26	0:21:44
Lochgoilhead	56N10	4w54	0:19:36
Lochinver	58N09	5w15	0:21:00
Lochmaben	55N08	3w27	0:13:48
Lochranza	55N42	5w18	0:21:12
Lochwinnoch	55N48	4w39	0:18:36
Lockerbie	55N07	3w22	0:13:28
Longmorn	57N36	3w17	0:13:08
Lossiemouth	57N43	3w18	0:13:12
Lumphanan	57N07	2w41	0:10:44
Lumsden	57N15	2w52	0:11:28
Luncarty	56N27	3w28	0:13:52
Luthrie	56N21	3w05	0:12:20
Lybster	58N18	3w13	0:12:52
Macduff	57N40	2w29	0:09:56
Mallaig	57N00	5w50	0:23:20
Markinch	56N12	3w08	0:12:32
Marypark	57N26	3w21	0:13:24
Marywell	57N02	2w42	0:10:48
Mauchline	55N31	4w24	0:17:36
Maud	57N31	2w06	0:08:24
Maxwelltown	55N04	3w38	0:14:32
Maybole	55N21	4w41	0:18:44
Meigle	56N35	3w09	0:12:36
Melbost	58N15	6w22	0:25:28
Melby House	60N18	1w39	0:06:36
Mellon Udrigle	57N55	5w39	0:22:36
Melrose	55N36	2w44	0:10:56
Melviag	57N48	5w49	0:23:16
Melvich	58N33	3w55	0:15:40
Memsie	57N39	2w02	0:08:08
Methil	56N10	3w01	0:12:04
Methlick	57N25	2w14	0:08:56
Methyen	56N25	3w34	0:14:16
Migvie	57N08	2w56	0:11:44
Millport	55N46	4w55	0:19:40
Milngavie	55N57	4w20	0:17:20
Minard	56N07	5w15	0:21:00
Minnigaff	54N58	4w30	0:18:00
Mintlaw	57N31	2w00	0:08:00
Moffat	55N20	3w27	0:13:48
Moniaive	55N12	3w55	0:15:40
Monifieth	56N29	2w49	0:11:16
Monimail	56N18	3w08	0:12:32
Montrose	56N43	2w29	0:09:56
Monymusk	57N13	2w31	0:10:04
Monzie	56N24	3w48	0:15:12
Mossbank	60N27	1w12	0:04:48
Motherwell	55N48	4w00	0:16:00
Muasdale	55N36	5w41	0:22:44
Muirdrum	56N31	2w42	0:10:48
Muirkirk	55N31	4w04	0:16:16
Muir of Ord	57N31	4w27	0:17:48
Muirtown	56N16	3w45	0:15:00
Mulben	57N31	3w06	0:12:24
Munlochy	57N32	4w15	0:17:00
Musselburgh	55N57	3w04	0:12:16
Muthill	56N19	3w50	0:15:20
Mybster	58N27	3w25	0:13:40
Nairn	57N35	3w53	0:15:32
Naust	57N47	5w39	0:22:36
Neilston	55N47	4w27	0:17:48
Nethy Bridge	57N16	3w38	0:14:32
New Abbey	54N59	3w38	0:14:32
Newburgh	56N20	3w15	0:13:00
Newburgh	57N18	2w00	0:08:00
Newcastleton	55N11	2w49	0:11:16
New Cumnock	55N24	4w12	0:16:48
New Deer	57N30	2w12	0:08:48
New Galloway	55N05	4w10	0:16:40
Newmachar	57N16	2w11	0:08:44
Newmains	55N47	3w53	0:15:32
Newmilns	55N37	4w20	0:17:20
Newport-On-Tay	56N26	2w55	0:11:40
Newtongrange	55N52	3w04	0:12:16
Newtonmore	57N04	4w08	0:16:32
Newton Stewart	54N57	4w29	0:17:56
Newtown Saint Boswells	55N34	2w40	0:10:40
Nigg	57N43	4w00	0:16:00
North Berwick	56N04	2w44	0:10:56
North Queensferry	56N01	3w25	0:13:40
North Tolsta	58N20	6w13	0:24:52
Northwaa	59N16	2w17	0:09:08
Oban	56N25	5w29	0:21:56
Ochiltree	55N28	4w23	0:17:32
Oldmeldrum	57N20	2w20	0:09:20
Onich	56N42	5w13	0:20:52
Opinan	57N43	5w47	0:23:08
Ormiston	55N56	2w40	0:10:40
Oykel Bridge	57N58	4w43	0:18:52
Paisley	55N50	4w26	0:17:44
Path of Condie	56N15	3w30	0:14:00
Peat Inn	56N17	2w53	0:11:32
Peebles	55N39	3w12	0:12:48
Penicuik	55N50	3w14	0:12:56
Perth	56N24	3w28	0:13:52
Peterculter	57N05	2w16	0:09:04
Peterhead	57N30	1w49	0:07:16
Pierowall	59N20	2w59	0:11:56
Pinwherry	55N09	4w50	0:19:20
Pitlochry	56N43	3w45	0:15:00
Pittenweem	56N12	2w44	0:10:56
Polbain	58N02	5w23	0:21:32
Poolewe	57N45	5w37	0:22:28
Port Askaig	55N51	6w07	0:24:28
Port Bannatyne	55N52	5w05	0:20:20
Port Ellen	55N39	6w12	0:24:48
Port Glasgow	55N57	4w41	0:18:44
Portknockie	57N41	2w51	0:11:24
Port Logan	54N43	4w56	0:19:44
Portmahomack	57N49	3w50	0:15:20
Portnaguiran	58N17	6w13	0:24:52
Portnahaven	55N41	6w31	0:26:04
Portobello	55N58	3w07	0:12:28
Port of Ness	58N29	6w13	0:24:52
Portpatrick	54N51	5w07	0:20:28
Portree	57N24	6w12	0:24:48
Port Seton	55N58	2w57	0:11:48
Portsoy	57N41	2w41	0:10:44
Port William	54N46	4w35	0:18:20
Prestonpans	55N57	3w00	0:12:00
Prestwick	55N30	4w37	0:18:28
Queensferry	55N59	3w25	0:13:40
Quoyness	58N54	3w18	0:13:12
Rackwick	58N52	3w23	0:13:32
Ramasaig	57N24	6w44	0:26:56
Ranfurly	55N52	4w33	0:18:12
Rapness	59N14	2w51	0:11:24
Rathen	57N38	2w02	0:08:08
Reay	58N33	3w47	0:15:08
Redland	59N05	3w05	0:12:20
Reiss	58N28	3w10	0:12:40
Renfrew	55N53	4w24	0:17:36
Reston	55N51	2w11	0:08:44
Rhynie	57N19	2w50	0:11:20
Ringford	54N54	4w03	0:16:12
Rodel	57N41	7w05	0:28:20
Rogart	58N00	4w08	0:16:32
Rosehearty	57N42	2w07	0:08:28
Rosyth	56N03	3w26	0:13:44
Rothes	57N31	3w13	0:12:52
Rothesay	55N51	5w03	0:20:12
Roxburgh	55N34	2w30	0:10:00
Rumbling Bridge	56N10	3w35	0:14:20
Rutherglen	55N50	4w12	0:16:48
Saint Andrews	56N20	2w48	0:11:12
Saint Combs	57N39	1w54	0:07:36
Saint Fillans	56N23	4w07	0:16:28
Saint Margaret's Hope	58N49	2w57	0:11:48
Saint Monance	56N12	2w46	0:11:04
Salen	56N43	5w47	0:23:08
Salen	56N31	5w57	0:23:48
Saltcoats	55N38	4w47	0:19:08
Sandbank	55N59	4w58	0:19:52
Sandhead	54N48	4w58	0:19:52
Sandness	60N17	1w38	0:06:32
Sandwick	60N00	1w15	0:05:00
Sanquhar	55N22	3w56	0:15:44
Sarclet	58N22	3w07	0:12:28
Scalasaig	56N04	6w11	0:24:44
Scalloway	60N08	1w18	0:05:12
Scardroy	57N31	4w59	0:19:56
Scarinish	56N29	6w48	0:27:12
Scourie	58N20	5w08	0:20:32
Selkirk	55N33	2w50	0:11:20
Shiel Bridge	57N12	5w25	0:21:40
Shieldaig	57N31	5w39	0:22:36
Shinness	58N05	4w28	0:17:52
Shotts	55N49	3w48	0:15:12
Skelmorlie	55N51	4w53	0:19:32
Sollas	57N39	7w21	0:29:24
Sorbie	54N48	4w26	0:17:44
Sorn	55N30	4w18	0:17:12
Sortat	58N33	3w13	0:12:52
Southend	55N20	5w38	0:22:32
Spean Bridge	56N53	4w54	0:19:36
Spittal of Glenshee	56N48	3w28	0:13:52
Staffin	57N37	6w12	0:24:48
Stanley	56N28	3w27	0:13:48
Staxigoe	58N28	3w04	0:12:16
Stenhousemuir	56N02	3w48	0:15:12
Stevenston	55N39	4w45	0:19:00
Stewarton	55N41	4w31	0:18:04
Stirling	56N07	3w57	0:15:48
Stoer	58N12	5w20	0:21:20
Stonehaven	56N38	2w13	0:08:52
Stonehouse	55N43	4w00	0:16:00
Stornoway	58N12	6w23	0:25:32
Strachan	57N01	2w32	0:10:08
Strachur	56N10	5w04	0:20:16
Stranraer	54N55	5w02	0:20:08
Strathaven	55N40	4w04	0:16:16
Strathdon	57N11	3w02	0:12:08
Strathkanaird	57N59	5w11	0:20:44
Strathmiglo	56N16	3w16	0:13:04
Strathpeffer	57N35	4w33	0:18:12
Strichen	57N34	2w05	0:08:20
Stromeferry	57N21	5w34	0:22:16
Stromness	58N57	3w18	0:13:12
Strontian	56N41	5w44	0:22:56
Struy	57N24	4w39	0:18:36
Swinton	55N43	2w15	0:09:00
Syre	58N22	4w14	0:16:56
Tain	57N48	4w04	0:16:16
Talisker	57N17	6w27	0:25:48
Talladale	57N42	5w29	0:21:56
Talmine	58N31	4w26	0:17:44
Tarbert	55N52	5w26	0:21:44
Tarbert	57N54	6w49	0:27:16
Tarbet	56N12	4w43	0:18:52
Tarbolton	55N31	4w29	0:17:56
Tarfside	56N54	2w50	0:11:20
Tarland	57N08	2w52	0:11:28
Tarves	57N22	2w13	0:08:52
Taynuilf	56N25	5w14	0:20:56
Tayport	57N27	2w53	0:11:32
Teangue	57N07	5w50	0:23:20
Teviothead	55N21	2w56	0:11:44
Thornhill	55N15	3w46	0:15:04
Thurso	58N35	3w32	0:14:08
Tibbermore	56N22	3w32	0:14:08
Tillicoultry	56N09	3w45	0:15:00
Tillyfourie	57N11	2w35	0:10:20
Tobermory	56N37	6w05	0:24:20
Toberonochy	56N13	5w38	0:22:32
Tolob	59N53	1w19	0:05:16
Tomatin	57N20	3w59	0:15:56
Tomdoun	57N04	5w03	0:20:12
Tomich	57N18	4w48	0:19:12
Tomintoul	57N14	3w22	0:13:28
Tomnavoulin	57N18	3w19	0:13:16
Tongue	58N28	4w25	0:17:40
Torphins	57N06	2w37	0:10:28
Torridon	57N33	5w31	0:22:04
Torrin	57N12	6w02	0:24:08
Toscaig	57N24	5w50	0:23:20
Tranent	55N57	2w58	0:11:52
Tresta	60N14	1w21	0:05:24
Troon	55N32	4w40	0:18:40
Turriff	57N32	2w28	0:09:52
Tyndrum	56N27	4w44	0:18:56
Uddingston	55N50	4w06	0:16:24
Uig	57N35	6w22	0:25:28
Uig	58N12	7w00	0:28:00
Ullapool	57N54	5w10	0:20:40
Ulsta	60N30	1w09	0:04:36
Vickie	59N53	1w18	0:05:12
Walls	60N14	1w35	0:06:20
Wasbister	59N10	3w07	0:12:28
Waterside	55N21	4w28	0:17:52
West Calder	55N52	3w35	0:14:20
Westerdale	58N27	3w30	0:14:00
West Kilbride	55N42	4w51	0:19:24
West Linton	55N46	3w22	0:13:28
Whauphill	54N49	4w29	0:17:56
Whitburn	55N52	3w42	0:14:48
Whitehall	59N07	2w37	0:10:28
Whitehouse	57N13	2w37	0:10:28
Whithorn	54N44	4w25	0:17:40
Whiting Bay	55N29	5w06	0:20:24
Wick	58N26	3w06	0:12:24
Wigtown	54N52	4w26	0:17:44
Wilkhaven	57N52	3w45	0:15:00
Wishaw	55N47	3w56	0:15:44
Wormit	56N25	2w59	0:11:56
Yarrow	55N32	3w01	0:12:04

SENEGAL

SÉNÉGAL

Time Table
Before 1/Jan/1912 LMT
Begin Standard 15w00
1/Jan/1912 0:00 1:00
Begin Standard 0w00
1/Jun/1941 0:00 0:00

Place	Lat	Long	Offset
Bakel	14N54	12w27	0:49:48
Bala	14N02	13w10	0:52:40
Bignona	12N49	16w14	1:04:56
Bokolako	13N36	12w33	0:50:12
Coki	15N30	15w59	1:03:56
Dagana	16N31	15w30	1:02:00
Dahra	15N21	15w29	1:01:56
Dakar	14N40	17w26	1:09:44
Daoudi	14N08	13w58	0:55:52
Dara	15N21	15w29	1:01:56
Darou Mousti	15N03	16w03	1:04:12
Dialakoto	13N19	13w18	0:53:12
Diamounguel	15N06	12w55	0:51:40
Diembéring	12N28	16w47	1:07:08
Diouloulou	13N03	16w36	1:06:24
Diourbel	14N40	16w15	1:05:00
Fafakourou	13N04	14w34	0:58:16
Fété Bowé	14N56	13w30	0:54:00
Foundiougne	14N08	16w28	1:05:52
Gamon	13N20	12w55	0:51:40
Gossas	14N30	16w04	1:04:16
Goudiry	14N11	12w43	0:50:52
Guinguinéo	14N16	15w57	1:03:48
Joal	14N10	16w51	1:07:24
Joal Fadiout	14N10	16w51	1:07:24
Kaffrine	14N06	15w33	1:02:12
Kaolack	14N09	16w04	1:04:16
Kébémer	15N22	16w27	1:05:48
Kédougou	12N33	12w11	0:48:44
Khombole	14N46	16w42	1:06:48
Khossanto	13N08	11w58	0:47:52
Kidira	14N28	12w13	0:48:52
Koki	15N30	15w59	1:03:56
Kolda	12N53	14w57	0:59:48
Kossanto	13N08	11w58	0:47:52
Koulia Ba	14N11	14w28	0:57:52
Koumbakara	12N42	14w29	0:57:56
Koumpenntoum	13N59	14w34	0:58:16
Koumpentoum	13N59	14w34	0:58:16
Koungheul	13N59	14w48	0:59:12
Koussanar	13N52	14w05	0:56:20
Koussane	14N08	12w26	0:49:44
Koutia Ba	14N11	14w28	0:57:52
Linguère	15N24	15w07	1:00:28
Louga	15N37	16w13	1:04:52
Maka	13N40	14w17	0:57:08
Mako	12N52	12w21	0:49:24
Marssassoum	12N50	16w00	1:04:00
Matam	15N40	13w15	0:53:00
Mbacké	14N48	15w55	1:03:40
Mbar	14N32	15w46	1:03:04
Mboro	15N09	16w54	1:07:36
Mbour	14N24	16w58	1:07:52
Médina Gonassé	13N08	13w45	0:55:00
Médina Saback	13N36	15w35	1:02:20
Mékhé	15N07	16w38	1:06:32
Nafadji	12N37	11w37	0:46:28
Namari	15N05	13w39	0:54:36
Nayé	14N25	12w12	0:48:48
Ndande	15N16	16w30	1:06:00
Ngoui	16N09	13w55	0:55:40
Niokolo Koba	13N04	12w43	0:50:52
Nioro du Rip	13N45	15w48	1:03:12
Podor	16N40	14w57	0:59:48
Ranérou	15N18	13w58	0:55:52
Richard-Toll	16N28	15w41	1:02:44
Ross-Béthio	16N16	16w08	1:04:32
Rufisque	14N43	17w17	1:09:08
Saint-Louis	16N02	16w30	1:06:00
Saraya	12N50	11w45	0:47:00
Sédhiou	12N44	15w33	1:02:12
Simenti	13N00	13w25	0:53:40
Sokone	13N53	16w22	1:05:28
Tambacounda	13N47	13w40	0:54:40
Thiès	14N48	16w56	1:07:44
Tiadiaye	14N25	16w42	1:06:48
Tiankoye	12N35	12w40	0:50:40
Tièl	14N56	15w04	1:00:16
Tilogne	15N58	13w36	0:54:24
Tivaouane	14N57	16w49	1:07:16
Tobor	12N39	16w16	1:05:04
Touba	14N51	15w53	1:03:32
Toubéré Bafal	14N23	13w32	0:54:08
Vélingara	15N00	14w40	0:58:40
Vélingara	13N09	14w07	0:56:28
Yang Yang	15N35	15w21	1:01:24
Ziguinchor	12N35	16w16	1:05:04

SEYCHELLES

SEYCHELLEN

Time Table
Before 1/Jun/1906 LMT
Begin Standard 60E00
1/Jun/1906 0:00 -4:00

Place	Lat	Long	Offset
Aldabra Islands	9s25	46E22	-3:05:28
Alphonse Island	7s00	52E45	-3:31:00
Amirante Islands	6s00	53E10	-3:32:40
Assumption Island	9s45	46E30	-3:06:00
Astove Island	10s06	47E45	-3:11:00
Cerf Island	9s32	50E59	-3:23:56
Coetivy Island	7s08	56E16	-3:45:04
Cosmoledo Group	9s43	47E35	-3:10:20
Farquhar Group	10s10	51E10	-3:24:40
Île Desroches	5s52	53E30	-3:34:00
La Digue Island	4s21	55E50	-3:43:20
Mahé Island	4s40	55E28	-3:41:52
Platte Island	5s52	55E23	-3:41:32
Port Victoria → Victoria	4s38	55E27	-3:41:48
Praslin Island	4s19	55E44	-3:42:56
Providence Island	9s14	51E02	-3:24:08
Saint Pierre Island	9s28	50E41	-3:22:44
Silhouette Island	4s29	55E14	-3:40:56
Victoria	4s38	55E27	-3:41:48

SIERRA LEONE

SIERRA LEONE

Time Table
Before 1/Jan/1882 LMT
Begin Standard 13w15
1/Jan/1882 0:00 0:53
Begin Standard 15w00
1/Jun/1913 0:00 1:00
1/Jun/1935 0:00 0:20
1/Oct/1935 0:00 1:00
1/Jun/1936 0:00 0:20
1/Oct/1936 0:00 1:00
1/Jun/1937 0:00 0:20
1/Oct/1937 0:00 1:00
1/Jun/1938 0:00 0:20
1/Oct/1938 0:00 1:00
1/Jun/1939 0:00 0:20
1/Oct/1939 0:00 1:00
1/Jun/1940 0:00 0:20
1/Oct/1940 0:00 1:00
1/Jun/1941 0:00 0:20
1/Oct/1941 0:00 1:00
1/Jun/1942 0:00 0:20
1/Oct/1942 0:00 1:00
Begin Standard 0w00
1/Jan/1957 0:00 0:00
1/Jun/1957 0:00 -1:00
1/Sep/1957 0:00 0:00
1/Jun/1958 0:00 -1:00
1/Sep/1958 0:00 0:00
1/Jun/1959 0:00 -1:00
1/Sep/1959 0:00 0:00
1/Jun/1960 0:00 -1:00
1/Sep/1960 0:00 0:00
1/Jun/1961 0:00 -1:00
1/Sep/1961 0:00 0:00
1/Jun/1962 0:00 -1:00
1/Sep/1962 0:00 0:00

Place	Lat	Long	Offset
Balia	9N20	10w57	0:43:48
Baoma	7N58	11w37	0:46:28
Batkanu	9N05	12w25	0:49:40
Bauya	8N11	12w34	0:50:16
Bo	7N56	11w21	0:45:24
Bonthe	7N32	12w30	0:50:00
Bumbuna	9N03	11w44	0:46:56
Daru	7N59	10w50	0:43:20
Falaba	9N51	11w19	0:45:16
Freetown	8N30	13w15	0:53:00
Gbangbama	7N42	12w19	0:49:16
Gbangbatok	7N48	12w23	0:49:32
Kabala	9N35	11w33	0:46:12
Kailahun	8N17	10w34	0:42:16
Kamakwie	9N30	12w14	0:48:56
Kambia	9N07	12w55	0:51:40
Kayima	8N53	11w10	0:44:40
Kenema	7N52	11w12	0:44:48
Kent	8N10	13w10	0:52:40
Koindu	8N26	10w19	0:41:16
Lungi	8N38	13w13	0:52:52
Lunsar	8N41	12w32	0:50:08
Mabonto	8N52	11w49	0:47:16
Magburaka	8N43	11w57	0:47:48
Makeni	8N53	12w03	0:48:12
Mange	8N55	12w51	0:51:24
Mano	8N02	12w06	0:48:24
Marampa	8N41	12w28	0:49:52
Masayama	8N15	10w49	0:43:16
Matru	7N36	12w11	0:48:44
Mongeri	8N19	11w44	0:46:56
Moyamba	8N10	12w26	0:49:44
Pendembu	8N06	10w42	0:42:48
Pendembu	9N06	12w12	0:48:48
Pepel	8N35	13w03	0:52:12
Port Loko	8N46	12w47	0:51:08
Pujehun	7N21	11w42	0:46:48
Russel	8N15	13w05	0:52:20
Sefadu	8N39	10w59	0:43:56
Segbwema	8N00	10w57	0:43:48
Shenge	7N55	12w57	0:51:48
Sulima	6N58	11w35	0:46:20
Sumbuya	7N39	11w58	0:47:52
Waterloo	8N20	13w04	0:52:16
Yele	8N25	11w50	0:47:20
Yengema	8N43	11w10	0:44:40
Yonibana	8N26	12w14	0:48:56
York	8N17	13w11	0:52:44
Zimi	7N19	11w18	0:45:12

SINGAPUR — SINGAPOUR — SINGAPORE

Time Table
Before 1/Jan/1880 LMT
Begin Standard 103E51
1/Jan/1880 0:00 -6:55
Begin Standard 105E00
1/Jun/1905 0:00 -7:00
Begin Standard 110E00
1/Jan/1933 0:00 -7:20
Begin Standard 135E00
15/Feb/1942 0:00 -9:00
Begin Standard 110E00
2/Sep/1945 0:00 -7:20
Begin Standard 112E30
1/Jan/1950 0:00 -7:30
Begin Standard 120E00
1/May/1982 0:00 -8:00

Ama Keng	1N24	103E42	-6:54:48
Bedok	1N19	103E57	-6:55:48
Bukit Panjang	1N23	103E46	-6:55:04
Bukit Timah	1N20	103E47	-6:55:08
Bulim	1N23	103E43	-6:54:52
Buona Vista	1N16	103E47	-6:55:08
Changi	1N23	103E59	-6:55:56
Choa Chu Kang	1N22	103E41	-6:54:44
Chong Pang	1N26	103E50	-6:55:20
Jalan Kayu	1N24	103E52	-6:55:28
Jurong	1N21	103E42	-6:54:48
Kampong Kranji	1N26	103E46	-6:55:04
Kampong Loyang	1N22	103E58	-6:55:52
Kampong Tanjong Keling	1N18	103E42	-6:54:48
Kranji	1N26	103E45	-6:55:00
Lokyang	1N20	103E41	-6:54:44
Mandai	1N25	103E45	-6:55:00
Nee Soon	1N24	103E49	-6:55:16
Pasir Panjang	1N17	103E47	-6:55:08
Paya Lebar	1N22	103E53	-6:55:32
Punggol	1N25	103E55	-6:55:40
Seletar	1N25	103E53	-6:55:32
Sembawang	1N27	103E50	-6:55:20
Serangoon	1N22	103E54	-6:55:36
Singapore	1N17	103E51	-6:55:24
Singapur → Singapore	1N17	103E51	-6:55:24
Thong Hoe	1N25	103E42	-6:54:48
Tuas	1N19	103E38	-6:54:32
Woodlands	1N27	103E46	-6:55:04
Yan Kit	1N22	103E58	-6:55:52
Yio Chu Kang	1N23	103E51	-6:55:24

ISLAS SALOMÓN — SALOMON-INSELN — ÎLES SALOMON — SOLOMON ISLANDS

Time Table
Before 1/Oct/1912 LMT
Begin Standard 165E00
1/Oct/1912 0:00 -11:00

DIVISIONS

1. Choiseul
2. Guadalcanal
3. Malaita
4. New Georgia
5. San Cristobal
6. Santa Isabel

Adam Port 3	9S34	161E33	-10:46:12
Aola 2	9S32	160E29	-10:41:56
Auki 3	8S46	160E42	-10:42:48
Avu Avu 2	9S50	160E23	-10:41:32
Bagarai 5	10S48	162E04	-10:48:16
Bambatana 1	7S02	156E48	-10:27:12
Bina 3	8S55	160E46	-10:43:04
Bola 2	9S37	160E39	-10:42:36
Choiseul Island 1	7S05	157E00	-10:28:00
Dadali 6	8S07	159E06	-10:36:24
Dala 3	8S35	160E40	-10:42:40
Fauabu 3	8S34	160E43	-10:42:52
Fual (Fula) 3	8S57	161E06	-10:44:24
Gatere 6	7S55	159E06	-10:36:24
Gizo 4	8S06	156E51	-10:27:24
Guadalcanal Island 2	9S32	160E12	-10:40:48
Henderson Field 2	9S26	160E27	-10:41:48
Honiara 2	9S26	159E57	-10:39:48
Inakona 2	9S49	160E02	-10:40:08
Kia 6	7S33	158E26	-10:33:44
Kira Kira 5	10S27	161E55	-10:47:40
Kolombagia 4	8S01	157E36	-10:30:24
Korrigole Harbour 6	8S03	158E59	-10:35:56
Lambeti 4	8S20	157E17	-10:29:08
Luti 1	7S14	156E59	-10:27:56
Malaita Island 3	9S00	161E00	-10:44:00
Manano (Manango) 1	6S51	157E58	-10:31:52
Manawai 3	9S05	161E11	-10:44:44
Maraugoa 5	10S26	161E27	-10:45:48
Maravari 4	7S51	156E42	-10:26:48
Maravovo 2	9S17	159E38	-10:38:32
Mbola 2	9S37	160E39	-10:42:36
Mundi Mundi 4	7S39	156E30	-10:26:00
New Georgia Island 4	8S15	157E30	-10:30:00
Nukiki 1	6S46	156E28	-10:25:52
Oteotea 3	9S05	161E11	-10:44:44
Papara 1	7S02	156E48	-10:27:12
Pukauli 2	9S50	160E23	-10:41:32
Rendova 4	8S27	157E18	-10:29:12
Ronroni 2	9S37	159E58	-10:39:52
San Cristobal Island 5	10S36	161E45	-10:47:00
Santa Isabel Island 6	8S00	159E00	-10:36:00
Sasamungga 1	7S02	156E47	-10:27:08
Sepi 6	8S33	159E50	-10:39:20
Siota 2	9S03	160E19	-10:41:16
Susubona 6	8S18	159E27	-10:37:48
Suu 3	9S10	160E56	-10:43:44
Tanabuli 6	8S24	159E49	-10:39:16
Tangarare 2	9S35	159E39	-10:38:36
Tomba-tomba 1	6S38	156E37	-10:26:28
Tulaghi 2	9S06	160E09	-10:40:36
Tulagi 2	9S06	160E09	-10:40:36
Tunnibuli 6	8S24	159E49	-10:39:16
Ugali 4	8S27	157E25	-10:29:40
Velaviruru 1	7S25	157E30	-10:30:00
Viru Harbour 4	8S30	157E45	-10:31:00
Visale 2	9S15	159E42	-10:38:48
Visale Mission 2	9S15	159E42	-10:38:48
Yandina 2	9S07	159E13	-10:36:52

SOOMAALIYEED — SOMALILAND — SOMALIE — SOMALIYA — SOMALIA

Time Table
Before 1/Nov/1893 LMT
Begin Standard 45E00
1/Nov/1893 0:00 -3:00
Begin Standard 37E29
1/Jan/1931 0:00 -2:30
Begin Standard 45E00
1/Jan/1957 0:00 -3:00

Abar Irir	4N53	46E10	-3:04:40
Abdul Ghadir	10N32	42E52	-2:51:28
Abou	4N21	43E03	-2:52:12
Adale	2N47	46E27	-3:05:48
Adego	8N58	49E35	-3:18:20
Afgoi	2N09	45E07	-3:00:28
Afgooye	2N09	45E07	-3:00:28
Afmadow	0N31	42E04	-2:48:16
Afmadu	0N31	42E04	-2:48:16
Ageraro	4N08	42E40	-2:50:40
Aggherar	4N03	42E40	-2:50:40
Ainabo	8N57	46E30	-3:06:00
‘Alula	11N58	50E48	-3:23:12
Ankhor	10N47	46E17	-3:05:08
Anole	2N01	42E20	-2:49:20
Arabei Dalon	3N34	46E30	-3:06:00
Arar Lugole	3N16	45E28	-3:01:52
Awal Aw Ballou	1N29	43E02	-2:52:08
Awdeyle	1N59	44E50	-2:59:20
Awdheegle	1N59	44E50	-2:59:20
Ba‘Adweyn	7N12	47E24	-3:09:36
Baardheere	2N20	42E17	-2:49:08
Baargaal	11N17	51E04	-3:24:16
Bacaadweeyn	7N12	47E32	-3:10:08
Bahado	5N48	47E11	-3:08:44
Baidoa	3N04	43E48	-2:55:12
Balad	2N22	45E25	-3:01:40
Balum	8N38	46E48	-3:07:12
Bardera	2N21	42E20	-2:49:20
Bargal	11N18	51E07	-3:24:28
Bawn	10N12	43E02	-2:52:08
Bederwanak	9N34	44E25	-2:57:40
Beira	6N59	47E20	-3:09:20
Beled Weyne	4N47	45E12	-3:00:48
Belet Uen → Beled Weyne	4N47	45E12	-3:00:48
Bender Beila	9N30	50E30	-3:22:00
Bender Cassim	11N17	49E11	-3:16:44
Bender Merhagno	11N39	50E25	-3:21:40
Berbera	10N25	45E02	-3:00:08
Bidi	1N00	42E40	-2:50:40
Bihen	10N38	48E24	-3:13:36
Bio Addo	8N16	49E52	-3:19:28
Bircao → Bur Gavo	1S10	41E50	-2:47:20
Bogon	2N56	42E00	-2:48:00
Bohol	5N43	46E10	-3:04:40
Bohotleh Wein	8N16	46E24	-3:05:36
Borama	9N58	43E07	-2:52:28
Bosaso	11N13	49E08	-3:16:32
Brava	1N05	44E02	-2:56:08
Bud Bud	4N15	46E30	-3:06:00
Bug Atoti	10N41	50E45	-3:23:00
Bulhale	5N27	46E33	-3:06:12
Bulhar	10N23	44E27	-2:57:48
Bulo Burti	3N52	45E40	-3:02:40
Bulo Gedudo	2N59	43E00	-2:52:00
Buqda ‘Aqable	4N04	45E21	-3:01:24
Buqda Kosar	4N35	44E59	-2:59:56
Buran	10N10	48E48	-3:15:12
Burao	9N30	45E30	-3:02:00
Burao Kibir	8N42	45E23	-3:01:32
Bur Gavo	1S10	41E50	-2:47:20
Bur Gibi	3N57	45E07	-3:00:28
Bur Hakkaba	2N43	44E10	-2:56:40
Buro	11N26	49E42	-3:18:48
Candala → Qandala	11N28	49E52	-3:19:28

SOMALIA SOMALIYA SOMALIE SOMALILAND SOOMAALIYEED

Ceemadle	5N14	46E56	-3:07:44
Ceerigaabo	10N37	47E22	-3:09:28
Ceg	8N58	45E20	-3:01:20
Chisimaio → Kismaayo	0S22	42E32	-2:50:08
Ciraadhame	10N30	49E22	-3:17:28
Comar Gambon	3N10	45E47	-3:03:08
Daba Gorayale	8N42	44E55	-2:59:40
Dabaro	6N21	48E43	-3:14:52
Daborow	6N21	48E43	-3:14:52
Dadle	5N20	46E58	-3:07:52
Dal Goble	9N52	49E50	-3:19:20
Dancug	10N58	49E04	-3:16:16
Dankug	10N58	49E04	-3:16:16
Dante	10N25	51E16	-3:25:04
Daragodleh	10N10	44E51	-2:59:24
Darboruk	9N44	44E31	-2:58:04
Darburruk	9N44	44E31	-2:58:04
Davegoriale	8N45	44E50	-2:59:20
Degla Reidab	2N51	42E18	-2:49:12
Dero Eri	9N01	46E43	-3:06:52
Dhiinsoor	2N24	42E59	-2:51:56
Dhurbo	11N37	50E20	-3:21:20
Dhuudo	9N20	50E12	-3:20:48
Dhuusa Mareeb	5N31	46E24	-3:05:36
Dif	1N00	41E00	-2:44:00
Dinach	9N15	50E37	-3:22:28
Dinsor	2N28	43E00	-2:52:00
Dirri	4N20	46E37	-3:06:28
Doigab	0N59	43E38	-2:54:32
Dolo	4N13	42E08	-2:48:32
Domadare	1N50	41E13	-2:44:52
Doolow	4N10	42E05	-2:48:20
Doygaab	0N59	43E32	-2:54:08
Duca degli	2N46	45E30	-3:02:00
Dudo	9N20	50E14	-3:20:56
Dujuma	1N15	42E34	-2:50:16
Dujuuma	1N15	42E34	-2:50:16
Dul Madoba	9N08	45E58	-3:03:52
Durbo	11N30	50E18	-3:21:12
Egerta	2N04	43E11	-2:52:44
Egherta	2N04	43E11	-2:52:44
Eik	8N58	45E09	-3:00:36
Eil	8N00	49E51	-3:19:24
El-Adde	2N35	46E09	-3:04:36
El-Aden Hindi	2N18	42E00	-2:48:00
El-Afwein	9N55	47E14	-3:08:56
El-Avagi	3N36	46E57	-3:07:48
Elayu	11N13	49E00	-3:16:00
El-Berde	4N52	43E40	-2:54:40
El-Bur	4N40	46E40	-3:06:40
El Dab	8N58	46E38	-3:06:32
El Dambahaddo	3N17	46E40	-3:06:40
El-Don Far	10N35	49E02	-3:16:08
El Dudu	2N37	41E46	-2:47:04
El-Hamurre	7N11	48E55	-3:15:40
El-Uarre	3N41	45E20	-3:01:20
El-Wak	2N50	41E03	-2:44:12
El-Wanot	4N07	47E07	-3:08:28
El-Warre	3N39	45E18	-3:01:12
Emadle	5N13	46E56	-3:07:44
Erigavo	10N37	47E24	-3:09:36
Eyl	7N59	49E49	-3:19:16
Faafaxdhuun	2N13	41E37	-2:46:28
Fafadur	2N11	41E32	-2:46:08
Feerfeer	8N30	47E55	-3:11:40
Ferfer	5N06	45E09	-3:00:36
Gabah	8N08	50E02	-3:20:08
Gabal	8N30	47E55	-3:11:40
Galgasc	0N14	41E37	-2:46:28
Galgash	0N14	41E37	-2:46:28
Galka'Yo	6N47	47E26	-3:09:44
Gal Tardo	3N34	45E58	-3:03:52
Garacad	6N57	49E19	-3:17:16
Garad	6N54	49E20	-3:17:20
Garadag	9N26	46E52	-3:07:28
Garbahaarey	3N19	42E13	-2:48:52
Garba Harre	3N20	42E17	-2:49:08
Gardo	9N30	49E03	-3:16:12
Garmal	8N35	50E19	-3:21:16
Garoe	8N24	48E29	-3:13:56
Garoowe	8N24	48E29	-3:13:56
Gelib → Jilib	0N29	42E46	-2:51:04
Gellinsoor	6N26	46E42	-3:06:48
Gellinsor	6N26	46E42	-3:06:48
Gel Turfo	3N05	45E58	-3:03:52
Giumbo → Jumboo	0S15	42E38	-2:50:32
Godalo	4N28	43E24	-2:53:36
Godinlabe	5N54	46E38	-3:06:32
Godinlave	5N54	46E38	-3:06:32
Goff	2N39	41E00	-2:44:00
Gofoundurei	4N31	46E46	-3:07:04
Goluin	1N40	44E35	-2:58:20
Golweyn	1N40	44E35	-2:58:20
Gorfoundurei	4N30	46E41	-3:06:44
Halin	9N08	48E47	-3:15:08
Handa	10N40	51E07	-3:24:28
Hando	10N39	51E08	-3:24:32
Harardera	4N32	47E53	-3:11:32
Hardiro	9N03	49E54	-3:19:36
Hargeysa	9N35	44E04	-2:56:16
Hariyo	5N00	47E23	-3:09:32
Heis	10N50	46E54	-3:07:36
Hobyo	5N21	48E32	-3:14:08
Hordio	10N32	51E08	-3:24:32
Horio	5N00	47E26	-3:09:44
Hudun	9N08	47E32	-3:10:08
Huguf	9N59	45E50	-3:03:20
Hurdiyo	10N33	51E08	-3:24:32
Ida	0N14	42E15	-2:49:00
Iddan	6N06	48E59	-3:15:56
Iidaan	6N06	48E59	-3:15:56
Ilad	10N09	47E52	-3:11:28
Iredame	10N29	49E21	-3:17:24
Isha Badoia	3N08	43E39	-2:54:36
Iskushuban	10N17	50E14	-3:20:56
Jamaame (Margherita)	0N04	42E46	-2:51:04
Jamame	0N04	42E46	-2:51:04
Jannaale	1N48	44E42	-2:58:48
Jannale	1N48	44E42	-2:58:48
Jersale	2N41	45E26	-3:01:44
Jialalassi	3N25	45E40	-3:02:40
Jibagalle	8N04	48E39	-3:14:36
Jibaganleh	8N05	48E37	-3:14:28
Jibalei	10N09	50E53	-3:23:32
Jigley	4N25	45E22	-3:01:28
Jiiqley	4N25	45E22	-3:01:28
Jilib	0N29	42E46	-2:51:04
Jire	5N22	48E05	-3:12:20
Johar	2N48	45E33	-3:02:12
Jontoy	0S05	42E35	-2:50:20
Jowhar	2N46	45E31	-3:02:04
Jumbo	0S15	42E38	-2:50:32
Jumboo	0S15	42E38	-2:50:32
Kabanjifa	3N34	43E30	-2:54:00
Kalis	8N23	49E05	-3:16:20
Kam Summa	0N15	42E47	-2:51:08
Kamsuuma	0N15	42E47	-2:51:08
Karin	10N51	45E47	-3:03:08
Kelyehed	8N46	49E12	-3:16:48
Kelyexeed	8N46	49E12	-3:16:48
Kenaf	1N37	41E36	-2:46:24
Kismaayo	0S22	42E32	-2:50:08
Kismayu	0S22	42E32	-2:50:08
Koraa Shiir	3N18	46E16	-3:05:04
Kor Aban	3N58	42E44	-2:50:56
Korashir	3N20	46E22	-3:05:28
Kotton	9N35	50E28	-3:21:52
Kursole	2N16	45E28	-3:01:52
Kurtumo	7N28	49E00	-3:16:00
Laas Caanood	8N28	47E21	-3:09:24
Laas Dawaco	10N28	49E05	-3:16:20
Laas Dhaareed	10N10	45E59	-3:03:56
Laas Qoray	11N10	48E13	-3:12:52
Las Anod	8N26	47E24	-3:09:36
Las Dawa'o	10N28	49E03	-3:16:12
Las Dureh	10N10	46E01	-3:04:04
Las Khoreh	11N10	48E13	-3:12:52
Lugh Ganane	3N56	42E32	-2:50:08
Luuq	3N48	42E33	-2:50:12
Madamarodi	2N37	44E37	-2:58:28
Madaxmaroodi	2N39	44E36	-2:58:24
Mahadday Weyn	2N58	45E32	-3:02:08
Mahadday Weyne	2N58	45E32	-3:02:08
Mait	10N57	47E06	-3:08:24
Manas	2N57	43E28	-2:53:52
Mareg	3N47	47E18	-3:09:12
Margherita → Jamaame	0N04	42E45	-2:51:00
Marka	1N43	44E53	-2:59:32
Maydh	11N00	47E07	-3:08:28
Meleden	10N25	49E51	-3:19:24
Meledin	10N25	49E51	-3:19:24
Merca → Marka	1N43	44E53	-2:59:32
Mereeg	3N46	47E18	-3:09:12
Merin Gubai	1N26	44E20	-2:57:20
Moccoidumis	1N36	44E26	-2:57:44
Mogadiscio → Muqdisho	2N04	45E22	-3:01:28
Mogadishu → Muqdisho	2N04	45E22	-3:01:28
Mokkoidumis	1N40	44E32	-2:58:08
Mooti	0N35	41E56	-2:47:44
Moqokorei	4N04	46E08	-3:04:32
Muqdisho (Mogadishu)	2N04	45E22	-3:01:28
Murcanyo	11N41	50E27	-3:21:48
Nabadid	9N39	43E28	-2:53:52
Obbia	5N20	48E38	-3:14:32
Oddur	4N10	43E53	-2:55:32
Odweina	9N23	45E04	-3:00:16
'Omar Gambon	3N12	45E50	-3:03:20
Ood Weyne	9N25	45E04	-3:00:16
Orgof	3N03	41E44	-2:46:56
Qandala	11N28	49E52	-3:19:28
Qaradog	9N30	46E57	-3:07:48
Qardho	9N30	49E05	-3:16:20
Rabaable	8N17	48E18	-3:13:12
Rabableh	8N17	48E18	-3:13:12
Rocca Littorio	6N46	47E26	-3:09:44
Saba Wanak	10N33	44E08	-2:56:32
Salagle	1N50	42E17	-2:49:08
Salahin	2N57	46E26	-3:05:44
Samaso	3N12	43E44	-2:54:56
Saranley	2N22	42E17	-2:49:08
Seemade	7N10	48E36	-3:14:24
Semmade	7N10	48E39	-3:14:36
Serenli	2N22	42E20	-2:49:20
Seylac	11N21	43E29	-2:53:56
Shawo	3N26	45E21	-3:01:24
Sidimo	2N27	41E58	-2:47:52
Sijerdero	8N47	48E02	-3:12:08
Silil	10N59	43E26	-2:53:44
Sillil	10N59	43E26	-2:53:44
Sinadhago	5N22	46E20	-3:05:20
Sinadogo	5N22	46E20	-3:05:20
Sinujif	8N33	48E59	-3:15:56
Solola	0N07	41E31	-2:46:04
Sooyaac	0N03	42E17	-2:49:08
Soya'	0N01	42E20	-2:49:20
Taleex	9N09	48E26	-3:13:44
Taleh	9N12	48E23	-3:13:32
Tarba	0N48	42E39	-2:50:36
Tarri	0N42	41E38	-2:46:32
Tarri Mashen	0N45	41E50	-2:47:20
Tayeegle	4N02	44E31	-2:58:04
Tayegle	4N02	44E31	-2:58:04
Ted	4N24	43E55	-2:55:40
Ted Ceidaar Dabole	4N24	43E55	-2:55:40
Tohen	11N42	51E17	-3:25:08
Tootias	3N57	43E57	-2:55:48
Tosilei	1N25	41E24	-2:45:36
Totias	3N57	43E58	-2:55:52
Waajid	3N48	43E15	-2:53:00
Wadamago	8N55	46E17	-3:05:08
Wallo	9N25	48E55	-3:15:40
Wajid	3N50	43E14	-2:52:56
Wakalla Wen	2N00	42E30	-2:50:00
Wakalla Yero	1N47	42E42	-2:50:48
Wanle Iten	2N38	44E55	-2:59:40
Wanle Weyne	2N37	44E54	-2:59:36
War Galla	1N10	41E11	-2:44:44
Wargalo	6N17	47E31	-3:10:04
Warinchiui	3N29	42E43	-2:50:52
Warshiikh	2N18	45E48	-3:03:12
Warshikh	2N18	45E48	-3:03:12
Warti Kogon	3N10	45E02	-3:00:08
Wassage	2N56	46E02	-3:04:08
Weel Shimbirro	2N23	44E16	-2:57:04
Wel Koban	2N33	44E20	-2:57:20
Welo	9N27	48E57	-3:15:48
Wel Shimbiro	2N23	44E16	-2:57:04
Weregta	1N30	42E28	-2:49:52
Xaafuun	10N25	51E16	-3:25:04
Xalin	9N06	48E37	-3:14:28
Xarardheere	4N39	47E51	-3:11:24
Xiis	10N53	46E54	-3:07:36
Xuddun	9N09	47E28	-3:09:52
Xuddur	4N07	43E54	-2:55:36
Yaaq-Baraawe	1N57	43E11	-2:52:44
Yageg	3N16	44E00	-2:56:00
Yak Monis	0N37	41E25	-2:45:40
Yaq Braway	2N00	43E45	-2:55:00
Yeed	4N33	43E02	-2:52:08
Yoontow	0S08	42E34	-2:50:16
Zauel	3N33	43E45	-2:55:00
Zawel	3N33	43E47	-2:55:08
Zeila (Zaila)	11N21	43E30	-2:54:00

Time Table # 1
Before 8/Feb/1892 LMT
Begin Standard 22E30
8/Feb/1892 0:00 -1:30
Begin Standard 30E00
1/Mar/1903 0:00 -2:00
20/Sep/1942 2:00 -3:00
21/Mar/1943 2:00 -2:00
19/Sep/1943 2:00 -3:00
19/Mar/1944 2:00 -2:00
....
Time Table # 2
Before 1/Jan/1881 LMT
Begin Standard 31E03
1/Jan/1881 0:00 -2:04
Begin Standard 30E00
1/Sep/1894 0:00 -2:00
27/Jul/1942 2:00 -3:00
21/Mar/1943 2:00 -2:00
19/Sep/1943 2:00 -3:00
19/Mar/1944 2:00 -2:00
....
Time Table # 3
Before 1/Jan/1881 LMT
Begin Standard 26E13
1/Jan/1881 0:00 -1:45
Begin Standard 22E30
8/Feb/1892 0:00 -1:30
Begin Standard 30E00
1/Mar/1903 0:00 -2:00
20/Sep/1942 2:00 -3:00
21/Mar/1943 2:00 -2:00
19/Sep/1943 2:00 -3:00
19/Mar/1944 2:00 -2:00

Aalwynsfontein 1 30s27 18E38 -1:14:32
Aansluit 1 26s44 22E28 -1:29:52
Aberdeen 1 32s29 24E03 -1:36:12
Abrahamsdam 1 29s08 22E39 -1:30:36
Acornhoek 1 24s37 31E02 -2:04:08
Acton Homes 2 28s36 29E26 -1:57:44
Addo 1 33s32 25E45 -1:43:00
Adelaide 1 32s42 26E20 -1:45:20
Adendorp 1 32s20 24E33 -1:38:12
Aggeneis 1 29s03 18E51 -1:15:24
Agulhas 1 34s50 20E00 -1:20:00
Albert Falls 2 29s27 30E25 -2:01:40
Albertinia 1 34s13 21E36 -1:26:24
Alberton 1 26s16 28E08 -1:52:32
Albertynsville 1 26s17 27E52 -1:51:28
Alcockspruit 2 27s55 30E01 -2:00:04
Alexander Bay 1 28s40 16E30 -1:06:00
Alexandra 1 26s06 28E05 -1:52:20
Alexandria 1 33s39 26E24 -1:45:36
Alice 1 32s47 26E50 -1:47:20
Alicedale 1 33s18 26E05 -1:44:20
Aliwal North 1 30s45 26E45 -1:47:00
Allanridge 3 27s55 26E44 -1:46:56
Alldays 1 22s44 29E04 -1:56:16
Amalia 1 27s16 25E03 -1:40:12
Amatikulu 2 29s06 31E27 -2:05:48
Amersfoort 1 26s59 29E53 -1:59:32
Amsterdam 1 26s35 30E45 -2:03:00
Ancona 3 27s40 26E32 -1:46:08
Andalusia → Jan Kempdorp
1 27s55 24E51 -1:39:24
Antwerp 1 26s06 28E10 -1:52:40
Anysberg 1 33s31 20E46 -1:23:04
Appleby 1 27s39 22E36 -1:30:24
Argent 1 26s04 28E50 -1:55:20
Arlington 3 28s06 27E54 -1:51:36
Ascent 3 27s12 29E03 -1:56:12
Ashton 1 33s50 20E05 -1:20:20
Askham 1 26s59 20E47 -1:23:08
Askraal 1 34s09 20E52 -1:23:28
Augrabies 1 28s37 20E20 -1:21:20
Aurora 1 32s42 18E29 -1:13:56
Austin's Post 3 29s32 25E49 -1:43:16
Avondrust 1 34s21 21E51 -1:27:24
Avontuur 1 33s44 23E11 -1:32:44
Baardskeerdersbos
1 34s34 19E35 -1:18:20
Babanango 2 28s30 31E00 -2:04:00
Badplaas 1 25s57 30E35 -2:02:20
Bakenkop 1 28s01 23E02 -1:32:08
Bakerville 1 26s00 26E06 -1:44:24
Bakoondfontein 1 32s43 22E30 -1:30:00
Balfour 1 26s44 28E31 -1:54:04
Ballengeich 2 27s52 29E59 -1:59:56
Balmoral 1 25s52 28E59 -1:55:56
Baltimore 1 23s15 28E20 -1:53:20
Bapsfontein 1 26s08 28E25 -1:53:40
Baragwanath 1 26s16 27E59 -1:51:56
Barberton 1 25s48 31E03 -2:04:12
Barkly East 1 30s58 27E33 -1:50:12
Barkly West 1 28s05 24E31 -1:38:04
Baroe 1 33s13 24E33 -1:38:12
Barrydale 1 33s55 20E43 -1:22:52
Bathurst 1 33s30 26E50 -1:47:20
Battlemount 1 26s57 23E46 -1:35:04
Bayala 2 27s47 32E08 -2:08:32
Beaufort West 1 32s18 22E36 -1:30:24
Bedford 1 32s41 26E05 -1:44:20
Beestekraal 1 25s23 27E38 -1:50:32
Beginsel 1 26s57 20E39 -1:22:36
Bekkersdal 1 26s18 27E42 -1:50:48
Belcobos 1 27s10 24E00 -1:36:00
Belfast 1 25s43 30E03 -2:00:12
Bell 1 33s15 27E23 -1:49:32
Bellville 1 33s53 18E36 -1:14:24
Belmont 1 29s28 24E22 -1:37:28
Benoni 1 26s19 28E27 -1:53:48
Benoni South 1 26s13 28E18 -1:53:12
Benoni-Suid 1 26s13 28E18 -1:53:12
Bergplaas 1 33s54 22E40 -1:30:40
Bergville 2 28s52 29E18 -1:57:12
Berlin 1 32s54 27E35 -1:50:20
Bernhardina 3 27s53 28E40 -1:54:40
Bethal 1 26s27 29E28 -1:57:52
Bethelsdorp 1 33s52 25E34 -1:42:16
Bethesdaweg 1 31s55 24E45 -1:39:00
Bethlehem 1 27s10 24E00 -1:36:00
Bethlehem 3 28s15 28E15 -1:53:00
Bethulie 3 30s32 25E59 -1:43:56
Betty's Bay 1 34s22 18E52 -1:15:28
Biesiesvlei 1 26s22 25E55 -1:43:40
Bilkfontein 1 27s50 23E56 -1:35:44
Bisho 1 32s50 27E20 -1:49:20
Bitterfontein 1 31s00 18E32 -1:14:08
Biyela 2 27s47 32E08 -2:08:32
Bizana 1 30s58 29E52 -1:59:28
Blackheath 1 26s08 27E58 -1:51:52
Bladgrond 1 28s52 19E57 -1:19:48
Blanco 1 33s57 22E24 -1:29:36
Bloedrivier 2 27s53 30E30 -2:02:00
Bloedrivier 2 28s06 30E33 -2:02:12
Bloekomspruit 1 26s45 28E21 -1:53:24
Bloemfontein 3 29s12 26E07 -1:44:28
Bloemhof 1 27s38 25E32 -1:42:08
Blouberg 1 23s08 28E56 -1:55:44
Bloubergstrand 1 33s47 18E28 -1:13:52
Bochum 1 23s17 29E07 -1:56:28
Boerboonfontein 1 33s43 20E32 -1:22:08
Boesmansriviermond
1 33s42 26E39 -1:46:36
Boetsap 1 27s59 24E30 -1:38:00
Bokfontein 1 32s48 19E16 -1:17:04
Bokhara 1 27s57 20E30 -1:22:00
Boksburg 1 26s12 28E14 -1:52:56
Boksburg-Noord 1 26s12 28E15 -1:53:00
Boksburg North 1 26s12 28E15 -1:53:00
Boksburg South 1 26s14 28E15 -1:53:00
Boksburg West 1 26s13 28E14 -1:52:56
Bon Accord 1 25s38 28E11 -1:52:44
Bonaero Park 1 26s07 28E16 -1:53:04
Bonnievale 1 33s57 20E06 -1:20:24
Boomrivier 1 29s33 20E27 -1:21:48
Boons 1 25s59 27E13 -1:48:52
Bordeaux 1 26s06 28E01 -1:52:04
Boshoek 1 25s30 27E09 -1:48:36
Boshof 3 28s34 25E04 -1:40:16
Boskop 1 26s34 27E08 -1:48:32
Boskuil 1 27s23 25E51 -1:43:24
Botersleegte 1 30s35 21E22 -1:25:28
Botha's Hill 2 29s45 30E45 -2:03:00
Bothaville 3 27s27 26E36 -1:46:24
Bo-Wadrif 1 32s26 20E07 -1:20:28
Brackenhurst 1 26s19 28E06 -1:52:24
Brakpan 1 26s13 28E20 -1:53:20
Brakpoort 1 31s20 23E22 -1:33:28
Brakputs 1 29s29 18E24 -1:13:36
Brandfort 3 28s47 26E30 -1:46:00
Brandkop 1 31s13 19E13 -1:16:52
Brandvlei 1 30s25 20E30 -1:22:00
Brandvlei 1 26s07 27E39 -1:50:36
Braunschweig 1 32s48 27E22 -1:49:28
Bredasdorp 1 34s32 20E02 -1:20:08
Bredell 1 26s05 28E17 -1:53:08
Breidbach 1 32s54 27E27 -1:49:48
Brenthurst 1 26s16 28E23 -1:53:32
Brentwood Park 1 26s08 28E18 -1:53:12
Brereton Park 1 26s55 30E30 -2:02:00
Breyten 1 26s16 30E00 -2:00:00
Brits 1 25s42 27E45 -1:51:00
Britstown 1 30s37 23E30 -1:34:00
Britten 1 27s42 25E17 -1:41:08
Broedersput 1 26s49 25E08 -1:40:32
Bronkhorstspruit
1 25s50 28E43 -1:54:52
Broodsnyersplaas
1 26s03 29E29 -1:57:56
Broteni 2 29s38 29E42 -1:58:48
Buchufontein 1 30s18 19E36 -1:18:24
Bultfontein 3 28s20 26E05 -1:44:20
Bulwater 1 32s29 21E48 -1:27:12
Bulwer 2 29s46 29E47 -1:59:08
Bundu 1 29s45 22E02 -1:28:08
Burgersdorp 1 31s00 26E20 -1:45:20
Burger Township 1 26s05 27E46 -1:51:04
Butterworth 1 32s23 28E04 -1:52:16
Buxton 1 27s38 24E42 -1:38:48
Cala 1 31s30 27E37 -1:50:28
Caledon 1 34s12 19E23 -1:17:32
Calitzdorp 1 33s33 21E42 -1:26:48
Calvinia 1 31s25 19E45 -1:19:00
Camden 1 26s38 30E07 -2:00:28
Campbell 1 28s48 23E44 -1:34:56
Camperdown 2 29s42 30E33 -2:02:12
Candover 2 27s28 31E57 -2:07:48
Cape Town (Kaapstad)
1 33s55 18E22 -1:13:28
Cap, Le → Cape Town
1 33s55 18E22 -1:13:28
Cardington 1 27s11 23E30 -1:34:00
Carletonville 1 26s23 27E22 -1:49:28
Carnarvon 1 30s56 22E08 -1:28:32
Carolina 1 26s05 30E06 -2:00:24
Cathcart 1 32s18 27E09 -1:48:36
Cedarmont 1 26s50 29E01 -1:56:04
Cedarville 1 30s23 29E03 -1:56:12
Ceres 1 33s21 19E18 -1:17:12
Chamdor 1 26s08 27E48 -1:51:12
Charl Cilliers 1 26s39 29E12 -1:56:48
Charlestown 2 27s30 29E55 -1:59:40
Chrissiesmeer 1 26s16 30E13 -2:00:52
Christiana 1 27s52 25E08 -1:40:32
Cinderella 1 26s15 28E16 -1:53:04
Citrusdal 1 32s36 19E00 -1:16:00
Ciudad del Cabo → Cape Town
1 33s55 18E22 -1:13:28
Clanwilliam 1 32s11 18E54 -1:15:36
Clarens 3 28s30 28E29 -1:53:56
Clifford 1 31s04 27E28 -1:49:52
Clocolan 3 29s00 27E30 -1:50:00
Cloverdene 1 26s09 28E22 -1:53:28
Clydesdale 3 26s54 27E55 -1:51:40
Coalbrook 3 26s51 27E53 -1:51:32
Coalville 1 26s01 29E10 -1:56:40
Cofimvaba 1 32s00 27E35 -1:50:20
Colenso 2 28s50 29E44 -1:58:56
Colesberg 1 30s45 25E05 -1:40:20
Coligny 1 26s17 26E15 -1:45:00
Commondale 1 27s20 30E56 -2:03:44
Comptonville 1 26s17 27E58 -1:51:52
Conway 1 31s43 25E16 -1:41:04
Cookhouse 1 32s44 25E48 -1:43:12
Cornelia 3 27s13 28E52 -1:55:28
Cradock 1 32s08 25E36 -1:42:24
Crafthole 1 26s24 24E03 -1:36:12
Creighton 2 30s01 29E51 -1:59:24
Cullinan 1 25s40 28E32 -1:54:08
Daggafontein 1 26s18 28E28 -1:53:52
Daleside 1 26s30 28E04 -1:52:16
Dalton 2 29s20 30E40 -2:02:40
Dalview 1 26s15 28E21 -1:53:24
Danielskuil 1 28s11 23E33 -1:34:12
Dannhauser 2 28s04 30E04 -2:00:16
Darling 1 33s23 18E23 -1:13:32
Darnall 2 29s23 31E18 -2:05:12
Daskop 1 33s44 22E43 -1:30:52
Dassiefontein 1 31s35 24E25 -1:37:40
Davel 1 26s24 29E40 -1:58:40
Daveyton Location
1 26s09 28E25 -1:53:40
De Aar 1 30s39 24E00 -1:36:00
Dealesville 3 28s40 25E37 -1:42:28
De Doorns 1 33s28 19E41 -1:18:44
Deelfontein 1 30s59 23E48 -1:35:12
Deelpan 1 26s19 25E36 -1:42:24
De Hoek 1 32s57 18E46 -1:15:04
Delareyville 1 26s44 25E29 -1:41:56
Delmas 1 26s08 28E43 -1:54:52
Delportshoop 1 28s22 24E20 -1:37:20
De Naauwte 1 30s08 21E42 -1:26:48
Deneysville 3 26s53 28E06 -1:52:24
Derby 1 25s55 27E02 -1:48:08
Derdepoort 1 24s42 26E20 -1:45:20
De Rust 1 33s30 22E32 -1:30:08
Despatch 1 33s46 25E30 -1:42:00
Devon 1 26s21 28E48 -1:55:12
Dewetsdorp 3 29s33 26E34 -1:46:16
Dibeng 1 27s35 22E54 -1:31:36
Dicks 2 27s43 30E10 -2:00:40
Die Boss 1 31s59 19E44 -1:18:56
Diemansputs 1 29s54 21E33 -1:26:12
Dirkiesdorp 1 27s10 30E25 -2:01:40
Dirkiesrus 1 26s20 24E44 -1:38:56
Discovery 1 26s10 27E54 -1:51:36
Donegal 1 26s10 23E58 -1:35:52
Donkerpoort 3 30s32 25E30 -1:42:00
Donnybrook 2 29s53 29E48 -1:59:12
Doorndam 1 28s03 21E03 -1:24:12
Dordrecht 1 31s20 27E03 -1:48:12
Doringbaai 1 31s48 18E15 -1:13:00
Douglas 1 29s04 23E46 -1:35:04
Dover 3 27s02 27E46 -1:51:04
Duiwelskloof 1 23s42 30E06 -2:00:24
Dullstroom 1 25s27 30E07 -2:00:28
Dundee 2 28s12 30E16 -2:01:04
Dunvegan 1 26s09 28E09 -1:52:36
Durban 2 29s55 30E56 -2:03:44
Durbanville 1 33s50 18E39 -1:14:36
Dwyka 1 33s02 21E30 -1:26:00
Dysselsdorp 1 33s34 22E28 -1:29:52
East London (Oos-Londen)
1 33s00 27E55 -1:51:40
Edenburg 3 29s45 25E56 -1:43:44
Edendale 2 29s39 30E18 -2:01:12
Edenvale 1 26s08 28E09 -1:52:36
Edenvale Location
1 26s08 28E11 -1:52:44
Edenville 3 27s37 27E34 -1:50:16
Elandsbaai 1 32s19 18E21 -1:13:24
Elandsfontein 1 26s10 28E12 -1:52:48
Elandskraal 2 28s28 30E32 -2:02:08
Elandsvlei 1 32s19 19E33 -1:18:12
Eldoradopark 1 26s18 27E53 -1:51:32
Eleasar 1 26s40 26E53 -1:47:32
Eleazer 1 26s40 26E53 -1:47:32
Elim 1 34s35 19E45 -1:19:00
Elliot 1 31s18 27E50 -1:51:20
Elliotdale 1 31s55 28E38 -1:54:32
Ellisras 1 23s40 27E46 -1:51:04
Elsburg 1 26s15 28E12 -1:52:48
Elspark 1 26s16 28E14 -1:52:56
Empangeni 2 28s50 31E48 -2:07:12
Engcobo 1 31s37 28E00 -1:52:00
Ermelo 1 26s34 29E58 -1:59:52
Eshowe 2 28s58 31E29 -2:05:56
Esperanza 2 30s21 30E40 -2:02:40
Estancia 1 26s17 29E52 -1:59:28
Estcourt 2 29s01 29E52 -1:59:28
Evaton 1 26s31 27E54 -1:51:36
Ewbank 1 26s14 23E35 -1:34:20
Excelda 1 32s16 22E08 -1:28:32
Excelsior 3 28s56 27E06 -1:48:24
Fauresmith 3 29s42 25E21 -1:41:24
Felixton 2 28s50 31E53 -2:07:32
Ferndale 1 26s05 27E59 -1:51:56
Ferreira 3 29s13 26E10 -1:44:40
Ficksburg 3 28s57 27E50 -1:51:20
Finaalspan 1 26s17 28E15 -1:53:00
Finsbury 1 26s13 27E39 -1:50:36
Flagstaff 1 31s05 29E29 -1:57:56
Florentia 1 26s16 28E08 -1:52:32
Florida 1 26s11 27E55 -1:51:40
Florisbad 3 28s46 26E06 -1:44:24
Fochville 1 26s30 27E30 -1:50:00
Fontainebleau 1 26s07 27E59 -1:51:56
Fort Beaufort 1 32s46 26E40 -1:46:40

SOUTH AFRICA SUDÁFRICA AFRIQUE DU SUD SÜDAFRIKA SUID-AFRIKA

Place		Lat	Long	Time
Fort Nottingham	2	29s25	29E55	-1:59:40
Fouriesburg	3	28s38	28E14	-1:52:56
Fourteen Streams	1	28s04	24E53	-1:39:32
Frankfort	3	27s17	28E30	-1:54:00
Frankfort	1	32s44	27E26	-1:49:44
Franklin	1	30s18	29E30	-1:58:00
Franschhoek	1	33s55	19E09	-1:16:36
Fraserburg	1	31s55	21E30	-1:26:00
Frere	2	28s52	29E47	-1:59:08
Friedesheim	3	27s55	26E43	-1:46:52
Ga-Mankoeng	1	23s57	29E42	-1:58:48
Gamoep	1	29s55	18E25	-1:13:40
Gannahoek	1	26s44	24E08	-1:36:32
Gannapan	1	30s23	22E12	-1:28:48
Gansbaai	1	34s35	19E22	-1:17:28
Ganyesa	1	26s35	24E10	-1:36:40
Garies	1	30s30	18E00	-1:12:00
Garskolk	1	30s41	22E02	-1:28:08
Geduld	1	26s15	28E25	-1:53:40
Geluk	1	27s01	24E18	-1:37:12
Geluksburg	2	28s30	29E33	-1:58:12
Genadendal	1	34s02	19E33	-1:18:12
Geneva	3	27s50	27E08	-1:48:32
George	1	33s58	22E24	-1:29:36
Gerdau	1	26s28	26E06	-1:44:24
Gerdview	1	26s10	28E11	-1:52:44
Germiston	1	26s13	28E10	-1:52:40
Germiston South	1	26s15	28E10	-1:52:40
Geysdorp	1	26s32	25E18	-1:41:12
Gingindlovu	2	29s02	31E30	-2:06:00
Glen Avon	1	31s43	26E12	-1:44:48
Glencoe	2	28s12	30E07	-2:00:28
Glenside	2	29s25	30E47	-2:03:08
Glenvista	1	26s17	28E13	-1:52:52
Gluckstadt	2	27s57	31E02	-2:04:08
Goedemoed	3	30s33	26E26	-1:45:44
Golela	1	27s20	31E55	-2:07:40
Gonubie	1	32s57	28E01	-1:52:04
Gonubie Mouth	1	32s57	28E01	-1:52:04
Good Hope	1	31s51	21E55	-1:27:40
Goodhouse	1	28s57	18E13	-1:12:52
Gordon's Bay	1	34s10	18E52	-1:15:28
Gouda	1	33s19	19E04	-1:16:16
Graaff-Reinet	1	32s14	24E32	-1:38:08
Graafwater	1	32s00	18E37	-1:14:28
Grabouw	1	34s09	19E02	-1:16:08
Grahamstad → Grahamstown	1	33s19	26E31	-1:46:04
Grahamstown	1	33s19	26E31	-1:46:04
Granaatboskolk	1	30s02	19E51	-1:19:24
Grasbult	1	30s52	21E47	-1:27:08
Graskop	1	24s58	30E49	-2:03:16
Grasmere	1	26s26	27E52	-1:51:28
Gravelotte	1	23s56	30E34	-2:02:16
Greenhills	1	26s10	27E40	-1:50:40
Greenlands	3	27s07	27E40	-1:50:40
Greenside	1	26s09	28E01	-1:52:04
Greylingstad	1	26s44	28E45	-1:55:00
Greyton	1	34s04	19E38	-1:18:32
Greytown	2	29s07	30E30	-2:02:00
Griekwastad	1	28s49	23E15	-1:33:00
Groblersdal	1	25s15	29E25	-1:57:40
Groblershoop	1	28s55	20E59	-1:23:56
Groenvlei	2	27s27	30E13	-2:00:52
Grondneus	1	28s06	20E48	-1:23:12
Groot-Brakrivier	1	34s01	21E46	-1:27:04
Groot Elandsvlei	1	26s08	27E40	-1:50:40
Groot-Marico	1	25s37	26E26	-1:45:44
Grootpan	1	25s58	26E33	-1:46:12
Grootvlei	1	26s44	28E32	-1:54:08
Haarlem	1	33s44	23E20	-1:33:20
Haenertsburg	1	24s00	29E50	-1:59:20
Haga-Haga	1	32s46	28E14	-1:52:56
Hamberg	1	26s11	27E53	-1:51:32
Hamburg	1	33s17	27E28	-1:49:52
Hammonia	3	28s43	27E49	-1:51:16
Hankey	1	33s50	24E52	-1:39:28
Hanover	1	31s04	24E29	-1:37:56
Hanover Road	1	30s58	24E33	-1:38:12
Harding	2	30s34	29E58	-1:59:52
Harrismith	3	28s18	29E03	-1:56:12
Hartbeesfontein	1	26s42	26E26	-1:45:44
Hartbeespoort	1	25s44	27E52	-1:51:28
Hartswater	1	27s34	24E43	-1:38:52
Hattingspruit	2	28s09	30E11	-2:00:44
Hauptsrus	1	26s33	26E18	-1:45:12
Heidelberg	1	34s06	20E59	-1:23:56
Heidelberg	1	26s32	28E18	-1:53:12
Heilbron	3	27s21	27E58	-1:51:52
Helpmekaar	2	28s29	30E29	-2:01:56
Hendrina	1	26s11	29E45	-1:59:00
Hennenman	3	27s59	27E01	-1:48:04
Herbertsdale	1	34s01	21E46	-1:27:04
Hermanus	1	34s25	19E16	-1:17:04
Hermon	1	33s27	18E59	-1:15:56
Hertzogville	3	28s08	25E33	-1:42:12
Heuningspruit	3	27s26	27E28	-1:49:52
Higgs' Hope	1	29s19	23E16	-1:33:04
Hillandale	1	33s06	20E36	-1:22:24
Himeville	2	29s44	29E31	-1:58:04
Hlabisa	2	28s08	31E52	-2:07:28
Hlobane	2	27s42	31E00	-2:04:00
Hluhluwe	2	28s01	32E15	-2:09:00
Hofmeyr	1	31s39	25E50	-1:43:20
Holgate	1	33s59	22E21	-1:29:24
Hondeklipbaai	1	30s20	17E18	-1:09:12
Honderfontein	1	32s12	21E22	-1:25:28
Honeydew	1	26s05	27E55	-1:51:40
Hoogte	3	27s28	28E03	-1:52:12
Hoopstad	3	27s54	25E58	-1:43:52
Hopefield	1	33s04	18E22	-1:13:28
Hopetown	1	29s34	24E03	-1:36:12
Hotazel	1	27s15	23E00	-1:32:00
Hottentotskloof	1	33s15	19E40	-1:18:40
Houtkop	1	26s36	27E52	-1:51:28
Houtkraal	1	30s23	24E05	-1:36:20
Howick	2	29s28	30E14	-2:00:56
Humansdorp	1	34s02	24E46	-1:39:04
Hutchinson	1	31s30	23E09	-1:32:36
Idutywa	1	32s02	28E16	-1:53:04
Ilinge	1	31s59	27E02	-1:48:08
Illovo	2	30s05	30E50	-2:03:20
Impendle	2	29s37	29E55	-1:59:40
Inanda	1	26s07	28E03	-1:52:12
Indwe	1	31s27	27E23	-1:49:32
Ingogo	2	27s32	29E56	-1:59:44
Ingwavuma	2	27s09	32E00	-2:08:00
Irene	1	25s51	28E13	-1:52:52
Isando	1	26s09	28E12	-1:52:48
Isipingo Beach	2	29s59	30E57	-2:03:48
Iswepe	1	26s50	30E31	-2:02:04
Ixopo	2	30s08	30E00	-2:00:00
Jabavu	1	26s15	27E53	-1:51:32
Jacobsdal	3	29s13	24E41	-1:38:44
Jagersfontein	3	29s44	25E29	-1:41:56
Jamestown	1	31s06	26E45	-1:47:00
Jan Kempdorp (Andalusia)	1	27s55	24E51	-1:39:24
Jansenville	1	32s57	24E40	-1:38:40
Johannesburg	1	26s15	28E00	-1:52:00
Jonkersberg	1	33s55	22E15	-1:29:00
Joubertina	1	33s50	23E51	-1:35:24
Juriesfontein	1	31s40	22E08	-1:28:32
Kaalspruit	3	29s15	26E10	-1:44:40
Kaapmuiden	1	25s33	31E20	-2:05:20
Kaapstad → Cape Town	1	33s55	18E22	-1:13:28
Kakamas	1	28s45	20E33	-1:22:12
Kalkmond	1	28s40	20E26	-1:21:44
Kalkstasie	1	30s00	18E55	-1:15:40
Kameel	1	26s38	24E58	-1:39:52
Kamieskroon	1	30s09	17E56	-1:11:44
Kanoneiland	1	28s39	21E05	-1:24:20
Kapstadt → Cape Town	1	33s55	18E22	-1:13:28
Kareedouw	1	33s57	24E18	-1:37:12
Karos	1	28s24	21E35	-1:26:20
Kasuka	1	33s40	26E41	-1:46:44
Keimoes	1	28s41	21E00	-1:24:00
Kei Mouth	1	32s41	28E22	-1:53:28
Kei Road	1	32s42	27E32	-1:50:08
Keiskammahoek	1	32s41	27E09	-1:48:36
Kempton Park	1	26s06	28E14	-1:52:56
Kendal	1	26s04	28E58	-1:55:52
Kendrew	1	32s32	24E30	-1:38:00
Kenhardt	1	29s19	21E12	-1:24:48
Kentani	1	32s31	28E19	-1:53:16
Kestell	3	28s19	28E38	-1:54:32
Keurboomsrivier	1	34s00	23E24	-1:33:36
Kew	1	26s08	28E06	-1:52:24
Khandla	2	28s37	31E05	-2:04:20
Kidd's Beach	1	33s09	27E42	-1:50:48
Kimberley	1	28s43	24E46	-1:39:04
Kingsley	2	27s55	30E33	-2:02:12
Kingswood	1	27s29	25E46	-1:43:04
King William's Town	1	32s51	27E22	-1:49:28
Kinross	1	26s22	29E03	-1:56:12
Kirkwood	1	33s22	25E15	-1:41:00
Klaarstroom	1	33s20	22E32	-1:30:08
Klawer	1	31s44	18E36	-1:14:24
Kleinbegin	1	28s50	21E36	-1:26:24
Klein Elandsvlei	1	26s09	27E39	-1:50:36
Kleinmond	1	34s21	19E03	-1:16:12
Klein-Soutpan	1	30s26	22E26	-1:29:44
Klerksdorp	1	26s58	26E39	-1:46:36
Klerkskraal	1	26s15	27E10	-1:48:40
Klipbakken	1	28s50	21E21	-1:25:24
Klipdale	1	34s19	19E57	-1:19:48
Klipplaat	1	33s02	24E21	-1:37:24
Klippoortje	1	26s17	28E14	-1:52:56
Kliprivierssoog	1	26s18	27E53	-1:51:32
Kliptown	1	26s17	27E53	-1:51:32
Klipwerf	1	31s09	19E52	-1:19:28
Knapdaar	1	30s43	26E09	-1:44:36
Knoppiesfontein	1	26s05	28E25	-1:53:40
Knysna	1	34s02	23E02	-1:32:08
Kocksoord	1	26s13	27E39	-1:50:36
Koegas	1	29s16	22E20	-1:29:20
Koekenaap	1	31s30	18E18	-1:13:12
Koffiefontein	3	29s30	25E00	-1:40:00
Kokstad	1	30s32	29E29	-1:57:56
Komatipoort	1	25s25	31E55	-2:07:40
Komga	1	32s35	27E55	-1:51:40
Komkans	1	31s16	18E09	-1:12:36
Kommadagga	1	33s09	25E55	-1:43:40
Kommandodrif	3	27s30	26E14	-1:44:56
Kommandokraal	1	33s06	22E51	-1:31:24
Kommetjie	1	34s08	18E21	-1:13:24
Koopan-Noord	1	26s53	20E41	-1:22:44
Koopan-Suid	1	27s15	20E22	-1:21:28
Koopmansfontein	1	28s14	24E01	-1:36:04
Koosfontein	1	27s22	25E27	-1:41:48
Kootjieskolk	1	31s15	20E21	-1:21:24
Koppies	3	27s20	27E30	-1:50:00
Korga	1	30s12	20E28	-1:21:52
Koringberg	1	33s01	18E40	-1:14:40
Koringplaas	1	32s48	20E58	-1:23:52
Koster	1	25s57	26E42	-1:46:48
Kowie → Port Alfred	1	33s36	26E55	-1:47:40
Kraaifontein	1	33s50	18E43	-1:14:52
Kraal	1	26s34	28E26	-1:53:44
Kraankuil	1	29s52	24E10	-1:36:40
Kranskop	2	29s00	30E47	-2:03:08
Kriel	1	26s16	29E14	-1:56:56
Kroondal	1	25s45	27E19	-1:49:16
Kroonstad	3	27s46	27E12	-1:48:48
Krugersdorp	1	26s05	27E35	-1:50:20
Krugersdorp West	1	26s06	27E45	-1:51:00
Kruidfontein	1	32s51	21E57	-1:27:48
Kruisfontein	1	34s00	24E43	-1:38:52
Kruisrivier	1	33s26	21E55	-1:27:40
Kruisvallei	1	33s53	23E10	-1:32:40
Kuruman	1	27s28	23E28	-1:33:52
Kwa-Mbonambi	2	28s36	32E05	-2:08:20
Kwa-Thema	1	26s18	28E23	-1:53:32
Ladismith	1	33s30	21E16	-1:25:04
Ladybrand	3	29s19	27E25	-1:49:40
Lady Frere	1	31s44	27E16	-1:49:04
Lady Grey	1	30s45	27E13	-1:48:52
Ladysmith	2	28s34	29E45	-1:59:00
Laingsburg	1	33s11	20E51	-1:23:24
Lakefield	1	26s11	28E18	-1:53:12
Lakeside	1	26s06	28E09	-1:52:36
Lambertsbaai → Lambert's Bay	1	32s05	18E17	-1:13:08
Lambert's Bay	1	32s05	18E17	-1:13:08
Lambrechts Drift	1	28s31	21E43	-1:26:52
Lambton	1	26s15	28E10	-1:52:40
Langebaan	1	33s06	18E02	-1:12:08
Langklip	1	28s12	20E20	-1:21:20
Largo	1	26s16	28E31	-1:54:04
Le Cap → Cape Town	1	33s55	18E22	-1:13:28
Leeudoringstad	1	27s15	26E10	-1:44:40
Leeu-Gamka	1	32s47	21E59	-1:27:56
Leipoldtville	1	32s14	18E30	-1:14:00
Lekkeroog	1	30s43	20E00	-1:20:00
Lemoenshoek	1	33s51	20E51	-1:23:24
Lenz	1	26s19	27E49	-1:51:16
Leslie	1	26s27	28E55	-1:55:40
Letjiesbos	1	32s34	22E16	-1:29:04
Lewisham	1	26s07	27E49	-1:51:16
Libode	1	31s33	29E02	-1:56:08
Lichtenburg	1	26s08	26E08	-1:44:32
Lidgetton	2	29s25	30E05	-2:00:20
Lindley	3	27s56	27E57	-1:51:48
Linmeyer	1	26s16	28E04	-1:52:16
Lockwillow	1	26s17	27E50	-1:51:20
Loeriesfontein	1	30s56	19E26	-1:17:44
Lohatlha	1	28s02	23E04	-1:32:16
Lombardy	1	26s07	28E08	-1:52:32
Lothair	1	26s26	30E27	-2:01:48
Louis Trichardt	1	23s01	29E43	-1:58:52
Louisvale	1	28s33	21E12	-1:24:48
Louwsburg	2	27s37	31E07	-2:04:28
Lower Loteni	2	29s32	29E36	-1:58:24
Loxton	1	31s30	22E22	-1:29:28
Luckhoff	3	29s44	24E43	-1:38:52
Luipaardsvlei	1	26s16	27E42	-1:50:48
Lusikisiki	1	31s25	29E30	-1:58:00
Lutzputs	1	28s03	20E40	-1:22:40
Lutzville	1	31s33	18E22	-1:13:28
Lydenburg	1	25s10	30E29	-2:01:56
Lyttelton	1	25s50	28E11	-1:52:44
Machadodorp	1	25s40	30E14	-2:00:56
Macleantown	1	32s47	27E45	-1:51:00
Maclear	1	31s02	28E23	-1:53:32
Madibogo	1	26s25	25E10	-1:40:40
Mafeking	1	25s53	25E39	-1:42:36
Mafikeng	1	25s53	25E39	-1:42:36
Magudu	2	27s31	31E40	-2:06:40
Mahlabatini	2	27s37	31E42	-2:06:48
Mahlabatini	2	28s14	31E30	-2:06:00
Mahlangasi	2	27s37	31E42	-2:06:48
Maizefield	1	26s28	29E31	-1:58:04
Makwassie	1	27s26	26E00	-1:44:00
Malgas	1	34s18	20E35	-1:22:20
Malmesbury	1	33s28	18E44	-1:14:56
Malvern East	1	26s12	28E08	-1:52:32
Mamre	1	33s30	18E29	-1:13:56
Mansieville Location	1	26s05	27E45	-1:51:00
Mapleton	1	26s20	28E14	-1:52:56
Mapumulo	2	29s11	31E02	-2:04:08
Maputa	1	26s59	32E46	-2:11:04
Maraisburg	1	26s11	27E56	-1:51:44
Marble Hall	1	24s57	29E13	-1:56:52
Marburg	2	30s44	30E26	-2:01:44
Mareetsane	1	26s09	25E25	-1:41:40
Margate	2	30s53	30E21	-2:01:24
Marianhill	2	29s52	30E50	-2:03:20
Mariannhill	2	29s52	30E50	-2:03:20
Marikana	1	25s42	27E30	-1:50:00
Maritzburg → Pietermaritzburg	2	29s37	30E16	-2:01:04
Marquard	3	28s54	27E28	-1:49:52
Marydale	1	29s23	22E05	-1:28:20
Matatiele	1	30s24	28E43	-1:54:52
Matsap	1	28s38	22E47	-1:31:08
McGregor	1	33s57	19E50	-1:19:20
Mdantsana	1	32s56	27E42	-1:50:48
Meadowlands	1	26s13	27E54	-1:51:36
Melkbosstrand	1	33s43	18E27	-1:13:48
Melmoth	2	28s38	31E24	-2:05:36
Memel	3	27s43	29E30	-1:58:00
Meredale	1	26s17	27E59	-1:51:56
Merriman	1	31s13	23E38	-1:34:32
Merwede	1	31s38	23E48	-1:35:12
Merweville	1	32s40	21E31	-1:26:04
Mesa	1	26s29	26E59	-1:47:56
Messina	1	22s23	30E00	-2:00:00
Meyerton	1	26s33	28E01	-1:52:04
Mica	1	24s10	30E48	-2:03:12
Middelburg	1	31s30	25E00	-1:40:00
Middelburg	1	25s47	29E28	-1:57:52
Middelpos	1	31s55	20E13	-1:20:52
Middelvlei	1	26s14	27E38	-1:50:32

Middelwit 1 24s58 27E00 -1:48:00
Middenin 3 27s43 28E02 -1:52:08
Mid Illovo 2 29s59 30E25 -2:01:40
Midway 1 26s18 27E51 -1:51:24
Migdol 1 26s54 25E27 -1:41:48
Minard 1 31s17 27E35 -1:50:20
Mjanyana 1 31s50 28E10 -1:52:40
Mkuze 2 27s10 32E00 -2:08:00
Modderbee 1 26s10 28E24 -1:53:36
Modderfontein 1 26s05 28E10 -1:52:40
Modderrivier 1 29s02 24E38 -1:38:32
Mofolo 1 26s14 27E53 -1:51:32
Molteno 1 31s22 26E22 -1:45:28
Mondeor 1 26s17 28E00 -1:52:00
Montagu 1 33s45 20E08 -1:20:32
Monument 1 26s06 27E43 -1:50:52
Mooirivier 2 29s13 29E50 -1:59:20
Mooketsi 1 23s35 30E05 -2:00:20
Moolman 1 27s10 30E53 -2:03:32
Moorreesburg 1 33s08 18E40 -1:14:40
Mopane 1 22s37 29E52 -1:59:28
Morgan's Bay 1 32s43 28E20 -1:53:20
Morgenzon 1 26s45 29E36 -1:58:24
Moroka 1 26s16 27E52 -1:51:28
Morokweng 1 26s12 23E45 -1:35:00
Mosselbaai (Mossel Bay)
1 34s11 22E08 -1:28:32
Mount Alida 2 29s09 30E18 -2:01:12
Mount Ayliff 1 30s54 29E20 -1:57:20
Mount Fletcher 1 30s40 28E30 -1:54:00
Mount Frere 1 31s00 28E58 -1:55:52
Mount Prospect 2 27s29 29E53 -1:59:32
Mount Stewart 1 33s10 24E26 -1:37:44
Mqanduli 1 31s48 28E46 -1:55:04
Mtubatuba 2 28s30 32E08 -2:08:32
Mtunzini 2 28s57 31E46 -2:07:04
Muiskraal 1 33s56 21E13 -1:24:52
Muldersvlei 1 30s41 22E13 -1:28:52
Murraysburg 1 31s58 23E47 -1:35:08
Mynfontein 1 30s55 23E57 -1:35:48
Nababiep 1 29s36 17E46 -1:11:04
Naboomspruit 1 24s32 28E36 -1:54:24
Namies 1 29s18 19E13 -1:16:52
Nancefield 1 26s17 27E53 -1:51:32
Napier 1 34s29 19E53 -1:19:32
Natalspruit 1 26s19 28E09 -1:52:36
Nelspoort 1 32s07 23E00 -1:32:00
Nelspoortjie 1 29s58 22E25 -1:29:40
Nelspruit 1 25s30 30E58 -2:03:52
Newcastle 2 27s49 29E55 -1:59:40
New Ermelo 1 26s32 30E02 -2:00:08
New Hanover 2 29s28 30E28 -2:01:52
New Machavie 1 26s48 26E57 -1:47:48
Newmarket 1 26s17 28E08 -1:52:32
New Redruth 1 26s16 28E07 -1:52:28
Ngome 2 27s46 31E28 -2:05:52
Ngqeleni 1 31s40 29E02 -1:56:08
Ngweni 2 27s56 32E15 -2:09:00
Nhlazatshe 2 28s10 31E14 -2:04:56
Niekerkshoop 1 29s19 22E51 -1:31:24
Nieu Bethesda 1 31s51 24E34 -1:38:16
Nieuwoudtville 1 31s23 19E07 -1:16:28
Nigel 1 26s30 28E28 -1:53:52
Nkandla 2 28s37 31E05 -2:04:20
Nkwalini 2 28s45 31E33 -2:06:12
Noenieput 1 27s29 20E06 -1:20:24
Nondweni 2 28s11 30E49 -2:03:16
Nongoma 2 27s58 31E35 -2:06:20
Normandien 2 27s57 29E47 -1:59:08
Northam 1 25s03 27E11 -1:48:44
North Germiston 1 26s14 28E09 -1:52:36
Northmead 1 26s10 28E20 -1:53:20
Norvalspont 1 30s38 25E27 -1:41:48
Nottingham Road 2 29s22 30E00 -2:00:00
Noupoort 1 31s10 24E57 -1:39:48
Nous 1 28s44 19E52 -1:19:28
Nqamakwe 1 32s12 27E56 -1:51:44
Nqutu 2 28s13 30E32 -2:02:08
N'Rougas 1 29s07 21E09 -1:24:36
Nseleni 2 28s33 31E39 -2:06:36
Ntambanana 2 28s36 31E45 -2:07:00
Nufcor 1 26s17 27E44 -1:50:56
Nuwerus 1 31s08 18E24 -1:13:36
Nylstroom 1 24s42 28E20 -1:53:20
Obobogorap 1 27s18 20E04 -1:20:16
Ockies 1 31s31 21E41 -1:26:44
Odendaalsrus 3 27s48 26E45 -1:47:00
Ogies 1 26s02 29E04 -1:56:16
Ohrigstad 1 24s49 30E33 -2:02:12
Okiep 1 29s39 17E53 -1:11:32
Olifantshoek 1 27s57 22E42 -1:30:48
Omdraaisvlei 1 30s08 23E08 -1:32:32
Onderstedorings 1 30s13 20E37 -1:22:28
Onseepkans 1 28s46 19E14 -1:16:56
Oos-Londen → East London
1 33s00 27E55 -1:51:40
Orangeville 3 27s00 28E15 -1:53:00
Oranjefontein 1 23s25 27E41 -1:50:44
Oranjerivier 1 29s40 24E12 -1:36:48
Oranjeville 3 27s00 28E15 -1:53:00
Orkney 1 27s00 26E39 -1:46:36
Orlando 1 26s14 27E55 -1:51:40
Orlando West Extension
1 26s15 27E54 -1:51:36
Oshoek 1 26s13 30E59 -2:03:56
Ottosdal 1 26s58 26E00 -1:44:00
Ottoshoop 1 25s45 25E59 -1:43:56
Oudtshoorn 1 33s35 22E14 -1:28:56
Paarl 1 33s45 18E56 -1:15:44
Pacaltsdorp 1 34s00 22E28 -1:29:52
Palmford 1 27s11 29E42 -1:58:48
Pampoenpoort 1 31s03 22E40 -1:30:40
Paradise Hill 1 26s18 28E00 -1:52:00
Parkdene 1 26s14 28E16 -1:53:04
Parkhill Gardens
1 26s14 28E11 -1:52:44
Park Rynie 2 30s25 30E35 -2:02:20
Parow 1 33s53 18E37 -1:14:28
Parys 3 26s56 27E26 -1:49:44
Patensie 1 33s46 24E49 -1:39:16
Paterson 1 33s26 25E58 -1:43:52
Paulpietersburg 2 27s30 30E51 -2:03:24
Paul Roux 3 28s18 27E59 -1:51:56
Paynesville 1 26s14 28E28 -1:53:52
Peachdale 1 26s30 24E42 -1:38:48
Pearston 1 32s35 25E08 -1:40:32
Peddie 1 33s14 27E07 -1:48:28
Pella 1 29s01 19E06 -1:16:24
Penge 1 24s22 30E13 -2:00:52
Perdekop 1 27s13 29E38 -1:58:32
Petersfield 1 26s14 28E26 -1:53:44
Petit 1 26s06 28E22 -1:53:28
Petrusburg 3 29s08 25E27 -1:41:48
Petrus Steyn 3 27s38 28E08 -1:52:32
Petrusville 1 30s05 24E41 -1:38:44
Phalaborwa 1 23s55 31E13 -2:04:52
Philadelphia 1 33s40 18E36 -1:14:24
Philippolis 3 30s19 25E13 -1:40:52
Philipstown 1 30s26 24E29 -1:37:56
Pienaarsrivier 1 25s15 28E18 -1:53:12
Pietermaritzburg
2 29s37 30E16 -2:01:04
Pietersburg 1 23s54 29E25 -1:57:40
Pietersfield 1 26s14 28E26 -1:53:44
Piet Retief 2 27s01 30E50 -2:03:20
Piketberg 1 32s54 18E46 -1:15:04
Pilgrim's Rest 1 24s55 30E44 -2:02:56
Pimville 1 26s18 27E54 -1:51:36
Pinetown 2 29s52 30E46 -2:03:04
Platrand 1 27s08 29E29 -1:57:56
Plettenbergbaai 1 34s04 23E22 -1:33:28
Pofadder 1 29s10 19E22 -1:17:28
Pomeroy 2 28s33 30E26 -2:01:44
Pomfret 1 25s50 23E32 -1:34:08
Pomona Estates 1 26s06 28E15 -1:53:00
Poortjie 1 30s13 22E44 -1:30:56
Port Alfred (Kowie)
1 33s36 26E55 -1:47:40
Port Edward 2 31s02 30E13 -2:00:52
Port Elizabeth 1 33s58 25E40 -1:42:40
Porterville 1 33s00 19E00 -1:16:00
Port Nolloth 1 29s17 16E51 -1:07:24
Port Saint Johns
1 31s38 29E33 -1:58:12
Port Shepstone 2 30s46 30E22 -2:01:28
Postmasburg 1 28s18 23E05 -1:32:20
Potchefstroom 1 26s46 27E01 -1:48:04
Potfontein 1 30s12 24E08 -1:36:32
Potgietersrus 1 24s15 28E55 -1:55:40
Potsdam 1 32s56 27E42 -1:50:48
Pretoria 1 25s45 28E10 -1:52:40
Pretoriusvlei 1 28s30 22E59 -1:31:56
Prieska 1 29s40 22E42 -1:30:48
Primrose 1 26s12 28E10 -1:52:40
Prince Albert 1 33s13 22E02 -1:28:08
Prince Albert Road
1 33s01 21E40 -1:26:40
Prince Alfred Hamlet
1 33s18 19E20 -1:17:20
Prinskof 1 32s06 20E53 -1:23:32
Protea 1 26s17 27E51 -1:51:24
Protem 1 34s16 20E05 -1:20:20
Pudimoe 1 27s26 24E44 -1:38:56
Punda Milia 1 22s40 31E05 -2:04:20
Putfontein 1 26s08 28E24 -1:53:36
Putfontein Landbouhoewes
1 26s08 28E24 -1:53:36
Putsonderwater 1 29s09 21E51 -1:27:24
Qamata 1 32s00 27E21 -1:49:24
Queenstown 1 31s52 26E52 -1:47:28
Qumbu 1 31s10 28E48 -1:55:12
Raceview 1 26s17 28E08 -1:52:32
Ramsgate 2 30s56 30E19 -2:01:16
Randburg 1 26s06 27E59 -1:51:56
Randfontein 1 26s11 27E42 -1:50:48
Randgate 1 26s11 27E41 -1:50:44
Ravenswood 1 26s11 28E15 -1:53:00
Rawsonville 1 33s41 19E20 -1:17:20
Rayton 1 24s45 28E32 -1:54:08
Rayton 1 25s45 28E32 -1:54:08
Recife 1 34s02 25E44 -1:42:56
Reddersburg 3 29s38 26E07 -1:44:28
Redelinghuys 1 32s30 18E33 -1:14:12
Redlands 1 29s52 22E57 -1:31:48
Reef Point 1 34s11 24E36 -1:38:24
Regents Park 1 26s15 28E04 -1:52:16
Regina 1 27s02 26E30 -1:46:00
Reitz 3 27s53 28E31 -1:54:04
Reivilo 1 27s36 24E08 -1:36:32
Remhoogte 1 29s33 23E01 -1:32:04
Republic Observatory
1 26s11 28E05 -1:52:20
Rhodes 1 30s47 27E59 -1:51:56
Rhodes Park 1 26s12 28E06 -1:52:24
Richard's Bay 2 28s47 32E06 -2:08:24
Richmond 1 31s23 23E56 -1:35:44
Richmond 1 26s19 28E13 -1:52:52
Richmond 2 29s54 30E08 -2:00:32
Riebeek-Kasteel 1 33s23 18E53 -1:15:32
Riebeek-Oos 1 33s10 26E10 -1:44:40
Riebeek-Wes 1 33s21 18E52 -1:15:28
Riet 1 29s00 23E54 -1:35:36
Rietbron 1 32s54 23E10 -1:32:40
Rietfontein 1 26s44 20E01 -1:20:04
Riethuiskraal 1 34s20 21E22 -1:25:28
Rietspruit 1 26s06 27E39 -1:50:36
Rietvlei 1 30s29 29E51 -1:59:24
Ritchie 1 29s02 24E38 -1:38:32
Rivasdale 1 26s17 27E56 -1:51:44
Riversdale 1 34s07 21E15 -1:25:00
River View 2 28s27 32E10 -2:08:40
Riviersonderend 1 34s09 19E55 -1:19:40
Roadside 3 27s31 28E52 -1:55:28
Robertsham 1 26s15 28E00 -1:52:00
Robertson 1 33s46 19E50 -1:19:20
Robinson 1 26s09 27E43 -1:50:52
Roelofskamp 1 26s10 24E24 -1:37:36
Roggeveldberge 1 32s17 20E08 -1:20:32
Roksana 1 26s07 28E04 -1:52:16
Rondebult 1 26s18 28E14 -1:52:56
Rongola 1 27s22 31E37 -2:06:28
Roodepoort-Maraisberg
1 26s11 27E54 -1:51:36
Roodepoort-Maraisburg
1 26s11 27E54 -1:51:36
Rooiberge 3 28s27 28E26 -1:53:44
Rooidam 1 28s07 21E15 -1:25:00
Rooiduinepunt 1 31s57 18E17 -1:13:08
Rooilyf 1 28s49 21E57 -1:27:48
Roosboom 2 28s36 29E44 -1:58:56
Rorke's Drift 2 28s20 30E32 -2:02:08
Rosboom 2 28s36 29E44 -1:58:56
Rosebank 1 26s09 28E02 -1:52:08
Rosedene 1 32s01 22E07 -1:28:28
Rosendal 3 28s30 27E55 -1:51:40
Roseneath 1 26s17 28E11 -1:52:44
Rosettenville 1 26s15 28E03 -1:52:12
Rosherville Dam 1 26s14 28E07 -1:52:28
Rosmead 1 31s29 25E08 -1:40:32
Rossouw 1 31s09 27E18 -1:49:12
Rostrataville 1 26s49 25E39 -1:42:36
Rostraville 1 26s49 25E39 -1:42:36
Rouxville 3 30s29 26E46 -1:47:04
Rowhill 1 26s14 28E26 -1:53:44
Royal Natal Natl Park
2 28s45 28E57 -1:55:48
Rustenburg 1 25s37 27E08 -1:48:32
Rustfontein 1 30s28 29E17 -1:57:08
Rustig 1 27s22 27E09 -1:48:36
Rusville 1 26s10 28E18 -1:53:12
Rutig 1 27s22 27E09 -1:48:36
Rykaartspos 1 26s32 26E39 -1:46:36
Rynfield 1 26s09 28E20 -1:53:20
Sabie 1 25s10 30E48 -2:03:12
Saint Faith's 2 30s30 30E12 -2:00:48
Saint Lucia Estuary
2 28s22 32E25 -2:09:40
Saint Marks 1 32s01 27E22 -1:49:28
Sakrivier 1 30s54 20E28 -1:21:52
Saldanha 1 33s00 17E56 -1:11:44
Salem 1 33s28 26E29 -1:45:56
Salt Lake 1 29s16 24E00 -1:36:00
Sandheuwel 1 31s46 20E48 -1:23:12
Sand River Valley
2 28s28 29E33 -1:58:12
Sandspruit 1 27s18 29E48 -1:59:12
Sannieshof 1 26s30 25E47 -1:43:08
Saracen 1 27s16 24E02 -1:36:08
Saron 1 33s11 19E01 -1:16:04
Sasolburg 3 26s48 27E45 -1:51:00
Satara 1 24s29 31E47 -2:07:08
Satarar Uskamp 1 24s29 31E47 -2:07:08
Schapenrust 1 26s16 28E22 -1:53:28
Schmidtsdrif 1 28s41 24E02 -1:36:08
Schoombee 1 31s28 25E30 -1:42:00
Schweizer-Reneke
1 27s11 25E18 -1:41:12
Scottburgh 2 30s19 30E40 -2:02:40
Seekoegat 1 33s03 22E31 -1:30:04
Selcourt 1 26s18 28E27 -1:53:48
Selection Park 1 26s18 28E27 -1:53:48
Senekal 3 28s30 27E32 -1:50:08
Setlagodi 1 26s16 25E06 -1:40:24
Settlers 1 25s02 28E30 -1:54:00
Severn 1 26s36 22E52 -1:31:28
Seweweekspoort 1 33s22 21E25 -1:25:40
Seymour 1 32s33 26E46 -1:47:04
Sezela 2 30s24 30E42 -2:02:48
Shakaskraal 2 29s26 31E14 -2:04:56
Shannon 3 29s08 26E18 -1:45:12
Sheepmoor 1 26s42 30E13 -2:00:52
Shingwidzi 1 23s05 31E25 -2:05:40
Shongwe 2 27s24 32E25 -2:09:40
Sibasa 1 22s53 30E33 -2:02:12
Sihlepu 2 27s42 32E06 -2:08:24
Silverfields 1 26s07 27E49 -1:51:16
Silver Streams 1 28s20 23E33 -1:34:12
Simonstad 1 34s14 18E26 -1:13:44
Simonstown 1 34s14 18E26 -1:13:44
Sinclair 1 26s07 28E24 -1:53:36
Sishen 1 27s55 22E59 -1:31:56
Skerpioensdrif 1 31s05 21E33 -1:26:12
Skipskop 1 34s33 20E25 -1:21:40
Skoenmakerskop 1 34s02 25E33 -1:42:12
Skuilte 1 26s07 28E19 -1:53:16
Skukuza 1 25s01 31E38 -2:06:32
Slurry 1 25s49 25E52 -1:43:28
Smithfield 3 30s09 26E30 -1:46:00
Sodium 1 30s11 23E09 -1:32:36
Soekmekaar 1 23s28 29E58 -1:59:52
Solheim 1 26s11 28E10 -1:52:40
Somerset East 1 32s42 25E35 -1:42:20
Somerset West 1 34s08 18E50 -1:15:20
Sononder 1 29s43 21E51 -1:27:24
Sonop 1 25s39 27E42 -1:50:48
Sonskyn 1 30s47 26E28 -1:45:52
Sonstraal 1 27s07 22E28 -1:29:52
South Crest 1 26s15 28E07 -1:52:28
Southcrest 1 26s15 28E07 -1:52:28
South Germiston 1 26s15 28E10 -1:52:40
Soutpan 3 28s43 26E04 -1:44:16
Soweto 1 26s14 27E54 -1:51:36
Spreeufontein 1 33s22 20E45 -1:23:00
Springbok 1 29s43 17E55 -1:11:40

SOUTH AFRICA SUDÁFRICA AFRIQUE DU SUD SÜDAFRIKA SUID-AFRIKA

Place		Lat	Long	Offset
Springfield	1	29s02	22E53	-1:31:32
Springfontein	3	30s19	25E36	-1:42:24
Springs	1	26s13	28E25	-1:53:40
Standerton	1	26s58	29E07	-1:56:28
Stanford	1	34s26	19E29	-1:17:56
Stanger	2	29s27	31E14	-2:04:56
Steel's Drift	3	27s21	29E30	-1:58:00
Steinkopf	1	29s18	17E43	-1:10:52
Stella	1	26s38	24E48	-1:39:12
Stellenbosch	1	33s58	18E50	-1:15:20
Sterkaar	1	31s05	23E42	-1:34:48
Sterkspruit	1	30s32	27E22	-1:49:28
Sterkstroom	1	31s32	26E32	-1:46:08
Sterling	1	31s16	21E28	-1:25:52
Steynsburg	1	31s15	25E49	-1:43:16
Steynsrus	3	27s58	27E33	-1:50:12
Steytlerville	1	33s21	24E21	-1:37:24
Stilbaai	1	34s24	21E26	-1:25:44
Stilfontein	1	26s50	26E50	-1:47:20
Stintonville	1	26s14	28E13	-1:52:52
Stoffberg	1	25s29	29E49	-1:59:16
Stormsrivier	1	33s59	23E52	-1:35:28
Stormsvlei	1	34s05	20E06	-1:20:24
Strand	1	34s06	18E50	-1:15:20
Strubenvale	1	26s16	28E28	-1:53:52
Struisbaai	1	34s49	20E04	-1:20:16
Struisbelt	1	26s19	28E29	-1:53:56
Struisbult	1	26s19	28E29	-1:53:56
Strydenburg	1	29s58	23E40	-1:34:40
Strydomsvlei	1	33s10	23E03	-1:32:12
Strydpoort	1	27s00	25E58	-1:43:52
Stutterheim	1	32s33	27E28	-1:49:52
Suidvaal	1	26s52	29E47	-1:59:08
Sundra	1	26s11	28E33	-1:54:12
Sunnyridge	1	26s10	28E11	-1:52:44
Sutherland	1	32s24	20E40	-1:22:40
Suurbekom	1	26s19	27E44	-1:50:56
Suurbraak	1	34s00	20E39	-1:22:36
Swartberg	1	30s15	29E23	-1:57:32
Swartplaas	1	26s08	26E57	-1:47:48
Swartruggens	1	25s40	26E42	-1:46:48
Swellendam	1	34s02	20E26	-1:21:44
Syferbult	1	26s00	27E20	-1:49:20
Tabankulu	1	30s58	29E19	-1:57:16
Talana	2	28s10	30E15	-2:01:00
Tarkastad	1	32s00	26E16	-1:45:04
Taung	1	27s33	24E47	-1:39:08
Tembisa	1	25s58	28E14	-1:52:56
Tendeka	2	27s44	30E54	-2:03:36
Thaba Nchu	3	29s17	26E52	-1:47:28
Thabazimbi	1	24s41	27E21	-1:49:24
Theunissen	3	28s30	26E41	-1:46:44
Thohoyandou	1	23s00	30E29	-2:01:56
Thornhill	1	26s07	28E09	-1:52:36
Three Sisters	1	31s54	23E06	-1:32:24
Tlhakgameng	1	26s27	24E21	-1:37:24
Tlhakmeng	1	26s27	24E21	-1:37:24
Tom Burke	1	23s05	28E00	-1:52:00
Tongaat	2	29s37	31E03	-2:04:12
Tosca	1	25s53	23E58	-1:35:52
Touwsrivier	1	33s20	20E00	-1:20:00
Trichardt	1	26s28	29E13	-1:56:52
Trompsburg	3	30s01	25E46	-1:43:04
Trooilapspan	1	28s40	21E25	-1:25:40
Tsembeyi	1	31s36	27E03	-1:48:12
Tshidilamolomo	1	25s50	24E41	-1:38:44
Tsineng	1	27s06	23E04	-1:32:16
Tsolo	1	31s18	28E37	-1:54:28
Tsomo	1	32s00	27E42	-1:50:48
Tugela	2	29s09	31E29	-2:05:56
Tugela Beach	2	29s12	31E31	-2:06:04
Tugela Ferry	2	28s44	30E27	-2:01:48
Tulbagh	1	33s17	19E09	-1:16:36
Tulpfontein	1	32s44	19E43	-1:18:52
Tweeling	3	27s38	28E31	-1:54:04
Twee Rivieren	1	26s27	20E37	-1:22:28
Tweespruit	3	29s11	27E01	-1:48:04
Tylden	1	32s07	27E05	-1:48:20
Tzaneen	1	23s50	30E09	-2:00:36
Ubombo	2	27s33	32E00	-2:08:00
Ugie	1	31s10	28E13	-1:52:52
Uitenhage	1	33s40	25E28	-1:41:52
Uitspanning	1	26s46	29E56	-1:59:44
Ulco	1	28s21	24E15	-1:37:00
Ulundi	2	28s17	31E26	-2:05:44
Umbogintwini	2	30s00	30E58	-2:03:52
Umhlanga Rocks	2	29s43	31E06	-2:04:24
Umkomaas	2	30s15	30E42	-2:02:48
Umtata	1	31s35	28E47	-1:55:08
Umtentweni	2	30s42	30E28	-2:01:52
Umzimkulu	1	30s16	29E56	-1:59:44
Umzinto	2	30s22	30E33	-2:02:12
Underberg	2	29s50	29E22	-1:57:28
Uniondale	1	33s40	23E08	-1:32:32
Upington	1	28s25	21E15	-1:25:00
Utrecht	2	27s38	30E20	-2:01:20
Uvongo Beach	2	30s51	30E23	-2:01:32
Vaalwater	1	24s20	28E03	-1:52:12
Valhalla	1	25s49	28E08	-1:52:32
Valstruisleegte	1	33s05	23E28	-1:33:52
Vanderbijlpark	1	26s42	27E54	-1:51:36
Vandykpark	1	26s16	28E19	-1:53:16
Van Reenen	2	28s22	29E24	-1:57:36
Van Reenen's Plaats	1	30s55	21E14	-1:24:56
Vanrhynsdorp	1	31s36	18E44	-1:14:56
Vanstadensrus	3	29s59	27E02	-1:48:08
Vanwyksdorp	1	33s46	21E28	-1:25:52
Vanwyksvlei	1	30s18	21E49	-1:27:16
Vanzylsrus	1	26s52	22E04	-1:28:16
Velddrif	1	32s47	18E11	-1:12:44
Ventersburg	3	28s09	27E08	-1:48:32
Ventersdorp	1	26s17	26E48	-1:47:12
Venterspos	1	26s18	27E39	-1:50:36
Venterspos Location	1	26s18	27E42	-1:50:48
Venterspos West	1	26s16	27E38	-1:50:32
Venterstad	1	30s47	25E48	-1:43:12
Vereeniging	1	26s38	27E57	-1:51:48
Verkeerdevlei	3	28s48	26E48	-1:47:12
Verkykerskop	3	27s54	29E17	-1:57:08
Vermaaklikheid	1	34s19	21E01	-1:24:04
Vermaas	1	26s30	25E59	-1:43:56
Verneukpan	1	30s00	21E00	-1:24:00
Versien	3	27s05	27E52	-1:51:28
Verulam	2	29s45	31E02	-2:04:08
Victoria West	1	31s25	23E04	-1:32:16
Vierfontein	3	27s03	26E46	-1:47:04
Viljoensdrif	3	26s44	27E55	-1:51:40
Viljoenshof	1	34s40	19E42	-1:18:48
Viljoenskroon	3	27s12	27E00	-1:48:00
Viljoenspos	2	27s35	30E30	-2:02:00
Villiers	3	27s03	28E35	-1:54:20
Villiersdorp	1	34s00	19E19	-1:17:16
Vinkekuil	1	32s42	20E27	-1:21:48
Virginia	3	28s12	26E49	-1:47:16
Vishoek	1	34s07	18E27	-1:13:48
Vleikolk	1	29s43	20E50	-1:23:20
Volksrust	1	27s24	29E53	-1:59:32
Voordeelspan	1	29s05	21E32	-1:26:08
Vosburg	1	30s33	22E52	-1:31:28
Vossman's Beacon	1	26s11	30E40	-2:02:40
Vrede	3	27s30	29E06	-1:56:24
Vredefort	3	27s02	27E20	-1:49:20
Vredenburg	1	32s54	17E59	-1:11:56
Vredendal	1	31s41	18E35	-1:14:20
Vroeggedeel	1	28s02	22E32	-1:30:08
Vroeunspan	1	27s50	20E24	-1:21:36
Vryburg	1	26s55	24E45	-1:39:00
Vryheid	2	27s52	30E38	-2:02:32
Wadeville	1	26s16	28E11	-1:52:44
Waenhuiskrans	1	34s41	20E14	-1:20:56
Wakkerstroom	2	27s24	30E10	-2:00:40
Walvisbaai (Walvis Bay)	1	22s59	14E31	-0:58:04
Walvis Bay → Walvisbaai	1	22s59	14E31	-0:58:04
Wanda	3	29s36	24E28	-1:37:52
Warden	3	27s56	29E00	-1:56:00
Warmbad	1	24s55	28E15	-1:53:00
Warm Baths → Warmbad	1	24s55	28E15	-1:53:00
Warrenton	1	28s09	24E47	-1:39:08
Wartburg	2	29s25	30E35	-2:02:20
Wasbank	2	28s24	30E05	-2:00:20
Waterdale	1	30s40	24E02	-1:36:08
Waterford	1	33s05	25E00	-1:40:00
Waterkloof	3	30s19	25E18	-1:41:12
Waterval-Boven	1	25s40	30E20	-2:01:20
Wattville	1	26s13	28E18	-1:53:12
Waverley	1	31s58	26E28	-1:45:52
Weenen	2	28s57	30E03	-2:00:12
Wegdras	1	28s50	21E52	-1:27:28
Welgedag	1	26s12	28E30	-1:54:00
Welkom	3	27s59	26E45	-1:47:00
Wellington	1	33s38	18E57	-1:15:48
Welverdiend	1	26s23	27E16	-1:49:04
Wentworth Park	1	26s07	27E48	-1:51:12
Wepener	3	29s46	27E00	-1:48:00
Wesselsbron	3	27s50	26E23	-1:45:32
Wesselsvlei	1	27s23	23E47	-1:35:08
Westhuyzen	1	27s30	25E27	-1:41:48
Westleigh	3	27s31	27E21	-1:49:24
Westonaria	1	26s19	27E41	-1:50:44
West Rand	1	26s07	27E45	-1:51:00
Whittlesea	1	32s10	26E50	-1:47:20
Wilderness	1	34s00	22E36	-1:30:24
Wildfontein	1	31s04	24E50	-1:39:20
Williston	1	31s20	20E53	-1:23:32
Willowdene	1	26s18	29E57	-1:59:48
Willowmore	1	33s17	23E29	-1:33:56
Willowvale	1	32s16	28E30	-1:54:00
Wilpoort	1	27s10	26E08	-1:44:32
Winburg	3	28s37	27E00	-1:48:00
Windsorton	1	28s16	24E44	-1:38:56
Winkelpos	3	27s35	26E49	-1:47:16
Winterton	2	28s46	29E35	-1:58:20
Winton	1	27s29	22E34	-1:30:16
Witbank	1	25s56	29E07	-1:56:28
Witdraai	1	26s58	20E45	-1:23:00
Witfield	1	26s11	28E12	-1:52:48
Withok	1	26s18	28E23	-1:53:32
Witpoort	1	27s10	26E08	-1:44:32
Witpoortje	1	26s08	27E50	-1:51:20
Witrivier	1	24s40	31E00	-2:04:00
Witsand	1	34s24	20E50	-1:23:20
Wolmaransstad	1	27s12	26E13	-1:44:52
Wolseley	1	33s26	19E12	-1:16:48
Wolvenspruit	3	28s50	25E32	-1:42:08
Wolwehoek	3	26s55	27E48	-1:51:12
Wonderkop	3	27s50	27E26	-1:49:44
Wooldridge	1	33s13	27E15	-1:49:00
Worcester	1	33s39	19E27	-1:17:48
Wuppertal	1	32s15	19E15	-1:17:00
Wychwood	1	26s12	28E08	-1:52:32
Wydegeleë	1	34s23	20E26	-1:21:44
Wydgelee	1	34s23	20E26	-1:21:44
Wynberg	1	34s02	18E28	-1:13:52
Zaaimansdal	1	33s35	23E22	-1:33:28
Zastron	3	30s18	27E07	-1:48:28
Zeerust	1	25s33	26E06	-1:44:24
Zoar	1	33s30	21E28	-1:25:52
Zooafskolk	1	29s56	20E24	-1:21:36
Zungwini	2	27s34	30E53	-2:03:32
Zuurbekom	1	26s19	27E49	-1:51:16

SOUTH GEORGIA SOUTH GEORGIA

Time Table
Before 1/Jan/1890 LMT
Begin Standard 30E00
1/Jan/1890 0:00 -2:00

Place	Lat	Long	Offset
Grytviken	54s16	36w32	2:26:08
Husvik Harbor	54s10	36w45	2:27:00
Prince Olaf Harbor	54s03	37w09	2:28:36

Time Table # 1

Before 2/May/1924 LMT
Begin Standard 150E00
2/May/1924 0:00 -10:00
1/Apr/1981 0:00 -11:00
1/Oct/1981 0:00 -10:00
1/Apr/1982 0:00 -11:00
1/Oct/1982 0:00 -10:00
1/Apr/1983 0:00 -11:00
1/Oct/1983 0:00 -10:00
1/Apr/1984 0:00 -11:00
30/Sep/1984 3:00 -10:00
31/Mar/1985 2:00 -11:00
29/Sep/1985 3:00 -10:00
30/Mar/1986 2:00 -11:00
28/Sep/1986 3:00 -10:00
29/Mar/1987 2:00 -11:00
27/Sep/1987 3:00 -10:00
27/Mar/1988 2:00 -11:00
25/Sep/1988 3:00 -10:00
26/Mar/1989 2:00 -11:00
24/Sep/1989 3:00 -10:00
25/Mar/1990 2:00 -11:00
30/Sep/1990 3:00 -10:00
29/Mar/1992 2:00 -11:00
27/Sep/1992 3:00 -10:00
28/Mar/1993 2:00 -11:00
26/Sep/1993 3:00 -10:00
27/Mar/1994 2:00 -11:00
25/Sep/1994 3:00 -10:00
26/Mar/1995 2:00 -11:00
24/Sep/1995 3:00 -10:00
31/Mar/1996 2:00 -11:00
29/Sep/1996 3:00 -10:00
30/Mar/1997 2:00 -11:00
28/Sep/1997 3:00 -10:00
29/Mar/1998 2:00 -11:00
27/Sep/1998 3:00 -10:00
28/Mar/1999 2:00 -11:00
26/Sep/1999 3:00 -10:00
26/Mar/2000 2:00 -11:00
24/Sep/2000 3:00 -10:00

Time Table # 2

Before 2/May/1924 LMT
Begin Standard 180E00
2/May/1924 0:00 -12:00
Begin Standard 195E00
1/Mar/1957 0:00 -13:00
1/Apr/1981 0:00 -14:00
1/Oct/1981 0:00 -13:00
1/Apr/1982 0:00 -14:00
1/Oct/1982 0:00 -13:00
1/Apr/1983 0:00 -14:00
1/Oct/1983 0:00 -13:00
1/Apr/1984 0:00 -14:00
30/Sep/1984 3:00 -13:00
31/Mar/1985 2:00 -14:00
29/Sep/1985 3:00 -13:00
30/Mar/1986 2:00 -14:00
28/Sep/1986 3:00 -13:00
29/Mar/1987 2:00 -14:00
27/Sep/1987 3:00 -13:00
27/Mar/1988 2:00 -14:00
25/Sep/1988 3:00 -13:00
26/Mar/1989 2:00 -14:00
24/Sep/1989 3:00 -13:00
25/Mar/1990 2:00 -14:00
30/Sep/1990 3:00 -13:00
Begin Standard 180E00
29/Sep/1991 3:00 -12:00
29/Mar/1992 2:00 -13:00
27/Sep/1992 3:00 -12:00
28/Mar/1993 2:00 -13:00
26/Sep/1993 3:00 -12:00
27/Mar/1994 2:00 -13:00
25/Sep/1994 3:00 -12:00
26/Mar/1995 2:00 -13:00
24/Sep/1995 3:00 -12:00
31/Mar/1996 2:00 -13:00
29/Sep/1996 3:00 -12:00
30/Mar/1997 2:00 -13:00
28/Sep/1997 3:00 -12:00
29/Mar/1998 2:00 -13:00
27/Sep/1998 3:00 -12:00
28/Mar/1999 2:00 -13:00
26/Sep/1999 3:00 -12:00
26/Mar/2000 2:00 -13:00
24/Sep/2000 3:00 -12:00

Time Table # 3

Before 2/May/1924 LMT
Begin Standard 165E00
2/May/1924 0:00 -11:00
Begin Standard 180E00
1/Mar/1957 0:00 -12:00
Begin Standard 195E00
1/Apr/1981 0:00 -14:00
1/Oct/1981 0:00 -13:00
1/Apr/1982 0:00 -14:00
1/Oct/1982 0:00 -13:00
1/Apr/1983 0:00 -14:00
1/Oct/1983 0:00 -13:00
1/Apr/1984 0:00 -14:00
30/Sep/1984 3:00 -13:00
31/Mar/1985 2:00 -14:00
29/Sep/1985 3:00 -13:00
30/Mar/1986 2:00 -14:00
28/Sep/1986 3:00 -13:00
29/Mar/1987 2:00 -14:00
27/Sep/1987 3:00 -13:00
27/Mar/1988 2:00 -14:00
25/Sep/1988 3:00 -13:00
26/Mar/1989 2:00 -14:00
24/Sep/1989 3:00 -13:00
25/Mar/1990 2:00 -14:00
30/Sep/1990 3:00 -13:00
Begin Standard 180E00
29/Sep/1991 3:00 -12:00
29/Mar/1992 2:00 -13:00
27/Sep/1992 3:00 -12:00
28/Mar/1993 2:00 -13:00
26/Sep/1993 3:00 -12:00
27/Mar/1994 2:00 -13:00
25/Sep/1994 3:00 -12:00
26/Mar/1995 2:00 -13:00
24/Sep/1995 3:00 -12:00
31/Mar/1996 2:00 -13:00
29/Sep/1996 3:00 -12:00
30/Mar/1997 2:00 -13:00
28/Sep/1997 3:00 -12:00
29/Mar/1998 2:00 -13:00
27/Sep/1998 3:00 -12:00
28/Mar/1999 2:00 -13:00
26/Sep/1999 3:00 -12:00
26/Mar/2000 2:00 -13:00
24/Sep/2000 3:00 -12:00

Time Table # 4

Before 2/May/1924 LMT
Begin Standard 165E00
2/May/1924 0:00 -11:00
Begin Standard 180E00
1/Mar/1957 0:00 -12:00
1/Apr/1981 0:00 -13:00
1/Oct/1981 0:00 -12:00
1/Apr/1982 0:00 -13:00
1/Oct/1982 0:00 -12:00
1/Apr/1983 0:00 -13:00
1/Oct/1983 0:00 -12:00
1/Apr/1984 0:00 -13:00
30/Sep/1984 3:00 -12:00
31/Mar/1985 2:00 -13:00
29/Sep/1985 3:00 -12:00
30/Mar/1986 2:00 -13:00
28/Sep/1986 3:00 -12:00
29/Mar/1987 2:00 -13:00
27/Sep/1987 3:00 -12:00
27/Mar/1988 2:00 -13:00
25/Sep/1988 3:00 -12:00
26/Mar/1989 2:00 -13:00
24/Sep/1989 3:00 -12:00
25/Mar/1990 2:00 -13:00
30/Sep/1990 3:00 -12:00
Begin Standard 165E00
29/Sep/1991 3:00 -11:00
29/Mar/1992 2:00 -12:00
27/Sep/1992 3:00 -11:00
28/Mar/1993 2:00 -12:00
26/Sep/1993 3:00 -11:00
27/Mar/1994 2:00 -12:00
25/Sep/1994 3:00 -11:00
26/Mar/1995 2:00 -12:00
24/Sep/1995 3:00 -11:00
31/Mar/1996 2:00 -12:00
29/Sep/1996 3:00 -11:00
30/Mar/1997 2:00 -12:00
28/Sep/1997 3:00 -11:00
29/Mar/1998 2:00 -12:00
27/Sep/1998 3:00 -11:00
28/Mar/1999 2:00 -12:00
26/Sep/1999 3:00 -11:00
26/Mar/2000 2:00 -12:00
24/Sep/2000 3:00 -11:00

Time Table # 5

Before 2/May/1924 LMT
Begin Standard 165E00
2/May/1924 0:00 -11:00
Begin Standard 180E00
1/Mar/1957 0:00 -12:00
Begin Standard 165E00
1/Apr/1981 0:00 -12:00
1/Oct/1981 0:00 -11:00
1/Apr/1982 0:00 -12:00
1/Oct/1982 0:00 -11:00
1/Apr/1983 0:00 -12:00
1/Oct/1983 0:00 -11:00
1/Apr/1984 0:00 -12:00
30/Sep/1984 3:00 -11:00
31/Mar/1985 2:00 -12:00
29/Sep/1985 3:00 -11:00
30/Mar/1986 2:00 -12:00
28/Sep/1986 3:00 -11:00
29/Mar/1987 2:00 -12:00
27/Sep/1987 3:00 -11:00
27/Mar/1988 2:00 -12:00
25/Sep/1988 3:00 -11:00
26/Mar/1989 2:00 -12:00
24/Sep/1989 3:00 -11:00
25/Mar/1990 2:00 -12:00
30/Sep/1990 3:00 -11:00
29/Mar/1992 2:00 -12:00
27/Sep/1992 3:00 -11:00
28/Mar/1993 2:00 -12:00
26/Sep/1993 3:00 -11:00
27/Mar/1994 2:00 -12:00
25/Sep/1994 3:00 -11:00
26/Mar/1995 2:00 -12:00
24/Sep/1995 3:00 -11:00
31/Mar/1996 2:00 -12:00
29/Sep/1996 3:00 -11:00
30/Mar/1997 2:00 -12:00
28/Sep/1997 3:00 -11:00
29/Mar/1998 2:00 -12:00
27/Sep/1998 3:00 -11:00
28/Mar/1999 2:00 -12:00
26/Sep/1999 3:00 -11:00
26/Mar/2000 2:00 -12:00
24/Sep/2000 3:00 -11:00

Time Table # 6

Before 2/May/1924 LMT
Begin Standard 150E00
2/May/1924 0:00 -10:00
Begin Standard 165E00
1/Mar/1957 0:00 -11:00
1/Apr/1981 0:00 -12:00
1/Oct/1981 0:00 -11:00
1/Apr/1982 0:00 -12:00
1/Oct/1982 0:00 -11:00
1/Apr/1983 0:00 -12:00
1/Oct/1983 0:00 -11:00
1/Apr/1984 0:00 -12:00
30/Sep/1984 3:00 -11:00
31/Mar/1985 2:00 -12:00
29/Sep/1985 3:00 -11:00
30/Mar/1986 2:00 -12:00
28/Sep/1986 3:00 -11:00
29/Mar/1987 2:00 -12:00
27/Sep/1987 3:00 -11:00
27/Mar/1988 2:00 -12:00
25/Sep/1988 3:00 -11:00
26/Mar/1989 2:00 -12:00
24/Sep/1989 3:00 -11:00
25/Mar/1990 2:00 -12:00
30/Sep/1990 3:00 -11:00
Begin Standard 150E00
29/Sep/1991 3:00 -10:00
29/Mar/1992 2:00 -11:00
27/Sep/1992 3:00 -10:00
28/Mar/1993 2:00 -11:00
26/Sep/1993 3:00 -10:00
27/Mar/1994 2:00 -11:00
25/Sep/1994 3:00 -10:00
26/Mar/1995 2:00 -11:00
24/Sep/1995 3:00 -10:00
31/Mar/1996 2:00 -11:00
29/Sep/1996 3:00 -10:00
30/Mar/1997 2:00 -11:00
28/Sep/1997 3:00 -10:00
29/Mar/1998 2:00 -11:00
27/Sep/1998 3:00 -10:00
28/Mar/1999 2:00 -11:00
26/Sep/1999 3:00 -10:00
26/Mar/2000 2:00 -11:00
24/Sep/2000 3:00 -10:00

Time Table # 7

Before 2/May/1924 LMT
Begin Standard 150E00
2/May/1924 0:00 -10:00
Begin Standard 135E00
1/Jan/1951 0:00 -9:00
Begin Standard 150E00
1/Mar/1957 0:00 -10:00
1/Apr/1981 0:00 -11:00
1/Oct/1981 0:00 -10:00
1/Apr/1982 0:00 -11:00
1/Oct/1982 0:00 -10:00
1/Apr/1983 0:00 -11:00
1/Oct/1983 0:00 -10:00
1/Apr/1984 0:00 -11:00
30/Sep/1984 3:00 -10:00
31/Mar/1985 2:00 -11:00
29/Sep/1985 3:00 -10:00
30/Mar/1986 2:00 -11:00
28/Sep/1986 3:00 -10:00
29/Mar/1987 2:00 -11:00
27/Sep/1987 3:00 -10:00
27/Mar/1988 2:00 -11:00
25/Sep/1988 3:00 -10:00
26/Mar/1989 2:00 -11:00
24/Sep/1989 3:00 -10:00
25/Mar/1990 2:00 -11:00
30/Sep/1990 3:00 -10:00
Begin Standard 135E00
29/Sep/1991 3:00 -9:00
29/Mar/1992 2:00 -10:00
27/Sep/1992 3:00 -9:00
28/Mar/1993 2:00 -10:00
26/Sep/1993 3:00 -9:00
27/Mar/1994 2:00 -10:00
25/Sep/1994 3:00 -9:00
26/Mar/1995 2:00 -10:00
24/Sep/1995 3:00 -9:00
31/Mar/1996 2:00 -10:00
29/Sep/1996 3:00 -9:00
30/Mar/1997 2:00 -10:00
28/Sep/1997 3:00 -9:00
29/Mar/1998 2:00 -10:00
27/Sep/1998 3:00 -9:00
28/Mar/1999 2:00 -10:00
26/Sep/1999 3:00 -9:00
26/Mar/2000 2:00 -10:00
24/Sep/2000 3:00 -9:00

Time Table # 8

Before 2/May/1924 LMT
Begin Standard 135E00
2/May/1924 0:00 -9:00
Begin Standard 150E00
1/Jan/1951 0:00 -10:00
Begin Standard 165E00
1/Mar/1957 0:00 -11:00
1/Apr/1981 0:00 -12:00
1/Oct/1981 0:00 -11:00
1/Apr/1982 0:00 -12:00
1/Oct/1982 0:00 -11:00
1/Apr/1983 0:00 -12:00
1/Oct/1983 0:00 -11:00
1/Apr/1984 0:00 -12:00
30/Sep/1984 3:00 -11:00
31/Mar/1985 2:00 -12:00
29/Sep/1985 3:00 -11:00
30/Mar/1986 2:00 -12:00
28/Sep/1986 3:00 -11:00
29/Mar/1987 2:00 -12:00
27/Sep/1987 3:00 -11:00
27/Mar/1988 2:00 -12:00
25/Sep/1988 3:00 -11:00
26/Mar/1989 2:00 -12:00
24/Sep/1989 3:00 -11:00
25/Mar/1990 2:00 -12:00
30/Sep/1990 3:00 -11:00
Begin Standard 150E00
29/Sep/1991 3:00 -10:00
29/Mar/1992 2:00 -11:00
27/Sep/1992 3:00 -10:00
28/Mar/1993 2:00 -11:00
26/Sep/1993 3:00 -10:00
27/Mar/1994 2:00 -11:00
25/Sep/1994 3:00 -10:00
26/Mar/1995 2:00 -11:00
24/Sep/1995 3:00 -10:00
31/Mar/1996 2:00 -11:00
29/Sep/1996 3:00 -10:00
30/Mar/1997 2:00 -11:00
28/Sep/1997 3:00 -10:00
29/Mar/1998 2:00 -11:00
27/Sep/1998 3:00 -10:00
28/Mar/1999 2:00 -11:00
26/Sep/1999 3:00 -10:00
26/Mar/2000 2:00 -11:00
24/Sep/2000 3:00 -10:00

Time Table # 9

Before 1/Jan/1880 LMT
Begin Standard 30E15
1/Jan/1880 0:00 -2:01
1/Jul/1917 23:00 -3:01
28/Dec/1917 0:00 -2:01
31/May/1918 22:00 -4:01
17/Sep/1918 0:00 -3:01
31/May/1919 23:00 -4:01
Begin Standard 45E00
1/Jul/1919 2:00 -4:00
16/Aug/1919 0:00 -3:00
14/Feb/1921 23:00 -4:00
20/Mar/1921 23:00 -5:00
1/Sep/1921 0:00 -4:00
1/Oct/1921 0:00 -3:00
Begin Standard 30E00
1/Oct/1922 0:00 -2:00
Begin Standard 45E00
21/Jun/1930 0:00 -3:00
1/Apr/1981 0:00 -4:00
1/Oct/1981 0:00 -3:00
1/Apr/1982 0:00 -4:00
1/Oct/1982 0:00 -3:00
1/Apr/1983 0:00 -4:00
1/Oct/1983 0:00 -3:00
1/Apr/1984 0:00 -4:00
30/Sep/1984 3:00 -3:00
31/Mar/1985 2:00 -4:00
29/Sep/1985 3:00 -3:00
30/Mar/1986 2:00 -4:00
28/Sep/1986 3:00 -3:00
29/Mar/1987 2:00 -4:00
27/Sep/1987 3:00 -3:00
27/Mar/1988 2:00 -4:00
25/Sep/1988 3:00 -3:00
26/Mar/1989 2:00 -4:00
24/Sep/1989 3:00 -3:00
25/Mar/1990 2:00 -4:00
30/Sep/1990 3:00 -3:00
Begin Standard 30E00
29/Sep/1991 3:00 -2:00
29/Mar/1992 2:00 -3:00
27/Sep/1992 3:00 -2:00
28/Mar/1993 2:00 -3:00
26/Sep/1993 3:00 -2:00
27/Mar/1994 2:00 -3:00
25/Sep/1994 3:00 -2:00
26/Mar/1995 2:00 -3:00
24/Sep/1995 3:00 -2:00
31/Mar/1996 2:00 -3:00
29/Sep/1996 3:00 -2:00
30/Mar/1997 2:00 -3:00
28/Sep/1997 3:00 -2:00
29/Mar/1998 2:00 -3:00
27/Sep/1998 3:00 -2:00
28/Mar/1999 2:00 -3:00
26/Sep/1999 3:00 -2:00
26/Mar/2000 2:00 -3:00
24/Sep/2000 3:00 -2:00

Time Table # 10

Before 2/May/1924 LMT
Begin Standard 135E00
2/May/1924 0:00 -9:00
Begin Standard 150E00
1/Mar/1957 0:00 -10:00
Begin Standard 165E00
1/Apr/1981 0:00 -12:00
1/Oct/1981 0:00 -11:00
1/Apr/1982 0:00 -12:00
1/Oct/1982 0:00 -11:00
1/Apr/1983 0:00 -12:00
1/Oct/1983 0:00 -11:00
1/Apr/1984 0:00 -12:00
30/Sep/1984 3:00 -11:00
31/Mar/1985 2:00 -12:00
29/Sep/1985 3:00 -11:00
30/Mar/1986 2:00 -12:00
28/Sep/1986 3:00 -11:00
29/Mar/1987 2:00 -12:00
27/Sep/1987 3:00 -11:00
27/Mar/1988 2:00 -12:00
25/Sep/1988 3:00 -11:00
26/Mar/1989 2:00 -12:00
24/Sep/1989 3:00 -11:00
25/Mar/1990 2:00 -12:00
30/Sep/1990 3:00 -11:00
Begin Standard 150E00
29/Sep/1991 3:00 -10:00
29/Mar/1992 2:00 -11:00
27/Sep/1992 3:00 -10:00
28/Mar/1993 2:00 -11:00
26/Sep/1993 3:00 -10:00
27/Mar/1994 2:00 -11:00
25/Sep/1994 3:00 -10:00
26/Mar/1995 2:00 -11:00
24/Sep/1995 3:00 -10:00
31/Mar/1996 2:00 -11:00
29/Sep/1996 3:00 -10:00
30/Mar/1997 2:00 -11:00
28/Sep/1997 3:00 -10:00
29/Mar/1998 2:00 -11:00
27/Sep/1998 3:00 -10:00
28/Mar/1999 2:00 -11:00
26/Sep/1999 3:00 -10:00
26/Mar/2000 2:00 -11:00
24/Sep/2000 3:00 -10:00

Time Table # 11

Before 2/May/1924 LMT
Begin Standard 135E00
2/May/1924 0:00 -9:00
Begin Standard 150E00
1/Mar/1957 0:00 -10:00
1/Apr/1981 0:00 -11:00
1/Oct/1981 0:00 -10:00
1/Apr/1982 0:00 -11:00
1/Oct/1982 0:00 -10:00
1/Apr/1983 0:00 -11:00
1/Oct/1983 0:00 -10:00
1/Apr/1984 0:00 -11:00
30/Sep/1984 3:00 -10:00
31/Mar/1985 2:00 -11:00
29/Sep/1985 3:00 -10:00
30/Mar/1986 2:00 -11:00
28/Sep/1986 3:00 -10:00
29/Mar/1987 2:00 -11:00
27/Sep/1987 3:00 -10:00
27/Mar/1988 2:00 -11:00
25/Sep/1988 3:00 -10:00
26/Mar/1989 2:00 -11:00
24/Sep/1989 3:00 -10:00
25/Mar/1990 2:00 -11:00
30/Sep/1990 3:00 -10:00
Begin Standard 135E00
29/Sep/1991 3:00 -9:00
29/Mar/1992 2:00 -10:00
27/Sep/1992 3:00 -9:00
28/Mar/1993 2:00 -10:00
26/Sep/1993 3:00 -9:00
27/Mar/1994 2:00 -10:00
25/Sep/1994 3:00 -9:00
26/Mar/1995 2:00 -10:00
24/Sep/1995 3:00 -9:00
31/Mar/1996 2:00 -10:00
29/Sep/1996 3:00 -9:00
30/Mar/1997 2:00 -10:00
28/Sep/1997 3:00 -9:00
29/Mar/1998 2:00 -10:00
27/Sep/1998 3:00 -9:00
28/Mar/1999 2:00 -10:00
26/Sep/1999 3:00 -9:00
26/Mar/2000 2:00 -10:00
24/Sep/2000 3:00 -9:00

Time Table # 12

Before 2/May/1924 LMT
Begin Standard 135E00
2/May/1924 0:00 -9:00
Begin Standard 120E00
1/Jan/1951 0:00 -8:00
Begin Standard 135E00
1/Mar/1957 0:00 -9:00
Begin Standard 150E00
1/Apr/1981 0:00 -11:00
1/Oct/1981 0:00 -10:00
1/Apr/1982 0:00 -11:00
1/Oct/1982 0:00 -10:00
1/Apr/1983 0:00 -11:00
1/Oct/1983 0:00 -10:00
1/Apr/1984 0:00 -11:00
30/Sep/1984 3:00 -10:00
31/Mar/1985 2:00 -11:00
29/Sep/1985 3:00 -10:00
30/Mar/1986 2:00 -11:00
28/Sep/1986 3:00 -10:00
29/Mar/1987 2:00 -11:00
27/Sep/1987 3:00 -10:00
27/Mar/1988 2:00 -11:00
25/Sep/1988 3:00 -10:00
26/Mar/1989 2:00 -11:00
24/Sep/1989 3:00 -10:00
25/Mar/1990 2:00 -11:00
30/Sep/1990 3:00 -10:00
Begin Standard 135E00
29/Sep/1991 3:00 -9:00
29/Mar/1992 2:00 -10:00
27/Sep/1992 3:00 -9:00
28/Mar/1993 2:00 -10:00
26/Sep/1993 3:00 -9:00
27/Mar/1994 2:00 -10:00
25/Sep/1994 3:00 -9:00
26/Mar/1995 2:00 -10:00
24/Sep/1995 3:00 -9:00
31/Mar/1996 2:00 -10:00
29/Sep/1996 3:00 -9:00
30/Mar/1997 2:00 -10:00
28/Sep/1997 3:00 -9:00

29/Mar/1998 2:00 -10:00
27/Sep/1998 3:00 -9:00
28/Mar/1999 2:00 -10:00
26/Sep/1999 3:00 -9:00
26/Mar/2000 2:00 -10:00
24/Sep/2000 3:00 -9:00
....

Time Table # 13
Before 2/May/1924 LMT
Begin Standard 135E00
2/May/1924 0:00 -9:00
Begin Standard 120E00
1/Jan/1951 0:00 -8:00
Begin Standard 135E00
1/Mar/1957 0:00 -9:00
1/Apr/1981 0:00 -10:00
1/Oct/1981 0:00 -9:00
1/Apr/1982 0:00 -10:00
1/Oct/1982 0:00 -9:00
1/Apr/1983 0:00 -10:00
1/Oct/1983 0:00 -9:00
1/Apr/1984 0:00 -10:00
30/Sep/1984 3:00 -9:00
31/Mar/1985 2:00 -10:00
29/Sep/1985 3:00 -9:00
30/Mar/1986 2:00 -10:00
28/Sep/1986 3:00 -9:00
29/Mar/1987 2:00 -10:00
27/Sep/1987 3:00 -9:00
27/Mar/1988 2:00 -10:00
25/Sep/1988 3:00 -9:00
26/Mar/1989 2:00 -10:00
24/Sep/1989 3:00 -9:00
25/Mar/1990 2:00 -10:00
30/Sep/1990 3:00 -9:00
Begin Standard 120E00
29/Sep/1991 3:00 -8:00
29/Mar/1992 2:00 -9:00
27/Sep/1992 3:00 -8:00
28/Mar/1993 2:00 -9:00
26/Sep/1993 3:00 -8:00
27/Mar/1994 2:00 -9:00
25/Sep/1994 3:00 -8:00
26/Mar/1995 2:00 -9:00
24/Sep/1995 3:00 -8:00
31/Mar/1996 2:00 -9:00
29/Sep/1996 3:00 -8:00
30/Mar/1997 2:00 -9:00
28/Sep/1997 3:00 -8:00
29/Mar/1998 2:00 -9:00
27/Sep/1998 3:00 -8:00
28/Mar/1999 2:00 -9:00
26/Sep/1999 3:00 -8:00
26/Mar/2000 2:00 -9:00
24/Sep/2000 3:00 -8:00
....

Time Table # 14
Before 2/May/1924 LMT
Begin Standard 135E00
2/May/1924 0:00 -9:00
Begin Standard 150E00
1/Mar/1957 0:00 -10:00
Begin Standard 135E00
1/Apr/1981 0:00 -10:00
1/Oct/1981 0:00 -9:00
1/Apr/1982 0:00 -10:00
1/Oct/1982 0:00 -9:00
1/Apr/1983 0:00 -10:00
1/Oct/1983 0:00 -9:00
1/Apr/1984 0:00 -10:00
30/Sep/1984 3:00 -9:00
31/Mar/1985 2:00 -10:00
29/Sep/1985 3:00 -9:00
30/Mar/1986 2:00 -10:00
28/Sep/1986 3:00 -9:00
29/Mar/1987 2:00 -10:00
27/Sep/1987 3:00 -9:00
27/Mar/1988 2:00 -10:00
25/Sep/1988 3:00 -9:00
26/Mar/1989 2:00 -10:00
24/Sep/1989 3:00 -9:00
25/Mar/1990 2:00 -10:00
30/Sep/1990 3:00 -9:00
29/Mar/1992 2:00 -10:00
27/Sep/1992 3:00 -9:00
28/Mar/1993 2:00 -10:00
26/Sep/1993 3:00 -9:00
27/Mar/1994 2:00 -10:00
25/Sep/1994 3:00 -9:00
26/Mar/1995 2:00 -10:00
24/Sep/1995 3:00 -9:00
31/Mar/1996 2:00 -10:00
29/Sep/1996 3:00 -9:00
30/Mar/1997 2:00 -10:00
28/Sep/1997 3:00 -9:00
29/Mar/1998 2:00 -10:00
27/Sep/1998 3:00 -9:00
28/Mar/1999 2:00 -10:00
26/Sep/1999 3:00 -9:00
26/Mar/2000 2:00 -10:00
24/Sep/2000 3:00 -9:00
....

Time Table # 15
Before 2/May/1924 LMT
Begin Standard 120E00
2/May/1924 0:00 -8:00
Begin Standard 135E00
1/Jan/1951 0:00 -9:00
Begin Standard 150E00
1/Mar/1957 0:00 -10:00
Begin Standard 135E00
1/Apr/1981 0:00 -10:00
1/Oct/1981 0:00 -9:00
1/Apr/1982 0:00 -10:00
1/Oct/1982 0:00 -9:00
1/Apr/1983 0:00 -10:00
1/Oct/1983 0:00 -9:00
1/Apr/1984 0:00 -10:00
30/Sep/1984 3:00 -9:00
31/Mar/1985 2:00 -10:00
29/Sep/1985 3:00 -9:00
30/Mar/1986 2:00 -10:00
28/Sep/1986 3:00 -9:00
29/Mar/1987 2:00 -10:00
27/Sep/1987 3:00 -9:00
27/Mar/1988 2:00 -10:00
25/Sep/1988 3:00 -9:00
26/Mar/1989 2:00 -10:00
24/Sep/1989 3:00 -9:00
25/Mar/1990 2:00 -10:00
30/Sep/1990 3:00 -9:00
29/Mar/1992 2:00 -10:00
27/Sep/1992 3:00 -9:00
28/Mar/1993 2:00 -10:00
26/Sep/1993 3:00 -9:00
27/Mar/1994 2:00 -10:00
25/Sep/1994 3:00 -9:00
26/Mar/1995 2:00 -10:00
24/Sep/1995 3:00 -9:00
31/Mar/1996 2:00 -10:00
29/Sep/1996 3:00 -9:00
30/Mar/1997 2:00 -10:00
28/Sep/1997 3:00 -9:00
29/Mar/1998 2:00 -10:00
27/Sep/1998 3:00 -9:00
28/Mar/1999 2:00 -10:00
26/Sep/1999 3:00 -9:00
26/Mar/2000 2:00 -10:00
24/Sep/2000 3:00 -9:00
....

Time Table # 16
Before 2/May/1924 LMT
Begin Standard 120E00
2/May/1924 0:00 -8:00
Begin Standard 135E00
1/Mar/1957 0:00 -9:00
1/Apr/1981 0:00 -10:00
1/Oct/1981 0:00 -9:00
1/Apr/1982 0:00 -10:00
1/Oct/1982 0:00 -9:00
1/Apr/1983 0:00 -10:00
1/Oct/1983 0:00 -9:00
1/Apr/1984 0:00 -10:00
30/Sep/1984 3:00 -9:00
31/Mar/1985 2:00 -10:00
29/Sep/1985 3:00 -9:00
30/Mar/1986 2:00 -10:00
28/Sep/1986 3:00 -9:00
29/Mar/1987 2:00 -10:00
27/Sep/1987 3:00 -9:00
27/Mar/1988 2:00 -10:00
25/Sep/1988 3:00 -9:00
26/Mar/1989 2:00 -10:00
24/Sep/1989 3:00 -9:00
25/Mar/1990 2:00 -10:00
30/Sep/1990 3:00 -9:00
Begin Standard 120E00
29/Sep/1991 3:00 -8:00
29/Mar/1992 2:00 -9:00
27/Sep/1992 3:00 -8:00
28/Mar/1993 2:00 -9:00
26/Sep/1993 3:00 -8:00
27/Mar/1994 2:00 -9:00
25/Sep/1994 3:00 -8:00
26/Mar/1995 2:00 -9:00
24/Sep/1995 3:00 -8:00
31/Mar/1996 2:00 -9:00
29/Sep/1996 3:00 -8:00
30/Mar/1997 2:00 -9:00
28/Sep/1997 3:00 -8:00
29/Mar/1998 2:00 -9:00
27/Sep/1998 3:00 -8:00
28/Mar/1999 2:00 -9:00
26/Sep/1999 3:00 -8:00
26/Mar/2000 2:00 -9:00
24/Sep/2000 3:00 -8:00
....

Time Table # 17
Before 2/May/1924 LMT
Begin Standard 120E00
2/May/1924 0:00 -8:00
1/Apr/1981 0:00 -9:00
1/Oct/1981 0:00 -8:00
1/Apr/1982 0:00 -9:00
1/Oct/1982 0:00 -8:00
1/Apr/1983 0:00 -9:00
1/Oct/1983 0:00 -8:00
1/Apr/1984 0:00 -9:00
30/Sep/1984 3:00 -8:00
31/Mar/1985 2:00 -9:00
29/Sep/1985 3:00 -8:00
30/Mar/1986 2:00 -9:00
28/Sep/1986 3:00 -8:00
29/Mar/1987 2:00 -9:00
27/Sep/1987 3:00 -8:00
27/Mar/1988 2:00 -9:00
25/Sep/1988 3:00 -8:00
26/Mar/1989 2:00 -9:00
24/Sep/1989 3:00 -8:00
25/Mar/1990 2:00 -9:00
30/Sep/1990 3:00 -8:00
29/Mar/1992 2:00 -9:00
27/Sep/1992 3:00 -8:00
28/Mar/1993 2:00 -9:00
26/Sep/1993 3:00 -8:00
27/Mar/1994 2:00 -9:00
25/Sep/1994 3:00 -8:00
26/Mar/1995 2:00 -9:00
24/Sep/1995 3:00 -8:00
31/Mar/1996 2:00 -9:00
29/Sep/1996 3:00 -8:00
30/Mar/1997 2:00 -9:00
28/Sep/1997 3:00 -8:00
29/Mar/1998 2:00 -9:00
27/Sep/1998 3:00 -8:00
28/Mar/1999 2:00 -9:00
26/Sep/1999 3:00 -8:00
26/Mar/2000 2:00 -9:00
24/Sep/2000 3:00 -8:00
....

Time Table # 18
Before 2/May/1924 LMT
Begin Standard 105E00
2/May/1924 0:00 -7:00
Begin Standard 135E00
1/Mar/1957 0:00 -9:00
1/Apr/1981 0:00 -10:00
1/Oct/1981 0:00 -9:00
1/Apr/1982 0:00 -10:00
1/Oct/1982 0:00 -9:00
1/Apr/1983 0:00 -10:00
1/Oct/1983 0:00 -9:00
1/Apr/1984 0:00 -10:00
30/Sep/1984 3:00 -9:00
31/Mar/1985 2:00 -10:00
29/Sep/1985 3:00 -9:00
30/Mar/1986 2:00 -10:00
28/Sep/1986 3:00 -9:00
29/Mar/1987 2:00 -10:00
27/Sep/1987 3:00 -9:00
27/Mar/1988 2:00 -10:00
25/Sep/1988 3:00 -9:00
26/Mar/1989 2:00 -10:00
24/Sep/1989 3:00 -9:00
25/Mar/1990 2:00 -10:00
30/Sep/1990 3:00 -9:00
Begin Standard 120E00
29/Sep/1991 3:00 -8:00
29/Mar/1992 2:00 -9:00
27/Sep/1992 3:00 -8:00
28/Mar/1993 2:00 -9:00
26/Sep/1993 3:00 -8:00
27/Mar/1994 2:00 -9:00
25/Sep/1994 3:00 -8:00
26/Mar/1995 2:00 -9:00
24/Sep/1995 3:00 -8:00
31/Mar/1996 2:00 -9:00
29/Sep/1996 3:00 -8:00
30/Mar/1997 2:00 -9:00
28/Sep/1997 3:00 -8:00
29/Mar/1998 2:00 -9:00
27/Sep/1998 3:00 -8:00
28/Mar/1999 2:00 -9:00
26/Sep/1999 3:00 -8:00
26/Mar/2000 2:00 -9:00
24/Sep/2000 3:00 -8:00
....

Time Table # 19
Before 2/May/1924 LMT
Begin Standard 105E00
2/May/1924 0:00 -7:00
Begin Standard 120E00
1/Mar/1957 0:00 -8:00
Begin Standard 105E00
1/Apr/1981 0:00 -8:00
1/Oct/1981 0:00 -7:00
1/Apr/1982 0:00 -8:00
1/Oct/1982 0:00 -7:00
1/Apr/1983 0:00 -8:00
1/Oct/1983 0:00 -7:00
1/Apr/1984 0:00 -8:00
30/Sep/1984 3:00 -7:00
31/Mar/1985 2:00 -8:00
29/Sep/1985 3:00 -7:00
30/Mar/1986 2:00 -8:00
28/Sep/1986 3:00 -7:00
29/Mar/1987 2:00 -8:00
27/Sep/1987 3:00 -7:00
27/Mar/1988 2:00 -8:00
25/Sep/1988 3:00 -7:00
26/Mar/1989 2:00 -8:00
24/Sep/1989 3:00 -7:00
25/Mar/1990 2:00 -8:00
30/Sep/1990 3:00 -7:00
29/Mar/1992 2:00 -8:00
27/Sep/1992 3:00 -7:00
28/Mar/1993 2:00 -8:00
26/Sep/1993 3:00 -7:00
27/Mar/1994 2:00 -8:00
25/Sep/1994 3:00 -7:00
26/Mar/1995 2:00 -8:00
24/Sep/1995 3:00 -7:00
31/Mar/1996 2:00 -8:00
29/Sep/1996 3:00 -7:00
30/Mar/1997 2:00 -8:00
28/Sep/1997 3:00 -7:00
29/Mar/1998 2:00 -8:00
27/Sep/1998 3:00 -7:00
28/Mar/1999 2:00 -8:00
26/Sep/1999 3:00 -7:00
26/Mar/2000 2:00 -8:00
24/Sep/2000 3:00 -7:00
....

Time Table # 20
Before 1/Jan/1880 LMT
Begin Standard 104E20
1/Jan/1880 0:00 -6:57
Begin Standard 105E00
2/May/1924 0:00 -7:00
Begin Standard 120E00
1/Mar/1957 0:00 -8:00
1/Apr/1981 0:00 -9:00
1/Oct/1981 0:00 -8:00
1/Apr/1982 0:00 -9:00
1/Oct/1982 0:00 -8:00
1/Apr/1983 0:00 -9:00
1/Oct/1983 0:00 -8:00
1/Apr/1984 0:00 -9:00
30/Sep/1984 3:00 -8:00
31/Mar/1985 2:00 -9:00
29/Sep/1985 3:00 -8:00
30/Mar/1986 2:00 -9:00
28/Sep/1986 3:00 -8:00
29/Mar/1987 2:00 -9:00
27/Sep/1987 3:00 -8:00
27/Mar/1988 2:00 -9:00
25/Sep/1988 3:00 -8:00
26/Mar/1989 2:00 -9:00
24/Sep/1989 3:00 -8:00
25/Mar/1990 2:00 -9:00
30/Sep/1990 3:00 -8:00
Begin Standard 105E00
29/Sep/1991 3:00 -7:00
29/Mar/1992 2:00 -8:00
27/Sep/1992 3:00 -7:00
28/Mar/1993 2:00 -8:00
26/Sep/1993 3:00 -7:00
27/Mar/1994 2:00 -8:00
25/Sep/1994 3:00 -7:00
26/Mar/1995 2:00 -8:00
24/Sep/1995 3:00 -7:00
31/Mar/1996 2:00 -8:00
29/Sep/1996 3:00 -7:00
30/Mar/1997 2:00 -8:00
28/Sep/1997 3:00 -7:00
29/Mar/1998 2:00 -8:00
27/Sep/1998 3:00 -7:00
28/Mar/1999 2:00 -8:00
26/Sep/1999 3:00 -7:00
26/Mar/2000 2:00 -8:00
24/Sep/2000 3:00 -7:00
....

Time Table # 21
Before 2/May/1924 LMT
Begin Standard 90E00
2/May/1924 0:00 -6:00
Begin Standard 105E00
1/Mar/1957 0:00 -7:00
1/Apr/1981 0:00 -8:00
1/Oct/1981 0:00 -7:00
1/Apr/1982 0:00 -8:00
1/Oct/1982 0:00 -7:00
1/Apr/1983 0:00 -8:00
1/Oct/1983 0:00 -7:00
1/Apr/1984 0:00 -8:00
30/Sep/1984 3:00 -7:00
31/Mar/1985 2:00 -8:00
29/Sep/1985 3:00 -7:00
30/Mar/1986 2:00 -8:00
28/Sep/1986 3:00 -7:00
29/Mar/1987 2:00 -8:00
27/Sep/1987 3:00 -7:00
27/Mar/1988 2:00 -8:00
25/Sep/1988 3:00 -7:00
26/Mar/1989 2:00 -8:00
24/Sep/1989 3:00 -7:00
25/Mar/1990 2:00 -8:00
30/Sep/1990 3:00 -7:00
Begin Standard 90E00
29/Sep/1991 3:00 -6:00
29/Mar/1992 2:00 -7:00
27/Sep/1992 3:00 -6:00
28/Mar/1993 2:00 -7:00
26/Sep/1993 3:00 -6:00
27/Mar/1994 2:00 -7:00
25/Sep/1994 3:00 -6:00
26/Mar/1995 2:00 -7:00
24/Sep/1995 3:00 -6:00
31/Mar/1996 2:00 -7:00
29/Sep/1996 3:00 -6:00
30/Mar/1997 2:00 -7:00
28/Sep/1997 3:00 -6:00
29/Mar/1998 2:00 -7:00
27/Sep/1998 3:00 -6:00
28/Mar/1999 2:00 -7:00
26/Sep/1999 3:00 -6:00
26/Mar/2000 2:00 -7:00
24/Sep/2000 3:00 -6:00
....

Time Table # 22
Before 2/May/1924 LMT
Begin Standard 75E00
2/May/1924 0:00 -5:00
Begin Standard 90E00
1/Jan/1951 0:00 -6:00
Begin Standard 105E00
1/Mar/1957 0:00 -7:00
1/Apr/1981 0:00 -8:00
1/Oct/1981 0:00 -7:00
1/Apr/1982 0:00 -8:00
1/Oct/1982 0:00 -7:00
1/Apr/1983 0:00 -8:00
1/Oct/1983 0:00 -7:00
1/Apr/1984 0:00 -8:00
30/Sep/1984 3:00 -7:00
31/Mar/1985 2:00 -8:00
29/Sep/1985 3:00 -7:00
30/Mar/1986 2:00 -8:00
28/Sep/1986 3:00 -7:00
29/Mar/1987 2:00 -8:00
27/Sep/1987 3:00 -7:00
27/Mar/1988 2:00 -8:00
25/Sep/1988 3:00 -7:00
26/Mar/1989 2:00 -8:00
24/Sep/1989 3:00 -7:00
25/Mar/1990 2:00 -8:00
30/Sep/1990 3:00 -7:00
Begin Standard 90E00
29/Sep/1991 3:00 -6:00
29/Mar/1992 2:00 -7:00
27/Sep/1992 3:00 -6:00
28/Mar/1993 2:00 -7:00
26/Sep/1993 3:00 -6:00
27/Mar/1994 2:00 -7:00
25/Sep/1994 3:00 -6:00
26/Mar/1995 2:00 -7:00
24/Sep/1995 3:00 -6:00
31/Mar/1996 2:00 -7:00
29/Sep/1996 3:00 -6:00
30/Mar/1997 2:00 -7:00
28/Sep/1997 3:00 -6:00
29/Mar/1998 2:00 -7:00
27/Sep/1998 3:00 -6:00
28/Mar/1999 2:00 -7:00
26/Sep/1999 3:00 -6:00
26/Mar/2000 2:00 -7:00
24/Sep/2000 3:00 -6:00
....

Time Table # 23
Before 2/May/1924 LMT
Begin Standard 75E00
2/May/1924 0:00 -5:00
Begin Standard 90E00
21/Jun/1930 0:00 -6:00
Begin Standard 105E00
1/Mar/1957 0:00 -7:00
1/Apr/1981 0:00 -8:00
1/Oct/1981 0:00 -7:00
1/Apr/1982 0:00 -8:00
1/Oct/1982 0:00 -7:00
1/Apr/1983 0:00 -8:00
1/Oct/1983 0:00 -7:00
1/Apr/1984 0:00 -8:00
30/Sep/1984 3:00 -7:00
31/Mar/1985 2:00 -8:00
29/Sep/1985 3:00 -7:00
30/Mar/1986 2:00 -8:00
28/Sep/1986 3:00 -7:00
29/Mar/1987 2:00 -8:00
27/Sep/1987 3:00 -7:00
27/Mar/1988 2:00 -8:00
25/Sep/1988 3:00 -7:00
26/Mar/1989 2:00 -8:00
24/Sep/1989 3:00 -7:00
25/Mar/1990 2:00 -8:00
30/Sep/1990 3:00 -7:00
Begin Standard 90E00
29/Sep/1991 3:00 -6:00
29/Mar/1992 2:00 -7:00
27/Sep/1992 3:00 -6:00
28/Mar/1993 2:00 -7:00
26/Sep/1993 3:00 -6:00
27/Mar/1994 2:00 -7:00
25/Sep/1994 3:00 -6:00
26/Mar/1995 2:00 -7:00
24/Sep/1995 3:00 -6:00
31/Mar/1996 2:00 -7:00
29/Sep/1996 3:00 -6:00
30/Mar/1997 2:00 -7:00
28/Sep/1997 3:00 -6:00
29/Mar/1998 2:00 -7:00
27/Sep/1998 3:00 -6:00
28/Mar/1999 2:00 -7:00
26/Sep/1999 3:00 -6:00
26/Mar/2000 2:00 -7:00
24/Sep/2000 3:00 -6:00
....

Time Table # 24
Before 2/May/1924 LMT
Begin Standard 75E00
2/May/1924 0:00 -5:00
Begin Standard 90E00
1/Mar/1957 0:00 -6:00
1/Apr/1981 0:00 -7:00
1/Oct/1981 0:00 -6:00
1/Apr/1982 0:00 -7:00
1/Oct/1982 0:00 -6:00
1/Apr/1983 0:00 -7:00
1/Oct/1983 0:00 -6:00
1/Apr/1984 0:00 -7:00
30/Sep/1984 3:00 -6:00
31/Mar/1985 2:00 -7:00
29/Sep/1985 3:00 -6:00
30/Mar/1986 2:00 -7:00
28/Sep/1986 3:00 -6:00
29/Mar/1987 2:00 -7:00
27/Sep/1987 3:00 -6:00
27/Mar/1988 2:00 -7:00
25/Sep/1988 3:00 -6:00
26/Mar/1989 2:00 -7:00
24/Sep/1989 3:00 -6:00
25/Mar/1990 2:00 -7:00
30/Sep/1990 3:00 -6:00
Begin Standard 75E00
29/Sep/1991 3:00 -5:00
29/Mar/1992 2:00 -6:00
27/Sep/1992 3:00 -5:00
28/Mar/1993 2:00 -6:00
26/Sep/1993 3:00 -5:00
27/Mar/1994 2:00 -6:00
25/Sep/1994 3:00 -5:00
26/Mar/1995 2:00 -6:00
24/Sep/1995 3:00 -5:00
31/Mar/1996 2:00 -6:00
29/Sep/1996 3:00 -5:00
30/Mar/1997 2:00 -6:00
28/Sep/1997 3:00 -5:00
29/Mar/1998 2:00 -6:00
27/Sep/1998 3:00 -5:00
28/Mar/1999 2:00 -6:00
26/Sep/1999 3:00 -5:00
26/Mar/2000 2:00 -6:00
24/Sep/2000 3:00 -5:00
....

Time Table # 25

Before 2/May/1924 LMT
Begin Standard 75E00
2/May/1924 0:00 -5:00
Begin Standard 90E00
1/Mar/1957 0:00 -6:00
Begin Standard 75E00
1/Apr/1981 0:00 -6:00
1/Oct/1981 0:00 -5:00
1/Apr/1982 0:00 -6:00
1/Oct/1982 0:00 -5:00
1/Apr/1983 0:00 -6:00
1/Oct/1983 0:00 -5:00
1/Apr/1984 0:00 -6:00
30/Sep/1984 3:00 -5:00
31/Mar/1985 2:00 -6:00
29/Sep/1985 3:00 -5:00
30/Mar/1986 2:00 -6:00
28/Sep/1986 3:00 -5:00
29/Mar/1987 2:00 -6:00
27/Sep/1987 3:00 -5:00
27/Mar/1988 2:00 -6:00
25/Sep/1988 3:00 -5:00
26/Mar/1989 2:00 -6:00
24/Sep/1989 3:00 -5:00
25/Mar/1990 2:00 -6:00
30/Sep/1990 3:00 -5:00
29/Mar/1992 2:00 -6:00
27/Sep/1992 3:00 -5:00
28/Mar/1993 2:00 -6:00
26/Sep/1993 3:00 -5:00
27/Mar/1994 2:00 -6:00
25/Sep/1994 3:00 -5:00
26/Mar/1995 2:00 -6:00
24/Sep/1995 3:00 -5:00
31/Mar/1996 2:00 -6:00
29/Sep/1996 3:00 -5:00
30/Mar/1997 2:00 -6:00
28/Sep/1997 3:00 -5:00
29/Mar/1998 2:00 -6:00
27/Sep/1998 3:00 -5:00
28/Mar/1999 2:00 -6:00
26/Sep/1999 3:00 -5:00
26/Mar/2000 2:00 -6:00
24/Sep/2000 3:00 -5:00
....

Time Table # 26
Before 2/May/1924 LMT
Begin Standard 105E00
2/May/1924 0:00 -7:00
1/Apr/1981 0:00 -8:00
1/Oct/1981 0:00 -7:00
1/Apr/1982 0:00 -8:00
1/Oct/1982 0:00 -7:00
1/Apr/1983 0:00 -8:00
1/Oct/1983 0:00 -7:00
1/Apr/1984 0:00 -8:00
30/Sep/1984 3:00 -7:00
31/Mar/1985 2:00 -8:00
29/Sep/1985 3:00 -7:00
30/Mar/1986 2:00 -8:00
28/Sep/1986 3:00 -7:00
29/Mar/1987 2:00 -8:00
27/Sep/1987 3:00 -7:00
27/Mar/1988 2:00 -8:00
25/Sep/1988 3:00 -7:00
26/Mar/1989 2:00 -8:00
24/Sep/1989 3:00 -7:00
25/Mar/1990 2:00 -8:00
30/Sep/1990 3:00 -7:00
29/Mar/1992 2:00 -8:00
27/Sep/1992 3:00 -7:00
28/Mar/1993 2:00 -8:00
26/Sep/1993 3:00 -7:00
27/Mar/1994 2:00 -8:00
25/Sep/1994 3:00 -7:00
26/Mar/1995 2:00 -8:00
24/Sep/1995 3:00 -7:00
31/Mar/1996 2:00 -8:00
29/Sep/1996 3:00 -7:00
30/Mar/1997 2:00 -8:00
28/Sep/1997 3:00 -7:00
29/Mar/1998 2:00 -8:00
27/Sep/1998 3:00 -7:00
28/Mar/1999 2:00 -8:00
26/Sep/1999 3:00 -7:00
26/Mar/2000 2:00 -8:00
24/Sep/2000 3:00 -7:00
....

Time Table # 27
Before 1/Jan/1880 LMT
Begin Standard 131E56
1/Jan/1880 0:00 -8:48
Begin Standard 135E00
2/May/1924 0:00 -9:00
Begin Standard 150E00
1/Mar/1957 0:00 -10:00
1/Apr/1981 0:00 -11:00
1/Oct/1981 0:00 -10:00
1/Apr/1982 0:00 -11:00
1/Oct/1982 0:00 -10:00
1/Apr/1983 0:00 -11:00
1/Oct/1983 0:00 -10:00
1/Apr/1984 0:00 -11:00
30/Sep/1984 3:00 -10:00
31/Mar/1985 2:00 -11:00
29/Sep/1985 3:00 -10:00
30/Mar/1986 2:00 -11:00
28/Sep/1986 3:00 -10:00
29/Mar/1987 2:00 -11:00
27/Sep/1987 3:00 -10:00
27/Mar/1988 2:00 -11:00
25/Sep/1988 3:00 -10:00
26/Mar/1989 2:00 -11:00
24/Sep/1989 3:00 -10:00
25/Mar/1990 2:00 -11:00
30/Sep/1990 3:00 -10:00
Begin Standard 135E00
29/Sep/1991 3:00 -9:00
29/Mar/1992 2:00 -10:00
27/Sep/1992 3:00 -9:00
28/Mar/1993 2:00 -10:00
26/Sep/1993 3:00 -9:00
27/Mar/1994 2:00 -10:00
25/Sep/1994 3:00 -9:00
26/Mar/1995 2:00 -10:00
24/Sep/1995 3:00 -9:00
31/Mar/1996 2:00 -10:00
29/Sep/1996 3:00 -9:00
30/Mar/1997 2:00 -10:00
28/Sep/1997 3:00 -9:00
29/Mar/1998 2:00 -10:00
27/Sep/1998 3:00 -9:00
28/Mar/1999 2:00 -10:00
26/Sep/1999 3:00 -9:00
26/Mar/2000 2:00 -10:00
24/Sep/2000 3:00 -9:00
....

Time Table # 28
Before 2/May/1924 LMT
Begin Standard 60E00
2/May/1924 0:00 -4:00
Begin Standard 90E00
1/Mar/1957 0:00 -6:00
Begin Standard 75E00
1/Apr/1981 0:00 -6:00
1/Oct/1981 0:00 -5:00
1/Apr/1982 0:00 -6:00
1/Oct/1982 0:00 -5:00
1/Apr/1983 0:00 -6:00
1/Oct/1983 0:00 -5:00
1/Apr/1984 0:00 -6:00
30/Sep/1984 3:00 -5:00
31/Mar/1985 2:00 -6:00
29/Sep/1985 3:00 -5:00
30/Mar/1986 2:00 -6:00
28/Sep/1986 3:00 -5:00
29/Mar/1987 2:00 -6:00
27/Sep/1987 3:00 -5:00
27/Mar/1988 2:00 -6:00
25/Sep/1988 3:00 -5:00
26/Mar/1989 2:00 -6:00
24/Sep/1989 3:00 -5:00
25/Mar/1990 2:00 -6:00
30/Sep/1990 3:00 -5:00
29/Mar/1992 2:00 -6:00
27/Sep/1992 3:00 -5:00
28/Mar/1993 2:00 -6:00
26/Sep/1993 3:00 -5:00
27/Mar/1994 2:00 -6:00
25/Sep/1994 3:00 -5:00
26/Mar/1995 2:00 -6:00
24/Sep/1995 3:00 -5:00
31/Mar/1996 2:00 -6:00
29/Sep/1996 3:00 -5:00
30/Mar/1997 2:00 -6:00
28/Sep/1997 3:00 -5:00
29/Mar/1998 2:00 -6:00
27/Sep/1998 3:00 -5:00
28/Mar/1999 2:00 -6:00
26/Sep/1999 3:00 -5:00
26/Mar/2000 2:00 -6:00
24/Sep/2000 3:00 -5:00
....

Time Table # 29
Before 2/May/1924 LMT
Begin Standard 60E00
2/May/1924 0:00 -4:00
Begin Standard 75E00
1/Mar/1957 0:00 -5:00
Begin Standard 45E00
1/Apr/1981 0:00 -4:00
1/Oct/1981 0:00 -3:00
1/Apr/1982 0:00 -4:00
1/Oct/1982 0:00 -3:00
1/Apr/1983 0:00 -4:00
1/Oct/1983 0:00 -3:00
1/Apr/1984 0:00 -4:00
30/Sep/1984 3:00 -3:00
31/Mar/1985 2:00 -4:00
29/Sep/1985 3:00 -3:00
30/Mar/1986 2:00 -4:00
28/Sep/1986 3:00 -3:00
29/Mar/1987 2:00 -4:00
27/Sep/1987 3:00 -3:00
27/Mar/1988 2:00 -4:00
25/Sep/1988 3:00 -3:00
26/Mar/1989 2:00 -4:00
24/Sep/1989 3:00 -3:00
25/Mar/1990 2:00 -4:00
30/Sep/1990 3:00 -3:00
29/Mar/1992 2:00 -4:00
27/Sep/1992 3:00 -3:00
28/Mar/1993 2:00 -4:00
26/Sep/1993 3:00 -3:00
27/Mar/1994 2:00 -4:00
25/Sep/1994 3:00 -3:00
26/Mar/1995 2:00 -4:00
24/Sep/1995 3:00 -3:00
31/Mar/1996 2:00 -4:00
29/Sep/1996 3:00 -3:00
30/Mar/1997 2:00 -4:00
28/Sep/1997 3:00 -3:00
29/Mar/1998 2:00 -4:00
27/Sep/1998 3:00 -3:00
28/Mar/1999 2:00 -4:00
26/Sep/1999 3:00 -3:00
26/Mar/2000 2:00 -4:00
24/Sep/2000 3:00 -3:00
....

Time Table # 30
Before 2/May/1924 LMT
Begin Standard 60E00
2/May/1924 0:00 -4:00
Begin Standard 75E00
1/Mar/1957 0:00 -5:00
1/Apr/1981 0:00 -6:00
1/Oct/1981 0:00 -5:00
1/Apr/1982 0:00 -6:00
1/Oct/1982 0:00 -5:00
1/Apr/1983 0:00 -6:00
1/Oct/1983 0:00 -5:00
1/Apr/1984 0:00 -6:00
30/Sep/1984 3:00 -5:00
31/Mar/1985 2:00 -6:00
29/Sep/1985 3:00 -5:00
30/Mar/1986 2:00 -6:00
28/Sep/1986 3:00 -5:00
29/Mar/1987 2:00 -6:00
27/Sep/1987 3:00 -5:00
27/Mar/1988 2:00 -6:00
25/Sep/1988 3:00 -5:00
26/Mar/1989 2:00 -6:00
24/Sep/1989 3:00 -5:00
25/Mar/1990 2:00 -6:00
30/Sep/1990 3:00 -5:00
Begin Standard 60E00
29/Sep/1991 3:00 -4:00
29/Mar/1992 2:00 -5:00
27/Sep/1992 3:00 -4:00
28/Mar/1993 2:00 -5:00
26/Sep/1993 3:00 -4:00
27/Mar/1994 2:00 -5:00
25/Sep/1994 3:00 -4:00
26/Mar/1995 2:00 -5:00
24/Sep/1995 3:00 -4:00
31/Mar/1996 2:00 -5:00
29/Sep/1996 3:00 -4:00
30/Mar/1997 2:00 -5:00
28/Sep/1997 3:00 -4:00
29/Mar/1998 2:00 -5:00
27/Sep/1998 3:00 -4:00
28/Mar/1999 2:00 -5:00
26/Sep/1999 3:00 -4:00
26/Mar/2000 2:00 -5:00
24/Sep/2000 3:00 -4:00
....

Time Table # 31
Before 2/May/1924 LMT
Begin Standard 60E00
2/May/1924 0:00 -4:00
Begin Standard 75E00
1/Mar/1957 0:00 -5:00
Begin Standard 90E00
1/Apr/1981 0:00 -7:00
1/Oct/1981 0:00 -6:00
1/Apr/1982 0:00 -7:00
1/Oct/1982 0:00 -6:00
1/Apr/1983 0:00 -7:00
1/Oct/1983 0:00 -6:00
1/Apr/1984 0:00 -7:00
30/Sep/1984 3:00 -6:00
31/Mar/1985 2:00 -7:00
29/Sep/1985 3:00 -6:00
30/Mar/1986 2:00 -7:00
28/Sep/1986 3:00 -6:00
29/Mar/1987 2:00 -7:00
27/Sep/1987 3:00 -6:00
27/Mar/1988 2:00 -7:00
25/Sep/1988 3:00 -6:00
26/Mar/1989 2:00 -7:00
24/Sep/1989 3:00 -6:00
25/Mar/1990 2:00 -7:00
30/Sep/1990 3:00 -6:00
Begin Standard 75E00
29/Sep/1991 3:00 -5:00
29/Mar/1992 2:00 -6:00
27/Sep/1992 3:00 -5:00
28/Mar/1993 2:00 -6:00
26/Sep/1993 3:00 -5:00
27/Mar/1994 2:00 -6:00
25/Sep/1994 3:00 -5:00
26/Mar/1995 2:00 -6:00
24/Sep/1995 3:00 -5:00
31/Mar/1996 2:00 -6:00
29/Sep/1996 3:00 -5:00
30/Mar/1997 2:00 -6:00
28/Sep/1997 3:00 -5:00
29/Mar/1998 2:00 -6:00
27/Sep/1998 3:00 -5:00
28/Mar/1999 2:00 -6:00
26/Sep/1999 3:00 -5:00
26/Mar/2000 2:00 -6:00
24/Sep/2000 3:00 -5:00
....

Time Table # 32
Before 2/May/1924 LMT
Begin Standard 45E00
2/May/1924 0:00 -3:00
Begin Standard 60E00
1/Mar/1957 0:00 -4:00
Begin Standard 75E00
1/Apr/1981 0:00 -6:00
1/Oct/1981 0:00 -5:00
1/Apr/1982 0:00 -6:00
1/Oct/1982 0:00 -5:00
1/Apr/1983 0:00 -6:00
1/Oct/1983 0:00 -5:00
1/Apr/1984 0:00 -6:00
30/Sep/1984 3:00 -5:00
31/Mar/1985 2:00 -6:00
29/Sep/1985 3:00 -5:00
30/Mar/1986 2:00 -6:00
28/Sep/1986 3:00 -5:00
29/Mar/1987 2:00 -6:00
27/Sep/1987 3:00 -5:00
27/Mar/1988 2:00 -6:00
25/Sep/1988 3:00 -5:00
26/Mar/1989 2:00 -6:00
24/Sep/1989 3:00 -5:00
25/Mar/1990 2:00 -6:00
30/Sep/1990 3:00 -5:00
Begin Standard 60E00
29/Sep/1991 3:00 -4:00
29/Mar/1992 2:00 -5:00
27/Sep/1992 3:00 -4:00
28/Mar/1993 2:00 -5:00
26/Sep/1993 3:00 -4:00
27/Mar/1994 2:00 -5:00
25/Sep/1994 3:00 -4:00
26/Mar/1995 2:00 -5:00
24/Sep/1995 3:00 -4:00
31/Mar/1996 2:00 -5:00
29/Sep/1996 3:00 -4:00
30/Mar/1997 2:00 -5:00
28/Sep/1997 3:00 -4:00
29/Mar/1998 2:00 -5:00
27/Sep/1998 3:00 -4:00
28/Mar/1999 2:00 -5:00
26/Sep/1999 3:00 -4:00
26/Mar/2000 2:00 -5:00
24/Sep/2000 3:00 -4:00
....

Time Table # 33
Before 1/Jan/1880 LMT
Begin Standard 44E49
1/Jan/1880 0:00 -2:59
Begin Standard 45E00
2/May/1924 0:00 -3:00
Begin Standard 60E00
1/Mar/1957 0:00 -4:00
1/Apr/1981 0:00 -5:00
1/Oct/1981 0:00 -4:00
1/Apr/1982 0:00 -5:00
1/Oct/1982 0:00 -4:00
1/Apr/1983 0:00 -5:00
1/Oct/1983 0:00 -4:00
1/Apr/1984 0:00 -5:00
30/Sep/1984 3:00 -4:00
31/Mar/1985 2:00 -5:00
29/Sep/1985 3:00 -4:00
30/Mar/1986 2:00 -5:00
28/Sep/1986 3:00 -4:00
29/Mar/1987 2:00 -5:00
27/Sep/1987 3:00 -4:00
27/Mar/1988 2:00 -5:00
25/Sep/1988 3:00 -4:00
26/Mar/1989 2:00 -5:00
24/Sep/1989 3:00 -4:00
25/Mar/1990 2:00 -5:00
30/Sep/1990 3:00 -4:00
Begin Standard 45E00
29/Sep/1991 3:00 -3:00
29/Mar/1992 2:00 -4:00
27/Sep/1992 3:00 -3:00
28/Mar/1993 2:00 -4:00
26/Sep/1993 3:00 -3:00
27/Mar/1994 2:00 -4:00
25/Sep/1994 3:00 -3:00
26/Mar/1995 2:00 -4:00
24/Sep/1995 3:00 -3:00
31/Mar/1996 2:00 -4:00
29/Sep/1996 3:00 -3:00
30/Mar/1997 2:00 -4:00
28/Sep/1997 3:00 -3:00
29/Mar/1998 2:00 -4:00
27/Sep/1998 3:00 -3:00
28/Mar/1999 2:00 -4:00
26/Sep/1999 3:00 -3:00
26/Mar/2000 2:00 -4:00
24/Sep/2000 3:00 -3:00
....

Time Table # 34
Before 2/May/1924 LMT
Begin Standard 45E00
2/May/1924 0:00 -3:00
Begin Standard 60E00
1/Mar/1957 0:00 -4:00
1/Apr/1981 0:00 -5:00
1/Oct/1981 0:00 -4:00
1/Apr/1982 0:00 -5:00
1/Oct/1982 0:00 -4:00
1/Apr/1983 0:00 -5:00
1/Oct/1983 0:00 -4:00
1/Apr/1984 0:00 -5:00
30/Sep/1984 3:00 -4:00
31/Mar/1985 2:00 -5:00
29/Sep/1985 3:00 -4:00
30/Mar/1986 2:00 -5:00
28/Sep/1986 3:00 -4:00
29/Mar/1987 2:00 -5:00
27/Sep/1987 3:00 -4:00
27/Mar/1988 2:00 -5:00
25/Sep/1988 3:00 -4:00
26/Mar/1989 2:00 -5:00
24/Sep/1989 3:00 -4:00
25/Mar/1990 2:00 -5:00
30/Sep/1990 3:00 -4:00
Begin Standard 45E00
29/Sep/1991 3:00 -3:00
29/Mar/1992 2:00 -4:00
27/Sep/1992 3:00 -3:00
28/Mar/1993 2:00 -4:00
26/Sep/1993 3:00 -3:00
27/Mar/1994 2:00 -4:00
25/Sep/1994 3:00 -3:00
26/Mar/1995 2:00 -4:00
24/Sep/1995 3:00 -3:00
31/Mar/1996 2:00 -4:00
29/Sep/1996 3:00 -3:00
30/Mar/1997 2:00 -4:00
28/Sep/1997 3:00 -3:00
29/Mar/1998 2:00 -4:00
27/Sep/1998 3:00 -3:00
28/Mar/1999 2:00 -4:00
26/Sep/1999 3:00 -3:00
26/Mar/2000 2:00 -4:00
24/Sep/2000 3:00 -3:00
....

Time Table # 35
Before 1/Jan/1880 LMT
Begin Standard 24E45
1/Jan/1880 0:00 -1:39
Begin Standard 15E00
1/Feb/1918 0:00 -1:00
15/Apr/1918 23:00 -2:00
16/Sep/1918 3:00 -1:00
Begin Standard 24E45
1/Jul/1919 0:00 -1:39
Begin Standard 30E00
1/May/1921 0:00 -2:00
6/Aug/1940 0:00 -3:00
Begin Standard 15E00
15/Sep/1941 0:00 -2:00
2/Nov/1942 3:00 -1:00
29/Mar/1943 2:00 -2:00
4/Oct/1943 3:00 -1:00
3/Apr/1944 2:00 -2:00
Begin Standard 30E00
22/Sep/1944 0:00 -3:00
Begin Standard 45E00
1/Jan/1946 0:00 -3:00
1/Apr/1981 0:00 -4:00
1/Oct/1981 0:00 -3:00
1/Apr/1982 0:00 -4:00
1/Oct/1982 0:00 -3:00
1/Apr/1983 0:00 -4:00
1/Oct/1983 0:00 -3:00
1/Apr/1984 0:00 -4:00
30/Sep/1984 3:00 -3:00
31/Mar/1985 2:00 -4:00
29/Sep/1985 3:00 -3:00
30/Mar/1986 2:00 -4:00
28/Sep/1986 3:00 -3:00
29/Mar/1987 2:00 -4:00
27/Sep/1987 3:00 -3:00
27/Mar/1988 2:00 -4:00
25/Sep/1988 3:00 -3:00
Begin Standard 30E00
26/Mar/1989 2:00 -3:00
24/Sep/1989 3:00 -2:00
25/Mar/1990 2:00 -3:00
30/Sep/1990 3:00 -2:00
31/Mar/1991 2:00 -3:00
29/Sep/1991 3:00 -2:00
29/Mar/1992 2:00 -3:00
27/Sep/1992 3:00 -2:00
28/Mar/1993 2:00 -3:00
26/Sep/1993 3:00 -2:00
27/Mar/1994 2:00 -3:00
25/Sep/1994 3:00 -2:00
26/Mar/1995 2:00 -3:00
24/Sep/1995 3:00 -2:00
31/Mar/1996 2:00 -3:00
29/Sep/1996 3:00 -2:00
30/Mar/1997 2:00 -3:00
28/Sep/1997 3:00 -2:00
29/Mar/1998 2:00 -3:00
27/Sep/1998 3:00 -2:00
28/Mar/1999 2:00 -3:00
26/Sep/1999 3:00 -2:00
26/Mar/2000 2:00 -3:00
24/Sep/2000 3:00 -2:00
....

Time Table # 36
Before 1/Jan/1880 LMT
Begin Standard 24E06
1/Jan/1880 0:00 -1:36
15/Apr/1918 2:00 -2:36
16/Sep/1918 3:00 -1:36
1/Apr/1919 2:00 -2:36
22/May/1919 3:00 -1:36
Begin Standard 30E00
11/May/1926 0:00 -2:00
5/Aug/1940 0:00 -3:00
Begin Standard 15E00
1/Jul/1941 0:00 -2:00
2/Nov/1942 3:00 -1:00
29/Mar/1943 2:00 -2:00
4/Oct/1943 3:00 -1:00
3/Apr/1944 2:00 -2:00
Begin Standard 30E00
8/Aug/1944 0:00 -3:00
Begin Standard 45E00
1/Jan/1946 0:00 -3:00
1/Apr/1981 0:00 -4:00
1/Oct/1981 0:00 -3:00
1/Apr/1982 0:00 -4:00
1/Oct/1982 0:00 -3:00
1/Apr/1983 0:00 -4:00
1/Oct/1983 0:00 -3:00
1/Apr/1984 0:00 -4:00
30/Sep/1984 3:00 -3:00
31/Mar/1985 2:00 -4:00
29/Sep/1985 3:00 -3:00
30/Mar/1986 2:00 -4:00
28/Sep/1986 3:00 -3:00
29/Mar/1987 2:00 -4:00
27/Sep/1987 3:00 -3:00
27/Mar/1988 2:00 -4:00
25/Sep/1988 3:00 -3:00
26/Mar/1989 2:00 -4:00
24/Sep/1989 3:00 -3:00
25/Mar/1990 2:00 -4:00
30/Sep/1990 3:00 -3:00
Begin Standard 30E00

29/Sep/1991 3:00 -2:00
29/Mar/1992 2:00 -3:00
27/Sep/1992 3:00 -2:00
28/Mar/1993 2:00 -3:00
26/Sep/1993 3:00 -2:00
27/Mar/1994 2:00 -3:00
25/Sep/1994 3:00 -2:00
26/Mar/1995 2:00 -3:00
24/Sep/1995 3:00 -2:00
31/Mar/1996 2:00 -3:00
29/Sep/1996 3:00 -2:00
30/Mar/1997 2:00 -3:00
28/Sep/1997 3:00 -2:00
29/Mar/1998 2:00 -3:00
27/Sep/1998 3:00 -2:00
28/Mar/1999 2:00 -3:00
26/Sep/1999 3:00 -2:00
26/Mar/2000 2:00 -3:00
24/Sep/2000 3:00 -2:00
....

Time Table # 37

Before 1/Jan/1880 LMT
Begin Standard 21E00
1/Jan/1880 0:00 -1:24
Begin Standard 23E54
1/Jan/1917 0:00 -1:36
Begin Standard 15E00
10/Oct/1919 0:00 -1:00
Begin Standard 30E00
12/Jul/1920 0:00 -2:00
Begin Standard 15E00
9/Oct/1920 0:00 -1:00
Begin Standard 30E00
3/Aug/1940 0:00 -3:00
Begin Standard 15E00
24/Jun/1941 0:00 -2:00
2/Nov/1942 3:00 -1:00
29/Mar/1943 2:00 -2:00
4/Oct/1943 3:00 -1:00
3/Apr/1944 2:00 -2:00
Begin Standard 30E00
1/Aug/1944 0:00 -3:00
Begin Standard 45E00
1/Jan/1946 0:00 -3:00
1/Apr/1981 0:00 -4:00
1/Oct/1981 0:00 -3:00
1/Apr/1982 0:00 -4:00
1/Oct/1982 0:00 -3:00
1/Apr/1983 0:00 -4:00
1/Oct/1983 0:00 -3:00
1/Apr/1984 0:00 -4:00
30/Sep/1984 3:00 -3:00
31/Mar/1985 2:00 -4:00
29/Sep/1985 3:00 -3:00
30/Mar/1986 2:00 -4:00
28/Sep/1986 3:00 -3:00
29/Mar/1987 2:00 -4:00
27/Sep/1987 3:00 -3:00
27/Mar/1988 2:00 -4:00
25/Sep/1988 3:00 -3:00
26/Mar/1989 2:00 -4:00
24/Sep/1989 3:00 -3:00
25/Mar/1990 2:00 -4:00
30/Sep/1990 3:00 -3:00
Begin Standard 30E00
29/Sep/1991 3:00 -2:00
29/Mar/1992 2:00 -3:00
27/Sep/1992 3:00 -2:00
28/Mar/1993 2:00 -3:00
26/Sep/1993 3:00 -2:00
27/Mar/1994 2:00 -3:00
25/Sep/1994 3:00 -2:00
26/Mar/1995 2:00 -3:00
24/Sep/1995 3:00 -2:00
31/Mar/1996 2:00 -3:00
29/Sep/1996 3:00 -2:00
30/Mar/1997 2:00 -3:00
28/Sep/1997 3:00 -2:00
29/Mar/1998 2:00 -3:00
27/Sep/1998 3:00 -2:00
28/Mar/1999 2:00 -3:00
26/Sep/1999 3:00 -2:00
26/Mar/2000 2:00 -3:00
24/Sep/2000 3:00 -2:00
....

Time Table # 38

Before 1/Apr/1893 LMT
Begin Standard 15E00
1/Apr/1893 0:00 -1:00
30/Apr/1916 23:00 -2:00
1/Oct/1916 1:00 -1:00
16/Apr/1917 2:00 -2:00
17/Sep/1917 3:00 -1:00
15/Apr/1918 2:00 -2:00
16/Sep/1918 3:00 -1:00
1/Apr/1940 2:00 -2:00
2/Nov/1942 3:00 -1:00
29/Mar/1943 2:00 -2:00
4/Oct/1943 3:00 -1:00
3/Apr/1944 2:00 -2:00
4/Oct/1944 2:00 -1:00
Begin Standard 30E00
1/Jan/1945 0:00 -2:00
28/Apr/1945 24:00 -3:00
31/Oct/1945 24:00 -2:00
Begin Standard 45E00
1/Jan/1946 0:00 -3:00
1/Apr/1981 0:00 -4:00
1/Oct/1981 0:00 -3:00
1/Apr/1982 0:00 -4:00
1/Oct/1982 0:00 -3:00
1/Apr/1983 0:00 -4:00
1/Oct/1983 0:00 -3:00
1/Apr/1984 0:00 -4:00
30/Sep/1984 3:00 -3:00
31/Mar/1985 2:00 -4:00
29/Sep/1985 3:00 -3:00
30/Mar/1986 2:00 -4:00
28/Sep/1986 3:00 -3:00
29/Mar/1987 2:00 -4:00
27/Sep/1987 3:00 -3:00
27/Mar/1988 2:00 -4:00
25/Sep/1988 3:00 -3:00
26/Mar/1989 2:00 -4:00
24/Sep/1989 3:00 -3:00
25/Mar/1990 2:00 -4:00
30/Sep/1990 3:00 -3:00
Begin Standard 30E00
29/Sep/1991 3:00 -2:00
29/Mar/1992 2:00 -3:00
27/Sep/1992 3:00 -2:00
28/Mar/1993 2:00 -3:00
26/Sep/1993 3:00 -2:00
27/Mar/1994 2:00 -3:00
25/Sep/1994 3:00 -2:00
26/Mar/1995 2:00 -3:00
24/Sep/1995 3:00 -2:00
31/Mar/1996 2:00 -3:00
29/Sep/1996 3:00 -2:00
30/Mar/1997 2:00 -3:00
28/Sep/1997 3:00 -2:00
29/Mar/1998 2:00 -3:00
27/Sep/1998 3:00 -2:00
28/Mar/1999 2:00 -3:00
26/Sep/1999 3:00 -2:00
26/Mar/2000 2:00 -3:00
24/Sep/2000 3:00 -2:00
....

Time Table # 39

Before 1/Jan/1880 LMT
Begin Standard 37E42
1/Jan/1880 0:00 -2:31
1/Jul/1917 23:00 -3:31
28/Dec/1917 0:00 -2:31
31/May/1918 22:00 -4:31
17/Sep/1918 0:00 -3:31
31/May/1919 23:00 -4:31
Begin Standard 45E00
1/Jul/1919 2:00 -4:00
16/Aug/1919 0:00 -3:00
14/Feb/1921 23:00 -4:00
20/Mar/1921 23:00 -5:00
1/Sep/1921 0:00 -4:00
1/Oct/1921 0:00 -3:00
Begin Standard 30E00
1/Oct/1922 0:00 -2:00
Begin Standard 45E00
21/Jun/1930 0:00 -3:00
1/Apr/1981 0:00 -4:00
1/Oct/1981 0:00 -3:00
1/Apr/1982 0:00 -4:00
1/Oct/1982 0:00 -3:00
1/Apr/1983 0:00 -4:00
1/Oct/1983 0:00 -3:00
1/Apr/1984 0:00 -4:00
30/Sep/1984 3:00 -3:00
31/Mar/1985 2:00 -4:00
29/Sep/1985 3:00 -3:00
30/Mar/1986 2:00 -4:00
28/Sep/1986 3:00 -3:00
29/Mar/1987 2:00 -4:00
27/Sep/1987 3:00 -3:00
27/Mar/1988 2:00 -4:00
25/Sep/1988 3:00 -3:00
26/Mar/1989 2:00 -4:00
24/Sep/1989 3:00 -3:00
25/Mar/1990 2:00 -4:00
30/Sep/1990 3:00 -3:00
Begin Standard 30E00
29/Sep/1991 3:00 -2:00
29/Mar/1992 2:00 -3:00
27/Sep/1992 3:00 -2:00
28/Mar/1993 2:00 -3:00
26/Sep/1993 3:00 -2:00
27/Mar/1994 2:00 -3:00
25/Sep/1994 3:00 -2:00
26/Mar/1995 2:00 -3:00
24/Sep/1995 3:00 -2:00
31/Mar/1996 2:00 -3:00
29/Sep/1996 3:00 -2:00
30/Mar/1997 2:00 -3:00
28/Sep/1997 3:00 -2:00
29/Mar/1998 2:00 -3:00
27/Sep/1998 3:00 -2:00
28/Mar/1999 2:00 -3:00
26/Sep/1999 3:00 -2:00
26/Mar/2000 2:00 -3:00
24/Sep/2000 3:00 -2:00
....

Time Table # 40

Before 1/Jan/1880 LMT
Begin Standard 37E42
1/Jan/1880 0:00 -2:31
1/Jul/1917 23:00 -3:31
28/Dec/1917 0:00 -2:31
31/May/1918 22:00 -4:31
17/Sep/1918 0:00 -3:31
31/May/1919 23:00 -4:31
1/Jul/1919 2:00 -3:31
16/Aug/1919 0:00 -2:31
14/Feb/1921 23:00 -3:31
20/Mar/1921 23:00 -4:31
1/Sep/1921 0:00 -3:31
1/Oct/1921 0:00 -2:31
Begin Standard 30E00
2/May/1924 0:00 -2:00
Begin Standard 45E00
21/Jun/1930 0:00 -3:00
Begin Standard 60E00
1/Mar/1957 0:00 -4:00
Begin Standard 45E00
1/Apr/1981 0:00 -4:00
1/Oct/1981 0:00 -3:00
1/Apr/1982 0:00 -4:00
1/Oct/1982 0:00 -3:00
1/Apr/1983 0:00 -4:00
1/Oct/1983 0:00 -3:00
1/Apr/1984 0:00 -4:00
30/Sep/1984 3:00 -3:00
31/Mar/1985 2:00 -4:00
29/Sep/1985 3:00 -3:00
30/Mar/1986 2:00 -4:00
28/Sep/1986 3:00 -3:00
29/Mar/1987 2:00 -4:00
27/Sep/1987 3:00 -3:00
27/Mar/1988 2:00 -4:00
25/Sep/1988 3:00 -3:00
26/Mar/1989 2:00 -4:00
24/Sep/1989 3:00 -3:00
25/Mar/1990 2:00 -4:00
30/Sep/1990 3:00 -3:00
29/Mar/1992 2:00 -4:00
27/Sep/1992 3:00 -3:00
28/Mar/1993 2:00 -4:00
26/Sep/1993 3:00 -3:00
27/Mar/1994 2:00 -4:00
25/Sep/1994 3:00 -3:00
26/Mar/1995 2:00 -4:00
24/Sep/1995 3:00 -3:00
31/Mar/1996 2:00 -4:00
29/Sep/1996 3:00 -3:00
30/Mar/1997 2:00 -4:00
28/Sep/1997 3:00 -3:00
29/Mar/1998 2:00 -4:00
27/Sep/1998 3:00 -3:00
28/Mar/1999 2:00 -4:00
26/Sep/1999 3:00 -3:00
26/Mar/2000 2:00 -4:00
24/Sep/2000 3:00 -3:00
....

Time Table # 41

Before 1/Jan/1880 LMT
Begin Standard 37E42
1/Jan/1880 0:00 -2:31
1/Jul/1917 23:00 -3:31
28/Dec/1917 0:00 -2:31
31/May/1918 22:00 -4:31
17/Sep/1918 0:00 -3:31
31/May/1919 23:00 -4:31
1/Jul/1919 2:00 -3:31
16/Aug/1919 0:00 -2:31
14/Feb/1921 23:00 -3:31
20/Mar/1921 23:00 -4:31
1/Sep/1921 0:00 -3:31
1/Oct/1921 0:00 -2:31
Begin Standard 45E00
2/May/1924 0:00 -3:00
Begin Standard 60E00
1/Mar/1957 0:00 -4:00
Begin Standard 45E00
1/Apr/1981 0:00 -4:00
1/Oct/1981 0:00 -3:00
1/Apr/1982 0:00 -4:00
1/Oct/1982 0:00 -3:00
1/Apr/1983 0:00 -4:00
1/Oct/1983 0:00 -3:00
1/Apr/1984 0:00 -4:00
30/Sep/1984 3:00 -3:00
31/Mar/1985 2:00 -4:00
29/Sep/1985 3:00 -3:00
30/Mar/1986 2:00 -4:00
28/Sep/1986 3:00 -3:00
29/Mar/1987 2:00 -4:00
27/Sep/1987 3:00 -3:00
27/Mar/1988 2:00 -4:00
25/Sep/1988 3:00 -3:00
26/Mar/1989 2:00 -4:00
24/Sep/1989 3:00 -3:00
25/Mar/1990 2:00 -4:00
30/Sep/1990 3:00 -3:00
29/Mar/1992 2:00 -4:00
27/Sep/1992 3:00 -3:00
28/Mar/1993 2:00 -4:00
26/Sep/1993 3:00 -3:00
27/Mar/1994 2:00 -4:00
25/Sep/1994 3:00 -3:00
26/Mar/1995 2:00 -4:00
24/Sep/1995 3:00 -3:00
31/Mar/1996 2:00 -4:00
29/Sep/1996 3:00 -3:00
30/Mar/1997 2:00 -4:00
28/Sep/1997 3:00 -3:00
29/Mar/1998 2:00 -4:00
27/Sep/1998 3:00 -3:00
28/Mar/1999 2:00 -4:00
26/Sep/1999 3:00 -3:00
26/Mar/2000 2:00 -4:00
24/Sep/2000 3:00 -3:00
....

Time Table # 42

Before 1/Jan/1880 LMT
Begin Standard 37E42
1/Jan/1880 0:00 -2:31
1/Jul/1917 23:00 -3:31
28/Dec/1917 0:00 -2:31
31/May/1918 22:00 -4:31
17/Sep/1918 0:00 -3:31
31/May/1919 23:00 -4:31
1/Jul/1919 2:00 -3:31
16/Aug/1919 0:00 -2:31
14/Feb/1921 23:00 -3:31
20/Mar/1921 23:00 -4:31
1/Sep/1921 0:00 -3:31
1/Oct/1921 0:00 -2:31
Begin Standard 45E00
2/May/1924 0:00 -3:00
Begin Standard 60E00
1/Mar/1957 0:00 -4:00
1/Apr/1981 0:00 -5:00
1/Oct/1981 0:00 -4:00
1/Apr/1982 0:00 -5:00
1/Oct/1982 0:00 -4:00
1/Apr/1983 0:00 -5:00
1/Oct/1983 0:00 -4:00
1/Apr/1984 0:00 -5:00
30/Sep/1984 3:00 -4:00
31/Mar/1985 2:00 -5:00
29/Sep/1985 3:00 -4:00
30/Mar/1986 2:00 -5:00
28/Sep/1986 3:00 -4:00
29/Mar/1987 2:00 -5:00
27/Sep/1987 3:00 -4:00
27/Mar/1988 2:00 -5:00
25/Sep/1988 3:00 -4:00
26/Mar/1989 2:00 -5:00
24/Sep/1989 3:00 -4:00
25/Mar/1990 2:00 -5:00
30/Sep/1990 3:00 -4:00
Begin Standard 45E00
29/Sep/1991 3:00 -3:00
29/Mar/1992 2:00 -4:00
27/Sep/1992 3:00 -3:00
28/Mar/1993 2:00 -4:00
26/Sep/1993 3:00 -3:00
27/Mar/1994 2:00 -4:00
25/Sep/1994 3:00 -3:00
26/Mar/1995 2:00 -4:00
24/Sep/1995 3:00 -3:00
31/Mar/1996 2:00 -4:00
29/Sep/1996 3:00 -3:00
30/Mar/1997 2:00 -4:00
28/Sep/1997 3:00 -3:00
29/Mar/1998 2:00 -4:00
27/Sep/1998 3:00 -3:00
28/Mar/1999 2:00 -4:00
26/Sep/1999 3:00 -3:00
26/Mar/2000 2:00 -4:00
24/Sep/2000 3:00 -3:00
....

Time Table # 43

Before 1/Jan/1880 LMT
Begin Standard 45E00
1/Jan/1880 0:00 -3:00
1/Jul/1917 23:00 -4:00
28/Dec/1917 0:00 -3:00
31/May/1918 22:00 -5:00
17/Sep/1918 0:00 -4:00
31/May/1919 23:00 -5:00
1/Jul/1919 2:00 -4:00
16/Aug/1919 0:00 -3:00
14/Feb/1921 23:00 -4:00
20/Mar/1921 23:00 -5:00
1/Sep/1921 0:00 -4:00
1/Oct/1921 0:00 -3:00
Begin Standard 60E00
1/Mar/1957 0:00 -4:00
Begin Standard 75E00
1/Apr/1981 0:00 -6:00
1/Oct/1981 0:00 -5:00
1/Apr/1982 0:00 -6:00
1/Oct/1982 0:00 -5:00
1/Apr/1983 0:00 -6:00
1/Oct/1983 0:00 -5:00
1/Apr/1984 0:00 -6:00
30/Sep/1984 3:00 -5:00
31/Mar/1985 2:00 -6:00
29/Sep/1985 3:00 -5:00
30/Mar/1986 2:00 -6:00
28/Sep/1986 3:00 -5:00
29/Mar/1987 2:00 -6:00
27/Sep/1987 3:00 -5:00
27/Mar/1988 2:00 -6:00
25/Sep/1988 3:00 -5:00
26/Mar/1989 2:00 -6:00
24/Sep/1989 3:00 -5:00
25/Mar/1990 2:00 -6:00
30/Sep/1990 3:00 -5:00
Begin Standard 60E00
29/Sep/1991 3:00 -4:00
29/Mar/1992 2:00 -5:00
27/Sep/1992 3:00 -4:00
28/Mar/1993 2:00 -5:00
26/Sep/1993 3:00 -4:00
27/Mar/1994 2:00 -5:00
25/Sep/1994 3:00 -4:00
26/Mar/1995 2:00 -5:00
24/Sep/1995 3:00 -4:00
31/Mar/1996 2:00 -5:00
29/Sep/1996 3:00 -4:00
30/Mar/1997 2:00 -5:00
28/Sep/1997 3:00 -4:00
29/Mar/1998 2:00 -5:00
27/Sep/1998 3:00 -4:00
28/Mar/1999 2:00 -5:00
26/Sep/1999 3:00 -4:00
26/Mar/2000 2:00 -5:00
24/Sep/2000 3:00 -4:00
....

Time Table # 44

Before 1/Jan/1880 LMT
Begin Standard 30E31
1/Jan/1880 0:00 -2:02
1/Jul/1917 23:00 -3:02
28/Dec/1917 0:00 -2:02
31/May/1918 22:00 -4:02
17/Sep/1918 0:00 -3:02
31/May/1919 23:00 -4:02
1/Jul/1919 2:00 -3:02
16/Aug/1919 0:00 -2:02
14/Feb/1921 23:00 -3:02
20/Mar/1921 23:00 -4:02
1/Sep/1921 0:00 -3:02
1/Oct/1921 0:00 -2:02
Begin Standard 30E00
2/May/1924 0:00 -2:00
Begin Standard 45E00
21/Jun/1930 0:00 -3:00
1/Apr/1981 0:00 -4:00
1/Oct/1981 0:00 -3:00
1/Apr/1982 0:00 -4:00
1/Oct/1982 0:00 -3:00
1/Apr/1983 0:00 -4:00
1/Oct/1983 0:00 -3:00
1/Apr/1984 0:00 -4:00
30/Sep/1984 3:00 -3:00
31/Mar/1985 2:00 -4:00
29/Sep/1985 3:00 -3:00
30/Mar/1986 2:00 -4:00
28/Sep/1986 3:00 -3:00
29/Mar/1987 2:00 -4:00
27/Sep/1987 3:00 -3:00
27/Mar/1988 2:00 -4:00
25/Sep/1988 3:00 -3:00
26/Mar/1989 2:00 -4:00
24/Sep/1989 3:00 -3:00
25/Mar/1990 2:00 -4:00
Begin Standard 30E00
17/Jul/1990 0:00 -3:00
30/Sep/1990 3:00 -2:00
29/Mar/1992 2:00 -3:00
27/Sep/1992 3:00 -2:00
28/Mar/1993 2:00 -3:00
26/Sep/1993 3:00 -2:00
27/Mar/1994 2:00 -3:00
25/Sep/1994 3:00 -2:00
26/Mar/1995 2:00 -3:00
24/Sep/1995 3:00 -2:00
31/Mar/1996 2:00 -3:00
29/Sep/1996 3:00 -2:00
30/Mar/1997 2:00 -3:00
28/Sep/1997 3:00 -2:00
29/Mar/1998 2:00 -3:00
27/Sep/1998 3:00 -2:00
28/Mar/1999 2:00 -3:00
26/Sep/1999 3:00 -2:00
26/Mar/2000 2:00 -3:00
24/Sep/2000 3:00 -2:00
....

Time Table # 45

Before 1/Jan/1880 LMT
Begin Standard 32E00
1/Jan/1880 0:00 -2:08
1/Jul/1917 23:00 -3:08
28/Dec/1917 0:00 -2:08
31/May/1918 22:00 -4:08
17/Sep/1918 0:00 -3:08
31/May/1919 23:00 -4:08
1/Jul/1919 2:00 -3:08
16/Aug/1919 0:00 -2:08
14/Feb/1921 23:00 -3:08
20/Mar/1921 23:00 -4:08
1/Sep/1921 0:00 -3:08
1/Oct/1921 0:00 -2:08
Begin Standard 30E00
2/May/1924 0:00 -2:00
Begin Standard 45E00
21/Jun/1930 0:00 -3:00
1/Apr/1981 0:00 -4:00
1/Oct/1981 0:00 -3:00
1/Apr/1982 0:00 -4:00
1/Oct/1982 0:00 -3:00
1/Apr/1983 0:00 -4:00
1/Oct/1983 0:00 -3:00
1/Apr/1984 0:00 -4:00
30/Sep/1984 3:00 -3:00
31/Mar/1985 2:00 -4:00
29/Sep/1985 3:00 -3:00
30/Mar/1986 2:00 -4:00
28/Sep/1986 3:00 -3:00
29/Mar/1987 2:00 -4:00
27/Sep/1987 3:00 -3:00
27/Mar/1988 2:00 -4:00
25/Sep/1988 3:00 -3:00
26/Mar/1989 2:00 -4:00
24/Sep/1989 3:00 -3:00
25/Mar/1990 2:00 -4:00
30/Sep/1990 3:00 -3:00
Begin Standard 30E00
29/Sep/1991 3:00 -2:00
29/Mar/1992 2:00 -3:00
27/Sep/1992 3:00 -2:00
28/Mar/1993 2:00 -3:00
26/Sep/1993 3:00 -2:00
27/Mar/1994 2:00 -3:00
25/Sep/1994 3:00 -2:00
26/Mar/1995 2:00 -3:00
24/Sep/1995 3:00 -2:00
31/Mar/1996 2:00 -3:00
29/Sep/1996 3:00 -2:00
30/Mar/1997 2:00 -3:00
28/Sep/1997 3:00 -2:00
29/Mar/1998 2:00 -3:00
27/Sep/1998 3:00 -2:00
28/Mar/1999 2:00 -3:00
26/Sep/1999 3:00 -2:00
26/Mar/2000 2:00 -3:00
24/Sep/2000 3:00 -2:00
....

Time Table # 46

Before 2/May/1924 LMT
Begin Standard 30E00
2/May/1924 0:00 -2:00
Begin Standard 45E00
21/Jun/1930 0:00 -3:00
1/Apr/1981 0:00 -4:00

1/Oct/1981	0:00	-3:00
1/Apr/1982	0:00	-4:00
1/Oct/1982	0:00	-3:00
1/Apr/1983	0:00	-4:00
1/Oct/1983	0:00	-3:00
1/Apr/1984	0:00	-4:00
30/Sep/1984	3:00	-3:00
31/Mar/1985	2:00	-4:00
29/Sep/1985	3:00	-3:00
30/Mar/1986	2:00	-4:00
28/Sep/1986	3:00	-3:00
29/Mar/1987	2:00	-4:00
27/Sep/1987	3:00	-3:00
27/Mar/1988	2:00	-4:00
25/Sep/1988	3:00	-3:00
26/Mar/1989	2:00	-4:00
24/Sep/1989	3:00	-3:00
25/Mar/1990	2:00	-4:00
30/Sep/1990	3:00	-3:00
Begin Standard		30E00
29/Sep/1991	3:00	-2:00
29/Mar/1992	2:00	-3:00
27/Sep/1992	3:00	-2:00
28/Mar/1993	2:00	-3:00
26/Sep/1993	3:00	-2:00
27/Mar/1994	2:00	-3:00
25/Sep/1994	3:00	-2:00
26/Mar/1995	2:00	-3:00
24/Sep/1995	3:00	-2:00
31/Mar/1996	2:00	-3:00
29/Sep/1996	3:00	-2:00
30/Mar/1997	2:00	-3:00
28/Sep/1997	3:00	-2:00
29/Mar/1998	2:00	-3:00
27/Sep/1998	3:00	-2:00
28/Mar/1999	2:00	-3:00
26/Sep/1999	3:00	-2:00
26/Mar/2000	2:00	-3:00
24/Sep/2000	3:00	-2:00

....

Time Table # 47

Before 2/May/1924		LMT
Begin Standard		45E00
2/May/1924	0:00	-3:00
Begin Standard		60E00
1/Mar/1957	0:00	-4:00
Begin Standard		45E00
1/Apr/1981	0:00	-4:00
1/Oct/1981	0:00	-3:00
1/Apr/1982	0:00	-4:00
1/Oct/1982	0:00	-3:00
1/Apr/1983	0:00	-4:00
1/Oct/1983	0:00	-3:00
1/Apr/1984	0:00	-4:00
30/Sep/1984	3:00	-3:00
31/Mar/1985	2:00	-4:00
29/Sep/1985	3:00	-3:00
30/Mar/1986	2:00	-4:00
28/Sep/1986	3:00	-3:00
29/Mar/1987	2:00	-4:00
27/Sep/1987	3:00	-3:00
27/Mar/1988	2:00	-4:00
25/Sep/1988	3:00	-3:00
26/Mar/1989	2:00	-4:00
24/Sep/1989	3:00	-3:00
25/Mar/1990	2:00	-4:00
30/Sep/1990	3:00	-3:00
29/Mar/1992	2:00	-4:00
27/Sep/1992	3:00	-3:00
28/Mar/1993	2:00	-4:00
26/Sep/1993	3:00	-3:00
27/Mar/1994	2:00	-4:00
25/Sep/1994	3:00	-3:00
26/Mar/1995	2:00	-4:00
24/Sep/1995	3:00	-3:00
31/Mar/1996	2:00	-4:00
29/Sep/1996	3:00	-3:00
30/Mar/1997	2:00	-4:00
28/Sep/1997	3:00	-3:00
29/Mar/1998	2:00	-4:00
27/Sep/1998	3:00	-3:00
28/Mar/1999	2:00	-4:00
26/Sep/1999	3:00	-3:00
26/Mar/2000	2:00	-4:00
24/Sep/2000	3:00	-3:00

DIVISIONS

1. Armenian SSR
2. Asian RSFSR
3. Azerbaijan SSR
4. Belorussian SSR
5. Estonian SSR
6. European RSFSR
7. Georgian SSR
8. Kaliningrad area
9. Kazakh SSR
10. Kirghiz SSR
11. Komandorskije Ostrova
12. Kuril Islands
13. Latvian SSR
14. Lithuanian SSR
15. Moldavian SSR
16. Nachicevanskaja ASSR
17. Novaja Zeml'a
18. Novosibirskije Ostrova
19. Ostrov Sachalin
20. Severnaja Zeml'a
21. Tajik SSR (Tadzhik)
22. Turkmen SSR
23. Ukrainian SSR
24. Uzbek SSR

Abagajtuj	2	16	49N35	117E49	-7:51:16
Abaj	2	21	50N27	85E05	-5:40:20
Abaj	9	24	49N38	72E52	-4:51:28
Abakan	2	21	53N43	91E26	-6:05:44
Abakanovo	6	40	59N18	37E39	-2:30:36
Abalak	2	30	58N08	68E36	-4:34:24
Aban	2	21	56N41	96E04	-6:24:16
Abaša	7	33	42N12	42E13	-2:48:52
Abastumani	7	33	41N46	42E50	-2:51:20
Abatskij	2	30	56N18	70E28	-4:41:52
Abaza	2	21	52N39	90E06	-6:00:24
Abdrachmanovo	6	41	54N46	52E30	-3:30:00
Abdulino	6	30	53N42	53E40	-3:34:40
Abdulovo	6	30	54N16	53E27	-3:33:48
Abez'	6	29	66N32	61E42	-4:06:48
Abinsk	6	47	44N52	38E09	-2:32:36
Abja-Paluoja	5	35	58N08	25E21	-1:41:24
Abramcevo	6	39	55N50	37E50	-2:31:20
Abramovka	6	41	51N12	41E01	-2:44:04
Abramovskaja	6	41	65N11	51E43	-3:26:52
Abrau-D'urso	6	47	44N43	37E37	-2:30:28
Abzanovo	6	30	53N50	58E36	-3:54:24
Ačchoj-Martan	6	47	43N11	45E18	-3:01:12
Ačči	24	24	39N57	68E14	-4:32:56
Achalciche	7	33	41N38	42E59	-2:51:56
Achali-Kindgi	7	33	42N48	41E16	-2:45:04
Achalkalaki	7	33	41N25	43E29	-2:53:56
Achangaran	24	24	40N54	69E37	-4:38:28
Achmeta	7	33	42N02	45E13	-3:00:52
Achsu	3	34	40N34	48E24	-3:13:36
Achtuba	6	34	51N37	44E22	-2:57:28
Achtubinsk	6	34	48N17	46E10	-3:04:40
Achty	6	47	41N28	47E43	-3:10:52
Achtyrka	23	45	50N19	34E55	-2:19:40
Achtyrskij	6	47	44N52	38E20	-2:33:20
Ači	10	24	41N17	73E02	-4:52:08
Acikak	2	20	54N11	106E18	-7:05:12
Ačikulak	6	47	44N34	44E50	-2:59:20
Ačimovy Vtoryje	2	25	60N04	75E12	-5:00:48
Ačinsk	2	21	56N17	90E30	-6:02:00
Ačisaj	9	24	43N35	68E53	-4:35:32
Ačisu	6	47	42N38	47E40	-3:10:40
Ačit	2	30	56N48	57E54	-3:51:36
Ačujevo	6	47	45N43	37E45	-2:31:00
Acvež	6	42	58N21	47E46	-3:11:04
Adak	6	29	66N30	59E38	-3:58:32
Adamovka	6	30	51N32	59E56	-3:59:44
Adamovskoje	6	39	54N52	35E57	-2:23:48
Adaševo	6	41	53N56	44E19	-2:57:16
Adigeni	7	33	41N42	42E42	-2:50:48
Adimi	2	11	47N20	138E56	-9:15:44
Adler	6	47	43N27	39E55	-2:39:40
Adrasman	21	24	40N38	69E58	-4:39:52
Adrianovka	2	16	51N34	114E30	-7:38:00
Adujevo	6	39	54N59	35E59	-2:23:56
Adutiškis	14	37	55N09	26E36	-1:46:24
Adyge	6	47	44N19	41E57	-2:47:48
Adyk	6	47	45N48	45E38	-3:02:32
Adžikend	3	34	40N31	46E21	-3:05:24
Adžima	2	11	48N08	139E40	-9:18:40
Adz'vavom	6	29	66N36	59E12	-3:56:48
Aegviidu	5	35	59N17	25E37	-1:42:28
Aeroflotskij	23	45	45N03	34E01	-2:16:04
Afanasjevka	6	40	50N47	38E36	-2:34:24
Afanasjevo	6	39	54N20	37E01	-2:28:04
Afanasjevo	6	39	55N18	36E12	-2:24:48
Afanasjevskoje	2	30	56N49	58E17	-3:53:08
Afipskij	6	47	44N55	38E50	-2:35:20
Afonicha	6	29	68N13	53E17	-3:33:08
Afrikanda	6	9	67N25	32E43	-2:10:52
Aga	2	16	51N12	115E10	-7:40:40
Agačag	9	24	44N03	71E58	-4:47:52
Agadyr'	9	24	48N17	72E53	-4:51:32
Agafonovka	6	34	50N36	47E26	-3:09:44
Agapa	2	21	71N27	89E15	-5:57:00
Agapovka	2	30	53N18	59E28	-3:57:52
Agara	7	33	42N03	43E49	-2:55:16
Agdam	3	34	39N59	46E57	-3:07:48
Agdaš	3	34	40N38	47E28	-3:09:52
Agdžabedi	3	34	40N03	47E28	-3:09:52
Agejevo	6	39	54N10	36E29	-2:25:56
Aginskoje	2	21	55N15	94E55	-6:19:40
Aginskoje	2	16	51N06	114E32	-7:38:08
Agnije-Afanasjevskij	2	11	51N57	138E45	-9:15:00
Agrafenovka	6	40	47N45	39E29	-2:37:56
Agraf'novka	6	40	47N45	39E29	-2:37:56
Agryz	6	41	56N33	53E00	-3:32:00
Agvali	6	47	42N33	46E06	-3:04:24
Aim	2	11	58N50	134E12	-8:56:48
Ainaži	13	36	57N52	24E21	-1:37:24
Aizpute	13	36	56N43	21E38	-1:26:32
Ajaguz	9	24	47N56	80E23	-5:21:32
Ajan	2	11	56N27	138E10	-9:12:40
Ajan	2	20	54N43	110E55	-7:23:40
Ajbas	9	32	47N51	49E37	-3:18:28
Ajdabul'	9	24	52N42	68E59	-4:35:56
Ajdar	6	40	50N03	38E56	-2:35:44
Ajdarly	9	30	44N32	65E50	-4:23:20
Ajdar-Nikolajevka	23	45	48N58	38E58	-2:35:52
Ajdyrlinskij	6	30	52N03	59E50	-3:59:20
Ajkino	6	41	62N15	49E56	-3:19:44
Ajni	21	24	39N23	68E32	-4:34:08
Ajrum	1	34	41N13	44E53	-2:59:32
Ajryk	9	24	50N30	76E48	-5:07:12
Ajsary	9	24	53N18	71E52	-4:47:28
Ajutinskij	6	40	47N46	40E08	-2:40:32
Akatjevo	6	39	54N59	38E45	-2:35:00
Akatova	6	39	55N09	31E48	-2:07:12
Akbajtal	21	24	38N32	73E49	-4:55:16
Akbeit	9	24	51N38	70E02	-4:40:08
Akbulak	6	30	51N01	55E37	-3:42:28
Akbulak	9	24	49N26	80E28	-5:21:52
Akčatau	9	24	47N59	74E02	-4:56:08
Akči	9	24	44N00	76E20	-5:05:20
Akdala	9	24	45N02	74E35	-4:58:20
Ak-Dovurak	2	21	51N16	90E31	-6:02:04
Akespe	9	30	46N48	60E31	-4:02:04
Akima	2	16	53N06	115E44	-7:42:56
Akimovka	23	45	46N42	35E09	-2:20:36
Akjar	6	30	51N50	58E14	-3:52:56
Akkala	24	30	43N43	59E31	-3:58:04
Akkani	2	2	65N30	171w10	11:24:40
Akkerman → Belgorod-Dnestrovskij	23	45	46N12	30E20	-2:01:20
Akkermanovka	6	30	51N14	58E15	-3:53:00
Akkol'	9	24	45N02	75E40	-5:02:40
Akkol'	9	24	43N25	70E47	-4:43:08
Akkol'skij	9	24	52N12	75E05	-5:00:20
Ak-Kul'	10	24	41N41	74E16	-4:57:04
Akmolinsk	9	24	51N10	71E30	-4:46:00
Akmuz	10	24	41N16	76E09	-5:04:36
Aknīste	13	36	56N10	25E45	-1:43:00
Akoba	9	32	49N28	47E25	-3:09:40
Akša	2	16	50N16	113E17	-7:33:08
Aksaj	9	30	51N09	53E00	-3:32:00
Aksaj	6	40	47N15	39E52	-2:39:28
Aksaj	9	24	43N22	70E12	-4:40:48
Aksakovo	6	30	54N02	54E09	-3:36:36
Aksarka	2	28	66N36	67E46	-4:31:04
Aksatau	9	30	49N23	54E36	-3:38:24
Aksenkino	6	32	53N59	53E06	-3:32:24
Aksenovo	6	39	55N40	38E15	-2:33:00
Aksentjevo	6	39	55N25	35E54	-2:23:36
Akšij	9	30	47N37	55E56	-3:43:44
Aksinjino	6	39	55N44	36E59	-2:27:56
Aksinjino	6	39	56N02	38E12	-2:32:48
Aks'onovo	2	19	58N51	101E43	-6:46:52
Aks'onovo-Zilovskoje	2	16	53N04	117E32	-7:50:08
Akstafa	3	34	41N08	45E28	-3:01:52
Aksu	9	24	52N28	71E59	-4:47:56
Aksu	9	24	45N37	79E30	-5:18:00
Aksu	9	30	50N56	53E06	-3:32:24
Aksuat	9	24	51N32	64E34	-4:18:16
Aksuat	9	24	47N45	82E40	-5:30:40
Aksuat	9	24	48N16	83E50	-5:35:20
Aksubajevo	6	41	54N52	50E50	-3:23:20
Aktal	10	24	41N25	75E03	-5:00:12
Aktanyš	6	30	55N43	54E05	-3:36:20
Aktaš	2	21	50N18	87E44	-5:50:56
Aktas	9	31	48N02	66E21	-4:25:24
Aktas	9	24	49N47	72E59	-4:51:56
Aktas	9	24	42N57	70E04	-4:40:16
Aktasty	9	30	50N44	61E43	-4:06:52
Aktau	9	24	50N16	73E02	-4:52:08
Akterek	9	24	43N22	75E18	-5:01:12
Akterek	10	24	42N14	77E45	-5:11:00
Aktobe	9	24	43N13	67E46	-4:31:04
Aktogaj	9	24	44N27	76E42	-5:06:48
Aktogaj	9	24	48N18	74E58	-4:59:52
Aktogaj	9	24	46N57	79E40	-5:18:40
Aktubek	9	24	48N37	71E06	-4:44:24
Akt'ubinsk	9	30	50N17	57E10	-3:48:40
Akt'ubinskij	6	41	54N49	52E47	-3:31:08
Aktumsyk	9	30	46N40	57E19	-3:49:16
Akt'uz	10	24	42N54	76E07	-5:04:28
Akuliči Pervyje	6	39	53N11	33E13	-2:12:52
Akulovo	6	39	55N31	36E42	-2:26:48
Akulovo	6	39	56N05	38E59	-2:35:56
Akuša	6	47	42N17	47E21	-3:09:24
Akuticha	2	21	52N27	84E29	-5:37:56
Akyr-T'ube	9	24	42N59	72E07	-4:48:28
Akžal	9	24	47N47	74E02	-4:56:08
Akžal	9	24	49N13	81E25	-5:25:40
Akžar	9	24	47N35	83E42	-5:34:48
Akžar	9	24	43N08	71E38	-4:46:32
Akžaryk	9	24	48N34	75E30	-5:02:00
Alabino	6	39	55N31	37E01	-2:28:04
Ala-Buka	10	24	41N23	71E30	-4:46:00
Alachadzy	7	33	43N14	40E18	-2:41:12
Aladino	6	39	54N49	38E12	-2:32:48
Aladjino	6	39	56N21	37E04	-2:28:16
Alagir	6	47	43N03	44E14	-2:56:56
Alajku	10	24	40N18	74E25	-4:57:40
Alajõe	5	35	59N01	27E26	-1:49:44
Alak'ul'a	6	9	59N44	29E56	-1:59:44
Alakurtti	6	9	66N57	30E18	-2:01:12
Alamedin	10	24	42N54	74E37	-4:58:28
Alapajevsk	2	30	57N52	61E42	-4:06:48
Alat	24	30	39N26	63E48	-4:15:12
Al'at	3	34	39N57	49E25	-3:17:40
Alatyr'	6	41	54N51	46E36	-3:06:24
Alaverdi	1	34	41N08	44E39	-2:58:36
Albazino	2	16	53N23	124E05	-8:16:20
Al'bertin	4	39	53N05	25E23	-1:41:32
Aldan	2	16	58N37	125E24	-8:21:36
Alechovščina	6	9	60N25	33E52	-2:15:28
Alejsk	2	21	52N28	82E45	-5:31:00
Aleksandrija	23	45	48N40	33E07	-2:12:28
Aleksandrijskaja	6	47	43N54	47E08	-3:08:32
Aleksandrinka	23	45	47N47	37E41	-2:30:44
Aleksandro-Kalinovo	23	45	48N25	37E40	-2:30:40
Aleksandro-Nevskaja	6	47	43N55	46E35	-3:06:20
Aleksandro-Nevskij	6	41	53N28	40E13	-2:40:52
Aleksandropol'	23	45	49N42	38E50	-2:35:20
Aleksandrov	6	39	56N24	38E43	-2:34:52
Aleksandrov Gaj	6	34	50N09	48E34	-3:14:16
Aleksandrovka	6	34	52N36	50E37	-3:22:28
Aleksandrovka	6	47	46N47	39E01	-2:36:04
Aleksandrovka	23	45	48N43	36E55	-2:27:40
Aleksandrovka	23	45	48N57	32E14	-2:08:56

Aleksandrovka 23
45 47N42 31E16 -2:05:04
Aleksandrovka 23
45 46N32 35E29 -2:21:56
Aleksandrovka 23
45 47N55 37E35 -2:30:20
Aleksandrovka 23
45 48N05 37E27 -2:29:48
Aleksandrovka 6
40 47N26 39E13 -2:36:52
Aleksandrovka 2
21 56N32 90E47 -6:03:08
Aleksandrovka 9
24 53N07 69E50 -4:39:20
Aleksandrovka 9
30 50N47 52E59 -3:31:56
Aleksandrovka 9
24 43N27 77E20 -5:09:20
Aleksandrovsk 23
45 48N35 39E12 -2:36:48
Aleksandrovskaja 6
9 60N03 29E59 -1:59:56
Aleksandrovskaja 6
9 59N44 30E21 -2:01:24
Aleksandrovskij 6
39 51N03 36E44 -2:26:56
Aleksandrovskij Šl'uz 2
21 59N26 89E20 -5:57:20
Aleksandrovskij Zavod 2
16 50N55 117E57 -7:51:48
Aleksandrovskoje 2
21 56N44 85E23 -5:41:32
Aleksandrovskoje 2
25 60N26 77E50 -5:11:20
Aleksandrovskoje 6
47 44N42 43E00 -2:52:00
Aleksandrovsk-Sachalinskij 19
8 50N54 142E10 -9:28:40
Aleksaškino 6 34 50N57 47E42 -3:10:48
Aleksejevka 6 34 52N35 51E17 -3:25:08
Aleksejevka 6 34 53N15 50E30 -3:22:00
Aleksejevka 6 41 53N02 42E46 -2:51:04
Aleksejevka 6 34 51N49 43E56 -2:55:44
Aleksejevka 6 34 52N18 48E01 -3:12:04
Aleksejevka 6 40 50N37 38E42 -2:34:48
Aleksejevka 23
45 47N14 36E32 -2:26:08
Aleksejevka 6 39 54N41 36E34 -2:26:16
Aleksejevka 6 40 47N38 38E49 -2:35:16
Aleksejevka 6 40 47N41 39E54 -2:39:36
Aleksejevka 23
45 49N25 38E46 -2:35:04
Aleksejevka 23
45 49N01 39E11 -2:36:44
Aleksejevka 2 23 52N30 79E33 -5:18:12
Aleksejevka 2 23 54N31 81E08 -5:24:32
Aleksejevka 2 24 55N22 72E03 -4:48:12
Aleksejevka 9 24 53N31 69E30 -4:38:00
Aleksejevka 9 24 51N59 70E59 -4:43:56
Aleksejevka 9 24 47N16 81E34 -5:26:16
Aleksejevka 9 24 48N25 85E40 -5:42:40
Aleksejevka 9 30 50N58 52E25 -3:29:40
Aleksejevo-Družkovka 23
45 48N34 37E36 -2:30:24
Aleksejevo-Lozovskoje 6
47 49N24 40E39 -2:42:36
Aleksejevo-Tuzlovka 6
40 47N50 39E24 -2:37:36
Aleksejevsk 2 20 57N50 108E23 -7:13:32
Aleksejevskaja 6
34 50N17 42E11 -2:48:44
Aleksejevskoje 6
41 55N18 50E06 -3:20:24
Aleksin 6 39 54N31 37E05 -2:28:20
Alešino 6 39 56N09 37E45 -2:31:00
Alešino 6 39 55N04 36E05 -2:24:20
Alešk1 6 41 51N38 41E46 -2:47:04
Aleškovo 6 39 54N53 36E23 -2:25:32
Alga 9 30 49N46 57E20 -3:49:20
Algabas 9 24 44N41 78E06 -5:12:24
Algabas 9 24 48N21 81E39 -5:26:36
Algabas 9 30 50N39 52E07 -3:28:28
Algači 2 16 50N43 117E47 -7:51:08
Algasovo 6 41 53N41 41E40 -2:46:40
Aliabad 3 34 41N29 46E37 -3:06:28
Ali-Bajramly 3
34 39N56 48E56 -3:15:44
Alibejli 3 34 41N23 46E49 -3:07:16
Alikovo 6 41 55N45 46E45 -3:07:00
Alimkent 24 24 40N58 69E11 -4:36:44
Allach-Jun' 2 11 61N08 138E03 -9:12:12
Alma-Ata 9 24 43N15 76E57 -5:07:48
Almalyk 24 24 40N50 69E35 -4:38:20
Almazar 24 24 40N59 68E54 -4:35:36
Almaznij 6 47 48N02 40E03 -2:40:12
Almaznyj 6 47 48N02 40E03 -2:40:12
Almazovo 6 39 55N51 38E02 -2:32:08
Al'menevo 2 30 54N57 63E34 -4:14:16
Al'metjevsk 6 41 54N53 52E20 -3:29:20
Al'mež 6 42 60N03 48E03 -3:12:12
Al'n'aš 6 30 56N44 54E43 -3:38:52
Alnaši 6 42 56N11 52E28 -3:29:52
Aloja 13 36 57N46 24E53 -1:39:32
Al'oškino 2 19 58N35 100E32 -6:42:08
Al'ošn'a 6 39 53N38 33E29 -2:13:56
Al'ošn'a 6 39 54N14 37E16 -2:29:04
Alovo 6 41 54N38 46E27 -3:05:48
Alsunga 13 36 56N59 21E34 -1:26:16
Altaj 2 21 53N27 91E48 -6:07:12
Altajskij 2 21 51N58 85E22 -5:41:28
Altan 2 18 49N31 111E32 -7:26:08
Altan 2 18 49N53 109E04 -7:16:16
Altata 6 34 51N07 48E44 -3:14:56
Altay 2 30 60N20 68E58 -4:35:52
Altuchovo 6 39 52N40 34E20 -2:17:20
Altyagač 3 34 40N50 48E54 -3:15:36
Altyaryk 24 24 40N23 71E30 -4:46:00
Altykarasu 9 30 49N12 55E52 -3:43:28
Altynaj 2 30 57N04 62E00 -4:08:00
Altynkul' 24 24 40N48 72E10 -4:48:40
Altynovka 23 44 51N27 33E10 -2:12:40
Altyntau 9 24 44N08 68E03 -4:32:12
Altyn-Topkan 21
24 40N38 69E35 -4:38:20
Alūksne 13 36 57N25 27E03 -1:48:12
Alunitdag 3 34 40N32 46E03 -3:04:12
Alupka 23 45 44N26 34E03 -2:16:12
Alušta 23 45 44N42 34E24 -2:17:36
Alygdžer 2 20 53N38 98E16 -6:33:04
Alypsatar 9 24 48N03 80E21 -5:21:24
Alytus 14 37 54N24 24E03 -1:36:12
Alzamaj 2 20 55N33 98E39 -6:34:36
Amangel'dy 9 31 50N10 65E13 -4:20:52
Amangel'dy 9 30 49N52 59E00 -3:56:00
Amangel'dy 9 24 43N43 71E07 -4:44:28
Amanotkel' 9 30 46N07 61E34 -4:06:16
Amantogaj 9 31 50N22 65E33 -4:22:12
Amasija 1 34 40N58 43E46 -2:55:04
Amazar 2 16 53N54 120E53 -8:03:32
Ambarčik 2 6 69N39 162E20-10:49:20
Ambarčik 2 21 55N09 95E46 -6:23:04
Ambarnyj 6 9 65N56 33E43 -2:14:52
Ambla 5 35 59N11 25E51 -1:43:24
Ambrolauri 7 33 42N31 43E09 -2:52:36
Amderma 6 29 69N45 61E39 -4:06:36
Amerevo 6 39 55N55 38E03 -2:32:12
Amga 2 16 60N53 132E00 -8:48:00
Amguema 2 2 66N58 179W16 11:57:04
Ammagan 24 30 38N56 67E15 -4:29:00
Amu-Darja 22 30 37N53 65E15 -4:21:00
Amursk 2 11 50N13 136E52 -9:07:28
Amvrosijevka 23
45 47N47 38E29 -2:33:56
Amz'a 6 30 56N13 54E23 -3:37:32
Anadyr' 2 2 64N45 177E29-11:49:56
Anaklia 7 33 42N24 41E34 -2:46:16
Ananjev 23 45 47N40 29E55 -1:59:40
Ananjevo 10 24 42N45 77E40 -5:10:40
Anapa 6 47 44N53 37E19 -2:29:16
Anar 9 24 50N38 72E27 -4:49:48
Anarchaj 9 24 44N02 75E15 -5:01:00
Anaš 2 21 54N52 91E00 -6:04:00
Anastasijevka 6
40 47N34 38E31 -2:34:04
Anastasijevskaja 6
47 45N13 37E53 -2:31:32
Anatoljevka 23
45 46N48 31E13 -2:04:52
Anciferovo 6 9 58N58 34E01 -2:16:04
Anciferovo 6 39 55N33 38E49 -2:35:16
Andižan 24 24 40N45 72E22 -4:49:28
Andomskij Pogost 6
40 61N14 36E36 -2:26:24
Andreapol' 6 39 56N39 32E15 -2:09:00
Andrejevka 6 30 55N42 54E23 -3:37:32
Andrejevka 6 32 52N19 51E55 -3:27:40
Andrejevka 23 45 49N32 36E38 -2:26:32
Andrejevka 23 45 47N06 36E35 -2:26:20
Andrejevka 6 39 55N07 38E37 -2:34:28
Andrejevka 6 39 55N59 37E08 -2:28:32
Andrejevka 23 45 47N28 37E39 -2:30:36
Andrejevka 23 45 48N49 37E33 -2:30:12
Andrejevka 9 24 52N59 67E23 -4:29:32
Andrejevka 9 24 45N50 80E35 -5:22:20
Andrejevo 6 40 55N56 41E08 -2:44:32
Andrejevo-Ivanovka 23
45 47N28 30E28 -2:01:52
Andrejevsk 2 17 58N06 114E08 -7:36:32
Andrejevskaja 6
47 47N21 43E02 -2:52:08
Andrejevskoje 6
39 54N23 36E12 -2:24:48
Andrejevskoje 6
39 56N24 39E01 -2:36:04
Andrejevskoje 6
39 55N46 36E35 -2:26:20
Andrejkoviči 6
39 52N25 33E00 -2:12:00
Andronovskoje 6
9 60N39 34E46 -2:19:04
Androsovka 6 34 52N41 49E35 -3:18:20
Andrupene 13 36 56N11 27E23 -1:49:32
Andr'ušino 2 30 59N12 62E59 -4:11:56
Andrušovka 23 44 50N01 29E01 -1:56:04
Andžijevskij 6
47 44N14 43E05 -2:52:20
Anga 2 20 53N58 106E12 -7:04:48
Angarsk 2 20 52N34 103E54 -6:55:36
Angaul 2 20 53N49 100E18 -6:41:12
Angren 24 24 41N01 70E12 -4:40:48
Anichovo 6 30 51N29 60E15 -4:01:00
Anikino 2 24 56N32 73E56 -4:55:44
Anikino 2 16 53N26 120E20 -8:01:20
Anikovo 6 41 59N23 43E45 -2:55:00
Aniskino 6 39 55N54 38E06 -2:32:24
Aniva 19 8 46N43 142E32 -9:30:08
Anjudin 6 29 62N33 58E12 -3:52:48
Ankata 9 32 50N44 51E34 -3:26:16
An'kovo 6 40 56N57 39E57 -2:39:48
Anna 6 41 51N29 40E25 -2:41:40
Annenskij Most 6
40 60N45 37E10 -2:28:40
Annenskoje 2 30 53N08 60E26 -4:01:44
Annino 6 9 59N46 30E03 -2:00:12
Anninskije Mineral'nyje Vody 2
11 52N44 140E12 -9:20:48
Anno-Rebrikovo 6
47 49N36 40E12 -2:40:48
Anopino 6 40 55N42 40E40 -2:42:40
Anpilogovo 6 39 51N47 36E01 -2:24:04
Antaliepté 14 37 55N40 25E51 -1:43:24
Antalovcy 23 44 48N38 22E31 -1:30:04
Antipino 6 39 55N55 33E16 -2:13:04
Antipino 2 30 57N49 66E34 -4:26:16
Antipovka 6 34 49N50 45E20 -3:01:20
Antoniny 23 44 49N49 26E52 -1:47:28
Antonov 23 44 49N37 29E47 -1:59:08
Antonovka 6 41 54N55 49E30 -3:18:00
Antonovka 9 24 53N19 68E26 -4:33:44
Antonovka 9 24 45N38 80E15 -5:21:00
Antonovo 9 32 49N23 51E47 -3:27:08
Antopol' 4 39 52N12 24E47 -1:39:08
Antracit 23 45 48N06 39E06 -2:36:24
Antratsit → Antracit 23
45 48N06 39E06 -2:36:24
Antropovo 6 41 58N26 43E00 -2:52:00
Antropovo 6 39 55N15 37E39 -2:30:36
Antsla 5 35 57N50 26E32 -1:46:08
Antun' 2 11 47N36 135E46 -9:03:04
Antuševo 6 41 59N59 42E18 -2:49:12
Antuševo 6 40 59N54 37E40 -2:30:40
Antykan 2 11 54N55 135E12 -9:00:48
Anučino 6 41 52N58 43E52 -2:55:28
Anučino 2 27 43N58 133E02 -8:52:08
An'ujsk 2 6 68N18 161E38-10:46:32
Anykščiai 14 37 55N32 25E06 -1:40:24
Anžero-Sudžensk 2
21 56N07 86E00 -5:44:00
Anzob 21 24 39N10 68E48 -4:35:12
Aparan 1 34 40N36 44E23 -2:57:32
Apastovo 6 41 55N11 48E30 -3:14:00
Apatity 6 9 67N34 33E18 -2:13:12
Ape 13 36 57N32 26E40 -1:46:40
Apostolovo 23 45 47N39 33E44 -2:14:56
Aprelevka 6 39 55N33 37E04 -2:28:16
Aprel'sk 2 17 58N10 114E34 -7:38:16
Aprel'skij 2 16 53N30 126E16 -8:25:04
Apšeronsk 6 47 44N28 39E44 -2:38:56
Arab-Jengidža 16
34 39N29 44E58 -2:59:52
Aral 10 24 42N32 72E40 -4:50:40
Aral 10 24 41N50 73E03 -4:52:12
Araldy 9 30 44N18 50E24 -3:21:36
Aral'sk 9 30 46N48 61E40 -4:06:40
Aralsul'fat 9 30 46N50 61E58 -4:07:52
Ararat 1 34 39N50 44E42 -2:58:48
Aravan 10 24 40N32 72E30 -4:50:00
Arbagar 2 16 51N56 116E15 -7:45:00
Arbaž 6 42 57N41 48E18 -3:13:12
Arbuzinka 23 45 47N53 31E19 -2:05:16
Arbuzovo 6 39 56N21 32E27 -2:09:48
Archangel → Archangel'sk 6
41 64N34 40E32 -2:42:08
Archangel'sk 6
41 64N34 40E32 -2:42:08
Archangel'skaja 6
47 45N41 40E15 -2:41:00
Archangel'skoje 6
47 44N37 44E05 -2:56:20
Archangel'skoje 6
41 55N13 44E05 -2:56:20
Archangel'skoje 6
42 54N26 48E40 -3:14:40
Archangel'skoje 6
41 51N27 40E55 -2:43:40
Archangel'skoje 6
39 53N16 37E42 -2:30:48
Archangel'skoje 6
39 55N19 35E58 -2:23:52
Archangel'skoje 6
39 55N47 37E18 -2:29:12
Archara 2 14 49N27 130E07 -8:40:28
Archipelag Nordenšel'da 2
21 76N45 96E00 -6:24:00
Archipelag Nordenšel'da Islands 2
21 76N45 96E00 -6:24:00
Archipo-Osipovka 6
47 44N22 38E33 -2:34:12
Archipovka 6 40 56N38 41E14 -2:44:56
Archipovo 6 41 66N26 45E52 -3:03:28
Archonskaja 6 47 43N07 44E30 -2:58:00
Arciz 23 45 46N00 29E26 -1:57:44
Ardatov 6 41 55N15 43E06 -2:52:24
Ardatov 6 41 54N51 46E13 -3:04:52
Ardon 6 47 43N12 44E18 -2:57:12
Arefjevo 2 21 57N01 90E40 -6:02:40
Argada 2 20 54N14 110E41 -7:22:44
Argajaš 2 30 55N29 60E52 -4:03:28
Argun 6 47 43N16 45E52 -3:03:28
Argut 9 24 49N51 87E03 -5:48:12
Ariadnoje 2 27 45N08 134E25 -8:57:40
Ariogala 14 37 55N16 23E30 -1:34:00
Aristovo 6 39 54N37 36E40 -2:26:40
Arja 6 41 57N30 46E00 -3:04:00
Arka 2 11 60N03 142E12 -9:28:48
Arkadak 6 34 51N58 43E28 -2:53:52
Arkalyk 9 31 50N13 66E50 -4:27:20
Arkhangel'sk → Archangel'sk 6
41 64N34 40E32 -2:42:08
Arkit 10 24 41N47 71E58 -4:47:52
Arktičeskogo Instituta Island 2
25 75N20 81E55 -5:27:40
Arktičeskogo Instituta, Ostrova 2
25 75N20 81E55 -5:27:40
Arktičeskogo Island 2
25 75N20 81E55 -5:27:40
Arktičeskogo, Ostrova 2
25 75N20 81E55 -5:27:40
Arkul' 6 42 57N17 50E03 -3:20:12
Arlan 6 30 55N58 54E15 -3:37:00
Arl'uk 2 21 55N26 84E50 -5:39:20
Arm'ansk 23 45 46N07 33E41 -2:14:44
Armavir 6 47 45N00 41E08 -2:44:32
Armizonskoje 2
30 55N57 67E42 -4:30:48

Arnejevo 6 39 54N58 37E35 -2:30:20
Ar'ofino 6 40 58N16 39E15 -2:37:00
Aromaševo 2 30 56N52 68E39 -4:34:36
Arpačin 6 40 47N14 40E11 -2:40:44
Aršan 2 20 51N54 102E27 -6:49:48
Aršan 2 20 53N54 99E54 -6:39:36
Aršan'-Zel'men' 6
47 47N36 44E36 -2:58:24
Arsenjev 2 27 44N10 133E15 -8:53:00
Arsenjevo 6 39 53N44 36E40 -2:26:40
Aršincevo 23 45 45N17 36E25 -2:25:40
Arsk 6 41 56N06 49E54 -3:19:36
Arslanbob 10 24 41N21 72E56 -4:51:44
Artašat 1 34 39N59 44E33 -2:58:12
Artemovsk → Art'omovsk 23
45 48N35 38E00 -2:32:00
Arti 2 30 56N26 58E32 -3:54:08
Artik 1 34 40N37 43E59 -2:55:56
Art'om 2 27 43N22 132E13 -8:48:52
Art'om-Ostrov 3
34 40N28 50E20 -3:21:20
Art'omovka 23 45 48N29 37E23 -2:29:32
Art'omovka 23 45 47N53 38E38 -2:34:32
Art'omovka 23 45 49N46 35E04 -2:20:16
Art'omovo 23 45 48N22 37E53 -2:31:32
Art'omovsk 23 45 48N27 38E42 -2:34:48
Art'omovsk 23 45 48N35 38E00 -2:32:00
Art'omovsk 2 21 54N21 93E26 -6:13:44
Art'omovskij 2
30 57N21 61E54 -4:07:36
Art'omovskij 2
17 58N12 114E45 -7:39:00
Art'omovskij 2
27 43N27 132E22 -8:49:28
Artybaš 2 21 51N48 87E16 -5:49:04
Artyk 2 6 64N12 145E06 -9:40:24
Arys' 9 24 42N26 68E48 -4:35:12
Arzamas 6 41 55N23 43E50 -2:55:20
Arzni 1 34 40N19 44E36 -2:58:24
Aša 2 30 55N00 57E16 -3:49:04
Ašagy-G'ojn'uk 3
34 41N18 47E00 -3:08:00
Ašap 6 30 57N07 56E30 -3:46:00
Asbest 2 30 57N00 61E30 -4:06:00
Aščerino 6 39 55N36 37E46 -2:31:04
Aščhabad 22 30 37N57 58E23 -3:53:32
Asekejevo 6 32 53N36 52E49 -3:31:16
Aseri 5 35 59N27 26E52 -1:47:28
Ashkhabad → Aščhabad 22
30 37N57 58E23 -3:53:32
Asino 2 21 57N00 86E09 -5:44:36
Ašitkovo 6 39 55N26 38E36 -2:34:24
Askanija-Nova 23
45 46N27 33E52 -2:15:28
Askino 6 30 56N05 56E34 -3:46:16
Askiz 2 21 53N08 90E32 -6:02:08
Ašlyk 2 30 57N33 68E40 -4:34:40
Aspindza 7 33 41N36 43E15 -2:53:00
Ašt 21 24 40N41 70E20 -4:41:20
Astachovo 23 45 47N52 39E37 -2:38:28
Astara 3 34 38N28 48E52 -3:15:28
Aštarak 1 34 40N18 44E22 -2:57:28
Astaškovo 6 39 55N32 38E38 -2:34:32
Astrachan' 6 34 46N21 48E03 -3:12:12
Astrachan-Bazar 3
34 39N14 48E31 -3:14:04
Astrachanka 9 24 51N33 69E47 -4:39:08
Astrachanskij 6
34 46N12 47E16 -3:09:04
Astrakhan → Astrachan' 6
34 46N21 48E03 -3:12:12
Asubulak 9 24 49N31 83E03 -5:32:12
Atabaj 9 24 43N30 68E20 -4:33:20
Atagaj 2 20 55N06 99E23 -6:37:32
Ataki 15 46 48N25 27E47 -1:51:08
Atalanka 2 20 54N50 103E05 -6:52:20
Atamanovka 2 16 51N56 113E37 -7:34:28
Atamanovo 2 21 56N24 93E36 -6:14:24
Atary 6 42 57N32 49E18 -3:17:12
At'aševo 6 41 54N36 46E06 -3:04:24
Atasu 9 24 48N42 71E38 -4:46:32
Atbasar 9 24 51N48 68E20 -4:33:20
Atbaši 10 24 41N10 75E48 -5:03:12
Atemar 6 41 54N11 45E24 -3:01:36
Atepcevo 6 39 55N20 36E46 -2:27:04
Atka 2 6 60N50 151E48-10:07:12
Atkarsk 6 34 51N52 45E00 -3:00:00
Atlasovo 19 8 46N01 142E09 -9:28:36
Atmanov Ugol 6
41 53N07 41E23 -2:45:32
Atmis 6 41 53N28 43E57 -2:55:48
Atnis 2 25 58N48 69E38 -4:38:32
At'urjevo 6 41 54N21 43E19 -2:53:16
Auce 13 36 56N28 22E53 -1:31:32
Auezov 9 24 49N46 81E38 -5:26:32
Auly 23 45 48N33 34E28 -2:17:52
Aurachmat 24 24 41N34 70E07 -4:40:28
Avadchara 7 33 43N31 40E39 -2:42:36
Aval' 24 24 40N19 71E50 -4:47:20
Avčala 7 33 41N48 44E48 -2:59:12
Avdejevka 23 45 48N08 37E46 -2:31:04
Avdotjino 23 45 47N55 37E51 -2:31:24
Avgustovka 6 34 52N16 50E44 -3:22:56
Avinurme 5 35 58N59 26E51 -1:47:24
Avranlo 7 33 41N39 43E52 -2:55:28
Aydere 22 30 38N24 56E45 -3:47:00
Azamatovo 6 30 53N18 53E28 -3:33:52
Azanka 2 30 58N02 64E48 -4:19:12
Azanovo 6 41 56N43 48E13 -3:12:52
Azejevo 6 41 54N41 42E02 -2:48:08
Azgir 9 32 47N50 47E54 -3:11:36
Azizbekov 1 34 39N40 45E30 -3:02:00
Aznakajevo 6 41 54N53 53E04 -3:32:16
Azov 6 40 47N07 39E25 -2:37:40
Azovskoje 23 45 45N34 34E34 -2:18:16

Babajevo 6 40 59N23 35E56 -2:23:44
Babajkovka 23 45 49N01 34E32 -2:18:08
Babajurt 6 47 43N36 46E47 -3:07:08
Babanka 23 45 48N43 30E26 -2:01:44
Babenki 6 39 55N21 37E11 -2:28:44
Babenkovo 23 45 49N15 37E21 -2:29:24
Babiči 4 39 52N17 30E00 -2:00:00
Babino 6 9 59N14 31E26 -2:05:44
Babino 6 41 59N50 40E49 -2:43:16
Babino 6 42 57N22 48E45 -3:15:00
Babino 6 39 56N44 34E17 -2:17:08
Babošino 6 39 54N13 37E08 -2:28:32
Babstovo 2 11 48N07 132E27 -8:49:48
Babuškin 2 20 51N41 105E54 -7:03:36
Babynino 6 39 54N23 35E43 -2:22:52
Bacaligo 7 33 42N33 44E57 -2:59:48
Bačalino 2 30 57N46 67E17 -4:29:08
Bacevići 4 39 53N24 29E14 -1:56:56
Bacharden 22 30 38N26 57E25 -3:49:40
Bachardok 22 30 38N46 58E30 -3:54:00
Bachčisaraj 23
45 44N45 33E51 -2:15:24
Bachmač 23 44 51N13 32E46 -2:11:04
Bachmetjevka 6
34 51N06 44E46 -2:59:04
Bachmutovka 23
45 48N52 39E03 -2:36:12
Bachmutovo 6 39 56N22 34E03 -2:16:12
Bacht 24 24 40N43 68E42 -4:34:48
Bachta 2 21 62N28 89E00 -5:56:00
Bachta 2 21 55N45 92E26 -6:09:44
Bachty 2 21 55N45 92E26 -6:09:44
Bachty 9 24 46N39 82E42 -5:30:48
Bačurka 6 29 68N32 56E57 -3:47:48
Bada 2 18 51N23 109E54 -7:19:36
Badam 9 24 42N23 69E15 -4:37:00
Badarma 2 20 57N46 102E36 -6:50:24
Baga-Burul 6 47 46N00 44E36 -2:58:24
Bagajevskij 6 40 47N19 40E23 -2:41:32
Bagan 2 23 54N06 77E40 -5:10:40
Bagana 6 42 54N22 51E25 -3:25:40
Bagara 24 24 40N55 68E26 -4:33:44
Bagdarin 2 20 54N26 113E36 -7:34:24
Bagerovo 23 45 45N23 36E17 -2:25:08
Bagmanl'ar 3 34 40N38 46E18 -3:05:12
Bagrationovsk 8
38 54N23 20E39 -1:22:36
Bagrinovcy 23 44 49N17 27E56 -1:51:44
Baikonur → Bajkonyr 9
31 47N50 66E03 -4:24:12
Bairkum 9 24 42N05 68E11 -4:32:44
Baisogala 14 37 55N38 23E43 -1:34:52
Bajan 3 34 40N34 46E09 -3:04:36
Bajanaul 9 24 50N47 75E42 -5:02:48
Bajandaj 2 20 53N04 105E30 -7:02:00
Bajangol 2 20 50N44 103E27 -6:53:48
Bajan-Gol 2 20 52N49 99E54 -6:39:36
Baj-Chak 2 21 51N13 94E34 -6:18:16
Bajčunas 9 30 47N14 52E55 -3:31:40
Bajčurovo 6 41 51N20 42E41 -2:50:44
Bajdonovo 2 20 54N17 104E38 -6:58:32
Bajer 2 20 55N44 99E30 -6:38:00
Bajevo 2 23 53N17 80E46 -5:23:04
Bajgakum 9 30 44N18 66E28 -4:25:52
Bajganin 9 30 48N43 55E53 -3:43:32
Bajgul 9 32 48N49 49E08 -3:16:32
Bajkadam 9 24 43N44 69E55 -4:39:40
Bajkal 2 20 51N53 104E47 -6:59:08
Bajkalovo 2 30 57N24 63E46 -4:15:04
Bajkalovo 2 30 57N45 67E40 -4:30:40
Bajkal'sk 2 20 51N33 104E05 -6:56:20
Bajkal'skoje 2
20 55N21 109E12 -7:16:48
Bajkit 2 21 61N41 96E25 -6:25:40
Bajkonyr 9 31 47N50 66E03 -4:24:12
Bajkovo 6 41 54N47 44E51 -2:59:24
Bajmak 6 30 52N36 58E19 -3:53:16
Bajnazar 9 24 48N32 73E42 -4:54:48
Bajrački 23 45 48N22 38E32 -2:34:08
Bajr'aki 6 41 54N43 53E24 -3:33:36
Bajram-Ali 22 30 37N37 62E10 -4:08:40
Bajsa 2 20 53N58 113E33 -7:34:12
Bajseit 9 24 43N35 78E20 -5:13:20
Baj-Sot 2 21 51N42 95E22 -6:21:28
Bajsun 24 30 38N14 67E12 -4:28:48
Bajtajlak 9 24 45N15 75E00 -5:00:00
Bajžansaj 9 24 43N13 69E56 -4:39:44
Bakal 2 30 54N56 58E48 -3:55:12
Bakaldy 6 41 55N39 44E44 -2:58:56
Bakaly 6 30 55N10 53E48 -3:35:12
Bakanas 9 24 44N50 76E15 -5:05:00
Bakbakty 9 24 44N35 76E40 -5:06:40
Bakčar 2 23 57N01 82E05 -5:28:20
Bakino 6 39 56N20 38E59 -2:35:56
Bakinskaja 6 47 44N46 39E18 -2:37:12
Baklanka 6 41 58N43 40E06 -2:40:24
Bakluši 6 34 52N07 43E22 -2:53:28
Bakou → Baku 3
34 40N23 49E51 -3:19:24
Bakovka 6 39 55N41 37E20 -2:29:20
Bakruz'ak 6 30 52N59 58E42 -3:54:48
Baksan 6 47 43N40 43E32 -2:54:08
Bakšejevo 6 39 55N44 39E53 -2:39:32
Bakšejevo 2 24 57N26 73E00 -4:52:00
Bakšty 4 39 53N56 26E11 -1:44:44
Baku 3 34 40N23 49E51 -3:19:24
Bakuriani 7 33 41N46 43E32 -2:54:08
Bakury 6 34 52N22 44E42 -2:58:48
Bakyrčik 9 24 49N46 81E38 -5:26:32
Bakyrly 9 24 44N21 67E48 -4:31:12
Balabanovo 6 39 55N11 36E40 -2:26:40
Balabino 23 45 47N44 35E13 -2:20:52
Balachany 3 34 40N29 49E54 -3:19:36
Balachčin 2 21 54N09 89E23 -5:57:32
Balachna 6 41 56N30 43E36 -2:54:24

Balachta 2 21 55N24 91E37 -6:06:28
Balad'ok 2 11 53N41 133E07 -8:52:28
Balagansk 2 20 53N57 103E02 -6:52:08
Balaj 2 21 55N52 93E59 -6:15:56
Balakirevo 6 39 56N30 38E51 -2:35:24
Balaklava 23 45 44N30 33E35 -2:14:20
Balakleja 23 44 49N14 31E44 -2:06:56
Balakleja 23 45 49N27 36E52 -2:27:28
Balakovo 6 34 52N02 47E47 -3:11:08
Balaši 6 34 51N24 49E55 -3:19:40
Balašicha 6 39 55N49 37E58 -2:31:52
Balašov 6 34 51N32 43E08 -2:52:32
Balbieriškis 14
37 54N32 23E52 -1:35:28
Balchaš 9 24 46N49 74E59 -4:59:56
Baldone 13 36 56N45 24E24 -1:37:36
Balej 2 16 51N36 116E38 -7:46:32
Balezino 6 42 57N58 53E00 -3:32:00
Balgazyn 2 21 51N08 95E00 -6:20:00
Balin 23 45 48N52 26E40 -1:46:40
Balkašino 9 24 52N31 68E46 -4:35:04
Balkhash → Balchaš 9
24 46N49 74E59 -4:59:56
Balki 23 45 47N23 34E57 -2:19:48
Balobanovo 6 39 55N51 38E14 -2:32:56
Baloži 13 36 56N53 24E06 -1:36:24
Balta 23 45 47N55 29E37 -1:58:28
Baltaj 6 34 52N28 46E38 -3:06:32
Baltasi 6 41 56N21 50E12 -3:20:48
Bălţi → Bel'cy 15
46 47N46 27E56 -1:51:44
Baltijsk (Pillau) 8
38 54N39 19E55 -1:19:40
Baltoji-Vokė 14
37 54N28 25E06 -1:40:24
Balvi 13 36 57N08 27E17 -1:49:08
Balygyčan 2 6 63N56 154E12-10:16:48
Balykči 24 24 40N54 71E50 -4:47:20
Balyksa 2 21 53N25 89E05 -5:56:20
Balykši 9 32 47N05 51E54 -3:27:36
Bal'zino 2 16 51N03 113E35 -7:34:20
Bambujka 2 20 55N47 115E48 -7:43:12
Bami 22 30 38N44 56E48 -3:47:12
B'andovan 3 34 39N46 49E23 -3:17:32
Bank 3 34 39N25 49E15 -3:17:00
Bannaja 2 20 57N05 108E12 -7:12:48
Bannikovo 2 30 56N07 70E17 -4:41:08
Bannovka 9 30 53N45 62E57 -4:11:48
Bannovskij 23 45 49N02 37E35 -2:30:20
Bar 23 44 49N04 27E40 -1:50:40
Bar 2 20 51N17 107E33 -7:10:12
Barabanovo 6 39 54N43 38E10 -2:32:40
Barabinsk 2 23 55N21 78E21 -5:13:24
Barakkol'skij 9
24 52N12 67E49 -4:31:16
Baran' 4 39 54N30 28E40 -1:54:40
Baran' 4 39 54N29 30E18 -2:01:12
Baranakovo 2 21 58N08 82E58 -5:31:52
Barancevo 6 39 55N04 37E38 -2:30:32
Baraniki 6 47 46N31 41E50 -2:47:20
Baranikovka 23
45 49N10 39E50 -2:39:20
Baranoviči 4 39 53N08 26E02 -1:44:08
Baranovka 23 44 50N18 27E40 -1:50:40
Baranovskoje 6
39 55N25 38E45 -2:35:00
Barany 6 42 57N38 52E16 -3:29:04
Barany 6 39 57N20 29E09 -1:56:36
Baraševo 6 41 54N32 42E53 -2:51:32
Baraši 23 44 50N43 28E01 -1:52:04
Baraški 6 41 65N40 52E10 -3:28:40
Bar'atino 6 39 54N19 34E31 -2:18:04
Bar'atino 6 39 54N43 36E49 -2:27:16
Barbaši 6 39 57N42 28E24 -1:53:36
Barčadiv 21 24 38N19 72E29 -4:49:56
Barchaticha 6 41 57N34 45E13 -3:00:52
Barda 6 30 56N54 55E38 -3:42:32
Barda 3 34 40N23 47E08 -3:08:32
Barguzin 2 20 53N37 109E37 -7:18:28
Barilo-Krepinskaja 6
40 47N45 39E32 -2:38:08
Barisacho 7 33 42N28 44E54 -2:59:36
Barkava 13 36 56N43 26E36 -1:46:24
Barluk 2 20 54N32 101E43 -6:46:52
Barmaševo 23 45 47N07 32E26 -2:09:44
Barnaul 2 21 53N22 83E45 -5:35:00
Baršatas 9 24 48N13 78E21 -5:13:24
Baršin 9 24 49N45 69E36 -4:38:24
Barskaun 10 24 42N10 77E37 -5:10:28
Barsuki 6 39 54N15 37E30 -2:30:00
Barvenkovo 23 45 48N54 37E02 -2:28:08
Barvicha 6 39 55N44 37E16 -2:29:04
Barybino 6 39 55N16 37E54 -2:31:36
Barybino 6 39 54N56 37E47 -2:31:08
Barykino 23 45 49N17 38E24 -2:33:36
Barykovo 6 39 54N38 38E48 -2:35:12
Baryn1no 6 39 55N47 36E21 -2:25:24
Baryš 6 34 53N39 47E08 -3:08:32
Baryševka 23 44 50N22 31E19 -2:05:16
Baryševo 2 21 54N58 83E11 -5:32:44
Baryšniki 6 41 56N57 46E33 -3:06:12
Barzas 2 21 55N43 86E19 -5:45:16
Basakin 6 34 48N11 42E18 -2:49:12
Bašanta 6 47 46N05 41E56 -2:47:44
Basargečar 1 34 40N11 45E43 -3:02:52
Basid 21 24 38N07 72E09 -4:48:36
Basjanovskij 2
30 58N19 60E44 -4:02:56
Baskakovka 6 39 54N36 34E19 -2:17:16
Baškend 3 34 40N38 45E32 -3:02:08
Baškino 6 39 55N18 36E41 -2:26:44
Baskuduk 9 30 49N43 61E32 -4:06:08
Baš-Kugandy 10
24 42N00 74E39 -4:58:36
Bašmakovo 6 41 53N12 43E02 -2:52:08

Baštanka 23 45 47N24 32E25 -2:09:40
Batagaj 2 11 67N38 134E38 -8:58:32
Batagaj-Alyta 2 11 67N48 130E25 -8:41:40
Batagol 2 20 52N22 100E45 -6:43:00
Batajsk 6 40 47N10 39E44 -2:38:56
Bataly 9 30 52N52 62E00 -4:08:00
Batama 2 20 53N53 101E36 -6:46:24
Batamaj 2 14 63N31 129E27 -8:37:48
Batamšinskij 9 30 50N36 58E16 -3:53:04
Bateckij 6 9 58N39 30E19 -2:01:16
Batken 10 24 40N03 70E50 -4:43:20
Batumi 7 33 41N38 41E38 -2:46:32
Baturin 23 44 51N21 32E51 -2:11:24
Baturino 6 39 55N35 37E31 -2:30:04
Baturino 2 21 57N48 85E12 -5:40:48
Baturinskaja 6 47 45N47 39E22 -2:37:28
Batyrevo 6 41 55N04 47E38 -3:10:32
Baunt 2 20 55N16 113E08 -7:32:32
Bauska 13 36 56N24 24E14 -1:36:56
Bautino 9 30 44N33 50E15 -3:21:00
Bavleny 6 39 56N24 39E34 -2:38:16
Bavly 6 41 54N25 53E17 -3:33:08
Bavtugaj 6 47 43N11 46E49 -3:07:16
Baykonur → Bajkonyr 9 31 47N50 66E03 -4:24:12
Bazalija 23 44 49N43 26E27 -1:45:48
Bazar 2 16 53N58 116E05 -7:44:20
Bazarčaj 1 34 39N40 45E48 -3:03:12
Bazar-Kurgan 10 24 41N02 72E45 -4:51:00
Bazarnyje Mataki 6 41 54N56 49E56 -3:19:44
Bazarnyj Karabulak 6 34 52N16 46E25 -3:05:40
Bazarnyj Syzgan 6 34 53N45 46E46 -3:07:04
Bazarovo 6 39 54N47 38E10 -2:32:40
Bazaršolan 9 32 49N04 51E56 -3:27:44
Bazartobe 9 32 49N23 51E50 -3:27:20
Bažigan 6 47 44N33 45E41 -3:02:44
Bazkovskaja 6 47 49N36 41E43 -2:46:52
Bazoj 2 23 55N45 83E22 -5:33:28
Bebelevo 6 39 54N32 36E30 -2:26:00
Bednodemjanovsk 6 41 53N56 43E10 -2:52:40
Bedoba 2 21 58N48 97E12 -6:28:48
Begičevskij 6 39 53N47 38E15 -2:33:00
Begoml' 4 39 54N44 28E04 -1:52:16
Begovat → Bekabad 24 24 40N13 69E14 -4:36:56
Begun' 23 44 51N24 28E17 -1:53:08
Begunici 6 9 59N35 29E19 -1:57:16
Begunicy 6 9 59N35 29E19 -1:57:16
Beja 2 21 53N03 90E54 -6:03:36
Bejneu 9 30 45N15 55E07 -3:40:28
Bejtonovo 2 16 53N14 124E27 -8:17:48
Bekabad 21 24 40N13 69E14 -4:36:56
Bekasovo 6 39 55N26 36E49 -2:27:16
Bek Budi 24 30 38N50 65E48 -4:23:12
Bekdaš 22 30 41N34 52E32 -3:30:08
Beketovo 2 16 53N13 125E01 -8:20:04
Beklemiševo 6 34 53N52 47E25 -3:09:40
Beklemiševo 2 16 52N07 112E40 -7:30:40
Bekovo 6 41 52N28 43E43 -2:54:52
Bektyševo 6 39 56N34 39E14 -2:36:56
Bel'agaš 9 24 50N48 80E44 -5:22:56
Belaja 6 39 51N03 35E43 -2:22:52
Belaja 6 42 57N59 51E42 -3:26:48
Belaja Ber'ozka 6 39 52N23 33E29 -2:13:56
Belaja Cerkov' 23 44 49N49 30E07 -2:00:28
Belaja Cholunica 6 42 58N50 50E48 -3:23:12
Belaja Gora 6 9 58N31 31E45 -2:07:00
Belaja Kalitva 6 47 48N11 40E46 -2:43:04
Belaja Krinica 23 45 47N21 33E10 -2:12:40
Belaja Krinica 23 44 50N38 29E29 -1:57:56
Bel'ajevka 6 30 57N28 55E28 -3:41:52
Bel'ajevka 6 30 51N24 56E26 -3:45:44
Bel'ajevka 23 45 46N29 30E12 -2:00:48
Bel'ajevo 6 39 55N31 31E06 -2:04:24
Bel'aninovo 6 39 55N57 37E39 -2:30:36
Bel'anskij 6 47 47N45 41E33 -2:46:12
Belaya Tserkov'→ Belaja Cerkov' 23 44 49N49 30E07 -2:00:28
Bel'cy 15 46 47N46 27E56 -1:51:44
Bel'd'ažki 6 39 52N39 35E42 -2:22:48
Belebej 6 30 54N07 54E07 -3:36:28
Belebelka 6 39 57N34 30E56 -2:03:44
Belenichino 6 39 50N56 36E37 -2:26:28
Belen'koje 23 45 47N37 35E03 -2:20:12
Belen'koje 23 45 48N46 37E38 -2:30:32
Belgorod 6 39 50N36 36E35 -2:26:20
Belgorod-Dnestrovskij 23 45 46N12 30E20 -2:01:20
Belica 6 39 51N07 35E34 -2:22:16
Beliči 23 44 50N29 30E19 -2:01:16
Belick 4 39 52N55 30E27 -2:01:48
Belickoje 23 45 48N25 37E13 -2:28:52
Beliki 23 45 49N15 34E16 -2:17:04
Belinskij 6 41 52N58 43E26 -2:53:44
Belka 23 44 50N49 28E11 -1:52:44
Bel'kovo 6 39 56N15 38E48 -2:35:12
Bellyk 2 21 54N32 91E17 -6:05:08
Beloglazovo 2 24 56N05 72E40 -4:50:40
Belogorje 6 41 50N30 40E01 -2:40:04
Belogorje 23 44 50N01 26E25 -1:45:40
Belogorka 9 30 50N42 53E27 -3:33:48
Belogornoje 6 34 52N25 47E35 -3:10:20
Belogorode 6 39 54N23 38E31 -2:34:04
Belogorodka 23 44 50N00 26E39 -1:46:36
Belogorovka 23 45 48N55 38E15 -2:33:00
Belogorsk 23 45 45N03 34E36 -2:18:24
Belogorsk 2 21 55N05 88E28 -5:53:52
Belogorsk 2 14 50N57 128E25 -8:33:40
Belogorskij 9 24 49N27 83E10 -5:32:40
Belogorskoje 6 34 53N35 48E12 -3:12:48
Beloguša 4 39 51N57 26E56 -1:47:44
Belojarsk 2 21 53N28 83E54 -5:35:36
Belojarskij 2 30 56N45 61E24 -4:05:36
Beloje 23 45 48N31 39E04 -2:36:16
Beloje 9 24 48N55 82E58 -5:31:52
Beloje 6 40 58N23 39E24 -2:37:36
Beloje 6 39 51N03 35E43 -2:22:52
Belokany 3 34 41N43 46E26 -3:05:44
Belokoroviči 23 44 51N07 28E02 -1:52:08
Belokurakino 23 45 49N33 38E44 -2:34:56
Belokuricha 2 21 51N59 84E59 -5:39:56
Beloluck 23 45 49N41 39E02 -2:36:08
Belomestnaja 6 39 52N24 37E37 -2:30:28
Belomestnaja Dvojn'a 6 41 52N42 41E03 -2:44:12
Belomorsk 6 40 64N32 34E48 -2:19:12
Beloomut 6 39 54N57 39E20 -2:37:20
Beloozersk 4 39 52N28 25E11 -1:40:44
Belopolje 23 45 51N09 34E18 -2:17:12
Belorečensk 6 47 44N46 39E52 -2:39:28
Beloreck 6 30 53N58 58E24 -3:53:36
Beloščelje 6 41 64N52 46E56 -3:07:44
Belousovka 23 44 49N57 32E20 -2:09:20
Belousovka 9 24 50N08 82E33 -5:30:12
Belousovo 6 39 55N05 36E40 -2:26:40
Bel'ov 6 39 53N48 36E08 -2:24:32
Belovo 2 23 52N57 82E16 -5:29:04
Belovo 2 21 54N25 86E18 -5:45:12
Belovodsk 23 45 49N12 39E35 -2:38:20
Belovodskoje 10 24 42N50 74E06 -4:56:24
Beloz'orje 23 44 49N29 31E35 -2:06:20
Beloz'orje 23 44 49N18 31E54 -2:07:36
Beloz'orka 23 45 46N37 32E27 -2:09:48
Beloz'orsk 6 40 60N02 37E48 -2:31:12
Beloz'orskoje 23 45 48N33 37E04 -2:28:16
Bel'skaja Vol'a 23 44 51N27 25E49 -1:43:16
Bel'skoje 2 21 57N49 92E09 -6:08:36
Bel'skoje 6 40 54N44 40E22 -2:41:28
Bel'tsy → Bel'cy 15 46 47N46 27E56 -1:51:44
Bel'tyrskij 2 21 53N02 90E16 -6:01:04
Belugino 6 39 54N47 37E54 -2:31:36
Belušje 6 41 66N54 47E31 -3:10:04
Belyj 6 39 55N50 32E56 -2:11:44
Belyje Berega 6 39 53N12 34E40 -2:18:40
Belyje Kolodezi 6 39 54N55 38E42 -2:34:48
Belyje Stolby 6 39 55N20 37E52 -2:31:28
Belyje Vody 9 24 42N25 69E50 -4:39:20
Belyj Gorodok 6 39 56N58 37E30 -2:30:00
Belyj Jar 6 34 53N57 48E58 -3:15:52
Belyj Jar 2 21 53N36 91E24 -6:05:36
Belyj Jar 2 21 58N26 85E01 -5:40:04
Belyj Kalodez' 6 40 50N02 38E40 -2:34:40
Belyj Kolodez' 23 45 50N12 37E08 -2:28:32
Belyj Rast 6 39 56N08 37E26 -2:29:44
Belyniči 4 39 53N59 29E42 -1:58:48
Belynkoviči 4 39 53N15 32E08 -2:08:32
Belz 23 44 50N23 24E01 -1:36:04
Bemyž 6 42 56N08 51E44 -3:26:56
Ben'akoni 4 39 54N15 25E22 -1:41:28
Bendery 15 46 46N48 29E29 -1:57:56
Bēne 13 36 56N29 23E04 -1:32:16
Berčogur 9 30 48N25 58E44 -3:54:56
Berd 1 34 40N53 45E23 -3:01:32
Berd'ansk 23 45 46N45 36E49 -2:27:16
Berd'auš 2 30 55N09 59E09 -3:56:36
Berdičev 23 44 49N54 28E36 -1:54:24
Berdigest'ach 2 16 62N06 126E40 -8:26:40
Berdniki 6 41 57N25 46E33 -3:06:12
Berdsk 2 21 54N47 83E02 -5:32:08
Berd'užje 2 30 55N48 68E19 -4:33:16
Berdyansk → Berd'ansk 23 45 46N45 36E49 -2:27:16
Bere 22 30 39N47 58E06 -3:52:24
Beregajevo 2 21 57N10 87E32 -5:50:08
Beregomet 23 44 48N12 25E21 -1:41:24
Beregovo 23 44 48N13 22E39 -1:30:36
Beregovoj 2 24 55N12 73E12 -4:52:48
Berendejevo 6 39 56N36 39E01 -2:36:04
Berestečko 23 44 50N23 25E07 -1:40:28
Berezajka 6 39 57N59 33E54 -2:15:36
Berezan' 23 44 50N19 31E30 -2:06:00
Berezanskaja 6 47 45N43 39E34 -2:38:16
Berežany 23 44 49N27 24E56 -1:39:44
Berezdov 23 44 50N27 27E05 -1:48:20
Berezino 4 39 54N54 28E12 -1:52:48
Berezino 9 32 50N06 48E52 -3:15:28
Berezino 23 45 46N14 29E12 -1:56:48
Berezino 4 39 53N49 28E59 -1:55:56
Berezna 23 44 51N34 31E47 -2:07:08
Berezn'agi 6 47 49N59 41E06 -2:44:24
Berezn'aki 23 44 49N09 31E57 -2:07:48
Berezn'aki 23 44 49N51 33E01 -2:12:04
Bereznegovatoje 23 45 47N20 32E49 -2:11:16
Berežnica 23 44 51N27 26E27 -1:45:48
Bereznik 6 41 62N51 42E40 -2:50:40
Berezniki 6 30 59N24 56E46 -3:47:04
Berikul'skij 2 21 55N32 88E08 -5:52:32
Beringa Island 11 4 55N12 166E00-11:04:00
Beringa, Ostrov 11 4 55N12 166E00-11:04:00
Beringovskij 2 2 63N03 179E19-11:57:16
Berislav 23 45 46N51 33E26 -2:13:44
Berkakit 2 16 56N34 124E48 -8:19:12
Berngardovka 6 9 60N01 30E36 -2:02:24
Ber'ostovica 4 39 53N07 23E58 -1:35:52
Ber'oza 23 44 51N44 33E52 -2:15:28
Ber'oza 4 39 52N32 24E59 -1:39:56
Ber'ozno 23 44 51N00 26E45 -1:47:00
Ber'ožnoje 6 40 59N55 39E17 -2:37:08
Ber'ozovaja Rudka 23 44 50N19 32E14 -2:08:56
Ber'ozovka 6 30 57N37 57E18 -3:49:12
Ber'ozovka 6 29 65N00 56E26 -3:45:44
Ber'ozovka 6 34 52N06 45E07 -3:00:28
Ber'ozovka 23 45 47N49 32E28 -2:09:52
Ber'ozovka 23 45 45N35 33E20 -2:13:20
Ber'ozovka 23 45 47N12 30E55 -2:03:40
Ber'ozovka 6 40 53N26 38E53 -2:35:32
Ber'ozovka 4 39 53N43 25E30 -1:42:00
Ber'ozovka 6 9 59N56 30E49 -2:03:16
Ber'ozovka 2 21 51N51 82E58 -5:31:52
Ber'ozovka 2 21 56N03 93E07 -6:12:28
Ber'ozovka 2 23 54N02 76E35 -5:06:20
Ber'ozovka 2 23 59N24 82E38 -5:30:32
Ber'ozovka 2 17 57N46 116E09 -7:44:36
Ber'ozovka 2 15 50N35 127E52 -8:31:28
Ber'ozovka 9 30 51N11 53E16 -3:33:04
Ber'ozovka 6 30 59N35 56E02 -3:44:08
Ber'ozovo 6 39 54N03 36E24 -2:25:36
Ber'ozovo 6 39 54N19 38E17 -2:33:08
Ber'ozovo 2 28 63N56 65E02 -4:20:08
Ber'ozovo 6 34 51N56 48E28 -3:13:52
Ber'ozovo 23 44 51N35 27E20 -1:49:20
Ber'ozovskaja 6 34 50N16 43E59 -2:55:56
Ber'ozovskij 2 21 55N39 86E16 -5:45:04
Ber'ozovskij R'adok 6 9 58N06 34E29 -2:17:56
Ber'ozovskoje 2 21 55N50 89E36 -5:58:24
Beršad' 23 45 48N23 29E30 -1:58:00
Bersut 6 41 55N32 50E54 -3:23:36
Besedino 6 39 51N42 36E28 -2:25:52
Besedy 6 39 55N37 37E47 -2:31:08
Bešenkoviči 4 39 55N03 29E27 -1:57:48
Beškent 24 30 38N49 65E39 -4:22:36
Beškube 24 24 39N50 68E18 -4:33:12
Beslan 6 47 43N12 44E33 -2:58:12
Beslenej 6 47 44N14 41E44 -2:46:56
Besp'atovo 6 39 54N45 38E54 -2:35:36
Bessarabka 23 45 46N20 28E58 -1:55:52
Bessarabka 2 24 53N37 73E17 -4:53:08
Bessonovka 6 41 53N18 45E03 -3:00:12
Best'ach 2 16 61N52 129E55 -8:39:40
Bestamak 9 30 49N43 55E07 -3:40:28
Bestamak 9 24 49N13 78E21 -5:13:24
Bestobe 9 24 52N30 73E05 -4:52:20
Bestuževo 6 41 61N37 43E58 -2:55:52
Betlica 6 39 54N01 33E57 -2:15:48
Bežanicy 6 39 56N58 29E53 -1:59:32
Bezdež 4 39 52N19 25E18 -1:41:12
Bežeck 6 39 57N47 36E39 -2:26:36
Bezenčuk 6 34 52N59 49E26 -3:17:44
Bezmein 22 30 38N05 58E12 -3:52:48
Bezmenšur 6 42 56N29 51E17 -3:25:08
Bežta 6 47 42N08 46E08 -3:04:32
Bezym'anka 6 34 49N56 43E15 -2:53:00
Bezym'annaja 6 34 51N20 46E26 -3:05:44
Bezymennoje 23 45 47N06 37E56 -2:31:44
Bezzubovo 6 39 55N27 38E55 -2:35:40
Biaza 2 23 56N38 78E18 -5:13:12
Bibir'ovo 6 39 54N28 33E08 -2:12:32
Biča 2 24 57N53 70E37 -4:42:28
Bičevinka 6 40 59N44 37E40 -2:30:40
Bičura 2 20 50N36 107E35 -7:10:20
Bičurina 6 30 56N51 55E25 -3:41:40
Bidžan 2 11 47N58 131E58 -8:47:52
Bigosovo 4 39 55N49 27E43 -1:50:52
Bijsk 2 21 52N34 85E15 -5:41:00
Bikbulovo 6 41 55N39 53E26 -3:33:44
Bikin 2 11 46N48 134E16 -8:57:04
Bikl'an' 6 41 55N37 52E10 -3:28:40
Bil'arsk 6 41 54N58 50E22 -3:21:28
Bil'asuvar 3 34 39N24 48E24 -3:13:36
Bil'čir 2 18 51N02 110E34 -7:22:16
Binagadi 3 34 40N28 49E49 -3:19:16
Bira 2 11 49N15 137E16 -9:09:04
Bira 2 11 49N02 132E30 -8:50:00
Birakan 2 11 49N01 131E42 -8:46:48
Birandža 2 11 54N35 136E18 -9:05:12
Birikčul' 2 21 53N20 89E56 -5:59:44
Biril'ussy 2 21 57N07 90E32 -6:02:08
Birlik 9 24 44N05 73E31 -4:54:04
Birlik 9 32 47N28 50E32 -3:22:08
Birmaj 3 34 39N46 47E56 -3:11:44
Birobidžan 2 11 48N08 132E57 -8:51:48

Birofel'd 2 11 48N26 132E47 -8:51:08
Birsk 6 30 55N25 55E32 -3:42:08
Birštonas 14 37 54N37 24E02 -1:36:08
Bir'učij 6 40 46N53 39E33 -2:38:12
Bir'ukovo 23 45 47N57 39E44 -2:38:56
Bir'ul'ka 2 20 53N52 106E21 -7:05:24
Bir'usa 2 21 57N10 96E30 -6:26:00
Bir'usinsk 2 20 55N57 97E49 -6:31:16
Biržai 14 37 56N12 24E45 -1:39:00
Biserovo 6 39 55N47 38E07 -2:32:28
Biskamža 2 21 53N30 89E30 -5:58:00
Bitca 6 39 55N34 37E37 -2:30:28
Bitik 9 32 50N09 50E30 -3:22:00
Biysk → Bijsk 2 21 52N34 85E15 -5:41:00
Biz'aki 6 41 55N56 52E28 -3:29:52
Biz'ar 6 30 57N31 56E09 -3:44:36
Bižbul'ak 6 30 53N43 54E16 -3:37:04
Blagodarnoje 9 24 47N03 82E10 -5:28:40
Blagodarnyj 6 47 45N06 43E27 -2:53:48
Blagodatnoje 6 39 51N32 34E54 -2:19:36
Blagodatnoje 23 45 47N42 37E25 -2:29:40
Blagodatnoje 23 45 47N53 38E29 -2:33:56
Blagodatnoje 9 24 51N18 72E49 -4:51:16
Blagodatovka 6 34 52N14 50E27 -3:21:48
Blagoveščenka 9 24 54N22 66E58 -4:27:52
Blagoveščenka 6 34 51N19 44E03 -2:56:12
Blagoveščenka 2 23 52N50 79E52 -5:19:28
Blagoveščensk 6 30 55N01 55E59 -3:43:56
Blagoveščensk 2 15 50N17 127E32 -8:30:08
Blagoveščenskoje 2 30 58N08 62E58 -4:11:52
Blagoveščenskoje 9 24 43N18 74E12 -4:56:48
Blinovskij 6 34 49N23 42E19 -2:49:16
Blizn'uki 23 45 48N52 36E33 -2:26:12
Bobr 4 39 54N20 29E16 -1:57:04
Bobrikovo 23 45 47N56 39E13 -2:36:52
Bobrinec 23 45 48N03 32E09 -2:08:36
Bobrka 23 44 49N38 24E18 -1:37:12
Bobrov 6 41 51N06 40E02 -2:40:08
Bobrovica 23 44 50N44 31E22 -2:05:28
Bobrujsk 4 39 53N09 29E14 -1:56:56
Bočejkovo 4 39 55N01 29E09 -1:56:36
Bochan 2 20 53N09 103E48 -6:55:12
Bodajbo 2 17 57N51 114E10 -7:36:40
Bogataja Černeščina 23 45 48N59 35E35 -2:22:20
Bogatiščevo-Jepišino 6 39 54N47 38E25 -2:33:40
Bogatoje 6 34 53N04 51E24 -3:25:36
Bogatyje Saby 6 41 56N01 50E27 -3:21:48
Bogatyr' 6 34 53N25 50E02 -3:20:08
Bogatyrevo 9 32 50N22 48E46 -3:15:04
Bogdanovič 2 30 56N47 62E01 -4:08:04
Bogdanovka 7 33 41N18 43E35 -2:54:20
Bogdanovka 6 34 52N42 50E46 -3:23:04
Bogdanovka 6 32 52N10 52E37 -3:30:28
Bogembaj 9 24 52N29 72E20 -4:49:20
Boget 9 32 49N40 47E59 -3:11:56
Bogoduchov 23 45 50N10 35E30 -2:22:00
Bogol'ubovo 6 39 56N13 40E31 -2:42:04
Bogol'ubovo 6 39 55N32 32E57 -2:11:48
Bogorodčany 23 44 48N48 24E32 -1:38:08
Bogorodick 6 39 53N46 38E08 -2:32:32
Bogorodickoje 6 47 46N20 41E10 -2:44:40
Bogorodičnoje 23 45 49N01 37E30 -2:30:00
Bogorodsk 6 41 62N16 52E28 -3:29:52
Bogorodsk 6 41 56N06 43E31 -2:54:04
Bogorodskoje 6 39 55N26 36E14 -2:24:56
Bogorodskoje 2 11 52N22 140E30 -9:22:00
Bogorodskoje 6 42 57N51 50E45 -3:23:00
Bogorodskoje 6 47 46N20 43E53 -2:55:32
Bogorodskoje 6 39 55N02 38E29 -2:33:56
Bogotol 2 21 56N12 89E33 -5:58:12
Bogovarovo 6 41 58N59 47E01 -3:08:04
Bograd 2 21 54N13 90E51 -6:03:24
Bogučany 2 21 58N23 97E29 -6:29:56
Bogučar 6 47 49N57 40E33 -2:42:12
Bogunaj 2 21 56N14 94E35 -6:18:20
Boguševsk 4 39 54N51 30E13 -2:00:52
Boguslav 23 44 49N33 30E53 -2:03:32
Bogušovsk 4 39 54N51 30E13 -2:00:52
Bogustan 24 24 41N41 70E05 -4:40:20
Bojarka 23 44 50N19 30E19 -2:01:16
Bojarkino 6 39 54N57 38E31 -2:34:04
Bojarsk 2 20 56N19 106E04 -7:04:16
Bojevo 6 41 51N24 39E19 -2:37:16
Bokino 6 41 52N38 41E26 -2:45:44
Boko 9 24 49N05 81E38 -5:26:32
Bokonbajevskoje 10 24 42N07 77E00 -5:08:00
Bokovo-Antratsit → Antracit 23 45 48N06 39E06 -2:36:24
Bokovo Platovo 23 45 48N07 39E01 -2:36:04
Bokovskaja 6 47 49N15 41E49 -2:47:16
Boksitogorsk 6 9 59N28 33E51 -2:15:24
Bolčary 2 30 59N49 68E48 -4:35:12
Bolchov 6 39 53N27 36E01 -2:24:04
Bolchuny 6 34 47N59 46E25 -3:05:40
Boldasevo 6 41 54N43 45E33 -3:02:12
Bol'džuan 21 24 38N19 69E40 -4:38:40
Bolechov 23 44 49N04 23E52 -1:35:28
Bolgrad 23 45 45N41 28E36 -1:54:24
Bolnisi 7 33 41N28 44E33 -2:58:12
Bolochovo 6 39 54N05 37E50 -2:31:20
Bologoje 6 39 57N54 34E02 -2:16:08
Bologovo 6 39 56N54 31E42 -2:06:48
Bolon' 2 11 49N55 136E07 -9:04:28
Bolotino 15 46 47N42 27E21 -1:49:24
Bolotnoje 2 21 55N41 84E23 -5:37:32
Boloto 6 39 54N10 36E20 -2:25:20
Bolotovskoje 2 30 58N33 62E28 -4:09:52
Bol'šaja 6 41 59N36 41E48 -2:47:12
Bol'šaja 6 47 45N59 42E42 -2:50:48
Bol'šaja Atn'a 6 41 56N15 49E27 -3:17:48
Bol'šaja Ber'ostovica 4 39 53N11 24E01 -1:36:04
Bol'šaja Blagoveščenka 23 45 46N51 34E03 -2:16:12
Bol'šaja Brembola 6 39 56N45 38E55 -2:35:40
Bol'šaja Bukon' 9 24 48N53 82E43 -5:30:52
Bol'šaja Černigovka 6 34 52N07 50E52 -3:23:28
Bol'šaja Chalan' 6 39 50N56 37E26 -2:29:44
Bol'šaja Chundala 6 9 60N04 34E18 -2:17:12
Bol'šaja Čurakovka 9 30 53N03 64E20 -4:17:20
Bol'šaja Damba 9 32 46N57 51E47 -3:27:08
Bol'šaja Dmitrijevka 6 34 51N21 45E15 -3:01:00
Bol'šaja Dora 6 40 59N05 37E38 -2:30:32
Bol'šaja Džalga 6 47 45N59 42E41 -2:50:44
Bol'šaja Glušica 6 34 52N24 50E28 -3:21:52
Bol'šaja Ižora 6 9 59N56 29E34 -1:58:16
Bol'šaja Kamenka 6 34 53N39 50E31 -3:22:04
Bol'šaja Kandala 6 42 54N32 49E22 -3:17:28
Bol'šaja Karpunicha 6 41 57N42 45E20 -3:01:20
Bol'šaja Kaskara 2 30 57N11 65E58 -4:23:52
Bol'šaja Ket' 2 21 57N39 91E45 -6:07:00
Bol'šaja Kirsanovka 6 40 47N40 38E54 -2:35:36
Bol'šaja Lipovica 6 41 52N33 41E20 -2:45:20
Bol'šaja Martynovka 6 47 47N17 41E40 -2:46:40
Bol'šaja Mošanica 4 39 53N58 29E37 -1:58:28
Bol'šaja Murta 2 21 56N55 93E07 -6:12:28
Bol'šaja Norja 6 42 56N41 52E43 -3:30:52
Bol'šaja Ol'šanka 6 34 51N32 44E17 -2:57:08
Bol'šaja Orlovka 6 47 47N20 41E16 -2:45:04
Bol'šaja Pas'ma 6 41 58N38 43E53 -2:55:32
Bol'šaja Rečka 2 20 51N57 104E44 -6:58:56
Bol'šaja Ržaksa 6 41 52N08 42E13 -2:48:52
Bol'šaja Sosnova 6 30 57N40 54E36 -3:38:24
Bol'šaja Talovaja 6 47 46N58 40E37 -2:42:28
Bol'šaja Tarel' 2 20 53N45 106E40 -7:06:40
Boi'šaja Tavoložka 6 34 52N07 49E04 -3:16:16
Bol'šaja Tavolžka 6 34 52N07 49E04 -3:16:16
Bol'šaja Uča 6 42 56N37 52E05 -3:28:20
Bol'šaja Usa 6 30 56N44 55E06 -3:40:24
Bol'šaja Višera 6 9 58N55 32E08 -2:08:32
Bol'šaja Vladimirovka 9 24 50N53 79E31 -5:18:04
Bol'šakovo 6 39 55N54 37E17 -2:29:08
Bol'šakovo 8 38 54N53 21E40 -1:26:40
Bol'šečernigovka 23 45 48N57 39E25 -2:37:40
Bol'šekrepinskaja 6 40 47N36 39E22 -2:37:28
Bol'šelig 6 41 62N07 52E25 -3:29:40
Bol'šenarymskoje 9 24 49N16 84E32 -5:38:08
Bol'šerečje 2 24 56N06 74E38 -4:58:32
Bol'šereck 2 4 52N25 156E24-10:25:36
Bol'šetroickoje 6 39 50N33 37E17 -2:29:08
Bol'šeustjikinskoje 6 30 55N57 58E16 -3:53:04
Bol'ševik 2 6 62N44 147E30 -9:50:00
Bol'ševik 4 39 52N34 30E53 -2:03:32
Bol'ševik 6 9 59N49 30E30 -2:02:00
Bol'ševik Island 20 19 78N40 102E30 -6:50:00
Bol'ševik, Ostrov 20 19 78N40 102E30 -6:50:00
Bol'šije Algaši 6 41 55N22 46E29 -3:05:56
Bol'šije Avt'uki 4 39 52N04 29E32 -1:58:08
Bol'šije Belyniči 6 39 54N38 38E50 -2:35:20
Bol'šije Berezniki 6 41 54N11 45E58 -3:03:52
Bol'šije Gorki 6 9 59N42 29E51 -1:59:24
Bol'šije Gorki 6 39 56N28 35E51 -2:23:24
Bol'šije Kajbicy 6 41 55N25 48E13 -3:12:52
Bol'šije Kl'uči 6 41 55N59 48E47 -3:15:08
Bol'šije Kl'učišči 6 42 54N08 48E14 -3:12:56
Bol'šije Michalicyny 6 42 58N29 48E14 -3:12:56
Bol'šije Ozerki 6 34 52N36 46E33 -3:06:12
Bol'šije Pom'aly 6 41 56N42 46E40 -3:06:40
Bol'šije Ručji 6 39 56N36 36E58 -2:27:52
Bol'šije Saly 6 40 47N24 39E41 -2:38:44
Bol'šije Tarchany 6 41 54N42 48E34 -3:14:16
Bol'šije Ugli 2 20 57N47 112E51 -7:31:24
Bol'šije Uki 2 24 56N57 72E37 -4:50:28
Bol'šije Ždanovy 6 42 58N40 49E05 -3:16:20
Bol'šoj 6 34 50N13 43E26 -2:53:44
Bol'šoj Bukon' 9 24 48N53 82E43 -5:30:52
Bol'šoje Aksu 9 24 43N20 79E35 -5:18:20
Bol'šoje Aleksejevskoje 6 39 55N14 38E12 -2:32:48
Bol'šoje Boldino 6 41 54N59 45E19 -3:01:16
Bol'šoje Bun'kovo 6 39 55N51 38E37 -2:34:28
Bol'šoje Goloustnoje 2 20 52N01 105E25 -7:01:40
Bol'šoje Gorodišče 6 39 50N37 37E06 -2:28:24
Bol'šoje Gorodišče 6 39 57N17 30E31 -2:02:04
Bol'šoje Ignatovo 6 41 55N02 45E34 -3:02:16
Bol'šoje Kibejevo 6 41 56N55 47E05 -3:08:20
Bol'šoje Korovino 6 40 54N30 39E02 -2:36:08
Bol'šoje Kozino 6 41 56N24 43E46 -2:55:04
Bol'šoje Manuškino 6 9 59N53 30E49 -2:03:16
Bol'šoje Michajlovskoje 6 39 56N47 38E04 -2:32:16
Bol'šoje Mikuškino 6 34 53N56 51E42 -3:26:48
Bol'šoje Muraškino 6 41 55N47 44E46 -2:59:04
Bol'šoje Nagatkino 6 42 54N31 47E58 -3:11:52
Bol'šoje Nurkejevo 6 41 55N22 52E40 -3:30:40
Bol'šoje Nyrsy 6 41 55N44 50E19 -3:21:16
Bol'šoje Ogar'ovo 6 39 53N33 37E43 -2:30:52
Bol'šoje Pikino 6 41 56N25 44E22 -2:57:28
Bol'šoje Polpino 6 39 53N14 34E30 -2:18:00
Bol'šoje Ramenje 6 9 58N21 36E40 -2:26:40
Bol'šoje Rybuškino 6 41 55N25 45E48 -3:03:12
Bol'šoje Sazonovo 6 42 58N06 53E21 -3:33:24
Bol'šoje Selo 6 40 57N43 38E56 -2:35:44
Bol'šoje Šem'akino 6 41 55N03 48E38 -3:14:32
Bol'šoje Soldatskoje 6 39 51N21 35E31 -2:22:04
Bol'šoje Sudačje 6 34 50N49 44E05 -2:56:20
Bol'šoje Uro 2 20 53N32 109E48 -7:19:12
Bol'šoje Zagorje 6 39 57N51 28E57 -1:55:48
Bol'šoje Žokovo 6 40 54N35 38E57 -2:35:48
Bol'šoj Kamen' 2 27 43N06 132E21 -8:49:24

Bol'šoj Kandarat' 6
42 54N25 47E00 -3:08:00
Bol'šoj Karagaj 2
30 57N57 70E15 -4:41:00
Bol'šoj Ketmen' 9
24 43N27 80E24 -5:21:36
Bol'šoj Kujaš 2
30 55N50 61E06 -4:04:24
Bol'šoj Kuvaj 6
42 54N37 47E05 -3:08:20
Bol'šoj Lug 2 20 52N07 104E10 -6:56:40
Bol'šoj Melik 6
34 51N38 43E18 -2:53:12
Bol'šoj Onguren 2
20 53N38 107E36 -7:10:24
Bol'šoj Porog 2
21 52N35 92E18 -6:09:12
Bol'šoj Šagan 9
32 50N57 51E08 -3:24:32
Bol'šoj Simonogont 6
9 59N50 29E49 -1:59:16
Bol'šoj Sorokino 2
30 56N38 69E53 -4:39:32
Bol'šoj Suchodol 23
45 48N25 39E53 -2:39:32
Bol'šoj Sundyr' 6
41 56N07 46E46 -3:07:04
Bol'šoj Tal'cy 6
9 59N13 33E00 -2:12:00
Bol'šoj Tolkaj 6
34 53N30 51E57 -3:27:48
Bol'šoj Uluj 2
21 56N39 90E36 -6:02:24
Bol'šoj Uzigont 6
9 59N48 29E53 -1:59:32
Bol'šoj Vjass 6
41 53N48 45E30 -3:02:00
Bol'šoj Vlasjevo 2
11 53N24 140E55 -9:23:40
Bol'šovcy 23 44 49N12 24E44 -1:38:56
Boltino 6 39 55N58 37E41 -2:30:44
Bolyčevo 6 39 55N46 35E43 -2:22:52
Bomnak 2 14 54N46 128E51 -8:35:24
Bondari 6 41 52N57 42E04 -2:48:16
Bondar'ov 23 45 49N22 39E10 -2:36:40
Bondar'ovka 23
45 49N23 39E37 -2:38:28
Bond'užskij 6 41 55N54 52E20 -3:29:20
Bor 6 41 63N00 42E38 -2:50:32
Bor 6 41 56N22 44E05 -2:56:20
Bordunskij 10 24 42N40 75E37 -5:02:28
Borilovo 6 39 53N22 35E58 -2:23:52
Borinskoje 6 40 52N27 39E22 -2:37:28
Borislav 23 44 49N16 23E27 -1:33:48
Borisoglebsk 6
41 51N23 42E06 -2:48:24
Borisoglebskij 6
40 57N16 39E09 -2:36:36
Borisov 23 44 50N11 26E31 -1:46:04
Borisov 4 39 54N15 28E30 -1:54:00
Borisovka 6 39 50N36 36E01 -2:24:04
Borisovka 6 41 52N50 39E58 -2:39:52
Borisovo 6 39 55N25 36E03 -2:24:12
Borisovo-Sudskoje 6
40 59N54 36E01 -2:24:04
Borisovskaja 6
40 60N12 39E48 -2:39:12
Borispol' 23 44 50N21 30E57 -2:03:48
Borki 23 45 49N42 36E02 -2:24:08
Borki 2 23 59N08 82E15 -5:29:00
Borkoviči 4 39 55N40 28E20 -1:53:20
Borod'anka 23 44 50N39 29E56 -1:59:44
Borodino 6 39 56N53 37E00 -2:28:00
Borodino 2 21 55N55 94E55 -6:19:40
Borodino 23 45 46N18 29E13 -1:56:52
Borodino 6 39 55N32 35E50 -2:23:20
Borodulicha 9 24 50N43 80E55 -5:23:40
Borodulino 6 30 57N59 54E20 -3:37:20
Borogoncy 2 13 62N42 131E08 -8:44:32
Boroml'a 23 45 50N37 34E59 -2:19:56
Boron'ki 4 39 53N09 32E08 -2:08:32
Borovaja 23 44 50N12 30E07 -2:00:28
Borovaja 23 45 49N24 37E40 -2:30:40
Boroviči 6 9 58N24 33E55 -2:15:40
Borovl'anka 2 21 52N38 84E29 -5:37:56
Borovoj 6 42 59N55 51E38 -3:26:32
Borovoje 23 44 51N06 27E13 -1:48:52
Borovoje 9 24 53N04 70E19 -4:41:16
Borovsk 6 39 55N12 36E30 -2:26:00
Borovskaja 6 41 60N46 41E06 -2:44:24
Borovskij 2 30 57N03 65E44 -4:22:56
Borovskoj 9 30 53N48 64E12 -4:16:48
Borovskoje 23 45 48N51 38E34 -2:34:16
Borovskoje 2 23 52N39 82E08 -5:28:32
Borovucha 4 39 55N36 28E37 -1:54:28
Borozdino 6 39 54N07 38E22 -2:33:28
Borščov 23 45 48N48 26E03 -1:44:12
Borščovo 6 39 56N30 36E51 -2:27:24
Borskoje 6 34 53N02 51E43 -3:26:52
Bortniči 23 44 50N22 30E41 -2:02:44
Borto 2 20 53N35 111E53 -7:27:32
Borz'a 2 16 50N24 116E31 -7:46:04
Borzna 23 44 51N15 32E25 -2:09:40
Boržomi 7 33 41N50 43E21 -2:53:24
Bosaga 9 24 47N55 72E58 -4:51:52
Boškajnar 21 24 38N13 68E51 -4:35:24
Bošn'akovo 19 8 49N38 142E10 -9:28:40
Bosogo 10 24 41N09 76E25 -5:05:40
Bostandyk 9 32 49N38 48E54 -3:15:36
Botejevo 23 45 46N41 35E52 -2:23:28
Botlich 6 47 42N39 46E14 -3:04:56
Botovo 6 39 56N03 38E26 -2:33:44
Boty 2 16 52N24 118E32 -7:54:08
Bozšakol' 9 24 51N50 74E20 -4:57:20
Braclav 23 45 48N50 28E55 -1:55:40

Bragin 4 39 51N47 30E14 -2:00:56
Braginovka 23 45 48N29 36E21 -2:25:24
Brailov 23 44 49N06 28E09 -1:52:36
Br'andino 6 42 54N23 49E23 -3:17:32
Br'anka 2 21 59N08 93E27 -6:13:48
Br'anka 23 45 48N29 38E39 -2:34:36
Br'ansk 6 39 53N15 34E22 -2:17:28
Braslav 4 39 55N38 27E02 -1:48:08
Bratol'ubovka 9
24 51N13 66E46 -4:27:04
Bratsk 2 20 56N05 101E48 -6:47:12
Bratskaja Kada 2
20 55N02 102E06 -6:48:24
Bratskoje 23 45 47N52 31E34 -2:06:16
Bravica 15 46 47N22 28E26 -1:53:44
Bredy 2 30 52N26 60E21 -4:01:24
Brejtovo 6 40 58N18 37E52 -2:31:28
Brest 4 39 52N06 23E42 -1:34:48
Bričany 15 46 48N22 27E04 -1:48:16
Brlik 9 24 44N05 73E31 -4:54:04
Brlik 9 24 43N40 73E49 -4:55:16
Brocēni 13 36 56N42 22E35 -1:30:20
Brodokalmak 2 30 55N35 62E06 -4:08:24
Brody 23 44 50N06 25E10 -1:40:40
Bronevskaja 6 40 61N43 39E10 -2:36:40
Bronickaja Guta 23
44 50N56 27E19 -1:49:16
Bronnicy 6 39 55N25 38E16 -2:33:04
Bronnikovo 2 30 58N32 68E25 -4:33:40
Bronnoje 4 39 52N19 30E29 -2:01:56
Brošnev-Osada 23
44 49N00 24E13 -1:36:52
Brovary 23 44 50N31 30E46 -2:03:04
Broža 4 39 52N57 29E07 -1:56:28
Br'uchoveckaja 6
47 45N48 38E59 -2:35:56
Brus'any 6 34 53N13 49E24 -3:17:36
Brusilov 23 44 50N17 29E32 -1:58:08
Brusovo 6 39 57N51 35E24 -2:21:36
Bryansk → Br'ansk 6
39 53N15 34E22 -2:17:28
Brykalansk 6 29 65N30 54E12 -3:36:48
Brykovka 6 34 52N32 48E35 -3:14:20
Bryli 4 39 53N54 30E33 -2:02:12
Bryn'kovskaja 6
47 46N02 38E35 -2:34:20
Brzešč Nad Bugiem → Brest 4
39 52N06 23E42 -1:34:48
Bučač 23 44 49N04 25E23 -1:41:32
Buchara 24 30 39N48 64E25 -4:17:40
Bučmany 23 44 51N04 28E04 -1:52:16
Budagovo 2 20 54N38 100E08 -6:40:32
Buda-Kosel'ovo 4
39 52N43 30E34 -2:02:16
Budarin 6 47 47N54 42E36 -2:50:24
Budarino 9 32 50N31 51E04 -3:24:16
Budogošč' 6 9 59N17 32E27 -2:09:48
Budogoviščí 6 39 53N36 36E18 -2:25:12
Bud'onnovka 9 30 50N52 52E48 -3:31:12
Bud'onnovsk 6 47 44N46 44E09 -2:56:36
Bud'onnovskaja 6
47 46N56 41E33 -2:46:12
Bud'onnyj 10 24 42N30 72E35 -4:50:20
Bud'onnyj 6 40 47N27 39E46 -2:39:04
Budslav 4 39 54N47 27E27 -1:49:48
Budy 23 45 49N53 36E02 -2:24:08
Budylka 23 45 50N30 34E26 -2:17:44
Bugajevka 23 45 49N39 39E42 -2:38:48
Bugajevka 23 45 49N28 37E23 -2:29:32
Bugajevka 23 45 48N25 38E53 -2:35:32
Bugrino 6 41 68N48 49E09 -3:16:36
Bugry 6 9 58N46 35E15 -2:21:00
Bugry 6 9 60N04 30E24 -2:01:36
Bugul'dejka 2 20 52N33 106E05 -7:04:20
Bugul'ma 6 41 54N33 52E48 -3:31:12
Buguruslan 6 32 53N39 52E26 -3:29:44
Buinsk 6 41 55N12 47E03 -3:08:12
Buinsk 6 41 54N57 48E17 -3:13:08
Buj 6 41 58N30 41E30 -2:46:00
Bujaki 6 42 59N03 48E40 -3:14:40
Bujnaksk 6 47 42N49 47E07 -3:08:28
Bujnoviči 4 39 51N52 28E33 -1:54:12
Bujukly 19 8 49N30 142E47 -9:31:08
Buka 24 24 40N48 69E11 -4:36:44
Bukačača 2 16 52N59 116E55 -7:47:40
Bukačevcy 23 44 49N15 24E29 -1:37:56
Bukan' 6 39 53N55 34E42 -2:18:48
Bukanovskaja 6
34 49N42 42E18 -2:49:12
Bukarevo 6 39 55N57 36E44 -2:26:56
Bukhara → Buchara 24
30 39N48 64E25 -4:17:40
Bukrino 6 39 54N48 36E14 -2:24:56
Bukuka 2 16 51N11 116E39 -7:46:36
Bukukun 2 18 49N27 111E08 -7:24:32
Bulajevo 9 24 54N54 70E26 -4:41:44
Bulak 2 16 51N02 115E21 -7:41:24
Bulanaš 2 30 57N16 62E00 -4:08:00
Bulanicha 2 21 52N48 84E57 -5:39:48
Bulava 2 11 51N55 140E25 -9:21:40
Bulavinovka 23
45 49N25 38E58 -2:35:52
Buldurtinskij 9
30 50N05 53E11 -3:32:44
Bulgakovka 23 45 49N11 38E33 -2:34:12
Bulgakovo 6 39 55N14 32E08 -2:08:32
Bulugansk 2 20 52N24 110E23 -7:21:32
Bulyčevo 6 39 55N06 37E15 -2:29:00
Bunaj 21 24 38N26 71E32 -4:46:08
Bun'atino 6 39 56N24 37E15 -2:29:00
Bund'ur 2 23 57N32 82E01 -5:28:04
Bunyrevo 6 39 54N34 37E09 -2:28:36
Buolkalach 2 16 72N56 119E50 -7:59:20
Bur 2 20 58N47 107E01 -7:08:04
Buraly 6 41 55N04 52E52 -3:31:28

Buran 9 24 48N04 85E15 -5:41:00
Burangulovo 6 30 53N26 58E23 -3:53:32
Burankol' 9 30 46N14 54E12 -3:36:48
Burannoje 6 30 50N59 54E28 -3:37:52
Buraševo 6 39 56N44 35E52 -2:23:28
Burcevo 6 39 55N02 38E09 -2:32:36
Burdalyk 22 30 38N25 64E20 -4:17:20
Bureja 2 14 49N52 129E48 -8:39:12
Burga 6 9 58N45 32E29 -2:09:56
Burkit 9 32 47N03 50E42 -3:22:48
Burla 2 23 53N19 78E21 -5:13:24
Burli 9 30 53N36 61E55 -4:07:40
Burli 9 30 51N25 52E44 -3:30:56
Burlit 2 11 46N33 134E14 -8:56:56
Burluk 6 34 50N34 44E33 -2:58:12
Burmakino 6 40 57N27 40E20 -2:41:20
Burnoje 9 24 42N37 70E46 -4:43:04
Burno-Okt'abr'skoje 9
24 42N42 70E49 -4:43:16
Buron 6 47 42N48 44E03 -2:56:12
Bursol' 2 23 53N11 78E27 -5:13:48
Burštyn 23 44 49N17 24E37 -1:38:28
Burukan 2 11 53N02 136E03 -9:04:12
Buruldaj 10 24 42N48 75E52 -5:03:28
Burundaj 9 24 43N23 76E51 -5:07:24
Burundučicha 6
41 58N21 46E07 -3:04:28
Buryn' 23 44 51N13 33E49 -2:15:16
Busk 23 44 49N58 24E37 -1:38:28
Buskul' 9 30 53N45 61E12 -4:04:48
Busse 2 16 51N16 126E58 -8:27:52
Busskoje 6 47 43N50 44E37 -2:58:28
Buston 24 30 40N04 64E49 -4:19:16
Buston 21 24 40N31 69E19 -4:37:16
Buštyna 23 44 48N04 23E27 -1:33:48
Bušuicha 6 41 59N02 40E26 -2:41:44
Bušulej 2 16 52N45 117E13 -7:48:52
Buta 6 41 55N02 51E57 -3:27:48
Butka 2 30 56N47 63E47 -4:15:08
Butuj 2 20 53N27 112E22 -7:29:28
Buturlino 6 41 55N34 44E55 -2:59:40
Buturlino 6 39 54N55 37E29 -2:29:56
Buturlinovka 6
47 50N50 40E36 -2:42:24
Butylicy 6 40 55N32 41E31 -2:46:04
Buyun Uzun 22 30 39N13 63E19 -4:13:16
Bužaninovo 6 39 56N23 38E18 -2:33:12
Bužarovo 6 39 55N59 36E47 -2:27:08
Buzinovka 6 34 48N32 43E53 -2:55:32
Buzlanovo 6 39 55N46 37E13 -2:28:52
Buzovna 3 34 40N31 50E04 -3:20:16
Buzuluk 6 32 52N47 52E15 -3:29:00
Buzuluk 9 24 51N55 66E16 -4:25:04
Bychov 4 39 53N32 30E12 -2:00:48
Byčicha 4 39 55N41 29E58 -1:59:52
Byčki 6 41 53N38 40E54 -2:43:36
Byčki 6 39 54N15 34E39 -2:18:36
Bygi 6 42 57N13 53E44 -3:34:56
Bykov 19 8 47N21 142E32 -9:30:08
Bykovec 15 46 47N13 28E27 -1:53:48
Bykovka 23 44 50N17 27E58 -1:51:52
Bykovka 6 39 55N29 37E40 -2:30:40
Bykovo 6 39 54N01 37E54 -2:31:36
Bykovo 6 39 55N37 38E04 -2:32:16
Bykovo 6 34 49N47 45E22 -3:01:28
Bylbasovka 23 45 48N51 37E30 -2:30:00
Bylkyldak 9 24 48N38 75E16 -5:01:04
Byrka 2 16 50N39 118E31 -7:54:04
Bystrovka 10 24 42N47 75E43 -5:02:52
Bystryj 2 24 57N50 73E58 -4:55:52
Bytča 4 39 54N18 28E24 -1:53:36
Byten' 4 39 52N54 25E29 -1:41:56
Bytkov 23 44 48N38 24E26 -1:37:44
Bytoš' 6 39 53N50 34E06 -2:16:24
Byvalki 4 39 51N51 30E37 -2:02:28
Čaa-Chol' 2 21 51N32 92E23 -6:09:32
Čaadajevka 6 41 53N09 45E56 -3:03:44
Čaadajevo 6 40 55N40 42E02 -2:48:08
Čabanovka 23 45 49N02 38E46 -2:35:04
Caca 6 34 48N11 44E40 -2:58:40
Cachkadzor 1 34 40N33 44E43 -2:58:52
Čadan 2 21 51N17 91E35 -6:06:20
Čadobec 2 19 58N40 98E51 -6:35:24
Čadyr-Lunga 15
46 46N03 28E47 -1:55:08
Cagan-Aman 6 34 47N34 46E43 -3:06:52
Čagda 2 13 58N45 130E37 -8:42:28
Cageri 7 33 42N39 42E45 -2:51:00
Čagoda 6 40 59N10 35E17 -2:21:08
Cagveri 7 33 41N48 43E29 -2:53:56
Čajan 9 24 43N02 69E23 -4:37:32
Čajek 10 24 41N56 74E30 -4:58:00
Čajkovskij 6 30 56N47 54E09 -3:36:36
Cakir 2 20 50N27 103E35 -6:54:20
Čakva 7 33 41N44 41E45 -2:47:00
Čalba 2 14 52N43 131E27 -8:45:48
Čaldonka 2 16 53N47 119E12 -7:56:48
Calendžicha 7 33 42N37 42E04 -2:48:16
Calka 7 33 41N37 44E05 -2:56:20
Čalkojdy 10 24 40N44 73E39 -4:54:36
Čal'mny-Varre 6
9 67N10 37E33 -2:30:12
Čalna 6 9 61N55 34E01 -2:16:04
Čalpy 6 41 55N05 53E06 -3:32:24
Čaltyr' 6 40 47N17 39E30 -2:38:00
Čamčakly 22 30 37N56 63E06 -4:12:24
Čamyndy 10 24 41N37 74E20 -4:57:20
Čamzinka 6 41 54N24 45E47 -3:03:08
Čančur 2 20 53N49 106E59 -7:07:56
Čangyrtas 10 24 40N53 72E50 -4:51:20
Čany 2 23 55N19 76E46 -5:07:04
Čapajev 9 32 50N12 51E10 -3:24:40
Čapajevka 23 45 47N29 36E20 -2:25:20
Čapajevka 6 39 54N38 35E50 -2:23:20
Čapajevka 23 44 49N33 32E06 -2:08:24

Čapajevka 23 44 49N23 30E26 -2:01:44
Čapajevo 23 45 49N21 35E54 -2:23:36
Čapajevo 9 32 50N12 51E10 -3:24:40
Čapajevsk 6 34 52N58 49E41 -3:18:44
Capel'ka 6 9 58N03 28E59 -1:55:56
Čaplejevka 23 44 51N43 33E12 -2:12:48
Čaplinka 23 45 46N23 33E32 -2:14:08
Čaplino 23 45 48N09 36E14 -2:24:56
Čaplino 2 2 64N25 172W15 11:29:00
Čaplygin 6 41 53N14 39E58 -2:39:52
Čara 2 16 56N54 118E12 -7:52:48
Čarach 2 30 59N03 62E15 -4:09:00
Čardak 24 24 41N37 69E56 -4:39:44
Čardara 9 24 41N17 67E55 -4:31:40
Čardžou 22 30 39N06 63E34 -4:14:16
Čarencavan 1 34 40N24 44E38 -2:58:32
Carevščina 6 34 52N27 46E43 -3:06:52
Caričanka 23 45 48N57 34E29 -2:17:56
Caricyn → Volgograd 6
34 48N44 44E25 -2:57:40
Čarkesar 24 24 41N02 70E53 -4:43:32
Čaronda 6 40 60N34 38E59 -2:35:56
Car'ov 6 34 48N40 45E22 -3:01:28
Car'ovščina 6 41 53N37 44E45 -2:59:00
Čarozero 6 40 60N28 38E39 -2:34:36
Čaršanga 22 30 37N30 66E01 -4:24:04
Čarsk 9 24 49N35 81E05 -5:24:20
Čartak 24 24 41N05 71E50 -4:47:20
Čarymovo 2 23 58N31 77E42 -5:10:48
Čaryn 9 24 43N46 79E24 -5:17:36
Čaryškoje 2 21 51N24 83E35 -5:34:20
Čascy 6 39 55N37 36E52 -2:27:28
Čašniki 4 39 54N52 29E08 -1:56:32
Čašnikovo 6 39 55N59 37E25 -2:29:40
Časov Jar 23 45 48N35 37E50 -2:31:20
Časovo 6 41 62N01 50E36 -3:22:24
Častoje 6 39 54N11 37E47 -2:31:08
Častooz'ornoje 2
30 55N34 67E53 -4:31:32
Častyje 6 30 57N19 54E59 -3:39:56
Čatyrtaš 10 24 40N55 76E26 -5:05:44
Čausovo 6 39 54N49 36E55 -2:27:40
Čausy 4 39 53N48 30E58 -2:03:52
Čauvaj 10 24 40N08 72E13 -4:48:52
Čavan'ga 6 9 66N06 37E47 -2:31:08
Čavka 7 33 41N44 41E45 -2:47:00
Čavlisaj 24 24 41N08 69E44 -4:38:56
Cchaltubo 7 33 42N20 42E35 -2:50:20
Cchinvali 7 33 42N13 43E56 -2:55:44
Cchorocku 7 33 42N32 42E07 -2:48:28
Cchunkuri 7 33 42N23 42E34 -2:50:16
Čebarkul' 2 30 54N58 60E25 -4:01:40
Čeboksary 6 41 56N09 47E15 -3:09:00
Čebotovka 6 47 48N42 39E51 -2:39:24
Čebotovka 6 47 48N41 40E00 -2:40:00
Cebrikovo 23 45 47N09 30E06 -2:00:24
Čebsara 6 40 59N12 38E50 -2:35:20
Čeburgol' 6 47 45N34 38E07 -2:32:28
Čečel'nik 23 45 48N14 29E21 -1:57:24
Čečersk 4 39 52N55 30E55 -2:03:40
Čečeviči 4 39 53N31 29E51 -1:59:24
Čechov 6 39 55N09 37E27 -2:29:48
Čechov 19 8 47N28 141E59 -9:27:56
Čečorsk 4 39 52N55 30E55 -2:03:40
Čečujsk 2 20 58N05 108E42 -7:14:48
Čeder 2 21 51N25 94E45 -6:19:00
Čeganly 6 30 53N54 53E34 -3:34:16
Čegdomyn 2 11 51N07 133E05 -8:52:20
Čegem Pervyj 6
47 43N34 43E35 -2:54:20
Čegitun' 2 2 66N34 171W06 11:24:24
Čeil'dag 3 34 40N17 49E18 -3:17:12
Čekalin 6 39 54N06 36E15 -2:25:00
Čekan 6 41 54N51 53E34 -3:34:16
Čekanovskij 2 20 56N13 101E25 -6:45:40
Čekmaguš 6 30 55N08 54E40 -3:38:40
Čekšino 6 41 59N39 40E33 -2:42:12
Čekujevo 6 40 63N34 38E56 -2:35:44
Čekunda 2 11 50N48 132E10 -8:48:40
Čel'abinsk 2 30 55N10 61E24 -4:05:36
Čelbasskaja 6 47 45N59 39E22 -2:37:28
Čeleken 22 30 39N26 53E07 -3:32:28
Čelina 6 47 46N32 41E02 -2:44:08
Čelinnoje 2 21 53N04 85E40 -5:42:40
Čelinnoje 2 30 54N31 63E39 -4:14:36
Čelinnyj 6 47 46N40 44E32 -2:58:08
Čelinograd 9 24 51N10 71E30 -4:46:00
Čelkar 9 30 47N50 59E36 -3:58:24
Čelmozero 6 9 64N18 31E48 -2:07:12
Čelno-Veršiny 6
42 54N26 51E06 -3:24:24
Čelobitjevo 6 39 55N55 37E40 -2:30:40
Čel'uš 2 21 51N32 87E46 -5:51:04
Čemal 2 21 51N25 86E01 -5:44:04
Čembilej 6 41 55N19 45E43 -3:02:52
Čemer 23 44 51N07 31E13 -2:04:52
Čemerisy 4 39 51N42 30E24 -2:01:36
Čemerovcy 23 44 49N01 26E21 -1:45:24
Čemolgan 9 24 43N23 76E37 -5:06:28
Čenča 2 20 55N57 110E59 -7:23:56
Čency 6 39 56N03 36E01 -2:24:04
Čengel'dy 9 24 41N51 68E59 -4:35:56
Čengel'dy 9 24 43N59 77E26 -5:09:44
Central'nyj 2 21 58N45 84E28 -5:37:52
Central'nyj 2 23 57N41 80E57 -5:23:48
Central'nyj 6 40 53N41 39E38 -2:38:32
Central'nyj 2 21 55N12 87E40 -5:50:40
Čepca 6 42 57N54 53E25 -3:33:40
Čepeckij 6 42 58N29 51E12 -3:24:48
Čepel' 23 45 49N19 36E55 -2:27:40
Čepel'ovo 6 39 55N11 37E30 -2:30:00
Čerdakly 6 42 54N23 48E51 -3:15:24
Čerdojak 9 24 48N48 84E00 -5:36:00
Čerdyn' 6 30 60N23 56E24 -3:45:36
Čereja 4 39 54N37 29E17 -1:57:08

Čeremchovo 2 20 53N09 103E05 -6:52:20
Čeremisinovo 6
39 51N54 37E15 -2:29:00
Čeremšan 6 41 55N15 48E07 -3:12:28
Čeremšan 6 41 54N40 51E30 -3:26:00
Čeremšanka 6 30 56N07 60E19 -4:01:16
Čeremšanka 2 23 59N10 76E51 -5:07:24
Čeremšany 2 27 44N42 135E43 -9:02:52
Čerepanovka 6 42 57N07 54E10 -3:36:40
Čerepanovo 2 21 54N13 83E22 -5:33:28
Čerepet' 6 39 54N07 36E23 -2:25:32
Čerepovec 6 40 59N08 37E54 -2:31:36
Čerevkovka 23 45 48N50 37E40 -2:30:40
Čerevkovo 6 41 61N46 45E12 -3:00:48
Čerga 2 21 51N35 85E38 -5:42:32
Čerikov 4 39 53N34 31E23 -2:05:32
Čerkašina 2 20 58N37 108E30 -7:14:00
Čerkasovo 6 39 54N33 36E48 -2:27:12
Čerkasskoje 23
45 48N35 38E56 -2:35:44
Čerkasskoje 23
45 48N50 37E23 -2:29:32
Čerkasskoje 6 34 52N26 47E13 -3:08:52
Čerkassy 23 44 49N26 32E04 -2:08:16
Čerkassy 6 40 52N41 38E43 -2:34:52
Čerkesovskij 6
34 50N41 42E34 -2:50:16
Čerkessk 6 47 44N14 42E04 -2:48:16
Čerkizovo 6 39 55N58 37E48 -2:31:12
Čerkizovo 6 39 55N57 37E22 -2:29:28
Čerkizovo 6 39 55N12 38E45 -2:35:00
Čerkovišče 6 39 55N54 30E51 -2:03:24
Čerlak 2 24 54N09 74E48 -4:59:12
Čerlakskij 2 24 53N47 74E31 -4:58:04
Čermen 6 47 43N11 44E42 -2:58:48
Čermoz 6 30 58N53 56E08 -3:44:32
Čern' 6 39 53N27 36E55 -2:27:40
Čern'achov 23 44 50N27 28E39 -1:54:36
Čern'achovsk (Insterburg) 8
38 54N38 21E49 -1:27:16
Černaja 23 45 47N37 29E20 -1:57:20
Čern'ajevo 2 16 52N45 126E00 -8:24:00
Černak 9 24 43N24 68E02 -4:32:08
Čern'anka 6 39 50N55 37E49 -2:31:16
Černăuţi → Černovcy 23
44 48N18 25E56 -1:43:44
Černava 6 40 53N37 39E09 -2:36:36
Černavčicy 4 39 52N13 23E44 -1:34:56
Černavka 6 34 52N18 47E14 -3:08:56
Černavka 6 41 52N11 42E25 -2:49:40
Černeckoje 6 39 55N15 37E20 -2:29:20
Černelica 23 44 48N48 25E26 -1:41:44
Černevcy 23 45 48N33 28E09 -1:52:36
Černigov 23 44 51N30 31E18 -2:05:12
Černigovka 2 14 49N37 129E57 -8:39:48
Černigovka 2 27 44N21 132E33 -8:50:12
Černigovka 23 45 47N13 36E14 -2:24:56
Černigovka 9 24 50N28 71E27 -4:45:48
Černigovskaja 6
47 44N41 39E40 -2:38:40
Černobaj 23 44 49N41 32E19 -2:09:16
Černobyl 23 44 51N17 30E15 -2:01:00
Černogolovka 6
39 56N00 38E22 -2:33:28
Černogorsk 2 21 53N49 91E18 -6:05:12
Černokol'skaja 2
24 56N42 72E49 -4:51:16
Černorečenskoje 9
24 43N00 74E55 -4:59:40
Černorečje 6 47 43N15 45E41 -3:02:44
Černovcy 23 44 48N18 25E56 -1:43:44
Černovka 2 23 56N47 76E28 -5:05:52
Černovka 2 15 51N43 128E12 -8:32:48
Čern'ovo 6 9 58N39 28E14 -1:52:56
Čern'ovo 6 39 54N43 38E36 -2:34:24
Čern'ovo 6 39 55N50 37E18 -2:29:12
Černovskije Kopi 2
16 52N00 113E15 -7:33:00
Černovskoje 6 42 58N42 47E23 -3:09:32
Černovskoje 6 30 57N29 54E36 -3:38:24
Černucha 6 41 55N36 43E46 -2:55:04
Černuchi 23 44 50N16 32E57 -2:11:48
Černuchino 23 45 48N19 38E30 -2:34:00
Černuška 6 30 56N29 56E03 -3:44:12
Černuška 2 20 52N58 101E55 -6:47:40
Černyševsk 2 16 52N35 117E00 -7:48:00
Černyševskij 2
18 63N00 112E15 -7:29:00
Černyškovskij 6
34 48N27 42E14 -2:48:56
Čer'omuchova 6
41 54N57 51E09 -3:24:36
Čerskij 2 6 68N45 161E45-10:47:00
Čertkovo 6 47 49N23 40E10 -2:40:40
Čertolino 6 39 56N12 33E54 -2:15:36
Čertomlyk 23 45 47N37 34E09 -2:16:36
Čerusti 6 39 55N33 40E01 -2:40:04
Červ'anka 2 20 57N41 99E33 -6:38:12
Červen' 4 39 53N42 28E26 -1:53:44
Červl'onnaja 6
47 43N30 45E54 -3:03:36
Červonaja Kamenka 23
45 48N38 33E26 -2:13:44
Červonoarmejsk 23
44 50N08 25E16 -1:41:04
Červonoarmejsk 23
44 50N28 28E14 -1:52:56
Červonoarmejskoje 23
45 45N47 28E44 -1:54:56
Červonoarmejskoje 23
45 47N57 35E27 -2:21:48
Červonograd 23
44 50N24 24E14 -1:36:56
Červonogranitnoje 23
44 50N34 28E33 -1:54:12

Červonoje 23 44 51N46 34E04 -2:16:16
Červonoje 23 44 49N57 28E53 -1:55:32
Červonopartizansk 23
45 48N04 39E50 -2:39:20
Červonyj Donec 23
45 49N29 36E34 -2:26:16
Cēsis 13 36 57N18 25E15 -1:41:00
Česma 2 30 53N50 60E40 -4:02:40
Cesvaine 13 36 56N58 26E19 -1:45:16
Cetatea Albă → Belgorod-Dnestrovskij 23
45 46N12 30E20 -2:01:20
Četbulak 10 24 41N17 73E58 -4:55:52
Četyrboki 23 44 50N02 27E01 -1:48:04
Chabaricha 6 41 65N50 52E16 -3:29:04
Chabarovo 6 29 69N39 60E24 -4:01:36
Chabarovsk 2 11 48N27 135E06 -9:00:24
Chabarowsk → Chabarovsk 2
11 48N27 135E06 -9:00:24
Chabary 2 23 53N37 79E33 -5:18:12
Chabez 6 47 44N02 41E47 -2:47:08
Chaboje 6 9 59N53 30E46 -2:03:04
Chačmas 3 34 41N28 48E48 -3:15:12
Chada-Bulak 2 16 50N38 116E18 -7:45:12
Chadyžensk 6 47 44N25 39E33 -2:38:12
Chadžalmachi 6
47 42N26 47E13 -3:08:52
Chaiši 7 33 42N57 42E12 -2:48:48
Chait 21 24 39N11 70E53 -4:43:32
Chajdarken 10 24 39N57 71E21 -4:45:24
Chaldan 3 34 40N43 47E15 -3:09:00
Chalilovo 6 30 51N24 58E04 -3:52:16
Chalkabad 24 30 42N42 59E43 -3:58:52
Chal'mer-Ju 6 29 67N58 64E50 -4:19:20
Chalturin 6 42 58N33 48E50 -3:15:20
Chalturino 23 45 49N31 35E17 -2:21:08
Chamamatjurt 6
47 43N36 46E30 -3:06:00
Chamamat'urt 6
47 43N36 46E30 -3:06:00
Chamza Chakimzada 24
24 40N26 71E30 -4:46:00
Chanabadskij 24
24 40N49 72E58 -4:51:52
Chanda 2 20 55N00 107E14 -7:08:56
Chandagajty 2 21 50N44 92E03 -6:08:12
Chandyga 2 12 62N40 135E36 -9:02:24
Changa 9 30 44N27 50E36 -3:22:24
Changokurt 2 30 61N58 64E18 -4:17:12
Chani 2 16 57N05 120E58 -8:03:52
Chanino 6 39 54N13 36E37 -2:26:28
Chanlar 3 34 40N34 46E20 -3:05:20
Chantau 9 24 44N13 73E51 -4:55:24
Chanty-Mansijsk 2
25 61N00 69E06 -4:36:24
Chanž'onkovo 23
45 48N06 38E06 -2:32:24
Chapčeranga 2 18 49N42 112E24 -7:29:36
Chapry 6 40 47N14 39E31 -2:38:04
Charabali 6 34 47N24 47E16 -3:09:04
Charagun 2 18 51N36 111E05 -7:24:20
Charal 2 21 51N58 96E39 -6:26:36
Charanor 2 16 50N05 116E40 -7:46:40
Charauz 2 20 52N16 106E17 -7:05:08
Charazargaj 2 20 52N57 104E41 -6:58:44
Charbala 2 16 64N07 120E19 -8:01:16
Charbatovo 2 20 53N46 106E00 -7:04:00
Charcyzsk 23 45 48N02 38E09 -2:32:36
Chardzhou → Čardžou 22
30 39N06 63E34 -4:14:16
Charik 2 20 54N15 101E39 -6:46:36
Charino 6 41 59N57 43E44 -2:54:56
Charino 6 39 54N33 37E52 -2:31:28
Charistvala 7 33 42N26 43E02 -2:52:08
Charitonovo 6 41 61N27 47E28 -3:09:52
Charitonovo 6 39 56N52 36E44 -2:26:56
Char'kin 9 32 48N46 51E49 -3:27:16
Char'kov (Kharkov) 23
45 50N00 36E15 -2:25:00
Charkow → Char'kov 23
45 50N00 36E15 -2:25:00
Charlovka 6 9 68N47 37E15 -2:29:00
Charlu 6 9 61N48 30E52 -2:03:28
Charovsk 6 41 59N59 40E11 -2:40:44
Charutajuvom 6
29 66N49 59E30 -3:58:00
Chasavjurt 6 47 43N15 46E37 -3:06:28
Chasav'urt 6 47 43N15 46E37 -3:06:28
Chašdala 24 30 39N42 67E07 -4:28:28
Chašuri 7 33 42N00 43E36 -2:54:24
Chasurta 2 20 52N17 108E52 -7:15:28
Chatanga 2 19 71N58 102E30 -6:50:00
Chatun' 6 39 55N00 37E50 -2:31:20
Chatyrka 2 2 62N03 175E15-11:41:00
Chavast 24 24 40N13 68E50 -4:35:20
Chavertovo 6 40 54N17 39E12 -2:36:48
Chavki 6 39 54N20 38E13 -2:32:52
Cheboksary → Čeboksary 6
41 56N09 47E15 -3:09:00
Chel'ul'ja 6 9 61N44 30E41 -2:02:44
Chelyabinsk → Čel'abinsk 2
30 55N10 61E24 -4:05:36
Cheremkhovo → Čeremchovo 2
20 53N09 103E05 -6:52:20
Cherepovets → Čerepovec 6
40 59N08 37E54 -2:31:36
Cherkassy → Čerkassy 23
44 49N26 32E04 -2:08:16
Cherkessk → Čerkessk 6
47 44N14 42E04 -2:48:16
Chernigov → Černigov 23
44 51N30 31E18 -2:05:12
Chernobyl 23 44 51N17 30E15 -2:01:00
Chernogorsk → Černogorsk 2
21 53N49 91E18 -6:05:12

Place	Zone	Latitude	Longitude	Time
Chernovtsy → Černovcy 23	44	48N18	25E56	-1:43:44
Chernoye 6	40	56N15	43E24	-2:53:36
Cherpuči 2	11	53N01	138E52	-9:15:28
Cherson 23	45	46N38	32E35	-2:10:20
Chiitola 6	9	61N16	29E38	-1:58:32
Chilly 3	34	39N25	49E05	-3:16:20
Chilok 2	18	51N21	110E28	-7:21:52
Chilovo 6	39	57N46	29E23	-1:57:32
Chimkent → Čimkent 9	24	42N18	69E36	-4:38:24
Chimki 6	39	55N54	37E26	-2:29:44
Chingansk 2	11	49N07	131E11	-8:44:44
Chirchik → Čirčik 24	24	41N29	69E35	-4:38:20
Chirovo 6	9	58N56	33E24	-2:13:36
Chirsa 7	33	41N31	46E06	-3:04:24
Chirvosti 6	9	59N57	30E37	-2:02:28
Chişinău → Kišin'ov 15	46	47N00	28E50	-1:55:20
Chislaviči 6	39	54N11	32E10	-2:08:40
Chist'akovo → Torez 23	45	48N01	38E37	-2:34:28
Chistopol → Čistopol' 6	41	55N21	50E37	-3:22:28
Chistyakovo → Torez 23	45	48N01	38E37	-2:34:28
Chita → Čita 2	16	52N03	113E30	-7:34:00
Chiv 6	47	41N46	47E54	-3:11:36
Chiva 24	30	41N24	60E22	-4:01:28
Chkalov → Orenburg 6	30	51N54	55E06	-3:40:24
Chlebnikovo 6	41	56N38	49E56	-3:19:44
Chlebnikovo 6	39	55N58	37E31	-2:30:04
Chlebodarnyj 6	47	46N41	40E50	-2:43:20
Chlebodarovka 23	45	47N29	37E23	-2:29:32
Chlevnoje 6	40	52N12	39E05	-2:36:20
Chmelevicy 6	41	57N45	46E22	-3:05:28
Chmelevo 6	39	56N09	39E08	-2:36:32
Chmelevoje 23	45	48N34	31E24	-2:05:36
Chmelita 6	39	55N25	33E53	-2:15:32
Chmel'nickij 23	44	49N25	27E00	-1:48:00
Chmel'nik 23	44	49N33	27E57	-1:51:48
Chmel'niki 6	39	56N52	38E13	-2:32:52
Chobeju 2	30	64N53	60E10	-4:00:40
Chobi 7	33	42N21	41E53	-2:47:32
Chochloma 6	41	56N58	43E54	-2:55:36
Chochol'skij 6	40	51N34	38E45	-2:35:00
Chodarus 2	20	52N36	99E19	-6:37:16
Chodorov 23	44	49N24	24E17	-1:37:08
Chodosy 4	39	53N56	31E29	-2:05:56
Chodovaja Griva 6	42	57N08	50E16	-3:21:04
Chodovaricha 6	29	68N57	53E40	-3:34:40
Chodžaimetk 21	24	39N37	69E14	-4:36:56
Chodžakala 22	30	38N43	56E20	-3:45:20
Chodžejli 24	30	42N48	59E25	-3:57:40
Chogot 2	20	53N15	105E52	-7:03:28
Chojniki 4	39	51N53	29E56	-1:59:44
Cholbon 2	16	51N53	116E15	-7:45:00
Choldarkipčak 21	24	39N51	68E52	-4:35:28
Cholm 6	39	57N09	31E11	-2:04:44
Cholmeč' 4	39	52N09	30E37	-2:02:28
Cholmogorovka 9	24	44N25	78E31	-5:14:04
Cholmogorskaja 6	41	63N49	40E39	-2:42:36
Cholmogory 6	41	64N15	41E40	-2:46:40
Cholmsk 19	8	47N03	142E03	-9:28:12
Cholmskij 6	47	44N52	38E24	-2:33:36
Cholmy 23	44	51N52	32E36	-2:10:24
Cholmy 6	39	54N56	38E33	-2:34:12
Cholm-Žirkovskij 6	39	55N31	33E29	-2:13:56
Cholodnaja Balka 23	45	48N02	38E04	-2:32:16
Cholopeniči 4	39	54N31	28E58	-1:55:52
Choltobino 6	39	54N11	38E28	-2:33:52
Choltoson 2	20	50N20	103E20	-6:53:20
Choluj 6	40	56N34	41E53	-2:47:32
Choluj 6	40	56N04	42E08	-2:48:32
Chomičev 6	34	48N11	45E01	-3:00:04
Chomutec 23	44	50N06	33E44	-2:14:56
Chomutovka 6	39	51N56	34E33	-2:18:12
Chomutovo 6	39	52N51	37E27	-2:29:48
Chomutovo 2	20	52N28	104E25	-6:57:40
Chomutovskaja 6	40	47N03	40E04	-2:40:16
Chon'atino 6	39	55N11	38E07	-2:32:28
Choncholoj 2	20	51N08	108E14	-7:12:56
Chonuu 2	6	66N27	143E06	-9:32:24
Chor 2	11	47N53	134E58	-8:59:52
Chorejver 6	29	67N25	58E03	-3:52:12
Chori 7	33	41N37	45E59	-3:03:56
Chorinsk 2	20	52N10	109E46	-7:19:04
Chorlovo 6	39	55N20	38E49	-2:35:16
Chorog 21	24	37N31	71E33	-4:46:12
Chorol 23	44	49N47	33E17	-2:13:08
Chorol' 2	27	44N25	132E04	-8:48:16
Chorošovo 6	39	55N08	38E47	-2:35:08
Chorostkov 23	44	49N13	25E55	-1:43:40
Chosedachard 6	29	67N02	59E22	-3:57:28
Chošeutovo 6	34	47N02	47E50	-3:11:20
Chosrech 6	47	41N59	47E18	-3:09:12
Chosta 6	47	43N33	39E53	-2:39:32
Choten' 23	45	51N07	34E46	-2:19:04
Chotešov 23	44	51N43	24E47	-1:39:08
Chotilovo 6	39	57N44	34E05	-2:16:20
Chotimsk 4	39	53N26	32E35	-2:10:20
Chotin 23	45	48N29	26E30	-1:46:00
Chotisino 6	39	54N24	36E33	-2:26:12
Chot'kovo 6	39	52N56	35E23	-2:21:32
Chot'kovo 6	39	56N15	38E00	-2:32:00
Chot'kovo 6	39	53N46	35E14	-2:20:56
Chotovn'a 4	39	53N17	30E32	-2:02:08
Chotuš' 6	39	54N32	37E44	-2:30:56
Chotynec 6	39	53N08	35E24	-2:21:36
Chotyniči 4	39	52N38	26E18	-1:45:12
Chovaling 21	24	38N21	69E58	-4:39:52
Chovu-Aksy 2	21	51N11	93E53	-6:15:32
Chrapun' 4	39	51N42	27E29	-1:49:56
Chr'aščevka 6	34	53N48	49E06	-3:16:24
Chrebtovo 6	39	56N35	38E16	-2:33:04
Chrenovoje 6	41	51N07	40E17	-2:41:08
Chreščatij 23	45	49N37	39E42	-2:38:48
Christinovka 23	45	48N49	29E58	-1:59:52
Christišče 23	45	48N55	37E30	-2:30:00
Christoforovka 23	45	47N59	33E05	-2:12:20
Christoforovo 6	42	60N53	47E13	-3:08:52
Chromtau 9	30	50N17	58E27	-3:53:48
Chrustal'nyj 2	27	44N24	135E06	-9:00:24
Chuchra 23	45	50N13	34E49	-2:19:16
Chučni 6	47	41N57	47E55	-3:11:40
Chudat 3	34	41N38	48E42	-3:14:48
Chudojelan' 2	20	54N42	99E37	-6:38:28
Chulo 7	33	41N41	42E18	-2:49:12
Chumalag 6	47	43N14	44E28	-2:57:52
Chunzach 6	47	42N33	46E43	-3:06:52
Churmuli 2	11	51N00	136E50	-9:07:20
Chušenga 2	18	51N27	110E55	-7:23:40
Chusovoy → Čusovoj 6	30	58N17	57E49	-3:51:16
Chust 23	44	48N10	23E18	-1:33:12
Chutor-Michajlovskij 23	44	52N03	33E56	-2:15:44
Chutorskoj 6	47	46N52	42E59	-2:51:56
Chužir 2	20	53N11	107E20	-7:09:20
Chvalynsk 6	34	52N30	48E07	-3:12:28
Chvančkara 7	33	42N34	43E01	-2:52:04
Chvastoviči 6	39	53N28	35E06	-2:20:24
Chvatovka 6	34	52N21	46E34	-3:06:16
Chvojnaja 6	9	58N54	34E32	-2:18:08
Chvorost'anka 6	34	52N36	48E59	-3:15:56
Chvostovo 19	8	46N08	142E14	-9:28:56
Chyrov 23	44	49N33	22E49	-1:31:16
Čiatura 7	33	42N17	43E17	-2:53:08
Čibargata 24	24	41N08	69E48	-4:39:12
Čibisovka 6	41	50N47	40E05	-2:40:20
Čibižek 2	21	54N27	93E40	-6:14:40
Čičatka 2	16	54N03	121E18	-8:05:12
Čichačovo 6	39	57N17	29E54	-1:59:36
Čichačovo 2	11	51N50	141E07	-9:24:28
Čichareši 7	33	42N48	43E03	-2:52:12
Čiganak 6	34	51N47	43E18	-2:53:12
Čiganak 9	24	45N06	73E58	-4:55:52
Čiganaki 6	34	47N57	43E05	-2:52:20
Čigirin 23	44	49N04	32E40	-2:10:40
Čigorak 6	41	51N26	42E09	-2:48:36
Čiili 9	30	44N10	66E45	-4:27:00
Čijen 9	24	43N08	75E55	-5:03:40
Čik 2	23	55N01	82E27	-5:29:48
Čikan 2	20	54N54	105E39	-7:02:36
Čikišl'ar 22	30	37N34	53E55	-3:35:40
Čikoj 2	20	50N16	106E54	-7:07:36
Čikola 6	47	43N12	43E55	-2:55:40
Čilekovo 6	34	47N50	43E30	-2:54:00
Čil'gazi 21	24	40N10	70E39	-4:42:36
Čilik 9	30	51N07	54E07	-3:36:28
Čilik 9	24	43N36	78E15	-5:13:00
Čimbaj 24	30	42N57	59E47	-3:59:08
Čimion 24	24	40N16	71E31	-4:46:04
Čimišlija 15	46	46N32	28E44	-1:54:56
Čimkent 9	24	42N18	69E36	-4:38:24
Čimkorgon 10	24	42N50	75E30	-5:02:00
Čiml'ansk 6	47	47N38	42E04	-2:48:16
Činabad 24	24	40N52	71E58	-4:47:52
Činadijevo 23	44	48N30	22E50	-1:31:20
Cinandali 7	33	41N53	45E34	-3:02:16
Činaz 24	24	40N56	68E45	-4:35:00
Cingaly 2	25	60N13	69E45	-4:39:00
Čingis 2	21	54N08	81E41	-5:26:44
Čingistaj 9	24	49N13	85E55	-5:43:40
Činišeucy 15	46	47N42	28E52	-1:55:28
Činja-Voryk 6	29	63N13	52E38	-3:30:32
Cipikan 2	20	54N55	113E21	-7:33:24
Čir 6	34	48N29	43E10	-2:52:40
Čiragidzor 3	34	40N27	46E19	-3:05:16
Čirčik 24	24	41N29	69E35	-4:38:20
Čirgalandy 2	21	50N36	97E20	-6:29:20
Čirikovo 6	39	55N23	37E14	-2:28:56
Čismena 6	39	56N02	36E13	-2:24:52
Čišmy 6	30	54N35	55E20	-3:41:20
Čistoje 6	40	56N32	43E02	-2:52:08
Čistooz'ornoje 2	23	54N43	76E33	-5:06:12
Čistopol' 6	41	55N21	50E37	-3:22:28
Čistopolje 6	40	47N31	39E27	-2:37:48
Čistopolje 9	24	52N34	67E15	-4:29:00
Čistovodovka 23	45	49N24	37E20	-2:29:20
Čita 2	16	52N03	113E30	-7:34:00
Citeli-Ckaro 7	33	41N28	46E07	-3:04:28
Civil'sk 6	41	55N53	47E29	-3:09:56
Čiža 6	41	67N06	44E19	-2:57:16
Čiža Vtoraja 9	32	50N52	49E40	-3:18:40
Čkalovo 9	24	53N38	70E24	-4:41:36
Čkalovo 23	45	46N28	34E11	-2:16:44
Čkalov → Orenburg 6	30	51N54	55E06	-3:40:24
Čkalovsk 21	24	40N13	69E50	-4:39:20
Čkalovsk 6	40	56N46	43E16	-2:53:04
Čkalovsk 9	24	41N15	68E00	-4:32:00
Čkalovskij 6	39	55N54	38E04	-2:32:16
Čoboty 6	39	55N39	37E21	-2:29:24
Čochatauri 7	33	42N01	42E15	-2:49:00
Čodro 2	21	50N50	88E34	-5:54:16
Čoktal 10	24	42N36	76E44	-5:06:56
Čokurdach 2	6	70N38	147E55	-9:51:40
Čolpon 10	24	42N12	75E28	-5:01:52
Čolpon-Ata 10	24	42N40	77E06	-5:08:24
Čon-Saryoj 10	24	42N37	76E53	-5:07:32
Čop 23	44	48N26	22E10	-1:28:40
Čopoviči 23	44	50N49	27E58	-1:51:52
Čorku 21	24	39N58	70E33	-4:42:12
Čormoz 6	30	58N53	56E08	-3:44:32
Čornaja 6	29	68N35	56E30	-3:46:00
Čornaja 6	39	55N45	38E04	-2:32:16
Čornaja 23	45	47N37	29E20	-1:57:20
Čornaja Cholunica 6	42	58N51	51E42	-3:26:48
Čornaja Gr'az' 6	39	54N58	36E48	-2:27:12
Čornaja Gr'az' 6	39	55N58	37E19	-2:29:16
Čornaja Gr'az' 6	39	54N31	35E52	-2:23:28
Čornaja Rečka 6	9	59N56	30E58	-2:03:52
Čornaja Sloboda 6	40	60N48	37E46	-2:31:04
Čornobajevka 23	45	46N42	32E32	-2:10:08
Čornoje 6	41	57N32	46E25	-3:05:40
Čornoje 9	24	51N44	77E34	-5:10:16
Čornolesskoje 6	47	44N42	43E42	-2:54:48
Čornomorskij 6	47	44N51	38E29	-2:33:56
Čornomorskoje 23	45	45N30	32E42	-2:10:48
Čornomorskoje 23	45	45N03	35E58	-2:23:52
Čornoreck 9	24	52N45	76E40	-5:06:40
Čornyj Jar 6	34	48N04	46E08	-3:04:32
Čornyj Mys 6	9	68N20	38E37	-2:34:28
Čornyj Mys 2	23	55N33	80E04	-5:20:16
Čornyj Ostrov 23	44	49N32	26E46	-1:47:04
Čornyj Otrog 6	30	51N55	55E59	-3:43:56
Čornyj Rynok 6	47	44N24	46E33	-3:06:12
Čortkov 23	44	49N01	25E48	-1:43:12
Čoruch-Dajron 21	24	40N24	69E40	-4:38:40
Crimea 6	47	47N40	40E46	-2:43:04
Ču 9	24	43N36	73E45	-4:55:00
Čubaricha 2	30	57N37	68E22	-4:33:28
Čubarovo 6	39	55N12	36E56	-2:27:44
Čublas 6	41	64N44	45E00	-3:00:00
Čučeviči 4	39	52N35	26E52	-1:47:28
Čuchloma 6	41	58N45	42E41	-2:50:44
Čučkovo 6	41	54N17	41E26	-2:45:44
Čučkovo 6	41	59N36	41E14	-2:44:56
Čučuleny 15	46	47N02	28E22	-1:53:28
Cudachar 6	47	42N21	47E11	-3:08:44
Čudin 4	39	52N44	26E59	-1:47:56
Čudnov 23	44	50N04	28E06	-1:52:24
Čudovo 6	9	59N07	31E41	-2:06:44
Čufarovo 6	42	54N06	47E19	-3:09:16
Čugujev 23	45	49N50	36E41	-2:26:44
Čugujevka 2	27	44N08	133E53	-8:55:32
Čugunaš 2	21	52N52	87E46	-5:51:04
Čuja 2	20	59N12	112E25	-7:29:40
Čukurčak 10	24	41N47	71E07	-4:44:28
Cukurino 23	45	48N05	37E18	-2:29:12
Čulak-Kurgan 9	24	43N46	69E12	-4:36:48
Čul'man 2	16	56N52	124E52	-8:19:28
Culukidze 7	33	42N20	42E25	-2:49:40
Čulym 2	23	55N06	80E58	-5:23:52
Čum 6	29	67N06	63E07	-4:12:28
Čumakovo 2	23	55N41	79E02	-5:16:08
Cuman' 23	44	50N49	25E53	-1:43:32
Čumbur-Kosa 6	47	46N57	38E53	-2:35:32
Čumikan 2	11	54N42	135E19	-9:01:16
Čundža 9	24	43N32	79E28	-5:17:52
Čunojar 2	21	57N27	97E18	-6:29:12
Čunskij 2	20	56N05	99E41	-6:38:44
Čunskij 2	20	57N26	97E31	-6:30:04
Čuny 6	40	59N39	36E04	-2:24:16
Čupa 6	9	66N16	33E00	-2:12:00
Čupachovka 23	45	50N23	34E36	-2:18:24
Čupalejka 6	41	55N11	42E33	-2:50:12
Čuprovo 6	41	64N14	46E36	-3:06:24
Čur 6	42	57N07	52E58	-3:31:52
Čuračiki 6	41	55N44	47E26	-3:09:44
Čurapča 2	13	62N00	132E24	-8:49:36
Čurbek 10	24	39N59	69E56	-4:39:44
Curib 6	47	42N14	46E49	-3:07:16
Čuroviči 6	39	52N10	32E01	-2:08:04
C'urupinsk 23	45	46N37	32E43	-2:10:52
Čusovoj 6	30	58N17	57E49	-3:51:16
Čust 24	24	41N00	71E15	-4:45:00
Čutejevo 6	41	55N16	47E47	-3:11:08
Čutovo 23	45	49N43	35E10	-2:20:40
Čutyr' 6	42	57N24	53E17	-3:33:08
Cvetkovo 23	44	49N11	31E33	-2:06:12

Cvetnogorsk 2 21 54N14 90E27 -6:01:48
Cvetnoje 23 45 48N57 32E29 -2:09:56
Cybulev 23 44 49N06 29E50 -1:59:20
Czernowitz → Černovcy 23
44 48N18 25E56 -1:43:44
D'adino 2 20 55N44 105E45 -7:03:00
Dagda 13 36 56N06 27E32 -1:50:08
Dagestanskije Ogni 6
47 42N07 48E12 -3:12:48
Dagomys 6 47 43N40 39E41 -2:38:44
Dal'mamedli 3 34 40N42 46E34 -3:06:16
Dalmatovo 2 30 56N16 62E56 -4:11:44
Dal'n'aja 19 8 45N56 142E04 -9:28:16
Dal'n'aja Muja 2
20 54N21 103E37 -6:54:28
Dal'negorsk 2 27 44N35 135E35 -9:02:20
Dal'neje-Konstantinovo 6
41 55N49 44E06 -2:56:24
Dal'nerečensk 2
27 45N55 133E43 -8:54:52
Dal'ne-Rusanovo 6
39 54N15 36E45 -2:27:00
Dal'nik 23 45 46N28 30E34 -2:02:16
Dal'stroja 2 2 68N19 177W39 11:50:36
Dambuki 2 14 54N21 127E38 -8:30:32
Dangara 21 24 38N06 69E22 -4:37:28
Dangara 24 24 40N35 70E54 -4:43:36
Danilov 6 41 58N12 40E12 -2:40:48
Danilovka 6 41 52N33 45E23 -3:01:32
Danilovka 6 34 50N21 44E06 -2:56:24
Danilovo 6 39 55N40 38E46 -2:35:04
Danilovskoje 6
39 56N48 35E45 -2:23:00
Danki 6 39 54N55 37E34 -2:30:16
Dankov 6 40 53N15 39E08 -2:36:32
Darasun 2 16 51N40 114E00 -7:36:00
Daraut-Kurgan 10
24 39N33 72E13 -4:48:52
Darbaza 9 24 41N35 69E02 -4:36:08
Darbėnai 14 37 56N01 21E15 -1:25:00
Darčeli 7 33 42N27 41E42 -2:46:48
Darjevka 6 40 47N42 39E41 -2:38:44
Darjinskij 9 24 49N04 72E56 -4:51:44
Darjinskoje 9 32 51N20 51E44 -3:26:56
Darovoje 6 39 54N34 38E22 -2:33:28
Darvaza 22 30 40N11 58E24 -3:53:36
Dašava 23 44 49N16 24E01 -1:36:04
Dašev 23 44 49N00 29E26 -1:57:44
Daškesan 3 34 40N30 46E04 -3:04:16
Daškovka 4 39 53N44 30E13 -2:00:52
Dastakert 1 34 39N23 46E02 -3:04:08
Daštidžum 21 24 38N01 70E12 -4:40:48
Daštioburdon 21
24 39N24 69E04 -4:36:16
D'at'kovo 6 39 53N36 34E20 -2:17:20
D'atlovići 4 39 52N20 26E50 -1:47:20
D'atlovo 6 39 56N14 36E16 -2:25:04
D'atlovo 4 39 53N28 25E24 -1:41:36
Datta 2 11 49N18 140E22 -9:21:28
Daugai 14 37 54N22 24E20 -1:37:20
Daugavpils 13 36 55N53 26E32 -1:46:08
Daurija 2 16 49N56 116E52 -7:47:28
Daurskoje 2 21 55N14 92E05 -6:08:20
Davenda 2 16 53N33 119E18 -7:57:12
David-Gorodok 4
39 52N03 27E14 -1:48:56
Davido-Nikol'skoje 23
45 48N30 39E50 -2:39:20
Davlekanovo 6 30 54N13 55E03 -3:40:12
Davydkovo 6 39 56N17 36E49 -2:27:16
Davydkovo 6 39 55N35 37E12 -2:28:48
Davydov Brod 23
45 47N14 33E12 -2:12:48
Davydovka 6 41 51N10 39E25 -2:37:40
Davydovo 6 39 55N37 38E52 -2:35:28
Davydovskoje 6
39 55N52 36E48 -2:27:12
Debal'cevo 23 45 48N20 38E24 -2:33:36
Debesy 6 42 57N39 53E49 -3:35:16
Dedenevo 6 39 56N15 37E31 -2:30:04
Dedilovskije Vyselki 6
39 54N20 38E03 -2:32:12
Dedinovo 6 39 55N03 39E07 -2:36:28
Dedoviči 6 39 57N32 29E56 -1:59:44
Dedovsk 6 39 55N52 37E07 -2:28:28
Degeres 9 24 43N14 75E49 -5:03:16
Degt'ari 23 44 50N35 32E45 -2:11:00
Degt'arsk 2 30 56N42 60E06 -4:00:24
Degtevo 6 47 49N11 40E39 -2:42:36
Dejnau 22 30 39N15 63E11 -4:12:44
De-Kastri 2 11 51N28 140E47 -9:23:08
Del'atiči 4 39 53N47 25E59 -1:43:56
Del'atin 23 44 48N32 24E37 -1:38:28
Delingde 2 16 70N08 114E00 -7:36:00
Demaki 6 42 58N26 51E43 -3:26:52
Dem'ansk 6 39 57N38 32E28 -2:09:52
Demidov 6 39 55N16 31E31 -2:06:04
Demidovka 23 44 50N25 25E20 -1:41:20
Demidovo 6 40 59N17 38E17 -2:33:08
Demjanovka 9 30 54N04 65E22 -4:21:28
Demjanovo 6 42 60N22 47E03 -3:08:12
Demjansk 6 39 57N38 32E28 -2:09:52
Demjanskoje 2 30 59N36 69E18 -4:37:12
Demjas 6 34 51N13 49E08 -3:16:32
Demurino 23 45 48N10 36E29 -2:25:56
Denau 22 30 38N16 67E54 -4:31:36
Denežnikovo 6 39 55N26 38E07 -2:32:28
Denežnikovo 23
45 49N02 38E57 -2:35:48
Deniskoviči 6 39 52N19 31E43 -2:06:52
Deniskoviči 4 39 52N44 26E41 -1:46:44
Denisovka 6 29 66N14 55E20 -3:41:20
Denisovka 9 30 52N28 61E46 -4:07:04
Denisovo 6 39 54N28 37E51 -2:31:24
Den'kovo 6 39 56N01 36E21 -2:25:24
Deražn'a 23 44 49N16 27E26 -1:49:44
Derbent 6 47 42N03 48E18 -3:13:12
Derbeškinskij 6
41 55N52 53E30 -3:34:00
Derbetovka 6 47 45N48 43E05 -2:52:20
Derečin 4 39 53N15 24E55 -1:39:40
Derev'anka 6 9 61N34 34E27 -2:17:48
Dergači 6 34 51N14 48E46 -3:15:04
Dergači 23 45 50N07 36E07 -2:24:28
Derkul 9 32 51N16 51E18 -3:25:12
Dernoviči 4 39 51N36 29E43 -1:58:52
Der'uzino 6 39 56N18 38E16 -2:33:04
Deržavino 6 32 53N13 52E22 -3:29:28
Deržavinsk 9 24 51N03 66E19 -4:25:16
Deržavinskij 9
24 51N03 66E19 -4:25:16
Desna 23 44 50N56 30E46 -2:03:04
Detčino 6 39 54N49 36E19 -2:25:16
Detskosel'skij 6
9 59N44 30E28 -2:01:52
Dev'atern'a 6 42 56N12 53E24 -3:33:36
Dev'atiny 6 40 60N56 36E46 -2:27:04
Devladovo 23 45 48N07 33E45 -2:15:00
Didbiran 2 11 51N58 139E20 -9:17:20
Dievenišk̇ės 14
37 54N12 25E37 -1:42:28
Digomi 7 33 41N47 44E44 -2:58:56
Digora 6 47 43N10 44E09 -2:56:36
Diirmentobe 9 30 45N44 63E37 -4:14:28
Dijag 6 29 65N48 57E39 -3:50:36
Dikaja 6 40 59N15 39E30 -2:38:00
Dikan'ka 23 45 49N49 34E32 -2:18:08
Dikli 13 36 57N35 25E06 -1:40:24
Dikson 2 22 73N30 80E35 -5:22:20
Diližan 1 34 40N45 44E52 -2:59:28
Dimitrov 23 45 48N15 37E18 -2:29:12
Dimitrovgrad 6
42 54N14 49E39 -3:18:36
Dimitrovskoje 24
24 40N16 69E03 -4:36:12
Dinamo 6 34 50N15 41E38 -2:46:32
Dinskaja 6 47 45N13 39E14 -2:36:56
Disna 4 39 55N33 28E10 -1:52:40
Divejevo 6 41 55N03 43E15 -2:53:00
Divenskaja 6 9 59N12 30E01 -2:00:04
Diviči 3 34 41N12 48E59 -3:15:56
Divin 4 39 51N58 24E35 -1:38:20
Divizija 23 45 45N57 29E59 -1:59:56
Divnogorsk 2 21 55N58 92E22 -6:09:28
Divnoje 6 47 45N55 43E22 -2:53:28
Djakonovo 6 39 54N34 38E20 -2:33:20
Djakovka 6 34 50N43 46E46 -3:07:04
Djakovo 23 45 47N57 39E09 -2:36:36
Djalal-Abad → Džalal-Abad 10
24 40N56 73E00 -4:52:00
Djambul → Džambul 9
24 42N54 71E22 -4:45:28
Dmanisi 7 33 41N22 44E12 -2:56:48
Dmitr'ašovka 6
40 52N09 39E04 -2:36:16
Dmitrijevka 2 23 55N10 75E36 -5:02:24
Dmitrijevka 9 24 43N30 77E02 -5:08:08
Dmitrijevka 23
45 48N55 39E10 -2:36:40
Dmitrijevka 23
45 47N56 38E56 -2:35:44
Dmitrijev-L'govskij 6
39 52N08 35E05 -2:20:20
Dmitrijevskij 9
30 49N08 57E50 -3:51:20
Dmitrijevskoje 6
47 45N48 41E54 -2:47:36
Dmitrijevskoje 6
39 54N40 37E38 -2:30:32
Dmitrijev Usad 6
41 54N14 43E18 -2:53:12
Dmitrijev Usad 6
41 54N08 43E08 -2:52:32
Dmitrijevy Gory 6
40 55N12 41E47 -2:47:08
Dmitrov 6 39 56N21 37E31 -2:30:04
Dmitrovcy 6 39 55N16 38E55 -2:35:40
Dmitroviči 4 39 53N59 29E06 -1:56:24
Dmitrovka 23 45 45N29 35E04 -2:20:16
Dmitrovka 23 45 46N51 36E35 -2:26:20
Dmitrovka 23 45 48N48 32E44 -2:10:56
Dmitrovskij Pogost 6
39 55N19 39E49 -2:39:16
Dmitrovsk-Orlovskij 6
39 52N30 35E09 -2:20:36
Dmuchajlovka 23
45 49N03 34E46 -2:19:04
Dnepr'any 23 45 46N44 33E16 -2:13:04
Dneprodzeržinsk 23
45 48N30 34E37 -2:18:28
Dnepropetrovsk 23
45 48N27 34E59 -2:19:56
Dneprovka 23 45 47N26 34E38 -2:18:32
Dneprovskoje 6
39 55N40 33E55 -2:15:40
Dniepropetrovsk → Dnepropetrovsk 23
45 48N27 34E59 -2:19:56
Dno 6 39 57N50 29E59 -1:59:56
Dobele 13 36 56N37 23E16 -1:33:04
Dobr'anka 6 30 58N27 56E24 -3:45:36
Dobr'anka 23 44 52N04 31E11 -2:04:44
Dobr'anka 23 45 48N21 30E54 -2:03:36
Dobrinka 6 34 48N49 42E58 -2:51:52
Dobrinka 6 34 50N49 41E51 -2:47:24
Dobrinka 6 41 52N09 40E29 -2:41:56
Dobroje 6 39 57N06 32E02 -2:08:08
Dobroje 6 41 55N52 39E48 -2:39:12
Dobromil' 23 44 49N34 22E47 -1:31:08
Dobropolje 23 45 48N28 37E05 -2:28:20
Doboslavka 4 39 52N24 26E15 -1:45:00
Dobrotvor 23 44 50N14 24E22 -1:37:28
Dobrovelíčkovka 23
45 48N23 31E11 -2:04:44
Dobrovolje 23 45 48N41 36E37 -2:26:28
Dobrovol'sk 8 38 54N46 22E31 -1:30:04
Dobruš 4 39 52N25 31E19 -2:05:16
Dobryn' 4 39 51N46 29E12 -1:56:48
D'ogtevo 6 47 49N11 40E39 -2:42:36
D'ogtevo 6 47 49N10 40E39 -2:42:36
Dokšicy 4 39 54N54 27E46 -1:51:04
Dokšukino 6 47 43N33 43E50 -2:55:20
Dokučajevsk 23
45 47N44 37E40 -2:30:40
Dol'a 23 45 47N53 37E41 -2:30:44
Dolgaja 2 30 55N49 64E15 -4:17:00
Dolgen'koje 23
45 49N01 37E19 -2:29:16
Dolgij Most 2 21 56N45 96E48 -6:27:12
Dolginovo 4 39 54N39 27E29 -1:49:56
Dolgoje 6 39 52N04 37E34 -2:30:16
Dolgoprudnyj 6
39 55N56 37E31 -2:30:04
Dolgorukovo 6 40 52N19 38E21 -2:33:24
Dolgoščelje 6 41 66N03 43E24 -2:53:36
Dolina 23 45 48N59 37E27 -2:29:48
Dolinnyj 9 30 51N16 52E11 -3:28:44
Dolinovskoje 23
45 48N36 38E33 -2:34:12
Dolinsk 19 8 47N21 142E48 -9:31:12
Dolinskaja 23 45 48N07 32E44 -2:10:56
Dolmatovka 23 45 46N13 32E26 -2:09:44
Dolmatovskij 6
40 57N29 42E18 -2:49:12
Dolon 9 24 50N40 79E18 -5:17:12
Dol'skoje 6 39 54N47 36E26 -2:25:44
Dolžak 23 45 48N41 26E32 -1:46:08
Dolžanskaja 6 47 46N37 37E48 -2:31:12
Dolžanskaja 23
45 48N03 39E39 -2:38:36
Dolžicy 6 9 58N00 29E51 -1:59:24
Dolžicy 6 9 58N31 29E08 -1:56:32
Dolžik 23 45 50N13 35E55 -2:23:40
Domacha 6 39 52N28 34E58 -2:19:52
Domačovo 4 39 51N44 23E37 -1:34:28
Domanevka 23 45 47N37 30E58 -2:03:52
Domaniči 6 39 53N02 33E25 -2:13:40
Domaška 6 34 53N00 50E47 -3:23:08
Dombaj 6 47 43N17 41E37 -2:46:28
Dombarovskij 6
30 50N46 59E32 -3:58:08
Domnino 6 39 54N10 38E11 -2:32:44
Domodedovo 6 39 55N26 37E46 -2:31:04
Doncovka 23 45 49N35 39E16 -2:37:04
Dond'ušany 15 46 48N15 27E37 -1:50:28
Doneck 6 47 48N21 40E02 -2:40:08
Doneck 23 45 48N00 37E48 -2:31:12
Donetsk → Doneck 23
45 48N00 37E48 -2:31:12
Donjezk → Doneck 23
45 48N00 37E48 -2:31:12
Donskoj 6 39 53N58 38E20 -2:33:20
Donskoj 6 40 47N25 40E14 -2:40:56
Donskoje 6 40 52N37 39E00 -2:36:00
Donskoje 23 45 47N31 37E33 -2:30:12
Donskoje 6 47 45N21 41E59 -2:47:56
Dorino 6 39 56N28 36E09 -2:24:36
Dormidontovka 2
11 47N45 134E57 -8:59:48
Dorochovo 6 39 55N33 36E23 -2:25:32
Dorogobuž 6 39 54N55 33E18 -2:13:12
Dorošata 6 42 57N21 51E08 -3:24:32
Dorošicha 6 39 56N52 35E50 -2:23:20
Dorpat → Tartu 5
35 58N23 26E43 -1:46:52
Dosatuj 2 16 50N23 118E38 -7:54:32
Dosčatoje 6 40 55N23 42E07 -2:48:28
Dossor 9 30 47N32 53E01 -3:32:04
Dotnuva 14 37 55N21 23E54 -1:35:36
Dovbyš 23 44 50N22 27E59 -1:51:56
Dovol'noje 2 23 54N30 79E40 -5:18:40
Dovsk 4 39 53N09 30E28 -2:01:52
Drabov 23 44 49N58 32E08 -2:08:32
Drakino 6 39 54N52 37E17 -2:29:08
Dranda 7 33 42N53 41E09 -2:44:36
Dretun 4 39 55N41 29E13 -1:56:52
Drezna 6 39 55N44 38E51 -2:35:24
Dribin 4 39 54N08 31E06 -2:04:24
Drobylevo 6 39 55N44 35E53 -2:23:32
Drobyš'ovo 23 45 49N02 37E44 -2:30:56
Drobyšovo 2 24 53N58 74E40 -4:58:40
Drogičin 4 39 52N11 25E09 -1:40:36
Drogobyč 23 44 49N21 23E30 -1:34:00
Drohobycz → Drogobyč 23
44 49N21 23E30 -1:34:00
Drokija 15 46 48N03 27E48 -1:51:12
Droskovo 6 39 52N31 37E05 -2:28:20
Drov'anaja 2 16 51N35 113E02 -7:32:08
Drožžanoje 6 41 54N44 47E34 -3:10:16
Druja 4 39 55N47 27E27 -1:49:48
Druskininkai 14
37 54N01 23E58 -1:35:52
Družba 6 39 55N53 37E45 -2:31:00
Družba 9 24 45N15 82E26 -5:29:44
Družba 23 44 52N03 33E56 -2:15:44
Družina 2 6 68N14 145E18 -9:41:12
Družkovka 23 45 48N37 37E33 -2:30:12
Družnaja Gorka 6
9 59N17 30E08 -2:00:32
Dubenskij 6 30 51N27 56E38 -3:46:32
Dubinino 6 39 56N09 37E01 -2:28:04
Dubjazy 6 41 56N08 49E13 -3:16:52
Dubki 6 9 60N00 30E00 -2:00:00
Dubki 6 39 55N41 37E14 -2:28:56
Dubna 6 39 54N09 36E58 -2:27:52
Dubna 6 39 56N44 37E10 -2:28:40

SOVIET UNION SOJUZ SOVETSKICH UNION SOCIALISTES RUSSIA U.S.S.R.

Dubnevo 6 39 55N06 38E08 -2:32:32
Dubno 23 44 50N26 25E44 -1:42:56
Dub'onki 6 41 54N27 46E18 -3:05:12
Dubossary 15 46 47N16 29E08 -1:56:32
Dubovaja Rošča 6 39 53N11 36E04 -2:24:16
Dubov'azovka 23 44 51N08 33E22 -2:13:28
Dubovići 23 44 51N38 33E35 -2:14:20
Dubovka 6 34 49N03 44E50 -2:59:20
Dubovka 6 41 51N26 41E25 -2:45:40
Dubovoje 6 41 53N08 40E05 -2:40:20
Dubovskij 6 41 56N21 46E48 -3:07:12
Dubovskoje 6 47 47N25 42E46 -2:51:04
Dubovyj Ovrag 6 34 48N20 44E37 -2:58:28
Dubovyj Umet 6 34 52N59 50E17 -3:21:08
Dubrova 4 39 51N47 28E13 -1:52:52
Dubrova 4 39 52N25 29E58 -1:59:52
Dubrova 6 30 56N59 54E33 -3:38:12
Dubrova 6 30 57N42 55E01 -3:40:04
Dubrovica 23 44 51N34 26E34 -1:46:16
Dubroviči 6 40 54N39 39E56 -2:39:44
Dubrovicy 6 39 56N46 39E10 -2:36:40
Dubrovino 2 21 55N28 83E17 -5:33:08
Dubrovka 6 39 53N42 33E30 -2:14:00
Dubrovka 6 9 59N51 30E56 -2:03:44
Dubrovka 6 40 59N13 36E13 -2:24:52
Dubrovka 6 39 54N44 36E21 -2:25:24
Dubrovka 23 45 47N54 39E02 -2:36:08
Dubrovki 6 41 53N49 43E19 -2:53:16
Dubrovno 4 39 54N35 30E41 -2:02:44
Dubrovnoje 2 30 57N58 69E25 -4:37:40
Dubrovnoje 9 24 54N49 68E06 -4:32:24
Dubrovo 6 9 59N51 33E34 -2:14:16
Dubrovskoje 2 20 58N45 111E10 -7:24:40
Dubunskaja 9 24 43N46 80E13 -5:20:52
Duchana 21 30 38N02 68E13 -4:32:52
Duchovnickoje 6 34 52N28 48E15 -3:13:00
Duchovščina 6 39 55N12 32E25 -2:09:40
Dudačkino 6 9 59N57 32E53 -2:11:32
Dudčany 23 45 47N12 33E46 -2:15:04
Dudinka 2 21 69N25 86E15 -5:45:00
Dudkin 6 47 47N53 40E32 -2:42:08
Dudorovskij 6 39 53N40 35E22 -2:21:28
Due 19 8 50N50 142E06 -9:28:24
Dugino 6 40 47N09 39E27 -2:37:48
Dugna 6 39 54N25 36E51 -2:27:24
Dūkštas 14 37 55N32 26E20 -1:45:20
Dul'apino 6 40 57N15 40E49 -2:43:16
Dul'durga 2 16 50N41 113E36 -7:34:24
Dulovka 6 39 57N32 28E20 -1:53:20
Duminiči 6 39 53N55 35E06 -2:20:24
Dünaburg → Daugavpils 13 36 55N53 26E32 -1:46:08
Dunaj 6 9 59N58 30E56 -2:03:44
Dunaj 2 27 42N52 132E22 -8:49:28
Dunajevcy 23 45 48N54 26E51 -1:47:24
Dunajevo 2 16 52N05 117E02 -7:48:08
Dundaga 13 36 57N31 22E21 -1:29:24
Dunilovo 6 40 57N00 41E27 -2:45:48
Dunilovo 6 40 57N46 38E55 -2:35:40
Dupl'atka 6 34 51N07 42E20 -2:49:20
Dupli 6 39 54N21 36E54 -2:27:36
Durasovka 6 34 51N41 44E55 -2:59:40
Durbe 13 36 56N35 21E21 -1:25:24
D'urbel'džin 10 24 41N16 74E57 -4:59:48
Durlešty 15 46 47N02 28E45 -1:55:00
Durnikino 6 34 51N39 42E49 -2:51:16
D'urt'uli 6 30 55N29 54E52 -3:39:28
Dušak 22 30 37N13 60E02 -4:00:08
Dušanbe 21 24 38N35 68E48 -4:35:12
Dušekan 2 20 60N39 109E03 -7:16:12
Dušeti 7 33 42N06 44E42 -2:58:48
Dusetos 14 37 55N45 25E51 -1:43:24
Dushanbe → Dušanbe 21 24 38N35 68E48 -4:35:12
Dušonovo 6 39 56N04 38E18 -2:33:12
Dutovo 6 29 63N47 56E35 -3:46:20
Duvan 6 30 55N42 57E54 -3:51:36
Duvannyj 3 34 40N06 49E24 -3:17:36
Dvinsk → Daugavpils 13 36 55N53 26E32 -1:46:08
Dvojnovskij 6 34 51N03 42E27 -2:49:48
Dvorcy 6 39 54N37 36E00 -2:24:00
Dvorec 2 26 58N23 99E56 -6:39:44
Dvoriši 6 9 58N12 35E13 -2:20:52
Dvornikovo 6 39 55N30 38E38 -2:34:32
Dvulučnoje 6 39 50N02 38E02 -2:32:08
Dylym 6 47 43N04 46E38 -3:06:32
Dymer 23 44 50N47 30E18 -2:01:12
Džabžur 1 34 40N54 43E58 -2:55:52
Džalagaš 9 30 45N05 64E40 -4:18:40
Džalal-Abad 10 24 40N56 73E00 -4:52:00
Džalinda 2 16 53N29 123E54 -8:15:36
Džamašuj 24 24 40N52 71E28 -4:45:52
Džambejty 9 30 50N16 52E35 -3:30:20
Džambul 9 32 47N34 50E12 -3:20:48
Džambul 9 24 42N54 71E22 -4:45:28
Džambul 9 24 47N12 71E42 -4:46:48
Džanga 22 30 40N00 53E03 -3:32:12
Džangi-Džol 10 24 41N36 72E08 -4:48:32
Džankoj 23 45 45N43 34E24 -2:17:36
Džansugurov 9 24 45N24 79E29 -5:17:56
Džanybek 9 32 49N25 46E51 -3:07:24
Džardžan 2 13 68N43 124E02 -8:16:08
Dzaudzhikau → Ordžonikidze 6 47 43N03 44E40 -2:58:40
Džaur 2 11 50N02 138E30 -9:14:00
Džava 7 33 42N24 43E54 -2:55:36
Džazator 9 24 49N45 87E23 -5:49:32
Džebel 22 30 39N38 54E14 -3:36:56
Džebrail 3 34 39N23 47E02 -3:08:08
Džergetal 10 24 41N30 75E47 -5:03:08
Džermuk 1 34 39N51 45E41 -3:02:44
Dzerzhinsk → Dzeržinsk 6 40 56N15 43E24 -2:53:36
Dzeržinsk 4 39 53N41 27E08 -1:48:32
Dzeržinsk 23 45 48N26 37E50 -2:31:20
Dzeržinsk 6 40 56N15 43E24 -2:53:36
Dzeržinsk 23 44 50N09 27E56 -1:51:44
Dzeržinskij 6 39 55N38 37E50 -2:31:20
Dzeržinskij 2 21 54N01 90E12 -6:00:48
Dzeržinskij 23 45 48N02 39E26 -2:37:44
Dzeržinskoje 2 21 56N49 95E18 -6:21:12
Dzeržinskoje 9 24 45N50 81E07 -5:24:28
Džetygara 9 30 52N11 61E12 -4:04:48
Džetyoguz 10 24 42N27 78E14 -5:12:56
Džetysaj 24 24 40N47 68E16 -4:33:04
Džezdy 9 24 48N04 67E05 -4:28:20
Džezkazgan 9 24 47N53 67E27 -4:29:48
Džezkazgan 9 24 47N47 67E46 -4:31:04
Dzhalilabad 3 34 39N14 48E31 -3:14:04
Dzhambul → Džambul 9 24 42N54 71E22 -4:45:28
Džilav 21 24 39N19 67E45 -4:31:00
Džilga 9 24 41N43 69E01 -4:36:04
Džirgatal' 21 24 39N13 71E12 -4:44:48
Džizak 24 24 40N06 67E50 -4:31:20
Džubga 6 47 44N20 38E43 -2:34:52
Džūkste 13 36 56N47 23E15 -1:33:00
Džul'fa 1 34 38N58 45E38 -3:02:32
Džumabazar 24 30 39N31 67E13 -4:28:52
Džurin 23 45 48N41 28E18 -1:53:12
Džurun 9 30 49N15 57E37 -3:50:28
Džusaly 9 30 45N28 64E05 -4:16:20
Džvari 7 33 42N43 42E04 -2:48:16
Dzygovka 23 45 48N22 28E19 -1:53:16
Ebenrode → Nesterov 8 38 54N38 22E34 -1:30:16
Echabi 19 8 53N30 142E59 -9:31:56
Ečmiadzin 1 34 40N10 44E18 -2:57:12
Edisseja 6 47 44N03 44E33 -2:58:12
Egoryevsk → Jegorjevsk 6 39 55N23 39E02 -2:36:08
Egvekinot 2 2 66N19 179W10 11:56:40
Eišiškės 14 37 54N10 25E00 -1:40:00
Eisk → Jejsk 6 47 46N42 38E16 -2:33:04
Ekaterinburg → Sverdlovsk 2 30 56N51 60E36 -4:02:24
Ekaterinodar → Krasnodar 6 47 45N02 39E00 -2:36:00
Ekaterinoslav → Dnepropetrovsk 23 45 48N27 34E59 -2:19:56
Ekibastuz 9 24 51N42 75E22 -5:01:28
Ekimčan 2 14 53N04 132E58 -8:51:52
Ekonda 2 19 65N47 105E17 -7:01:08
El'ban 2 11 50N06 136E31 -9:06:04
El'brusskij 6 47 43N38 42E10 -2:48:40
El'buzd 6 40 46N53 39E41 -2:38:44
El'dikan 2 12 60N48 135E11 -9:00:44
Eleja 13 36 56N26 23E42 -1:34:48
Elektrogorsk 6 39 55N53 38E47 -2:35:08
Elektrostal' 6 39 55N47 38E28 -2:33:52
Elektrougli 6 39 55N43 38E13 -2:32:52
Elektrozavod 6 30 52N34 54E01 -3:36:04
Elets → Jelec 6 40 52N37 38E30 -2:34:00
Elisenvaara 6 9 61N25 29E46 -1:59:04
Elista 6 47 46N16 44E14 -2:56:56
El'ton 6 34 49N08 46E50 -3:07:20
Elva 5 35 58N13 26E25 -1:45:40
Emba 9 30 48N50 58E08 -3:52:32
Emi 2 26 50N36 97E49 -6:31:16
Emmaste 5 35 58N42 22E36 -1:30:24
Emmaus 6 39 56N47 36E07 -2:24:28
Engažimo 2 17 57N51 114E56 -7:39:44
Engel's 6 34 51N30 46E07 -3:04:28
Engel's'ovo 23 45 48N22 39E23 -2:37:32
Engure 13 36 57N10 23E13 -1:32:52
Enmelen 2 2 65N01 175W54 11:43:36
Enurmino 2 2 66N57 171W49 11:27:16
Erdnijevskij 6 47 46N52 46E17 -3:05:08
Ērgļi 13 36 56N54 25E38 -1:42:32
Erivan → Jerevan 1 34 40N11 44E30 -2:58:00
Erken-Jurt 6 47 44N27 41E54 -2:47:36
Ertil' 6 41 51N51 40E49 -2:43:16
Erzin 2 21 50N15 95E10 -6:20:40
Eskilkan 9 24 43N12 68E31 -4:34:04
Espe 9 24 43N52 74E10 -4:56:40
Essentuki → Jessentuki 6 47 44N03 42E51 -2:51:24
Etyka 2 16 51N00 116E50 -7:47:20
Evensk 2 5 61N57 159E14-10:36:56
Evpatoria → Jevpatorija 23 45 45N12 33E22 -2:13:28
Ezere 13 36 56N26 22E22 -1:29:28
Ežerėlis 14 37 54N53 23E37 -1:34:28
Ežva 6 41 61N47 50E40 -3:22:40
Fabričnyj 9 24 43N11 76E24 -5:05:36
Fajansovyj 6 39 54N04 34E24 -2:17:36
Fajzabad 21 24 38N34 69E19 -4:37:16
Fakejev 9 32 48N57 49E56 -3:19:44
Fakel 6 42 57N38 53E02 -3:32:08
Falenki 6 42 58N22 51E35 -3:26:20
Falešty 15 46 47N34 27E43 -1:50:52
Fal'šivyj Gelendžik 6 47 44N31 38E09 -2:32:36
Fanipol' 4 39 53N45 27E20 -1:49:20
Farab 21 24 39N14 67E28 -4:29:52
Farbovano 23 44 50N09 31E51 -2:07:24
Fariš 24 30 40N35 66E52 -4:27:28
Faščovka 23 45 48N16 38E37 -2:34:28
Fastov 23 44 50N06 29E55 -1:59:40
Fastoveckaja 6 47 45N56 40E09 -2:40:36
Fat'ož 6 39 52N07 35E52 -2:23:28
Faustovo 6 39 55N26 38E29 -2:33:56
Fedorino 6 39 55N08 36E06 -2:24:24
Fedosejevka 6 47 46N53 44E00 -2:56:00
Fedosejevskaja 6 41 62N07 40E42 -2:42:48
Fedosicha 2 23 54N47 81E54 -5:27:36
Fedosjino 6 39 55N08 38E30 -2:34:00
Fedotovo 6 39 55N41 39E12 -2:36:48
Fenino 6 39 55N44 37E57 -2:31:48
Feodosija 23 45 45N02 35E23 -2:21:32
Fergana 24 24 40N23 71E46 -4:47:04
Feršampenuaz 2 30 53N32 59E51 -3:59:24
Ferzikovo 6 39 54N32 36E45 -2:27:00
Fetisovo 9 30 42N46 52E38 -3:30:32
Filatova Gora 6 39 57N40 28E10 -1:52:40
Filimonki 6 39 55N33 37E21 -2:29:24
Filimonovo 2 21 56N12 95E28 -6:21:52
Filippovka 6 34 53N59 49E46 -3:19:04
Filippovo 6 42 58N18 50E30 -3:22:00
Filippovskoje 6 39 56N06 38E37 -2:34:28
Filippovskoje 6 39 56N48 39E07 -2:36:28
Filonovskaja 6 34 50N34 42E46 -2:51:04
Finejevo 6 39 56N02 38E53 -2:35:32
Firovo 6 39 57N29 33E40 -2:14:40
Firsanovka 6 39 55N57 37E15 -2:29:00
Firsovo 2 16 52N20 118E06 -7:52:24
Fir'uza 22 30 37N56 58E04 -3:52:16
Fischhausen → Primorsk 8 38 54N44 20E01 -1:20:04
Fizuli 3 34 39N37 47E08 -3:08:32
Florešty 15 46 47N53 28E17 -1:53:08
F'odorovka 6 40 47N20 38E23 -2:33:32
F'odorovka 9 30 53N38 62E42 -4:10:48
F'odorovka 9 24 53N22 76E18 -5:05:12
F'odorovka 9 30 51N09 51E59 -3:27:56
F'odorovka 2 23 56N05 78E49 -5:15:16
F'odorovka 6 30 53N11 55E11 -3:40:44
F'odorovka 6 34 53N28 49E38 -3:18:32
F'odorovka 6 32 52N21 52E55 -3:31:40
F'odorovka 23 45 49N23 35E07 -2:20:28
F'odorovka 23 45 47N33 36E33 -2:26:12
F'odorovka 6 39 56N15 37E14 -2:28:56
F'odorovskoje 6 39 56N08 38E04 -2:32:16
F'odorovskoje 6 39 56N07 38E52 -2:35:28
F'odorovskoje 6 39 56N44 36E58 -2:27:52
Fogelevo 9 24 42N03 69E32 -4:38:08
Foki 6 30 56N42 54E21 -3:37:24
Fokino 6 39 53N27 34E24 -2:17:36
Fomin 6 47 46N58 43E38 -2:54:32
Fominiči 6 39 54N07 34E41 -2:18:44
Fominki 6 40 55N57 42E22 -2:49:28
Fominskaja 6 41 61N17 48E40 -3:14:40
Fominskoje 6 40 58N59 39E06 -2:36:24
Fomkino 6 42 54N25 50E30 -3:22:00
Fornosovo 6 9 59N35 30E35 -2:02:20
Forpost 2 24 56N47 72E10 -4:48:40
Fort-Ševčenko 9 30 44N31 50E16 -3:21:04
Fosforitnyj 6 39 55N19 38E54 -2:35:36
Fr'anovo 6 39 56N08 38E27 -2:33:48
Fr'azino 6 39 55N58 38E04 -2:32:16
Frolišči 6 40 56N25 42E39 -2:50:36
Frolišči 6 39 56N18 39E13 -2:36:52
Frolovo 6 34 49N47 43E39 -2:54:36
Frunze 10 24 40N07 71E44 -4:46:56
Frunze 10 24 42N54 74E36 -4:58:24
Frunze 23 45 46N16 34E52 -2:19:28
Frunze 23 45 48N40 38E45 -2:35:00
Frunzovka 23 45 47N20 29E44 -1:58:56
Furmanov 6 40 57N15 41E07 -2:44:28
Furmanovka 9 24 44N17 72E57 -4:51:48
Furmanovo 9 32 49N42 49E28 -3:17:52
Gad'ač 23 45 50N22 34E00 -2:16:00
Gadiloviči 4 39 53N05 30E16 -2:01:04
Gadrut 3 34 39N32 47E02 -3:08:08
Gafurov 21 24 40N14 69E44 -4:38:56
Gagarin 6 39 55N33 35E00 -2:20:00
Gagino 6 41 55N14 45E02 -3:00:08
Gagra 7 33 43N20 40E15 -2:41:00
Gaigalava 13 36 56N40 27E18 -1:49:12
Gaj 6 30 51N27 58E27 -3:53:48
Gajny 6 30 60N15 54E15 -3:37:00
Gajsin 23 45 48N48 29E24 -1:57:36
Gajutino 6 40 58N42 38E32 -2:34:08
Gajvoron 23 45 48N22 29E52 -1:59:28
Gakugsa 6 40 61N34 36E26 -2:25:44
Galaassija 24 30 39N52 64E27 -4:17:48
Galanovo 6 42 56N09 54E07 -3:36:28
Gali 7 33 42N38 41E44 -2:46:56
Galič 6 41 58N23 42E21 -2:49:24
Galič 23 44 49N08 24E43 -1:38:52
Galkino 2 30 55N36 62E55 -4:11:40
Galkino 9 24 52N14 78E20 -5:13:20
Galkino 6 39 54N46 35E49 -2:23:16
Gall'aaral 24 24 40N02 67E35 -4:30:20

Gamalejevka 6 32 52N16 53E26 -3:33:44
Gancevici 4 39 52N45 26E26 -1:45:44
Ganči 21 24 39N58 69E08 -4:36:32
Gandzha → Kirovabad 3 34 40N40 46E22 -3:05:28
Ganišob 21 24 39N03 70E47 -4:43:08
Gannovka 23 45 48N33 38E35 -2:34:20
Gantiadi 7 33 43N24 40E06 -2:40:24
Gan'uškino 9 32 46N36 49E16 -3:17:04
Garbokaraj 2 20 54N09 99E52 -6:39:28
Garcevo 6 39 52N45 32E59 -2:11:56
Gardabani 7 33 41N28 45E06 -3:00:24
Gardinas → Grodno 4 39 53N41 23E50 -1:35:20
Garga 2 20 54N26 110E33 -7:22:12
Gargždai 14 37 55N43 21E24 -1:25:36
Gari 2 30 59N26 62E21 -4:09:24
Garliava 14 37 54N49 23E52 -1:35:28
Garm 21 24 39N02 70E22 -4:41:28
Gasan-Kuli 22 30 37N27 53E59 -3:35:56
Gaspra 23 45 44N27 34E07 -2:16:28
Gastello 19 8 49N07 142E58 -9:31:52
Gatčina 6 9 59N34 30E08 -2:00:32
Gaujiena 13 36 57N30 26E40 -1:46:40
Gavrilov-Jam 6 40 57N18 39E51 -2:39:24
Gavrilovka 23 45 48N37 37E31 -2:30:04
Gavrilovka Vtoraja 6 41 52N53 42E46 -2:51:04
Gavrilov Posad 6 40 56N33 40E07 -2:40:28
Gavry 6 39 56N55 27E53 -1:51:32
Gazalkent 24 24 41N33 69E47 -4:39:08
Gazimurskij Zavod 2 16 51N33 118E22 -7:53:28
Gaznau 24 24 40N10 71E02 -4:44:08
Gden' 4 39 51N20 30E25 -2:01:40
Gdov 6 9 58N44 27E48 -1:51:12
Gebi 7 33 42N46 43E30 -2:54:00
Gegečkori 7 33 42N25 42E22 -2:49:28
Gelendžik 6 47 44N33 38E06 -2:32:24
Gelgaudiškis 14 37 55N05 23E00 -1:32:00
Gel'm'azov 23 44 49N49 31E49 -2:07:16
General'skoje 6 40 47N28 39E35 -2:38:20
Geničesk 23 45 46N11 34E48 -2:19:12
Geokčaj 3 34 40N39 47E44 -3:10:56
Geok-Tepe 22 30 38N09 57E58 -3:51:52
Georgijevka 6 34 53N18 51E01 -3:24:04
Georgijevka 23 45 48N26 39E17 -2:37:08
Georgijevka 9 24 49N19 81E35 -5:26:20
Georgijevka 9 24 43N03 74E43 -4:58:52
Georgijevka 9 24 42N11 70E00 -4:40:00
Georgijevsk 6 47 44N09 43E28 -2:53:52
Georgiu-Dež (Liski) 6 41 50N59 39E30 -2:38:00
Gerasimovka 2 25 58N37 71E53 -4:47:32
Gerca 23 45 48N09 26E16 -1:45:04
Gerge'bil 6 47 42N31 47E05 -3:08:20
Germanoviči 4 39 55N25 27E44 -1:50:56
Giaginskaja 6 47 44N53 40E05 -2:40:20
Gidajevo 6 42 59N57 52E22 -3:29:28
Gidrotorf 6 41 56N28 43E33 -2:54:12
Giedraičiai 14 37 55N05 25E15 -1:41:00
Gigant 6 47 46N30 41E20 -2:45:20
Gimoly 6 9 63N03 32E19 -2:09:16
Girvas 6 9 62N30 33E40 -2:14:40
Gissar 21 24 38N33 68E35 -4:34:20
Gižduvan 24 30 40N06 64E41 -4:18:44
Gižiga 2 5 62N03 160E30-10:42:00
Glad' 6 9 59N07 32E06 -2:08:24
Gl'ad'anskoje 2 30 54N54 65E06 -4:20:24
Gladkovka 23 45 46N23 32E36 -2:10:24
Glaževo 6 9 59N41 32E05 -2:08:20
Glazok 6 41 53N06 40E42 -2:42:48
Glazov 6 42 58N09 52E40 -3:30:40
Glazovo 6 39 54N47 37E34 -2:30:16
Glazovo 6 39 55N38 35E46 -2:23:04
Glazovo 6 39 54N57 37E22 -2:29:28
Glazunovka 6 39 52N30 36E19 -2:25:16
Glazunovskaja 6 34 49N50 42E51 -2:51:24
Glebovka 6 47 46N38 39E59 -2:39:56
Glebovo 6 39 56N54 37E43 -2:30:52
Glebovo 6 39 56N39 38E42 -2:34:48
Glin'any 23 44 49N49 24E30 -1:38:00
Glinka 6 39 54N39 32E52 -2:11:28
Glinkovo 9 24 42N55 69E40 -4:38:40
Globino 23 44 49N23 33E17 -2:13:08
Glod'any 15 46 47N47 27E31 -1:50:04
Glotovka 6 34 53N57 46E42 -3:06:48
Glotovo 6 41 63N30 49E23 -3:17:32
Glubokij 6 47 48N31 40E19 -2:41:16
Glubokij 2 14 52N53 129E44 -8:38:56
Glubokij 6 47 47N01 42E47 -2:51:08
Glubokoje 6 39 54N32 38E32 -2:34:08
Glubokoje 9 24 50N06 82E19 -5:29:16
Glubokoje 4 39 55N08 27E41 -1:50:44
Gluchov 23 44 51N41 33E53 -2:15:32
Gluchovo 6 39 55N46 37E16 -2:29:04
Gluša 4 39 53N05 28E52 -1:55:28
Glusk 4 39 52N54 28E41 -1:54:44
Gluškeviči 23 44 51N34 27E47 -1:51:08
Gluškovo 6 39 51N22 34E38 -2:18:32
Glybokaja 23 44 48N07 25E56 -1:43:44
Gmelinka 6 34 50N24 46E54 -3:07:36
Gnezdovo 6 39 54N47 31E47 -2:07:08
Gnilec 6 39 52N22 36E01 -2:24:04
Gnivan' 23 44 49N06 28E20 -1:53:20
Gobustan 3 34 40N06 49E24 -3:17:36
Godunovo 6 39 56N29 39E02 -2:36:08

Gogolevka 6 39 54N17 31E58 -2:07:52
Gogolevo 23 44 49N56 33E48 -2:15:12
Golaja Pristan' 23 45 46N31 32E31 -2:10:04
Gol'čicha 2 21 71N43 83E36 -5:34:24
Golicyno 6 41 53N38 44E07 -2:56:28
Golicyno 6 39 55N37 36E59 -2:27:56
Golicyno 6 39 55N58 40E26 -2:41:44
Goljevo 6 39 55N48 37E19 -2:29:16
Gol'movskij 23 45 48N25 38E05 -2:32:20
Goloby 23 44 51N06 24E59 -1:39:56
Golovačovka 9 24 42N52 71E13 -4:44:52
Golovanevsk 23 45 48N23 30E28 -2:01:52
Golovanovo 6 40 54N55 40E27 -2:41:48
Golovanovo 6 42 56N09 54E07 -3:36:28
Golovčin 4 39 54N04 29E55 -1:59:40
Golovčino 6 39 50N32 35E47 -2:23:08
Golovinka 6 47 43N48 39E28 -2:37:52
Golovino 6 39 55N58 40E26 -2:41:44
Golovino 6 39 56N01 39E11 -2:36:44
Golovinščino 6 41 53N18 43E59 -2:55:56
Golovinskaja 2 20 53N26 102E43 -6:50:52
Golovnino 6 39 54N23 36E10 -2:24:40
Golovno 23 44 51N21 24E04 -1:36:16
Golovskoje 2 20 55N30 105E32 -7:02:08
Gol'šany 4 39 54N15 26E01 -1:44:04
Gol't'ajevo 6 39 55N13 36E02 -2:24:08
Gol't'avino 2 26 58N26 98E27 -6:33:48
Golubi 6 41 59N28 41E39 -2:46:36
Golubinskij 6 34 48N52 43E34 -2:54:16
Golubovka 23 45 48N53 35E19 -2:21:16
Golubovka 9 24 53N09 74E12 -4:56:48
Golumet' 2 20 53N03 102E21 -6:49:24
Golynki 6 39 54N52 31E23 -2:05:32
Golyšmanovo 2 30 56N28 68E38 -4:34:32
Golyšmanovo 2 30 56N23 68E23 -4:33:32
Gomel' 4 39 52N25 31E00 -2:04:00
Gonam 2 11 57N21 131E12 -8:44:48
Gončarovka 6 40 50N32 39E28 -2:37:52
Gonochovo 2 23 52N57 81E20 -5:25:20
Gonža 2 16 53N36 125E19 -8:21:16
Gora 6 41 60N02 41E43 -2:46:52
Gor'ačegorsk 2 21 55N24 88E55 -5:55:40
Gor'ačij Kl'uč 6 47 44N37 39E07 -2:36:28
Gor'ačinsk 2 20 52N59 108E18 -7:13:12
Goradiz 3 34 39N27 47E20 -3:09:20
Gor'any 4 39 55N25 29E02 -1:56:08
Gorbačevo Michajlovka 23 45 47N50 38E00 -2:32:00
Gorbatov 6 40 56N08 43E04 -2:52:16
Gorbatovka 6 41 56N15 43E45 -2:55:00
Gorbica 2 16 53N06 119E13 -7:56:52
Gorboviči 4 39 53N49 30E41 -2:02:44
Gorčucha 6 41 57N43 43E43 -2:54:52
Gordejevka 6 39 52N59 31E58 -2:07:52
Gorelki 6 39 54N15 37E37 -2:30:28
Goreloje 6 41 52N57 41E28 -2:45:52
Goreloje 7 33 41N14 43E42 -2:54:48
Gorelovo 6 9 59N47 30E08 -2:00:32
Gorenki 6 39 55N48 37E55 -2:31:40
Gori 7 33 41N58 44E07 -2:56:28
Goricy 6 39 57N09 36E44 -2:26:56
Goris 1 34 39N31 46E23 -3:05:32
Gor'kaja Balka 6 47 44N17 43E59 -2:55:56
Gorki 6 39 54N18 36E08 -2:24:32
Gorki 6 39 55N32 37E45 -2:31:00
Gorki 6 41 57N38 45E05 -3:00:20
Gorki 4 39 54N17 30E59 -2:03:56
Gorki → Gor'kij 6 41 56N20 44E00 -2:56:00
Gor'kij (Gorky) 6 41 56N20 44E00 -2:56:00
Gorki Vtoryje 6 39 55N44 37E11 -2:28:44
Gor'kiy → Gor'kij 6 41 56N20 44E00 -2:56:00
Gor'kovskoje 2 24 55N22 74E24 -4:57:36
Gorky → Gor'kij 6 41 56N20 44E00 -2:56:00
Gorlovka 7 33 41N14 43E42 -2:54:48
Gorlovka 23 45 48N18 38E03 -2:32:12
Gorlovo 6 40 53N50 39E02 -2:36:08
Gorn'ackij 6 29 67N32 64E03 -4:16:12
Gorn'ackij 6 47 48N17 40E55 -2:43:40
Gorn'ackoje 23 45 47N42 34E08 -2:16:32
Gornaja Prolejka 6 34 49N24 44E59 -2:59:56
Gorn'ak 6 40 53N36 39E29 -2:37:56
Gorn'ak 23 45 48N04 37E24 -2:29:36
Gorn'ak 2 23 51N00 81E29 -5:25:56
Gorn'ak 23 44 50N20 24E10 -1:36:40
Gorno-Altajsk 2 21 51N58 85E58 -5:43:52
Gornoje 9 24 48N29 85E00 -5:40:00
Gornopravdinsk 2 25 60N07 69E54 -4:39:36
Gornostajevka 23 45 47N01 33E44 -2:14:56
Gorno-Vod'anoje 6 34 49N16 44E56 -2:59:44
Gornovodnoje 2 27 43N42 134E44 -8:58:56
Gornozavodsk 6 30 58N20 58E32 -3:54:08
Gornozavodsk 19 8 46N34 141E49 -9:27:16

Gornyj 2 11 50N48 136E29 -9:05:56
Gornyj 2 27 44N57 133E59 -8:55:56
Gornyj 6 34 51N46 48E34 -3:14:16
Gornyj Balyklej 6 34 49N34 45E04 -3:00:16
Gornyje Kl'uči 2 27 45N12 133E31 -8:54:04
Gorochov 23 44 50N30 24E45 -1:39:00
Gorochovatka 23 45 49N21 37E31 -2:30:04
Gorochovec 6 40 56N12 42E40 -2:50:40
Gorochovje 6 39 56N31 30E29 -2:01:56
Gorodec 4 39 52N58 30E21 -2:01:24
Gorodec 4 39 53N33 30E02 -2:00:08
Gorodec 6 41 56N38 43E30 -2:54:00
Gorodec 23 44 51N17 26E19 -1:45:16
Gorodec 6 9 58N32 29E47 -1:59:08
Gorodec 4 39 52N12 24E40 -1:38:40
Gorodeja 4 39 53N19 26E32 -1:46:08
Gorodenka 23 44 48N41 25E29 -1:41:56
Gorodišče 23 45 49N03 39E38 -2:38:32
Gorodišče 6 41 53N17 45E42 -3:02:48
Gorodišče 6 34 48N48 44E29 -2:57:56
Gorodišče 6 40 51N09 38E04 -2:32:16
Gorodišče 23 44 49N17 31E27 -2:05:48
Gorodišče 6 9 59N38 32E08 -2:08:32
Gorodišče 4 39 53N19 26E00 -1:44:00
Gorodišče 4 39 53N44 29E48 -1:59:12
Gorodišče 6 39 54N53 38E13 -2:32:52
Gorodišče 6 39 56N47 38E52 -2:35:28
Gorodišče 23 45 48N19 38E39 -2:34:36
Gorodišči 6 39 55N52 39E05 -2:36:20
Gorodkovka 23 45 48N23 28E42 -1:54:48
Gorodn'a 6 39 54N57 38E49 -2:35:16
Gorodn'a 6 39 56N43 36E19 -2:25:16
Gorodn'a 23 44 51N53 31E36 -2:06:24
Gorodnica 23 44 50N48 27E20 -1:49:20
Gorodno 6 39 57N32 29E35 -1:58:20
Gorodok 23 44 49N47 23E39 -1:34:36
Gorodok 4 39 55N28 29E59 -1:59:56
Gorodok 23 44 49N10 26E34 -1:46:16
Gorod'onka 23 44 48N41 25E29 -1:41:56
Goršečnoje 6 40 51N32 38E02 -2:32:08
Gorskaja 6 9 60N03 29E59 -1:59:56
Gorskoje 23 45 48N46 38E30 -2:34:00
Gorškovo 6 39 54N26 37E59 -2:31:56
Gory 4 39 54N16 31E13 -2:04:52
Gory 9 32 48N38 51E46 -3:27:04
Gošča 23 44 50N36 26E41 -1:46:44
Gostagajevskaja 6 47 45N01 37E30 -2:30:00
Gostilovo 6 39 55N18 38E36 -2:34:24
Gostiščevo 6 39 50N47 36E39 -2:26:36
Gosudarev Bajrak 23 45 48N21 38E08 -2:32:32
Gotešty 15 46 46N09 28E10 -1:52:40
Gotoputovo 2 30 56N46 70E10 -4:40:40
Gotval'd 23 45 49N40 36E19 -2:25:16
Grabc'ovo 6 39 54N34 36E22 -2:25:28
Grabovo 9 24 53N07 74E52 -4:59:28
Gračevka 6 39 55N06 36E49 -2:27:16
Gračev Kust 6 34 51N59 49E50 -3:19:20
Grachovo 6 42 56N04 51E58 -3:27:52
Grači 6 34 49N49 43E33 -2:54:12
Gračov 6 47 49N26 41E32 -2:46:08
Gračovka 6 32 52N57 52E52 -3:31:28
Gračovka 6 41 52N07 40E01 -2:40:04
Gračov Kust 6 34 51N59 49E50 -3:19:20
Gr'adcy 6 39 56N24 31E55 -2:07:40
Gradižsk 23 44 49N13 33E07 -2:12:28
Grajvoron 6 39 50N28 35E39 -2:22:36
Gramoteino 2 21 54N31 86E22 -5:45:28
Grandiči 4 39 53N43 23E49 -1:35:16
Granitnoje 23 45 47N27 37E52 -2:31:28
Granitogorsk 9 24 42N44 73E27 -4:53:48
Granki 6 39 54N51 31E27 -2:05:48
Granov 23 45 48N52 29E34 -1:58:16
Gr'azi 6 41 52N29 39E57 -2:39:48
Gr'aznoje 6 40 54N02 39E07 -2:36:28
Gr'aznovo 6 39 54N18 36E49 -2:27:16
Gr'aznovo 6 39 55N57 37E34 -2:30:16
Gr'aznyj Irtek 6 32 51N56 53E11 -3:32:44
Gr'azovec 6 41 58N53 40E14 -2:40:56
Grebenka 23 44 50N07 32E25 -2:09:40
Grebnevo 6 39 55N58 38E05 -2:32:20
Greb'onki 23 44 49N57 30E12 -2:00:48
Grečiškino 23 45 48N52 38E54 -2:35:36
Grejdernoje 6 47 46N53 45E01 -3:00:04
Grekov 6 34 47N24 43E41 -2:54:44
Grekovo 6 47 48N54 40E14 -2:40:56
Grem'ačevo 6 39 54N14 36E15 -2:25:00
Grem'ačij 2 20 57N01 108E12 -7:12:48
Grem'ačinsk 6 30 58N34 57E51 -3:51:24
Grem'ačinsk 2 20 52N48 107E57 -7:11:48
Grem'ačje 6 40 51N29 39E00 -2:36:00
Gremicha 6 9 68N03 39E27 -2:37:48
Gressk 4 39 53N10 27E29 -1:49:56
Gribanovskij 6 41 51N27 41E58 -2:47:52
Gribovka 6 39 54N19 38E27 -2:33:48
Gricev 23 44 49N58 27E14 -1:48:56
Grigoriopol' 15 46 47N10 29E18 -1:57:12
Grigorjevka 6 40 47N27 38E23 -2:33:32
Grigorjevka 10 24 42N43 77E30 -5:10:00
Grigorjevka 23 45 46N17 33E44 -2:14:56
Grigorjevskoje 6 39 54N49 37E59 -2:31:56
Grigorjevskoje 6 39 54N48 39E15 -2:37:00
Grigorovka 23 44 50N05 30E39 -2:02:36

Grigorovka 6 39 54N38 36E20 -2:25:20
Grigorovka 23 44 51N03 32E51 -2:11:24
Grigorovo 6 39 56N42 37E35 -2:30:20
Grigorovskoje 6 39 54N17 36E21 -2:25:24
Grimajlov 23 44 49N20 26E01 -1:44:04
Grin'ava 15 46 47N59 24E49 -1:39:16
Grin'ovo 6 39 52N35 33E04 -2:12:16
Grišino 6 39 56N13 37E40 -2:30:40
Griškovcy 23 44 49N56 28E36 -1:54:24
Grivenskaja 6 47 45N38 38E09 -2:32:36
Grobina 13 36 56N33 21E10 -1:24:40
Grodekovo 9 24 42N49 71E29 -4:45:56
Grodno 4 39 53N41 23E50 -1:35:20
Grodovka 23 45 48N15 37E23 -2:29:32
Grodz'anka 4 39 53N33 28E45 -1:55:00
Gromoslavka 6 34 48N12 43E37 -2:54:28
Gromovka 23 45 46N19 34E06 -2:16:24
Grossevīči 2 11 47N59 139E30 -9:18:00
Groznoje 10 24 42N36 71E12 -4:44:48
Groznyj 6 47 43N20 45E42 -3:02:48
Groznyy → Groznyj 6 47 43N20 45E42 -3:02:48
Grun' 23 45 50N16 34E36 -2:18:24
Gruševka 6 47 47N55 40E40 -2:42:40
Gruševskaja 6 40 47N26 39E57 -2:39:48
Grušino 6 41 59N27 44E09 -2:56:36
Gruzdžiai 14 37 56N06 23E16 -1:33:04
Gruznovka 2 20 55N09 105E12 -7:00:48
Gruzskaja Balka 6 47 46N25 40E19 -2:41:16
Gruzskoje 23 45 48N33 37E18 -2:29:12
Gruzsko-Zor'anskoje 23 45 47N56 38E06 -2:32:24
Gubacha 6 30 58N52 57E36 -3:50:24
Gubany 6 39 56N37 30E40 -2:02:40
Gubari 6 41 51N32 42E33 -2:50:12
Gubinicha 23 45 48N48 35E15 -2:21:00
Gubino 6 34 53N19 48E44 -3:14:56
Gubino 6 39 55N42 39E07 -2:36:28
Gubkin 6 39 51N18 37E32 -2:30:08
Gudauta 7 33 43N06 40E37 -2:42:28
Gudermes 6 47 43N20 46E08 -3:04:32
Guga 2 11 52N43 137E35 -9:10:20
Gukas'an 7 34 41N03 43E52 -2:55:28
Gukovo 6 47 48N03 39E56 -2:39:44
Gul'a 2 16 54N41 121E01 -8:04:04
Gul'aj-Borisovka 6 47 46N38 40E13 -2:40:52
Gul'ajpole 23 45 47N38 36E16 -2:25:04
Gulbene 13 36 57N11 26E45 -1:47:00
Gul'ča 10 24 40N19 73E26 -4:53:44
Gulistan 24 24 40N30 68E46 -4:35:04
Gul'ripš 7 33 42N57 41E06 -2:44:24
Gul'ripši 7 33 42N57 41E06 -2:44:24
Gul'šad 9 24 46N39 74E24 -4:57:36
Gumbinnen → Gusev 8 38 54N36 22E12 -1:28:48
Gunda 2 20 52N47 111E44 -7:26:56
Gunib 6 47 42N25 46E57 -3:07:48
Gura 6 42 57N18 51E25 -3:25:40
Gura-Galbena 15 46 46N43 28E42 -1:54:48
Guran 2 20 54N46 100E38 -6:42:32
Gurdžaani 7 33 41N43 45E48 -3:03:12
Gurejev 6 47 47N21 43E16 -2:53:04
G'urg'an 3 34 40N23 50E19 -3:21:16
Gurjev 9 32 47N07 51E56 -3:27:44
Gurjevo 6 39 54N42 36E28 -2:25:52
Gurjevsk 2 21 54N17 85E56 -5:43:44
Gurjevsk (Neuhausen) 8 38 54N47 20E38 -1:22:32
Gurievo 6 9 59N28 28E54 -1:55:36
Gurskoje 2 11 50N21 138E12 -9:12:48
Gurzuf 23 45 44N33 34E17 -2:17:08
Gusar 21 24 39N28 67E50 -4:31:20
Gušari 21 24 38N55 68E51 -4:35:24
Gusarka 23 45 47N23 36E31 -2:26:04
Gus'atin 23 44 49N05 26E11 -1:44:44
Gus'-Chrustal'nyj 6 40 55N37 40E40 -2:42:40
Guselka 6 34 50N27 45E09 -3:00:36
Gusev 6 47 48N27 40E32 -2:42:08
Gusev (Gumbinnen) 8 38 54N36 22E12 -1:28:48
Gusevo 6 39 56N06 33E21 -2:13:24
Gusevskij 6 40 55N40 40E34 -2:42:16
Gusino 6 39 54N44 31E22 -2:05:28
Gusinoje Ozero 2 20 51N09 106E10 -7:04:40
Gusinoozersk 2 20 51N17 106E30 -7:06:00
Guskef 21 24 39N02 69E20 -4:37:20
Gus'-Khrustal'nyy → Gus'-Chrustal'nyj 6 40 55N37 40E40 -2:42:40
Gus'-železnyj 6 40 55N03 41E10 -2:44:40
Gutaj 2 18 49N59 108E12 -7:12:48
Guty 23 45 50N08 35E21 -2:21:24
Guzar 24 30 38N36 66E15 -4:25:00
Gvardejsk (Tapiau) 8 38 54N39 21E05 -1:24:20
Gvardejskoje 23 45 45N07 34E01 -2:16:04
Gvardejskoje 23 45 48N44 35E19 -2:21:16
Gvardejskoje 23 44 49N20 26E42 -1:46:48
Gvazda 6 41 50N44 40E30 -2:42:00
Gvozdec 23 44 48N34 25E17 -1:41:08
Gybdan 6 42 56N33 51E39 -3:26:36
Gyda 2 25 70N52 78E30 -5:14:00
Gyrbovec 15 46 46N50 29E21 -1:57:24
Gžatsk 2 23 55N42 78E11 -5:12:44
Gžel' 6 39 55N36 38E24 -2:33:36

Gzhatsk → Gagarin 6 39 55N33 35E00 -2:20:00
Haapsalu 5 35 58N56 23E33 -1:34:12
Haljala 5 35 59N26 26E16 -1:45:04
Hardteck → Krasnolesje 8 38 54N24 22E23 -1:29:32
Haselberg → Krasnoznamensk 8 38 54N57 22E30 -1:30:00
Heiligenbeil → Mamonovo 8 38 54N28 19E57 -1:19:48
Heinrichswalde → Slavsk 8 38 55N03 21E41 -1:26:44
Hullo 5 35 59N00 23E14 -1:32:56
Ibresi 6 41 55N18 47E03 -3:08:12
Ičera 2 20 58N32 109E47 -7:19:08
Ičn'a 23 44 50N52 32E24 -2:09:36
Idel' 6 40 64N08 34E14 -2:16:56
Idrica 6 39 56N21 28E53 -1:55:32
Idrinskoje 2 21 54N21 92E07 -6:08:28
Idževan 1 34 40N53 45E07 -3:00:28
Iecava 13 36 56N36 24E12 -1:36:48
Igarka 2 21 67N28 86E35 -5:46:20
Igdy 22 30 39N54 56E54 -3:47:36
Igirma 2 20 56N59 103E37 -6:54:28
Iglino 6 30 54N50 56E26 -3:45:44
Iglovo 6 39 55N47 36E40 -2:26:40
Ignacej 15 46 47N41 28E40 -1:54:40
Ignalina 14 37 55N21 26E10 -1:44:40
Ignašino 2 16 53N28 122E24 -8:09:36
Ignatjevcy 6 42 57N32 51E39 -3:26:36
Ignatovka 6 34 53N57 47E38 -3:10:32
Ignatovo 6 39 56N10 37E32 -2:30:08
Igodovo 6 41 58N01 42E21 -2:49:24
Igra 6 42 57N33 53E04 -3:32:16
Igumnovo 6 39 55N37 38E18 -2:33:12
Igžej 2 20 53N59 103E10 -6:52:40
Iisaku 5 35 59N06 27E19 -1:49:16
Ika 2 20 59N18 106E12 -7:04:48
Ikej 2 20 54N12 100E04 -6:40:16
Iki-Burul 6 47 45N49 44E39 -2:58:36
Ikon-Chal' 6 47 44N18 41E55 -2:47:40
Ikr'anoje 6 34 46N06 47E45 -3:11:00
Ikša 6 39 56N10 37E31 -2:30:04
Ilanskij 2 21 56N14 96E03 -6:24:12
Ilbenge 2 16 62N49 124E24 -8:17:36
Ilek 6 32 51N30 53E22 -3:33:28
Ilevskij Pogost 6 41 60N41 43E46 -2:55:04
Ileza 6 41 60N43 43E54 -2:55:36
Ilijsk 9 24 43N53 77E10 -5:08:40
Ilimsk 2 20 56N46 103E52 -6:55:28
Ilinka 6 39 54N04 38E12 -2:32:48
Ilir 2 20 55N13 100E40 -6:42:40
Ilja 4 39 54N25 27E18 -1:49:12
Iljak 2 25 60N11 77E59 -5:11:56
Iljič 24 24 40N50 68E47 -4:33:48
Iljičevsk 16 34 39N33 44E58 -2:59:52
Iljičovsk 23 45 46N18 30E39 -2:02:36
Iljincy 23 44 49N07 29E12 -1:56:48
Iljinka 6 47 48N32 41E05 -2:44:20
Iljino 6 39 55N57 31E40 -2:06:40
Iljinskij 6 30 58N35 55E41 -3:42:44
Iljinskij 6 9 61N02 32E41 -2:10:44
Iljinskij 6 39 55N37 38E06 -2:32:24
Iljinskij 2 16 52N05 114E10 -7:36:40
Iljinskij 19 8 47N58 142E12 -9:28:48
Iljinskij Pogost 6 39 55N28 38E54 -2:35:36
Iljinskoje 6 41 58N47 44E36 -2:58:24
Iljinskoje 6 39 53N14 35E26 -2:21:44
Iljinskoje 6 39 57N19 38E32 -2:34:08
Iljinskoje 6 39 54N59 36E11 -2:24:44
Iljinskoje 6 39 56N34 35E57 -2:23:48
Iljinskoje 6 39 55N46 37E15 -2:29:00
Iljinskoje 6 42 56N29 52E49 -3:31:16
Iljinskoje 6 39 56N58 37E11 -2:28:44
Iljinskoje-Chovanskoje 6 40 56N58 39E46 -2:39:04
Iljinsko-Podomskoje 6 41 61N08 47E56 -3:11:44
Iljinsko-Zaborskoje 6 41 57N16 44E23 -2:57:32
Il'ka 2 20 51N43 108E32 -7:14:08
Il'kino 6 40 55N13 41E36 -2:46:24
Illarionovo 23 45 48N25 35E16 -2:21:04
Il'mino 6 41 53N47 45E40 -3:02:40
Ilovajsk 23 45 47N56 38E13 -2:32:52
Ilovatka 6 34 50N31 45E55 -3:03:40
Ilovka 6 40 50N43 38E38 -2:34:32
Ilovl'a 6 34 49N18 43E59 -2:55:56
Il'pyrskij 2 4 59N56 164E10-10:56:40
Il'skij 6 47 44N51 38E35 -2:34:20
Ilūkste 13 36 55N58 26E18 -1:45:12
Ima 2 20 55N13 115E55 -7:43:40
Imantau 9 24 52N58 68E22 -4:33:28
Imavere 5 35 58N44 25E48 -1:43:12
Imeni Abaja 9 24 50N44 69E30 -4:38:00
Imeni Babuškina 6 41 59N45 43E07 -2:52:28
Imeni Čapajeva 9 24 43N28 76E50 -5:07:20
Imeni C'urupy 6 39 55N30 38E39 -2:34:36
Imeni Džambula 9 24 45N26 74E24 -4:57:36
Imeni Džambula 9 24 47N43 74E09 -4:56:36
Imeni Frunze 9 24 46N23 77E20 -5:09:20
Imeni Il-Go Okt'abr'a 2 16 55N54 119E36 -7:58:24
Imeni Kalinina 10 24 41N28 76E22 -5:05:28

Imeni Kalinina 9 24 43N16 74E03 -4:56:12
Imeni Kalinina 6 32 51N51 52E43 -3:30:52
Imeni Kalinina 24 30 43N40 59E07 -3:56:28
Imeni Karla Libknechta 6 39 51N37 35E27 -2:21:48
Imeni Kirova 9 24 46N27 77E13 -5:08:52
Imeni Leninskogo Komsomola 9 24 50N45 66E44 -4:26:56
Imeni Marta 9 30 46N57 58E58 -3:55:52
Imeni Michajla Ivanoviča Kalinina 6 41 57N59 45E07 -3:00:28
Imeni Panfilova 9 24 43N23 77E07 -5:08:28
Imeni Poliny Osipenko 2 11 52N25 136E28 -9:05:52
Imeni Sardarova Karachana 21 24 38N26 68E46 -4:35:04
Imeni Seredy 6 40 46N52 40E03 -2:40:12
Imeni Ševčenko 9 30 45N58 61E04 -4:04:16
Imeni Stepana Razina 6 41 54N54 44E18 -2:57:12
Imeni Tel'mana 2 11 48N36 134E59 -8:59:56
Imeni Timir'azeva 9 30 53N39 65E31 -4:22:04
Imeni Vladimira Iljiča Lenina 6 34 53N36 46E58 -3:07:52
Imeni Vorovskogo 6 40 55N43 41E06 -2:44:24
Imeni Vorovskogo 6 39 55N43 38E20 -2:33:20
Imeni XXI Partsjezda 9 24 50N43 67E50 -4:31:20
Imeni Žel'abova 6 40 58N57 36E36 -2:26:24
Imišli 3 34 39N52 48E04 -3:12:16
Impilachti 6 9 61N40 31E04 -2:04:16
In'a 2 21 53N31 82E40 -5:30:40
In'a 2 21 50N48 86E37 -5:46:28
In'a 2 7 59N24 144E48 -9:39:12
In'akino 6 41 54N26 41E07 -2:44:28
Inarigda 2 20 63N14 107E27 -7:09:48
Inčoun 2 2 66N18 170W17 11:21:08
Incy 6 41 65N48 40E26 -2:41:44
Inderborskij 9 32 48N33 51E44 -3:26:56
Indiga 6 41 67N41 49E00 -3:16:00
Indom 6 29 64N36 55E22 -3:41:28
Indura 4 39 53N27 23E53 -1:35:32
Ingička 24 30 39N52 67E20 -4:29:20
Ingulec 23 45 47N43 33E14 -2:12:56
Ingulo-Kamenka 23 45 48N17 32E30 -2:10:00
Inguzet 2 21 58N50 83E52 -5:35:28
Innokentjevka 2 11 49N42 136E57 -9:07:48
Innokentjevskij 2 11 48N37 140E10 -9:20:40
Innolovo 6 9 59N47 29E59 -1:59:56
Inokovka 6 41 52N33 42E34 -2:50:16
Inozemcevo 6 47 44N06 43E06 -2:52:24
Insar 6 41 53N52 44E21 -2:57:24
Insterburg → Čern'achovsk 8 38 54N38 21E49 -1:27:16
Inta 6 29 66N02 60E08 -4:00:32
Inza 6 34 53N51 46E21 -3:05:24
Inžavino 6 41 52N19 42E30 -2:50:00
Inzer 6 30 54N14 57E34 -3:50:16
Iolotan' 22 30 37N18 62E21 -4:09:24
Iordan 24 24 39N58 71E46 -4:47:04
Iory 21 24 39N30 67E53 -4:31:32
Iovlevo 6 39 56N10 38E20 -2:33:20
Ipat 6 29 66N13 56E33 -3:46:12
Ipatovo 6 47 45N43 42E53 -2:51:32
Irajol' 6 29 64N27 55E08 -3:40:32
Irba 2 26 58N07 99E00 -6:36:00
Irbejskoje 2 21 55N39 95E28 -6:21:52
Irbit 2 30 57N41 63E03 -4:12:12
Irdyn' 23 44 49N23 31E44 -2:06:56
Irgakly 6 47 44N22 44E45 -2:59:00
Irgiz 9 30 48N37 61E16 -4:05:04
Iriklinskij 6 30 51N39 58E38 -3:54:32
Irkeštam 10 24 39N41 73E55 -4:55:40
Irkinejevo 2 21 58N30 96E49 -6:27:16
Irklijev 23 44 49N32 32E18 -2:09:12
Irklijevskaja 6 47 45N51 39E39 -2:38:36
Irkoutsk → Irkutsk 2 20 52N16 104E20 -6:57:20
Irkutsk 2 20 52N16 104E20 -6:57:20
Irpen' 23 44 50N31 30E15 -2:01:00
Iršava 23 44 48N20 23E03 -1:32:12
Irtyš 2 24 54N29 74E22 -4:57:28
Irtyšsk 9 24 53N21 75E27 -5:01:48
Irubaj 9 32 50N11 51E21 -3:25:24
Is 2 30 58N48 59E43 -3:58:52
Isakly 6 42 54N08 51E32 -3:26:08
Isakovka 2 24 55N45 74E24 -4:57:36
Isakovo 6 39 54N36 37E02 -2:28:08
Isakovo 6 39 55N59 37E23 -2:29:32
Isakovo 6 39 55N11 34E40 -2:18:40
Isakovo 6 41 60N30 41E13 -2:44:52
Is'angulovo 6 30 52N12 56E36 -3:46:24
Iščerskaja 6 47 43N43 45E08 -3:00:32
Išejevka 6 42 54N25 48E16 -3:13:04
Isenbajevo 6 41 56N03 53E25 -3:33:40
Isetskoje 2 30 56N29 65E21 -4:21:24
Isfana 10 24 39N50 69E31 -4:38:04
Isfara 21 24 40N07 70E38 -4:42:32

Isil'kul' 2 24 54N55 71E16 -4:45:04
Išim 2 30 56N09 69E27 -4:37:48
Išimbaj 6 30 53N28 56E02 -3:44:08
Išimka 9 24 51N24 67E08 -4:28:32
Isinga 2 20 52N55 112E00 -7:28:00
Iskandar 24 24 41N36 69E43 -4:38:52
Iškejevo 6 41 55N51 50E56 -3:23:44
Iske R'az'ap 6 42 54N36 49E42 -3:18:48
Iski-Naukat 10 24 40N16 72E36 -4:50:24
Iskininskij 9 30 47N13 52E41 -3:30:44
Iskitim 2 21 54N38 83E18 -5:33:12
Ismailly 3 34 40N47 48E09 -3:12:36
Ismailovo 6 30 55N34 54E39 -3:38:36
Issa 6 41 53N52 44E51 -2:59:24
Issyk 9 24 43N22 77E28 -5:09:52
Istisu 3 34 39N57 45E59 -3:03:56
Istobensk 6 42 58N25 48E48 -3:15:12
Istobnoje 6 39 51N08 37E21 -2:29:24
Istobnoje 6 40 51N16 38E39 -2:34:36
Istra 6 39 55N55 36E52 -2:27:28
Itaka 2 16 53N53 118E42 -7:54:48
Itatka 2 21 56N49 85E37 -5:42:28
Itatskij 2 21 56N04 89E05 -5:56:20
Itlar' 6 39 56N51 39E17 -2:37:08
Itum-Kale 6 47 42N43 45E35 -3:02:20
Iturup Island 12 8 44N54 147E30 -9:50:00
Iturup, Ostrov 12 8 44N54 147E30 -9:50:00
Iul'tin 2 2 67N50 178W48 11:55:12
Ivacevići 4 39 52N43 25E21 -1:41:24
Ivačovo 6 40 60N32 36E22 -2:25:28
Ivancevo 6 39 55N58 36E07 -2:24:28
Ivancovo 6 39 56N39 35E50 -2:23:20
Ivane-Puste 23 45 48N39 26E11 -1:44:44
Ivangorod 6 9 59N24 28E10 -1:52:40
Ivanica 23 44 50N47 32E36 -2:10:24
Ivaniči 23 44 50N39 24E20 -1:37:20
Ivanišči 6 39 55N46 40E26 -2:41:44
Ivanišči 6 39 56N36 35E13 -2:20:52
Ivankov 23 44 50N56 29E54 -1:59:36
Ivankovcy 2 11 49N06 134E28 -8:57:52
Ivan'kovo 6 39 54N44 37E57 -2:31:48
Ivan'kovskij 6 40 56N39 40E05 -2:40:20
Ivano-Frankovo 23 44 49N55 23E43 -1:34:52
Ivano-Frankovsk 23 44 48N55 24E43 -1:38:52
Ivanopol' 23 44 49N52 28E12 -1:52:48
Ivanopolje 23 45 48N28 37E46 -2:31:04
Ivano-Šamševo 6 40 46N52 39E54 -2:39:36
Ivanov 23 44 49N28 28E21 -1:53:24
Ivanovka 6 41 52N15 41E35 -2:46:20
Ivanovka 23 45 46N43 34E33 -2:18:12
Ivanovka 23 45 46N58 30E28 -2:01:52
Ivanovka 23 45 48N14 38E58 -2:35:52
Ivanovka 23 45 47N35 37E19 -2:29:16
Ivanovka 2 14 50N22 128E02 -8:32:08
Ivanovka 2 27 43N58 132E30 -8:50:00
Ivanovka 10 24 42N54 75E05 -5:00:20
Ivanovka 6 30 52N51 53E48 -3:35:12
Ivanovka 6 34 51N54 43E46 -2:55:04
Ivanovo 6 40 57N00 40E59 -2:43:56
Ivanovo 4 39 52N09 25E32 -1:42:08
Ivanovo-Voznesensk → Ivanovo 6 40 57N00 40E59 -2:43:56
Ivanovskaja 6 30 60N48 55E52 -3:43:28
Ivanovskaja 6 47 45N17 38E29 -2:33:56
Ivanovskoje 6 39 56N23 37E07 -2:28:28
Ivanovskoje 6 9 59N46 30E47 -2:03:08
Ivanovskoje 6 39 51N37 34E57 -2:19:48
Ivanovskoje 6 9 59N17 28E49 -1:55:16
Ivanovskoje 6 39 55N05 37E50 -2:31:20
Ivanovskoje 6 39 54N55 36E50 -2:27:20
Ivanovskoje 6 39 55N52 36E55 -2:27:40
Ivan-Ozero 6 39 54N04 38E20 -2:33:20
Ivantejevka 6 34 52N16 49E07 -3:16:28
Ivantejevka 6 39 55N58 37E55 -2:31:40
Ivantejevo 6 39 57N48 33E09 -2:12:36
Ivdel' 2 30 60N42 60E24 -4:01:36
Ivenec 4 39 53N53 26E45 -1:47:00
Ivje 4 39 53N56 25E46 -1:43:04
Ivn'a 6 39 51N04 36E08 -2:24:32
Ivnica 23 44 50N09 29E03 -1:56:12
Ivolginsk 2 20 51N45 107E14 -7:08:56
Ivot 23 44 51N58 33E28 -2:13:52
Ivot 6 39 53N42 34E12 -2:16:48
Iwanowo → Ivanovo 6 40 57N00 40E59 -2:43:56
Iz'aslav 23 44 50N07 26E51 -1:47:24
Izberbaš 6 47 42N33 47E52 -3:11:28
Izd'oškovo 6 39 55N08 33E37 -2:14:28
Izendy 9 30 45N48 59E28 -3:57:52
Iževsk 6 42 56N51 53E14 -3:32:56
Iževskoje 6 40 54N34 40E53 -2:43:32
Izhevsk → Iževsk 6 42 56N51 53E14 -3:32:56
Ižma 6 29 65N02 53E55 -3:35:40
Izmail 23 45 45N21 28E50 -1:55:20
Izmajlovo 6 34 53N43 47E14 -3:08:56
Izmalkovo 6 39 52N41 37E58 -2:31:52
Ižmorskij 2 21 56N11 86E38 -5:46:32
Iznoski 6 39 54N59 35E19 -2:21:16
Izoplit 6 39 56N38 36E12 -2:24:48
Iz'um 23 45 49N12 37E19 -2:29:16
Izumrud 2 30 57N05 61E23 -4:05:32
Izvarino 23 45 48N17 39E52 -2:39:28
Izvestij CIK Islands 2 25 75N55 82E30 -5:30:00
Izvestij CIK, Ostrova 2 25 75N55 82E30 -5:30:00
Izvestkovyj 2 11 48N59 131E33 -8:46:12
Jabločnoje 23 45 50N18 35E14 -2:20:56
Jabločnyj 19 8 47N10 142E04 -9:28:16
Jablonov 23 44 48N24 24E57 -1:39:48
Jablonovo 2 16 51N51 112E49 -7:31:16
Jachniki 23 44 50N26 33E10 -2:12:40
Jachroma 6 39 56N17 37E30 -2:30:00
Jadrin 6 41 55N56 46E12 -3:04:48
Jadromino 6 39 55N57 36E36 -2:26:24
Jaduty 23 44 51N22 32E19 -2:09:16
Jagodnoje 6 34 53N36 49E04 -3:16:16
Jagodnoje 2 6 62N33 149E40 -9:58:40
Jagodnyj 2 30 59N44 65E04 -4:20:16
Jagotin 23 44 50N17 31E46 -2:07:04
Jagunovskij 2 21 55N17 85E59 -5:43:56
Jaisan 9 30 50N51 56E14 -3:44:56
Jaja 2 21 56N12 86E26 -5:45:44
Jaji'u 2 21 51N48 87E36 -5:50:24
Jajpan 24 24 40N23 70E48 -4:43:12
Jajsan 9 30 50N51 56E14 -3:44:56
Jajva 6 30 59N20 57E15 -3:49:00
Jakkonen 6 9 66N33 29E52 -1:59:28
Jakovleviči 4 39 54N20 30E31 -2:02:04
Jakovlevka 2 27 44N26 133E28 -8:53:52
Jakovlevo 6 39 54N48 37E26 -2:29:44
Jakša 6 29 61N48 56E49 -3:47:16
Jakšanga 6 41 58N23 45E56 -3:03:44
Jakšur-Bodja 6 42 57N11 53E09 -3:32:36
Jakutsk 2 16 62N00 129E40 -8:38:40
Jalama 3 34 41N44 48E34 -3:14:16
Jalan' 2 21 58N21 91E53 -6:07:32
Jal'čiki 6 41 55N09 48E01 -3:12:04
Jal'gelevo 6 9 59N44 29E57 -1:59:48
Jalta 23 45 46N58 37E16 -2:29:04
Jalta (Yalta) 23 45 44N30 34E10 -2:16:40
Jaltuškov 23 45 48N58 27E30 -1:50:00
Jalutorovsk 2 30 56N40 66E18 -4:25:12
Jam 6 39 55N29 37E45 -2:31:00
Jam 24 24 40N07 68E11 -4:32:44
Jama 23 45 48N52 38E06 -2:32:24
Jamanchalinka 9 32 47N40 51E35 -3:26:20
Jamarovka 2 18 50N38 110E16 -7:21:04
Jamašurma 6 41 55N58 49E36 -3:18:24
Jaminsk 4 39 52N46 28E16 -1:53:04
Jaminskij 6 34 50N21 42E14 -2:48:56
Jam-Ižora 6 9 59N42 30E36 -2:02:24
Jamki 2 30 59N33 66E47 -4:27:08
Jamkino 6 39 55N55 38E24 -2:33:36
Jamm 6 9 58N26 28E03 -1:52:12
Jampol' 23 45 48N16 28E17 -1:53:08
Jampol' 23 45 48N56 37E58 -2:31:52
Jampol' 23 44 49N58 26E14 -1:44:56
Jampol' 23 44 51N57 33E46 -2:15:04
Jamsk 2 6 59N35 154E10-10:16:40
Jamskaja Sloboda 6 39 55N29 36E01 -2:24:04
Jamuga 6 39 56N24 36E40 -2:26:40
Janajkino 9 32 50N43 51E06 -3:24:24
Janaul 6 30 56N16 54E56 -3:39:44
Jandrakinot 2 2 64N54 172W32 11:30:08
Jangarej 6 29 68N46 61E25 -4:05:40
Jangel'skij 2 30 53N08 58E59 -3:55:56
Jangiabad 24 24 41N08 70E05 -4:40:20
Jangi-Bazar 10 24 41N40 70E53 -4:43:32
Jangijer 24 24 40N17 68E50 -4:35:20
Jangijul' 24 24 41N07 69E03 -4:36:12
Jangikišlak 24 30 40N25 67E10 -4:28:40
Jangikurgan 24 24 40N34 71E09 -4:44:36
Jangikurgan 24 24 41N12 71E44 -4:46:56
Jangulovo 6 41 56N26 50E25 -3:21:40
Janino 6 9 59N56 30E36 -2:02:24
Janov 23 44 49N28 28E21 -1:53:24
Janoviči 4 39 55N17 30E42 -2:02:48
Janskij 2 11 68N28 134E48 -8:59:12
Jantarnyj 8 38 54N52 19E57 -1:19:48
Jantikovo 6 41 55N32 47E48 -3:11:12
Janvarcevo 9 32 51N26 52E15 -3:29:00
Jany-Kurgan 9 30 43N55 67E15 -4:29:00
Japtiksal'a 2 25 69N21 72E32 -4:50:08
Jar 6 42 58N15 52E06 -3:28:24
Jaramor 6 41 56N07 48E44 -3:14:56
Jaransk 6 42 57N19 47E54 -3:11:36
Jarcevo 6 39 55N04 32E41 -2:10:44
Jardymly 3 34 38N55 48E15 -3:13:00
Jarega 6 29 63N27 53E26 -3:33:44
Jaremča 23 44 48N27 24E33 -1:38:12
Jaren'ga 6 29 63N27 53E26 -3:33:44
Jarenga 6 41 62N43 49E30 -3:18:00
Jarensk 6 41 62N11 49E02 -3:16:08
Jargara 15 46 46N27 28E27 -1:53:48
Jarkino 2 19 59N08 99E23 -6:37:32
Jarkovo 2 30 57N24 67E05 -4:28:20
Jarkul'-Mat'uškino 2 23 55N51 76E06 -5:04:24
Jarmolincy 23 44 49N12 26E50 -1:47:20
Jarochta 2 19 58N58 98E58 -6:35:52
Jaropolec 6 39 56N08 35E49 -2:23:16
Jaroslavec 23 44 51N33 33E40 -2:14:40
Jaroslavl' 6 40 57N37 39E52 -2:39:28
Jaroslavskaja 6 47 44N36 40E27 -2:41:48
Jaroslavskij 2 27 44N10 132E13 -8:48:52
Jarovaja 23 45 49N03 37E37 -2:30:28
Jar-Sale 2 25 66N50 70E50 -4:43:20
Jarsomovy 2 25 60N15 73E38 -4:54:32
Järva-Jaani 5 35 59N02 25E53 -1:43:32
Järvakandi 5 35 58N47 24E49 -1:39:16
Jašalta 6 47 46N20 42E17 -2:49:08
Jasašnaja Tašla 6 34 53N55 48E16 -3:13:04
Jasenki 6 40 51N32 38E12 -2:32:48
Jasenovoje 6 39 54N10 36E47 -2:27:08
Jasenovskij 23 45 48N10 39E10 -2:36:40
Jasenskaja 6 47 46N22 38E16 -2:33:04
Jasin'a 23 44 48N16 24E20 -1:37:20
Jasinovataja 23 45 48N08 37E51 -2:31:24
Jasinovka 23 45 48N08 37E57 -2:31:48
Jaškino 2 21 55N54 85E26 -5:41:44
Jaškul' 6 47 46N11 45E21 -3:01:24
Jasnogorka 23 45 48N47 37E33 -2:30:12
Jasnogorsk 6 39 54N29 37E42 -2:30:48
Jasnomorskij 19 8 46N45 141E54 -9:27:36
Jasnyj 6 30 51N04 59E58 -3:59:52
Jasnyj 2 14 53N17 127E59 -8:31:56
Jastrebovka 6 39 51N27 37E32 -2:30:08
Jastrebovka 6 39 54N36 36E24 -2:25:36
Jaungulbene 13 36 57N04 26E36 -1:46:24
Jaunjelgava 13 36 56N37 25E05 -1:40:20
Jaunpiebalga 13 36 57N11 26E03 -1:44:12
Jaunpils 13 36 56N44 23E01 -1:32:04
Javan 21 24 38N19 69E02 -4:36:08
Javas 6 41 54N26 42E51 -2:51:24
Javkino 23 45 47N16 32E37 -2:10:28
Javlenka 9 24 54N21 68E27 -4:33:48
Javorov 23 44 49N56 23E23 -1:33:32
Jaz 6 41 54N54 45E13 -3:00:52
Jažalbicy 6 9 58N02 32E58 -2:11:52
Jazevec 6 41 65N43 46E30 -3:06:00
Jazjavan 24 24 40N39 71E44 -4:46:56
Jažma 6 41 66N56 44E29 -2:57:56
Jazovaja 9 24 49N27 85E20 -5:41:20
Jazykovo 6 42 54N18 47E24 -3:09:36
Jechegnadzor 1 34 39N46 45E21 -3:01:24
Jedarma 2 20 58N44 102E36 -6:50:24
Jedelevo 6 34 53N24 47E45 -3:11:00
Jedincy 15 46 48N10 27E19 -1:49:16
Jedisa 7 33 42N31 44E16 -2:57:04
Jednevo 6 39 56N06 36E14 -2:24:56
Jedogon 2 20 54N15 100E15 -6:41:00
Jedrovo 6 39 57N55 33E38 -2:14:32
Jefimovka 6 32 52N13 52E03 -3:28:12
Jefimovskij 6 9 59N30 35E02 -2:20:08
Jefremov 6 39 53N09 38E07 -2:32:28
Jefremova 6 39 56N13 38E59 -2:35:56
Jefremovka 6 40 47N19 38E29 -2:33:56
Jefremovo-Stepanovka 6 47 48N43 40E50 -2:43:20
Jefremovskaja 6 39 55N25 38E59 -2:35:56
Jegindybulak 9 24 49N45 76E23 -5:05:32
Jegindybulak 9 24 48N42 81E48 -5:27:12
Jegorjevka 2 15 50N42 127E42 -8:30:48
Jegorjevsk 6 39 55N23 39E02 -2:36:08
Jejsk 6 47 46N42 38E16 -2:33:04
Jēkabpils 13 36 56N29 25E51 -1:43:24
Jekaterinburg → Sverdlovsk 2 30 56N51 60E36 -4:02:24
Jekaterinino 6 39 55N49 33E58 -2:15:52
Jekaterininskoje 2 24 56N53 74E34 -4:58:16
Jekaterinoslav → Dnepropetrovsk 23 45 48N27 34E59 -2:19:56
Jekaterinoslavka 2 14 50N23 129E08 -8:36:32
Jekaterinovka 6 34 52N03 44E21 -2:57:24
Jekaterinovka 6 47 46N42 38E46 -2:35:04
Jekaterinovka 6 40 47N33 38E23 -2:33:32
Jekaterinovka 9 24 54N36 70E58 -4:43:52
Jekaterinovka 6 34 53N04 49E28 -3:17:52
Jekaterinovka 6 47 46N32 41E42 -2:46:48
Jekaterinovskaja 6 47 46N20 39E58 -2:39:52
Jekimoviči 6 39 54N07 33E18 -2:13:12
Jekpindykurylys 9 32 47N49 47E17 -3:09:08
Jelabuga 6 41 55N47 52E04 -3:28:16
Jelan' 6 47 48N41 39E47 -2:39:08
Jelan' 2 30 57N39 63E42 -4:14:48
Jelan' 6 34 52N13 44E11 -2:56:44
Jelan' 6 34 50N57 43E44 -2:54:56
Jelancy 2 20 52N49 106E25 -7:05:40
Jelanec 23 45 47N42 31E51 -2:07:24
Jelanka 2 24 55N37 75E18 -5:01:12
Jelan'-Koleno 6 41 51N09 41E14 -2:44:56
Jelan'-Kolenovskij 6 41 51N10 41E10 -2:44:40
Jelat'ma 6 40 54N58 41E45 -2:47:00
Jelaur 6 41 54N34 50E21 -3:21:24
Jelaur 6 34 53N50 48E48 -3:15:12
Jelchovka 6 34 53N51 50E18 -3:21:12
Jel'covka 2 21 53N15 86E15 -5:45:00
Jel'cy 6 39 56N40 33E51 -2:15:24
Jel'cy 6 39 56N11 38E46 -2:35:04

Jelec 6	40	52N37	38E30	-2:34:00
Jeleckij 6	29	67N03	64E10	-4:16:40
Jelenskij 6	39	53N29	35E23	-2:21:32
Jelgava 13	36	56N39	23E42	-1:34:48
Jelgavkrasti 13	36	57N28	24E26	-1:37:44
Jelisejevka 23	45	47N02	36E24	-2:25:36
Jelizarovo 6	41	58N33	44E50	-2:59:20
Jelizarovo 23	45	48N12	34E33	-2:18:12
Jelizavetgradka 23	45	48N48	32E24	-2:09:36
Jelizavetinka 6	30	51N46	59E45	-3:59:00
Jelizavetinka 9	24	51N28	71E12	-4:44:48
Jelizavetopol'skoje 2	30	52N51	60E36	-4:02:24
Jelizavetovka 6	47	46N39	38E53	-2:35:32
Jelizovo 4	39	53N24	29E01	-1:56:04
Jel'n'a 6	39	54N35	33E11	-2:12:44
Jelnat' 6	40	57N20	42E49	-2:51:16
Jel'niki 6	41	54N37	43E53	-2:55:32
Jel'onovka 23	45	47N50	37E40	-2:30:40
Jel'onovka 23	45	48N39	38E01	-2:32:04
Jelošnoje 2	30	55N27	66E44	-4:26:56
Jelovo 6	30	57N03	54E54	-3:39:36
Jelšanka 6	34	51N49	46E23	-3:05:32
Jelšanka 6	34	52N35	47E59	-3:11:56
Jelšanka Pervaja 6	32	52N53	52E02	-3:28:08
Jel'sk 4	39	51N48	29E09	-1:56:36
Jemantajevo 6	30	53N34	53E50	-3:35:20
Jemanželinsk 2	30	54N45	61E20	-4:05:20
Jemca 6	41	63N04	40E20	-2:41:20
Jemeljanovka 23	45	45N32	34E53	-2:19:32
Jemeljanovo 2	21	56N11	92E40	-6:10:40
Jemel'stan 6	41	61N13	52E29	-3:29:56
Jemil'čino 23	44	50N52	27E48	-1:51:12
Jenakijevo 23	45	48N14	38E13	-2:32:52
Jenbek 9	24	48N53	77E12	-5:08:48
Jendongin 2	20	53N27	113E01	-7:32:04
Jenisejsk 2	21	58N27	92E10	-6:08:40
Jenotajevka 6	34	47N15	47E03	-3:08:12
Jen'uka 2	16	57N58	121E42	-8:06:48
Jepač 6	29	66N58	61E22	-4:05:28
Jepichin 6	34	48N16	45E14	-3:00:56
Jepifan' 6	39	53N49	38E33	-2:34:12
Jerachtur 6	40	54N43	41E09	-2:44:36
Jerbent 22	30	39N19	58E36	-3:54:24
Jerbogačon 2	20	61N16	108E00	-7:12:00
Jercevo 6	41	60N48	40E05	-2:40:20
Jerdenevo 6	39	54N55	36E27	-2:25:48
Jeremejevka 6	40	46N58	39E33	-2:38:12
Jeremejevo 6	39	55N57	37E01	-2:28:04
Jeremino 6	39	56N27	37E58	-2:31:52
Jerevan 1	34	40N11	44E30	-2:58:00
Jergač 6	30	57N28	56E39	-3:46:36
Jergeninskij 6	47	47N07	44E28	-2:57:52
Jerki 23	45	48N59	31E00	-2:04:00
Jermak 9	24	52N02	76E55	-5:07:40
Jermakovo 6	34	53N11	49E38	-3:18:32
Jermakovskaja 6	47	48N03	41E17	-2:45:08
Jermakovskoje 2	21	53N16	92E24	-6:09:36
Jermekejevo 6	30	54N05	53E40	-3:34:40
Jermentau 9	24	51N38	73E10	-4:52:40
Jermica 6	29	66N56	52E15	-3:29:00
Jermilovka 2	24	57N40	72E55	-4:51:40
Jermiš' 6	41	54N46	42E16	-2:49:04
Jermolajevo 6	30	52N43	55E48	-3:43:12
Jermolajevo 2	21	55N13	92E10	-6:08:40
Jermolino 6	39	56N48	37E49	-2:31:16
Jermolino 2	30	57N20	64E43	-4:18:52
Jermolino 6	39	55N12	36E36	-2:26:24
Jermolino 6	39	55N57	36E54	-2:27:36
Jerofej Pavlovič 2	16	53N58	122E01	-8:08:04
Jer'omino 2	23	58N35	79E25	-5:17:40
Jeropol 2	3	65N15	168E40	-11:14:40
Jerši 6	39	54N24	34E12	-2:16:48
Jeršiči 6	39	53N40	32E44	-2:10:56
Jeršov 6	34	51N20	48E17	-3:13:08
Jeršovka 9	30	54N07	64E59	-4:19:56
Jeršovo 6	39	55N46	36E52	-2:27:28
Jeršovskij 2	30	52N29	59E08	-3:56:32
Jertarskij 2	30	56N47	64E18	-4:17:12
Jertom 6	41	63N32	47E48	-3:11:12
Jertoma 6	41	63N32	47E48	-3:11:12
Jerykly 6	41	55N11	51E26	-3:25:44
Jesaulovka 23	45	48N03	39E02	-2:36:08
Jesenoviči 6	39	57N17	34E14	-2:16:56
Jesensaj 9	32	49N54	51E28	-3:25:52
Ješera 7	33	43N04	40E55	-2:43:40
Jesil' 9	24	51N58	66E24	-4:25:36
Jes'ki 6	39	57N56	36E23	-2:25:32
Jessej 2	19	68N29	102E10	-6:48:40
Jessentuki 6	47	44N03	42E51	-2:51:24
Jevgaščino 2	24	56N26	74E41	-4:58:44
Jevgenjevka 9	24	43N31	77E40	-5:10:40
Jevlach 3	34	40N36	47E09	-3:08:36
Jevlaš'ovo 6	41	53N07	46E51	-3:07:24
Jevpatorija 23	45	45N12	33E22	-2:13:28
Jevra 2	30	59N56	64E27	-4:17:48
Jevsug 23	45	49N13	39E18	-2:37:12
Jezeriščе 4	39	55N50	29E59	-1:59:56
Ježicha 6	42	58N06	47E40	-3:10:40
Ježovo 6	42	58N02	52E14	-3:28:56
Jieznas 14	37	54N36	24E10	-1:36:40
Jõgeva 5	35	58N45	26E24	-1:45:36
Jonava 14	37	55N05	24E17	-1:37:08
Joniškėlis 14	37	56N02	24E10	-1:36:40
Joniškis 14	37	56N14	23E37	-1:34:28
J'orzovka 6	34	48N56	44E38	-2:58:32
Joškar-Ola 6	41	56N38	47E52	-3:11:28
Juanlatgale 6	39	57N04	27E56	-1:51:44
Juchnov 6	39	54N45	35E14	-2:20:56
Juchoviči 4	39	56N02	28E39	-1:54:36
Judinki 6	39	54N37	37E17	-2:29:08
Judinki 6	39	55N27	35E48	-2:23:12
Judino 6	39	54N09	38E19	-2:33:16
Judino 6	39	55N40	37E12	-2:28:48
Judino 6	41	55N51	48E55	-3:15:40
Judino 6	40	58N43	39E17	-2:37:08
Jug 6	30	57N43	56E10	-3:44:40
Jugo-Kamskij 6	30	57N42	55E35	-3:42:20
Jukamenskoje 6	42	57N53	52E15	-3:29:00
Juksa 2	21	56N55	85E10	-5:40:40
Juksejevo 6	30	59N52	54E19	-3:37:16
Jukta 2	19	63N23	105E41	-7:02:44
Juldybajevo 6	30	52N20	57E52	-3:51:28
Juma 6	9	65N07	33E16	-2:13:04
Jumaguzino 6	30	52N54	56E23	-3:45:32
Jumaševo 6	30	54N59	54E25	-3:37:40
Juodkrantė 14	37	55N33	21E08	-1:24:32
Juodupė 14	37	56N05	25E37	-1:42:28
Jur 2	11	59N52	137E39	-9:10:36
Juratiški 4	39	54N02	25E54	-1:43:36
Jurbarkas 14	37	55N05	22E48	-1:31:12
Jurcevo 6	9	60N02	32E36	-2:10:24
Jurenino 6	41	59N24	42E47	-2:51:08
Jureviči 4	39	51N57	29E32	-1:58:08
Jurga 2	21	55N42	84E51	-5:39:24
Jurgamyš 2	30	55N21	64E28	-4:17:52
Jurino 6	41	56N18	46E18	-3:05:12
Jurja 6	42	59N03	49E14	-3:16:56
Jurjevec 6	41	57N18	43E06	-2:52:24
Jurjevka 23	45	48N44	36E02	-2:24:08
Jurjevka 23	45	48N30	39E00	-2:36:00
Jurjev-Pol'skij 6	39	56N30	39E41	-2:38:44
Jurjevskoje 6	39	55N05	36E13	-2:24:52
Jurjev → Tartu 5	35	58N23	26E43	-1:46:52
Jurla 6	30	59N17	54E19	-3:37:16
Jurlovo 6	39	55N24	37E16	-2:29:04
Jurlovo 6	39	55N19	35E52	-2:23:28
Jūrmala 13	36	56N58	23E42	-1:34:48
Jurovo 6	39	55N30	38E22	-2:33:28
Jurovo 6	41	57N30	43E50	-2:55:20
Jurovo 23	44	51N22	27E50	-1:51:20
Jurovskoje 2	30	59N29	69E02	-4:36:08
Jurty 2	20	56N03	97E37	-6:30:28
Jur'uzan' 2	30	54N52	58E26	-3:53:44
Jušala 2	30	57N04	64E17	-4:17:08
Jus'ki 6	42	56N39	53E05	-3:32:20
Juškovo 6	41	59N46	45E11	-3:00:44
Juškozero 6	9	64N44	32E06	-2:08:24
Justa 6	47	47N07	46E18	-3:05:12
Jus'va 6	30	58N56	54E57	-3:39:48
Jutaza 6	41	54N35	53E16	-3:33:04
Juuru 5	35	59N04	24E59	-1:39:56
Juža 6	40	56N35	42E01	-2:48:04
Južno-Aleksandrovka 2	21	55N51	96E10	-6:24:40
Južno-Jenisejskij 2	21	58N48	94E39	-6:18:36
Južno-Sachalinsk 19	8	46N58	142E42	-9:30:48
Južno-Suchokumsk 6	47	44N37	45E34	-3:02:16
Južno-Ural'sk 2	30	54N26	61E15	-4:05:00
Južnyj 9	24	49N21	73E01	-4:52:04
Južnyj 6	41	56N08	44E09	-2:56:36
Južnyj 6	47	47N20	41E51	-2:47:24
Južnyj 2	21	53N14	83E42	-5:34:48
Južnyj 2	30	53N33	60E02	-4:00:08
Južnyj-Alamyšik 24	24	40N46	72E38	-4:50:32
Južnyj Prijut 7	33	43N12	41E55	-2:47:40
Juzovka → Doneck 23	45	48N00	37E48	-2:31:12
Kaachka 22	30	37N21	59E36	-3:58:24
Kaarli 5	35	59N24	26E27	-1:45:48
Kaban' 9	24	54N39	66E28	-4:25:52
Kabanje 23	45	49N13	38E12	-2:32:48
Kabanovka 6	34	53N39	51E18	-3:25:12
Kabanovo 2	24	55N20	70E52	-4:43:28
Kabansk 2	20	52N03	106E39	-7:06:36
Kabardinka 6	47	44N39	37E57	-2:31:48
Kablukovo 6	39	56N50	36E12	-2:24:48
Kablukovo 6	39	56N02	38E10	-2:32:40
Kača 23	45	44N47	33E32	-2:14:08
Kačalinskaja 6	34	49N07	44E03	-2:56:12
Kačanovo 6	39	57N28	27E46	-1:51:04
Kacbachskij 2	30	52N58	59E40	-3:58:40
Kačerginė 14	37	54N56	23E44	-1:34:56
Kachati 7	33	42N30	41E46	-2:47:04
Kachi 3	34	41N26	46E56	-3:07:44
Kachib 6	47	42N25	46E36	-3:06:24
Kachovka 23	45	46N47	33E30	-2:14:00
K'achta 2	20	50N26	106E25	-7:05:40
Kačiry 9	24	53N05	76E07	-5:04:28
Kačkanar 2	30	58N42	59E38	-3:58:32
Kačkarovka 23	45	47N06	33E44	-2:14:56
Kačug 2	20	53N58	105E52	-7:03:28
Kadeshiki 6	42	58N08	49E11	-3:16:44
Kadijevka 23	45	48N34	38E40	-2:34:40
Kadiyevka → Kadijevka 23	45	48N34	38E40	-2:34:40
Kadnikov 6	41	59N30	40E20	-2:41:20
Kadnikovskij 6	41	60N19	40E15	-2:41:00
Kadom 6	41	54N34	42E30	-2:50:00
Kadoškino 6	41	54N01	44E25	-2:57:40
Kaduj 6	40	59N12	37E09	-2:28:36
Kadyj 6	41	57N47	43E11	-2:52:44
Kadykčan 2	6	63N02	146E50	-9:47:20
Kadyšovo 6	42	54N20	46E45	-3:07:00
Kadžaran 1	34	39N11	46E08	-3:04:32
Kadžerom 6	29	64N41	55E54	-3:43:36
Kadži-Saj 10	24	42N08	77E10	-5:08:40
Kafan 1	34	39N11	46E08	-3:04:32
Kafan 1	34	39N13	46E24	-3:05:36
Kagal'nickaja 6	40	46N53	40E09	-2:40:36
Kagal'nik 6	40	47N05	39E19	-2:37:16
Kagan 24	30	39N43	64E33	-4:18:12
Kagarlyk 23	44	49N51	30E50	-2:03:20
Kagul 15	46	45N54	28E11	-1:52:44
Käina 5	35	58N50	22E45	-1:31:00
Kainda 10	24	42N50	73E41	-4:54:44
Kairy 23	45	46N57	33E43	-2:14:52
Kaišiadorys 14	37	54N52	24E27	-1:37:48
Kajasan 2	30	55N12	62E16	-4:09:04
Kajasula 6	47	44N19	44E59	-2:59:56
Kajgy 9	24	50N55	64E43	-4:18:52
Kajmanačicha 9	24	53N32	75E11	-5:00:44
Kajmonovo 2	20	56N50	104E54	-6:59:36
Kajmysovy 2	25	59N48	76E31	-5:06:04
Kajnar 9	24	49N12	77E25	-5:09:40
Kajrakkum 21	24	40N16	69E49	-4:39:16
Kajrakty 9	24	48N31	73E14	-4:52:56
Kajsackoje 6	34	49N44	46E51	-3:07:24
Kakino 6	41	55N12	44E53	-2:59:32
Kalač 6	47	50N25	41E01	-2:44:04
Kalačinsk 2	24	55N03	74E34	-4:58:16
Kalač-Kurtlak 6	47	49N00	42E26	-2:49:44
Kalač-Na-Donu 6	34	48N43	43E31	-2:54:04
Kalai-Chumb 21	24	38N28	70E46	-4:43:04
Kalai-Mor 22	30	35N39	62E33	-4:10:12
Kalais 6	41	52N38	42E38	-2:50:32
Kalajka 2	20	58N28	111E46	-7:27:04
Kalakan 2	20	55N08	116E45	-7:47:00
Kalančak 23	45	46N16	33E17	-2:13:08
Kalanguj 2	16	51N01	116E31	-7:46:04
Kalaraš 15	46	47N16	28E19	-1:53:16
Kalašnikovo 6	39	57N17	35E13	-2:20:52
Kalauri 7	33	41N49	45E42	-3:02:48
Kalaus-Kr'akovka 23	45	48N46	38E52	-2:35:28
Kal'azin 6	39	57N15	37E52	-2:31:28
Kaleščatovka 23	45	49N35	39E55	-2:39:40
Kalevala 6	9	65N13	31E08	-2:04:32
Kalga 2	16	50N57	118E48	-7:55:12
Kalgačicha 6	40	63N20	36E44	-2:26:56
Kalikino 6	30	52N55	54E05	-3:36:20
Kalikino 6	41	52N57	39E50	-2:39:20
Kalinin 6	47	47N11	42E10	-2:48:40
Kalinin 6	39	56N52	35E55	-2:23:40
Kalininabad 21	24	39N45	69E08	-4:36:32
Kaliningrad 6	39	55N55	37E49	-2:31:16
Kaliningrad (Königsberg) 8	38	54N43	20E30	-1:22:00
Kalinino 6	47	45N07	39E00	-2:36:00
Kalinino 23	45	47N27	37E28	-2:29:52
Kalinino 2	14	49N24	129E20	-8:37:20
Kalinino 1	34	41N07	44E17	-2:57:08
Kalinino 6	30	57N20	56E20	-3:45:20
Kalinino 6	34	46N21	48E53	-3:15:32
Kalininsk 6	34	51N30	44E28	-2:57:52
Kalininsk 10	24	42N29	72E06	-4:48:24
Kalininskaja 6	47	47N52	42E15	-2:49:00
Kalininskaja 6	47	45N29	38E40	-2:34:40
Kalininskij 23	45	48N01	39E36	-2:38:24
Kalininskoje 23	45	47N07	32E59	-2:11:56
Kalininskoje 10	24	42N50	73E49	-4:55:16
Kalinkoviči 4	39	52N08	29E21	-1:57:24
Kalinovka 23	44	49N27	28E32	-1:54:08
Kalinovka 9	30	49N58	55E22	-3:41:28
Kalinovka 6	39	51N54	34E28	-2:17:52
Kalinovka 23	44	50N14	30E14	-2:00:56
Kalinovo 6	39	54N54	37E17	-2:29:08
Kalinovo 23	45	48N34	38E31	-2:34:04
Kalistraticha 2	21	52N59	83E35	-5:34:20
Kalkaman 9	24	51N58	76E02	-5:04:08
Kallaste 5	35	58N39	27E09	-1:48:36
Kalmakkora 9	24	44N03	78E44	-5:14:56
Kalmyckije Mysy 2	23	51N53	82E16	-5:29:04
Kalmykov 6	34	49N01	42E49	-2:51:16
Kalmykovka 23	45	49N17	38E39	-2:34:36
Kalmykovka 23	45	49N17	39E52	-2:39:28
Kalmykovo 9	32	49N03	51E47	-3:27:08
Kalnciems 13	36	56N50	23E37	-1:34:28
Kal'niboloto 23	45	48N44	31E00	-2:04:00
Kalnibolotskaja 6	47	46N01	40E28	-2:41:52
Kaltan 2	21	53N30	87E17	-5:49:08

Kal'tino 6	9	59N58	30E40	-2:02:40
Kaluga 6	39	54N31	36E16	-2:25:04
Kalugino 6	39	54N59	37E11	-2:28:44
Kalugino 9	32	48N22	51E33	-3:26:12
Kaluš 23	44	49N03	24E23	-1:37:32
Kalvarija 14	37	54N21	23E14	-1:32:56
K'alvaz 3	34	38N39	48E18	-3:13:12
Kama 6	42	56N19	54E06	-3:36:24
Kama 2	30	60N08	62E10	-4:08:40
Kamajai 14	37	55N49	25E30	-1:42:00
Kambarka 6	42	56N17	54E12	-3:36:48
Kambja 5	35	58N14	26E42	-1:46:48
Kamen' 4	39	55N01	28E53	-1:55:32
Kamenec 4	39	52N24	23E49	-1:35:16
Kamenec-Podol'skij 23	45	48N41	26E36	-1:46:24
Kamenka 6	9	59N59	30E53	-2:03:32
Kamenka 2	21	58N33	95E51	-6:23:24
Kamenka 9	24	52N22	69E04	-4:36:16
Kamenka 2	11	44N28	136E01	-9:04:04
Kamenka 9	32	51N07	50E19	-3:21:16
Kamenka 9	24	42N55	72E50	-4:51:20
Kamenka 6	41	65N54	44E05	-2:56:20
Kamenka 6	41	56N11	45E35	-3:02:20
Kamenka 6	40	57N23	41E49	-2:47:16
Kamenka 6	41	53N13	44E03	-2:56:12
Kamenka 6	41	52N04	41E49	-2:47:16
Kamenka 6	40	50N43	39E25	-2:37:40
Kamenka 23	44	49N02	32E06	-2:08:24
Kamenka 15	46	48N03	28E42	-1:54:48
Kamenka 6	39	54N43	38E19	-2:33:16
Kamenka 6	39	56N11	37E18	-2:29:12
Kamenka 6	39	55N13	36E59	-2:27:56
Kamenka 23	45	49N38	39E22	-2:37:28
Kamenka 23	45	49N07	37E18	-2:29:12
Kamenka 23	45	47N25	37E42	-2:30:48
Kamenka-Bugskaja 23	44	50N07	24E20	-1:37:20
Kamenka-Dneprovskaja 23	45	47N29	34E25	-2:17:40
Kamen'-Kaširskij 23	44	51N38	24E58	-1:39:52
Kamen'-Na-Obi 2	21	53N47	81E20	-5:25:20
Kamennogorsk 6	9	60N58	29E07	-1:56:28
Kamennoje 23	44	51N31	27E38	-1:50:32
Kamennoje 23	45	47N53	35E25	-2:21:40
Kamennomostskij 6	47	44N18	40E12	-2:40:48
Kamennyj Brod 23	44	50N25	27E49	-1:51:16
Kamennyj Brod 6	40	47N26	39E51	-2:39:24
Kamennyj Jar 6	34	48N27	45E34	-3:02:16
Kamenolomni 6	40	47N40	40E13	-2:40:52
Kamen'-Rybolov 2	27	44N46	132E02	-8:48:08
Kamensk 2	20	51N58	106E36	-7:06:24
Kamenskij 6	34	50N53	45E29	-3:01:56
Kamenskoje 2	4	62N30	166E12	-11:04:48
Kamenskoje 23	45	45N49	29E16	-1:57:04
Kamenskoje 6	39	55N16	36E50	-2:27:20
Kamensk-Šachtinskij 6	47	48N21	40E19	-2:41:16
Kamensk-Ural'skij 2	30	56N28	61E54	-4:07:36
Kameškovo 6	40	56N21	41E00	-2:44:00
Kaminskij 6	40	57N10	41E28	-2:45:52
Kamniokan 2	20	56N17	111E57	-7:27:48
Kamo 1	34	40N22	45E08	-3:00:32
Kamskij 6	42	60N04	53E13	-3:32:52
Kamskoje Ustje 6	41	55N13	49E16	-3:17:04
Kamyšet 2	20	55N12	98E42	-6:34:48
Kamyšev 6	47	46N39	42E38	-2:50:32
Kamyšev 6	47	46N53	42E31	-2:50:04
Kamyševacha 23	45	47N43	35E32	-2:22:08
Kamyševacha 23	45	48N42	38E23	-2:33:32
Kamyševatskaja 6	47	46N25	37E57	-2:31:48
Kamyševskaja 6	47	47N37	41E49	-2:47:16
Kamyšin 6	34	50N06	45E24	-3:01:36
Kamyškurgon 21	24	40N34	70E24	-4:41:36
Kamyšla 6	42	54N07	52E10	-3:28:40
Kamyšlov 2	30	56N52	62E43	-4:10:52
Kamyslybas 9	30	46N11	61E57	-4:07:48
Kamyšnoje 9	30	51N58	61E47	-4:07:08
Kamyšovyj 6	47	46N26	45E12	-3:00:48
Kamyš-Zar'a 23	45	47N19	36E42	-2:26:48
Kamyz'ak 6	34	46N07	48E05	-3:12:20
Kanadej 6	34	53N10	47E30	-3:10:00
Kanajevka 6	41	53N07	45E35	-3:02:20
Kanajevka 6	34	52N12	49E40	-3:18:40
Kananikol'skoje 6	30	52N47	57E29	-3:49:56
Kanaš 6	41	55N31	47E30	-3:10:00
Kanava 6	29	61N07	54E58	-3:39:52
Kanava 6	47	47N13	45E24	-3:01:36
Kanavka 6	34	50N19	48E33	-3:14:12
Kandabulak 6	34	53N58	50E44	-3:22:56
Kandagač 9	30	49N28	57E25	-3:49:40
Kandalakša 6	9	67N09	32E21	-2:09:24
Kandat 2	21	57N08	89E02	-5:56:08
Kandava 13	36	57N05	22E49	-1:31:16
Kandry 6	30	54N34	54E07	-3:36:28
Kanevskaja 6	47	46N05	38E57	-2:35:48
Kangalassy 2	16	62N23	129E59	-8:39:56
Kangaz 15	46	46N07	28E33	-1:54:12
Kangil 2	16	52N15	116E20	-7:45:20
Kangly 24	24	40N07	67E54	-4:31:36
Kanibadam 21	24	40N17	70E25	-4:41:40
Kanin Nos 6	41	68N39	43E14	-2:52:56
Kankunskij 2	16	57N37	126E08	-8:24:32
Kan'ov 23	44	49N44	31E28	-2:05:52
Kan'ovka 6	9	67N08	39E40	-2:38:40
Kansaj 21	24	40N30	69E41	-4:38:44
Kansk 2	21	56N13	95E41	-6:22:44
Kant 10	24	42N55	74E55	-4:59:40
Kantemirovka 6	40	49N41	39E51	-2:39:24
Kantemirovka 9	24	42N51	70E20	-4:41:20
Kantubek 24	30	45N07	59E16	-3:57:04
Kan'utino 6	39	55N33	33E14	-2:12:56
Kanzanavolok 6	40	62N23	36E58	-2:27:52
Kapal 9	24	45N08	79E03	-5:16:12
Kapčagaj 9	24	43N53	77E12	-5:08:48
Kapitanovka 23	45	48N54	31E42	-2:06:48
Kapkataš 10	24	40N23	74E20	-4:57:20
Kapkinka 6	34	48N08	43E51	-2:55:24
Kaporskoje 6	9	59N45	29E58	-1:59:52
Kapralicha 2	30	56N11	67E15	-4:29:00
Kapsukas 14	37	54N33	23E21	-1:33:24
Kapustin Jar 6	34	48N36	45E45	-3:03:00
Kapustino 23	45	48N57	31E14	-2:04:56
Kapyrevščina 6	39	55N15	32E53	-2:11:32
Kara 2	28	69N14	65E00	-4:20:00
Karaaul 9	24	48N57	79E15	-5:17:00
Karabagl'ar 16	34	39N26	45E12	-3:00:48
Kara-Balta 10	24	42N50	73E52	-4:55:28
Kara-Balty 10	24	42N50	73E52	-4:55:28
Karabanovo 6	39	56N19	38E42	-2:34:48
Karabaš 6	41	54N42	52E36	-3:30:24
Karabaš 2	30	55N29	60E14	-4:00:56
Karabau 9	30	48N26	52E54	-3:31:36
Karabekaul 22	30	38N30	64E08	-4:16:32
Karabudachkent 6	47	42N41	47E34	-3:10:16
Karabula 2	21	58N08	97E23	-6:29:32
Karabulak 9	24	42N32	69E46	-4:39:04
Karabulak 10	24	39N51	69E38	-4:38:32
Karabulak 9	24	44N54	78E30	-5:14:00
Karabulak 9	24	47N34	84E41	-5:38:44
Karabutak 9	30	49N59	60E10	-4:00:40
Karačajevsk 6	47	43N45	41E54	-2:47:36
Karačala 3	34	39N48	48E57	-3:15:48
Karačev 6	39	53N07	35E00	-2:20:00
Karachtaj 24	24	40N55	69E46	-4:39:04
Karači 6	42	57N59	50E28	-3:21:52
Karaftit 2	20	54N12	111E54	-7:27:36
Karagaj 6	30	58N16	54E56	-3:39:44
Karagaj 9	32	48N39	47E38	-3:10:32
Karagajly 9	24	49N20	75E48	-5:03:12
Karaganda 9	24	49N50	73E10	-4:52:40
Karagel 22	30	39N23	53E11	-3:32:44
Karagičevskij 6	34	50N11	42E55	-2:51:40
Karagužicha 9	24	50N47	83E00	-5:32:00
Karaičev 6	47	48N37	42E13	-2:48:52
Karaidel' 6	30	55N50	56E53	-3:47:32
Karaidel'skij 6	30	55N49	57E05	-3:48:20
Karajantak 24	24	40N03	67E54	-4:31:36
Karakabak 9	24	50N33	75E09	-5:00:36
Karakain 10	24	41N26	74E19	-4:57:16
Kara-Kala 22	30	38N26	56E18	-3:45:12
Karakastek 9	24	43N08	76E06	-5:04:24
Karakavak 10	24	39N41	72E43	-4:50:52
Karakendža 21	24	39N14	71E31	-4:46:04
Karakolka 10	24	41N32	77E23	-5:09:32
Karaksar 2	16	51N16	115E58	-7:43:52
Karakul' 21	24	39N02	73E33	-4:54:12
Karakul' 24	30	39N32	63E50	-4:15:20
Karakul' 2	24	57N26	70E51	-4:43:24
Kara-Kul'dža 10	24	40N37	73E35	-4:54:20
Karakulino 6	42	56N01	53E43	-3:34:52
Karakul'skoje 2	30	54N04	62E26	-4:09:44
Karakum 9	24	46N49	79E33	-5:18:12
Karalat 6	34	45N55	48E18	-3:13:12
Karalon 2	20	57N02	115E52	-7:43:28
Karam 2	20	55N09	107E37	-7:10:28
Karamurt 9	24	42N19	69E58	-4:39:52
Karamyševo 2	19	57N34	100E55	-6:43:40
Karamyševo 6	39	57N45	28E45	-1:55:00
Karamyševo 6	39	54N46	36E07	-2:24:28
Karamzino 6	39	56N00	34E33	-2:18:12
Karaoba 9	30	53N17	65E06	-4:20:24
Karaoba 9	30	47N03	56E20	-3:45:20
Karaoj 9	24	45N54	74E45	-4:59:00
Karaozek 9	24	43N43	77E23	-5:09:32
Karaozek 9	30	45N03	65E18	-4:21:12
Karaozek 24	30	43N16	58E40	-3:54:40
Karapyši 23	44	49N38	30E47	-2:03:08
Karaš 6	39	56N54	39E24	-2:37:36
Karasaj 10	24	41N34	77E49	-5:11:16
Karašengel' 9	24	47N29	75E35	-5:02:20
Karaskan 24	24	41N03	71E49	-4:47:16
Karasu 3	34	40N11	48E41	-3:14:44
Karasu 10	24	43N03	73E57	-4:55:48
Karasu 9	30	52N40	65E28	-4:21:52
Karasu 9	30	51N20	62E21	-4:09:24
Karasuk 2	23	53N44	78E02	-5:12:08
Karata 6	47	42N35	46E21	-3:05:24
Karatal 9	24	45N07	77E54	-5:11:36
Karatal 9	24	47N36	85E12	-5:40:48
Karatau 9	24	43N10	70E28	-4:41:52
Karatobe 9	30	49N41	53E31	-3:34:04
Karatogaj 9	30	48N42	59E40	-3:58:40
Karaton 9	30	46N25	53E30	-3:34:00
Kara-T'ube 9	30	49N41	53E31	-3:34:04
Karaturuk 9	24	43N33	77E59	-5:11:56
Karatuzskoje 2	21	53N36	92E53	-6:11:32
Karaul 2	21	70N06	83E08	-5:32:32
Karaulkel'dy 9	30	48N43	55E53	-3:43:32
Karault'ob'o 10	24	40N33	75E57	-5:03:48
Karauzak 24	30	42N59	60E02	-4:00:08
Karauzek 6	34	47N15	48E25	-3:13:40
Karavan 10	24	41N30	71E45	-4:47:00
Karavannoje 6	34	45N59	47E08	-3:08:32
Karavannoje 6	42	57N47	47E41	-3:10:44
Karažal 9	24	48N02	70E49	-4:43:16
Kärdla 5	35	59N00	22E45	-1:31:00
Kardymovo 6	39	54N54	32E26	-2:09:44
Kardžin 6	47	43N16	44E16	-2:57:04
Kareli 7	33	42N01	43E54	-2:55:36
Karel'skij Gorodok 6	9	58N04	36E30	-2:26:00
Karepino 6	30	61N02	57E02	-3:48:08
Kärevere 5	35	58N26	26E29	-1:45:56
Kargali 6	41	55N12	50E54	-3:23:36
Kargalinskaja 6	47	43N44	46E30	-3:06:00
Karganaj 2	2	65N21	175E25	-11:41:40
Kargapolje 2	30	55N57	64E27	-4:17:48
Kargasok 2	23	59N07	80E53	-5:23:32
Kargat 2	23	55N10	80E17	-5:21:08
Karginskaja 6	47	49N21	41E38	-2:46:32
Kargopol' 6	40	61N30	38E58	-2:35:52
Karino 6	39	54N42	38E56	-2:35:44
Karinskoje 6	39	55N42	36E41	-2:26:44
Karintorf 6	42	58N33	50E11	-3:20:44
Karjepolje 6	41	65N34	43E40	-2:54:40
Karkalaj 6	42	57N00	52E24	-3:29:36
Karkaralinsk 9	24	49N23	75E21	-5:01:24
Kärla 5	35	58N20	22E15	-1:29:00
Karlo-Libknechtovsk 23	45	48N42	38E04	-2:32:16
Karlo-Marksovo 23	45	48N16	38E09	-2:32:36
Karlovka 23	45	49N27	35E08	-2:20:32
Karluk 2	20	53N27	105E58	-7:03:52
Karl'uk 24	30	38N12	67E42	-4:30:48
Karmanovka 9	32	49N24	50E22	-3:21:28
Karmanovo 6	39	55N52	34E52	-2:19:28
Karnauchovka 23	45	48N28	34E44	-2:18:56
Karniki 6	39	54N12	38E05	-2:32:20
Karpinsk 2	30	59N45	60E01	-4:00:04
Karpogory 6	41	64N00	44E24	-2:57:36
Karpovka 23	45	49N10	37E43	-2:30:52
Karpovka 23	45	47N57	39E36	-2:38:24
Karpovo 6	40	60N02	36E43	-2:26:52
Karpovo 6	39	55N35	38E34	-2:34:16
Karpunicha 6	41	57N42	45E20	-3:01:20
Karpuninskij 2	30	58N43	61E50	-4:07:20
Karša 9	32	49N48	51E27	-3:25:48
Karsakpaj 9	31	47N49	66E41	-4:26:44
Kārsava 13	36	56N47	27E40	-1:50:40
Karši 24	30	38N53	65E48	-4:23:12
Karsovaj 6	42	58N14	53E11	-3:32:44
Karsun 6	42	54N11	46E59	-3:07:56
Kartajol' 6	29	64N32	53E14	-3:32:56
Kartaly 2	30	53N03	60E40	-4:02:40
Käru 5	35	58N50	25E11	-1:40:44
Karvala 6	9	59N41	30E09	-2:00:36
Karym 2	30	60N07	66E41	-4:26:44
Karymskoje 2	16	51N37	114E21	-7:37:24
Karymskoje 2	20	54N07	101E49	-6:47:16
Karza 2	23	58N35	80E50	-5:23:20
Karzachi 7	33	41N15	43E16	-2:53:04
Kasan 24	30	39N02	65E35	-4:22:20
Kasan → Kazan' 6	41	55N49	49E08	-3:16:32
Kasansaj 24	24	41N15	71E32	-4:46:08
Kašary 6	47	49N03	41E00	-2:44:00
Kasilovo 6	39	50N38	35E37	-2:22:28
Kasimov 6	40	54N56	41E24	-2:45:36
Kašin 6	39	57N21	37E37	-2:30:28
Kašira 6	39	54N51	38E10	-2:32:40
Kaskabulak 9	24	49N34	79E52	-5:19:28
Kaskana 24	24	40N45	69E36	-4:38:24
Kaskelen 9	24	43N12	76E37	-5:06:28
Kasli 2	30	55N53	60E46	-4:03:04
Kasn'a 6	39	55N24	34E20	-2:17:20
Kašperovka 23	44	49N26	29E41	-1:58:44
Kaspi 7	33	41N57	44E25	-2:57:40
Kaspijsk 6	47	42N52	47E38	-3:10:32
Kaspijskij 6	47	45N22	47E24	-3:09:36
Kaspl'a 6	39	55N00	31E38	-2:06:32
Kastornoje 6	40	51N50	38E06	-2:32:24
Kasum-Ismailov 3	34	40N36	46E47	-3:07:08
Kasumkent 6	47	41N41	48E07	-3:12:28
Kata 2	20	58N46	102E40	-6:50:40
Katajevo 2	18	50N57	108E41	-7:14:44
Katajsk 2	30	56N18	62E35	-4:10:20
Katangli 19	8	51N42	143E14	-9:32:56
Katašin 6	39	52N36	32E10	-2:08:40
Katav-Ivanovsk 2	30	54N45	58E12	-3:52:48
Katech 3	34	41N39	46E34	-3:06:16
Katerinopol' 23	45	48N56	30E59	-2:03:56
Katešovo 6	39	54N08	37E00	-2:28:00
Katni 6	42	57N59	47E46	-3:11:04
Katon-Karagaj 9	24	49N11	85E37	-5:42:28

Katričev 6 34 49N23 45E33 -3:02:12
Kattakurgan 24 30 39N55 66E15 -4:25:00
Katta-Taldyk 10 24 40N19 73E12 -4:52:48
Katunino 6 41 58N01 45E39 -3:02:36
Katunki 6 40 56N50 43E14 -2:52:56
Kaunas 14 37 54N54 23E54 -1:35:36
Kaušany 15 46 46N38 29E25 -1:57:40
Kavača 2 4 60N16 169E51-11:19:24
Kavalerovo 2 27 44N15 135E04 -9:00:16
Kaverino 6 41 54N10 41E47 -2:47:08
Kaverino 6 39 56N11 36E15 -2:25:00
Kavykuči-Gazimurskije 2 16 51N22 118E10 -7:52:40
Kazach 3 34 41N06 45E22 -3:01:28
Kazachstan 9 30 51N09 53E00 -3:32:00
Kazačij 6 40 46N58 40E03 -2:40:12
Kazačinskoje 2 21 57N49 93E17 -6:13:08
Kazačinskoje 2 20 56N16 107E36 -7:10:24
Kazačja Lopan' 23 45 50N21 36E11 -2:24:44
Kazačje 2 11 70N44 136E13 -9:04:52
Kazačji Lageri 23 45 46N42 32E59 -2:11:56
Kazačka 6 34 51N28 43E56 -2:55:44
Kazackij 9 30 49N20 58E31 -3:54:04
Kazackoje 23 44 51N18 33E29 -2:13:56
Kazakdarja 24 30 43N27 59E46 -3:59:04
Kazakevičevo 2 11 48N17 134E46 -8:59:04
Kazaki 6 40 52N38 38E16 -2:33:04
Kazaklija 15 46 46N00 28E37 -1:54:28
Kazal'cevo 2 23 59N18 80E30 -5:22:00
Kazalinsk 9 30 45N46 62E07 -4:08:28
Kazan' 6 41 55N49 49E08 -3:16:32
Kazanbulak 3 34 40N38 46E41 -3:06:44
Kazandžik 22 30 39N16 55E32 -3:42:08
Kazanka 23 45 47N50 32E49 -2:11:16
Kazanka 9 24 53N20 67E27 -4:29:48
Kazanovka 6 39 53N46 38E34 -2:34:16
Kazanskaja 6 47 49N48 41E09 -2:44:36
Kazanskoje 6 39 54N59 37E39 -2:30:36
Kazanskoje 2 30 55N38 69E14 -4:36:56
Kazarman 10 24 41N24 74E03 -4:56:12
Kazatin 23 44 49N43 28E50 -1:55:20
Kazatkul' 2 23 55N02 76E03 -5:04:12
Kazbegi 7 33 42N39 44E39 -2:58:36
Kazgorodok 9 24 52N53 70E42 -4:42:48
Kazgorodok 9 24 49N56 71E36 -4:46:24
Kažim 6 41 60N20 51E30 -3:26:00
Kazi-Magomed 3 34 40N03 48E56 -3:15:44
Kazinka 6 39 50N14 37E50 -2:31:20
Kazinka 6 40 52N32 39E42 -2:38:48
Kazlu Rūda 14 37 54N46 23E30 -1:34:00
Kaz'minskoje 6 47 44N35 41E41 -2:46:44
Kaznačejevo 6 39 54N31 37E16 -2:29:04
Kaztalovka 9 32 49N46 48E42 -3:14:48
Kazy 22 30 39N13 57E30 -3:50:00
Kazym 2 30 63N40 67E14 -4:28:56
Keb'uty 6 47 45N50 44E14 -2:56:56
Keče 9 24 43N14 71E22 -4:45:28
Kedabek 3 34 40N34 45E49 -3:03:16
Kėdainiai 14 37 55N17 24E00 -1:36:00
Kedon 2 5 64N08 159E14-10:36:56
Kedrovka 2 21 55N32 86E03 -5:44:12
Kedvavom 6 29 64N15 53E27 -3:33:48
Kega 6 40 65N10 36E54 -2:27:36
Kegejli 24 30 42N45 59E35 -3:58:20
Kegičovka 23 45 49N17 35E46 -2:23:04
Kegums 13 36 56N46 24E45 -1:39:00
Kehra 5 35 59N20 25E20 -1:41:20
Keila 5 35 59N18 24E25 -1:37:40
Kelasuri 7 33 43N08 41E13 -2:44:52
Kel'badžar 3 34 40N07 46E02 -3:04:08
Kel'd'ušovo 6 41 55N01 44E59 -2:59:56
Keles 24 24 41N24 69E12 -4:36:48
Kelif 22 30 37N21 66E15 -4:25:00
Kellerovka 9 24 53N50 69E17 -4:37:08
Kelmė 14 37 55N38 22E56 -1:31:44
Kel'mency 23 45 48N27 26E50 -1:47:20
Kel'temašat 9 24 42N30 70E17 -4:41:08
Kem' 6 40 64N57 34E36 -2:18:24
Kemerovo 2 21 55N20 86E05 -5:44:20
Keml'a 6 41 54N42 45E15 -3:01:00
Kenaral 10 24 42N32 72E08 -4:48:32
Kenašči 9 30 50N32 53E20 -3:33:20
Kendyrlik 9 24 47N30 85E12 -5:40:48
Kenes 9 24 43N41 67E49 -4:31:16
Kenes 9 24 43N59 73E35 -4:54:20
Kenga 2 23 57N27 80E57 -5:23:48
Kenimekh 24 30 40N15 65E05 -4:20:20
Kense 9 24 46N49 68E20 -4:33:20
Kentau 9 24 43N36 68E36 -4:34:24
Kepina 6 41 65N24 41E50 -2:47:20
Kerč' 23 45 45N22 36E27 -2:25:48
Kerčel' 2 30 59N18 64E46 -4:19:04
Kerčemja 6 29 61N28 53E50 -3:35:20
Kerčevskij 6 30 59N55 56E17 -3:45:08
Kerch → Kerč' 23 45 45N22 36E27 -2:25:48
Keret' 6 9 66N16 33E34 -2:14:16
Kerga 6 41 62N39 46E00 -3:04:00
Kergez 3 34 40N18 49E38 -3:18:32
Kerki 6 29 63N43 54E05 -3:36:20
Kerki 22 30 37N50 65E12 -4:20:48
Keros 6 43 60N44 52E50 -3:31:20
Kerpinen' 15 46 46N47 28E22 -1:53:28
Kerva 6 39 55N37 39E35 -2:38:20
Kerženec 6 41 56N28 44E26 -2:57:44
Keskozero 6 9 61N24 33E12 -2:12:48
Kes'ma 6 9 58N27 37E04 -2:28:16
Kesova Gora 6 39 57N35 37E17 -2:29:08
Kesten'ga 6 9 65N55 31E47 -2:07:08
Ketoj Island 12 8 47N20 152E28-10:09:52
Ketoj, Ostrov 12 8 47N20 152E28-10:09:52
Ketovo 2 30 55N21 65E18 -4:21:12
Keul' 2 20 58N25 102E49 -6:51:16
Kevdo-Mel'sitovo 6 41 53N09 43E54 -2:55:36
Kevsala 6 47 45N48 42E41 -2:50:44
Kez 6 42 57N53 53E43 -3:34:52
Kežma 2 19 58N59 101E09 -6:44:36
Khanty-Mansiysk → Chanty-Mansijsk 2 25 61N00 69E06 -4:36:24
Kharkov → Char'kov 23 45 50N00 36E15 -2:25:00
Kherson → Cherson 23 45 46N38 32E35 -2:10:20
Khimki → Chimki 6 39 55N54 37E26 -2:29:44
Khiva → Chiva 24 30 41N24 60E22 -4:01:28
Khmel'nitskiy → Chmel'nickij 23 44 49N25 27E00 -1:48:00
Khorog → Chorog 21 24 37N31 71E33 -4:46:12
Kichčik 12 8 53N24 156E03-10:24:12
Kickany 15 46 46N47 29E36 -1:58:24
Kičkino 6 47 47N05 44E02 -2:56:08
Kičma 6 42 57N12 48E55 -3:15:40
Kicman' 23 44 48N27 25E44 -1:42:56
Kičmengskij Gorodok 6 41 59N59 45E48 -3:03:12
Kiev → Kijev 23 44 50N26 30E31 -2:02:04
Kiew → Kijev 23 44 50N26 30E31 -2:02:04
Kiik 9 24 47N31 72E55 -4:51:40
Kiikkaškan 9 24 49N28 77E04 -5:08:16
Kijaly 9 24 54N17 69E41 -4:38:44
Kijasovo 6 42 56N21 53E07 -3:32:28
Kijev (Kiev) 23 44 50N26 30E31 -2:02:04
Kijevka 9 24 50N16 71E34 -4:46:16
Kijevka 6 47 46N05 42E57 -2:51:48
Kijevka 6 34 50N46 48E28 -3:13:52
Kijevskoje 6 47 45N03 37E52 -2:31:28
Kijkašor 6 41 60N46 49E24 -3:17:36
Kijma 9 24 51N35 67E34 -4:30:16
Kikerino 6 9 59N28 29E35 -1:58:20
Kikimorka 6 42 58N10 49E27 -3:17:48
Kiknur 6 42 57N19 47E14 -3:08:56
Kikvidze 6 34 50N53 42E46 -2:51:04
Kikvidze 6 34 50N44 43E03 -2:52:12
Kil'dinstroj 6 9 68N48 33E06 -2:12:24
Kilemary 6 41 56N47 46E52 -3:07:28
Kilija 23 45 45N27 29E16 -1:57:04
Kilingi-Nõmme 5 35 58N09 24E58 -1:39:52
Kil'mez' 6 42 57N04 51E21 -3:25:24
Kimil'tej 2 20 54N08 101E59 -6:47:56
Kimovsk 6 39 53N58 38E32 -2:34:08
Kimry 6 39 56N52 37E21 -2:29:24
Kindel'a 6 32 51N36 52E58 -3:31:52
Kindikan 2 20 56N02 115E15 -7:41:00
Kinel' 6 34 53N14 50E39 -3:22:36
Kinel'-Čerkassy 6 34 53N29 51E29 -3:25:56
Kinel'-Čerkasy 6 34 53N29 51E29 -3:25:56
Kinešma 6 40 57N26 42E09 -2:48:36
Kingisepp 6 9 59N22 28E36 -1:54:24
Kingiseppa 6 9 59N22 28E36 -1:54:24
Kintus 2 25 60N09 71E25 -4:45:40
Kiperčeny 15 46 47N32 28E50 -1:55:20
Kipijevo 6 29 65N40 54E30 -3:38:00
Kir'a 6 41 55N04 46E53 -3:07:32
Kirbla 5 35 58N44 23E57 -1:35:48
Kirda 24 24 41N06 69E00 -4:36:00
Kirejevo 6 34 50N01 44E29 -2:57:56
Kirejevsk 6 39 53N56 37E56 -2:31:44
Kirejkovo 6 39 53N38 35E49 -2:23:16
Kirensk 2 20 57N46 108E08 -7:12:32
Kirgili 24 24 40N24 71E43 -4:46:52
Kirgiz-Mijaki 6 30 53N38 54E47 -3:39:08
Kirikovka 23 45 50N22 35E07 -2:20:28
Kirillov 6 40 59N52 38E23 -2:33:32
Kirillovka 6 39 55N57 37E20 -2:29:20
Kirillovo 6 41 57N07 45E27 -3:01:48
Kirillovo 6 41 53N47 42E40 -2:50:40
Kirillovskoje 6 9 60N28 29E17 -1:57:08
Kiriši 6 9 59N27 32E02 -2:08:08
Kirjanovskaja Kontora 2 20 58N18 104E13 -6:56:52
Kirov 6 42 58N38 49E42 -3:18:48
Kirov 6 39 54N05 34E20 -2:17:20
Kirovabad 3 34 40N40 46E22 -3:05:28
Kirovakan 1 34 40N48 44E30 -2:58:00
Kirovgrad 2 30 57N26 60E04 -4:00:16
Kirovka 9 24 47N07 82E00 -5:28:00
Kirovo 23 45 47N41 35E46 -2:23:04
Kirovo 23 45 48N50 38E03 -2:32:12
Kirovo 2 30 55N33 63E46 -4:15:04
Kirovo 24 24 40N26 70E34 -4:42:16
Kirovo 23 44 51N29 29E24 -1:57:36
Kirovo-Čepeck 6 42 58N33 50E01 -3:20:04
Kirovograd 23 45 48N30 32E18 -2:09:12
Kirovsk 23 45 49N01 37E56 -2:31:44
Kirovsk 23 45 48N38 38E39 -2:34:36
Kirovsk 6 9 59N52 31E00 -2:04:00
Kirovsk 22 30 37N42 60E23 -4:01:32
Kirovsk 3 34 38N48 48E43 -3:14:52
Kirovsk 6 9 67N37 33E35 -2:14:20
Kirovsk 4 39 53N16 29E29 -1:57:56
Kirovskij 12 8 54N18 155E47-10:23:08
Kirovskij 9 24 44N52 78E12 -5:12:48
Kirovskij 2 15 54N26 126E55 -8:27:40
Kirovskij 2 27 45N07 133E30 -8:54:00
Kirovskij 3 34 40N26 49E51 -3:19:24
Kirovskoje 23 45 48N33 34E53 -2:19:32
Kirovskoje 23 45 45N14 35E13 -2:20:52
Kirovskoje 23 45 48N09 38E21 -2:33:24
Kirovskoje 10 24 42N39 71E35 -4:46:20
Kirpičnyj Zavod 6 9 60N01 30E48 -2:03:12
Kirpil'skaja 6 47 45N23 39E43 -2:38:52
Kirs 6 42 59N21 52E14 -3:28:56
Kirsanov 6 41 52N38 42E43 -2:50:52
Kirsanovka 6 32 52N30 52E53 -3:31:32
Kirza 2 23 54N14 81E40 -5:26:40
Kiržač 6 39 56N09 38E52 -2:35:28
Kišaly 6 41 54N23 43E12 -2:52:48
Kiselevsk → Kisel'ovsk 2 21 54N00 86E39 -5:46:36
Kisel'ovka 6 47 47N18 44E07 -2:56:28
Kisel'ovsk 2 21 54N00 86E39 -5:46:36
Kishinev → Kišin'ov 15 46 47N00 28E50 -1:55:20
Kišin 23 44 51N08 27E41 -1:50:44
Kišin'ov (Kishinev) 15 46 47N00 28E50 -1:55:20
Kisl'akovka 23 45 46N44 31E59 -2:07:56
Kisl'akovskaja 6 47 46N27 39E40 -2:38:40
Kislovka 23 45 49N38 37E53 -2:31:32
Kislovo 6 34 49N54 45E25 -3:01:40
Kislovodsk 6 47 43N55 42E44 -2:50:56
Kisnema 6 40 60N20 37E39 -2:30:36
Kista 6 47 46N05 43E06 -2:52:24
Kistendej 6 34 52N08 43E39 -2:54:36
Kistruss 6 40 54N28 40E34 -2:42:16
Kitenevo 6 39 56N21 36E13 -2:24:52
Kivak 2 2 64N16 172W57 11:31:48
Kivercy 23 44 50N50 25E27 -1:41:48
Kiveriči 6 39 57N22 36E36 -2:26:24
Kiviõli 5 35 59N21 26E57 -1:47:48
Kizel 6 30 59N03 57E40 -3:50:40
Kizevatovo 6 41 53N13 45E18 -3:01:12
Kiziljurt 6 47 43N12 46E53 -3:07:32
Kizil'skoje 2 30 52N44 58E54 -3:55:36
Kizil'unt 6 47 43N12 46E53 -3:07:32
Kižinga 2 20 51N51 109E55 -7:19:40
Kizl'ar 6 47 43N50 46E40 -3:06:40
Kizner 6 42 56N17 51E31 -3:26:04
Kiz'oma 6 41 61N08 44E50 -2:59:20
Kizyl-Ajak 22 30 37N40 65E23 -4:21:32
Kizyl-Arvat 22 30 38N58 56E15 -3:45:00
Kizyl-Atrek 22 30 37N36 54E46 -3:39:04
Kizyl-Su 22 30 39N48 53E01 -3:32:04
Kladbišči 6 41 55N32 45E33 -3:02:12
Kladkovo 6 39 55N24 38E51 -2:35:24
Klaipėda (Memel) 14 37 55N43 21E07 -1:24:28
Kl'as'ma 6 39 55N59 37E50 -2:31:20
Kl'asticy 4 39 55N53 28E36 -1:54:24
Kl'avlino 6 42 54N17 52E01 -3:28:04
Kl'az'ma 6 39 55N58 37E27 -2:29:48
Kleck 4 39 53N04 26E38 -1:46:32
Klementjevka 9 24 50N16 80E56 -5:23:44
Klementjevo 6 39 55N38 36E01 -2:24:04
Klenovka 6 30 57N45 54E19 -3:37:16
Klenovo 6 39 55N19 37E21 -2:29:24
Klesov 23 44 51N19 26E54 -1:47:36
Kletn'a 6 39 53N23 33E12 -2:12:48
Kletskaja 6 34 49N19 43E04 -2:52:16
Kletskij 6 34 49N19 43E04 -2:52:16
Kletsko-Počtovskij 6 34 49N36 43E03 -2:52:12
Klevan' 23 44 50N44 26E02 -1:44:08
Klevenka 6 34 52N07 49E33 -3:18:12
Kličev 4 39 53N29 29E21 -1:57:24
Klička 2 16 50N26 118E00 -7:52:00
Klimino 2 19 58N39 98E42 -6:34:48
Klimoviči 4 39 53N37 31E58 -2:07:52
Klimovo 6 39 52N23 32E11 -2:08:44
Klimovo 6 39 55N22 38E52 -2:35:28
Klimovsk 6 39 55N22 37E32 -2:30:08
Klimovskoje 6 39 54N42 37E48 -2:31:12
Klimov Zavod 6 39 54N50 34E55 -2:19:40
Klin 6 39 56N20 36E44 -2:26:56
Klin 6 39 55N19 36E20 -2:25:20
Klin-Bel'din 6 39 54N45 39E13 -2:36:52
Klincovka 6 34 51N41 49E11 -3:16:44
Klincy 6 39 52N47 32E14 -2:08:56
Klinkino 23 45 47N17 38E15 -2:33:00
Klintsy → Klincy 6 39 52N47 32E14 -2:08:56
Kliškovcy 23 45 48N26 26E15 -1:45:00
Klobuticy 6 9 58N35 29E35 -1:58:20
Klooga 5 35 59N19 24E16 -1:37:04
Kl'učevaja 6 41 65N16 41E32 -2:46:08
Kl'učevskij 2 16 53N33 119E26 -7:57:44
Kl'uči 6 34 51N59 46E31 -3:06:04
Kl'uči 6 34 51N26 45E11 -3:00:44
Kl'uči 2 4 56N18 160E51-10:43:24
Kl'uči 2 23 52N16 79E10 -5:16:40
Kl'učovka 6 30 51N22 55E48 -3:43:12
Kl'učovka 10 24 42N34 71E48 -4:47:12

Place	Zone	Lat	Long	Time
Klukhori 6	47	43N47	41E54	-2:47:36
Kl'ukvenka 2	21	58N34	85E55	-5:43:40
Kn'aginino 6	41	55N49	45E03	-3:00:12
Kn'ažaja-Bajgora 6	41	52N23	40E02	-2:40:08
Kn'azevka 2	24	57N35	74E10	-4:56:40
Kn'ažji Gory 6	39	56N05	35E14	-2:20:56
Kn'ažovo 6	41	59N40	43E54	-2:55:36
Knevicy 6	39	57N56	32E14	-2:08:56
Kob' 2	20	55N25	101E24	-6:45:36
Kob'aj 2	16	63N34	126E30	-8:26:00
Kobel'aki 23	45	49N09	34E12	-2:16:48
Kobi 7	33	42N33	44E32	-2:58:08
Koboldo 2	14	52N58	132E42	-8:50:48
Kobona 6	9	60N01	31E36	-2:06:24
Koboža 6	9	58N49	35E01	-2:20:04
Kobra 6	41	60N03	50E44	-3:22:56
Kobrin 4	39	52N13	24E21	-1:37:24
Kobrinskoje 6	9	59N25	30E07	-2:00:28
Kobuleti 7	33	41N50	41E47	-2:47:08
Kobyl'nik 4	39	54N56	26E41	-1:46:44
Kobyžča 23	44	50N49	31E30	-2:06:00
Kočelajevo 6	41	54N01	44E02	-2:56:08
Kočemary 6	40	54N50	40E58	-2:43:52
Kočen'ajevka 6	34	53N52	46E59	-3:07:56
Kočen'ga 6	41	60N09	43E33	-2:54:12
Kočenga 2	20	55N55	104E06	-6:56:24
Kočerdyk 2	30	54N35	62E58	-4:11:52
Kočerga 2	20	55N15	103E46	-6:55:04
Kočerov 23	44	50N21	29E21	-1:57:24
Kočetovka 6	41	55N16	46E07	-3:04:28
Kočetovka 6	41	52N58	40E29	-2:41:56
Kočevar 6	41	60N26	42E11	-2:48:44
Kočevo 6	30	59N36	54E18	-3:37:12
Kochanoviči 4	39	55N52	28E08	-1:52:32
Kochanovo 4	39	54N28	30E01	-2:00:04
Kochma 6	40	56N56	41E06	-2:44:24
Kočki 2	23	52N24	80E40	-5:22:40
Kočki 2	23	54N20	80E29	-5:21:56
Kočkor-Ata 10	24	41N04	72E29	-4:49:56
Kočkorka 10	24	42N14	75E45	-5:03:00
Kočkurovo 6	41	54N02	45E26	-3:01:44
Kočmes 6	29	66N12	60E44	-4:02:56
Kočon'ovo 2	23	55N02	82E12	-5:28:48
Kočubej 6	47	44N24	46E33	-3:06:12
Kočubejevskoje 6	47	44N41	41E41	-2:46:44
Kodačdikost 6	29	63N11	55E49	-3:43:16
Kodino 6	40	63N43	39E41	-2:38:44
Kodra 23	44	50N36	29E34	-1:58:16
Kodyma 23	45	48N07	29E07	-1:56:28
Kodžori 7	33	41N40	44E41	-2:58:44
Kohila 5	35	59N10	24E45	-1:39:00
Kohtla-Järve 5	35	59N24	27E15	-1:49:00
Koigi 5	35	58N50	25E45	-1:43:00
Kojandy 9	24	49N51	75E40	-5:02:40
Kojda 6	41	66N23	42E31	-2:50:04
Kojgorodok 6	41	60N26	50E58	-3:23:52
Kojsary 10	24	42N33	78E10	-5:12:40
Kojsug 6	40	47N07	39E41	-2:38:44
Kojtaš 24	30	40N11	67E19	-4:29:16
K'okajgyr 10	24	40N43	75E37	-5:02:28
Kokalaat 9	31	49N47	64E15	-4:17:00
Kokand 24	24	40N33	70E57	-4:43:48
Kokankišlak 24	24	40N56	72E30	-4:50:00
K'okbel' 10	24	40N17	72E55	-4:51:40
Kokčetav 9	24	53N17	69E25	-4:37:40
Kok-Jangak 10	24	41N02	73E12	-4:52:48
Koknese 13	36	56N39	25E29	-1:41:56
Kokorevka 6	39	52N35	34E16	-2:17:04
Kokoškino 6	39	55N38	37E11	-2:28:44
Kokoškinskij 6	39	55N38	37E11	-2:28:44
Kokpaš 2	21	51N12	87E45	-5:51:00
Kokpekty 9	24	48N45	82E24	-5:29:36
Kokšamary 6	41	56N10	47E45	-3:11:00
Koksaraj 9	24	42N40	68E08	-4:32:32
Koksovyj 6	47	48N12	40E39	-2:42:36
Koksu 9	24	44N59	77E56	-5:11:44
Koksu 9	24	41N27	68E01	-4:32:04
Koktal 9	24	44N09	79E48	-5:19:12
Koktas 9	24	47N33	70E55	-4:43:40
Kok-Taš 10	24	41N12	72E25	-4:49:40
Koktas 9	24	45N59	73E32	-4:54:08
Kokterek 9	32	49N25	49E15	-3:17:00
Koktubek 9	30	48N07	56E51	-3:47:24
Kokuj 2	16	52N13	117E33	-7:50:12
Kokžar 9	30	49N01	60E10	-4:00:40
Kola 6	9	68N53	33E01	-2:12:04
Kol'adovka 23	45	49N05	39E12	-2:36:48
Kolageran 1	34	40N58	44E37	-2:58:28
Kolbači 2	16	54N22	123E02	-8:12:08
Kolbasna 15	46	47N47	29E13	-1:56:52
Kolbasnaja 15	46	47N47	29E13	-1:56:52
Kolbča 4	39	53N39	29E14	-1:56:56
Kolchozabad 21	24	37N27	68E31	-4:34:04
Kol'covo 6	39	54N27	36E40	-2:26:40
Kol'čuga 6	39	55N43	37E12	-2:28:48
Kol'čugino 6	39	56N18	39E23	-2:37:32
Koleno 6	34	51N52	44E07	-2:56:28
Kolga 5	35	59N32	25E42	-1:42:48
Koli 6	9	59N30	34E30	-2:18:00
Kolka 13	36	57N45	22E35	-1:30:20
Kolki 23	44	51N37	26E37	-1:46:28
Kolki 23	44	51N07	25E41	-1:42:44
Kolmogorovo 2	21	59N15	91E20	-6:05:20
Kolobovo 6	40	56N42	41E21	-2:45:24
Kolodn'a 6	39	54N48	32E09	-2:08:36
Kologriv 6	41	58N51	44E17	-2:57:08
Kologrivovka 6	34	51N44	45E20	-3:01:20
Kolojar 6	34	52N34	46E58	-3:07:52
Kolokol'covka 6	34	52N36	49E48	-3:19:12
Kolokol'covka 6	34	51N12	44E36	-2:58:24
Kolomak 23	45	49N50	35E18	-2:21:12
Kolomea → Kolomyja 23	44	48N32	25E04	-1:40:16
Kolomenskaja Sloboda 6	39	54N22	38E15	-2:33:00
Kolomna 6	39	55N05	38E49	-2:35:16
Kolomyja 23	44	48N32	25E04	-1:40:16
Kol'osnoje 23	45	46N02	29E56	-1:59:44
Kolosovka 2	24	56N28	73E36	-4:54:24
Kolovertnoje 9	32	50N36	51E06	-3:24:24
Kolpaševo 2	21	58N20	82E50	-5:31:20
Kolpino 6	9	59N45	30E36	-2:02:24
Kolpny 6	39	52N15	37E02	-2:28:08
Kol'togan 9	30	43N51	67E25	-4:29:40
Koltovskaja 6	41	52N47	44E16	-2:57:04
Koltubanovskij 6	32	52N57	52E02	-3:28:08
Koltuši 6	9	59N56	30E40	-2:02:40
Kol'ubakino 6	39	55N40	36E32	-2:26:08
Kol'upanovo 6	39	54N26	36E14	-2:24:56
Koluškino 6	47	48N39	40E56	-2:43:44
Koluton 9	24	51N43	69E25	-4:37:40
Kolyberovo 6	39	55N16	38E44	-2:34:56
Kolyčevo 6	39	55N30	37E52	-2:31:28
Kolymskaja 2	6	68N44	158E44	-10:34:56
Kolyšlej 6	41	52N42	44E32	-2:58:08
Kolyšovo 6	39	54N54	36E57	-2:27:48
Kolyvan' 2	21	51N18	82E34	-5:30:16
Kolyvan' 2	23	55N18	82E45	-5:31:00
Koma 2	21	55N02	91E19	-6:05:16
Komariči 6	39	52N27	34E47	-2:19:08
Komarin 4	39	51N26	30E31	-2:02:04
Komarniki 23	44	49N00	23E04	-1:32:16
Komarno 23	44	49N38	23E42	-1:34:48
Komarovka 23	44	51N14	32E07	-2:08:28
Komarovo 6	9	58N39	33E26	-2:13:44
Komarovy 2	25	60N26	75E50	-5:03:20
Kominternovskoje 23	45	46N49	30E56	-2:03:44
Komissarovka 23	45	48N23	38E32	-2:34:08
Komissarovka 6	47	48N07	40E09	-2:40:36
Komissarovo 2	27	44N59	131E46	-8:47:04
Komissarovskij 6	47	47N29	42E59	-2:51:56
Kommunal'naja 2	16	52N03	115E06	-7:40:24
Kommunar 6	41	58N10	43E33	-2:54:12
Kommunar 2	21	54N20	89E18	-5:57:12
Kommunarka 6	39	55N34	37E29	-2:29:56
Kommunarsk 23	45	48N30	38E47	-2:35:08
Kommunary 6	9	60N54	29E47	-1:59:08
Kompanejevka 23	45	48N15	32E12	-2:08:48
Komrat 15	46	46N18	28E38	-1:54:32
Komsomolabad 21	24	38N52	69E57	-4:39:48
Komsomolec 9	30	53N45	62E02	-4:08:08
Komsomolec Island 20	19	80N30	95E00	-6:20:00
Komsomolec, Ostrov 20	19	80N30	95E00	-6:20:00
Komsomol'sk 2	21	55N38	88E11	-5:52:44
Komsomol'sk 2	21	57N27	86E02	-5:44:08
Komsomol'sk 6	40	57N02	40E21	-2:41:24
Komsomol'sk 22	30	39N02	63E36	-4:14:24
Komsomol'skij 9	30	47N20	53E42	-3:34:48
Komsomol'skij 19	8	50N22	142E10	-9:28:40
Komsomol'skij 23	45	47N40	37E26	-2:29:44
Komsomol'skij 6	41	54N27	45E49	-3:03:16
Komsomol'skij 9	24	51N40	66E39	-4:26:36
Komsomol'sk-Na-Amure 2	11	50N35	137E02	-9:08:08
Komsomol'sk-Na-Ust'urte 22	30	44N03	58E20	-3:53:20
Komsomol'skoje 6	41	55N16	47E33	-3:10:12
Komsomol'skoje 6	34	50N46	47E03	-3:08:12
Komsomol'skoje 23	45	49N35	36E30	-2:26:00
Komsomol'skoje 23	44	49N43	28E40	-1:54:40
Komsomol'skoje 23	45	47N40	38E05	-2:32:20
Komsomol'skoje 2	20	52N29	111E06	-7:24:24
Komyšn'a 23	44	50N12	33E41	-2:14:44
Konagkend 3	34	41N04	48E37	-3:14:28
Konakovo 6	39	56N42	36E46	-2:27:04
Končanskoje-Suvorovskoje 6	9	58N39	34E04	-2:16:16
Konceba 23	45	48N07	29E56	-1:59:44
Konda 2	30	61N20	63E58	-4:15:52
Kondega 6	9	60N14	33E30	-2:14:00
Kondinskoje 2	30	59N40	67E22	-4:29:28
Kondol' 6	41	52N49	45E03	-3:00:12
Kondopoga 6	9	62N12	34E17	-2:17:08
Kondratjevo 6	9	60N38	28E08	-1:52:32
Kondratjevo 2	20	57N21	98E11	-6:32:44
Kondrovka 6	41	54N36	43E17	-2:53:08
Kondrovo 6	39	54N48	35E56	-2:23:44
Konecbor 6	29	64N52	57E44	-3:50:56
Konergino 2	2	65N54	178W50	11:55:20
Königsberg → Kaliningrad 8	38	54N43	20E30	-1:22:00
Kon'-Kolodez' 6	40	52N08	39E11	-2:36:44
Kon'kovo 23	45	47N20	38E10	-2:32:40
Konkudera 2	20	57N33	112E30	-7:30:00
Konobejevo 6	39	55N24	38E40	-2:34:40
Konoša 6	41	60N58	40E15	-2:41:00
Konotop 23	44	51N14	33E12	-2:12:48
Konovalovka 6	34	53N06	51E34	-3:26:16
Kon'ovo 2	30	56N18	70E43	-4:42:52
Kon'ovo 6	40	62N08	39E16	-2:37:04
Konstantinovka 6	42	56N41	50E53	-3:23:32
Konstantinovka 23	45	49N57	35E07	-2:20:28
Konstantinovka 23	45	47N51	31E09	-2:04:36
Konstantinovka 23	45	48N32	37E43	-2:30:52
Konstantinovka 23	45	47N52	37E24	-2:29:36
Konstantinovka 6	9	59N47	30E08	-2:00:32
Konstantinovo 6	39	56N33	38E02	-2:32:08
Konstantinovsk 6	47	47N35	41E06	-2:44:24
Konstantinovskij 6	47	47N35	41E06	-2:44:24
Konstantinovskij 6	40	57N50	39E36	-2:38:24
Konstantinovskije Porogi 6	40	60N34	37E04	-2:28:16
Kontejevo 6	41	58N26	41E21	-2:45:24
Kon'uchovo 9	24	55N08	70E38	-4:42:32
Konyr 9	30	50N25	53E25	-3:33:40
Konyrat 9	32	49N36	47E01	-3:08:04
Konyrolen 9	24	44N16	79E19	-5:17:16
Konyševka 6	39	51N51	35E18	-2:21:12
Konystanu 9	30	48N51	53E20	-3:33:20
Koonga 5	35	58N35	24E12	-1:36:48
Koosa 5	35	58N33	27E07	-1:48:28
Kopa 9	24	43N32	75E50	-5:03:20
Kopajgorod 23	45	48N51	27E48	-1:51:12
Kopanbulak 9	24	48N56	80E52	-5:23:28
Kopanovka 6	34	47N27	46E48	-3:07:12
Kopanskaja 6	47	46N17	38E29	-2:33:56
Kopapan 9	32	50N20	50E26	-3:21:44
Kopatkeviči 4	39	52N19	28E49	-1:55:16
Kopceviči 4	39	52N14	28E19	-1:53:16
Kopejsk 2	30	55N07	61E37	-4:06:28
Kopeysk → Kopejsk 2	30	55N07	61E37	-4:06:28
Kopjevo 2	21	55N03	89E50	-5:59:20
Kopnino 6	39	56N53	38E29	-2:33:56
Koporje 6	9	59N44	29E01	-1:56:04
Koppi 2	11	48N32	140E07	-9:20:28
Kopt'ovo 6	40	56N43	40E31	-2:42:04
Kopyčincy 23	44	49N06	25E55	-1:43:40
Kopyl' 4	39	53N09	27E05	-1:48:20
Kopylovka 2	23	58N40	82E22	-5:29:28
Kopylovo 6	41	60N35	45E02	-3:00:08
Kopylovo 6	39	56N26	36E25	-2:25:40
Kopys' 4	39	54N19	30E18	-2:01:12
Korablino 6	41	53N55	40E01	-2:40:04
Kor'akovka 9	24	52N24	77E08	-5:08:32
Kor'ažma 6	41	61N18	47E06	-3:08:24
Korcevo 6	41	58N52	42E13	-2:48:52
Korcovo 6	41	58N52	42E13	-2:48:52
Kordovo 2	21	54N06	93E17	-6:13:08
Korec 23	44	50N37	27E09	-1:48:36
Korekozevo 6	39	54N20	36E11	-2:24:44
Korelakša 6	9	65N33	32E22	-2:09:28
Koreliči 4	39	53N34	26E08	-1:44:32
Korenkovo 23	45	45N07	36E24	-2:25:36
Koren'ovo 6	39	55N40	38E00	-2:32:00
Koren'ovo 6	39	51N25	34E55	-2:19:40
Korenovsk 6	47	45N29	39E28	-2:37:52
Korf 2	4	60N19	165E50	-11:03:20
Korfovskij 2	11	48N13	135E03	-9:00:12
Korgašino 6	39	54N45	37E41	-2:30:44
Kõrgessaare 5	35	58N59	22E28	-1:29:52
Korkino 2	30	54N54	61E23	-4:05:32
Korkino 2	20	54N23	105E14	-7:00:56
Korl'aki 6	42	57N06	46E57	-3:07:48
Korliki 2	25	61N31	82E22	-5:29:28
Korma 4	39	53N08	30E48	-2:03:12
Korma 4	39	52N21	31E31	-2:06:04
Kormilovka 2	24	55N00	74E06	-4:56:24
Kormovoje 6	47	46N17	43E30	-2:54:00
Kornejevka 6	34	51N45	48E46	-3:15:04
Kornejevka 9	24	54N01	68E27	-4:33:48
Kornejevka 9	24	50N12	74E19	-4:57:16
Kornešty 15	46	47N22	27E59	-1:51:56
Kornilovo 2	23	53N32	81E05	-5:24:20
Kornin 23	44	50N06	29E32	-1:58:08
Kornouchovo 6	41	55N33	49E53	-3:19:32
Korn'ovo 6	9	60N03	30E45	-2:03:00
Koroča 6	39	50N48	37E11	-2:28:44
Korol'ovo 23	44	48N09	23E08	-1:32:32
Korol'ovščina 6	39	55N49	31E45	-2:07:00
Kor'onevo 6	39	55N40	38E00	-2:32:00
Korop 23	44	51N34	32E56	-2:11:44
Korosten' 23	44	50N57	28E39	-1:54:36
Korostyšev 23	44	50N19	29E03	-1:56:12
Korotkova 2	20	56N43	107E55	-7:11:40
Korotojak 6	40	50N59	39E10	-2:36:40
Korotovo 6	40	58N57	37E28	-2:29:52
Korotyš 6	39	52N22	37E27	-2:29:48

Korovincy 23 44 50N48 33E45 -2:15:00
Korovino 6 32 53N49 53E03 -3:32:12
Korovino 6 39 51N25 36E45 -2:27:00
Korsakov 19 8 46N38 142E46 -9:31:04
Korsakovo 6 39 53N16 37E21 -2:29:24
Korševo 6 41 51N11 40E07 -2:40:28
Korsun' 23 45 48N12 38E05 -2:32:20
Koršunovo 2 20 58N37 110E10 -7:20:40
Korsun'-Ševčenkovskij 23 44 49N26 31E16 -2:05:04
Kortelisy 23 44 51N51 24E25 -1:37:40
Kortilisy 23 44 51N51 24E25 -1:37:40
Kortkeros 6 41 61N49 51E28 -3:25:52
Kor'ukovka 23 44 51N46 32E14 -2:08:56
Koryst' 23 44 50N35 27E01 -1:48:04
Koržeuc' 15 46 48N13 27E02 -1:48:08
Korževka 6 42 54N12 46E22 -3:05:28
Kosa 6 30 59N56 54E55 -3:39:40
Kosa 2 20 54N47 108E52 -7:15:28
Koš-Agač 2 21 50N00 88E40 -5:54:40
Kosaja Gora 6 39 54N07 37E33 -2:30:12
Košankol' 9 32 49N56 48E11 -3:12:44
Koščagyl 9 30 46N51 53E48 -3:35:12
Kose 5 35 59N11 25E10 -1:40:40
Koševelka 6 39 55N09 38E05 -2:32:20
Košelicha 6 41 55N02 43E33 -2:54:12
Koškerovo 6 39 55N38 38E22 -2:33:28
Kosikovo 6 41 59N52 43E23 -2:53:32
Kosino 6 42 58N23 51E17 -3:25:08
Kosino 6 39 55N43 37E52 -2:31:28
Kosju 6 29 65N38 59E03 -3:56:12
Kosjuvom 6 29 66N17 59E50 -3:59:20
Koškar 9 30 47N27 53E29 -3:33:56
Koški 6 42 54N12 50E28 -3:21:52
Koškino 6 41 56N20 50E49 -3:23:16
Koskol' 9 31 49N31 67E05 -4:28:20
Koskuduk 9 24 44N06 77E22 -5:09:28
Koslan 6 41 63N28 48E52 -3:15:28
Kosmynino 6 40 57N35 40E46 -2:43:04
Kosogor 6 42 57N07 47E34 -3:10:16
Kosolapovo 6 41 56N57 49E37 -3:18:28
Kosov 23 44 48N19 25E05 -1:40:20
Kossovo 4 39 52N45 25E09 -1:40:36
Koš-Tegirmen 10 24 42N47 73E53 -4:55:32
Kosterevo 6 39 55N56 39E37 -2:38:28
Kostešty 15 46 46N52 28E44 -1:54:56
Kostino 6 39 56N18 37E43 -2:30:52
Kostino 6 39 55N55 37E51 -2:31:24
Kostino 6 34 52N11 51E20 -3:25:20
Kostino 6 32 52N24 51E39 -3:26:36
Kostino-Otdelec 6 41 51N33 41E26 -2:45:44
Kost'kovo 6 9 60N02 33E14 -2:12:56
Košt'ob'o 10 24 41N06 74E15 -4:57:00
Kostomukša 6 9 64N41 30E49 -2:03:16
Kostopol' 23 44 50N53 26E26 -1:45:44
Kostriževka 23 44 48N38 25E41 -1:42:44
Kostroma 6 40 57N46 40E55 -2:43:40
Kostrovo 6 39 55N53 36E42 -2:26:48
Kost'ukoviči 4 39 53N20 32E03 -2:08:12
Kost'ukovka 4 39 52N32 30E56 -2:03:44
Kot'ajevka 9 32 46N33 48E46 -3:15:04
Kotel'nič 6 42 58N18 48E20 -3:13:20
Kotel'niki 6 39 55N39 37E52 -2:31:28
Kotel'nikovo 6 34 47N38 43E09 -2:52:36
Kotel'nyj Island 18 1 75N45 138E44 -9:14:56
Kotel'nyj, Ostrov 18 1 75N45 138E44 -9:14:56
Kotel'va 23 45 50N05 34E45 -2:19:00
Kotikovo 19 8 49N08 144E13 -9:36:52
Kotkino 6 41 67N02 51E03 -3:24:12
Kotl'akovo 6 39 56N17 35E49 -2:23:16
Kotlas 6 41 61N16 46E35 -3:06:20
Kotly 6 9 59N36 28E45 -1:55:00
Kotorovo 6 40 54N54 41E35 -2:46:20
Kotovka 23 45 49N08 34E57 -2:19:48
Kotovo 6 34 50N18 44E50 -2:59:20
Kotovsk 15 46 46N49 28E34 -1:54:16
Kotovsk 6 41 52N36 41E32 -2:46:08
Kotovsk 23 45 47N45 29E33 -1:58:12
Kot'užen' 15 46 47N51 28E36 -1:54:24
Kounradskij 9 24 46N59 75E00 -5:00:00
Kourak 2 21 54N50 84E40 -5:38:40
Kova 2 19 58N18 100E21 -6:41:24
Kovaksa 6 41 55N31 43E30 -2:54:00
Koval'ovka 23 45 47N16 31E43 -2:06:52
Kovarskas 14 37 55N26 24E55 -1:39:40
Kovarzino 6 40 60N09 38E33 -2:34:12
Kovdor 6 9 67N34 30E22 -2:01:28
Kovel' 23 44 51N14 24E41 -1:38:44
Kovernino 6 41 57N07 43E49 -2:55:16
Kovno → Kaunas 14 37 54N54 23E54 -1:35:36
Kovpyta 23 44 51N23 30E50 -2:03:20
Kovrina Vtoraja 6 47 47N01 41E44 -2:46:56
Kovrov 6 40 56N22 41E18 -2:45:12
Kovševata 23 44 49N29 30E38 -2:02:32
Kovylkin 6 47 48N16 41E28 -2:45:52
Kovylkino 6 41 54N02 43E56 -2:55:44
Kovža 6 40 61N09 38E58 -2:35:52
Kovžinskij Zavod 6 40 60N24 37E04 -2:28:16
Kowel → Kovel' 23 44 51N14 24E41 -1:38:44
Koža 6 42 57N47 48E57 -3:15:48
Kožanka 23 44 49N58 29E46 -1:59:04
Kožany 6 39 52N48 31E44 -2:06:56
Koz'any 4 37 55N18 26E52 -1:47:28
Kozdinga 6 41 63N43 47E32 -3:10:08
Kozelec 23 44 50N55 31E08 -2:04:32
Kozel'ščina 23 45 49N13 33E51 -2:15:24
Kozel'sk 6 39 54N02 35E48 -2:23:12
Koževnikovo 2 23 56N16 84E00 -5:36:00
Kožim 6 29 65N48 59E28 -3:57:52
Kozin 23 44 50N14 30E39 -2:02:36
Kozino 6 39 55N54 37E11 -2:28:44
Kozlov 23 44 49N33 25E20 -1:41:20
Kozlov Bereg 6 9 58N57 27E44 -1:50:56
Kozlovka 6 41 55N52 48E14 -3:12:56
Kozlovka 6 41 52N33 45E41 -3:02:44
Kozlovka 6 41 51N39 41E16 -2:45:04
Kozlovka 6 47 50N52 40E27 -2:41:48
Kozlovo 6 39 57N34 35E29 -2:21:56
Kozlovo 6 39 56N31 36E16 -2:25:04
Kozlovščina 4 39 53N19 25E18 -1:41:12
Koz'mino 6 41 61N56 48E19 -3:13:16
Koz'modemjansk 6 41 56N20 46E36 -3:06:24
Koz'mogorodskoje 6 41 65N32 44E55 -2:59:40
Kozova 23 44 49N26 25E09 -1:40:36
Kožpos'olok 6 40 63N10 38E06 -2:32:24
Kožuchovo 6 39 55N43 37E54 -2:31:36
Kozul'ka 2 21 56N10 91E24 -6:05:36
Kožurla 2 23 55N21 79E02 -5:16:08
Krainka 6 39 54N07 36E21 -2:25:24
Krai-Russkije 6 42 57N23 46E50 -3:07:20
Krajčikovo 2 24 56N16 73E20 -4:53:20
Krajeva 2 27 44N54 131E08 -8:44:32
Krajneje 6 47 47N29 46E01 -3:04:04
Krajnovka 6 47 43N57 47E24 -3:09:36
Krakovec 23 44 49N57 23E07 -1:32:28
Krakovo 6 34 53N36 50E51 -3:23:24
Kramatorsk 23 45 48N43 37E32 -2:30:08
Kransaja Pol'ana 6 47 43N41 40E13 -2:40:52
Krapivinskij 2 21 55N00 86E49 -5:47:16
Krapivna 6 39 53N38 35E31 -2:22:04
Krasavino 6 41 60N58 46E26 -3:05:44
Krasavka 6 34 51N11 43E24 -2:53:36
Krasilov 23 44 49N39 26E59 -1:47:56
Krasino 17 29 70N45 54E27 -3:37:48
Krasivka 6 41 52N16 42E31 -2:50:04
Krasivoje 9 24 51N54 66E46 -4:27:04
Kraskino 2 27 42N44 130E48 -8:43:12
Kraskovo 6 39 55N39 37E59 -2:31:56
Krāslava 13 36 55N54 27E10 -1:48:40
Krasnaja Gora 6 39 53N01 31E37 -2:06:28
Krasnaja Gora 6 40 60N16 35E42 -2:22:48
Krasnaja Gorbatka 6 40 55N52 41E46 -2:47:04
Krasnaja Gorka 6 40 56N12 43E04 -2:52:16
Krasnaja Jaranga 2 2 65N40 172W50 11:31:20
Krasnaja Jaruga 6 39 50N48 35E39 -2:22:36
Krasnaja Pachra 6 39 55N27 37E17 -2:29:08
Krasnaja Pol'ana 6 42 56N15 51E09 -3:24:36
Krasnaja Pol'ana 6 30 52N13 53E38 -3:34:32
Krasnaja Pol'ana 6 47 46N06 41E30 -2:46:00
Krasnaja Pol'ana 23 45 47N33 37E05 -2:28:20
Krasnaja Poljana 6 47 43N41 40E13 -2:40:52
Krasnaja Popovka 23 45 49N08 38E09 -2:32:36
Krasnaja Sloboda 4 39 52N51 27E10 -1:48:40
Krasnaja Sloboda 3 34 41N24 48E31 -3:14:04
Krasnaja Talovka 23 45 48N51 39E51 -2:39:24
Krasnaja Vol'a 4 39 52N23 27E04 -1:48:16
Krasnaja Zar'a 6 39 52N47 37E41 -2:30:44
Krasn'anka 6 34 51N04 47E56 -3:11:44
Krasneno 2 2 64N38 174E48-11:39:12
Krasnoarmejsk 23 45 48N17 37E11 -2:28:44
Krasnoarmejsk 6 34 51N02 45E42 -3:02:48
Krasnoarmejsk 6 39 56N08 38E08 -2:32:32
Krasnoarmejskaja 6 47 45N23 38E12 -2:32:48
Krasnoarmejskij 6 47 47N01 42E12 -2:48:48
Krasnoarmejskij 2 4 69N35 172E00-11:28:00
Krasnoarmejskoje 23 45 47N14 37E56 -2:31:44
Krasnoarmejskoje 6 41 55N46 47E11 -3:08:44
Krasnoarmejskoje 6 34 52N44 50E02 -3:20:08
Krasnoborsk 6 41 61N34 45E53 -3:03:32
Krasnoborsk 6 34 53N46 48E04 -3:12:16
Krasnobrodskij 2 21 54N10 86E28 -5:45:52
Krasnodar 6 47 45N02 39E00 -2:36:00
Krasnodarskij 23 45 48N15 39E51 -2:39:24
Krasnodon 23 45 48N17 39E48 -2:39:12
Krasnofarfornyj 6 9 59N08 31E51 -2:07:24
Krasnoflotskoje 6 47 50N04 41E14 -2:44:56
Krasnogorka 9 24 43N15 75E10 -5:00:40
Krasnogorodskoje 6 39 56N50 28E17 -1:53:08
Krasnogorovka 23 45 48N00 37E31 -2:30:04
Krasnogorsk 6 39 55N50 37E20 -2:29:20
Krasnogorsk 19 8 48N24 142E06 -9:28:24
Krasnogorskij 24 24 41N09 69E39 -4:38:36
Krasnogorskij 6 41 56N09 48E20 -3:13:20
Krasnogorskij 2 30 54N36 61E15 -4:05:00
Krasnogorskoje 6 42 57N42 52E30 -3:30:00
Krasnogorskoje 2 21 52N18 86E12 -5:44:48
Krasnogovardejskij 2 30 57N22 62E20 -4:09:20
Krasnograd 23 45 49N22 35E27 -2:21:48
Krasnogvardejsk 24 30 39N46 67E16 -4:29:04
Krasnogvardejskij 6 39 54N04 37E46 -2:31:04
Krasnogvardejskij 9 24 51N24 69E18 -4:37:12
Krasnogvardejskoje 9 24 51N24 69E18 -4:37:12
Krasnogvardejskoje 6 47 45N51 41E31 -2:46:04
Krasnogvardejskoje 6 40 50N39 38E24 -2:33:36
Krasnogvardejskoje 23 45 45N29 34E17 -2:17:08
Krasnoil'sk 23 44 48N01 25E34 -1:42:16
Krasnojar 9 32 48N54 51E46 -3:27:04
Krasnojarka 2 24 55N20 73E04 -4:52:16
Krasnojarka 2 30 59N26 60E30 -4:02:00
Krasnojarovo 2 14 51N27 128E28 -8:33:52
Krasnojarsk 2 21 56N01 92E50 -6:11:20
Krasnojarskij 6 30 51N58 59E55 -3:59:40
Krasnoje 6 39 54N26 38E38 -2:34:32
Krasnoje 23 45 48N23 39E31 -2:38:04
Krasnoje 23 45 48N25 37E19 -2:29:16
Krasnoje 2 21 54N37 85E23 -5:41:32
Krasnoje 6 42 59N12 47E49 -3:11:16
Krasnoje 6 40 50N56 38E41 -2:34:44
Krasnoje 6 40 50N21 38E50 -2:35:20
Krasnoje 6 47 46N44 39E34 -2:38:16
Krasnoje 15 46 46N38 29E50 -1:59:20
Krasnoje 6 39 53N06 33E55 -2:15:40
Krasnoje 6 40 52N51 38E47 -2:35:08
Krasnoje 4 39 54N14 27E05 -1:48:20
Krasnoje Echo 6 40 55N48 40E42 -2:42:48
Krasnoje Gorodišče 6 40 54N04 38E44 -2:34:56
Krasnoje-Na-Volge 6 40 57N31 41E14 -2:44:56
Krasnoje Selo 6 9 59N44 30E05 -2:00:20
Krasnoje Selo 6 47 48N02 45E13 -3:00:52
Krasnoje Selo 6 47 48N46 42E20 -2:49:20
Krasnoje Znam'a 6 39 57N26 35E13 -2:20:52
Krasnoje Znam'a 22 30 36N58 62E30 -4:10:00
Krasnokamsk 6 30 58N04 55E48 -3:43:12
Krasnokutsk 9 24 53N01 75E59 -5:03:56
Krasnokutsk 23 45 50N06 35E09 -2:20:36
Krasnokutskoje 9 24 53N01 75E59 -5:03:56
Krasnolesje (Hardteck) 8 38 54N24 22E23 -1:29:32
Krasnolesnyj 6 41 51N53 39E35 -2:38:20
Krasnoluki 4 39 54N37 28E50 -1:55:20
Krasnomajskij 6 39 57N37 34E22 -2:17:28
Krasnookt'abr'skij 10 24 42N50 74E18 -4:57:12
Krasnookt'abr'skij 6 41 56N40 47E45 -3:11:00
Krasnookt'abr'skij 6 34 48N53 44E45 -2:59:00
Krasnoostrovskij 6 9 60N18 28E40 -1:54:40
Krasnopavlovka 23 45 49N08 36E19 -2:25:16
Krasnoperekopsk 23 45 45N57 33E47 -2:15:08
Krasnopolje 23 45 50N46 35E16 -2:21:04
Krasnopolje 4 39 53N20 31E24 -2:05:36
Krasnorečenskij 2 27 44N41 135E14 -9:00:56
Krasnoščelje 6 9 67N21 37E02 -2:28:08
Krasnoščokovo 2 21 51N40 82E45 -5:31:00
Krasnosel'kup 2 25 65N41 82E28 -5:29:52
Krasnosel'sk 1 34 40N36 45E21 -3:01:24
Krasnosel'skoje 23 45 45N25 32E42 -2:10:48

Krasnoslobodsk 6 41 54N26 43E48 -2:55:12
Krasnoslobodsk 6 34 48N42 44E34 -2:58:16
Krasnotorka 23 45 48N41 37E31 -2:30:04
Krasnoturansk 2 21 54N16 91E29 -6:05:56
Krasnoturjinsk 2 30 59N46 60E12 -4:00:48
Krasnoufimsk 2 30 56N37 57E46 -3:51:04
Krasnoural'sk 2 30 58N21 60E03 -4:00:12
Krasnousol'skij 6 30 53N54 56E27 -3:45:48
Krasnovidovo 6 41 55N21 49E04 -3:16:16
Krasnovišersk 6 30 60N23 56E59 -3:47:56
Krasnovka 6 47 48N47 40E07 -2:40:28
Krasnovka 23 45 47N24 37E26 -2:29:44
Krasnovodsk 22 30 40N00 53E00 -3:32:00
Krasnoyarsk → Krasnojarsk 2 21 56N01 92E50 -6:11:20
Krasnozatonskij 6 41 61N41 50E58 -3:23:52
Krasnozavodsk 6 39 56N27 38E13 -2:32:52
Krasnoznamensk (Haselberg) 8 38 54N57 22E30 -1:30:00
Krasnoznamenskij 9 24 51N03 69E30 -4:38:00
Krasnoz'orskoje 2 23 53N59 79E14 -5:16:56
Krasnyj 6 39 54N34 31E26 -2:05:44
Krasnyj 19 8 46N15 141E15 -9:25:00
Krasnyj Aul 9 24 51N03 81E02 -5:24:08
Krasnyj Bazar 3 34 39N41 46E58 -3:07:52
Krasnyj Bogatyr' 6 40 56N02 41E08 -2:44:32
Krasnyj Bor 6 9 59N41 30E41 -2:02:44
Krasnyj Bor 6 41 55N17 43E59 -2:55:56
Krasnyj Bor 6 41 55N53 53E06 -3:32:24
Krasnyj Cholm 6 9 58N03 37E07 -2:28:28
Krasnyj Cholm 6 30 51N35 54E09 -3:36:36
Krasnyj Cholm 6 41 54N11 40E42 -2:42:48
Krasnyj Chuduk 6 34 46N18 46E56 -3:07:44
Krasnyj Čikoj 2 18 50N22 108E15 -7:13:00
Krasnyje Baki 6 41 57N08 45E10 -3:00:40
Krasnyje Barrikady 6 34 46N14 47E53 -3:11:32
Krasnyje Četai 6 41 55N42 46E09 -3:04:36
Krasnyje Gory 6 9 58N57 29E29 -1:57:56
Krasnyje Okny 23 45 47N32 29E27 -1:57:48
Krasnyje Partizany 23 44 50N57 31E47 -2:07:08
Krasnyje Tkači 6 40 57N30 39E45 -2:39:00
Krasnyj Gorodok 6 39 57N11 33E44 -2:14:56
Krasnyj Gul'aj 6 42 54N01 48E22 -3:13:28
Krasnyj Jar 6 34 51N38 46E25 -3:05:40
Krasnyj Jar 6 34 50N37 45E47 -3:03:08
Krasnyj Jar 6 34 50N42 44E46 -2:59:04
Krasnyj Jar 2 21 55N54 86E57 -5:47:48
Krasnyj Jar 2 24 55N14 72E56 -4:51:44
Krasnyj Jar 2 21 57N07 84E33 -5:38:12
Krasnyj Jar 9 24 53N20 69E14 -4:36:56
Krasnyj Jar 6 34 46N33 48E21 -3:13:24
Krasnyj Jar 6 34 53N30 50E22 -3:21:28
Krasnyj Kl'č 6 30 55N26 56E12 -3:44:48
Krasnyj Kut 6 34 50N57 46E58 -3:07:52
Krasnyj Kut 23 45 48N12 38E48 -2:35:12
Krasnyj Liman 6 41 51N32 39E50 -2:39:20
Krasnyj Liman 23 45 48N59 37E49 -2:31:16
Krasnyj Log 6 41 51N23 39E46 -2:39:04
Krasnyj Luč 6 39 57N04 30E05 -2:00:20
Krasnyj Luč 23 45 48N08 38E56 -2:35:44
Krasnyj Majak 6 40 56N03 41E23 -2:45:32
Krasnyj Manyč 6 47 46N59 41E07 -2:44:28
Krasnyj Manyč 6 47 46N33 42E10 -2:48:40
Krasnyj Manyč 6 47 45N31 44E42 -2:58:48
Krasnyj Meliorator 6 34 50N02 46E06 -3:04:24
Krasnyj Okt'abr' 23 45 48N15 38E12 -2:32:48
Krasnyj Okt'abr' 23 45 48N56 39E23 -2:37:32
Krasnyj Okt'abr' 2 30 55N37 64E48 -4:19:12
Krasnyj Okt'abr' 9 24 46N50 75E59 -5:03:56
Krasnyj Okt'abr' 6 34 51N33 45E42 -3:02:48
Krasnyj Okt'abr' 6 40 56N06 41E23 -2:45:32
Krasnyj Okt'abr' 6 39 56N07 38E53 -2:35:32
Krasnyj Okt'abr' 6 39 55N37 36E30 -2:26:00
Krasnyj Oskol 23 45 49N11 37E26 -2:29:44
Krasnyj Partizan 6 47 46N20 43E10 -2:52:40
Krasnyj Perekop 23 45 46N41 33E46 -2:15:04
Krasnyj Profintern 6 40 57N45 40E27 -2:41:48
Krasnyj Rog 6 39 52N57 33E45 -2:15:00
Krasnyj Steklovar 6 41 56N13 48E47 -3:15:08
Krasnyj Sulin 6 40 47N54 40E03 -2:40:12
Krasnyj Tekstil'ščik 6 34 51N23 45E50 -3:03:20
Krasnyj Tkač 6 39 55N28 39E05 -2:36:20
Krasnyy Luch → Krasnyj Luč 23 45 48N08 38E56 -2:35:44
Krasucha 6 39 57N23 33E12 -2:12:48
Kras'ukovskaja 6 40 47N31 40E06 -2:40:24
Kražiai 14 37 55N36 22E40 -1:30:40
Krečetovo 6 40 60N56 38E30 -2:34:00
Krečevicy 6 9 58N37 31E21 -2:05:24
Kremenčug 23 45 49N04 33E25 -2:13:40
Kremenec 23 44 50N07 25E45 -1:43:00
Kremennaja 23 45 49N03 38E14 -2:32:56
Kremen'ovka 23 45 47N20 37E29 -2:29:56
Kremenskoj 6 47 47N49 41E08 -2:44:32
Kremenskoje 6 39 55N06 35E57 -2:23:48
Kremges 23 45 49N04 33E15 -2:13:00
Krepenskij 23 45 48N06 39E03 -2:36:12
Krešchonka 2 23 55N52 80E06 -5:20:24
Krestcy 6 9 58N15 32E31 -2:10:04
Krestcy 6 40 58N23 39E00 -2:36:00
Krestjanskij 24 24 40N32 69E02 -4:36:08
Krestjanskoje 6 47 45N34 42E56 -2:51:44
Krest-Major 2 6 67N37 144E45 -9:39:00
Krestovaja Guba 17 29 74N07 55E33 -3:42:12
Krestovo-Gorodišče 6 42 54N10 48E36 -3:14:24
Kresty 6 39 55N16 37E06 -2:28:24
Kretinga 14 37 55N53 21E13 -1:24:52
Krevo 4 39 54N19 26E17 -1:45:08
Kričov 4 39 53N42 31E43 -2:06:52
Krimskij 6 47 47N39 40E44 -2:42:56
Krinicčno-Lugskoje 6 40 47N45 39E12 -2:36:48
Krinički 23 45 48N22 34E27 -2:17:48
Kriničnaja 23 45 48N08 38E02 -2:32:08
Kriničnoje 23 45 45N32 28E40 -1:54:40
Kriul'any 15 46 47N13 29E09 -1:56:36
Kriuša 6 39 54N28 36E24 -2:25:36
Kriv'ačka 6 41 58N40 45E27 -3:01:48
Krivaja Ruda 23 44 49N31 32E59 -2:11:56
Kriv'anskaja 6 40 47N24 40E10 -2:40:40
Krivcy 6 39 55N28 38E12 -2:32:48
Krivič 4 39 54N43 27E17 -1:49:08
Krivinka 9 24 51N08 78E10 -5:12:40
Krivoj Buzan 6 34 46N31 48E33 -3:14:12
Krivoje Ozero 23 45 47N56 30E21 -2:01:24
Krivoj Rog 23 45 47N55 33E21 -2:13:24
Krivonosovo 6 40 49N55 39E16 -2:37:04
Krivorožje 6 47 48N51 40E45 -2:43:00
Krivorožje 23 45 48N31 38E40 -2:34:40
Krivošeino 2 23 57N20 83E57 -5:35:48
Krivošin 4 39 52N52 26E08 -1:44:32
Krivoy Rog → Krivoj Rog 23 45 47N55 33E21 -2:13:24
Kriwoi-Rog → Krivoj Rog 23 45 47N55 33E21 -2:13:24
Krizskoje 23 45 49N28 39E38 -2:38:32
Krolevec 23 44 51N33 33E23 -2:13:32
Kromy 6 39 52N43 35E46 -2:23:04
Kronoki 2 4 54N36 161E10 -10:44:40
Kronštadt 6 9 59N59 29E45 -1:59:00
Kropotkin 6 47 45N26 40E34 -2:42:16
Kropotkin 2 17 58N30 115E17 -7:41:08
Kropufino 6 40 60N23 39E10 -2:36:40
Krošn'a 23 44 50N18 28E39 -1:54:36
Krotovka 6 34 53N18 51E12 -3:24:48
Krotovo 2 30 56N57 69E20 -4:37:20
Kr'učkov 6 34 48N01 45E40 -3:02:40
Kr'učkovo 6 39 57N03 35E34 -2:22:16
Krugloje 4 39 54N15 29E48 -1:59:12
Krugloje 6 40 47N01 39E15 -2:37:00
Kruglozernyj 9 32 51N06 51E17 -3:25:08
Krugloz'ornoje 2 23 55N13 79E01 -5:16:04
Krugloz'ornyj 9 32 51N06 51E17 -3:25:08
Kruglyži 6 42 58N31 47E42 -3:10:48
Kr'ukov 6 47 47N24 42E28 -2:49:52
Kr'ukovo 2 4 66N30 159E31 -10:38:04
Kr'ukovo 6 39 55N59 37E10 -2:28:40
Kr'ukovo 6 39 55N28 36E32 -2:26:08
Kr'ukovo 6 40 47N40 39E13 -2:36:52
Krulevščina 4 39 55N02 27E45 -1:51:00
Krupec 6 39 51N38 34E21 -2:17:24
Krupki 4 39 54N19 29E08 -1:56:32
Krušinovka 4 39 53N14 29E50 -1:59:20
Krutaja 6 29 63N02 54E38 -3:38:32
Krutaja 2 23 57N24 76E27 -5:05:48
Krutaja Gorka 2 24 55N25 73E15 -4:53:00
Krutcy 6 39 57N10 29E23 -1:57:32
Krutec 6 40 60N17 39E25 -2:37:40
Krutec 6 39 56N10 38E33 -2:34:12
Kruticha 2 21 53N58 81E14 -5:24:56
Kruticha 2 23 56N49 77E10 -5:08:40
Krutinka 2 24 56N01 71E31 -4:46:04
Krutoje 6 39 52N26 37E28 -2:29:52
Krutoj Log 6 30 57N53 58E14 -3:52:56
Krutoj Majdan 6 41 55N35 44E04 -2:56:16
Krutyje Verchi 6 39 54N19 36E26 -2:25:44
Krylovskaja 6 47 46N07 39E19 -2:37:16
Krym 6 40 47N19 39E31 -2:38:04
Krymsk 6 47 44N56 37E59 -2:31:56
Krymskij 6 47 47N40 40E46 -2:43:04
Krymskoje 23 45 48N45 38E48 -2:35:12
Kryžopol' 23 45 48N23 28E52 -1:55:28
Ksaverovka 23 44 50N03 30E12 -2:00:48
Ksenjevka 2 16 53N34 118E44 -7:54:56
Ksenofontova 6 30 60N58 56E12 -3:44:48
Kšenskij 6 39 51N52 37E43 -2:30:52
Kstovo 6 41 56N11 44E11 -2:56:44
Kuba 3 34 41N22 48E31 -3:14:04
Kubatly 3 34 39N22 46E34 -3:06:16
Kubenskoje 6 40 59N26 39E40 -2:38:40
Kubinka 6 39 55N35 36E43 -2:26:52
Kubuchaj 2 16 50N30 114E48 -7:39:12
Kučema 6 41 65N37 42E28 -2:49:52
Kučen'ajevo 6 41 54N44 46E24 -3:05:36
Kuchterin Lug 2 14 52N25 128E05 -8:32:20
Kuchtinka 6 39 54N29 38E10 -2:32:40
Kučino 6 39 55N45 37E58 -2:31:52
Kučkak 21 24 40N15 70E20 -4:41:20
Kučki 6 41 53N01 44E29 -2:57:56
Kudara 2 20 52N13 106E39 -7:06:36
Kudara 21 24 38N25 72E41 -4:50:44
Kudara-Somon 2 20 50N10 107E25 -7:09:40
Kudejevskij 6 30 54N52 56E46 -3:47:04
Kudever' 6 39 56N47 29E23 -1:57:32
Kudinovo 6 39 55N45 38E12 -2:32:48
Kudirkos Naumiestis 14 37 54N46 22E53 -1:31:32
Kudrovo 6 9 59N54 30E31 -2:02:04
Kudymkar 6 30 59N01 54E37 -3:38:28
Kugaly 9 24 44N29 78E40 -5:14:40
Kugarčino 6 41 55N33 50E29 -3:21:56
Kugej 6 40 46N53 39E19 -2:37:16
Kugesi 6 41 56N02 47E18 -3:09:12
Kuibyschew → Kujbyšev 6 34 53N12 50E09 -3:20:36
Kuivastu 5 35 58N35 23E22 -1:33:28
Kuja 6 29 67N46 53E10 -3:32:40
Kuja 6 41 65N05 40E06 -2:40:24
Kujbyšev 2 23 55N27 78E19 -5:13:16
Kujbyšev 6 34 53N12 50E09 -3:20:36
Kujbyšev 6 41 54N57 49E05 -3:16:20
Kujbyševka 23 45 47N37 31E42 -2:06:48
Kujbyševo 23 45 44N38 33E52 -2:15:28
Kujbyševo 23 45 47N22 36E39 -2:26:36
Kujbyševo 6 40 47N49 38E55 -2:35:40
Kujbyševo 24 24 40N22 71E17 -4:45:08
Kujbyševskij 9 24 53N15 66E51 -4:27:24
Kujbyševskij 21 24 37N52 68E44 -4:34:56
Kujbyševskij Zaton 6 41 55N09 49E12 -3:16:48
Kujeda 6 30 56N26 55E35 -3:42:20
Kujgan 9 24 45N25 74E10 -4:56:40
Kujgenkol' 9 32 49N17 47E59 -3:11:56
Kuj'uk 24 24 41N15 69E20 -4:37:20
Kujman' 6 40 52N52 39E16 -2:37:04
Kujtun 2 20 54N21 101E29 -6:45:56
Kukan 2 11 49N12 133E28 -8:53:52
Kukarino 6 39 55N31 35E59 -2:23:56
Kukmor 6 41 56N13 50E54 -3:23:36
Kukoboj 6 41 58N42 39E54 -2:39:36
Kukol' 6 9 59N52 32E35 -2:10:20
Kukuj 6 9 59N21 32E33 -2:10:12
Kukuštan 6 30 57N38 56E30 -3:46:00
Kul'ab 21 24 37N55 69E46 -4:39:04
Kulagi 6 39 52N56 32E24 -2:09:36
Kulaj 2 24 57N42 75E15 -5:01:00
Kulakovo 6 39 55N06 37E28 -2:29:52
Kulakovo 2 21 58N06 93E57 -6:15:48
Kulakši 9 30 47N12 55E24 -3:41:36
Kulanak 10 24 41N22 75E31 -5:02:04
Kulandy 9 30 46N08 59E31 -3:58:04
Kular 2 11 70N41 134E22 -8:57:28
Kulautuva 14 37 54N58 23E38 -1:34:32
Kul'či 2 11 53N33 139E36 -9:18:24
Kuldīga 13 36 56N58 21E59 -1:27:56
Kul'dur 2 11 49N13 131E38 -8:46:32
Kulebaki 6 40 55N24 42E32 -2:50:08
Kulejevo 2 23 59N40 80E59 -5:23:56
Kulešovka 6 40 47N05 39E33 -2:38:12
Kulevčinskij 2 30 53N12 61E26 -4:05:44
Kulgunino 6 30 53N35 56E56 -3:47:44
Kuligi 6 42 58N11 53E46 -3:35:04
Kulikov 23 44 49N58 24E04 -1:36:16
Kulikovka 6 34 52N14 47E36 -3:10:24
Kulikovka 23 44 51N23 31E37 -2:06:28

Kulikovo 6 41 52N14 39E35 -2:38:20
Kulikovskij 6 34 50N51 42E34 -2:50:16
Kullamaa 5 35 58N53 24E05 -1:36:20
Kuloj 6 41 64N58 43E28 -2:53:52
Kuloj 6 41 61N02 42E29 -2:49:56
Kuloli 21 24 39N22 68E03 -4:32:12
Kulotino 6 9 58N27 33E21 -2:13:24
Kul'pino 6 39 56N18 37E09 -2:28:36
Kul'sary 9 30 46N59 54E01 -3:36:04
Kultuk 2 20 51N44 103E42 -6:54:48
Kulunda 2 23 52N35 78E57 -5:15:48
Kulyab 21 24 37N55 69E46 -4:39:04
Kumakanda 2 16 52N44 116E55 -7:47:40
Kumara 2 16 51N37 126E47 -8:27:08
Kumbel' 10 24 42N30 73E11 -4:52:44
Kum-Dag 22 30 39N16 54E35 -3:38:20
Kumeny 6 42 58N07 49E56 -3:19:44
Kumertau 6 30 52N46 55E47 -3:43:08
Kuminovskoje 2 30 57N48 64E07 -4:16:28
Kuminskij 2 30 58N40 66E04 -4:24:16
Kumli 6 47 43N58 46E04 -3:04:16
Kumora 2 20 55N53 111E13 -7:24:52
Kumuch 6 47 42N11 47E07 -3:08:28
Kumylženskaja 6 34 49N53 42E36 -2:50:24
Kunašak 2 30 55N43 61E36 -4:06:24
Kunašir Island 12 8 44N10 146E00 -9:44:00
Kunašir, Ostrov 12 8 44N10 146E00 -9:44:00
Kun'batar 6 47 44N17 45E34 -3:02:16
Kunda 5 35 59N29 26E32 -1:46:08
Kundat 2 21 55N14 87E51 -5:51:24
Kungrad 24 30 43N06 58E54 -3:55:36
Kungur 6 30 57N25 56E57 -3:47:48
Kuni Vyselki 6 39 54N18 38E41 -2:34:44
Kunja 6 39 56N18 30E59 -2:03:56
Kunje 23 45 49N23 37E15 -2:29:00
Kunost' 6 40 60N01 37E38 -2:30:32
Kuntiki 2 23 58N29 76E24 -5:05:36
Kuolajarvi 6 9 66N58 29E12 -1:56:48
Kup'ansk 23 45 49N42 37E38 -2:30:32
Kupanskoje 6 39 56N51 38E43 -2:34:52
Kup'ansk-Uzlovoj 23 45 49N39 37E39 -2:30:36
Kupava 6 34 51N07 42E57 -2:51:48
Kupavna 6 39 55N45 38E08 -2:32:32
Kupičev 23 44 51N00 24E44 -1:38:56
Kupino 2 23 54N22 77E18 -5:09:12
Kupiškis 14 37 55N50 24E58 -1:39:52
Kupuri 2 14 54N44 130E30 -8:42:00
Kur'ačeje 23 45 48N10 39E37 -2:38:28
Kur'ačevka 23 45 49N39 38E42 -2:34:48
Kur'ačevka 23 45 49N22 39E36 -2:38:24
Kurach 6 47 41N36 47E46 -3:11:04
Kurachovka 23 45 48N02 37E23 -2:29:32
Kurachovo 23 45 47N59 37E16 -2:29:04
Kuragaty 9 24 43N06 72E59 -4:51:56
Kuragino 2 21 53N53 92E40 -6:10:40
Kuraj 2 21 56N42 95E29 -6:21:56
Kurajlysaj 9 30 50N07 51E51 -3:27:24
Kurakino 6 41 52N33 44E03 -2:56:12
Kurakino 6 39 54N30 35E48 -2:23:12
Kurakovo 6 39 54N05 37E14 -2:28:56
Kuram 9 24 43N33 78E08 -5:12:32
Kurašasaj 9 30 50N18 56E55 -3:47:40
Kurba 6 40 57N34 39E32 -2:38:08
Kurbatovo 2 21 55N34 91E10 -6:04:40
Kurbulik 2 20 53N45 108E57 -7:15:48
Kurčaloj 6 47 43N12 46E05 -3:04:20
Kurchatov 6 39 51N39 35E36 -2:22:24
Kurčum 9 24 48N37 83E40 -5:34:40
Kurdaj 9 24 43N21 74E59 -4:59:56
K'urdamir 3 34 40N21 48E08 -3:12:32
Kurdgelauri 7 33 41N58 45E32 -3:02:08
Kurd'umovka 23 45 48N28 37E59 -2:31:56
Kurejskaja 2 20 58N56 111E20 -7:25:20
Kuren' 23 44 51N09 32E44 -2:10:56
Kurenec 4 39 54N33 26E57 -1:47:48
Kuressaae 5 35 58N15 22E29 -1:29:56
Kurgal'džino 9 24 50N36 70E01 -4:40:04
Kurgal'džinskij 9 24 50N36 70E01 -4:40:04
Kurgan 2 30 55N26 65E18 -4:21:12
Kurgan-T'ube 21 24 37N50 68E48 -4:35:12
Kurgasyn 9 31 49N15 66E43 -4:26:52
Kurgatej 2 20 54N23 99E27 -6:37:48
Kurgolovo 6 9 59N46 28E06 -1:52:24
Kurilovka 6 34 50N44 48E02 -3:12:08
Kuril'sk 12 8 45N14 147E53 -9:51:32
Kurja 6 29 61N42 57E09 -3:48:36
Kurja 2 21 51N36 82E19 -5:29:16
Kurjanovskaja 6 41 60N19 41E33 -2:46:12
Kurkino 6 40 53N26 38E40 -2:34:40
Kurkino 6 39 55N53 37E23 -2:29:32
Kurkliai 14 37 55N25 25E03 -1:40:12
Kurlackoje 6 40 47N21 39E03 -2:36:12
Kurleja 2 16 52N11 119E11 -7:56:44
Kurlin 6 32 51N48 51E00 -3:24:00
Kurlovskij 6 40 55N27 40E36 -2:42:24
Kurmanajevka 6 34 49N53 42E36 -2:50:24
Kurmanajevka 6 32 52N31 52E06 -3:28:24
Kurmankol' 9 32 49N09 48E27 -3:13:48
Kurmenty 10 24 42N48 78E15 -5:13:00
Kuropatkino 6 47 46N32 45E20 -3:01:20
Kuropatkino 24 30 39N57 67E27 -4:29:48
Kurort-Darasun 2 16 51N12 113E44 -7:34:56
Kurovo 6 39 55N49 36E00 -2:24:00
Kurovskoje 6 39 55N34 38E55 -2:35:40
Kursavka 6 47 44N28 42E31 -2:50:04
Kuršėnai 14 37 56N00 22E56 -1:31:44
Kursk 6 39 51N42 36E12 -2:24:48
Kurskaja 6 47 44N03 44E27 -2:57:48
Kurtamyš 2 30 54N55 64E27 -4:17:48
Kurtino 6 39 54N59 38E17 -2:33:08
Kurumkan 2 20 54N18 110E18 -7:21:12
Kurunzulaj 2 16 51N00 117E10 -7:48:40
Kurusaj 21 24 40N35 69E24 -4:37:36
Kurylys 9 30 48N38 60E47 -4:03:08
Kusa 2 30 55N20 59E29 -3:57:56
Kušalino 6 39 57N07 36E05 -2:24:20
Kuščovskaja 6 47 46N33 39E37 -2:38:28
Kušen'ki 23 45 48N53 34E07 -2:16:28
Kuška 22 30 35N16 62E20 -4:09:20
Kuškušara 6 41 64N58 40E21 -2:41:24
Kušmurun 9 30 52N27 64E36 -4:18:24
Kušnarenkovo 6 30 55N06 55E22 -3:41:28
Kušnica 23 44 48N27 23E14 -1:32:56
Kustanaj 9 30 53N10 63E35 -4:14:20
Kustar'ovka 6 41 54N16 42E16 -2:49:04
Kušugum 23 45 47N42 35E14 -2:20:56
Kušumskij 6 34 51N38 48E21 -3:13:24
K'us'ur 2 14 70N39 127E15 -8:29:00
Kušva 2 30 58N18 59E45 -3:59:00
Kutais 6 47 44N32 39E18 -2:37:12
Kutaisi 7 33 42N15 42E40 -2:50:40
Kutejnikovo 23 45 47N49 38E18 -2:33:12
Kutejnikovo 6 40 47N34 39E46 -2:39:04
Kutima 2 20 57N10 108E16 -7:13:04
Kutkašen 3 34 40N59 47E50 -3:11:20
Kutluškino 6 41 55N14 50E24 -3:21:36
Kutomara 2 16 51N06 118E49 -7:55:16
Kuttuzi 6 9 59N45 30E04 -2:00:16
Kutukovo 6 40 54N26 40E31 -2:42:04
Kutulik 2 20 53N21 102E48 -6:51:12
Kuty 23 44 48N16 25E10 -1:40:40
Kuuli-Majak 22 30 40N14 52E42 -3:30:48
Kuva 24 24 40N32 72E05 -4:48:20
Kuvak-Nikol'skoje 6 41 53N37 43E30 -2:54:00
Kuvandyk 6 30 51N28 57E21 -3:49:24
Kuvasaj 24 24 40N18 71E58 -4:47:52
Kuvšinovo 6 39 57N02 34E10 -2:16:40
Kuybyshev → Kujbyšev 6 34 53N12 50E09 -3:20:36
Kuzaranda 6 9 62N22 35E37 -2:22:28
Kuzedejevo 2 21 53N20 87E10 -5:48:40
Kuzemin 23 45 50N09 34E39 -2:18:36
Kuzemino 23 45 50N09 34E39 -2:18:36
Kuzemovka 23 45 49N31 37E59 -2:31:56
Kužener 6 41 56N48 48E56 -3:15:44
Kuženkino 6 39 57N44 33E59 -2:15:56
Kuzkejevo 6 41 55N46 52E48 -3:31:12
Kuz'miniči 6 39 54N16 33E42 -2:14:48
Kuzmino 6 39 55N09 37E53 -2:31:32
Kuz'mino 6 39 56N36 37E55 -2:31:40
Kuzmiščevo 6 39 54N46 37E12 -2:28:48
Kuz'movka 2 21 62N19 92E02 -6:08:08
Kuznečicha 6 41 54N43 49E38 -3:18:32
Kuznečikovo 6 39 56N13 36E35 -2:26:20
Kuzneck 6 41 53N07 46E36 -3:06:24
Kuzneck → Novokuzneck 2 21 53N45 87E06 -5:48:24
Kuznečnoje 6 9 61N09 29E52 -1:59:28
Kuznecova 2 27 46N16 138E03 -9:12:12
Kuznecovka 6 39 56N18 28E33 -1:54:12
Kuznecovo 6 39 55N27 36E57 -2:27:48
Kuznecovo 2 30 59N15 63E28 -4:13:52
Kuznecovo 6 39 55N30 38E21 -2:33:24
Kuznecovo-Michajlovka 23 45 47N27 38E13 -2:32:52
Kuznecovskij 6 47 47N25 40E57 -2:43:48
Kuznecy 6 39 55N51 38E40 -2:34:40
Kuznetsk → Kuzneck 6 41 53N07 46E36 -3:06:24
Kuznetsovsk 23 44 51N22 25E53 -1:43:32
Kuzomen' 6 41 64N17 42E53 -2:51:32
Kuzomen' 6 9 66N17 36E54 -2:27:36
Kuzovatovo 6 34 53N33 47E41 -3:10:44
Kvaisi 7 33 42N31 43E40 -2:54:40
Kvareli 7 33 41N56 45E54 -3:03:36
Kvarsa 6 42 56N58 53E57 -3:35:48
Kvašenki 6 39 56N48 37E33 -2:30:12
Kvitok 2 20 56N03 98E30 -6:34:00
Kybartai 14 37 54N39 22E45 -1:31:00
Kykva 6 42 57N22 53E50 -3:35:20
Kyn 6 30 57N52 58E38 -3:54:32
Kyra 2 18 49N36 111E58 -7:27:52
Kyrčany 6 42 57N37 50E10 -3:20:40
Kyren 2 20 51N41 102E08 -6:48:32
Kyrkkazyk 10 24 42N30 72E20 -4:49:20
Kyrta 6 29 64N04 57E42 -3:50:48
Kyrykkuduk 9 32 49N51 51E54 -3:27:36
Kyštovka 2 23 56N33 76E38 -5:06:32
Kyštym 2 30 55N42 60E34 -4:02:16
Kysykkamys 9 32 49N14 50E19 -3:21:16
Kytlym 2 30 59N30 59E12 -3:56:48
Kytmanovo 2 21 53N28 85E28 -5:41:52
Kyzas 2 21 52N20 89E20 -5:57:20
Kyzyl 2 21 51N42 94E27 -6:17:48
Kyzylagaš 9 24 45N54 81E37 -5:26:28
Kyzylaryk 9 24 43N57 70E42 -4:42:48
Kyzylbejit 10 24 41N30 72E24 -4:49:36
Kyzyl-Chaja 2 21 50N03 89E54 -5:59:36
Kyzyl-Džar 10 24 41N17 72E02 -4:48:08
Kyzylemgek 10 24 41N57 74E56 -4:59:44
Kyzylespe 9 24 47N27 73E53 -4:55:32
Kyzyl-Kija 10 24 40N16 72E08 -4:48:32
Kyzyl-Kommuna 9 24 48N44 67E32 -4:30:08
Kyzylkup 22 30 40N38 53E58 -3:35:52
Kyzyl-Mažalyk 2 21 51N10 90E32 -6:02:08
Kyzylmazar 21 24 39N39 68E25 -4:33:40
Kyzyloba 9 32 49N37 50E38 -3:22:32
Kyzyltau 9 24 47N53 72E05 -4:48:20
Kyzylt'ob'o 10 24 42N13 75E16 -5:01:04
Kyzyltu 9 24 47N43 75E42 -5:02:48
Kyzyltu 10 24 42N11 76E40 -5:06:40
Kyzyltu 9 30 47N46 59E08 -3:56:32
Kyzyluj 9 31 48N07 65E28 -4:21:52
Kyzylžar 9 24 48N17 69E39 -4:38:36
Kzyl-Kuga 9 30 48N28 53E01 -3:32:04
Kzyl-Orda 9 30 44N48 65E28 -4:21:52
Kzyltu 9 24 53N38 72E20 -4:49:20
Labinsk 6 47 44N38 40E44 -2:42:56
Labytnangi 2 28 66N39 66E21 -4:25:24
Lač 6 29 63N18 54E28 -3:37:52
Lachdenpochja 6 9 61N31 30E08 -2:00:32
L'achi 6 40 55N20 41E56 -2:47:44
Lachia 1 34 39N38 46E32 -3:06:08
L'achoviči 4 39 53N02 26E16 -1:45:04
L'achoviči 4 39 52N23 27E55 -1:51:40
L'achovskije Islands 18 1 73N30 141E00 -9:24:00
L'achovskije Ostrova 18 1 73N30 141E00 -9:24:00
Lachva 4 39 52N13 27E04 -1:48:16
Lackoje 6 40 58N05 38E08 -2:32:32
Ladan 23 44 50N31 32E35 -2:10:20
L'adiny 6 40 61N33 38E20 -2:33:20
Ladovskaja Balka 6 47 45N38 41E25 -2:45:40
Ladožskaja 6 47 45N19 39E54 -2:39:36
Ladožskoje Ozero 6 9 60N08 31E04 -2:04:16
Laduškin 8 38 54N36 20E11 -1:20:44
Ladva 6 9 61N21 34E34 -2:18:16
Ladva-Vetka 6 9 61N21 34E27 -2:17:48
Ladvozero 6 9 65N00 29E50 -1:59:20
L'ady 6 9 58N38 28E47 -1:55:08
L'ady 6 39 54N36 31E10 -2:04:40
Ladyženka 9 24 51N00 68E42 -4:34:48
Ladyžin 23 45 48N41 29E15 -1:57:00
Ladžanurges 7 33 42N37 42E50 -2:51:20
Lagič 3 34 40N51 48E24 -3:13:36
Lagodechi 7 33 41N49 46E18 -3:05:12
Lagolovo 6 9 59N42 30E00 -2:00:00
L'agušje 2 23 54N24 77E59 -5:11:56
Laiševo 6 41 55N24 49E32 -3:18:08
Lajkovo 6 39 55N42 37E13 -2:28:52
Lajtamak 2 30 58N25 67E25 -4:29:40
Lajturi 7 33 41N55 41E55 -2:47:40
Lakedemonovka 6 40 47N12 38E33 -2:34:12
L'aki 3 34 40N34 47E26 -3:09:44
Lakinsk 6 39 56N01 39E57 -2:39:48
Lakinskij 6 39 56N01 39E57 -2:39:48
L'alino 6 40 54N29 39E06 -2:36:24
Lal'sk 6 42 60N44 47E34 -3:10:16
L'ambir' 6 41 54N17 45E07 -3:00:28
L'amca 6 40 64N27 37E04 -2:28:16
L'amen'ga 6 41 59N51 44E31 -2:58:04
Lamskoje 6 39 52N57 38E02 -2:32:08
Lančchuti 7 33 42N06 42E01 -2:48:04
Lančin 23 44 48N34 24E45 -1:39:00
Landina 2 30 59N12 67E02 -4:28:08
L'angar 10 24 40N25 73E07 -4:52:28
L'angar 21 24 37N02 72E42 -4:50:48
L'angasovo 6 42 58N32 49E30 -3:18:00
Lannaja 23 45 49N21 35E16 -2:21:04
Lanovcy 23 44 49N52 26E05 -1:44:20
L'apičev 6 34 48N30 43E32 -2:54:08
Lapino 6 39 54N57 37E49 -2:31:16
Laplandija 6 9 68N16 33E19 -2:13:16
Lapominka 6 41 64N48 40E28 -2:41:52
Lapšanga 6 41 57N27 45E03 -3:00:12
Larga 15 46 48N23 26E50 -1:47:20
Larino 23 45 47N53 37E56 -2:31:44
Larjak 2 25 61N16 80E15 -5:21:00
Larjan 6 9 59N30 33E47 -2:15:08
L'aščevka 23 44 49N33 32E41 -2:10:44
Lašino 6 42 58N16 49E59 -3:19:56
L'askel'a 6 9 61N45 30E59 -2:03:56
L'askoviči 4 39 52N07 28E09 -1:52:36
Lašma 6 40 54N56 41E09 -2:44:36
Lašmanka 6 41 54N44 51E28 -3:25:52
Latjuga 6 41 64N16 48E46 -3:15:04
Latnaja 6 40 51N43 38E55 -2:35:40
Latonovo 6 40 47N29 38E38 -2:34:32
Laukuva 14 37 55N37 22E14 -1:28:56
Laul'u 2 27 45N46 135E16 -9:01:04
Laut 2 30 59N18 66E02 -4:24:08
Lavassaare 5 35 58N31 24E22 -1:37:28
Lavela 6 41 63N38 45E31 -3:02:04
Lavrentija 2 2 65N35 171W00 11:24:00
Laž 6 42 57N11 49E14 -3:16:56
Lazarev 2 11 52N13 141E32 -9:26:08
Lazarevo 6 42 56N49 50E15 -3:21:00
Lazarevskoje 6 47 43N55 39E20 -2:37:20
Lazdijai 14 37 54N14 23E31 -1:34:04
Lazo 2 27 43N25 133E55 -8:55:40
Lazorki 23 44 50N06 32E39 -2:10:36
Leb'ažje 6 42 57N25 49E32 -3:18:08
Leb'ažje 2 30 55N16 66E29 -4:25:56
Leb'ažje 9 24 51N28 77E46 -5:11:04
Lebed'an' 6 40 53N01 39E09 -2:36:36

Lebedevka 6 34 51N06 47E09 -3:08:36
Lebedevka 2 30 56N48 66E57 -4:27:48
Lebedevka 9 30 50N09 54E07 -3:36:28
Lebedi 6 39 51N17 37E38 -2:30:32
Lebedin 23 45 48N59 31E31 -2:06:04
Lebedin 23 45 50N36 34E30 -2:18:00
Lebedino 6 41 55N14 49E50 -3:19:20
Lechta 6 41 60N49 48E28 -3:13:52
Ledkovo 6 41 67N14 50E30 -3:22:00
Lehtse 5 35 59N15 25E50 -1:43:20
Leipalingis 14 37 54N05 23E51 -1:35:24
Leisi 5 35 58N34 22E39 -1:30:36
Lejasciems 13 36 57N17 26E35 -1:46:20
Lel'čicy 4 39 51N47 28E19 -1:53:16
Lemberg → L'vov 23 44 49N50 24E00 -1:36:00
Lemeškino 6 34 51N01 44E27 -2:57:48
Lemešovka 23 44 52N04 31E38 -2:06:32
Lemmatsi 5 35 58N20 26E37 -1:46:28
Lendery 6 9 63N26 31E03 -2:04:12
Lenger 9 24 42N12 69E54 -4:39:36
Leninabad 21 24 40N17 69E37 -4:38:28
Leninakan 1 34 40N48 43E50 -2:55:20
Lenindžol 10 24 41N03 72E38 -4:50:32
Leningori 7 33 42N07 44E29 -2:57:56
Leningrad 6 9 59N55 30E15 -2:01:00
Leningrado → Leningrad 6 9 59N55 30E15 -2:01:00
Leningradskaja 6 47 46N19 39E24 -2:37:36
Leningradskij 21 24 38N06 70E01 -4:40:04
Leningradskoje 9 24 53N33 71E35 -4:46:20
Lenino 23 45 45N18 35E47 -2:23:08
Leninogorsk 6 41 54N36 52E30 -3:30:00
Leninogorsk 9 24 50N27 83E32 -5:34:08
Leninpol' 10 24 42N29 71E55 -4:47:40
Leninsk 9 30 45N40 63E20 -4:13:20
Leninsk 6 47 46N08 43E46 -2:55:04
Leninsk 6 34 48N42 45E11 -3:00:44
Leninsk 23 45 45N16 35E54 -2:23:36
Leninsk 2 30 54N55 59E54 -3:59:36
Leninsk 24 24 40N38 72E15 -4:49:00
Leninskaja Sloboda 6 41 56N05 44E28 -2:57:52
Leninskij 6 47 46N31 44E28 -2:57:52
Leninskij 6 41 56N34 45E56 -3:03:44
Leninskij 15 46 47N53 28E23 -1:53:32
Leninskij 6 39 54N18 37E28 -2:29:52
Leninskij 23 45 48N05 39E31 -2:38:04
Leninskij 9 24 52N13 76E47 -5:07:08
Leninsk-Kuzneckij 2 21 54N38 86E10 -5:44:40
Leninskoje 9 32 49N03 49E56 -3:19:44
Leninskoje 10 24 40N42 73E11 -4:52:44
Leninskoje 24 24 41N45 69E23 -4:37:32
Leninskoje 9 30 54N04 65E22 -4:21:28
Leninskoje 23 45 45N16 35E54 -2:23:36
Leninskoje 6 42 58N19 47E06 -3:08:24
Leninskoje 23 44 51N27 33E18 -2:13:12
Leninskoje 9 30 50N44 57E53 -3:51:32
Leninskoje 2 11 47N56 132E38 -8:50:32
Leninžol 9 32 49N20 47E05 -3:08:20
Len'ki 2 23 52N57 80E26 -5:21:44
Lenkoran' 3 34 38N45 48E50 -3:15:20
Lensk 2 16 61N00 114E50 -7:39:20
Lenskoje 2 30 58N09 63E11 -4:12:44
Lentechi 7 33 42N48 42E44 -2:50:56
Lentvaris 14 37 54N39 25E03 -1:40:12
Leonicha 6 40 59N37 38E51 -2:35:24
Leonidovo 19 8 49N17 142E50 -9:31:20
Leonovo 6 39 55N26 38E42 -2:34:48
Leontjevka 9 24 43N03 69E50 -4:39:20
Leontjevo 6 40 58N58 36E37 -2:26:28
Leovo 15 46 46N29 28E15 -1:53:00
Lepel' 4 39 54N53 28E42 -1:54:48
Lepeški 6 39 56N05 38E07 -2:32:28
Lepl'avo 23 44 49N48 31E32 -2:06:08
Lepsinsk 9 24 45N32 80E37 -5:22:28
Lepsy 9 24 46N18 78E20 -5:13:20
Lepsy 9 24 46N15 78E55 -5:15:40
Lerik 3 34 38N46 48E25 -3:13:40
Lermontovka 2 11 47N10 134E20 -8:57:20
Leščinovka 23 45 49N16 34E14 -2:16:56
Lesken 6 47 43N16 43E48 -2:55:12
Les'ki 23 44 49N19 32E13 -2:08:52
Lesnaja 4 39 52N59 25E46 -1:43:04
Lesnoj 6 41 54N11 40E27 -2:41:48
Lesnoj 2 30 56N57 67E15 -4:29:00
Lesnoje 6 9 58N17 35E32 -2:22:08
Lesnoje Konobejevo 6 41 54N02 41E55 -2:47:40
Lesnoje Mat'unino 6 34 53N27 47E26 -3:09:44
Lesnoj Gorodok 6 39 55N39 37E13 -2:28:52
Lesnyje Pol'any 6 42 58N58 52E26 -3:29:44
Lesnyje Pol'any 6 39 55N57 37E53 -2:31:32
Lesogorsk 6 41 55N06 43E56 -2:55:44
Lesogorsk 2 20 56N03 99E33 -6:38:12
Lesogorsk 19 8 49N27 142E08 -9:28:32
Lesogorskij 6 9 61N02 28E53 -1:55:32
Lesopil'noje 2 11 46N44 134E20 -8:57:20
Lesosibirsk 2 21 58N16 92E29 -6:09:56
Lesovščina 23 44 50N47 28E35 -1:54:20
Lesozavodsk 2 27 45N28 133E27 -8:53:48
Lesozavodskij 6 9 66N44 32E49 -2:11:16
Lešukonskoje 6 41 64N54 45E40 -3:02:40

Lesunovo 6 41 55N40 43E07 -2:52:28
Letičev 23 44 49N23 27E37 -1:50:28
Letka 6 41 59N36 49E22 -3:17:28
Letn'aja Zolotica 6 40 64N57 36E50 -2:27:20
Letnerečenskij 6 40 64N17 34E23 -2:17:32
Letovo 6 39 55N34 37E24 -2:29:36
Levaši 6 47 42N27 47E20 -3:09:20
Levdym 2 30 60N29 66E19 -4:25:16
Levicha 2 30 57N36 59E55 -3:59:40
Levino 6 40 60N29 37E30 -2:30:00
Levokumskoje 6 47 44N48 44E39 -2:58:36
Lev Tolstoj 6 40 53N13 39E27 -2:37:48
Leža 6 41 58N56 40E45 -2:43:00
Ležn'ovo 6 40 56N46 40E53 -2:43:32
L'gov 6 39 51N43 35E17 -2:21:08
Libau → Liepāja 13 36 56N31 21E01 -1:24:04
Lichoslavl' 6 39 57N07 35E28 -2:21:52
Lichovka 23 45 48N41 33E55 -2:15:40
Lichovskoj 6 47 48N07 40E12 -2:40:48
Lid' 6 9 59N39 35E05 -2:20:20
Lida 4 39 53N53 25E18 -1:41:12
Lielvārde 13 36 56N43 24E51 -1:39:24
Liepāja 13 36 56N31 21E01 -1:24:04
Liepna 13 36 57N25 27E25 -1:49:40
Ligačovo 6 39 55N56 37E15 -2:29:00
Līgatne 13 36 57N14 25E02 -1:40:08
Ligovka 23 45 49N08 36E03 -2:24:12
Ligovo 6 9 60N13 31E48 -2:07:12
Lihula 5 35 58N41 23E50 -1:35:20
Likėnai 14 37 56N12 24E37 -1:38:28
Likino 6 39 55N38 37E08 -2:28:32
Likino-Dulevo 6 39 55N43 38E58 -2:35:52
Liman 6 34 45N47 47E14 -3:08:56
Liman 23 45 49N36 36E27 -2:25:48
Liman 23 45 45N41 29E45 -1:59:00
Liman 23 45 49N21 38E57 -2:35:48
Limanskoje 23 45 46N38 30E00 -2:00:00
Limbaži 13 36 57N31 24E42 -1:38:48
Linachamari 6 9 69N40 31E20 -2:05:20
Linda 6 41 56N37 44E07 -2:56:28
Linevo 21 54N05 83E24 -5:33:36
Linksmakalnis 14 37 54N45 23E55 -1:35:40
Linkuva 14 37 56N05 23E59 -1:35:56
Linovica 23 44 50N28 32E22 -2:09:28
Lin'ovo 6 34 50N53 44E51 -2:59:24
Liozno 4 39 55N02 30E48 -2:03:12
Lipcy 23 45 50N13 36E25 -2:25:40
Lipeck 6 40 52N37 39E35 -2:38:20
Lipeckoje Vtoroje 23 45 47N46 29E41 -1:58:44
Lipetsk → Lipeck 6 40 52N37 39E35 -2:38:20
Lipicy 6 39 53N22 37E17 -2:29:08
Lipin Bor 6 40 60N16 37E57 -2:31:48
Lipkany 15 46 48N16 26E48 -1:47:12
Lipki 6 39 53N58 37E42 -2:30:48
Lipniški 4 39 54N00 25E37 -1:42:28
Lipovaja Dolina 23 44 50N35 33E48 -2:15:12
Lipovcy 2 27 44N11 131E44 -8:46:56
Lipovec 23 44 49N14 29E03 -1:56:12
Lipovka 6 34 52N26 46E11 -3:04:44
Lipovka 6 34 49N46 44E46 -2:59:44
Lipovka 6 41 50N52 40E02 -2:40:08
Lisakovsk 9 30 52N36 62E37 -4:10:28
Lisavy 6 39 56N33 38E32 -2:34:08
Lisec 23 44 48N52 24E36 -1:38:24
Lisičansk 23 45 48N55 38E26 -2:33:44
Lisichansk → Lisičansk 23 45 48N55 38E26 -2:33:44
Lisicy 6 39 56N47 36E21 -2:25:24
Lisij Nos 6 9 60N01 30E00 -2:00:00
Lisja 6 30 57N15 54E22 -3:37:28
Liski 6 41 50N56 39E29 -2:37:56
Liski → Georgiu-Dež 41 50N59 39E30 -2:38:00
Lišn'ovka 23 44 51N28 25E25 -1:41:40
Lista 6 34 47N44 45E54 -3:03:36
Listv'anka 2 20 51N52 104E51 -6:59:24
Listv'anskij 2 21 54N27 83E29 -5:33:56
Litin 23 44 49N20 28E05 -1:52:20
Litke 2 11 53N57 140E15 -9:21:00
Litovko 2 11 49N15 135E11 -9:00:44
Litvinovka 6 47 48N24 40E53 -2:43:32
Litvinovka 23 45 49N18 39E27 -2:37:48
Litvinovo 6 40 59N34 38E01 -2:32:04
Litvinskoje 9 24 50N42 72E42 -4:50:48
Livadija 2 27 42N50 132E39 -8:50:36
Līvāni 13 36 56N22 26E11 -1:44:44
Livanovka 9 30 52N06 61E59 -4:07:56
Livenka 6 40 50N26 38E18 -2:33:12
Livenka 6 41 50N44 40E14 -2:40:56
Livny 6 39 52N25 37E37 -2:30:28
Lizino 23 45 49N33 38E51 -2:35:24
Lizinovka 6 40 50N08 39E28 -2:37:52
Ljalovo 6 39 56N03 37E14 -2:28:56
Loban 6 41 65N44 45E25 -3:01:40
Lobanovo 6 39 53N04 38E14 -2:32:56
Lobanovskije Vyselki 6 40 54N18 38E58 -2:35:52
Lobaski 6 41 54N38 45E09 -3:00:36
Lobkoviči 4 39 53N50 31E45 -2:07:00
Lobn'a 6 39 56N01 37E30 -2:30:00
Lobskoje 6 9 62N45 35E16 -2:21:04
Lobva 2 30 59N12 60E30 -4:02:00
Lochino 6 39 55N42 37E19 -2:29:16
Lochvica 23 44 50N22 33E16 -2:13:04

Lodejnoje Pole 6 9 60N44 33E30 -2:14:00
Lodejnoje Polje 6 9 60N44 33E30 -2:14:00
Log 6 34 49N29 43E52 -2:55:28
Logačovka 6 32 52N23 52E21 -3:29:24
Logduz 6 41 60N00 44E41 -2:58:44
Loginovo 6 39 55N42 38E44 -2:34:56
Logišin 4 39 52N20 25E59 -1:43:56
Logojsk 4 39 54N12 27E49 -1:51:16
Logovskij 6 34 48N26 43E23 -2:53:32
Lojev 4 39 51N56 30E46 -2:03:04
Lojga 6 41 61N05 44E37 -2:58:28
Lojno 6 42 59N44 52E39 -3:30:36
Lokači 23 44 50N44 24E39 -1:38:36
Lokbatan 3 34 40N20 49E43 -3:18:52
Lokn'a 6 39 56N50 30E09 -2:00:36
Lokot' 6 39 52N34 34E34 -2:18:16
Lokot' 2 23 51N11 81E11 -5:24:44
Loksa 5 35 59N35 25E45 -1:43:00
Loktyši 4 39 52N50 26E43 -1:46:52
Lom 6 40 57N54 39E12 -2:36:48
Lomakino 24 24 40N05 68E10 -4:32:40
Lomonosov 6 9 59N55 29E46 -1:59:04
Lomonosovskij 9 30 52N50 66E28 -4:25:52
Lomovatka 23 45 48N27 38E34 -2:34:16
Lomovoje 6 41 64N01 40E40 -2:42:40
Lomy 2 16 52N17 117E59 -7:51:56
Lončakovo 2 11 47N05 134E10 -8:56:40
Londoko 2 11 49N02 131E59 -8:47:56
Longasy 6 9 61N58 35E09 -2:20:36
Loo 6 47 43N43 39E36 -2:38:24
Lopandino 6 39 52N28 34E49 -2:19:16
Lopanka 6 47 46N24 40E59 -2:43:56
Lopar'ovo 6 41 58N20 42E41 -2:50:44
Lopatiči 4 39 53N34 30E53 -2:03:32
Lopatin 23 44 50N13 24E50 -1:39:20
Lopatin 6 47 43N53 47E41 -3:10:44
Lopatino 6 41 52N37 45E47 -3:03:08
Lopatino 6 39 54N45 37E00 -2:28:00
Lopatino 19 8 48N24 142E15 -9:29:00
Lopatinskij 6 39 55N21 38E34 -2:34:16
Lopatovo 6 39 56N08 29E12 -1:56:48
Lopotovo 6 39 56N04 36E49 -2:27:16
Lopšen'ga 6 40 64N58 37E41 -2:30:44
Lopt'uga 6 41 63N16 47E56 -3:11:44
Lopuchovka 6 34 51N59 44E42 -2:58:48
Lopuchovka 6 34 50N37 44E29 -2:57:56
Lorino 2 2 65N30 171W43 11:26:52
Losevo 6 41 50N40 40E02 -2:40:08
Losinoborskaja 2 21 58N27 89E28 -5:57:52
Losino-Petrovskij 6 39 55N52 38E12 -2:32:48
Losinovka 23 44 50N51 31E54 -2:07:36
Loškar'ovka 23 45 47N57 34E12 -2:16:48
Los'mino 6 39 55N04 34E24 -2:17:36
Lošnica 4 39 54N17 28E46 -1:55:04
Lotošino 6 39 56N14 35E38 -2:22:32
Louchi 6 9 66N04 33E00 -2:12:00
Lovcy 6 39 55N00 39E15 -2:37:00
Lovozero 6 9 65N00 29E50 -1:59:20
Lovozero 6 9 68N00 35E00 -2:20:00
Ložnikovo 2 24 56N54 73E56 -4:55:44
Ložnikovo 2 16 51N22 117E03 -7:48:12
Lozno-Aleksandrovka 23 45 49N50 38E44 -2:34:56
Loznoje 6 34 49N17 44E26 -2:57:44
Lozovaja 23 45 48N54 36E20 -2:25:20
Lozovaja 23 45 49N28 37E54 -2:31:36
Lozovaja 9 24 53N17 77E45 -5:11:00
Lozovoje 23 44 49N18 27E18 -1:49:12
Lozovoje 23 45 49N13 37E36 -2:30:24
Lozovskij 23 45 48N33 38E54 -2:35:36
L'uban' 6 9 59N21 31E13 -2:04:52
L'uban' 4 39 52N37 29E08 -1:56:32
L'uban' 4 39 52N48 27E59 -1:51:56
Lubāna 13 36 56N54 26E43 -1:46:52
Lub'any 6 42 56N02 51E24 -3:25:36
L'ubar 23 44 49N55 27E44 -1:50:56
L'ubašovka 23 45 47N51 30E15 -2:01:00
L'ubča 4 39 53N45 26E03 -1:44:12
L'ubeč 23 44 51N42 30E39 -2:02:36
L'ubercy 6 39 55N41 37E53 -2:31:32
L'ubešov 23 44 51N46 25E31 -1:42:04
L'ubickoje 6 34 51N46 49E19 -3:17:16
L'ubim 6 41 58N22 40E41 -2:42:44
L'ubimovka 9 24 52N15 66E45 -4:27:00
L'ubimovka 6 39 51N31 35E37 -2:22:28
L'ubimovka 23 45 46N47 33E34 -2:14:16
L'ubimyj 23 45 47N53 39E28 -2:37:52
L'ubino 2 21 57N30 88E47 -5:55:08
L'ubinskij 2 24 55N09 72E42 -4:50:48
L'ubnica 6 39 57N58 32E42 -2:10:48
Lubny 23 44 50N01 33E00 -2:12:00
L'ubochna 6 39 53N31 34E23 -2:17:32
L'uboml' 23 44 51N14 24E01 -1:36:04
L'ubostan' 6 39 51N19 35E44 -2:22:56
L'ubotin 23 45 49N57 35E57 -2:23:48
L'ubučany 6 39 55N15 37E33 -2:30:12
L'ubytino 6 9 58N49 33E23 -2:13:32
Lučak 24 30 38N23 67E25 -4:29:40
Luch 6 40 57N01 42E15 -2:49:00
Luchovicy 6 39 54N59 39E03 -2:36:12
Lučin 4 39 53N01 30E01 -2:00:04
Luck 23 44 50N44 25E20 -1:41:20
L'udinovo 6 39 53N52 34E27 -2:17:48
L'udkovo 6 39 54N36 34E43 -2:18:52
Ludoni 6 9 58N12 29E21 -1:57:24
Ludwigsort → Laduškin 8 38 54N36 20E11 -1:20:44
Ludza 13 36 56N33 27E43 -1:50:52
Luga 6 9 58N44 29E52 -1:59:28

Place		Lat.	Long.	Time
Luganskoje 23	45	48N26	38E15	-2:33:00
Lugansk → Vorošilovgrad 23	45	48N34	39E20	-2:37:20
Luginino 6	39	57N43	35E17	-2:21:08
Luginy 23	44	51N04	28E24	-1:53:36
Lugovaja Subbota 2	30	59N52	69E45	-4:39:00
Lugovoj 2	30	59N44	65E55	-4:23:40
Lugovoj 9	24	42N56	72E45	-4:51:00
Lugovoje 9	24	42N55	72E43	-4:50:52
Lugovskij 2	20	58N02	112E54	-7:31:36
Lugovskoje 6	34	50N38	46E28	-3:05:52
L'uk 6	42	56N55	52E48	-3:31:12
Lukačok 2	14	53N03	132E16	-8:49:04
Luk'anovo 6	39	54N52	37E25	-2:29:40
Lukašin 1	34	40N12	44E01	-2:56:04
Lukaškin Jar 2	23	60N20	78E24	-5:13:36
Lukašovka 6	39	51N38	35E35	-2:22:20
Luki 4	39	53N29	26E15	-1:45:00
Lukino 6	39	55N26	37E04	-2:28:16
Lukino 6	39	55N50	36E49	-2:27:16
Luknovo 6	40	56N12	42E03	-2:48:12
Lukojanov 6	41	55N02	44E30	-2:58:00
Lukoškino 6	39	55N19	37E16	-2:29:04
Lukov 23	44	51N13	24E19	-1:37:16
Lukovskaja 6	34	50N35	41E52	-2:47:28
Lumbovka 6	9	67N44	40E30	-2:42:00
Lunin 4	39	52N18	26E38	-1:46:32
Luninec 4	39	52N15	26E48	-1:47:12
Lunino 6	41	53N35	45E14	-3:00:56
Lunino 6	39	54N09	38E29	-2:33:56
Lunno 4	39	53N27	24E16	-1:37:04
Lusakert 1	34	40N23	44E36	-2:58:24
L'usino 4	39	52N38	26E31	-1:46:04
L'uten'ka 23	45	50N13	34E02	-2:16:08
Lutsk → Luck 23	44	50N44	25E20	-1:41:20
Lutugino 23	45	48N24	39E13	-2:36:52
Luza 6	40	62N42	37E06	-2:28:24
Luza 6	42	60N39	47E10	-3:08:40
Luža 6	9	59N58	31E56	-2:07:44
Lužki 4	39	55N21	27E52	-1:51:28
Lužki 6	39	54N51	37E36	-2:30:24
L'va Tolstogo 6	39	54N37	36E03	-2:24:12
L'vov 23	44	49N50	24E00	-1:36:00
L'vovskij 6	39	55N19	37E31	-2:30:04
Lwów → L'vov 23	44	49N50	24E00	-1:36:00
Lyčkovo 23	45	49N06	35E12	-2:20:48
Lyčkovo 6	39	57N55	32E24	-2:09:36
Lykošino 6	9	58N07	33E43	-2:14:52
Lymbel'karamo 2	21	60N15	83E32	-5:34:08
Lymkoj 2	25	59N31	70E22	-4:41:28
Lynga 6	42	57N17	53E04	-3:32:16
Lyntupy 4	39	55N03	26E19	-1:45:16
Lysaja Gora 23	45	48N11	31E06	-2:04:24
Lys'anka 23	44	49N16	30E50	-2:03:20
Lyskovo 6	41	56N04	45E02	-3:00:08
Lysogorka 6	40	47N42	39E12	-2:36:48
Lys'va 6	30	58N07	57E47	-3:51:08
Lysyje Gory 6	34	51N32	44E46	-2:59:04
Lytkarino 6	39	55N35	37E54	-2:31:36
Lyubertsy → L'ubercy 6	39	55N41	37E53	-2:31:32
Maardu 5	35	59N28	25E02	-1:40:08
Mača 2	16	59N54	117E35	-7:50:20
Mačecha 6	34	50N48	43E17	-2:53:08
Mačechi 23	45	49N31	34E26	-2:17:44
Machačkala 6	47	42N58	47E30	-3:10:00
Machalino 6	41	53N05	46E14	-3:04:56
Macharadze 7	33	41N56	42E00	-2:48:00
Machindžauri 7	33	41N40	41E43	-2:46:52
Machmud-Mekteb 6	47	44N26	45E13	-3:00:52
Machn'ovo 2	30	58N27	61E42	-4:06:48
Machorovka 9	24	54N17	69E41	-4:38:44
Machtaly 9	24	41N22	68E02	-4:32:08
Mačkassy 6	41	52N46	45E34	-3:02:16
M'ačkovo 6	39	55N13	38E40	-2:34:40
M'ačkovo 6	39	56N21	39E03	-2:36:12
Madagiz 3	34	40N19	46E44	-3:06:56
Madajevo 6	41	54N48	44E31	-2:58:04
M'adel' 4	39	54N53	26E57	-1:47:48
Madenijet 9	24	47N53	78E37	-5:14:28
Madona 13	36	56N51	26E13	-1:44:52
Madora 4	39	53N09	30E11	-2:00:44
Madžalis 6	47	42N08	47E50	-3:11:20
Magadan 2	6	59N34	150E48	-10:03:12
Magansk 2	21	55N52	93E15	-6:13:00
Magaramkent 6	47	41N37	48E21	-3:13:24
Magdagači 2	16	53N27	125E48	-8:23:12
Magdalinovka 23	45	48N55	34E54	-2:19:36
Magerov 23	44	50N08	23E43	-1:34:52
M'aglovo 6	9	59N53	30E41	-2:02:44
Magnitka 2	30	55N21	59E43	-3:58:52
Magnitogorsk 2	30	53N27	59E04	-3:56:16
Magnitostroj 6	32	51N43	53E05	-3:32:20
Mago 2	11	53N15	140E13	-9:20:52
M'agozero 6	9	60N21	34E50	-2:19:20
Maišiagala 14	37	54N52	25E04	-1:40:16
Majačnyj 6	30	52N41	55E44	-3:42:56
Majaki 23	45	46N25	30E16	-2:01:04
Majaki 23	45	48N57	37E37	-2:30:28
Majakovskij 7	33	42N06	42E48	-2:51:12
Majchura 21	24	39N02	68E35	-4:34:20
Majdantal 9	24	43N41	68E02	-4:32:08
Majja 2	16	61N44	130E18	-8:41:12
Majkain 9	24	51N27	75E52	-5:03:28
Majkop 6	47	44N35	40E07	-2:40:28
Majkor 6	30	59N01	55E54	-3:43:36
Majlibaš 9	30	45N49	62E39	-4:10:36
Majli-Saj 10	24	41N17	72E29	-4:49:56
Majmak 10	24	42N40	71E15	-4:45:00
Majna 2	21	53N00	91E28	-6:05:52
Majna 6	42	54N07	47E37	-3:10:28
Majno-Gytkino 2	2	63N36	176E30	-11:46:00
Majsk 2	23	57N49	77E16	-5:09:04
Majskij 2	14	52N18	129E38	-8:38:32
Majskij 2	11	49N00	140E10	-9:20:40
Majskij 6	47	43N38	44E04	-2:56:16
Majskij 6	40	47N43	40E03	-2:40:12
Majskoje 9	24	50N55	78E15	-5:13:00
Majskoje 6	39	56N08	37E55	-2:31:40
Majtan 9	24	45N46	74E20	-4:57:20
Majtobe 9	24	43N01	70E35	-4:42:20
Makanči 9	24	46N48	82E00	-5:28:00
Makarakskij 2	21	55N36	88E03	-5:52:12
Makar-Ib 6	41	63N39	49E24	-3:17:36
Makaricha 6	29	66N15	58E20	-3:53:20
Makarje 6	42	58N35	48E11	-3:12:44
Makarjev 6	41	57N52	43E48	-2:55:12
Makarjevo 6	41	56N06	45E06	-3:00:24
Makarov 19	8	48N38	142E48	-9:31:12
Makarov 23	44	50N28	29E49	-1:59:16
Makarovo 2	20	57N29	107E52	-7:11:28
Makarovo 6	34	52N18	43E20	-2:53:20
Makarovo 6	39	54N22	36E40	-2:26:40
Makaševka 6	41	51N30	42E36	-2:50:24
Makat 9	30	47N39	53E19	-3:33:16
Makejevka 23	44	50N40	31E50	-2:07:20
Makejevka 23	45	48N02	37E58	-2:31:52
Makejevka 23	45	49N14	37E59	-2:31:56
Makeyevka → Makejevka 23	45	48N02	37E58	-2:31:52
Makhachkala → Machačkala 6	47	42N58	47E30	-3:10:00
M'akino 6	39	55N48	37E22	-2:29:28
Makinsk 9	24	52N37	70E26	-4:41:44
M'akiševo 6	39	56N34	28E53	-1:55:32
M'akit 2	6	61N24	152E09	-10:08:36
Makkavejevo 2	16	51N44	113E58	-7:35:52
Maklakovo 2	21	58N16	92E29	-6:09:56
Makopse 6	47	43N59	39E13	-2:36:52
Makošino 23	44	51N27	32E18	-2:09:12
Makovskoje 2	21	58N12	90E52	-6:03:28
M'aksa 6	40	58N54	38E12	-2:32:48
Maksatica 6	39	57N48	35E53	-2:23:32
Maksimicha 2	20	53N15	108E43	-7:14:52
Maksimkin Jar 2	21	58N42	86E48	-5:47:12
Maksimoviči 23	44	51N13	29E37	-1:58:28
Maksimovka 2	27	46N04	137E51	-9:11:24
Maksimovka 6	34	52N59	51E10	-3:24:40
Maksimovka 23	45	47N38	37E34	-2:30:16
Maksimovo 6	39	56N20	35E58	-2:23:52
Makušino 2	30	55N13	67E13	-4:28:52
Malachovka 6	39	55N39	38E00	-2:32:00
Malachovo 6	39	54N45	37E27	-2:29:48
Malachovo 6	39	54N22	37E31	-2:30:04
Malachovskij 6	47	49N08	41E43	-2:46:52
Mal'agurt 6	42	57N39	52E32	-3:30:08
Malaja Beloz'orka 23	45	47N14	34E56	-2:19:44
Malaja Bessergenovka 6	40	47N09	38E36	-2:34:24
Malaja Borščovka 6	39	56N33	36E53	-2:27:32
Malaja Bykovka 6	34	51N54	47E45	-3:11:00
Malaja Devica 23	44	50N41	32E10	-2:08:40
Malaja Doroginka 6	40	54N06	38E56	-2:35:44
Malaja Dubna 6	39	55N52	38E58	-2:35:52
Malaja Ižmora 6	41	53N32	42E48	-2:51:12
Malaja Janisol' 23	45	47N22	37E20	-2:29:20
Malaja Jekaterinovka 6	34	51N26	44E17	-2:57:08
Malaja Orlovka 6	47	47N18	41E24	-2:45:36
Malaja Pera 6	29	64N11	54E47	-3:39:08
Malaja Serdoba 6	41	52N28	44E56	-2:59:44
Malaja Tokmačevka 23	45	47N32	35E54	-2:23:36
Malaja Višera 6	9	58N51	32E14	-2:08:56
Malaja Viska 23	45	48N39	31E38	-2:06:32
Mal'cevo 6	39	55N56	37E57	-2:31:48
Mal'čevskaja 6	47	49N04	40E21	-2:41:24
Mal'čevsko-Polnenskaja 6	47	48N58	40E12	-2:40:48
Malejevka 23	45	47N29	32E43	-2:10:52
Malek 24	24	40N47	68E37	-4:34:28
Malen'ga 6	40	63N50	36E25	-2:25:40
Maleta 2	18	50N50	108E25	-7:13:40
Malgobek 6	47	43N32	44E34	-2:58:16
Malin 23	44	50N46	29E15	-1:57:00
Malinki 6	40	54N05	38E59	-2:35:56
Malinniki 6	39	56N17	38E24	-2:33:36
Malino 6	39	55N06	38E11	-2:32:44
Malino 6	39	55N58	37E13	-2:28:52
Malinovka 2	21	53N24	87E17	-5:49:08
Malinovka 6	34	51N47	43E26	-2:53:44
Malinovka 23	45	49N47	36E43	-2:26:52
Malivo 6	39	55N07	39E02	-2:36:08
Malka 2	4	53N20	157E30	-10:30:00
Malka 6	47	43N47	43E21	-2:53:24
Malmyž 6	42	56N31	50E41	-3:22:44
Maloarchangel'sk 6	39	52N24	36E30	-2:26:00
Maloarchangel'skoje 2	18	50N24	108E50	-7:15:20
Malodel'skaja 6	34	50N11	43E53	-2:55:32
Maloduša 4	39	52N09	30E14	-2:00:56
Malojaroslavec 6	39	55N01	36E28	-2:25:52
Malojaz 6	30	55N13	58E09	-3:52:36
Maloje Goloustnoje 2	20	52N18	105E18	-7:01:12
Malojekaterinovka 23	45	47N39	35E16	-2:21:04
Maloje Kozino 6	41	56N26	43E41	-2:54:44
Maloje Ščerbedino 6	47	47N56	44E41	-2:58:44
Maloje-Ščerbedino 6	34	51N59	42E50	-2:51:20
Maloje Skuratovo 6	39	53N33	37E00	-2:28:00
Malokirsanovka 6	40	47N28	38E31	-2:34:04
Malokrasnojarka 2	23	56N28	76E01	-5:04:04
Malomichajlovka 23	45	48N06	36E23	-2:25:32
Malonabatovskij 6	34	48N57	43E40	-2:54:40
Malor'azancevo 23	45	48N53	38E23	-2:33:32
Malorita 4	39	51N47	24E05	-1:36:20
Malorossijskij 9	30	53N12	62E30	-4:10:00
Malošujka 6	40	63N45	37E22	-2:29:28
Malta 13	36	56N21	27E10	-1:48:40
Malybaj 9	24	43N30	78E25	-5:13:40
Malyje Alabuchi 6	41	51N33	42E10	-2:48:40
Malyje Derbety 6	47	47N56	44E41	-2:58:44
Malyje Gorod'atiči 4	39	52N33	28E20	-1:53:20
Malyje Jaguri 6	47	45N26	43E01	-2:52:04
Malyje Kamkaly 9	24	44N44	71E31	-4:46:04
Malyje Karmakuly 17	29	72N23	52E44	-3:30:56
Malyje Porogi 6	9	59N47	30E42	-2:02:48
Malyj Sarybulak 9	24	52N10	72E35	-4:50:20
Malyn' 6	39	54N36	38E40	-2:34:40
Malyševo 6	39	57N50	35E36	-2:22:24
Mama 2	20	58N18	112E54	-7:31:36
Mamadyš 6	41	55N44	51E25	-3:25:40
Mamakan 2	17	57N48	114E01	-7:36:04
Mamedkala 6	47	42N10	48E06	-3:12:24
Maml'utka 9	24	54N57	68E35	-4:34:20
Mamonovo 6	39	55N41	37E19	-2:29:16
Mamonovo (Heiligenbeil) 8	38	54N28	19E57	-1:19:48
Mamontovo 2	23	52N43	81E37	-5:26:28
Mamontovo 2	23	51N45	81E25	-5:25:40
Mamraš 6	47	41N44	48E19	-3:13:16
Mamykovo 6	41	54N38	50E37	-3:22:28
Mamyl' 6	29	61N57	56E41	-3:46:44
Manajenki 6	39	53N42	36E27	-2:25:48
Maneviči 23	44	51N17	25E33	-1:42:12
Manglisi 7	33	41N43	44E24	-2:57:36
Mangut 2	16	49N46	112E38	-7:30:32
Mangut 2	24	55N47	70E46	-4:43:04
Manily 2	4	62N29	165E36	-11:02:24
Manino 6	39	53N58	34E20	-2:17:20
Mankanaj 9	30	48N58	60E58	-4:03:52
Mankent 9	24	42N25	69E50	-4:39:20
Man'kovka 23	45	48N58	30E20	-2:01:20
Man'kovka 23	45	49N34	38E27	-2:33:48
Man'kovo 6	47	49N24	40E17	-2:41:08
Man'kovo-Ber'ozovskaja 6	47	48N47	41E33	-2:46:12
Mansurovo 6	39	55N52	36E36	-2:26:24
Manturovo 6	41	58N20	44E46	-2:59:04
Manturovo 6	39	51N28	37E07	-2:28:28
Manuilovskaja 6	41	60N29	40E40	-2:42:40
Manz'a 2	21	58N29	96E15	-6:25:00
Manželija 23	45	49N19	33E38	-2:14:32
Manzurka 2	20	53N30	106E04	-7:04:16
Maraldy 9	24	52N26	77E45	-5:11:00
Maralik 1	34	40N35	43E52	-2:55:28
Marasany 6	30	57N27	54E25	-3:37:40
Maraza 3	34	40N33	48E56	-3:15:44
Marcevo 6	40	47N15	38E53	-2:35:32
Marcha 2	16	60N37	123E18	-8:13:12
Marchamat 24	24	40N30	72E19	-4:49:16
Marčichina Buda 23	44	51N58	34E03	-2:16:12
Marčugi 6	39	55N21	38E33	-2:34:12
Mardakert 3	34	40N12	46E48	-3:07:12
Mardarovka 23	45	47N32	29E44	-1:58:56
Marevo 6	39	57N19	32E05	-2:08:20
Marfinka 6	40	47N36	38E32	-2:34:08
Marfino 6	34	46N25	48E44	-3:14:56
Marganec 23	45	47N38	34E40	-2:18:40
Margaritovka 6	47	46N55	38E52	-2:35:28

Margelan → Margilan 24
24 40N28 71E44 -4:46:56
Margilan 24 24 40N28 71E44 -4:46:56
Marica 6 39 51N45 35E16 -2:21:04
Mariec 6 41 56N32 49E50 -3:19:20
Mariinsk 2 21 56N13 87E45 -5:51:00
Mariinskoje 2 11 51N43 140E13 -9:20:52
Marijec 6 41 56N32 49E50 -3:19:20
Mari-Malmyž 6 42 56N30 50E52 -3:23:28
Marinovka 6 34 48N41 43E49 -2:55:16
Marinovka 23 45 47N46 30E53 -2:03:32
Marinovka 23 45 47N54 38E51 -2:35:24
Marinskij Posad 6
41 56N07 47E43 -3:10:52
Mariškino 6 39 55N21 38E37 -2:34:28
Mari-Turek 6 41 56N47 49E36 -3:18:24
Mariupol' → Ždanov 23
45 47N06 37E33 -2:30:12
Märjamaa 5 35 58N54 24E26 -1:37:44
Marjanovka 2 24 54N58 72E38 -4:50:32
Marjanovka 23 44 50N28 24E48 -1:39:12
Marjanskaja 6 47 45N06 38E38 -2:34:32
Marjevka 9 24 53N46 67E24 -4:29:36
Marjina Gorka 4
39 53N31 28E09 -1:52:36
Marjinka 23 45 47N56 37E31 -2:30:04
Marjino 6 39 55N52 37E18 -2:29:12
Marjino 2 11 48N31 130E38 -8:42:32
Marjino 6 39 54N28 37E12 -2:28:48
Marjino 6 9 59N50 29E56 -1:59:44
Marjino 6 9 59N54 31E00 -2:04:00
Marjinskaja 6 47 43N53 43E29 -2:53:56
Marjinsko 6 9 58N49 28E32 -1:54:08
Markansu 21 24 39N18 73E20 -4:53:20
Markelovo 2 23 56N42 83E33 -5:34:12
Markovka 23 45 49N31 39E34 -2:38:16
Markovo 2 20 57N20 107E04 -7:08:16
Markovo 2 3 64N40 170E25-11:21:40
Markovo 6 40 57N01 40E30 -2:42:00
Markovo 6 39 55N52 39E17 -2:37:08
Marks 6 34 51N42 46E46 -3:07:04
Markulešty 15 46 47N52 28E14 -1:52:56
Marneuli 7 33 41N28 44E50 -2:59:20
Mars'aty 2 30 60N05 60E29 -4:01:56
Martemjanovskij 2
23 55N54 80E22 -5:21:28
Martisovo 6 39 56N34 31E55 -2:07:40
Martovaja 23 45 49N57 36E57 -2:27:48
Martuk 9 30 50N46 56E31 -3:46:04
Martuni 1 34 40N08 45E19 -3:01:16
Martuni 3 34 39N48 47E06 -3:08:24
Martynoviči 23
44 51N17 29E37 -1:58:28
Martynovka 23 44 49N38 31E18 -2:05:12
Martynovo 9 32 50N43 50E23 -3:21:32
Martynovskij 6
34 50N29 42E18 -2:49:12
Marusino 6 39 55N42 37E59 -2:31:56
Maruškino 6 39 55N36 37E12 -2:28:48
Mary 22 30 37N36 61E50 -4:07:20
Masak 9 24 43N37 78E18 -5:13:12
Masally 3 34 39N03 48E40 -3:14:40
Maševka 23 45 49N26 34E52 -2:19:28
Maševo 23 44 52N06 32E48 -2:11:12
Masis 1 34 40N00 44E29 -2:57:56
Maškino 6 39 54N53 36E08 -2:24:32
Maškoviči 6 39 54N11 36E17 -2:25:08
Masl'anino 2 21 54N20 84E13 -5:36:52
Masl'anskaja 2
30 55N56 70E08 -4:40:32
Maslova 6 9 59N47 30E48 -2:03:12
Maslovka 6 41 51N33 39E14 -2:36:56
Maslovo 2 30 60N07 60E30 -4:02:00
Massandra 23 45 44N32 34E12 -2:16:48
Massiaru 5 35 58N00 24E35 -1:38:20
Maštaga 3 34 40N32 50E00 -3:20:00
Mataj 9 24 45N53 78E43 -5:14:52
Matani 7 33 42N06 45E13 -3:00:52
Matča 21 24 39N27 69E39 -4:38:36
M'atlevo 6 39 54N54 35E39 -2:22:36
Matočkin Šar 17
29 73N16 56E27 -3:45:48
Maturino 6 40 59N06 37E55 -2:31:40
Matusov 23 44 49N03 31E34 -2:06:16
Matvejevka 6 30 53N32 53E29 -3:33:56
Matvejev-Kurgan 6
40 47N35 38E52 -2:35:28
Matvejevo 6 30 57N47 57E51 -3:51:24
Matvejevo 6 41 58N38 43E30 -2:54:00
Matyševo 6 34 50N49 44E12 -2:56:48
Maykop → Majkop 6
47 44N35 40E07 -2:40:28
Maza 6 41 57N14 44E13 -2:56:52
Mazanovo 2 14 51N40 128E52 -8:35:28
Mazarsu 10 24 41N56 72E40 -4:50:40
Mažeikiai 14 37 56N19 22E20 -1:29:20
Mazirbe 13 36 57N41 22E21 -1:29:24
Mazsalaca 13 36 57N52 25E03 -1:40:12
Mazul'skij 2 21 56N16 90E28 -6:01:52
Mcensk 6 39 53N17 36E35 -2:26:20
Meana 22 30 36N55 60E30 -4:02:00
Mečebilovo 23 45 49N04 36E41 -2:26:44
Mečetinskaja 6
47 46N46 40E27 -2:41:48
Mečetka 6 41 50N54 40E05 -2:40:20
Mechel'ta 6 47 42N48 46E30 -3:06:00
Mechonskoje 2 30 56N09 64E34 -4:18:16
Mechren'ga 6 41 61N46 40E57 -2:43:48
Mečigmen 2 2 65N28 172W05 11:28:20
Medenica 23 44 49N26 23E45 -1:35:00
Medininkai 14 37 54N32 25E40 -1:42:40
Mednogorsk 6 30 51N24 57E37 -3:50:28
Mednoje 6 39 56N56 35E29 -2:21:56
Mednyj Island 11
4 54N45 167E35-11:10:20
Mednyj, Ostrov 11
4 54N45 167E35-11:10:20
Medvedevo 2 25 60N37 77E21 -5:09:24
Medvedevo 6 41 56N37 47E47 -3:11:08
Medvedevo 6 41 60N02 43E01 -2:52:04
Medvedevskoje 6
40 58N58 35E58 -2:23:52
Medvedickij 6 34 50N47 44E43 -2:58:52
Medvedok 6 42 57N23 50E05 -3:20:20
Medvedovskaja 6
47 45N27 39E01 -2:36:04
Medvenka 6 39 51N26 36E07 -2:24:28
Medvenka 6 39 54N15 37E42 -2:30:48
Medvežinka 23 45 48N10 39E31 -2:38:04
Medvežjegorsk 6
9 62N55 34E23 -2:17:32
Medvežji Oz'ora 6
39 55N52 37E59 -2:31:56
Medvežskaja 6 29 64N57 57E34 -3:50:16
Medvin 23 44 49N23 30E47 -2:03:08
Medyn' 6 39 54N58 35E52 -2:23:28
Medžibož 23 44 49N26 27E25 -1:49:40
Meget 2 20 52N24 104E03 -6:56:12
Megra 6 41 66N09 41E37 -2:46:28
Megra 6 40 60N10 37E13 -2:28:52
Megri 1 34 38N56 46E16 -3:05:04
Mehikoorma 5 35 58N14 27E28 -1:49:52
Mejnypil'gyno 2
2 62N32 177E02-11:48:08
Mel'cany 6 41 54N28 44E43 -2:58:52
Melechovo 6 40 56N17 41E17 -2:45:08
Meleck 2 21 57N25 90E12 -6:00:48
Meleješt' 15 46 46N59 29E33 -1:58:12
Melekess 6 42 54N14 49E39 -3:18:36
Melenki 6 40 55N20 41E38 -2:46:32
Meleškoviči 4 39 51N56 28E59 -1:55:56
Meleuz 6 30 52N58 55E55 -3:43:40
Mel'guny 6 41 52N09 40E52 -2:43:28
Melichovo 6 39 50N42 36E48 -2:27:12
Melichovo 6 39 55N07 37E39 -2:30:36
Melitopol' 23 45 46N50 35E22 -2:21:28
Mel'nica-Podol'skaja 23
45 48N37 26E10 -1:44:40
Mel'nikovo 2 23 56N34 84E05 -5:36:20
Mel'nikovo 21 24 40N19 70E19 -4:41:16
Melovatka 23 45 49N21 38E11 -2:32:44
Melovoje 23 45 49N22 40E06 -2:40:24
Memel → Klaipėda 14
37 55N43 21E07 -1:24:28
Mena 23 44 51N31 32E13 -2:08:52
Menčikury 23 45 47N04 34E48 -2:19:12
Mendelejevsk 6
41 55N54 52E20 -3:29:20
Mend'ukino 6 39 54N47 38E51 -2:35:24
Men'uša 6 9 58N23 30E42 -2:02:48
Menzelinsk 6 41 55N43 53E08 -3:32:32
Mereckij 9 24 43N48 74E42 -4:58:48
Merefa 23 45 49N49 36E03 -2:24:12
Mereny 15 46 46N58 29E04 -1:56:16
Mergenevo 9 32 49N56 51E17 -3:25:08
Merke 9 24 42N52 73E11 -4:52:44
Merkinė 14 37 54N10 24E10 -1:36:40
Merkuloviči 4 39 52N58 30E36 -2:02:24
Merlejevo 6 39 55N05 37E13 -2:28:52
Mer'oža 6 40 59N02 36E23 -2:25:32
Mērsrags 13 36 57N21 23E07 -1:32:28
Merv → Mary 22
30 37N36 61E50 -4:07:20
Mery 6 39 55N49 36E36 -2:26:24
Mes'agutovo 6 30 55N35 58E20 -3:53:20
Meščerino 6 39 53N37 37E23 -2:29:32
Meščerino 6 39 55N11 38E21 -2:33:24
Meščerskij 6 39 55N40 37E25 -2:29:40
Meščerskoje 6 39 55N17 37E38 -2:30:32
Meščovsk 6 39 54N19 35E17 -2:21:08
Meščura 6 41 63N20 50E52 -3:23:28
Meškuičiai 14 37 56N05 23E28 -1:33:52
Mestia 7 33 43N03 42E43 -2:50:52
Metallostroj 6 9 59N47 30E33 -2:02:12
Metechi 7 33 41N55 44E21 -2:57:24
Meždurečensk 2
21 53N42 88E03 -5:52:12
Meždurečenskij 2
30 59N36 65E53 -4:23:32
Mezen' 6 41 65N50 44E13 -2:56:52
Meževaja 23 45 48N16 36E44 -2:26:56
Mežgorje 23 44 48N32 23E30 -1:34:00
Mezinovskij 6 40 55N30 40E21 -2:41:24
Mežirič 23 45 50N43 34E29 -2:17:56
Mežoz'ornyj 2 30 54N09 59E23 -3:57:32
Mgači 19 8 51N05 142E17 -9:29:08
Mglin 6 39 53N04 32E51 -2:11:24
Miass 2 30 54N59 60E06 -4:00:24
Mičavičevnik 6
29 64N14 57E58 -3:51:52
Micha-Cchakaja 7
33 42N17 42E04 -2:48:16
Michajlo-Kocubinskoje 23
44 51N27 31E04 -2:04:16
Michajlov 6 40 54N14 39E02 -2:36:08
Michajlovka 23
45 47N16 35E14 -2:20:56
Michajlovka 23
45 48N30 38E54 -2:35:36
Michajlovka 23
45 48N09 37E22 -2:29:28
Michajlovka 23
45 48N44 37E16 -2:29:04
Michajlovka 6 9 60N04 30E14 -2:00:56
Michajlovka 6 9 59N43 30E01 -2:00:04
Michajlovka 2 23 51N49 79E45 -5:19:00
Michajlovka 2 23 56N26 78E53 -5:15:32
Michajlovka 9 24 53N51 76E32 -5:06:08
Michajlovka 2 20 50N26 104E10 -6:56:40
Michajlovka 2 20 55N30 114E09 -7:36:36
Michajlovka 2 16 51N07 119E20 -7:57:20
Michajlovka 2 20 52N57 103E18 -6:53:12
Michajlovka 2 14 49N13 129E56 -8:39:44
Michajlovka 2 27 43N56 132E00 -8:48:00
Michajlovka 9 24 42N50 75E42 -5:02:48
Michajlovka 10
24 42N37 78E20 -5:13:20
Michajlovka 9 24 43N06 71E36 -4:46:24
Michajlovka 6 34 47N38 46E54 -3:07:36
Michajlovka 6 34 50N05 43E15 -2:53:00
Michajlovka 6 40 49N53 39E38 -2:38:32
Michajlovka 23
45 49N19 36E28 -2:25:52
Michajlovo 6 41 56N56 45E04 -3:00:16
Michajlovo-Aleksandrovskij 6
47 49N13 40E15 -2:41:00
Michajlovskaja 6
34 50N58 41E52 -2:47:28
Michajlovskij 2
23 51N41 79E47 -5:19:08
Michajlovskij 9
30 50N17 55E23 -3:41:32
Michajlovskij 6
41 56N11 45E47 -3:03:08
Michajlovskij 6
41 60N05 43E29 -2:53:56
Michajlovskoje 6
39 55N50 36E20 -2:25:20
Michajlovskoje 6
39 55N35 37E35 -2:30:20
Michajlovskoje 6
41 56N11 45E47 -3:03:08
Michajlovskoje 6
40 58N23 37E40 -2:30:40
Michalevo 6 39 55N27 38E26 -2:33:44
Michali 6 39 55N17 39E05 -2:36:20
Michalkovo 6 39 54N11 37E33 -2:30:12
Michanoviči 4 39 53N45 27E40 -1:50:40
Michejevo 2 20 57N10 104E53 -6:59:32
Michel'sona 6 39 55N42 37E54 -2:31:36
Michel'sonovskij 6
39 55N42 37E54 -2:31:36
Micheta 7 33 41N52 44E44 -2:58:56
Michnevo 6 39 55N07 37E58 -2:31:52
Michninskaja 6
41 60N26 46E14 -3:04:56
Michurinsk → Mičurinsk 6
41 52N54 40E30 -2:42:00
Mičurinsk 6 41 52N54 40E30 -2:42:00
Mignoviči 6 39 54N16 31E34 -2:06:16
Migulinskaja 6
47 49N42 41E16 -2:45:04
Mijaly 9 30 48N57 53E42 -3:34:48
Mikaševiči 4 39 52N13 27E28 -1:49:52
Mikoyan 16 34 39N45 45E20 -3:01:20
Mikšino 6 39 57N15 35E43 -2:22:52
Mikulincy 23 44 49N24 25E38 -1:42:32
Mikulino 6 39 55N02 31E07 -2:04:28
Mikun' 6 41 62N21 50E06 -3:20:24
Milaševiči 23 44 51N39 27E56 -1:51:44
Mil'atino 6 39 54N29 34E18 -2:17:12
Mil'atino 6 39 55N41 35E48 -2:23:12
Mil'kovo 2 4 54N43 158E37-10:34:28
Millerovo 6 47 48N55 40E25 -2:41:40
Millerovo 6 40 47N49 39E15 -2:37:00
Millionnyj 2 16 54N30 126E19 -8:25:16
Miloslaviči 4 39 53N41 32E15 -2:09:00
Miloslavskoje 6
40 53N34 39E24 -2:37:36
Mil'utinskaja 6
47 48N38 41E40 -2:46:40
Minbulak 10 24 41N30 75E53 -5:03:32
Mind'ak 6 30 54N02 58E48 -3:55:12
Mindživan 3 34 39N03 46E42 -3:06:48
Mineral'nyje Vody 6
47 44N12 43E08 -2:52:32
Mingečaur 3 34 40N45 47E03 -3:08:12
Mingrel'skaja 6
47 45N01 38E20 -2:33:20
Minjar 2 30 55N04 57E33 -3:50:12
Min'kovo 6 41 59N42 43E28 -2:53:52
Minkulincy 23 44 49N24 25E38 -1:42:32
Min-Kuš 10 24 41N41 74E28 -4:57:52
Minsk 4 39 53N54 27E34 -1:50:16
Minulovo 6 9 60N03 30E45 -2:03:00
Minur'uk 10 24 40N56 73E22 -4:53:28
Minusinsk 2 21 53N43 91E42 -6:06:48
Minžir 15 46 46N40 28E19 -1:53:16
Miory 4 39 55N37 27E38 -1:50:32
Mir 4 39 53N27 26E28 -1:45:52
Miraki 24 30 39N02 67E10 -4:28:40
Mir-Bašir 3 34 40N20 46E55 -3:07:40
Mireny 15 46 46N58 29E04 -1:56:16
Mirgorod 23 44 49N58 33E36 -2:14:24
Mirgorodka 9 30 50N58 53E33 -3:34:12
Mirnoje Ozero 2
23 57N44 78E45 -5:15:00
Mirnyj 2 16 62N33 113E53 -7:35:32
Mirnyj 6 34 53N30 50E18 -3:21:12
Mirnyj 23 44 50N57 28E34 -1:54:16
Mironovka 23 44 49N39 30E59 -2:03:56
Mironovo 2 20 58N19 109E38 -7:18:32
Mironovskij 23
45 48N29 38E17 -2:33:08
Miropol' 23 44 50N07 27E41 -1:50:44
Miropolje 23 45 51N02 35E16 -2:21:04
Mirovoje 23 45 47N45 34E45 -2:19:00
Mirovskoje 23 45 48N05 33E23 -2:13:32
Mirza-Aki 10 24 40N45 73E25 -4:53:40
Mirzaani 7 33 41N23 46E09 -3:04:36
Misailovo 6 39 55N34 37E49 -2:31:16
Mišelevka 2 20 52N51 103E09 -6:52:36
Mišicha 2 20 51N38 105E35 -7:02:20
Misirevo 6 39 56N16 36E45 -2:27:00
Miškino 6 9 59N42 30E45 -2:03:00

Miškino 2 30 55N20 63E55 -4:15:40
Mišn'ovo 6 39 53N58 36E21 -2:25:24
Mišurin Rog 23 45 48N50 33E58 -2:15:52
Mišutino 6 40 59N31 36E01 -2:24:04
Mišutino 6 39 56N23 38E06 -2:32:24
Mit'ajevo 6 39 55N16 36E32 -2:26:08
Mit'ajevo 2 30 60N17 61E06 -4:04:24
Mit'akino 6 39 54N24 38E50 -2:35:20
Mit'akinskaja 6 47 48N36 39E47 -2:39:08
Mitau → Jelgava 13 36 56N39 23E42 -1:34:48
Mitino 6 39 55N51 37E21 -2:29:24
Mitiškovo 6 39 54N40 33E31 -2:14:04
Mitrofanovka 6 40 49N58 39E42 -2:38:48
Mitrofanovo 6 29 63N13 56E00 -3:44:00
Mius 6 34 51N26 47E56 -3:11:44
Miusinsk 23 45 48N05 38E53 -2:35:32
Miževiči 4 39 52N59 25E05 -1:40:20
Mizoč 23 44 50N24 26E09 -1:44:36
Mlinov 23 44 50N31 25E37 -1:42:28
Močalejevka 6 34 53N38 51E46 -3:27:04
Močališče 6 41 56N21 48E23 -3:13:32
Močily 6 39 54N20 38E41 -2:34:44
Mogdy 2 11 50N35 133E51 -8:55:24
Mogilev → Mogil'ov 4 39 53N54 30E21 -2:01:24
Mogil'ov 23 45 48N52 34E29 -2:17:56
Mogil'ov 4 39 53N54 30E21 -2:01:24
Mogil'ov-Podol'skij 23 45 48N27 27E48 -1:51:12
Mogoča 2 16 53N44 119E44 -7:58:56
Mogočin 2 23 57N43 83E34 -5:34:16
Mogojto 2 20 54N25 110E27 -7:21:48
Mogojtuj 2 16 51N17 114E55 -7:39:40
Mogzon 2 18 51N45 111E58 -7:27:52
Moinkum 9 24 43N48 73E41 -4:54:44
Mointy 9 24 47N13 73E21 -4:53:24
Mõisaküla 5 35 58N06 25E11 -1:40:44
Moisejeviči 4 39 53N13 28E17 -1:53:08
Moisejevka 23 45 49N14 39E51 -2:39:24
Moisejevka 2 23 58N05 76E16 -5:05:04
Moisejevo Alabuška 6 41 51N54 42E06 -2:48:24
Mojnalyk 2 21 51N18 95E33 -6:22:12
Mokino 6 42 57N27 49E11 -3:16:44
Moklakan 2 16 54N56 118E56 -7:55:44
Mokraja Jel'muta 6 47 46N51 41E41 -2:46:44
Mokraja Ol'chovka 6 34 50N28 44E59 -2:59:56
Mokrany 4 39 51N50 24E14 -1:36:56
Mokro-Jelančik 23 45 47N42 38E31 -2:34:04
Mokrous 6 34 51N14 47E37 -3:10:28
Mokrousovo 2 30 55N48 66E45 -4:27:00
Mokrušinskoje 2 21 57N31 93E11 -6:12:44
Mokryj Gašun 6 47 46N53 42E45 -2:51:00
Mokryj Kor 6 39 54N34 37E58 -2:31:52
Mokšan 6 41 53N26 44E37 -2:58:28
Mokvin 23 44 50N57 26E48 -1:47:12
Molčanovka 6 47 46N52 38E37 -2:34:28
Molčanovo 2 23 57N35 83E48 -5:35:12
Moldary 9 24 50N47 78E29 -5:13:56
Molėtai 14 37 55N14 25E25 -1:41:40
Moločansk 23 45 47N12 35E36 -2:22:24
Moločnoje 6 40 59N17 39E41 -2:38:44
Molodečno 4 39 54N19 26E49 -1:47:16
Molodi 6 39 55N17 37E31 -2:30:04
Molodogvardejsk 23 45 48N20 39E40 -2:38:40
Molodoj Tud 6 39 56N26 33E36 -2:14:24
Molod'ožnyj 2 11 50N23 136E48 -9:07:12
Molokovo 6 9 58N10 36E45 -2:27:00
Molokovo 6 39 55N34 37E52 -2:31:28
Molotkoviči 4 39 52N07 25E56 -1:43:44
Molotov → Perm' 6 30 58N00 56E15 -3:45:00
Molotovsk → Severodvinsk 6 40 64N34 39E50 -2:39:20
Molvoticy 6 39 57N25 32E20 -2:09:20
Molžaninovo 6 39 55N56 37E22 -2:29:28
Monachovo 23 45 48N09 38E07 -2:32:28
Monakino 2 27 43N24 133E29 -8:53:56
Monaš 9 32 46N58 50E36 -3:22:24
Monastyrišče 23 44 49N00 29E49 -1:59:16
Monastyriska 23 44 49N06 25E11 -1:40:44
Monastyrščina 6 39 54N21 31E50 -2:07:20
Mončegorsk 6 9 67N54 32E58 -2:11:52
Mondy 2 20 51N40 100E59 -6:43:56
Monetnyj 2 30 57N03 60E53 -4:03:32
Mongoj 2 20 53N57 113E50 -7:35:20
Monino 6 39 55N50 38E11 -2:32:44
Mõniste 5 35 57N35 26E33 -1:46:12
Monogarovo 6 39 54N42 38E45 -2:35:00
Montaj-Taš 9 24 42N06 68E58 -4:35:52
Mor'akovskij Zaton 2 21 56N45 84E41 -5:38:44
Morcy 6 34 51N18 47E51 -3:11:24
Mordino 6 41 61N21 51E52 -3:27:28
Mordovo 6 34 51N07 45E48 -3:03:12
Mordovo 6 41 52N05 40E46 -2:43:04
Mordovo-Adel'akovo 6 34 53N47 51E36 -3:26:24
Mordovskij Buguruslan 6 32 53N48 52E31 -3:30:04
Mordves 6 39 54N34 38E13 -2:32:52
Morec 6 34 51N03 44E03 -2:56:12
Morga 6 41 54N26 46E29 -3:05:56
Morgauši 6 41 55N58 46E47 -3:07:08
Morino 6 39 57N54 30E22 -2:01:28
Morki 6 41 56N25 49E01 -3:16:04
Morkiny Gory 6 39 57N33 36E18 -2:25:12
Mormal' 4 39 52N45 29E53 -1:59:32
Moroč' 4 39 52N34 27E36 -1:50:24
Morošečnoje 2 4 56N24 156E12 -10:24:48
Morovsk 23 44 51N06 30E50 -2:03:20
Morozkovo 2 30 59N29 61E01 -4:04:04
Morozovka 6 40 50N09 39E38 -2:38:32
Morozovka 23 45 49N28 39E54 -2:39:36
Morozovsk 6 47 48N22 41E50 -2:47:20
Morozovskaja 6 41 61N10 50E18 -3:21:12
Moršansk 6 41 53N26 41E49 -2:47:16
Morščichino 6 39 55N56 37E20 -2:29:20
Morskaja Masel'ga 6 9 63N06 34E54 -2:19:36
Morty 6 41 55N49 51E44 -3:26:56
Morženga 6 41 59N37 40E12 -2:40:48
Mosal'sk 6 39 54N29 34E59 -2:19:56
Mošanicy 6 39 54N56 38E23 -2:33:32
Moscou → Moskva 6 39 55N45 37E35 -2:30:20
Moscow → Moskva 6 39 55N45 37E35 -2:30:20
Moscú → Moskva 6 39 55N45 37E35 -2:30:20
Mošenskoje 6 9 58N31 34E35 -2:18:20
Moskal'vo 19 8 53N35 142E30 -9:30:00
Moskau → Moskva 6 39 55N45 37E35 -2:30:20
Moškino 6 41 57N45 45E20 -3:01:20
Moškovo 2 21 55N18 83E37 -5:34:28
Moskovskaja Slav'anka 6 9 59N45 30E30 -2:02:00
Moskva (Moscow) 6 39 55N45 37E35 -2:30:20
Mošny 23 44 49N32 31E44 -2:06:56
Mošok 6 40 55N48 41E17 -2:45:08
Mosolovo 6 41 54N17 40E32 -2:42:08
Mosovsk 2 20 51N44 105E53 -7:03:32
Mospino 23 45 47N53 38E03 -2:32:12
Mosta 6 40 56N32 42E10 -2:48:40
Mostiska 23 44 49N48 23E09 -1:32:36
Mostki 23 45 49N19 38E30 -2:34:00
Mostok 4 39 53N59 30E28 -2:01:52
Mostovaja 6 39 56N13 33E08 -2:12:32
Mostovoje 23 45 47N24 30E59 -2:03:56
Mostovskoj 6 47 44N25 40E48 -2:43:12
Mostovskoje 2 30 55N46 66E22 -4:25:28
Mosty 4 39 53N25 24E32 -1:38:08
Motol' 4 39 52N19 25E36 -1:42:24
Motorki 6 42 56N53 51E29 -3:25:56
Motorovo 2 24 56N31 71E10 -4:44:40
Motovilovo 6 41 55N36 43E51 -2:55:24
Motygino 2 21 58N11 94E40 -6:18:40
Motyklejka 2 6 59N26 148E38 -9:54:32
Motyžin 23 44 50N23 29E55 -1:59:40
Motyzlej 6 41 54N54 42E54 -2:51:36
Možajevka 6 47 48N44 39E45 -2:39:00
Možajsk 6 39 55N30 36E01 -2:24:04
Možajskij 6 9 59N43 30E07 -2:00:28
Možarovka 6 30 51N09 59E05 -3:56:20
Možarov Majdan 6 41 55N37 45E53 -3:03:32
Možary 6 41 53N53 41E02 -2:44:08
Mozdok 6 47 43N44 44E38 -2:58:32
Možga 6 42 56N23 52E17 -3:29:08
Mozolevo 6 9 59N19 33E51 -2:15:24
Mozuli 6 39 56N36 28E11 -1:52:44
Mozyr' 4 39 52N03 29E14 -1:56:56
Mrakovo 6 30 52N43 56E38 -3:46:32
Mšinskaja 6 9 59N01 29E57 -1:59:48
Msta 6 39 57N55 34E29 -2:17:56
Mstera 6 40 56N23 41E56 -2:47:44
Mstislavl' 4 39 54N02 31E42 -2:06:48
Mstiž 4 39 54N34 28E10 -1:52:40
Mtsensk → Mcensk 6 39 53N17 36E35 -2:26:20
Muchanovo 6 39 56N31 38E20 -2:33:20
Muchen 2 11 48N10 136E13 -9:04:52
Muchino 6 42 58N11 51E02 -3:24:08
Muchino 2 16 52N16 127E14 -8:28:56
Muchor-Konduj 2 16 52N25 113E16 -7:33:04
Muchoršibir' 2 20 51N03 107E50 -7:11:20
Muchrani 7 33 41N56 44E35 -2:58:20
Muchtadir 3 34 41N41 48E46 -3:15:04
Muchtolovo 6 41 55N27 43E13 -2:52:52
Mučikan 2 16 53N02 120E27 -8:01:48
Mučkapskij 6 41 51N52 42E28 -2:49:52
Mučkas 6 41 64N02 48E27 -3:13:48
M'uc'ucl'u 3 34 40N28 47E55 -3:11:40
Mudjuga 6 40 63N46 39E15 -2:37:00
Mugodžarskaja 9 30 48N36 58E27 -3:53:48
Mugrejevskij 6 40 56N36 42E21 -2:49:24
Mugur-Aksy 2 21 50N21 90E30 -6:02:00
Muja 2 20 56N24 115E39 -7:42:36
Mujezerskij 6 9 63N57 31E55 -2:07:40
Mujnak 24 30 43N48 59E02 -3:56:08
Mukačevo 23 44 48N27 22E45 -1:31:00
Mukry 22 30 37N36 65E44 -4:22:56
Mukur 9 30 48N03 54E30 -3:38:00
Mulaly 9 24 45N27 78E19 -5:13:16
Mul'da 6 29 67N28 63E34 -4:14:16
Mullovka 6 42 54N13 49E25 -3:17:40
Mumra 6 34 45N47 47E41 -3:10:44
Munajly 9 30 46N47 54E31 -3:38:04
Mundybaš 2 21 53N14 87E19 -5:49:16
Munkács → Mukačevo 23 44 48N27 22E45 -1:31:00
Munozero 6 9 67N05 34E12 -2:16:48
Muraši 6 42 59N24 48E55 -3:15:40
Muraški 6 39 55N59 37E45 -2:31:00
Muratkovo 2 30 58N26 62E23 -4:09:32
Muratovo 23 45 48N48 38E45 -2:35:00
Muravjovka 2 14 49N50 127E44 -8:30:56
Muravjovo 6 39 56N14 34E14 -2:16:56
Murgab 21 24 38N10 73E59 -4:55:56
Murinja 2 20 54N47 107E21 -7:09:24
Murino 6 9 60N03 30E27 -2:01:48
Murino 2 20 51N30 104E23 -6:57:32
Murmansk 6 9 68N58 33E05 -2:12:20
Murmino 6 40 54N36 40E03 -2:40:12
Murom 6 40 55N34 42E02 -2:48:08
Muromcevo 2 24 56N23 75E14 -5:00:56
Murovanyje Kurilovcy 23 45 48N43 27E31 -1:50:04
Murukta 2 19 67N46 102E01 -6:48:04
Musl'umovo 6 41 55N18 53E12 -3:32:48
Mustafino 6 30 55N01 53E38 -3:34:32
Mustajevo 6 32 51N48 53E25 -3:33:40
Mustajõe 5 35 57N59 26E58 -1:47:52
Mustjala 5 35 58N28 22E14 -1:28:56
Mustla 5 35 58N14 25E52 -1:43:28
Mustvee 5 35 58N51 26E56 -1:47:44
Mutoraj 2 19 61N20 100E30 -6:42:00
Mužač' 6 39 54N22 36E21 -2:25:24
Muži 2 28 65N22 64E40 -4:18:40
Mužiči 6 47 43N03 44E59 -2:59:56
Mužiksu 9 24 47N42 84E58 -5:39:52
Myjeldino 6 29 61N46 54E48 -3:39:12
Myjlybulak 9 24 48N57 75E13 -5:00:52
Myla 6 41 65N25 50E48 -3:23:12
Myl'džino 2 23 59N03 78E29 -5:13:56
Mynaral 9 24 45N25 73E41 -4:54:44
Myšega 6 39 54N31 37E02 -2:28:08
Myski 2 21 53N42 87E48 -5:51:12
Myškino 6 40 57N47 38E27 -2:33:48
Mys Šmidta 2 2 68N56 179W26 11:57:44
Mys Vchodnoj 2 21 73N53 86E43 -5:46:52
Mysy 6 30 60N34 53E57 -3:35:48
Mys Želanija 17 29 76N56 68E35 -4:34:20
Myt 6 40 56N48 42E21 -2:49:24
Mytišči 6 39 55N55 37E46 -2:31:04
Mytishchi → Mytišči 6 39 55N55 37E46 -2:31:04
Mytišino 6 39 54N48 34E01 -2:16:04
Myzovo 23 44 51N22 24E31 -1:38:04
Naberežnoje 6 39 55N57 37E58 -2:31:52
Naberežnyje Čelny 6 41 55N42 52E19 -3:29:16
Načalovo 6 34 46N20 48E11 -3:12:44
Nachabino 6 39 55N51 37E11 -2:28:44
Nachičevan' 16 34 39N13 45E24 -3:01:36
Nachodka 2 27 42N48 132E52 -8:51:28
Nadeždinskoje 2 11 48N18 133E11 -8:52:44
Nadporožje 6 9 60N28 34E17 -2:17:08
Nadterečnaja 6 47 43N37 45E22 -3:01:28
Nadvoicy 6 9 63N52 34E15 -2:17:00
Nadvornaja 23 44 48N38 24E34 -1:38:16
Nadym 2 25 65N35 72E42 -4:50:48
Nadyrovo 6 41 54N53 52E28 -3:29:52
Naftalan 3 34 40N31 46E50 -3:07:20
Nagavskaja 6 34 47N47 42E50 -2:51:20
Nagibino 2 24 55N46 72E43 -4:50:52
Nagol'no-Tarasovka 23 45 48N00 39E29 -2:37:56
Nagorje 6 39 56N55 38E16 -2:33:04
Nagornoje 23 45 45N26 28E27 -1:53:48
Nagornyj 6 9 59N43 30E16 -2:01:04
Nagornyj 2 16 55N58 124E57 -8:19:48
Nagorsk 6 42 59N18 50E48 -3:23:12
Nagorskoje 6 39 56N54 38E06 -2:32:24
Najstenjarvi 6 9 62N16 32E38 -2:10:32
Nalchik → Nal'čik 6 47 43N29 43E37 -2:54:28
Nal'čik 6 47 43N29 43E37 -2:54:28
Namangan 24 24 41N00 71E40 -4:46:40
Namdanak 24 24 41N11 69E42 -4:38:48
Naminga 2 16 56N33 118E41 -7:54:44
N'andoma 6 41 61N40 40E12 -2:40:48
Napalkovo 2 25 70N03 73E47 -4:55:08
Napareuli 7 33 42N03 45E31 -3:02:04
Napas 2 23 59N53 81E58 -5:27:52
Narasun 2 16 50N06 112E58 -7:31:52
Narazeni 7 33 42N27 41E57 -2:47:48
Nariman 10 24 40N34 72E48 -4:51:12
Narimanabad 3 34 38N53 48E52 -3:15:28
Narjan-Mar 6 29 67N39 53E00 -3:32:00
Narma 6 41 54N46 42E01 -2:48:04
Narmušad' 6 40 54N40 41E07 -2:44:28
Narodiči 23 44 51N13 29E03 -1:56:12
Naro-Fominsk 6 39 55N23 36E43 -2:26:52
Naro-Osakovo 6 39 55N33 36E33 -2:26:12
Narovčat 6 41 53N52 43E41 -2:54:44
Narovl'a 4 39 51N48 29E29 -1:57:56
Nartkala 6 47 43N33 43E50 -2:55:20
Naruksovo 6 41 54N37 44E33 -2:58:12
Narva 5 35 59N23 28E12 -1:52:48
Narva 2 21 55N25 93E39 -6:14:36
Narva-Jõesuu 5 35 59N27 28E03 -1:52:12
Narvan 24 30 40N15 67E12 -4:28:48
Narym 2 23 58N58 81E30 -5:26:00
Naryn 2 21 50N13 96E27 -6:25:48
Naryn 10 24 41N26 75E59 -5:03:56

Narynkol 9 24 42N43 80E12 -5:20:48
Naryškino 6 41 52N27 43E41 -2:54:44
Naryškino 6 39 52N58 35E44 -2:22:56
Nasadkino 6 39 56N29 37E21 -2:29:24
Naskaftym 6 41 52N57 45E38 -3:02:32
Nasosnyj 3 34 40N37 49E34 -3:18:16
Nasriddinbek 24 24 40N41 71E55 -4:47:40
Nastasjino 6 39 54N28 38E16 -2:33:04
Nastaška 23 44 49N39 30E19 -2:01:16
Nasva 6 39 56N35 30E10 -2:00:40
Nataljevka 6 40 47N10 38E29 -2:33:56
Nataljin Jar 6 34 51N46 50E35 -3:22:20
Nataljino 6 34 52N56 49E02 -3:16:08
Natuchajevskaja 6 47 44N54 37E34 -2:30:16
Nau 21 24 40N09 69E22 -4:37:28
Naučnyj 23 45 44N44 34E01 -2:16:04
Naugol'noje 6 39 56N22 38E11 -2:32:44
Naujamiestis 14 37 55N41 24E04 -1:36:16
Naujoji Akmenė 14 37 56N19 22E55 -1:31:40
Naukan 2 2 66N01 169W43 11:18:52
Naumovščina 6 9 58N23 28E20 -1:53:20
Naunak 2 23 59N00 80E13 -5:20:52
Naurskaja 6 47 43N38 45E19 -3:01:16
Nauški 2 20 50N28 106E07 -7:04:28
Navašino 6 40 55N32 42E12 -2:48:48
Navesnoje 6 39 52N17 37E57 -2:31:48
Navl'a 6 39 52N51 34E30 -2:18:00
Navoi 24 30 40N15 65E15 -4:21:00
Navoloki 6 40 57N28 41E59 -2:47:56
Nazarjevo 6 39 55N22 36E24 -2:25:36
Nazarjevo 6 39 55N59 37E16 -2:29:04
Nazarovo 2 21 56N01 90E26 -6:01:44
Nazarovskij 6 47 49N33 40E56 -2:43:44
Nazija 6 9 59N50 31E35 -2:06:20
Nazimicha 6 39 55N59 38E08 -2:32:32
Nazimovo 2 21 59N30 90E58 -6:03:52
Nazina 2 23 60N07 78E52 -5:15:28
Nazran' 6 47 43N13 44E46 -2:59:04
Nazyvajevsk 2 24 55N34 71E21 -4:45:24
Nebit-Dag 22 30 39N30 54E22 -3:37:28
Nebolči 6 9 59N08 33E18 -2:13:12
Nebyloje 6 39 56N22 39E59 -2:39:56
Nečajannoje 23 45 46N57 31E33 -2:06:12
Nečajevka 6 41 53N17 44E27 -2:57:48
Nečajevo 6 39 54N42 37E23 -2:29:32
Nechajevskaja 6 34 50N25 41E44 -2:46:56
Nechajevskij 6 34 50N25 41E44 -2:46:56
Nechvorošča 23 45 49N09 34E44 -2:18:56
Nedančiči 23 44 51N30 30E37 -2:02:28
Nedel'noje 6 39 54N50 36E39 -2:26:36
Nedrigajlov 23 44 50N50 33E53 -2:15:32
Nefedjevo 6 39 54N39 37E56 -2:31:44
Nef'odovo 2 25 58N48 72E34 -4:50:16
Nefteabad 21 24 40N12 70E34 -4:42:16
Neftečala 3 34 39N23 49E16 -3:17:04
Neftegorsk 6 47 44N22 39E42 -2:38:48
Neftekamsk 6 30 56N06 54E17 -3:37:08
Neftekumsk 6 47 44N45 44E48 -2:59:12
Negoreloje 4 39 53N36 27E04 -1:48:16
Neja 6 41 58N18 43E54 -2:55:36
Nekl'udovo 6 41 56N24 43E59 -2:55:56
Nekrasino 6 39 56N18 36E33 -2:26:12
Nekrasovka 6 39 55N41 37E56 -2:31:44
Nekrasovo 6 34 51N10 45E18 -3:01:12
Nekrasovo 6 40 54N30 38E57 -2:35:48
Nekrasovskoje 6 40 57N41 40E22 -2:41:28
Nel'aty 2 20 56N29 115E41 -7:42:44
Nelidovo 6 39 56N13 32E46 -2:11:04
Nel'kan 2 11 57N40 136E13 -9:04:52
Nel'ma 2 11 47N39 139E09 -9:16:36
Nema 6 42 57N31 50E31 -3:22:04
Neman (Ragnit) 8 38 55N02 22E02 -1:28:08
Nemčinovka 6 39 55N43 37E23 -2:29:32
Nemenčinė 14 37 54N51 25E29 -1:41:56
Nemeriči 6 39 53N51 33E59 -2:15:56
Nemirov 23 44 50N07 23E25 -1:33:40
Nemirov 23 45 48N58 28E50 -1:55:20
Nemirovo 6 39 55N54 36E12 -2:24:48
Nemoviči 23 44 51N16 26E38 -1:46:32
Nenaševo 6 39 54N34 37E28 -2:29:52
Nepecino 6 39 55N12 38E37 -2:34:28
Nerčinsk 2 16 51N58 116E35 -7:46:20
Nerčinskij Zavod 2 16 51N19 119E36 -7:58:24
Nerechta 6 40 57N28 40E34 -2:42:16
Nereta 13 36 56N13 25E18 -1:41:12
Nerevoznoje 6 42 56N53 53E54 -3:35:36
Neringa 8 38 55N18 21E01 -1:24:04
Nerl' 6 40 56N40 40E24 -2:41:36
Nerl' 6 39 57N03 37E59 -2:31:56
Neroj 2 20 54N28 97E49 -6:31:16
Nes' 6 41 66N37 44E36 -2:58:24
Neščeretovo 23 45 49N24 38E48 -2:35:12
Neškan 2 2 67N03 173W01 11:32:04
Nesterkovo 6 9 59N10 30E33 -2:02:12
Nesterov 23 44 50N04 23E58 -1:35:52
Nesterov (Ebenrode) 8 38 54N38 22E34 -1:30:16
Nesterovka 6 30 52N26 53E42 -3:34:48
Nesterovo 2 20 52N22 107E53 -7:11:32
Nesterovo 6 41 54N31 41E49 -2:47:16
Nesterovo 6 39 56N45 36E30 -2:26:00
Nestiary 6 41 56N34 45E21 -3:01:24
Nestoita 23 45 47N47 29E21 -1:57:24
Nesvetaj 6 40 47N27 39E40 -2:38:40
Nesviž 4 39 53N13 26E40 -1:46:40
Neuhausen → Gurjevsk 8 38 54N47 20E38 -1:22:32
Neukuhren → Pionerskij 8 38 54N57 20E20 -1:21:20
Neval'cevo 2 23 58N38 81E53 -5:27:32
Nevanka 2 20 56N30 98E54 -6:35:36
Nevel' 6 39 56N02 29E55 -1:59:40
Nevel'sk 19 8 46N40 141E53 -9:27:32
Never 2 16 53N58 124E05 -8:16:20
Neverkino 6 41 52N47 46E44 -3:06:56
Neverovo 6 41 55N07 44E24 -2:57:36
Nevežkino 6 41 53N07 43E19 -2:53:16
Nevinnomyssk 6 47 44N38 41E56 -2:47:44
Nevjansk 2 30 57N32 60E13 -4:00:52
Nevon 2 20 58N07 102E49 -6:51:16
Nevskoje 6 9 58N08 30E26 -2:01:44
Nezamajevskaja 6 47 46N09 40E16 -2:41:04
Nezavertajlovka 15 46 46N37 29E56 -1:59:44
Nežin 23 44 51N03 31E54 -2:07:36
Nezlobnaja 6 47 44N08 43E23 -2:53:32
Neznanovo 6 41 54N02 40E06 -2:40:24
Nīca 13 36 56N19 21E04 -1:24:16
Nidž 3 34 40N56 47E41 -3:10:44
Nikel' 6 9 69N24 30E12 -2:00:48
Nikel'tau 9 30 50N23 58E13 -3:52:52
Nikiforovo 6 39 55N50 38E05 -2:32:20
Nikitovka 6 40 50N23 38E25 -2:33:40
Nikitovka 23 45 48N21 38E02 -2:32:08
Nikitskoje 6 39 55N18 38E28 -2:33:52
Nikitskoje 6 39 55N13 35E46 -2:23:04
Nikolajev 23 44 49N32 23E58 -1:35:52
Nikolajev 23 45 46N58 32E00 -2:08:00
Nikolajevka 23 45 46N23 29E24 -1:57:36
Nikolajevka 23 45 47N33 30E25 -2:01:40
Nikolajevka 23 44 51N04 34E02 -2:16:08
Nikolajevka 6 40 47N18 38E50 -2:35:20
Nikolajevka 23 45 48N46 38E20 -2:33:20
Nikolajevka 23 45 47N39 37E41 -2:30:44
Nikolajevka 23 45 48N51 37E46 -2:31:04
Nikolajevka 2 21 56N29 95E06 -6:20:24
Nikolajevka 2 23 54N57 75E44 -5:02:56
Nikolajevka 9 24 49N10 81E59 -5:27:56
Nikolajevka 2 20 55N46 98E10 -6:32:40
Nikolajevka 2 11 48N34 134E47 -8:59:08
Nikolajevka 6 34 46N21 47E44 -3:10:56
Nikolajevka 6 34 52N28 49E14 -3:16:56
Nikolajevka 6 34 52N11 48E04 -3:12:16
Nikolajevka 6 34 53N08 47E12 -3:08:48
Nikolajevka 23 45 47N38 33E12 -2:12:48
Nikolajevka 23 45 47N06 34E14 -2:16:56
Nikolajevka 23 45 44N58 33E37 -2:14:28
Nikolajevo 6 9 58N16 29E29 -1:57:56
Nikolajevo-Kozlovskij 6 40 47N13 38E21 -2:33:24
Nikolajevskaja 6 47 47N37 41E29 -2:45:56
Nikolajevskij 6 34 50N01 45E28 -3:01:52
Nikolajevsk-Na-Amure 2 11 53N08 140E44 -9:22:56
Nikolajevskoje 2 16 52N21 117E00 -7:48:00
Nikolajevskoje 6 47 45N08 39E36 -2:38:24
Nikolajevskoje 2 18 51N04 111E48 -7:27:12
Nikolayev → Nikolajev 23 45 46N58 32E00 -2:08:00
Nikolo-Berezovec 6 41 58N38 42E17 -2:49:08
Nikolo-Ber'ozovka 6 30 56N08 54E09 -3:36:36
Nikolo-Chovanskoje 6 39 55N36 37E27 -2:29:48
Nikologory 6 40 56N09 41E59 -2:47:56
Nikolo-Kropotki 6 39 56N44 37E55 -2:31:40
Nikolo-L'vovsk 2 27 43N54 131E23 -8:45:32
Nikolo-Makarovo 6 41 57N38 43E34 -2:54:16
Nikol'sk 6 41 59N30 45E27 -3:01:48
Nikol'sk 6 41 53N45 46E05 -3:04:20
Nikol'skij 6 9 60N55 34E00 -2:16:00
Nikol'skij 9 24 47N55 67E28 -4:29:52
Nikol'skij 2 30 56N18 68E58 -4:35:52
Nikol'skij Toržok 6 40 59N53 38E46 -2:35:04
Nikol'skoje 6 41 52N37 43E49 -2:55:16
Nikol'skoje 6 47 50N35 41E10 -2:44:40
Nikol'skoje 6 39 52N39 36E04 -2:24:16
Nikol'skoje 6 39 55N26 35E04 -2:20:16
Nikol'skoje 6 41 59N23 44E36 -2:58:24
Nikol'skoje 6 41 59N30 42E32 -2:50:08
Nikol'skoje 6 39 54N51 35E53 -2:23:32
Nikol'skoje 6 39 54N27 36E24 -2:25:36
Nikol'skoje 6 39 54N30 36E50 -2:27:20
Nikol'skoje 6 39 54N03 37E10 -2:28:40
Nikol'skoje 6 39 54N18 35E53 -2:23:32
Nikol'skoje 6 39 55N37 36E41 -2:26:44
Nikol'skoje 6 39 55N15 36E04 -2:24:16
Nikol'skoje 6 39 56N09 36E43 -2:26:52
Nikol'skoje 6 39 55N53 36E26 -2:25:44
Nikol'skoje 23 45 47N46 37E18 -2:29:12
Nikol'skoje 6 9 59N41 30E47 -2:03:08
Nikol'skoje 6 39 55N46 37E54 -2:31:36
Nikol'skoje 2 23 57N12 84E21 -5:37:24
Nikol'skoje 11 4 55N12 166E00-11:04:00
Nikol Skoje 6 30 52N02 55E43 -3:42:52
Nikol'skoje 6 34 47N46 46E24 -3:05:36
Nikol'skoje-Na-Čeremšane 6 42 54N03 49E14 -3:16:56
Nikol'skoje-Na-Dnepre 23 45 48N12 35E12 -2:20:48
Nikol'skoje-Ur'upino 6 39 55N48 37E13 -2:28:52
Nikonorovka 6 47 49N07 39E59 -2:39:56
Nikonova Gora 6 40 60N22 36E07 -2:24:28
Nikonovskoje 6 39 55N17 38E10 -2:32:40
Nikopol' 23 45 47N35 34E25 -2:17:40
Nikulino 6 39 56N48 35E50 -2:23:20
Nikulino 6 41 58N05 44E14 -2:56:56
Nikulino 6 39 55N16 33E46 -2:15:04
Nikulkino 6 39 56N07 38E38 -2:34:32
Nikul'skoje 6 39 55N10 38E41 -2:34:44
Nimančik 2 11 52N09 133E47 -8:55:08
Niny 6 47 44N29 43E57 -2:55:48
Nisporeny 15 46 47N06 28E11 -1:52:44
Nītaure 13 36 57N10 25E10 -1:40:40
Nivnoje 6 39 53N11 32E35 -2:10:20
Nivskij 6 9 67N16 32E23 -2:09:32
Niža 6 41 66N20 43E16 -2:53:04
Nižankoviči 23 44 49N40 22E47 -1:31:08
Nizhniy Tagil → Nižnij Tagil 2 30 57N55 59E57 -3:59:48
Nizhny Novgorod → Gor'kij 6 41 56N20 44E00 -2:56:00
Nižin 4 39 52N38 28E10 -1:52:40
Nizino 6 9 59N50 29E53 -1:59:32
Nižn'aja 6 41 56N34 49E07 -3:16:28
Nižn'aja Čvorovaja 2 23 59N11 77E31 -5:10:04
Nižnaja Dobrinka 6 34 50N18 45E42 -3:02:48
Nižn'aja Duvanka 23 45 49N35 38E10 -2:32:40
Nižn'aja-Gerasimovka 23 45 48N46 39E44 -2:38:56
Nižn'aja Grajvoronka 6 39 51N47 37E45 -2:31:00
Nižn'aja Irga 2 30 56N51 57E26 -3:49:44
Nižn'aja Karelina 2 20 57N55 107E44 -7:10:56
Nižn'aja Krynka 23 45 48N07 38E11 -2:32:44
Nižnaja Matrenka 6 41 52N16 40E06 -2:40:24
Nižn'aja-Ol'chovaja 23 45 48N44 39E35 -2:38:20
Nižn'aja Omka 2 24 55N26 74E55 -4:59:40
Nizn'aja Omra 6 29 62N46 55E46 -3:43:04
Nižn'aja Ošma 6 41 55N44 51E18 -3:25:12
Nižn'aja Peša 6 41 66N43 47E36 -3:10:24
Nižn'aja Pojma 2 21 56N11 97E13 -6:28:52
Nižn'aja Pokrovka 6 34 51N40 50E07 -3:20:28
Nižn'aja Šachtama 2 16 51N24 117E40 -7:50:40
Nižn'aja Salda 2 30 58N05 60E43 -4:02:52
Nižn'aja Syzran' 6 34 53N04 48E34 -3:14:16
Nižn'aja Tavda 2 30 57N40 66E12 -4:24:48
Nižn'aja Tojma 6 41 62N24 44E10 -2:56:40
Nižn'aja Tura 2 30 58N37 59E49 -3:59:16
Nižn'aja Vol'dža 2 23 58N19 79E20 -5:17:20
Nižn'aja Zaimka 2 20 56N09 98E14 -6:32:56
Nižneangarsk 2 20 55N47 109E33 -7:18:12
Nižnebakanskij 6 47 44N52 37E52 -2:31:28
Nižne-Baranikovka 6 47 49N05 39E51 -2:39:24
Nižnečujskij 10 24 43N12 74E21 -4:57:24
Nižnedevick 6 40 51N33 38E20 -2:33:20
Nižnegnutov 6 34 48N02 42E22 -2:49:28
Nižnegorskij 23 45 45N27 34E44 -2:18:56
Nižneilimsk 2 20 57N11 103E16 -6:53:04
Nižneje 23 45 48N46 38E37 -2:34:28
Nižneje Al'kejevo 6 41 54N46 50E03 -3:20:12
Nižn'eje Gir'unino 2 16 51N12 116E58 -7:47:52
Nižneje Kučukovo 6 41 56N13 52E57 -3:31:48
Nižneje M'ačkovo 6 39 55N33 37E59 -2:31:56

Nižneje Platino 23 45 48N48 39E30 -2:38:00
Nižneje Romanovo 2 30 59N47 69E35 -4:38:20
Nižneje Sančelejevo 6 34 53N40 49E27 -3:17:48
Nižnekamsk 6 41 55N32 51E58 -3:27:52
Nižnekamskij 6 41 55N32 51E58 -3:27:52
Nižnekundr'učen-Skaja 6 47 47N45 40E57 -2:43:48
Nižnelemskij 6 29 64N01 56E16 -3:45:04
Nižne-Mit'akin Pervyj 6 47 48N41 40E02 -2:40:08
Nižne-Nagol'naja 6 47 49N00 39E59 -2:39:56
Nižneoz'ornoje 6 30 51N37 53E56 -3:35:44
Nižne-Podpol'nyj 6 40 47N12 40E01 -2:40:04
Nižne-Pokrovka 23 45 49N13 38E38 -2:34:32
Nižnetambovskoje 2 11 50N54 138E13 -9:12:52
Nižne-T'oploje 23 45 48N48 39E23 -2:37:32
Nižnetroickij 6 30 54N20 53E41 -3:34:44
Nižneudinsk 2 20 54N54 99E03 -6:36:12
Nižnij Baskunčak 6 34 48N13 46E50 -3:07:20
Nižnij Casučej 2 16 50N31 115E08 -7:40:32
Nižnij Čir 6 34 48N22 43E03 -2:52:12
Nižnij Čulym 2 23 54N37 78E56 -5:15:44
Nižnije Černi 6 34 47N41 43E26 -2:53:44
Nižnije Čeršely 6 41 54N40 52E08 -3:28:32
Nižnije Ostrovcy 6 39 55N35 38E01 -2:32:04
Nižnije Sergi 2 30 56N40 59E18 -3:57:12
Nižnije Serogozy 23 45 46N50 34E23 -2:17:32
Nižnije Timers'any 6 42 54N34 47E45 -3:11:00
Nižnije V'azovyje 6 41 55N49 48E32 -3:14:08
Nižnij Ingaš 2 21 56N12 96E31 -6:26:04
Nižnij Kisl'aj 6 41 50N50 40E11 -2:40:44
Nižnij Kuranach 2 16 58N49 125E32 -8:22:08
Nižnij Lomov 6 41 53N32 43E41 -2:54:44
Nižnij Mamon 6 47 50N11 40E30 -2:42:00
Nižnij Odec 6 29 63N40 54E52 -3:39:28
Nižnij Odes 6 29 63N40 54E52 -3:39:28
Nižnij Ol'šan 6 40 50N45 38E55 -2:35:40
Nižnij P'andž 21 24 37N08 68E32 -4:34:08
Nižnij Paramonov 6 47 47N57 41E55 -2:47:40
Nižnij Rogačik 23 45 47N21 34E02 -2:16:08
Nižnij Serebr'akov 6 47 47N58 41E02 -2:44:08
Nižnij Škaft 6 41 53N36 45E40 -3:02:40
Nižnij Stan 2 16 52N18 115E44 -7:42:56
Nižnij Tagil 2 30 57N55 59E57 -3:59:48
Nižnij Takanyš 6 41 55N57 51E04 -3:24:16
Nižnij Ufalej 2 30 55N55 59E59 -3:59:56
Nižnij V'aloz'orskij 6 9 66N44 35E10 -2:20:40
Nižnyj Nagol'čik 23 45 48N01 39E04 -2:36:16
Nizy 23 45 50N47 34E46 -2:19:04
Nogajsk 23 45 46N44 36E20 -2:25:20
Noginsk 6 39 55N51 38E27 -2:33:48
Nogliki 19 8 51N48 143E10 -9:32:40
Nojember'an 1 34 41N12 45E01 -3:00:04
Nolinsk 6 42 57N33 49E57 -3:19:48
Nonburg 6 41 65N34 50E32 -3:22:08
Nor Ačin 1 34 40N19 44E35 -2:58:20
Nordenšel'da, Archipelag 2 21 76N45 96E00 -6:24:00
Nordenšel'da Islands 2 21 76N45 96E00 -6:24:00
Nordvik 2 19 74N02 111E32 -7:26:08
Noril'sk 2 21 69N20 88E06 -5:52:24
Norsk 2 14 52N20 129E55 -8:39:40
Nosova 2 30 59N30 63E13 -4:12:52
Nosovaja 6 29 68N15 54E35 -3:38:20
Nosovaja 6 41 57N15 45E35 -3:02:20
Nosovka 23 44 50N55 31E35 -2:06:20
Nosovo 6 39 57N07 27E50 -1:51:20
Nosovo 6 40 47N16 38E40 -2:34:40
Nosovščina 6 40 62N56 37E03 -2:28:12
Nošul' 6 41 60N09 49E28 -3:17:52
Novabad 21 24 39N01 70E09 -4:40:36
Novabad 21 24 38N37 68E45 -4:35:00
Novaja 6 39 55N13 38E54 -2:35:36
Novaja 6 39 55N48 38E03 -2:32:12
Novaja Astrachan' 23 45 49N07 38E36 -2:34:24

Novaja Belaja 6 40 49N46 39E11 -2:36:44
Novaja Belokorovīči 23 44 51N07 28E02 -1:52:08
Novaja Binaradka 6 34 53N48 49E56 -3:19:44
Novaja Borovaja 23 44 50N42 28E39 -1:54:36
Novaja Čigla 6 41 51N13 40E28 -2:41:52
Novaja Derevn'a 6 40 54N01 38E53 -2:35:32
Novaja Derevn'a 2 20 57N15 103E08 -6:52:32
Novaja Ivanovka 23 45 45N55 29E05 -1:56:20
Novaja Janisol' 23 45 47N17 37E16 -2:29:04
Novaja Kachovka 23 45 46N45 33E23 -2:13:32
Novaja Kalitva 6 41 50N06 40E01 -2:40:04
Novaja Kazmaska 6 42 56N49 53E31 -3:34:04
Novaja Kriuša 6 47 50N16 41E16 -2:45:04
Novaja Ladoga 6 9 60N05 32E16 -2:09:04
Novaja L'al'a 2 30 59N03 60E36 -4:02:24
Novaja Majačka 23 45 46N36 33E14 -2:12:56
Novaja Maluksa 6 9 59N39 31E21 -2:05:24
Novaja Malykla 6 42 54N13 49E57 -3:19:48
Novaja Mojgora 6 39 54N27 38E32 -2:34:08
Novaja Odessa 23 45 47N19 31E47 -2:07:08
Novaja Porubežka 6 34 51N45 49E40 -3:18:40
Novaja Praga 23 45 48N33 32E54 -2:11:36
Novaja Ropša 6 9 59N45 29E53 -1:59:32
Novaja Sibir' Island 18 1 75N00 149E00 -9:56:00
Novaja Sibir', Ostrov 18 1 75N00 149E00 -9:56:00
Novaja Sloboda 23 44 51N23 34E08 -2:16:32
Novaja Slobodka 6 39 54N56 36E47 -2:27:08
Novaja Šul'ba 9 24 50N33 81E20 -5:25:20
Novaja Uda 2 20 54N07 103E33 -6:54:12
Novaja Ušica 23 45 48N49 27E16 -1:49:04
Novaja Usman' 6 41 51N37 39E24 -2:37:36
Novaja Vodolaga 23 45 49N43 35E52 -2:23:28
Novaja Zburjevka 23 45 46N28 32E24 -2:09:36
Novaja Zeml'a 17 29 74N07 55E33 -3:42:12
Novaja Zeml'a Islands 17 29 74N07 55E33 -3:42:12
Novgorod 6 9 58N31 31E17 -2:05:08
Novgorodka 23 45 48N21 32E39 -2:10:36
Novgorod-Severskij 23 44 51N59 33E16 -2:13:04
Novgorodskoje 23 45 48N20 37E50 -2:31:20
Novičicha 2 23 52N13 81E24 -5:25:36
Novikovo 2 23 58N15 80E39 -5:22:36
Novikovo 19 8 46N23 143E20 -9:33:20
Novinka 6 9 59N49 33E20 -2:13:20
Novka 4 39 55N27 30E24 -2:01:36
Novki 6 40 56N22 41E06 -2:44:24
Novl'anka 6 40 55N48 41E44 -2:46:56
Novlenskoje 6 40 59N37 39E20 -2:37:20
Novoachtyrka 23 45 48N55 38E49 -2:35:16
Novoajdar 23 45 48N57 39E00 -2:36:00
Novoaleksandrovka 6 32 51N56 52E26 -3:29:44
Novoaleksandrovka 23 45 48N17 39E37 -2:38:28
Novoaleksandrovka 23 45 49N08 39E17 -2:37:08
Novoaleksandrovka 9 24 51N47 68E49 -4:35:16
Novoaleksandrovo 6 39 55N59 37E33 -2:30:12
Novoaleksandrovsk 6 47 45N29 41E16 -2:45:04
Novoaleksandrov-Skaja 6 47 45N29 41E16 -2:45:04
Novoaleksejevka 9 30 52N56 64E41 -4:18:44
Novoaleksejevka 9 24 52N47 74E54 -4:59:36
Novoaleksejevka 9 30 50N08 55E39 -3:42:36
Novoaleksejevka 23 45 46N06 32E30 -2:10:00
Novoaleksejevka 23 45 46N13 34E39 -2:18:36
Novoaltajsk 2 21 53N24 83E58 -5:35:52
Novoamvrosijevskoje 23 45 47N49 38E29 -2:33:56
Novoanninskij 6 34 50N32 42E41 -2:50:44

Novoarchangel'sk 23 45 48N39 30E48 -2:03:12
Novoarchangel'skoje 6 39 55N55 37E33 -2:30:12
Novoasbest 2 30 57N44 60E45 -4:03:00
Novoazorskoje 23 45 47N08 38E05 -2:32:20
Novoazovsk 23 45 47N08 38E05 -2:32:20
Novobachmutovka 23 45 48N15 37E48 -2:31:12
Novobatajsk 6 40 46N54 39E47 -2:39:08
Novobelaja 23 45 49N49 39E18 -2:37:12
Novobessergenovka 6 40 47N11 38E51 -2:35:24
Novobogatinskoje 9 32 47N22 51E11 -3:24:44
Novobogdanovka 23 45 47N06 35E29 -2:21:56
Novobogordskoje 6 30 53N11 53E56 -3:35:44
Novobogorodskoje 6 30 53N11 53E56 -3:35:44
Novoborovaja 23 45 49N15 38E33 -2:34:12
Novobratcevskij 6 39 55N51 37E23 -2:29:32
Novoburejskij 2 14 49N49 129E54 -8:39:36
Novočeboksarsk 6 41 56N08 47E30 -3:10:00
Novo Čeremšansk 6 42 54N21 50E10 -3:20:40
Novočerkassk 6 40 47N25 40E06 -2:40:24
Novočernorečenskij 2 21 56N16 91E06 -6:04:24
Novocharitonovo 6 39 55N35 38E30 -2:34:00
Novocherkassk → Novočerkassk 6 40 47N25 40E06 -2:40:24
Novochop'orsk 6 41 51N07 41E37 -2:46:28
Novochop'orskij 6 41 51N06 41E33 -2:46:12
Novociml'anskaja 6 47 47N59 42E17 -2:49:08
Novodanilovka 23 45 46N38 35E00 -2:20:00
Novoderev'ankov-Skaja 6 47 46N19 38E45 -2:35:00
Novoderkul 23 45 49N08 39E38 -2:38:32
Novodevičje 6 34 53N37 48E52 -3:15:28
Novodolinka 9 24 51N12 72E33 -4:50:12
Novodolinskij 9 24 49N44 72E45 -4:51:00
Novodoroninskoje 2 18 51N08 112E08 -7:28:32
Novodružesk 23 45 48N58 38E21 -2:33:24
Novodubovoje 6 40 52N19 39E13 -2:36:52
Novodugino 6 39 55N38 34E18 -2:17:12
Novodvinsk 6 41 64N26 40E47 -2:43:08
Novodžereljevskaja 6 47 45N46 38E41 -2:34:44
Novoekonomičeskoje 23 45 48N18 37E15 -2:29:00
Novofetinino 6 39 56N14 39E17 -2:37:08
Novogaritovo 6 41 52N47 40E07 -2:40:28
Novogorbovo 6 39 55N43 36E29 -2:25:56
Novogornyj 2 30 55N37 60E47 -4:03:08
Novograd-Volynskij 23 44 50N36 27E36 -1:50:24
Novogrigorjevka 23 45 46N24 34E59 -2:19:56
Novogrigorjevskaja 6 34 49N26 43E37 -2:54:28
Novogrigorjevskoje 6 47 44N25 43E51 -2:55:24
Novogrodovka 23 45 48N13 37E20 -2:29:20
Novogroznenskij 6 47 43N15 46E15 -3:05:00
Novogrudok 4 39 53N36 25E50 -1:43:20
Novogupalovka 23 45 48N02 35E26 -2:21:44
Novoignatjevka 23 45 47N38 37E41 -2:30:44
Novoiljinsk 2 20 51N42 108E41 -7:14:44
Novoiljinskij 6 30 57N54 55E30 -3:42:00
Novoivanovka 9 24 43N08 71E26 -4:45:44
Novoivanovka 23 44 49N44 33E28 -2:13:52
Novoivanovka 23 45 47N41 38E23 -2:33:32
Novoivanovskoje 6 39 55N43 37E22 -2:29:28
Novoizborsk 6 39 57N50 27E59 -1:51:56
Novojampol' 2 14 52N55 127E38 -8:30:32
Novojamskoje 6 39 52N14 34E28 -2:17:52
Novoje 6 39 55N38 38E55 -2:35:40
Novoje 2 30 58N53 68E40 -4:34:40
Novoje Alechnovo 6 39 56N02 36E49 -2:27:16
Novojegorjevskoje 2 23 51N46 80E53 -5:23:32
Novojekaterinovka 23 45 47N43 38E07 -2:32:28
Novoje Koval'ovo 6 9 59N59 30E34 -2:02:16

Novoje Leušino 6 40 56N48 40E32 -2:42:08
Novojel'n'a 4 39 53N28 25E35 -1:42:20
Novojenisejsk 2 21 58N16 92E24 -6:09:36
Novoje Pavšino 6 39 54N15 37E07 -2:28:28
Novoje Zarečje 6 39 57N43 34E22 -2:17:28
Novokačalinsk 2 27 45N06 132E01 -8:48:04
Novokadinsk 2 20 54N46 101E24 -6:45:36
Novokamala 2 21 55N58 94E58 -6:19:52
Novokarasuk 2 24 56N16 71E46 -4:47:04
Novokaširovo 6 41 54N58 52E32 -3:30:08
Novokaširsk 6 39 54N51 38E15 -2:33:00
Novokazalinsk 9 30 45N50 62E10 -4:08:40
Novokijevskij 6 34 50N27 43E08 -2:52:32
Novokorsunskaja 6 47 45N38 39E09 -2:36:36
Novokrasn'anka 23 45 49N08 38E18 -2:33:12
Novokrasnoje 23 45 48N01 31E21 -2:05:24
Novokručininskij 2 16 51N46 113E48 -7:35:12
Novokubanka 9 24 51N40 70E44 -4:42:56
Novokujbyševsk 6 34 53N07 49E58 -3:19:52
Novokurovka 2 11 48N51 134E20 -8:57:20
Novokuzneck 2 21 53N45 87E06 -5:48:24
Novokuznetsk → Novokuzneck 2 21 53N45 87E06 -5:48:24
Novolakskoje 6 47 43N07 46E29 -3:05:56
Novoleuškovskaja 6 47 45N59 39E58 -2:39:52
Novolimarevka 23 45 49N17 39E36 -2:38:24
Novolukoml' 4 39 54N40 29E08 -1:56:32
Novol'vovsk 6 40 53N55 38E47 -2:35:08
Novomalorossijskaja 6 47 45N38 39E53 -2:39:32
Novomansurkino 6 34 53N52 51E52 -3:27:28
Novomargaritovka 6 47 46N54 38E50 -2:35:20
Novomariinka 2 21 55N27 96E01 -6:24:04
Novomarkovka 9 24 51N44 72E17 -4:49:08
Novomel'nikov 6 47 43N56 45E09 -3:00:36
Novomelovatka 6 47 50N27 40E46 -2:43:04
Novomelovoje 6 40 51N23 38E13 -2:32:52
Novomichajlovka 23 45 47N51 37E29 -2:29:56
Novomichajlovka 2 23 55N13 81E57 -5:27:48
Novomichajlovskij 6 47 44N15 38E51 -2:35:24
Novomichajlovskij 6 30 53N54 54E08 -3:36:32
Novomichajlovskoje 6 47 44N15 38E51 -2:35:24
Novomichajlovskoje 6 39 55N25 37E10 -2:28:40
Novominskaja 6 47 46N19 38E57 -2:35:48
Novomirgorod 23 45 48N47 31E39 -2:06:36
Novomoskovsk 23 45 48N37 35E12 -2:20:48
Novomoskovsk 6 39 54N05 38E13 -2:32:52
Novomyšastovskaja 6 47 45N12 38E35 -2:34:20
Novonagajevo 6 30 55N56 54E15 -3:37:00
Novonikolajevka 23 45 46N13 32E45 -2:11:00
Novonikolajevka 23 45 47N59 35E55 -2:23:40
Novonikolajevka 6 40 46N59 39E36 -2:38:24
Novonikolajevka 9 24 42N26 70E28 -4:41:52
Novonikolajevskij 6 34 50N58 42E22 -2:49:28
Novonikolayevsk → Novosibirsk 2 21 55N02 82E55 -5:31:40
Novonikol'skoje 6 39 55N50 37E15 -2:29:00
Novonikol'skoje 6 34 49N09 45E00 -3:00:00
Novonikol'skoje 2 23 59N46 79E12 -5:16:48
Novonikol'skoje 6 9 59N25 33E13 -2:12:52
Novonikol'skoje 23 45 49N21 39E51 -2:39:24
Novoomel'kovo 23 45 49N08 39E05 -2:36:20
Novoorsk 6 30 51N23 58E58 -3:55:52
Novopavlovka 2 18 51N13 109E14 -7:16:56
Novopavlovskaja 6 47 43N58 43E38 -2:54:32
Novopavlovskoje 2 18 50N56 111E35 -7:26:20
Novopetrovo 2 30 57N11 69E10 -4:36:40
Novopetrovskoje 6 39 55N59 36E28 -2:25:52
Novopiscovo 6 40 57N19 41E54 -2:47:36
Novopodrezkovo 6 39 55N57 37E21 -2:29:24
Novopokrovka 9 24 50N41 80E28 -5:21:52
Novopokrovka 2 27 45N52 134E28 -8:57:52
Novopokrovka 10 24 42N52 74E45 -4:59:00
Novopokrovka 23 45 48N03 34E37 -2:18:28
Novopokrovka 9 24 53N43 67E45 -4:31:00
Novopokrovskoje 6 34 51N35 43E36 -2:54:24
Novopolevodino 6 34 51N46 47E29 -3:09:56
Novopolock 4 39 55N31 28E38 -1:54:32
Novopskov 23 45 49N33 39E05 -2:36:20
Novorajčichinsk 2 14 49N47 129E38 -8:38:32
Novor'ažsk 6 41 53N44 40E07 -2:40:28
Novorepnoje 6 34 51N06 48E24 -3:13:36
Novorossijka 10 24 42N44 76E07 -5:04:28
Novorossijsk 6 47 44N45 37E45 -2:31:00
Novorossijskoje 9 30 50N13 58E00 -3:52:00
Novorossiysk → Novorossijsk 6 47 44N45 37E45 -2:31:00
Novorossoš' 23 45 49N32 39E15 -2:37:00
Novorudnyj 6 30 51N30 58E10 -3:52:40
Novorybinka 9 24 51N51 71E14 -4:44:56
Novorybnoje 2 19 72N50 105E50 -7:03:20
Novoržev 6 39 57N02 29E20 -1:57:20
Novošachtinsk 6 40 47N47 39E56 -2:39:44
Novosaratovka 6 9 59N50 30E32 -2:02:08
Novoščerbinovskaja 6 47 46N28 38E38 -2:34:32
Novosel'e 2 23 54N10 76E53 -5:07:32
Novoselenginsk 2 20 51N06 106E37 -7:06:28
Novoselica 23 45 48N14 26E17 -1:45:08
Novoselickoje 6 47 44N45 43E26 -2:53:44
Novoselišče 23 44 49N48 25E03 -1:40:12
Novoselje 6 9 59N48 30E05 -2:00:20
Novoselki 6 39 55N08 37E33 -2:30:12
Novoselki 6 39 54N49 38E55 -2:35:40
Novosel'nyj 9 30 50N00 54E38 -3:38:32
Novoselovka Pervaja 23 45 48N12 37E31 -2:30:04
Novoselovo 6 39 56N04 39E04 -2:36:16
Novoselovo 2 21 55N04 91E07 -6:04:28
Novosel'skoje 23 45 45N20 28E33 -1:54:12
Novosemejkino 6 34 53N23 50E22 -3:21:28
Novosergijevka 6 30 52N06 53E39 -3:34:36
Novosergijevka 6 9 59N54 30E34 -2:02:16
Novoseslavino 6 41 53N21 40E26 -2:41:44
Novošešminsk 6 41 55N04 51E15 -3:25:00
Novoshakhtinsk → Novošachtinsk 6 40 47N47 39E56 -2:39:44
Novosibirsk 2 21 55N02 82E55 -5:31:40
Novosil' 6 39 52N58 37E03 -2:28:12
Novosil'skoje 6 40 51N56 38E31 -2:34:04
Novosokol'niki 6 39 56N21 30E10 -2:00:40
Novos'olki 4 39 52N02 24E21 -1:37:24
Novos'olki 6 39 56N01 33E37 -2:14:28
Novos'olki 4 39 52N24 28E33 -1:54:12
Novos'olki 6 9 59N42 30E17 -2:01:08
Novos'olki 6 40 55N48 42E41 -2:50:44
Novos'olki 6 40 54N50 39E46 -2:39:04
Novos'olovka 23 45 49N04 37E42 -2:30:48
Novos'olovo 2 21 55N04 91E07 -6:04:28
Novos'olovo 2 20 56N04 107E42 -7:10:48
Novos'olovskoje 23 45 45N26 33E34 -2:14:16
Novospasovka 6 40 47N42 39E04 -2:36:16
Novospasskoje 6 34 53N08 47E45 -3:11:00
Novostrel'covka 23 45 49N20 39E55 -2:39:40
Novostrojevo (Trempen) 8 38 54N27 21E50 -1:27:20
Novosvetlovka 23 45 48N30 39E30 -2:38:00
Novosysojevka 2 27 44N14 133E22 -8:53:28
Novotavolžanka 6 39 50N22 36E50 -2:27:20
Novotitarovskaja 6 47 45N14 39E00 -2:36:00
Novotroick 2 23 56N11 78E41 -5:14:44
Novotroickoje 23 45 47N43 37E35 -2:30:20
Novotroickoje 2 23 56N11 78E41 -5:14:44
Novotroickoje 9 24 43N42 73E46 -4:55:04
Novotroickoje 6 42 58N28 47E06 -3:08:24
Novotroickoje 23 45 46N22 34E20 -2:17:20
Novo-Troitsk → Novotroick 6 30 51N12 58E20 -3:53:20
Novotulka 6 34 52N38 48E45 -3:15:00
Novotulka 6 34 50N50 47E34 -3:10:16
Novotul'skij 6 39 54N10 37E43 -2:30:52
Novoukolovo 6 40 51N02 38E25 -2:33:40
Novoukrainka 23 45 48N19 31E32 -2:06:08
Novouljanovsk 6 42 54N08 48E24 -3:13:36
Novoural'sk 6 30 51N15 57E16 -3:49:04
Novouzensk 6 34 50N28 48E08 -3:12:32
Novovaršavka 2 24 54N11 74E42 -4:58:48
Novovasiljevka 23 45 46N51 36E46 -2:27:04
Novovasiljevka 23 45 46N48 35E44 -2:22:56
Novov'atsk 6 42 58N29 49E44 -3:18:56
Novov'azniki 6 40 56N12 42E10 -2:48:40
Novovolynsk 23 44 50N50 24E05 -1:36:20
Novovoroncovka 23 45 47N29 33E54 -2:15:36
Novovoronežskij 6 41 51N16 39E11 -2:36:44
Novovoskresenovka 10 24 42N50 73E32 -4:54:08
Novovoskresenskoje 23 45 47N21 33E37 -2:14:28
Novozacharkino 6 34 52N11 48E29 -3:13:56
Novozagorje 6 39 55N39 38E38 -2:34:32
Novozavidovskij 6 39 56N33 36E26 -2:25:44
Novožilovskaja 6 41 64N50 51E20 -3:25:20
Novozizevka 6 34 50N48 49E08 -3:16:32
Novozybkov 6 39 52N32 31E56 -2:07:44
Novyj 2 21 55N39 86E39 -5:46:36
Novyj Afon 7 33 43N06 40E48 -2:43:12
Novyj Bor 6 29 66N43 52E16 -3:29:04
Novyj Bug 23 45 47N41 32E30 -2:10:00
Novyj Bujan 6 34 53N41 50E04 -3:20:16
Novyj Bykov 23 44 50N36 31E39 -2:06:36
Novyj Dvor 4 39 52N50 24E21 -1:37:24
Novyje Ajbesi 6 41 54N49 47E02 -3:08:08
Novyje Aneny 15 46 46N52 29E14 -1:56:56
Novyje Basy 23 45 50N53 34E51 -2:19:24
Novyje Burasy 6 34 52N08 46E06 -3:04:24
Novyje Denisoviči 4 39 54N12 29E13 -1:56:52
Novyje Gorki 6 40 56N42 41E06 -2:44:24
Novyje Maty 6 30 55N15 54E04 -3:36:16
Novyje Salty 6 41 54N06 53E26 -3:33:44
Novyje Senžary 23 45 49N21 34E19 -2:17:16
Novyje Z'atcy 6 42 57N27 52E36 -3:30:24
Novyj Jaryčev 23 44 49N55 24E18 -1:37:12
Novyj Jegorlyk 6 47 46N24 41E54 -2:47:36
Novyj Karačaj 6 47 43N49 41E56 -2:47:44
Novyj Karamass 6 41 56N11 48E58 -3:15:52
Novyj Kiner 6 41 56N24 49E44 -3:18:56
Novyj Multan 6 42 57N09 52E19 -3:29:16
Novyj Nekouz 6 40 57N54 38E04 -2:32:16
Novyj Oskol 6 39 50N46 37E53 -2:31:32
Novyj Pogost 4 39 55N30 27E29 -1:49:56
Novyj Port 2 25 67N40 72E52 -4:51:28
Novyj Put' 9 24 43N29 73E52 -4:55:28
Novyj Ropsk 6 39 52N18 32E19 -2:09:16
Novyj Stan 6 39 56N18 37E00 -2:28:00
Novyj Svet 23 45 47N48 38E00 -2:32:00
Novyj Tap 2 30 57N04 67E49 -4:31:16
Novyj Tevriz 2 23 59N04 78E08 -5:12:32
Novyj Torjal 6 41 57N00 48E44 -3:14:56
Novyj Vas'ugan 2 23 58N34 76E29 -5:05:56
Novy Torjal 6 41 57N00 48E44 -3:14:56
Nowokusnezk → Novokuzneck 2 21 53N45 87E06 -5:48:24
Nowosibirsk → Novosibirsk 2 21 55N02 82E55 -5:31:40
Nožaj-Jurt 6 47 43N05 46E24 -3:05:36
Nucha → Šeki 3 34 41N12 47E12 -3:08:48
N'uchča 6 41 63N27 46E28 -3:05:52
N'učpas 6 41 60N51 51E18 -3:25:12
Nudol'-Šarino 6 39 56N06 36E31 -2:26:04
Nudž 3 34 40N56 47E41 -3:10:44

Nuia 5 35 58N04 25E33 -1:42:12
N'uja 2 16 60N32 116E14 -7:44:56
N'uksenica 6 41 60N25 44E13 -2:56:52
Nukus 24 30 42N50 59E29 -3:57:56
Nul'vand 21 24 38N16 70E32 -4:42:08
Numto 2 25 63N40 71E20 -4:45:20
Nun'amo 2 2 65N37 170W40 11:22:40
Nunligran 2 2 64N48 175W24 11:41:36
Nura 9 30 48N53 62E20 -4:09:20
N'urba 2 16 63N17 118E20 -7:53:20
Nurek 21 24 38N23 69E19 -4:37:16
Nurlat 6 42 54N26 50E46 -3:23:04
Nurlaty 6 41 55N37 48E18 -3:13:12
Nušpoly 6 39 56N39 37E44 -2:30:56
Nutepel'men 2 2 67N26 174W56 11:39:44
Nutepelmen 2 2 65N31 178W30 11:54:00
N'uvčim 6 41 61N22 50E42 -3:22:48
Nyda 2 25 66N36 72E54 -4:51:36
Nylga 6 42 56N46 52E22 -3:29:28
Nylga 2 15 51N38 127E35 -8:30:20
Nyrov 6 30 60N42 56E40 -3:46:40
Nyš 19 8 51N31 142E46 -9:31:04
Nyša 6 42 56N23 51E51 -3:27:24
Nytva 6 30 57N56 55E20 -3:41:20
Nyvrovo 19 8 54N19 142E36 -9:30:24
Občuga 4 39 54N30 29E22 -1:57:28
Obeliai 14 37 55N56 25E48 -1:43:12
Obertin 23 44 48N42 25E11 -1:40:44
Obichody 23 44 51N02 28E59 -1:55:56
Obi-Garm 21 24 38N43 69E42 -4:38:48
Obikanda 24 30 39N10 67E10 -4:28:40
Obil'noje 6 47 47N31 44E25 -2:57:40
Objačevo 6 41 60N20 49E34 -3:18:16
Oblastnaja 6 42 56N59 52E37 -3:30:28
Oblivskaja 6 47 48N32 42E30 -2:50:00
Oblučje 2 11 49N03 131E04 -8:44:16
Obninsk 6 39 55N05 36E37 -2:26:28
Obojan' 6 39 51N13 36E16 -2:25:04
Obol' 4 39 55N22 29E17 -1:57:08
Oboldino 6 39 55N53 37E56 -2:31:44
Obolon' 23 44 49N36 32E52 -2:11:28
Oboz'orskij 6 41 63N28 40E18 -2:41:12
Obrazcovo-Travino 6 34 45N58 48E02 -3:12:08
Obrovo 4 39 52N30 25E34 -1:42:16
Obručevka 9 24 42N30 69E05 -4:36:20
Obryvistoje 19 8 48N46 144E40 -9:38:40
Obšarovka 6 34 53N07 48E52 -3:15:28
Obtovo 23 44 51N37 33E13 -2:12:52
Obuchov 23 44 50N08 30E37 -2:02:28
Obuchova 6 39 56N06 32E22 -2:09:28
Obuchoviči 23 44 51N00 29E46 -1:59:04
Obuchovka 9 24 46N13 81E05 -5:24:20
Obuchovo 6 39 55N50 38E16 -2:33:04
Obuchovo 6 39 56N09 36E55 -2:27:40
Obuškovo 6 39 55N47 37E02 -2:28:08
Obvinsk 6 30 58N29 54E51 -3:39:24
Obžericha 6 40 57N11 42E58 -2:51:52
Očakov 23 45 46N37 31E33 -2:06:12
Očamčira 7 33 42N44 41E28 -2:45:52
Očamčire 7 33 42N44 41E28 -2:45:52
Očchamuri 7 33 41N52 41E50 -2:47:20
Očer 6 30 57N53 54E42 -3:38:48
Očeretino 23 45 48N14 37E36 -2:30:24
Ocha 19 8 53N34 142E56 -9:31:44
Ochansk 6 30 57N43 55E23 -3:41:32
Ochotsk 2 7 59N23 143E18 -9:33:12
Ochvat 6 39 56N46 32E27 -2:09:48
Odesa → Odessa 23 45 46N28 30E44 -2:02:56
Odessa 23 45 46N28 30E44 -2:02:56
Odesskoje 2 24 54N13 72E58 -4:51:52
Odincovo 6 39 54N40 38E00 -2:32:00
Odincovo 6 39 55N41 37E17 -2:29:08
Odojev 6 39 53N56 36E41 -2:26:44
Ogibalovo 6 40 60N34 39E40 -2:38:40
Ogni 2 21 51N54 83E31 -5:34:04
Ogn'ov Jar 2 23 58N23 76E29 -5:05:56
Ogn'ovka 9 24 49N36 83E25 -5:33:40
Ogodža 2 14 52N44 132E31 -8:50:04
Ogorodnoje 23 45 45N53 28E50 -1:55:20
Ogre 13 36 56N51 24E36 -1:38:24
Ojm'akon 2 6 63N28 142E49 -9:31:16
Ojok 2 20 52N35 104E27 -6:57:48
Ojtal 9 24 42N55 73E17 -4:53:08
Ojtal 10 24 40N24 74E06 -4:56:24
Okhotsk → Ochotsk 2 7 59N23 143E18 -9:33:12
Okino-Kl'uči 2 20 50N36 107E06 -7:08:24
Okladnevo 6 9 58N36 33E39 -2:14:36
Oknica 15 46 48N24 27E29 -1:49:56
Okno 23 44 48N34 25E58 -1:43:52
Okonešnikovo 2 24 54N50 75E05 -5:00:20
Oksovskij 6 40 62N37 39E55 -2:39:40
Okt'abr' 9 24 43N41 77E12 -5:08:48
Okt'abr' 6 39 57N50 37E26 -2:29:44
Okt'abr' 9 30 45N45 61E34 -4:06:16
Okt'abr'sk 9 30 49N28 57E25 -3:49:40
Okt'abr'sk 6 34 53N11 48E40 -3:14:40
Okt'abr'skij 6 47 44N56 39E00 -2:36:00
Okt'abr'skij 6 39 50N26 36E22 -2:25:28
Okt'abr'skij 6 40 53N47 39E29 -2:37:56
Okt'abr'skij 4 39 52N38 28E53 -1:55:32
Okt'abr'skij 6 39 55N37 37E58 -2:31:52
Okt'abr'skij 6 40 54N14 38E54 -2:35:36
Okt'abr'skij 6 40 47N28 40E04 -2:40:16
Okt'abr'skij 9 30 52N35 62E40 -4:10:40
Okt'abr'skij 9 24 49N38 83E35 -5:34:20
Okt'abr'skij 2 16 50N04 118E04 -7:52:16
Okt'abr'skij 2 20 56N05 99E26 -6:37:44
Okt'abr'skij 2 14 53N01 128E37 -8:34:28
Okt'abr'skij 2 11 49N02 140E11 -9:20:44
Okt'abr'skij 21 24 38N33 68E22 -4:33:28
Okt'abr'skij 6 30 56N31 57E12 -3:48:48
Okt'abr'skij 6 41 61N04 43E08 -2:52:32
Okt'abr'skij 6 42 59N29 48E50 -3:15:20
Okt'abr'skij 6 30 54N28 53E28 -3:33:52
Okt'abr'skij 6 41 56N17 44E12 -2:56:48
Okt'abr'skij 6 40 57N08 40E20 -2:41:20
Okt'abr'skij 6 41 58N19 44E19 -2:57:16
Okt'abr'skij 6 42 56N35 53E58 -3:35:52
Okt'abr'skij 6 34 47N58 43E38 -2:54:32
Okt'abr'skoje 6 41 52N54 46E30 -3:06:00
Okt'abr'skoje 23 45 48N38 33E04 -2:12:16
Okt'abr'skoje 23 45 45N18 34E09 -2:16:36
Okt'abr'skoje 6 41 52N18 39E44 -2:38:56
Okt'abr'skoje 23 45 48N28 37E22 -2:29:28
Okt'abr'skoje 2 25 62N28 66E03 -4:24:12
Okt'abr'skoje 2 30 54N26 62E44 -4:10:56
Okt'abr'skoje 9 24 52N07 65E40 -4:22:40
Okt'abr'skoje 6 30 52N20 55E30 -3:42:00
Okt'abr'skoje 6 47 45N37 42E49 -2:51:16
Oktember'an 1 34 40N09 44E02 -2:56:08
Oktyabr'skiy → Okt'abr'skij 6 30 54N28 53E28 -3:33:52
Okulovka 6 9 58N26 33E18 -2:13:12
Okumi 7 33 42N43 41E45 -2:47:00
Okun'ov Nos 6 29 66N15 52E28 -3:29:52
Ola 2 6 59N35 151E17 -10:05:08
Olarevo 6 41 59N22 40E04 -2:40:16
Ol'chi 6 41 53N53 41E28 -2:45:52
Ol'chovatka 6 40 50N18 39E17 -2:37:08
Ol'chovatka 23 45 48N15 38E25 -2:33:40
Ol'chovka 2 30 56N22 63E46 -4:15:04
Ol'chovka 6 34 49N52 44E34 -2:58:16
Ol'chovoje 23 45 48N40 39E34 -2:38:16
Olema 6 41 64N30 46E08 -3:04:32
Olenegorsk 6 9 68N09 33E15 -2:13:00
Olenevka 23 45 45N23 32E32 -2:10:08
Olenica 6 9 66N29 35E20 -2:21:20
Olenino 6 39 56N12 33E29 -2:13:56
Olenja Rečka 2 21 52N48 93E14 -6:12:56
Olen'kovo 6 39 54N34 38E06 -2:32:24
Olen'ok 2 16 68N33 112E18 -7:29:12
Olenty 9 30 50N02 52E07 -3:28:28
Olesko 23 44 49N58 24E53 -1:39:32
Olevsk 23 44 51N13 27E39 -1:50:36
Ol'ga 2 27 43N45 135E18 -9:01:12
Ol'ginka 6 47 44N14 38E53 -2:35:32
Ol'ginka 23 45 47N42 37E31 -2:30:04
Ol'gino 2 24 54N59 71E54 -4:47:36
Ol'gino 2 16 52N53 125E47 -8:23:08
Ol'ginskaja 6 47 45N57 38E34 -2:34:16
Ol'ginskaja 6 40 47N11 39E56 -2:39:44
Ol'gopol' 23 45 48N12 29E29 -1:57:56
Ol'govo 6 39 56N16 37E21 -2:29:24
Oliki 6 9 59N46 29E55 -1:59:40
Olinsk 2 16 52N24 116E13 -7:44:52
Olišovka 23 44 51N13 31E18 -2:05:12
Oloči 2 16 51N21 119E55 -7:59:40
Ol'okminsk 2 16 60N24 120E24 -8:01:36
Olonec 6 9 61N00 32E57 -2:11:48
Olonki 2 20 52N54 103E45 -6:55:00
Olov'annaja 2 2 66N10 178W59 11:55:56
Olov'annaja 2 16 50N56 115E35 -7:42:20
Ol'ša 6 39 54N51 31E52 -2:07:28
Ol'šana 23 45 50N48 34E02 -2:16:08
Ol'šana 23 44 49N13 31E13 -2:04:52
Ol'šana 23 45 49N47 37E46 -2:31:04
Ol'šanka 23 45 48N14 30E52 -2:03:28
Ol'šanka 6 39 51N46 35E25 -2:21:40
Ol'šany 23 45 50N03 35E53 -2:23:32
Ol'šany 4 39 52N05 27E20 -1:49:20
Olsufjevo 6 39 53N36 33E40 -2:14:40
Olychovatka 23 45 50N12 37E31 -2:30:04
Olyka 23 44 50N42 25E51 -1:43:24
Olym 6 40 51N42 38E10 -2:32:40
Ol'zony 2 20 52N57 105E15 -7:01:00
Omalo 7 33 42N23 45E38 -3:02:32
Omčak 2 6 61N38 147E55 -9:51:40
Omčaly 22 30 40N47 53E43 -3:34:52
Omel'nik 23 45 49N12 33E32 -2:14:08
Omsino 6 42 58N36 50E28 -3:21:52
Omsk 2 24 55N00 73E24 -4:53:36
Omsukčan 2 6 62N32 155E48 -10:23:12
Omutinskij 2 30 56N31 67E41 -4:30:44
Omutninsk 6 42 58N40 52E12 -3:28:48
Onega 6 40 63N55 38E05 -2:32:20
Onekotan Island 12 8 49N25 154E45 -10:19:00
Onekotan, Ostrov 12 8 49N25 154E45 -10:19:00
Ongudaj 2 21 50N45 86E09 -5:44:36
Oni 7 33 42N34 43E27 -2:53:48
Onochoj 2 20 51N58 108E01 -7:12:04
Onor 19 8 50N11 142E40 -9:30:40
Onufrijevka 23 45 48N54 33E26 -2:13:44
Onufrijevo 6 39 55N51 36E31 -2:26:04
Opalicha 6 39 55N49 37E15 -2:29:00
Oparino 6 42 59N52 48E17 -3:13:08
Opečenskij Posad 6 9 58N16 34E07 -2:16:28
Opočka 6 39 56N43 28E38 -1:54:32
Opošn'a 23 45 49N58 34E37 -2:18:28
Opsa 4 39 55N32 26E47 -1:47:08
Oranki 6 41 55N53 43E44 -2:54:56
Oranžerei 6 34 45N50 47E36 -3:10:24
Oratov 23 44 49N12 29E32 -1:58:08
Orda 6 30 57N12 56E54 -3:47:36
Ordubad 16 34 38N56 46E02 -3:04:08
Ordynskoje 2 23 54N22 81E56 -5:27:44
Ordzhonikidze → Jenakijevo 23 45 48N14 38E13 -2:32:52
Ordzhonikidze → Ordžonikidze 6 47 43N03 44E40 -2:58:40
Ordžonikidze 24 24 41N21 69E22 -4:37:28
Ordžonikidze 9 30 52N28 61E46 -4:07:04
Ordžonikidze 23 45 47N40 34E04 -2:16:16
Ordžonikidze 23 45 44N57 35E22 -2:21:28
Ordžonikidze 6 47 43N03 44E40 -2:58:40
Ordžonikidze 3 34 40N53 47E23 -3:09:32
Ordžonikidze 7 33 42N01 43E12 -2:52:48
Ordžonikidzeabad 21 24 38N34 69E01 -4:36:04
Ordžonikidzevskaja 6 47 43N18 45E03 -3:00:12
Ordžonikidzevskij 2 21 54N46 88E59 -5:55:56
Ordžonikidzevskij 6 47 43N51 41E54 -2:47:36
Orechov 23 45 47N34 35E47 -2:23:08
Orechovka 6 34 52N56 48E14 -3:12:56
Orechovka 23 45 48N17 39E13 -2:36:52
Orechovo 6 41 58N28 41E58 -2:47:52
Orechovo-Zujevo 6 39 55N49 38E59 -2:35:56
Orechovsk 4 39 54N41 30E30 -2:02:00
Oredež 6 9 58N49 30E20 -2:01:20
Orekhovo-Zuyevo → Orechovo-Zujevo 6 39 55N49 38E59 -2:35:56
Orel → Or'ol 6 39 52N59 36E05 -2:24:20
Orenburg 6 30 51N54 55E06 -3:40:24
Oreški 6 39 55N43 36E21 -2:25:24
Orgejev 15 46 47N23 28E48 -1:55:12
Orgtrud 6 40 56N12 40E37 -2:42:28
Oriči 6 42 58N24 49E05 -3:16:20
Orinin 23 45 48N46 26E24 -1:45:36
Orissaare 5 35 58N34 23E05 -1:32:20
Orl'a 4 39 53N30 24E59 -1:39:56
Orlik 2 20 52N30 99E55 -6:39:40
Orlik 9 32 48N17 51E32 -3:26:08
Orlinga 2 20 56N03 105E53 -7:03:32
Orlov Gaj 6 34 50N57 48E12 -3:12:48
Orlovka 2 21 59N03 85E59 -5:43:56
Orlovka 6 41 51N02 40E32 -2:42:08
Orlovka 23 44 51N54 32E47 -2:11:08
Orlovka 23 45 45N40 33E21 -2:13:24
Orlovka 23 45 48N10 37E39 -2:30:36
Orlovo 6 41 51N45 39E35 -2:38:20
Orlovo 6 39 55N38 37E23 -2:29:32
Orlovskij 6 47 46N52 42E03 -2:48:12
Oročen 2 16 58N28 125E26 -8:21:44
Or'ol 6 39 52N59 36E05 -2:24:20
Or'ol 6 30 59N21 56E35 -3:46:20
Oron 2 17 57N11 116E28 -7:45:52
Orša 4 39 54N30 30E24 -2:01:36
Oršanka 6 41 56N55 47E53 -3:11:32
Orsk 6 30 51N12 58E34 -3:54:16
Ortonura 10 24 41N29 76E12 -5:04:48
Ortoterek 10 24 41N56 71E21 -4:45:24
Orto-Tokoj 10 24 42N21 76E01 -5:04:04
Orudjevo 6 39 56N26 37E32 -2:30:08
Oržev 23 44 50N45 26E07 -1:44:28
Orževka 6 41 52N43 42E55 -2:51:40
Oržica 23 44 49N48 32E42 -2:10:48
Oš 10 24 40N33 72E48 -4:51:12
Osa 6 30 57N17 55E26 -3:41:44
Osa 2 20 53N24 103E53 -6:55:32
Osakarovka 9 24 50N32 72E39 -4:50:36
Osanovo 6 39 54N12 38E41 -2:34:44
Oščepkovo 2 30 56N29 70E42 -4:42:48
Osečenka 6 39 57N33 34E48 -2:19:12
Osejevskaja 6 39 55N53 38E10 -2:32:40
Ošejkino 6 39 56N15 35E54 -2:23:36
Osetrovo 2 20 56N47 105E47 -7:03:08
Osh → Oš 10 24 40N33 72E48 -4:51:12
Osinki 6 34 52N51 49E30 -3:18:00
Osinniki 6 42 58N03 47E02 -3:08:08

Osinniki 2	21	53N37	87E21	-5:49:24
Osinovka 2	18	50N34	109E27	-7:17:48
Osinovka 2	20	56N19	101E56	-6:47:44
Osinovka 23	45	49N34	39E05	-2:36:20
Osintorf 4	39	54N42	30E39	-2:02:36
Osipenko → Berd'ansk 23	45	46N45	36E49	-2:27:16
Osipoviči 4	39	53N18	28E38	-1:54:32
Osipovo Selo 6	39	56N51	30E30	-2:02:00
Os'kino 6	40	51N14	39E02	-2:36:08
Oskolkovo 6	29	67N58	53E42	-3:34:48
Oskuj 6	9	59N17	32E05	-2:08:20
Ošm'any 4	39	54N25	25E56	-1:43:44
Os'mino 6	9	59N01	29E06	-1:56:24
Ošoba 21	24	40N44	70E26	-4:41:44
Ossora 2	4	59N20	163E13	-10:52:52
Ošta 6	40	60N49	35E32	-2:22:08
Ostapje 23	44	49N33	33E46	-2:15:04
Ostaškov 6	39	57N09	33E06	-2:12:24
Ostašovo 6	39	55N52	35E52	-2:23:28
Oster 23	44	50N57	30E53	-2:03:32
Oster 6	39	54N01	32E48	-2:11:12
Ostki 23	44	51N16	27E22	-1:49:28
Ost'or 6	39	54N01	32E48	-2:11:12
Ost'or 23	44	50N57	30E53	-2:03:32
Ostrog 23	44	50N20	26E31	-1:46:04
Ostrogožsk 6	40	50N52	39E05	-2:36:20
Ostrokonje 6	41	59N52	42E02	-2:48:08
Ostrošickij Gorodok 4	39	54N04	27E42	-1:50:48
Ostrov 4	39	52N53	25E59	-1:43:56
Ostrov 6	39	55N35	37E51	-2:31:24
Ostrov 6	39	57N20	28E22	-1:53:28
Ostrov 6	40	60N34	37E55	-2:31:40
Ostrov'anskij 6	47	46N45	42E13	-2:48:52
Ostrovcy 6	39	55N35	38E01	-2:32:04
Ostrovec 4	39	54N37	25E57	-1:43:48
Ostrovki 6	9	59N48	30E50	-2:03:20
Ostrovno 4	39	55N08	29E53	-1:59:32
Ostrovskaja 6	34	50N26	44E27	-2:57:48
Ostrovskoje 6	40	57N48	42E15	-2:49:00
Ostrov-Zalit 6	9	58N01	28E04	-1:52:16
Ostryna 4	39	53N44	24E32	-1:38:08
Osuga 6	39	56N02	34E18	-2:17:12
Osveja 4	39	56N01	28E06	-1:52:24
Ošvor 6	29	66N58	62E53	-4:11:32
Otar 9	24	43N33	75E13	-5:00:52
Otepää 5	35	58N03	26E30	-1:46:00
Otjassy 6	41	53N14	41E39	-2:46:36
Otorma 6	41	53N32	42E32	-2:50:08
Otradnaja 6	47	44N23	41E31	-2:46:04
Otradnoje 6	9	59N47	30E49	-2:03:16
Otradnyj 6	34	53N22	51E21	-3:25:24
Ottuk 10	24	42N18	76E18	-5:05:12
Ottuk 10	24	41N38	75E51	-5:03:24
Otyn'a 23	44	48N44	24E51	-1:39:24
Ovčinino 6	39	56N02	39E03	-2:36:12
Ovcyno 6	9	59N48	30E37	-2:02:28
Ovidiopol' 23	45	46N17	30E27	-2:01:48
Ovinišče 6	9	58N22	37E02	-2:28:08
Ovino 6	9	59N41	33E11	-2:12:44
Oviši 13	36	57N34	21E45	-1:27:00
Ovruč 23	44	51N21	28E49	-1:55:16
Ovs'anikovo 6	41	60N09	45E16	-3:01:04
Ovs'anka 2	21	55N57	92E33	-6:10:12
Ovs'anka 2	16	53N35	126E57	-8:27:48
Ovs'annikovo 6	39	56N54	37E33	-2:30:12
Ovstug 6	39	53N24	33E52	-2:15:28
Oymyakon → Ojm'akon 2	6	63N28	142E49	-9:31:16
Oyrot-Tura 2	21	51N58	85E57	-5:43:48
Ozariči 4	39	52N28	29E16	-1:57:04
Ozd'atiči 4	39	54N06	28E50	-1:55:20
Ozek 9	30	46N35	60E41	-4:02:44
Ozereckoje 6	39	56N04	37E23	-2:29:32
Ožerelje 6	39	54N48	38E17	-2:33:08
Ožerelki 6	39	55N51	38E52	-2:35:28
Ozerišče 6	39	54N48	33E13	-2:12:52
Ozerki 2	21	53N38	83E44	-5:34:56
Ozerki 6	30	51N13	53E56	-3:35:44
Ozerki 6	34	51N32	45E16	-3:01:04
Ozerki 6	34	52N01	45E29	-3:01:56
Ozerki 6	9	59N54	30E44	-2:02:56
Ozernoje 23	44	50N11	28E42	-1:54:48
Ozernovskij 2	4	51N30	156E31	-10:26:04
Ozernyj 2	2	66N24	179W06	11:56:24
Ozero 6	41	56N58	44E43	-2:58:52
Ozery 6	39	54N51	38E34	-2:34:16
Ozgoryš 10	24	41N15	74E45	-4:59:00
Ozinki 6	34	51N12	49E45	-3:19:00
Oz'ornaja 6	30	51N08	60E50	-4:03:20
Oz'ornaja 9	30	53N25	63E15	-4:13:00
Oz'ornoje 2	30	56N48	71E15	-4:45:00
Oz'ornoje 6	32	51N46	51E28	-3:25:52
Oz'ornoje 6	34	51N41	44E55	-2:59:40
Oz'ornyj 6	30	51N08	60E50	-4:03:20
Oz'ornyj 6	40	57N10	40E59	-2:43:56
Oz'orsk 23	44	51N43	26E24	-1:45:36
Oz'orsk 8	38	54N25	22E01	-1:28:04
Oz'orskij 19	8	46N36	143E08	-9:32:32
Oz'ory 4	39	53N43	24E11	-1:36:44
Pabradė 14	37	54N59	25E44	-1:42:56
Pačelma 6	41	53N15	43E21	-2:53:24
Pačelma 6	41	53N20	43E20	-2:53:20
Pachača 2	4	60N34	169E03	-11:16:12
Pachomovo 6	39	54N38	37E33	-2:30:12
Pachotnyj Ugol 6	41	52N58	41E56	-2:47:44
Pachtaabad 21	24	38N28	68E10	-4:32:40
Padany 6	9	63N17	33E22	-2:13:28
Padovka 6	34	52N28	49E31	-3:18:04
Padunskaja 2	21	55N02	85E02	-5:40:08
Pagėgiai 14	37	55N09	21E54	-1:27:36
Paide 5	35	58N54	25E33	-1:42:12
Paj 6	9	61N13	34E24	-2:17:36
Pajtug 24	24	40N53	72E15	-4:49:00
Pakruojis 14	37	55N58	23E52	-1:35:28
Palamuse 5	35	58N41	26E35	-1:46:20
Palana 2	4	59N07	159E58	-10:39:52
Palanga 14	37	55N55	21E03	-1:24:12
Palatcy 9	24	49N09	83E43	-5:34:52
Palatka 2	6	60N06	150E54	-10:03:36
Pal'co 6	39	53N17	34E56	-2:19:44
Paldiski 5	35	59N20	24E06	-1:36:24
Palech 6	40	56N48	41E51	-2:47:24
Palivere 5	35	58N59	23E52	-1:35:28
Palkino 6	41	58N15	42E56	-2:51:44
Palkino 6	39	57N32	28E01	-1:52:04
Pallasovka 6	34	50N03	46E53	-3:07:32
P'al'ma 6	40	62N26	35E53	-2:23:32
Palmnicken → Jantarnyj 8	38	54N52	19E57	-1:19:48
Paločka 2	21	58N25	84E32	-5:38:08
Paluga 6	41	65N16	45E11	-3:00:44
Palvantaš 24	24	40N34	72E12	-4:48:48
Palvart 22	30	38N11	64E34	-4:18:16
Pam'ati 13 Borcov 2	21	56N13	92E20	-6:09:20
Pam'atnaja 2	30	56N01	65E42	-4:22:48
Pam'at' Parižskoj Kommuny 6	41	56N06	44E31	-2:58:04
Pančevo 23	45	48N44	31E51	-2:07:24
Pandėlys 14	37	56N01	25E13	-1:40:52
Panevėžys 14	37	55N44	24E21	-1:37:24
Panfilov 9	24	44N10	80E01	-5:20:04
Panfilovo 6	34	50N26	42E55	-2:51:40
Panika 9	32	50N59	50E11	-3:20:44
Panino 6	41	51N38	40E08	-2:40:32
Panino 6	39	56N25	34E34	-2:18:16
Panino-Nesterovo 6	39	55N23	38E11	-2:32:44
Pankratovo 6	41	59N10	43E30	-2:54:00
Panovo 6	41	59N48	46E27	-3:05:48
Panovo 2	19	58N58	101E58	-6:47:52
Pansionat 6	39	55N59	37E41	-2:30:44
Pantajevka 23	45	48N41	32E53	-2:11:32
Pantelejmonovka 23	45	48N12	37E59	-2:31:56
Pan'utino 23	45	48N56	36E17	-2:25:08
Panyčevo 2	23	57N05	81E49	-5:27:16
Pap 24	24	40N53	71E07	-4:44:28
Papilė 14	37	56N09	22E48	-1:31:12
Papulovo 6	42	60N34	48E00	-3:12:00
Parabel' 2	23	58N43	81E31	-5:26:04
Paradino 4	39	53N59	31E51	-2:07:24
Parafijevka 23	44	50N53	32E38	-2:10:32
Paragačaj 16	34	39N07	45E56	-3:03:44
Paramušir Island 12	8	50N40	156E08	-10:24:32
Paramušir, Ostrov 12	8	50N40	156E08	-10:24:32
Paran'ga 6	41	56N43	49E24	-3:17:36
Parbig 2	23	57N14	81E24	-5:25:36
Parchomenko 23	45	48N34	39E43	-2:38:52
Parchomovka 23	45	50N08	35E01	-2:20:04
Paren' 2	4	62N28	163E05	-10:52:20
Parfenjevo 6	41	61N21	42E43	-2:50:52
Parfenjevo 6	41	58N29	43E25	-2:53:40
Parfentevo 6	39	55N06	38E49	-2:35:16
Parfino 6	39	57N58	31E41	-2:06:44
Pargolovo 6	9	60N04	30E18	-2:01:12
Pariči 4	39	52N48	29E25	-1:57:40
Parkany 15	46	46N49	29E31	-1:58:04
Parkent 24	24	41N18	69E40	-4:38:40
Pärnu 5	35	58N24	24E32	-1:38:08
Pärnu-Jaagupi 5	35	58N37	24E30	-1:38:00
Paromaj 19	8	52N50	143E02	-9:32:08
Paršino 2	20	59N10	111E48	-7:27:12
Pärsti 5	35	58N25	25E32	-1:42:08
Partizansk 2	27	43N08	133E09	-8:52:36
Partizanskoje 2	21	55N30	94E24	-6:17:36
Parutino 23	45	46N43	31E53	-2:07:32
Pasanauri 7	33	42N21	44E41	-2:58:44
Pašija 6	30	58N26	58E16	-3:53:04
Pašino 2	21	55N11	83E00	-5:32:00
Paškovo 6	41	53N39	42E25	-2:49:40
Paškovo 2	11	48N54	130E42	-8:42:48
Paškovskij 6	47	45N02	39E06	-2:36:24
Pašn'a 6	29	63N21	56E28	-3:45:52
Pašozero 6	9	60N02	34E37	-2:18:28
Pašskij Perevoz 6	9	60N24	32E59	-2:11:56
Pašukovo 6	39	55N55	38E16	-2:33:04
Pasvalys 14	37	56N04	24E24	-1:37:36
P'atichatki 23	45	48N24	33E42	-2:14:48
P'atigorsk 6	47	44N03	43E04	-2:52:16
P'atimar 9	32	49N31	50E32	-3:22:08
P'atnica 6	39	54N46	38E09	-2:32:36
P'atnica 6	39	56N05	36E48	-2:27:12
P'atnickoje 6	39	50N25	37E51	-2:31:24
P'atnickoje 6	39	54N20	35E53	-2:23:32
Patokino 6	39	56N27	39E06	-2:36:24
P'atovskij 6	39	54N41	36E04	-2:24:16
Pavda 2	30	59N15	59E30	-3:58:00
Pavel'cevo 6	39	56N15	36E26	-2:25:44
Pavelec 6	40	53N50	39E16	-2:37:04
Pävilosta 13	36	56N53	21E14	-1:24:56
Pavino 6	41	59N07	46E07	-3:04:28
Pavliščevo 6	39	55N11	35E59	-2:23:56
Pavliščevo 6	39	55N34	35E59	-2:23:56
Pavlodar 9	24	52N18	76E57	-5:07:48
Pavlograd 23	45	48N32	35E53	-2:23:32
Pavlogradka 2	24	54N12	73E33	-4:54:12
Pavlopol' 23	45	47N16	37E47	-2:31:08
Pavlovka 6	30	55N25	56E33	-3:46:12
Pavlovka 6	30	51N55	54E47	-3:39:08
Pavlovka 6	34	52N41	47E09	-3:08:36
Pavlovka 23	45	47N45	37E14	-2:28:56
Pavlovka 23	45	48N08	39E33	-2:38:12
Pavlovka 23	45	49N36	38E42	-2:34:48
Pavlovo 6	40	55N58	43E04	-2:52:16
Pavlovo 6	41	60N05	45E17	-3:01:08
Pavlovo 6	9	59N56	30E40	-2:02:40
Pavlovo 6	9	59N49	30E54	-2:03:36
Pavlovsk 6	41	50N27	40E08	-2:40:32
Pavlovsk 6	9	59N41	30E27	-2:01:48
Pavlovsk 2	21	53N20	82E59	-5:31:56
Pavlovskaja 6	47	46N08	39E48	-2:39:12
Pavlovskaja Sloboda 6	39	55N49	37E05	-2:28:20
Pavlovskij 6	30	57N50	54E51	-3:39:24
Pavlovskij 9	30	52N32	63E06	-4:12:24
Pavlovskij Posad 6	39	55N47	38E40	-2:34:40
Pavlyš 23	45	48N55	33E21	-2:13:24
Pavšino 6	39	55N49	37E21	-2:29:24
Pavšozero 6	40	60N38	35E34	-2:22:16
Pavy 6	9	58N03	29E30	-1:58:00
P'ažijeva Sel'ga 6	9	61N29	34E29	-2:17:56
Pčevža 6	9	59N23	32E20	-2:09:20
Pečenegi 23	45	49N52	36E55	-2:27:40
Pečenežin 23	44	48N32	24E54	-1:39:36
Pečenga 6	9	69N33	31E07	-2:04:28
Pečerniki 6	40	54N39	39E14	-2:36:56
Pečernikovskije Vyselki 6	40	54N10	39E10	-2:36:40
Pechra-Jakovlevskaja 6	39	55N48	37E58	-2:31:52
Pechra-Pokrovskoje 6	39	55N50	37E57	-2:31:48
Pechu 7	33	43N24	40E49	-2:43:16
Peči 6	41	54N48	44E19	-2:57:16
Pečicy 6	39	55N36	38E27	-2:33:48
Pečora 6	29	65N10	57E11	-3:48:44
Pečora 23	45	48N52	28E42	-1:54:48
Pečory 6	39	57N49	27E36	-1:50:24
Pegyš 6	41	63N26	50E30	-3:22:00
Peklino 6	39	53N33	33E32	-2:14:08
Pektubajevo 6	41	57N02	48E23	-3:13:32
Pel'a-Chovanskaja 6	41	54N36	44E56	-2:59:44
Pelagejevka 23	45	48N06	38E36	-2:34:24
Peleduj 2	16	59N36	112E45	-7:31:00
Pelenija 15	46	47N53	27E50	-1:51:20
Pel'ušn'a 6	9	58N56	32E52	-2:11:28
Pelym 2	30	59N38	63E05	-4:12:20
Pemzašen 1	34	40N35	43E57	-2:55:48
Pen'agino 6	39	55N50	37E21	-2:29:24
Pen'akša 6	41	56N22	44E56	-2:59:44
Pendžikent 21	24	39N29	67E35	-4:30:20
Penkino 6	39	54N50	38E53	-2:35:32
Peno 6	39	56N55	32E45	-2:11:00
Pen'ok 2	23	55N30	81E34	-5:26:16
Peny 6	39	51N04	35E54	-2:23:36
Penza 6	41	53N13	45E00	-3:00:00
Penzino 6	34	52N07	50E27	-3:21:48
Perchuškovo 6	39	55N41	37E10	-2:28:40
Perebrody 23	44	51N43	27E00	-1:48:00
Perečin 23	44	48N44	22E26	-1:29:44
Peredel 6	39	55N12	35E41	-2:22:44
Peredel'cy 6	39	55N36	37E21	-2:29:24
Peredelkino 6	39	55N39	37E21	-2:29:24
Peregino 6	39	57N27	31E21	-2:05:24
Pereginskoje 23	44	48N49	24E12	-1:36:48
Peregonovka 23	45	48N32	30E31	-2:02:04
Perejaslav-Chmel'nickij 23	44	50N06	31E30	-2:06:00
Perejaslavka 2	11	47N58	135E06	-9:00:24
Perejaslavskaja 6	47	45N51	39E02	-2:36:08
Perejezdnoje 23	45	48N47	38E04	-2:32:16
Perejež'na 6	42	59N43	48E12	-3:12:48
Perekopnoje 6	34	51N13	48E04	-3:12:16
Perekopovka 23	44	50N37	33E25	-2:13:40
Perekopskaja 6	34	49N21	43E20	-2:53:20
Perelazi 6	39	53N02	31E28	-2:05:52
Perelazovskij 6	34	49N09	42E33	-2:50:12
Perelazy 6	39	53N02	31E28	-2:05:52
Perelešino 6	41	51N44	40E07	-2:40:28
Perelesinskij 6	41	51N44	40E07	-2:40:28
Perel'ub 6	34	51N52	50E22	-3:21:28
Perem'otnoje 9	32	51N11	50E49	-3:23:16
Peremyšl' 6	39	54N16	36E10	-2:24:40
Peremyšl'any 23	44	49N41	24E33	-1:38:12
Pereputje 19	8	46N17	141E54	-9:27:36
Pererov 4	39	52N04	28E00	-1:52:00
Pereščepino 23	45	49N01	35E22	-2:21:28
Pereščepnoje 6	34	50N32	45E06	-3:00:24
Pereslavl'-Zalesskij 6	39	56N44	38E51	-2:35:24
Peresypkino Pervoje 6	41	52N55	42E55	-2:51:40

Peretrusovo 6 39 56N51 36E53 -2:27:32
Pereval'sk 23 45 48N26 38E47 -2:35:08
Perevolockij 6 30 51N32 55E06 -3:40:24
Perevoz 6 41 55N36 44E32 -2:58:08
Perevoz 6 9 59N43 30E47 -2:03:08
Perevoz 2 17 59N00 116E57 -7:47:48
Perl'ovka 6 40 51N51 38E51 -2:35:24
Perm' 6 30 58N00 56E15 -3:45:00
Permas 6 41 59N20 45E34 -3:02:16
Permisi 6 41 54N06 45E48 -3:03:12
Pernovo 6 39 55N58 39E10 -2:36:40
Peršaj 4 39 54N02 26E41 -1:46:44
Peršotravensk 23 45 48N22 36E24 -2:25:36
Peršotravensk 23 44 50N12 27E39 -1:50:36
Peršotravnevoje 23 45 48N22 36E24 -2:25:36
Peršotravnevoje 23 44 51N24 28E53 -1:55:32
Peršotravnevoje 23 45 47N03 37E18 -2:29:12
Pertominsk 6 40 64N47 38E25 -2:33:40
Pertovo 6 41 54N22 41E31 -2:46:04
Pervaja Maja 9 24 48N55 67E25 -4:29:40
Pervesinka 6 34 52N13 43E15 -2:53:00
Pervoavgustovskij 6 39 52N14 35E03 -2:20:12
Pervoje Pole 2 2 63N05 179E19-11:57:16
Pervomajka 23 45 49N09 37E58 -2:31:52
Pervomajka 9 24 51N17 70E08 -4:40:32
Pervomajsk 23 45 48N04 30E52 -2:03:28
Pervomajsk 23 45 48N37 38E35 -2:34:20
Pervomajsk 23 45 49N05 39E37 -2:38:28
Pervomajsk 2 21 58N02 94E05 -6:16:20
Pervomajsk 6 41 54N53 43E49 -2:55:16
Pervomajskij 6 41 64N26 40E47 -2:43:08
Pervomajskij 6 34 53N22 51E38 -3:26:32
Pervomajskij 6 34 51N22 48E54 -3:15:36
Pervomajskij 6 41 53N15 40E18 -2:41:12
Pervomajskij 23 45 49N24 36E12 -2:24:48
Pervomajskij 6 39 54N04 32E29 -2:09:56
Pervomajskij 4 39 53N54 25E23 -1:41:32
Pervomajskij 6 39 55N57 37E52 -2:31:28
Pervomajskij 6 39 54N03 37E32 -2:30:08
Pervomajskij 6 39 55N32 37E09 -2:28:36
Pervomajskij 23 45 47N58 38E47 -2:35:08
Pervomajskij 2 30 54N52 61E08 -4:04:32
Pervomajskij 2 30 59N29 61E24 -4:05:36
Pervomajskij 2 16 51N44 115E39 -7:42:36
Pervomajskij 10 24 42N51 74E04 -4:56:16
Pervomajskij 6 30 51N32 55E06 -3:40:24
Pervomajskij 6 30 53N41 55E57 -3:43:48
Pervomajskoje 6 47 48N50 41E14 -2:44:56
Pervomajskoje 6 34 51N28 47E37 -3:10:28
Pervomajskoje 6 34 50N56 46E46 -3:07:04
Pervomajskoje 23 45 45N43 33E51 -2:15:24
Pervomajskoje 6 39 52N56 33E36 -2:14:24
Pervomajskoje 2 21 53N45 84E08 -5:36:32
Pervomajskoje 2 21 57N06 86E12 -5:44:48
Pervomajskoje 9 24 42N05 69E53 -4:39:32
Pervomajskoje 6 41 55N05 47E22 -3:09:28
Pervomajskoje 6 47 46N03 42E13 -2:48:52
Pervomajskoje 6 47 46N21 43E37 -2:54:28
Pervomaskij 6 30 53N41 55E57 -3:43:48
Pervoural'sk 2 30 56N54 59E58 -3:59:52
Pervušino 6 41 58N02 41E56 -2:47:44
Pes' 6 9 58N55 34E19 -2:17:16
Pesčanaja 23 45 48N08 29E44 -1:58:56
Pesčanka 6 34 51N18 43E40 -2:54:40
Pesčanka 23 45 48N12 28E53 -1:55:32
Pesčanoje 6 40 62N09 35E48 -2:23:12
Pesčanoje 23 44 49N44 31E50 -2:07:20
Pesčanoje 23 45 49N34 37E51 -2:31:24
Pesčanoje 9 24 53N01 76E19 -5:05:16
Pesčanokopskoje 6 47 46N12 41E04 -2:44:16
Pesčanyj 23 45 47N02 37E28 -2:29:52
Pesjane 6 39 56N01 38E48 -2:35:12
Peski 6 41 51N16 42E27 -2:49:48
Peski 23 44 50N23 33E27 -2:13:48
Peski 4 39 53N21 24E38 -1:38:32
Peski 6 39 55N13 38E46 -2:35:04
Peški 6 39 56N08 37E04 -2:28:16
Peski 23 45 49N26 38E59 -2:35:56
Peski-Rad'kovskije 23 45 49N17 37E36 -2:30:24
Peskovatskoje 6 39 54N03 36E16 -2:25:04
Peskovka 6 42 59N04 52E22 -3:29:28
Peskovka 23 44 50N42 29E38 -1:58:32
Peškovo 6 40 47N02 39E24 -2:37:36
Peškovo Grecovo 6 39 54N26 37E36 -2:30:24
Peškovskoje 9 30 53N45 62E23 -4:09:32
Pesočenskij 6 39 54N10 36E06 -2:24:24
Pesočin 23 45 49N57 36E06 -2:24:24
Pesočn'a 6 41 54N07 40E50 -2:43:20
Pesočnoje 6 40 58N01 39E10 -2:36:40
Pesočnoje 4 39 53N20 27E06 -1:48:24
Pesočnyj 6 9 60N07 30E08 -2:00:32
Pest'aki 6 40 56N43 42E40 -2:50:40
Pestovo 6 41 57N12 46E44 -3:06:56
Pestovo 6 9 58N36 35E48 -2:23:12
Pestravka 6 34 52N24 49E58 -3:19:52
Pestrecy 6 41 55N46 49E39 -3:18:36
Pestrikovo 6 39 55N05 38E53 -2:35:32
Petrecovo 6 30 61N18 57E07 -3:48:28
Petrikov 4 39 52N08 28E30 -1:54:00
Petrikovka 23 45 48N43 34E37 -2:18:28
Petriščevo 6 39 54N37 36E57 -2:27:48
Petriščevo 6 39 55N30 36E18 -2:25:12
Petrodvorec 6 9 59N53 29E54 -1:59:36
Petrograd → Leningrad 6 9 59N55 30E15 -2:01:00
Petrokrepost' 6 9 59N57 31E02 -2:04:08
Petrominsk 6 40 64N47 38E25 -2:33:40
Petropavlovka 6 47 50N06 40E54 -2:43:36
Petropavlovka 23 45 48N27 36E26 -2:25:44
Petropavlovka 23 45 49N43 37E42 -2:30:48
Petropavlovka 2 20 50N38 105E19 -7:01:16
Petropavlovsk 6 30 56N20 57E09 -3:48:36
Petropavlovsk 9 24 54N54 69E06 -4:36:24
Petropavlovsk-Kamčatskij 2 4 53N01 158E39-10:34:36
Petropavlovskoje 2 21 52N04 84E08 -5:36:32
Petropavlovskoje 2 20 58N13 108E59 -7:15:56
Petro-Slav'anka 6 9 59N48 30E31 -2:02:04
Petrovka 6 34 53N13 51E58 -3:27:52
Petrovka 23 45 46N54 30E44 -2:02:56
Petrovka 23 45 48N53 39E52 -2:39:28
Petrovka 23 45 48N48 39E16 -2:37:04
Petrovo 23 45 48N20 33E16 -2:13:04
Petrovo 6 9 58N22 35E09 -2:20:36
Petrovo 6 39 55N00 38E08 -2:32:32
Petrovo 2 20 54N30 105E15 -7:01:00
Petrovo-Dal'neje 6 39 55N45 37E11 -2:28:44
Petrovsk 6 34 52N19 45E23 -3:01:32
Petrovskaja 6 47 45N25 37E57 -2:31:48
Petrovskij 6 40 56N39 40E19 -2:41:16
Petrovskij 6 34 50N45 41E59 -2:47:56
Petrovskij 6 39 54N29 36E59 -2:27:56
Petrovskoje 6 39 57N01 39E16 -2:37:04
Petrovskoje 23 45 49N10 36E54 -2:27:36
Petrovskoje 6 39 55N27 38E21 -2:33:24
Petrovskoje 6 39 55N32 36E59 -2:27:56
Petrovskoje 23 45 48N18 38E52 -2:35:28
Petrovskoje 6 39 55N36 37E53 -2:31:32
Petrovskoje 6 41 52N39 40E15 -2:41:00
Petrovsk-Zabajkal'skij 2 18 51N17 108E50 -7:15:20
Petrov Val 6 34 50N09 45E12 -3:00:48
Petrozavodsk 6 9 61N47 34E20 -2:17:20
Petrun' 6 29 66N28 60E43 -4:02:52
Petrušino 6 9 59N48 30E50 -2:03:20
Petuchovo 2 30 55N06 67E58 -4:31:52
Petuški 6 39 55N55 39E28 -2:37:52
Pevek 2 4 69N42 170E17-11:21:08
Pezas 2 21 54N39 87E46 -5:51:04
Peženga 6 41 59N10 44E16 -2:57:04
Pičajevo 6 41 53N15 42E12 -2:48:48
Pičeury 6 41 54N19 45E50 -3:03:20
Pichtovka 2 23 56N00 82E42 -5:30:48
Pičkir'ajevo 6 41 54N12 42E27 -2:49:48
Picunda 7 33 43N12 40E21 -2:41:24
Pigari 6 34 51N24 49E42 -3:18:48
Pikal'ovo 6 9 59N31 34E06 -2:16:24
Pikkola 6 9 59N42 30E08 -2:00:32
Pil'dozero 6 9 65N43 33E28 -2:13:52
Pil'gyn 2 2 69N18 179W08 11:56:32
Pillau → Baltijsk 8 38 54N39 19E55 -1:19:40
Pil'na 6 41 55N33 45E55 -3:03:40
Piltene 13 36 57N13 21E40 -1:26:40
Pil'ugino 6 32 53N25 52E26 -3:29:44
Pinčuga 2 21 58N23 96E59 -6:27:56
Pinduši 6 9 62N56 34E35 -2:18:20
Pinega 6 41 64N42 43E19 -2:53:16
Pinerovka 6 34 51N34 43E04 -2:52:16
Pinsk 4 39 52N07 26E04 -1:44:16
Pin'ug 6 42 60N15 47E48 -3:11:12
Pionerskij (Neukuhren) 8 38 54N57 20E20 -1:21:20
Pir'atin 23 44 50N15 32E30 -2:10:00
Piroči 6 39 55N04 38E57 -2:35:48
Pirogovka 23 44 51N54 33E18 -2:13:12
Pirogovskij 6 39 55N59 37E44 -2:30:56
Pirovskoje 2 21 57N37 92E16 -6:09:04
Pirsagat 3 34 39N54 49E24 -3:17:36
Pisarevka 6 47 49N53 40E12 -2:40:48
Piščalje 6 42 58N14 48E42 -3:14:48
Piscovo 6 40 57N11 40E32 -2:42:08
Pis'mennoje 23 45 48N13 35E48 -2:23:12
Pišnur 6 42 57N47 47E58 -3:11:52
Pitelino 6 41 54N34 41E49 -2:47:16
Piterka 6 34 50N42 47E27 -3:09:48
Pitim 6 41 53N12 42E21 -2:49:24
Pitk'aranta 6 9 61N34 31E27 -2:05:48
Pivan' 2 11 50N29 137E06 -9:08:24
Pižanka 6 42 57N28 48E33 -3:14:12
Pižma 6 41 57N52 47E06 -3:08:24
Pjalka 6 9 66N43 40E59 -2:43:56
Plachino 6 40 54N28 39E20 -2:37:20
Plachtejevka 23 45 46N07 29E43 -1:58:52
Plaksino 6 39 56N11 30E42 -2:02:48
Planerskoje 23 45 44N57 35E14 -2:20:56
Plast 2 30 54N22 60E50 -4:03:20
Plastovo 6 39 54N17 37E03 -2:28:12
Plastun 2 11 44N45 136E19 -9:05:16
Plastunovskaja 6 47 45N18 39E16 -2:37:04
Platnirovskaja 6 47 45N23 39E23 -2:37:32
Platono-Petrovka 6 40 46N59 39E28 -2:37:52
Platonovka 6 41 52N43 41E57 -2:47:48
Platovo 6 47 48N05 39E53 -2:39:32
Pļaviņas 13 36 56N37 25E43 -1:42:52
Plavsk 6 39 53N43 37E18 -2:29:12
Plechanovo 6 39 54N14 37E33 -2:30:12
Plechanovskoje 6 41 52N39 39E50 -2:39:20
Plechovo 6 39 51N07 35E18 -2:21:12
Pleščenicy 4 39 54N25 27E50 -1:51:20
Pleseck 6 41 62N43 40E20 -2:41:20
Plešivka 6 39 54N23 37E09 -2:28:36
Pletenevka 6 39 54N31 36E06 -2:24:24
Plet'onyj Tašlyk 23 45 48N29 31E40 -2:06:40
Plintovka 6 9 60N01 30E46 -2:03:04
Pliski 23 44 51N07 32E24 -2:09:36
Pliskov 23 44 49N23 29E18 -1:57:12
Plodorodnoje 6 47 46N44 41E06 -2:44:24
Pl'os 6 40 57N27 41E31 -2:46:04
Ploskij 6 47 46N17 40E15 -2:41:00
Ploskoje 6 40 52N45 38E21 -2:33:24
Ploskoš' 6 39 56N46 31E16 -2:05:04
Pl'oso 6 40 59N47 35E43 -2:22:52
Plotbišče 6 42 56N50 50E35 -3:22:20
Plotina 6 47 48N33 40E05 -2:40:20
Plotnica 4 39 52N03 26E39 -1:46:36
Plungė 14 37 55N55 21E51 -1:27:24
Pl'usa 6 9 58N26 29E21 -1:57:24
Pl'uskovo 6 39 52N46 33E49 -2:15:16
Pobedino 19 8 49N51 142E49 -9:31:16
Počajev 23 44 50N01 25E31 -1:42:04
Počegda 6 41 62N42 43E23 -2:53:32
Počep 6 39 52N56 33E27 -2:13:48
Počepy 4 39 53N17 31E20 -2:05:20
Pochvistnevo 6 34 53N38 52E08 -3:28:32
Počinki 6 41 54N42 44E51 -2:59:24
Počinnaja Sopka 6 9 58N25 34E22 -2:17:28
Počinok 6 39 54N25 32E27 -2:09:48
Podbel'skaja 6 34 53N37 51E50 -3:27:20
Podberezje 6 39 56N57 30E38 -2:02:32
Podberezje 6 39 56N46 37E10 -2:28:40
Podborki 6 39 54N11 35E56 -2:23:44
Podborovje 6 9 59N30 35E02 -2:20:08
Podbuž 23 44 49N22 23E15 -1:33:00
Podbužje 6 39 53N30 34E56 -2:19:44
Podčerje 6 29 63N57 57E34 -3:50:16
Podchožeje 6 39 54N19 38E34 -2:34:16
Podčinnyj 6 34 50N52 45E13 -3:00:52
Poddemjur 6 29 64N05 53E26 -3:33:44
Poddolgoje 6 39 53N12 38E04 -2:32:16
Poddorje 6 39 57N28 31E07 -2:04:28
Podgajcy 23 44 49N16 25E08 -1:40:32
Podgorenskij 6 41 50N24 39E39 -2:38:36
Podgornaja 6 47 50N28 41E10 -2:44:40
Podgornoje 6 41 51N43 39E07 -2:36:28
Podgornoje 6 41 50N27 39E37 -2:38:28
Podgornoje 2 23 57N47 82E36 -5:30:24
Podgornoje 9 24 42N55 72E25 -4:49:40
Podgornoje 6 47 46N33 43E07 -2:52:28
Podgorodnaja 23 45 48N07 30E51 -2:03:24
Podgorodnoje 23 45 48N34 35E08 -2:20:32
Podjom-Michajlovka 6 34 52N49 50E32 -3:22:08
Podkamen' 23 44 49N57 25E19 -1:41:16
Podkamennaja Tunguska 2 21 61N36 90E09 -6:00:36
Podlesnoje 6 34 51N50 47E03 -3:08:12
Podlesnoje 23 45 48N47 32E15 -2:09:00
Podlopatki 2 20 50N55 107E05 -7:08:20
Podmošje 6 39 56N23 37E24 -2:29:36
Podol'sk 6 39 55N26 37E33 -2:30:12
Podora 6 29 62N22 54E19 -3:37:16
Podosinovec 6 42 60N17 47E04 -3:08:16
Podoz'orskij 6 40 57N14 40E20 -2:41:20

Podporožje 6 9 60N53 34E07 -2:16:28
Podrezčicha 6 42 59N22 51E28 -3:25:52
Podstepnyj 9 32 51N08 51E28 -3:25:52
Podsvilje 4 39 55N09 27E58 -1:51:52
Podt'osovo 2 21 58N36 92E06 -6:08:24
Pod'uga 6 41 61N06 40E53 -2:43:32
Poduškino 6 39 55N43 37E17 -2:29:08
Podvoločisk 23 44 49N33 26E09 -1:44:36
Podymachino 2 20 56N59 106E11 -7:04:44
Podyvotje 6 39 52N03 34E08 -2:16:32
Pogar 6 39 52N33 33E16 -2:13:04
Pogibi 19 8 52N12 141E42 -9:26:48
Pogodajev 9 32 51N37 51E04 -3:24:16
Pogoreloje Gorodišče 6 39 56N08 34E56 -2:19:44
Pogost 6 40 57N39 42E33 -2:50:12
Pogost 4 39 52N51 27E39 -1:50:36
Pogost 4 39 53N51 29E09 -1:56:36
Pogost 6 39 56N52 39E04 -2:36:16
Pogožeje 6 39 51N36 37E16 -2:29:04
Pograničnoje 6 34 50N32 48E38 -3:14:32
Pograničnyj 6 47 46N57 45E46 -3:03:04
Pograničnyj 2 27 44N25 131E24 -8:45:36
Pogrebišče 23 44 49N29 29E16 -1:57:04
Pogromnoje 6 32 52N35 52E32 -3:30:08
Pogruznaja 6 42 54N14 50E29 -3:21:56
Pöide 5 35 58N31 23E03 -1:32:12
Poim 6 41 53N01 43E11 -2:52:44
Poiseevo 6 41 55N32 53E30 -3:34:00
Poisevo 6 41 55N32 53E30 -3:34:00
Pojarkovo 2 14 49N38 128E38 -8:34:32
Pokatejeva 2 21 56N59 97E25 -6:29:40
Pokatilovka 9 24 45N23 80E10 -5:20:40
Pokatilovka 9 30 51N06 51E53 -3:27:32
Pokojnoje 6 47 44N48 44E16 -2:57:04
Pokol'ubiči 4 39 52N30 31E02 -2:04:08
Pokrov 6 39 55N55 39E10 -2:36:40
Pokrovka 9 24 49N28 81E28 -5:25:52
Pokrovka 2 27 43N57 131E39 -8:46:36
Pokrovka 10 24 42N20 78E01 -5:12:04
Pokrovka 10 24 42N45 71E36 -4:46:24
Pokrovka 6 34 48N22 46E04 -3:04:16
Pokrovka 6 32 53N47 53E19 -3:33:16
Pokrovka 23 45 47N59 36E14 -2:24:56
Pokrovka 9 24 54N17 68E15 -4:33:00
Pokrovo-Kirejevo 23 45 47N38 38E16 -2:33:04
Pokrovsk 2 16 61N29 129E06 -8:36:24
Pokrovskaja Arčada 6 41 52N56 44E13 -2:56:52
Pokrovskij 23 45 46N32 31E38 -2:06:32
Pokrovskoje 23 45 49N44 38E13 -2:32:52
Pokrovskoje 6 39 52N38 36E51 -2:27:24
Pokrovskoje 6 39 56N25 37E03 -2:28:12
Pokrovskoje 6 39 55N53 36E19 -2:25:16
Pokrovskoje 6 40 47N25 38E54 -2:35:36
Pokrovskoje 23 45 48N37 38E09 -2:32:36
Pokrovskoje 6 9 59N44 30E46 -2:03:04
Pokrovskoje 2 30 57N14 66E48 -4:27:12
Pokrovskoje 23 45 47N59 36E14 -2:24:56
Pokrovskoje 6 41 54N04 43E37 -2:54:28
Pokrovskoje 6 41 53N54 40E26 -2:41:44
Pokrovsk-Ural'skij 2 30 60N10 59E49 -3:59:16
Pokur 2 25 61N02 75E26 -5:01:44
Pola 6 39 57N56 31E50 -2:07:20
Pol'arnik 2 2 66N58 179W20 11:57:20
Pol'arnyj 2 2 69N10 178E48 -11:55:12
Pol'arnyj 6 9 69N12 33E22 -2:13:28
Poldnevica 6 41 58N37 46E38 -3:06:32
Pol'dorak 21 24 39N25 69E56 -4:39:44
Polesje 4 39 53N05 31E17 -2:05:08
Polessk (Labiau) 8 38 54N52 21E05 -1:24:20
Polesskoje 23 44 51N14 29E22 -1:57:28
Polevaja 6 39 51N37 36E30 -2:26:00
Polevskoj 2 30 56N26 60E11 -4:00:44
Politotdel'skoje 6 40 47N33 39E05 -2:36:20
Polivanovo 6 34 53N36 47E23 -3:09:32
Pol'kino 2 19 71N10 99E13 -6:36:52
Pol'noje-Jaltunovo 6 41 53N59 41E52 -2:47:28
Polnovo-Seliger 6 39 57N32 32E55 -2:11:40
Polock 4 39 55N31 28E46 -1:55:04
Polock 2 30 52N46 59E42 -3:58:48
Pologi 23 45 47N29 36E15 -2:25:00
Pologoje Zajmišče 6 34 48N29 45E57 -3:03:48
Pologrudovo 2 24 57N07 74E13 -4:56:52
Polom 6 42 59N13 50E50 -3:23:20
Polom 6 42 57N47 53E29 -3:33:56
Polonnoje 23 44 50N07 27E30 -1:50:00
Pološkovo 6 39 54N08 35E53 -2:23:32
Polotn'anyj 6 39 54N45 36E00 -2:24:00
Polotsk → Polock 4 39 55N31 28E46 -1:55:04
Polovinkino 23 45 49N14 38E55 -2:35:40
Polovinnoje 2 30 54N43 63E50 -4:15:20
Polovinnoje 2 23 53N46 79E15 -5:17:00
Polovo 6 39 57N03 32E27 -2:09:48
Poltava 23 45 49N35 34E34 -2:18:16
Poltavka 2 24 54N22 71E45 -4:47:00
Poltevy Pen'ki 6 41 54N35 42E06 -2:48:24
Põltsamaa 5 35 58N38 25E58 -1:43:52
Poludino 9 24 54N51 69E55 -4:39:40
Polunočnoje 2 30 60N52 60E25 -4:01:40
Polur'adinki 6 39 54N51 38E41 -2:34:44
Poluškino 6 39 55N41 38E05 -2:32:20
Põlva 5 35 58N03 27E03 -1:48:12
Polynnoje 6 34 46N51 46E56 -3:07:44
Polysajevo 2 21 54N35 86E14 -5:44:56
Pominovo 6 39 55N26 39E11 -2:36:44
Pomor'any 23 44 49N38 24E56 -1:39:44
Pomošnaja 23 45 48N14 31E26 -2:05:44
Pomozdino 6 29 62N12 54E06 -3:36:24
Pompejevka 2 11 48N23 130E46 -8:43:04
Ponazyrevo 6 41 58N21 46E19 -3:05:16
Ponežukaj 6 47 44N53 39E22 -2:37:28
Pon'goma 6 40 65N21 34E25 -2:17:40
Poninka 23 44 50N12 27E32 -1:50:08
Ponino 6 42 58N16 52E49 -3:31:16
Ponizovje 6 39 55N17 31E04 -2:04:16
Ponoj 6 9 67N05 41E07 -2:44:28
Ponomar'ovka 6 30 53N19 54E08 -3:36:32
Ponomar'ovka 2 23 56N08 82E23 -5:29:32
Ponornica 23 44 51N43 32E49 -2:11:16
Pontonnyj 6 9 59N47 30E38 -2:02:32
Ponyri 6 39 52N19 36E20 -2:25:20
Popasnaja 23 45 48N37 38E20 -2:33:20
Popasnoje 23 45 48N48 35E31 -2:22:04
Popel'n'a 23 44 49N57 29E27 -1:57:48
Popel'nastoje 23 45 48N39 33E43 -2:14:52
Poperečnoje 2 20 52N23 110E42 -7:22:48
Popigaj 2 19 71N55 110E47 -7:23:08
Popki 6 34 50N11 44E30 -2:58:00
Poplevinskij 6 40 53N41 39E33 -2:38:12
Popova 2 27 42N58 131E42 -8:46:48
Popovka 6 47 49N14 41E12 -2:44:48
Popovka 6 40 60N08 39E21 -2:37:24
Popovkino 6 39 56N07 36E01 -2:24:04
Poputnaja 6 47 44N31 41E27 -2:45:48
Porchov 6 39 57N46 29E34 -1:58:16
Porečje 6 39 55N43 35E33 -2:22:12
Porečje 6 39 56N06 30E29 -2:01:56
Porečje 4 39 53N55 24E07 -1:36:28
Porečje Rybnoje 6 40 57N06 39E23 -2:37:32
Poreckoje 6 41 55N12 46E20 -3:05:20
Porez 6 42 57N40 51E10 -3:24:40
Porjaguba 6 9 66N47 33E45 -2:15:00
Porog 6 40 63N50 38E29 -2:33:56
Porog 6 9 59N16 33E24 -2:13:36
Porogi 6 9 59N46 30E47 -2:03:08
Poronajsk 19 8 49N14 143E04 -9:32:16
Poroškovo 23 44 48N41 22E45 -1:31:00
Porosozero 6 9 62N43 32E42 -2:10:48
Porozovo 4 39 52N56 24E22 -1:37:28
Porožskij 2 20 56N04 101E46 -6:47:04
Port-Iljič 3 34 38N53 48E48 -3:15:12
Port-Katon 6 47 46N52 38E46 -2:35:04
Port-Vladimir 6 9 69N25 33E06 -2:12:24
Porzdni 6 40 57N00 42E33 -2:50:12
Poščharv 21 24 38N24 71E10 -4:44:40
Pošechonje-Volodarsk 6 40 58N30 39E07 -2:36:28
Posevnaja 2 21 54N18 83E20 -5:33:20
Posjet 2 27 42N39 130E50 -8:43:20
Pos'olki 6 41 53N08 46E29 -3:05:56
Pos'olok 6 9 59N43 30E12 -2:00:48
Pospelicha 2 23 51N57 81E46 -5:27:04
Postavy 4 39 55N07 26E50 -1:47:20
P'ostraja Dresva 2 6 61N34 156E41 -10:26:44
Potanino 6 9 60N16 32E47 -2:11:08
Potapovo Vtoroje 6 39 55N56 37E58 -2:31:52
Poti 7 33 42N09 41E40 -2:46:40
Potijevka 23 44 50N37 28E58 -1:55:52
Povenec 6 9 62N51 34E45 -2:19:00
Poverennyj 6 47 46N45 43E12 -2:52:48
Povetkino 6 39 54N20 38E23 -2:33:32
Povorino 6 41 51N12 42E14 -2:48:56
Povorsk 23 44 51N16 25E07 -1:40:28
Požarskoje 2 27 46N16 134E04 -8:56:16
Pozdejevka 2 14 50N36 128E56 -8:35:44
Požva 6 30 59N05 56E05 -3:44:20
Pr'adovka 23 45 48N55 34E41 -2:18:44
Pr'amicyno 6 39 51N39 35E56 -2:23:44
Praskoveja 6 47 44N43 44E12 -2:56:48
Praskovejevka 23 45 48N40 38E00 -2:32:00
Pravda 19 8 47N00 142E01 -9:28:04
Pravdinsk 6 41 56N32 43E34 -2:54:16
Pravdinsk 8 38 54N27 21E01 -1:24:04
Pravdinskij 6 39 56N04 37E51 -2:31:24
Pr'aža 6 9 61N42 33E35 -2:14:20
Prečistoje 6 41 58N27 40E19 -2:41:16
Prečistoje 6 39 55N41 34E56 -2:19:44
Prečistoje 6 39 55N31 32E22 -2:09:28
Predgornoje 9 24 47N10 81E02 -5:24:08
Predivinsk 2 21 57N04 93E27 -6:13:48
Predmostnoje 23 45 45N57 34E37 -2:18:28
Pregradnaja 6 47 43N58 41E12 -2:44:48
Pregradnoje 6 47 45N49 41E45 -2:47:00
Preila 14 37 55N22 21E04 -1:24:16
Preiļi 13 36 56N18 26E43 -1:46:52
Preobraženije 2 27 42N57 133E55 -8:55:40
Preobraženoje 23 45 49N32 38E10 -2:32:40
Preobraženovka 2 11 48N04 131E55 -8:47:40
Presnogor'kovka 9 30 54N30 65E45 -4:23:00
Presnovka 9 24 54N40 67E09 -4:28:36
Preussisch Eylau → Bagrationovsk 8 38 54N23 20E39 -1:22:36
Priargunsk 2 16 50N27 119E00 -7:56:00
Priazovskoje 23 45 46N43 35E38 -2:22:32
Pribylovo 6 9 60N26 28E40 -1:54:40
Pridneprovsk 23 45 48N24 35E09 -2:20:36
Priekule 13 36 56N26 21E35 -1:26:20
Priekulė 14 37 55N33 21E19 -1:25:16
Prienai 14 37 54N38 23E57 -1:35:48
Priiskovyj 2 21 54N39 88E42 -5:54:48
Priiskovyj 2 16 51N57 116E39 -7:46:36
Prijutnoje 6 47 46N06 43E31 -2:54:04
Prijutovo 6 30 53N54 53E56 -3:35:44
Prikolotnoje 23 45 50N09 37E21 -2:29:24
Prikumsk 6 47 44N46 44E09 -2:56:36
Prilepy 6 39 54N03 37E42 -2:30:48
Priluki 23 44 50N36 32E24 -2:09:36
Priluki 6 41 59N16 39E53 -2:39:32
Priluki 6 39 54N51 37E53 -2:31:32
Primorje (Warnicken) 8 38 54N57 20E02 -1:20:08
Primorka 6 40 47N16 39E03 -2:36:12
Primorsk 6 34 49N16 45E03 -3:00:12
Primorsk 8 38 54N44 20E01 -1:20:04
Primorsk 6 9 60N22 28E36 -1:54:24
Primorsk 3 34 40N13 49E33 -3:18:12
Primorsk 23 45 46N44 36E20 -2:25:20
Primorskij 23 45 45N07 35E29 -2:21:56
Primorskij 2 27 43N07 131E38 -8:46:32
Primorsko-Achtarsk 6 47 46N03 38E11 -2:32:44
Primorskoje 23 45 47N11 37E42 -2:30:48
Priozernyj 6 47 47N23 45E14 -3:00:56
Prioz'ornyj 9 24 47N50 84E13 -5:36:52
Prioz'orsk 6 9 61N02 30E04 -2:00:16
Priputni 23 44 50N57 32E14 -2:08:56
Prirečje 2 20 55N07 101E03 -6:44:12
Prirečnyj 9 30 51N03 52E26 -3:29:44
Priselje 6 39 55N09 32E49 -2:11:16
Prišib 23 45 47N16 35E21 -2:21:24
Prišib 3 34 39N08 48E36 -3:14:24
Prislon 6 39 56N48 37E16 -2:29:04
Pristan'-Prževal'sk 10 24 42N34 78E18 -5:13:12
Pristen' 6 39 51N15 36E41 -2:26:44
Pristen' 23 45 49N36 37E38 -2:30:32
Priural'nyj 9 30 51N29 53E06 -3:32:24
Privetnoje 23 45 44N50 34E41 -2:18:44
Privodino 6 41 61N05 46E28 -3:05:52
Privokzal'nyj 6 39 55N59 35E56 -2:23:44
Privokzal'nyj 2 30 58N53 60E43 -4:02:52
Privolje 23 45 49N01 38E18 -2:33:12
Privolje 23 45 48N52 37E16 -2:29:04
Privol'naja 6 47 46N09 38E42 -2:34:48
Privol'noje 6 34 50N57 46E06 -3:04:24
Privol'noje 23 45 47N29 32E17 -2:09:08
Privolžje 6 34 52N52 48E37 -3:14:28
Privolžsk 6 40 57N23 41E17 -2:45:08
Privolžskij 6 34 46N24 48E00 -3:12:00
Privolžskij 6 34 51N24 46E02 -3:04:08
Privolžskoje 6 34 51N06 45E57 -3:03:48
Prochladnoje 9 24 48N30 82E41 -5:30:44
Prochladnyj 6 47 43N46 44E00 -2:56:00
Prochorkino 2 23 59N34 79E26 -5:17:44
Prochorovka 6 39 54N07 38E11 -2:32:44
Prognoj 6 47 48N45 39E51 -2:39:24
Progress 2 14 49N42 129E39 -8:38:36
Prokopjeva 2 19 58N03 100E39 -6:42:36
Prokopjevsk 2 21 53N53 86E45 -5:47:00
Prokopyevsk → Prokopjevsk 2 21 53N53 86E45 -5:47:00
Prokuševo 6 9 59N55 34E56 -2:19:44
Prokutkino 2 30 56N19 69E46 -4:39:04
Prokutskoje 2 30 56N19 69E46 -4:39:04
Proletarij 6 9 58N26 31E44 -2:06:56
Proletarsk 6 47 46N42 41E44 -2:46:56
Proletarsk 23 45 48N56 38E23 -2:33:32
Proletarsk 21 24 40N10 69E30 -4:38:00
Proletarskaja 6 47 46N42 41E44 -2:46:56
Proletarskij 6 39 50N47 35E47 -2:23:08
Proletarskij 6 39 55N01 37E23 -2:29:32
Prolysovo 6 39 52N54 34E09 -2:16:36
Promyšlennaja 2 21 54N55 85E40 -5:42:40
Promyšlennovskij 2 21 55N29 86E12 -5:44:48
Promyšlennyj 6 29 67N35 63E55 -4:15:40
Promyslovka 6 34 45N44 47E10 -3:08:40
Pron'a Gorodišče 6 40 54N15 38E43 -2:34:52
Pronin 6 34 49N12 42E11 -2:48:44
Pronsk 6 40 54N07 39E37 -2:38:28
Prorva 9 30 46N03 53E15 -3:33:00
Proryvnoje 2 30 54N23 64E26 -4:17:44
Pros'anaja 23 45 48N07 36E23 -2:25:32
Pros'anov 23 45 49N42 35E47 -2:23:08
Proskoveja 6 47 44N43 44E12 -2:56:48
Proskurov → Chmel'nickij 23 44 49N25 27E00 -1:48:00
Prosnica 6 42 58N26 50E15 -3:21:00
Protasovo 6 39 54N48 38E35 -2:34:20

Protasovo 6 39 54N11 37E00 -2:28:00
Protasovo 6 39 56N08 37E36 -2:30:24
Protasy 4 39 52N47 29E05 -1:56:20
Protva 6 39 55N01 36E41 -2:26:44
Providenija 2 2 64N23 173W18 11:33:12
Prud'anka 23 45 50N14 36E09 -2:24:36
Prudentov 6 34 49N39 46E19 -3:05:16
Prudišči 6 39 54N24 38E26 -2:33:44
Prudki 6 39 54N46 36E29 -2:25:56
Prudy 4 39 53N47 26E32 -1:46:08
Pružany 4 39 52N33 24E28 -1:37:52
Prževal'sk 10 24 42N29 78E24 -5:13:36
Pšagar 24 24 39N58 68E08 -4:32:32
Psebaj 6 47 44N07 40E47 -2:43:08
Pselec 6 39 51N17 36E32 -2:26:08
Pskem 24 24 41N56 70E22 -4:41:28
Pskent 24 24 40N54 69E20 -4:37:20
Pskov 6 39 57N50 28E20 -1:53:20
Ptič' 4 39 52N09 28E52 -1:55:28
Pučež 6 40 56N59 43E11 -2:52:44
Puchoviči 4 39 53N32 28E15 -1:53:00
Pudem 6 42 58N18 52E10 -3:28:40
Pudino 2 23 57N34 79E24 -5:17:36
Pudož 6 40 61N48 36E32 -2:26:08
Pugačov 6 34 52N01 48E50 -3:15:20
Pugač'ovo 6 42 56N35 53E02 -3:32:08
Puhja 5 35 58N20 26E19 -1:45:16
Puir 2 11 53N10 141E25 -9:25:40
Puksoozero 6 41 62N38 40E36 -2:42:24
Pul'chakim 24 30 38N10 67E21 -4:29:24
Pulichatum 22 30 35N57 61E07 -4:04:28
Pul'mo 23 44 51N31 23E47 -1:35:08
Pulon'ga 6 9 66N17 40E02 -2:40:08
Pumsi 6 42 57N12 51E39 -3:26:36
Punduga 6 41 60N08 40E12 -2:40:48
Pungan 24 24 40N45 70E49 -4:43:16
Purdoški 6 41 54N40 43E32 -2:54:08
Purech 6 40 56N39 43E05 -2:52:20
Puronga 6 41 60N09 40E54 -2:43:36
Puščino 6 39 54N50 37E36 -2:30:24
Pushkin → Puškin 6
9 59N43 30E25 -2:01:40
Puškar'ovka 23
45 48N40 34E16 -2:17:04
Puškin 6 9 59N43 30E25 -2:01:40
Puškino 6 34 51N14 46E59 -3:07:56
Puškino 6 39 56N01 37E51 -2:31:24
Puškino 6 39 56N36 35E46 -2:23:04
Puškino 3 34 39N27 48E33 -3:14:12
Puškinskij 6 9 59N43 30E18 -2:01:12
Puškinskije Gory 6
39 57N01 28E54 -1:55:36
Püssi 5 35 59N24 27E01 -1:48:04
Pustin' 6 40 59N54 35E32 -2:22:08
Pustomyty 23 44 49N42 23E56 -1:35:44
Pustoš' 6 41 60N07 42E45 -2:51:00
Pustoška 6 39 56N20 29E22 -1:57:28
Pustozersk 6 29 67N33 52E27 -3:29:48
Put'atin 2 27 42N52 132E25 -8:49:40
Put'atino 6 41 54N10 41E07 -2:44:28
Putila 23 44 48N01 25E03 -1:40:12
Putilkovo 6 39 55N52 37E23 -2:29:32
Putincevo 9 24 49N50 84E22 -5:37:28
Putivl' 23 44 51N21 33E52 -2:15:28
Puurmani 5 35 58N34 26E17 -1:45:08
Pyatigorsk → P'atigorsk 6
47 44N03 43E04 -2:52:16
Pyčas 6 42 56N29 52E28 -3:29:52
Pyrkino 6 41 53N29 45E07 -3:00:28
Pyšma 2 30 56N56 63E13 -4:12:52
Pytalovo 6 39 57N04 27E56 -1:51:44
Raasiku 5 35 59N22 25E11 -1:40:44
R'abcevo 6 39 54N39 32E19 -2:09:16
Rabočeostrovsk 6
40 64N59 34E48 -2:19:12
Rabočij 2 23 59N07 79E00 -5:16:00
Rabotki 6 41 56N03 44E38 -2:58:32
R'abovskij 6 34 50N01 41E53 -2:47:32
Rach'a 6 9 60N05 30E49 -2:03:16
Rachmanovka 6 34 51N57 49E29 -3:17:56
Rachmanovka 23
45 47N48 33E13 -2:12:52
Rachmanovo 6 39 55N44 38E37 -2:34:28
Rachny Lesovyje 23
45 48N47 28E29 -1:53:56
Rachov 23 44 48N03 24E12 -1:36:48
R'ad 6 39 57N56 35E04 -2:20:16
Radčenskoje 6 47 49N48 40E32 -2:42:08
Radechov 23 44 50N18 24E37 -1:38:28
Radiščevo 6 34 52N51 47E53 -3:11:32
Rad'kovka 6 39 51N06 36E58 -2:27:52
Radofinnikovo 6
9 59N09 30E55 -2:03:40
Radogošča 6 9 59N47 34E51 -2:19:24
Radoj'a 15 46 47N44 28E09 -1:52:36
Radomka 23 44 51N56 32E32 -2:10:08
Radomyšl' 23 44 50N30 29E14 -1:56:56
Radoškoviči 4 39 54N09 27E14 -1:48:56
Radovicy 6 39 55N06 39E32 -2:38:08
Radul' 23 44 51N49 30E42 -2:02:48
Radun' 4 39 54N03 25E00 -1:40:00
Radušnoje 23 45 47N49 33E29 -2:13:56
Radutino 6 39 52N39 33E57 -2:15:48
Radvaniči 4 39 52N02 24E02 -1:36:08
Radviliškis 14
37 55N50 23E31 -1:34:04
Radykovskoje 6
47 45N56 41E57 -2:47:48
Rafalovka 23 44 51N22 25E52 -1:43:28
Ragnit → Neman 8
38 55N02 22E02 -1:28:08
Ragozino 2 23 59N15 77E52 -5:11:28
Raguli 6 47 45N38 43E42 -2:54:48
Raguva 14 37 55N34 24E36 -1:38:24

Raj-Aleksandrovka 23
45 48N48 37E51 -2:31:24
Rajčichinsk 2 14 49N46 129E25 -8:37:40
Rajevskij 6 30 54N04 54E56 -3:39:44
Rajgorod 6 34 48N26 44E55 -2:59:40
Rajgorodka 23 45 49N22 37E57 -2:31:48
Rajgorodka 23 45 48N50 39E04 -2:36:16
Rajgorodok 23 45 48N54 37E43 -2:30:52
Rajgorodok 9 30 48N48 52E53 -3:31:32
Rajkuzi 6 9 59N47 29E57 -1:59:48
Rajskoje 23 45 48N34 37E25 -2:29:40
Rakitnoje 6 39 50N51 35E50 -2:23:20
Rakitnoje 23 44 49N42 30E27 -2:01:48
Rakitnoje 23 44 51N17 27E14 -1:48:56
Rakitnoje 2 27 45N36 134E17 -8:57:08
Rakke 5 35 58N59 26E15 -1:45:00
Rakša 6 41 53N33 41E37 -2:46:28
Raksakiny 2 25 60N37 73E52 -4:55:28
Rakuša 9 30 47N03 52E47 -3:31:08
Rakvere 5 35 59N22 26E20 -1:45:20
Ramasucha 6 39 52N46 33E33 -2:14:12
Ramenje 6 41 60N17 43E46 -2:55:04
Ramenje 6 39 56N34 37E13 -2:28:52
Ramenskoje 6 39 55N34 38E14 -2:32:56
Rameški 6 39 57N21 36E03 -2:24:12
Ramit 21 24 38N44 69E17 -4:37:08
Ramon' 6 41 51N54 39E20 -2:37:20
Ramuševo 6 39 57N50 31E37 -2:06:28
Ramygala 14 37 55N31 24E18 -1:37:12
Ramzaj 6 41 53N18 44E44 -2:58:56
Rancevo 6 39 56N56 34E03 -2:16:12
Rancevo 6 39 56N40 33E02 -2:12:08
Rangkul' 21 24 38N29 74E22 -4:57:28
Ranino 6 41 52N58 40E15 -2:41:00
Ranneje 6 32 51N29 52E37 -3:30:28
Rannij 6 32 51N29 52E37 -3:30:28
Rapatovo 6 30 55N04 54E37 -3:38:28
Räpina 5 35 58N06 27E27 -1:49:48
Rapkan 24 24 40N22 70E40 -4:42:40
Rapla 5 35 59N01 24E47 -1:39:08
Rarz 21 24 39N23 68E44 -4:34:56
Raseiniai 14 37 55N24 23E07 -1:32:28
Raševka 23 44 50N14 33E54 -2:15:36
Raškov 15 46 47N57 28E50 -1:55:20
R'asna 4 39 54N01 31E12 -2:04:48
R'asnopol' 23 45 47N04 31E12 -2:04:48
Raspopinskaja 6
34 49N24 42E52 -2:51:28
Rasskazovka 6 39 55N38 37E20 -2:29:20
Rasskazovo 6 41 52N40 41E53 -2:47:32
Rassua Island 12
8 47N45 153E01 -10:12:04
Rassua, Ostrov 12
8 47N45 153E01 -10:12:04
Rassudovo 6 39 55N29 36E54 -2:27:36
Rassvet 6 47 43N58 46E44 -3:06:56
Rassypnaja 6 30 51N35 53E37 -3:34:28
Rassypnoje 23 45 48N08 38E34 -2:34:16
Rastorgujevo 6
39 55N33 37E41 -2:30:44
Rastovcy 6 39 56N39 37E35 -2:30:20
Rastunovo 6 39 55N16 37E50 -2:31:20
Ratčino 6 41 53N02 39E55 -2:39:40
Ratčino 6 39 55N16 38E39 -2:34:36
Rat'kovo 6 39 56N01 38E38 -2:34:32
Ratno 23 44 51N40 24E31 -1:38:04
Ratomka 4 39 53N56 27E21 -1:49:24
Rauna 13 36 57N20 25E43 -1:42:52
Raupal'an 2 2 65N28 171W59 11:27:56
Rava-Russkaja 23
44 50N14 23E37 -1:34:28
Ravat 10 24 39N54 70E12 -4:40:48
Ravnina 22 30 37N57 62E40 -4:10:40
R'azan' 6 40 54N38 39E44 -2:38:56
R'azancevo 6 39 56N42 39E12 -2:36:48
R'azanovo 6 39 55N29 37E31 -2:30:04
Razbegaj 6 9 59N47 29E56 -1:59:44
Razdan 1 34 40N30 44E46 -2:59:04
Razdel'naja 23
45 46N51 30E05 -2:00:20
Razdolinsk 2 21 58N25 94E38 -6:18:32
Razdolje 2 20 52N27 103E13 -6:52:52
Razdol'noje 2 27 43N30 131E52 -8:47:28
Razdol'noje 23
45 45N47 33E29 -2:13:56
Razdol'noje 23
45 47N37 38E01 -2:32:04
Razdol'nyj 6 47 46N38 42E57 -2:51:48
Razdorskaja 6 47 47N33 40E38 -2:42:32
Razdory 23 45 48N21 35E42 -2:22:48
Razdory 6 39 55N45 37E18 -2:29:12
R'aženoje 6 40 47N31 38E52 -2:35:28
Raževo 2 30 56N09 68E25 -4:33:40
Razmachnino 2 16 51N47 115E28 -7:41:52
Razmitelevo 6 9 59N54 30E41 -2:02:44
Raznočinovka 6
34 46N37 47E57 -3:11:48
Raznomojka 6 30 52N29 55E52 -3:43:28
R'ažsk 6 41 53N43 40E04 -2:40:16
Razvil'noje 6 47 46N14 41E18 -2:45:12
Reboly 6 9 63N50 30E47 -2:03:08
Rebricha 2 23 53N05 82E20 -5:29:20
Rečane 6 39 56N25 31E39 -2:06:36
Rečica 4 39 51N52 26E48 -1:47:12
Rečica 4 39 52N22 30E25 -2:01:40
Rečki 23 45 51N07 34E30 -2:18:00
Redkino 6 39 56N38 36E17 -2:25:08
Redut 9 32 47N22 51E53 -3:27:32
Regozero 6 9 65N28 31E10 -2:04:40
Remennicy 6 39 56N43 36E36 -2:26:24
Remontnoje 6 47 46N33 43E39 -2:54:36
Rencēni 13 36 57N44 25E26 -1:41:44
Renda 13 36 57N09 22E22 -1:29:28
Reni 23 45 45N27 28E17 -1:53:08
Repetek 22 30 38N34 63E11 -4:12:44

Repino 6 9 60N10 29E52 -1:59:28
Repjovka 6 34 53N09 48E06 -3:12:24
Repjovka 6 40 51N05 38E39 -2:34:36
Repki 23 44 51N48 31E05 -2:04:20
Repolka 6 9 59N16 29E34 -1:58:16
Repolovo 2 25 60N40 69E50 -4:39:20
Rešetilovka 23
45 49N34 34E04 -2:16:16
Rešetnikovo 6 39 56N27 36E34 -2:26:16
Rešma 6 40 57N24 42E34 -2:50:16
Rešn'ovka 23 44 49N47 27E25 -1:49:40
Rešoty 6 39 57N09 28E30 -1:54:00
Rettichovka 2 27 44N10 132E47 -8:51:08
Reutov 6 39 55N46 37E52 -2:31:28
Rev'akino 6 39 54N22 37E40 -2:30:40
Reval → Tallinn 5
35 59N25 24E45 -1:39:00
Revda 6 9 67N58 34E32 -2:18:08
Revda 2 30 56N48 59E57 -3:59:48
Rež 2 30 57N23 61E24 -4:05:36
Rēzekne 13 36 56N30 27E19 -1:49:16
Rezeny 15 46 46N46 28E54 -1:55:36
Rezina 15 46 47N44 28E58 -1:55:52
Rezino 2 24 55N51 75E18 -5:01:12
Rhev 6 39 56N15 34E20 -2:17:20
Rietavas 14 37 55N44 21E56 -1:27:44
Rīga 13 36 56N57 24E06 -1:36:24
Riga 2 20 56N36 106E17 -7:05:08
Riguldi 5 35 59N08 23E33 -1:34:12
Rimsko-Korsakovka 6
34 51N34 48E31 -3:14:04
Risti 5 35 58N59 24E03 -1:36:12
Ristna 5 35 58N56 22E05 -1:28:20
Ročegda 6 41 62N42 43E23 -2:53:32
Rodakovo 23 45 48N33 39E02 -2:36:08
Rodinka 6 41 57N24 43E34 -2:54:16
Rodino 6 41 58N57 44E59 -2:59:56
Rodino 2 23 52N30 80E15 -5:21:00
Rodionovo-Nesvetajskaja 6
40 47N36 39E42 -2:38:48
Rodionovo-Nesvetajskoje 6
40 47N36 39E42 -2:38:48
Rodn'a 6 39 56N22 34E55 -2:19:40
Rodničok 6 34 51N26 42E54 -2:51:36
Rodniki 6 40 57N06 41E44 -2:46:56
Rodniki 6 39 55N39 38E04 -2:32:16
Rodnikovskij 9
30 50N39 57E12 -3:48:48
Rodostov 4 39 51N58 24E57 -1:39:48
Rogačevo 6 39 56N26 37E10 -2:28:40
Rogačov 4 39 53N05 30E03 -2:00:12
Rogačovka 6 41 51N30 39E34 -2:38:16
Rogalik 6 47 48N56 40E03 -2:40:12
Rogan' 23 45 49N54 36E29 -2:25:56
Rogatin 23 44 49N25 24E37 -1:38:28
Rognedino 6 39 53N48 33E33 -2:14:12
Rogovatoje 6 40 51N14 38E22 -2:33:28
Rogovo 6 39 55N13 37E05 -2:28:20
Rogovskaja 6 47 45N44 38E44 -2:34:56
Rogovskoje 6 42 58N33 50E43 -3:22:52
Rogožkino 6 40 47N10 39E21 -2:37:24
Rogozov 23 44 50N14 31E03 -2:04:12
Roja 13 36 57N30 22E49 -1:31:16
Roja 23 45 47N59 37E20 -2:29:20
Roji'anka 23 45 46N17 29E46 -1:59:04
Rokiškis 14 37 55N58 25E35 -1:42:20
Romankovcy 23 45 48N29 27E13 -1:48:52
Romanova 2 20 57N04 103E24 -6:53:36
Romanovka 6 34 49N47 45E05 -3:00:20
Romanovka 6 9 60N03 30E42 -2:02:48
Romanovka 2 23 54N38 76E03 -5:04:12
Romanovka 2 20 53N14 112E46 -7:31:04
Romanovka 6 34 51N24 47E23 -3:09:32
Romanovka 6 34 51N45 42E45 -2:51:00
Romanovo 2 23 52N37 81E14 -5:24:56
Romanovo 2 30 59N09 61E30 -4:06:00
Romanovo 6 39 56N39 39E14 -2:36:56
Romanovo 2 23 53N58 80E30 -5:22:00
Romaški 6 34 50N13 46E41 -3:06:44
Romaškino 6 32 52N29 51E48 -3:27:12
Romaškovo 6 39 55N44 37E20 -2:29:20
Rometan 24 30 39N56 64E23 -4:17:32
Romit 21 24 38N44 69E17 -4:37:08
Romny 23 44 50N45 33E30 -2:14:00
Romny 2 14 50N44 129E15 -8:37:00
Romodan 23 44 49N59 33E19 -2:13:16
Romodanovo 6 41 54N26 45E20 -3:01:20
Ronga 6 41 56N43 48E32 -3:14:08
Rõngu 5 35 58N09 26E15 -1:45:00
Ropaži 13 36 57N08 24E30 -1:38:00
Ropča 6 41 63N02 52E16 -3:29:04
Ropša 6 9 59N44 29E52 -1:59:28
Rošal' 6 39 55N40 39E51 -2:39:24
Rošča 6 39 54N47 36E51 -2:27:24
Roščino 6 9 60N15 29E37 -1:58:28
Rosl'akovo 6 9 69N03 33E09 -2:12:36
Rosl'atino 6 41 59N46 44E15 -2:57:00
Roslavl' 6 39 53N57 32E52 -2:11:28
Rošore 21 24 38N20 72E19 -4:49:16
Ross' 4 39 53N17 24E24 -1:37:36
Rossasna 4 39 54N39 30E53 -2:03:32
Rossitten → Rybačij 8
38 55N09 20E51 -1:23:24
Rossony 4 39 55N53 28E49 -1:55:16
Rossoš' 6 40 51N08 38E29 -2:33:56
Rossoš' 6 40 50N12 39E34 -2:38:16
Roštkala 21 24 37N16 71E49 -4:47:16
Rostov 6 40 57N11 39E25 -2:37:40
Rostov-Na-Donu 6
40 47N14 39E42 -2:38:48
Rosvinskoje 6 29 66N32 52E26 -3:29:44
Rovbick 4 39 52N40 24E05 -1:36:20
Rovbickskaja 4
39 52N40 24E05 -1:36:20
Roven'ki 6 40 49N56 38E54 -2:35:36

Roven'ki 23 45 48N05 39E21 -2:37:24
Rovenskaja Sloboda 4 39 52N13 30E19 -2:01:16
Rovno 23 44 50N37 26E15 -1:45:00
Rovnoje 10 24 42N53 73E32 -4:54:08
Rovnoje 6 34 50N47 46E05 -3:04:20
Rovnoje 23 45 48N15 31E45 -2:07:00
Roždestvenka 9 24 50N52 71E22 -4:45:28
Roždestvenka 2 23 55N21 77E29 -5:09:56
Roždestvenka 2 30 55N42 70E00 -4:40:00
Roždestveno 6 39 56N51 36E33 -2:26:12
Roždestveno 6 39 55N57 36E23 -2:25:32
Roždestveno 6 34 53N15 50E04 -3:20:16
Roždestveno 6 40 57N44 37E57 -2:31:48
Roždestvenskaja Chava 6 41 51N38 39E40 -2:38:40
Roždestvenskoje 6 41 51N14 42E10 -2:48:40
Roždestvenskoje 6 41 58N09 45E35 -3:02:20
Roždestvenskoje 6 41 52N47 42E10 -2:48:40
Roždestvo 6 39 57N36 33E48 -2:15:12
Rožišče 23 44 50N54 25E15 -1:41:00
Rožki 6 42 56N41 50E31 -3:22:04
Rožkov 9 30 51N39 52E19 -3:29:16
Rožn'atov 23 44 48N56 24E09 -1:36:36
Rozovka 23 45 47N23 37E04 -2:28:16
Rtiščevo 6 34 52N16 43E47 -2:55:08
Rubanovka 23 45 47N00 34E10 -2:16:40
Rubcovsk 2 23 51N33 81E10 -5:24:40
Rubcy 23 45 49N12 37E33 -2:30:12
Rubel' 4 39 51N58 27E04 -1:48:16
Rubežka 9 32 51N26 51E59 -3:27:56
Rubežnoje 23 45 49N01 38E23 -2:33:32
Rubl'ovka 23 45 49N15 33E19 -2:13:16
Rubl'ovo 6 39 55N47 37E21 -2:29:24
Rubtsovsk → Rubcovsk 2 23 51N33 81E10 -5:24:40
Rucava 13 36 56N09 21E10 -1:24:40
Ruchan' 6 39 53N33 32E48 -2:11:12
Ručjuvom 6 29 66N42 61E08 -4:04:32
Rudensk 4 39 53N36 27E52 -1:51:28
Rūdiškės 14 37 54N31 24E50 -1:39:20
Rudki 23 44 49N39 23E29 -1:33:56
Rudkino 6 40 51N27 39E01 -2:36:04
Rudn'a 6 34 50N48 44E33 -2:58:12
Rudn'a 6 39 54N57 31E06 -2:04:24
Rudnaja Pristan' 2 27 44N22 135E48 -9:03:12
Rudnevo 6 39 54N44 38E09 -2:32:36
Rudnica 23 45 48N15 28E55 -1:55:40
Rudničnyj 2 30 59N42 60E18 -4:01:12
Rudničnyj 9 24 44N40 78E55 -5:15:40
Rudničnyj 6 42 59N38 52E27 -3:29:48
Rudničnyj 2 21 56N08 86E12 -5:44:48
Rudnyj 9 30 52N57 63E07 -4:12:28
Rudnyj 2 27 44N21 134E58 -8:59:52
Rudovka 6 41 53N07 42E23 -2:49:32
Rudovka 23 45 49N24 38E27 -2:33:48
Rugāji 13 36 57N00 27E08 -1:48:32
Ruguj 6 9 59N28 32E50 -2:11:20
Rūjiena 13 36 57N54 25E21 -1:41:24
Rum'ancevo 6 39 55N38 37E26 -2:29:44
Rum'ancevo 6 39 55N58 36E32 -2:26:08
R'uminskoje 6 39 56N31 38E47 -2:35:08
R'umki 6 9 59N47 30E02 -2:00:08
Rundēni 13 36 56N16 27E50 -1:51:20
Rušan 21 24 37N58 71E30 -4:46:00
Rusanov 23 44 50N29 31E09 -2:04:36
Rusanovka 23 44 50N32 33E44 -2:14:56
Rusavkina-Popovščina 6 39 55N42 38E04 -2:32:16
Rusnė 14 37 55N18 21E22 -1:25:28
Russka 6 9 58N59 28E30 -1:54:00
Russkaja Bujlovka 6 41 50N22 40E03 -2:40:12
Russkaja Gavan' 17 29 76N10 62E35 -4:10:20
Russkaja Pol'ana 2 24 53N47 73E53 -4:55:32
Russkaja Talovka 9 32 49N59 49E05 -3:16:20
Russkaja Žuravka 6 47 50N21 40E33 -2:42:12
Russkij 2 27 43N03 131E50 -8:47:20
Russkij Aktaš 6 41 55N02 52E07 -3:28:28
Russkij Brod 6 39 52N36 37E22 -2:29:28
Russkij Kameškir 6 41 52N52 46E06 -3:04:24
Russkij Pervyj 6 47 43N50 44E37 -2:58:28
Russkij Turek 6 42 57N03 50E13 -3:20:52
Russkij Vožoj 6 42 56N57 53E22 -3:33:28
Russkoje 6 40 47N45 38E56 -2:35:44
Russkoje-Dobrino 6 42 54N22 52E28 -3:29:52
Russko-Vysockoje 6 9 59N42 29E56 -1:59:44
Rustajskij 6 41 56N31 44E49 -2:59:16
Rustavi 7 33 41N33 45E02 -3:00:08
Rutčenkovo 23 45 47N57 37E44 -2:30:56
Rutul 6 47 41N33 47E25 -3:09:40
Ruza 6 39 55N42 36E12 -2:24:48
Ruzajevka 6 41 54N04 44E57 -2:59:48
Ruzajevka 9 24 52N49 66E57 -4:27:48
Ružany 4 39 52N52 24E53 -1:39:32
Ružičnaja 23 44 49N24 26E58 -1:47:52
Ružin 23 44 49N43 29E14 -1:56:56
Ryazan'→ R'azan' 6 40 54N38 39E44 -2:38:56
Rybačje 9 24 46N27 81E32 -5:26:08
Rybačje 10 24 42N26 76E12 -5:04:48
Rybakovka 23 45 46N37 31E20 -2:05:20
Rybinsk 6 40 58N03 38E52 -2:35:28
Rybinskije Budy 6 39 51N13 35E57 -2:23:48
Rybinskoje 2 21 55N47 94E47 -6:19:08
Rybkino 6 41 54N15 43E46 -2:55:04
Rybnaja Sloboda 6 41 55N28 50E09 -3:20:36
Rybnica 15 46 47N45 29E01 -1:56:04
Rybnoje 6 40 54N44 39E30 -2:38:00
Rybnoje 2 21 58N08 94E30 -6:18:00
Rybnovsk 19 8 53N12 141E50 -9:27:20
Rybuška 6 34 51N17 45E26 -3:01:44
Ryčkovo 2 30 58N09 61E43 -4:06:52
Rykonec 6 40 59N33 36E34 -2:26:16
Rylovīči 6 39 52N31 32E04 -2:08:16
Ryl'sk 6 39 51N36 34E43 -2:18:52
Rynok 6 34 45N39 47E34 -3:10:16
Ryškany 15 46 47N58 27E32 -1:50:08
Ržaksa 6 41 52N09 42E02 -2:48:08
Ržaksa-Vyselki 6 41 52N09 42E02 -2:48:08
Ržanica 6 39 53N26 33E55 -2:15:40
Ržava 6 39 51N14 36E43 -2:26:52
Ržev 6 39 56N16 34E20 -2:17:20
Ržiščov 23 44 49N58 31E03 -2:04:12
Sääre 5 35 57N56 22E02 -1:28:08
Saatly 3 34 39N56 48E23 -3:13:32
Sabajevo 6 41 53N59 45E43 -3:02:52
Šabanovo 6 39 55N38 38E43 -2:34:52
Sabažo 7 33 42N14 41E48 -2:47:12
Šabel'kovka 23 45 48N45 37E29 -2:29:56
Šabel'sk 6 47 46N51 38E29 -2:33:56
Sabicy 6 9 58N50 29E18 -1:57:12
Sabile 13 36 57N03 22E35 -1:30:20
Sabirabad 3 34 40N01 48E29 -3:13:56
Sablinskoje 6 47 44N31 43E14 -2:52:56
Šablykino 6 39 52N51 35E12 -2:20:48
Šabo 23 45 46N08 30E23 -2:01:32
Sabunči 3 34 40N26 49E56 -3:19:44
Saburovo 6 39 55N53 37E16 -2:29:04
Sabyndy 9 24 50N53 70E33 -4:42:12
Sačchere 7 33 42N21 43E23 -2:53:32
Sachalin, Ostrov 8 51N00 143E00 -9:32:00
Šachand 24 24 40N54 71E28 -4:45:52
Šachbuz 16 34 39N25 45E34 -3:02:16
Sachnovščina 23 45 49N08 35E53 -2:23:32
Šachovskaja 6 39 56N02 35E29 -2:21:56
Šachrichan 24 24 40N44 72E03 -4:48:12
Šachrinau 21 24 38N34 68E20 -4:33:20
Šachrisabz 24 30 39N03 66E50 -4:27:20
Šachristan 21 24 39N47 68E49 -4:35:16
Šachrovka 6 42 58N34 52E12 -3:28:48
Šachterskij 2 2 64N42 177E40-11:50:40
Šachtinsk 9 24 49N40 72E37 -4:50:28
Šachtnoje 23 45 47N57 38E17 -2:33:08
Šacht'orsk 23 45 48N03 38E28 -2:33:52
Šacht'orsk 19 8 49N11 142E07 -9:28:28
Šachty 6 40 47N42 40E13 -2:40:52
Šachunja 6 41 57N40 46E37 -3:06:28
Šack 6 41 54N01 41E43 -2:46:52
Šack 23 44 51N31 23E57 -1:35:48
Šack 4 39 53N25 27E41 -1:50:44
Sadčikovka 9 30 53N01 63E27 -4:13:48
Sadon 6 47 42N51 44E00 -2:56:00
Sadovoje 6 47 47N46 44E30 -2:58:00
Sadovoje 6 47 46N56 44E23 -2:57:32
Sadovoje Pervoje 6 41 51N33 40E29 -2:41:56
Šadrina 2 14 51N33 130E22 -8:41:28
Šadrino 2 21 55N52 91E06 -6:04:24
Šadrinsk 2 30 56N05 63E38 -4:14:32
Safakulevo 2 30 54N59 62E33 -4:10:12
Safonovo 6 41 65N42 47E39 -3:10:36
Safonovo 6 39 55N06 33E15 -2:13:00
Safonovo 6 39 55N33 38E17 -2:33:08
Saga 9 30 49N25 55E17 -3:41:08
Saga 9 31 50N23 64E15 -4:17:00
Šagalakasa 9 32 46N54 50E43 -3:22:52
Sagaredžo 7 33 41N44 45E20 -3:01:20
Sagiz 9 30 47N31 53E16 -3:33:04
Sagiz 9 30 48N12 54E56 -3:39:44
Šagonar 2 21 51N32 92E48 -6:11:12
Sagunovka 23 44 49N17 32E23 -2:09:32
Saguny 6 41 50N36 39E43 -2:38:52
Sagutjevo 6 39 52N28 33E28 -2:13:52
Šaim 2 30 60N21 64E14 -4:16:56
Saint Petersburg → Leningrad 6 9 59N55 30E15 -2:01:00
Sajak 9 24 47N02 77E22 -5:09:28
Sajanogorsk 2 21 53N08 91E29 -6:05:56
Sajantuj 2 20 51N44 107E30 -7:10:00
Sajasan 6 47 43N03 46E17 -3:05:08
Sajat 22 30 38N47 63E53 -4:15:32
Sajchin 9 32 48N50 46E47 -3:07:08
Šajgino 6 41 57N46 46E51 -3:07:24
Šajmak' 21 24 37N27 74E44 -4:58:56
Sajram 9 24 42N18 69E45 -4:39:00
Sajukino 6 41 52N47 41E59 -2:47:56
Sakar 22 30 38N56 63E45 -4:15:00
Sakar-Čaga 22 30 37N38 61E40 -4:06:40
Sakhalin 8 51N00 143E00 -9:32:00
Sakhalin Island 8 51N00 143E00 -9:32:00
Saki 23 45 45N09 33E35 -2:14:20
Šakiai 14 37 54N57 23E03 -1:32:12
Šal'a 2 30 57N15 58E43 -3:54:52
Salacgrīva 13 36 57N45 24E21 -1:37:24
Salair 2 21 54N13 85E47 -5:43:08
Salakas 14 37 55N35 26E08 -1:44:32
Šalakuša 6 41 62N15 40E17 -2:41:08
Salantai 14 37 56N04 21E32 -1:26:08
Salar 24 24 41N21 69E22 -4:37:28
Salarjovo 6 39 55N37 37E26 -2:29:44
Salauš 6 41 55N59 52E53 -3:31:32
Salavat 6 30 53N21 55E55 -3:43:40
Salazgor' 6 41 54N07 43E09 -2:52:36
Salba 2 21 53N14 92E36 -6:10:24
Šalčininkai 14 37 54N18 25E23 -1:41:32
Šaldaj 9 24 51N56 78E48 -5:15:12
Šaldež 6 41 56N52 44E46 -2:59:04
Saldus 13 36 56N40 22E30 -1:30:00
Salechard 2 28 66N33 66E40 -4:26:40
Šalgačova 6 40 62N19 39E35 -2:38:20
Salgan 6 41 55N14 45E30 -3:02:00
Šalgija 9 24 47N35 70E36 -4:42:24
Šali 6 47 43N08 45E54 -3:03:36
Šali 6 41 55N41 49E40 -3:18:40
Salikovo 6 39 55N30 36E13 -2:24:52
Šalinskoje 2 21 55N43 93E46 -6:15:04
Saljany 3 34 39N34 48E58 -3:15:52
Šalkar 9 30 50N32 51E51 -3:27:24
Šalkar 9 32 48N03 48E56 -3:15:44
Salme 5 35 58N10 22E15 -1:29:00
Salmi 6 9 61N22 31E53 -2:07:32
Sal'nica 23 44 49N44 28E02 -1:52:08
Salobel'ak 6 42 57N07 48E05 -3:12:20
Salomatino 6 34 50N01 44E50 -2:59:20
Saloslovo 6 39 55N42 37E09 -2:28:36
Sal'sk 6 47 46N28 41E33 -2:46:12
Šal'skij 6 40 61N48 35E58 -2:23:52
Saltanovka 6 39 52N47 34E17 -2:17:08
Saltykovka 6 39 55N46 37E55 -2:31:40
Saltykovka 6 34 52N07 44E05 -2:56:20
Šalygino 23 44 51N34 34E07 -2:16:28
Samagaltaj 2 21 50N36 95E03 -6:20:12
Šamaldy-Saj 10 24 41N12 72E11 -4:48:44
Samara → Kujbyšev 6 34 53N12 50E09 -3:20:36
Samarga 2 11 47N17 138E48 -9:15:12
Samarka 2 27 44N44 134E13 -8:56:52
Samarkand 24 30 39N40 66E48 -4:27:12
Samarskoje 9 24 49N00 83E23 -5:33:32
Samarskoje 6 30 52N02 58E10 -3:52:40
Samarskoje 6 40 46N56 39E41 -2:38:44
Šamary 2 30 57N21 58E14 -3:52:56
Sambek 6 40 47N45 39E48 -2:39:12
Sambek 6 40 47N20 39E01 -2:36:04
Sambor 23 44 49N32 23E11 -1:32:44
Šamchor 3 34 40N50 46E02 -3:04:08
Samet' 6 40 57N49 40E44 -2:42:56
Samoded 6 41 63N38 40E29 -2:41:56
Samofalovka 6 34 48N57 44E13 -2:56:52
Samojlovka 6 34 51N12 43E43 -2:54:52
Samosdelka 6 34 46N02 47E53 -3:11:32
Samotevīči 4 39 53N13 31E50 -2:07:20
Šamovo 4 39 54N12 31E22 -2:05:28
Samovol'no-Ivanovka 6 34 52N33 50E53 -3:23:32
S'amozero 6 9 61N54 33E18 -2:13:12
Sam Pervyj 9 30 45N28 56E06 -3:44:24
Šampur 6 41 52N19 41E37 -2:46:28
Šamrajevka 23 44 49N46 29E49 -1:59:16
Samsonovka 9 24 42N44 70E32 -4:42:08
Samtredia 7 33 42N10 42E20 -2:49:20
Samus' 2 21 56N46 84E44 -5:38:56
S'amža 6 41 60N01 41E02 -2:44:08
Sančursk 6 42 56N57 47E15 -3:09:00
Sandata 6 47 46N16 41E46 -2:47:04
Sandogora 6 41 58N12 40E59 -2:43:56
Sandovo 6 9 58N28 36E25 -2:25:40
Šandrovka 23 45 48N57 35E46 -2:23:04
Sandykači 22 30 36N33 62E34 -4:10:16
Šangaly 6 41 61N08 43E19 -2:53:16
Sangar 2 14 63N55 127E31 -8:30:04
Sangtuda 21 24 38N04 69E04 -4:36:16
Sangvor 21 24 38N53 71E06 -4:44:24
Sangvor 21 24 38N47 71E12 -4:44:48
Sanino 6 9 59N50 29E54 -1:59:36
Saperkino 6 42 54N05 51E38 -3:26:32
Šapki 6 9 59N36 31E14 -2:04:56
Šapkino 6 41 51N42 42E24 -2:49:36
Šapkovo 6 40 54N34 39E10 -2:36:40
Šapkovo 6 39 55N47 33E20 -2:13:20
Sap'ornaja 6 9 59N46 30E41 -2:02:44
Sap'ornyj 6 9 59N46 30E41 -2:02:44
Saporoschje → Zaporožje 23 45 47N50 35E10 -2:20:40
Sapožok 6 41 53N56 40E41 -2:42:44
Šapša 6 9 60N34 34E01 -2:16:04
Šapsugskaja 6 47 44N45 38E05 -2:32:20
Sara 6 42 54N38 46E46 -3:07:04
Sarai 6 41 53N44 41E00 -2:44:00
Sarajčik 9 32 47N30 51E43 -3:26:52
Saraj-Gir 6 30 53N36 53E24 -3:33:36
Sarajskij 6 47 47N19 40E45 -2:43:00
Sarala 2 21 54N52 89E14 -5:56:56
Šaraldaj 2 20 51N01 107E38 -7:10:32
Saralžinskaja 9 32 49N12 48E55 -3:15:40
Saran' 9 24 49N46 72E52 -4:51:28
Šaran 6 30 54N49 54E00 -3:36:00
Šaranbaš-Kn'azevo 6 30 54N58 54E09 -3:36:36
Šaranga 6 41 57N11 46E34 -3:06:16
Saranpaul' 2 28 64N14 60E53 -4:03:32
Saransk 6 41 54N11 45E11 -3:00:44
Šarapovo 6 39 55N11 37E16 -2:29:04
Šarapovo 6 41 55N17 44E42 -2:58:48
Sarapul 6 42 56N28 53E48 -3:35:12

Name		Lat	Long	Time
Sarapul'skoje 2	11	48N52	135E59	-9:03:56
Sarata 23	45	46N02	29E38	-1:58:32
Šara-Togot 2	20	53N01	106E43	-7:06:52
Saratov 6	34	51N34	46E02	-3:04:08
Saratovka 6	30	51N12	54E54	-3:39:36
Sarbaj 6	34	53N39	51E34	-3:26:16
Šarčino 2	23	53N09	81E45	-5:27:00
Šardonem' 6	41	63N56	44E37	-2:58:28
Sargatskoje 2	24	55N37	73E30	-4:54:00
Šargol'džin 2	16	52N21	114E42	-7:38:48
Šargorod 23	45	48N44	28E05	-1:52:20
Šargun 22	30	38N37	67E53	-4:31:32
Saripul' 21	24	38N26	70E08	-4:40:32
Šarja 6	41	58N24	45E30	-3:02:00
Šarkan 6	42	57N18	53E53	-3:35:32
Sarkand 9	24	45N26	79E54	-5:19:36
Šarkovščina 4	39	55N22	27E28	-1:49:52
Šarlauk 22	30	38N13	55E38	-3:42:32
Šarlyk 6	30	52N55	54E35	-3:38:20
Sarmakovo 6	47	43N43	43E12	-2:52:48
Sarmanovo 6	41	55N15	52E36	-3:30:24
Šarnutovskij 6	47	47N40	43E46	-2:55:04
Sarny 23	44	51N21	26E36	-1:46:24
Šarovka 23	45	50N01	35E27	-2:21:48
Sarpa 6	47	47N07	45E29	-3:01:56
Šarpajevka 6	47	48N34	40E59	-2:43:56
Sars 6	30	56N33	57E07	-3:48:28
Sartičala 7	33	41N43	45E10	-3:00:40
Sartol'gen 9	32	48N57	47E03	-3:08:12
Saru 10	24	42N20	77E55	-5:11:40
Sarvadyk 6	47	46N07	44E07	-2:56:28
Saryagač 9	24	41N27	69E10	-4:36:40
Saryassija 24	30	38N25	67E57	-4:31:48
Sarybarak 9	24	43N24	71E30	-4:46:00
Sarybasat 9	30	46N38	60E27	-4:01:48
Sarybulak 10	24	40N54	73E49	-4:55:16
Sarybulak 9	24	49N27	76E27	-5:05:48
Sarychosor 21	24	38N32	69E49	-4:39:16
Sarydala 24	24	41N11	70E27	-4:41:48
Saryg-Sep 2	21	51N30	95E36	-6:22:24
Sarykoby 9	24	43N44	72E35	-4:50:20
Sarykomej 9	24	45N12	74E11	-4:56:44
Sarymogol 10	24	39N55	72E47	-4:51:08
Saryozek 9	24	44N22	77E59	-5:11:56
Šarypovo 2	21	55N33	89E12	-5:56:48
Saryšagan 9	24	46N07	73E38	-4:54:32
Sarysu 9	24	48N23	69E59	-4:39:56
Sary-Taš 10	24	39N44	73E15	-4:53:00
Sarytau 9	24	49N54	76E41	-5:06:44
Saryžaz 9	24	42N55	79E38	-5:18:32
Saskylach 2	16	71N55	114E01	-7:36:04
Sasovo 6	41	54N21	41E54	-2:47:36
S'as'stroj 6	9	60N08	32E34	-2:10:16
Sastobe 9	24	42N34	70E00	-4:40:00
Sasykoli 6	34	47N33	47E00	-3:08:00
Šatalovka 6	40	51N09	38E16	-2:33:04
Šatalovo 6	39	54N20	32E27	-2:09:48
Satanov 23	44	49N15	26E16	-1:45:04
Satis 6	41	55N02	43E48	-2:55:12
Satka 2	30	55N03	59E01	-3:56:04
Šatki 6	41	55N11	44E08	-2:56:32
Šatovo 6	39	54N56	37E14	-2:28:56
Šatrovo 2	30	56N31	64E38	-4:18:32
Šatura 6	39	55N34	39E32	-2:38:08
Šaturtorf 6	39	55N34	39E26	-2:37:44
Šaul'der 9	24	42N47	68E24	-4:33:36
Saulkrasti 13	36	57N17	24E25	-1:37:40
Šaum'ani 7	33	41N21	44E46	-2:59:04
Šaum'anovsk 3	34	40N26	46E34	-3:06:16
Saura 9	30	44N14	50E50	-3:23:20
Sauran 9	24	43N29	67E50	-4:31:20
Sauškin 6	34	49N30	43E32	-2:54:08
S'ava 6	41	58N01	46E22	-3:05:28
Saviči 4	39	52N25	29E03	-1:56:12
Saviči 4	39	51N37	30E17	-2:01:08
Savincy 23	45	49N24	37E04	-2:28:16
Savinka 6	40	54N27	38E52	-2:35:28
Savinka 6	34	50N06	47E06	-3:08:24
Savino 6	40	56N35	41E13	-2:44:52
Savino-Borisovskaja 6	41	62N38	44E34	-2:58:16
Savinsk 2	11	52N10	140E23	-9:21:32
Savinskij 6	41	62N58	40E08	-2:40:32
Sav'olovo 6	39	56N52	37E22	-2:29:28
Savran' 23	45	48N09	30E04	-2:00:16
Savruši 6	41	55N02	50E40	-3:22:40
S'avta 6	29	67N08	61E45	-4:07:00
Savvatejevka 2	20	52N20	103E39	-6:54:36
Savvino 6	39	56N33	37E47	-2:31:08
Savvino 6	39	55N43	36E48	-2:27:12
Savvo-Borz'a 2	16	50N46	118E18	-7:53:12
Sayansk 2	20	54N02	102E06	-6:48:24
Sazdy 9	32	46N57	49E19	-3:17:16
Sazdy 9	30	47N22	61E48	-4:07:12
Sažino 2	30	56N20	58E11	-3:52:44
Sazonovo 6	40	59N04	35E14	-2:20:56
Šazud 21	24	37N43	72E11	-4:48:44
Ščapino 2	4	55N19	159E25	-10:37:40
Ščapov 9	32	51N01	51E11	-3:24:44
Ščapovo 6	39	55N09	38E11	-2:32:44
Sčastje 23	45	48N44	39E14	-2:36:56
Ščedrin 4	39	52N53	29E33	-1:58:12
Ščedrovka 6	47	49N30	40E17	-2:41:08
Ščeglovo 6	9	60N02	30E46	-2:03:04
Ščeljajur 6	29	65N21	53E21	-3:33:24
Ščelkovo 6	39	55N55	38E00	-2:32:00
Ščemilovo 6	39	55N48	38E05	-2:32:20
Ščerbakovo 2	24	56N01	73E29	-4:53:56
Ščerbakovo 2	5	65N15	160E30	-10:42:00
Ščerbakty 9	24	52N29	78E09	-5:12:36
Ščerbinka 6	39	55N31	37E35	-2:30:20
Ščerbinovka 23	45	48N26	37E50	-2:31:20
Schaut 6	47	43N43	42E32	-2:50:08
Schodn'a 6	39	55N57	37E18	-2:29:12
Ščigry 6	39	51N53	36E55	-2:27:40
Ščitkoviči 4	39	53N13	27E59	-1:51:56
Ščokino 6	39	54N01	37E31	-2:30:04
Ščolkovo 6	39	55N55	38E00	-2:32:00
Ščors 23	44	51N49	31E59	-2:07:56
Ščorsk 23	45	48N22	34E06	-2:16:24
Ščot'ovo 23	45	48N09	39E04	-2:36:16
Ščučin 4	39	53N36	24E45	-1:39:00
Ščučinsk 9	24	52N56	70E12	-4:40:48
Ščučje 2	30	55N17	63E59	-4:15:56
Ščučje 6	41	51N45	40E29	-2:41:56
Ščučje Ozero 6	30	56N28	56E38	-3:46:32
Ščukino 6	39	54N28	37E01	-2:28:04
Ščurovo 6	39	55N03	38E49	-2:35:16
Šebalin 6	47	47N22	43E36	-2:54:24
Šebalino 2	21	51N17	85E40	-5:42:40
Šebalino 6	34	48N16	43E21	-2:53:24
Šebekino 6	39	50N25	36E56	-2:27:44
Šebelinka 23	45	49N27	36E30	-2:26:00
Šeberta 2	20	54N40	99E54	-6:39:36
Sebež 6	39	56N17	28E29	-1:53:56
Šebunino 19	8	46N27	141E51	-9:27:24
Sečenovo 6	41	55N13	45E54	-3:03:36
Šechman' 6	41	52N32	40E29	-2:41:56
Seda 14	37	56N10	22E04	-1:28:16
Seda 13	36	57N40	25E46	-1:43:04
Sedanovo 2	20	56N58	101E22	-6:45:28
Sedel'nikovo 2	24	56N57	75E18	-5:01:12
Sedn'ov 23	44	51N39	31E34	-2:06:16
Šedok 6	47	44N13	40E52	-2:43:28
Sedovo 23	45	47N03	38E10	-2:32:40
Sedovo-Vasiljevka 23	45	47N14	38E08	-2:32:32
Sedtim 6	29	66N25	56E20	-3:45:20
Šeduva 14	37	55N46	23E46	-1:35:04
Segeža 6	9	63N44	34E19	-2:17:16
Šegmas 6	41	64N43	49E14	-3:16:56
Šegovary 6	41	62N23	42E57	-2:51:48
Seitovka 6	34	46N43	48E03	-3:12:12
Sejmčan 2	6	62N53	152E26	-10:09:44
Šejno 6	41	53N22	43E12	-2:52:48
Sekači 6	34	50N30	43E37	-2:54:28
Šeki (Nucha) 3	34	41N12	47E12	-3:08:48
Sekretarka 6	41	52N36	44E11	-2:56:44
Šekšema 6	41	58N22	45E11	-3:00:44
Šeksna 6	40	59N13	38E30	-2:34:00
Šelabolicha 2	21	53N25	82E37	-5:30:28
Šelajevo 2	20	56N56	97E42	-6:30:48
Šelanger 6	41	56N13	48E16	-3:13:04
Sel'atin 15	46	47N53	25E12	-1:40:48
Sel'co 6	39	53N22	34E06	-2:16:24
Sel'co 6	41	63N18	41E22	-2:45:28
Sel'cy 6	9	59N57	30E43	-2:02:52
Sel'cy 6	39	57N57	35E59	-2:23:56
Selec 6	39	52N33	33E35	-2:14:20
Selec-Cholopejev 4	39	53N23	30E24	-2:01:36
Šelechov 2	20	52N13	104E08	-6:56:32
Selečn'a 6	39	52N23	34E23	-2:17:32
Selemdžinsk 2	14	52N36	131E08	-8:44:32
Šelemeti 6	42	57N27	48E07	-3:12:28
Selenduma 2	20	50N55	106E10	-7:04:40
Selenginsk 2	20	52N06	107E01	-7:08:04
Selezen'ovo 6	41	59N12	42E18	-2:49:12
Selezen'ovo 6	9	60N45	28E39	-1:54:36
Selezni 6	39	55N39	31E29	-2:05:56
Selezni 6	41	52N48	41E15	-2:45:00
Selezn'ovo 6	9	60N45	28E39	-1:54:36
Sel'gon 2	11	49N36	135E26	-9:01:44
Selichino 2	11	50N22	137E38	-9:10:32
Šelichovo 2	20	55N42	97E41	-6:30:44
Selidovo 23	45	48N08	37E18	-2:29:12
Seliksa 6	41	53N13	45E18	-3:01:12
Selišče 6	39	56N53	33E16	-2:13:04
Selišče 6	41	64N58	46E18	-3:05:12
Selitrennoje 6	34	47N11	47E27	-3:09:48
Selivanovskaja 6	47	48N52	41E42	-2:46:48
Seližarovo 6	39	56N51	33E27	-2:13:48
Šelkovka 6	39	55N32	36E22	-2:25:28
Šelkovskaja 6	47	43N30	46E22	-3:05:28
Šelopugino 2	16	51N39	117E33	-7:50:12
Selty 6	42	57N19	52E10	-3:28:40
Sel'vačevo 6	39	55N25	37E57	-2:31:48
Šemacha 3	34	40N38	48E39	-3:14:36
Šemacha 2	30	56N15	59E16	-3:57:04
Šemanicha 6	41	57N18	45E24	-3:01:36
Semcy 6	39	52N51	33E28	-2:13:52
Semejkino 23	45	48N19	39E32	-2:38:08
Semeliškės 14	37	54N40	24E40	-1:38:40
Semenovka 23	44	49N36	33E10	-2:12:40
Semertak 2	14	52N57	132E34	-8:50:16
Šemetovo 6	39	54N28	38E30	-2:34:00
Semeževo 4	39	52N58	27E00	-1:48:00
Semibalki 6	40	47N00	39E03	-2:36:12
Semibratovo 6	40	57N18	39E32	-2:38:08
Semibugry 6	34	46N11	48E16	-3:13:04
Semides'atnoje 6	40	51N21	38E44	-2:34:56
Semigorsk 2	20	56N42	104E41	-6:58:44
Semijarka 9	24	50N54	78E20	-5:13:20
Semikarakorsk 6	47	47N31	40E48	-2:43:12
Semikarakorskij 6	47	47N31	40E48	-2:43:12
Semilej 6	41	53N57	45E21	-3:01:24
Semilovo 6	40	55N04	42E10	-2:48:40
Semiluki 6	40	51N41	39E02	-2:36:08
Semiozerje 2	18	49N52	110E23	-7:21:32
Semioz'ornoje 9	30	52N22	64E08	-4:16:32
Semioz'ornyj 2	16	53N44	120E25	-8:01:40
Semipalatinsk 9	24	50N28	80E13	-5:20:52
Semipolka 9	24	54N07	67E16	-4:29:04
Semipolki 23	44	50N43	30E56	-2:03:44
Semizbugy 9	24	50N12	74E48	-4:59:12
Semjany 6	41	56N02	45E59	-3:03:56
Seml'ovo 6	39	55N03	33E58	-2:15:52
Šemonaicha 9	24	50N39	81E54	-5:27:36
Sem'ono-Aleksandrovka 6	41	51N03	40E12	-2:40:48
Sem'onov 6	41	56N48	44E30	-2:58:00
Sem'onovka 23	44	52N10	32E35	-2:10:20
Sem'onovka 9	24	51N20	70E46	-4:43:04
Sem'onovka 10	24	42N43	77E32	-5:10:08
Sem'onovka 23	44	49N36	33E10	-2:12:40
Sem'onovskoje 6	39	55N03	37E46	-2:31:04
Sem'onovskoje 6	39	55N18	38E21	-2:33:24
Šemordan 6	41	56N11	50E26	-3:21:44
Šemurša 6	41	54N53	47E32	-3:10:08
Šemyšejka 6	41	52N54	45E24	-3:01:36
Semža 6	41	66N09	44E08	-2:56:32
Šenber 9	31	49N46	66E09	-4:24:36
Šenbertal 9	30	48N43	60E20	-4:01:20
Senča 23	44	50N16	33E20	-2:13:20
Šender 9	31	49N46	66E09	-4:24:36
Šengel'šij 9	30	48N33	57E28	-3:49:52
Sengilej 6	34	53N58	48E46	-3:15:04
Senkevičevka 23	44	50N32	25E02	-1:40:08
Sen'kovo 23	45	49N31	37E43	-2:30:52
Šenkursk 6	41	62N08	42E53	-2:51:32
Sennaja 6	47	45N15	37E01	-2:28:04
Senno 4	39	54N49	29E43	-1:58:52
Sennoj 6	34	50N16	43E37	-2:54:28
Sennoj 6	34	52N11	46E57	-3:07:48
Šentala 6	42	54N27	51E29	-3:25:56
Sentas 9	24	49N19	82E28	-5:29:52
Sentelek 2	21	51N13	83E44	-5:34:56
Šepetovka 23	44	50N11	27E04	-1:48:16
Sepyč 6	30	58N11	54E08	-3:36:32
Šerabad 24	30	37N40	67E01	-4:28:04
Serafimovič 6	34	49N36	42E43	-2:50:52
Šeragul 2	20	54N29	100E56	-6:43:44
Šerbakul' 2	24	54N38	72E24	-4:49:36
Serdež 6	42	57N17	48E17	-3:13:08
Serditoje 23	45	48N02	38E24	-2:33:36
Serdobsk 6	41	52N28	44E13	-2:56:52
Serebr'anka 2	24	57N13	70E42	-4:42:48
Serebr'anka 23	45	48N55	38E08	-2:32:32
Serebr'anka 6	39	55N45	37E55	-2:31:40
Serebr'ansk 9	24	49N43	83E20	-5:33:20
Serebr'anyje Prudy 6	39	54N28	38E44	-2:34:56
Serebrovo 2	20	55N24	97E52	-6:31:28
Serechoviči 23	44	51N25	24E40	-1:38:40
Sereda 6	39	55N54	35E31	-2:22:04
Sereda 6	41	58N00	40E27	-2:41:48
Seredejskij 6	39	54N03	35E14	-2:20:56
SeredIči 6	39	53N35	35E51	-2:23:24
Seredina-Buda 23	44	52N11	34E01	-2:16:04
Serednikovo 6	39	55N56	37E14	-2:28:56
Serednikovo 6	39	55N15	39E40	-2:38:40
Seredn'ovo 6	39	55N35	37E18	-2:29:12
Seredžius 14	37	55N05	23E25	-1:33:40
Šeregeš 2	21	52N57	88E02	-5:52:08
Šeremetjevka 6	41	55N23	51E32	-3:26:08
Šeremetjevskij 6	39	55N59	37E30	-2:30:00
Šereševo 4	39	52N33	24E13	-1:36:52
Ser'ga 6	30	57N46	56E52	-3:47:28
Sergač 6	41	55N32	45E28	-3:01:52
Sergeja Kirova Islands 2	21	77N12	89E30	-5:58:00
Sergeja Kirova, Ostrova 2	21	77N12	89E30	-5:58:00
Sergejeviči 4	39	53N30	27E45	-1:51:00
Sergejevka 2	27	44N22	131E39	-8:46:36
Sergejevka 2	27	43N21	133E22	-8:53:28
Sergejevka 23	45	48N40	37E22	-2:29:28
Sergejevka 9	24	53N51	67E25	-4:29:40
Sergejevka 9	24	51N39	68E13	-4:32:52
Sergejevo 2	21	57N18	86E02	-5:44:08
Sergijevka 6	41	51N46	41E05	-2:44:20
Sergijevskaja 6	41	60N16	43E54	-2:55:36
Sergijevskaja 6	34	50N16	43E47	-2:55:08
Sergijevskij 6	32	51N56	51E54	-3:27:36
Sergili 24	24	41N13	69E14	-4:36:56
Sergino 2	30	62N30	65E38	-4:22:32
Sergokala 6	47	42N27	47E40	-3:10:40
Serjol 6	41	60N02	48E58	-3:15:52
Serkovo 6	39	54N28	38E46	-2:35:04
Šerlovaja Gora 2	16	50N34	116E15	-7:45:00
Serman 6	41	53N34	46E22	-3:05:28
Serniki 23	44	51N49	26E14	-1:44:56
Sernovodsk 6	34	53N56	51E17	-3:25:08
Sernur 6	41	56N56	49E09	-3:16:36
Sernyy Zavod 22	30	39N59	58E50	-3:55:20
Ser'odka 6	9	58N10	28E12	-1:52:48

Seroglazka 6 34 47N01 47E29 -3:09:56
Ser'ogovo 6 41 62N20 50E36 -3:22:24
Serov 2 30 59N29 60E31 -4:02:04
Serovo 24 24 40N27 71E12 -4:44:48
Serpejsk 6 39 54N20 34W59 2:19:56
Serpnevoje 23 45 46N18 29E02 -1:56:08
Serpuchov 6 39 54N55 37E25 -2:29:40
Serpukhov → Serpuchov 6 39 54N55 37E25 -2:29:40
Šerstin 4 39 52N39 31E03 -2:04:12
Šerstobitovo 2 23 57N16 78E52 -5:15:28
Seryševo 2 14 51N08 128E20 -8:33:20
Sešan 2 2 66N46 171W26 11:25:44
Sešča 6 39 53N45 33E23 -2:13:32
Seščinskij 6 39 53N45 33E23 -2:13:32
Šestakovka 23 45 48N32 31E58 -2:07:52
Šestakovo 2 20 56N29 103E59 -6:55:56
Šestakovo 6 39 56N21 35E49 -2:23:16
Šestern'a 23 45 47N33 33E16 -2:13:04
Sestroreck 6 9 60N06 29E58 -1:59:52
Šešurga 6 42 57N29 47E35 -3:10:20
Šėta 14 37 55N17 24E15 -1:37:00
Setraki 6 47 49N23 40E49 -2:43:16
Sevan 1 34 40N34 44E57 -2:59:48
Sevastopol' 23 45 44N36 33E32 -2:14:08
Sevastopol'skij 9 30 53N08 65E44 -4:22:56
Ševčenko 9 30 43N35 51E05 -3:24:20
Ševčenkovo 23 45 45N33 29E20 -1:57:20
Ševčenkovo 23 44 51N40 33E39 -2:14:36
Ševčenkovo 23 45 49N41 37E10 -2:28:40
Ševčenkovo Vtoroje 23 45 47N29 36E08 -2:24:32
Ševelevskaja 6 41 60N52 44E12 -2:56:48
Ševelevskij Majdan 6 41 54N25 42E15 -2:49:00
Severnaja Zeml'a 20 19 79N30 98E00 -6:32:00
Severnaja Zeml'a Islands 20 19 79N30 98E00 -6:32:00
Severnoje 6 41 58N02 41E26 -2:45:44
Severnoje 6 32 54N06 52E32 -3:30:08
Severnoje 6 47 44N49 42E51 -2:51:24
Severnoje 23 45 48N04 38E44 -2:34:56
Severnoje 2 23 56N21 78E23 -5:13:32
Severnyj 6 39 55N56 37E33 -2:30:12
Severnyj 6 29 67N38 64E06 -4:16:24
Severnyj Kommunar 6 30 58N23 54E02 -3:36:08
Severnyj Prijut 6 47 43N16 41E51 -2:47:24
Severodoneck 23 45 48N58 38E27 -2:33:48
Severodvinsk 6 40 64N34 39E50 -2:39:20
Severo-Jenisejskij 2 21 60N22 93E01 -6:12:04
Severo-Kuril'sk 12 8 50N40 156E08-10:24:32
Severomorsk 6 9 69N05 33E24 -2:13:36
Severoural'sk 2 30 60N09 59E57 -3:59:48
Severo-Zadonsk 6 40 54N02 38W24 2:33:36
Severskaja 6 47 44N51 38E42 -2:34:48
Severucha 2 30 58N28 63E25 -4:13:40
Sevsk 6 39 52N09 34E30 -2:18:00
Ševykan 2 20 54N20 106E49 -7:07:16
Šežim 6 29 62N07 58E21 -3:53:24
Shadrinsk → Šadrinsk 2 30 56N05 63E38 -4:14:32
Shakhty → Šachty 6 40 47N42 40E13 -2:40:52
Shchekino → Ščokino 6 39 54N01 37E31 -2:30:04
Shchelkovo → Ščelkovo 6 39 55N55 38E00 -2:32:00
Shcherbakov → Rybinsk 6 40 58N03 38E52 -2:35:28
Sheki → Šeki 3 34 41N12 47E12 -3:08:48
Shostka → Šostka 23 44 51N52 33E30 -2:14:00
Shuya → Šuja 6 9 61N55 34E12 -2:16:48
Sialejevskaja P'atina 6 41 53N49 44E32 -2:58:08
Šiaškotan Island 12 8 48N49 154E06-10:16:24
Šiaškotan, Ostrov 12 8 48N49 154E06-10:16:24
Šiauliai 14 37 55N56 23E19 -1:33:16
Šiazan' 3 34 41N05 49E06 -3:16:24
Sibaj 6 30 52N42 58E39 -3:54:36
Šibbe 10 24 39N53 72E05 -4:48:20
Sibiči 2 27 46N04 135E22 -9:01:28
Sibircevo 2 27 44N12 132E26 -8:49:44
Šichany 6 34 52N07 47E13 -3:08:52
Šichtovo 6 39 55N43 32E18 -2:09:12
Sidel'kino 6 42 54N32 51E08 -3:24:32
Sidorovo 6 41 58N48 40E58 -2:43:52
Sidory 6 34 50N08 43E19 -2:53:16
Sig 6 40 65N35 34E13 -2:16:52
Šigali 6 41 55N33 48E02 -3:12:08
Siglan 2 6 59N02 152E25-10:09:40
Signachi 7 33 41N37 45E54 -3:03:36
Šigony 6 34 53N23 48E42 -3:14:48
Sigulda 13 36 57N09 24E51 -1:39:24
Šiiči 4 39 52N15 29E14 -1:56:56
Sija 6 41 63N38 41E38 -2:46:32
Sikt'ach 2 13 69N55 125E02 -8:20:08
Šila 2 21 56N33 93E02 -6:12:08
Šilalė 14 37 55N28 22E12 -1:28:48
Šil'da 6 30 51N46 59E45 -3:59:00
Šilikty 9 24 47N10 84E32 -5:38:08
Šilka 2 16 51N51 116E02 -7:44:08
Sillamäe 5 35 59N24 27E45 -1:51:00
Šil'naja Balka 9 32 50N34 49E01 -3:16:04
Šiloviči 6 39 55N24 32E33 -2:10:12
Šilovka 6 42 54N03 48E40 -3:14:40
Šilovo 6 39 55N00 33E46 -2:15:04
Šilovo 6 41 54N19 40E53 -2:43:32
Šilutė 14 37 55N21 21E29 -1:25:56
Sim 2 30 54N59 57E41 -3:50:44
Sima 6 39 56N41 39E33 -2:38:12
Simanoviči 4 39 53N05 28E38 -1:54:32
Simanovsk 2 15 52N00 127E42 -8:30:48
Simbirsk → Uljanovsk 6 42 54N20 48E24 -3:13:36
Simeiz 23 45 44N26 34E01 -2:16:04
Simferopol' 23 45 44N57 34E06 -2:16:24
Simnas 14 37 54N24 23E39 -1:34:36
Simoneti 7 33 42N14 42E52 -2:51:28
Simonicha 6 42 56N31 53E50 -3:35:20
Simoniči 4 39 51N53 28E04 -1:52:16
Šimorskoje 6 40 55N19 42E02 -2:48:08
Šimsk 6 9 58N13 30E43 -2:02:52
Simušir Island 12 8 46N58 152E02-10:08:08
Simušir, Ostrov 12 8 46N58 152E02-10:08:08
Sinatle 7 33 42N28 43E04 -2:52:16
Sin'avka 4 39 52N58 26E29 -1:45:56
Sin'avka 6 40 47N17 39E17 -2:37:08
Sinda 2 11 48N57 136E18 -9:05:12
Sindi 5 35 58N24 24E40 -1:38:40
Sindor 6 41 62N50 51E57 -3:27:48
Sinegorje 6 42 59N42 50E40 -3:22:40
Sinegorsk 19 8 47N10 142E30 -9:30:00
Sinegorskij 6 47 48N00 40E53 -2:43:32
Sinel'nikovo 23 45 48N20 35E31 -2:22:04
Sinen'kije 6 34 51N15 45E46 -3:03:04
Sinevir 23 44 48N30 23E38 -1:34:32
Sinevka 23 45 50N33 34E06 -2:16:24
Sinez'orki 6 39 53N02 34E26 -2:17:44
Šingoža 9 24 47N45 80E40 -5:22:40
Sinicha 23 45 49N31 37E34 -2:30:16
Sinije Lip'agi 6 40 51N23 38E29 -2:33:56
Sin'kovo 6 39 56N26 36E04 -2:24:16
Sin'kovo 6 39 54N37 38E56 -2:35:44
Sin'kovo 6 39 56N23 37E19 -2:29:16
Šinkovo 6 39 56N03 31E31 -2:06:04
Sinskoje 2 16 61N08 126E48 -8:27:12
Sin'uga 2 17 57N45 115E13 -7:40:52
Šipicyno 2 23 56N04 77E18 -5:09:12
Šipicyno 6 41 61N17 46E28 -3:05:52
Šipilovo 6 39 54N49 37E32 -2:30:08
Šipoteny 15 46 47N18 28E11 -1:52:44
Šipovatoje 23 45 49N56 37E24 -2:29:36
Šipunovo 2 23 52N13 82E17 -5:29:08
Šira 2 21 54N29 89E56 -5:59:44
Šir'aj 6 34 49N34 44E07 -2:56:28
Šir'ajevo 23 45 47N23 30E13 -2:00:52
Širdkoje 23 45 48N08 34E49 -2:19:16
Širega 6 41 60N10 41E15 -2:45:00
Šireniki 2 2 64N25 173W57 11:35:48
Širinguši 6 41 53N51 42E46 -2:51:04
Širmovka 23 44 49N34 29E06 -1:56:24
Širokaja Pad' 19 8 50N14 142E09 -9:28:36
Širokij 2 14 49N45 129E30 -8:38:00
Širokij Bujerak 6 34 52N07 47E46 -3:11:04
Širokino 23 45 47N06 37E49 -2:31:16
Širokoje 23 45 47N58 38E13 -2:32:52
Širokoje 23 45 47N41 33E14 -2:12:56
Širokolanovka 23 45 47N10 31E24 -2:05:36
Širokovo 2 20 55N27 99E23 -6:37:32
Širotino 23 45 48N55 38E31 -2:34:04
Širotino 4 39 55N23 29E37 -1:58:28
Širotinskaja 6 34 49N16 43E39 -2:54:36
Širvintos 14 37 55N03 24E57 -1:39:48
Šišaki 23 44 49N53 34E00 -2:16:00
Šišakovo 6 41 60N02 41E30 -2:46:00
Šiševka 6 40 58N52 38E52 -2:35:28
Sisian 1 34 39N32 46E02 -3:04:08
Šišicy 4 39 53N13 27E32 -1:50:08
Šiškejevo 6 41 54N12 44E45 -2:59:00
Šiškino 2 16 52N18 113E35 -7:34:20
Šišlovo 6 39 54N14 38E33 -2:34:12
Šitkino 2 20 56N23 98E21 -6:33:24
Sitkovcy 23 45 48N54 37E12 -1:56:48
Sitn'a-Ščelkanovo 6 39 54N58 37E59 -2:31:56
Sitniki 6 41 56N27 44E06 -2:56:24
Sitnikovo 2 30 56N23 67E53 -4:31:32
Sivaki 2 16 52N39 126E45 -8:27:00
Sivašskoje 23 45 46N23 34E34 -2:18:16
Siverskij 6 9 59N21 30E05 -2:00:20
Sivkovo 6 39 55N26 35E53 -2:23:32
Sivomaskinskij 6 29 66N40 62E35 -4:10:20
Siz'absk 6 29 65N05 53E49 -3:35:16
Sizaja 2 19 58N07 100E38 -6:42:32
Siziman 2 11 50N43 140E26 -9:21:44
Sjanovo 6 39 54N59 37E25 -2:29:40
Skadovsk 23 45 46N08 32E54 -2:11:36
Skaistkalne 13 36 56N23 24E39 -1:38:36
Skala-Podol'skaja 23 45 48N51 26E12 -1:44:48
Skalat 23 44 49N26 25E59 -1:43:56
Skalino 6 41 58N32 40E13 -2:40:52
Skal'nyj 6 30 58N22 57E59 -3:51:56
Skaudvilė 14 37 55N24 22E35 -1:30:20
Skidel' 4 39 53N34 24E15 -1:37:00
Škin' 6 39 55N11 38E30 -2:34:00
Sklad 2 16 71N55 123E33 -8:14:12
Šklov 4 39 54N13 30E18 -2:01:12
Skole 23 44 49N02 23E29 -1:33:56
Skomorošk1 6 39 54N05 36E57 -2:27:48
Skomorošk1 23 44 49N20 29E26 -1:57:44
Skopin 6 40 53N51 39E33 -2:38:12
Skorodnoje 4 39 51N38 28E49 -1:55:16
Skorodnoje 6 39 51N05 37E14 -2:28:56
Skotovataja 23 45 48N13 37E54 -2:31:36
Škotovo 2 27 43N20 132E21 -8:49:24
Skovorodino 2 16 53N59 123E55 -8:15:40
Skripl1vka 6 39 57N32 30E38 -2:02:32
Skrīveri 13 36 56N39 25E08 -1:40:32
Skrudaliena 13 36 55N49 26E43 -1:46:52
Skrunda 13 36 56N41 22E01 -1:28:04
Škunovka 6 30 50N45 55E27 -3:41:48
Skuodas 14 37 56N16 21E32 -1:26:08
Skuratovskij 6 39 54N07 37E36 -2:30:24
Škurinskaja 6 47 46N35 39E22 -2:37:28
Škurišenskaja 6 34 49N52 42E57 -2:51:48
Skvira 23 44 49N44 29E40 -1:58:40
Sladkij 6 47 46N10 42E17 -2:49:08
Sladkovo 2 30 55N32 70E20 -4:41:20
Slagoviščí 6 39 53N57 35E54 -2:23:36
Slancy 6 9 59N06 28E04 -1:52:16
Slaščevskaja 6 34 49N52 42E21 -2:49:24
Slastucha 6 34 51N57 44E32 -2:58:08
Slatino 23 45 50N12 36E11 -2:24:44
Slautnoje 2 4 63N00 167E59-11:11:56
Slava 2 14 52N08 129E24 -8:37:36
Slav'anka 2 27 42N53 131E21 -8:45:24
Slav'anka 24 24 40N40 68E32 -4:34:08
Slav'anka 23 45 48N24 36E43 -2:26:52
Slav'anogorsk 23 45 49N02 37E31 -2:30:04
Slav'anoserbsk 23 45 48N42 38E59 -2:35:56
Slav'ansk 23 45 48N52 37E37 -2:30:28
Slav'ansk-Na-Kubani 6 47 45N15 38E08 -2:32:32
Slavgorod 23 45 50N36 35E21 -2:21:24
Slavgorod 4 39 53N27 31E00 -2:04:00
Slavgorod 2 23 53N00 78E40 -5:14:40
Slavgorod 23 45 48N06 35E31 -2:22:04
Slavitino 6 39 56N41 39E13 -2:36:52
Slavkino 6 34 52N58 47E11 -3:08:44
Slavkoviči 6 39 57N39 29E05 -1:56:20
Slavnoje 4 39 54N18 29E27 -1:57:48
Slavsk (Heinrichswalde) 8 38 55N03 21E41 -1:26:44
Slavskoje 23 44 48N49 23E24 -1:33:36
Slavuta 23 44 50N18 26E52 -1:47:28
Slednevo 6 39 56N25 38E36 -2:34:24
Sled'uki 4 39 53N35 30E22 -2:01:28
Slepino 6 9 59N11 29E02 -1:56:08
Sloboda 23 44 51N11 33E37 -2:14:28
Sloboda 6 39 55N30 31E51 -2:07:24
Sloboda 4 39 53N58 28E08 -1:52:32
Sloboda 6 41 51N09 40E17 -2:41:08
Slobodka 4 39 55N41 27E11 -1:48:44
Slobodka 6 39 54N22 37E33 -2:30:12
Slobodka 23 45 47N53 29E21 -1:57:24
Slobodskoj 6 42 58N42 50E12 -3:20:48
Slobodzeja 15 46 46N44 29E43 -1:58:52
Slobodzeja-Mare 15 46 45N34 28E12 -1:52:48
Slobodzeja-Prut 15 46 45N34 28E12 -1:52:48
Slonim 4 39 53N06 25E19 -1:41:16
Slonovka 6 39 50N39 37E45 -2:31:00
Slovečno 23 44 51N23 28E21 -1:53:24
Slovinka 6 41 58N02 43E07 -2:52:28
Sluck 4 39 53N01 27E33 -1:50:12
Sl'ud'anka 2 20 51N38 103E42 -6:54:48
Sludy 6 40 58N52 36E52 -2:27:28
Šl'uz-Mokr'aki 2 21 59N17 88E50 -5:55:20
Smachtino 6 39 54N51 36E25 -2:25:40
Smalininkai 14 37 55N05 22E35 -1:30:20
Smela 23 44 49N14 31E53 -2:07:32
Smeloje 23 44 50N55 33E36 -2:14:24
Šmel'ovka 6 42 54N47 49E11 -3:16:44
Smidovič 2 11 48N36 133E49 -8:55:16
Šmidta → Mys Šmidta 2 2 68N56 179W26 11:57:44
Smiloviči 4 39 53N45 28E01 -1:52:04
Smiltene 13 36 57N26 25E56 -1:43:44
Smirnovskij 9 24 54N31 69E25 -4:37:40
Smirnych 19 8 49N43 142E38 -9:30:32
Smol'anica 4 39 52N42 24E38 -1:38:32
Smol'aninovo 2 27 43N19 132E28 -8:49:52
Smol'any 4 39 54N36 30E04 -2:00:16
Smolensk 6 39 54N47 32E03 -2:08:12
Smolenskoje 2 21 52N20 85E05 -5:40:20
Smoleviči 4 39 54N02 28E05 -1:52:20
Smolovka 4 39 55N33 30E13 -2:00:52
Smorgon' 4 39 54N29 26E24 -1:45:36
Smorodovka 6 39 57N08 29E52 -1:59:28
Smotrič 23 45 48N56 26E34 -1:46:16
Smuskovoje 6 47 47N20 45E55 -3:03:40
Smyčka 6 39 56N04 35E56 -2:23:44
Smyšl'ajevka 6 34 53N15 50E22 -3:21:28

Sn'adin 4 39 52N04 28E19 -1:53:16
Snagost' 6 39 51N21 34E54 -2:19:36
Šn'ajevo 6 34 52N34 46E11 -3:04:44
Sn'atyn 23 44 48N28 25E34 -1:42:16
Snežnoje 23 45 48N01 38E46 -2:35:04
Snigir'ovka 23
45 47N06 32E47 -2:11:08
Snov 4 39 53N13 26E24 -1:45:36
Sobič 23 44 51N52 33E14 -2:12:56
Sobinka 6 39 55N59 40E01 -2:40:04
Sobolekovo 6 41 55N39 51E53 -3:27:32
Sobolev 6 32 51N56 51E43 -3:26:52
Sobolevka 23 45 48N36 29E30 -1:58:00
Sobolevo 6 39 55N31 38E43 -2:34:52
Sobolino 2 16 53N23 119E42 -7:58:48
Socgorodok 6 39 50N11 38E09 -2:32:36
Soch 24 24 39N57 71E08 -4:44:32
Sochi → Soči 6
47 43N35 39E45 -2:39:00
Sochondo 2 16 51N49 112E32 -7:30:08
Soči 6 47 43N35 39E45 -2:39:00
Sofijevka 23 45 46N33 34E03 -2:16:12
Sofijevka 23 45 48N04 33E52 -2:15:28
Sofijevskij 23
45 48N12 38E52 -2:35:28
Sofijsk 2 11 52N15 133E58 -8:55:52
Sofijsk 2 11 51N34 139E52 -9:19:28
Sofjanga 6 9 65N52 31E15 -2:05:00
Sofje-Kondratjevka 23
45 48N18 38E12 -2:32:48
Sofjino 6 39 55N30 38E11 -2:32:44
Sofrino 6 39 56N09 37E56 -2:31:44
Sofronovo 6 40 59N48 36E54 -2:27:36
Sogda 2 11 50N24 132E12 -8:48:48
Sojana 6 41 65N48 43E20 -2:53:20
Sojda 6 40 61N11 37E40 -2:30:40
Šojna 6 41 67N52 44E08 -2:56:32
Sokal' 23 44 50N29 24E17 -1:37:08
Sokir'any 23 45 48N27 27E25 -1:49:40
Sokirincy 23 44 50N42 32E46 -2:11:04
Sokol 2 13 72N24 126E48 -8:27:12
Sokol 19 8 47N14 142E45 -9:31:00
Sokol 6 41 59N28 40E10 -2:40:40
Sokolka 6 41 55N34 51E30 -3:26:00
Sokol'nikovo 6
39 55N21 35E49 -2:23:16
Sokologornoje 23
45 46N29 34E58 -2:19:52
Sokolova-Gora 23
44 50N19 28E36 -1:54:24
Sokolova Pustyn' 6
39 54N51 38E03 -2:32:12
Sokolovka 9 24 55N06 69E12 -4:36:48
Sokolovo 2 21 52N33 84E46 -5:39:04
Sokolovo 6 29 65N21 56E57 -3:47:48
Sokolovo 6 41 52N49 42E26 -2:49:44
Sokolovo 6 39 52N55 34E39 -2:18:36
Sokolovo 6 39 56N02 36E55 -2:27:40
Sokolovo-Kundr'učenskij 6
40 47N50 39E57 -2:39:48
Sokol'skoje 6 41 57N08 43E13 -2:52:52
Šokpar 9 24 43N49 74E21 -4:57:24
Sokrutovka 6 34 47N54 46E33 -3:06:12
Sokša 6 41 58N24 42E27 -2:49:48
Sokuluk 10 24 42N52 74E18 -4:57:12
Sokur 2 21 55N13 83E13 -5:32:52
Sokur 6 34 52N01 45E48 -3:03:12
Sol' 23 45 48N43 38E02 -2:32:08
Šolaksaj 9 24 51N45 64E48 -4:19:12
Sol'cy 6 9 58N08 30E20 -2:01:20
Soldatskaja 6 47 43N48 43E49 -2:55:16
Soldatskoje 24
24 40N52 68E56 -4:35:44
Soldatsko-Stepnoje 6
34 49N32 45E30 -3:02:00
Solenoje 6 47 46N14 42E32 -2:50:08
Solenoje Zajmišče 6
34 47N56 46E07 -3:04:28
Solginskij 6 41 61N05 41E19 -2:45:16
Soligalič 6 41 59N05 42E17 -2:49:08
Soligorsk 4 39 52N48 27E32 -1:50:08
Solikamsk 6 30 59N39 56E47 -3:47:08
Šollar 3 34 41N40 48E38 -3:14:32
Solncedar 6 47 44N34 38E01 -2:32:04
Solncevo 6 39 55N39 37E24 -2:29:36
Solnečnogorsk 6
39 56N11 36E59 -2:27:56
Šolochovskij 6
47 48N18 41E03 -2:44:12
Solodča 6 34 49N39 44E17 -2:57:08
Solodniki 6 34 48N25 45E16 -3:01:04
Šologoncy 2 16 66N13 114E14 -7:36:56
Solomennikova 2
21 58N20 89E02 -5:56:08
Solomennoje 6 9 61N51 34E19 -2:17:16
Solonešnoje 2 21 51N40 84E21 -5:37:24
Solonka 6 34 50N13 41E28 -2:45:52
Sol'onoje 6 47 44N03 40E53 -2:43:32
Sol'onoje 23 45 49N18 37E39 -2:30:36
Sol'onoje 23 45 48N13 34E52 -2:19:28
Sol'onoje Ozero 23
45 45N53 34E27 -2:17:48
Sol'onoje Zajmišče 6
34 47N56 46E07 -3:04:28
Solotča 6 40 54N48 39E51 -2:39:24
Solotobe 9 30 44N38 66E05 -4:24:20
Solotvin 23 44 48N42 24E25 -1:37:40
Solotvina 15 46 47N57 23E52 -1:35:28
Solovjovka 6 9 60N46 30E09 -2:00:36
Solovjovsk 2 16 54N14 124E26 -8:17:44
Solovjovsk 2 16 49N55 115E42 -7:42:48
Solton 2 21 52N50 86E28 -5:45:52
Sol'vyčegodsk 6
41 61N21 46E52 -3:07:28
Soly 4 39 54N31 26E11 -1:44:44

Solza 6 40 64N33 39E29 -2:37:56
Sõmerpalu 5 35 57N51 26E48 -1:47:12
Somino 6 9 59N21 34E52 -2:19:28
Somnitel'nyj 2
11 52N12 139E04 -9:16:16
Somovo 6 39 52N53 34E58 -2:19:52
Somovo 6 41 51N44 39E23 -2:37:32
Šomyškol' 9 30 46N30 59E53 -3:59:32
Sonduga 6 41 60N08 41E55 -2:47:40
Šonguj 6 9 68N47 33E00 -2:12:00
Sonkovo 6 39 57N47 37E09 -2:28:36
Sonostrov 6 9 66N09 34E10 -2:16:40
Sopki 6 39 57N06 30E55 -2:03:40
Sopockin 4 39 53N50 23E39 -1:34:36
Šoptykol' 9 24 51N16 75E45 -5:03:00
Šorapani 7 33 42N05 43E05 -2:52:20
Soročinka 9 32 47N30 51E44 -3:26:56
Soročinsk 6 32 52N26 53E10 -3:32:40
Soročkino 2 30 57N02 68E52 -4:35:28
Sorok 2 20 52N20 100E12 -6:40:48
Soroki 15 46 48N09 28E17 -1:53:08
Sorokino 2 21 55N52 93E15 -6:13:00
Sorokino 2 21 54N13 91E31 -6:06:04
Sorokino 2 21 53N45 84E58 -5:39:52
Sorokošiči 23 44 51N12 30E35 -2:02:20
Sorovskije 2 25 59N53 71E34 -4:46:16
Sorsk 2 21 54N01 90E12 -6:00:48
Šorsu 24 24 40N17 70E48 -4:43:12
Šortandy 9 24 51N42 71E00 -4:44:00
Sortavala 6 9 61N42 30E41 -2:02:44
Sorviži 6 42 57N52 48E32 -3:14:08
Sosedka 6 41 53N15 42E40 -2:50:40
Sosedno 6 9 58N14 28E42 -1:54:48
Sosenki 6 39 55N34 37E26 -2:29:44
Šoška 6 41 62N42 50E40 -3:22:40
Soskovo 6 39 52N45 35E23 -2:21:32
Sosnica 23 44 51N32 32E28 -2:09:52
Sosnicy 6 39 57N38 30E25 -2:01:40
Sosnogorsk 6 29 63N37 53E51 -3:35:24
Sosnovaja Maza 6
34 52N30 47E53 -3:11:32
Sosnovec 6 40 64N26 34E27 -2:17:48
Sosnovica 6 41 60N21 40E50 -2:43:20
Sosnovka 6 42 54N06 46E38 -3:06:32
Sosnovka 6 39 54N31 38E08 -2:32:32
Sosnovka 6 39 54N54 38E41 -2:34:44
Sosnovka 2 23 59N10 81E18 -5:25:12
Sosnovka 9 24 51N26 79E28 -5:17:52
Sosnovka 2 20 54N09 109E35 -7:18:20
Sosnovka 10 24 42N40 73E55 -4:55:40
Sosnovka 6 41 52N26 43E29 -2:53:56
Sosnovka 6 9 66N30 40E32 -2:42:08
Sosnovka 6 41 56N13 47E13 -3:08:52
Sosnovka 6 42 57N48 51E43 -3:26:52
Sosnovka 6 42 56N17 51E17 -3:25:08
Sosnovka 6 41 53N14 41E22 -2:45:28
Sosnovka 6 42 57N16 53E31 -3:34:04
Sosnovo 6 9 60N33 30E15 -2:01:00
Sosnovo 6 30 56N42 54E35 -3:38:20
Sosnovoborsk 6
41 53N18 46E16 -3:05:04
Sosnovoje 23 44 50N49 27E00 -1:48:00
Sosnovo-Oz'orskoje 2
20 52N31 111E30 -7:26:00
Sosnovskij 2 24 54N36 73E10 -4:52:40
Sosnovskoje 6 41 55N48 43E10 -2:52:40
Sosnovyj Bor 6 9 59N55 29E07 -1:56:28
Sosnovyj Bor 6
30 57N07 55E03 -3:40:12
Sosnovyj Solonec 6
34 53N17 49E33 -3:18:12
Šostka 23 44 51N52 33E30 -2:14:00
Sos'va 2 28 63N40 62E06 -4:08:24
Sos'va 2 30 59N10 61E50 -4:07:20
Sotnicyno 6 41 54N17 41E49 -2:47:16
Sovetabad 21 24 40N14 69E44 -4:38:56
Sovetabad 24 24 40N48 72E58 -4:51:52
Sovetašen 1 34 40N06 44E33 -2:58:12
Sovetašen 1 34 39N50 45E03 -3:00:12
Sovetka 6 40 47N30 39E15 -2:37:00
Sovetsk 6 39 53N56 37E39 -2:30:36
Sovetsk (Tilsit) 8
38 55N05 21E53 -1:27:32
Sovetsk 6 42 57N37 48E58 -3:15:52
Sovetskaja 6 47 44N02 44E03 -2:56:12
Sovetskaja 6 47 49N00 42E07 -2:48:28
Sovetskaja 6 47 44N46 41E11 -2:44:44
Sovetskaja Gavan' 2
11 48N58 140E18 -9:21:12
Sovetskij 6 30 51N04 56E29 -3:45:56
Sovetskij 6 41 56N46 48E32 -3:14:08
Sovetskij 23 45 45N20 34E56 -2:19:44
Sovetskij 6 9 60N32 28E41 -1:54:44
Sovetskij 21 24 38N02 69E35 -4:38:20
Sovetskoje 6 40 50N21 39E01 -2:36:04
Sovetskoje 6 47 43N19 43E36 -2:54:24
Sovetskoje 6 47 42N52 45E41 -3:02:44
Sovetskoje 9 24 42N17 70E15 -4:41:00
Sovetskoje 6 47 47N18 44E31 -2:58:04
Sovetskoje 6 34 51N27 46E44 -3:06:56
Šovgenovskij 6
47 45N02 40E14 -2:40:56
Sovpolje 6 41 65N18 43E55 -2:55:40
Sozimskij 6 42 59N44 52E16 -3:29:04
Šožma 6 41 61N56 40E15 -2:41:00
Spas-Demensk 6
39 54N25 34E01 -2:16:04
Spas-Klepiki 6
40 55N08 40E13 -2:40:52
Spass 6 39 55N55 35E55 -2:23:40
Spassk-Dal'nij 2
27 44N37 132E48 -8:51:12
Spasskij 2 30 53N42 59E12 -3:56:48
Spasskij Zavod 9
24 49N32 73E17 -4:53:08

Spasskoje 6 39 53N06 36E24 -2:25:36
Spasskoje 6 39 54N05 38E28 -2:33:52
Spasskoje 6 41 55N52 45E42 -3:02:48
Spassk-R'azanskij 6
40 54N24 40E23 -2:41:32
Spas-Zaulok 6 39 56N29 36E34 -2:26:16
Spevakovka 23 45 49N03 38E54 -2:35:36
Špikov 23 45 48N46 28E35 -1:54:20
Spirovo 6 39 57N26 34E59 -2:19:56
Spitak 1 34 40N51 44E16 -2:57:04
Splavnucha 6 34 51N05 45E22 -3:01:28
Spoği 13 36 56N05 26E44 -1:46:56
Spokojnaja 6 47 44N15 41E25 -2:45:40
Špola 23 44 49N01 31E24 -2:05:36
Spornoje 2 6 62N20 151E03-10:04:12
Sporovo 4 39 52N25 25E20 -1:41:20
Šramkovka 23 44 50N10 32E05 -2:08:20
Sredn'aja Achtuba 6
34 48N43 44E52 -2:59:28
Sredn'aja Ol'okma 2
16 55N26 120E33 -8:02:12
Srednegorje 6 9 60N34 29E25 -1:57:40
Srednekolymsk 2
6 67N27 153E41-10:14:44
Srednij Ikorec 6
41 51N05 39E45 -2:39:00
Srednij Kalar 2
16 55N51 117E24 -7:49:36
Srednij Urgal 2
11 51N09 132E59 -8:51:56
Srednij Vas'ugan 2
23 59N16 78E15 -5:13:00
Srednyj 23 45 48N09 39E50 -2:39:20
Sretensk 2 16 52N15 117E43 -7:50:52
Sretenskoje 2 21 56N28 96E25 -6:25:40
Stachanov 23 45 48N34 38E40 -2:34:40
Staicele 13 36 57N50 24E45 -1:39:00
Stajki 23 44 50N05 30E54 -2:03:36
Stalinabad → Dušanbe 21
24 38N35 68E48 -4:35:12
Stalingrad → Volgograd 6
34 48N44 44E25 -2:57:40
Stalino → Doneck 23
45 48N00 37E48 -2:31:12
Stalinogorsk → Novomoskovsk 6
39 54N05 38E13 -2:32:52
Stalinsk → Novokuzneck 2
21 53N45 87E06 -5:48:24
Stancija-Gorčakovo 24
24 40N25 71E45 -4:47:00
Stancionno-Ojašinskij 2
21 55N28 83E53 -5:35:32
Staničnо-Luganskoje 23
45 48N39 39E30 -2:38:00
Stanislav 23 45 46N34 32E09 -2:08:36
Stanislavčik 23
45 48N58 28E07 -1:52:28
Stanislav → Ivano-Frankovsk 23
44 48N55 24E43 -1:38:52
Stanisławów → Ivano-Frankovsk 23
44 48N55 24E43 -1:38:52
Stanovoj Kolodez' 6
39 52N51 36E16 -2:25:04
Star' 6 39 53N37 34E09 -2:16:36
Staraja 6 9 59N55 30E38 -2:02:32
Staraja Belica 4
39 54N42 29E38 -1:58:32
Staraja Belica 6
39 51N59 35E13 -2:20:52
Staraja Belogorka 6
32 52N05 53E17 -3:33:08
Staraja Duginka 6
40 54N20 38E45 -2:35:00
Staraja Kriuša 6
47 50N12 41E09 -2:44:36
Staraja Kulatka 6
34 52N43 47E37 -3:10:28
Staraja Kupavna 6
39 55N48 38E10 -2:32:40
Staraja Kupavnal 6
39 55N48 38E10 -2:32:40
Staraja Majačka 23
45 46N30 33E11 -2:12:44
Staraja Majna 6
42 54N36 48E57 -3:15:48
Staraja Poltavka 6
34 50N28 46E28 -3:05:52
Staraja Porubežka 6
34 52N03 49E11 -3:16:44
Staraja Račejka 6
34 53N22 48E03 -3:12:12
Staraja Rudn'a 4
39 52N50 30E17 -2:01:08
Staraja Russa 6
9 58N00 31E23 -2:05:32
Staraja Ruza 6
39 55N39 36E20 -2:25:20
Staraja Sachča 6
42 54N25 49E58 -3:19:52
Staraja Sin'ava 23
44 49N36 27E37 -1:50:28
Staraja Sitn'a 6
39 54N56 38E09 -2:32:36
Staraja Terizmorga 6
41 54N16 44E32 -2:58:08
Staraja Toropa 6
39 56N17 31E40 -2:06:40
Staraja Ušica 23
45 48N35 27E07 -1:48:28
Staraja Veduga 6
40 51N48 38E31 -2:34:04
Staraja Vičuga 6
40 57N16 41E53 -2:47:32
Staraja Vyževka 23
44 51N27 24E24 -1:37:36

Starbejevo 6 39 55N55 37E28 -2:29:52
Starčenkovo 23 45 47N17 36E59 -2:27:56
Starica 6 39 56N30 34E56 -2:19:44
Starica 6 9 59N04 29E30 -1:58:00
Starica 6 34 48N13 45E56 -3:03:44
Starij R'ad 6 9 58N05 34E54 -2:19:36
Starina 6 41 59N37 44E42 -2:58:48
Starnikovo 6 39 55N22 38E24 -2:33:36
Staroalejskoje 2 23 51N00 82E01 -5:28:04
Starobačaty 2 21 54N14 86E07 -5:44:28
Starobaltačevo 6 30 56N01 55E56 -3:43:44
Starobel'sk 23 45 49N16 38E56 -2:35:44
Starobeševo 23 45 47N44 38E03 -2:32:12
Starobin 4 39 52N44 27E28 -1:49:52
Staročerkasskaja 6 40 47N15 40E03 -2:40:12
Starocuruchajtuj 2 16 50N12 119E15 -7:57:00
Staroderev'ankov-Skaja 6 47 46N08 38E58 -2:35:52
Starodub 6 39 52N35 32E46 -2:11:04
Starod'umejevo 6 30 55N16 54E22 -3:37:28
Starogan'kino 6 34 53N55 52E15 -3:29:00
Staroignatjevka 23 45 47N32 37E47 -2:31:08
Staroje 6 41 59N16 40E40 -2:42:40
Staroje Bojsarovo 6 41 55N31 53E54 -3:35:36
Staroje Drožžanoje 6 41 54N44 47E34 -3:10:16
Staroje Ibrajkino 6 41 54N52 51E02 -3:24:08
Staroje Jaškino 6 32 52N49 52E57 -3:31:48
Staroje Jermakovo 6 42 54N04 51E59 -3:27:56
Staroje Oleničevo 6 47 45N34 47E11 -3:08:44
Staroje Rachino 6 9 58N08 32E39 -2:10:36
Staroje Šajgovo 6 41 54N18 44E26 -2:57:44
Staroje Šajmurzino 6 41 54N45 47E58 -3:11:52
Staroje Selo 4 39 55N14 29E54 -1:59:36
Staroje Sindrovo 6 41 54N25 44E06 -2:56:24
Staroje Slavkino 6 41 52N34 45E08 -3:00:32
Staroje Ustje 6 41 53N28 41E51 -2:47:24
Starojurjevo 6 41 53N21 40E42 -2:42:48
Starokazačje 23 45 46N21 29E59 -1:59:56
Starokonstantinov 23 44 49N46 27E13 -1:48:52
Starokuručevo 6 30 55N09 54E04 -3:36:16
Starolaspa 23 45 47N34 37E59 -2:31:56
Staroleuškovskaja 6 47 45N59 39E44 -2:38:56
Staromichajlovka 23 45 47N58 37E36 -2:30:24
Starominskaja 6 47 46N31 39E04 -2:36:16
Staromlinovka 23 45 47N42 36E49 -2:27:16
Staromušta 6 30 55N49 54E14 -3:36:56
Staronikolajevo 6 39 55N37 36E16 -2:25:04
Staro-Podgorodneje 6 39 54N46 38E57 -2:35:48
Staropokrovka 10 24 42N50 75E18 -5:01:12
Staroščerbinovskaja 6 47 46N37 38E40 -2:34:40
Staroseslavino 6 41 53N12 40E25 -2:41:40
Starošešminsk 6 41 55N22 51E15 -3:25:00
Starosoldatskoje 2 24 56N12 72E37 -4:50:28
Starosubchangulovo 6 30 53N06 57E26 -3:49:44
Starotimoškino 6 34 53N43 47E32 -3:10:08
Starotitarovskaja 6 47 45N14 37E09 -2:28:36
Staroutkinsk 2 30 57N14 59E20 -3:57:20
Staroverovka 23 45 49N33 35E42 -2:22:48
Starožilovo 6 40 54N14 39E55 -2:39:40
Starožil'sk 6 41 56N34 47E17 -3:09:08
Starožil'skij 6 41 56N34 47E17 -3:09:08
Staryj Ajbesi 6 41 54N57 47E03 -3:08:12
Staryj-Ajdar 23 45 48N43 39E11 -2:36:44
Staryj Bagr'až 6 41 54N54 51E39 -3:26:36
Staryj Bir'uz'ak 6 47 44N47 46E54 -3:07:36
Staryj Bol'ševik 6 39 55N57 37E47 -2:31:08
Staryj Čartorijsk 23 44 51N15 25E54 -1:43:36
Staryj Chop'or 6 34 51N30 42E58 -2:51:52
Staryj Čindant 2 16 50N33 115E33 -7:42:12
Staryje Burasy 6 34 52N16 46E09 -3:04:36
Staryje Dorogi 4 39 53N02 28E16 -1:53:04
Staryje Maty 6 30 55N14 53E55 -3:35:40
Staryje Popel'uchi 23 45 48N18 28E55 -1:55:40
Staryje Senžary 23 45 49N25 34E27 -2:17:48
Staryje Turdaki 6 41 53N55 45E29 -3:01:56
Staryje Z'atcy 6 42 57N21 52E39 -3:30:36
Staryj Kazangal 9 32 50N15 47E39 -3:10:36
Staryj Kistruss 6 40 54N28 40E34 -2:42:16
Staryj Krym 23 45 47N10 37E30 -2:30:00
Staryj Krym 23 45 45N03 35E05 -2:20:20
Staryj Lesken 6 47 43N20 43E55 -2:55:40
Staryj Medved' 6 9 58N18 30E30 -2:02:00
Staryj Merčik 23 45 49N58 35E46 -2:23:04
Staryj Oskol 6 39 51N19 37E51 -2:31:24
Staryj Sambor 23 44 49N27 22E59 -1:31:56
Staryj Tukšum 6 34 53N42 48E33 -3:14:12
Stavišče 23 44 49N23 30E12 -2:00:48
Stavnoje 23 44 48N59 22E40 -1:30:40
Stavropol' 6 47 45N02 41E59 -2:47:56
Stavropol → Toljatti 6 34 53N31 49E26 -3:17:44
Stavrovo 6 39 56N08 40E00 -2:40:00
Stebl'ov 23 44 49N24 31E06 -2:04:24
Stegalovka 6 40 52N24 38E19 -2:33:16
Stekl'anka 6 41 59N08 41E37 -2:46:28
Steklino 6 39 56N51 32E10 -2:08:40
Steksovo 6 41 55N17 43E25 -2:53:40
Stende 13 36 57N09 22E33 -1:30:12
Stepan' 23 44 51N10 26E18 -1:45:12
Stepanakert 3 34 39N49 46E44 -3:06:56
Stepanavan 1 34 41N00 44E23 -2:57:32
Stepancevo 6 39 56N22 36E10 -2:24:40
Stepancevo 6 40 56N08 41E42 -2:46:48
Stepancy 23 44 49N42 31E18 -2:05:12
Stepano-Krynka 23 45 47N55 38E21 -2:33:24
Stepanovka 23 45 50N58 34E37 -2:18:28
Stepanovka 2 30 57N13 67E26 -4:29:44
Stepanovka 6 32 52N04 53E02 -3:32:08
Stepanovo 6 39 55N43 38E28 -2:33:52
Stepanovskoje 6 39 55N47 37E10 -2:28:40
Stepan Razin 3 34 40N24 49E59 -3:19:56
Stepanščino 6 39 55N15 38E30 -2:34:00
Stepn'ak 9 24 52N50 70E50 -4:43:20
Stepnoj 6 34 48N56 45E36 -3:02:24
Stepnoje 6 47 44N17 44E36 -2:58:24
Stepnoje 6 34 51N24 46E52 -3:07:28
Stepurino 6 39 56N24 35E16 -2:21:04
Sterlibaševo 6 30 53N28 55E15 -3:41:00
Sterlitamak 6 30 53N37 55E58 -3:43:52
Šterovka 23 45 48N19 38E57 -2:35:48
Stežki 6 41 53N06 41E13 -2:44:52
Stiene 13 36 57N26 24E34 -1:38:16
Stodolišči 4 39 51N44 28E30 -1:54:00
Stodolišče 6 39 54N11 32E39 -2:10:36
Stojba 2 14 52N49 131E43 -8:46:52
Stolbcy 4 39 53N29 26E44 -1:46:56
Stolbišči 6 41 55N39 49E14 -3:16:56
Stolboucha 9 24 49N59 84E30 -5:38:00
Stolbovo 6 39 52N38 34E47 -2:19:08
Stolbun 4 39 52N48 31E25 -2:05:40
Stolin 4 39 51N53 26E51 -1:47:24
Stol'noje 23 44 51N31 31E55 -2:07:40
Stolpino 6 40 57N24 42E55 -2:51:40
Štormovo 23 45 49N06 38E55 -2:35:40
Storoževaja 6 47 43N53 41E27 -2:45:48
Storoževsk 6 41 61N57 52E16 -3:29:04
Storožinec 23 44 48N10 25E43 -1:42:52
Stradeč' 4 39 51N56 23E40 -1:34:40
Straženy 15 46 47N08 28E36 -1:54:24
Straševiči 6 39 56N49 34E36 -2:18:24
Strel'covka 23 45 49N18 39E52 -2:39:28
Streleckije Vyselki 6 40 54N12 38E57 -2:35:48
Strelica 6 40 51N37 38E55 -2:35:40
Strelka 2 21 58N05 93E01 -6:12:04
Strelka-Čun'a 2 19 61N45 102E48 -6:51:12
Strelkovo 6 39 55N28 37E37 -2:30:28
Strelkovoje 23 45 45N54 34E53 -2:19:32
Strel'na 6 9 59N51 30E02 -2:00:08
Strel'na 6 9 66N06 38E40 -2:34:40
Strel'skaja 6 42 59N28 47E47 -3:11:08
Stremilovo 6 39 55N09 37E09 -2:28:36
Strenči 13 36 57N37 25E41 -1:42:44
Strešen' 15 46 47N08 28E36 -1:54:24
Strešin 4 39 52N43 30E05 -2:00:20
Strižavka 23 44 49N19 28E28 -1:53:52
Striži 6 42 58N30 49E13 -3:16:52
Stroitel' 6 39 50N47 36E26 -2:25:44
Stromyn' 6 39 56N03 38E29 -2:33:56
Strugi-Krasnyje 6 9 58N17 29E06 -1:56:24
Strunino 6 39 56N23 38E34 -2:34:16
Strupna 6 39 54N43 38E48 -2:35:12
Stryj 23 44 49N15 23E51 -1:35:24
Stučka 13 36 56N38 25E13 -1:40:52
Studenec 6 41 54N52 48E16 -3:13:04
Stud'onoje 6 32 51N36 53E10 -3:32:40
Stud'onoje 2 23 53N37 77E31 -5:10:04
Stud'onok 23 44 51N42 34E07 -2:16:28
Stupino 6 39 54N53 38E05 -2:32:20
Styla 23 45 47N41 37E50 -2:31:20
Šubač 6 40 60N22 38E14 -2:32:56
Subačius 14 37 55N46 24E47 -1:39:08
Šubarkuduk 9 30 49N13 56E34 -3:46:16
Šubarši 9 30 48N35 57E12 -3:48:48
Subata 13 36 56N01 25E56 -1:43:44
Subbotino 2 21 53N04 91E55 -6:07:40
Subchankulovo 6 30 54N34 53E49 -3:35:16
Suchaja 2 20 52N32 107E06 -7:08:24
Suchana 2 16 68N45 118E00 -7:52:00
Suchan → Partizansk 2 27 43N08 133E09 -8:52:36
Suchiniči 6 39 54N06 35E20 -2:21:20
Suchobezvodnoje 6 41 57N03 44E50 -2:59:20
Suchoborka 6 42 59N06 49E58 -3:19:52
Suchodol 6 39 54N27 37E22 -2:29:28
Suchodol 6 34 53N55 51E14 -3:24:56
Suchodol'skij 6 39 53N43 38E17 -2:33:08
Suchoj 6 47 47N06 41E21 -2:45:24
Suchoj Log 2 30 56N55 62E01 -4:08:04
Suchoj Pit 2 21 58N48 92E49 -6:11:16
Suchorečka 6 32 52N49 52E27 -3:29:48
Suchotinka 6 41 52N31 41E35 -2:46:20
Suchotinskij 6 47 47N18 44E31 -2:58:04
Suchoverkovo 6 39 56N37 35E35 -2:22:20
Suchov Pervyj 6 34 49N59 43E28 -2:53:52
Suchumi 7 33 43N01 41E02 -2:44:08
Šučje 6 41 51N45 40E29 -2:41:56
Suda 6 40 59N09 37E33 -2:30:12
Sudaj 6 41 58N58 43E08 -2:52:32
Sudak 23 45 44N52 34E59 -2:19:56
Sudbišči 6 39 52N57 37E39 -2:30:36
Sud'bodarovka 6 30 52N19 54E07 -3:36:28
Sudislavl' 6 40 57N53 41E43 -2:46:52
Sudnikovo 6 39 55N53 36E02 -2:24:08
Sudogda 6 40 55N57 40E50 -2:43:20
Sudovaja Višn'a 23 44 49N49 23E22 -1:33:28
Sudža 6 39 51N12 35E16 -2:21:04
Sufi-Kurgan 10 24 40N02 73E30 -4:54:00
Sugandy 9 24 43N27 74E38 -4:58:32
Šugnou 21 24 38N35 70E20 -4:41:20
Sugonovo 6 39 54N41 36E41 -2:26:44
Šugozero 6 9 59N55 34E12 -2:16:48
Šugurovo 6 41 54N31 52E06 -3:28:24
Sugurovo 6 41 53N25 46E29 -3:05:56
Šuja 6 40 56N50 41E23 -2:45:32
Šuja 6 9 61N55 34E12 -2:16:48
Šujskoje 6 41 59N22 40E59 -2:43:56
Sukhumi → Suchumi 7 33 43N01 41E02 -2:44:08
Sukkozero 6 9 63N11 32E18 -2:09:12
Sukmanovka 6 41 51N47 41E34 -2:46:16
Sukovo 6 39 54N54 38E19 -2:33:16
Sukroml'a 6 39 56N53 34E44 -2:18:56
Suksun 6 30 57N07 57E24 -3:49:36
Sulak 6 47 43N16 47E32 -3:10:08
Sulak 6 34 51N52 48E21 -3:13:24
Suleja 6 30 55N09 58E50 -3:55:20
Šul'ginka 23 45 49N08 38E56 -2:35:44
Šul'gino 6 39 55N50 35E55 -2:23:40
Šul'gino 6 39 54N33 37E35 -2:30:20
Sulin 6 47 48N54 40E07 -2:40:28
Sulinskij 6 40 47N52 40E06 -2:40:24
Sultan-Saly 6 40 47N21 39E35 -2:38:20
Sul'ukta 10 24 39N56 69E34 -4:38:16
Sulusaj 24 30 38N50 67E05 -4:28:20
Suly 9 24 53N45 66E30 -4:26:00
Šum 2 21 54N51 95E18 -6:21:12
Šum 6 9 59N52 31E46 -2:07:04
Šum'ači 6 39 53N52 32E25 -2:09:40
Šumanaj 24 30 42N37 59E08 -3:56:32
Šumarokovo 6 39 55N46 35E55 -2:23:40
Šum'atino 6 39 55N00 36E21 -2:25:24
Šumbut 6 41 55N33 50E41 -3:22:44
Šumek 9 24 48N42 85E32 -5:42:08
Šumerl'a 6 41 55N30 46E26 -3:05:44
Sumgait 3 34 40N36 49E38 -3:18:32
Šumicha 2 30 55N14 63E19 -4:13:16
Šumilino 4 39 55N18 29E37 -1:58:28
Šumilinskaja 6 47 49N58 41E26 -2:45:44
Sumki 2 30 55N03 65E44 -4:22:56
Sumkino 2 30 58N09 68E21 -4:33:24
Sumsar 10 24 41N18 71E19 -4:45:16
S'umsi 6 42 57N07 51E37 -3:26:28
Šumskij 2 20 54N48 99E09 -6:36:36
Šumskij Posad 6 40 64N15 35E25 -2:21:40
Šumskoje 23 44 50N07 26E07 -1:44:28

Šumšu Island 12
8 50N40 156E08-10:24:32
Šumšu, Ostrov 12
8 50N40 156E08-10:24:32
Sumy 2 23 54N48 80E26 -5:21:44
Sumy 23 45 50N55 34E45 -2:19:00
Suna 6 42 57N51 50E05 -3:20:20
Šungaj 9 32 48N32 46E46 -3:07:04
Suntar 2 16 62N10 117E40 -7:50:40
Suojarvi 6 9 62N05 32E21 -2:09:24
Suordach 2 11 66N43 132E04 -8:48:16
Suponevo 6 39 53N12 34E18 -2:17:12
Sura 6 41 53N53 45E45 -3:03:00
Šurab 21 24 40N03 70E33 -4:42:12
Surami 7 33 42N01 43E34 -2:54:16
Šuran 6 41 55N22 49E50 -3:19:20
Surava 6 41 52N57 41E18 -2:45:12
Suraž 4 39 55N25 30E44 -2:02:56
Suraž 6 39 53N01 32E24 -2:09:36
Surchan 9 32 46N39 49E38 -3:18:32
Surchdara 21 24 38N37 69E55 -4:39:40
Šurči 22 30 37N59 67E47 -4:31:08
Surgut 2 25 61N14 73E20 -4:53:20
Surgut 6 34 53N55 51E14 -3:24:56
Šurinda 2 20 55N13 113E23 -7:33:32
S'urkum 2 11 50N08 140E31 -9:22:04
Šurma 6 42 56N58 50E21 -3:21:24
Surovatficha 6 41 55N45 43E56 -2:55:44
Surovikino 6 34 48N36 42E51 -2:51:24
Surovo 2 20 55N37 105E36 -7:02:24
Sursk 6 41 53N04 45E42 -3:02:48
Surskij Majdan 6
41 55N01 46E32 -3:06:08
Surskoje 6 42 54N30 46E44 -3:06:56
Šuryškary 2 28 65N54 65E22 -4:21:28
Susamyr 10 24 42N09 73E58 -4:55:52
Susanino 6 41 58N09 41E36 -2:46:24
Susanino 6 9 59N30 30E22 -2:01:28
Susanino 2 11 52N47 140E06 -9:20:24
Šušary 6 9 59N48 30E23 -2:01:32
Šušary 6 9 59N46 30E21 -2:01:24
Šušenskoje 2 21 53N19 91E58 -6:07:52
Susleny 15 46 47N25 28E59 -1:55:56
Suslonger 6 41 56N18 48E13 -3:12:52
Sušn'aki Pervoje 2
21 57N53 88E47 -5:55:08
Šustikovo 6 39 55N17 35E59 -2:23:56
Susuman 2 6 62N47 148E10 -9:52:40
Sut-Chol' 2 21 51N24 91E17 -6:05:08
Suure-Jaani 5 35 58N33 25E28 -1:41:52
Suvainiškis 14
37 56N10 25E17 -1:41:08
Šuvel'an 3 34 40N30 50E09 -3:20:36
Suvo 2 20 53N39 110E00 -7:20:00
Suvorka 2 20 56N33 103E24 -6:53:36
Suvorov 6 39 54N07 36E30 -2:26:00
Suvorovo 6 39 56N07 35E54 -2:23:36
Suvorovo 23 45 45N34 28E59 -1:55:56
Suykbulak 9 24 49N48 80E50 -5:23:20
Suzak 9 24 44N07 68E28 -4:33:52
Suzdal' 6 40 56N25 40E26 -2:41:44
S'uzikozero 6 40 61N48 37E20 -2:29:20
Suz'omka 6 39 52N19 34E05 -2:16:20
S'uz'um 6 42 58N02 47E32 -3:10:08
Suzun 2 21 53N47 82E19 -5:29:16
Sval'ava 23 44 48N33 22E59 -1:31:56
Švarcevskij 6 39 54N06 37E59 -2:31:56
Švaricha 6 42 57N33 49E37 -3:18:28
Svataj 2 6 67N57 151E54-10:07:36
Sv'atogorskaja 23
45 49N04 37E32 -2:30:08
Sv'atoslavka 6
34 51N20 43E26 -2:53:44
Svatovo 23 45 49N23 38E13 -2:32:52
Sveča 6 42 58N16 47E32 -3:10:08
Svėdasai 14 37 55N41 25E22 -1:41:28
Švėkšna 14 37 55N31 21E37 -1:26:28
Sven' 6 39 53N09 34E21 -2:17:24
Švenčionėliai 14
37 55N10 26E00 -1:44:00
Švenčionys 14 37 55N07 26E10 -1:44:40
Šventoji 14 37 56N02 21E05 -1:24:20
Sverbejevo 2 16 53N36 123E15 -8:13:00
Sverdlovo 6 39 56N38 36E37 -2:26:28
Sverdlovo 6 34 51N16 44E34 -2:58:16
Sverdlovsk 2 30 56N51 60E36 -4:02:24
Sverdlovsk 23 45 48N05 39E40 -2:38:40
Svessa 23 44 51N57 33E54 -2:15:36
Svetilovtči 4 39 52N48 31E19 -2:05:16
Svetlaja 2 27 46N33 138E18 -9:13:12
Svetlanovo 23 45 48N42 38E28 -2:33:52
Svetlogorsk 4 39 52N38 29E42 -1:58:48
Svetlogorsk 8 38 54N57 20E10 -1:20:40
Svetlograd 6 47 45N20 42E40 -2:50:40
Svetloje 6 42 57N03 53E38 -3:34:32
Svetlovodsk 23
45 49N04 33E15 -2:13:00
Svetlyj 6 30 50N47 60E53 -4:03:32
Svetlyj 8 38 54N41 20E08 -1:20:32
Svetlyj 2 17 58N26 115E55 -7:43:40
Svetlyj Jar 6 34 48N29 44E46 -2:59:04
Svetogorsk 6 9 61N07 28E51 -1:55:24
Svežen'kaja 6 41 54N01 42E26 -2:49:44
Svir' 4 39 54N51 26E24 -1:45:36
Svirica 6 9 60N29 32E51 -2:11:24
Svirsk 2 20 53N04 103E21 -6:53:24
Svir'stroj 6 9 60N48 33E43 -2:14:52
Sviščovka 6 41 52N51 43E44 -2:54:56
Svisloč' 4 39 53N26 28E59 -1:55:56
Svisloč' 4 39 53N02 24E06 -1:36:24
Svistunovka 23
45 49N29 38E20 -2:33:20
Svitino 6 39 54N54 35E49 -2:23:16
Svoboda 6 47 47N12 40E39 -2:42:36
Svoboda 6 39 51N58 36E17 -2:25:08
Svobodnaja 19 8 46N48 143E23 -9:33:32
Svobodnoje 23 45 47N32 37E34 -2:30:16
Svobodnyj 2 15 51N24 128E08 -8:32:32
Svobodnyj 6 34 52N20 46E22 -3:05:28
Svobodnyj Port 23
45 46N20 31E51 -2:07:24
Svojna 6 39 54N09 36E39 -2:26:36
Swerdlowsk → Sverdlovsk 2
30 56N51 60E36 -4:02:24
Syalach 2 13 66N12 124E00 -8:16:00
Syčova 2 30 57N35 69E20 -4:37:20
Syčovka 6 39 55N50 34E17 -2:17:08
Syktyvkar 6 41 61N40 50E46 -3:23:04
Syloga 6 41 63N50 43E39 -2:54:36
Sym 2 21 60N20 88E23 -5:53:32
Syn'a 6 29 65N22 57E42 -3:50:48
Synkovo 6 39 55N21 37E38 -2:30:32
Syntul 6 40 55N00 41E18 -2:45:12
Synžereja 15 46 47N38 28E09 -1:52:36
Syrčan 6 42 57N22 50E15 -3:21:00
Syrdarja 24 24 40N52 68E38 -4:34:32
Syrdarjinskij 9
24 41N15 68E00 -4:32:00
Syrskij 6 40 52N34 39E29 -2:37:56
Sysert' 2 30 56N29 60E49 -4:03:16
Systyg-Chem 2 21 52N40 95E30 -6:22:00
Syt'kovo 6 39 56N31 34E01 -2:16:04
Syzran' 6 34 53N09 48E27 -3:13:48
Tabat 2 21 52N57 90E43 -6:02:52
Tabor 2 6 71N16 150E12-10:00:48
Tabory 2 30 58N31 64E33 -4:18:12
Tabuny 2 23 52N46 78E45 -5:15:00
T'ačev 23 44 48N02 23E34 -1:34:16
Tachiataš 24 30 42N22 59E35 -3:58:20
Tachta 2 11 53N08 139E53 -9:19:32
Tachta 6 47 45N54 42E07 -2:48:28
Tachta-Bazar 22
30 35N57 62E50 -4:11:20
Tachtabrod 9 24 52N38 67E34 -4:30:16
Tachtakupyr 24
30 43N02 60E17 -4:01:08
Tachtamygda 2 16 54N06 123E34 -8:14:16
Tacinskij 6 47 48N13 41E17 -2:45:08
Tadžikabad 21 24 39N07 70E50 -4:43:20
Tagaj 6 42 54N18 47E39 -3:10:36
Tagan 2 23 54N57 77E18 -5:09:12
Taganrog 6 40 47N12 38E56 -2:35:44
T'aginka 23 45 46N47 33E04 -2:12:16
Tagna 2 20 53N36 101E54 -6:47:36
T'agun 2 21 53N56 85E38 -5:42:32
Taimba 2 19 60N18 98E58 -6:35:52
Tajbola 6 9 68N26 33E19 -2:13:16
Tajdakovo 6 39 54N29 37E32 -2:30:08
Tajga 2 21 56N04 85E37 -5:42:28
Tajginka 2 30 55N37 60E30 -4:02:00
Tajlakdžegen 24
30 43N54 60E29 -4:01:56
Tajlakovy 2 25 59N20 74E04 -4:56:16
Tajna 2 21 56N27 95E30 -6:22:00
Tajninka 6 39 55N54 37E45 -2:31:00
Tajožnyj 2 21 56N09 94E29 -6:17:56
Tajšet 2 20 55N57 98E00 -6:32:00
Tajsojgan 9 30 48N19 53E29 -3:33:56
Tajturka 2 20 52N51 103E28 -6:53:52
Tajura 2 20 57N00 106E35 -7:06:20
Tajžina 2 21 53N38 87E28 -5:49:52
Takčijan 24 30 38N32 68E03 -4:32:12
Takeli 21 24 40N30 69E25 -4:37:40
Takob 21 24 38N50 68E57 -4:35:48
Taksino 6 39 56N19 36E10 -2:24:40
Talakan 2 11 49N38 133E18 -8:53:12
Talakovka 23 45 47N10 37E43 -2:30:52
Talalajevka 23
44 50N51 33E08 -2:12:32
Talandža 2 11 49N27 131E35 -8:46:20
Talap 9 32 48N26 48E03 -3:12:12
Talas 10 24 42N32 72E14 -4:48:56
Taldan 2 16 53N40 124E48 -8:19:12
Taldom 6 39 56N44 37E32 -2:30:08
Taldyapan 9 32 49N46 50E14 -3:20:56
Taldyapan 9 32 48N07 47E08 -3:08:32
Taldykuduk 9 32 50N09 49E33 -3:18:12
Taldy-Kurgan 9
24 45N00 78E23 -5:13:32
Talgar 9 24 43N18 77E18 -5:09:12
Talica 6 42 58N01 51E30 -3:26:00
Talica 6 41 58N44 41E34 -2:46:16
Talica 2 30 57N00 63E43 -4:14:52
Talickij Čamlyk 6
41 52N02 40E32 -2:42:08
Tal'ka 4 39 53N22 28E21 -1:53:24
Tallinn 5 35 59N25 24E45 -1:39:00
Tally 6 32 53N08 53E04 -3:32:16
Talmazy 15 46 46N38 29E40 -1:58:40
Tal'menka 2 21 53N51 83E35 -5:34:20
Tal'niki 2 20 52N47 102E24 -6:49:36
Tal'noje 23 45 48N53 30E42 -2:02:48
Taloje 2 21 55N24 95E40 -6:22:40
Talovaja 6 41 51N06 40E44 -2:42:56
Talovka 2 23 51N27 81E54 -5:27:36
Talovka 2 21 57N10 93E09 -6:12:36
Talovka 9 32 50N25 47E35 -3:10:20
Talovka 6 47 44N14 46E36 -3:06:24
Talovka 6 34 49N58 45E01 -3:00:04
Talovoje 23 45 48N18 39E40 -2:38:40
Talsi 13 36 57N15 22E36 -1:30:24
Talšik 9 23 53N42 71E53 -4:47:32
Talvik'ul'a 6 9 68N45 29E19 -1:57:16
Taly 6 41 49N51 40E04 -2:40:16
Talyzino 6 41 55N06 45E49 -3:03:16
Tamala 6 41 52N33 43E16 -2:53:04
Taman' 6 47 45N13 36E43 -2:26:52
Tambej 2 25 71N30 71E50 -4:47:20
Tambov 6 41 52N43 41E25 -2:45:40
Tambovka 2 14 50N06 128E04 -8:32:16
Tambovka 6 34 47N18 47E23 -3:09:32
Tamga 10 24 42N09 77E32 -5:10:08
Tamga 2 27 45N34 133E36 -8:54:24
Tamica 6 40 64N10 38E05 -2:32:20
Tamir 2 20 50N24 107E25 -7:09:40
Tamsalu 5 35 59N10 26E06 -1:44:24
Tanchoj 2 20 51N33 105E07 -7:00:28
Tandaj 9 32 47N33 51E30 -3:26:00
Tanga 2 18 51N02 111E33 -7:26:12
Tanguj 2 20 55N23 100E58 -6:43:52
Tansyk 9 24 47N20 79E52 -5:19:28
Tapa 5 35 59N16 25E58 -1:43:52
Tapiau → Gvardejsk 8
38 54N39 21E05 -1:24:20
Tara 2 24 56N54 74E22 -4:57:28
Tarakanovka 6 39 55N07 35E44 -2:22:56
Taraklija 15 46 46N34 29E06 -1:56:24
Taraklija 15 46 45N54 28E38 -1:54:32
Taranovka 23 45 49N37 36E08 -2:24:32
Taraščа 23 44 49N34 30E29 -2:01:56
Tarasovka 6 39 55N58 37E50 -2:31:20
Tarasovka 23 45 48N21 37E33 -2:30:12
Tarasovka 6 47 49N28 40E05 -2:40:20
Tarasovka 23 45 49N40 38E23 -2:33:32
Tarasovo 2 20 55N52 107E48 -7:11:12
Tarasovo 6 41 66N13 46E39 -3:06:36
Tarasovo 6 41 62N49 41E10 -2:44:40
Tarasovo 6 42 58N18 48E45 -3:15:00
Tarasovskij 6 47 48N43 40E22 -2:41:28
Tarbagataj 2 20 51N30 107E22 -7:09:28
Tarbagataj 2 20 52N07 109E12 -7:16:48
Tarbagataj 2 18 51N12 109E05 -7:16:20
Tarchovka 6 9 60N04 29E58 -1:59:52
Tareja 2 21 73N20 90E37 -6:02:28
Tarkazy 6 30 53N52 53E39 -3:34:36
Tarki 6 47 42N56 47E30 -3:10:00
Tarko-Sale 2 25 64N55 77E49 -5:11:16
T'arlevo 6 9 59N42 30E27 -2:01:48
Tarnogskij Gorodok 6
41 60N29 43E33 -2:54:12
Tarnopol → Ternopol' 23
44 49N34 25E36 -1:42:24
Tarta 22 30 40N02 52E46 -3:31:04
Tartu 5 35 58N23 26E43 -1:46:52
Tarumovka 6 47 44N03 46E33 -3:06:12
Tarusa 6 39 54N43 37E11 -2:28:44
Tarutino 6 39 55N07 36E56 -2:27:44
Tarutino 23 45 46N12 29E09 -1:56:36
Tarza 6 41 62N30 40E25 -2:41:40
Tas 9 32 48N27 51E02 -3:24:08
Tašanta 9 24 49N43 89E11 -5:56:44
Tasaral 9 24 46N20 73E58 -4:55:52
Tašauz 22 30 41N50 59E58 -3:59:52
Tasbuget 9 30 44N48 65E33 -4:22:12
Taschkent → Taškent 24
24 41N20 69E18 -4:37:12
Tasejevo 2 21 57N12 94E54 -6:19:36
Tašelan 2 20 51N45 108E55 -7:15:40
Tashkent → Taškent 24
24 41N20 69E18 -4:37:12
Taširovo 6 39 55N25 36E39 -2:26:36
Taskajevo 2 23 55N06 78E36 -5:14:24
Taškent 24 24 41N20 69E18 -4:37:12
Taškepri 22 30 36N18 62E38 -4:10:32
Taskesken 9 24 47N15 80E44 -5:22:56
Taš-Kumyr 10 24 41N21 72E14 -4:48:56
Taškyja 10 24 40N16 74E19 -4:57:16
Tašla 6 32 51N47 52E46 -3:31:04
Tasoba 9 32 49N47 49E52 -3:19:28
Taštagol 2 21 52N47 87E53 -5:51:32
Taštyp 2 21 52N48 89E54 -5:59:36
Tatal 6 47 47N17 46E16 -3:05:04
Tatarbunary 23
45 45N49 29E36 -1:58:24
Tatarinka 6 39 55N58 33E54 -2:15:36
Tatarino 6 40 50N36 39E07 -2:36:28
Tatarinovo 6 39 56N34 38E25 -2:33:40
Tatarinovo 6 39 55N13 37E56 -2:31:44
Tatarka 2 24 53N58 75E05 -5:00:20
Tatarka 4 39 53N16 28E48 -1:55:12
Tatarsk 2 23 55N13 75E58 -5:03:52
Tatarskij Kandyz 6
41 54N07 53E07 -3:32:28
Tatarskij Sajman 6
34 53N18 47E07 -3:08:28
Tatarskoje-Maklakovo 6
41 55N48 45E34 -3:02:16
Tataurovo 6 42 57N48 49E34 -3:18:16
Tataurovo 6 41 58N44 43E20 -2:53:20
Tataurovo 2 16 51N37 112E56 -7:31:44
Tatiščevo 6 39 56N24 37E31 -2:30:04
Tatiščevo 6 34 51N40 45E35 -3:02:20
Tatty 9 24 43N12 73E19 -4:53:16
Tau 9 32 49N40 47E17 -3:09:08
Taučik 9 30 44N21 51E19 -3:25:16
Tauragė 14 37 55N15 22E17 -1:29:08
Taurak 2 21 51N35 85E01 -5:40:04
Taurovo 2 25 59N36 73E18 -4:53:12
Tauz 3 34 41N00 45E38 -3:02:32
Tavajza 2 11 45N12 136E44 -9:06:56
Tavda 2 30 58N03 65E15 -4:21:00
Tavil'dara 21 24 38N43 70E28 -4:41:52
Tavn-Gašun 6 47 46N01 45E55 -3:03:40
Tavolžan 9 24 52N44 77E27 -5:09:48
Tavričanka 2 27 43N22 131E52 -8:47:28
Tavričeskoje 2
24 54N35 73E38 -4:54:32
Tavry 6 9 59N55 30E42 -2:02:48
T'ažinskij 2 21 56N07 88E31 -5:54:04
Tazovskij 2 25 67N28 78E42 -5:14:48
Tbilisi 7 33 41N43 44E49 -2:59:16
Tbilisskaja 6 47 45N23 40E12 -2:40:48
Tcheljabinsk → Čel'abinsk 2
30 55N10 61E24 -4:05:36
Teberda 6 47 43N28 41E45 -2:47:00

Techtin 4 39 53N51 29E44 -1:58:56
Tedžen 22 30 37N23 60E31 -4:02:04
Tedženstroj 22 30 36N55 60E53 -4:03:32
Teeli 2 21 51N07 90E14 -6:00:56
Tegistyk 9 24 44N02 68E22 -4:33:28
Tejkovo 6 40 56N52 40E34 -2:42:16
Tekeli 9 24 44N48 78E57 -5:15:48
Tekstil'ščiki 6 39 55N57 37E49 -2:31:16
Telavi 7 33 41N55 45E28 -3:01:52
Tel'čje 6 39 53N21 36E20 -2:25:20
Telechany 4 39 52N31 25E51 -1:43:24
Telegino 6 41 52N55 44E34 -2:58:16
Telemba 2 20 52N43 113E16 -7:33:04
Telenešty 15 46 47N30 28E22 -1:53:28
Teli 2 21 51N07 90E14 -6:00:56
Telikovka 6 34 52N35 48E17 -3:13:08
Telizi 6 9 59N42 29E59 -1:59:56
Tel'ma 2 20 52N43 103E41 -6:54:44
Tel'mana 23 45 48N30 39E18 -2:37:12
Tel'manovo 23 45 47N24 38E02 -2:32:08
Tel'novskij 19 8 49N22 142E05 -9:28:20
Telšiai 14 37 55N59 22E15 -1:29:00
Teluša 4 39 53N03 29E31 -1:58:04
Tem' 2 20 55N21 100E44 -6:42:56
Tem'asovo 6 30 52N59 58E06 -3:52:24
Temir 9 30 49N08 57E06 -3:48:24
Temirgojevskaja 6 47 45N07 40E16 -2:41:04
Temirlanovka 9 24 42N36 69E17 -4:37:08
Temirtau 9 24 50N05 72E56 -4:51:44
Temirtau 2 21 53N08 87E28 -5:49:52
Temnikov 6 41 54N38 43E12 -2:52:48
Temnikovo 6 39 55N43 38E01 -2:32:04
Tempy 6 39 56N38 37E18 -2:29:12
Temr'uk 6 47 45N17 37E23 -2:29:32
Ten'gušev o 6 41 54N46 42E44 -2:50:56
Tenkeli 2 10 70N01 140E58 -9:23:52
Ten'ki 6 41 55N26 49E00 -3:16:00
Teofipol' 23 44 49N50 26E25 -1:45:40
Teplik 23 45 48N40 29E44 -1:58:56
Teplooz'orsk 2 11 49N00 131E48 -8:47:12
Teplovka 6 32 51N33 51E33 -3:26:12
Teplovo 6 41 55N25 42E56 -2:51:44
Ter'ajevo 6 39 56N11 36E07 -2:24:28
Terbuny 6 40 52N08 38E17 -2:33:08
Terebovl'a 23 44 49N18 25E43 -1:42:52
Terebuš 6 39 54N16 38E09 -2:32:36
Terebutinec 6 9 59N01 33E39 -2:14:36
Terechovka 4 39 52N13 31E27 -2:05:48
Terechovo 6 39 55N50 35E45 -2:23:00
Terek 10 24 40N01 73E33 -4:54:12
Terek 6 47 43N29 44E08 -2:56:32
Terekli-Mekteb 6 47 44N10 45E53 -3:03:32
Terek-Saj 10 24 41N32 71E09 -4:44:36
Terekty 9 32 48N34 49E02 -3:16:08
Teren'ga 6 34 53N42 48E24 -3:13:36
Terenino 6 39 54N31 33E35 -2:14:20
Terenkuduk 9 32 48N24 47E11 -3:08:44
Terensaj 6 30 51N36 59E31 -3:58:04
Terenuzek 9 30 45N05 64E59 -4:19:56
Teresva 23 44 48N01 23E42 -1:34:48
Tergauči 24 24 41N11 71E30 -4:46:00
Terib'orka 6 9 69N08 35E08 -2:20:32
Termez 24 30 37N14 67E16 -4:29:04
Ternej 2 11 45N03 136E37 -9:06:28
Ternopol' 23 44 49N34 25E36 -1:42:24
Ternovatoje 23 45 47N50 36E09 -2:24:36
Ternovka 6 34 51N19 42E56 -2:51:44
Ternovka 6 41 51N40 41E37 -2:46:28
Ternovka 23 45 47N02 32E01 -2:08:04
Ternovka 23 45 48N32 29E58 -1:59:52
Ternovka 6 41 53N09 45E02 -3:00:08
Ternovoje 6 34 51N03 43E43 -2:54:52
Ternovskaja 6 47 45N53 40E24 -2:41:36
Tersa 6 34 50N53 43E48 -2:55:12
Tersa 6 34 52N05 47E32 -3:10:08
Teržola 7 33 42N12 42E59 -2:51:56
Teša 6 40 55N30 42E50 -2:51:20
Tesovo 6 39 55N34 36E05 -2:24:20
Tetijev 23 44 49N23 29E41 -1:58:44
Tetri-Ckaro 7 33 41N34 44E28 -2:57:52
Tet'uši 6 41 54N57 48E50 -3:15:20
Tet'ušskoje 6 42 54N18 48E03 -3:12:12
Tevli 4 39 52N20 24E15 -1:37:00
Tevriz 2 24 57N34 72E24 -4:49:36
Thorez → Torez 23 45 48N01 38E37 -2:34:28
Tianeti 7 33 42N07 44E59 -2:59:56
Tibel'ti 2 20 51N46 103E11 -6:52:44
Tichmenevo 19 8 49N12 142E54 -9:31:36
Tichmenevo 6 40 58N00 38E36 -2:34:24
Tichon 6 41 59N23 46E38 -3:06:32
Tichonova Pustyn' 6 39 54N38 36E09 -2:24:36
Tichonoviči 23 44 51N56 32E09 -2:08:36
Tichonovka 2 20 53N13 104E13 -6:56:52
Tichookeanskij 2 27 43N00 132E24 -8:49:36
Tichoreck 6 47 45N51 40E09 -2:40:36
Tichtozero 6 9 65N35 30E27 -2:01:48
Tichvin 6 9 59N39 33E31 -2:14:04
Tiflis → Tbilisi 7 33 41N43 44E49 -2:59:16
Tigil' 2 4 57N48 158E40-10:34:40
Tikhoretsk → Tichoreck 6 47 45N51 40E09 -2:40:36
Tikša 6 9 64N07 32E27 -2:09:48
Tiksi 2 14 71N36 128E48 -8:35:12

Tiligulo-Berezanka 23 45 46N52 31E24 -2:05:36
Tiliktino 6 39 56N06 36E36 -2:26:24
Tilsit → Sovetsk 8 38 55N05 21E53 -1:27:32
Tim 6 39 51N37 37E07 -2:28:28
Timaricha 6 41 57N33 44E47 -2:59:08
Timaševo 6 39 55N08 36E29 -2:25:56
Timaševo 6 34 53N21 51E12 -3:24:48
Timaševsk 6 47 45N37 38E57 -2:35:48
Timaševskaja 6 47 45N37 38E57 -2:35:48
Timel'ga 2 23 58N53 76E42 -5:06:48
Timir'azevo 8 38 55N05 21E37 -1:26:28
Timir'azevskij 2 21 56N29 84E54 -5:39:36
Timirevo 6 39 55N08 39E10 -2:36:40
Timkoviči 4 39 53N03 27E00 -1:48:00
Timkovo 6 39 55N56 38E37 -2:34:28
Timonovo 6 39 56N13 37E02 -2:28:08
Timošino 6 40 60N05 36E10 -2:24:40
Timošino 6 41 57N50 44E25 -2:57:40
Timovo 6 41 53N17 43E41 -2:54:44
Timšer 6 29 62N06 54E40 -3:38:40
Timur 9 24 42N50 68E26 -4:33:44
Tinskoj 2 21 56N10 96E55 -6:27:40
Tiraspol' 15 46 46N51 29E38 -1:58:32
Tirl'anskij 6 30 54N14 58E35 -3:54:20
Tirullai 14 37 55N47 23E22 -1:33:28
Tiskino 2 21 58N05 83E10 -5:32:40
Tiškovka 23 45 48N29 30E56 -2:03:44
Tiškovo 6 39 56N05 37E44 -2:30:56
Tiškovo 6 34 46N02 48E36 -3:14:24
Tišnevo 6 39 55N10 36E17 -2:25:08
Tisul' 2 21 55N45 88E19 -5:53:16
Tit-Ary 2 16 71N58 127E01 -8:28:04
Titovka 6 47 48N59 39E44 -2:38:56
Titovo 6 41 53N17 43E41 -2:54:44
Titovo 6 39 54N19 36E56 -2:27:44
Titovo 6 39 55N35 39E07 -2:36:28
Tkibuli 7 33 42N21 42E59 -2:51:56
Tkvarčeli 7 33 42N51 41E41 -2:46:44
Tl'ančetamak 6 41 55N28 52E37 -3:30:28
Tl'arata 6 47 42N07 46E22 -3:05:28
Tloch 6 47 42N38 46E28 -3:05:52
Tlumač 23 44 48N52 25E01 -1:40:04
Tobašino 6 41 56N56 47E40 -3:10:40
Tobekuduk 9 30 49N50 54E15 -3:37:00
Tobol 9 30 52N40 62E39 -4:10:36
Tobol'sk 2 30 58N12 68E16 -4:33:04
Tobseda 6 29 68N36 52E14 -3:28:56
Toburdanovo 6 41 55N22 47E38 -3:10:32
Tochoj 2 20 50N30 105E00 -7:00:00
Tochta 6 41 62N14 48E48 -3:15:12
Tochtamyš 21 24 37N50 74E39 -4:58:36
Tockoje 6 32 52N32 52E45 -3:31:00
Toganas 9 30 50N49 52E02 -3:28:08
Togliatti → Toljatti 6 34 53N31 49E26 -3:17:44
Togučin 2 21 55N16 84E23 -5:37:32
Togur 2 21 58N24 82E49 -5:31:16
Toguzbulak 10 24 42N06 76E44 -5:06:56
Togyz 9 30 47N34 60E33 -4:02:12
Tojtepa 24 24 41N03 69E22 -4:37:28
Tokarevka 9 24 50N08 73E12 -4:52:48
Tokar'ovka 6 41 51N59 41E09 -2:44:36
Tokar'ovo 6 39 55N17 35E04 -2:20:16
Tokar'ovo 6 39 55N38 37E55 -2:31:40
Tokko 2 16 59N59 119E52 -7:59:28
Tokma 2 20 58N13 105E42 -7:02:48
Tokmak 10 24 42N55 75E18 -5:01:12
Tokmak 23 45 47N15 35E43 -2:22:52
Tokovskoje 23 45 47N38 33E59 -2:15:56
Toksovo 6 9 60N09 30E31 -2:02:04
Toktogul 10 24 41N50 72E50 -4:51:20
Tokur 2 14 53N10 132E53 -8:51:32
Tolbuchino 6 40 57N51 40E03 -2:40:12
Tole 9 24 42N40 70E08 -4:40:32
Toljatti (Togliatti) 6 34 53N31 49E26 -3:17:44
Tol'ka 2 25 64N02 81E55 -5:27:40
Tolmači 6 39 57N26 35E41 -2:22:44
Tolmačovo 6 9 58N52 29E55 -1:59:40
Toločin 4 39 54N25 29E42 -1:58:48
Tolomo 2 11 50N03 137E45 -9:11:00
Tol'skij Majdan 6 41 54N57 44E39 -2:58:36
Tolstoje 23 44 48N50 25E44 -1:42:56
Tolstopal'cevo 6 39 55N38 37E13 -2:28:52
Tolvajarvi 6 9 62N17 31E27 -2:05:48
Tolyatti → Toljatti 6 34 53N31 49E26 -3:17:44
Tolybaj 9 30 50N31 62E19 -4:09:16
Tomakovka 23 45 47N48 34E44 -2:18:56
Tomar 9 24 46N24 75E03 -5:00:12
Tomari 19 8 47N47 142E03 -9:28:12
Tomarovka 6 39 50N41 36E14 -2:24:56
Tomašgorod 23 44 51N19 27E02 -1:48:08
Tomašpol' 23 45 48N33 28E31 -1:54:04
Tomilino 6 39 55N39 37E57 -2:31:48
T'omkino 6 39 55N05 35E01 -2:20:04
Tommot 2 16 58N58 126E19 -8:25:16
T'omnyj 2 16 53N24 118E31 -7:54:04
Tompa 2 20 55N08 109E47 -7:19:08
Tomptokan 2 11 57N06 133E59 -8:55:56
Tomsk 2 21 56N30 84E58 -5:39:52
Tonež 4 39 51N49 27E48 -1:51:12
Tonkino 6 41 57N23 46E28 -3:05:52
Tonšajevo 6 41 57N44 47E00 -3:08:00
Toora-Chem 2 21 52N28 96E17 -6:25:08
Tootsi 5 35 58N34 24E47 -1:39:08
Topar 9 24 49N32 72E50 -4:51:20
Topčicha 2 21 52N49 83E10 -5:32:40

Topkanovo 6 39 54N43 38E29 -2:33:56
Topki 2 21 55N16 85E36 -5:42:24
T'oploje 6 40 53N13 38E53 -2:35:32
T'oploje 6 39 53N37 37E36 -2:30:24
T'oplyj Stan 6 34 53N58 50E10 -3:20:40
Topoli 9 32 47N59 51E36 -3:26:24
Toporok 6 9 58N33 33E28 -2:13:52
Topsa 6 41 62N39 43E34 -2:54:16
Torbejevo 6 39 54N44 36E11 -2:24:44
Torbejevo 6 41 54N05 43E15 -2:53:00
Torbino 6 9 58N35 32E53 -2:11:32
Torchany 6 41 55N34 46E36 -3:06:24
Torčin 23 44 50N46 24E59 -1:39:56
Torej 2 20 50N33 104E50 -6:59:20
Torez 23 45 48N01 38E37 -2:34:28
Torgo 2 17 58N28 119E50 -7:59:20
Toriki 6 9 59N47 30E07 -2:00:28
Torkoviči 6 9 58N52 30E20 -2:01:20
Torlino 2 30 58N53 63E46 -4:15:04
Tormosin 6 34 48N12 42E42 -2:50:48
Torna 6 41 68N04 44E10 -2:56:40
T'orny 23 45 48N09 33E33 -2:14:12
T'orny 23 44 50N59 33E59 -2:15:56
T'orny 23 45 49N05 37E57 -2:31:48
Torom 2 11 54N32 135E50 -9:03:20
Toropec 6 39 56N30 31E39 -2:06:36
Toropovo 6 39 54N21 36E07 -2:24:28
Torošino 6 39 57N56 28E36 -1:54:24
Torosozero 6 40 62N30 38E10 -2:32:40
Toruajgyr 10 24 42N32 76E26 -5:05:44
Tõrva 5 35 58N00 25E56 -1:43:44
Tory 2 20 51N47 103E00 -6:52:00
Toržok 6 39 57N03 34E58 -2:19:52
Toškovskij 23 45 48N46 38E34 -2:34:16
Tosno 6 9 59N33 30E53 -2:03:32
T'osovo 6 39 55N37 34E30 -2:18:00
T'osovo-Netyl'skij 6 9 58N57 31E04 -2:04:16
T'osovskij 6 9 58N48 30E52 -2:03:28
Tõstamaa 5 35 58N20 24E00 -1:36:00
Tostu 10 24 41N34 71E34 -4:46:16
Totban 9 32 46N47 49E06 -3:16:24
T'otkino 6 39 51N17 34E16 -2:17:04
Tot'ma 6 41 59N57 42E45 -2:51:00
Tova 6 41 65N58 40E45 -2:43:00
Tovarkovo 6 39 54N42 35E57 -2:23:48
Tovarkovskij 6 39 53N40 38E14 -2:32:56
Tpig 6 47 41N47 47E36 -3:10:24
Trakai 14 37 54N38 24E56 -1:39:44
Trakt 6 41 62N44 51E11 -3:24:44
Trasna 6 39 54N45 38E42 -2:34:48
Tregubovo 6 9 58N59 31E33 -2:06:12
Tremino 2 20 56N42 98E04 -6:32:16
Trempen → Novostrojevo 8 38 54N27 21E50 -1:27:20
Treščevo 6 39 54N11 37E55 -2:31:40
Treskino 6 41 52N40 44E40 -2:58:40
Trialeti 7 33 41N33 44E07 -2:56:28
Triduby 23 45 48N06 30E24 -2:01:36
Trilesy 23 44 49N59 29E50 -1:59:20
Tripolje 23 44 50N07 30E46 -2:03:04
Tr'ochizbenka 23 45 48N45 38E58 -2:35:52
Tr'ochsv'atskoje 6 39 56N29 37E03 -2:28:12
Troica 6 40 54N24 40E14 -2:40:56
Troick 2 21 57N25 94E50 -6:19:20
Troick 2 30 54N06 61E35 -4:06:20
Troickaja 6 47 45N08 38E07 -2:32:28
Troickij 6 34 50N14 43E05 -2:52:20
Troickij 9 30 50N41 54E38 -3:38:32
Troickij 2 30 57N03 63E43 -4:14:52
Troickij 2 20 54N36 113E09 -7:32:36
Troickij 6 34 50N14 43E03 -2:52:12
Troickije Rosl'ai 6 41 53N21 41E24 -2:45:36
Troickij Sungur 6 34 53N17 47E37 -3:10:28
Troickij Zavod 2 20 53N27 102E09 -6:48:36
Troicko-Charcyzsk 23 45 47N58 38E16 -2:33:04
Troickoje 6 41 51N17 41E28 -2:45:52
Troickoje 23 45 49N55 38E19 -2:33:16
Troickoje 23 45 47N38 30E19 -2:01:16
Troickoje 6 39 55N23 37E25 -2:29:40
Troickoje 6 39 54N52 37E07 -2:28:28
Troickoje 6 40 47N22 38E53 -2:35:32
Troickoje 23 45 48N32 38E23 -2:33:32
Troickoje 2 21 52N58 84E40 -5:38:40
Troickoje 2 11 49N27 136E36 -9:06:24
Troickoje 6 30 59N07 58E25 -3:53:40
Troickoje 6 30 52N19 56E23 -3:45:32
Troickoje 6 47 46N26 44E15 -2:57:00
Troickoje 6 34 53N22 48E23 -3:13:32
Troickoje 6 32 53N06 52E32 -3:30:08
Troickoje 6 32 53N23 52E48 -3:31:12
Troicko-Pečorsk 6 29 62N44 56E06 -3:44:24
Trojanov 23 44 50N07 28E31 -1:54:04
Trojanovka 23 44 51N20 25E17 -1:41:08
Trojebratskij 9 24 54N28 66E01 -4:24:04
Trojekurovo 6 41 53N25 39E43 -2:38:52
Trojekurovo 6 40 53N00 38E58 -2:35:52
Troparevo 6 39 55N23 35E54 -2:23:36
Troškovo 6 41 57N19 46E05 -3:04:20
Troškūnai 14 37 55N36 24E51 -1:39:24
Trosna 6 39 52N26 35E46 -2:23:04
Trost'anec 23 45 48N31 29E12 -1:56:48
Trost'anec 23 45 50N28 34E59 -2:19:56
Trubč'ovsk 6 39 52N37 33E44 -2:14:56
Trubetčino 6 40 52N53 39E33 -2:38:12

Trubino 6	39	55N59	38E08	-2:32:32
Trubino 6	39	54N58	36E42	-2:26:48
Trud 6	39	57N37	33E58	-2:15:52
Trudfront 6	34	45N56	47E41	-3:10:44
Trudnovo 2	21	56N39	91E30	-6:06:00
Trudovaja 23	45	48N21	38E04	-2:32:16
Trudovoj 9	24	53N15	66E51	-4:27:24
Trudovoj 6	32	51N42	52E43	-3:30:52
Trunovskoje 6	47	45N29	42E08	-2:48:32
Trušeny 15	46	47N04	28E41	-1:54:44
Truskavec 23	44	49N16	23E33	-1:34:12
Truslejka 6	34	53N54	46E24	-3:05:36
Tryškiai 14	37	56N04	22E35	-1:30:20
Tsaritsyn → Volgograd 6	34	48N44	44E25	-2:57:40
Tskhinvali → Cchinvali 7	33	42N13	43E56	-2:55:44
Tuapse 6	47	44N07	39E05	-2:36:20
Tuba 2	20	57N24	102E48	-6:51:12
T'ub'ak-Čekurča 6	41	56N05	49E56	-3:19:44
Tubinskij 6	30	52N53	58E13	-3:52:52
T'uchtet 2	21	56N32	89E19	-5:57:16
Tučkovo 6	39	55N36	36E28	-2:25:52
Tudu 5	35	59N11	26E51	-1:47:24
Tugolesskij Bor 6	39	55N33	39E49	-2:39:16
Tugolukovo 6	41	51N56	41E40	-2:46:40
Tugulym 2	30	57N04	64E39	-4:18:36
Tugur 2	11	53N48	136E48	-9:07:12
Tuguša 2	21	55N57	96E26	-6:25:44
Tugutuj 2	20	52N40	104E50	-6:59:20
Tuim 2	21	54N20	89E55	-5:59:40
T'ujabuguz 24	24	40N58	69E15	-4:37:00
Tujemojnak 9	31	49N20	62E55	-4:11:40
Tujmazy 6	30	54N36	53E42	-3:34:48
Tukaj 2	21	55N24	90E49	-6:03:16
T'ukalinsk 2	24	55N52	72E12	-4:48:48
Tukan 6	30	53N50	57E26	-3:49:44
Tukolon' 2	20	55N24	107E42	-7:10:48
Tukuj-Mekteb 6	47	44N20	45E11	-3:00:44
Tukums 13	36	57N00	23E10	-1:32:40
Tula 6	39	54N12	37E37	-2:30:28
T'ul'apsy 2	21	57N28	89E38	-5:58:32
Tul'čin 23	45	48N39	28E52	-1:55:28
T'ulek 10	24	41N56	75E41	-5:02:44
T'ul'gan 6	30	52N22	56E12	-3:44:48
Tul'goviči 4	39	51N47	29E38	-1:58:32
T'uljapsy 2	21	57N28	89E38	-5:58:32
T'ul'kino 6	30	59N49	56E30	-3:46:00
T'ul'kubas 9	24	42N28	70E02	-4:40:08
Tul'skij 6	47	44N31	40E10	-2:40:40
Tulun 2	20	54N35	100E33	-6:42:12
Tuma 6	40	55N09	40E34	-2:42:16
Tumak 6	34	46N14	48E31	-3:14:04
Tumalykol' 9	30	48N21	60E03	-4:00:12
Tuman'an 1	34	41N00	44E40	-2:58:40
Tumanovo 6	39	55N25	34E39	-2:18:36
Tumanskij 2	2	63N58	178E12	-11:52:48
Tumany 2	6	60N56	155E56	-10:23:44
T'um'ati → Sklad 2	16	71N55	123E33	-8:14:12
Tumbotino 6	40	55N59	43E02	-2:52:08
T'umen' 2	30	57N09	65E32	-4:22:08
T'umen'-Aryk 9	30	44N02	67E01	-4:28:04
T'umencevo 2	23	53N20	81E31	-5:26:04
Tumenskoje 6	39	55N00	38E32	-2:34:08
Tumutuk 6	41	55N02	53E19	-3:33:16
T'unež 6	39	54N37	38E29	-2:33:56
Tungokočen 2	16	53N33	115E36	-7:42:24
Tunka 2	20	51N45	102E42	-6:50:48
Tuobuja 2	16	62N00	122E02	-8:08:08
Tuoj-Chaja 2	18	62N32	111E18	-7:25:12
T'up 10	24	42N44	78E22	-5:13:28
Tupičov 23	44	51N46	31E26	-2:05:44
Tupik 2	16	54N26	119E57	-7:59:48
Tura 2	19	64N17	100E15	-6:41:00
Turan 2	21	52N08	93E55	-6:15:40
Turan 2	20	51N38	101E40	-6:46:40
Turbov 23	44	49N21	28E44	-1:54:56
Turčasovo 6	40	63N06	39E12	-2:36:48
Turdej 6	39	53N22	38E01	-2:32:04
Turgaj 9	24	51N46	72E44	-4:50:56
Turgaj 9	31	49N38	63E28	-4:13:52
Turgen' 9	24	43N24	77E36	-5:10:24
Turgenevka 2	20	53N02	105E41	-7:02:44
Turgenevo 6	41	54N50	46E19	-3:05:16
Turginovo 6	39	56N30	36E00	-2:24:00
Turgojak 2	30	55N10	60E07	-4:00:28
Turgoš 6	9	59N18	35E10	-2:20:40
Türi 5	35	58N48	25E26	-1:41:44
Turij Rog 2	11	45N14	131E58	-8:47:52
Turijsk 23	44	51N07	24E31	-1:38:04
Turilovka 6	47	49N06	40E13	-2:40:52
Turinsk 2	30	58N03	63E42	-4:14:48
Turinskaja Sloboda 2	30	57N37	64E25	-4:17:40
Turka 2	20	52N57	108E13	-7:12:52
Turka 23	44	49N10	23E02	-1:32:08
Turkestan 9	24	43N18	68E15	-4:33:00
Turki 6	34	51N59	43E16	-2:53:04
Turkmen-Kala 22	30	37N26	62E20	-4:09:20
Turlan 9	24	43N36	69E03	-4:36:12
Turmantas 14	37	55N42	26E27	-1:45:48
Turočak 2	21	52N16	87E08	-5:48:32
Turopin 23	44	51N00	24E27	-1:37:48
Turov 4	39	52N04	27E44	-1:50:56
Turovo 6	39	54N52	37E49	-2:31:16
Turša 6	41	56N56	47E40	-3:10:40
Tursunzade 21	24	38N32	68E13	-4:32:52
Turuchansk 2	21	65N49	87E59	-5:51:56
Turuntajevo 2	20	52N12	107E37	-7:10:28
Turuntajevo 2	21	56N38	85E59	-5:43:56
Tutajev 6	40	57N53	39E32	-2:38:08
Tutkaul 21	24	38N18	69E17	-4:37:08
T'ut'kovo 6	39	54N37	38E32	-2:34:08
Tutura 2	20	54N46	105E15	-7:01:00
T'uva-Guba 6	9	69N08	33E32	-2:14:08
Tuža 6	42	57N37	47E57	-3:11:48
T'uzbel' 10	24	40N34	73E21	-4:53:24
Tuzly 23	45	45N52	30E05	-2:00:20
Tvardica 15	46	46N09	28E58	-1:55:52
Tver → Kalinin 6	39	56N52	35E55	-2:23:40
Tybju 6	41	60N37	50E20	-3:21:20
Tygda 2	16	53N07	126E20	-8:25:20
Tylovaj 6	42	57N30	53E47	-3:35:08
Tymovskoje 19	8	50N51	142E39	-9:30:36
Tymsk 2	23	59N24	80E18	-5:21:12
Tyndinskij 2	16	55N10	124E43	-8:18:52
Tynica 23	44	51N08	32E54	-2:11:36
Typta 2	20	54N35	104E31	-6:58:04
Tyr 2	11	52N57	139E48	-9:19:12
Tyret' 2	20	53N41	102E19	-6:49:16
Tyrgetuj 2	16	51N27	113E46	-7:35:04
Tyrka 2	20	54N30	107E09	-7:08:36
Tyrma 2	11	50N03	132E12	-8:48:48
Tyrnovo 15	46	48N10	27E40	-1:50:40
Tyrnyauz 6	47	43N23	42E56	-2:51:44
Tysmenica 23	44	48N54	24E49	-1:39:16
Tytuvėnai 14	37	55N36	23E12	-1:32:48
Tyumen'→ T'umen' 2	30	57N09	65E32	-4:22:08
Tyvrov 23	44	49N01	28E30	-1:54:00
Ubinskoje 2	23	55N19	79E41	-5:18:44
Ubur-Tochtor 2	16	50N06	113E37	-7:34:28
Uč-Adži 22	30	38N05	62E48	-4:11:12
Učaly 2	30	54N19	59E27	-3:57:48
Učami 2	21	63N50	96E29	-6:25:56
Učaral 9	24	46N10	80E56	-5:23:44
Ucholovo 6	41	53N47	40E29	-2:41:56
Uchta 6	29	63N33	53E38	-3:34:32
Uchta 6	40	61N12	38E32	-2:34:08
Uchtoma 6	40	60N10	38E02	-2:32:08
Učinskij Ryboučastok 2	30	60N02	65E10	-4:20:40
Učkupr'uk 24	24	40N33	71E04	-4:44:16
Učkurgan 24	24	41N07	72E05	-4:48:20
Učterek 10	24	41N45	73E12	-4:52:48
Učujevskij Majdan 6	41	54N33	44E30	-2:58:00
Udarnyj 19	8	49N07	142E09	-9:28:36
Udel'naja 6	39	55N38	38E03	-2:32:12
Udimskij 6	41	61N09	45E52	-3:03:28
Udoml'a 6	39	57N52	35E01	-2:20:04
Udskoje 2	11	54N32	134E26	-8:57:44
Udy 23	45	50N24	36E03	-2:24:12
Udža 2	16	71N14	117E10	-7:48:40
Udžary 3	34	40N31	47E39	-3:10:36
Uelen 2	2	66N10	169W48	11:19:12
Uel'kal' 2	2	65N32	179E17	-11:57:08
Ufa 6	30	54N44	55E56	-3:43:44
Ufra 22	30	40N00	53E02	-3:32:08
Ugāle 13	36	57N16	22E02	-1:28:08
Uglegorsk 19	8	49N02	142E03	-9:28:12
Uglegorsk 23	45	48N19	38E17	-2:33:08
Uglekamensk 2	27	43N13	133E11	-8:52:44
Uglezavodsk 19	8	47N21	142E38	-9:30:32
Uglič 6	39	57N32	38E19	-2:33:16
Uglovaja 6	42	57N01	52E57	-3:31:48
Uglovka 6	9	58N14	33E31	-2:14:04
Uglovoje 2	27	43N20	132E06	-8:48:24
Uglovskoje 2	23	51N23	80E12	-5:20:48
Ugly-Zavod 23	44	52N11	32E53	-2:11:32
Ugnev 23	44	50N23	23E44	-1:34:56
Ugodiči 6	40	57N10	39E30	-2:38:00
Ugodskij Zavod 6	39	55N02	36E45	-2:27:00
Ugolnyy 2	2	63N03	179E03	-11:56:12
Ugra 6	39	54N47	34E17	-2:17:08
Ugrojedy 23	45	50N52	35E17	-2:21:08
Ugr'umovo 6	39	55N09	37E40	-2:30:40
Uguj 2	23	56N02	76E03	-5:04:12
Ug'ut 10	24	41N24	74E50	-4:59:20
Uil 9	30	49N05	54E40	-3:38:40
Uinskoje 6	30	56N53	56E35	-3:46:20
Ujaly 9	30	44N37	60E57	-4:03:48
Ujar 2	21	55N48	94E20	-6:17:20
Ujemskij 6	41	64N29	40E50	-2:43:20
Ujgursaj 24	24	40N53	71E03	-4:44:12
Ujskoje 2	30	54N22	60E00	-4:00:00
Uk 2	20	55N04	98E52	-6:35:28
Uka 2	4	57N50	162E06	-10:48:24
Ukhta → Uchta 6	29	63N33	53E38	-3:34:32
Ukmergė 14	37	55N15	24E45	-1:39:00
Ukrainka 2	24	54N39	71E20	-4:45:20
Ukrainsk 23	45	48N06	37E18	-2:29:12
Uks'anskoje 2	30	55N57	63E01	-4:12:04
Uktuz 2	30	55N38	68E30	-4:34:00
Uktym 6	41	62N38	48E52	-3:15:28
Ukurejskij 2	16	52N24	116E49	-7:47:16
Ukyr 2	18	49N28	108E52	-7:15:28
Ula-Chuduk 6	47	47N39	45E34	-3:02:16
Ulanbel' 9	24	44N48	71E10	-4:44:40
Ulan-Erge 6	47	46N19	44E53	-2:59:32
Ulanov 23	44	49N42	28E08	-1:52:32
Ulanovo 23	44	51N46	34E18	-2:17:12
Ulanovskij 6	39	54N04	37E51	-2:31:24
Ulan-Ude 2	20	51N50	107E37	-7:10:28
Ulan-Ušotej 2	20	50N45	105E29	-7:01:56
Ul'ašovo 6	29	65N27	56E57	-3:47:48
Ul'atuj 2	16	51N09	116E14	-7:44:56
Ul'ba 9	24	50N16	83E22	-5:33:28
Ul'chun-Partija 2	16	49N56	112E46	-7:31:04
Ulety 2	18	51N22	112E29	-7:29:56
Ulgajsyn 9	30	49N38	60E17	-4:01:08
Ulja 2	11	58N51	141E50	-9:27:20
Uljanino 6	39	55N21	38E26	-2:33:44
Uljanovka 23	45	48N20	30E13	-2:00:52
Uljanovka 23	45	50N58	34E18	-2:17:12
Uljanovka 6	9	59N38	30E46	-2:03:04
Uljanovo 24	24	40N07	68E30	-4:34:00
Uljanovo 6	39	53N43	35E32	-2:22:08
Uljanovsk 6	42	54N20	48E24	-3:13:36
Uljanovskoje 19	8	46N17	142E13	-9:28:52
Uljanovskoje 9	24	50N02	73E42	-4:54:48
Ul'kan 2	20	57N14	107E19	-7:09:16
Ulla 4	39	55N14	29E15	-1:57:00
Ulu 2	16	60N19	127E24	-8:29:36
Ulunchan 2	20	54N51	111E02	-7:24:08
Ulunga 2	27	46N31	136E56	-9:07:44
Ulutau 9	31	48N39	67E01	-4:28:04
Ulyanovsk → Uljanovsk 6	42	54N20	48E24	-3:13:36
Umal'tinskij 2	11	51N56	133E36	-8:54:24
Uman' 23	45	48N44	30E14	-2:00:56
Umancevo 6	47	47N44	44E16	-2:57:04
Umba 6	9	66N41	34E15	-2:17:00
Um'ot 6	41	52N31	42E58	-2:51:52
Um'ot 6	41	54N08	42E42	-2:50:48
Uncukul' 6	47	42N42	46E48	-3:07:12
Unda 2	16	51N42	116E56	-7:47:44
Undory 6	42	54N37	48E25	-3:13:40
Uneča 6	39	52N50	32E40	-2:10:40
Ungeny 15	46	47N12	27E48	-1:51:12
Ungurkuj 2	20	50N27	106E58	-7:07:52
Ungvár → Užgorod 23	44	48N37	22E18	-1:29:12
Uni 6	42	57N46	51E30	-3:26:00
Unica 6	9	62N38	34E38	-2:18:32
Unkurda 2	30	55N48	59E24	-3:57:36
Unža 6	41	58N01	44E01	-2:56:04
Unže-Pavinskaja 2	30	58N53	64E02	-4:16:08
Uojan 2	20	56N07	111E38	-7:26:32
Uporovo 2	30	56N18	66E17	-4:25:08
Urachi 6	47	42N21	47E36	-3:10:24
Uraj 2	30	60N08	64E48	-4:19:12
Urakan 2	20	58N38	106E01	-7:04:04
Uralo-Kl'uči 2	21	56N03	97E28	-6:29:52
Uralovo 23	44	52N11	33E34	-2:14:16
Ural'skij 6	32	51N36	51E40	-3:26:40
Ura-T'ube 21	24	39N55	68E59	-4:35:56
Urazmetovo 6	30	53N49	55E25	-3:41:40
Urazovka 6	41	55N24	45E38	-3:02:32
Urazovo 6	39	50N07	38E04	-2:32:16
Urda 9	32	48N47	47E26	-3:09:44
Urdoma 6	41	61N47	48E32	-3:14:08
Urdžar 9	24	47N05	81E38	-5:26:32
Urečje 4	39	52N57	27E54	-1:51:36
Ureki 7	33	41N59	41E46	-2:47:04
Ureliki 2	2	64N23	173W15	11:33:00
Uren' 6	41	57N28	45E49	-3:03:16
Urga 24	30	43N35	58E30	-3:54:00
Urgenč 24	30	41N33	60E38	-4:02:32
Urgut 24	30	39N23	67E15	-4:29:00
Urickij 9	30	53N19	65E34	-4:22:16
Urickoje 9	30	53N19	65E34	-4:22:16
Urickoje 6	40	52N02	38E11	-2:32:44
Urkarach 6	47	42N11	47E38	-3:10:32
Urluk 2	18	50N03	107E55	-7:11:40
Urman 6	30	54N52	56E52	-3:47:28
Urmary 6	41	55N42	47E57	-3:11:48
Urmetan 21	24	39N27	68E17	-4:33:08
Urožajnoje 6	47	44N47	44E55	-2:59:40
Uršel'skij 6	39	55N41	40E13	-2:40:52
Ursk 2	21	54N27	85E24	-5:41:36
Urtazym 6	30	52N12	58E50	-3:55:20
Urul'ga 2	16	51N45	114E47	-7:39:08
Ur'ung-Chaja 2	16	72N48	113E23	-7:33:32
Urup 6	47	43N52	41E09	-2:44:36
Ur'upino 2	16	52N46	120E00	-8:00:00
Ur'upinsk 6	34	50N47	41E59	-2:47:56
Urup Island 12	8	46N00	150E00	-10:00:00
Urup, Ostrov 12	8	46N00	150E00	-10:00:00
Uruša 2	16	54N03	122E54	-8:11:36
Urus-Martan 6	47	43N08	45E32	-3:02:08
Urusovo 6	39	54N15	38E26	-2:33:44
Urussu 6	41	54N36	53E24	-3:33:36
Uryl' 9	24	49N15	86E20	-5:45:20
Uryv 6	40	51N07	39E10	-2:36:40
Urzajbaš 6	30	54N43	54E23	-3:37:32
Uržum 6	42	57N08	50E00	-3:20:00
Usa 2	21	54N03	88E45	-5:55:00
Ušači 4	39	55N11	28E37	-1:54:28
Ušaki 6	9	59N29	30E59	-2:03:56
Ušakovka 6	47	48N48	39E48	-2:39:12
Ušakovo 2	16	51N55	126E34	-8:26:16
Ušakovo 2	24	56N22	75E41	-5:02:44
Usanovy 2	25	59N28	73E24	-4:53:36
Ušaral 9	24	43N54	70E42	-4:42:48
Uščerpje 6	39	52N43	31E53	-2:07:32
Usinsk 6	29	65N58	56E39	-3:46:36
Uskovo 6	39	55N56	37E19	-2:29:16
Usman' 2	11	51N29	134E00	-8:56:00
Usman' 6	41	52N02	39E44	-2:38:56
Usmanka 6	34	52N49	51E42	-3:26:48
Usmat 24	24	39N44	67E40	-4:30:40
Usmyn' 6	39	55N52	31E09	-2:04:36
Usolje 6	39	56N49	38E40	-2:34:40
Usolje 6	30	59N25	56E41	-3:46:44
Usolje 6	34	53N23	49E05	-3:16:20

Usolje-Sibirskoje 2 20 52N47 103E38 -6:54:32
Usovo 6 39 55N44 37E13 -2:28:52
Uspenka 23 45 48N23 39E10 -2:36:40
Uspenka 23 45 47N43 38E42 -2:34:48
Uspenka 9 24 52N54 77E25 -5:09:40
Uspenka 6 34 50N38 41E28 -2:45:52
Uspenovka 9 30 51N16 53E36 -3:34:24
Uspenskij 9 24 48N42 72E40 -4:50:40
Uspenskoje 6 39 55N43 37E04 -2:28:16
Ušsaj 24 30 43N50 58E53 -3:55:32
Ussurijsk 2 27 43N48 131E59 -8:47:56
Usta 6 41 57N26 45E40 -3:02:40
Ust'-Ajsk 6 30 56N07 57E40 -3:50:40
Ust'-Bagar'ak 2 30 56N08 61E52 -4:07:28
Ust'-Barguzin 2 20 53N27 108E59 -7:15:56
Ust'-Belaja 2 2 65N30 173E20-11:33:20
Ust'-Bol'šereck 2 4 52N48 156E14-10:24:56
Ust'-B'ur' 2 21 53N49 90E15 -6:01:00
Ust'-Buzulukskaja 6 34 50N12 42E10 -2:48:40
Ust'-Bystr'anskaja 6 47 47N49 41E03 -2:44:12
Ust'-Čaja 2 23 58N17 82E38 -5:30:32
Ust'-Čaryšskaja Pristan' 2 21 52N24 83E39 -5:34:36
Ust'-Čaun 2 4 68N47 170E30-11:22:00
Ust'-Choperskaja 6 34 49N36 42E24 -2:49:36
Ust'-Cil'ma 6 41 65N27 52E06 -3:28:24
Ust'-Čižapka 2 23 59N02 79E37 -5:18:28
Ust'-Čorna 23 44 48N18 23E56 -1:35:44
Ust'-Čornaja 2 16 52N57 119E02 -7:56:08
Ust'-Dolyssy 6 39 56N09 29E39 -1:58:36
Ust'-Doneckij 6 47 47N39 40E52 -2:43:28
Ust'-Džegutinskaja 6 47 44N05 41E58 -2:47:52
Ust'-Elegest 2 21 51N32 94E05 -6:16:20
Ust'gr'aznucha 6 34 50N28 45E26 -3:01:44
Ust'-Il'a 2 16 50N25 113E41 -7:34:44
Ust'-Ilga 2 20 55N00 105E02 -7:00:08
Ust'-Ilimsk 2 20 58N00 102E39 -6:50:36
Ustilug 23 44 50N51 24E09 -1:36:36
Ust'-Ilyč 6 29 62N32 56E41 -3:46:44
Ustinovka 23 45 48N49 38E34 -2:34:16
Ustinovka 23 45 47N57 32E32 -2:10:08
Ust'-Išim 2 24 57N44 71E10 -4:44:40
Ust'-Izes 2 23 55N56 76E56 -5:07:44
Ust'-Ižora 6 9 59N48 30E36 -2:02:24
Ust'-Javron'ga 6 41 63N25 44E21 -2:57:24
Ustje 6 39 55N16 36E20 -2:25:20
Ustje 2 21 57N46 94E42 -6:18:48
Ustje 6 40 57N47 39E47 -2:39:08
Ustje 6 9 60N49 32E49 -2:11:16
Ustje 6 40 59N38 39E43 -2:38:52
Ustje-Kirovskoje 6 9 58N45 35E55 -2:23:40
Ust'-K'achta 2 20 50N32 106E16 -7:05:04
Ust'-Kajtym 2 21 57N23 95E28 -6:21:52
Ust'-Kalmanka 2 21 52N07 83E19 -5:33:16
Ust'-Kamčatsk 2 4 56N15 162E30-10:50:00
Ust'-Kamenogorsk 9 24 49N58 82E38 -5:30:32
Ust'-Kan 2 21 50N57 84E45 -5:39:00
Ust'-Kan 2 21 56N31 93E48 -6:15:12
Ust'-Karenga 2 16 54N26 116E30 -7:46:00
Ust'-Karsk 2 16 52N43 118E48 -7:55:12
Ust'-Katav 2 30 54N56 58E10 -3:52:40
Ust'-Kemčug 2 21 57N13 90E30 -6:02:00
Ust'-Kil'mez' 6 42 56N57 50E30 -3:22:00
Ust'-Kišert' 6 30 57N22 57E15 -3:49:00
Ust'-Koksa 2 21 50N18 85E36 -5:42:24
Ust'-Kujda 2 11 70N01 135E36 -9:02:24
Ust'-Kulom 6 29 61N42 53E40 -3:34:40
Ust'-Kurd'um 6 34 51N39 46E12 -3:04:48
Ust'-Kurenga 2 24 57N27 75E34 -5:02:16
Ust'-Kut 2 20 56N46 105E40 -7:02:40
Ust'-Labinsk 6 47 45N13 39E42 -2:38:48
Ust'-Lubija 2 16 52N36 120E16 -8:01:04
Ust'-Luga 6 9 59N40 28E15 -1:53:00
Ust'-Lyža 6 29 65N44 56E36 -3:46:24
Ust'-Maja 2 12 60N25 134E32 -8:58:08
Ust'-Manja 2 30 62N11 60E20 -4:01:20
Ust'-Naryk 2 21 54N20 87E25 -5:49:40
Ust'-Nemda 6 42 57N03 50E22 -3:21:28
Ust'-Nera 2 6 64N34 143E12 -9:32:48
Ust'-Niman 2 11 51N23 132E42 -8:50:48
Ust'-N'ukža 2 16 56N34 121E37 -8:06:28
Uštobe 9 24 45N16 78E00 -5:12:00
Ust'-Omčug 2 6 61N09 149E38 -9:58:32
Ust'-Ordynskij 2 20 52N48 104E45 -6:59:00
Ust'-Oz'ornaja 2 16 50N42 117E06 -7:48:24
Ust'-Oz'ornoje 2 21 58N54 87E48 -5:51:12
Ust'-Paden'ga 6 41 61N53 42E36 -2:50:24
Ust'-Pečengskoje 6 41 59N47 42E37 -2:50:28
Ust'-Pinega 6 41 64N11 41E56 -2:47:44
Ust'-Pit 2 21 58N59 91E44 -6:06:56
Ust'-Pogožje 6 34 49N28 44E38 -2:58:32
Ustreka 6 9 58N38 34E33 -2:18:12
Ust'-Reki 6 41 62N12 46E45 -3:07:00
Ust'-Sara 6 9 60N13 33E57 -2:15:48
Ust'-Ščerbedino 6 34 51N53 42E52 -2:51:28
Ust'-Šonoša 6 41 61N10 41E18 -2:45:12
Ust'-Sumy 2 23 54N48 80E26 -5:21:44
Ust'-Tara 2 24 56N41 74E39 -4:58:36
Ust'-Tarka 2 23 55N34 75E42 -5:02:48
Ust'-Tašino 2 14 51N07 129E35 -8:38:20
Ust'-Tygda 2 14 52N35 127E53 -8:31:32
Ust'-Tym 2 23 59N26 80E08 -5:20:32
Ust'-Tyrma 2 11 50N29 131E18 -8:45:12
Ust'uckoje 6 9 58N32 35E20 -2:21:20
Ust'-Uda 2 20 54N10 103E03 -6:52:12
Ust'-Ulagan 2 21 50N38 87E58 -5:51:52
Ust'-Umal'ta 2 11 51N39 133E18 -8:53:12
Ust'-Undurga 2 16 53N07 118E04 -7:52:16
Ust'-Unja 6 29 61N48 57E48 -3:51:12
Ust'-Urgal 2 11 51N09 132E33 -8:50:12
Ust'-Us 2 21 52N07 92E17 -6:09:08
Ust'-Usa 6 29 65N59 56E54 -3:47:36
Ust'-Uza 6 41 52N58 45E17 -3:01:08
Ust'užna 6 40 58N51 36E26 -2:25:44
Ust'-Vichoreva 2 20 56N47 101E24 -6:45:36
Ust'-Voja 6 29 64N27 57E40 -3:50:40
Ust'-Vyjskaja 6 41 62N57 46E41 -3:06:44
Ust'-Vym' 6 41 62N14 50E24 -3:21:36
Ust'-Zaza 2 20 53N10 111E40 -7:26:40
Ust'-Žuja 2 17 58N48 118E12 -7:52:48
Usuch-Čaj 6 47 41N25 47E53 -3:11:32
Usugli 2 16 52N39 115E16 -7:41:04
Ušumun 2 16 52N49 126E27 -8:25:48
Ušur 6 42 57N47 52E58 -3:31:52
Usv'aty 6 39 55N45 30E45 -2:03:00
Utata 2 20 50N51 102E45 -6:51:00
Utena 14 37 55N30 25E36 -1:42:24
Utevka 6 34 52N57 50E58 -3:23:52
Ut'ma 2 24 57N35 71E45 -4:47:00
Utorgoš 6 9 58N17 30E15 -2:01:00
Utta 6 47 46N23 46E01 -3:04:04
Uulu 5 35 58N17 24E35 -1:38:20
Uva 6 42 56N59 52E13 -3:28:52
Uvaroviči 4 39 52N36 30E44 -2:02:56
Uvarovka 6 39 55N32 35E37 -2:22:28
Uvarovo 6 41 51N59 42E15 -2:49:00
Uvat 2 30 59N09 68E54 -4:35:36
Uvel'skij 2 30 54N26 61E22 -4:05:28
Užanicha 2 23 54N41 81E02 -5:24:08
Uzas 2 23 57N04 76E55 -5:07:40
Užava 13 36 57N14 21E27 -1:25:48
Uzda 4 39 53N27 27E13 -1:48:52
Uzgen 10 24 40N46 73E18 -4:53:12
Užgorod 23 44 48N37 22E18 -1:29:12
Uzin 23 44 49N50 30E24 -2:01:36
Uzkij Lug 2 20 50N42 108E01 -7:12:04
Uzlovaja 6 39 53N59 38E10 -2:32:40
Uzmorje 6 34 51N15 45E55 -3:03:40
Uz'ukovo 6 34 53N38 49E43 -3:18:52
Uzun 24 30 38N22 68E03 -4:32:12
Uzunagač 2 30 56N28 67E18 -4:29:12
Uzunagač 9 24 43N13 76E20 -5:05:20
Uzunkuduk 24 30 40N33 67E11 -4:28:44
Uzunovo 6 39 54N32 38E37 -2:34:28
Užur 2 21 55N20 89E50 -5:59:20
Užventis 14 37 55N47 22E39 -1:30:36
Vabalninkas 14 37 55N58 24E45 -1:39:00
Vabkent 24 30 40N02 64E30 -4:18:00
Vača 6 40 55N48 42E46 -2:51:04
Vachrušev 19 8 48N59 142E58 -9:31:52
Vachruševo 23 45 48N10 38E46 -2:35:04
Vachtan 6 41 57N58 46E42 -3:06:48
Vači 6 47 42N05 47E13 -3:08:52
Vad 6 41 55N32 44E12 -2:56:48
Vadino 6 39 55N16 33E16 -2:13:04
Vadinsk 6 41 53N43 43E04 -2:52:16
Vagaj 2 30 57N56 69E01 -4:36:04
Vagaj 2 30 56N28 67E18 -4:29:12
Väike-Maarja 5 35 59N08 26E15 -1:45:00
Vaiņode 13 36 56N26 21E50 -1:27:20
Vajgač 6 29 70N25 58E46 -3:55:04
Valaam 6 9 61N23 30E57 -2:03:48
Valamaz 6 42 57N32 52E05 -3:28:20
Valdaj 6 39 57N59 33E14 -2:12:56
Valdaj 6 40 63N26 35E30 -2:22:00
Valdemārpils 13 36 57N22 22E35 -1:30:20
Valentin 2 27 43N08 134E17 -8:57:08
Valentinovka 6 39 55N55 37E56 -2:31:44
Valga 13 36 57N47 26E02 -1:44:08
Valka 13 36 57N46 26E00 -1:44:00
V'alki 6 39 55N39 38E05 -2:32:20
Valki 23 45 49N50 35E37 -2:22:28
Valkininkas 14 37 54N21 24E50 -1:39:20
Valle 13 36 56N30 24E44 -1:38:56
Valmiera 13 36 57N33 25E24 -1:41:36
Valok 23 45 45N47 34E57 -2:19:48
Valujec 6 39 52N46 33E23 -2:13:32
Valujevka 6 47 46N44 43E43 -2:54:52
Valujevo 6 39 55N35 37E21 -2:29:24
Valujki 6 39 50N13 38E08 -2:32:32
Vanavara 2 19 60N22 102E16 -6:49:04
Vanč 21 24 38N23 71E26 -4:45:44
Vandam 3 34 40N57 47E57 -3:11:48
Vändra 5 35 58N39 25E02 -1:40:08
Vandžiogala 14 37 55N07 23E58 -1:35:52
Vani 7 33 42N06 42E30 -2:50:00
Vanino 2 11 49N05 140E15 -9:21:00
Vankarem 2 2 67N51 175W50 11:43:20
Vannovka 9 24 42N32 70E21 -4:41:24
Vanskoje 6 40 58N56 36E52 -2:27:28
Vapn'arka 23 45 48N32 28E44 -1:54:56
Varakļāni 13 36 56N37 26E44 -1:46:56
Varandej 6 29 68N48 58E00 -3:52:00
Varciche 7 33 42N08 42E43 -2:50:52
Vardenik 1 34 40N08 45E27 -3:01:48
Vardenis 1 34 40N11 45E43 -3:02:52
Varegovo 6 40 57N47 39E17 -2:37:08
Varėna 14 37 54N13 24E34 -1:38:16
Varenikovskaja 6 47 45N07 37E37 -2:30:28
Varenovka 6 40 47N18 39E02 -2:36:08
Varfolomejevka 6 34 50N01 48E12 -3:12:48
Vargaši 2 30 55N23 65E48 -4:23:12
Varlamovo 2 30 54N38 60E40 -4:02:40
Varna 2 30 53N24 60E58 -4:03:52
Varnavino 6 41 57N24 45E04 -3:00:16
Varniai 14 37 55N45 22E22 -1:29:28
Värska 5 35 57N58 27E38 -1:50:32
Vartašen 3 34 41N06 47E28 -3:09:52
V'artsil'a 6 9 62N11 30E41 -2:02:44
Varva 23 44 50N31 32E41 -2:10:44
Varvarovka 23 45 49N05 38E24 -2:33:36
Varvarovka 23 45 48N42 36E02 -2:24:08
Varvarovka 23 45 49N33 35E12 -2:20:48
Varzi 6 41 56N03 52E50 -3:31:20
Varzino 6 9 68N19 38E19 -2:33:16
Varzob 21 24 38N46 68E49 -4:35:16
Varzuga 6 9 67N24 36E32 -2:26:08
Varzyk 24 24 41N07 71E14 -4:44:56
Vasalemma 5 35 59N14 24E18 -1:37:12
Vasileviči 4 39 52N14 29E49 -1:59:16
Vasiliški 4 39 53N47 24E51 -1:39:24
Vasiljevka 2 11 46N52 134E03 -8:56:12
Vasiljevka 4 39 52N15 31E31 -2:06:04
Vasiljevka 23 45 47N26 35E16 -2:21:04
Vasiljevo 6 41 55N52 48E42 -3:14:48
Vasiljevo 6 40 60N46 38E59 -2:35:56
Vasiljevskij Moch 6 39 57N01 35E55 -2:23:40
Vasiljevskoje 6 41 56N31 45E49 -3:03:16
Vasiljevskoje 6 39 55N00 37E25 -2:29:40
Vasiljevskoje 6 39 56N20 37E54 -2:31:36
Vasiljevskoje 6 40 56N56 41E40 -2:46:40
Vasil'kov 23 44 50N12 30E19 -2:01:16
Vasil'kovka 23 45 48N13 36E02 -2:24:08
Vasil'sursk 6 41 56N08 46E01 -3:04:04
Vasis 2 24 57N22 74E44 -4:58:56
Vaskelovo 6 9 60N22 30E22 -2:01:28
Vas'kin Bor 2 30 58N20 65E28 -4:21:52
Vaškovci 23 45 48N24 27E08 -1:48:32
Vaškovcy 23 44 48N23 25E30 -1:42:00
Vastseliina 5 35 57N44 27E17 -1:49:08
Vas'unino 6 39 55N15 37E01 -2:28:04
Vašutino 6 39 55N56 37E26 -2:29:44
V'atka → Kirov 6 42 58N38 49E42 -3:18:48
V'atskije Pol'any 6 42 56N14 51E04 -3:24:16
V'atskoje 6 40 57N52 40E16 -2:41:04
V'atskoje 2 11 48N44 135E43 -9:02:52
Vatulino 6 39 55N39 36E09 -2:24:36
Vatutino 23 44 49N02 31E04 -2:04:16
Vaulovo 6 39 56N09 39E17 -2:37:08
Vavož 6 42 56N47 51E55 -3:27:40
V'aža 6 47 49N16 41E01 -2:44:04
V'azemskij 2 11 47N32 134E48 -8:59:12
Važgort 6 41 64N01 47E02 -3:08:08
V'az'ma 6 39 55N13 34E18 -2:17:12
V'azniki 6 40 56N15 42E10 -2:48:40
V'azovaja 6 41 57N39 45E44 -3:02:56
V'azovka 6 34 51N48 45E47 -3:03:08
V'azovka 6 34 52N52 48E24 -3:13:36
V'azovka 6 34 50N52 43E57 -2:55:48
V'azovka 6 34 48N19 45E36 -3:02:24
V'azovoje 6 39 51N09 37E01 -2:28:04
V'azovoje 6 39 51N54 36E59 -2:27:56
V'azovok 23 44 49N11 31E25 -2:05:40
V'azyn' 4 39 54N25 27E10 -1:48:40
Vecpiebalga 13 36 57N08 25E50 -1:43:20
Vecumnieki 13 36 56N36 24E31 -1:38:04
Vedi 1 34 39N56 44E42 -2:58:48
Vednoje 6 39 57N08 36E10 -2:24:40
Vedomša 6 39 56N44 38E21 -2:33:24
Vedrovo 6 40 57N33 42E52 -2:51:28
Veisiejai 14 37 54N06 23E42 -1:34:48
Vejčin 4 39 52N27 28E10 -1:52:40
Vejdelevka 6 40 50N09 38E27 -2:33:48
Vekšor 6 41 60N33 49E26 -3:17:44
Velegož 6 39 54N42 37E16 -2:29:04
Velet'ma 6 40 55N20 42E25 -2:49:40
Velevščina 4 39 54N44 28E35 -1:54:20
Vel'gija 6 9 58N23 33E59 -2:15:56
Veličkovo 6 39 54N59 36E46 -2:27:04
Velikaja 2 2 64N04 176E12-11:44:48
Velikaja 6 42 59N13 49E04 -3:16:16

Velikaja Aleksandrovka 23 45 47N20 33E18 -2:13:12
Velikaja Bagačka 23 44 49N47 33E43 -2:14:52
Velikaja Beloz'orka 23 45 47N16 34E42 -2:18:48
Velikaja Danilovka 23 45 50N04 36E19 -2:25:16
Velikaja Dymerka 23 44 50N36 30E55 -2:03:40
Velikaja Gluša 23 44 51N49 25E02 -1:40:08
Velikaja Kema 2 11 45N30 137E12 -9:08:48
Velikaja Kochnovka 23 45 49N07 33E27 -2:13:48
Velikaja Korenicha 23 45 46N57 31E54 -2:07:36
Velikaja Kosnica 23 45 48N09 28E27 -1:53:48
Velikaja Lepeticha 23 45 47N11 33E56 -2:15:44
Velikaja Michajlovka 23 45 47N04 29E52 -1:59:28
Velikaja Novos'olka 23 45 47N50 36E50 -2:27:20
Velikaja Pisarevka 23 45 50N26 35E28 -2:21:52
Velikaja Rublevka 23 45 49N53 34E49 -2:19:16
Velikaja Vradijevka 23 45 47N52 30E35 -2:02:20
Velikij Ber'oznyj 23 44 48N53 22E27 -1:29:48
Velikij Bor 4 39 52N02 29E56 -1:59:44
Velikij Burluk 23 45 50N05 37E24 -2:29:36
Velikij Buruluk 23 45 50N05 37E24 -2:29:36
Velikij Byčkov 15 46 47N58 24E03 -1:36:12
Velikij Chutor 23 44 49N52 32E06 -2:08:24
Velikij Dvor 6 39 56N46 37E25 -2:29:40
Velikije Borki 23 44 49N32 25E45 -1:43:00
Velikije Dederkaly 23 44 50N02 26E07 -1:44:28
Velikije Kopani 23 45 46N29 32E59 -2:11:56
Velikije Korovincy 23 44 49N59 28E17 -1:53:08
Velikije Krynki 23 44 49N27 33E29 -2:13:56
Velikije Lučki 23 44 48N26 22E35 -1:30:20
Velikije Luki 6 39 56N20 30E32 -2:02:08
Velikije Mosty 23 44 50N14 24E06 -1:36:24
Velikije Soročincy 23 44 50N03 33E56 -2:15:44
Velikij Gluboček 23 44 49N37 25E32 -1:42:08
Velikij Log 23 45 48N15 39E33 -2:38:12
Velikij žvančik 23 45 48N46 26E59 -1:47:56
Velikoarchan-Gel'skoje 6 41 50N51 40E46 -2:43:04
Velikockoje 23 45 49N21 40E02 -2:40:08
Velikodolinskoje 23 45 46N21 30E35 -2:02:20
Velikodvorskaja 6 41 60N18 41E58 -2:47:52
Velikodvorskij 6 40 55N15 40E41 -2:42:44
Velikoje 6 40 59N32 36E59 -2:27:56
Velikoje 6 40 57N21 39E47 -2:39:08
Velikookt'abr'skij 6 39 57N26 33E49 -2:15:16
Velikoploskoje 23 45 47N01 29E40 -1:58:40
Velikorusskoje 2 24 54N39 74E38 -4:58:32
Velikovisočnoje 6 29 67N16 52E01 -3:28:04
Velikovo 6 41 59N18 42E08 -2:48:32
Velimče 23 44 51N36 24E44 -1:38:56
Veliž 6 39 55N38 31E12 -2:04:48
Veližany 2 30 57N34 65E49 -4:23:16
Veljaminovo 6 39 55N53 36E52 -2:27:28
Veljaminovo 6 39 55N12 37E52 -2:31:28
Vel'sk 6 41 61N05 42E05 -2:48:20
Vel't 6 41 68N03 49E55 -3:19:40
Vendičany 23 45 48N37 27E48 -1:51:12
Venev 6 39 54N21 38E16 -2:33:04
Vengerovka 23 45 48N43 38E24 -2:33:36
Vengerovo 2 23 55N41 76E45 -5:07:00
Ventspils 13 36 57N24 21E36 -1:26:24
Veprik 23 45 50N23 34E11 -2:16:44
Verba 23 44 50N17 25E37 -1:42:28
Verbilki 6 39 56N32 37E36 -2:30:24
Verbinskij 6 40 47N53 40E02 -2:40:08
Verbl'užka 23 45 48N23 32E54 -2:11:36
Verbovskij 6 40 55N32 42E00 -2:48:00
Verch'aja Irmen' 2 23 54N35 82E14 -5:28:56
Verchazovka 6 34 50N56 48E46 -3:15:04
Vercheje Talyzino 6 41 55N06 45E49 -3:03:16
Verchn'ačka 23 45 48N49 30E02 -2:00:08
Verchn'aja Amga 2 16 59N30 126E08 -8:24:32
Verchnaja Buzinovka 6 34 49N04 43E12 -2:52:48
Verchn'aja Čebula 2 21 56N02 87E36 -5:50:24
Verchn'aja Chava 6 41 51N50 39E56 -2:39:44
Verchn'aja Chila 2 16 52N06 115E54 -7:43:36
Verchn'aja Chortica 23 45 47N51 35E01 -2:20:04
Verchn'aja Čuginka 23 45 48N55 39E39 -2:38:36
Verchnaja Dobrinka 6 34 50N46 45E03 -3:00:12
Verchn'aja Gniluša 6 47 50N16 40E23 -2:41:32
Verchn'aja Grajvoronka 6 39 51N41 37E46 -2:31:04
Verchn'aja Inta 6 29 66N00 60E20 -4:01:20
Verchn'aja Irmen' 2 23 54N35 82E14 -5:28:56
Verchnaja Maza 6 34 52N58 47E56 -3:11:44
Verchn'aja Orl'anka 6 34 53N44 51E04 -3:24:16
Verchn'aja Pyšma 2 30 56N55 60E37 -4:02:28
Verchn'aja Salda 2 30 58N02 60E33 -4:02:12
Verchn'aja Serebr'akovka 6 47 47N21 42E14 -2:48:56
Verchn'aja Sin'ačicha 2 30 57N59 61E40 -4:06:40
Verchn'aja Sysert' 2 30 56N26 60E46 -4:03:04
Verchn'aja Tarka 2 23 56N37 77E30 -5:10:00
Verchnaja Tereška 6 34 52N54 47E24 -3:09:36
Verchn'aja Tišanka 6 41 51N19 40E32 -2:42:08
Verchn'aja Tojma 6 41 62N13 45E00 -3:00:00
Verchn'aja Troica 6 39 57N15 37E08 -2:28:32
Verchn'aja Tura 2 30 58N22 59E49 -3:59:16
Verchn'aja Zaimka 2 20 55N51 110E09 -7:20:36
Verchn'aja Zima 2 20 53N48 101E47 -6:47:08
Verchneaks'onovskij 6 34 48N21 42E38 -2:50:32
Verchne-Anikin 6 47 48N09 39E59 -2:39:56
Verchnebakanskij 6 47 44N52 37E39 -2:30:36
Verchneber'ozovskij 9 24 50N17 82E13 -5:28:52
Verchnebuzanskij 6 34 46N38 48E02 -3:12:08
Verchnecaricynskij 6 34 48N23 43E57 -2:55:48
Verchnedneprovsk 23 45 48N39 34E21 -2:17:24
Verchnedneprovskij 6 39 54N59 33E21 -2:13:24
Verchneduvannyj 23 45 48N20 39E48 -2:39:12
Verchnedvinsk 4 39 55N47 27E56 -1:51:44
Verchneimbatskoje 2 21 63N11 87E58 -5:51:52
Verchnejarkejev 6 30 55N27 54E19 -3:37:16
Verchnejarkejevo 6 30 55N27 54E19 -3:37:16
Verchneje 23 45 48N53 38E28 -2:33:52
Verchneje šachlovo 6 39 55N02 37E15 -2:29:00
Verchneje Sinevidnoje 23 44 49N06 23E34 -1:34:16
Verchnemakejevka 6 47 49N10 41E03 -2:44:12
Verchnesadovoje 23 45 44N42 33E42 -2:14:48
Verchnesjezžeje 6 34 52N44 51E15 -3:25:00
Verchnespasskoje 6 41 52N39 41E47 -2:47:08
Verchne-T'oploje 23 45 48N51 39E26 -2:37:44
Verchnetulomskij 6 9 68N38 31E45 -2:07:00
Verchneural'sk 2 30 53N53 59E13 -3:56:52
Verchneusinskoje 2 21 52N14 93E01 -6:12:04
Verchnevil'ujsk 2 16 63N27 120E18 -8:01:12
Verchnevolynskoje 24 24 40N43 68E51 -4:35:24
Verchnij Amyl 2 21 53N08 94E30 -6:18:00
Verchnij Avz'an 6 30 53N32 57E33 -3:50:12
Verchnij Balyklej 6 34 49N34 45E10 -3:00:40
Verchnij Baskunčak 6 34 48N14 46E44 -3:06:56
Verchnij Byk 6 47 50N43 41E14 -2:44:56
Verchnije Dvoriki 6 39 56N28 38E22 -2:33:28
Verchnije Kigi 6 30 55N25 58E37 -3:54:28
Verchnije Korobki 6 34 50N19 44E38 -2:58:32
Verchnije Lipki 6 34 49N38 43E51 -2:55:24
Verchnije Tatyšly 6 30 56N17 55E52 -3:43:28
Verchnij Ikorec 6 41 51N11 39E46 -2:39:04
Verchnij-Karačan 6 41 51N24 41E46 -2:47:04
Verchnij Krasnyj Pereval 2 11 46N33 134E37 -8:58:28
Verchnij Kužebar 2 21 53N22 93E15 -6:13:00
Verchnij Landech 6 40 56N51 42E36 -2:50:24
Verchnij Leb'ažinskij 6 34 46N45 47E50 -3:11:20
Verchnij Lomov 6 41 53N28 43E34 -2:54:16
Verchnij Lomovec 6 40 52N13 38E37 -2:34:28
Verchnij Mamon 6 47 50N10 40E23 -2:41:32
Verchnij Most 6 39 57N31 28E50 -1:55:20
Verchnij Nejvinskij 2 30 57N17 60E09 -4:00:36
Verchnij Petr'ak 2 23 57N29 77E30 -5:10:00
Verchnij Rogačik 23 45 47N14 34E21 -2:17:24
Verchnij šergol'džin 2 18 50N12 108E20 -7:13:20
Verchnij Tagil 2 30 57N22 59E56 -3:59:44
Verchnij Takermen' 6 41 55N39 52E43 -3:30:52
Verchnij Ufalej 2 30 56N04 60E14 -4:00:56
Verchnij Ul'chun 2 16 49N34 112E32 -7:30:08
Verchnij Uslon 6 41 55N47 48E57 -3:15:48
Verchnyje Nikul'asy 6 9 60N25 30E45 -2:03:00
Verchnyj Nagol'čik 23 45 48N05 39E06 -2:36:24
Verchojansk 2 11 67N35 133E27 -8:53:48
Verchol'ensk 2 20 54N06 105E35 -7:02:20
Verchopuja 6 41 61N34 41E31 -2:46:04
Verchošižemje 6 42 58N01 49E07 -3:16:28
Verchososna 6 40 50N44 38E14 -2:32:56
Verchoturje 2 30 58N52 60E48 -4:03:12
Verchoturovo 2 21 58N22 95E21 -6:21:24
Verchovažje 6 41 60N45 42E00 -2:48:00
Verchovcevo 23 45 48N29 34E14 -2:16:56
Verchovina 23 44 48N09 24E47 -1:39:08
Verchovino 6 41 59N33 43E19 -2:53:16
Verchovje 6 39 52N49 37E14 -2:28:56
Verchovl'an' 6 39 55N03 38E21 -2:33:24
Verchozim 6 41 52N56 46E23 -3:05:32
Verchubinka 9 24 50N29 82E26 -5:29:44
Verduga 6 9 58N46 29E12 -1:56:48
Vereb'jo 6 9 58N41 32E42 -2:10:48
Vereja 6 39 55N37 38E02 -2:32:08
Vereja 6 39 55N46 39E06 -2:36:24
Vereja 6 39 55N21 36E11 -2:24:44
Veremejki 4 39 53N46 31E15 -2:05:00
Vereščagino 2 21 64N14 87E37 -5:50:28
Vereščagino 6 30 58N05 54E40 -3:38:40
Veresoč' 23 44 51N19 31E46 -2:07:04
Veretje 6 39 54N08 36E17 -2:25:08
Vergulevka 23 45 48N24 38E32 -2:34:08
Verigino 6 39 56N42 38E08 -2:32:32
Verin Talin 1 34 40N23 43E53 -2:55:32
Veriora 5 35 58N00 27E21 -1:49:24
Verkhneudinsk → Ulan-Ude 2 20 51N50 107E37 -7:10:28
Verkhniy Ufaley → Verchnij Ufalej 2 30 56N04 60E14 -4:00:56
Verkhnyaya Salda → Verchn'aja Salda 2 30 58N02 60E33 -4:02:12
Verkhoyansk → Verchojansk 2 11 67N35 133E27 -8:53:48
Veršina Tei 2 21 53N20 89E36 -5:58:24
Veršino-Darasunskij 2 16 52N20 115E32 -7:42:08
Veršino-šachtaminskij 2 16 51N21 117E50 -7:51:20
Vert'ačij 6 34 48N57 43E53 -2:55:32
Vertijevka 23 44 51N10 31E51 -2:07:24
Vertkovo 6 39 56N07 36E25 -2:25:40
Vertlinskoje 6 39 56N14 36E58 -2:27:52
Veseja 4 39 53N04 27E41 -1:50:44
Veselinovo 23 45 47N21 31E14 -2:04:56
Veselovskoje 2 23 54N00 78E43 -5:14:52
Vešenskaja 6 47 49N38 41E43 -2:46:52
Vesjegonsk 6 9 58N40 37E16 -2:29:04
Veškajma 6 42 54N03 47E08 -3:08:32
Veškajma 6 42 54N04 47E02 -3:08:08
Veški 6 39 55N56 37E37 -2:30:28
Ves'olaja Gora 23 45 48N43 39E16 -2:37:04

Ves'olaja Rošča 9
24 53N47 76E22 -5:05:28
Ves'oloje 6 34 50N17 45E15 -3:01:00
Ves'oloje 23 45 47N01 34E55 -2:19:40
Ves'oloje 6 40 47N10 38E45 -2:35:00
Ves'oloje 9 24 43N19 77E06 -5:08:24
Ves'olo-Voznesenka 6
40 47N09 38E20 -2:33:20
Ves'olyj 6 40 47N20 39E18 -2:37:12
Ves'olyj 6 47 47N06 40E45 -2:43:00
Ves'olyje Terny 23
45 48N07 33E32 -2:14:08
Ves'olyj Jar 2
23 51N18 81E07 -5:24:28
Ves'olyj Jar 2
27 43N57 135E28 -9:01:52
Ves'olyj Podol 23
44 49N36 33E16 -2:13:04
Ves'olyj Podol 9
30 53N31 65E54 -4:23:36
Vetčin 4 39 52N27 28E10 -1:52:40
Vetju 6 41 62N57 50E44 -3:22:56
Vetka 4 39 52N33 31E10 -2:04:40
Vetl'anka 6 34 52N52 51E09 -3:24:36
Vetluga 6 41 57N51 45E47 -3:03:08
Vetlužskij 6 41 58N23 45E26 -3:01:44
Vetlužskij 6 41 57N11 45E07 -3:00:28
Vetoškino 6 42 57N18 49E44 -3:18:56
Vetrino 4 39 55N25 28E28 -1:53:52
Viatka → Kirov 6
42 58N38 49E42 -3:18:48
Viborg → Vyborg 6
9 60N42 28E45 -1:55:00
Vichorevka 2 20 56N12 101E09 -6:44:36
Vichuga → Vičuga 6
40 57N13 41E56 -2:47:44
Vičuga 6 40 57N13 41E56 -2:47:44
Vidim 2 20 56N29 103E09 -6:52:36
Vidlica 6 9 61N10 32E21 -2:09:24
Vidnoje 6 39 55N34 37E41 -2:30:44
Vidogošči 6 39 56N42 36E23 -2:25:32
Vidzy 4 39 55N24 26E38 -1:46:32
Viekšniai 14 37 56N16 22E31 -1:30:04
Viesīte 13 36 56N21 25E33 -1:42:12
Vievis 14 37 54N46 24E48 -1:39:12
Vigala 5 35 58N43 24E22 -1:37:28
Viipuri → Vyborg 6
9 60N42 28E45 -1:55:00
Viivikonna 5 35 59N19 27E42 -1:50:48
Viktor 6 29 66N09 58E07 -3:52:28
Viktorovka 9 30 52N51 62E32 -4:10:08
Vikulovo 2 30 56N49 70E37 -4:42:28
Vil'a 6 40 55N15 42E13 -2:48:52
Viļaka 13 36 57N11 27E41 -1:50:44
Viļāni 13 36 56N33 26E57 -1:47:48
Vil'ča 23 44 51N22 29E24 -1:57:36
Vilejka 4 39 54N30 26E53 -1:47:32
Vilenki 6 40 54N16 38E55 -2:35:40
Vil'gort 6 30 60N34 56E24 -3:45:36
Vil'gort 6 41 61N35 50E40 -3:22:40
Viljandi 5 35 58N22 25E36 -1:42:24
Vilkaviškis 14
37 54N39 23E02 -1:32:08
Vilkija 14 37 55N03 23E35 -1:34:20
Vilkovo 23 45 45N25 29E35 -1:58:20
Vilna → Vilnius 14
37 54N41 25E19 -1:41:16
Vilnius 14 37 54N41 25E19 -1:41:16
Vil'ujsk 2 16 63N45 121E35 -8:06:20
Vil'va 6 30 58N37 56E52 -3:47:28
Vin'kovcy 23 44 49N02 27E14 -1:48:56
Vinnica 23 44 49N14 28E29 -1:53:56
Vinniki 23 44 49N48 24E08 -1:36:32
Vinnitsa → Vinnica 23
44 49N14 28E29 -1:53:56
Vinogradov 23 44 48N09 23E02 -1:32:08
Vinogradovo 6 39 55N57 37E32 -2:30:08
Vinogradovo 6 39 55N25 38E32 -2:34:08
Vinogrobol' 6 39 51N51 36E26 -2:25:44
Viny 6 9 58N22 32E13 -2:08:52
Vinzili 2 30 56N58 65E46 -4:23:04
Virandozero 6 40 64N05 35E58 -2:23:52
Virbalis 14 37 54N38 22E49 -1:31:16
Virtsu 5 35 58N34 23E31 -1:34:04
Viru-Jaagupi 5
35 59N15 26E28 -1:45:52
Viru-Nigula 5 35 59N27 26E41 -1:46:44
Visim 2 30 57N39 59E30 -3:58:00
Viškil' 6 42 58N05 48E19 -3:13:16
Visl'ajevo 6 39 54N25 36E43 -2:26:52
Visn'aki 6 39 55N47 37E54 -2:31:36
Višn'akovo 6 39 55N45 38E10 -2:32:40
Višnevčik 23 44 49N02 26E28 -1:45:52
Visnevo 4 39 54N08 26E14 -1:44:56
Višnevoje 23 45 48N27 33E56 -2:15:44
Višnevoje 6 41 52N38 43E26 -2:53:44
Višn'ovec 23 44 49N54 25E45 -1:43:00
Višn'ovka 15 46 46N20 28E26 -1:53:44
Višn'ovka 9 24 50N49 72E12 -4:48:48
Vistina 6 9 59N47 28E29 -1:53:56
Vit'azevka 23 45 48N01 31E53 -2:07:32
Vitebsk 4 39 55N12 30E11 -2:00:44
Vitim 2 16 59N28 112E34 -7:30:16
Vitimskij 2 20 58N14 113E18 -7:33:12
Vizinga 6 41 61N05 50E04 -3:20:16
Vižnica 23 44 48N15 25E12 -1:40:48
Vjuny 2 23 55N31 82E55 -5:31:40
Vladikavkaz → Ordžonikidze 6
47 43N03 44E40 -2:58:40
Vladimir 6 39 56N10 40E25 -2:41:40
Vladimirec 23 44 51N25 26E08 -1:44:32
Vladimirovka 23
45 47N44 37E23 -2:29:32
Vladimirovka 9
30 53N28 64E02 -4:16:08
Vladimirovka 9
32 50N51 51E08 -3:24:32
Vladimirovka 23
45 47N32 32E55 -2:11:40
Vladimirskij Tupik 6
39 55N42 33E18 -2:13:12
Vladimirskoje 6
41 56N49 45E07 -3:00:28
Vladimir-Volynskij 23
44 50N51 24E20 -1:37:20
Vladivostok 2 27 43N10 131E56 -8:47:44
Vladyčnoje 6 41 58N49 39E29 -2:37:56
Vlaskovo 6 39 56N11 36E31 -2:26:04
Vlasovo 2 11 70N48 135E00 -9:00:00
Vlasovo 6 39 56N38 38E14 -2:32:56
Vlazoviči 6 39 53N01 32E18 -2:09:12
Vnukovo 6 39 55N38 37E16 -2:29:04
Vochrinka 6 39 55N24 38E18 -2:33:12
Vochtoga 6 41 58N47 41E07 -2:44:28
Vodnyj 6 29 63N32 53E18 -3:33:12
Vodosalma 6 9 64N29 30E44 -2:02:56
Vodovatovo 6 41 55N24 43E34 -2:54:16
Vodzimonje 6 42 56N49 51E38 -3:26:32
Vognema 6 40 59N59 38E10 -2:32:40
Võhma 5 35 58N38 25E33 -1:42:12
Voinka 23 45 45N52 33E59 -2:15:56
Vojevodskoje 2
21 52N47 85E35 -5:42:20
Vojkovo 23 45 48N00 38E02 -2:32:08
Vojkovo 23 45 45N31 33E52 -2:15:28
Vojkovskij 23 45 47N46 38E20 -2:33:20
Vojnica 6 9 65N12 30E15 -2:01:00
Vojnilov 23 44 49N08 24E30 -1:38:00
Voj-Vož 6 29 62N56 54E56 -3:39:44
Voj-Vož 6 29 64N20 55E03 -3:40:12
Volčanka 6 34 52N33 49E59 -3:19:56
Volčansk 2 30 59N56 60E04 -4:00:16
Volčansk 23 45 50N18 36E57 -2:27:48
Volčejarovka 23
45 48N50 38E22 -2:33:28
Volčenskij 6 47 48N14 40E07 -2:40:28
Volchov 6 9 59N55 32E20 -2:09:20
Volčicha 2 23 52N02 80E23 -5:21:32
Volčje 23 44 49N14 22E53 -1:31:32
Volčki 6 41 52N29 40E42 -2:42:48
Volga 6 40 57N57 38E24 -2:33:36
Volgino 6 9 58N27 33E52 -2:15:28
Volgodonsk 6 47 47N33 42E08 -2:48:32
Volgograd (Stalingrad) 6
34 48N44 44E25 -2:57:40
Volgorečensk 6
40 57N30 41E02 -2:44:08
Vol'ka 4 39 52N47 25E39 -1:42:36
Volkovincy 23 44 49N13 27E39 -1:50:36
Volkovo 6 39 55N46 36E15 -2:25:00
Volkovo 6 41 59N15 41E27 -2:45:48
Volkovskoje 6 39 54N49 37E13 -2:28:52
Volkovysk 4 39 53N10 24E28 -1:37:52
Vol'naja Gorka 6
9 58N43 30E51 -2:03:24
Vol'nogorsk 23
45 48N29 34E01 -2:16:04
Vol'noje 6 34 47N09 47E38 -3:10:32
Vol'noje 2 24 54N17 71E21 -4:45:24
Volnovacha 23 45 47N36 37E31 -2:30:04
Vol'nyj 6 47 45N55 45E14 -3:00:56
Voločajevka Vtoraja 2
11 48N34 134E34 -8:58:16
Voločanka 2 21 71N00 94E28 -6:17:52
Voločisk 23 44 49N32 26E11 -1:44:44
Volockaja 6 41 60N17 42E59 -2:51:56
Volodarka 2 21 52N43 83E38 -5:34:32
Volodarka 23 44 49N31 29E55 -1:59:40
Volodarsk 23 45 48N06 39E35 -2:38:20
Volodarsk 6 40 56N13 43E10 -2:52:40
Volodarskij 6 39 55N30 37E57 -2:31:48
Volodarskij 6 34 46N24 48E32 -3:14:08
Volodarskoje 9
24 53N18 68E08 -4:32:32
Volodarskoje 23
45 47N12 37E20 -2:29:20
Volodarsk-Volynskij 23
44 50N37 28E25 -1:53:40
Volodino 2 23 57N06 83E54 -5:35:36
Vologda 6 41 59N12 39E55 -2:39:40
Voloje 6 39 54N09 34E35 -2:18:20
Volokolamsk 6 39 56N02 35E57 -2:23:48
Volokonovka 6 39 50N29 37E51 -2:31:24
Volokovaja 6 41 66N28 48E10 -3:12:40
Volonga 6 41 67N07 47E41 -3:10:44
Volontirovka 15
46 46N26 29E37 -1:58:28
Vološino 6 40 47N31 39E40 -2:38:40
Vološino 6 47 48N55 39E56 -2:39:44
Vološka 6 40 61N20 40E06 -2:40:24
Vološno 6 9 58N29 28E29 -1:53:56
Volosoviči 4 39 54N46 28E50 -1:55:20
Volosovo 6 9 59N26 29E29 -1:57:56
Volosskaja Balaklejka 23
45 49N37 37E20 -2:29:20
Volot 6 39 57N56 30E42 -2:02:48
Volovec 23 44 48N43 23E11 -1:32:44
Volovo 6 39 53N35 38E02 -2:32:08
Volovo 6 39 52N03 37E53 -2:31:32
Vložin 4 39 54N05 26E32 -1:46:08
Vol'sk 6 34 52N02 47E23 -3:09:32
Vol'teva 6 41 64N30 44E12 -2:56:48
Volyncy 4 39 55N42 28E11 -1:52:44
Volyncy 6 41 57N48 45E28 -3:01:52
Volynka 23 44 51N37 32E26 -2:09:44
Volzhskiy → Volžskij 6
34 48N50 44E44 -2:58:56
Volžsk 6 41 55N53 48E21 -3:13:24
Volžskij 6 34 48N50 44E44 -2:58:56
Volžskij 6 34 53N27 50E07 -3:20:28
Vondanka 6 42 59N07 47E49 -3:11:16
Võnnu 5 35 58N17 27E05 -1:48:20
Vonozero 6 9 60N22 34E26 -2:17:44
Vorbjovo 2 20 57N23 102E18 -6:49:12
Vorga 6 39 53N45 32E45 -2:11:00
Vorkuta 6 29 67N27 63E58 -4:15:52
Vorn'any 4 39 54N44 26E01 -1:44:04
Vorobjevka 6 47 50N39 40E56 -2:43:44
Vorobjevo 2 23 56N08 76E32 -5:06:08
Vorobjevo 6 39 56N11 35E45 -2:23:00
Vorobji 6 39 55N09 36E48 -2:27:12
Vorobjovka 6 47 50N38 40E56 -2:43:44
Vorob'jovo 6 41 59N38 40E55 -2:43:40
Vorobjovo 23 45 45N20 33E15 -2:13:00
Vorochta 23 44 48N18 24E36 -1:38:24
Voron' 4 39 55N00 28E39 -1:54:36
Voroncovka 9 24 48N49 81E32 -5:26:08
Voroncovka 2 20 58N51 112E56 -7:31:44
Voroncovka 6 41 50N37 40E21 -2:41:24
Voroncovka 23 45 45N51 33E47 -2:15:08
Voroncovka 2 30 59N39 60E14 -4:00:56
Voroncovo 6 39 57N18 28E42 -1:54:48
Voroncovo 6 40 55N16 40E27 -2:41:48
Voronej → Voronež 6
41 51N40 39E10 -2:36:40
Voronež 23 44 51N46 33E28 -2:13:52
Voronež 6 41 51N40 39E10 -2:36:40
Voronezh → Voronež 6
41 51N40 39E10 -2:36:40
Voronino 6 39 56N24 36E52 -2:27:28
Voronjo 6 41 58N00 42E01 -2:48:04
Voronjo 6 9 68N27 35E21 -2:21:24
Voronki 6 39 55N48 37E16 -2:29:04
Voron'ki 23 44 50N14 33E02 -2:12:08
Voronkovo 23 45 47N43 29E08 -1:56:32
Voronok 6 39 52N23 32E40 -2:10:40
Voronovica 23 44 49N06 28E41 -1:54:44
Voronovkova Niva 6
39 57N04 29E16 -1:57:04
Voronovo 2 23 56N01 83E52 -5:35:28
Voronovo 4 39 54N09 25E19 -1:41:16
Voronovo 6 39 55N19 37E10 -2:28:40
Voropajevo 4 39 55N09 27E13 -1:48:52
Voroshilovsk → Kommunarsk 23
45 48N30 38E47 -2:35:08
Voroshilovsk → Stavropol' 6
47 45N02 41E59 -2:47:56
Voroshilov → Ussurijsk 2
27 43N48 131E59 -8:47:56
Vorošilovgrad (Lugansk) 23
45 48N34 39E20 -2:37:20
Vorotajevka 6 34 51N56 47E16 -3:09:04
Vorotynec 6 41 56N04 45E52 -3:03:28
Vorotynsk 6 39 54N25 36E05 -2:24:20
Vorožba 23 45 51N12 34E14 -2:16:56
Vorožejka 2 21 58N12 90E02 -6:00:08
Vorsma 6 40 55N59 43E16 -2:53:04
Võru 5 35 57N50 27E01 -1:48:04
Voruch 21 24 39N52 70E35 -4:42:20
Vorzel' 23 44 50N33 30E09 -2:00:36
Voschod 6 47 47N24 41E50 -2:47:20
Vosja 6 41 59N01 41E11 -2:44:44
Voskresenka 2 16 53N15 119E31 -7:58:04
Voskresenka 6 34 51N01 46E28 -3:05:52
Voskresenki 6 39 54N57 38E04 -2:32:16
Voskresenovskoje 6
9 59N43 30E47 -2:03:08
Voskresensk 6 39 55N19 38E42 -2:34:48
Voskresenskoje 23
45 47N02 32E09 -2:08:36
Voskresenskoje 6
40 53N12 38E43 -2:34:52
Voskresenskoje 6
40 58N54 38E36 -2:34:24
Voskresenskoje 6
40 59N26 37E56 -2:31:44
Voskresenskoje 6
40 57N49 37E40 -2:30:40
Voskresenskoje 6
39 54N07 37E07 -2:28:28
Voskresenskoje 6
39 56N20 38E29 -2:33:56
Voskresenskoje 6
30 53N08 56E10 -3:44:40
Voskresenskoje 6
41 56N51 45E26 -3:01:44
Voskresenskoje 6
34 51N51 46E56 -3:07:44
Vossijatskoje 23
45 47N41 32E07 -2:08:28
Vostočnaja Kambal'nica 6
41 68N18 46E00 -3:04:00
Vostočno-Kounradskij 9
24 47N02 75E07 -5:00:28
Vostočnyj 2 30 58N48 61E52 -4:07:28
Vostočnyj 19 8 53N29 143E03 -9:32:12
Vostočnyj 19 8 48N17 142E34 -9:30:16
Vostočnyj 6 39 55N47 37E49 -2:31:16
Vostr'akovo 6 39 55N23 37E49 -2:31:16
Vostrecovo 2 27 45N53 134E58 -8:59:52
Vostrovo 2 23 52N09 80E38 -5:22:32
Votkinsk 6 42 57N03 53E59 -3:35:56
Vot'pa 2 30 60N13 62E57 -4:11:48
Vožajol' 6 41 62N50 51E17 -3:25:08
Vožd' Proletariata 6
39 55N26 39E19 -2:37:16
Vozdviženka 23
45 47N46 36E05 -2:24:20
Vozdviženka 6 30 53N10 54E14 -3:36:56
Vozdviženskoje 6
39 56N12 38E04 -2:32:16
Vozdviženskoje 6
41 56N58 45E37 -3:02:28
Vozdviženskoje 6
47 45N50 43E40 -2:54:40

Vožega 6 41 60N29 40E12 -2:40:48
Vožgaly 6 42 58N09 50E11 -3:20:44
Vožgora 6 41 64N32 48E25 -3:13:40
Voznesenje 6 9 61N01 35E27 -2:21:48
Voznesenka 9 24 52N24 70E12 -4:40:48
Voznesenka 23 45 46N51 35E26 -2:21:44
Voznesenovka 6 47 46N16 44E21 -2:57:24
Voznesensk 23 45 47N34 31E20 -2:05:20
Voznesenskoje 6 47 45N49 43E25 -2:53:40
Voznesenskoje 6 41 54N54 42E46 -2:51:04
Vozroždenije 6 34 52N42 48E12 -3:12:48
Vozžajevka 2 14 50N44 128E41 -8:34:44
Vračevo 6 39 54N53 39E10 -2:36:40
Vrubovka 23 45 48N44 38E20 -2:33:20
Vrubovskij 23 45 48N26 39E07 -2:36:28
Vschody 6 39 54N42 34E06 -2:16:24
Vsevoložsk 6 9 60N01 30E40 -2:02:40
Vtoroje Potapovo 6 39 55N56 37E58 -2:31:52
Vtoryje Levyje Lamki 6 41 53N17 41E04 -2:44:16
Vuadil' 24 24 40N11 71E43 -4:46:52
Vulkanešty 15 46 45N41 28E24 -1:53:36
Vurnary 6 41 55N29 46E58 -3:07:52
Vvedenka 9 30 54N03 63E45 -4:15:00
Vvedenovka 2 15 51N19 128E12 -8:32:48
Vvedenskoje 6 39 55N42 36E54 -2:27:36
Vyatka → Kirov 6 42 58N38 49E42 -3:18:48
Vyaz'ma → V'az'ma 6 39 55N13 34E18 -2:17:12
Vyazniki → V'azniki 6 40 56N15 42E10 -2:48:40
Vyborg 6 9 60N42 28E45 -1:55:00
Vyčegodskij 6 41 61N16 46E48 -3:07:12
Vydrino 2 20 56N50 99E02 -6:36:08
Vydrino 2 20 51N27 104E39 -6:58:36
Vygoda 23 44 48N56 23E55 -1:35:40
Vygoniči 6 39 53N08 34E05 -2:16:20
Vygoniščí 4 39 52N37 25E55 -1:43:40
Vyjezdnoje 6 41 55N23 43E47 -2:55:08
Vyježžij Log 2 21 54N58 93E57 -6:15:48
Vyksa 6 40 55N18 42E11 -2:48:44
Vylkovo 2 23 53N05 81E26 -5:25:44
Vyntja 2 30 60N31 67E18 -4:29:12
Vypolzovo 6 39 57N53 33E42 -2:14:48
Vyrica 6 9 59N25 30E21 -2:01:24
Vyša 6 41 53N52 42E24 -2:49:36
Vyšelej 6 41 53N26 45E29 -3:01:56
Vyselki 6 47 45N35 39E38 -2:38:32
Vyšestebl ijevskaja 6 47 45N12 37E00 -2:28:00
Vyšgorodok 6 39 57N02 28E01 -1:52:04
Vyška 22 30 39N20 54E08 -3:36:32
Vyška 6 39 57N31 35E57 -2:23:48
Vyskod' 6 39 57N46 30E04 -2:00:16
Vyškov 6 39 52N29 31E41 -2:06:44
Vyšneol'šanoje 6 39 52N08 37E39 -2:30:36
Vyšnij Voločok 6 39 57N35 34E34 -2:18:16
Vysock 6 9 60N36 28E34 -1:54:16
Vysock 23 44 51N43 26E39 -1:46:36
Vysokaja Gora 6 41 55N56 49E19 -3:17:16
Vysokiniči 6 39 54N54 36E55 -2:27:40
Vysokogornyj 2 11 50N09 139E09 -9:16:36
Vysokogorsk 2 27 44N23 135E23 -9:01:32
Vysokoje 9 24 42N30 70E32 -4:42:08
Vysokoje 6 39 56N43 34E55 -2:19:40
Vysokoje 6 39 54N02 33E44 -2:14:56
Vysokoje 4 39 52N22 23E22 -1:33:28
Vysokoje 6 39 54N30 37E03 -2:28:12
Vysokoje 6 39 55N59 37E09 -2:28:36
Vysokopolje 23 45 47N29 33E32 -2:14:08
Vysokovsk 6 39 56N19 36E33 -2:26:12
Vysšaja Dubečn'a 23 44 50N44 30E40 -2:02:40
Vystupoviči 23 44 51N34 29E04 -1:56:16
Vytegra 6 40 61N00 36E24 -2:25:36
Vzmorje 19 8 47N51 142E31 -9:30:04
Vzvad 6 9 58N10 31E29 -2:05:56
Warnicken → Primorje 8 38 54N57 20E02 -1:20:08
Wilna → Vilnius 14 37 54N41 25E19 -1:41:16
Windau → Ventspils 13 36 57N24 21E36 -1:26:24
Wladiwostok → Vladivostok 2 27 43N10 131E56 -8:47:44
Wolgograd → Volgograd 6 34 48N44 44E25 -2:57:40
Woronesch → Voronež 6 41 51N40 39E10 -2:36:40
Yakutsk → Jakutsk 2 16 62N00 129E40 -8:38:40
Yalta → Jalta 23 45 44N30 34E10 -2:16:40
Yangi-Yul'→ Jangijul' 24 24 41N07 69E03 -4:36:12
Yegor'yevsk → Jegorjevsk 6 39 55N23 39E02 -2:36:08
Yekaterinburg → Sverdlovsk 2 30 56N51 60E36 -4:02:24
Yekaterinodar → Krasnodar 6 47 45N02 39E00 -2:36:00
Yekaterinoslav → Dnepropetrovsk 23 45 48N27 34E59 -2:19:56
Yelets → Jelec 6 40 52N37 38E30 -2:34:00
Yenakiyevo → Jenakijevo 23 45 48N14 38E13 -2:32:52
Yerevan → Jerevan 1 34 40N11 44E30 -2:58:00
Yessentuki → Jessentuki 6 47 44N03 42E51 -2:51:24
Yevpatoriya → Jevpatorija 23 45 45N12 33E22 -2:13:28
Yeysk → Jejsk 6 47 46N42 38E16 -2:33:04
Ylakiai 14 37 56N17 21E51 -1:27:24
Yndin 6 29 61N24 55E10 -3:40:40
Yntaly 9 24 48N58 70E55 -4:43:40
Ynykčanskij 2 11 60N15 137E43 -9:10:52
Yoshkar-Ola → Joškar-Ola 6 41 56N38 47E52 -3:11:28
Yurga → Jurga 2 21 55N42 84E51 -5:39:24
Yuryev → Tartu 5 35 58N23 26E43 -1:46:52
Yuzhno-Sakhalinsk → Južno-Sachalinsk 19 8 46N58 142E42 -9:30:48
Yuzovka → Doneck 23 45 48N00 37E48 -2:31:12
Zaajatskaja 9 30 52N53 61E35 -4:06:20
Zaamin 24 24 39N58 68E24 -4:33:36
Zabajkal'sk 2 16 49N38 117E19 -7:49:16
Žabasak 9 30 50N21 61E40 -4:06:40
Žabinka 4 39 52N12 24E01 -1:36:04
Zabituj 2 20 53N16 102E50 -6:51:20
Žabje 23 44 48N11 24E46 -1:39:04
Zabolotje 6 39 56N40 38E06 -2:32:24
Zabolotje 23 44 51N38 24E15 -1:37:00
Zabolotje 4 39 52N40 28E34 -1:54:16
Zabolotje 4 39 53N56 24E46 -1:39:04
Zabolotje 6 40 54N24 38E54 -2:35:36
Zabolotje 6 39 55N32 38E12 -2:32:48
Zabolotov 23 44 48N29 25E16 -1:41:04
Zaborje 4 39 55N55 29E19 -1:57:16
Zaborje 6 39 55N23 37E47 -2:31:08
Zaborje 6 39 53N06 31E42 -2:06:48
Zaborje 6 39 54N51 32E41 -2:10:44
Zaborje 6 39 55N24 31E34 -2:06:16
Zabory 6 39 55N58 32E17 -2:09:08
Zaburunje 9 32 46N44 50E09 -3:20:36
Zabyčanje 4 39 53N25 31E52 -2:07:28
Začepilovka 23 45 49N12 35E14 -2:20:56
Zacharkovo 6 39 55N47 37E19 -2:29:16
Zacharovo 6 39 56N31 36E44 -2:26:56
Zacharovo 6 40 54N22 39E17 -2:37:08
Zacharvan' 6 29 66N21 55E48 -3:43:12
Zachidnoje 23 44 51N29 31E15 -2:05:00
Zachmet 22 30 37N43 62E30 -4:10:00
Zachožje 6 9 59N44 30E51 -2:03:24
Zachrebetnoje 6 9 69N00 36E25 -2:25:40
Začistje 4 39 54N24 28E45 -1:55:00
Zadonsk 6 40 52N23 38E57 -2:35:48
Žadovo 23 44 52N03 32E39 -2:10:36
Zaerap 6 40 59N18 36E37 -2:26:28
Zafarabad 21 24 40N11 68E51 -4:35:24
Žagare 14 37 56N21 23E15 -1:33:00
Zagnitkov 23 45 48N03 28E54 -1:55:36
Zagor'anskij 6 39 55N55 37E55 -2:31:40
Zagorsk 6 39 56N18 38E08 -2:32:32
Zagorskij 19 8 47N19 142E28 -9:29:52
Zagryzovo 23 45 49N31 37E43 -2:30:52
Zagustaj 2 20 51N58 110E45 -7:23:00
Zaigrajevo 2 20 51N50 108E16 -7:13:04
Žailma 9 24 43N46 69E47 -4:39:08
Žailma 9 30 51N32 61E37 -4:06:28
Zaimka 2 19 58N41 100E40 -6:42:40
Zainsk 6 41 55N18 52E06 -3:28:24
Zajarsk 2 20 56N10 102E52 -6:51:28
Zajcevka 6 40 49N41 40E00 -2:40:00
Zajcevo 23 45 48N24 38E02 -2:32:08
Zajcevo 23 45 48N32 38E04 -2:32:16
Zajcevo 6 39 55N39 37E11 -2:28:44
Zajcevo 6 39 54N08 37E26 -2:29:44
Zajkany 15 46 47N59 27E22 -1:49:28
Zaj-Karataj 6 41 54N42 52E22 -3:29:28
Zajmo-Obryv 6 40 47N02 39E19 -2:37:16
Zajsan 9 24 47N28 84E55 -5:39:40
Žajsk 6 40 55N54 42E32 -2:50:08
Zakamensk 2 20 50N23 103E17 -6:53:08
Zakataly 3 34 41N38 46E39 -3:06:36
Zakatnyj 6 47 46N32 44E04 -2:56:16
Zakotnoje 23 45 48N54 37E58 -2:31:52
Zakotnoje 23 45 49N28 38E58 -2:35:52
Žaksy 9 24 51N55 67E20 -4:29:20
Žalanaš 9 24 51N55 65E02 -4:20:08
Zalari 2 20 53N34 102E32 -6:50:08
Zalegošč' 6 39 52N56 36E53 -2:27:32
Zaleščiki 23 44 48N38 25E44 -1:42:56
Zalesje 6 9 58N42 36E10 -2:24:40
Zalesje 8 38 54N51 21E32 -1:26:08
Zalesovo 2 21 54N00 84E47 -5:39:08
Zalizničnoje 23 45 47N53 33E29 -2:13:56
Založcy 23 44 49N48 25E24 -1:41:36
Žaltyr 9 24 51N40 69E50 -4:39:20
Zalučje 6 39 57N40 31E46 -2:07:04
Žamankak 9 32 48N56 48E45 -3:15:00
Zamarino 6 39 54N18 37E11 -2:28:44
Žambaj 9 32 47N11 50E34 -3:22:16
Zameženaja 6 41 65N02 51E50 -3:27:20
Zamglaj 23 44 51N49 31E13 -2:04:52
Zamjany 6 34 46N50 47E40 -3:10:40
Zamožnoje 23 45 47N19 37E49 -2:31:16
Zamševa 2 21 59N07 89E14 -5:56:56
Zamzor 2 20 55N21 98E35 -6:34:20
Žanadarja 9 30 44N45 64E40 -4:18:40
Žanašu 9 32 47N27 48E31 -3:14:04
Žanatalap 9 24 47N06 84E13 -5:36:52
Žanatalap 9 30 47N11 61E52 -4:07:28
Žanatarlyk 9 24 44N16 73E12 -4:52:48
Zanevka 6 9 59N56 30E31 -2:02:04
Zangelan 3 34 39N06 46E39 -3:06:36
Žangiztobe 9 24 49N16 81E18 -5:25:12
Žanterek 9 30 47N57 54E21 -3:37:24
Zaokskij 6 39 54N44 37E24 -2:29:36
Zaokskoje 6 39 54N44 37E24 -2:29:36
Zaostroviči 4 39 52N54 26E47 -1:47:08
Zaostrovje 6 9 60N38 33E16 -2:13:04
Zaostrovje 6 9 60N50 30E22 -2:01:28
Zaoz'orje 6 39 55N34 38E02 -2:32:08
Zaoz'orje 6 39 57N12 38E15 -2:33:00
Zaoz'ornyj 2 21 55N58 94E42 -6:18:48
Zapadnaja Dvina 6 39 56N16 32E04 -2:08:16
Zaplavnoje 6 34 48N43 45E01 -3:00:04
Zaplavnoje 6 34 52N58 51E44 -3:26:56
Zapl'usje 6 9 58N26 29E43 -1:58:52
Zapokrovskij 2 16 50N50 119E05 -7:56:20
Zapol'arnyj 6 29 67N30 63E42 -4:14:48
Zapol'arnyj 6 9 69N26 30E48 -2:03:12
Zapolje 6 9 58N23 29E41 -1:58:44
Zaporojie → Zaporožje 23 45 47N50 35E10 -2:20:40
Zaporozh'ye → Zaporožje 23 45 47N50 35E10 -2:20:40
Zaporožje 23 45 48N14 38E41 -2:34:44
Zaporožje 23 45 47N50 35E10 -2:20:40
Zaporožskaja 6 47 45N23 36E52 -2:27:28
Zapovednoje 8 38 55N04 21E24 -1:25:36
Zapovednyj 2 27 42N52 133E45 -8:55:00
Zaprudn'a 6 39 56N34 37E26 -2:29:44
Zarajsk 6 39 54N46 38E53 -2:35:32
Zarasai 14 37 55N44 26E15 -1:45:00
Žarbulak 9 24 46N05 82E04 -5:28:16
Zardaly 10 24 39N38 70E57 -4:43:48
Zardob 3 34 40N13 47E43 -3:10:52
Zarečensk 6 9 66N40 31E23 -2:05:32
Zarečje 6 39 56N52 33E50 -2:15:20
Zarečje 6 41 58N56 39E40 -2:38:40
Zarečje 6 39 55N41 37E23 -2:29:32
Zarečje 6 41 63N08 44E46 -2:59:04
Zarečnoje 23 44 51N48 26E06 -1:44:24
Zarečnyj 6 40 53N45 39E35 -2:38:20
Zarečnyj 6 40 57N28 42E18 -2:49:12
Zarečnyj 6 41 53N13 45E13 -3:00:52
Zarinskaja 2 21 53N43 84E58 -5:39:52
Žarkamys 9 30 47N56 56E26 -3:45:44
Žarkova 2 21 58N00 87E17 -5:49:08
Žarkovskij 6 39 55N52 32E17 -2:09:08
Žarma 9 24 48N48 80E50 -5:23:20
Žarsuat 9 24 46N27 80E48 -5:23:12
Zarubino 2 27 42N40 131E04 -8:44:16
Zarubino 6 9 58N44 33E28 -2:13:52
Žaryk 9 24 48N52 72E51 -4:51:24
Žaryn' 6 39 53N47 33E04 -2:12:16
Zasa 13 36 56N17 25E58 -1:43:52
Zašejek 6 9 67N25 32E28 -2:09:52
Žaškov 23 44 49N15 30E06 -2:00:24
Zaslavl' 4 39 54N01 27E15 -1:49:00
Zasosna 6 40 50N37 38E23 -2:33:32
Žastalap 9 32 49N11 50E24 -3:21:36
Zastava 6 41 59N12 46E46 -3:07:04
Zastavna 23 44 48N31 25E50 -1:43:20
Zasulje 4 39 53N34 26E50 -1:47:20
Zasulje 6 41 64N41 47E48 -3:11:12
Zatišje 23 45 47N19 29E51 -1:59:24
Z'at'kovo 2 23 53N36 80E20 -5:21:20
Zatobol'sk 9 30 53N12 63E43 -4:14:52
Zaton 2 21 53N18 83E49 -5:35:16
Zavalje 23 45 48N13 30E01 -2:00:04
Zaval'noje 6 41 52N02 39E51 -2:39:24
Zavetnoje 6 47 47N07 43E52 -2:55:28
Zavety Iljiča 2 11 49N02 140E17 -9:21:08
Zavidovka 6 40 54N16 38E49 -2:35:16
Zavidovo 6 39 56N32 36E32 -2:26:08
Zavitinsk 2 14 50N07 129E27 -8:37:48
Zavjalovo 2 21 54N30 82E27 -5:29:48
Zavjalovo 6 42 56N47 53E23 -3:33:32
Zavod Michajlovskij 6 30 56N32 54E17 -3:37:08
Zavodo-Petrovskij 2 30 56N50 66E45 -4:27:00
Zavodoukovsk 2 30 56N33 66E32 -4:26:08
Zavodouspenskoje 2 30 56N51 65E00 -4:20:00
Zavodskoj 2 21 53N04 84E25 -5:37:40
Zavodskoj 6 47 48N24 40E19 -2:41:16
Zavolžje 6 41 56N37 43E26 -2:53:44
Zavolžsk 6 40 57N30 42E10 -2:48:40
Zavolžskoje 6 34 46N59 47E37 -3:10:28
Zavoronežskoje 6 41 52N53 40E33 -2:42:12
Zavorovo 6 39 55N20 38E13 -2:32:52
Zban 9 31 48N53 63E58 -4:15:52
Zbaraž 23 44 49N39 25E47 -1:43:08
Zborov 23 44 49N39 25E08 -1:40:32
Ždanov 23 45 47N06 37E33 -2:30:12
Ždanova 2 21 58N37 88E58 -5:55:52
Ždanovo 23 45 48N14 34E44 -2:18:56
Ždanovsk 3 34 39N47 47E37 -3:10:28
Ždany 23 44 50N12 33E13 -2:12:52
Zdolbunov 23 44 50N31 26E15 -1:45:00
Zebl'aki 6 41 58N23 45E45 -3:03:00
Žegalovo 6 39 55N54 37E59 -2:31:56

Name	Reg.	Lat.	Long.	Time
žegalovo 6	41	54N43	43E25	-2:53:40
žegdoči 2	16	53N20	120E49	-8:03:16
Zeja 2	16	53N45	127E15	-8:29:00
žel'abino 6	39	55N52	37E11	-2:28:44
žel'abužskaja 6	39	54N36	36E32	-2:26:08
želannoje 23	45	48N13	37E25	-2:29:40
želdybino 6	39	56N14	39E02	-2:36:08
Zelencovo 6	41	59N52	44E59	-2:59:56
Zelenec 6	29	62N29	55E16	-3:41:04
Zelenga 6	34	46N11	48E37	-3:14:28
Zelenoborskij 6	9	66N49	32E18	-2:09:12
Zelenogorsk 6	9	60N12	29E42	-1:58:48
Zelenogradsk 8	38	54N58	20E29	-1:21:56
Zelenovka 23	45	46N59	36E14	-2:24:56
železinka 9	24	53N32	75E18	-5:01:12
železn'a 6	39	54N31	37E28	-2:29:52
železnodorožnyj 6	39	55N45	38E01	-2:32:04
železnodorožnyj 24	30	43N04	58E50	-3:55:20
železnodorožnyj 6	29	67N58	64E38	-4:18:32
železnodorožnyj 6	41	62N35	50E55	-3:23:40
železnodorožnyj 8	38	54N22	21E19	-1:25:16
železnogorsk 6	39	52N22	35E23	-2:21:32
železnogorsk-Ilimskij 2	20	56N37	104E08	-6:56:32
železnoje 23	45	48N19	37E51	-2:31:24
Zel'onaja Rošča 6	40	47N07	40E13	-2:40:52
Zel'onaja Rošča 6	41	54N29	52E02	-3:28:08
Zel'onaja Rošča 6	9	60N10	29E08	-1:56:32
Zel'onodol'sk 6	41	55N51	48E33	-3:14:12
Zel'onoje 23	45	47N43	33E12	-2:12:48
Zel'onoje Ozero 2	16	53N40	116E36	-7:46:24
Zel'onyj 9	32	51N10	50E41	-3:22:44
Zel'onyj 9	32	48N07	51E31	-3:26:04
Zel'onyj Bor 4	39	54N01	28E28	-1:53:52
želudok 4	39	53N36	24E59	-1:39:56
želva 14	37	55N13	25E06	-1:40:24
Zel'va 4	39	53N09	24E49	-1:39:16
žemaičiu Naumiestis 14	37	55N22	21E42	-1:26:48
žembejtinskij 9	30	50N30	52E39	-3:30:36
Zembin 4	39	54N22	28E13	-1:52:52
žemčug 2	20	51N41	102E24	-6:49:36
Zemcy 6	39	56N15	32E23	-2:09:32
Zemetčino 6	41	53N30	42E38	-2:50:32
Zeml'ansk 6	40	51N54	38E44	-2:34:56
Zemo-Kedi 7	33	41N26	46E24	-3:05:36
žemovo 6	39	54N45	38E49	-2:35:16
Zen'kov 23	45	50N13	34E22	-2:17:28
Zenzeli 6	34	45N56	47E03	-3:08:12
Zeravšan 21	24	39N11	68E40	-4:34:40
žerdevka 6	41	51N51	41E28	-2:45:52
Zerenda 9	24	52N55	69E10	-4:36:40
Zergenta 6	47	47N42	45E12	-3:00:48
Zernograd 6	47	46N50	40E19	-2:41:16
žernovka 6	39	54N49	37E46	-2:31:04
žešart 6	41	62N05	49E34	-3:18:16
Zestafoni 7	33	42N07	43E02	-2:52:08
žest'anka 6	34	51N36	49E24	-3:17:36
žestoki 6	39	56N19	36E22	-2:25:28
žestylevo 6	39	56N24	37E39	-2:30:36
žetybaj 9	32	48N51	48E04	-3:12:16
Zgurovka 23	44	50N31	31E46	-2:07:04
Zhdanov → ždanov 23	45	47N06	37E33	-2:30:12
Zhitomir → žitomir 23	44	50N16	28E40	-1:54:40
Zhukovskiy → žukovskij 6	39	55N35	38E08	-2:32:32
žičicy 6	39	55N07	31E17	-2:05:08
židačov 23	44	49N23	24E08	-1:36:32
Ziddi 21	24	39N03	68E48	-4:35:12
žideli 9	24	48N40	70E29	-4:41:56
Zid'ki 23	45	49N42	36E21	-2:25:24
žiežmariai 14	37	54N48	24E27	-1:37:48
žigajlovka 23	45	50N38	35E07	-2:20:28
žigalgan 9	30	44N36	50E46	-3:23:04
žigalovo 2	20	54N48	105E08	-7:00:32
žigansk 2	13	66N45	123E20	-8:13:20
Zigazinskij 6	30	53N50	57E20	-3:49:20
žigulevsk 6	34	53N25	49E27	-3:17:48
žiguli 6	34	53N22	49E19	-3:17:16
Zijančurino 6	30	51N33	56E55	-3:47:40
žijenkum 9	24	42N50	69E00	-4:36:00
Zikejevo 6	39	53N44	34E52	-2:19:28
Zilair 6	30	52N14	57E30	-3:50:00
žilaja Kosa 9	30	46N49	53E12	-3:32:48
žilaja Tambica 6	40	62N32	36E09	-2:24:36
žilino 8	38	54N54	21E56	-1:27:44
žiloj Bor 6	9	59N06	34E37	-2:18:28
žil'ovo 6	39	54N59	38E02	-2:32:08
Zilupe 13	36	56N23	28E07	-1:52:28
Zima 2	20	53N55	102E04	-6:48:16
Zimn'ackij 6	34	49N44	42E53	-2:51:32
Zimogorje 23	45	48N35	38E56	-2:35:44
Zimonino 6	39	53N47	31E52	-2:07:28
Zimovniki 6	47	47N08	42E28	-2:49:52
Zimovskoje 2	21	57N31	86E52	-5:47:28
Zin'kov 23	44	49N04	27E04	-1:48:16
žipkovšino 2	16	51N52	112E59	-7:31:56
žir'akovo 2	30	57N53	65E37	-4:22:28
žir'atino 6	39	53N15	33E44	-2:14:56
Zirgan 6	30	53N14	55E55	-3:43:40
žirnov 6	47	48N13	41E06	-2:44:24
žirnovsk 6	34	51N00	44E46	-2:59:04
žiroškino 6	39	55N22	38E03	-2:32:12
žiteli 6	41	65N04	47E26	-3:09:44
žitjevo 6	41	59N54	41E06	-2:44:24
žitkoviči 4	39	52N14	27E54	-1:51:36
žitkovo 6	9	60N42	29E20	-1:57:20
žitkur 6	34	48N57	46E17	-3:05:08
žitnoje 6	34	45N49	47E41	-3:10:44
žitomir 23	44	50N16	28E40	-1:54:40
žizdra 6	39	53N45	34E44	-2:18:56
žižica 6	39	56N17	31E21	-2:05:24
Zlatoust 2	30	55N10	59E40	-3:58:40
Zlatoustovsk 2	14	52N58	133E38	-8:54:32
žlobin 4	39	52N54	30E03	-2:00:12
Zlydnev 6	34	48N46	45E48	-3:03:12
Zlynka 6	39	52N25	31E44	-2:06:56
Zlynka 23	45	48N28	31E32	-2:06:08
Zmeinogorsk 2	23	51N10	82E13	-5:28:52
žmerinka 23	44	49N02	28E06	-1:52:24
Zmijov 23	45	49N40	36E19	-2:25:16
Zmijovka 6	39	52N40	36E23	-2:25:32
Zmi'ovka 6	39	52N40	36E23	-2:25:32
Znamenka 2	21	53N32	91E54	-6:07:36
Znamenka 9	24	50N05	79E32	-5:18:08
Znamenka 2	20	54N42	104E50	-6:59:20
Znamenka 6	41	52N24	41E26	-2:45:44
Znamenka 23	45	48N43	32E40	-2:10:40
Znamenka 6	39	54N54	34E34	-2:18:16
Znamenka 23	45	48N51	37E22	-2:29:28
Znamenka 2	23	53N10	79E30	-5:18:00
Znamenka Vtoraja 23	45	48N43	32E35	-2:10:20
Znamensk 8	38	54N37	21E13	-1:24:52
Znamenskoje 6	39	53N17	35E41	-2:22:44
Znamenskoje 6	39	55N45	37E09	-2:28:36
Znamenskoje 2	24	57N08	73E55	-4:55:40
Znamenskoje 6	41	53N19	42E57	-2:51:48
Znob'-Novgorodskoje 23	44	52N16	33E36	-2:14:24
Zod 3	34	40N12	45E52	-3:03:28
žodino 4	39	54N06	28E21	-1:53:24
žodiški 4	39	54N38	26E26	-1:45:44
Zol'noje 6	34	53N27	49E48	-3:19:12
Zoločov 23	44	49N47	24E52	-1:39:28
Zoločov 23	45	50N17	35E59	-2:23:56
Zolotaja Gora 2	16	54N16	126E36	-8:26:24
Zolotari 6	34	49N46	46E21	-3:05:24
Zolotar'ovka 6	41	53N04	45E20	-3:01:20
Zolotkovo 6	40	55N32	41E06	-2:44:24
Zolotniki 23	44	49N17	25E23	-1:41:32
Zolotoje 23	45	48N41	38E31	-2:34:04
Zolotoje 6	34	50N51	45E53	-3:03:32
Zolotoj Kolodec 23	45	48N32	37E15	-2:29:00
Zolotoj Potok 23	44	48N54	25E20	-1:41:20
Zolotonoša 23	44	49N40	32E02	-2:08:08
Zolotucha 6	34	47N49	46E44	-3:06:56
Zolotuchino 6	39	52N05	36E23	-2:25:32
ž'oltoje 23	45	48N39	39E07	-2:36:28
žoltoje 23	45	47N47	33E50	-2:15:20
žoltoje 23	45	48N30	33E31	-2:14:04
žoltyje Vody 23	45	48N21	33E31	-2:14:04
žolymbet 9	24	51N45	71E44	-4:46:56
Zorinsk 23	45	48N25	38E34	-2:34:16
Zoti 7	33	41N53	42E28	-2:49:52
Zovka 6	9	58N26	28E52	-1:55:28
žovnino 23	44	49N23	32E41	-2:10:44
žovten' 23	45	47N14	30E20	-2:01:20
žovten' 23	44	49N03	24E45	-1:39:00
žovtnevoje 23	45	49N39	34E09	-2:16:36
žovtnevoje 23	45	50N57	34E22	-2:17:28
žovtnevoje 23	44	51N15	28E07	-1:52:28
žovtnevoje 23	45	46N52	32E02	-2:08:08
Zozov 23	44	49N19	29E01	-1:56:04
žuanbalyk 9	30	45N04	61E51	-4:07:24
žuantobe 9	24	44N45	68E54	-4:35:36
Zubcov 6	39	56N10	34E34	-2:18:16
Zubkoviči 23	44	51N02	27E41	-1:50:44
Zubova Pol'ana 6	41	54N04	42E51	-2:51:24
Zubovka 6	42	54N16	51E06	-3:24:24
Zubovo 6	40	60N19	36E57	-2:27:48
Zubovo 6	41	56N52	44E08	-2:56:32
Zubovo 6	39	54N33	35E29	-2:21:56
Zugdeli 2	20	55N03	111E10	-7:24:40
Zugdidi 7	33	42N30	41E53	-2:47:32
Zugres 23	45	48N01	38E15	-2:33:00
Zui 6	39	57N06	31E37	-2:06:28
Zuja 23	45	45N03	34E20	-2:17:20
Zujevka 23	45	48N04	38E15	-2:33:00
Zujevka 6	42	58N25	51E10	-3:24:40
Z'ukajka 6	30	58N12	54E43	-3:38:52
žukopa 6	39	56N33	32E42	-2:10:48
žukovka 2	21	56N05	91E42	-6:06:48
žukovka 6	39	53N32	33E44	-2:14:56
žukovka 6	39	55N44	37E15	-2:29:00
žukovskaja 6	47	47N37	42E28	-2:49:52
žukovskij 6	39	55N35	38E08	-2:32:32
žukovskoje 6	47	46N05	41E21	-2:45:24
žulanka 2	23	54N22	80E36	-5:22:24
žuldyz 9	32	49N16	49E30	-3:18:00
žulebino 6	39	55N42	37E51	-2:31:24
Z'ul'z'a 2	16	52N33	116E13	-7:44:52
žumala 9	32	50N29	49E47	-3:19:08
žura 15	46	47N31	29E04	-1:56:16
Zura 6	42	57N37	53E26	-3:33:44
žuraviči 4	39	53N15	30E33	-2:02:12
žuraviči 23	44	50N59	25E43	-1:42:52
žuravl'ovka 9	24	51N57	69E56	-4:39:44
žuravl'ovka 23	45	48N13	38E58	-2:35:52
žurban 2	14	54N12	127E56	-8:31:44
žutovo Vtoroje 6	34	47N49	43E51	-2:55:24
Z'uzel'skij 2	30	56N29	60E07	-4:00:28
Z'uzino 6	39	55N40	38E07	-2:32:28
žuzymdyk 9	24	43N05	69E08	-4:36:32
Zv'agino 6	39	55N59	37E48	-2:31:12
Zvannoje 6	39	51N23	34E33	-2:18:12
Zvenigorod 6	39	55N44	36E51	-2:27:24
Zvenigorodka 23	44	49N04	30E57	-2:03:48
Zvenigovo 6	41	55N58	48E02	-3:12:08
Zverevo 6	47	48N01	40E07	-2:40:28
Zverinogolovskoje 2	30	54N28	64E50	-4:19:20
Zvezdnyj 2	20	56N49	106E27	-7:05:48
Zyr'anka 2	6	65N45	150E51	-10:03:24
Zyr'anovsk 9	24	49N43	84E20	-5:37:20
Zyr'anovskij 2	30	57N46	61E42	-4:06:48
Zyr'anskoje 2	21	56N50	86E38	-5:46:32
Zyryanovsk → Zyr'anovsk 9	24	49N43	84E20	-5:37:20

SPAIN ESPAGNE SPANIEN ESPAÑA

Time Table # 1

Date	Time	Offset
Before	1/Jan/1901	LMT
Begin Standard		0w00
1/Jan/1901	0:00	0:00
5/May/1917	23:00	-1:00
6/Oct/1917	24:00	0:00
15/Apr/1918	23:00	-1:00
6/Oct/1918	24:00	0:00
5/Apr/1919	23:00	-1:00
6/Oct/1919	24:00	0:00
16/Apr/1924	23:00	-1:00
4/Oct/1924	24:00	0:00
17/Apr/1926	23:00	-1:00
2/Oct/1926	24:00	0:00
9/Apr/1927	23:00	-1:00
1/Oct/1927	24:00	0:00
14/Apr/1928	23:00	-1:00
6/Oct/1928	24:00	0:00
20/Apr/1929	23:00	-1:00
6/Oct/1929	24:00	0:00
22/May/1937	23:00	-1:00
2/Oct/1937	24:00	0:00
22/Mar/1938	23:00	-1:00
1/Oct/1938	24:00	0:00
15/Apr/1939	23:00	-1:00
7/Oct/1939	24:00	0:00
16/Mar/1940	23:00	-1:00
2/May/1942	23:00	-2:00
1/Sep/1942	24:00	-1:00
17/Apr/1943	23:00	-2:00
3/Oct/1943	24:00	-1:00
15/Apr/1944	23:00	-2:00
10/Oct/1944	24:00	-1:00
14/Apr/1945	23:00	-2:00
30/Sep/1945	1:00	-1:00
13/Apr/1946	23:00	-2:00
Begin Standard		15E00
29/Sep/1946	24:00	-1:00
30/Apr/1949	23:00	-2:00
30/Sep/1949	1:00	-1:00
13/Apr/1974	23:00	-2:00
6/Oct/1974	1:00	-1:00
12/Apr/1975	23:00	-2:00
5/Oct/1975	1:00	-1:00
27/Mar/1976	23:00	-2:00
26/Sep/1976	1:00	-1:00
2/Apr/1977	23:00	-2:00
25/Sep/1977	1:00	-1:00
2/Apr/1978	2:00	-2:00
1/Oct/1978	1:00	-1:00
1/Apr/1979	2:00	-2:00
30/Sep/1979	3:00	-1:00
6/Apr/1980	2:00	-2:00
28/Sep/1980	3:00	-1:00
29/Mar/1981	2:00	-2:00
27/Sep/1981	3:00	-1:00
28/Mar/1982	2:00	-2:00
26/Sep/1982	3:00	-1:00
27/Mar/1983	2:00	-2:00
25/Sep/1983	3:00	-1:00
25/Mar/1984	2:00	-2:00
30/Sep/1984	3:00	-1:00
31/Mar/1985	2:00	-2:00
29/Sep/1985	3:00	-1:00
30/Mar/1986	2:00	-2:00
28/Sep/1986	3:00	-1:00
29/Mar/1987	2:00	-2:00
27/Sep/1987	3:00	-1:00
27/Mar/1988	2:00	-2:00
25/Sep/1988	3:00	-1:00
26/Mar/1989	2:00	-2:00
24/Sep/1989	3:00	-1:00
25/Mar/1990	2:00	-2:00
30/Sep/1990	3:00	-1:00
31/Mar/1991	2:00	-2:00
29/Sep/1991	3:00	-1:00
29/Mar/1992	2:00	-2:00
27/Sep/1992	3:00	-1:00
28/Mar/1993	2:00	-2:00
26/Sep/1993	3:00	-1:00
27/Mar/1994	2:00	-2:00
25/Sep/1994	3:00	-1:00
26/Mar/1995	2:00	-2:00
24/Sep/1995	3:00	-1:00
31/Mar/1996	2:00	-2:00
29/Sep/1996	3:00	-1:00
30/Mar/1997	2:00	-2:00
28/Sep/1997	3:00	-1:00
29/Mar/1998	2:00	-2:00
27/Sep/1998	3:00	-1:00
28/Mar/1999	2:00	-2:00
26/Sep/1999	3:00	-1:00
26/Mar/2000	2:00	-2:00
24/Sep/2000	3:00	-1:00

Time Table # 2

Date	Time	Offset
Before	1/Jan/1901	LMT
Begin Standard		0w00
1/Jan/1901	0:00	0:00
5/May/1917	23:00	-1:00
6/Oct/1917	24:00	0:00
15/Apr/1918	23:00	-1:00
6/Oct/1918	24:00	0:00
5/Apr/1919	23:00	-1:00
6/Oct/1919	24:00	0:00
16/Apr/1924	23:00	-1:00
4/Oct/1924	24:00	0:00
17/Apr/1926	23:00	-1:00
2/Oct/1926	24:00	0:00
9/Apr/1927	23:00	-1:00
1/Oct/1927	24:00	0:00
14/Apr/1928	23:00	-1:00
6/Oct/1928	24:00	0:00
20/Apr/1929	23:00	-1:00
6/Oct/1929	24:00	0:00
16/Jun/1937	23:00	-1:00
2/Oct/1937	24:00	0:00
2/Apr/1938	23:00	-1:00
30/Apr/1938	23:00	-2:00
2/Oct/1938	24:00	-1:00
28/Mar/1939	24:00	0:00
15/Apr/1939	23:00	-1:00
7/Oct/1939	24:00	0:00
16/Mar/1940	23:00	-1:00
2/May/1942	23:00	-2:00
1/Sep/1942	24:00	-1:00
17/Apr/1943	23:00	-2:00
3/Oct/1943	24:00	-1:00
15/Apr/1944	23:00	-2:00
10/Oct/1944	24:00	-1:00
14/Apr/1945	23:00	-2:00
30/Sep/1945	1:00	-1:00
13/Apr/1946	23:00	-2:00
Begin Standard		15E00
29/Sep/1946	24:00	-1:00
30/Apr/1949	23:00	-2:00
30/Sep/1949	1:00	-1:00
13/Apr/1974	23:00	TT#1

Time Table # 3

Date	Time	Offset
Before	1/Jan/1901	LMT
Begin Standard		0w00
1/Jan/1901	0:00	0:00
5/May/1917	23:00	-1:00
6/Oct/1917	24:00	0:00
15/Apr/1918	23:00	-1:00
6/Oct/1918	24:00	0:00
5/Apr/1919	23:00	-1:00
6/Oct/1919	24:00	0:00
16/Apr/1924	23:00	-1:00
4/Oct/1924	24:00	0:00
17/Apr/1926	23:00	-1:00
2/Oct/1926	24:00	0:00
9/Apr/1927	23:00	-1:00
1/Oct/1927	24:00	0:00
14/Apr/1928	23:00	-1:00
6/Oct/1928	24:00	0:00
20/Apr/1929	23:00	-1:00
6/Oct/1929	24:00	0:00
16/Jun/1937	23:00	-1:00
2/Oct/1937	24:00	0:00
22/Mar/1938	23:00	-1:00
1/Oct/1938	24:00	0:00
15/Apr/1939	23:00	-1:00
7/Oct/1939	24:00	0:00
16/Mar/1940	23:00	-1:00
2/May/1942	23:00	-2:00
1/Sep/1942	24:00	-1:00
17/Apr/1943	23:00	-2:00
3/Oct/1943	24:00	-1:00
15/Apr/1944	23:00	-2:00
10/Oct/1944	24:00	-1:00
14/Apr/1945	23:00	-2:00
30/Sep/1945	1:00	-1:00
13/Apr/1946	23:00	-2:00
Begin Standard		15E00
29/Sep/1946	24:00	-1:00
30/Apr/1949	23:00	-2:00
30/Sep/1949	1:00	-1:00
13/Apr/1974	23:00	TT#1

Time Table # 4

Date	Time	Offset
Before	1/Jan/1901	LMT
Begin Standard		0w00
1/Jan/1901	0:00	0:00
5/May/1917	23:00	-1:00
6/Oct/1917	24:00	0:00
15/Apr/1918	23:00	-1:00
6/Oct/1918	24:00	0:00
5/Apr/1919	23:00	-1:00
6/Oct/1919	24:00	0:00
16/Apr/1924	23:00	-1:00
4/Oct/1924	24:00	0:00
17/Apr/1926	23:00	-1:00
2/Oct/1926	24:00	0:00
9/Apr/1927	23:00	-1:00
1/Oct/1927	24:00	0:00
14/Apr/1928	23:00	-1:00
6/Oct/1928	24:00	0:00
20/Apr/1929	23:00	-1:00
6/Oct/1929	24:00	0:00
16/Jun/1937	23:00	-1:00
2/Oct/1937	24:00	0:00
2/Apr/1938	23:00	-1:00
30/Apr/1938	23:00	-2:00
17/Jun/1938	0:00	-1:00
1/Oct/1938	24:00	0:00
15/Apr/1939	23:00	-1:00
7/Oct/1939	24:00	0:00
16/Mar/1940	23:00	-1:00
2/May/1942	23:00	-2:00
1/Sep/1942	24:00	-1:00
17/Apr/1943	23:00	-2:00
3/Oct/1943	24:00	-1:00
15/Apr/1944	23:00	-2:00
10/Oct/1944	24:00	-1:00
14/Apr/1945	23:00	-2:00
30/Sep/1945	1:00	-1:00
13/Apr/1946	23:00	-2:00
Begin Standard		15E00
29/Sep/1946	24:00	-1:00
30/Apr/1949	23:00	-2:00
30/Sep/1949	1:00	-1:00
13/Apr/1974	23:00	TT#1

Time Table # 5

Date	Time	Offset
Before	1/Jan/1901	LMT
Begin Standard		0w00
1/Jan/1901	0:00	0:00
5/May/1917	23:00	-1:00
6/Oct/1917	24:00	0:00
15/Apr/1918	23:00	-1:00
6/Oct/1918	24:00	0:00
5/Apr/1919	23:00	-1:00
6/Oct/1919	24:00	0:00
16/Apr/1924	23:00	-1:00
4/Oct/1924	24:00	0:00
17/Apr/1926	23:00	-1:00
2/Oct/1926	24:00	0:00
9/Apr/1927	23:00	-1:00
1/Oct/1927	24:00	0:00
14/Apr/1928	23:00	-1:00
6/Oct/1928	24:00	0:00
20/Apr/1929	23:00	-1:00
6/Oct/1929	24:00	0:00
16/Jun/1937	23:00	-1:00
2/Oct/1937	24:00	0:00
2/Apr/1938	23:00	-1:00
30/Apr/1938	23:00	-2:00
2/Oct/1938	24:00	-1:00
26/Jan/1939	0:00	0:00
15/Apr/1939	23:00	-1:00
7/Oct/1939	24:00	0:00
16/Mar/1940	23:00	-1:00
2/May/1942	23:00	-2:00
1/Sep/1942	24:00	-1:00
17/Apr/1943	23:00	-2:00
3/Oct/1943	24:00	-1:00
15/Apr/1944	23:00	-2:00
10/Oct/1944	24:00	-1:00
14/Apr/1945	23:00	-2:00
30/Sep/1945	1:00	-1:00
13/Apr/1946	23:00	-2:00
Begin Standard		15E00
29/Sep/1946	24:00	-1:00
30/Apr/1949	23:00	-2:00
30/Sep/1949	1:00	-1:00
13/Apr/1974	23:00	TT#1

Time Table # 6

Date	Time	Offset
Before	1/Mar/1922	LMT
Begin Standard		15w00
1/Mar/1922	0:00	1:00
Begin Standard		0w00
30/Sep/1946	1:00	0:00
6/Apr/1980	0:00	-1:00
28/Sep/1980	1:00	0:00
29/Mar/1981	1:00	-1:00
27/Sep/1981	2:00	0:00
28/Mar/1982	1:00	-1:00
26/Sep/1982	2:00	0:00
27/Mar/1983	1:00	-1:00
25/Sep/1983	2:00	0:00
25/Mar/1984	1:00	-1:00
30/Sep/1984	2:00	0:00
31/Mar/1985	1:00	-1:00
29/Sep/1985	2:00	0:00
30/Mar/1986	1:00	-1:00
28/Sep/1986	2:00	0:00
29/Mar/1987	1:00	-1:00
27/Sep/1987	2:00	0:00
27/Mar/1988	1:00	-1:00
25/Sep/1988	2:00	0:00
26/Mar/1989	1:00	-1:00
24/Sep/1989	2:00	0:00
25/Mar/1990	1:00	-1:00
30/Sep/1990	2:00	0:00
31/Mar/1991	1:00	-1:00
29/Sep/1991	2:00	0:00
29/Mar/1992	1:00	-1:00
27/Sep/1992	2:00	0:00
28/Mar/1993	1:00	-1:00
26/Sep/1993	2:00	0:00
27/Mar/1994	1:00	-1:00
25/Sep/1994	2:00	0:00
26/Mar/1995	1:00	-1:00
24/Sep/1995	2:00	0:00
31/Mar/1996	1:00	-1:00
29/Sep/1996	2:00	0:00
30/Mar/1997	1:00	-1:00
28/Sep/1997	2:00	0:00
29/Mar/1998	1:00	-1:00
27/Sep/1998	2:00	0:00
28/Mar/1999	1:00	-1:00
26/Sep/1999	2:00	0:00
26/Mar/2000	1:00	-1:00
24/Sep/2000	2:00	0:00

Time Table # 7

Date	Time	Offset
Before	1/Jan/1901	LMT
Begin Standard		0w00
1/Jan/1901	0:00	0:00
6/May/1918	23:00	-1:00
7/Oct/1918	23:00	0:00
16/Apr/1924	23:00	-1:00
4/Oct/1924	23:00	0:00
17/Apr/1926	23:00	-1:00
2/Oct/1926	23:00	0:00
9/Apr/1927	23:00	-1:00
1/Oct/1927	23:00	0:00
14/Apr/1928	23:00	-1:00
6/Oct/1928	23:00	0:00
3/Jun/1967	12:00	-1:00
1/Oct/1967	0:00	0:00
24/Jun/1974	0:00	-1:00
1/Sep/1974	0:00	0:00
1/May/1976	0:00	-1:00
1/Aug/1976	0:00	0:00
1/May/1977	0:00	-1:00
28/Sep/1977	0:00	0:00
1/Jun/1978	0:00	-1:00
4/Aug/1978	0:00	0:00
Begin Standard		15E00
16/Mar/1984	0:00	-1:00
30/Mar/1986	2:00	TT#1

DIVISIONS

1. Mainland
2. Balearic Islands (Baleares)
3. Canary Islands
4. Spanish Morocco

Place	TT	Lat	Long	Offset
Abéjar 1	1	41N48	2w47	0:11:08
Abenójar 1	2	38N53	4w21	0:17:24
Adanero 1	1	40N56	4w36	0:18:24
Adra 1	2	36N44	3w01	0:12:04
Ágreda 1	1	41N51	1w56	0:07:44
Aguilar 1	1	37N31	4w39	0:18:36
Águilas 1	2	37N24	1w35	0:06:20
Ajalvir 1	2	40N32	3w29	0:13:56
Alagón 1	1	41N46	1w07	0:04:28
Alameda 1	1	37N12	4w39	0:18:36
Alarcón 1	2	39N33	2w05	0:08:20
Alayor 2	1	39N56	4E08	-0:16:32
Albacete 1	2	38N59	1w51	0:07:24
Alba de Tormes 1	1	40N49	5w31	0:22:04
Albaida 1	2	38N51	0w31	0:02:04
Albarracín 1	1	40N25	1w26	0:05:44
Alberique 1	2	39N07	0w31	0:02:04
Albocácer 1	4	40N21	0E02	-0:00:08
Albuñol 1	2	36N47	3w12	0:12:48
Alburquerque 1	1	39N13	7w00	0:28:00
Alcalá de Guadaira 1	1	37N20	5w50	0:23:20
Alcalá de Henares 1	2	40N29	3w22	0:13:28
Alcalá la Real 1	1	37N28	3w56	0:15:44
Alcanar 1	4	40N33	0E29	-0:01:56
Alcañices 1	1	41N42	6w21	0:25:24
Alcañiz 1	4	41N03	0w08	0:00:32
Alcántara 1	1	39N43	6w53	0:27:32
Alcantarilla 1	2	37N58	1w13	0:04:52
Alcaraz 1	2	38N40	2w29	0:09:56
Alcaudete 1	1	37N36	4w05	0:16:20
Alcázar de San Juan 1	2	39N24	3w12	0:12:48
Alcira 1	2	39N09	0w26	0:01:44
Alcobendas 1	2	40N32	3w38	0:14:32
Alcolea del Pinar 1	1	41N02	2w28	0:09:52
Alconchel 1	1	38N31	7w04	0:28:16
Alcorcón 1	2	40N21	3w50	0:15:20
Alcoy 1	2	38N42	0w28	0:01:52
Alcubierre 1	4	41N48	0w27	0:01:48
Alcudia 2	1	39N52	3E07	-0:12:28
Alella 1	5	41N30	2E18	-0:09:12
Alfambra 1	1	40N33	1w02	0:04:08
Alfaro 1	1	42N11	1w45	0:07:00
Alfarrás 1	5	41N49	0E35	-0:02:20
Algeciras 1	1	36N08	5w30	0:22:00
Algemesí 1	2	39N11	0w26	0:01:44
Alginet 1	2	39N16	0w28	0:01:52
Algorta 1	3	43N22	3w01	0:12:04
Alhama de Granada 1	1	37N00	3w59	0:15:56
Alhama de Murcia 1	2	37N51	1w25	0:05:40
Alhaurín el Grande 1	1	36N38	4w41	0:18:44
Alía 1	1	39N27	5w13	0:20:52
Aliaga 1	4	40N40	0w42	0:02:48
Alicante 1	2	38N21	0w29	0:01:56
Aliseda 1	1	39N26	6w41	0:26:44
Allariz 1	1	42N11	7w48	0:31:12
Almadén 1	2	38N46	4w50	0:19:20
Almadén de la Plata 1	1	37N52	6w04	0:24:16
Almagro 1	2	38N53	3w43	0:14:52
Almansa 1	2	38N52	1w05	0:04:20
Almanza 1	1	42N39	5w02	0:20:08
Almazán 1	1	41N29	2w32	0:10:08
Almazora 1	4	39N57	0w03	0:00:12
Almenar de Soria 1	1	41N41	2w12	0:08:48
Almendralejo 1	1	38N41	6w24	0:25:36
Almería 1	2	36N50	2w27	0:09:48
Almodóvar del Campo 1	2	38N43	4w10	0:16:40
Almonte 1	1	37N15	6w31	0:26:04
Almudébar 1	1	42N03	0w35	0:02:20
Almuñécar 1	1	36N43	3w41	0:14:44
Álora 1	1	36N48	4w42	0:18:48
Alosno 1	1	37N33	7w07	0:28:28
Alsasua 1	1	42N54	2w10	0:08:40
Amposta 1	4	40N43	0E35	-0:02:20
Amurrio 1	3	43N04	3w00	0:12:00
Anchuras 1	1	39N29	4w50	0:19:20
Andújar 1	2	38N03	4w04	0:16:16
Antequera 1	1	37N01	4w33	0:18:12
Aoíz 1	1	42N47	1w22	0:05:28
Aracena 1	1	37N53	6w33	0:26:12
Aranda de Duero 1	1	41N41	3w41	0:14:44
Aranjuez 1	1	40N02	3w36	0:14:24
Archidona 1	1	37N05	4w23	0:17:32
Arcos de la Frontera 1	1	36N45	5w48	0:23:12
Arenas de San Pedro 1	1	40N12	5w05	0:20:20
Arenys de Mar 1	5	41N35	2E33	-0:10:12
Arévalo 1	1	41N04	4w43	0:18:52
Argamasilla de Alba 1	2	39N07	3w06	0:12:24
Arganda 1	1	40N18	3w26	0:13:44
Argentona 1	5	41N33	2E24	-0:09:36
Arizgoiti 1	3	43N13	2w54	0:11:36
Arjona 1	2	37N56	4w03	0:16:12
Arnedo 1	1	42N13	2w06	0:08:24
Arrecife 3	6	28N57	13w32	0:54:08
Arroyo de la Luz 1	1	39N29	6w35	0:26:20

Artá 2 1 39N42 3E21 -0:13:24
Arzúa 1 1 42N56 8W09 0:32:36
Aspe 1 2 38N21 0W46 0:03:04
Astillero 1 3 43N24 3W49 0:15:16
Astorga 1 1 42N27 6W03 0:24:12
Astudillo 1 1 42N12 4W18 0:17:12
Ateca 1 1 41N20 1W47 0:07:08
Atienza 1 1 41N12 2W52 0:11:28
Ávila 1 1 40N39 4W42 0:18:48
Avilés 1 3 43N33 5W55 0:23:40
Ayamonte 1 1 37N13 7W24 0:29:36
Ayora 1 2 39N04 1W03 0:04:12
Azaila 1 4 41N17 0W29 0:01:56
Azpeitia 1 1 43N11 2W16 0:09:04
Azuaga 1 1 38N16 5W41 0:22:44
Badajoz 1 1 38N53 6W58 0:27:52
Badalona 1 5 41N27 2E15 -0:09:00
Baena 1 1 37N37 4W19 0:17:16
Baeza 1 2 37N59 3W28 0:13:52
Bailén 1 2 38N06 3W46 0:15:04
Balaguer 1 5 41N47 0E49 -0:03:16
Balazote 1 2 38N53 2W08 0:08:32
Balearen 2 1 39N30 3E00 -0:12:00
Baleares 2 1 39N30 3E00 -0:12:00
Baléares, Îles 2
1 39N30 3E00 -0:12:00
Baleares, Islas 2
1 39N30 3E00 -0:12:00
Balearic Islands 2
1 39N30 3E00 -0:12:00
Baltanás 1 1 41N56 4W15 0:17:00
Bande 1 1 42N02 7W58 0:31:52
Bañolas 1 5 42N07 2E46 -0:11:04
Baños de Cerrato 1
1 41N55 4W28 0:17:52
Barbadillo del Mercado 1
1 42N02 3W21 0:13:24
Barbastro 1 4 42N02 0E08 -0:00:32
Barbate de Franco 1
1 36N12 5W55 0:23:40
Barcarrota 1 1 38N31 6W51 0:27:24
Barcelona 1 5 41N23 2E11 -0:08:44
Barcelone → Barcelona 1
5 41N23 2E11 -0:08:44
Bargas 1 1 39N56 4W03 0:16:12
Barrax 1 2 39N03 2W12 0:08:48
Barriada Pomar Alto 1
5 41N29 2E14 -0:08:56
Basella 1 5 42N01 1E18 -0:05:12
Bayo 1 1 43N09 8W58 0:35:52
Bayona 1 1 42N07 8W51 0:35:24
Baza 1 2 37N29 2W46 0:11:04
Beasain 1 1 43N03 2W11 0:08:44
Beas de Segura 1
2 38N15 2W53 0:11:32
Becerreá 1 1 42N51 7W10 0:28:40
Béjar 1 1 40N23 5W46 0:23:04
Belalcázar 1 2 38N34 5W10 0:20:40
Belchite 1 4 41N18 0W45 0:03:00
Bélmez 1 1 38N16 5W12 0:20:48
Belmonte 1 1 43N17 6W14 0:24:56
Belmonte 1 2 39N34 2W42 0:10:48
Belorado 1 1 42N25 3W11 0:12:44
Belvís 1 2 40N33 3W33 0:14:12
Belvís de la Jara 1
1 39N45 4W57 0:19:48
Benabarre 1 4 42N07 0E29 -0:01:56
Benamejí 1 1 37N16 4W32 0:18:08
Benavente 1 1 42N00 5W41 0:22:44
Benicarló 1 4 40N25 0E26 -0:01:44
Benidorm 1 2 38N32 0W08 0:00:32
Benisa 1 2 38N34 0E03 -0:00:12
Berga 1 5 42N06 1E51 -0:07:24
Berja 1 2 36N51 2W57 0:11:48
Berlanga de Duero 1
1 41N28 2W51 0:11:24
Bermeo 1 3 43N26 2W43 0:10:52
Bermillo de Sayago 1
1 41N22 6W06 0:24:24
Betanzos 1 1 43N17 8W12 0:32:48
Bétera 1 2 39N35 0W27 0:01:48
Bilbao 1 3 43N15 2W58 0:11:52
Binéfar 1 4 41N51 0E18 -0:01:12
Blanes 1 5 41N41 2E48 -0:11:12
Boadilla del Monte 1
2 40N24 3W53 0:15:32
Boiro 1 1 42N39 8W54 0:35:36
Bolaños de Calatrava 1
2 38N54 3W40 0:14:40
Bollullos par del Condado 1
1 37N20 6W32 0:26:08
Boltaña 1 4 42N27 0E04 -0:00:16
Borja 1 1 41N50 1W32 0:06:08
Borjas Blancas 1
5 41N31 0E52 -0:03:28
Brenes 1 1 37N33 5W52 0:23:28
Brihuega 1 2 40N45 2W52 0:11:28
Briviesca 1 1 42N33 3W19 0:13:16
Broto 1 4 42N36 0W06 0:00:24
Brozas 1 1 39N37 6W46 0:27:04
Bujalance 1 1 37N54 4W22 0:17:28
Bujaraloz 1 4 41N30 0W09 0:00:36
Bullas 1 2 38N03 1W40 0:06:40
Buñol 1 2 39N25 0W47 0:03:08
Burgos 1 1 42N21 3W42 0:14:48
Burjasot 1 2 39N31 0W25 0:01:40
Burriana 1 4 39N53 0W05 0:00:20
Cabeza del Buey 1
2 38N43 5W13 0:20:52
Cabra 1 1 37N28 4W27 0:17:48
Cabras 3 6 28N28 13W51 0:55:24
Cabrera de Mataró 1
5 41N32 2E24 -0:09:36
Cabrils 1 5 41N32 2E22 -0:09:28
Cáceres 1 1 39N29 6W22 0:25:28

Cadaqués 1 5 42N17 3E17 -0:13:08
Cadix → Cádiz 1 1 36N32 6W18 0:25:12
Cádiz 1 1 36N32 6W18 0:25:12
Calahorra 1 1 42N18 1W58 0:07:52
Calamocha 1 1 40N55 1W18 0:05:12
Calañas 1 1 37N39 6W53 0:27:32
Calanda 1 4 40N56 0W14 0:00:56
Calatayud 1 1 41N21 1W38 0:06:32
Caldas de Reyes 1
1 42N36 8W38 0:34:32
Calella 1 5 41N37 2E40 -0:10:40
Callosa de Ensarriá 1
2 38N39 0W07 0:00:28
Callosa de Segura 1
2 38N08 0W52 0:03:28
Calpe 1 2 38N39 0E03 -0:00:12
Camariñas 1 1 43N07 9W10 0:36:40
Camas 1 1 37N24 6W02 0:24:08
Cambados 1 1 42N30 8W48 0:35:12
Cambrils 1 5 41N04 1E03 -0:04:12
Campanario 1 1 38N52 5W37 0:22:28
Campillo de Llerena 1
1 38N30 5W50 0:23:20
Campillos 1 1 37N03 4W51 0:19:24
Campo de Criptana 1
2 39N24 3W07 0:12:28
Canarias, Islas 3
6 28N00 15W30 1:02:00
Canary Islands 3
6 28N00 15W30 1:02:00
Cañaveras 1 2 40N22 2W24 0:09:36
Candás 1 3 43N35 5W46 0:23:04
Candeleda 1 1 40N09 5W14 0:20:56
Cañete 1 2 40N03 1W35 0:06:20
Canfranc 1 1 42N43 0W31 0:02:04
Cangas 1 1 42N16 8W47 0:35:08
Cangas de Narcea 1
3 43N11 6W33 0:26:12
Cangas de Onís 1
3 43N21 5W07 0:20:28
Canjáyar 1 2 37N00 2W44 0:10:56
Can Rull 1 5 41N33 2E05 -0:08:20
Cantalejo 1 1 41N15 3W55 0:15:40
Caravaca 1 2 38N06 1W51 0:07:24
Carballino 1 1 42N26 8W04 0:32:16
Carballo 1 1 43N13 8W41 0:34:44
Carboneras de Guadazaon 1
2 39N53 1W48 0:07:12
Carcagente 1 2 39N08 0W27 0:01:48
Carcastillo 1 1 42N23 1W26 0:05:44
Cardeña 1 2 38N13 4W19 0:17:16
Cariñena 1 1 41N20 1W13 0:04:52
Carlet 1 2 39N14 0W31 0:02:04
Carmona 1 1 37N28 5W38 0:22:32
Carrión de los Condes 1
1 42N20 4W36 0:18:24
Carrizo 1 1 42N35 5W50 0:23:20
Cartagena 1 2 37N36 0W59 0:03:56
Cartaya 1 1 37N17 7W09 0:28:36
Casa de la Torrecilla 1
2 40N19 3W37 0:14:28
Casar de Cáceres 1
1 39N34 6W25 0:25:40
Casas Ibáñez 1 2 39N17 1W28 0:05:52
Casasimarro 1 2 39N22 2W02 0:08:08
Casavieja 1 1 40N17 4W46 0:19:04
Caspe 1 4 41N14 0W02 0:00:08
Castellbisbal 1 5 41N29 1E59 -0:07:56
Castelldefels 1 5 41N17 1E59 -0:07:56
Castellón de la Plana 1
4 39N59 0W02 0:00:08
Castellote 1 4 40N48 0W19 0:01:16
Castro del Río 1
1 37N41 4W28 0:17:52
Castrojeriz 1 1 42N17 4W08 0:16:32
Castronuño 1 1 41N23 5W16 0:21:04
Castropol 1 1 43N32 7W02 0:28:08
Castro-Urdiales 1
3 43N23 3W13 0:12:52
Castuera 1 1 38N43 5W33 0:22:12
Catarroja 1 2 39N24 0W24 0:01:36
Cazalla de la Sierra 1
1 37N56 5W45 0:23:00
Cazorla 1 2 37N55 3W00 0:12:00
Cebreros 1 1 40N27 4W28 0:17:52
Cedeira 1 1 43N39 8W03 0:32:12
Cehegín 1 2 38N06 1W48 0:07:12
Celanova 1 1 42N09 7W58 0:31:52
Cervelló 1 5 41N24 1E57 -0:07:48
Cervera 1 5 41N40 1E17 -0:05:08
Cervera del Río Alhama 1
1 42N01 1W57 0:07:48
Cervera de Pisuerga 1
1 42N52 4W30 0:18:00
Cervo 1 1 43N40 7W25 0:29:40
Ceuta 4 7 35N53 5W19 0:21:16
Chantada 1 1 42N37 7W46 0:31:04
Chelva 1 2 39N45 0W59 0:03:56
Chiclana de la Frontera 1
1 36N25 6W08 0:24:32
Chinchón 1 2 40N08 3W25 0:13:40
Chincilla de Monte Aragón 1
2 38N55 1W43 0:06:52
Chiva 1 2 39N28 0W43 0:02:52
Ciempozuelos 1 1 40N10 3W37 0:14:28
Cieza 1 2 38N14 1W25 0:05:40
Cifuentes 1 2 40N47 2W37 0:10:28
Cilleruelo de Bezana 1
3 42N58 3W51 0:15:24
Cistierna 1 1 42N48 5W07 0:20:28
Ciudadela 2 1 40N02 3E50 -0:15:20
Ciudad Real 1 2 38N59 3W56 0:15:44
Ciudad Rodrigo 1
1 40N36 6W32 0:26:08
Cobeña 1 2 40N34 3W30 0:14:00

Cocentaina 1 2 38N45 0W26 0:01:44
Cofrentes 1 2 39N14 1W04 0:04:16
Cogolludo 1 1 40N57 3W05 0:12:20
Coín 1 1 36N40 4W45 0:19:00
Colmenar 1 1 36N54 4W20 0:17:20
Colmenar de Oreja 1
2 40N06 3W23 0:13:32
Colmenar Viejo 1
2 40N40 3W46 0:15:04
Columbretes, Islas
1 39N52 0E40 -0:02:40
Constantina 1 1 37N52 5W37 0:22:28
Consuegra 1 2 39N28 3W36 0:14:24
Corcubión 1 1 42N57 9W11 0:36:44
Córdoba 1 1 37N53 4W46 0:19:04
Cordova → Córdoba 1
1 37N53 4W46 0:19:04
Coria 1 1 39N59 6W32 0:26:08
Coria del Río 1 1 37N16 6W03 0:24:12
Cornellá 1 5 41N21 2E05 -0:08:20
Corral de Almaguer 1
2 39N46 3W11 0:12:44
Cortegana 1 1 37N55 6W49 0:27:16
Corunna → La Coruña 1
1 43N22 8W23 0:33:32
Coslada 1 2 40N26 3W34 0:14:16
Crevillente 1 2 38N15 0W48 0:03:12
Cuéllar 1 1 41N24 4W19 0:17:16
Cuenca 1 2 40N04 2W08 0:08:32
Cuevas del Almanzora 1
2 37N18 1W53 0:07:32
Cúllar de Baza 1
2 37N35 2W34 0:10:16
Cullera 1 2 39N10 0W15 0:01:00
Curtis 1 1 43N07 8W03 0:32:12
Daganzo de Arriba 1
2 40N33 3W27 0:13:48
Daimiel 1 2 39N04 3W37 0:14:28
Dalías 1 2 36N49 2W52 0:11:28
Daroca 1 1 41N07 1W25 0:05:40
Denia 1 2 38N51 0E07 -0:00:28
Dolores 1 2 38N08 0W46 0:03:04
Don Benito 1 1 38N57 5W52 0:23:28
Dos Hermanas 1 1 37N17 5W55 0:23:40
Dragonera, Isla 2
1 39N35 2E19 -0:09:16
Durango 1 3 43N10 2W37 0:10:28
Durón 1 2 40N38 2W43 0:10:52
Écija 1 1 37N32 5W05 0:20:20
Éibar 1 1 43N11 2W28 0:09:52
Ejea de los Caballeros 1
1 42N08 1W08 0:04:32
El Arahal 1 1 37N16 5W33 0:22:12
El Arrabal Torrelletas 1
5 41N21 1E57 -0:07:48
El Barco de Avila 1
1 40N21 5W31 0:22:04
El Barco de Valdeorras 1
1 42N25 6W59 0:27:56
El Bonillo 1 2 38N57 2W32 0:10:08
El Burgo de Osma 1
1 41N35 3W04 0:12:16
Elche 1 2 38N15 0W42 0:02:48
Elche de la Sierra 1
2 38N27 2W03 0:08:12
Elda 1 2 38N29 0W47 0:03:08
El Ferrol del Caudillo 1
1 43N29 8W14 0:32:56
El Grove 1 1 42N30 8W52 0:35:28
El Molinillo 1 2 39N28 4W13 0:16:52
El Negralejo 1 2 40N24 3W31 0:14:04
El Porcal 1 1 40N18 3W32 0:14:08
El Puente del Arzobispo 1
1 39N48 5W10 0:20:40
El Puerto de Santa María 1
1 36N36 6W13 0:24:52
Embid 1 1 40N58 1W43 0:06:52
Enguera 1 2 38N59 0W41 0:02:44
Épila 1 1 41N36 1W17 0:05:08
Escalona 1 1 40N10 4W24 0:17:36
Escorial → San Lorenzo de El Escorial 1
1 40N35 4W09 0:16:36
Espejo 1 1 37N41 4W33 0:18:12
Esplugas 1 5 41N22 2E05 -0:08:20
Estella 1 1 42N40 2W02 0:08:08
Estepa 1 1 37N18 4W54 0:19:36
Estepona 1 1 36N26 5W08 0:20:32
Falset 1 5 41N08 0E49 -0:03:16
Famadas 1 5 41N21 2E05 -0:08:20
Felanitx 2 1 39N28 3E08 -0:12:32
Fermoselle 1 1 41N19 6W23 0:25:32
Fernán-Núñez 1 1 37N40 4W43 0:18:52
Ferrol → El Ferrol del Caudillo 1
1 43N29 8W14 0:32:56
Figueras 1 5 42N16 2E58 -0:11:52
Fonsagrada 1 1 43N08 7W04 0:28:16
Formentera 2 1 38N42 1E28 -0:05:52
Fraga 1 4 41N31 0E21 -0:01:24
Frechilla 1 1 42N08 4W50 0:19:20
Fregenal de la Sierra 1
1 38N10 6W39 0:26:36
Fuencaliente 1 2 38N24 4W18 0:17:12
Fuenlabrada 1 1 40N17 3W48 0:15:12
Fuensalida 1 1 40N03 4W12 0:16:48
Fuente de Cantos 1
1 38N15 6W18 0:25:12
Fuente-obejuna 1
1 38N16 5W25 0:21:40
Fuentesaúco 1 1 41N14 5W30 0:22:00
Fuentes de Ebro 1
4 41N31 0W38 0:02:32
Gádor 1 2 36N57 2W29 0:09:56
Galaroza 1 1 37N55 6W42 0:26:48
Gallur 1 1 41N52 1W19 0:05:16
Gandesa 1 4 41N03 0E26 -0:01:44

Gandía 1 2 38N58 0W11 0:00:44
Garrovillas 1 1 39N43 6W33 0:26:12
Gaucín 1 1 36N31 5W19 0:21:16
Gavá 1 5 41N18 2E01 -0:08:04
Gérgal 1 2 37N07 2W33 0:10:12
Gerona 1 5 41N59 2E49 -0:11:16
Getafe 1 2 40N18 3W43 0:14:52
Gibraleón 1 1 37N23 6W58 0:27:52
Gijón 1 1 43N32 5W40 0:22:40
Ginzo de Limia 1
1 42N03 7W43 0:30:52
Gondomar 1 1 42N07 8W45 0:35:00
Grado 1 1 43N23 6W04 0:24:16
Granada 1 1 37N13 3W41 0:14:44
Granadella 1 4 41N21 0E40 -0:02:40
Grandas 1 1 43N13 6W52 0:27:28
Grañén 1 4 41N56 0W22 0:01:28
Granollers 1 5 41N37 2E18 -0:09:12
Grazalema 1 1 36N46 5W22 0:21:28
Guadalajara 1 2 40N38 3W10 0:12:40
Guadalcanal 1 1 38N06 5W49 0:23:16
Guadix 1 2 37N18 3W08 0:12:32
Guardo 1 1 42N47 4W50 0:19:20
Guareña 1 1 38N51 6W06 0:24:24
Guernica y Luno 1
3 43N19 2W41 0:10:44
Guijuelo 1 1 40N33 5W40 0:22:40
Guitiriz 1 1 43N11 7W54 0:31:36
Haro 1 1 42N35 2W51 0:11:24
Hellín 1 2 38N31 1W41 0:06:44
Herencia 1 2 39N21 3W22 0:13:28
Herrera del Duque 1
2 39N10 5W03 0:20:12
Herrera de Pisuerga 1
1 42N36 4W20 0:17:20
Hervás 1 1 40N16 5W51 0:23:24
Híjar 1 4 41N10 0W27 0:01:48
Hinojosa del Duque 1
2 38N30 5W09 0:20:36
Hospital de Orbigo 1
1 42N28 5W53 0:23:32
Hospitalet 1 5 41N22 2E08 -0:08:32
Hoyos 1 1 40N10 6W43 0:26:52
Huelma 1 2 37N39 3W27 0:13:48
Huelva 1 1 37N16 6W57 0:27:48
Huércal-Overa 1 2 37N23 1W57 0:07:48
Huesca 1 1 42N08 0W25 0:01:40
Huéscar 1 2 37N49 2W32 0:10:08
Huete 1 2 40N08 2W41 0:10:44
Húmera 1 2 40N26 3W47 0:15:08
Ibiza 2 1 38N54 1E26 -0:05:44
Ibiza Island 2 1 39N00 1E25 -0:05:40
Igualada 1 5 41N35 1E38 -0:06:32
Illescas 1 1 40N07 3W50 0:15:20
Inca 2 1 39N43 2E54 -0:11:36
Infiesto 1 3 43N21 5W22 0:21:28
Iniesta 1 2 39N26 1W45 0:07:00
Irún 1 1 43N21 1W47 0:07:08
Irurzun 1 1 42N55 1W50 0:07:20
Isaba 1 1 42N52 0W55 0:03:40
Isla Cristina 1 1 37N12 7W19 0:29:16
Isla Dragonera 2
1 39N35 2E19 -0:09:16
Isla Ibiza 2 1 39N00 1E25 -0:05:40
Islas Baleares 2
1 39N30 3E00 -0:12:00
Islas Columbretes
1 39N52 0E40 -0:02:40
Iznalloz 1 2 37N23 3W31 0:14:04
Jaca 1 1 42N34 0W33 0:02:12
Jadraque 1 1 40N55 2W55 0:11:40
Jaén 1 2 37N46 3W47 0:15:08
Jaraicejo 1 1 39N40 5W49 0:23:16
Jaraiz de la Vera 1
1 40N04 5W45 0:23:00
Jarandilla 1 1 40N08 5W39 0:22:36
Játiva 1 2 38N59 0W31 0:02:04
Jávea 1 2 38N47 0E10 -0:00:40
Jerez de la Frontera 1
1 36N41 6W08 0:24:32
Jerez de los Caballeros 1
1 38N19 6W46 0:27:04
Jijona 1 2 38N32 0W30 0:02:00
Jimena de la Frontera 1
1 36N26 5W27 0:21:48
Jódar 1 2 37N50 3W21 0:13:24
Jumilla 1 2 38N29 1W17 0:05:08
La Albuera 1 1 38N43 6W49 0:27:16
La Aldehuela 1 2 40N18 3W36 0:14:24
La Algaba 1 1 37N28 6W01 0:24:04
La Almarcha 1 2 39N41 2W22 0:09:28
La Almunia de Doña Godina 1
1 41N29 1W22 0:05:28
La Bañeza 1 1 42N18 5W54 0:23:36
La Bisbal 1 5 41N57 3E03 -0:12:12
La Campana 1 1 37N34 5W26 0:21:44
La Cañiza 1 1 42N13 8W16 0:33:04
La Carolina 1 2 38N15 3W37 0:14:28
La Coruña 1 1 43N22 8W23 0:33:32
La Creu 1 5 41N32 2E07 -0:08:28
La Estación 1 5 41N34 2E14 -0:08:56
La Estrada 1 1 42N41 8W29 0:33:56
La Floresta 1 5 41N27 2E04 -0:08:16
La Florida 1 5 41N31 2E12 -0:08:48
La Fregeneda 1 1 40N59 6W52 0:27:28
La Fuente de San Esteban 1
1 40N48 6W15 0:25:00
La Gallega 1 1 41N54 3W16 0:13:04
Lage 1 1 43N13 9W00 0:36:00
Laguardia 1 1 42N33 2W35 0:10:20
La Guardia 1 1 41N54 8W53 0:35:32
La Gudiña 1 1 42N04 7W08 0:28:32
La Laguna → San Cristóbal de la Lagun 3
6 28N29 16W19 1:05:16
Lalín 1 1 42N39 8W07 0:32:28

La Línea 1 1 36N10 5W19 0:21:16
La Llagosta 1 5 41N31 2E12 -0:08:48
La Marañosa 1 1 40N17 3W35 0:14:20
La Nava de Ricomalillo 1
1 39N39 4W59 0:19:56
Landete 1 2 39N54 1W22 0:05:28
Langreo → Sama (de Langreo) 1
3 43N18 5W41 0:22:44
La Orotava 3 6 28N23 16W31 1:06:04
La Palma 1 5 41N25 1E58 -0:07:52
La Palma del Condado 1
1 37N23 6W33 0:26:12
La Poveda 1 2 40N19 3W29 0:13:56
La Puebla 2 1 39N46 3E01 -0:12:04
La Puebla de Cazalla 1
1 37N14 5W19 0:21:16
La Puebla de Montalbán 1
1 39N52 4W21 0:17:24
Laracha 1 1 43N15 8W35 0:34:20
La Rambla 1 1 37N36 4W44 0:18:56
Laredo 1 3 43N24 3W25 0:13:40
La Robla 1 1 42N48 5W37 0:22:28
La Roca de la Sierra 1
1 39N07 6W41 0:26:44
La Roda 1 2 39N13 2W09 0:08:36
Las Cabezas de San Juan 1
1 36N59 5W56 0:23:44
La Solana 1 2 38N56 3W14 0:12:56
Las Palmas de Gran Canaria 3
6 28N06 15W24 1:01:36
Las Rozas de Madrid 1
2 40N29 3W52 0:15:28
La Unión 1 2 37N37 0W52 0:03:28
La Vecilla de Curueño 1
1 42N51 5W24 0:21:36
Lebrija 1 1 36N55 6W04 0:24:16
Ledesma 1 1 41N05 6W00 0:24:00
Leganés 1 2 40N19 3W45 0:15:00
León 1 1 42N36 5W34 0:22:16
Lepe 1 1 37N15 7W12 0:28:48
Lequeitio 1 3 43N22 2W30 0:10:00
Lérida 1 5 41N37 0E37 -0:02:28
Lerma 1 1 42N02 3W45 0:15:00
Les Fonts 1 5 41N32 2E02 -0:08:08
Lillo 1 2 39N43 3W18 0:13:12
Linares 1 2 38N05 3W38 0:14:32
Liria 1 2 39N38 0W36 0:02:24
Llanes 1 3 43N25 4W45 0:19:00
Llansá 1 5 42N22 3E09 -0:12:36
Llerena 1 1 38N14 6W01 0:24:04
Llivia 1 5 42N28 1E59 -0:07:56
Lluchmayor 2 1 39N29 2E54 -0:11:36
Lodosa 1 1 42N25 2W05 0:08:20
Logroño 1 1 42N28 2W27 0:09:48
Logrosán 1 1 39N20 5W29 0:21:56
Loja 1 1 37N10 4W09 0:16:36
Lora del Río 1 1 37N39 5W32 0:22:08
Lorca 1 2 37N40 1W42 0:06:48
Los Llanos (de Aridane) 3
6 28N39 17W54 1:11:36
Los Navalmorales 1
1 39N43 4W38 0:18:32
Los Palacios y Villafranca 1
1 37N10 5W56 0:23:44
Los Santos de Maimona 1
1 38N27 6W23 0:25:32
Los Yébenes 1 2 39N34 3W53 0:15:32
Lozoyuela 1 1 40N55 3W37 0:14:28
Luarca 1 1 43N32 6W32 0:26:08
Lucena 1 1 37N24 4W29 0:17:56
Lucena del Cid 1
4 40N08 0W17 0:01:08
Lugo 1 1 43N00 7W34 0:30:16
Lumbrales 1 1 40N56 6W43 0:26:52
Luque 1 1 37N33 4W16 0:17:04
Madrid 1 2 40N24 3W41 0:14:44
Madridejos 1 2 39N28 3W32 0:14:08
Madrigalejo 1 1 39N09 5W37 0:22:28
Madroñera 1 1 39N26 5W46 0:23:04
Maestu 1 1 42N44 2W27 0:09:48
Mahón 2 1 39N53 4E15 -0:17:00
Mahora 1 2 39N13 1W44 0:06:56
Majadahonda 1 2 40N29 3W52 0:15:28
Majorca 2 1 39N30 3E00 -0:12:00
Málaga 1 1 36N43 4W25 0:17:40
Malagón 1 2 39N10 3W51 0:15:24
Mallorca 2 1 39N30 3E00 -0:12:00
Mallorquinas 1 5 41N28 2E16 -0:09:04
Malpartida de Plasencia 1
1 39N59 6W02 0:24:08
Manacor 2 1 39N34 3E12 -0:12:48
Mancha Real 1 2 37N47 3W37 0:14:28
Manlléu 1 5 42N00 2E17 -0:09:08
Manresa 1 5 41N44 1E50 -0:07:20
Manzanares 1 2 39N00 3W22 0:13:28
Maqueda 1 1 40N04 4W22 0:17:28
Maranchón 1 1 41N03 2W12 0:08:48
Marbella 1 1 36N31 4W53 0:19:32
Marchena 1 1 37N20 5W24 0:21:36
Marín 1 1 42N23 8W42 0:34:48
Marquina-Jemein 1
1 43N16 2W30 0:10:00
Martorell 1 5 41N28 1E56 -0:07:44
Martorellas 1 5 41N32 2E14 -0:08:56
Martos 1 1 37N43 3W58 0:15:52
Masnou 1 5 41N29 2E19 -0:09:16
Maspalomas 3 6 27N45 15W34 1:02:16
Matabuena 1 1 41N10 3W40 0:14:40
Mataró 1 5 41N32 2E27 -0:09:48
Mazarrón 1 2 37N36 1W19 0:05:16
Medinaceli 1 1 41N10 2W26 0:09:44
Medina del Campo 1
1 41N18 4W55 0:19:40
Medina de Ríoseco 1
1 41N53 5W02 0:20:08

Medina-Sidonia 1
1 36N27 5W55 0:23:40
Mejorada del Campo 1
2 40N24 3W29 0:13:56
Melilla 4 7 35N19 2W58 0:11:52
Mellid 1 1 42N55 8W00 0:32:00
Menorca 2 1 40N00 4E00 -0:16:00
Mercader y Millás 1
5 41N21 2E05 -0:08:20
Mérida 1 1 38N55 6W20 0:25:20
Miajadas 1 1 39N09 5W54 0:23:36
Mieres 1 1 43N15 5W46 0:23:04
Minas de Ríotinto 1
1 37N42 6W35 0:26:20
Minglanilla 1 2 39N32 1W36 0:06:24
Mingorría 1 1 40N45 4W40 0:18:40
Minorca 2 1 40N00 4E00 -0:16:00
Miranda de Ebro 1
1 42N41 2W57 0:11:48
Moguer 1 1 37N16 6W50 0:27:20
Mojácar 1 2 37N08 1W51 0:07:24
Molina de Aragón 1
1 40N51 1W53 0:07:32
Molina de Segura 1
2 38N03 1W12 0:04:48
Molins de Rey 1 5 41N25 2E01 -0:08:04
Mollet 1 5 41N33 2E13 -0:08:52
Mombuey 1 1 42N02 6W20 0:25:20
Moncada 1 5 41N29 2E11 -0:08:44
Mondoñedo 1 1 43N26 7W22 0:29:28
Monesterio 1 1 38N05 6W16 0:25:04
Monforte de Lemos 1
1 42N31 7W30 0:30:00
Mongat 1 5 41N28 2E17 -0:09:08
Monóvar 1 2 38N26 0W50 0:03:20
Monreal 1 1 42N42 1W30 0:06:00
Monreal del Campo 1
1 40N47 1W21 0:05:24
Montalbán 1 4 40N50 0W48 0:03:12
Montánchez 1 1 39N13 6W09 0:24:36
Montblanch 1 5 41N22 1E10 -0:04:40
Montefrío 1 1 37N19 4W01 0:16:04
Montejicar 1 2 37N34 3W30 0:14:00
Montellano 1 1 37N00 5W34 0:22:16
Montflorit 1 5 41N29 2E08 -0:08:32
Montijo 1 1 38N55 6W37 0:26:28
Montilla 1 1 37N35 4W38 0:18:32
Montmeló 1 5 41N33 2E15 -0:09:00
Montornés del Vallés 1
5 41N33 2E16 -0:09:04
Montoro 1 2 38N01 4W23 0:17:32
Montuenga 1 1 41N03 4W37 0:18:28
Monzón 1 4 41N55 0E12 -0:00:48
Mora 1 2 39N41 3W46 0:15:04
Mora de Rubielos 1
4 40N15 0W45 0:03:00
Moral de Calatrava 1
2 38N50 3W35 0:14:20
Morasverdes 1 1 40N36 6W16 0:25:04
Moratalla 1 2 38N12 1W53 0:07:32
Morella 1 4 40N37 0W06 0:00:24
Morón de Almazán 1
1 41N25 2W25 0:09:40
Morón de la Frontera 1
1 37N08 5W27 0:21:48
Móstoles 1 2 40N19 3W51 0:15:24
Mota del Cuervo 1
2 39N30 2W52 0:11:28
Mota del Marqués 1
1 41N38 5W10 0:20:40
Motilla del Palancar 1
2 39N34 1W53 0:07:32
Motril 1 1 36N45 3W31 0:14:04
Mula 1 2 38N03 1W30 0:06:00
Munera 1 2 39N02 2W28 0:09:52
Muniesa 1 4 41N02 0W48 0:03:12
Murcia 1 2 37N59 1W07 0:04:28
Murguía 1 1 42N57 2W49 0:11:16
Murias de Paredes 1
3 42N51 6W11 0:24:44
Muros 1 1 42N47 9W02 0:36:08
Nadela 1 1 42N58 7W30 0:30:00
Nájera 1 1 42N25 2W44 0:10:56
Narón 1 1 43N32 8W10 0:32:40
Nava del Rey 1 1 41N20 5W05 0:20:20
Navahermosa 1 1 39N38 4W28 0:17:52
Navalcarnero 1 1 40N18 4W00 0:16:00
Navalmoral de la Mata 1
1 39N54 5W32 0:22:08
Navalvillar de Pela 1
1 39N06 5W28 0:21:52
Navia 1 1 43N32 6W43 0:26:52
Negreira 1 1 42N54 8W44 0:34:56
Nerja 1 1 36N44 3W52 0:15:28
Nerva 1 1 37N42 6W32 0:26:08
Níjar 1 2 36N58 2W12 0:08:48
Novelda 1 2 38N23 0W46 0:03:04
Noya 1 1 42N47 8W53 0:35:32
Nules 1 4 39N51 0W09 0:00:36
Ocaña 1 2 39N56 3W31 0:14:04
Olite 1 1 42N29 1W39 0:06:36
Oliva 1 2 38N55 0W07 0:00:28
Oliva de la Frontera 1
1 38N16 6W55 0:27:40
Olivenza 1 1 38N41 7W06 0:28:24
Olmedillo de Roa 1
1 41N47 3W56 0:15:44
Olmedo 1 1 41N23 4W41 0:18:44
Olot 1 5 42N11 2E29 -0:09:56
Olvera 1 1 36N56 5W16 0:21:04
Onda 1 4 39N58 0W15 0:01:00
Onteniente 1 2 38N49 0W37 0:02:28
Orcera 1 2 38N19 2W39 0:10:36
Ordenes 1 1 43N04 8W24 0:33:36
Orense 1 1 42N20 7W51 0:31:24

Place	Zone	Latitude	Longitude	Time
Orgaz 1	2	39N39	3w54	0:15:36
Orihuela 1	2	38N05	0w57	0:03:48
Orjiva 1	1	36N54	3w25	0:13:40
Orotava 3	6	28N25	16w32	1:06:08
Orrius 1	5	41N33	2E21	-0:09:24
Ortigueira 1	1	43N41	7w51	0:31:24
Osorno 1	1	42N24	4w22	0:17:28
Osuna 1	1	37N14	5w07	0:20:28
Oviedo 1	1	43N22	5w50	0:23:20
Padrón 1	1	42N44	8w40	0:34:40
Palamós 1	5	41N51	3E08	-0:12:32
Palanquinos 1	1	42N27	5w31	0:22:04
Palas del Rey 1	1	42N52	7w52	0:31:28
Palencia 1	1	42N01	4w32	0:18:08
Pallejá 1	5	41N25	2E00	-0:08:00
Palma del Río 1	1	37N42	5w17	0:21:08
Palma (de Mallorca) 2	1	39N34	2E39	-0:10:36
Pampeluna → Pamplona 1	1	42N49	1w38	0:06:32
Pamplona 1	1	42N49	1w38	0:06:32
Papiol 1	5	41N26	2E01	-0:08:04
Paracuellos de Jarama 1	2	40N30	3w32	0:14:08
Paradas 1	1	37N18	5w30	0:22:00
Paredes de Nava 1	1	42N09	4w41	0:18:44
Pastrana 1	2	40N25	2w55	0:11:40
Paterna 1	2	39N30	0w26	0:01:44
Pedro Muñoz 1	2	39N24	2w58	0:11:52
Pego 1	2	38N51	0w07	0:00:28
Peñafiel 1	1	41N36	4w07	0:16:28
Peñaranda de Bracamonte 1	1	40N54	5w12	0:20:48
Peñarroya-Pueblonuevo 1	1	38N18	5w16	0:21:04
Peñíscola 1	4	40N21	0E25	-0:01:40
Perales de Alfambra 1	1	40N38	1w00	0:04:00
Perales del Río 1	2	40N19	3w38	0:14:32
Piedrabuena 1	2	39N02	4w10	0:16:40
Piedrahita 1	1	40N28	5w19	0:21:16
Pina 1	4	41N29	0w32	0:02:08
Pinos-Puente 1	1	37N15	3w45	0:15:00
Plasencia 1	1	40N02	6w05	0:24:20
Pola de Laviana 1	3	43N15	5w34	0:22:16
Pola de Lena 1	3	43N10	5w49	0:23:16
Pola de Siero 1	3	43N23	5w40	0:22:40
Polinyá 1	5	41N33	2E10	-0:08:40
Polvoranca 1	2	40N19	3w48	0:15:12
Ponferrada 1	1	42N33	6w35	0:26:20
Pons 1	5	41N55	1E12	-0:04:48
Pont de Suert 1	4	42N24	0E45	-0:03:00
Pontevedra 1	1	42N26	8w38	0:34:32
Porcuna 1	1	37N52	4w11	0:16:44
Portugalete 1	3	43N19	3w01	0:12:04
Porzuna 1	2	39N09	4w09	0:16:36
Posadas 1	1	37N48	5w06	0:20:24
Potes 1	3	43N09	4w37	0:18:28
Pozo Alcón 1	2	37N42	2w56	0:11:44
Pozoblanco 1	2	38N22	4w51	0:19:24
Pozo-Cañada 1	2	38N48	1w45	0:07:00
Pozuelo de Alarcón 1	2	40N26	3w49	0:15:16
Prat de Llobregat 1	5	41N20	2E06	-0:08:24
Pravia 1	1	43N29	6w07	0:24:28
Premiá de Mar 1	5	41N29	2E21	-0:09:24
Priego 1	2	40N27	2w18	0:09:12
Priego de Córdoba 1	1	37N26	4w11	0:16:44
Puebla de Alcocer 1	2	38N59	5w15	0:21:00
Puebla de Don Fadrique 1	2	37N58	2w26	0:09:44
Puebla de Don Rodrigo 1	2	39N05	4w37	0:18:28
Puebla de Sanabria 1	1	42N03	6w38	0:26:32
Puebla de Trives 1	1	42N20	7w15	0:29:00
Puenteareas 1	1	42N11	8w30	0:34:00
Puente-Caldelas 1	1	42N23	8w30	0:34:00
Puente de Arganda 1	2	40N19	3w31	0:14:04
Puentedeume 1	1	43N24	8w10	0:32:40
Puente-Genil 1	1	37N23	4w47	0:19:08
Puente la Reina 1	1	42N40	1w49	0:07:16
Puerto del Rosario 3	6	28N30	13w52	0:55:28
Puerto de Pollensa 2	1	39N55	3E05	-0:12:20
Puertollano 1	2	38N41	4w07	0:16:28
Puerto Real 1	1	36N32	6w11	0:24:44
Puigcerdá 1	5	42N26	1E56	-0:07:44
Purchena 1	2	37N21	2w22	0:09:28
Quesada 1	2	37N51	3w04	0:12:16
Quintanar de la Orden 1	2	39N34	3w03	0:12:12
Quinto 1	4	41N25	0w29	0:01:56
Quiroga 1	1	42N29	7w16	0:29:04
Rábade 1	1	43N07	7w37	0:30:28
Ramales de la Victoria 1	3	43N15	3w27	0:13:48
Redondela 1	1	42N17	8w36	0:34:24
Reinosa 1	3	43N00	4w08	0:16:32
Reixach 1	5	41N30	2E12	-0:08:48
Rentería 1	1	43N19	1w54	0:07:36
Requena 1	2	39N29	1w06	0:04:24
Reus 1	5	41N09	1E07	-0:04:28
Revilla del Campo 1	1	42N13	3w32	0:14:08
Riaño 1	3	42N58	5w01	0:20:04
Riaza 1	1	41N17	3w28	0:13:52
Ribadavia 1	1	42N17	8w08	0:32:32
Ribadeo 1	1	43N32	7w02	0:28:08
Ribadesella 1	3	43N28	5w04	0:20:16
Ribas de Jarama 1	2	40N23	3w31	0:14:04
Ríópar 1	2	38N30	2w27	0:09:48
Ripoll 1	5	42N12	2E12	-0:08:48
Ripollet 1	5	41N30	2E10	-0:08:40
Rivas-Vaciamadrid 1	2	40N20	3w31	0:14:04
Roa 1	1	41N42	3w55	0:15:40
Robleda 1	1	40N23	6w36	0:26:24
Robledo 1	2	38N46	2w26	0:09:44
Rodalquilar 1	2	37N40	2w08	0:08:32
Roncesvalles 1	1	43N01	1w19	0:05:16
Ronda 1	1	36N44	5w10	0:20:40
Rota 1	1	36N37	6w21	0:25:24
Rubí 1	5	41N29	2E02	-0:08:08
Rute 1	1	37N19	4w22	0:17:28
Sabadell 1	5	41N33	2E06	-0:08:24
Sabiñánigo 1	1	42N31	0w22	0:01:28
Sacedón 1	2	40N29	2w43	0:10:52
Sada 1	1	43N21	8w15	0:33:00
Sádaba 1	1	42N17	1w16	0:05:04
Sagunto 1	4	39N41	0w16	0:01:04
Sahagún 1	1	42N22	5w02	0:20:08
Salamanca 1	1	40N58	5w39	0:22:36
Salas de los Infantes 1	1	42N01	3w17	0:13:08
Saldaña 1	1	42N31	4w44	0:18:56
Sama (de Langreo) 1	3	43N18	5w41	0:22:44
San Andrés de la Barca 1	5	41N27	1E59	-0:07:56
San Antonio Abad 2	1	38N58	1E18	-0:05:12
San Bartolomé de la Cuadra 1	5	41N26	2E02	-0:08:08
San Baudilio de Llobregat 1	5	41N21	2E03	-0:08:12
San Carlos de la Rápita 1	4	40N37	0E36	-0:02:24
San Clemente 1	2	39N24	2w26	0:09:44
San Clemente de Llobregat 1	5	41N20	2E00	-0:08:00
San Cristóbal de la Laguna 3	6	28N29	16w19	1:05:16
San Cugat del Vallés 1	5	41N28	2E05	-0:08:20
San Esteban de Gormaz 1	1	41N35	3w12	0:12:48
San Fausto de Campcentellas 1	5	41N31	2E14	-0:08:56
San Feliu de Guixols 1	5	41N47	3E02	-0:12:08
San Feliu de Llobregat 1	5	41N23	2E03	-0:08:12
San Fernando 1	1	36N28	6w12	0:24:48
San Fernando de Henares 1	2	40N26	3w32	0:14:08
San Ginés de Vilasar 1	5	41N31	2E22	-0:09:28
Sangüesa 1	1	42N35	1w17	0:05:08
San Ildefonso o La Granja 1	1	40N54	4w00	0:16:00
San Juan Bautista 2	1	39N05	1E30	-0:06:00
San Juan Despí 1	5	41N22	2E04	-0:08:16
San Juan de Vilasar 1	5	41N30	2E24	-0:09:36
San Justo Desvern 1	5	41N23	2E05	-0:08:20
San Lorenzo de El Escorial 1	1	40N35	4w09	0:16:36
San Lorenzo de la Parrilla 1	2	39N51	2w22	0:09:28
Sanlúcar de Barrameda 1	1	36N47	6w21	0:25:24
Sanlúcar la Mayor 1	1	37N23	6w12	0:24:48
San Marco 1	1	43N13	8w17	0:33:08
San Martín de Valdeiglesias 1	1	40N21	4w24	0:17:36
San Mateo 1	4	40N28	0E11	-0:00:44
San Miguel 3	6	28N05	16w37	1:06:28
San Nicolás 3	6	27N59	15w46	1:03:04
San Pedro de Premiá 1	5	41N31	2E21	-0:09:24
San Quirico de Tarrasa 1	5	41N32	2E05	-0:08:20
San Roque 1	1	36N13	5w24	0:21:36
San Sebastián 1	1	43N19	1w59	0:07:56
San Sebastián de la Gomera 3	6	28N06	17w06	1:08:24
San Sebastián de los Reyes 1	2	40N33	3w38	0:14:32
Santa Amalia 1	1	39N01	6w01	0:24:04
Santa Catalina de Armara 1	1	43N02	8w49	0:35:16
Santa Coloma de Cervelló 1	5	41N22	2E01	-0:08:04
Santa Coloma de Farnés 1	5	41N52	2E40	-0:10:40
Santa Coloma de Gramanet 1	5	41N27	2E13	-0:08:52
Santa Cruz de la Palma 3	6	28N41	17w45	1:11:00
Santa Cruz de la Zarza 1	2	39N58	3w10	0:12:40
Santa Cruz de Mudela 1	2	38N38	3w28	0:13:52
Santa Cruz de Tenerife 3	6	28N27	16w14	1:04:56
Santa Eugenia 1	1	42N33	9w00	0:36:00
Santa Eulalia 1	1	40N34	1w19	0:05:16
Santa Eulalia del Río 2	1	38N59	1E31	-0:06:04
Santa Fe 1	1	37N11	3w43	0:14:52
Santa María de Barbará 1	5	41N31	2E08	-0:08:32
Santa María la Real de Nieva 1	1	41N04	4w24	0:17:36
Santander 1	3	43N28	3w48	0:15:12
Santañy 2	1	39N22	3E07	-0:12:28
Santa Perpetua de Moguda 1	5	41N32	2E11	-0:08:44
Santa Quiteria 1	5	41N34	2E19	-0:09:16
Santiago → Santiago de Compostela 1	1	42N53	8w33	0:34:12
Santiago de Compostela 1	1	42N53	8w33	0:34:12
Santisteban del Puerto 1	2	38N15	3w12	0:12:48
Santo Domingo de la Calzada 1	1	42N26	2w57	0:11:48
Santoña 1	3	43N27	3w27	0:13:48
San Vicente de Alcántara 1	1	39N21	7w08	0:28:32
San Vicente de Baracaldo 1	3	43N18	2w59	0:11:56
San Vicente de la Barquera 1	3	43N26	4w24	0:17:36
San Vicente dels Horts 1	5	41N24	2E01	-0:08:04
Saragossa → Zaragoza 1	1	41N38	0w53	0:03:32
Sardanyola 1	5	41N30	2E09	-0:08:36
Sariñena 1	4	41N48	0w10	0:00:40
Sarria 1	1	42N47	7w24	0:29:36
Sedano 1	1	42N43	3w45	0:15:00
Segorbe 1	4	39N51	0w29	0:01:56
Segovia 1	1	40N57	4w07	0:16:28
Seo de Urgel 1	5	42N21	1E28	-0:05:52
Sepúlveda 1	1	41N18	3w45	0:15:00
Sequeros 1	1	40N31	6w01	0:24:04
Sestao 1	3	43N18	3w00	0:12:00
Sevilla 1	1	37N23	5w59	0:23:56
Seville → Sevilla 1	1	37N23	5w59	0:23:56
Sierra de Outes 1	1	42N51	8w54	0:35:36
Sigüenza 1	1	41N04	2w38	0:10:32
Sigües 1	1	42N38	1w00	0:04:00
Socuéllamos 1	2	39N17	2w48	0:11:12
Sóller 2	1	39N46	2E42	-0:10:48
Solsona 1	5	41N59	1E31	-0:06:04
Sonseca 1	2	39N42	3w57	0:15:48
Sorbas 1	2	37N07	2w07	0:08:28
Soria 1	1	41N46	2w28	0:09:52
Sort 1	5	42N24	1E08	-0:04:32
Sos del Rey Católico 1	1	42N30	1w13	0:04:52
Soto de Aldovea 1	2	40N26	3w27	0:13:48
Soto de Pajares 1	1	40N17	3w32	0:14:08
Sueca 1	2	39N12	0w19	0:01:16
Sumbilla 1	1	43N10	1w40	0:06:40
Tábara 1	1	41N49	5w57	0:23:48
Tabernes de Valldigna 1	2	39N04	0w16	0:01:04
Tafalla 1	1	42N31	1w40	0:06:40
Talarrubias 1	2	39N02	5w14	0:20:56
Talavera de la Reina 1	1	39N57	4w50	0:19:20
Tamarite de Litera 1	4	41N52	0E26	-0:01:44
Tarancón 1	2	40N01	3w00	0:12:00
Tarazona 1	1	41N54	1w44	0:06:56
Tarazona de la Mancha 1	2	39N15	1w55	0:07:40
Tardajos 1	1	42N21	3w49	0:15:16
Tarifa 1	1	36N01	5w36	0:22:24
Tarragona 1	5	41N07	1E15	-0:05:00
Tarrasa 1	5	41N34	2E01	-0:08:04
Tárrega 1	5	41N39	1E09	-0:04:36
Tauste 1	1	41N55	1w15	0:05:00
Teba 1	1	36N58	4w56	0:19:44
Telde 3	6	28N00	15w25	1:01:40
Tembleque 1	2	39N42	3w30	0:14:00
Tenerife (Santa Cruz de) 3	6	28N27	16w14	1:04:56
Teruel 1	1	40N21	1w06	0:04:24
Teyá 1	5	41N30	2E19	-0:09:16
Tiana 1	5	41N29	2E16	-0:09:04
Tierga 1	1	41N37	1w36	0:06:24
Tineo 1	1	43N20	6w25	0:25:40
Tobarra 1	2	38N35	1w41	0:06:44
Toledo 1	1	39N52	4w01	0:16:04
Tolosa 1	1	43N08	2w04	0:08:16
Tomelloso 1	2	39N10	3w01	0:12:04
Tordesillas 1	1	41N30	5w00	0:20:00
Toreno 1	1	42N42	6w30	0:26:00
Toro 1	1	41N31	5w24	0:21:36
Torquemada 1	1	42N02	4w19	0:17:16
Torre Baja 1	2	40N07	1w15	0:05:00
Torreblanca 1	4	40N13	0E12	-0:00:48
Torrecilla en Cameros 1	1	42N16	2w37	0:10:28
Torre del Campo 1	1	37N46	3w53	0:15:32
Torredonjimeno 1	1	37N46	3w57	0:15:48

SPAIN — ESPAGNE — SPANIEN — ESPAÑA

Place	Zone	Lat	Long	Time
Torrejoncillo 1	1	39N54	6W28	0:25:52
Torrejón de Ardoz 1	2	40N27	3W29	0:13:56
Torrelaguna 1	2	40N50	3W32	0:14:08
Torrelavega 1	3	43N21	4W03	0:16:12
Torrellas de Llobregat 1	5	41N21	1E59	-0:07:56
Torremolinos 1	1	36N37	4W30	0:18:00
Torrente 1	2	39N26	0W28	0:01:52
Torreperogil 1	2	38N02	3W17	0:13:08
Torrevieja 1	2	37N59	0W41	0:02:44
Torrijos 1	1	39N59	4W17	0:17:08
Torrox 1	1	36N46	3W58	0:15:52
Tortosa 1	4	40N48	0E31	-0:02:04
Totana 1	2	37N46	1W30	0:06:00
Tragacete 1	2	40N21	1W51	0:07:24
Traid 1	1	40N40	1W49	0:07:16
Tremp 1	5	42N10	0E54	-0:03:36
Treviño 1	1	42N44	2W45	0:11:00
Trigueros 1	1	37N23	6W50	0:27:20
Triste 1	1	42N23	0W43	0:02:52
Trujillo 1	1	39N28	5W53	0:23:32
Tudela 1	1	42N05	1W36	0:06:24
Tudela de Duero 1	1	41N35	4W35	0:18:20
Tuineje 3	6	28N19	14W03	0:56:12
Túy 1	1	42N03	8W38	0:34:32
Úbeda 1	2	38N01	3W22	0:13:28
Ubrique 1	1	36N41	5W27	0:21:48
Ugíjar 1	2	36N57	3W03	0:12:12
Ullastrell 1	5	41N31	1E58	-0:07:52
Urbanización La Pineda 1	5	41N16	2E00	-0:08:00
Utiel 1	2	39N34	1W12	0:04:48
Utrera 1	1	37N11	5W47	0:23:08
Valdepeñas 1	2	38N46	3W23	0:13:32
Valderas 1	1	42N05	5W27	0:21:48
Valderrobres 1	4	40N53	0E09	-0:00:36
Valdoviño 1	1	43N36	8W08	0:32:32
Valence → Valencia 1	2	39N28	0W22	0:01:28
Valencia 1	2	39N28	0W22	0:01:28
Valencia de Alcántata 1	1	39N25	7W14	0:28:56
Valencia de Don Juan 1	1	42N18	5W31	0:22:04
Valladolid 1	1	41N39	4W43	0:18:52
Vall de Uxó 1	4	39N49	0W14	0:00:56
Valldoreix 1	5	41N28	2E04	-0:08:16
Valle 1	3	43N14	4W18	0:17:12
Vallirana 1	5	41N23	1E56	-0:07:44
Vallromanas 1	5	41N32	2E18	-0:09:12
Valls 1	5	41N17	1E15	-0:05:00
Valmaseda 1	3	43N12	3W12	0:12:48
Valoria la Buena 1	1	41N48	4W32	0:18:08
Valverde 3	6	27N48	17W55	1:11:40
Valverde del Camino 1	1	37N34	6W45	0:27:00
Vejer de la Frontera 1	1	36N15	5W58	0:23:52
Vélez-Málaga 1	1	36N47	4W06	0:16:24
Vélez Rubio 1	2	37N39	2W04	0:08:16
Velilla de San Antonio 1	2	40N22	3W29	0:13:56
Vendrell 1	5	41N13	1E32	-0:06:08
Vera 1	2	37N15	1W52	0:07:28
Vergara 1	1	43N07	2W25	0:09:40
Verín 1	1	41N56	7W26	0:29:44
Viana del Bollo 1	1	42N11	7W06	0:28:24
Vich 1	5	41N56	2E15	-0:09:00
Viella 1	4	42N42	0E48	-0:03:12
Vigo 1	1	42N14	8W43	0:34:52
Viladecaballs 1	5	41N33	1E58	-0:07:52
Viladecáns 1	5	41N19	2E00	-0:08:00
Vilafranca del Panadés 1	5	41N21	1E42	-0:06:48
Vilanova de la Roca 1	5	41N33	2E17	-0:09:08
Villablino 1	3	42N56	6W19	0:25:16
Villacañas 1	2	39N38	3W20	0:13:20
Villacarriedo 1	3	43N14	3W48	0:15:12
Villacarrillo 1	2	38N07	3W05	0:12:20
Villacastín 1	1	40N47	4W25	0:17:40
Villada 1	1	42N15	4W58	0:19:52
Villa del Río 1	1	37N59	4W17	0:17:08
Villadiego 1	1	42N31	4W00	0:16:00
Villafranca del Bierzo 1	1	42N36	6W48	0:27:12
Villafranca de los Barros 1	1	38N34	6W20	0:25:20
Villagaracía 1	1	42N36	8W45	0:35:00
Villajoyosa 1	2	38N30	0W14	0:00:56
Villalba 1	1	43N18	7W41	0:30:44
Villalón de Campos 1	1	42N06	5W02	0:20:08
Villalpando 1	1	41N52	5W24	0:21:36
Villamartín 1	1	36N52	5W38	0:22:32
Villanueva de Córdoba 1	2	38N20	4W37	0:18:28
Villanueva de la Serana 1	1	38N58	5W48	0:23:12
Villanueva de la Sierra 1	1	40N12	6W24	0:25:36
Villanueva de los Infantes 1	2	38N44	2W59	0:11:56
Villanueva del Río y Minas 1	1	37N39	5W42	0:22:48
Villanueva y Geltrú 1	5	41N14	1E44	-0:06:56
Villarcayo 1	3	42N56	3W34	0:14:16
Villardefrades 1	1	41N43	5W15	0:21:00
Villar del Arzobispo 1	2	39N44	0W49	0:03:16
Villarreal 1	4	39N56	0W06	0:00:24
Villarrobledo 1	2	39N16	2W36	0:10:24
Villarrubia de los Ojos 1	2	39N13	3W36	0:14:24
Villasayas 1	1	41N21	2W37	0:10:28
Villaviciosa 1	3	43N29	5W26	0:21:44
Villaviciosa de Córdoba 1	1	38N05	5W01	0:20:04
Villena 1	2	38N38	0W51	0:03:24
Vimianzo 1	1	43N07	9W02	0:36:08
Vinaroz 1	4	40N28	0E29	-0:01:56
Vitigudino 1	1	41N01	6W26	0:25:44
Vitoria 1	1	42N51	2W40	0:10:40
Viver 1	4	39N55	0W36	0:02:24
Vivero 1	1	43N40	7W35	0:30:20
Xeres → Jerez de la Frontera 1	1	36N41	6W08	0:24:32
Yecla 1	2	38N37	1W07	0:04:28
Yeste 1	2	38N22	2W18	0:09:12
Zafra 1	1	38N25	6W25	0:25:40
Zalamea de la Serana 1	1	38N39	5W39	0:22:36
Zamora 1	1	41N30	5W45	0:23:00
Zaragoza 1	1	41N38	0W53	0:03:32
Zarauz 1	1	43N17	2W10	0:08:40
Zorita 1	1	39N17	5W42	0:22:48
Zuera 1	1	41N52	0W47	0:03:08

SRI LANKA — SERENDIB — CEYLON

Time Table

Date	Time	Offset
Before 1/Jan/1880	LMT	
Begin Standard		79E53
1/Jan/1880	0:00	-5:20
Begin Standard		82E30
1/Jan/1906	0:00	-5:30
5/Jan/1942	0:00	-6:00
1/Sep/1942	0:00	-6:30
16/Oct/1945	2:00	-5:30

Place	Lat	Long	Time
Ambalangoda	6N14	80E03	-5:20:12
Anuradhapura	8N21	80E23	-5:21:32
Badulla	6N59	81E03	-5:24:12
Batticaloa	7N43	81E42	-5:26:48
Chilaw	7N34	79E47	-5:19:08
Colombo	6N56	79E51	-5:19:24
Dehiwala-Mount Lavinia	6N51	79E52	-5:19:28
Galle	6N02	80E13	-5:20:52
Gampola	7N10	80E34	-5:22:16
Hambantota	6N07	81E07	-5:24:28
Jaffna	9N40	80E00	-5:20:00
Kalutara	6N35	79E58	-5:19:52
Kandy	7N18	80E38	-5:22:32
Kegalla	7N15	80E21	-5:21:24
Kotte	6N54	79E54	-5:19:36
Kurunegala	7N29	80E22	-5:21:28
Mannar	8N59	79E54	-5:19:36
Matale	7N28	80E37	-5:22:28
Matara	5N56	80E33	-5:22:12
Moratuwa	6N46	79E53	-5:19:32
Nawalapitiya	7N03	80E32	-5:22:08
Negombo	7N13	79E50	-5:19:20
Nuwara-Eliya	6N58	80E46	-5:23:04
Panadura	6N43	79E54	-5:19:36
Polonnaruwa	7N56	81E00	-5:24:00
Puttalam	8N02	79E49	-5:19:16
Ratnapura	6N41	80E24	-5:21:36
Sigiriya	7N57	80E45	-5:23:00
Talaimannar	9N05	79E44	-5:18:56
Tangalla	6N01	80E48	-5:23:12
Trincomalee	8N34	81E14	-5:24:56
Vavuniya	8N45	80E30	-5:22:00
Weligama	5N58	80E25	-5:21:40

Time Table
Before 1/Jan/1931 LMT
Begin Standard 30E00
1/Jan/1931 0:00 -2:00
1/May/1970 0:00 -3:00
15/Oct/1970 0:00 -2:00
30/Apr/1971 0:00 -3:00
15/Oct/1971 0:00 -2:00
30/Apr/1972 0:00 -3:00
15/Oct/1972 0:00 -2:00
29/Apr/1973 0:00 -3:00
15/Oct/1973 0:00 -2:00
28/Apr/1974 0:00 -3:00
15/Oct/1974 0:00 -2:00
27/Apr/1975 0:00 -3:00
15/Oct/1975 0:00 -2:00
25/Apr/1976 0:00 -3:00
15/Oct/1976 0:00 -2:00
24/Apr/1977 0:00 -3:00
15/Oct/1977 0:00 -2:00
30/Apr/1978 0:00 -3:00
15/Oct/1978 0:00 -2:00
29/Apr/1979 0:00 -3:00
15/Oct/1979 0:00 -2:00
27/Apr/1980 0:00 -3:00
15/Oct/1980 0:00 -2:00
26/Apr/1981 0:00 -3:00
15/Oct/1981 0:00 -2:00
25/Apr/1982 0:00 -3:00
15/Oct/1982 0:00 -2:00
24/Apr/1983 0:00 -3:00
15/Oct/1983 0:00 -2:00
29/Apr/1984 0:00 -3:00
15/Oct/1984 0:00 -2:00
28/Apr/1985 0:00 -3:00
15/Oct/1985 0:00 -2:00

Place	Lat	Long	Offset
'Abd Allāh	13N30	23E02	-1:32:08
Abekr	12N43	28E55	-1:55:40
Abelek	7N23	28E46	-1:55:04
'Ābidīn	13N33	29E38	-1:58:32
'Abīdīyah	18N14	33E57	-2:15:48
'Abrī	11N40	30E28	-2:01:52
'Abrī	20N48	30E20	-2:01:20
Abū Dawm	16N16	32E36	-2:10:24
Abū Dīs	19N08	33E34	-2:14:16
Abū Dulayq	15N54	33E49	-2:15:16
Abū Gelba	13N11	31E52	-2:07:28
Abū Ḥamad	19N32	33E19	-2:13:16
Abū Ḥarāz	12N58	29E52	-1:59:28
Abū Ḥarāz	19N04	32E07	-2:08:28
Abū Jābirah	11N04	26E51	-1:47:24
Abū Jubayhah	11N27	31E14	-2:04:56
Abū Kulaywāt	12N20	26E00	-1:44:00
Abū Maṭāriq	10N58	26E17	-1:45:08
Abū Na'āmah	12N44	34E08	-2:16:32
Abū Shanab	10N47	29E32	-1:58:08
Abū Shanab	13N57	27E47	-1:51:08
Abū Ṭunayṭin	14N24	31E01	-2:04:04
Abū Zabad	12N21	29E15	-1:57:00
Abwong	9N07	32E12	-2:08:48
Abyaḍ	13N46	26E28	-1:45:52
Abyei	9N36	28E26	-1:53:44
Achol	6N34	31E31	-2:06:04
Adarama	17N05	34E54	-2:19:36
Adarot	17N50	36E07	-2:24:28
Ad-Dabbah	18N03	30E57	-2:03:48
Ad-Dāmir	17N35	33E58	-2:15:52
Ad-Du'ayn	11N26	26E09	-1:44:36
Ad-Duwaym	14N00	32E19	-2:09:16
Adok	8N11	30E19	-2:01:16
Agalak	11N01	32E42	-2:10:48
Agaru	10N59	34E44	-2:18:56
Agogo	7N49	28E52	-1:55:28
Ajok	9N15	28E27	-1:53:48
'Akasha East	21N05	30E43	-2:02:52
Akobo	7N47	33E01	-2:12:04
Akop	8N21	29E05	-1:56:20
Akot	6N33	30E03	-2:00:12
Al-'Abbāsīyah	12N10	31E18	-2:05:12
Al-Ait	12N22	27E27	-1:49:48
Al-'Aṭrūn	18N11	26E36	-1:46:24
Al-Barun	11N44	33E30	-2:14:00
Al-Bauga	18N16	33E55	-2:15:40
Al-Fāshir	13N38	25E21	-1:41:24
Al-Fifi	10N03	25E01	-1:40:04
Al-Garef	12N03	34E19	-2:17:16
Al-Gebir	13N43	29E49	-1:59:16
Al-Hajālīj	14N36	31E54	-2:07:36
Al-Ḥawātah	13N25	34E38	-2:18:32
Al-Ḥillah	13N27	27E08	-1:48:32
Al-Ḥuḍayb	13N00	32E50	-2:11:20
Al-Ḥuṣayḥiṣah	14N44	33E18	-2:13:12
Al-Jabalayn	12N36	32E48	-2:11:12
Al-Jaylī	16N01	32E36	-2:10:24
Al-Jubayn	12N07	35E10	-2:20:40
Al-Junaynah	13N27	22E27	-1:29:48
Al-Kāb	19N18	32E43	-2:10:52
Al-Kāmilīn	15N05	33E11	-2:12:44
Al-Karabah	18N33	33E42	-2:14:48
Al-Kawah	13N44	32E30	-2:10:00
Al-Khandaq	18N36	30E34	-2:02:16
Al-Kharṭūm	15N36	32E32	-2:10:08
Al-Kharṭūm Baḥrī	15N38	32E33	-2:10:12
Al-Lagowa	11N24	29E08	-1:56:32
Al-Layyah	16N16	35E25	-2:21:40
Al-Mafāzah	13N36	34E33	-2:18:12
Al-Manāqil	14N15	32E59	-2:11:56
Al-Masīd	15N15	32E57	-2:11:48
Al-Matammah	16N43	33E22	-2:13:28
Al-Matnah	13N47	35E03	-2:20:12
Al-Muglad	11N02	27E44	-1:50:56
Al-Musallamīyah	14N34	33E21	-2:13:24
Al-Qaḍārif	14N02	35E24	-2:21:36
Al-Quṭaynah	14N52	32E21	-2:09:24
Al-Quwaysī	13N20	34E05	-2:16:20
Al-Ubayyiḍ	13N11	30E13	-2:00:52
Al-Uḍayyah	12N03	28E17	-1:53:08
Aluk	8N26	27E27	-1:49:48
Al-Wazz	15N01	30E10	-2:00:40
Amadi	5N31	30E20	-2:01:20
'Amārat Abū Sinn	15N21	35E45	-2:23:00
'Amar Jadīd	14N28	25E14	-1:40:56
'Amm-Adām	16N22	36E06	-2:24:24
Angarbaka	9N44	24E44	-1:38:56
An-Nawfalāb	15N52	32E32	-2:10:08
An-Nuhūd	12N42	28E26	-1:53:44
'Aqīq	18N14	38E12	-2:32:48
Araka	4N20	30E23	-2:01:32
Aramtalla	6N47	29E13	-1:56:52
Argo	19N31	30E25	-2:01:40
Aroma	15N49	36E08	-2:24:32
Ar-Rahad	12N43	30E39	-2:02:36
Ar-Rank	11N45	32E48	-2:11:12
Ar-Ru'At	12N21	32E17	-2:09:08
Ar-Ruṣayriṣ	11N51	34E23	-2:17:32
Ar-Uṣayriṣ	11N51	34E23	-2:17:32
Ash-Shurayk	18N48	33E34	-2:14:16
As-Sa'Ata	13N37	29E59	-1:59:56
Aṣ-Ṣāfiyah	15N31	30E07	-2:00:28
Aṣ-Ṣufayyah	15N30	34E42	-2:18:48
As-Sumayḥ	9N49	27E39	-1:50:36
'Aṭbarah	17N42	33E59	-2:15:56
Attir	6N04	30E50	-2:03:20
Aṭ-Ṭuwayshah	12N21	26E32	-1:46:08
Aworo Kit	10N59	32E38	-2:10:32
Ayod	8N07	31E26	-2:05:44
Ayom	7N52	28E23	-1:53:32
Az-Zaydāb	17N26	33E53	-2:15:32
Babanūsah	11N20	27E48	-1:51:12
Bagawi	12N19	34E21	-2:17:24
Bangjang	11N23	32E42	-2:10:48
Bārah	13N42	30E22	-2:01:28
Barakah	10N58	27E59	-1:51:56
Barbar	18N01	33E59	-2:15:56
Bardai	12N43	21E53	-1:27:32
Bargnop	9N30	28E28	-1:53:52
Belabolo	8N57	25E51	-1:43:24
Belbubulo	9N57	34E04	-2:16:16
Belichifor	6N33	33E16	-2:13:04
Bentiu	9N14	29E50	-1:59:20
Beringil	12N10	25E41	-1:42:44
Betbetti	15N06	24E12	-1:36:48
Bint Goda	13N17	31E33	-2:06:12
Bobuk	11N30	34E05	-2:16:20
Boli	6N01	28E43	-1:54:52
Bongak	7N27	33E14	-2:12:56
Bor	6N12	31E33	-2:06:12
Buddu	11N54	24E08	-1:36:32
Bunduqiyah	5N06	30E53	-2:03:32
Buram	10N49	25E10	-1:40:40
Būr Sūdān (Port Sudan)	19N37	37E14	-2:28:56
Chaka	4N49	31E14	-2:04:56
Daga Post	9N12	33E58	-2:15:52
Dagash	19N22	33E24	-2:13:36
Daghfalī	19N17	32E30	-2:10:00
Dalāmī	11N52	30E28	-2:01:52
Dalqū	20N07	30E37	-2:02:28
Dam Gamad	13N17	27E28	-1:49:52
Dango	10N00	24E45	-1:39:00
Daqqāq	12N56	26E58	-1:47:52
Darāfisah	13N23	31E59	-2:07:56
Dari	5N48	30E21	-2:01:24
Dār Zubi	13N07	23E40	-1:34:40
Dawrah	12N22	24E19	-1:37:16
Daym Zubayr	7N43	26E13	-1:44:52
Derudeb	17N32	36E06	-2:24:24
Dibs	12N34	24E14	-1:36:56
Dikala	4N41	31E23	-2:05:32
Dilling	12N03	29E39	-1:58:36
Dimo	5N19	29E10	-1:56:40
Dirrah	13N37	26E06	-1:44:24
Dīsah	12N02	34E19	-2:17:16
Dodo Goei	5N57	27E26	-1:49:44
Doka	13N31	35E46	-2:23:04
Dongola → Dunqulah	19N10	30E29	-2:01:56
Duhi	7N07	28E45	-1:55:00
Duk Fadiat	7N45	31E25	-2:05:40
Duk Faiwil	7N30	31E29	-2:05:56
Dunkuj	12N50	32E49	-2:11:16
Dunqulah	19N10	30E29	-2:01:56
Dunqulah al-Qadīmah	18N13	30E45	-2:03:00
Dunqunāb	21N06	37E05	-2:28:20
El-Karafab	18N10	31E36	-2:06:24
El-Obeid → Al-Ubayyiḍ	13N11	30E13	-2:00:52
Eriba	16N37	36E04	-2:24:16
Erkowit	18N46	37E07	-2:28:28
Ermil Post	13N37	27E36	-1:50:24
Es-Suki	13N20	33E54	-2:15:36
Faddoi	8N07	32E07	-2:08:28
Fadit	9N58	32E13	-2:08:52
Fagwir	9N33	30E25	-2:01:40
Fakī Ṣādiq	12N08	23E55	-1:35:40
Fakrinkotti	18N01	31E20	-2:05:20
Fangak	9N04	30E53	-2:03:32
Fathai	8N05	31E48	-2:07:12
Fongfong	12N56	23E14	-1:32:56
Gabir	8N35	24E40	-1:38:40
Gabras	10N16	26E14	-1:44:56
Gadamai	17N09	36E06	-2:24:24
Gadein	8N11	28E44	-1:54:56
Gaghamni	11N41	28E19	-1:53:16
Galegu	12N36	35E02	-2:20:08
Gambi Aṭrash	10N03	33E47	-2:15:08
Gebeit Mine	21N03	36E19	-2:25:16
Ghābat al-'Arab	9N02	29E29	-1:57:56
Gharig	10N47	27E33	-1:50:12
Ghubaysh	12N09	27E21	-1:49:24
Gizen	10N49	34E48	-2:19:12
Gobur	4N20	31E04	-2:04:16
Gogrial	8N32	28E07	-1:52:28
Goshabi	17N58	31E06	-2:04:24
Gossinga	8N39	25E59	-1:43:56
Gulnam	6N55	29E30	-1:58:00
Habīlah	12N41	22E33	-1:30:12
Hadalīya	16N10	36E06	-2:24:24
Ḥajar Banga	11N30	23E00	-1:32:00
Ḥalā'ib	22N13	36E38	-2:26:32
Halasa	14N26	30E39	-2:02:36
Ḥamad	15N19	33E43	-2:14:52
Ḥamrat ash-Shaykh	14N35	27E58	-1:51:52
Handub	19N14	37E16	-2:29:04
Hārūn	11N20	25E43	-1:42:52
Haybān	11N13	30E31	-2:02:04
Hūdī	17N42	34E17	-2:17:08
Ḥufrat an-Naḥās	9N45	24E19	-1:37:16
Ḥukūmah	13N52	36E07	-2:24:28
Ḥumaydah	14N22	22E31	-1:30:04
Ḥusheib	14N54	35E07	-2:20:28
Ibba	4N48	29E06	-1:56:24
Imasa	18N01	36E12	-2:24:48
'Iyāl Bakhīt	13N25	28E41	-1:54:44
Jabal al-Awliyā'	15N14	32E30	-2:10:00
Jabal Dūd	13N25	33E09	-2:12:36
Jabal Qerri	16N15	32E48	-2:11:12
Jefawa	10N57	23E48	-1:35:12
Jelli	5N22	31E48	-2:07:12
Jerbar	5N39	31E05	-2:04:20
Jidād	11N05	24E44	-1:38:56
Jirbān	11N03	30E36	-2:02:24
Jokau	8N24	33E49	-2:15:16
Jūbā	4N51	31E37	-2:06:28
Jubayt	18N57	36E50	-2:27:20
Jughna	12N24	25E06	-1:40:24
Kabkābīyah	13N39	24E05	-1:36:20
Kabna	19N10	32E41	-2:10:44
Kabr	10N54	26E50	-1:47:20
Kabūshīyah	16N53	33E42	-2:14:48
Kadodo	11N04	29E31	-1:58:04
Kāduqlī	11N01	29E43	-1:58:52
Kafia Kingi	9N16	24E25	-1:37:40
Kagmar	14N24	30E25	-2:01:40
Kaiedin	9N45	32E11	-2:08:44
Kajo Kaji	3N53	31E40	-2:06:40
Kākā	10N36	32E11	-2:08:44
Kan	9N01	31E47	-2:07:08
Kanafis	9N48	25E40	-1:42:40
Kapoeta	4N47	33E35	-2:14:20
Karmah	19N38	30E25	-2:01:40
Karora	17N42	38E22	-2:33:28
Karotho Post	5N11	35E50	-2:23:20
Kas	12N30	24E17	-1:37:08
Kassalā	15N28	36E24	-2:25:36
Kassinger	18N45	31E54	-2:07:36
Kawm	13N31	22E50	-1:31:20
Keri Kera	12N21	32E46	-2:11:04
Keyala	4N27	32E52	-2:11:28
Khartoum → Al-Kharṭūm	15N36	32E32	-2:10:08
Khartoum North → Al-Kharṭūm Bahri	15N38	32E33	-2:10:12
Khartum → Al-Kharṭūm	15N36	32E32	-2:10:08
Khashm al-Qirbah	14N58	35E55	-2:23:40
Khashum	12N27	28E02	-1:52:08
Khogali	6N08	27E47	-1:51:08
Khuwayy	13N05	29E14	-1:56:56
Kigille	8N40	34E02	-2:16:08
Kiteiyab	17N12	33E43	-2:14:52
Kodok	9N53	32E07	-2:08:28
Kokka	20N00	30E35	-2:02:20
Kongor	7N10	31E21	-2:05:24
Korgus	19N13	33E29	-2:13:56
Kosha	20N49	30E32	-2:02:08
Kubbī	11N08	25E14	-1:40:56
Kubbum	11N47	23E47	-1:35:08
Kuḥaylī	19N25	32E50	-2:11:20
Kulaykilī	11N21	25E36	-1:42:24
Kumbar	12N03	30E16	-2:01:04
Kuraymah	18N33	31E51	-2:07:24
Kurmuk	10N33	34E17	-2:17:08
Kūrtī	18N07	31E33	-2:06:12
Kuru	7N43	26E31	-1:46:04
Kūstī	13N10	32E40	-2:10:40
Kutum	14N12	24E40	-1:38:40
Kwajok	8N19	28E00	-1:52:00
Lafon	5N02	32E27	-2:09:48
Latiri	9N10	25E43	-1:42:52
Leho	7N07	33E52	-2:15:28
Liwan	4N54	35E40	-2:22:40
Logirim	4N43	33E14	-2:12:56
Logo	5N20	30E18	-2:01:12
Loka	4N16	31E01	-2:04:04
Lol	6N26	29E37	-1:58:28
Longairo	4N30	32E17	-2:09:08
Loronyo	4N39	32E38	-2:10:32
Lowelli	5N59	33E45	-2:15:00
Lukka	14N33	23E42	-1:34:48
Maar	6N54	31E33	-2:06:12
Mabrūk	8N07	29E25	-1:57:40
Madbar	6N19	30E40	-2:02:40
Madeir	7N50	29E12	-1:56:48
Madol	9N02	27E46	-1:51:04
Magwe	4N08	32E17	-2:09:08
Majeigha	11N33	24E40	-1:38:40
Majrūr	14N01	30E27	-2:01:48
Malakāl	9N31	31E39	-2:06:36
Malawiya	15N16	36E12	-2:24:48
Malek	6N04	31E36	-2:06:24
Malha Wells	15N08	26E12	-1:44:48
Malūṭ	10N26	32E12	-2:08:48
Malwal	9N19	31E35	-2:06:20
Ma'mūn	12N15	22E41	-1:30:44
Mapoi	5N28	27E40	-1:50:40
Marawī	18N29	31E49	-2:07:16

SUDAN SUDÁN SOUDAN AS-SŪDĀN

Place	Lat	Long	Time
Marīdī	4N55	29E28	-1:57:52
Markundi	11N33	23E49	-1:35:16
Mashar	9N14	26E52	-1:47:28
Mashra'Ar-Raqq	8N25	29E16	-1:57:04
Mashra'ur-Raqq	8N25	29E16	-1:57:04
Mbia	6N15	29E19	-1:57:16
Mboro	6N18	28E45	-1:55:00
Medi	5N04	30E44	-2:02:56
Meheisa	19N37	32E57	-2:11:48
Meiyino	6N12	34E40	-2:18:40
Mellit	14N08	25E33	-1:42:12
Menawashei	12N40	24E59	-1:39:56
Minkamman	6N03	31E32	-2:06:08
Miskī	14N51	24E13	-1:36:52
Mismār	18N13	35E38	-2:22:32
Misterei	13N07	22E09	-1:28:36
Mitatib	16N03	36E11	-2:24:44
Modo	5N29	30E38	-2:02:32
Mogogh	8N26	31E19	-2:05:16
Moingbi	5N46	28E49	-1:55:16
Mongalla	5N12	31E46	-2:07:04
Mortesoro	10N12	34E09	-2:16:36
Mowein	7N36	28E11	-1:52:44
Mu'Allaqah	13N28	23E57	-1:35:48
Muḥammad Qawl	20N54	37E05	-2:28:20
Mulwad	18N39	30E35	-2:02:20
Mumu	12N06	23E42	-1:34:48
Muqaṭṭa'	14N40	35E51	-2:23:24
Murnei	12N57	22E52	-1:31:28
Muru	6N36	29E15	-1:57:00
Mvolo	6N03	29E56	-1:59:44
Na'ām	9N42	28E27	-1:53:48
Nabalat al-Ḥajanah	13N13	29E02	-1:56:08
Nadi	18N40	33E42	-2:14:48
Nagichot	4N16	33E34	-2:14:16
Nakape	5N47	28E37	-1:54:28
Nāṣir	8N36	33E04	-2:12:16
Naui	18N28	30E43	-2:02:52
New Alfa	15N10	35E40	-2:22:40
Ngangala	4N42	31E55	-2:07:40
Ngoboli	4N57	32E37	-2:10:28
Ngop	6N16	30E12	-2:00:48
Niaro	10N38	31E31	-2:06:04
Nimule	3N36	32E03	-2:08:12
Nyala	12N03	24E53	-1:39:32
Nyamlell	9N07	26E58	-1:47:52
Nyerol	8N41	32E02	-2:08:08
Nyiel	6N06	31E13	-2:04:52
Ogr	12N02	27E06	-1:48:24
Omdurman → Umm Durmān	15N38	32E30	-2:10:00
Opari	3N56	32E03	-2:08:12
Orarak	6N15	32E23	-2:09:32
Pakeng	6N55	30E40	-2:02:40
Paloich	6N45	30E08	-2:00:32
Paloich	10N28	32E32	-2:10:08
Panyang	10N04	29E58	-1:59:52
Pathiong	6N46	30E54	-2:03:36
Peper	7N04	33E00	-2:12:00
Pibor Post	6N48	33E08	-2:12:32
Poko	5N38	31E50	-2:07:20
Port Sudan → Būr Sūdān	19N37	37E14	-2:28:56
Qala' an-Naḥl	13N38	34E57	-2:19:48
Qallābāt	12N43	23E26	-1:33:44
Qallābāt	12N58	36E09	-2:24:36
Qantur	9N45	25E52	-1:43:28
Qawz Rajab	16N04	35E34	-2:22:16
Qurdūd	10N17	29E56	-1:59:44
Qurrāṣah	14N38	32E12	-2:08:48
Rabak	13N09	32E44	-2:10:56
Raffili Mission	6N53	27E58	-1:51:52
Raga	8N28	25E41	-1:42:44
Rahad al-Baraī	11N18	23E53	-1:35:32
Rajāj	10N55	24E43	-1:38:52
Rashād	11N51	31E04	-2:04:16
Riangnom	9N55	30E01	-2:00:04
Rombari	4N33	31E02	-2:04:08
Ruboani	8N06	30E45	-2:03:00
Rufā'Ah	14N46	33E22	-2:13:28
Rumbek	6N48	29E41	-1:58:44
Sahaba	18N55	30E28	-2:01:52
Salālah	21N19	36E13	-2:24:52
Salim	12N52	28E40	-1:54:40
Sallūm	19N23	37E06	-2:28:24
Sannār	13N33	33E38	-2:14:32
Sāqiat al-'Abd	20N48	30E19	-2:01:16
Sawākin	19N07	37E20	-2:29:20
Sawdirī	14N25	29E05	-1:56:20
Seilo	12N20	23E50	-1:35:20
Shambat	15N40	32E32	-2:10:08
Shambe	7N07	30E46	-2:03:04
Shandī	16N42	33E26	-2:13:44
Shatawī	14N39	32E06	-2:08:24
Sherab	10N43	24E47	-1:39:08
Shibarni	14N50	24E25	-1:37:40
Shigaib	15N01	23E36	-1:34:24
Shuwak	14N23	35E52	-2:23:28
Sinjah	13N09	33E56	-2:15:44
Sinkāt	18N50	36E50	-2:27:20
Sirsiri	4N24	31E53	-2:07:32
Siyeteb	18N00	35E01	-2:20:04
Sumayḥ	12N43	30E50	-2:03:20
Sunjikāy	12N20	29E46	-1:59:04
Suq'At al-Jamal	12N48	27E42	-1:50:48
Talawdī	10N38	30E23	-2:01:32
Tali Post	5N54	30E47	-2:03:08
Tambura	5N36	27E28	-1:49:52
Tandaltī	13N01	31E52	-2:07:28
Taqāṭu' hayyā	18N20	36E22	-2:25:28
Ṭawkar	18N26	37E44	-2:30:56
Ṭayyārah	13N12	30E47	-2:03:08
Tehamiyam	18N20	36E32	-2:26:08
Tereida	10N35	31E17	-2:05:08
Thar Nhom	7N26	30E29	-2:01:56
Thorial	8N40	29E56	-1:59:44
Tibari	5N01	31E43	-2:06:52
Timinar	19N02	30E29	-2:01:56
Tior	6N23	31E11	-2:04:44
Togni	18N04	35E13	-2:20:52
Toinya	6N17	29E44	-1:58:56
Tolwa	6N38	32E37	-2:10:28
Tombe	5N49	31E41	-2:06:44
Tonga	9N28	31E03	-2:04:12
Tonj	7N17	28E45	-1:55:00
Torit	4N24	32E34	-2:10:16
Trinkitat	18N41	37E43	-2:30:52
Tullus	11N03	24E33	-1:38:12
Tumbur	4N20	31E34	-2:06:16
Tungaru	10N14	30E42	-2:02:48
Twong	8N18	28E20	-1:53:20
Ughaybish	10N52	31E05	-2:04:20
Ulu	10N43	33E29	-2:13:56
Umm Badr	14N14	27E57	-1:51:48
Umm Bayyū'D	12N05	31E40	-2:06:40
Umm Bel	13N32	28E04	-1:52:16
Umm Boim	11N43	25E57	-1:43:48
Umm Dabbī	14N37	30E23	-2:01:32
Umm Dam	13N45	30E59	-2:03:56
Umm Dhibbān	14N14	29E37	-1:58:28
Umm Dhibbān	15N26	32E51	-2:11:24
Umm Digulgulaya	10N29	24E57	-1:39:48
Umm Durmān (Omdurman)	15N38	32E30	-2:10:00
Umm Jamālah	11N27	28E12	-1:52:48
Umm Kaddādah	13N36	26E42	-1:46:48
Umm Kuwaykah	13N00	32E17	-2:09:08
Umm Mirdi	18N59	33E32	-2:14:08
Umm Qantur	14N17	31E22	-2:05:28
Umm Qurayn	9N58	28E55	-1:55:40
Umm Ruwābah	12N54	31E13	-2:04:52
Umm Sayyālah	14N25	31E10	-2:04:40
Umm Shalīl	10N51	23E42	-1:34:48
Umm Shanqah	13N14	27E14	-1:48:56
Umm Shuṭūr	7N17	33E14	-2:12:56
Uphal	6N58	34E16	-2:17:04
Uwayl	8N46	27E24	-1:49:36
Vuya	5N21	29E40	-1:58:40
Wad al-Ḥaddād	13N49	33E32	-2:14:08
Wad Bandah	13N06	27E57	-1:51:48
Wad Ban Naqa	16N30	33E08	-2:12:32
Wad Ḥāmid	16N30	32E48	-2:11:12
Wādī Ḥalfā'	21N56	31E20	-2:05:20
Wad Madanī	14N25	33E28	-2:13:52
Wal Athiang	7N42	29E40	-1:58:40
Wa'Th	8N10	32E07	-2:08:28
Wāw	7N42	28E00	-1:52:00
Wawa	20N26	30E21	-2:01:24
Wayi	5N11	30E10	-2:00:40
Wedweil	9N00	27E12	-1:48:48
Winejok	9N01	27E34	-1:50:16
Woi	7N53	31E10	-2:04:40
Wuneba	4N50	30E20	-2:01:20
Wun Rog	9N00	28E21	-1:53:24
Yambio	4N34	28E23	-1:53:32
Ya'Qūb	12N29	25E11	-1:40:44
Yei	4N05	30E40	-2:02:40
Yirol	6N33	30E30	-2:02:00
Yirwa	7N47	27E15	-1:49:00
Zakfero	12N10	27E35	-1:50:20
Zalingei	12N54	23E29	-1:33:56
Zingwanda	7N10	27E56	-1:51:44

SURINAME DUTCH GUIANA

Time Table
Before 1/Jan/1911 LMT
Begin Standard 55w13
1/Jan/1911 0:00 3:41
Begin Standard 55w09
1/Jan/1935 0:00 3:41
Begin Standard 52w30
1/Oct/1945 0:00 3:30
Begin Standard 45w00
1/Oct/1984 0:00 3:00

Place	Lat	Long	Time
Albina	5N30	54w03	3:36:12
Berg en Dal	5N09	55w04	3:40:16
Brokopondo	5N04	54w58	3:39:52
Charlottenburg	5N51	54w46	3:39:04
Coronie	5N52	56w23	3:45:32
Groningen	5N48	55w28	3:41:52
Kwakoegron	5N15	55w20	3:41:20
Moengo	5N37	54w24	3:37:36
Nieuw Amsterdam	5N53	55w05	3:40:20
Nieuw Nickerie	5N57	56w59	3:47:56
Onverwacht	5N36	55w12	3:40:48
Paramaribo	5N50	55w10	3:40:40
Paranam	5N37	55w06	3:40:24
Republiek	5N30	55w15	3:41:00
Totness	5N53	56w19	3:45:16
Wageningen	5N46	56w41	3:46:44

SWAZILANDIA SWASILAND SWAZILAND

Time Table
Before 1/Mar/1903 LMT
Begin Standard 30E00
1/Mar/1903 0:00 -2:00

Place	Lat	Long	Offset
Balegane	26S04	31E34	-2:06:16
Big Bend	26S50	31E57	-2:07:48
Bunya	26S32	31E01	-2:04:04
Burntop	26S49	30E54	-2:03:36
Forbes Reef	26S10	31E05	-2:04:20
Goedgegun	27S06	31E12	-2:04:48
Gollel	27S20	31E55	-2:07:40
Havelock	25S56	31E06	-2:04:24
Hlatikulu	27S00	31E25	-2:05:40
Hluti	27S13	31E35	-2:06:20
Lobamba	26S27	31E12	-2:04:48
Mahamba	27S07	31E10	-2:04:40
Malkerns	26S32	31E11	-2:04:44
Maloma	27S00	31E40	-2:06:40
Mankaiana	26S42	31E00	-2:04:00
Manzini	26S30	31E25	-2:05:40
Matsapa	26S29	31E23	-2:05:32
Mbabane	26S18	31E06	-2:04:24
Mhlume	26S02	31E50	-2:07:20
Mlawula	26S11	32E01	-2:08:04
Mliba	26S14	31E36	-2:06:24
Mpaka	26S26	31E47	-2:07:08
Nsoko	27S02	31E57	-2:07:48
Piggs Peak	25S38	31E15	-2:05:00
Sipofaneni	26S41	31E41	-2:06:44
Sitobela	26S53	31E36	-2:06:24
Stegi	26S32	31E58	-2:07:52
Tshaneni	26S00	31E47	-2:07:08

SVERIGE SCHWEDEN SUÈDE SUECIA SWEDEN

Time Table
Before 31/May/1878 LMT
Begin Standard 18E03
31/May/1878 0:00 -1:12
Begin Standard 15E00
1/Jan/1900 1:00 -1:00
14/Apr/1916 23:00 -2:00
30/Sep/1916 24:00 -1:00
6/Apr/1980 2:00 -2:00
28/Sep/1980 3:00 -1:00
29/Mar/1981 2:00 -2:00
27/Sep/1981 3:00 -1:00
28/Mar/1982 2:00 -2:00
26/Sep/1982 3:00 -1:00
27/Mar/1983 2:00 -2:00
25/Sep/1983 3:00 -1:00
25/Mar/1984 2:00 -2:00
30/Sep/1984 3:00 -1:00
31/Mar/1985 2:00 -2:00
29/Sep/1985 3:00 -1:00
30/Mar/1986 2:00 -2:00
28/Sep/1986 3:00 -1:00
29/Mar/1987 2:00 -2:00
27/Sep/1987 3:00 -1:00
27/Mar/1988 2:00 -2:00
25/Sep/1988 3:00 -1:00
26/Mar/1989 2:00 -2:00
24/Sep/1989 3:00 -1:00
25/Mar/1990 2:00 -2:00
30/Sep/1990 3:00 -1:00
31/Mar/1991 2:00 -2:00
29/Sep/1991 3:00 -1:00
29/Mar/1992 2:00 -2:00
27/Sep/1992 3:00 -1:00
28/Mar/1993 2:00 -2:00
26/Sep/1993 3:00 -1:00
27/Mar/1994 2:00 -2:00
25/Sep/1994 3:00 -1:00
26/Mar/1995 2:00 -2:00
24/Sep/1995 3:00 -1:00
31/Mar/1996 2:00 -2:00
29/Sep/1996 3:00 -1:00
30/Mar/1997 2:00 -2:00
28/Sep/1997 3:00 -1:00
29/Mar/1998 2:00 -2:00
27/Sep/1998 3:00 -1:00
28/Mar/1999 2:00 -2:00
26/Sep/1999 3:00 -1:00
26/Mar/2000 2:00 -2:00
24/Sep/2000 3:00 -1:00

Place	Lat	Long	Offset
Abbekås	55N24	13E36	-0:54:24
Abisko	68N20	18E51	-1:15:24
Åby	58N40	16E11	-1:04:44
Åbyggeby	60N44	17E07	-1:08:28
Åbytorp	59N07	15E04	-1:00:16
Adolfsberg	59N15	15E10	-1:00:40
Åhus	55N55	14E17	-0:57:08
Åkarp	55N39	13E07	-0:52:28
Åker	59N15	17E05	-1:08:20
Åkerby	60N25	17E46	-1:11:04
Åkersberga	59N29	18E18	-1:13:12
Alanäs	64N10	15E42	-1:02:48
Ålberga	58N44	16E34	-1:06:16
Alby	62N30	15E28	-1:01:52
Alfta	61N21	16E05	-1:04:20
Älgarås	58N48	14E14	-0:56:56
Alingsås	57N56	12E31	-0:50:04
Älmhult	56N33	14E08	-0:56:32
Älmsta	59N58	18E48	-1:15:12
Almunge	59N53	18E03	-1:12:12
Alnarp	55N39	13E05	-0:52:20
Alsike	59N45	17E45	-1:11:00
Ålstäket	59N20	18E28	-1:13:52
Alster	59N24	13E36	-0:54:24
Alsterbro	56N57	15E55	-1:03:40
Älta	59N16	18E11	-1:12:44
Alunda	60N04	18E05	-1:12:20
Älvängen	57N58	12E07	-0:48:28
Älvdalen	61N14	14E02	-0:56:08
Alvesta	56N54	14E33	-0:58:12
Alvik	62N25	17E24	-1:09:36
Älvkarleby	60N34	17E27	-1:09:48
Älvkarleö bruk	60N32	17E24	-1:09:36
Älvros	62N03	14E39	-0:58:36
Älvsbyn	65N39	20E59	-1:23:56
Åmål	59N03	12E42	-0:50:48
Ambjörby	60N30	13E10	-0:52:40
Ammarnäs	65N56	16E09	-1:04:36
Åmmeberg	58N52	15E00	-1:00:00
Åmotfors	59N46	12E22	-0:49:28
Åmsele	64N32	19E20	-1:17:20
Ånäset	64N16	21E03	-1:24:12
Anderslöv	55N26	13E22	-0:53:28
Anderstorp	57N17	13E38	-0:54:32
Aneby	57N50	14E48	-0:59:12
Ånge	62N31	15E37	-1:02:28
Ängelholm	56N15	12E51	-0:51:24
Ängelsberg	59N58	16E00	-1:04:00
Ängsö	59N32	16E51	-1:07:24
Anjan	63N41	12E49	-0:51:16
Ankarsrum	57N42	16E19	-1:05:16
Anttis	67N16	22E52	-1:31:28
Äppelbo	60N30	14E00	-0:56:00
Arboga	59N24	15E50	-1:03:20
Arbrå	61N29	16E23	-1:05:32
Åre	63N24	13E04	-0:52:16
Arild	56N16	12E34	-0:50:16
Årjäng	59N23	12E08	-0:48:32
Arjeplog	66N00	17E58	-1:11:52
Arkösund	58N30	16E56	-1:07:44
Ärla	59N17	16E40	-1:06:40
Arlöv	55N39	13E05	-0:52:20
Årnäs	58N41	13E35	-0:54:20
Årsta havsbad	59N05	18E10	-1:12:40
Årsunda	60N32	16E44	-1:06:56
Arvidsjaur	65N35	19E07	-1:16:28
Arvika	59N39	12E36	-0:50:24
Åsarna	62N39	14E21	-0:57:24
Asarum	56N12	14E50	-0:59:20
Åsbro	59N00	15E03	-1:00:12
Åseda	57N10	15E20	-1:01:20
Åsele	64N10	17E20	-1:09:20
Åsensbruk	58N48	12E25	-0:49:40
Åshammar	60N39	16E32	-1:06:08
Askersund	58N53	14E54	-0:59:36
Äsköping	59N09	16E04	-1:04:16
Åsljunga	56N19	13E22	-0:53:28
Asmundtorp	55N53	12E56	-0:51:44
Aspö	59N29	17E02	-1:08:08
Åstorp	56N08	12E57	-0:51:48
Åtvidaberg	58N12	16E00	-1:04:00
Avesta	60N09	16E12	-1:04:48
Backberg	60N37	16E37	-1:06:28
Backe	63N49	16E24	-1:05:36
Bäckefors	58N48	12E10	-0:48:40
Bäckehagen	60N39	15E34	-1:02:16
Bäckhammar	59N10	14E11	-0:56:44
Baggeryd	57N30	14E07	-0:56:28
Baggetorp	59N01	16E04	-1:04:16
Ballingslöv	56N13	13E51	-0:55:24
Bålsta	59N35	17E30	-1:10:00
Bankeryd	57N51	14E07	-0:56:28
Bäsna	60N32	15E12	-1:00:48
Båstad	56N26	12E51	-0:51:24
Bastuträsk	64N47	20E02	-1:20:08
Beddinge läge	55N21	13E29	-0:53:56
Bengtsfors	59N02	12E13	-0:48:52
Berga	59N21	16E26	-1:05:44
Bergby	60N56	17E02	-1:08:08
Bergkvara	56N23	16E05	-1:04:20
Bergsäng	60N06	13E33	-0:54:12
Bergsbrunna	59N49	17E43	-1:10:52
Bergshamra	59N38	18E37	-1:14:28
Bergsjö	61N59	17E04	-1:08:16
Bergvreten	60N31	16E26	-1:05:44
Berthåga	59N52	17E35	-1:10:20
Bie	59N05	16E12	-1:04:48
Billeberga	55N53	13E00	-0:52:00
Billesholm	56N03	13E00	-0:52:00
Billinge	55N58	13E21	-0:53:24
Billingsfors	58N59	12E15	-0:49:00
Bispberg	60N22	15E47	-1:03:08
Bispgården	63N02	16E37	-1:06:28
Bjärnum	56N17	13E42	-0:54:48
Bjärred	55N43	13E01	-0:52:04
Bjärsjölagård	55N44	13E41	-0:54:44
Bjästa	63N12	18E30	-1:14:00
Björbo	60N28	14E42	-0:58:48
Björklinge	60N02	17E33	-1:10:12
Björknäs	59N19	18E14	-1:12:56
Björkvik	58N50	16E31	-1:06:04
Björna	63N34	18E33	-1:14:12
Björndammen	59N12	16E49	-1:07:16
Björneborg	59N15	14E15	-0:57:00
Björnlunda	59N04	17E09	-1:08:36
Bjurholm	63N56	19E13	-1:16:52
Bjuv	56N05	12E54	-0:51:36
Blombacka	59N37	13E47	-0:55:08
Blomstermåla	56N59	16E20	-1:05:20
Blötberget	60N07	15E04	-1:00:16
Böda	57N15	17E03	-1:08:12
Boda	61N01	15E13	-1:00:52
Bodafors	57N30	14E42	-0:58:48
Boda Glasbruk	56N44	15E40	-1:02:40
Bodåsgruvan	60N25	16E26	-1:05:44
Boden	65N50	21E42	-1:26:48
Bofors	59N20	14E32	-0:58:08
Boliden	64N52	20E23	-1:21:32
Bollmora	59N15	18E13	-1:12:52
Bollnäs	61N21	16E25	-1:05:40
Bollstabruk	63N00	17E39	-1:10:36
Bollstanäs	59N30	17E56	-1:11:44
Bomhus	60N41	17E13	-1:08:52
Bona	58N34	15E03	-1:00:12
Bönan	60N44	17E18	-1:09:12
Borås	57N43	12E55	-0:51:40
Borensberg	58N34	15E17	-1:01:08
Borggård	58N44	15E32	-1:02:08
Borgholm	56N53	16E39	-1:06:36
Borlänge	60N29	15E25	-1:01:40
Borrby	55N27	14E10	-0:56:40
Bosjökloster	55N54	13E31	-0:54:04
Botkyrka	59N14	17E49	-1:11:16
Boxholm	58N12	15E03	-1:00:12
Braås	57N04	15E03	-1:00:12
Bräcke	62N43	15E27	-1:01:48
Brålanda	58N34	12E22	-0:49:28
Brastad	58N23	11E29	-0:45:56
Brattfors	59N40	14E01	-0:56:04
Bredaryd	57N10	13E44	-0:54:56
Bredbyn	63N27	18E06	-1:12:24
Bredsjö	59N50	14E44	-0:58:56
Brevens bruk	59N01	15E35	-1:02:20
Brevik	59N21	18E12	-1:12:48
Brickebacken	59N15	15E15	-1:01:00
Bro	59N31	17E38	-1:10:32
Broby	56N15	14E05	-0:56:20
Broddbo	59N59	16E28	-1:05:52
Bromölla	56N04	14E28	-0:57:52
Brötjärna	60N30	15E01	-1:00:04
Brunflo	63N05	14E49	-0:59:16
Brunna	59N51	17E26	-1:09:44
Brunnsvik	60N12	15E08	-1:00:32
Bunge	57N51	19E01	-1:16:04
Bunkeflo strand	55N33	12E57	-0:51:48
Bureå	64N37	21E12	-1:24:48
Burgsvik	57N03	18E16	-1:13:04
Burträsk	64N31	20E39	-1:22:36
Buskhyttan	58N40	16E56	-1:07:44
By	60N12	16E28	-1:05:52
Bydalen	63N06	13E47	-0:55:08
Bygdeå	64N04	20E51	-1:23:24
Byske	64N57	21E12	-1:24:48
Byxelkrok	57N20	17E00	-1:08:00
Calmar → Kalmar	56N40	16E22	-1:05:28
Charlottenberg	59N53	12E17	-0:49:08
Dala-Floda	60N31	14E47	-0:59:08
Dala-Husby	60N21	16E00	-1:04:00
Dala-Järna	60N33	14E21	-0:57:24
Dalarö	59N08	18E24	-1:13:36
Dalby	55N40	13E20	-0:53:20
Dalkarlsberg	59N26	14E51	-0:59:24
Dalsjöfors	57N43	13E05	-0:52:20
Dals-Långed	58N55	12E18	-0:49:12
Danderyd	59N25	18E01	-1:12:04
Dannemora	60N11	17E49	-1:11:16
Degeberga	55N50	14E05	-0:56:20
Degerfors	59N14	14E26	-0:57:44
Degerhamn	56N21	16E24	-1:05:36
Deje	59N36	13E28	-0:53:52
Delsbo	61N48	16E35	-1:06:20
Dingtuna	59N34	16E22	-1:05:28
Diö	56N38	14E13	-0:56:52
Djura	60N37	15E00	-1:00:00
Djurås	60N33	15E08	-1:00:32
Djurmo	60N33	15E10	-1:00:40
Djurö	59N19	18E41	-1:14:44
Djursholm	59N24	18E05	-1:12:20
Domnarvet	60N30	15E27	-1:01:48
Domsjö	63N15	18E43	-1:14:52
Dorotea	64N16	16E24	-1:05:36
Dösjebro	55N49	13E01	-0:52:04
Duved	63N24	12E52	-0:51:28

Place	Lat.	Long.	Time
Ed	58N55	11E55	-0:47:40
Edebäck	60N04	13E33	-0:54:12
Edebo	60N01	18E34	-1:14:16
Edsbro	59N54	18E29	-1:13:56
Edsbruk	58N02	16E28	-1:05:52
Edsbyn	61N23	15E49	-1:03:16
Edsgatan	59N26	13E33	-0:54:12
Ekeby	56N00	12E58	-0:51:52
Ekenässjön	57N30	15E00	-1:00:00
Eket	56N15	13E11	-0:52:44
Ekolsund	59N37	17E22	-1:09:28
Eksjö	57N40	14E57	-0:59:48
Eldforsen	60N26	14E13	-0:56:52
Emmaboda	56N38	15E32	-1:02:08
Enånger	61N32	17E00	-1:08:00
Enbacka	60N25	15E36	-1:02:24
Enköping	59N38	17E04	-1:08:16
Enstaberga	58N45	16E51	-1:07:24
Ervalla	59N22	15E15	-1:01:00
Eskilstuna	59N22	16E30	-1:06:00
Eslöv	55N50	13E20	-0:53:20
Essvik	62N19	17E24	-1:09:36
Estocolmo → Stockholm			
	59N20	18E03	-1:12:12
Everöd	55N54	14E06	-0:56:24
Fagersta	60N00	15E47	-1:03:08
Fagerviken	60N33	17E45	-1:11:00
Falkenberg	56N54	12E28	-0:49:52
Falköping	58N10	13E31	-0:54:04
Falla	58N41	15E45	-1:03:00
Falsterbo	55N24	12E50	-0:51:20
Falun	60N36	15E38	-1:02:32
Fanthyttan	59N40	15E06	-1:00:24
Färgelanda	58N34	11E59	-0:47:56
Färila	61N48	15E51	-1:03:24
Färjestaden	56N39	16E27	-1:05:48
Färna	59N47	15E51	-1:03:24
Fårösund	57N52	19E03	-1:16:12
Farsta	59N14	18E04	-1:12:16
Fellingsbro	59N26	15E35	-1:02:20
Figeholm	57N22	16E33	-1:06:12
Filipstad	59N43	14E10	-0:56:40
Finja	56N10	13E41	-0:54:44
Finnerödja	58N56	14E26	-0:57:44
Finnhamn	59N28	18E50	-1:15:20
Finspång	58N43	15E47	-1:03:08
Finsta	59N44	18E30	-1:14:00
Fiskebäckskil	58N15	11E27	-0:45:48
Fittja	59N15	17E52	-1:11:28
Fjällåsen	67N29	20E10	-1:20:40
Fjällbacka	58N36	11E17	-0:45:08
Fjärdhundra	59N47	16E56	-1:07:44
Fjugesta	59N10	14E52	-0:59:28
Flacksta	59N23	16E27	-1:05:48
Flen	59N04	16E35	-1:06:20
Floby	58N08	13E20	-0:53:20
Floda	57N48	12E22	-0:49:28
Floda	59N04	16E21	-1:05:24
Flyinge	55N45	13E21	-0:53:24
Folkärna	60N09	16E19	-1:05:16
Föllinge	63N40	14E37	-0:58:28
Fors	60N13	16E18	-1:05:12
Forsbacka	60N37	16E53	-1:07:32
Forserum	57N42	14E28	-0:57:52
Forshaga	59N32	13E28	-0:53:52
Forsmark	60N22	18E09	-1:12:36
Frånö	62N54	17E50	-1:11:20
Fränsta	62N30	16E09	-1:04:36
Fredrika	64N05	18E24	-1:13:36
Fredriksberg	60N08	14E23	-0:57:32
Fristad	57N50	13E01	-0:52:04
Fritsla	57N33	12E47	-0:51:08
Frösön	63N11	14E32	-0:58:08
Frostavallen	55N58	13E30	-0:54:00
Frövi	59N28	15E22	-1:01:28
Funäsdalen	62N32	12E33	-0:50:12
Furudal	61N10	15E08	-1:00:32
Furulund	55N46	13E04	-0:52:16
Furusund	59N40	18E55	-1:15:40
Furuvik	60N39	17E20	-1:09:20
Gäddede	64N30	14E09	-0:56:36
Gagnef	60N35	15E04	-1:00:16
Gällivare	67N07	20E45	-1:23:00
Gällö	62N55	15E14	-1:00:56
Gamla Uppsala	59N54	17E38	-1:10:32
Gamleby	57N54	16E24	-1:05:36
Gårdsjö	58N52	14E19	-0:57:16
Gårdskär	60N37	17E35	-1:10:20
Garpenberg	60N19	16E12	-1:04:48
Garphyttan	59N19	14E56	-0:59:44
Gävle	60N40	17E10	-1:08:40
Gefle → Gävle	60N40	17E10	-1:08:40
Gemla	56N52	14E38	-0:58:32
Genarp	55N36	13E23	-0:53:32
Getinge	56N49	12E44	-0:50:56
Gideåvallen	63N29	18E58	-1:15:52
Gimo	60N11	18E11	-1:12:44
Gislaved	57N18	13E32	-0:54:08
Gislövs läge	55N21	13E14	-0:52:56
Gisslarbo	59N38	15E49	-1:03:16
Glanshammar	59N19	15E24	-1:01:36
Glimåkra	56N18	14E08	-0:56:32
Glimmingehus	55N30	14E13	-0:56:52
Glommersträsk	65N16	19E38	-1:18:32
Glumslöv	55N56	12E48	-0:51:12
Gnarp	62N03	17E16	-1:09:04
Gnesta	59N03	17E18	-1:09:12
Gnosjö	57N22	13E44	-0:54:56
Godegård	58N44	15E09	-1:00:36
Göksholm	59N16	15E33	-1:02:12
Gonäs	60N09	15E06	-1:00:24
Göteborg (Gothenburg)			
	57N43	11E58	-0:47:52
Götene	58N32	13E29	-0:53:56
Gothem	57N35	18E43	-1:14:52
Gothenburg → Göteborg			
	57N43	11E58	-0:47:52
Gräddö	59N46	19E02	-1:16:08
Granbergsdal	59N24	14E35	-0:58:20
Grangärde	60N16	14E59	-0:59:56
Grängesberg	60N05	14E59	-0:59:56
Gränna	58N01	14E28	-0:57:52
Granön	64N15	19E19	-1:17:16
Gräsö	60N21	18E28	-1:13:52
Grästorp	58N20	12E40	-0:50:40
Grebbestad	58N42	11E15	-0:45:00
Grillby	59N37	17E15	-1:09:00
Grisslehamn	60N06	18E50	-1:15:20
Grums	59N21	13E06	-0:52:24
Grytgöl	58N48	15E33	-1:02:12
Grythyttan	59N42	14E32	-0:58:08
Guldsmedshyttan	59N42	15E06	-1:00:24
Gullholmen	58N11	11E24	-0:45:36
Gullspång	58N59	14E06	-0:56:24
Gunnarn	65N00	17E40	-1:10:40
Gunnebo	57N43	16E32	-1:06:08
Gusselby	59N39	15E14	-1:00:56
Gustavsberg	59N19	18E23	-1:13:32
Gusum	58N16	16E29	-1:05:56
Gysinge	60N17	16E53	-1:07:32
Gyttorp	59N31	14E58	-0:59:52
Habo	57N55	14E04	-0:56:16
Hackås	62N55	14E31	-0:58:04
Hagfors	60N02	13E42	-0:54:48
Håksberg	60N11	15E12	-1:00:48
Hällabrottet	59N07	15E12	-1:00:48
Hällberga	59N19	16E36	-1:06:24
Hällbybrunn	59N24	16E25	-1:05:40
Hällefors	59N47	14E30	-0:58:00
Hälleforsnäs	59N10	16E30	-1:06:00
Hällekis	58N38	13E25	-0:53:40
Hallen	63N11	14E05	-0:56:20
Hällestad	58N44	15E34	-1:02:16
Hällnäs	64N19	19E38	-1:18:32
Hallsberg	59N04	15E07	-1:00:28
Hållsta	59N18	16E27	-1:05:48
Hallstahammar	59N37	16E13	-1:04:52
Hallstavik	60N03	18E36	-1:14:24
Halmstad	56N39	12E50	-0:51:20
Hälsingborg → Helsingborg			
	56N03	12E42	-0:50:48
Halvarsgårdarna	60N24	15E23	-1:01:32
Hamburgsund	58N33	11E16	-0:45:04
Hammar	58N49	14E57	-0:59:48
Hammarby	60N33	16E34	-1:06:16
Hammarn	59N45	14E30	-0:58:00
Hammarö	59N20	13E31	-0:54:04
Hammarstrand	63N06	16E21	-1:05:24
Hammerdal	63N36	15E21	-1:01:24
Hampetorp	59N09	15E40	-1:02:40
Hamra	61N39	15E00	-1:00:00
Handen	59N10	18E08	-1:12:32
Handöl	63N16	12E26	-0:49:44
Haparanda	65N50	24E10	-1:36:40
Härad	59N23	16E55	-1:07:40
Harbo	60N06	17E12	-1:08:48
Harg	59N49	18E57	-1:15:48
Harg	60N11	18E24	-1:13:36
Hargshamn	60N10	18E28	-1:13:52
Härkeberga	59N42	17E11	-1:08:44
Harlösa	55N43	13E32	-0:54:08
Harmånger	61N56	17E13	-1:08:52
Harnäs	60N39	17E22	-1:09:28
Härnevi	59N44	17E05	-1:08:20
Härnösand	62N38	17E56	-1:11:44
Harstena	58N16	17E01	-1:08:04
Hasselfors	59N05	14E39	-0:58:36
Hässleholm	56N09	13E46	-0:55:04
Hästbo	60N27	16E27	-1:05:48
Haverö	62N24	15E05	-1:00:20
Hävla	58N55	15E52	-1:03:28
Heby	59N56	16E53	-1:07:32
Hede	62N25	13E30	-0:54:00
Hedemora	60N17	15E59	-1:03:56
Hedesunda	60N24	16E59	-1:07:56
Helsingborg	56N03	12E42	-0:50:48
Hemse	57N14	18E22	-1:13:28
Herräng	60N08	18E39	-1:14:36
Herrljunga	58N05	13E02	-0:52:08
Herrskogen	59N32	16E15	-1:05:00
Herstadberg	58N38	16E10	-1:04:40
Hille	60N44	17E11	-1:08:44
Hittarp	56N06	12E38	-0:50:32
Hjo	58N18	14E17	-0:57:08
Hjortkvarn	58N53	15E25	-1:01:40
Hofors	60N33	16E17	-1:05:08
Höganäs	56N12	12E33	-0:50:12
Högbo	60N40	16E48	-1:07:12
Högfors	59N59	15E01	-1:00:04
Högsby	57N10	16E02	-1:04:08
Högsjö	59N02	15E41	-1:02:44
Hohultslätt	56N58	15E39	-1:02:36
Höje	59N54	13E33	-0:54:12
Hökåsen	59N40	16E35	-1:06:20
Hököpinge	55N30	13E00	-0:52:00
Höljes	60N54	12E36	-0:50:24
Höllviksnäs	55N25	12E57	-0:51:48
Holmsund	63N42	20E21	-1:21:24
Hölö	59N01	17E35	-1:10:20
Hönö	57N42	11E39	-0:46:36
Höör	55N56	13E32	-0:54:08
Hörby	55N51	13E39	-0:54:36
Hörken	60N02	14E56	-0:59:44
Horndal	60N18	16E25	-1:05:40
Hörnefors	63N38	19E54	-1:19:36
Hörningsholm	59N03	17E40	-1:10:40
Hosjö	60N35	15E46	-1:03:04
Hotagen	63N59	14E15	-0:57:00
Hoting	64N07	16E10	-1:04:40
Hova	58N52	14E13	-0:56:52
Hovmantorp	56N47	15E08	-1:00:32
Hovsta	59N21	15E13	-1:00:52
Huddinge	59N14	17E59	-1:11:56
Huddunge	60N03	16E59	-1:07:56
Hudiksvall	61N44	17E07	-1:08:28
Hult	58N40	16E07	-1:04:28
Hultsfred	57N29	15E50	-1:03:20
Hunnebostrand	58N27	11E18	-0:45:12
Husby-Långhundra	59N45	18E01	-1:12:04
Huskvarna	57N48	14E16	-0:57:04
Husum	63N20	19E10	-1:16:40
Hyllinge	56N06	12E51	-0:51:24
Hyllstofta	56N08	13E16	-0:53:04
Hyltebruk	57N00	13E14	-0:52:56
Idkerberget	60N23	15E14	-1:00:56
Idre	61N52	12E43	-0:50:52
Igelfors	58N51	15E41	-1:02:44
Iggesund	61N38	17E04	-1:08:16
Ingelstad	56N45	14E55	-0:59:40
Ingvallsbenning	60N15	15E53	-1:03:32
Insjön	60N41	15E05	-1:00:20
Intränget	60N20	16E09	-1:04:36
Jäder	59N25	16E41	-1:06:44
Jäderfors	60N41	16E40	-1:06:40
Jakobsberg	59N26	17E50	-1:11:20
Järbo	60N43	16E36	-1:06:24
Järfälla	59N24	17E50	-1:11:20
Järlåsa	59N53	17E12	-1:08:48
Järna	59N06	17E34	-1:10:16
Järpen	63N21	13E29	-0:53:56
Järvsö	61N43	16E10	-1:04:40
Jävre	65N09	21E59	-1:27:56
Jokkmokk	66N37	19E50	-1:19:20
Jönåker	58N44	16E40	-1:06:40
Jönköping	57N47	14E11	-0:56:44
Jonstorp	56N14	12E40	-0:50:40
Jordbro	59N09	18E07	-1:12:28
Jörn	65N04	20E02	-1:20:08
Junsele	63N41	16E54	-1:07:36
Jursla	58N40	16E11	-1:04:44
Kåbdalis	66N10	20E00	-1:20:00
Kåge	64N50	20E59	-1:23:56
Kågeröd	56N01	13E06	-0:52:24
Kälarne	62N59	16E05	-1:04:20
Kalix	65N51	23E08	-1:32:32
Källfallet	59N50	15E31	-1:02:04
Kallhäll	59N27	17E48	-1:11:12
Kallinge	56N14	15E17	-1:01:08
Kalmar	56N40	16E22	-1:05:28
Kantorp	59N01	16E28	-1:05:52
Kapellskär	59N43	19E04	-1:16:16
Kappelshamn	57N51	18E47	-1:15:08
Karbenning	60N02	16E04	-1:04:16
Kårberg	58N58	14E57	-0:59:48
Kårböle	61N59	15E19	-1:01:16
Karby	59N34	18E13	-1:12:52
Karesuando	68N25	22E30	-1:30:00
Karlholmsbruk	60N31	17E35	-1:10:20
Karlsborg	58N32	14E31	-0:58:04
Karlsborg	65N48	23E17	-1:33:08
Karlsby	58N38	15E08	-1:00:32
Karlshamn	56N10	14E51	-0:59:24
Karlskoga	59N20	14E31	-0:58:04
Karlskrona	56N10	15E35	-1:02:20
Karlstad	59N22	13E30	-0:54:00
Karmansbo	59N42	15E44	-1:02:56
Kärrgruvan	60N05	15E56	-1:03:44
Kårsta	59N39	18E14	-1:12:56
Kärsta	59N40	16E49	-1:07:16
Karungi	66N03	23E57	-1:35:48
Kåseberga	55N23	14E04	-0:56:16
Katrineholm	59N00	16E12	-1:04:48
Kattarp	56N09	12E46	-0:51:04
Katthammarsvik	57N26	18E50	-1:15:20
Kävlinge	55N48	13E06	-0:52:24
Kil	59N30	13E19	-0:53:16
Kilafors	61N14	16E34	-1:06:16
Kilsmo	59N04	15E31	-1:02:04
Kimstad	58N32	15E58	-1:03:52
Kinna	57N30	12E41	-0:50:44
Kiruna	67N51	20E16	-1:21:04
Kisa	57N59	15E37	-1:02:28
Kivik	55N41	14E15	-0:57:00
Klågerup	55N36	13E15	-0:53:00
Klagshamn	55N32	12E55	-0:51:40
Klagstorp	55N24	13E22	-0:53:28
Klimpfjäll	65N04	14E52	-0:59:28
Klintehamn	57N24	18E12	-1:12:48
Klippan	56N08	13E06	-0:52:24
Kloten	59N54	15E17	-1:01:08
Knäred	56N32	13E19	-0:53:16
Knislinge	56N11	14E05	-0:56:20
Knivsta	59N43	17E48	-1:11:12
Knutby	59N55	18E15	-1:13:00
Kolbäck	59N34	16E15	-1:05:00
Kolmården	58N40	16E23	-1:05:32
Kolsva	59N36	15E50	-1:03:20
Köping	59N31	16E00	-1:04:00
Köpmanholmen	63N10	18E34	-1:14:16
Kopparberg	59N52	14E59	-0:59:56
Koppom	59N43	12E09	-0:48:36
Korså	60N38	16E08	-1:04:32
Korselbränna	64N27	15E35	-1:02:20
Korsnäs	60N35	15E43	-1:02:52
Koskullskulle	67N12	20E50	-1:23:20
Kosta	56N51	15E23	-1:01:32
Kramfors	62N56	17E47	-1:11:08
Krångede	63N09	16E05	-1:04:20
Krapperup	56N16	12E31	-0:50:04
Kristdala	57N24	16E11	-1:04:44
Kristianopel	56N15	16E02	-1:04:08
Kristianstad	56N02	14E08	-0:56:32
Kristineberg	65N04	18E35	-1:14:20
Kristinehamn	59N20	14E07	-0:56:28
Krokek	58N40	16E24	-1:05:36

Krokom	63N19	14E30	-0:58:00
Krylbo	60N08	16E13	-1:04:52
Kumla	59N08	15E08	-1:00:32
Kummelnäs	59N21	18E17	-1:13:08
Kungälv	57N52	11E58	-0:47:52
Kungsängen	59N29	17E45	-1:11:00
Kungsbacka	57N29	12E04	-0:48:16
Kungsgården	60N36	16E37	-1:06:28
Kungshamn	58N22	11E15	-0:45:00
Kungsör	59N25	16E05	-1:04:20
Kvarnsveden	60N31	15E24	-1:01:36
Kvarntorp	59N08	15E15	-1:01:00
Kvarsebo	58N39	16E39	-1:06:36
Kvicksund	59N27	16E19	-1:05:16
Kvidinge	56N08	13E04	-0:52:16
Kvikkjokk	66N55	17E50	-1:11:20
Kvissleby	62N17	17E21	-1:09:24
Kvistbro	59N09	14E49	-0:59:16
Kyrkheden	60N10	13E29	-0:53:56
Läckö	58N41	13E13	-0:52:52
Lagan	56N55	13E59	-0:55:56
Laholm	56N31	13E02	-0:52:08
Laisvall	66N05	17E10	-1:08:40
Lammhult	57N10	14E35	-0:58:20
Landsbro	57N22	14E54	-0:59:36
Landskrona	55N52	12E50	-0:51:20
Långban	59N51	14E15	-0:57:00
Långsele	63N11	17E04	-1:08:16
Långshyttan	60N27	16E01	-1:04:04
Lannabruk	59N14	14E56	-0:59:44
Lännaholm	59N53	17E57	-1:11:48
Lärbro	57N47	18E47	-1:15:08
Lästringe	58N54	17E18	-1:09:12
Laxå	58N59	14E37	-0:58:28
Leksand	60N44	14E59	-0:59:56
Leksberg	59N41	13E49	-0:55:16
Lenhovda	57N00	15E17	-1:01:08
Lerberget	56N11	12E33	-0:50:12
Lerum	57N46	12E16	-0:49:04
Lesjöfors	59N59	14E11	-0:56:44
Lessebo	56N45	15E16	-1:01:04
Lickershamn	57N50	18E31	-1:14:04
Liden	62N42	16E48	-1:07:12
Lidingö	59N22	18E08	-1:12:32
Lidköping	58N30	13E10	-0:52:40
Liljendal	60N08	14E04	-0:56:16
Lilla Edet	58N08	12E08	-0:48:32
Lillån	59N19	15E13	-1:00:52
Lillhärdal	61N51	14E04	-0:56:16
Lima	60N56	13E26	-0:53:44
Limmared	57N32	13E21	-0:53:24
Linanäs	59N28	18E31	-1:14:04
Linderöd	55N56	13E49	-0:55:16
Lindesberg	59N35	15E15	-1:01:00
Lindesnäs	60N20	14E32	-0:58:08
Lindfors	59N36	13E49	-0:55:16
Lindholmen	59N35	18E06	-1:12:24
Lindö	58N37	16E15	-1:05:00
Lindome	57N34	12E05	-0:48:20
Lingbo	61N03	16E41	-1:06:44
Linköping	58N25	15E37	-1:02:28
Lit	63N19	14E49	-0:59:16
Ljugarn	57N19	18E42	-1:14:48
Ljunga	58N31	16E21	-1:05:24
Ljungaverk	62N29	16E03	-1:04:12
Ljungby	56N50	13E56	-0:55:44
Ljungbyhed	56N04	13E12	-0:52:48
Ljungbyholm	56N38	16E10	-1:04:40
Ljungdalen	62N51	12E47	-0:51:08
Ljungsbro	58N31	15E30	-1:02:00
Ljungskile	58N14	11E55	-0:47:40
Ljusdal	61N50	16E05	-1:04:20
Ljusfallshammar	58N47	15E29	-1:01:56
Ljusne	61N13	17E08	-1:08:32
Löberöd	55N47	13E30	-0:54:00
Löddeköpinge	55N46	13E01	-0:52:04
Loka brunn	59N36	14E28	-0:57:52
Lomma	55N41	13E05	-0:52:20
Lönsboda	56N24	14E19	-0:57:16
Los	61N44	15E10	-1:00:40
Lotorp	58N44	15E50	-1:03:20
Lövånger	64N22	21E18	-1:25:12
Lövstabruk	60N24	17E53	-1:11:32
Ludgo	58N55	17E08	-1:08:32
Ludvika	60N09	15E11	-1:00:44
Lugnås	58N39	13E42	-0:54:48
Luleå	65N34	22E10	-1:28:40
Lumsheden	60N43	16E15	-1:05:00
Lund	55N42	13E11	-0:52:44
Lundsberg	59N30	14E10	-0:56:40
Luspebryggan	67N01	19E51	-1:19:24
Lyckeby	56N12	15E39	-1:02:36
Lycksele	64N36	18E40	-1:14:40
Lyrestad	58N48	14E04	-0:56:16
Lysekil	58N16	11E26	-0:45:44
Malå	65N11	18E44	-1:14:56
Målilla	57N23	15E48	-1:03:12
Malmbäck	57N35	14E28	-0:57:52
Malmberget	67N10	20E40	-1:22:40
Malmköping	59N08	16E44	-1:06:56
Malmö	55N36	13E00	-0:52:00
Malmslätt	58N25	15E30	-1:02:00
Malung	60N40	13E44	-0:54:56
Månkarbo	60N14	17E28	-1:09:52
Mariannelund	57N37	15E34	-1:02:16
Mariedamm	58N51	15E09	-1:00:36
Mariefred	59N16	17E13	-1:08:52
Marieholm	55N52	13E09	-0:52:36
Mariestad	58N43	13E51	-0:55:24
Markaryd	56N26	13E36	-0:54:24
Marma	61N16	16E52	-1:07:28
Marma	60N30	17E25	-1:09:40
Märsta	59N37	17E51	-1:11:24
Marstrand	57N53	11E35	-0:46:20
Marviken	58N34	16E51	-1:07:24
Matfors	62N21	17E02	-1:08:08
Matsknutsgårdarna	60N28	15E22	-1:01:28
Medevi	58N40	14E57	-0:59:48
Mehede	60N27	17E24	-1:09:36
Mellansel	63N26	18E19	-1:13:16
Mellerud	58N42	12E28	-0:49:52
Mellösa	59N06	16E33	-1:06:12
Mjälgen	60N33	15E07	-1:00:28
Mjällom	62N59	18E26	-1:13:44
Mjölby	58N19	15E08	-1:00:32
Mockfjärd	60N30	14E58	-0:59:52
Moheda	57N00	14E34	-0:58:16
Moholm	58N37	14E02	-0:56:08
Möklinta	60N05	16E32	-1:06:08
Molkom	59N36	13E43	-0:54:52
Mölle	56N17	12E29	-0:49:56
Mollösund	58N04	11E28	-0:45:52
Mölnbo	59N03	17E25	-1:09:40
Mölndal	57N39	12E01	-0:48:04
Mölnlycke	57N39	12E09	-0:48:36
Mölntorp	59N33	16E15	-1:05:00
Mönsterås	57N02	16E26	-1:05:44
Mora	61N00	14E33	-0:58:12
Moraby	60N23	15E35	-1:02:20
Mörarp	56N04	12E52	-0:51:28
Mörbylånga	56N31	16E23	-1:05:32
Morgårdshammar	60N09	15E23	-1:01:32
Morgongåva	59N56	16E57	-1:07:48
Mörlunda	57N19	15E51	-1:03:24
Mörrum	56N11	14E45	-0:59:00
Mosås	59N12	15E08	-1:00:32
Motala	58N33	15E03	-1:00:12
Motjärnshyttan	59N56	13E58	-0:55:52
Mullhyttan	59N09	14E41	-0:58:44
Mullsjö	57N55	13E53	-0:55:32
Munka-Ljungby	56N15	12E58	-0:51:52
Munkedal	58N29	11E41	-0:46:44
Munkerud	59N50	13E31	-0:54:04
Munkfors	59N50	13E32	-0:54:08
Munksund	65N17	21E29	-1:25:56
Munktorp	59N32	16E08	-1:04:32
Myckelgensjö	63N34	17E37	-1:10:28
Nacka	59N18	18E10	-1:12:40
Naglarby	60N25	15E34	-1:02:16
Närkes Marieberg	59N12	15E10	-1:00:40
Nås	60N27	14E29	-0:57:56
Näs	58N41	15E50	-1:03:20
Näsåker	63N26	16E54	-1:07:36
Nässjö	57N39	14E41	-0:58:44
Nävekvarn	58N38	16E49	-1:07:16
Nedre Soppero	68N01	21E44	-1:26:56
Njurunda	62N16	17E22	-1:09:28
Nora	59N31	15E02	-1:00:08
Norberg	60N04	15E56	-1:03:44
Nordanholen	60N30	14E57	-0:59:48
Nordingrå	62N56	18E16	-1:13:04
Nordmaling	63N34	19E30	-1:18:00
Nordmark	59N50	14E06	-0:56:24
Norrahammar	57N42	14E06	-0:56:24
Norra Rörum	56N01	13E30	-0:54:00
Norrboda	60N28	18E25	-1:13:40
Norrfjärden	65N25	21E27	-1:25:48
Norrköping	58N36	16E11	-1:04:44
Norrskedika	60N17	18E17	-1:13:08
Norrsundet	60N56	17E08	-1:08:32
Norrtälje	59N46	18E42	-1:14:48
Norsjö	64N55	19E29	-1:17:56
Nossebro	58N11	12E43	-0:50:52
Nybro	56N45	15E54	-1:03:36
Nyhammar	60N17	14E58	-0:59:52
Nyhyttan	59N40	14E48	-0:59:12
Nyköping	58N45	17E00	-1:08:00
Nykroppa	59N38	14E18	-0:57:12
Nykvarn	59N11	17E26	-1:09:44
Nyland	63N00	17E46	-1:11:04
Nynäshamn	58N54	17E57	-1:11:48
Nyvång	56N08	12E54	-0:51:36
Obbola	63N42	20E19	-1:21:16
Ockelbo	60N53	16E43	-1:06:52
Öckerö	57N43	11E39	-0:46:36
Ödåkra	56N06	12E44	-0:50:56
Ödeby	59N24	15E25	-1:01:40
Odensbacken	59N10	15E32	-1:02:08
Ödeshög	58N14	14E39	-0:58:36
Offerdal	63N28	14E00	-0:56:00
Öje	60N49	13E51	-0:55:24
Olofström	56N16	14E30	-0:58:00
Olshammar	58N45	14E48	-0:59:12
Opsaheden	60N28	13E59	-0:55:56
Örbyhus	60N14	17E42	-1:10:48
Örebro	59N17	15E13	-1:00:52
Öregrund	60N20	18E26	-1:13:44
Örkelljunga	56N17	13E17	-0:53:08
Ornäs	60N31	15E32	-1:02:08
Örnsköldsvik	63N18	18E43	-1:14:52
Orrefors	56N50	15E45	-1:03:00
Orsa	61N07	14E37	-0:58:28
Örsundsbro	59N44	17E18	-1:09:12
Örtofta	55N47	13E14	-0:52:56
Örträsk	64N08	18E59	-1:15:56
Osby	56N22	13E59	-0:55:56
Osbyholm	55N51	13E36	-0:54:24
Oskar-Fredriksborg	59N24	18E26	-1:13:44
Oskarshamn	57N16	16E26	-1:05:44
Oskarström	56N48	12E58	-0:51:52
Ösmo	58N59	17E54	-1:11:36
Östanå	59N33	18E35	-1:14:20
Östanå	60N38	16E48	-1:07:12
Östanbyn	60N39	16E48	-1:07:12
Östansjö	59N03	14E59	-0:59:56
Österbybruk	60N12	17E54	-1:11:36
Österbymo	57N50	15E16	-1:01:04
Österfärnebo	60N18	16E48	-1:07:12
Österhaninge	59N08	18E12	-1:12:48
Österlövsta	60N26	17E47	-1:11:08
Österskär	59N28	18E18	-1:13:12
Östersund	63N11	14E39	-0:58:36
Östervåla	60N11	17E11	-1:08:44
Östhammar	60N16	18E22	-1:13:28
Östmark	60N17	12E45	-0:51:00
Östraby	55N46	13E41	-0:54:44
Östra Grevie	55N28	13E08	-0:52:32
Östra Husby	58N35	16E33	-1:06:12
Östra Ljungby	56N11	13E04	-0:52:16
Ottenby	56N14	16E25	-1:05:40
Otterbäcken	58N57	14E02	-0:56:08
Övedskloster	55N41	13E38	-0:54:32
Överkalix	66N21	22E56	-1:31:44
Övertorneå	66N23	23E40	-1:34:40
Överum	57N59	16E19	-1:05:16
Oviken	62N59	14E24	-0:57:36
Oxelösund	58N40	17E06	-1:08:24
Oxie	55N33	13E04	-0:52:16
Pajala	67N11	23E22	-1:33:28
Pålsboda	59N04	15E20	-1:01:20
Partille	57N44	12E07	-0:48:28
Påryd	56N34	15E55	-1:03:40
Påskallavik	57N10	16E27	-1:05:48
Penningby	59N41	18E40	-1:14:40
Persberg	59N45	14E15	-0:57:00
Pershagen	59N10	17E39	-1:10:36
Pershyttan	59N30	15E00	-1:00:00
Perstorp	56N08	13E23	-0:53:32
Piteå	65N20	21E30	-1:26:00
Polcirkeln	66N34	21E05	-1:24:20
Råå	56N00	12E44	-0:50:56
Råda	60N00	13E36	-0:54:24
Rågsveden	60N29	14E05	-0:56:20
Rämmen	60N07	14E08	-0:56:32
Ramnäs	59N46	16E12	-1:04:48
Ramsberg	59N46	15E17	-1:01:08
Ramsele	63N33	16E29	-1:05:56
Rämshyttan	60N18	15E13	-1:00:52
Ramsjö	62N11	15E39	-1:02:36
Ramvik	62N49	17E51	-1:11:24
Rånäs	59N48	18E17	-1:13:08
Råneå	65N52	22E18	-1:29:12
Ransäter	59N46	13E26	-0:53:44
Ransta	59N48	16E38	-1:06:32
Råö	57N24	11E56	-0:47:44
Rasbo	59N57	17E53	-1:11:32
Rätansbyn	62N29	14E32	-0:58:08
Rättvik	60N53	15E06	-1:00:24
Rejmyra	58N50	15E55	-1:03:40
Rekarne	59N26	16E20	-1:05:20
Rensjön	68N05	19E49	-1:19:16
Repbäcken	60N31	15E20	-1:01:20
Resarö	59N26	18E20	-1:13:20
Riddarhyttan	59N48	15E33	-1:02:12
Riksgränsen	68N24	18E12	-1:12:48
Rimbo	59N45	18E22	-1:13:28
Rimforsa	58N08	15E40	-1:02:40
Risbäck	64N42	15E32	-1:02:08
Risinge	58N42	15E51	-1:03:24
Robertsfors	64N11	20E51	-1:23:24
Robertsholm	60N35	76E16	-5:05:04
Röbrinken	58N36	15E53	-1:03:32
Rockhammar	59N32	15E26	-1:01:44
Röfors	58N57	14E37	-0:58:28
Röke	56N14	13E30	-0:54:00
Romakloster	57N31	18E27	-1:13:48
Romfartuna	59N44	16E35	-1:06:20
Romme	60N26	15E30	-1:02:00
Ronehamn	57N10	18E29	-1:13:56
Ronneby	56N12	15E18	-1:01:12
Rönneshytta	58N56	15E02	-1:00:08
Rönninge	59N12	17E44	-1:10:56
Rörbäcksnäs	61N08	12E49	-0:51:16
Rosersberg	59N35	17E53	-1:11:32
Roslags-Bro	59N50	18E44	-1:14:56
Roslags-Näsby	59N26	18E04	-1:12:16
Rosshyttan	60N04	16E21	-1:05:24
Rossön	63N55	16E21	-1:05:24
Röstånga	56N00	13E17	-0:53:08
Rundvik	63N32	19E26	-1:17:44
Runhällen	60N02	16E49	-1:07:16
Ryd	56N28	14E41	-0:58:44
Rydaholm	56N59	14E16	-0:57:04
Rydbo	59N28	18E11	-1:12:44
Rydsgård	55N28	13E35	-0:54:20
Sädvaluspen	66N24	16E51	-1:07:24
Säffle	59N08	12E56	-0:51:44
Sala	59N55	16E36	-1:06:24
Salbohed	59N55	16E19	-1:05:16
Salem	59N13	17E44	-1:10:56
Sälen	61N10	13E16	-0:53:04
Saltsjöbaden	59N17	18E18	-1:13:12
Sandared	57N43	12E47	-0:51:08
Sandarne	61N16	17E10	-1:08:40
Sandhamn	59N17	18E55	-1:15:40
Sandslån	63N01	17E47	-1:11:08
Sandviken	60N37	16E46	-1:07:04
Sannahed	59N06	15E09	-1:00:36
Särna	61N41	13E08	-0:52:32
Säter	60N21	15E45	-1:03:00
Sätrabrunn	59N51	16E27	-1:05:48
Sävar	63N54	20E34	-1:22:16
Sävsjö	57N25	14E40	-0:58:40
Saxdalen	60N09	14E57	-0:59:48
Seskarön	65N44	23E44	-1:34:56
Siggebohyttan	59N37	15E01	-1:00:04
Sigtuna	59N37	17E43	-1:10:52
Sikfors	59N48	14E35	-0:58:20
Siljansnäs	60N45	14E42	-0:58:48
Silverdalen	57N32	15E44	-1:02:56
Simonstorp	58N47	16E09	-1:04:36
Simpnäs	59N52	19E04	-1:16:16
Simrishamn	55N33	14E20	-0:57:20
Singö	60N10	18E44	-1:14:56

SWEDEN SUECIA SUÈDE SCHWEDEN SVERIGE

Place	Lat	Long	Time
Själevad	63N18	18E36	-1:14:24
Sjöbo	55N38	13E42	-0:54:48
Sjösa	58N46	17E04	-1:08:16
Sjötorp	58N50	13E59	-0:55:56
Skagersvik	58N58	14E06	-0:56:24
Skälderviken	56N17	12E50	-0:51:20
Skänninge	58N24	15E05	-1:00:20
Skanör	55N25	12E52	-0:51:28
Skara	58N22	13E25	-0:53:40
Skärblacka	58N34	15E54	-1:03:36
Skärhamn	58N00	11E33	-0:46:12
Skarhult	55N49	13E23	-0:53:32
Skärplinge	60N28	17E46	-1:11:04
Skattkärr	59N25	13E41	-0:54:44
Skebobruk	59N58	18E36	-1:14:24
Skebokvarn	59N04	16E42	-1:06:48
Skegrie	55N24	13E04	-0:52:16
Skellefteå	64N46	20E57	-1:23:48
Skelleftehamn	64N41	21E14	-1:24:56
Skene	57N29	12E38	-0:50:32
Skepptuna	59N43	18E05	-1:12:20
Skillingaryd	57N26	14E05	-0:56:20
Skinnskatteberg	59N50	15E41	-1:02:44
Skivarp	55N25	13E34	-0:54:16
Skoby	60N02	18E01	-1:12:04
Skoghall	59N19	13E26	-0:53:44
Skogstorp	59N20	16E28	-1:05:52
Sköldinge	59N02	16E26	-1:05:44
Sköllersta	59N09	15E20	-1:01:20
Skolsta	59N40	17E14	-1:08:56
Skövde	58N24	13E50	-0:55:20
Skromberga	56N00	12E58	-0:51:52
Skruv	56N41	15E22	-1:01:28
Skulforp	58N21	13E49	-0:55:16
Skultuna	59N43	16E25	-1:05:40
Skurup	55N28	13E30	-0:54:00
Skutskär	60N38	17E25	-1:09:40
Skyllberg	58N57	14E59	-0:59:56
Skyttorp	60N05	17E44	-1:10:56
Slagnäs	65N34	18E05	-1:12:20
Slite	57N43	18E48	-1:15:12
Smålandsstenar	57N10	13E24	-0:53:36
Smedby	58N33	16E16	-1:05:04
Smedjebacken	60N08	15E25	-1:01:40
Smögen	58N21	11E13	-0:44:52
Smygehamn	55N21	13E22	-0:53:28
Söderbärke	60N05	15E33	-1:02:12
Söderby-Karl	59N53	18E41	-1:14:44
Söderfors	60N23	17E14	-1:08:56
Söderhamn	61N18	17E03	-1:08:12
Söderköping	58N29	16E18	-1:05:12
Södertälje	59N12	17E37	-1:10:28
Södra Åby	55N23	13E18	-0:53:12
Södra Råda	59N01	14E10	-0:56:40
Södra Sandby	55N43	13E20	-0:53:20
Södra Vi	57N45	15E48	-1:03:12
Sofiero	56N05	12E39	-0:50:36
Solberg	63N47	17E38	-1:10:32
Sollefteå	63N10	17E16	-1:09:04
Sollentuna	59N28	17E54	-1:11:36
Solna	59N22	18E01	-1:12:04
Solvarbo	60N24	15E40	-1:02:40
Sölvesborg	56N03	14E33	-0:58:12
Sonstorp	58N45	15E36	-1:02:24
Söråker	62N31	17E30	-1:10:00
Sörberge	62N31	17E22	-1:09:28
Sörforsa	61N40	17E00	-1:08:00
Sorsele	65N30	17E30	-1:10:00
Sörstafors	59N35	16E13	-1:04:52
Sorunda	59N01	17E48	-1:11:12
Sörvik	60N11	15E09	-1:00:36
Sösdala	56N02	13E40	-0:54:40
Sövestad	55N30	13E47	-0:55:08
Sparreholm	59N04	16E49	-1:07:16
Spillersboda	59N42	18E51	-1:15:24
Staffanstorp	55N38	13E13	-0:52:52
Stäket	59N28	17E48	-1:11:12
Stallarholmen	59N22	17E12	-1:08:48
Ställberg	59N59	14E55	-0:59:40
Ställdalen	59N56	14E56	-0:59:44
Stånga	57N17	18E28	-1:13:52
Stångby	55N46	13E10	-0:52:40
Stavsnäs	59N17	18E41	-1:14:44
Stegeborg	58N26	16E35	-1:06:20
Stehag	55N54	13E23	-0:53:32
Stensätra	60N36	16E44	-1:06:56
Stensele	65N05	17E09	-1:08:36
Stenstorp	58N16	13E43	-0:54:52
Stenungsund	58N05	11E49	-0:47:16
Stidsvig	56N12	13E08	-0:52:32
Stigtomta	58N48	16E47	-1:07:08
Stjärnhov	59N05	17E00	-1:08:00
Stjärnsund	60N26	16E12	-1:04:48
Stjärnsund	58N51	14E55	-0:59:40
Stockamöllan	55N57	13E22	-0:53:28
Stockby	59N20	17E41	-1:10:44
Stockholm	59N20	18E03	-1:12:12
Stocksund	59N23	18E04	-1:12:16
Stöde	62N25	16E35	-1:06:20
Stöllet	60N24	13E16	-0:53:04
Storå	59N43	15E08	-1:00:32
Stora Mellösa	59N13	15E30	-1:02:00
Stora Skedvi	60N24	15E48	-1:03:12
Stora Sundby	59N16	16E07	-1:04:28
Stora Vika	58N56	17E48	-1:11:12
Storfors	59N32	14E16	-0:57:04
Storlien	63N19	12E06	-0:48:24
Stornorrforsen	63N52	20E03	-1:20:12
Storuman	65N06	17E06	-1:08:24
Storvik	60N35	16E32	-1:06:08
Storvreta	59N58	17E42	-1:10:48
Strängnäs	59N23	17E02	-1:08:08
Strångsjö	58N54	16E12	-1:04:48
Stråssa	59N45	15E13	-1:00:52
Striberg	59N33	14E56	-0:59:44
Strömsberg	60N24	17E35	-1:10:20
Strömsbro	60N42	17E10	-1:08:40
Strömsbruk	61N53	17E19	-1:09:16
Strömsholm	59N32	16E15	-1:05:00
Strömsnäsbruk	56N33	13E43	-0:54:52
Strömstad	58N56	11E10	-0:44:40
Strömsund	63N51	15E35	-1:02:20
Strövelstorp	56N09	12E49	-0:51:16
Studsvik	58N46	17E23	-1:09:32
Stugun	63N10	15E36	-1:02:24
Sundby	59N23	17E03	-1:08:12
Sundbyberg	59N22	17E58	-1:11:52
Sundbyholm	59N27	16E37	-1:06:28
Sundsbruk	62N27	17E22	-1:09:28
Sundsvall	62N23	17E18	-1:09:12
Sunnansjö	60N13	14E57	-0:59:48
Sunne	59N50	13E09	-0:52:36
Sunnemo	59N53	13E43	-0:54:52
Sunnersta	59N48	17E39	-1:10:36
Surahammar	59N43	16E13	-1:04:52
Surte	57N49	12E01	-0:48:04
Svalöv	55N55	13E06	-0:52:24
Svaneholm	55N30	13E28	-0:53:52
Svängsta	56N16	14E46	-0:59:04
Svanskog	59N11	12E33	-0:50:12
Svappavaara	67N39	21E04	-1:24:16
Svärdsjö	60N45	15E55	-1:03:40
Svartå	59N08	14E31	-0:58:04
Svarte	55N25	13E43	-0:54:52
Svärtinge	58N39	16E00	-1:04:00
Svedala	55N30	13E14	-0:52:56
Sveg	62N02	14E21	-0:57:24
Svenljunga	57N30	13E07	-0:52:28
Svennevad	59N01	15E22	-1:01:28
Svenstorp	55N46	13E15	-0:53:00
Svinesund	59N06	11E16	-0:45:04
Syssleback	60N44	12E52	-0:51:28
Taberg	57N41	14E05	-0:56:20
Taberg	59N50	14E08	-0:56:32
Täby	59N30	18E03	-1:12:12
Tågarp	55N56	12E57	-0:51:48
Tällberg	60N49	15E00	-1:00:00
Tånga	56N12	12E46	-0:51:04
Tännäs	62N27	12E40	-0:50:40
Tanumshede	58N44	11E19	-0:45:16
Tärendö	67N10	22E38	-1:30:32
Tärnaby	65N43	15E16	-1:01:04
Tärnsjö	60N09	16E56	-1:07:44
Tåsjö	64N13	15E54	-1:03:36
Teckomatorp	55N52	13E05	-0:52:20
Tensta	60N02	17E40	-1:10:40
Tibro	58N26	14E10	-0:56:40
Tidaholm	58N11	13E57	-0:55:48
Tidö	59N30	16E28	-1:05:52
Tierp	60N20	17E30	-1:10:00
Tillberga	59N41	16E37	-1:06:28
Timmernabben	56N58	16E26	-1:05:44
Tingsryd	56N32	14E59	-0:59:56
Tingstäde	57N44	18E36	-1:14:24
Tjällmo	58N43	15E21	-1:01:24
Tjörnarp	56N00	13E37	-0:54:28
Tobo	60N16	17E39	-1:10:36
Töcksfors	59N30	11E50	-0:47:20
Tollarp	55N56	13E59	-0:55:56
Tomelilla	55N33	13E57	-0:55:48
Tönnet	60N14	13E30	-0:54:00
Töre	65N54	22E39	-1:30:36
Töreboda	58N43	14E08	-0:56:32
Torekov	56N26	12E37	-0:50:28
Torhamn	56N05	15E50	-1:03:20
Tormestorp	56N07	13E44	-0:54:56
Torsåker	60N31	16E29	-1:05:56
Torsås	56N24	16E00	-1:04:00
Torsby	60N08	13E00	-0:52:00
Torshälla	59N25	16E28	-1:05:52
Torsö	58N47	13E48	-0:55:12
Torup	56N58	13E05	-0:52:20
Torup	55N34	13E12	-0:52:48
Träkvista	59N16	17E17	-1:11:08
Tranås	58N03	14E59	-0:59:56
Tranemo	57N29	13E21	-0:53:24
Trängslet	61N25	13E40	-0:54:40
Transtrand	61N05	13E19	-0:53:16
Träslövsläge	57N04	12E16	-0:49:04
Trehörningsjö	63N42	18E48	-1:15:12
Trelleborg	55N22	13E10	-0:52:40
Trolleholm	55N54	13E15	-0:53:00
Trollhättan	58N16	12E18	-0:49:12
Trosa	58N54	17E33	-1:10:12
Tullgarn	58N57	17E35	-1:10:20
Tullinge	59N12	17E53	-1:11:32
Tumba	59N12	17E49	-1:11:16
Tuna-Hästberg	60N20	15E11	-1:00:44
Tungelsta	59N06	18E02	-1:12:08
Turinge	59N12	17E27	-1:09:48
Tyfors	60N09	14E12	-0:56:48
Tygelsjö	55N31	13E00	-0:52:00
Tylla	60N28	15E33	-1:02:12
Tylösand	56N39	12E44	-0:50:56
Tyngsjö	60N18	13E53	-0:55:32
Tynnelsö	59N25	17E06	-1:08:24
Tyresö	59N14	18E18	-1:13:12
Tyringe	56N10	13E35	-0:54:20
Tystberga	58N52	17E15	-1:09:00
Uddeholm	60N01	13E37	-0:54:28
Uddevalla	58N21	11E55	-0:47:40
Ullervad	58N40	13E52	-0:55:28
Ullvi	59N42	16E37	-1:06:28
Ulricehamn	57N47	13E25	-0:53:40
Ulvshyttan	60N18	15E22	-1:01:28
Umeå	63N50	20E15	-1:21:00
Umfors	65N56	15E00	-1:00:00
Umnäs	65N24	16E10	-1:04:40
Undenäs	58N39	14E25	-0:57:40
Undersåker	63N20	13E23	-0:53:32
Untraverket	60N25	17E18	-1:09:12
Upplanda	60N14	17E44	-1:10:56
Upplands Väsby	59N31	17E54	-1:11:36
Uppsala	59N52	17E38	-1:10:32
Upsala → Uppsala	59N52	17E38	-1:10:32
Vä	55N59	14E05	-0:56:20
Vad	60N02	15E39	-1:02:36
Vadsbro	58N58	16E36	-1:06:24
Vadstena	58N27	14E54	-0:59:36
Vaggeryd	57N30	14E07	-0:56:28
Vagnhärad	58N55	17E30	-1:10:00
Vålådalen	63N10	12E57	-0:51:48
Vålberg	59N24	13E12	-0:52:48
Valbo	60N40	17E04	-1:08:16
Valdemarsvik	58N12	16E36	-1:06:24
Valla	59N02	16E23	-1:05:32
Vallåkra	55N58	12E52	-0:51:28
Vallentuna	59N32	18E05	-1:12:20
Valsjöbyn	64N04	14E08	-0:56:32
Valskog	59N27	15E57	-1:03:48
Våmhus	61N08	14E28	-0:57:52
Vänersborg	58N22	12E19	-0:49:16
Vännäs	63N55	19E45	-1:19:00
Vansbro	60N31	14E13	-0:56:52
Vara	58N16	12E57	-0:51:48
Varberg	57N06	12E15	-0:49:00
Vårgårda	58N02	12E48	-0:51:12
Vargön	58N22	12E22	-0:49:28
Värnamo	57N11	14E02	-0:56:08
Varnhem	58N23	13E39	-0:54:36
Värö	57N16	12E11	-0:48:44
Vårsta	59N10	17E48	-1:11:12
Väse	59N23	13E57	-0:55:48
Västanfors	59N59	15E49	-1:03:16
Västerås	59N37	16E33	-1:06:12
Västerby	60N19	15E55	-1:03:40
Västerfärnebo	59N57	16E17	-1:05:08
Västerhaninge	59N07	18E06	-1:12:24
Västervik	57N45	16E38	-1:06:32
Västra Torup	56N09	13E29	-0:53:56
Vattholma	60N01	17E44	-1:10:56
Vaxholm	59N24	18E20	-1:13:20
Växjö	56N52	14E49	-0:59:16
Veberöd	55N38	13E29	-0:53:56
Veddige	57N16	12E19	-0:49:16
Vedevåg	59N32	15E17	-1:01:08
Vejbystrand	56N19	12E45	-0:51:00
Vellinge	55N28	13E01	-0:52:04
Vemdalen	62N27	13E52	-0:55:28
Vendel	60N10	17E36	-1:10:24
Vendelsö	59N12	18E12	-1:12:48
Venjan	60N57	13E55	-0:55:40
Vetlanda	57N26	15E04	-1:00:16
Vidsel	65N51	20E24	-1:21:36
Vik	59N44	17E28	-1:09:52
Vika	60N31	15E42	-1:02:48
Viken	56N09	12E34	-0:50:16
Vikmanshyttan	60N17	15E49	-1:03:16
Vilhelmina	64N37	16E39	-1:06:36
Vimmerby	57N40	15E51	-1:03:24
Vindeln	64N12	19E44	-1:18:56
Vingåker	59N02	15E52	-1:03:28
Vinslöv	56N06	13E55	-0:55:40
Vintrosa	59N15	14E57	-0:59:48
Virsbo	59N52	16E02	-1:04:08
Virserum	57N19	15E35	-1:02:20
Visby	57N38	18E18	-1:13:12
Viskafors	57N38	12E50	-0:51:20
Vislanda	56N47	14E27	-0:57:48
Vissefjärda	56N32	15E35	-1:02:20
Vittinge	59N54	17E04	-1:08:16
Vittsjö	56N20	13E40	-0:54:40
Vivsta	62N29	17E19	-1:09:16
Vollsjö	55N42	13E46	-0:55:04
Vrena	58N52	16E41	-1:06:44
Vretstorp	59N02	14E52	-0:59:28
Vrigstad	57N21	14E28	-0:57:52
Vuoggatjålme	66N36	16E22	-1:05:28
Wisby → Visby	57N38	18E18	-1:13:12
Ystad	55N25	13E49	-0:55:16
Ytterharnäs	60N39	17E21	-1:09:24
Ytterhogdal	62N12	14E51	-0:59:24
Yttermalung	60N35	13E50	-0:55:20
Ytterselö	59N23	17E15	-1:09:00
Yxsjöberg	60N03	14E46	-0:59:04
Zinkgruvan	58N49	15E05	-1:00:20

SCHWEIZ SUIZA SVIZZERA SUISSE SWITZERLAND

Time Table # 1
Before 1/Jun/1894 LMT
Begin Standard 15E00
1/Jun/1894 0:00 -1:00
5/May/1941 2:00 -2:00
6/Oct/1941 0:00 -1:00
4/May/1942 2:00 -2:00
5/Oct/1942 0:00 -1:00
29/Mar/1981 2:00 -2:00
27/Sep/1981 3:00 -1:00
28/Mar/1982 2:00 -2:00
26/Sep/1982 3:00 -1:00
27/Mar/1983 2:00 -2:00
25/Sep/1983 3:00 -1:00
25/Mar/1984 2:00 -2:00
30/Sep/1984 3:00 -1:00
31/Mar/1985 2:00 -2:00
29/Sep/1985 3:00 -1:00
30/Mar/1986 2:00 -2:00
28/Sep/1986 3:00 -1:00
29/Mar/1987 2:00 -2:00
27/Sep/1987 3:00 -1:00
27/Mar/1988 2:00 -2:00
25/Sep/1988 3:00 -1:00
26/Mar/1989 2:00 -2:00
24/Sep/1989 3:00 -1:00
25/Mar/1990 2:00 -2:00
30/Sep/1990 3:00 -1:00
31/Mar/1991 2:00 -2:00
29/Sep/1991 3:00 -1:00
29/Mar/1992 2:00 -2:00
27/Sep/1992 3:00 -1:00
28/Mar/1993 2:00 -2:00
26/Sep/1993 3:00 -1:00
27/Mar/1994 2:00 -2:00
25/Sep/1994 3:00 -1:00
26/Mar/1995 2:00 -2:00
24/Sep/1995 3:00 -1:00
31/Mar/1996 2:00 -2:00
29/Sep/1996 3:00 -1:00
30/Mar/1997 2:00 -2:00
28/Sep/1997 3:00 -1:00
29/Mar/1998 2:00 -2:00
27/Sep/1998 3:00 -1:00
28/Mar/1999 2:00 -2:00
26/Sep/1999 3:00 -1:00
26/Mar/2000 2:00 -2:00
24/Sep/2000 3:00 -1:00
....

Time Table # 2
Before 12/Sep/1848 LMT
Begin Standard 7E26
12/Sep/1848 0:00 -0:30
Begin Standard 15E00
1/Jun/1894 0:00 -1:00
5/May/1941 2:00 -2:00
6/Oct/1941 0:00 -1:00
4/May/1942 2:00 -2:00
5/Oct/1942 0:00 -1:00
29/Mar/1981 2:00 -2:00
27/Sep/1981 3:00 -1:00
28/Mar/1982 2:00 -2:00
26/Sep/1982 3:00 -1:00
27/Mar/1983 2:00 -2:00
25/Sep/1983 3:00 -1:00
25/Mar/1984 2:00 -2:00
30/Sep/1984 3:00 -1:00
31/Mar/1985 2:00 -2:00
29/Sep/1985 3:00 -1:00
30/Mar/1986 2:00 -2:00
28/Sep/1986 3:00 -1:00
29/Mar/1987 2:00 -2:00
27/Sep/1987 3:00 -1:00
27/Mar/1988 2:00 -2:00
25/Sep/1988 3:00 -1:00
26/Mar/1989 2:00 -2:00
24/Sep/1989 3:00 -1:00
25/Mar/1990 2:00 -2:00
30/Sep/1990 3:00 -1:00
31/Mar/1991 2:00 -2:00
29/Sep/1991 3:00 -1:00
29/Mar/1992 2:00 -2:00
27/Sep/1992 3:00 -1:00
28/Mar/1993 2:00 -2:00
26/Sep/1993 3:00 -1:00
27/Mar/1994 2:00 -2:00
25/Sep/1994 3:00 -1:00
26/Mar/1995 2:00 -2:00
24/Sep/1995 3:00 -1:00
31/Mar/1996 2:00 -2:00
29/Sep/1996 3:00 -1:00
30/Mar/1997 2:00 -2:00
28/Sep/1997 3:00 -1:00
29/Mar/1998 2:00 -2:00
27/Sep/1998 3:00 -1:00
28/Mar/1999 2:00 -2:00
26/Sep/1999 3:00 -1:00
26/Mar/2000 2:00 -2:00
24/Sep/2000 3:00 -1:00

Place	TT	Lat	Long	Offset
Aadorf	2	47N30	8E54	-0:35:36
Aarau	2	47N23	8E03	-0:32:12
Aarberg	2	47N03	7E16	-0:29:04
Aarburg	2	47N19	7E54	-0:31:36
Aarwangen	2	47N15	7E46	-0:31:04
Acquarossa	2	46N28	8E57	-0:35:48
Adelboden	2	46N30	7E33	-0:30:12
Adliswil	2	47N19	8E32	-0:34:08
Aesch	2	47N28	7E36	-0:30:24
Aeschi	2	46N40	7E42	-0:30:48
Affoltern am Albis	2	47N17	8E27	-0:33:48
Agno	2	46N00	8E54	-0:35:36
Aigle	2	46N19	6E58	-0:27:52
Airolo	2	46N32	8E37	-0:34:28
Allaman	2	46N28	6E24	-0:25:36
Alle	2	47N26	7E08	-0:28:32
Allschwil	2	47N33	7E33	-0:30:12
Alpnachstad	2	46N57	8E17	-0:33:08
Altdorf	2	46N53	8E39	-0:34:36
Altstätten	2	47N23	9E33	-0:38:12
Alvaneu-Bad	2	46N40	9E39	-0:38:36
Amden	2	47N09	9E11	-0:36:44
Amriswil	2	47N33	9E18	-0:37:12
Amsoldingen	2	46N43	7E35	-0:30:20
Amsteg	2	46N46	8E41	-0:34:44
Andeer	2	46N36	9E26	-0:37:44
Andelfingen	2	47N36	8E41	-0:34:44
Andermatt	2	46N38	8E36	-0:34:24
Appenzell	2	47N20	9E25	-0:37:40
Apples	2	46N34	6E25	-0:25:40
Aquila	2	46N31	8E57	-0:35:48
Arbedo	2	46N12	9E03	-0:36:12
Arbon	2	47N31	9E26	-0:37:44
Ardez	2	46N46	10E11	-0:40:44
Ardon	2	46N13	7E15	-0:29:00
Arlesheim	2	47N30	7E37	-0:30:28
Arolla	2	46N02	7E29	-0:29:56
Arosa	2	46N47	9E41	-0:38:44
Arth	2	47N04	8E31	-0:34:04
Ascona	2	46N09	8E46	-0:35:04
Ausserferrera	2	46N33	9E26	-0:37:44
Avenches	2	46N53	7E02	-0:28:08
Ayer	2	46N11	7E36	-0:30:24
Baar	2	47N12	8E32	-0:34:08
Baden	2	47N29	8E18	-0:33:12
Bad Ragaz	2	47N00	9E30	-0:38:00
Bâle → Basel	2	47N33	7E35	-0:30:20
Balgach	2	47N25	9E35	-0:38:20
Balsthal	2	47N19	7E42	-0:30:48
Bargen	2	47N48	8E37	-0:34:28
Basel (Bâle)	2	47N33	7E35	-0:30:20
Bassecourt	2	47N20	7E15	-0:29:00
Bätterkinden	2	47N08	7E32	-0:30:08
Baulmes	2	46N48	6E32	-0:26:08
Bauma	2	47N23	8E53	-0:35:32
Beatenberg	2	46N42	7E48	-0:31:12
Beckenried	2	46N58	8E29	-0:33:56
Beinwil	2	47N22	7E35	-0:30:20
Beinwil am See	2	47N16	8E13	-0:32:52
Bellelay	2	47N16	7E10	-0:28:40
Bellinzona	2	46N11	9E02	-0:36:08
Belp	2	46N53	7E30	-0:30:00
Bergün	2	46N38	9E45	-0:39:00
Bern (Berne)	2	46N57	7E26	-0:29:44
Berna → Bern	2	46N57	7E26	-0:29:44
Berne → Bern	2	46N57	7E26	-0:29:44
Beromünster	2	47N12	8E11	-0:32:44
Bex	2	46N15	7E01	-0:28:04
Biasca	2	46N22	8E58	-0:35:52
Biel (Bienne)	2	47N10	7E12	-0:28:48
Bienne → Biel	2	47N10	7E12	-0:28:48
Bière	2	46N33	6E20	-0:25:20
Bignasco	2	46N20	8E36	-0:34:24
Binningen	2	47N32	7E34	-0:30:16
Bischofszell	2	47N29	9E15	-0:37:00
Bivio	2	46N28	9E38	-0:38:32
Blatten	2	46N25	7E50	-0:31:20
Blonay	2	46N28	6E54	-0:27:36
Boltigen	2	46N38	7E24	-0:29:36
Bonaduz	2	46N49	9E25	-0:37:40
Boncourt	2	47N30	6E56	-0:27:44
Bonfol	2	47N29	7E09	-0:28:36
Boudry	2	46N57	6E50	-0:27:20
Bourg-Saint-Pierre	2	45N57	7E12	-0:28:48
Braunwald	2	46N56	9E00	-0:36:00
Bremgarten	2	47N21	8E21	-0:33:24
Breno	2	46N02	8E53	-0:35:32
Brienz	2	46N46	8E03	-0:32:12
Brig	2	46N19	8E00	-0:32:00
Brione	2	46N18	8E47	-0:35:08
Brissago	2	46N07	8E43	-0:34:52
Broc	2	46N36	7E06	-0:28:24
Brugg	2	47N29	8E12	-0:32:48
Brunnen	2	47N00	8E36	-0:34:24
Brunni	2	47N03	8E42	-0:34:48
Brusio	2	46N14	10E07	-0:40:28
Bubendorf	2	47N27	7E44	-0:30:56
Buchs	2	47N23	8E04	-0:32:16
Buchs	2	47N10	9E28	-0:37:52
Bülach	2	47N31	8E32	-0:34:08
Bulle	2	46N37	7E04	-0:28:16
Buochs	2	46N58	8E22	-0:33:28
Büren an der Aare	2	47N08	7E23	-0:29:32
Burgdorf	2	47N04	7E37	-0:30:28
Bürglen	2	46N53	8E40	-0:34:40
Bürglen	2	47N33	9E09	-0:36:36
Camedo	2	46N09	8E37	-0:34:28
Campo Blenio	2	46N34	8E56	-0:35:44
Campocologno	2	46N13	10E08	-0:40:32
Capolago	2	45N55	8E59	-0:35:56
Carouge	1	46N11	6E09	-0:24:36
Cazis	2	46N43	9E25	-0:37:40
Celerina	2	46N31	9E51	-0:39:24
Cevio	2	46N19	8E36	-0:34:24
Cham	2	47N11	8E28	-0:33:52
Champéry	2	46N10	6E52	-0:27:28
Champex	2	46N02	7E07	-0:28:28
Chancy	1	46N08	6E00	-0:24:00
Charmey	2	46N38	7E10	-0:28:40
Château d'Oex	2	46N28	7E08	-0:28:32
Châtel-Saint-Denis	2	46N32	6E54	-0:27:36
Chavornay	2	46N43	6E34	-0:26:16
Chêne-Bourg	1	46N12	6E12	-0:24:48
Cheseaux	2	46N35	6E36	-0:26:24
Chexbres	2	46N29	6E47	-0:27:08
Chiasso	2	45N50	9E01	-0:36:04
Chippis	2	46N17	7E33	-0:30:12
Chur	2	46N51	9E32	-0:38:08
Churwalden	2	46N47	9E33	-0:38:12
Cimalmotto	2	46N17	8E29	-0:33:56
Coire → Chur	2	46N51	9E32	-0:38:08
Collombey	2	46N16	6E57	-0:27:48
Colombier	2	46N58	6E52	-0:27:28
Comologno	2	46N12	8E34	-0:34:16
Compatsch	2	46N58	10E25	-0:41:40
Concise	2	46N51	6E43	-0:26:52
Coppet	1	46N19	6E12	-0:24:48
Cossonay	2	46N37	6E31	-0:26:04
Court	2	47N14	7E20	-0:29:20
Couvet	2	46N56	6E38	-0:26:32
Crans	2	46N19	7E28	-0:29:52
Crassier	2	46N22	6E11	-0:24:44
Cresta	2	46N28	9E31	-0:38:04
Cully	2	46N29	6E44	-0:26:56
Curaglia	2	46N41	8E51	-0:35:24
Dagmersellen	2	47N13	7E59	-0:31:56
Davos	2	46N48	9E50	-0:39:20
Delémont	2	47N22	7E21	-0:29:24
Dielsdorf	2	47N29	8E27	-0:33:48
Diepoldsau	2	47N23	9E38	-0:38:32
Diessenhofen	2	47N41	8E45	-0:35:00
Dietikon	2	47N24	8E24	-0:33:36
Disentis	2	46N43	8E51	-0:35:24
Domat/Ems	2	46N50	9E28	-0:37:52
Dombresson	2	47N04	6E58	-0:27:52
Dongio	2	46N27	8E58	-0:35:52
Dornach	2	47N29	7E37	-0:30:28
Döttingen	2	47N34	8E16	-0:33:04
Dübendorf	2	47N25	8E38	-0:34:32
Dürrenboden	2	46N57	8E50	-0:35:20
Dussnang	2	47N26	8E58	-0:35:52
Ebnat	2	47N15	9E08	-0:36:32
Echallens	2	46N38	6E38	-0:26:32
Eglisau	2	47N34	8E32	-0:34:08
Egnach	2	47N33	9E23	-0:37:32
Einsiedeln	2	47N08	8E45	-0:35:00
Elm	2	46N55	9E11	-0:36:44
Embrach	2	47N30	8E36	-0:34:24
Emmenbrücke	2	47N04	8E17	-0:33:08
Engelberg	2	46N49	8E25	-0:33:40
Engwilen	2	47N37	9E05	-0:36:20
Ennenda	2	47N01	9E05	-0:36:20
Entlebuch	2	47N00	8E04	-0:32:16
Eriswil	2	47N05	7E51	-0:31:24
Erlach	2	47N03	7E06	-0:28:24
Ermatingen	2	47N41	9E06	-0:36:24
Erstfeld	2	46N49	8E39	-0:34:36
Escholzmatt	2	46N55	7E56	-0:31:44
Estavayer-Le-Lac	2	46N51	6E50	-0:27:20
Euseigne	2	46N10	7E25	-0:29:40
Evionnaz	2	46N11	7E01	-0:28:04
Evolène	2	46N07	7E30	-0:30:00
Faido	2	46N29	8E48	-0:35:12
Feldis	2	46N48	9E26	-0:37:44
Ferret	2	45N55	7E06	-0:28:24
Fiesch	2	46N20	8E10	-0:32:40
Filzbach	2	47N07	9E08	-0:36:32
Flawil	2	47N24	9E12	-0:36:48
Fleurier	2	46N54	6E35	-0:26:20
Flims	2	46N50	9E17	-0:37:08
Flüelen	2	46N54	8E38	-0:34:32
Flühli	2	46N53	8E01	-0:32:04
Flums	2	47N05	9E20	-0:37:20
Frauenfeld	2	47N34	8E54	-0:35:36
Freiburg → Fribourg	2	46N48	7E09	-0:28:36
Fribourg (Freiburg)	2	46N48	7E09	-0:28:36
Frick	2	47N31	8E01	-0:32:04
Frutigen	2	46N35	7E39	-0:30:36
Fuldera	2	46N37	10E22	-0:41:28
Fusio	2	46N27	8E40	-0:34:40
Gadmen	2	46N44	8E21	-0:33:24
Gais	2	47N22	9E27	-0:37:48
Gams	2	47N12	9E28	-0:37:52
Gandria	2	46N01	9E00	-0:36:00
Gänsbrunnen	2	47N16	7E28	-0:29:52
Gelfingen	2	47N13	8E16	-0:33:04
Gelterkinden	2	47N28	7E51	-0:31:24
Geneva → Genève	1	46N12	6E09	-0:24:36
Genève (Geneva)	1	46N12	6E09	-0:24:36
Genf → Genève	1	46N12	6E09	-0:24:36
Gerlafingen	2	47N10	7E34	-0:30:16
Gersau	2	47N00	8E32	-0:34:08
Gerzensee	2	46N51	7E33	-0:30:12
Ginebra → Genève	1	46N12	6E09	-0:24:36
Giornico	2	46N24	8E52	-0:35:28
Giswil	2	46N50	8E11	-0:32:44
Gland	2	46N26	6E16	-0:25:04
Glaris → Glarus	2	47N02	9E04	-0:36:16
Glarus	2	47N02	9E04	-0:36:16
Glattfelden	2	47N33	8E30	-0:34:00
Gletsch	2	46N34	8E22	-0:33:28
Goldau	2	47N03	8E33	-0:34:12
Goppenstein	2	46N22	7E45	-0:31:00
Gordola	2	46N11	8E52	-0:35:28
Göschenen	2	46N40	8E35	-0:34:20
Gossau	2	47N25	9E15	-0:37:00
Grächen	2	46N12	7E50	-0:31:20
Grandson	2	46N49	6E38	-0:26:32
Granges → Grenchen	2	47N11	7E24	-0:29:36
Greifensee	2	47N22	8E41	-0:34:44
Grenchen	2	47N11	7E24	-0:29:36
Grimmialp	2	46N34	7E29	-0:29:56
Grindelwald	2	46N37	8E02	-0:32:08
Grolley	2	46N50	7E05	-0:28:20
Grosshöchstetten	2	46N55	7E38	-0:30:32
Gruyères	2	46N35	7E05	-0:28:20
Gstaad	2	46N28	7E17	-0:29:08
Gsteig	2	46N23	7E16	-0:29:04
Guttannen	2	46N39	8E18	-0:33:12
Gwatt	2	46N43	7E38	-0:30:32
Hallau	2	47N42	8E27	-0:33:48
Hasle	2	47N01	7E39	-0:30:36
Heiden	2	47N27	9E33	-0:38:12
Henniez	2	46N44	6E54	-0:27:36
Herisau	2	47N23	9E17	-0:37:08
Herznach	2	47N28	8E03	-0:32:12
Herzogenbuchsee	2	47N12	7E41	-0:30:44
Hindelbank	2	47N03	7E32	-0:30:08
Hinterrhein	2	46N32	9E12	-0:36:48
Hinwil	2	47N18	8E51	-0:35:24
Hochdorf	2	47N10	8E17	-0:33:08
Horgen	2	47N15	8E36	-0:34:24
Horw	2	47N01	8E18	-0:33:12
Hospental	2	46N37	8E34	-0:34:16
Hundwil	2	47N22	9E19	-0:37:16
Huttwil	2	47N07	7E51	-0:31:24
Iferten → Yverdon	2	46N47	6E39	-0:26:36
Ilanz	2	46N46	9E12	-0:36:48
Il Fuorn	2	46N40	10E12	-0:40:48
Indemini	2	46N06	8E50	-0:35:20
Innerferrera	2	46N31	9E28	-0:37:52
Innerthal	2	47N06	8E56	-0:35:44
Innertkirchen	2	46N42	8E14	-0:32:56
Ins	2	47N00	7E06	-0:28:24
Interlaken	2	46N41	7E51	-0:31:24

SWITZERLAND SUISSE SVIZZERA SUIZA SCHWEIZ

Place		Lat.	Long.	Time
Intragna	2	46N10	8E42	-0:34:48
Iseltwald	2	46N43	7E58	-0:31:52
Isone	2	46N08	8E59	-0:35:56
Jegenstorf	2	47N03	7E30	-0:30:00
Jenaz	2	46N55	9E45	-0:39:00
Kallnach	2	47N01	7E14	-0:28:56
Kaltbrunn	2	47N12	9E02	-0:36:08
Kandersteg	2	46N30	7E40	-0:30:40
Kerzers	2	46N58	7E12	-0:28:48
Kesswil	2	47N36	9E20	-0:37:20
Kiental	2	46N35	7E43	-0:30:52
Kilchberg	2	47N19	8E33	-0:34:12
Kirchberg	2	47N05	7E35	-0:30:20
Kirchberg	2	47N25	9E03	-0:36:12
Kleinlützel	2	47N26	7E25	-0:29:40
Klingnau	2	47N35	8E15	-0:33:00
Klosters	2	46N54	9E53	-0:39:32
Kloten	2	47N27	8E35	-0:34:20
Koblenz	2	47N37	8E14	-0:32:56
Köniz	2	46N56	7E25	-0:29:40
Konolfingen	2	46N53	7E38	-0:30:32
Kreuzlingen	2	47N39	9E11	-0:36:44
Kriens	2	47N02	8E17	-0:33:08
Küblis	2	46N55	9E47	-0:39:08
Küsnacht	2	47N19	8E35	-0:34:20
Küssnacht am Rigi	2	47N05	8E27	-0:33:48
Küttigen	2	47N25	8E03	-0:32:12
La Brévine	2	46N59	6E36	-0:26:24
La Chaux-De-Fonds	2	47N06	6E50	-0:27:20
Lachen	2	47N12	8E51	-0:35:24
Lancy	1	46N11	6E07	-0:24:28
Landquart	2	46N58	9E33	-0:38:12
La Neuveville	2	47N04	7E06	-0:28:24
Langenbruck	2	47N21	7E46	-0:31:04
Langenthal	2	47N13	7E47	-0:31:08
Langnau	2	46N57	7E47	-0:31:08
Langwies	2	46N49	9E43	-0:38:52
Lantsch	2	46N41	9E34	-0:38:16
La Punt	2	46N35	9E55	-0:39:40
La Roche	2	46N42	7E08	-0:28:32
La Sagne	2	47N03	6E48	-0:27:12
La Sarraz	2	46N40	6E31	-0:26:04
La Tour-De-Peilz	2	46N27	6E49	-0:27:16
Latterbach	2	46N40	7E35	-0:30:20
Läufelfingen	2	47N24	7E51	-0:31:24
Laufen	2	47N25	7E30	-0:30:00
Laufenburg (Baden)	2	47N33	8E04	-0:32:16
Lauis → Lugano	2	46N01	8E58	-0:35:52
Laupen	2	46N54	7E14	-0:28:56
Lausanne	2	46N31	6E38	-0:26:32
Lauterbrunnen	2	46N36	7E55	-0:31:40
Lavin	2	46N46	10E06	-0:40:24
Le Brassus	2	46N35	6E13	-0:24:52
Le Châble	2	46N05	7E12	-0:28:48
Le Châtelard	2	46N04	6E58	-0:27:52
Le Locle	2	47N03	6E45	-0:27:00
Lengnau	2	47N11	7E22	-0:29:28
Lenk	2	46N28	7E27	-0:29:48
Le Noirmont	2	47N13	6E58	-0:27:52
Lenzburg	2	47N23	8E11	-0:32:44
Lenzerheide (Lai)	2	46N44	9E33	-0:38:12
Le Pont	2	46N40	6E20	-0:25:20
Le Prese	2	46N18	10E04	-0:40:16
Les Diablerets	2	46N21	7E10	-0:28:40
Les Haudères	2	46N05	7E31	-0:30:04
Les Marécottes	2	46N07	7E00	-0:28:00
Les Mosses	2	46N24	7E07	-0:28:28
Les Ponts-De-Martel	2	46N54	6E41	-0:26:44
Les Verrières	2	46N54	6E30	-0:26:00
Leuk	2	46N19	7E38	-0:30:32
Leukerbad	2	46N23	7E38	-0:30:32
Leysin	2	46N21	7E01	-0:28:04
Lichtensteig	2	47N19	9E05	-0:36:20
Liestal	2	47N29	7E44	-0:30:56
Linthal	2	46N55	9E00	-0:36:00
L'Isle	2	46N37	6E25	-0:25:40
Littau	2	47N03	8E16	-0:33:04
Locarno	2	46N10	8E48	-0:35:12
Lucens	2	46N42	6E50	-0:27:20
Lucerne → Luzern	2	47N03	8E18	-0:33:12
Lugano	2	46N01	8E58	-0:35:52
Luggarus → Locarno	2	46N10	8E48	-0:35:12
Lumbrein	2	46N41	9E08	-0:36:32
Lungern	2	46N47	8E10	-0:32:40
Lutry	2	46N30	6E41	-0:26:44
Lützelflüh	2	47N00	7E41	-0:30:44
Luzern	2	47N03	8E18	-0:33:12
Lyss	2	47N04	7E18	-0:29:12
Macolin	2	47N09	7E14	-0:28:56
Maggia	2	46N15	8E42	-0:34:48
Maienfeld	2	47N00	9E32	-0:38:08
Maloja	2	46N24	9E41	-0:38:44
Malvaglia	2	46N25	8E59	-0:35:56
Männedorf	2	47N15	8E42	-0:34:48
Marbach	2	46N52	7E55	-0:31:40
Märstetten	2	47N36	9E04	-0:36:16
Martigny	2	46N06	7E04	-0:28:16
Martina	2	46N53	10E30	-0:42:00
Mauensee	2	47N10	8E04	-0:32:16
Meilen	2	47N16	8E38	-0:34:32
Meiringen	2	46N43	8E12	-0:32:48
Melchtal	2	46N50	8E17	-0:33:08
Melide	2	45N57	8E57	-0:35:48
Mels	2	47N03	9E25	-0:37:40
Mendrisio	2	45N52	8E59	-0:35:56
Menziken	2	47N14	8E12	-0:32:48
Merishausen	2	47N45	8E37	-0:34:28
Mesocco	2	46N23	9E14	-0:36:56
Meyrin	1	46N14	6E05	-0:24:20
Möhlin	2	47N34	7E51	-0:31:24
Mollis	2	47N05	9E04	-0:36:16
Montana	2	46N18	7E29	-0:29:56
Montbovon	2	46N29	7E03	-0:28:12
Montfaucon	2	47N17	7E03	-0:28:12
Monthey	2	46N15	6E57	-0:27:48
Montreux	2	46N26	6E55	-0:27:40
Morcote	2	45N56	8E55	-0:35:40
Morges	2	46N31	6E30	-0:26:00
Moudon	2	46N40	6E48	-0:27:12
Moutier	2	47N17	7E23	-0:29:32
Mulegns	2	46N33	9E37	-0:38:28
Münchenbuchsee	2	47N01	7E27	-0:29:48
Münchenstein	2	47N31	7E37	-0:30:28
Münsingen	2	46N53	7E34	-0:30:16
Münster	2	46N29	8E16	-0:33:04
Münsterlingen	2	47N38	9E14	-0:36:56
Muotathal	2	46N59	8E46	-0:35:04
Murgenthal	2	47N16	7E50	-0:31:20
Muri	2	46N56	7E29	-0:29:56
Muri	2	47N16	8E21	-0:33:24
Mürren	2	46N34	7E54	-0:31:36
Murten	2	46N56	7E07	-0:28:28
Müstair	2	46N37	10E27	-0:41:48
Muttenz	2	47N32	7E39	-0:30:36
Näfels	2	47N06	9E04	-0:36:16
Naters	2	46N20	7E59	-0:31:56
Nendaz	2	46N11	7E18	-0:29:12
Nesslau	2	47N13	9E13	-0:36:52
Netstal	2	47N03	9E03	-0:36:12
Neuchâtel	2	46N59	6E56	-0:27:44
Neuenburg → Neuchâtel	2	46N59	6E56	-0:27:44
Neuenegg	2	46N54	7E18	-0:29:12
Neuhausen	2	47N41	8E37	-0:34:28
Neu Sankt Johann	2	47N14	9E12	-0:36:48
Nidau	2	47N07	7E14	-0:28:56
Niederbipp	2	47N16	7E39	-0:30:36
Niederurnen	2	47N07	9E03	-0:36:12
Niederwald	2	46N26	8E12	-0:32:48
Niederweningen	2	47N30	8E23	-0:33:32
Nyon	2	46N23	6E14	-0:24:56
Oberägeri	2	47N08	8E37	-0:34:28
Oberdiessbach	2	46N51	7E38	-0:30:32
Oberengstringen	2	47N25	8E28	-0:33:52
Oberhofen	2	46N44	7E40	-0:30:40
Oberried	2	46N44	7E58	-0:31:52
Oberriet	2	47N19	9E33	-0:38:12
Oberuzwil	2	47N26	9E08	-0:36:32
Oberwald	2	46N32	8E21	-0:33:24
Oensingen	2	47N17	7E44	-0:30:56
Oftringen	2	47N19	7E56	-0:31:44
Olivone	2	46N32	8E57	-0:35:48
Ollon	2	46N18	7E00	-0:28:00
Olten	2	47N21	7E54	-0:31:36
Orbe	2	46N43	6E32	-0:26:08
Oron-La-Ville	2	46N34	6E50	-0:27:20
Orsières	2	46N02	7E09	-0:28:36
Osogna	2	46N18	9E00	-0:36:00
Ostermundigen	2	46N58	7E29	-0:29:56
Palézieux	2	46N33	6E50	-0:27:20
Parpan	2	46N46	9E33	-0:38:12
Payerne	2	46N49	6E56	-0:27:44
Peseux	2	46N59	6E53	-0:27:32
Pfäfers	2	46N59	9E30	-0:38:00
Pfäffikon	2	47N22	8E47	-0:35:08
Pfäffikon	2	47N12	8E46	-0:35:04
Pfaffnau	2	47N14	7E54	-0:31:36
Pfyn	2	47N36	8E57	-0:35:48
Pieterlen	2	47N11	7E20	-0:29:20
Piotta	2	46N31	8E40	-0:34:40
Plaffeien	2	46N44	7E17	-0:29:08
Platta	2	46N40	8E51	-0:35:24
Ponte Tresa	2	45N58	8E52	-0:35:28
Pontresina	2	46N28	9E53	-0:39:32
Porrentruy	2	47N25	7E05	-0:28:20
Poschiavo	2	46N18	10E04	-0:40:16
Posieux	2	46N46	7E06	-0:28:24
Pratteln	2	47N31	7E42	-0:30:48
Preda	2	46N36	9E46	-0:39:04
Prilly	2	46N32	6E36	-0:26:24
Promontogno	2	46N21	9E34	-0:38:16
Pully	2	46N31	6E39	-0:26:36
Rafz	2	47N37	8E32	-0:34:08
Ramosch	2	46N50	10E22	-0:41:28
Randa	2	46N07	7E47	-0:31:08
Rapperswil	2	47N14	8E50	-0:35:20
Raron	2	46N19	7E48	-0:31:12
Regensdorf	2	47N26	8E28	-0:33:52
Reichenau	2	46N49	9E24	-0:37:36
Reichenbach	2	46N38	7E42	-0:30:48
Reigoldswil	2	47N24	7E41	-0:30:44
Reinach	2	47N30	7E35	-0:30:20
Reinach	2	47N15	8E11	-0:32:44
Renens	2	46N32	6E35	-0:26:20
Rheineck	2	47N28	9E35	-0:38:20
Rheinfelden	2	47N33	7E48	-0:31:12
Riaz	2	46N38	7E04	-0:28:16
Richisau	2	47N02	8E54	-0:35:36
Richterswil	2	47N13	8E42	-0:34:48
Riddes	2	46N10	7E13	-0:28:52
Riederalp	2	46N23	8E01	-0:32:04
Riehen	2	47N35	7E39	-0:30:36
Riggisberg	2	46N48	7E29	-0:29:56
Rolle	2	46N28	6E20	-0:25:20
Romainmôtier	2	46N42	6E29	-0:25:56
Romanshorn	2	47N34	9E22	-0:37:28
Romont	2	46N42	6E55	-0:27:40
Rona	2	46N34	9E38	-0:38:32
Ronco	2	46N08	8E44	-0:34:56
Root	2	47N07	8E23	-0:33:32
Rorschach	2	47N29	9E30	-0:38:00
Rossa	2	46N22	9E08	-0:36:32
Röthenbach	2	46N51	7E45	-0:31:00
Rothrist	2	47N19	7E53	-0:31:32
Rougemont	2	46N29	7E12	-0:28:48
Roveredo	2	46N14	9E08	-0:36:32
Rue	2	46N37	6E50	-0:27:20
Rümlang	2	47N27	8E32	-0:34:08
Rüti	2	47N16	8E51	-0:35:24
Saanen	2	46N29	7E16	-0:29:04
Saanenmöser	2	46N31	7E18	-0:29:12
Saas Almagell	2	46N07	7E58	-0:31:52
Saas Fee	2	46N07	7E55	-0:31:40
Saas Grund	2	46N08	7E56	-0:31:44
Sachseln	2	46N52	8E15	-0:33:00
Saignelégier	2	47N15	7E00	-0:28:00
Saint-Aubin	2	46N54	6E47	-0:27:08
Saint-Blaise	2	47N01	6E59	-0:27:56
Saint-Cergue	2	46N27	6E09	-0:24:36
Sainte-Croix	2	46N49	6E31	-0:26:04
Saint-Gall → Sankt Gallen	2	47N25	9E23	-0:37:32
Saint-Gingolph	2	46N24	6E52	-0:27:28
Saint-Imier	2	47N09	7E00	-0:28:00
Saint-Luc	2	46N13	7E36	-0:30:24
Saint-Maurice	2	46N13	7E00	-0:28:00
Saint-Moritz → Sankt Moritz	2	46N30	9E50	-0:39:20
Saint-Prex	2	46N29	6E28	-0:25:52
Saint-Ursanne	2	47N22	7E10	-0:28:40
Salavaux	2	46N55	7E02	-0:28:08
Samedan	2	46N33	9E52	-0:39:28
Samnaun	2	46N56	10E22	-0:41:28
San Bernardino	2	46N28	9E12	-0:36:48
San Carlo	2	46N25	8E32	-0:34:08
San Gion	2	46N38	8E50	-0:35:20
Sankt Antönien	2	46N58	9E49	-0:39:16
Sankt Gallen	2	47N25	9E23	-0:37:32
Sankt Margrethen	2	47N27	9E36	-0:38:24
Sankt Moritz	2	46N30	9E50	-0:39:20
Sankt Niklaus	2	46N11	7E48	-0:31:12
Sankt Peterzell	2	47N19	9E11	-0:36:44
San Murezzan → Sankt Moritz	2	46N30	9E50	-0:39:20
Santa Maria	2	46N16	9E09	-0:36:36
Santa Maria	2	46N36	10E24	-0:41:36
Sargans	2	47N03	9E26	-0:37:44
Sarnen	2	46N54	8E15	-0:33:00
Sattel	2	47N05	8E42	-0:34:48
Savièse	2	46N16	7E20	-0:29:20
Savognin	2	46N36	9E36	-0:38:24
Saxon	2	46N09	7E11	-0:28:44
Schaffhausen	2	47N42	8E38	-0:34:32
S-Chanf	2	46N36	9E59	-0:39:56
Schangnau	2	46N50	7E52	-0:31:28
Schiers	2	46N59	9E41	-0:38:44
Schinznach Bad	2	47N27	8E10	-0:32:40
Schleitheim	2	47N45	8E29	-0:33:56
Schlieren	2	47N24	8E27	-0:33:48
Schöftland	2	47N18	8E03	-0:32:12
Schönenwerd	2	47N22	8E00	-0:32:00
Schuls → Scuol	2	46N48	10E18	-0:41:12
Schüpfheim	2	46N57	8E01	-0:32:04
Schwanden	2	47N00	9E04	-0:36:16
Schwarzenburg	2	46N49	7E21	-0:29:24
Schwarzsee	2	46N40	7E20	-0:29:20
Schwyz	2	47N02	8E40	-0:34:40
Scuol (Schuls)	2	46N48	10E18	-0:41:12
Sedrun	2	46N41	8E46	-0:35:04
Seeberg	2	47N09	7E40	-0:30:40
Seen	2	47N29	8E46	-0:35:04
Seengen	2	47N19	8E13	-0:32:52
Seewis	2	47N00	9E32	-0:38:08
Sempach	2	47N08	8E11	-0:32:44
Sennwald	2	47N16	9E30	-0:38:00
Seon	2	47N21	8E10	-0:32:40
Sertig-Dörfli	2	46N44	9E51	-0:39:24
Seuzach	2	47N32	8E44	-0:34:56
Sevelen	2	47N07	9E29	-0:37:56
Siebnen	2	47N11	8E54	-0:35:36
Sierre	2	46N18	7E32	-0:30:08
Signau	2	46N55	7E43	-0:30:52
Sigriswil	2	46N43	7E42	-0:30:48
Sils im Engadin	2	46N22	9E46	-0:39:04
Silvaplana	2	46N26	9E47	-0:39:08
Sins	2	47N11	8E23	-0:33:32
Sion (Sitten)	2	46N14	7E21	-0:29:24
Sirnach	2	47N28	9E00	-0:36:00
Sisikon	2	46N57	8E42	-0:34:48
Sissach	2	47N28	7E49	-0:31:16
Sitten → Sion	2	46N14	7E21	-0:29:24
Soazza	2	46N22	9E13	-0:36:52
Soleure → Solothurn	2	47N13	7E32	-0:30:08
Solothurn	2	47N13	7E32	-0:30:08
Somvix	2	46N44	8E56	-0:35:44
Sonceboz	2	47N11	7E11	-0:28:44
Sonogno	2	46N21	8E47	-0:35:08
Sörenberg	2	46N50	8E03	-0:32:12
Sottens	2	46N39	6E44	-0:26:56
Speicher	2	47N24	9E27	-0:37:48
Spiez	2	46N41	7E39	-0:30:36
Splügen	2	46N33	9E20	-0:37:20
Stäfa	2	47N15	8E44	-0:34:56
Stalden	2	46N14	7E52	-0:31:28
Stammheim	2	47N38	8E47	-0:35:08
Stans	2	46N57	8E22	-0:33:28
Stansstad	2	46N59	8E20	-0:33:20
Steckborn	2	47N40	8E55	-0:35:40
Steffisburg	2	46N47	7E39	-0:30:36
Steg	2	47N21	8E56	-0:35:44
Stein	2	47N33	7E58	-0:31:52
Stein am Rhein	2	47N40	8E51	-0:35:24
Stöckalp	2	46N48	8E17	-0:33:08
Suhr	2	47N22	8E05	-0:32:20

SCHWEIZ SUIZA SVIZZERA SUISSE SWITZERLAND

Place		Lat	Long	Offset
Sumiswald	2	47N02	7E45	-0:31:00
Sursee	2	47N10	8E06	-0:32:24
Susch	2	46N46	10E04	-0:40:16
Tarasp	2	46N38	10E25	-0:41:40
Täuffelen	2	47N04	7E12	-0:28:48
Tavanasa	2	46N45	9E04	-0:36:16
Tavannes	2	47N13	7E12	-0:28:48
Tenigerbad	2	46N42	8E57	-0:35:48
Tesserete	2	46N04	8E58	-0:35:52
Teufen	2	47N23	9E23	-0:37:32
Thalkirch	2	46N38	9E16	-0:37:04
Thalwil	2	47N17	8E34	-0:34:16
Thayngen	2	47N45	8E42	-0:34:48
Thoune → Thun	2	46N45	7E37	-0:30:28
Thun	2	46N45	7E37	-0:30:28
Thusis	2	46N42	9E26	-0:37:44
Tiefencastel	2	46N40	9E35	-0:38:20
Trachselwald	2	47N01	7E45	-0:31:00
Tramelan	2	47N13	7E06	-0:28:24
Trasadingen	2	47N40	8E26	-0:33:44
Trimbach	2	47N22	7E54	-0:31:36
Trin	2	46N50	9E22	-0:37:28
Trogen	2	47N24	9E28	-0:37:52
Trun	2	46N45	8E58	-0:35:52
Tschamut	2	46N40	8E42	-0:34:48
Turbenthal	2	47N27	8E51	-0:35:24
Turtmann	2	46N18	7E41	-0:30:44
Twann	2	47N06	7E10	-0:28:40
Unterägeri	2	47N08	8E35	-0:34:20
Unterbäch	2	46N17	7E48	-0:31:12
Unterschächen	2	46N52	8E47	-0:35:08
Unterseen	2	46N41	7E51	-0:31:24
Unterterzen	2	47N07	9E15	-0:37:00
Unterwasser	2	47N12	9E19	-0:37:16
Urnäsch	2	47N19	9E17	-0:37:08
Uster	2	47N21	8E43	-0:34:52
Utzenstorf	2	47N08	7E33	-0:30:12
Uznach	2	47N14	9E00	-0:36:00
Valangin	2	47N01	6E54	-0:27:36
Valbella	2	46N45	9E33	-0:38:12
Vallorbe	2	46N43	6E22	-0:25:28
Vals Platz	2	46N37	9E11	-0:36:44
Vättis	2	46N55	9E27	-0:37:48
Vaulruz	2	46N37	6E59	-0:27:56
Verbier	2	46N06	7E13	-0:28:52
Vergeletto	2	46N14	8E36	-0:34:24
Vernayaz	2	46N08	7E02	-0:28:08
Vernier	1	46N13	6E06	-0:24:24
Versoix	1	46N16	6E10	-0:24:40
Vésenaz	1	46N14	6E12	-0:24:48
Vevey	2	46N28	6E51	-0:27:24
Vex	2	46N13	7E24	-0:29:36
Vicosoprano	2	46N22	9E37	-0:38:28
Villars	2	46N18	7E04	-0:28:16
Villeneuve	2	46N24	6E55	-0:27:40
Villmergen	2	47N21	8E15	-0:33:00
Vinadi	2	46N55	10E29	-0:41:56
Vira	2	46N08	8E51	-0:35:24
Visp	2	46N18	7E53	-0:31:32
Vissoie	2	46N13	7E36	-0:30:24
Vitznau	2	47N01	8E29	-0:33:56
Vouvry	2	46N20	6E53	-0:27:32
Vrin	2	46N39	9E06	-0:36:24
Vuitebœuf	2	46N37	6E34	-0:26:16
Wädenswil	2	47N14	8E40	-0:34:40
Wald	2	47N17	8E55	-0:35:40
Waldenburg	2	47N23	7E45	-0:31:00
Waldstatt	2	47N21	9E17	-0:37:08
Walenstadt	2	47N07	9E19	-0:37:16
Wallisellen	2	47N25	8E36	-0:34:24
Wangen an der Aare	2	47N14	7E39	-0:30:36
Wängi	2	47N30	8E57	-0:35:48
Wangs	2	47N02	9E26	-0:37:44
Wasen	2	47N03	7E48	-0:31:12
Wassen	2	46N42	8E36	-0:34:24
Wattenwil	2	46N46	7E30	-0:30:00
Wattwil	2	47N18	9E06	-0:36:24
Weggis	2	47N02	8E26	-0:33:44
Weinfelden	2	47N34	9E06	-0:36:24
Weissenburg	2	46N39	7E28	-0:29:52
Weisstannen	2	46N59	9E21	-0:37:24
Wengen	2	46N36	7E56	-0:31:44
Wettingen	2	47N28	8E19	-0:33:16
Wetzikon	2	47N19	8E47	-0:35:08
Wiedlisbach	2	47N15	7E39	-0:30:36
Wiesen	2	46N43	9E43	-0:38:52
Wil	2	47N27	9E03	-0:36:12
Wildegg	2	47N25	8E11	-0:32:44
Wildhaus	2	47N12	9E22	-0:37:28
Willisau	2	47N07	8E00	-0:32:00
Wimmis	2	46N41	7E38	-0:30:32
Windisch	2	47N29	8E13	-0:32:52
Winterthur	2	47N30	8E43	-0:34:52
Wohlen	2	47N21	8E17	-0:33:08
Wolfenschiessen	2	46N55	8E24	-0:33:36
Wolhusen	2	47N04	8E04	-0:32:16
Worb	2	46N56	7E34	-0:30:16
Würenlingen	2	47N32	8E16	-0:33:04
Wynigen	2	47N06	7E40	-0:30:40
Yverdon	2	46N47	6E39	-0:26:36
Yvonand	2	46N48	6E45	-0:27:00
Zell	2	47N09	7E55	-0:31:40
Zermatt	2	46N02	7E45	-0:31:00
Zernez	2	46N43	10E05	-0:40:20
Zillis	2	46N38	9E27	-0:37:48
Zinal	2	46N08	7E38	-0:30:32
Zizers	2	46N56	9E34	-0:38:16
Zofingen	2	47N18	7E57	-0:31:48
Zollikofen	2	47N00	7E28	-0:29:52
Zollikon	2	47N20	8E35	-0:34:20
Zoug → Zug	2	47N10	8E31	-0:34:04
Zuchwil	2	47N12	7E33	-0:30:12
Zug	2	47N10	8E31	-0:34:04
Zuoz	2	46N36	9E58	-0:39:52
Zürich	2	47N23	8E32	-0:34:08
Zurigo → Zürich	2	47N23	8E32	-0:34:08
Zurzach	2	47N35	8E18	-0:33:12
Zweisimmen	2	46N33	7E22	-0:29:28

AS-SŪRĪYAH SYRIEN SYRIE SIRIA SYRIA

Time Table # 1

Before 1/Jan/1920 LMT

Begin Standard 30E00

Date	Time	Offset
1/Jan/1920	0:00	-2:00
18/Apr/1920	2:00	-3:00
3/Oct/1920	2:00	-2:00
17/Apr/1921	2:00	-3:00
2/Oct/1921	2:00	-2:00
16/Apr/1922	2:00	-3:00
1/Oct/1922	2:00	-2:00
15/Apr/1923	2:00	-3:00
7/Oct/1923	2:00	-2:00
29/Apr/1962	2:00	-3:00
1/Oct/1962	2:00	-2:00
1/May/1963	2:00	-3:00
30/Sep/1963	2:00	-2:00
1/May/1964	2:00	-3:00
1/Oct/1964	2:00	-2:00
1/May/1965	2:00	-3:00
30/Sep/1965	2:00	-2:00
24/Apr/1966	2:00	-3:00
1/Oct/1966	2:00	-2:00
1/May/1967	2:00	-3:00
1/Oct/1967	2:00	-2:00
1/May/1968	2:00	-3:00
1/Oct/1968	2:00	-2:00
1/May/1969	2:00	-3:00
1/Oct/1969	2:00	-2:00
1/May/1970	2:00	-3:00
1/Oct/1970	2:00	-2:00
1/May/1971	2:00	-3:00
1/Oct/1971	2:00	-2:00
1/May/1972	2:00	-3:00
1/Oct/1972	2:00	-2:00
1/Apr/1973	2:00	-3:00
1/Oct/1973	2:00	-2:00
1/May/1974	2:00	-3:00
1/Oct/1974	2:00	-2:00
1/May/1975	2:00	-3:00
1/Oct/1975	2:00	-2:00
1/May/1976	2:00	-3:00
1/Oct/1976	2:00	-2:00
1/May/1977	2:00	-3:00
1/Sep/1977	2:00	-2:00
1/May/1978	2:00	-3:00
1/Sep/1978	2:00	-2:00
9/Apr/1983	2:00	-3:00
1/Oct/1983	2:00	-2:00
9/Apr/1984	2:00	-3:00
1/Oct/1984	2:00	-2:00
16/Feb/1986	2:00	-3:00
19/Oct/1986	2:00	-2:00
1/Mar/1987	2:00	-3:00
31/Oct/1987	2:00	-2:00
15/Mar/1988	2:00	-3:00
31/Oct/1988	2:00	-2:00
31/Mar/1989	2:00	-3:00
1/Oct/1989	2:00	-2:00
1/Apr/1990	2:00	-3:00
30/Sep/1990	2:00	-2:00
1/Apr/1991	2:00	-3:00
30/Sep/1991	2:00	-2:00
....		

Time Table # 2

Before 1/Jan/1920 LMT

Begin Standard 30E00

Date	Time	Offset
1/Jan/1920	0:00	-2:00
18/Apr/1920	2:00	-3:00
3/Oct/1920	2:00	-2:00
17/Apr/1921	2:00	-3:00
2/Oct/1921	2:00	-2:00
16/Apr/1922	2:00	-3:00
1/Oct/1922	2:00	-2:00
15/Apr/1923	2:00	-3:00
7/Oct/1923	2:00	-2:00
29/Apr/1962	2:00	-3:00
1/Oct/1962	2:00	-2:00
1/May/1963	2:00	-3:00
30/Sep/1963	2:00	-2:00
1/May/1964	2:00	-3:00
1/Oct/1964	2:00	-2:00
1/May/1965	2:00	-3:00
30/Sep/1965	2:00	-2:00
24/Apr/1966	2:00	-3:00
1/Oct/1966	2:00	-2:00
1/May/1967	2:00	-3:00
1/Jul/1967	0:00	-2:00
7/Jul/1974	0:00	-3:00
13/Oct/1974	0:00	-2:00
20/Apr/1975	0:00	-3:00
31/Aug/1975	0:00	-2:00
14/Apr/1985	0:00	-3:00
15/Sep/1985	0:00	-2:00
18/May/1986	0:00	-3:00
7/Sep/1986	0:00	-2:00
15/Apr/1987	0:00	-3:00
13/Sep/1987	0:00	-2:00
9/Apr/1988	0:00	-3:00
3/Sep/1988	0:00	-2:00
29/Apr/1989	0:00	-3:00
2/Sep/1989	0:00	-2:00
25/Mar/1990	0:00	-3:00
26/Aug/1990	0:00	-2:00
10/Mar/1991	0:00	-3:00
1/Sep/1991	0:00	-2:00

DIVISIONS

1. Syria

2. Golan Heights (annexed to Israel 196

Place		Lat	Long	Offset
‘Abbādah 1	1	33N30	36E33	-2:26:12
Abū Kamāl 1	1	34N27	40E55	-2:43:40
Ad-Dānā 1	1	36N13	36E46	-2:27:04
Ad-Dayr 1	1	32N28	36E27	-2:25:48
Ad-Dīmās 1	1	33N35	36E05	-2:24:20
‘Adhrā’ 1	1	33N37	36E30	-2:26:00
‘Afrīn 1	1	36N31	36E52	-2:27:28
‘Āhirah 1	1	32N53	36E28	-2:25:52
‘Ajamī 1	1	36N28	37E42	-2:30:48
Akhtarīn 1	1	36N31	37E20	-2:29:20
Al-‘Āl 2	2	32N48	35E44	-2:22:56
Al-‘Ānāt 1	1	32N21	36E48	-2:27:12
Al-‘Anz 1	1	32N23	36E38	-2:26:32
Al-Arak 1	1	34N38	38E35	-2:34:20
Al-‘Ashārah 1	1	34N55	40E34	-2:42:16
Al-Atārib 1	1	36N08	36E49	-2:27:16
Al-Bāb 1	1	36N22	37E31	-2:30:04
Al-Baṭrūnah 1	1	33N39	36E02	-2:24:08
Al-Buṭaynah 1	1	32N57	36E42	-2:26:48
Alep → Ḥalab 1	1	36N12	37E10	-2:28:40
Aleppo → Ḥalab 1	1	36N12	37E10	-2:28:40
Al-Ghārīyah 1	1	32N23	36E39	-2:26:36
Al-Ghizlānīyah 1	1	33N23	36E27	-2:25:48
Al-Ḥaffah 1	1	35N35	36E02	-2:24:08
Al-Ḥafīr al-Fawqānī 1	1	33N42	36E28	-2:25:52
Al-Ḥamīdīyah 1	1	34N43	35E56	-2:23:44
Al-Ḥarāk 1	1	32N44	36E18	-2:25:12
Al-Ḥārrah 1	1	33N03	36E00	-2:24:00
Al-Ḥasakah 1	1	36N29	40E45	-2:43:00
Al-Hījānah 1	1	33N21	36E33	-2:26:12
Al-Jibāb 1	1	33N06	36E15	-2:25:00
Al-Junaynah 1	1	32N54	36E44	-2:26:56
Al-Kafr 1	1	32N38	36E38	-2:26:32
Al-Kawm 1	1	35N11	38E52	-2:35:28
Al-Khushnīyah 2	2	33N00	35E48	-2:23:12
Al-Kiswah 1	1	33N21	36E14	-2:24:56
Al-Lādhiqīyah (Latakia) 1	1	35N31	35E47	-2:23:08
Al-Majdal 1	1	32N47	36E30	-2:26:00
Al-Mashqūq 1	1	32N24	36E43	-2:26:52
Al-Mashrafah 1	1	34N50	36E52	-2:27:28
Al-Mayādīn 1	1	35N01	40E27	-2:41:48
Al-Mazzah 1	1	33N30	36E15	-2:25:00
Al-Mismīyah 1	1	33N08	36E23	-2:25:32
Al-Mu‘Aẓẓamīyah 1	1	33N45	36E39	-2:26:36
Al-Musayfirah 1	1	32N37	36E20	-2:25:20
Al-Mushannaf 1	1	32N44	36E46	-2:27:04
Al-Mutā‘Iyah 1	1	32N29	36E17	-2:25:08
Al-Qābūn 1	1	33N33	36E20	-2:25:20
Al-Qadam 1	1	33N28	36E17	-2:25:08
Al-Qāmishlī 1	1	37N02	41E14	-2:44:56
Al-Qaryatayn 1	1	34N14	37E14	-2:28:56
Al-Qunayṭirah 1	1	33N07	35E49	-2:23:16
Al-Qurayyah 1	1	32N32	36E36	-2:26:24
Al-Quṣayr 1	1	34N31	36E35	-2:26:20
Al-Quṭayfah 1	1	33N44	36E36	-2:26:24
‘Āmūdā 1	1	37N05	40E54	-2:43:36
An-Nabk 1	1	34N01	36E44	-2:26:56
An-Nakhl 1	1	33N00	36E07	-2:24:28
An-Nāmir 1	1	32N47	36E13	-2:24:52
An-Nāṣirīyah 1	1	33N52	36E49	-2:27:16
‘Aqrabā 1	1	33N06	36E00	-2:24:00
Arīḥā 1	1	35N48	35E36	-2:22:24
Ar-Rafīd 1	1	32N57	35E53	-2:23:32
Ar-Raqqah 1	1	35N56	39E01	-2:36:04
Ar-Rastān 1	1	34N55	36E44	-2:26:56
Ar-Ruḥaybah 1	1	33N45	36E42	-2:26:48
Ar-Rushaydah 1	1	32N40	36E50	-2:27:20
Ash-Shaykh Miskīn 1	1	32N49	36E09	-2:24:36
Ash-Shaykh Sa‘D 1	1	32N50	36E02	-2:24:08
As-Sabkhah 1	1	35N48	39E15	-2:37:00
As-Safīrah 1	1	36N04	37E22	-2:29:28
‘Assāl al-Ward 1	1	33N52	36E24	-2:25:36
As-Salamīyah 1	1	35N01	37E03	-2:28:12
‘Assān 1	1	36N05	37E14	-2:28:56
Aṣ-Ṣanamayn 1	1	33N05	36E10	-2:24:40
Aṣ-Ṣaqlabīyah 1	1	35N22	36E23	-2:25:32
As-Sijn 1	1	32N47	36E28	-2:25:52
As-Sukhnah 1	1	34N52	38E52	-2:35:28
As-Summāqīyāt 1	1	32N26	36E24	-2:25:36
Aṣ-Ṣuwār 1	1	35N30	40E39	-2:42:36
As-Suwaydā’ 1	1	32N42	36E34	-2:26:16
Ath-Tha‘Lah 1	1	32N42	36E26	-2:25:44
At-Tall 1	1	33N36	36E18	-2:25:12
Aṭ-Ṭayyibah 1	1	32N33	36E14	-2:24:56
Aṭ-Ṭayyibah 1	1	32N48	36E46	-2:27:04
‘Ayn al-‘Arab 1	1	36N54	38E21	-2:33:24
‘Ayn Dīwār 1	1	37N17	42E11	-2:48:44
‘Ayrah 1	1	32N37	36E32	-2:26:08

SYRIA SIRIA SYRIE SYRIEN AS-SŪRĪYAH

Name		Lat	Long	Offset
A'Zāz 1	1	36N35	37E03	-2:28:12
Az-Zabdānī 1	1	33N43	36E05	-2:24:20
Az-Zarbah 1	1	36N04	36E59	-2:27:56
Baddā 1	1	33N41	36E26	-2:25:44
Bāniyās 1	1	35N11	35E57	-2:23:48
Bāniyās 2	2	33N15	35E41	-2:22:44
Barzah 1	1	33N34	36E19	-2:25:16
Bayt Jinn 1	1	33N19	35E53	-2:23:32
Bayyā'īyah al-Kabīrah 1	1	35N42	37E09	-2:28:36
Bulbul 1	1	36N46	36E49	-2:27:16
Burāq 1	1	33N10	36E29	-2:25:56
Buraykah 1	1	32N50	36E34	-2:26:16
Burj Islām 1	1	35N41	35E48	-2:23:12
Burj Ṣāfītā 1	1	34N49	36E07	-2:24:28
Buṣayrah 1	1	35N09	40E26	-2:41:44
Buṣrá al-Ḥarīrī (Bosor) 1	1	32N50	36E20	-2:25:20
Buṣrá ash-Shām 1	1	32N31	36E29	-2:25:56
Buṭayḥah 2	2	32N56	35E53	-2:23:32
Buwayḍān 1	1	33N12	36E26	-2:25:44
Dablān 1	1	34N52	40E34	-2:42:16
Dā'īl 1	1	32N45	36E08	-2:24:32
Dāmā 1	1	32N57	36E25	-2:25:40
Damas → Dimashq 1	1	33N30	36E18	-2:25:12
Damasco → Dimashq 1	1	33N30	36E18	-2:25:12
Damascus → Dimashq 1	1	33N30	36E18	-2:25:12
Damaskus → Dimashq 1	1	33N30	36E18	-2:25:12
Dar'ā 1	1	32N37	36E06	-2:24:24
Dārayyā 1	1	33N27	36E15	-2:25:00
Darbāsīyah 1	1	37N04	40E39	-2:42:36
Darkūsh 1	1	35N59	36E23	-2:25:32
Dār Ta'Izzah 1	1	36N17	36E51	-2:27:24
Dayr 'Alī 1	1	33N17	36E18	-2:25:12
Dayr 'Aṭīyah 1	1	34N06	36E46	-2:27:04
Dayr az-Zawr 1	1	35N20	40E09	-2:40:36
Dayr Ḥāfir 1	1	36N09	37E42	-2:30:48
Dayrīk 1	1	37N10	42E08	-2:48:32
Dayr Qānūn 1	1	33N36	36E08	-2:24:32
Deir-es-Zor → Dayr az-Zawr 1	1	35N20	40E09	-2:40:36
Deraa → Dar'ā 1	1	32N37	36E06	-2:24:24
Dibbīn 1	1	32N26	36E34	-2:26:16
Dimashq (Damascus) 1	1	33N30	36E18	-2:25:12
Djerablous → Jarābulus 1	1	36N49	38E01	-2:32:04
Dulq Maghār 1	1	36N22	38E39	-2:34:36
Dūmā 1	1	33N35	36E24	-2:25:36
Ḍumayr 1	1	33N38	36E40	-2:26:40
Ḍummar 1	1	33N32	36E14	-2:24:56
Esh-Sham → Dimashq 1	1	33N30	36E18	-2:25:12
Fīq 2	2	32N47	35E42	-2:22:48
Furqlus 1	1	34N36	37E05	-2:28:20
Ghabāghib 1	1	33N10	36E13	-2:24:52
Ghārīyat al-Gharbīyah 1	1	32N41	36E13	-2:24:52
Ghārīyat ash-Sharqīyah 1	1	32N40	36E16	-2:25:04
Ghaṣm 1	1	32N33	36E22	-2:25:28
Ghunthur 1	1	34N23	37E09	-2:28:36
Haffe → Al-Ḥaffah 1	1	35N35	36E02	-2:24:08
Ḥalab (Aleppo) 1	1	36N12	37E10	-2:28:40
Ḥalbūn 1	1	33N40	36E15	-2:25:00
Haleb → Ḥalab 1	1	36N12	37E10	-2:28:40
Ḥamāh 1	1	35N08	36E45	-2:27:00
Ḥammām at-Turkumān 1	1	36N32	39E03	-2:36:12
Ḥarastā al-Baṣal 1	1	33N34	36E22	-2:25:28
Ḥārim 1	1	36N12	36E31	-2:26:04
Ḥārithān 1	1	36N16	37E05	-2:28:20
Ḥarrān al-'Awāmīd 1	1	33N27	36E34	-2:26:16
Ḥimṣ (Homs) 1	1	34N44	36E43	-2:26:52
Ḥīnah 1	1	33N21	35E56	-2:23:44
Ḥirjillah 1	1	33N22	36E18	-2:25:12
Ḥisyah 1	1	34N24	36E45	-2:27:00
Homs → Ḥimṣ 1	1	34N44	36E43	-2:26:52
Ibta' 1	1	32N47	36E09	-2:24:36
Idlib 1	1	35N55	36E38	-2:26:32
Imtān 1	1	32N24	36E49	-2:27:16
Izra' 1	1	32N51	36E15	-2:25:00
Jabā 1	1	33N10	35E56	-2:23:44
Jablah 1	1	35N21	35E55	-2:23:40
Jarābulus 1	1	36N49	38E01	-2:32:04
Jaramānah 1	1	33N29	36E21	-2:25:24
Jawbar 1	1	33N31	36E19	-2:25:16
Jayrūd 1	1	33N49	36E44	-2:26:56
Jisr ash-Shughūr 1	1	35N48	36E19	-2:25:16
Jubb al-Jarrāḥ 1	1	34N49	37E19	-2:29:16
Jubbātā al-Khashab 1	1	33N13	35E49	-2:23:16
Judaydat al-Khās 1	1	33N24	36E33	-2:26:12
Judaydat 'Arṭūz 1	1	33N26	36E10	-2:24:40
Juwayzah 2	2	33N02	35E51	-2:23:24
Kafr Naffākh 2	2	33N04	35E44	-2:22:56
Kafr Nāsij 1	1	33N09	36E03	-2:24:12
Kafr Sūsah 1	1	33N29	36E16	-2:25:04
Kafr Takhārīm 1	1	36N07	36E31	-2:26:04
Kanākir 1	1	33N15	36E05	-2:24:20
Kasrat Muraybiṭ 1	1	36N02	38E08	-2:32:32
Kassab 1	1	35N56	35E59	-2:23:56
Khabab 1	1	33N00	36E16	-2:25:04
Khalkhalah 1	1	33N04	36E32	-2:26:08
Khān Abū Shāmāt 1	1	33N40	36E54	-2:27:36
Khān Arnabah 1	1	33N11	35E53	-2:23:32
Khān Shaykhūn 1	1	35N26	36E38	-2:26:32
Kharabā 1	1	32N34	36E27	-2:25:48
Khirbat al-Ghazālah 1	1	32N44	36E12	-2:24:48
Khirbat 'Awwād 1	1	32N19	36E43	-2:26:52
Khisfīn 2	2	32N51	35E49	-2:23:16
Knaddah 1	1	35N45	36E12	-2:24:48
Kufayr Yabūs 1	1	33N42	36E01	-2:24:04
Lāhitah 1	1	32N59	36E35	-2:26:20
Latakia → Al-Lādhiqīyah 1	1	35N31	35E47	-2:23:08
Ma'Arrat an-Nu'Mān 1	1	35N38	36E40	-2:26:40
Ma'Arrat Miṣrīn 1	1	36N01	36E40	-2:26:40
Ma'Arrat Ṣaydnāyā 1	1	33N41	36E23	-2:25:32
Maḍāyā 1	1	33N41	36E06	-2:24:24
Maḥajjah 1	1	32N57	36E14	-2:24:56
Mallāḥ 1	1	32N30	36E51	-2:27:24
Ma'Lūlā 1	1	33N50	36E33	-2:26:12
Manbij 1	1	36N31	37E57	-2:31:48
Manṣūrah 2	2	33N08	35E48	-2:23:12
Māri' 1	1	36N28	37E11	-2:28:44
Marmarītā 1	1	34N47	36E15	-2:25:00
Mas'Adah (Cæsarea Philippi) 2	2	33N14	35E45	-2:23:00
Maskanah 1	1	36N01	38E05	-2:32:20
Maṣyāf 1	1	35N03	36E21	-2:25:24
Māyir 1	1	36N23	37E02	-2:28:08
Mazra'At-Bayt Jinn 1	1	33N19	35E55	-2:23:40
Minīn 1	1	33N39	36E18	-2:25:12
Mughr 2	2	33N05	35E43	-2:22:52
Muḥradah 1	1	35N15	36E35	-2:26:20
Mukharram al-Fawqānī 1	1	34N49	37E04	-2:28:16
Mutbīn 1	1	33N09	36E15	-2:25:00
Muzayrīb 1	1	32N42	36E01	-2:24:04
Najhā 1	1	33N23	36E22	-2:25:28
Naṣīb 1	1	32N33	36E11	-2:24:44
Nawá 1	1	32N53	36E03	-2:24:12
Nu'Aymah 1	1	32N38	36E10	-2:24:40
Palmyra → Tudmur 1	1	34N33	38E17	-2:33:08
Qabbāsīn 1	1	36N25	37E34	-2:30:16
Qan'Abah 2	2	33N08	35E40	-2:22:40
Qanāyah 1	1	33N01	36E11	-2:24:44
Qārā 1	1	34N09	36E44	-2:26:56
Qāsim 1	1	32N59	36E05	-2:24:20
Qaṭanā 1	1	33N26	36E05	-2:24:20
Qaṭmā 1	1	36N36	36E57	-2:27:48
Qayṭah 1	1	33N04	36E08	-2:24:32
Qiṣrāyā 1	1	34N53	36E26	-2:25:44
Qudaym 1	1	35N03	38E25	-2:33:40
Rānkūs 1	1	33N45	36E23	-2:25:32
Ra's al-'Ayn 1	1	36N51	40E04	-2:40:16
Ruḍaymah Lioūa 1	1	33N01	36E35	-2:26:20
Ṣadad 1	1	34N18	36E56	-2:27:44
Ṣāfītā → Burj Ṣāfītā 1	1	34N49	36E07	-2:24:28
Saḥam al-Jawlān 1	1	32N46	35E56	-2:23:44
Sahwat al-Qamḥ 1	1	32N36	36E23	-2:25:32
Sālah 1	1	32N38	36E46	-2:27:04
Ṣalkhad 1	1	32N29	36E43	-2:26:52
Ṡalqīn 1	1	36N08	36E27	-2:25:48
Salūq 'Atīq 1	1	36N36	39E07	-2:36:28
Samj 1	1	32N27	36E30	-2:26:00
Sarāqib 1	1	35N52	36E48	-2:27:12
Sa'Sa' 1	1	33N17	36E02	-2:24:08
Ṣaydnāyā 1	1	33N42	36E22	-2:25:28
Ṡhaddādī 1	1	36N02	40E45	-2:43:00
Sha'F 1	1	32N38	36E51	-2:27:24
Shahba 1	1	32N51	36E37	-2:26:28
Shaqqā 1	1	32N53	36E42	-2:26:48
Shaqrā' 1	1	32N54	36E14	-2:24:56
Shaykh al-Ḥadīd 1	1	36N30	36E35	-2:26:20
Shinīrah 1	1	32N22	36E45	-2:27:00
Shinshār 1	1	34N36	36E44	-2:26:56
Shuyūkh al-Fawqanī 1	1	36N46	38E03	-2:32:12
Sirghāyā 1	1	33N48	36E09	-2:24:36
Ṣūrān 1	1	36N34	37E13	-2:28:52
Ṣūrān 1	1	35N17	36E45	-2:27:00
Ṡuwaydah 1	1	35N46	39E38	-2:38:32
Suwaydā' → As-Suwaydā' 1	1	32N42	36E34	-2:26:16
Tabaqah 1	1	35N52	38E34	-2:34:16
Ṭafas 1	1	32N44	36E04	-2:24:16
Ṫall al-Abyaḍ 1	1	36N41	38E57	-2:35:48
Tall Bīsah 1	1	34N50	36E44	-2:26:56
Tall Kalakh 1	1	34N40	36E15	-2:25:00
Tall Kūshik 1	1	36N48	42E04	-2:48:16
Tall Rif'At 1	1	36N28	37E06	-2:28:24
Tall Salḥab 1	1	35N15	36E22	-2:25:28
Tall Tamir 1	1	36N39	40E22	-2:41:28
Ṭarṭūs 1	1	34N53	35E53	-2:23:32
Ṫasīl 1	1	32N50	35E58	-2:23:52
Tibnah 1	1	32N59	36E13	-2:24:52
Ṭīsīyah 1	1	32N24	36E27	-2:25:48
Ṫiyās 1	1	34N33	37E40	-2:30:40
Tudmur (Palmyra) 1	1	34N33	38E17	-2:33:08
Umm Walad 1	1	32N39	36E26	-2:25:44
'Urmān 1	1	32N30	36E45	-2:27:00
'Uwaynāt 1	1	35N43	36E05	-2:24:20
Yabrūd 1	1	33N58	36E40	-2:26:40
Yādūdah 1	1	32N40	36E04	-2:24:16
Zakīyah 1	1	33N20	36E08	-2:24:32

TAIWAN TAIWÁN FORMOSA REPUBLIC OF CHINA T'AIWAN

Time Table
Before 1/Jan/1896 LMT
Begin Standard 120E00

Date	Time	Offset
1/Jan/1896	0:00	-8:00
1/May/1945	0:00	-9:00
1/Oct/1945	0:00	-8:00
1/May/1946	0:00	-9:00
1/Oct/1946	0:00	-8:00
1/May/1947	0:00	-9:00
1/Oct/1947	0:00	-8:00
1/May/1948	0:00	-9:00
1/Oct/1948	0:00	-8:00
1/May/1949	0:00	-9:00
1/Oct/1949	0:00	-8:00
1/May/1950	0:00	-9:00
1/Oct/1950	0:00	-8:00
1/May/1951	0:00	-9:00
1/Oct/1951	0:00	-8:00
1/Mar/1952	0:00	-9:00
1/Nov/1952	0:00	-8:00
1/Apr/1953	0:00	-9:00
1/Nov/1953	0:00	-8:00
1/Apr/1954	0:00	-9:00
1/Nov/1954	0:00	-8:00
1/Apr/1955	0:00	-9:00
1/Oct/1955	0:00	-8:00
1/Apr/1956	0:00	-9:00
1/Oct/1956	0:00	-8:00
1/Apr/1957	0:00	-9:00
1/Oct/1957	0:00	-8:00
1/Apr/1958	0:00	-9:00
1/Oct/1958	0:00	-8:00
1/Apr/1959	0:00	-9:00
1/Oct/1959	0:00	-8:00
1/Jun/1960	0:00	-9:00
1/Oct/1960	0:00	-8:00
1/Jun/1961	0:00	-9:00
1/Oct/1961	0:00	-8:00
1/Apr/1974	0:00	-9:00
1/Oct/1974	0:00	-8:00
1/Apr/1975	0:00	-9:00
1/Oct/1975	0:00	-8:00
30/Jun/1980	0:00	-9:00
30/Sep/1980	0:00	-8:00

Name	Lat	Long	Offset
Changhua	24N05	120E32	-8:02:08
Ch'angpin	23N19	121E27	-8:05:48
Ch'aochou	22N33	120E32	-8:02:08
Ch'ech'eng	22N05	120E42	-8:02:48
Ch'engtzuliao	25N06	121E27	-8:05:48
Chiahsien	23N05	120E35	-8:02:20
Chiai	23N29	120E27	-8:01:48
Chiali	23N10	120E10	-8:00:40
Chiaohsi	24N49	121E46	-8:07:04
Chiaopan	24N50	121E21	-8:05:24
Chiapaot'ai	24N11	121E00	-8:04:00
Chichi	23N50	120E47	-8:03:08
Chihpen	22N42	121E02	-8:04:08
Ch'ihshang	23N07	121E12	-8:04:48
Chihtungtsun	22N44	120E14	-8:00:56
Ch'iku	23N08	120E07	-8:00:28
Chilung (Keelung)	25N08	121E44	-8:06:56
Ch'ingt'ung	25N02	121E43	-8:06:52
Chinkuashih	25N07	121E51	-8:07:24
Chinshan	25N13	121E38	-8:06:32
Chinshui	24N36	120E53	-8:03:32
Ch'ishan	22N53	120E28	-8:01:52
Ch'itu	25N06	121E43	-8:06:52
Chunan	24N41	120E52	-8:03:28
Chungho	25N00	121E30	-8:06:00
Chungli	24N57	121E13	-8:04:52
Chungliao	22N41	121E28	-8:05:52
Chungp'u	23N25	120E31	-8:02:04
Chushan	23N45	120E40	-8:02:40

T'AIWAN REPUBLIC OF CHINA FORMOSA TAIWÁN TAIWAN

Place	Lat	Long	Time
Chutung	24N44	121E05	-8:04:20
Chuwei	25N08	121E27	-8:05:48
Erhlin	23N54	120E22	-8:01:28
Erhshui	23N49	120E36	-8:02:24
Fangliao	22N22	120E35	-8:02:20
Fangshan	22N16	120E39	-8:02:36
Fenglin	23N45	121E26	-8:05:44
Fengpin	23N36	121E31	-8:06:04
Fengyüan	24N15	120E43	-8:02:52
Fuli	23N11	121E14	-8:04:56
Hsichih	25N04	121E39	-8:06:36
Hsientung	25N09	121E44	-8:06:56
Hsihu	23N58	120E28	-8:01:52
Hsilo	23N48	120E27	-8:01:48
Hsinch'eng	24N08	121E39	-8:06:36
Hsinchu	24N48	120E58	-8:03:52
Hsinchuang	25N02	121E27	-8:05:48
Hsinhua	23N02	120E18	-8:01:12
Hsinshih	23N05	120E17	-8:01:08
Hsintien	24N57	121E32	-8:06:08
Hsiyü	23N36	119E30	-7:58:00
Hsüehchia	23N14	120E10	-8:00:40
Hualien	23N59	121E36	-8:06:24
Huhsi	23N35	119E39	-7:58:36
Hungmao	24N55	120E58	-8:03:52
Huoshaoliao	25N00	121E45	-8:07:00
Huwei	23N43	120E26	-8:01:44
Ilan	24N46	121E45	-8:07:00
Jenli	23N15	120E08	-8:00:32
Juisui	23N30	121E21	-8:05:24
Kangshan	22N48	120E17	-8:01:08
Kaohiung → Kaohsiung	22N38	120E17	-8:01:08
Kaohsiung	22N38	120E17	-8:01:08
Kaohsiunghsien	22N38	120E21	-8:01:24
Keelung → Chilung	25N08	121E44	-8:06:56
Kiirun → Chilung	25N08	121E44	-8:06:56
K'ouhu	23N35	120E11	-8:00:44
Kuanhsi	24N48	121E10	-8:04:40
Kuanmiao	22N58	120E19	-8:01:16
Kuanshan	23N03	121E09	-8:04:36
Kuanyin	25N02	121E04	-8:04:16
Kunghsi	24N37	121E16	-8:05:04
Kung-Pei-Tien	25N06	121E38	-8:06:32
Kuohsing	24N02	120E51	-8:03:24
Laohuk'ou	24N53	121E03	-8:04:12
Likang	22N47	120E29	-8:01:56
Linyüan	22N30	120E23	-8:01:32
Liufentzu	24N57	121E35	-8:06:20
Lotung	24N41	121E46	-8:07:04
Luchou	25N05	121E28	-8:05:52
Lukang	24N03	120E25	-8:01:40
Luliao	25N07	121E39	-8:06:36
Lungt'an	24N52	121E12	-8:04:48
Luyeh	22N55	121E08	-8:04:32
Makung (P'enghu)	23N34	119E34	-7:58:16
Malienkang	25N10	121E39	-8:06:36
Matou	23N11	120E14	-8:00:56
Meinung	22N54	120E32	-8:02:08
Miaoli	24N34	120E49	-8:03:16
Mucha	24N59	121E34	-8:06:16
Nanao	24N28	121E48	-8:07:12
Nanchuang	24N36	120E59	-8:03:56
Nanhsi	23N11	120E29	-8:01:56
Nant'ou	23N55	120E41	-8:02:44
Neihu	25N05	121E34	-8:06:16
Neishuishan	25N09	121E43	-8:06:52
Nuannuan	25N06	121E44	-8:06:56
Paiho	23N21	120E25	-8:01:40
Paisha	23N40	119E35	-7:58:20
Panch'iao	25N01	121E27	-8:05:48
Peikang	23N34	120E18	-8:01:12
Peinan	22N47	121E07	-8:04:28
P'ingtung	22N40	120E29	-8:01:56
P'otzu	23N28	120E14	-8:00:56
Puli	23N58	120E57	-8:03:48
Putai	23N23	120E09	-8:00:36
Sanchih	25N16	121E30	-8:06:00
Sanchung	25N04	121E30	-8:06:00
Sanch'ungch'iao	25N12	121E35	-8:06:20
Sangchungshih	25N04	121E29	-8:05:56
Sanhsing	24N40	121E39	-8:06:36
Sani	24N25	120E46	-8:03:04
Shenk'eng	25N00	121E36	-8:06:24
Shihti	25N02	121E44	-8:06:56
Shihting	24N59	121E39	-8:06:36
Shoufeng	23N52	121E30	-8:06:00
Shuang-Hsi	25N01	121E39	-8:06:36
Ssuchunghsi	22N06	120E44	-8:02:56
Suao	24N36	121E51	-8:07:24
Tachia	24N21	120E37	-8:02:28
Tachoshui	24N20	121E44	-8:06:56
Tafanlieh	21N58	120E46	-8:03:04
Tahsi	24N57	121E53	-8:07:32
Tahu	24N26	120E52	-8:03:28
Taichu → T'aichung	24N09	120E41	-8:02:44
T'aichung	24N09	120E41	-8:02:44
Taihoku → T'aipei	25N03	121E30	-8:06:00
T'aihsi	23N42	120E11	-8:00:44
T'aima	22N37	120E59	-8:03:56
T'ainan	23N00	120E12	-8:00:48
T'ainanhsien	23N18	120E19	-8:01:16
T'aipei	25N03	121E30	-8:06:00
T'aipeihsien	25N01	121E27	-8:05:48
T'aitung	22N45	121E09	-8:04:36
Takao → Kaohsiung	22N38	120E17	-8:01:08
Takow → Kaohsiung	22N38	120E17	-8:01:08
Tanshui	25N10	121E26	-8:05:44
Tashuik'u	25N13	121E30	-8:06:00
Tawu	22N22	120E54	-8:03:36
Tayüan	25N04	121E11	-8:04:44
T'ienchung	23N52	120E35	-8:02:20
T'ouch'eng	24N52	121E49	-8:07:16
Touliu	23N43	120E32	-8:02:08
Tounan	23N41	120E28	-8:01:52
Ts'aot'un	23N59	120E41	-8:02:44
Tsoying	22N41	120E17	-8:01:08
T'uch'ang	24N35	121E29	-8:05:56
T'uch'eng	24N59	121E26	-8:05:44
Tungho	22N58	121E18	-8:05:12
Tungkang	22N28	120E26	-8:01:44
Tungshih	24N15	120E49	-8:03:16
Wanli	25N11	121E41	-8:06:44
Wuch'i	24N16	120E31	-8:02:04
Wulai	24N52	121E33	-8:06:12
Yehliu	25N12	121E41	-8:06:44
Yenshuichen	23N20	120E16	-8:01:04
Yüanli	24N27	120E39	-8:02:36
Yüanlin	23N58	120E34	-8:02:16
Yüli	23N20	121E18	-8:05:12
Yungho	25N01	121E31	-8:06:04

TANZANIE ZANZIBAR TANGANYIKA TANSANIA TANZANIA

Time Table # 1		
Before	1/Jan/1931	LMT
Begin Standard		37E30
1/Jan/1931	0:00	-2:30
Begin Standard		45E00
1/Jan/1940	0:00	-3:00
....		

Time Table # 2		
Before	1/Jan/1931	LMT
Begin Standard		45E00
1/Jan/1931	0:00	-3:00
Begin Standard		41E15
1/Jan/1948	0:00	-2:45
Begin Standard		45E00
1/Jan/1961	0:00	-3:00

Place	Table	Lat	Long	Time
Arusha	2	3S22	36E41	-2:26:44
Arusha Chini	2	3S35	37E20	-2:29:20
Babati	2	4S13	35E45	-2:23:00
Bagamoyo	2	6S26	38E54	-2:35:36
Bahi	2	5S59	35E19	-2:21:16
Banagi	2	2S16	34E51	-2:19:24
Barikiwa	2	9S28	37E54	-2:31:36
Bereku	2	4S27	35E44	-2:22:56
Bigwa	2	7S13	39E09	-2:36:36
Biharamulo	2	2S38	31E20	-2:05:20
Bugene	2	1S35	31E08	-2:04:32
Bukene	2	4S14	32E53	-2:11:32
Bukima	2	1S48	33E25	-2:13:40
Bukoba	2	1S20	31E49	-2:07:16
Bukombe	2	3S31	32E03	-2:08:12
Bunazi	2	1S13	31E24	-2:05:36
Bungu	2	7S38	39E03	-2:36:12
Chake Chake	2	5S15	39E46	-2:39:04
Chamba	2	11S35	36E58	-2:27:52
Chinunje	2	11S19	37E19	-2:29:16
Chipogolo	2	6S52	36E02	-2:24:08
Chiwanda	2	11S22	34E54	-2:19:36
Chunya	2	8S32	33E25	-2:13:40
Chwaka	2	6S10	39E26	-2:37:44
Dareda	2	4S13	35E33	-2:22:12
Dar es Salaam	2	6S48	39E17	-2:37:08
Daressalam → Dar Es Salaam	2	6S48	39E17	-2:37:08
Dodoma	2	6S11	35E45	-2:23:00
Dongobesh	2	4S04	35E23	-2:21:32
Farkwa	2	5S24	35E36	-2:22:24
Galula	2	8S36	33E02	-2:12:08
Geita	2	2S52	32E10	-2:08:40
Gulwe	2	6S30	36E29	-2:25:56
Gumbiro	2	10S16	35E39	-2:22:36
Handeni	2	5S26	38E01	-2:32:04
Hedaru	2	4S30	37E54	-2:31:36
Hogoro	2	5S57	36E27	-2:25:48
Ibiri	2	4S56	32E33	-2:10:12
Ibondo	2	2S38	32E40	-2:10:40
Idodi	2	7S47	35E11	-2:20:44
Ifakara	2	8S08	36E41	-2:26:44
Igalula	2	5S14	33E00	-2:12:00
Igalula	2	5S38	32E38	-2:10:32
Igarukiro	2	3S08	33E31	-2:14:04
Igawa	2	8S35	34E28	-2:17:52
Ikoma	2	2S04	34E37	-2:18:28
Ikungu	2	1S34	33E40	-2:14:40
Ilagala	2	5S12	29E50	-1:59:20
Ilongero	2	4S40	34E52	-2:19:28
Inyonga	2	6S43	32E04	-2:08:16
Ipala	2	4S30	32E53	-2:11:32
Ipokera	2	8S03	35E41	-2:22:44
Ipole	2	5S47	32E44	-2:10:56
Iringa	2	7S46	35E42	-2:22:48
Isaka	2	3S54	32E56	-2:11:44
Isebania	2	1S15	34E33	-2:18:12
Iseke	2	6S25	35E01	-2:20:04
Isenyela	2	8S36	33E30	-2:14:00
Iseramagazi	2	4S40	32E09	-2:08:36
Issuna	2	5S23	34E46	-2:19:04
Itaka	2	8S52	32E47	-2:11:08
Itigi	2	5S42	34E29	-2:17:56
Itobo	2	4S10	33E01	-2:12:04
Itungi Port	2	9S35	33E56	-2:15:44
Kahama	2	3S50	32E36	-2:10:24
Kahe	2	3S30	37E26	-2:29:44
Kalema	2	1S12	31E50	-2:07:20
Kaliua	2	5S04	31E48	-2:07:12
Kamachumu	2	1S35	31E37	-2:06:28
Karema	2	6S49	30E26	-2:01:44
Karungu	2	1S08	33E59	-2:15:56
Kasanga	2	8S28	31E09	-2:04:36
Kashasha	2	1S44	31E37	-2:06:28
Kasulu	2	4S34	30E06	-2:00:24
Katale	2	4S59	31E03	-2:04:12
Katuma	2	6S10	30E34	-2:02:16
Kengeja	2	5S25	39E44	-2:38:56
Kharumwa	2	3S12	32E39	-2:10:36
Kibaha	2	6S46	38E55	-2:35:40
Kibara	2	2S09	33E27	-2:13:48
Kibau Iyayi	2	8S52	34E32	-2:18:08
Kibaya	2	5S18	36E34	-2:26:16
Kiberashi	2	5S23	37E26	-2:29:44
Kiberege	2	7S57	36E52	-2:27:28
Kibiti	2	7S44	38E57	-2:35:48
Kibondo	2	3S35	30E42	-2:02:48
Kibwesa	2	6S28	29E57	-1:59:48
Kidatu	2	7S42	36E57	-2:27:48
Kidete	2	6S25	37E16	-2:29:04
Kidugallo	2	6S47	38E12	-2:32:48
Kigoma	2	4S52	29E38	-1:58:32
Kigwa	2	5S10	33E08	-2:12:32
Kihundo	2	9S25	38E59	-2:35:56
Kihurio	2	4S28	38E04	-2:32:16
Kikale	2	7S50	39E12	-2:36:48
Kilimatinde	2	5S51	34E57	-2:19:48
Kilindoni	2	7S55	39E39	-2:38:36
Kiloli	2	6S50	33E23	-2:13:32
Kilondo	2	9S46	34E21	-2:17:24
Kilosa	2	6S50	36E59	-2:27:56
Kilwa Kisiwani	2	8S58	39E30	-2:38:00
Kilwa Kivinje	2	8S45	39E24	-2:37:36
Kilwa Masoko	2	8S56	39E31	-2:38:04
Kimamba	2	6S47	37E08	-2:28:32
Kimande	2	7S22	35E30	-2:22:00
Kinesi	2	1S28	33E52	-2:15:28
Kintinku	2	5S53	35E14	-2:20:56
Kinyangiri	2	4S27	34E37	-2:18:28
Kipanga	2	6S14	35E21	-2:21:24
Kipatimu	2	8S29	38E56	-2:35:44
Kipembawe	2	7S39	33E24	-2:13:36
Kipili	2	7S26	30E36	-2:02:24
Kirurumo	2	5S53	34E11	-2:16:44
Kisaki	2	7S28	37E36	-2:30:24
Kisarawe	2	6S54	39E04	-2:36:16
Kishanda	2	1S42	31E34	-2:06:16
Kisiju	2	7S24	39E20	-2:37:20
Kisiwani	2	4S08	37E57	-2:31:48
Kiswere	2	9S26	39E33	-2:38:12
Kitangari	2	10S39	39E20	-2:37:20
Kitaya	2	10S39	40E10	-2:40:40
Kitunda	2	6S48	33E13	-2:12:52
Kizimkazi	1	6S27	39E28	-2:37:52
Koani	1	6S08	39E17	-2:37:08
Koga	2	6S14	32E25	-2:09:40
Kolo	2	4S44	35E50	-2:23:20
Konde	2	4S57	39E45	-2:39:00
Kondoa	2	4S54	35E47	-2:23:08
Kongwa	2	6S12	36E25	-2:25:40
Korogwe	2	5S09	38E29	-2:33:56
Kumsenga	2	3S47	30E25	-2:01:40

TANZANIA TANSANIA TANGANYIKA ZANZIBAR TANZANIE

Kwachaga	2	5S38	38E08	-2:32:32
Kwa Mtoro	2	5S14	35E26	-2:21:44
Kwangwazi	2	7S47	38E15	-2:33:00
Kyaka	2	1S16	31E25	-2:05:40
Lembeni	2	3S47	37E37	-2:30:28
Likuyu	2	10S20	36E14	-2:24:56
Lindi	2	10S00	39E43	-2:38:52
Lisitu	2	9S39	34E39	-2:18:36
Litoo	2	9S54	38E24	-2:33:36
Liuli	2	11S05	34E38	-2:18:32
Liwale	2	9S46	37E56	-2:31:44
Liwale Chini	2	9S41	38E01	-2:32:04
Loiborsoit	2	3S52	36E26	-2:25:44
Loliondo	2	2S03	35E37	-2:22:28
Longido	2	2S44	36E41	-2:26:44
Luganga	2	7S31	35E32	-2:22:08
Luguru	2	2S55	33E58	-2:15:52
Lukumburu	2	9S45	35E09	-2:20:36
Lunguya	2	3S23	32E24	-2:09:36
Lupembe	2	9S15	35E15	-2:21:00
Lupiro	2	8S23	36E40	-2:26:40
Lusahunga	2	2S52	31E15	-2:05:00
Lushoto	2	4S47	38E17	-2:33:08
Mabuki	2	2S59	33E11	-2:12:44
Madaba	2	8S40	37E47	-2:31:08
Madibira	2	8S12	34E49	-2:19:16
Mahenge	2	7S38	36E16	-2:25:04
Mahenge	2	8S41	36E43	-2:26:52
Mahuta	2	10S52	39E27	-2:37:48
Makanya	2	4S20	37E51	-2:31:24
Makasuko	2	6S00	34E56	-2:19:44
Makere	2	4S17	30E25	-2:01:40
Makongolosi	2	8S24	33E09	-2:12:36
Makuliro	2	9S35	37E26	-2:29:44
Makumbako	2	8S51	34E50	-2:19:20
Makuyuni	2	3S33	36E06	-2:24:24
Malagarasi	2	5S06	30E50	-2:03:20
Malangali	2	8S34	34E51	-2:19:24
Malinyi	2	8S56	36E08	-2:24:32
Malolo	2	7S18	36E35	-2:26:20
Mambali	2	4S33	32E41	-2:10:44
Manda	2	7S58	32E26	-2:09:44
Manda	2	8S30	32E44	-2:10:56
Manda	2	10S28	34E35	-2:18:20
Mantare	2	2S43	33E13	-2:12:52
Manyoni	2	5S45	34E50	-2:19:20
Mapinga	2	6S36	39E04	-2:36:16
Marungu	2	3S44	30E48	-2:03:12
Masasi	2	10S43	38E48	-2:35:12
Matombo	2	7S03	37E46	-2:31:04
Maurui	2	5S07	38E23	-2:33:32
Mbalizi	2	8S56	33E22	-2:13:28
Mbamba Bay	2	11S17	34E46	-2:19:04
Mbate	2	8S52	39E10	-2:36:40
Mbemba	2	10S03	38E36	-2:34:24
Mbeya	2	8S54	33E27	-2:13:48
Mbinga	2	10S56	35E01	-2:20:04
Mbirira	2	4S21	30E10	-2:00:40
Mbogo	2	7S26	33E26	-2:13:44
Mbulu	2	3S51	35E32	-2:22:08
Mchinga	2	9S44	39E42	-2:38:48
Mchungo	2	7S42	39E17	-2:37:08
Mdandu	2	9S09	34E42	-2:18:48
Meia Meia	2	5S49	35E48	-2:23:12
Mgeta	2	8S19	36E08	-2:24:32
Mikese	2	6S46	37E54	-2:31:36
Mikindani	2	10S17	40E07	-2:40:28
Mikumi	2	7S24	36E59	-2:27:56
Milumba	2	7S06	31E04	-2:04:16
Mingoyo	2	10S06	39E38	-2:38:32
Mkalama	2	4S07	34E38	-2:18:32
Mkata	2	5S47	38E17	-2:33:08
Mkokotoni	1	5S52	39E15	-2:37:00
Mkulwe	2	8S35	32E19	-2:09:16
Mkwaja	2	5S47	38E51	-2:35:24
Mkwaya	2	10S06	39E40	-2:38:40
Mnazi	2	8S54	39E06	-2:36:24
Mohoro	2	8S08	39E10	-2:36:40
Mombo	2	4S53	38E17	-2:33:08
Mondo	2	4S59	35E54	-2:23:36
Morogoro	2	6S49	37E40	-2:30:40
Moshi	2	3S21	37E20	-2:29:20
Mpanda	2	6S22	31E02	-2:04:08
Mpui	2	8S21	31E50	-2:07:20
Mpwapwa	2	6S21	36E29	-2:25:56
Mrijo	2	5S10	36E15	-2:25:00
Msagali	2	6S21	36E18	-2:25:12
Msata	2	6S20	38E23	-2:33:32
Mtakuja	2	7S22	30E37	-2:02:28
Mtama	2	10S18	39E22	-2:37:28
Mtowabaga	2	2S30	35E53	-2:23:32
Mtwara	2	10S16	40E11	-2:40:44
Mtyangimbori	2	10S16	35E31	-2:22:04
Mugombazi	2	5S50	30E14	-2:00:56
Muheza	2	5S10	38E47	-2:35:08
Muhutwe	2	1S33	31E42	-2:06:48
Muleba	2	1S49	31E40	-2:06:40
Musasa	2	3S21	31E33	-2:06:12
Musoma	2	1S30	33E48	-2:15:12
Mvomero	2	6S20	37E25	-2:29:40
Mvuha	2	7S12	37E51	-2:31:24
Mwadui	2	3S33	33E36	-2:14:24
Mwanza	2	2S31	32E54	-2:11:36
Mwaya	2	9S33	33E57	-2:15:48
Mwaya	2	8S55	36E50	-2:27:20
Mwimbi	2	8S39	31E40	-2:06:40
Mwitikira	2	6S31	35E39	-2:22:36
Mzenga	2	6S56	38E43	-2:34:52
Mziha	2	5S54	37E47	-2:31:08
Naberera	2	4S12	36E56	-2:27:44
Nachingwea	2	10S23	38E46	-2:35:04
Nagaga	2	10S54	39E07	-2:36:28
Namanga	2	2S33	36E46	-2:27:04
Namanyere	2	7S31	31E03	-2:04:12
Nanjirinji	2	9S39	39E04	-2:36:16
Nansio	2	2S08	33E03	-2:12:12
Ndala	2	4S46	33E16	-2:13:04
Nduguti	2	4S18	34E42	-2:18:48
Ndumbwe	2	10S14	39E58	-2:39:52
Newala	2	10S56	39E18	-2:37:12
Ngara	2	2S28	30E39	-2:02:36
Ngarimbi	2	8S28	38E36	-2:34:24
Ngasamo	2	2S33	33E53	-2:15:32
Ngerengere	2	6S45	38E07	-2:32:28
Ngomba	2	8S23	32E53	-2:11:32
Ngoywa	2	5S56	32E48	-2:11:12
Ngunga	2	3S41	33E34	-2:14:16
Njinjo	2	8S48	38E54	-2:35:36
Njombe	2	9S20	34E46	-2:19:04
Nkonko	2	6S20	34E58	-2:19:52
Nkutuyu → Tukuyu	2	9S15	33E38	-2:14:32
Nondwa	2	6S26	35E20	-2:21:20
Ntumba	2	8S20	32E05	-2:08:20
Nungwe	2	2S46	32E01	-2:08:04
Nyahanga	2	2S23	33E33	-2:14:12
Nyahua	2	5S24	33E19	-2:13:16
Nyakabindi	2	2S38	33E59	-2:15:56
Nyakakiri	2	2S15	31E28	-2:05:52
Nyakanazi	2	3S00	31E15	-2:05:00
Nyamtumbo	2	10S29	36E02	-2:24:08
Nyamwage	2	8S08	39E00	-2:36:00
Nyandekwa	2	3S55	32E30	-2:10:00
Nyilumba	2	10S29	40E20	-2:41:20
Nzega	2	4S13	33E11	-2:12:44
Nzima	2	3S03	32E48	-2:11:12
Nzubuka	2	4S45	32E50	-2:11:20
Oldeani	2	3S21	35E33	-2:22:12
Pangani	2	5S26	38E58	-2:35:52
Puge	2	4S45	33E07	-2:12:28
Ruanda	2	10S33	34E57	-2:19:48
Rudewa	2	10S06	34E39	-2:18:36
Runazi	2	2S47	31E28	-2:05:52
Runere	2	3S06	33E16	-2:13:04
Rungwa	2	7S21	31E40	-2:06:40
Rungwa	2	6S57	33E31	-2:14:04
Rungwe	2	9S10	33E36	-2:14:24
Ruponda	2	10S15	38E42	-2:34:48
Ruvu	2	6S48	38E39	-2:34:36
Sadani	2	6S03	38E47	-2:35:08
Salawe	2	3S19	32E52	-2:11:28
Same	2	4S04	37E44	-2:30:56
Sao Hill	2	8S20	35E12	-2:20:48
Saranda	2	5S43	34E59	-2:19:56
Seke	2	3S20	33E31	-2:14:04
Sekenke	2	4S16	34E10	-2:16:40
Shanwa	2	3S10	33E46	-2:15:04
Shinyanga	2	3S40	33E26	-2:13:44
Shirati	2	1S08	33E59	-2:15:56
Sikonge	2	5S38	32E46	-2:11:04
Simba	2	1S44	34E13	-2:16:52
Simba Sirori	2	1S44	34E13	-2:16:52
Simbo	2	4S53	29E44	-1:58:56
Simbo	2	4S40	33E27	-2:13:48
Singida	2	4S49	34E45	-2:19:00
Sitalike	2	6S38	31E08	-2:04:32
Somanga	2	8S24	39E17	-2:37:08
Songea	2	10S41	35E39	-2:22:36
Sudi	2	10S06	39E57	-2:39:48
Suguti	2	1S44	33E39	-2:14:36
Sumbawanga	2	7S58	31E37	-2:06:28
Tabora	2	5S01	32E48	-2:11:12
Tandala	2	9S23	34E14	-2:16:56
Tanga	2	5S04	39E06	-2:36:24
Taveta	2	9S01	35E37	-2:22:28
Tukuyu	2	9S15	33E39	-2:14:36
Tunduru	2	11S07	37E21	-2:29:24
Tutubu	2	5S30	32E41	-2:10:44
Ujiji	2	4S55	29E41	-1:58:44
Ulaya	2	7S04	36E54	-2:27:36
Urambo	2	5S04	32E03	-2:08:12
Uruwira	2	6S27	31E21	-2:05:24
Ushashi	2	2S00	33E57	-2:15:48
Ushetu	2	4S10	32E16	-2:09:04
Usoke	2	5S06	32E20	-2:09:20
Ussure	2	4S39	34E23	-2:17:32
Utegi	2	1S20	34E35	-2:18:20
Utengule	2	8S57	35E50	-2:23:20
Utete	2	7S59	38E47	-2:35:08
Uvinza	2	5S06	30E22	-2:01:28
Wete	2	5S04	39E43	-2:38:52
Wiedhaven	1	10S28	34E34	-2:18:16
Zanzibar	1	6S10	39E11	-2:36:44
Zinga Mulike	2	9S09	38E44	-2:34:56

THAILAND TAILANDIA THAÏLANDE SIAM MUANG THAI

Time Table
Before 1/Jan/1880 LMT
Begin Standard 100E31
1/Jan/1880 0:00 -6:42
Begin Standard 105E00
1/Apr/1920 0:00 -7:00

Amnat Charoen	15N51	104E38	-6:58:32
Ang Thong	14N35	100E27	-6:41:48
Ao Luk	8N23	98E43	-6:34:52
Aranyaprathet	13N41	102E30	-6:50:00
Bacho	6N37	101E39	-6:46:36
Ban Aen	18N02	98E37	-6:34:28
Ban Baen Phichit	13N50	100E40	-6:42:40
Ban Bang Chan	13N49	100E42	-6:42:48
Ban Bang O	13N53	100E36	-6:42:24
Ban Bang Phli Yai	13N36	100E42	-6:42:48
Ban Bang Phraek	13N53	100E26	-6:41:44
Ban Bang Pu	13N31	100E39	-6:42:36
Ban Bua Chum	15N15	101E12	-6:44:48
Ban Bung Fang Nok	13N48	100E43	-6:42:52
Ban Bung Na Rang	16N11	100E09	-6:40:36
Ban Dan	15N19	105E30	-7:02:00
Ban Dan Lan Hoi	17N00	99E35	-6:38:20
Ban Don → Surat Thani	9N08	99E19	-6:37:16
Ban Don Muang	13N55	100E36	-6:42:24
Bang Kapi	13N46	100E39	-6:42:36
Bang Khen	13N52	100E36	-6:42:24
Bang Khun Thian	13N42	100E28	-6:41:52
Bangkok → Krung Thep	13N45	100E31	-6:42:04
Bang Krathum	16N34	100E18	-6:41:12
Bang Kruai	13N48	100E29	-6:41:56
Bang Lamung	12N58	100E54	-6:43:36
Bang Mun Nak	16N02	100E23	-6:41:32
Bang Pa In	14N14	100E35	-6:42:20
Bang Saphan	11N12	99E31	-6:38:04
Ban Hat Yai → Hat Yai	7N01	100E28	-6:41:52
Ban Ha Yaek Pak Kret	13N54	100E31	-6:42:04
Ban Hom	15N33	98E46	-6:35:04
Ban Hong	18N18	98E50	-6:35:20
Ban Huai Yang	11N36	99E40	-6:38:40
Ban Hua Lamphu Thong	13N32	100E38	-6:42:32
Ban Kaeng Khoi	14N35	101E01	-6:44:04
Ban Kai Kiang	14N57	99E12	-6:36:48
Ban Khan Na Yao	13N47	100E41	-6:42:44
Ban Khlong Bua Loi	13N41	100E41	-6:42:44
Ban Khlong Kua	6N57	100E08	-6:40:32
Ban Khlong Samrong	13N39	100E36	-6:42:24
Ban Khlong Song	13N51	100E43	-6:42:52
Ban Khok Bao Sao	13N52	100E39	-6:42:36
Ban Khuan Mao	7N58	99E37	-6:38:28
Ban Kota Baru	6N27	101E21	-6:45:24
Ban Krang	12N52	99E18	-6:37:12
Ban Kruat	14N25	103E07	-6:52:28
Ban Kum Daeng	13N53	100E36	-6:42:24
Ban Laem Sing	13N30	100E34	-6:42:16
Ban Lat Phrao	13N47	100E36	-6:42:24
Ban Le Kathe	15N49	98E53	-6:35:32
Ban Luk Kho	13N34	100E27	-6:41:48
Ban Mae La Luang	18N32	97E56	-6:31:44
Ban Mae Mo	18N15	99E42	-6:38:48
Ban Muang Yot	19N22	100E34	-6:42:16
Ban Na Kha	9N26	98E28	-6:33:52
Ban Nam Chan	18N01	103E53	-6:55:32
Ban Nam Thaeng	15N34	105E30	-7:02:00
Ban Na San	8N48	99E22	-6:37:28
Ban Nong Lumphuk	14N40	102E43	-6:50:52
Ban Nong Takhian	13N08	101E24	-6:45:36
Ban O Pao	13N50	100E38	-6:42:32
Ban Pak Bong	18N32	98E56	-6:35:44

Place	Lat.	Long.	Time
Ban Pak Chan	10N32	98E51	-6:35:24
Ban Pak Nam	10N26	99E15	-6:37:00
Ban Pak Phraek	8N13	100E12	-6:40:48
Ban Phai	16N04	102E44	-6:50:56
Ban Phai	17N33	103E00	-6:52:00
Ban Phe	12N38	101E26	-6:45:44
Ban Pho	13N36	101E05	-6:44:20
Banphot Phisai	15N56	99E59	-6:39:56
Ban Phraek Kasa	13N34	100E38	-6:42:32
Ban Pong	13N49	99E53	-6:39:32
Ban Rai	15N05	99E31	-6:38:04
Ban Ron Phibun	8N09	99E51	-6:39:24
Ban Saen To	16N05	99E51	-6:39:24
Ban Sakhla	13N32	100E30	-6:42:00
Ban Salik	18N30	100E45	-6:43:00
Ban Sam Phan	8N33	99E09	-6:36:36
Ban Samrong	14N23	102E50	-6:51:20
Ban Song Kong	13N53	100E34	-6:42:16
Ban Sop Huai Hai	19N33	98E05	-6:32:20
Ban Sum Sui	14N28	99E05	-6:36:20
Ban Takhlo	15N27	100E44	-6:42:56
Ban Tamru	13N31	100E41	-6:42:44
Ban Tao Pun	13N53	100E41	-6:42:44
Ban Tong Khop	17N04	104E16	-6:57:04
Ban Ya Plong	8N53	98E35	-6:34:20
Betong	5N45	101E05	-6:44:20
Bo Phloi	14N19	99E31	-6:38:04
Borabu	16N02	103E07	-6:52:28
Bua Yai	15N35	102E25	-6:49:40
Bung Kan	18N23	103E37	-6:54:28
Buriram	15N00	103E07	-6:52:28
Cha-Am	12N48	99E58	-6:39:52
Chachoengsao	13N42	101E05	-6:44:20
Chae Hom	18N43	99E35	-6:38:20
Chai Badan	15N04	101E05	-6:44:20
Chainat	15N11	100E08	-6:40:32
Chaiya	9N23	99E14	-6:36:56
Chaiyaphum	15N48	102E02	-6:48:08
Chakkarat	15N00	102E16	-6:49:04
Chana	6N55	100E44	-6:42:56
Chanthaburi	12N36	102E09	-6:48:36
Chaturat	15N34	101E51	-6:47:24
Chawang	8N25	99E30	-6:38:00
Chiang Dao	19N22	98E58	-6:35:52
Chiang Kham	19N32	100E18	-6:41:12
Chiang Khan	17N52	101E36	-6:46:24
Chiang Khian	19N37	100E00	-6:40:00
Chiang Mai	18N47	98E59	-6:35:56
Chiang Rai	19N54	99E50	-6:39:20
Chiang Saen	20N16	100E05	-6:40:20
Chom Thong	18N25	98E41	-6:34:44
Chon Buri	13N22	100E59	-6:43:56
Chon Daen	16N11	100E51	-6:43:24
Chum Phae	16N32	102E06	-6:48:24
Chumphon	10N30	99E10	-6:36:40
Chumphon Buri	15N21	103E24	-6:53:36
Chum Saeng	15N54	100E19	-6:41:16
Dan Sai	17N17	101E09	-6:44:36
Den Chai	17N59	100E04	-6:40:16
Det Udom	14N54	105E05	-7:00:20
Fang	19N55	99E13	-6:36:52
Hadyai → Hat Yai	7N01	100E28	-6:41:52
Hat Yai	7N01	100E28	-6:41:52
Hot	18N06	98E36	-6:34:24
Hua Hin	12N34	99E58	-6:39:52
Huai Yot	7N45	99E37	-6:38:28
Hua Sai	8N02	100E18	-6:41:12
Kabin Buri	13N59	101E43	-6:46:52
Kalasin	16N29	103E30	-6:54:00
Kamphaeng Phet	16N28	99E30	-6:38:00
Kanchanaburi	14N01	99E32	-6:38:08
Kanchanadit	9N10	99E28	-6:37:52
Kantang	7N25	99E31	-6:38:04
Kantharalak	14N39	104E39	-6:58:36
Kapoe	9N35	98E40	-6:34:40
Kaset Sombun	16N17	101E57	-6:47:48
Khao Saming	12N21	102E27	-6:49:48
Khao Yoi	13N14	99E50	-6:39:20
Khemmarat	16N03	105E13	-7:00:52
Khiri Mat	16N50	99E48	-6:39:12
Khlong Khlung	16N12	99E43	-6:38:52
Khlong Thom	7N56	99E09	-6:36:36
Khlong Yai	11N46	102E54	-6:51:36
Khlung	12N27	102E14	-6:48:56
Khok Kloi	8N17	98E19	-6:33:16
Khok Pho	6N43	101E06	-6:44:24
Khok Samrong	15N04	100E44	-6:42:56
Khon Kaen	16N26	102E50	-6:51:20
Khu Khan	14N42	104E12	-6:56:48
Khun Yuam	18N49	97E57	-6:31:48
Klaeng	12N47	101E39	-6:46:36
Ko Kha	18N11	99E24	-6:37:36
Korat → Nakhon Ratchasima	14N58	102E07	-6:48:28
Kosum Phisai	16N13	103E01	-6:52:04
Krabi	8N04	98E55	-6:35:40
Krung Thep (Bangkok)	13N45	100E31	-6:42:04
Kuchinarai	16N32	104E04	-6:56:16
Kumphawapi	17N07	103E01	-6:52:04
Laem Ngop	12N10	102E26	-6:49:44
Lampang	18N18	99E31	-6:38:04
Lamphun	18N35	99E01	-6:36:04
Lang Suan	9N57	99E04	-6:36:16
Lap Lae	17N39	100E02	-6:40:08
Laun	10N07	98E46	-6:35:04
Li	17N48	98E57	-6:35:48
Loei	17N29	101E35	-6:46:20
Lom Kao	16N53	101E14	-6:44:56
Lom Sak	16N47	101E15	-6:45:00
Long	18N05	99E50	-6:39:20
Lop Buri	14N48	100E37	-6:42:28
Mae Hong Son	19N16	97E56	-6:31:44
Mae Ramat	16N58	98E31	-6:34:04
Mae Rim	18N54	98E57	-6:35:48
Mae Sariang	18N10	97E56	-6:31:44
Mae Sot	16N43	98E34	-6:34:16
Mae Tha	18N28	99E08	-6:36:32
Maha Sarakham	16N11	103E18	-6:53:12
Makham	12N40	102E12	-6:48:48
Muang Sam Sip	15N31	104E44	-6:58:56
Mukdahan	16N32	104E43	-6:58:52
Nakhon Nayok	14N12	101E13	-6:44:52
Nakhon Pathom	13N49	100E03	-6:40:12
Nakhon Phanom	17N24	104E47	-6:59:08
Nakhon Ratchasima	14N58	102E07	-6:48:28
Nakhon Sawan	15N41	100E07	-6:40:28
Nakhon Si Thammarat	8N26	99E58	-6:39:52
Nakhon Thai	17N07	100E50	-6:43:20
Nam Pat	17N43	100E41	-6:42:44
Nam Phong	16N42	102E52	-6:51:28
Nam Tok	14N14	99E04	-6:36:16
Nan	18N47	100E47	-6:43:08
Nang Rong	14N38	102E48	-6:51:12
Na Noi	18N19	100E43	-6:42:52
Narathiwat	6N26	101E50	-6:47:20
Na Thawi	6N45	100E42	-6:42:48
Ngao	18N46	99E59	-6:39:56
Nong Bua Lamphu	17N11	102E25	-6:49:40
Nong Han	17N21	103E07	-6:52:28
Nong Khai	17N52	102E44	-6:50:56
Nonthaburi	13N50	100E29	-6:41:56
Non Thai	15N12	102E19	-6:49:16
Pai	19N19	98E27	-6:33:48
Pak Kret	13N55	100E30	-6:42:00
Pak Phanang	8N21	100E12	-6:40:48
Pak Phayun	7N21	100E19	-6:41:16
Pak Thong Chai	14N43	102E01	-6:48:04
Pathiu	10N42	99E19	-6:37:16
Pathum Thani	14N01	100E32	-6:42:08
Pattani	6N52	101E16	-6:45:04
Phan	19N28	99E43	-6:38:52
Phanat Nikhom	13N27	101E11	-6:44:44
Phangnga	8N28	98E32	-6:34:08
Phanom Thuan	14N07	99E42	-6:38:48
Phan Thong	13N28	101E06	-6:44:24
Phasi Charoen	13N43	100E26	-6:41:44
Phato	9N48	98E48	-6:35:12
Phatthalung	7N37	100E05	-6:40:20
Phayao	19N10	99E55	-6:39:40
Phet Buri	13N06	99E57	-6:39:48
Phetchabun	16N25	101E08	-6:44:32
Phibun Mangsahan	15N14	105E14	-7:00:56
Phichai	17N17	100E05	-6:40:20
Phichit	16N26	100E22	-6:41:28
Phimai	15N13	102E30	-6:50:00
Phitsanulok	16N50	100E15	-6:41:00
Phon	15N49	102E36	-6:50:24
Phon Phisai	18N01	103E05	-6:52:20
Phrae	18N09	100E08	-6:40:32
Phra Nakhon → Krung Thep	13N45	100E31	-6:42:04
Phra Nakhon Si Ayutthaya	14N21	100E33	-6:42:12
Phran Kratai	16N40	99E36	-6:38:24
Phrao	19N22	99E13	-6:36:52
Phra Phutthabat	14N43	100E48	-6:43:12
Phra Pradaeng	13N40	100E32	-6:42:08
Phrom Phiram	17N02	100E12	-6:40:48
Phuket	7N53	98E24	-6:33:36
Phutthaisong	15N32	103E01	-6:52:04
Pong	19N10	100E17	-6:41:08
Prachantakham	14N04	101E31	-6:46:04
Prachin Buri	14N03	101E22	-6:45:28
Prachuap Khiri Khan	11N49	99E48	-6:39:12
Prakhon Chai	14N37	103E05	-6:52:20
Pran Buri	12N23	99E55	-6:39:40
Rangae	6N17	101E44	-6:46:56
Ranong	9N58	98E38	-6:34:32
Ranot	7N46	100E19	-6:41:16
Rasi Salai	15N20	104E09	-6:56:36
Rat Burana	13N41	100E30	-6:42:00
Rattanaburi	15N19	103E51	-6:55:24
Rattaphum	7N08	100E16	-6:41:04
Rayong	12N40	101E17	-6:45:08
Roi Et	16N03	103E40	-6:54:40
Sa	18N34	100E45	-6:43:00
Sadao	6N38	100E26	-6:41:44
Sai Buri	6N42	101E37	-6:46:28
Sai Yok	14N07	99E08	-6:36:32
Sa Kaeo	13N49	102E04	-6:48:16
Sakon Nakhon	17N10	104E09	-6:56:36
Sam Ngao	17N15	99E01	-6:36:04
Samut Prakan	13N36	100E36	-6:42:24
Samut Sakhon	13N32	100E17	-6:41:08
Samut Songkhram	13N24	100E00	-6:40:00
Sangkhai	14N39	103E52	-6:55:28
Sangkhla	15N07	98E28	-6:33:52
Sara Buri	14N32	100E55	-6:43:40
Saraphi	18N43	99E03	-6:36:12
Sattahip	12N40	100E54	-6:43:36
Satun	6N37	100E04	-6:40:16
Sawankhalok	17N19	99E50	-6:39:20
Sawi	10N14	99E07	-6:36:28
Selaphum	16N02	103E57	-6:55:48
Si Chon	9N00	99E54	-6:39:36
Sikao	7N34	99E21	-6:37:24
Si Khiu	14N53	101E44	-6:46:56
Sing Buri	14N53	100E25	-6:41:40
Singora → Songkhla	7N12	100E36	-6:42:24
Si Prachan	14N37	100E09	-6:40:36
Si Racha	13N10	100E56	-6:43:44
Sisaket	15N07	104E20	-6:57:20
Si Satchanalai	17N31	99E46	-6:39:04
Song	18N28	100E11	-6:40:44
Songkhla	7N12	100E36	-6:42:24
Song Phi Nong	14N13	100E03	-6:40:12
Sop Prap	17N53	99E20	-6:37:20
Sukhothai	17N01	99E49	-6:39:16
Sungai Kolok	6N02	101E58	-6:47:52
Sung Noen	14N54	101E50	-6:47:20
Suphan Buri	14N28	100E07	-6:40:28
Surat Thani (Ban Don)	9N08	99E19	-6:37:16
Surin	14N53	103E29	-6:53:56
Suwannaphum	15N33	103E47	-6:55:08
Tak	16N52	99E08	-6:36:32
Tak Bai	6N16	102E03	-6:48:12
Ta Khli	15N15	100E21	-6:41:24
Takua Pa	8N53	98E21	-6:33:24
Taling Chan	13N46	100E27	-6:41:48
Taphan Hin	16N13	100E26	-6:41:44
Thai Muang	8N24	98E16	-6:33:04
Thalang	8N01	98E19	-6:33:16
Tha Li	17N37	101E25	-6:45:40
Tha Pla	17N48	100E32	-6:42:08
Tha Sala	8N40	99E56	-6:39:44
Tha Tako	15N38	100E29	-6:41:56
That Phanom	16N57	104E44	-6:58:56
Tha Tum	15N19	103E41	-6:54:44
Tha Uthen	17N34	104E36	-6:58:24
Thepha	6N52	100E58	-6:43:52
Thoen	17N36	99E12	-6:36:48
Thon Buri	13N43	100E29	-6:41:56
Thong Pha Phum	14N44	98E38	-6:34:32
Thun Chang	19N25	100E53	-6:43:32
Thung Song	8N09	99E41	-6:38:44
Thung Wa	7N06	99E46	-6:39:04
Trang	7N33	99E36	-6:38:24
Trat	12N14	102E30	-6:50:00
Ubon Ratchathani	15N14	104E54	-6:59:36
Udon Thani	17N26	102E46	-6:51:04
Uthai Thani	15N22	100E03	-6:40:12
U Thong	14N22	99E54	-6:39:36
Uthumphon Phisai	15N05	104E08	-6:56:32
Uttaradit	17N38	100E06	-6:40:24
Wang Chin	17N53	99E37	-6:38:28
Wang Noi	14N13	100E44	-6:42:56
Wang Saphung	17N18	101E46	-6:47:04
Wang Thong	16N50	100E26	-6:41:44
Wanon Niwat	17N38	103E46	-6:55:04
Warin Chamrap	15N12	104E53	-6:59:32
Wiang Pa Pao	19N22	99E30	-6:38:00
Wiang Phan	20N26	99E53	-6:39:32
Wichian Buri	15N39	101E07	-6:44:28
Yala	6N33	101E18	-6:45:12
Yaring	6N52	101E22	-6:45:28
Yasothon	15N45	104E08	-6:56:32

TOGO — RÉPUBLIQUE TOGOLAISE — TOGO

Time Table
Before 1/Jan/1893 LMT
Begin Standard 0w00
1/Jan/1893 0:00 0:00

Place	Lat	Long	Offset
Adéta	7N08	0E44	-0:02:56
Agbélouvé	6N40	1E10	-0:04:40
Akaba	7N57	1E03	-0:04:12
Anécho	6N14	1E36	-0:06:24
Anié	7N45	1E12	-0:04:48
Atakpamé	7N32	1E08	-0:04:32
Badou	7N35	0E36	-0:02:24
Bafilo	9N21	1E16	-0:05:04
Bassari	9N15	0E47	-0:03:08
Blitta	8N19	0E59	-0:03:56
Bogou	10N39	0E11	-0:00:44
Dapango	10N52	0E12	-0:00:48
Fazao	8N42	0E46	-0:03:04
Guérin Kouka	9N41	0E37	-0:02:28
Kabou	9N27	0E49	-0:03:16
Kambolé	8N45	1E36	-0:06:24
Kandé	9N57	1E03	-0:04:12
Klouto	6N57	0E34	-0:02:16
Kouniohou	7N40	0E48	-0:03:12
Lama-Kara	9N33	1E12	-0:04:48
Lomé	6N08	1E13	-0:04:52
Mandouri	10N51	0E49	-0:03:16
Niamtougou	9N46	1E06	-0:04:24
Nuatja	6N57	1E10	-0:04:40
Pagouda	9N45	1E19	-0:05:16
Palimé	6N54	0E38	-0:02:32
Porto-Séguro	6N12	1E29	-0:05:56
Sansanné-Mango	10N21	0E28	-0:01:52
Sokodé	8N59	1E08	-0:04:32
Sotouboua	8N34	0E59	-0:03:56
Tabligbo	6N35	1E30	-0:06:00
Tchamba	9N02	1E25	-0:05:40
Tsévié	6N25	1E13	-0:04:52

TOKELAU ISLANDS — UNION ISLANDS

Time Table
Before 1/Jan/1901 LMT
Begin Standard 150w00
1/Jan/1901 0:00 10:00

Place	Lat	Long	Offset
Atafu Island	8s33	172w30	11:30:00
Fakaofo Island	9s22	171w14	11:24:56
Manihiki Island	10s24	161w01	10:44:04
Nassau Island	11s33	165w25	11:01:40
Nukunonu Island	9s12	171w54	11:27:36
Penrhyn Island	9s00	158w00	10:32:00
Pukapuka	10s53	165w49	11:03:16
Tongareva Island (Penrhyn)	9s00	158w00	10:32:00

TONGA — FRIENDLY ISLANDS — TONGATAPU

Time Table
Before 1/Jan/1901 LMT
Begin Standard 185E00
1/Jan/1901 0:00 -12:20
Begin Standard 195E00
1/Oct/1968 0:00 -13:00

DIVISIONS

1. Ata Island
2. Ata Island
3. Eua Island
4. Tafahi Island
5. Toku Island
6. Tongatapu Islands
7. Vava'u Islands

Place	Lat	Long	Offset
Ata Island 1	22s20	176w12	11:44:48
Ata Island 2	21s03	175w00	11:40:00
Eua Island 3	21s22	174w56	11:39:44
Fatuma 6	21s13	175w07	11:40:28
Fatumu 6	21s13	175w07	11:40:28
Fuaamotu 6	21s16	175w08	11:40:32
Houma 6	21s09	175w19	11:41:16
Houma 3	21s19	174w57	11:39:48
Huma 3	21s19	174w57	11:39:48
Kolonga 6	21s08	175w04	11:40:16
Kolovai 6	21s06	175w20	11:41:20
Mua 6	21s11	175w07	11:40:28
Nukualofa 6	21s08	175w12	11:40:48
Nukunuku 6	21s08	175w18	11:41:12
Ohonua 3	21s20	174w57	11:39:48
Pea 6	21s10	175w14	11:40:56
Tafahi Island 4	15s51	173w43	11:34:52
Toku Island 5	18s10	174w11	11:36:44
Tongatapu Islands 6	21s10	175w10	11:40:40
Vava'u Islands 7	18s36	174w00	11:36:00

TRANSKEI — TRANSKEI

Time Table
Before 8/Feb/1892 LMT
Begin Standard 22E30
8/Feb/1892 0:00 -1:30
Begin Standard 30E00
1/Mar/1903 0:00 -2:00
20/Sep/1942 2:00 -3:00
21/Mar/1943 2:00 -2:00
19/Sep/1943 2:00 -3:00
19/Mar/1944 2:00 -2:00

Place	Lat	Long	Offset
Bizana	30s58	29E52	-1:59:28
Butterworth	32s23	28E04	-1:52:16
Cala	31s30	27E37	-1:50:28
Cofimvaba	32s00	27E35	-1:50:20
Elliotdale	31s55	28E38	-1:54:32
Engcobo	31s37	28E00	-1:52:00
Flagstaff	31s05	29E29	-1:57:56
Idutywa	32s02	28E16	-1:53:04
Kentani	32s31	28E19	-1:53:16
Lady Frere	31s44	27E16	-1:49:04
Libode	31s33	29E02	-1:56:08
Lusikisiki	31s25	29E30	-1:58:00
Mjanyana	31s50	28E10	-1:52:40
Mount Ayliff	30s54	29E20	-1:57:20
Mount Fletcher	30s40	28E30	-1:54:00
Mount Frere	31s00	28E58	-1:55:52
Mqanduli	31s48	28E46	-1:55:04
Ngqeleni	31s40	29E02	-1:56:08
Nqamakwe	32s12	27E56	-1:51:44
Port Saint Johns	31s38	29E33	-1:58:12
Qamata	32s00	27E21	-1:49:24
Qumbu	31s10	28E48	-1:55:12
Rietvlei	30s29	29E51	-1:59:24
Sterkspruit	30s32	27E22	-1:49:28
Tabankulu	30s58	29E19	-1:57:16
Tsembeyi	31s36	27E03	-1:48:12
Tsolo	31s18	28E37	-1:54:28

TRANSKEI

TRANSKEI

Place	Lat	Long	Offset
Tsomo	32s00	27e42	-1:50:48
Umtata	31s35	28e47	-1:55:08
Umzimkulu	30s16	29e56	-1:59:44
Willowvale	32s16	28e30	-1:54:00

TRINITÉ-ET-TOBAGO — TRINIDAD AND TOBAGO

Time Table
Before 2/Mar/1912 LMT
Begin Standard 60w00
2/Mar/1912 0:00 4:00

DIVISIONS

1. Tobago
2. Trinidad

Place	Lat	Long	Offset
Arima 2	10n38	61w17	4:05:08
Basse Terre 2	10n08	61w18	4:05:12
Blanchisseuse 2	10n47	61w18	4:05:12
Bonasse 2	10n05	61w52	4:07:28
Chaguanas 2	10n31	61w25	4:05:40
Claxton Bay 2	10n20	61w28	4:05:52
Débé 2	10n12	61w27	4:05:48
Guayaguayare 2	10n08	61w02	4:04:08
La Brea 2	10n15	61w37	4:06:28
Moriah 1	11n15	60w43	4:02:52
Pierreville 2	10n18	61w01	4:04:04
Plymouth 1	11n13	60w47	4:03:08
Point Fortin 2	10n11	61w41	4:06:44
Port of Spain 2	10n39	61w31	4:06:04
Princes Town 2	10n16	61w23	4:05:32
Puerto Espãna → Port of Spain 2	10n39	61w31	4:06:04
Redhead 2	10n47	60w57	4:03:48
Rio Claro 2	10n18	61w11	4:04:44
Roxborough 1	11n15	60w35	4:02:20
San Fernando 2	10n17	61w28	4:05:52
Sangre Grande 2	10n35	61w07	4:04:28
Scarborough 1	11n11	60w44	4:02:56
Siparia 2	10n08	61w30	4:06:00
Speyside 1	11n18	60w32	4:02:08
Toco 2	10n50	60w57	4:03:48
Tunapuna 2	10n38	61w23	4:05:32

TUNISIE — TUNESIEN — TUNIS — TÚNEZ — TUNISIA

Time Table
Before 12/May/1881 LMT
Begin Standard 2e20
12/May/1881 0:00 -0:09
Begin Standard 15e00
9/Mar/1911 0:00 -1:00
15/Apr/1939 23:00 -2:00
18/Nov/1939 24:00 -1:00
25/Feb/1940 23:00 -2:00
6/Oct/1941 0:00 -1:00
8/Mar/1942 24:00 -2:00
2/Nov/1942 3:00 -1:00
29/Mar/1943 2:00 -2:00
17/Apr/1943 2:00 -1:00
25/Apr/1943 2:00 -2:00
4/Oct/1943 2:00 -1:00
3/Apr/1944 2:00 -2:00
8/Oct/1944 0:00 -1:00
2/Apr/1945 2:00 -2:00
16/Sep/1945 3:00 -1:00
30/Apr/1977 0:00 -2:00
24/Sep/1977 1:00 -1:00
1/May/1978 0:00 -2:00
1/Oct/1978 1:00 -1:00
1/Jun/1988 0:00 -2:00
25/Sep/1988 1:00 -1:00
26/Mar/1989 0:00 -2:00
24/Sep/1989 1:00 -1:00
1/May/1990 0:00 -2:00
30/Sep/1990 1:00 -1:00
31/Mar/1991 0:00 -2:00
29/Sep/1991 1:00 -1:00

Place	Lat	Long	Offset
Aïn Djelloula	35n48	9e51	-0:39:24
Aïn Draham	36n47	8e42	-0:34:48
Ariana	36n52	10e12	-0:40:48
Bechater	37n18	9e45	-0:39:00
Béja	36n44	9e11	-0:36:44
Ben Gardane	33n08	11e13	-0:44:52
Ben Ghardane	33n08	11e13	-0:44:52
Binzert (Bizerte)	37n17	9e52	-0:39:28
Bordj Sidi Toui	32n44	11e22	-0:45:28
Bou Arada	36n20	9e38	-0:38:32
Bou Ficha	36n18	10e29	-0:41:56
Bou Hadjar	35n42	10e48	-0:43:12
Bou Salem	36n36	8e59	-0:35:56
Carthage	36n51	10e21	-0:41:24
Cekhira	34n17	10e06	-0:40:24
Chebba	35n14	10e02	-0:40:08
Crétéville	36n40	10e20	-0:41:20
Dehibat	32n01	10e42	-0:42:48
Djebel Abiod	36n58	9e05	-0:36:20
Djebeniana	35n02	10e55	-0:43:40
Djebibina	36n07	10e06	-0:40:24
Djemmal	35n38	10e46	-0:43:04
Djenein	31n44	10e09	-0:40:36
Djeradou	36n15	10e23	-0:41:32
Djerba	32n53	10e52	-0:43:28
Douz	33n28	9e01	-0:36:04
Ebba Ksour	35n57	8e50	-0:35:20
El Alia	37n10	10e03	-0:40:12
El Aroussa	36n22	9e28	-0:37:52
El Djem	35n18	10e43	-0:42:52
El Fahs	36n22	9e55	-0:39:40
El Haouaria	37n03	11e02	-0:44:08
El Jem	35n18	10e43	-0:42:52
El Kairouan	35n41	10e07	-0:40:28
El Kantara	33n41	10e55	-0:43:40
El Kasserine	35n11	8e48	-0:35:12
El Kef	36n11	8e43	-0:34:52
El Krib	36n19	9e09	-0:36:36
Ellès	35n57	9e06	-0:36:24
El Maharès	34n32	10e30	-0:42:00
El Mahdia	35n30	11e04	-0:44:16
El Metlaoui	34n20	8e24	-0:33:36
El Moknine	35n38	10e54	-0:43:36
Enfida	36n07	10e23	-0:41:32
Es-Sekhira	34n17	10e06	-0:40:24
Es Sers	36n04	9e02	-0:36:08
Es Smala es Souassi	35n21	10e33	-0:42:12
Fériana	34n57	8e34	-0:34:16
Ferryville → Menzel Bourguiba	37n10	9e48	-0:39:12
Fondouk el Aouareb	35n34	9e46	-0:39:04
Fort Saint	30n19	9e30	-0:38:00
Gabès	33n53	10e07	-0:40:28
Gafour	36n18	9e19	-0:37:16
Gafsa	34n25	8e48	-0:35:12
Ghardimaou	36n26	8e27	-0:33:48
Graïba	34n30	10e13	-0:40:52
Grombalia	36n36	10e30	-0:42:00
Hadjeb el Aïoun	35n24	9e33	-0:38:12
Haffouz	35n38	9e41	-0:38:44
Haïdra	35n34	8e27	-0:33:48
Hammamet	36n24	10e37	-0:42:28
Hammam Lif	36n44	10e20	-0:41:20
Hergla	36n02	10e31	-0:42:04
Jebeniana	35n02	10e55	-0:43:40
Jemmal	35n38	10e46	-0:43:04
Jendouba (Souk el Arba)	36n30	8e47	-0:35:08
Kaala Djerda	35n40	8e36	-0:34:24
Kairouan → El Kairouan	35n41	10e07	-0:40:28
Kalaa Kebira	35n52	10e32	-0:42:08
Kalaa Srira	35n49	10e33	-0:42:12
Kasserine → El Kasserine	35n11	8e48	-0:35:12
Kebili	33n42	8e58	-0:35:52
Kelibia	36n51	11e06	-0:44:24
Kesra	35n49	9e22	-0:37:28
Korba	36n35	10e52	-0:43:28
Korbous	36n49	10e35	-0:42:20
Ksar Hellal	35n39	10e54	-0:43:36
Ksar Rhilane	33n00	9e38	-0:38:32
Ksour Essaf	35n25	11e00	-0:44:00
La Goulette	36n49	10e18	-0:41:12
La Marsa	36n53	10e20	-0:41:20
Le Kef → El Kef	36n11	8e43	-0:34:52
Mabeul	36n27	10e46	-0:43:04
Mahdia	35n30	11e04	-0:44:16
Mahres	34n32	10e30	-0:42:00
Maktar	35n51	9e12	-0:36:48
Makthar	35n51	9e12	-0:36:48
Manouba	36n50	10e06	-0:40:24
Mateur	37n03	9e40	-0:38:40
Matmata	33n33	9e58	-0:39:52
Médenine	33n21	10e30	-0:42:00
Medjez el Bab	36n39	9e37	-0:38:28
Mejez el Bab	36n39	9e37	-0:38:28
Menzel Bourguiba	37n10	9e48	-0:39:12
Menzel Bou Zelfa	36n41	10e36	-0:42:24
Menzel Djemil	37n14	9e55	-0:39:40
Menzel Temime	36n47	10e59	-0:43:56
Metlaoui	34n20	8e24	-0:33:36
Moknine	35n38	10e54	-0:43:36
Monastir	35n47	10e50	-0:43:20
Msaken	35n44	10e35	-0:42:20
Nabeul	36n27	10e44	-0:42:56
Nebeur	36n17	8e47	-0:35:08
Nefta	33n52	7e33	-0:30:12
Oued Meliz	36n27	8e34	-0:34:16
Oued Zarga	36n40	9e25	-0:37:40
Porto Farina	37n10	10e12	-0:40:48
Protville	36n54	10e01	-0:40:04
Ras Djebel	37n13	10e09	-0:40:36
Remada	32n19	10e24	-0:41:36
Robâa Oued Yahia	36n05	9e35	-0:38:20
Sakiet Sidi Youssef	36n13	8e22	-0:33:28
Sbeïtla	35n14	9e08	-0:36:32
Sbiba	35n33	9e05	-0:36:20
Sfax	34n44	10e46	-0:43:04
Sidi Ali Ben Nasrallah	35n15	9e50	-0:39:20
Sidi Bou Zid	35n02	9e30	-0:38:00
Sidi Daoud	37n00	10e55	-0:43:40
Siliana	36n05	9e22	-0:37:28
Soliman	36n42	10e30	-0:42:00
Souk-el-Arba → Jendouba	36n30	8e47	-0:35:08
Sousse	35n49	10e38	-0:42:32
Tabarka	36n57	8e45	-0:35:00
Tadjerouine	35n54	8e34	-0:34:16
Takrouna	36n09	10e20	-0:41:20
Tameghza	34n23	7e57	-0:31:48
Tamerza	34n23	7e57	-0:31:48
Tataouine	32n56	10e27	-0:41:48
Tébourba	36n49	9e51	-0:39:24
Téboursouk	36n28	9e15	-0:37:00
Testour	36n33	9e27	-0:37:48
Thala	35n35	8e40	-0:34:40
Tozeur	33n55	8e08	-0:32:32
Túnez → Tunis	36n48	10e11	-0:40:44
Tunis	36n48	10e11	-0:40:44
Utique	37n03	10e03	-0:40:12
Zaghouan	36n24	10e09	-0:40:36
Zaouiet Azmour	36n55	11e01	-0:44:04
Zaouiet el Mgaïz	36n56	10e50	-0:43:20
Zarzis	33n30	11e07	-0:44:28
Zriba	36n20	10e16	-0:41:04

TURKEY TURQUÍA TURQUIE TÜRKEI TÜRKIYE

Time Table # 1

Date	Time	Offset
Before 1/Jan/1880 LMT		
Begin Standard		29E14
1/Jan/1880	0:00	-1:57
Begin Standard		30E00
1/Oct/1910	0:00	-2:00
1/May/1916	0:00	-3:00
1/Oct/1916	0:00	-2:00
28/Mar/1920	0:00	-3:00
25/Oct/1920	0:00	-2:00
3/Apr/1921	0:00	-3:00
3/Oct/1921	0:00	-2:00
26/Mar/1922	0:00	-3:00
8/Oct/1922	0:00	-2:00
13/May/1924	0:00	-3:00
1/Oct/1924	0:00	-2:00
1/May/1925	0:00	-3:00
1/Oct/1925	0:00	-2:00
1/Dec/1940	0:00	-3:00
21/Sep/1941	0:00	-2:00
1/Apr/1942	0:00	-3:00
31/Oct/1942	24:00	-2:00
2/Apr/1945	0:00	-3:00
7/Oct/1945	24:00	-2:00
31/May/1946	24:00	-3:00
30/Sep/1946	24:00	-2:00
19/Apr/1947	24:00	-3:00
4/Oct/1947	24:00	-2:00
17/Apr/1948	24:00	-3:00
2/Oct/1948	24:00	-2:00
9/Apr/1949	24:00	-3:00
1/Oct/1949	24:00	-2:00
18/Apr/1950	24:00	-3:00
7/Oct/1950	24:00	-2:00
21/Apr/1951	24:00	-3:00
7/Oct/1951	24:00	-2:00
14/Jul/1962	24:00	-3:00
7/Oct/1962	24:00	-2:00
14/May/1964	24:00	-3:00
30/Sep/1964	24:00	-2:00
2/May/1970	24:00	-3:00
3/Oct/1970	24:00	-2:00
1/May/1971	24:00	-3:00
2/Oct/1971	24:00	-2:00
6/May/1972	24:00	-3:00
7/Oct/1972	24:00	-2:00
3/Jun/1973	1:00	-3:00
4/Nov/1973	3:00	-2:00
31/Mar/1974	2:00	-3:00
3/Nov/1974	5:00	-2:00
30/Mar/1975	0:00	-3:00
26/Oct/1975	0:00	-2:00
1/Jun/1976	0:00	-3:00
31/Oct/1976	0:00	-2:00
3/Apr/1977	0:00	-3:00
16/Oct/1977	0:00	-2:00
2/Apr/1978	0:00	-3:00
Begin Standard		45E00
15/Oct/1978	0:00	-3:00
1/Apr/1979	3:00	-4:00
14/Oct/1979	24:00	-3:00
6/Apr/1980	3:00	-4:00
12/Oct/1980	24:00	-3:00
29/Mar/1981	3:00	-4:00
11/Oct/1981	24:00	-3:00
28/Mar/1982	3:00	-4:00
10/Oct/1982	24:00	-3:00
31/Jul/1983	0:00	-4:00
2/Oct/1983	0:00	-3:00
Begin Standard		30E00
20/Apr/1985	0:00	-3:00
28/Sep/1985	0:00	-2:00
30/Mar/1986	2:00	-3:00
28/Sep/1986	3:00	-2:00
29/Mar/1987	2:00	-3:00
27/Sep/1987	3:00	-2:00
27/Mar/1988	2:00	-3:00
25/Sep/1988	3:00	-2:00
26/Mar/1989	2:00	-3:00
24/Sep/1989	3:00	-2:00
25/Mar/1990	2:00	-3:00
30/Sep/1990	3:00	-2:00
31/Mar/1991	2:00	-3:00
29/Sep/1991	3:00	-2:00
29/Mar/1992	2:00	-3:00
27/Sep/1992	3:00	-2:00
28/Mar/1993	2:00	-3:00
26/Sep/1993	3:00	-2:00
27/Mar/1994	2:00	-3:00
25/Sep/1994	3:00	-2:00
26/Mar/1995	2:00	-3:00
24/Sep/1995	3:00	-2:00
31/Mar/1996	2:00	-3:00
29/Sep/1996	3:00	-2:00
30/Mar/1997	2:00	-3:00
28/Sep/1997	3:00	-2:00
29/Mar/1998	2:00	-3:00
27/Sep/1998	3:00	-2:00
28/Mar/1999	2:00	-3:00
26/Sep/1999	3:00	-2:00
26/Mar/2000	2:00	-3:00
24/Sep/2000	3:00	-2:00

....

Time Table # 2

Date	Time	Offset
Before 1/Jan/1880 LMT		
Begin Standard		29E14
1/Jan/1880	0:00	-1:57
Begin Standard		30E00
1/Oct/1910	0:00	-2:00
28/Mar/1920	0:00	-3:00
25/Oct/1920	0:00	-2:00
3/Apr/1921	0:00	-3:00
3/Oct/1921	0:00	-2:00
26/Mar/1922	0:00	-3:00
8/Oct/1922	0:00	-2:00
13/May/1924	0:00	-3:00
1/Oct/1924	0:00	-2:00
1/May/1925	0:00	-3:00
1/Oct/1925	0:00	-2:00
1/Dec/1940	0:00	-3:00
21/Sep/1941	0:00	-2:00
1/Apr/1942	0:00	-3:00
31/Oct/1942	24:00	-2:00
2/Apr/1945	0:00	-3:00
7/Oct/1945	24:00	-2:00
31/May/1946	24:00	-3:00
30/Sep/1946	24:00	-2:00
19/Apr/1947	24:00	-3:00
4/Oct/1947	24:00	-2:00
17/Apr/1948	24:00	-3:00
2/Oct/1948	24:00	-2:00
9/Apr/1949	24:00	-3:00
1/Oct/1949	24:00	-2:00
18/Apr/1950	24:00	-3:00
7/Oct/1950	24:00	-2:00
21/Apr/1951	24:00	-3:00
7/Oct/1951	24:00	-2:00
14/Jul/1962	24:00	-3:00
7/Oct/1962	24:00	-2:00
14/May/1964	24:00	-3:00
30/Sep/1964	24:00	-2:00
2/May/1970	24:00	-3:00
3/Oct/1970	24:00	-2:00
1/May/1971	24:00	-3:00
2/Oct/1971	24:00	-2:00
6/May/1972	24:00	-3:00
7/Oct/1972	24:00	-2:00
3/Jun/1973	1:00	-3:00
4/Nov/1973	3:00	-2:00
31/Mar/1974	2:00	-3:00
3/Nov/1974	5:00	-2:00
30/Mar/1975	0:00	-3:00
26/Oct/1975	0:00	-2:00
1/Jun/1976	0:00	-3:00
31/Oct/1976	0:00	-2:00
3/Apr/1977	0:00	-3:00
16/Oct/1977	0:00	-2:00
2/Apr/1978	0:00	-3:00
Begin Standard		45E00
15/Oct/1978	0:00	-3:00
1/Apr/1979	3:00	-4:00
14/Oct/1979	24:00	-3:00
6/Apr/1980	3:00	-4:00
12/Oct/1980	24:00	-3:00
29/Mar/1981	3:00	-4:00
11/Oct/1981	24:00	-3:00
28/Mar/1982	3:00	-4:00
10/Oct/1982	24:00	-3:00
31/Jul/1983	0:00	-4:00
2/Oct/1983	0:00	-3:00
Begin Standard		30E00
20/Apr/1985	0:00	-3:00
28/Sep/1985	0:00	-2:00
30/Mar/1986	2:00	-3:00
28/Sep/1986	3:00	-2:00
29/Mar/1987	2:00	-3:00
27/Sep/1987	3:00	-2:00
27/Mar/1988	2:00	-3:00
25/Sep/1988	3:00	-2:00
26/Mar/1989	2:00	-3:00
24/Sep/1989	3:00	-2:00
25/Mar/1990	2:00	-3:00
30/Sep/1990	3:00	-2:00
31/Mar/1991	2:00	-3:00
29/Sep/1991	3:00	-2:00
29/Mar/1992	2:00	-3:00
27/Sep/1992	3:00	-2:00
28/Mar/1993	2:00	-3:00
26/Sep/1993	3:00	-2:00
27/Mar/1994	2:00	-3:00
25/Sep/1994	3:00	-2:00
26/Mar/1995	2:00	-3:00
24/Sep/1995	3:00	-2:00
31/Mar/1996	2:00	-3:00
29/Sep/1996	3:00	-2:00
30/Mar/1997	2:00	-3:00
28/Sep/1997	3:00	-2:00
29/Mar/1998	2:00	-3:00
27/Sep/1998	3:00	-2:00
28/Mar/1999	2:00	-3:00
26/Sep/1999	3:00	-2:00
26/Mar/2000	2:00	-3:00
24/Sep/2000	3:00	-2:00

....

Time Table # 3

Date	Time	Offset
Before 1/Jan/1880 LMT		
Begin Standard		29E14
1/Jan/1880	0:00	-1:57
Begin Standard		30E00
1/Oct/1910	0:00	-2:00
1/Dec/1940	0:00	-3:00
21/Sep/1941	0:00	-2:00
1/Apr/1942	0:00	-3:00
31/Oct/1942	24:00	-2:00
2/Apr/1945	0:00	-3:00
7/Oct/1945	24:00	-2:00
31/May/1946	24:00	-3:00
30/Sep/1946	24:00	-2:00
19/Apr/1947	24:00	-3:00
4/Oct/1947	24:00	-2:00
17/Apr/1948	24:00	-3:00
2/Oct/1948	24:00	-2:00
9/Apr/1949	24:00	-3:00
1/Oct/1949	24:00	-2:00
18/Apr/1950	24:00	-3:00
7/Oct/1950	24:00	-2:00
21/Apr/1951	24:00	-3:00
7/Oct/1951	24:00	-2:00
14/Jul/1962	24:00	-3:00
7/Oct/1962	24:00	-2:00
14/May/1964	24:00	-3:00
30/Sep/1964	24:00	-2:00
2/May/1970	24:00	-3:00
3/Oct/1970	24:00	-2:00
1/May/1971	24:00	-3:00
2/Oct/1971	24:00	-2:00
6/May/1972	24:00	-3:00
7/Oct/1972	24:00	-2:00
3/Jun/1973	1:00	-3:00
4/Nov/1973	3:00	-2:00
31/Mar/1974	2:00	-3:00
3/Nov/1974	5:00	-2:00
30/Mar/1975	0:00	-3:00
26/Oct/1975	0:00	-2:00
1/Jun/1976	0:00	-3:00
31/Oct/1976	0:00	-2:00
3/Apr/1977	0:00	-3:00
16/Oct/1977	0:00	-2:00
2/Apr/1978	0:00	-3:00
Begin Standard		45E00
15/Oct/1978	0:00	-3:00
1/Apr/1979	3:00	-4:00
14/Oct/1979	24:00	-3:00
6/Apr/1980	3:00	-4:00
12/Oct/1980	24:00	-3:00
29/Mar/1981	3:00	-4:00
11/Oct/1981	24:00	-3:00
28/Mar/1982	3:00	-4:00
10/Oct/1982	24:00	-3:00
31/Jul/1983	0:00	-4:00
2/Oct/1983	0:00	-3:00
Begin Standard		30E00
20/Apr/1985	0:00	-3:00
28/Sep/1985	0:00	-2:00
30/Mar/1986	2:00	-3:00
28/Sep/1986	3:00	-2:00
29/Mar/1987	2:00	-3:00
27/Sep/1987	3:00	-2:00
27/Mar/1988	2:00	-3:00
25/Sep/1988	3:00	-2:00
26/Mar/1989	2:00	-3:00
24/Sep/1989	3:00	-2:00
25/Mar/1990	2:00	-3:00
30/Sep/1990	3:00	-2:00
31/Mar/1991	2:00	-3:00
29/Sep/1991	3:00	-2:00
29/Mar/1992	2:00	-3:00
27/Sep/1992	3:00	-2:00
28/Mar/1993	2:00	-3:00
26/Sep/1993	3:00	-2:00
27/Mar/1994	2:00	-3:00
25/Sep/1994	3:00	-2:00
26/Mar/1995	2:00	-3:00
24/Sep/1995	3:00	-2:00
31/Mar/1996	2:00	-3:00
29/Sep/1996	3:00	-2:00
30/Mar/1997	2:00	-3:00
28/Sep/1997	3:00	-2:00
29/Mar/1998	2:00	-3:00
27/Sep/1998	3:00	-2:00
28/Mar/1999	2:00	-3:00
26/Sep/1999	3:00	-2:00
26/Mar/2000	2:00	-3:00
24/Sep/2000	3:00	-2:00

DIVISIONS

1. Asian

2. European

Place	Table	Lat	Long	Offset
Abşeker 1	3	38N55	39E11	-2:36:44
Acıgöl 1	3	38N35	34E31	-2:18:04
Acıpayam 1	3	37N25	29E22	-1:57:28
Adagide 1	3	38N06	28E02	-1:52:08
Adala 1	3	38N34	28E17	-1:53:08
Adana 1	3	37N01	35E18	-2:21:12
Adapazarı 1	3	40N46	30E24	-2:01:36
Adilcevaz 1	3	38N44	42E44	-2:50:56
Adıyaman 1	3	37N46	38E17	-2:33:08
Adrianople → Edirne 2	2	41N40	26E34	-1:46:16
Afşin 1	3	38N15	36E55	-2:27:40
Afyon 1	3	38N45	30E33	-2:02:12
Afyonkarahisar → Afyon 1	3	38N45	30E33	-2:02:12
Ağcakışla 1	3	39N33	36E22	-2:25:28
Ağın 1	3	38N57	38E43	-2:34:52
Ağlasun 1	3	37N40	30E32	-2:02:08
Agri → Karaköse 1	3	39N44	43E03	-2:52:12
Ağva 1	3	41N09	29E50	-1:59:20
Ağvaniş 1	3	40N04	38E37	-2:34:28
Ahalt 1	3	40N50	41E33	-2:46:12
Ahırlı 1	3	38N37	26E31	-1:46:04
Ahırlı 1	3	37N14	32E08	-2:08:32
Ahlât 1	3	38N45	42E29	-2:49:56
Ahmetli 1	3	38N31	27E57	-1:51:48
Akbaba 1	3	41N09	29E06	-1:56:24
Akçaabat 1	3	41N02	39E34	-2:38:16
Akçadağ 1	3	38N21	37E59	-2:31:56
Akçakale 1	3	36N41	38E56	-2:35:44
Akçakoca 1	3	41N05	31E09	-2:04:36
Akçakoyunlu 1	3	36N46	37E38	-2:30:32
Akçaova 1	3	37N30	28E02	-1:52:08
Akçaova 1	3	41N03	29E57	-1:59:48
Akdağ 1	3	40N43	36E00	-2:24:00
Akdağmadeni 1	3	39N40	35E54	-2:23:36
Akhisar 1	3	38N55	27E51	-1:51:24
Akkışla 1	3	39N00	36E11	-2:24:44
Akköy 1	3	37N29	27E15	-1:49:00
Akmeşe 1	3	40N51	30E12	-2:00:48
Akpınar 1	3	37N34	38E13	-2:32:52
Akpınar 1	3	39N17	33E40	-2:14:40
Aksaray 1	3	38N23	34E03	-2:16:12
Akşehir 1	3	38N21	31E25	-2:05:40
Akseki 1	3	37N02	31E48	-2:07:12
Aktepe 1	3	36N44	36E27	-2:25:48
Akviran 1	3	40N54	29E30	-1:58:00
Akviran 1	3	37N27	32E23	-2:09:32
Akyazı 1	3	40N41	30E37	-2:02:28
Alaca 1	3	40N10	34E51	-2:19:24
Alacahan 1	3	39N07	37E37	-2:30:28
Alaçalı 1	3	41N11	29E27	-1:57:48
Alaçam 1	3	41N37	35E37	-2:22:28
Alaçatı 1	3	38N16	26E23	-1:45:32
Alakilise 1	3	39N56	38E38	-2:34:32
Alanya 1	3	36N33	32E01	-2:08:04
Alaplı 1	3	41N11	31E24	-2:05:36
Alaşehir 1	3	38N21	28E32	-1:54:08
Alemdar 1	3	41N03	29E14	-1:56:56
Alenz 1	3	37N51	41E36	-2:46:24
Alexandretta → İskenderun 1	3	36N37	36E07	-2:24:28
Aliağaçiftliği 1	3	38N48	26E59	-1:47:56
Alibahadır 1	3	41N11	29E12	-1:56:48
Alibardak 1	3	38N06	40E25	-2:41:40
Alibeyköy 2	1	41N04	28E56	-1:55:44
Alıcık 1	3	40N49	35E21	-2:21:24
Almus 1	3	40N23	36E55	-2:27:40
Alos 1	3	38N07	39E32	-2:38:08
Alpu 1	3	39N47	30E58	-2:03:52
Altintaş 1	3	39N04	30E07	-2:00:28
Altunoluk 1	3	39N34	26E44	-1:46:56
Altunova 1	3	39N13	26E47	-1:47:08
Alucra 1	3	40N20	38E46	-2:35:04
Amasra 1	3	41N45	32E24	-2:09:36
Amasya 1	3	40N39	35E51	-2:23:24
Anadolufeneri 1	3	41N12	29E09	-1:56:36
Anamur 1	3	36N06	32E50	-2:11:20
Andırın 1	3	37N34	36E20	-2:25:20
Angora → Ankara 1	3	39N56	32E52	-2:11:28
Ankara 1	3	39N56	32E52	-2:11:28
Antakya (Antioch) 1	3	36N14	36E07	-2:24:28
Antalya 1	3	36N53	30E42	-2:02:48
Antioch → Antakya 1	3	36N14	36E07	-2:24:28
Araban 1	3	37N26	37E41	-2:30:44
Araç 1	3	41N15	33E21	-2:13:24
Araklı 1	3	40N57	40E03	-2:40:12
Arapkir 1	3	39N03	38E30	-2:34:00
Ardahan 1	3	41N07	42E41	-2:50:44
Ardanuç 1	3	41N08	42E04	-2:48:16
Ardasa 1	3	40N35	39E18	-2:37:12
Ardeşen 1	3	41N12	41E00	-2:44:00
Argıthanı 1	3	38N17	31E43	-2:06:52
Armutlu 1	3	40N31	28E50	-1:55:20
Arpaçay 1	3	40N52	43E20	-2:53:20
Arsin 1	3	40N58	39E56	-2:39:44
Arsuz 1	3	36N27	35E51	-2:23:24
Artova 1	3	40N03	36E19	-2:25:16
Artvin 1	3	41N11	41E49	-2:47:16
Aşağıçığıl 1	3	38N03	31E52	-2:07:28
Aşağıhanik 1	3	37N43	39E59	-2:39:56
Asağı İhtik 1	3	39N38	38E49	-2:35:16
Asagı Kuluşağı 1	3	38N39	38E39	-2:34:36
Aşağılahan 1	3	38N50	39E59	-2:39:56
Aşağı Mestikân 1	3	38N25	38E46	-2:35:04
Aşkale 1	3	39N55	40E42	-2:42:48
Aslanapa 1	3	39N13	29E52	-1:59:28
Asmaca 1	3	37N53	35E58	-2:23:52
Aşutka 1	3	39N09	38E37	-2:34:28
Atabey 1	3	37N57	30E39	-2:02:36
Atışalan 2	1	41N03	28E52	-1:55:28
Atışmektebi 1	3	40N55	29E11	-1:56:44
Atkaracalar 1	3	40N50	33E04	-2:12:16
Avanos 1	3	38N43	34E51	-2:19:24
Avnik 1	3	39N50	41E59	-2:47:56
Ayancık 1	3	41N57	34E36	-2:18:24
Ayaş 1	3	40N01	32E21	-2:09:24
Ayazağa 2	1	41N06	28E59	-1:55:56
Aydın 1	3	37N51	27E51	-1:51:24
Aydıncık 1	3	36N08	33E19	-2:13:16
Ayınkâf 1	3	37N34	41E10	-2:44:40
Aynı 1	3	37N43	41E55	-2:47:40
Ayrancı 1	3	37N22	33E42	-2:14:48
Ayvacık 1	3	39N36	26E24	-1:45:36
Ayvacık 1	3	41N00	36E39	-2:26:36
Ayvalı 1	3	38N44	37E38	-2:30:32
Ayvalık 1	3	39N18	26E41	-1:46:44
Azakpert 1	3	39N14	40E30	-2:42:00
Azdavay 1	3	41N39	33E18	-2:13:12
Babadağ 1	3	37N48	28E52	-1:55:28
Babaeski 2	2	41N26	27E06	-1:48:24
Bademli 1	3	37N02	32E41	-2:10:44
Bafra 1	3	41N34	35E56	-2:23:44
Bağarası 1	3	37N42	27E33	-1:50:12
Bağlum 1	3	40N03	32E51	-2:11:24
Bahce 1	3	37N14	36E34	-2:26:16
Bahçeköy 2	1	41N11	28E59	-1:55:56

Bahemdan 1 3 38N19 41E09 -2:44:36
Bahser 1 3 37N57 39E18 -2:37:12
Bakırköy 2 1 40N59 28E52 -1:55:28
Bâlâ 1 3 39N34 33E08 -2:12:32
Balcı 1 3 38N43 34E06 -2:16:24
Balıkesir 1 3 39N39 27E53 -1:51:32
Balışıh 1 3 39N56 33E43 -2:14:52
Ballı 2 2 40N50 27E03 -1:48:12
Balya 1 3 39N45 27E35 -1:50:20
Banarlı 2 2 41N04 27E20 -1:49:20
Banaz 1 3 38N46 29E46 -1:59:04
Bandırma 1 3 40N20 27E58 -1:51:52
Barak 1 3 36N51 37E59 -2:31:56
Barbaros 2 2 40N54 27E27 -1:49:48
Bardız 1 3 40N26 42E20 -2:49:20
Barla 1 3 38N01 30E47 -2:03:08
Bartın 1 3 41N38 32E21 -2:09:24
Basbirin 1 3 37N19 41E38 -2:46:32
Başıbüyük 1 3 40N57 29E08 -1:56:32
Başkale 1 3 38N02 44E00 -2:56:00
Başköy 1 3 39N53 44E32 -2:58:08
Başmakcı 1 3 37N54 30E01 -2:00:04
Başnık 1 3 38N07 40E44 -2:42:56
Başpınar 1 3 39N12 38E42 -2:34:48
Batırga 1 3 36N24 36E11 -2:24:44
Batman 1 3 37N52 41E07 -2:44:28
Bayat 1 3 38N59 30E56 -2:03:44
Bayat 1 3 40N39 34E15 -2:17:00
Bayburt 1 3 40N16 40E15 -2:41:00
Bayındır 1 3 38N13 27E40 -1:50:40
Bayraktar 1 3 39N41 42E08 -2:48:32
Bayramıç 1 3 39N48 26E37 -1:46:28
Bayramören 1 3 40N57 33E12 -2:12:48
Bebekler 1 3 37N21 30E04 -2:00:16
Bebeli 1 3 36N41 35E27 -2:21:48
Bedirli 1 3 39N35 36E38 -2:26:32
Bekilli 1 3 38N14 29E26 -1:57:44
Bekirhan 1 3 38N10 41E19 -2:45:16
Belen 1 3 36N32 36E10 -2:24:40
Belören 1 3 40N51 33E30 -2:14:00
Belveren 1 3 37N39 37E34 -2:30:16
Bereketli 1 3 40N31 37E18 -2:29:12
Bergama 1 3 39N07 27E11 -1:48:44
Bergos 1 3 40N14 26E36 -1:46:24
Beşiri 1 3 37N55 41E18 -2:45:12
Besni 1 3 37N41 37E52 -2:31:28
Beşpınar 1 3 41N09 35E14 -2:20:56
Beyazköy 2 2 41N21 27E42 -1:50:48
Beyçayırı 1 3 40N15 26E55 -1:47:40
Beyce 1 3 39N54 29E00 -1:56:00
Beycuma 1 3 41N19 31E59 -2:07:56
Beydili 1 3 40N10 31E01 -2:04:04
Beykoz 1 3 41N08 29E05 -1:56:20
Beylikahır 1 3 39N42 31E13 -2:04:52
Beypazarı 1 3 40N10 31E56 -2:07:44
Beypınarı 1 3 39N31 37E44 -2:30:56
Beyşehir 1 3 37N41 31E43 -2:06:52
Biga 1 3 40N13 27E14 -1:48:56
Bigadiç 1 3 39N23 28E08 -1:52:32
Bilecik 1 3 40N09 29E59 -1:59:56
Bingöl 1 3 38N53 40E29 -2:41:56
Birecik 1 3 37N02 37E58 -2:31:52
Birik 1 3 39N01 38E15 -2:33:00
Birimşe 1 3 38N03 38E32 -2:34:08
Bismil 1 3 37N51 40E40 -2:42:40
Bitlis 1 3 38N22 42E06 -2:48:24
Bodrum 1 3 37N02 27E26 -1:49:44
Boğazkale 1 3 40N02 34E37 -2:18:28
Boğazköy 2 1 41N11 28E46 -1:55:04
Boğazlıyan 1 3 39N12 35E15 -2:21:00
Boğlan 1 3 38N58 41E03 -2:44:12
Böğürtlen 1 3 37N10 38E04 -2:32:16
Bolayır 2 2 40N31 26E45 -1:47:00
Bolu 1 3 40N44 31E37 -2:06:28
Bolvadin 1 3 38N42 31E04 -2:04:16
Bombat 1 3 38N08 42E14 -2:48:56
Bor 1 3 37N54 34E34 -2:18:16
Borkça 1 3 41N22 41E40 -2:46:40
Borlu 1 3 38N44 28E27 -1:53:48
Bornova 1 3 38N27 27E14 -1:48:56
Boyabat 1 3 41N28 34E47 -2:19:08
Boyali 1 3 41N02 33E19 -2:13:16
Boyalık 2 2 41N15 28E37 -1:54:28
Bozburun 1 3 36N41 28E04 -1:52:16
Bozdoğan 1 3 37N40 28E19 -1:53:16
Bozkır 1 3 37N11 32E15 -2:09:00
Bozkurt 1 3 37N49 29E37 -1:58:28
Bozüyük 1 3 39N54 30E03 -2:00:12
Bozyaka 1 3 37N08 31E12 -2:04:48
Bucak 1 3 37N28 30E36 -2:02:24
Bucakkışla 1 3 36N57 33E02 -2:12:08
Bulancak 1 3 40N57 38E14 -2:32:56
Bulanık 1 3 39N05 42E15 -2:49:00
Buldan 1 3 38N03 28E51 -1:55:24
Bünyan 1 3 38N51 35E52 -2:23:28
Burç 1 3 37N02 37E10 -2:28:40
Burdur 1 3 37N43 30E17 -2:01:08
Burhaniye 1 3 37N57 28E45 -1:55:00
Burhaniye 1 3 39N30 26E58 -1:47:52
Bursa 1 3 40N11 29E04 -1:56:16
Büyükada 1 3 40N52 29E07 -1:56:28
Büyükarmudan 1 3 39N35 38E26 -2:33:44
Büyükbakkal 1 3 40N59 29E11 -1:56:44
Büyükçekmece 2 2 41N01 28E34 -1:54:16
Buyuk Doğanca 2 2 41N11 26E25 -1:45:40
Büyükkale 1 3 38N01 27E34 -1:50:16
Büyükkarıştıran 2
2 41N18 27E32 -1:50:08
Büyük Lâçin 1 3 40N47 34E54 -2:19:36
Cabirülensar 1 3 37N00 38E59 -2:35:56
Cacas 1 3 38N23 41E17 -2:45:08
Çağış 1 3 39N30 28E01 -1:52:04
Çağlarca 1 3 39N05 39E10 -2:36:40
Çağrankaya 1 3 40N47 40E33 -2:42:12
Çakıralan 1 3 41N10 35E47 -2:23:08
Çakmak 1 3 37N37 34E19 -2:17:16
Çal 1 3 38N05 29E24 -1:57:36
Çala 1 3 41N05 43E21 -2:53:24
Çaldere 1 3 40N49 37E01 -2:28:04
Çaldıran 1 3 39N09 43E55 -2:55:40
Çalgan 1 3 37N35 38E19 -2:33:16
Çalı 1 3 40N10 28E54 -1:55:36
Çaltılıbük 1 3 39N57 28E36 -1:54:24
Çamardı 1 3 37N50 35E00 -2:20:00
Camiçi 1 3 40N40 37E00 -2:28:00
Camiyanı 1 3 40N52 38E38 -2:34:32
Çamlıbel 1 3 40N05 36E29 -2:25:56
Çamlıca 2 2 40N46 26E39 -1:46:36
Çamlıdere 1 3 40N30 32E29 -2:09:56
Çan 1 3 40N02 27E03 -1:48:12
Çan 1 3 39N09 40E13 -2:40:52
Çanakkale 1 3 40N09 26E24 -1:45:36
Çandarlı 1 3 38N56 26E56 -1:47:44
Çandır 1 3 40N16 33E29 -2:13:56
Çandır 1 3 39N15 35E32 -2:22:08
Çankırı 1 3 40N36 33E37 -2:14:28
Çardak 1 3 38N06 36E49 -2:27:16
Çardi 1 3 39N41 29E10 -1:56:40
Çarşamba 1 3 41N12 36E44 -2:26:56
Çat 1 3 39N40 41E00 -2:44:00
Çatak 1 3 38N01 43E07 -2:52:28
Çatalan 1 3 37N14 35E16 -2:21:04
Çatalca 2 2 41N09 28E27 -1:53:48
Çatalzeytin 1 3 41N57 34E13 -2:16:52
Çavdır 1 3 37N09 29E42 -1:58:48
Çavuş 1 3 37N36 31E56 -2:07:44
Çavuşlar 1 3 40N43 32E04 -2:08:16
Çay 1 3 38N35 31E02 -2:04:08
Çaycuma 1 3 41N25 32E05 -2:08:20
Çayırhan 1 3 40N06 31E37 -2:06:28
Çayırlı 1 3 39N48 40E01 -2:40:04
Çayırlıahmetçiler 1
3 40N58 31E27 -2:05:48
Çayırşeyhi 1 3 39N18 35E40 -2:22:40
Çayra 1 3 40N41 39E06 -2:36:24
Cebeciköy 2 1 41N07 28E52 -1:55:28
Ceceli 1 3 39N43 33E52 -2:15:28
Çekmeköy 1 3 41N03 29E10 -1:56:40
Celâlli 1 3 39N42 37E26 -2:29:44
Çelebiler 1 3 41N26 32E57 -2:11:48
Çelikhân 1 3 38N02 38E15 -2:33:00
Çeltik 1 3 41N11 32E19 -2:09:16
Çeltikçi 1 3 40N20 32E28 -2:09:52
Çeltikçi 1 3 37N32 30E29 -2:01:56
Cemilbey 1 3 40N21 35E04 -2:20:16
Çemişgezek 1 3 39N04 38E55 -2:35:40
Çerkeş 1 3 40N50 32E54 -2:11:36
Çerkezköy 2 2 41N17 28E00 -1:52:00
Çermik 1 3 38N09 39E27 -2:37:48
Çeşme 1 3 38N18 26E19 -1:45:16
Çetinkaya 1 3 39N15 37E38 -2:30:32
Cevizli 1 3 37N12 31E45 -2:07:00
Cevizlik 1 3 40N48 39E38 -2:38:32
Ceyhan 1 3 37N04 35E47 -2:23:08
Ceylânpınar 1 3 36N51 40E02 -2:40:08
Cide 1 3 41N54 33E00 -2:12:00
Çiftalan 2 1 41N15 28E54 -1:55:36
Çiftehan 1 3 37N31 34E46 -2:19:04
Çifteler 1 3 39N22 31E03 -2:04:12
Çiftlik 1 3 40N08 39E27 -2:37:48
Çiftlik 1 3 38N11 34E30 -2:18:00
Cihangir 1 3 40N03 29E07 -1:56:28
Çıksı 1 3 38N30 40E55 -2:43:40
Çilader 1 3 41N02 37E06 -2:28:24
Çıldır 1 3 41N08 43E07 -2:52:28
Çinar 1 3 37N44 40E25 -2:41:40
Çınarcık 1 3 40N39 29E06 -1:56:24
Çine 1 3 37N36 28E04 -1:52:16
Cingife 1 3 37N20 37E33 -2:30:12
Çırçır 1 3 40N04 36E48 -2:27:12
Çivril 1 3 38N18 29E45 -1:59:00
Cizre 1 3 37N20 42E12 -2:48:48
Çobanlar 1 3 38N41 30E47 -2:03:08
Çoğun 1 3 39N20 34E08 -2:16:32
Çokak 1 3 37N45 36E19 -2:25:16
Çolaklı 1 3 38N22 38E33 -2:34:12
Çonlu 1 3 40N13 28E06 -1:52:24
Constantinople → İstanbul 1
1 41N01 28E58 -1:55:52
Çorlu 2 2 41N09 27E48 -1:51:12
Çorum 1 3 39N14 28E27 -1:53:48
Çorum 1 3 40N33 34E58 -2:19:52
Çubuk 1 3 40N15 33E02 -2:12:08
Çukurca 1 3 37N15 43E37 -2:54:28
Cülmen 1 3 37N19 38E48 -2:35:12
Cumalı 1 3 36N42 27E27 -1:49:48
Cumaovası 1 3 38N15 27E09 -1:48:36
Çumra 1 3 37N34 32E48 -2:11:12
Çungüş 1 3 38N13 39E17 -2:37:08
Daday 1 3 41N28 33E28 -2:13:52
Dağkızılca 1 3 38N18 27E24 -1:49:36
Dalama 1 3 37N47 28E04 -1:52:16
Dalavakasır 1 3 37N14 41E45 -2:47:00
Damar 1 3 41N15 41E34 -2:46:16
Damıar 1 3 41N15 41E34 -2:46:16
Darende 1 3 38N34 37E30 -2:30:00
Darıca 1 3 40N45 29E23 -1:57:32
Datça 1 3 36N45 27E40 -1:50:40
Davulga 1 3 38N58 31E23 -2:05:32
Davutlar 1 3 37N43 27E17 -1:49:08
Dazkırı 1 3 37N55 29E52 -1:59:28
Dedeköy 1 3 37N58 29E36 -1:58:24
Dedeli 1 3 39N11 43E05 -2:52:20
Değirmendere 1 3 38N07 27E09 -1:48:36
Delice 1 3 39N58 34E02 -2:16:08
Deliilyas 1 3 39N20 36E48 -2:27:12
Deliktaş 1 3 39N21 37E13 -2:28:52
Demirci 1 3 39N03 28E40 -1:54:40
Demircidere 1 3 37N33 27E50 -1:51:20
Demirköy 2 2 41N49 27E45 -1:51:00
Demirtaş 1 3 40N16 29E06 -1:56:24
Denizli 1 3 37N46 29E06 -1:56:24
Derbesiye 1 3 37N06 40E40 -2:42:40
Dereishaklı 1 3 41N03 39E08 -2:36:32
Dereköy 2 2 41N56 27E21 -1:49:24
Dereköy 1 3 39N16 27E19 -1:49:16
Dereköy 1 3 40N08 37E47 -2:31:08
Dereli 1 3 40N45 38E27 -2:33:48
Dereseki 1 3 41N08 29E08 -1:56:32
Derik 1 3 37N22 40E17 -2:41:08
Derinkuyu 1 3 38N23 34E45 -2:19:00
Deşt 1 3 39N10 39E49 -2:39:16
Destek 1 3 40N51 36E12 -2:24:48
Devecikonağı 1 3 39N55 28E34 -1:54:16
Develi 1 3 38N23 35E30 -2:22:00
Devrek 1 3 41N13 31E57 -2:07:48
Devrekâni 1 3 41N36 33E51 -2:15:24
Digor 1 3 40N23 43E24 -2:53:36
Dih 1 3 37N46 42E11 -2:48:44
Dikbıyık 1 3 41N13 36E38 -2:26:32
Dikili 1 3 39N04 26E53 -1:47:32
Dikmen 1 3 39N53 32E50 -2:11:20
Dimetoka 1 3 40N16 27E17 -1:49:08
Dinar 1 3 38N04 30E10 -2:00:40
Dineksaray 1 3 37N23 32E37 -2:10:28
Direkli 1 3 39N43 36E40 -2:26:40
Dişidi 1 3 38N47 39E00 -2:36:00
Divriği 1 3 39N23 38E07 -2:32:28
Diyadin 1 3 39N33 43E41 -2:54:44
Diyarbakır 1 3 37N55 40E14 -2:40:56
Dodurga 1 3 39N48 29E55 -1:59:40
Doğanbey 1 3 37N37 27E11 -1:48:44
Doğanbey 1 3 38N04 26E53 -1:47:32
Doğanbey 1 3 37N48 31E54 -2:07:36
Doğançay 1 3 40N37 30E20 -2:01:20
Doğanhisar 1 3 38N09 31E41 -2:06:44
Doğanşehir 1 3 38N06 37E53 -2:31:32
Doğubayazıt 1 3 39N32 44E08 -2:56:32
Dokmetepe 1 3 40N19 36E18 -2:25:12
Dolaybaköy 1 3 40N54 29E15 -1:57:00
Domaniç 1 3 39N48 29E37 -1:58:28
Dörtyol 1 3 36N52 36E12 -2:24:48
Dudullu 1 3 41N02 29E09 -1:56:36
Duğur 1 3 41N31 42E42 -2:50:48
Dümeli 1 3 40N32 33E31 -2:14:04
Dumlupınar 1 3 38N52 30E00 -2:00:00
Durağan 1 3 41N25 35E04 -2:20:16
Durak 1 3 39N42 28E17 -1:53:08
Dursunbey 1 3 39N35 28E38 -1:54:32
Düzce 1 3 40N50 31E10 -2:04:40
Eceabat 2 2 40N11 26E21 -1:45:24
Edincik 1 3 40N20 27E51 -1:51:24
Edirne 2 2 41N40 26E34 -1:46:16
Edremit 1 3 39N35 27E01 -1:48:04
Efkere 1 3 38N47 35E40 -2:22:40
Eğil 1 3 38N15 40E05 -2:40:20
Eğret 1 3 38N57 30E18 -2:01:12
Eğridir 1 3 37N52 30E51 -2:03:24
Eğriköy 1 3 38N44 27E21 -1:49:24
Eksere 1 3 36N48 32E01 -2:08:04
Elâzığ 1 3 38N41 39E14 -2:36:56
Elbaşı 1 3 38N41 35E59 -2:23:56
Elbeyli 1 3 36N41 37E26 -2:29:44
Elbistan 1 3 38N13 37E12 -2:28:48
Elemi 1 3 41N04 35E30 -2:22:00
Eleşkirt 1 3 39N48 42E42 -2:50:48
Elki 1 3 37N34 43E10 -2:52:40
Elmadağ (Küçükyozgat) 1
3 39N55 33E15 -2:13:00
Elmalı 1 3 36N44 29E56 -1:59:44
Emet 1 3 39N20 29E15 -1:57:00
Emiralem 1 3 38N36 27E09 -1:48:36
Emirdağ 1 3 39N01 31E10 -2:04:40
Emirhan 1 3 39N42 37E46 -2:31:04
Emrekom 1 3 39N58 41E57 -2:47:48
Enez 2 2 40N44 26E04 -1:44:16
Erbaa 1 3 40N42 36E36 -2:26:24
Erciş 1 3 39N02 43E22 -2:53:28
Erdek 1 3 40N24 27E48 -1:51:12
Erdemli 1 3 36N37 34E18 -2:17:12
Ereğli 1 3 37N31 34E04 -2:16:16
Ereğli 1 3 41N17 31E25 -2:05:40
Erenköy 1 3 40N58 38E08 -2:32:32
Ergani 1 3 38N17 39E46 -2:39:04
Erkilet 1 3 38N49 35E27 -2:21:48
Ermelik 1 3 39N42 39E02 -2:36:08
Ermenak 1 3 36N38 32E54 -2:11:36
Ertuğrul 1 3 39N34 27E43 -1:50:52
Erzincan 1 3 39N44 39E29 -2:37:56
Erzurum 1 3 39N55 41E17 -2:45:08
Esbiye 1 3 40N57 38E44 -2:34:56
Esenler 2 1 41N02 28E51 -1:55:24
Esenli 1 3 40N41 37E24 -2:29:36
Esesi 1 3 39N49 39E19 -2:37:16
Esirgâh 1 3 39N48 38E52 -2:35:28
Eskiköy 1 3 36N36 30E34 -2:02:16
Eski Malatya 1 3 38N26 38E23 -2:33:32
Eskipazar 1 3 40N58 32E33 -2:10:12
Eskişehir 1 3 39N46 30E32 -2:02:08
Eşme 1 3 38N24 28E59 -1:55:56
Esmirna → İzmir 1
3 38N25 27E09 -1:48:36
Estambul → İstanbul 1
1 41N01 28E58 -1:55:52
Etili 1 3 39N59 26E54 -1:47:36
Etimesğut 1 3 39N57 32E40 -2:10:40
Everek 1 3 38N23 35E30 -2:22:00
Eymir 1 3 40N02 35E14 -2:20:56
Ezine 1 3 39N47 26E20 -1:45:20
Ezinepazarı 1 3 40N34 36E09 -2:24:36
Fak 1 3 37N51 39E05 -2:36:20
Fakılı 1 3 39N13 35E00 -2:20:00
Fariske 1 3 36N37 32E38 -2:10:32
Fatikli 1 3 36N08 36E12 -2:24:48
Fatsa 1 3 41N02 37E31 -2:30:04

TURKEY TURQUÍA TURQUIE TÜRKEI TÜRKIYE

Felâhiye 1	3	39N06	35E35	-2:22:20
Fethiye 1	3	36N37	29E07	-1:56:28
Fevzipaşa 1	3	37N07	36E37	-2:26:28
Finike 1	3	36N18	30E09	-2:00:36
Foça 1	3	38N39	26E46	-1:47:04
Gallipoli → Gelibolu 2	2	40N24	26E40	-1:46:40
Gaman 1	3	41N10	36E20	-2:25:20
Gaziantep 1	3	37N05	37E22	-2:29:28
Gazipaşa 1	3	36N17	32E20	-2:09:20
Gebeler 1	3	39N26	29E00	-1:56:00
Gebeme 1	3	40N38	37E48	-2:31:12
Gebze 1	3	40N48	29E25	-1:57:40
Gediz 1	3	39N02	29E25	-1:57:40
Gelegra 1	3	40N01	31E50	-2:07:20
Gelenbe 1	3	39N10	27E50	-1:51:20
Gelendost 1	3	38N07	31E01	-2:04:04
Gelibolu (Gallipoli) 2	2	40N24	26E40	-1:46:40
Gelveri 1	3	38N17	34E23	-2:17:32
Gemerek 1	3	39N11	36E05	-2:24:20
Gemlik 1	3	40N26	29E09	-1:56:36
Genç 1	3	38N46	40E35	-2:42:20
Gencek 1	3	37N27	31E33	-2:06:12
Gercüş 1	3	37N34	41E23	-2:45:32
Gerede 1	3	40N48	32E12	-2:08:48
Gerger 1	3	38N02	39E02	-2:36:08
Geriş 1	3	36N58	31E44	-2:06:56
Germencik 1	3	37N51	27E37	-1:50:28
Germili 1	3	39N06	38E49	-2:35:16
Germiter 1	3	38N28	37E36	-2:30:24
Gerze 1	3	41N48	35E12	-2:20:48
Gevaş 1	3	38N16	43E07	-2:52:28
Geyikli 1	3	39N48	26E12	-1:44:48
Geyve 1	3	40N30	30E18	-2:01:12
Giresun 1	3	40N55	38E24	-2:33:36
Girimira 1	3	37N07	41E26	-2:45:44
Göbel 1	3	40N00	28E09	-1:52:36
Göçbeyli 1	3	39N13	27E25	-1:49:40
Gödene 1	3	36N34	30E21	-2:01:24
Gökçe 2	2	40N11	25E55	-1:43:40
Gökçen 1	3	38N07	27E53	-1:51:32
Gökdere 1	3	38N44	40E13	-2:40:52
Gökdere 1	3	40N29	36E47	-2:27:08
Göksun 1	3	38N03	36E30	-2:26:00
Göktepe 1	3	37N15	28E36	-1:54:24
Gölbası 1	3	37N50	37E40	-2:30:40
Gölbaşı 1	3	39N48	32E49	-2:11:16
Gölcuk 1	3	39N18	27E59	-1:51:56
Gölcük 1	3	40N44	29E48	-1:59:12
Gölköy 1	3	40N42	37E38	-2:30:32
Göllet 1	3	40N45	42E18	-2:49:12
Gölmarmara 1	3	38N42	27E56	-1:51:44
Gölpazarı 1	3	40N15	30E19	-2:01:16
Gölveren 1	3	37N48	33E52	-2:15:28
Gömele 1	3	41N02	30E34	-2:02:16
Gönen 1	3	40N06	27E39	-1:50:36
Gördes 1	3	38N54	28E18	-1:53:12
Görele 1	3	41N02	39E00	-2:36:00
Görukle 1	3	40N14	28E50	-1:55:20
Göykazi 1	3	36N14	29E59	-1:59:56
Göynücek 1	3	40N24	35E32	-2:22:08
Göynük 1	3	40N24	30E47	-2:03:08
Gözne 1	3	36N59	34E34	-2:18:16
Gücük 1	3	38N12	37E29	-2:29:56
Güdül 1	3	40N13	32E15	-2:09:00
Gülebağdı 1	3	39N52	39E50	-2:39:20
Güllük 1	3	37N14	27E36	-1:50:24
Gülnar 1	3	36N20	33E25	-2:13:40
Gülpınar 1	3	39N32	26E07	-1:44:28
Gülşehir 1	3	38N45	34E38	-2:18:32
Gümgüm 1	3	39N10	41E28	-2:45:52
Gümüşhacıköy 1	3	40N53	35E14	-2:20:56
Gümüşhane 1	3	40N27	39E29	-2:37:56
Gümüşköy 2	1	41N14	28E58	-1:55:52
Gündüzlü 1	3	40N53	37E43	-2:30:52
Güney 1	3	38N09	29E05	-1:56:20
Güngören 2	1	41N01	28E53	-1:55:32
Güre 1	3	38N39	29E10	-1:56:40
Gürsu 1	3	40N13	29E12	-1:56:48
Gürün 1	3	38N43	37E17	-2:29:08
Güvem 1	3	40N36	32E40	-2:10:40
Güzelbahçe 1	3	38N21	26E54	-1:47:36
Güzelsu 1	3	36N54	31E53	-2:07:32
Hacıbektaş 1	3	38N57	34E35	-2:18:20
Hacihamza 1	3	41N05	34E28	-2:17:52
Hacıishaklı 1	3	36N11	33E40	-2:14:40
Hacıköy 1	3	40N04	35E31	-2:22:04
Hacılar 1	3	38N39	35E27	-2:21:48
Hadım 1	3	36N59	32E28	-2:09:52
Hafik 1	3	39N52	37E24	-2:29:36
Hafızbey 1	3	37N12	30E31	-2:02:04
Hakkâri 1	3	37N34	43E45	-2:55:00
Halfeti 1	3	37N15	37E52	-2:31:28
Halimiye 1	3	36N40	32E45	-2:11:00
Halkalı 2	1	41N02	28E47	-1:55:08
Hamam 1	3	39N30	35E24	-2:21:36
Hamamözü 1	3	40N48	35E02	-2:20:08
Hamidiye 2	2	41N09	26E40	-1:46:40
Hamo 1	3	39N36	38E11	-2:32:44
Hamur 1	3	39N36	42E59	-2:51:56
Hani 1	3	38N24	40E24	-2:41:36
Hanköyü 1	3	38N35	39E04	-2:36:16
Hanobası 1	3	38N35	33E50	-2:15:20
Hanönü 1	3	41N38	34E28	-2:17:52
Harbiye 1	3	36N11	36E05	-2:24:20
Harfaz 1	3	38N01	41E19	-2:45:16
Harhur 1	3	37N49	42E20	-2:49:20
Harmanlı 1	3	37N51	37E45	-2:31:00
Harran 1	3	36N51	39E00	-2:36:00
Hart 1	3	40N24	40E09	-2:40:36
Haruniye 1	3	37N17	36E27	-2:25:48
Hasançelebi 1	3	38N58	37E54	-2:31:36
Hasankale → Pasinler 1	3	39N59	41E41	-2:46:44
Hasankeyf 1	3	37N43	41E25	-2:45:40
Hasayaz 1	3	40N15	33E20	-2:13:20
Hasbek 1	3	39N33	35E33	-2:22:12
Hashır 1	3	37N54	42E36	-2:50:24
Hasköy 2	2	41N38	26E41	-1:46:44
Hasköy 1	3	40N59	42E52	-2:51:28
Hasras 1	3	37N57	42E16	-2:49:04
Hassa 1	3	36N50	36E29	-2:25:56
Hatip 1	3	37N46	32E25	-2:09:40
Hatunsaray 1	3	37N35	32E21	-2:09:24
Havilhanları 1	3	38N09	41E47	-2:47:08
Havran 1	3	39N33	27E06	-1:48:24
Havsa 2	2	41N33	26E49	-1:47:16
Havza 1	3	40N58	35E41	-2:22:44
Haydaran 1	3	39N14	39E43	-2:38:52
Haydarlı 1	3	38N16	30E23	-2:01:32
Haymana 1	3	39N27	32E30	-2:10:00
Hayrabolu 2	2	41N12	27E06	-1:48:24
Hayrat 1	3	40N40	40E24	-2:41:36
Hazak 1	3	37N21	41E54	-2:47:36
Hazro 1	3	38N15	40E47	-2:43:08
Hazzo 1	3	38N11	41E29	-2:45:56
Hekimhan 1	3	38N49	37E56	-2:31:44
Hendek 1	3	40N48	30E45	-2:03:00
Hereke 1	3	40N48	29E39	-1:58:36
Herheri 1	3	37N41	39E00	-2:36:00
Hezan 1	3	38N21	40E38	-2:42:32
Himmetdede 1	3	38N55	35E07	-2:20:28
Hınıs 1	3	39N22	41E44	-2:46:56
Hinzik 1	3	40N08	40E58	-2:43:52
Hisarköy 1	3	39N48	29E37	-1:58:28
Hisarönu 1	3	41N33	32E02	-2:08:08
Hivris 1	3	38N18	42E10	-2:48:40
Hocaköy 1	3	41N03	30E17	-2:01:08
Hocaköy 1	3	37N08	32E16	-2:09:04
Hocalar 1	3	38N34	30E00	-2:00:00
Hocalı 1	3	38N41	27E41	-1:50:44
Hoka 1	3	40N21	40E55	-2:43:40
Hoketçe 1	3	38N16	36E13	-2:24:52
Holhol 1	3	39N14	40E03	-2:40:12
Homa 1	3	38N14	30E01	-2:00:04
Honaz 1	3	37N45	29E17	-1:57:08
Hopa 1	3	41N25	41E24	-2:45:36
Horasan 1	3	40N03	42E11	-2:48:44
Horsunlu 1	3	37N55	28E36	-1:54:24
Horzum 1	3	37N10	29E30	-1:58:00
Hoşalay 1	3	42N00	33E27	-2:13:48
Hotamış 1	3	37N36	33E13	-2:12:52
Hoyran 1	3	38N19	30E59	-2:03:56
Hozat 1	3	39N07	39E14	-2:36:56
Hundezler 1	3	40N40	40E24	-2:41:36
Hunut 1	3	40N39	41E09	-2:44:36
Hüseyinli 1	3	40N21	33E59	-2:15:56
Hüvek 1	3	37N22	38E31	-2:34:04
Hüyük 1	3	37N57	31E37	-2:06:28
İbradı 1	3	37N06	31E36	-2:06:24
İbrala 1	3	37N09	33E31	-2:14:04
İbriktepe 2	2	41N00	26E30	-1:46:00
İçme 1	3	38N37	39E34	-2:38:16
Iğdır 1	3	40N16	35E38	-2:22:32
Iğdır 1	3	39N55	44E02	-2:56:08
İğneada 2	2	41N52	27E58	-1:51:52
İhsangazi 1	3	41N11	33E33	-2:14:12
İkitelli 2	1	41N04	28E47	-1:55:08
İkizce 1	3	39N36	32E40	-2:10:40
İkizdere 1	3	40N47	40E33	-2:42:12
Ilgaz 1	3	40N56	33E38	-2:14:32
Ilgın 1	3	38N17	31E55	-2:07:40
İliç 1	3	39N28	38E34	-2:34:16
Ilıca 1	3	39N52	27E46	-1:51:04
Ilıca 1	3	39N57	41E07	-2:44:28
İlisira 1	3	37N12	33E02	-2:12:08
İlyasbey 1	3	40N13	29E52	-1:59:28
İmamlar 1	3	40N47	30E59	-2:03:56
İmerhav 1	3	41N25	42E14	-2:48:56
İmranlı 1	3	39N54	38E07	-2:32:28
İmron 1	3	38N12	38E53	-2:35:32
İncesu 1	3	38N38	35E11	-2:20:44
İncirliova 1	3	37N50	27E43	-1:50:52
İnderesi 1	3	37N50	35E40	-2:22:40
İnebolu 1	3	41N58	33E46	-2:15:04
İnece 2	2	41N41	27E04	-1:48:16
İnecik 2	2	40N56	27E16	-1:49:04
İnegöl 1	3	40N05	29E31	-1:58:04
İnekollar 1	3	39N33	28E56	-1:55:44
İnevi 1	3	38N40	32E56	-2:11:44
İnhisar 1	3	40N03	30E23	-2:01:32
İnönü 1	3	39N48	30E09	-2:00:36
İntepe 1	3	40N00	26E20	-1:45:20
İpkaiye 1	3	40N12	27E06	-1:48:24
İpsala 2	2	40N55	26E23	-1:45:32
İpsile 1	3	40N14	37E33	-2:30:12
İresi 1	3	39N09	39E53	-2:39:32
İşcehisar 1	3	38N51	30E45	-2:03:00
Işıklı 1	3	38N19	29E51	-1:59:24
İskenderun 1	3	36N37	36E07	-2:24:28
İskilip 1	3	40N45	34E29	-2:17:56
İslâhiye 1	3	37N03	36E36	-2:26:24
İsmailli 1	3	38N56	27E13	-1:48:52
İspanak 1	3	38N52	37E07	-2:28:28
Isparta 1	3	37N46	30E33	-2:02:12
İspir 1	3	40N29	41E00	-2:44:00
İstanbul 1	1	41N01	28E58	-1:55:52
İstilli 1	3	37N14	41E04	-2:44:16
İvrindi 1	3	39N34	27E29	-1:49:56
İzmir 1	3	38N25	27E09	-1:48:36
İzmit (Kocaeli) 1	3	40N46	29E55	-1:59:40
İznik 1	3	40N26	29E43	-1:58:52
Kabadüz 1	3	40N53	37E56	-2:31:44
Kabalı 1	3	41N52	35E05	-2:20:20
Kabilcevaz 1	3	38N20	41E25	-2:45:40
Kadıköy 2	2	40N46	26E46	-1:47:04
Kadınhanı 1	3	38N15	32E14	-2:08:56
Kadirli 1	3	37N23	36E05	-2:24:20
Kadışehri 1	3	40N00	35E49	-2:23:16
Kâğıthane 2	1	41N04	28E58	-1:55:52
Kağızman 1	3	40N09	43E08	-2:52:32
Kalacık 1	3	37N17	39E02	-2:36:08
Kalamaki 1	3	36N15	29E24	-1:57:36
Kalan 1	3	39N07	39E32	-2:38:08
Kale 1	3	37N26	28E51	-1:55:24
Kale 1	3	40N23	39E39	-2:38:36
Kalecik 1	3	40N06	33E25	-2:13:40
Kaman 1	3	39N22	33E44	-2:14:56
Kamarik 1	3	39N37	39E18	-2:37:12
Kâmil 1	3	41N07	34E47	-2:19:08
Kandıra 1	3	41N04	30E09	-2:00:36
Kangal 1	3	39N15	37E24	-2:29:36
Kânireş 1	3	39N18	41E01	-2:44:04
Kanlıavşar 1	3	37N13	38E16	-2:33:04
Karaali 1	3	39N40	32E57	-2:11:48
Karabiğa 1	3	40N24	27E18	-1:49:12
Karabük 1	3	41N12	32E37	-2:10:28
Karabulduk 1	3	40N50	38E34	-2:34:16
Karaca 1	3	40N12	39E08	-2:36:32
Karacabey 1	3	40N13	28E21	-1:53:24
Karacadağ 2	2	41N57	27E40	-1:50:40
Karacaköy 2	2	41N24	28E22	-1:53:28
Karacali 1	3	40N53	37E17	-2:29:08
Karacasu 1	3	37N43	28E37	-1:54:28
Karacaviran 1	3	39N44	38E08	-2:32:32
Karacaviran 1	3	37N33	39E22	-2:37:28
Karaçayır 1	3	39N55	37E01	-2:28:04
Karaçürun 1	3	37N35	38E57	-2:35:48
Karadere 1	3	40N59	30E50	-2:03:20
Karadoğan 1	3	40N25	31E51	-2:07:24
Karadoruk 1	3	38N53	37E22	-2:29:28
Karahallı 1	3	38N20	29E32	-1:58:08
Karaisalı 1	3	37N16	35E03	-2:20:12
Karakecili 1	3	39N36	33E23	-2:13:32
Karaköse 1	3	39N44	43E03	-2:52:12
Karakulak 1	3	39N59	40E01	-2:40:04
Karakurt 1	3	40N10	42E36	-2:50:24
Karamağara 1	3	39N42	35E31	-2:22:04
Karaman 1	3	37N05	29E20	-1:57:20
Karaman 1	3	37N11	33E14	-2:12:56
Karamanlı 1	3	37N22	29E49	-1:59:16
Karamürsel 1	3	40N42	29E36	-1:58:24
Karanti 1	3	40N15	27E07	-1:48:28
Karaoglan 1	3	39N14	39E13	-2:36:52
Karapınar 1	3	37N43	33E33	-2:14:12
Karapınar 1	3	41N30	32E12	-2:08:48
Karaşar 1	3	40N20	32E00	-2:08:00
Karasu 1	3	41N06	30E41	-2:02:44
Karataş 1	3	36N36	35E21	-2:21:24
Karaurğan 1	3	40N15	42E17	-2:49:08
Karayaka 1	3	40N45	36E37	-2:26:28
Karayün 1	3	39N41	37E19	-2:29:16
Karbeyaz 1	3	36N02	36E12	-2:24:48
Kargı 1	3	41N08	34E30	-2:18:00
Kars 1	3	40N36	43E05	-2:52:20
Karsantı 1	3	37N33	35E24	-2:21:36
Karşıyaka 1	3	38N27	27E07	-1:48:28
Kartal 1	3	40N53	29E10	-1:56:40
Kaş 1	3	36N12	29E38	-1:58:32
Kaşçiftliği 1	3	36N36	29E45	-1:59:00
Kasır 1	3	37N10	40E52	-2:43:28
Kasrik 1	3	38N13	41E54	-2:47:36
Kastamonu 1	3	41N22	33E47	-2:15:08
Kavacık 1	3	39N40	28E30	-1:54:00
Kavak 1	3	38N24	39E26	-2:37:44
Kavak 1	3	41N05	36E03	-2:24:12
Kavak 1	3	39N18	37E30	-2:30:00
Kavakköy 1	3	40N13	27E46	-1:51:04
Kavaklıdere 1	3	37N26	28E22	-1:53:28
Kayadibi 1	3	39N29	36E43	-2:26:52
Kayadibi 1	3	39N55	34E15	-2:17:00
Kayaş 1	3	39N56	32E58	-2:11:52
Kaymakçı 1	3	38N10	28E08	-1:52:32
Kaymaz 1	3	39N31	31E11	-2:04:44
Kaynak 1	3	37N43	39E37	-2:38:28
Kayseri 1	3	38N43	35E30	-2:22:00
Kazancı 1	3	36N30	32E53	-2:11:32
Kazanlı 1	3	36N50	34E45	-2:19:00
Keban 1	3	38N48	38E45	-2:35:00
Keçiborlu 1	3	37N57	30E18	-2:01:12
Keferdiz 1	3	38N19	39E03	-2:36:12
Keles 1	3	39N55	29E14	-1:56:56
Kemah 1	3	39N36	39E02	-2:36:08
Kemaliye 1	3	39N16	38E29	-2:33:56
Kemalpaşa 1	3	41N30	41E30	-2:46:00
Kemalpaşa 1	3	38N25	27E26	-1:49:44
Kemer 1	3	36N38	29E21	-1:57:24
Kemerburgaz 2	1	41N09	28E54	-1:55:36
Kemerhisar 1	3	37N49	34E36	-2:18:24
Kepsut 1	3	39N41	28E09	-1:52:36
Kerburan 1	3	37N33	41E44	-2:46:56
Keşan 2	2	40N51	26E37	-1:46:28
Keşap 1	3	40N55	38E31	-2:34:04
Keşirlik 2	2	41N58	27E12	-1:48:48
Keskin 1	3	39N41	33E37	-2:14:28
Kestep 1	3	36N27	29E16	-1:57:04
Keysun 1	3	37N34	37E50	-2:31:20
Kiği 1	3	39N19	40E21	-2:41:24
Kığzı 1	3	38N18	43E25	-2:53:40
Kılaban 1	3	37N27	42E51	-2:51:24
Kılandıras 1	3	38N34	30E11	-2:00:44
Kılbasan 1	3	37N20	33E12	-2:12:48
Kilimli 1	3	41N28	31E50	-2:07:20
Kılınç 1	3	40N38	29E23	-1:57:32
Kilis 1	3	36N44	37E05	-2:28:20
Kınık 1	3	39N05	27E23	-1:49:32
Kiranlık 1	3	39N07	41E41	-2:46:44
Kiraz 1	3	38N13	28E13	-1:52:52
Kirazlı 1	3	40N02	26E41	-1:46:44
Kirçal 1	3	41N39	35E16	-2:21:04
Kırcasalih 2	2	41N23	26E48	-1:47:12
Kireç 1	3	39N33	28E22	-1:53:28
Kirec 1	3	40N59	39E10	-2:36:40

Kirgali 1 3 37N55 40E00 -2:40:00
Kırıkhan 1 3 39N32 41E20 -2:45:20
Kırıkhan 1 3 36N32 36E19 -2:25:16
Kırıkkale 1 3 39N50 33E31 -2:14:04
Kırka 1 3 39N17 30E33 -2:02:12
Kırkağaç 1 3 39N06 27E40 -1:50:40
Kırklareli 2 2 41N44 27E12 -1:48:48
Kırmıt 1 3 37N11 35E41 -2:22:44
Kırşehir 1 3 39N09 34E10 -2:16:40
Kisha 1 3 40N28 41E28 -2:45:52
Kısırkaya 2 1 41N14 28E58 -1:55:52
Kısırmandıra 2 1 41N14 28E49 -1:55:16
Kıskanlı 1 3 39N32 41E58 -2:47:52
Kışla 1 3 40N51 30E57 -2:03:48
Kıyıköy 2 2 41N38 28E05 -1:52:20
Kızılcabölük 1 3 37N37 29E01 -1:56:04
Kızılcahamam 1 3 40N28 32E39 -2:10:36
Kızılçakçak 1 3 40N46 43E37 -2:54:28
Kızıldikme 1 3 39N05 37E01 -2:28:04
Kızılhisar 1 3 37N33 29E18 -1:57:12
Kızıloğlan 1 3 41N20 34E52 -2:19:28
Kızıltepe 1 3 37N12 40E36 -2:42:24
Kızılveran 1 3 40N27 34E28 -2:17:52
Kızılviran 1 3 37N52 32E07 -2:08:28
Kızılyaka 1 3 37N09 32E54 -2:11:36
Kocaali 1 3 41N03 30E52 -2:03:28
Kocaaliler 1 3 37N19 30E44 -2:02:56
Kocaeli → İzmit 1
3 40N46 29E55 -1:59:40
Koçali 1 3 37N55 38E15 -2:33:00
Koçarlı 1 3 37N45 27E42 -1:50:48
Kocasinan 2 1 41N01 28E50 -1:55:20
Kölük 1 3 37N46 38E36 -2:34:24
Kömürcüpınar 2 1 41N15 28E51 -1:55:24
Konakpınar 1 3 39N26 27E53 -1:51:32
Konstantinopel → İstanbul 1
1 41N01 28E58 -1:55:52
Konya 1 3 37N52 32E31 -2:10:04
Köprüören 1 3 39N30 29E47 -1:59:08
Korgan 1 3 40N44 37E13 -2:28:52
Korkuteli 1 3 37N04 30E13 -2:00:52
Körsüleymanlı 1 3 38N17 38E01 -2:32:04
Korucu 1 3 39N28 27E22 -1:49:28
Köse 1 3 40N13 39E39 -2:38:36
Kösefakılı 1 3 39N36 34E09 -2:16:36
Köşk 1 3 37N51 28E03 -1:52:12
Kosor 1 3 40N39 42E39 -2:50:36
Kösreli 1 3 37N11 35E59 -2:23:56
Kotum 1 3 38N25 42E18 -2:49:12
Köyceğiz 1 3 36N57 28E41 -1:54:44
Koyulhisar 1 3 40N18 37E51 -2:31:24
Koyuneli 1 3 39N50 27E15 -1:49:00
Köyyeri 1 3 38N30 36E30 -2:26:00
Kozağacı 1 3 39N24 31E50 -2:07:20
Kozaklı 1 3 39N14 34E49 -2:19:16
Kozan 1 3 37N27 35E49 -2:23:16
Kozlu 1 3 41N26 31E46 -2:07:04
Kozlu 1 3 40N37 36E30 -2:26:00
Küçükbahce 1 3 38N33 26E24 -1:45:36
Küçükbakkal 1 3 40N58 29E06 -1:56:24
Küçükçekmece 2 1 40N59 28E46 -1:55:04
Küçükköy 2 1 41N04 28E54 -1:55:36
Küçükkuyu 1 3 39N32 26E36 -1:46:24
Küfre 1 3 38N02 42E00 -2:48:00
Kula 1 3 38N32 28E40 -1:54:40
Kulu 1 3 39N06 33E05 -2:12:20
Kumköy 2 1 41N15 29E02 -1:56:08
Kumluca 1 3 36N22 30E18 -2:01:12
Kumluca 1 3 41N27 32E28 -2:09:52
Küplü 2 2 41N07 26E21 -1:45:24
Küplu 1 3 40N06 30E00 -2:00:00
Küre 1 3 41N48 33E43 -2:14:52
Kurşunlu 1 3 40N51 33E16 -2:13:04
Kurşunlu 1 3 38N40 37E51 -2:31:24
Kurtalan 1 3 37N57 41E42 -2:46:48
Kürteşe 1 3 41N14 33E44 -2:14:56
Kurthasanlı 1 3 38N20 32E11 -2:08:44
Kurucaşile 1 3 41N50 32E43 -2:10:52
Kuruçay 1 3 39N39 38E29 -2:33:56
Kuşadası 1 3 37N51 27E15 -1:49:00
Kütahya 1 3 39N25 29E59 -1:59:56
Kuyucak 1 3 37N51 38E21 -2:33:24
Kuyucak 1 3 37N55 28E28 -1:53:52
Kuztekke 1 3 41N48 33E16 -2:13:04
Kuzucubelen 1 3 36N51 34E27 -2:17:48
Lâdik 1 3 40N55 35E55 -2:23:40
Lâlapaşa 2 2 41N50 26E44 -1:46:56
Lâleli 1 3 41N03 37E37 -2:30:28
Lâpseki 1 3 40N20 26E41 -1:46:44
Levent 1 3 38N27 37E52 -2:31:28
Leyne 1 3 37N22 28E02 -1:52:08
Lice 1 3 38N28 40E39 -2:42:36
Lüleburgaz 2 2 41N24 27E21 -1:49:24
Maan 1 3 36N51 38E50 -2:35:20
Macar 1 3 37N06 30E56 -2:03:44
Macun 1 3 36N58 30E50 -2:03:20
Maden 1 3 38N23 39E40 -2:38:40
Madenhanları 1 3 40N11 40E25 -2:41:40
Mağara 1 3 36N43 33E52 -2:15:28
Mahmudiye 1 3 39N30 31E00 -2:04:00
Mahmutbey 2 1 41N03 28E49 -1:55:16
Mahmutşevketpaşa 1
3 41N09 29E11 -1:56:44
Malabadi 1 3 38N09 41E12 -2:44:48
Malatya 1 3 38N21 38E19 -2:33:16
Malazgirt 1 3 39N09 42E31 -2:50:04
Malkara 2 2 40N53 26E54 -1:47:36
Maltepe 1 3 40N02 27E58 -1:51:52
Maltepe 1 3 40N55 29E08 -1:56:32
Mamure 1 3 40N08 35E18 -2:21:12
Manastırbükü 1 3 40N48 38E56 -2:35:44
Manavgat 1 3 36N47 31E26 -2:05:44
Manisa 1 3 38N36 27E26 -1:49:44
Maraş 1 3 37N36 36E55 -2:27:40
Mardin 1 3 37N18 40E44 -2:42:56

Mareşalçakmak 1 3 39N22 39E13 -2:36:52
Marmara Ereğlisi 2
2 40N58 27E57 -1:51:48
Marmaris 1 3 36N51 28E16 -1:53:04
Maserti 1 3 37N24 40E58 -2:43:52
Mecidiye 2 2 40N38 26E32 -1:46:08
Mecidiye 1 3 38N53 27E42 -1:50:48
Meçitözü 1 3 40N31 35E19 -2:21:16
Mecrihan 1 3 37N08 39E03 -2:36:12
Mehmetkân 1 3 38N26 41E17 -2:45:08
Melefan 1 3 38N11 41E34 -2:46:16
Menemen 1 3 38N36 27E04 -1:48:16
Mengen 1 3 40N59 31E37 -2:06:28
Menteşpiri 1 3 41N41 32E39 -2:10:36
Meram 1 3 37N50 32E27 -2:09:48
Mercümüt 1 3 38N25 39E04 -2:36:16
Merdinik 1 3 40N48 42E36 -2:50:24
Mersin 1 3 36N48 34E38 -2:18:32
Merzifon 1 3 40N53 35E29 -2:21:56
Meşkinan 1 3 37N18 40E22 -2:41:28
Mesudiye 1 3 40N28 37E46 -2:31:04
Meydan 1 3 38N21 41E47 -2:47:08
Meydancik 1 3 41N25 42E14 -2:48:56
Mezraa 1 3 41N12 35E08 -2:20:32
Midyat 1 3 37N25 41E23 -2:45:32
Mihalıççık 1 3 39N52 31E30 -2:06:00
Mihmandar 1 3 36N52 35E18 -2:21:12
Milâs 1 3 37N19 27E47 -1:51:08
Mirtağ 1 3 38N23 41E56 -2:47:44
Mirvan 1 3 38N33 39E48 -2:39:12
Misk 1 3 38N48 42E13 -2:48:52
Misli 1 3 38N10 34E52 -2:19:28
Mizar 1 3 37N26 39E26 -2:37:44
Mollahasan 1 3 39N22 42E37 -2:50:28
Mollakendi 1 3 38N36 39E20 -2:37:20
Mordoğan 1 3 38N30 26E37 -1:46:28
Mucur 1 3 39N04 34E23 -2:17:32
Mudanya 1 3 40N22 28E52 -1:55:28
Mudurnu 1 3 40N28 31E13 -2:04:52
Muğla 1 3 37N12 28E22 -1:53:28
Mumcular 1 3 37N05 27E40 -1:50:40
Muncusun 1 3 38N54 35E38 -2:22:32
Muradiye 1 3 38N59 43E46 -2:55:04
Muradiye 1 3 38N39 27E21 -1:49:24
Muratlı 2 2 41N10 27E30 -1:50:00
Mürefte 2 2 40N40 27E14 -1:48:56
Murgul 1 3 41N17 41E46 -2:47:04
Mürsel 1 3 39N11 37E59 -2:31:56
Mürşitpınar 1 3 36N54 38E19 -2:33:16
Muş 1 3 38N44 41E30 -2:46:00
Musabeyli 1 3 39N51 34E37 -2:18:28
Musazade 1 3 41N22 41E16 -2:45:04
Müsgebi 1 3 37N02 27E21 -1:49:24
Mustafakemalpaşa 1
3 40N02 28E24 -1:53:36
Musun 1 3 39N42 43E49 -2:55:16
Mut 1 3 36N39 33E27 -2:13:48
Mutmur 1 3 38N51 38E31 -2:34:04
Naipli 1 3 39N48 27E13 -1:48:52
Naipli 1 3 40N19 38E07 -2:32:28
Nallıhan 1 3 40N11 31E21 -2:05:24
Namrun 1 3 37N09 34E36 -2:18:24
Narince 1 3 37N52 38E46 -2:35:04
Narlı 1 3 37N27 37E09 -2:28:36
Narman 1 3 40N21 41E52 -2:47:28
Navşar 1 3 37N18 44E35 -2:58:20
Nazilli 1 3 37N55 28E21 -1:53:24
Nazımiye 1 3 39N11 39E50 -2:39:20
Nevşehir 1 3 38N38 34E43 -2:18:52
Niğde 1 3 37N59 34E42 -2:18:48
Niksar 1 3 40N36 36E58 -2:27:52
Nizip 1 3 37N01 37E46 -2:31:04
Nurettin 1 3 39N14 42E25 -2:49:40
Nurhak 1 3 37N58 37E25 -2:29:40
Nusaybin 1 3 37N03 41E13 -2:44:52
Obruk 1 3 38N10 33E12 -2:12:48
Odayeri 2 1 41N14 28E51 -1:55:24
Ödemiş 1 3 38N13 27E59 -1:51:56
Of 1 3 40N57 40E18 -2:41:12
Oğnut 1 3 39N08 40E53 -2:43:32
Oğuz 1 3 39N32 38E51 -2:35:24
Oğuzeli 1 3 36N59 37E30 -2:30:00
Okam 1 3 40N53 42E36 -2:50:24
Oltu 1 3 40N33 41E59 -2:47:56
Olur 1 3 40N50 42E08 -2:48:32
Ömerin 1 3 37N18 42E04 -2:48:16
Ömerköy 1 3 39N48 28E03 -1:52:12
Ömerli 1 3 41N05 29E19 -1:57:16
Ordu 1 3 35N56 36E01 -2:24:04
Ordu 1 3 41N00 37E53 -2:31:32
Örencik 1 3 39N16 29E33 -1:58:12
Orhangazi 1 3 40N30 29E18 -1:57:12
Orhanlar 1 3 39N54 27E37 -1:50:28
Örkenez 1 3 38N12 31E17 -2:05:08
Ormanlı 1 3 41N10 31E39 -2:06:36
Orta 1 3 40N38 33E06 -2:12:24
Ortaca 1 3 36N49 28E47 -1:55:08
Ortaklar 1 3 37N53 27E30 -1:50:00
Ortaköy 1 3 40N17 35E16 -2:21:04
Ortaköy 1 3 38N44 34E03 -2:16:12
Ortaköy 1 3 38N00 34E23 -2:17:32
Ortaköy 1 3 40N27 38E02 -2:32:08
Osmancık 1 3 40N59 34E49 -2:19:16
Osmaneli 1 3 40N22 30E01 -2:00:04
Osmaniye 1 3 37N05 36E14 -2:24:56
Osmanlı 1 3 41N52 34E37 -2:18:28
Osmanpaşa 1 3 39N38 34E58 -2:19:52
Ovacık 1 3 41N05 32E55 -2:11:40
Pah 1 3 39N08 30E10 -2:00:40
Pah 1 3 39N08 39E40 -2:38:40
Palamut 1 3 38N59 27E41 -1:50:44
Palu 1 3 38N42 39E57 -2:39:48
Pamukova 1 3 40N31 30E09 -2:00:36
Panlı 1 3 38N52 33E56 -2:15:44
Parona 1 3 37N31 41E58 -2:47:52

Paşavenk 1 3 38N53 39E29 -2:37:56
Pasinler (Hasankale) 1
3 39N59 41E41 -2:46:44
Pasur 1 3 38N30 41E02 -2:44:08
Patnos 1 3 39N14 42E52 -2:51:28
Payamlı 1 3 37N01 38E35 -2:34:20
Payas 1 3 36N47 36E10 -2:24:40
Pazar 1 3 41N11 40E53 -2:43:32
Pazar 1 3 40N17 36E18 -2:25:12
Pazarcık 1 3 40N00 29E54 -1:59:36
Pazarcık 1 3 37N31 37E19 -2:29:16
Pazarköy 1 3 40N55 32E11 -2:08:44
Pazarköy 1 3 39N51 27E24 -1:49:36
Pazarviran 1 3 38N41 36E11 -2:24:44
Pazaryeri 1 3 38N05 28E14 -1:52:56
Pazaryeri 1 3 41N57 34E01 -2:16:04
Peçenek 1 3 40N25 32E19 -2:09:16
Pehlivanköy 2 2 41N21 26E55 -1:47:40
Pendik 1 3 40N53 29E13 -1:56:52
Perşembe 1 3 41N04 37E46 -2:31:04
Pertek 1 3 38N50 39E22 -2:37:28
Petnahor 2 1 41N11 28E53 -1:55:32
Pınar 1 3 37N02 27E57 -1:51:48
Pınarbaşı 1 3 41N36 33E07 -2:12:28
Pınarbaşı 1 3 38N44 36E24 -2:25:36
Pınarhisar 2 2 41N37 27E30 -1:50:00
Pirahmet 1 3 38N11 39E51 -2:39:24
Piran 1 3 38N22 40E04 -2:40:16
Pirinççiköy 2 1 41N10 28E50 -1:55:20
Pirlerkondu 1 3 36N55 32E31 -2:10:04
Piyadin 1 3 37N01 29E58 -1:59:52
Polatlı 1 3 39N36 32E09 -2:08:36
Polenezköy 1 3 41N07 29E12 -1:56:48
Polos 2 2 41N50 27E04 -1:48:16
Poyraz 1 3 41N12 29E07 -1:56:28
Pozantı 1 3 37N25 34E52 -2:19:28
Pulur 1 3 40N10 39E53 -2:39:32
Ravlı 1 3 40N08 33E06 -2:12:24
Refahiye 1 3 39N54 38E46 -2:35:04
Reis 1 3 38N16 31E35 -2:06:20
Reşadiye 1 3 40N24 37E21 -2:29:24
Reşadiye 1 3 41N05 29E15 -1:57:00
Reyhanlı 1 3 36N18 36E32 -2:26:08
Rivaköy 1 3 41N13 29E12 -1:56:48
Rize 1 3 41N02 40E31 -2:42:04
Rumelifeneri 2 1 41N14 29E06 -1:56:24
Rumkiğ 1 3 39N00 39E18 -2:37:12
Şabanözü 1 3 40N29 33E18 -2:13:12
Sabuncu 1 3 39N33 30E12 -2:00:48
Safraköy 2 1 41N00 28E47 -1:55:08
Safranbolu 1 3 41N15 32E45 -2:11:00
Şahin 2 2 41N01 26E50 -1:47:20
Saimbeyli 1 3 38N00 36E06 -2:24:24
Salanda 1 3 38N50 34E32 -2:18:08
Salavat 1 3 41N53 34E55 -2:19:40
Salihli 1 3 38N29 28E09 -1:52:36
Salıpazarı 1 3 40N54 31E58 -2:07:52
Salmanlı 1 3 40N55 30E18 -2:01:12
Samandağı 1 3 36N07 35E56 -2:23:44
Samandıra 1 3 40N59 29E13 -1:56:52
Samatlar 1 3 41N14 33E07 -2:12:28
Sambayat 1 3 37N41 38E03 -2:32:12
Şamlı 1 3 39N48 27E51 -1:51:24
Şamrah 1 3 37N30 40E30 -2:42:00
Samsat 1 3 37N30 38E31 -2:34:04
Samsun 1 3 41N17 36E20 -2:25:20
Samutlu 1 3 39N44 32E22 -2:09:28
Sandıklı 1 3 38N28 30E17 -2:01:08
Sapanca 1 3 40N41 30E16 -2:01:04
Şaphane 1 3 39N01 29E14 -1:56:56
Saray 2 2 41N26 27E55 -1:51:40
Sarayakpınar 2 2 41N46 26E29 -1:45:56
Saraycık 1 3 40N57 35E08 -2:20:32
Sarayköy 1 3 37N55 28E58 -1:55:52
Sarayönü 1 3 38N17 32E25 -2:09:40
Sarıgazi 1 3 41N01 29E12 -1:56:48
Sarıgöl 1 3 38N14 28E43 -1:54:52
Sarıkamış 1 3 40N20 42E35 -2:50:20
Sarıkaya 1 3 38N47 32E15 -2:09:00
Sarıköy 1 3 40N12 27E36 -1:50:24
Sarıoğlan 1 3 39N05 35E59 -2:23:56
Sarıoğlan 1 3 37N12 32E33 -2:10:12
Sarısu 1 3 39N01 42E55 -2:51:40
Sarıyer 2 1 41N10 29E03 -1:56:12
Şarkîkaraağaç 1 3 38N04 31E23 -2:05:32
Şarkışla 1 3 39N21 36E26 -2:25:44
Şarköy 2 2 40N37 27E06 -1:48:24
Şaruhanlı 1 3 38N44 27E34 -1:50:16
Satırlar 1 3 37N30 29E46 -1:59:04
Savaştepe 1 3 39N22 27E40 -1:50:40
Savcılıbüyükoba 1
3 39N14 33E41 -2:14:44
Savur 1 3 37N33 40E53 -2:43:32
Scutari → Üsküdar 1
3 41N01 29E01 -1:56:04
Seben 1 3 40N24 31E34 -2:06:16
Şebinkarahisar 1
3 40N18 38E26 -2:33:44
Şefaatli 1 3 39N31 34E46 -2:19:04
Seferihisar 1 3 38N11 26E51 -1:47:24
Seki 1 3 36N24 29E13 -1:56:52
Selçuk 1 3 37N56 27E22 -1:49:28
Selendi 1 3 38N46 27E53 -1:51:32
Selepür 1 3 39N36 39E54 -2:39:36
Selimiye 1 3 37N24 27E40 -1:50:40
Senirkent 1 3 38N07 30E33 -2:02:12
Şenköy 1 3 36N05 36E05 -2:24:20
Serdar 1 3 37N08 36E27 -2:25:48
Şereflikoçhisar 1
3 38N56 33E33 -2:14:12
Sergen 2 2 41N42 27E42 -1:50:48
Sevir 1 3 39N12 38E13 -2:32:52
Şevketiye 1 3 40N05 27E51 -1:51:24
Seydim 1 3 40N33 34E45 -2:19:00
Seydişehir 1 3 37N25 31E51 -2:07:24

TURKEY TURQUÍA TURQUIE TÜRKEI TÜRKIYE

Seyitgazi 1	3	39N27	30E43	-2:02:52
Sihiyan 1	3	37N53	41E46	-2:47:04
Şıhlar 1	3	40N43	38E21	-2:33:24
Şıhraş 1	3	37N28	42E13	-2:48:52
Siirt 1	3	37N56	41E57	-2:47:48
Şile 1	3	41N11	29E36	-1:58:24
Silifke 1	3	36N22	33E56	-2:15:44
Silivri 2	2	41N04	28E15	-1:53:00
Sille 1	3	37N56	32E26	-2:09:44
Silvan (Miyafarkin) 1	3	38N08	41E01	-2:44:04
Simav 1	3	39N05	28E59	-1:55:56
Şimiz 1	3	37N49	41E22	-2:45:28
Sinan 1	3	37N52	41E00	-2:44:00
Sinan 1	3	38N06	38E45	-2:35:00
Sinanpaşa 1	3	38N45	30E15	-2:01:00
Sincan 1	3	39N28	37E54	-2:31:36
Sındıran 1	3	39N17	32E41	-2:10:44
Sındırgı 1	3	39N14	28E10	-1:52:40
Sinekçi 1	3	40N16	27E24	-1:49:36
Sinekli 2	2	41N14	28E12	-1:52:48
Sinop 1	3	42N01	35E09	-2:20:36
Şipek 1	3	40N14	41E29	-2:45:56
Sirkeli 1	3	40N09	32E52	-2:11:28
Sivas 1	3	39N45	37E02	-2:28:08
Sivaslı 1	3	38N30	29E42	-1:58:48
Siverek 1	3	37N45	39E19	-2:37:16
Sivrice 1	3	38N27	39E19	-2:37:16
Sivrihisar 1	3	39N27	31E34	-2:06:16
Smyrna → İzmir 1	3	38N25	27E09	-1:48:36
Soğanlı 1	3	40N55	29E12	-1:56:48
Söğüt 1	3	40N00	30E11	-2:00:44
Söğütalan 1	3	40N03	28E34	-1:54:16
Söğütlü 1	3	40N54	30E29	-2:01:56
Söke 1	3	37N45	27E24	-1:49:36
Soma 1	3	39N10	27E36	-1:50:24
Sorgun 1	3	39N49	35E11	-2:20:44
Şuhut 1	3	38N32	30E33	-2:02:12
Sulakyurt 1	3	40N10	33E44	-2:14:56
Süleymanlı 1	3	37N54	36E50	-2:27:20
Sultançiftlikköy 1	3	41N02	29E11	-1:56:44
Sultandağı 1	3	38N32	31E14	-2:04:56
Sultanhanı 1	3	38N15	33E33	-2:14:12
Sultanhisar 1	3	37N53	28E10	-1:52:40
Sülüklü 1	3	39N05	30E58	-2:03:52
Suluova (Suluca) 1	3	40N47	35E42	-2:22:48
Sulusaray 1	3	40N00	36E06	-2:24:24
Sungurlu 1	3	40N10	34E23	-2:17:32
Sürgü 1	3	38N01	37E59	-2:31:56
Sürgücü 1	3	37N35	40E44	-2:42:56
Sürüç 1	3	36N58	38E24	-2:33:36
Suşehri 1	3	40N11	38E06	-2:32:24
Susurluk 1	3	39N54	28E10	-1:52:40
Susuzmüsellim 2	2	41N06	27E03	-1:48:12
Sütçüler 1	3	37N30	30E59	-2:03:56
Suvarlı 1	3	37N32	37E38	-2:30:32
Taflan 1	3	41N25	36E09	-2:24:36
Tahir 1	3	38N47	38E17	-2:33:08
Tahtaköprü 1	3	39N57	29E39	-1:58:36
Tanır 1	3	38N26	36E55	-2:27:40
Tanyeri 1	3	39N36	39E54	-2:39:36
Tap 1	3	38N29	41E49	-2:47:16
Taraklı 1	3	40N24	30E29	-2:01:56
Tarsus 1	3	36N55	34E53	-2:19:32
Taşağıl 2	2	41N31	27E07	-1:48:28
Taşağıl 1	3	36N55	31E14	-2:04:56
Taşçı 1	3	38N13	35E48	-2:23:12
Taşkesen 1	3	39N43	41E29	-2:45:56
Taşköprü 1	3	41N30	34E14	-2:16:56
Taşova 1	3	40N46	36E20	-2:25:20
Taşrumi 1	3	38N48	44E04	-2:56:16
Tasucu 1	3	36N19	33E53	-2:15:32
Tatarlar 2	2	41N46	26E55	-1:47:40
Tatvan 1	3	38N30	42E16	-2:49:04
Tavas 1	3	37N34	29E04	-1:56:16
Tavsalayihüseyan 1	3	38N38	40E32	-2:42:08
Tavşanlı 1	3	39N33	29E30	-1:58:00
Tavsi 1	3	37N56	38E39	-2:34:36
Tefen 1	3	41N19	32E08	-2:08:32
Tefenni 1	3	37N18	29E47	-1:59:08
Teke 1	3	41N04	29E39	-1:58:36
Tekirdağ 2	2	40N59	27E31	-1:50:04
Tekke 1	3	40N43	36E12	-2:24:48
Tekkiraz 1	3	40N59	37E08	-2:28:32
Tekman 1	3	39N38	41E31	-2:46:04
Tepe 1	3	37N48	40E47	-2:43:08
Tercan 1	3	39N47	40E24	-2:41:36
Terme 1	3	41N12	36E59	-2:27:56
Teştik 1	3	40N08	38E45	-2:35:00
Til 1	3	38N44	41E49	-2:47:16
Timar 1	3	38N49	43E27	-2:53:48
Tire 1	3	38N04	27E45	-1:51:00
Tirebolu 1	3	41N00	38E48	-2:35:12
Tirilye 1	3	40N23	28E47	-1:55:08
Tokaris 1	3	37N45	38E50	-2:35:20
Tokat 1	3	40N19	36E34	-2:26:16
Toklar 1	3	38N26	36E01	-2:24:04
Tomarza 1	3	38N27	35E49	-2:23:16
Tomek 1	3	38N02	32E41	-2:10:44
Tömük 1	3	36N41	34E22	-2:17:28
Tonya 1	3	40N53	39E16	-2:37:04
Toprakkale 1	3	37N06	36E07	-2:24:28
Torbalı 1	3	38N10	27E21	-1:49:24
Tortum 1	3	40N19	41E35	-2:46:20
Tosköy 1	3	41N27	35E54	-2:23:36
Tosya 1	3	41N01	34E02	-2:16:08
Trabzon 1	3	41N00	39E43	-2:38:52
Trebizond → Trabzon 1	3	41N00	39E43	-2:38:52
Tug 1	3	38N27	42E16	-2:49:04
Tuht 1	3	40N46	33E47	-2:15:08
Tunçbilek 1	3	39N37	29E29	-1:57:56
Tunceli 1	3	39N07	39E32	-2:38:08
Turgut 1	3	38N37	31E49	-2:07:16
Turgutlu 1	3	38N30	27E43	-1:50:52
Turhal 1	3	40N24	36E06	-2:24:24
Turkoğlu 1	3	37N31	36E49	-2:27:16
Türüşmek 1	3	39N03	39E32	-2:38:08
Tut 1	3	37N48	37E55	-2:31:40
Tutak 1	3	39N32	42E46	-2:51:04
Tuzla 1	3	36N42	35E05	-2:20:20
Tuzluca 1	3	40N03	43E40	-2:54:40
Tuzlukçu 1	3	38N28	31E38	-2:06:32
Üçköşe 1	3	40N13	41E00	-2:44:00
Ula 1	3	37N05	28E26	-1:53:44
Ulaş 1	3	39N27	37E03	-2:28:12
Ulubey 1	3	38N25	29E18	-1:57:12
Uluborlu 1	3	38N05	30E28	-2:01:52
Ulukışla 1	3	37N33	34E30	-2:18:00
Ulus 1	3	41N35	32E39	-2:10:36
Umraniye 1	3	38N37	30E48	-2:03:12
Umraniye 1	3	41N01	29E05	-1:56:20
Umurlu 1	3	37N50	27E58	-1:51:52
Ünye 1	3	41N08	37E17	-2:29:08
Urfa 1	3	37N08	38E46	-2:35:04
Ürgüp 1	3	38N38	34E56	-2:19:44
Urla 1	3	38N18	26E46	-1:47:04
Ürmeli 1	3	40N55	37E32	-2:30:08
Uşak 1	3	38N41	29E25	-1:57:40
Üsküdar 1	3	41N01	29E01	-1:56:04
Uskumuruköy 2	1	41N12	29E01	-1:56:04
Üstükran 1	3	39N16	41E17	-2:45:08
Üzümlü 1	3	37N32	31E37	-2:06:28
Üzümlü 1	3	36N44	29E14	-1:56:56
Uzunköprü 2	2	41N16	26E41	-1:46:44
Uzunkuyu 1	3	38N17	26E33	-1:46:12
Valir 1	3	38N48	40E41	-2:42:44
Van 1	3	38N28	43E20	-2:53:20
Varto 1	3	39N10	41E28	-2:45:52
Vaskovan 1	3	38N57	38E57	-2:35:48
Vezirköprü 1	3	41N09	35E28	-2:21:52
Viranşehir 1	3	39N00	36E39	-2:26:36
Viranşehir 1	3	37N13	39E45	-2:39:00
Vize 2	2	41N34	27E45	-1:51:00
Yağcılar 1	3	39N25	28E23	-1:53:32
Yahyalı 1	3	38N07	35E22	-2:21:28
Yaka 1	3	41N15	34E01	-2:16:04
Yakacık 1	3	40N55	29E13	-1:56:52
Yakapınar 1	3	37N00	35E36	-2:22:24
Yalakdereköy 1	3	40N36	29E33	-1:58:12
Yalova 1	3	40N39	29E15	-1:57:00
Yalvaç 1	3	38N17	31E11	-2:04:44
Yarbasan 1	3	38N59	28E49	-1:55:16
Yarma 1	3	37N49	32E54	-2:11:36
Yatağan 1	3	37N20	28E09	-1:52:36
Yavi 1	3	39N48	36E13	-2:24:52
Yaylak 1	3	37N23	38E20	-2:33:20
Yazıhan 1	3	38N36	38E11	-2:32:44
Yeniçağa 1	3	40N46	32E02	-2:08:08
Yenice 1	3	39N45	28E55	-1:55:40
Yenice 1	3	39N55	27E18	-1:49:12
Yenice 1	3	36N59	35E03	-2:20:12
Yenicekale 1	3	37N37	36E37	-2:26:28
Yeniceoba 1	3	38N53	32E48	-2:11:12
Yenifoça 1	3	38N44	26E51	-1:47:24
Yeniköy 1	3	37N04	30E36	-2:02:24
Yeniköy 1	3	39N46	28E00	-1:52:00
Yenimehmetli 1	3	39N26	32E10	-2:08:40
Yenipazar 1	3	37N48	28E12	-1:52:48
Yenipazar 1	3	40N11	30E31	-2:02:04
Yenişehir 1	3	40N16	29E39	-1:58:36
Yerkesik 1	3	37N07	28E17	-1:53:08
Yerköy 1	3	39N38	34E29	-2:17:56
Yeşilhisar 1	3	38N21	35E06	-2:20:24
Yeşilkent 1	3	36N59	36E10	-2:24:40
Yeşilköy 2	1	40N57	28E49	-1:55:16
Yeşilyurt 1	3	38N18	38E15	-2:33:00
Yiğitaliler 1	3	39N52	26E37	-1:46:28
Yıldızeli 1	3	39N52	36E38	-2:26:32
Yozgat 1	3	39N50	34E48	-2:19:12
Yukarıbey 1	3	39N15	27E06	-1:48:24
Yukarı Ezbider 1	3	40N06	38E21	-2:33:24
Yumurtalık 1	3	36N49	35E45	-2:23:00
Yunak 1	3	38N49	31E45	-2:07:00
Yürük 2	2	40N56	27E04	-1:48:16
Zanapa 1	3	37N25	34E13	-2:16:52
Zara 1	3	39N55	37E46	-2:31:04
Zekeriyaköy 2	1	41N11	29E01	-1:56:04
Zeligar 1	3	38N04	41E49	-2:47:16
Zerenik 1	3	39N20	39E05	-2:36:20
Zevker 1	3	40N00	38E51	-2:35:24
Zeytindağ 1	3	38N58	27E04	-1:48:16
Zile 1	3	40N18	35E54	-2:23:36
Zir 1	3	39N59	33E21	-2:13:24
Zivarık 1	3	38N19	32E53	-2:11:32
Zivint 1	3	37N13	30E18	-2:01:12
Zok 1	3	38N02	41E33	-2:46:12
Zonguldak 1	3	41N27	31E49	-2:07:16

TURKS AND CAICOS ÎLES TURQUES ET CAÏQUES ISLAS TURCAS Y CAICOS

Time Table		
Before 1/Jan/1890 LMT		
Begin Standard	76w48	
1/Jan/1890	0:00	5:07
Begin Standard	75w00	
1/Feb/1912	0:00	5:00
29/Apr/1979	2:00	4:00
28/Oct/1979	2:00	5:00
27/Apr/1980	2:00	4:00
26/Oct/1980	2:00	5:00
26/Apr/1981	2:00	4:00
25/Oct/1981	2:00	5:00
25/Apr/1982	2:00	4:00
31/Oct/1982	2:00	5:00
24/Apr/1983	2:00	4:00
30/Oct/1983	2:00	5:00
29/Apr/1984	2:00	4:00
28/Oct/1984	2:00	5:00
28/Apr/1985	2:00	4:00
27/Oct/1985	2:00	5:00
27/Apr/1986	2:00	4:00
26/Oct/1986	2:00	5:00
5/Apr/1987	2:00	4:00
25/Oct/1987	2:00	5:00
3/Apr/1988	2:00	4:00
30/Oct/1988	2:00	5:00
2/Apr/1989	2:00	4:00
29/Oct/1989	2:00	5:00
1/Apr/1990	2:00	4:00
28/Oct/1990	2:00	5:00
7/Apr/1991	2:00	4:00
27/Oct/1991	2:00	5:00
5/Apr/1992	2:00	4:00
25/Oct/1992	2:00	5:00
4/Apr/1993	2:00	4:00
31/Oct/1993	2:00	5:00
3/Apr/1994	2:00	4:00
30/Oct/1994	2:00	5:00
2/Apr/1995	2:00	4:00
29/Oct/1995	2:00	5:00
7/Apr/1996	2:00	4:00
27/Oct/1996	2:00	5:00
6/Apr/1997	2:00	4:00
26/Oct/1997	2:00	5:00
5/Apr/1998	2:00	4:00
25/Oct/1998	2:00	5:00
4/Apr/1999	2:00	4:00
31/Oct/1999	2:00	5:00
2/Apr/2000	2:00	4:00
29/Oct/2000	2:00	5:00

Grand Turk	21N28	71w08	4:44:32
Kew	21N54	72w02	4:48:08
Middle Caicos Island	21N47	71w43	4:46:52
North Caicos Island	21N56	71w59	4:47:56
Providenciales Island	21N47	72w17	4:49:08
Turks Islands	21N24	71w07	4:44:28
West Caicos Island	21N39	72w28	4:49:52

ELLICE ISLANDS — LAGOON ISLANDS — TUVALU ISLANDS

Time Table
Before 1/Jan/1901 LMT
Begin Standard 180E00
1/Jan/1901 0:00 -12:00

Place	Lat	Long	Offset
Funafuti Island	8S31	179E13	-11:56:52
Nanomea Island	5S39	176E08	-11:44:32
Nanumanga Island	6S18	176E20	-11:45:20
Niutao Island	6S06	177E17	-11:49:08
Nui Island	7S15	177E10	-11:48:40
Nukufetau Island	8S00	178E22	-11:53:28
Nukulailai Island	9S23	179E52	-11:59:28
Nurakita Island	10S45	179E30	-11:58:00
Vaitupu Island	7S28	178E41	-11:54:44

UGANDA — OUGANDA — UGANDA

Time Table
Before 1/Jul/1928 LMT
Begin Standard 45E00
1/Jul/1928 0:00 -3:00
Begin Standard 37E30
1/Jan/1930 0:00 -2:30
Begin Standard 41E15
1/Jan/1948 0:00 -2:45
Begin Standard 45E00
1/Jan/1957 0:00 -3:00

Place	Lat	Long	Offset
Aber	2N12	32E21	-2:09:24
Adilang	2N44	33E29	-2:13:56
Adjumani	3N22	31E47	-2:07:08
Aduku	2N01	32E43	-2:10:52
Aloi	2N17	33E10	-2:12:40
Amudat	1N57	34E57	-2:19:48
Amuria	2N01	33E38	-2:14:32
Anyeke	2N24	32E31	-2:10:04
Arua	3N01	30E55	-2:03:40
Atiak	3N15	32E07	-2:08:28
Biso	1N46	31E25	-2:05:40
Bombo	0N35	32E32	-2:10:08
Buganga	0S03	31E59	-2:07:56
Bugiri	0N34	33E45	-2:15:00
Bukuya	0N41	31E50	-2:07:20
Bushenyi	0S32	30E11	-2:00:44
Busia	0N28	34E05	-2:16:20
Butemba	1N09	31E36	-2:06:24
Butiaba	1N49	31E19	-2:05:16
Entebbe	0N04	32E28	-2:09:52
Fort Portal	0N40	30E17	-2:01:08
Gulu	2N47	32E18	-2:09:12
Hoima	1N26	31E21	-2:05:24
Ibanda	0S08	30E29	-2:01:56
Iganga	0N37	33E29	-2:13:56
Jinja	0N26	33E12	-2:12:48
Kaabong	3N31	34E08	-2:16:32
Kabale	1S15	29E59	-1:59:56
Kagulu	1N15	33E18	-2:13:12
Kaliro	0N54	33E30	-2:14:00
Kampala	0N19	32E25	-2:09:40
Kamuli	0N57	33E07	-2:12:28
Kapchorwa	1N24	34E27	-2:17:48
Kasese	0N10	30E05	-2:00:20
Katakwi	1N55	33E57	-2:15:48
Kibanga Port	0N11	32E52	-2:11:28
Kiboga	1N02	30E58	-2:03:52
Kikagati	1S02	30E40	-2:02:40
Kilembe	0N12	30E00	-2:00:00
Kinoni	0S39	30E27	-2:01:48
Kiryandongo	1N53	32E03	-2:08:12
Kisizi	1S00	29E56	-1:59:44
Kisoro	1S17	29E41	-1:58:44
Kitgum	3N18	32E53	-2:11:32
Koboko	3N25	30E58	-2:03:52
Kotido	3N00	34E06	-2:16:24
Kumi	1N29	33E56	-2:15:44
Kyegegwa	0N29	31E03	-2:04:12
Kyenjojo	0N37	30E38	-2:02:32
Kyotera	0S33	31E19	-2:05:16
Lira	2N15	32E54	-2:11:36
Loyoro	3N21	34E16	-2:17:04
Lyantonde	0S24	31E09	-2:04:36
Madi Opei	3N37	33E05	-2:12:20
Magoro	1N44	34E06	-2:16:24
Majanji	0N15	33E59	-2:15:56
Masaka	0S20	31E44	-2:06:56
Masindi	1N41	31E43	-2:06:52
Masindi Port	1N42	32E05	-2:08:20
Mbale	1N05	34E10	-2:16:40
Mbarara	0S37	30E39	-2:02:36
Mbirizi	0S23	31E27	-2:05:48
Mityana	0N24	32E03	-2:08:12
Mjanji	0N15	33E59	-2:15:56
Moroto	2N32	34E39	-2:18:36
Moyo	3N39	31E43	-2:06:52
Mpigi	0N13	32E42	-2:10:48
Mubende	0N35	31E23	-2:05:32
Mwerasandu	0S59	30E23	-2:01:32
Nabiswera	1N28	32E16	-2:09:04
Nakasongola	1N19	32E28	-2:09:52
Namasagali	1N01	32E57	-2:11:48
Ngora	1N27	33E46	-2:15:04
Ntusi	0N03	31E13	-2:04:52
Okollo	2N40	31E08	-2:04:32
Pabo	3N00	32E09	-2:08:36
Padibe	3N28	32E50	-2:11:20
Pakwach	2N28	31E30	-2:06:00
Palabek	3N26	32E34	-2:10:16
Pallisa	1N10	33E42	-2:14:48
Patonga	2N46	33E18	-2:13:12
Port Bell	0N17	32E39	-2:10:36
Rhino Camp	2N58	31E24	-2:05:36
Rubona	0N33	30E10	-2:00:40
Rukungiri	0S48	29E55	-1:59:40
Rwashamaire	0S49	30E08	-2:00:32
Sanje	0S46	31E30	-2:06:00
Sembabule	0S05	31E27	-2:05:48
Soroti	1N43	33E37	-2:14:28
Tororo	0N42	34E11	-2:16:44
Ukuti	3N39	33E32	-2:14:08
Zulia	4N10	34E01	-2:16:04

ITTIHĀD AL-IMĀRĀT AL-‘ARABĪYAH — UNITED ARAB EMIRATES

Time Table
Before 1/Jan/1920 LMT
Begin Standard 60E00
1/Jan/1920 0:00 -4:00

Place	Lat	Long	Offset
Abu Dhabi → Abū Ẓaby	24N28	54E22	-3:37:28
Abū Ẓaby	24N28	54E22	-3:37:28
Al-Buraymī	24N15	55E45	-3:43:00
Al-Fujayrah	25N06	56E21	-3:45:24
Ash-Shāriqah	25N22	55E23	-3:41:32
Ḍadnah	25N33	56E21	-3:45:24
Dibay → Dubayy	25N18	55E18	-3:41:12
Dubai → Dubayy	25N18	55E18	-3:41:12
Dubayy	25N18	55E18	-3:41:12
Ra's al-Khaymah	25N47	55E57	-3:43:48
‘Ujmān	25N25	55E27	-3:41:48
Umm al-Qaywayn	25N35	55E34	-3:42:16

ESTADOS UNIDOS — ÉTATS-UNIS — UNITED STATES OF AMERICA

No entries in this volume. See THE AMERICAN ATLAS, 5th Edition, ACS Publications.

URUGUAY

URUGUAY

Time Table # 1

Date	Time	Offset
Before 28/Jun/1898 LMT		
Begin Standard		56w11
28/Jun/1898	0:00	3:45
Begin Standard		52w30
1/May/1920	0:00	3:30
2/Oct/1923	0:00	3:00
1/Apr/1924	0:00	3:30
1/Oct/1924	0:00	3:00
1/Apr/1925	0:00	3:30
1/Oct/1925	0:00	3:00
1/Apr/1926	0:00	3:30
29/Oct/1933	0:00	3:00
1/Apr/1934	0:00	3:30
28/Oct/1934	0:00	3:00
1/Apr/1935	0:00	3:30
27/Oct/1935	0:00	3:00
30/Mar/1936	0:00	3:30
1/Nov/1936	0:00	3:00
28/Mar/1937	0:00	3:30
31/Oct/1937	0:00	3:00
27/Mar/1938	0:00	3:30
30/Oct/1938	0:00	3:00
26/Mar/1939	0:00	3:30
29/Oct/1939	0:00	3:00
31/Mar/1940	0:00	3:30
27/Oct/1940	0:00	3:00
30/Mar/1941	0:00	3:30
1/Aug/1941	0:00	3:00
1/Jan/1942	0:00	3:30
Begin Standard		45w00
14/Dec/1942	0:00	2:00
14/Mar/1943	0:00	3:00
24/May/1959	0:00	2:00
15/Nov/1959	0:00	3:00
17/Jan/1960	0:00	2:00
6/Mar/1960	0:00	3:00
4/Apr/1965	0:00	2:00
26/Sep/1965	0:00	3:00
1/Apr/1966	0:00	2:00
31/Oct/1966	0:00	3:00
1/Apr/1967	0:00	2:00
31/Oct/1967	0:00	3:00
27/May/1968	0:00	2:30
2/Dec/1968	0:00	3:00
27/May/1969	0:00	2:30
2/Dec/1969	0:00	3:00
27/May/1970	0:00	2:30
2/Dec/1970	0:00	3:00
24/Apr/1972	0:00	2:00
15/Aug/1972	0:00	3:00
10/Mar/1974	0:00	2:30
22/Dec/1974	0:00	2:00
1/Oct/1976	0:00	3:00
4/Dec/1977	0:00	2:00
1/Apr/1978	0:00	3:00
1/Oct/1979	0:00	2:00
1/May/1980	0:00	3:00
14/Dec/1987	0:00	2:00
14/Mar/1988	0:00	3:00
11/Dec/1988	0:00	2:00
12/Mar/1989	0:00	3:00
29/Oct/1989	0:00	2:00
4/Mar/1990	0:00	3:00

....

Time Table # 2

Date	Time	Offset
Before 28/Jun/1898 LMT		
Begin Standard		56w11
28/Jun/1898	0:00	3:45
Begin Standard		52w30
1/May/1920	0:00	3:30
29/Oct/1933	0:00	3:00
1/Apr/1934	0:00	3:30
28/Oct/1934	0:00	3:00
1/Apr/1935	0:00	3:30
27/Oct/1935	0:00	3:00
30/Mar/1936	0:00	3:30
1/Nov/1936	0:00	3:00
28/Mar/1937	0:00	3:30
31/Oct/1937	0:00	3:00
27/Mar/1938	0:00	3:30
30/Oct/1938	0:00	3:00
26/Mar/1939	0:00	3:30
29/Oct/1939	0:00	3:00
31/Mar/1940	0:00	3:30
27/Oct/1940	0:00	3:00
30/Mar/1941	0:00	3:30
1/Aug/1941	0:00	3:00
1/Jan/1942	0:00	3:30
Begin Standard		45w00
14/Dec/1942	0:00	2:00
14/Mar/1943	0:00	3:00
24/May/1959	0:00	2:00
15/Nov/1959	0:00	3:00
17/Jan/1960	0:00	2:00
6/Mar/1960	0:00	3:00
4/Apr/1965	0:00	2:00
26/Sep/1965	0:00	3:00
1/Apr/1966	0:00	2:00
31/Oct/1966	0:00	3:00
1/Apr/1967	0:00	2:00
31/Oct/1967	0:00	3:00
27/May/1968	0:00	2:30
2/Dec/1968	0:00	3:00
27/May/1969	0:00	2:30
2/Dec/1969	0:00	3:00
27/May/1970	0:00	2:30
2/Dec/1970	0:00	3:00
24/Apr/1972	0:00	2:00
15/Aug/1972	0:00	3:00
10/Mar/1974	0:00	2:30
22/Dec/1974	0:00	2:00
1/Oct/1976	0:00	3:00
4/Dec/1977	0:00	2:00
1/Apr/1978	0:00	3:00
1/Oct/1979	0:00	2:00
1/May/1980	0:00	3:00
14/Dec/1987	0:00	2:00
14/Mar/1988	0:00	3:00
11/Dec/1988	0:00	2:00
12/Mar/1989	0:00	3:00
29/Oct/1989	0:00	2:00
4/Mar/1990	0:00	3:00

Place	Table	Latitude	Longitude	Offset
Abayuba	1	34s51	56w14	3:44:56
Achar	2	32s25	56w10	3:44:40
Agraciada	2	33s48	58w15	3:53:00
Aguas Corrientes	2	34s31	56w24	3:45:36
Aiguá	2	34s12	54w45	3:39:00
Algorta	2	32s25	57w23	3:49:32
Ansina	2	31s54	55w28	3:41:52
Arapey	2	30s58	57w32	3:50:08
Arroyo Grande → Ismael Cortinas	2	33s58	57w06	3:48:24
Artigas	2	30s24	56w28	3:45:52
Artilleros	2	34s22	57w34	3:50:16
Atlántida	2	34s46	55w45	3:43:00
Baltasar Brum	2	30s44	57w19	3:49:16
Barker	2	34s16	57w27	3:49:48
Belén	2	30s47	57w47	3:51:08
Bella Unión	2	30s15	57w35	3:50:20
Bifurcación	2	34s19	56w48	3:47:12
Boca del Rosario	2	34s26	57w17	3:49:08
Cañada Nieto	2	33s43	58w05	3:52:20
Canelones	2	34s32	56w17	3:45:08
Capilla de Farruco	2	32s53	55w25	3:41:40
Capurro	2	34s25	56w28	3:45:52
Cardal	2	34s18	56w24	3:45:36
Cardona	2	33s53	57w23	3:49:32
Cardozo	2	32s38	56w21	3:45:24
Carlos Reyles	2	33s03	56w29	3:45:56
Carmelo	2	34s00	58w17	3:53:08
Carmen	2	33s15	56w01	3:44:04
Castillo	2	33s53	57w40	3:50:40
Castillos	2	34s12	53w50	3:35:20
Casupá	2	34s07	55w39	3:42:36
Cebollatí	2	33s16	53w47	3:35:08
Cerro Chato	2	33s06	55w08	3:40:32
Cerro Colorado	2	33s52	55w33	3:42:12
Cerro Vera	2	33s11	57w28	3:49:52
Chamizo	2	34s10	56w41	3:46:44
Chapicuy	2	31s39	57w54	3:51:36
Chuy	2	33s41	53w27	3:33:48
Colla	2	34s04	57w21	3:49:24
Colón	2	33s53	54w43	3:38:52
Colón	1	34s48	56w14	3:44:56
Colonia del Sacramento	2	34s28	57w51	3:51:24
Colonia Lavalleja	2	31s06	57w01	3:48:04
Colonia Nicolich	1	34s50	56w02	3:44:08
Colonia Valdense	2	34s20	57w14	3:48:56
Conchillas	2	34s15	58w04	3:52:16
Constitución	2	31s05	57w50	3:51:20
Costa de San José	2	33s51	56w53	3:47:32
Cuaró	2	30s37	56w54	3:47:36
Cufré	2	34s12	57w06	3:48:24
Curtina	2	32s09	56w07	3:44:28
Dieciocho de Julio	2	33s41	53w33	3:34:12
Dolores	2	33s33	58w13	3:52:52
Drabble → José Enrique Rodó	2	33s41	57w34	3:50:16
Durazno	2	33s22	56w31	3:46:04
Ecilda Paullier	2	34s22	57w04	3:48:16
El Cerro	2	34s00	58w15	3:53:00
Florencio Sánchez	2	33s53	57w24	3:49:36
Florida	2	34s06	56w13	3:44:52
Fomento	2	34s26	57w14	3:48:56
Fraile Muerto	2	32s31	54w32	3:38:08
Francia	2	32s33	56w37	3:46:28
Fray Bentos	2	33s08	58w18	3:53:12
Fray Marcos	2	34s11	55w44	3:42:56
Garzón	2	34s36	54w33	3:38:12
General Enrique Martínez	2	33s12	53w48	3:35:12
Goñi	2	33s31	56w24	3:45:36
González	2	34s14	56w52	3:47:28
Greco	2	32s48	57w03	3:48:12
Guichón	2	32s21	57w12	3:48:48
Isla Mala	2	34s12	56w21	3:45:24
Isla Patrulla	2	32s59	54w35	3:38:20
Ismael Cortinas (Arroyo Grande)	2	33s58	57w06	3:48:24
Ituzaingó	2	34s25	56w26	3:45:44
Joanicó	2	34s36	56w15	3:45:00
Joaquín Suárez	2	34s44	56w02	3:44:08
José Batlle y Ordóñez	2	33s28	55w07	3:40:28
José Enrique Rodó (Drabble)	2	33s41	57w34	3:50:16
José Pedro Varela	2	33s27	54w32	3:38:08
Juan L. Lacaze	2	34s26	57w27	3:49:48
La Cruz	2	33s56	56w15	3:45:00
La Mariscala	2	34s03	54w47	3:39:08
La Paloma	2	34s40	54w10	3:36:40
La Paz	1	34s46	56w15	3:45:00
La Paz	2	34s21	57w18	3:49:12
Lascano	2	33s40	54w12	3:36:48
Las Piedras	1	34s44	56w13	3:44:52
Laureles	2	31s22	55w51	3:43:24
Lavalleja → Minas	2	34s23	55w14	3:40:56
Libertad	2	34s38	56w39	3:46:36
Lorenzo Geyres (Queguay)	2	32s05	57w55	3:51:40
Los Cerrillos	2	34s37	56w22	3:45:28
Mal Abrigo	2	34s09	56w57	3:47:48
Maldonado	2	34s54	54w57	3:39:48
Manga	1	34s49	56w06	3:44:24
Melo	2	32s22	54w11	3:36:44
Mendoza	2	34s17	56w13	3:44:52
Mercedes	2	33s16	58w01	3:52:04
Merinos	2	32s24	56w54	3:47:36
Miguelete	2	34s01	57w39	3:50:36
Minas	2	34s23	55w14	3:40:56
Minas de Corrales	2	31s35	55w28	3:41:52
Montevideo	1	34s53	56w11	3:44:44
Nueva Helvecia	2	34s19	57w13	3:48:52
Nueva Palmira	2	33s53	58w25	3:53:40
Nuevo Berlín	2	32s59	58w03	3:52:12
Ombúes de Lavalle	2	33s55	57w47	3:51:08
Palermo	2	33s48	55w59	3:43:56
Palmitas	2	33s31	57w49	3:51:16
Pan de Azúcar	2	34s48	55w14	3:40:56
Pando	2	34s43	55w57	3:43:48
Paso del Cerro	2	31s29	55w50	3:43:20
Paso de los Toros	2	32s49	56w31	3:46:04
Paysandú	2	32s19	58w05	3:52:20
Piedras Coloradas	2	32s23	57w36	3:50:24
Piedra Sola	2	32s04	56w21	3:45:24
Pintado	2	33s50	56w18	3:45:12
Piraraj á	2	33s44	54w45	3:39:00
Piriápolis	2	34s54	55w17	3:41:08
Plácido Rosas	2	32s45	53w44	3:34:56
Polanco	2	33s54	55w09	3:40:36
Progreso	2	34s40	56w13	3:44:52
Pueblo Nuevo	2	34s26	56w29	3:45:56
Punta del Este	2	34s58	54w57	3:39:48
Puntas del Sauce	2	33s51	57w01	3:48:04
Quebracho	2	31s57	57w53	3:51:32
Queguay → Lorenzo Geyres	2	32s05	57w55	3:51:40
Rafael Perazza	2	34s32	56w47	3:47:08
Real de San Carlos	2	34s26	57w53	3:51:32
Retamosa	2	33s35	54w44	3:38:56
Riachuelo	2	34s28	57w43	3:50:52
Río Branco	2	32s34	53w25	3:33:40
Rivera	2	30s54	55w31	3:42:04
Rocha	2	34s29	54w20	3:37:20
Rodríguez	2	34s23	56w33	3:46:12
Rosario	2	34s19	57w21	3:49:24
Rossell y Rius	2	33s11	55w42	3:42:48
Salto	2	31s23	57w58	3:51:52
San Antonio	2	31s22	57w48	3:51:12
San Antonio	2	34s27	56w05	3:44:20
San Carlos	2	34s48	54w55	3:39:40
San Gregorio	2	32s37	55w40	3:42:40
San Gregorio	2	33s57	56w45	3:47:00
San Javier	2	32s41	58w08	3:52:32
San José de Mayo	2	34s20	56w42	3:46:48
San Martín	2	33s45	57w37	3:50:28
San Pedro	2	34s21	57w51	3:51:24
San Pedro de Arriba	2	34s18	57w47	3:51:08
San Ramón	2	34s18	55w58	3:43:52
Santa Catalina	2	33s49	57w29	3:49:56
Santa Clara de Olimar	2	32s55	54w58	3:39:52
Santa Lucía	2	34s27	56w24	3:45:36
Santa Rosa	2	34s30	56w03	3:44:12
Santiago Vázquez	1	34s48	56w21	3:45:24
Sarandí del Yí	2	33s21	55w38	3:42:32
Sarandí Grande	2	33s44	56w20	3:45:20
Sauce	2	34s39	56w04	3:44:16
Solís	2	34s36	55w29	3:41:56
Soriano	2	33s24	58w19	3:53:16
Tacuarembó	2	31s44	55w59	3:43:56
Tala	2	34s21	55w46	3:43:04
Tarariras	2	34s17	57w37	3:50:28
Terminal	2	34s09	57w31	3:50:04
Toledo	1	34s45	56w05	3:44:20
Tomás Gomensoro	2	30s26	57w26	3:49:44
Tranqueras	2	31s12	55w45	3:43:00
Treinta y Tres	2	33s14	54w23	3:37:32
Tres Árboles	2	32s24	56w43	3:46:52
Trinidad	2	33s32	56w54	3:47:36
Valle Edén	2	31s50	56w09	3:44:36
Veinticinco de Agosto	2	34s24	56w25	3:45:40
Veinticinco de Mayo	2	34s12	56w22	3:45:28
Velázquez	2	34s02	54w17	3:37:08
Vergara	2	32s56	53w57	3:35:48
Vichadero	2	31s48	54w43	3:38:52
Villa Alejandrina	2	33s46	58w21	3:53:24
Yaguarí	2	31s31	54w58	3:39:52
Young	2	32s41	57w38	3:50:32

NEW HEBRIDES — NOUVELLES HÉBRIDES — VANUATU

Time Table
Before 13/Jan/1912 LMT
Begin Standard 165E00

Date	Time	Offset
13/Jan/1912	0:00	-11:00
25/Sep/1983	0:00	-12:00
25/Mar/1984	0:00	-11:00
23/Oct/1984	0:00	-12:00
24/Mar/1985	0:00	-11:00
29/Sep/1985	0:00	-12:00
23/Mar/1986	0:00	-11:00
28/Sep/1986	0:00	-12:00
29/Mar/1987	0:00	-11:00
27/Sep/1987	0:00	-12:00
27/Mar/1988	0:00	-11:00
25/Sep/1988	0:00	-12:00
26/Mar/1989	0:00	-11:00
24/Sep/1989	0:00	-12:00
25/Mar/1990	0:00	-11:00
23/Sep/1990	0:00	-12:00
24/Mar/1991	0:00	-11:00
29/Sep/1991	0:00	-12:00
29/Mar/1992	0:00	-11:00
27/Sep/1992	0:00	-12:00
28/Mar/1993	0:00	-11:00
26/Sep/1993	0:00	-12:00
27/Mar/1994	0:00	-11:00
25/Sep/1994	0:00	-12:00
26/Mar/1995	0:00	-11:00
24/Sep/1995	0:00	-12:00
31/Mar/1996	0:00	-11:00
29/Sep/1996	0:00	-12:00
30/Mar/1997	0:00	-11:00
28/Sep/1997	0:00	-12:00
29/Mar/1998	0:00	-11:00
27/Sep/1998	0:00	-12:00
28/Mar/1999	0:00	-11:00
26/Sep/1999	0:00	-12:00
26/Mar/2000	0:00	-11:00

DIVISIONS

1. Ambrim Island
2. Aneityum Island
3. Efate Island
4. Epi Island
5. Eromanga Island
6. Espíritu Santo Island
7. Maewo Island
8. Malekula Island
9. Oba Island
10. Pentecost Island
11. Santa María Island
12. Tana Island
13. Torres Islands
14. Vanua Lava Island

Place	Latitude	Longitude/Offset
Ambrim Island 1	16s15	168E10-11:12:40
Aname 2	20s08	169E47-11:19:08
Aneityum Island 2	20s12	169E45-11:19:00
Anelgauhat 2	20s14	169E44-11:18:56
Anelngauhat 2	20s14	169E44-11:18:56
Autoua 8	16s21	167E45-11:11:00
Banks Islands 6	13s50	167E30-11:10:00
Dillon Bay 5	18s46	168E58-11:15:52
Duin Dui 9	15s24	167E46-11:11:04
Efate Island 3	17s40	168E25-11:13:40
Epi Island 4	16s43	168E15-11:13:00
Eromanga Island 5	18s45	169E05-11:16:20
Espíritu Santo Island 6	15s50	166E50-11:07:20
Forari 3	17s39	168E32-11:14:08
Ipota 5	18s48	169E16-11:17:04
Isangel 12	19s32	169E16-11:17:04
Lamap 6	16s26	167E43-11:10:52
Lamenu 4	16s34	168E11-11:12:44
Lenakel 12	19s32	169E16-11:17:04
Loanatit 12	19s22	169E14-11:16:56
Lolowai 9	15s18	168E00-11:12:00
Losolava 11	14s11	167E34-11:10:16
Luganville 6	15s32	167E08-11:08:32
Maewo Island 7	15s10	168E10-11:12:40
Malau 6	15s10	166E48-11:07:12
Malekula Island 8	16s15	167E30-11:10:00
Marino 7	15s00	168E09-11:12:36
Narovorovo 7	15s13	168E09-11:12:36
Nasawa 7	15s13	168E09-11:12:36
Nazareth 10	15s29	168E10-11:12:40
Nazareth 9	15s21	167E50-11:11:20
Nduindui 9	15s24	167E46-11:11:04
New Hebrides Islands	16s00	167E00-11:08:00
Nokuku 6	14s53	166E35-11:06:20
Norsup 8	16s05	167E23-11:09:32
Nul 4	16s49	168E24-11:13:36
Oba Island 9	15s25	167E50-11:11:20
Pallier 6	14s53	166E35-11:06:20
Pentecost Island 10	15s42	168E10-11:12:40
Port Patrick 2	20s08	169E47-11:19:08
Port Patterson 14	13s49	167E33-11:10:12
Port Sandwich 8	16s25	167E48-11:11:12
Port Stanley 8	16s03	167E25-11:09:40
Port Vila 3	17s44	168E19-11:13:16
Pusei 6	15s22	166E36-11:06:24
Retelimba 8	16s06	167E25-11:09:40
Sakau 4	16s49	168E24-11:13:36
Santa María Island 11	14s15	167E30-11:10:00
Santo 6	15s32	167E08-11:08:32
Talomako 6	15s10	166E48-11:07:12
Tana Island 12	19s30	169E20-11:17:20
Tanoriki 7	14s59	168E09-11:12:36
Torari 3	17s39	168E32-11:14:08
Torres Islands 13	13s15	166E37-11:06:28
Vaimali 4	16s34	168E11-11:12:44
Vanua Lava Island 14	13s48	167E28-11:09:52
Ver 11	14s11	167E34-11:10:16
Vila 3	17s44	168E19-11:13:16
Vunmarama 10	15s29	168E10-11:12:40
Walurigi 9	15s21	167E50-11:11:20
Whitesands 12	19s28	169E25-11:17:40
Wusi 6	15s22	166E36-11:06:24

VENDA — VENDA

Time Table
Before 8/Feb/1892 LMT
Begin Standard 22E30
8/Feb/1892 0:00 -1:30
Begin Standard 30E00
1/Mar/1903 0:00 -2:00
20/Sep/1942 2:00 -3:00
21/Mar/1943 2:00 -2:00
19/Sep/1943 2:00 -3:00
19/Mar/1944 2:00 -2:00

Place	Latitude	Longitude	Offset
Sibasa	22s53	30E33	-2:02:12
Thohoyandou	23s00	30E29	-2:01:56

VENEZUELA — VENEZUELA

Time Table
Before 1/Jan/1890 LMT
Begin Standard 66w55
1/Jan/1890 0:00 4:28
Begin Standard 67w30
12/Feb/1912 0:00 4:30
Begin Standard 60w00
1/Jan/1965 0:00 4:00

Place	Latitude	Longitude	Offset
Acarigua	9N33	69w12	4:36:48
Achaguas	7N46	68w14	4:32:56
Agua Negra	10N28	67w01	4:28:04
Altagracía de Orituco	9N52	66w23	4:25:32
Alto de Ña Paula	10N24	66w48	4:27:12
Anaco	9N27	64w28	4:17:52
Angostura → Ciudad Bolívar	8N08	63w33	4:14:12
Apurito	7N56	68w27	4:33:48
Arabelo	4N55	64w13	4:16:52
Aragua de Barcelona	9N28	64w49	4:19:16
Aragua de Maturín	9N58	63w29	4:13:56
Araure	9N34	69w13	4:36:52
Araya	10N34	64w15	4:17:00
Arichuna	7N42	67w08	4:28:32
Arismendi	8N29	68w22	4:33:28
Aroa	10N26	68w54	4:35:36
Bachaquero	9N56	71w08	4:44:32
Bailadores	8N15	71w50	4:47:20
Barcelona	10N08	64w42	4:18:48
Barinas	8N38	70w12	4:40:48
Barinitas	8N45	70w25	4:41:40
Barquisimeto	10N04	69w19	4:37:16
Barrancas	8N46	70w06	4:40:24
Barrancas	8N42	62w11	4:08:44
Baruta	10N26	66w53	4:27:32
Bejuma	10N11	68w16	4:33:04
Bergantín	10N01	64w22	4:17:28
Betijoque	9N23	70w44	4:42:56
Biscucuy	9N22	69w59	4:39:56
Bobures	9N15	71w11	4:44:44
Boca del Pozo	11N00	64w23	4:17:32
Boconó	9N15	70w16	4:41:04
Bruzual	8N03	69w19	4:37:16
Cabeza de Tigre	10N28	66w46	4:27:04
Cabimas	10N23	71w28	4:45:52
Cabruta	7N38	66w15	4:25:00
Cabure	11N08	69w38	4:38:32
Cagua	10N11	67w27	4:29:48
Caicara	7N37	66w10	4:24:40
Caicara de Maturín	9N49	63w36	4:14:24
Calabozo	8N56	67w26	4:29:44
Camaguán	8N06	67w36	4:30:24
Cambural	10N26	66w59	4:27:56
Cantaura	9N19	64w21	4:17:24
Capatárida	11N11	70w37	4:42:28
Caraballeda	10N37	66w50	4:27:20
Caracas	10N30	66w56	4:27:44
Carache	9N38	70w14	4:40:56
Cariaco	10N29	63w33	4:14:12
Caricuao	10N27	66w59	4:27:56

Caripe 10N12 63W29 4:13:56
Caripito 10N08 63W06 4:12:24
Carite 10N24 67W01 4:28:04
Carora 10N11 70W05 4:40:20
Carúpano 10N40 63W14 4:12:56
Casanay 10N30 63W25 4:13:40
Casigua (El Cubo) 8N46 72W30 4:50:00
Catamare 10N36 67W02 4:28:08
Catia La Mar 10N36 67W02 4:28:08
Cazorla 8N01 67W00 4:28:00
Chacao 10N30 66W51 4:27:24
Chaguaramas 9N20 66W16 4:25:04
Chichiriviche 10N56 68W16 4:33:04
Chivacoa 10N10 68W54 4:35:36
Churuguara 10N49 69W32 4:38:08
Ciudad Bolívar 8N08 63W33 4:14:12
Ciudad Bolivia 8N21 70W34 4:42:16
Ciudad de Guayana → Ciudad Guayana 8N22 62W40 4:10:40
Ciudad Guayana 8N22 62W40 4:10:40
Ciudad Ojeda (Lagunillas) 10N12 71W19 4:45:16
Ciudad Piar 7N27 63W19 4:13:16
Clarines 9N56 65W10 4:20:40
Cojedes 9N37 68W55 4:35:40
Colonia Agrícola Turén 9N15 69W05 4:36:20
Coporito 8N56 62W00 4:08:00
Coro 11N25 69W41 4:38:44
Cúa 10N10 66W54 4:27:36
Cují 10N28 67W02 4:28:08
Cumaná 10N28 64W10 4:16:40
Cumanacoa 10N15 63W55 4:15:40
Cunaviche 7N22 67W25 4:29:40
Curiapo 8N33 61W00 4:04:00
Curumo 10N27 66W52 4:27:28
Dabajuro 11N02 70W40 4:42:40
Dolores 8N18 69W34 4:38:16
Ejido 8N33 71W14 4:44:56
El Aguacate 10N28 66W59 4:27:56
El Amparo de Apure 7N06 70W45 4:43:00
El Baúl 8N57 68W17 4:33:08
El Callao 7N21 61W49 4:07:16
El Calverio 8N59 67W00 4:28:00
El Caribe 10N37 66W50 4:27:20
El Carmen 10N24 67W01 4:28:04
El Carmen 10N24 66W50 4:27:20
El Cojo 10N37 66W53 4:27:32
El Corozo 10N35 66W58 4:27:52
El Cubo → Casigua 8N46 72W30 4:50:00
El Dorado 6N44 61W38 4:06:32
El Encantado 10N27 66W47 4:27:08
El Guanábano 10N24 67W01 4:28:04
El Guapo 10N09 65W58 4:23:52
El Guarapo 10N36 66W58 4:27:52
El Guayabo 8N37 72W20 4:49:20
El Hatillo 10N26 66W49 4:27:16
El Limoncito 10N29 66W47 4:27:08
El Manteco 7N27 62W32 4:10:08
El Mijao 10N23 66W48 4:27:12
El Oasis 10N35 66W59 4:27:56
Elorza 7N03 69W31 4:38:04
El Oso 4N59 65W25 4:21:40
El Otro Lado 10N24 66W49 4:27:16
El Palmar 7N58 61W53 4:07:32
El Palmar 10N38 66W52 4:27:28
El Pao 8N01 62W38 4:10:32
El Pao 9N38 68W08 4:32:32
El Paradero 10N38 69W32 4:38:08
El Paují 10N26 66W49 4:27:16
El Perú 7N19 61W49 4:07:16
El Pilar 10N32 63W09 4:12:36
El Rastro 9N03 67W27 4:29:48
El Samán de Apure 7N55 68W44 4:34:56
El Sitio 10N28 66W46 4:27:04
El Socorro 8N59 65W44 4:22:56
El Sombrero 9N23 67W03 4:28:12
El Tigre 8N55 64W15 4:17:00
El Tigrito → San José de Guanipa 8N54 64W09 4:16:36
El Tocuyo 9N47 69W48 4:39:12
El Vigía 8N38 71W39 4:46:36
El Yagual 7N29 68W25 4:33:40
El Zamural 10N27 67W00 4:28:00
El Zig-Zag 10N33 66W58 4:27:52
Encontrados 9N03 72W14 4:48:56
Esmeralda 3N10 65W33 4:22:12
Espino 8N34 66W01 4:24:04
Gato Negro 10N33 66W57 4:27:48
Gavilán 10N24 66W51 4:27:24
Guacara 10N14 67W53 4:31:32
Guanare 9N03 69W45 4:39:00
Guanarito 8N42 69W12 4:36:48
Guanta 10N14 64W36 4:18:24
Guaracarumbo 10N34 66W59 4:27:56
Guarenas 10N28 66W37 4:26:28
Guarico 9N32 69W48 4:39:12
Guasdualito 7N15 70W44 4:42:56
Guasipati 7N28 61W54 4:07:36
Guatire 10N28 66W32 4:26:08
Guayabal 8N00 67W24 4:29:36
Guayana → Ciudad Guayana 8N22 62W40 4:10:40
Güiria 10N34 62W18 4:09:12
Higuerote 10N29 66W06 4:24:24
Irapa 10N34 62W35 4:10:20
Juangriego 11N05 63W57 4:15:48
Jusepín 9N45 63W31 4:14:04
La Asunción 11N02 63W53 4:15:32
La Boyera 10N23 66W57 4:27:48
La Boyera 10N25 66W50 4:27:20
La Ceiba 9N28 71W04 4:44:16
La Chivera 10N37 66W54 4:27:36
La Concepción 10N38 71W50 4:47:20
La Cumbre 10N32 66W57 4:27:48
La Dolorita 10N29 66W47 4:27:08
La Estrella 10N25 66W48 4:27:12
La Fría 8N13 72W15 4:49:00
La Grita 8N08 71W59 4:47:56
La Guaira 10N36 66W56 4:27:44
Lagunillas 8N31 71W24 4:45:36
Lagunillas → Ciudad Ojeda 10N12 71W19 4:45:16
La Majada 10N27 67W01 4:28:04
La Paragua 6N50 63W20 4:13:20
Las Adjuntas 10N26 67W01 4:28:04
Las Bonitas 7N52 65W40 4:22:40
Las Flores 10N34 66W56 4:27:44
Las Mayas 10N26 66W56 4:27:44
Las Mercedes 9N07 66W24 4:25:36
Las Minas 10N27 66W52 4:27:28
Las Vegas 9N35 68W37 4:34:28
La Tiama 10N26 66W46 4:27:04
La Trinidad 10N27 66W52 4:27:28
La Trinidad de Orichuna 7N07 69W45 4:39:00
La Unión 8N13 67W46 4:31:04
La Unión 10N25 66W48 4:27:12
La Urbana 7N08 66W56 4:27:44
La Vela 11N27 69W34 4:38:16
La Victoria 10N14 67W20 4:29:20
Lezama 9N43 66W24 4:25:36
Libertad 8N20 69W37 4:38:28
Libertad 9N23 68W44 4:34:56
Lira 10N26 66W46 4:27:04
Los Aguacates 10N35 66W48 4:27:12
Los Dos Caminos 10N31 66W50 4:27:20
Los Naranjos 10N27 66W48 4:27:12
Los Taques 11N50 70W16 4:41:04
Los Teques 10N21 67W02 4:28:08
Luepa 5N43 61W31 4:06:04
Maca 10N28 66W48 4:27:12
Macarao 10N26 67W02 4:28:08
Machiques 10N04 72W34 4:50:16
Macuro 10N39 61W56 4:07:44
Macuto 10N37 66W53 4:27:32
Maiquetía 10N36 66W57 4:27:48
Mamera 10N27 66W59 4:27:56
Mantecal 7N33 69W09 4:36:36
Mapire 7N45 64W42 4:18:48
Maracaibo 10N40 71W37 4:46:28
Maracay 10N15 67W36 4:30:24
Maripa 7N26 65W09 4:20:36
Maroa 2N43 67W33 4:30:12
Maturín 9N45 63W11 4:12:44
Mene de Mauroa 10N43 71W01 4:44:04
Mene Grande 9N49 70W56 4:43:44
Mérida 8N36 71W08 4:44:32
Moitaco 8N01 64W21 4:17:24
Montalbancito 10N28 66W59 4:27:56
Morganito 5N04 67W44 4:30:56
Morón 10N29 68W11 4:32:44
Motatán 9N24 70W36 4:42:24
Mucuchíes 8N45 70W55 4:43:40
Naranjal 10N28 67W02 4:28:08
Nirgua 10N09 68W34 4:34:16
Ocumare del Tuy 10N07 66W46 4:27:04
Onoto 9N36 65W12 4:20:48
Ortiz 9N37 67W17 4:29:08
Ospino 9N18 69W27 4:37:48
Palmar de Cariaco 10N34 66W55 4:27:40
Palmarito 7N37 70W10 4:40:40
Palo Negro 10N11 67W33 4:30:12
Papelón 10N27 66W47 4:27:08
Paraguaipoa 11N21 71W57 4:47:48
Parapara 9N44 67W18 4:29:12
Pariaguán 8N51 64W43 4:18:52
Pedernales 9N58 62W16 4:09:04
Pedregal 11N01 70W08 4:40:32
Petare 10N29 66W49 4:27:16
Píritu 11N22 69W08 4:36:32
Píritu 9N23 69W12 4:36:48
Porlamar 10N57 63W51 4:15:24
Pozuelos 10N11 64W39 4:18:36
Pregonero 8N01 71W46 4:47:04
Pueblo Nuevo 11N58 69W55 4:39:40
Puerto Ayacucho 5N40 67W35 4:30:20
Puerto Cabello 10N28 68W01 4:32:04
Puerto Cumarebo 11N29 69W21 4:37:24
Puerto de Nutrias 8N05 69W18 4:37:12
Puerto la Cruz 10N13 64W38 4:18:32
Puerto Ordaz → Ciudad Guayana 8N22 62W40 4:10:40
Puerto Páez 6N13 67W28 4:29:52
Puerto Píritu 10N04 65W03 4:20:12
Punta de Mata 9N43 63W38 4:14:32
Punta Piedras 10N54 64W06 4:16:24
Punto Fijo 11N42 70W13 4:40:52
Quíbor 9N56 69W37 4:38:28
Quiriquire 9N59 63W13 4:12:52
Río Caribe 10N42 63W07 4:12:28
Río Grande 10N35 66W57 4:27:48
Rosario 10N19 72W19 4:49:16
Rubio 7N43 72W22 4:49:28
Sabana de Mendoza 9N26 70W46 4:43:04
Sabaneta 8N46 69W56 4:39:44
Sacupana 8N35 61W39 4:06:36
Samariapo 5N15 67W48 4:31:12
San Antonio de Galipán 10N33 66W53 4:27:32
San Antonio del Golfo 10N27 63W50 4:15:20
San Antonio del Táchira 7N50 72W27 4:49:48
San Antonio de Tamanaco 9N41 66W03 4:24:12
San Carlos 9N40 68W36 4:34:24
San Carlos del Zulia 9N01 71W55 4:47:40
San Carlos de Río Negro 1N55 67W04 4:28:16
San Cristóbal 7N46 72W14 4:48:56
San Felipe 10N20 68W44 4:34:56
San Fernando de Apure 7N54 67W28 4:29:52
San Fernando de Atabapo 4N03 67W42 4:30:48
San José 10N34 66W57 4:27:48
San José de Galipán 10N35 66W54 4:27:36
San José de Gauribe 9N52 65W48 4:23:12
San José de Guanipa 8N54 64W09 4:16:36
San José de Río Chico 10N18 65W59 4:23:56
San José de Tiznados 9N23 67W33 4:30:12
San Juan de Colón 8N02 72W16 4:49:04
San Juan de Dios 10N35 66W55 4:27:40
San Juan de los Cayos 11N10 68W25 4:33:40
San Juan de los Morros 9N55 67W21 4:29:24
San Juan de Payara 7N39 67W36 4:30:24
San Lorenzo 9N47 71W04 4:44:16
San Luis 11N07 69W42 4:38:48
San Mateo 9N45 64W33 4:18:12
San Pedro 8N50 71W58 4:47:52
San Rafael 10N58 71W44 4:46:56
Santa Ana de Barcelona 9N19 64W39 4:18:36
Santa Bárbara 3N57 67W06 4:28:24
Santa Bárbara 7N47 71W10 4:44:40
Santa Cruz 8N25 71W39 4:46:36
Santa Cruz 10N26 67W01 4:28:04
Santa Elena de Uairén 4N37 61W08 4:04:32
Santa Lucía 8N07 69W46 4:39:04
Santa María de Ipire 8N49 65W19 4:21:16
Santa Rita 10N32 71W32 4:46:08
Santa Rosa 8N26 69W24 4:37:36
Santa Rosa 10N30 66W46 4:27:04
Santa Rosa de Amanadona 1N29 66W55 4:27:40
Santa Rosalía 9N02 69W01 4:36:04
Santa Teresa del Tuy 10N14 66W40 4:26:40
San Timoteo 9N48 71W04 4:44:16
San Tomé 8N58 64W08 4:16:32
Santo Tomás 8N53 64W33 4:18:12
Santo Tomé de Guayana → Ciudad Guayan 8N22 62W40 4:10:40
Sarare 9N47 69W10 4:36:40
Sinamaica 11N05 71W51 4:47:24
Siquisique 10N34 69W42 4:38:48
Soledad 8N10 63W34 4:14:16
Tanaguarena 10N37 66W49 4:27:16
Táriba 7N49 72W13 4:48:52
Temblador 8N59 62W44 4:10:56
Tía Juana 10N16 71W22 4:45:28
Timotes 8N59 70W44 4:42:56
Tinaco 9N42 68W26 4:33:44
Tinaquillo 9N55 68W18 4:33:12
Tocuyo de la Costa 11N02 68W23 4:33:32
Torunos 8N30 70W04 4:40:16
Tovar 8N20 71W46 4:47:04
Trujillo 9N22 70W26 4:41:44
Tucacas 10N48 68W19 4:33:16
Tucupido 9N17 65W47 4:23:08
Tucupita 9N04 62W03 4:08:12
Tumeremo 7N18 61W30 4:06:00
Upata 8N01 62W24 4:09:36
Uracoa 9N00 62W21 4:09:24
Ureña 7N55 72W28 4:49:52
Valencia 10N11 68W00 4:32:00
Valera 9N19 70W37 4:42:28
Valle de Guanape 9N54 65W41 4:22:44
Valle de la Pascua 9N13 66W00 4:24:00
Victorino 2N48 67W50 4:31:20
Villa Bruzual 9N20 69W06 4:36:24
Villa de Cura 10N02 67W29 4:29:56
Yaguaraparo 10N34 62W49 4:11:16
Yaritagua 10N05 69W08 4:36:32
Yavita 2N55 67W26 4:29:44
Yoco 10N36 62W24 4:09:36
Yumare 10N37 68W41 4:34:44
Zaraza 9N21 65W19 4:21:16

Time Table
Before 9/Jun/1906 LMT
Begin Standard 106E35
9/Jun/1906 0:00 -7:06
Begin Standard 105E00
11/Mar/1911 0:01 -7:00
Begin Standard 120E00
1/May/1912 0:00 -8:00
Begin Standard 105E00
1/May/1931 0:00 -7:00

DIVISIONS

1. North Vietnam
2. South Vietnam

Place	Lat	Long	Offset
An-Hai 2	15N13	108E56	-7:15:44
An-Loc 2	11N39	106E36	-7:06:24
An-Nhon 2	13N53	109E06	-7:16:24
An-Tan 2	15N26	108E39	-7:14:36
An-Tuc (An-Khe) 2	13N57	108E39	-7:14:36
Ap-Ba-Tien 2	10N44	106E36	-7:06:24
Ap-Binh-Quoi 2	10N48	106E36	-7:06:24
Ap-Binh-Thanh 2	11N11	108E42	-7:14:48
Ap-Talai 2	11N24	107E23	-7:09:32
Ap-Tan-Hoa 2	10N45	106E35	-7:06:20
Ap-Tan-My 2	11N43	108E49	-7:15:16
Bac-Giang 1	21N16	106E12	-7:04:48
Bach-Ma 2	16N12	107E52	-7:11:28
Bac-Kan 1	22N08	105E50	-7:03:20
Bac-Lieu (Vinh-Loi) 2	9N17	105E44	-7:02:56
Bac-Ninh 1	21N11	106E03	-7:04:12
Bac-Quang 1	22N29	104E52	-6:59:28
Ba-Don 1	17N45	106E27	-7:05:48
Ba-Dong 2	9N40	106E34	-7:06:16
Bai-Thuong 1	19N54	105E23	-7:01:32
Ba-Na 2	15N59	107E59	-7:11:56
Ban-Bat 2	13N13	108E39	-7:14:36
Ban-Blech 2	13N12	108E13	-7:12:52
Ban-Don 2	12N53	107E48	-7:11:12
Ban-M'diap 2	12N56	108E43	-7:14:52
Ban-M'drack 2	12N42	108E47	-7:15:08
Bao-Ha 1	22N11	104E21	-6:57:24
Bao-Lac 1	22N57	105E40	-7:02:40
Bao-Loc 2	11N32	107E48	-7:11:12
Ba-Queo 2	10N48	106E38	-7:06:32
Ba-To 2	14N46	108E44	-7:14:56
Ba-Tri 2	10N02	106E36	-7:06:24
Ben-Cat 2	11N09	106E36	-7:06:24
Ben-Giang 2	15N41	107E47	-7:11:08
Ben-Thuy 1	18N39	105E42	-7:02:48
Bien-Hoa (Bianhoa) 2	10N57	106E49	-7:07:16
Binh-Ca 1	21N48	105E18	-7:01:12
Binh-Chanh 2	10N40	106E34	-7:06:16
Binh-Gia 1	21N59	106E21	-7:05:24
Binh-Hung-Hoa 2	10N49	106E37	-7:06:28
Binh-Khe 2	13N57	108E51	-7:15:24
Binh-Kieu 2	15N35	108E04	-7:12:16
Binh-Son 2	15N18	108E46	-7:15:04
Binh-Trung 2	10N47	106E46	-7:07:04
Bo-Duc (Bu-Dop) 2	11N58	106E48	-7:07:12
Bong-Mieu 2	15N25	108E24	-7:13:36
Bo-Trach 1	17N35	106E32	-7:06:08
Buon-Bu-N'jang 2	12N06	107E40	-7:10:40
Buon-Mrong 2	12N48	108E28	-7:13:52
Buon-Ngo 2	12N30	108E28	-7:13:52
Buon-Thach-Hom 2	12N17	108E48	-7:15:12
Buon-Ya-Soup 2	13N05	107E52	-7:11:28
Cai-Nuoc 2	8N56	105E01	-7:00:04
Ca-Mau → Quan-Long 2	9N11	105E08	-7:00:32
Cam-Lo 2	16N49	106E59	-7:07:56
Cam-Pha 1	21N01	107E19	-7:09:16
Cam-Ranh 2	11N54	109E09	-7:16:36
Cam-Xuyen 1	18N15	106E00	-7:04:00
Can-Tho 2	10N02	105E47	-7:03:08
Cao-Bang 1	22N40	106E15	-7:05:00
Cao-Lanh 2	10N27	105E38	-7:02:32
Cap-Saint-Jacques → Vung-Tau 2	10N21	107E04	-7:08:16
Chanh-Hung 2	10N44	106E41	-7:06:44
Chapa 1	22N21	103E50	-6:55:20
Chau-Phu 2	10N42	105E07	-7:00:28
Cho-Chu 1	21N54	105E39	-7:02:36
Cholon 2	10N45	106E40	-7:06:40
Cho-Moi 2	10N33	105E24	-7:01:36
Cho-Moi 2	10N51	106E38	-7:06:32
Chon-Thanh 2	11N24	106E36	-7:06:24
Con-Cuong 1	19N02	104E54	-6:59:36
Cua-Lo 1	18N49	105E43	-7:02:52
Cua-Rao 1	19N16	104E27	-6:57:48
Dak-Gle 2	15N11	107E48	-7:11:12
Dak-To 2	14N42	107E51	-7:11:24
Da-Lat 2	11N56	108E25	-7:13:40
Dam-Doi 2	8N50	105E15	-7:01:00
Da-Nang 2	16N04	108E13	-7:12:52
Dien-Bien-Phu 1	21N23	103E01	-6:52:04
Di-Linh 2	11N35	108E04	-7:12:16
Dinh-Ca 1	21N45	106E03	-7:04:12
Dinh-Lap 1	21N33	107E06	-7:08:24
Dinh-Nam → Nam-Dinh 1	20N25	106E10	-7:04:40
Don-Duong 2	11N51	108E35	-7:14:20
Dong-Hai 2	12N34	109E14	-7:16:56
Dong-Hoi 1	17N29	106E36	-7:06:24
Dong-Khe 1	22N26	106E27	-7:05:48
Dong-Trieu 1	21N05	106E31	-7:06:04
Dong-Van 1	23N16	105E22	-7:01:28
Do-Son 1	20N42	106E47	-7:07:08
Duong-Dong 2	10N13	103E58	-6:55:52
Gia-Dinh 2	10N48	106E42	-7:06:48
Gia-Rai 2	9N14	105E28	-7:01:52
Go-Cong 2	10N50	106E50	-7:07:20
Go-Vap 2	10N49	106E41	-7:06:44
Ha-Dong 1	20N58	105E46	-7:03:04
Ha-Giang 1	22N50	104E59	-6:59:56
Hai-Duong 1	20N56	106E19	-7:05:16
Hai-Phong 1	20N52	106E41	-7:06:44
Ham-Tan 2	10N40	107E46	-7:11:04
Ha-Noi 1	21N02	105E51	-7:03:24
Ha-Tan 1	18N30	105E20	-7:01:20
Ha-Tien 2	10N23	104E29	-6:57:56
Ha-Tinh 1	18N20	105E54	-7:03:36
Hau-Bon (Cheo-Reo) 2	13N24	108E27	-7:13:48
Hau-Duc 2	15N20	108E13	-7:12:52
Hiale 2	15N55	107E34	-7:10:16
Hoa-Binh 1	20N50	105E20	-7:01:20
Hoa-Da 2	11N11	108E33	-7:14:12
Hoai-Nhon 2	14N26	109E01	-7:16:04
Hoa-Thoi 2	10N44	106E35	-7:06:20
Hoi-An 2	15N52	108E19	-7:13:16
Hoi-Xuan 1	20N22	105E07	-7:00:28
Hon-Chong 2	10N10	104E37	-6:58:28
Hon-Gai 1	20N57	107E05	-7:08:20
Hong-Ngu 2	10N48	105E21	-7:01:24
Hue 2	16N28	107E36	-7:10:24
Hung-Long 2	10N40	106E39	-7:06:36
Hung-Yen 1	20N39	106E04	-7:04:16
Huong-Hoa 2	16N37	106E45	-7:07:00
Huong-Khe 1	18N13	105E41	-7:02:44
Huong-Thuy 2	16N25	107E40	-7:10:40
Kannack 2	14N07	108E37	-7:14:28
Ke-Sach 2	9N46	105E59	-7:03:56
Khanh-Hoa 2	12N15	109E06	-7:16:24
Khanh-Hung 2	9N36	105E58	-7:03:52
Khe-Bo 1	19N08	104E41	-6:58:44
Kien-Binh 2	9N55	105E19	-7:01:16
Kien-Hung 2	9N43	105E17	-7:01:08
Kinh-Duc 2	11N49	107E58	-7:11:52
Kontum 2	14N21	108E00	-7:12:00
Kwinhon → Qui-Nhon 2	13N46	109E14	-7:16:56
Ky-Anh 1	18N05	106E18	-7:05:12
Lac-Giao 2	12N40	108E03	-7:12:12
Lai-Chau 1	22N02	103E10	-6:52:40
Lang-Mo 1	17N14	106E27	-7:05:48
Lang-Phuoc-Hai 2	10N26	107E18	-7:09:12
Lang-Son 1	21N50	106E44	-7:06:56
Lao-Bao 2	16N37	106E36	-7:06:24
Lao-Cai 1	22N30	103E57	-6:55:48
Lich-Hoi-Thuong 2	9N26	106E08	-7:04:32
Lien-Huong 2	11N13	108E44	-7:14:56
Linh-Cam 1	18N31	105E34	-7:02:16
Loc-Ninh 2	11N51	106E36	-7:06:24
Long-Thanh 2	10N47	106E57	-7:07:48
Long-Truong 2	10N49	106E49	-7:07:16
Long-Xuyen 2	10N23	105E25	-7:01:40
Mo-Cay 2	10N08	106E20	-7:05:20
Moc-Chau 1	20N51	104E37	-6:58:28
Mo-Duc 2	14N57	108E53	-7:15:32
Mong-Cai 1	21N32	107E58	-7:11:52
Muong-Hinh 1	19N49	105E03	-7:00:12
Muong-Sen 1	19N24	104E08	-6:56:32
Muong-Te 1	22N28	102E37	-6:50:28
My-Tho 2	10N21	106E21	-7:05:24
Nam-Can 2	8N46	104E59	-6:59:56
Nam-Dinh 1	20N25	106E10	-7:04:40
Na-San 1	21N12	104E02	-6:56:08
Nghia-Hanh 2	15N03	108E47	-7:15:08
Nghia-Hung 1	19N18	105E26	-7:01:44
Nghia-Lo 1	21N36	104E31	-6:58:04
Nha-Be 2	10N42	106E44	-7:06:56
Nha-Nam 1	21N27	106E06	-7:04:24
Nha-Trang 2	12N15	109E11	-7:16:44
Nhon-Trach 2	10N43	106E51	-7:07:24
Ninh-Binh 1	20N15	105E59	-7:03:56
Ninh-Hoa 2	12N29	109E08	-7:16:32
On 1	21N40	106E35	-7:06:20
Phan-Rang 2	11N34	108E59	-7:15:56
Phan-Thiet 2	10N56	108E06	-7:12:24
Phat-Diem 1	20N06	106E06	-7:04:24
Phong-Tho 1	22N32	103E21	-6:53:24
Phu-Cat 2	14N01	109E03	-7:16:12
Phu-Cuong 2	10N58	106E39	-7:06:36
Phu-Huu 1	18N58	105E31	-7:02:04
Phu-Huu 2	10N43	106E47	-7:07:08
Phu-Loc 2	16N16	107E53	-7:11:32
Phu-Ly 1	20N32	105E56	-7:03:44
Phu-My 2	14N10	109E03	-7:16:12
Phung-Hiep 2	9N49	105E50	-7:03:20
Phuoc-Binh 2	11N50	106E58	-7:07:52
Phuoc Khanh 2	10N40	106E48	-7:07:12
Phuoc-Le 2	10N30	107E10	-7:08:40
Phuoc-Long 2	9N26	105E28	-7:01:52
Phuoc-Long-Xa 2	10N49	106E46	-7:07:04
Phuoc-Luong 2	10N45	106E48	-7:07:12
Phu-Tho 1	21N24	105E13	-7:00:52
Phu-Tho-Hoa 2	10N46	106E38	-7:06:32
Phu-Vang 2	16N31	107E37	-7:10:28
Phu-Vinh 2	9N56	106E20	-7:05:20
Phu-Yen 1	21N16	104E39	-6:58:36
Pimah 2	15N36	107E25	-7:09:40
Pleiku 2	13N59	108E00	-7:12:00
Quang-Ngai 2	15N07	108E48	-7:15:12
Quan-Long (Ca-Mau) 2	9N11	105E08	-7:00:32
Que-Son 2	15N40	108E14	-7:12:56
Qui-Chau 1	19N33	105E06	-7:00:24
Quinh-Luu 1	19N10	105E42	-7:02:48
Qui-Nhon 2	13N46	109E14	-7:16:56
Rach-Gia 2	10N01	105E05	-7:00:20
Ron 1	17N53	106E27	-7:05:48
Sa-Dec 2	10N18	105E46	-7:03:04
Sai-Gon → Thanh-Pho Ho Chi Minh 2	10N45	106E40	-7:06:40
Sam-Son 1	19N44	105E54	-7:03:36
Soc-Giang 1	22N54	106E01	-7:04:04
Song-Cau 2	13N27	109E13	-7:16:52
Son-Ha 2	15N03	108E34	-7:14:16
Son-Hoa 2	13N02	108E58	-7:15:52
Son-La 1	21N19	103E54	-6:55:36
Son-Tay 1	21N08	105E30	-7:02:00
Ta-Khoa 1	21N13	104E18	-6:57:12
Tam-Ky 2	15N34	108E29	-7:13:56
Tam-Quan 2	14N35	109E03	-7:16:12
Tan-An 2	8N46	105E11	-7:00:44
Tan-An 2	10N32	106E25	-7:05:40
Tan-Binh 2	10N48	106E40	-7:06:40
Tan-Chau 2	10N48	105E15	-7:01:00
Tang-Nhon-Phu 2	10N50	106E47	-7:07:08
Tan-Kien 2	10N42	106E35	-7:06:20
Tan-Qui-Dong 2	10N44	106E42	-7:06:48
Tan-Thoi-Nhut 2	10N50	106E36	-7:06:24
Tan-Thuan-Dong 2	10N45	106E44	-7:06:56
Tay-Ninh 2	11N18	106E06	-7:04:24
Thach-By 2	14N40	109E04	-7:16:16
Thai-Binh 1	20N27	106E20	-7:05:20
Thai-Nguyen 1	21N36	105E50	-7:03:20
Thang-Binh 2	15N44	108E22	-7:13:28
Thanh-Hoa 1	19N48	105E46	-7:03:04
Thanh-My-Tay 2	10N49	106E46	-7:07:04
Thanh-Pho Ho Chi Minh (Sai-Gon) 2	10N45	106E40	-7:06:40
Than-Uyen 1	22N00	103E54	-6:55:36
That-Khe 1	22N16	106E28	-7:05:52
Thoi-Binh 2	9N21	105E05	-7:00:20
Thong-Tay-Hoi 2	10N50	106E39	-7:06:36
Thon-Lac-Nghiep 2	11N20	108E54	-7:15:36
Thot-Not 2	10N16	105E32	-7:02:08
Thuan-Chau 1	21N26	103E41	-6:54:44
Thu-Duc 2	10N51	106E45	-7:07:00
Tien-Yen 1	21N20	107E24	-7:09:36
Tinh-Bien 2	10N36	104E57	-6:59:48
Tourane → Da-Nang 2	16N04	108E13	-7:12:52
Tou-Rout 2	16N24	107E00	-7:08:00
Tra-Cu 2	9N42	106E16	-7:05:04
Tri-Ton 2	10N25	105E00	-7:00:00
Truc-Giang 2	10N14	106E23	-7:05:32
Trung-Luong 2	13N57	109E15	-7:17:00
Tsinh-Ho 1	22N22	103E14	-6:52:56
Tua-Chua 1	21N55	103E21	-6:53:24
Tuan-Giao 1	21N35	103E25	-6:53:40
Tuy-An 2	13N17	109E16	-7:17:04
Tuyen-Hoa 1	17N50	106E10	-7:04:40
Tuyen-Quang 1	21N49	105E13	-7:00:52
Tuy-Hoa 2	13N05	109E18	-7:17:12
Van-Ninh (Van-Gia) 2	12N42	109E14	-7:16:56
Viet-Tri 1	21N18	105E26	-7:01:44
Vinh 1	18N40	105E40	-7:02:40
Vinh-Chau 2	9N19	105E59	-7:03:56
Vinh-Linh 1	17N04	107E02	-7:08:08
Vinh-Loc 2	10N49	106E34	-7:06:16
Vinh-Long 2	10N15	105E58	-7:03:52
Vinh-Tuy 1	17N24	106E36	-7:06:24
Vinh-Tuy 2	9N37	105E22	-7:01:28
Vu-Liet 1	18N43	105E23	-7:01:32
Vung-Tau (Cap-Saint-Jacques) 2	10N21	107E04	-7:08:16
Xa-Muong-Man 2	10N58	108E01	-7:12:04
Xa-Vo-Dat 2	11N09	107E31	-7:10:04
Xom-Binh-Phuoc 2	10N40	106E47	-7:07:08
Xom-Long-Moc 1	18N51	105E01	-7:00:04
Xom-Xoai-Minh 2	10N42	106E50	-7:07:20
Xuan-Loc 2	10N56	107E14	-7:08:56
Xuan-Thoi-Thuong 2	10N52	106E34	-7:06:16
Xuyen-Moc 2	10N34	107E25	-7:09:40
Yen-Bai 1	21N42	104E52	-6:59:28
Yen-Chau 1	21N03	104E18	-6:57:12

VIRGIN ISLANDS — ÎLES VIERGES — JUNGFERNINSELN — ISLAS VIRGENES

Time Table
Before 1/Jul/1911 LMT
Begin Standard 60w00
1/Jul/1911 0:01 4:00

DIVISIONS

1. British Virgins
2. U S Virgins (American)

Place	Div	Lat	Long	Offset
Charlotte Amalie	2	18N21	64w56	4:19:44
Christiansted	2	17N45	64w42	4:18:48
Cruz Bay	2	18N20	64w48	4:19:12
East End	2	18N21	64w40	4:18:40
Frederiksted	2	17N43	64w53	4:19:32
Kingshill	2	17N44	64w48	4:19:12
Nadir	2	18N19	64w53	4:19:32
Road Town	1	18N27	64w37	4:18:28
Saint Thomas → Charlotte Amalie	2	18N21	64w56	4:19:44
Spanish Town	1	18N27	64w26	4:17:44

WAKE ISLAND — ÎLE DE WAKE — WAKE — ISLA WAKE

Time Table
Before 1/Jan/1901 LMT
Begin Standard 180E00
1/Jan/1901 0:00 -12:00

Place	Lat	Long	Offset
Flipper Point	19N18	166E35	-11:06:20
Heel Point	19N19	166E37	-11:06:28
Kuku Point	19N18	166E34	-11:06:16
Peacock Point	19N16	166E37	-11:06:28
Peale Island	19N19	166E35	-11:06:20
Settlement	19N18	166E37	-11:06:28
Toki Point	19N19	166E35	-11:06:20
Wake Island	19N17	166E37	-11:06:28
Wilkes Island	19N18	166E34	-11:06:16

WALES — GALLES — CYMRU — GALES

Time Table # 1
Before 1/Jan/1848 LMT
Begin Standard 0w00

Date	Time	Offset
1/Jan/1848	0:00	0:00
3/Apr/1921	2:00	-1:00
3/Oct/1921	3:00	0:00
26/Mar/1922	2:00	-1:00
8/Oct/1922	3:00	0:00
22/Apr/1923	2:00	-1:00
16/Sep/1923	3:00	0:00
13/Apr/1924	2:00	-1:00
21/Sep/1924	3:00	0:00
19/Apr/1925	2:00	-1:00
4/Oct/1925	3:00	0:00
18/Apr/1926	2:00	-1:00
3/Oct/1926	3:00	0:00
10/Apr/1927	2:00	-1:00
2/Oct/1927	3:00	0:00
22/Apr/1928	2:00	-1:00
7/Oct/1928	3:00	0:00
21/Apr/1929	2:00	-1:00
6/Oct/1929	3:00	0:00
13/Apr/1930	2:00	-1:00
5/Oct/1930	3:00	0:00
19/Apr/1931	2:00	-1:00
4/Oct/1931	3:00	0:00
17/Apr/1932	2:00	-1:00
2/Oct/1932	3:00	0:00
9/Apr/1933	2:00	-1:00
8/Oct/1933	3:00	0:00
22/Apr/1934	2:00	-1:00
7/Oct/1934	3:00	0:00
14/Apr/1935	2:00	-1:00
6/Oct/1935	3:00	0:00
19/Apr/1936	2:00	-1:00
4/Oct/1936	3:00	0:00
18/Apr/1937	2:00	-1:00
3/Oct/1937	3:00	0:00
10/Apr/1938	2:00	-1:00
2/Oct/1938	3:00	0:00
16/Apr/1939	2:00	-1:00
19/Nov/1939	3:00	0:00
25/Feb/1940	2:00	-1:00
4/May/1941	2:00	-2:00
10/Aug/1941	3:00	-1:00
5/Apr/1942	2:00	-2:00
9/Aug/1942	3:00	-1:00
4/Apr/1943	2:00	-2:00
15/Aug/1943	3:00	-1:00
2/Apr/1944	2:00	-2:00
17/Sep/1944	3:00	-1:00
2/Apr/1945	2:00	-2:00
15/Jul/1945	3:00	-1:00
7/Oct/1945	3:00	0:00
14/Apr/1946	2:00	-1:00
6/Oct/1946	3:00	0:00
16/Mar/1947	2:00	-1:00
13/Apr/1947	2:00	-2:00
10/Aug/1947	3:00	-1:00
2/Nov/1947	3:00	0:00
14/Mar/1948	2:00	-1:00
31/Oct/1948	3:00	0:00
3/Apr/1949	2:00	-1:00
30/Oct/1949	3:00	0:00
16/Apr/1950	2:00	-1:00
22/Oct/1950	3:00	0:00
15/Apr/1951	2:00	-1:00
21/Oct/1951	3:00	0:00
20/Apr/1952	2:00	-1:00
26/Oct/1952	3:00	0:00
19/Apr/1953	2:00	-1:00
4/Oct/1953	3:00	0:00
11/Apr/1954	2:00	-1:00
3/Oct/1954	3:00	0:00
17/Apr/1955	2:00	-1:00
2/Oct/1955	3:00	0:00
22/Apr/1956	2:00	-1:00
7/Oct/1956	3:00	0:00
14/Apr/1957	2:00	-1:00
6/Oct/1957	3:00	0:00
20/Apr/1958	2:00	-1:00
5/Oct/1958	3:00	0:00
19/Apr/1959	2:00	-1:00
4/Oct/1959	3:00	0:00
10/Apr/1960	2:00	-1:00
2/Oct/1960	3:00	0:00
26/Mar/1961	2:00	-1:00
29/Oct/1961	3:00	0:00
25/Mar/1962	2:00	-1:00
28/Oct/1962	3:00	0:00
31/Mar/1963	2:00	-1:00
27/Oct/1963	3:00	0:00
22/Mar/1964	2:00	-1:00
25/Oct/1964	3:00	0:00
21/Mar/1965	2:00	-1:00
24/Oct/1965	3:00	0:00
20/Mar/1966	2:00	-1:00
23/Oct/1966	3:00	0:00
19/Mar/1967	2:00	-1:00
29/Oct/1967	3:00	0:00
Begin Standard		15E00
18/Feb/1968	2:00	-1:00
Begin Standard		0w00
31/Oct/1971	3:00	0:00
19/Mar/1972	2:00	-1:00
29/Oct/1972	3:00	0:00
18/Mar/1973	2:00	-1:00
28/Oct/1973	3:00	0:00
17/Mar/1974	2:00	-1:00
27/Oct/1974	3:00	0:00
16/Mar/1975	2:00	-1:00
26/Oct/1975	3:00	0:00
21/Mar/1976	2:00	-1:00
24/Oct/1976	3:00	0:00
20/Mar/1977	2:00	-1:00
23/Oct/1977	3:00	0:00
19/Mar/1978	2:00	-1:00
29/Oct/1978	3:00	0:00
18/Mar/1979	2:00	-1:00
28/Oct/1979	3:00	0:00
16/Mar/1980	2:00	-1:00
26/Oct/1980	3:00	0:00
29/Mar/1981	1:00	-1:00
25/Oct/1981	2:00	0:00
28/Mar/1982	1:00	-1:00
24/Oct/1982	2:00	0:00
27/Mar/1983	1:00	-1:00
23/Oct/1983	2:00	0:00
25/Mar/1984	1:00	-1:00
28/Oct/1984	2:00	0:00
31/Mar/1985	1:00	-1:00
27/Oct/1985	2:00	0:00
30/Mar/1986	1:00	-1:00
26/Oct/1986	2:00	0:00
29/Mar/1987	1:00	-1:00
25/Oct/1987	2:00	0:00
27/Mar/1988	1:00	-1:00
23/Oct/1988	2:00	0:00
26/Mar/1989	1:00	-1:00
29/Oct/1989	2:00	0:00
25/Mar/1990	1:00	-1:00
28/Oct/1990	2:00	0:00
31/Mar/1991	1:00	-1:00
27/Oct/1991	2:00	0:00
29/Mar/1992	1:00	-1:00
25/Oct/1992	2:00	0:00
28/Mar/1993	1:00	-1:00
24/Oct/1993	2:00	0:00
27/Mar/1994	1:00	-1:00
23/Oct/1994	2:00	0:00
26/Mar/1995	1:00	-1:00
29/Oct/1995	2:00	0:00
31/Mar/1996	1:00	-1:00
27/Oct/1996	2:00	0:00
30/Mar/1997	1:00	-1:00
26/Oct/1997	2:00	0:00
29/Mar/1998	1:00	-1:00
25/Oct/1998	2:00	0:00
28/Mar/1999	1:00	-1:00
24/Oct/1999	2:00	0:00
26/Mar/2000	1:00	-1:00
29/Oct/2000	2:00	0:00

Time Table # 2
Before 1/Jan/1855 LMT
Begin Standard 0w00

Date	Time	Offset
1/Jan/1855	0:00	0:00
3/Apr/1921	2:00	TT#1

Place	TT	Lat	Long	Offset
Aberaman	1	51N42	3w25	0:13:40
Aberavon → Port Talbot	1	51N36	3w47	0:15:08
Aberayron	1	52N15	4w15	0:17:00
Abercarn	1	51N39	3w08	0:12:32
Aberdare	1	51N43	3w27	0:13:48
Aberdaron	1	52N49	4w43	0:18:52
Aberdovey	1	52N33	4w02	0:16:08
Aberdulais	1	51N41	3w48	0:15:12
Abergavenny	1	51N50	3w00	0:12:00
Abergele	1	53N17	3w34	0:14:16
Abergwynfi	1	51N40	3w35	0:14:20
Abergynolwyn	1	52N40	3w58	0:15:52
Aberporth	1	52N09	4w33	0:18:12
Abersoch	1	52N50	4w29	0:17:56
Abersychan	1	51N44	3w04	0:12:16
Abertillery	1	51N45	3w09	0:12:36
Aberystwyth	1	52N25	4w05	0:16:20
Amlwch	1	53N25	4w20	0:17:20
Ammanford	1	51N48	3w59	0:15:56
Angle	2	51N41	5w06	0:20:24
Bagillt	1	53N16	3w10	0:12:40
Bala	1	52N54	3w35	0:14:20
Bangor	1	53N13	4w08	0:16:32
Bargoed	1	51N43	3w15	0:13:00
Barmouth	1	52N43	4w03	0:16:12
Barry	1	51N24	3w18	0:13:12
Beaumaris	1	53N16	4w05	0:16:20
Beddgelert	1	53N01	4w06	0:16:24
Bedwas	1	51N35	3w13	0:12:52
Benllech	1	53N19	4w13	0:16:52
Bethesda	1	53N11	4w03	0:16:12
Betws-Y-Coed	1	53N05	3w48	0:15:12
Blaenau Ffestiniog	1	52N59	3w56	0:15:44
Blaenavon	1	51N48	3w05	0:12:20
Blaina	1	51N46	3w10	0:12:40
Borth	1	52N29	4w03	0:16:12
Brechfa	1	51N54	4w36	0:18:24
Brecknock → Brecon	2	51N57	3w24	0:13:36
Brecon	2	51N57	3w24	0:13:36
Bridgend	1	51N31	3w35	0:14:20
Briton Ferry	1	51N38	3w49	0:15:16
Bronllys	1	52N01	3w16	0:13:04
Brymbo	1	53N06	3w04	0:12:16
Brynamman	1	51N49	3w52	0:15:28
Bryncethin	1	51N33	3w34	0:14:16
Brynford	1	53N16	3w14	0:12:56
Brynmawr	1	51N49	3w11	0:12:44
Buckley	1	53N09	3w04	0:12:16
Builth Wells	1	52N09	3w24	0:13:36
Burry Port	1	51N42	4w15	0:17:00
Bwlch	1	51N54	3w15	0:13:00
Caergwrle	1	53N07	3w03	0:12:12
Caerleon	1	51N37	2w57	0:11:48
Caernarvon	1	53N08	4w16	0:17:04
Caerphilly	1	51N35	3w14	0:12:56
Caersws	1	52N31	3w25	0:13:40
Caldicot	1	51N36	2w45	0:11:00
Camrose	1	51N51	5w01	0:20:04
Capel Curig	1	53N06	3w54	0:15:36
Cardiff	1	51N29	3w13	0:12:52
Cardigan	1	52N06	4w40	0:18:40
Carmarthen	1	51N52	4w19	0:17:16
Carmel	1	53N17	3w15	0:13:00
Carnarvon → Caernarvon	1	53N08	4w16	0:17:04
Carno	1	52N33	3w31	0:14:04
Cemmaes	1	52N37	3w42	0:14:48
Cerrigydrudion	1	53N02	3w33	0:14:12
Chepstow	1	51N39	2w41	0:10:44

GALES CYMRU GALLES WALES

Chirk	1	52N56	3w03	0:12:12
Clydach	1	51N43	3w50	0:15:20
Clynnog-Fawr	1	53N01	4w23	0:17:32
Colwyn Bay	1	53N18	3w43	0:14:52
Connah's Quay	1	53N13	3w03	0:12:12
Conway	1	53N17	3w50	0:15:20
Corwen	1	52N59	3w22	0:13:28
Cowbridge	1	51N28	3w27	0:13:48
Cray	1	51N55	3w36	0:14:24
Criccieth	1	52N55	4w14	0:16:56
Crickhowell	1	51N53	3w07	0:12:28
Crymmych	1	51N59	4w40	0:18:40
Cwmbran	1	51N39	3w00	0:12:00
Cynwyl Elfed	1	51N55	4w22	0:17:28
Dale	1	51N43	5w11	0:20:44
Deganwy	1	53N18	3w47	0:15:08
Denbigh	1	53N11	3w25	0:13:40
Devils's Bridge	1	52N23	3w51	0:15:24
Dinas	1	52N00	4w54	0:19:36
Dinas Powis	1	51N26	3w14	0:12:56
Dolgarrog	1	53N11	3w51	0:15:24
Dolgellau	1	52N44	3w53	0:15:32
Dolwyddelan	1	53N03	3w53	0:15:32
East Aberthaw	1	51N23	3w22	0:13:28
Ebbw Vale	1	51N47	3w12	0:12:48
Fairbourne	1	52N41	4w03	0:16:12
Ffestiniog	1	52N58	3w55	0:15:40
Fishguard	1	51N59	4w59	0:19:56
Flint	1	53N15	3w07	0:12:28
Forden	1	52N36	3w08	0:12:32
Gaerwen	1	53N13	4w16	0:17:04
Gilwern	1	51N51	3w06	0:12:24
Glanamman	1	51N48	3w54	0:15:36
Glan-Y-Don	1	53N19	3w15	0:13:00
Glynneath	1	51N46	3w38	0:14:32
Goodwick	1	52N00	5w00	0:20:00
Gorsedd	1	53N17	3w16	0:13:04
Gorseinon	1	51N40	4w02	0:16:08
Gowerton	1	51N39	4w01	0:16:04
Greenfield	1	53N18	3w13	0:12:52
Guilsfield	1	52N42	3w09	0:12:36
Gwalchmai	1	53N15	4w25	0:17:40
Halkyn	1	53N14	3w11	0:12:44
Harlech	1	52N52	4w07	0:16:28
Haverfordwest	1	51N49	4w58	0:19:52
Hawarden	1	53N11	3w02	0:12:08
Hay-On-Wye	1	52N04	3w07	0:12:28
Hendy	1	51N43	4w04	0:16:16
Hengoed	1	51N39	3w10	0:12:40
Hirwaun	1	51N45	3w30	0:14:00
Holt	1	53N05	2w53	0:11:32
Holyhead	1	53N19	4w38	0:18:32
Holywell	1	53N17	3w13	0:12:52
Johnston	2	51N46	5w00	0:20:00
Kerry	1	52N30	3w16	0:13:04
Kidwelly	1	51N45	4w18	0:17:12
Knighton	1	52N21	3w03	0:12:12
Lampeter	1	52N07	4w05	0:16:20
Laugharne	1	51N47	4w28	0:17:52
Letterston	1	51N56	5w00	0:20:00
Llanaber	1	52N45	4w05	0:16:20
Llanaelhaiarn	1	52N59	4w24	0:17:36
Llanarth	1	52N12	4w18	0:17:12
Llanarthney	1	51N52	4w09	0:16:36
Llanbedrog	1	52N52	4w29	0:17:56
Llanbister	1	52N21	3w27	0:13:48
Llanboidy	1	51N54	4w36	0:18:24
Llanbrynmair	1	52N37	3w57	0:15:48
Llanbyther	1	52N04	4w09	0:16:36
Llandaff	1	51N30	3w14	0:12:56
Llanddewi Brefi	1	52N10	3w57	0:15:48
Llandeilo	1	51N52	3w59	0:15:56
Llandinam	1	52N29	3w26	0:13:44
Llandissilio	1	51N53	4w44	0:18:56
Llandovery	1	51N59	3w48	0:15:12
Llandrindod Wells	1	52N15	3w23	0:13:32
Llandudno	1	53N19	3w49	0:15:16
Llandybie	1	51N50	4w00	0:16:00
Llandyssul	1	52N02	4w19	0:17:16
Llanelli	1	51N42	4w10	0:16:40
Llanelltyd	1	52N45	3w54	0:15:36
Llanenddwyn	1	52N49	4w06	0:16:24
Llanerchymedd	1	53N20	4w22	0:17:28
Llanfaethlu	1	53N21	4w32	0:18:08

Llanfair Caereinion	1	52N39	3w20	0:13:20
Llanfairfechan	1	53N15	3w58	0:15:52
Llanfairpwllgwyngyll	1	53N13	4w12	0:16:48
Llanfrynach	2	51N56	3w21	0:13:24
Llanfyllin	1	52N46	3w17	0:13:08
Llanfynydd	1	51N56	4w06	0:16:24
Llanfyrnach	1	51N57	4w35	0:18:20
Llangadog	1	51N56	3w53	0:15:32
Llangefni	1	53N16	4w18	0:17:12
Llangennech	1	51N41	4w04	0:16:16
Llangollen	1	52N58	3w10	0:12:40
Llangranog	1	52N09	4w29	0:17:56
Llangurig	1	52N25	3w36	0:14:24
Llangwryfon	1	52N19	4w03	0:16:12
Llangynog	1	52N50	3w25	0:13:40
Llanharan	1	51N33	3w25	0:13:40
Llanidloes	1	52N27	3w32	0:14:08
Llanilar	1	52N21	4w01	0:16:04
Llanllyfni	1	53N03	4w17	0:17:08
Llanon	1	52N17	4w10	0:16:40
Llanpumsaint	1	51N56	4w18	0:17:12
Llanrhaeadr-Ym-Mochnant	1	52N51	3w17	0:13:08
Llanrhidian	1	51N37	4w11	0:16:44
Llanrhystyd	1	52N18	4w09	0:16:36
Llanrwst	1	53N08	3w48	0:15:12
Llansantffraid-Ym-Mechain	1	52N47	3w08	0:12:32
Llansawel	1	52N01	4w00	0:16:00
Llantrisant	1	51N33	3w23	0:13:32
Llantwit Major	1	51N25	3w30	0:14:00
Llanuwchllyn	1	52N52	3w41	0:14:44
Llanwenog	1	52N06	4w12	0:16:48
Llanwrda	1	51N58	3w53	0:15:32
Llanwrtyd Wells	1	52N07	3w38	0:14:32
Llay	1	53N06	2w59	0:11:56
Llyswen	1	52N02	3w17	0:13:08
Loughor	1	51N40	4w04	0:16:16
Machynlleth	1	52N35	3w51	0:15:24
Maenclochog	1	51N54	4w48	0:19:12
Maesteg	1	51N37	3w40	0:14:40
Manorbier	1	51N39	4w48	0:19:12
Margam	1	51N34	3w44	0:14:56
Mathry	1	51N57	5w05	0:20:20
Menai Bridge	1	53N14	4w10	0:16:40
Merthyr Tydfil	1	51N46	3w23	0:13:32
Milford Haven	2	51N40	5w02	0:20:08
Mmanford	1	51N48	3w59	0:15:56
Mold	1	53N10	3w08	0:12:32
Monmouth	1	51N50	2w43	0:10:52
Montgomery	1	52N33	3w03	0:12:12
Morfa Nefyn	1	52N56	4w33	0:18:12
Mostyn	1	53N19	3w16	0:13:04
Mountain Ash	1	51N42	3w24	0:13:36
Nannerch	1	53N13	3w15	0:13:00
Narberth	1	51N48	4w45	0:19:00
Neath	1	51N40	3w48	0:15:12
Nefyn	1	52N57	4w31	0:18:04
Newborough	1	53N09	4w22	0:17:28
Newbridge on Wye	1	52N13	3w27	0:13:48
Newcastle Emlyn	1	52N02	4w28	0:17:52
Newchurch	1	52N09	3w08	0:12:32
Newport	1	52N01	4w51	0:19:24
Newport	1	51N35	3w00	0:12:00
New Quay	1	52N13	4w22	0:17:28
Newtown	1	52N32	3w19	0:13:16
New Tredegar	1	51N43	3w14	0:12:56
Neyland	1	51N43	4w57	0:19:48
Northop	1	53N12	3w08	0:12:32
Ogmore Vale	1	51N38	3w31	0:14:04
Old Colwyn	1	53N18	3w43	0:14:52
Painscastle	1	52N07	3w12	0:12:48
Pembrey	1	51N42	4w16	0:17:04
Pembroke	1	51N41	4w55	0:19:40
Pembroke Dock	1	51N42	4w56	0:19:44
Penarth	1	51N27	3w11	0:12:44
Pencader	1	52N01	4w16	0:17:04
Pencoed	1	51N32	3w30	0:14:00
Penmaenmawr	1	53N16	3w54	0:15:36
Penrhyn Bay	1	53N19	3w45	0:15:00
Penrhyndeudraeth	1	52N56	4w04	0:16:16
Pentraeth	1	53N17	4w12	0:16:48
Pentre Halkyn	1	53N15	3w12	0:12:48

Penygroes	1	53N04	4w17	0:17:08
Penygroes	1	51N49	4w02	0:16:08
Pontardawe	1	51N44	3w51	0:15:24
Pontardulais	1	51N43	4w03	0:16:12
Ponterwyd	1	52N25	3w50	0:15:20
Pontrhydfendigaid	1	52N17	3w51	0:15:24
Pontyberem	1	51N17	4w09	0:16:36
Pontycymmer	1	51N37	3w34	0:14:16
Pontypool	1	51N43	3w02	0:12:08
Pontypridd	1	51N37	3w22	0:13:28
Porteynon	1	51N33	4w13	0:16:52
Porth	1	51N38	3w25	0:13:40
Porthcawl	1	51N29	3w43	0:14:52
Portmadoc	1	52N55	4w08	0:16:32
Port Talbot	1	51N36	3w47	0:15:08
Prestatyn	1	53N20	3w24	0:13:36
Presteigne	1	52N17	3w00	0:12:00
Pumpsaint	1	52N03	3w58	0:15:52
Pwllheli	1	52N53	4w25	0:17:40
Pyle	1	51N32	3w42	0:14:48
Queensferry	1	53N12	3w01	0:12:04
Raglan	1	51N47	2w51	0:11:24
Resolven	1	51N42	3w42	0:14:48
Rhayader	1	52N18	3w30	0:14:00
Rhdsneigr	1	53N14	4w31	0:18:04
Rhondda	1	51N40	3w27	0:13:48
Rhosesmor	1	53N12	3w10	0:12:40
Rhosllanerchrugog	1	53N00	3w03	0:12:12
Rhos-On-Sea	1	53N19	3w45	0:15:00
Rhossilli	1	51N34	4w17	0:17:08
Rhuddlan	1	53N18	3w27	0:13:48
Rhyl	1	53N19	3w29	0:13:56
Rhymney	1	51N46	3w18	0:13:12
Risca	1	51N37	3w07	0:12:28
Ruabon	1	52N59	3w02	0:12:08
Rumney	1	51N31	3w07	0:12:28
Ruthin	1	53N07	3w18	0:13:12
Saint Arvans	1	51N40	2w41	0:10:44
Saint Asaph	1	53N16	3w26	0:13:44
Saint Athan	1	51N24	3w25	0:13:40
Saint Bride's Major	1	51N28	3w38	0:14:32
Saint Clears	1	51N50	4w30	0:18:00
Saint David's	1	51N54	5w16	0:21:04
Saint Dogmaels	1	52N05	4w40	0:18:40
Saundersfoot	1	51N43	4w43	0:18:52
Sealand	1	53N12	2w58	0:11:52
Senghenydd	1	51N36	3w16	0:13:04
Sennybridge	1	51N57	3w34	0:14:16
Seven Sisters	1	51N46	3w43	0:14:52
Shotton	1	53N12	3w02	0:12:08
Skewen	1	51N40	3w51	0:15:24
Solva	1	51N52	5w11	0:20:44
Swansea	1	51N38	3w57	0:15:48
Talgarreg	1	52N08	4w18	0:17:12
Talgarth	1	52N00	3w15	0:13:00
Talsarnau	1	52N54	4w03	0:16:12
Talybont	1	52N29	3w59	0:15:56
Tenby	1	51N41	4w43	0:18:52
The Mumbles	1	51N34	4w00	0:16:00
Tintern Parva	1	51N42	2w40	0:10:40
Tonyrefail	1	51N36	3w25	0:13:40
Trawsfynydd	1	52N54	3w55	0:15:40
Tredegar	1	51N47	3w16	0:13:04
Tregaron	1	52N13	3w55	0:15:40
Treharris	1	51N41	3w16	0:13:04
Tremadoc	1	52N56	4w09	0:16:36
Tudweiliog	1	52N54	4w35	0:18:20
Tywyn	1	52N35	4w05	0:16:20
Usk	1	51N43	2w54	0:11:36
Walwen	1	53N14	3w15	0:13:00
Welshpool	1	52N40	3w09	0:12:36
Whitchurch	1	51N33	3w14	0:12:56
Whitland	1	51N50	4w37	0:18:28
Wolf's Castle	1	51N54	4w58	0:19:52
Wrexham	1	53N03	3w00	0:12:00
Ysbyty Ystwyth	1	52N20	3w48	0:15:12
Ystalyfera	1	51N47	3w47	0:15:08
Ystrad Aeron	1	52N11	4w11	0:16:44
Ystradfellte	1	51N48	3w34	0:14:16
Ystradgynlais	1	51N47	3w45	0:15:00

WALLIS AND FUTUNA

WALLIS AND FUTUNA

Time Table
Before 1/Jan/1901 LMT
Begin Standard 180E00
1/Jan/1901 0:00 -12:00

Place	Lat	Long	LMT
Futuna Island	14S15	178W09	11:52:36
Horne, Îles de	14S16	178W05	11:52:20
Wallis, Îles	13S18	176W10	11:44:40

YEMEN — YÉMEN — JEMEN — YEMEN ARAB REPUBLIC — AL-YAMAN

Time Table
Before 1/Jan/1950 LMT
Begin Standard 45E00
1/Jan/1950 0:00 -3:00

Place	Lat	Long	LMT
'Adan (Aden)	12N45	45E12	-3:00:48
Aden	12N45	45E12	-3:00:48
Aḩwar	13N31	46E42	-3:06:48
Al-Buzūn	15N35	50E55	-3:23:40
Al-Farḑah	14N51	48E27	-3:13:48
Al-Fāzah	14N08	43E05	-2:52:20
Al-Ghayḑah	16N12	52E15	-3:29:00
Al-Ghulayfiqah	14N27	43E02	-2:52:08
Al-Ḩawrah	13N49	47E37	-3:10:28
Al-Ḩawţah	15N50	48E27	-3:13:48
Al-Ḩudaydah	14N48	42E57	-2:51:48
Al-Ḩumayshah	13N41	45E52	-3:03:28
Al-Ḩumayshī	13N41	45E52	-3:03:28
Al-Ḩuwaymī	14N05	47E44	-3:10:56
Al-'Irqah	13N30	47E22	-3:09:28
Al-Kawd	13N05	45E22	-3:01:28
Al-Khuraybah	15N06	48E19	-3:13:16
Al-Luḩayyah	15N42	42E42	-2:50:48
Al-Maghārīm	15N01	47E51	-3:11:24
Al-Mukallā	14N32	49E08	-3:16:32
Al-Mukhā (Mocha)	13N19	43E15	-2:53:00
'Amd	15N18	48E00	-3:12:00
Anşāb	14N31	46E30	-3:06:00
Ar-Rawḑah	14N28	47E17	-3:09:08
Ar-Rāwuk	15N45	48E54	-3:15:36
Ash-Shiḩr	14N44	49E35	-3:18:20
Aş-Şadārah	14N30	48E04	-3:12:16
As-Şalīf	15N18	42E40	-2:50:40
As-Salīmah	14N02	45E46	-3:03:04
As-Sufāl	14N06	48E42	-3:14:48
'Ataq	14N33	46E48	-3:07:12
At-Tubah	12N40	43E30	-2:54:00
Az-Zaydīyah	15N18	43E04	-2:52:16
Bājil	15N04	43E16	-2:53:04
Bayḩā al-Qişād	14N48	45E43	-3:02:52
Bayḩān al-Qaşād	14N48	45E43	-3:02:52
Bayt al-Faqīh	14N32	43E20	-2:53:20
Bi'r 'Alī	14N01	48E19	-3:13:16
Burūm	14N22	48E57	-3:15:48
Buzu	15N35	50E55	-3:23:40
Dhamār	14N46	44E23	-2:57:32
Dhubāb	12N56	43E25	-2:53:40
Fayrā	13N17	43E25	-2:53:40
Fazeka	14N08	43E05	-2:52:20
Ghayl Bā Wazīr	14N48	49E21	-3:17:24
Ghulayfiqah	14N27	43E02	-2:52:08
Ḩabbān	14N21	47E05	-3:08:20
Ḣadībū	12N38	54E02	-3:36:08
Hanīn	15N50	48E19	-3:13:16
Ḩaraḑ	16N28	43E04	-2:52:16
Ḩarīb	14N57	45E30	-3:02:00
Ḣarrah	14N57	50E19	-3:21:16
Ḣaynin	15N50	48E19	-3:13:16
Ḩişn al-'Abr	16N05	47E22	-3:09:28
Ḩişn al-Qarn	15N11	49E05	-3:16:20
Ḣodeida → Al-Ḩudaydah	14N48	42E57	-2:51:48
Ibb	14N01	44E10	-2:56:40
'Iyādh	14N59	46E51	-3:07:24
Kawkabān	15N40	43E52	-2:55:28
Khamir	16N05	43E55	-2:55:40
Khawrah	14N26	46E09	-3:04:36
Laḩij	13N02	44E54	-2:59:36
Lawdar	13N53	45E52	-3:03:28
Madīnat ash-Sha'B	12N50	44E56	-2:59:44
Manākhah	15N07	43E44	-2:54:56
Manwakh	16N50	48E05	-3:12:20
Ma'rib	15N30	45E20	-3:01:20
Māwiyah	13N35	44E21	-2:57:24
Mawshij	13N43	43E17	-2:53:08
Maydī	16N20	42E46	-2:51:04
Mijdaḩah	14N00	48E26	-3:13:44
Minwakh	16N50	48E05	-3:12:20
Mocha → Al-Mukhā	13N19	43E15	-2:53:00
Mukallā → Al-Mukallā	14N32	49E08	-3:16:32
Musaymīr	13N27	44E37	-2:58:28
Mutayyin	15N59	43E04	-2:52:16
Nişāb	14N31	46E30	-3:06:00
Nūsa	14N00	46E43	-3:06:52
Nūsah	14N00	46E43	-3:06:52
Perim	12N38	43E25	-2:53:40
Qabr Hūd	16N08	49E37	-3:18:28
Qa'ţabah	13N51	44E42	-2:58:48
Qishn	15N26	51E40	-3:26:40
Ramādah	13N38	43E56	-2:55:44
Ridā'	14N38	44E54	-2:59:36
Şa'Dah	16N52	43E37	-2:54:28
Şalīf	15N18	42E40	-2:50:40
Şan'ā'	15N23	44E12	-2:56:48
Şanāw	17N50	51E00	-3:24:00
Sayḩūt	15N12	51E14	-3:24:56
Say'ūn	15N56	48E47	-3:15:08
Saywūn	15N56	48E47	-3:15:08
Shabwah	15N22	47E01	-3:08:04
Shaqrā'	13N21	45E42	-3:02:48
Shaykh 'Uthmān	12N52	44E59	-2:59:56
Shibām	15N56	48E38	-3:14:32
Shuqrā'	13N21	45E42	-3:02:48
Sīdī Tha'Am	16N12	44E41	-2:58:44
Sūq-'Abs	15N59	43E04	-2:52:16
Suquţrā (Socotra)	12N40	54E03	-3:36:12
Ta'Izz	13N38	44E04	-2:56:16
Tamnum	15N07	50E49	-3:23:16
Tamrida (Suquţrā)	12N40	54E03	-3:36:12
Tarīm	16N03	48E59	-3:15:56
Thamnūn	15N07	50E49	-3:23:16
Turbah	12N40	43E30	-2:54:00
'Umrān	15N50	43E56	-2:55:44
Yarīm	14N29	44E21	-2:57:24
Yashbum	14N19	46E56	-3:07:44
Zabīd	14N10	43E17	-2:53:08
Zamakh	16N30	47E35	-3:10:20
Zilme	16N25	43E49	-2:55:16

YUGOSLAVIA — YOUGOSLAVIE — JUGOSLAWIEN — JUGOSLAVIJA

Time Table
Before 1/Jan/1884 LMT
Begin Standard 15E00

Date	Time	Offset
1/Jan/1884	0:00	-1:00
18/Apr/1941	23:00	-2:00
2/Nov/1942	3:00	-1:00
29/Mar/1943	2:00	-2:00
3/Oct/1943	3:00	-1:00
3/Apr/1944	2:00	-2:00
3/Oct/1944	3:00	-1:00
8/May/1945	2:00	-2:00
16/Sep/1945	3:00	-1:00
27/Mar/1983	2:00	-2:00
25/Sep/1983	3:00	-1:00
25/Mar/1984	2:00	-2:00
30/Sep/1984	3:00	-1:00
31/Mar/1985	2:00	-2:00
29/Sep/1985	3:00	-1:00
30/Mar/1986	2:00	-2:00
28/Sep/1986	3:00	-1:00
29/Mar/1987	2:00	-2:00
27/Sep/1987	3:00	-1:00
27/Mar/1988	2:00	-2:00
25/Sep/1988	3:00	-1:00
26/Mar/1989	2:00	-2:00
24/Sep/1989	3:00	-1:00
25/Mar/1990	2:00	-2:00
30/Sep/1990	3:00	-1:00
31/Mar/1991	2:00	-2:00
29/Sep/1991	3:00	-1:00
29/Mar/1992	2:00	-2:00
27/Sep/1992	3:00	-1:00
28/Mar/1993	2:00	-2:00
26/Sep/1993	3:00	-1:00
27/Mar/1994	2:00	-2:00
25/Sep/1994	3:00	-1:00
26/Mar/1995	2:00	-2:00
24/Sep/1995	3:00	-1:00
31/Mar/1996	2:00	-2:00
29/Sep/1996	3:00	-1:00
30/Mar/1997	2:00	-2:00
28/Sep/1997	3:00	-1:00
29/Mar/1998	2:00	-2:00
27/Sep/1998	3:00	-1:00
28/Mar/1999	2:00	-2:00
26/Sep/1999	3:00	-1:00
26/Mar/2000	2:00	-2:00
24/Sep/2000	3:00	-1:00

Place	Lat	Long	LMT
Ada	45N48	20E08	-1:20:32
Agram → Zagreb	45N48	15E58	-1:03:52
Ajdovščina	45N53	13E53	-0:55:32
Aleksinac	43N32	21E43	-1:26:52
Alibunar	45N05	20E58	-1:23:52
Andrijevica	42N44	19E46	-1:19:04
Anhovo	46N03	13E37	-0:54:28
Apatin	45N40	18E59	-1:15:56
Aranđelovac	44N18	20E35	-1:22:20
Babina Greda	45N07	18E33	-1:14:12
Bačka Palanka	45N15	19E24	-1:17:36
Bačka Topola	45N49	19E38	-1:18:32
Bački Petrovac	45N22	19E35	-1:18:20
Baderna	45N12	13E46	-0:55:04
Bajina Bašta	43N58	19E34	-1:18:16
Bajmok	45N58	19E25	-1:17:40
Bale	45N02	13E48	-0:55:12
Banja Luka	44N46	17E11	-1:08:44
Bar	42N05	19E05	-1:16:20
Baška	44N58	14E46	-0:59:04
Batina	45N51	18E51	-1:15:24
Bečej	45N37	20E03	-1:20:12
Bela Crkva	44N54	21E26	-1:25:44
Bela Palanka	43N13	22E19	-1:29:16
Belgrad → Beograd	44N50	20E30	-1:22:00
Belgrade → Beograd	44N50	20E30	-1:22:00
Belgrado → Beograd	44N50	20E30	-1:22:00
Beli Manastir	45N46	18E36	-1:14:24
Beltinci	46N36	16E15	-1:05:00
Benkovac	44N02	15E37	-1:02:28
Beograd (Belgrade)	44N50	20E30	-1:22:00
Berovo	41N42	22E51	-1:31:24
Bihać	44N49	15E52	-1:03:28
Bijeljina	44N45	19E13	-1:16:52
Bijelo Polje	43N02	19E44	-1:18:56
Bileća	42N53	18E26	-1:13:44
Biograd	43N56	15E27	-1:01:48
Bitola	41N01	21E20	-1:25:20
Bitolj → Bitola	41N01	21E20	-1:25:20
Bjelovar	45N54	16E51	-1:07:24
Blace	43N17	21E18	-1:25:12
Blagaj	43N15	17E50	-1:11:20
Bled	46N22	14E06	-0:56:24
Bogomila	41N36	21E28	-1:25:52
Bohinjska Bistrica	46N17	13E57	-0:55:48
Bol	43N16	16E40	-1:06:40
Bor	44N05	22E07	-1:28:28
Bosanska Dubica	45N11	16E49	-1:07:16
Bosanska Gradiška	45N09	17E15	-1:09:00
Bosanska Krupa	44N53	16E10	-1:04:40
Bosanski Novi	45N03	16E23	-1:05:32
Bosanski Petrovac	44N33	16E22	-1:05:28
Bosanski Šamac	45N03	18E28	-1:13:52
Bosansko Grahovo	44N11	16E22	-1:05:28
Bosilegrad	42N29	22E28	-1:29:52
Bovec	46N20	13E33	-0:54:12
Brčko	44N53	18E48	-1:15:12
Brestanica	45N59	15E29	-1:01:56
Brežice	45N54	15E36	-1:02:24

Brinje 45N00 15E08 -1:00:32
Brioni 44N55 13E46 -0:55:04
Brod 41N31 21E12 -1:24:48
Brtonigla 45N23 13E38 -0:54:32
Brza Palanka 44N28 22E27 -1:29:48
Bugojno 44N03 17E27 -1:09:48
Buje 45N24 13E40 -0:54:40
Busovača 44N06 17E53 -1:11:32
Čačak 43N53 20E21 -1:21:24
Čajniče 43N33 19E04 -1:16:16
Čakovec 46N23 16E26 -1:05:44
Čapljina 43N07 17E42 -1:10:48
Cavtat 42N35 18E13 -1:12:52
Cazin 44N58 15E57 -1:03:48
Čazma 45N45 16E37 -1:06:28
Celje 46N14 15E16 -1:01:04
Čemerno 43N11 18E37 -1:14:28
Čepovan 46N03 13E47 -0:55:08
Cerknica 45N48 14E22 -0:57:28
Cerna 45N11 18E42 -1:14:48
Cetinje 42N23 18E55 -1:15:40
Cres 44N58 14E25 -0:57:40
Crikvenica 45N11 14E42 -0:58:48
Črna 46N28 14E51 -0:59:24
Črnomelj 45N34 15E11 -1:00:44
Crvenka 45N39 19E28 -1:17:52
Čuprija 43N56 21E23 -1:25:32
Čurug 45N29 20E04 -1:20:16
Đakovica 42N23 20E25 -1:21:40
Đakovo 45N19 18E25 -1:13:40
Dalj 45N29 18E59 -1:15:56
Darda 45N37 18E41 -1:14:44
Daruvar 45N36 17E13 -1:08:52
Debar 41N31 20E30 -1:22:00
Deliblato 44N50 21E03 -1:24:12
Delnice 45N24 14E48 -0:59:12
Derventa 44N58 17E55 -1:11:40
Despotovac 44N05 21E33 -1:26:12
Dimitrovgrad 43N01 22E47 -1:31:08
Doboj 44N44 18E06 -1:12:24
Domžale 46N08 14E36 -0:58:24
Donja Stubica 45N59 15E58 -1:03:52
Donji Vakuf 44N09 17E25 -1:09:40
Dragvograd 46N35 15E02 -1:00:08
Drniš 43N51 16E09 -1:04:36
Drvar 44N22 16E24 -1:05:36
Dubica 45N11 16E48 -1:07:12
Dubrovnik 42N38 18E07 -1:12:28
Duga Resa 45N27 15E30 -1:02:00
Đurđevac 46N03 17E04 -1:08:16
Dutovlje 45N46 13E50 -0:55:20
Duvno 43N43 17E14 -1:08:56
Erdevik 45N07 19E25 -1:17:40
Esseg → Osijek 45N33 18E41 -1:14:44
Eszék → Osijek 45N33 18E41 -1:14:44
Fažana 44N55 13E49 -0:55:16
Fiume → Rijeka 45N20 14E27 -0:57:48
Foča 43N31 18E46 -1:15:04
Fojnica 43N58 17E54 -1:11:36
Gacko 43N10 18E32 -1:14:08
Gaj 45N29 17E02 -1:08:08
Galižana 44N56 13E52 -0:55:28
Garešnica 45N35 16E56 -1:07:44
Gevgelija 41N08 22E30 -1:30:00
Glamoč 44N03 16E51 -1:07:24
Glina 45N20 16E06 -1:04:24
Gnjilane 42N28 21E29 -1:25:56
Goražde 43N40 18E56 -1:15:44
Gorjani 45N24 18E21 -1:13:24
Gornja Radgona 46N41 16E00 -1:04:00
Gornji Grad 46N18 14E49 -0:59:16
Gornji Milanovac 44N01 20E27 -1:21:48
Gornji Vakuf 43N56 17E35 -1:10:20
Gospić 44N33 15E23 -1:01:32
Gostivar 41N47 20E54 -1:23:36
Gračac 44N18 15E51 -1:03:24
Gračanica 44N42 18E19 -1:13:16
Gradačac 44N53 18E26 -1:13:44
Grdelica 42N54 22E04 -1:28:16
Grubišno Polje 45N42 17E10 -1:08:40
Herceg-Novi 42N27 18E32 -1:14:08
Hodoš 46N50 16E20 -1:05:20
Hvar 43N10 16E27 -1:05:48
Idrija 46N00 14E01 -0:56:04
Ilirska Bistrica 45N34 14E15 -0:57:00
Imotski 43N27 17E13 -1:08:52
Inđija 45N03 20E05 -1:20:20
Istok 42N47 20E29 -1:21:56
Ivanec 46N13 16E08 -1:04:32
Ivangrad 42N50 19E52 -1:19:28
Ivanić Grad 45N42 16E24 -1:05:36
Ivanjica 43N35 20E14 -1:20:56
Izola 45N32 13E40 -0:54:40
Jablanac 44N42 14E54 -0:59:36
Jablanica 43N39 17E45 -1:11:00
Jajce 44N21 17E16 -1:09:04
Janja 44N40 19E15 -1:17:00
Janjina 42N56 17E26 -1:09:44
Jaša Tomić 45N27 20E51 -1:23:24
Jastrebarsko 45N40 15E39 -1:02:36
Jesenice 46N27 14E04 -0:56:16
Kačanik 42N13 21E14 -1:24:56
Kalinovik 43N31 18E26 -1:13:44
Kamnik 46N13 14E37 -0:58:28
Kanal 46N05 13E38 -0:54:32
Kanfanar 45N07 13E51 -0:55:24
Kanjiža 46N04 20E04 -1:20:16
Kaptol 45N26 17E44 -1:10:56
Karlobag 44N32 15E05 -1:00:20
Karlovac 45N29 15E34 -1:02:16
Kavadarci 41N26 22E00 -1:28:00
Kičevo 41N31 20E57 -1:23:48
Kikinda 45N50 20E28 -1:21:52
Kistanje 43N59 15E58 -1:03:52
Kladanj 44N13 18E41 -1:14:44

Kladovo 44N37 22E37 -1:30:28
Ključ 44N32 16E47 -1:07:08
Knić 43N55 20E43 -1:22:52
Knin 44N02 16E12 -1:04:48
Knjaževac 43N34 22E16 -1:29:04
Kobarid 46N15 13E35 -0:54:20
Kočani 41N55 22E25 -1:29:40
Kočevje 45N38 14E52 -0:59:28
Kolašin 42N49 19E31 -1:18:04
Komen 45N49 13E44 -0:54:56
Konjic 43N39 17E57 -1:11:48
Koper 45N33 13E44 -0:54:56
Koprivnica 46N10 16E50 -1:07:20
Korčula 42N58 17E08 -1:08:32
Kosovska Mitrovica 42N53 20E52 -1:23:28
Kostajnica 45N14 16E33 -1:06:12
Kotor 42N25 18E46 -1:15:04
Kotoriba 46N21 16E49 -1:07:16
Kotor Varoš 44N37 17E23 -1:09:32
Kovin 44N45 20E59 -1:23:56
Kozarac 44N58 16E51 -1:07:24
Kragujevac 44N01 20E55 -1:23:40
Krainburg → Kranj 46N15 14E21 -0:57:24
Kraljevica 45N16 14E34 -0:58:16
Kraljevo 43N43 20E41 -1:22:44
Kranj 46N15 14E21 -0:57:24
Kranjska Gora 46N29 13E47 -0:55:08
Krapina 46N10 15E52 -1:03:28
Kratovo 42N05 22E11 -1:28:44
Krepoljin 44N16 21E37 -1:26:28
Kriva Palanka 42N12 22E20 -1:29:20
Križevci 46N02 16E33 -1:06:12
Krško 45N58 15E29 -1:01:56
Kruševac 43N35 21E20 -1:25:20
Kruševo 41N22 21E14 -1:24:56
Kučevo 44N27 21E44 -1:26:56
Kula 45N36 19E32 -1:18:08
Kulen Vakuf 44N34 16E06 -1:04:24
Kumanovo 42N08 21E43 -1:26:52
Kupres 44N00 17E17 -1:09:08
Kuršumlija 43N08 21E17 -1:25:08
Kutina 45N29 16E46 -1:07:04
Labin 45N05 14E07 -0:56:28
Laibach → Ljubljana 46N03 14E31 -0:58:04
Laško 46N09 15E14 -1:00:56
Lenart 46N35 15E50 -1:03:20
Leskovac 42N59 21E57 -1:27:48
Lešnica 44N39 19E19 -1:17:16
Lištica 43N23 17E36 -1:10:24
Litija 46N03 14E50 -0:59:20
Livno 43N50 17E01 -1:08:04
Ljubija 44N56 16E37 -1:06:28
Ljubinje 42N57 18E05 -1:12:20
Ljubljana 46N03 14E31 -0:58:04
Ljubovija 44N11 19E22 -1:17:28
Ljubuški 43N12 17E33 -1:10:12
Ljutomer 46N31 16E12 -1:04:48
Log pod Mangartom 46N24 13E36 -0:54:24
Lokve 46N01 13E49 -0:55:16
Loznica 44N32 19E13 -1:16:52
Lubiana → Ljubljana 46N03 14E31 -0:58:04
Ludbreg 46N15 16E37 -1:06:28
Maglaj 44N33 18E06 -1:12:24
Makarska 43N18 17E02 -1:08:08
Marburg an der Drau → Maribor 46N33 15E39 -1:02:36
Maria-Theresiopel → Subotica 46N06 19E39 -1:18:36
Maribor 46N33 15E39 -1:02:36
Medveđa 42N50 21E35 -1:26:20
Metković 43N03 17E39 -1:10:36
Metlika 45N39 15E19 -1:01:16
Miničevo 43N41 22E18 -1:29:12
Mionica 44N15 20E05 -1:20:20
Miren 45N54 13E37 -0:54:28
Mislinja 46N28 15E14 -1:00:56
Mladenovac 44N26 20E42 -1:22:48
Modriča 44N57 18E18 -1:13:12
Mojstrana 46N27 13E56 -0:55:44
Monastir → Bitola 41N01 21E20 -1:25:20
Mostar 43N20 17E49 -1:11:16
Most na Soči 46N09 13E44 -0:54:56
Motovun 45N20 13E50 -0:55:20
Mrkonjić Grad 44N25 17E05 -1:08:20
Mrkopalj 45N19 14E51 -0:59:24
Murska Sobota 46N40 16E10 -1:04:40
Mursko središče 46N31 16E27 -1:05:48
Muta 46N37 15E10 -1:00:40
Na Logu 46N23 13E45 -0:55:00
Našice 45N29 18E06 -1:12:24
Negotin 44N14 22E32 -1:30:08
Neusatz → Novi Sad 45N15 19E50 -1:19:20
Nevesinje 43N15 18E07 -1:12:28
Nikšić 42N46 18E56 -1:15:44
Niš 43N19 21E54 -1:27:36
Nish → Niš 43N19 21E54 -1:27:36
Nova Gorica 45N57 13E39 -0:54:36
Nova Gradiška 45N16 17E23 -1:09:32
Nova Varoš 43N28 19E48 -1:19:12
Novi Bečej 45N36 20E08 -1:20:32
Novigrad 45N19 13E34 -0:54:16
Novigrad 44N11 15E33 -1:02:12
Novi Pazar 43N08 20E31 -1:22:04
Novi Sad 45N15 19E50 -1:19:20
Novi Vinodolski 45N08 14E48 -0:59:12
Novo Mesto 45N48 15E10 -1:00:40
Novska 45N21 16E59 -1:07:56
Obrenovac 44N39 20E12 -1:20:48
Obrovac 44N12 15E41 -1:02:44
Odžaci 45N30 19E16 -1:17:04
Ogulin 45N16 15E14 -1:00:56

Ohrid 41N07 20E47 -1:23:08
Okučani 45N16 17E12 -1:08:48
Omišalj 45N13 14E34 -0:58:16
Opatija 45N21 14E19 -0:57:16
Orahovica 45N31 17E53 -1:11:32
Ormož 46N25 16E09 -1:04:36
Osečina 44N23 19E36 -1:18:24
Osijek 45N33 18E41 -1:14:44
Osipaonica 44N33 21E04 -1:24:16
Otočac 44N52 15E14 -1:00:56
Pag 44N27 15E04 -1:00:16
Pakrac 45N26 17E12 -1:08:48
Pančevo 44N52 20E39 -1:22:36
Paračin 43N52 21E24 -1:25:36
Pazin 45N14 13E56 -0:55:44
Peč 42N40 20E19 -1:21:16
Pehčevo 41N46 22E54 -1:31:36
Perlez 45N12 20E24 -1:21:36
Perušić 44N39 15E23 -1:01:32
Pesnica 46N36 15E41 -1:02:44
Petrinja 45N26 16E17 -1:05:08
Petrovac 44N22 21E27 -1:25:48
Petrovgrad → Zrenjanin 45N23 20E24 -1:21:36
Piran 45N32 13E34 -0:54:16
Pirot 43N09 22E35 -1:30:20
Pitomača 45N57 17E14 -1:08:56
Plaški 45N05 15E22 -1:01:28
Plav 42N36 19E56 -1:19:44
Plave 46N02 13E36 -0:54:24
Pleternica 45N17 17E48 -1:11:12
Pljevlja 43N21 19E21 -1:17:24
Ploče 43N04 17E26 -1:09:44
Podgorica → Titograd 42N26 19E14 -1:16:56
Podkoren 46N30 13E45 -0:55:00
Podravska Slatina 45N42 17E42 -1:10:48
Podujevo 42N55 21E11 -1:24:44
Pola → Pula 44N52 13E50 -0:55:20
Poreč 45N13 13E37 -0:54:28
Portorož 45N31 13E36 -0:54:24
Postojna 45N47 14E13 -0:56:52
Požarevac 44N37 21E11 -1:24:44
Požega 43N50 20E02 -1:20:08
Pragersko 46N23 15E40 -1:02:40
Preko 44N05 15E11 -1:00:44
Preševo 42N18 21E39 -1:26:36
Priboj 43N35 19E31 -1:18:04
Prijedor 44N59 16E43 -1:06:52
Prijepolje 43N23 19E39 -1:18:36
Prilep 41N20 21E33 -1:26:12
Priština 42N39 21E10 -1:24:40
Prizren 42N12 20E44 -1:22:56
Prnjavor 44N52 17E40 -1:10:40
Prokuplje 43N14 21E36 -1:26:24
Prozor 43N49 17E37 -1:10:28
Ptuj 46N25 15E52 -1:03:28
Pučišča 43N21 16E44 -1:06:56
Pula 44N52 13E50 -0:55:20
Pulj → Pula 44N52 13E50 -0:55:20
Rab 44N46 14E46 -0:59:04
Radeče 46N04 15E11 -1:00:44
Radenci 46N38 16E03 -1:04:12
Radlje ob Dravi 46N37 15E13 -1:00:52
Radoviš 41N38 22E28 -1:29:52
Radovljica 46N21 14E11 -0:56:44
Ragusa → Dubrovnik 42N38 18E07 -1:12:28
Raška 43N17 20E37 -1:22:28
Rateče 46N30 13E43 -0:54:52
Ravna Gora 45N23 14E57 -0:59:48
Ražanj 43N40 21E33 -1:26:12
Resen 41N05 21E00 -1:24:00
Ribnica 45N44 14E44 -0:58:56
Rieka → Rijeka 45N20 14E27 -0:57:48
Rijeka 45N20 14E27 -0:57:48
Rogaška Slatina 46N14 15E38 -1:02:32
Rogatica 43N48 19E00 -1:16:00
Rovinj 45N05 13E38 -0:54:32
Rožaj 42N50 20E10 -1:20:40
Rudo 43N37 19E22 -1:17:28
Ruma 45N00 19E49 -1:19:16
Šabac 44N45 19E42 -1:18:48
Sali 43N56 15E10 -1:00:40
Samobor 45N48 15E43 -1:02:52
Sanski Most 44N46 16E40 -1:06:40
Sarajevo 43N52 18E25 -1:13:40
Sarayevo → Sarajevo 43N52 18E25 -1:13:40
Šavnik 42N57 19E05 -1:16:20
Savudrija 45N30 13E30 -0:54:00
Sebenico → Šibenik 43N44 15E54 -1:03:36
Senj 44N59 14E54 -0:59:36
Senta 45N56 20E04 -1:20:16
Šentjur 46N13 15E24 -1:01:36
Serayevo → Sarajevo 43N52 18E25 -1:13:40
Sežana 45N42 13E52 -0:55:28
Šibenik 43N44 15E54 -1:03:36
Šid 45N08 19E13 -1:16:52
Silba 44N23 14E42 -0:58:48
Sinj 43N42 16E38 -1:06:32
Sisak 45N29 16E23 -1:05:32
Sjenica 43N16 20E00 -1:20:00
Škofije 45N34 13E48 -0:55:12
Škofja Loka 46N10 14E18 -0:57:12
Skopje 41N59 21E26 -1:25:44
Skradin 43N49 15E56 -1:03:44
Slano 42N47 17E54 -1:11:36
Slavonska Požega 45N20 17E41 -1:10:44
Slavonski Brod 45N10 18E01 -1:12:04
Slovenjgradec 46N31 15E05 -1:00:20
Slovenska Bistrica 46N23 15E34 -1:02:16

YUGOSLAVIA — YOUGOSLAVIE — JUGOSLAWIEN — JUGOSLAVIJA

Place	Lat	Long	Offset
Slunj	45N07	15E35	-1:02:20
Smederevo	44N40	20E56	-1:23:44
Smederevska Palanka	44N22	20E58	-1:23:52
Soča	46N20	13E39	-0:54:36
Sodražica	45N46	14E38	-0:58:32
Sombor	45N46	19E07	-1:16:28
Šoštanj	46N23	15E03	-1:00:12
Spalato → Split	43N31	16E27	-1:05:48
Split	43N31	16E27	-1:05:48
Srbobran	45N33	19E48	-1:19:12
Sremska Mitrovica	44N58	19E37	-1:18:28
Sremski Karlovci	45N12	19E57	-1:19:48
Srpska Crnja	45N43	20E42	-1:22:48
Stalać	43N40	21E25	-1:25:40
Stara Fužina	46N17	13E54	-0:55:36
Stara Pazova	44N59	20E10	-1:20:40
Stari Bar	42N06	19E08	-1:16:32
Stari Grad	43N11	16E36	-1:06:24
Štip	41N44	22E12	-1:28:48
Stolac	43N05	17E58	-1:11:52
Ston	42N50	17E42	-1:10:48
Struga	41N11	20E40	-1:22:40
Strumica	41N26	22E38	-1:30:32
Subotica	46N06	19E39	-1:18:36
Suhopolje	45N48	17E30	-1:10:00
Supetar	43N23	16E33	-1:06:12
Surdulica	42N41	22E10	-1:28:40
Sveti Nikole	41N52	21E58	-1:27:52
Sveti Petar u Šumi	45N11	13E52	-0:55:28
Svetozarevo	43N58	21E16	-1:25:04
Svilajnac	44N14	21E13	-1:24:52
Szabadka → Subotica	46N06	19E39	-1:18:36
Temerin	45N24	19E53	-1:19:32
Tešanj	44N37	18E00	-1:12:00
Teslić	44N37	17E51	-1:11:24
Tetovo	42N01	20E58	-1:23:52
Tijesno	43N48	15E39	-1:02:36
Titel	45N12	20E18	-1:21:12
Titograd	42N26	19E14	-1:16:56
Titova Korenica	44N45	15E43	-1:02:52
Titovo Užice	43N51	19E51	-1:19:24
Titov Veles	41N41	21E48	-1:27:12
Tolmin	46N11	13E44	-0:54:56
Travnik	44N14	17E40	-1:10:40
Trbovlje	46N10	15E03	-1:00:12
Trebinje	42N43	18E20	-1:13:20
Trgovište	42N21	22E05	-1:28:20
Trogir	43N31	16E15	-1:05:00
Trpanj	43N00	17E17	-1:09:08
Trstenik	43N37	21E00	-1:24:00
Tržič	46N22	14E19	-0:57:16
Tutin	42N59	20E20	-1:21:20
Tuzla	44N32	18E41	-1:14:44
Udbina	44N32	15E46	-1:03:04
Újvidék → Novi Sad	45N15	19E50	-1:19:20
Ulcinj	41N55	19E11	-1:16:44
Umag	45N25	13E32	-0:54:08
Uroševac	42N22	21E09	-1:24:36
Ušće	43N28	20E37	-1:22:28
Üsküb → Skopje	41N59	21E26	-1:25:44
Uzdin	45N12	20E38	-1:22:32
Užice → Titovo Užice	43N51	19E51	-1:19:24
Valandovo	41N19	22E34	-1:30:16
Valjevo	44N16	19E53	-1:19:32
Valpovo	45N39	18E26	-1:13:44
Varaždin	46N19	16E20	-1:05:20
Vareš	44N09	18E19	-1:13:16
Varvarin	43N43	21E19	-1:25:16
Vela Luka	42N58	16E43	-1:06:52
Velenje	46N21	15E06	-1:00:24
Velika Gorica	45N43	16E05	-1:04:20
Velika Plana	44N20	21E04	-1:24:16
Velike Lašče	45N50	14E38	-0:58:32
Veliki Bečkerek → Zrenjanin	45N23	20E24	-1:21:36
Veliko Gradište	44N45	21E32	-1:26:08
Veli Lošinj	44N31	14E30	-0:58:00
Versec → Vršac	45N07	21E18	-1:25:12
Vinica	45N28	15E15	-1:01:00
Vinkovci	45N17	18E49	-1:15:16
Vipava	45N51	13E58	-0:55:52
Virje	46N04	16E59	-1:07:56
Virovitica	45N50	17E23	-1:09:32
Virpazar	42N15	19E05	-1:16:20
Vis	43N03	16E12	-1:04:48
Višegrad	43N47	19E17	-1:17:08
Visoko	43N59	18E11	-1:12:44
Vitanje	46N23	15E18	-1:01:12
Vižinada	45N20	13E46	-0:55:04
Vladičin Han	42N42	22E04	-1:28:16
Vlasenica	44N11	18E56	-1:15:44
Vlasotince	42N58	22E08	-1:28:32
Voćin	45N37	17E32	-1:10:08
Vodnjan	44N57	13E51	-0:55:24
Vojnić	45N19	15E42	-1:02:48
Vranje	42N33	21E54	-1:27:36
Vrbas	45N35	19E39	-1:18:36
Vrbovec	45N53	16E25	-1:05:40
Vrbovsko	45N23	15E05	-1:00:20
Vrginmost	45N21	15E52	-1:03:28
Vrhnika	45N58	14E18	-0:57:12
Vrlika	43N55	16E24	-1:05:36
Vrnograč	45N10	15E57	-1:03:48
Vršac	45N07	21E18	-1:25:12
Vrsar	45N08	13E37	-0:54:28
Vučitrn	42N49	20E58	-1:23:52
Vukovar	45N21	19E00	-1:16:00
Žabari	44N21	21E13	-1:24:52
Žabljak	43N09	19E07	-1:16:28
Zadar	44N07	15E14	-1:00:56
Žaga	46N18	13E29	-0:53:56
Zagabria → Zagreb	45N48	15E58	-1:03:52
Zagreb	45N48	15E58	-1:03:52
Žagubica	44N13	21E48	-1:27:12
Zaječar	43N54	22E17	-1:29:08
Žalec	46N15	15E10	-1:00:40
Zara → Zadar	44N07	15E14	-1:00:56
Zavidovići	44N27	18E09	-1:12:36
Železnik	44N43	20E23	-1:21:32
Zelina	45N58	16E15	-1:05:00
Zemun	44N51	20E25	-1:21:40
Zenica	44N12	17E55	-1:11:40
Žirje Island	43N40	15E39	-1:02:36
Žirje, Otok	43N40	15E39	-1:02:36
Zlarin	43N42	15E50	-1:03:20
Zlatar	46N06	16E05	-1:04:20
Žminj	45N09	13E55	-0:55:40
Zrenjanin	45N23	20E24	-1:21:36
Županja	45N04	18E42	-1:14:48
Žužemberk	45N50	14E56	-0:59:44
Zvornik	44N23	19E06	-1:16:24

ZAIRE — BELGIAN CONGO — ZAÏRE

Time Table # 1
Before 9/Nov/1897 LMT
Begin Standard 15E00
9/Nov/1897 0:00 -1:00
....

Time Table # 2
Before 9/Nov/1897 LMT
Begin Standard 15E00
9/Nov/1897 0:00 -1:00
Begin Standard 30E00
25/Apr/1920 0:00 -2:00
....

Time Table # 3
Before 9/Nov/1897 LMT
Begin Standard 15E00
9/Nov/1897 0:00 -1:00
Begin Standard 30E00
14/Jun/1935 0:00 -2:00

Place	Time Table	Lat	Long	Offset
Aba	3	3N52	30E14	-2:00:56
Abiengama	3	2N35	27E46	-1:51:04
Abumombazi	3	3N42	22E10	-1:28:40
Adi	3	3N24	30E48	-2:03:12
Adranga	3	2N54	30E26	-2:01:44
Adusa	3	1N23	28E01	-1:52:04
Aketi	3	2N44	23E46	-1:35:04
Akula	1	2N22	20E11	-1:20:44
Albertville → Kalemie	2	5S56	29E12	-1:56:48
Amadi	3	3N35	26E47	-1:47:08
Amamula	3	0S18	27E50	-1:51:20
Andudu	3	2N29	28E41	-1:54:44
Ango	3	4N02	25E52	-1:43:28
Angu	3	3N33	24E28	-1:37:52
Angumu	3	0S07	27E42	-1:50:48
Ankoro	2	6S45	26E57	-1:47:48
Anzi	3	0S52	23E24	-1:33:36
Api	3	3N40	25E26	-1:41:44
Asani	2	4S25	29E05	-1:56:20
Avakubi	3	1N20	27E34	-1:50:16
Azile	3	3N32	29E52	-1:59:28
Babeyru	3	1N52	27E27	-1:49:48
Badakani	1	4S46	14E52	-0:59:28
Bafuku	3	4N15	27E54	-1:51:36
Bafwabaka	3	2N07	27E40	-1:50:40
Bafwabalinga	3	0N51	27E04	-1:48:16
Bafwaboli	3	0N39	26E10	-1:44:40
Bafwangbe	3	1N39	26E51	-1:47:24
Bafwapada	3	0N56	26E57	-1:47:48
Bafwasende	3	1N05	27E16	-1:49:04
Bafwasomboli	3	1N27	27E01	-1:48:04
Bagata	1	3S44	17E57	-1:11:48
Bagbele	3	4N21	29E17	-1:57:08
Bakambe	2	5S39	23E37	-1:34:28
Bakwa-Kenge	2	4S51	22E04	-1:28:16
Bakwanga → Mbuji-Mayi	2	6S09	23E38	-1:34:32
Balaka	1	4S51	19E57	-1:19:48
Balangala	1	0N24	19E45	-1:19:00
Balena	1	0N55	20E00	-1:20:00
Balobe	3	0N05	28E00	-1:52:00
Bamata	3	1S00	21E06	-1:24:24
Bamba	1	5S45	18E23	-1:13:32
Bambesa	3	3N28	25E43	-1:42:52
Bambili	3	3N39	26E07	-1:44:28
Bambinga	1	3S42	18E54	-1:15:36
Bambula	3	1S17	25E38	-1:42:32
Banalia	3	1N33	25E20	-1:41:20
Banana	1	6S01	12E24	-0:49:36
Banda	3	4N11	27E04	-1:48:16
Bandundu	1	3S18	17E20	-1:09:20
Banga	2	5S27	20E28	-1:21:52
Banguru	3	0N27	27E17	-1:49:08
Bankana	1	4S25	16E11	-1:04:44
Bankumuna	1	4S28	19E57	-1:19:48
Banningville → Bandundu	1	3S18	17E20	-1:09:20
Baraka	2	4S06	29E06	-1:56:24
Bari	1	3N19	19E23	-1:17:32
Baringa	1	6S17	16E55	-1:07:40
Baringa	3	0N45	20E52	-1:23:28
Basankusu	1	1N14	19E48	-1:19:12
Basekpio	3	4N44	24E40	-1:38:40
Basoko	3	1N14	23E36	-1:34:24
Basongo	2	4S20	20E24	-1:21:36
Batama	3	0N56	26E39	-1:46:36
Baya	2	11S52	27E27	-1:49:48
Baya	1	4N57	19E43	-1:18:52
Befale	3	0N28	20E58	-1:23:52
Befori	3	0N06	22E17	-1:29:08
Bela	3	0N38	29E14	-1:56:56
Belondo	1	0S16	19E31	-1:18:04
Belonge	1	2S06	19E32	-1:18:08
Bena-Dibele	2	4S07	22E50	-1:31:20
Bena-Leka	2	5S08	22E10	-1:28:40
Bena-Tshadi	2	4S40	22E49	-1:31:16
Bendela	1	3S18	17E36	-1:10:24
Bengamisa	3	0N57	25E10	-1:40:40
Beni	2	0N30	29E28	-1:57:52
Beno	1	3S37	17E48	-1:11:12
Betamba	1	2S13	21E23	-1:25:32
Betumbe-Bongo	1	2S11	18E46	-1:15:04
Bibanga	2	6S15	23E56	-1:35:44
Bikoro	1	0S45	18E07	-1:12:28
Bili	3	4N09	25E10	-1:40:40
Binga	3	2N23	20E30	-1:22:00
Bingi	2	0S24	29E05	-1:56:20
Binza	1	4S21	15E14	-1:00:56
Biodi	3	3N19	28E35	-1:54:20
Biondo	3	0S23	25E13	-1:40:52
Birava	2	2S21	28E54	-1:55:36
Bishanga	2	4S31	21E02	-1:24:08
Boa	2	10S32	28E06	-1:52:24
Bodalangi	3	3N14	22E14	-1:28:56
Bodjoki	3	2N59	22E18	-1:29:12
Bodjokola	3	3N54	20E17	-1:21:08
Boende	3	0S13	20E52	-1:23:28
Bofoku	3	0S57	20E53	-1:23:32
Boga	3	1N03	29E56	-1:59:44
Bogbonga	1	1N35	19E25	-1:17:40
Bogilima	1	3N34	19E16	-1:17:04
Bogoro	3	1N24	30E17	-2:01:08
Bokada	1	4N08	19E23	-1:17:32
Bokala	1	3S07	17E02	-1:08:08
Bokala	1	2N03	18E59	-1:15:56
Bokatola	1	0S38	18E46	-1:15:04
Bokela	3	1S08	21E56	-1:27:44
Bokode	1	3N58	19E29	-1:17:56
Bokondji	1	2N22	18E42	-1:14:48
Bokondo	3	0N15	22E32	-1:30:08
Bokota	3	0S51	22E18	-1:29:12
Bokote	1	0S05	20E08	-1:20:32
Bokungu	3	0S41	22E19	-1:29:16
Bolama	3	1N57	22E58	-1:31:52
Boleko	1	1S31	19E53	-1:19:32
Bolia	1	1S36	18E23	-1:13:32
Bolingo	2	3S30	21E43	-1:26:52
Bolobo	1	2S10	16E14	-1:04:56
Bololo	2	3S50	21E08	-1:24:32
Bolomba	1	0N29	19E12	-1:16:48
Bolombo	2	3S59	21E22	-1:25:28
Bolondo	1	0N27	20E01	-1:20:04
Boma	1	5S51	13E03	-0:52:12
Bomaneh	3	1N18	23E47	-1:35:08
Bomate	1	1S10	19E41	-1:18:44
Bombakabo	1	3N04	19E42	-1:18:48
Bombimba	1	0N31	19E24	-1:17:36
Bombo-Kasanji	2	5S54	21E51	-1:27:24
Bomboma	1	2N25	18E54	-1:15:36
Bombo-Makuka	1	5S26	16E19	-1:05:16
Bombombwa	3	1N21	25E30	-1:42:00
Bomili	3	1N40	27E01	-1:48:04
Bomongiri	3	1S57	21E13	-1:24:52
Bomongo	1	1N22	18E21	-1:13:24
Bomputu	1	0S20	20E06	-1:20:24
Bondo	3	1S22	23E53	-1:35:32
Bondo	3	3N49	23E40	-1:34:40
Bongandanga	3	1N30	21E03	-1:24:12
Bongo	1	3N01	20E06	-1:20:24
Bongo I	1	3N01	20E06	-1:20:24
Bongo II	1	1S47	17E41	-1:10:44
Bongolu	3	2N48	22E29	-1:29:56
Booke	1	2S33	22E00	-1:28:00

Place		Lat	Long	Time
Bosambi	3	2N24	22E39	-1:30:36
Bosenge	3	1N18	22E19	-1:29:16
Bosobolo	1	4N11	19E54	-1:19:36
Boso-Djafo	1	1N06	19E14	-1:16:56
Bososama	1	4N18	20E00	-1:20:00
Botola	1	1S17	18E13	-1:12:52
Boyabo	1	3N43	18E46	-1:15:04
Boyasengese	3	3N29	20E33	-1:22:12
Boyenge	1	0N25	18E51	-1:15:24
Boyera	1	0S38	19E25	-1:17:40
Bozene	1	2N56	19E12	-1:16:48
Buburu	1	1N26	18E03	-1:12:12
Budi	2	3S04	23E56	-1:35:44
Budjala	1	2N39	19E42	-1:18:48
Bukama	2	9S12	25E51	-1:43:24
Bukavu	2	2S30	28E52	-1:55:28
Bukumbirwa	2	0S46	28E44	-1:54:56
Bukunga	2	7S41	25E56	-1:43:44
Bulukuto	3	0S12	21E42	-1:26:48
Bulungu	2	6S04	21E54	-1:27:36
Bulungu	1	4S33	18E36	-1:14:24
Bumba	3	2N11	22E28	-1:29:52
Bumbo	2	7S04	21E57	-1:27:48
Bumbo	1	6S55	19E16	-1:17:04
Buna	1	3S15	18E59	-1:15:56
Bunia	3	1N34	30E15	-2:01:00
Bunianga	1	3S34	20E06	-1:20:24
Bunkeya	2	10S07	27E17	-1:49:08
Busanga	3	0S51	22E04	-1:28:16
Busangu	2	8S32	25E31	-1:42:04
Businga	3	3N20	20E53	-1:23:32
Busu-Adula	3	2N05	21E40	-1:26:40
Busu-Djanoa	3	1N43	21E23	-1:25:32
Busu-Melo	3	1N48	20E15	-1:21:00
Buta	3	2N48	24E44	-1:38:56
Butembo	2	0N09	29E17	-1:57:08
Butsha	3	0N57	29E13	-1:56:52
Buye	3	4N38	27E30	-1:50:00
Bwasa	1	3S53	18E25	-1:13:40
Bwendi	3	4N01	26E41	-1:46:44
Colon Koret	3	0N34	23E28	-1:33:52
Coquilhatville → Mbandaka				
	1	0N04	18E16	-1:13:04
Costermansville → Bukavu				
	2	2S30	28E52	-1:55:28
Dakwa	3	4N00	26E26	-1:45:44
Dekese	2	3S27	21E24	-1:25:36
Demba	2	5S30	22E16	-1:29:04
Dembia	3	3N31	25E50	-1:43:20
Denge	3	3N34	28E14	-1:52:56
Dibaya	2	6S30	22E57	-1:31:48
Digba	3	4N24	25E47	-1:43:08
Dilolo	2	10S42	22E20	-1:29:20
Dimbelenge	2	5S33	23E07	-1:32:28
Dinga	1	5S19	16E34	-1:06:16
Dingba	3	3N24	27E55	-1:51:40
Dingila	3	3N39	26E22	-1:45:28
Diobo	3	2N16	20E29	-1:21:56
Djabir	3	0N32	24E05	-1:36:20
Djamba	2	9S49	22E07	-1:28:28
Djelo-Binza	1	4S23	15E16	-1:01:04
Djokupunda	2	5S27	20E58	-1:23:52
Djolu	3	0N37	22E21	-1:29:24
Djombo	3	1N21	20E22	-1:21:28
Djugu	3	1N55	30E30	-2:02:00
Domiongo	2	4S37	21E15	-1:25:00
Dongo	1	2N43	18E24	-1:13:36
Dongobe	3	4N37	23E12	-1:32:48
Doromo	3	3N49	26E17	-1:45:08
Doruma	3	4N44	27E42	-1:50:48
Dubele	3	2N54	29E33	-1:58:12
Dubie	2	8S33	28E32	-1:54:08
Dula	3	4N41	20E22	-1:21:28
Duma	3	4N57	27E19	-1:49:16
Dungu	3	3N37	28E34	-1:54:16
Duru	3	4N14	28E45	-1:55:00
Ebabaka	1	2S30	18E19	-1:13:16
Ebangalakata	3	0S29	21E29	-1:25:56
Ebonda	3	2N12	22E21	-1:29:24
Egbunda	3	2N44	27E12	-1:48:48
Ekanga	2	2S23	23E14	-1:32:56
Ekoli	3	0S23	24E16	-1:37:04
Ekombe	3	1N16	21E36	-1:26:24
Ekuku	3	0S42	21E38	-1:26:32
Ekuta	1	2N59	18E42	-1:14:48
Elila	2	2S43	25E53	-1:43:32
Elingampangu	2	2S03	24E02	-1:36:08
Elipa	3	0S53	24E34	-1:38:16
Élisabethville → Lubumbashi				
	2	11S40	27E28	-1:49:52
Embondo	1	0N15	19E38	-1:18:32
Enyamba	2	3S40	24E58	-1:39:52
Eranga	1	1S52	18E56	-1:15:44
Esambo	2	3S40	23E24	-1:33:36
Esebi	3	2N57	30E39	-2:02:36
Etoile	2	11S38	27E34	-1:50:16
Etoka	3	0N10	23E23	-1:33:32
Etondo	2	7S46	23E36	-1:34:24
Etuku	2	3S43	25E44	-1:42:56
Evungu	2	4S27	25E12	-1:40:48
Faradje	3	3N44	29E43	-1:58:52
Fataki	2	4S46	28E11	-1:52:44
Fatunda	1	4S08	17E13	-1:08:52
Feshi	1	6S07	18E10	-1:12:40
Fizi	2	4S18	28E57	-1:55:48
Gabia	1	4S34	17E07	-1:08:28
Ganda	3	4N05	23E32	-1:34:08
Gandajika	2	6S45	23E57	-1:35:48
Gangala-Na-Bodio				
	3	3N41	29E08	-1:56:32
Gangwa	2	3S30	20E55	-1:23:40
Gazi	3	1N04	24E31	-1:38:04
Gbwado	3	3N54	20E46	-1:23:04
Gemena	1	3N15	19E46	-1:19:04
Geti	3	1N13	30E12	-2:00:48
Gilima	3	3N55	28E22	-1:53:28
Giro	3	3N08	29E15	-1:57:00
Gitambo	3	4N21	24E45	-1:39:00
Goma	2	1S41	29E14	-1:56:56
Gombari	3	2N43	29E04	-1:56:16
Gombe	1	0S42	17E35	-1:10:20
Gongo-Yembe	1	1S58	18E40	-1:14:40
Guba	2	10S40	26E26	-1:45:44
Gumba	3	2N57	21E26	-1:25:44
Gundji	3	2N05	21E27	-1:25:48
Gungi	1	6S21	19E15	-1:17:00
Gungu	1	5S44	19E19	-1:17:16
Gwalangu	1	2N19	18E11	-1:12:44
Gwane	3	4N43	25E50	-1:43:20
Gwobu	3	2N37	26E13	-1:44:52
Hembe	3	1N54	22E42	-1:30:48
Iba	1	3S05	17E38	-1:10:32
Ibaka	2	4S16	23E12	-1:32:48
Ibambi	3	2N22	27E37	-1:50:28
Ibanshe	2	4S58	21E30	-1:26:00
Ibeke Gembo	1	1S24	18E51	-1:15:24
Ibembo	3	2N38	23E37	-1:34:28
Idiofa	1	5S02	19E36	-1:18:24
Ikali	1	2S02	21E02	-1:24:08
Ikela	3	1S11	23E16	-1:33:04
Ikamba	1	4S22	15E16	-1:01:04
Ikozi	2	2S32	27E37	-1:50:28
Ila	2	2S53	21E05	-1:24:20
Ilebo (Port-Francqui)				
	2	4S19	20E35	-1:22:20
Ilu	3	4N12	23E02	-1:32:08
Imbonga	1	0S43	19E46	-1:19:04
Imbundi	1	5S44	16E16	-1:05:04
Imese	1	2N07	18E06	-1:12:24
Inganda	3	0S05	20E57	-1:23:48
Ingende	1	0S15	18E57	-1:15:48
Inketete	2	2S37	21E53	-1:27:32
Inongo	1	1S57	18E16	-1:13:04
Irebu	1	0S37	17E45	-1:11:00
Irumu	3	1N27	29E52	-1:59:28
Isaka	1	2S35	18E48	-1:15:12
Isaka-Buku	2	3S55	22E03	-1:28:12
Isandja Etat	2	2S59	22E00	-1:28:00
Isanga	3	1S26	22E18	-1:29:12
Isangi	3	0N46	24E15	-1:37:00
Ishenga Oswe	2	3S46	22E34	-1:30:16
Isiro (Paulis)	3	2N47	27E37	-1:50:28
Itipo	1	0S50	18E35	-1:14:20
Itoko	3	1S00	21E45	-1:27:00
Itula	2	3S29	27E52	-1:51:28
Jadotville → Likasi				
	2	10S59	26E44	-1:46:56
Kabalo	2	6S03	26E55	-1:47:40
Kabambare	2	4S42	27E43	-1:50:52
Kabeya	2	5S40	27E58	-1:51:52
Kabinda	2	6S08	24E29	-1:37:56
Kabobo	2	5S07	29E03	-1:56:12
Kabondo-Dianda	2	8S53	25E40	-1:42:40
Kabongo	2	7S19	25E35	-1:42:20
Kabongo	2	8S43	28E11	-1:52:44
Kabotshome	2	3S46	26E54	-1:47:36
Kabunda	2	12S25	29E22	-1:57:28
Kabunga	2	1S42	28E08	-1:52:32
Kabwanga	2	7S01	22E37	-1:30:28
Kabwe-Katanda	2	7S59	24E29	-1:37:56
Kafakumba	2	9S41	23E44	-1:34:56
Kafumba	1	5S23	18E55	-1:15:40
Kafwira	2	12S10	27E33	-1:50:12
Kahemba	1	7S17	19E00	-1:16:00
Kahia	2	6S21	28E24	-1:53:36
Kai-Ndunda	1	5S42	12E42	-0:50:48
Kakelwe	2	4S49	29E00	-1:56:00
Kakenge	2	4S51	21E55	-1:27:40
Kalama	2	2S55	28E33	-1:54:12
Kalamba	1	0S26	18E17	-1:13:08
Kalehe	2	2S06	28E55	-1:55:40
Kalema	2	4S08	24E15	-1:37:00
Kalemie (Albertville)				
	2	5S56	29E12	-1:56:48
Kalima	2	2S34	26E37	-1:46:28
Kaloko	2	6S47	25E48	-1:43:12
Kalole	2	3S42	27E22	-1:49:28
Kalonda	1	4S48	17E33	-1:10:12
Kalonga	2	9S10	27E25	-1:49:40
Kalundu	2	3S26	29E08	-1:56:32
Kama	2	3S32	27E07	-1:48:28
Kamana	2	5S59	24E56	-1:39:44
Kamango	2	0N39	29E53	-1:59:32
Kambove	2	10S52	26E38	-1:46:32
Kambuye	2	7S18	22E50	-1:31:20
Kamenda	2	6S28	24E33	-1:38:12
Kamina	2	8S44	25E00	-1:40:00
Kamituga	2	3S04	28E11	-1:52:44
Kampene	2	3S36	26E40	-1:46:40
Kamudilo	2	7S42	27E18	-1:49:12
Kamwandu	2	6S04	22E42	-1:30:48
Kananga (Luluabourg)				
	2	5S54	22E25	-1:29:40
Kanda-Kanda	2	6S56	23E36	-1:34:24
Kandala	1	6S02	19E24	-1:17:36
Kangowa	2	9S55	22E48	-1:31:12
Kaniama	2	7S31	24E11	-1:36:44
Kaniamba	2	7S27	26E57	-1:47:48
Kaniepa	2	9S00	27E21	-1:49:24
Kansenia	2	10S19	26E02	-1:44:08
Kanzenze	2	10S31	25E12	-1:40:48
Kapanga	2	8S21	22E35	-1:30:20
Kapanga	1	5S04	16E58	-1:07:52
Kapema	2	10S42	28E24	-1:53:36
Kapia	1	4S17	19E46	-1:19:04
Kapona	2	7S11	29E09	-1:56:36
Kapulo	2	8S18	29E15	-1:57:00
Karawa	3	3N20	20E18	-1:21:12
Karibumba	2	0N22	29E22	-1:57:28
Kasaji	2	10S22	23E27	-1:33:48
Kasangale	2	6S20	22E42	-1:30:48
Kasangulu	1	4S36	15E10	-1:00:40
Kasenga	2	10S22	28E38	-1:54:32
Kasenyi	3	1N24	30E26	-2:01:44
Kasese	2	1S38	27E07	-1:48:28
Kasinge	2	6S20	26E59	-1:47:56
Kasongo	2	4S27	26E40	-1:46:40
Kasongo-Lunda	1	6S28	16E49	-1:07:16
Kasumba	2	12S12	27E48	-1:51:12
Katako-Kombe	2	3S24	24E25	-1:37:40
Katanda	2	0S50	29E22	-1:57:28
Katanti	2	2S18	27E08	-1:48:32
Katapakishi	2	8S15	22E49	-1:31:16
Katompi	2	6S11	26E20	-1:45:20
Katopa	2	2S45	25E06	-1:40:24
Katshungu	2	2S27	27E23	-1:49:32
Katumba	2	7S45	25E18	-1:41:12
Kayembe-Mukulu	2	9S03	23E57	-1:35:48
Kayombo	2	9S36	25E37	-1:42:28
Kayuyu	2	3S39	26E21	-1:45:24
Kaziza	2	10S42	23E52	-1:35:28
Kazumba	2	6S25	22E02	-1:28:08
Kenge	1	4S52	16E59	-1:07:56
Kenia	1	2S43	17E04	-1:08:16
Kialwe	2	9S22	27E08	-1:48:32
Kiama	1	7S15	17E44	-1:10:56
Kiambi	2	7S20	28E01	-1:52:04
Kibamba	2	4S53	26E33	-1:46:12
Kibanseke	1	4S26	15E23	-1:01:32
Kibanseke I	1	4S26	15E23	-1:01:32
Kibenga	1	7S55	17E35	-1:10:20
Kibila	2	8S14	26E23	-1:45:32
Kibombo	2	3S54	25E55	-1:43:40
Kienge	2	10S34	27E33	-1:50:12
Kikimi	1	4S26	15E25	-1:01:40
Kikombo	1	5S59	18E09	-1:12:36
Kikombo	1	5S40	18E48	-1:15:12
Kikongo	1	4S16	17E11	-1:08:44
Kikwit	1	5S02	18E49	-1:15:16
Kilembe	1	5S42	19E55	-1:19:40
Kilima	2	0S59	29E12	-1:56:48
Kilomines	3	1N48	30E14	-2:00:56
Kilwa	2	9S18	28E25	-1:53:40
Kima	2	1S26	26E43	-1:46:52
Kimbanda	1	4S07	17E59	-1:11:56
Kimbongo	1	6S08	18E01	-1:12:04
Kimbwala	1	4S22	15E12	-1:00:48
Kimpangu	1	5S51	15E01	-1:00:04
Kimuenza	1	4S27	15E17	-1:01:08
Kimvula	1	5S44	15E58	-1:03:52
Kimwanga	2	7S08	28E42	-1:54:48
Kinda	2	9S18	25E04	-1:40:16
Kinda	2	4S47	21E48	-1:27:12
Kindele	2	8S39	24E11	-1:36:44
Kindu	2	2S57	25E56	-1:43:44
Kingoma	1	5S11	13E34	-0:54:16
Kingoma-Ngoma	1	5S50	16E49	-1:07:16
Kingombe	2	3S56	26E35	-1:46:20
Kingombe	2	7S24	26E11	-1:44:44
Kingunda	1	6S34	16E58	-1:07:52
Kingungi	1	5S24	17E56	-1:11:44
Kinschasa → Kinshasa				
	1	4S18	15E18	-1:01:12
Kinshasa (Léopoldville)				
	1	4S18	15E18	-1:01:12
Kintobongo-Bunge				
	2	8S54	26E23	-1:45:32
Kinzia	1	3S36	18E26	-1:13:44
Kipandi	1	5S19	16E46	-1:07:04
Kipushi	2	11S46	27E14	-1:48:56
Kipushia	2	6S10	25E12	-1:40:48
Kipushia	2	12S58	29E30	-1:58:00
Kiri	1	1S27	19E00	-1:16:00
Kirotshe	2	1S37	29E02	-1:56:08
Kirundu	3	0S44	25E32	-1:42:08
Kisambo	1	6S25	18E14	-1:12:56
Kisanga	3	2N29	26E35	-1:46:20
Kisangani (Stanleyville)				
	3	0S30	25E12	-1:40:48
Kisantu	1	5S07	15E05	-1:00:20
Kisengwa	2	6S00	25E50	-1:43:20
Kishi	2	10S04	26E26	-1:45:44
Kisia	1	4S35	18E22	-1:13:28
Kitanda	2	6S36	26E27	-1:45:48
Kitanda	2	9S59	27E28	-1:49:52
Kitangua	2	6S17	20E22	-1:21:28
Kitenda	1	6S53	17E21	-1:09:24
Kitengo	2	7S26	24E08	-1:36:32
Kitshua-Nseke	1	4S26	19E36	-1:18:24
Kitu	2	7S38	27E42	-1:50:48
Kitutu	2	3S17	28E05	-1:52:20
Kobo	1	4S54	17E09	-1:08:36
Kodi	2	3S34	22E12	-1:28:48
Kokola	2	0N47	29E36	-1:58:24
Kolambo	2	7S34	21E58	-1:27:52
Kole	3	2N07	25E26	-1:41:44
Kole	2	3S27	22E29	-1:29:56
Kolwezi	2	10S43	25E28	-1:41:52
Komeshia	2	8S01	27E07	-1:48:28
Kondolole	3	1N20	25E58	-1:43:52
Kongolo	2	5S26	24E49	-1:39:16
Kongolo	2	5S23	27E00	-1:48:00
Koni	2	10S42	27E15	-1:49:00
Kumu	3	3N04	25E09	-1:40:36
Kunda	2	3S57	26E35	-1:46:20
Kungu	1	2N47	19E12	-1:16:48
Kuntshankoie	2	3S20	23E34	-1:34:16
Kunzulu	1	3S29	16E09	-1:04:36
Kutu	1	2S44	18E09	-1:12:36
Kutu-Moke	1	3S12	17E21	-1:09:24
Kwamouth	1	3S10	16E12	-1:04:48
Lambo Katenga	2	5S02	28E48	-1:55:12
Langa-Langa	1	3S54	15E56	-1:03:44
Lebo	3	4N29	23E57	-1:35:48
Lediba	1	3S03	16E32	-1:06:08

Place	Zone	Lat.	Long.	Time
Leguga	3	3N23	25E02	-1:40:08
Lekotero	3	0S46	23E51	-1:35:24
Lemba-Gaba	1	4S27	15E18	-1:01:12
Lemfu	1	5S18	15E13	-1:00:52
Lengulu	3	3N15	26E30	-1:46:00
Léopoldville → Kinshasa				
	1	4S18	15E18	-1:01:12
Libanga	1	0N19	18E41	-1:14:44
Libenge	1	3N39	18E38	-1:14:32
Liboko	3	2N43	21E28	-1:25:52
Libunga	3	1N49	26E35	-1:46:20
Lienart	3	3N04	25E31	-1:42:04
Lifanga	3	0N19	21E57	-1:27:48
Lifoku	3	0S04	21E18	-1:25:12
Ligasa	3	0N42	23E45	-1:35:00
Likako	3	0N15	21E00	-1:24:00
Likasi (Jadotville)				
	2	10S59	26E44	-1:46:56
Likati	3	3N21	23E53	-1:35:32
Likete	3	0S43	21E25	-1:25:40
Likimi	3	2N50	20E45	-1:23:00
Lilanga	3	0S34	23E55	-1:35:40
Lilenga	3	0N54	22E06	-1:28:24
Lingomo	3	0N38	21E59	-1:27:56
Lingwala	1	4S22	15E17	-1:01:08
Lioko	3	0N02	22E04	-1:28:16
Lioko	3	1N25	23E07	-1:32:28
Lisala	3	2N09	21E31	-1:26:04
Litoko	3	1S13	24E47	-1:39:08
Loango Buele	1	5S10	12E59	-0:51:56
Lodja	2	3S29	23E26	-1:33:44
Loengo	2	4S45	26E27	-1:45:48
Loka	1	0N20	17E57	-1:11:48
Lokako	1	2S14	21E45	-1:27:00
Lokalema	3	1N59	22E17	-1:29:08
Lokandu	2	2S31	25E47	-1:43:08
Lokofa-Bokolongo				
	1	0N12	19E22	-1:17:28
Lokolama	1	2S34	19E53	-1:19:32
Lokolenge	3	1N11	22E40	-1:30:40
Lolengi	3	0N07	20E59	-1:23:56
Lolingo	3	0N55	22E38	-1:30:32
Lolo	3	2N13	23E00	-1:32:00
Lolwa	3	1N22	29E31	-1:58:04
Lomela	2	2S18	23E17	-1:33:08
Londo	3	2N03	25E43	-1:42:52
Lonkala	2	4S37	23E14	-1:32:56
Loto	2	2S49	22E29	-1:29:56
Lowa	3	1S24	25E51	-1:43:24
Lua	1	5S18	16E06	-1:04:24
Luali	1	5S06	12E29	-0:49:56
Luanza	2	8S42	28E42	-1:54:48
Luashi	2	10S56	23E37	-1:34:28
Lubamiti	1	2S29	17E47	-1:11:08
Lubefu	2	4S43	24E25	-1:37:40
Lubile	2	2S55	26E45	-1:47:00
Lubondai	2	6S34	22E39	-1:30:36
Lubondoi	2	8S02	26E31	-1:46:04
Lubudi	2	9S57	25E58	-1:43:52
Lubudi	2	6S51	21E18	-1:25:12
Lubue	1	4S09	19E52	-1:19:28
Lubumbaschi → Lubumbashi				
	2	11S40	27E28	-1:49:52
Lubumbashi (élisabethville)				
	2	11S40	27E28	-1:49:52
Lubunda	2	5S10	26E40	-1:46:40
Lubutu	2	0S44	26E35	-1:46:20
Luebo	2	5S21	21E25	-1:25:40
Lueki	2	3S22	25E51	-1:43:24
Luemba	2	3S42	28E40	-1:54:40
Luena	2	9S27	25E47	-1:43:08
Lueta	2	7S19	22E06	-1:28:24
Lufupa	2	10S37	24E56	-1:39:44
Luishia	2	11S10	27E02	-1:48:08
Luiza	2	7S12	22E25	-1:29:40
Luizi	2	6S03	27E28	-1:49:52
Lukala	1	5S31	14E32	-0:58:08
Lukanga	1	1S00	18E08	-1:12:32
Lukanga	1	1S41	18E09	-1:12:36
Lukolela	2	5S23	24E32	-1:38:08
Lukolela	1	1S03	17E12	-1:08:48
Lukula	1	5S23	12E57	-0:51:48
Lukuni	1	5S52	17E11	-1:08:44
Lula	1	5S22	16E02	-1:04:08
Lulonga	1	0N37	18E23	-1:13:32
Luluabourg → Kananga				
	2	5S54	22E25	-1:29:40
Lumuna	2	3S46	26E24	-1:45:36
Lunia-Bubi	2	7S30	24E49	-1:39:16
Luofu	2	0S10	29E14	-1:56:56
Luozi	1	4S57	14E08	-0:56:32
Luputa	2	7S10	23E42	-1:34:48
Lusaka	2	7S10	29E27	-1:57:48
Lusambo	2	4S58	23E27	-1:33:48
Lusanga	1	4S50	18E44	-1:14:56
Lusangaye	2	4S54	26E00	-1:44:00
Lusangi	2	4S37	27E08	-1:48:32
Luseke	2	2S51	23E08	-1:32:32
Lusengo	1	1N46	19E29	-1:17:56
Lutshi	2	4S09	26E30	-1:46:00
Luvua	2	8S48	25E19	-1:41:16
Mabanga	1	1N30	19E06	-1:16:24
Mabenga-Cité	1	3S39	18E40	-1:14:40
Mabenge	3	4N14	24E09	-1:36:36
Maboma	3	2N32	28E13	-1:52:52
Mabwe	2	8S39	26E31	-1:46:04
Madia	2	7S08	26E00	-1:44:00
Madibi	1	4S18	18E24	-1:13:36
Madimba	1	4S58	15E08	-1:00:32
Maduda	1	4S55	13E06	-0:52:24
Maduo	3	1S24	20E44	-1:22:56
Maganga	3	0N51	26E22	-1:45:28
Mahagi	3	2N18	30E59	-2:03:56
Mahagi Port	3	2N09	31E14	-2:04:56
Maie	3	2N46	30E34	-2:02:16
Makanza	1	1N36	19E07	-1:16:28
Makaw	1	3S29	18E19	-1:13:16
Makaya	1	3S22	18E02	-1:12:08
Makoka	2	2S34	25E29	-1:41:56
Makongo	3	3N25	26E22	-1:45:28
Makoro	3	3N08	29E44	-1:58:56
Makumbi	2	5S51	20E41	-1:22:44
Makwende-Bayo	2	7S08	28E06	-1:52:24
Malandji	2	5S56	22E18	-1:29:12
Malela	2	2S28	26E09	-1:44:36
Malela	2	4S22	26E08	-1:44:32
Malengoya	3	3N32	25E25	-1:41:40
Mali	2	2S48	26E08	-1:44:32
Maloba	2	6S18	27E39	-1:50:36
Malonga	2	10S24	23E10	-1:32:40
Maluku-Maes	1	4S06	15E31	-1:02:04
Mambasa	3	1N21	29E03	-1:56:12
Mangala	3	1N02	23E50	-1:35:20
Mange	3	0N54	20E30	-1:22:00
Mangombe	2	1S25	26E54	-1:47:36
Mangungu	1	5S13	19E35	-1:18:20
Mani	2	6S27	25E20	-1:41:20
Manono	2	7S18	27E25	-1:49:40
Mantantale	1	2S10	20E06	-1:20:24
Mapanda	2	9S32	24E16	-1:37:04
Marchal	1	5S16	14E58	-0:59:52
Masi-Manimba	1	4S46	17E55	-1:11:40
Masisi	2	1S24	28E49	-1:55:16
Massina	1	4S22	15E22	-1:01:28
Masuika	2	7S37	22E32	-1:30:08
Mata	2	7S53	21E58	-1:27:52
Matadi	1	5S49	13E27	-0:53:48
Mateko	1	4S03	18E55	-1:15:40
Mato	2	8S01	24E55	-1:39:40
Mawa	3	2N43	26E42	-1:46:48
Mawiwi	3	3N06	27E40	-1:50:40
Mayamba	1	4S46	16E52	-1:07:28
Mayoko	3	1S05	23E49	-1:35:16
Mbali	1	2S50	16E12	-1:04:48
Mbandaka (Coquilhatville)				
	1	0N04	18E16	-1:13:04
Mbanza-Ngungu	1	5S15	14E52	-0:59:28
Mboie	2	6S56	21E54	-1:27:36
Mboli	3	4N08	23E09	-1:32:36
Mbuji-Mayi (Bakwanga)				
	2	6S09	23E38	-1:34:32
Mbulula	2	5S26	27E26	-1:49:44
Mbuma	3	3N32	24E50	-1:39:20
Medje	3	2N25	27E18	-1:49:12
Metsera	2	2S35	26E07	-1:44:28
Mikope	2	5S03	20E48	-1:23:12
Minga	2	11S08	27E57	-1:51:48
Misoke	2	1S06	28E38	-1:54:32
Mitwaba	2	8S38	27E20	-1:49:20
Moanza	1	5S25	17E30	-1:10:00
Moba	2	7S03	29E47	-1:59:08
Mobayi-Mbongo	3	4N18	21E11	-1:24:44
Mobeka	1	1N53	19E46	-1:19:04
Modjamboli	3	2N28	22E06	-1:28:24
Mogalo	1	3N10	19E04	-1:16:16
Mohangi	2	0N03	29E05	-1:56:20
Mokambo	2	12S25	28E21	-1:53:24
Mokaria	3	2N00	23E20	-1:33:20
Mokimbo	2	6S20	28E42	-1:54:48
Mokolo	1	1N57	18E05	-1:12:20
Mokombe	3	0S14	23E48	-1:35:12
Moku	3	2N57	29E22	-1:57:28
Mokumbusu	3	1N44	21E04	-1:24:16
Molanda	3	2N28	20E48	-1:23:12
Molegbe	3	4N14	20E53	-1:23:32
Moliro	2	8S13	30E34	-2:02:16
Molowaie	2	5S47	23E20	-1:33:20
Moma	3	1S36	23E57	-1:35:48
Mombango	3	1N45	24E26	-1:37:44
Mombongo	3	1N39	23E09	-1:32:36
Mompono	3	0N04	21E48	-1:27:12
Mondimbi	3	1N43	22E58	-1:31:52
Mondombe	3	0S53	22E45	-1:31:00
Monga	3	4N12	22E49	-1:31:16
Mongai-Musenge	1	4S04	19E34	-1:18:16
Mongandjo	3	1N21	24E20	-1:37:20
Mongbwalu	3	1N57	30E02	-2:00:08
Monie	1	4S00	17E22	-1:09:28
Monkoto	3	1S38	20E39	-1:22:36
Monveda	3	2N57	21E27	-1:25:48
Mpala	2	6S45	29E31	-1:58:04
Mpese	1	5S14	15E33	-1:02:12
Mpoka	1	1S26	17E02	-1:08:08
Muanda	1	5S56	12E21	-0:49:24
Muhala	2	5S40	28E43	-1:54:52
Muhulu	2	1S03	27E17	-1:49:08
Mukebo	2	6S49	28E03	-1:52:12
Mukomwenze	2	6S52	27E16	-1:49:04
Mulonda Funda	2	11S06	25E28	-1:41:52
Mulongo	2	7S50	27E00	-1:48:00
Muma	3	3N24	23E15	-1:33:00
Mume	2	9S40	27E26	-1:49:44
Mungbere	3	2N38	28E30	-1:54:00
Mununzi	3	0N36	29E15	-1:57:00
Musa	1	2N40	19E18	-1:17:12
Musadi	2	2S34	22E47	-1:31:08
Musao	2	7S43	26E17	-1:45:08
Mushenge	2	4S32	21E21	-1:25:24
Mushie	1	3S01	16E54	-1:07:36
Musoshi	2	11S54	27E46	-1:51:04
Mutanda	1	5S17	16E34	-1:06:16
Mutiko	2	1S39	28E12	-1:52:48
Mutombo-Mukulu	2	7S58	24E00	-1:36:00
Mutoto	2	5S42	22E42	-1:30:48
Mutshatsha	2	10S39	24E27	-1:37:48
Muyumba	2	7S15	26E59	-1:47:56
Mwadi-Kalumba	1	7S53	18E46	-1:15:04
Mwango	2	6S51	24E13	-1:36:52
Mwanza	2	7S54	26E45	-1:47:00
Mwehu	2	5S44	26E40	-1:46:40
Mweka	2	4S51	21E34	-1:26:16
Mwemena	2	10S19	27E28	-1:49:52
Mwenda	2	12S01	28E44	-1:54:56
Mwendjila	1	7S12	18E51	-1:15:24
Mwene-Ditu	2	7S03	23E27	-1:33:48
Mwenga	2	3S02	28E26	-1:53:44
Mwepo	2	11S56	26E11	-1:44:44
Mwetshi	2	4S42	22E39	-1:30:36
Mwilambwe	2	8S07	25E00	-1:40:00
Namoya	2	4S01	27E34	-1:50:16
Napopo	3	4N12	28E02	-1:52:08
Nasondoye	2	10S22	25E06	-1:40:24
Ndu	3	4N41	22E49	-1:31:16
Nduye	3	1N50	29E01	-1:56:04
Nekalagba	3	2N50	28E01	-1:52:04
Ngale	3	2N56	21E20	-1:25:20
Ngali	1	2S27	19E20	-1:17:20
Ngele	3	0S29	20E25	-1:21:40
Ngidinga	1	5S37	15E17	-1:01:08
Ngombe	2	6S35	20E42	-1:22:48
Ngombe	1	4S24	15E11	-1:00:44
Ngote	3	2N14	30E48	-2:03:12
Niabembe	2	2S14	27E44	-1:50:56
Niangara	3	3N42	27E52	-1:51:28
Nia-Nia	3	1N24	27E36	-1:50:24
Niapu	3	2N25	26E28	-1:45:52
Niemba	2	5S57	28E26	-1:53:44
Nioka	3	2N10	30E39	-2:02:36
Nioki	1	2S43	17E41	-1:10:44
Nkoso	2	2S42	22E39	-1:30:36
Nkoto	1	1S56	19E41	-1:18:44
Nkunga	1	4S41	18E34	-1:14:16
Nsontin	1	3S09	18E00	-1:12:00
Ntandembele	1	2S11	17E08	-1:08:32
Nundu	2	3S49	29E05	-1:56:20
Nyavikungu	2	11S26	25E54	-1:43:36
Nyunzu	2	5S57	28E01	-1:52:04
Nziro	3	3N17	24E06	-1:36:24
Obokote	2	0S52	26E19	-1:45:16
Okoka	2	2S57	23E27	-1:33:48
Okolo	2	3S46	23E55	-1:35:40
Ombwe	2	4S22	25E35	-1:42:20
Onadikondo	2	3S52	24E10	-1:36:40
Onema	2	4S33	24E31	-1:38:04
Ongoka	3	1S23	26E02	-1:44:08
Onko	1	4S07	19E59	-1:19:56
Opala	3	0S37	24E21	-1:37:24
Opienge	3	0N12	27E30	-1:50:00
Oria	3	3N17	30E41	-2:02:44
Oshwe	1	3S24	19E30	-1:18:00
Palanganene	1	6S26	18E50	-1:15:20
Panga	3	1N51	26E25	-1:45:40
Pangi	2	3S11	26E38	-1:46:32
Pania-Mutombo	2	5S11	23E51	-1:35:24
Panu	1	3S48	19E07	-1:16:28
Panzi	1	7S13	17E58	-1:11:52
Parka	3	4N31	27E20	-1:49:20
Paulis → Isiro	3	2N47	27E37	-1:50:28
Pena-Lunanga	2	4S16	28E10	-1:52:40
Penge	2	5S31	24E37	-1:38:28
Pepa	2	7S42	29E47	-1:59:08
Pia	3	4N00	26E17	-1:45:08
Piana Mwanga	2	7S40	28E10	-1:52:40
Pimu-Lendo	3	1N46	20E54	-1:23:36
Pinga	2	1S01	28E42	-1:54:48
Pogoso	1	6S46	17E12	-1:08:48
Poko	3	3N09	26E53	-1:47:32
Pomongo	1	5S00	19E08	-1:16:32
Ponthierville → Ubundu				
	3	0S21	25E29	-1:41:56
Popokabaka	1	5S42	16E35	-1:06:20
Port-Francqui → Ilebo				
	2	4S19	20E35	-1:22:20
Pumbi	3	3N26	22E11	-1:28:44
Punia	2	1S28	26E27	-1:45:48
Pweto	2	8S28	28E54	-1:55:36
Rifflart	1	4S25	15E21	-1:01:24
Risasi	3	0S25	25E44	-1:42:56
Roa	3	3N49	24E56	-1:39:44
Rona	3	2N14	30E52	-2:03:28
Rubi	3	2N49	25E14	-1:40:56
Rutshuru	2	1S11	29E27	-1:57:48
Sabuka	1	4S27	15E10	-1:00:40
Sakania	2	12S45	28E34	-1:54:16
Salimi	2	9S24	23E35	-1:34:20
Samangwa	2	4S24	24E10	-1:36:40
Samba	2	4S38	26E22	-1:45:28
Samba	3	0N14	21E19	-1:25:16
Sampwe	2	9S20	27E26	-1:49:44
Samusele	2	10S06	24E05	-1:36:20
Sandoa	2	9S41	22E52	-1:31:28
Sanga	2	7S02	28E21	-1:53:24
Sangwa	2	5S30	26E00	-1:44:00
Sapindji	2	9S39	23E12	-1:32:48
Sapwe	2	10S57	28E10	-1:52:40
Seke-Banza	1	5S20	13E16	-0:53:04
Selembao	1	4S22	15E17	-1:01:08
Selenge	1	1S58	18E11	-1:12:44
Semendua	1	3S11	18E05	-1:12:20
Sentery	2	5S22	25E45	-1:43:00
Senza	3	3N02	26E19	-1:45:16
Shabunda	2	2S42	27E20	-1:49:20
Shambi	3	1S49	22E39	-1:30:36
Shambuanda	2	6S38	20E13	-1:20:52
Shangalume	2	10S49	26E34	-1:46:16
Shinkolobwe	2	11S02	26E35	-1:46:20
Simba	3	0N36	22E55	-1:31:40
Sokele	2	9S55	24E36	-1:38:24
Sola	2	5S09	27E06	-1:48:24
Sona-Bata	1	4S54	15E09	-1:00:36
Songololo	1	5S42	14E02	-0:56:08
Songwe	2	3S24	26E16	-1:45:04
Songwe	2	12S25	29E40	-1:58:40
Stanleyville → Kisangani				
	3	0N30	25E12	-1:40:48

ZAÏRE BELGIAN CONGO ZAIRE

Name	Zone	Lat	Long	Offset
Sulia	2	1S32	26E33	-1:46:12
Sundi-Lutete	1	4S34	14E14	-0:56:56
Swa-Tenda	1	7S09	17E07	-1:08:28
Takundi	1	4S45	16E34	-1:06:16
Tapili	3	3N25	27E40	-1:50:40
Tembe	2	0S16	28E14	-1:52:56
Tenke	2	10S35	26E07	-1:44:28
Tenke	2	11S26	26E45	-1:47:00
Teturi	3	1N04	29E08	-1:56:32
Thysville → Mbanza-Ngungu	1	5S15	14E52	-0:59:28
Titule	3	3N17	25E32	-1:42:08
Todro	3	3N21	30E14	-2:00:56
Tolo	1	2S56	18E34	-1:14:16
Tshabuta	2	7S47	23E16	-1:33:04
Tshela	1	4S59	12E56	-0:51:44
Tshibeke	2	2S44	28E36	-1:54:24
Tshibinda	2	2S19	28E45	-1:55:00
Tshibomba	2	9S02	22E34	-1:30:16
Tshikapa	2	6S25	20E48	-1:23:12
Tshilenge	2	6S15	23E46	-1:35:04
Tshimbulu	2	6S29	22E51	-1:31:24
Tshindjamba	2	10S54	22E41	-1:30:44
Tshinota	2	7S01	20E57	-1:23:48
Tshinsenda	2	12S18	27E58	-1:51:52
Tshisuku	2	6S26	19E55	-1:19:40
Tshitadi	2	6S45	21E45	-1:27:00
Tshoa	1	5S34	12E41	-0:50:44
Tshofa	2	5S14	25E15	-1:41:00
Tshumbiri	1	2S39	16E14	-1:04:56
Tua	1	3S38	16E36	-1:06:24
Tukpo	3	4N25	25E52	-1:43:28
Tweya	1	0S54	19E05	-1:16:20
Ubili	2	1S07	26E55	-1:47:40
Ubondo	3	0S52	25E37	-1:42:28
Ubundu (Ponthierville)	3	0S21	25E29	-1:41:56
Ulamba	2	9S07	23E40	-1:34:40
Utamba	2	1S06	26E50	-1:47:20
Utu	2	1S45	27E54	-1:51:36
Uvira	2	3S24	29E08	-1:56:32
Virungu	2	7S04	29E46	-1:59:04
Vitshumbi	2	0S41	29E23	-1:57:32
Wafania	3	1S21	20E20	-1:21:20
Waika	2	2S21	25E43	-1:42:52
Waka	1	0S48	20E10	-1:20:40
Waka	3	1N01	20E13	-1:20:52
Wake	1	0S48	20E10	-1:20:40
Walikale	2	1S25	28E03	-1:52:12
Wamba	3	2N09	28E00	-1:52:00
Wanga	3	2N58	29E13	-1:56:52
Wanie-Rukula	3	0N15	25E32	-1:42:08
Wapinda	3	3N41	22E48	-1:31:12
Watsa	3	3N03	29E32	-1:58:08
Watsi Kengo	3	0S48	20E33	-1:22:12
Watu	1	3S18	20E03	-1:20:12
Wauwa	3	3N27	27E21	-1:49:24
Wema	3	0S26	21E38	-1:26:32
Wendji	1	0S04	18E10	-1:12:40
Wenge	3	0N03	24E01	-1:36:04
Wusanga	2	3S22	22E50	-1:31:20
Yaenengu	3	2N28	23E15	-1:33:00
Yagonde	3	0N02	22E41	-1:30:44
Yahila	3	0N13	24E28	-1:37:52
Yahuma	3	1N05	23E13	-1:32:52
Yakoma	3	4N05	22E27	-1:29:48
Yakuluku	3	4N20	28E48	-1:55:12
Yali	3	0N04	21E03	-1:24:12
Yalikamba	3	1S17	22E30	-1:30:00
Yalikomba	3	1S17	22E30	-1:30:00
Yalisere	3	0N11	22E33	-1:30:12
Yalufi	3	0N45	24E26	-1:37:44
Yambata	3	2N26	21E58	-1:27:52
Yamboyo	3	0N40	22E18	-1:29:12
Yambuya	3	1N16	24E33	-1:38:12
Yandja	1	1S41	17E43	-1:10:52
Yandongi	3	2N51	22E16	-1:29:04
Yangambi	3	0N47	24E28	-1:37:52
Yangarakata	3	3N01	30E28	-2:01:52
Yapehe	3	0S13	24E27	-1:37:48
Yasa	2	3S42	21E24	-1:25:36
Yasa-Lokwa	1	5S15	19E24	-1:17:36
Yasendu	3	0N27	24E20	-1:37:20
Yayama	3	1S16	23E07	-1:32:28
Yekumbo	3	1S02	23E27	-1:33:48
Yindi	3	1N35	27E40	-1:50:40
Yokamba	3	0N01	22E17	-1:29:08
Yokana	3	0N45	22E53	-1:31:32
Yoko	1	2S36	20E06	-1:20:24
Yokolo	3	0S36	23E04	-1:32:16
Yolombo	3	1S32	23E15	-1:33:00
Yolonga	3	1S36	23E12	-1:32:48
Yumbi	2	1S14	26E14	-1:44:56
Yumbi	1	1S53	16E32	-1:06:08
Zobia	3	2N58	25E56	-1:43:44
Zongo	1	4N21	18E36	-1:14:24
Zongwe	2	5S05	27E55	-1:51:40

ZAMBIE NORTHERN RHODESIA SAMBIA ZAMBIA

Time Table
Before 1/Mar/1903 LMT
Begin Standard 30E00
1/Mar/1903 0:00 -2:00

Name	Lat	Long	Offset
Abercorn → Mbala	8S50	31E22	-2:05:28
Balovale	13S33	23E06	-1:32:24
Bancroft → Chililabombwe	12S18	27E43	-1:50:52
Batoka	16S47	27E15	-1:49:00
Bowwood	17S07	26E17	-1:45:08
Broken Hill → Kabwe	14S27	28E27	-1:53:48
Bwana Mkubwa	13S01	28E42	-1:54:48
Chadiza	14S05	32E28	-2:09:52
Chalabesa	11S22	31E01	-2:04:04
Chambishi	12S40	28E03	-1:52:12
Chasefu	11S55	33E08	-2:12:32
Chasefu Mission	11S55	33E08	-2:12:32
Chavuma	13S05	22E40	-1:30:40
Chibwe	14S12	28E31	-1:54:04
Chiengi	8S39	29E10	-1:56:40
Chikoa	13S24	32E07	-2:08:28
Chikote	15S52	26E54	-1:47:36
Chilanga	15S34	28E17	-1:53:08
Chililabombwe (Bancroft)	12S18	27E43	-1:50:52
Chilonga	12S03	31E21	-2:05:24
Chilubula Mission	10S09	31E00	-2:04:00
Chimpembe	9S31	29E33	-1:58:12
Chingola	12S32	27E52	-1:51:28
Chinsali	10S34	32E03	-2:08:12
Chinyama Litapi	13S31	22E21	-1:29:24
Chipata (Fort Jameson)	13S39	32E40	-2:10:40
Chipili	10S44	29E04	-1:56:16
Chisamba	14S58	28E23	-1:53:32
Chitambo	12S55	30E39	-2:02:36
Chitokoloki	13S50	23E13	-1:32:52
Choma	16S48	26E59	-1:47:56
Feira	15S37	30E25	-2:01:40
Fiwila Mission	13S58	29E36	-1:58:24
Fort Jameson → Chipata	13S39	32E40	-2:10:40
Fort Rosebery → Mansa	11S12	28E53	-1:55:32
Gwembe	16S30	27E35	-1:50:20
Ibwe Munyama	16S09	28E34	-1:54:16
Ilondola Mission	10S42	31E47	-2:07:08
Ingwe	13S02	26E25	-1:45:40
Isoka	10S10	32E35	-2:10:20
Kabwe (Broken Hill)	14S27	28E27	-1:53:48
Kafinda	12S39	30E20	-2:01:20
Kafue	15S47	28E11	-1:52:44
Kafulwe Mission	9S00	29E02	-1:56:08
Kalabo	14S57	22E40	-1:30:40
Kalene Hill	11S11	24E10	-1:36:40
Kalinku	11S12	33E12	-2:12:48
Kalomo	17S02	26E30	-1:46:00
Kalulushi	12S50	28E03	-1:52:12
Kalundu	10S16	29E24	-1:57:36
Kamapanda	12S00	24E10	-1:36:40
Kambanga	13S23	23E03	-1:32:12
Kambole Mission	8S46	30E46	-2:03:04
Kangombe	14S03	23E40	-1:34:40
Kanona	13S04	30E38	-2:02:32
Kansanshi	12S05	26E26	-1:45:44
Kapatu	9S43	30E42	-2:02:48
Kapiri Mposhi	13S58	28E41	-1:54:44
Kasabi	14S48	23E42	-1:34:48
Kasama	10S13	31E12	-2:04:48
Kasempa	13S27	25E50	-1:43:20
Kashitu	13S42	28E40	-1:54:40
Kataba	16S05	25E10	-1:40:40
Katete	14S05	32E07	-2:08:28
Katima Mulilo	17S27	24E14	-1:36:56
Kawama Mission	10S04	28E37	-1:54:28
Kawambwa	9S47	29E05	-1:56:20
Kayambi	9S27	31E58	-2:07:52
Kazembe	12S11	32E37	-2:10:28
Kazungula	17S45	25E20	-1:41:20
Kitwe	12S49	28E13	-1:52:52
Lakulu	14S22	23E17	-1:33:08
Lealui	15S10	23E02	-1:32:08
Livingstone	17S50	25E53	-1:43:32
Luampa	15S03	24E28	-1:37:52
Luanshya	13S08	28E24	-1:53:36
Lukulu	14S25	23E12	-1:32:48
Lumwana	11S50	25E10	-1:40:40
Lundazi	12S19	33E13	-2:12:52
Lusaka	15S25	28E17	-1:53:08
Lusongwa	12S58	24E16	-1:37:04
Luwingu	10S15	29E55	-1:59:40
Magoye	16S00	27E37	-1:50:28
Makoli	17S27	26E05	-1:44:20
Mankoya	14S47	24E48	-1:39:12
Mansa (Fort Rosebery)	11S12	28E53	-1:55:32
Mapanza	16S15	26E55	-1:47:40
Mapanza Mission	16S15	26E55	-1:47:40
Masuku	17S12	27E07	-1:48:28
Mayoba	17S13	26E16	-1:45:04
Mazabuka	15S51	27E46	-1:51:04
Mbala (Abercorn)	8S50	31E22	-2:05:28
Mbereshi Mission	9S45	28E46	-1:55:04
Mbindawina	15S57	23E18	-1:33:12
Mfuwe	13S04	31E46	-2:07:04
Mkushi	13S40	29E20	-1:57:20
Mkushi River	13S32	29E45	-1:59:00
Mongu	15S15	23E09	-1:32:36
Monze	16S16	27E28	-1:49:52
Mpika	11S54	31E26	-2:05:44
Mporokoso	9S23	30E05	-2:00:20
Mpulungu	8S46	31E07	-2:04:28
Msoro	13S36	31E55	-2:07:40
Msoro Mission	13S36	31E55	-2:07:40
Mufulira	12S33	28E14	-1:52:56
Mujimbeji Mission	12S11	24E57	-1:39:48
Mukinge Hill	13S29	25E52	-1:43:28
Mukuku	12S09	29E49	-1:59:16
Mukwela	17S02	26E39	-1:46:36
Mulobezi	16S48	25E09	-1:40:36
Mulungushi	14S40	28E50	-1:55:20
Mumbwa	14S59	27E04	-1:48:16
Mushima	14S13	25E05	-1:40:20
Musofu Mission	13S31	29E02	-1:56:08
Mutanda Mission	12S24	26E16	-1:45:04
Muzoka	16S41	27E19	-1:49:16
Mwanangumune	15S31	23E30	-1:34:00
Mwanza	17S02	24E27	-1:37:48
Mwinilunga	11S44	24E26	-1:37:44
Nakonde	9S20	32E42	-2:10:48
Nalolo	15S35	23E07	-1:32:28
Nalusa	14S55	22E13	-1:28:52
Namwala	15S45	26E26	-1:45:44
Nangoma	15S30	23E08	-1:32:32
Nangweshi	16S26	23E17	-1:33:08
Nanzhila	16S05	26E07	-1:44:28
Nanzila	16S05	26E07	-1:44:28
Nawinda Kuta	16S25	24E28	-1:37:52
Nchanga	12S30	27E53	-1:51:32
Nchelenge	9S20	28E50	-1:55:20
Ndabala	13S28	29E50	-1:59:20
Ndola	12S58	28E38	-1:54:32
Ngosa Farm	12S18	27E28	-1:49:52
Ngwerere	15S18	28E20	-1:53:20
Nkala Mission	15S55	26E00	-1:44:00
Nuala	13S27	28E16	-1:53:04
Nyakulenga	13S03	23E29	-1:33:56
Nyanji Mission	14S23	31E48	-2:07:12
Nyimba	14S35	30E52	-2:03:28
Old Mkushi	14S22	29E22	-1:57:28
Pemba	16S31	27E22	-1:49:28
Petauke	14S15	31E20	-2:05:20
Piccadilly Circus	13S56	29E24	-1:57:36
Rosa	9S38	31E21	-2:05:24
Rufunsa	15S05	29E40	-1:58:40
Samfya	11S21	29E32	-1:58:08
Senanga	16S06	23E16	-1:33:04
Senga Hill	9S22	31E12	-2:04:48
Senkobo	17S38	25E58	-1:43:52
Serenje	13S15	30E14	-2:00:56
Sesheke	17S29	24E18	-1:37:12
Sikalongo	16S46	27E07	-1:48:28
Sikelenge	14S50	24E14	-1:36:56
Sioma	16S39	23E30	-1:34:00
Solwezi	12S11	26E25	-1:45:40
Tara	16S56	26E47	-1:47:08
Ushaa	14S55	23E18	-1:33:12
Walamba	13S29	28E45	-1:55:00
Zimba	17S19	26E13	-1:44:52

ZIMBABWE

SOUTHERN RHODESIA

Time Table
Before 1/Mar/1903 LMT
Begin Standard 30E00
1/Mar/1903 0:00 -2:00

Antelope Mine	21s02	28E27	-1:53:48
Arcturus	17s47	31E20	-2:05:20
Avondale	17s43	30E58	-2:03:52
Balla Balla	20s26	29E02	-1:56:08
Bambezi	20s00	28E56	-1:55:44
Bannockburn	20s16	29E51	-1:59:24
Battlefields	18s31	29E52	-1:59:28
Beatrice	18s15	30E55	-2:03:40
Beitbridge	22s13	30E00	-2:00:00
Belingwe	20s30	29E53	-1:59:32
Bembesi	20s00	28E56	-1:55:44
Bikita	20s06	31E41	-2:06:44
Bindura	17s19	31E20	-2:05:20
Blue Gum Mine	18s25	29E25	-1:57:40
Bradley Institute	17s02	31E27	-2:05:48
Buhera	19s18	31E29	-2:05:56
Bulawayo	20s09	28E36	-1:54:24
Chakari	18s05	29E51	-1:59:24
Chatsworth	19s38	31E13	-2:04:52
Chegutu	18s10	30E14	-2:00:56
Chibi	20s19	30E30	-2:02:00
Chinhoyi	17s22	30E12	-2:00:48
Chipinga	20s12	32E38	-2:10:32
Chipinge	20s12	32E38	-2:10:32
Chipuriro	16s39	30E42	-2:02:48
Chiredzi	21s03	31E45	-2:07:00
Chirundu	15s59	28E54	-1:55:36
Chivhu	19s01	30E53	-2:03:32
Colleen Bawn	21s00	29E13	-1:56:52
Concession	17s22	30E57	-2:03:48
Craigmore	20s28	32E50	-2:11:20
Dahlia	18s35	27E08	-1:48:32
Darwendale	17s43	30E33	-2:02:12
Dete	18s38	26E50	-1:47:20
Dett	18s38	26E50	-1:47:20
Duchess Hill	18s18	30E13	-2:00:52
Eiffel Flats	18s15	29E59	-1:59:56
Enkeldoorn	19s01	30E53	-2:03:32
Esigodini	20s18	28E56	-1:55:44
Essexvale	20s18	28E56	-1:55:44
Featherstone	18s42	30E49	-2:03:16
Felixburg	19s29	30E51	-2:03:24
Figtree	20s24	28E21	-1:53:24
Filabusi	20s34	29E20	-1:57:20
Fort Rixon	20s01	29E18	-1:57:12
Fort Victoria	20s05	30E50	-2:03:20
Gaths Mine	20s00	30E31	-2:02:04
Gatooma	18s21	29E55	-1:59:40
Glenclova	19s59	31E26	-2:05:44
Glendale	17s21	31E04	-2:04:16
Gokwe	18s07	28E58	-1:55:52
Gutu	19s38	31E10	-2:04:40
Gwai	19s15	27E42	-1:50:48
Gwanda	20s57	29E01	-1:56:04
Gwelo	19s27	29E49	-1:59:16
Harare (Salisbury)	17s50	31E03	-2:04:12
Hartley	18s10	30E14	-2:00:56
Headlands	18s14	32E03	-2:08:12
Heany Junction	20s06	28E54	-1:55:36
Highfield	17s50	31E00	-2:04:00
Hunters Road	19s09	29E48	-1:59:12
Inyanga	18s13	32E46	-2:11:04
Inyantue	18s32	26E41	-1:46:44
Inyati	19s39	28E54	-1:55:36
Inyazura	18s43	32E10	-2:08:40
Jumbo	17s28	30E55	-2:03:40
Kariba	16s30	28E45	-1:55:00
Kariyangwe	17s57	27E30	-1:50:00
Karoi	16s50	29E40	-1:58:40
Kennedy	18s52	27E10	-1:48:40
Keynshamburg	19s15	29E39	-1:58:36
Kezi	20s58	28E32	-1:54:08
Kildonan	17s21	30E37	-2:02:28
Lalapanzi	19s16	30E15	-2:01:00
Legion Mine	21s23	28E33	-1:54:12
Lions Den	17s16	30E02	-2:00:08
Lukosi	18s30	26E30	-1:46:00
Lupani	18s54	27E44	-1:50:56
Macheke	18s05	31E51	-2:07:24
Makaha	17s17	32E37	-2:10:28
Makwiro	17s58	30E28	-2:01:52
Marandellas	18s10	31E36	-2:06:24
Marshbrook	18s34	31E03	-2:04:12
Marula	20s26	28E06	-1:52:24
Maryland	17s39	30E29	-2:01:56
Mashaba	20s02	30E29	-2:01:56
Masuie	18s05	25E45	-1:43:00
Matetsi	18s16	25E56	-1:43:44
Matopos	20s24	28E28	-1:53:52
Mazunga	21s45	29E52	-1:59:28
Melfort	17s59	31E19	-2:05:16
Melsetter	19s48	32E50	-2:11:20
Miami	16s40	29E46	-1:59:04
Mneni	20s38	30E03	-2:00:12
Mount Selinda	20s25	32E43	-2:10:52
Mphoengs	21s10	27E51	-1:51:24
Mrewa	17s39	31E47	-2:07:08
Mtoko	17s24	32E13	-2:08:52
Munene	20s38	30E03	-2:00:12
Murewa	17s39	31E47	-2:07:08
Mutambara	19s36	32E33	-2:10:12
Mutare	18s58	32E40	-2:10:40
Mutoko	17s24	32E13	-2:08:52
Mvuma	19s19	30E35	-2:02:20
Mwenezi	21s22	30E45	-2:03:00
Ngamo	19s08	27E32	-1:50:08
Ngomahuru	20s26	30E43	-2:02:52
Nkai	19s00	28E54	-1:55:36
Nkayi	19s00	28E54	-1:55:36
Norton	17s53	30E42	-2:02:48
Nuanetsi	21s22	30E45	-2:03:00
Nyamandhlovu	19s50	28E16	-1:53:04
Nyanda	20s05	30E50	-2:03:20
Nyazura	18s43	32E10	-2:08:40
Odzi	18s58	32E23	-2:09:32
Penhalonga	18s54	32E40	-2:10:40
Plumtree	20s30	27E50	-1:51:20
Que Que	18s55	29E49	-1:59:16
Redcliff	19s02	29E50	-1:59:20
Rusambo	16s35	32E12	-2:08:48
Rusape	18s32	32E07	-2:08:28
Rutenga	21s08	30E45	-2:03:00
Sakubva	19s00	32E10	-2:08:40
Salisbury → Harare	17s50	31E03	-2:04:12
Sambawizi	18s21	26E16	-1:45:04
Sawmills	19s31	28E02	-1:52:08
Selukwe	19s40	30E00	-2:00:00
Shabani	20s20	30E02	-2:00:08
Shamva	17s18	31E34	-2:06:16
Shangani	19s47	29E22	-1:57:28
Shurugwi	19s40	30E00	-2:00:00
Sinoia	17s22	30E12	-2:00:48
Sipolilo	16s39	30E42	-2:02:48
Somabula	19s41	29E41	-1:58:44
Tandaai	19s36	32E48	-2:11:12
Tandai	19s36	32E48	-2:11:12
The Range	19s00	31E04	-2:04:16
Tjolotjo	19s47	27E46	-1:51:04
Tuli	21s59	29E15	-1:57:00
Turk Mine	19s45	28E50	-1:55:20
Umguza	19s25	27E51	-1:51:24
Umniati	18s39	29E49	-1:59:16
Umtali	18s58	32E40	-2:10:40
Umvuma	19s19	30E35	-2:02:20
Victoria Falls	17s56	25E50	-1:43:20
Wanderer	19s37	29E59	-1:59:56
Wankie	18s22	26E29	-1:45:56
Wedza	18s35	31E35	-2:06:20
West Nicholson	21s06	29E25	-1:57:40
Zaka	20s20	31E29	-2:05:56
Zawi	17s13	30E02	-2:00:08
Zvishavane	20s20	30E02	-2:00:08

INDEX ITA - KOR

INDEX PAC - QAT

INDEX ZAN - ZYP

COUNTRIES BY CONTINENT

BIBLIOGRAPHY

Astronomic Institute of Brazil. *Hora de verão no Brasil.*

Astro-Psychological Problems. journal, Gauquelin, Françoise, ed, Paris.

Bordoni, Grazia. "The Legal Time in Italy", vol 1 no. 2. March 1983.

Gauquelin, Françoise. "The Legal Time in France", vol 1, no. 3. June 1983.

Prager, Maria. "Time Changes in Austria", vol 1, no. 4. September 1983.

Karlinski, Marius. "Time Changes in Poland", vol 2, no. 1. December 1983.

Keller, Michael. "Time Changes in Switzerland", vol 2, no. 2. March 1984.

de Pablos, Jose Luis San Miguel. "Time Changes in Spain", vol 2, no. 3. June 1984.

Gauquelin, Françoise with Fr. Jacob. "Time Changes in Germany", vol 2, no. 4. September 1984.

Skapski, Jan Sar. "More Precision About Time Changes in Poland", vol 3, no. 1. January 1985.

The Book of Calendars. Edited by Frank Parise. New York: Facts On File, 1982.

Blumenson, Martin. *The Duel for France 1944.* Houghton Mifflin, 1963.

Chandu, Jack F. *Time Changes in the World.* Deventer: Uitgeverij Ankh-Hermes bv, 1984.

The Daily News Almanac and Year-Book 1922. Chicago.

Encyclopedia Brittanica 1984 Book of the Year: Events of 1983.

Michel, Henri. *The Second World War.* Praeger, 1975.

Le Corre, Henri. *Régimes Horaires pour l'Europe et l'Afrique.* Éditions Traditionnelles. Paris, 1982.

Doane, Doris C. *Time Changes in the World.* American Federation of Astrologers, Inc., 1982.

______. *Time Changes in Canada and Mexico.* American Federation of Astrologers, Inc., 1982.

Gauquelin, Françoise Schneider. *Problèmes De L'Heure Résolus en Astrologie.* Paris: La Grande Conjunction, 1987.

Hammond Family Reference World Atlas. Garden City: Doubleday & Company, Inc., 1972.

Hammond's Comparative World Atlas: Desk Edition. New York: C. S. Hammond & Company, 1950.

Hare, Humphrey. *France Reborn.* Scribner's, 1964.

The Middle East and North Africa 1984-85. 31st ed. London: Europa Publications Limited, 1984.

The New International Atlas. Rand McNally, 1982 and 1984.

Official Airline Guide. Oakbrook, Il: The Reuben H. Donnelley Corp., 1956 - 1985.

Polich, Wendel. "Hora de Verano en la Republica Argentina." *In Tablas de Casas Astrologicas.* Ediciones Regulus.

Reader's Digest Almanac and Yearbook 1970. Pleasantville: The Reader's Digest Association, 1970.

Scobel, A. *Andrees Allgemeiner Handatlas.* Verlag von Velhagen und Klasing. Bielefeld und Leptiz. 1899.

The Official Guide of the Railways. . . of the United States. . . 1931-1969 Editions. New York: National Railway Publication Co., 1868.

Webster's New Geographical Dictionary. Springfield: Merriam-Webster Inc., 1984.

The World Almanac and Book of Facts 1985. New York: Newspaper Enterprise Association Inc., 1984.

Worldmark Encyclopedia of the Nations. 6th ed. 5 vols. New York: Worldmark Press, Ltd., 1984.